WHAT'S IN THE FOUNDATION DIRECTORY?

The Foundation Directory provides information on the finances, governance, and giving interests of the nation's 10,000 largest grantmaking foundations—those foundations who were among the top 10,000 in terms of awards made in the latest fiscal year of record. The information in The Foundation Directory is based either on reports received directly from the foundations or on the most current public records available.

The Foundation Directory is arranged alphabetically by state and, within states, by foundation name. Each entry includes the foundation's name and address, financial data for the latest available year of record, a description of funding interests, a list of officers and trustees, and the foundation's IRS Employer Identification Number. Where applicable, additional information is provided on the types of grants or other forms of support awarded, restrictions on the giving program by geographic or subject area, application procedures and deadlines, and the number of staff members the foundation employs. When available, a selected list of up to ten grants reported during a given fiscal year is included.

When using The Foundation Directory to identify potential funding sources, grantseekers are urged to read each foundation description carefully to determine the nature of the grantmaker's interests and to note any restrictions on giving that would prevent the foundation from considering their proposal. Some foundations limit their giving to a particular subject field or geographic area; others are unable to provide certain types of support, such as funds for buildings and equipment or for general operating budgets. Even when a foundation has not provided an explicit limitations statement, restrictions on giving may exist. This is often the case with entries updated from public records. Further research into the giving patterns of these foundations is necessary before applying for funds.

INDEXES

Seven indexes to the descriptive entries are provided to assist grantseekers and other users of The Foundation Directory:

- The **Index to Donors, Officers, Trustees** is an alphabetical list of individual and corporate donors, officers, and members of governing boards whose names appear in The Foundation Directory entries.

- The **Geographic Index** lists foundations by the states and cities in which they are located, with cross-references to foundations located elsewhere that have made substantial grants in a particular state.

- The **International Giving Index** provides access to foundations whose giving interests extend beyond the United States. A complete alphabetical list of countries, continents, and regions is provided at the beginning of the index. Under each country, continent, or region, entry numbers are listed by the state location and abbreviated name of the foundation.

- The **Types of Support Index** provides access to foundation entries by the specific types of support the foundation awards. A glossary of the forms of support included appears at the beginning of this index. Under each type of support term, entry numbers are listed by the state location and abbreviated name of the foundation.

- The **Subject Index** provides access to giving interests of foundations based on the "Fields of Interest" section of their entries. A list of the subject terms used is provided at the beginning of this index. Under each subject term, entry numbers are listed by the state location and abbreviated name of the foundation.

- The index of **Foundations New to the Edition** is a listing of foundations that appear in the current edition of The Foundation Directory but had not met criteria for inclusion in the previous edition. The descriptive entries for these foundations are highlighted with a star (☆).

- The **Foundation Name Index** is an alphabetical list of all foundations with entries in The Foundation Directory. Former names of foundations appear with "see" references to the appropriate entry numbers. This index also provides references to Appendix A, which lists foundations that appeared in the previous edition but have since terminated or otherwise become ineligible for inclusion.

In the Geographic Index, Types of Support Index, and Subject Index, foundations that award grants on a national, regional, or international basis are listed in boldface type. The other foundations generally limit their giving to the city or state in which they are located.

APPENDIXES

- **Appendix A** lists foundations described in the previous edition of The Foundation Directory that do not have entries in the current edition because they have terminated operations, merged with another foundation, ceased grantmaking, or changed their legal status.

- **Appendix B** lists foundations that have made a significant amount of grants, but are excluded because they contribute only to a few specified beneficiaries or to the support of a single institution.

**FOUNDATION
CENTER**

Knowledge to build on.

THE
FOUNDATION
DIRECTORY

29th Edition

FOUNDATION
CENTER
Knowledge to build on.

THE FOUNDATION DIRECTORY

29th Edition
2007

David G. Jacobs
Senior Editor

CONTRIBUTING STAFF

Senior Vice President for Information Resources and Publishing	Rick Schoff
Senior Director of Database Publishing	Jeffrey A. Falkenstein
Regional Product Manager	Margaret Mary Feczko
Director of Grants Processing	Rebecca MacLean
Grants Processing Supervisor	Denise McLeod
Information Control Manager	Yinebon Iniya
Assistant Editor	Regina Judith Faighes
Senior Editorial Associates	Jeanette L. Boulanger
Joseph W. Guastella
Editorial Associates	Charlene Feeley
Adrian Palacios
Rita C. Tobiasen
Editorial Assistants	Lauren Braithwaite
Jody Kitcher
David Rosado
Eliza Stein
Erma Williams
Editor, Corporate Foundations	David L. Clark
Editor, Community Foundations	Jonathan Miller
Editorial Consultant	Melissa R. Douglas
Publishing Database Administrator	Kathye Giesler
System Administrator	Emmy So
Communications Project Manager	Cheryl Loe
Production Manager	Christine Innamorato
Programmer	Mirek Drozdzowski

The editor gratefully acknowledges the many other Foundation Center staff who contributed support, encouragement, and information that was indispensable to the preparation of this volume. Special mention should also be made of the staff members of the New York, Washington, DC, Cleveland, San Francisco, and Atlanta libraries who assisted in tracking changes in foundation information. We would like to express our appreciation as well to the many foundations that cooperated fully in updating information prior to the compilation of *The Foundation Directory*.

CONTENTS

INTRODUCTION

The Foundation Directory is the definitive annual reference source for information about private and community grantmaking foundations in the United States. It is used by fundseekers, foundation and government officials, scholars, journalists, and others generally interested in foundation giving in this country.

THE 2007 EDITION

The 2007 Edition is the twenty-ninth complete revision of The Foundation Directory since the volume was first published by the Foundation Center in 1960. This year's edition of the Directory contains information on the 10,000 largest grantmaking foundations in the US. These foundations awarded the most dollars in total giving during the most current fiscal year of record.[1] (Entries for the next 10,000 largest grantmaking foundations in the U.S. during the most current fiscal year of record can be found in a companion volume, Foundation Directory Part 2). Entries in this volume hold a combined total assets value of more than $475 billion (86.4 percent of all foundation assets) and awarded grants totaling over $31 billion (87.5 percent of all foundation giving) in the latest year of record (Table 1).

SELECTED GRANTS

To illustrate a foundation's giving pattern, up to 10 selected grants to recipient organizations have been provided whenever possible (Grants to individuals are not listed). Of the 10,000 entries in this volume, 5,849 (58.4 percent) include lists of selected grants. In all, 52,543 grants are included, totaling over $8.5 billion in support to organizations. These grants may serve to illustrate fields of interest and geographic preferences. In general, however, the selected grants represent large awards and may not reveal the full spectrum of programs and giving interests of a foundation. The complete descriptive entry should always be carefully examined to determine a foundation's current funding emphasis, and, where available, the "average" grant amount noted in the fiscal information section should be consulted to ascertain the typical range of grants awarded.

FOUNDATIONS NEW TO THE FOUNDATION DIRECTORY

There are 1,694 foundations in the 2007 edition that were not listed in the 2006 edition (Table 2). Of these, 1,502 (88.7 percent) are independent foundations, 119 (7.0 percent) are company-sponsored foundations, 15 (0.9 percent) are community foundations, and 58 (3.4 percent) are grantmaking operating foundations. One hundred and twenty-six of the newly added foundations hold assets of $20 million or more (Table 6), but, like other foundations in The Foundation Directory, the majority fall into the $1 million to $10 million asset range. Foundations new to The Foundation Directory can be identified by a star (☆) in their descriptive entries. Users with a particular interest in these newly qualifying foundations will find them listed separately in the index of Foundations New to the Edition.

WHAT IS A FOUNDATION?

The Foundation Directory includes those organizations meeting the Foundation Center's definition of a private or community foundation and which were among the top 10,000 annual givers in the latest year of record. The Center defines a foundation as a nongovernmental, nonprofit organization with its own funds (usually from a single source, either an individual, family, or corporation) and program managed by its own trustees and directors that was established to maintain or aid educational, social, charitable, religious, or other activities serving the common welfare, primarily by making grants to other nonprofit organizations.

The Foundation Directory does not include organizations whose giving is restricted by charter to one or more specified organizations; foundations that function as endowments for special purposes within and under the governance of a parent institution, such as a college or church; operating foundations that do not maintain active grantmaking programs; organizations that act as associations for industrial or other special groups; or organizations that make general appeals to the public for funds. Lists of private foundations that meet the criteria for The Foundation Directory but which are excluded for the reasons cited above are provided in the Appendixes.

---

[1]In addition, The Foundation Directory includes entries for 3 large organizations that are not private foundations, but closely resemble them in form and function: Howard Hughes Medical Institute, classified by the IRS as a Medical Research Organization, The California HealthCare Foundation, which is classified as a public charity, and The Pew Charitable Trusts, which was reorganized as a public charity in 2004. These organizations resemble private foundations in that they do not make appeals to the public for donations, and aid charitable purposes through grantmaking in accordance with an IRS payout requirement. These entries are omitted from the statistical tables and summaries in this edition.

TYPES OF FOUNDATIONS

Foundations included in this volume fall into one of four categories:

Independent Foundation: A fund or endowment designated by the Internal Revenue Service as a private foundation under the law, the primary function of which is the making of grants. The assets of most independent foundations are derived from the gift of an individual or family. Some function under the direction of family members and are known as "family foundations." Depending on their range of giving, independent foundations may also be known as "general purpose" or "special purpose" foundations.

Company-Sponsored Foundation: A private foundation under the tax law deriving its funds from a profit-making company or corporation but independently constituted, the purpose of which is to make grants, usually on a broad basis although not without regard for the business interests of the corporation. Company-sponsored foundations are legally distinct from contributions programs administered within the corporation directly from corporate funds. Direct corporate giving programs are not listed in *The Foundation Directory*. The Foundation Center's *National Directory of Corporate Giving,* Twelfth Edition, published in 2006, includes complete corporate giving profiles on over 3,700 companies.

Operating Foundation: A fund or endowment designated under the tax law by the Internal Revenue Service as a private operating foundation, the primary purpose of which is to operate research, social welfare, or other programs determined by its governing body or charter. Most operating foundations award few or no grants to outside organizations, and therefore those do not appear in *The Foundation Directory*.

Community Foundation: In its general charitable purposes, a community foundation is much like a private foundation; its funds, however, are derived from many donors rather than a single source, as is usually the case with private foundations. Further, community foundations are usually classified under the tax law as public charities and are therefore subject to different rules and regulations than those which govern private foundations. Public charities other than community foundations are not included in *The Foundation Directory*.

FIGURE A. General Characteristics of Four Types of Foundations

Foundation Type	Description	Source of Funds	Decision-Making Activity	Grantmaking Requirements	Reporting
Independent Foundation	An independent grant-making organization established to aid social, educational, religious, or other charitable activities.	Endowment generally derived from a single source such as an individual, a family, or a group of individuals. Contributions to endowment limited as to tax deductibility.	Decisions may be made by donor or members of the donor's family; by an independent board of directors or trustees; or by a bank or trust officer acting on the donor's behalf.	Broad discretionary giving allowed but may have specific guidelines and give only in a few specific fields. About 70% limit their giving to local area.	Annual information returns (990-PF) filed with IRS must be made available to public. A small percentage issue separately printed annual reports.
Company-Sponsored Foundation	Legally an independent grantmaking organization with close ties to the corporation providing funds.	Endowment and annual contributions from a profit-making corporation. May maintain small endowment and pay out most of contributions received annually in grants, or may maintain endowment to cover contributions in years when corporate profits are down.	Decisions made by board of directors often composed of corporate officials, but which may include individuals with no corporate affiliation. Decisions may also be made by local company officials.	Giving tends to be in fields related to corporate activities or in communities where corporation operates. Usually give more grants but in smaller dollar amounts than independent foundations.	Same as above.
Operating Foundation	An organization that uses its resources to conduct research or provide a direct service.	Endowment usually provided from a single source, but eligible for maximum deductible contributions from public.	Decisions generally made by independent board of directors.	Makes few, if any grants. Grants generally related directly to the foundation's program.	Same as above.
Community Foundation	A publicly sponsored organization that makes grants for social, educational, religious, or other charitable purposes in a specific community or region.	Contributions received from many donors. Usually eligible for maximum tax deductible contributions from public.	Decisions made by board of directors representing the diversity of the community.	Grants generally limited to charitable organizations in local community.	IRS 990 return available to public. Many publish full guidelines or annual reports.

SOURCES OF INFORMATION

The entries in *The Foundation Directory* are revised and updated on an ongoing basis, using the newest and most complete information available. This information is either provided by the foundation itself, or it comes from available public records. The main source of information are the foundations' tax returns, the form 990-PF. Other public sources of information used in this edition include updates from foundation Web sites, annual reports, press releases and newspaper articles. In addition, the Foundation Center offers private foundations several ways to alert us to newer and more current information. Entries in the book are prepared and sent to the individual foundations for verification. In 2006, 1,767 responded to these requests. In addition, 46 foundations sent either full or partial information updates via Foundation Center electronic reporting applications (Foundation Finder and Foundation Directory Online Updater) available on the Foundation Center's Web site (foundationcenter.org). For grantmakers who do not respond to our requests for information, entries were prepared from the most recent IRS tax return available as of January 2007. These entries are indicated in *The Foundation Directory*, by the symbol (◇) following the foundation name.

The Internet has become an important and effective research tool, enabling staff to learn more about foundations and their grantmaking activities. This edition contains 2,091 entries with a URL (Internet web site address), and an additional 430 that report having an e-mail address.

A breakdown of the 10,000 foundations by fiscal year-end date reveals the following: 425 foundations (4.2 percent) with 2006 fiscal data, 7,182 foundations (71.8 percent) with 2005 fiscal data, 1,995 foundations (19.9 percent) with 2004 fiscal data, and 398 foundations (3.9 percent) with 2003 fiscal data. Thus, 2006 and 2005 fiscal information is reported for 76 percent of the foundations listed. Of the 100 largest foundations, 97 percent are represented by 2006 or 2005 fiscal data (Tables 4 and 5). Even when more recent financial information was not available, foundation addresses, contacts, program information, and application procedures reflect the latest updates received by the Center through January, 2007.

TABLE 1. **Aggregate Fiscal Data by Foundation Type** (All dollar figures expressed in thousands)

Foundation Type	Number of Foundations	%	Assets	%	Gifts Received	%	Total Giving*	%	Qualifying Distributions	%	Loans
Independent	8,413	84.1	$395,209,778	83.1	$12,622,445	50.9	$21,853,756	68.6	$23,986,704	68.2	$177,364
Company-Sponsored	918	9.2	16,156,180	3.4	3,788,350	15.3	3,842,059	12.1	4,009,149	11.4	9,372
Community	424	4.2	43,681,430	9.2	5,480,825	22.1	3,183,230	10.0	3,269,901	9.3	9,347
Operating	245	2.5	20,434,004	4.3	2,915,026	11.8	2,980,963	9.4	3,927,856	11.2	6,876
Total	**10,000**	**100.0**	**$475,481,392**	**100.0**	**$24,806,645**	**100.0**	**$31,860,008**	**100.0**	**$35,193,610**	**100.0**	**$202,958**

Note: Figures may not add up due to rounding.

*Throughout this introduction,, "Total Giving" figures include grants,, scholarships,, employee matching gifts,, and other amounts reported as "Grants and Contributions Paid During the Year" on the 990-PF reporting form. Loan amounts including program-related investments (PRIs) are indicated separately. Total giving does not include all qualifying distributions under the tax law, e.g., loans, PRIs,, and program or other administrative expenses.

TABLE 2. **Aggregate Fiscal Data for Foundations New to *The Foundation Directory* by Foundation Type** (All dollar figures expressed in thousands)

Foundation Type	Number of Foundations	%	Assets	%	Gifts Received	%	Total Giving*	%	Qualifying Distributions	%	Loans
Independent	1,502	88.7	$13,036,574	92.2	$2,843,480	81.6	$1,275,737	73.9	$1,338,325	73.5	$15
Company-Sponsored	119	7.0	674,584	4.8	213,904	6.1	96,030	5.6	97,316	5.3	0
Community	15	0.9	127,171	0.9	33,447	1.0	8,621	0.5	9,548	0.5	0
Operating	58	3.4	307,105	2.2	394,998	11.3	346,518	20.1	374,980	20.6	0
Total	**1,694**	**100.0**	**$14,145,434**	**100.0**	**$3,485,830**	**100.0**	**$1,726,907**	**100.0**	**$1,820,169**	**100.0**	**$15**

Note: Figures may not add up due to rounding.

*Throughout this introduction, "Total Giving" figures include grants, scholarships, employee matching gifts, and other amounts reported as "Grants and Contributions Paid During the Year" on the 990-PF reporting form. Loan amounts including program-related investments (PRIs) are indicated separately. Total giving does not include all qualifying distributions under the tax law, e.g., loans, PRIs, and program or other administrative expenses.

TABLE 3. Fiscal Data of Foundations by Region and State (Dollar figures expressed in thousands)

Region	Number of Foundations	%	Assets	%	Gifts Received	%	Expenditures	%	Total Giving	%
NORTHEAST	**3,382**	**33.8**	**$140,105,355**	**29.5**	**$ 7,866,648**	**31.7**	**$13,099,479**	**34.2**	**$11,198,156**	**35.1**
New England	**777**	**7.8**	**20,395,142**	**4.3**	**1,424,016**	**5.7**	**1,924,191**	**5.0**	**1,622,047**	**5.1**
Connecticut	209	2.1	5,244,393	1.1	498,529	2.0	634,157	1.7	567,602	1.8
Maine	38	0.4	1,198,144	0.3	57,482	0.2	95,696	0.2	79,316	0.2
Massachusetts	449	4.5	11,496,186	2.4	713,255	2.9	1,001,325	2.6	813,395	2.6
New Hampshire	26	0.3	771,311	0.2	30,060	0.1	61,338	0.2	48,179	0.2
Rhode Island	48	0.5	1,507,047	0.3	105,244	0.4	116,162	0.3	101,031	0.3
Vermont	7	0.1	178,062	0.0	19,447	0.1	15,513	0.0	12,524	0.0
Middle Atlantic	**2,605**	**26.1**	**119,710,212**	**25.2**	**6,442,632**	**26.0**	**11,175,288**	**29.2**	**9,576,108**	**30.1**
New Jersey	361	3.6	17,351,998	3.6	2,668,461	10.8	3,373,941	8.8	3,121,049	9.8
New York	1,801	18.0	82,665,720	17.4	3,241,428	13.1	6,295,542	16.4	5,161,386	16.2
Pennsylvania	443	4.4	19,692,495	4.1	532,743	2.1	1,505,805	3.9	1,293,673	4.1
MIDWEST	**2,242**	**22.4**	**99,800,841**	**21.0**	**4,873,196**	**19.6**	**7,961,060**	**20.8**	**6,799,956**	**21.3**
East North Central	**1,594**	**15.9**	**75,326,378**	**15.8**	**2,961,696**	**11.9**	**5,599,859**	**14.6**	**4,798,756**	**15.1**
Illinois	515	5.2	19,554,504	4.1	670,674	2.7	1,369,468	3.6	1,181,415	3.7
Indiana	165	1.7	14,712,406	3.1	449,317	1.8	1,049,266	2.7	916,750	2.9
Michigan	278	2.8	22,809,593	4.8	697,759	2.8	1,629,996	4.3	1,350,527	4.2
Ohio	400	4.0	12,837,253	2.7	768,354	3.1	1,031,544	2.7	888,520	2.8
Wisconsin	236	2.4	5,412,622	1.1	375,592	1.5	519,585	1.4	461,543	1.4
West North Central	**648**	**6.5**	**24,474,463**	**5.1**	**1,911,500**	**7.7**	**2,361,201**	**6.2**	**2,001,200**	**6.3**
Iowa	86	0.9	2,092,496	0.4	178,625	0.7	189,786	0.5	168,574	0.5
Kansas	61	0.6	1,498,025	0.3	64,269	0.3	116,865	0.3	101,388	0.3
Minnesota	242	2.4	10,659,701	2.2	464,351	1.9	863,458	2.3	669,613	2.1
Missouri	160	1.6	7,584,738	1.6	597,740	2.4	911,677	2.4	807,408	2.5
Nebraska	79	0.8	2,240,234	0.5	571,816	2.3	248,058	0.6	228,153	0.7
North Dakota	8	0.1	140,893	0.0	11,818	0.0	9,896	0.0	7,556	0.0
South Dakota	12	0.1	258,375	0.1	22,881	0.1	21,460	0.1	18,508	0.1
SOUTH	**2,529**	**25.3**	**99,557,024**	**20.9**	**6,225,899**	**25.1**	**8,081,618**	**21.1**	**6,777,923**	**21.3**
South Atlantic	**1,525**	**15.3**	**56,742,637**	**11.9**	**3,109,006**	**12.5**	**4,658,839**	**12.2**	**3,866,262**	**12.1**
Delaware	78	0.8	3,043,367	0.6	69,210	0.3	225,988	0.6	194,689	0.6
District of Columbia	102	1.0	4,485,440	0.9	295,416	1.2	453,901	1.2	342,673	1.1
Florida	443	4.4	13,100,299	2.8	636,490	2.6	1,023,697	2.7	854,277	2.7
Georgia	221	2.2	8,474,770	1.8	640,096	2.6	765,593	2.0	651,982	2.0
Maryland	204	2.0	10,596,273	2.2	462,288	1.9	777,988	2.0	632,893	2.0
North Carolina	209	2.1	9,297,849	2.0	595,921	2.4	867,698	2.3	760,804	2.4
South Carolina	59	0.6	1,313,830	0.3	70,465	0.3	105,293	0.3	88,159	0.3
Virginia	181	1.8	5,730,240	1.2	207,538	0.8	385,251	1.0	292,977	0.9
West Virginia	28	0.3	700,569	0.1	131,582	0.5	53,431	0.1	47,809	0.2
East South Central	**278**	**2.8**	**7,296,080**	**1.5**	**431,032**	**1.7**	**650,230**	**1.7**	**562,077**	**1.8**
Alabama	77	0.8	1,323,269	0.3	66,238	0.3	117,656	0.3	101,835	0.3
Kentucky	52	0.5	1,344,333	0.3	59,152	0.2	102,035	0.3	85,611	0.3
Mississippi	38	0.4	790,101	0.2	31,272	0.1	71,508	0.2	56,144	0.2
Tennessee	111	1.1	3,838,378	0.8	274,370	1.1	359,031	0.9	318,687	1.0
West South Central	**726**	**7.3**	**35,518,306**	**7.5**	**2,685,860**	**10.8**	**2,772,549**	**7.2**	**2,349,584**	**7.4**
Arkansas	35	0.4	2,291,690	0.5	618,696	2.5	420,629	1.1	404,542	1.3
Louisiana	63	0.6	2,000,772	0.4	80,197	0.3	128,211	0.3	97,622	0.3
Oklahoma	73	0.7	7,570,538	1.6	911,587	3.7	396,900	1.0	309,619	1.0
Texas	555	5.6	23,655,306	5.0	1,075,380	4.3	1,826,809	4.8	1,537,801	4.8
WEST	**1,842**	**18.4**	**135,987,528**	**28.6**	**5,833,916**	**23.5**	**9,135,046**	**23.9**	**7,080,704**	**22.2**
Mountain	**422**	**4.2**	**18,414,286**	**3.9**	**1,275,569**	**5.1**	**1,271,515**	**3.3**	**1,045,794**	**3.3**
Arizona	70	0.7	3,171,550	0.7	747,376	3.0	197,163	0.5	157,384	0.5
Colorado	146	1.5	6,729,699	1.4	240,794	1.0	483,865	1.3	381,563	1.2
Idaho	17	0.2	931,749	0.2	10,408	0.0	54,897	0.1	48,713	0.1
Montana	11	0.1	257,346	0.1	6,078	0.0	20,867	0.1	16,428	0.1
Nevada	59	0.6	3,513,361	0.7	91,288	0.4	235,097	0.6	207,766	0.7
New Mexico	38	0.4	1,070,070	0.2	36,606	0.1	80,011	0.2	56,226	0.2
Utah	54	0.5	1,760,272	0.4	74,509	0.3	136,777	0.4	121,717	0.4
Wyoming	27	0.3	980,240	0.2	68,510	0.3	62,837	0.2	55,997	0.2
Pacific	**1,420**	**14.2**	**117,573,242**	**24.7**	**4,558,346**	**18.4**	**7,863,531**	**20.5**	**6,034,910**	**18.9**
Alaska	8	0.1	640,226	0.1	18,130	0.1	38,592	0.1	30,092	0.1
California	1,141	11.4	75,458,030	15.9	3,672,943	14.8	5,152,704	13.5	3,984,980	12.5
Hawaii	32	0.3	1,022,806	0.2	40,374	0.2	75,403	0.2	60,123	0.2
Oregon	75	0.8	3,601,193	0.8	153,139	0.6	263,973	0.7	230,762	0.7
Washington	164	1.6	36,850,986	7.8	673,760	2.7	2,332,858	6.1	1,728,954	5.4
CARIBBEAN	**5**	**0.1**	**30,645**	**0.0**	**6,987**	**0.0**	**5,986**	**0.0**	**3,269**	**0.0**
Puerto Rico	2	0.0	26,349	0.0	4,471	0.0	3,821	0.0	1,217	0.0
Virgin Islands	3	0.0	4,296	0.0	2,516	0.0	2165	0.0	2,053	0.0
SOUTH PACIFIC	**0**	**0.0**	**0**	**0.0**	**0**	**0.0**	**0**	**0.0**	**0**	**0.0**
American Samoa	0	0.0	0	0.0	0	0.0	0	0.0	0	0.0
Total	**10,000**	**100.0**	**$475,481,392**	**100.0**	**$24,806,645**	**100.0**	**$38,283,189**	**100.0**	**$31,860,008**	**100.0**

Note: Figures may not add up due to rounding.

TABLE 4. 100 Largest Foundations by Assets

Name	Assets	Total Giving	Fiscal Date	Name	Assets	Total Giving	Fiscal Date
1. Bill & Melinda Gates Foundation	$29,153,508,829	$1,356,250,292	12/31/05	52. The Freedom Forum, Inc.[3]	$1,071,127,819	$ 28,368,456	12/31/05
2. The Ford Foundation	11,615,906,693	516,907,177	09/30/05	53. Greater Kansas City Community Foundation	1,013,035,000	140,702,000	12/31/05
3. J. Paul Getty Trust[1]	9,618,627,974	22,778,357	06/30/05	54. Howard Heinz Endowment	948,757,866	39,413,997	12/31/05
4. The Robert Wood Johnson Foundation	9,359,361,000	372,500,000	12/31/05	55. The Ahmanson Foundation	938,348,497	41,218,405	10/31/05
5. Lilly Endowment Inc.	8,360,760,584	427,465,199	12/31/05	56. The Joyce Foundation	892,492,212	30,571,102	12/31/05
6. W. K. Kellogg Foundation	7,799,270,734	262,809,343	08/31/06	57. Conrad N. Hilton Foundation	889,768,444	39,108,321	02/28/06
7. The William and Flora Hewlett Foundation	7,336,131,000	319,916,093	12/31/05	58. The San Francisco Foundation	883,443,000	68,100,000	06/30/06
8. The David and Lucile Packard Foundation	5,788,480,930	150,115,645	12/31/05	59. The Meadows Foundation, Inc.	876,650,177	26,038,090	12/31/05
9. The Andrew W. Mellon Foundation	5,586,112,000	199,340,000	12/31/05	60. The Packard Humanities Institute[4]	858,955,029	13,555,364	12/31/05
10. John D. and Catherine T. MacArthur Foundation	5,490,449,000	194,500,000	12/31/05	61. Open Society Institute	858,935,162	45,565,966	12/31/05
11. Gordon and Betty Moore Foundation	5,308,627,945	218,758,756	12/31/05	62. Barr Foundation	857,054,761	37,643,680	12/31/05
12. The California Endowment	3,729,571,524	153,242,789	02/28/05	63. The Columbus Foundation and Affiliated Organizations	850,089,853	65,626,215	12/31/05
13. The Rockefeller Foundation	3,417,557,613	111,083,354	12/31/05	64. The Oregon Community Foundation	850,034,138	40,478,757	12/31/05
14. The Starr Foundation	3,344,801,753	159,130,952	12/31/05	65. Weingart Foundation	839,604,507	40,561,794	06/30/06
15. The Annie E. Casey Foundation	3,152,516,760	173,118,671	12/31/05	66. Broad Foundation	835,659,229	40,992,554	12/31/05
16. The Kresge Foundation	3,032,422,497	149,831,151	12/31/05	67. Rockefeller Brothers Fund, Inc.	815,561,407	23,769,840	12/31/05
17. The Duke Endowment	2,708,834,085	125,629,926	12/31/05	68. Hall Family Foundation	814,088,561	29,628,310	12/31/05
18. The Annenberg Foundation	2,539,268,854	273,414,830	06/30/06	69. The Edna McConnell Clark Foundation	808,121,944	31,175,454	09/30/05
19. Charles Stewart Mott Foundation	2,480,562,766	113,334,381	12/31/05	70. Bush Foundation	796,152,567	30,363,717	11/30/05
20. Casey Family Programs[2]	2,265,711,291	8,248,714	12/31/05	71. The Henry Luce Foundation, Inc.	792,916,471	35,954,289	12/31/05
21. Tulsa Community Foundation	2,264,564,027	29,572,740	12/31/05	72. Horace W. Goldsmith Foundation	788,615,258	37,495,001	12/31/05
22. Carnegie Corporation of New York	2,244,208,247	91,053,489	09/30/05	73. Longwood Foundation, Inc.	785,221,853	30,528,172	09/30/05
23. The Harry and Jeanette Weinberg Foundation, Inc.	2,154,005,108	93,630,682	02/28/06	74. The J. E. and L. E. Mabee Foundation, Inc.	769,999,802	36,532,800	08/31/06
24. John S. and James L. Knight Foundation	2,071,507,291	92,577,162	12/31/05	75. Boston Foundation, Inc.	769,807,869	63,914,314	06/30/06
25. The McKnight Foundation	2,050,595,000	90,710,176	12/31/05	76. Surdna Foundation, Inc.	769,100,511	30,608,760	06/30/05
26. Robert W. Woodruff Foundation, Inc.	1,950,691,385	101,030,268	12/31/05	77. Community Foundation Silicon Valley	760,821,244	75,366,593	06/30/05
27. Doris Duke Charitable Foundation	1,920,145,122	62,691,247	12/31/05	78. M. J. Murdock Charitable Trust	758,617,116	26,176,683	12/31/05
28. The New York Community Trust	1,897,604,374	136,970,963	12/31/05	79. The Lynde and Harry Bradley Foundation, Inc.	755,894,000	34,737,079	12/31/05
29. Richard King Mellon Foundation	1,882,031,732	74,356,247	12/31/05	80. Fred C. and Katherine B. Andersen Foundation	752,341,252	25,349,733	12/31/05
30. Ewing Marion Kauffman Foundation	1,860,797,344	50,603,728	06/30/05	81. Burroughs Wellcome Fund	702,980,765	24,350,797	08/31/06
31. The Cleveland Foundation	1,716,136,165	66,421,855	12/31/05	82. Communities Foundation of Texas, Inc.	699,873,000	59,931,000	06/30/06
32. The James Irvine Foundation	1,610,480,320	73,123,056	12/31/05	83. The Pittsburgh Foundation	690,511,755	31,466,977	12/31/05
33. Alfred P. Sloan Foundation	1,581,350,875	61,165,933	12/31/05	84. Hartford Foundation for Public Giving	664,546,568	24,763,885	12/31/05
34. Houston Endowment Inc.	1,512,185,118	51,642,096	12/31/05	85. Marguerite Casey Foundation	663,183,945	27,687,400	12/31/05
35. The Chicago Community Trust	1,503,994,247	75,988,536	09/30/05	86. The Minneapolis Foundation	654,649,964	37,154,937	03/31/06
36. The Wallace Foundation	1,447,299,661	56,665,282	12/31/05	87. The AVI CHAI Foundation	653,609,340	30,655,330	12/31/05
37. W. M. Keck Foundation	1,333,252,000	65,350,257	12/31/05	88. Community Foundation for Greater Atlanta, Inc.	638,817,268	89,391,237	06/30/06
38. Walton Family Foundation, Inc.	1,328,793,250	157,989,927	12/31/05	89. Jack Kent Cooke Foundation	637,795,172	15,759,958	05/31/06
39. The Samuel Roberts Noble Foundation, Inc.	1,269,572,071	6,829,697	12/31/05	90. The Commonwealth Fund	634,403,522	15,229,313	06/30/06
40. The William Penn Foundation	1,253,208,618	64,641,331	12/31/05	91. Wayne & Gladys Valley Foundation	623,762,552	23,117,765	09/30/05
41. Lumina Foundation for Education, Inc.	1,235,598,231	48,457,322	12/31/05	92. The Saint Paul Foundation, Inc.	617,910,511	34,675,706	12/31/05
42. The Michael and Susan Dell Foundation	1,226,020,349	56,238,527	12/31/05	93. Peninsula Community Foundation	614,336,446	92,331,777	12/31/05
43. The Brown Foundation, Inc.	1,223,019,722	68,356,805	06/30/06	94. The John A. Hartford Foundation, Inc.	614,197,200	26,333,414	12/31/05
44. Donald W. Reynolds Foundation	1,204,806,991	69,203,364	12/31/05	95. The Robert A. Welch Foundation	611,141,615	27,393,359	08/31/06
45. The Moody Foundation	1,158,543,467	15,803,315	12/31/05	96. The Picower Foundation	604,882,964	27,662,893	12/31/05
46. California Community Foundation	1,152,601,808	91,367,805	06/30/06	97. William Randolph Hearst Foundation	597,342,514	26,991,685	12/31/05
47. Marin Community Foundation	1,125,930,427	51,649,386	06/30/06	98. McCune Foundation	585,046,089	27,309,409	09/30/05
48. Freeman Foundation	1,105,466,120	42,067,148	12/31/05	99. Kate B. Reynolds Charitable Trust	569,540,075	19,327,315	08/31/06
49. Daniels Fund	1,090,055,954	44,947,978	12/31/05	100. J. Bulow Campbell Foundation	561,671,985	28,891,099	12/31/05
50. John Templeton Foundation	1,080,335,362	44,321,264	12/31/05				
51. The California Wellness Foundation	1,072,427,215	48,410,903	12/31/05				

[1] J. Paul Getty Trust is an operating foundation and most of its qualifying distributions are paid out for administration of operating programs and not for grants. Total giving includes only grants and grant-related expenses as reported. In 2005, program amounts totaled over $187 million.

[2] Casey Family Programs is an operating foundation and most of its qualifying distributions are paid out for administration of operating programs and not for grants. Total giving includes only grants and grant-related expenses as reported. In 2005, program amounts totaled over $86 million.

[3] The Freedom Forum, Inc. is an operating foundation and most of its qualifying distributions are paid out for administration of operating programs and not for grants. Total giving includes only grants and grant-related expenses as reported. In 2005, program amounts totaled over $10 million.

[4] The Packard Humanities Institute is an operating foundation and most of its qualifying distributions are paid out for administration of operating programs and not for grants. Total giving includes only grants and grant-related expenses as reported. In 2005, program amounts totaled over $62 million.

TABLE 6. Foundations New to *The Foundation Directory* with Assets Over $20 Million (All dollar figures expressed in thousands)

	Name	State	Established Year	Type of Foundation*	Fiscal Date	Assets	Gifts Received	Total Giving
1.	Leon Levy Foundation	NY	2005	IF	03/31/05	$533,617	$535,207	$ 1,522
2.	Mt. Cuba Center, Inc.	DE	1953	IF	12/31/05	309,949	0	3,605
3.	Flight Attendant Medical Research Institute, Inc.	FL	2000	IF	09/30/05	299,116	0	21,339
4.	Paso del Norte Health Foundation	TX	1995	IF	12/31/04	192,024	0	7,1423
5.	The USAA Foundation, Inc.	TX	2004	CS	06/30/05	152,337	200	651
6.	Robert Mapplethorpe Foundation, Inc.	NY	1988	IF	05/31/05	145,731	0	512
7.	J.A. Wedum Foundation	MN	1959	IF	12/31/04	142,784	157	875
8.	The Rosalinde and Arthur Gilbert Foundation	CA	2002	IF	12/31/04	141,079	28,655	4,397
9.	Williamsburg Community Health Foundation	VA	1996	IF	12/31/05	127,631	0	5,074
10.	The Terry Foundation	TX	1986	IF	12/31/05	124,110	402	7,264
11.	The Samuel and Jean Frankel Jewish Heritage Foundation	MI	2004	IF	12/31/05	107,606	61,625	3,954
12.	Welborn Baptist Foundation, Inc.	IN	1999	IF	12/31/05	107,342	3	3,193
13.	Westlake Health Foundation	IL	1998	IF	12/31/05	105,340	0	4,511
14.	Yellow Chair Foundation	NY	2000	IF	12/31/04	102,222	57,070	3,225
15.	Koret Fund	CA	2004	IF	12/31/05	101,704	41,475	4,773
16.	Richard & Susan Smith 1990 Charitable Trust	MA	1990	FM	12/31/05	99,617	52,033	910
17.	Gary Karlin Michelson, M.D. Charitable Foundation, Inc.	CA	1995	IF	12/31/05	97,808	102,674	4,126
18.	Edgerton Foundation	CA	2001	IF	06/30/05	97,433	0	524
19.	The Laszlo N. Tauber Family Foundation	MD	2004	FM	12/31/05	94,242	68,500	2,122
20.	Thomas Spiegel Family Foundation	CA	2004	IF	12/31/04	91,826	0	3,788
21.	Soros Charitable Foundation	NY	1992	IF	11/30/05	90,731	0	4,100
22.	The Tabasgo Foundation	CA	2005	IF	12/31/05	89,890	95,558	8,314
23.	The Price Family Charitable Fund	CA	1983	FM	12/31/05	87,834	2	800
24.	Google Foundation	CA	2004	CS	12/31/05	84,911	90,000	5,450
25.	Lola G. Duff & William H. Duff II Scholarship	OH		IF	03/31/05	79,955	0	2,047
26.	Mr. & Mrs. Samuel Oschin Family Foundation	CA	2004	FM	09/30/05	76,039	13,605	5,008
27.	John E. Fetzer Memorial Trust Fund	MI	1991	IF	06/30/05	75,804	1,000	3,000
28.	Irene S. Scully Family Foundation	CA	2004	IF	12/31/04	72,147	64,640	1,488
29.	The Joseph and Robert Cornell Memorial Foundation	NY		IF	12/31/05	71,418	0	3,853
30.	Charles T. Bauer Foundation	TX	2004	IF	12/31/05	64,701	3,869	450
31.	John E. Morgan Roundation, Inc.	NY		IF	12/31/04	64,607	0	1,524
32.	The Joan Mitchell Foundation, Inc.	NY		IF	12/31/05	61,363	399	745
33.	Marge & Charles J. Schott Foundation	OH	1980	IF	06/30/05	59,065	48,821	1,148
34.	The Anna and John J. Sie Foundation	CO	2003	IF	12/31/05	57,047	0	801
35.	Kalmanovitz Charitable Foundation	CA	2001	IF	06/30/05	55,613	0	700
36.	Nanci's Animal Rights Foundation, Inc.	FL		IF	06/30/05	55,487	25,002	10,000
37.	Brookfield Arts Foundation, Inc.	MA	1995	OP	12/31/05	54,033	10,475	15,459
38.	John William Pope Foundation	NC	1986	IF	06/30/05	53,580	3,862	7,408
39.	Francqui Foundation	NY		IF	12/31/05	53,571	0	847
40.	Mithun Family Foundation	MN	1986	IF	12/31/05	53,411	43,374	450
41.	Phoenixville Community Health Foundation	PA	1997	IF	06/30/05	52,395	2	1,422
42.	T. Gary and Kathleen Rogers Private Family Foundation	CA	2003	IF	12/31/05	52,263	13,256	1,686
43.	Building Hope...A Charter School Facilities Fund	DC	2003	OP	12/31/04	51,297	28,563	379
44.	Omidyar Network Fund, Inc.	CA	2004	IF	12/31/04	49,448	57,029	8,071
45.	BayTree Fund	CA	2004	IF	12/31/05	49,040	0	1,822
46.	Seedlings Foundation	CT	2002	IF	12/31/05	48,656	7,450	3,559
47.	Morgan Family Foundation	OH	2003	FM	11/30/05	47,455	0	2,083
48.	The Boeing Company Charitable Trust	WA	1952	CS	12/31/05	47,445	2,622	3,864
49.	The Soros Foundation-Hungary, Inc.	NY	1983	IF	12/31/04	47,364	0	20,991
50.	The Robert Kravis and Kimberly Kravis Foundation	NY	1998	IF	11/30/05	47,083	0	6,301
51.	The Ludcke Foundation	MA	1991	IF	12/31/05	46,791	8,601	793
52.	Heimbinder Family Foundation	OH	1989	IF	12/31/05	45,658	0	409
53.	Texas Pioneer Foundation	TX		IF	06/30/05	44,975	36,242	345
54.	The Warwick Foundation of Bucks County	PA	2001	IF	12/31/05	44,849	0	1,234
55.	M. G. Davis Trust	NY		IF	12/31/04	43,536	0	1,800
56.	Gerald and Henrietta Rauenhorst Foundation, Inc.	FL	2004	IF	12/31/05	43,445	11,955	864
57.	Carl & Roberta Deutsch Foundation	CA	1997	IF	12/31/05	42,953	20,000	1,028
58.	Krauss, Miller, Lutz Charitable Trust Foundation, Inc.	FL	2003	IF	12/31/05	42,950	0	3,940
59.	Robert C. & Adele R. Schiff Family Foundation	OH	2002	IF	11/30/05	42,626	31,325	400
60.	Edmund and Jeannik Littlefield Foundation	CA	1958	FM	12/31/05	42,450	0	2,617
61.	The GFC Foundation	UT	1994	IF	06/30/05	41,801	11,631	389
62.	Sara Giles Moore Foundation	GA	1997	FM	12/31/05	40,960	31,494	1,400
63.	The Provident Bank Foundation	NJ	2003	CS	12/31/04	38,429	0	2,333
64.	Avery-Tsui Foundation	CA	2004	IF	12/31/05	37,883	0	1,891

*Type of foundation codes: OP=Operating foundation; IF=Independent foundation; CS=Company-sponsored foundation; CM=Community foundation.

TABLE 6. (Continued)

Name	State	Established Year	Type of Foundation*	Fiscal Date	Assets	Gifts Received	Total Giving
65. Enlight Foundation	CA	2004	IF	12/31/05	$37,804	$ 0	$ 810
66. The Morey Foundation	MI	1990	IF	12/31/05	37,432	0	423
67. Robert and Michelle Diener Foundation	TX	2001	IF	12/31/05	36,682	0	819
68. Melmac Education Foundation	ME	2001	IF	12/31/05	35,989	0	1,352
69. Patrick G. & Shirley W. Ryan Foundation	IL	1984	IF	11/30/05	35,682	47	349
70. Tennessee Health Foundation, Inc.	TN	2003	IF	12/31/05	35,655	23,300	1,078
71. The William R. Orthwein, Jr. & Laura Rand Orthwein Foundation	MO		IF	11/30/05	35,276	98	1,450
72. The Countess Moira Charitable Foundation	NY	2000	IF	06/30/05	34,791	31,682	605
73. Franklin Benevolent Corporation	CA	1998	IF	12/31/04	33,396	0	1,511
74. Dugas Family Foundation	TN	1998	IF	12/31/04	33,136	1,840	1,857
75. The Barnett and Annalee Newman Foundation	DE	1996	IF	12/31/05	32,539	0	938
76. The Paul & Elisabeth Merage Family Foundation	CA	2002	IF	12/31/05	31,180	0	1,427
77. The Peter and Carmen Lucia Buck Foundation	NY	1999	FM	06/30/05	31,096	20,000	338
78. The Angell Foundation	CA		IF	06/30/05	29,543	12,100	1,007
79. The Nicholas Foundation	CA	1998	IF	12/31/05	29,462	66	2,890
80. The Lindmor Foundation	NY	1991	IF	12/31/05	28,779	5,082	894
81. Dolan Family Foundation	NY	1987	FM	11/30/05	28,716	90	1,817
82. Northwest Health Foundation Fund, II	OR	2000	IF	12/31/05	28,507	81	3,060
83. The Orokawa Foundation, Inc.	MD	2005	IF	06/30/05	28,433	27,975	700
84. The Pauley Family Foundation	VA	1993	FM	12/31/05	28,141	0	1,158
85. The Catalyst Fund	ME		IF	12/31/04	27,204	0	442
86. George R. Johnson Family Foundation	TN	2004	IF	12/31/05	26,798	0	1,387
87. Keystone Nazareth Charitable Foundation	PA		CS	12/31/04	26,788	0	749
88. Hirsch Family Foundation	TX	2004	IF	12/31/05	26,333	8,173	907
89. Irene W. & Guy L. Anderson Children's Foundation	CA	1970	IF	11/30/05	26,141	0	688
90. Leo Adler Community Trust	OR	1993	IF	06/30/05	25,749	0	1,113
91. The Jim Moran Foundation, Inc.	FL	2000	CS	12/31/04	25,566	9,398	1,056
92. The Edith Glick Shoolman Children's Foundation	NY		IF	12/31/05	25,458	1,066	455
93. Sweet Water Trust	MA	1991	FM	12/31/05	25,003	0	1,240
94. Naddisy Foundation, Inc.	NY	2002	IF	12/31/05	24,821	0	1,141
95. North Dade Medical Foundation, Inc.	FL	1997	IF	09/30/05	24,343	533	12,965
96. Gould Family Foundation	NY	2003	IF	12/31/05	24,283	0	825
97. The Precourt Foundation	CO	1994	IF	12/31/05	24,002	19,979	454
98. The John P. Ellbogen Foundation	WY	2003	IF	12/31/05	23,622	1,000	823
99. John C. Hench Foundation	CA	1990	IF	11/30/05	23,615	18,235	425
100. Change Happens Foundation	HI	2001	IF	12/31/05	23,445	4,690	724
101. The Robert A. Waidner Foundation	MD	2001	IF	12/31/05	23,150	0	5,446
102. The Boyd Foundation	NV	1986	OP	12/31/05	23,063	0	375
103. The Blank Family Foundation, Inc.	FL	2002	IF	12/31/04	22,991	5,543	850
104. Edward S. Moore Family Foundation, Inc.	NY	2005	IF	03/31/05	22,777	0	765
105. Common Stream, Inc.	MA		IF	12/31/05	22,462	0	1,640
106. The Roger and Rosemary Enrico Foundation	TX	2000	IF	12/31/05	22,460	0	906
107. William C. Dowling Jr. Foundation	NY	2003	IF	12/31/05	22,300	50	1,067
108. Rosaria P. Haugland Foundation	OR	2003	IF	09/30/05	22,261	3,652	1,646
109. The Dow Foundation	NJ		IF	11/30/05	21,998	17,996	1,036
110. Andre & Katherine Merage Foundation of Nevada	CA	2002	IF	12/31/05	21,551	0	990
111. The Harry T. Mangurian, Jr. Foundation, Inc.	NY	1999	IF	12/31/05	21,496	0	520
112. Hickey Family Foundation	AZ	2004	IF	12/31/05	21,449	21,890	500
113. Keith & Mary Kay McCaw Family Foundation	WA	1995	FM	12/31/05	21,245	9,000	563
114. Laura G. Turner Charitable Foundation, Inc.	TN	1989	IF	12/31/05	21,141	0	540
115. The Fran and Warren Rupp Foundation	MN	1977	FM	12/31/05	21,113	24	712
116. The Almar Foundation	LA	1997	FM	12/31/05	21,098	307	373
117. Oppenheimer Brothers Foundation	CA	2001	IF	12/31/05	20,966	586	1,185
118. The Charlesmead Foundation, Inc.	RI	1987	FM	11/30/05	20,839	0	622
119. B. B. Owen Trust	TX	1974	IF	09/30/05	20,808	0	420
120. The Park Foundation	OH	2004	CS	12/31/05	20,795	103	574
121. Kentucky Fund for Healthy Living, Inc.	KY	2003	IF	03/31/05	20,498	0	1,453
122. Martha Sue Parr Trust	WI		IF	03/31/05	20,482	10,307	553
123. M.D.C. Holdings, Inc. Charitable Foundation	CO	1999	CS	12/31/04	20,303	6,300	405
124. Willard and Pat Walker Charitable Foundation, Inc.	AR	2003	IF	12/31/05	20,223	23,699	20,404
125. Edward and Hannah M. Rutledge Charities, Inc.	WI	1911	IF	05/31/06	20,116	2	319
126. J. L. Williams Foundation, Inc.	TX	2000	IF	12/31/05	20,027	0	468

*Type of foundation codes: OP=Operating foundation; IF=Independent foundation; CS=Company-sponsored foundation; CM=Community foundation.

TABLE 7. Foundations by Asset Categories (All dollar figures expressed in thousands)

Asset Category	Number of Foundations	%	Assets	%	Gifts Received	%	Total Giving	%	Grants*	%
$100 million and over	643	6.4	$330,878,463	69.6	$ 9,662,530	39.0	$15,529,432	48.7	$15,214,142	52.8
$50 to $100 million	648	6.5	44,935,443	9.5	3,399,786	13.7	2,963,273	9.3	2,869,800	10.0
$25 to $50 million	1,137	11.4	39,671,057	8.3	2,677,497	10.8	2,791,814	8.8	2,704,802	9.4
$10 to $25 million	2,585	25.9	40,736,184	8.6	2,898,725	11.7	3,374,678	10.6	3,109,540	10.8
$5 to $10 million	1,892	18.9	14,141,702	3.0	1,588,331	6.4	1,827,210	5.7	1,783,867	6.2
$1 to $5 million	1,729	17.3	4,693,388	1.0	2,010,634	8.1	2,370,011	7.4	1,725,639	6.0
Under $1 million	1,366	13.7	425,155	0.1	2,569,143	10.4	3,003,591	9.4	1,390,965	4.8
Total	**10,000**	**100.0**	**$475,481,392**	**100.0**	**$24,806,645**	**100.0**	**$31,860,008**	**100.0**	**$28,798,754**	**100.0**

Note: Figures may not add up due to rounding.
*"Grants" figures represent grants paid to organizations.

TABLE 8. Foundations New to *The Foundation Directory* by Asset Categories (All dollar figures expressed in thousands)

Asset Category	Number of Foundations	%	Assets	%	Gifts Received	%	Total Giving	%	Grants*	%
$100 million and over	15	0.9	$ 2,692,593	19.0	$ 724,795	20.8	$ 72,039	4.2	$ 72,039	5.1
$50 to $100 million	28	1.7	1,998,089	14.1	665,636	19.1	88,546	5.1	85,731	6.1
$25 to $50 million	50	3.0	1,823,078	12.9	359,348	10.3	98,651	5.7	97,384	6.9
$10 to $25 million	234	13.8	3,497,294	24.7	593,019	17.0	264,948	15.3	262,051	18.6
$5 to $10 million	360	21.3	2,574,204	18.2	285,720	8.2	200,211	11.6	197,890	14.1
$1 to $5 million	530	31.3	1,406,275	9.9	332,876	9.5	366,831	21.2	360,265	25.6
Under $1 million	477	28.2	153,901	1.1	524,437	15.0	635,681	36.8	332,830	23.6
Total	**1,694**	**100.0**	**$14,145,434**	**100.0**	**$3,485,830**	**100.0**	**$1,726,907**	**100.0**	**$1,408,190**	**100.0**

Note: Figures may not add up due to rounding.
*"Grants" figures represent grants paid to organizations.

TABLE 9. Independent Foundations by Asset Categories (All dollar figures expressed in thousands)

Asset Category	Number of Foundations	%	Assets	%	Gifts Received	%	Total Giving	%	Grants*	%
$100 million and over	511	6.1	$272,352,232	68.9	$ 4,673,057	37.0	$12,070,020	55.2	$11,877,397	55.4
$50 to $100 million	533	6.3	37,046,195	9.4	2,068,941	16.4	1,951,511	8.9	1,914,520	8.9
$25 to $50 million	961	11.4	33,443,723	8.5	1,610,894	12.8	1,911,887	8.7	1,869,568	8.7
$10 to $25 million	2,264	26.9	35,565,240	9.0	1,833,950	14.5	2,447,165	11.2	2,385,826	11.1
$5 to $10 million	1,678	19.9	12,583,079	3.2	825,082	6.5	1,162,846	5.3	1,141,149	5.3
$1 to $5 million	1,423	16.9	3,883,410	1.0	902,447	7.1	1,252,180	5.7	1,229,097	5.7
Under $1 million	1,043	12.4	335,898	0.1	708,073	5.6	1,058,147	4.8	1,040,431	4.8
Total	**8,413**	**100.0**	**$395,209,778**	**100.0**	**$12,622,445**	**100.0**	**$21,853,756**	**100.0**	**$21,457,988**	**100.0**

Note: Figures may not add up due to rounding.
*"Grants" figures represent grants paid to organizations.

TABLE 10. Company-Sponsored Foundations by Asset Categories (All dollar figures expressed in thousands)

Asset Category	Number of Foundations	%	Assets	%	Gifts Received	%	Total Giving	%	Grants*	%
$100 million and over	33	3.6	$ 6,043,846	37.4	$ 692,895	18.3	$ 818,046	21.3	$ 740,313	22.1
$50 to $100 million	50	5.4	3,292,247	20.4	747,427	19.7	700,754	18.2	654,021	19.5
$25 to $50 million	79	8.6	2,762,390	17.1	695,010	18.3	594,224	15.5	560,084	16.7
$10 to $25 million	154	16.8	2,453,907	15.2	541,679	14.3	550,280	14.3	504,644	15.1
$5 to $10 million	131	14.3	940,710	5.8	233,163	6.2	211,871	5.5	196,472	5.9
$1 to $5 million	227	24.7	592,166	3.7	411,261	10.9	460,764	12.0	428,348	12.8
Under $1 million	244	26.6	70,914	0.4	466,915	12.3	506,119	13.2	262,832	7.9
Total	**918**	**100.0**	**$16,156,180**	**100.0**	**$3,788,350**	**100.0**	**$3,842,059**	**100.0**	**$3,346,714**	**100.0**

Note: Figures may not add up due to rounding.
*"Grants" figures represent grants paid to organizations.

TABLE 11. Community Foundations by Asset Categories (All dollar figures expressed in thousands)

Asset Category	Number of Foundations	%	Assets	%	Gifts Received	%	Total Giving	%	Grants*	%
$100 million and over	82	19.3	$34,265,639	78.4	$4,251,194	77.6	$2,485,948	78.1	$2,448,721	78.5
$50 to $100 million	52	12.3	3,756,669	8.6	480,689	8.8	276,729	8.7	270,562	8.7
$25 to $50 million	89	21.0	3,175,034	7.3	360,004	6.6	217,690	6.8	208,322	6.7
$10 to $25 million	118	27.8	2,010,085	4.6	264,732	4.8	136,869	4.3	127,691	4.1
$5 to $10 million	50	11.8	379,894	0.9	86,873	1.6	38,206	1.2	36,811	1.2
$1 to $5 million	29	6.8	91,752	0.2	34,570	0.6	24,357	0.8	22,512	0.7
Under $1 million	4	0.9	2,357	0.0	2,762	0.1	3,432	0.1	3,264	0.1
Total	**424**	**100.0**	**$43,681,430**	**100.0**	**$5,480,825**	**100.0**	**$3,183,230**	**100.0**	**$3,117,882**	**100.0**

Note: Figures may not add up due to rounding.
*"Grants" figures represent grants paid to organizations.

TABLE 12. Operating Foundations by Asset Categories (All dollar figures expressed in thousands)

Asset Category	Number of Foundations	%	Assets	%	Total Giving*	%	Progam Amount	%
$100 million and over	17	6.9	$18,216,746	89.1	$ 155,417	5.2	$498,778	73.9
$50 to $100 million	13	5.3	840,332	4.1	34,279	1.1	89,564	13.3
$25 to $50 million	8	3.3	289,909	1.4	68,013	2.3	25,943	3.8
$10 to $25 million	49	20.0	706,952	3.5	240,364	8.1	26,190	3.9
$5 to $10 million	33	13.5	238,019	1.2	414,286	13.9	10,725	1.6
$1 to $5 million	50	20.4	126,060	0.6	632,711	21.2	13,373	2.0
Under $1 million	75	30.6	15,986	0.1	1,435,892	48.2	10,462	1.5
Total	**245**	**100.0**	**$20,434,004**	**100.0**	**$2,980,963**	**100.0**	**$675,035**	**100.0**

Note: Figures may not add up due to rounding.
*Throughout this introduction, "Total Giving" figures include grants, scholarships, employee matching gifts, and other amounts reported as "Grants and Contributions Paid During the Year" on the 990-PF reporting form. Loan amounts including program-related investments (PRIs) are indicated separately. Total giving does not include all qualifying distributions under the tax law, e.g., loans, PRIs, and program or other administrative expenses.

HOW TO USE
THE FOUNDATION DIRECTORY

The Foundation Directory is one of the first tools grantseekers should use to identify foundations that might be interested in funding their project or organization. It provides basic descriptions and current fiscal data for the nation's largest foundations—those foundations who were among the top 10,000 in terms of awards made in the latest fiscal year record. In addition, indexes help to identify foundations that may have giving interests in particular subject fields or geographic areas, or that provide specific types of support.

Researchers, journalists, grantmakers, and others interested in the philanthropic field use The Foundation Directory to get a broad overview of current foundation activities nationally or within a particular geographic region, or to gather facts about one or more specific foundations.

When using The Foundation Directory to identify potential funding sources, grantseekers are urged to read each foundation description carefully to determine the nature of the grantmaker's interests and to note any restrictions on giving that would prevent the foundation from considering their proposal. Many foundations limit their giving to a particular subject field or geographic area; others are unable to provide certain types of support, such as funds for buildings and equipment or for general operating budgets. Even when a foundation has not provided an explicit limitations statement, restrictions on giving may exist. This is often the case with entries updated from public records. Further research into the giving patterns of these foundations is necessary before applying for funds.

ARRANGEMENT

The Foundation Directory is arranged alphabetically by state and, within states, by foundation name. Each descriptive entry is assigned a sequence number; references in the indexes are to these entry numbers.

WHAT'S IN AN ENTRY?

There are 34 basic data elements that could be included in a Foundation Directory entry. The content of entries varies widely due to differences in the size and nature of foundation programs and the availability of information from foundations. Specific data elements that could be included are:

1. The full legal **name of the foundation.**

2. The **former name** of the foundation.

3. The **street address, city,** and **zip code** of the foundation's principal office.

4. The **telephone number** of the foundation.

5. The name and title of the **contact person** of the foundation.

6. Any **additional address** (such as a separate application address) supplied by the foundation. Additional telephone or Fax numbers as well as E-mail and/or URL addresses also may be listed here.

7. **Establishment data,** including the legal form (usually a trust or corporation) and the year and state in which the foundation was established.

8. The **donor(s)** or principal contributor(s) to the foundation, including individuals, families, and corporations. If a donor is deceased, the symbol ‡ follows the name.

9. **Foundation type:** community, company-sponsored, independent, or operating.

10. The **year-end date** of the foundation's accounting period for which financial data is supplied.

11. **Assets:** the total value of the foundation's investments at the end of the accounting period. In a few instances, foundations that act as "pass-throughs" for annual corporate or individual gifts report zero assets.

12. **Asset type:** generally, assets are reported at market value (M) or ledger value (L).

13. **Gifts received:** the total amount of new capital received by the foundation in the year of record.

14. **Expenditures:** total disbursements of the foundation, including overhead expenses (salaries; investment, legal, and other professional fees; interest; rent; etc.) and federal excise taxes, as well as the total amount paid for grants, scholarships, and matching gifts.

15. The total amount of **qualifying distributions** made by the foundation in the year of record. This figure includes all grants paid, qualifying administrative expenses, loans and program-related investments, set-asides, and amounts paid to acquire assets used directly in carrying out charitable purposes.

16. The dollar value and number of **grants paid** during the year, with the largest grant paid **(high)** and smallest grant paid **(low).** When supplied by the foundation, the average range of grant payments is also indicated. Grant figures generally do not include commitments for future payment or

amounts spent for grants to individuals, employee matching gifts, loans, or foundation-administered programs.

17. The total dollar value of **set-asides** made by the foundation during the year. Although set-asides count as qualifying distributions toward the foundation's annual payout requirement, they are distinct from any amounts listed as grants paid.

18. The total amount and number of **grants made directly to or on behalf of individuals,** including scholarships, fellowships, awards, and medical payments. When supplied by the foundation, high, low, and average range are also indicated.

19. The dollar amount and number of **employee matching gifts** awarded, generally by company-sponsored foundations.

20. The total dollars expended for **programs administered by the foundation** and the number of foundation-administered programs. These programs can include museums or other institutions supported exclusively by the foundation, research programs administered by the foundation, etc.

21. The dollar amount and number of **loans** made to nonprofit organizations by the foundation. These can include program-related investments, emergency loans to help nonprofits that are waiting for grants or other income payments, etc. When supplied by the foundation, high, low, and average range are also indicated.

22. The number of **loans to individuals** and the total amount loaned. When supplied by the foundation, high, low, and average range are also indicated.

23. The monetary value and number of **in-kind gifts**.

24. The **purpose and activities,** in general terms, of the foundation. This statement reflects funding interests as expressed by the foundation or, if no foundation statement is available, an analysis of the actual grants awarded by the foundation during the most recent two-year period for which public records exist. Many foundations leave statements of purpose intentionally broad, indicating only the major program areas within which they fund. More specific areas of interest can often be found in the "Fields of Interest" section of the entry.

25. The **fields of interest** reflected in the foundation's giving program. The terminology used in this section conforms to the Foundation Center's Grants Classification System (GCS). The terms also provide access to foundation entries through the Subject Index at the back of the volume.

26. The **international giving interests** of the foundation.

27. The **type of support** (such as endowment funds, building/renovation, equipment, fellowships, etc.) offered by the foundation. Definitions of the terms used to describe the forms of support available are provided at the beginning of the Types of Support Index at the back of this volume.

28. Any stated **limitations** on the foundation's giving program, including geographic preferences, restrictions by subject focus or type of recipient, or specific types of support the foundation cannot provide. It is noted here if a foundation does not accept unsolicited applications.

29. **Publications** or other printed materials distributed by the foundation that describe its activities and giving program. These can include annual or multi-year reports, newsletters, corporate giving reports, informational brochures, grant lists, etc. It is also noted whether a foundation will send copies of its IRS information return (Form 990-PF) on request.

30. **Application information,** including the preferred form of application, the number of copies of proposals requested, application deadlines, frequency and dates of board meetings, and the general amount of time the foundation requires to notify applicants of the board's decision. Some foundations have indicated that their funds are currently committed to ongoing projects.

31. The names and titles of **officers, principal administrators, trustees, or directors,** and members of other governing bodies. An asterisk (*) following the individual's name indicates an officer who is also a trustee or director.

32. The number of professional and support **staff** employed by the foundation, and an indication of part-time or full-time status of these employees, as reported by the foundation.

33. **EIN:** the Employer Identification Number assigned to the foundation by the Internal Revenue Service for tax purposes. This number can be useful when ordering or searching for the foundation's annual information return, Form 990-PF.

34. A list of **selected grants**. Up to ten grants reported during a given fiscal year may be provided. Grants to individuals are not included.

INDEXES

Seven indexes to the descriptive entries are provided at the back of the book to assist grantseekers and other users of *The Foundation Directory:*

1. The **Index to Donors, Officers, Trustees** is an alphabetical list of individual and corporate donors, officers, and members of governing boards whose names appear in *The Foundation Directory* entries. Many grantseekers find this index helpful in determining whether current or prospective members of their own governing boards, alumni of their schools, or current contributors are affiliated with any foundations.

2. The **Geographic Index** references foundation entries by the state and city in which the foundation maintains its principal offices. The index includes "see also" references at the end of each state section to indicate foundations that have made substantial grants in that state but are located elsewhere. Foundations that award grants on a national, regional, or international basis are indicated in bold type. The remaining foundations generally limit their giving to the state or city in which they are located.

3. The **International Giving Index** provides access to foundations whose giving interests extend beyond the United States. A complete alphabetical list of countries, continents, and regions is provided at the beginning of the index. Under each country, continent, or region, entry numbers are listed by the state location and abbreviated

name of the foundation. Organizations whose programs benefit foreign countries should use this index to identify funders with similar geographic interests.

4. The **Types of Support Index** provides access to foundation entries by the specific types of support the foundation awards. A glossary of the forms of support listed appears at the beginning of the index. Under each type of support term, entry numbers are listed by the state location and abbreviated name of the foundation. Foundations that award grants on a national, regional, or international basis are indicated in bold type. When using this index, grantseekers should focus on foundations located in their own state that offer the specific type of support needed, or on foundations listed in bold type if their program has national impact.

5. The **Subject Index** provides access to the giving interests of foundations based on the "Fields of Interest" sections of their entries. The terminology in the index conforms to the Foundation Center's Grants Classification System (GCS). A complete alphabetical list of the subject headings in the current edition is provided at the beginning of the index as well as "see also" references to related subject areas included in this volume. Under each subject term, entry numbers are listed by the state location and abbreviated name of the foundation. As in the Types of Support Index, foundations that award grants on a national, regional, or international basis are indicated in bold type. Again, grantseekers should focus on foundations located in their own state that have shown an interest in their subject area, or on foundations listed in bold type if their program is national in scope.

6. The index of **Foundations New to the Edition** is a listing of foundations that appear in the current edition of *The Foundation Directory* but had not met criteria for inclusion in the previous edition. The descriptive entries for these foundations are highlighted with a star (☆).

7. The **Foundation Name Index** is an alphabetical list of all foundations appearing in the *Directory*. Former names of foundations appear with "see" references to the appropriate entry numbers. This index also provides references to Appendix A, which lists foundations that appeared in the previous edition but have since terminated or otherwise become ineligible for inclusion.

APPENDIXES

In addition to the descriptive entries and indexes, *The Foundation Directory* includes two appendixes. Appendix A lists foundations described in the previous edition of the *The Foundation Directory* that do not have entries in the current edition because they have terminated operations, merged with another foundation, ceased grantmaking, or changed their legal status. Appendix B lists those foundations that are excluded because they contribute only to a few specified beneficiaries or to the support of a single institution.

RESEARCHING FOUNDATIONS

Foundations receive many thousands of requests each year. Most of these requests are declined because there are never enough funds to go around or because the application clearly falls outside the foundation's fields of interest. Sometimes the qualifications of the staff are not well established; the budget or the means of evaluating the project may not be presented convincingly; or the organization may not have asked itself whether it is especially suited to make a contribution to the solution of the problem, whether it can provide the service proposed, or whether others are not already effectively engaged in the same activity.

The first step in researching foundation funding support, then, is to analyze your own program and organization to determine the need you plan to address, the audience you will serve, and the amount and type of support you need. Become familiar with the basic facts about foundations in general as well as how they operate. Consider other sources of funding, such as individual contributors, government grants, earned income possibilities, and so on. Although foundations are an important source of support for nonprofit organizations, their giving represents a relatively small percentage of the total philanthropic dollars contributed annually, and an even smaller percentage of the total when government grants and earned income are included.

Once you have determined the amount and type of support you need and the reasons why you are seeking foundation support, *The Foundation Directory* can help you to develop an initial list of foundations that might be interested in funding your project. In determining whether or not it is appropriate to approach a particular foundation with a grant request, keep in mind the following questions:

1. Has the foundation demonstrated a real commitment to funding in your subject area?

2. Does it seem likely that the foundation will make a grant in your geographic area?

3. Does the amount of money you are requesting fit within the foundation's grant range?

4. Does the foundation have any policy prohibiting grants for the type of support you are requesting?

5. Does the foundation prefer to make grants that cover the full cost of a project or does it favor projects where other foundations or funding sources share the cost?

6. What types of organizations does the foundation tend to support?

7. Does the foundation have specific application deadlines and procedures or does it review proposals continuously?

Some of these questions can be answered from the information provided in *The Foundation Directory,* but grantseekers will almost always want to consult a few additional resources before submitting a request for funding. If the foundation issues an annual report, application guidelines, or other printed materials describing its program, it is advisable to obtain copies and study them carefully before preparing your proposal. If the foundation has a Web site, studying it is essential. The foundation's annual information return (Form 990-PF) includes a list of all grants paid by the foundation, as well as basic data about its finances, officers, and giving policies.

THE FOUNDATION DIRECTORY PART 2

The Foundation Directory Part 2 provides information on the second tier of U.S. grantmaking foundations, those among the next 10,000 largest annual givers. *The Foundation Directory Part 2* serves as a guide to smaller but significant grantmakers whose charitable giving often supports local organizations. Together *The Foundation Directory* and *The Foundation Directory Part 2* constitute the standard reference work for information on 20,000 of the largest active grantmaking foundations in the United States.

THE FOUNDATION DIRECTORY SUPPLEMENT

The Foundation Directory Supplement, published six months after *The Foundation Directory* and *The Foundation Directory Part 2,* contains entries that have had substantial changes since the publication of those volumes. New information is highlighted in boldface type in the entries.

THE FOUNDATION 1000

The Foundation Center's annual publication, *The Foundation 1000,* describes in detail the 1,000 largest U.S. foundations, and, with the exception of publications issued directly by those foundations, provides the most complete source of information available on this group. *The Foundation Directory* foundations that are described more fully in *The Foundation 1000* are indicated by the symbol ▼ next to their entry. The Center also publishes a number of other reference tools that provide information on private philanthropy, as well as *Foundation Fundamentals,* a guidebook to funding research strategies. Copies of all Center print and electronic publications, as well as other relevant state and local foundation directories, are available for free examination at Foundation Center libraries and Cooperating Collections, which are listed at the end of this introduction.

GLOSSARY

The following list includes important terms used by grantmakers and grantseekers. A number of sources have been consulted in compiling this glossary, including *The Handbook on Private Foundations,* 3rd Edition, by David F. Freeman, John A. Edie, Jane C. Nober, and the Council on Foundations (Washington, DC, 2005); *The Law of Tax-Exempt Organizations,* 8th Edition, by Bruce R. Hopkins (Hoboken, NJ: John Wiley & Sons, 2003); and the *AFP Fund-Raising Dictionary,* (2003).

Annual Report: A *voluntary* report issued by a foundation or corporation that provides financial data and descriptions of grantmaking activities. Annual reports vary in format from simple typewritten documents listing the year's grants to detailed publications that provide substantial information about the grantmaking program.

Assets: The amount of capital or principal—money, stocks, bonds, real estate, or other resources—controlled by the foundation or corporate giving program. Generally, assets are invested and the income is used to make grants.

Beneficiary: In philanthropic terms, the donee or grantee receiving funds from a foundation or corporate giving program is the beneficiary, although society benefits as well. Foundations whose legal terms of establishment restrict their giving to one or more named beneficiaries are not included in this publication.

Bricks and Mortar: An informal term for grants for buildings or construction projects.

Capital Support: Funds provided for endowment purposes, buildings, construction, or equipment, and including, for example, grants for "bricks and mortar."

Challenge Grant: A grant awarded that will be paid only if the donee organization is able to raise additional funds from another source(s). Challenge grants are often used to stimulate giving from other donors. (*See also* **Matching Grant**)

Community Foundation: A 501(c)(3) organization that makes grants for charitable purposes in a specific community or region. Funds are usually derived from many donors and held in an endowment independently administered; income earned by the endowment is then used to make grants. Although a few community foundations may be classified by the IRS as private foundations, most are classified as public charities eligible for maximum income tax-deductible contributions from the general public. (*See also* **501(c)(3); Public Charity**)

Community Fund: An organized community program which makes annual appeals to the general public for funds that are usually not retained in an endowment but are used for the ongoing operational support of local social and health service agencies. (*See also* **Federated Giving Program**)

Company-Sponsored Foundation (also referred to as Corporate Foundation): A private foundation whose grant funds are derived primarily from the contributions of a profit-making business organization. The company-sponsored foundation may maintain close ties with the donor company, but it is an independent organization with its own endowment and is subject to the same rules and regulations as other private foundations. (*See also* **Private Foundation**)

Cooperative Venture: A joint effort between or among two or more grantmakers (including foundations, corporations, and government agencies). Partners may share in funding responsibilities or contribute information and technical resources.

Corporate Giving Program: A grantmaking program established and administered within a profit-making company. Corporate giving programs do not have a separate endowment and their annual grant totals are generally more directly related to current profits. They are not subject to the same reporting requirements as private foundations. Some companies make charitable contributions through both a corporate giving program and a company-sponsored foundation.

Distribution Committee: The board responsible for making grant decisions. For community foundations, it is intended to be broadly representative of the community served by the foundation.

Donee: The recipient of a grant. (Also known as the grantee or the beneficiary.)

Donor: The individual or organization that makes a grant or contribution. (Also known as the grantor.)

Employee Matching Gift: A contribution to a charitable organization by a company employee that is matched by a similar contribution from the employer. Many corporations have employee matching gift programs in higher education that stimulate their employees to give to the college or university of their choice.

Endowment: Funds intended to be kept permanently and invested to provide income for continued support of an organization.

Expenditure Responsibility: In general, when a private foundation makes a grant to an organization that is not classified by the IRS as a "public charity," the foundation is required by law to provide some assurance that the funds will be used for the intended charitable purposes. Special reports on such grants must be filed with the IRS. Most grantee organizations are public charities and many foundations do not make "expenditure responsibility" grants.

Family Foundation: An independent private foundation whose funds are derived from members of a single family. Family members often serve as officers or board members of the foundation and have a significant role in grantmaking decisions. (See also **Operating Foundation; Private Foundation; Public Charity**)

Federated Giving Program: A joint fundraising effort usually administered by a nonprofit "umbrella" organization which in turn distributes contributed funds to several nonprofit agencies. United Way and community chests or funds, the United Jewish Appeal and other religious appeals, the United Negro College Fund, and joint arts councils are examples of federated giving programs. (See also **Community Fund**)

501(c)(3): The section of the Internal Revenue code that defines nonprofit, charitable (as broadly defined), tax-exempt organizations; 501(c)(3) organizations are further defined as public charities, private operating foundations, and private non-operating foundations. (See also **Operating Foundation; Private Foundation; Public Charity**)

Form 990-PF: The annual information return that all private foundations must submit to the IRS each year and which is also filed with appropriate state officials. The form requires information on the foundation's assets, income, operating expenses, contributions and grants, paid staff and salaries, program funding areas, grantmaking guidelines and restrictions, and grant application procedures.

General Purpose Foundation: An independent private foundation that awards grants in many different fields of interest. (See also **Special Purpose Foundation**)

General Purpose Grant: A grant made to further the general purpose or work of an organization, rather than for a specific purpose or project. (See also **Operating Support Grant**)

Grantee Financial Report: A report detailing how grant funds were used by an organization. Many corporations require this kind of report from grantees. A financial report generally includes a listing of all expenditures from grant funds as well as an overall organizational financial report covering revenue and expenses, assets and liabilities.

Grassroots Fundraising: Efforts to raise money from individuals or groups from the local community on a broad basis. Usually an organization's own constituents— people who live in the neighborhood served or clients of the agency's services—are the sources of these funds. Grassroots fundraising activities include membership drives, raffles, auctions, benefits, and a range of other activities.

Independent Foundation: A grantmaking organization usually classified by the IRS as a private foundation. Independent foundations may also be known as family foundations, general purpose foundations, special purpose foundations, or private non-operating foundations. The Foundation Center defines independent foundations and company-sponsored foundations separately; however, federal law normally classifies both as private, non-operating foundations subject to the same rules and requirements. (See also **Private Foundation**)

In-Kind Contributions: Contributions of equipment, supplies, or other property as distinguished from monetary grants. Some organizations may also donate space or staff time as an in-kind contribution.

Matching Grant: A grant that is made to match funds provided by another donor. (See also **Challenge Grant; Employee Matching Gift**)

Operating Foundation: A 501(c)(3) organization classified by the IRS as a private foundation whose primary purpose is to conduct research, social welfare, or other programs determined by its governing body or establishment charter. Some grants may be made, but the sum is generally small relative to the funds used for the foundation's own programs. (See also **501(c)(3)**)

Operating Support Grant: A grant to cover the regular personnel, administrative, and other expenses of an existing program or project. (See also **General Purpose Grant**)

Payout Requirement: The minimum amount that private foundations are required to expend for charitable purposes (includes grants and, within certain limits, the administrative cost of making grants). In general, a private foundation must meet or exceed an annual payout requirement of five percent of the average market value of the foundation's assets.

Private Foundation: A nongovernmental, nonprofit organization with funds (usually from a single source, such as an individual, family, or corporation) and program managed by its own trustees or directors that was established to maintain or aid social, educational, religious or other charitable activities serving the common welfare, primarily through the making of grants. "Private foundation" also means an organization that is tax-exempt under code section 501(c)(3) and is classified by the IRS as a private foundation as defined in the code. The code definition usually, but not always, identifies a foundation with the characteristics first described. (See also **501(c)(3); Public Charity**)

Program Amount: Funds that are expended to support a particular program administered internally by the foundation or corporate giving program.

Program Officer: A staff member of a foundation who reviews grant proposals and processes applications for the board of trustees. Only a small percentage of foundations have program officers.

Program-Related Investment (PRI): A loan or other investment (as distinguished from a grant) made by a foundation or corporate giving program to another organization for a project related to the grantmaker's stated charitable purpose and interests. Program-related investments are often made from a revolving fund; the foundation generally expects to receive its money back with interest or some other form of return at less than current market rates, and it then becomes available for further program-related investments.

Proposal: A written application, often with supporting documents, submitted to a foundation or corporate giving program in requesting a grant. Preferred procedures and formats vary. Consult published guidelines.

Public Charity: In general, an organization that is tax-exempt under code section 501(c)(3) and is classified by the IRS as a public charity and not a private foundation. Public charities generally derive their funding or support primarily from the general public in carrying out their social, educational, religious, or other charitable activities serving the common welfare. Some public charities engage in grantmaking activities, although most engage in direct service or other tax-exempt activities. Public charities are eligible for maximum income tax-deductible contributions from the public and are not subject to the same rules and restrictions as private foundations. Some are also referred to as "public foundations" or "publicly supported organizations" and may use the term "foundation" in their names. (*See also* **501(c)(3); Private Foundation**)

Qualifying Distributions: Expenditures of private foundations used to satisfy the annual payout requirement. These can include grants, reasonable administrative expenses, set-asides, loans and program-related investments, and amounts paid to acquire assets used directly in carrying out exempt purposes.

Query Letter: A brief letter outlining an organization's activities and its request for funding sent to a foundation or corporation to determine whether it would be appropriate to submit a full grant proposal. Many grantmakers prefer to be contacted in this way before receiving a full proposal.

RFP: Request For Proposal. When the government issues a new contract or grant program, it sends out RFPs to agencies that might be qualified to participate. The RFP lists project specifications and application procedures. A few foundations occasionally use RFPs in specific fields, but most prefer to consider proposals that are initiated by applicants.

Seed Money: A grant or contribution used to start a new project or organization. Seed grants may cover salaries and other operating expenses of a new project.

Set-Asides: Funds set aside by a foundation for a specific purpose or project that are counted as qualifying distributions toward the foundation's annual payout requirement. Amounts for the project must be paid within five years of the first set-aside.

Special Purpose Foundation: A private foundation that focuses its grantmaking activities in one or a few special areas of interest. For example, a foundation may only award grants in the area of cancer research or child development. (*See also* **General Purpose Foundation**)

Technical Assistance: Operational or management assistance given to nonprofit organizations. It can include fundraising assistance, budgeting and financial planning, program planning, legal advice, marketing, and other aids to management. Assistance may be offered directly by a foundation or corporate staff member, or be offered in the form of a grant to pay for the services of an outside consultant. (*See also* **In-Kind Contributions**)

Trustee: A member of a governing board. A foundation's board of trustees meets to review grant proposals and make decisions. Often also referred to as a "director" or "board member."

TABLE 5. 100 Largest Foundations by Total Giving

Name	Total Giving	Assets	Fiscal Date	Name	Total Giving	Assets	Fiscal Date
1. Bill & Melinda Gates Foundation	$1,356,250,292	$29,153,508,829	12/31/05	46. Community Foundation Silicon Valley	$75,366,593	$ 760,821,244	06/30/05
2. The Bristol-Myers Squibb Patient Assistance Foundation, Inc.	582,106,194	2,208,209	12/31/05	47. Richard King Mellon Foundation	74,356,247	1,882,031,732	12/31/05
3. Merck Patient Assistance Program, Inc.	533,118,219	0	12/31/05	48. The James Irvine Foundation	73,123,056	1,610,480,320	12/31/05
4. The Ford Foundation	516,907,177	11,615,906,693	09/30/05	49. GE Foundation	70,635,496	3,677,622	12/31/05
5. Lilly Endowment Inc.	427,465,199	8,360,760,584	12/31/05	50. Donald W. Reynolds Foundation	69,203,364	1,204,806,991	12/31/05
6. Janssen Ortho Patient Assistance Foundation, Inc.	387,671,696	5,858,833	12/31/05	51. Citigroup Foundation	68,436,019	64,789,440	12/31/04
7. The Robert Wood Johnson Foundation	372,500,000	9,359,361,000	12/31/05	52. The Brown Foundation, Inc.	68,356,805	1,223,019,722	06/30/06
				53. The San Francisco Foundation	68,100,000	883,443,000	06/30/06
8. The William and Flora Hewlett Foundation	319,916,093	7,336,131,000	12/31/05	54. The Cleveland Foundation	66,421,855	1,716,136,165	12/31/05
9. The Annenberg Foundation	273,414,830	2,539,268,854	06/30/06	55. The Columbus Foundation and Affiliated Organizations	65,626,215	850,089,853	12/31/05
10. W. K. Kellogg Foundation	262,809,343	7,799,270,734	08/31/06	56. W. M. Keck Foundation	65,350,257	1,333,252,000	12/31/05
11. Wyeth Pharmaceutical Assistance	247,184,612	0	12/31/05	57. The Wells Fargo Foundation	65,007,124	554,108,137	12/31/05
12. Gordon and Betty Moore Foundation	218,758,756	5,308,627,945	12/31/05	58. The William Penn Foundation	64,641,331	1,253,208,618	12/31/05
13. Aventis Pharmaceuticals Health Care Foundation	217,845,821	0	12/31/05	59. Boston Foundation, Inc.	63,914,314	769,807,869	06/30/06
				60. ExxonMobil Foundation	63,660,965	110,612,415	12/31/05
14. The Andrew W. Mellon Foundation	199,340,000	5,586,112,000	12/31/05	61. Doris Duke Charitable Foundation	62,691,247	1,920,145,122	12/31/05
15. John D. and Catherine T. MacArthur Foundation	194,500,000	5,490,449,000	12/31/05	62. Koret Foundation	61,855,026	247,754,640	12/31/05
16. Genentech Access To Care Foundation	194,079,971	0	12/31/05	63. Verizon Foundation	61,834,820	382,799,097	12/31/05
17. The Roche Patient Assistance Foundation	174,463,465	0	12/31/05	64. Alfred P. Sloan Foundation	61,165,933	1,581,350,875	12/31/05
18. The Annie E. Casey Foundation	173,118,671	3,152,516,760	12/31/05	65. The Judith Rothschild Foundation	60,855,837	27,524,343	12/31/05
19. The Starr Foundation	159,130,952	3,344,801,753	12/31/05	66. Communities Foundation of Texas, Inc.	59,931,000	699,873,000	06/30/06
20. Walton Family Foundation, Inc.	157,989,927	1,328,793,250	12/31/05	67. The Susan Thompson Buffett Foundation	59,683,343	318,521,200	12/31/05
21. Wal-Mart Foundation	154,537,406	18,881,075	01/31/05	68. Foundation for the Carolinas	59,551,103	424,272,918	12/31/05
22. The California Endowment	153,242,789	3,729,571,524	02/28/05	69. Johnson & Johnson Family of Companies Contribution Fund	59,399,325	74,824,234	12/31/05
23. The David and Lucile Packard Foundation	150,115,645	5,788,480,930	12/31/05	70. The Wachovia Foundation, Inc.	57,363,628	70,227,017	12/31/05
24. The Kresge Foundation	149,831,151	3,032,422,497	12/31/05	71. The JPMorgan Chase Foundation	56,786,083	122,701,486	12/31/04
25. Boehringer Ingelheim Cares Foundation, Inc.	147,996,554	18,549,163	12/31/05	72. The Wallace Foundation	56,665,282	1,447,299,661	12/31/05
26. Lilly Cares Foundation, Inc.	146,701,709	1,377	12/31/04	73. The Michael and Susan Dell Foundation	56,238,527	1,226,020,349	12/31/05
27. Greater Kansas City Community Foundation	140,702,000	1,013,035,000	12/31/05	74. Omaha Community Foundation	53,598,735	393,005,266	12/31/05
28. The New York Community Trust	136,970,963	1,897,604,374	12/31/05	75. The Robert W. Wilson Charitable Trust	52,452,518	166,865,173	12/31/05
29. The Duke Endowment	125,629,926	2,708,834,085	12/31/05	76. Marin Community Foundation	51,649,386	1,125,930,427	06/30/06
30. The Bank of America Charitable Foundation, Inc.	123,287,819	41,742,644	12/31/05	77. Houston Endowment Inc.	51,642,096	1,512,185,118	12/31/05
31. Charles Stewart Mott Foundation	113,334,381	2,480,562,766	12/31/05	78. Ewing Marion Kauffman Foundation	50,603,728	1,860,797,344	06/30/05
32. The Rockefeller Foundation	111,083,354	3,417,557,613	12/31/05	79. Merck-Schering Plough Patient Assistance Program	48,702,436	0	12/31/05
33. Greater Houston Community Foundation	109,144,475	199,126,686	12/31/05	80. Lumina Foundation for Education, Inc.	48,457,322	1,235,598,231	12/31/05
34. Betty and George Kaiser Foundation	105,657,775	609,348	12/31/05	81. The California Wellness Foundation	48,410,903	1,072,427,215	12/31/05
35. Robert W. Woodruff Foundation, Inc.	101,030,268	1,950,691,385	12/31/05	82. AT&T Foundation	47,556,509	194,083,201	12/31/05
36. The Harry and Jeanette Weinberg Foundation, Inc.	93,630,682	2,154,005,108	02/28/06	83. The Baltimore Community Foundation	46,272,563	166,036,468	12/31/05
37. John S. and James L. Knight Foundation	92,577,162	2,071,507,291	12/31/05	84. Avon Foundation	45,974,681	52,373,251	12/31/05
38. Peninsula Community Foundation	92,331,777	614,336,446	12/31/05	85. The Seattle Foundation	45,948,620	473,444,919	12/31/05
39. California Community Foundation	91,367,805	1,152,601,808	06/30/06	86. Open Society Institute	45,565,966	858,935,162	12/31/05
40. The Community Foundation for the National Capital Region	91,235,382	346,982,198	03/31/06	87. Daniels Fund	44,947,978	1,090,055,954	12/31/05
41. Carnegie Corporation of New York	91,053,489	2,244,208,247	09/30/05	88. John Templeton Foundation	44,321,264	1,080,335,362	12/31/05
42. The McKnight Foundation	90,710,176	2,050,595,000	12/31/05	89. Genzyme Charitable Foundation, Inc.	43,689,150	0	12/31/05
43. Community Foundation for Greater Atlanta, Inc.	89,391,237	638,817,268	06/30/06	90. The San Diego Foundation	43,516,000	484,163,000	06/30/06
				91. Skirball Foundation	43,269,726	230,578,263	12/31/05
				92. Intel Foundation	43,102,949	77,744,647	12/31/05
44. Ford Motor Company Fund	77,916,903	107,283,149	12/31/04	93. The Lenfest Foundation, Inc.	42,717,807	122,341,875	06/30/05
45. The Chicago Community Trust	75,988,536	1,503,994,247	09/30/05	94. Freeman Foundation	42,067,148	1,105,466,120	12/31/05
				95. The Merck Company Foundation	41,596,595	124,449,548	12/31/05
				96. The Ahmanson Foundation	41,218,405	938,348,497	10/31/05
				97. Yawkey Foundation II	41,114,600	458,492,742	12/31/05
				98. Broad Foundation	40,992,554	835,659,229	12/31/05
				99. Weingart Foundation	40,561,794	839,604,507	06/30/06
				100. The Oregon Community Foundation	40,478,757	850,034,138	12/31/05

ABBREVIATIONS

The following lists contain standard abbreviations frequently used by the Foundation Center's editorial staff. These abbreviations are used most frequently in the addresses of grantmakers and the titles of corporate and grantmaker officers.

STREET ABBREVIATIONS

1st	First*	N.E.	Northeast
2nd	Second*	N.W.	Northwest
3rd	Third*	No.	Number
Apt.	Apartment	Pkwy.	Parkway
Ave.	Avenue	Pl.	Place
Bldg.	Building	Plz.	Plaza
Blvd.	Boulevard	R.R.	Rural Route
Cir.	Circle	Rd.	Road
Ct.	Court	Rm.	Room
Ctr.	Center	Rte.	Route
Dept.	Department	S.	South
Dr.	Drive	S.E.	Southeast
E.	East	S.W.	Southwest
Expwy.	Expressway	Sq.	Square
Fl.	Floor	St.	Saint
Ft.	Fort	St.	Street
Hwy.	Highway	Sta.	Station
Ln.	Lane	Ste.	Suite
M.C.	Mail Code	Terr.	Terrace
M.S.	Mail Stop	Tpke.	Turnpike
Mt.	Mount	Univ.	University
N.	North	W.	West

*Numerics used always

TWO LETTER STATE AND TERRITORY ABBREVIATIONS

AK	Alaska	NC	North Carolina
AL	Alabama	ND	North Dakota
AR	Arkansas	NE	Nebraska
AZ	Arizona	NH	New Hampshire
CA	California	NJ	New Jersey
CO	Colorado	NM	New Mexico
CT	Connecticut	NV	Nevada
DC	District of Columbia	NY	New York
DE	Delaware	OH	Ohio
FL	Florida	OK	Oklahoma
GA	Georgia	OR	Oregon
HI	Hawaii	PA	Pennsylvania
IA	Iowa	PR	Puerto Rico
ID	Idaho	RI	Rhode Island
IL	Illinois	SC	South Carolina
IN	Indiana	SD	South Dakota
KS	Kansas	TN	Tennessee
KY	Kentucky	TX	Texas
LA	Louisiana	UT	Utah
MA	Massachusetts	VA	Virginia
MD	Maryland	VI	Virgin Islands
ME	Maine	VT	Vermont ·
MI	Michigan	WA	Washington
MN	Minnesota	WI	Wisconsin
MO	Missouri	WV	West Virginia
MS	Mississippi	WY	Wyoming
MT	Montana		

ABBREVIATIONS USED FOR OFFICER TITLES

Acctg.	Accounting	Govt.	Government
ADM.	Admiral	Hon.	Judge
Admin.	Administration	Inf.	Information
Admin.	Administrative	Int.	Internal
Admin.	Administrator	Intl.	International
Adv.	Advertising	Jr.	Junior
Amb.	Ambassador	Lt.	Lieutenant
Assn.	Association	Ltd.	Limited
Assoc(s).	Associate(s)	Maj.	Major
Asst.	Assistant	Mfg.	Manufacturing
Bro.	Brother	Mgmt.	Management
C.A.O.	Chief Accounting Officer	Mgr.	Manager
C.A.O.	Chief Administration Officer	Mktg.	Marketing
		Msgr.	Monsignor
C.E.O.	Chief Executive Officer	Mt.	Mount
C.F.O.	Chief Financial Officer	Natl.	National
C.I.O.	Chief Information Officer	Off.	Officer
		Opers.	Operations
C.I.O.	Chief Investment Officer	Org.	Organization
		Plan.	Planning
C.O.O.	Chief Operating Officer	Pres.	President
Capt.	Captain	Prog(s).	Program(s)
Chair.	Chairperson	RADM.	Rear Admiral
Col.	Colonel	Rels.	Relations
Comm.	Committee	Rep.	Representative
Comms.	Communications	Rev.	Reverend
Commo.	Commodore	Rt. Rev.	Right Reverend
Compt.	Comptroller	Secy.	Secretary
Cont.	Controller	Secy.-Treas.	Secretary-Treasurer
Contrib(s).	Contribution(s)		
Coord.	Coordinator	Sen.	Senator
Corp.	Corporate, Corporation	Soc.	Society
Co(s).	Company(s)	Sr.	Senior
Dep.	Deputy	Sr.	Sister
Devel.	Development	Supvr.	Supervisor
Dir.	Director	Svc(s).	Service(s)
Distrib(s).	Distribution(s)	Tech.	Technology
Div.	Division	Tr.	Trustee
Exec.	Executive	Treas.	Treasurer
Ext.	External	Univ.	University
Fdn.	Foundation	V.P.	Vice President
Fr.	Father	VADM.	Vice Admiral
Genl.	General	Vice-Chair.	Vice Chairperson
Gov.	Governor		

ADDITIONAL ABBREVIATIONS

E-mail	Electronic mail
FAX	Facsimile
LOI	Letter of Inquiry
RFP	Request for Proposals
SASE	Self-Addressed Stamped Envelope
TDD, TTY	Telecommunication Device for the Deaf
Tel.	Telephone
URL	Uniform Resource Locator (web site)

Jan.	January
Feb.	February
Mar.	March
Apr.	April
Aug.	August
Sept.	September
Oct.	October
Nov.	November
Dec.	December

RESOURCES OF THE FOUNDATION CENTER

The Foundation Center is a national service organization founded and supported by foundations to provide a single authoritative source of information on foundation and corporate giving. The Center's programs are designed to help grantseekers select those funders that may be most interested in their projects from more than 88,000 active U.S. grantmakers. Among its primary activities toward this end are offering searchable databases online and on CD-ROM as well as publishing print directories covering foundation and corporate philanthropy; disseminating information on grantmaking, grantseeking, and related subjects through its site on the internet; offering educational courses and workshops; and maintaining a network of regional centers and Cooperating Collections nationwide.

Databases and publications of the Foundation Center are the primary working tools of every serious grantseeker. They are also used by grantmakers, scholars, journalists, and legislators—in short, by anyone seeking any type of factual information on philanthropy. All private foundations and a significant number of corporate grantmakers and public charities actively engaged in grantmaking, regardless of size or geographic location, are included in one or more of the Center's databases or publications.

For those who wish to access information on grantmakers and their grants electronically, *Foundation Directory Online* offers five plans to meet the needs of grantseekers—from *Basic,* featuring profiles of the 10,000 largest U.S. foundations to *Professional,* our most comprehensive option with more than 88,000 funders, nearly 800,000 grants, and 360,000+ IRS 990s. The Center also issues *FC Search: The Foundation Center's Database on CD-ROM* containing the full universe of more than 88,000 foundations, grantmaking public charities, corporate givers and more than 350,000 recent grants.

Foundation Center print publications include directories that describe specific funders, characterizing their program interests and providing fiscal and personnel data; grants indexes that list and classify by subject recent foundation and corporate awards; fundraising and nonprofit management guides; and research reports on the field.

In addition, the Center's award-winning web site features a wide array of free information about the philanthropic community. The Foundation Center's electronic and print products may be ordered from the Foundation Center, 79 Fifth Avenue, New York, NY 10003-3076, or online at our web site. For more information about any aspect of the Center's products or services or for the name of the Center's library collection nearest you, call (800) 424-9836, or visit us on the web at foundationcenter.org.

ONLINE DATABASES

FOUNDATION DIRECTORY ONLINE SUBSCRIPTION PLANS

Foundation Directory Online Basic
Search for foundation funding prospects from among the nation's largest 10,000 foundations and search the index of more than 70,000 names of trustees, officers, and donors. Perform searches using up to twelve search fields.
MONTHLY SUBSCRIPTIONS START AT $19.95 PER MONTH
ANNUAL SUBSCRIPTIONS START AT $195 PER YEAR

Foundation Directory Online Plus
Plus service allows users to search the 10,000 largest foundations in the U.S. and the index of more than 70,000 names of trustees, officers, and donors—plus 790,000+ grants awarded by major foundations.
MONTHLY SUBSCRIPTIONS START AT $29.95 PER MONTH
ANNUAL SUBSCRIPTIONS START AT $295 PER YEAR

Foundation Directory Online Premium
In addition to featuring 20,000 of the nation's large and mid-sized foundations and an index of more than 120,000 names of trustees, officers, and donors—*Premium* service includes a searchable database of 880,000+ grants awarded by major U.S. foundations.
MONTHLY SUBSCRIPTIONS START AT $59.95 PER MONTH
ANNUAL SUBSCRIPTIONS START AT $595 PER YEAR

Foundation Directory Online Platinum
Search our entire universe of U.S. foundations, corporate giving programs, and grantmaking public charities—more than 88,000 funders in all. In addition to more funders, you'll get access to more in-depth data and an index of more than 400,000 names of trustees, officers, and donors. This service also includes a searchable file of over 900,000 grants awarded by the largest U.S. foundations.
MONTHLY SUBSCRIPTIONS START AT $149.95 PER MONTH
ANNUAL SUBSCRIPTIONS START AT $995 PER YEAR

Foundation Directory Online Professional
Foundation Directory Online Professional provides top-tier intelligence on grantmakers and their grants. *Professional* features our most comprehensive database, updated weekly: 88,000 funders, over 900,000 grants, and 400,000 trustee, officer, and donor names—fully-indexed—plus a fully Keyword-searchable database of 360,000+ 990s for grantmaking organizations, and unique funder portfolios including foundation news, RFPs, key staff affiliations, and full-color grant distribution charts.
MONTHLY SUBSCRIPTIONS START AT $179.95 PER MONTH
ANNUAL SUBSCRIPTIONS START AT $1,295 PER YEAR

PLEASE VISIT FCONLINE.FOUNDATIONCENTER.ORG TO SUBSCRIBE.

Corporate Giving Online

Find out who's making corporate grants and in-kind donations. Search profiles of more than 3,700 companies, 3,000 company-sponsored foundations, 1,400 direct giving programs, and descriptions of nearly 125,000 grants. Updated weekly, users may choose from 30 search fields in three separate search screens—plus, free text search to find any word or phrase in a record.

MONTHLY SUBSCRIPTIONS START AT $59.95 PER MONTH
ANNUAL SUBSCRIPTIONS START AT $595 PER YEAR

Foundation Grants to Individuals Online

Foundation Grants to Individuals Online features more than 6,200 foundation funding sources for individual grantseekers in education, research, arts and culture, or for special needs. Updated quarterly, users may choose from up to nine different search fields to discover prospective funders. Foundation records contain current, authoritative data on the funder, including the name, address, and contact information; fields of interest; types of support; application information; and descriptions of funding opportunities for individual grantseekers.

ONE-MONTH SUBSCRIPTION: $9.95
THREE-MONTH SUBSCRIPTION: $26.95
ANNUAL SUBSCRIPTION: $99.95
PLEASE VISIT GTIONLINE.FOUNDATIONCENTER.ORG TO SUBSCRIBE.

CD-ROMs

FC SEARCH: The Foundation Center's Database on CD-ROM, Version 11.0

The Foundation Center's comprehensive database of grantmakers and their associated grants can be accessed in this fully searchable CD-ROM format. *FC Search* contains more than 88,000 grantmaker records, including all known active foundations and corporate giving programs in the United States. It also includes more than 350,000 newly reported grants from the largest foundations and the names of more than 400,000 trustees, officers, and donors which can be quickly linked to their foundation affiliations. Users can also link from *FC Search* to the Web sites of 7,900+ grantmakers and 2,900+ corporations.

Grantseekers and other researchers may select multiple criteria and create customized prospect lists that can be printed or saved. Basic or Advanced search modes and special search options enable users to make searches as broad or as specific as required. Up to 21 different criteria may be selected:

- grantmaker name
- grantmaker type
- grantmaker city
- grantmaker state
- geographic focus
- fields of interest
- type of support
- total assets
- total giving
- trustees, officers, and donors
- establishment date
- corporate name
- corporate location
- recipient name
- recipient city
- recipient state
- recipient type
- subjects
- grant amount
- year grant authorized
- text search

FC Search is a user friendly, yet sophisticated fundraising research tool. It has been developed with both the novice and experienced researcher in mind. Assistance is available through Online Help, a *User Manual* that accompanies *FC Search,* as well as through a free User Hotline.

APRIL 2007 / STANDALONE (SINGLE USER) VERSION: $1,195
LOCAL AREA NETWORK (2–8 USERS IN ONE BUILDING) VERSION: $1,895
ADDITIONAL COPIES OF USER MANUAL: $19.95
Prices include fall 2007 Update disk plus one User Manual.

DIRECTORY OF MISSOURI GRANTMAKERS ON CD-ROM

This CD-ROM provides a comprehensive, searchable database of grantmakers in the state or that have an interest in Missouri nonprofits—more than 1,400 foundations, corporate giving programs and public charities—from the largest grantmakers to local family foundations. Missouri nonprofit fundraisers can facilitate their funding research with entries that include giving amounts, fields of interest, purpose statements, selected grants, application guidelines, and contact information.

JUNE 2007 / ISBN 1-59542-157-2 / $75

GUIDE TO GREATER WASHINGTON D.C. GRANTMAKERS ON CD-ROM, Version 5.0

Compiled with the assistance of Washington Grantmakers, this CD-ROM covers more than 2,700 grantmakers located in the D.C. region or that have an interest in DC-area nonprofits. Users can generate prospect lists using 12 search fields. Grantmaker portraits feature crucial information: address, phone number, contact name, financial data, giving limitations, and names of key officials. For the first time, this CD-ROM features a separate searchable Grants database including summaries of close to 20,000 grants awarded to nonprofits in the Washington, DC area, or from funders in the region.

JULY 2007 / SINGLE USER / ISBN 1-59542-145-9/ $75

GUIDE TO OHIO GRANTMAKERS ON CD-ROM, Version 4.0

This CD-ROM features a searchable Foundation database, including profiles of more than 4,000 foundations with over 400 funders outside the state that award grants in Ohio. A separate searchable Grants database includes more than 30,000 summaries of grants awarded in Ohio nonprofits or from Ohio funders. Produced in collaboration with the Ohio Grantmakers Forum and the Ohio Association of Nonprofit Organizations.

MAY 2007 / ISBN 1-59542-134-3/ $125

SYSTEM CONFIGURATIONS FOR CD-ROM PRODUCTS

- Windows-based PC
- Microsoft 95 or above
- Pentium microprocessor
- 64mb memory

Internet access required to access grantmaker web sites and Foundation Center web site.

GRANTMAKER DIRECTORIES

THE FOUNDATION DIRECTORY, 2007 Edition

The Foundation Directory has been widely known and respected in the field for more than 40 years. It includes the latest information on the 10,000 largest U.S. foundations based on total giving.

Each *Directory* entry contains information on application procedures, giving limitations, types of support awarded, the publications of each foundation, and foundation staff. In addition, each entry features such vital data as the grantmaker's giving interests, financial data, grant amounts, address, and telephone number. This edition includes more than 52,000 selected grants. The Foundation Center works closely with foundations to ensure the accuracy and timeliness of the information provided.

The *Directory* includes indexes by foundation name; subject areas of interest; names of donors, officers, and trustees; geographic location; international interests; types of support awarded; and grantmakers new to the volume. Also included are analyses of the foundation community by geography, asset and grant size, and the different foundation types.

APRIL 2007 / ISBN 1-59542-124-6 / $215 / PUBLISHED ANNUALLY

THE FOUNDATION DIRECTORY PART 2, 2007 Edition

The Foundation Directory Part 2 brings you the same thorough coverage for the next largest set of 10,000 foundations. It includes *Directory*-level information on mid-sized foundations, an important group of grantmakers responsible for millions of dollars in funding annually. Essential data on foundations is included along with more than 49,000 recently awarded foundation grants, providing an excellent overview of the foundations' giving interests. Quick access to foundation entries is facilitated by seven indexes, including foundation name; subject areas of interest; names of donors, officers, and trustees; geographic location; international interests; types of support awarded; and grantmakers new to the volume.
APRIL 2007 / ISBN 1-59542-125-4 / $185 / PUBLISHED ANNUALLY

THE FOUNDATION DIRECTORY SUPPLEMENT, 2007 Edition

The Foundation Directory Supplement provides new information on *Foundation Directory* and *Foundation Directory Part 2* grantmakers six months after those volumes are published. The *Supplement* ensures that users of the *Directory* and *Directory Part 2* always have the latest addresses, contact names, policy statements, application guidelines, and financial data for the foundations they're approaching for funding.
SEPTEMBER 2007 / ISBN 1-59542-139-4/ $125 / PUBLISHED ANNUALLY

GUIDE TO FUNDING FOR INTERNATIONAL AND FOREIGN PROGRAMS, 8th Edition

The *Guide to Funding for International and Foreign Programs* covers more than 1,400 grantmakers interested in funding projects with an international focus, both within the U.S. and abroad. Program areas covered include international relief, disaster assistance, human rights, civil liberties, community development, education, and more. The volume also includes descriptions of more than 9,300 recently awarded grants.
MAY 2006 / ISBN 1-59542-088-6 / $125

GUIDE TO U.S. FOUNDATIONS, THEIR TRUSTEES, OFFICERS, AND DONORS, 2007 Edition

This fundraising reference tool provides fundraisers with current, accurate information on more than 73,000 private and community foundations in the U.S. The three-volume set also includes a master list of the names of the people who establish, oversee, and manage those institutions so that fundraisers can discover the philanthropic connections of current donors, board members, volunteers, and prominent families in their geographic area. Each entry includes asset and giving amounts as well as geographic limitations, allowing fundraisers to quickly determine whether or not to pursue a particular grant source.

The *Guide to U.S. Foundations* is the only source of published data on thousands of local foundations. (It includes over 50,000 grantmakers not covered in other print publications.) Each entry also tells you whether you can find more extensive information on the grantmaker in another Foundation Center reference work.
APRIL 2007/ 1-59542-126-2 / $395 / PUBLISHED ANNUALLY

THE FOUNDATION 1000, 2006/2007 Edition

The Foundation 1000 provides access to extensive and accurate information on 1,000 of the largest foundations in the country. *Foundation 1000* grantmakers hold over $320 billion in assets and awarded over 200,000 grants worth over $18 billion to nonprofit organizations nationwide in the most current year of record.
The Foundation 1000 provides thorough analyses of 1,000 of the largest foundations and their grant programs, including all the data fundraisers need when applying for grants from these top-level foundations. Each multi-page foundation profile features a full foundation portrait, a detailed breakdown of the foundation's grant programs, and extensive lists of recently awarded foundation grants.

Five indexes target potential funders in a variety of ways: by subject field, type of support, geographic location, international giving, and the names of foundation officers, donors, and trustees.
OCTOBER 2006 / ISBN 1-59542-103-3 / $295 / PUBLISHED ANNUALLY

NATIONAL DIRECTORY OF CORPORATE GIVING, 12th Edition

The *National Directory of Corporate Giving* offers authoritative information on over 4,300 company-sponsored foundations, grantmaking public charities, and direct corporate giving programs. It features detailed portraits of over 3,000 company-sponsored foundations and grantmaking public charities plus nearly 1,400 direct corporate giving programs.

Fundraisers will find essential information on these corporate grantmakers, including application information, key personnel, types of support generally awarded, giving limitations, financial data, and purpose and activities statements. Also included in the 12th Edition are more than 7,500 selected grants, providing the best indication of a grantmaker's funding priorities by identifying nonprofits it has already funded. The volume also provides data on the companies that sponsor foundations, grantmaking public charities, and direct-giving programs. Each entry gives the company's name and address, a listing of its types of business, its financial data (complete with *Forbes* and *Fortune* ratings), a listing of its subsidiaries, divisions, plants, and offices, and a charitable-giving statement.

The *National Directory of Corporate Giving* features an extensive bibliography to guide you to further research on corporate funding. Seven essential indexes target funding prospects by geographic region; international giving; types of support; subject area; officers, donors, and trustees; types of business; and corporation and corporate grantmaker name.
AUGUST 2006/ ISBN 1-59542-098-3 / $195 / PUBLISHED ANNUALLY

FOUNDATION GRANTS TO INDIVIDUALS, 16th Edition

The only publication devoted entirely to foundation grant opportunities for qualified individual applicants, the 16th Edition of this volume features more than 6,000 entries, all of which profile grantmaker giving to individuals. Entries include grantmaker addresses and telephone numbers, financial data, giving limitations, and application guidelines. This volume will save individual grantseekers countless hours of research. Indexes include:

- ◆ Geographic Focus
- ◆ International Focus
- ◆ Company Name
- ◆ Specific Schools
- ◆ Type of Support
- ◆ Subject
- ◆ Grantmaker Name

JULY 2007 / ISBN 1-59542-137-8 / $65 / PUBLISHED ANNUALLY

GRANT GUIDES

Designed for fundraisers who work within defined fields of nonprofit development, the *Grant Guides* series lists actual foundation grants of $10,000 or more in 12 key areas of grantmaking.

Each title in the series affords immediate access to the names, addresses, and giving limitations of the foundations listed. The grant descriptions provide fundraisers with the grant recipient's name and location; the amount of the grant; the date the grant was authorized; and a description of the grant's intended use.

In addition, each *Grant Guide* includes three indexes: by the type of organization generally funded by the grantmaker, the subject focus of the foundation's grants, and the geographic area in which the foundation has already funded projects.

Each *Grant Guide* also includes a concise overview of the foundation spending patterns within the specified field. The introduction uses a series of statistical tables to document such important findings as 1) the 25 top funders in the given area of interest (by total dollar amount of grants); 2) the 15 largest grants reported; 3) the total dollar amount and number of grants awarded for specific types of support, recipient organization type, and population group; and 4) the total grant dollars received in each U.S. state and many foreign countries.
2006–2007 EDITIONS / $75 EACH / SERIES PUBLISHED ANNUALLY IN DECEMBER

FUNDRAISING GUIDES

FOUNDATION FUNDAMENTALS, 8th Edition
Foundation Fundamentals, often used as a basic primer in academic programs on the nonprofit sector, has been thoroughly updated to introduce beginners to the world of foundations. While prior editions of this guide focused on effective use of print resources, this edition places particular emphasis on harnessing electronic databases and the Web to uncover information on grantmakers and their grants. Research strategies are explored that utilize subject, geographic and types of support approaches to finding funders. In addition, the guide features chapters on planning a funding research strategy, corporate giving, and presenting ideas to funders. A variety of worksheets and illustrations are provided throughout the text. The expanded and updated bibliography includes the latest publications as well as descriptions of the most relevant web sites.
SEPTEMBER 2007 / ISBN 1-59542-156-4 / $24.95

THE FOUNDATION CENTER'S GRANTS CLASSIFICATION SYSTEM INDEXING MANUAL WITH THESAURUS, Revised Edition
A complete "how-to" guide, the *Grants Classification Manual* is an excellent resource for any organization that wants to classify foundation grants or their recipients. The *Manual* includes a complete set of classification codes to facilitate precise tracking of grants and recipients by subject, recipient type, and population categories. It also features a revised thesaurus to help identify the "official" terms and codes that represent thousands of subject areas and recipient types in the Center's system of grants classification.
MAY 1995 / ISBN 0-87954-644-1 / $95

THE FOUNDATION CENTER'S GUIDE TO GRANTSEEKING ON THE WEB, Revised Edition
Packed with a wealth of information, the *Guide to Grantseeking on the Web* provides both novice and experienced Web users with a gateway to the numerous online resources available to grantseekers. Foundation Center staff experts have team-authored this guide, contributing their extensive knowledge of Web content as well as their tips and strategies on how to evaluate and use Web-based funding materials. Presented in a concise, "how-to" style, the *Guide* will introduce you to the Web and structure your funding research with a toolkit of resources. These resources include foundation and corporate Web sites, searchable databases for grantseeking, government funding sources, online journals, and interactive services on the Web for grantseekers.
SEPTEMBER 2003 / BOOK / ISBN 1-931923-67-1 / $29.95
CD-ROM / ISBN 1-931923-73-6 / $29.95
BOOK AND CD-ROM / $49.95

THE FOUNDATION CENTER'S GUIDE TO PROPOSAL WRITING, 5th Edition
The *Guide* is a comprehensive manual on the strategic thinking and mechanics of proposal writing. It covers each step of the process, from pre-proposal planning to the writing itself to the essential post-grant follow-up. The book features many extracts from actual grant proposals and also includes candid advice from grantmakers on the "do's and don'ts" of proposal writing. Written by a professional fundraiser who has been creating successful proposals for more than 30 years, *The Foundation Center's Guide to Proposal Writing* offers the kind of valuable tips and in-depth, practical instruction that no other source provides.
MARCH 2007 / ISBN 1-59542-129-7 / $34.95

THE FOUNDATION CENTER'S GUIDE TO WINNING PROPOSALS
The *Guide to Winning Proposals* features 20 grant proposals reprinted in their entirety that have been funded by some of today's most influential grantmakers.

To represent the diversity of nonprofits throughout the country, proposals have been selected from large and small, local and national organizations, and for many different support purposes, including basic budgetary support, special projects, construction, staff positions, and more. The *Guide to Winning Proposals* also includes actual letters of inquiry, budgets, cover letters, and supplementary documents needed to develop a complete proposal.
OCTOBER 2003 / ISBN 1-931923-47-7 / $34.95

THE FOUNDATION CENTER'S GUIDE TO WINNING PROPOSALS II
A companion to *Guide to Winning Proposals,* volume II features 31 compelling grant proposals from some of the nation's most influential funders. Each proposal, reprinted in its entirety, includes a critique by the decision-maker who approved the grant. The accompanying commentary points to the strengths and weaknesses of each proposal and provides insight into what makes some proposals more successful than others. In addition to cover letters and budgets, volume II includes winning proposals for general operating support, special projects, and and other topics.
OCTOBER 2005 / ISBN 1-59542-054-1 / $34.95

GUÍA PARA ESCRIBIR PROPUESTAS
The Spanish language edition of the 3rd edition of the *Guide to Proposal Writing* includes a special appendix listing consultants and technical assistance providers who can help Spanish speakers craft proposals in English, or give advice on fundraising.
MARCH 2003 / ISBN 1-931923-16-7 / $34.95

SECURING YOUR ORGANIZATION'S FUTURE: A Complete Guide to Fundraising Strategies, Revised Edition
by Michael Seltzer
In this completely updated edition, Michael Seltzer acts as your personal fundraising consultant. Beginners get bottom-line facts and easy-to-follow worksheets; veteran fundraisers receive a complete review of the basics plus new money-making ideas. Seltzer supplements his text with an extensive bibliography of selected readings and resource organizations. Highly recommended for use as a text in nonprofit management programs at colleges and universities.
FEBRUARY 2001 / ISBN 0-87954-900-9 / $34.95

RAISE MORE MONEY FOR YOUR NONPROFIT ORGANIZATION: A Guide to Evaluating and Improving Your Fundraising
by Anne L. New
In *Raise More Money,* Anne New sets guidelines for a fundraising program that will benefit the incipient as well as the established nonprofit organization. The author divides her text into three sections: "The Basics," which delineates the necessary steps a nonprofit must take before launching a development campaign; "Fundraising Methods," which encourages organizational self-analysis and points the way to an effective program involving many sources of funding; and "Fundraising Resources," a 20-page bibliography that highlights useful research and funding directories.
JANUARY 1991 / ISBN 0-87954-388-A / $14.95

NONPROFIT MANAGEMENT GUIDES

THE 21ST CENTURY NONPROFIT
by Paul B. Firstenberg
In *The 21st Century Nonprofit,* Paul B. Firstenberg provides nonprofit managers with the know-how to make their organizations effective agents of change. *The 21st Century Nonprofit* encourages managers to adopt strategies developed by the for-profit sector in recent years. These strategies will help them to expand their revenue base by diversifying grant sources, exploit the possibilities of for-profit enterprises, and develop human resources by learning how to attract and retain talented people. The book also explores the nature of leadership through short profiles of three nonprofit CEOs.
JULY 1996 / ISBN 0-87954-672-7 / $34.95

AMERICA'S NONPROFIT SECTOR: A Primer, 2nd Edition
by Lester M. Salamon
In this revised edition of his classic book, Lester M. Salamon clarifies the basic structure and role of the nonprofit sector in the U.S. He places the nonprofit sector into context in relation to the government and business sectors. He also shows how the position of the nonprofit sector has changed over time, both generally and in the major fields in which the sector is active. Illustrated with numerous charts and tables, Salamon's book is an easy-to-understand primer for government officials, journalists, and students—in short, for anyone who wants to comprehend the makeup of America's nonprofit sector.
FEBRUARY 1999 / ISBN 0-87954-801-0 / $14.95

BEST PRACTICES OF EFFECTIVE NONPROFIT ORGANIZATIONS: A Practitioner's Guide
by Philip Bernstein
This volume provides guidance for any nonprofit professional eager to advance their organization's goals. Philip Bernstein has drawn on his own extensive experience as a nonprofit executive, consultant, and volunteer to produce this review of "best practices" adopted by successful nonprofit organizations. Topics include defining purposes and goals, creating comprehensive financing plans, evaluating services, and effective communication.
FEBRUARY 1997 / ISBN 0-87954-755-3 / $29.95

THE BOARD MEMBER'S BOOK: Making a Difference in Voluntary Organizations, 3rd Edition
by Brian O'Connell
The revised and expanded edition of this popular title by former Independent Sector President, Brian O'Connell, is a guide to the issues, challenges, and possibilities that emerge from the interchange between a nonprofit organization and its board. O'Connell offers practical advice on how to be a more effective board member as well as on how board members can help their organizations make a difference.
MARCH 2003 / ISBN 1-931923-17-5 / $29.95

CAREERS FOR DREAMERS AND DOERS: A Guide to Management Careers in the Nonprofit Sector
by Lilly Cohen and Dennis R. Young
A timeless guide to management positions in the nonprofit world, *Careers for Dreamers and Doers* offers practical advice for starting a job search and suggests strategies used by successful managers throughout the voluntary sector.
NOVEMBER 1989 / ISBN 0-87954-294-2 / $29.95

ECONOMICS FOR NONPROFIT MANAGERS
by Dennis R. Young and Richard Steinberg
In *Economics for Nonprofit Managers,* Young and Steinberg treat micro-economic analysis as an indispensable skill for nonprofit managers. They introduce and explain concepts such as opportunity cost, analysis at the margin, market equilibrium, market failure, and cost-benefit analysis. This volume also focuses on issues of particular concern to nonprofits, such as the economics of fundraising and volunteer recruiting, the regulatory environment, the impact of competition on nonprofit performance, interactions among sources of revenue, and more.
JULY 1995 / ISBN 0-87954-610-7 / $34.95

EFFECTIVE ECONOMIC DECISION-MAKING BY NONPROFIT ORGANIZATIONS
by Dennis R. Young
Editor Dennis R. Young offers useful, practical guidelines to support today's nonprofit managers in their efforts to maximize the effectiveness with which their organizations employ their valuable resources. A group of expert authors explores core operating decisions that face all organizations and provides solutions that are unique to nonprofits of any size. Chapters cover such decision-making areas as pricing of services, compensation of staff, outsourcing, fundraising expenditures, and investment and disbursement of funds. Published by the National Center on Nonprofit Enterprise and the Foundation Center.
DECEMBER 2003 / ISBN 1-931923-69-8 / $34.95

INVESTING IN CAPACITY BUILDING: A Guide To High-impact Approaches
by Barbara Blumenthal
This publication by Barbara Blumenthal offers guidance to grantmakers and consultants in designing better approaches to helping nonprofits, while showing nonprofit managers how to obtain more effective assistance. Based on interviews with more than 100 grantmakers, intermediaries, and consultants; 30 evaluations of capacity building programs; and a review of research on capacity building; *Investing in Capacity Building: A Guide to High-Impact Approaches* identifies the most successful strategies for helping nonprofits improve organizational performance.
SEPTEMBER 2003 / ISBN 1-931923-65-5 / $34.95

THE NONPROFIT ENTREPRENEUR: Creating Ventures to Earn Income
Edited by Edward Skloot
In a well-organized topic-by-topic approach to nonprofit venturing, nonprofit consultant and entrepreneur Edward Skloot demonstrates how nonprofits can launch successful earned-income enterprises without compromising their missions. Skloot has compiled a collection of writings by the nation's top practitioners and advisors in nonprofit enterprise. Topics covered include legal issues, marketing techniques, business planning, avoiding the pitfalls of venturing for smaller nonprofits, and a special section on museums and their retail operations.
SEPTEMBER 1988 / ISBN 0-87954-239-X / $19.95

A NONPROFIT ORGANIZATION OPERATING MANUAL:
Planning for Survival and Growth
by Arnold J. Olenick and Philip R. Olenick

This straightforward, all-inclusive desk manual for nonprofit executives covers all aspects of starting and managing a nonprofit. The authors discuss legal problems, obtaining tax exemption, organizational planning and development, and board relations; operational, proposal, cash, and capital budgeting; marketing, grant proposals, fundraising, and for-profit ventures; computerization; and tax planning and compliance.
JULY 1991 / ISBN 0-87954-293-4 / $29.95

PEOPLE POWER: Service, Advocacy, Empowerment
by Brian O'Connell

People Power, a selection of O'Connell's most powerful writings, provides thought-provoking commentary on the nonprofit world. The 25+ essays included in this volume range from keen analyses of the role of voluntarism in American life, to sound advice for nonprofit managers, to suggestions for developing and strengthening the nonprofit sector of the future.
OCTOBER 1994 / ISBN 0-87954-563-1 / $24.95

PHILANTHROPY'S CHALLENGE
Building Nonprofit Capacity Through Venture Grantmaking
by Paul B. Firstenberg

In this book, Paul Firstenberg challenges grantors to proactively assist grantee management as the way to maximize the social impact of nonprofit programs, while showing grantseekers how the growing grantor emphasis on organizational capacity building will impact their efforts to win support. The author draws on his years of experience working in both nonprofit and for-profit organizations to explore the roles of grantor and grantee within various models of venture grantmaking. A full chapter is devoted to governance issues and responsibilities.
JANUARY 2003 / SOFTBOUND: ISBN 1-931923-15-9 / $29.95
HARDBOUND: ISBN 1-931923-53-1 / $39.95

PROMOTING ISSUES AND IDEAS: A Guide to Public Relations for Nonprofit Organizations, Third Edition
by M Booth & Associates
Available June 2007. For details and to order, visit: foundationcenter.org/marketplace.

SUCCEEDING WITH CONSULTANTS:
Self-Assessment for the Changing Nonprofit
by Barbara Kibbe and Fred Setterberg

This inspirational book, written by Barbara Kibbe and Fred Setterberg and supported by the David and Lucile Packard Foundation, guides nonprofits through the process of selecting and utilizing consultants to strengthen their organizations' operations. The book emphasizes self assessment tools and covers six different areas in which a nonprofit organization might benefit from a consultant's advice: governance, planning, fund development, financial management, public relations and marketing, and quality assurance.
APRIL 1992 / ISBN 0-87954-450-3 / $19.95

WISE DECISION-MAKING IN UNCERTAIN TIMES
Using Nonprofit Resources Effectively

Demands on nonprofit services have escalated within the context of economic downturns and reduced government funding in the post-9/11 economy. In this new environment, nonprofit managers must develop strategies to steer their organizations through profound transformations in programs, operations, fund development, and financing. In this essential guide, a team of experts evaluates entrepreneurial approaches, market engagement and competition, managing for performance and integrity, understanding and managing risk, managing fiscal stress, investment strategies, institutional collaboration and transformation, mobilizing for public sector support, and holistic grantmaking.
AUGUST 2006 / ISBN 1-59542-099-1 / $34.95

RESEARCH REPORTS

ARTS FUNDING IV: An Update on Foundation Trends

Prepared in cooperation with Grantmakers in the Arts, this report provides a framework for understanding trends in foundation funding for arts and culture through 2001. Based on a sample of 800+ foundations, it compares growth in arts funding with other sources of public and private support, examines changes in giving for specific arts disciplines, analyzes giving patterns by region, and explores shifts in the types of support funders award.
JULY 2003 / ISBN 1-931923-48-5 / $19.95

CALIFORNIA FOUNDATIONS
A Profile of the State's Grantmaking Community

Based on a Foundation Center survey, this report covers the latest foundation trends in California. Starting with an introductory essay on the overall health of California philanthropy, it illuminates critical issues facing these funders. It then provides an overview of California foundations that focuses on changes in their resources from 1999 to 2004, estimates 2005 giving, and discusses the outlook for giving in 2006; and a detailed analysis of the 2004 giving priorities. Prepared in cooperation with the University of Southern California Center on Philanthropy and Public Policy.
NOVEMBER 2006 / ISBN 1-59542-104-1 / $24.95

FAMILY FOUNDATIONS: A Profile of Funders and Trends

Prepared in cooperation with the National Center for Family Philanthropy, *Family Foundations* is an essential resource for anyone interested in understanding the fastest growing segment of foundation philanthropy. The report provides a comprehensive measurement of the size and scope of the U.S. family foundation community. Through the use of objective and subjective criteria, the report identifies the number of family foundations and their distribution by region and state, size, geographic focus, and decade of establishment; and includes analyses of staffing and public reporting by these funders. *Family Foundations* also examines trends in giving by a sample of larger family foundations between 1993 and 1998 and compares these patterns with independent foundations overall.
AUGUST 2000 / ISBN 0-87954-917-3 / $19.95

FOUNDATIONS TODAY SERIES, 2007 Edition

The *Foundations Today Series* provides the latest information on foundation growth and trends in foundation giving.
THREE BOOK SET / ISBN 1-59542-127-B / $95

Foundation Giving Trends: Update on Funding Priorities—Examines 2005 grantmaking patterns of a sample of more than 1,000 larger U.S. foundations and compares current giving priorities with trends since 1980.
FEBRUARY 2007 / ISBN 1-59542-127-0 / $45

Foundation Growth and Giving Estimates: Current Outlook—Provides a first look at estimates of foundation giving for 2006 and final statistics on actual giving and assets for 2005. Presents new top 100 foundation lists.
APRIL 2007 / ISBN 1-59542-132-7 / $20

Foundation Yearbook: Facts and Figures on Private and Community Foundations—Documents the growth in number, giving, and assets of all active U.S. foundations from 1975 through 2005.
JUNE 2007 / ISBN 1-59542-135-1 / $45

INTERNATIONAL GRANTMAKING III:
An Update on U.S. Foundation Trends

Prepared in cooperation with the Council on Foundations as an update to the 2000 *International Grantmaking II* study, this report examines perspectives on the post-9/11 funding climate and the current outlook for the field based on a 2004 survey of more than 65 leading U.S. international grantmakers. It also documents actual trends in international giving based on the grants of over 600 larger U.S. foundations. In particular, the study analyzes shifts in giving priorities, countries/regions targeted for support, and the impact of large new funders.
NOVEMBER 2004 / ISBN 1-59542-008-8 / $40

THE PRI DIRECTORY: Charitable Loans and Other
Program-Related Investments by Foundations, 2nd Edition

Certain foundations have developed an alternative financing approach—known as program-related investing—for supplying capital to the nonprofit sector. PRIs have been used to support community revitalization, low-income housing, microenterprise development, historic preservation, human services, and more. This directory lists leading PRI providers and includes tips on how to seek out and manage PRIs. Foundation listings include funder name and state; recipient name, city, and state (or country); and a description of the project funded. There are several helpful indexes by foundation/recipient location, subject/type of support, and recipient name, as well as an index to donors, officers, and trustees.
SEPTEMBER 2003 / ISBN 1-931923-49-3 / $75

NEW YORK METROPOLITAN AREA FOUNDATIONS:
A Profile of the Grantmaking Community

Prepared in cooperation with the New York Regional Association of Grantmakers, this study examines the size, scope, and giving patterns of foundations based in the eight-county New York metropolitan area. It documents the New York area's share of all U.S. foundations; details the growth of area foundations through 2000; profiles area foundations by type, size, and geographic focus; compares broad giving trends of New York area and all U.S. foundations between 1992 and 2000; and examines giving by non-New York area grantmakers to recipients in the New York area.
DECEMBER 2002 / ISBN 1-931923-52-3/ $24.95

SOCIAL JUSTICE GRANTMAKING

Independent Sector and the Foundation Center have partnered in developing this groundbreaking research, resulting in a quantitative study of social justice funding by 1,000 of the largest private and community foundations in the U.S. *Social Justice Grantmaking* is the first study to benchmark foundation funding for nonprofit organizations working to make structural changes that increase opportunities for those who are least well off economically, socially, or politically. Presented here for the first time: a definition of the social justice grantmaking field developed by grantmakers and practitioners; profiles of the top social justice funders; principle grantmaking priorities and funding trends; geographic distribution of funding within and outside of the U.S. Through interviews with key funders, the report also lends perspective on the motivations and challenges faced by social justice funders. From economic development to healthcare to civil and human rights, this report will enhance both the practice and understanding of social justice philanthropy.
AUGUST 2005 / ISBN 1-59542-052-5/ $24.95

SOUTHEASTERN FOUNDATIONS II: A Profile of the Region's
Grantmaking Community, 2nd Edition

Produced in cooperation with the Southeastern Council of Foundations, *Southeastern Foundations II* provides a detailed examination of foundation philanthropy in the 12-state Southeast region. The report includes an overview of the Southeast's share of all U.S. foundations, measures the growth of Southeastern foundations since 1992, profiles Southeastern funders by type, size, and geographic focus, compares broad giving trends of Southeastern and all U.S. foundations in 1992 and 1997, and details giving by non-Southeastern grantmakers to recipients in the region.
NOVEMBER 1999 / ISBN 0-87954-775-8 / $19.95
MEMBERSHIP PROGRAM

ASSOCIATES PROGRAM

Essential facts and figures are at your fingertips through this e-mail and toll-free telephone reference service, helping you to:
◆ Identify potential sources of foundation and corporate funding for your organization; and
◆ Gather important information to use in targeting and presenting your proposals effectively.

An annual $995 membership in the Associates Program gives you vital information on a timely basis, saving you hundreds of hours of research time. As a member, you may place an unlimited number of requests for assistance. Our staff will refer to any print or online resource available to us in any of our five library/learning centers.

Members also receive a special monthly e-newsletter and have access to an exclusive extranet site, which provides news that includes information about the newest foundations, changes at more established foundations, special discounts and invitations to members-only briefings, and more.

Since the mid-1970s, thousands of professional fundraisers have discovered the Associates Program to be a highly reliable and extremely cost-effective service. In times when budgets are tight, nonprofit staffers wearing many hats at once find it especially useful. For more information, call (800) 634-2953 or visit us online to learn how we can serve your specific needs.

FOUNDATION CENTER'S WEB SITE

foundationcenter.org

The premier online source for fundraising information you can trust and tools you can use, our site is updated and expanded daily, providing grantseekers, grantmakers, researchers, journalists, and the general public with easy access to valuable resources. Registered visitors receive news, announcements, and job alerts based on their region and subject interests.

GET STARTED

◆ Find answers to questions about seeking funds, nonprofit management, and how to start a nonprofit organization. Search comprehensive FAQs, ask our Online Librarian a question by e-mail, or find a reference guide to meet your needs.
◆ Learn about foundations and fundraising, proposal writing, nonprofit management, and how to use our tools and resources. You'll find books, free orientations, training courses, and online tutorials to help your nonprofit.
◆ See the full curriculum of training courses—at locations nationwide and online—to get you started or to develop your expertise in grantseeking and nonprofit management. Visit often for dates and locations of classroom courses.

◆ Visit our regional center homepages to find out what's happening at Foundation Center locations in Atlanta, Cleveland, New York, San Francisco, and Washington, DC. Find a library near you among our network of more than more than 300 cooperating collections throughout the U.S.

FINDING FUNDERS

◆ Look up nonprofit organizations with our free Foundation Finder tool that will help you find addresses, web sites and fiscal data. Or use our 990 Finder to access IRS returns for foundations and nonprofits.

◆ Check statistics . . . national, state, and metropolitan area data on U.S. foundations and their grants is at your fingertips. You'll learn about the assets and giving of the nation's grantmaking foundations, how they distribute their grant dollars, and the top recipients of their gifts.

◆ Identify funding sources with monthly or annual subscriptions to *Foundation Directory Online,* the leading grantseeking database on the web. Search up to 88,000 comprehensive foundation and corporate giver profiles and nearly 800,000 grant descriptions.

GAIN KNOWLEDGE

◆ Find information on grantmakers using our online, print, and CD-ROM directories. Learn the skills you need to write a winning proposal or ensure the future of your nonprofit through Foundation Center books and training courses.

◆ Access Research Studies to discover the latest data available on U.S. foundation philanthropy. Our research staff analyzes and interprets the data we collect on foundations. Learn about national and regional trends, and get the latest statistics on foundation giving.

◆ Search the *Catalog of Nonprofit Literature,* a bibliographic database of nearly 25,000 entries on the field of philanthropy—more than 17,000 include abstracts. Or look up a foundation-sponsored report on a topic of interest in PubHub.

◆ Get the news you need from *Philanthropy News Digest* (PND), a daily digest of philanthropy-related articles. Read interviews with leaders, look for RFPs, learn from the experts, and share ideas with others in the field.

LEARN AT YOUR OWN PACE WITH ONLINE TRAINING.

The Foundation Center's online training courses include:

◆ Grantseeking Basics for Nonprofit Organizations—Designed for anyone in the nonprofit sector who wants to learn more about identifying and researching foundations as potential sources of funding.

◆ Proposal Writing: The Statement of Need—Designed for beginners as well as experienced grantseekers, this course will help you construct a compelling statement of need.

◆ Proposal Writing: The Project Description—Designed for grantseekers at any level of experience, this course explores every aspect of drafting a compelling project description—from stating objectives to outlining key components.

◆ Proposal Writing: The Budget—Designed for beginning fundraisers who want to master the art of preparing project budgets for proposals to private foundations and corporations.

◆ NEW! Proposal Writing: The Comprehensive Course—Designed to help development professionals master the art of proposal writing, step-by-step, through each section of a proposal—from the executive summary to the conclusion and packaging the proposal—with lessons on cover letters and format options.

FOUNDATION CENTER

Cooperating Collections
Free Funding Information Centers

For free fundraising information and other funding-related technical assistance, visit our Cooperating Collections nationwide. Located in libraries, nonprofit resource centers, or other agencies, Cooperating Collections provide visitors with free access to core Foundation Center electronic and print resources and fundraising research guidance, along with access to the Internet and our searchable databases. Many offer workshops and programs for local nonprofits. For the most current contact information, visit foundationcenter.org/collections or call (800) 424-9836. Individual Collection hours vary, so please confirm specifics before paying a visit. No appointment is necessary, and no fee is charged for use of Foundation Center resources.

ALABAMA

Birmingham: Birmingham Public Library, Government Documents Dept., 2100 Park Place (205) 226-3620

Huntsville: Huntsville-Madison County Public Library, Information and Periodicals Dept., 915 Monroe St. (256) 532-5940

Mobile: Mobile Public Library, West Regional Library, 5555 Grelot Rd. (251) 340-8555

Montgomery: Auburn University at Montgomery Library, 74-40 East Dr. (334) 244-3200

ALASKA

Anchorage: Consortium Library, 3211 Providence Dr. (907) 786-1848

Juneau: Juneau Public Library, 292 Marine Way (907) 586-5267

ARIZONA

Flagstaff: Flagstaff City-Coconino County Public Library, 300 W. Aspen Ave. (928) 779-7670

Phoenix: Phoenix Public Library, Information Services Dept., 1221 N. Central Ave. (602) 262-4636

Tucson: Pima County Public Library, 101 N. Stone Ave. (520) 791-4393

Yuma: Yuma County Library District, 350 3rd Ave. (928) 782-1871

ARKANSAS

Fort Smith: University of Arkansas—Fort Smith, Boreham Library, 5210 Grand Ave. (479) 788-7204

Little Rock: Central Arkansas Library System, 100 Rock St. (501) 918-3000

CALIFORNIA

Bakersfield: Kern County Library, Beale Memorial Library, 701 Truxtun Ave. (661) 868-0701

Bayside: Humboldt Area Foundation, Rooney Resource Center, 373 Indianola Rd. (707) 442-2993

Camarillo: Ventura County Community Foundation, Resource Center for Nonprofit Organizations, 1317 Del Norte Rd., Ste. 150 (805) 988-0196

Fairfield: Solano Community Foundation, 1261 Travis Blvd, Ste. 320 (707) 399-3846

Fresno: Fresno Nonprofit Advancement Council, 1752 L St. (559) 264-1513

Lompoc: Lompoc Public Library, 501 E. North Ave. (805) 875-8789

Long Beach: Long Beach Nonprofit Partnership, 3635 Atlantic Ave. (562) 290-0018

Los Angeles: Center for Nonprofit Management in Southern California, Nonprofit Resource Library, 1000 N. Alameda St. (213) 687-9511

Los Angeles: Southern California Library for Social Studies and Research, 6120 S. Vermont Ave. (323) 759-6063

Milpitas: Compasspoint Nonprofit Services, Nonprofit Development Library, 600 Valley Way, Ste. A (408) 719-1400

Moreno Valley: Resource Center for Nonprofits, 21250 Box Springs Rd., Ste. 211 (951) 686-2890

North Hills: Los Angeles Public Library, Mid-Valley Regional Branch Library, 16244 Nordhoff St. (818) 895-3654

Pasadena: Flintridge Foundation, Philanthropy Resource Center, 1040 Lincoln Ave., Ste. 100 (626) 449-0839

Redding: Shasta Regional Community Foundation, Center for Nonprofit Resources, 2280 Benton Dr., Bldg. C, Ste. A (530) 244-1219

Richmond: Richmond Public Library, 352 Civic Center Plaza (510) 620-6561

Riverside: Riverside Public Library, 3581 Mission Inn Ave. (951) 826-5201

Sacramento: Nonprofit Resource Center, 828 I St., 2nd Fl. (916) 264-2772

San Diego: Nonprofit Management Solutions, 8265 Vickers St., Ste. C (858) 292-5702

San Diego: San Diego Foundation, Funding Information Center, 2508 Historic Decatur, Ste. 200 (619) 235-2300

San Francisco (Regional Foundation Center): The Foundation Center, 312 Sutter St., Ste. 606 (415) 397-0902

San Pedro: Los Angeles Public Library, San Pedro Regional Branch, 931 S. Gaffey St. (310) 548-7779

Santa Ana: Volunteer Center Orange County, 1901 E. 4th St., Ste. 100 (714) 953-5757

Santa Barbara: Santa Barbara Public Library, 40 E. Anapamu St. (805) 962-7653

Santa Monica: Santa Monica Public Library, 601 Santa Monica Blvd. (310) 458-8600

Santa Rosa: Sonoma County Library, 3rd and E Sts. (707) 545-0831

Seaside: Seaside Branch Library, 550 Harcourt Ave. (831) 899-2055

Sonora: Sierra Nonprofit Support Center, 39 N. Washington St. #F (209) 533-1093

Soquel: Community Foundation of Santa Cruz, 2425 Porter St., Ste. 17 (831) 477-0800

Ukiah: Catalyst (North Coast Opportunities), 413 N. State St. (707) 462-2984

Victorville: High Desert Resource Network, Victorville City Library, 15011 Circle Dr. (760) 949-2930

COLORADO

Colorado Springs: El Pomar Nonprofit Resource Center, Penrose Library, 20 N. Cascade Ave. (719) 531-6333

Denver: Denver Public Library, 10 W. 14th Ave. Pkwy. (720) 865-1111

Durango: Durango Public Library, 1188 E. 2nd Ave. (970) 375-3380

Greeley: Weld Library District, Farr Branch Library, 1939 61st Ave. (970) 506-8518

Pueblo: Pueblo-City County Library District, 100 E. Abriendo Ave. (719) 562-5600

CONNECTICUT

Greenwich: Greenwich Library, 101 W. Putnam Ave. (203) 622-7900

Resources include

- Foundation Directory Online Professional *or* FC Search: The Foundation Center's Database on CD-ROM
- The Foundation Directory, Part 2, and Supplement
- Foundation Fundamentals
- Foundations Today Series
- Foundation Grants to Individuals
- Foundation Grants to Individuals Online
- The Foundation Center's Guide to Proposal Writing
- Guía para escribir propuestas
- The Foundation Center's Guides to Winning Proposals
- Guide to U.S. Foundations, Their Trustees, Officers, and Donors
- National Directory of Corporate Giving
- Guide to Funding for International & Foreign Programs
- Board Member's Book
- Securing Your Organization's Future

Foundation Center locations

Main
New York:
79 Fifth Ave., 2nd Fl.
(212) 620-4230

Regional Centers
Atlanta:
Hurt Bldg., 50 Hurt Plaza
Ste. 150, Grand Lobby
(404) 880-0094

Cleveland:
Kent H. Smith Library
1422 Euclid Ave., Ste. 1600
(216) 861-1934

San Francisco:
312 Sutter St., Ste. 606
(415) 397-0902

Washington, DC:
1627 K St., NW, 3rd Fl.
(202) 331-1400

Hartford: Hartford Public Library, 500 Main St. (860) 695-6295

New Haven: New Haven Free Public Library, 133 Elm St. (203) 946-7431

Westport: Westport Public Library, Arnold Bernhard Plaza, 20 Jesup Rd. (203) 291-4840

DELAWARE

Dover: Dover Public Library, 45 S. State St. (302) 736-7030

Newark: University of Delaware, Hugh Morris Library, 181 S. College Ave. (302) 831-2432

Wilmington: Nonprofit Community Resource Center, Community Services Bldg., 100 W. 10th St., Ste. 812 (302) 573-4475

DISTRICT OF COLUMBIA

Washington, DC (Regional Foundation Center): The Foundation Center, 1627 K St., NW, 3rd Fl. (202) 331-1400

FLORIDA

Bartow: Bartow Public Library, 2151 S. Broadway Ave. (863) 534-0131

Boca Raton: Junior League of Boca Raton, 261 NW 13th St. (561) 620-2553

Daytona Beach: Volusia County Library Center, City Island, 105 E. Magnolia Ave. (386) 257-6036

Fort Lauderdale: Nova Southeastern University, Library, Research, and Information Technology Center, 3100 Ray Ferrero Jr. Blvd. (954) 262-4613

Fort Pierce: Indian River Community College, Learning Resources Center, 3209 Virginia Ave. (772) 462-7600

Gainesville: Alachua County Library District, 401 E. University Ave. (352) 334-3900

Jacksonville: Jacksonville Public Library, Nonprofit Resource Center, 303 N. Laura St. (904) 630-2665

Miami: Miami-Dade Public Library, Humanities/Social Science Dept., 101 W. Flagler St. (305) 375-5575

Orlando: Orange County Library System, Social Sciences Dept., 101 E. Central Blvd. (407) 835-7323

Sarasota: Selby Public Library, 1331 1st St. (941) 861-1100

Tallahassee: State Library of Florida, R.A. Gray Building, 500 S. Bronough St. (850) 245-6600

Tampa: Hillsborough County Public Library Cooperative, John F. Germany Public Library, 900 N. Ashley Dr. (813) 273-3652

West Palm Beach: Community Foundation for Palm Beach and Martin Counties, 700 S. Dixie Highway, Ste. 200 (561) 659-6800

GEORGIA

Atlanta: Atlanta-Fulton Public Library System, One Margaret Mitchell Square, Ivan Allen Jr. Reference Dept. (404) 730-1900

Atlanta (Regional Foundation Center): The Foundation Center, Hurt Bldg., 50 Hurt Plaza, Ste. 150, Grand Lobby (404) 880-0094

Augusta: Georgia Center for Nonprofits, East Central Georgia Regional Office, Enterprise Mill, 1450 Greene St., Ste. 160 (706) 823-9718

Brunswick: Coastal Georgia Nonprofit Center, 1311 Union St. (912) 265-1850

Gainesville: Hall County Library System, 127 Main St. NW (770) 532-3311

Macon: Methodist Home, Rumford Center, 304 Pierce Ave., 1st Fl. (478) 751-2800

Savannah: Georgia Center for Nonprofits, Coastal Georgia Regional Office, 428 Bull St. (912) 234-9688

Thomasville: Thomas County Public Library, 201 N. Madison St. (229) 225-5252

HAWAII

Honolulu: University of Hawaii at Manoa, Hamilton Library, Business, Humanities, and Social Sciences Dept., 2550 The Mall (808) 956-7214

IDAHO

Boise: Boise Public Library, Funding Information Center, 715 S. Capitol Blvd. (208) 384-4024

Caldwell: Caldwell Public Library, 1010 Dearborn St. (208) 459-3242

Pocatello: Marshall Public Library, 113 S. Garfield (208) 232-1263

ILLINOIS

Carbondale: Carbondale Public Library, 405 W. Main St. (618) 457-0354

Chicago: Donors Forum of Chicago Library, 208 S. LaSalle, Ste. 735 (312) 578-0175

Evanston: Evanston Public Library, 1703 Orrington Ave. (847) 866-0300

Quincy: John Wood Community College, 1301 S. 48th St. (217) 224-6500

Rock Island: Rock Island Public Library, 401 19th St. (309) 732-7323

Springfield: University of Illinois at Springfield, Central Illinois Nonprofit Resources Center, Brookens Library, One University Plaza, MS BRK 140 (217) 206-6633

INDIANA

Evansville: Evansville Vanderburgh Public Library, 200 SE Martin Luther King Jr. Blvd. (812) 428-8218

Fort Wayne: Allen County Public Library, 200 E. Berry St. (260) 421-1238

Indianapolis: First Samuel Missionary Baptist Church, 1402 N. Belleview Place (317) 635-1942

Indianapolis: Indianapolis-Marion County Public Library, 202 N. Alabama St. (317) 269-1700

Muncie: Muncie Public Library, 2005 S. High St. (765) 747-8204

Terre Haute: Vigo County Public Library, One Library Square (812) 232-1113

Valparaiso: Valparaiso University, The Christopher Center for Library and Information Resources, 1410 Chapel Dr. (219) 464-5364

IOWA

Cedar Rapids: Cedar Rapids Public Library, 500 1st St. SE (319) 398-5123

Council Bluffs: Council Bluffs Public Library, 400 Willow Ave. (712) 323-7553

Creston: Southwestern Community College, Learning Resource Center, 1501 W. Townline Rd. (641) 782-7081

Des Moines: Des Moines Public Library, 1000 Grand Ave. (515) 283-4152

Sioux City: Sioux City Public Library, Siouxland Funding Research Center, 529 Pierce St. (712) 255-2933

KANSAS

Colby: Pioneer Memorial Library, 375 W. 4th St. (785) 460-4470

Dodge City: Dodge City Public Library, 1001 2nd Ave. (620) 225-0248

Ellis: Ellis Public Library, 907 Washington (785) 726-3464

Lakin: Kearny County Library, 101 E. Prairie (620) 355-6674

Liberal: Liberal Memorial Library, 519 N. Kansas (620) 626-0180

Salina: Salina Public Library, 301 W. Elm (785) 825-4624

Topeka: Topeka and Shawnee County Public Library, Adult Services, 1515 SW 10th Ave. (785) 580-4400

Wichita: Wichita Public Library, 223 S. Main St. (316) 261-8500

KENTUCKY

Bowling Green: Western Kentucky University, Helm-Cravens Library, 110 Helm Library (270) 745-6163

Covington: Kenton County Public Library, 502 Scott Blvd. (859) 962-4060

Lexington: Lexington Public Library, 140 E. Main St. (859) 231-5520

Louisville: Louisville Free Public Library, 301 York St. (502) 574-1617

Somerset: Pulaski County Public Library, 107 N. Main St. (606) 679-8401

LOUISIANA

Alexandria: Community Development Works, 1101 4th St., Ste. 101B (318) 443-7880

Baton Rouge: East Baton Rouge Parish Library, River Center Branch, 120 St. Louis St. (225) 389-4967

Baton Rouge: Louisiana Association of Nonprofit Organizations, 700 N. 10th St., Ste. 250 (225) 343-5266

DeRidder: Beauregard Parish Library, 205 S. Washington Ave. (337) 463-6217

Lake Charles: Louisiana Association of Nonprofit Organizations, 220 Louie St. (337) 310-9540

Monroe: Ouachita Parish Public Library, 1800 Stubbs Ave. (318) 327-1490

New Orleans: Louisiana Association of Nonprofit Organizations, 1824 Oretha Castle Haley Blvd. (504) 309-2081

New Orleans: New Orleans Public Library, Business and Science Division, 219 Loyola Ave. (504) 596-2580

Shreveport: Louisiana Association of Nonprofit Organizations, 2924 Knight St., Ste. 406 (318) 865-5510

Shreveport: Shreve Memorial Library, 424 Texas St. (318) 226-5894

MAINE

Portland: University of Southern Maine, Maine Philanthropy Center, Glickman Family Library, 314 Forest Ave., Room 321 (207) 780-5039

MARYLAND

Baltimore: Enoch Pratt Free Library, Social Science and History Dept., 400 Cathedral St. (410) 396-5320

Salisbury: Community Foundation of the Eastern Shore, 1324 Belmont Ave., Ste. 401 (410) 724-9911

Wye Mills: Chesapeake College Library, 1000 College Dr. (410) 827-5860

MASSACHUSETTS

Boston: Associated Grant Makers, 55 Court St., Ste. 520 (617) 426-2606

Boston: Boston Public Library, Social Sciences Reference Dept., 700 Boylston St. (617) 536-5400

Pittsfield: Berkshire Athenaeum, One Wendell Ave. (413) 499-9480

Springfield: Springfield City Library, 220 State St. (413) 263-6828

Worcester: Worcester Public Library, Grants Resource Center, 3 Salem Square (508) 799-1654

MICHIGAN

Alpena: Alpena County Library, 211 N. 1st St. (989) 356-6188

Ann Arbor: University of Michigan, Harlan Hatcher Graduate Library, 920 N. University (734) 615-8610

Battle Creek: Willard Public Library, Nonprofit and Funding Resource Collections, 7 W. Van Buren St. (269) 968-3284

Detroit: Wayne State University, Purdy/Kresge Library, 134 Purdy/Kresge Library (313) 577-6424

East Lansing: Michigan State University, Funding Center, 100 Library (517) 432-6123

Farmington Hills: Farmington Community Library, 32737 W. 12 Mile Rd. (248) 553-0300

Flint: Flint Public Library, 1026 E. Kearsley St. (810) 232-7111

Grand Rapids: Grand Rapids Public Library, 111 Library St. NE (616) 988-5400

Marquette: Peter White Public Library, 217 N. Front St. (906) 226-4311

Petoskey: Petoskey Public Library, 500 E. Mitchell St. (231) 758-3100

Saginaw: Hoyt Public Library, 505 Janes Ave. (989) 755-0904

Scottville: West Shore Community College Library, 3000 N. Stiles Rd. (231) 845-6211

Traverse City: Traverse Area District Library, 610 Woodmere Ave. (231) 932-8500

MINNESOTA

Brainerd: Brainerd Public Library, 416 S. 5th St. (218) 829-5574

Duluth: Duluth Public Library, 520 W. Superior St. (218) 723-3802

Marshall: Southwest State University, University Library, N. Highway 23 (507) 537-6108

Minneapolis: Minneapolis Public Library, 300 Nicollet Mall (612) 630-6000

Rochester: Rochester Public Library, 101 2nd St. SE (507) 285-8002

St. Paul: St. Paul Public Library, 90 W. 4th St. (651) 266-7000

MISSISSIPPI

Hattiesburg: Library of Hattiesburg, Petal and Forrest County, 329 Hardy St. (601) 582-4461

Jackson: Jackson/Hinds Library System, 300 N. State St. (601) 968-5803

MISSOURI

Kansas City: Kansas City Public Library, 14 W. 10th St. (816) 701-3400

Kansas City: University of Missouri–Kansas City, Council on Philanthropy, 4747 Troost Ave., Ste. 207 (816) 235-6259

Springfield: Springfield-Greene County Library, 4653 S. Campbell (417) 874-8110

St. Louis: St. Louis Public Library, 1301 Olive St. (314) 241-2288

St. Peters: St. Charles City–County Library District, 427 Spencer Rd. (636) 447-2320

MONTANA

Baker: Fallon County Library, 6 W. Fallon Ave. (406) 778-7160

Billings: Montana State University–Billings, Library-Special Collections, 1500 University Dr. (406) 657-2262

Libby: Lincoln County Public Libraries, Libby Public Library, 220 W. 6th St. (406) 293-2778

Missoula: The University of Montana, Mansfield Library, 32 Campus Dr. #9936 (406) 243-6800

NEBRASKA

Cambridge: Butler Memorial Library, 621 Penn St. (308) 697-3836

Lincoln: University of Nebraska–Lincoln, Love Library (402) 472-2526

Omaha: Omaha Public Library, Social Science Dept., 215 S. 15th St. (402) 444-4826

NEVADA

Elko: Great Basin College Library, 1500 College Parkway (775) 753-2222

Las Vegas: Clark County Library, 1401 E. Flamingo Rd. (702) 507-3400

Reno: Washoe County Library, 301 S. Center St. (775) 327-8300

NEW HAMPSHIRE

Concord: Concord Public Library, 45 Green St. (603) 225-8670

Plymouth: Plymouth State University, Herbert H. Lamson Library (603) 535-2258

NEW JERSEY

Elizabeth: Free Public Library of Elizabeth, 11 S. Broad St. (908) 354-6060

Randolph: County College of Morris, Learning Resource Center, 214 Center Grove Rd. (973) 328-5296

Trenton: New Jersey State Library, Funding Information Center, 185 W. State St. (609) 292-6220

Vineland: Cumberland County College, Center for Leadership, Community and Neighborhood Development, 3322 College Dr. (856) 691-8600

Washington: Warren County Community College Library, 475 Rte. 57 W. (908) 835-9222

NEW MEXICO

Albuquerque: Albuquerque/Bernalillo County Library System, 501 Copper Ave. NW (505) 768-5141

Santa Fe: New Mexico State Library, 1209 Camino Carlos Rey (505) 476-9702

NEW YORK

Albany: New York State Library, Cultural Education Center, Empire State Plaza (518) 474-5355

Binghamton: Broome County Public Library, 185 Court St. (607) 778-6400

Bronx: New York Public Library, Bronx Library Center, 310 E. Kingsbridge Rd. (718) 579-4244

Brooklyn: Brooklyn Public Library, Social Sciences/Philosophy Division, Grand Army Plaza (718) 230-2122

Buffalo: Buffalo and Erie County Public Library, Business, Science, and Technology Dept., One Lafayette Square (716) 858-8900

Corning: Southeast Steuben County Library, 300 Nasser Civic Center Plaza (607) 936-3713

Holbrook: Sachem Public Library, 150 Holbrook Rd. (631) 588-5024

Huntington: Huntington Public Library, 338 Main St. (631) 427-5165

Jamaica: Queens Borough Public Library, Social Sciences Division, 89-11 Merrick Blvd. (718) 990-0700

Levittown: Levittown Public Library, One Bluegrass Lane (516) 731-5728

New York (Main Foundation Center Library): The Foundation Center, 79 Fifth Ave., 2nd Fl. (212) 620-4230

Poughkeepsie: Adriance Memorial Library, Special Services Dept., 93 Market St. (845) 485-3445

Riverhead: Riverhead Free Library, 330 Court St. (631) 727-3228

Rochester: Rochester Public Library, Grants Information Center, 115 South Ave. (585) 428-8120

Staten Island: New York Public Library, St. George Library Center, 5 Central Ave. (718) 442-8560

Syracuse: Onondaga County Public Library, 447 S. Salina St. (315) 435-1900

Utica: Utica Public Library, 303 Genesee St. (315) 735-2279

White Plains: White Plains Public Library, 100 Martine Ave. (914) 422-1480

Yonkers: Yonkers Public Library, Riverfront Library, One Larkin Center (914) 337-1500

NORTH CAROLINA

Asheville: Community Foundation of Western North Carolina, Pack Memorial Library, 67 Haywood St. (828) 250-4711

Charlotte: Public Library of Charlotte and Mecklenburg County, 310 N. Tryon St. (704) 336-2725

Durham: Durham County Public Library, 300 N. Roxboro St. (919) 560-0100

Raleigh: Cameron Village Library, Wake County Public Libraries, 1930 Clark Ave. (919) 856-6710

Wilmington: New Hanover County Public Library, 201 Chestnut St. (910) 798-6301

Winston-Salem: Forsyth County Public Library, 660 W. 5th St. (336) 727-2264

NORTH DAKOTA

Bismarck: Bismarck Public Library, 515 N. 5th St. (701) 222-6410

Fargo: Fargo Public Library, 102 N. 3rd St. (701) 241-1491

Minot: Minot Public Library, 516 2nd Ave. SW (701) 852-1045

OHIO

Akron: Akron-Summit County Public Library, 60 S. High St. (330) 643-9000

Canton: Stark County District Library, 715 Market Ave. N. (330) 452-0665

Cincinnati: Public Library of Cincinnati and Hamilton County, Grants Resource Center, 800 Vine St. (513) 369-6900

Cleveland (Regional Foundation Center): The Foundation Center, Kent H. Smith Library, 1422 Euclid Ave., Ste. 1600 (216) 861-1934

Columbus: Columbus Metropolitan Library, Business and Technology Dept., 96 S. Grant Ave. (614) 645-2590

Dayton: Dayton Metro Library, Grants Information Center, 215 E. 3rd St. (937) 227-9500

Elyria: Elyria Public Library, West River Branch, 1194 W. River Road N. (440) 324-9827

Lima: Lima Public Library, 650 W. Market St. (419) 228-5113

Mansfield: Mansfield/Richland County Public Library, 43 W. 3rd St. (419) 521-3110

Painesville: Morley Library, 184 Phelps St. (440) 352-3383

Piqua: Edison Community College Library, 1973 Edison Dr. (937) 778-7950

Portsmouth: Portsmouth Public Library, 1220 Gallia St. (740) 354-5688

Toledo: Toledo-Lucas County Public Library, Social Sciences Dept., 325 N. Michigan St. (419) 259-5207

Youngstown: Public Library of Youngstown and Mahoning County, 305 Wick Ave. (330) 744-8636

OKLAHOMA

Oklahoma City: Oklahoma City University, Dulaney Browne Library, 2501 N. Blackwelder (405) 521-5822

Tulsa: Tulsa City-County Library, 400 Civic Center (918) 596-7977

OREGON

Eugene: University of Oregon, Knight Library, 1501 Kincaid (541) 346-3053

Klamath Falls: Oregon Institute of Technology Library, 3201 Campus Dr. (541) 885-1000

Medford: Jackson County Library Services, 205 S. Central Ave. (541) 774-8689

Portland: Multnomah County Library, Government Documents, 801 SW 10th Ave. (503) 988-5123

Salem: Oregon State Library, 250 Winter St. NE (503) 378-4243

PENNSYLVANIA

Allentown: Allentown Public Library, 1210 Hamilton St. (610) 820-2400

Bethlehem: Northampton Community College, Paul and Harriett Mack Library, 3835 Green Pond Rd. (610) 861-5360

Blue Bell: Montgomery County Community College, The Brendlinger Library, 340 DeKalb Pike (215) 641-6596

Erie: Erie County Library System, 160 E. Front St. (814) 451-6927

Harrisburg: Dauphin County Library System, East Shore Area Library, 4501 Ethel St. (717) 652-9380

Hazleton: Hazleton Area Public Library, 55 N. Church St. (570) 454-2961

Honesdale: Wayne County Public Library, 1406 N. Main St. (570) 253-1220

Lancaster: Lancaster Public Library, 125 N. Duke St. (717) 394-2651

Philadelphia: Free Library of Philadelphia, Regional Foundation Center, 1901 Vine St., 2nd Fl. (215) 686-5423

Philadelphia: The Johnson-UGO Foundation Library, Johnson Memorial UMC Education Building, 3117 Longshore Ave. (215) 338-4487

Pittsburgh: Carnegie Library of Pittsburgh, 612 Smithfield St. (412) 281-7143

Pittston: Nonprofit and Community Assistance Center, 1151 Oak St. (570) 655-5581

Reading: Reading Public Library, 100 S. 5th St. (610) 655-6355

Williamsport: James V. Brown Library, 19 E. 4th St. (570) 326-0536

York: Martin Library, 159 E. Market St. (717) 846-5300

PUERTO RICO

Santurce: Universidad Del Sagrado Corazón, M.M.T. Guevara Library (787) 728-1515

RHODE ISLAND

Providence: Providence Public Library, 150 Empire St. (401) 455-8088

SOUTH CAROLINA

Anderson: Anderson County Library, 300 N. McDuffie St. (864) 260-4500

Charleston: Charleston County Library, 68 Calhoun St. (843) 805-6930

Columbia: South Carolina State Library, 1500 Senate St. (803) 734-8026

Greenville: Greenville County Library System, 25 Heritage Green Place (864) 242-5000

Spartanburg: Spartanburg County Public Libraries, 151 S. Church St. (864) 596-3500

SOUTH DAKOTA

Madison: Dakota State University, Nonprofit Management Institute, 820 N. Washington (605) 367-5100

Pierre: South Dakota State Library, 800 Governors Dr. (605) 773-3131 or (800) 423-6665 (within South Dakota)

Rapid City: Rapid City Public Library, 610 Quincy St. (605) 394-4171

Spearfish: Black Hills State University, E.Y. Berry Library-Learning Center, 1200 University St., Unit 9676 (605) 642-6834

TENNESSEE

Chattanooga: United Way of Greater Chattanooga, Center for Nonprofits, 630 Market St. (423) 752-0300

Johnson City: Johnson City Public Library, 100 W. Millard St. (423) 434-4450

Knoxville: Knox County Public Library, 500 W. Church Ave. (865) 215-8751

Memphis: The Alliance for Nonprofit Excellence, 606 S. Mendenhall, Ste. 108 (901) 684-6605

Memphis: Memphis Public Library and
Information Center, 3030 Poplar Ave.
(901) 415-2734

Nashville: Nashville Public Library, 615
Church St. (615) 862-5800

TEXAS

Amarillo: Amarillo Area Foundation, Grants
Center, 801 S. Filmore, Ste. 700
(806) 376-4521

Austin: Hogg Foundation for Mental Health,
Regional Foundation Library, 3001 Lake
Austin Blvd., 4th Fl. (512) 471-5041 or
(888) 404-4336 (toll free)

Beaumont: Beaumont Public Library, 801
Pearl St. (409) 838-6606

Corpus Christi: Corpus Christi Public Library,
Funding Information Center, 805 Comanche
St. (361) 880-7000

Dallas: Dallas Public Library, Urban
Information, 1515 Young St.
(214) 670-1400

Edinburg: Southwest Border Nonprofit
Resource Center, 1201 W. University Dr.
(956) 292-7566

El Paso: University of Texas at El Paso,
Community Non-Profit Grant Library, 500 W.
University, Benedict Hall, Room 103
(915) 747-5672

Fort Worth: Funding Information Center of Fort
Worth, 329 S. Henderson St.
(817) 334-0228

Houston: Houston Public Library, Bibliographic
Information Center, 500 McKinney St.
(832) 393-1313

Houston: United Way of the Texas Gulf Coast,
50 Waugh Dr. (713) 685-2300

Laredo: Laredo Public Library, Nonprofit
Management and Volunteer Center, 1120 E.
Calton Rd. (956) 795-2400

Longview: Longview Public Library, 222 W.
Cotton St. (903) 237-1350

Lubbock: Lubbock Area Foundation, Inc.,
1655 Main St., Ste. 202 (806) 762-8061

North Richland Hills: North Richland Hills
Public Library, 6720 NE Loop 820
(817) 427-6800

San Antonio: Nonprofit Resource Center of
Texas, 7404 Highway 90 W.
(210) 227-4333

Tyler: Nonprofit Development Center of United
Way of Tyler/Smith County, 4000 Southpark
Dr. (903) 581-6376

Waco: WACO-McLennan County Library, 1717
Austin Ave. (254) 750-5941

Wichita Falls: Nonprofit Management Center
of Wichita Falls, 2301 Kell Blvd., Ste. 218
(940) 322-4961

UTAH

Moab: Grand County Public Library, 257 E.
Center St. (435) 259-5421

Salt Lake City: Salt Lake City Public Library,
210 E. 400 S. (801) 524-8200

Salt Lake City: Utah Nonprofits Association,
175 S. Main St., Ste. 750
(801) 596-1800

VERMONT

Middlebury: Ilsley Public Library, 75 Main St.
(802) 388-4095

Montpelier: Vermont Dept. of Libraries,
Reference and Law Information Services,
109 State St. (802) 828-3261

VIRGINIA

Abingdon: Washington County Public Library,
205 Oak Hill St. (276) 676-6222

Fairfax: Fairfax County Public Library, 12000
Government Center Parkway, Ste. 329
(703) 324-3100

Hampton: Hampton Public Library, 4207
Victoria Blvd. (757) 727-1314

Hopewell: Appomattox Regional Library
System, 245 E. Cawson St.
(804) 458-0110

Richmond: Richmond Public Library, Business,
Science and Technology, 101 E. Franklin St.
(804) 646-7223

Roanoke: Roanoke City Public Library System,
Main Library, 706 S. Jefferson St.
(540) 853-2471

WASHINGTON

Kennewick: Mid-Columbia Library, 1620 S.
Union St. (509) 783-7878

Redmond: Redmond Regional Library,
Nonprofit and Philanthropy Resource
Center, 15990 NE 85th St.
(425) 885-1861

Seattle: Seattle Public Library, Fundraising
Resource Center, 1000 4th Ave.
(206) 386-4636

Spokane: Spokane Public Library, Funding
Information Center, 906 W. Main Ave.
(509) 444-5300

Tacoma: University of Washington Tacoma
Library, 1902 Commerce St.
(253) 692-4440

WEST VIRGINIA

Charleston: Kanawha County Public Library,
123 Capitol St. (304) 343-4646

Parkersburg: West Virginia University at
Parkersburg, 300 Campus Dr.
(304) 424-8260

Shepherdstown: Shepherd University, Ruth A.
Scarborough Library, 301 N. King St.
(304) 876-5420

Wheeling: Wheeling Jesuit University, Bishop
Hodges Library, 316 Washington Ave.
(304) 243-2226

WISCONSIN

Madison: University of Wisconsin–Madison,
Memorial Library, Grants Information Center,
728 State St., Room 262 (608) 262-3242

Milwaukee: Marquette University, Raynor
Memorial Library, Funding Information
Center, 1355 W. Wisconsin Ave.
(414) 288-1515

Stevens Point: University of
Wisconsin–Stevens Point, Library
Foundation Collection, 900 Reserve St.
(715) 346-2540

WYOMING

Cheyenne: Laramie County Community
College, Ludden Library, 1400 E. College
Dr. (307) 778-1206

Gillette: Campbell County Public Library, 2101
4-J Rd. (307) 687-0115

Jackson: Teton County Library, 125 Virginian
Lane (307) 733-2164

Sheridan: Sheridan County Fulmer Public
Library, 335 W. Alger St. (307) 674-8585

FOUNDATION CENTER
Knowledge to build on.

About the Foundation Center Established in 1956 and today
supported by more than 600 foundations, the Foundation Center is the
nation's leading authority on organized philanthropy, connecting
nonprofits and the grantmakers supporting them to tools they can use
and information they can trust. The Center maintains the most
comprehensive database on U.S. grantmakers and their grants and
conducts research on trends in foundation growth and giving. We also
operate education and outreach programs that help nonprofit
organizations obtain the resources they need. Our web site receives
more than 40,000 visits each day, and thousands of people are served
in our five regional learning centers and through our national network of
more than 300 Cooperating Collections. For more information, visit
foundationcenter.org or call (212) 620-4230.

Interested in Becoming a Cooperating Collection?
Cooperating Collections provide under-resourced and underserved
populations across the U.S. with crucial information and education. To
expand the network in regions where nonprofit communities are most in
need of Foundation Center resources, we welcome proposals from
qualified institutions—public, academic, or special libraries; community
foundations; nonprofit resource centers; and other technical assistance
providers—that can partner with us to help grantseekers succeed. If you
are interested in establishing a Collection in your area or would like to
learn more about the program, please visit foundationcenter.org/
collections or contact: Coordinator of Cooperating Collections,
Foundation Center, 79 Fifth Avenue, New York, NY 10003 (e-mail:
ccmail@foundationcenter.org).

DESCRIPTIVE DIRECTORY

DESCRIPTIVE DIRECTORY

ALABAMA

1

Alabama Power Foundation, Inc. ▼
600 N. 18th St.
P.O. Box 2641
Birmingham, AL 35291-0011 (205) 257-2508
FAX: (205) 257-1860; URL: http://
www.southerncompany.com/alpower/foundation

Established in 1989 in AL.
Donors: Alabama Power Co.; Elmer Harris; Glenda Harris; Bruce Hutchins; Priscilla Hutchins.
Foundation type: Company-sponsored foundation.
Financial data (yr. ended 12/31/05): Assets, $149,168,819 (M); gifts received, $56,476; expenditures, $10,043,231; qualifying distributions, $9,284,434; giving activities include $6,820,917 for 1,425 grants (high: $517,568; low: $62), and $113,500 for 226 grants to individuals (high: $1,000; low: $500).
Purpose and activities: The foundation supports organizations involved with education, the environment, and community development.
Fields of interest: Education; Environment; Community development; Federated giving programs.
Type of support: Endowments; General/operating support; Capital campaigns; Seed money; Scholarship funds; Employee-related scholarships; Matching/challenge support.
Limitations: Giving limited to AL. No support for religious organizations or fraternal, athletic, or veterans' organizations. No grants to individuals (except for employee-related scholarships), or for fundraising or general operating support for United Way-supported organizations.
Publications: Application guidelines; Annual report (including application guidelines); Grants list; Informational brochure (including application guidelines).
Application information: Application form not required.
  Initial approach: Letter of inquiry
  Copies of proposal: 1
  Deadline(s): Feb. 1, May 1, Aug. 1, and Nov. 1
  Board meeting date(s): Quarterly
  Final notification: 3 months
Officers and Directors:* Robert Holmes, Jr.,* Chair.; William B. Johnson,* Pres.; William E. Zales, Jr., Secy.; Art P. Beattie,* Treas.; Robin A. Hurst; William B. Hutchins III; C. Alan Martin; Charles D. McCrary; Rodney O. Mundy; Michael D. Scott; Steve R. Spencer; Jerry L. Stewart.
Number of staff: 4 full-time professional; 2 full-time support.
EIN: 570901832
Selected grants: The following grants were reported in 2005.
$517,568 to United Way of Central Alabama, Birmingham, AL. For general operating support.
$411,783 to Birmingham Urban Revitalization Partnership, Birmingham, AL. For general operating support.
$150,000 to Mobile Carnival Association, Mobile, AL. For capital support.
$121,000 to Scholarship Program Administrators, Nashville, TN. For program support.
$100,000 to Birmingham Civil Rights Institute, Birmingham, AL. For capital support.

$100,000 to Childrens Harbor, Alexander City, AL. For capital support.
$25,000 to Alabama-Tombigbee Regional Commission, Camden, AL. For project.
$23,200 to United Way, Wiregrass, Dothan, AL. For general operating support.
$15,000 to Chickasaw Civic Theater, Chickasaw, AL. For capital support.
$11,000 to Samford University, Birmingham, AL. For general operating support.

2

Alfa Foundation ✧
P.O. Box 11189
Montgomery, AL 36111-0189 (334) 613-4498
Contact: David R. Proctor

Established in 1996 in AL.
Donors: Alfa Mutual Insurance Co.; Alfa Mutual Fire Insurance Co.
Foundation type: Company-sponsored foundation.
Financial data (yr. ended 10/31/05): Assets, $21,893,391 (M); gifts received, $990,005; expenditures, $1,263,933; qualifying distributions, $1,103,750; giving activities include $1,103,750 for 24 grants (high: $300,000; low: $2,500).
Purpose and activities: The foundation supports community foundations and organizations involved with higher education.
Fields of interest: Higher education; Foundations (community).
Type of support: General/operating support.
Limitations: Giving limited to AL. No grants to individuals.
Application information: Application form not required.
  Deadline(s): None
Officers: Jerry A. Newby, Pres.; C. Lee Ellis, Exec. V.P.; H. Al Scott, Secy.; Stephen G. Rutledge, Treas.
EIN: 721373145
Selected grants: The following grants were reported in 2004.
$220,393 to United Way.
$50,000 to Alabama Institute for Deaf and Blind, Talladega, AL.
$50,000 to Athens State University, Athens, AL.
$40,000 to YMCA of Montgomery, Montgomery, AL.
$25,000 to Community Care Network, Montgomery, AL.
$25,000 to Tuskegee University, Tuskegee, AL.
$10,000 to Insurance Education Foundation, Indianapolis, IN.
$5,000 to Childrens Harbor, Alexander City, AL.

3

Alpha Foundation, Inc. ▼ ✧
159 Stoneway Trail
Madison, AL 35758
Contact: Lonnie S. McMillian, Dir.

Donor: Lonnie S. McMillian.
Foundation type: Operating foundation.
Financial data (yr. ended 12/31/05): Assets, $50,139,209 (M); expenditures, $617,663; qualifying distributions, $617,663; giving activities include $443,540 for 17 grants (high: $210,000; low: $100; average: $10,000–$55,000).
Purpose and activities: Giving primarily for biotechnology research as well as for education including a medical school and children services.

Fields of interest: Historic preservation/historical societies; Elementary school/education; Higher education; Medical school/education; Human services; Children, services; Science.
Limitations: Giving primarily in AL.
Application information:
  Initial approach: Letter
  Deadline(s): None
Directors: Barbara M. Fisk; Emily M. Key; Helen W. McMillian; Lonnie S. McMillian; Susan M. Whitehead; John R. Wynn.
EIN: 631188643
Selected grants: The following grants were reported in 2004.
$2,500,000 to Hudson-Alpha Institute for Biotechnology, Huntsville, AL. 2 grants: $2,000,000, $500,000
$1,000,000 to University of Alabama, School of Medicine, Tuscaloosa, AL.
$10,000 to Georgia Tech Alumni Association, Atlanta, GA.
$10,000 to Rainbow Elementary School, Madison, AL.

4

Altec/Styslinger Foundation ✧
210 Inverness Center Dr.
Birmingham, AL 35242

Established in 1997 in AL.
Donors: Lee J. Styslinger, Jr.; Altec Industries, Inc.; Global Rental Co.
Foundation type: Independent foundation.
Financial data (yr. ended 12/31/05): Assets, $5,731,264 (M); gifts received, $3,014,399; expenditures, $502,959; qualifying distributions, $468,000; giving activities include $468,000 for 60 grants (high: $50,000; low: $500).
Purpose and activities: Giving primarily for arts and culture, education, health associations, human services, children and youth services, and religion.
Fields of interest: Performing arts; Arts; Higher education; Education; Environment; Animals/ wildlife; Health organizations, association; Youth development, centers/clubs; Human services; Children/youth, services; Federated giving programs; Religion.
Limitations: Applications not accepted. Giving on a national basis. No grants to individuals.
Application information: Contributes only to pre-selected organizations.
Officers and Directors:* Lee J. Styslinger, Jr.,* Chair.; Lee J. Styslinger III,* Pres.; J. Don Williams, Secy.
EIN: 721372302

5

AmSouth Bancorporation Foundation ✧
c/o AmSouth Bank
P.O. Box 11647
Birmingham, AL 35202-1647 (205) 326-5305
Contact: Ann Wells, Treas.

Established in 1997 in AL.
Donors: AmSouth Bank; AmSouth Bancorporation.
Foundation type: Company-sponsored foundation.
Financial data (yr. ended 12/31/04): Assets, $38,292 (M); gifts received, $1,061,250; expenditures, $1,032,629; qualifying distributions, $1,031,813; giving activities include $1,031,813 for 834 grants (high: $100,000; low: $25).

Purpose and activities: The foundation supports organizations involved with arts and culture, education, the environment, health, human services, and community development.
Fields of interest: Museums; Arts; Education; Environment; Health care; Human services; Community development.
Type of support: General/operating support; Employee matching gifts.
Limitations: Giving primarily in AL, FL, GA, and TN. No support for religious organizations not of direct benefit to the entire community, political organizations, or alumni groups. No grants to individuals, or for cultural or social events.
Application information: Application form required.
   Initial approach: Contact foundation for application form
   Deadline(s): Feb. 1, May 1, Aug. 1, and Nov. 1
Officers and Trustees:* Stephen A. Yoder,* Pres.; Douglas J. Jackson,* V.P.; Dale M. Herbert, Secy.; Ann E. Wells, Treas.; Sloan D. Gibson IV; C. Dowd Ritter; AmSouth Bank.
EIN: 631144265

6

The Charlie and Beth Anderson Family Foundation ✦

(formerly The Charles C. and Beth Anderson Family Foundation)
c/o Martin R. Abroms
P.O. Box 1426
Florence, AL   35631

Established in 1999 in TN.
Donors: Charles C. Anderson, Jr.; Beth B. Anderson; Charles C. Anderson.
Foundation type: Independent foundation.
Financial data (yr. ended 12/31/05): Assets, $3,507,128 (M); gifts received, $102,521; expenditures, $1,279,698; qualifying distributions, $1,277,668; giving activities include $1,275,000 for 8 grants (high: $1,000,000; low: $5,000).
Fields of interest: Historic preservation/historical societies; Secondary school/education; Higher education; Libraries (public); Education; Athletics/sports, school programs; Boys & girls clubs; Human services; Children, services; Christian agencies & churches.
Limitations: Applications not accepted. Giving primarily in TN. No grants to individuals.
Application information: Contributes only to pre-selected organizations.
Directors: Martin R. Abroms; Charles C. Anderson, Jr.
EIN: 621795976

7

The Anderson Foundation ✦

1901 6th Ave. N., No. 2900
Birmingham, AL   35203

Established in 1991 in AL.
Donors: Anderson News Co.; American Promotional Events, Inc.; Treat Entertainment, Inc.; Promotion, Inc.; Anderson Management Svcs.; Anderson Merchandisers.
Foundation type: Company-sponsored foundation.
Financial data (yr. ended 12/31/04): Assets, $1,563,130 (M); gifts received, $504,005; expenditures, $478,073; qualifying distributions,

$476,577; giving activities include $474,000 for 12 grants (high: $150,000; low: $1,000).
Purpose and activities: The foundation supports organizations involved with arts and culture, education, health, and human services.
Fields of interest: Arts; Higher education; Education; Health care; Human services.
Limitations: Applications not accepted. Giving primarily in AL, CA, CT, and GA. No grants to individuals.
Application information: Contributes only to pre-selected organizations.
Directors: Charles C. Anderson; Charles C. Anderson, Jr.; Clyde B. Anderson; Harold M. Anderson; Joel R. Anderson; Terry C. Anderson; Gerald H. Daugherty.
EIN: 631045859

8

The Ard Family Foundation ✦

2129 Montgomery Hwy.
Birmingham, AL   35209

Established in 2002 in AL.
Donors: George Garrabant Ard; James Ard.
Foundation type: Operating foundation.
Financial data (yr. ended 12/31/05): Assets, $1,319,583 (M); gifts received, $1,362,656; expenditures, $874,850; qualifying distributions, $873,165; giving activities include $873,165 for 43 grants (high: $145,000; low: $100).
Fields of interest: Health organizations, association; Human services; Public affairs; Christian agencies & churches.
Limitations: Applications not accepted. Giving primarily in AL. No grants to individuals.
Application information: Contributes only to pre-selected organizations.
Officers: George Garrabant Ard, Pres.; Katherine L. Ard, V.P. and Secy.
EIN: 431990285

9

The Aaron Aronov Family Foundation ✦ ☆

3500 Eastern Blvd.
Montgomery, AL   36116

Established in 1992 in AL.
Donor: Marjorie Aronov.
Foundation type: Independent foundation.
Financial data (yr. ended 12/31/05): Assets, $2,441 (M); gifts received, $429,600; expenditures, $439,473; qualifying distributions, $438,795; giving activities include $438,795 for 42 grants (high: $100,000; low: $25).
Purpose and activities: Funding primarily for arts and culture, and medical research.
Fields of interest: Arts; Education; Health organizations, association; Medical research, institute; Human services.
Limitations: Applications not accepted. Giving primarily in AL. No grants to individuals.
Application information: Contributes only to pre-selected organizations.
Officer and Directors:* Marjorie Aronov,* Chair.; Jake F. Aronov; Owen W. Aronov; Teri A. Grusin.
EIN: 631063087
Selected grants: The following grants were reported in 2004.
$56,000 to Montgomery Museum of Fine Arts, Montgomery, AL.

$9,000 to University of Alabama, Tuscaloosa, AL. 3 grants: $2,000, $5,000, $2,000
$5,000 to Huntingdon College, Montgomery, AL.
$5,000 to Montgomery Academy, Montgomery, AL.
$4,901 to Atlanta Scholars Kollel, Atlanta, GA.
$100 to Montgomery County Historical Society, Montgomery, AL.

10

George W. Barber, Jr. Foundation ✦ ☆

27 Inverness Ctr. Pkwy.
Birmingham, AL   35242

Established in 1986 in AL.
Donor: George W. Barber, Jr.
Foundation type: Independent foundation.
Financial data (yr. ended 12/31/05): Assets, $8,864,357 (M); expenditures, $435,772; qualifying distributions, $426,562; giving activities include $426,562 for 9 grants (high: $355,562; low: $1,000).
Purpose and activities: Giving primarily to a museum; some giving for health care and children's services.
Fields of interest: Museums; Arts; Education; Environment, natural resources; Environment; Animals/wildlife, preservation/protection; Health care; Health organizations, association; Children/youth, services.
Limitations: Applications not accepted. Giving primarily in AL. No grants to individuals.
Application information: Contributes only to pre-selected organizations.
Officers: B. Austin Cunningham, Pres.; James N. Hicks, V.P.; T. Paul Sanford, Secy.-Treas.
Director: George W. Barber, Jr.
EIN: 630941684

11

Bashinsky Foundation, Inc. ✦

3432 E. Briarcliff Rd.
Birmingham, AL   35223

Established in 1988 in AL.
Donors: SYB, Inc.; Joann Bashinsky; Sloan Y. Bashinsky, Sr.
Foundation type: Company-sponsored foundation.
Financial data (yr. ended 12/31/05): Assets, $13,811,455 (M); expenditures, $724,388; qualifying distributions, $690,240; giving activities include $635,490 for 9 grants (high: $300,000; low: $2,000), and $54,750 for 22 grants to individuals (high: $3,000; low: $2,500).
Purpose and activities: The foundation supports organizations involved with higher education and human services.
Fields of interest: Higher education; Human services.
Type of support: General/operating support; Employee-related scholarships.
Limitations: Giving limited to areas of company operations, with emphasis on the South. No grants to individuals (except for employee-related scholarships).
Application information: Application form required.
   Initial approach: Contact foundation for application form
   Deadline(s): Mar. 1 to request application form; Mar. 30 for submission

---

Officers: Sloan Y. Bashinsky, Sr., Chair.; John S. Stein, Pres.; Joann Bashinsky, V.P. and Treas.; John P. McKleroy, Jr., Secy.
EIN: 630968201

12

The J. L. Bedsole Foundation ▼ ✧
P.O. Box 1137
Mobile, AL   36633   (251) 432-3369
Contact: Mabel B. Ward, Exec. Dir.
FAX: (251) 432-1134;
E-mail: info@jlbedsolefoundation.org; URL: http://www.jlbedsolefoundation.org

Established in 1949.
Donor: J.L. Bedsole‡.
Foundation type: Independent foundation.
Financial data (yr. ended 12/31/04): Assets, $80,444,473 (M); expenditures, $5,304,402; qualifying distributions, $4,231,796; giving activities include $3,110,669 for 58 grants (high: $500,000; low: $175; average: $5,000–$100,000), and $767,250 for 166 grants to individuals (high: $9,000; low: $500; average: $1,000–$6,000).
Purpose and activities: The foundation's primary interest is the support of educational institutions in Alabama, as well as civic and economic development which is generally limited to southwest Alabama. The arts, social services, and health programs receive limited grants.
Fields of interest: Arts; Elementary/secondary education; Higher education; Hospitals (general); Human services; Economic development.
Type of support: General/operating support; Capital campaigns; Building/renovation; Publication; Scholarship funds; Scholarships—to individuals.
Limitations: Giving limited to Mobile, Baldwin, Clarke, Monroe, and Washington counties, AL. No grants to individuals (except for J.L. Bedsole Scholarships and awards).
Publications: Application guidelines.
Application information: Requests from non-resident applicants not considered or acknowledged. Application form not required.
Initial approach: 1- to 2-page pre-proposal letter
Copies of proposal: 1
Board meeting date(s): Feb., Apr., June, Sept., and Dec.
Final notification: Following distribution committee meetings
Officers and Distribution Committee:* T. Massey Bedsole,* Chair.; Mabel B. Ward,* Exec. Dir.; M. Palmer Bedsole, Jr.; Travis M. Bedsole, Jr.; T. Bestor Ward III; John White-Spunner; Robert J. Williams.
Trustee: AmSouth Bank.
Number of staff: 1 full-time support; 4 part-time support.
EIN: 237225708
Selected grants: The following grants were reported in 2004.
$500,000 to Center for the Living Arts, Mobile, AL. For operating support.
$250,000 to Mobile Carnival Association, Mobile, AL. For capital support.
$250,000 to UMS-Wright Preparatory School, Mobile, AL. For capital support for Raising the Bar Campaign.
$216,000 to MLK Avenue Redevelopment Corporation, Mobile, AL. 2 grants: $146,000 (For operating support), $70,000 (For operating support for Children's Defense Fund Freedom School).

$210,000 to Chamber of Commerce Foundation, Mobile Area, Mobile, AL. For operating support.
$200,000 to Alabama High School of Mathematics and Science, Mobile, AL. For capital support.
$150,000 to Spring Hill College, Mobile, AL. For capital support.
$127,498 to Explore Center, Mobile, AL. For capital support.
$56,831 to Chamber of Commerce, Mobile Area, Mobile, AL. For JL Bedsole International Program Scholarships.

13

Mary K. Archibald Blount Foundation ✧
4119 Old Leeds Ln.
Birmingham, AL   35213
Contact: Kay Blount Miles

Donor: Mary K. Archibald‡.
Foundation type: Independent foundation.
Financial data (yr. ended 12/31/03): Assets, $9,351,012 (M); gifts received, $100,876; expenditures, $434,959; qualifying distributions, $404,714; giving activities include $404,714 for 5 grants (high: $285,714; low: $14,000).
Fields of interest: Elementary/secondary education; Cancer; AIDS.
Application information:
Initial approach: Letter
Deadline(s): None
Officers and Trustees:* Katherine B. Miles,* Chair., Pres., and Treas.; Thomas A. Blount,* Secy.; Joseph W. Blount; S. Roberts Blount; Winton M. Blount III.
EIN: 630823583

14

The Blount Foundation, Inc. ✧
8665 Old Marsh Way
Montgomery, AL   36117   (334) 244-4391
Contact: D. Joseph McInnes, Pres.

Incorporated in 1970 in AL.
Donors: Blount, Inc.; Roberts and Mildred Blount Foundation.
Foundation type: Company-sponsored foundation.
Financial data (yr. ended 12/31/05): Assets, $473,337 (M); expenditures, $652,032; qualifying distributions, $537,360; giving activities include $537,360 for 24 grants (high: $100,000; low: $500).
Purpose and activities: The foundation supports organizations involved with arts and culture, education, health, and civic affairs.
Fields of interest: Museums; Arts; Higher education; Education; Health care; Public affairs.
Type of support: General/operating support; Building/renovation; Equipment; Endowments; Publication; Scholarship funds; Research; Employee matching gifts; Matching/challenge support.
Limitations: Giving primarily in areas of company operations in AL. No support for certain religious or sectarian organizations or governmental or quasi-governmental agencies. No grants to individuals, or for demonstration projects, conferences, seminars, or courtesy advertising; no loans; no in-kind gifts.
Publications: Informational brochure (including application guidelines).
Application information: Proposals should be no longer than 2 to 3 pages. Application form not required.

Initial approach: Proposal
Copies of proposal: 1
Deadline(s): None
Board meeting date(s): As needed
Final notification: 12 weeks following board meeting
Officers: D. Joseph McInnes,* Pres.; Truitt K. Johnson, V.P.; Aubrey M. Dubose, Secy.-Treas.
Number of staff: 1 full-time professional; 1 full-time support.
EIN: 636050260

15

Herman & Emmie Bolden Foundation ✧
P.O. Box 360028
Birmingham, AL   35236   (205) 988-8989
Contact: Herman D. Bolden, V.P.

Established in 1982 in AL.
Donors: Herman D. Bolden; Southern Coach Manufacturing Co., Inc.
Foundation type: Independent foundation.
Financial data (yr. ended 6/30/05): Assets, $4,895,263 (M); expenditures, $642,083; qualifying distributions, $618,600; giving activities include $618,600 for 27 grants (high: $188,100; low: $100).
Purpose and activities: Giving primarily for children's services, and to health associations, education, and churches.
Fields of interest: Education; Health organizations, association; Cancer; Cancer research; Human services; Federated giving programs; Protestant agencies & churches.
Limitations: Giving primarily in AL. No grants to individuals.
Application information: Application form not required.
Deadline(s): None
Officers: Emmie C. Bolden, Pres.; Herman D. Bolden, V.P.; Stanley C. Bolden, Secy.
EIN: 630828670
Selected grants: The following grants were reported in 2005.
$188,100 to University of Alabama, Comprehensive Center, Birmingham, AL. For general support.
$155,000 to Dawson Memorial Baptist Church, Birmingham, AL. For general support.
$59,500 to American Cancer Society, Birmingham, AL. For general support.
$55,000 to Evergreen United Methodist Church, Chapel Hill, NC. For general support.
$51,000 to Arthritis Foundation, Montgomery, AL. For general support.
$37,000 to United Way of Central Alabama, Birmingham, AL. For general support.
$22,950 to Huntingdon College, Montgomery, AL. For general support.
$15,500 to Crippled Childrens Foundation, Birmingham, AL. For general support.
$8,500 to Goodfellows Fund, Monroe, LA. For general support.
$5,000 to Leukemia & Lymphoma Society, Birmingham, AL. For general support.

16

The Harry B. & Jane H. Brock Foundation ◇

(formerly The Brock Foundation)
P.O. Box 11643
Birmingham, AL 35202 (205) 939-0236
Contact: Harry B. Brock, Jr., Pres.

Established in 1985 in AL.
Donor: Harry B. Brock, Jr.
Foundation type: Independent foundation.
Financial data (yr. ended 12/31/05): Assets,
$7,900,079 (M); expenditures, $408,149;
qualifying distributions, $371,582; giving activities
include $370,475 for 41 grants (high: $41,163;
low: $400; average: $5,000–$10,000).
Purpose and activities: Primary areas of interest
include community development, community funds,
social services, and cancer treatment and research.
Fields of interest: Higher education; Education;
Environment, natural resources; Environment;
Cancer; Cancer research; Recreation; Children/
youth, services; Community development;
Federated giving programs; Social sciences;
General charitable giving.
Type of support: General/operating support; Annual
campaigns; Capital campaigns; Endowments;
Program development; Research.
Limitations: Giving primarily in AL. No grants to
individuals.
Publications: Application guidelines.
Application information: Application form not
required.
Initial approach: Letter
Copies of proposal: 3
Deadline(s): Nov. 1
Board meeting date(s): Dec.
Final notification: After board meeting
Officers and Directors:* Harry B. Brock, Jr.,* Pres.;
Jane H. Brock,* V.P.; Carolyn F. Robertson,* Secy.;
Harry B. Brock III; Stanley M. Brock; Barrett B.
MacKay.
EIN: 630926012
Selected grants: The following grants were reported
in 2005.
$41,163 to Samford University, Birmingham, AL.
$38,782 to Mountain Brook Baptist Church,
Birmingham, AL.
$25,000 to Birmingham Zoo, Birmingham, AL.
$20,000 to Childrens Hospital of Alabama,
Birmingham, AL.
$14,380 to University of Alabama, Tuscaloosa, AL.
$10,000 to Methodist Home for the Aging,
Birmingham, AL.
$10,000 to Ronald McDonald House Charities of
Alabama, Birmingham, AL.
$5,000 to McCallie School, Chattanooga, TN.
$2,500 to Humane Society of Shelby County,
Columbiana, AL.
$2,250 to Joyce Meyer Ministries, Fenton, MO.

17

The Joseph S. Bruno Charitable Foundation ◇

P.O. Box 530727
Birmingham, AL 35253-0727 (205) 879-0799
Contact: Jera G. Stribling, Exec. Dir.
FAX: (205) 879-4899; E-mail: jstribling@jsbcf.org

Established in 1985 in AL.
Foundation type: Independent foundation.

Financial data (yr. ended 11/30/05): Assets,
$11,371,143 (M); expenditures, $646,775;
qualifying distributions, $540,536; giving activities
include $448,550 for 40 grants (high: $50,000;
low: $2,000).
Fields of interest: Arts; Education; Health care;
Community development; Religion.
Type of support: Annual campaigns; Capital
campaigns; Building/renovation; Equipment;
Endowments; Program development; Seed money;
Scholarship funds; Program evaluation; Matching/
challenge support.
Limitations: Giving primarily in Birmingham, AL. No
grants to individuals.
Publications: Informational brochure (including
application guidelines).
Application information: Application form not
required.
Initial approach: Letter
Copies of proposal: 1
Deadline(s): Mar. 1 and Sept. 1
Board meeting date(s): Apr. and Oct.
Officers: Robert A. Sprain, Jr., V.P. and Secy.; Benny
M. LaRussa, Jr., V.P. and Treas.; Jera G. Stribling,
Exec. Dir.
Directors: Norm Davis; Anne B. LaRussa; Marian
Phillips.
Number of staff: 1 full-time professional; 1 part-time
support.
EIN: 630936234
Selected grants: The following grants were reported
in 2005.
$315,000 to Birmingham Civil Rights Institute,
Birmingham, AL.
$50,000 to Birmingham Zoo, Birmingham, AL.
$30,000 to Saint Vincents Foundation, Birmingham,
AL.
$20,000 to Ronald McDonald House Charities of
Alabama, Birmingham, AL.
$20,000 to Saint Francis Xavier Catholic Church,
Birmingham, AL.
$15,000 to Alabama Symphony Orchestra,
Birmingham, AL.
$13,550 to McWane Center, Birmingham, AL.
$10,000 to Childrens Dance Foundation,
Birmingham, AL.
$10,000 to Sixteenth Street Foundation,
Birmingham, AL.
$5,000 to Exceptional Foundation, Birmingham, AL.

18

The Caring Foundation

450 Riverchase Pkwy. E.
Birmingham, AL 35244
Contact: James M. Brown, Sr. V.P., Blue Cross and
Blue Shield of Alabama, Inc.

Established in 1990 in AL.
Donor: Blue Cross and Blue Shield of Alabama, Inc.
Foundation type: Company-sponsored foundation.
Financial data (yr. ended 12/31/05): Assets,
$29,476,175 (M); expenditures, $3,614,794;
qualifying distributions, $3,517,541; giving
activities include $3,516,195 for 259 grants (high:
$792,870; low: $50).
Purpose and activities: The foundation supports
organizations involved with education, health,
safety, and children and youth.
Fields of interest: Education; Hospitals (general);
Health care; Safety, education; Children/youth,
services; Federated giving programs.
Type of support: General/operating support;
Program development.

Limitations: Giving primarily in AL. No grants to
individuals, or for capital campaigns.
Application information: Application form not
required.
Initial approach: Proposal
Copies of proposal: 1
Deadline(s): None
Board meeting date(s): 4th Wed. in Apr.
Final notification: 1 to 2 months
Officers and Directors:* M. Eugene Moor, Jr.,*
Chair.; G. Phillip Pope,* Pres.; Terry Kellogg, V.P.
and Treas.; A. Grey Till, Jr., Secy.; Donald M. Ball;
Raymond J. Browne, M.D.; Kenneth Hubbard; W.
Charles Mayer; William J. Stevens.
EIN: 631035261
Selected grants: The following grants were reported
in 2004.
$1,075,349 to Alabama Child Caring Foundation,
Birmingham, AL.
$462,000 to United Way of Madison County,
Huntsville, AL.
$218,750 to Alabama Poison Control Systems,
Tuscaloosa, AL.
$205,000 to Childrens Hospital of Alabama,
Birmingham, AL.
$65,000 to Auburn University Foundation, Auburn,
AL.
$62,000 to University of Alabama, Tuscaloosa, AL.
$50,000 to Alabama Partnership for Children,
Montgomery, AL.
$45,000 to American Red Cross, Mobile, AL.
$32,250 to YMCA of Metropolitan Birmingham,
Birmingham, AL.
$25,000 to Alabama High School of Mathematics
and Science, Mobile, AL.

19

Carson Pirie Scott Foundation ◇

750 Lakeshore Pkwy.
Birmingham, AL 35211
Contact: Edward P. Carroll, Pres.

Incorporated in 1959 in IL.
Donors: Carson Pirie Scott & Co.; Carson
International, Inc.
Foundation type: Company-sponsored foundation.
Financial data (yr. ended 12/31/05): Assets,
$503,827 (M); expenditures, $368,892; qualifying
distributions, $366,107; giving activities include
$366,107 for 141 grants (high: $58,417; low:
$100).
Purpose and activities: The foundation supports
organizations involved with arts and culture,
education, health, youth development, and
community development.
Fields of interest: Arts; Education; Hospitals
(general); Health care; Health organizations; Youth
development; Community development; Federated
giving programs; Government/public administration.
Type of support: Continuing support; Building/
renovation.
Limitations: Applications not accepted. Giving
primarily in areas of company operations, with
emphasis on Chicago, IL. No grants to individuals,
or for endowments or research; no loans; no
matching gifts.
Publications: Program policy statement.
Application information: Contributes only to
pre-selected organizations.
Board meeting date(s): 3rd Mon. in May

Officers and Directors:* Edward P. Carroll, Pres.; Charles J. Hansen,* V.P.; Brian J. Martin, V.P.; Michael R. MacDonald,* Secy.
EIN: 366112629
Selected grants: The following grants were reported in 2004.
$57,636 to United Way of Greater Milwaukee, Milwaukee, WI.
$26,000 to Medical College of Wisconsin, Milwaukee, WI.
$16,000 to United Way of Central Minnesota, Saint Cloud, MN.
$11,609 to United Way of Central Iowa, Des Moines, IA.
$11,048 to United Way of Rock River Valley, Rockford, IL.
$10,291 to United Way of Metropolitan Chicago, Chicago, IL.
$4,554 to United Way of the Midlands, Omaha, NE.
$4,531 to United Way of the DuPage Area, Oak Brook, IL.
$3,622 to United Way of Northwest Illinois, Freeport, IL.
$1,259 to United Way of Siouxland, Sioux City, IA.

20
Central Alabama Community Foundation, Inc. ✧

(formerly Montgomery Area Community Foundation, Inc.)
P.O. Box 427
Montgomery, AL 36101-0427 (334) 264-6223
FAX: (334) 263-6225; E-mail: cacf@bellsouth.net;
URL: http://www.cacfinfo.org

Established in 1987 in AL.
Foundation type: Community foundation.
Financial data (yr. ended 12/31/04): Assets, $27,809,922 (M); gifts received, $12,144,567; expenditures, $2,784,041; giving activities include $1,880,041 for grants.
Purpose and activities: The foundation was created by and for the people of central Alabama. Individuals and corporate donors make gifts and bequests of any size for the betterment of the community. Through the grants program, the foundation addresses a wide variety of needs and opportunities, supporting programs and projects in education, human services, health, cultural arts, and other civic concerns.
Fields of interest: Arts; Education; Health care; Human services; Nonprofit management; Community development.
Type of support: Program development; Seed money; Scholarship funds; Technical assistance; Scholarships—to individuals; Matching/challenge support.
Limitations: Giving limited to Autauga, Elmore, Lowndes, Macon, and Montgomery counties, AL. No grants to individuals (except for designated scholarship funds limited to local area residents).
Publications: Application guidelines; Annual report; Newsletter.
Application information: RFP available in mid-July. Visit foundation Web site for application forms, guidelines, and deadlines per grant type. Application form required.
Initial approach: Letter
Copies of proposal: 2
Deadline(s): Varies with area
Final notification: Mar. and Nov.
Officers and Directors:* Winton M. Blount III,* Pres.; Elizabeth T. Emmet,* V.P.; Rhonda L. Sibley,*

Secy.-Treas.; Carol W. Butler, Exec. Dir.; Carl Barranco; Larry Bern; LaBarron Boone; Cedric Bradford; Elton N. Dean, Sr.; W. Inge Hill, Jr.; Debbie Hobbs; William F. Joseph; Margaret B. Lowder; Mac McLeod; Caroline B. Novak; Sim Penton; Ray Petty; Dee Russell; James Scott; Christopher S. Simmons; Kathy Sawyer; Albert Striplin; John Trotman, Sr.; Ken Upchurch III; Ronnie J. Wynn.
Number of staff: 4 full-time professional; 1 full-time support.
EIN: 630842355

21
Christian Workers Foundation of Alabama, Inc.

5181 Desoto Caverns Pkwy.
Childersburg, AL 35044-9713
Contact: Allen Mathis

Established in 2001 in AL.
Donor: Allen W. Mathis, Jr.
Foundation type: Independent foundation.
Financial data (yr. ended 6/30/05): Assets, $12,398,434 (M); gifts received, $2,858,506; expenditures, $631,666; qualifying distributions, $450,000; giving activities include $450,000 for 17 grants (high: $135,000; low: $5,000).
Purpose and activities: The foundation supports evangelical para-church organizations that board members have a relationship with.
Fields of interest: Christian agencies & churches.
Limitations: Applications not accepted. Giving on a national basis. No grants to individuals.
Application information: Contributes only to pre-selected organizations.
Board meeting date(s): Apr. or May
Trustee: Allen W. Mathis III.
EIN: 311745056
Selected grants: The following grants were reported in 2004.
$79,000 to InterVarsity Christian Fellowship/USA, Madison, WI.
$67,000 to Miracle of Nazareth International Foundation, Mishawaka, IN.
$37,000 to Young Life, Colorado Springs, CO.
$28,000 to Moody Bible Institute of Chicago, Chicago, IL.
$25,000 to Knollwood Christian School, Sylacauga, AL.
$15,000 to Campus Outreach, Birmingham, AL.
$10,000 to Campus Crusade for Christ International, Orlando, FL.
$10,000 to Westminster Theological Seminary, Glenside, PA.
$5,000 to Fellowship of Christian Athletes, Montgomery, AL.
$5,000 to Ute Trail Ranch Foundation, Dallas, TX.

22
The Comer Foundation ✧

31 Inverness Center Pkwy., Ste. 50
Birmingham, AL 35242-4842
Contact: Shirley Ogburn, Admin.
FAX: (205) 408-9834;
E-mail: comerfoundation@aol.com

Incorporated in 1945 in AL.
Donors: Avondale Mills; Comer-Avondale Mills, Inc.; Cowikee Mills.
Foundation type: Independent foundation.

Financial data (yr. ended 12/31/03): Assets, $13,250,923 (M); expenditures, $852,721; qualifying distributions, $824,266; giving activities include $724,600 for 27 grants (high: $70,000; low: $100).
Purpose and activities: Emphasis on higher and other education; support also for health, recreation, human services, and cultural programs.
Fields of interest: Elementary/secondary education; Higher education; Education; Health care; Recreation; Human services.
Limitations: Giving primarily in AL. No grants to individuals.
Application information: Application form not required.
Initial approach: Letter
Copies of proposal: 1
Deadline(s): None
Board meeting date(s): Quarterly
Officers and Trustees:* Gillian C. Goodrich,* Chair.; Shirley Ogburn, Admin.; Richard J. Comer, Jr.; Francis H. Crockard; Hugh Comers Nabers, Jr.; Jane B. Selfe.
Number of staff: 1 full-time professional.
EIN: 636004424
Selected grants: The following grants were reported in 2003.
$100,000 to Childrens Hospital of Alabama, Birmingham, AL. For establishment of research and innovation center.
$56,000 to Auburn University, Auburn, AL. For scholarships.
$50,000 to Mountain Brook Library Foundation, Mountain Brook, AL. For support of plant expansion.
$37,500 to University of Alabama, Tuscaloosa, AL. For scholarships.
$20,000 to Birmingham-Southern College, Birmingham, AL. For scholarships.
$18,750 to University of Montevallo, Montevallo, AL. For scholarships.
$15,000 to Childrens Harbor, Alexander City, AL. For program support.
$15,000 to Jacksonville State University, Jacksonville, AL. For scholarships.
$7,500 to Alabama State University, Montgomery, AL. For scholarships.
$7,500 to Central Alabama Community College, Alexander City, AL. For scholarships.

23
Community Foundation of Calhoun County ✧

(formerly Calhoun County Community Foundation)
1000 Quintard Ave., Ste. 307
P.O. Box 1826
Anniston, AL 36202 (256) 231-5160
Contact: Wayne Carmello-Harper, C.E.O.; For grant requests: Eula Tatman, Dir., Grants and Progs.
FAX: (256) 231-5161;
E-mail: info@yourcommunityfirst.org; URL: http://www.yourcommunityfirst.org/

Established in 1997 in AL; reorganized as a community foundation in 1999.
Foundation type: Community foundation.
Financial data (yr. ended 9/30/05): Assets, $17,949,654 (M); gifts received, $1,392,834; expenditures, $1,093,521; giving activities include $521,782 for grants.
Purpose and activities: The foundation awards grants in the following general areas: projects that directly serve persons who are unable to afford basic

medical care; projects that benefit the general public through health education; and projects that promote or improve healthcare. The foundation also awards several scholarships and grants from various donor funds.

Fields of interest: Arts; Child development, education; Education; Health care; Mental health, treatment; Human services.

Type of support: General/operating support; Building/renovation; Equipment; Emergency funds; Program development; Conferences/seminars; Publication; Scholarship funds; Research; Technical assistance; Matching/challenge support.

Limitations: Giving to organizations who provide services to residents of Calhoun County, AL. No support for religious organizations for religious purposes or to influence elections. No grants to individuals (except for scholarships), or for organizations operating less than one year, endowments, special events or fundraising campaigns, or capital campaigns.

Publications: Application guidelines; Annual report; Financial statement; Grants list; Informational brochure; Newsletter.

Application information: The foundation reviews Letters of Proposal and determines which organizations receive an invitation to submit a grant application; grant applications are not accepted without official invitation from foundation. Visit foundation Web site for application form and guidelines. Application form required.

  Initial approach: Submit Letter of Proposal (no longer than 3 pages)
  Copies of proposal: 10
  Deadline(s): May 15 for Letter of Proposal (with Sept. 1 application due date) and Nov. 15 (with Mar. 1 application due date)
  Board meeting date(s): Quarterly
  Final notification: First week of May and Nov.

Officers and Directors:* Terry Childers,* Chair.; J.B. Freeman,* Vice-Chair.; Wayne Carmello-Harper, C.E.O. and Pres.; Betty Hill Jackson,* Secy.; Forrest French,* Treas.; James S. Daniel, M.D.; Vikki Floyd; Leon Garrett; Janice Hudson; James Mullis, Jr., M.D.; Robert Smith; Wesley Smith, M.D.; Esta Spector; Arthur F. Toole III, M.D.; Martha Vandervoort; Maj. Genl. Gerald G. Watson.

Number of staff: 3 full-time professional; 1 part-time professional.

EIN: 630308398

24
The Community Foundation of Greater Birmingham ▼ ◇

(formerly The Greater Birmingham Foundation)
2100 First Ave. N., Ste. 700
Birmingham, AL 35203 (205) 328-8641
Contact: Kate Nielsen, Pres.; For grants: Patti Whitt, Sr. Prog. Off.
FAX: (205) 328-6576;
E-mail: info@foundationbirmingham.org; Additional E-mail: patti@foundationbirmingham.org;
URL: http://www.foundationbirmingham.org

Established in 1959 in AL by resolution and declaration of trust; corporate side established in 1997.

Foundation type: Community foundation.

Financial data (yr. ended 12/31/04): Assets, $125,430,040 (M); gifts received, $5,288,383; expenditures, $10,807,075; giving activities

include $9,258,875 for 543 grants (high: $225,000; low: $135).

Purpose and activities: The foundation seeks to make life better in the greater Birmingham, AL, area, by connecting caring people and key resources with community needs, today and tomorrow. Primary areas of interest include arts and culture, education, the environment, health, human services and strengthening families, and supportive communities.

Fields of interest: Arts, artist's services; Arts; Higher education; Libraries/library science; Education, drop-out prevention; Education, reading; Education; Environment, toxics; Environment, beautification programs; Environment; Reproductive health, prenatal care; Health care, insurance; Health care; Substance abuse, prevention; Recreation, parks/playgrounds; Neighborhood centers; Children, day care; Family services; Family services, parent education; Family services, adolescent parents; Human services, emergency aid; Aging, centers/services; Human services; Nonprofit management; Community development; Public affairs; Economically disadvantaged.

Type of support: Capital campaigns; Building/renovation; Equipment; Program development; Publication; Seed money; Curriculum development; Matching/challenge support.

Limitations: Giving limited to Blount, Jefferson, Shelby, St. Clair, and Walker counties, AL. No support for religious organizations or for religious purposes (except from Advised Funds). No grants to individuals directly, or for endowment funds, operating budgets, deficit reduction, national fundraising drives, conference or seminar expenses, benefit tickets, or replacement of government funding cuts.

Publications: Application guidelines; Annual report; Financial statement; Grants list; Informational brochure; Newsletter.

Application information: Visit foundation Web site for proposal summary form and application guidelines. Agencies that have not applied to the foundation before must attend an Overview Session before submitting a proposal. Application form required.

  Initial approach: Telephone or e-mail
  Copies of proposal: 3
  Deadline(s): Mar. 15 and Sept. 15
  Board meeting date(s): Biannually (May and Nov.) for distribution of unrestricted funds; other meetings as needed
  Final notification: May and Dec.

Officers and Directors:* Jeffrey H. Cohn, M.D.*, Chair.; Van L. Richey,* Vice-Chair.; Kate Nielsen, Pres.; James A. King III, V.P., Devel.; Karen Rolen, V.P., Initiatives and Progs.; Wendy Rodde, C.F.O.; Kirkwood R. Balton; Ralph D. Cook; H. Corbin Day; Edward M. Friend III; Gillian White Goodrich; M. Miller Gorrie; Thomas H. Lowder; Carl E. "Eddie" Miller III; Margaret M. Porter; Carole W. Samuelson, M.D.; William E. Smith, Jr.; Odessa Woolfolk.

Trustee Banks: AmSouth Bank; Canterbury Trust Company; Compass Bank; CB&T; National Bank of Commerce; Regions Bank; The Trust Co. of Sterne, Agee and Leach; Wachovia Bank, N.A.

Number of staff: 8 full-time professional; 1 part-time professional; 3 full-time support; 1 part-time support.

EIN: 631209631

25
The Community Foundation of South Alabama

(formerly The Mobile Community Foundation)
154-A St. Louis St.
Mobile, AL 36602 (251) 438-5591
Contact: Thomas H. Davis, Jr., Exec. Dir.
FAX: (251) 438-5592;
E-mail: info@communityendowment.com;
Application address: P.O. Box 990, Mobile, AL 36601-0990; Additional E-mail: tdavis@communityendowment.com; URL: http://www.communityendowment.com

Incorporated in 1976 in AL.

Foundation type: Community foundation.

Financial data (yr. ended 9/30/05): Assets, $44,818,298 (M); gifts received, $6,379,253; expenditures, $6,103,551; giving activities include $4,322,645 for 458 grants.

Purpose and activities: The foundation strengthens the future of nonprofit organizations in Southwest Alabama by encouraging gifts, large and small from all segments of the community. Giving primarily for philanthropy and voluntarism, education, arts and recreation, health and human services and community and civic affairs. Visit the foundation's Web site for special grant application information and requirements available to nonprofits through the Hurricane Katrina Relief Fund, a collaborative effort of the foundation, the United Way of Southwest Alabama, and WKRG-TV5 to assist agencies servicing hurricane victims in Alabama, Mississippi and Louisiana.

Fields of interest: Visual arts; Performing arts; Performing arts, dance; Arts; Education; Environment; Health care; Crime/violence prevention; Crime/violence prevention, abuse prevention; Disasters, Hurricane Katrina; Recreation; Human services; Community development, citizen coalitions; Community development, neighborhood associations; Philanthropy/voluntarism.

Type of support: General/operating support; Annual campaigns; Building/renovation; Emergency funds; Program development; Seed money; Scholarship funds; In-kind gifts; Matching/challenge support.

Limitations: Giving primarily in the eight counties of southwestern AL: Baldwin, Choctaw, Clarke, Conecuh, Escambia, Mobile, Monroe, and Washington. No support for religious organizations for religious purposes. No grants to individuals, or for national fundraising drives, conference or seminar expenses, tickets for charity benefits, or budget deficits.

Publications: Application guidelines; Annual report; Financial statement; Informational brochure (including application guidelines); Newsletter.

Application information: Visit foundation Web site for full application form and guidelines. Application form required.

  Initial approach: Submit application form and attachments
  Copies of proposal: 9
  Deadline(s): Feb. 1 for Arts and Oct. 2 for Education
  Board meeting date(s): Quarterly
  Final notification: Apr. for Arts and Dec. for Education

Officers and Directors:* G. Porter Brock, Jr.,* Pres.; Ron Melton,* V.P.; Michael S. Marshall,* Secy.; George V. Davis,* Treas.; Thomas H. Davis, Jr., Exec. Dir.; Walter A. Bell; Yuell Busey; Murray E. Cape; J. Gary Cooper; Barbara Drummond; Dr.

Bernard H. Eichold, II; Robert M. Hodgson; Kimberly H. Jardine; Vivian G. Johnston, Jr.; Neil Kennedy; John R. McNeil; Herbert A. Meisler; Mrs. Arlene Mitchell; Thomas E. Mitchell; Norman D. Pitman, Jr.; Mary Powell; Mrs. Edna Rivers; John Saint; Irving Silver; Luis M. Williams; Robert J. Williams; Winston Williams; Raymond R. Wingard.
Number of staff: 2 full-time professional; 2 full-time support; 1 part-time support.
EIN: 630695166

26
Community Foundation of Southeast Alabama ✧

(formerly Wiregrass Community Foundation)
179 Honeysuckle Rd., Ste. 5
P.O. Box 1422
Dothan, AL 36302-1422 (334) 671-1059
FAX: (334) 793-0627; URL: http://www.cfsea.org

Established in 1995 in AL.
Foundation type: Community foundation.
Financial data (yr. ended 12/31/04): Assets, $619,911 (M); gifts received, $99,856; expenditures, $360,028; giving activities include $332,751 for grants.
Purpose and activities: The mission of the Community Foundation of Southeast Alabama is to identify and connect caring people and their resources with community needs, today and tomorrow.
Fields of interest: Humanities; Arts; Education; Environment; Health care; Human services; Economic development; Religion.
Limitations: Giving limited to the five-county Wiregrass region of Coffee, Dale, Geneva, Henry, and Houston counties, AL. No grants to individuals.
Application information:
  Initial approach: Contact foundation
Officers and Trustees: Bill Flowers,* Chair. and Treas.; Barbara Everett,* Vice-Chair.; David C. Jamison,* Pres. and Secy.; Loretta Baker; E.E. "Top" Bishop, Jr.; Brent Browning; Jane Brunson; Joe Copeland; Phil Forrester; David Hansen; Sean Hara; David Herndon; David C. Jamison; David Johnston; David "Mit" Kirkland; Davis Malone; Nadine Marley; Mark O'Mary; Bill Parker; Jim Rudd; Morris Slingluff; Ralph Smith; Neil Strickland; Mary Alice Veal; Francina Williams.
Number of staff: 2 part-time professional; 2 part-time support.
EIN: 631126660

27
Community Foundation of West Alabama ✧

P.O. Box 3033
Tuscaloosa, AL 35403 (205) 366-0698
Contact: Glenn Taylor, Exec. Dir.
E-mail: CFOWA@bellsouth.net; URL: http://www.thecfwa.org

Established in 1999 in AL.
Foundation type: Community foundation.
Financial data (yr. ended 12/31/05): Assets, $4,615,658 (M); gifts received, $3,324,640; expenditures, $525,028; giving activities include $460,659 for grants.
Purpose and activities: The foundation seeks to connect people and resources to the real needs of the community. The foundation strives to help build

partnerships between donors, nonprofit organizations and the community at large in order to strengthen and enhance the quality of life of the people of western AL.
Fields of interest: Humanities; Arts; Education; Environment; Health care; Disasters, Hurricane Katrina; Recreation; Residential/custodial care, hospices; Aging, centers/services; Human services; Community development; Federated giving programs; Children/youth.
Limitations: Giving limited to western AL, including Bibb, Fayette, Green, Hale, Lamar, Pickens, Sumter, and Tuscaloosa. No support for religious organizations for religious purposes. No grants to individuals (except for scholarships), or for dinners, balls, or other ticketed events, or endowments.
Application information: Visit foundation Web site for application form and guidelines. Application form required.
  Initial approach: Submit application form and attachments
  Copies of proposal: 1
  Deadline(s): Apr. 1 and Oct. 1
  Board meeting date(s): May and Nov.
  Final notification: May and Nov.
Officers and Directors: Davis S. "Buddy" Burton, Jr.,* Chair.; Laura Gregory McKane,* Chair., Grants; Thomas A. Nettles IV,* Pres.; William A. Tate,* V.P.; Gina Miers,* Secy.; William W. Walker, Jr.,* Treas.; Glenn Taylor, Exec. Dir.; John L. Blackburn; Joseph D. "Jody" Blackburn; Pierce Boyd; Sam Faucett; James I. Harrison III; Anne Moman; Gordon Rosen; Charles Storey.
EIN: 631225003

28
Compass Bank Foundation ✧

(formerly Central Bank Foundation)
P.O. Box 10566, M.C. AL/BI/CH/ACT
Birmingham, AL 35296
Contact: Jerry W. Powell, Tr.
Application address: 15 S. 20th St., Birmingham, AL 35233, tel.: (205) 297-3960

Established in 1981 in AL.
Donor: Compass Bank.
Foundation type: Company-sponsored foundation.
Financial data (yr. ended 12/31/05): Assets, $6,823,686 (M); gifts received, $3,406,789; expenditures, $3,411,294; qualifying distributions, $3,409,694; giving activities include $3,409,694 for 447 grants (high: $666,000; low: $25).
Purpose and activities: The foundation supports organizations involved with arts and culture, higher education, and public policy.
Fields of interest: Performing arts, orchestra (symphony); Performing arts, opera; Arts; Higher education; American Red Cross; Federated giving programs; Public policy, research.
Type of support: General/operating support; Annual campaigns; Program development; Scholarship funds; Sponsorships; Employee-related scholarships; Matching/challenge support.
Limitations: Giving primarily in AL, AZ, CO, FL, NM, and TX. No support for religious organizations. No grants to individuals (except for employee-related scholarships).
Application information:
  Initial approach: Contact foundation for application information
Officer and Trustees: Garrett R. Hegel, Pres.; D. Paul Jones, Jr.; Jerry W. Powell.
EIN: 630823545

Selected grants: The following grants were reported in 2004.
$334,000 to University of Houston-University Park, Bauer College of Business, Houston, TX.
$100,000 to University of Alabama, Birmingham, AL. 2 grants: $50,000 each
$80,000 to Economic Development Partnership of Alabama Foundation, Birmingham, AL.
$60,000 to Alabama Symphony Orchestra, Birmingham, AL.
$50,000 to Houston Grand Opera, Houston, TX.
$25,000 to American Red Cross, National Headquarters, DC.
$25,000 to Museum of Fine Arts, Houston, Houston, TX.
$25,000 to University of North Florida, Coggin College of Business, Jacksonville, FL.
$22,000 to Schultz Center for Teaching and Leadership, Jacksonville, FL.

29
Corman Foundation, Inc. ✧

P.O. Drawer 1268
Atmore, AL 36504
Contact: Charles R. Dettling, Exec. Dir.
E-mail: cdellting@trinsic.com; Additional e-mail: lparsons@trinsic.com; URL: http://www.cormanfoundation.org

Established in 1993 in AL.
Donors: James F. Corman; Jane D. Corman.
Foundation type: Independent foundation.
Financial data (yr. ended 12/31/04): Assets, $7,326,854 (M); expenditures, $2,016,506; qualifying distributions, $1,808,465; giving activities include $1,686,006 for 19 grants (high: $1,104,275; low: $210).
Purpose and activities: Giving limited to major Evangelical Christian ministries involved in evangelism, discipleship, leadership training, development, and church planting.
Fields of interest: Christian agencies & churches.
International interests: Eastern Europe; India; Latin America; Soviet Union (Former); Western Africa.
Type of support: General/operating support; Continuing support; Program development; Conferences/seminars; Internship funds; Technical assistance; Consulting services; Matching/challenge support.
Limitations: Applications not accepted. Giving on an international basis, primarily in Eastern Europe, Eurasia, India and surrounding areas, and parts of western Africa. No support for colleges, schools, local organizations, or directly to foreign charities. No grants to individuals, or for domestic church construction.
Application information: Unsolicited requests for funds not accepted.
  Board meeting date(s): Every other Thurs.
Officers and Directors: James F. Corman,* Pres.; Jane D. Corman,* Secy.-Treas.; Charles R. Dettling,* Exec. Dir.
Number of staff: 1 full-time professional; 2 part-time professional.
EIN: 631084918
Selected grants: The following grants were reported in 2004.
$1,104,275 to Campus Crusade for Christ International, Orlando, FL. For family ministry.
$131,250 to Impact Movement, Orlando, FL. For foreign mission.
$85,505 to Evangelism Explosion International, Fort Lauderdale, FL. For family ministry.

$70,500 to Mission to the World, Lawrenceville, GA. For foreign mission.

$53,169 to Christian Business Mens Committee of U.S.A., Chattanooga, TN. For family ministry.

$41,300 to Jesus Video Project, San Bernardino, CA. For family ministry.

$37,000 to Faith Comes By Hearing International Foundation, Albuquerque, NM. For foreign mission.

$25,000 to Grace Community Church, Mobile, AL. For family ministry.

$22,750 to Campus Outreach, Birmingham, AL. For family ministry.

$20,184 to Trans World Radio, Cary, NC. For foreign mission.

30
Crampton Trust ✧

c/o Regions Bank
P.O. Box 2527
Mobile, AL 36622 (251) 690-1411
Contact: J.D. Peake, Jr.

Established in 1993 in AL.
Donor: Katharine C. Cochrane†.
Foundation type: Independent foundation.
Financial data (yr. ended 12/31/05): Assets, $19,516,607 (M); expenditures, $1,131,416; qualifying distributions, $936,732; giving activities include $926,639 for 36 grants (high: $100,000; low: $2,750; average: $3,000–$25,000).
Purpose and activities: Giving primarily for arts and culture, a public library, education, and health and human services.
Fields of interest: Museums (art); Arts; Libraries (public); Education; Health care; Health organizations, association; Food banks; Human services; Children/youth, services.
Type of support: General/operating support; Capital campaigns; Building/renovation; Equipment; Endowments; Program-related investments/loans.
Limitations: Giving primarily limited to southwestern AL, including Baldwin, Clarke, Escambia, Mobile, Monroe and Washington counties. No grants to individuals.
Application information: Application form not required.
  Initial approach: Letter
  Deadline(s): None
Distribution Committee: Gilbert F. Dukes, Jr.; John C. Johnson; Mabel B. Ward.
Trustee: Regions Bank.
EIN: 636181261
Selected grants: The following grants were reported in 2003.
$189,507 to Center for the Living Arts, Mobile, AL. For preservation and expansion.
$150,000 to UMS-Wright Preparatory School, Mobile, AL. For capital campaign.
$92,000 to Mobile Museum of Art, Mobile, AL. For capital campaign.
$78,192 to University of South Alabama, Mobile, AL. 3 grants: $40,000 (For medical scholarship), $5,000 (For Cancer Research Institute equipment purchase), $33,192 to College of Medicine (For professorship).
$35,000 to University of Mobile, Mobile, AL. For computer system.
$25,000 to Spring Hill College, Mobile, AL. For library capital campaign.
$25,000 to Tuskegee University, Tuskegee, AL. For legacy campaign.

$15,000 to American Red Cross, Mobile, AL. For Disaster Response Program.

31
The Daniel Foundation of Alabama ▼

820 Shades Creek Pkwy., Ste. 1200
Birmingham, AL 35209
Contact: Maria S. Kennedy

Established in 1978 in AL as partial successor to the Daniel Foundation.
Foundation type: Independent foundation.
Financial data (yr. ended 12/31/05): Assets, $115,598,465 (M); expenditures, $5,633,561; qualifying distributions, $5,427,500; giving activities include $5,427,500 for 199 grants.
Purpose and activities: Emphasis on higher education and cultural organizations.
Fields of interest: Arts; Higher education; Education; Health care; Human services.
Limitations: Giving primarily in the southeastern U.S., with emphasis on AL.
Publications: Application guidelines; Annual report.
Application information: Guidelines must be requested each time prior to submitting a proposal. Application form required.
  Initial approach: Letter
  Copies of proposal: 5
  Deadline(s): 15th of the month prior to board meeting
  Board meeting date(s): Mar., July and Nov.
  Final notification: Varies
Officers and Directors: * Charles W. Daniel,* Chair.; Lyndra P. Daniel,* Pres.; Marion Daniel Head, V.P.; James F. Hughey, Jr.,* V.P.; Maria Kennedy,* Exec. Dir.
Number of staff: 1 part-time professional; 1 part-time support.
EIN: 630736444
Selected grants: The following grants were reported in 2005.
$500,000 to Citadel, The, Charleston, SC.
$350,000 to Mayo Foundation, Rochester, MN.
$250,000 to Discovery 2000, McWane Center, Birmingham, AL.
$200,000 to Birmingham Museum of Art, Birmingham, AL.
$200,000 to Salvation Army.
$150,000 to Troy University, Troy, AL.
$25,000 to Birmingham Landmarks, Pelham, AL.
$25,000 to Cornerstone Schools of Alabama, Birmingham, AL.
$20,000 to Jubilee Community Center, Montgomery, AL.
$10,000 to Giving Flite, Birmingham, AL.

32
The Dixon Foundation

2830 Cahaba Rd.
Birmingham, AL 35223

Established in 1986 in AL.
Foundation type: Operating foundation.
Financial data (yr. ended 12/31/04): Assets, $14,180,328 (M); expenditures, $1,361,301; qualifying distributions, $719,315; giving activities include $526,580 for 53 grants (high: $109,420; low: $64), and $167,764 for foundation-administered programs.
Purpose and activities: Primarily awards grants to ministers of the North Alabama Conference of the United Methodist Church for continuing study and programs; support also for health organizations, medical research, and children's services.
Fields of interest: Adult/continuing education; Pediatrics; Health organizations; Medical research; Children/youth, services; Protestant agencies & churches.
Type of support: Continuing support; Program development; Fellowships; Research; Grants to individuals.
Limitations: Giving primarily to residents and organizations in AL.
Application information: Application form not required.
  Initial approach: Letter
  Deadline(s): None
  Board meeting date(s): Usually 3 times per year
Officers and Directors: * Edwin M. Dixon,* Pres.; David E. Dixon, V.P. and Treas.; Alice D. Grotnes, V.P.
Number of staff: 2 part-time professional.
EIN: 630944809
Selected grants: The following grants were reported in 2003.
$105,725 to Highlands United Methodist Church, Birmingham, AL.
$94,132 to University of Alabama, Birmingham, AL. 2 grants: $40,008 (For junior faculty research), $54,124 (For Dixon Post Doctoral Fellowship program).
$21,438 to New Life Harvest Ministries, Birmingham, AL. For Children's Ministries.
$20,000 to United Way of Central Alabama, Birmingham, AL.
$15,500 to Camp Smile-A-Mile, Birmingham, AL. For Children with Cancer.
$12,000 to First Priority of Alabama, Birmingham, AL.
$11,450 to Auburn University Foundation, Auburn, AL.
$10,455 to Purdue Foundation, West Lafayette, IN.
$5,000 to McWane Center, Birmingham, AL.

33
Curtis Finlay Foundation, Inc. ✧

P.O. Box 298
Brewton, AL 36427 (251) 867-7706
Contact: Richard D. Finlay, Dir.

Established in AL.
Donor: Curtis Finlay†.
Foundation type: Independent foundation.
Financial data (yr. ended 12/31/05): Assets, $11,020,321 (M); expenditures, $665,304; qualifying distributions, $515,000; giving activities include $459,000 for 50 grants (high: $50,000; low: $250), and $41,000 for 12 grants to individuals (high: $4,000; low: $1,000).
Purpose and activities: Scholarships only to residents of Escambia County, AL, attending accredited preparatory schools, four-year colleges or universities, or Jefferson Davis Community College, AL; giving also for the arts and human services.
Fields of interest: Arts, government agencies; Higher education; Education; Human services; American Red Cross; YM/YWCAs & YM/YWHAs; Community development, neighborhood development; Federated giving programs.
Type of support: General/operating support; Scholarship funds; Scholarships—to individuals.
Limitations: Giving limited to AL. Scholarships limited to residents of Escambia County, AL; giving to organizations primarily in Brewton, AL.

Application information: Application form not required.

    Deadline(s): None

Directors: Richard D. Finlay; Sally Finlay; Paul D. Owens, Jr.

EIN: 631080992

34

Founders Charitable Foundation, Inc. ✧ ☆

2140 11th Ave. S., Ste. 402
Birmingham, AL 35205 (205) 212-5353
Contact: William K. Nicrosi

Established in 2001 in AL.

Donors: Michael B. Patton; Timothy R. Smith; Carl O. Black; Marilyn S. Black; William B. Israel.

Foundation type: Independent foundation.

Financial data (yr. ended 12/31/05): Assets, $1,551,588 (M); gifts received, $164,790; expenditures, $429,698; qualifying distributions, $414,904; giving activities include $414,904 for 41 grants (high: $55,000; low: $80).

Fields of interest: Environment; Health organizations, association; Human services; Children/youth, services; Christian agencies & churches.

Application information: Application form required.

    Initial approach: Letter

    Deadline(s): None

Directors: William K. Nicrosi II; Kenneth H. Polk.

EIN: 631263667

Selected grants: The following grants were reported in 2005.

$12,000 to American Red Cross.
$10,000 to Mountain Brook City Schools, Mountain Brook, AL.
$10,000 to Salvation Army.
$4,000 to Childrens Hospital.
$4,000 to Rhodes College, Memphis, TN.
$3,000 to First Baptist Church.
$2,000 to Center for Children and Young Adults, Marietta, GA.
$1,250 to New York Fellowship, New York, NY.
$500 to Creative Montessori School, Homewood, AL.

35

The Frank and Fred Friedman Family Foundation ✧

(formerly The Frank and Fred Friedman Foundation)
c/o Fred H. Friedman
P.O. Box 430229
Birmingham, AL 35243-1229
E-mail: fredf3443@aol.com

Established in 1990 in AL.

Donor: Frank Friedman.

Foundation type: Independent foundation.

Financial data (yr. ended 3/31/06): Assets, $11,958,743 (M); gifts received, $19,233; expenditures, $1,010,873; qualifying distributions, $734,502; giving activities include $734,502 for 49 grants (high: $437,694; low: $100).

Fields of interest: Education; Health care; Jewish agencies & temples.

Type of support: Annual campaigns; Capital campaigns; Building/renovation; Curriculum development; Matching/challenge support.

Limitations: Applications not accepted. Giving limited to Birmingham, AL, and the surrounding counties. No grants to individuals.

Application information: Contributes only to pre-selected organizations.

    Board meeting date(s): Biannually

Officers and Directors:* Fred H. Friedman,* Pres. and Treas.; Brenda Friedman,* Secy.; Jordan Friedman; Leah Friedman.

EIN: 630921651

36

The James I. Harrison Family Foundation ✧

6745 Emerald Ln.
Tuscaloosa, AL 35406 (205) 342-3246
Contact: James I. Harrison, Jr., Pres.

Established in 1997 in GA.

Donor: James I. Harrison, Jr.

Foundation type: Independent foundation.

Financial data (yr. ended 12/31/05): Assets, $17,901,743 (M); gifts received, $250; expenditures, $1,017,513; qualifying distributions, $908,680; giving activities include $907,400 for 14 grants (high: $600,000; low: $500).

Purpose and activities: Giving primarily to charitable organizations in Tuscaloosa County, AL. Most grants are awarded based on the proactive efforts of the foundation president.

Fields of interest: Elementary/secondary education; Higher education; Health organizations, association; Youth development, centers/clubs; Human services.

Limitations: Giving generally limited to Tuscaloosa County, AL.

Application information:

    Initial approach: Telephone or written request

    Deadline(s): None

Officer: James I. Harrison, Jr., Pres. and Secy.-Treas.

Director: Peggy T. Harrison.

Trustee: Lazard Freres & Co.

EIN: 582327810

37

Hearin-Chandler Foundation ✧

(formerly Chandler Foundation)
P.O. Box 81328
Mobile, AL 36689 (251) 344-9970
Contact: Luis M. Williams, Tr.

Established in 1963 in AL.

Donors: Ralph B. Chandler†; William J. Hearin†.

Foundation type: Independent foundation.

Financial data (yr. ended 12/31/05): Assets, $27,391,377 (M); expenditures, $1,464,999; qualifying distributions, $1,106,782; giving activities include $1,041,877 for 34 grants (high: $250,000; low: $1,000).

Purpose and activities: Giving primarily to cultural institutions; giving also for education, the environment, and human services.

Fields of interest: Museums; Performing arts; Arts; Higher education; Libraries (public); Botanical gardens; Environment, beautification programs; Human services; Community development; Christian agencies & churches; Women.

Type of support: Scholarship funds; Program development; Matching/challenge support; General/operating support; Equipment; Endowments; Capital campaigns; Building/renovation.

Limitations: Giving primarily in Mobile County, AL. No grants to individuals.

Application information: Application form not required.

    Initial approach: Letter

    Copies of proposal: 1

    Deadline(s): Oct. 1

    Board meeting date(s): Dec.

    Final notification: Jan. of the next calendar year

Trustee: Luis M. Williams.

Number of staff: 1 part-time professional.

EIN: 636075470

Selected grants: The following grants were reported in 2003.

$100,000 to Mercy Medical, Daphne, AL.
$100,000 to Providence Hospital Foundation, Mobile, AL.
$100,000 to Spring Hill College, Mobile, AL.
$75,000 to University of Mobile, Mobile, AL.
$50,000 to Dauphin Island Sea Lab, Dauphin Island, AL.
$50,000 to Mobile Association for the Blind, Mobile, AL.
$40,000 to Home of Grace for Women, Eight Mile, AL.
$35,000 to University of Montevallo, Montevallo, AL.
$20,000 to Edith Murphy Foundation, Mobile, AL.
$10,000 to United Cerebral Palsy of Mobile, Mobile, AL.

38

Ronne & Donald Hess Foundation

(formerly Ronne & Donald Hess Charitable Foundation)
505 N. 20th St., Ste. 1015
Birmingham, AL 35203
Contact: Susan Swartz

Established in 1985 in AL.

Donors: Ronne Hess; Donald Hess.

Foundation type: Independent foundation.

Financial data (yr. ended 12/31/05): Assets, $4,189,551 (M); gifts received, $640,538; expenditures, $1,241,622; qualifying distributions, $1,212,454; giving activities include $1,212,454 for 80 grants (high: $190,304; low: $250; average: $1,000–$5,000).

Fields of interest: Arts; Higher education; Human services; Jewish agencies & temples.

Type of support: Annual campaigns; Capital campaigns; Building/renovation.

Limitations: Applications not accepted. Giving primarily in AL. No grants to individuals.

Application information: Unsolicited requests for funds not accepted.

    Board meeting date(s): Varies

Officers and Directors:* Ronne Hess,* Pres.; Donald Hess,* V.P. and Secy.-Treas.; Alan Z. Engel,* V.P.; Heidi C. Hess.

Number of staff: 1 part-time support.

EIN: 630916545

39

Hill Crest Foundation, Inc. ✧

P.O. Box 530507
Mountain Brook, AL 35253
Contact: Charles R. Terry Sr., Chair.

Established in 1967 in AL.

Foundation type: Independent foundation.

Financial data (yr. ended 6/30/05): Assets, $37,072,992 (M); expenditures, $1,972,752; qualifying distributions, $1,701,760; giving activities include $1,640,150 for 72 grants (high: $200,000; low: $1,000).

Purpose and activities: Giving primarily for health associations, human services and education; some funding also for the arts.

Fields of interest: Arts; Higher education; Education; Hospitals (general); Health care; Health organizations, association; Human services; Children/youth, services; Community development.

Type of support: Capital campaigns; Building/renovation; Equipment; Endowments; Program development; Professorships; Publication; Seed money; Scholarship funds; Research; Technical assistance; Matching/challenge support.

Limitations: Giving limited to AL. No grants to individuals.

Application information: Application form not required.

  Initial approach: Letter
  Copies of proposal: 4
  Deadline(s): None
  Board meeting date(s): Quarterly

Officer and Trustees:* Charles R. Terry, Sr.,* Chair.; Bill D. Eddleman; W. Price Hightower; Willard L. Hurley; William W. Walker.

Number of staff: 2 full-time professional.

EIN: 630516927

Selected grants: The following grants were reported in 2004.

$100,000 to Alabama Childrens Hospital Foundation, Birmingham, AL.

$100,000 to Birmingham Zoo, Birmingham, AL.

$100,000 to KID One Transport System, Birmingham, AL.

$100,000 to University of Alabama, School of Social Work, Tuscaloosa, AL.

$100,000 to University of Alabama, Department of Neurobiology, Birmingham, AL.

$50,000 to Auburn University, Auburn, AL.

$25,000 to Alabama School of Fine Arts Foundation, Birmingham, AL.

$10,000 to Center for Urban Missions, Birmingham, AL.

$7,500 to Arthritis Foundation, Montgomery, AL.

$3,000 to Muscular Dystrophy Association, Mobile, AL.

40

The Hugh Kaul Foundation ✧

P.O. Box 11426
Birmingham, AL 35202 (205) 326-5382
Contact: Carla B. Gale, V.P. and Trust Off., AmSouth Bank

Established in 1989 in AL.

Donor: Hugh Kaul‡.

Foundation type: Independent foundation.

Financial data (yr. ended 12/31/05): Assets, $64,283,053 (M); expenditures, $3,279,021; qualifying distributions, $3,025,454; giving activities include $2,999,891 for 48 grants (high: $650,000; low: $5,000; average: $50,000–$100,000).

Purpose and activities: Giving primarily for arts, education, children and youth services, family services, and community development.

Fields of interest: Arts; Education; Children/youth, services; Family services; Community development.

Type of support: Publication; Program evaluation; Professorships; Matching/challenge support;

Management development/capacity building; Land acquisition; General/operating support; Equipment; Curriculum development; Annual campaigns; Capital campaigns; Building/renovation; Program development; Seed money.

Limitations: Giving limited to Jefferson, Clay and Coosa counties, and the greater metropolitan Birmingham, AL, area. No support for religious organizations. No grants to individuals.

Publications: Application guidelines.

Application information: Application form not required.

  Initial approach: Proposal
  Copies of proposal: 11
  Deadline(s): Mar. 15 and Sept. 15
  Board meeting date(s): May and Nov.
  Final notification: May 31 and Dec. 15

Distribution Committee: W. Houston Blount; Nancy Dunlap; John Kaul Greene; Beverly P. Head III; Hillery Head; Don James; John McMahon, Jr.; Sam Yates.

Trustee: AmSouth Bank.

EIN: 636158725

Selected grants: The following grants were reported in 2005.

$650,000 to University of Alabama, Birmingham, AL.

$150,000 to United Cerebral Palsy of Greater Birmingham, Birmingham, AL.

$125,000 to Black Warrior-Cahaba Rivers Land Trust, Birmingham, AL.

$100,000 to Alabama Symphony Association, Birmingham, AL.

$100,000 to Entrepreneurial Center, Birmingham, AL.

$100,000 to YMCA of Metropolitan Birmingham, Birmingham, AL.

$74,190 to Birmingham Botanical Society, Birmingham, AL.

$50,000 to Regional Cultural Alliance of Greater Birmingham, Birmingham, AL.

$40,000 to Salvation Army of Birmingham, Birmingham, AL.

$35,000 to Better Basics, Birmingham, AL.

41

The Kimerling Foundation, Inc. ✧ ☆

P.O. Box 131423
Birmingham, AL 35213-6423

Incorporated in 1969 in AL.

Donors: Max L. Kimerling; Hyman Kimerling; M. Kimerling & Sons, Inc.; Alabama Oxygen Co., Inc.

Foundation type: Independent foundation.

Financial data (yr. ended 7/31/06): Assets, $833,789 (M); expenditures, $635,120; qualifying distributions, $634,000; giving activities include $634,000 for grants.

Purpose and activities: Giving primarily for Jewish agencies.

Fields of interest: Hospitals (general); Human services; Jewish federated giving programs; Jewish agencies & temples.

Limitations: Applications not accepted. Giving primarily in Birmingham, AL. No grants to individuals.

Application information: Contributes only to pre-selected organizations.

Officers: Joseph Kimerling, Pres.; Jonathan Kimerling, V.P.; David Kimerling, Secy.

EIN: 237015591

42

The J. K. Lowder Family Foundation ✧

(formerly James K. and Margaret Lowder Foundation)
2000 Interstate Park Dr.
Montgomery, AL 36109

Established in 1995 in AL.

Donors: James K. Lowder; Catherine Lowder; Colonial Company.

Foundation type: Independent foundation.

Financial data (yr. ended 12/31/04): Assets, $11,199,414 (M); gifts received, $515,522; expenditures, $569,080; qualifying distributions, $492,755; giving activities include $492,755 for 26 grants (high: $115,000; low: $5).

Purpose and activities: Giving primarily for the arts, education, and youth services.

Fields of interest: Museums (art); Performing arts, dance; Performing arts, theater; Performing arts, orchestra (symphony); Elementary school/education; Theological school/education; Scholarships/financial aid; Education; Boys & girls clubs; Human services; American Red Cross; YM/YWCAs & YM/YWHAs; Foundations (community); Federated giving programs; Christian agencies & churches.

Limitations: Applications not accepted. Giving primarily in AL. No grants to individuals.

Application information: Contributes only to pre-selected organizations.

Officers: James K. Lowder, Pres.; Margaret B. Lowder, V.P. and Secy.

Director: Thomas H. Lowder.

EIN: 631139499

43

Robert and Charlotte Lowder Foundation ✧

2080 Bell Rd.
Montgomery, AL 36117

Established in 1995 in AL.

Donors: Robert E. Lowder; Catherine Lowder.

Foundation type: Independent foundation.

Financial data (yr. ended 12/31/05): Assets, $137,120 (M); gifts received, $1,446,000; expenditures, $1,472,147; qualifying distributions, $1,392,430; giving activities include $1,392,430 for 29 grants (high: $600,000; low: $250).

Purpose and activities: Giving primarily for higher education and to Presbyterian churches; funding also for health associations, and children, youth, and social services.

Fields of interest: Higher education; Health organizations, association; Human services; American Red Cross; Children/youth, services; Federated giving programs; Protestant agencies & churches.

Limitations: Applications not accepted. Giving primarily in Auburn and Montgomery, AL. No grants to individuals.

Application information: Contributes only to pre-selected organizations.

Officers and Directors:* Robert E. Lowder, Pres.; Charlotte G. Lowder, V.P. and Secy.; Mary Catherine L. Struble,* Treas.; Bryan T. Cotney.

EIN: 631139624

Selected grants: The following grants were reported in 2004.

$255,000 to Moorings Presbyterian Church, Naples, FL.

$105,000 to Memorial Presbyterian Church, Montgomery, AL.

$75,000 to Child Protect, Montgomery, AL.

$50,000 to Judson College, Marion, AL.

$25,000 to Montgomery Area Council on Aging, Montgomery, AL.

$7,000 to Hospice of Montgomery, Montgomery, AL.

$5,000 to University of Alabama, Tuscaloosa, AL.

44

The Thomas H. and Jarman F. Lowder Foundation ✧

38 Country Club Rd.

Birmingham, AL   35213

Established in 1995 in AL.

Donors: Thomas H. Lowder; Jarman F. Lowder; Catherine Lowder.

Foundation type: Independent foundation.

Financial data (yr. ended 12/31/04): Assets, $17,449,422 (M); gifts received, $3,427,925; expenditures, $880,011; qualifying distributions, $724,438; giving activities include $724,438 for 38 grants (high: $230,000; low: $88).

Purpose and activities: Giving primarily for education, human services, and federated giving programs; funding also for children and youth services, animal welfare, and to Christian and Roman Catholic organizations and churches.

Fields of interest: Higher education; Education; Animal welfare; Human services; Children/youth, services; Foundations (community); Federated giving programs; Christian agencies & churches; Roman Catholic agencies & churches.

Limitations: Applications not accepted. Giving primarily in Birmingham, AL. No grants to individuals.

Application information: Contributes only to pre-selected organizations.

Officers: Thomas H. Lowder, Pres. and Treas.; Jarman F. Lowder, V.P. and Secy.

EIN: 631139498

45

The Jane K. Lowe Charitable Foundation ✧

P.O. Box 348

Huntsville, AL   35804-0348   (256) 531-1231

E-mail: janelowe@hiwaay.net; URL: http://www.lowefoundation.org

Established in 1998 in AL.

Donor: Jane K. Lowe†.

Foundation type: Independent foundation.

Financial data (yr. ended 12/31/05): Assets, $37,835,960 (M); gifts received, $140,089; expenditures, $2,026,592; qualifying distributions, $1,658,093; giving activities include $1,658,093 for 23 grants (high: $580,333; low: $21,324).

Purpose and activities: Giving primarily for education and youth organizations.

Fields of interest: Higher education; Education; Health care; Boys & girls clubs; Human services; Children/youth, services.

Type of support: General/operating support; Program development; Scholarship funds.

Limitations: Giving primarily in Madison County, AL. No support for religious organizations for projects that primarily benefit their own members or adherence. No grants to individuals, or for conferences, seminars, special events, productions, performances or debt.

Publications: Application guidelines.

Application information: Application form not required.

Initial approach: Proposal

Copies of proposal: 3

Deadline(s): June 1

Final notification: On or before July 15

Trustees: W.F. Sanders, Jr.; B.R. Smith; John R. Wynn.

Number of staff: 1 full-time professional.

EIN: 636203439

46

The Ben May Charitable Trust ✧

c/o AmSouth Bank

P.O. Box 1628

Mobile, AL   36633-1628

Contact: Mr. Vivian G. Johnston, Jr., Chair., Distrib. Comm.

Application address: P.O. Box 123, Mobile, AL 36601-0123, tel.: (251) 432-5511

Established in 1971 in AL.

Foundation type: Independent foundation.

Financial data (yr. ended 12/31/05): Assets, $12,385,874 (M); expenditures, $700,992; qualifying distributions, $627,396; giving activities include $542,000 for 46 grants (high: $100,000; low: $1,000; average: $5,000–$10,000).

Fields of interest: Arts; Higher education; Education; Alzheimer's disease research; Human services; Children, services; Foundations (community); Christian agencies & churches; Protestant agencies & churches; Jewish agencies & temples.

Limitations: Giving primarily in AL; some giving nationally, with emphasis on NY. No grants to individuals.

Application information: Application form not required.

Deadline(s): None

Distribution Committee: Vivian G. Johnston, Jr., Chair.; Hon. William Brevard Hand; Martin Perlman, M.D.

Trustee: AmSouth Bank.

EIN: 237145009

47

Mayer Electric Supply Foundation, Inc. ✧

P.O. Box 1328

Birmingham, AL   35201

Established about 1966.

Donors: Charles A. Collat; Mayer Electric Supply Co., Inc.

Foundation type: Independent foundation.

Financial data (yr. ended 11/30/05): Assets, $5,268,950 (M); gifts received, $874,370; expenditures, $460,333; qualifying distributions, $428,125; giving activities include $428,125 for 4 grants (high: $265,000; low: $20,000).

Purpose and activities: Giving primarily for human services and Jewish organizations and temples.

Fields of interest: Higher education; Human services; Federated giving programs; Jewish agencies & temples.

Limitations: Giving primarily in Birmingham, AL. No grants to individuals.

Application information:

Initial approach: Letter

Deadline(s): None

Officers and Directors:* Charles A. Collat,* Pres.; James T. Summerlin,* V.P.; Patsy W. Collat,* Secy.

EIN: 630505982

48

The Violet H. McLendon Educational Fund ✧

c/o Wachovia Bank, N.A

P.O. Box 809

Dothan, AL   36302

Established in 1989 in AL.

Foundation type: Independent foundation.

Financial data (yr. ended 12/31/05): Assets, $6,505,848 (M); expenditures, $372,933; qualifying distributions, $336,456; giving activities include $336,456 for 4 grants (high: $256,348; low: $8,010).

Purpose and activities: Support primarily for college scholarship funds.

Fields of interest: Higher education, college (community/junior); Protestant agencies & churches.

Type of support: Scholarship funds.

Limitations: Giving primarily AL, FL, and GA. No grants to individuals.

Application information:

Initial approach: Letter

Deadline(s): None

Trustee: Wachovia Bank, N.A.

EIN: 636160114

49

D. W. McMillan Foundation ✧

329 Belleville Ave.

Brewton, AL   36426-2039

Contact: Ed Leigh McMillan II, Tr.

Application address: P.O. Box 867, Brewton, AL 36427

Established in 1956 in AL.

Donor: D.W. McMillan Trust.

Foundation type: Independent foundation.

Financial data (yr. ended 12/31/05): Assets, $26,556,148 (M); expenditures, $1,439,727; qualifying distributions, $1,292,039; giving activities include $1,250,000 for 46 grants (high: $100,000; low: $3,000).

Purpose and activities: Aid to poor and needy people, including welfare and medical aid, through grants to local health and welfare organizations; limited to programs giving direct aid.

Fields of interest: Hospitals (general); Health care; Mental health/crisis services; Health organizations, association; Human services; Children/youth, services; Residential/custodial care, hospices; Homeless, human services; Disabilities, people with; Economically disadvantaged; Homeless.

Type of support: Continuing support; Emergency funds.

Limitations: Giving limited to Escambia County, AL, and Escambia County, FL.

Application information: Application form not required.

Initial approach: Letter

Copies of proposal: 1

Deadline(s): None

Board meeting date(s): Dec. 1

Final notification: Dec. 31

Trustees: John David Finlay, Jr.; Michael N. Hoke; Ed Leigh McMillan II; Allison R. Sinrod.

Number of staff: 2 part-time support.
EIN: 636044830

50
McWane Foundation

P.O. Box 43327
Birmingham, AL 35243-0327 (205) 414-3100
Contact: A. Michelle Clemon

Established in 1961.
Donor: McWane, Inc.
Foundation type: Company-sponsored foundation.
Financial data (yr. ended 12/31/05): Assets,
$592,275 (M); gifts received, $2,067,261;
expenditures, $2,143,980; qualifying distributions,
$2,143,135; giving activities include $2,143,135
for 64 grants (high: $1,000,000; low: $100).
Purpose and activities: The foundation supports
organizations involved with arts and culture,
education, health, human services, and community
development.
Fields of interest: Museums; Arts; Higher
education; Education; Health care; Children/youth,
services; Human services; Community
development.
Limitations: Giving primarily in AL. No grants to
individuals.
Application information: Application form not
required.
  Initial approach: Proposal
  Copies of proposal: 1
  Deadline(s): None
Trustees: John McMahon; C. Phillip McWane.
EIN: 636044384
Selected grants: The following grants were reported
in 2005.
$1,000,000 to McWane Center, Birmingham, AL.
$200,000 to YMCA of Metropolitan Birmingham,
  Birmingham, AL.
$122,000 to Joseph H. Firth Youth Center,
  Phillipsburg, NJ.
$53,180 to Literacy Council of Central Alabama,
  Birmingham, AL.
$50,000 to American Red Cross, Birmingham, AL.
$47,250 to Regional Cultural Alliance of Greater
  Birmingham, Birmingham, AL.
$42,000 to Birmingham-Southern College,
  Birmingham, AL.
$30,000 to Alabama Symphony Orchestra,
  Birmingham, AL.
$25,000 to Douglas Elementary School, Douglas,
  AL.
$24,000 to Auburn University, Auburn, AL.

51
The Tom & Amy Methvin Foundation ✧

c/o Thomas J. Methvin
272 Commerce St.
Montgomery, AL 36104
Application address: c/o Tom and Amy Methvin,
9829 Wynchase Cir., Montgomery, AL 36117

Established in 2000 in AL.
Donors: Amy Methvin; Tom Methvin.
Foundation type: Independent foundation.
Financial data (yr. ended 12/31/05): Assets,
$622,232 (M); gifts received, $150,000;
expenditures, $445,705; qualifying distributions,
$439,873; giving activities include $434,773 for
121 grants (high: $25,000; low: $50), and $5,100

for 11 grants to individuals (high: $1,000; low:
$200).
Fields of interest: Medical research, institute;
Human services; Children/youth, services; Christian
agencies & churches.
Application information: Application form not
required.
  Initial approach: Letter
  Deadline(s): None
Officers: Thomas J. Methvin, Pres.; Amy Methvin,
Secy.-Treas.
EIN: 631258474
Selected grants: The following grants were reported
in 2005.
$15,000 to Community Care Network, Montgomery,
  AL. 2 grants: $5,000, $10,000
$10,000 to Child Evangelism Fellowship,
  Warrenton, MO.
$5,000 to Childrens Protective Association,
  Montgomery, AL.
$5,000 to Lifeline Childrens Services, Birmingham,
  AL.
$4,500 to Family Sunshine Center Foundation,
  Montgomery, AL.
$3,500 to Habitat for Humanity International. 2
  grants: $2,500, $1,000
$2,000 to YMCA.
$1,000 to Fellowship of Christian Athletes, Kansas
  City, MO.

52
Robert R. Meyer Foundation ✧

c/o AmSouth Bank
P.O. Box 11426
Birmingham, AL 35202
Contact: Carla B. Gale, V.P. and Trust Off., AmSouth
Bank

Trust established in 1942 in AL.
Donors: Robert R. Meyer†; John E. Meyer†.
Foundation type: Independent foundation.
Financial data (yr. ended 12/31/04): Assets,
$41,737,149 (M); expenditures, $2,177,532;
qualifying distributions, $2,002,544; giving
activities include $1,932,266 for 57 grants (high:
$200,000; low: $5,000).
Purpose and activities: Aid largely to local health
and welfare organizations, educational institutions,
and cultural organizations selected by an advisory
committee.
Fields of interest: Education; Hospitals (general);
Health care; Health organizations, association;
Human services.
Type of support: General/operating support;
Continuing support; Management development/
capacity building; Building/renovation; Equipment;
Land acquisition; Program development;
Publication; Curriculum development; Scholarship
funds; Research; Technical assistance; Program
evaluation; Matching/challenge support.
Limitations: Giving limited to the metropolitan
Birmingham, AL, area. No grants to individuals, or
for endowment funds.
Publications: Application guidelines.
Application information: Application form not
required.
  Initial approach: Proposal (no more than 4 pages)
  Copies of proposal: 7
  Deadline(s): Mar. 15 and Sept. 15
  Board meeting date(s): June and Dec.
  Final notification: Mid June and mid Dec.
Advisory Committee: Raymond Harbert; Elmer E.
Harris; Gaynell Hendricks; William M. Spencer III.

Trustee: AmSouth Bank.
EIN: 636019645

53
A. S. Mitchell Foundation, Inc. ✧

(formerly The Mitchell Foundation, Inc.)
P.O. Box 1126
Mobile, AL 36633

Incorporated in 1957 in AL.
Donors: A.S. Mitchell†; Mrs. A.S. Mitchell†.
Foundation type: Independent foundation.
Financial data (yr. ended 1/31/05): Assets,
$17,042,831 (M); expenditures, $985,469;
qualifying distributions, $860,857; giving activities
include $740,000 for 48 grants (high: $100,000;
low: $1,000).
Purpose and activities: Giving primarily for
education, as well as for historical preservation,
human services and for United Methodist Church
support.
Fields of interest: Museums (art); Museums
(natural history); Historic preservation/historical
societies; Arts; Elementary/secondary education;
Higher education; Education; Environment, natural
resources; Animals/wildlife; Human services; YM/
YWCAs & YM/YWHAs; Children/youth, services;
Developmentally disabled, centers & services;
Protestant agencies & churches.
Limitations: Applications not accepted. Giving
primarily in AL. No grants to individuals.
Application information: Contributes only to
pre-selected organizations.
  Board meeting date(s): Quarterly
Officers and Directors:* Augustine Meaher III,*
Pres.; Frank B. Vinson, Jr.,* V.P.; David D. Dukes,*
Secy.-Treas.; Hon. William Brevard Hand; Joseph L.
Meaher; Kenneth G. Vinson.
Number of staff: 1 full-time support.
EIN: 630368954

54
Gloria Narramore Moody Foundation,
Inc. ✧ ☆

201 Marina Dr., Apt. 805
Tuscaloosa, AL 35406 (205) 349-3466
Application address: P.O. Box 1029, Tuscaloosa, AL
35403-1029

Established in 1990 in AL.
Donor: Frank M. Moody, Sr.†.
Foundation type: Independent foundation.
Financial data (yr. ended 12/31/05): Assets,
$4,907,889 (M); gifts received, $5,210,213;
expenditures, $655,923; qualifying distributions,
$610,075; giving activities include $610,075 for
grants.
Purpose and activities: Giving to higher education,
the arts and culture, and public services.
Fields of interest: Performing arts; Performing arts,
music; Performing arts, orchestra (symphony);
Humanities; Higher education; Libraries (public).
Type of support: General/operating support;
Continuing support; Capital campaigns; Building/
renovation; Endowments; Program development;
Fellowships; Grants to individuals.
Limitations: Giving primarily in AL.
Publications: Application guidelines; Financial
statement.
Application information:

Initial approach: Letter
Deadline(s): None
Officers: Gloria N. Moody, Pres.; Celeste Burnum, V.P.; Hugh Rowe Thomas, V.P.; Larry W. O'Neal, Treas.
Number of staff: 1 part-time professional.
EIN: 634020569
Selected grants: The following grants were reported in 2004.
$155,027 to Alabama Symphony Orchestra, Birmingham, AL.
$25,000 to Alabama Shakespeare Festival, Montgomery, AL.
$15,000 to Birmingham Museum of Art, Birmingham, AL.
$10,000 to Birmingham Childrens Theater, Birmingham, AL.
$10,000 to From the Top, Boston, MA.
$10,000 to United Cerebral Palsy, DC.
$1,000 to Birmingham Civil Rights Institute, Birmingham, AL.
$500 to Hebron Baptist Church, Dacula, GA.

55

Moore Family Foundation, Inc. ✧ ☆
8326 Enterprise Ave. N.E.
Tuscaloosa, AL 35405
Contact: Elaine Moore, Secy.
FAX: (205) 752-2313; *E-mail:* jcmoore@dbtech.net

Established in 1997 in AL.
Donor: James C. Moore.
Foundation type: Independent foundation.
Financial data (yr. ended 12/31/05): Assets, $2,384,827 (M); gifts received, $4,800; expenditures, $418,827; qualifying distributions, $375,199; giving activities include $375,199 for grants.
Purpose and activities: Giving primarily for Christian organizations. Some funding also for education.
Fields of interest: Education; Christian agencies & churches.
Type of support: Continuing support; Endowments.
Limitations: Giving primarily in AL, AZ, and NC. No grants to individuals.
Application information: Application form required.
Copies of proposal: 1
Board meeting date(s): Quarterly
Officer: Elaine Moore, Secy.
EIN: 631185433
Selected grants: The following grants were reported in 2004.
$7,500 to Evangel Bible Translators, Irvine, CA.
$2,000 to First Baptist Church, Tuscaloosa, AL.
$1,500 to Hospice of West Alabama, Tuscaloosa, AL.
$250 to University of Alabama, Tuscaloosa, AL.

56

The Patterson Family Charitable Foundation ✧
4 Church St.
Birmingham, AL 35213
Contact: Thomas L. Patterson, Dir.

Established in 2000 in AL.
Donor: Thomas L. Patterson.
Foundation type: Independent foundation.
Financial data (yr. ended 12/31/05): Assets, $1,777,520 (M); expenditures, $449,014; qualifying distributions, $418,308; giving activities

include $418,308 for 6 grants (high: $170,500; low: $1,000).
Purpose and activities: Giving primarily to a university and an Episcopal church.
Fields of interest: Higher education; Health care; Children/youth, services; Protestant agencies & churches.
Limitations: Giving primarily in AL. No grants to individuals.
Application information: Application form not required.
Initial approach: Letter
Deadline(s): None
Directors: April Suzanne Benetollo; Jens-Peter Berndt; Amy Elizabeth Knowles; Carolyn L. Patterson; Thomas L. Patterson.
EIN: 631262324
Selected grants: The following grants were reported in 2003.
$100,000 to University of Alabama, Tuscaloosa, AL. 2 grants: $32,500 to Blackburn Institute (For general support), $67,500 (For general support).
$50,000 to Saint Thomas Episcopal Church, Birmingham, AL. For general support.
$1,000 to Crippled Childrens Foundation, Birmingham, AL. For general support.
$1,000 to YMCA of Pawtucket, Pawtucket, RI. For general support.

57

Pleiad Foundation ✧
2140 Warwick Dr.
Birmingham, AL 35209
Contact: Carrie C. McMahon, Pres.

Established in 1995 in AL.
Donors: Betty T. McMahon; John J. McMahon, Jr.; David A. McMahon; Joel W. McMahon; John J. McMahon III; Buffalo News, Inc.; McCloud Investments.
Foundation type: Independent foundation.
Financial data (yr. ended 12/31/05): Assets, $4,290,909 (M); gifts received, $332,000; expenditures, $673,962; qualifying distributions, $628,709; giving activities include $628,709 for 28 grants (high: $200,000; low: $500).
Purpose and activities: Giving primarily to Episcopal churches and schools, as well as to a United Methodist church; funding also for education, an athletic facility fund, and the arts.
Fields of interest: Arts; Higher education; Education; Foundations (public); Federated giving programs; Protestant agencies & churches.
Limitations: Giving limited to Birmingham, AL.
Application information: Application form not required.
Deadline(s): None
Officer: Carrie C. McMahon, Pres.
Directors: Ashley R. McMahon; Betty T. McMahon; David A. McMahon; Joel W. McMahon; John J. McMahon, Jr.; John J. McMahon III.
EIN: 631159236

58

Protective Life Foundation ✧
P.O. Box 2606
Birmingham, AL 35202 (205) 268-4434
Contact: Kate H. Cotton, Exec. Dir.
FAX: (205) 268-5547;
E-mail: kate.cotton@protective.com; *URL:* http://www.protective.com/default.asp?id=4

Established in 1994 in AL.
Donor: Protective Life Insurance Co.
Foundation type: Company-sponsored foundation.
Financial data (yr. ended 12/31/05): Assets, $0 (M); gifts received, $2,605,000; expenditures, $2,618,975; qualifying distributions, $2,567,473; giving activities include $2,567,473 for 198 grants (high: $262,500).
Purpose and activities: The foundation supports organizations involved with arts and culture, education, health, youth development, youth, community development, and civic affairs.
Fields of interest: Arts; Education, reading; Education; Health care; Youth development; Youth, services; Community development; Public affairs.
Type of support: General/operating support; Annual campaigns; Capital campaigns; Program development; Scholarship funds; Research; Sponsorships; Employee matching gifts; Grants to individuals.
Limitations: Giving primarily in the metropolitan Birmingham, AL, area. Generally, no support for K-12 public or private schools, churches, public facilities, or state organizations, or foundations. Generally, no grants for animal-related causes or sporting events.
Publications: Application guidelines; Annual report.
Application information: Application form not required.
Initial approach: Proposal
Copies of proposal: 1
Deadline(s): Feb. 20, May 25, Aug. 25, and Nov. 10
Board meeting date(s): Mar., June, Sept., and Dec.
Final notification: Varies
Officers and Directors:* John D. Johns,* Pres.; Kate H. Cotton,* Exec. Dir.; Allen W. Ritchie,* Treas.; Charles D. Evers, Jr.
Number of staff: 1 part-time professional.
EIN: 631129596
Selected grants: The following grants were reported in 2005.
$262,500 to United Way of Central Alabama, Birmingham, AL. For corporate gift.
$240,000 to University of Alabama, Birmingham, AL. 2 grants: $15,000 to School of Business (For Blazer Fund), $225,000 to Capital Campaign (For clinical initiative awards).
$75,000 to American Red Cross, Birmingham, AL. For Hurricane Katrina relief.
$75,000 to University of Alabama, Blackburn Institute, Tuscaloosa, AL. To endow Protective Life Government Experience initiative.
$60,000 to Birmingham Civil Rights Institute, Birmingham, AL. For Expanding the Legacy capital campaign.
$50,000 to Childrens Hospital and Health System, Milwaukee, WI. For capital campaign for The Children's Center for Research and Innovation.
$50,000 to Entrepreneurial Center, Birmingham, AL. For campus campaign.
$30,000 to YMCA of Metropolitan Birmingham, Birmingham, AL. For capital campaign, teen programming for the Western Branch and Strong Kids annual program.
$16,667 to Virginia Samford Theater, Birmingham, AL. For capital campaign.

59
Belle G. Roberts Charitable Trust ✦ ☆
c/o Regions Bank, Trust Dept.
P.O. Box 2527
Mobile, AL 36622

Established in 2002 in AL.
Donors: Belle G. Roberts†; Harriet Davis Irrevocable Trust.
Foundation type: Independent foundation.
Financial data (yr. ended 3/31/05): Assets, $15,430,111 (M); expenditures, $922,720; qualifying distributions, $740,897; giving activities include $709,904 for 2 grants (high: $354,952; low: $354,952).
Fields of interest: Higher education; Health care.
Limitations: Applications not accepted. Giving primarily in AL. No grants to individuals.
Application information: Contributes only to pre-selected organizations.
Trustees: J. Manson Murray; Regions Bank.
EIN: 726214520

60
Benjamin and Roberta Russell Foundation ✦
(formerly Benjamin and Roberta Russell Educational and Charitable Foundation, Inc.)
P.O. Box 369
Alexander City, AL 35011-0369
Contact: James D. Nabors, Secy.-Treas.

Incorporated in 1944 in AL.
Donor: Benjamin Russell.
Foundation type: Independent foundation.
Financial data (yr. ended 12/31/05): Assets, $16,191,992 (M); expenditures, $967,214; qualifying distributions, $814,096; giving activities include $814,096 for 17 grants (high: $216,556; low: $4,000).
Purpose and activities: Giving for higher and public education, youth programs, and a hospital.
Fields of interest: Higher education; Education; Hospitals (general); Youth development, services; Children/youth, services.
Type of support: General/operating support; Scholarship funds.
Limitations: Applications not accepted. Giving limited to AL; scholarship funds limited to Tallapoosa and Coosa counties. No grants to individuals (except for scholarships).
Application information: Unsolicited requests for funds not accepted.
Officers and Directors:* Nancy R. Gwaltney,* Pres.; Benjamin Russell,* V.P.; James D. Nabors,* Secy.-Treas.; Earl C. Baumgardner; Roberta A. Baumgardner; Tommy Bice; James W. Brown, Jr.; Julia Goree; Adelia R. Hendrix.
EIN: 630393126
Selected grants: The following grants were reported in 2003.
$200,000 to Childrens Harbor, Alexander City, AL.
$195,532 to Scholarships Inc., Green Bay, WI.
$35,000 to Central Alabama Community College, Alexander City, AL.
$35,000 to University of Alabama, Birmingham, AL.
$30,000 to Arise Citizens Policy Project, Montgomery, AL.
$25,000 to Lyman Ward Military Academy, Camp Hill, AL.
$20,000 to Multiple Sclerosis Society, National, Birmingham, AL.

$10,000 to Boys and Girls Clubs of America, Alexander City, AL.
$10,000 to Camp ASCCA (Alabamas Special Camp for Children and Adults) - Easter Seals, Jacksons Gap, AL.

61
Saks Incorporated Foundation ✦
750 Lakeshore Pkwy., Tax Dept.
Birmingham, AL 35211
Application address: c/o Ken Metzner, 12 E. 49th St., New York, NY 10017

Established in 1998 in AL.
Donors: Donald Hess; Saks Inc.; Colonial Properties; Polo Ralph Lauren Corp.; Advance Magazine Group.
Foundation type: Company-sponsored foundation.
Financial data (yr. ended 1/28/06): Assets, $1,850,673 (M); gifts received, $663,000; expenditures, $1,069,794; qualifying distributions, $964,000; giving activities include $709,500 for 77 grants (high: $50,000; low: $500), and $254,500 for 117 grants to individuals (high: $3,000; low: $1,000).
Purpose and activities: The foundation supports organizations involved with arts and culture, education, health, and human services.
Fields of interest: Visual arts, design; Museums (art); Performing arts, ballet; Performing arts, orchestra (symphony); Arts; Education; Health care; Cancer research; AIDS research; Human services; Federated giving programs.
Type of support: Continuing support; Annual campaigns; Capital campaigns; Emergency funds; Research; Employee-related scholarships.
Limitations: Applications not accepted. Giving primarily in AL, FL, GA, and NY. No grants to individuals (except for employee-related scholarships).
Application information: Contributes only through employee-related scholarships and to pre-selected organizations.
Officers: R. Brad Martin, Pres.; Brian J. Martin, Exec. V.P. and Secy.; James A. Coggin, Exec. V.P.; James S. Scully, Sr. V.P. and Treas.; Charles J. Hansen, Sr. V.P.
EIN: 631207483
Selected grants: The following grants were reported in 2005.
$180,300 to Scholarship Program Administrators, Nashville, TN.
$100,000 to Entertainment Industry Foundation, Los Angeles, CA.
$50,000 to Breast Cancer Research Foundation, New York, NY.
$35,000 to Mosaic Foundation, McLean, VA.
$26,000 to National Underground Railroad Freedom Center, Cincinnati, OH.
$25,000 to Portland Art Museum, Portland, OR.
$20,000 to Alabama Shakespeare Festival, Montgomery, AL.
$12,500 to University of Memphis Foundation, Memphis, TN.
$10,000 to Educational Foundation for the Fashion Industries, New York, NY.
$10,000 to Metropolitan Opera, New York, NY.

62
Richard M. Scrushy Charitable Foundation, Inc. ✦
2310 Marin Dr.
Birmingham, AL 35243

Established in 1997 in AL.
Donor: Richard M. Scrushy.
Foundation type: Independent foundation.
Financial data (yr. ended 12/31/05): Assets, $8,197,003 (M); expenditures, $858,203; qualifying distributions, $749,727; giving activities include $715,591 for 25 grants (high: $164,000; low: $16; average: $2,000–$10,000).
Purpose and activities: Giving primarily for Protestant ministries and organizations including United Methodist, Baptist, Lutheran, and Pentecostal churches.
Fields of interest: Education; Health organizations, association; Human services; Protestant agencies & churches.
Limitations: Applications not accepted. Giving primarily in Birmingham, AL. No grants to individuals.
Application information: Contributes only to pre-selected organizations.
Directors: Amy Scrushy Adams; Christa E. Scrushy; Richard M. Scrushy.
EIN: 721374013

63
Sybil H. Smith Charitable Trust ✦
169 Dauphin St., Ste. 320
Mobile, AL 36602 (251) 343-0185
Contact: Ann Smith Bedsole, Chair.

Established in 1983 in AL.
Donor: Sybil H. Smith†.
Foundation type: Independent foundation.
Financial data (yr. ended 7/31/05): Assets, $21,569,359 (M); expenditures, $1,246,887; qualifying distributions, $1,164,386; giving activities include $1,009,837 for 34 grants (high: $300,500; low: $500).
Purpose and activities: Giving primarily for education and human services; some emphasis in funding for the arts.
Fields of interest: Arts; Education; Human services; Community development.
Type of support: Annual campaigns; Capital campaigns; Building/renovation; Equipment; Consulting services; Matching/challenge support.
Limitations: Giving primarily in the 1st Congressional District of Mobile, AL. No grants to individuals.
Publications: Annual report; Grants list.
Application information: Application form not required.
  Initial approach: Letter
  Copies of proposal: 5
  Deadline(s): None
  Board meeting date(s): 1st Mon. in Feb., May, Aug., and Nov.
Committee Members: Ann Smith Bedsole, Chair.; Raine Demas; John H. Martin III; Mary Martin Riser.
Trustee: Whitney Bank of Alabama.
Number of staff: 1 full-time professional.
EIN: 636128407
Selected grants: The following grants were reported in 2003.
$500,000 to Center for the Living Arts, Mobile, AL.

$125,000 to Franklin Primary Health Center, Mobile, AL.

$35,000 to Nature Conservancy, Birmingham, AL.

$25,000 to Explore Center, Gulf Coast Exploreum Museum of Science, Mobile, AL.

$25,000 to Monroe Health Foundation, Monroeville, AL.

$16,720 to Historic Mobile Preservation Society, Mobile, AL.

$15,180 to Bayside Academy, Daphne, AL.

$10,000 to Monroe County Public Library, Monroeville, AL.

$9,121 to Family Counseling Center of Mobile, Mobile, AL.

$8,000 to Jumbo Shrimp Theater, Summerdale, AL.

64
The Mary Elizabeth Stallworth Foundation Trust ◇ ☆
P.O. Box 724
Monroeville, AL 36461 (251) 575-4021
Contact: David F. Steele, Tr.

Established in 1995 in AL.
Donor: Mary E. Stallworth†.
Foundation type: Independent foundation.
Financial data (yr. ended 12/31/04): Assets, $8,737,387 (M); expenditures, $585,380; qualifying distributions, $329,830; giving activities include $329,830 for grants.
Purpose and activities: Giving primarily for education, medical care and rehabilitation.
Fields of interest: Education, single organization support; Higher education, college; Education; Medical care, rehabilitation; YM/YWCAs & YM/YWHAs.
Limitations: Giving primarily in AL.
Application information: Application form not required.
Deadline(s): None
Trustees: Kenneth Howard; David F. Steele; F.S. Steele.
EIN: 631153060
Selected grants: The following grants were reported in 2004.
$125,000 to Huntingdon College, Montgomery, AL.
$10,000 to Auburn University Foundation, Auburn, AL.
$10,000 to Judson College, Marion, AL.
$5,000 to American Cancer Society, Birmingham, AL.
$4,580 to Monroe County Heritage Museum, Monroeville, AL.
$1,000 to United Methodist Childrens Home, Selma, AL.

65
Stephens Foundation ◇ ☆
P.O. Box 1943
Birmingham, AL 35201-1943

Established in 1991.
Foundation type: Independent foundation.
Financial data (yr. ended 12/31/05): Assets, $2,148,872 (M); expenditures, $1,209,744; qualifying distributions, $1,209,000; giving activities include $1,209,000 for grants.
Purpose and activities: Giving primarily to the Alabama Symphony endowment; some giving to education.

Fields of interest: Performing arts, orchestra (symphony); Education.
Type of support: General/operating support.
Limitations: Applications not accepted. Giving limited to Birmingham, AL. No grants to individuals.
Application information: Contributes only to pre-selected organizations.
Officers: James T. Stephens, Pres.; Dell S. Brooke, Secy.; Elton B. Stephens, Jr., Treas.
Trustee: Jane S. Comer.
EIN: 631035698
Selected grants: The following grants were reported in 2004.
$200,000 to University of Alabama, Alys Robinson Stephens Performing Arts Center, Tuscaloosa, AL.

66
Strain Foundation ◇
4412 Corinth Dr.
Birmingham, AL 35213-1816
Contact: Juanelle D. Strain, Dir.

Established around 1994 in AL.
Donors: John T. Strain; Juanelle D. Strain.
Foundation type: Independent foundation.
Financial data (yr. ended 10/31/05): Assets, $6,417,126 (M); expenditures, $1,516,730; qualifying distributions, $1,516,730; giving activities include $1,504,000 for 2 grants (high: $1,500,000; low: $4,000).
Purpose and activities: Giving primarily to a university.
Fields of interest: Higher education; Human services.
Limitations: Giving primarily in Birmingham, AL. No grants to individuals.
Application information:
Initial approach: Letter
Deadline(s): None
Directors: Janet Strain McDonald; John T. Strain; Juanelle D. Strain; Julia Strain.
EIN: 631108283
Selected grants: The following grants were reported in 2003.
$220,000 to Parkinson Association of Alabama, Birmingham, AL.
$25,000 to Lakeshore Foundation, Birmingham, AL.
$20,000 to Childrens Hospital and Health System, Milwaukee, WI. For research.
$20,000 to Leukemia & Lymphoma Society, Birmingham, AL. For research.
$10,000 to American Heart Association, Birmingham, AL. For research.
$10,000 to Birmingham Museum of Art, Birmingham, AL.
$10,000 to Cahaba River Society, Birmingham, AL.
$7,500 to Collins Chapel Baptist Church, Jemison, AL.
$5,000 to Birmingham Botanical Society, Birmingham, AL.
$5,000 to Canterbury United Methodist Church, Birmingham, AL.

67
The Thompson Foundation, Inc. ◇
2830 Cahaba Rd.
Birmingham, AL 35223

Established in 1997 in AL.

Donors: Lisa Thompson; Michael D. Thompson; Thompson Tractor Co.
Foundation type: Independent foundation.
Financial data (yr. ended 12/31/05): Assets, $4,244,625 (M); gifts received, $2,085,914; expenditures, $1,416,975; qualifying distributions, $1,379,423; giving activities include $1,366,203 for 194 grants (high: $175,000; low: $50).
Purpose and activities: Giving for art and cultural programs, education, youth services, and health associations; funding also for health and social services.
Fields of interest: Arts; Higher education; Education; Environment; Health organizations, association; Disasters, fire prevention/control; Human services; Children/youth, services; Federated giving programs; Christian agencies & churches.
Limitations: Applications not accepted. Giving primarily in AL. No grants to individuals.
Application information: Contributes only to pre-selected organizations.
Officers and Directors:* Michael D. Thompson,* Pres.; Hall W. Thompson, Jr.,* V.P.; Lisa Thompson-Smith,* Secy.; Betty D. Morrison, Exec. Dir.; Netagene Ray Thompson; Patricia Thompson.
EIN: 721389140
Selected grants: The following grants were reported in 2003.
$117,000 to United Way of Central Alabama, Birmingham, AL.
$104,000 to Birmingham Zoo, Birmingham, AL.
$98,000 to University of Alabama, Tuscaloosa, AL. 2 grants: $75,000, $23,000
$50,000 to United Cerebral Palsy of Greater Birmingham, Birmingham, AL. 2 grants: $25,000 each
$35,000 to Auburn University, Auburn, AL.
$30,462 to Alabama Symphony Orchestra, Birmingham, AL.
$15,000 to Cathedral Church of the Advent, Birmingham, AL.
$10,000 to Alabama School of Fine Arts, Birmingham, AL.

68
The Joseph Treadwell Charitable Foundation ◇
c/o BancTrust Co.
P.O. Box 3067
Mobile, AL 36652

Established in 1988 in AL.
Donor: Joseph Treadwell†.
Foundation type: Independent foundation.
Financial data (yr. ended 12/31/05): Assets, $8,900,764 (M); expenditures, $629,607; qualifying distributions, $466,874; giving activities include $466,874 for 18 grants (high: $105,000; low: $270; average: $10,000–$25,000).
Purpose and activities: Giving primarily for education, health and human services.
Fields of interest: Higher education; Health care; Mental health/crisis services; Health organizations, association; Health organizations, formal/general education; Human services; Children, services; Residential/custodial care.
Limitations: Applications not accepted. Giving primarily in AL. No grants to individuals.
Application information: Contributes only to pre-selected organizations.
Managers: Vincent F. Kilborn; Ralph "Sonny" Middleton; John H. Wilson.

Trustee: BancTrust Co.
EIN: 570880131
Selected grants: The following grants were reported in 2005.
$105,000 to Salvation Army.
$98,108 to University of South Alabama, Mobile, AL.
$20,000 to Mercy Medical, Daphne, AL.
$10,000 to Independent Living Center, Birmingham, AL.
$10,000 to Volunteer Mobile, Mobile, AL.
$7,000 to Edith Murphy Foundation, Mobile, AL.
$3,000 to Survivors of Mental Illness Outreach, Mobile, AL.
$500 to Coast Guard Mutual Assistance, Arlington, VA.
$270 to American Red Cross.

69
William D. Trippe Trust, Inc. ✧
c/o Regions Bank
P.O. Box 2527
Mobile, AL 36622-0001
Application address: c/o Glenn T. York, Pres., P.O. Box 246, Cedartown, GA 30125, tel.: (770) 748-3427

Established in 1996 in GA.
Foundation type: Independent foundation.
Financial data (yr. ended 12/31/05): Assets, $8,995,670 (M); expenditures, $468,009; qualifying distributions, $417,505; giving activities include $412,575 for 3 grants (high: $392,615; low: $7,800).
Purpose and activities: Primarily supports the Polk County, GA, school district, and community projects in the city of Cedartown, GA.
Fields of interest: Elementary/secondary education; Community development; Foundations (community).
Limitations: Giving limited to Polk County, GA. No grants to individuals.
Application information:
  Initial approach: Standard format
  Deadline(s): None
Officer and Directors:* Glenn T. York,* Pres.; James J. Carter, Jr.; Lloyd H. Gray, Jr.; George E. Mundy; Jane C. Wyatt; Michael H. York, Sr.
EIN: 586301950
Selected grants: The following grants were reported in 2003.
$396,645 to Cedartown, City of, Cedartown, GA. 3 grants: $250,000 (For new facility for Boys and Girls Club), $100,000 (For Beautification Project), $46,645 (For Veterans Memorial Park).
$9,657 to Polk School District, Cedartown, GA. For playground equipment.

70
Union Planters Community Foundation ✧
c/o Regions Financial Corp.
417 N. 20th St., Ste. 1600
Birmingham, AL 35203

Established in 1998 in TN.
Donors: Union Planters Corp.; Union Planters Holding Corp.; Union Planters Bank.
Foundation type: Company-sponsored foundation.
Financial data (yr. ended 12/31/04): Assets, $530,880 (M); gifts received, $2,078,624; expenditures, $3,231,890; qualifying distributions,

$3,231,890; giving activities include $3,231,890 for 722+ grants (high: $175,000).
Purpose and activities: The foundation supports organizations involved with arts and culture, education, health, human services, community development, civic affairs, and religion.
Fields of interest: Arts; Education; Health care; Human services; Community development; Federated giving programs; Government/public administration; Religion.
Limitations: Applications not accepted. Giving on a national basis. No grants to individuals.
Application information: Contributes only to pre-selected organizations.
Officers and Directors:* Jackson W. Moore,* Pres.; E. James House,* Secy.; Bobby L. Doxey, Treas.; Brad L. Champlin; John V. White, Jr.
EIN: 311635388
Selected grants: The following grants were reported in 2004.
$100,000 to Nashville Symphony, Nashville, TN.
$56,000 to Orange Bowl Committee, Miami, FL.
$50,000 to United Way of the Mid-South, Memphis, TN.
$32,500 to Indianapolis Zoological Society, Indianapolis, IN.
$10,000 to Cuban American National Council, Miami, FL.
$10,000 to University of Illinois, Springfield, IL.
$5,000 to Adventure Science Center, Nashville, TN.
$4,486 to United Way of Anderson County, Oak Ridge, TN.
$2,500 to Vincennes University Foundation, Vincennes, IN.
$2,000 to YMCA, Jackson Metropolitan, Jackson, MS.

71
Samuel E. Upchurch, Jr. Charitable Foundation ✧ ☆
3828 Forest Glen Dr.
Birmingham, AL 35213-3916

Established in 1992 in AL.
Donor: Samuel E. Upchurch, Jr.
Foundation type: Independent foundation.
Financial data (yr. ended 12/31/05): Assets, $2,226,131 (M); gifts received, $545,808; expenditures, $465,308; qualifying distributions, $457,600; giving activities include $457,600 for grants.
Fields of interest: Higher education; Law school/education; Federated giving programs; Christian agencies & churches.
Limitations: Applications not accepted. Giving primarily in AL. No grants to individuals.
Application information: Contributes only to pre-selected organizations.
Directors: John S.P. Samford; Cheryl V. Upchurch; Samuel E. Upchurch, Jr.
EIN: 631083893
Selected grants: The following grants were reported in 2004.
$67,000 to University of Alabama, School of Law, Tuscaloosa, AL. For general support.
$15,000 to Davidson College, Davidson, NC. For general support.
$15,000 to United Way of Central Alabama, Birmingham, AL. For general support.
$10,000 to Washington and Lee University, Lexington, VA. For general support.
$5,000 to Linly Heflin Unit, Birmingham, AL. For general support.

$1,000 to Big Springs Baptist Church, AL. For general support.
$1,000 to Birmingham Museum of Art, Birmingham, AL. For general support.
$1,000 to Community Ministry for Girls, Birmingham, AL. For general support.
$1,000 to Elam Baptist Church, Tallassee, AL. For general support.

72
Lanny S. Vines Foundation ✧ ☆
3600 Redmont Rd.
Birmingham, AL 35213

Established in 1996 in AL.
Donor: Lanny S. Vines.
Foundation type: Independent foundation.
Financial data (yr. ended 12/31/05): Assets, $72,911 (M); gifts received, $750,000; expenditures, $897,035; qualifying distributions, $846,390; giving activities include $846,390 for grants.
Fields of interest: Arts; Education; Health organizations, association; Human services.
Limitations: Applications not accepted. Giving primarily in AL. No grants to individuals.
Application information: Contributes only to pre-selected organizations.
Director: Lanny S. Vines.
EIN: 570899717

73
Vulcan Materials Company Foundation ✧
P.O. Box 385014
Birmingham, AL 35238-5014 (205) 298-3222
Contact: Carol Maxwell, Secy.-Treas.
E-mail: giving@vmcmail.com; URL: http://www.vulcanmaterials.com/social.asp?content=vulcan

Established in 1987 in AL.
Donors: Vulcan Materials Co.; Vulcan Lands Inc.; Calmat Co.
Foundation type: Company-sponsored foundation.
Financial data (yr. ended 11/30/05): Assets, $6,960,642 (M); expenditures, $3,264,817; qualifying distributions, $3,264,817; giving activities include $3,224,422 for 839 grants (high: $122,500; low: $50).
Purpose and activities: The foundation supports organizations involved with K-12 and higher education and environmental stewardship. Special emphasis is directed toward programs designed to promote math, science, engineering, and business education.
Fields of interest: Education, reform; Elementary/secondary education; Higher education; Engineering school/education; Environment; Business/industry; Science, formal/general education; Mathematics.
Type of support: General/operating support; Continuing support; Annual campaigns; Capital campaigns; Endowments; Program development; Seed money; Scholarship funds; Employee volunteer services; Employee-related scholarships; In-kind gifts; Matching/challenge support.
Limitations: Giving on a national basis in areas of company operations. No support for political organizations, athletic, labor, fraternal, or veterans' organizations, or discriminatory organizations. No grants to individuals (except for employee-related scholarships), or for telephone or mass mail

appeals, testimonial dinners, or sectarian religious activities.

Publications: Annual report (including application guidelines).

Application information: Proposals should be no longer than 1 to 2 pages. Application form not required.

Initial approach: Proposal to nearest company division; proposal to foundation for organizations located in the Birmingham, AL, area

Copies of proposal: 1

Deadline(s): None

Board meeting date(s): Quarterly

Officers and Trustees:* Donald M. James,* Chair.; William F. Denson III,* Pres.; David A. Donaldson, V.P.; Carol Maxwell, Secy.-Treas.; Guy M. Badgett III; J. Wayne Houston; Bradley C. Rosenwald; Daniel F. Sansone.

Number of staff: 1 full-time professional; 1 part-time support.

EIN: 630971859

Selected grants: The following grants were reported in 2005.

$162,500 to United Way of Central Alabama, Birmingham, AL. 2 grants: $40,000, $122,500

$100,000 to Samford University, Vulcan Materials Center for Environmental Stewardship and Education, Birmingham, AL.

$62,500 to University of Alabama, Tuscaloosa, AL. For Crimson Tradition Fund.

$50,000 to Alabama Symphony Orchestra, Birmingham, AL.

$48,366 to American Red Cross, National Headquarters, DC. 2 grants: $36,410 (For National Disaster Relief Fund), $11,956 (For National Disaster Relief Fund).

$25,000 to Birmingham Museum of Art, Birmingham, AL.

$15,000 to Alabama People Against a Littered State, Montgomery, AL.

$14,324 to Miller Association of Parents and Teachers, Lafayette, IN.

74

Allyrae Wallace Educational Trust ✧

P.O. Box 433

Camden, AL 36726 (334) 682-4155

Contact: Haas Strother, Tr.

Established in 1996 in AL.

Foundation type: Independent foundation.

Financial data (yr. ended 12/31/04): Assets, $7,920,257 (M); expenditures, $426,396; qualifying distributions, $367,864; giving activities include $367,864 for grants to individuals.

Purpose and activities: The foundation awards cash scholarships to Wilcox County residents to attend college or vocational school.

Type of support: Scholarships—to individuals.

Limitations: Giving limited to residents of Wilcox County, AL, who are making progress toward a college degree.

Application information: Application form not required.

Deadline(s): None

Trustees: R.J. Browder; Haas Strother.

EIN: 636192432

75

Susan Mott Webb Charitable Trust ✧

P.O. Box 11647

Birmingham, AL 35202-1647 (205) 801-0380

Contact: Laura Wainwright, V.P., AmSouth Bank

E-mail: cgale@amsouth.com

Established in 1978 in AL.

Donor: Susan Mott Webb†.

Foundation type: Independent foundation.

Financial data (yr. ended 12/31/05): Assets, $17,294,751 (M); expenditures, $991,670; qualifying distributions, $886,767; giving activities include $871,550 for grants.

Purpose and activities: Emphasis on supporting charitable organizations in the Birmingham, AL, area only.

Fields of interest: Arts; Education; Animals/wildlife; Health care; Human services; Youth, services; Urban/community development; Christian agencies & churches; General charitable giving; Homeless.

Type of support: General/operating support; Continuing support; Annual campaigns; Capital campaigns; Building/renovation; Equipment; Endowments; Emergency funds; Program development; Publication; Curriculum development; Internship funds; Technical assistance.

Limitations: Giving limited to the greater Birmingham, AL, area. No grants to individuals, or for scholarships or fellowships; no loans.

Publications: Application guidelines.

Application information: Call to obtain guidelines. Application form not required.

Initial approach: Letter or proposal

Copies of proposal: 6

Deadline(s): Apr. 1 and Oct. 1

Board meeting date(s): June and Dec.

Final notification: June 30 and Dec. 31

Trustees: Nina Botsford; Stewart Dansby; Suzanne Dansby Phelps; Charles B. Webb, Jr.; AmSouth Bank.

EIN: 636112593

76

Working Woman's Home Association, Inc. ✧ ☆

2473 Rosemont Pl.

Montgomery, AL 36106

Foundation type: Independent foundation.

Financial data (yr. ended 1/31/06): Assets, $7,506,440 (M); expenditures, $399,986; qualifying distributions, $321,673; giving activities include $321,673 for grants.

Fields of interest: Arts; Education; Youth development; Human services; Family services; Christian agencies & churches.

Limitations: Applications not accepted. No grants to individuals.

Application information: Contributes only to pre-selected organizations.

Officers: Peggy Joseph, Pres.; Carol Brewbaker, V.P.; Tutter Rogers, Secy.; Mary Lou Evans, Treas.

Directors: Martha Allen; Burke Chambers; Beth Dubina; Mary Coleman Hester; and 5 additional directors.

EIN: 630302186

Selected grants: The following grants were reported in 2006.

$27,750 to Family Sunshine Center Foundation, Montgomery, AL.

$20,000 to Nellie Burge Community Center, Montgomery, AL.

$15,000 to Montgomery Cancer Wellness Foundation, Montgomery, AL.

$10,787 to Child Protect, Montgomery, AL.

$10,000 to Aid to Inmate Mothers, Montgomery, AL.

$10,000 to Childrens Protective Association, Montgomery, AL.

$7,000 to Boy Scouts of America, Anchorage, AK.

$5,184 to Jubilee Community Center, Montgomery, AL.

$3,550 to American Red Cross.

77

The Wyker Family Foundation ✧ ☆

P.O. Box 2717

Decatur, AL 35602

Application address: c/o J.W. Wyker, III, Tr., 2211 Century Ct. S.E., Decatur, AL 35601

Established in 2001 in AL.

Donor: J.W. Wyker, Jr.

Foundation type: Independent foundation.

Financial data (yr. ended 12/31/05): Assets, $382,559 (M); expenditures, $402,819; qualifying distributions, $401,843; giving activities include $401,843 for 17 grants (high: $389,788; low: $50).

Purpose and activities: Giving primarily to Christian organizations; funding also for youth and social services.

Fields of interest: Boy scouts; Youth development; Foundations (private grantmaking); Religious federated giving programs; Christian agencies & churches.

Type of support: General/operating support.

Application information: Application form not required.

Deadline(s): None

Trustees: Isobel Wyker Fulkerson; J.W. Wyker III.

EIN: 696001620

ALASKA

78
The Alaska Community Foundation ✧ ☆
301 W. Northern Lights Blvd., Ste. 408
Anchorage, AK 99503 (907) 334-6700
Contact: Marcia Hastings, Exec. Dir.
FAX: (907) 334-5780;
E-mail: mhastings@alaskacf.org; URL: http://
www.alaskacf.org

Incorporated in 1995.
Foundation type: Community foundation.
Financial data (yr. ended 12/31/05): Assets,
$17,451,951 (M); gifts received, $6,298,886;
expenditures, $1,008,138; giving activities include
$575,426 for grants.
Purpose and activities: The foundation is a
nonprofit public charity promoting personal
philanthropy and providing financial management,
strategic development and donor development
services to communities, organizations and donors
across AK.
Fields of interest: Scholarships/financial aid;
Human services; Community development.
Type of support: Capital campaigns; Emergency
funds; Program development; Seed money;
Scholarship funds; Matching/challenge support.
Limitations: Giving generally limited to AK. No
support for religious organizations for religious
purposes. No grants for unrestricted funds,
operating funds, endowments, overhead costs,
fundraising activities, sponsorships, membership
solicitations, debt reduction, or funding after the
fact.
Publications: Annual report; Grants list;
Informational brochure.
Application information: Visit foundation Web site
for application guidelines. Application form not
required.
    Initial approach: Letter of inquiry (no longer than
        2 pages)
    Copies of proposal: 1
    Deadline(s): Apr. 15
    Board meeting date(s): Monthly
    Final notification: July
Officers and Directors:* Jo Michalski,* Chair.; Leo
Bustad,* Co. Vice-Chair.; Rick Nerland,*
Co-Vice-Chair.; Carol Simonetti, C.E.O.; Margaret
Price,* Secy.; Allan Johnston,* Treas.; Marcia
Hastings, Exec. Dir.; Carla Beam; Ken Castner;
Morgan Christen; Susan Behlke Foley; Pat Gamble;
Jack Griffin; Joan McCoy; Sharon Richards; Debby
Sedwick; Thelma Snow-Jackson; Reed Stoops; J.C.
"Chris" Swalling; Garret Wong.
Number of staff: 1 full-time professional; 1 part-time
professional; 1 full-time support.
EIN: 920155067

79
Alaska Conservation Foundation ✧
441 W. 5th Ave., Ste. 402
Anchorage, AK 99501-2340 (907) 276-1917
Contact: Deborah L. Williams, Exec. Dir.; For grants:
Julie Jessen, Assoc. Prog. Off.
FAX: (907) 274-4145; E-mail: acfinfo@akcf.org;
Grant request E-mail: jjessen@akcf.org; URL: http://
www.akcf.org

Established in 1980 in AK.
Foundation type: Community foundation.
Financial data (yr. ended 6/30/04): Assets,
$8,076,254 (M); gifts received, $6,613,811;
expenditures, $4,908,064; giving activities include
$1,822,718 for 214 grants (high: $130,000; low:
$75), $8,145 for 6 grants to individuals (high:
$3,000; low: $500), and $2,333,116 for
foundation-administered programs.
Purpose and activities: Awards grants to protect the
integrity of Alaskan ecosystems and promote
sustainable livelihoods among Alaskan
communities and peoples; awards to honor
outstanding environmental volunteer activists and
professionals, and to sustain community
development.
Fields of interest: Environment, research;
Environment, natural resources; Environmental
education; Environment; Animals/wildlife,
preservation/protection; Animals/wildlife,
sanctuaries; Economic development; Community
development; Social sciences, public policy; Public
affairs, information services.
Type of support: General/operating support;
Continuing support; Equipment; Emergency funds;
Program development; Conferences/seminars;
Publication; Internship funds; Technical assistance;
Consulting services; Program evaluation; Grants to
individuals; Scholarships—to individuals;
Matching/challenge support.
Limitations: Giving primarily in AK. No grants for
annual campaigns, deficit financing, building funds,
land acquisition, renovation projects, general or
special endowments, or exchange programs; no
student loans.
Publications: Application guidelines; Annual report;
Financial statement; Grants list; Informational
brochure; Newsletter; Program policy statement.
Application information: Visit foundation Web site
for grant guidelines. Application form required.
    Initial approach: Letter or telephone
    Copies of proposal: 1
    Deadline(s): Varies
    Board meeting date(s): Feb., May, and Sept.
    Final notification: 2 weeks after board meeting
Officers and Directors:* Ken Leghorn,* Chair.; Bill
Lazar,* Vice-Chair., National Trustees; Helen
Nienhueser,* Vice-Chair.; Nina Miller Heyano,*
Secy.; Barb Seibel, C.F.O.; Deborah L. Williams,
Exec. Dir.; David Rockefeller, Jr., Advisor; Jonathan
Blattmachr, Counsel; Thomas A. Barron; RaeShaun
Bibbs; Robert Bundy; David Cline; Wallace Cole;
April Crosby; Bert Fingerhut; David Hardenberg;
Vernita Herdman; Jennifer Huntington; Carol Kasza;
Doug McConnell; Scott Nathan; Susan Cohn
Schultz; John Sisk; Ted Smith; Stacy Studebaker;
Adam Wolfensohn.
Number of staff: 18 full-time professional; 3
part-time professional; 2 full-time support; 1
part-time support.
EIN: 920061466
Selected grants: The following grants were reported
in 2005.
$75,000 to Alaska Conservation Solutions,
    Anchorage, AK. For work on global warming. For
    grant made through Climate Change program.
$66,740 to Alaska Marine Conservation Council,
    Anchorage, AK. For Friends of Bristol Bay project.
    Grant made through Alaska Coalition.
$66,000 to Green Corps, Boston, MA. For Green
    Corps organizers. Grant made through Alaska
    Coalition.

$60,000 to Oceana, DC. For conservation of North
    Pacific Marine Ecosystem. Grant made through
    Alaska Oceans Program.
$50,000 to Alaska Center for the Environment,
    Anchorage, AK. For building in-state support.
    Grant made through Alaska Oceans Program.
$50,000 to Alaska Coalition, DC. For grasstops
    organizing.
$50,000 to Earthjustice, Juneau, AK. For legal
    support to Alaska Rainforest Campaign. Grant
    made through Alaska Rainforest Campaign.
$50,000 to Southeast Alaska Conservation Council,
    Juneau, AK. To coordinate statewide
    transportation efforts. Grant made through
    Alaska Coalition.
$46,000 to Alaska Wilderness League, DC. For
    slideshow outreach. Grant made through Alaska
    Coalition.
$20,000 to Alaska Conservation Voters, Anchorage,
    AK. For operating support.

80
Arctic Education Foundation ✧
3900 C St., Ste. 801
Anchorage, AK 99503 (907) 852-8633
Contact: Leona Okakok
FAX: (907) 852-2774; E-mail: lokakok@asrc.com;
Application address: P.O. Box 129, Barrow, AK
99723; Additional tel.: (800) 770-2772; Additional
E-mail: dcook@asrc.com; URL: http://
www.arcticed.com

Established in 1978 in AK.
Donors: Arctic Slope Regional Corp.; Chevron
U.S.A., Inc.; BP Alaska; Shell Oil Co.; Amoco Corp.;
Piqunik Management Corp.; UIC Construction.
Foundation type: Company-sponsored foundation.
Financial data (yr. ended 12/31/03): Assets,
$581,823 (M); gifts received, $724,186;
expenditures, $417,598; qualifying distributions,
$408,073; giving activities include $408,073 for
236 grants to individuals (high: $5,025; low: $50).
Purpose and activities: The foundation awards
college scholarships to Inupiat Natives of the Arctic
Slope Region of Alaska and their descendants.
Fields of interest: Native Americans/American
Indians.
Type of support: Scholarships—to individuals.
Limitations: Giving primarily in AK.
Publications: Annual report.
Application information: Application form required.
    Initial approach: Download application form and
        mail to foundation
    Deadline(s): Mar. 1, June 1, Aug. 1, and Dec. 1
    Board meeting date(s): Jan. and Aug.
Officer: Crawford Patkotak, Secy.-Treas.
Directors: George T. Kaleak, Sr.; Molly Pederson;
George Sielak.
Number of staff: 1 full-time professional.
EIN: 920068447

81
Atwood Foundation, Inc.
2000 Atwood Dr.
Anchorage, AK 99517-1333 (907) 274-4900
Contact: Robert N. Reeves, Pres.
E-mail: atwoodfoundation@gci.net

Established in 1962 in AK.
Donors: Robert B. Atwood; Anchorage Times
Publishing Co.

Foundation type: Independent foundation.
Financial data (yr. ended 12/31/04): Assets, $23,036,043 (M); gifts received, $1,970,000; expenditures, $1,263,370; qualifying distributions, $1,132,008; giving activities include $977,010 for 18 grants (high: $255,000; low: $2,500).
Purpose and activities: Giving primarily for higher education and the arts.
Fields of interest: Performing arts centers; Higher education; Athletics/sports, Special Olympics.
Limitations: Giving primarily in Anchorage, AK. No grants to individuals.
Publications: Annual report.
Application information: Application form required.
 Initial approach: Letter
 Copies of proposal: 1
 Deadline(s): Dec. 31
 Board meeting date(s): Quarterly
 Final notification: 90 days
Officers: Ed Rasmuson, Chair.; William J. Tobin, Vice-Chair.; Robert N. Reeves, Pres.; David Tobin, Secy.; Gloria Allen, Treas.
Directors: Nancy Harbour.
Number of staff: 1 full-time professional; 1 part-time support.
EIN: 926002571
Selected grants: The following grants were reported in 2004.
$255,000 to Alaska Center for the Performing Arts, Anchorage, AK. For program support.
$201,250 to Alaska Zoo, Anchorage, AK. For program support.
$200,000 to Alaska Pacific University, Anchorage, AK. For program support.
$120,000 to University of Alaska Anchorage, Anchorage, AK. For program support.
$25,000 to Alaska Botanical Garden, Anchorage, AK. For program support.
$25,000 to Alaska Moving Image, Anchorage, AK. For program support.
$25,000 to Anchorage Opera, Anchorage, AK. For program support.
$24,260 to Dollars for Dogs, Anchorage, AK. For program support.
$21,000 to Food Bank of Alaska, Anchorage, AK. For program support.
$20,000 to Alaska Theater of Youth, Anchorage, AK. For program support.

82
The Carr Foundation, Inc. ✧
550 W. 7th Ave., Ste. 1540
Anchorage, AK 99501

Established in 1990 in AK.
Donor: L.J. Carr.
Foundation type: Independent foundation.
Financial data (yr. ended 12/31/05): Assets, $4,710,657 (M); gifts received, $635,473; expenditures, $366,074; qualifying distributions, $342,026; giving activities include $340,000 for 31 grants (high: $100,000; low: $500).
Purpose and activities: Giving primarily for Roman Catholic organizations; funding also for education, the arts, and social services.
Fields of interest: Performing arts, music; Performing arts, opera; Arts; Higher education; Education; Human services; Roman Catholic agencies & churches.
Limitations: Applications not accepted. Giving primarily in AK. No grants to individuals.
Application information: Contributes only to pre-selected organizations.

Officers: L.J. Carr, Pres.; Wilma Carr, V.P.; Jacqueline Carr, Secy.-Treas.
EIN: 920135110
Selected grants: The following grants were reported in 2004.
$90,000 to Alaska Pacific University, Anchorage, AK.
$25,000 to Eisenhower Medical Center Foundation, Rancho Mirage, CA.
$15,000 to Brother Francis House, Anchorage, AK.
$12,500 to Ted Stevens Foundation, Anchorage, AK.
$11,500 to Clare House, Anchorage, AK.
$11,000 to Catholic Social Services, Anchorage, AK. For McAuley Manor.
$10,000 to Anchorage Concert Association, Anchorage, AK.
$10,000 to Anchorage Senior Center, Anchorage, AK.

83
The CIRI Foundation ✧
(also known as The Cook Inlet Region, Inc. Foundation)
3600 San Jeronimo Dr., Ste. 256
Anchorage, AK 99508-2870 (907) 793-3575
FAX: (907) 793-3585;
E-mail: tcf@thecirifoundation.org; Additional tel.: (800) 764-3382; URL: http://www.thecirifoundation.org

Established in 1982 in AK.
Donor: Cook Inlet Region, Inc.
Foundation type: Company-sponsored foundation.
Financial data (yr. ended 12/31/04): Assets, $50,138,747 (M); gifts received, $359,327; expenditures, $2,479,009; qualifying distributions, $2,245,921; giving activities include $479,964 for 14 grants (high: $68,600; low: $1,500), and $1,055,543 for 327 grants to individuals (high: $9,000; low: $105).
Purpose and activities: The foundation supports organizations involved with Alaska Native heritage and education and awards scholarships, grants, and fellowships to Alaska Natives.
Fields of interest: Arts, cultural/ethnic awareness; Education; Native Americans/American Indians.
Type of support: Continuing support; Program development; Fellowships; Research; Grants to individuals; Scholarships—to individuals.
Limitations: Giving primarily in the Cook Inlet Region, AK. No grants for endowments, buildings or equipment, completed projects, re-granting, or lobbying or propaganda efforts; no loans.
Publications: Application guidelines; Informational brochure (including application guidelines); Multi-year report; Program policy statement.
Application information: Visit Web site for deadlines for Kenai Natives Association Scholarship and Grant Fund, Salamatof Native Association, Inc. Scholarship and Grant Program, Tyonek Native Corporation Scholarship and Grant Fund, Ninilchik Native Association, Inc. Scholarship and Vocational Grant Fund, the Cap Lathrop Endowment Scholarship Fund, the Howard Rock Foundation Scholarship Program, named scholarships, and project grants. Statements of purpose should be no longer than 500 words for new applicants; 300 words for repeat applicants. Organizations receiving project grants are asked to submit a final report. The foundation may request additional information at a later date for project grants. Application form required.

Initial approach: Download application form and mail or fax proposal and application form to foundation; contact foundation or visit Web site for application information for George Miller, Jr. Management Leadership Endowment Fund
Copies of proposal: 1
Deadline(s): Mar. 31, June 30, Sept. 30, and Dec. 1 for education grants, fellowships, and Jump Start; June 1 and Dec. 1 for General Semester Scholarships; June 1 for Special Excellence Scholarships, Excellence Scholarships, and Achievement Scholarships
Board meeting date(s): Quarterly
Final notification: 30 to 40 days following deadlines for project grants
Officers and Directors:* Ronald Perry,* Chair.; Sharon Gagnon, Ph.D.*, Vice-Chair.; Susan A. Anderson, C.E.O. and Pres.; Craig Floerchinger,* Secy.-Treas.; Penny Carty; Britton E. Crosly; Robert Gottstein; Shirley Holloway, Ph.D.; Sharon Huhndorf, Ph.D.; Elaine Maimon, Ph.D.; Sophie Minich; Rayna Neumiller; Gregory Razo; Deanna Sackett; Jacklyn Sallee.
Number of staff: 6
EIN: 920087914
Selected grants: The following grants were reported in 2004.
$68,600 to Chickaloon, Village of, Chickaloon, AK.
$66,000 to Salamatof Tribal Council, Kenai, AK.
$65,000 to Koahnic Broadcast Corporation, Anchorage, AK.
$60,000 to Kenaitze Indian Tribe, Kenai, AK.
$56,000 to Sheldon Jackson College, Sitka, AK.
$50,000 to Alaska Native Heritage Center, Anchorage, AK.
$50,000 to Cook Inlet Tribal Council, Anchorage, AK.
$25,864 to Alutiiq Heritage Foundation, Kodiak, AK.
$10,000 to Alaska Robotics Education Association, Anchorage, AK.
$10,000 to Project GRAD Kenai Peninsula, Homer, AK.

84
The Doyon Foundation ✧
1 Doyon Pl., Ste. 300
Fairbanks, AK 99701 (888) 478-4755
FAX: (905) 459-2065;
E-mail: foundation@doyon.com; Additional tel.: (907) 459-2050; URL: http://www.doyonfoundation.com/

Established in 1988 in AK.
Donor: Doyon Ltd.
Foundation type: Company-sponsored foundation.
Financial data (yr. ended 6/30/05): Assets, $8,334,048 (M); gifts received, $1,528,638; expenditures, $1,705,020; qualifying distributions, $338,822; giving activities include $9,298 for 1 grant, and $329,524 for 511 grants to individuals (high: $3,910; low: $141).
Purpose and activities: The foundation supports organizations involved with Native Americans. Special emphasis is directed toward programs designed to strengthen Native culture and heritage through education; and improve the quality of life for Alaska Native people.
Fields of interest: Arts, cultural/ethnic awareness; Native Americans/American Indians.
Type of support: General/operating support; Internship funds; Scholarships—to individuals.
Limitations: Giving primarily in AK.

Publications: Application guidelines; Annual report; Newsletter.

Application information: Application form required.

Initial approach: Download application form and mail to foundation

Deadline(s): Mar. 15, June 15, Sept. 15, and Nov. 15 for vocational scholarships; June 15 and Nov. 15 for college scholarships and scholarships for certificate degrees

Board meeting date(s): Quarterly

Officers and Directors:* Dawn Dinwoodie,* Pres.; Shane Derendoff,* V.P.; Sarah Sherry,* Secy.-Treas.; Josephine Malemute; Jennifer Maguire.

Number of staff: 2 full-time professional.

EIN: 943089624

85

Rasmuson Foundation ▼

301 W. Northern Lights Blvd., Ste. 400
Anchorage, AK 99503   (907) 297-2700
Contact: Diane S. Kaplan, C.E.O. and Pres.
FAX: (907) 297-2770;
E-mail: rasmusonfdn@rasmuson.org; URL: http://www.rasmuson.org

Established in 1955 in AK.

Donors: Elmer E. Rasmuson‡; Jenny Rasmuson‡.

Foundation type: Independent foundation.

Financial data (yr. ended 12/31/05): Assets, $527,896,528 (M); expenditures, $26,444,354; qualifying distributions, $24,086,158; giving activities include $24,086,158 for grants.

Purpose and activities: The foundation is a catalyst to promote a better life for Alaskans. Programmatic interests include arts & culture, health, social services, organizational capacity building, community development, recreation, and education.

Fields of interest: Arts; Education; Health care; Recreation; Human services; Children/youth, services; Aging, centers/services; Women, centers/services; Community development; Native Americans/American Indians.

Type of support: Management development/capacity building; Equipment; Land acquisition; Program development; Seed money; Curriculum development; Technical assistance; Program-related investments/loans; Matching/challenge support.

Limitations: Giving limited to AK. No support for K-12 education or religious organizations. No grants to individuals, scholarships, endowments, deficits or debt reduction, fundraising events, indirect or overhead costs; or for operating funds.

Publications: Application guidelines; Grants list; Informational brochure (including application guidelines); Newsletter.

Application information: All application forms available on Web site. Application form required.

Initial approach: E-mail, telephone, or proposal
Copies of proposal: 2
Deadline(s): None
Board meeting date(s): Summer and winter
Final notification: Varies

Officers and Directors:* Edward B. Rasmuson,* Chair.; Cathryn Rasmuson,* Vice-Chair.; Diane S. Kaplan, C.E.O. and Pres.; Mary Louise Rasmuson,* Secy.-Treas.; Jeff Clarke, C.A.O.; Rob Allen; Hon. Morgan Christen; Doug Eby; Adam Gibbons; Lile R. Gibbons; Nadine Hargesheimer; Natasha von Imhof; Judy Rasmuson; John Wanamaker.

Trustee: Wells Fargo Bank, N.A.

Number of staff: 12 full-time professional; 1 part-time support.

EIN: 916340739

Selected grants: The following grants were reported in 2005.

$1,176,050 to Petersburg, City of, Petersburg, AK. For construction of aquatic center.

$1,024,971 to Central Peninsula Health Centers, Kenai, AK. 2 grants: $1,000,000 (For construction of community health center), $24,971 (For network infrastructure upgrade).

$1,000,000 to Cook Inlet Housing Authority, Anchorage, AK. For completion of low-income housing project.

$900,000 to Foraker Group, Anchorage, AK. For Foraker Sustaining Support Initiative, capacity building award to strengthen and expand technical assistance opportunities for Alaska's nonprofit community, payable over 3 years.

$852,500 to Alaska Natural History Association, Anchorage, AK. To acquire Rapuzzi Collection of Gold Rush-era buildings and artifacts.

$735,489 to Food Bank of Alaska, Anchorage, AK. For blueprint to end hunger in Alaska.

$363,341 to New Koliganek Village Council, Koliganek, AK. For construction of family resource center and clinic, payable over 2 years.

$100,000 to Simonian Little League, Anchorage, AK. For construction of concession building and ballfield amenities at Abbott Loop Community Park.

$22,098 to McCarthy-Kennicott Historical Museum, Glennallen, AK. For continued renovation of museum facility for improved accessibility (to ADA standards) and appearance.

ARIZONA

86

A.P.S. Foundation, Inc. ✧

P.O. Box 53999, M.S. 9557
Phoenix, AZ 85072-3999
Contact: Terry DeValle, Contribs. Coord.
E-mail: sandie.jones@aps.com; *URL:* http://
www.aps.com/general_info/aboutaps_14.html

Established in 1981 in AZ.
Donor: Arizona Public Service Co.
Foundation type: Company-sponsored foundation.
Financial data (yr. ended 12/31/05): Assets,
$22,443,654 (L); expenditures, $1,793,500;
qualifying distributions, $1,793,500; giving
activities include $1,793,500 for 54 grants (high:
$250,000; low: $2,500).
Purpose and activities: The foundation supports
organizations involved with arts and culture,
education, the environment, health, human
services, and community development.
Fields of interest: Arts; Education; Environment;
Hospitals (general); Health organizations,
association; Children/youth, services; Human
services; Civil rights, minorities; Community
development; Economically disadvantaged.
Type of support: General/operating support; Capital
campaigns; Matching/challenge support.
Limitations: Giving primarily in AZ. No support for
charter schools or religious, political, fraternal,
legislative, or lobbying organizations. No grants to
individuals, or for travel-related or hotel expenses.
Application information: Application form not
required.
  Initial approach: Proposal
  Final notification: 30 to 60 days
Officers and Directors:* William J. Post,* Chair. and
Pres.; Jack E. Davis,* V.P.; Armando B. Flores,*
V.P.; James M. Levine,* V.P.; Nancy C. Loftin,*
Secy.-Treas.
Number of staff: 2 full-time professional; 1 part-time
support.
EIN: 953735903
Selected grants: The following grants were reported
in 2004.
$250,000 to University of Arizona Foundation,
  Tucson, AZ. For Technology and Management
  Fund.
$100,000 to Phoenix Art Museum, Phoenix, AZ. 2
  grants: $50,000 each
$75,000 to Human Services Campus, Phoenix, AZ.
$60,000 to Fresh Start Womens Foundation,
  Phoenix, AZ.
$50,000 to Arizona Project ChalleNGe, Queen
  Creek, AZ.
$35,000 to HomeBase Youth Services, Phoenix, AZ.
$30,000 to West Valley Fine Arts Council, Litchfield
  Park, AZ.
$25,000 to Alliance for Audience, Phoenix, AZ.
$25,000 to Coconino Community College, Page, AZ.

87

Arizona Community Foundation ▼ ✧

2201 E. Camelback Rd., Ste. 202
Phoenix, AZ 85016 (602) 381-1400
Contact: Sharon Landis, Sr. V.P., Finance and
Admin.

FAX: (602) 381-1575;
E-mail: slandis@azfoundation.org; Additional tel.:
(800) 222-8221; Grant application E-mail:
grants@azfoundation.org; URL: http://
www.azfoundation.org

Incorporated in 1978 in AZ.
Donors: L. Dilatush†; Bert A. Getz; G.R. Herberger;
R. Kieckhefer; Newton Rosenzweig†.
Foundation type: Community foundation.
Financial data (yr. ended 12/31/05): Assets,
$502,887,302 (M); gifts received, $98,926,655;
expenditures, $33,943,138; giving activities
include $25,249,128 for 2,638+ grants.
Purpose and activities: The foundation provides
support for both individual community and broader
statewide needs in a wide range of areas including
the arts and culture, public education, the
environment, youth development, community
building, and health and human services.
Fields of interest: Visual arts, architecture;
Performing arts; Arts; Education, public education;
Education, early childhood education; Child
development, education; Higher education; Adult
education—literacy, basic skills & GED; Education,
reading; Education; Environment, natural resources;
Environment; Health care; Substance abuse,
services; Mental health/crisis services; Health
organizations, association; AIDS; AIDS research;
Legal services; Employment; Housing/shelter,
development; Housing/shelter; Disasters,
Hurricane Katrina; Boys & girls clubs; Children/
youth, services; Child development, services; Family
services; Homeless, human services; Human
services; Rural development; Community
development; Engineering/technology; Science;
Government/public administration; Public affairs;
Aging; Disabilities, people with; Minorities;
Economically disadvantaged; Homeless.
Type of support: General/operating support;
Continuing support; Building/renovation;
Equipment; Emergency funds; Program
development; Publication; Seed money; Scholarship
funds; Research; Technical assistance; Matching/
challenge support.
Limitations: Giving limited to AZ. No support for
religious organizations for religious purposes. No
grants to individuals (except for scholarships), travel
to or support of conferences, fundraising campaigns
and expenses, debt reduction, or capital grants;
generally, no loans.
Publications: Application guidelines; Annual report;
Financial statement; Informational brochure;
Newsletter; Program policy statement.
Application information: Visit foundation Web site
for application and guidelines per grant type.
Application form required.
  Initial approach: Complete online grant
    application
  Deadline(s): Varies
  Board meeting date(s): Quarterly
  Final notification: 60 days
Officers and Directors:* Gerald "Jerry" Bisgrove,*
Chair.; Richard Silverman,* Vice-Chair.; Robert L.
King, C.E.O. and Pres.; Deborah Whitehurst, Exec.
V.P., Ext. Affairs; Sharon Landis, Sr. V.P., Finance
and Admin.; Sandy Doubleday, V.P., Mktg. and
Comms.; Marilyn Harris,* Secy.; William J.
Hodges,* Treas.; Kerrie Bainum, Cont.; Bert A.
Getz,* Chair. Emeritus; Ellen Steele Allare; Dr.
William V. Andrew; Tony Astorga; Betsy Bayless;
Susan Budinger; Ernest Calderon; Mike Cohn; Jack
Davis; Robert M. Delgado; Robert S. Diamond;
Bennett Dorrance; Howard R. Emden; Carol Parry

Fox; John C. Giles; John Gogolak; John V. Gosule;
Sharon Harper; Jerry Hirsh; Russell L. Jones;
Michael E. Kelly; Neal Kurn; Grace Y. Lau; Marjorie
McClanahan; Denise Resnik; Lisa Shover; Richard
Snell; Hal Tashman; Richard H. Whitney; Peterson
Zah.
Number of staff: 25 full-time professional; 2
part-time professional; 8 full-time support; 3
part-time support.
EIN: 860348306
Selected grants: The following grants were reported
in 2005.
$80,000 to Youth Count, Prescott, AZ. 2 grants:
  $50,000 (For Communities for All Ages),
  $30,000 (For Communities for All Ages).
$50,000 to Arizonas Children Association, Phoenix,
  AZ. For Communities for All Ages.
$50,000 to Big Brothers Big Sisters of Northeastern
  Arizona, Show Low, AZ. For Communities for all
  Ages.
$20,000 to Temple University, Philadelphia, PA. For
  Communities for All Ages.
$15,000 to Arizona Alliance for Arts Education,
  Phoenix, AZ. For Arts Education Technical
  Assistance.
$15,000 to Bisbee Unified School District No. 2,
  Bisbee, AZ. For Arts in Schools, Arts in
  Communities.
$15,000 to Del E. Webb Center for the Performing
  Arts, Wickenburg, AZ. For Arts in Schools, Arts in
  Community.
$15,000 to Gila Valley Arts Council, Safford, AZ. For
  Arts in Schools, Arts in Communities.
$15,000 to Happy Tails, Phoenix, AZ. For Hearing
  Dog Training for Hearing Impaired.

88

Aurora Foundation ▼ ✧

4835 E. Exeter Blvd.
Phoenix, AZ 85018-2940

Established in 1997 in AZ.
Donor: John G. Sperling.
Foundation type: Independent foundation.
Financial data (yr. ended 12/31/04): Assets,
$178,703,210 (M); expenditures, $20,301,239;
qualifying distributions, $20,296,239; giving
activities include $20,236,680 for 4 grants (high:
$15,079,750; low: $300,000).
Purpose and activities: Giving primarily for a
community foundation, medical research, and an
agricultural experiment station; funding also for a
Hispanic-American organization.
Fields of interest: Medical research, institute;
Agriculture/food; Foundations (community);
Hispanics/Latinos.
Type of support: General/operating support.
Limitations: Applications not accepted. Giving
primarily in AZ and TX. No grants to individuals.
Application information: Contributes only to
pre-selected organizations.
Trustee: John G. Sperling.
EIN: 860873239
Selected grants: The following grants were reported
in 2004.
$4,556,930 to Kronos Longevity Research Institute,
  Phoenix, AZ. For medical research.

89
Howard R. & Joy M. Berlin Foundation ✧
2007 Smoketree Dr.
P.O. Box 3731
Carefree, AZ 85377-3731

Established in 1994 in DE.
Donors: Howard R. Berlin; Joy M. Berlin.
Foundation type: Independent foundation.
Financial data (yr. ended 9/30/05): Assets,
$7,292,454 (M); gifts received, $280;
expenditures, $406,089; qualifying distributions,
$379,025; giving activities include $379,025 for 19
grants (high: $200,000; low: $20).
Purpose and activities: Giving primarily for art and
culture, education, and human services.
Fields of interest: Arts; Education; Health
organizations, association; Human services.
Limitations: Applications not accepted. No grants to
individuals.
Application information: Contributes only to
pre-selected organizations.
Officers and Directors:* Howard R. Berlin,* Pres.;
Joy M. Berlin,* V.P. and Secy.; Howard R. Berlin, Jr.
EIN: 223330579

90
**The Joseph & Mary Cacioppo
  Foundation** ✧
c/o Michael-Anne Young
4769 E. Camp Lowell Dr.
Tucson, AZ 85712

Incorporated in 1983 in AZ.
Foundation type: Independent foundation.
Financial data (yr. ended 6/30/05): Assets,
$8,222,270 (M); gifts received, $146,496;
expenditures, $685,545; qualifying distributions,
$617,040; giving activities include $439,097 for
192 grants (high: $3,079; low: $1,540).
Limitations: Applications not accepted. No grants to
individuals.
Application information: Unsolicited requests or
proposals will not be accepted.
Officers and Trustees:* Charles R. Young,* 1st
V.P.; Merry S. Lewis, Secy.; Charles R. Young II,*
Treas.; Michael-Anne Young, Exec. Dir.; Elizabeth
Day; Laura Wilband.
EIN: 860465698

91
**Community Foundation for Southern
  Arizona** ✧
2250 E. Broadway Blvd.
Tucson, AZ 85719-6014 (520) 770-0800
Contact: Steve Alley, C.E.O.
FAX: (520) 770-1500;
E-mail: philanthropy@cfsoaz.org; Additional E-mails:
bbrown@cfsoaz.org and salley@cfsoaz.org;
URL: http://www.cfsoaz.org

Established in 1980 in AZ.
Foundation type: Community foundation.
Financial data (yr. ended 6/30/05): Assets,
$75,423,339 (M); gifts received, $8,638,923;
expenditures, $6,558,179; giving activities include
$4,881,549 for grants.
Purpose and activities: The mission of the
foundation is to work with charitably minded
individuals and organizations to strengthen
southern AZ communities, now and for generations

to come. The foundation also administers a variety
of donor-initiated funds and conducts competitive
scholarship and grant rounds.
Fields of interest: Arts; Education; Environment;
Health care; AIDS; Recreation; Children/youth,
services; Human services; Community
development.
International interests: Mexico.
Type of support: Program development; Scholarship
funds; Research; Scholarships—to individuals;
Matching/challenge support.
Limitations: Giving limited to southern AZ, with
particular emphasis on Pima and Santa Cruz
counties. No support for sectarian organizations or
individual schools (except for special literacy
grants). No grants to individuals (except
scholarships), or for operating expenses,
endowment building, capital campaigns, debt
retirement, research or fundraising events.
Publications: Application guidelines; Annual report;
Financial statement; Informational brochure.
Application information: Visit foundation Web site
for grant application and guidelines per grant type.
Application form required.
  Initial approach: Letter of inquiry
  Deadline(s): Varies
  Board meeting date(s): Bimonthly
  Final notification: 60 days
Officers and Trustees:* Robert H. Friesen,* Chair.;
Carmen Marriott,* 1st Vice-Chair.; James J.
Glasser,* 2nd Vice-Chair.; Steve Alley, C.E.O. and
Pres.; Judith Brown,* Secy.; Gerald T. Miron,*
Treas.; Mary B. Brown; Shirley J. Chann; Michael A.
Chihak; John L. Claps; Carl Cooper; Nancy Davis;
Patricia G. Escher; Bill Gaylord; Cindy Godwin; Noel
D. Matkin; Bradley Jon Nystedt; Jonathan
Rothschild; Anita Royal; Thomas Warne.
Number of staff: 5 full-time professional; 10 full-time
support; 2 part-time support.
EIN: 942681765

92
Cooper Family Foundation ✧
c/o Snell & Wilmer
1 Arizona Ctr.
Phoenix, AZ 85004-0001
Contact: David E. Weiss, Dir.

Established in 1998 in AZ.
Donors: John Cooper; Mary Cooper; John and Mary
Logser Charitable Lead Trust; John and Mary Cooper
Charitable Lead Annuity Trust.
Foundation type: Independent foundation.
Financial data (yr. ended 12/31/03): Assets,
$4,036,599 (M); gifts received, $3,859,158;
expenditures, $675,392; qualifying distributions,
$658,475; giving activities include $651,000 for 27
grants (high: $200,000; low: $1,000).
Purpose and activities: Giving primarily for human
services, and religious purposes, particularly a
Baptist church.
Fields of interest: Arts councils; Education; Health
organizations, association; Food banks; Human
services; Children/youth, services; Federated giving
programs; Christian agencies & churches;
Protestant agencies & churches.
Application information:
  Initial approach: Letter
  Deadline(s): None
Directors: Christine Cooper; Gary Cooper; David E.
Weiss.
EIN: 860905824

Selected grants: The following grants were reported
in 2003.
$200,000 to Mount Zion Baptist Church.
$55,000 to Crisis Nursery, Phoenix, AZ.
$30,000 to Boy Scouts of America, Four Lakes
  Council, Madison, WI.
$30,000 to Boys and Girls Clubs of Tioga County,
  Owego, NY.
$20,000 to Saint Marys Food Bank, Phoenix, AZ.
$15,000 to Downtown Urban Community Kids,
  Phoenix, AZ.
$10,000 to Broadway Cares/Equity Fights AIDS,
  New York, NY.
$10,000 to Tioga County Council on the Arts,
  Owego, NY.
$5,000 to Arizona Recreation Center for the
  Handicapped (ARCH), Phoenix, AZ.
$5,000 to Coburn Free Library, Owego, NY.

93
Frederick Gardner Cottrell Foundation ✧
c/o Gary M. Munsinger, Pres.
101 N. Wilmot Rd., Ste. 600
Tucson, AZ 85711-3365

Established in 1998 in AZ.
Donor: Research Corporation Technologies, Inc.
Foundation type: Independent foundation.
Financial data (yr. ended 12/31/05): Assets,
$1,334,294 (M); expenditures, $976,665;
qualifying distributions, $969,635; giving activities
include $966,000 for 14 grants (high: $200,000;
low: $500).
Purpose and activities: Giving to educational and
scientific organizations to advance research and
chair teaching positions.
Fields of interest: Higher education; Eye research;
Marine science; Science.
Limitations: Applications not accepted. Giving
primarily in Woods Hole, MA, Hunt Valley, MD,
Brunswick, ME, and Houston, TX. No grants to
individuals.
Application information: Unsolicited requests for
funds not accepted.
Officers: Gary Munsinger, Pres.; Rebecca Buescher,
Secy.; Linda Tansik, Treas.
Directors: Shaun A. Kirkpatrick; Christopher P.
Martin; John Schaefer; G. King Walters; R. Scott
Pyron.
EIN: 860940147

94
**Lawrence T. and Janet T. Dee
  Foundation** ✧
c/o Wells Fargo Bank, N.A.
P.O. Box 53456, MAC S4035-014
Phoenix, AZ 85072
Application address: c/o Wells Fargo Bank
Northwest, N.A., Attn.: David L. Buchman, V.P. and
Relationship Mgr., P.O. Box 25491, Salt Lake City,
UT 84125, tel.: (801) 246-1436

Established in 1971 in UT.
Donors: L.T. Dee†; Janet T. Dee†.
Foundation type: Independent foundation.
Financial data (yr. ended 12/31/05): Assets,
$13,579,987 (M); expenditures, $691,308;
qualifying distributions, $615,606; giving activities
include $595,500 for 96 grants (high: $50,000;
low: $1,000).

Purpose and activities: Support for healthcare services, education, cultural programs, including the fine and performing arts, and community and social service agencies.

Fields of interest: Visual arts; Performing arts; Arts; Child development, education; Higher education; Education; Medical care, rehabilitation; Health care; Medical research, institute; Human services; Children/youth, services; Child development, services; Family services.

Type of support: General/operating support; Annual campaigns; Building/renovation; Equipment; Endowments; Program development; Scholarship funds; Research; Matching/challenge support.

Limitations: Giving primarily in Salt Lake City and Ogden, UT. No grants to individuals; no loans.

Publications: Application guidelines.

Application information: Application form not required.

Initial approach: Letter
Copies of proposal: 2
Deadline(s): None, but suggest no later than Sept. 30
Board meeting date(s): Mar., June, and Sept.

Trustee: Wells Fargo Bank, N.A.

EIN: 876150803

Selected grants: The following grants were reported in 2005.

$97,500 to University of Utah, Salt Lake City, UT. 3 grants: $40,000, $7,500, $50,000

$35,000 to Nature Conservancy, Salt Lake City, UT.

$20,000 to Utah Symphony and Opera, Salt Lake City, UT.

$15,000 to Midtown Community Health Center, Ogden, UT.

$7,500 to Childrens Center, Salt Lake City, UT.

$5,000 to Eccles Community Art Center, Ogden, UT.

$5,000 to Friends for Sight, Salt Lake City, UT.

$5,000 to Ronald McDonald House Charities of the Intermountain Area, Salt Lake City, UT.

95

Dorrance Family Foundation ✧

7600 E. Doubletree Ranch Rd., Ste. 300
Scottsdale, AZ 85258 (480) 367-7000
Contact: Bennett Dorrance, Pres.

Established in 1991 in AZ.

Donor: Bennett Dorrance.

Foundation type: Independent foundation.

Financial data (yr. ended 12/31/04): Assets, $41,702,863 (M); gifts received, $150,000; expenditures, $4,028,878; qualifying distributions, $3,142,192; giving activities include $3,142,192 for 44 grants (high: $1,026,000; low: $250; average: $1,000–$25,000).

Purpose and activities: Giving primarily for education and arts and cultural programs.

Fields of interest: Museums (science/technology); Arts; Elementary/secondary education; Higher education, college.

Limitations: Giving primarily in AZ. No grants to individuals.

Application information:

Initial approach: Letter
Deadline(s): None

Officers and Directors: * Bennett Dorrance, * Pres.; Bennett Dorrance, Jr., * V.P.; Jacquelynn W. Dorrance, * Secy.-Treas.

Number of staff: 1 full-time professional.

EIN: 860691863

Selected grants: The following grants were reported in 2004.

$1,026,000 to Phoenix Art Museum, Phoenix, AZ. For matching grant for endowment and Costume Institute.

$303,000 to Bourgade Catholic High School, Phoenix, AZ. For scholarship program.

$25,500 to Arizona Science Center, Phoenix, AZ. To enhance science learning across Arizona.

$25,000 to Big Brothers Big Sisters of Central Arizona, Phoenix, AZ. For Marie Bartlett Heard Elementary School Site-Based Mentoring Program.

$20,000 to Heard Museum, Phoenix, AZ. For reinstallation of signature galleries and for Circle of Giving.

$10,000 to Boys Hope Girls Hope of Arizona, Phoenix, AZ. To provide stable home, quality education, and chance to succeed with at-risk youth.

$10,000 to Ho Chi Minh City University of Technology, Ho Chi Minh City, Vietnam. For scholarship program.

96

Dougherty Foundation, Inc. ✧

3507 N. Central, Ste. 404
Phoenix, AZ 85012-2020 (602) 264-7478
Contact: Linda M. Czarnecki, Secy.-Treas.

Incorporated in 1954 in AZ.

Donors: M.J. Dougherty†; Mrs. M.J. Dougherty†.

Foundation type: Independent foundation.

Financial data (yr. ended 12/31/05): Assets, $6,880,042 (M); expenditures, $466,522; qualifying distributions, $436,359; giving activities include $203,115 for 25 grants to individuals (high: $23,000; low: $500), and $119,750 for 19 loans to individuals (high: $36,250; low: $500).

Purpose and activities: Gives student loans for students attending participating AZ schools. Students may not apply directly.

Type of support: Fellowships; Student loans—to individuals.

Limitations: Applications not accepted. Giving limited to AZ schools. No grants to individuals directly.

Publications: Financial statement; Informational brochure.

Application information: Unsolicited requests for funds not accepted.

Board meeting date(s): Quarterly and as required

Officers and Directors: * James P. Walsh, * Pres.; Catherine R. Eden, * V.P.; John A. LaSota, Jr., * V.P.; Mary Martha Prince, * V.P.; Linda M. Czarnecki, Secy.-Treas.

Number of staff: 1 full-time professional; 4 part-time professional.

EIN: 866051637

97

Alberta B. Farrington Foundation ✧

7570 N. Silvercrest Way
Paradise Valley, AZ 85253
Contact: Harry J. Cavanagh, Pres.

Established in 1992 in AZ.

Donor: Alberta B. Farrington†.

Foundation type: Independent foundation.

Financial data (yr. ended 12/31/05): Assets, $16,868,944 (M); expenditures, $866,933; qualifying distributions, $603,722; giving activities include $560,550 for grants.

Purpose and activities: Giving primarily to Roman Catholic agencies, churches, and schools, as well as for golfing, higher education, health associations, social services, and children and youth services.

Fields of interest: Higher education; Botanical gardens; Health organizations, association; Food banks; Athletics/sports, golf; Human services; Children/youth, services; Federated giving programs; Roman Catholic agencies & churches.

Limitations: Giving primarily in AZ. No grants to individuals.

Application information: Application form not required.

Deadline(s): None

Officers: Harry J. Cavanagh, Pres.; Geri J. Cavanagh, Secy.-Treas.

Directors: Harry J. Cavanagh, Jr.; Jamie Hufford; Denise Scott.

EIN: 860717723

Selected grants: The following grants were reported in 2004.

$125,000 to Arizona State University Foundation, Tempe, AZ. 2 grants: $100,000, $25,000

$75,000 to Saint Marys High School, Phoenix, AZ.

$50,000 to Banner Health Foundation of Arizona, Phoenix, AZ.

$50,000 to Junior Golf Association of Arizona, Phoenix, AZ.

$50,000 to Villa de Marie Academy, Phoenix, AZ.

$40,000 to Saint Josephs Catholic Church, Phoenix, AZ.

$30,000 to Desert Botanical Garden, Phoenix, AZ.

$25,000 to Career Concepts for Youth, Phoenix, AZ.

$20,000 to Diocese of Phoenix, Phoenix, AZ.

98

The Flinn Foundation ▼ ✧

1802 N. Central Ave.
Phoenix, AZ 85004-1506 (602) 744-6800
Contact: John W. Murphy, C.E.O.

FAX: (602) 744-6815; E-mail: info@flinn.org; E-mail for scholarship information: fscholars@flinn.org; URL: http://www.flinn.org

Established in 1965 in AZ.

Donors: Irene Flinn†; Robert S. Flinn, M.D.†.

Foundation type: Independent foundation.

Financial data (yr. ended 12/31/05): Assets, $181,299,956 (M); expenditures, $12,699,774; qualifying distributions, $11,919,010; giving activities include $8,901,789 for 29 grants (high: $4,000,000; low: $3,000; average: $10,000–$487,561), $540,000 for grants to individuals, and $86,451 for 1 foundation-administered program.

Purpose and activities: To improve the quality of life in Arizona by improving the competitiveness of Arizona's biomedical/research enterprise; by strengthening universities through an undergraduate scholarship program for outstanding high school students; and by furthering the artistic mission and strengthening the institutional capacity of principal visual and performing arts organizations.

Fields of interest: Arts; Higher education; Medical research, institute; Biological sciences.

Type of support: Program development; Seed money; Scholarship funds; Research.

Limitations: Giving limited to AZ. No grants for building projects, purchase of equipment, endowment projects, annual fundraising campaigns, ongoing operating expenses or deficit needs; requests to support conferences and workshops, publications, or the production of films and video are considered only when these activities are an integral component of a larger foundation initiative.

Publications: Annual report; Financial statement; Newsletter; Occasional report.

Application information: Applications accepted for Flinn Scholarship only. Grants awarded through RFP or invitation. Application form required.

Initial approach: Scholarship application form and information available on foundation Web site

Board meeting date(s): Quarterly

Officers and Directors:* David J. Gullen, M.D.*, Chair.; Lisa Wilkinson-Fannin, M.D.*, Vice-Chair.; John W. Murphy, C.E.O. and Pres.; Don P. Snider, V.P. and C.F.O.; Saundra E. Johnson, V.P., Strategic Devel. and Comms.; William A. Read, Ph.D., V.P., Research and Technology; Jay S. Ruffner,* Secy.; Rosellen C. Papp,* Treas.; Robert A. Brooks, M.D., Hon. Dir.; Donald K. Buffmire, M.D., Hon. Dir.; David R. Frazer, Hon. Dir.; Merlin W. Kampfer, M.D., Hon. Dir.; Edward V. O'Malley, Jr., Hon. Dir.; A.J. Pfister, Hon. Dir.; Linda J. Blessing, Ph.D.; Drew M. Brown; Eric M. Reiman, M.D.; W. Scott Robertson, M.D.; Steven M. Wheeler.

Number of staff: 10 full-time professional; 6 full-time support.

EIN: 860421476

Selected grants: The following grants were reported in 2004.

$600,000 to Battelle Memorial Institute, Columbus, OH. For research and program support in AZ bioscience sector.

$217,600 to Maricopa Partnership for Arts and Culture, Phoenix, AZ. For start-up activities.

$95,776 to University of Arizona Foundation, Tucson, AZ. 2 grants: $23,776 (For Donald K, Buffmire Visiting Lectureship), $72,000 (For scholarships).

$79,800 to Arizona State University, Tempe, AZ. 2 grants: $15,000 (For Arizona Consortium for Medicine, Society and Values), $64,800 (For scholarships).

$66,523 to Institute of International Education, New York, NY. For seminar in Budapest, Hungary, and Romania for Flinn Scholars.

$39,000 to Churchill College, Churchill College, Cambridge, England. For Swanson International Scholarship.

$25,000 to Maricopa Community Colleges District, Tempe, AZ. For honorary grant for general support.

$10,000 to National Arts Strategies, DC. For executive program for arts leaders.

99
The Gagarin Trust ◇

27514 N. Azathlan Dr.
Rio Verde, AZ 85263
Contact: Odile Segal, Tr.

Established in 1997 in CT.
Donors: Andrew Gagarin; Jamie Gagarin.
Foundation type: Independent foundation.
Financial data (yr. ended 12/31/05): Assets, $5,243,654 (M); expenditures, $1,514,678; qualifying distributions, $1,471,383; giving activities include $1,434,926 for 4 grants (high: $956,493; low: $6,000).
Purpose and activities: Giving primarily for education, particularly international education; giving also to a fund for international nonprofit development to fight poverty.

Fields of interest: Human services; International affairs, public education; Foundations (private grantmaking).
Type of support: General/operating support.
Limitations: Applications not accepted. Giving on a national basis. No grants to individuals.
Application information: Contributes only to pre-selected organizations.
Trustee: Odile Segal; Nancy Wiltsek; Vincent McGee.
EIN: 066419374

100
Gesner-Johnson Foundation ◇

3440 E. Tonto Dr.
Phoenix, AZ 85044
Contact: Marcia Campbell, Treas.
E-mail: azmarcia@cox.net; Application address: c/o Paul C. Johnson, Kelley Blue Book, 195 Technology Dr., Irvine, CA 92618

Established in 1997 in MN.
Donors: Lloyd P. Johnson; Rosalind G. Johnson‡.
Foundation type: Independent foundation.
Financial data (yr. ended 12/31/03): Assets, $12,129,877 (M); gifts received, $442,179; expenditures, $693,743; qualifying distributions, $630,284; giving activities include $627,251 for 21 grants (high: $50,000; low: $7,500).
Purpose and activities: Each grant is intended to create a significant difference in the receiving organization, with funds designated for specific projects that will have a lasting impact on the community served.
Fields of interest: Arts; Education; Health care; Protestant agencies & churches.
Type of support: Building/renovation; Equipment.
Limitations: Applications not accepted. Giving to Phoenix, AZ, Los Angeles, CA, and Seattle, WA. No grants for general operating expense.
Application information: Unsolicited requests for funds will not be accepted.
Board meeting date(s): Usually June 1 to Dec. 1
Officers and Directors:* Paul C. Johnson,* Chair.; Russell Johnson,* Secy.; Marcia Campbell,* Treas.
Number of staff: None.
EIN: 411890875
Selected grants: The following grants were reported in 2003.

$50,000 to Evergreen School, Shoreline, WA. For general support.

$50,000 to Kidspace, A Participatory Museum, Pasadena, CA. For general support.

$50,000 to Mayfield Junior School of the Holy Child Jesus, Pasadena, CA. For Excellence in Education capital campaign.

$49,050 to Save the Family Foundation, Mesa, AZ. For general support.

$41,488 to Boys and Girls Clubs of Pasadena, Pasadena, CA. To purchase vans.

$40,953 to Stardust Non-Profit Building Supplies, Mesa, AZ. For general support.

$34,500 to Central Area Youth Association (CAYA), Seattle, WA. For general support.

$32,750 to Valley Youth Theater, Phoenix, AZ. For general support.

$30,000 to Northland Family Help Center, Flagstaff, AZ. To purchase van.

$20,000 to New Horizons for Learning, Seattle, WA. To purchase van.

101
Globe Foundation ◇

c/o Lynn Getz-Schmidt
6730 N. Scottsdale Rd., Ste. 250
Scottsdale, AZ 85253-4424 (480) 991-0500

Established in 1958 in IL.
Donors: Bert A. Getz; George F. Getz, Jr.‡.
Foundation type: Independent foundation.
Financial data (yr. ended 12/31/05): Assets, $27,094,868 (M); gifts received, $2,092,722; expenditures, $2,981,475; qualifying distributions, $1,388,135; giving activities include $1,386,843 for 64 grants (high: $200,000; low: $25).
Purpose and activities: Giving primarily for publicly supported community organizations and institutions, with emphasis on youth, cultural organizations, and hospitals.
Fields of interest: Museums; Arts; Environment; Hospitals (general); Health care; Children/youth, services; Community development; Aging.
Type of support: General/operating support; Continuing support; Annual campaigns; Capital campaigns; Building/renovation; Equipment; Endowments; Program development; Professorships; Curriculum development; Research; Employee matching gifts; Matching/challenge support.
Limitations: Applications not accepted. Giving on a national basis. No support for privately supported groups. No grants to individuals.
Application information: Contributes only to pre-selected organizations.
Board meeting date(s): Apr. and Oct.
Officers and Directors:* Bert A. Getz,* C.E.O. and Pres.; Lynn Getz-Schmidt,* V.P. and Exec. Dir.; Bert A. Getz, Jr.,* V.P.; George F. Getz,* Secy.; Michael J. Olsen, Treas.; Rock S. Edwards; James L. Johnson.
EIN: 366054050

102
The George Mason Green & Lois C. Green Foundation ◇

2440 E. Broadway
Tucson, AZ 85719 (520) 791-3939
Contact: Linda Lohse, Secy.

Established in 1986 in AZ.
Donors: Lois C. Green‡; G.M. Green Unitrust; George Mason Green‡.
Foundation type: Independent foundation.
Financial data (yr. ended 12/31/05): Assets, $14,518,933 (M); gifts received, $152,104; expenditures, $1,184,375; qualifying distributions, $1,108,903; giving activities include $1,060,876 for 12 grants (high: $200,000; low: $4,050).
Fields of interest: Arts; Human services; Children/youth, services.
Type of support: General/operating support; Annual campaigns; Capital campaigns; Building/renovation; Endowments; Emergency funds.
Limitations: Giving primarily in Tucson, AZ. No grants to individuals.
Application information: Application form not required.
Initial approach: Letter
Copies of proposal: 1
Deadline(s): None
Officers: Florence Lohse, V.P.; Linda Lohse, Secy.; Robert Lohse, Pres.; Thomas Lohse, Treas.
EIN: 742379340

103
Bruce T. Halle Family Foundation ✧
20225 N. Scottsdale Rd.
Scottsdale, AZ   85255
Contact: Diane M. Halle, Pres.

Established in 2002 in AZ.
Donors: Bruce T. Halle, Sr.; Reinalt-Thomas Corporation.
Foundation type: Independent foundation.
Financial data (yr. ended 12/31/05): Assets, $19 (M); gifts received, $2,298,431; expenditures, $2,315,410; qualifying distributions, $2,315,388; giving activities include $2,288,000 for 78 grants (high: $322,000; low: $250).
Purpose and activities: Giving primarily for health care including health organizations, education, the arts, children, youth, women, and social services.
Fields of interest: Museums (art); Museums (specialized); Performing arts; Arts; Elementary/secondary education; Higher education; Education; Hospitals (specialty); Health care, infants; Health organizations, association; Medical research, association; Food banks; Human services; Children/youth, services; Foundations (community); Roman Catholic agencies & churches; Women.
Limitations: Giving primarily in AZ; some funding nationally, particularly in CA and CO. No grants to individuals.
Application information: Application form not required.
Initial approach: Letter
Deadline(s): Mar. 15 and Sept. 15
Officers and Directors:* Bruce T. Halle, Sr.,* Chair.; Diane M. Halle,* Pres.; Bruce T. Halle, Jr.,* V.P.; Susan Halle,* V.P.; Lisa Halle Pederson,* Secy.; Michael S. Zuieback,* Treas.
EIN: 460469787
Selected grants: The following grants were reported in 2004.
$310,000 to Childhelp USA, Scottsdale, AZ. For general support.
$250,000 to University of Arizona, Eller College, Tucson, AZ. For Distinguished Scholars Fund.
$200,000 to Center for the Future of Arizona, Phoenix, AZ. For educational support.
$134,500 to Celebrity Fight Night Foundation, Phoenix, AZ. For medical research.
$110,000 to Mission of Mercy Arizona Mobile Clinic, Phoenix, AZ.
$107,500 to Scottsdale Healthcare Foundation, Scottsdale, AZ. For safety programs.
$105,000 to Center for Integrative Medicine, Tucson, AZ. For fellows program.
$100,000 to Barrow Neurological Foundation, Phoenix, AZ. For medical support.
$100,000 to Holy Redeemer High School, Detroit, MI.
$100,000 to SouthGate Church, Phoenix, AZ. For general support.

104
The Robert and Marie Hansen Foundation ✧
12475 N. Rancho Vistoso Blvd., Ste. 155
Oro Valley, AZ   85755-1895
Contact: Debra Pickett

Established in 2002 in AZ.
Donors: Paul T. Clifton; John P. Hansen; Karen A. Clifton; Mark W. Hansen.
Foundation type: Independent foundation.

Financial data (yr. ended 6/30/06): Assets, $8,013,914 (M); gifts received, $1,432,314; expenditures, $534,409; qualifying distributions, $375,900; giving activities include $375,900 for 18 grants (high: $125,000; low: $1,000).
Fields of interest: Education; Human services; Public affairs; Roman Catholic agencies & churches.
Type of support: Research; Program development; Curriculum development; Annual campaigns.
Limitations: Applications not accepted. No grants for capital campaigns.
Application information: Unsolicited requests for funds not accepted.
Board meeting date(s): Oct. 15
Trustees: Paul T. Clifton; Marie E. Hansen; Robert A. Hansen.
EIN: 866309859

105
Help From Above ✧ ☆
4001 W Indian School Rd., Ste. A
Phoenix, AZ   85019

Foundation type: Independent foundation.
Financial data (yr. ended 3/31/06): Assets, $1,085,420 (M); gifts received, $1,100,000; expenditures, $679,946; qualifying distributions, $670,946; giving activities include $650,121 for 31 grants (high: $155,573; low: $500), and $20,815 for 5 grants to individuals (high: $5,000; low: $500).
Purpose and activities: Giving primarily to Christian agencies, churches, and schools, and to food banks. Support also to individuals, for assistance with living expenses.
Fields of interest: Elementary/secondary education; Food banks; Human services; Christian agencies & churches.
Type of support: Grants to individuals.
Limitations: Applications not accepted. Giving primarily in AZ and CA.
Application information: Unsolicited requests for funds not accepted.
Officers: John W. Kenyon III, Pres.; Daniel A. Bang, Secy.-Treas.
Director: Suzanne Escobar Kenyon.
EIN: 861048274

106
Herberger Foundation ✧
10881 N. Scottsdale Rd., Ste. 200
Scottsdale, AZ   85254

Established in 1961 in AZ.
Donors: G.R. Herberger‡; Mrs. G.R. Herberger‡; Gary K. Herberger; G.R. Herberger Revocable Trust.
Foundation type: Independent foundation.
Financial data (yr. ended 12/31/05): Assets, $22,079,777 (M); gifts received, $3,068,813; expenditures, $1,012,410; qualifying distributions, $982,810; giving activities include $981,000 for 16 grants (high: $700,000; low: $1,000).
Purpose and activities: Giving primarily for the arts and education.
Fields of interest: Arts, association; Museums (art); Arts; Higher education; Education; Health care; Human services; Children/youth, services.
Limitations: Applications not accepted. Giving primarily in AZ, with emphasis on Phoenix; some giving also in MN. No grants to individuals; no loans or program-related investments.

Application information: Contributes only to pre-selected organizations. Unsolicited requests for funds not accepted.
Officers and Directors:* Gary K. Herberger,* C.E.O. and Pres.; Judd R. Herberger,* V.P.; Doris Schlacter,* Secy.-Treas.
EIN: 866050190
Selected grants: The following grants were reported in 2005.
$700,000 to Saint Cloud State University Foundation, Saint Cloud, MN.
$100,000 to Phoenix Symphony Association, Phoenix, AZ.
$25,000 to Phoenix Theater, Phoenix, AZ.
$10,000 to Ballet Arizona, Phoenix, AZ.
$10,000 to Phoenix Art Museum, Phoenix, AZ.

107
The Hermundslie Foundation ✧
3762 N. Harrison Rd.
Tucson, AZ   85749-8742   (520) 789-8501
Contact: Gerold D. Hermundslie, Pres.

Established in 1968 in AZ.
Foundation type: Independent foundation.
Financial data (yr. ended 12/31/05): Assets, $21,434,263 (M); expenditures, $1,415,915; qualifying distributions, $983,971; giving activities include $983,971 for 9 grants (high: $500,000; low: $16,000).
Purpose and activities: Giving primarily for education, medical research, and religion.
Fields of interest: Education; Health care; Health organizations, association; Alzheimer's disease; Diabetes; Medical research, institute; Federated giving programs; Christian agencies & churches.
Type of support: Research.
Application information:
Initial approach: Letter
Deadline(s): None
Officer: Gerold D. Hermundslie, Pres.
Directors: Gloria Fitzgerald; Carol Hermundslie; John Hubbard.
EIN: 237001359

108
Hickey Family Foundation ✧ ☆
6333 N. Scottsdale Rd.
Scottsdale, AZ   85250
Contact: Nancy E. Baldwin, Tr.

Established in 2004 in AZ.
Donor: Francis G. Hickey, Jr.
Foundation type: Independent foundation.
Financial data (yr. ended 12/31/05): Assets, $21,448,578 (M); gifts received, $21,890,000; expenditures, $647,538; qualifying distributions, $607,478; giving activities include $500,000 for 5 grants (high: $100,000; low: $100,000).
Fields of interest: Higher education; Youth development, services; Youth, services.
Application information:
Initial approach: Letter
Deadline(s): None
Trustee: Nancy E. Baldwin.
Agent: Citibank, N.A.
EIN: 866331657

109

IFS Family Foundation, Inc. ✧
7716 E. Black Mountain Rd.
Scottsdale, AZ 85262
Contact: Irwin F. Smith, Pres.

Established in 1999 in CT.
Donor: Irwin F. Smith.
Foundation type: Independent foundation.
Financial data (yr. ended 12/31/05): Assets,
$8,016,011 (M); expenditures, $542,478;
qualifying distributions, $422,651; giving activities
include $422,651 for 20 grants (high: $200,000;
low: $100).
Fields of interest: Arts; Higher education; Hospitals
(general); Health organizations, association; Human
services; Children/youth, services.
Limitations: Giving on a national basis, with some
emphasis on AZ, WA, and WI.
Application information:
Initial approach: Letter
Deadline(s): None
Officers: Irwin F. Smith, Pres. and Treas.; Linda S.
Smith, V.P. and Secy.; Stephen D. Smith, V.P.;
Susan N. Smith, V.P.
EIN: 061552716
Selected grants: The following grants were reported
in 2005.
$200,000 to University of Wisconsin Childrens
Hospital, Madison, WI.
$20,000 to Ronald McDonald House.
$15,000 to Bowdoin College, Brunswick, ME.
$5,000 to AmeriCares, Stamford, CT.
$100 to American Indian Relief Council, Warrenton,
VA.

110

Jasam Foundation Fund B
1002 N. Dalian Pl.
Tucson, AZ 85748-2070
Contact: Joan D. Guylas, Admin.

Established in 2002 in AR.
Foundation type: Independent foundation.
Financial data (yr. ended 12/31/05): Assets,
$8,775,624 (M); expenditures, $412,234;
qualifying distributions, $347,292; giving activities
include $347,292 for 17 grants (high: $121,688;
low: $950).
Purpose and activities: Giving to support U.S.
troops.
Fields of interest: Hospitals (general); Human
services; Children/youth, services; Christian
agencies & churches.
Limitations: Applications not accepted. Giving
limited to western MI, and the greater Tucson, AZ,
area. No grants to individuals.
Application information: Contributes only to
pre-selected organizations.
Board meeting date(s): Varies
Officer: Joan D. Guylas, Admin.
Number of staff: 1 part-time support.
EIN: 383637370

111

The Jazzbird Foundation ✧
9820 E. Thompson Peak Pkwy., No. 801
Scottsdale, AZ 85255

Established in 1994 in AZ.

Donors: Gretchen F. Ravenscroft; Robert C.
Ravenscroft.
Foundation type: Independent foundation.
Financial data (yr. ended 12/31/05): Assets,
$158,610 (M); gifts received, $881,900;
expenditures, $870,964; qualifying distributions,
$855,400; giving activities include $855,400 for 21
grants (high: $119,600; low: $6,000).
Purpose and activities: Giving primarily for
education, and to Lutheran and other Christian
organizations and churches.
Fields of interest: Higher education; Theological
school/education; Christian agencies & churches;
Protestant agencies & churches.
Limitations: Applications not accepted. Giving
primarily in AZ. No grants to individuals.
Application information: Contributes only to
pre-selected organizations.
Officers and Directors:* Robert B. Ravenscroft,*
Pres.; Gretchen F. Ravenscroft,* V.P.; Lori Geare,*
Secy.; Steve F. Buel, Treas.
EIN: 860745156
Selected grants: The following grants were reported
in 2004.
$163,500 to Majesty Foundation, Grosse Pointe
Farms, MI.
$50,000 to Claremont School of Theology,
Claremont, CA.
$40,000 to Luis Palau Evangelistic Association,
Portland, OR.
$40,000 to Minden Opera House, Minden, NE.
$33,000 to Arizona State University, Tempe, AZ.
$20,000 to El Dorado Community Church, El
Dorado, CA.
$10,000 to Northwestern University, Evanston, IL.

112

**Arthur L. "Bud" Johnson in Memory of
Elaine V. Johnson Foundation**
(also known as Arthur L. & Elaine V. Johnson
Foundation)
1095 E. Oakland Ct.
Gilbert, AZ 85296 (480) 632-8693
Contact: David Hammerslag, Managing Tr.
FAX: (480) 545-8949;
E-mail: info@aljfoundation.org; *URL:* http://
www.aljfoundation.org

Established in 1990 in IL.
Donor: Arthur L. Johnson†.
Foundation type: Independent foundation.
Financial data (yr. ended 12/31/05): Assets,
$13,244,531 (M); expenditures, $712,583;
qualifying distributions, $520,604; giving activities
include $505,155 for 12 grants (high: $161,120;
low: $400).
Purpose and activities: Giving aid to organizations
that use animals to assist the physically
handicapped and also giving for nature conservancy.
Fields of interest: Environment; Animals/wildlife,
training; Animals/wildlife; Physically disabled.
Type of support: Management development/
capacity building; Capital campaigns; Building/
renovation; Equipment; Land acquisition; Program
development; Conferences/seminars; Seed money;
Research; Consulting services; Program evaluation;
Matching/challenge support.
Limitations: Giving primarily on a national basis. No
grants to individuals.
Publications: Application guidelines; Grants list.
Application information: Application form not
required.

Initial approach: Letter
Copies of proposal: 2
Deadline(s): None
Board meeting date(s): Various
Final notification: 90-120 days from receipt
Trustees: David Hammerslag; Sally Hammerslag.
EIN: 363739494

113

J. W. Kieckhefer Foundation ✧
116 E. Gurley St.
P.O. Box 1151
Prescott, AZ 86302
Contact: John I. Kieckhefer, Tr.; Eugene P. Polk, Tr.

Trust established in 1953 in AZ.
Donor: John W. Kieckhefer†.
Foundation type: Independent foundation.
Financial data (yr. ended 12/31/05): Assets,
$47,779,608 (M); expenditures, $1,330,333;
qualifying distributions, $788,350; giving activities
include $788,350 for 54 grants (high: $50,000;
low: $500).
Purpose and activities: Emphasis on medical
research, hospices and health agencies; family
planning and services, the handicapped, and other
social services; education, including medical and
other higher education; youth and child welfare
agencies; ecology and conservation; community
funds; and cultural programs.
Fields of interest: Arts; Higher education; Medical
school/education; Education; Environment, natural
resources; Environment; Reproductive health, family
planning; Medical care, rehabilitation; Health care;
Health organizations, association; Medical
research, institute; Food services; Human services;
Children/youth, services; Family services;
Residential/custodial care, hospices; Federated
giving programs; Marine science; Public policy,
research.
Type of support: General/operating support;
Continuing support; Annual campaigns; Building/
renovation; Equipment; Land acquisition;
Endowments; Emergency funds; Program
development; Conferences/seminars; Publication;
Research; Matching/challenge support.
Limitations: Applications not accepted. No grants to
individuals.
Application information: Contributes mostly to
pre-selected organizations. Internally initiated
grants comprise virtually all of the current
grantmaking of the foundation.
Board meeting date(s): Quarterly, and as required
Trustees: John I. Kieckhefer; Eugene P. Polk.
EIN: 866022877
Selected grants: The following grants were reported
in 2003.
$75,000 to Yavapai Regional Medical Center,
Prescott, AZ. For capital campaign.
$50,000 to Arizona Community Foundation,
Phoenix, AZ. For endowment fund.
$50,000 to Mayo Foundation, Scottsdale, AZ. For
Comprehensive Cancer Center.
$35,000 to Arizona Friends of Foster Children
Foundation, Phoenix, AZ. Toward permanent
endowment fund.
$35,000 to Arizona State University, Tempe, AZ. For
general support.
$25,000 to Hospital for Special Surgery, New York,
NY. For endowment.
$20,000 to Yavapai County Health Department,
Prescott, AZ. For Robert Wood Johnson

Foundation Local Initiatives Funding Partners Program.

$15,000 to Tumbleweed Center for Youth Development, Phoenix, AZ. For general support.

$15,000 to YMCA, Southwest Valley Regional, Goodyear, AZ. Toward the furnishings and fixtures campaign.

$10,000 to Salvation Army of Phoenix, Phoenix, AZ. For general support.

114

The Lisa and Robert Laizure Foundation ✧
14945 W. Jomax Rd.
Surprise, AZ   85387-6223

Established in 1999 in AZ.
Donors: Robert S. Laizure; Lisa S. Laizure.
Foundation type: Independent foundation.
Financial data (yr. ended 12/31/04): Assets, $1,370,006 (M); gifts received, $12,050; expenditures, $984,969; qualifying distributions, $947,762; giving activities include $931,942 for 23 grants (high: $540,000; low: $1,000), and $15,820 for foundation-administered programs.
Fields of interest: Youth, services; Christian agencies & churches.
Limitations: Applications not accepted. Giving primarily AZ, with emphasis on Phoenix. No grants to individuals.
Application information: Contributes only to pre-selected organizations.
Officers: Robert S. Laizure, Pres.; Lisa S. Laizure, V.P.
EIN: 860940164

115

William S. and Ina Levine Foundation ✧ ☆
1702 E. Highland Ave., Ste. 310
Phoenix, AZ   85016

Established in 1997 in AZ.
Foundation type: Independent foundation.
Financial data (yr. ended 5/31/05): Assets, $3,123,754 (M); expenditures, $1,300,419; qualifying distributions, $1,295,867; giving activities include $1,295,867 for 81 grants (high: $125,000; low: $500).
Fields of interest: Arts; Education; Health care; Health organizations, association; Human services; Jewish agencies & temples.
Limitations: Applications not accepted. Giving primarily in AZ. No grants to individuals.
Application information: Contributes only to pre-selected organizations.
Officer and Directors:* William S. Levine,* Pres.; Jay David Levine; Jonathan L. Levine*; Julie Schoen.
EIN: 860866703
Selected grants: The following grants were reported in 2005.
$250,000 to Jewish Federation of Greater Phoenix, Phoenix, AZ. 2 grants: $125,000 each
$175,000 to King David School, Scottsdale, AZ. 3 grants: $75,000, $25,000, $75,000
$50,000 to American Heart Association, Tempe, AZ.
$50,000 to American Jewish Committee, New York, NY.
$50,000 to Simon Wiesenthal Center, Los Angeles, CA.
$25,000 to Joseph Kushner Hebrew Academy, Livingston, NJ.
$10,000 to Yeshiva of Flatbush, Brooklyn, NY.

116

T. W. Lewis Foundation ✧ ☆
850 W. Elliot Rd., Ste. 101
Tempe, AZ   85284-1202   (480) 820-0807
FAX: (480) 820-1445;
E-mail: twlfoundation@twlewis.com; Additional E-mail: info@twlewis.com; URL: http://www.twlewisfoundation.org/

Established in 2000 in AZ.
Donors: Janet R. Lewis; Thomas W. Lewis.
Foundation type: Independent foundation.
Financial data (yr. ended 12/31/05): Assets, $8,090,711 (M); gifts received, $2,600,005; expenditures, $808,008; qualifying distributions, $758,206; giving activities include $758,206 for grants.
Purpose and activities: Giving primarily to programs that improve the quality of life for people in need, with a special focus on the needs and education of children. The foundation also offers a scholarship program, designed to assist outstanding Maricopa County, AZ, high school students in attending college and furthering their education.
Fields of interest: Education; Children, services.
Limitations: Giving on a national basis, with emphasis on AZ; scholarships limited to Maricopa County, AZ, high school students.
Publications: Grants list.
Application information: Application form not required.
Initial approach: Letter, E-mail, or telephone
Officers: Thomas W. Lewis, Pres. and Treas.; Janet R. Lewis, V.P. and Secy.
Director: Thomas W. Lewis, Jr.
EIN: 860989236
Selected grants: The following grants were reported in 2003.
$20,000 to University of Kentucky, Lexington, KY. For RJL scholarship.
$10,000 to Aid to Adoption of Special Kids (AASK), Phoenix, AZ. For Christmas party and foster home needs.
$10,000 to Child Crisis Center-East Valley, Mesa, AZ. For general support.
$10,000 to Phoenix Childrens Hospital Foundation, Phoenix, AZ. For general support.
$10,000 to University of North Carolina, Business school, Chapel Hill, NC.
$8,811 to Big Brothers Big Sisters of Central Arizona, Phoenix, AZ. For fundraiser.
$5,000 to United Cerebral Palsy Association of Central Arizona, Phoenix, AZ. For general support.
$5,000 to YMCA, Ahwatukee Foothills, Phoenix, AZ.
$2,500 to Chandler Education Foundation, Chandler, AZ. For Golf Tournament.
$1,000 to Communities in Schools of Arizona, Arizona Mentoring Partnership, Tempe, AZ.

117

The Ronald and Maxine Linde Foundation
c/o Maxine H. Linde
3300 E. Stanford Dr.
Paradise Valley, AZ   85253-7527

Established in 1989 in IL.
Donors: Ronald K. Linde; Maxine H. Linde.
Foundation type: Independent foundation.
Financial data (yr. ended 2/28/06): Assets, $20,012,285 (M); expenditures, $948,689; qualifying distributions, $899,995; giving activities include $896,150 for 8 grants (high: $800,000; low: $6,500).
Purpose and activities: Giving primarily for higher education.
Fields of interest: Higher education; Scholarships/financial aid.
Type of support: General/operating support; Capital campaigns; Building/renovation; Endowments; Publication; Scholarship funds; Research; Matching/challenge support.
Limitations: Applications not accepted. Giving primarily in CA. No grants to individuals.
Application information: Contributes only to pre-selected organizations.
Board meeting date(s): 1st Mon. in May
Officers and Directors:* Ronald K. Linde,* Chair. and Secy.-Treas.; Maxine H. Linde,* Pres.; Jennings J. Newcom; Lester G. Traub.
EIN: 363635349
Selected grants: The following grants were reported in 2006.
$50,000 to California Institute of Technology, Pasadena, CA. For general support.
$25,000 to Keck Graduate Institute of Applied Life Sciences, Claremont, CA. For student scholarships.
$9,000 to University of Iowa Foundation, Iowa City, IA. For research publication.
$8,000 to Fidelity Investments Charitable Gift Fund, Boston, MA. For general support.
$2,500 to Textile Museum, DC. For journal publication.
$1,000 to University of Southern California, Los Angeles, CA. For student scholarships.
$650 to Foundation for Research and Conservation of Andean Monuments, New York, NY. For research dissemination.

118

John F. Long Foundation, Inc. ✧
P.O. Box 14029
Phoenix, AZ   85063   (602) 272-0421, ext. 506
FAX: (623) 846-7208;
E-mail: foundation@jflong.com; Application address: c/o Jacob F. Long, 5035 W. Camelback Rd., Phoenix, AZ 85063, tel.: (602) 272-0421; URL: http://www.jflong.com/foundation.htm

Established in 1959.
Donor: John F. Long.
Foundation type: Independent foundation.
Financial data (yr. ended 4/30/06): Assets, $6,677,563 (M); expenditures, $457,774; qualifying distributions, $424,704; giving activities include $399,929 for 172 grants (high: $16,684; low: $150).
Purpose and activities: The foundation looks for groups who are working to help themselves, their own communities, and help others like themselves through self-empowering, community organizing efforts. The foundation's approach to grant requests focuses on fostering local neighborhood vitality and excellence.
Fields of interest: Arts; Elementary/secondary education; Human services; Children/youth, services; Family services; Christian agencies & churches; Protestant agencies & churches.
Limitations: Giving primarily in Phoenix, AZ. No grants to individuals.
Application information: Application guidelines and questionnaire available on foundation Web site. Grant requests exceeding $1,000 must be accompanied by financial reports for the past and current fiscal year, and a list of past donors going

back no more than 2 years. Application form required.

Initial approach: E-mail, fax, or letter requesting application form
Deadline(s): None

Director: John F. Long.
Trustee: Jacob F. Long.
EIN: 866052431
Selected grants: The following grants were reported in 2005.

$20,500 to West Valley Child Crisis Center, Glendale, AZ.
$8,100 to Phoenix Day, Phoenix, AZ.
$6,974 to Boys and Girls Club, Tri-City West, Phoenix, AZ.
$6,340 to Alhambra Education Partnerships, Phoenix, AZ.
$5,187 to West Valley Fine Arts Council, Litchfield Park, AZ.
$5,000 to Homeward Bound, Phoenix, AZ.
$4,100 to Westside Food Bank, Sun City, AZ.
$2,000 to Peoria Educational Enrichment Foundation, Peoria, AZ.
$1,500 to Arizona Science Center, Phoenix, AZ.
$1,000 to Power Paws Assistance Dogs, Phoenix, AZ.

119
The David and Lura Lovell Foundation ◇
2995 E. Manzanita Ridge Pl.
Tucson, AZ 85718
Contact: Lura M. Lovell, Pres.

Established in 1993 in OH.
Donors: Lura M. Lovell; David C. Lovell‡.
Foundation type: Independent foundation.
Financial data (yr. ended 12/31/04): Assets, $10,961,128 (M); gifts received, $64,000; expenditures, $785,959; qualifying distributions, $607,993; giving activities include $607,993 for 18 grants (high: $250,000; low: $5,000).
Purpose and activities: Giving primarily for the mentally ill and for Roman Catholic education; funding also for integrative medicine, education about mental illness, and spiritual education.
Fields of interest: Higher education; Mental health/crisis services; Human services, mind/body enrichment; Developmentally disabled, centers & services; Roman Catholic agencies & churches.
Type of support: General/operating support; Continuing support; Endowments; Program development; Publication; Scholarship funds.
Limitations: Applications not accepted. Giving primarily in Tucson, AZ, Minneapolis, MN, and Toledo, OH. No grants to individuals.
Application information: Unsolicited requests for funds not accepted.
Board meeting date(s): June and Dec.
Officers and Trustees:* Lura M. Lovell,* Pres.; Ann Moushey,* Secy.; Stephen J. Lovell; Jodee Robertson.
EIN: 341733685

120
The Kemper and Ethel Marley Foundation ▼ ◇
P.O. Box 10392
Phoenix, AZ 85064
Contact: Daniel Corrigan, V.P.

Established in 1990 in AZ.

Donors: Ethel Marley‡; Kemper Marley Trust.
Foundation type: Independent foundation.
Financial data (yr. ended 2/28/05): Assets, $115,203,079 (M); gifts received, $5,527,910; expenditures, $7,942,115; qualifying distributions, $6,508,481; giving activities include $6,487,298 for 31 grants (high: $2,610,000; low: $1,000; average: $12,000–$500,000).
Purpose and activities: Giving primarily for higher education, human service organizations, the arts, and a zoo.
Fields of interest: Museums; Historic preservation/historical societies; Higher education; Zoos/zoological societies; Youth, services.
Type of support: General/operating support.
Limitations: Applications not accepted. Giving limited to AZ. No support for animal welfare organizations. No grants to individuals.
Application information: Contributes only to pre-selected organizations.
Officers and Directors:* Daniel Corrigan,* V.P.; Stephen M. Corrigan,* V.P.; Nancy Elitharp Ball,* Treas.
EIN: 860653091
Selected grants: The following grants were reported in 2005.

$2,610,000 to Surprise, City of, Surprise, AZ. For capital support.
$500,000 to Brophy College Preparatory, Phoenix, AZ. For capital support.
$500,000 to Lincoln Health Foundation, Phoenix, AZ. For capital support.
$500,000 to Phoenix Art Museum, Phoenix, AZ. For capital support.
$400,000 to Arizona Zoological Society, Phoenix Zoo, Phoenix, AZ. For capital support.
$350,000 to Xavier College Preparatory School, Phoenix, AZ. For capital support.
$175,000 to Arizona State University Foundation, Tempe, AZ. For capital support.
$165,500 to Arizona Science Center, Phoenix, AZ. For operating support.
$50,000 to Heard Museum, Phoenix, AZ. For capital support.
$50,000 to Ronald McDonald House, Phoenix, AZ. For capital support.

121
Marshall Foundation ◇
P.O. Box 3306
Tucson, AZ 85722   (520) 622-8613
Contact: Jane McCollum

Incorporated in 1930 in AZ.
Donor: Louise F. Marshall‡.
Foundation type: Independent foundation.
Financial data (yr. ended 12/31/05): Assets, $20,491,018 (M); expenditures, $2,590,788; qualifying distributions, $749,588; giving activities include $710,681 for 48 grants (high: $299,098; low: $100).
Purpose and activities: Giving primarily for higher education, and the arts; funding also for human services, Jewish organizations, as well as to a United Methodist church.
Fields of interest: Higher education; Human services; Protestant agencies & churches; Jewish agencies & temples.
Type of support: Capital campaigns; Building/renovation; Scholarship funds.
Limitations: Giving limited to Pima County, AZ. No grants to individuals, or for operational support, or annual support.

Publications: Annual report; Informational brochure.
Application information: Funding to new recipients is limited due to large-scale commitments to the University of Arizona Scholarship Fund and the University Medical Center Artificial Heart Laboratory as well as other long-term commitments. Application form required.
Initial approach: Letter
Copies of proposal: 2
Deadline(s): Quarterly: Feb. 1, May 1, Aug. 1 and Nov. 1
Board meeting date(s): Monthly
Officers and Directors:* Charles Jackson,* C.E.O. and Pres.; George Steele,* V.P.; Samuel Chang, Secy.; Anne Nelson, Treas.
Number of staff: 2 full-time professional; 1 part-time professional; 4 full-time support.
EIN: 860102198

122
Dorothy D. and Joseph A. Moller Foundation
P.O. Box 626
Scottsdale, AZ 85252
Contact: Dorothy D. Moller, Tr.

Established in 1987 in AZ.
Donors: Dorothy D. Moller; Joseph A. Moller‡.
Foundation type: Independent foundation.
Financial data (yr. ended 12/31/05): Assets, $10,808,143 (M); gifts received, $101,933; expenditures, $430,816; qualifying distributions, $406,750; giving activities include $396,230 for 19 grants (high: $130,000; low: $500).
Fields of interest: Media/communications; Higher education; Education; Animal welfare; Legal services, public interest law; Public affairs, research; Public affairs, formal/general education; Public affairs, political organizations.
Limitations: Applications not accepted. Giving on a national basis. No grants to individuals.
Application information: Contributes only to pre-selected organizations.
Trustee: Dorothy D. Moller.
EIN: 746355685
Selected grants: The following grants were reported in 2004.

$130,000 to George Mason University Foundation, Fairfax, VA. For general support.
$130,000 to Hillsdale College, Hillsdale, MI. For general support.
$130,000 to Principia Corporation, Saint Louis, MO. For general support.
$124,200 to Young Americas Foundation, Herndon, VA. For general support.
$120,000 to Heritage Foundation, DC. For general support.
$50,000 to Arizona Animal Welfare League, Phoenix, AZ. For general support.
$50,000 to Goldwater Institute, Phoenix, AZ. For general support.
$50,000 to Palmer R. Chitester Fund, Erie, PA. For general support.
$40,000 to Media Research Center, Alexandria, VA. For general support.
$25,000 to Leadership Institute, Arlington, VA. For general support.

123
Moreno Family Foundation ◇
2555 E. Camelback Rd., Ste. 780
Phoenix, AZ 85016

Established in 1998 in AZ.
Donors: Arturo Moreno; Carole Moreno.
Foundation type: Independent foundation.
Financial data (yr. ended 12/31/05): Assets, $5,326,095 (L); gifts received, $4,624,885; expenditures, $802,504; qualifying distributions, $768,863; giving activities include $768,863 for 49 grants (high: $333,600; low: $100).
Purpose and activities: Giving primarily to community centers and services, and for education, and youth and health services.
Fields of interest: Education; Health organizations, research; Boys & girls clubs; Children/youth, services; Federated giving programs; Jewish federated giving programs; Christian agencies & churches; Jewish agencies & temples.
Limitations: Applications not accepted. Giving primarily in Phoenix, AZ. No grants to individuals.
Application information: Contributes only to pre-selected organizations.
Officer: Fernando Pacheco, Mgr.
Directors: Arturo Moreno; Carole Moreno.
EIN: 860918198

124
Margaret T. Morris Foundation ◇
P.O. Box 592
Prescott, AZ 86302
Contact: Thomas E. Polk, Tr.

Established in 1967.
Donor: Margaret T. Morris†.
Foundation type: Independent foundation.
Financial data (yr. ended 12/31/05): Assets, $16,322,703 (M); expenditures, $759,162; qualifying distributions, $718,246; giving activities include $711,550 for 47 grants (high: $100,000; low: $350).
Purpose and activities: Support for the performing arts and other cultural programs, education, with emphasis on higher education, youth and child welfare, family planning, medical research and education, the environment and animal welfare, and social services, primarily those benefiting the handicapped.
Fields of interest: Museums; Performing arts; Performing arts, music; Arts; Higher education; Medical school/education; Education; Environment; Animal welfare; Reproductive health, family planning; Mental health/crisis services; Medical research, institute; Human services; Children/youth, services; Residential/custodial care, hospices; Homeless, human services; Marine science; Disabilities, people with; Economically disadvantaged; Homeless.
Type of support: General/operating support; Capital campaigns; Building/renovation; Land acquisition; Endowments; Debt reduction; Program development; Scholarship funds; Matching/challenge support.
Limitations: Applications not accepted. Giving primarily in AZ. No support for religious organizations or their agencies. No grants to individuals; no loans.

Application information: Internally initiated grants comprise virtually all of the current grantmaking of the foundation.
  Board meeting date(s): Aug., Dec., and as required
Trustees: Richard L. Menschel; Eugene P. Polk; Thomas E. Polk.
EIN: 866057798

125
C. W. and Modene Neely Charitable Foundation ◇
660 W. Elliot Rd.
Gilbert, AZ 85233

Established in 1996.
Donor: C.W. Neely Administrative Trust.
Foundation type: Independent foundation.
Financial data (yr. ended 12/31/05): Assets, $10,918,752 (M); expenditures, $617,079; qualifying distributions, $570,106; giving activities include $482,500 for 31 grants (high: $100,000; low: $2,500), and $50,000 for 1 loan/program-related investment.
Purpose and activities: Giving primarily for health care and to religious organizations.
Fields of interest: Hospitals (general); Hospitals (specialty); Cancer; Christian agencies & churches.
Type of support: General/operating support; Emergency funds; Program development; Seed money; Scholarship funds.
Limitations: Giving primarily in AZ.
Application information: Application form not required.
  Initial approach: Letter
  Deadline(s): None
  Board meeting date(s): Jan., May and Nov.
Officers: Richard N. Morrison,* Pres.; June Morrison, V.P.; Gail McCracken,* Secy.
Board Member: Michael Elliot.
Number of staff: 1 part-time professional.
EIN: 860854513

126
Otto & Edna Neely Foundation ◇
325 N. Alma School Rd., Ste. 1
Chandler, AZ 85224-4379 (480) 917-0767

Established in 1988 in AZ.
Foundation type: Independent foundation.
Financial data (yr. ended 12/31/05): Assets, $18,347,286 (M); expenditures, $1,018,746; qualifying distributions, $800,895; giving activities include $683,286 for 57 grants (high: $90,750; low: $1,000).
Purpose and activities: Giving primarily for higher and other education, as well as for children, youth and social services, and for Presbyterian and United Methodist churches; funding also for an arts and entertainment alliance.
Fields of interest: Arts, alliance; Elementary/secondary education; Higher education; Human services; Children/youth, services; Protestant agencies & churches.
Limitations: Giving primarily in AZ.
Application information:
  Initial approach: Letter
  Deadline(s): None
Officers and Directors:* Joe S. Reynolds,* Pres.; Clifford W. Saylor,* 1st V.P.; Harley Christian,* Secy.-Treas. and Mgr.; Gregory L. Bamford; Steve

Haase; Norman L. Knox; Robert H. Neill; Logan W. Stillwell.
EIN: 860581770

127
Noah's Family Foundation ◇
c/o Jonah Shacknai
8125 N. Hayden Rd.
Scottsdale, AZ 85258

Established in 1997 in AZ.
Donors: Jonah Shacknai; Paterna Enterprises, LLP.
Foundation type: Independent foundation.
Financial data (yr. ended 12/31/05): Assets, $1,984,594 (M); expenditures, $585,185; qualifying distributions, $571,073; giving activities include $570,163 for 13 grants (high: $255,580; low: $288).
Fields of interest: Elementary/secondary education; Higher education; Health organizations, association; Autism research; Human services; Jewish agencies & temples; Disabilities, people with.
Limitations: Applications not accepted. Giving primarily in AZ. No grants to individuals.
Application information: Contributes only to pre-selected organizations.
Officers and Director:* Jonah Shacknai,* Pres.; Howard J. Luber, M.D., Secy.-Treas.
EIN: 860887816
Selected grants: The following grants were reported in 2003.
$25,000 to National Public Radio, DC.
$20,000 to Crisis Nursery, Phoenix, AZ.
$10,000 to Delta Society, Renton, WA.
$10,000 to Phoenix Country Day School, Phoenix, AZ.
$2,500 to Communities in Schools of Arizona, Phoenix, AZ.
$2,500 to Jewish Federation of Greater Phoenix, Phoenix, AZ.
$1,000 to Brophy College Preparatory, Phoenix, AZ.
$1,000 to Childhelp USA, Scottsdale, AZ.
$1,000 to United Cerebral Palsy, DC.
$150 to Fertile Hope, New York, NY.

128
The John and Sophie Ottens Foundation
P.O. Box 4389
Sedona, AZ 86340-4389 (970) 626-5310
Contact: Henry O. Hooper, Pres.
E-mail: hoh@independence.net; *Application address:* P.O. Box 429, Ridgeway, CO 81432; tel.: (970) 626-5310

Established in 1998 in AZ.
Donors: John Ottens†; Sophie Ottens†.
Foundation type: Independent foundation.
Financial data (yr. ended 1/31/06): Assets, $23,317,699 (M); expenditures, $986,703; qualifying distributions, $702,780; giving activities include $702,780 for 14 grants (high: $196,000; low: $5,000).
Purpose and activities: Giving for the physical or mental rehabilitation of Native Americans; giving also for education, health professions, and social work for Native Americans.
Fields of interest: Higher education, college; Hospitals (general); Medical research; Native Americans/American Indians.

Type of support: General/operating support;
Continuing support; Equipment; Program
development; Curriculum development; Internship
funds; Scholarship funds; Technical assistance.
Limitations: Giving limited to AZ, CO, NM, and UT.
Publications: Application guidelines; Newsletter.
Application information: Application form not
required.
  Initial approach: E-mail, letter, or telephone
  Copies of proposal: 1
  Deadline(s): None
  Board meeting date(s): June and Sept.
  Final notification: within 30 days
Officers and Directors:* Henry O. Hooper,* Pres.;
Steven K. Aronoff,* Secy.-Treas.; Cynthia Aronoff;
Jeanne R. Hooper.
Number of staff: 2 part-time professional; 1
part-time support.
EIN: 860911121
Selected grants: The following grants were reported
in 2005.
$520,350 to Northern Arizona University
  Foundation, Flagstaff, AZ. 9 grants: $23,850,
  $52,000, $17,000, $28,000, $80,000,
  $40,000, $45,500, $74,000, $160,000
$22,550 to Saint Michaels Indian School, Saint
  Michaels, AZ.

129

Phelps Dodge Foundation ✧
1 N. Central Ave.
Phoenix, AZ   85004   (602) 366-8050
FAX: (602) 366-7323;
E-mail: communityaffairs@phelpsdodge.com;
Additional tel.: (800) 528-1182, ext. 8050;
URL: http://www.phelpsdodge.com/
Community-Environment/CommunityRelations/
CharitableGiving/

Incorporated in 1953 in NY.
Donor: Phelps Dodge Corp.
Foundation type: Company-sponsored foundation.
Financial data (yr. ended 12/31/03): Assets,
$17,243,258 (M); expenditures, $997,039;
qualifying distributions, $961,529; giving activities
include $717,508 for 45 grants, and $238,296 for
employee matching gifts.
Purpose and activities: The foundation supports
organizations involved with arts and culture,
education, health, and human services.
Fields of interest: Arts; Higher education;
Education; Health care; Human services.
Type of support: General/operating support;
Continuing support; Annual campaigns; Scholarship
funds; Employee matching gifts; Matching/
challenge support.
Limitations: Giving primarily in areas of company
operations, with emphasis on AZ and NM. No
support for religious organizations or fraternal,
veterans', labor, or political organizations. No grants
to individuals, or for start-up needs, emergency
needs, travel, medical procedures, advertising,
lobbying, debt reduction, capital campaigns or
equipment, research, special projects, or
conferences; no loans.
Publications: Corporate report.
Application information: E-mailed proposals should
be in MS Word format. Application form not required.
  Initial approach: Mail or E-mail proposal to
    foundation
  Copies of proposal: 1
  Deadline(s): None

  Board meeting date(s): May
  Final notification: 2 to 3 months
Officers: David Pulatie, Pres.; G.W. Stevens, V.P.
and Treas.; Tracy L. Bame, V.P.; Mary K. Sterling,
Secy.
Directors: S. David Colton; Ramiro Peru.
Number of staff: 2 part-time professional; 1
part-time support.
EIN: 136077350

130

The Virginia G. Piper Charitable Trust ▼
6720 N. Scottsdale Rd., Ste. 350
Scottsdale, AZ   85253   (480) 948-5853
Contact: Judy Jolley Mohraz Ph.D., C.E.O. and Pres.
FAX: (480) 348-1316; E-mail: info@pipertrust.org;
URL: http://www.pipertrust.org

Established in 1995.
Donor: Virginia G. Piper‡.
Foundation type: Independent foundation.
Financial data (yr. ended 3/31/05): Assets,
$552,859,276 (M); gifts received, $169,655;
expenditures, $28,758,070; qualifying
distributions, $24,759,794; giving activities include
$21,684,642 for 230 grants (high: $2,000,000;
low: $410; average: $500–$250,000), $27,270 for
128 employee matching gifts, and $465,008 for 3
foundation-administered programs.
Purpose and activities: The trust seeks to enhance
and strengthen the quality of life for the people in
Maricopa County through support of healthcare and
medical research, children, older adults, arts and
culture, education and religious organizations.
Fields of interest: Arts; Youth development, adult &
child programs; Aging, centers/services; Youth.
Type of support: Technical assistance; Program
development; Matching/challenge support;
General/operating support; Fellowships;
Equipment; Endowments; Continuing support;
Capital campaigns; Building/renovation; Employee
matching gifts.
Limitations: Giving primarily in Maricopa County, AZ.
No support for private foundations, or for start-ups.
No grants to individuals.
Publications: Annual report; Biennial report; Grants
list; Occasional report.
Application information: The Summary Form can be
filled in online from the foundation's Web site.
Applications should be directed to the Grants
Manager. Organizations must have been in
operation for 3 years. Application form required.
  Initial approach: Letter of inquiry (2 pages) and
    Summary Form (from foundation Web site)
  Copies of proposal: 1
  Deadline(s): None
  Board meeting date(s): 3 times per year
  Final notification: 3 to 6 months
Officers: Judy Jolley Mohraz, Ph.D., C.E.O. and
Pres.; Mary Jane Rynd, Exec. V.P. and C.F.O.; Lynn
R. Hoffman, Cont.
Trustees: James D. Bruner; Jose A. Cardenas; Paul
N. Critchfield; Arthur W. DeCabooter; Laura R.
Grafman; Sharon C. Harper; Steven J. Zabilski.
Number of staff: 8 full-time professional; 6 full-time
support; 1 part-time support.
EIN: 866247076
Selected grants: The following grants were reported
in 2005.
$4,550,000 to Scottsdale Healthcare Foundation,
  Scottsdale, AZ. To create Scottsdale Clinical
  Research Institute to increase clinical trials for
  new cancer drugs, recruit and retain talent, work

in concert with Translational Genomics Research
  Institute, and build alliances in biomedical
  industry.
$3,000,000 to Maricopa Partnership for Arts and
  Culture, Phoenix, AZ. For efforts to strengthen
  arts and cultural organizations and link vital
  cultural community to regional economic
  development.
$3,000,000 to Saint Vincent de Paul Society,
  Phoenix, AZ. For endowment and to provide
  challenge grant for medical and dental clinics.
$1,000,000 to Saint Josephs Foundation, Phoenix,
  AZ. For capital project that includes new
  children's cardiac intensive care unit and
  expansion and rehabilitation of existing neonatal
  intensive care unit.
$547,644 to Tempe, City of, Community Services
  Department, Tempe, AZ. For implementation of
  Life Options/Next Chapter project for older adults
  to explore options including health, wellness,
  education, and volunteer and paid opportunities.
$533,946 to Mesa Community College, Mesa, AZ.
  For implementation of Life Options/Next Chapter
  project for older adults to explore options
  including health, wellness, education, and
  volunteer and paid opportunities.
$347,010 to Scottsdale Community College,
  Community College District, Scottsdale, AZ. For
  implementation of Life Options/Next Chapter
  project for older adults to explore options
  including health, wellness, education, volunteer
  and paid opportunities.
$201,000 to Mayo Clinic Arizona, Scottsdale, AZ.
  For implementation of Healthy Steps program to
  enhance child development practices of family
  physicians.
$200,000 to Phoenix Theater, Phoenix, AZ. For
  upgraded ticketing, telephone, and accounting
  system software to increase efficiency and
  patron services.
$130,000 to Phoenix Childrens Hospital
  Foundation, Phoenix, AZ. To expand and enhance
  pediatric resident and physician training in
  Healthy Steps program.

131

The Pocono Charitable Foundation ✧
P.O. Box 65929
Tucson, AZ   85728-5929   (520) 465-6725

Established in 2001 in AZ.
Donors: James D. Toole; Molly C. Toole.
Foundation type: Independent foundation.
Financial data (yr. ended 12/31/05): Assets,
$129,353 (M); gifts received, $308,750;
expenditures, $527,948; qualifying distributions,
$526,009; giving activities include $526,009 for 29
grants (high: $204,332; low: $500).
Fields of interest: Elementary/secondary
education; Education; Human services; Children/
youth, services; Roman Catholic agencies &
churches.
Limitations: Giving primarily in AZ.
Application information: Application form not
required.
  Initial approach: Letter
  Deadline(s): None
Officers and Directors:* James D. Toole,* Pres.;
Molly C. Toole,* V. P.; Elizabeth Toole Goodrow,*
Secy.; Thomas D. Toole,* Treas.; Molly Toole
Roman; James D. Toole III.
EIN: 861045072

132
James Arthur Rae Charitable Trust ◇ ☆
7521 E. 1st St.
Scottsdale, AZ   85251

Established in 1998 in AZ.
Donor: Maryland Investments, Inc.
Foundation type: Independent foundation.
Financial data (yr. ended 12/31/05): Assets, $7,395,557 (M); expenditures, $618,103; qualifying distributions, $433,927; giving activities include $418,604 for 2 grants (high: $393,604; low: $25,000).
Fields of interest: Children/youth, services; Christian agencies & churches.
Limitations: Applications not accepted. Giving on a national basis. No grants to individuals.
Application information: Contributes only to pre-selected organizations.
Trustees: Carlos Wagner; Maryland, LLC.
EIN: 860937247

133
David E. Reese Family Foundation ◇
7348 Red Ledge Dr.
Paradise Valley, AZ   85253-2880

Established in 1994 in AZ.
Donors: David E. Reese; Caleb F. Reese; Everett D. Reese II; Everett Reese†.
Foundation type: Independent foundation.
Financial data (yr. ended 12/31/04): Assets, $20,411,634 (M); expenditures, $993,760; qualifying distributions, $954,000; giving activities include $954,000 for 32 grants (high: $189,500; low: $1,000).
Fields of interest: Arts; Higher education; Education; Environment, land resources; Environment; Human services; Foundations (private grantmaking); Foundations (community).
Limitations: Applications not accepted. Giving primarily in Scottsdale and Phoenix, AZ; some giving also in MI. No grants to individuals.
Application information: Contributes only to pre-selected organizations.
Officers: David E. Reese, Pres.; Louise R. Reese, V.P. and Secy.; Everett D. Reese, Treas.
EIN: 860763892
Selected grants: The following grants were reported in 2003.
$250,000 to Denison University, Granville, OH.
$151,000 to Arizona Community Foundation, Phoenix, AZ.
$100,000 to Grand Traverse Regional Land Conservancy, Traverse City, MI.
$100,000 to Lawrenceville School, Lawrenceville, NJ.
$50,000 to Heard Museum, Phoenix, AZ.
$50,000 to Wheaton Club Philadelphia, Philadelphia, PA.
$25,000 to Hospice of the Valley, Phoenix, AZ.
$25,000 to Humane Society, Arizona, Phoenix, AZ.
$25,000 to Painted Turtle, Santa Monica, CA.
$10,000 to Phoenix Art Museum, Phoenix, AZ.

134
Research Corporation ▼
4703 E. Camp Lowell Dr., Ste. 201
Tucson, AZ   85712   (520) 571-1111
Contact: Daniel Gasch, C.F.O.

FAX: (520) 571-1119; E-mail: awards@rescorp.org; URL: http://www.rescorp.org

Incorporated in 1912 in NY.
Donors: Rachel Brown†; Frederick Gardner Cottrell†; Elizabeth Hazen†; Donald F. Jones†; Edward C. Kendall†; Paul C. Mangelsdorf; Charles H. Townes; Robert E. Waterman†; Robert R. Williams†; Robert B. Woodward†.
Foundation type: Operating foundation.
Financial data (yr. ended 12/31/05): Assets, $157,293,030 (M); expenditures, $10,854,341; qualifying distributions, $9,998,099; giving activities include $5,599,843 for 277 grants (high: $100,000; low: $95; average: $5,000–$35,000).
Purpose and activities: To advance academic science research and teaching. The awards programs include the Cottrell College Science Awards, Cottrell Scholars Awards, Research Innovation Awards, Research Opportunity Awards and Special Opportunities in Science Awards and are open to U.S. and Canadian colleges and universities to support basic research in the physical sciences (physics, chemistry and astronomy).
Fields of interest: Astronomy; Chemistry; Physics; Science.
Type of support: Program development; Research.
Limitations: Giving only in the U.S. and Canada. No grants to individuals directly, or for building or endowment funds, indirect costs, common supplies and services, tuition, research leave to start new projects, faculty academic year salaries, post-doctoral or graduate student stipends, secretarial assistance, general support, scholarships, fellowships, publications, travel expenses to scientific meetings or to research facilities, or matching gifts; no loans.
Publications: Application guidelines; Annual report; Newsletter; Occasional report.
Application information: Only online applications will be accepted. Application form required.
   Initial approach: For Department Development Prog.: Letter of inquiry or telephone call; For all other programs: Fill out application request form on foundation Web site or request by phone
   Deadline(s): Cottrell College Science Awards: target dates - May 15 and Nov. 15; Research Opportunity Awards nominations: May 1 and Oct. 1; Special Opportunities in Science Awards and Cottrell Scholars Awards: none; Research Innovation Awards: May 1
   Board meeting date(s): Feb., Apr., and Nov.
   Final notification: Differs by program
Officers and Directors: Stuart B. Crampton,* Chair.; James M. Gentile, Ph.D.*, Pres.; Raymond Kellman, Ph.D., V.P.; Robert B. Hallock, Secy.; Daniel Gasch, C.F.O.; Suzanne D. Jaffe,* Treas.; R. Palmer Baker, Jr., Dir. Emeritus; Carlyle G. Caldwell, Dir. Emeritus; Paul J. Collins, Dir. Emeritus; Burt N. Dorsett, Dir. Emeritus; William G. Hendrickson, Dir. Emeritus; John W. Johnstone, Jr., Dir. Emeritus; Colin B. Mackay, Dir. Emeritus; S. Dillon Ripley, Dir. Emeritus; Frederick Seitz, Dir. Emeritus; George L. Shinn, Dir. Emeritus; G. King Walters, Dir. Emeritus; Patricia C. Barron; Peter K. Dorhout; Robert Holland, Jr.; Brent Iverson; Gayle P.W. Jackson; Patrick S. Osmer; John P. Schaefer.
Advisory Committee: Mark E. Bussell; Donald R. Deardorff; Susan M. Kauzlarich; John T. Koh; Elizabeth McCormack; Michael A. Morrison; Mats A. Selen; Thomas D. Tullius.

Number of staff: 9 full-time professional; 5 full-time support.
EIN: 131963407
Selected grants: The following grants were reported in 2005.
$100,000 to Massachusetts Institute of Technology, Department of Physics, Cambridge, MA. For Cottrell Scholar Award for research, searching for hidden order in exotic superconductors by scanning tunneling microscopy.
$100,000 to New York University, Department of Chemistry, New York, NY. For Cottrell Scholar Award for research, control of protein-protein interactions with artificial alpha helics and innovations in teaching and implementation of organic chemistry.
$100,000 to Northwestern University, Department of Chemistry, Evanston, IL. For Cottrell Scholar Award for research, nanoscaffolds for the growth and manipulation of chemical and biological structures at the single component level.
$100,000 to Southern Illinois University, Department of Chemistry and Biochemistry, Carbondale, IL. For Cottrell Scholar Award for research, enhancing NMR signals from biomolecular, organic, and polymer thin films using optical nuclear polarization.
$100,000 to University of Chicago, Department of Chemistry, Chicago, IL. For Cottrell Scholar Award for research, chemical crosslinking method to study DNA repair/modification proteins.
$100,000 to University of Illinois at Urbana-Champaign, Department of Chemistry, Urbana, IL. For Cottrell Scholar Award for research, science beyond the limits of diffraction and disciplinary borders: 3 D magic-angle spinning NMR and the liberal arts.
$100,000 to University of Montreal, Department of Physics, Montreal, Canada. For Cottrell Scholar Award for research, white dwarf stars as cosmochronometers and distance indicators.
$100,000 to University of Ottawa, Department of Chemistry, Ottawa, Canada. For Cottrell Scholar Award for research, preventing catalyst decomposition and achieving reactivity in the direct arylation and animation of C-H bonds.
$100,000 to University of Wisconsin, Department of Chemistry, Madison, WI. For Cottrell Scholar Award for research, regulation of bacterial communication pathways with synthetic ligands.
$37,665 to Mount Saint Vincent University, Department of Chemistry, Halifax, Canada. For Cottrell College Science Award for research, Synthesis and catalytic applications of novel bidentate N-heterocyclic carbenes (NHCs) in aerobic oxidation of alcohols.

135
LaNelle Robson Foundation ◇
9532 E. Riggs Rd.
Sun Lakes, AZ   85248-7411   (480) 895-9200
Contact: Edward J. Robson, Pres.

Established in 1987 in AZ.
Donors: Sun Lakes Marketing LP; Robson Communities, Inc.; Saddlebrooke Development Co.; Pebblecreek Properties LP; Scott Management Co.
Foundation type: Independent foundation.
Financial data (yr. ended 1/31/05): Assets, $2,055,047 (M); gifts received, $520,000; expenditures, $583,916; qualifying distributions,

$573,848; giving activities include $573,251 for 31 grants (high: $93,200; low: $100).
Purpose and activities: Giving primarily for education, health associations, and children, youth and social services.
Fields of interest: Performing arts, orchestra (symphony); Arts; Higher education; Education; Hospitals (general); Health organizations, association; Boys & girls clubs; Human services; Children/youth, services; Federated giving programs.
Limitations: Giving primarily in AZ, with some emphasis on Phoenix. No grants to individuals.
Application information: Application form not required.
  Initial approach: Proposal
  Copies of proposal: 1
  Deadline(s): None
Officers and Directors:* Edward J. Robson, Pres.; Steven S. Robson,* V.P. and Treas.; Mark E. Robson,* V.P.; Kimberly A. Robson-Ortiz,* V.P.; Lynda Robson-Weiser,* Secy.; Robert D. Robson.
EIN: 742461052
Selected grants: The following grants were reported in 2004.
$100,000 to Colorado College, Colorado Springs, CO.
$44,126 to Boys and Girls Clubs of Metropolitan Phoenix, Phoenix, AZ.
$30,000 to Brophy College Preparatory, Phoenix, AZ.
$28,990 to HomeBase Youth Services, Phoenix, AZ.
$24,645 to Arizona State University Foundation, Tempe, AZ.
$20,000 to Humane Society, Arizona, Phoenix, AZ.
$20,000 to Neighbors Who Care, Reston, VA.
$12,500 to University of Arizona Foundation, Tucson, AZ.
$11,500 to Sun Angel Foundation, Phoenix, AZ.
$10,000 to All Saints Episcopal Church, Phoenix, AZ.

136

Rodel Foundation ◇
6720 N. Scottsdale Rd., Ste. 380
Scottsdale, AZ 85253

Established in 1999 in AZ; reorganized in 2004.
Donors: William D. Budinger; Donald V. Budinger.
Foundation type: Independent foundation.
Financial data (yr. ended 12/31/04): Assets, $58,893,266 (M); expenditures, $1,427,437; qualifying distributions, $1,301,965; giving activities include $1,210,000 for 8 grants (high: $900,000; low: $5,000).
Fields of interest: Environment; Children/youth, services; Social sciences, public policy; Public policy, research.
Limitations: Applications not accepted. Giving on a national basis, with some emphasis on AZ, CO and Washington, DC. No grants to individuals.
Application information: Contributes only to pre-selected organizations.
Trustees: Donald V. Budinger; William D. Budinger; Susan B. Loncki.
EIN: 861015598
Selected grants: The following grants were reported in 2003.
$1,000,000 to Arizona Center for Public Policy, Phoenix, AZ.
$210,000 to Aspen Institute, Aspen, CO.
$100,000 to Whispering Hope Ranch Foundation, Payson, AZ.

$75,000 to Aspen Youth Experience, Aspen, CO.
$75,000 to Grand Canyon Trust, Flagstaff, AZ.
$52,042 to Mathematics, Engineering, Science Achievement (MESA), Salt Lake City, UT.
$50,000 to Delaware Community Foundation, Wilmington, DE.
$25,000 to Phoenix Country Day School, Phoenix, AZ.
$23,000 to Coronado Library, Coronado, CA.
$20,000 to Arizona Community Foundation, Phoenix, AZ.

137

The Jess & Sheila Schwartz Family Foundation ◇
15 Biltmore Estates Dr.
Phoenix, AZ 85016-2821   (602) 274-7955
Contact: Sheila Schwartz, Pres.

Established in 1999 in AZ.
Donor: Sheila Schwartz.
Foundation type: Independent foundation.
Financial data (yr. ended 12/31/05): Assets, $1,461 (M); gifts received, $1,766,000; expenditures, $1,766,176; qualifying distributions, $1,756,795; giving activities include $1,756,795 for 18 grants (high: $750,000; low: $3,000).
Fields of interest: Secondary school/education; Education; Jewish federated giving programs; Jewish agencies & temples.
Limitations: Giving primarily in AZ.
Application information: Application form not required.
  Initial approach: Proposal
  Deadline(s): None
Officers and Directors:* Sheila Schwartz,* Pres.; Frank L. Schwartz,* Secy.-Treas.; Lesley Schwartz Hammer; Abby I. Schwartz.
EIN: 860942313
Selected grants: The following grants were reported in 2005.
$750,000 to Jess Schwartz Jewish Community High School, Phoenix, AZ. For operating support.
$325,000 to Partnership for Excellence in Jewish Education, Boston, MA.
$155,000 to King David School, Scottsdale, AZ.
$140,000 to Weizmann Institute of Science, Rehovot, Israel. For scholarships.
$100,000 to Phoenix Hebrew Academy, Phoenix, AZ.
$72,000 to Jewish Federation of Greater Phoenix, Phoenix, AZ. For program support.
$50,000 to American Society for Technion-Israel Institute of Technology, New York, NY.
$23,795 to Jewish Community Day School Scholarship Fund, Scottsdale, AZ. For scholarships.
$12,000 to Bar-Ilan University, Ramat Gan, Israel. For doctoral fellowship.
$10,000 to Jewish Community Foundation of Greater Phoenix, Scottsdale, AZ. For scholarships.

138

The Mary Elizabeth Dee Shaw Charitable Trust ◇
c/o Wells Fargo Bank Northwest, N.A.
P.O. Box 53456, MAC S4035-014
Phoenix, AZ 85072
Application address: c/o Jack D. Lampros, P.O. Box 9936, Ogden, UT 84409, tel.: (801) 626-9531

Trust established in 1959 in UT.
Donor: Mary Elizabeth Dee Shaw†.
Foundation type: Independent foundation.
Financial data (yr. ended 12/31/05): Assets, $11,470,476 (M); expenditures, $622,780; qualifying distributions, $587,799; giving activities include $558,889 for 1 grant.
Purpose and activities: Giving primarily to the McKay Dee Foundation in Ogden UT.
Fields of interest: Hospitals (general).
Limitations: Giving limited to UT. No grants to individuals.
Application information: Funds largely committed for the foreseeable future. New grantmaking will be severely limited.
  Initial approach: Letter
  Deadline(s): None
Officers and Directors:* Jack D. Lampros,* Chair.; Dean W. Herst,* Vice-Chair.; C.W. Stromberg,* Vice-Chair.; Mary L. Barker,* Secy.; O. Rex Child,* Treas.
Trustees: Thomas D. Dee II; Joseph F. Hansen; Wells Fargo Bank Northwest, N.A.; and 4 additional trustees.
EIN: 876116370

139

Solheim Foundation ◇
c/o Karsten Louis Solheim
P.O. Box 84558
Phoenix, AZ 85071-4558   (602) 687-5248

Established in 1985 in AZ.
Donors: Karsten Solheim†; Louise C. Solheim; Karsten Manufacturing Co.
Foundation type: Independent foundation.
Financial data (yr. ended 6/30/05): Assets, $387,538 (M); expenditures, $1,672,794; qualifying distributions, $1,636,011; giving activities include $1,615,750 for 10 grants (high: $1,000,000; low: $750).
Purpose and activities: Giving primarily for Christian education, missions, and other related activities.
Fields of interest: Higher education; Health organizations, association; Human services; Christian agencies & churches.
Limitations: Applications not accepted. Giving on a national basis. No grants to individuals.
Application information: Contributes only to pre-selected organizations.
Trustees: Stacey Pauwels; Allan D. Solheim; David Solheim; Joy Solheim; Karsten Louis Solheim; Louise C. Solheim.
EIN: 742378207
Selected grants: The following grants were reported in 2003.
$100,000 to Jesus Video Project, Birmingham, AL. For general support.
$85,000 to International Foundation, DC. For Future Generations Ministries.
$25,000 to College Golf Fellowship, Flower Mound, TX. For general support.
$25,000 to Dawn Ministries, Colorado Springs, CO. For general support.
$25,000 to Links Players International, Fresno, CA. For general support.
$25,000 to Phoenix Gospel Mission, Phoenix, AZ. For general support.
$20,000 to Latin American Mission, Miami, FL. For general support.
$15,000 to Junior Achievement of Arizona, Tempe, AZ. For general support.

$10,000 to Luis Palau Evangelistic Association, Portland, OR. For general support.
$450 to Arizona School Choice Trust, Phoenix, AZ. For general support.

140
Soling Family Foundation ✧ ☆
11051 E. Placita Cumbia
Tucson, AZ 85730

Established in 1985 in NY.
Donor: Chester P. Soling.
Foundation type: Independent foundation.
Financial data (yr. ended 5/31/05): Assets, $537,425 (M); gifts received, $25,288; expenditures, $379,346; qualifying distributions, $316,375; giving activities include $316,375 for 19 grants (high: $150,000; low: $75).
Fields of interest: Media/communications; Performing arts; Elementary/secondary education; Botanical gardens.
Limitations: Applications not accepted. Giving primarily in MA and NY. No grants to individuals.
Application information: Contributes only to pre-selected organizations.
Officers: Chester P. Soling, Pres.; Cevin Soling, Secy.
EIN: 133288798
Selected grants: The following grants were reported in 2005.
$5,000 to Tucson Symphony Society, Tucson, AZ.
$200 to Tucson Botanical Gardens, Tucson, AZ. 2 grants: $100 each
$100 to Brooklyn Technical High School, Brooklyn, NY.
$100 to Epilepsy Foundation, Landover, MD.

141
Stardust Foundation, Inc. ✧
6730 N. Scottsdale Rd., Ste. 230
Scottsdale, AZ 85253 (480) 607-5800
Contact: Fdn. Mgr.

Established in 1993 in AZ as successor to the Bisgrove Foundation.
Donors: Gerald Bisgrove; Bisgrove Foundation.
Foundation type: Independent foundation.
Financial data (yr. ended 12/31/05): Assets, $558,879,204 (M); gifts received, $583,287,904; expenditures, $4,786,496; qualifying distributions, $4,541,561; giving activities include $4,519,723 for 98 grants (high: $1,000,000; low: $16).
Purpose and activities: Giving primarily for affordable housing, neighborhood development, and youth and families.
Fields of interest: Housing/shelter, expense aid; Children/youth, services; Community development.
Limitations: Giving primarily in Phoenix and Scottsdale, AZ.
Application information:
  Initial approach: Letter
  Deadline(s): Sept. 30
Officers and Trustee:* Gerald Bisgrove,* Pres.; Debra Bisgrove, V.P. and Secy.; Jon Munson, Treas.
EIN: 860735230

142
The Steele Foundation, Inc.
702 E. Osborn Rd., Ste. 200
Phoenix, AZ 85014-5215
Contact: Gail Flinn, C.F.O.
E-mail: steele@bcattorneys.com; Additional address: P.O. Box 1112, Phoenix, AZ 85001

Established in 1980 in AZ.
Donors: Horace Steele†; Ethel Steele†.
Foundation type: Independent foundation.
Financial data (yr. ended 12/31/04): Assets, $76,092,428 (M); expenditures, $3,929,416; qualifying distributions, $3,583,687; giving activities include $3,391,347 for 67 grants (high: $300,000; low: $150; average: $5,000–$100,000).
Purpose and activities: Primary areas of interest are education and medical research. Giving is limited to organizations within the state of Arizona.
Fields of interest: Education; Health care; Medical research, institute.
Type of support: General/operating support; Building/renovation; Capital campaigns; Endowments; Research.
Limitations: Applications not accepted. Giving only in AZ. No support for political organizations. No grants to individuals.
Application information: Contributes only to pre-selected organizations.
Officers and Directors:* Daniel Cracchiolo,* Pres.; Gail Flinn,* Secy. and C.F.O.; Andrea Cracchiolo III, M.D.; Marianne Cracchiolo Mago; Bryant Stocks.
Number of staff: 1 full-time professional; 1 part-time professional.
EIN: 953466880
Selected grants: The following grants were reported in 2004.
$250,000 to Xavier College Preparatory School, Phoenix, AZ. For capital campaign.
$200,000 to University of Arizona Health Sciences Center, Steele Children's Research Center, Tucson, AZ. For Horace Steele Chair for pediatric research.
$150,000 to Arizona Hospital and Healthcare Association (AZHHA), Morrison Institute for Health Studies, Tempe, AZ. For research and literature on healthcare industry in Arizona.
$125,000 to Seton Catholic High School, Chandler, AZ. For capital campaign.
$110,000 to Barrow Neurological Foundation, Phoenix, AZ. For fellowship, research and education programs.
$100,000 to All Saints Episcopal Day School, Phoenix, AZ. For Campus Improvement Plan.
$100,000 to Brophy College Preparatory, Phoenix, AZ. For capital campaign.
$100,000 to Law College Association of the University of Arizona, Tucson, AZ. For Chester Smith Professorship and Evo DeConcini Professorship.
$50,000 to Ronald McDonald House, Phoenix, AZ. For expansion.
$50,000 to Saints Simon and Jude Elementary School, Phoenix, AZ. For capital campaign.

143
Sterne-Elder Memorial Trust ✧ ☆
c/o Wells Fargo Bank, N.A.
P.O. Box 53456, MAC S4035-014
Phoenix, AZ 85072
Contact: Michael J. Love, V.P., Wells Fargo Bank, N.A.

Established in 1977 in CO.
Donors: Charles S. Sterne†; Dorothy Sterne†.
Foundation type: Independent foundation.
Financial data (yr. ended 3/31/05): Assets, $8,375,078 (M); gifts received, $46,800; expenditures, $715,725; qualifying distributions, $596,524; giving activities include $398,642 for 1 grant.
Purpose and activities: Giving primarily for health and human service organizations in Denver, CO.
Type of support: General/operating support; Continuing support; Annual campaigns; Capital campaigns; Endowments; Matching/challenge support.
Limitations: Applications not accepted. Giving primarily in Denver, CO. No grants to individuals.
Application information: Contributes only to pre-selected organizations.
Trustee: Wells Fargo Bank, N.A.
Number of staff: 1 part-time professional.
EIN: 846143172

144
Winifred L. Stevens Foundation ✧
18839 N. Celosia Ln.
Surprise, AZ 85387
Contact: John V. Stevens Sr., Pres.

Established in 1996 in CA.
Donors: Linda S. Spady; Falcon's Flight, Inc.
Foundation type: Independent foundation.
Financial data (yr. ended 12/31/05): Assets, $29,947,353 (M); gifts received, $435,653; expenditures, $1,068,705; qualifying distributions, $1,034,214; giving activities include $1,034,214 for 21 grants (high: $456,000; low: $3,500; average: $10,000–$100,000).
Purpose and activities: Funding primarily for a Seventh Day-Adventist church and other religious organizations.
Fields of interest: Animals/wildlife, preservation/protection; Human services; Protestant agencies & churches; Religion.
Limitations: Applications not accepted. Giving primarily in CA. No grants to individuals.
Application information: Contributes only to pre-selected organizations.
Officers and Directors:* John V. Stevens, Sr.,* Pres.; Linda S. Spady,* V.P.; John V. Stevens, Jr.,* Secy.
EIN: 954505998

145
Ruth McCormick Tankersley Charitable Trust ✧
3430 E. Sunrise Dr., Ste. 200
Tucson, AZ 85718-3236 (520) 792-1181
Contact: Richard Duffield, Tr.

Established in 1994 in AZ.
Foundation type: Independent foundation.
Financial data (yr. ended 12/31/05): Assets, $7,420,945 (M); expenditures, $459,642; qualifying distributions, $455,352; giving activities include $388,980 for 19 grants (high: $100,000; low: $5,000).
Purpose and activities: Giving primarily for education, especially for literacy programs; funding also for human services.
Fields of interest: Education; Hospitals (general); Human services.

Limitations: Giving on a national basis, with some emphasis on FL and TX.
Application information: The trust has a proposal sheet which applicants may use. Application form not required.
Deadline(s): None
Trustees: Richard Duffield; Kristie Miller; Mark McCormick Miller; Daniel Norton; Charles R. Player, Jr.; Burton Rubin; Tiffany T. Wolfe.
EIN: 866224242
Selected grants: The following grants were reported in 2004.
$75,000 to Girl Scouts of the U.S.A.. 2 grants: $20,000, $55,000
$50,000 to FINCA International, DC.
$41,500 to Saint Marys Hall, San Antonio, TX. 2 grants: $10,000, $31,500
$40,000 to Trinity University, San Antonio, TX. 2 grants: $10,000, $30,000
$32,500 to Humane Society of Austin, Austin, TX.
$6,000 to Humane Society of Tampa Bay, Tampa, FL.
$5,000 to College Bound, DC.

146
Torhjelm Foundation ◆
7201 E. Camelback Rd., Ste. 305
Scottsdale, AZ 85251-3318 (480) 874-2389
Contact: Gary Torhjelm, Pres. and Treas.

Established in 1987 in AZ.
Donors: Gary Torhjelm; Donna Torhjelm.
Foundation type: Independent foundation.
Financial data (yr. ended 12/31/05): Assets, $51,640 (M); gifts received, $1,255,000; expenditures, $1,205,700; qualifying distributions, $1,205,700; giving activities include $1,203,850 for 27 grants (high: $428,000; low: $50).
Fields of interest: Human services; Christian agencies & churches.
Limitations: Giving on a national basis, with emphasis on AZ. No grants to individuals.
Application information:
Initial approach: Proposal
Deadline(s): None
Officers and Directors: * Gary Torhjelm, * Pres. and Treas.; Donna Torhjelm, * V.P. and Secy.; David R. Berezan.
EIN: 860565535
Selected grants: The following grants were reported in 2005.
$428,000 to Samaritans Purse, Boone, NC.
$152,000 to Billy Graham Evangelistic Association, Minneapolis, MN.
$137,000 to Focus on the Family, Colorado Springs, CO.
$62,500 to Alliance Defense Fund, Scottsdale, AZ.
$55,000 to Scottsdale Healthcare Foundation, Scottsdale, AZ.
$15,500 to Life Outreach International, Fort Worth, TX.
$10,500 to Phoenix Rescue Mission, Phoenix, AZ.
$7,000 to Voice of the Martyrs, Bartlesville, OK.
$1,000 to Evangelism Explosion International, Fort Lauderdale, FL.

147
Trend Homes Foundation ◆ ☆
890 W. Elliot Rd., No. 102
Gilbert, AZ 85233

Established in 2004 in AZ.
Donors: Stan Porter; R. Gordon Porter; J. Merrill Funk; Wayne Porter; Amy Riding; Shawn Porter; Denise Aubrey; Scott Porter.
Foundation type: Independent foundation.
Financial data (yr. ended 12/31/05): Assets, $0 (M); expenditures, $1,620,104; qualifying distributions, $1,620,104; giving activities include $1,620,104 for 1 grant.
Fields of interest: Mormon agencies & churches.
Limitations: Applications not accepted. No grants to individuals.
Application information: Contributes only to pre-selected organizations.
Officer: Reed Porter, Pres.
Directors: J. Merrill Funk; Mark Funk; J. Stanton Porter; R. Gordon Porter; Shawn Porter.
EIN: 201722163

148
University of Phoenix Alumni Network ◆
(formerly University of Phoenix Network for Professional Development)
4615 E. Elwood St.
Phoenix, AZ 85040-1958 (800) 795-2586
Contact: Terri Bishop

Established in 1979 as Phoenix Institute of Education and Arts, Inc.
Foundation type: Operating foundation.
Financial data (yr. ended 8/31/05): Assets, $378,043 (M); gifts received, $643,873; expenditures, $816,697; qualifying distributions, $815,261; giving activities include $466,508 for grants to individuals.
Purpose and activities: Giving for higher education.
Fields of interest: Higher education, college.
Type of support: Scholarships—to individuals.
Limitations: Applications not accepted. Giving limited to Phoenix, AZ.
Officers: Todd Nelson, Pres.; Bill Brebaugh, Secy.; Larry Fleischer, Treas.; Lyn Marquis, Exec. Dir.
Directors: Carrie Fries; Laura Palmer Noone; Shannon T. Wilson.
EIN: 953366652

149
The Viad Corp Fund ◆ ☆
(formerly The Dial Corp Fund)
Viad Corporate Ctr., M.S. 0949
1850 N. Central Ave.
Phoenix, AZ 85004 (602) 207-7538
Contact: John P. Hughes
E-mail: jhughes@viad.com

Established in 1987 in AZ.
Donors: The Dial Corp; Viad Corp.
Foundation type: Company-sponsored foundation.
Financial data (yr. ended 12/31/05): Assets, $404,823 (M); expenditures, $511,372; qualifying distributions, $510,880; giving activities include $510,880 for grants.
Purpose and activities: The fund supports organizations involved with health and human services.
Fields of interest: Health care; Children/youth, services; Human services.
Limitations: Applications not accepted. Giving primarily in Phoenix, AZ.
Publications: Corporate giving report.

Application information: Contributes only to pre-selected organizations.
Officers and Directors: * Suzanne Pearl, * Chair., C.E.O. and Pres.; Scott E. Sayre, V.P. and Secy.; Ellen M. Ingersoll, V.P. and Treas.
EIN: 742499884
Selected grants: The following grants were reported in 2005.
$50,000 to Nevada Cancer Institute, Las Vegas, NV.
$17,000 to United Cerebral Palsy, DC.
$15,000 to Arizona Voice for Crime Victims, Phoenix, AZ.
$15,000 to Boys and Girls Clubs of Metropolitan Phoenix, Phoenix, AZ.
$5,000 to Camp Fire USA.
$5,000 to Childhelp USA, Scottsdale, AZ.
$5,000 to March of Dimes Birth Defects Foundation, White Plains, NY.
$5,000 to Urban League.
$3,000 to Arizona Kidney Foundation, Phoenix, AZ.
$2,500 to Salvation Army.

150
Del E. Webb Foundation ◆
101 Saguaro Dr.
P.O. Box 3350
Wickenburg, AZ 85358 (928) 684-7223
Contact: Marjorie Johnson, Secy.

Incorporated in 1960 in AZ.
Donor: Del E. Webb‡.
Foundation type: Independent foundation.
Financial data (yr. ended 12/31/05): Assets, $49,992,398 (M); expenditures, $2,906,630; qualifying distributions, $2,555,465; giving activities include $2,089,160 for 31 grants (high: $500,000; low: $15,000).
Purpose and activities: The foundation primarily applies its resources to preserve and enrich the benefits derived from improved and expanded medical services and medical research to residents of AZ, CA, and NV.
Fields of interest: Higher education; Hospitals (general); Health care; Health organizations, association; Medical research, institute.
Limitations: Giving primarily in AZ, CA, and NV. No support for government agencies, sectarian or religious organizations, or pass-through organizations. No grants to individuals, or for deficit financing or indirect costs.
Application information: Application form required.
Initial approach: Letter
Copies of proposal: 4
Deadline(s): Feb. 28 and Aug. 31
Board meeting date(s): Apr. and Oct.
Final notification: Following board meeting
Officers and Directors: * Robert H. Johnson, * Pres.; Lawrence A. Johnson, * V.P.; Marjorie Johnson, * Secy.; Del V. Werderman, * Treas.; Owens F. Childress.
Number of staff: 2
EIN: 866052737
Selected grants: The following grants were reported in 2005.
$500,000 to Sun Health Foundation, Sun City, AZ. For expansion of DEW Memorial Hospital.
$300,000 to Burnham Institute, La Jolla, CA. For research.
$250,000 to Saint Rose Dominican Hospital, Henderson, NV. To build medical center.
$100,000 to John Tracy Clinic, Los Angeles, CA. For hearing program for children from birth to kindergarten.

$100,000 to Nevada Cancer Institute, Las Vegas, NV. To build cancer center.

$100,000 to Yavapai College, Prescott, AZ. For day care and education center.

$80,000 to Recording for the Blind and Dyslexic, Phoenix, AZ. For reading program.

$66,400 to Foundation for the Retarded of the Desert, Palm Desert, CA. To purchase buses.

$50,000 to Verdugo Hills Hospital Foundation, Glendale, CA. To upgrade equipment.

$25,000 to Arthritis Foundation, Phoenix, AZ. For research.

151
Weberg Trust
(formerly Weberg Foundation)
c/o John P. Weberg
32883 N. 70th St.
Scottsdale, AZ 85262
FAX: (480) 488-5818; E-mail: jwebarg@netcom.com

Established in 1999 in CO; reorganized in 2004. The entity was originally known as Weberg Foundation.
Donors: John P. Weberg; Jacqueline Weberg.
Foundation type: Independent foundation.
Financial data (yr. ended 12/31/05): Assets, $56,433,195 (M); expenditures, $5,496,522; qualifying distributions, $5,002,088; giving activities include $4,862,642 for grants.
Purpose and activities: Support for microenterprise development worldwide.
Limitations: Applications not accepted. Giving primarily in Africa and Southeast Asia. No grants to individuals.
Application information: Contributes only to pre-selected organizations.
Officer: John P. Weberg; Jacqueline Weber.
EIN: 206382151
Selected grants: The following grants were reported in 2005.

$3,145,000 to Opportunity International, Oak Brook, IL. 4 grants: $495,000 (For start-up work in Rwanda and Kenya), $2,000,000 (For general support), $150,000 (For microenterprise program to help the poor), $500,000 to Women's Opportunity Fund (For LEAD (Leadership, Empowerment, Access and Development) campaign challenge grant).

$1,000,000 to World Vision, Federal Way, WA. 3 grants: $500,000 (For grants for Rwanda and Kenya), $200,000 (For capital support for Small Enterprise Development Agency (SEDA) affiliate in Tanzania), $300,000 (For microenterprise program to help the poor).

$400,000 to World Relief, Baltimore, MD. 2 grants: $200,000 (For work of SoFMEDA in northeast India), $200,000 (For microenterprise program to help the poor).

$200,000 to Hope International, Lancaster, PA. For projects in Afghanistan and Congo.

152
Robert T. Wilson Foundation ✧
P.O. Box 399
Flagstaff, AZ 86002-0399
Contact: Richard F. Wilson, Pres.

Established in 1954 in TX; incorporated in 1963.
Donors: Richard F. Wilson; Jean H. Wilson; Suzanne C. Wilson†; and other members of the Wilson family.
Foundation type: Operating foundation.
Financial data (yr. ended 12/31/05): Assets, $3,436,551 (M); gifts received, $416,715; expenditures, $557,402; qualifying distributions, $455,058; giving activities include $455,058 for 3 grants (high: $447,558; low: $2,500).
Fields of interest: Higher education; Animal welfare; Human services; International relief.
Type of support: Emergency funds; Program development; Seed money; Scholarship funds; Matching/challenge support.
Limitations: Giving primarily in AZ. No grants to individuals, or for building or endowment funds or operating budgets; no loans.
Publications: Application guidelines.
Application information: Application form not required.
　Initial approach: Letter
　Copies of proposal: 1
　Deadline(s): None
　Board meeting date(s): July and as required
Officers: Richard F. Wilson, Pres.; Jean H. Wilson, Secy.-Treas.

Number of staff: 1 full-time professional; 1 full-time support.
EIN: 860264036

153
WWJD Foundation ✧
c/o R. Dale Lillard
2412 W. Huntington Dr.
Tempe, AZ 85282

Established in 2003 in AZ.
Foundation type: Independent foundation.
Financial data (yr. ended 12/31/04): Assets, $7,633 (M); gifts received, $490,000; expenditures, $553,819; qualifying distributions, $553,819; giving activities include $553,648 for 1 grant.
Fields of interest: Elementary/secondary education.
Limitations: Applications not accepted. Giving primarily in AZ. No grants to individuals.
Application information: Unsolicited requests for funds not accepted.
Officer: R. Dale Lillard, Pres.
EIN: 870690583

154
James C. and Louise A. Wyant Foundation ✧
1881 N. King St.
Tucson, AZ 85749

Donors: James C. Wyant; Louise A. Wyant.
Foundation type: Independent foundation.
Financial data (yr. ended 12/31/05): Assets, $5,093,878 (M); expenditures, $1,054,589; qualifying distributions, $1,000,000; giving activities include $1,000,000 for 1 grant.
Fields of interest: Higher education.
Limitations: Applications not accepted. No grants to individuals.
Application information: Contributes only to pre-selected organizations.
Officer and Trustees: * James C. Wyant,* Pres.; Clair F. Wyant.
EIN: 860939044

ARKANSAS

155
Ben J. Altheimer Charitable Foundation, Inc. ✧

425 W. Capitol, Ste. 1800
Little Rock, AR 72201
Contact: John S. Selig, Pres. and Secy.-Treas.

Established in 1995 in AR.
Donors: Ben J. Altheimer, Jr.†; The Ben J. Altheimer Foundation; Ben J. Altheimer Trust.
Foundation type: Independent foundation.
Financial data (yr. ended 12/31/05): Assets, $1,942,403 (M); expenditures, $554,782; qualifying distributions, $535,538; giving activities include $535,538 for 13 grants (high: $200,000; low: $2,935; average: $25,000–$100,000).
Purpose and activities: Funding primarily for higher education and medical research.
Fields of interest: Arts; Higher education; Law school/education; Medical school/education; Education; Medical care, community health systems; Hospitals (specialty); Allergies; Pediatrics; Community development.
Type of support: General/operating support; Capital campaigns; Scholarship funds; Scholarships—to individuals.
Limitations: Giving primarily in AR. No grants to individuals (except for scholarships).
Application information:
  Initial approach: Letter
Officers: John S. Selig, Pres. and Secy.-Treas.; William H. Bowen, V.P.; Michael J. Selig, V.P.
EIN: 710769229
Selected grants: The following grants were reported in 2003.
$101,130 to Arkansas Childrens Hospital, Little Rock, AR. For scholarships.
$100,000 to Florence Crittenton Home, Little Rock, AR.
$77,062 to Altheimer, City of, Altheimer, AR.
$50,000 to University of Arkansas for Medical Sciences Foundation, Little Rock, AR.
$43,000 to Hendrix College, Conway, AR. For Minority Advancement Program.
$41,865 to Pathways to College, Altheimer, AR.
$15,000 to Arts and Science Center for Southeast Arkansas, Pine Bluff, AR. For expansion of its school tour programs.
$1,735 to Boy Scouts of America, Quapaw Area Council, Little Rock, AR.

156
Arkansas Community Foundation, Inc. ▼

700 S. Rock St.
Little Rock, AR 72202 (501) 372-1116
Contact: Pat Lile, C.E.O.; For grants: Cecilia Patterson, Prog. Dir.
FAX: (501) 372-1166; E-mail: arcf@arcf.org; Additional tel.: (888) 220-2723; Additional E-mail: plile@arcf.org; Grant application E-mail: cpatterson@arcf.org; URL: http://www.arcf.org

Established in 1976 in AR.
Foundation type: Community foundation.
Financial data (yr. ended 6/30/05): Assets, $86,570,758 (M); gifts received, $15,888,681;

expenditures, $5,476,232; giving activities include $3,894,810 for 1,526 grants.
Purpose and activities: The foundation seeks to inspire people and communities to build and distribute charitable funds for Good, for Arkansas, for Ever.
Fields of interest: Humanities; Arts; Higher education; Libraries/library science; Education; Environment; Animal welfare; Health care; Youth development; Human services; Community development; Religion.
Type of support: General/operating support; Continuing support; Endowments; Program development; Conferences/seminars; Publication; Seed money; Scholarship funds; Research; Technical assistance.
Limitations: Giving limited to AR. No support for multi-year commitments. No grants to individuals, or for operating expenses, debt elimination, capital improvements, building, property, computer systems or emergency.
Publications: Annual report; Financial statement; Grants list; Informational brochure; Newsletter; Occasional report.
Application information: Visit foundation Web site for application information.
  Initial approach: Contact Prog. Dir.
  Copies of proposal: 2
  Board meeting date(s): Feb., May, Sept., and Nov.
Officers and Directors:* Jim Ross,* Chair.; J. Baxter Sharp III,* 1st Vice-Chair.; Cindy Pugh,* 2nd Vice-Chair.; Pat Lile, C.E.O. and Pres.; Heather Larkin Eason, Exec. V.P.; Helen Stout, C.F.O. and C.O.O.; Mary Ann Ritter Arnold,* Secy.; Jim Williamson,* Treas.; Jerry Adams; Sharon Allen; Ted Belden; John Chamberlin; Murray Claycomb; Mary Elizabeth Eldridge; Glenn Freeman; Ted Gammill; Al Hampton; Harold Hardwick; William Haught; Bob Holmes; Don Livingston; Dr. Mahlon Maris; David Matthews; Thomas McGill; Steve Nipper; Larry Ross; John Steuri; Margaret Wills; Peggy Wright.
Number of staff: 7 full-time professional; 4 full-time support.
EIN: 521055743
Selected grants: The following grants were reported in 2005.
$364,000 to University of Arkansas at Fayetteville Foundation, Fayetteville, AR. 4 grants: $150,000 to College of Agriculture (For teaching auditorium), $100,000 (For endowment to keep Agri auditorium technology up to date), $64,000 (To SAE Fraternity for renovation of student housing), $50,000 (For Endowed Chancellor's Scholarship).
$35,000 to Hot Springs School District, Hot Springs, AR. For Hot Springs Technology Institute.
$30,000 to Central Arkansas Library System, Little Rock, AR. For development of Arkansas Studies Curriculum at Butler Center, particularly to finalize materials for 2nd, 3rd, and 4th grades.
$26,250 to Phillips Community College Foundation, Helena, AR. For scholarships for associate nursing students, Med Lab Techs and LPNs.
$25,000 to Indiana University, School of Medicine, Indianapolis, IN. For scholarship fund.
$25,000 to Positive Atmosphere Reaches Kids (PARK) Foundation, Little Rock, AR. For intensive after-school tutoring program for at-risk students.
$25,000 to University of Arkansas for Medical Sciences, Center for Psychiatric Research, Educational and Clinical Care, Little Rock, AR. For capital support for new facility and to provide psychiatric treatment.

157
Blue & You Foundation for a Healthier Arkansas

(formerly ABC Foundation)
USAble Corporate Ctr.
320 W. Capitol, Ste. 200
Little Rock, AR 72201 (501) 378-3300
Contact: Patrick O'Sullivan, Exec. Dir.
FAX: (501) 378-2051;
E-mail: posullivan@arkbluecross.com; Additional tel.: (501) 378-2221; URL: http://www.blueandyoufoundationarkansas.org

Established in 2001 in AR.
Donor: Arkansas Blue Cross and Blue Shield.
Foundation type: Company-sponsored foundation.
Financial data (yr. ended 12/31/05): Assets, $33,410,600 (M); expenditures, $1,728,517; qualifying distributions, $1,554,451; giving activities include $1,554,451 for 23 grants (high: $150,000; low: $16,789).
Purpose and activities: The foundation supports programs designed to affect health care delivery, health care policy, and health care economics in Arkansas.
Fields of interest: Health care, reform; Health care.
Type of support: Research; Program evaluation; Program development; General/operating support.
Limitations: Giving limited to AR. No support for private foundations, organizations with a contractual relationship with Arkansas Blue Cross and Blue Shield, political or lobbying organizations, fraternal, athletic, or social organizations, or religious organizations not of direct benefit to the entire community. No grants to individuals, or for fundraising events or celebrations, capital campaigns or endowments, facilities or equipment, conferences, indirect costs, or tobacco-related programs.
Publications: Application guidelines; Grants list; Program policy statement.
Application information: Support is limited to 2 years in length. Proposals should be no longer than 4 to 6 pages. Application form required.
  Initial approach: Download application form and mail proposal and application form to foundation
  Copies of proposal: 2
  Deadline(s): July 16
  Final notification: Nov.
Officers and Directors: Robert D. Cabe, Chair.; Lee Douglass, Secy.; P. Mark White, Treas.; Patrick O'Sullivan, Exec. Dir.; Carolyn Blakely, Ph.D.; Sybil Jordan Hampton; Mahlon Maris, M.D.; Hayes C. McClerkin; George K. Mitchell, M.D.; Robert L. Shoptaw.
Number of staff: 2 full-time professional.
EIN: 710862108
Selected grants: The following grants were reported in 2006.
$150,000 to Greater Texarkana Peoples Clinic, Texarkana, TX.
$149,974 to Arkansas Childrens Hospital Foundation, Little Rock, AR. For Community-Focused School-Based Obesity Prevention Program.
$107,510 to Arkansas Educational Telecommunications Network Foundation, Conway, AR. For Fighting Fat television program.
$98,760 to Saint Francis House, Community Clinic, Springdale, AR. For Prenatal Pathways Program.
$90,000 to Arkansas Delta Rural Development Network, Fall and Spring Arkansas Institute, Clinton, AR.

$88,482 to University of Arkansas, Agriculture Cooperative Extension, Little Rock, AR. For Arkansas HOPE Project.

$84,957 to Arkansas Human Development Corporation, Little Rock, AR. For Promotoras de Salud Project.

$84,400 to Crowleys Ridge Rural Health Coalition, Paragould, AR. For Medicine Assistance Program.

$68,292 to Ozark Health Medical Center, Clinton, AR. For Fit Families Program.

$65,000 to Good Samaritan Clinic, Fort Smith, AR. For Coping with Hypertension and Diabetes Program.

158
Bodenhamer Foundation ◇
P.O. Box 7588
Little Rock, AR 72217

Established in 1986 in AR.
Donor: Lee Bodenhamer.
Foundation type: Independent foundation.
Financial data (yr. ended 11/30/05): Assets, $3,898,310 (M); expenditures, $3,874,601; qualifying distributions, $3,853,320; giving activities include $3,853,320 for 9 grants (high: $3,845,880; low: $440).
Fields of interest: Higher education; Education; Health care; Eye research.
Limitations: Applications not accepted. Giving primarily in AR. No grants to individuals.
Application information: Contributes only to pre-selected organizations.
Trustee: Lee Bodenhamer.
EIN: 752070352

159
Bradberry Family Foundation ◇ ☆
One W. Mountain St., Ste. 300
Fayetteville, AR 72701

Established in 1997 in AR.
Donors: Edwin G. Bradberry; Karlee Bradberry.
Foundation type: Independent foundation.
Financial data (yr. ended 12/31/05): Assets, $241,721 (M); expenditures, $336,091; qualifying distributions, $329,744; giving activities include $329,744 for grants.
Fields of interest: Higher education; Human services; Christian agencies & churches.
Type of support: General/operating support.
Limitations: Applications not accepted. Giving primarily in AR. No grants to individuals.
Application information: Contributes only to pre-selected organizations.
Trustees: Edwin G. Bradberry; John G. Bradberry; Karlee Bradberry; Robert W. Bradberry; William B. Bradberry; Rebecca Ann Moody; Karolyn C. Wolverton.
EIN: 626318708
Selected grants: The following grants were reported in 2004.
$200,000 to University of Arkansas, Fayetteville, AR.
$2,000 to Fayetteville Community Foundation, Fayetteville, AR.
$2,000 to Marymount Manhattan College, New York, NY. For Writing Center.
$1,000 to Boy Scouts of America, Greater Alabama Council, Birmingham, AL.
$1,000 to Feed the Children, Oklahoma City, OK.

$1,000 to Heifer Project International, Little Rock, AR.
$1,000 to Mosaic Manhattan Church, New York, NY.
$1,000 to Sacred Heart Church, Camden, NJ.

160
East Arkansas Business Development Council, Inc. ◇ ☆
P.O. Box 1970
Jonesboro, AR 72403 (870) 935-2871
Contact: Sherry Stringer, Pres.

Donor: Jonesboro Central Planning Assoc.
Foundation type: Independent foundation.
Financial data (yr. ended 12/31/04): Assets, $4,191,505 (M); gifts received, $40,500; expenditures, $3,414,995; qualifying distributions, $3,145,169; giving activities include $3,145,169 for 3 grants (high: $2,970,169; low: $75,000), and $269,024 for 4 foundation-administered programs.
Purpose and activities: Applicants must engage in activities designed to create jobs; to assist in the development of business in the eastern AR, area; to provide and promote educational opportunities to members and potential members of the workforce in the eastern AR, area; and to aid, assist, and foster the development and improvement of Jonesboro, AR, and other communities in the eastern AR, area.
Fields of interest: Education; Employment; Community development.
Limitations: Giving primarily in eastern AR.
Application information: All applications must be reviewed and approved by the Board of Directors.
Initial approach: To be determined by the Board of Directors
Deadline(s): To be set by the Board of Directors
Officers: Sherry Stringer, Pres.; Bob Schuchardt, V.P.; Sam Hummelstein, Secy.
Directors: Nancy Chrisman; Niel Crowson; Jan Duggar; Wallace Fowler; John Freeman; Charles Frierson; Gregg Goodner; Steve Seitz.
EIN: 710655498

161
Charles A. Frueauff Foundation, Inc. ▼
3 Financial Ctr.
900 S. Shackleford, Ste. 300
Little Rock, AR 72211 (501) 219-1410
Contact: Sue M. Frueauff, C.A.O.
URL: http://www.frueaufffoundation.com

Incorporated in 1950 in NY.
Donor: Charles A. Frueauff†.
Foundation type: Independent foundation.
Financial data (yr. ended 12/31/05): Assets, $113,147,673 (M); expenditures, $6,337,387; qualifying distributions, $5,821,784; giving activities include $5,367,500 for 147 grants (high: $300,000; low: $2,500; average: $20,000–$100,000), and $1,928 for 3 foundation-administered programs.
Purpose and activities: Support for health, including hospitals, mental health, and other health services; welfare purposes, including services to children, the indigent, and the handicapped; and private four-year higher education.
Fields of interest: Higher education; Hospitals (general); Health care; Human services; Children/youth, services.

Type of support: Technical assistance; Emergency funds; General/operating support; Continuing support; Annual campaigns; Capital campaigns; Building/renovation; Equipment; Endowments; Program development; Scholarship funds; Matching/challenge support.
Limitations: Giving limited to the U.S. with emphasis on east of the Rockies, the South, and Northeast. No grants to individuals, primary or secondary schools, colleges and universities, churches, multi-year grants, fundraising drives, or special events.
Publications: Grants list; Informational brochure (including application guidelines).
Application information: Application form not required.
Initial approach: Letter or telephone
Copies of proposal: 1
Deadline(s): Submit proposal in letter form between Jan. 1 and Mar. 15 for Mar. 15 deadline or between June 1 and Sept. 15 for Sept. 15 deadline. Do not submit proposal between Sept. 15 and Jan. 1
Board meeting date(s): May and Nov.
Final notification: After May and Nov. meetings
Officers and Trustees:* David A. Frueauff,* C.E.O. and Pres.; Anna Kay Frueauff-Williams,* V.P., Comms.; James P. Fallon,* C.F.O.; Sue M. Frueauff,* C.A.O.; A.C. McCully, M.D.*, Pres. Emeritus; Karl P. Fanning.
Number of staff: 3 full-time professional; 1 part-time professional.
EIN: 135605371
Selected grants: The following grants were reported in 2005.
$300,000 to Desert Caballeros Western Museum, Wickenburg, AZ. For renovation and expansion.
$150,000 to United Negro College Fund, Fairfax, VA. For student assistance.
$85,000 to Boys and Girls Club of the Arkansas River Valley, Russellville, AR. For program support and capital campaign.
$55,000 to Centers for Youth and Families, Little Rock, AR. For Parent Center.
$50,000 to Arkansas Childrens Hospital, Dental Department, Little Rock, AR.
$50,000 to Positive Atmosphere Reaches Kids (PARK) Foundation, Little Rock, AR. For program support.
$50,000 to Tallahassee Boys Choir, Tallahassee, FL. For internship and program support.
$35,000 to Rockhurst University, Kansas City, MO. For Center for Service Learning.
$32,000 to Neighbors Link Corporation, Mount Kisco, NY. For operating support.
$30,000 to Little Sisters of the Assumption Family Health Service, New York, NY. For home health care reimbursement.

162
The Thomas & Natalie Garrison Foundation ◇ ☆
2 N. College
Fayetteville, AR 72701

Established in 2003 in AR.
Donors: Thomas R. Garrison; Natalie Garrison.
Foundation type: Independent foundation.
Financial data (yr. ended 12/31/05): Assets, $991,814 (M); gifts received, $10,000; expenditures, $492,726; qualifying distributions, $478,550; giving activities include $478,550 for grants.

Fields of interest: Higher education; Children/youth, services; Christian agencies & churches.
Limitations: Applications not accepted. Giving primarily in AR. No grants to individuals.
Application information: Contributes only to pre-selected organizations.
Officers: Thomas R. Garrison, Pres.; Natalie Garrison, Secy.-Treas.
EIN: 030533020

163
Glass Family Foundation ◇
17 Glenbrook
Bentonville, AR   72712
Contact: David D. Glass, Dir.

Established in 2000 in AR.
Donor: David D. Glass.
Foundation type: Independent foundation.
Financial data (yr. ended 12/31/05): Assets, $13,051,805 (M); expenditures, $1,543,241; qualifying distributions, $1,543,105; giving activities include $1,542,000 for 12 grants (high: $500,000; low: $2,000).
Fields of interest: Education; Human services; Christian agencies & churches.
Limitations: Giving primarily in AR, MO, and TX. No grants to individuals.
Application information: Application form not required.
   Deadline(s): None
Officers and Directors:* Ruth A. Glass,* Pres.; Dayna A. Martz,* Secy.-Treas.; David D. Glass.
EIN: 710848400
Selected grants: The following grants were reported in 2004.
$550,000 to Benny Hinn Ministries, Irving, TX. To further religious ministries.
$200,000 to Benton County Sunshine School, Bentonville, AR. For general fund.
$200,000 to General Council of the Assemblies of God. For general fund.
$100,000 to Greater Houston Community Foundation, Houston, TX. For general fund.
$72,000 to Southwest Baptist University, Bolivar, MO. For general fund.
$50,000 to Make-A-Wish Foundation of America, Phoenix, AZ. For general fund.
$25,000 to Champions for Kids, Raleigh, NC. For general fund.
$25,000 to Cooper Institute for Aerobics Research, Dallas, TX. For general operating expenses.
$20,000 to Northwest Arkansas Childrens Shelter, Bentonville, AR. For general fund.
$10,000 to Kids Across America Foundation, Branson, MO. For general fund.

164
George and Linda Gleason Foundation ◇ ☆
P.O. Box 8811
Little Rock, AR   72231-8811   (501) 978-2200
Contact: George G. Gleason II, Tr.

Established in 1994 in AR.
Foundation type: Independent foundation.
Financial data (yr. ended 12/31/05): Assets, $1,360,099 (M); expenditures, $389,932; qualifying distributions, $389,030; giving activities include $389,030 for 29 grants (high: $85,090; low: $10).

Fields of interest: Arts; Education; Lung research; Human services; Family services; Christian agencies & churches.
Application information:
   Initial approach: Narrative
   Deadline(s): None
Trustees: George G. Gleason II; Linda D. Gleason.
EIN: 716169642
Selected grants: The following grants were reported in 2005.
$85,090 to Ministry to the Inner City, Little Rock, AR.
$35,048 to American Lung Association of Arkansas, Little Rock, AR. 2 grants: $24,998, $10,050
$15,075 to Seattle Treatment Education Project, Seattle, WA.
$10,000 to Fellowship of Christian Athletes, Kansas City, MO.
$7,705 to Campus Crusade for Christ. 2 grants: $2,680, $5,025
$5,025 to Hendrix College, Conway, AR.
$2,680 to Arkansas Independent Colleges and Universities, North Little Rock, AR.
$1,000 to Access Schools, Little Rock, AR.

165
The Hussman Foundation ◇ ☆
P.O. Box 2221
Little Rock, AR   72203   (501) 378-3400
Contact: Walter Hussman, Jr., Tr.

Established in 1984 in AR.
Donors: Wehco Video, Inc.; Walter Hussman, Jr.
Foundation type: Independent foundation.
Financial data (yr. ended 12/31/05): Assets, $7,210,364 (M); gifts received, $272,000; expenditures, $1,315,578; qualifying distributions, $1,315,578; giving activities include $1,314,271 for 16 grants (high: $1,000,000; low: $1,000).
Purpose and activities: Giving primarily to educational organizations.
Fields of interest: Media, journalism/publishing; Education; Children, services; Civil rights.
Limitations: Giving primarily in Little Rock, AR. No grants to individuals.
Application information: Application form not required.
   Initial approach: Letter
   Deadline(s): None
Trustees: Marilyn Augur; Walter Hussman, Jr.
EIN: 581605071

166
The Harvey and Bernice Jones Charitable Trust ◇
P.O. Box 2035
Springdale, AR   72765   (479) 756-0611
Contact: Joel Carver, Dir.

Established in 1989 in AR.
Foundation type: Independent foundation.
Financial data (yr. ended 11/30/05): Assets, $4,875,084 (M); expenditures, $899,900; qualifying distributions, $858,000; giving activities include $858,000 for 9 grants (high: $500,000).
Fields of interest: Higher education; Education; Health care; Health organizations, association; Heart & circulatory research; Children, services.
Limitations: Giving primarily in AR.
Application information: Application form not required.

Initial approach: Letter
Deadline(s): None
Board meeting date(s): Varies
Directors: Joel Carver; Dan Ferritor.
EIN: 716135580

167
The Murphy Foundation ◇
Union Bldg.
El Dorado, AR   71730-6133
Application address: c/o Brett Williamson, 200 N. Jefferson, Ste. 400, El Dorado, AR 71730, tel.: (870) 862-4961

Incorporated in 1958 in AR.
Donors: Charles H. Murphy, Jr.; members of the Murphy family.
Foundation type: Independent foundation.
Financial data (yr. ended 4/30/06): Assets, $64,112,252 (M); gifts received, $74,400; expenditures, $2,891,974; qualifying distributions, $2,746,795; giving activities include $2,553,501 for 52 grants (high: $908,091; low: $72), and $177,500 for 66 grants to individuals (high: $6,500; low: $1,000).
Purpose and activities: Emphasis on higher education, including scholarships; grants also for the arts.
Fields of interest: Arts; Higher education; Libraries/library science; Education; Health organizations, association; Boys & girls clubs; Boy scouts; Human services; Children/youth, services; Aging, centers/services; Federated giving programs.
Type of support: General/operating support; Annual campaigns; Endowments; Scholarships—to individuals.
Limitations: Giving primarily in southern AR for grants to organizations; giving limited to the southern AR area for grants to individuals.
Application information: Application form, including a copy of applicant's scholastic record, required for educational grants to individuals.
   Initial approach: Letter
   Copies of proposal: 1
   Deadline(s): Aug. 1 for educational grants
   Board meeting date(s): Semiannually
Officers and Directors:* R. Madison Murphy,* Pres.; Jerry W. Watkins,* V.P.; Brett Williamson, Secy.-Treas.
EIN: 716049826
Selected grants: The following grants were reported in 2006.
$908,091 to Hendrix College, Conway, AR. For operating support.
$509,577 to Tulane University, New Orleans, LA. 3 grants: $123,060 (For building renovations), $378,317 (For grant made in form of stock for educational fund), $8,200.
$501,414 to University of Arkansas for Medical Sciences, Little Rock, AR. For Center on Aging.
$60,000 to National Council on Economic Education, New York, NY. For operating support.
$25,000 to Barton Library, El Dorado, AR. For operating support.
$10,000 to Arkansas State Council on Economic Education, Little Rock, AR. For operating support.
$7,500 to American Lung Association of Arkansas, Little Rock, AR.
$200 to American Cancer Society, Little Rock, AR.

168
Robert D. & Barbara Nabholz Charitable Trust ✧

c/o Regions Bank
P.O. Box 279
Conway, AR 72033

Established in 2003 in AR.
Donor: Robert D. Nabholz†.
Foundation type: Independent foundation.
Financial data (yr. ended 12/31/04): Assets, $6,716,004 (M); gifts received, $8,308,509; expenditures, $1,724,931; qualifying distributions, $1,686,666; giving activities include $1,686,666 for 8 grants (high: $1,305,000; low: $6,666).
Fields of interest: Elementary/secondary education; Higher education; Human services.
Limitations: Applications not accepted. Giving primarily in AR. No grants to individuals.
Application information: Contributes only to pre-selected organizations.
Directors: Susan N. Denys; David J. Nabholz; John P. Nabholz; Nancy A. Nabholz; R. Dan Nabholz; Timothy A. Nabholz.
Trustee: Regions Bank.
EIN: 736337547

169
Northwest Arkansas Community Foundation

800 Founders Park Dr. E.
Springdale, AR 72762 (479) 361-4624
FAX: (479) 361-5094;
E-mail: info@nwacommunityfoundation.org;
URL: http://www.nwacommunityfoundation.org

Established in 1999 in AR.
Foundation type: Community foundation.
Financial data (yr. ended 12/31/05): Assets, $11,592,100 (M); gifts received, $3,297,877; expenditures, $1,673,323; giving activities include $1,421,469 for 204 grants (high: $200,000; low: $100), and $35,066 for 31 grants to individuals (high: $3,000; low: $500).
Purpose and activities: The foundation is a collection of funds built through charitable contributions dedicated to improving the quality of life for the people in the Northwest AR community.
Fields of interest: Arts; Higher education; Education; Health care; Human services; Community development.
Type of support: Scholarships—to individuals; General/operating support; Annual campaigns; Capital campaigns; Building/renovation; Equipment; Endowments; Program development; Conferences/seminars; Seed money; Curriculum development; Scholarship funds; Program evaluation.
Limitations: Applications not accepted. Giving limited to Benton, Carroll, Madison and Washington counties in northwest AR. No support for religious organizations. No grants to individuals (except for scholarships).
Publications: Biennial report; Informational brochure; Newsletter.
Application information:
  Board meeting date(s): Bimonthly
Officers and Directors:* Merry Lee Phillips,* Chair.; William "Jackson" Butt II,* Vice-Chair.; Nan Schoonover, C.F.O.; Ed Clifford,* Treas.; Suzanne Ward, Exec. Dir.; Fadil Bayyari; Don Blakeman; Joy Drummonds; Terry England; Daniel E. "Dan" Ferritor;

John Neihouse; Betsy Phillips; Julie Roblee; Bob Shaw; Mark Simmons; Dick Trammel; Walter Turnbow; Jim von Gremp; DeAnne F. Witherspoon; Donald "Buddy" Wray.
Number of staff: 4 full-time professional; 2 full-time support.
EIN: 311682365

170
The Pruet Foundation ✧ ☆

c/o Les Jerry
315 E. Oak St., Ste. 100
El Dorado, AR 71731-0031

Established in 1991 in AR.
Donor: Chesley Pruet.
Foundation type: Independent foundation.
Financial data (yr. ended 12/31/05): Assets, $1,627,333 (M); expenditures, $508,035; qualifying distributions, $500,000; giving activities include $500,000 for grants.
Fields of interest: Education; Cancer; Protestant agencies & churches.
Limitations: Applications not accepted. Giving primarily in AR. No grants to individuals.
Application information: Contributes only to pre-selected organizations.
Officers and Directors:* Elizabeth J. Pruet, Pres.; Paula James,* V.P. and Secy.; Ann Calhoon,* V.P. and Treas.
EIN: 710710627

171
Rebsamen Fund ☆

11219 Financial Centre Pkwy., Ste. 303
Little Rock, AR 72211

Incorporated in 1944 in AR.
Donors: Rebsamen Insurance, Inc.; Ruth Remmel.
Foundation type: Independent foundation.
Financial data (yr. ended 12/31/04): Assets, $2,370,098 (M); expenditures, $812,924; qualifying distributions, $810,758; giving activities include $810,758 for 10 grants (high: $691,899; low: $1,000).
Purpose and activities: The foundation supports organizations involved with arts and culture, education, health, youth development, wildlife preservation, and human services.
Fields of interest: Historic preservation/historical societies; Arts; Higher education; Animals/wildlife, preservation/protection; Health care; Youth development; Human services; Federated giving programs.
Limitations: Giving primarily in AR.
Application information: Application form not required.
  Initial approach: Proposal
  Deadline(s): None
  Board meeting date(s): Quarterly
Officers: Mary R. Wohlleb, Pres.; Steve Bauman, V.P.; Ruth R. Remmel, V.P.; Raymond R. Remmel, Secy.-Treas.
EIN: 716053911

172
The Winthrop Rockefeller Foundation ▼ ✧

308 E. 8th St.
Little Rock, AR 72202-3999 (501) 376-6854
Contact: Prog. Mgr.

FAX: (501) 374-4797;
E-mail: programstaff@wrfoundation.org;
URL: http://www.wrfoundation.org

Incorporated in 1956 in AR as Rockwin Fund, Inc.; renamed in 1974.
Donor: Winthrop Rockefeller†.
Foundation type: Independent foundation.
Financial data (yr. ended 12/31/05): Assets, $139,724,120 (M); gifts received, $782,000; expenditures, $9,589,949; qualifying distributions, $8,784,100; giving activities include $6,928,101 for 43+ grants (high: $2,000,000; low: $13,265; average: $20,000–$264,500), $15,000 for 1 grant to an individual, $500 for 1 in-kind gift, and $125,000 for 1 loan/program-related investment.
Purpose and activities: The goals of the foundation are to: 1) encourage the development of Arkansas' ability to provide an equitable, quality education for all children; 2) strengthen the capacity of local communities to break the cycle of poverty by supporting projects that promote local economic development; and 3) nurture strong, broad-based grassroots leadership through the development of community-based organizations.
Fields of interest: Education, early childhood education; Higher education; Agriculture; Youth development, citizenship; Civil rights; Rural development; Community development; Economics; Public policy, research.
Type of support: In-kind gifts; Management development/capacity building; Program development; Seed money; Research; Program evaluation; Program-related investments/loans; Matching/challenge support.
Limitations: Giving limited to AR, or for projects that benefit AR. No grants to individuals, or for capital expenditures, fundraising campaigns, scientific research, operating support or endowments; no loans (except program-related investments).
Publications: Annual report; Financial statement; Grants list; Occasional report.
Application information: The foundation encourages electronic submission of concept papers via E-mail, however, hard copies must follow. Application form not required.
  Initial approach: Concept paper (no more than 4 pages)
  Copies of proposal: 1
  Deadline(s): None
  Board meeting date(s): Mar., June, Sept., and Dec.
  Final notification: Immediately after board approves funding
Officers and Directors:* J. Michael Jones, Chair.; Andrea M. Dobson, Co-Interim Pres., C.O.O. and C.F.O.; William F. Rahn, Co-Interim Pres. and Sr. Prog. Mgr.; Ivye Allen, Ph.D.; Kay Kelley Arnold; Overtis Hicks Brantley; Ralph D. Christy, Ph.D.; Mark C. Doromus; Greg Hartz; Al "Papa Rap" Lopez; Bob J. Nash; Daniel V. Rainey, Ph.D.; Mary Sanchez; Lori Villarosa.
Number of staff: 5 full-time professional; 4 full-time support.
EIN: 710285871
Selected grants: The following grants were reported in 2004.
$4,000,000 to Arkansas Community Foundation, Little Rock, AR. For science mini-grants for Arkansas public middle school teachers in Arkansas Community Foundation Affiliate communities, and building ACF endowment.

$2,916,190 to Yale University, New Haven, CT. For growth and sustainability of School of the 21st Century Network in Arkansas.

$358,086 to Catticus Corporation, Berkeley, CA. For videotape evaluation of middle school participants in University of Arkansas for Medical Sciences Summer Science Discovery Program, encouraging minority children to consider pursuing education and careers in health sciences.

$320,580 to University of Arkansas, Monticello, AR. For model project to improve writing skills for teachers seeking national board certification.

$143,796 to National Conference for Community and Justice, Arkansas Chapter, Little Rock, AR. For expansion and development of new delivery model for Unitown program.

$140,000 to University of Arkansas at Fayetteville Foundation, College of Education and Health Professions, Fayetteville, AR. For Arkansas A Plus Schools Network.

$135,775 to New York Foundation for the Arts, New York, NY. For production of video documentary and curriculum guide about Native Americans in Arkansas, 1800-1860.

$90,000 to Urban Institute, DC. For a portrait of immigrant population in Arkansas.

$60,000 to Arkansas Single Parent Scholarship Fund, Springdale, AR. For Arkansas Single Parent Scholarship fund business plan.

$60,000 to Mississippi County Arkansas Economic Opportunity Commission (MCAEOC), Blytheville, AR. For business plan.

173
Winthrop Rockefeller Trust ▼ ✧
2230 Cottondale Ln., Ste. 6
Little Rock, AR   72202   (501) 661-9294
Contact: Marion Burton, Tr.

Established in 1973 in AR.
Donor: Winthrop Rockefeller‡.
Foundation type: Independent foundation.
Financial data (yr. ended 6/30/05): Assets, $121,073,672 (M); expenditures, $7,311,121; qualifying distributions, $6,099,098; giving activities include $6,029,876 for 9 grants (high: $1,393,759; low: $151,580; average: $400,000–$600,000).
Purpose and activities: Support primarily for an agricultural development institute and a historic preservation foundation.
Fields of interest: Historic preservation/historical societies; Agriculture.
Type of support: General/operating support.
Limitations: Giving limited to AR. No grants to individuals.
Application information: Application form not required.
  Deadline(s): None
Officer: Donna Huckabee, C.E.O.
Trustees: Marion Burton; Donal C. O'Brien, Jr.; Robert Schults.
EIN: 716082655
Selected grants: The following grants were reported in 2005.
$2,334,663 to University of Arkansas Community College Morrilton, Morrilton, AR. 2 grants: $1,393,759 to Winthrop Rockefeller Center (For operating support), $940,904 to Winthrop Rockefeller Center (For capital support).
$946,604 to Winrock International, Morrilton, AR. For general support.

$797,000 to Winthrop Rockefeller Foundation, Little Rock, AR. For general support.
$600,000 to Audubon Arkansas, Little Rock, AR. For operating support.
$400,000 to Arkansas Childrens Hospital, Little Rock, AR. For special needs children.
$400,000 to Philander Smith College, Little Rock, AR. For program support.
$400,000 to University of Arkansas Foundation, Arkansas Centers for Health Improvement, Little Rock, AR. For general support.
$151,580 to Arkansas Aviation Historical Society, Aerospace Education Center, Little Rock, AR. For challenge grant for educational support.

174
The Ross Foundation ✧
P.O. Box 335
Arkadelphia, AR   71923-0335   (870) 246-9881
Contact: Mary Elizabeth Eldridge, Grants Off.

Established in 1966 in AR.
Donors: Esther C. Ross‡; Jane Ross‡.
Foundation type: Independent foundation.
Financial data (yr. ended 12/31/05): Assets, $86,776,593 (M); expenditures, $2,177,876; qualifying distributions, $12,547,942; giving activities include $540,832 for 25 grants (high: $139,247; low: $100).
Purpose and activities: Giving primarily for education, community development, and children and youth services.
Fields of interest: Arts, association; Higher education; Libraries (public); Education; Children/youth, services; Community development; Foundations (community); Federated giving programs.
Type of support: General/operating support; Building/renovation; Equipment; Endowments; Emergency funds; Program development; Publication; Seed money; Research; Consulting services; Matching/challenge support.
Limitations: Giving limited to Arkadelphia and Clark County, AR. No grants to individuals, or for scholarships or fellowships; no loans.
Publications: Application guidelines; Financial statement; Informational brochure (including application guidelines).
Application information: Application form required.
  Initial approach: Letter
  Copies of proposal: 6
  Deadline(s): None
  Board meeting date(s): 4th Tues. of Feb., May, Aug., and Nov.
  Final notification: 30 days
Officers and Trustees:* Ross M. Wipple,* Chair.; Mark Karnes, Mgr., Opers.; David Hunt, Mgr.; Peggy Clark; Toney McMillan; Robert C. Rhodes; Mary Whipple.
Number of staff: 4 full-time professional; 4 full-time support; 1 part-time support.
EIN: 716060574
Selected grants: The following grants were reported in 2004.
$296,033 to Arkadelphia Public Schools, Arkadelphia, AR. 3 grants: $285,233, $10,000, $800
$50,000 to Arkansas Sheriffs Youth Ranches, Batesville, AR.
$17,500 to Ouachita Baptist University, Arkadelphia, AR. 2 grants: $10,000, $7,500
$16,000 to United Way of Clark County, Arkadelphia, AR.

$2,500 to Wildwood Park for the Performing Arts, Little Rock, AR.
$1,000 to Conference of Southwest Foundations, Dallas, TX.

175
The Schmieding Foundation, Inc. ✧
P.O. Box 369
Springdale, AR   72765-0369
Contact: Gilda Underwood, Pres.

Established in 1990 in AR.
Donors: H.C. Schmieding‡; L.H. Schmieding.
Foundation type: Independent foundation.
Financial data (yr. ended 12/31/04): Assets, $23,046,256 (M); expenditures, $2,085,325; qualifying distributions, $1,592,092; giving activities include $1,592,092 for 110 grants (high: $833,115; low: $50), and $78,140 for 2 foundation-administered programs.
Fields of interest: Education; Hospitals (specialty); Human services; Children/youth, services; Christian agencies & churches.
Type of support: General/operating support; Continuing support; Building/renovation; Program development.
Limitations: Giving primarily in Washington and Benton counties, AR.
Application information: Application form required.
  Deadline(s): None
Officers: L.H. Schmieding, C.E.O.; Gilda Underwood, Pres.; Lance Taylor, V.P. and Secy.-Treas.
Directors: John Coan; Bob Rokeby; Helen Sharpe; Fred Smith; Patricia Williams; Robby Zink.
Number of staff: 2 part-time professional.
EIN: 237262279
Selected grants: The following grants were reported in 2004.
$445,112 to University of Arkansas for Medical Sciences Foundation, Little Rock, AR. 3 grants: $393,500, $26,612 (For playground equipment), $25,000 (For dermatology program).
$110,000 to Arkansas Childrens Hospital, Little Rock, AR. 2 grants: $10,000, $100,000
$22,000 to Salem Lutheran Church, Springdale, AR. For general fund and indebtedness.
$10,000 to Arkansas Childrens Hospital Foundation, Little Rock, AR.
$10,000 to Circle of Life Hospice, Springdale, AR.
$10,000 to Ozark Guidance Center, Springdale, AR.
$10,000 to Springdale High School Band Boosters, Springdale, AR.

176
Stella B. Smith Charitable Trust ✧
c/o Regions Bank, Trust Dept.
P.O. Box 1471
Little Rock, AR   72203-1471

Established around 1974.
Donor: Stella B. Smith.
Foundation type: Independent foundation.
Financial data (yr. ended 12/31/03): Assets, $15,677,405 (M); expenditures, $1,559,036; qualifying distributions, $836,965; giving activities include $729,209 for 31 grants (high: $99,500; low: $500).
Purpose and activities: Giving primarily for arts, education, health care and an Episcopal church.
Fields of interest: Arts; Higher education; Health care; Health organizations, association; Human

services; Foundations (community); Protestant agencies & churches.

Limitations: Applications not accepted. Giving primarily in AR. No grants to individuals.

Application information: Contributes only to pre-selected organizations.

Trustees: Maxine P. Hamilton; Catherine H. Mayton; Michael R. Mayton; Regions Bank.

EIN: 237365134

Selected grants: The following grants were reported in 2004.

$118,000 to University of Arkansas, Little Rock, AR.

$77,500 to Arkansas Symphony Orchestra, Little Rock, AR.

$74,934 to Access Schools, Little Rock, AR.

$67,500 to Episcopal Collegiate School Foundation, Little Rock, AR.

$54,612 to Second Presbyterian Church, Little Rock, AR.

$52,500 to Easter Seal Society of Arkansas, Little Rock, AR.

$50,000 to University of Central Arkansas, Conway, AR.

$42,000 to YMCA of Metropolitan Little Rock, Little Rock, AR.

$35,000 to American Heart Association, Little Rock, AR.

$30,000 to American Lung Association of Arkansas, Little Rock, AR.

177
The Soderquist Family Foundation ✧

c/o Donald G. Soderquist
201 S. 19th St., Ste. P
Rogers, AR 72758-1123

Established in 2001 in AR.

Donors: Donald G. Soderquist; M. David Sloane; Soderquist Char. Lead Annuity Tr.

Foundation type: Independent foundation.

Financial data (yr. ended 12/31/05): Assets, $13,244,736 (M); gifts received, $1,176,148; expenditures, $894,373; qualifying distributions, $602,105; giving activities include $602,105 for 17 grants (high: $130,000; low: $1,000).

Fields of interest: Higher education; Human services; Christian agencies & churches.

Limitations: Applications not accepted. Giving on a national basis. No grants to individuals.

Application information: Contributes only to pre-selected organizations.

Officers and Directors:* Donald G. Soderquist,* Pres.; Sandra Ford,* V.P.; Wendy Koons,* V.P.; Jeffrey Soderquist,* V.P.; Mark Soderquist,* V.P.; Joann Soderquist,* Secy.-Treas.

EIN: 731621266

178
The Roy & Christine Sturgis Charitable & Educational Trust ✧

P.O. Box 7599
Little Rock, AR 72217 (501) 664-8525
Contact: Barry Findley, Tr.

Established about 1979.

Donors: Roy Sturgis†; Christine Sturgis.

Foundation type: Independent foundation.

Financial data (yr. ended 12/31/05): Assets, $13,641,606 (M); expenditures, $563,992; qualifying distributions, $538,042; giving activities

include $460,192 for 23 grants (high: $64,211; low: $840).

Purpose and activities: Giving primarily for Baptist and other Christian organizations.

Fields of interest: Higher education; Education; Hospitals (general); Human services; Christian agencies & churches.

Limitations: Giving limited to AR. No grants to individuals.

Application information: Application form not required.

Initial approach: Proposal
Deadline(s): None

Trustees: Barry Findley; Brian Findley; Lisa Speer.

EIN: 710495345

179
Charles M. and Joan R. Taylor Foundation, Inc. ✧

200 Louisiana St.
Little Rock, AR 72201-2706

Established in 1997 in AR.

Donor: Charles M. Taylor Irrevocable Trust.

Foundation type: Independent foundation.

Financial data (yr. ended 12/31/03): Assets, $21,571,578 (M); gifts received, $92,000; expenditures, $602,615; qualifying distributions, $522,765; giving activities include $515,000 for 8 grants (high: $100,000; low: $15,000).

Purpose and activities: Funding primarily for Alzheimer's disease and arthritis, health care, higher education, and Episcopal churches.

Fields of interest: Media, television; Higher education; Arthritis; Alzheimer's disease; Protestant agencies & churches.

Type of support: Continuing support; Land acquisition; Endowments; Program development; Scholarship funds.

Limitations: Applications not accepted. Giving primarily in AR. No grants to individuals.

Application information: Contributes only to pre-selected organizations.

Directors: Hanna Goss; Sarah Hopkins; Rev. Alfred Shands III; Phoebe Shelby Strudwick; Julia Joan Taylor.

EIN: 710799820

Selected grants: The following grants were reported in 2004.

$50,000 to Arkansas Childrens Hospital Foundation, Little Rock, AR. For Child Life and Institutional Design programs.

$50,000 to Berea College, Berea, KY. For student life scholarships for nursing.

$50,000 to Canine Companions for Independence, Santa Rosa, CA. For program support.

$50,000 to Charlevoix County Community Foundation, East Jordan, MI. For Grandview Medical Centers Alzheimer's Unit.

$50,000 to Historic Arkansas Museum, Little Rock, AR. For living history program.

$50,000 to Nature Conservancy, Little Rock, AR. For program support.

$50,000 to Nature Conservancy, Lexington, KY. For program support.

$50,000 to Tip of the Mitt Watershed Council, Petoskey, MI.

$50,000 to Twentieth Century Club Hope Lodge, Little Rock, AR. For renovations, repairs, and maintenance of building.

$50,000 to Wings of Mercy, Holland, MI. For program support.

180
Tenenbaum Foundation ✧ ☆

P.O. Box 15128, GMF
Little Rock, AR 72231-5128 (501) 945-0881
Contact: R.J. Wills, Tr.

Established about 1967 in AR.

Donors: J.M. Tenenbaum; A. Tenenbaum Co., Inc.; Arkansas Aluminum Alloys, Inc.

Foundation type: Independent foundation.

Financial data (yr. ended 12/31/05): Assets, $3,786,112 (M); gifts received, $1,000,000; expenditures, $570,803; qualifying distributions, $565,851; giving activities include $565,851 for grants.

Purpose and activities: Giving primarily for education, health associations, youth programs, human services, and Jewish organizations.

Fields of interest: Education; Health organizations, association; Boys clubs; Girls clubs; Boys & girls clubs; Human services; Jewish federated giving programs; Jewish agencies & temples.

Limitations: Giving primarily in AR. No grants to individuals.

Application information:

Initial approach: Letter
Deadline(s): None

Trustees: Harold Tenenbaum; R.J. Wills.

EIN: 716061727

Selected grants: The following grants were reported in 2003.

$78,000 to Jewish Federation of Arkansas, Little Rock, AR.

$20,000 to Baptist Health Foundation, Little Rock, AR.

$10,000 to Good Shepherd Ecumenical Retirement Center, Little Rock, AR.

$5,500 to Boys and Girls Club of Little Rock, Little Rock, AR.

$5,500 to University of Arkansas for Medical Sciences Foundation, Little Rock, AR.

$5,000 to Pulaski Technical College, North Little Rock, AR.

$2,500 to United Way of Pulaski County, Little Rock, AR.

$1,500 to Arkansas Childrens Hospital, Little Rock, AR.

$200 to Arkansas Food Bank Network, Little Rock, AR.

$200 to Youth Home, Little Rock, AR.

181
Trinity Foundation

P.O. Box 7008
Pine Bluff, AR 71611-7008
Contact: Drew Atkinson, Secy.

Incorporated about 1952 in AR.

Donors: Pine Bluff Sand & Gravel Co.; McGeorge Contracting Co.; Cornerstone Farm & Gin Co.; Standard Investment Co.; Harvey W. McGeorge†.

Foundation type: Independent foundation.

Financial data (yr. ended 9/30/05): Assets, $19,842,358 (M); expenditures, $1,264,424; qualifying distributions, $1,155,850; giving activities include $985,050 for 41 grants (high: $243,750; low: $2,000), and $170,800 for grants to individuals.

Purpose and activities: Giving primarily for education, youth services, and student scholarships.

Fields of interest: Arts; Higher education; Scholarships/financial aid; Education; Environment; Boys & girls clubs; Children/youth, services.
Type of support: General/operating support; Scholarships—to individuals.
Limitations: Giving primarily in central AR. No grants to individuals directly.
Application information: Scholarship application information available only at guidance offices of public high schools in Pine Bluff, Little Rock, Benton, and Bauxite, AR. Application form not required.
Initial approach: Letter
Deadline(s): Apr. 10 of senior year in high school for scholarships
Board meeting date(s): Varies
Final notification: 3 to 6 months
Officers: Scott McGeorge, Pres.; Haskel Dickinson, V.P.; Wallace P. McGeorge III, V.P.; Drew Atkinson, Secy.; Gerald Majors, Treas.
Number of staff: None.
EIN: 716050288
Selected grants: The following grants were reported in 2005.
$243,750 to Little Rock Public Education Foundation, Little Rock, AR. For general support.
$100,000 to Hendrix College, Conway, AR. For Building Fund.
$100,000 to Jefferson Foundation, Pine Bluff, AR. For general support.
$100,000 to William J. Clinton Presidential Foundation, Little Rock, AR. For general support.
$50,000 to Saint Andrews Church, Little Rock, AR. For general support.
$45,000 to Literacy Council of Jefferson County, Pine Bluff, AR. For general support.
$40,000 to Arkansas Childrens Hospital, Little Rock, AR. For general support.
$30,000 to University of Arkansas Foundation, Little Rock, AR. For general support.
$16,000 to Saint Vincent Health System, Little Rock, AR. For medical clinic.
$2,000 to Rotary Club International, Little Rock, AR.

182
Tyson Foundation, Inc. ✧
P.O. Box 2020
Springdale, AR 72765 (479) 290-4955
Contact: Shelby Rogers, Pres.

Established in 1970 in AR.
Donor: Don Tyson.
Foundation type: Independent foundation.
Financial data (yr. ended 12/31/05): Assets, $28,078,888 (M); expenditures, $1,599,932; qualifying distributions, $1,442,617; giving activities include $133,500 for 9 grants (high: $30,000; low: $1,000), and $1,304,308 for grants to individuals.
Purpose and activities: Primary area of interest is education, including scholarships available to individuals majoring in certain areas of agriculture, business, engineering, computer science, and nursing. Scholarships awarded only to employees of Tyson Foods, Inc. and their dependents.
Fields of interest: Arts; Higher education; Education; Hospitals (general); Boys & girls clubs; Family services.
Type of support: Capital campaigns; Equipment; Scholarships—to individuals.
Limitations: Applications not accepted. Giving primarily in areas where company employees live in AR, Modesto, CA, and Chicago, IL; giving also to

areas of AK, AL, FL, GA, IN, KY, MD, MN, MO, MS, NC, OK, OR, PA, TN, TX, VA, and WA.
Application information: Unsolicited requests for funds not accepted. Scholarships awarded to employees of Tyson Foods, Inc. and their families.
Board meeting date(s): Biannually
Officer: Shelby Rogers, Pres.
Trustees: James B. Blair; Harry C. Erwin III.
Number of staff: 1 full-time professional; 1 part-time professional; 1 part-time support.
EIN: 237087948

183
Union County Community Foundation, Inc. ✧
P.O. Box 148
El Dorado, AR 71731-0148
Contact: Elise Drake, Dir.

Established in 1996 in AR.
Foundation type: Community foundation.
Financial data (yr. ended 9/30/05): Assets, $10,702,037 (M); gifts received, $449,459; expenditures, $625,800; giving activities include $423,703 for 42 grants (high: $102,220; low: $225), and $98,424 for 52 grants to individuals (high: $18,500; low: $250).
Purpose and activities: The foundation provides a charitable vehicle that accepts, invests and distributes resources according to the donors' wishes. Giving also to individuals for scholarships.
Fields of interest: Historic preservation/historical societies; Scholarships/financial aid; Education; Human services; Community development; Protestant agencies & churches.
Type of support: Employee matching gifts; In-kind gifts.
Limitations: Applications not accepted. Giving limited to the El Dorado, AR, area.
Publications: Financial statement; Grants list; Newsletter.
Officers and Board Members:* Jerry Watkins,* Chair.; Clara Jones,* Vice-Chair.; David Rothwell,* Secy.; John McFarland,* Treas.; Andy Allen; Bob Brown; Melissa Jerry; Lenore Newsome; Jeff Nolan; Marc Parnell; Bob Risor; Joyce Rutledge; Joy Sugg; Ann Wilson.
Number of staff: 1 full-time professional; 1 full-time support.
EIN: 311500805

184
Wal-Mart Foundation ▼
(also known as SAM'S CLUB Foundation)
702 S.W. 8th St.
Bentonville, AR 72716-0150 (800) 530-9925
Contact: Brad Fisher, Dir.
FAX: (479) 273-6850; URL: http://www.walmartfoundation.org

Established in 1979 in AR.
Donor: Wal-Mart Stores, Inc.
Foundation type: Company-sponsored foundation.
Financial data (yr. ended 1/31/05): Assets, $18,881,075 (M); gifts received, $148,447,653; expenditures, $155,212,734; qualifying distributions, $155,210,734; giving activities include $154,033,905 for 147,518 grants (high: $6,084,000; low: $1), and $503,501 for 98 grants to individuals (high: $100,000; low: $1).

Purpose and activities: The foundation supports organizations involved with education, the environment, health, substance abuse, hunger, safety, children and youth, community development, senior citizens, and minorities and awards college scholarships.
Fields of interest: Elementary/secondary education; Higher education; Adult education—literacy, basic skills & GED; Education, reading; Education; Environment; Health care; Substance abuse, services; Alcoholism; Food services; Safety/disasters; Children/youth, services; Economic development; Community development; Federated giving programs; Aging; Minorities.
Type of support: Employee volunteer services; Scholarship funds; Employee matching gifts; Employee-related scholarships; Scholarships—to individuals; Matching/challenge support.
Limitations: Giving primarily in areas of company operations. No support for faith-based organizations not of direct benefit to the entire community or political organizations. No grants for research, endowments, annual meetings, capital campaigns, conferences, travel, fundraising dinners or galas, cultural performances, or film or video projects.
Publications: Informational brochure.
Application information:
Initial approach: Contact nearest company store for application information
Deadline(s): Contact high school counselor for deadline for Sam Walton Community Scholarships
Board meeting date(s): Mar., May, Aug., and Nov.
Trustees: Lawrence V. Jackson; Thomas M. Schoewe; H. Lee Scott, Jr.
Number of staff: 8 full-time professional; 14 full-time support.
EIN: 716107283
Selected grants: The following grants were reported in 2005.
$6,084,000 to Scholarship Program Administrators, Nashville, TN. For Sam Walton Community Scholarships.
$5,000,000 to Mercy Medical Clinics, Rogers, AR.
$2,000,000 to American Red Cross, National Headquarters, DC.
$1,351,200 to Veterans of Foreign Wars Foundation, Kansas City, MO. 2 grants: $20,000, $1,331,200
$750,000 to Community Foundation for the National Capital Region, DC.
$332,444 to Charities Funds Transfer, Alexandria, VA. For matching contribution.
$25,000 to Arkansas Childrens Hospital Foundation, Little Rock, AR.
$15,000 to Metropolitan Emergency Support Services.
$10,000 to Mamie P. Whitesides Elementary School, Mount Pleasant, SC. For Teacher of the Year award.

185
Willard and Pat Walker Charitable Foundation, Inc. ▼ ✧ ☆
61 E. Sunbridge, Ste. 1
Fayetteville, AR 72703
Contact: Deborah Walker, Vice-Chair.
Application address: P.O. Box 10500, Fayetteville, AR 72703-0043; tel.: (479) 582-2310

Established in 2003 in AR; funded in 2004 from the transfer of assets from Willard and Pat Walker Charitable Foundation Trust.

Donors: Amy S. Walker; Willard and Pat Walker Charitable Foundation Trust.

Foundation type: Independent foundation.

Financial data (yr. ended 12/31/05): Assets, $20,222,875 (M); gifts received, $23,698,969; expenditures, $20,571,021; qualifying distributions, $20,540,993; giving activities include $20,404,063 for 63 grants (high: $5,000,000; low: $300).

Fields of interest: Higher education; Education; Health organizations; Children/youth, services; Residential/custodial care, hospices.

Type of support: Continuing support; Capital campaigns; Building/renovation; Equipment; Endowments.

Limitations: Giving primarily in AR. No grants to individuals.

Application information: Audio and videotapes will not be accepted. Only 1 application per organization per year.

   Initial approach: Letter (not to exceed 3 pages)
   Deadline(s): Quarterly

Officers: Deborah A. Walker, Vice-Chair.; Amy S. Walker, Pres.; John M. Walker, Secy.-Treas.

EIN: 200235689

186

Walton Family Foundation, Inc. ▼ ✧

P.O. Box 2030
Bentonville, AR 72712 (479) 464-1570
Contact: Buddy D. Philpot, Exec. Dir.
FAX: (479) 464-1580; URL: http://www.wffhome.com

Established in 1987 in AR.

Donors: Sam M. Walton†; Helen R. Walton; John T. Walton†; Walton Enterprises, LLC.

Foundation type: Independent foundation.

Financial data (yr. ended 12/31/05): Assets, $1,328,793,250 (M); gifts received, $415,157,921; expenditures, $161,327,512; qualifying distributions, $157,989,927; giving activities include $157,989,927 for grants.

Purpose and activities: Giving primarily for systemic reform of primary education (K-12).

Fields of interest: Elementary/secondary education; Child development, education.

Type of support: Employee-related scholarships; Program-related investments/loans; Scholarships—to individuals.

Limitations: Applications not accepted. Giving primarily in AR, with emphasis on the Mississippi River's delta region of AR and MS. No support for non-established medical research programs. No grants to individuals (except for scholarships for children of Wal-Mart associates), or for endowments for operations, church-related construction projects, travel expenses for groups to compete or perform, or start-up funds.

Application information: Generally contributes only to pre-selected organizations.

Officers and Directors:* Jim C. Walton,* Secy.-Treas.; Buddy D. Philpot, Exec. Dir.; Carrie W. Penner; Alice A. Walton; Alice L. Walton; Benjamin S. Walton; John T. Walton; S. Robson Walton; Samuel R. Walton; Steuart L. Walton; Thomas L. Walton.

Number of staff: 5 full-time professional; 2 full-time support.

EIN: 133441466

187

Bob White Memorial Foundation ☆

(also known as BWMF Farm)
P.O. Box 537
Eudora, AR 71640-9419
Contact: Rebecca A. Poole, Secy.

Established in 1982 in AR.

Donor: J. Austin White.

Foundation type: Independent foundation.

Financial data (yr. ended 12/31/05): Assets, $4,645,231 (M); expenditures, $605,714; qualifying distributions, $350,300; giving activities include $350,300 for grants.

Purpose and activities: To support a better standard of living in Eudora and Chicot County, AR.

Fields of interest: Human services; Community development.

Type of support: General/operating support; Building/renovation; Endowments; Scholarship funds.

Limitations: Giving primarily in Chicot County, AR and the immediate area of the southeast AR geographical region. No grants to individuals.

Publications: Application guidelines; Annual report.

Application information: Application form required.

   Initial approach: Letter
   Copies of proposal: 1
   Deadline(s): Sept. 1
   Board meeting date(s): 2nd Thurs. of each month
   Final notification: 3 months

Officer and Trustees:* Rebecca A. Poole,* Secy.; Reynold Meyer; Craig Stephenson; Stephen Tisdale.

Number of staff: 1 full-time support.

EIN: 311041899

Selected grants: The following grants were reported in 2004.

$107,300 to Southeast Arkansas Regional Community Foundation, Eudora, AR. For operating support for Austin White Cultural Center.

$40,000 to Ross Van Ness-Wellford Volunteer Fire Department, Eudora, AR. To purchase fire fighting equipment.

$17,500 to Chicot Memorial Hospital foundation, Lake Village, AR. To purchase equipment.

$7,500 to Eudora Christian School, Eudora, AR.

$7,500 to University of Arkansas at Monticello Foundation, Monticello, AR. For scholarships.

$5,000 to Fawnwood Volunteer Fire Department, Lake Village, AR. To purchase fire fighting equipment.

$500 to Delta Mens Association, Eudora, AR. For Arkansas Childrens Hospital.

$300 to Association of Small Foundations, DC.

188

Whitt Foundation ✧ ☆

8904 Moody Rd.
Fort Smith, AR 72903

Established in 1998.

Foundation type: Independent foundation.

Financial data (yr. ended 12/31/05): Assets, $913,495 (M); expenditures, $328,868; qualifying distributions, $328,868; giving activities include $324,009 for 10 grants (high: $100,000; low: $1,500).

Fields of interest: Higher education, university; Education; Crime/law enforcement; Boys & girls clubs; Federated giving programs; Protestant agencies & churches.

Limitations: Giving primarily in Fort Smith, AR.

Application information: Application form not required.

   Deadline(s): None

Officers: Christopher M. Whitt, Pres.; David Whitt, V.P.; John Whitt, Secy.-Treas.

EIN: 710811940

Selected grants: The following grants were reported in 2004.

$100,000 to Trinity Educational Trust, Fort Smith, AR.

$10,000 to Bost Lifebridge.

$10,000 to Boys and Girls Club, Fort Smith, Fort Smith, AR.

$10,000 to Central Presbyterian Church of Forth Smith, Fort Smith, AR.

$10,000 to Grace Community Church, Fort Smith, AR.

$10,000 to United Way of Fort Smith Area, Fort Smith, AR.

$5,000 to Bost School for Limited Children, Fort Smith, AR.

$500 to Good Samaritan Clinic, Fort Smith, AR.

189

Windgate Charitable Foundation, Inc. ▼ ✧

P.O. Box 826
Siloam Springs, AR 72761-0826
(479) 524-9829
Contact: John E. Brown, III, Exec. Dir.

Established in 1993 in AR.

Donor: Dorothea W. Hutcheson†.

Foundation type: Independent foundation.

Financial data (yr. ended 12/31/05): Assets, $63,758,463 (M); expenditures, $19,763,023; qualifying distributions, $19,537,896; giving activities include $19,394,794 for 174 grants (high: $4,028,724; low: $500; average: $10,000–$100,000).

Purpose and activities: Giving primarily to promote art and craft education, and projects that strengthen marriage and family relationships. Limited giving also to programs that serve children and Christian higher education.

Fields of interest: Arts education; Children/youth, services; Family services.

Type of support: Program development; Matching/challenge support.

Limitations: Giving on a national basis with emphasis on the Midwest and Southwest. No support for private religious schools or churches. No grants to individuals, or for undesignated annual funds, debt retirement, completed projects, or group travel for performance or competition.

Publications: Application guidelines; Program policy statement.

Application information: Application form not required.

   Initial approach: 2-page letter
   Copies of proposal: 1
   Deadline(s): None
   Board meeting date(s): Varies
   Final notification: 4 to 6 months

Officer: John E. Brown III, Exec. Dir.

Directors: Robyn Horn; Karen Hutcheson; Mary E. Hutcheson; Richard Hutcheson; William L. Hutcheson.

Number of staff: 2

EIN: 710723781

Selected grants: The following grants were reported in 2005.

$4,028,724 to University of Arkansas, College of Education and Health Professions, Department of Education Reform, Fayetteville, AR.

$3,539,363 to University of Arkansas for Medical Sciences, Little Rock, AR. For endowment and scholarships.

$1,003,412 to John Brown University, Art Department, Siloam Springs, AR. For endowment fund.

$1,003,321 to Penland School of Crafts, Penland, NC. For challenge grant.

$1,001,300 to University of Arkansas at Fayetteville Foundation, Fayetteville, AR. 2 grants: $500,650 (For Great Expectations Arkansas), $500,650 (For Arkansas A Plus Schools, as part of Great Expectations).

$125,000 to University of Central Oklahoma, Edmond, OK.

$120,000 to University of Arkansas, College of Education and Health Professions, Little Rock, AR. For Great Expectations Arkansas Masters of Arts Scholars.

$55,000 to Clear Spring School, Eureka Springs, AR. For Wisdom of the Hands.

$48,670 to Purchase College Foundation, Purchase, NY. For scholarships and Visiting Artist Program.

CALIFORNIA

190
324 Foundation ✧ ☆
(formerly The K-Swiss Foundation)
31248 Oak Crest Dr.
Westlake Village, CA 91361-4643
Contact: Janice L. Smith

Established in 1994 in CA.
Donor: K-Swiss Inc.
Foundation type: Company-sponsored foundation.
Financial data (yr. ended 12/31/05): Assets, $1,778,791 (M); gifts received, $150,000; expenditures, $513,602; qualifying distributions, $512,375; giving activities include $512,375 for grants.
Purpose and activities: The foundation supports Jewish agencies and temples and organizations involved with education and health.
Fields of interest: Education; Health organizations, association; Federated giving programs; Jewish federated giving programs; Jewish agencies & temples.
Type of support: General/operating support.
Limitations: Applications not accepted. Giving primarily in areas of company operations. No grants to individuals.
Application information: Contributes only to pre-selected organizations.
Officers: Steven Nichols, Chair.; George Powlick, Treas.
Directors: David Nichols; Harriet Nichols.
EIN: 954422206
Selected grants: The following grants were reported in 2003.
$66,000 to Anti-Defamation League of Bnai Brith, New York, NY. For general support.
$37,000 to Jewish Federation Council of Greater Los Angeles, Los Angeles, CA. For capital campaign.
$10,000 to Los Angeles Philharmonic, Los Angeles, CA. For general support.
$10,000 to United States Holocaust Memorial Museum, DC. For general support.
$6,750 to University of Southern California, Los Angeles, CA. For general support.
$5,250 to Cedars-Sinai Medical Center, Los Angeles, CA. For general support.
$1,500 to Lupus Foundation of America, Los Angeles, CA. For general support.
$1,000 to Multiple Sclerosis Society, National, New York, NY. For general support.
$1,000 to Telluride Medical Center, Telluride, CO. For capital support.
$1,000 to United Negro College Fund, Fairfax, VA. For general support.

191
A-T Medical Research Foundation
5241 Round Meadow Rd.
Hidden Hills, CA 91302-1163
Contact: Pamela J. Smith, Pres. and C.F.O.

Established in 1983 in CA.
Donors: George A. Smith†; Pamela J. Smith.
Foundation type: Operating foundation.
Financial data (yr. ended 9/30/05): Assets, $316,133 (M); gifts received, $927,473;

expenditures, $853,429; qualifying distributions, $783,742; giving activities include $549,000 for 3 grants.
Purpose and activities: Grants to individuals on an international basis only for medical research relating to ataxia-telangiectasia.
Fields of interest: Medical research, institute.
Type of support: Seed money; Research.
Limitations: Applications not accepted. Giving on a national and international basis. No support for religious or political organizations. No grants to individuals directly, or for scholarships; no student loans.
Publications: Annual report; Informational brochure; Newsletter.
Application information: Unsolicited requests for funds not accepted.
Officer: Pamela J. Smith, Pres. and C.F.O.
Directors: David Haskell; Lois Rosen.
EIN: 953882022
Selected grants: The following grants were reported in 2004.
$190,000 to Tel Aviv University, Tel Aviv, Israel. .
$187,500 to University of California, Berkeley, CA.
$35,000 to Benaroya Research Institute at Virgina Mason, Seattle, WA.

192
Aaroe Associates Charitable Foundation, Inc. ✧
12544 High Bluff Rd., Ste. 420
San Diego, CA 92130

Established in 1995 in CA.
Donor: John Aaroe & Assocs.
Foundation type: Independent foundation.
Financial data (yr. ended 4/30/05): Assets, $67,796 (M); gifts received, $470,115; expenditures, $500,524; qualifying distributions, $500,513; giving activities include $499,630 for 209 grants (high: $35,000; low: $200).
Purpose and activities: Giving primarily for education, the arts, as well as children, youth, family and social services, including a center for blind children.
Fields of interest: Performing arts; Arts; Elementary/secondary education; Education; Environment, natural resources; Animals/wildlife; Hospitals (general); Health care; Health organizations, association; AIDS research; Recreation, camps; Youth development; Human services; Children/youth, services; Family services; Blind/visually impaired.
Limitations: Applications not accepted. Giving primarily in CA. No grants to individuals.
Application information: Contributes only to pre-selected organizations.
Officers: Steve Games, Pres.; Nyda Jones-Church, Secy.-Treas.
EIN: 954528536

193
The Thomas C. Ackerman Foundation
101 W. Broadway, Ste. 900
San Diego, CA 92101-3391
Contact: Lynne Newman, Admin.
FAX: (619) 698-8051;
E-mail: info@ackermanfoundation.org; URL: http://www.ackermanfoundation.org

Established in 1991 in CA.

Donor: Thomas C. Ackerman, Jr.†.
Foundation type: Independent foundation.
Financial data (yr. ended 12/31/05): Assets, $7,668,422 (M); expenditures, $670,256; qualifying distributions, $438,175; giving activities include $438,175 for 48 grants (high: $25,000; low: $500).
Purpose and activities: The Thomas C. Ackerman Foundation is committed to helping youth achieve success in their early education, whether they are college-bound or entering the work force directly after high school. The foundation believes that a well-rounded kindergarten through twelfth-grade education including music, arts, culture, math and science is essential to helping students fulfill their future roles as parents/professionals and citizens. Support for organizations involved with arts and culture, education, health and human services, and community development. The foundation also supports well-rounded kindergarten through twelfth-grade educational programs that include music, arts, culture, math and science.
Fields of interest: Arts; Elementary/secondary education; Secondary school/education; Education; Health care; Human services; Community development.
Type of support: General/operating support; Management development/capacity building; Equipment; Program development; Seed money; Curriculum development; Scholarship funds; Program evaluation; Matching/challenge support.
Limitations: Giving primarily in San Diego County, CA. No support for religious organizations for religious purposes, or for international organizations, or medical/biological research organizations. No grants to individuals, or for continuing support, conferences or symposia.
Publications: Application guidelines; Annual report; Grants list.
Application information: Guidelines for completing Letter of Intent are available on foundation Web site. Full proposals accepted only after approval of letter of intent. Application form required.
> *Initial approach:* Applicants must electronically submit an initial 2-page Letter of Intent (LOI) to be considered for a grant
> *Copies of proposal:* 3
> *Deadline(s):* Application deadlines available on foundation Web site
> *Board meeting date(s):* Quarterly
> *Final notification:* Within 30 days of board meeting
Officers and Directors:* Robert G. Copeland,* Pres.; Joanne Pastula,* V.P.; Kenneth G. Coveney,* Secy.; H. Michael Collins, Treas.; Christopher C. Calkins; Gail K. Naughton; John G. Rebelo.
Number of staff: 1 full-time professional.
EIN: 330477490
Selected grants: The following grants were reported in 2005.
$50,000 to Junior Achievement.
$25,000 to Francis Parker School, San Diego, CA.
$25,000 to San Diego Natural History Museum, San Diego, CA.
$23,000 to Lux Art Institute, Encinitas, CA.
$15,000 to San Diego City Schools, San Diego, CA.
$10,000 to Boy Scouts of America, Anchorage, AK.
$10,000 to Human Development Foundation, Encinitas, CA.
$10,000 to YMCA.
$7,500 to San Diego Performing Arts League, San Diego, CA.
$5,000 to Hope Through Housing Foundation, Rancho Cucamonga, CA.

194
Adams Fund ✧ ☆
915 Wilshire Blvd., Ste. 1760
Los Angeles, CA 90017

Established in 1959 in CA.
Donors: Morgan Adams, Jr.; Suzanne V. Parry; Adams Plaza; Nash Mariposa, Ltd.; John King Adams.
Foundation type: Independent foundation.
Financial data (yr. ended 12/31/04): Assets, $1,462,070 (M); gifts received, $1,203,700; expenditures, $652,663; qualifying distributions, $629,282; giving activities include $629,282 for 58 grants (high: $161,200; low: $100).
Fields of interest: Arts; Education; Human services; YM/YWCAs & YM/YWHAs; Philanthropy/voluntarism.
Type of support: General/operating support; Publication.
Limitations: Applications not accepted. Giving primarily in CA. No grants to individuals.
Application information: Contributes only to pre-selected organizations.
Trustees: David V. Adams; John K. Adams; Richard E. Beth; Mary Adams O'Connell.
Number of staff: 2 part-time support.
EIN: 956015986

195
Adventist World Charitable Trust ✧ ☆
332 W. F St., Ste. A
Oakdale, CA 95361
Application address: c/o Ingrid K. Bloomquist, 1260 W. Crescent Ave., Redlands, CA 92373

Donors: Olov A. Blomquist; Willma Blomquist; Edald Loaser.
Foundation type: Independent foundation.
Financial data (yr. ended 9/30/05): Assets, $460,899 (M); gifts received, $5,000; expenditures, $524,489; qualifying distributions, $432,881; giving activities include $432,881 for grants.
Purpose and activities: Support primarily for Seventh Day Adventist Churches.
Fields of interest: Christian agencies & churches.
Application information: Application form not required.
  Deadline(s): None
Trustees: Ingrid K. Blomquist; Linnea Torkelsen; Max C. Torkelsen.
EIN: 946544104
Selected grants: The following grants were reported in 2004.
$223,216 to Seventh-Day Adventist Church.

196
The Agouron Institute ▼ ✧
1055 E. Colorado Blvd., Ste. 250
Pasadena, CA 91106

Foundation type: Independent foundation.
Financial data (yr. ended 6/30/05): Assets, $84,974,188 (M); expenditures, $5,529,063; qualifying distributions, $4,553,258; giving activities include $3,829,529 for 19 grants (high: $1,251,706; low: $5,000; average: $47,000–$448,000).
Purpose and activities: Giving primarily for scientific research and education.

Fields of interest: Higher education; Education; Science, research; Biological sciences.
Limitations: Applications not accepted. Giving primarily on a national and international basis, including Stockholm, Sweden, and Cambridge, United Kingdom.
Application information: Contributes only to pre-selected organizations.
Officers: Melvin Simon, Chair.; John Abelson, Pres.; Willis Wood, Secy.-Treas.
Directors: Phillip H. Abelson; Gustaf Arrhenius; Gary Friedman; Theodor Friedman; Gordon Gill; David Hirsch; Peter Johnson; Deborah Spector.
EIN: 953248387
Selected grants: The following grants were reported in 2005.
$1,251,706 to California Institute of Technology, Pasadena, CA. For scientific research and education.
$557,510 to University of San Diego, San Diego, CA. For scientific research and education.
$448,000 to Helen Hay Whitney Foundation, New York, NY. For scientific fellowships.
$361,000 to University of Southern California, Wrigley Institute for Environmental Studies, Los Angeles, CA. For scientific research and education.
$355,713 to Universidad de Concepcion, Concepcion, Chile. For scientific research and education.
$265,350 to Jane Coffin Childs Memorial Fund for Medical Research, New Haven, CT. For scientific fellowships.
$112,750 to Medical Research Council, Molecular Biology Department, London, England. For scientific research and education.
$100,000 to National Academy of Sciences, DC. For scientific research and education.
$53,000 to Carnegie Institution of Washington, DC. For scientific research and education.
$10,000 to Scripps Research Institute, La Jolla, CA. For scientific research and education.

197
Ahmanson Charitable Community Trust
2699 White Rd., Ste. 101
Irvine, CA 92614

Established in 2001 in CA.
Donors: Howard F. Ahmanson, Jr.; Roberta G. Ahmanson.
Foundation type: Independent foundation.
Financial data (yr. ended 12/31/05): Assets, $2,914 (M); gifts received, $2,451,000; expenditures, $2,454,661; qualifying distributions, $2,454,385; giving activities include $2,430,754 for 33 grants (high: $400,000; low: $5,000; average: $10,000–$150,000).
Limitations: Applications not accepted. No grants to individuals.
Application information: Contributes only to pre-selected organizations.
Trustees: Howard F. Ahmanson, Jr.; Roberta G. Ahmanson.
EIN: 330946961
Selected grants: The following grants were reported in 2003.
$351,540 to Survivors of the Shoah Visual History Foundation, Los Angeles, CA.
$50,000 to Discovery Institute, Seattle, WA.
$41,000 to University of Maryland-College Park Foundation, College Park, MD.

$20,000 to Foundation for Children and Families of Iowa, Des Moines, IA.
$20,000 to Orange County Rescue Mission, Tustin, CA.
$15,000 to West Chester University of Pennsylvania, West Chester, PA.
$10,000 to Childrens Scholarship Fund, Southern California, Los Angeles, CA.
$5,000 to Hoyt Sherman Place Foundation, Des Moines, IA.
$1,000 to Gingerbread House Nursery School, Ida Grove, IA.
$1,000 to Orchard Place, Des Moines, IA.

198
The Ahmanson Foundation ▼
9215 Wilshire Blvd.
Beverly Hills, CA 90210 (310) 278-0770
Contact: Leonard E. Walcott, Jr., V.P.
E-mail: info@theahmansonfoundation.org;
URL: http://www.theahmansonfoundation.org

Incorporated in 1952 in CA.
Donors: Howard F. Ahmanson†; Dorothy G. Sullivan†; William H. Ahmanson; Robert H. Ahmanson.
Foundation type: Independent foundation.
Financial data (yr. ended 10/31/05): Assets, $938,348,497 (M); expenditures, $47,027,434; qualifying distributions, $42,824,004; giving activities include $41,218,405 for 506 grants (high: $2,000,000; low: $1,000; average: $10,000–$100,000).
Purpose and activities: Emphasis on education at all levels, the arts and humanities, health and medicine, and a broad range of human service programs.
Fields of interest: Visual arts; Museums; Performing arts; Humanities; Arts; Elementary school/education; Secondary school/education; Higher education; Nursing school/education; Adult education—literacy, basic skills & GED; Libraries/library science; Education, reading; Education; Health care; Health organizations, association; Biomedicine; Crime/violence prevention, domestic violence; Human services; Youth, services; Homeless, human services; Minorities; Economically disadvantaged; Homeless.
Type of support: Capital campaigns; Building/renovation; Equipment; Land acquisition; Scholarship funds; Technical assistance.
Limitations: Giving primarily in southern CA, with emphasis on the Los Angeles area. No support for religious organizations for sectarian purposes, or advocacy or political organizations. No grants to individuals, or generally for continuing support, endowed chairs, annual campaigns, deficit financing, professorships, internships, fellowships, film production, media projects, seminars, general research and development, workshops, studies, surveys, operational support of regional and national charities, underwriting, or exchange programs; no loans.
Publications: Application guidelines; Annual report (including application guidelines).
Application information: Application form not required.
  Initial approach: Letter of inquiry or proposal
  Copies of proposal: 1
  Deadline(s): None
  Board meeting date(s): 4 times annually
  Final notification: 60 to 90 days

Officers and Trustees: * Robert H. Ahmanson,* Pres.; Leonard E. Walcott, Jr., V.P. and Managing Dir.; William Hayden Ahmanson,* V.P.; William Howard Ahmanson,* V.P.; Robert F. Erburu,* V.P.; Karen A. Hoffman,* Secy. and Sr. Prog. Off.; Kristen K. O'Connor, C.F.O. and Treas.; Howard F. Ahmanson, Jr.; Lloyd E. Cotsen; Robert M. DeKruif; Stephen D. Rountree.
Number of staff: 12 full-time professional; 1 full-time support.
EIN: 956089998
Selected grants: The following grants were reported in 2004.
$3,500,000 to Autry National Center of the American West, Los Angeles, CA. 2 grants: $3,000,000 (Toward construction of new facility, payable over 3 years), $500,000 (For additional conservation/preservation of Southwest Collection).
$2,700,000 to Museum Associates, Los Angeles, CA. 2 grants: $1,950,000 (For acquisition of Houdon's sculpture Seated Voltaire for Los Angeles County Museum of Art, payable over 2 years), $750,000 (For acquisition of painting by Ubaldo Gandolfi, Selene and Endymion, c. 1780).
$1,500,000 to California Science Center Foundation, Los Angeles, CA. Toward World of Ecology.
$1,500,000 to UCLA Foundation, School of Medicine, Los Angeles, CA. For additional support toward Replacement Hospital.
$1,000,000 to K C E T Community Television of Southern California, Los Angeles, CA. Toward new PBS Hollywood Presents, Series II.
$1,000,000 to University of Southern California, College of Letters, Arts and Sciences, Los Angeles, CA. For additional support toward construction of Molecular and Computational Biology Building.
$750,000 to Pueblo Nuevo Development, Los Angeles, CA. Toward property acquisition and construction of Camino Nuevo Charter Academy High School.
$500,000 to Huntington Library, Art Collections and Botanical Gardens, San Marino, CA. For planning and implementation of renovation of Mansion.

199
Akonadi Foundation ◇
469 9th St., Ste. 210
Oakland, CA 94607 (510) 663-3867
Contact: Quinn Delaney, Pres.
E-mail: info@akonadi.org; URL: http://www.akonadi.org

Established in 1999 in CA.
Donor: Quinn Delaney.
Foundation type: Independent foundation.
Financial data (yr. ended 12/31/05): Assets, $15,179,876 (M); gifts received, $4,775,000; expenditures, $2,130,481; qualifying distributions, $2,005,693; giving activities include $1,913,250 for 49 grants (high: $210,000; low: $2,500).
Purpose and activities: The mission of the foundation is to work with others to eliminate racism, with a focus on structural and institutional racism.
Fields of interest: Civil rights, race/intergroup relations.
Limitations: Giving primarily in the San Francisco Bay Area, CA. No support for organizations which provide local programming in areas outside of northern CA. No grants to individuals.

Publications: Grants list.
Application information: Full proposals are by invitation only. Application information is available on foundation Web site.
   Initial approach: Letter of interest (not exceeding 2 pages)
   Deadline(s): None for letters of intent
Officers: Quinn Delaney, Pres.; Wayne Jordan, Secy.
Number of staff: 1 part-time support.
EIN: 943329873
Selected grants: The following grants were reported in 2004.
$70,000 to Legal Services for Prisoners with Children, San Francisco, CA.
$52,700 to Applied Research Center, Oakland, CA.
$50,150 to Legal Aid Society-Employment Law Center, San Francisco, CA.
$50,000 to Global Rights, DC.
$50,000 to Immigrant Legal Resource Center, San Francisco, CA.
$40,250 to Center for Third World Organizing, Oakland, CA.
$40,000 to International Indian Treaty Council, San Francisco, CA.
$40,000 to Wildflowers Institute, San Francisco, CA.
$30,000 to Center for New Community, Chicago, IL.
$30,000 to Latino Issues Forum, San Francisco, CA.

200
The Al-Ameen Foundation ◇
1301 Ocean Ave.
Santa Monica, CA 90401 (310) 394-2791
Contact: Ahmad Adaya, Pres.

Established in 1998 in CA.
Donor: Ahmad Adaya.
Foundation type: Independent foundation.
Financial data (yr. ended 12/31/03): Assets, $3,477,882 (M); gifts received, $1,000,000; expenditures, $659,038; qualifying distributions, $652,381; giving activities include $652,381 for grants.
Fields of interest: Secondary school/education; Education; Islam.
International interests: Pakistan.
Limitations: Applications not accepted. Giving primarily in CA.
Application information: Contributes only to pre-selected organizations.
Officers: Ahmad Adaya, Pres.; Tehmina Tannir, Secy.; Gazala Shauk, C.F.O.
Directors: Amina Adaya; Salim Adaya; Nargis Dada; Nasreen Haroon; Ruksana Mohammed.
EIN: 954698812

201
Alafi Family Foundation ☆
P.O. Box 7338
Berkeley, CA 94707
Contact: Margaret Alafi, Pres.

Established in 1999 in CA.
Foundation type: Independent foundation.
Financial data (yr. ended 12/31/05): Assets, $2,870,921 (M); gifts received, $200; expenditures, $479,984; qualifying distributions, $478,697; giving activities include $478,697 for 25 grants (high: $220,000; low: $100).
Purpose and activities: Giving primarily for the performing arts, learning disorders, child abuse

prevention, women who are homeless, and biological research on mental disorders.
Fields of interest: Performing arts; Mental health/crisis services; Learning disorders; Neuroscience research; Crime/violence prevention, child abuse; Women, centers/services; Homeless.
Type of support: Matching/challenge support; Grants to individuals; Conferences/seminars; Equipment; Internship funds; Scholarship funds; Research; Scholarships—to individuals.
Limitations: Giving primarily in northern CA. No support for religious or political organizations.
Application information: Application form not required.
   Initial approach: Letter (1-2 pages)
   Copies of proposal: 1
   Deadline(s): None
   Board meeting date(s): Jan. 5, Mar. 6, and Sept. 28
   Final notification: 2-3 weeks
Officers: Margaret Alafi, Pres.; Chris Alafi, V.P.; Shireen Alafi, Secy.; Moshe Alafi, C.F.O.
Number of staff: 4 part-time professional; 1 part-time support.
EIN: 943343568

202
Allequash Foundation ◇
15 S. Raymond Ave., Ste. 202
Pasadena, CA 91105

Established in 1961 in CA.
Donors: Alexander P. Hixon†; Midland Investment Co.; Adelaide F. Hixon.
Foundation type: Independent foundation.
Financial data (yr. ended 12/31/05): Assets, $1,138,865 (M); expenditures, $781,531; qualifying distributions, $759,559; giving activities include $759,559 for 42 grants (high: $500,000; low: $50).
Purpose and activities: Giving primarily for higher education, the arts and media, global activism/affairs, women and families, and youth development.
Fields of interest: Media, radio; Arts; Higher education; Education; Human services; Women, centers/services; International affairs; Federated giving programs; Christian agencies & churches.
Limitations: Applications not accepted. Giving primarily in CA. No grants to individuals.
Application information: Contributes only to pre-selected organizations.
Officers and Director: * Adelaide F. Hixon,* Pres.; Gene Murray, Secy.-Treas.
EIN: 956050003
Selected grants: The following grants were reported in 2004.
$301,000 to Huntington Memorial Hospital, Huntington, IN.
$200,000 to Desmond Tutu Peace Foundation, New York, NY.
$100,000 to Esalen Institute, Big Sur, CA.
$2,000 to Direct Relief International, Santa Barbara, CA.
$2,000 to Human Rights Watch, New York, NY.
$500 to Young and Healthy, Pasadena, CA.

203
The Allergan Foundation ✧
2525 Dupont Dr.
P.O. Box 19534, M.C. T2-7D
Irvine, CA 92623-9534
Contact: Shawn McPherson, Admin.
URL: http://www.allerganfoundation.org

Established in 1998 in GA.
Donor: Allergan, Inc.
Foundation type: Company-sponsored foundation.
Financial data (yr. ended 12/31/04): Assets,
$15,877,230 (M); gifts received, $1,278,000;
expenditures, $2,230,804; qualifying distributions,
$2,145,963; giving activities include $2,119,498
for grants.
Purpose and activities: The foundation supports
organizations involved with arts and culture,
education, health, human services, community
development, and civic affairs.
Fields of interest: Arts; Education; Health care;
Human services; Community development;
Federated giving programs; Public affairs.
Publications: Annual report.
Application information: Application form required.
Initial approach: Download application form and
mail to foundation
Copies of proposal: 1
Deadline(s): May 15 through July 15
Agent: Wachovia Bank, N.A.
EIN: 330794475
Selected grants: The following grants were reported
in 2003.
$150,000 to University of California at Irvine
Foundation, Irvine, CA.
$10,000 to C-Change, DC.
$10,000 to Chapman University, Orange, CA.
$5,000 to Center for the Partially Sighted, Los
Angeles, CA.
$5,000 to Glaucoma Research and Education
Group, San Francisco, CA.
$2,000 to Alzheimers Disease and Related
Disorders Association, Orange, CA.
$2,000 to Blind Childrens Learning Center of Orange
County, Santa Ana, CA.
$2,000 to California Literacy, Pasadena, CA.
$2,000 to California Society for Biomedical
Research, Sacramento, CA.
$2,000 to Tustin Public Schools Foundation, Tustin,
CA.

204
Alliance Healthcare Foundation
9325 Sky Park Ct., Ste. 350
San Diego, CA 92123 (858) 874-3788
Contact: Yolanda Boyd, Grants Admin.
FAX: (858) 874-3656;
E-mail: AllianceHealthcareFoundation@alliancehf.or
g; Address letter of intent to: Linda Lloyd, Dr. P.H.,
V.P., Progs.; Grant Contact for inquiries: Yolanda
Boyd, Grants Admin., tel.: (858) 614-4885, E-mail:
yboyd@alliancehf.org; URL: http://
www.alliancehf.org

Established in 1988 in CA; converted to
Independent foundation as a result of sale of
Community Care Network, Inc. to Value Health in
1994.
Donors: Charles Robins; Margaret Muench;
Kathleen Briggs; National AIDS Fund; AIDS Walk San
Diego, Inc.
Foundation type: Independent foundation.

Financial data (yr. ended 6/30/05): Assets,
$74,548,320 (M); gifts received, $556,188;
expenditures, $3,487,178; qualifying distributions,
$3,284,230; giving activities include $2,079,376
for 75 grants.
Purpose and activities: The mission of the Alliance
Healthcare Foundation is to promote quality health
care in the San Diego, CA, region, with special
emphasis on the medically underserved. We
accomplish this through collaborative grantmaking,
advocacy and education.
Fields of interest: Health care; Mental health/crisis
services, public policy; AIDS; Crime/violence
prevention.
Type of support: General/operating support;
Program development; Seed money; Technical
assistance; Program evaluation.
Limitations: Giving limited to San Diego and Imperial
counties, CA. No grants to individuals, lobbying,
capital campaigns, or construction or renovation.
Publications: Application guidelines; Financial
statement; Grants list; Informational brochure;
Multi-year report (including application guidelines);
Newsletter; Occasional report.
Application information: Eligible organizations may
be invited to submit a full proposal. Application
guidelines available on foundation Web site.
Application form not required.
Initial approach: 3- to 4-page letter of intent
Deadline(s): None
Board meeting date(s): Feb., May, Aug., and Nov.
Final notification: 4-6 weeks
Officers and Trustees: B. Kathlyn Mead,* Chair.;
Irma Cota,* Vice-Chair.; Ruth Lyn Riedel, Ph.D.*,
C.E.O. and Pres.; Linda S. Lloyd, Dr. P.H., V.P.,
Progs.; Elizabeth McPhail,* Treas.; Robert B.
McCray; Rosemary Johnson, M.D.; Phyllis Quan; Joe
Ramsdel, M.D.; Donna J. Walker.
Number of staff: 7 full-time professional.
EIN: 330340635

205
Allianz Foundation for North America ✧
777 San Marin Dr., Ste. A21
Novato, CA 94998
Contact: Rev. Christopher Worthley, Exec. Dir.
E-mail: christopher_worthley@azoac.com;
URL: http://www.allianzgroup.com/foundation-na

Established as a company-sponsored foundation in
2002 in CA by a company incorporated in Germany.
Donor: Allianz AG.
Foundation type: Independent foundation.
Financial data (yr. ended 12/31/05): Assets, $70
(M); gifts received, $360,141; expenditures,
$360,141; qualifying distributions, $360,141;
giving activities include $360,141 for 13 grants
(high: $50,000; low: $12,500).
Purpose and activities: Giving to empower young
people to shape a secure future for themselves and
their communities in which they live by helping them
become successful, self-reliant and socially
conscious.
Fields of interest: Children/youth, services.
Type of support: Program development.
Limitations: Giving on a national basis with an
emphasis on major metropolitan areas. No support
for political parties, candidates or partisan political
organizations, sectarian religious purposes,
fraternal and veteran organizations, fundraising
events, trips or tours, sporting events, or for
advertising. No grants to individuals, or for capital
campaigns, endowments, or medical research.

Publications: Application guidelines.
Application information: Grant guidelines and
application procedures available on foundation Web
site. Application form not required.
Initial approach: One-page project concept paper
to Exec. Dir. before submitting proposal.
Preferably e-mailed
Deadline(s): None
Board meeting date(s): Annually prior to June
Officers and Board Members: Jan Carendi,* Chair.
and Pres.; Emilio Galli-Zugaro,* Exec. V.P.; Richard
Hayes, V.P.; Peter Huehne,* C.F.O.; Katherine K.
Crocker, Secy.; Phyllis Secosky, Treas.; Rev.
Christopher Worthley,* Exec. Dir.; Sabia Schwarzer.
EIN: 680493856

206
The Alon Family Foundation ✧
20384 Glasgow Dr.
Saratoga, CA 95070-4324

Established in 1994 in CA.
Donors: Ruth Alon; Zvi Alon.
Foundation type: Independent foundation.
Financial data (yr. ended 10/31/05): Assets,
$2,791,886 (M); expenditures, $377,805;
qualifying distributions, $355,938; giving activities
include $346,928 for 17 grants (high: $214,288;
low: $100).
Fields of interest: Jewish agencies & temples.
Limitations: Applications not accepted. No grants to
individuals.
Application information: Contributes only to
pre-selected organizations.
Officer: Zvi Alon, Pres.
EIN: 770389665

207
The Alpert & Alpert Foundation ✧
1815 S. Soto St.
Los Angeles, CA 90023-4210 (323) 265-4040
Contact: Jake J. Farber, Pres.

Established in 1974 in CA.
Donors: Raymond Alpert; Jake J. Farber; Alpert &
Alpert Iron & Metal, Inc.; Vista Metals Corp.; V.S.
Trading.
Foundation type: Company-sponsored foundation.
Financial data (yr. ended 6/30/05): Assets,
$308,857 (M); gifts received, $1,700,000;
expenditures, $1,612,200; qualifying distributions,
$1,612,200; giving activities include $1,612,200
for 7 grants (high: $727,500; low: $200).
Purpose and activities: The foundation supports
community foundations and organizations involved
with higher education and Judaism.
Fields of interest: Higher education; Foundations
(community); Jewish federated giving programs;
Jewish agencies & temples.
Type of support: General/operating support.
Limitations: Giving primarily in Long Beach and Los
Angeles, CA. No grants to individuals.
Application information:
Initial approach: Contact foundation for
application information
Deadline(s): None
Officers and Directors: Jake J. Farber,* Pres.; Alan
Alpert,* V.P.; Howard Farber,* V.P.; Raymond
Alpert,* Secy.-Treas.
EIN: 237388729

Selected grants: The following grants were reported in 2005.

$727,500 to Raymond and Barbara Alpert Foundation, Long Beach, CA. For unrestricted support.

$700,000 to Jewish Community Foundation, Los Angeles, CA. For unrestricted support.

$77,500 to Jewish Federation of Greater Long Beach and West Orange County, Long Beach, CA. For unrestricted support.

$55,000 to Jewish Federation Council of Greater Los Angeles, Los Angeles, CA. For unrestricted support.

$50,000 to American Associates, Ben-Gurion University of the Negev, Los Angeles, CA. For unrestricted support.

$2,000 to Theodore Roosevelt Senior High School, Los Angeles, CA. For unrestricted support.

$200 to King David School, Scottsdale, AZ. For unrestricted support.

208
The Herb Alpert Foundation ✧
c/o Rona Sebastian, Pres.
1414 6th St.
Santa Monica, CA 90401

Established in 1988 in CA.
Donor: Herb Alpert.
Foundation type: Independent foundation.
Financial data (yr. ended 12/31/04): Assets, $43,503,849 (M); gifts received, $39,986; expenditures, $4,052,395; qualifying distributions, $3,101,547; giving activities include $3,101,547 for 35 grants (high: $759,478; low: $400).
Purpose and activities: Support primarily for education and the arts.
Fields of interest: Arts education; Arts; Education; Youth development.
Type of support: Seed money; Program development; General/operating support.
Limitations: Applications not accepted. Giving on a national basis, with an emphasis on Los Angeles, CA. No grants to individuals (except for awards program).
Application information: Contributes only to pre-selected organizations.
Officers: Herb Alpert, Chair.; Lani Hall Alpert, Vice-Chair.; Rona Sebastian, Pres.; Werner Wolfen, Secy.
Number of staff: 1 full-time professional; 1 full-time support.
EIN: 954191227

209
Raymond & Barbara Alpert Foundation ✧ ☆
5521 E. La Pasada St.
Long Beach, CA 90815-4320
Contact: Raymond Alpert, Pres.

Established in 1996 in CA.
Donors: Raymond Alpert; Barbara Alpert; Philip Waldman; Teri Alpert.
Foundation type: Independent foundation.
Financial data (yr. ended 12/31/05): Assets, $2,169,464 (M); gifts received, $600,450; expenditures, $418,845; qualifying distributions, $418,845; giving activities include $418,845 for 84 grants (high: $202,000; low: $50).

Fields of interest: Health organizations, association; Jewish agencies & temples.
Limitations: Giving primarily in Long Beach, CA. No grants to individuals.
Application information:
Initial approach: Letter
Deadline(s): None
Officers: Raymond Alpert, Pres.; Barbara Alpert, C.F.O. and Treas.
EIN: 954541253
Selected grants: The following grants were reported in 2004.

$110,000 to Morasha Jewish Day School, Rancho Santa Margarita, CA.
$60,000 to Jewish Federation.
$20,150 to Alpe X Jewish Community.
$6,400 to Temple Israel, Long Beach, CA.
$2,200 to Jewish Vocational Service.
$1,170 to Jewish National Fund, New York, NY.
$500 to Family Service Agency.
$215 to Bnai Brith Youth Organization, San Mateo, CA.
$100 to American Jewish Committee, Los Angeles, CA.
$50 to Long Beach Public Library Foundation, Long Beach, CA.

210
The Lisa & Steve Altman Family Foundation ✧ ☆
17728 Old Winery Way
Poway, CA 92064

Foundation type: Independent foundation.
Financial data (yr. ended 12/31/05): Assets, $1,369,778 (M); gifts received, $876,280; expenditures, $470,537; qualifying distributions, $461,244; giving activities include $461,244 for grants.
Fields of interest: Education; Human services; Jewish federated giving programs; Protestant agencies & churches; Jewish agencies & temples.
Limitations: Applications not accepted. No grants to individuals.
Application information: Contributes only to pre-selected organizations.
Trustees: Lisa Altman; Steve Altman.
EIN: 582667016

211
Jenifer Altman Foundation
P.O. Box 29209
San Francisco, CA 94129 (415) 561-2182
Contact: Ashley Iwanaga
FAX: (415) 561-6480; E-mail: info@jaf.org;
URL: http://www.jaf.org

Established in 1991 in CA.
Donors: Jenifer Altman†; Pinewood Foundation.
Foundation type: Independent foundation.
Financial data (yr. ended 6/30/05): Assets, $13,424,313 (M); expenditures, $1,186,806; qualifying distributions, $706,739; giving activities include $411,500 for 14 grants.
Purpose and activities: The foundation is dedicated to the vision of a socially just and ecologically sustainable future through program interests in environmental health and mind-body health. Funding priorities also include environmental protection, health and environmental research, environmental justice and community coalitions. In the wake of

Hurricanes Katrina and Rita, the foundation expanded its work with grantees and colleagues in the region.
Fields of interest: Environment; Disasters, Hurricane Katrina.
Type of support: General/operating support; Continuing support.
Limitations: Giving on a local, national and international basis, with some emphasis on the Gulf Coast region of the U.S.
Publications: Application guidelines; Grants list; Program policy statement.
Application information: Application guidelines and application cover sheet available on foundation Web site. Application form required.
Initial approach: Letter
Copies of proposal: 1
Deadline(s): None
Board meeting date(s): Fall and spring
Final notification: Generally within 3 months
Officers and Directors:* Michael Lerner, Ph.D.*, Pres.; Catherine Porter,* Secy.; Albert Wells,* Treas.; Anne Bartley; John Peterson Myers.
Number of staff: 2 full-time professional; 1 part-time professional; 1 full-time support.
EIN: 943146675
Selected grants: The following grants were reported in 2004.
$300,000 to Commonweal, Bolinas, CA.
$5,000 to Coastal Health Alliance, Point Reyes Station, CA.

212
Maurice Amado Foundation
3940 Laurel Canyon Blvd., No. 809
Studio City, CA 91604 (818) 980-9190
Contact: Pam Kaizer, Exec. Dir.
FAX: (818) 980-9190;
E-mail: pkaizer@mauriceamadofdn.org; URL: http://www.mauriceamadofdn.org

Incorporated in 1961 in CA.
Donor: Maurice Amado†.
Foundation type: Independent foundation.
Financial data (yr. ended 11/30/05): Assets, $31,585,762 (M); expenditures, $1,483,371; qualifying distributions, $1,235,131; giving activities include $1,063,175 for 77 grants (high: $62,000; low: $500).
Purpose and activities: Support primarily for activities that promote Sephardic Jewish culture and heritage.
Fields of interest: Arts; Education; Jewish agencies & temples.
Type of support: General/operating support; Continuing support; Program development; Publication; Curriculum development; Research.
Limitations: Giving on a national basis, with some emphasis on Los Angeles, CA, and New York, NY. No grants to individuals directly.
Publications: Application guidelines; Grants list; Informational brochure (including application guidelines).
Application information: Check foundation Web site for guidelines. Letter should be on organizational letterhead. When sending public relations materials, please include five copies. Application form not required.
Initial approach: Letter or telephone
Copies of proposal: 5
Deadline(s): Aug. 30 and Feb. 15
Board meeting date(s): Biannually
Final notification: Late Nov. and late May

Officers and Directors:* Ralph D. Amado,* Pres.; Bernice Amado,* V.P. and Secy.; Samuel R. Tarica,* V.P.; Pam Kaizer, Exec. Dir.; Ralph A. Amado; Victor Lavis; Susan Malcolm; Mark Tarica.
Number of staff: 1 part-time professional.
EIN: 956041700

213
Amar Foundation ◇

c/o McCabe & Totah, LLP
1760 The Almeda, Ste. 300
San Jose, CA 95126

Established in 1987 in CA.
Donors: Neeru Khosla; Vinod Khosla.
Foundation type: Independent foundation.
Financial data (yr. ended 12/31/04): Assets, $8,325,359 (M); expenditures, $1,390,608; qualifying distributions, $1,281,713; giving activities include $1,281,703 for 10 grants (high: $300,000; low: $19,300).
Purpose and activities: Giving primarily for education, and to organizations concerning India.
Fields of interest: Education; Human services; Children, services; International affairs.
International interests: India.
Limitations: Applications not accepted. Giving primarily in CA. No grants to individuals.
Application information: Contributes only to pre-selected organizations.
Officers and Director:* Neeru Khosla,* Pres.; Vinod Khosla, Secy.
EIN: 943055731
Selected grants: The following grants were reported in 2004.
$360,000 to Global Peace Networks, Santa Clara, CA.
$300,000 to DonorsChoose, New York, NY. For Bay Area expansion project.
$300,000 to Grameen Foundation USA, DC. For general support.
$167,000 to Stanford Center for Economic Policy Research, Stanford, CA.
$65,400 to Nueva School, Hillsborough, CA. For general support.
$25,000 to American Indiana Foundation, Milpitas, CA. For general support.
$25,000 to Pacific Vascular Research Foundation, San Francisco, CA. For general support.
$20,000 to Stanford University, School of Engineering, Stanford, CA.
$19,300 to United States Ski and Snowboard Association, Park City, UT. For general support.

214
Amateur Athletic Foundation of Los Angeles

2141 W. Adams Blvd.
Los Angeles, CA 90018-2040 (323) 730-4600
Contact: F. Patrick Escobar, V.P., Grants and Progs.
FAX: (323) 730-9637; E-mail: info@aafla.org;
URL: http://www.aafla.org

Established in 1982 in CA.
Donor: Los Angeles Olympic Organizing Comm.
Foundation type: Independent foundation.
Financial data (yr. ended 12/31/05): Assets, $156,187,554 (M); expenditures, $10,952,598; qualifying distributions, $9,265,628; giving activities include $5,461,940 for 180 grants (high: $3,000,000; low: $118; average: $1,000–

$35,000), and $2,605,504 for 4 foundation-administered programs.
Purpose and activities: Support for youth sports programs, especially in areas where the risk of delinquency is high. Special attention to sectors of the population underserved by current sports programs: girls, minorities, and the disabled.
Fields of interest: Athletics/sports, training; Athletics/sports, amateur leagues; Youth development; Youth, services; Girls.
Type of support: Capital campaigns; Building/renovation; Equipment; Program development; Matching/challenge support.
Limitations: Giving limited to eight southern CA counties. No grants to individuals, endowments, travel outside of southern CA, single, public, or private school facilities or programs not including sports schools, routine operating expenses, purchase of land, debt recovery (or incurring debt liability).
Publications: Application guidelines; Biennial report; Biennial report (including application guidelines).
Application information: Application form not required.
  Initial approach: Proposal
  Copies of proposal: 3
  Deadline(s): None
  Board meeting date(s): 3 times per year
  Final notification: 4 weeks
Officers and Directors:* Peter V. Ueberroth,* Chair.; Anita L. DeFrantz,* Pres.; Conrad R. Freund, C.O.O.; F. Patrick Escobar, V.P., Grants and Progs.; Wayne Wilson, V.P., Education Services; John E. Bryson; Yvonne Brathwaite Burke; Jae Min Chang; James L. Easton; Janet Evans; Priscilla Florence; Robert V. Graziano; Rafer Johnson; Maureen Kindel; Thomas E. Larkin, Jr.; Charles D. Miller; Peter O'Malley; Joan A. Payden; Amy Quinn; Frank M. Sanchez; Gilbert R. Vasquez; David L. Wolper; John Ziffren.
Number of staff: 18 full-time professional; 3 part-time professional.
EIN: 953792725
Selected grants: The following grants were reported in 2005.
$450,000 to Kids In Sports, Los Angeles, CA.
$366,988 to LAs BEST (Better Educated Students for Tomorrow), Los Angeles, CA.
$200,000 to Tiger Woods Foundation, Los Alamitos, CA. For putting course at the new Tiger Woods Learning Center.
$82,000 to Woodley Park Archers, Northridge, CA. For implementing a mobile archery program at park sites throughout Los Angeles.
$60,000 to King Harbor Youth Foundation, Redondo Beach, CA. For learn-to-sail program.
$50,000 to YMCA, Channel Islands, Santa Barbara, CA. For gymnasium floor at new facility.
$20,849 to Youth Mentoring Connection, Los Angeles, CA. For surf and snowboarding program.
$19,100 to Samoan National Nurses Association, Carson, CA. For volleyball program.
$19,008 to Boys and Girls Club, Burbank, Burbank, CA. For after-school soccer program at Washington, Miller Elementary Schools and Luther Middle School.
$13,705 to Diamond Bar Little League, Diamond Bar, CA. For new fence to protect Stephens Fields.

215
American Foundation for Courtesy and Grooming ◇

(formerly DL Foundation)
10100 Santa Monica Blvd., Ste. 1300
Los Angeles, CA 90067

Established in 1993 in NY.
Donor: David Letterman.
Foundation type: Independent foundation.
Financial data (yr. ended 12/31/04): Assets, $41,428 (M); gifts received, $637,062; expenditures, $622,938; qualifying distributions, $622,938; giving activities include $622,913 for 46 grants (high: $230,000; low: $100).
Purpose and activities: Giving primarily for children's services and education.
Fields of interest: Media, television; Performing arts centers; Historic preservation/historical societies; Arts; Elementary/secondary education; Higher education; Education; Environment, natural resources; Cancer research; Parkinson's disease research; Human services; Children, services; Residential/custodial care.
Limitations: Applications not accepted. Giving primarily in IN and NY; limited giving nationally. No grants to individuals.
Application information: Contributes only to pre-selected organizations.
Officers: David Letterman, Pres.; M.M. Mulrooney, Secy.; F. Nigro, Treas.
EIN: 223250026
Selected grants: The following grants were reported in 2003.
$230,000 to Child Advocates. For general support.
$40,000 to Ball State University Foundation, Muncie, IN. For general support.
$35,000 to Indianapolis Art Center, Indianapolis, IN. For general support.
$25,000 to Indiana School for the Deaf, Indianapolis, IN. For general support.
$25,000 to Nineveh-Hensley-Jackson United School Corporation, Trafalgar, IN. For general support.
$10,000 to Marion County Child Advocacy Center, Indianapolis, IN. For general support.
$10,000 to Muscular Dystrophy Family Foundation, Indianapolis, IN. For general support.
$10,000 to Riley Childrens Foundation, Indianapolis, IN. For general support.
$3,500 to Hole in the Wall Gang Fund, New Haven, CT. For general support.
$900 to Choteau High School, Choteau, MT. For general support.

216
American Friends of the Citizens Empowerment Center in Israel ◇

9420 Wilshire Blvd., 4th Fl.
Beverly Hills, CA 90212
FAX: (310) 300-4101; E-mail: ceci@cecisrael.org;
URL: http://www.cecisrael.org

Established in 2003 in CA.
Donors: Eli Sassouni; Ebrahim Simhaee; Parviz Nazarian; Nahai Insurance Services.
Foundation type: Independent foundation.
Financial data (yr. ended 12/31/04): Assets, $130,116 (M); gifts received, $608,160; expenditures, $690,633; qualifying distributions, $357,000; giving activities include $102,000 for 2 grants, and $255,000 for 1 foundation-administered program.

Purpose and activities: The organization is dedicated to initiating and establishing learning centers for the purpose of education and research in governance and voting systems.
Fields of interest: Education; International affairs; Jewish agencies & temples.
International interests: Israel.
Limitations: Applications not accepted. Giving primarily in Tel Aviv, Israel; some funding in Sherman Oaks, CA. No grants to individuals.
Application information: Contributes only to pre-selected organizations.
Officers and Directors:* Parviz Nazarian,* C.E.O.; Brian Weiner,* Secy.; Yoav Peled,* C.F.O.; and 21 additional directors.
EIN: 320050648

217

American Honda Foundation ✧
1919 Torrance Blvd., M.S. 100-1W-5A
Torrance, CA 90501   (310) 781-4090
Contact: Kathryn A. Carey, Mgr.
FAX: (310) 781-4270;
E-mail: kathryn_carey@ahm.honda.com; Application address: P.O. Box 2205, Torrance, CA 90509-2205; URL: http://corporate.honda.com/america/philanthropy.aspx?id=ahf

Established in 1984 in CA.
Donor: American Honda Motor Co., Inc.
Foundation type: Company-sponsored foundation.
Financial data (yr. ended 3/31/04): Assets, $31,493,533 (M); gifts received, $1,000,000; expenditures, $1,600,852; qualifying distributions, $1,350,206; giving activities include $1,350,206 for 26 grants.
Purpose and activities: The foundation supports organizations involved with education, the environment, employment, human services, science, minorities, Native Americans, and economically disadvantaged people.
Fields of interest: Education, association; Education, early childhood education; Elementary school/education; Secondary school/education; Vocational education; Higher education; Education; Environment, natural resources; Environment; Employment, services; Employment; Children/youth, services; Human services; Physical/earth sciences; Chemistry; Mathematics; Physics; Engineering/technology; Biological sciences; Science; Minorities; Native Americans/American Indians; Economically disadvantaged.
Type of support: General/operating support; Continuing support; Program development; Seed money; Curriculum development; Matching/challenge support.
Limitations: Giving on a national basis. No support for religious, political, veterans', or fraternal organizations, private foundations, labor groups, or arts and culture or health organizations. No grants to individuals, or for trips, general operating support for hospitals, building or renovation, youth recreational activities, annual campaigns, fundraising, student foreign exchange programs, sponsorships, corporate memberships, medical or educational research, conferences or seminars, disaster relief, beauty or talent contests, or welfare or social issues; no small business loans.
Publications: Application guidelines; Biennial report (including application guidelines); Grants list; Informational brochure (including application guidelines); Multi-year report; Program policy statement.

Application information: Application form required.
Initial approach: Download application form and mail proposal and application form to application address
Copies of proposal: 1
Deadline(s): Nov. 1, Feb. 1, May 1, and Aug. 1
Board meeting date(s): Jan., Apr., July, and Oct.
Final notification: 2 months
Officers and Directors:* Hiroshi Soda,* Pres.; Gary Kessler,* V.P.; Thomas Ross,* Secy.-Treas.; Kathryn A. Carey, Exec. Dir.; Kent Dellinger; Abrahm Dent; Lou Juneman; Wade Terry; Jeanette Tomikawa.
Number of staff: 4 full-time professional.
EIN: 953924667
Selected grants: The following grants were reported in 2005.
$100,000 to Sequatchie County Schools, Dunlap, TN.
$80,000 to Galef Institute, Los Angeles, CA.
$75,000 to Kiss Institute for Practical Robotics, Norman, OK.
$75,000 to Texas State University, San Marcos, TX.
$60,000 to Urban Education Partnership, Los Angeles, CA.
$50,080 to Charles R. Drew University of Medicine and Science, Los Angeles, CA.
$50,000 to Music Intelligence Neural Development (MIND) Institute, Costa Mesa, CA.
$50,000 to School on Wheels, Malibu, CA.
$42,740 to National Wildlife Federation, Boulder, CO.
$40,950 to Metropolitan School District of Washington Township, Indianapolis, IN.

218

Amerman Family Foundation ✧
P.O. Box 479
Santa Ysabel, CA 92070

Established in 1997 in CA.
Donors: Jerome T. Amerman; John W. Amerman.
Foundation type: Independent foundation.
Financial data (yr. ended 12/31/05): Assets, $3,822,623 (M); expenditures, $580,510; qualifying distributions, $479,500; giving activities include $479,500 for 9 grants (high: $100,000; low: $30,000).
Purpose and activities: Giving primarily for higher education, children and youth services, a children's hospital, and to a zoological society; funding also for an equine retirement foundation.
Fields of interest: Higher education; Education; Zoos/zoological societies; Hospitals (specialty); Substance abuse, prevention; Substance abuse, treatment; Human services; Children/youth, services.
Limitations: Applications not accepted. Giving primarily in CA. No grants to individuals.
Application information: Contributes only to pre-selected organizations.
Officers: John W. Amerman, Pres.; Anne H. Thompson, Secy.; Jerome T. Amerman, Treas.
Directors: Anne J. Amerman; Garrett J. Amerman; Glenn Bozarth; John Conners.
EIN: 330757355
Selected grants: The following grants were reported in 2004.
$100,000 to University of Kentucky, Lexington, KY.
$93,500 to Zoological Society of San Diego, San Diego, CA.

$50,000 to Mattel Childrens Hospital at the University of California at Los Angeles, Los Angeles, CA.
$50,000 to Phoenix House, New York, NY.
$30,200 to University of Florida, Gainesville, FL.
$22,000 to California Equine Retirement Foundation, Winchester, CA.

219

Amgen Foundation, Inc. ▼
1 Amgen Center Dr., M.S. 28-1-B
Thousand Oaks, CA 91320-1799
(805) 447-4056
FAX: (805) 449-6757;
E-mail: amgenfoundation@amgen.com; URL: http://www.amgen.com/citizenship/foundation.html

Established in 1991 in CA.
Donor: Amgen Inc.
Foundation type: Company-sponsored foundation.
Financial data (yr. ended 12/31/05): Assets, $108,573,406 (M); gifts received, $25,521,417; expenditures, $17,708,665; qualifying distributions, $16,541,439; giving activities include $16,541,439 for grants.
Purpose and activities: The foundation supports organizations involved with arts and culture, science education, health, human services, and community development.
Fields of interest: Arts; Education; Health care, equal rights; Health care; Human services; Community development; Science.
Type of support: Research; Endowments; Capital campaigns; Program evaluation; Program development; General/operating support; Employee matching gifts.
Limitations: Giving primarily in areas of company operations in CA, CO, PR, RI, and WA; giving also to regional and national organizations. No support for religious organizations not of direct benefit to the entire community, political organizations, labor unions or fraternal, service, or veterans' organizations, international organizations, private foundations, or discriminatory organizations. No grants to individuals, or for fundraising or sports-related events, corporate sponsorships, or lobbying activities.
Publications: Application guidelines; Annual report.
Application information: Support is limited to 1 contribution per organization during any given year. Application form required.
Initial approach: Complete online application form
Deadline(s): None
Board meeting date(s): Quarterly
Officer and Directors:* Jean J. Lim,* Pres.; Fabrizio Bonanni; H. Christian Fibiger; Brian M. McNamee; Richard D. Nanula; Phyllis Piano; David J. Scott; Helen I. Torley.
EIN: 770252898
Selected grants: The following grants were reported in 2004.
$1,500,000 to Boys and Girls Clubs of Conejo and Las Virgenes, Calabasas, CA.
$1,000,000 to American Health Quality Foundation, DC.
$1,000,000 to California Science Center Foundation, Los Angeles, CA.
$1,000,000 to UCLA Foundation, Los Angeles, CA.
$500,000 to Childrens Charities Foundation, DC.
$452,797 to Cancer Research and Prevention Foundation, Alexandria, VA.
$35,000 to Impact on Education, Boulder, CO.

$25,000 to Performing Arts Center of Los Angeles
County, Los Angeles, CA.
$20,000 to Boys and Girls Club of Santa Clara
Valley, Santa Paula, CA.
$20,000 to Estes Park Medical Center Foundation,
Estes Park, CO.

220
Anaheim Community Foundation ✧
200 S. Anaheim Blvd., Ste. 433
Anaheim, CA 92805-3820 (714) 765-4419
Contact: Terry D. Lowe, C.E.O.; For grant requests:
Nancy Lerner Boone, Recreation Svcs. Mgr.
FAX: (714) 765-4454;
E-mail: messageto@anaheimcommfound.org;
Additional tel.: (714) 765-5250; URL: http://
www.anaheimcommfound.org

Established in 1984 in CA.
Foundation type: Community foundation.
Financial data (yr. ended 6/30/05): Assets,
$794,262 (M); gifts received, $342,661;
expenditures, $363,735; giving activities include
$352,064 for grants.
Purpose and activities: The foundation seeks to: 1)
encourage community participation, partnerships,
and collaboration that result in successful
responses to community challenges and
opportunities; 2) strengthen community-based
organizations that effectively address community
needs, promote volunteerism, and provide
community leadership; 3) promote
community-building programs and events that
inspire community pride and unity; and 4) provide
individuals and business opportunities to make
charitable investments that directly benefit the
Anaheim community.
Fields of interest: Arts; Libraries/library science;
Environment; Medical care, rehabilitation;
Substance abuse, services; Crime/violence
prevention, youth; Athletics/sports, Special
Olympics; Youth development, services; Youth
development; Human services, emergency aid;
Aging, centers/services; Human services; Youth;
Aging.
Type of support: General/operating support;
Emergency funds; Program development;
Scholarships—to individuals.
Limitations: Giving limited to the Anaheim, CA, area.
No support for religious or proselytizing activities.
Publications: Application guidelines; Annual report;
Informational brochure.
Application information: Visit foundation Web site
for application form and guidelines. Application form
required.
  Initial approach: Telephone to determine eligibility
  Copies of proposal: 5
  Deadline(s): Feb. 28 for grants; Mar. 18 for
    scholarships
  Board meeting date(s): 1st Mon. of each month
Officers and Directors:* Terry D. Lowe,* C.E.O.;
Bruce Solari,* Pres.; Marcie Edwards,* V.P.;
Michael Ambrosi,* Secy.; Steve Faessel,* Secy.;
Jeffery Hunter,* C.F.O.; Sarah Alevizon; Suzi Brown;
Nathan Jurczyk; Charles Malley; Dawn E. Miller;
Michael D. Neben; Al R. Peraza; Irv Pickler; Joaquin
Quesada; Michael Rubin; Jim Ruth; Bernard
Schneider; Greg Smith; Jacquelyn Terrell; Frances
Wiseman.
EIN: 330033023

221
Irene W. & Guy L. Anderson Children's
Foundation ☆
c/o Rita Grazdan
1111 Tahquitz Canyon Way, Ste. 109
Palm Springs, CA 92262 (760) 318-8146
FAX: (760) 318-8155;
E-mail: andersongrants@aol.com; URL: http://
www.andersongrants.org

Established in 1970 in CA.
Foundation type: Independent foundation.
Financial data (yr. ended 11/30/05): Assets,
$26,141,222 (M); expenditures, $2,301,457;
qualifying distributions, $813,539; giving activities
include $687,850 for 58 grants (high: $29,200;
low: $200).
Purpose and activities: The foundation makes grant
money available to any non-profit group or
organization in the Coachella Valley whose purpose
is to meet the unmet needs of the youth of the
Coachella Valley.
Fields of interest: Education; Youth development;
Youth, services; Family services.
Type of support: General/operating support;
Continuing support; Program development; Program
evaluation.
Limitations: Giving limited to the Coachella Valley,
CA. No grants to individuals.
Publications: Grants list; Newsletter.
Application information: See foundation Web site
for additional application information. Application
form required.
  Initial approach: Request application
  Copies of proposal: 8
  Deadline(s): June
Trustee: William A. Schlesinger.
Number of staff: 2 full-time professional; 7 part-time
professional.
EIN: 237089096

222
A. Gary Anderson Family Foundation ✧
300 S. Harbor Blvd., Ste. 1010
Anaheim, CA 92805
Contact: Erin J. Lastinger, C.E.O.

Established in 1992 in CA.
Donor: Anderson Family Administrative Trust.
Foundation type: Independent foundation.
Financial data (yr. ended 12/31/03): Assets,
$73,246,862 (M); gifts received, $521,463;
expenditures, $3,715,107; qualifying distributions,
$3,162,691; giving activities include $2,665,064
for 54 grants (high: $500,000; low: $50; average:
$1,000–$25,000).
Fields of interest: Arts; Higher education; Human
services.
Limitations: Giving primarily in CA. No grants to
individuals.
Application information: Application form required.
  Initial approach: Letter
  Copies of proposal: 5
  Deadline(s): None
Officers and Trustees:* Erin Jette Lastinger,*
C.E.O. and Pres.; Erik Kjell Anderson,* V.P.; Nancy
S. Larson, Treas.; Gary N. Babick; Daniel S. Coelho;
Frank E. O'Bryan.
EIN: 330550267
Selected grants: The following grants were reported
in 2004.

$522,000 to Big Brothers/Big Sisters. 4 grants:
  $500,000, $6,000, $6,000, $10,000
$300,000 to Chapman University, Orange, CA.
$125,000 to Canyon Acres Childrens Services,
  Anaheim, CA.
$30,000 to Seabury Hall, Makawao, HI.

223
The Angelica Foundation ✧ ☆
P.O. Box 675814
Rancho Santa Fe, CA 92067-5814
(858) 756-6756

Established in 1994 in CA.
Donors: Ruben and Elizabeth Ransing Trust; The
Keller Group Investment.
Foundation type: Independent foundation.
Financial data (yr. ended 12/31/05): Assets,
$6,006,108 (M); gifts received, $305,340;
expenditures, $937,540; qualifying distributions,
$630,664; giving activities include $317,121 for 26
grants (high: $108,000; low: $11).
Purpose and activities: Giving primarily to support
progressive organizations working for democratic
change, environmental sustainability, and social
justice.
Fields of interest: Arts; Higher education, university;
Education; Environment, forests; Environment;
Human services; International human rights.
International interests: Latin America; Mexico.
Type of support: Annual campaigns.
Limitations: Applications not accepted. No support
for public education, political organizations, or
programs promoting religious doctrines. No grants
to individuals, or for academic scholarships,
conferences, or fundraising events.
Publications: Annual report.
Officers and Directors: Suzanne D. Gollin,* Pres.;
James D. Gollin,* Secy.-Treas.; Christopher Brown;
Nancy Harris Campbell; Nina Royal; Gladys Schmidt.
Number of staff: 1 part-time professional; 2
part-time support.
EIN: 330632647
Selected grants: The following grants were reported
in 2004.
$157,268 to Tides Foundation, San Francisco, CA.
  3 grants: $149,768, $2,500, $5,000
$16,000 to Center for Economic Justice,
  Albuquerque, NM.
$14,335 to Threshold Foundation, San Francisco,
  CA. 2 grants: $4,335, $10,000
$10,000 to Permacultura America Latina, Santa Fe,
  NM.
$6,000 to League of Conservation Voters, DC.
$4,500 to Ruckus Society, Berkeley, CA.
$1,000 to Friends of the River, Sacramento, CA.

224
The Angell Foundation ✧ ☆
10880 Wilshire Blvd., Ste. 920
Los Angeles, CA 90024 (310) 475-9700
Contact: Perry Oretzky, Pres.

Donor: Angell Family Trust.
Foundation type: Independent foundation.
Financial data (yr. ended 6/30/05): Assets,
$29,542,514 (M); gifts received, $12,100,000;
expenditures, $1,181,094; qualifying distributions,
$1,094,222; giving activities include $1,007,450
for 17+ grants (high: $600,000).

Purpose and activities: Giving limited to youth, education, spirituality, the arts, and social justice in southern CA and in New England.
Fields of interest: Arts; Education; Civil rights, advocacy; Spirituality; Youth.
Limitations: Giving primarily in southern CA and New England.
Application information:
Initial approach: Initial contact letter
Deadline(s): None
Officers: Perry Oretzky, Pres.; Marian Bukrinsky, Secy.
EIN: 010789717

225
Appleton Foundation ◇
c/o Bruce Alexander Gaguine
P.O. Box 1460
Santa Cruz, CA 95061

Established in 1998 in CA.
Donors: Alexander Gaguine; Jane Yett; John Hellwig; John Gaguine; Benito Gaguine.
Foundation type: Independent foundation.
Financial data (yr. ended 12/31/05): Assets, $53,043 (M); expenditures, $880,008; qualifying distributions, $847,152; giving activities include $847,152 for 58 grants (high: $350,000; low: $500).
Fields of interest: Education; Environment; Health care; Human services; International affairs; Community development.
Type of support: General/operating support.
Limitations: Applications not accepted. Giving primarily in CA, Washington, DC, and NY; funding also in Medellin, Colombia; San Jose, Costa Rica; Guayaquil, Ecuador; Mexico City, Mexico; and Managua, Nicaragua. No grants to individuals.
Application information: Contributes only to pre-selected organizations.
Officers: Alexander Gaguine, Pres.; Jane Yett, Secy.
Director: John Hellwig.
EIN: 911792407

226
The Applied Materials Foundation ▼ ◇
c/o Mike O'Farrell
3050 Bowers Ave., M.S. 2033
Santa Clara, CA 95054

Established in 1994.
Donor: Applied Materials, Inc.
Foundation type: Company-sponsored foundation.
Financial data (yr. ended 10/31/04): Assets, $3,755,883 (M); expenditures, $7,408,551; qualifying distributions, $7,407,063; giving activities include $7,407,063 for 174 grants (high: $862,000; low: $100).
Purpose and activities: The foundation supports organizations involved with arts and culture, education, and human services.
Fields of interest: Arts; Education; Human services.
Limitations: Applications not accepted. Giving primarily in CA. No grants to individuals.
Application information: Contributes only to pre-selected organizations.
Officers: James C. Morgan, Pres.; Michael K. O'Farrell, V.P.; Charmaine Mesina, Secy.; George Davis, C.F.O.
EIN: 770386898

Selected grants: The following grants were reported in 2004.
$862,000 to Cornell University, College of Engineering, Ithaca, NY. For Teaching Laboratory.
$400,000 to Housing Trust of Santa Clara County, San Jose, CA. For 2 Plus 2 Equals 2000 Campaign.
$350,000 to East Side Union High School District, San Jose, CA. For Center for Professional Excellence, continuing education for adults and continuous improvement for staff.
$250,000 to National Hispanic University, San Jose, CA. For Building Today, Shaping Tomorrow.
$218,703 to World Reach, Bethesda, MD. 2 grants: $118,563 (For general support), $100,140 (For general support).
$190,000 to Second Harvest Food Bank of Santa Clara and San Mateo Counties, San Jose, CA. For Holiday Food Drive.
$130,000 to Arts Council Silicon Valley, San Jose, CA. For Excellence in the Arts Fund.
$50,000 to Teach for America, Emeryville, CA. For general support.
$28,500 to University of Texas, School of Engineering, Austin, TX. For engineering program.

227
The Aquila Foundation ◇ ☆
P.O. Box 6278
Oakland, CA 94608
Contact: Ron J. Boehm, Pres.

Established in 1992 in CA.
Donor: Trans-Box Systems, Inc.
Foundation type: Company-sponsored foundation.
Financial data (yr. ended 9/30/04): Assets, $30,451 (M); gifts received, $387,154; expenditures, $380,245; qualifying distributions, $380,245; giving activities include $318,545 for 3 + grants.
Purpose and activities: The foundation supports Christian agencies and churches and organizations involved with education and other areas.
Fields of interest: Education; Christian agencies & churches; General charitable giving.
Limitations: Giving primarily in HI and OR.
Application information: Application form not required.
Initial approach: Proposal
Deadline(s): None
Officers: Ron J. Boehm, Pres.; Charlotte Boehm, V.P.; Linda Critchfield, Secy.; Bob Willis, Treas.
EIN: 943162459

228
Aramont Foundation ◇
c/o Gibson Dunn & Crutcher, LLP
2029 Century Park E., Ste. 4000
Los Angeles, CA 90067-3026

Established in 2003 in CA.
Donor: Jeronimo Arango.
Foundation type: Independent foundation.
Financial data (yr. ended 12/31/05): Assets, $6,140,320 (M); expenditures, $471,678; qualifying distributions, $450,045; giving activities include $450,000 for grants.
Purpose and activities: Support for institutions of higher learning.
Fields of interest: Higher education.

Limitations: Applications not accepted. Giving on a national basis, with some emphasis on CA and MA. No grants to individuals.
Application information: Contributes only to pre-selected organizations.
Trustees: Javier F. Arango; William Stinehart, Jr.
EIN: 686230212

229
Arata Brothers Trust ◇
P.O. Box 430
Sacramento, CA 95812-0430

Trust established in 1976 in CA.
Foundation type: Independent foundation.
Financial data (yr. ended 12/31/05): Assets, $8,205,741 (M); expenditures, $677,111; qualifying distributions, $479,500; giving activities include $479,500 for 58 grants (high: $40,000; low: $750).
Purpose and activities: Giving primarily for health, education, religious organizations and social services.
Fields of interest: Arts; Elementary/secondary education; Law school/education; Education; Health care; Health organizations, association; Medical research, institute; Human services; Children/youth, services; Christian agencies & churches; Blind/visually impaired.
Type of support: General/operating support.
Limitations: Giving primarily in CA, with emphasis on Sacramento. No grants to individuals.
Application information: Application form not required.
Initial approach: Letter
Deadline(s): None
Trustees: Francis B. Dillon; Renato R. Parenti; Mark Sewell.
EIN: 237204615

230
Aratani Foundation ◇
23505 Crenshaw Blvd., No. 230
Torrance, CA 90505
Contact: George T. Aratani, Pres.

Established in 1992 in CA.
Donors: George T. Aratani; Sakaye I. Aratani.
Foundation type: Independent foundation.
Financial data (yr. ended 12/31/03): Assets, $31,175,916 (M); expenditures, $948,612; qualifying distributions, $731,362; giving activities include $731,362 for 75 grants (high: $164,982; low: $82).
Purpose and activities: Giving primarily to Japanese-American cultural organizations.
Fields of interest: Museums; Education; Health care; Recreation; Religion.
Type of support: General/operating support; Continuing support; Income development; Management development/capacity building; Annual campaigns; Capital campaigns; Building/renovation; Endowments; Program development; Conferences/seminars; Seed money; Curriculum development; Fellowships; Scholarship funds; Exchange programs.
Limitations: Giving primarily in Los Angeles, CA. No grants to individuals.
Application information: Application outline is available. Application form not required.
Initial approach: Letter

Copies of proposal: 1
Deadline(s): None
Board meeting date(s): As needed
Officers: George T. Aratani, Pres.; Tets Murata, V.P.; Sakaye I. Aratani, Secy.
Number of staff: 1 full-time professional; 3 full-time support.
EIN: 954377347
Selected grants: The following grants were reported in 2003.
$164,924 to Japanese American Cultural and Community Center, Los Angeles, CA.
$150,258 to California State Polytechnic University, Pomona, CA.
$50,000 to University of California, Los Angeles, CA.
$17,000 to Asian Pacific American Legal Center of Southern California, Los Angeles, CA.
$10,000 to National Japanese American Memorial Foundation, DC.
$5,000 to Japanese Community Pioneer Social Service Center, Los Angeles, CA.
$5,000 to Morikami Museum and Japanese Gardens, Delray Beach, FL.
$2,604 to Japanese Chamber of Commerce, New York, NY.
$2,500 to Asian Pacific Community Fund of Southern California, Los Angeles, CA.
$1,750 to Little Tokyo Service Center, Los Angeles, CA.

231

The Loreen Arbus Foundation ✧
c/o Michael Schneider & Co.
137 Spinnaker Mall
Marina Del Rey, CA 90292

Established in 2004 in CA.
Donor: Loreen Arbus.
Foundation type: Independent foundation.
Financial data (yr. ended 12/31/05): Assets, $528,534 (M); gifts received, $1,298,786; expenditures, $977,606; qualifying distributions, $977,606; giving activities include $548,738 for 57 grants (high: $135,697; low: $40).
Purpose and activities: Giving primarily for medical research and for support for women in the arts, media, and business industries, with an emphasis on equity and workforce preparedness.
Fields of interest: Museums; Higher education; Health organizations, association; Medical research, institute; Human services; Women, centers/services.
Limitations: Applications not accepted. Giving primarily in Los Angeles, CA and in New York, NY. No grants to individuals.
Application information: Contributes only to pre-selected organizations.
Officers: Loreen Arbus, Pres.; Norman Fox, V.P.; Holly Toplitzky, Secy.-Treas.
EIN: 753126107

232

Archstone Foundation
401 E. Ocean Blvd., Ste. 1000
Long Beach, CA 90802-4933 (562) 590-8655
Contact: E. Thomas Brewer, Dir., Progs.
FAX: (562) 495-0317;
E-mail: archstone@archstone.org; URL: http://www.archstone.org

Established in 1985 in CA; created as a result of the conversion of the nonprofit FHP health maintenance organization; status changed to a private foundation in 1998.
Foundation type: Independent foundation.
Financial data (yr. ended 6/30/05): Assets, $117,280,783 (M); expenditures, $6,229,571; qualifying distributions, $6,128,091; giving activities include $4,724,580 for 95 grants (high: $586,761; low: $600; average: $1,000–$90,000).
Purpose and activities: Giving toward the preparation of society in meeting the needs of an aging population. The majority of the foundation's resources are allocated to programs that address elder abuse prevention, fall prevention among the elderly, end-of-life issues, and emerging needs within the field of aging.
Fields of interest: Geriatrics; Gerontology; Aging.
Type of support: Program development; Conferences/seminars; Publication; Curriculum development; Technical assistance; Program evaluation.
Limitations: Giving primarily in southern CA. No support for biomedical research. No grants to individuals, or for capital expenditures, or bricks and mortar, or building campaigns, endowments or for fundraising.
Publications: Application guidelines; Annual report (including application guidelines); Occasional report.
Application information: Full proposal will be requested by the foundation. Proposals by fax not accepted. Copy of the proposal on CD-ROM is requested in MS Word. See foundation Web site for letter of inquiry grant application coversheet, application guidelines, procedures, and forms. Application form required.
Initial approach: Letter of inquiry
Copies of proposal: 1
Deadline(s): See foundation Web site for deadlines
Board meeting date(s): Quarterly
Final notification: Approximately 1 month response time to letter of inquiry
Officers and Directors:* Hon. John T. Knox,* Chair.; Joseph F. Prevratil,* C.E.O. and Pres.; Mary Ellen Kullman, V.P.; Len Hughes Andrus, M.D.; Robert C. Maxson, Ed.D.; J. W. Peltason, Ph.D.; Hon. Renee B. Simon; Mark Douglas Smith, M.D.; Rahamin "Rocky" Suares; Hon. Harriett M. Wieder.
Number of staff: 5 full-time professional; 1 full-time support.
EIN: 330133359
Selected grants: The following grants were reported in 2005.
$674,822 to University of California, Los Angeles, CA. 2 grants: $88,061 (To expand memory training program for seniors), $586,761 (To develop Fall Prevention Center of Excellence).
$306,000 to California State University, Fullerton, CA. To develop Fall Prevention Center of Excellence.
$194,555 to City of Hope National Medical Center, Duarte, CA. To offer End-of-Life Nursing Education Consortium training program in Southern California.
$177,965 to California State University at Long Beach Foundation, Long Beach, CA. For statewide geriatric workforce development project.
$121,500 to Alzheimers Association of Los Angeles, Riverside and San Bernadino Counties, Los Angeles, CA. To continue services for

individuals and their families with early stage Alzheimer's disease.
$112,365 to Community Hospital of Long Beach, Long Beach, CA. To continue Intergenerational Resource Center.
$104,400 to Little Tokyo Service Center, Los Angeles, CA. For expansion of services to low-income seniors in Los Angeles County.
$96,750 to Elizabeth Hospice Foundation, Escondido, CA. To continue complementary therapies training program for hospice volunteers and staff.
$36,000 to Info Link Orange County, Costa Mesa, CA. For development of information and referral services for older adults in Orange County.

233

Argosy Foundation ✧
345 California St., 27th Fl.
San Francisco, CA 94104

Donor: Carter P. Thacher.
Foundation type: Independent foundation.
Financial data (yr. ended 12/31/04): Assets, $4,100,494 (M); gifts received, $106,338; expenditures, $471,731; qualifying distributions, $444,361; giving activities include $441,100 for 54 grants (high: $200,000; low: $250).
Purpose and activities: Giving primarily for arts and culture, higher education, and human services.
Fields of interest: Museums (art); Arts; Higher education; Education; Human services.
Limitations: Applications not accepted. Giving primarily in CA, with emphasis on San Francisco. No grants to individuals.
Application information: Contributes only to pre-selected organizations.
Officers: Carter P. Thacher, Pres.; Mary Wilbur Thacher, V.P.; Robert L. Schmalz, Secy.; Herbert B. Tully, C.F.O.
EIN: 943294950

234

The Argyros Foundation ✧
949 S. Coast Dr., No. 600
Costa Mesa, CA 92626 (714) 481-5000
Contact: Daniel Russo, Treas. and Tr.

Established in 1979 in CA.
Donors: George L. Argyros; The Argyros Charitable Trusts; GLA Foundation; HBI Financial Inc.
Foundation type: Independent foundation.
Financial data (yr. ended 7/31/05): Assets, $106,879,420 (M); gifts received, $7,597,013; expenditures, $4,423,202; qualifying distributions, $3,948,882; giving activities include $3,770,502 for 83 grants (high: $1,680,204; low: $99; average: $2,000–$50,000).
Purpose and activities: Giving primarily to arts and cultural programs, education, health care, youth development, and human services.
Fields of interest: Arts; Education; Eye research; Youth development, services; Children/youth, services; Marine science.
Type of support: Program development; Scholarship funds.
Limitations: Giving primarily in Orange County, CA. No grants to individuals.
Application information: Requests for funding from organizations outside the Orange County, CA, area not considered.

Initial approach: Proposal
Deadline(s): June 1
Officers and Trustees: George L. Argyros,* C.E.O. and Secy.; Julie A. Argyros, Pres.; Daniel Russo,* Treas.; Carol Campbell, Exec. Dir.; Stephanie Gehl; Melissa Mitchell.
EIN: 953421867
Selected grants: The following grants were reported in 2005.
$1,680,204 to Horatio Alger Association of Distinguished Americans, Alexandria, VA.
$791,955 to South Coast Repertory Theater, Costa Mesa, CA.
$251,000 to Saint Pauls Greek Orthodox Church, Irvine, CA.
$83,333 to Rice University, Houston, TX.
$62,000 to Orange County Performing Arts Center, Costa Mesa, CA.
$55,000 to Hellenic College/Holy Cross, Brookline, MA.
$49,650 to Chapman University, Orange, CA.
$26,384 to Pegasus School, Huntington Beach, CA.
$25,000 to New York University, New York, NY.
$11,000 to National Museum of Women in the Arts, DC.

235

Arkay Foundation ◇

1120 Forest Ave., No. 344
Pacific Grove, CA   93950
Contact: Stephen B. Kahn, Pres.
E-mail: info@arkayfoundation.org; *URL:* http://www.arkayfoundation.org

Established in 1995 in CA.
Donor: Stephen B. Kahn.
Foundation type: Independent foundation.
Financial data (yr. ended 10/31/05): Assets, $16,133 (M); gifts received, $500,000; expenditures, $502,552; qualifying distributions, $488,534; giving activities include $427,930 for 46 grants (high: $123,430; low: $100).
Purpose and activities: Giving primarily for issues of social justice, public health, women's concerns, voter engagement and civic participation.
Fields of interest: Arts; Environment, alliance; Human services; Women, centers/services; Civil rights; Public affairs, citizen participation.
Type of support: General/operating support; Program development; Seed money; Research; Technical assistance.
Limitations: Applications not accepted. Giving on a national basis.
Application information: Proposals accepted by invitation only; trustees initiate grants. The foundation does not give priority to local programs located in the Carmel/Monterey, CA, area, unless there is evidence that the local program has the potential for leveraging change and having a wide-spread impact. See foundation Web site for complete information.
Officers and Directors: Stephen B. Kahn,* Pres.; Marian Penn,* Secy.-Treas.; Susan Reed Clark; David M. Goldschmidt; Cecelia Hurwich; Karen M. Kahn.
EIN: 770404924
Selected grants: The following grants were reported in 2004.
$100,000 to Center for Community Change, DC. For general support.
$25,000 to Alliance for Justice, DC. For general support.

$25,000 to International Forum on Globalization, San Francisco, CA. For general support.
$25,000 to Project Vote, Columbus, OH. For general support.
$25,000 to Public Employees for Environmental Responsibility (PEER), DC. For combating dirty science.
$21,000 to Center for Public Interest Research, Boston, MA.
$20,000 to Lewis and Clark College, Portland, OR. For fighting cynicism building trust project.
$15,000 to California State University at Monterey Bay Foundation, Seaside, CA.
$15,000 to Climate Policy Center, DC.
$10,000 to Big Sur Land Trust, Carmel, CA. For general support.

236

Arntz Family Foundation

(formerly Eugene S. Arntz Foundation)
P.O. Box 10396
San Rafael, CA   94912
Contact: Nancy Rosa
E-mail: nancy@arntzfamilyfoundation.org;
URL: http://www.arntzfamilyfoundation.org

Established in 1994 in CA.
Donors: Eugene S. Arntz‡; K. Allan Arntz; Thomas E. Arntz; Donald M. Arntz.
Foundation type: Independent foundation.
Financial data (yr. ended 9/30/05): Assets, $13,471,104 (M); gifts received, $66,772; expenditures, $629,631; qualifying distributions, $581,497; giving activities include $493,520 for 68 grants (high: $40,000; low: $150).
Purpose and activities: The purpose of the foundation is to support environmental organizations, with an emphasis on those organizations that work toward systematic change and sustainability, particularly where the areas of environment and economic development come together.
Fields of interest: Environment.
International interests: Central America; Mexico.
Type of support: General/operating support; Program development.
Limitations: Applications not accepted. No grants to individuals.
Publications: Grants list.
Application information: Contributes only to pre-selected organizations. Unsolicited requests for funds not accepted.
Board meeting date(s): Feb. and July
Trustees: Donald M. Arntz; K. Allan Arntz; Katherine Arntz; Thomas E. Arntz.
Number of staff: 1 part-time professional.
EIN: 686109096
Selected grants: The following grants were reported in 2005.
$40,000 to Ecologic Development Fund, Cambridge, MA.
$38,400 to Seacology, Berkeley, CA.
$25,000 to Rocky Mountain Institute, Snowmass, CO.
$20,000 to Natural Step, San Francisco, CA.
$18,500 to Earth Island Institute, San Francisco, CA.
$15,000 to Population Communications International, New York, NY.
$15,000 to World Wildlife Fund, DC.
$10,750 to Trees, Water and People, Fort Collins, CO.
$5,000 to Hesperian Foundation, Berkeley, CA.

$1,000 to Predator Conservation Alliance, Bozeman, MT.

237

John Arrillaga Foundation ◇

2560 Mission College Blvd., Ste. 101
Santa Clara, CA   95054   (408) 980-0130
Contact: John Arrillaga, Pres.

Established around 1978 in CA.
Donors: John Arrillaga; Imperial Promenade Assocs., LLC.
Foundation type: Independent foundation.
Financial data (yr. ended 9/30/05): Assets, $38,396,596 (M); gifts received, $8,896,754; expenditures, $2,266,227; qualifying distributions, $2,074,921; giving activities include $2,074,921 for 29 grants (high: $1,913,695; low: $250).
Fields of interest: Arts; Higher education; Health organizations, association; Human services.
Type of support: Continuing support; Program development.
Limitations: Giving primarily in CA, with some emphasis on Stanford.
Application information: Application form not required.
Initial approach: Letter
Deadline(s): None
Officers and Directors: John Arrillaga,* Pres.; Laura Arrillaga,* Secy.; John Arrillaga, Jr.,* Treas.
EIN: 942460896
Selected grants: The following grants were reported in 2004.
$669,192 to Stanford University Hospital, Stanford, CA. 2 grants: $659,192, $10,000
$100,000 to California Family Foundation, Palo Alto, CA.
$10,000 to Christmas Bureau of Palo Alto, Palo Alto, CA.
$5,000 to Palo Alto Community Child Care, Palo Alto, CA.

238

Craig S. Atkins Foundation ◇ ☆

18201 Von Karman, Ste. 150
Irvine, CA   92612   (949) 705-5600
Contact: Craig S. Atkins, Pres.

Established in 2001.
Donor: Craig S. Atkins.
Foundation type: Independent foundation.
Financial data (yr. ended 12/31/05): Assets, $1,472,855 (M); gifts received, $1,702,176; expenditures, $1,124,696; qualifying distributions, $1,122,800; giving activities include $1,122,800 for 5 grants (high: $1,120,000; low: $100).
Fields of interest: Environment; Human services; Protestant agencies & churches.
Limitations: Giving primarily in CA. No grants to individuals.
Application information: Application form not required.
Initial approach: Letter
Deadline(s): None
Officers: Craig S. Atkins, Pres.; Mackey O'Donnell, Secy.
EIN: 912171384

239
Atkinson Foundation
1720 S. Amphlett Blvd., Ste. 100
San Mateo, CA 94402-2710
Contact: Elizabeth H. Curtis, Admin.
E-mail: atkinfdn@aol.com; Tel./Fax: (650) 357-1101

Incorporated in 1939 in CA.
Donors: George H. Atkinson†; Mildred M. Atkinson†.
Foundation type: Independent foundation.
Financial data (yr. ended 12/31/05): Assets, $19,062,396 (M); expenditures, $1,156,365; qualifying distributions, $1,033,443; giving activities include $942,194 for 116 grants (high: $60,000; low: $971).
Purpose and activities: Primary areas of interest include the disadvantaged and the homeless, child welfare, family planning, and the handicapped. Broad purposes are to help people reach their highest potential and to reach self-sufficiency. Giving for social services, including youth and the aged, education, family planning programs, and international development programs.
Fields of interest: Child development, education; Secondary school/education; Vocational education; Higher education; Adult education—literacy, basic skills & GED; Reproductive health, family planning; Substance abuse, services; Mental health/crisis services; AIDS; Alcoholism; Crime/violence prevention, youth; Food services; Human services; Children/youth, services; Child development, services; Family services; Residential/custodial care, hospices; Aging, centers/services; Minorities/immigrants, centers/services; Homeless, human services; International economic development; Disabilities, people with; Women; Economically disadvantaged.
International interests: Central America; Mexico.
Type of support: General/operating support; Continuing support; Income development; Program development; Seed money; Scholarship funds; Technical assistance.
Limitations: Giving limited for the benefit of San Mateo County, CA, for social welfare, secondary schools, colleges, and church activities. Some international grantmaking (through U.S.-based nonprofit organizations) in Mexico and Central America, for technical assistance, population issues, economic development, and water and food resources. No support for sports groups, or national or statewide umbrella organizations. No grants to individuals directly (including scholarships), or for research or doctoral study, annual campaigns, travel to conferences or events, media presentations, or fundraising events; no loans.
Publications: Application guidelines; Annual report (including application guidelines).
Application information: Contact the foundation to obtain the required Proposal Cover Sheet. Application form required.
  Initial approach: Letter or telephone
  Copies of proposal: 1
  Deadline(s): First of each month immediately prior to the 4 quarterly meeting months: (Feb. 1, May 1, Aug. 1, and Nov. 1)
  Board meeting date(s): Mar., June, Sept., and Dec.
  Final notification: Within 3 months
Officers and Directors:* Linda L. Lanier,* Pres.; Ray N. Atkinson,* V.P.; James C. Ingwersen,* Secy.; James R. Avedisian,* Treas.; Elizabeth H. Curtis,* Admin.; Jean S. Atkinson; William W. Crandall, Jr.; Dirk Damonte; John E. Herrell.

Number of staff: 1 full-time professional.
EIN: 946075613
Selected grants: The following grants were reported in 2005.
$67,500 to Pacific School of Religion, Berkeley, CA. 2 grants: $7,500, $60,000
$15,000 to Church World Service, Elkhart, IN.
$15,000 to North Peninsula Neighborhood Services Center, South San Francisco, CA.
$15,000 to Samaritan House, San Mateo, CA.
$12,000 to Vida Verde Nature Education, Half Moon Bay, CA.
$10,000 to Boys and Girls Club of the Peninsula, Redwood City, CA.
$10,000 to Court Appointed Special Advocates (CASA), New York, NY.
$10,000 to Mid-Peninsula Housing Services Corporation, Redwood City, CA.
$7,500 to Strategies for International Development, Arlington, VA.

240
Myrtle L. Atkinson Foundation ✧
5 Pembroke Pl.
Menlo Park, CA 94025-5859
Contact: Myrtle W. Harris, Pres.

Incorporated in 1939 in NV.
Donor: E.A. Whitsett†.
Foundation type: Independent foundation.
Financial data (yr. ended 12/31/04): Assets, $9,743,436 (M); expenditures, $458,251; qualifying distributions, $422,550; giving activities include $422,550 for 64 grants (high: $20,000; low: $1,000).
Purpose and activities: To teach, promulgate and disseminate the gospel of Jesus Christ throughout the world and also to unite in Christian Fellowship the large number of consecrated Christians in the various evangelical churches; to encourage and promote religious, scientific, technical and all other kinds of education, enlightenment and research. Giving mainly for capital funds for Christian churches and evangelism; support also for local and international relief and welfare agencies, literacy, hospices, and hunger.
Fields of interest: Theological school/education; Adult education—literacy, basic skills & GED; Education, reading; Education; Food services; Human services; Residential/custodial care, hospices; Christian agencies & churches; Protestant agencies & churches; Minorities.
Type of support: Research; Capital campaigns; Building/renovation; Endowments.
Limitations: Applications not accepted. Giving primarily in CA and on the West Coast. No grants to individuals.
Application information: Unsolicited requests for funds not accepted.
  Board meeting date(s): Summer
Officers and Directors:* M.W. Harris,* Pres.; R. Harris,* V.P.; W.N. Harris,* Secy.-Treas.; J. Harris; J. Whitsett.
EIN: 956047161

241
The Atlas Family Foundation
(formerly Richard & Lezlie Atlas Foundation)
P.O. Box 25338
Los Angeles, CA 90025-0338
Contact: Richard S. Atlas, Tr.

E-mail: Thejmint@aol.com; URL: http://www.atlasfamilyfoundation.org

Established in 1985 in CA.
Donors: Richard S. Atlas; Lezlie Atlas.
Foundation type: Independent foundation.
Financial data (yr. ended 2/28/05): Assets, $6,002,553 (M); expenditures, $803,949; qualifying distributions, $770,991; giving activities include $640,932 for 55 grants (high: $60,000; low: $200).
Purpose and activities: Giving primarily for early childhood education, parenting education, and early child development, pre-natal to age 3, and vulnerable children and families in Los Angeles County, CA.
Fields of interest: Education, early childhood education; Child development, education; Mental health, association; Child development, services.
Type of support: Program evaluation; Management development/capacity building; Matching/challenge support; Conferences/seminars; General/operating support; Continuing support; Annual campaigns; Program development; Technical assistance.
Limitations: Applications not accepted. Giving primarily in Los Angeles, CA.
Application information: Contributes only to pre-selected organizations. Unsolicited requests for funds not considered.
  Board meeting date(s): Varies
Trustees: Lezlie Atlas; Richard S. Atlas; Michael G. O'Brien; Michelle Atlas O'Brien; Allison Atlas Tannenbaum; David Tannenbaum.
Number of staff: 2 part-time professional.
EIN: 942988629
Selected grants: The following grants were reported in 2005.
$75,000 to Los Angeles Child Guidance Clinic, Los Angeles, CA. For general support.
$60,000 to Blind Childrens Center, Los Angeles, CA. For general support.
$60,000 to Saint Joseph Center, Venice, CA. For general support.
$60,000 to Venice Family Clinic, Venice, CA. For general support.
$60,000 to Westside Childrens Center, Culver City, CA. For general support.
$50,000 to Camino Nuevo Charter Academy, Los Angeles, CA. For general support.
$50,000 to Para Los Ninos, Los Angeles, CA. For general support.
$40,000 to Long Beach Day Nursery, Long Beach, CA. For general support.
$25,000 to Kayne-ERAS Center, Culver City, CA. For general support.
$24,000 to University of California, Los Angeles, CA. For general support.

242
The Auen Foundation ✧
(formerly The Auen-Bergen Foundation)
P.O. Box 13390
Palm Desert, CA 92255-3390

Established in 1992 in CA.
Donor: H.N. and Frances C. Berger Foundation.
Foundation type: Independent foundation.
Financial data (yr. ended 12/31/05): Assets, $37,390,387 (M); expenditures, $1,527,031; qualifying distributions, $1,525,700; giving activities include $1,087,800 for 51 grants (high:

$200,000; low: $1,000), $35,435 for 1 in-kind gift, and $2,846 for 1 loan/program-related investment.
Fields of interest: Arts; Higher education; Education; Health care; Substance abuse, treatment; Health organizations, association; AIDS research; Human services; YM/YWCAs & YM/YWHAs; Residential/custodial care, hospices; Aging, centers/services; Religion.
Type of support: General/operating support; Equipment; Program-related investments/loans.
Limitations: Applications not accepted. Giving primarily in CA, with emphasis on Palm Desert and Palm Springs. No grants to individuals.
Application information: Contributes only to pre-selected organizations.
Trustee: Ronald M. Auen.
EIN: 954325051
Selected grants: The following grants were reported in 2003.
$204,749 to University of Idaho, College of Agriculture, Moscow, ID. For Hot Springs Ranch Lease.
$60,000 to Salk Institute for Biological Studies, San Diego, CA. For research.
$50,000 to Desert AIDS Project, Palm Springs, CA. For senior programs.
$30,000 to University of Southern California, Los Angeles, CA. For Bridging the Generation Gap.
$20,000 to ACT for Multiple Sclerosis, Palm Desert, CA. To help underwrite portion of event.
$17,500 to Alzheimers Association, Palm Desert, CA. For Care Consultation Program.
$15,000 to Cove Communities Senior Association, Palm Desert, CA. For Meals on Wheels.
$15,000 to Inner-City Arts, Los Angeles, CA. For Family Days.
$10,000 to Arrowhead Arts Association, Blue Jay, CA. For intergenerational programs.
$10,000 to Children Affected by AIDS Foundation, Los Angeles, CA. For scholarships.

243
Autry Foundation ✧
4383 Colfax Ave.
Studio City, CA 91604 (818) 752-7770
Contact: Jacqueline Autry, Pres.

Established in 1974 in CA.
Donors: Gene Autry†; Jacqueline Autry.
Foundation type: Independent foundation.
Financial data (yr. ended 12/31/05): Assets, $14,910,116 (M); expenditures, $2,625,416; qualifying distributions, $2,160,343; giving activities include $2,160,343 for 28 grants (high: $1,005,000; low: $100).
Purpose and activities: The foundation provides support to the Autry Museum of Western Heritage, with limited giving to various other charities of interest to the board only.
Fields of interest: Museums; Human services; Children/youth, services; Aging, centers/services.
Limitations: Giving limited to the Los Angeles, CA, area, and Riverside and Orange counties. No grants to individuals.
Application information: Application form not required.
  Initial approach: Letter on organization's letterhead
  Copies of proposal: 1
  Deadline(s): None
  Board meeting date(s): Varies
Officers and Directors:* Jacqueline Autry,* Pres.; Joanne D. Hale,* V.P.; Maxine Hansen, Secy.;

Stanley Schneider,* Treas.; Karla Buhlman; David W. Cartwright.
EIN: 237433359

244
Avery Dennison Foundation ✧ ☆
(formerly Avery International Foundation)
150 N. Orange Grove Blvd.
Pasadena, CA 91103
Contact: Joyce Reid, Admin., Contribs.

Established in 1977.
Donor: Avery Dennison Corp.
Foundation type: Company-sponsored foundation.
Financial data (yr. ended 12/31/04): Assets, $8,120,059 (M); expenditures, $339,138; qualifying distributions, $336,500; giving activities include $336,500 for 16 grants (high: $95,000; low: $2,500).
Purpose and activities: The foundation supports organizations involved with arts and culture, education, human services, and civic affairs.
Fields of interest: Arts; Education, reform; Business school/education; Education; Human services; Federated giving programs; Public affairs.
Type of support: Fellowships; Scholarship funds; Capital campaigns; Building/renovation; Program development.
Limitations: Giving primarily in areas of company operations, with emphasis on CA; giving also to national organizations. No support for service clubs or veterans' or fraternal organizations, churches or religious organizations, private foundations, political organizations or candidates, or United Way-supported organizations (over 30 percent of budget). No grants to individuals, or for beauty or talent contests, political activities, or general operating support for hospitals.
Application information: Support is limited to 1 contribution per organization during any given year. Multi-year funding is not automatic. Application form not required.
  Initial approach: Proposal
  Final notification: 3 to 6 months
Officers and Trustees:* Robert G. Van Schoonenberg,* Pres.; Diane B. Dixon,* Secy.; Judith K. Gain, Treas.; Karyn E. Rodriguez.
EIN: 953251844
Selected grants: The following grants were reported in 2004.
$95,000 to Institute for Educational Advancement, South Pasadena, CA.
$75,000 to Art Center College of Design, Pasadena, CA.
$20,000 to Harvard University, Cambridge, MA.
$10,000 to Case Western Reserve University, Cleveland, OH.
$10,000 to Rose Bowl Aquatics Center, Pasadena, CA.
$6,000 to Junior Achievement.
$5,000 to United Way.
$5,000 to Western Justice Center Foundation, Pasadena, CA.

245
Avery-Tsui Foundation ✧ ☆
2618 Canyon Ave.
San Diego, CA 92123

Established in 2004 in CA.
Donor: The R. Stanton Avery Foundation.

Foundation type: Independent foundation.
Financial data (yr. ended 12/31/05): Assets, $37,883,220 (M); expenditures, $2,429,870; qualifying distributions, $2,022,833; giving activities include $1,890,500 for 14 grants (high: $500,000; low: $1,000).
Purpose and activities: Giving primarily for education and the arts, as well as for Chinese cultural and educational organizations, and social services.
Fields of interest: Arts, cultural/ethnic awareness; Arts; Elementary/secondary education; Higher education; Law school/education; Libraries (academic/research); Human services; Philanthropy/voluntarism.
Limitations: Applications not accepted. Giving primarily in CA, with emphasis on San Diego, and New York, NY.
Application information: Contributes only to pre-selected organizations.
Officers and Directors:* Dennis S. Avery,* Pres.; Sally Tsui Wong-Avery,* V.P.; Natasha Wong,* Secy.
EIN: 656431837

246
The Avis Family Foundation ✧
c/o myCFO, Inc.
1700 Seaport Blvd., 4th Fl.
Redwood City, CA 94063

Established in 2000 in CA.
Donors: Anne R. Avis; Gregory M. Avis.
Foundation type: Independent foundation.
Financial data (yr. ended 12/31/04): Assets, $14,905,636 (M); gifts received, $999,216; expenditures, $652,268; qualifying distributions, $591,500; giving activities include $580,000 for 1 grant.
Fields of interest: Federated giving programs.
Limitations: Applications not accepted. Giving primarily in Boston, MA. No grants to individuals.
Application information: Contributes only to pre-selected organizations.
Officers: Gregory M. Avis, Pres.; Anne R. Avis, Secy.
EIN: 770546893
Selected grants: The following grants were reported in 2004.
$580,000 to Williams College, Williamstown, MA.

247
The Ayrshire Foundation
301 E. Colorado Blvd., No. 802
Pasadena, CA 91101
Contact: Margaret G. Boyer, Pres.
E-mail: info@AyrshireFoundation.org; URL: http://www.ayrshirefoundation.org

Established in 1998 in CA.
Donor: James N. Gamble†.
Foundation type: Independent foundation.
Financial data (yr. ended 5/31/05): Assets, $19,104,187 (M); expenditures, $1,156,518; qualifying distributions, $1,052,573; giving activities include $1,034,500 for 15 grants (high: $275,000; low: $10,000).
Purpose and activities: Giving primarily for health care, including a hospital, and a cancer center; some giving also for education, the arts, and youth and social services.

Fields of interest: Arts; Education; Environment; Health care; Children/youth, services; Community development; Aging.
Type of support: Capital campaigns; Building/renovation; Equipment; Land acquisition; Endowments; Program development; Conferences/seminars; Professorships; Film/video/radio; Seed money; Scholarship funds; Matching/challenge support.
Limitations: Giving primarily in CA. No grants for continuing support.
Publications: Annual report; Grants list.
Application information: Unsolicited requests for funds not accepted. Application form not required.
Initial approach: Varies
Copies of proposal: 1
Deadline(s): Mar. 15 and Sept. 15
Board meeting date(s): May and Oct.
Final notification: One month or less
Officers and Directors: Margaret G. Boyer,* Pres.; Tracy G. Hirrel,* V.P.; Susan T. House, Secy.; Richard J. Hirrel,* Treas.; Peter S. Boyer.
Number of staff: 1 full-time professional.
EIN: 954690418
Selected grants: The following grants were reported in 2004.
$100,000 to Northern Michigan Hospital Foundation, Petoskey, MI. For general support.
$100,000 to University of Southern California Kenneth Norris Jr. Cancer Hospital, Los Angeles, CA. For general support.
$75,000 to California Academy of Sciences, San Francisco, CA. For general support.
$74,450 to Kidspace, A Participatory Museum, Pasadena, CA. For general support.
$50,000 to Cathedral School for Boys, San Francisco, CA. For general support.
$50,000 to Mayfield Junior School of the Holy Child Jesus, Pasadena, CA. For general support.
$50,000 to Monte Vista Grove Homes, Pasadena, CA. For general support.
$30,000 to Haight Ashbury Food Program, San Francisco, CA. For general support.
$15,000 to Magic Theater, San Francisco, CA. For general support.
$10,000 to Planned Parenthood of Pasadena, Pasadena, CA. For general support.

248
Azus Foundation, Inc. ✧
1567 E. 25th St.
Los Angeles, CA 90011-1813

Established in 1979.
Donors: Al Azus; Alna Envelope Co.
Foundation type: Independent foundation.
Financial data (yr. ended 12/31/05): Assets, $902,825 (M); gifts received, $20,000; expenditures, $541,985; qualifying distributions, $541,985; giving activities include $539,437 for 23 + grants (high: $101,300).
Purpose and activities: Giving primarily for Jewish organizations and human services.
Fields of interest: Health care; Health organizations, association; Human services; Children/youth, services; Jewish federated giving programs; Jewish agencies & temples.
Limitations: Applications not accepted. Giving on a national basis. No grants to individuals.
Application information: Contributes only to pre-selected organizations.
Manager: Al Azus.

Number of staff: 2 part-time support.
EIN: 953386905

249
William Babcock Memorial Endowment ✧
305 San Anselmo Ave., Ste. 219
San Anselmo, CA 94960
Contact: Lynne Walsh, Exec. Dir.

Established in 1954 in CA; incorporated in 1959.
Foundation type: Independent foundation.
Financial data (yr. ended 2/28/05): Assets, $4,845,790 (L); gifts received, $357,450; expenditures, $841,068; qualifying distributions, $774,486; giving activities include $620,685 for 309 grants to individuals (high: $75,000; low: $34).
Purpose and activities: Grants or loans only for Marin County, CA residents for medical expenses that are extremely excessive in relation to income and are not covered by public programs or health insurance.
Fields of interest: Health care.
Type of support: Grants to individuals.
Limitations: Giving limited to Marin County, CA. Generally no support for organizations.
Publications: Application guidelines.
Application information: Documents providing proof of residency in Marin County, CA, are required. Application form required.
Initial approach: Telephone
Deadline(s): None
Board meeting date(s): Monthly
Final notification: By letter
Officers and Directors: Gary Runes,* Pres.; Marjorie Belknap, M.D.*, V.P.; Valerie Stilson, R.N.*, Secy.; David Costanza, M.D.*, Treas.; Lynne Walsh, Exec. Dir.; Jeffrey Allen; Joane Berry; Michael Osborne, M.D.; Richard Riede.
Number of staff: 1 full-time professional; 1 full-time support; 1 part-time support.
EIN: 941367170

250
Gerson Bakar Foundation ✧
1 Lombard St., Ste. 202
San Francisco, CA 94111

Established in 1984 in CA.
Donor: Gerson Bakar.
Foundation type: Independent foundation.
Financial data (yr. ended 12/31/05): Assets, $57,957,477 (M); gifts received, $2,770,766; expenditures, $2,700,700; qualifying distributions, $2,298,288; giving activities include $2,116,042 for 62 grants (high: $500,000; low: $25).
Fields of interest: Museums (art); Higher education; Education; Animals/wildlife; Health organizations, association; Human services; Federated giving programs.
Limitations: Applications not accepted. Giving primarily in the San Francisco Bay Area, CA; some giving nationally. No grants to individuals.
Application information: Contributes only to pre-selected organizations.
Officers and Directors: Gerson Bakar, Chair.; Barbara Bass Bakar, Pres.; Richard L. Greene,* Secy.; Nalraj Goundar, Treas.; William Coblentz; Phyllis Cook; Warren Hellman.
EIN: 942949602
Selected grants: The following grants were reported in 2004.

$500,000 to University of California at San Francisco Foundation, San Francisco, CA.
$400,000 to United Way of the Bay Area, San Francisco, CA.
$65,500 to American Conservatory Theater, San Francisco, CA.
$25,000 to University of California, San Francisco, CA.
$2,500 to Smith College, Northampton, MA.
$1,951 to Holy Names High School, Oakland, CA.
$250 to Saint Johns College, Santa Fe, NM.
$250 to Theater Rhinoceros, San Francisco, CA.

251
Bob Baker Foundation, Inc. ✧
591 Camino de la Reina, Ste. 1100.
San Diego, CA 92108-3113

Established in 1987 in CA.
Donors: Bob Baker Enterprises, Inc.; Robert H. Baker; Rekab Properties.
Foundation type: Independent foundation.
Financial data (yr. ended 6/30/05): Assets, $839,930 (M); gifts received, $1,155,000; expenditures, $1,406,797; qualifying distributions, $1,399,901; giving activities include $1,381,917 for 31 grants (high: $300,000; low: $200).
Purpose and activities: The foundation supports Christian agencies and churches and organizations involved with education, the environment, health, children and youth, human services, and community development.
Fields of interest: Higher education; Education; Environment; Hospitals (general); Health care; Children/youth, services; Homeless, human services; Human services; Community development; Christian agencies & churches.
Type of support: Annual campaigns; Building/renovation; Scholarship funds.
Limitations: Giving primarily in San Diego, CA. No grants to individuals.
Application information:
Board meeting date(s): Annually
Trustees: Michael V. Baker; Robert H. Baker; Thomas J. Solomon.
EIN: 330265135
Selected grants: The following grants were reported in 2004.
$200,000 to Diocese of San Diego, San Diego, CA. To help build high schools.
$105,700 to University of San Diego, San Diego, CA. For remembrance scholarship fund, Science and Technology Center building fund, and President's Club.
$85,000 to Academy of Our Lady of Peace, San Diego, CA. For Saint Therese state project and amphitheater construction.
$55,350 to Mercy Hospital Foundation, San Diego, CA. For heart care center campaign and fundraisers.
$30,000 to Saint Vincent de Paul Society, San Diego, CA. For transportation needs.
$17,500 to Interfaith Community Services, Escondido, CA.
$10,000 to Nativity Prep Academy, San Diego, CA.
$5,000 to Scripps Foundation for Medicine and Science, San Diego, CA. For San Diego Fire and Rescue Helicopter Fundraiser.
$1,000 to Childrens Hospital Foundation, San Diego, CA. For fundraiser.
$1,000 to Zoological Society of San Diego, San Diego, CA. For Pride of the Park fundraiser.

252
The R. C. Baker Foundation
P.O. Box 6150
Orange, CA   92863-6150
Contact: Frank L. Scott, Chair.

Trust established in 1952 in CA.
Donor: R.C. Baker, Sr.✝.
Foundation type: Independent foundation.
Financial data (yr. ended 12/31/05): Assets,
$31,674,568 (M); expenditures, $1,745,316;
qualifying distributions, $1,559,118; giving
activities include $1,437,000 for 98 grants (high:
$400,000; low: $250).
Purpose and activities: Emphasis on higher
education, including scholarships administered by
selected colleges and universities; some support for
hospitals and health agencies, cultural programs,
and social service and youth agencies.
Fields of interest: Visual arts; Museums; Performing
arts; Arts; Education, association; Education, fund
raising/fund distribution; Higher education;
Education; Hospitals (general); Health care; Mental
health/crisis services; Medical research, institute;
Food services; Youth development, services; Human
services; Children/youth, services; Leadership
development; Disabilities, people with.
Type of support: General/operating support;
Continuing support; Annual campaigns; Capital
campaigns; Building/renovation; Equipment;
Emergency funds; Program development; Research.
Limitations: Giving limited to the western U.S. No
grants to individuals, or for endowment funds; no
loans.
Application information: Application form not
required.
  Initial approach: Cover letter with proposal
  Copies of proposal: 1
  Deadline(s): Submit proposal preferably in Apr. or
  Sept.; deadline May 1 and Oct. 1
  Board meeting date(s): June and Nov.
Officers and Trustees:* Frank L. Scott,* Chair.;
Ronald Turner,* Vice-Chair.; James H. Hickey; Larry
Scott, Jr.; Joe Shelton.
Corporate Trustee: Bank of America, N.A.
Number of staff: 1 full-time support.
EIN: 951742283
Selected grants: The following grants were reported
in 2004.
$75,000 to Harvey Mudd College, Claremont, CA.
$50,000 to Columbus Community Hospital,
  Columbus, TX.
$25,000 to Anaheim Memorial Medical Center,
  Anaheim, CA.
$25,000 to Doheny Eye Institute, Los Angeles, CA.
$23,000 to YMCA.
$22,500 to YMCA of Orange, Orange, CA.
$20,000 to College of the Desert Foundation, Palm
  Desert, CA.
$15,000 to Cystic Fibrosis Foundation, Los Angeles,
  CA.
$11,000 to YMCA of Greater Whittier, Whittier, CA.
$5,000 to Communities in Schools, San Francisco,
  CA.

253
The Baker Street Foundation ◇
135 Main St., Ste. 1140
San Francisco, CA   94105

Established in 1993 in CA.
Donor: Mary M. Miner.
Foundation type: Independent foundation.

Financial data (yr. ended 12/31/03): Assets,
$62,501,115 (M); expenditures, $3,054,678;
qualifying distributions, $2,920,259; giving
activities include $2,915,000 for 45 grants (high:
$600,000; low: $5,000; average: $20,000–
$100,000).
Purpose and activities: Funding primarily for
education, medical research, human services, and
arts and culture.
Fields of interest: Arts; Elementary/secondary
education; Higher education; Libraries/library
science; Health care; Medical research; Human
services.
Limitations: Applications not accepted. Giving
primarily in San Francisco, CA. No grants to
individuals.
Application information: Contributes only to
pre-selected organizations.
Officers and Directors:* Mary M. Miner,* Pres.;
Helen Sedwick,* Secy.; Roy Bukstein,* C.F.O.;
Justine Miner; Nicola Miner.
EIN: 943192365

254
The Bandai Foundation ◇
5551 Katella Ave.
Cypress, CA   90630
Application address: c/o The Carmen Group, 1301
K St. N.W., Ste. 800 E., Washington, DC 20005

Established in 1995 in CA.
Foundation type: Operating foundation.
Financial data (yr. ended 12/31/04): Assets,
$9,953,174 (M); expenditures, $492,149;
qualifying distributions, $434,481; giving activities
include $348,000 for 3 grants (high: $275,000;
low: $3,000).
Purpose and activities: The foundation is focusing
their resources on promoting the U.S. Marine Corps
Toys for Tots campaign.
Fields of interest: Children/youth, services.
Limitations: Giving primarily in CA and NY.
Application information: Application form not
required.
  Deadline(s): None
Officers: Masaaki Tsuji, Chair. and Pres.; Kunio
Ikoma, Secy.-Treas.
EIN: 330655933
Selected grants: The following grants were reported
in 2004.
$275,000 to Elizabeth Glaser Pediatric AIDS
  Foundation, Santa Monica, CA.
$70,000 to Toys R Us Childrens Fund, New York,
  NY.
$3,000 to Ronald McDonald House of Orange
  County, Orange, CA.

255
The William C. Bannerman Foundation
9255 Sunset Blvd., Ste. 400
West Hollywood, CA   90069   (310) 273-9933
Contact: Elliot Ponchick, Pres.

Established in 1958 in CA.
Foundation type: Independent foundation.
Financial data (yr. ended 4/30/05): Assets,
$9,595,846 (M); expenditures, $702,039;
qualifying distributions, $536,282; giving activities
include $446,373 for 45 grants (high: $100,000;
low: $250).

Purpose and activities: Giving for education, women
and children, and the environment.
Fields of interest: Secondary school/education;
Education; Environment; Children, services;
Women.
Type of support: General/operating support; Annual
campaigns; Capital campaigns; Building/
renovation; Equipment; Program development; Seed
money; Matching/challenge support.
Limitations: Giving limited to the Los Angeles, CA,
area. No support for political organizations, or for
religious or medical/health organizations, or for
universities. No grants to individuals.
Publications: Application guidelines.
Application information: Application form not
required.
  Initial approach: 2-page letter
  Deadline(s): Oct. 31
  Board meeting date(s): July and Mar.
  Final notification: Mar. 15
Officers and Directors:* Elliot Ponchick,* Pres.; E.T.
Ponchick,* V.P. and Secy.-Treas.
Number of staff: 1 part-time professional.
EIN: 956061353
Selected grants: The following grants were reported
in 2004.
$35,000 to Cabrillo Marine Aquarium, Friends of,
  San Pedro, CA.
$15,000 to Good Shepherd Shelter, Los Angeles,
  CA.
$15,000 to Rainbow Services, San Pedro, CA.
$13,000 to Youth Communication Chicago Center,
  Chicago, IL.
$12,500 to Historical Society of Southern
  California, Los Angeles, CA.
$10,000 to Children of the Night, Van Nuys, CA.
$10,000 to Long Beach BLAST-Better Learning After
  School Today, Long Beach, CA.
$10,000 to Union of Concerned Scientists,
  Cambridge, MA.
$10,000 to Urban Education Partnership, Los
  Angeles, CA.
$10,000 to Women for Women International, DC.

256
Joseph L. Barbonchielli and Marie and Manuel B. Perez Foundation ◇
44 Montgomery St., No. 3585
San Francisco, CA   94104   (415) 433-5446
Contact: Clifton W. Ohman, Pres.

Donor: Joseph L. Barbonchielli Trust.
Foundation type: Independent foundation.
Financial data (yr. ended 9/30/05): Assets,
$6,991,316 (M); expenditures, $368,798;
qualifying distributions, $365,400; giving activities
include $365,400 for 14 grants (high: $50,000;
low: $10,400).
Purpose and activities: Giving limited to the elderly
and needy who live in their own residences, for
health and human services.
Fields of interest: Health care, home services;
Human services; Aging; Economically
disadvantaged.
Limitations: Giving limited to the San Francisco, CA,
area.
Application information: Application form not
required.
  Initial approach: Letter
  Deadline(s): None

Officers and Trustees:* Clifton W. Ohman,* Pres.; Patricia Olcomendy,* Secy.-Treas.; Mary K. Lopez,* C.F.O.; Jeffrey A. Hawkins.
EIN: 943343590

257
The Coeta and Donald Barker Foundation

(formerly The Donald R. Barker Foundation)
P.O. Box 936
Rancho Mirage, CA 92270-0936
Contact: Joan K. Damiani, Exec. Admin.

Established in 1977 in OR.
Donor: Donald R. Barker†.
Foundation type: Independent foundation.
Financial data (yr. ended 11/30/05): Assets, $10,166,987 (M); expenditures, $601,514; qualifying distributions, $595,514; giving activities include $496,575 for 161 grants (high: $200,000; low: $100), and $8,000 for 2 employee matching gifts.
Purpose and activities: Giving primarily for education, conservation, health care and social services.
Fields of interest: Arts; Secondary school/education; Higher education; Environment, natural resources; Environment; Hospitals (general); Health care; Mental health/crisis services; Health organizations, association; Heart & circulatory diseases; Medical research, institute; Heart & circulatory research; Children/youth, services; Family services; Community development; Disabilities, people with.
Type of support: General/operating support; Continuing support; Building/renovation; Equipment; Endowments; Program development; Scholarship funds.
Limitations: Giving limited to CA and OR. No support for sectarian religious purposes, or for agencies that rely on federal or tax dollars for their principal support. No grants to individuals or for conferences, or operational deficits.
Publications: Application guidelines.
Application information:
  Board meeting date(s): May and Oct.
Officer and Trustees:* Nancy G. Harris,* Chair.; John D. Brennan; Vernon Gleaves; Dana E. Newquist; Jim Richards.
Number of staff: 1 full-time professional; 1 part-time support.
EIN: 930698411

258
Barth Family Foundation ◇ ☆

433 N. Camden Dr., Ste. 1070
Beverly Hills, CA 90210

Established in 2001 in CA.
Donor: Robert Barth.
Foundation type: Independent foundation.
Financial data (yr. ended 12/31/05): Assets, $2,771,675 (M); gifts received, $350,000; expenditures, $402,635; qualifying distributions, $400,300; giving activities include $400,300 for 10 grants (high: $100,000; low: $1,800).
Fields of interest: Health organizations, association; Cancer.
Limitations: Applications not accepted. No grants to individuals.
Application information: Contributes only to pre-selected organizations.

Officers: Robert Barth, Pres.; Suzanne Barth, Secy.
EIN: 912171985

259
The Bartman Foundation ◇

11777 San Vicente Blvd., No. 600
Los Angeles, CA 90049-5051

Established in 1969 in CA.
Donors: N. Bartman†; Cecile C. Bartman.
Foundation type: Independent foundation.
Financial data (yr. ended 12/31/05): Assets, $10,513,376 (M); gifts received, $318,627; expenditures, $956,704; qualifying distributions, $824,675; giving activities include $823,325 for 115 grants (high: $100,000; low: $100).
Purpose and activities: Giving primarily for education; funding also for human services, medical research, community development, and federated giving programs.
Fields of interest: Arts; Higher education; Libraries/library science; Education; Health care; Health organizations, association; Medical research, institute; Cancer research; Human services; Children/youth, services; Community development; Federated giving programs; Religion.
Limitations: Applications not accepted. Giving primarily in CA. No grants to individuals.
Application information: Contributes only to pre-selected organizations.
Trustee: Cecile C. Bartman.
EIN: 237005283
Selected grants: The following grants were reported in 2004.
$310,000 to Los Angeles County Museum of Art, Los Angeles, CA.
$62,500 to Pomona College, Claremont, CA.
$50,000 to Library Foundation of Los Angeles, Los Angeles, CA.
$25,000 to Prostate Cancer Foundation, Santa Monica, CA.
$20,000 to Los Angeles Free Clinic, Los Angeles, CA.
$15,000 to Los Angeles Philharmonic Association, Los Angeles, CA.
$10,000 to University of Chicago, Chicago, IL.
$10,000 to Venice Family Clinic, Venice, CA.
$5,000 to K C E T Community Television of Southern California, Los Angeles, CA.
$5,000 to Stop Cancer, Los Angeles, CA.

260
Battle Family Foundation ☆

c/o A. George Battle
35 Vicente Rd.
Berkeley, CA 94705
E-mail: sb@skipbattle.com

Established in 1999 in CA.
Donor: A. George Battle.
Foundation type: Independent foundation.
Financial data (yr. ended 12/31/04): Assets, $2,969,495 (M); gifts received, $1,982,175; expenditures, $365,705; qualifying distributions, $362,918; giving activities include $360,000 for 3 grants (high: $325,000; low: $10,000).
Purpose and activities: Giving primarily for higher education; some funding also for the arts.
Fields of interest: Arts; Higher education.
International interests: Africa.

Limitations: Applications not accepted. No grants to individuals.
Application information: Contributes only to pre-selected organizations.
Officers: A. George Battle, Pres.; Emily T. Battle, V.P. and Treas.; Daniel K. Battle, Secy.
EIN: 943350554

261
Evalyn M. Bauer Foundation ◇

(formerly M. R. Bauer Foundation)
c/o James Ackerman
1 World Trade Center, No. 1440
Long Beach, CA 90831-1440

Established in 1955 in IL; reorganized in 1995 in CA.
Donors: M.R. Bauer†; Evelyn M. Bauer†.
Foundation type: Independent foundation.
Financial data (yr. ended 12/31/05): Assets, $34,593,108 (M); expenditures, $1,966,385; qualifying distributions, $1,759,295; giving activities include $1,630,350 for grants.
Purpose and activities: Grants primarily for higher education, including medical and legal education, hospitals, cultural programs, and social service and youth agencies.
Fields of interest: Arts; Higher education; Law school/education; Medical school/education; Hospitals (general); Human services; Children/youth, services.
Type of support: General/operating support; Professorships; Research.
Limitations: Applications not accepted. Giving primarily in CA. No grants to individuals.
Application information: Contributes only to pre-selected organizations.
Officers and Directors:* Loraine S. Ackerman,* Pres.; Lee Ackerman, V.P.; Nancy Gains, Secy. and C.F.O.
EIN: 330669419

262
K. & F. Baxter Family Foundation, Inc. ◇

P.O. Box 13053
Berkeley, CA 94712-4053 (510) 524-8145
Contact: Stacey K. Bell, Exec. Dir.
FAX: (510) 524-4101;
E-mail: kfbaxterfound@aol.com; *URL:* http://www.kfbaxterfoundation.com

Established in 1997 in CA.
Donor: Frank E. Baxter.
Foundation type: Independent foundation.
Financial data (yr. ended 12/31/05): Assets, $1,496,286 (M); expenditures, $579,434; qualifying distributions, $531,546; giving activities include $521,546 for 15 grants (high: $100,000; low: $3,816), and $5,550 for 3 grants to individuals (high: $2,800; low: $750).
Purpose and activities: The foundation supports creating successful schools for low income children and acknowledging, supporting and celebrating biracial children, including support for preschool scholarships, early childhood education, and charter schools.
Fields of interest: Education, research; Education, single organization support; Education, public education; Elementary/secondary education; Children, day care.

Type of support: General/operating support; Equipment; Program development; Publication; Curriculum development; Research; Program evaluation.
Limitations: Giving limited to schools located within the geographic areas of the following school districts: Berkeley, Oakland, West Contra Costa, and Los Angeles, CA. All other grants may be nationwide. No support for early childhood programs or for biracial research.
Publications: Application guidelines; Grants list; Occasional report.
Application information: Proposals must address all questions and areas of the preliminary proposal idea. Scholarship guidelines available on foundation Web site. Application form not required.
  Initial approach: Telephone call or e-mail proposal idea, 3 weeks before proposals are due
  Copies of proposal: 4
  Deadline(s): Feb. 1 and Aug. 1
  Board meeting date(s): Mar. and Sept.
  Final notification: Apr. 15 and Oct. 15
Officers: Frank E. Baxter, Pres. and Secy.; Stacey K. Bell, Exec. Dir.
Directors: Pamela A. Riley; Stacy Thompson.
Number of staff: 1 part-time professional.
EIN: 954633505

263
The Donald E. and Delia B. Baxter Foundation ◇
171 Saxony Rd., Ste. 113
Encinitas, CA 92024

Incorporated in 1959 in CA.
Donor: Delia B. Baxter.
Foundation type: Independent foundation.
Financial data (yr. ended 12/31/05): Assets, $26,474,457 (M); expenditures, $1,687,004; qualifying distributions, $1,489,000; giving activities include $1,489,000 for 4 grants (high: $650,000; low: $51,000).
Purpose and activities: Giving primarily for educational and scientific institutions for research and development of medicine, instruments, and fluids for alleviating pain and protecting and prolonging human life.
Fields of interest: Medical school/education; Medical research, institute.
Type of support: Building/renovation; Professorships; Fellowships; Scholarship funds; Research.
Limitations: Applications not accepted. Giving primarily in CA and KY. No grants to individuals.
Application information: Grants initiated by the foundation's board. Unsolicited requests for funds not accepted.
Officers: Donald B. Haake, Pres.; Jane H. Russell, V.P. and Secy.; H.R. Haake, Treas.
Directors: Kelly Haake; Martha B. Haake; James Russell.
EIN: 956029555

264
Greater Bay Bancorp Foundation ◇
1900 University Ave., 6th Fl.
East Palo Alto, CA 94303   (650) 838-6142
Contact: Ervie L. Smith, Dir.
URL: http://www.gbbk.com/foundation/foundation_about.html

Established in 1998 in CA.
Donor: Greater Bay Bancorp.
Foundation type: Company-sponsored foundation.
Financial data (yr. ended 12/31/04): Assets, $174,038 (M); gifts received, $901,330; expenditures, $1,860,341; qualifying distributions, $1,782,452; giving activities include $1,782,452 for grants.
Purpose and activities: The foundation supports organizations involved with arts and culture, education, the environment, health, human services, and senior citizens.
Fields of interest: Arts; Education; Environment; Health care; Youth, services; Aging, centers/services; Human services; Aging.
Type of support: General/operating support; Endowments; Program development; Conferences/seminars; Curriculum development; Fellowships; Scholarship funds; Employee matching gifts.
Limitations: Giving primarily in the Greater Bay Area, CA. No support for religious, political, or fraternal organizations. No grants to individuals.
Publications: Application guidelines; Annual report; Informational brochure.
Application information: Application form required.
  Initial approach: Download application form and mail to foundation
  Copies of proposal: 1
  Deadline(s): Feb. 15, May 15, Aug. 15, and Nov. 15
  Board meeting date(s): Mar., June, Sept., and Dec.
Officers and Trustees:* Duncan L. Matteson,* Chair.; Bryon A. Scordelis, Pres.; Colleen Anderson, V.P.; Kamran Husain, V.P.; Carleen Maniglia, Secy. and Admin.; Mark T. Eschen, Cont.; C. Donald Allen; Lawrence A. Aufmuth; Susan Ford Dorsey; David L. Kalkbrenner; Linda R. Meier; Donald H. Seiler.
Number of staff: 1 full-time professional; 1 part-time support.
EIN: 770474639
Selected grants: The following grants were reported in 2004.
$40,000 to Lenders for Community Development, San Jose, CA.
$21,950 to Boys and Girls Club of the Peninsula, Redwood City, CA.
$20,000 to San Jose State University Foundation, San Jose, CA.
$13,900 to Sequoia Hospital Foundation, Redwood City, CA.
$9,060 to Valle Monte League, Sunnyvale, CA.
$5,000 to Asian Health Services, Oakland, CA.
$4,520 to Peninsula Volunteers, Menlo Park, CA.
$2,500 to Alameda County Library Foundation, Fremont, CA.
$2,500 to Building Futures Now, Los Altos, CA.
$1,000 to Las Trampas School, Lafayette, CA.

265
BayTree Fund ◇ ☆
c/o Eugene Lewis & Associates
44 E. Foothill Blvd., Ste. 100
Arcadia, CA 91006

Established in 2004 in CA.
Donor: R. Stanton Avery Foundation.
Foundation type: Independent foundation.
Financial data (yr. ended 12/31/05): Assets, $49,039,906 (M); expenditures, $2,394,232; qualifying distributions, $1,919,972; giving activities include $1,822,150 for 12+ grants (high: $500,000).

Fields of interest: Media/communications; Public affairs.
Limitations: Applications not accepted. No grants to individuals.
Application information: Contributes only to pre-selected organizations.
Officers and Director:* Judith Avery,* Pres.; John Lewis, Secy.-Treas.
EIN: 260084354

266
Beagle Charitable Foundation ◇
c/o Harvey Armstrong, myCFO, Inc.
1700 Seaport Blvd., 4th Fl.
Redwood City, CA 94063

Established in 1999 in WA.
Donor: Joy D. Covey.
Foundation type: Independent foundation.
Financial data (yr. ended 3/31/05): Assets, $8,197,534 (M); gifts received, $316,930; expenditures, $394,025; qualifying distributions, $389,028; giving activities include $379,000 for 20 grants (high: $145,500; low: $1,000).
Fields of interest: Higher education; Environment, natural resources; Environment; Health care; Foundations (public).
Limitations: Applications not accepted. Giving on a national basis. No grants to individuals.
Application information: Contributes only to pre-selected organizations.
Officers: Joy D. Covey, Pres.; Lee S. Gerstein, V.P.; Harvey L. Armstrong, Secy.
EIN: 770529181

267
The Frances and William H. Beattie Foundation ◇
(formerly The Beattie Foundation)
c/o CGTC
333 S. Hope St., 34th Fl.
Los Angeles, CA 90071

Donor: William H. Beattie†.
Foundation type: Independent foundation.
Financial data (yr. ended 12/31/05): Assets, $6,205,665 (M); expenditures, $935,536; qualifying distributions, $838,028; giving activities include $825,700 for 26 grants (high: $60,000; low: $2,500).
Purpose and activities: Giving primarily for higher education; also giving for the performing arts and conservation.
Fields of interest: Performing arts; Higher education; Education; Environment, natural resources; Housing/shelter, development; YM/YWCAs & YM/YWHAs.
Limitations: Applications not accepted. Giving primarily in Asheville, NC and the Greenville, SC, area. No grants to individuals.
Application information: Contributes only to pre-selected organizations.
Advisory Committee: Joel B. Adams, Jr.; Marla T. Adams; Dorothy B. Hamill.
Trustee: Capital Guardian Trust Co.
EIN: 576113645
Selected grants: The following grants were reported in 2005.
$20,000 to Pack Place Performing Arts, Asheville, NC.

$17,000 to North Carolina Center for International Understanding, Raleigh, NC.

$10,000 to Nature Conservancy, Durham, NC.

$10,000 to Southern Environmental Law Center, Chapel Hill, NC.

$10,000 to YMCA of Western North Carolina, Asheville, NC.

$5,000 to Children First of Buncombe County, Asheville, NC.

$5,000 to Mountain Housing Opportunities, Asheville, NC.

$5,000 to North Carolina Outward Bound School, Asheville, NC.

$5,000 to Pisgah Legal Services, Asheville, NC.

$3,000 to Hospitality House of Asheville, Asheville, NC.

268

Beavers Charitable Trust ◇ ☆

2053 Grant Rd., PMB 370
Los Altos, CA 94024-6913 (650) 694-4834
FAX: (650) 694-4836;
E-mail: thebeavers@sbcglobal.net; URL: http://www.thebeavers.org/trust.html

Established in 1977 in CA.

Donors: The Beavers, Inc.; Corey Delta Constructors; Kellogg LLC; Granite Construction Co.; S & W Scott Foundation; Traylor Brothers, Inc.; Tutor-Saliba; The Dutra Group.

Foundation type: Independent foundation.

Financial data (yr. ended 4/30/06): Assets, $8,282,838 (M); gifts received, $1,034,000; expenditures, $413,618; qualifying distributions, $355,000; giving activities include $355,000 for grants.

Purpose and activities: Awards grants to higher education institutions offering engineering degrees.

Fields of interest: Higher education; Engineering school/education.

Type of support: Endowments; Scholarship funds; Matching/challenge support.

Limitations: Applications not accepted. Giving on a national basis. No grants to individuals.

Application information: Contributes only to pre-selected organizations.

Board meeting date(s): Jan., Apr., Aug., and Oct.

Officer and Trustees:* Lynn E. Barr,* Chair.; Sam E. Baker, Jr.; John Callan; Thomas R. Draeger; Ronald M. Fedrick; Gerard M. Kenny; Ralph G. Larison; Thomas W. Traylor.

Number of staff: 1 full-time professional; 1 part-time support.

EIN: 953605104

Selected grants: The following grants were reported in 2004.

$100,000 to California State University, School of Engineering, Chico, CA. For scholarships.

$20,000 to California State Polytechnic University, Pomona, CA. For scholarships.

$20,000 to University of Hawaii, Honolulu, HI. For scholarships.

$20,000 to University of Notre Dame, Notre Dame, IN. For scholarships.

$20,000 to Washington State University, Pullman, WA. For scholarships.

269

Bechtel Group Foundation

(formerly Bechtel Foundation)
50 Beale St.
San Francisco, CA 94105 (415) 768-1842
Contact: Marthe Patterson, Comms. and Grants Off.
E-mail: becfoun@bechtel.com; Application address:
P.O. Box 193965, San Francisco, CA 94119-3965;
URL: http://www.bechtel.com/foundation.htm

Incorporated in 1953 in CA.

Donors: Bechtel Group, Inc.; Bechtel Power Corp.; Bechtel Systems of Infrastructure, Inc.; Bechtel Corp.

Foundation type: Company-sponsored foundation.

Financial data (yr. ended 12/31/05): Assets, $13,864,953 (M); gifts received, $4,422,087; expenditures, $3,278,170; qualifying distributions, $3,135,494; giving activities include $3,135,494 for 440 grants (high: $840,600; low: $100).

Purpose and activities: The foundation supports organizations involved with arts and culture, education, human services, engineering and construction business, and public policy research.

Fields of interest: Arts; Higher education; Business school/education; Engineering school/education; Education; Human services; Federated giving programs; Science, formal/general education; Mathematics; Engineering; Public policy, research.

Type of support: General/operating support; Program development; Scholarship funds; Employee volunteer services; Employee matching gifts; Employee-related scholarships.

Limitations: Giving on a national and international basis in areas of company operations. No support for religious organizations. No grants to individuals (except for employee-related scholarships), or for endowments or special projects.

Application information: Application form not required.

Initial approach: Proposal
Deadline(s): None
Board meeting date(s): Annually
Final notification: Varies

Officers and Directors:* R.P. Bechtel,* Chair.; J.P. Laspa, Pres.; R.M. Burt,* Sr. V.P.; M.S. Knox, Principal V.P. and Treas.; Adrian Zaccaria.

Number of staff: 1 full-time professional; 1 part-time professional; 1 full-time support; 1 part-time support.

EIN: 946078120

Selected grants: The following grants were reported in 2005.

$840,600 to American Red Cross.

$155,000 to United Way of the Bay Area, San Francisco, CA.

$60,000 to Scholarship America, Saint Peter, MN.

$50,000 to JASON Foundation for Education, Needham Heights, MA.

$30,425 to Stanford University, Stanford, CA.

$7,500 to United Way of Frederick County, Frederick, MD.

$6,000 to Montgomery Hospice Society, Rockville, MD.

$5,000 to American Geological Institute Foundation, Alexandria, VA.

$3,000 to Salvation Army.

$500 to College of Saint Elizabeth, Morristown, NJ.

270

S. D. Bechtel, Jr. Foundation ▼ ◇

(formerly Elizabeth and Stephen Bechtel, Jr. Foundation)
P.O. Box 193809
San Francisco, CA 94119-3809 (415) 284-8572
Contact: Kay Barthold, Asst.
FAX: (415) 284-8571;
E-mail: esb@fremontgroup.com

Incorporated in 1957 in CA.

Donors: S.D. Bechtel, Jr.; Elizabeth H. Bechtel.

Foundation type: Independent foundation.

Financial data (yr. ended 12/31/04): Assets, $121,401,259 (M); gifts received, $16,901,860; expenditures, $5,023,963; qualifying distributions, $4,293,536; giving activities include $3,929,532 for 201 grants (high: $200,000; low: $550; average: $1,000–$50,000).

Purpose and activities: The purpose of the foundation is to support well-managed nonprofit organizations that provide quality programs and create significant sustained benefits primarily in the areas of engineering and science, conservation, youth development and education, and preventive health care programs and research. The foundation also supports civic and cultural institutions in the San Francisco Bay Area.

Fields of interest: Engineering school/education; Education; Animals/wildlife, preservation/protection; Youth development, services; Engineering/technology; Engineering; Science; Leadership development.

Type of support: General/operating support; Continuing support; Annual campaigns; Capital campaigns; Building/renovation; Land acquisition; Program development; Curriculum development; Scholarship funds; Research; Program evaluation; Matching/challenge support.

Limitations: Applications not accepted. Giving primarily in the San Francisco Bay Area and northern CA. No grants to individuals, or for tenured or contract positions, endowment activities, or underwriting/sponsoring events.

Application information: Contributes only to pre-selected organizations.

Board meeting date(s): Late spring and early winter

Officers and Directors:* S.D. Bechtel, Jr., Pres.; Nancy S. Hair, V.P. and Secy.-Treas.; Lauren B. Dachs, V.P. and Exec. Dir.; Elizabeth H. Bechtel,* V.P.; Alan M. Dachs; Nonie B. Ramsay.

Number of staff: 1 full-time professional; 3 part-time professional; 1 full-time support.

EIN: 946066138

Selected grants: The following grants were reported in 2004.

$200,000 to Purdue University, West Lafayette, IN. For capital support.

$200,000 to Thacher School, Ojai, CA. For capital support.

$100,000 to California Academy of Sciences, San Francisco, CA. For capital support.

$100,000 to California Conservation Fund, San Francisco, CA. For capital support.

$75,000 to Boy Scouts of America, San Francisco Bay Area Council, San Leandro, CA. For capital support.

$50,000 to Audubon California, Sacramento, CA. For capital support.

$15,000 to American Society for Engineering Education, DC. For program support.

$15,000 to Property and Environment Research Center, Bozeman, MT. For program support.

$15,000 to San Francisco Conservation Corps, San Francisco, CA. For program support.

$5,000 to National Trust for Historic Preservation, San Francisco, CA. For program support.

271
Newton and Rochelle Becker Family Foundation ✧
700 Larkspur Landing Cir., Ste. 199
Larkspur, CA 94939

Established in 1999 in CA.
Donors: Newton D. Becker; Rochelle Becker; Hochberg Family Foundation.
Foundation type: Independent foundation.
Financial data (yr. ended 9/30/05): Assets, $13,104,564 (M); gifts received, $5,000; expenditures, $3,326,188; qualifying distributions, $3,207,679; giving activities include $3,083,928 for 29 grants (high: $2,274,580; low: $500; average: $10,000–$291,000), and $89,661 for 4 foundation-administered programs.
Fields of interest: Media/communications; Media, film/video; International affairs; Jewish federated giving programs; Jewish agencies & temples.
Limitations: Applications not accepted. No grants to individuals.
Application information: Contributes only to pre-selected organizations.
Officers: Newton D. Becker, Pres.; David E. Becker, V.P., Secy. and C.F.O.
Directors: Rochelle Becker; Laura Becker Mintzer.
EIN: 954765920
Selected grants: The following grants were reported in 2005.
$291,000 to Middle East Media Research Institute, DC.
$61,848 to Foundation for the Defense of Democracies, DC.
$55,000 to Zionist Organization of America, New York, NY.
$30,000 to Center for the Study of Popular Culture, Los Angeles, CA.
$25,000 to Center for Security Policy, DC.
$25,000 to Jewish Institute for National Security Affairs, DC.
$10,000 to Washington Institute for Near East Policy, DC.
$2,500 to Stephen S. Wise Temple, Los Angeles, CA.

272
Arnold and Mabel Beckman Foundation ▼
100 Academy Dr.
Irvine, CA 92617 (949) 721-2222
Contact: Jacqueline Dorrance, Exec. Dir.
FAX: (949) 721-2225; Mailing address: P.O. Box 13219, Newport Beach, CA 92658; e-mail (for Kathlene Williams, Exec. Asst.): k.williams@beckman-foundation.com; URL: http://www.beckman-foundation.com

Incorporated in 1977 in CA.
Donors: Arnold O. Beckman†; Mabel M. Beckman†; Conexant.
Foundation type: Independent foundation.
Financial data (yr. ended 8/31/05): Assets, $533,551,993 (M); gifts received, $127,068,810; expenditures, $19,291,290; qualifying distributions, $18,310,199; giving activities include

$17,245,476 for 187 grants (high: $1,750,000; low: $25; average: $5,000–$80,000).
Purpose and activities: The foundation makes grants to nonprofit research institutions to promote research in chemistry and life sciences, broadly interpreted, to foster the invention of methods, instruments, and materials that will open new avenues of research in science.
Fields of interest: Cancer; Eye diseases; Heart & circulatory diseases; Biomedicine; Medical research, institute; Cancer research; Eye research; Heart & circulatory research; AIDS research; Science; Marine science; Physical/earth sciences; Chemistry; Physics; Engineering/technology; Biological sciences.
Type of support: Research; Employee matching gifts; Grants to individuals.
Limitations: Giving primarily in the U.S. No support for political or religious purposes, or for research that does not fall within the foundation's areas of interest. No grants to individuals (except for Beckman Young Investigator's Program), or for dinners, mass mailings, or fundraising campaigns; no loans.
Publications: Application guidelines; Program policy statement.
Application information: Grant policy and procedure information is available from the foundation. Application form required.
> *Initial approach:* Pre-proposal letter not to exceed 3 pages
> *Copies of proposal:* 1
> *Deadline(s):* Oct. 1
> *Board meeting date(s):* Quarterly
> *Final notification:* Apr. or May

Officers and Directors:* George L. Argyros,* Chair.; Gavin Herbert, Sr.,* Vice-Chair.; Theodore L. Brown, Ph.D.*, Secy.; Gary T. Wescombe, Ph.D.*, Treas.; Jacqueline Dorrance, Exec. Dir.; Arnold W. Beckman; G. Patricia Beckman; Gerald E. Gallwas; Harry B. Gray, Ph.D.; Gary H. Hunt; William H. May.
Number of staff: 1 full-time professional; 3 full-time support.
EIN: 953169713
Selected grants: The following grants were reported in 2005.
$1,838,000 to Cold Spring Harbor Laboratory, Cold Spring Harbor, NY. 2 grants: $88,000, $1,750,000 (For general support).
$1,732,000 to California Institute of Technology, Pasadena, CA.
$1,732,000 to University of Illinois at Urbana-Champaign, Beckman Institute for Advanced Science and Technology, Urbana, IL.
$1,155,000 to Stanford University, Beckman Center for Molecular and Genetic Medicine, Stanford, CA.
$866,000 to Beckman Research Institute of the City of Hope, Duarte, CA. For research.
$333,333 to University of Pennsylvania, Philadelphia, PA.
$333,333 to University of Southern California, Norris Cancer Center, Los Angeles, CA.
$117,000 to Santa Ana Unified School District, Santa Ana, CA.
$80,000 to University of Michigan, Ann Arbor, MI.

273
Milo W. Bekins Foundation ✧
5000 Birch Ave., 10th Fl.
Newport Beach, CA 92660

Trust established in 1953 in CA.

Donors: Milo W. Bekins†; The Bekins Co.
Foundation type: Independent foundation.
Financial data (yr. ended 12/31/04): Assets, $6,340,290 (M); expenditures, $434,330; qualifying distributions, $347,231; giving activities include $338,000 for 20 grants (high: $35,000; low: $1,000).
Purpose and activities: Giving primarily to health organizations, including children's hospitals, and including services for people who are blind; funding also for children and youth services, and social services.
Fields of interest: Higher education; Education; Hospitals (general); Hospitals (specialty); Eye diseases; Human services; Children/youth, services; Federated giving programs.
Type of support: Scholarship funds.
Limitations: Applications not accepted. Giving primarily in CA, with emphasis on Los Angeles. No grants to individuals.
Application information: Contributes only to pre-selected organizations.
Trustees: Jacqueline Bekins; Michael Bekins; Richard Bekins; Virginia Bekins Daum.
EIN: 956039745
Selected grants: The following grants were reported in 2004.
$30,000 to Doheny Eye Institute, Los Angeles, CA.
$30,000 to Pacific Lodge Youth Services, Woodland Hills, CA.
$30,000 to University of Redlands, Redlands, CA.
$16,000 to Pepperdine University, Malibu, CA.
$15,000 to SoundArt Foundation, Philmont, NY.
$10,000 to House Ear Institute, Los Angeles, CA.
$5,000 to American Cancer Society, Oakland, CA.
$1,000 to Lance Armstrong Foundation, Austin, TX.
$1,000 to Lawrence Hall of Science, Berkeley, CA.

274
Bell Charitable Foundation ✧
P.O. Box 642
Rancho Santa Fe, CA 92067

Established in 1994 in CA.
Donor: Bell Family Trust.
Foundation type: Independent foundation.
Financial data (yr. ended 10/31/05): Assets, $7,091,577 (M); expenditures, $394,502; qualifying distributions, $394,502; giving activities include $388,805 for 67 grants (high: $60,000; low: $200).
Purpose and activities: Giving primarily for Parkinson's disease research; funding also for medical research, youth programs, and education.
Fields of interest: Education; Health care; Medical research, institute; Parkinson's disease research; Children/youth, services; Disabilities, people with.
Limitations: Applications not accepted. Giving primarily in San Diego County, CA. No grants to individuals.
Application information: Contributes only to pre-selected organizations. Unsolicited requests for funds not accepted or acknowledged.
Officers and Directors:* Martha A. Bell,* Pres.; Kathleen Bell-Flynn,* V.P.; Steve Flynn*, Secy.
EIN: 330640946
Selected grants: The following grants were reported in 2005.
$10,000 to Burn Institute, San Diego, CA.
$10,000 to Council for National Policy, Arlington, VA.
$7,500 to Boy Scouts of America, San Diego, CA.

$7,500 to North Coast Repertory Theater, Solana Beach, CA.

$5,000 to Community Resource Center, Encinitas, CA.

$5,000 to Elizabeth Hospice, Escondido, CA.

$5,000 to Freedom Alliance, Dulles, VA.

$5,000 to Landmark Legal Foundation, Leesburg, VA.

$5,000 to Pacific Justice Institute, Citrus Heights, CA.

$5,000 to Point Loma Nazarene University, San Diego, CA.

275

Bella Vista Foundation

(formerly Kirkwood Family Foundation)
1660 Bush St., Ste. 300
San Francisco, CA 94109 (415) 561-6540
Contact: Mary L. Gregory, Exec. Dir.
FAX: (415) 561-6477; URL: http://www.pfs-llc.net/bellavista/index.html

Established in 1999 in CA.
Foundation type: Independent foundation.
Financial data (yr. ended 12/31/05): Assets, $48,811,129 (M); expenditures, $2,315,015; qualifying distributions, $2,045,122; giving activities include $1,798,627 for grants.
Purpose and activities: The foundation maintains a two-part grantmaking focus to fund programs that address fundamental causes of societal problems, rather than programs that seek to remedy the effects of those programs. Through its Early Childhood Development Focus Area, the foundation funds programs addressing the social, emotional, cognitive, and physical needs of children in the 45 months from conception to age three, particularly those that help parents improve their parenting/nurturing skills. Under its Ecosystem Restoration Grants, the foundation focuses on protecting, restoring, and revitalizing high priority watershed ecosystems in California and Oregon. Within these key watersheds, the foundation's priorities are promoting the sustainable management of forest and agricultural land, revitalizing streams, and restoring riparian areas, with the goal of enhancing and maintaining self-sustaining watershed ecosystems.
Fields of interest: Education, early childhood education; Environment, natural resources; Children, services; Child development, services; Family services, parent education.
Type of support: General/operating support; Program development.
Limitations: Giving primarily in Marin, San Francisco, San Mateo and Santa Clara counties (in area of early childhood development) and in California and Oregon (environmental restoration projects). No support for the arts or sectarian religious purposes. No grants to individuals, or for benefit events. Generally, no grants for medical research, health care, publications, or video production (except under special circumstances and only in the early childhood development focus area).
Application information: Please check foundation Web site for current grantmaking information and guidelines.
Board meeting date(s): Fall
Officers and Directors:* Robert C. Kirkwood,* Pres.; Susan K. Koe,* V.P.; John H. Kirkwood,* Secy.; Jean K. Casey,* C.F.O.; Mary L. Gregory, Exec. Dir.; Jean G. Doyle.
EIN: 943345967

Selected grants: The following grants were reported in 2005.

$100,000 to Edgewood Center for Children and Families, San Francisco, CA. For continued support of KinStart program, helping grandparents or other relative caregivers who are raising children ages 0-3 in San Mateo County and San Francisco.

$75,000 to Pacific Forest Trust, San Francisco, CA. To continue acquistion, landowner outreach and community building activities in McCloud Forest as part of Headwaters of Biodiversity: Klamath-Siskiyou Conservation Project.

$75,000 to Raising A Reader - San Francisco, San Francisco, CA. To provide access to this shared books program for children ages 0-5 in San Francisco.

$75,000 to Trust for Public Land, Western Region, San Francisco, CA. For Phase II of Sierra Checkerboard Initiative, during which TPL will develop land realignment solutions, including acquisitions, land exchanges, conservation easements, and management agreements.

$75,000 to World Wildlife Fund, DC. For restoration of fish passage on Little Butte Creek, tributary system in Rogue River, with ultimate goal of providing fish access to 1,000 miles of prime riverine habitat by 2007.

$66,333 to Parents Leadership Institute, Palo Alto, CA. To use core Parenting by Connection curriculum to create handbook, reader and teacher's guide, run pilot classes for parents, and create certification procedure for trainers.

$60,000 to Mattole Restoration Council, Petrolia, CA. For riparian and forest restoration projects including fuel reduction projects, in Mattole River Watershed in Northern California.

$60,000 to Nature Conservancy, San Francisco, CA. For development of restoration plan for Upper Pajaro River floodplain, 20,000 acres site, which was once vast network of wetlands that connected Mt. Hamilton Range and Santa Cruz Mountains.

$60,000 to Prenatal to Three Initiative, San Mateo, CA. For continued support to parent education classes (Strengthening MultiCultural Families) and Touchpoints support groups for parents with children prenatal to three.

$55,000 to Florence Crittenton Services, San Francisco, CA. For Parent and Family Resource Center providing parenting education through group settings and individualized consultation.

276

The Legler Benbough Foundation

2550 5th Ave., Ste. 132
San Diego, CA 92103-6622 (619) 235-8099
Contact: Peter K. Ellsworth, Pres.
FAX: (619) 235-8077; URL: http://www.benboughfoundation.org

Established in 1985 in CA.
Donor: Legler Benbough†.
Foundation type: Independent foundation.
Financial data (yr. ended 12/31/05): Assets, $43,459,072 (M); expenditures, $2,289,405; qualifying distributions, $1,900,301; giving activities include $1,747,989 for 47 grants (high: $100,000; low: $5,000).
Purpose and activities: Giving to improve the quality of life and opportunity for people in the city of San Diego, CA, by support of 1), cultural organizations located in Balboa Park, 2) non-profit research

organizations located near the Univ. of California, and 3) health, education and welfare projects in the Market Creek area of the Diamond Neighborhoods of San Diego.
Fields of interest: Museums; Education; Hospitals (general); Health care; Medical research; Youth development; Children/youth, services; Community development.
Type of support: General/operating support; Continuing support; Program development; Scholarship funds; Research; Program-related investments/loans; Matching/challenge support.
Limitations: Giving limited to within the city of San Diego, CA. No support for religious, political, AIDS, or homeless organizations. No grants to individuals or for capital campaigns, or the performing or modern arts.
Publications: Application guidelines.
Application information: Application form required.
Initial approach: Letter to request application
Copies of proposal: 1
Deadline(s): Mar. 15 and Sept. 15
Board meeting date(s): Quarterly
Final notification: Apr. 15 and Oct. 15
Officers and Directors:* Peter K. Ellsworth,* Pres.; Thomas E. Cisco,* V.P. and Secy.-Treas.; Hugh C. Carter; Frederick P. Crowell; John G. Rebelo, Jr.
Number of staff: 2 full-time professional.
EIN: 330105049
Selected grants: The following grants were reported in 2004.

$200,000 to Zoological Society of San Diego, San Diego, CA.

$125,000 to Neurosciences Institute, San Diego, CA.

$100,000 to Sharp HealthCare Foundation, San Diego, CA.

$85,000 to Reuben H. Fleet Science Center, San Diego, CA.

$50,000 to Balboa Park Cultural Partnership, San Diego, CA.

$50,000 to Sidney Kimmel Cancer Center, San Diego, CA.

$45,000 to Museum of Photographic Arts, San Diego, CA.

$30,000 to Elementary Institute of Science, San Diego, CA.

$30,000 to San Diego Family Justice Center, San Diego, CA.

$28,000 to Childrens Hospital and Health Center, San Diego, CA.

277

Beneto Foundation ◇

P.O. Box 980220
West Sacramento, CA 95798-0220

Established in 1997 in CA.
Donor: Stephen Beneto.
Foundation type: Independent foundation.
Financial data (yr. ended 12/31/04): Assets, $3,082,169 (M); gifts received, $120,000; expenditures, $790,007; qualifying distributions, $781,000; giving activities include $781,000 for 17 grants (high: $500,000; low: $500).
Purpose and activities: Giving primarily for children and youth services, as well as for health associations, particularly an institute for research in neurodevelopmental disorders; funding also for human services, and Roman Catholic higher education.
Fields of interest: Higher education; Health care, association; Hospitals (general); Neuroscience

research; Human services; Children/youth, services.

Limitations: Applications not accepted. No grants to individuals.

Application information: Contributes only to pre-selected organizations.

Officers and Directors:* Stephen Beneto, Chair. and Pres.; Velma Masterson,* Secy.-Treas.; Darlene Beneto; Lucille R. Friday; Gene Hume; Paul Marchi; Nina Pucci.

EIN: 680397473

Selected grants: The following grants were reported in 2003.

$30,000 to Childrens Receiving Home of Sacramento, Sacramento, CA. For children's programs.

$30,000 to Sacramento Childrens Home, Sacramento, CA. For children's programs.

$10,000 to Mercy Foundation, Rancho Cordova, CA. For community health services.

$10,000 to Shriners Hospitals for Children, Tampa, FL.

$10,000 to SUCCEED Program, Sacramento, CA.

$5,000 to Sacramento Loaves and Fishes, Sacramento, CA. For meal and shelter programs.

$4,500 to University of California, MIND Institute, Davis, CA. For program support.

$1,000 to Okizu Foundation, Novato, CA. For program support.

$1,000 to Saint Jude Childrens Research Hospital, Memphis, TN.

$750 to West Sacramento Teen Center, West Sacramento, CA. For community programs.

278
The Benificus Foundation ✧
(formerly Vallejo Ventures Private Foundation)
2995 Woodside Rd., No. 400-402
Woodside, CA 94062

Established in 1997 in CA.

Donors: Ann Howland Doerr; L. John Doerr.

Foundation type: Independent foundation.

Financial data (yr. ended 9/30/05): Assets, $53,215,625 (M); gifts received, $57,944; expenditures, $2,118,137; qualifying distributions, $1,762,750; giving activities include $1,759,500 for 14 grants (high: $1,000,000; low: $5,000).

Fields of interest: Media, television; Education; Hospitals (general); Health organizations, association; Cystic fibrosis research; Foundations (private grantmaking).

Limitations: Applications not accepted. Giving primarily in CA; some funding nationally. No grants to individuals.

Application information: Contributes only to pre-selected organizations.

Officers: L. John Doerr III, Pres.; Ann Howland Doerr, V.P. and Secy.-Treas.

EIN: 770444504

Selected grants: The following grants were reported in 2005.

$1,000,000 to Stanford Hospital and Clinics, Stanford, CA.

$300,000 to Grameen Foundation USA, DC.

$202,000 to Aspen Institute, Aspen, CO.

$50,000 to NetDay, Irvine, CA.

$25,000 to Rice University, Houston, TX.

$25,000 to Santa Clara University, Santa Clara, CA.

$10,000 to Raphael House, San Francisco, CA.

$5,000 to Aspen Center for Environmental Studies, Aspen, CO.

279
The Bennett Family Foundation ✧ ☆
777 S. Ham Ln., Ste. L
Lodi, CA 95241

Donor: Dennis Bennett.

Foundation type: Independent foundation.

Financial data (yr. ended 12/31/05): Assets, $256,303 (M); gifts received, $330,000; expenditures, $324,415; qualifying distributions, $322,180; giving activities include $322,180 for 9 + grants (high: $276,900).

Fields of interest: Higher education; Human services; Christian agencies & churches.

Limitations: Giving primarily in CA, with emphasis on Lodi.

Application information:
Initial approach: Letter

Officer: Dennis Bennett, Pres. and Treas.

EIN: 431967486

280
Alain Ralphs Benson Foundation ✧ ☆
1411 Tenth St.
Coronado, CA 92118

Established in 2005 in CA.

Foundation type: Operating foundation.

Financial data (yr. ended 12/31/05): Assets, $2,642,072 (M); gifts received, $3,304,009; expenditures, $682,148; qualifying distributions, $681,987; giving activities include $579,734 for 2 + grants (high: $572,536).

Fields of interest: Children/youth, services; Children, services.

Limitations: Applications not accepted. Giving primarily in CA and in Mexico. No grants to individuals.

Application information: Unsolicited requests for funds not accepted.

Officers: Anthony W. Ralphs, Pres.; Maria De Pillar Ralphs, C.F.O.

Trustees: Harriet H. Carter; Bernadatte M. Ralphs; Carlos Vega.

EIN: 202143546

281
H. N. & Frances C. Berger Foundation ▼ ✧
P.O. Box 13390
Palm Desert, CA 92255-3390   (760) 341-5293
Contact: Christopher M. McGuire, V.P.

Established in 1993 in CA, AZ, and TX.

Foundation type: Independent foundation.

Financial data (yr. ended 12/31/04): Assets, $497,568,470 (M); expenditures, $29,772,354; qualifying distributions, $27,868,134; giving activities include $24,092,018 for 91 grants (high: $14,400,000; low: $750; average: $15,000–$250,000), and $1,409,650 for 2 foundation-administered programs.

Purpose and activities: Emphasis on higher education, cultural programs, public health organizations, and hospitals. Committed to long-term support of present donees.

Fields of interest: Arts; Higher education; Hospitals (general); Health care; Health organizations, association.

Limitations: Applications not accepted. Giving primarily in CA.

Application information: Contributes only to pre-selected organizations.

Board meeting date(s): Semiannually, and as required

Officers and Directors:* Ronald M. Auen,* Pres.; John N. Berger,* V.P.; Darrell Burrage,* V.P.; Christopher M. McGuire,* V.P.; Douglass Vance,* V.P.; Joan C. Auen,* Secy.-Treas.; Lewis Webb, Jr.

EIN: 521757452

Selected grants: The following grants were reported in 2004.

$14,400,000 to Xavier College Preparatory High School, Palm Desert, CA. To purchase land to construct high school.

$3,434,820 to Corporation for Education Network Initiatives in California (CENIC), Cypress, CA. For fiber optic network infrastructure serving Coachella Valley educational institutions.

$800,000 to Appalachian College Association, Berea, KY. For continuation of Student Faculty Travel programs.

$500,000 to Huntington Hospital, Pasadena, CA. For acquisition and enhancement of radiation therapy equipment.

$325,000 to Teammates for Kids, Littleton, CO. For construction of Mount Sinai Hospital Zone in New York.

$250,000 to Mission Healthcare Foundation, Asheville, NC. For construction of Pediatric Outpatient Center.

$200,000 to University of San Diego, Hahn School of Nursing, San Diego, CA. For establishment of endowed scholarship for Masters and Doctoral students.

$50,000 to Burchette Conners Ellington Herford and Lynch Memorial College, New Rochelle, NY. For FBI Agents Memorial College Education Fund.

$48,735 to Stroke Recovery Center, Palm Springs, CA. For stroke rehabilitation program.

$25,000 to Desert Forum, Palm Springs, CA. For Desert Town Hall Speakers Series.

282
Erik E. and Edith H. Bergstrom Foundation, A Charitable Trust ✧
P.O. Box 520
Palo Alto, CA 94302-0520
Contact: Edith H. Bergstrom, Dir.

Newly formed in 2002 in CA; previously Erik E. and Edith H. Bergstrom Foundation, Inc.

Donors: Edith H. Bergstrom; Erik E. Bergstrom.

Foundation type: Independent foundation.

Financial data (yr. ended 9/30/05): Assets, $79,133,241 (M); expenditures, $4,896,579; qualifying distributions, $3,951,497; giving activities include $3,891,613 for 14 grants (high: $710,475; low: $2,500; average: $110,000–$572,400).

Purpose and activities: Giving primarily for international affairs.

Fields of interest: Health care; Family services; International agricultural development; International economic development; International affairs.

Limitations: Applications not accepted. Giving primarily in the U.S., Mexico and Central America. No grants to individuals.

Application information: Contributes only to pre-selected organizations.

Directors: Edith H. Bergstrom; Erik E. Bergstrom.

EIN: 912155835

283
Berkshire Foundation
P.O. Box 221432
Carmel, CA 93922

Established in 1996 in CA.
Donors: Roberta Buffett Bialek; Hilton Bialek†; Berkshire Hathaway Inc.
Foundation type: Independent foundation.
Financial data (yr. ended 12/31/05): Assets, $5,941,492 (M); expenditures, $382,674; qualifying distributions, $377,487; giving activities include $375,000 for 6 grants (high: $150,000; low: $25,000).
Purpose and activities: Giving primarily for education and human services.
Fields of interest: Education; Human services; Civil liberties, reproductive rights.
Limitations: Applications not accepted. Giving primarily in CA. No grants to individuals.
Application information: Contributes only to pre-selected organizations.
Officers: Roberta Buffett Bialek, Pres.; Susan S. Lansbury, Secy.-Treas.
Directors: Carolyn B. Akcan; Cynthia S. Zak.
EIN: 770438710

284
The Lowell Berry Foundation
3685 Mt. Diablo Blvd., Ste. 269
Lafayette, CA 94549 (925) 284-4427
Contact: Katherine Sanders, Office Mgr.; For religious grants: Patricia Berry Conklin; For social service grants: Barbara Berry Corneille

Incorporated in 1950 in CA.
Donors: Lowell W. Berry†; Farm Service Co.; The Best Fertilizer Co. of Texas.
Foundation type: Independent foundation.
Financial data (yr. ended 12/31/05): Assets, $26,174,080 (M); expenditures, $1,610,751; qualifying distributions, $1,579,955; giving activities include $1,489,333 for grants.
Purpose and activities: Support for evangelical Christian religious programs; non-religious grants are focused on social services. Grants also for education, youth agencies, and health associations.
Fields of interest: Arts; Education; Human services; Children/youth, services; Christian agencies & churches.
Type of support: General/operating support; Continuing support; Program development; Conferences/seminars; Scholarship funds.
Limitations: Giving primarily in Contra Costa and Alameda counties, CA. No support for newly established organizations. No grants to individuals, or for building or capital funds, equipment, seed money, or land acquisition.
Publications: Grants list; Informational brochure (including application guidelines).
Application information: Application form not required.
Initial approach: Letter or telephone for application guidelines
Copies of proposal: 1
Deadline(s): None
Board meeting date(s): Quarterly
Final notification: 3 to 4 months for religious grants; 3 to 4 months for social service grants
Officers and Directors:* Larry R. Langdon,* Pres.; Patricia Berry Conklin,* V.P.; Barbara Berry Corneille,* Secy.; Gary L. Depolo,* Treas.; John D.

Asher; Jami S. Kane; Jayne S. Mordell; Annette S. Robison.
Number of staff: 1 part-time support.
EIN: 946108391

285
Betterworld Together Foundation ◇
c/o Diane Garrett
1 Betterworld Cir., Ste. 200
Temecula, CA 92590

Established in 2000 in CA.
Donors: Paul Garrett; The Garrett Group, LLC.
Foundation type: Independent foundation.
Financial data (yr. ended 12/31/04): Assets, $725,322 (M); gifts received, $1,357,193; expenditures, $656,705; qualifying distributions, $322,621; giving activities include $322,621 for 34 grants (high: $100,000; low: $1,000).
Fields of interest: Libraries (public); Foundations (community).
Limitations: Giving primarily in CA. No grants to individuals.
Application information: Unsolicited requests for funds not accepted.
Officer: Diane Garrett, Exec. Dir.
Director: Paul Garrett.
EIN: 330884474

286
Burton G. Bettingen Corporation ◇
134 S. Mansfield Ave.
Los Angeles, CA 90036-3019 (323) 938-8478
Contact: Patricia A. Brown, Exec. Dir.
FAX: (323) 938-8479; E-mail: burtonbet@aol.com

Established in 1984 in CA.
Donor: Burton G. Bettingen†.
Foundation type: Independent foundation.
Financial data (yr. ended 9/30/04): Assets, $14,007,009 (M); gifts received, $1,482,145; expenditures, $2,219,427; qualifying distributions, $2,058,305; giving activities include $1,769,000 for 12 grants (high: $1,100,000; low: $100).
Purpose and activities: Support primarily for social services, with emphasis on street children.
Fields of interest: Human services; Children/youth, services; Family services.
Type of support: General/operating support; Capital campaigns.
Limitations: Giving primarily in southern CA. No grants to individuals, or for general fundraising events, conferences, seminars, dinners, or mass mailings.
Application information:
Initial approach: Letter
Board meeting date(s): Mar.
Officers and Directors:* Sandra G. Nowicki,* Chair. and Pres.; Patricia A. Brown,* Secy.-Treas. and Exec. Dir.; W.M. Lyles IV; George D. O'Neill, Jr.; George J. Parnassus.
Number of staff: 1 full-time professional; 1 part-time support.
EIN: 953942826
Selected grants: The following grants were reported in 2003.
$500,000 to North Country School, Lake Placid, NY.
$250,000 to Pueblo Nuevo Development, Los Angeles, CA.
$200,500 to Aviva Family and Childrens Services, Los Angeles, CA.

$200,000 to Childrens Bureau of Southern California, Los Angeles, CA.
$120,000 to United Negro College Fund, Fairfax, VA.
$100,225 to Catholic Charities of the Archdiocese of Los Angeles, Los Angeles, CA.
$100,000 to Childrens Hospital Los Angeles, Los Angeles, CA.
$100,000 to Los Angeles County High School for the Arts, Los Angeles, CA.
$100,000 to Phoenix House of California, Sylmar, CA.
$100,000 to Saint Johns Health Center, Santa Monica, CA.

287
Bickerstaff Family Foundation ◇
(also known as Caring Kids)
3052 Burney Pl.
Los Alamitos, CA 90720 (562) 430-5420
Contact: Deborah J. Bickerstaff, Pres.

Established in 2000 in CA.
Donors: Deborah J. Bickerstaff; Glen E. Bickerstaff.
Foundation type: Independent foundation.
Financial data (yr. ended 12/31/04): Assets, $14,483,316 (M); gifts received, $6,241,013; expenditures, $1,484,828; qualifying distributions, $1,413,105; giving activities include $1,413,105 for 20 grants (high: $651,000; low: $2,500).
Fields of interest: Education; Hospitals (general); Cancer research; Children/youth, services; Religion; Homeless.
Limitations: Giving primarily in CA. No grants to individuals.
Application information:
Deadline(s): None
Officers: Deborah J. Bickerstaff, Pres.; Glen E. Bickerstaff, Secy.
EIN: 954819633

288
Susan & Charlie Bickerton Foundation ◇ ☆
P.O. Box 14666
Oakland, CA 94614-2666

Established in 1998 in CA.
Donors: Susan Bickerton; Charlie Bickerton.
Foundation type: Independent foundation.
Financial data (yr. ended 12/31/05): Assets, $492,262 (M); expenditures, $369,526; qualifying distributions, $738,303; giving activities include $368,777 for 2 grants (high: $351,000; low: $17,777).
Fields of interest: Education.
Type of support: General/operating support.
Limitations: Applications not accepted. Giving primarily in CA. No grants to individuals.
Application information: Contributes only to pre-selected organizations.
Director: Charlie Bickerton.
EIN: 943315137

289
The Bilger Foundation ◇ ☆
480 Bel Air Rd.
Los Angeles, CA 90077

Established in 1990 in CA.
Donors: Arthur Bilger; Dahlia Bilger.

Foundation type: Independent foundation.
Financial data (yr. ended 12/31/05): Assets, $5,264,007 (M); gifts received, $887,850; expenditures, $444,549; qualifying distributions, $413,651; giving activities include $413,651 for 56 grants (high: $45,510; low: $100).
Purpose and activities: Giving for Jewish organizations and health associations.
Fields of interest: Arts; Education; Health organizations, association; Human services; Children/youth, services; Jewish federated giving programs; Jewish agencies & temples.
Limitations: Applications not accepted. Giving on a national basis. No grants to individuals.
Application information: Contributes only to pre-selected organizations.
Officer: Arthur Bilger, Pres.
EIN: 226524956
Selected grants: The following grants were reported in 2004.
$17,000 to American Jewish Committee, New York, NY.
$15,000 to Camp Ronald McDonald for Good Times, Los Angeles, CA.
$10,110 to Center for Early Education, West Hollywood, CA.
$10,000 to Marlborough School, Los Angeles, CA.
$6,000 to Urban Gateways: The Center for Arts in Education, Chicago, IL.
$5,000 to Academy for Jewish Religion, Riverdale, NY.
$5,000 to Alliance for Childrens Rights, Los Angeles, CA.
$5,000 to Food Allergy Initiative, New York, NY.
$4,000 to Los Angeles County Museum of Art, Los Angeles, CA.

290
Sheri Biller & Les Biller Family Foundation ✧ ☆

P.O. Box 63954
San Francisco, CA 94163
Application address: Wells Fargo Bank, N.A., P.O. Box 20160, Long Beach, CA 90801

Established in 2001 in CA.
Donors: Les Biller; Sheri Biller.
Foundation type: Independent foundation.
Financial data (yr. ended 12/31/05): Assets, $11,565,207 (M); gifts received, $402,381; expenditures, $1,002,990; qualifying distributions, $918,039; giving activities include $868,805 for 24 grants (high: $525,500; low: $500).
Purpose and activities: Giving to enhance the quality of life in the community through support of: 1) women's organizations which relieve suffering, defend rights, and improve living conditions of women in areas of abuse, health, vocational, legal assistance and family planning; 2) higher education for children of immigrants, in which the foundation funds, through a third party organization cadidate selection process, the higher education expenses of children of immigrants, immigrant (resident) children, and naturalized citizen children; 3) disadvantaged youth programs which focus on education, mentoring, developing leadership skills, encouraging community services and building self-esteem; and 4) theater arts programs in general education, the opera, theatrical arts, and in particular, youth performing arts that serve the needs of disadvantaged youth.
Limitations: Giving primarily in Los Angeles, CA. No support for projects outside the stated areas of

interest, pilot or seed programs unless the Founding Trustee is actively involved, or for organizations determined to be unhealthy or financially unstable. No grants to individuals, or for requests less than $1,000, or for more than directed by the Trust document.
Application information: For contributions of $100,000 or more, the foundation requires two years of audited financial statements and tax returns, a site visit completed by a trustee representative, and a detailed follow-up reporting on project expenditure and achievement.
  Initial approach: Letter
  Deadline(s): Nov. 1
Trustees: Les Biller; Sheri Biller.
EIN: 841608504

291
Binder Foundation ✧

11111 Santa Monica Blvd., Ste. 1850
Los Angeles, CA 90025

Established in 1997 in CA.
Donors: Adele Binder; Gordon M. Binder.
Foundation type: Independent foundation.
Financial data (yr. ended 12/31/05): Assets, $22,826,026 (M); gifts received, $5,200; expenditures, $1,187,579; qualifying distributions, $1,065,033; giving activities include $1,055,333 for 16 grants (high: $358,333; low: $1,000).
Fields of interest: Arts, association; Performing arts, orchestra (symphony); Higher education; Business school/education; Human services; Public policy, research.
Limitations: Applications not accepted. Giving primarily in CA; some funding also in Washington, DC, MA and NY. No grants to individuals.
Application information: Contributes only to pre-selected organizations.
Trustees: Adele Binder; Gordon M. Binder.
EIN: 954635806

292
The Bireley Foundation ✧ ☆

130 N. Brand Blvd., Ste. 405
Glendale, CA 91203-2617
Contact: John M. Carmack, Secy. and C.F.O.

Incorporated in 1960 in CA.
Donors: Frank W. Bireley; and members of the Bireley Family.
Foundation type: Independent foundation.
Financial data (yr. ended 12/31/05): Assets, $3,869,417 (M); expenditures, $2,170,082; qualifying distributions, $2,050,036; giving activities include $2,050,036 for grants.
Purpose and activities: Giving primarily for health associations and human services; funding also for the arts and the United Way.
Fields of interest: Performing arts; Arts; Higher education; Education; Health care; Health organizations, association; Cancer; Autism; Medical research, institute; Cancer research; Housing/shelter; Human services; Federated giving programs.
Type of support: General/operating support; Annual campaigns; Building/renovation; Equipment; Seed money; Research; Matching/challenge support.
Limitations: Giving primarily in FL. No grants to individuals.

Application information: Application form not required.
  Initial approach: Letter or proposal
  Copies of proposal: 2
  Deadline(s): None
  Board meeting date(s): 6 times a year
Officers: Frank W. Bireley, C.E.O. and Pres.; William Robert Bireley, V.P.; Christine Bireley Oliver, V.P.; John M. Carmack, Secy. and C.F.O.
EIN: 956029475
Selected grants: The following grants were reported in 2003.
$63,000 to Lee Memorial Health System Foundation, Fort Myers, FL.
$50,000 to Patrons of the Pratt Society, Homer, AK.
$44,000 to United Way of Lee County, Fort Myers, FL.
$15,000 to Habitat for Humanity of Lee County, North Fort Myers, FL.
$10,000 to Pioneer Theater Company, Salt Lake City, UT.
$5,000 to Shelter Ministries of Dallas, Dallas, TX.
$5,000 to YWCA of Salt Lake City, Salt Lake City, UT.
$2,500 to Florida Gulf Coast University, Fort Myers, FL.
$2,000 to Candlelighters of Southwest Florida, Fort Myers, FL.
$2,000 to Lee County Public Schools Foundation, Fort Myers, FL.

293
The Stanley and Joyce Black Family Foundation ✧ ☆

433 N. Camden Dr., Ste. 1070
Beverly Hills, CA 90210

Established in 1989 in CA.
Donors: Stanley Black; Joyce Black.
Foundation type: Independent foundation.
Financial data (yr. ended 12/31/05): Assets, $11,124,072 (M); gifts received, $1,247,878; expenditures, $625,106; qualifying distributions, $589,863; giving activities include $586,240 for 119 grants (high: $50,000; low: $25).
Fields of interest: Arts; Education; Human services; Jewish federated giving programs; Jewish agencies & temples.
Limitations: Applications not accepted. Giving primarily in CA. No grants to individuals.
Application information: Contributes only to pre-selected organizations.
Directors: Jack Black; Joyce Black; Stanley Black; Janis Goldman; Jill Zalben.
EIN: 954259961
Selected grants: The following grants were reported in 2004.
$50,000 to Cedars-Sinai Medical Center, Los Angeles, CA.
$50,000 to Childrens Hospital Los Angeles, Los Angeles, CA.
$50,000 to Los Angeles Jewish Home for the Aging, Reseda, CA.
$20,000 to Chabad of California, Los Angeles, CA. 2 grants: $10,000 each
$10,000 to University Synagogue, Los Angeles, CA.
$10,000 to Zimmer Jewish Discovery Childrens Museum, Los Angeles, CA.
$3,150 to Los Angeles Philharmonic, Los Angeles, CA.
$1,000 to Jewish Family Service of Los Angeles, Los Angeles, CA.
$1,000 to Los Angeles Free Clinic, Los Angeles, CA.

294
The Aaron and Marie Blackman Foundation, Inc. ✧
423 Broadway, Rm. 706
Millbrae, CA 94030
Contact: Milton Jacobs, Pres.

Established in 1989 in CA.
Donor: Marie Blackman.
Foundation type: Independent foundation.
Financial data (yr. ended 12/31/04): Assets, $7,949,161 (M); expenditures, $528,473; qualifying distributions, $483,092; giving activities include $439,700 for 56 grants (high: $80,000; low: $500).
Purpose and activities: Giving primarily to Jewish organizations, temples, and schools.
Fields of interest: Education; Human services; Aging, centers/services; Jewish agencies & temples.
International interests: Israel.
Limitations: Giving primarily in CA; some giving in Israel. No grants to individuals.
Application information: Application form not required.
   Deadline(s): None
Officers and Directors:* Milton Jacobs,* Pres.; Elizabeth Landers,* Secy.; Herbert Meiberger; Matook Nissim; Peter Samuels; Ron Solomon; Stuart Weinstein.
EIN: 943105905

295
Sam & Rie Bloomfield Foundation, Inc. ✧
1600 Dove St., No. 330
Newport Beach, CA 92660-1418

Established in 1958 in KS.
Donors: Sam Bloomfield†; Rie Bloomfield.
Foundation type: Independent foundation.
Financial data (yr. ended 11/30/05): Assets, $12,096,994 (M); expenditures, $772,866; qualifying distributions, $643,550; giving activities include $552,476 for 20 grants (high: $255,000; low: $750).
Purpose and activities: Giving primarily for a children's museum and science center, as well as to other museums, and arts and culture; funding also for higher education and human services.
Fields of interest: Museums (art); Museums (science/technology); Museums (specialized); Performing arts, orchestra (symphony); Higher education; Human services; Jewish agencies & temples.
Limitations: Applications not accepted. Giving primarily in Wichita, KS. No grants to individuals.
Application information: Contributes only to pre-selected organizations.
Officers and Trustees:* William L. Lucas,* Secy.; Alan L. McKay,* Secy.; Verlon L. McKay,* Treas.
EIN: 956074613
Selected grants: The following grants were reported in 2005.
$255,000 to Exploration Place, Wichita, KS.
$50,000 to Wichita Art Museum Foundation, Wichita, KS.
$25,000 to Friends University, Wichita, KS.
$20,000 to Wichita State University, Wichita, KS. 2 grants: $10,000 each
$2,500 to Opera Kansas, Wichita, KS.
$2,000 to Kansas Aviation Museum, Wichita, KS.
$2,000 to San Diego Aerospace Museum, San Diego, CA.

296
Blue Shield of California Foundation ▼
(formerly California Physicians' Service Foundation)
50 Beale St.
San Francisco, CA 94105-1819 (415) 229-5785
Contact: Crystal Hayling M.D., Pres. and C.E.O.; Brittany Imwalle, Dir., Finance and Admin.
FAX: (415) 229-6268;
E-mail: bscf@blueshieldcafoundation.org;
URL: http://www.blueshieldcafoundation.org/

Established in 1981 as a grantmaking public charity; status changed to company-sponsored foundation in 2004.
Donor: California Physicians' Service Agency Inc.
Foundation type: Company-sponsored foundation.
Financial data (yr. ended 12/31/05): Assets, $58,331,780 (M); gifts received, $29,829,415; expenditures, $23,611,919; qualifying distributions, $23,050,720; giving activities include $21,674,334 for 404 grants (high: $4,000,000; low: $2,000), and $32,000 for 16 grants to individuals (high: $2,500; low: $1,500).
Purpose and activities: The foundation supports organizations involved with health, domestic violence, and medical technology.
Fields of interest: Health care, alliance; Health care, equal rights; Health care; Crime/violence prevention, domestic violence; Family services, domestic violence; Science; Economically disadvantaged.
Type of support: General/operating support; Management development/capacity building; Program development; Scholarship funds; Research; Employee-related scholarships.
Limitations: Giving limited to CA. No support for religious organizations not of direct benefit to the entire community or political candidates or organizations. No grants to individuals (except for employee-related scholarships), or for political causes or campaigns.
Publications: Application guidelines; Annual report; Financial statement; Grants list; Informational brochure.
Application information: Application form required.
   Initial approach: Complete online application form
   Deadline(s): Rolling
   Board meeting date(s): Quarterly
   Final notification: 90 days
Officers and Trustees:* Ezra C. Davidson, Jr., M.D.*, Chair.; Crystal Hayling, M.D.*, Pres. and C.E.O.; Belva Davis; Thomas W. Epstein; Heidi Kunz; Aliza Lifshitz, M.D.; Esta Soler.
Number of staff: 9 full-time professional; 3 full-time support.
EIN: 942822302
Selected grants: The following grants were reported in 2004.
$2,900,000 to L.A. Care Health Plan, Los Angeles, CA. 2 grants: $2,000,000 (For Los Angeles Children's Health Initiative Coalition), $900,000 (For insurance premiums for low-income families).
$500,000 to Alameda Alliance for Health, Alameda, CA. For Family Care Premiums.
$100,000 to Violence Intervention Program (VIP) Community Mental Health Center, Los Angeles, CA. For intervention and prevention of family violence among foster care youth.
$87,500 to Organizacion en California de Lideres Campesinas, Pomona, CA. For domestic violence prevention and education for farmworker women.
$85,000 to Community Overcoming Relationship Abuse (CORA), San Mateo, CA. For information technology capacity support.
$70,000 to STAND Against Domestic Violence, Concord, CA. For Adelante Familia Outreach to Latino community.
$60,000 to Womens Educational Media, San Francisco, CA. For Let's Get Real California Training Project.
$20,000 to Mendocino Coast Clinics, Fort Bragg, CA. For core support.
$15,000 to YWCA of San Diego County, San Diego, CA.

297
Blum Family Foundation ✧
909 Montgomery St., Ste. 400
San Francisco, CA 94133

Established in 2002 in CA.
Donor: Richard C. Blum.
Foundation type: Independent foundation.
Financial data (yr. ended 12/31/05): Assets, $393,590 (M); gifts received, $1,049,009; expenditures, $663,823; qualifying distributions, $659,387; giving activities include $554,130 for 36 grants (high: $218,309; low: $100).
Fields of interest: Arts; Cancer research; Human services; Foundations (private grantmaking).
Limitations: Applications not accepted. No grants to individuals.
Application information: Contributes only to pre-selected organizations.
Officer: Richard C. Blum, Chair.
Director: Erica Stone.
EIN: 954894347
Selected grants: The following grants were reported in 2004.
$205,642 to American Himalayan Foundation, San Francisco, CA.
$101,209 to Aspen Institute, DC.
$25,000 to Asia Society, New York, NY.
$12,000 to Foundation for the People of Burma, San Francisco, CA.
$10,000 to Together for Peace Foundation, DC.

298
Blume Foundation ✧
85 El Cerrito Ave.
Hillsborough, CA 94010

Established in 1957 in CA.
Donors: John A. Blume; Ruth C. Blume†.
Foundation type: Independent foundation.
Financial data (yr. ended 11/30/05): Assets, $22,628,470 (M); expenditures, $1,304,717; qualifying distributions, $1,150,000; giving activities include $1,150,000 for 24 grants (high: $300,000; low: $5,000).
Purpose and activities: Giving primarily for higher education; support also for animal welfare, health, and medical research.
Fields of interest: Higher education, university; Hospitals (general); Health organizations, association; Neuroscience; Neuroscience research; Boys & girls clubs; Human services; Foundations (public).
Limitations: Applications not accepted. Giving primarily in CA. No grants to individuals.

Application information: Contributes only to pre-selected organizations.

  Board meeting date(s): Nov.

Officer: Jene S. Blume, Pres.

EIN: 946073163

Selected grants: The following grants were reported in 2004.

$600,000 to Stanford University, Stanford, CA. 2 grants: $300,000 each

$100,000 to Peninsula Humane Society and Society for the Prevention of Cruelty to Animals, San Mateo, CA.

$50,000 to Boys and Girls Club Foundation, Mid-Peninsula, San Mateo, CA.

$45,000 to Mills-Peninsula Hospital Foundation, Burlingame, CA.

$40,000 to American Cancer Society, San Mateo, CA.

$30,000 to K Q E D, San Francisco, CA.

$20,000 to Church of Jesus Christ of Latter Day Saints.

$20,000 to Planned Parenthood.

$20,000 to Salvation Army, San Mateo County, Redwood City, CA.

299
Boeckmann Charitable Foundation ✧

15505 Roscoe Blvd.

North Hills, CA   91343   (818) 787-3800

Contact: Herbert F. Boeckmann II, C.E.O.; Jane Boeckmann, Secy.

Established in 1982 in CA.

Donors: Herbert F. Boeckmann II; Jane Boeckmann.

Foundation type: Independent foundation.

Financial data (yr. ended 11/30/05): Assets, $1,635,232 (M); gifts received, $100,000; expenditures, $765,576; qualifying distributions, $760,470; giving activities include $760,470 for grants.

Purpose and activities: Giving primarily for religion and human services.

Fields of interest: Children/youth, services; Protestant agencies & churches; Religion.

Limitations: Giving primarily in CA.

Application information:

  Initial approach: Letter

  Deadline(s): None

Officers: Herbert F. Boeckmann II, C.E.O.; Jane Boeckmann, Secy.

EIN: 953806976

Selected grants: The following grants were reported in 2003.

$638,700 to Church on the Way, Van Nuys, CA.

$100,000 to Promise Keepers, Denver, CO.

$66,500 to High Adventure Ministries, Simi Valley, CA.

$65,500 to Boy Scouts of America, Western Los Angeles County Council, Van Nuys, CA.

$37,500 to Sierra Canyon High School Foundation, Chatsworth, CA.

$25,000 to Northwestern University, Evanston, IL.

$25,000 to United States Center for World Mission, Pasadena, CA.

$25,000 to Valley Presbyterian Hospital Foundation, Van Nuys, CA.

$20,000 to Horatio Alger Association of Distinguished Americans, Alexandria, VA.

$10,000 to American Cancer Society, Culver City, CA.

300
David Bohnett Foundation

245 S. Beverly Dr.

Beverly Hills, CA   90212   (310) 276-0001

Contact: Michael Fleming, Exec. Dir.

FAX: (310) 276-0007;

E-mail: mfpfleming@yahoo.com; URL: http://www.bohnettfoundation.org/

Established in 1999 in CA and DE.

Donor: David C. Bohnett.

Foundation type: Independent foundation.

Financial data (yr. ended 12/31/05): Assets, $33,559,519 (M); gifts received, $4,220,200; expenditures, $2,399,139; qualifying distributions, $2,138,279; giving activities include $1,939,353 for 173 grants (high: $100,000; low: $100).

Purpose and activities: The purpose of the foundation is to improve society through social activism. The foundation supports: 1) Positive portrayals of gays and lesbians in the media; 2) The reduction and elimination of the manufacture and sale of handguns; 3) Eliminating the rare animal trade; 4) The development of mass-transit and non-fossil fuel transportation; and 5) Voter registration activities.

Fields of interest: Media/communications; Human services; Civil rights, gays/lesbians; Civil rights, voter education; LGBTQ.

Type of support: General/operating support; Program development.

Limitations: Giving on a national basis, with emphasis on southern CA. No grants to individuals, or for videos or other film productions.

Publications: Grants list.

Application information: Application deadlines and information available on Web site. Application form required.

  Initial approach: Through foundation Web site

  Copies of proposal: 1

  Deadline(s): Jan. 31 and July 31

  Board meeting date(s): Twice a year

  Final notification: 4 months

Officers: David C. Bohnett, Chair.; Liz Atherton, Cont.; Michael Fleming, Exec. Dir.

Board of Advisors: Gwen Baba; Christopher Caldwell; Rich Llewellyn; Ed Pierce; Rob Saltzman.

Number of staff: 1 full-time professional; 1 part-time support.

EIN: 954735846

Selected grants: The following grants were reported in 2004.

$100,000 to Los Angeles Gay and Lesbian Center, Los Angeles, CA.

$100,000 to Proteus Fund, Amherst, MA.

$50,000 to Gay and Lesbian Leadership Institute, DC.

$50,000 to Lambda Legal Defense and Education Fund, New York, NY.

$35,000 to Servicemembers Legal Defense Network, DC.

$25,000 to Astraea Lesbian Foundation for Justice, New York, NY.

$25,000 to Educational Fund to Stop Gun Violence, DC.

$25,000 to Outfest, Los Angeles, CA.

$10,000 to Gay and Lesbian Adolescent Social Services (GLASS), West Hollywood, CA.

$5,000 to Museum of Television and Radio, Beverly Hills, CA.

301
The Bolthouse Foundation ▼

2000 Oak St., Ste. 200

Bakersfield, CA   93301-3058

Contact: Fred Green, Exec. Dir.

URL: http://www.thebolthousefoundation.org

Established in 1988 in CA.

Donors: William Bolthouse Farms, Inc.; Weyerhaeuser Corporation.

Foundation type: Independent foundation.

Financial data (yr. ended 12/31/04): Assets, $935,531 (M); gifts received, $5,306,949; expenditures, $5,872,275; qualifying distributions, $5,872,275; giving activities include $5,871,407 for 33 grants (high: $974,350; low: $15,000; average: $50,000–$200,000).

Purpose and activities: The foundation's purpose is to glorify the Lord Jesus Christ by supporting charitable and religious organizations whose ministry, goals, and operating principles are consistent with evangelical Christianity as described in the foundation's statement of faith.

Fields of interest: Theological school/education; Christian agencies & churches.

Limitations: Giving on a national and international basis. No support for private foundations. No grants to individuals.

Application information: The foundation does not accept unsolicited grant inquires by mail. For further information see the foundation Web site.

  Initial approach: See grant inquing tab on the foundation website

  Board meeting date(s): Apr.

Officers and Trustees:* William J. Bolthouse,* Pres.; Anthony L. Leggio,* Secy.; Stewart Fleeman,* Treas.; Fred Green, Exec. Dir.

Number of staff: 1 part-time support.

EIN: 770186343

Selected grants: The following grants were reported in 2004.

$974,350 to World Vision International, Monrovia, CA. To provide agricultural consulting in Romania and for Orphan Care Kids Club.

$612,000 to Masters College, Santa Clarita, CA. For Music Center and coach.

$500,000 to Bakersfield Christian High School, Bakersfield, CA. For scholarships.

$500,000 to Citivision, New York, NY. For multi-purpose center.

$300,000 to Lake Ann Baptist Camp, Lake Ann, MI. For Welcome Center.

$200,000 to Capitol Ministries, Santa Clarita, CA. To expand ministry.

$200,000 to Family Research Council, DC. For Center for Marriage and Family.

$184,000 to Cedarville University, Cedarville, OH. For scholarships.

$164,400 to Walk Thru the Bible Ministries, Atlanta, GA. For work in East Asia.

$100,000 to Caleb Project, Littleton, CO. For film project.

302
The Otis Booth Foundation ✧

10431 Bellagio Rd.

Los Angeles, CA   90077

Established in 1967 in CA.

Donor: Berkshire Hathaway Inc.

Foundation type: Independent foundation.

Financial data (yr. ended 11/30/05): Assets, $14,384,343 (M); expenditures, $760,405;

qualifying distributions, $760,405; giving activities include $760,220 for 25 grants (high: $100,000; low: $1,000).

Purpose and activities: Giving primarily for museums, as well as for education, and health.

Fields of interest: Museums (natural history); Museums (specialized); Education; Hospitals (general); Medical research; Federated giving programs.

Limitations: Applications not accepted. Giving in the U.S., primarily in CA. No grants to individuals.

Application information: Contributes only to pre-selected organizations.

Officers and Trustees: * Otis Booth, Jr.,* Pres.; Charles T. Munger,* V.P. and Treas.; Richard D. Esbenshade, Secy.-Treas.

EIN: 956140019

303

Booth Heritage Foundation, Inc. ◇

c/o Goodfriend and Jacobs
1299 Ocean Ave., Ste. 333
Santa Monica, CA 90401

Established in 2000 in CA.

Donors: David Booth; Suzanne Deal Booth.

Foundation type: Independent foundation.

Financial data (yr. ended 1/31/05): Assets, $2,533,895 (M); gifts received, $4,285,190; expenditures, $2,461,742; qualifying distributions, $2,461,593; giving activities include $2,461,593 for 65 grants (high: $1,300,000; low: $50).

Purpose and activities: Giving primarily for higher education and the arts.

Fields of interest: Museums; Museums (art); Arts; Higher education; Education; Human services; Children/youth, services; Jewish federated giving programs.

Limitations: Applications not accepted. Giving primarily in CA and IL; some giving in NY. No grants to individuals.

Application information: Contributes only to pre-selected organizations.

Officers and Directors: * Suzanne Deal Booth,* Pres.; David Booth,* Secy. and C.F.O.

EIN: 954785406

Selected grants: The following grants were reported in 2005.

$511,175 to Saint Matthews Parish School, Pacific Palisades, CA.

$200,000 to Los Angeles County Museum of Art, Los Angeles, CA.

$100,000 to American Academy in Rome, New York, NY.

$26,500 to California Institute of the Arts, Valencia, CA.

$11,000 to Geffen Playhouse, Los Angeles, CA.

$10,000 to J. Paul Getty Museum, Malibu, CA.

$7,500 to Los Angeles Conservancy, Los Angeles, CA.

$3,000 to Friends of Florence, DC.

$1,000 to University of the Arts, Philadelphia, PA.

$1,000 to Wonder of Reading, Los Angeles, CA.

304

Albert & Elaine Borchard Foundation, Inc. ◇

22055 Clarendon St., Ste. 210
Woodland Hills, CA 91367-6355

Established in 1978 in CA.

Donors: B. Lawrence Brennan; Robert K. Johnson; Richard E. Kipper; O.W. Moyle III; Alzheimer's Association.

Foundation type: Independent foundation.

Financial data (yr. ended 7/31/05): Assets, $19,800,002 (M); expenditures, $1,544,329; qualifying distributions, $874,845; giving activities include $690,101 for 56 grants (high: $36,000; low: $500).

Purpose and activities: Giving primarily for legal services, including legal services for the elderly; funding also for higher education, and children, youth and social services.

Fields of interest: Higher education; Legal services; Disasters, preparedness/services; Human services; Children/youth, services; Aging, centers/services; Homeless, human services; International relief, 2004 tsunami.

Type of support: Scholarship funds.

Limitations: Giving primarily in CA; some funding nationally, particularly in UT. No grants to individuals.

Application information:
Initial approach: Proposal
Copies of proposal: 3
Deadline(s): None

Officers and Directors: * Willard A. Beling,* Chair.; Edward D. Spurgeon,* Pres.; Betty Beling; Carol Spurgeon.

EIN: 953294377

Selected grants: The following grants were reported in 2004.

$48,334 to University of Southern California, Los Angeles, CA. 2 grants: $33,334 to Keck School of Medicine (For expanding research programs), $15,000 (For Borchard Russian Exchange Program).

$30,000 to National Senior Citizens Law Center, DC. For capacity development.

$25,000 to University of California, Los Angeles, CA. For Compagnie de Hanneton-Junebug Symphony at Freud playhouse.

$25,000 to University of California, Irvine, CA. For conference on Impact of Global Change on Biological Diversity and Ecosystem Health.

$10,000 to Achievement Rewards for College Scientists (ARCS) Foundation, Los Angeles, CA. For scholarship.

$10,000 to Alzheimers Association, Chicago, IL. For programs for prevention and treatment of Alzheimers disease.

$10,000 to American Red Cross, Los Angeles, CA. For Southern California disaster relief for wild fire victims.

$10,000 to Habitat for Humanity International, Los Angeles, CA. For homebuilding projects in Compton, Santa Monica, and Los Angeles.

$10,000 to Planned Parenthood of Los Angeles, Los Angeles, CA. For education and outreach programs.

305

Louis L. Borick Foundation ◇

7800 Woodley Ave.
Van Nuys, CA 91406-1788 (818) 902-2562
Contact: Louis L. Borick, Pres.

Established in 1997 in CA.

Donor: Louis L. Borick.

Foundation type: Independent foundation.

Financial data (yr. ended 12/31/05): Assets, $15,327,690 (M); expenditures, $810,747; qualifying distributions, $780,925; giving activities

---

include $779,675 for 142 grants (high: $50,000; low: $25).

Purpose and activities: Giving primarily for health associations, children, youth and social services, and Jewish organizations.

Fields of interest: Higher education; Health organizations, association; Cancer research; Human services; Children/youth, services; Federated giving programs; Jewish federated giving programs; Military/veterans' organizations; Jewish agencies & temples.

Limitations: Giving primarily in CA. No grants to individuals.

Application information:
Initial approach: Letter
Deadline(s): Nov. 30

Officer and Directors: * Louis L. Borick,* Pres.; Steven J. Borick.

Trustees: Robert Borick; Linda Borick Davidson.

EIN: 954635770

Selected grants: The following grants were reported in 2003.

$50,000 to United Way, Inc., Los Angeles, CA.

$26,000 to Scleroderma Research Foundation, San Francisco, CA.

$25,000 to American Red Cross, CA.

$25,000 to Loyola Marymount University, Los Angeles, CA.

$12,000 to Childrens Hospital Los Angeles, Los Angeles, CA.

$10,000 to Concern Foundation, Beverly Hills, CA.

$10,000 to Heart of Los Angeles Youth, Los Angeles, CA.

$10,000 to Jewish Family Service of Los Angeles, Los Angeles, CA.

$10,000 to Los Angeles Jewish Home for the Aging, Reseda, CA.

$10,000 to Weingart Center, Los Angeles, CA.

306

Borina Charitable Trust ◇

P.O. Box 1076
Aptos, CA 95001-1076

Established in 2003 in CA.

Foundation type: Independent foundation.

Financial data (yr. ended 12/31/04): Assets, $12,020,260 (M); expenditures, $758,192; qualifying distributions, $578,441; giving activities include $578,406 for 3 grants (high: $300,000; low: $25,000).

Fields of interest: Elementary/secondary education; Human services; Community development.

Limitations: Applications not accepted. Giving primarily in CA. No grants to individuals.

Application information: Contributes only to pre-selected organizations.

Trustees: Sheila Burke; William F. Locke-Paddon.

EIN: 686219922

307

Borina Foundation ◇

P.O. Box 1076
Aptos, CA 95001

Established in 2003 in CA.

Foundation type: Independent foundation.

Financial data (yr. ended 12/31/05): Assets, $15,671,728 (M); expenditures, $1,010,064; qualifying distributions, $712,767; giving activities

---

include $701,756 for 18 grants (high: $300,000; low: $500).

Purpose and activities: Giving primarily for education, including Roman Catholic schools.

Fields of interest: Historic preservation/historical societies; Elementary/secondary education; Law school/education; Human services; Community development; Foundations (community).

Limitations: Applications not accepted. Giving primarily in CA. No grants to individuals.

Application information: Unsolicited requests for funds not accepted.

Officers: William F. Locke-Paddon, Pres.; Sheila Burke, C.F.O.

EIN: 680515701

308

The James G. Boswell Foundation ✧

101 W. Walnut St.
Pasadena, CA   91103-3636   (626) 583-3002

Incorporated in 1947 in CA.

Donor: James G. Boswell‡.

Foundation type: Independent foundation.

Financial data (yr. ended 12/31/05): Assets, $91,065,601 (M); expenditures, $4,597,764; qualifying distributions, $4,471,715; giving activities include $4,314,315 for 16 grants (high: $1,000,000; low: $7,000; average: $50,000–$400,000).

Purpose and activities: Giving primarily for education, health, youth development, agricultural education, and the environment.

Fields of interest: Higher education; Education; Environment; Hospitals (general); Health care; Health organizations, association; Agriculture; Children/youth, services.

Type of support: General/operating support; Continuing support; Annual campaigns; Scholarship funds.

Limitations: Applications not accepted. Giving primarily in CA.

Application information: Contributes only to pre-selected organizations.

Board meeting date(s): Feb. and as required

Officers and Trustees:* James W. Boswell,* Pres.; Susan W. Dulin,* V.P.; R. Sherman Railsback,* Secy.; R. Kenneth Dulin; Ross Hall.

EIN: 956047326

Selected grants: The following grants were reported in 2005.

$1,000,000 to California Agricultural Leadership Foundation, Sacramento, CA. For endowment fund.

$1,000,000 to Kaweah Delta Hospital Foundation, Visalia, CA. For capital campaign.

$800,000 to Corcoran Community Supporting Organization, Corcoran, CA. For operating support for Corcoran YMCA.

$400,000 to Eastlake Educational Foundation, Chula Vista, CA. For operating support.

$400,000 to Little League Baseball, Chula Vista, CA. For capital campaign.

$150,000 to International Agri-Center, Tulare, CA. For capital campaign.

309

The Bothin Foundation ✧

1660 Bush St., Ste. 300
San Francisco, CA   94109   (415) 561-6540, ext. 205

Contact: Eric Sloan, Sr. Prog. Off.

FAX: (415) 561-6477; E-mail: esloan@pfs-llc.net;
URL: http://www.pfs-llc.net/bothin/index.html

Incorporated in 1917 in CA.

Donors: Henry E. Bothin†; Ellen Chabot Bothin†; Genevieve Bothin de Limur‡.

Foundation type: Independent foundation.

Financial data (yr. ended 12/31/04): Assets, $37,114,673 (M); expenditures, $2,100,251; qualifying distributions, $1,705,010; giving activities include $1,428,229 for 100 grants (high: $125,000; low: $1,500).

Purpose and activities: Support for organizations providing direct services to low-income, at-risk children, youth and families, the elderly, and disabled. To a limited extent, grants may also be made to environmental agencies and arts organizations that serve youth predominately. The foundation prefers to make grants for capital, building, and equipment needs.

Fields of interest: Environment; Human services; Children/youth, services; Child development, services; Family services; Aging, centers/services; Homeless, human services; Disabilities, people with.

Type of support: Capital campaigns; Building/renovation; Equipment.

Limitations: Giving primarily in CA, with emphasis on San Francisco, Marin, Sonoma and San Mateo counties. No support for religious organizations, or educational institutions (except those directly aiding the developmentally or learning disabled). No grants to individuals, or for general operating funds, endowment funds, program support, scholarships, fellowships, medical research conferences or for production or distribution of films or other media presentations; no loans.

Publications: Application guidelines; Annual report; Grants list.

Application information: The Board prefers that three full years elapse between grants. The foundation has ceased its grantmaking in Santa Barbara. See Web site for details. Application form not required.

Initial approach: Letter on organizational letterhead, containing a brief outline of the project

Copies of proposal: 1

Deadline(s): None

Board meeting date(s): Feb., May, and Oct.

Final notification: 2 to 3 months

Officers and Directors:* Genevieve di San Faustino,* Pres.; A. Michael Casey,* V.P. and Treas.; Jessica Galloway, Secy.; Lyman H. Casey; Shannon Casey; Jay Jacobs; Gordon E Miller; Suzie Pollak; Carol K. Prince.

EIN: 941196182

Selected grants: The following grants were reported in 2005.

$175,000 to Families on Track, South San Francisco, CA. 2 grants: $50,000 (For emergency grant for closing costs), $125,000 (For emergency grant for closing costs).

$25,000 to Marine Mammal Center, Sausalito, CA. Toward construction of Discovery Classroom in New Marine Science Community Education Center.

$25,000 to Saint Francis Foundation, San Francisco, CA. Toward capital campaign to build and equip new Emergency Department.

$25,000 to San Francisco Conservatory of Music, San Francisco, CA. Toward capital campaign for relocation to building in Civic Center.

$25,000 to Tenderloin Neighborhood Development Corporation, San Francisco, CA. To purchase office furniture for agency providing affordable housing for low-income people.

$25,000 to Womens Initiative for Self Employment, San Francisco, CA. To purchase furniture and equipment for use in entrepreneurial training program for low-income women.

$20,000 to ARC San Francisco, San Francisco, CA. Toward replacement of roof.

$20,000 to Becoming Independent, Santa Rosa, CA. To purchase document shredder for agency providing employment for people with developmental disabilities.

$20,000 to Commonweal, Bolinas, CA. Toward office renovations for agency serving cancer patients and at-risk children.

310

Bowes Family Foundation ✧ ☆

177 Steuart St., Ste. 700
San Francisco, CA   94105

Donor: John Bowes.

Foundation type: Independent foundation.

Financial data (yr. ended 6/30/05): Assets, $2,909,985 (M); gifts received, $98,750; expenditures, $651,375; qualifying distributions, $590,465; giving activities include $588,716 for 39 grants (high: $125,000; low: $50).

Fields of interest: Arts; Elementary/secondary education; Education; Cancer; Human services.

Limitations: Applications not accepted. Giving primarily in San Francisco, CA. No grants to individuals.

Application information: Contributes only to pre-selected organizations.

Officers and Directors:* Frances F. Bowes,* Chair. and V.P.; John G. Bowes,* Pres.; Diana B. Weller, Secy.; Elena B. Marano; Alexandria B. Williamson.

EIN: 200489340

311

William K. Bowes, Jr. Foundation ▼

c/o Pacific Foundation Services
1660 Bush St., Ste. 300
San Francisco, CA   94109

Established in 1991 in CA.

Donor: William K. Bowes, Jr.

Foundation type: Independent foundation.

Financial data (yr. ended 12/31/04): Assets, $221,819,316 (M); gifts received, $114,419,573; expenditures, $9,667,714; qualifying distributions, $8,453,609; giving activities include $7,796,390 for 35 grants (high: $2,600,000; low: $250; average: $100,000–$300,000).

Purpose and activities: Giving primarily for museums, higher education, health care and/or patient services, cancer research, adoption, and religion.

Fields of interest: Museums; Higher education; Health care, patient services; Cancer research; Human services; Religion.

Type of support: General/operating support; Building/renovation; Scholarship funds.
Limitations: Applications not accepted. Giving primarily in CA. No grants to individuals.
Application information: Contributes only to pre-selected organizations.
Officers: William K. Bowes, Jr., Pres.; John M. Bryan, Secy.-Treas.; Ronald J. Henrickson, C.F.O.
EIN: 943148482
Selected grants: The following grants were reported in 2004.
$2,600,000 to Exploratorium, San Francisco, CA. For general operating support, for capital campaign, and for internships.
$920,000 to Stanford University, Stanford, CA. 2 grants: $720,000 (For Media Fellowship at Hoover Institution and for Fellowship Fund), $200,000 (For President's Fund and for Ruth Garland Bowes Scholarship).
$627,500 to Asian Art Museum of San Francisco, San Francisco, CA. For general operating support and for renovations.
$564,140 to University of California at San Francisco Foundation, San Francisco, CA. 2 grants: $314,140 (For Angiogenesis Fund at Cancer Center), $250,000 (For Raising Hope at Mission Bay Cancer Center).
$500,000 to San Francisco Opera Association, San Francisco, CA. For general operating support.
$400,000 to United Religions Initiative (URI), San Francisco, CA. For general operating support.
$176,000 to University of California, Berkeley, CA. For Incentive Awards.
$100,000 to Creative Capital Foundation, New York, NY. For general operating support and for grants to artists.

312
Bowman Family Foundation ✧
c/o Paul Perez
1875 S. Grant St., Ste. 600
San Mateo, CA 94402

Established in 2001 in CA.
Donors: Lawrence Bowman; Mark Hurley.
Foundation type: Independent foundation.
Financial data (yr. ended 5/31/05): Assets, $4,368,450 (M); gifts received, $600,000; expenditures, $473,569; qualifying distributions, $473,569; giving activities include $458,500 for 8 grants.
Fields of interest: Hospitals (general); Human services; Foundations (private grantmaking); Christian agencies & churches.
Limitations: Applications not accepted. Giving primarily in CA. No grants to individuals.
Application information: Contributes only to pre-selected organizations.
Officers: Lawrence Bowman, C.E.O. and Pres.; Paul Perez, Secy. and C.F.O.
EIN: 943380924

313
The Herbert & Marigrace Boyer Foundation ✧
c/o Robert Stenson, C.P.A.
700 Larkspur Landing Cir., Ste. 105
Larkspur, CA 94939-1710

Established in 1986 in CA.
Donors: Herbert W. Boyer; Marigrace Boyer.

Foundation type: Independent foundation.
Financial data (yr. ended 12/31/05): Assets, $2,206,908 (M); expenditures, $685,084; qualifying distributions, $650,000; giving activities include $650,000 for 2 grants (high: $400,000; low: $250,000).
Purpose and activities: Giving primarily to a medical school.
Fields of interest: Higher education; Medical school/education.
Type of support: Building/renovation; Scholarship funds.
Limitations: Applications not accepted. Giving primarily in New Haven, CT. No grants to individuals.
Application information: Contributes only to pre-selected organizations.
Officers: Herbert W. Boyer, Pres.; Marigrace Boyer, Secy.; Robert T. Stenson, C.F.O.
EIN: 680118055
Selected grants: The following grants were reported in 2004.
$400,000 to Yale University, School of Medicine, New Haven, CT. For building expansion fund.
$250,000 to University of Pittsburgh, Pittsburgh, PA. For endowment of teaching position in molecular biology.
$2,500 to Trout Unlimited, Montana Regional Office, Helena, MT.

314
BP Foundation ✧
212 Granada Dr.
Corte Madera, CA 94925-2010
Application address: c/o Scholarship Foundation of Santa Barbara, 2253 Las Positas Rd., Santa Barbara, CA 93105, tel.: (805) 687-6065, FAX: (805) 687-6031, URL: http://www.sbscholarship.org; or P.O. Box 3620, Santa Barbara, CA 93130

Established in 2001 in CA.
Donor: Kathryn B. Partridge†.
Foundation type: Independent foundation.
Financial data (yr. ended 12/31/05): Assets, $23,347,344 (M); expenditures, $1,327,244; qualifying distributions, $1,141,785; giving activities include $960,000 for grants.
Purpose and activities: Scholarship awards to graduating students who will be attending Santa Barbara College.
Fields of interest: Scholarships/financial aid.
Type of support: Scholarships—to individuals.
Limitations: Giving primarily in Santa Barbara, CA.
Application information: Application form required.
Deadline(s): None
Trustees: Carolyn Bartolomel; Sherry Partridge Kimball; Charles Kent Partridge; Charles W. Partridge; Herbert Scott Partridge.
EIN: 776203456
Selected grants: The following grants were reported in 2004.
$675,000 to Scholarship Foundation of Santa Barbara, Santa Barbara, CA.
$5,000 to Music Academy of the West, Santa Barbara, CA.
$2,000 to Girls Inc. of Greater Santa Barbara, Santa Barbara, CA.
$2,000 to Ojai Festivals, Ojai, CA.
$1,000 to Foundation for the Performing Arts Center, San Luis Obispo, CA.

315
The Bradley Foundation ✧ ☆
1672 Main St., Ste. E-364
Ramona, CA 92065
Contact: Barbara Teets

Established in 1997.
Donor: W.R. Bradley.
Foundation type: Independent foundation.
Financial data (yr. ended 12/31/05): Assets, $5,595,969 (M); gifts received, $1,478; expenditures, $937,399; qualifying distributions, $891,881; giving activities include $640,000 for 27 grants (high: $150,000; low: $2,500), and $193,000 for 11 grants to individuals (high: $40,000; low: $3,000).
Fields of interest: Education; Human services; Children/youth, services; Family services, domestic violence; Christian agencies & churches.
Type of support: General/operating support; Grants to individuals.
Limitations: Giving primarily in CA, with emphasis on San Diego; some funding nationally.
Application information:
Initial approach: Letter
Deadline(s): None
Officer: W.R. Bradley, Pres.
EIN: 330771070

316
The Brandenburg Family Foundation ✧
1122 Willow St., Ste. 200
San Jose, CA 95125
Contact: Lee H. Brandenburg, Pres.

Established in 1997 in CA.
Donors: Lee H. Brandenburg; Diane M. Brandenburg; Eric L. Brandenburg.
Foundation type: Independent foundation.
Financial data (yr. ended 12/31/05): Assets, $108 (M); gifts received, $392,350; expenditures, $397,343; qualifying distributions, $397,343; giving activities include $395,938 for 35 grants (high: $50,000; low: $500).
Purpose and activities: Giving for community services, art and cultural programs, education, youth services, and health services.
Fields of interest: Performing arts, ballet; Performing arts, theater; Arts; Education, formal/general education; Higher education; Education; Heart & circulatory diseases; Youth development; YM/YWCAs & YM/YWHAs.
Limitations: Giving primarily in San Jose, CA.
Application information:
Initial approach: Letter
Deadline(s): None
Officers: Lee H. Brandenburg, Pres.; Eric L. Brandenburg, V.P.; Ronald Zraick, Jr., Secy.
Directors: William B. Baron; Diane M. Brandenburg; Karen Brandenburg; William L. Brandenburg; Melodee Dunlap.
EIN: 770444869
Selected grants: The following grants were reported in 2004.
$150,000 to Ronald McDonald House.
$100,000 to Montalvo Association, Saratoga, CA.
$50,000 to United Way.
$12,000 to Salvation Army.
$10,000 to Arthur Szyk Society, Burlingame, CA.

317

Brandes Family Foundation ✧
P.O. Box 535
Rancho Santa Fe, CA 92067-0535

Established in 1996 in CA.
Donors: Charles Brandes; Linda Brandes.
Foundation type: Independent foundation.
Financial data (yr. ended 12/31/04): Assets, $22,761,788 (M); gifts received, $85,194; expenditures, $515,194; qualifying distributions, $476,905; giving activities include $464,734 for 14 grants (high: $321,560; low: $20).
Purpose and activities: Giving primarily for youth and family services.
Fields of interest: Education; Animals/wildlife; Health care; Health organizations, association; Youth development; Human services; Family services.
Limitations: Giving on a national basis. No grants to individuals.
Application information:
  Initial approach: Letter
  Deadline(s): None
Officer: Charles Brandes, Treas.
EIN: 330709977
Selected grants: The following grants were reported in 2003.
$333,000 to Salk Institute for Biological Studies, San Diego, CA.
$114,000 to Helen Woodward Animal Center, Rancho Santa Fe, CA.
$100,200 to Lux Art Institute, Encinitas, CA.
$2,000 to Boys and Girls Clubs of Greater San Diego, San Diego, CA.
$2,000 to Humane Society of San Diego, San Diego, CA.
$1,000 to Make-A-Wish Foundation of America, Phoenix, AZ.
$1,000 to Rolling Readers USA, San Diego, CA.
$500 to San Diego Food Bank, San Diego, CA.
$500 to San Diego Rescue Mission, San Diego, CA.
$440 to Maryland Avenue School, Milwaukee, WI.

318

Braun/Brown Family Foundation ✧ ☆
c/o Howard and Howard, C.P.A., Inc.
16255 Ventura Blvd., Ste. 700
Encino, CA 91436

Established in 2001 in CA.
Donors: David Braun; Sherri Brown.
Foundation type: Independent foundation.
Financial data (yr. ended 6/30/05): Assets, $175,092 (M); gifts received, $303,603; expenditures, $347,231; qualifying distributions, $344,539; giving activities include $344,539 for 16 grants (high: $203,200; low: $350).
Fields of interest: Elementary/secondary education; Human services; Jewish agencies & temples.
Limitations: Applications not accepted. Giving primarily in CA. No grants to individuals.
Application information: Contributes only to pre-selected organizations.
Trustee: David Braun.
EIN: 010571310
Selected grants: The following grants were reported in 2005.
$3,000 to New Israel Fund, Los Angeles, CA.
$2,000 to University of Judaism, Los Angeles, CA.
$2,000 to Viewpoint Educational Foundation, Calabasas, CA.

$1,000 to UNICEF, New York, NY.

319

The Bravo Foundation ✧
(formerly Everhealth Foundation)
2727 Camino Del Rio S., Ste. 137
San Diego, CA 92108 (760) 740-6630
Contact: Michael B. Lopez, C.E.O. and Pres.
E-mail: mblopez@bravofdn.com

Established in 1997 in CA.
Foundation type: Independent foundation.
Financial data (yr. ended 12/31/05): Assets, $14,691,903 (M); expenditures, $826,971; qualifying distributions, $719,944; giving activities include $499,300 for 83 grants (high: $25,000; low: $365).
Purpose and activities: The foundation awards grants only to human service organizations which serve the poor and disadvantaged, with special focus on the Hispanic community.
Fields of interest: Elementary/secondary education; Law school/education; Education; Health organizations, association; Human services; Children/youth, services; Aging, centers/services; Roman Catholic agencies & churches.
Limitations: Applications not accepted. Giving limited to San Diego, Imperial, and Riverside counties, CA, and CO. No support for religious or political purposes. No grants to individuals, or for capital campaigns, endowment funds, research, deficit budgets, conferences, transportation and lodging, testimonial dinners, ceremonies, or for publications or media projects.
Application information: Unsolicited requests for funds not accepted.
Officers: Michael B. Lopez, C.E.O. and Pres.; Lisa Garcia Ruiz, Secy.; Geoffrey Sando, Treas.
Director: J. Leanne Debora.
Number of staff: 1 full-time professional; 1 full-time support.
EIN: 952160081

320

The Donald Bren Foundation ✧
P.O. Box 3090
Newport Beach, CA 92658-3090

Established in 1986 in CA.
Donor: Donald L. Bren.
Foundation type: Independent foundation.
Financial data (yr. ended 11/30/05): Assets, $8,607,454 (M); expenditures, $809,698; qualifying distributions, $806,598; giving activities include $800,000 for 2 grants (high: $700,000; low: $100,000).
Purpose and activities: Giving primarily for higher education.
Fields of interest: Higher education.
Type of support: Endowments; Professorships.
Limitations: Applications not accepted. Giving primarily in CA. No grants to individuals.
Application information: Contributes only to pre-selected organizations.
Officers and Directors:* Donald L. Bren,* Chair. and C.E.O.; John A. Flynn, Exec. V.P., Secy., and C.F.O.; M.A. Pope, Sr. V.P.; Michael McKee; Gerald Parsky; Frank Quinlan; Stan Ross; Peter Ueberroth; Ray L. Watson; Hon. Pete Wilson.
EIN: 954094426

Selected grants: The following grants were reported in 2004.
$3,000,000 to University of California, Santa Barbara, CA.
$2,645,000 to University of California at Irvine Foundation, Irvine, CA.
$700,000 to Irvine Public Schools Foundation, Irvine, CA.
$250,000 to Chapman University, Orange, CA.
$200,000 to Marine Corps University, Quantico, VA.

321

The Mervyn L. Brenner Foundation, Inc. ✧
30 Van Ness Ave., Ste. 3600
San Francisco, CA 94102

Incorporated in 1961 in CA.
Donor: Mervyn L. Brenner‡.
Foundation type: Independent foundation.
Financial data (yr. ended 8/31/05): Assets, $7,134,659 (M); expenditures, $1,048,170; qualifying distributions, $1,020,511; giving activities include $1,018,581 for 185 grants (high: $80,000; low: $500).
Purpose and activities: Giving primarily for education; some funding also for arts and culture, health and human services, and religious organizations.
Fields of interest: Museums; Museums (specialized); Performing arts; Historic preservation/historical societies; Arts; Elementary/secondary education; Education, early childhood education; Higher education; Law school/education; Libraries/library science; Education; Environment, natural resources; Animal welfare; Reproductive health, family planning; Mental health/crisis services; Health organizations, association; Boys & girls clubs; Human services; YM/YWCAs & YM/YWHAs; Children/youth, services; Family services; Jewish agencies & temples; Aging.
Type of support: General/operating support; Annual campaigns.
Limitations: Applications not accepted. Giving primarily in CA. No grants to individuals.
Application information: Contributes only to pre-selected organizations.
Officers: John R. Gentry, Pres.; Paul E. Buechner, V.P.; Jane T. Schueler, V.P.; Marc H. Monheimer, Secy.; Robert K. Taylor, Treas.
EIN: 946088679

322

Bright Family Foundation
1620 N. Carpenter Rd., Bldg. B
Modesto, CA 95351
Contact: Calvin E. Bright, Pres.

Established in 1986 in CA.
Donor: Calvin E. Bright.
Foundation type: Independent foundation.
Financial data (yr. ended 12/31/05): Assets, $9,933,260 (M); gifts received, $500,000; expenditures, $697,091; qualifying distributions, $410,177; giving activities include $408,900 for 47 grants (high: $42,000; low: $500).
Purpose and activities: Giving primarily for education, including scholarship grants, and for medical research, and Christian organizations and churches.

Fields of interest: Arts; Higher education; Medical school/education; Human services; Children/youth, services; Christian agencies & churches.

Type of support: Fellowships; General/operating support; Building/renovation; Scholarship funds; In-kind gifts.

Limitations: Giving primarily in Stanislaus County, CA, within a 50-mile radius of Modesto.

Application information: Application form not required.

> *Initial approach:* Letter on organization letterhead
> *Copies of proposal:* 1
> *Deadline(s):* Dec. 1
> *Board meeting date(s):* Dec.
> *Final notification:* By Dec. 31; positive responses only

Officers and Directors:* Calvin E. Bright,* Pres.; Carol Bright Tougas,* Secy.-Treas.; Susan B. Hunter.

EIN: 770126942

Selected grants: The following grants were reported in 2005.

$50,000 to California State University, Stanislaus, Turlock, CA. 2 grants: $20,000, $30,000

$42,000 to Modesto Junior College, Modesto, CA.

$25,000 to Central West Ballet, Modesto, CA. 2 grants: $20,000, $5,000

$20,000 to Community Hospice, Modesto, CA.

$20,000 to Emanuel Medical Center, Turlock, CA.

$20,000 to Memorial Hospital Foundation, Modesto, CA.

$20,000 to Slavic Gospel Association, Loves Park, IL.

$5,000 to Brigham Young University, Provo, UT.

323

The Broad Art Foundation ✧

10900 Wilshire Blvd., 12th Fl.
Los Angeles, CA 90024-6532
Contact: Eli Broad, Tr.
URL: http://www.broadartfoundation.org

Established in 1984 in CA.

Donors: Eli Broad; Edythe L. Broad.

Foundation type: Operating foundation.

Financial data (yr. ended 12/31/05): Assets, $323,079,536 (M); gifts received, $287,763; expenditures, $8,497,870; qualifying distributions, $17,505,343; giving activities include $1,513,135 for 63 grants (high: $150,000; low: $100; average: $1,000–$50,000), and $15,932,130 for 3 foundation-administered programs.

Purpose and activities: The foundation lends art to museums.

Fields of interest: Museums (art); Arts.

Type of support: General/operating support.

Limitations: Applications not accepted. Giving primarily in CA and NY. No grants to individuals.

Publications: Informational brochure.

Application information: Contributes only to pre-selected organizations.

Trustee: Eli Broad.

Number of staff: 2 full-time professional; 1 part-time professional; 1 part-time support.

EIN: 954664939

Selected grants: The following grants were reported in 2004.

$85,000 to Museum of Modern Art, New York, NY. 2 grants: $35,000, $50,000

$48,680 to Metropolitan Museum of Art, New York, NY.

$30,000 to Solomon R. Guggenheim Foundation, New York, NY.

$25,000 to American Friends of the Israel Museum, New York, NY.

$10,500 to Americans for the Arts, New York, NY.

$10,000 to American Friends of Versailles, Chicago, IL.

$10,000 to Jewish Museum, New York, NY.

$9,558 to Los Angeles County Museum of Art, Los Angeles, CA.

$5,000 to Creative Capital Foundation, New York, NY.

324

Broad Foundation ▼

10900 Wilshire Blvd., 12th Fl.
Los Angeles, CA 90024-6532 (310) 954-5050
Contact: Wendy Jones, Grants Coord.
FAX: (310) 954-5051;
E-mail: info@broadfoundation.org; E-mail for grant information: grants@broadfoundation.org;
URL: http://www.broadfoundation.org/

Established in 1999 in CA; As of Jan 1, 2007, the Eli & Edythe L. Broad Foundation merged into the Broad Foundation.

Donors: Eli Broad; U.S. Department of Education.

Foundation type: Independent foundation.

Financial data (yr. ended 12/31/05): Assets, $835,659,229 (M); gifts received, $200,102,468; expenditures, $52,572,393; qualifying distributions, $46,383,619; giving activities include $40,992,554 for 75 grants (high: $10,000,000; low: $2,000), and $500,000 for 1 foundation-administered program.

Purpose and activities: The foundation's mission is to dramatically improve K-12 urban public education through better governance, management, and labor relations.

Fields of interest: Elementary/secondary school reform.

Limitations: Giving on a national basis. No grants to individuals.

Publications: Annual report.

Application information: See foundation Web site for list of eligible urban school districts. Application form not required.

> *Initial approach:* Concept paper (no more than 3 pages)
> *Copies of proposal:* 1
> *Deadline(s):* Rolling basis
> *Final notification:* Within 60 days

Officers: Kevin Hall, C.O.O.; Dan Katzu, Managing Dir.; Robin Kramer, Sr. Dir.

Trustees: Edythe L. Broad; Eli Broad.

Number of staff: 9 full-time professional; 5 full-time support.

EIN: 954686318

Selected grants: The following grants were reported in 2004.

$5,000,000 to Council of Chief State School Officers, DC. To develop and implement SchoolMatters.com, national education data website.

$2,800,000 to Pacific Charter School Development, Compton, CA. For charter school facilities development in Los Angeles.

$2,200,000 to NewSchools Venture Fund, San Francisco, CA. 2 grants: $700,000 (For Green Dot Public Schools), $1,500,000 (For Aspire Public Schools).

$2,039,791 to Broad Center for the Management of School Systems, Los Angeles, CA. To train individuals interested in becoming educational

leaders in urban school districts throughout the country.

$2,000,000 to New Leaders for New Schools, New York, NY. For national program to attract, prepare and support new generation of principals for urban schools.

$1,775,932 to University of San Diego, San Diego, CA. To support district principal training in partnership with San Diego City Schools.

$1,642,000 to National Center for Educational Accountability, Austin, TX. 2 grants: $1,000,000 to Just for the Kids (For School Information Partnership, national public-private partnership to assist states in effectively using internet-based education data reporting and analysis to raise student achievement), $642,000 to Just for the Kids (For analysis and collection of data necessary for Broad Prize for Urban Education).

$1,125,000 to Clark County School District, Las Vegas, NV. For partnership with Edison Schools to improve student achievement at elementary and middle schools.

325

Broad Reach Foundation

2118 Wilshire Blvd., No. 383
Santa Monica, CA 90403

Established in 2001 in CA.

Donors: David K. Richards; Carol A. Richards.

Foundation type: Independent foundation.

Financial data (yr. ended 12/31/04): Assets, $50,661,193 (M); gifts received, $10,032,431; expenditures, $2,306,265; qualifying distributions, $2,061,761; giving activities include $2,035,000 for 9 grants (high: $1,550,000; low: $5,000).

Limitations: Applications not accepted. No grants to individuals.

Application information: Contributes only to pre-selected organizations.

> *Board meeting date(s):* As needed

Officers and Directors:* Carol A. Richards,* Pres.; David K. Richards,* Treas.

EIN: 954861421

326

Dana & Albert R. Broccoli Charitable Foundation ✧

2400 Broadway, Rm. 310
Santa Monica, CA 90404

Established in 1980 in CA.

Donors: Albert R. Broccoli†; Dana Broccoli.

Foundation type: Independent foundation.

Financial data (yr. ended 12/31/04): Assets, $15,934,338 (M); gifts received, $2,563,039; expenditures, $1,009,718; qualifying distributions, $999,000; giving activities include $999,000 for 20 grants (high: $500,000; low: $1,000).

Purpose and activities: Giving primarily for higher education, and for arts education, and other art and cultural programs; funding also for hospitals, and social services.

Fields of interest: Arts education; Media, film/video; Museums (specialized); Arts; Higher education; Hospitals (general); Boys & girls clubs; Human services.

Type of support: General/operating support; Scholarship funds.

Limitations: Applications not accepted. Giving primarily in CA. No grants to individuals.
Application information: Contributes only to pre-selected organizations.
Officers and Directors:* Michael G. Wilson,* Pres.; Barbara Broccoli,* V.P.; David Pope,* Secy.; Christina Broccoli; Tom Camp; Burton Forester.
EIN: 953502889

327

Brooks-Mathews Foundation ◊
4725 Thornton Ave.
Fremont, CA 94536 (510) 797-7980
Contact: John Brooks, Pres.

Established in 1959.
Donors: John Brooks; Barbara Brooks; Susan Jane Moldow; William Mathews Brooks.
Foundation type: Independent foundation.
Financial data (yr. ended 12/31/05): Assets, $941,366 (M); gifts received, $460,000; expenditures, $372,486; qualifying distributions, $360,200; giving activities include $360,200 for 21 grants (high: $100,000; low: $250).
Purpose and activities: Funding primarily for education, including a medical school, as well as for the arts and culture, health care, and human services.
Fields of interest: Museums (art); Arts; Education; Hospitals (general); Human services.
Type of support: General/operating support.
Limitations: Giving primarily in CA; some funding nationally.
Application information:
  Initial approach: Letter
  Deadline(s): None
Officers and Directors:* John Brooks, Pres.; Barbara Brooks,* V.P.; William Mathews Brooks,* V.P.
EIN: 946098103

328

Brotman Foundation of California ◊
11845 W. Olympic Blvd., Ste. 845
Los Angeles, CA 90064
Contact: Michael B. Sherman, Pres.

Established in 1964.
Foundation type: Independent foundation.
Financial data (yr. ended 12/31/03): Assets, $7,105,796 (M); expenditures, $528,187; qualifying distributions, $415,594; giving activities include $341,355 for 68 grants (high: $25,000; low: $355).
Purpose and activities: Giving mainly for children, health and medical research; some support for arts, education, and environmental organizations.
Fields of interest: Arts; Education; Environment; Health care; Health organizations, association; AIDS; Medical research, institute; AIDS research; Children/youth, services.
Type of support: General/operating support; Continuing support; Conferences/seminars; Research.
Limitations: Giving primarily in southern CA. No grants to individuals.
Application information: Application form not required.
  Initial approach: Letter
  Copies of proposal: 1
  Deadline(s): None

Board meeting date(s): 3rd Wed. of each month
Final notification: 1-2 weeks
Officers and Director:* Michael B. Sherman, Pres.; Lowell Marks,* Secy.; Toni Brotman, Treas.
EIN: 956094639
Selected grants: The following grants were reported in 2003.
$25,000 to Cedars-Sinai Research for Womens Cancers, Los Angeles, CA.
$25,000 to Museum of Contemporary Art (MOCA), Los Angeles, CA.
$15,000 to Elizabeth Glaser Pediatric AIDS Foundation, Santa Monica, CA.
$7,500 to Library Foundation of Los Angeles, Los Angeles, CA.
$5,000 to Blind Childrens Center, Los Angeles, CA.
$5,000 to Children of the Night, Van Nuys, CA.
$2,500 to Boys and Girls Club of Los Angeles, Eastside, Los Angeles, CA.
$2,500 to Childrens Craniofacial Association, Dallas, TX.
$2,500 to Scleroderma Research Foundation, San Francisco, CA.
$1,000 to Los Angeles County Museum of Art, Los Angeles, CA.

329

The Robert Brownlee Foundation ◊ ☆
1280 Space Park Way, Ste. 104
Mountain View, CA 94043
Contact: Robert T. Borawski, Pres.

Established in 1986.
Donor: Robert G. Brownlee‡.
Foundation type: Independent foundation.
Financial data (yr. ended 9/30/05): Assets, $626,944 (M); expenditures, $417,443; qualifying distributions, $412,236; giving activities include $405,500 for 14 grants (high: $125,000; low: $3,000).
Purpose and activities: Grants to non-profit organizations that provide hands-on, interactive, science programs for pre-college youth.
Fields of interest: Science.
Type of support: General/operating support; Continuing support; Equipment.
Limitations: Giving primarily in the San Francisco Bay Area, CA. No grants to individuals.
Publications: Informational brochure.
Application information: Limited funding for new requests. Science programs must be primarily youth-oriented projects to be considered for funding. Preference given to small regional organizations with annual operating budgets of less than $300,000. Unsolicited grant requests are acceptable but not favored. Application form not required.
  Initial approach: Letter
  Copies of proposal: 6
  Deadline(s): Jan. 31 and July 31
  Board meeting date(s): Mar. and Sept.
  Final notification: 30 days after board meetings
Officers and Directors:* Robert Borawski,* Pres.; James Ingram, V.P. and Secy.; Edith Eddy,* V.P.; James R. Murphy, V.P.; Leonard Simon,* V.P.; Randall Blair,* C.F.O. and Treas.
EIN: 770131702
Selected grants: The following grants were reported in 2005.
$125,000 to Trust for Hidden Villa, Los Altos Hills, CA.
$50,000 to Resource Area for Teachers, San Jose, CA.

$25,000 to Marine Science Institute, Redwood City, CA.
$25,000 to Youth Science Institute, Los Gatos, CA.
$20,000 to Exploratorium, San Francisco, CA.
$16,500 to Happy Hollow Corporation, San Jose, CA.
$14,000 to Pacific Environmental Education Center, Fort Bragg, CA.
$5,000 to Marine Mammal Center, Sausalito, CA.
$5,000 to Randall Museum, San Francisco, CA.
$5,000 to Wilderness Society, DC.

330

The Frank H. and Eva B. Buck Foundation
P.O. Box 5610
Vacaville, CA 95696-5610 (707) 446-7700
Contact: Robert Walker, Exec. Dir.
FAX: (707) 446-7766;
E-mail: rwalker@buckfoundation.org; URL: http://www.buckfoundation.org

Established in 1989 in CA.
Donor: Eva Benson Buck‡.
Foundation type: Independent foundation.
Financial data (yr. ended 3/31/06): Assets, $57,873,558 (M); expenditures, $5,608,912; qualifying distributions, $4,882,634; giving activities include $649,451 for 28 grants (high: $100,000; low: $150; average: $1,000–$75,000), and $3,862,474 for 129 grants to individuals (high: $85,070; low: $260; average: $22,150–$48,935).
Purpose and activities: Awards scholarships to residents of Contra Costa, Napa, Sacramento, San Joaquin, Solano, and Yolo counties, CA; grants program focuses on education in these six counties.
Fields of interest: Education.
Type of support: General/operating support; Management development/capacity building; Annual campaigns; Capital campaigns; Building/renovation; Equipment; Program development; Conferences/seminars; Curriculum development; Internship funds; Technical assistance; Grants to individuals; Scholarships—to individuals; Matching/challenge support.
Limitations: Giving limited to Contra Costa, Napa, Sacramento, San Joaquin, Solano, and Yolo counties, CA.
Publications: Application guidelines; Informational brochure; Newsletter.
Application information: Applicants need to submit a short information application (2 pages) prior to the complete application. Complete applications are accepted by invitation only. Application form required for scholarship program. Application is available online. Submission should also include teacher's assessment and parental authorization for release of school records. Application form required.
  Initial approach: Letter or e-mail
  Deadline(s): Jan. 15 and July 15 for grants
  Board meeting date(s): Varies
Officers and Directors:* Christian P. Erdman,* Pres.; Stacey B. Morris,* Secy.; Walter Buck,* Treas.; Carol Franc Buck; Paul Buck.
Number of staff: 3 full-time professional; 1 full-time support; 2 part-time support.
EIN: 770233870
Selected grants: The following grants were reported in 2006.
$100,000 to Lafayette Community Foundation, Lafayette, CA.
$75,000 to Explorit Science Center, Davis, CA.

$50,000 to Junior Achievement of the Bay Area, South San Francisco, CA.

$35,000 to Mount Diablo Unified School District, Concord, CA.

$25,000 to Bring Me A Book Foundation, Mountain View, CA.

$15,000 to Solano Community Foundation, Fairfield, CA.

$10,000 to Crocker Art Museum, Sacramento, CA.

$5,810 to Council on Foundations, DC.

331
The Henry W. Bull Foundation ✧

c/o Santa Barbara Bank & Trust
P.O. Box 2340
Santa Barbara, CA 93120-2340
(805) 899-8405
Contact: Janice Gibbons, V.P. and Sr. Trust Off.

Trust established in 1960 in CA.

Donor: Maud L. Bull‡.

Foundation type: Independent foundation.

Financial data (yr. ended 12/31/05): Assets, $8,873,267 (M); expenditures, $473,881; qualifying distributions, $434,526; giving activities include $428,470 for 114 grants (high: $30,000; low: $270; average: $2,000–$5,000).

Purpose and activities: Giving primarily for the arts, education and health and human services.

Fields of interest: Performing arts, music; Arts; Education; Health care; Health organizations, association; Christian agencies & churches; Disabilities, people with.

Type of support: General/operating support; Continuing support; Annual campaigns; Capital campaigns; Building/renovation; Equipment; Program development; Research; Matching/challenge support.

Limitations: Giving on a national basis. No grants to individuals or private foundations.

Publications: Application guidelines.

Application information: Application form not required.

Initial approach: Proposal
Copies of proposal: 1
Deadline(s): Apr. 1 and Sept. 1
Board meeting date(s): 2 times per year
Final notification: Positive replies only

Trustees: Frederic Astaire, Jr.; Roy Gaskin; Peter Potter; Santa Barbara Bank & Trust.

Number of staff: 2 part-time support.

EIN: 956062058

332
Bruce and Anne Bundy Foundation ✧

c/o Union Bank of California, N.A.
18300 Von Karman Ave., Ste. 340
Irvine, CA 92612

Established in 1993 in CA.

Donors: Anne S. Bundy‡; Bruce Bundy‡.

Foundation type: Independent foundation.

Financial data (yr. ended 8/31/05): Assets, $9,859,158 (M); expenditures, $585,261; qualifying distributions, $491,179; giving activities include $461,912 for 8 grants (high: $100,000; low: $7,748).

Purpose and activities: Giving primarily for medical research, including 2 prestigious biomedical institutes, as well as for services for people who are blind, including a center for blind children; funding also to an ear institute and for human services.

Fields of interest: Alzheimer's disease; Human services; Biological sciences; Blind/visually impaired; Deaf/hearing impaired.

Type of support: Research.

Limitations: Applications not accepted. Giving limited to southern CA. No grants to individuals.

Application information: Contributes only to pre-selected organizations.

Board meeting date(s): July

Trustees: Douglas Nosworthy; Union Bank of California, N.A.

EIN: 946659802

Selected grants: The following grants were reported in 2003.

$100,000 to House Ear Institute, Los Angeles, CA.

$100,000 to Salk Institute for Biological Studies, San Diego, CA.

$100,000 to University of California, Los Angeles, CA.

$45,000 to Blind Childrens Center, Los Angeles, CA.

$35,000 to John Douglas French (JDF) Foundation for Alzheimers Disease Research, Los Angeles, CA.

$27,000 to Braille Institute of America, Los Angeles, CA.

$25,000 to Goodwill Industries of Orange County, Santa Ana, CA.

$19,000 to Guide Dogs of America, Sylmar, CA.

$18,387 to John Tracy Clinic, Los Angeles, CA.

$10,000 to Beverly Hospital Foundation, Montebello, CA.

333
The Bunker Foundation ✧

(formerly The Susan Ingemanson McNealy Foundation)
P.O. Box 223609
Carmel, CA 93922-3609

Established in 1994 in CA.

Donors: Scott McNealy; Susan McNealy; Susan Ingemanson.

Foundation type: Independent foundation.

Financial data (yr. ended 11/30/05): Assets, $8,775,794 (M); expenditures, $501,625; qualifying distributions, $501,480; giving activities include $499,500 for 24 grants (high: $100,000; low: $500).

Purpose and activities: Giving primarily for education, and health and social services.

Fields of interest: Arts; Education; Hospitals (general); Health organizations, association; Human services; Protestant agencies & churches.

Limitations: Applications not accepted. Giving primarily in CA; giving also in CO, MA, and MI. No grants to individuals.

Application information: Contributes only to pre-selected organizations.

Officer and Directors:* Susan Ingemanson,* Pres.; Paul Ingemanson.

EIN: 943215751

Selected grants: The following grants were reported in 2005.

$100,000 to AmeriCares, Stamford, CT.

$100,000 to CHP 11-99 Foundation, Norwalk, CA.

$50,000 to Kettering University, Flint, MI.

$40,000 to San Francisco 49ers Academy, East Palo Alto, CA.

$30,000 to United Way, CA.

$16,000 to Stanford University, Stanford, CA.

334
Burch Family Foundation ✧ ☆

1301 Delresto Dr.
Beverly Hills, CA 90210
Contact: Robert D. Burch, Tr.

Established in 1984 in CA.

Donor: Robert D. Burch.

Foundation type: Independent foundation.

Financial data (yr. ended 5/31/06): Assets, $5,814,477 (M); expenditures, $547,344; qualifying distributions, $541,587; giving activities include $541,587 for 32 grants (high: $398,800; low: $100).

Purpose and activities: Giving primarily for higher education, the arts, and social services including a rescue mission.

Fields of interest: Arts; Elementary/secondary education; Higher education; Law school/education; Digestive disorders research; Human services; Homeless, human services; Social sciences; Public policy, research; Public affairs, reform.

Type of support: General/operating support; Continuing support; Annual campaigns; Endowments; Program development; Professorships.

Limitations: Giving primarily in CA; some funding also in Washington, DC, and Arlington, VA. No grants to individuals.

Application information: Application form not required.

Initial approach: Letter
Deadline(s): None

Trustee: Robert D. Burch.

EIN: 953924403

Selected grants: The following grants were reported in 2005.

$200,000 to University of California, Berkeley, CA.

$35,100 to Cato Institute, DC.

$11,500 to Citizens Against Government Waste, DC.

$10,000 to Chandler School, Pasadena, CA.

$5,000 to Fulfillment Fund, Los Angeles, CA.

$5,000 to Tax Foundation, DC.

$2,000 to Independent Institute, Oakland, CA.

$1,000 to Carleton College, Northfield, MN.

$1,000 to Reason Foundation, Los Angeles, CA.

$500 to Harvard-Westlake School, North Hollywood, CA.

335
Leslie and Walter Burlock Foundation ✧ ☆

c/o Walter E. Burlock, Jr.
126 Commonwealth Ave.
San Francisco, CA 94118

Established in 1995 in NY.

Donor: Walter E. Burlock, Jr.

Foundation type: Independent foundation.

Financial data (yr. ended 11/30/05): Assets, $618,671 (M); gifts received, $508,634; expenditures, $356,537; qualifying distributions, $352,200; giving activities include $352,200 for grants.

Fields of interest: Education; Human services.

Type of support: General/operating support.

Limitations: Applications not accepted. Giving primarily in ME and NY. No grants to individuals.

Application information: Contributes only to pre-selected organizations.

Trustees: Walter E. Burlock, Jr.; Leslie Walker.

EIN: 133865445

Selected grants: The following grants were reported in 2004.

$50,000 to Bay School of San Francisco, San Francisco, CA.

$50,000 to University of California at San Francisco Foundation, Langley Porter Psychiatric Institute, San Francisco, CA.

$25,000 to Bowdoin College, Brunswick, ME.

$5,000 to Haleakala, The Kitchen, New York, NY.

$4,600 to Gateway High School, San Francisco, CA.

$3,000 to Boys and Girls Clubs of San Francisco, San Francisco, CA.

$2,380 to California Academy of Sciences, San Francisco, CA.

$2,000 to Curtis Memorial Library, Brunswick, ME.

$1,000 to Oxbow School, Napa, CA.

$500 to YMCA, Bath Area Family, Bath, ME.

336
Andrew H. Burnett Foundation ✧
114 E. De La Guerra St., Ste. 3
Santa Barbara, CA 93101 (805) 963-8822
Contact: Allen W. Finger, Pres.

Established in 1998 in CA.
Donor: Helen P. Burnett.
Foundation type: Independent foundation.
Financial data (yr. ended 6/30/05): Assets, $2,189,713 (M); expenditures, $645,024; qualifying distributions, $570,758; giving activities include $525,000 for 57 grants (high: $60,000; low: $2,000).
Purpose and activities: Giving primarily for art and culture, with emphasis on music, aid for people in need, the environment, and health.
Fields of interest: Museums; Performing arts, music; Arts; Education; Environment; Hospitals (general); Health care; Human services; Children/youth, services; Family services; Residential/custodial care, senior continuing care.
Limitations: Giving limited to residents of the Santa Barbara, Goleta, and Carpinteria, CA, area. No grants to individuals.
Application information: Application form required.
Deadline(s): Apr. 1
Officers and Directors:* Allen W. Finger,* Pres.; Joanne S. Rapp,* Secy.; Arthur R. Gaudi,* C.F.O.
EIN: 770492768
Selected grants: The following grants were reported in 2004.

$60,000 to Santa Barbara Center for the Performing Arts, Santa Barbara, CA. For general support.

$25,000 to Community Arts Music Association of Santa Barbara, Santa Barbara, CA. For general support.

$10,000 to Cancer Center of Santa Barbara, Santa Barbara, CA. For general support.

$8,000 to Community Environmental Council, Santa Barbara, CA. For general support.

$8,000 to Environmental Defense Center, Santa Barbara, CA. For general support.

$8,000 to Sansum Medical Research Foundation, Santa Barbara, CA. For general support.

$5,000 to Casa Serena, Santa Barbara, CA. For general support.

$5,000 to Domestic Violence Solutions for Santa Barbara County, Santa Barbara, CA. For general support.

$5,000 to Santa Barbara Chamber Orchestra Society, Santa Barbara, CA. For general support.

$2,000 to Prime Time Band, Santa Barbara, CA. For general support.

337
Burnham Foundation ✧
110 W. A St., Ste. 900
San Diego, CA 92101

Established in 1980 in CA.
Donors: Malin Burnham; Burnham Way.
Foundation type: Independent foundation.
Financial data (yr. ended 12/31/05): Assets, $8,262,852 (L); expenditures, $1,088,289; qualifying distributions, $932,657; giving activities include $932,657 for 92 grants (high: $250,000; low: $25).
Purpose and activities: Giving primarily for higher education, as well as for health associations, children, youth and social services, YMCAs, and to the United Way.
Fields of interest: Arts; Secondary school/education; Higher education; Health organizations, association; Cancer research; Human services; YM/YWCAs & YM/YWHAs; Children/youth, services; Federated giving programs.
Limitations: Applications not accepted. Giving primarily in CA. No grants to individuals.
Application information: Contributes only to pre-selected organizations.
Officers and Directors:* Malin Burnham,* Pres.; Roberta Burnham,* V.P.; Alan Scharsu, Secy.; Kit Sparks, Treas.; Robert Brettbard; Pauline Des Granges; Robert Lauer.
EIN: 953565278
Selected grants: The following grants were reported in 2003.

$2,001,000 to University of California at San Diego Foundation, La Jolla, CA.

$11,500 to University of San Diego, San Diego, CA.

$9,935 to Junior Achievement of San Diego, San Diego, CA.

$8,000 to California State University, San Marcos, CA.

$4,000 to San Diego State University Foundation, San Diego, CA.

$2,500 to Elderhelp of San Diego, San Diego, CA.

$1,512 to Sheepfold Home for Battered Women and Children, Orange, CA.

$500 to UCLA Foundation, Los Angeles, CA.

$200 to Family Health Centers of San Diego, San Diego, CA.

$100 to International Wildlife Education and Conservation, Create-A-Smile Animal Assisted Therapy, Santa Monica, CA.

338
Fritz B. Burns Foundation ▼ ✧
4001 W. Alameda Ave., Ste. 203
Burbank, CA 91505-4338 (818) 840-8802
Contact: Joseph E. Rawlinson, Pres.

Incorporated in 1955 in CA.
Donor: Fritz B. Burns†.
Foundation type: Independent foundation.
Financial data (yr. ended 9/30/05): Assets, $155,934,330 (M); expenditures, $9,177,312; qualifying distributions, $7,499,869; giving activities include $7,326,000 for 90 grants (high: $1,001,000; low: $1,000).
Purpose and activities: Grants primarily for education, hospitals and medical research organizations; support also for Roman Catholic religious associations and schools, social welfare agencies, and church support.
Fields of interest: Higher education; Education; Hospitals (general); Medical research, institute;

Human services; Roman Catholic federated giving programs; Roman Catholic agencies & churches.
Type of support: Program-related investments/loans.
Limitations: Giving primarily in the Los Angeles, CA, area. No support for private foundations. No grants to individuals.
Application information:
Initial approach: Letter
Deadline(s): Sept. 30
Board meeting date(s): Feb., May, Aug., and Nov.
Final notification: Approvals in Nov., payments made in Feb.
Officers and Directors:* Joseph E. Rawlinson,* Pres.; W.K. Skinner,* V.P. and Secy.-Treas.; Don Freeberg; Rex J. Rawlinson; Edward F. Slattery.
EIN: 943218106
Selected grants: The following grants were reported in 2005.

$2,001,000 to Loyola Marymount University, Los Angeles, CA. 2 grants: $1,000,000 to Law School, $1,001,000

$500,000 to Thomas Aquinas College, Santa Paula, CA.

$260,000 to Saint Annes Maternity Home, Los Angeles, CA.

$250,000 to Saint Joseph Medical Center, Burbank, CA.

$150,000 to American Red Cross, Los Angeles, CA.

$150,000 to Little Sisters of the Poor, San Pedro, CA. For Jeanne Jugan Residence.

$101,000 to Union Rescue Mission, Los Angeles, CA.

$50,000 to Meet Each Need with Dignity (MEND), Pacoima, CA.

$50,000 to Notre Dame Academy, Los Angeles, CA.

339
Byer Foundation ✧
66 Potrero Ave.
San Francisco, CA 94103 (415) 626-7844
Contact: Allan G. Byer, Tr.

Established in 1995 in CA.
Donor: Allan G. Byer.
Foundation type: Independent foundation.
Financial data (yr. ended 12/31/05): Assets, $752,439 (M); expenditures, $505,253; qualifying distributions, $504,468; giving activities include $504,468 for 35 grants (high: $116,210; low: $500).
Purpose and activities: Giving primarily to Jewish agencies and temples, and Jewish federated giving programs; funding also for health associations, particularly for cancer research.
Fields of interest: Arts; Higher education; Hospitals (general); Health organizations, association; Cancer research; Human services; Aging, centers/services; Jewish federated giving programs; Jewish agencies & temples.
Limitations: Giving primarily in CA. No grants to individuals.
Application information:
Initial approach: Letter
Deadline(s): None
Trustees: Allan G. Byer; Marian Byer.
EIN: 943216991
Selected grants: The following grants were reported in 2005.

$116,210 to Peninsula Temple Sholom, Burlingame, CA.

$6,500 to Giants Community Fund, San Francisco, CA.

$5,000 to American Red Cross.

$5,000 to San Francisco Symphony, San Francisco, CA.

$2,500 to Eisenhower Medical Center Foundation, Rancho Mirage, CA.

$1,500 to San Domenico School, San Anselmo, CA.

$1,000 to Arizona Science Center, Phoenix, AZ.

$1,000 to Institute on Aging, San Francisco, CA.

$500 to Cincinnati Association for the Blind, Cincinnati, OH.

$500 to Mission Hospice of San Mateo County, San Mateo, CA.

340
C.S. Fund

469 Bohemian Hwy.
Freestone, CA 95472 (707) 874-2942
Contact: Roxanne Turnage, Exec. Dir.
FAX: (707) 874-1734; E-mail: inquiries@csfund.org;
URL: http://www.csfund.org

Established in 1981 in CA as "pass through" fund for annual gifts of donors.

Donors: Maryanne Mott; Herman Warsh†.
Foundation type: Independent foundation.
Financial data (yr. ended 10/31/05): Assets, $3,685,373 (M); gifts received, $1,403,345; expenditures, $2,155,800; qualifying distributions, $2,246,234; giving activities include $1,231,616 for grants.
Purpose and activities: A private foundation, giving for programs with national or international impact; specific areas of funding include biotechnology, economic globalizations, food sovereignty, and civil liberties.
Type of support: General/operating support; Continuing support; Conferences/seminars; Publication; Research; Technical assistance; Matching/challenge support.
Limitations: Giving primarily on a national basis. No grants for endowment funds, capital ventures, emergency requests, or video or film production.
Publications: Application guidelines; Grants list.
Application information: A hard copy of the letter of inquiry is preferred over fax or e-mail. If the letter of inquiry describing the project falls within the foundation's area of interest, a full proposal will be invited. Application guidelines and procedures available on foundation Web site. Application form not required.
Initial approach: Letter of inquiry, not to exceed 3 pages
Copies of proposal: 1
Deadline(s): None, for letter of inquiry
Officers and Directors:* Michael Warsh,* Pres.; Marise Meynet Stewart,* V.P.; Maryanne Mott,* Secy.; Roxanne Turnage, Exec. Dir.; Corinne Meadows-Efram; Teresa Robinson.
Number of staff: 3 full-time professional; 3 part-time support.
EIN: 953607882
Selected grants: The following grants were reported in 2005.
$120,000 to Institute for Agriculture and Trade Policy, Minneapolis, MN. 2 grants: $60,000 each
$75,000 to Tides Center, San Francisco, CA.
$60,000 to International Forum on Globalization, San Francisco, CA.
$50,000 to Friends of the Earth, DC.
$50,000 to International Center for Technology Assessment, DC.
$50,000 to Science and Environmental Health Network, Ames, IA.

$40,000 to Center for International Environmental Law, DC.

$40,000 to Earthjustice, Oakland, CA.

$10,000 to EarthRights International, DC.

341
CAA Foundation ◇

c/o Bruce E. King
9830 Wilshire Blvd.
Beverly Hills, CA 90212

Established in 1995 in CA.

Donors: Creative Artists Agency, LLC; Robert Goldman; Bruce King; Richard Lovett.
Foundation type: Company-sponsored foundation.
Financial data (yr. ended 11/30/04): Assets, $173,486 (M); gifts received, $577,630; expenditures, $699,876; qualifying distributions, $621,353; giving activities include $621,353 for 28 grants (high: $120,000; low: $1,087).
Purpose and activities: The foundation supports organizations involved with arts and culture, education, housing, human services, and community development.
Fields of interest: Arts; Education; Housing/shelter; Human services; Community development.
Limitations: Applications not accepted. Giving primarily in CA. No grants to individuals.
Application information: Contributes only to pre-selected organizations.
Officers and Directors:* Richard Lovett,* Pres.; Michelle Kydd,* Secy.; Bruce E. King,* C.F.O.
EIN: 954556189
Selected grants: The following grants were reported in 2003.
$60,000 to Venice High School, Venice, CA. For Holiday program.
$36,153 to Mark Twain Middle School, Los Angeles, CA. For holiday program and back to school party.
$25,031 to Museum of Contemporary Art (MOCA), Los Angeles, CA. For J. Moloney Fund.
$25,000 to Childrens Burn Foundation, Sherman Oaks, CA.
$20,600 to Coeur d Alene Avenue Elementary School, Venice, CA. For holiday program.
$12,000 to Art Center College of Design, Pasadena, CA. For Arts scholarship.
$12,000 to Otis College of Art and Design, Los Angeles, CA. For arts scholarship.
$12,000 to UCLA Foundation, Los Angeles, CA. For Arts scholarship.
$11,500 to PENCIL Foundation, Nashville, TN.
$6,000 to L.A. Works, Los Angeles, CA.

342
Cacique Foundation ◇

14940 Proctor Ave.
City of Industry, CA 91746-3219
Contact: Angelo P. Gonzalez
Scholarship address: c/o Mount Sac Fdn. office on the campus of Mount San Antonio College, 1100 N. Grand Ave., Walnut, CA 91789; tel.: (909) 594-5611; FAX: (909) 468-4064; E-mail: foundation@mtsca.edu; URL: http://www.mtsacfoundation.org

Established in 1996 in CA.

Donors: Cacique, Inc.; Cacique Distributors, U.S.
Foundation type: Independent foundation.
Financial data (yr. ended 12/31/04): Assets, $9,088 (M); gifts received, $678,050;

expenditures, $807,434; qualifying distributions, $805,934; giving activities include $740,615 for 55 grants (high: $250,000; low: $95).
Purpose and activities: Giving primarily for education, health associations, human services, Roman Catholic churches and organizations, and to Latino organizations. Scholarships are available to individuals who are either graduate teen mothers sponsored by the Buenanueva Fdn., employees of Cacique, Inc., or single parents, and who are enrolled as full-time students. GPA and/or financial need may be considered.
Fields of interest: Performing arts; Elementary/secondary education; Higher education; Education; Health organizations, association; Human services; Foundations (community); Roman Catholic agencies & churches; Hispanics/Latinos.
Limitations: Giving primarily in CA.
Application information: Scholarship funds are available to individuals for study at Mount San Antonio College (Mt. Sac). The program is administered by the Mount Sac Foundation. Cacique currently donates $5,000 per year toward these scholarships. Application form required.
Initial approach: Send for application
Copies of proposal: 1
Deadline(s): June 28, (for scholarship program)
Officers: Gilbert L. De Cardenas, Chair.; Jennie De Cardenas, Pres.; Charles "Chuck" Aedo, V.P.; Ana De Cardenas-Raptis, Secy.; Orlando Ortega, C.F.O.
EIN: 954518246
Selected grants: The following grants were reported in 2003.
$1,000,000 to City of Hope, Los Angeles, CA.
$264,955 to Holy Family Church, South Pasadena, CA. For capital campaign.
$100,000 to Cedars-Sinai Medical Center, Los Angeles, CA. For research.
$48,770 to Buena Nueva Foundation, Pasadena, CA. For educational support for unwed mothers.
$25,000 to Center for the Partially Sighted, Los Angeles, CA.
$1,500 to California Community Foundation, Los Angeles, CA. For Mario Cruz Scholarship Fund.
$1,500 to Casa de San Gabriel Community Center, San Gabriel, CA.
$1,000 to Saint Jude Childrens Research Hospital, Memphis, TN.
$900 to Mayfield Junior School of the Holy Child Jesus, Pasadena, CA. For annual campaign.
$300 to Boy Scouts of America, Costa Mesa, CA.

343
Caddock Foundation, Inc. ◇

1717 Chicago Ave.
Riverside, CA 92507
Contact: Richard E. Caddock, Jr., Treas.

Incorporated in 1968 in CA.

Foundation type: Independent foundation.
Financial data (yr. ended 12/31/05): Assets, $1,840,307 (M); expenditures, $828,965; qualifying distributions, $823,450; giving activities include $823,450 for 17 grants (high: $360,000; low: $1,350).
Purpose and activities: Grants to Evangelical Christian religious associations and activities, including bible studies.
Fields of interest: Christian agencies & churches.
Type of support: General/operating support; Continuing support; Program evaluation.
Limitations: Applications not accepted. No grants to individuals.

Application information: Contributes only to pre-selected organizations.
Officers: John B. Caddock, Pres.; James C. Caddock, V.P.; Sue Brinkman, Secy.; Richard E. Caddock, Jr., Treas.
EIN: 952559728

344
Cadence Foundation ✧ ☆
c/o Kathryn Wheeler
555 River Oaks Pkwy.
San Jose, CA 95134

Foundation type: Independent foundation.
Financial data (yr. ended 12/31/05): Assets, $133,136 (M); gifts received, $975,104; expenditures, $977,054; qualifying distributions, $977,054; giving activities include $973,886 for 5 grants (high: $880,451; low: $4,610).
Fields of interest: Youth development; Human services; Foundations (public).
Limitations: Applications not accepted. Giving primarily in CA and MA; funding also in Rockville, MD. No grants to individuals.
Application information: Contributes only to pre-selected organizations.
Officers and Directors:* William Porter,* Pres.; John Paul Bruno,* V.P. and Treas.; James Cowie,* Secy.; Kathryn Wheeler.
EIN: 300127470

345
California Community Foundation ▼
445 S. Figueroa St., Ste. 3400
Los Angeles, CA 90071 (213) 413-4130
Contact: Alvertha Penny, V.P., Progs.; Vera de Vera, Dir., Grants; Daphny Toussaint, Grants Specialist
FAX: (213) 383-2046; E-mail: info@ccf-la.org;
URL: http://www.calfund.org

Established in 1915 in CA by bank resolution.
Foundation type: Community foundation.
Financial data (yr. ended 6/30/06): Assets, $1,152,601,808 (M); gifts received, $466,617,193; expenditures, $102,710,737; giving activities include $91,367,805 for grants, and $2,536,303 for 4 loans/program-related investments (high: $2,000,000; low: $100,000).
Purpose and activities: The mission of the foundation is to strengthen Los Angeles communities through effective philanthropy and civic engagement. The foundation makes multi-year grants (usually two years) in four main areas: arts and human development, education, health and neighborhood revitalization.
Fields of interest: Arts; Education, early childhood education; Elementary school/education; Education; Animal welfare; Health care; AIDS; AIDS research; Crime/violence prevention, domestic violence; Employment; Housing/shelter, development; Children/youth, services; Aging, centers/services; Human services; Civil rights, race/intergroup relations; Community development; Public affairs; Aging; Disabilities, people with; Asians/Pacific Islanders; African Americans/ Blacks; Hispanics/Latinos; Native Americans/ American Indians; Women; AIDS, people with; LGBTQ; Immigrants/refugees; Economically disadvantaged; Homeless.
Type of support: General/operating support; Capital campaigns; Continuing support; Management

development/capacity building; Program development; Scholarship funds; Research; Technical assistance; Consulting services; Program evaluation; Program-related investments/loans; Employee matching gifts; Matching/challenge support.
Limitations: Giving limited to Los Angeles County, CA. No support for sectarian purposes. No grants to individuals (except fellowships for artists or scholarships), or for annual campaigns, equipment, endowment funds, debt reduction, operating budgets, re-granting, fellowships, films, conferences, dinners, or special events.
Publications: Application guidelines; Annual report (including application guidelines); Financial statement; Informational brochure; Newsletter.
Application information: Visit foundation Web site for application forms and guidelines. Applicants will receive written notification that either invites or discourages the submission of a full grant application based on Letter of Intent. Application form required.
> *Initial approach:* Submit Letter of Intent
> *Copies of proposal:* 1
> *Deadline(s):* Apr. 1, Aug. 1, and Dec. 1 for Letter of Intent; Feb. 1, June 1, and Oct. 1 for full grant application
> *Board meeting date(s):* Mar., June, Oct., and Dec.
> *Final notification:* Within 4 to 6 weeks for Letter of Intent determination; Mar., June, and Oct. for grants

Officers and Board of Governors:* Dorothy Avila Courtney,* Chair.; Antonia Hernandez,* C.E.O. and Pres.; Joe Lumarda, Exec. V.P. and C.O.O.; Steve Cobb, V.P. and C.F.O.; Alvertha Penny, V.P., Progs.; Denise Trinh, Cont.; Jane G. Pisano, Chair. Emeritus; Reveta Bowers; Bruce C. Corwin; Jane B. Eisner; David W. Fleming; Dennis Gertmenian; Ronald E. Gother; John Kobara; Joanne Corday Kozberg; Ki Suh Park; Carolina Reyes, M.D.; James M. Rosser; Thomas Schumacher; Robert Segal; William E.B. Siart; Sheldon M. Stone; Cynthia Telles; Tom Unterman.
Number of staff: 31 full-time professional; 13 full-time support.
EIN: 953510055
Selected grants: The following grants were reported in 2006.
$4,000,000 to Childrens Health Initiative of Greater Los Angeles, Los Angeles, CA. For health insurance costs for children living at or below 200% of federal poverty level in Centinela Medical Fund's priority areas.
$250,000 to Arroyo Vista Family Health Center, Los Angeles, CA. For relocation and renovation of Lincoln Heights community clinic that serves uninsured and underinsured residents.
$225,000 to Corporation for Supportive Housing, Oakland, CA. For general operating support of affordable housing intermediary that provides technical assistance and financial support to Los Angeles area nonprofit organizations that develop permanent supportive housing for low-income individuals and families.
$143,853 to JWCH Institute, Los Angeles, CA. For new health services at recently reopened Bell Gardens Health Center.
$120,000 to East Los Angeles Community Corporation, Los Angeles, CA. For general operating support for agency's predevelopment, land acquisition and affordable housing development activites in Boyle Heights and East Los Angeles.

$100,000 to Los Angeles Coalition to End Hunger and Homelessness, Los Angeles, CA. For housing policy advocacy efforts of Save Section 8 Coalition.
$100,000 to Music Intelligence Neural Development (MIND) Institute, Costa Mesa, CA. For collaboration with Long Beach Unified School District to establish Math and Music program at six low-income elementary schools.
$95,000 to University of California, Los Angeles, CA. For principal and teacher training program that seeks to improve student achievement and increase parent involvement at three Baldwin Park elementary schools.
$80,000 to Jovenes, Los Angeles, CA. For operating support to expand level of services for homeless immigrant and foster care youth.
$40,000 to Parent Institute for Quality Education, San Diego, CA. For training courses for low-income parents to help them navigate public school system and promote parent-teacher collaboration.

346
The California Endowment ▼ ✧
1000 N. Alameda St.
Los Angeles, CA 90012 (800) 449-4149
FAX: (213) 928-8801;
E-mail: questions@calendow.org; URL: http:// www.calendow.org

Established in 1996 in CA; converted from Blue Cross of California.
Foundation type: Independent foundation.
Financial data (yr. ended 2/28/05): Assets, $3,729,571,524 (M); expenditures, $216,017,001; qualifying distributions, $215,323,851; giving activities include $152,970,674 for 1,650 grants (high: $4,237,500; low: $100; average: $1,000–$500,000), $272,115 for employee matching gifts, $2,481,303 for foundation-administered programs and $200,000 for loans/program-related investments.
Purpose and activities: To expand access to affordable, quality health care for underserved individuals and communities and to promote fundamental improvements in the health status of all Californians.
Fields of interest: Health care, equal rights; Health care; Minorities; Economically disadvantaged.
Type of support: Management development/ capacity building; General/operating support; Building/renovation; Conferences/seminars; Technical assistance; Program evaluation; Program-related investments/loans; Employee matching gifts.
Limitations: Giving primarily in CA. No support for political purposes, medical or scientific research, or uncompensated care for direct clinical services. No grants to individuals for scholarships; fellowships or grants, or for endowments, operating deficits or retirement of debt, media projects not part of a broader project or strategy, medical supplies, laboratory fees, X-ray services, medications, vaccines or prescriptions; capital funding for purchase, construction or renovation of facilities or other physical infrastructure; indirect costs that exceed 15% of the total of requested personnel and operating costs.
Publications: Application guidelines; Annual report; Occasional report.

Application information: See foundation Web site for grant application guide and downloadable grant application coversheet. Application form required.

Initial approach: Application including application coversheet

Copies of proposal: 4

Deadline(s): None

Board meeting date(s): Feb., Apr., July, Oct. and Dec. (Optional)

Final notification: Four months

Officers and Directors:* Arthur Chen, M.D.*, Chair.; Daniel Boggan,* Vice-Chair.; Robert K. Ross, M.D.*, C.E.O. and Pres.; Irene M. Ibarra, Exec. V.P.; Michael J. Januzik, V.P. and C.F.O.; Brytain Ashford, V.P., Human Resources; Dennis Hunt, V.P., Comms. and Public Affairs; Alonzo Louis Plough, Ph.D., V.P., Progs., Planning, and Eval.; Kathleen Brown; John E. Bryson; Jesse Casso, Jr.; Tessie Guillermo; Beverly Hamilton; James Keddy; James Lewis Kyle II, M.D.; Maurice Lim Miller; Hugo Morales; E. Lewis Reid; Rita Scardaci; Cynthia Ann Telles, Ph.D.; Fernando M. Torres-Gill, Ph.D.; Maria Tripp; Winnie O. Willis, Sc.D.

Number of staff: 168 full-time professional; 11 full-time support; 2 part-time support.

EIN: 954523232

Selected grants: The following grants were reported in 2005.

$4,294,537 to Children Now, Oakland, CA. To expand 100 Percent Campaign, policy and advocacy activities which serve as anchor in support of Children's Coverage Program to achieve health coverage for all children in California.

$4,056,779 to Public Health Institute, Building Communities for Healthy Eating and Physical Activity Program Office, Oakland, CA. To provide program support and coordination of statewide technical assistance providers for up to five local collaboratives working to increase opportunities for physical activity and healthy eating for children and families in targeted neighborhoods, and to advance policy agenda that supports community-based public health and increased resources for primary prevention.

$3,383,088 to University of California, Los Angeles, CA. To increase availability, accessibility and utility of California Health Interview Survey (CHIS) 2005 health data by collecting oversamples of key populations, administering specific survey topics that support California Endowment program interests, conducting and publishing studies on asthma, diabetes and access to health insurance and health care, and broadly disseminating survey data and studies to community-based organizations, state and local officials, researchers and decision-makers.

$2,600,000 to Rural Community Assistance Corporation, West Sacramento, CA. For Agricultural Worker Community Health and Housing Assistance Program, strategic partnership with Agricultural Worker Health Initiative's Poder Popular Program to provide management assistance, training, and related technical support with primary focus on improving local community infrastructure and housing for agricultural workers in California.

$1,869,555 to University of California, San Francisco, CA. To implement key organizational change strategies in LEADing Organizational Change-Advancing Quality Through Culturally Responsive Care, initiative to integrate culturally and linguistically appropriate services into public hospitals and health systems in California.

$1,203,950 to California Teachers Association, Burlingame, CA. To expand Teachers for Healthy Kids, teacher-to-parent outreach program to increase children's enrollment in free and low-cost health coverage programs in targeted low-income school districts in California.

$1,000,000 to K C E T Community Television of Southern California, Los Angeles, CA. For public health policy television programming aimed at increasing California residents' participation in health policy advocacy, and increasing awareness of health policy issues among California policymakers in order to have impact on local and statewide policy change.

$988,000 to National Public Radio, DC. For increased coverage of health care issues affecting minorities and underserved populations in California including coverage on disparities in health status and treatment; access to quality, affordable health care; obesity prevention; and children's health issues.

$955,725 to Institute for Health Policy Solutions, DC. Toward development of local children's health initiatives throughout state and to facilitate transfer of innovation and best practices from local programs statewide to advance health coverage for all children in California.

$950,000 to Santa Clara Family Health Foundation, Campbell, CA. To provide one year of full medical, dental and vision coverage through Healthy Kids program to uninsured, ineligible children 6-18 years of age in Santa Clara County.

347

California HealthCare Foundation

476 9th St.
Oakland, CA 94607 (510) 238-1040
Contact: Lisa Kang, Dir., Grants Admin.
FAX: (510) 238-1388; E-mail: info@chcf.org;
URL: http://www.chcf.org

Established in 1996 in CA; converted from Blue Cross of California.

Financial data (yr. ended 2/28/06): Assets, $899,734,292 (M); expenditures, $56,646,293; giving activities include $44,187,033 for 373 grants (high: $2,221,042; low: $630; average: $10,000–$200,000), and $826,674 for 36 grants to individuals (high: $135,539; low: $421).

Purpose and activities: The foundation's mission is to expand access to affordable, quality health care for underserved individuals and communities, and to promote fundamental improvements in the health status of the people of California. The foundation commissions research and analysis, publishes and disseminates information, convenes stakeholders, and funds the development of programs and models aimed at improving the healthcare delivery and financing systems.

Fields of interest: Health care, HMOs; Health care, insurance; Health care; Health organizations, public policy; Health organizations, public education.

Type of support: Program development; Research; Program evaluation.

Limitations: Giving primarily in CA. No grants for general operating expenses, capital campaigns, annual campaigns, building, purchases or renovations, direct clinical care costs, or equipment.

Publications: Informational brochure (including application guidelines); Occasional report.

Application information: Projects must have potential to inform or impact health care access and

health policy issues in California; Application form required only for RFPs; See Web site for latest information including available publications. Application form not required.

Initial approach: Letter of intent

Copies of proposal: 2

Deadline(s): None

Board meeting date(s): Quarterly

Final notification: 6-8 weeks from receipt

Officers and Directors:* A. Eugene Washington, Jr., M.D., M.Sc.*, Chair.; Monica C. Lozano, Vice-Chair.; Mark Douglas Smith, M.D., C.E.O. and Pres.; Napoleon Brandford III; Geoffrey Cowan; Ralph P. Garcia; Pamela Joyner; Harry W. Low; Ian Morrison, Ph.D., M.A.; Walter W. "Bill" Noce, Jr.; Sheryl Pressler.

Number of staff: 37 full-time professional; 3 part-time professional; 9 full-time support; 1 part-time support.

EIN: 954523231

348

California Masonic Foundation ◇

1111 California St.
San Francisco, CA 94108
Contact: Angel Alvarez-Mapp, Coord.
E-mail: foundation@Freemason.org; URL: http://www.freemason.org

Incorporated in 1969 in CA.

Donor: Grand Lodge F & AM of California.

Foundation type: Independent foundation.

Financial data (yr. ended 6/30/05): Assets, $16,751,369 (M); gifts received, $5,404,510; expenditures, $1,998,267; qualifying distributions, $1,547,132; giving activities include $1,069,132 for 19 grants, $478,000 for 99 grants to individuals, and $95,934 for 2 foundation-administered programs.

Purpose and activities: Support for education, including scholarships to high school graduating seniors who are U.S. citizens residing in CA, and in need of financial aid for full-time undergraduate study at accredited institutions of higher learning.

Type of support: General/operating support; Scholarships—to individuals.

Limitations: Giving limited to CA.

Publications: Application guidelines.

Application information: The scholarship application form is available on Web site between Sept. 1 to Feb. 15. Students must apply on line. No hard copies will be mailed from this office. Application form required.

Initial approach: Online

Copies of proposal: 1

Deadline(s): Feb. 15

Officer and Trustees:* John F. Lowe,* Pres.; and 7 additional trustees.

Number of staff: 1 full-time support.

EIN: 237013074

349

California Space Grant Foundation ◇

(doing business as Discovery Space Technology Center)
8340 Clairemont Mesa Blvd., Ste. 203
San Diego, CA 92111 (619) 944-2555
Contact: Philip E. Smith, C.E.O.
FAX: (858) 569-8637; E-mail: info@csgf.org;
Northern CA address: c/o NASA AMES Research

Park, P.O. Box 433, Moffett Field, CA 94035; URL: http://www.csgf.org

Established in 2002 in CA.
Donors: NASA Ames Research Center; Education Associates Program; NASA Dryden Flight Research Center; NASA Langley Research Center; Pioneer Space Center; I2 Cam UC Davis; National Oceanic & Atmospheric Administration; Sandia National Laboratories.
Foundation type: Independent foundation.
Financial data (yr. ended 12/31/05): Assets, $367,769 (M); gifts received, $4,441,659; expenditures, $4,409,304; qualifying distributions, $4,411,667; giving activities include $84,229 for 11 grants (high: $38,000; low: $500), and $1,348,595 for 198 grants to individuals (high: $28,592; low: $125).
Purpose and activities: The foundation is organized to enable students of all ethnic and financial backgrounds to attain high skill technical and professional careers through education and exciting programs. The foundation creates, facilitates, manages, and integrates K-12, college and university, and life-long learning opportunities built around real world space, land, and sea projects.
Fields of interest: Education; Science, public education; Space/aviation; Science.
Type of support: Fellowships.
Limitations: Giving primarily in CA.
Application information: Application form not required.
  Initial approach: Letter
  Deadline(s): None
Officers: Philip E. Smith, C.E.O.; James Grady, C.O.O.; Claudia von Wilpert, C.F.O.
Directors: William Boyd; Paul Coleman; Susan Dong; Michael Wiskerchen.
EIN: 943031747

350
The California Wellness Foundation ▼
6320 Canoga Ave., Ste. 1700
Woodland Hills, CA   91367-7111
(818) 702-1900
Contact: Joan C. Hurley, Dir., Grants Mgmt.
FAX: (818) 702-1999; E-mail: tcwf@tcwf.org; Branch Office address: 575 Market St., Ste. 1850, San Francisco, CA 94105, tel.: (415) 908-3000, fax: (415) 908-3001; URL: http://www.tcwf.org

Established in 1991 in CA; converted from Health Net HMO.
Donor: Health Net Corp.
Foundation type: Independent foundation.
Financial data (yr. ended 12/31/05): Assets, $1,072,427,215 (M); expenditures, $59,061,006; qualifying distributions, $55,566,775; giving activities include $48,036,901 for 425 grants (high: $1,000,000; low: $1,050; average: $10,000–$150,000), $187,500 for 9 grants to individuals (high: $25,000; low: $12,500), and $186,502 for 139 employee matching gifts.
Purpose and activities: The foundation's mission is to improve the health of the people of California by making grants for health promotion, wellness education and disease prevention. The foundation pursues the following goals through grantmaking: 1) to address the particular health needs of traditionally underserved populations, including low-income individuals, people of color, youth and residents of rural areas; 2) to support and strengthen nonprofit organizations that seek to improve the health of underserved populations; 3) to recognize and encourage leaders who are working to increase health and wellness within their communities; and 4) to inform the development of public policies that promote wellness and enhance access to preventive health care.
Fields of interest: Medical care, community health systems; Public health; Public health, occupational health; Mental health/crisis services; Crime/violence prevention; Youth development, services; Children/youth, services; Youth, pregnancy prevention; Family services; Leadership development; Aging.
Type of support: Technical assistance; General/operating support; Continuing support; Program development; Conferences/seminars; Publication; Seed money; Research; Program evaluation; Employee matching gifts; Grants to individuals.
Limitations: Giving limited to CA; national organizations providing services in CA are also considered. No support for religious or sectarian organizations. No grants to individuals (except for research fellowships and awards), or for annual fund drives, building campaigns, major equipment, or biomedical research.
Publications: Annual report; Annual report (including application guidelines); Informational brochure; Newsletter (including application guidelines); Occasional report.
Application information: Application form not required.
  Initial approach: 1- to 2-page letter
  Deadline(s): Varies
  Board meeting date(s): Quarterly
  Final notification: 4 to 6 months
Officers and Directors:* Douglas X. Patino, Ph.D.*, Chair.; Stewart Kwoh,* Vice-Chair.; Gary L. Yates,* C.E.O. and Pres.; Magdalena Beltran-Del Olmo, V.P., Comms.; Margaret W. Minnich, V.P., Finance and Admin.; Cristina M. Regalado, V.P., Progs.; David S. Barlow; Ezra C. Davidson, Jr., M.D.; Elizabeth M. Gomez; Barbara S. Marshall; Earl G. Mink; Peggy Saika; Barbara C. Staggers, M.D.; Luz Vega-Marquis.
Number of staff: 19 full-time professional; 2 part-time professional; 18 full-time support; 2 part-time support.
EIN: 954292101
Selected grants: The following grants were reported in 2006.
$400,000 to San Diego County Office of Education, San Diego, CA. For establishing gang and violence prevention services.
$300,000 to Maternal Outreach Management System (MOMS), Santa Ana, CA. For operating support.
$255,000 to Pajaro Valley Community Health Trust, Watsonville, CA. For diabetes prevention and treatment services for local farmworkers.
$225,000 to Operation Safe House, Riverside, CA. For operating support.
$200,000 to California Health Care Safety-Net Institute, Oakland, CA. For operating support.
$200,000 to Occidental College, Pollution Prevention Center, Los Angeles, CA. For phasing out toxic and smog-forming chemicals in dry cleaning industry.
$175,000 to United African American Ministerial Action Council (UAAMAC), San Diego, CA. For Medical Advocacy Program to provide healthcare access to formerly incarcerated males.
$150,000 to Alliance for Rural Community Health, Ukiah, CA. For Empowerment Through Education program to provide scholarships to minority employees.
$150,000 to People Resources, Woodland, CA. For operating support.
$150,000 to West County Health Centers, Guerneville, CA. For core operating support for Community Health Access for Rural Teens program, to educate teens in rural western Sonoma County about healthy lifestyle choices and healthy sexuality.

351
The Callison Foundation
969G Edgewater Blvd., PMB 148
Foster City, CA   94404
Contact: Gerald Hing, Secy.

Established in 1965 in CA.
Donor: Fred W. Callison†.
Foundation type: Independent foundation.
Financial data (yr. ended 12/31/05): Assets, $8,213,844 (M); expenditures, $451,300; qualifying distributions, $360,500; giving activities include $360,500 for 26 grants (high: $15,000; low: $7,500).
Purpose and activities: Giving primarily for the arts and education.
Fields of interest: Arts; Education; Community development; Science; Religion.
Type of support: General/operating support; Scholarship funds.
Limitations: Giving primarily in the San Francisco Bay Area, CA. No grants to individuals.
Application information: Application form required.
  Initial approach: Letter of intent
  Copies of proposal: 4
  Deadline(s): July 1
  Board meeting date(s): Varies
Officers and Directors:* Mort Pactor,* Pres.; Gerald Hing,* Secy.; Peter O'Hara,* Treas.
EIN: 946127962
Selected grants: The following grants were reported in 2005.
$15,000 to Aim High for High School, San Francisco, CA. For summer program expansion and strategic plan implementation.
$15,000 to Bay Area Youth (BAY) Fund for Education, San Francisco, CA.
$15,000 to Central City Hospitality House, San Francisco, CA. For arts program.
$15,000 to Jamestown Community Center, San Francisco, CA. For educational enrichment and academic support for grades 3-12.
$13,000 to College Preparatory School, Oakland, CA. For scholarships.
$10,000 to Creative Arts Charter School, San Francisco, CA. For Emotional Wellness Program to support at-risk students.
$10,000 to East Palo Alto Kids Foundation, Palo Alto, CA.
$10,000 to Experience Corps, Palo Alto, CA.
$10,000 to Family Builders By Adoption, Oakland, CA.
$10,000 to First Place Fund for Youth, Oakland, CA. For Emancipation Specialist Program to provide case management for high-risk foster youth in group homes.
$10,000 to Girls Inc. of Alameda County, San Leandro, CA. For Eureka Program to provide math, science and technology-based training and internships for high school girls.
$10,000 to Give2Asia, San Francisco, CA. For Tsunami Recovery Fund.

$7,500 to Marine Mammal Center, Sausalito, CA. Expansion of Whale Bus outreach program.

$5,000 to American Red Cross, San Francisco, CA. For Hurricane Katrina support.

352

The Campbell Family Foundation ✧

305 Churchill Ave.
Palo Alto, CA 94301

Established in 1999 in CA.
Donors: William V. Campbell; Roberta Campbell.
Foundation type: Independent foundation.
Financial data (yr. ended 12/31/05): Assets, $23,456,466 (M); gifts received, $11,535,533; expenditures, $5,736,849; qualifying distributions, $5,547,758; giving activities include $5,540,630 for 24 grants (high: $5,000,000; low: $5,000).
Purpose and activities: Giving primarily to Roman Catholic schools, children and youth services, and to a computer history museum.
Fields of interest: Museums (specialized); Higher education; Education; Youth development; Children/youth, services.
Limitations: Applications not accepted. Giving primarily in CA, some funding in NY and PA. No grants to individuals.
Application information: Contributes only to pre-selected organizations.
Officers: William V. Campbell, Pres.; Roberta Campbell, Secy.-Treas.
Director: Tom Baenziger.
EIN: 770517945

353

Frank A. Campini Foundation ✧

220 Sansome St., Ste. 700
San Francisco, CA 94104
Contact: Paul J. Ruby, Pres.

Established in 1960 in CA.
Donor: Frank A. Campini†.
Foundation type: Independent foundation.
Financial data (yr. ended 12/31/05): Assets, $23,453,817 (M); expenditures, $1,131,948; qualifying distributions, $1,002,000; giving activities include $963,000 for 66 grants (high: $100,000; low: $1,000).
Fields of interest: Museums; Education; Cancer; AIDS; Medical research, institute; Cancer research; AIDS research; Human services.
Limitations: Giving primarily in the San Francisco Bay Area, CA. No support for religious organizations. No grants to individuals.
Application information: Application form not required.
  Initial approach: Letter
  Copies of proposal: 1
  Deadline(s): Oct. 1
  Board meeting date(s): Dec.
Officers and Directors:* Paul J. Ruby,* Pres.; Hendrika C. Neys,* Exec. V.P.
EIN: 946107956
Selected grants: The following grants were reported in 2003.
$100,000 to Boys and Girls Clubs of San Francisco, San Francisco, CA. For operating support.
$50,000 to Family House, San Francisco, CA. For capital campaign.

$5,000 to Crohns and Colitis Foundation of America, Northern California Chapter, San Francisco, CA. For general support.

$5,000 to Edgewood Center for Children and Families, San Francisco, CA. For general support.

$5,000 to Family Link, San Francisco, CA. For general operating support.

$5,000 to Huckleberry Youth Programs, San Francisco, CA. For general support.

$5,000 to Judah L. Magnes Museum, Berkeley, CA. For operating support.

$5,000 to San Francisco Museum of Modern Art, San Francisco, CA. For general support.

$2,000 to National Lymphedema Network, Oakland, CA. For general support.

$2,000 to Presidio World College, San Francisco, CA. For general support.

354

Iris & B. Gerald Cantor Foundation

(formerly The B. G. Cantor Art Foundation)
1180 South Beverly Dr., Ste. 321
Los Angeles, CA 90035
Contact: Judith Sobol, Exec. Dir.
FAX: (310) 277-4296; E-mail: jsobol@ibgcf.org;
URL: http://www.cantorfoundation.org

Established in 1978 in CA.
Donors: B. Gerald Cantor†; Iris Cantor; Cantor Fitzgerald, LP; Cantor Fitzgerald Inc.; Amethyst, Inc.
Foundation type: Independent foundation.
Financial data (yr. ended 4/30/05): Assets, $53,272,421 (M); gifts received, $257,079; expenditures, $1,356,626; qualifying distributions, $1,352,251; giving activities include $814,272 for grants.
Purpose and activities: Giving primarily for exhibitions of and research about the work of Rodin, as well as for medical research, art museums, and women's health care.
Fields of interest: Museums; Hospitals (general); Health care; Medical research, institute.
Type of support: General/operating support; Continuing support; Annual campaigns; Capital campaigns; Building/renovation; Endowments; Professorships; Publication; Fellowships; Scholarship funds; Research; Grants to individuals; Scholarships—to individuals; Matching/challenge support.
Limitations: Giving primarily in CA and NY, or for Rodin studies at Musee Rodin in Paris, France.
Application information: Applicants are required to have a preliminary discussion with foundation staff prior to writing a proposal. Application form not required.
  Initial approach: E-mail inquiry
  Copies of proposal: 10
  Board meeting date(s): Quarterly
  Final notification: 6 months
Officers and Directors:* Iris Cantor,* Chair. and Pres.; Suzanne Fisher,* Secy.; Joel Rothstein,* Treas.; Judith Sobol,* Exec. Dir.; Randi Ross Aitken; Michele Geller; Monica Ross Muhart.
Number of staff: 1 full-time professional; 1 part-time professional; 1 full-time support.
EIN: 136227347

355

The Cantus Fund ✧

1481 Sage Canyon Rd.
St. Helena, CA 94574-9714
Contact: Janet Pagano, Dir.

Established in 2002 in CA.
Donors: Dana Johnson; Mark Nelson.
Foundation type: Independent foundation.
Financial data (yr. ended 12/31/05): Assets, $41,999,773 (M); expenditures, $1,668,447; qualifying distributions, $1,614,517; giving activities include $1,401,081 for 36 grants (high: $300,000; low: $250).
Purpose and activities: Giving primarily for the performing arts, particularly the symphony and other music events; funding also for health associations, particularly a heart fund for babies, education, family services and community development.
Fields of interest: Performing arts; Performing arts, music; Performing arts, orchestra (symphony); Elementary/secondary education; Health organizations, association; Children, services; Family services; Community development; Foundations (community).
Limitations: Applications not accepted. Giving primarily in Napa County, CA. No grants to individuals.
Application information: Contributes only to pre-selected organizations.
Officers and Directors:* Mark Nelson,* Pres.; Dana Johnson,* Secy.-Treas.; Janet Pagano.
Number of staff: 1 full-time professional; 1 full-time support; 1 part-time support.
EIN: 020630178

356

Capdevila/Gillespie Foundation ✧ ☆

720 Golden Park Ave.
San Diego, CA 92106

Established in 1998 in CA.
Donors: Martin J. Capdevilla; Wendy Gillespie Capdevilla; Ron McMahon; David Ruyle; Mary Ruyle.
Foundation type: Independent foundation.
Financial data (yr. ended 12/31/05): Assets, $640,639 (M); gifts received, $490,000; expenditures, $537,989; qualifying distributions, $537,710; giving activities include $536,000 for 8 grants (high: $500,000; low: $1,000).
Fields of interest: Youth development.
Type of support: General/operating support.
Limitations: Applications not accepted. Giving primarily in Chula Vista, Rancho Santa Fe, and San Diego, CA. No grants to individuals.
Application information: Contributes only to pre-selected organizations.
Officers and Directors:* Wendy Gillespie Capdevilla,* C.E.O.; Martin J. Capdevilla,* C.F.O. and Secy.
EIN: 330795195

357

The Capital Group Companies Charitable Foundation ▼

11100 Santa Monica Blvd., 9th Fl.
Los Angeles, CA 90025-3384

Established in 1997 in CA.
Donors: Capital Management Services, Inc.; Capital Bank & Trust Co.; The Capital Group Cos., Inc.;

Capital Research & Management Co.; Capital International, Inc.
Foundation type: Company-sponsored foundation.
Financial data (yr. ended 6/30/05): Assets, $141,254,474 (M); gifts received, $81,170,850; expenditures, $18,544,885; qualifying distributions, $17,107,432; giving activities include $17,093,132 for 4,502 grants (high: $333,900; low: $50).
Purpose and activities: The foundation supports organizations involved with arts and culture, education, and human services.
Fields of interest: Museums; Performing arts, music; Arts; Higher education; Education; Children, services; Family services; Human services.
Limitations: Applications not accepted. Giving on a national and internationl basis. No support for religious, political, or fraternal organizations or professional organizations. No grants to individuals.
Application information: Contributes only to pre-selected organizations.
Officers and Directors:* James M. Brown,* Chair.; Naomi Kobayashi, Secy.; Edith H.L. Van Huss, C.F.O.; James B. Lovelace; Theodore R. Samuels.
EIN: 954658856
Selected grants: The following grants were reported in 2005.
$333,900 to Harvey Mudd College, Claremont, CA.
$236,700 to K C E T Community Television of Southern California, Los Angeles, CA.
$100,000 to Doctors Without Borders USA, New York, NY.
$100,000 to International Rescue Committee, New York, NY.
$50,400 to For Love of Children (FLOC), DC.
$25,000 to Direct Relief International, Santa Barbara, CA.
$15,000 to City of Hope, Los Angeles, CA.
$15,000 to Hebrew Union College-Jewish Institute of Religion, Skirball Cultural Center, Los Angeles, CA.
$14,200 to Sexual Minority Youth Assistance League, DC.
$10,380 to Trinity College, Hartford, CT.

358
The Truman Capote Literary Trust ✧
c/o F. Altman & Co.
9255 Sunset Blvd., Ste. 901
Los Angeles, CA   90069
Application address: c/o Alan U. Schwartz, 11355 W. Olympic Blvd., 10th Fl., Los Angeles, CA 90064

Established in 1993 in CA.
Foundation type: Independent foundation.
Financial data (yr. ended 12/31/03): Assets, $9,008,836 (M); expenditures, $535,923; qualifying distributions, $410,756; giving activities include $316,120 for 4 grants (high: $131,320; low: $21,800).
Purpose and activities: Giving to institutions of higher education for creative writing and literary criticism fellowships.
Fields of interest: Higher education.
Type of support: Fellowships.
Limitations: Giving on a national basis. No grants to individuals.
Application information:
  Initial approach: Letter on organization letterhead
  Deadline(s): None
Trustee: Alan U. Schwartz.
EIN: 956957275

359
The Carnegie Foundation for the Advancement of Teaching
51 Vista Ln.
Stanford, CA   94305   (650) 566-5100
FAX: (650) 326-0278; URL: http:// www.carnegiefoundation.org

Incorporated in 1906 under an Act of Congress.
Donors: Andrew Carnegie†; Atlantic Philanthropies, Inc.; The William and Flora Hewlett Foundation; Carnegie Corporation of New York; The Ford Foundation; Lumina Foundation for Education; TIAA-CREF; Spencer Foundation; Gates Foundation; Goldman Fund; Lilly Endowment; Gordon Russell.
Foundation type: Operating foundation.
Financial data (yr. ended 6/30/05): Assets, $126,023,145 (M); gifts received, $5,826,802; expenditures, $11,004,142; qualifying distributions, $10,605,157; giving activities include $629,120 for 18 grants (high: $50,000; low: $1,678), and $5,933,023 for 4 foundation-administered programs.
Purpose and activities: The foundation's current mission is to do all things necessary to encourage, uphold, and dignify the profession of teaching. Present emphasis is on education research.
Fields of interest: Education, research; Elementary/ secondary education; Higher education; Graduate/ professional education; Education.
Type of support: Research.
Limitations: Applications not accepted. No grants to individuals.
Publications: Annual report; Informational brochure.
Application information: Contributes only to pre-selected organizations.
Officers: Lee Shulman, Pres.; Patricia Hutchings, V.P.; Stephanie Waldman, Secy.; Ann Fitzgerald, Treas.
Trustees: John D. Bransford; Rebecca Chopp; K. Patricia Cross; Yehuda Elkana; Bernadine Chuck Fong; Susan H. Fuhrman; Louis M. Gomez; Nils Hasselmo; Janet L. Holmgren; Deborah Meier; Richard A. Middleton; Renee A. Moore; Lynn Olson; Eduardo J. Padron; Gordon Russell; Catherine R. Stimson; David S. Tatel; Nina Zolt.
Number of staff: 25 full-time professional; 26 full-time support.
EIN: 131623924
Selected grants: The following grants were reported in 2005.
$50,000 to College of the Desert, Palm Desert, CA.
$50,000 to Merced College, Merced, CA.
$49,992 to San Francisco Community College District, San Francisco, CA.
$49,126 to Laney College, Oakland, CA.
$47,950 to Pasadena City College Foundation, Pasadena, CA.
$42,250 to University of Pennsylvania, Philadelphia, PA.
$20,000 to Association of American Colleges and Universities, DC.
$7,500 to Education Writers Association, DC.
$7,500 to Mills College, Oakland, CA.

360
Carpenter Family Childrens Foundation, Inc. ✧ ☆
2500 Border Links Dr.
Visalia, CA   93291

Established in 2001 in CA.

Donor: T. Michael Carpenter.
Foundation type: Independent foundation.
Financial data (yr. ended 6/30/06): Assets, $779,422 (M); gifts received, $245,152; expenditures, $389,659; qualifying distributions, $373,954; giving activities include $367,509 for 13 grants (high: $280,000; low: $250).
Limitations: *Applications not accepted. No grants to* individuals.
Application information: Contributes only to pre-selected organizations.
Officers: T. Michael Carpenter, Chair.; Todd C. Carpenter, Pres.; Joan M. Carpenter, Secy.; William N. Dillberg, C.F.O.
Director: Philip T. Hornburg.
EIN: 770587663

361
The Carsey Family Foundation ✧
c/o Capell Rudolph
11601 Wilshire Blvd., Ste. 1840
Los Angeles, CA   90025

Established in 1988 in CA.
Donors: Marcia L. Carsey; John J. Carsey†.
Foundation type: Independent foundation.
Financial data (yr. ended 9/30/05): Assets, $240,350 (M); gifts received, $1,665,000; expenditures, $1,874,846; qualifying distributions, $1,871,500; giving activities include $1,871,500 for 29 grants (high: $760,000; low: $1,000; average: $1,000–$100,000).
Purpose and activities: Giving primarily for higher education, as well as for children, youth and social services, and federated giving programs.
Fields of interest: Performing arts centers; Higher education; Education; Big Brothers/Big Sisters; Human services; Children/youth, services; Federated giving programs; Women.
Type of support: General/operating support; Building/renovation.
Limitations: Applications not accepted. Giving primarily in CA. No grants to individuals.
Application information: Contributes only to pre-selected organizations.
Officers: Marcia L. Carsey, Pres.; Frederick A. Richman, Secy.
EIN: 954135538
Selected grants: The following grants were reported in 2005.
$760,000 to University of New Hampshire Foundation, Durham, NH.
$252,500 to Campbell Hall, North Hollywood, CA.
$142,500 to Boch Center for the Performing Arts, Mashpee, MA.
$10,000 to DreamCatchers, Malibu, CA.
$5,000 to Los Angeles Leadership Academy, Los Angeles, CA.
$4,000 to American Red Cross, Los Angeles, CA.
$1,500 to Los Angeles Child Development Center, Los Angeles, CA.
$1,000 to National Council for Families and Television, Los Angeles, CA.

362
John W. Carson Foundation, Inc. ✧
c/o Lexington Financial Mgmt., LLC
9350 Wilshire Blvd., Ste. 250
Beverly Hills, CA   90212

Established in 1981 in CA.

Donor: John W. Carson.
Foundation type: Independent foundation.
Financial data (yr. ended 11/30/05): Assets, $1,014,398 (M); expenditures, $3,223,124; qualifying distributions, $3,214,706; giving activities include $3,175,000 for 5 grants (high: $3,000,000; low: $5,000).
Purpose and activities: Giving primarily for health services, children and youth services, education, and for social services.
Fields of interest: Education; Health organizations, association; Human services; Children/youth, services; Federated giving programs.
Type of support: General/operating support; Building/renovation.
Limitations: Applications not accepted. Giving primarily in CA and NE. No grants to individuals.
Application information: Contributes only to pre-selected organizations. Unsolicited applications not considered.
Officers and Director:* Jeffrey Sotzing, Chair. and Pres.; Allan L. Alexander,* Secy.; Lawrence L. Witzer, C.F.O. and Treas.
EIN: 953714138

363
The Caruso Family Foundation ◇
101 The Grove Dr.
Los Angeles, CA 90036
Contact: David J. Liston, Secy. and C.F.O.

Established in 1991 in CA.
Donors: Marc A. Caruso; Rick J. Caruso; Christina Stewart; Marvin Rapaport; Henry J. Caruso.
Foundation type: Independent foundation.
Financial data (yr. ended 12/31/05): Assets, $904,173 (M); gifts received, $781,452; expenditures, $673,761; qualifying distributions, $672,644; giving activities include $672,644 for 16 + grants (high: $211,000).
Purpose and activities: Giving primarily for education including a law school as well as for health care including medical research, and human services.
Fields of interest: Secondary school/education; Higher education; Law school/education; Education; Ear & throat research; Crime/law enforcement; Human services; Children/youth, services; Federated giving programs; Jewish agencies & temples.
Type of support: General/operating support; Continuing support; Building/renovation; Curriculum development.
Limitations: Giving primarily in CA. No grants to individuals.
Application information: Application form not required.
  Initial approach: 1-page proposal
  Copies of proposal: 5
  Board meeting date(s): Dec. 1
  Final notification: Jan. 31
Officers and Trustees:* Rick J. Caruso,* Pres.; Christina J. Caruso,* V.P.; Marc A. Caruso,* V.P.; David J. Liston, Secy. and C.F.O.; Gloria G. Caruso; Henry J. Caruso; Tina P. Caruso.
EIN: 954317077
Selected grants: The following grants were reported in 2004.
$211,364 to Pepperdine University, School of Law, Malibu, CA. For unrestricted support.
$155,000 to Brentwood School, Los Angeles, CA. For unrestricted support.

$106,594 to House Ear Institute, Los Angeles, CA. For Hearing Disorder Research.
$15,000 to Los Angeles Police Foundation, Los Angeles, CA. For unrestricted support.
$13,995 to Saint Francis High School, La Canada Flintridge, CA. For unrestricted support.
$11,000 to Alternative Living for the Aging, West Hollywood, CA. For unrestricted support.
$10,000 to American Jewish Committee, New York, NY. For unrestricted support.
$10,000 to Saint Johns Health Center, Santa Monica, CA. For unrestricted support.
$10,000 to WeSpark, Sherman Oaks, CA. For unrestricted support.
$6,000 to World Affairs Council of Los Angeles, Los Angeles, CA. For unrestricted support.

364
Cassin Educational Initiative Foundation ◇
3000 Sand Hill Rd., Bldg. 3, Ste. 210
Menlo Park, CA 94025
Contact: Jeffrey D. Thielman, Exec. Dir.
Additional address: 106A Kenny Cottle, Stuart House, 885 Centre St., Newton, MA 02459, tel.: (617) 244-8512, FAX: (617) 244-8747, E-mail: thielman@bc.edu; URL: http://www.cassinfoundation.org/

Established in 2000.
Donors: Brendan J. Cassin; Isabel Cassin.
Foundation type: Independent foundation.
Financial data (yr. ended 6/30/05): Assets, $3,724,429 (M); expenditures, $3,120,784; qualifying distributions, $2,947,223; giving activities include $2,801,142 for 34 grants (high: $250,000; low: $7,500; average: $50,000–$100,000), and $879,597 for 4 foundation-administered programs.
Purpose and activities: The Cassin Educational Initiative Foundation is committed to helping religious congregations, dioceses and other groups begin Nativity/San Miguel and Cristo Rey schools in communities challenged by low educational attainment and limited academic options.
Fields of interest: Education; Religion.
Limitations: Applications not accepted. Giving on a national basis. No grants to individuals.
Application information: Contributes only to pre-selected organizations.
Officers: Brendan J. Cassin, Chair. and Pres.; Idabel Cassin, Secy.-Treas.; Jeffrey D. Thielman, Exec. Dir.
EIN: 943376336
Selected grants: The following grants were reported in 2004.
$424,000 to North Cambridge Catholic High School, Cambridge, MA. For operating support.
$395,000 to Cristo Rey Network, Chicago, IL.
$350,000 to Notre Dame High School, Lawrence, MA. For operating support.
$300,000 to Saint Martin de Porres High School, Waukegan, IL. For operating support.
$300,000 to San Miguel High School, Tucson, AZ. For operating support.
$260,000 to Cristo Rey High School, New York, NY. For operating support.
$254,800 to Arrupe Jesuit High School, Denver, CO. For operating support.
$200,000 to Juan Diego Catholic High School, Draper, UT. For operating support.
$200,000 to Verbum Dei High School, Los Angeles, CA. For operating support.

$150,000 to Saint Martin de Porres High School, Cleveland, OH. For operating support.

365
The Cassin Foundation ◇ ☆
3000 Sand Hill Rd., Bldg. 3, Ste. 210
Menlo Park, CA 94025

Established in 1996 in CA.
Donors: Brendan J. Cassin; Isabel B. Cassin.
Foundation type: Independent foundation.
Financial data (yr. ended 6/30/05): Assets, $1,159,576 (M); expenditures, $536,239; qualifying distributions, $527,000; giving activities include $527,000 for 18 grants (high: $275,000; low: $1,000).
Purpose and activities: Giving primarily for education.
Fields of interest: Performing arts, music; Elementary/secondary education; Higher education; Education; Human services; Children/youth, services; Roman Catholic federated giving programs.
Limitations: Applications not accepted. Giving primarily in CA. No grants to individuals.
Application information: Contributes only to pre-selected organizations.
Officers: Brendan J. Cassin, Chair. and Pres.; Isabel B. Cassin, V.P. and Secy.-Treas.
EIN: 943258882

366
George V. and Rena G. Castagnola Family Foundation ◇ ☆
2791 Sycamore Canyon Rd.
Santa Barbara, CA 93108-1916
Contact: Virginia Castagnola Hunter, Chair.

Foundation type: Independent foundation.
Financial data (yr. ended 6/30/06): Assets, $502,775 (M); expenditures, $537,868; qualifying distributions, $530,362; giving activities include $530,362 for 46 grants (high: $239,498; low: $75).
Fields of interest: Museums; Performing arts; Higher education; Environment; International affairs, arms control; International affairs; Civil rights.
Type of support: Continuing support; Land acquisition; Endowments; Program development; Conferences/seminars; Publication; Seed money; Research.
Limitations: Applications not accepted. Giving on a national and international basis. No grants to individuals.
Application information: Contributes only to pre-selected organizations. Unsolicited requests for funds will not be considered or acknowledged.
Officers: Virginia Castagnola Hunter, Chair. and Pres.; Renee Castagnola, Secy. and C.F.O.
EIN: 770358709
Selected grants: The following grants were reported in 2003.
$20,000 to Community Arts Music Association of Santa Barbara, Santa Barbara, CA. For general support.
$15,000 to Santa Barbara Museum of Natural History, Santa Barbara, CA. For general support.
$7,200 to Nuclear Age Peace Foundation, Santa Barbara, CA. For general support.
$5,000 to National Geographic Society, DC. For general support.

$5,000 to Ojai Festivals, Ojai, CA. For general support.

$5,000 to Santa Barbara Maritime Museum, Santa Barbara, CA. For general support.

$5,000 to Space Information Laboratories, Space Endeavour Center, Vandenberg AFB, CA. For space education youth programs.

$4,000 to American Himalayan Foundation, San Francisco, CA. For general support.

$3,100 to Crane Country Day School, Santa Barbara, CA. For general support.

$2,500 to Conservation International, DC. For general support.

367
Caufield Family Foundation ◇
4 Embarcadero Ctr., Ste. 3620
San Francisco, CA   94111

Established in 1993 in CA.
Donor: Frank J. Caufield.
Foundation type: Independent foundation.
Financial data (yr. ended 6/30/05): Assets, $3,033,397 (M); expenditures, $416,099; qualifying distributions, $373,840; giving activities include $330,190 for 58 grants (high: $85,350; low: $100).
Purpose and activities: Giving primarily for child abuse prevention, education, and the arts.
Fields of interest: Museums; Arts; Education; Environment; Health organizations; Crime/violence prevention, child abuse; Human services; Children/youth, services; Civil rights, immigrants; Federated giving programs.
Limitations: Applications not accepted. Giving primarily in San Francisco, CA; some funding nationally. No grants to individuals.
Application information: Contributes only to pre-selected organizations.
Officers: Frank J. Caufield, Pres.; Frank R. Caufield, V.P.; Kirsten N. Caufield, V.P.; Kimberley R. Burke, Secy.-Treas.
EIN: 943187012

368
The CEC Foundation ◇ ☆
c/o John R. Fuqua
P.O. Box 1324
Los Alamitos, CA   90720-2420

Established in 1999 in CA.
Donor: Carol Electric, Inc.
Foundation type: Operating foundation.
Financial data (yr. ended 12/31/05): Assets, $1,234,403 (M); gifts received, $494,500; expenditures, $1,175,245; qualifying distributions, $1,169,155; giving activities include $1,169,155 for 16 grants (high: $1,000,000; low: $1,500).
Fields of interest: Human services; Christian agencies & churches.
Limitations: Applications not accepted. Giving primarily in CA. No grants to individuals.
Application information: Unsolicited requests for funds not accepted.
Officers: John R. Fuqua, Pres.; Ronald J. Hathaway, Secy.; Allen W. Moffitt, Treas.
EIN: 330859870

369
Hugh Stuart Center Charitable Trust ◇
96 N. 3rd St., No. 500
San Jose, CA   95112   (408) 293-0463
Contact: Louis O'Neal, Tr.; Arthur K. Lund, Tr.

Trust established in 1977 in CA.
Donor: Hugh Stuart Center‡.
Foundation type: Independent foundation.
Financial data (yr. ended 12/31/05): Assets, $21,874,232 (M); expenditures, $1,152,518; qualifying distributions, $919,316; giving activities include $738,457 for 80 grants (high: $65,000; low: $450).
Purpose and activities: Giving to arts and culture, including radio underwriting and public television, education, health and human services, and police activity leagues.
Fields of interest: Media, television; Media, radio; Arts; Elementary/secondary education; Higher education; Health care; Medical research, institute; Youth development, centers/clubs; Human services.
Type of support: Annual campaigns; Equipment; Program development; Matching/challenge support.
Limitations: Giving primarily in Santa Clara County and San Jose, CA. No grants to individuals.
Publications: Informational brochure.
Application information: Application form not required.
   Copies of proposal: 1
   Deadline(s): None
   Board meeting date(s): Varies
   Final notification: Positive responses only
Trustees: Arthur K. Lund; Louis O'Neal.
EIN: 942455308
Selected grants: The following grants were reported in 2004.
$65,500 to Santa Clara University, Santa Clara, CA. For general support.
$50,000 to Naval Postgraduate School (NPS) Foundation, Monterey, CA. For general support.
$44,748 to Spartan Foundation, San Jose, CA. For general support.
$35,000 to San Jose State University, San Jose, CA. For general support.
$35,000 to Scripps Clinic and Research Foundation, La Jolla, CA. For general support.
$25,000 to Committee of 200 Foundation, Chicago, IL. For general support.
$20,000 to California History Center Foundation, Cupertino, CA. For general support.
$20,000 to Lake Tahoe Shakespeare Festival, Incline Village, NV. For general support.
$20,000 to West Hills Community College, Coalinga, CA. For general support.
$15,000 to San Francisco Opera, San Francisco, CA. For general support.

370
Centofante Foundation ◇ ☆
225 Ave. I, Ste. 300
P.O. Box 7000-997
Redondo Beach, CA   90277

Established in 1989 in CA.
Donors: Albert J. Centofante; Mary J. Centofante; Cenco Capital Co.; Michelle A. Katnik.
Foundation type: Independent foundation.
Financial data (yr. ended 12/31/05): Assets, $1,233,715 (M); gifts received, $200,000; expenditures, $358,835; qualifying distributions,

$357,500; giving activities include $357,500 for 6 grants (high: $150,000; low: $5,000).
Fields of interest: Higher education, university; Libraries/library science; Education; Hospitals (general); Roman Catholic agencies & churches.
Limitations: Applications not accepted. Giving limited to Los Angeles, CA. No grants to individuals.
Application information: Contributes only to pre-selected organizations.
Officers: Mary J. Centofante, Pres.; Linda M. Wenglikowski, Secy.
Trustees: Albert T. Centofante; James P. Centofante; Jane F. Centofante; Michelle A. Katnik.
EIN: 330361839
Selected grants: The following grants were reported in 2004.
$83,000 to Little Company of Mary Hospital, Torrance, CA.
$37,400 to University of Southern California, Los Angeles, CA. 2 grants: $12,400 (For swim team), $25,000 (For band).
$20,000 to Paulist Communications, Los Angeles, CA.
$10,000 to Saint Raphael School, Los Angeles, CA.
$5,000 to Saint Lawrence Martyr Catholic Church, Redondo Beach, CA.

371
Chais Family Foundation ▼ ◇
c/o Mantovani
16530 Ventura Blvd., Ste. 611
Encino, CA   91436

Established in 1985.
Donors: Stanley Chais; Pamela Chais.
Foundation type: Independent foundation.
Financial data (yr. ended 5/31/05): Assets, $119,880,092 (M); gifts received, $330,642; expenditures, $6,386,128; qualifying distributions, $6,176,800; giving activities include $6,176,800 for 42 grants (high: $1,400,000; low: $300; average: $1,000–$200,000).
Purpose and activities: Giving primarily for education, and for Jewish agencies and organizations.
Fields of interest: Higher education; Theological school/education; Education; Environment, natural resources; Jewish federated giving programs; Jewish agencies & temples.
International interests: Israel.
Limitations: Applications not accepted. Giving primarily in Los Angeles, CA, and New York, NY; some giving in Washington, DC and Chicago, IL. No grants to individuals.
Application information: Contributes only to pre-selected organizations.
Officers and Directors:* Stanley Chais,* Chair.; Emily Chais,* V.P.; Mark Chais,* V.P.; William Chais,* V.P.; Pamela Chais,* Secy. and C.F.O.
EIN: 954017323
Selected grants: The following grants were reported in 2005.
$1,400,000 to Jewish Community Foundation.
$750,000 to American Friends of Israel Arts and Science Academy, Chicago, IL.
$366,000 to American Friends of Interdisciplinary Center Herzliya, New York, NY.
$350,000 to American Society for Technion-Israel Institute of Technology, Los Angeles, CA.
$328,000 to Hillel: The Foundation for Jewish Campus Life, DC.
$270,000 to American Committee for Tel Aviv Foundation, New York, NY.

$200,000 to Israel Education Fund, New York, NY.

$175,000 to American Associates of the Haifa Foundation, Beverly Hills, CA.

$150,000 to Jewish Television Network, Beverly Hills, CA.

$25,000 to United Jewish Communities, New York, NY.

372
Chambers Family Foundation ✧

c/o myCFO, Inc.
P.O. Box 10194, Dept. 12
Palo Alto, CA 94303

Established in 1997 in CA.

Donors: Constance E. Chambers; John T. Chambers.

Foundation type: Independent foundation.

Financial data (yr. ended 12/31/05): Assets, $16,542,475 (M); expenditures, $470,812; qualifying distributions, $360,000; giving activities include $360,000 for 3 grants (high: $250,000; low: $10,000).

Fields of interest: Historic preservation/historical societies; Higher education; Boys & girls clubs; YM/YWCAs & YM/YWHAs.

Limitations: Applications not accepted. Giving primarily in CA and NY. No grants to individuals.

Application information: Contributes only to pre-selected organizations.

Trustees: Constance E. Chambers; John T. Chambers.

EIN: 770443168

Selected grants: The following grants were reported in 2003.

$25,000 to Lucile Packard Foundation for Childrens Health, Palo Alto, CA. For general support.

$20,000 to InnVision the Way Home, San Jose, CA. For general support.

$20,000 to Palo Alto Partners in Education, Palo Alto, CA. For general support.

$20,000 to Second Harvest Food Bank of Santa Clara and San Mateo Counties, San Jose, CA. For general support.

$10,000 to Adolescent Counseling Services, Palo Alto, CA. For general support.

$10,000 to Child Advocates of Santa Clara and San Mateo Counties, Milpitas, CA. For general support.

$10,000 to Childrens Health Council, Palo Alto, CA. For general support.

$10,000 to University Club of Palo Alto Scholarship Fund, Palo Alto, CA. For general support.

$10,000 to YMCA of the Mid-Peninsula, Palo Alto, CA. For general support.

$5,000 to Forever Young Foundation, Mesa, AZ. For general support.

373
Change a Life Foundation

24331 Muirlands Blvd., No. 4-308
Lake Forest, CA 92630   (949) 788-9999
Contact: Lisa C. Fujimoto, Exec. Dir.
FAX: (949) 788-9266; E-mail: info@changealife.org;
URL: http://www.changealife.org

Established in 2000 in CA.

Foundation type: Independent foundation.

Financial data (yr. ended 12/31/04): Assets, $110,944 (M); gifts received, $3,150,000; expenditures, $3,388,819; qualifying distributions,

$3,035,974; giving activities include $3,035,974 for 127 grants (high: $337,541; low: $1,044; average: $10,000–$100,000).

Purpose and activities: The Change a Life Foundation's founder has a unique philanthropic vision, which is an altruistic compassion for mankind and a heart-filled desire to help individuals in need. His vision is to help people directly who are in their most desperate hour with little or no resources to help themselves. The ultimate mission of the founder is to inspire and challenge grant recipients to follow his charitable example, and one day repay the favor by helping others in need. The foundation will continue to honor its founder and donor by fulfilling his mission to better society by anonymously helping one person at a time.

Fields of interest: Human services.

Type of support: Equipment; Emergency funds; Scholarship funds; Grants to individuals; Scholarships—to individuals.

Limitations: Applications not accepted. Giving limited to southern CA.

Publications: Annual report.

Application information: Unsolicited requests for funds are not accepted though the foundation will accept organizational information for review. Guidelines available on foundation Web site apply only to pre-selected organizations that have a case-management component to their programs.

Board meeting date(s): Mar., May, July, Sept., Nov.

Officers: Richard E. Tomlin, Jr., Pres.; Lisa C. Fujimoto, Exec. V.P. and Exec. Dir.; Andy Bui, Treas.

Number of staff: 1 full-time professional; 2 part-time professional.

EIN: 330935713

Selected grants: The following grants were reported in 2004.

$337,541 to Orange County Community Foundation, Irvine, CA.

$187,063 to Partners in Care Foundation, San Fernando, CA.

$122,904 to Orangewood Childrens Foundation, Santa Ana, CA.

$111,244 to Habitat for Humanity, South Bay-Long Beach, Long Beach, CA.

$100,344 to Junior Blind of America, Los Angeles, CA.

$83,303 to United Cerebral Palsy Association of San Diego County, San Diego, CA.

$77,578 to Blind Childrens Learning Center of Orange County, Santa Ana, CA.

$11,963 to Saint Joseph Hospital, Eureka, CA.

$11,145 to South Bay Community Services Center, Chula Vista, CA.

$9,375 to California State University, Long Beach, CA.

374
The William McCaskey Chapman and Adaline Dinsmore Chapman Foundation

P.O. Box 221982
Carmel, CA 93922-1982
Contact: Emily Hull-Parsons, Exec. Dir.
E-mail for Emily Hull-Parsons:
ehparsons@sbcglobal.net; Tel./FAX: (831) 626-8370; URL: http://www.smallfoundations.org/webpage/chapmanhome.htm

Established in 1983 in CA.

Donor: Adaline Dinsmore Chapman†.

Foundation type: Independent foundation.

Financial data (yr. ended 9/30/05): Assets, $11,578,186 (M); expenditures, $1,005,530; qualifying distributions, $831,618; giving activities include $734,200 for 44 grants (high: $57,000; low: $1,500).

Purpose and activities: Contributions limited to educational organizations for K-12 levels in the coastal areas of Monterey County, CA, from Marina through Big Sur.

Fields of interest: Arts education; Performing arts, theater; Performing arts, music; Elementary/secondary education; Education, early childhood education; Secondary school/education; Education.

Type of support: General/operating support; Scholarship funds.

Limitations: Giving limited to the coastal towns of Monterey County, CA, from Marina to Big Sur. No grants to individuals.

Publications: Annual report; Informational brochure (including application guidelines).

Application information: Grantees are normally asked to match grants dollar for dollar. Grant application form available on foundation Web site. Application form required.

Initial approach: Request application form
Copies of proposal: 1
Deadline(s): Mar. 1
Board meeting date(s): Monthly (normally the 4th Mon.)
Final notification: May 1

Officers and Trustees:* Thomas E. McCullogh,* Chair.; Robert G. Gard, Jr.,* Secy.; Sarah Lane Bonner,* Treas.; Emily Hull-Parsons, Exec. Dir.; Laurence P. Horan.

Number of staff: 1 part-time professional.

EIN: 770011251

Selected grants: The following grants were reported in 2005.

$57,000 to Friends of Monterey Academy of Oceanographic Sciences, Monterey, CA.

$40,000 to Chartwell School, Seaside, CA.

$25,000 to Los Arboles Middle School, Marina, CA.

$23,000 to Youth Music Monterey, Monterey, CA.

$20,000 to Palma High School, Salinas, CA.

$20,000 to Santa Catalina School, Monterey, CA.

$20,000 to York School, Monterey, CA.

$18,000 to Bay View Elementary School, Santa Cruz, CA.

$13,000 to Pacific Repertory Theater, Carmel, CA.

$10,000 to Monterey Jazz Festival, Monterey, CA.

375
Chartwell Charitable Foundation ▼ ✧

1999 Ave. of the Stars, Ste. 3050
Los Angeles, CA 90067-4613   (310) 556-7600

Established in 1998 in CA.

Donor: A. Jerrold Perenchio.

Foundation type: Independent foundation.

Financial data (yr. ended 12/31/05): Assets, $1,624 (M); gifts received, $10,079,000; expenditures, $10,112,524; qualifying distributions, $10,082,664; giving activities include $10,071,750 for 232 grants (high: $1,000,000; low: $500; average: $10,000–$100,000).

Purpose and activities: Giving primarily for health care and to children's organizations.

Fields of interest: Hospitals (general); Children/youth, services.

Limitations: Giving primarily in CA and NY.

Application information:
Initial approach: Letter
Deadline(s): None

Officers: A. Jerrold Perenchio, Chair. and Exec. V.P.; Margaret A. Perenchio, Pres.; Robert V. Cahill, V.P.; Michael A. Enright, Treas.

EIN: 954679659

Selected grants: The following grants were reported in 2005.

$1,000,000 to Henry Mancini Institute, Culver City, CA. 2 grants: $500,000 each

$1,000,000 to Save the Children Federation, Westport, CT.

$500,000 to American Red Cross, Los Angeles, CA.

$500,000 to DonorsChoose Los Angeles, Los Angeles, CA.

$250,000 to Art Center College of Design, Pasadena, CA.

$25,000 to American Australian Association, New York, NY.

$25,000 to Library Foundation of Los Angeles, Los Angeles, CA.

$25,000 to Performing Arts Center of Los Angeles County, Los Angeles, CA. For Spotlight Awards.

$10,000 to Midnight Mission, Los Angeles, CA.

376
Cesar E. Chavez Community Development Fund ◇

(formerly Martin Luther King Farm Worker Fund)
P.O. Box 62
Keene, CA 93531

Established around 1975 in CA.

Foundation type: Independent foundation.

Financial data (yr. ended 12/31/03): Assets, $7,188,516 (M); expenditures, $547,593; qualifying distributions, $474,697; giving activities include $474,697 for 3 grants (high: $234,697; low: $90,000).

Purpose and activities: Giving primarily for food services and to farm workers.

Fields of interest: Agriculture, farm bureaus/granges; Food services.

Limitations: Applications not accepted. Giving primarily in Keene, CA. No grants to individuals.

Application information: Contributes only to pre-selected organizations.

Officer: Paul Chavez, Chair.

Trustees: Marcos Camacho; Richard Chavez; Dolores Huerta; Cecilia Ruiz.

EIN: 942311424

Selected grants: The following grants were reported in 2003.

$234,697 to National Farm Workers Service Center, Keene, CA. For general support.

$150,000 to Cesar E. Chavez Foundation, Glendale, CA. For general support.

$90,000 to Stonybrook Corporation, Keene, CA. For general support.

377
Cheeryble Foundation ◇

c/o Flekman, Baren & Co.
9171 Wilshire Blvd., Ste. 400
Beverly Hills, CA 90210 (310) 274-5847
Contact: Zora Charles, Pres.

Established in 1987 in CA.

Donors: Les Charles; Zora Charles.

Foundation type: Independent foundation.

Financial data (yr. ended 12/31/05): Assets, $2,578,372 (M); gifts received, $1,000,000; expenditures, $617,925; qualifying distributions,

$617,616; giving activities include $588,155 for 66 grants (high: $100,000; low: $100).

Fields of interest: Museums (art); Higher education; Animals/wildlife, association; Reproductive health, family planning; Cancer research; Boys & girls clubs; Human services; Federated giving programs.

Type of support: General/operating support.

Limitations: Giving primarily in CA, with some emphasis on Santa Barbara. No grants to individuals.

Application information: Application form not required.

Initial approach: Letter
Deadline(s): None

Officers: Zora Charles, Pres. and Secy.; Les Charles, C.F.O.

EIN: 954121906

378
The Cheesecake Factory-Oscar and Evelyn Overton Charitable Foundation ◇ ☆

26901 Malibu Hills Rd.
Calabasas Hills, CA 91301

Established in 2001 in NV.

Donor: David Overton.

Foundation type: Independent foundation.

Financial data (yr. ended 12/31/05): Assets, $223,144 (M); gifts received, $499,260; expenditures, $534,234; qualifying distributions, $534,174; giving activities include $425,000 for 5 grants (high: $202,000; low: $1,000).

Fields of interest: Cancer research; Jewish agencies & temples; Homeless.

Type of support: General/operating support.

Limitations: Applications not accepted. Giving in the U.S., primarily in CA. No grants to individuals.

Application information: Contributes only to pre-selected organizations.

Officers and Directors:* David Overton, Pres.; Debby Zurzolo,* Secy.; Michael Dixon,* Treas.; Linda Candioty; Sheila Overton.

EIN: 880508407

Selected grants: The following grants were reported in 2004.

$140,000 to City of Hope National Medical Center, Duarte, CA.

$30,000 to Stellaris Health Network, Armonk, NY.

$1,000 to Los Angeles Jewish Home for the Aging, Reseda, CA.

379
Chesed Foundation ◇

12121 Wilshire Blvd., Ste. 1400
Los Angeles, CA 90025 (310) 207-1000
Contact: Hooshang Namvar, Secy.

Established in 1998 in CA.

Donors: Mousa Namvar; Ezri Namvar; Namco Capital Grp., Inc.; Woodman Partners, LLC; New Life Holdings, LLC; Pico 26, LLC; Pacesetter Fabrics; Equimax Mortgage, Inc.; Wilshire 19, LLC; Namco Insurance; Roxy 15 LLC; Trifish LLC; Lacy 20, Inc.; La Brea Property, LLC; Magdiel LLC; Maram Holdings LLC.

Foundation type: Independent foundation.

Financial data (yr. ended 12/31/04): Assets, $454,425 (M); gifts received, $617,382; expenditures, $462,142; qualifying distributions, $455,922; giving activities include $455,922 for grants.

Fields of interest: Human services; Jewish agencies & temples.

Limitations: Giving primarily in CA. No grants to individuals.

Application information: Application form not required.

Deadline(s): None

Officers: Mousa Namvar, Pres.; Hooshang Namvar, Secy.

Directors: Ezri Namvar; Homayoun Namvar; Ramin Namvar.

EIN: 954672577

380
ChevronTexaco Foundation ◇

(formerly Texaco Foundation)
6001 Bollinger Canyon Rd., Rm. A2328
San Ramon, CA 94583

Incorporated in 1979 in DE.

Donors: Texaco Inc.; ChevronTexaco Corp.; Chevron Corp.

Foundation type: Company-sponsored foundation.

Financial data (yr. ended 12/31/04): Assets, $696,302 (M); expenditures, $435,820; qualifying distributions, $403,379; giving activities include $393,379 for 3 grants (high: $250,100; low: $11,299).

Purpose and activities: The foundation supports hospitals and organizations involved with arts and culture, education, the environment, health, human services, and civil rights.

Fields of interest: Performing arts, music; Arts; Education, equal rights; Education, early childhood education; Elementary school/education; Higher education; Education; Environment; Health care; Human services; Civil rights, public education; Science, public education; Mathematics.

Type of support: Program development; Seed money; Curriculum development; Fellowships; Scholarship funds; Research.

Limitations: Giving primarily in areas of company operations; giving also to national organizations. No support for religious organizations, private foundations, or fraternal, social, or veterans' organizations. No grants to individuals, or for general operating support, non-hospital capital campaigns, endowments, films, videos, or television projects, courtesy advertising, social functions, commemorative journals, meetings, or political activities; no loans.

Publications: Annual report; Informational brochure.

Application information: Application form not required.

Initial approach: Proposal
Deadline(s): None

Officer: J.W. Rhodes.

Number of staff: 3

EIN: 133007516

Selected grants: The following grants were reported in 2003.

$750,000 to Community Foundation for the National Capital Region, DC. For Moving Forward Employment and Educational Opportunities for Immigrant Families.

$684,000 to Columbia University, Oral History Research Office, New York, NY. For Oral History Telling Lives Project: September 11 Stories.

$340,000 to WAVE (Work, Achievement, Values and Education), DC. For District of Columbia Homeland Security Academy to assist displaced youth in DC.

$272,700 to Scholarship America, Saint Peter, MN. 2 grants: $142,810 (For financial support and to recognize excellence in children of eligible employees), $129,890 (For financial support and to recognize excellence in children of eligible employees).

$150,000 to Nature Conservancy, Baton Rouge, LA. For Touch Science. Walk on the Wild Side, It's our Nature.

$125,000 to Nature Conservancy of Texas, San Antonio, TX. For Touch Science Mad Island Costal Connect.

$100,000 to Active Voice, San Francisco, CA. For Islam project.

$100,000 to Educators for Social Responsibility, Cambridge, MA. For Teaching for Understanding in Secondary Classrooms Post-September 11 Project.

$74,000 to Japanese American Citizens League, San Francisco, CA. For what it means to be an American project.

381
Children's Educational Opportunity Foundation ✦ ☆
60 Bowling Dr.
Oakland, CA 94618
Scholarship address: c/o Admin., P.O. Box 21456, Oakland, CA 94620, tel.: (510) 483-7971

Established in 1997 in CA.
Donors: Christopher H. Berg; Nancy M. Berg; Walter Meier; Mrs. Walter Meier; Ruth A. Berg Revocable Trust; Banbury Fund; The Clorox Company Foundation.
Foundation type: Operating foundation.
Financial data (yr. ended 6/30/05): Assets, $575 (M); gifts received, $291,300; expenditures, $350,514; qualifying distributions, $350,514; giving activities include $345,780 for 229 grants to individuals.
Purpose and activities: Awards available only to low-income families who live in Oakland, CA, with children in grades K-8, to attend the private school of their choice.
Type of support: Scholarships—to individuals.
Limitations: Giving limited to residents of Oakland, CA.
Application information: Applications to be submitted with copies of current-year income tax returns. Award payments are made to student's choice of school. Application form required.
Deadline(s): None
Officers: Ruth A. Berg, Pres.; Christopher H. Berg, Secy.; Nancy M. Berg, Treas.
Directors: Ces Butner; Kate Ernst; Kurt Herzog; Ann Manchester, Ed.D.; Merrill Schwartz.
EIN: 943201181
Selected grants: The following grants were reported in 2005.
$40,500 to Saint Bernard School, Philadelphia, PA.
$6,000 to Clara Mohammed School, Milwaukee, WI.
$2,280 to Saint Theresas School, Austin, TX.
$1,500 to Julia Morgan School for Girls, Oakland, CA.
$1,500 to Northern Light School, Oakland, CA.

382
Chintu Gudiya Foundation ✦ ☆
453 Lincoln Ave.
Alameda, CA 94501

Established in 1999 in CA.
Donor: Donald Ajit Lobo.
Foundation type: Independent foundation.
Financial data (yr. ended 6/30/05): Assets, $11,536,674 (M); expenditures, $524,295; qualifying distributions, $485,582; giving activities include $485,582 for 13 grants (high: $200,000; low: $250).
Fields of interest: Education; Environment, natural resources; Environmental education; Human services; Women, centers/services.
Limitations: Applications not accepted. Giving primarily in CA. No grants to individuals.
Application information: Contributes only to pre-selected organizations.
Officers and Directors:* Donald Ajit Lobo,* Pres.; Mari Grace Tilos,* Secy.-Treas.
EIN: 943315265
Selected grants: The following grants were reported in 2005.
$200,000 to DASRA, Mumbai (Bombay), India. .
$5,000 to Becoming Independent, Santa Rosa, CA.
$5,000 to OpNet, San Francisco, CA.
$1,000 to Equality California, San Francisco, CA.

383
The Chiron Charitable Foundation ✦
4560 Horton St.
Emeryville, CA 94608
FAX: (510) 601-6952;
E-mail: chiron_foundation@chiron.com

Established in 2003 in CA.
Donor: Chiron Corp.
Foundation type: Company-sponsored foundation.
Financial data (yr. ended 12/31/04): Assets, $2,689,892 (M); expenditures, $1,354,546; qualifying distributions, $1,354,100; giving activities include $1,345,050 for 43 grants (high: $78,000; low: $5,000).
Purpose and activities: The foundation supports organizations involved with cultural and ethnic awareness, education, disabled children, health, cancer, employment training, hunger, housing, and economically disadvantaged people. Special emphasis is directed toward programs designed to provide benefit to those who would not otherwise receive it, including minorities, indigent adults, at-risk children and youth, and people groups in the developing world; improve the availability of and access to the highest standards of care in disease prevention, treatment, and management; and improve patient outcomes through improved communication between health care providers and patients.
Fields of interest: Arts, cultural/ethnic awareness; Scholarships/financial aid; Education; Health care, equal rights; Health care, blood supply; Public health, communicable diseases; Health care; Health organizations, alliance; Health organizations, public education; Cancer; Cancer research; Employment, training; Food services; Housing/shelter; Science, formal/general education; Mathematics; Children; Youth; Adults; Disabilities, people with; Physically disabled; Mentally disabled; Minorities; Indigenous people; Economically disadvantaged.
Type of support: General/operating support; Program development; Research.
Limitations: Giving limited to the San Francisco East Bay Area (Alameda, Contra Costa, and Solano counties), CA, Philadelphia, PA, and Seattle, WA, for education and community health and human

services; giving on a national and international basis for health. No support for religious, fraternal, service, or veterans' organizations, teacher organizations, municipal or for-profit hospitals, labor unions, government departments, discriminatory organizations, political organizations, or sports teams. No grants to individuals, or for alumni drives, memorials, capital campaigns, travel, individual fundraising activities, athletic competitions, conferences, advertising or media productions, or fundraising events or dinners.
Publications: Application guidelines; Grants list.
Application information: Application form required.
Initial approach: Download application form and E-mail, fax, or mail to foundation
Officers: Jay Grover, Pres.; William Waller, Secy.; Joel Jung, Treas.
EIN: 200500318

384
The Christensen Fund ▼
394 University Ave.
Palo Alto, CA 94301 (650) 323-8700
Contact: Lourdes Inga, Grants Admin.
FAX: (650) 462-8602;
E-mail: info@christensenfund.org; URL: http://www.christensenfund.org

Incorporated in 1957 in CA.
Donors: Allen D. Christensen†; Carmen M. Christensen.
Foundation type: Independent foundation.
Financial data (yr. ended 12/31/04): Assets, $116,648,219 (M); gifts received, $1,600,000; expenditures, $8,993,979; qualifying distributions, $7,757,240; giving activities include $5,406,869 for 93 grants (high: $100,000; low: $4,000; average: $10,000–$75,000).
Purpose and activities: The fund believes in the power of biological and cultural diversity to sustain and enrich a world faced with great change and uncertainty. Focus is on "bio-cultural" - the rich but neglected adaptive interweave of people and place, culture and ecology. The fund's mission is to buttress the efforts of people and institutions who believe in a biodiverse world infused with artistic expression and work to secure ways of life and landscapes that are beautiful, bountiful and resilient. The fund pursues this mission through place-based work in the region chosen for their potential to withstand and recover from the global erosion of diversity. Focus is on backing the efforts of locally-recognized community custodians of this heritage, and their alliances with scholars, artists, advocates and others. International efforts are also funded to help build global understanding of these issues. The fund works primarily through capacity and network building, knowledge generation, collaboration and mission-related investments.
Fields of interest: Arts, cultural/ethnic awareness; Visual arts; Museums; Environment, research; Environment, natural resources; Environment; Biological sciences.
International interests: Asia; Australia; Ethiopia; Mexico; Turkey.
Type of support: Conferences/seminars; Continuing support; Equipment; Program development; Seed money; Fellowships; Research; Program evaluation; Matching/challenge support.
Limitations: Giving primarily in the Southwest (Four Corners region), northern Mexico (including the Colorado Plateau and Delta, the Pueblo and Hispanic communities of the Rio Arriba/Rio Grande,

the Sonoran Desert on both sides of the Mexican-U.S. border and east of the Colorado River, and the Sierra Tarahumara Montane West), Central Asia (the mountains and associated valleys of northeastern Turkey, the Kyrgyz Republic, and Tajikistan), the Rift Valley (especially southwest Ethiopia and adjacent areas of northern Kenya) and Northern Australia (especially Arhem Land, Far Northern Queensland, and the Kimberley and Torres Strait Islands). No grants to individuals, or for capital funds, or building or renovation funding; no loans.

Publications: Grants list.

Application information: Please refer to the fund's Web site for guidelines and program areas. For events such as conferences and workshops, apply at least four months in advance of their starting date to enable timely review and grant processing. Application form required.

Initial approach: Initial inquiry or pre-proposal as outlined on fund's Web site

Copies of proposal: 1

Deadline(s): submit pre-proposal by Mar. 31 (for 1st half of calendar year) or Aug. 31 (for 2nd half of calendar year

Board meeting date(s): Quarterly

Final notification: Bi-annual cycle

Officers and Directors:* C. Diane Christensen,* Chair. and Pres.; Thomas K. Seligman, V.P.; Tara Diann Stein,* Secy.; Kenneth Kirshenbaum,* Treas.; Kenneth Wilson, Ph.D., Exec. Dir.; E. Walter Coward, Jr., Ph.D.; Rodolfo Dirzo; Winona LaDuke; John G. Robinson.

Number of staff: 8 full-time professional; 1 part-time support.

EIN: 946055879

Selected grants: The following grants were reported in 2003.

$2,216,509 to Wildlife Conservation Society, Bronx, NY. 2 grants: $1,966,509 (For endowment challenge grant to support program for graduate training in conservation for nationals of less developed countries), $250,000 (For Phase II of WCS-Papua New Guinea biological training and conservation capacity building program in Papua New Guinea that mentors promising students in scientific research methods and reporting).

$400,000 to Missouri Botanical Garden, Saint Louis, MO. For Christensen Fund Program for Tropical Plant Conservation, integrated research and training program that focuses on tropical Andean countries and extends support to undergraduates.

$304,500 to Tides Foundation, San Francisco, CA. For Genesis project, photographic essay to focus attention on origins and importance of biological and cultural diversity.

$230,000 to Terralingua, DC. For Phase II of Global Biocultural Diversity Assessment (GBCDA) Program.

$193,200 to Society for Conservation Biology, Arlington, VA. For travel, accommodations and membership for non-USA members in order to increase international representation and participation.

$130,000 to Worldwide Indigenous Science Network, Lahaina, HI. For research and travel to design collaborative, inter-disciplinary program and interpretative materials on relationships between Anglo-Saxon artistic expression and biological and cultural landscapes.

$100,000 to Indigenous Language Institute, Santa Fe, NM. To explore use of technology for indigenous language revitalization in U.S. with symposium, Ancient Voices, Modern Tools, for

Annual Youth Language Fair, and core support during period of financial transition.

$100,000 to International Association for the Study of Common Property, Gary, IN. For travel support for annual conference participants from Ethiopia, Turkey, Central Asia and Aboriginal Australia and Papua New Guinea.

$100,000 to International Society of Ethnobiology, Athens, GA. Toward establishment of Darrell Posey Fellowship for Ethnoecology and Traditional Resource Rights, fellowship and small grants program, and for administrative support systems required for development.

385
Louis J. Christopher Memorial Charity Fund ✧

c/o Wells Fargo Bank, N.A.
Box 63954, MAC A0330-011
San Francisco, CA 94163

Established in 2002 in CA.

Foundation type: Independent foundation.

Financial data (yr. ended 12/31/05): Assets, $15,282,830 (M); expenditures, $843,775; qualifying distributions, $767,932; giving activities include $744,455 for 6 grants (high: $227,431; low: $62,013).

Purpose and activities: Giving primarily for higher education and hospitals, particularly to a children's hospital and for orthopedic research.

Fields of interest: Higher education, university; Hospitals (general); Health organizations, association; Orthopedics; Residential/custodial care, hospices.

Limitations: Applications not accepted. Giving primarily in Los Angeles, CA; minor giving outside the U.S. No grants to individuals.

Application information: Contributes only to pre-selected organizations.

Trustee: Wells Fargo Bank, N.A.

EIN: 956019838

Selected grants: The following grants were reported in 2003.

$171,937 to Childrens Hospital Los Angeles, Los Angeles, CA.

$164,250 to Los Angeles Orthopaedic Hospital Foundation, Los Angeles, CA.

$69,759 to University of Southern California, Los Angeles, CA.

$57,350 to Elks of Los Angeles Foundation Fund, Los Angeles, CA.

$52,627 to Loyola Marymount University, Los Angeles, CA.

$46,882 to Saint Christophers Hospice, London, England. .

386
Chrysopolae Foundation ✧

P.O. Box 10174
San Rafael, CA 94912

Established in 1997 in CA.

Donors: Lawrence Charles Ford†; Lawrence Charles Ford, Jr; Cynthia Carroll.

Foundation type: Independent foundation.

Financial data (yr. ended 12/31/04): Assets, $9,917,473 (M); gifts received, $3,507,659; expenditures, $1,541,431; qualifying distributions, $1,476,087; giving activities include $1,468,526

for 23 grants (high: $1,172,916; low: $500), and $2,300 for 8 grants to individuals.

Purpose and activities: The foundation awards scholarships to former Tamsical High School Team Program students attending an accredited undergraduate college only.

Fields of interest: Higher education; Medical research, institute.

Limitations: Applications not accepted. Giving primarily in CA.

Application information: Unsolicited requests for funds not accepted.

Officers: Lawrence Charles Ford, Jr., Pres.; Cynthia Carroll, Secy.-Treas.

EIN: 943265060

Selected grants: The following grants were reported in 2004.

$1,172,916 to Vanguard Charitable Endowment Program, Southeastern, PA.

$50,000 to Huntingtons Disease Society of America, New York, NY. For medical research.

$34,800 to Tamiscal High School, Larkspur, CA. For general support.

$19,000 to Thacher School, Ojai, CA. For general support.

$16,250 to 826 Valencia, San Francisco, CA. For general support.

$10,000 to Children of Shelters, San Francisco, CA. For general support.

$10,000 to Marin Country Day School, Corte Madera, CA. For general support.

$10,000 to NARAL Pro-Choice America Foundation, DC. For general support.

$7,500 to Reading Tree, San Francisco, CA. For general support.

$5,000 to Sierra Club Foundation, San Francisco, CA. For general support.

387
Arthur & Carlyse Ciocca Charitable Foundation ✧

240 Stockton St., Ste. 800
San Francisco, CA 94108

Established in 1997 in CA.

Donors: Arthur Ciocca; Carlyse Ciocca.

Foundation type: Independent foundation.

Financial data (yr. ended 12/31/04): Assets, $8,792,532 (M); gifts received, $3,805,667; expenditures, $1,769,286; qualifying distributions, $1,761,000; giving activities include $1,761,000 for 25 grants.

Purpose and activities: Giving primarily for federated giving programs, as well as for education, medical centers, and social services.

Fields of interest: Education; Hospitals (general); Human services; Federated giving programs.

Limitations: Applications not accepted. Giving primarily in San Francisco, CA, and Alexandria, VA. No grants to individuals.

Application information: Contributes only to pre-selected organizations.

Officers: Carlyse Ciocca, Pres.; Arthur Ciocca, Secy.

EIN: 943279919

Selected grants: The following grants were reported in 2004.

$1,000,000 to University of San Francisco, San Francisco, CA.

$50,000 to Basic Fund, San Francisco, CA.

$5,000 to Hillsdale College, Hillsdale, MI.

$5,000 to Students in Free Enterprise, Springfield, MO.

$2,000 to Breakthrough Collaborative, San Francisco, CA.

388
Cisco Systems Foundation ▼ ✧
170 W. Tasman Dr.
San Jose, CA   95134-1706
E-mail: ciscofoundation@cisco.com; E-mail for product donations:
dicountech_cisco@techsoup.org; URL: http://www.cisco.com/go/foundation

Established in 1997 in CA.
Donor: Cisco Systems, Inc.
Foundation type: Company-sponsored foundation.
Financial data (yr. ended 7/31/05): Assets, $104,695,664 (M); expenditures, $11,615,924; qualifying distributions, $10,795,228; giving activities include $5,147,688 for 181 grants (high: $499,379; low: $2,550), and $5,426,065 for 25 employee matching gifts.
Purpose and activities: The foundation supports organizations involved with arts education, education, health, hunger, housing, and human services.
Fields of interest: Arts education; Elementary/secondary education; Vocational education; Adult/continuing education; Education; Health care; Food services; Housing/shelter; Human services.
Type of support: General/operating support; Continuing support; Employee matching gifts.
Limitations: Giving primarily in CA. No support for religious or sectarian organizations. No grants to individuals, or for capital campaigns, start-up needs, research, athletic events, fundraising events, conferences, seminars, or field trips.
Publications: Annual report; Financial statement; Grants list; IRS Form 990-PF.
Application information: Support is limited to 1 contribution per organization during any given year for 3 years for San Jose Impact Grants. Multi-year funding is not automatic. Organizations receiving San Jose Impact Grants are asked to provide periodic progress reports. Application form required.
Initial approach: Complete online application form
Deadline(s): Mar. 15 to Apr. 30 and Oct. 15 to Nov. 30 for San Jose Impact Grants
Officer: Michael Yutrzenka, Exec. Dir.
Trustees: Larry R. Carter; John T. Chambers; Duncan Mitchell; John P. Morgridge; Tae Yao.
EIN: 770443347
Selected grants: The following grants were reported in 2005.
$499,379 to Community Voice Mail National Office, Seattle, WA. For Unity Project.
$469,640 to Save the Children Federation, Westport, CT. For U.S. Programs Rural Education Initiative/Cisco Center for Technological Excellence.
$308,000 to City Year, Boston, MA. For program support.
$250,000 to Acumen Fund, New York, NY. For Scaling Successful Approaches for the Bottom of the Pyramid.
$250,000 to Digital Opportunity Trust, Ottawa, Canada. For global netcorps program.
$250,000 to Network for Good, Vienna, VA. For enhancing nonprofits' adoption of online tools.
$200,000 to Habitat for Humanity International, Americus, GA. For Cisco Tsunami Rebuilding grant.
$15,000 to Bay Area School Reform Collaborative, San Francisco, CA. For Leadership Networks.

$15,000 to United InnoWorks Academy, Potomac, MD. For National InnoWorks Mentor Training Summit.
$12,000 to Next Door Solutions to Domestic Violence, San Jose, CA. For Youth and Children's Services.

389
The Clorox Company Foundation ▼ ✧
1221 Broadway
Oakland, CA   94612-1888   (510) 208-3223
E-mail: cloroxfndt@eastbaycf.org; Mailing address: c/o East Bay Community Foundation, De Domenico Bldg., 200 Frank Ogawa Plz., Oakland, CA 94612;
URL: http://www.thecloroxcompany.com/community/index.html

Incorporated in 1980 in CA.
Donor: The Clorox Co.
Foundation type: Company-sponsored foundation.
Financial data (yr. ended 6/30/05): Assets, $5,947,741 (M); gifts received, $2,038,265; expenditures, $5,017,748; qualifying distributions, $5,017,748; giving activities include $4,733,551 for 69 grants (high: $1,635,561).
Purpose and activities: The foundation supports organizations involved with arts and culture, K-12 education, disaster relief, youth development, and civic affairs. Grants are administered by the East Bay Community Foundation.
Fields of interest: Arts; Elementary/secondary education; Disasters, preparedness/services; Youth development; Voluntarism promotion; Public affairs.
Type of support: Donated products; General/operating support; Emergency funds; Program development; Scholarship funds; Employee volunteer services; Employee matching gifts.
Limitations: Giving primarily in areas of company operations, with emphasis on the Oakland, CA, area; giving on a national and international basis for disaster relief. No support for national organizations, religious organizations not of direct benefit to the entire community, political parties, candidates, or organizations, or exclusive membership organizations. No grants to individuals, or for fundraising, athletic events or league sponsorships, travel, advertising or promotional sponsorships, tickets, conferences, conventions, meetings, or similar events, media production, political activities, dues, debt reduction, capital campaigns, or individual school projects.
Publications: Application guidelines; Annual report (including application guidelines).
Application information: Unsolicited requests for scholarship funds are not accepted. Application form required.
Initial approach: Complete online application form
Deadline(s): July 1, Oct. 1, Jan. 1, and Apr. 1; between Oct. 1 and Feb. 1 for Arts Mini-Grants Initiative
Board meeting date(s): Mar. and Sept.
Final notification: 2 months following deadlines
Officers and Trustees:* Gerald E. Johnston,* Chair.; Steven S. Silberblatt,* Pres.; Jacqueline P. Kane,* V.P. and Secy.; Daniel J. Heinrich,* V.P. and Treas.; James A. Hasler; Patricia F. Martin; Soraya M. Wright.
EIN: 942674980
Selected grants: The following grants were reported in 2005.
$2,385,991 to JK Group, Plainsboro, NJ. 5 grants: $113,664 (For corporate employee GIFT

---

campaign match), $206,315 (For corporate employee GIFT campaign match), $244,856 (For corporate employee GIFT campaign match), $185,595 (For corporate employee GIFT campaign match), $1,635,561 (For GIFT campaign employee donations).
$477,500 to East Bay Community Foundation, Oakland, CA. 3 grants: $47,500 (For education grants), $130,000 (For education grants), $300,000 (For Oakland Unified School District redesign project).
$125,000 to American Red Cross, Bay Area Chapter, San Francisco, CA. For South Asia relief efforts.
$125,000 to United States Fund for UNICEF, New York, NY. For rebuilding schools after tsunami.

390
CNC Foundation ✧ ☆
1423 Hamilton Ave.
Palo Alto, CA   94301

Established in 1998 in CA.
Donors: Charles T. Munger; Charlotte Lowell.
Foundation type: Independent foundation.
Financial data (yr. ended 12/31/05): Assets, $53,357 (M); gifts received, $53,387; expenditures, $370,596; qualifying distributions, $365,465; giving activities include $365,465 for 99 grants (high: $30,000; low: $10).
Fields of interest: Higher education; Health organizations, association; Human services; Christian agencies & churches.
Limitations: Applications not accepted. No grants to individuals.
Application information: Contributes only to pre-selected organizations.
Trustees: Charlotte Lowell; Charles T. Munger, Jr.
EIN: 776160567
Selected grants: The following grants were reported in 2005.
$30,000 to International Justice Mission, Alexandria, VA.
$15,000 to Bayshore Christian Ministries, East Palo Alto, CA.
$10,000 to Freedom Alliance, Dulles, VA.
$10,000 to Mendenhall Ministries, Mendenhall, MS.
$10,000 to Village Enterprise Fund, San Carlos, CA.
$8,000 to Salvation Army.
$6,000 to Campus Crusade for Christ.
$6,000 to Hoover Institution on War, Revolution and Peace, Stanford, CA.
$5,000 to Wycliffe Bible Translators, Orlando, FL.
$850 to YMCA.

391
Vincent J. Coates Foundation ✧
1080 Leonello Ave.
Los Altos, CA   94024

Established in 2000 in CA.
Donor: Vincent J. Coates.
Foundation type: Independent foundation.
Financial data (yr. ended 12/31/05): Assets, $14,154,950 (M); expenditures, $4,154,008; qualifying distributions, $4,153,206; giving activities include $4,150,000 for 3 grants (high: $2,000,000; low: $150,000).
Purpose and activities: Giving primarily for higher education, including university support for basic

---

molecular and cellular research, a bioscience center, and neurological research; funding also for human services.

Fields of interest: Higher education; Medical research, institute; Biomedicine research; Neuroscience research; Employment; Human services.

Limitations: Applications not accepted. Giving primarily in Stanford, CA, and Boston, MA; some funding also in Westport, CT.

Application information: Contributes only to pre-selected organizations.

Officers: Vincent J. Coates, Pres.; Stella Coates, V.P. and Secy.-Treas.

Directors: John Coates; Norman Coates; Darryl Manning.

EIN: 770533167

Selected grants: The following grants were reported in 2003.

$550,000 to Salk Institute for Biological Studies, San Diego, CA. To purchase mass spectrometer equipment.

$329,056 to University of San Francisco Foundation, San Francisco, CA. For Malaria research fund.

$318,000 to University of California at San Francisco Foundation, San Francisco, CA. For Microscopy fund.

$300,000 to Foundation for Neurologic Diseases, Newburyport, MA. For research fund for Neurological diseases.

$300,000 to Stanford University, Stanford, CA.

$300,000 to Yale University, New Haven, CT. For research.

$125,000 to Dress for Success Mid-Fairfield County, Westport, CT.

$900 to Westport Rotary Foundation, Westport, CT. For Rotary Polio Plus Campaign.

392
The Cobb Foundation ✧ ☆
44 E. Foothill Blvd., Ste. 100
Arcadia, CA   91006

Established in 2005 in CA.
Foundation type: Independent foundation.
Financial data (yr. ended 9/30/05): Assets, $5,737,347 (M); gifts received, $6,316,712; expenditures, $753,750; qualifying distributions, $751,580; giving activities include $743,500 for grants.
Fields of interest: Human services; Homeless, human services.
Limitations: Applications not accepted. Giving primarily in CA. No grants to individuals.
Application information: Contributes only to pre-selected organiations.
Officers and Directors:* Mark Silk,* C.E.O.; Sarah Silk,* Secy.
EIN: 542161288

393
Lynne Cohen Foundation for Ovarian Cancer Research ✧
P.O. Box 7128
Santa Monica, CA   90406-7128   (877) 682-7911
Contact: Amy Cohen Epstein
FAX: (310) 571-9126; E-mail: Amy@lcfocr.org; additional E-mail: trudy@lcfocr.org; URL: http://www.lynnecohenfoundation.org/

Established in 1998 in CA.
Foundation type: Independent foundation.
Financial data (yr. ended 12/31/04): Assets, $240,412 (M); gifts received, $592,178; expenditures, $1,189,262; qualifying distributions, $1,187,417; giving activities include $628,130 for 4 grants (high: $266,667; low: $82,878).
Purpose and activities: To fund traditional projects as well as complimentary therapies aimed at helping women who have ovarian cancer. The foundation is dedicated to finding an early detection test for ovarian cancer, to establishing high risk clinics for women with family members with ovarian and/or breast cancer, and to finding better clinical treatments for women with the disease.
Fields of interest: Higher education, university; Cancer; Cancer research; Women.
Type of support: Research.
Limitations: Giving primarily in New York, NY, and Houston, TX.
Application information:
    Initial approach: Letter
    Deadline(s): None
Officers: Amy Cohen Epstein, Pres.; Erin Cohen, V.P.; Whitney Rosenson, Secy. and C.F.O.
Board of Advisors: Robert Cohen; Nancy Cord; Gary Freeman.
EIN: 954668714

394
Colburn Foundation ▼
1000 Wilshire Blvd., Ste. 340
Los Angeles, CA   90017
E-mail: admin@colburnfoundation.org

Established in 1999 in CA.
Donor: Richard D. Colburn‡.
Foundation type: Independent foundation.
Financial data (yr. ended 12/31/05): Assets, $156,397,526 (M); expenditures, $7,969,096; qualifying distributions, $7,114,260; giving activities include $6,552,705 for 34 grants.
Purpose and activities: Giving primarily for classical music in Southern California.
Fields of interest: Performing arts, music; Performing arts, orchestra (symphony).
Type of support: General/operating support; Scholarship funds.
Limitations: Applications not accepted. Giving primarily in southern CA. No support for 501c(3) organizations. No grants to individuals.
Application information: Contributes only to pre-selected organizations.
    Board meeting date(s): Quarterly basis, 2nd Tues. of each quarter
Officers and Directors:* Robert Egelston,* Chair.; Christine Eberhardt, Cont.; Allison Sampson, Exec. Dir.; Robert Attiyeh; Edmund Edelman; Carol Colburn Hogel; Eugene Krieger; Arvind Manocha.
Number of staff: 1 full-time professional; 2 part-time professional.
EIN: 954693145
Selected grants: The following grants were reported in 2005.
$3,260,000 to Colburn School of the Performing Arts, Los Angeles, CA.
$1,065,000 to Los Angeles Philharmonic, Los Angeles, CA.
$800,000 to Los Angeles Opera Company, Los Angeles, CA.
$351,475 to Apollo Amused, Santa Monica, CA. For general support.

$183,730 to Da Camera Society of Texas, Houston, TX. For general support.
$100,000 to Los Angeles Chamber Orchestra Society, Los Angeles, CA.
$100,000 to Los Angeles Master Chorale, Los Angeles, CA. For general support.
$100,000 to Pennsylvania Ballet, Philadelphia, PA. For general support.
$70,000 to Philharmonic Society of Orange County, Irvine, CA. For general support.
$20,000 to Santa Fe Opera, Santa Fe, NM.

395
The Tara Colburn Fund ✧
418 S. Lucerne Blvd.
Los Angeles, CA   90020
Contact: N. Ciriello

Established in 1988 in CA.
Donor: Tara G. Colburn.
Foundation type: Independent foundation.
Financial data (yr. ended 12/31/05): Assets, $69,331 (M); gifts received, $4,256,778; expenditures, $8,969,307; qualifying distributions, $8,679,247; giving activities include $8,679,247 for 1 grant.
Purpose and activities: To sponsor musical education and the arts.
Fields of interest: Performing arts, opera; Arts.
Limitations: Giving primarily in Los Angeles, CA.
Application information:
    Initial approach: Letter or proposal
    Deadline(s): None
Directors: Olga Chernov; Nicholas G. Ciriello; Mary Lou Raucci; Alexander Simitch.
EIN: 954139380

396
The Collins Family Foundation ✧
c/o Quintile Wealth Mgmt., LLC
11150 Santa Monica Blvd., Ste. 400
Los Angeles, CA   90025

Established in 1997 in CA.
Donors: David C. Collins; Mary C. Collins.
Foundation type: Independent foundation.
Financial data (yr. ended 12/31/04): Assets, $2,509,310 (M); gifts received, $10; expenditures, $364,728; qualifying distributions, $348,758; giving activities include $351,482 for 14 grants (high: $150,000; low: $204).
Purpose and activities: Giving primarily for education, including a college-preparatory day school, and a law school; funding also for human services.
Fields of interest: Elementary/secondary education; Higher education; Law school/education; Education; Human services.
Limitations: Applications not accepted. Giving primarily in CA, with emphasis on Los Angeles. No grants to individuals.
Application information: Contributes only to pre-selected organizations.
Officers: Mary C. Collins, Pres.; David C. Collins, Secy. and C.F.O.
Director: Stephen A. Kroft.
EIN: 954618828

397
The Carol & James Collins Foundation
6101 W. Centinela Ave., Ste. 100
Culver City, CA 90230-6337
Contact: Cathy Hession, Exec. Dir.
E-mail: cathy@jamesacollins.com

Established in 1985 in CA; reincorporated in DE in 2002.
Donors: James A. Collins; Carol L. Collins.
Foundation type: Independent foundation.
Financial data (yr. ended 9/30/05): Assets, $9,772,446 (M); gifts received, $4,671,850; expenditures, $436,244; qualifying distributions, $390,744; giving activities include $317,730 for 33 grants (high: $15,000; low: $500).
Purpose and activities: The foundation's mission is to enrich the lives of children, youth, and families, particularly the underserved, in the southern CA, area. The foundation gives to organizations that give people the tools to become educated, healthy, self-reliant, and contributing members of our society. Also giving to after-school programs.
Fields of interest: Education; Human services.
Type of support: General/operating support; Continuing support; Capital campaigns; Building/ renovation; Equipment; Program development; Curriculum development; Matching/challenge support.
Limitations: Giving limited to southern CA. No grants to individuals.
Publications: Informational brochure (including application guidelines).
Application information: After receipt of letter of inquiry, an invitation to submit grant proposal is decided upon. Application form required.
  Initial approach: Letter of Inquiry
  Copies of proposal: 1
  Deadline(s): Mar. 1, June 1, Sept. 1, and Dec. 1
  Board meeting date(s): Feb., May, Aug., and Nov.
  Final notification: Quarterly
Officers: James A. Collins, Chair.; Cathleen Collins Hession, Pres. and Secy.-Treas.
Directors: Carol L. Collins; Melissa Collins Gudim; Kelly L. Collins.
Number of staff: 1 full-time professional.
EIN: 300100019
Selected grants: The following grants were reported in 2005.
$15,000 to Heart of Los Angeles Youth, Los Angeles, CA.
$15,000 to Kids Included Together San Diego, San Diego, CA.
$10,000 to Accelerated School, Los Angeles, CA.
$10,000 to Inner-City Arts, Los Angeles, CA.
$10,000 to LAs BEST (Better Educated Students for Tomorrow), Los Angeles, CA.
$10,000 to Para Los Ninos, Los Angeles, CA.
$10,000 to Sound Art, Los Angeles, CA.
$10,000 to United States Olympic Committee, Los Angeles, CA.
$10,000 to Westside Childrens Center, Culver City, CA.
$10,000 to Wonder of Reading, Los Angeles, CA.

398
Colombo Charitable Trust ◇
(formerly Elsie T. & Josephine Colombo Charitable Trust)
c/o Bank of the West, Trust Dept.
P.O. Box 1121
San Jose, CA 95108
Application address: c/o Bank of the West, Attn.: Alan Hemstad, Asst. V.P. and Trust Off., 1165 Lincoln Ave., Ste 225, San Jose, CA 95125-3038

Established in 1993 in CA.
Donor: Elsie T. Colombo.
Foundation type: Independent foundation.
Financial data (yr. ended 12/31/03): Assets, $5,033,328 (M); gifts received, $362,859; expenditures, $362,653; qualifying distributions, $331,358; giving activities include $320,000 for 14 grants (high: $34,000; low: $6,000).
Fields of interest: Health care; Diabetes; Human services; Christian agencies & churches.
Limitations: Giving primarily in CA. No grants to individuals.
Application information:
  Initial approach: Letter
  Deadline(s): None
Trustee: Bank of the West.
EIN: 776098160
Selected grants: The following grants were reported in 2004.
$24,000 to Our Lady of Fatima Villa, Saratoga, CA.
$22,000 to Marthas Kitchen, San Jose, CA.
$22,000 to Sacred Heart Nativity School, San Jose, CA.
$20,000 to Parents Helping Parents, Santa Clara, CA.
$16,000 to Sequoia Hospital Foundation, Redwood City, CA.
$13,000 to Hospice of the Valley, San Jose, CA.
$7,100 to Books Aloud, San Jose, CA.
$5,400 to SEE International, Santa Barbara, CA.

399
Columbia Foundation ▼
1016 Lincoln Blvd., Ste. 205
P.O. Box 29470
San Francisco, CA 94129 (415) 561-6880
Contact: Susan Reed Clark, Exec. Dir.
FAX: (415) 561-6883; *E-mail:* info@columbia.org;
URL: http://www.columbia.org

Incorporated in 1940 in CA.
Donors: Madeleine H. Russell†; Christine H. Russell.
Foundation type: Independent foundation.
Financial data (yr. ended 5/31/05): Assets, $73,328,611 (M); gifts received, $31,819; expenditures, $4,509,327; qualifying distributions, $3,748,727; giving activities include $3,235,767 for 122 grants (high: $240,000; low: $800; average: $1,000–$50,000).
Purpose and activities: While the foundation's broad philanthropic purpose has given it flexibility to respond to changing social conditions, it has nevertheless maintained its long-standing interest in world peace, human rights, the environment, cross-cultural and international understanding, the quality of urban life, and the arts. Within each of these areas the board of directors sets new priorities as conditions change.
Fields of interest: Arts; Environment, natural resources; Environment; Animals/wildlife, preservation/protection; Agriculture/food; Civil

rights, advocacy; Civil liberties, advocacy; Civil liberties, right to die; Urban/community development; Social sciences.
International interests: England.
Type of support: General/operating support; Continuing support; Building/renovation; Program development; Publication; Seed money; Curriculum development; Research.
Limitations: Giving primarily in the San Francisco Bay Area, CA. Some foundation-initiated giving in the United Kingdom and other countries for the arts. No support for private foundations, institutions supported by federated campaigns or heavily subsidized by government funds, or projects in medicine or religion. No grants to individuals, or for scholarships, fellowships, ongoing programs, or operating budgets of established agencies.
Publications: Annual report (including application guidelines); Grants list; Program policy statement (including application guidelines).
Application information: Grants to programs based in the United Kingdom or other countries are initiated by the foundation; unsolicited proposals are not considered. Proposals sent by fax or E-mail not considered; they should be 2-sided and reproduced on recycled paper. Further guidelines available on foundation Web site. Application form required.
  Initial approach: Application form, 2-page summary, and proposal narrative
  Copies of proposal: 1
  Deadline(s): Arts and Culture: Apr. 1; Human Rights: Aug. 1; Sustainable Communities and Economies: Dec. 1
  Board meeting date(s): 4 times per year
  Final notification: 10 weeks after deadline
Officers and Directors:* Christine H. Russell,* Pres.; Charles P. Russell,* Secy.; Alice C. Russell-Shapiro,* Treas.; Susan Reed Clark, Exec. Dir.
Number of staff: 3 full-time professional; 1 full-time support.
EIN: 941196186
Selected grants: The following grants were reported in 2004.
$250,000 to Proteus Fund, Amherst, MA. For Civil Marriage Collaborative, donor-advised grant making program supported by institutional donors to bolster strategic state and local efforts to strengthen broad and diverse grassroots constituency to achieve civil marriage equality in the U. S. and to oppose efforts to limit or deny civil marriage rights to lesbian, gay, bisexual, and transgender people.
$155,000 to Creative Work Fund, San Francisco, CA. For final grant to provide funds for individuals artists to create new art works in collaboration with other artists or community organizations.
$150,000 to California Polytechnic State University, Sustainable Agriculture Resource Center, San Luis Obispo, CA. To develop Institute on Sustainable Agriculture within College of Agriculture.
$100,000 to Compassion and Choices, Portland, OR. For end-of-life education and advocacy programs in California, payable over 2 years.
$100,000 to Death with Dignity National Center, Portland, OR. To defend Oregon death with dignity law from Federal challenge and to educate Federal officials about benefits of the law, payable over 2 years.
$100,000 to Gay-Straight Alliance Network, San Francisco, CA. For continuing programmatic and

organizational development, payable over 2 years.

$75,000 to Los Cenzontles Mexican Arts Center, San Pablo, CA. For organizational development to increase revenue from ticket income, marketing of products, corporate sponsorships of major events, and major donor campaign.

$75,000 to San Francisco Opera, San Francisco, CA. For annual support and transition funding.

$70,000 to Redefining Progress, Oakland, CA. For Scenarios for Sustainability: Forecasting the Economic, Social, and Environmental Impacts of Land Use Planning that will provide concrete tools (Genuine Progress Indicator and the Ecological Footprint) to help city planners, elected officials, and the public make better informed land-use decisions to strengthen economy of San Francisco Bay Area while reducing region's Ecological Footprint.

$60,000 to National Center for Lesbian Rights, San Francisco, CA. For Safe Homes Project to improve care of lesbian, gay, bisexual, transgendered, and queer/questioning youth in California's foster care and juvenile justice systems.

400
Commercial Capital Bank Community Foundation ◇ ☆
8105 Irvine Ctr. Dr., 15th Fl.
Irvine, CA   92618

Established in 2004 in CA.
Donor: Hawthorne Financial Corp. and Subs.
Foundation type: Independent foundation.
Financial data (yr. ended 12/31/05): Assets, $2,239,140 (M); expenditures, $631,582; qualifying distributions, $622,167; giving activities include $622,167 for grants.
Fields of interest: Education; Medical research; Human services; Children/youth, services; Human services; Jewish federated giving programs; Jewish agencies & temples.
Limitations: Applications not accepted. Giving primarily in CA. No grants to individuals.
Application information: Contributes only to pre-selected organizations.
Officers and Directors: * David S. Depillo,* Pres.; Stephen H. Gordon,* C.E.O; Richard A. Sanchez,* Secy.; Christopher G. Hagerty,* C.F.O.
EIN: 030542086

401
Community Foundation for Monterey County ▼ ◇
2354 Garden Rd.
Monterey, CA   93940   (831) 375-9712
Contact: Todd Lueders, C.E.O.; For grants: Jackie Wendland, Grants Mgr.; For grants: Jeff S. Bryant, Sr. Prog. Off.
FAX: (831) 375-4731; E-mail: info@cfmco.org; Additional Address: 945 S. Main, Ste. 205, Salinas, CA 93901; Additional E-mails: jackie@cfmco.org and jeff@cfmco.org; URL: http://www.cfmco.org

Incorporated in 1945 in CA.
Foundation type: Community foundation.
Financial data (yr. ended 12/31/05): Assets, $97,412,700 (M); gifts received, $6,235,419; expenditures, $7,610,905; giving activities include $6,018,885 for 608 grants.

Purpose and activities: The foundation seeks to improve the quality of life in Monterey County by raising, managing, and distributing charitable funds to worthy organizations and by creating positive connections between donors and their interests. Primarily supports arts and cultural organizations, libraries, schools and other educational institutions, and human services organizations.
Fields of interest: Historic preservation/historical societies; Arts; Education; Environment; Animal welfare; Health care; Substance abuse, prevention; Employment; Housing/shelter; Human services; Community development; Youth; Aging.
Type of support: Continuing support; Capital campaigns; Building/renovation; Equipment; Emergency funds; Program development; Technical assistance; Consulting services; Matching/challenge support.
Limitations: Giving primarily in Monterey County, CA. No support for sectarian religious programs. No grants to individuals (except for scholarships), or for annual campaigns, deficit financing, operating costs, general endowments, fellowships, travel, research or publications.
Publications: Application guidelines; Annual report (including application guidelines); Informational brochure; Newsletter.
Application information: Visit foundation Web site for application forms and specific guidelines per grant type. Application form required.
  Initial approach: Telephone or e-mail
  Copies of proposal: 2
  Deadline(s): Jan. 3, May 1, and Aug. 7 for general endowment grants; varies for others
  Board meeting date(s): 4th Tues. of selected months
  Final notification: Late Apr., late Aug., and late Nov.
Officers and Directors: * Mary R. Wright,* Chair.; David G. Armanasco,* Vice-Chair.; C. Lee Cox,* Vice-Chair; Todd Lueders, C.E.O. and Pres.; Judy Sulsona, C.O.O. and Exec. V.P.; Richard Borda,* Secy.; F. Warren Wayland,* Treas.; Shreve "Mac" Archer; Nancy B. Ausonio; Jim Bogart; Thomas Bohnen; Jeanette Cisneros; Diane Cordero de Noriega; Valerie Golden; Carla Hudson; Roberta Huntington; Jeanne Landreth; Eric Miller; Mary Orradre; Carlos Ramos; Edward Valeau.
Number of staff: 14 full-time professional.
EIN: 941615897
Selected grants: The following grants were reported in 2005.

$34,000 to Police Activities League, Monterey County, Salinas, CA. For FLASH Program operating support.

$30,000 to Volunteer Center of Monterey County, Salinas, CA. For Caminos Program.

$28,000 to National Steinbeck Center, Salinas, CA. For Steinbeck Chair.

$23,000 to Central Coast Center for Independent Living, Salinas, CA. For conducting Housing Needs Survey for people with disabilities.

$20,000 to Alliance on Aging, Monterey, CA. For operating support.

$18,000 to Community Bridges, Watsonville, CA. For Agricultural Workers' Access to Health Project.

$17,550 to Meals on Wheels of the Monterey Peninsula, Pacific Grove, CA. For Investment in Independence program.

$15,000 to Chartwell School, Seaside, CA. To provide additional staffing to Boys and Girls Clubs homework centers.

$13,500 to Blind and Visually Impaired Center of Monterey County, Pacific Grove, CA. For VISTA (Visually-Impaired Students Technology Assistance) program.

$10,000 to Monterey County Cultural Council, Carmel, CA. For expansion of Professional Artists in Schools program in Salinas Valley schools.

402
The Community Foundation of Mendocino County, Inc.
(formerly Mendocino County Community Foundation, Inc.)
135 W. Gobbi St., Ste. 204
Ukiah, CA   95482-5477   (707) 468-9882
Contact: Susanne Norgard, Exec. Dir.
FAX: (707) 468-5529;
E-mail: info@communityfound.org; URL: http://www.communityfound.org

Established in 1993 in CT.
Foundation type: Community foundation.
Financial data (yr. ended 6/30/05): Assets, $6,685,685 (M); gifts received, $1,339,676; expenditures, $681,674; giving activities include $376,892 for grants.
Purpose and activities: The foundation seeks to match donor's philanthropic interests with community needs and opportunities.
Fields of interest: Historic preservation/historical societies; Arts; Libraries/library science; Education; Environment; Health care; Recreation, parks/playgrounds; Recreation; Youth development, centers/clubs; Youth development, adult & child programs; Children/youth, services; Economic development; Community development; Economically disadvantaged.
Type of support: Emergency funds; Program development; Seed money; Scholarship funds; Technical assistance.
Limitations: Giving limited to Mendocino County, CA, and its service areas. No support for for-profit organizations. No grants to individuals (except for scholarships).
Publications: Annual report; Newsletter.
Application information: Visit foundation Web site for application form and guidelines. Faxed, e-mailed, or late submissions are not accepted. Application form required.
  Initial approach: Letter of inquiry on grant programs and opportunities
  Copies of proposal: 10
  Deadline(s): Varies by program
  Board meeting date(s): 1st Tues. monthly (except for July and Dec.)
  Final notification: Varies by program
Officers and Directors: * Claire Ellis,* Pres.; Jim Moorehead,* V.P.; Rudolph Light,* Secy.; John Knapp,* Treas.; Susanne Norgard, Exec. Dir.; Sharon Brewer; Conrad L. Cox; Guilford Dye; Jim Mayfield; Greg Nelson; Diane Pauli; Herbert E. Pruett; Francine Selim.
Number of staff: 1 full-time professional; 2 part-time professional.
EIN: 680330462

403
The Community Foundation of Santa Cruz County ◇

(formerly Greater Santa Cruz County Community Foundation)
2425 Porter St., Ste. 17
Soquel, CA 95073-2453   (831) 477-0800
Contact: Lance Linares, Exec. Dir.; For grants: Christina Cuevas, Prog. Dir.
FAX: (831) 477-0991; E-mail: info@cfscc.org; Additional E-mails: lance@cfscc.org and christina@cfscc.org; URL: http://www.cfscc.org

Incorporated in 1982 in CA.
Foundation type: Community foundation.
Financial data (yr. ended 12/31/04): Assets, $31,767,568 (M); gifts received, $4,478,557; expenditures, $4,177,776; giving activities include $3,004,904 for 350+ grants.
Purpose and activities: The purpose of the foundation is to strengthen the community, and to inspire philanthropy and community involvement in Santa Cruz County, CA.
Fields of interest: Historic preservation/historical societies; Arts; Education; Environment; Health care; Youth development; Human services; Community development.
Type of support: Continuing support; Management development/capacity building; Equipment; Emergency funds; Program development; Conferences/seminars; Seed money; Scholarship funds; Technical assistance; Program evaluation; Scholarships—to individuals; Matching/challenge support.
Limitations: Giving limited to Santa Cruz County, CA. No support for religious organizations for religious purposes or individual (public or private) schools, as distinct from a school district. No grants to individuals (except for scholarships from designated funds), or for annual campaigns, deficit financing, building or renovation funds, land acquisition, fellowships, research, endowments, fundraising events, or celebrations; no student loans.
Publications: Application guidelines; Annual report; Financial statement; Grants list.
Application information: Visit foundation Web site for application guidelines and specific deadlines. The foundation strongly encourages all potential applicants to attend one of the free grant application sessions; visit Web site for upcoming dates. Based upon review of letters of intent, the foundation will invite eligible organizations to submit a full proposal. Application form required.
  Initial approach: Letter of intent (no longer than 3 pages)
  Copies of proposal: 3
  Deadline(s): Feb. 13 for letter of intent; Apr. 24 for full proposal; Mar. 31 for scholarships
  Board meeting date(s): Quarterly
  Final notification: Within 6 weeks for letter of intent determination
Officers and Directors:* Jess Brown,* Pres.; Margaret A. Leonard,* V.P.; Karen A. Cogswell,* Secy.; Ralph Miljanich,* Treas.; Lance Linares, Exec. Dir.; Jack Baskin, Dir. Emeritus; Ian D. McPhail, Dir. Emeritus; Tom Brezsny; Pedro Castillo; Ceil Cirillo; Frederick H. Ebey; Ana Espinoza; Deidre Hamilton; Mary Hammer; William Kelsay; Leola Lapides; Eric F. Mendelson; Rachael A. Spencer; James C. Thompson; Rachel Wedeen; Jill G. Wilson; Donna Ziel.

Number of staff: 5 full-time professional; 2 part-time professional; 1 full-time support; 2 part-time support.
EIN: 942808039

404
Community Foundation of the Napa Valley ◇

3299 Claremont Way, Ste. 2
Napa, CA 94558   (707) 254-9565
FAX: (707) 254-7955; E-mail: info@cfnv.org; URL: http://www.cfnv.org

Established in 1994 in CA.
Foundation type: Community foundation.
Financial data (yr. ended 6/30/05): Assets, $10,294,542 (M); gifts received, $5,991,569; expenditures, $4,183,348; giving activities include $1,892,330 for 64+ grants (high: $261,165).
Purpose and activities: The mission of the foundation is to access, develop, and preserve community resources to meet community needs in Napa County, CA.
Fields of interest: Performing arts; Arts; Education; Environment; Health care; Youth, services; Human services.
Type of support: General/operating support; Program development; Seed money; Scholarship funds.
Limitations: Giving primarily in the Napa County, CA, area.
Publications: Annual report; Informational brochure; Multi-year report; Newsletter.
Application information: Visit foundation Web site for application guidelines. Application form not required.
  Initial approach: Letter
  Deadline(s): Mar. 1 for Napa Valley Fund for the Arts grants
  Board meeting date(s): Bimonthly
Officers and Board Members:* Harry T. Price,* Chair.; Terence Mulligan, Pres.; William H. Phelps,* Secy.; Glen Terry,* Treas.; Lauren Ackerman; Lisa Cort; Jamie Davies; J. Melville Engle; Mark Farley; Lorrain Kongsgaard; Dorothy Lind-Salmon; David Meyers; Janet Pagano; Richard E. Walton; Rabbi David White.
Number of staff: 2 full-time professional; 1 part-time professional.
EIN: 680349777

405
The Community Foundation Serving Riverside and San Bernardino Counties ◇

(formerly Community Foundation of Riverside County)
3880 Lemon St., Ste. 300
Riverside, CA 92501-3622   (909) 684-4194, ext. 14
Contact: Celia Cudiamat, V.P., Grant Progs.; For grants: Penny Beaulieu, Office Admin. Mgr.
FAX: (909) 684-1911;
E-mail: ccudiamat@thecommunityfoundation.net; Grant request E-mail: pbeaulieu@thecommunityfoundation.net; URL: http://www.thecommunityfoundation.net

Established as a trust in 1941 in CA.
Foundation type: Community foundation.

Financial data (yr. ended 12/31/05): Assets, $44,029,628 (M); gifts received, $2,230,136; expenditures, $4,341,219; giving activities include $3,533,351 for grants.
Purpose and activities: The foundation seeks to strengthen the community by meeting the needs and enhancing the lives of individuals in Riverside and San Bernardino counties, CA, in partnership with philanthropic individuals, community leaders, and the nonprofit sector. This is accomplished through building permanent endowments, making prudent grants for charitable causes, being a catalyst to solve community concerns and strengthening nonprofit organizations.
Fields of interest: Arts; Education; Health care; Youth development, adult & child programs; Children/youth, services; Family services; Human services; Public affairs.
Type of support: Equipment; Land acquisition; Emergency funds; Program development; Seed money; Scholarship funds; Program evaluation; Matching/challenge support.
Limitations: Giving primarily in Riverside and San Bernardino counties, CA. No support for sectarian programs, fraternal organizations, or school or college-based extracurricular activities. No grants to individuals (directly), or for ongoing operating expenses, deficits or existing obligations, endowment, capital fund, or annual fund appeals, capital campaigns, event sponsorship, or research.
Publications: Application guidelines; Annual report; Financial statement; Grants list; Informational brochure; Newsletter.
Application information: Visit foundation Web site for application form and guidelines; applicants must have been offering programs for at least 3 years. Application form required.
  Initial approach: Telephone or e-mail
  Copies of proposal: 1
  Deadline(s): Jan. for Community Impact grants; varies for others
  Board meeting date(s): Feb., Apr., June, Aug., Oct., and Dec.
  Final notification: Immediately after board meetings
Officers and Directors:* Lynn Bogh Baldi,* Chair.; Larry Sharp,* Vice-Chair.; Sheryl J. Alexander, C.E.O. and Pres.; Celia Cudiamat, V.P., Grant Progs.; Susan Kean, V.P., Devel.; Gloria Macias-Harrison,* Secy.; Kirk G. Stitt,* C.F.O.; Henry Coil; David Cornwall; Andrea Dutton; James Erickson; Marilyn Forst; Stanley M. Grube; Andrew T. Jessup, Sr.; Albert K. Karnig, Ph.D.; Hon. Patrick J. Morris; Rod Pacheco; Benita Roberts; Philip M. Savage III; Regina Stone; Hon. Grover Trask.
Number of staff: 5 full-time professional.
EIN: 330748536

406
Community Foundation Silicon Valley ▼ ◇

(formerly Community Foundation of Santa Clara County)
60 S. Market St., Ste. 1000
San Jose, CA 95113-1000   (408) 278-2200
Contact: Peter Hero, Pres.; For grant information meeting reservations: Lupe Barrera, Exec. Asst./ Receptionist; For Community Investment grants: Maya McCray, Prog. and Grants Svcs. Mgr.

Established in 1954 in CA; merged with the Peninsula Community Foundation in 2006.
Foundation type: Community foundation.

Financial data (yr. ended 6/30/05): Assets, $760,821,244 (M); gifts received, $140,184,428; expenditures, $86,305,391; giving activities include $75,366,593 for 4,644 grants (high: $1,000,000; low: $100).

Purpose and activities: The foundation seeks to be a leader for philanthropy. As such, the foundation catalyzes community change, brings people together to solve problems, and builds a permanent endowment for future regional needs.

Fields of interest: Visual arts; Performing arts; Performing arts, theater; Performing arts, music; Arts; Education, early childhood education; Elementary school/education; Secondary school/education; Higher education; Adult/continuing education; Adult education—literacy, basic skills & GED; Education, reading; Education; Environment; Health care; Mental health/crisis services; Health organizations, association; AIDS; AIDS research; Employment; Food services; Housing/shelter, development; Disasters, Hurricane Katrina; Youth, services; Residential/custodial care, hospices; Women, centers/services; Minorities/immigrants, centers/services; Homeless, human services; Human services; Community development; Federated giving programs; Engineering/technology; Public affairs; Minorities; Native Americans/American Indians; Women; Homeless.

Type of support: General/operating support; Emergency funds; Program development; Seed money; Scholarship funds; Technical assistance; Consulting services; Program-related investments/loans; Employee matching gifts; Grants to individuals; Matching/challenge support.

Limitations: Giving primarily in Santa Clara and southern San Mateo counties, CA.

Publications: Application guidelines; Annual report; Financial statement; Informational brochure; Newsletter.

Application information: The foundation has merged with the Peninsula Community Foundation. Visit www.siliconvalleycf.org for updated application information and guidelines.

Officers and Directors: Gregory M. Avis,* Chair.; J. Michael Patterson,* Vice-Chair.; Peter Hero, Pres.; Ellen Ammerman, C.F.O.; Anne M. Yamamoto,* Treas.; David Mitchell, Genl. Counsel; Laura K. Arrillaga; John Dean; Debra Engel; Jorge Fernandes; Kevin A. Fong; Greg Gallo; Narenda Gupta; William Johnson; Lata Krishnan; Jeff Skoll; John Michael Sobrato; Erika Williams.

Number of staff: 18 full-time professional; 31 full-time support.

EIN: 770066922

Selected grants: The following grants were reported in 2005.

$3,250,000 to National Hispanic University, San Jose, CA. 2 grants: $2,000,000, $1,250,000

$1,250,000 to Oakland Unified School District, Oakland, CA.

$1,000,000 to Edison Institute, Dearborn, MI.

$1,000,000 to NewSchools Venture Fund, San Francisco, CA.

$1,000,000 to Stanford University, Stanford, CA.

$949,000 to National Council for Science and the Environment, DC.

$899,650 to VMC Foundation, San Jose, CA.

$841,767 to Synopsys Silicon Valley Science and Technology Outreach Foundation, Mountain View, CA.

$700,000 to EdSource, Mountain View, CA.

407
Community Foundation Sonoma County ▼ ✧

(formerly The Sonoma County Community Foundation)
250 D St., Ste. 205
Santa Rosa, CA 95404-4773   (707) 579-4073
Contact: Kay M. Marquet, C.E.O.; For grants: Robert Judd, Dir., Progs.
FAX: (707) 579-4801;
E-mail: jharrison@sonomacf.org; Additional E-mail: kmarquet@sonomacf.org; Grant inquiry E-mail: rjudd@sonomacf.org; URL: http://www.sonomacf.org

Incorporated in 1983 in CA.

Foundation type: Community foundation.

Financial data (yr. ended 12/31/04): Assets, $99,400,199 (M); gifts received, $11,086,115; expenditures, $8,286,827; giving activities include $5,116,404 for 642+ grants (high: $200,000), and $595,965 for foundation-administered programs.

Purpose and activities: The foundation matches philanthropic interests with community needs by serving as a leader, resource, and catalyst to enrich quality of life; encouraging philanthropy at all levels; providing comprehensive donor services; and responding to changing community needs and opportunities.

Fields of interest: Humanities; Arts, artist's services; Arts; Education; Environmental education; Environment; Health care; Housing/shelter, temporary shelter; Housing/shelter; Children/youth, services; Women, centers/services; Homeless, human services; Human services; Community development; Children/youth.

Type of support: General/operating support; Continuing support; Endowments; Emergency funds; Program development; Seed money; Scholarship funds; Technical assistance; Consulting services; Program evaluation; Program-related investments/loans; Scholarships—to individuals; Matching/challenge support.

Limitations: Giving limited to Sonoma County, CA. No support for religious purposes or advocacy activities, or primary or secondary schools or their academic foundations. No grants to individuals (except for academic scholarships), or for fundraising events, annual fund campaigns, capital campaigns, conferences, or debt retirement; no loans (except program-related investments).

Publications: Application guidelines; Annual report; Financial statement; Informational brochure; Newsletter.

Application information: Visit foundation Web site for application forms, guidelines, and specific deadlines. Application form required.

Initial approach: Letter or telephone call to Prog. Off.

Deadline(s): Varies

Board meeting date(s): 1st Tues. of most months

Final notification: Varies

Officers and Directors: Herbert M. Dwight, Jr.,* Chair.; Jean Schulz,* Vice-Chair.; Kay M. Marquet, C.E.O. and Pres.; Paul DeMarco, V.P., Finance and Admin.; Kate Ecker, V.P., Devel.; Glenn Yamamoto,* Secy.; Christopher Dobson,* Treas.; Suzanne Adams, Cont.; Barbara Banke; Benny Bray; Demaris Brinton; Mary Caldwell, Ph.D.; Barbara Graves; Albert Handelmann; Lew Reid; Harry Richardson, M.D.; Francisco H. Vazquez, Ph.D.; David Voss.

Number of staff: 9 full-time professional; 3 full-time support; 1 part-time support.

EIN: 680003212

Selected grants: The following grants were reported in 2004.

$125,000 to California Parenting Institute, Santa Rosa, CA. For general support of Pediatric Dental Center.

$125,000 to Santa Rosa Symphony, Santa Rosa, CA. For general support.

$110,000 to Princeton University, Princeton, NJ. For annual giving, class of 1955.

$100,000 to Catholic Charities of the Diocese of Santa Rosa, Santa Rosa, CA. For general operating support.

$100,000 to Laguna de Santa Rosa Foundation, Sebastopol, CA. To develop fundraising program and begin planning work for Stone Farm project.

$100,000 to Petaluma Phoenix Center, Petaluma, CA. For building retrofit and other expenses.

$100,000 to Santa Rosa Memorial Hospital Foundation, Santa Rosa, CA. For adding to Emergency Room Trauma Center.

$90,000 to Luther Burbank Center for the Arts, Santa Rosa, CA. For capital improvements.

$75,000 to Filmmakers Collaborative, San Francisco, CA. For keystone funding for production of Restoring Eden for public television.

$50,000 to Actors Theater of Sonoma County, Santa Rosa, CA. For Sixth Street Playhouse building fund.

408
Compassion for Animals Foundation, Inc. ✧

3962 Landmark St.
Culver City, CA 90232-2315
Contact: Gilbert N. Michaels, Pres.

Established in 1986 in CA.

Donor: Gilbert N. Michaels.

Foundation type: Operating foundation.

Financial data (yr. ended 11/30/04): Assets, $1,234,917 (M); gifts received, $1,000,000; expenditures, $374,713; qualifying distributions, $374,713; giving activities include $368,500 for grants.

Purpose and activities: Giving strictly for the protection and advancement of animal rights and the prevention of cruelty to animals, through scientific research, literary and educational efforts, and charitable activities.

Fields of interest: Animal welfare.

Type of support: General/operating support.

Limitations: Giving on a national basis.

Application information: Application form not required.

Initial approach: Letter

Deadline(s): None

Officers: Gilbert N. Michaels, Pres.; Julie Javor, Secy.; Lonnie Horn, C.F.O.

EIN: 954082225

Selected grants: The following grants were reported in 2004.

$174,000 to Animals Voice, Chico, CA.

$50,000 to Humane Society.

$25,000 to Return to Freedom, Lompoc, CA.

$10,000 to Primarily Primates, San Antonio, TX.

$10,000 to Vegetarians International Voice for Animals (VIVA) USA, Davis, CA.

409

Compton Foundation, Inc. ▼ ✧
255 Shoreline Dr., Ste. 540
Redwood City, CA 94065 (650) 508-1181
Contact: Edith T. Eddy, Exec. Dir.
FAX: (650) 508-1191;
E-mail: info@comptonfoundation.org; URL: http://www.comptonfoundation.org

Incorporated in 1972 in NY as successor to the Compton Trust; reincorporated in 1992 in CA.
Donor: Members of the Compton family.
Foundation type: Independent foundation.
Financial data (yr. ended 12/31/04): Assets, $79,291,484 (M); gifts received, $2,065; expenditures, $8,209,192; qualifying distributions, $7,458,808; giving activities include $6,561,276 for 376 grants (high: $150,000; low: $200; average: $5,000–$100,000).
Purpose and activities: To coordinate the Compton family giving to community, national, and international programs in areas of its special interests, including peace and world order, population, and the environment. Other concerns include equal education opportunity, community welfare, and culture and the arts.
Fields of interest: Environment, natural resources; Environment; Reproductive health, family planning; International peace/security; International affairs, arms control; International affairs, foreign policy; Population studies.
International interests: Central America; Mexico; Sub-Saharan Africa.
Type of support: General/operating support; Continuing support; Land acquisition; Program development; Fellowships; Research; Consulting services; Program-related investments/loans; Matching/challenge support.
Limitations: Giving on an international basis to U.S.-based organizations for projects in Mexico, Central America, and Sub-Saharan Africa and on a national basis for programs in peace and population and the environment. Other funding limited to areas where board members reside: primarily San Francisco, Marin, and Santa Clara counties, CA. No grants to individuals, or for capital or building funds, no loans (except for program-related investments).
Publications: Biennial report; Financial statement; Informational brochure (including application guidelines).
Application information: Proposals submitted by fax or e-mail not accepted. Application form required.
  Initial approach: Brief 3- to 4-page proposal
  Copies of proposal: 1
  Deadline(s): Mar. 7 (for June meeting), Apr. 3 (for Emergency Contraception Initiative), and Sept. 7 (for Dec. meeting)
  Board meeting date(s): June and Dec.
  Final notification: 6 months
Officers and Directors:* Marshal J. Compton,* Pres.; W. Danforth Compton,* V.P.; Rebecca DiDomenico,* Secy.; Richard Morrison,* Treas.; Edith T. Eddy, Exec. Dir.; James R. Compton, Chair. Emeritus; Ann C. Stephens, Vice-Chair. Emeritus; Kennette M. Benedict; Michael Lerner; Stephen Perry; Lee Etta Powell; Carol C. Wall.
Number of staff: 4 full-time professional; 2 part-time support.
EIN: 943142932
Selected grants: The following grants were reported in 2004.
$300,000 to Rural Education Action Project, SmartMeme, Montpelier, VT. For peace and security programs.

$200,000 to Brotherhood/Sister Sol, New York, NY. For peace and security programs.
$200,000 to Ruckus Society, Berkeley, CA. For peace and security programs.
$150,000 to Brown University, Providence, RI. For population and reproductive health programs.
$147,085 to Public Health Institute, International Health Programs, Oakland, CA. For population and reproductive health programs.
$93,573 to Leadership Institute for Ecology and the Economy, Santa Rosa, CA. For general education support.
$50,000 to Local Initiative Support, Training and Education Network (LISTEN), DC. For peace and security programs.
$40,000 to Proteus Fund, Amherst, MA. For peace and security programs.
$30,000 to Pathfinder International, Watertown, MA. For population and reproductive health programs.
$25,000 to Public Citizen Foundation, DC. For environment and sustainability programs.

410

Condon Family Foundation ✧
710 Las Canoas Pl.
Santa Barbara, CA 93105

Established in 1995 in CA.
Donors: Thomas J. Condon; Julie H. Condon.
Foundation type: Independent foundation.
Financial data (yr. ended 12/31/05): Assets, $4,589,776 (M); gifts received, $600,000; expenditures, $514,209; qualifying distributions, $514,209; giving activities include $508,285 for 16 grants (high: $200,000; low: $500).
Purpose and activities: Giving for Roman Catholic churches and education and for lymphoma research.
Fields of interest: Higher education; Cancer research; Roman Catholic agencies & churches.
Limitations: Applications not accepted. Giving primarily in CA. No grants to individuals.
Application information: Contributes only to pre-selected organizations.
Officers: Thomas J. Condon, Pres. and C.I.O.; Christine Condon, Secy.; Thomas H. Condon, Treas.
Finance Comm: Julie H. Condon; Amy Saleh.
EIN: 954522880
Selected grants: The following grants were reported in 2003.
$200,000 to Cathedral of Our Lady of Angels, Los Angeles, CA. For capital campaign.
$100,000 to Institute for Advanced Catholic Studies, Greensburg, PA. For unrestricted support.
$50,000 to Chaminade College Preparatory School, Chatsworth, CA. For capital campaign.
$15,000 to University of Southern California, Los Angeles, CA. For annual fund campaign.

411

Confidence Foundation
625 Fair Oaks Ave., Ste. 360
South Pasadena, CA 91030-5813
Contact: Linda J. Blinkenberg, Pres.

Established in 1980 in CA.
Donors: N. Paul Whittier†; N. Paul Whittier Charitable Lead Trust.
Foundation type: Independent foundation.

Financial data (yr. ended 12/31/05): Assets, $51,737,505 (M); gifts received, $1,945,955; expenditures, $2,601,255; qualifying distributions, $2,413,407; giving activities include $2,220,316 for 115 grants (high: $200,000; low: $500).
Purpose and activities: Giving primarily for education, social services, youth, children, and families, health and medicine, and communities.
Fields of interest: Education, early childhood education; Secondary school/education; Education; Reproductive health, family planning; Health care; Medical research, institute; Youth development, citizenship; Human services; Family services; Science; Public policy, research; Leadership development; Minorities; Economically disadvantaged.
Type of support: Building/renovation; Program development; Seed money; Scholarship funds; Matching/challenge support.
Limitations: Giving primarily in Los Angeles, CA. No grants to individuals; no loans.
Application information: Grants usually initiated by the foundation. Application form not required.
  Initial approach: Letter of inquiry
  Copies of proposal: 1
  Deadline(s): None
  Board meeting date(s): As needed
Officers and Directors:* Linda J. Blinkenberg,* Pres. and C.F.O.; Michael J. Casey,* V.P. and Secy.; Arlo G. Sorensen,* V.P.; Cheyenna Whittier.
EIN: 953500483
Selected grants: The following grants were reported in 2004.
$100,000 to Saint Johns Well Child and Family Center, Los Angeles, CA.
$94,000 to McKinley Childrens Center, San Dimas, CA.
$50,000 to Whittier Institute for Diabetes and Endocrinology, La Jolla, CA.
$40,000 to Sandpoint Waldorf School, Sandpoint, ID.
$25,000 to Pasadena Conservatory of Music, Pasadena, CA.
$20,000 to Pacific Lodge Boys Home, Woodland Hills, CA.
$5,000 to Festival at Sandpoint, Sandpoint, ID.
$5,000 to Hospitaller Foundation of California, Los Angeles, CA.
$2,500 to Flintridge Sacred Heart Academy, La Canada Flintridge, CA.
$2,500 to USC/Norris Comprehensive Cancer Center, Los Angeles, CA.

412

Michael J. Connell Foundation ✧
225 S. Lake Ave., Ste. 271
Pasadena, CA 91101
Contact: Michael J. Connell, Pres.

Incorporated in 1931 in CA.
Donor: Michael J. Connell.
Foundation type: Independent foundation.
Financial data (yr. ended 6/30/05): Assets, $13,289,717 (M); expenditures, $748,091; qualifying distributions, $606,691; giving activities include $555,000 for 16 grants (high: $240,000; low: $1,000).
Purpose and activities: Giving generally restricted to programs initiated by the foundation in social, cultural, and educational and medical fields.
Fields of interest: Arts education; Performing arts, theater; Performing arts, orchestra (symphony); Arts; Elementary/secondary education; Higher

education; Education, reading; Education; Animals/wildlife, preservation/protection; Hospitals (specialty); Medical research; Human services; American Red Cross.

Type of support: Equipment; Program development; Fellowships; Internship funds.

Limitations: Giving primarily in southern CA, with emphasis on Los Angeles. No grants to individuals, or for building funds; no loans.

Publications: Financial statement.

Application information: Requests for grants are generally discouraged. Application form not required.

   Initial approach: Proposal
   Copies of proposal: 1
   Deadline(s): Feb. 15, May 15, Aug. 15, and Nov. 15
   Board meeting date(s): Mar., June, Sept. and Dec.
   Final notification: 3 months

Officers: Michael J. Connell, Pres.; Richard A. Wilson, V.P.; Richard A. Grant, Treas.

Director: Christopher Connell.

Number of staff: 1 full-time professional; 1 part-time professional.

EIN: 956000904

413
G.L. Connolly Foundation ✧ ☆
P.O. Box 6657
Moraga, CA 94570
Application address: c/o Thomas A. Connolly, 52 E. 81st St., New York, NY 10028 or Ronald G. Connolly, P.O. Box 6667, Moraga, CA 94570

Established in 2004 in DE.

Donor: The Laffey-Mchugh Foundation.

Foundation type: Independent foundation.

Financial data (yr. ended 12/31/05): Assets, $11,144,028 (M); expenditures, $397,250; qualifying distributions, $328,225; giving activities include $319,000 for 52 grants (high: $30,000; low: $1,000).

Fields of interest: Higher education; Human services; Children/youth, services; Social sciences, public policy; Roman Catholic agencies & churches.

Limitations: Giving primarily in New York, NY, and Washington, DC.

Application information:

   Initial approach: Letter
   Deadline(s): Apr. or Oct.

Officers: Ronald G. Connolly, Co-Pres.; Thomas A. Connolly, Co-Pres.

EIN: 200247328

414
The Sirpuhe & John Conte Foundation ✧
75-600 Beryl Ln.
Indian Wells, CA 92210-8620

Established in 1999 in CA.

Donors: John Conte†; Sirpuhe Conte.

Foundation type: Operating foundation.

Financial data (yr. ended 12/31/04): Assets, $7,301,364 (M); expenditures, $405,740; qualifying distributions, $352,049; giving activities include $347,250 for 23 grants (high: $62,000; low: $1,000).

Purpose and activities: Giving primarily for education, the arts, health care, and to Armenian churches and organizations.

Fields of interest: Arts; Education; Animal welfare; Health care; Religion.

Limitations: Applications not accepted. Giving primarily in CA.

Application information: Contributes only to pre-selected organizations.

Officers: Sirpuhe Conte, Pres.; Louise Danelian, V.P.; Joyce Stein, V.P.; George Phillips, Secy.

EIN: 330884049

Selected grants: The following grants were reported in 2003.

$60,000 to United Armenian Congregational Church, Los Angeles, CA.

$51,100 to Eisenhower Medical Center, Rancho Mirage, CA.

$30,000 to UCLA Foundation, Los Angeles, CA. For scholarships.

$25,000 to Armenian Assembly of America, Beverly Hills, CA.

$20,000 to McCallum Theater, Palm Desert, CA.

$10,000 to Virginia Waring International Piano Competition, Palm Desert, CA.

$10,000 to Young Musicians Foundation, Beverly Hills, CA.

$5,000 to Inner-City Arts, Los Angeles, CA.

$2,000 to Starkey Hearing Foundation, Eden Prairie, MN.

$1,000 to Braille Institute, Santa Barbara, CA.

415
The Scott Cook and Signe Otsby Charitable Foundation ✧
2995 Woodside Rd., Ste. 400-400
Woodside, CA 94062

Established in 2003 in CA.

Donors: Scott Cook; Signe Ostby.

Foundation type: Independent foundation.

Financial data (yr. ended 12/31/04): Assets, $16,410,756 (M); gifts received, $2,032,621; expenditures, $1,640,899; qualifying distributions, $1,274,418; giving activities include $1,268,500 for 11 grants (high: $1,000,000; low: $500).

Fields of interest: Education; Human services; Philanthropy/voluntarism; Protestant agencies & churches.

Limitations: Applications not accepted. Giving primarily in CA. No grants to individuals.

Application information: Unsolicited requests for funds not accepted.

Officers and Directors:* Signe Ostby,* Pres.; Sharon Cook Farney,* Secy.; Scott Cook,* C.F.O.

EIN: 200478828

416
Helen K. and James S. Copley Foundation ✧
(formerly James S. Copley Foundation)
7776 Ivanhoe Ave.
P.O. Box 1530
La Jolla, CA 92038-1530 (858) 454-0411

Incorporated in 1953 in CA.

Donors: The Copley Press Inc.; San Diego Union Shoe Fund.

Foundation type: Company-sponsored foundation.

Financial data (yr. ended 12/31/04): Assets, $23,476,605 (M); expenditures, $1,897,742; qualifying distributions, $1,674,043; giving activities include $1,632,610 for 191 grants (high: $500,000; low: $50).

Purpose and activities: The foundation supports museums, hospitals and hospices, and organizations involved with arts and culture, education, health, and community development.

Fields of interest: Media, journalism/publishing; Museums; Performing arts; Performing arts, dance; Performing arts, theater; Performing arts, music; Arts; Child development, education; Elementary school/education; Secondary school/education; Higher education; Adult education—literacy, basic skills & GED; Libraries/library science; Education, reading; Education; Hospitals (general); Health care; Substance abuse, services; Health organizations, association; AIDS; Recreation; Human services; Youth, services; Child development, services; Residential/custodial care, hospices; Aging, centers/services; Homeless, human services; Community development; Federated giving programs; Aging.

Type of support: Capital campaigns; Building/renovation; Equipment; Land acquisition; Endowments; Employee matching gifts.

Limitations: Giving primarily in San Diego, San Pedro, and Torrance, CA, Galesburg, Lincoln, Peoria, and Springfield, IL, and Canton, Dover, Massillon, and New Philadelphia, OH. No support for religious, fraternal, or athletic organizations, government agencies, local chapters of national organizations, public elementary or secondary schools, or public broadcasting systems. No grants to individuals, or for research, publications, conferences, general operating support, or large campaigns; no loans.

Publications: Informational brochure (including application guidelines).

Application information: Application form not required.

   Initial approach: Proposal
   Copies of proposal: 1
   Deadline(s): Jan. 2
   Board meeting date(s): Spring
   Final notification: 2 to 3 weeks following board meeting; otherwise within 1 week

Officers and Directors:* Helen K. Copley,* Chair.; David C. Copley,* Pres.; Robert F. Crouch, V.P.; Karl Zobell,* V.P.; Charles F. Patrick,* Treas.

EIN: 956051770

Selected grants: The following grants were reported in 2004.

$500,000 to La Jolla Playhouse, La Jolla, CA.

$200,000 to Museum of Photographic Arts, San Diego, CA.

$200,000 to United Way of San Diego County, San Diego, CA. 4 grants: $50,000 each

$50,000 to San Diego Opera Association, San Diego, CA.

$30,000 to San Diego Crew Classic, San Diego, CA.

$25,000 to Monarch School Project, San Diego, CA.

$20,000 to Zoological Society of San Diego, San Diego, CA.

417
The Corcoran Community Foundation ✧
P.O. Box 655
Corcoran, CA 93212

Incorporated in 1965 in CA.

Donors: W.W. Boswell; Mrs. W.W. Boswell.

Foundation type: Community foundation.

Financial data (yr. ended 12/31/05): Assets, $14,168,235 (M); gifts received, $1,372,086; expenditures, $1,352,514; giving activities include $1,094,024 for grants.

Purpose and activities: The purpose of the foundation is to receive contributions, gifts and bequests, and to distribute these funds for charitable, educational, religious and scientific purposes to improve the community of Corcoran, CA.
Fields of interest: Arts; Education; Human services; Community development.
Limitations: Giving limited to the Corcoran, CA, area.
Officers and Trustees:* Mary Wadsworth,* Pres.; Terry Kwast,* V.P.; Terrell Devaney,* Secy.; Jon Rachford,* Treas.; Steve Bonilla; James W. Boswell; Michael Boyett; Kirk Gilkey; Barbara Gomez; Ross F. Hall; Phillip Hansen; Jimmy Hesskett; Mike Nordstrom; Sidonio Palmerian; Jim Razor; Jeanette Todd.
Number of staff: 1 full-time professional.
EIN: 941608857

418
The Corrigan-Walla Foundation ◇
c/o Robert T. Borawski
1280 Space Park Way, Ste. 104
Mountain View, CA 94043

Established in 1993 in CA.
Donors: Sigrun Corrigan; Wilfred J. Corrigan.
Foundation type: Independent foundation.
Financial data (yr. ended 10/31/05): Assets, $7,858,958 (M); expenditures, $436,488; qualifying distributions, $426,900; giving activities include $402,500 for 25 grants (high: $75,000; low: $2,000).
Purpose and activities: Funding primarily for the arts.
Fields of interest: Performing arts, ballet; Performing arts, orchestra (symphony); Performing arts, opera; Arts; Residential/custodial care, group home.
Limitations: Applications not accepted. Giving primarily in CA. No grants to individuals.
Application information: Contributes only to pre-selected organizations.
Officers: Sigrun Corrigan, Pres.; Wilfred J. Corrigan, V.P.; Robert Borawski, Secy.
EIN: 770359520
Selected grants: The following grants were reported in 2004.
  $105,000 to San Francisco Symphony, San Francisco, CA.
  $75,000 to San Francisco Opera, San Francisco, CA.
  $10,000 to Community School of Music and Arts, Mountain View, CA.
  $10,000 to Saint Vincent de Paul Society, Los Angeles, CA.
  $10,000 to San Francisco Ballet, San Francisco, CA.
  $10,000 to Sequoia Hospital Foundation, Redwood City, CA.
  $5,000 to HOPE Rehabilitation Services, Santa Clara, CA.
  $5,000 to Trust for Hidden Villa, Los Altos Hills, CA.
  $3,000 to Marine Science Institute, Redwood City, CA.
  $3,000 to Resource Area for Teachers, San Jose, CA.

419
The Cortopassi Family Foundation ◇
(formerly The Capecchio Foundation)
11292 N. Alpine Rd.
Stockton, CA 95212

Established in 1990 in CA.
Donors: Dean A. Cortopassi; Joan A. Cortopassi; California Italian-American Cultural Institute, Inc.; UC Davis Foundation; Bank of Stockton.
Foundation type: Operating foundation.
Financial data (yr. ended 12/31/05): Assets, $18,568,413 (M); gifts received, $345,086; expenditures, $1,295,529; qualifying distributions, $1,270,077; giving activities include $1,212,782 for 76 grants (high: $170,000; low: $250).
Fields of interest: Performing arts; Performing arts, orchestra (symphony); Historic preservation/historical societies; Arts; Secondary school/education; Education, reading; Education; Environment, natural resources; Health organizations; Human services; Children/youth, services; Residential/custodial care, hospices; Federated giving programs.
Type of support: Scholarship funds.
Limitations: Applications not accepted. Giving primarily in Stockton, CA.
Application information: Unsolicited requests for funds not accepted.
Officers: Dean A. Cortopassi, Pres.; Donald Lenz, Secy.-Treas.
Director: Joan A. Cortopassi.
EIN: 680232655

420
Cortopassi Institute ◇
11292 N. Alpine Rd.
Stockton, CA 95212

Established in 2002 in CA.
Donors: Dean A. Cortopassi; Joan A. Cortopassi.
Foundation type: Independent foundation.
Financial data (yr. ended 12/31/05): Assets, $35,547,859 (M); gifts received, $1,985,039; expenditures, $1,338,126; qualifying distributions, $1,317,153; giving activities include $1,132,950 for 25 grants (high: $300,000; low: $2,000).
Purpose and activities: Giving primarily for school reform and public interest law.
Fields of interest: Elementary/secondary school reform; Legal services, public interest law.
Type of support: General/operating support.
Limitations: Applications not accepted. Giving on a national basis. No grants to individuals.
Application information: Contributes only to pre-selected organizations.
Officers and Trustees:* Dean A. Cortopassi, Pres.; Donald G. Lenz,* Secy.-Treas.; Gerald Barton; Jeffrey Colombini; Joan A. Cortopassi; Thomas Cortopassi; Kevin Huber.
EIN: 030412489

421
Cotsen Family Foundation ◇
12100 Wilshire Blvd., Ste. 905
Los Angeles, CA 90025-7100

Established in 1984 in CA.
Donor: Lloyd Cotsen.
Foundation type: Independent foundation.

Financial data (yr. ended 6/30/05): Assets, $83,638,209 (M); expenditures, $3,753,990; qualifying distributions, $3,753,990; giving activities include $2,186,731 for 6 grants (high: $2,066,731; low: $10,000).
Purpose and activities: Giving primarily for higher education, with emphasis on a university library.
Fields of interest: Museums; Arts; Elementary/secondary education; Higher education; Libraries (academic/research); Education.
Limitations: Applications not accepted. Giving on a national basis, with emphasis on Princeton, NJ. No grants to individuals.
Application information: Contributes only to pre-selected organizations.
Officers and Directors:* Lloyd Cotsen,* C.E.O. and Pres.; David Hardacre, V.P., and Secy.; Linda Tansey, C.F.O.; Judy Johnson, Exec. Dir.; Gary Hart; Nancy Ichinaga; Steve Lavine; Barry Munitz.
EIN: 953953038

422
The Countrywide Foundation ◇ ☆
5220 Las Virgenes Rd., M.S. AC-126
Calabasas, CA 91302

Donors: Stanford L. Kurland; J. Grant Couch, Jr.; Countrywide Home Loans, Inc.
Foundation type: Company-sponsored foundation.
Financial data (yr. ended 12/31/05): Assets, $48,507 (M); gifts received, $690,333; expenditures, $693,777; qualifying distributions, $693,777; giving activities include $693,777 for grants.
Limitations: Giving primarily in New York, NY.
Directors: Stanford L. Kurland; Anne D. McCallion; Angelo R. Mozilo; Sandor E. Samuels.
EIN: 954349038

423
S. H. Cowell Foundation ▼
120 Montgomery St., Ste. 2570
San Francisco, CA 94104 (415) 397-0285
Contact: Lise Maisano, Dir. of Grants
FAX: (415) 986-6786; URL: http://www.shcowell.org

Trust established in 1955 in CA.
Donor: S.H. Cowell†.
Foundation type: Independent foundation.
Financial data (yr. ended 12/31/04): Assets, $169,801,309 (M); expenditures, $7,749,358; qualifying distributions, $6,514,480; giving activities include $5,046,104 for 90 grants (high: $325,000; low: $1,000; average: $10,000–$150,000), and $84,144 for 49 employee matching gifts.
Purpose and activities: The goal of the foundation is to improve the quality of life of children and families living in poverty in northern California by making grants that directly support and strengthen children, families, and the neighborhoods where they live. Priority is given to communities where Cowell has made, or could make, place-based complementary grants in Northern California towns and neighborhoods where there is widespread and acute poverty and there are strong working relationships among residents and institutional leaders. The foundation funds efforts to increase a town or neighborhood's capacity to engage and serve its low-income families. These guidelines

apply across all of our program areas: Community Infrastructure including Affordable Housing, Family Resources Centers, K-12 Public Education, Responsive, and Youth Development.

Fields of interest: Education, early childhood education; Vocational education; Education; Housing/shelter; Youth development; Human services; Minorities; Economically disadvantaged.

Type of support: Capital campaigns; Building/renovation; Equipment; Land acquisition; Program development; Seed money; Consulting services; Program-related investments/loans; Employee matching gifts; Matching/challenge support.

Limitations: Giving limited to northern CA. No support for projects restricted to people with specific medical, physical, or health conditions, daycare centers, drug or alcohol abuse programs, environmental or conservation programs, health clinics or other medical service projects, political lobbying, population programs, post-secondary education, projects that are the responsibility of government agencies (except for school districts in the event of emergency funding and budget crises), or sectarian, politically partisan, or religious projects. No grants to individuals, or for general operating support, special events and conferences, books, films, videos, academic or medical research, or capital requests (when less than fifty percent of total funds have been raised).

Publications: Annual report.

Application information: Application form not required.

> *Initial approach:* Visit foundation Web site, then telephone inquiry
> *Copies of proposal:* 1
> *Deadline(s):* None
> *Board meeting date(s):* Bimonthly
> *Final notification:* 3 to 6 months

Officers and Directors:* Ann Alpers,* Pres.; Cora M. Tellez,* V.P.; Fredric C. Nelson,* Secy.; Greg Wendt,* Treas.; Jack W. Chu; Donald D. Roberts; Mary Lee Widener.

Number of staff: 9 full-time professional; 3 full-time support.

EIN: 941392803

Selected grants: The following grants were reported in 2004.

$285,000 to Pajaro Valley Unified School District, Watsonville, CA.

$250,000 to Planned Parenthood Mar Monte, San Jose, CA.

$140,000 to Vallejo Community Consortium, Vallejo, CA. For Fighting Back Partnership.

$137,500 to California Coalition for Rural Housing Project, Sacramento, CA.

$108,400 to Grafton Elementary School, Knights Landing, CA.

$71,000 to Near and Arnolds School of Performing Arts and Cultural Education (SPACE), Ukiah, CA.

$70,000 to Community Housing Development Corporation of North Richmond, Richmond, CA.

$64,255 to University of California, New Teacher Center, Santa Cruz, CA.

$60,000 to California State University Hayward Foundation, Hayward, CA.

$50,465 to Kings Beach Elementary School, Kings Beach, CA.

424
Richard & Jean Coyne Family Foundation ✧
110 Constitution Dr.
Menlo Park, CA 94025-1107 (650) 326-6040
Contact: Jean A. Coyne, Pres.

Established in 1991 in CA.
Donor: Jean A. Coyne.
Foundation type: Independent foundation.
Financial data (yr. ended 12/31/05): Assets, $5,140,325 (M); expenditures, $428,155; qualifying distributions, $424,000; giving activities include $424,000 for 16 grants (high: $50,000; low: $15,000).

Purpose and activities: The foundation funds programs in three areas: 1) college scholarships for students in the design and visual communications fields, 2) programs that help high school students develop portfolios to qualify for admission to art schools, and 3) programs that introduce grade-school children to the fields of design and advertising.

Fields of interest: Arts, multipurpose centers/programs; Arts education; Visual arts; Visual arts, design; Elementary/secondary education; Higher education.

Type of support: Scholarship funds.

Limitations: Giving on a national basis, with some emphasis on CA and New York, NY.

Application information:

> *Initial approach:* Letter
> *Deadline(s):* None

Officers: Jean A. Coyne, Pres.; Patrick S. Coyne, V.P.; Martha R. Coyne, Secy.; Eric P. Coyne, Treas.

Trustee: Arthur N. Inman.

EIN: 770259860

Selected grants: The following grants were reported in 2004.

$50,000 to Art Center College of Design, Pasadena, CA. For scholarships and art supply stipends.

$50,000 to Creatives for Causes, Hopkins, MN. For outreach program.

$30,000 to Visual Arts Foundation, New York, NY. For scholarships.

$25,000 to Cooper-Hewitt Museum, The Smithsonians National Museum of Design, New York, NY. For program support.

$20,000 to Art Directors Club, New York, NY. For career workshops.

$20,000 to California College of the Arts, Oakland, CA. For scholarships.

$20,000 to California Institute of the Arts, Valencia, CA. For scholarships.

$20,000 to Oxbow School, Napa, CA. For scholarships.

$15,400 to Corcoran School of Art, DC. For scholarships.

$15,000 to Light Bringer Project, Pasadena, CA. For program support.

425
The Sid and Jenny Craig Foundation ✧ ☆
P.O. Box 675532
Rancho Santa Fe, CA 92067

Established in 1991 in CA.
Donors: Sid Craig; Jenny Craig.
Foundation type: Independent foundation.
Financial data (yr. ended 12/31/05): Assets, $2,226,533 (M); expenditures, $1,058,605; qualifying distributions, $1,040,000; giving activities include $1,040,000 for grants.

Purpose and activities: Support primarily for educational programs for disadvantaged children.

Fields of interest: Education; Veterinary medicine; Disasters, 9/11/01; Children, services; Economically disadvantaged.

Limitations: Applications not accepted. Giving primarily in CA. No grants to individuals.

Application information: Contributes only to pre-selected organizations.

Officers: Sid Craig, C.E.O.; Jenny Craig, V.P. and C.F.O.; Marvin Sears, Secy.

EIN: 954344841

426
Crail-Johnson Foundation
222 W. 6th St., Ste. 1010
San Pedro, CA 90731 (310) 519-7413
Contact: Pat Christopher, Prog. Off.
FAX: (310) 519-7221;
E-mail: Pat-Christopher@crail-johnson.org;
Additional E-mail: carolyn-johnson@crail-johnson.org; URL: http://www.crail-johnson.org

Established in 1987 in CA.
Donors: Jerry L. Johnson†; Robert Johnson†; Robert Johnson Charitable Lead Trust.
Foundation type: Independent foundation.
Financial data (yr. ended 12/31/04): Assets, $17,859,235 (M); gifts received, $3,058,403; expenditures, $2,256,156; qualifying distributions, $2,201,156; giving activities include $2,100,985 for 117 grants (high: $250,000; low: $50).

Purpose and activities: The foundation promotes the well-being of children in need through the effective application of human and financial resources.

Fields of interest: Education, early childhood education; Child development, education; Elementary school/education; Education, reading; Health care; Children/youth, services; Child development, services; Family services; Science; Mathematics.

Type of support: General/operating support; Capital campaigns; Equipment; Emergency funds; Program development; Seed money; Curriculum development; Employee matching gifts; Matching/challenge support.

Limitations: Giving primarily in Los Angeles County and the greater Los Angeles, CA, area. Generally no support for athletic events, religious programs and causes, political causes, or for university level education. No grants to individuals, or for research.

Publications: Annual report (including application guidelines); Financial statement; Grants list.

Application information: See foundation Web site for annual report (including application guidelines and grants list). Please do not send unsolicited proposals with extensive attachments and/or videotapes. Application form required.

> *Initial approach:* Letter of inquiry (no more than 3 pages)
> *Copies of proposal:* 1
> *Deadline(s):* Varies
> *Board meeting date(s):* Quarterly

Officers and Directors:* Eric C. Johnson,* Chair.; Alan C. Johnson,* Pres.; Carolyn E. Johnson,* V.P.; Ann L. Johnson,* V.P.; Craig C. Johnson,* V.P.; Jack S. Peterson,* Secy.; S.L. Hutchison,* C.F.O.; John Berwald.

Number of staff: 1 full-time professional.

EIN: 330247161

Selected grants: The following grants were reported in 2004.

$300,000 to Boys and Girls Club. 2 grants: $100,000, $200,000
$250,000 to Accelerated School, Los Angeles, CA.
$150,000 to Boys and Girls Club of San Pedro, San Pedro, CA.
$50,000 to I Have A Dream Foundation, New York, NY.
$43,760 to Dramatic Results, Long Beach, CA.
$30,000 to Rainbow Services, San Pedro, CA.
$30,000 to YMCA.
$25,000 to Educating Young Minds, Los Angeles, CA.
$20,100 to Assistance League of Long Beach, Long Beach, CA.

427
Crawford Family Foundation ◇
520 Georgian Rd.
La Canada, CA   91011

Established in 1999 in CA.
Donors: Gordon Crawford; Dona Crawford.
Foundation type: Independent foundation.
Financial data (yr. ended 12/31/05): Assets, $3,657,316 (M); gifts received, $1,104,815; expenditures, $862,145; qualifying distributions, $856,938; giving activities include $856,938 for 62 grants (high: $150,000; low: $300; average: $1,000–$50,000).
Purpose and activities: Giving primarily for youth services, and health associations.
Fields of interest: Media, radio; Education; Environment, natural resources; Health organizations, association; Youth development; Human services; Christian agencies & churches.
Limitations: Applications not accepted. Giving primarily in CA. No grants to individuals.
Application information: Contributes only to pre-selected organizations.
Officers: Gordon Crawford, Pres.; Dona Crawford, V.P.; Orsi Z. Crawford, Secy.; Jeffrey G. Crawford, Treas.
EIN: 954737866

428
The Crean Foundation ◇
2300 Mesa Dr.
Newport Beach, CA   92660
Contact: Marc S. Goldin, C.F.O.

Established in 1981 in CA.
Donors: John C. Crean; Donna S. Crean.
Foundation type: Independent foundation.
Financial data (yr. ended 12/31/05): Assets, $83,875,256 (M); expenditures, $3,336,040; qualifying distributions, $2,814,440; giving activities include $2,814,440 for 34 grants (high: $2,000,000; low: $5,000; average: $10,000–$50,000).
Purpose and activities: Support primarily for higher education, hospitals, and human services.
Fields of interest: Higher education; Hospitals (general); Human services.
Type of support: General/operating support.
Limitations: Applications not accepted. Giving primarily in CA. No grants to individuals.
Application information: Contributes only to pre-selected organizations.

Officers: John C. Crean, Pres.; Andrew Crean, V.P.; Donna S. Crean, Secy.; Marc S. Goldin, C.F.O.
EIN: 953676334

429
The Mary A. Crocker Trust ◇
233 Post St., 2nd Fl.
San Francisco, CA   94108   (415) 982-0138
Contact: Barbaree Jernigan, Admin.

Trust established in 1889 in CA.
Donor: Mary A. Crocker‡.
Foundation type: Independent foundation.
Financial data (yr. ended 12/31/05): Assets, $13,748,277 (M); expenditures, $770,891; qualifying distributions, $719,763; giving activities include $572,500 for 41 grants (high: $50,000; low: $1,000).
Purpose and activities: Giving primarily for precollegiate education, forestry, the environment, and community relations.
Fields of interest: Elementary school/education; Secondary school/education; Education; Environment, natural resources; Environment; Agriculture; Youth, services; Voluntarism promotion.
Type of support: Program development; Seed money; Matching/challenge support.
Limitations: Giving primarily in the San Francisco Bay Area, CA. No support for sectarian purposes. No grants to individuals, or for operating budgets, continuing support, annual campaigns, deficit financing, building or endowment funds, capital campaigns, land acquisition, scholarships, fellowships, or conferences; no loans.
Publications: Application guidelines; Grants list; Program policy statement.
Application information: Application form required.
Initial approach: Letter
Copies of proposal: 1
Deadline(s): None
Board meeting date(s): 2 to 3 times a year
Final notification: 3 months
Officer: Tania W. Stepanian, Chair.
Trustees: Elizabeth Atcheson; Charles Crocker; Frederick W. Whitridge; Abigail H. Wilder.
Number of staff: 1 full-time professional.
EIN: 946051917

430
Crockett Community Foundation ◇
P.O. Box 155
Crockett, CA   94525   (510) 787-9708
Contact: Jeanne Owens

Established in 1994 in CA.
Foundation type: Community foundation.
Financial data (yr. ended 12/31/04): Assets, $2,555,660 (M); gifts received, $761,913; expenditures, $719,422; giving activities include $658,671 for 22 grants (high: $151,997; low: $55).
Purpose and activities: Giving to promote and improve the quality of life in Crockett, CA.
Fields of interest: Libraries/library science; Education; Environment; Safety/disasters, public policy; Recreation, community facilities; Youth development, adult & child programs; Aging, centers/services; Community development.
Type of support: General/operating support; Capital campaigns; Building/renovation; Equipment; Land acquisition; Program development; Seed money; Consulting services.

Limitations: Giving limited to Crockett, CA. No grants to individuals.
Application information: Application form required.
Initial approach: Letter
Copies of proposal: 8
Deadline(s): Mar. 31 and Sept. 30
Board meeting date(s): 1st Thurs. of each month
Final notification: June and Dec.
Officers and Directors:* Mervyn Silverman,* Chair.; Marybeth Carter, Pres.; Gerald Epperson, V.P.; Margaret Lopez Faria,* Secy.; Bud Burlison,* Treas.; Jay Gunkelman; Mary Wais.
EIN: 680348673

431
Croul Family Foundation ◇
1901 Bayadere Terr.
Corona del Mar, CA   92625
Contact: Spencer Behr Croul, Secy.
FAX: (949) 548-1026;
E-mail: Foundation@croul.com

Established in 1997 in CA.
Donor: John V. Croul.
Foundation type: Independent foundation.
Financial data (yr. ended 12/31/04): Assets, $17,212,660 (M); gifts received, $531,500; expenditures, $1,535,645; qualifying distributions, $1,500,433; giving activities include $1,329,148 for 85 grants (high: $595,000; low: $1,000), and $30,652 for 6 grants to individuals (high: $7,404; low: $3,650).
Purpose and activities: Dedicated to giving financial aid to organizations that assist people who have low incomes and who are economically disadvantaged.
Fields of interest: Education; Human services; Economically disadvantaged; Homeless.
Limitations: Giving limited to Los Angeles and Orange counties, CA.
Publications: Application guidelines; Program policy statement.
Officers and Trustees:* John V. Croul,* C.E.O.; Spencer Behr Croul,* Secy.; John Bradford Croul,* C.F.O.
Number of staff: 1 part-time support.
EIN: 330749543
Selected grants: The following grants were reported in 2003.
$173,200 to Claremont McKenna College, Claremont, CA.
$20,000 to Union Rescue Mission, Los Angeles, CA.
$10,000 to Goodwill Industries of Orange County, Santa Ana, CA.
$10,000 to Los Angeles Mission, Los Angeles, CA.
$10,000 to Someone Cares Soup Kitchen, Irvine, CA.
$5,000 to Adoption Guild of Southern Orange County, Newport Beach, CA.
$5,000 to Orange County Rescue Mission, Tustin, CA.
$5,000 to Second Harvest Food Bank, Los Angeles, CA.
$3,000 to A Place Called Home, Los Angeles, CA.
$2,000 to Beyond Shelter, Los Angeles, CA.

432
Roy E. Crummer Foundation ◇
130 Newport Center Dr., Ste. 140-B
Newport Beach, CA   92660-6923
(949) 644-4702

Established in 1964 in NV.
Donor: Jean Crummer Coburn.
Foundation type: Independent foundation.
Financial data (yr. ended 12/31/05): Assets, $6,551,478 (M); expenditures, $418,751; qualifying distributions, $328,000; giving activities include $328,000 for 115 grants (high: $25,000; low: $500).
Fields of interest: Arts; Secondary school/education; Higher education; Animal welfare; Health care; Health organizations, association; Human services.
Limitations: Giving primarily in CA. No grants to individuals.
Application information:
Initial approach: Letter
Deadline(s): Oct. 31
Officers and Trustees:* Roy E. Crummer,* Pres.; Donn J. Crummer,* V.P.; Margarite Brown,* Secy.-Treas.; Ian F. Gow; Lee D. Strom.
EIN: 886004422

433

John & Geraldine Cusenza Family Foundation ✧

578 W. Portrero Rd.
Hidden Valley, CA   91361-5013
Application address: 3835R E. Thousand Oaks Blvd., Ste. 257, Westlake Village, CA 91362

Established in 1995.
Donors: Geraldine Cusenza; John Cusenza.
Foundation type: Independent foundation.
Financial data (yr. ended 11/30/05): Assets, $7,402,044 (M); expenditures, $439,414; qualifying distributions, $350,475; giving activities include $350,475 for grants.
Purpose and activities: Giving primarily for children services.
Fields of interest: Hospitals (general); Cancer research; Breast cancer research; Kidney research; Human services; Children/youth, services; Roman Catholic agencies & churches.
Limitations: Giving primarily in CA. No grants to individuals.
Application information:
Initial approach: Letter
Deadline(s): None
Officers: Geraldine Cusenza, Pres.; John Cusenza, C.F.O.
EIN: 954556555
Selected grants: The following grants were reported in 2004.
$236,000 to Homeboy Industries, Los Angeles, CA. 3 grants: $5,000, $10,000, $221,000
$3,000 to Pace e Bene, Las Vegas, NV.
$1,000 to AIDS Service Center, Pasadena, CA.
$1,000 to National Italian American Foundation, DC.
$229 to K C E T Community Television of Southern California, Los Angeles, CA.

434

D & DF Foundation ▼ ✧

1 Maritime Plz., Ste. 1400
San Francisco, CA   94111

Established in 1986.
Donors: Donald G. Fisher; Doris F. Fisher.
Foundation type: Independent foundation.
Financial data (yr. ended 6/30/05): Assets, $83,073,615 (M); gifts received, $12,780,001;

expenditures, $14,873,296; qualifying distributions, $14,033,235; giving activities include $14,033,200 for 149 grants (high: $2,500,000; low: $500; average: $10,000–$500,000).
Purpose and activities: Giving primarily for education and art museums.
Fields of interest: Museums (art); Arts; Higher education; Education; Health organizations, association.
Limitations: Applications not accepted. Giving primarily in San Francisco, CA. No grants to individuals.
Application information: Contributes only to pre-selected organizations.
Officer: Jane Spray, Treas.
Trustees: Donald G. Fisher; Doris F. Fisher.
EIN: 943022002
Selected grants: The following grants were reported in 2005.
$2,500,000 to University of California at San Francisco Foundation, San Francisco, CA. For general support.
$2,000,000 to Stanford University, Stanford, CA. For Cancer Center.
$2,000,000 to Stanford University Hospital, Stanford, CA. For general support.
$1,000,000 to Princeton University, Princeton, NJ. For general support.
$537,940 to Boys and Girls Clubs of America, Atlanta, GA. For general support.
$500,000 to Music Concourse Community Partnership, San Francisco, CA. For general support.
$235,000 to San Francisco Symphony, San Francisco, CA. For general support.
$50,000 to Museum of Modern Art, New York, NY. For general support.
$30,000 to San Francisco Day School, San Francisco, CA. For general support.
$15,000 to San Francisco Free Clinic, San Francisco, CA. For general support.

435

A. M. Dachs Foundation

P.O. Box 193809
San Francisco, CA   94119-3809

Established in 1991 in CA.
Donor: Alan M. Dachs.
Foundation type: Independent foundation.
Financial data (yr. ended 12/31/05): Assets, $1,200,198 (M); gifts received, $1,903,150; expenditures, $724,151; qualifying distributions, $724,006; giving activities include $717,500 for 13 grants (high: $200,000; low: $2,500).
Fields of interest: Secondary school/education; Higher education, university; Human services.
Type of support: Capital campaigns; Building/renovation; Endowments; Scholarship funds.
Limitations: Applications not accepted. Giving in the U.S., primarily in CA and CT. No grants to individuals.
Application information: Contributes only to pre-selected organizations.
Officers and Directors:* Alan M. Dachs,* Pres.; Lauren B. Dachs,* V.P.; Nancy S. Hair, Secy.-Treas.; Deborah Duncan.
EIN: 943144688

436

Edward J. Daly Foundation ✧

c/o Michael Helms
111 Pine St., 18th Fl.
San Francisco, CA   94111

Established in 1962.
Donor: Edward J. Daly‡.
Foundation type: Independent foundation.
Financial data (yr. ended 12/31/03): Assets, $6,042,539 (M); expenditures, $383,699; qualifying distributions, $376,588; giving activities include $350,000 for 50 grants (high: $200,000; low: $500).
Purpose and activities: Giving primarily for glaucoma research, as well as for the arts, and human services.
Fields of interest: Arts; Education; Health care; Medical research, institute; Children/youth, services; Protestant agencies & churches.
Limitations: Applications not accepted. Giving primarily in CA, with emphasis on San Francisco. No grants to individuals.
Application information: Contributes only to pre-selected organizations.
Officers: June Berhendt, Pres.; Michael Helms, Secy.
EIN: 946109262
Selected grants: The following grants were reported in 2003.
$200,000 to Glaucoma Research and Education Group, San Francisco, CA.
$5,000 to Asian Art Museum Foundation of San Francisco, San Francisco, CA.
$5,000 to San Francisco Conservatory of Music, San Francisco, CA.
$3,000 to Edgewood Center for Children and Families, San Francisco, CA.
$3,000 to Larkin Street Youth Services, San Francisco, CA.
$2,500 to Project Open Hand, San Francisco, CA.
$2,000 to Self-Help for the Elderly, San Francisco, CA.
$1,000 to San Francisco Ballet, San Francisco, CA.
$1,000 to San Francisco Opera Guild, San Francisco, CA.
$1,000 to San Francisco Symphony, San Francisco, CA.

437

Robert and Carole Daly Foundation ✧

(formerly Robert Daly Foundation)
9460 Wilshire Blvd., Ste. 600
Beverly Hills, CA   90212

Established in 1987 in CA.
Donor: Robert Daly.
Foundation type: Independent foundation.
Financial data (yr. ended 12/31/04): Assets, $3,793,933 (M); expenditures, $666,069; qualifying distributions, $641,463; giving activities include $641,463 for 85 grants (high: $50,000; low: $250).
Purpose and activities: Giving primarily for the arts, as well as for education, health care, including children's health, and human services.
Fields of interest: Media, film/video; Arts; Higher education; Education; Environment; Hospitals (general); Health care; Health organizations, association; Cancer research; AIDS research; Diabetes research; Human services; Children/youth, services.

Type of support: General/operating support; Capital campaigns.
Limitations: Applications not accepted. Giving primarily in CA, with emphasis on Los Angeles, and New York, NY. No grants to individuals.
Application information: Contributes only to pre-selected organizations.
Trustee: Robert A. Daly.
EIN: 956875322
Selected grants: The following grants were reported in 2003.
$200,000 to American Film Institute, Los Angeles, CA. For general support.
$25,000 to New York University, Tisch School of the Arts, New York, NY. For general support.
$10,200 to Crossroads School for Arts and Sciences, Santa Monica, CA. For general support.
$10,000 to Motion Picture and Television Fund, Woodland Hills, CA. For general support.
$5,000 to Entertainment Industry Foundation, Los Angeles, CA. For general support.
$5,000 to Geffen Playhouse, Los Angeles, CA. For general support.
$5,000 to HELP Group: Health, Education, Learning and Psychology, Sherman Oaks, CA. For general support.
$2,500 to American Museum of the Moving Image, Astoria, NY. For general support.
$1,000 to Para Los Ninos, Los Angeles, CA. For general support.
$500 to Prostate Cancer Research Institute, Los Angeles, CA. For general support.

438
Danford Foundation ◇
P.O. Box 4609
Foster City, CA   94404-0609   (650) 349-4055
Contact: Katherine F. Fisher, Secy.

Established in CA in 1982.
Donor: Gladys B. Danford†.
Foundation type: Independent foundation.
Financial data (yr. ended 6/30/05): Assets, $17,585,336 (M); expenditures, $827,058; qualifying distributions, $816,808; giving activities include $696,100 for 77 grants (high: $45,000; low: $500).
Purpose and activities: Giving primarily for health associations and medical research, children, youth, and social services, particularly for food, housing, job training, services for the homeless, and substance abuse programs.
Fields of interest: Performing arts; Arts; Elementary/secondary education; Higher education; Libraries/library science; Education; Animal welfare; Hospitals (general); Health organizations, association; Eye diseases; Nerve, muscle & bone diseases; Health organizations; Medical research, association; Medical research, institute; Human services; Children/youth, services; Family services; Homeless, human services; Roman Catholic agencies & churches; Economically disadvantaged.
Type of support: Scholarship funds; Research; Equipment; Continuing support.
Limitations: Giving primarily in the San Francisco Bay Area, CA. No support for political organizations. No grants to individuals.
Publications: Annual report.
Application information: Application form not required.
Initial approach: Letter
Copies of proposal: 1

Deadline(s): None
Board meeting date(s): Every 4 months
Final notification: 30 days
Officers: Frank L. Hannig, Pres.; Betty Shehi, V.P.; Katherine F. Fisher, Secy.; George A. Fisher, C.F.O. and Treas.
EIN: 942819322
Selected grants: The following grants were reported in 2004.
$36,000 to Guide Dogs for the Blind, San Rafael, CA. For training of dog team.
$28,500 to Leukemia & Lymphoma Society, San Francisco, CA. For research.
$22,000 to Sequoia Hospital Foundation, Redwood City, CA. For medical equipment.
$20,000 to Stanford University, School of Medicine, Stanford, CA. For research.
$11,000 to Canine Companions for Independence, Santa Rosa, CA. For equipment purchase.
$10,000 to Special Olympics Northern California, Pleasant Hill, CA. For purchase of sports equipment.
$5,000 to Multiple Sclerosis Society, National, Oakland, CA. For research.
$5,000 to Ronald McDonald House at Childrens Hospital, Palo Alto, CA. Toward purchase of furniture.
$5,000 to Young Latino Leaders, Redwood City, CA. For youth programs.
$2,500 to Cystic Fibrosis Foundation, Oakland, CA. For research.

439
Danvera Foundation ◇
4906 Proctor Ave.
Walnut Creek, CA   94596-4137

Established in 2001 in CA.
Donor: Patrick J. Morrin.
Foundation type: Independent foundation.
Financial data (yr. ended 12/31/05): Assets, $6,961,838 (M); expenditures, $434,681; qualifying distributions, $406,530; giving activities include $404,000 for 8 grants (high: $225,000; low: $5,000; average: $25,000–$50,000).
Fields of interest: Arts; Higher education; Education.
Limitations: Applications not accepted. Giving primarily in CA and CO. No grants to individuals.
Application information: Contributes only to pre-selected organizations.
Officers: Patrick J. Morrin, Pres.; Janice Jagelski, Secy.-Treas.
EIN: 752979435
Selected grants: The following grants were reported in 2003.
$75,000 to University of San Diego, San Diego, CA. 2 grants: $25,000 (For scholarship program), $50,000 (For science lab in Shiley Science Center).
$25,000 to University of California at Santa Barbara Foundation, Santa Barbara, CA. For Schuyler Lecture Fund.
$20,000 to Grand County Historical Association, Hot Sulphur Springs, CO. For building support.
$20,000 to Music Center of Los Angeles County, Los Angeles, CA. For Disney Hall.
$5,000 to Womens Building, San Francisco, CA. For leadership program.

440
Hugh and Hazel Darling Foundation
520 S. Grand Ave., 7th Fl.
Los Angeles, CA   90071   (213) 683-5200
Contact: Richard L. Stack, Tr.

Established in 1988 in CA.
Donors: Hugh Darling†; Hazel Darling†.
Foundation type: Independent foundation.
Financial data (yr. ended 12/31/05): Assets, $30,121,366 (M); expenditures, $2,049,872; qualifying distributions, $1,929,642; giving activities include $1,800,000 for 40 grants (high: $300,000; low: $1,000).
Purpose and activities: Giving for support of education in California, with emphasis on legal education.
Fields of interest: Law school/education; Education.
Type of support: Capital campaigns; Building/ renovation; Equipment; Endowments; Scholarship funds; Matching/challenge support.
Limitations: Giving limited to CA. No grants to individuals.
Application information: Application form not required.
Initial approach: Letter
Copies of proposal: 1
Deadline(s): None
Board meeting date(s): Varies
Final notification: Varies
Trustee: Richard L. Stack.
Number of staff: 1 part-time support.
EIN: 956874901
Selected grants: The following grants were reported in 2003.
$250,000 to Azusa Pacific University, Azusa, CA. For building construction.
$250,000 to Chapman University, School of Law, Orange, CA. For library books.
$250,000 to Loyola Marymount University, School of Law, Los Angeles, CA. For building renovation.
$200,000 to University of San Francisco, San Francisco, CA. For building renovation.
$200,000 to University of Southern California, School of Law, Los Angeles, CA. For library renovation.
$100,000 to Pepperdine University, Malibu, CA. For scholarships.
$75,000 to University of West Los Angeles School of Law and Paralegal Studies, Inglewood, CA. For paralegal program.
$50,000 to Hope International University, Fullerton, CA. For building construction.
$50,000 to Mount Saint Marys College, Los Angeles, CA. For classroom renovation.
$50,000 to Pacific Research Institute for Public Policy, San Francisco, CA.

441
Dart-L Foundation ◇
4032 Wilshire Blvd., 6th Fl.
Los Angeles, CA   90010

Established in 1998 in CA.
Donors: Aaron Friedman; Ira David Friedman; Jacob Friedman; Lea Friedman; Ruchel Friedman Klavan; Libby Friedman Lehmann; Tzippy Friedman Notis.
Foundation type: Independent foundation.
Financial data (yr. ended 12/31/04): Assets, $64,240,160 (M); gifts received, $15,000,000; expenditures, $3,010,466; qualifying distributions,

$2,619,182; giving activities include $2,617,397 for 149 grants (high: $1,000,000; low: $54).

Purpose and activities: Giving primarily to Jewish agencies, temples and schools.

Fields of interest: Education; Jewish agencies & temples.

Limitations: Applications not accepted. Giving primarily in CA, with emphasis on Los Angeles, and New York, with emphasis on Brooklyn. No grants to individuals.

Application information: Contributes only to pre-selected organizations.

Officers and Directors:* Jacob Friedman, Pres.; Lea Friedman, V.P.; Ira David Friedman,* C.F.O; Aaron Friedman; Ruchel Friedman Klavan; Libby Friedman Lehmann; Tzippy Friedman Notis.

EIN: 954701699

Selected grants: The following grants were reported in 2003.

$500,000 to Yeshiva Rabbi Solomon Kluger, Brooklyn, NY.

$101,000 to Mosdos Spinka International, Brooklyn, NY.

$100,000 to Mesivta Kol Yaakov, New York, NY.

$100,000 to Notzer Chesed, New York, NY.

$3,000 to Bais Yaakov School for Girls, Los Angeles, CA.

$1,800 to Congregation Kehilas Yaakov, Los Angeles, CA.

$1,800 to Jewish Family Service of Los Angeles, Los Angeles, CA.

$1,000 to Beth Medrash Govoha, Brooklyn, NY.

$500 to Tomchei Shabbos of Los Angeles, Los Angeles, CA.

$50 to Yeshivat Hanegev, New York, NY.

442

The David Family Foundation, Inc. ✧

10960 Wilshire Blvd., Ste. 2150
Los Angeles, CA 90024

Established in 1998 in CA.

Donors: Larry David; Laurie David.

Foundation type: Independent foundation.

Financial data (yr. ended 12/31/05): Assets, $9,445 (M); gifts received, $1,197,000; expenditures, $1,223,597; qualifying distributions, $1,024,124; giving activities include $1,024,124 for 24 grants (high: $450,000; low: $500).

Purpose and activities: Giving for environmental conservation, the arts, education and youth services.

Fields of interest: Arts; Education; Environment; Hospitals (general); Children/youth, services.

Limitations: Applications not accepted. Giving primarily in CA; some funding also in MA. No grants to individuals.

Publications: Annual report.

Application information: Contributes only to pre-selected organizations.

Officers: Laurie David, Pres.; Larry David, Secy.; Matt Lichtenberg, C.F.O.

EIN: 954675258

443

The Ruth and Leo David Foundation ✧ ☆

2222 E. 17th St.
Santa Ana, CA 92705

Established in 2004 in CA.

Donor: Leo David.

Foundation type: Independent foundation.

Financial data (yr. ended 12/31/05): Assets, $343,224 (M); gifts received, $750,000; expenditures, $510,035; qualifying distributions, $506,400; giving activities include $506,400 for 2 grants (high: $500,000; low: $6,400).

Fields of interest: Performing arts, music; Jewish agencies & temples.

International interests: Israel.

Limitations: Applications not accepted. Giving primarily in CA. No grants to individuals.

Application information: Contributes only to pre-selected organizations.

Directors: Leo David; Ruth David.

EIN: 201199793

444

The Davidow Charitable Fund ✧

(formerly The Diana and Robert Davidow Foundation)

11601 Wilshire Blvd., Ste. 1820
Los Angeles, CA 90025

Established in 1986 in CA.

Donors: Robert A. Davidow; Diana R. Davidow.

Foundation type: Independent foundation.

Financial data (yr. ended 10/31/05): Assets, $7,423,593 (M); gifts received, $139,128; expenditures, $579,290; qualifying distributions, $545,185; giving activities include $531,475 for 146 grants (high: $75,000; low: $100).

Purpose and activities: Giving primarily for Jewish organizations, as well as for education, health associations, and children, youth and social services.

Fields of interest: Higher education; Education; Hospitals (general); Health organizations, association; Cancer; Cancer research; Human services; Jewish federated giving programs; Jewish agencies & temples.

Limitations: Applications not accepted. Giving primarily in CA and NY. No grants to individuals.

Application information: Contributes only to pre-selected organizations.

Officers: Robert A. Davidow, C.E.O. and Pres.; Diana R. Davidow, Secy. and C.F.O.

EIN: 330210307

Selected grants: The following grants were reported in 2005.

$75,000 to John Wayne Cancer Institute, Santa Monica, CA.

$25,000 to American Red Cross.

$10,000 to Cedars-Sinai Medical Center, Los Angeles, CA.

$10,000 to Cystic Fibrosis Foundation, Bethesda, MD.

$10,000 to Fulfillment Fund, Los Angeles, CA.

$10,000 to New School for Child Development, Van Nuys, CA.

$2,000 to American Friends of the Hebrew University, New York, NY.

$1,000 to Venice Family Clinic, Venice, CA.

$500 to American Heart Association, Dallas, TX.

$500 to Childhelp USA, Scottsdale, AZ.

445

The Davidson Family Foundation ✧

255 W. Julian St., Ste. 200
San Jose, CA 95110-2406

Established in 1992 in CA.

Donors: Charles W. Davidson; Anita Davidson.

Foundation type: Independent foundation.

Financial data (yr. ended 10/31/05): Assets, $15,837,333 (M); gifts received, $608,454; expenditures, $716,980; qualifying distributions, $696,548; giving activities include $695,485 for 75 grants (high: $165,000; low: $100).

Purpose and activities: Giving primarily to community services including a YMCA; funding also for education and the arts.

Fields of interest: Museums (specialized); Performing arts; Arts; Elementary/secondary education; Higher education; Engineering school/education; Education; Animal welfare; Health organizations, association; Medical research, association; Medical research, institute; Recreation; Human services; YM/YWCAs & YM/YWHAs; Federated giving programs.

Type of support: Annual campaigns; Scholarship funds; Research.

Limitations: Applications not accepted. Giving primarily in CA, with emphasis on San Jose. No grants to individuals.

Application information: Contributes only to pre-selected organizations.

Officers: Charles W. Davidson, Pres.; Gloria K. Chiang, V.P.; Patricia J. Propolanis, Secy.

EIN: 770325599

Selected grants: The following grants were reported in 2004.

$225,330 to San Jose State University, San Jose, CA. 2 grants: $33,980, $191,350 to College of Engineering

$150,150 to YWCA of Silicon Valley, San Jose, CA.

$50,000 to San Juan Bautista Child Development Center, San Jose, CA.

$25,000 to Via Rehabilitation Services, Santa Clara, CA.

$10,000 to Across the Bridge Foundation, Downtown College Preparatory, San Jose, CA.

$10,000 to American Bobsled Club, Salt Lake City, UT.

$10,000 to HOPE Rehabilitation Services, Santa Clara, CA.

$10,000 to San Jose Stage Company, San Jose, CA.

$8,000 to San Jose Conservation Corps and Charter School, San Jose, CA.

446

Louise M. Davies Foundation ✧

c/o Northern Trust of California, N.A.
180 Montgomery St., Ste. 1616
San Francisco, CA 94104

Established in 1974 in CA.

Donor: Louise M. Davies.

Foundation type: Independent foundation.

Financial data (yr. ended 12/31/05): Assets, $24,434,463 (M); expenditures, $1,375,479; qualifying distributions, $1,238,818; giving activities include $1,171,000 for 52 grants.

Purpose and activities: Giving primarily for Roman Catholic education as well as for the arts, with emphasis on the performing arts.

Fields of interest: Museums (art); Performing arts, orchestra (symphony); Performing arts, opera; Elementary/secondary education; Higher education; Education; Human services; Youth, services; Roman Catholic agencies & churches.

Type of support: General/operating support; Capital campaigns; Endowments; Scholarship funds.

Limitations: Applications not accepted. Giving primarily in San Francisco, CA. No grants to individuals.

Application information: Contributes only to pre-selected organizations.
Officers and Directors:* Philip Hudner, Jr.,* Pres.; Ann C. Matthews, Secy.-Treas.
EIN: 237359841
Selected grants: The following grants were reported in 2003.
$100,000 to Basic Fund, San Francisco, CA.
$75,000 to San Francisco Opera, San Francisco, CA.
$50,000 to California Historical Society, San Francisco, CA.
$50,000 to Marin Catholic High School, Kentfield, CA.
$50,000 to San Francisco Symphony, San Francisco, CA. For Louise M. Davies Guest Conductor Fund.
$35,000 to Thomas Aquinas School, Tahoe City, CA.
$30,000 to Merola Opera Program, San Francisco, CA. For Training Program.
$25,000 to Saint Martin de Porres School.
$25,000 to Trinity Grammar and Prep, Sacramento, CA.
$10,000 to Larkin Street Youth Services, San Francisco, CA.

447
Willametta K. Day Foundation ✧

c/o Oakmont Corp.
865 S. Figueroa St., Ste. 700
Los Angeles, CA 90017 (213) 891-6300
Contact: Jonathan D. Jaffrey, Secy.
Mailing address: P.O. Box 71289, Los Angeles, CA 90071

Trust established in 1954 in CA.
Donor: Willametta K. Day†.
Foundation type: Independent foundation.
Financial data (yr. ended 12/31/04): Assets, $61,538,682 (M); expenditures, $3,065,602; qualifying distributions, $2,297,205; giving activities include $1,934,276 for 105 grants (high: $333,750; low: $150).
Purpose and activities: Giving primarily for secondary and other education, with emphasis on an all-girls' boarding and day school in Glencoe, MD, as well as for the arts and cultural organizations, and health and human services.
Fields of interest: Museums; Arts; Secondary school/education; Higher education; Education; Hospitals (general); Health organizations, association; Human services; Jewish federated giving programs; Christian agencies & churches; Jewish agencies & temples.
Type of support: General/operating support.
Limitations: Giving on a national basis, with emphasis on CA, Glencoe, MD, and OR. No grants to individuals.
Publications: Financial statement.
Application information: Application form not required.
   Initial approach: Letter
   Copies of proposal: 1
   Deadline(s): Nov.
   Board meeting date(s): Annually
Officers: Robert A. Day, Jr., Chair.; Howard M. Day, Pres.; Jonathan D. Jaffrey, V.P. and Secy.; Tammis A. Day, V.P.; Theodore J. Day, V.P.
Trustees: Dorothy W. Day; Howard M. Day; Thomas Joseph Deegan-Day; Lucinda A. Fournier.
Number of staff: 2 full-time professional; 3 full-time support.
EIN: 956092476

Selected grants: The following grants were reported in 2003.
$1,125,000 to Oldfields School, Glencoe, MD.
$225,000 to Linfield College, McMinnville, OR.
$40,000 to University of Southern California, Los Angeles, CA.
$12,650 to Los Angeles Opera Company, Los Angeles, CA.
$7,500 to Elton John AIDS Foundation, Beverly Hills, CA.
$7,200 to Oregon State University, Corvallis, OR.
$3,000 to Stanford University, Law School, Stanford, CA.
$2,000 to Whittier College, Whittier, CA.
$1,500 to Midnight Mission, Los Angeles, CA.
$1,000 to Santa Clara University, Santa Clara, CA.

448
Marie C. de Dampierre Memorial Foundation

(formerly Christian de Guigne Memorial Foundation)
c/o O'Donnell, Waiss, Wall & Meschke
100 Broadway, 3rd Fl.
San Francisco, CA 94111
Contact: John A. Meschke, Secy.-Treas.

Established in 1960 in CA.
Foundation type: Independent foundation.
Financial data (yr. ended 12/31/05): Assets, $2,389,457 (M); expenditures, $536,198; qualifying distributions, $477,033; giving activities include $469,281 for 9 grants.
Purpose and activities: Support for higher and secondary education, hospitals, and health agencies; support also for a French medical institution.
Fields of interest: Secondary school/education; Higher education; Hospitals (general); Health care.
Type of support: General/operating support; Scholarship funds.
Limitations: Giving limited to the San Francisco Bay Area, CA. No grants to individuals, or for building funds, fellowships, matching gifts, or special projects; no loans.
Application information: Application form not required.
   Initial approach: Letter
   Copies of proposal: 3
   Deadline(s): Submit proposal any time except Nov. or Dec.; deadline Oct. 31
   Board meeting date(s): Dec.
   Final notification: 1 month
Officers and Directors:* Nicole de Sugny MacDonald,* Pres.; France de Sugny Bark,* V.P.; John A. Meschke,* Secy.-Treas.
EIN: 946076503
Selected grants: The following grants were reported in 2003.
$495,000 to University of San Francisco, San Francisco, CA.
$20,000 to Seton Medical Center, Daly City, CA.
$10,000 to Friendly Place, Oakland, CA.
$10,000 to Morning Star Outreach, Hayward, CA.

449
The Barbara Delano Foundation, Inc. ✧

(formerly The Barbara Gauntlett Foundation, Inc.)
450 Pacific Ave., Ste. 201
San Francisco, CA 94133 (415) 834-1758
Contact: Stephanie Carnow, Prog. Asst.

FAX: (415) 834-1759;
E-mail: bdfoundation@usa.net

Established in 1985 in NY.
Donor: Barbara Gauntlett†.
Foundation type: Independent foundation.
Financial data (yr. ended 12/31/04): Assets, $28,671,615 (M); expenditures, $2,573,487; qualifying distributions, $2,398,014; giving activities include $2,327,000 for 5 grants (high: $2,197,000; low: $5,000).
Purpose and activities: Support for endangered species protection in developing countries.
Fields of interest: Environment, natural resources; Environment, forests; Animals/wildlife, preservation/protection; Animals/wildlife, endangered species.
International interests: Africa; Asia; Developing countries; Global programs; Latin America; Russia.
Type of support: Equipment; Land acquisition; Emergency funds; Program development; Matching/challenge support.
Limitations: Giving for the benefit of developing nations only. No support for private foundations. No grants to individuals, or for research, film projects, conferences, administrative costs, large equipment purchases, for-profit organizations, wildlife sanctuaries, rescue centers or hospitals, or projects not specifically dedicated to wildlife conservation.
Application information: Application guidelines available on foundation Web site; proposals only considered after letter of request. Application form not required.
   Initial approach: Letter, fax or E-mail inquiry of no more than 2 pages
   Copies of proposal: 1
   Deadline(s): Sept. 1
   Board meeting date(s): Nov., Dec.
   Final notification: After board meeting
Officers and Directors:* Suwanna Gauntlett,* Pres.; Christopher C. Angell,* Secy.; Charles C. Goodfellow III,* Treas.; Jerome A. Manning; Neal P. Myerberg.
Number of staff: 1 full-time professional; 1 part-time professional.
EIN: 115238046
Selected grants: The following grants were reported in 2004.
$4,147,000 to WildAid, San Francisco, CA. 2 grants: $1,950,000, $2,197,000
$150,000 to Environmental Investigation Agency, DC. 2 grants: $70,000, $80,000
$30,000 to Sea Turtle Restoration Project, Forest Knolls, CA.
$25,000 to Tony Fitzjohn/George Adamson African Wildlife Preservation Trust, Los Angeles, CA.

450
Cecil B. DeMille Foundation ✧

223 W. Alameda Ave., Ste. 101
Burbank, CA 91502-2575
Contact: Cecilia DeMille Presley, Mgr.

Established in 1991 in CA.
Foundation type: Independent foundation.
Financial data (yr. ended 12/31/05): Assets, $10,913,957 (M); expenditures, $610,424; qualifying distributions, $557,059; giving activities include $527,791 for 19 grants (high: $205,000; low: $100).
Purpose and activities: Giving primarily to the arts, including to an academy of motion picture arts and sciences, and higher education.

Fields of interest: Media, film/video; Museums; Performing arts; Arts; Higher education; Medical school/education; Children/youth, services.
Limitations: Giving primarily in CA. No grants to individuals.
Application information: Application form not required.
  Initial approach: Letter
  Deadline(s): None
Managers: Peter DeMille Calvin; Joseph W. Harper, Jr.; Cecilia DeMille Presley.
EIN: 954268286

451
Carl & Roberta Deutsch Foundation ✧ ☆
2444 Wilshire Blvd., Ste. 600
Santa Monica, CA 90403 (310) 453-0055
Contact: William E. Holler, V.P.

Established in 1997 in CA.
Donors: Carl Deutsch; Roberta Deutsch.
Foundation type: Independent foundation.
Financial data (yr. ended 12/31/05): Assets, $42,953,176 (M); gifts received, $20,000,000; expenditures, $1,244,675; qualifying distributions, $1,027,685; giving activities include $1,027,685 for grants.
Purpose and activities: Giving for human services, education, art programs and women's services.
Fields of interest: Arts; Higher education; Higher education, college; Education; Boy scouts; Human services; Women.
Limitations: Giving primarily in CA. No grants to individuals.
Application information:
  Initial approach: Letter
  Deadline(s): None
Officers: Carl Deutsch, Pres.; William E. Holler, V.P. and Secy.-Treas.
EIN: 954610378
Selected grants: The following grants were reported in 2003.
$29,000 to Friends of the Child Advocates, Monterey Park, CA.
$25,000 to Gabriella Axelrad Education Foundation, Encino, CA.
$25,000 to Rape Foundation, North Hollywood, CA.
$20,000 to SHARE, Beverly Hills, CA.
$10,000 to Cabrillo Marine Aquarium, Friends of, San Pedro, CA.
$10,000 to Farm Hands, Beverly Hills, CA.
$8,500 to University of California, Oakland, CA.
$5,400 to Professional Dancers Society, Beverly Hills, CA.
$5,000 to Malibu Ballet Society, Malibu, CA.
$5,000 to Young Musicians Foundation, Beverly Hills, CA.

452
The DeVito/Perlman Family Foundation ✧
(formerly Culver Theatre Foundation)
3550 Wilshire Blvd., No. 840
Los Angeles, CA 90010-2409

Established in 1993 in CA.
Donors: Danny DeVito; Rhea Perlman DeVito.
Foundation type: Independent foundation.
Financial data (yr. ended 6/30/05): Assets, $2,147,158 (M); gifts received, $300; expenditures, $502,154; qualifying distributions,

$494,534; giving activities include $475,707 for 45 grants (high: $140,000; low: $100).
Purpose and activities: Giving primarily to a university; support also for children's services, including children's hospitals and health organizations; some funding for other health associations, as well as for family services, social services, including firefighters' and police officers' associations, and the arts.
Fields of interest: Arts; Higher education; Hospitals (specialty); Health organizations; AIDS research; Diabetes research; Human services; Children, services; Family services.
Limitations: Applications not accepted. Giving primarily in CA. No grants to individuals.
Application information: Contributes only to pre-selected organizations.
Officers: Danny DeVito, Pres. and Secy.; Rhea Perlman DeVito, V.P.
EIN: 954455931
Selected grants: The following grants were reported in 2004.
$63,333 to Oakwood School, North Hollywood, CA.
$15,000 to Childrens Hospital Los Angeles, Los Angeles, CA.
$15,000 to Elizabeth Glaser Pediatric AIDS Foundation, Santa Monica, CA.
$10,000 to Westside Childrens Center, Culver City, CA.
$5,000 to Alliance for Childrens Rights, Los Angeles, CA.
$5,000 to California Institute of the Arts, Valencia, CA.
$5,000 to Rape Foundation, North Hollywood, CA.
$5,000 to Venice Family Clinic, Venice, CA.
$1,000 to Beverly Hills Firemens Association, Beverly Hills, CA.
$1,000 to Ensemble Studio Theater, Los Angeles, CA.

453
The Dhont Family Foundation
2700 N. Main St., Ste. 1100
Santa Ana, CA 92705

Established in 1999 in CA.
Foundation type: Independent foundation.
Financial data (yr. ended 12/31/05): Assets, $22,238,476 (M); expenditures, $3,171,965; qualifying distributions, $975,000; giving activities include $975,000 for 16 grants (high: $275,000; low: $5,000).
Fields of interest: Higher education; Education; Hospitals (general); Human services; Youth, services.
Limitations: Applications not accepted. Giving primarily in CA. No grants to individuals.
Application information: Contributes only to pre-selected organizations.
Officers: Andre G. Dhont; Denis Lesenne; Robert E. Topp.
EIN: 330846817

454
Donald C. & Elizabeth M. Dickinson Foundation ✧
c/o '
P.O. Box 7078
Rancho Santa Fe, CA 92067
Contact: Martin C. Dickinson, Pres.

Established in 1995 in CA.
Donor: Elizabeth M. Dickinson.
Foundation type: Independent foundation.
Financial data (yr. ended 12/31/05): Assets, $34,596,905 (M); expenditures, $2,329,074; qualifying distributions, $2,197,450; giving activities include $2,168,500 for 23 grants (high: $575,000; low: $10,000; average: $25,000–$100,000).
Purpose and activities: Giving primarily for education and health and human services.
Fields of interest: Museums; Education; Hospitals (general); Medical research, association; Human services; Children/youth, services; Residential/custodial care, hospices; Foundations (community).
Limitations: Giving primarily in CA.
Application information: Application form not required.
  Initial approach: Letter
  Deadline(s): Aug. 31
Officers: Martin C. Dickinson, Pres.; Elizabeth D. Smoyer, V.P.; Barry C. Fitzpatrick, Secy.; Don Smoyer, Treas.
Directors: Kristopher Dickinson; John M. Seiber; Becky Welch.
EIN: 330653203
Selected grants: The following grants were reported in 2005.
$175,000 to San Diego Hospice Foundation, San Diego, CA.
$50,000 to Burn Institute, San Diego, CA.
$50,000 to Kraemer Endowment Foundation, El Cajon, CA.
$50,000 to Mercy Hospital Foundation, San Diego, CA.
$40,000 to Saturday Academy, Beaverton, OR.
$37,500 to San Diego Education Fund, San Diego, CA.
$31,000 to Helen Woodward Animal Center, Rancho Santa Fe, CA.
$25,000 to Athletes for Education, San Diego, CA.
$20,000 to Family Literacy Foundation, Solana Beach, CA.

455
Stanley Diller Charitable Foundation ✧
P.O. Box 36679
Los Angeles, CA 90036-0679 (310) 843-0411

Donors: Stanley Diller; The Goldrich Family Foundation.
Foundation type: Independent foundation.
Financial data (yr. ended 6/30/05): Assets, $374 (M); gifts received, $446,000; expenditures, $483,382; qualifying distributions, $478,491; giving activities include $478,491 for 33 grants (high: $55,000; low: $180).
Fields of interest: Jewish agencies & temples.
Limitations: Applications not accepted. Giving primarily in NY, with some giving in CA. No grants to individuals.
Application information: Contributes only to pre-selected organizations.
Officers: Stanley Diller, Pres.; Sheryl Rosenberg, Secy.-Treas.
EIN: 956136972

456
The Walt Disney Company
Foundation ▼ ◇
(formerly Disney Foundation)
500 S. Buena Vista St.
Burbank, CA 91521-3603
Contact: Tillie J. Baptie, Exec. Dir.
URL: http://disney.go.com/disneyhand/
contributions/wdcfoundation.html

Incorporated in 1951 in CA.
Donor: The Walt Disney Co.
Foundation type: Company-sponsored foundation.
Financial data (yr. ended 9/30/05): Assets,
$25,469,172 (M); gifts received, $27,033,533;
expenditures, $3,236,358; qualifying distributions,
$3,236,358; giving activities include $1,404,100
for 32 grants (high: $500,000; low: $1,000),
$1,476,759 for grants to individuals, and $299,734
for 477 employee matching gifts.
Purpose and activities: The foundation supports
organizations involved with arts and culture,
education, the environment, and human services.
Fields of interest: Arts; Education; Environment;
Human services; Voluntarism promotion.
Type of support: General/operating support;
Continuing support; Annual campaigns; Capital
campaigns; Program development; Scholarship
funds; Employee matching gifts; Employee-related
scholarships.
Limitations: Applications not accepted. Giving
primarily in areas of company operations, with
emphasis on Los Angeles and Orange County, CA,
Orange and Osceola counties, FL, and New York, NY.
No support for public agencies, educational
institutions, tax-supported organizations,
organizations supported by a consolidated giving
program already supported by the foundation, or
sectarian organizations. No grants to individuals
(except for employee-related scholarships), or for
endowments, building, start-up needs, research,
conferences, or general fund drives; no loans.
Publications: Financial statement.
Application information: Contributes only through
employee-related scholarships and to pre-selected
organizations.
Board meeting date(s): Annually between Jan. and
May
Officers: Marsha L. Reed, Secy.; Robert A. Iger,
Treas.; Tillie J. Baptie, Exec. Dir.
EIN: 956037079
Selected grants: The following grants were reported
in 2005.
$550,000 to California Institute of the Arts,
Valencia, CA. 2 grants: $50,000 to Character
Animation Program (For Character Animation
Program), $500,000 (For general operations).
$114,600 to Junior Achievement, National, New
York, NY.
$100,000 to California Science Center, Los
Angeles, CA.
$100,000 to Childrens Hospital of Orange County
(CHOC) Foundation, Orange, CA.
$100,000 to Entertainment Industry Foundation,
Los Angeles, CA.
$100,000 to National Hispanic Cultural Center
Foundation, Albuquerque, NM.
$50,000 to Motion Picture and Television Fund
Foundation, Woodland Hills, CA.
$25,000 to Ryman Arts, Los Angeles, CA.
$5,000 to Junior Achievement of Southern
California, Los Angeles, CA. For Junior
Achievement Scholarship Local Award.

457
The Walt and Lilly Disney Foundation ▼
(formerly The Lillian B. Disney Foundation)
c/o Diane Disney Miller, Pres.
P.O. Box 2566
San Anselmo, CA 94979-2566

Established in 1974 in CA.
Donor: Lillian B. Disney‡.
Foundation type: Independent foundation.
Financial data (yr. ended 12/31/04): Assets,
$230,284,955 (M); gifts received, $169,796;
expenditures, $10,019,397; qualifying
distributions, $9,133,151; giving activities include
$9,102,682 for 8 grants (high: $7,693,244; low:
$20,000; average: $50,000–$250,000).
Purpose and activities: Giving primarily for the arts,
education and human services.
Fields of interest: Arts; Education; Human services.
Type of support: General/operating support.
Limitations: Applications not accepted. Giving on a
national basis. No grants to individuals.
Application information: Contributes only to
pre-selected organizations.
Board meeting date(s): Annually
Officers: Diane Disney Miller, Pres.; Christopher D.
Miller, V.P.; Walter E.D. Miller, Secy.
EIN: 237425637
Selected grants: The following grants were reported
in 2004.
$7,943,244 to Los Angeles Philharmonic, Los
Angeles, CA. 2 grants: $250,000, $7,693,244
(For endowment fund. Grant made in form of
stock).
$700,000 to Ralph Lauren Center for Cancer Care
and Prevention, New York, NY. For medical
research.
$150,000 to Disney Elementary Magnet School,
Chicago, IL. For education in arts.
$139,438 to Thank You Walt Disney, Kansas City,
MO. For studio rehabilitation.
$100,000 to Research to Prevent Blindness, New
York, NY. For medical research.
$50,000 to Cregier Multiplex School, Chicago, IL.
For education in arts.
$20,000 to John Tracy Clinic, Los Angeles, CA. For
medical program in hearing loss.

458
DJ & T Foundation
c/o Prappas Co.
9201 Wilshire Blvd., No. 204
Beverly Hills, CA 90210 (310) 278-1160
Contact: William Prappas
E-mail: Will@prappascompany.com; *URL:* http://
www.djtfoundation.org

Established in 1994 in CA.
Donor: Robert W. Barker.
Foundation type: Independent foundation.
Financial data (yr. ended 5/31/05): Assets,
$22,174,928 (M); gifts received, $1,043,014;
expenditures, $2,329,430; qualifying distributions,
$2,319,940; giving activities include $2,247,729
for 1,790 grants (high: $250,000; low: $15).
Purpose and activities: Giving only to free or low
cost spay/neuter clinics or spay/neuter voucher
programs for companion dogs.
Fields of interest: Animal population control.
Type of support: General/operating support;
Continuing support; Capital campaigns; Building/
renovation; Equipment; Matching/challenge
support.

Limitations: Giving on a national basis. No grants to
individuals.
Application information: Application form available
on Web site. Application form required.
Initial approach: Request application
Copies of proposal: 1
Deadline(s): None
Board meeting date(s): As needed
Final notification: 2-4 months
Officers: Robert W. Barker, Pres.; Kent T. Valandra,
Secy.; Robert Louis Valandra, C.F.O.
Number of staff: 1 full-time support; 1 part-time
support.
EIN: 954499239
Selected grants: The following grants were reported
in 2004.
$26,597 to Humane Society of Tennessee Valley,
Knoxville, TN. For spaying and neutering
domestic animals.
$10,000 to Hounds Haven, Dillonvale, OH. For
spaying and neutering domestic animals.
$9,360 to Humane Society of Potsdam, Potsdam,
NY. For spaying and neutering domestic animals.
$7,500 to Arizona Animal Welfare League, Phoenix,
AZ. For spaying and neutering domestic animals.
$4,907 to Animal Defense League of Arizona,
Tucson, AZ. For spaying and neutering domestic
animals.
$3,955 to Humane Society of Southern Illinois,
Murphysboro, IL. For spaying and neutering
domestic animals.
$2,970 to Humane Society of Cherokee County,
Woodstock, GA. For spaying and neutering
domestic animals.
$2,821 to Animal Rescue Coalition, Sarasota, FL.
For spaying and neutering domestic animals.
$2,335 to Humane Society, Suncoast, Englewood,
FL. For spaying and neutering domestic animals.
$1,384 to Humane Society of Southwestern
Michigan, Benton Harbor, MI. For spaying and
neutering domestic animals.

459
Thelma Doelger Charitable Trust ◇
950 John Daly Blvd., Ste. 300
Daly City, CA 94015-3004 (650) 755-2333
Contact: D. Eugene Richard, Tr.

Established in 1995 in CA.
Foundation type: Independent foundation.
Financial data (yr. ended 6/30/05): Assets,
$14,249,720 (M); expenditures, $864,506;
qualifying distributions, $705,551; giving activities
include $606,000 for 24 grants (high: $75,000;
low: $3,000).
Purpose and activities: Giving primarily for animal
welfare, social services, a medical center, and
children and youth services.
Fields of interest: Museums; Higher education;
Animal welfare; Zoos/zoological societies;
Hospitals (general); Boys & girls clubs; Human
services; Children/youth, services.
Limitations: Giving limited to CA. No grants to
individuals.
Application information: Application form required.
Initial approach: Letter or telephone requesting
application form
Deadline(s): None
Trustees: Edward M. King; Howard E. Mason, Jr.; D.
Eugene Richard.
EIN: 943318483
Selected grants: The following grants were reported
in 2005.

$75,000 to Seton Medical Center, Daly City, CA.

$70,000 to Humane Society, Marin, Novato, CA.

$70,000 to Peninsula Humane Society and Society for the Prevention of Cruelty to Animals, San Mateo, CA.

$70,000 to San Francisco Society for the Prevention of Cruelty to Animals, San Francisco, CA.

$60,000 to Marine Mammal Center, Sausalito, CA.

$50,000 to Coyote Point Museum Association, San Mateo, CA.

$50,000 to San Francisco Zoological Society, San Francisco, CA.

$25,000 to Seton Medical Center Coastside, Moss Beach, CA.

$10,000 to Boys and Girls Club, Mid-Peninsula, San Mateo, CA.

$7,500 to Salvation Army of San Francisco, San Francisco, CA.

460
Carrie Estelle Doheny Foundation ▼ ✧

707 Wilshire Blvd., Ste. 4960
Los Angeles, CA 90017-9843 (213) 488-1122
Contact: Nina S. Shepherd, Secy.-Treas., C.F.O., and C.A.O.
FAX: (213) 488-1544;
E-mail: peggy@dohenyfoundation.org; URL: http://www.dohenyfoundation.org

Trust established in 1949 in CA.
Donor: Mrs. Edward L. Doheny‡.
Foundation type: Independent foundation.
Financial data (yr. ended 12/31/05): Assets, $168,245,329 (M); expenditures, $10,151,570; qualifying distributions, $8,609,105; giving activities include $8,084,551 for 310 grants (high: $1,700,000; low: $1,542; average: $5,000–$100,000).
Purpose and activities: The foundation was established for the advancement of education, medicine, religion, science; the improvement of the health and welfare of infants, children, adults, families, and the aged; the help and care of the sick, aged, and incapacitated; and the aid of the needy.
Fields of interest: Elementary/secondary education; Higher education; Hospitals (general); Eye diseases; Medical research, institute; Eye research; Children/youth, services; Family services; Aging, centers/services; Roman Catholic agencies & churches; Religion; Aging; Disabilities, people with.
Type of support: General/operating support; Continuing support; Annual campaigns; Capital campaigns; Building/renovation; Equipment; Emergency funds; Program development; Matching/challenge support.
Limitations: Giving primarily in the Los Angeles, CA, area. No support for tax-supported organizations, radio or television programs, or for political purposes. No grants to individuals, or for endowment funds, publications, travel, advertising, or scholarships.
Publications: Application guidelines; Annual report (including application guidelines); Grants list.
Application information: Application form required.
Initial approach: Telephone, E-mail or letter
Copies of proposal: 1
Deadline(s): None
Board meeting date(s): Monthly
Final notification: 2 to 3 months
Officers and Directors:* Robert A. Smith III,* Pres.; Austin F. Gavin,* V.P.; Nina S. Shepherd, Secy.-Treas., C.F.O., and C.A.O.; Robert F. Erburu;

George Gibbs; Joseph Nally; Rev. William Piletic, C.M.; Mrs. Terry Seidler.
Trustee: Carrie Estelle Doheny Foundation Corp.
Number of staff: 2 full-time professional; 1 part-time professional; 1 full-time support.
EIN: 952051633
Selected grants: The following grants were reported in 2004.
$1,000,000 to Doheny Eye Institute, Los Angeles, CA. For general operating support.
$725,000 to Archdiocese of Los Angeles, Los Angeles, CA. 3 grants: $400,000 (For construction of Our Lady of the Angels Cathedral), $25,000 (For scholarship funding), $300,000 (For maintenance and repair of poor inner city elementary schools).
$500,000 to Sisters of Social Service, Los Angeles, CA. For campaign to build assisted living facility, Motherhouse, Ministry Center, and meeting space.
$300,000 to Daughters of Charity of Saint Vincent de Paul, Los Altos Hills, CA. For renovation of bathrooms at Marillac and Marian Residences.
$120,000 to Mount Saint Marys College, Los Angeles, CA. For repairs and maintenance for Doheny campus.
$25,000 to Hospitaller Foundation of California, Los Angeles, CA. For construction of new Alzheimer's unit at retirement center.
$22,000 to Resurrection School, Los Angeles, CA. For Matching Grant Program.
$20,000 to Child SHARE Program, Glendale, CA. For expansion of foster parent support and retention program.

461
Dixon and Carol Doll Family Foundation ✧ ☆

2020 Broadway
San Francisco, CA 94115-1538 (650) 233-1400
Contact: Carol Ann Doll, Pres.

Established in 2000 in CA.
Donors: Carol Ann Doll; Dixon R. Doll.
Foundation type: Independent foundation.
Financial data (yr. ended 12/31/04): Assets, $5,236 (M); gifts received, $184,000; expenditures, $376,586; qualifying distributions, $367,306; giving activities include $370,150 for 31 + grants (high: $100,000).
Fields of interest: Arts; Education; Health organizations, association; Human services; Children/youth, services; Christian agencies & churches.
Limitations: Giving primarily in San Francisco, CA.
Application information: Application form required.
Deadline(s): None
Final notification: Within 2 months
Officers: Carol Ann Doll, Pres.; Dixon R. Doll, V.P. and Secy.-Treas.
EIN: 943346287

462
Dollens Family Foundation ✧ ☆

c/o Frank E. Clohan
550 Hamilton Ave., Ste. 300
Palo Alto, CA 94301

Established in 1996 in CA.
Donors: Ronald W. Dollens; Susan S. Dollens.
Foundation type: Independent foundation.

Financial data (yr. ended 10/31/05): Assets, $1,404,648 (M); gifts received, $1,499,680; expenditures, $1,346,555; qualifying distributions, $1,346,555; giving activities include $1,339,124 for 14 grants (high: $1,010,174; low: $200).
Fields of interest: Performing arts; Business school/education; Education, services; Federated giving programs; Jewish agencies & temples.
Limitations: Applications not accepted. Giving primarily in IN; some funding nationally. No grants to individuals.
Application information: Contributes only to pre-selected organizations.
Officers and Directors:* Ronald W. Dollens,* C.E.O.; Stephanie J. Dollens,* Secy.; Williams G. Dollens,* C.F.O.; Susan S. Dollens.
EIN: 352000508
Selected grants: The following grants were reported in 2003.
$60,000 to White Lick Heritage Commission, Avon, IN.
$50,100 to United Way of Central Indiana, Indianapolis, IN.
$50,000 to University of Indianapolis, Kelley School of Business, Indianapolis, IN.
$40,000 to Butler Foundation, Indianapolis, IN.
$5,000 to United Methodist Church, Sandborn, IN.
$4,560 to Purdue University, West Lafayette, IN.
$2,500 to Zionsville Presbyterian Church, Zionsville, IN.
$2,040 to Indiana Symphony Society, Indianapolis Symphony Orchestra, Indianapolis, IN.
$2,000 to Duke University, Durham, NC.
$1,250 to Purdue Foundation, West Lafayette, IN.

463
Dougherty Family Foundation ✧

5380 Arezzo Dr.
San Jose, CA 95138
Contact: Gregory Dougherty, Chair.

Established in 2001 in CA.
Donors: Gregory Dougherty; Nancy Dougherty.
Foundation type: Independent foundation.
Financial data (yr. ended 9/30/05): Assets, $11,155,032 (M); expenditures, $522,681; qualifying distributions, $511,300; giving activities include $511,100 for 14 grants (high: $302,900; low: $700).
Purpose and activities: Giving primarily for children's health care and services; some giving also for education, and the arts.
Fields of interest: Performing arts, theater (musical); Arts; Education; Hospitals (specialty); Health care; Health organizations, association; Children/youth, services; Family services; Roman Catholic agencies & churches.
Limitations: Giving primarily in CA.
Application information: Application form not required.
Initial approach: Letter
Deadline(s): None
Officers: Gregory Dougherty, Chair.; Nancy Dougherty, Secy. and C.F.O.
EIN: 912169485

464
Douglas Foundation ◇
(formerly Douglas Charitable Foundation)
c/o Anne Douglas
141 El Camino Dr., Ste. 209
Beverly Hills, CA 90212 (310) 274-5294

Established in 1964 in CA.
Donors: Kirk Douglas; Anne Douglas; Pepsico, Inc.
Foundation type: Independent foundation.
Financial data (yr. ended 12/31/05): Assets,
$22,255,492 (M); gifts received, $50,000;
expenditures, $1,772,499; qualifying distributions,
$1,657,247; giving activities include $1,613,963
for 70 grants (high: $500,000; low: $100).
Purpose and activities: Giving primarily for the arts
and education; some giving for Jewish agencies and
temples.
Fields of interest: Media, film/video; Performing
arts; Performing arts, theater; Arts; Education;
Hospitals (general); Health care; Human services;
Jewish federated giving programs; Jewish agencies
& temples.
Type of support: General/operating support.
Limitations: Applications not accepted. Giving
primarily in CA. No grants to individuals.
Application information: Contributes only to
pre-selected organizations.
Trustees: Anne Douglas; Kirk Douglas; Peter
Douglas; Anita May Rosenstein; Franklin F. Wallis.
EIN: 956096827
Selected grants: The following grants were reported
in 2003.
$500,000 to Center Theater Group of Los Angeles,
Los Angeles, CA.
$232,000 to American Friends of the Israel
Philharmonic Orchestra, Beverly Hills, CA.
$100,000 to Motion Picture and Television Fund,
Woodland Hills, CA.
$100,000 to Sinai Temple, Los Angeles, CA.
$40,000 to Chesed Foundation of America, New
York, NY.
$24,300 to Womens Guild Cedars-Sinai Medical
Center, Los Angeles, CA.
$13,500 to Los Angeles Gay and Lesbian Center,
Los Angeles, CA.
$11,000 to Crane Country Day School, Santa
Barbara, CA.
$10,000 to Desert Healthcare Foundation, Palm
Springs, CA.
$10,000 to Sansum Medical Research Foundation,
Santa Barbara, CA.

465
The Draper Foundation ◇
2882 Sand Hill Rd., Ste. 150
Menlo Park, CA 94025 (650) 233-9000
Contact: Tim C. Draper, Pres.

Established in 1996 in CA.
Donors: William Draper; Phyllis Draper; Tim Draper;
Melissa Draper; Polly Draper.
Foundation type: Independent foundation.
Financial data (yr. ended 9/30/05): Assets,
$6,854,778 (M); gifts received, $53,186;
expenditures, $3,642,429; qualifying distributions,
$7,080,705; giving activities include $3,538,276
for 54 grants (high: $2,500,000; low: $250).
Purpose and activities: Giving primarily for the arts,
education, medical research, and children and
social services.
Fields of interest: Arts; Higher education;
Education; Environment; Health organizations,

association; Medical research, institute; Human
services; Children, services; International affairs;
Federated giving programs.
Limitations: Giving on a national basis.
Application information:
Initial approach: Proposal
Deadline(s): None
Officers: Tim C. Draper, Pres.; Rebecca Draper,
Secy.; William Draper, C.F.O.
EIN: 943256415

466
The Draper Richards Foundation ◇
50 California St., Ste. 2925
San Francisco, CA 94111 (415) 616-4050
Contact: Jennifer Shilling Stein, Exec. Dir.; Anne
Marie Burgoyne, Dir.
FAX: (415) 616-4060;
E-mail: info@draperrichards.org; Application E-mail:
proposals@draperrichards.org; URL: http://
www.draperrichards.org/

Established in 2001 in CA.
Donors: William H. Draper III; Robin R. Donohoe.
Foundation type: Operating foundation.
Financial data (yr. ended 12/31/04): Assets,
$4,092,780 (M); gifts received, $2,520,000;
expenditures, $881,538; qualifying distributions,
$868,977; giving activities include $800,000 for 8
grants (high: $100,000; low: $100,000).
Purpose and activities: Awards fellowships to
selected social entrepreneurs with seed funding of
$100,000 annually for three years as well as
technical support. The Foundation only awards six
fellowships per year so that we can fully engage with
our portfolio of grantee organizations. The funds are
specifically and solely for entrepreneurs starting
new non-profit organizations that seek to solve
existing social problems in innovative new ways. The
Foundation will select proposals from a variety of
public service areas, including, but not limited to,
education, youth and families, the environment,
arts, health, and community and economic
development. The foundation does not fund
organizations later in their lifecycle.
Fields of interest: Arts; Education; Environment;
Health care; Crime/law enforcement; Employment;
Housing/shelter; Youth development, adult & child
programs; Human services; International affairs,
equal rights; International economic development;
Civil rights; Economic development; Nonprofit
management; Community development;
Philanthropy/voluntarism; Public affairs.
Type of support: General/operating support;
Management development/capacity building;
Program development; Seed money; Fellowships;
Technical assistance.
Limitations: Giving on a national or international
basis. No support for local community-based
organizations. No grants for research or
scholarships.
Publications: Application guidelines.
Application information: Please see foundation
Web site for submission guidelines. Application form
not required.
Initial approach: Brief proposal, no more than 3
pages
Copies of proposal: 1
Deadline(s): None
Final notification: Acknowledgement of receipt
within 14 business days
Officers: Jennifer Shilling Stein, Pres. and Exec. Dir.;
Cynthia Lam, Secy.-Treas.

Directors: Anne Marie Burgoyne; Robin R. Donohoe;
William H. Draper III.
Number of staff: 2 full-time professional.
EIN: 912172351

467
Drew Family Foundation ◇ ☆
528 Ramona St.
Palo Alto, CA 94301

Established in 2000 in CA.
Donors: John Drew; Ellen Drew.
Foundation type: Independent foundation.
Financial data (yr. ended 6/30/05): Assets,
$5,522,390 (M); gifts received, $890,000;
expenditures, $386,716; qualifying distributions,
$350,745; giving activities include $352,000 for 17
grants (high: $75,000; low: $1,000).
Fields of interest: Elementary/secondary
education; Higher education; Human services;
Children/youth, services.
Limitations: Applications not accepted. Giving
primarily on a national basis, with some emphasis
on CA, IL, and NY. No grants to individuals.
Application information: Contributes only to
pre-selected organizations.
Officers: Ellen Todd Drew, Pres.; John Drew,
Secy.-Treas.
EIN: 770552387
Selected grants: The following grants were reported
in 2005.
$75,000 to Saint Josephs Home of Springfield,
Springfield, IL.
$40,000 to Norwich University, Northfield, VT.
$21,000 to West Point Fund, West Point, NY.
$10,000 to Law Foundation of Silicon Valley, San
Jose, CA.
$10,000 to Los Altos Educational Foundation, Los
Altos, CA.
$10,000 to Salem College, Winston-Salem, NC.

468
**Dreyer's Grand Ice Cream Charitable
Foundation** ◇
5929 College Ave.
Oakland, CA 94618-1325 (510) 450-4586
Contact: Kelly M. Su'a, Secy.-Treas.
FAX: (510) 610-4400; URL: http://
www.dreyersinc.com/dreyersfoundation/index.asp

Established in 1987 as a company-sponsored
operating foundation.
Donor: Dreyer's Grand Ice Cream, Inc.
Foundation type: Operating foundation.
Financial data (yr. ended 12/31/04): Assets,
$19,387 (M); gifts received, $865,000;
expenditures, $875,416; qualifying distributions,
$865,285; giving activities include $592,207 for 25
grants (high: $25,000; low: $25).
Purpose and activities: The foundation supports
organizations involved with arts and culture,
education, health, youth development, and
community development and operates a bus
program available to schools and other nonprofit
organizations for field trips and cultural activities.
Fields of interest: Arts; Education; Health
organizations, association; Health organizations;
Youth development; Community development.
Limitations: Giving primarily in the Oakland, CA,
area. No support for political organizations. No
grants to individuals, or for raffle tickets, semi-pro

athletic sponsorships, benefit advertising, field trips, tours, independent film or video productions, endowments, political campaigns, or religious purposes.
Application information: Proposals should be no longer than 3 pages. Application form not required.
 Initial approach: Proposal
 Deadline(s): Jan. 15th for contributions of over $3,000
Officers: Diane McIntyre, Pres.; Dave Moirao, V.P.; Kelly M. Su'a, Secy.-Treas.
Directors: Margaret Harrington; Nancy Reed.
EIN: 943006987
Selected grants: The following grants were reported in 2005.
$35,000 to Teach for America, New York, NY.
$25,000 to Community Alliance for Learning, Berkeley, CA.
$20,000 to James Logan High School, Union City, CA.
$18,000 to East Bay Conservation Corps, Oakland, CA.
$15,000 to Chabot Space and Science Center, Oakland, CA.
$15,000 to East Oakland Boxing Association, Oakland, CA.
$15,000 to Junior Achievement of the Bay Area, South San Francisco, CA.
$15,000 to Junior League of Oakland - East Bay, Lafayette, CA.
$10,000 to Prospect Sierra School, El Cerrito, CA.
$3,000 to Willows Theater Company, Concord, CA.

469
Joseph Drown Foundation ▼
1999 Ave. of the Stars, Ste. 2330
Los Angeles, CA   90067   (310) 277-4488
Contact: Wendy Wachtell, V.P.
FAX: (310) 277-4573; E-mail: staff@jdrown.org;
URL: http://www.jdrown.org

Established in 1953 in CA.
Donor: Joseph W. Drown‡.
Foundation type: Independent foundation.
Financial data (yr. ended 3/31/06): Assets, $95,808,013 (M); expenditures, $6,521,501; qualifying distributions, $5,674,024; giving activities include $5,160,650 for 142 grants (high: $250,000; low: $5,000; average: $25,000–$100,000).
Purpose and activities: The goal of the foundation is to assist individuals in becoming successful, self-sustaining, contributing citizens. The foundation is interested in programs that break down any barrier that prevents a person from continuing to grow and learn. Grants primarily for education and health, community, and social services.
Fields of interest: Education, early childhood education; Elementary school/education; Education.
Type of support: General/operating support; Program development; Seed money; Scholarship funds; Matching/challenge support.
Limitations: Giving primarily in Los Angeles, CA. No support for religious purposes. No grants to individuals, or for endowments, capital campaigns, building funds, or seminars or conferences.
Publications: Informational brochure (including application guidelines).
Application information: Please do not send videos or materials that need to be returned. Application form not required.
 Initial approach: Proposal and letter

Copies of proposal: 1
Deadline(s): Jan. 15, Apr. 15, July 15, and Oct. 15
Board meeting date(s): Mar., June, Sept., and Dec.
Final notification: Immediately after board meeting
Officers and Directors:* Norman C. Obrow,* Chair. and Pres.; Thomas C. Marshall,* V.P.; Wendy Wachtell, V.P.; Philip S. Magaram,* Secy.-Treas.; Elaine Mahoney.
Number of staff: 3 full-time professional.
EIN: 956093178
Selected grants: The following grants were reported in 2006.
$250,000 to California State University, Performing Arts Center, Northridge, CA. For development and outreach.
$125,000 to University of California, School of Medicine, San Francisco, CA. For research in atrial and ventricular fibrillation.
$100,000 to Baruch College of the City University of New York, New York, NY. For faculty awards for excellence in teaching.
$100,000 to Betty Ford Center at Eisenhower Medical Center, Rancho Mirage, CA. For children's program.
$66,000 to Venice Family Clinic, Venice, CA. For Childhood Obesity Prevention, Detection and Management Program.
$50,000 to AIDS Research Alliance, West Hollywood, CA. For research on prostratin.
$35,000 to Family Unity International, Elm Grove, WI. For operating support of Working Boys Center.
$25,000 to Childrens Museum of Los Angeles, Los Angeles, CA. For operating support.
$25,000 to Saint Annes Maternity Home, Los Angeles, CA. For residential treatment program.
$25,000 to Sunny Hills Childrens Garden, San Anselmo, CA. For therapeutic education for children and teens at risk.

470
The Drum Foundation ◇
c/o The Botto Law Group
180 Montgomery St., 16th Fl.
San Francisco, CA   94104

Incorporated in 1956 in CA.
Donor: Frank G. Drum‡.
Foundation type: Independent foundation.
Financial data (yr. ended 12/31/04): Assets, $5,772,130 (M); expenditures, $519,940; qualifying distributions, $461,005; giving activities include $421,500 for 33 grants (high: $40,000; low: $2,500).
Purpose and activities: To aid Roman Catholic Church-related educational and charitable organizations, usually limited to the Archdiocese of San Francisco, including those supported by Mr. Drum during his lifetime.
Fields of interest: Elementary/secondary education; Higher education; Human services; Federated giving programs; Roman Catholic federated giving programs; Roman Catholic agencies & churches.
Type of support: General/operating support; Continuing support; Annual campaigns; Building/renovation; Equipment; Land acquisition; Debt reduction; Emergency funds; Program development; Conferences/seminars; Professorships; Publication; Seed money; Fellowships; Internship

funds; Scholarship funds; Research; Exchange programs.
Limitations: Applications not accepted. Giving primarily in the San Francisco Bay Area, CA. No grants to individuals, or for endowment funds or matching gifts.
Application information: Contributes only to pre-selected organizations.
 Board meeting date(s): As required
Officers and Directors:* Janet Abbott,* Pres.; Philip Hudner,* Secy.-Treas.
EIN: 946067469

471
The Durfee Foundation
1453 3rd St. Promenade, Ste. 312
Santa Monica, CA   90401
Contact: Claire Peeps
FAX: (310) 899-5121; E-mail: admin@durfee.org; Additional E-mail for Claire Peeps: Claire@durfee.org; URL: http://www.durfee.org

Established in 1969 in CA.
Foundation type: Independent foundation.
Financial data (yr. ended 12/31/05): Assets, $27,556,614 (M); expenditures, $1,549,482; qualifying distributions, $1,353,350; giving activities include $758,485 for 37 grants (high: $150,000; low: $1,000), $243,484 for 50 grants to individuals (high: $15,000; low: $775), and $51,837 for foundation-administered programs.
Purpose and activities: The purpose of the foundation is to support creative individuals and community-based leadership.
Fields of interest: Arts.
Type of support: General/operating support; Grants to individuals.
Limitations: Giving limited to Los Angeles, CA.
Publications: Application guidelines; Annual report; Informational brochure.
Application information: Details on application forms. Application form required.
 Initial approach: Visit Web site
 Deadline(s): Varies
 Board meeting date(s): 3 times annually
 Final notification: 4 to 6 weeks
Officers: Judith Avery, Chair.; Caroline D. Avery, Pres.; Michael A. Newkirk, V.P.; Halina Avery, Secy.; Diana McKee, Co-Treas.; Jonathan Newkirk, Co-Treas.
Number of staff: 2 full-time professional; 1 part-time professional; 2 part-time support.
EIN: 954856207

472
The Richard F. Dwyer and Eleanor W. Dwyer Fund for Excellence ◇ ☆
(formerly American Foundation for Oceanography)
c/o Allan Lasher
321 N. Las Casas Ave.
Pacific Palisades, CA   90272-3307

Established in 1953 in CA.
Donors: Darlene Lasher; Allan Lasher; Richard F. Dwyer.
Foundation type: Independent foundation.
Financial data (yr. ended 6/30/06): Assets, $7,224,103 (M); expenditures, $407,708; qualifying distributions, $368,004; giving activities include $368,004 for 17 grants (high: $344,954; low: $100).

Purpose and activities: Giving primarily to an organization which provides shelter and services for people who are low-income, homeless or mentally ill; funding also for health care, and children, youth, and social services.
Fields of interest: Education, single organization support; Education; Health care; Health organizations; Medical research, institute; Housing/shelter; Human services; Children/youth, services; Family services; Foundations (private grantmaking); Economically disadvantaged.
Limitations: Applications not accepted. Giving primarily in Los Angeles and Santa Monica, CA. No grants to individuals.
Application information: Contributes only to pre-selected organizations.
Officers and Directors:* Carole Greene,* Pres.; Allan Lasher,* V.P. and Secy.; Michael Parker,* Treas.; Warren E. Greene; Ann L. Parker.
EIN: 956027788
Selected grants: The following grants were reported in 2006.
$344,954 to Ocean Park Community Center, Santa Monica, CA.
$5,000 to Saint Joseph Center, Venice, CA.
$1,000 to Boys and Girls Club, Burbank, Burbank, CA.
$1,000 to California Literacy, Pasadena, CA.
$500 to A Window Between Worlds, Venice, CA.
$500 to Los Angeles Police Foundation, Los Angeles, CA.
$500 to University High School, Fresno, CA.

473
Margaret E. Early Medical Research Trust ✧
1055 W. 7th St., 29th Fl.
Los Angeles, CA 90017
Contact: Eli B. Dubrow, Tr.

Established in 1982.
Foundation type: Independent foundation.
Financial data (yr. ended 12/31/05): Assets, $11,976,376 (M); expenditures, $935,447; qualifying distributions, $874,843; giving activities include $748,379 for 10 grants (high: $75,000; low: $73,379).
Purpose and activities: Giving to institutions in the Los Angeles, CA, area, which have substantial research facilities for research into the causes and cures of cancer and related diseases.
Fields of interest: Cancer; Cancer research.
Type of support: Research.
Limitations: Giving limited to the greater Los Angeles, CA, area.
Application information: Written grant proposals based on National Institute of Health guidelines. Application form required.
  Initial approach: Proposal
  Copies of proposal: 10
Trustee: Eli B. Dubrow.
EIN: 953740506
Selected grants: The following grants were reported in 2003.
$298,000 to University of California, Los Angeles, CA. 6 grants: $48,000, $50,000 to School of Medicine, $50,000, $50,000, $50,000 to David Geffen School of Medicine, $50,000
$50,000 to California Institute for Cancer Research, Los Angeles, CA.
$50,000 to University of Southern California, Keck School of Medicine, Los Angeles, CA.

$49,800 to California Institute of Technology, Pasadena, CA.
$41,667 to City of Hope, Los Angeles, CA.

474
The East Bay Community Foundation
DeDomenico Bldg.
200 Frank H. Ogawa Plz.
Oakland, CA 94612 (510) 836-3223
Contact: Karen Stevenson, Pres.
FAX: (510) 836-3287; E-mail: info@eastbaycf.org; Grantmaking E-mails: program@eastbaycf.org and communityinvestment@eastbaycf.org; URL: http://www.eastbaycf.org

Established in 1928 in CA as The Alameda County Community Foundation by resolution and declaration of trust; revised in 1972 to include Contra Costa County.
Foundation type: Community foundation.
Financial data (yr. ended 6/30/05): Assets, $171,604,607 (M); gifts received, $67,920,307; expenditures, $27,398,235; giving activities include $19,569,747 for 1,788 grants (high: $3,155,097; low: $39).
Purpose and activities: The foundation connects donor interests to community needs and opportunities utilizing community knowledge and leadership. Priorities in grantmaking are arts and culture, community health, education and youth development, the environment, neighborhood and community building, and strengthening families.
Fields of interest: Arts; Education; Environmental education; Environment; Public health; Health care; Youth development; Family services; Community development; Youth; LGBTQ.
Type of support: General/operating support; Management development/capacity building; Program development; Seed money; Technical assistance; Program evaluation; Employee matching gifts; Matching/challenge support.
Limitations: Giving limited to Alameda and Contra Costa counties, CA. No support for religious organizations for religious purposes. No grants to individuals directly, or for building and endowment funds, capital expenditures, annual fund appeals, existing obligations, retroactive funding, deficit financing, fundraising events, and celebrations.
Publications: Application guidelines; Annual report; Informational brochure; Newsletter; Program policy statement.
Application information: Visit foundation Web site for application form and guidelines. Faxed applications are not accepted. Application form required.
  Initial approach: Submit application form and attachments
  Copies of proposal: 2
  Deadline(s): Rolling
  Board meeting date(s): May and Nov.
  Final notification: Within 4 to 6 months
Officers and Trustees:* James P. King,* Chair.; Michael Dalby, Chair. Elect; Stephen L. Hicks,* Vice-Chair.; Karen Stevenson, Pres.; Michael Petrini, Exec. V.P.; Carla Dartis, V.P., Community Investment; Chris Nicholson, V.P., Devel.; John Pachtner, V.P., External Affairs & Comms.; Maggie Parente, V.P., Human Resources & Admin.; Marcia Barinaga,* Secy.; James Bangura, Cont.; Michael M. Howe,* Pres. Emeritus; Lois DeDomenico,* Emeritus; Richard G. Heggie,* Emeritus; Deborah Alvarez-Rodriguez; Ronald D. Cordes; Edgar H. Grubb; Kathleen Huston; Patricia M. Jones; Craig

Lundin; Amy Slater; Timothy H. Smallsreed; Alfredo Terrazas.
Number of staff: 15 full-time professional; 1 part-time professional; 6 full-time support.
EIN: 946070996

475
Eaton Family Foundation, Inc. ✧ ☆
c/o Edward F. Eaton
85 Enterprise, Ste. 300
Aliso Viejo, CA 92656

Established in 2004 in CA and DE.
Donor: Edward F. Heaton.
Foundation type: Independent foundation.
Financial data (yr. ended 12/31/05): Assets, $476,185 (M); expenditures, $533,198; qualifying distributions, $531,500; giving activities include $531,500 for 6 grants (high: $300,000; low: $10,000).
Purpose and activities: Giving to Christian ministries and organizations, and children, youth, and social services, including a soup kitchen.
Fields of interest: Youth development, adult & child programs; Children/youth, services; Christian agencies & churches; Disabilities, people with.
Limitations: Applications not accepted. Giving primarily in Costa Mesa, CA. No grants to individuals.
Application information: Contributes only to pre-selected organizations.
Directors: Edward F. Heaton.
EIN: 201712897

476
The Harold Edelstein Foundation ✧
100 W. Broadway, Ste. 600
Glendale, CA 91210

Donor: Harold Edelstein Crut No. 2.
Foundation type: Independent foundation.
Financial data (yr. ended 12/31/03): Assets, $13,422,883 (M); gifts received, $222,128; expenditures, $1,371,617; qualifying distributions, $969,209; giving activities include $755,575 for 13 grants (high: $201,675; low: $2,500).
Purpose and activities: Giving primarily to Jewish organizations, as well as for social services; funding also for children and youth services, particularly a children's hospital.
Fields of interest: Hospitals (specialty); Food distribution, meals on wheels; Human services; Children/youth, services; Family services; Jewish federated giving programs; Jewish agencies & temples.
Limitations: Applications not accepted. Giving primarily in CA, with emphasis on Los Angeles. No grants to individuals.
Application information: Contributes only to pre-selected organizations.
Directors: Marvin G. Burns; Marvin Rothenberg; Frederick L. Simmons.
EIN: 954814292
Selected grants: The following grants were reported in 2004.
$342,130 to Korean American Family Service Center, Los Angeles, CA.
$150,000 to Israel Humanitarian Foundation, New York, NY.
$77,000 to Childrens Hospital, Rancho Santa Fe, CA.

$30,000 to Children of the Night, Van Nuys, CA.

$28,500 to Saint Vincent Senior Citizen Nutrition Program, Los Angeles, CA.

$28,000 to Las Familias del Pueblo, Los Angeles, CA.

$5,000 to Covenant House California, Hollywood, CA.

$5,000 to Kid Street Learning Center, Santa Rosa, CA.

$5,000 to Venice Family Clinic, Venice, CA.

477

Edgerton Foundation ✧ ☆

9454 Wilshire Blvd., 4th Fl.
Beverly Hills, CA 90212

Successor foundation established in 2001 in CA, NV, WA.

Donor: W. Alton Jones Foundation.

Foundation type: Independent foundation.

Financial data (yr. ended 6/30/05): Assets, $97,433,042 (M); expenditures, $1,773,842; qualifying distributions, $924,542; giving activities include $524,165 for 17 grants (high: $137,000; low: $30), and $143,344 for 1 foundation-administered program.

Fields of interest: Performing arts, theater; Performing arts, orchestra (symphony); Elementary/secondary education; Environment, legal rights; Environment, natural resources; Environment; Hospitals (specialty); International affairs.

Limitations: Applications not accepted. Giving primarily in Los Angeles, CA, and Washington, DC; some funding nationally. No grants to individuals.

Application information: Contributes only to pre-selected organizations.

Officers: Bradford W. Edgerton, M.D., Pres.; Louise D. Edgerton, Secy.-Treas.

EIN: 912160742

478

Joseph K. & Inez Eichenbaum Foundation ✧

(formerly J. K. & Inez Eichenbaum Foundation)
20501 Ventura Blvd., Ste. 325
Woodland Hills, CA 91364
Application address: c/o Joann Berry, Pres., 190 N. Canon Dr., Ste. 404, Beverly Hills, CA 90210

Established in 1971.

Donors: J.K. Eichenbaum†; Inez Eichenbaum.

Foundation type: Independent foundation.

Financial data (yr. ended 11/30/04): Assets, $22,557,619 (M); expenditures, $1,552,876; qualifying distributions, $1,028,106; giving activities include $969,664 for 117 grants (high: $125,000; low: $35).

Purpose and activities: Grants primarily for Jewish welfare and health associations; some giving for the arts and for animal welfare.

Fields of interest: Arts; Higher education; Animal welfare; Health organizations, association; Medical research, institute; Human services; Jewish federated giving programs; Jewish agencies & temples.

International interests: Israel.

Limitations: Giving primarily in CA. No grants to individuals, or for prizes; no loans.

Application information:
Initial approach: Letter on organization letterhead
Deadline(s): None

Officers: Joann Berry, Pres.; Daniel R. Swett, V.P.; Mark Comer, Treas.

Directors: Jody Berry; Anthony Boyar; Bram Goldsmith; Vicki Magasinn.

EIN: 956101264

Selected grants: The following grants were reported in 2003.

$125,000 to Tel Aviv University: American Council, New York, NY. For research for Alzheimer, AIDS, and other research.

$122,565 to SHARE, Beverly Hills, CA.

$100,000 to Kayne-ERAS Center, Culver City, CA.

$50,000 to Bancroft Neurohealth, Haddonfield, NJ.

$50,000 to Big Brothers/Big Sisters of Greater Los Angeles, Los Angeles, CA.

$15,000 to Casa Colina Centers for Rehabilitation Foundation, Pomona, CA.

$15,000 to United Jewish Fund of Greater Los Angeles, Los Angeles, CA.

$10,500 to Young Musicians Foundation, Beverly Hills, CA.

$10,200 to American Cancer Society, Atlanta, GA.

$10,000 to Thalians, The, Los Angeles, CA.

479

Harry and Hilda Eisen Family Foundation ✧

1811 Mountain Ave.
Norco, CA 92860

Established in 1991 in CA.

Donors: Harry Eisen; Hilda Eisen.

Foundation type: Independent foundation.

Financial data (yr. ended 12/31/05): Assets, $1,191,418 (M); gifts received, $500,000; expenditures, $468,731; qualifying distributions, $467,296; giving activities include $467,296 for 25 grants (high: $181,000; low: $500).

Fields of interest: Museums (history); Muscular dystrophy; Medical research; Human services; Jewish federated giving programs; Jewish agencies & temples.

Limitations: Applications not accepted. Giving primarily in CA. No grants to individuals.

Application information: Contributes only to pre-selected organizations.

Officers: Harry Eisen, Pres.; Hilda Eisen, V.P.

Director: Randy W. Miller.

EIN: 330492606

Selected grants: The following grants were reported in 2004.

$38,010 to City of Hope, Los Angeles, CA.

$10,000 to Congregation Beth Israel, Los Angeles, CA.

$6,860 to Boy Scouts of America, Redlands, CA.

$5,000 to California Foundation for Agriculture in the Classroom, Sacramento, CA.

$4,450 to Los Angeles Regional Foodbank, Los Angeles, CA.

$3,000 to National Conference for Community and Justice, New York, NY.

$2,000 to Raise Foundation, Tustin, CA.

480

Ben B. and Joyce E. Eisenberg Foundation ✧

12400 Wilshire Blvd., Ste. 1250
Los Angeles, CA 90025 (310) 820-1232
Contact: Richard A. Bender, Secy.-Treas.

Established in 1986 in CA.

Foundation type: Independent foundation.

Financial data (yr. ended 5/31/05): Assets, $50,377,051 (M); expenditures, $3,579,408; qualifying distributions, $4,514,361; giving activities include $2,514,361 for 40 grants (high: $260,000; low: $500).

Purpose and activities: Support primarily for Jewish education and Jewish giving; support also for medical research and care facilities and civic affairs.

Fields of interest: Higher education; Health care; Health organizations, association; Medical research, institute; Government/public administration; Jewish agencies & temples.

International interests: Israel.

Type of support: Continuing support; Annual campaigns; Research.

Limitations: Giving primarily in the Los Angeles, CA, area.

Application information:
Initial approach: Letter

Officers and Directors:* Joyce Eisenberg-Keefer,* Pres.; Richard A. Bender, Secy.-Treas.; Joyce Green; Edna Weiss.

Number of staff: 3 full-time support.

EIN: 990246427

Selected grants: The following grants were reported in 2005.

$226,550 to John Wayne Cancer Institute, Santa Monica, CA.

$55,500 to University of Judaism, Los Angeles, CA.

$31,050 to University Synagogue, Los Angeles, CA.

$18,000 to Valley Beth Shalom, Encino, CA.

481

The Eisner Foundation, Inc. ▼ ✧

9401 Wilshire Blvd., Ste. 760
Beverly Hills, CA 90212 (310) 777-3640
Contact: Laura W. Hobart, Exec. Dir.
FAX: (310) 777-3644; *URL:* http://www.eisnerfoundation.org

Established in 1996 in CA.

Donors: Michael D. Eisner; Jane B. Eisner.

Foundation type: Independent foundation.

Financial data (yr. ended 12/31/04): Assets, $130,986,581 (M); expenditures, $5,839,559; qualifying distributions, $5,332,568; giving activities include $5,064,479 for 129 grants (high: $2,000,000; low: $100; average: $1,000–$10,000).

Purpose and activities: Support for underserved children in Los Angeles and Orange counties, CA, specifically for learning differences, prevention of abuse and neglect, K-12 public education, and after-school programs, access to basic medical care, sports programs, and arts in education.

Fields of interest: Arts education; Elementary/secondary education; Health care; Crime/violence prevention, abuse prevention; Athletics/sports, school programs.

Type of support: General/operating support; Continuing support; Capital campaigns; Building/renovation; Equipment; Program development; Matching/challenge support.

Limitations: Giving limited to Los Angeles and Orange counties, CA. No support for sectarian purposes. Generally, no grants to individuals, annual campaigns, existing obligations, re-granting programs, sponsoring conferences or special events.

Application information: Full application form available on the foundation's Web site. Applications sent via fax or E-mail not accepted. Application form required.

Initial approach: Application
Copies of proposal: 2
Board meeting date(s): Mar., June, Sept., and Dec.

Officers and Directors:* Jane B. Eisner,* Pres.; Michael B. Eisner,* V.P.; Anders D. Eisner,* Secy.; Eric D. Eisner,* C.F.O.; Laura W. Hobart, Exec. Dir.; Michael D. Eisner.

Number of staff: 1 part-time professional; 1 part-time support.

EIN: 954607191

Selected grants: The following grants were reported in 2004.

$2,000,000 to California State University, Northridge, CA. For program support.

$1,319,852 to Cedars-Sinai Medical Center, Los Angeles, CA. 3 grants: $200,000 (For program support), $344,760 (For program support), $775,092 (For program support).

$250,000 to Project GRAD Los Angeles, North Hollywood, CA. For program support.

$200,000 to Denison University, Granville, OH. 2 grants: $100,000 each (For program support).

$50,000 to Childrens Hospital of Orange County (CHOC) Foundation, Orange, CA. For annual support.

$20,000 to Childrens Dental Center, Inglewood, CA. For program support.

$5,000 to Partnership for After School Education, New York, NY. For general support.

482
Eldorado Foundation ⬦

50 Lupine Ave., Apt. 3
San Francisco, CA 94118
Contact: Ava Jean Brumbaum, Secy.-Treas.

Established in 1964 in CA.
Foundation type: Independent foundation.
Financial data (yr. ended 12/31/05): Assets, $1,690,856 (M); expenditures, $440,337; qualifying distributions, $427,136; giving activities include $421,000 for 56 grants (high: $50,000; low: $1,000).
Fields of interest: Arts; Education; Environment, natural resources; Hospitals (general); Eye research; Human services; Christian agencies & churches; Protestant agencies & churches.
Type of support: Continuing support; Program development.
Limitations: Giving primarily in San Francisco, CA. No grants to individuals.
Application information: Limited funds available for grantmaking. Application form not required.
Initial approach: Letter
Copies of proposal: 1
Deadline(s): Apr. 1
Board meeting date(s): May
Officers and Directors:* Henry K. Evers, Pres.; Bruce Dohrmann,* V.P.; Ava Jean Brumbaum,* Secy.-Treas.; Peggy Merrifield.
Number of staff: None.
EIN: 946100642
Selected grants: The following grants were reported in 2005.

$50,000 to San Francisco Conservatory of Music, San Francisco, CA.

$38,000 to Meritus College Fund, San Francisco, CA.

$17,000 to Fromm Institute for Lifelong Learning, San Francisco, CA.

$15,000 to 826 Valencia, San Francisco, CA.

$10,000 to Mount Zion Health Fund, San Francisco, CA.

$7,500 to Edgewood Center for Children and Families, San Francisco, CA.

$5,000 to Asian Art Museum of San Francisco, San Francisco, CA.

$5,000 to Episcopal Community Services, San Diego, CA.

$5,000 to Exploratorium, San Francisco, CA.

$3,000 to Berkeley Repertory Theater, Berkeley, CA.

483
Energy Foundation ▼ ⬦

1012 Torney Ave., No. 1
San Francisco, CA 94129   (415) 561-6700
Contact: Eric Heitz, Pres.
FAX: (415) 561-6709; E-mail: energyfund@ef.org;
URL: http://www.ef.org

Established in 1991 in CA.
Donors: The Blue Moon Fund; The William and Flora Hewlett Foundation; John D. and Catherine T. MacArthur Foundation; The McKnight Foundation; Mertz Gilmore Foundation; The David and Lucile Packard Foundation; The Pew Charitable Trusts; The Rockefeller Foundation.
Foundation type: Independent foundation.
Financial data (yr. ended 12/31/05): Assets, $22,678,999 (M); gifts received, $27,585,414; expenditures, $27,140,969; qualifying distributions, $27,402,735; giving activities include $20,120,515 for 412 grants (high: $380,000; low: $1,000; average: $10,000–$100,000), and $1,704,345 for foundation-administered programs.
Purpose and activities: To assist in a transition to a sustainable energy future by promoting energy efficiency and renewable energy.
Fields of interest: Environment, energy.
International interests: China.
Type of support: Program development.
Limitations: Giving limited to the U.S. and China. No support for sectarian or religious purposes or political organizations. No grants to individuals, or for endowment funds, debt reduction, planning, renovation, maintenance, retrofit, or purchase of buildings, equipment purchases, land acquisition, general support grants, annual fundraising campaigns, research and development of technology, demonstration projects or capital construction.
Publications: Annual report (including application guidelines); Financial statement.
Application information: Application form required.
Initial approach: Letter of inquiry
Copies of proposal: 1
Deadline(s): At least 12 weeks in advance of next board meeting (for inclusion in a specific docket)
Board meeting date(s): 3rd week of Mar., 3rd week of June, and 1st week of Nov.
Final notification: Approximately 4 weeks
Officers and Directors:* Eric Heitz,* Pres.; Douglas Ogden, Exec. V.P. and Dir., CSEP; Robert O'Connor, V.P. and C.F.O.; Charlotte Pera, V.P. U.S. Operations; David Wooley, V.P., Domestic Policy Initiatives; Rosina Bierbaum; Robert Crane; Larry Goulder; Denis Hayes; James Lents; Alan Lloyd; Rose McKinney-James; Victor Rabinowitch; Phil Sharp; Susan F. Tierney; Michael Wang; Hongjun Zhang.
Number of staff: 26
EIN: 943126848

Selected grants: The following grants were reported in 2005.

$470,000 to Regulatory Assistance Project, Gardiner, ME. 2 grants: $250,000 (To educate utility regulators and key policymakers about benefits of energy efficiency standards and long-term resource planning, and to advocate for smart electric transmission growth), $220,000 (To provide international best-practice training and capacity building for China Sustainable Energy Program (CSEP)).

$380,000 to Union of Concerned Scientists, Cambridge, MA. For UCS Clean Vehicles Program.

$350,000 to Renewable Northwest Project, Portland, OR. To diversify electricity mix in Northwest so that 10 percent of supply comes from non-hydro renewable resources by 2010, payable over 2.25 years.

$325,000 to Natural Resources Defense Council, New York, NY. For work on Regional Greenhouse Gas Initiative and West Coast Governors' Global Warming Initiative.

$300,000 to Environmental Defense, New York, NY. To promote clean vehicle policies at federal level, in California, and in Connecticut.

$300,000 to Wind on the Wires, Saint Paul, MN. To continue working to overcome barriers to wind power in Midwest.

$275,000 to Environmental Law and Policy Center of the Midwest, Chicago, IL. To conduct research and encourage policy development on use of advanced biofuels.

$265,000 to Center for Public Interest Research, Boston, MA. For advocacy on Regional Greenhouse Gas Initiative by New England Climate Coalition.

$50,000 to Friends of the Earth, DC. To press for update to federal fuel economy test procedure and promote non-petroleum fuels in California.

484
Engemann Family Foundation ⬦ ☆

c/o Roger Engemann
600 N. Rosemead Blvd.
Pasadena, CA 91107

Established in 1998 in CA.
Donor: Roger Engemann.
Foundation type: Independent foundation.
Financial data (yr. ended 12/31/05): Assets, $4,846,094 (M); gifts received, $1,500,000; expenditures, $402,138; qualifying distributions, $394,000; giving activities include $394,000 for 12 grants (high: $250,000; low: $500).
Purpose and activities: Giving primarily for education, medical research, and human services.
Fields of interest: Arts; Libraries (public); Education; Hospitals (general); Human services.
Limitations: Applications not accepted. Giving primarily in CA. No grants to individuals.
Application information: Contributes only to pre-selected organizations.
Directors: Michele Engemann; Roger Engemann.
EIN: 954677701
Selected grants: The following grants were reported in 2004.

$55,000 to Scripps College, Claremont, CA.

$50,000 to Huntington Library, Art Collections and Botanical Gardens, San Marino, CA.

$10,000 to Altadena Guild of the Huntington Memorial Hospital, Duarte, CA.

$10,000 to Pasadena Playhouse State Theater of California, Pasadena, CA.
$6,000 to Recording for the Blind and Dyslexic, Los Angeles, CA.
$5,000 to Huntington Hospital, Pasadena, CA.
$5,000 to Pasadena Educational Foundation, Pasadena, CA.
$1,250 to Cheder Menachem, Los Angeles, CA.
$1,000 to Holy Family High School, Glendale, CA.
$1,000 to Hoover Institution on War, Revolution and Peace, Stanford, CA.

485
Robert & Mary Jane Engman Foundation ◇ ☆
43044 Business Park Dr.
Temecula, CA 92590-3614

Established in 2004 in CA.
Donors: Robert G. Engman; Mary Jane Engman.
Foundation type: Independent foundation.
Financial data (yr. ended 12/31/05): Assets, $1,208,672 (M); expenditures, $523,310; qualifying distributions, $520,350; giving activities include $520,350 for 33 grants (high: $135,000; low: $100; average: $1,000–$10,000).
Fields of interest: Animal welfare; Human services.
Limitations: Applications not accepted. Giving primarily in CA. No grants to individuals.
Application information: Contributes only to pre-selected organizations.
Officers and Directors:* Robert G. Engman,* Pres. and C.F.O.; Mary Jane Engman,* V.P. and Secy.; Carrie Leslie Engman; Elaine Engman; Karen M. Engman; Mark Glenn Engman; Jeffrey Holtzman.
EIN: 900063438

486
Enlight Foundation ◇ ☆
954 Roble Ridge Rd.
Palo Alto, CA 94306

Established in 2004 in CA.
Donor: Yong Ping Duan.
Foundation type: Independent foundation.
Financial data (yr. ended 12/31/05): Assets, $37,803,991 (M); expenditures, $830,748; qualifying distributions, $822,899; giving activities include $810,000 for 5 grants (high: $500,000; low: $5,000).
Fields of interest: Higher education; Human services.
Limitations: Applications not accepted. Giving primarily in CA. No grants to individuals.
Application information: Contributes only to pre-selected organizations.
Directors: Yong Ping Duan; Xin Liu.
EIN: 201063909

487
Environment Now Foundation
2515 Wilshire Blvd.
Santa Monica, CA 90403   (310) 829-5568
FAX: (310) 829-6820; URL: http://www.environmentnow.org

Established in 1989 in CA.
Donors: Frank G. Wells†; Luanne C. Wells.
Foundation type: Independent foundation.

Financial data (yr. ended 12/31/04): Assets, $35,251,440 (M); gifts received, $859,068; expenditures, $2,789,992; qualifying distributions, $2,758,536; giving activities include $1,041,482 for 48 grants (high: $118,796; low: $250).
Purpose and activities: The foundation's mission is to be an active leader in creating measurably effective environmental programs to protect and restore California's environment. Focus is on preservation of coasts and forests, and on reduction of air pollution and urban sprawl. The foundation's ultimate goal is to restore the balance and health of California's ecosystems.
Fields of interest: Environment, natural resources.
Type of support: General/operating support; Program development; Seed money; Matching/challenge support.
Limitations: Applications not accepted. Giving limited to CA. No support for projects unrelated to the environment. No grants to individuals.
Publications: Annual report.
Application information: Unsolicited requests for funds not accepted.
Officers and Directors:* Kevin Wells,* Pres.; Terry O'Day, Exec. Dir.; Dan Emmett; Paul Heeschen; Mary Nichols; Luanne C. Wells; Robert G. Wells.
Number of staff: 6 full-time professional; 1 part-time professional; 1 full-time support.
EIN: 954247242
Selected grants: The following grants were reported in 2003.
$326,018 to Energy Independence Now, Santa Barbara, CA.
$98,600 to Sequoia ForestKeeper, Kernville, CA.
$72,997 to Santa Barbara ChannelKeeper, Santa Barbara, CA.
$65,559 to Community Environmental Council, Santa Barbara, CA.
$57,500 to Coalition for Clean Air, Los Angeles, CA.
$54,852 to San Diego Coastkeeper, San Diego, CA.
$28,145 to GreenInfo Network, San Francisco, CA.
$24,327 to Wishtoyo Foundation, Oxnard, CA.
$5,088 to Mountains Restoration Trust, Malibu, CA.
$2,700 to Heal The Bay, Santa Monica, CA.

488
The Esseff Foundation ◇
790 Hampshire Rd., Unit E
Westlake Village, CA 91361-5933

Donors: George Esseff, Sr.; Rosemary Esseff, Inc.; Supra Alloys; George J. Esseff, Jr; Sheryl Lynn Esseff; Thomas Bunk; Larry Proffitt; Snappy Materials LLC.
Foundation type: Operating foundation.
Financial data (yr. ended 12/31/05): Assets, $405,071 (M); gifts received, $540,850; expenditures, $911,204; qualifying distributions, $805,765; giving activities include $737,437 for 62 grants (high: $265,000; low: $20).
Purpose and activities: Giving primarily to Roman Catholic organizations, and for affordable housing; funding also for higher education and human services.
Fields of interest: Higher education; Medical research; Housing/shelter; Human services; Military/veterans' organizations; Roman Catholic agencies & churches.
Limitations: Applications not accepted. Giving primarily in Arlington, VA, NE, and CA, with emphasis on Thousand Oaks. No grants to individuals.
Application information: Contributes only to pre-selected organizations.

Officers: George J. Esseff, Pres.; Rosemary C. Esseff, Secy.
EIN: 953447950
Selected grants: The following grants were reported in 2004.
$118,159 to Institute for Priestly Formation, Omaha, NE.
$52,250 to Many Mansions, Thousand Oaks, CA.
$41,565 to Kings College, Wilkes Barre, PA.
$41,205 to Salesian Missions, Arlington, VA.
$6,000 to Marywood University, Scranton, PA.
$3,100 to Legatus, Ann Arbor, MI.
$1,000 to College Misericordia, Dallas, PA.
$1,000 to Sisters of Notre Dame, Thousand Oaks, CA.
$500 to Saint Luke Productions, Beaverton, OR.
$75 to Saint Augustine Academy, Ventura, CA.

489
The Eucalyptus Foundation
P.O. Box 29550
San Francisco, CA 94129
Contact: Stephen Schwarz, Secy.
FAX: (415) 561-3347; Additional address for express mail/courier: 567 Ruger St., San Francisco, CA 94129

Established in 1991 in CA.
Donors: Frances K. Geballe; Theodore H. Geballe; Adam Geballe; Alison F. Geballe.
Foundation type: Independent foundation.
Financial data (yr. ended 6/30/05): Assets, $20,752,858 (M); gifts received, $2,000,000; expenditures, $1,584,915; qualifying distributions, $1,580,085; giving activities include $1,575,420 for 30 grants (high: $600,000; low: $500).
Purpose and activities: Giving primarily for community development and education.
Fields of interest: Education; Environment; Human services; Children/youth, services; Community development, neighborhood development; Economically disadvantaged.
Type of support: Research; General/operating support; Continuing support; Annual campaigns; Capital campaigns; Building/renovation; Curriculum development; Scholarship funds.
Limitations: Applications not accepted. No grants to individuals.
Application information: Contributes only to pre-selected organizations.
Board meeting date(s): June and as required
Officers and Directors:* Frances K. Geballe,* Pres.; Theodore H. Geballe,* V.P.; Stephen Schwarz, Secy.; Alison F. Geballe, C.F.O.; Adam P. Geballe; Gordon T. Geballe.
EIN: 943148772
Selected grants: The following grants were reported in 2004.
$600,000 to Hebrew Home for Aged Disabled, San Francisco, CA. For capital projects and endowment.
$200,000 to Yale University, School of Forestry and Environmental Studies, New Haven, CT. For industrial environmental management and industrial ecology programs.
$50,000 to Eastside College Preparatory School, East Palo Alto, CA. For general support.
$38,200 to Mid-Peninsula Education Center, Menlo Park, CA. For minority scholarships.
$30,000 to San Francisco Free Clinic, San Francisco, CA. For general support.
$20,000 to Save San Francisco Bay Association, Oakland, CA. For education initiatives.

$20,000 to Tenderloin Neighborhood Development Corporation, San Francisco, CA. For general support.

$5,000 to Architectural Foundation of San Francisco, San Francisco, CA. For general support.

$5,000 to Inmate Correctional Education Project, Foster City, CA. For incarcerated women with children program.

$5,000 to Western Center on Law and Poverty, Los Angeles, CA. For general support.

490
Everlasting Private Foundation ✧

c/o Annie M. H. Chan
19770 Stevens Creek Blvd.
Cupertino, CA   95014   (408) 343-1088

Established in 1996 in CA.
Donor: Annie M.H. Chan.
Foundation type: Operating foundation.
Financial data (yr. ended 12/31/05): Assets, $45,738,199 (M); expenditures, $2,151,520; qualifying distributions, $1,888,035; giving activities include $1,621,500 for 10 grants (high: $1,410,000; low: $500), and $176,452 for 1 foundation-administered program.
Purpose and activities: Giving to foster Christian beliefs through the operation of a camp that focuses on religious/biblical education; giving also to a Baptist church and seminary, and for education.
Fields of interest: Arts; Theological school/education; Education; Christian agencies & churches; Protestant agencies & churches.
Limitations: Applications not accepted. Giving primarily in CA. No grants to individuals.
Application information: Contributes only to pre-selected organizations.
Officers: Annie M.H. Chan, Pres.; Myong Shin Woo, Secy. and C.F.O.
Number of staff: 3 full-time professional; 2 part-time professional.
EIN: 770425562
Selected grants: The following grants were reported in 2003.
$2,149,000 to Ohana Foundation for Technical Development, Honolulu, HI. For general support.

$300,000 to Community Foundation Silicon Valley, San Jose, CA. For general support.

$50,000 to Kings Academy, Sunnyvale, CA. For general support.

$50,000 to Northwest Baptist Seminary, Tacoma, WA. For general support.

$2,500 to Foothill-De Anza Community Colleges Foundation, Los Altos Hills, CA. For general support.

$653 to Voice of the Martyrs, Bartlesville, OK. For general support.

491
Max Factor Family Foundation ✧

9777 Wilshire Blvd., Ste. 1011
Beverly Hills, CA   90212   (310) 274-8193

Trust established in 1941 in CA.
Donor: members of the Factor family.
Foundation type: Independent foundation.
Financial data (yr. ended 12/31/05): Assets, $11,080,090 (M); expenditures, $518,744; qualifying distributions, $473,112; giving activities

include $473,112 for 25 grants (high: $200,000; low: $1,000).
Fields of interest: Hospitals (general); Health organizations, association; Medical research, institute; Human services; Children/youth, services; Jewish federated giving programs.
Type of support: General/operating support; Continuing support; Building/renovation; Scholarship funds; Research.
Limitations: Applications not accepted. Giving primarily in Los Angeles, CA. No grants to individuals.
Application information: Contributes only to pre-selected organizations.
Trustees: Barbara F. Bentley; Gerald Factor; Max Factor III.
Number of staff: 3 part-time professional.
EIN: 956030779
Selected grants: The following grants were reported in 2003.
$200,000 to United Jewish Fund of Greater Los Angeles, Los Angeles, CA.

$53,912 to University of Southern California, Los Angeles, CA. 2 grants: $33,334 to School of Law, $20,578

$50,000 to Los Angeles Jewish Home for the Aging, Reseda, CA.

$50,000 to Public Health Foundation of Los Angeles County, Los Angeles, CA.

$46,900 to Cedars-Sinai Medical Center, Los Angeles, CA.

$30,959 to Childrens Hospital of Los Angeles Foundation, Los Angeles, CA.

$25,000 to Hope, City of, Hope, AR.

$25,000 to University of California, School of Medicine, Los Angeles, CA.

$20,242 to Venice Family Clinic, Venice, CA.

492
Fairchild-Martindale Foundation ✧

P.O. Box 11864
Santa Ana, CA   92711-1864

Established in 1969 in CA.
Donors: Elizabeth F. Martindale; Harry T. Martindale.
Foundation type: Independent foundation.
Financial data (yr. ended 12/31/05): Assets, $16,846,312 (M); expenditures, $1,198,680; qualifying distributions, $1,038,821; giving activities include $1,022,500 for 38 grants (high: $100,000; low: $2,500).
Purpose and activities: Giving primarily for education, health care, and the arts.
Fields of interest: Arts; Higher education; Health care; Health organizations; Children/youth, services.
Limitations: Applications not accepted. Giving primarily in CA. No grants to individuals.
Application information: Contributes only to pre-selected organizations.
Trustee: Stephen F. Keller.
EIN: 237001273
Selected grants: The following grants were reported in 2005.
$100,000 to Lehigh University, Bethlehem, PA.

$94,101 to Utah Symphony and Opera, Salt Lake City, UT.

$75,000 to Cathedral of Our Lady of Angels, Los Angeles, CA.

$50,000 to Childrens Hospital Los Angeles, Los Angeles, CA.

$50,000 to Hoover Institution on War, Revolution and Peace, Stanford, CA.

$50,000 to University of California at Berkeley Foundation, Berkeley, CA.

$50,000 to University of Utah, Salt Lake City, UT.

$25,000 to Heritage Foundation, DC.

$25,000 to Hoag Hospital Foundation, Newport Beach, CA.

$20,000 to Saint Annes Maternity Home, Los Angeles, CA.

493
Family First Foundation, Inc. ✧

5804 E. Slauson Ave.
Commerce, CA   90040

Established in 2002 in CA.
Donors: Hubert Guez; Roxanne Guez; Eduardo Verruno; Sanders Morris Harris; Tee-Teas, LLC.
Foundation type: Independent foundation.
Financial data (yr. ended 12/31/05): Assets, $50,981 (M); gifts received, $5,000; expenditures, $417,320; qualifying distributions, $417,320; giving activities include $411,501 for 12 grants (high: $186,000; low: $1,000; average: $3,150–$25,000).
Fields of interest: Elementary school/education; Education; Human services; Children, services; Family services; Jewish agencies & temples.
Limitations: Giving primarily in Los Angeles, CA; some giving also in Brooklyn, NY.
Officers: Frank Valensi, Pres.; Uri Harkham, Secy. and C.F.O.
EIN: 680533741

494
Fansler Foundation

5713 N. West St., Ste. 102
Fresno, CA   93711   (559) 432-0544
Contact: Marlene Fansler, Pres.

Established in 1984 in CA.
Donors: D. Paul Fansler†; Fansler Living Trust.
Foundation type: Independent foundation.
Financial data (yr. ended 10/31/05): Assets, $22,711,691 (M); gifts received, $3,000; expenditures, $1,359,707; qualifying distributions, $1,085,917; giving activities include $960,360 for 31 grants (high: $150,000; low: $250).
Purpose and activities: Giving primarily for education and health care, and social services, with emphasis on children and youth; some giving also for a family development center, and handicap accessibility facilities.
Fields of interest: Education, early childhood education; Health organizations, association; Cerebral palsy; Asthma; Crime/violence prevention, child abuse; Children/youth, services; Disabilities, people with.
Limitations: Giving primarily in the Fresno County, CA, area. No grants to individuals.
Publications: Application guidelines.
Application information: Contact the foundation for specifics to be covered, and required attachments. Application form required.
   Initial approach: Letter of intent, no more than 3-typewritten pages
   Copies of proposal: 6
   Deadline(s): Mar. 31 for funding by Oct. 31
   Board meeting date(s): As needed
   Final notification: July 31

Officer: Marlene Fansler, Pres.
Trustees: Bethanie Crabtree; Linda Duncan; Craig Saladino; Mark Schuh.
Number of staff: 2 full-time professional.
EIN: 770095125

495
Farallon Foundation
c/o Hugh W. Ditzler, Jr.
6114 LaSalle Ave., PMB Ste. 443
Oakland, CA   94611-2802
E-mail: FarallonFdn@aol.com

Established in 1972 in CA.
Donors: Hugh W. Ditzler, Jr.; Nancy M. Ditzler; Marian Zischke; Peter H. Zischke; John R. Shuman†; Josephine R. Shuman; W. James Lloyd; Pamela Lloyd; Gerald C. Down; William K. Steiner; Frances K. Lloyd†; Kate Ditzler; Karin Chamberlain; David Chamberlain; Marian Baldauf; Richard Reinhardt; Debra Perry; Mark Perry; Karen Nager; Charles Nager; Susan Wait; Bradford Wait; JoEllen Brean; Park T. Dingwell; Joseph Eldridge†; James G. Siler; Susan Siler; Robert Shuman; Laura Waste; William Waste†.
Foundation type: Independent foundation.
Financial data (yr. ended 12/31/05): Assets, $5,752,437 (M); gifts received, $419,380; expenditures, $385,789; qualifying distributions, $324,851; giving activities include $316,299 for 315 grants (high: $12,000; low: $20).
Purpose and activities: Support only for donor-advised organizations.
Fields of interest: Performing arts; Education; Hospitals (general); Salvation Army; Christian agencies & churches.
Limitations: Applications not accepted. Giving primarily in the western U.S. No grants to individuals.
Publications: Financial statement.
Application information: Unsolicited requests for funds not accepted. Disbursements only as recommended by donors.
  Board meeting date(s): Jan. and July
Officer and Directors:* Hugh W. Ditzler, Jr.,* Pres. and Mgr.; Hugh W. Ditzler III; Nancy M. Ditzler; Peter H. Zischke.
Number of staff: None.
EIN: 237216373

496
Farrell Family Foundation ◇
P.O. Box 1206
La Jolla, CA   92038

Established in 2001 in CA.
Donor: Peter C. Farrell.
Foundation type: Independent foundation.
Financial data (yr. ended 12/31/04): Assets, $3,052,905 (M); gifts received, $1,910,000; expenditures, $468,651; qualifying distributions, $433,609; giving activities include $393,700 for 21 grants (high: $250,000; low: $250).
Fields of interest: Education; Community development; Foundations (community).
Limitations: Applications not accepted. Giving primarily in CA. No grants to individuals.
Application information: Contributes only to pre-selected organizations.

Directors: Fiona Tudor, Exec. Dir.; Paul A. Farrell; Peter C. Farrell; Michael J. Farrell; Catherine A. Sertori.
EIN: 912167530
Selected grants: The following grants were reported in 2004.
$250,000 to San Diego Foundation, San Diego, CA.
$53,000 to San Diego Opera Association, San Diego, CA.
$12,500 to University of California at San Diego Foundation, La Jolla, CA.
$10,000 to Variety Childrens Lifeline, Solana Beach, CA.
$500 to Neurosciences Institute, San Diego, CA.
$250 to Zoological Society of San Diego, San Diego, CA.

497
Edward Fein Foundation ◇ ☆
(formerly Edward Feinstein Foundation)
21031 Ventura Blvd., Ste. 1000
Woodland Hills, CA   91364
URL: http://www.foundationcenter.org/grantmaker/fein/

Established in 1965 in NY.
Donor: Edward Fein.
Foundation type: Independent foundation.
Financial data (yr. ended 3/31/06): Assets, $8,263,221 (M); expenditures, $439,572; qualifying distributions, $436,200; giving activities include $436,200 for grants.
Purpose and activities: Giving primarily for higher education; funding also for regular education, human services, and Jewish organizations and temples.
Fields of interest: Higher education; Education; Legal services; Human services; Youth, services; Jewish federated giving programs; Jewish agencies & temples; Aging.
International interests: Israel.
Limitations: Applications not accepted. Giving primarily in AZ, CA and NV. No grants to individuals.
Application information: Contributes only to pre-selected organizations.
  Board meeting date(s): Jan.
Trustee: Edward Fein.
EIN: 136220451
Selected grants: The following grants were reported in 2005.
$101,300 to Brandeis University, Waltham, MA.
$75,000 to American Friends of the Hebrew University, New York, NY.
$40,000 to Poly Prep Country Day School, Brooklyn, NY.
$16,000 to Golden Slipper Club Camp, Bala Cynwyd, PA.
$11,000 to One Organization for the Needs of the Elderly, Van Nuys, CA.
$10,000 to Temple Bat Yam, Stateline, NV.
$5,000 to Social Venture Partners, Phoenix, AZ.
$4,500 to Seeds of Peace, New York, NY.
$2,000 to Hebrew Seniorlife, Boston, MA.
$200 to March of Dimes Birth Defects Foundation, White Plains, NY.

498
Feintech Family Foundation ◇
321 S. Beverly Dr., Ste. K
Beverly Hills, CA   90212

Established in 1950 in CA.
Donors: Evelyn M. Feintech; Irving Feintech; Norman Feintech; Liberty Building Co.
Foundation type: Independent foundation.
Financial data (yr. ended 9/30/05): Assets, $370,771 (M); gifts received, $251,948; expenditures, $749,105; qualifying distributions, $748,445; giving activities include $743,240 for 25 grants (high: $225,700; low: $100).
Purpose and activities: Giving primarily for medical research and health care, and for Jewish welfare and concerns; support also for the arts.
Fields of interest: Arts; Hospitals (general); Medical research, institute; Human services; Jewish federated giving programs; Jewish agencies & temples.
Limitations: Applications not accepted. Giving primarily in CA, with emphasis on Los Angeles. No grants to individuals.
Application information: Contributes only to pre-selected organizations.
Officers: Irving Feintech, Pres.; Evelyn M. Feintech, V.P.
Director: Celia Littenberg.
EIN: 956072287
Selected grants: The following grants were reported in 2003.
$123,200 to Cedars-Sinai Medical Center, Los Angeles, CA.
$53,900 to Stephen S. Wise Temple, Los Angeles, CA.
$50,500 to Music Center Foundation, Los Angeles, CA.
$50,375 to Jewish Federation Council of Greater Los Angeles, Los Angeles, CA.
$50,000 to Hebrew Union College-Jewish Institute of Religion, Los Angeles, CA.
$40,200 to Cheerful Helpers for Handicapped Children, Los Angeles, CA.
$35,000 to Shoah Foundation, Philadelphia, PA. For general support.
$25,000 to Anti-Defamation League of Bnai Brith, Los Angeles, CA.
$10,000 to Junior Blind of America, Los Angeles, CA.
$10,000 to Shanes Inspiration, Valley Village, CA.

499
Evelyn M. & Norman Feintech Family Foundation ◇ ☆
321 S. Beverly Dr., Ste. K
Beverly Hills, CA   90212

Established in 1990 in CA.
Donors: Irving Feintech; Evelyn M. Feintech; Norman Feintech; Lynn Diane Feintech; Shapell Industries.
Foundation type: Independent foundation.
Financial data (yr. ended 12/31/05): Assets, $4,411,907 (M); gifts received, $1,141,150; expenditures, $338,231; qualifying distributions, $337,267; giving activities include $330,292 for 37 grants (high: $101,950; low: $100).
Purpose and activities: Giving for art and cultural programs, health and human services, and for Jewish organizations.
Fields of interest: Performing arts; Arts; Higher education; Hospitals (general); Health care; Human services; Civil rights, women; Civil liberties, reproductive rights; Jewish agencies & temples.
Limitations: Applications not accepted. Giving primarily in CA. No grants to individuals.
Application information: Contributes only to pre-selected organizations.

Officers and Directors:* Evelyn M. Feintech,* Pres.; Irving Feintech, V.P.; Vivian A. Feintech, V.P.; Lynn Diane Feintech,* Secy.-Treas.
EIN: 954268945
Selected grants: The following grants were reported in 2004.
$103,250 to ODC San Francisco, San Francisco, CA. For general support.
$60,300 to Cheerful Helpers for Handicapped Children, Los Angeles, CA. For general support.
$26,500 to Cedars-Sinai Medical Center, Los Angeles, CA. For general support.
$18,000 to Jewish Federation Council of Greater Los Angeles, Los Angeles, CA. For general support.
$11,000 to Smile Train, New York, NY. For general support.
$10,000 to Los Angeles Opera Theater, Los Angeles, CA. For general support.
$5,000 to Save a Heart Foundation, Los Angeles, CA. For general support.
$1,000 to American Jewish Committee, New York, NY. For general support.
$1,000 to Los Angeles Master Chorale Association, Los Angeles, CA. For general support.
$1,000 to Revlon Run/Walk for Women, Santa Monica, CA. For general support.

500
Irving Feintech Family Foundation ◇ ☆
321 S. Beverly Dr., Ste. K
Beverly Hills, CA 90212

Established in 1990 in CA.
Donors: Irving Feintech; The Feintech Family Foundation; Liberty Building Co.; Shapell Industries.
Foundation type: Independent foundation.
Financial data (yr. ended 12/31/05): Assets, $4,058,693 (M); expenditures, $370,728; qualifying distributions, $368,769; giving activities include $358,035 for 20 grants (high: $75,000; low: $400).
Fields of interest: Arts; Higher education; Education; Hospitals (general); Medical research; Human services; Federated giving programs.
Limitations: Applications not accepted. Giving primarily in CA. No grants to individuals.
Application information: Contributes only to pre-selected organizations.
Officers and Director:* Irving Feintech,* Pres. and Treas.; Lisa A. Feintech, V.P. and Secy.; Wendy Feintech, V.P.
EIN: 954268946
Selected grants: The following grants were reported in 2004.
$75,000 to Anonymoose Foundation, Beverly Hills, CA. For general support.
$47,500 to Cedars-Sinai Medical Center, Los Angeles, CA. For general support.
$12,580 to Geffen Playhouse, Los Angeles, CA. For general support.
$10,000 to Lutheran World Relief, Baltimore, MD. For general support.
$5,000 to Los Angeles Free Clinic, Los Angeles, CA. For general support.
$5,000 to Los Angeles Master Chorale, Los Angeles, CA. For general support.
$5,000 to Teen Line, Los Angeles, CA. For general support.
$3,000 to Meals on Wheels of Los Angeles, Los Angeles, CA. For general support.
$2,760 to Puck-Lazaroff Charitable Foundation, Beverly Hills, CA. For general support.

$1,860 to Los Angeles Chamber Orchestra Society, Los Angeles, CA. For general support.

501
Femino Foundation
Three Pointe Dr., Ste. 300
Brea, CA 92821
Contact: Robert L. Bacon, Secy.
Additional address: P.O. Box 1285, Brea, CA 92822

Established in 1969 in CA.
Donors: James J. Femino; Sue Femino; Dominic Femino.
Foundation type: Independent foundation.
Financial data (yr. ended 9/30/05): Assets, $10,885,377 (M); gifts received, $395,000; expenditures, $472,181; qualifying distributions, $468,890; giving activities include $468,890 for 39 grants (high: $206,000; low: $25).
Purpose and activities: Support primarily for hospitals, health organizations, and institutions of medical research and education; support also for higher and other educational institutions, as well as for art, music and literature.
Fields of interest: Visual arts; Performing arts, music; Literature; Higher education; Medical school/education; Education; Health organizations, association; Medical research, institute; Engineering/technology; Science.
Type of support: Capital campaigns; Scholarship funds; Research.
Limitations: Applications not accepted. Giving primarily in southern CA. No grants to individuals.
Application information: Contributes only to pre-selected organizations. Unsolicited requests for funds not considered.
Officers and Trustees:* James J. Femino,* Pres.; Sue Femino,* V.P.; Robert L. Bacon,* Secy.; Frank P. Uehle,* Treas.; Marie Femino.
EIN: 237423792
Selected grants: The following grants were reported in 2005.
$100,000 to Childrens Hospital, Rancho Santa Fe, CA.
$8,875 to Polytechnic School, Pasadena, CA.
$3,300 to Salvation Army, Redding, CA.
$2,500 to Aquarium of the Pacific, Long Beach, CA.
$1,650 to Kidspace, A Participatory Museum, Pasadena, CA.
$1,000 to Casa Colina Centers for Rehabilitation Foundation, Pomona, CA.
$1,000 to Little Sisters of the Poor, San Pedro, CA.
$1,000 to Los Angeles Master Chorale, Los Angeles, CA.
$250 to Women at Work, Pasadena, CA.
$25 to Disabled American Veterans, Cincinnati, OH.

502
Bettye Poetz Ferguson Foundation ◇
425 California St., Ste. 2500
San Francisco, CA 94104
Contact: D. Keith Bilter, Tr.

Established in 1994 in CA.
Donor: Bettye Poetz Ferguson.
Foundation type: Independent foundation.
Financial data (yr. ended 12/31/05): Assets, $105,949 (M); gifts received, $500,000; expenditures, $494,440; qualifying distributions, $494,341; giving activities include $492,184 for 79

grants (high: $50,000; low: $100; average: $500–$10,000).
Fields of interest: Performing arts; Higher education; Human services.
Limitations: Applications not accepted. Giving limited to the San Francisco Bay Area, CA.
Application information: Unsolicited requests for funds not accepted.
Trustees: George Argyris; D. Keith Bilter; Bettye Poetz Ferguson.
EIN: 943192412

503
Eris & Larry Field Family Foundation ◇
433 N. Camden Dr., Ste. 820
Beverly Hills, CA 90210
Contact: Lawrence N. Field, Pres.

Established in 1983 in CA.
Donors: Lawrence N. Field; Eris M. Field.
Foundation type: Operating foundation.
Financial data (yr. ended 6/30/05): Assets, $359,854 (M); gifts received, $1,000,000; expenditures, $876,394; qualifying distributions, $820,473; giving activities include $820,473 for 67 grants (high: $256,750; low: $1,000).
Purpose and activities: Giving primarily for health, education, and Jewish organizations; funding also for the arts and human services.
Fields of interest: Performing arts; Performing arts centers; Arts; Higher education; Education; Hospitals (general); Human services; Foundations (private grantmaking); Jewish federated giving programs; Jewish agencies & temples.
Type of support: General/operating support.
Limitations: Giving primarily in the Los Angeles, CA, area.
Application information: Application form not required.
Deadline(s): None
Officers and Directors:* Lawrence N. Field,* Pres.; Eris M. Field,* V.P.; John Harrington, C.F.O.; Lisa S. Field; Robyn L. Field.
EIN: 953905829

504
The Frances K. & Charles D. Field Foundation ◇
155 Montgomery St., Ste. 404
San Francisco, CA 94104-4109

Established in CA.
Donor: The Frances K. Field Private Trust.
Foundation type: Independent foundation.
Financial data (yr. ended 12/31/05): Assets, $18,102,428 (M); expenditures, $1,060,219; qualifying distributions, $930,184; giving activities include $760,000 for 10 grants (high: $125,000; low: $25,000; average: $50,000–$100,000), $15,000 for 1 grant to an individual, and $100,000 for 1 employee matching gift.
Purpose and activities: Giving primarily to museums, the symphony, and the opera, including music education and opera training programs; funding also for a university's medical student scholarship fund.
Fields of interest: Arts, formal/general education; Museums; Performing arts, orchestra (symphony); Performing arts, opera; Child development, education; Higher education; Education.

Limitations: Applications not accepted. Giving primarily in San Francisco, CA; funding also in Bath, England. No grants to individuals.
Application information: Contributes only to pre-selected organizations.
Officers: Yeoryios Apallas, Pres.; John O. Jenkins, 1st V.P. and Secy.; Lawrence Drew, 2nd V.P. and Treas.
EIN: 680534344

505
The Charles D. and Frances K. Field Fund ✧ ☆
180 Montgomery St., Ste. 1616
San Francisco, CA 94104

Established in CA.
Foundation type: Independent foundation.
Financial data (yr. ended 12/31/05): Assets, $16,908,356 (M); expenditures, $981,191; qualifying distributions, $844,623; giving activities include $800,000 for 21 grants (high: $100,000; low: $5,000).
Fields of interest: Museums (art); Performing arts; Performing arts, opera; Arts; Education; Hospitals (general); Human services.
Limitations: Applications not accepted. Giving primarily in San Francisco, CA.
Application information: Contributes only to pre-selected organizations.
Officers and Directors:* Philip Hudner,* Pres.; Michael L. Helms,* Secy.; John F. Miller,* Treas.
EIN: 460497841

506
The Fieldstone Foundation ✧
14 Corporate Plz.
Newport Beach, CA 92660 (949) 759-5869
Contact: Janine Mason Barone, Exec. Dir.
E-mail: janineb@fieldstone-homes.com; Additional address: 5465 Morehouse Dr., Ste. 250, San Diego, CA 92121, tel.: (858) 404-8056; Additional E-mail: foundation@fieldstone-homes.com; URL: http://www.fieldstone-homes.com/foundation

Established in 1983 in CA.
Donor: Fieldstone Communities, Inc.
Foundation type: Company-sponsored foundation.
Financial data (yr. ended 12/31/05): Assets, $6,584,186 (M); gifts received, $1,432,782; expenditures, $1,218,125; qualifying distributions, $1,153,594; giving activities include $810,843 for grants.
Purpose and activities: The foundation supports organizations involved with arts and culture, education, domestic violence, human services, community development, and Christianity.
Fields of interest: Arts; Child development, education; Education; Crime/violence prevention, domestic violence; Children/youth, services; Child development, services; Homeless, human services; Human services; Community development; Christian agencies & churches.
Type of support: General/operating support; Program development; Employee matching gifts; Matching/challenge support.
Limitations: Applications not accepted. Giving limited to Orange, Riverside, San Bernardino, and San Diego counties, CA, and Salt Lake City, UT. No support for veterans' organizations, labor organizations, or fraternal organizations or athletic organizations not of direct benefit to the entire community. No grants for advertising, continuing support, or capital campaigns.
Application information: Contributes only to pre-selected organizations.
Officers: Peter M. Ochs, Chair.; Keith A. Johnson, Vice-Chair.; David R. Langlois, Pres.; Janine Mason Barone, Exec. Dir.; Rick Haugen, C.F.O.
Number of staff: 2 part-time professional; 1 part-time support.
EIN: 330103025

507
Ernest L. and Ruth W. Finley Foundation ✧ ☆
1400 N. Dutton Ave., Ste. 12
Santa Rosa, CA 95401-4644 (707) 545-3136
Contact: Evert B. Person, Tr.

Established in 1985 in CA.
Donors: Ernest L. Finley†; Ruth W. Finley†.
Foundation type: Independent foundation.
Financial data (yr. ended 8/31/06): Assets, $619,243 (M); gifts received, $472,550; expenditures, $449,953; qualifying distributions, $405,000; giving activities include $405,000 for grants.
Purpose and activities: Giving primarily for the performing and visual arts, social services, and religious endeavors.
Fields of interest: Arts; Human services; Children/youth, services; Family services; Government/public administration; Roman Catholic agencies & churches; Religion.
Type of support: General/operating support; Building/renovation; Endowments; Scholarship funds.
Limitations: Giving limited to Santa Rosa, CA. No grants to individuals.
Application information:
  Initial approach: Proposal
  Copies of proposal: 3
  Deadline(s): None
  Board meeting date(s): As required
Trustees: Brad Bollinger; William W. Godward; Evert B. Person; Norma J. Person.
EIN: 941694310

508
Firedoll Foundation ✧
1460 Maria Ln., Ste. 420
Walnut Creek, CA 94596
Contact: Neil Sims, Prog. Off.
E-mail: info@firedoll.org; URL: http://www.firedoll.org

Established in 1998 in CA.
Donor: Straus Family Trust.
Foundation type: Independent foundation.
Financial data (yr. ended 5/31/05): Assets, $6,352,489 (M); gifts received, $686,899; expenditures, $1,031,015; qualifying distributions, $1,000,246; giving activities include $995,319 for 96 grants (high: $30,000; low: $1,000).
Purpose and activities: The foundation offers grants to nonprofits in the areas of environmental conservation, immigrant/human rights, community development, Mid-East peace, and offers support for Bay Area non-profits servicing victims of traumatic brain injury.
Fields of interest: Environment, natural resources; Environment, water resources; Environment, forests; Animals/wildlife, fisheries; Housing/shelter, homeless; International peace/security; Civil rights, immigrants; Community development, small businesses.
International interests: Middle East.
Type of support: General/operating support; Continuing support; Capital campaigns; Building/renovation; Equipment; Land acquisition; Emergency funds; Program development; Seed money; Technical assistance; Program evaluation; Program-related investments/loans; Matching/challenge support.
Limitations: Giving primarily in the San Francisco Bay Area, CA, with emphasis on Alameda and Contra Costa counties; some giving to national organizations promoting environmental conservation. No grants to individuals or for the arts.
Publications: Application guidelines; Grants list; Program policy statement.
Application information: Consult application guidelines on Web site before sending proposals. Proposals not following guidelines will be returned. Application form required.
  Initial approach: E-mail or written letter of inquiry or proposal after consulting Web site
  Copies of proposal: 1
  Deadline(s): Between Oct. 1 and Dec. 31 for Environmental Conservation, Immigration/Human Rights and Community Development. No deadline for other areas
  Final notification: 6-10 weeks
Officers: Sandor Straus, Pres. and Treas.; Faye Straus, V.P. and Secy.
Number of staff: 1 full-time professional; 1 part-time professional.
EIN: 943301999
Selected grants: The following grants were reported in 2005.
$30,000 to Renaissance Entrepreneurship Center, San Francisco, CA.
$25,000 to Marine Mammal Center, Sausalito, CA.
$23,150 to Grassroots International, Boston, MA. 2 grants: $5,150, $18,000
$20,000 to Conservation Strategy Fund, Philo, CA.
$17,000 to Caribbean Conservation Corporation, Gainesville, FL.
$16,500 to International Institute of the East Bay, Oakland, CA.
$15,000 to Catholic Charities of the East Bay, Oakland, CA.
$15,000 to Northern California Community Loan Fund, San Francisco, CA.
$13,000 to Rainforest Action Network, San Francisco, CA.

509
Firelight Foundation ✧
740 Front St., Ste. 380
Santa Cruz, CA 95060 (831) 429-8750
Contact: Jennifer Astone, Dir.
FAX: (831) 429-2036;
E-mail: info@firelightfoundation.org; URL: http://www.firelightfoundation.org

Established in 1999 in CA.
Donors: David M. Katz; Kerry A. Olson.
Foundation type: Independent foundation.
Financial data (yr. ended 9/30/05): Assets, $11,778,721 (M); gifts received, $1,156,136; expenditures, $2,211,371; qualifying distributions,

$2,126,324; giving activities include $1,098,705 for 120 grants (high: $35,000; low: $1,300).

Purpose and activities: The mission of the Firelight Foundation is to support and advocate for the needs and rights of children who are orphaned or affected by HIV/AIDS in Sub-Saharan Africa. Firelight strives to increase the resources available to grassroots organizations that are strengthening the capacity of families and communities to care for children made vulnerable by HIV/AIDS.

Fields of interest: AIDS; Children/youth, services; Women, centers/services.

International interests: Lesotho; Malawi; Rwanda; South Africa; Sub-Saharan Africa; Tanzania; Zambia; Zimbabwe.

Type of support: General/operating support; Continuing support; Management development/capacity building; Building/renovation; Program development; Technical assistance.

Limitations: Giving in Sub-Saharan Africa; few grants to U.S.-based organizations. No grants to individuals, or for academic or medical research, endowments, or fundraisers.

Publications: Application guidelines; Annual report; Grants list; Informational brochure; Informational brochure (including application guidelines); Occasional report.

Application information: Application information available on foundation Web site. Application form required.

   Initial approach: Letter
   Deadline(s): See foundation Web site
   Board meeting date(s): Spring (Apr.) and fall (Sept.)
   Final notification: May and Nov.

Officers and Directors:* Kerry A. Olson, Ph.D.*, Pres.; David M. Katz,* V.P.; Debra Evans,* Secy.; Nancy Shallow, J.D.; Jim Hayes.

Number of staff: 6 full-time professional; 2 part-time support.

EIN: 770529657

510
Fireman's Fund Foundation ✧

(formerly Fireman's Fund Insurance Company Foundation)
777 San Marin Dr.
Novato, CA 94998
Contact: Phyllis Secosky, Secy. and Exec. Dir.

Incorporated in 1953 in CA. Status changed to company-sponsored operating foundation in 2004.

Donor: Fireman's Fund Insurance Co.

Foundation type: Operating foundation.

Financial data (yr. ended 12/31/05): Assets, $148,096 (M); gifts received, $577,873; expenditures, $439,393; qualifying distributions, $441,981; giving activities include $441,981 for 63 grants (high: $56,421; low: $2,060).

Purpose and activities: The foundation supports hospices and organizations involved with arts and culture, education, substance abuse, crime and violence, human services, civil rights, youth, senior citizens, disabled people, mentally disabled people, women, economically disadvantaged people, and homeless people.

Fields of interest: Arts; Education, equal rights; Child development, education; Education; Substance abuse, services; Crime/violence prevention, abuse prevention; Children/youth, services; Child development, services; Family services; Family services, domestic violence; Residential/custodial care, hospices; Human

services; Civil rights, equal rights; Voluntarism promotion; Youth; Aging; Disabilities, people with; Mentally disabled; Women; Economically disadvantaged; Homeless.

Type of support: Sponsorships; Employee matching gifts.

Limitations: Giving primarily in Marin and Sonoma counties, CA. No support for religious organizations not of direct benefit to the entire community, fraternal, veterans', sectarian, political, health, or national organizations, other grantmaking bodies, or organizations not registered with Guidestar.org. No grants to individuals, or for scholarships, capital campaigns, endowments, medical research, travel, advertising, subscription fees, admissions tickets, sporting events, benefit events, video or film production, or general operating support; no loans.

Application information: Application form required.

   Initial approach: Complete online application form
   Deadline(s): Apr. 1 and Oct. 1
   Board meeting date(s): May and Nov.
   Final notification: 3 months

Officers and Directors:* Janet S. Kloenhamer,* Chair.; Chuck Kaoitsky,* Pres.; Phyllis Secosky, Secy. and Exec. Dir.; Joseph Beneducci; Bruce F. Friedberg; Jill Paterson; Christopher Worthley.

Number of staff: 1 full-time professional.

EIN: 946078025

Selected grants: The following grants were reported in 2004.

$49,485 to Volunteer Center of Sonoma County, Santa Rosa, CA.

$16,540 to Center for Volunteer and Nonprofit Leadership of Marin, San Rafael, CA.

$15,000 to Bernard Osher Marin Jewish Community Center, San Rafael, CA.

$15,000 to Image for Success, San Rafael, CA.

$15,000 to Luther Burbank Memorial Foundation, Santa Rosa, CA.

$15,000 to Marin Interfaith Youth Outreach, San Rafael, CA.

$15,000 to Marin Symphony Association, San Rafael, CA.

$10,000 to Bay Area Discovery Museum, Sausalito, CA.

$10,000 to Full Circle Programs, San Rafael, CA.

$10,000 to Novato Youth Center, Novato, CA.

511
First American Financial Foundation ✧

1 First American Way
Santa Ana, CA 92707

Established in 1985 in CA.

Donor: The First American Corp.

Foundation type: Company-sponsored foundation.

Financial data (yr. ended 10/31/05): Assets, $3,469,826 (M); gifts received, $4,050,000; expenditures, $790,808; qualifying distributions, $790,751; giving activities include $790,751 for 52 grants (high: $220,000; low: $150).

Purpose and activities: The foundation supports organizations involved with arts and culture, education, human services, and neighborhood development.

Fields of interest: Performing arts centers; Arts; Higher education; Education; Boys & girls clubs; Boy scouts; Human services; Community development, neighborhood development.

Type of support: General/operating support.

Limitations: Applications not accepted. Giving primarily in CA. No grants to individuals.

Application information: Contributes only to pre-selected organizations.

Trustees: Donald P. Kennedy; Parker S. Kennedy; Thomas A. Klemens.

EIN: 330148572

Selected grants: The following grants were reported in 2005.

$220,000 to Orange County Performing Arts Center, Costa Mesa, CA.

$25,500 to Chapman University, Orange, CA.

$25,000 to Pacific Chorale, Santa Ana, CA.

$10,000 to Santa Ana College Foundation, Santa Ana, CA.

$5,000 to Business Committee for the Arts, Long Island City, NY.

$2,500 to Alvin Ailey Dance Foundation, New York, NY.

512
First Fruit, Inc. ✧ ☆

14 Corporate Plz.
Newport Beach, CA 92660   (949) 720-3774
Contact: Rob Martin, Exec. Dir.
FAX: (949) 760-5349; E-mail: info@firstfruit.org;
URL: http://www.firstfruit.org

Established in 1976 in CA.

Donors: Peter M. Ochs; Gail J. Ochs.

Foundation type: Independent foundation.

Financial data (yr. ended 12/31/05): Assets, $18,738,657 (M); gifts received, $800,000; expenditures, $2,499,652; qualifying distributions, $2,434,009; giving activities include $1,729,872 for 81 grants (high: $120,000; low: $2,000).

Purpose and activities: Grants are made only to organizations which engage in advancing the Gospel of Jesus Christ primarily in Third World countries. Preference is given to evangelical ministries, usually with strategic pioneering programs among peoples who have not had repeated contact with the Gospel message.

Fields of interest: Protestant agencies & churches.

International interests: Developing countries.

Type of support: General/operating support; Building/renovation; Equipment; Program development; Conferences/seminars; Seed money; Curriculum development; Research; Program evaluation; Matching/challenge support.

Limitations: Giving limited to non-developed or developing countries. No grants to individuals.

Application information: Application form not required.

   Initial approach: Letter of inquiry
   Copies of proposal: 1
   Deadline(s): None
   Board meeting date(s): Three times per year, as determined by the board

Officers and Directors:* Peter M. Ochs,* Pres.; Gail J. Ochs,* V.P.; Dennis W. Thome,* Secy.; Rick Haugen, Treas.; Rob Martin, Exec. Dir.; David W. Bennett.

Number of staff: 4 full-time professional; 1 part-time professional; 1 full-time support.

EIN: 953081605

Selected grants: The following grants were reported in 2004.

$112,000 to Luis Palau Evangelistic Association, Portland, OR.

$78,730 to Avant Ministries, Kansas City, MO.

$68,000 to Peter Deyneka Russian Ministries, Wheaton, IL.

$49,346 to Evangelism Resources, Lexington, KY.

$40,000 to John Stott Ministries, Carol Stream, IL.

$35,000 to Servant Partners, Pasadena, CA.
$32,000 to Partners International, Spokane, WA.
$24,000 to International Urban Associates, Seattle, WA.
$20,000 to Council of International Childrens Ministries, Boulder, CO.
$15,000 to Fourteen Four Group, Montrose, CA.

513
Kathryn C. Fishback Family Foundation, Inc. ✧ ☆
6692 La Jolla Scenic Dr. S.
La Jolla, CA   92037

Established in 1998 in CA.
Donor: Kathryn C. Fishback.
Foundation type: Independent foundation.
Financial data (yr. ended 12/31/05): Assets, $6,384 (M); gifts received, $315,000; expenditures, $339,757; qualifying distributions, $315,500; giving activities include $315,500 for grants.
Purpose and activities: Giving for the arts, hospitals, and health associations.
Fields of interest: Performing arts, opera; Arts; Hospitals (general); Health organizations, association.
Limitations: Applications not accepted. Giving primarily in CA. No grants to individuals.
Application information: Contributes only to pre-selected organizations.
Directors: Kathryn C. Fishback; Jeanne C. Jones; Brian E. Lewis.
EIN: 330854982
Selected grants: The following grants were reported in 2003.
$62,500 to San Diego Opera Association, San Diego, CA.
$60,000 to La Jolla Playhouse, La Jolla, CA.
$50,000 to Hoag Memorial Hospital Presbyterian, Women's Pavilion, Newport Beach, CA.
$40,000 to American Red Cross, Orange County Chapter, Santa Ana, CA.
$10,000 to Lance Armstrong Foundation, Austin, TX.
$10,000 to Whittier Institute for Diabetes and Endocrinology, La Jolla, CA.

514
Ella Fitzgerald Charitable Foundation
P.O. Box 1587
Pacific Palisades, CA   90272   (310) 826-3869
Contact: Fran E. Morris Rosman, Exec. Dir.
E-mail: ellafitzgerald@earthlink.net; URL: http://www.ellafitzgeraldfoundation.org

Established in 1993 in CA.
Donor: Ella Fitzgerald‡.
Foundation type: Independent foundation.
Financial data (yr. ended 12/31/04): Assets, $14,817,164 (M); gifts received, $1,000; expenditures, $997,193; qualifying distributions, $997,193; giving activities include $764,678 for 117+ grants (high: $37,000).
Purpose and activities: Giving primarily for education and human services.
Fields of interest: Performing arts, music; Education, reading; Eye diseases; Heart & circulatory diseases; Diabetes; Children/youth, services.
Type of support: Continuing support; Fellowships.

Limitations: Applications not accepted. Giving on a national basis, with strong emphasis on CA. No grants to individuals; no loans.
Publications: Occasional report.
Application information: Unsolicited requests for funds not accepted.
Board meeting date(s): Quarterly
Officers and Directors:* Richard D. Rosman,* Pres.; Fran E. Morris Rosman,* Exec. Dir.; Mary Olson Kromolowski; Perry Maguire; Joseph Pressutti.
Number of staff: 1 full-time professional; 1 part-time professional.
EIN: 954419236
Selected grants: The following grants were reported in 2003.
$32,930 to Smithsonian Institution, DC. For Ella in Hollywood exhibit.
$10,000 to Christopher Newport University, Newport News, VA.
$10,000 to RX for Reading, Los Angeles, CA.
$10,000 to University of Southern California, Los Angeles, CA.
$6,604 to PUENTE Learning Center: People United to Enrich the Neighborhood Through Education, Los Angeles, CA.
$6,283 to A Place Called Home, Los Angeles, CA.
$5,000 to Family Literacy Foundation, Solana Beach, CA.
$5,000 to Guide Dogs of America, Sylmar, CA.
$5,000 to Santa Monica/Malibu Unified School District, Santa Monica, CA.
$1,107 to Gardena High School, Gardena, CA.

515
Fitzpatrick Foundation ✧
1110 Burlingame Ave., Ste. 300
Burlingame, CA   94010   (650) 373-1040
Contact: Jodi Allison Jennings
FAX: (650) 373-1037;
E-mail: info@fitzpatrickfoundation.org; URL: http://www.fitzpatrickfoundation.org/

Established in 1999 in CA.
Donors: Patricia W. Fitzpatrick; Michael J. Fitzpatrick.
Foundation type: Independent foundation.
Financial data (yr. ended 12/31/05): Assets, $24,068,277 (M); gifts received, $793,563; expenditures, $1,187,361; qualifying distributions, $1,084,709; giving activities include $1,075,627 for 54 grants (high: $185,000; low: $500).
Purpose and activities: The primary interest of the Fitzpatrick Foundation is to support elementary and secondary school programs for students and educators, with a particular emphasis on programs serving economically disadvantaged youth in the San Francisco Bay Area. The foundation also supports professional development programs for educators with an emphasis on providing and applying technology skills in the classroom.
Fields of interest: Elementary school/education; Secondary school/education; Education; Boys & girls clubs.
Limitations: Giving primarily in the San Francisco Bay Area, CA. No grants to individuals, or for endowments or for annual fund drives.
Publications: Application guidelines.
Application information:
Initial approach: Letter on organization letterhead
Copies of proposal: 1
Deadline(s): 8 weeks prior to board meeting

Board meeting date(s): Quarterly
Final notification: Two weeks following board meeting
Officers: Patricia W. Fitzpatrick, Pres.; Michael J. Fitzpatrick, C.F.O.
Directors: Christopher Fitzpatrick; Kimberly Fitzpatrick; Michael J. Fitzpatrick, Jr.
EIN: 943347336

516
Five Bridges Foundation ✧
P.O. Box 194405
San Francisco, CA   94119-4405
E-mail: contact@fivebridges.org; URL: http://www.fivebridges.org

Established in 1998 in CA.
Foundation type: Independent foundation.
Financial data (yr. ended 9/30/05): Assets, $22,074,951 (M); expenditures, $1,655,915; qualifying distributions, $1,109,276; giving activities include $1,055,000 for 94 grants (high: $25,000; low: $5,000).
Purpose and activities: The foundation's mission is to promote and improve the quality of life for the residents of the greater San Francisco Bay Area, CA by funding organizations that have programs directed toward achievement of long-term, positive change, particularly in the areas of women's and children's health and welfare, education of young people, and other services to the disadvantaged and underprivileged.
Fields of interest: Education; Health care, infants; Health care; Health organizations, association; AIDS; Crime/violence prevention, youth; Crime/violence prevention, domestic violence; Legal services; Food banks; Human services; Children/youth, services; Children, services; Family services; Women, centers/services; Christian agencies & churches; Disabilities, people with; Substance abusers.
Limitations: Giving limited to the ten Bay Area counties of Alameda, Contra Costa, Marin, Napa, San Francisco, San Mateo, Santa Clara, Santa Cruz, Solano, and Sonoma, CA. No support for organizations that mainly distribute grants to other organizations. No grants to artistic and aesthetic programs, or for receptions, banquets, displays, shows, or other similar programs.
Publications: Application guidelines; Grants list.
Application information: See foundation Web site for application guidelines and procedures and to download the application form. Do not send materials by Special Delivery, Express Mail or by other forms of expedited mail. Grants will be made only for a single fiscal year (i.e. no multi-year grants). Application form required.
Initial approach: Preliminary proposal (no more than 2 pages) by letter or e-mail before submission of a full application form
Copies of proposal: 5
Deadline(s): June 15 and Nov. 30 for preliminary proposals; Jan. 15 and July 15 for applications
Board meeting date(s): Varies
Final notification: Mar. and Sept.
Officers and Directors:* Edward E. Kallgren,* Pres.; Chester MacPhee, Jr.,* V.P. and Secy.; Warren Blomseth,* V.P. and Treas.; Charles Kallgren,* V.P.
Number of staff: 4 part-time professional.
EIN: 940732210
Selected grants: The following grants were reported in 2005.

$25,000 to San Francisco Food Bank, San Francisco, CA.

$20,000 to Emergency Shelter Program, Hayward, CA.

$20,000 to Head-Royce School, Oakland, CA.

$20,000 to Phoenix Programs, Concord, CA.

$20,000 to San Francisco Community Clinic Consortium, San Francisco, CA.

$15,000 to Henry Ohlhoff House, San Francisco, CA.

$15,000 to Legal Community Against Violence, San Francisco, CA.

$10,000 to Alisa Ann Ruch Burn Foundation, San Francisco, CA.

$10,000 to Community Action Board of Santa Cruz County, Santa Cruz, CA.

$10,000 to Sunny Hills Childrens Garden, San Anselmo, CA.

517
Morgan Flagg Family Foundation ✧ ☆
(formerly Flagg Family Foundation)
3050 Citrus Cir., Ste. 125
Walnut Creek, CA   94598

Established in 1962 in CA.
Donor: Morgan Flagg.
Foundation type: Independent foundation.
Financial data (yr. ended 10/31/05): Assets, $705,805 (M); gifts received, $4,700; expenditures, $979,809; qualifying distributions, $979,808; giving activities include $978,330 for 16 grants (high: $540,000; low: $30).
Fields of interest: Visual arts; Museums (art); Higher education; Education.
Limitations: Applications not accepted. Giving primarily in San Francisco, CA. No grants to individuals.
Application information: Unsolicited requests for funds not accepted.
Officers and Directors:* Morgan Flagg, Pres.; Ann Johnson,* Secy.; James R. Flagg; M. Elizabeth Flagg.
EIN: 956047557

518
Fleishhacker Foundation
P.O. Box 29918
San Francisco, CA   94129-0918   (415) 561-5350
Contact: Christine Elbel, Exec. Dir.
FAX: (415) 561-5345;
E-mail: info@fleishhackerfoundation.org;
URL: http://www.fleishhackerfoundation.org

Incorporated in 1947 in CA.
Donors: Mortimer Fleishhacker, Sr.†; Mortimer Fleishhacker, Jr.†; Janet Fleishhacker Bates†.
Foundation type: Independent foundation.
Financial data (yr. ended 12/31/05): Assets, $15,812,925 (M); expenditures, $941,814; qualifying distributions, $874,658; giving activities include $632,900 for 111 grants (high: $20,000; low: $500), and $100,000 for 4 grants to individuals (high: $25,000; low: $25,000).
Purpose and activities: Grants to visual and performing arts organizations; support also for precollegiate education.
Fields of interest: Media, film/video; Visual arts; Museums; Performing arts; Performing arts, dance; Performing arts, theater; Performing arts, music;

Arts; Elementary school/education; Secondary school/education; Education; Minorities.
Type of support: General/operating support; Building/renovation; Equipment; Program development; Curriculum development; Fellowships; Technical assistance.
Limitations: Giving limited to the greater San Francisco Bay Area, CA. No grants for annual campaigns, endowments, large capital campaigns, deficit financing, fund raising events, matching gifts or scholarships; no loans.
Publications: Application guidelines; Grants list; Program policy statement.
Application information: Fellowships not open to individual application. Application form required.
   Initial approach: Full proposal
   Copies of proposal: 1
   Deadline(s): Usually Jan. 15 and July 15
   Board meeting date(s): Biannually
   Final notification: 3 to 4 months
Officers and Directors:* David Fleishhacker,* Pres.; John Ehrlich, Jr.,* V.P.; Deborah Sloss,* Secy.; Mortimer Fleishhacker,* Treas.; Christine Elbel, Exec. Dir.; Delia Fleishhacker Ehrlich; Jodi Ehrlich; Jeffrey Fleishhacker; William Fleishhacker; Lois Gordon; Edie Rindal; Hillary Sloss; Laura Sloss; Robin Strawbridge.
Number of staff: 1 full-time professional; 1 part-time support.
EIN: 946051048

519
Flextronics Foundation ✧
2090 Fortune Dr.
San Jose, CA   95131
Contact: Bob Zapotosky, Treas.
URL: http://www.flextronics.com/SocialResponsibility/Foundation/default.asp

Established in 2001 in CA.
Donor: Flextronics International U.S.A., Inc.
Foundation type: Company-sponsored foundation.
Financial data (yr. ended 12/31/04): Assets, $6,053,131 (M); expenditures, $379,714; qualifying distributions, $379,656; giving activities include $379,656 for grants.
Purpose and activities: The foundation supports organizations involved with education, safety and disasters, and children.
Fields of interest: Education; Safety/disasters, government agencies; Children, services.
Limitations: Giving on a national and international basis, with emphasis on areas of company operations. No support for religious or political organizations. No grants to individuals, or for advertising, athletic events or league sponsorships, conventions, conferences, meetings or seminars, clubs, contests, field trips, film and/or video projects, fundraising activities, marketing, sponsorships, or travel or similar activities.
Application information: Application form required.
   Initial approach: Complete online application form
Officers: Jim Sacherman, Pres.; Tim Stewart, Secy.; Bob Zapotosky, Treas.
EIN: 770567788
Selected grants: The following grants were reported in 2005.
$25,000 to American India Foundation, New York, NY.
$14,000 to World Vision India, India. .
$10,000 to Family Supportive Housing, San Jose, CA.

$10,000 to Housing Trust of Santa Clara County, San Jose, CA.
$5,000 to Estrella Family Services, San Jose, CA.
$5,000 to Next Door Solutions to Domestic Violence, San Jose, CA.
$5,000 to Rebuilding Together Peninsula, Menlo Park, CA.
$5,000 to Sacred Heart Community Service, San Jose, CA.
$3,000 to Catholic Relief Services, Baltimore, MD.
$1,000 to World Vision, Tacoma, WA.

520
Flintridge Foundation
1040 Lincoln Ave., Ste. 100
Pasadena, CA   91103   (626) 449-0839
Contact: Ms. J.L. Moseley, Managing Dir.
FAX: (626) 585-0011;
E-mail: Jack@FlintridgeFoundation.org; URL: http://www.flintridgefoundation.org

Established in 1984 in CA.
Donors: Francis Loring Moseley†; Louisa Moseley†.
Foundation type: Independent foundation.
Financial data (yr. ended 12/31/05): Assets, $9,703,414 (M); gifts received, $167,560; expenditures, $3,111,050; qualifying distributions, $2,154,651; giving activities include $522,085 for 41 grants (high: $20,000; low: $914).
Purpose and activities: The foundation currently awards grants in conservation and theater. The conservation program is directed towards grassroots environmental organizations working in the Pacific Northwest. The theater program focuses on collaborative ensembles. The community services program is built around the foundation's Philanthropy Resource Library and includes technical assistance in the forms of resource material, workshops, and staff assistance for local nonprofits, particularly focusing on those helping families.
Fields of interest: Performing arts, theater; Environment, natural resources; Environment, water resources; Environment, forests; Nonprofit management; Leadership development.
Type of support: General/operating support; Continuing support; Management development/capacity building; Program development; Conferences/seminars; Technical assistance; Consulting services.
Limitations: Applications not accepted. Giving limited to CA, OR, and WA.
Publications: Financial statement; Grants list; Informational brochure; Occasional report.
Application information: Unsolicited requests for funds not accepted.
   Board meeting date(s): 3 times per year
Officers and Directors:* Armando Gonzalez,* Pres.; Alexander Moseley,* V.P.; Mona Heinze,* Secy.; David Moseley,* Treas.; Josh Addison; Judith Johnson; Ernestine L. Moore; Cassandra Moseley; Sarah Sockit Moseley; Sue Webber.
Number of staff: 8 full-time professional; 1 part-time professional.
EIN: 953926331

521
Flora Family Foundation ▼
2121 Sand Hill Rd., Ste. 123
Menlo Park, CA   94025   (650) 233-1335
Contact: B. Stephen Toben, Pres.

FAX: (650) 233-1340; E-mail: info@florafamily.org; URL: http://www.florafamily.org

Established in 1998 in CA.
Donors: William Hewlett†; Flora Lamson Hewlett†.
Foundation type: Independent foundation.
Financial data (yr. ended 12/31/04): Assets, $108,983,918 (M); expenditures, $5,523,579; qualifying distributions, $5,151,347; giving activities include $4,816,400 for 238 grants (high: $125,000; low: $100; average: $1,000–$30,000).
Purpose and activities: Giving primarily for museums, higher education, the environment, health associations, disaster relief, children and social services, as well as services for women, philanthropy and federated giving programs.
Fields of interest: Museums; Higher education; Environment; Health care; Health organizations, association; Health organizations; Disasters, preparedness/services; Human services; Children, services; Women, centers/services; Federated giving programs; Philanthropy/voluntarism.
Type of support: Income development; General/operating support; Continuing support; Management development/capacity building; Annual campaigns; Capital campaigns; Building/renovation; Equipment; Land acquisition; Endowments; Debt reduction; Emergency funds; Program development; Conferences/seminars; Professorships; Publication; Seed money; Curriculum development; Fellowships; Internship funds; Scholarship funds; Research; Consulting services; Program evaluation; Employee matching gifts; Exchange programs; Matching/challenge support.
Limitations: Applications not accepted. No grants to individuals.
Application information: Contributes only to pre-selected organizations.
Board meeting date(s): Feb., June, and Oct.
Officers and Directors:* Susan S. Briggs,* Chair.; B. Stephen Toben,* Pres.; Patricia Gump, Corp. Secy.; Annette Rado, C.F.O.; Eric Gimon; Bill Hewlett; Kimberly Leilani Myers Hewlett; Walter Hewlett.
Number of staff: 1 full-time professional; 1 part-time professional; 1 part-time support.
EIN: 770500183
Selected grants: The following grants were reported in 2004.
$125,000 to Synergos Institute, New York, NY. For endowment.
$120,000 to Stanford University, Stanford, CA. 2 grants: $100,000 (For performance assessment), $20,000 to School of Education (For teacher performance assessment).
$100,000 to Global Fund for Women, San Francisco, CA. For endowment.
$100,000 to Pacific Institute for Studies in Development, Environment and Security, Oakland, CA. For sustainability program.
$75,000 to University School of Nashville, Nashville, TN. For general support.
$70,000 to Oregon Public Broadcasting, Portland, OR. For general support.
$20,000 to Ecotrust, Portland, OR. For Market Connections.
$17,300 to Tibet Fund, New York, NY. For Dalhousie project.
$10,000 to San Francisco Museum of Modern Art, San Francisco, CA. For education program.

522
Floyd Family Foundation
150 La Sandra Way
Portola Valley, CA 94028-7312
Contact: William S. Floyd, Pres.

Established in 1989 in CA.
Donors: William S. Floyd; Mary Bell Floyd†.
Foundation type: Independent foundation.
Financial data (yr. ended 6/30/06): Assets, $7,470,344 (M); gifts received, $214,896; expenditures, $475,318; qualifying distributions, $423,760; giving activities include $420,085 for 52 grants (high: $102,500; low: $250).
Purpose and activities: Giving primarily for education and human services.
Fields of interest: Education; Human services; Philanthropy/voluntarism.
Limitations: Applications not accepted. Giving on a national basis. No grants to individuals.
Application information: Contributes only to pre-selected organizations. Unsolicited requests for funds not considered.
Officers: William S. Floyd, Pres.; Jeanne Floyd Downs, V.P. and Secy.-Treas.
EIN: 943106119
Selected grants: The following grants were reported in 2005.
$162,750 to Avenidas, Palo Alto, CA. For capital campaign.
$63,500 to Childrens Health Council, Palo Alto, CA. For annual support.
$53,000 to University of California, Berkeley, CA. For annual support.
$18,125 to Stanford University, Stanford, CA. For annual support.
$10,000 to Valley Presbyterian Church, Portola Valley, CA. For annual support.
$5,100 to University of the Pacific, Stockton, CA. For annual support.
$5,000 to Hoover Institution on War, Revolution and Peace, Stanford, CA. For annual support.
$5,000 to Howard University, Department of Athletics, DC. For annual support.
$5,000 to Yosemite Foundation, San Francisco, CA. For annual support.
$3,000 to YMCA of Stanislaus County, Modesto, CA. For annual support.

523
The Fluor Foundation ◇
1 Enterprise Dr.
Aliso Viejo, CA 92656-2606 (949) 349-6797
Contact: Suzanne Huffmon Esber, Exec. Dir.
FAX: (949) 349-7175;
E-mail: community.relations@fluor.com;
URL: http://www.fluor.com/communities/default.asp

Incorporated in 1952 in CA.
Donor: Fluor Corp.
Foundation type: Company-sponsored foundation.
Financial data (yr. ended 12/31/05): Assets, $9,582,866 (M); gifts received, $3,234,934; expenditures, $3,130,600; qualifying distributions, $3,127,712; giving activities include $3,016,844 for 199 grants (high: $603,845; low: $200), and $110,868 for 194 employee matching gifts.
Purpose and activities: The foundation supports organizations involved with arts and culture, education, health, hunger, housing, youth development, human services, community development, volunteerism, and civic affairs.
Fields of interest: Arts education; Arts councils; Media, television; Media, radio; Visual arts; Museums; Performing arts; Performing arts, orchestra (symphony); Arts; Elementary/secondary education; Higher education; Engineering school/education; Education; Health care; Food services; Housing/shelter; Youth development, adult & child programs; Youth development; Family services; Human services, financial counseling; Human services, emergency aid; Human services; Economic development; Community development; Voluntarism promotion; Science, formal/general education; Mathematics; Engineering/technology; Public policy, research; Public affairs.
Type of support: Scholarships—to individuals; General/operating support; Annual campaigns; Capital campaigns; Building/renovation; Endowments; Program development; Scholarship funds; Research; Employee matching gifts; Employee-related scholarships.
Limitations: Giving primarily in areas of company operations, with some emphasis on Orange County, CA, Fernald, OH, San Juan, PR, Rumford, RI, Greenville, SC, Fort Bend County, TX, and Richland, WA. No support for sports organizations, veterans', fraternal, labor, or religious organizations, or lobbying or political organizations. No grants to individuals (except for employee scholarships), or for film production, publishing activities, sports programs, or lobbying or political campaigns.
Publications: Application guidelines; Financial statement; Informational brochure; Program policy statement.
Application information: Proposals should be no longer than 2 to 3 pages. Additional information may be requested at a later date. Application form not required.
Initial approach: Proposal to nearest company facility; proposal to foundation for organizations located in Orange County, CA
Copies of proposal: 1
Deadline(s): None
Board meeting date(s): Apr. and Oct.
Final notification: Within 2 months
Officers and Trustees:* Alan L. Boeckmann,* Chair.; J. Robert Fluor II,* Pres.; Lawrence N. Fisher, Secy.; Kevin Karkut, Treas.; Suzanne Huffmon Esber, Exec. Dir.; Steve Gilbert; John Hopkins; Mike Steuert; Mark Stevens; Dwayne Wilson.
EIN: 510196032

524
Kay Richard and Elizabeth Bates Flynt Foundation ◇ ☆
13350 Country Way
Los Altos Hills, CA 94022

Foundation type: Independent foundation.
Financial data (yr. ended 12/31/05): Assets, $3,158,064 (M); gifts received, $2,874,775; expenditures, $349,118; qualifying distributions, $341,900; giving activities include $341,900 for grants.
Fields of interest: Animals/wildlife, preservation/protection.
Limitations: Applications not accepted. Giving on a national basis, with some emphasis on CA. No grants to individuals.
Application information: Contributes only to pre-selected organizations.
Officer: Peggy Flynt Reavis, Secy. and C.F.O.
Trustee: Christine F. Hemrick.
EIN: 770498527

Selected grants: The following grants were reported in 2003.

$80,000 to African Wildlife Foundation, DC. For general support.

$55,000 to Wildlife Conservation Network, Los Altos, CA. For general support.

$1,700 to Wild Cat Education and Conservation Fund, Occidental, CA. For general support.

$500 to Drokpa A California Non Profit Public Benefit Corporation, San Francisco, CA. For general support.

525
R. Gwin Follis Foundation ◇

c/o James D. Follis
1750 Taylor St., Ste. 2203
San Francisco, CA 94133-3655
Contact: James G. Follis, Pres.
E-mail: jgfollis@pacbell.net

Established in 1963 in CA.
Donor: R. Gwin Follis.
Foundation type: Independent foundation.
Financial data (yr. ended 12/31/04): Assets, $2,952,903 (M); expenditures, $469,450; qualifying distributions, $465,349; giving activities include $464,309 for 19 grants (high: $112,500; low: $5,000).
Fields of interest: Media/communications; Arts; Education; Environment; Health organizations, association; Human services; Community development.
Type of support: General/operating support; Continuing support; Annual campaigns; Capital campaigns; Building/renovation; Conferences/seminars.
Limitations: Applications not accepted. Giving primarily in San Francisco, CA. No grants to individuals.
Application information: Unsolicited requests for funds not accepted.
Board meeting date(s): Varies
Officers and Directors:* Mary van Voorhees,* Chair.; James G. Follis,* Pres.; Willard R. Hurst,* Secy.-Treas.
Number of staff: 1
EIN: 946073028

526
The Foothills Foundation ◇ ☆

P.O. Box 193809
San Francisco, CA 94119-3809

Established in 1977 in CA.
Donor: Gary Hogan Bechtel.
Foundation type: Independent foundation.
Financial data (yr. ended 12/31/05): Assets, $5,608,789 (M); expenditures, $484,375; qualifying distributions, $482,602; giving activities include $475,000 for 13 grants (high: $100,000; low: $2,500).
Fields of interest: Secondary school/education; Education; Animal welfare; Human services; Children/youth, services; Foundations (private grantmaking).
Type of support: General/operating support; Annual campaigns; Capital campaigns.
Limitations: Applications not accepted. Giving primarily in CA. No grants to individuals.
Application information: Contributes only to pre-selected organizations.

Officers and Directors:* Gary Hogan Bechtel,* Pres.; Jacquie L. Bechtel, V.P.; George T. Argyris,* Secy.; Nancy S. Hair, Treas.
EIN: 942412392
Selected grants: The following grants were reported in 2004.

$92,000 to Mid-Peninsula High School, Menlo Park, CA. 3 grants: $25,000, $42,000, $25,000

$25,000 to University of the Pacific, Stockton, CA.

$2,500 to Best Friends, Beaver, PA.

527
Forest Lawn Foundation

625 Fair Oaks Ave., Ste. 360
South Pasadena, CA 91030
Contact: Linda J. Blinkenberg, Exec. Dir.

Incorporated in 1951 in CA.
Donors: Forest Lawn Co.; Hubert Eaton Estate Trust.
Foundation type: Independent foundation.
Financial data (yr. ended 12/31/05): Assets, $59,424,955 (M); expenditures, $3,674,997; qualifying distributions, $3,356,159; giving activities include $3,225,200 for 103 grants (high: $400,000; low: $1,000).
Purpose and activities: Giving primarily for education, youth organizations, hospices, hospitals, family services and homeless and emergency services in Los Angeles and Orange counties, CA. Programs that facilitate the prevention of or provide solutions to social problems are favored over those that address the consequences.
Fields of interest: Education; Hospitals (general); Food services; Human services; Children/youth, services; Family services; Human services, emergency aid; Residential/custodial care, hospices; Homeless, human services; Disabilities, people with; Homeless.
Type of support: General/operating support; Continuing support; Emergency funds; Program development; Matching/challenge support.
Limitations: Applications not accepted. Giving primarily in Los Angeles and Orange counties, CA, with priority given to Forest Lawn market areas. No support for federated appeals, political purposes, or projects or programs normally funded by the government, or arts and culture. No grants to individuals, or for endowment funds, or fundraising events.
Application information: Grants initiated by the foundation.
Board meeting date(s): Quarterly
Officers and Trustees:* John Llewellyn,* Chair. and C.E.O.; Timothy Applegate, Secy.; Russ Whittenberg, C.F.O.; Linda J. Blinkenberg, Exec. Dir.; Darin B. Drabing; Keith Renken; Philip V. Swan.
EIN: 956030792
Selected grants: The following grants were reported in 2004.

$200,000 to Childrens Bureau of Southern California, Los Angeles, CA.

$100,000 to Parent Institute for Quality Education, Los Angeles, CA.

$100,000 to YMCA of Metropolitan Los Angeles, Los Angeles, CA.

$92,000 to Learning for Life-Exploring Foundation of Orange County, Santa Ana, CA.

$40,000 to Boys and Girls Club, Variety, Los Angeles, CA.

$34,000 to Independent Colleges of Southern California, Los Angeles, CA.

$25,000 to Boys and Girls Club of Cypress, Cypress, CA.

$20,000 to Glendale Adventist Medical Center, Glendale, CA.

$15,000 to Downtown Womens Center, Los Angeles, CA.

$10,000 to Citrus Valley Medical Center, Covina, CA.

528
The Louis W. Foster and Gladyce L. Foster Family Foundation ◇

3213 Elvido Dr.
Los Angeles, CA 90049

Established in 1998 in CA.
Donor: Louis Foster†.
Foundation type: Independent foundation.
Financial data (yr. ended 6/30/05): Assets, $26,120,188 (M); expenditures, $1,384,892; qualifying distributions, $1,148,408; giving activities include $1,148,408 for 2 grants (high: $801,833; low: $346,575).
Fields of interest: Higher education; Housing/shelter, development.
Limitations: Applications not accepted. Giving primarily in Stanford, CA, and Americus, GA. No grants to individuals.
Application information: Contributes only to pre-selected organizations.
Officers: Greg Foster, Pres.; Judith Warren, Secy.; R. Scott Foster, M.D., Treas.
EIN: 954712250
Selected grants: The following grants were reported in 2003.

$1,010,887 to Stanford University, Stanford, CA.

529
Foundation for Deep Ecology ◇

1062 Fort Cronkhite
Sausalito, CA 94965 (415) 229-9339
Contact: Lizzie Udwin, Prog. Admin.
FAX: (415) 229-9340;
E-mail: info@deepecology.org; *URL:* http://www.deepecology.org

Established in 1989 in CA.
Donor: Douglas R. Tompkins.
Foundation type: Independent foundation.
Financial data (yr. ended 6/30/05): Assets, $53,974,718 (M); expenditures, $4,066,455; qualifying distributions, $3,678,279; giving activities include $2,732,181 for 31 grants (high: $2,100,000; low: $1,668), and $294,576 for 4 foundation-administered programs.
Purpose and activities: Focus on fundamental ecological issues: 1) protection of forests, aquatic ecosystems and other habitats, including wildlands philanthropy (buying land to save it), wilderness recovery (supporting the design and implementation of large-scale wilderness recovery networks), funding for activists fighting for full protection of species and ecosystems and funding for efforts to eliminate resource extraction on public lands; 2) support for alternative models of agriculture that support biodiversity, local self-reliance and healthy agrarian communities, support for efforts in the fight against industrial agriculture, and support for efforts to link conservationists with farmers and activists in order to integrate habitat preservation and restoration with diverse farming practices; 3)

campaigns for effective analysis, organizing and action in response to the rapid acceleration in macroeconomic trends toward global economic integration and free trade that has shifted real political power away from citizen democracies to global corporate bureaucracies, and the further centralization of global corporate power caused by new technological innovation. Supported projects include educational programs exposing the full consequences of the global economy and new free trade agreements, technological critiques and campaigns, and groups fighting large road-building, infrastructure, and dam projects.

Fields of interest: Environment, natural resources; Environment, land resources; Environment; Animals/wildlife, preservation/protection; Agriculture; International affairs.

International interests: Argentina; Chile; South America.

Type of support: General/operating support; Continuing support; Land acquisition; Program development; Conferences/seminars; Publication; Seed money; Grants to individuals.

Limitations: Applications not accepted. Giving primarily in South America (Chile and Argentina). No support for curriculum development or K-12 educational projects, or for businesses or debt. No grants for television, video, photography (visual arts) or film productions, research, or individual academic pursuits (including graduate work or scholarships).

Publications: Multi-year report.

Application information: Contributes only to pre-selected organizations. Unsolicited requests for funds will not be accepted.

Board meeting date(s): Annually

Officers and Directors:* Douglas R. Tompkins,* Pres.; Quincey Imhoff,* V.P.; Kris McDivitt Tompkins,* V.P.; Debra B. Ryker,* Secy.-Treas.

Number of staff: 3 full-time professional; 2 part-time professional; 3 full-time support.

EIN: 943106115

530
Foundation for Psycho-cultural Research ✧

736 El Medio Ave.
Pacific Palisades, CA   90272-3451
URL: http://www.thefpr.org/

Established in 2000 in CA.

Donors: Robert Lemelson; Susan Morse Lemelson.

Foundation type: Operating foundation.

Financial data (yr. ended 11/30/04): Assets, $15,150,527 (M); expenditures, $1,007,256; qualifying distributions, $880,061; giving activities include $499,070 for 3 grants (high: $254,783; low: $21,622), and $175,682 for 4 foundation-administered programs.

Purpose and activities: The mission of the foundation is to support and advance interdisciplinary research projects and scholarship at the intersection of psychology, culture, neuroscience and psychiatry, with an emphasis on psycho-cultural central, factors as not peripheral.

Fields of interest: Neuroscience; Science; Psychology/behavioral science.

Limitations: Applications not accepted. Giving on a national and international basis. No grants to individuals.

Application information: Contributes only to pre-selected organizations.

Officers and Directors:* Robert Lemelson, Ph.D.*, Pres.; Susan Morse Lemelson,* Secy.-Treas.;

Douglas Hollan, Ph.D.; Marvin Karno, M.D.; Beate Ritz-Barr, M.D.

EIN: 954774901

531
Foundation of the Pierre Fauchard Academy ✧

c/o Windes & McClaughry
P.O. Box 87
Long Beach, CA   90801-0087

Established in 1986 in CA.

Foundation type: Independent foundation.

Financial data (yr. ended 12/31/04): Assets, $6,998,677 (M); gifts received, $8,405; expenditures, $522,131; qualifying distributions, $425,693; giving activities include $289,693 for 31 grants (high: $46,500; low: $3,000), and $136,000 for grants to individuals.

Purpose and activities: Support primarily for dental schools and the study and research of dentistry.

Fields of interest: Dental school/education; Human services.

Type of support: Scholarships—to individuals.

Limitations: Applications not accepted. Giving on a national basis.

Application information: Unsolicited requests for funds not accepted.

Officers: Carl G. Lundgren, Co-Pres.; Michael J. Perpich, Co-Pres.; Malcolm David Campbell, V.P.; William Winspear, V.P.; Richard A. Kozal, Secy.; William B. Kort, Treas.; Frederick J. Halik, Exec. Dir.

Directors: C.F. Larry Barrett; Michael J. Cripton; Minoru Horiuchi; James E. Long; Gary Louder; Kevin L. Roach; Nicholas D. Saccone; Scott M. Welch.

EIN: 770120371

532
Four Friends Foundation ✧ ☆

2405 Briarcrest Rd.
Beverly Hills, CA   90210

Established in 1990 in CA.

Donors: Robert Shaye; Eva Shaye.

Foundation type: Independent foundation.

Financial data (yr. ended 12/31/05): Assets, $5,989,515 (M); expenditures, $454,192; qualifying distributions, $456,267; giving activities include $456,267 for grants.

Purpose and activities: Giving primarily for higher education and the arts.

Fields of interest: Arts; Higher education; Medical research, institute; Human services; Philanthropy/voluntarism.

International interests: Sweden.

Limitations: Applications not accepted. Giving on a national basis, with some emphasis on MI and New York, NY; funding also in Sweden. No grants to individuals.

Application information: Contributes only to pre-selected organizations.

Trustees: Eva Shaye; Katja Shaye; Robert Shaye.

EIN: 954292739

Selected grants: The following grants were reported in 2003.

$155,000 to University of Michigan, Ann Arbor, MI.

$25,000 to Inside Out Foundation, Los Angeles, CA.

$20,000 to Center for Mind-Body Medicine, DC.

$2,000 to Lincoln Center Theater, New York, NY.

$1,000 to Guild Hall, New York, NY.

$350 to Center for the Study of Popular Culture, Los Angeles, CA.

533
Franklin Benevolent Corporation ✧ ☆
(formerly Davies Medical Center)

770 Tamalpais Dr., Ste. 309
Corte Madera, CA   94925   (415) 945-0223
Contact: Gregory Monardo, Pres.
FAX: (415) 945-9115; URL: http://www.frankben.org

Established in 1998 in CA; converted from Davies Medical Center.

Foundation type: Independent foundation.

Financial data (yr. ended 12/31/04): Assets, $33,395,732 (M); expenditures, $2,508,582; qualifying distributions, $2,058,430; giving activities include $1,510,500 for 4 grants (high: $1,400,000; low: $5,000).

Purpose and activities: The corporation provides financial support to facilitate the delivery of healthcare services to the San Francisco community.

Fields of interest: Health care.

Limitations: Applications not accepted. Giving limited to San Francisco, CA. No grants to individuals.

Application information: Contributes only to pre-selected organizations.

Officers and Directors:* J. Edward Tippetts,* Vice-Chair.; Gregory Monardo,* Pres.; James Uyeda,* Secy.-Treas.; Cherie Mohrgeld, M.C.; Thomas Rodrigues; H. Marcia Smolens; Ralph A. Van Orsdel.

EIN: 940486350

534
The Fremont Bank Foundation ✧ ☆

39150 Fremont Blvd.
Fremont, CA   94538-1316

Established as a company-sponsored operating foundation in 1996 in CA.

Donor: Fremont Bank.

Foundation type: Operating foundation.

Financial data (yr. ended 12/31/05): Assets, $3,258,740 (M); gifts received, $884,236; expenditures, $587,313; qualifying distributions, $585,936; giving activities include $546,595 for grants.

Purpose and activities: The foundation supports organizations involved with arts and culture, education, health, human services, and Protestantism.

Fields of interest: Arts; Education; Health care; Human services; Protestant agencies & churches.

Limitations: Applications not accepted. Giving primarily in CA. No grants to individuals.

Application information: Contributes only to pre-selected organizations.

Officers: Hattie Hughes, Pres.; Alan Hyman, V.P.; Michael Wallace, Secy.

Director: Howard Hyman.

EIN: 943170075

Selected grants: The following grants were reported in 2004.

$87,000 to Stanford University, Stanford, CA. 2 grants: $50,000, $37,000

$32,000 to Boy Scouts of America, San Leandro, CA.

$30,000 to Spectrum Community Services, Hayward, CA.

$25,000 to Holy Names University, Oakland, CA.

$25,000 to Hunger Project, New York, NY.

$20,000 to Project Second Chance, Pleasant Hill, CA.

$16,000 to Valley Montessori School, Livermore, CA.

$10,000 to Kidango, Fremont, CA.

$5,000 to Tri-City Homeless Coalition, Fremont, CA.

535
The Fremont Group Foundation

P.O. Box 193809
San Francisco, CA 94119-3809
Contact: Nancy Hair
FAX: (415) 284-8128;
E-mail: nhair@fremontgroup.com; URL: http://www.fremontgroup.com/values/commitment.html

Established in 1996 in CA.
Donor: Fremont Sequoia Holding, L.P.
Foundation type: Company-sponsored foundation.
Financial data (yr. ended 12/31/04): Assets, $9,252,901 (M); gifts received, $1,000; expenditures, $503,775; qualifying distributions, $477,710; giving activities include $471,445 for 323 grants (high: $35,492; low: $25).
Purpose and activities: The foundation supports organizations involved with education and birth defects.
Fields of interest: Education; Genetics/birth defects; Boy scouts.
Limitations: Applications not accepted. Giving primarily in CA. No support for political or religious organizations or organizations involved with reproductive issues. No grants to individuals.
Application information: Contributes only to pre-selected organizations.
  Board meeting date(s): Twice per year
Officers and Directors:* Alan M. Dachs,* Pres.; Richard S. Kopf,* V.P. and Secy.; Lauren B. Dachs,* V.P.; Deborah L. Duncan, V.P.
Number of staff: 1 part-time support.
EIN: 333255428

536
Samuel H. French III and Katharine Weaver French Fund ◇

c/o Wells Fargo Bank, N.A.
4475 Executive Dr., 1st Fl.
San Diego, CA 92121 (858) 597-4307
Contact: Michael Campbell
E-mail: michael.j.campbell@wellsfargo.com;
Application address: Wells Fargo Bank, N.A., attn.: M. David Schmutz, 4475 Executive Dr., Ste. 100, San Diego, CA 92121; additional tel./FAX: (858) 597-4336

Established in 1986 in CA.
Foundation type: Independent foundation.
Financial data (yr. ended 5/31/05): Assets, $9,107,025 (M); expenditures, $648,621; qualifying distributions, $588,185; giving activities include $566,000 for 67 grants (high: $25,000; low: $2,500).
Purpose and activities: Support for a hospital, health organizations, child welfare and youth services, and the elderly.

Fields of interest: Hospitals (general); Health organizations, association; Children/youth, services; Aging, centers/services; Aging.
Type of support: Building/renovation; Equipment; Program development; Conferences/seminars; Scholarship funds; Research; Matching/challenge support.
Limitations: Giving limited to San Diego County, CA. No support for start-up organizations. No grants to individuals, or for salaries.
Publications: Annual report; Grants list; Informational brochure (including application guidelines).
Application information: Letter should also include 2 prior years' financials, along with the latest year's financial record. Please send E-mail first to obtain latest guidelines. Application form not required.
  Initial approach: Letter (on 8 1/2 x 11 paper)
  Copies of proposal: 6
  Deadline(s): Feb. 15, May 15, Aug. 15 and Nov. 15
  Board meeting date(s): Mar., June, Sept., and Dec.
  Final notification: 3-4 months
Trustee: Wells Fargo Bank, N.A.
EIN: 954111082
Selected grants: The following grants were reported in 2004.
$25,000 to Zoological Society of San Diego, San Diego, CA.
$15,000 to Reuben H. Fleet Science Center, San Diego, CA.
$11,000 to Interfaith Shelter Network, Santa Rosa, CA.
$10,000 to Leadership Institute of Chicago, Chicago, IL.
$10,000 to Linda Vista Health Care Center, San Diego, CA.
$10,000 to Salvation Army of San Diego, San Diego, CA.
$10,000 to San Diego State University Foundation, San Diego, CA.
$10,000 to Tri-City Hospital Foundation, Oceanside, CA.
$10,000 to Winston School of San Diego, Del Mar, CA.
$10,000 to YMCA of San Diego County, Ira C. Copley Family Branch, San Diego, CA.

537
Fresno Regional Foundation ◇

5260 N. Palm Ave., Ste. 228
Fresno, CA 93704 (559) 226-5600
Contact: Daniel G. DeSantis, C.E.O.
FAX: (559) 230-2078;
E-mail: info@fresnoregfoundation.org; Additional E-mail: frfdan@pacbell.net; URL: http://www.fresnoregfoundation.org

Established as a trust in 1966 in CA.
Foundation type: Community foundation.
Financial data (yr. ended 12/31/05): Assets, $22,790,471 (M); gifts received, $6,026,332; expenditures, $3,798,399; giving activities include $3,040,121 for grants.
Purpose and activities: The foundation provides opportunities for donors to achieve their charitable intentions by matching gifts with real needs. Grantmaking interests include health, the arts, civic projects, education, the environment, parks and music, and human services.
Fields of interest: Performing arts, music; Arts; Education; Environment; Health care; Recreation,

parks/playgrounds; Human services; Economic development; Government/public administration.
Type of support: Continuing support; Management development/capacity building; Equipment; Seed money; Program-related investments/loans.
Limitations: Giving primarily in the central San Joaquin Valley, CA, area, especially Fresno, Kings, Madera, Mariposa, Merced, and Tulare counties. No grants to individuals (except for scholarships), or for endowment funds.
Application information: Visit foundation Web site for application form and guidelines. Faxed or e-mailed applications are not accepted. Application form required.
  Initial approach: Submit application form and attachments
  Copies of proposal: 7
  Deadline(s): June
  Final notification: Aug.
Officers and Governors:* Daniel G. DeSantis,* C.E.O.; Morton G. Rosenstein, M.D.*, Pres.; Jeffery A. Jaech,* V.P.; Fausto Hinojosa,* Secy.; William Lucido,* Treas.; John Blossom, M.D.; Angie Cisneros; Walter Cucuk; Judy Ganulin; James Hallowell; John Hortsmann; Don Schafer; Patricia Tom; O. James Woodward III.
Trustee Bank: Wells Fargo Bank, N.A.
Number of staff: 4 full-time professional; 2 full-time support.
EIN: 770478025

538
Friedman Family Foundation

353 Folsom St.
San Francisco, CA 94105 (650) 342-8750
Contact: Lisa Kawahara
FAX: (866) 223-1078;
E-mail: info@friedmanfoundation.org; URL: http://www.friedmanfamilyfoundation.org

Established in 1964 in CA.
Donors: Phyllis K. Friedman; Howard Friedman†.
Foundation type: Independent foundation.
Financial data (yr. ended 2/28/05): Assets, $15,085,715 (M); expenditures, $1,313,950; qualifying distributions, $1,305,537; giving activities include $1,165,000 for 131 grants (high: $20,000; low: $300).
Purpose and activities: Support for programs which attempt to end the cycle of poverty, especially programs that provide tools, support, asset building, and opportunity to people in need in order to overcome the root causes of their poverty, and in which the people to be helped are part of the design and decision making of the organization or project. Preference is given to new and creative programs, and programs working for systemic change.
Fields of interest: Economic development; Community development; Economically disadvantaged; Homeless.
Type of support: General/operating support; Program development; Program-related investments/loans.
Limitations: Giving primarily in the San Francisco Bay Area, CA. No grants to individuals, or for films, videos, conferences, seminars, capital campaigns, scholarships, research, or special or fundraising events.
Publications: Grants list; Multi-year report (including application guidelines); Occasional report (including application guidelines).

Application information: Application guidelines available on foundation Web site. Fax submissions are not accepted. Application form required.
Initial approach: 2- 3-page letter
Copies of proposal: 1
Deadline(s): Varies; see Web site for current dates
Board meeting date(s): Varies, meets 3 times a year
Final notification: 4 to 6 months
Officers and Directors:* Phyllis K. Friedman,* Pres.; Eleanor Friedman,* V.P.; Robert E. Friedman,* Secy.; David A. Friedman,* Treas.
Number of staff: 1 part-time professional; 1 part-time support.
EIN: 946109692
Selected grants: The following grants were reported in 2004.
$20,000 to Asian Neighborhood Design, San Francisco, CA. For general support.
$20,000 to Association for Enterprise Opportunity, Arlington, VA. For general support.
$20,000 to Bay Area Organizing Committee, San Francisco, CA. For general support.
$20,000 to California Association for Microenterprise Opportunity (CAMEO), San Francisco, CA. For general support.
$20,000 to Catholic Charities of San Jose, San Jose, CA. For general support.
$20,000 to Coalition on Homelessness, San Francisco, CA. For general support.
$20,000 to First Nations Development Institute, Fredericksburg, VA. For general support.
$20,000 to Larkin Street Youth Center, San Francisco, CA. For general support.
$20,000 to San Francisco Organizing Project, San Francisco, CA. For general support.
$20,000 to Womens Action to Gain Economic Security (WAGES), Oakland, CA. For general support.

539
Morton & Marcine Friedman Foundation ◇
7750 College Town Dr., Ste. 300
Sacramento, CA 95826 (916) 381-9011
Contact: Morton Friedman, Pres.

Established in 1997 in CA.
Donors: Marcine Friedman; Morton L. Friedman.
Foundation type: Independent foundation.
Financial data (yr. ended 12/31/05): Assets, $6,711,577 (M); gifts received, $274,981; expenditures, $332,498; qualifying distributions, $328,995; giving activities include $328,995 for 44 grants (high: $113,000; low: $30).
Purpose and activities: Giving primarily for Jewish organizations and Jewish education, as well as for higher and other education, including a law school; funding also for the arts, particularly to art museums, and health and human services.
Fields of interest: Museums (art); Performing arts; Arts; Elementary/secondary education; Higher education; Health care; Medical research; Legal services, public interest law; Human services; Family services; Foundations (community); Jewish agencies & temples.
Type of support: General/operating support.
Limitations: Giving primarily in Sacramento, CA. No grants to individuals.
Application information:
Initial approach: Letter
Deadline(s): Mar. 1

Officers: Morton L. Friedman, Pres.; Marcine Friedman, Secy.
EIN: 680282444
Selected grants: The following grants were reported in 2005.
$113,000 to American Israel Education Foundation (AIEF), DC.
$7,500 to American Red Cross, National Headquarters, DC.
$1,500 to Center for Fathers and Families, Sacramento, CA.

540
Tully and Elise Friedman Fund
1 Maritime Plz., Ste. 1000
San Francisco, CA 94111

Established in 1997 in CA.
Donors: Tully M. Friedman; Elise D. Friedman.
Foundation type: Independent foundation.
Financial data (yr. ended 12/31/04): Assets, $2,195,183 (M); expenditures, $1,274,040; qualifying distributions, $1,271,690; giving activities include $1,269,895 for 31 grants (high: $435,000; low: $45).
Fields of interest: Museums (art); Arts; Elementary/secondary education; Human services.
Limitations: Applications not accepted.
Application information: Unsolicited requests for funds not accepted.
Officers: Tully M. Friedman, Pres.; Elise D. Friedman, V.P., Secy., and C.F.O.
EIN: 943264446
Selected grants: The following grants were reported in 2003.
$400,000 to Fine Arts Museums of San Francisco, San Francisco, CA. For New DeYoung Fund.
$250,000 to Asian Art Museum of San Francisco, San Francisco, CA. For general support.
$5,000 to Children Affected by AIDS Foundation, Los Angeles, CA. For general support.
$2,500 to Gateway High School, San Francisco, CA. For general support.
$1,000 to Children of Shelters, San Francisco, CA. For general support.
$1,000 to Multiple Sclerosis Society of Northern California, National, San Francisco, CA. For general support.
$650 to College Track, East Palo Alto, CA. For general support.
$500 to Junior League of San Francisco, San Francisco, CA. For general support.
$500 to Making Waves Education Program, Richmond, CA. For general support.
$500 to San Francisco Symphony, San Francisco, CA. For general support.

541
The Alfred & Hanna Fromm Fund ◇
80 E. Sir Francis Drake Blvd., No. 4D
Larkspur, CA 94939

Established in 1965 in CA.
Donors: Alfred Fromm†; Hanna Fromm.
Foundation type: Independent foundation.
Financial data (yr. ended 9/30/05): Assets, $14,683,988 (M); gifts received, $1,713,221; expenditures, $1,268,260; qualifying distributions, $1,198,935; giving activities include $1,180,000 for 6 grants (high: $600,000; low: $10,000).

Purpose and activities: Giving primarily to Jewish federated giving funds and for higher education, including an adult learning center taught by retired professors for retired residents of the San Francisco Bay Area, CA.
Fields of interest: Arts; Higher education; Adult/continuing education; Human services; Jewish federated giving programs; Jewish agencies & temples.
International interests: Israel.
Limitations: Applications not accepted. Giving primarily in Larkspur, and San Francisco, CA. No grants to individuals.
Application information: Contributes only to pre-selected organizations.
Officers and Directors:* Rabbi Brian L. Lurie, Pres.; David George Fromm, Secy.; Peter K. Maier,* Treas.
Agent: Suzanne Daggert.
EIN: 946100399

542
Fund for Nonviolence
303 Potero, No. 54
Santa Cruz, CA 95060 (831) 460-9321
Contact: Betsy Fairbanks, C.E.O. and Pres.
FAX: (831) 460-9137;
E-mail: mail@fundfornonviolence.org; URL: http://www.fundfornonviolence.org

Established in 1997 in CA.
Foundation type: Independent foundation.
Financial data (yr. ended 12/31/05): Assets, $4,289,408 (M); gifts received, $1,750,000; expenditures, $956,153; qualifying distributions, $795,647; giving activities include $818,576 for 66 grants (high: $5,000), and $50,000 for 1 loan to an individual.
Purpose and activities: The fund cultivates and supports community-based efforts to bring about social change that moves humanity towards a more just and compassionate co-existence. Emphasis on human rights, movement-building and advocacy in programs on (1) Prisons- primarily with CA focus and; (2) Commercial sexual exploitation of children and; (3) Latin America.
Fields of interest: International human rights; Civil rights, advocacy; Civil liberties, advocacy; Civil liberties, death penalty issues.
International interests: Latin America.
Type of support: Program-related investments/loans; General/operating support; Continuing support; Management development/capacity building; Program development; Conferences/seminars; Seed money; Technical assistance; Program evaluation.
Limitations: Giving on a national and international basis; giving through Prison Program primarily in CA. No support for direct services not in the context of social change. No grants for one time events or experiences without meaningful follow up; or for individually designed academic research or media projects.
Publications: Application guidelines; Grants list; Informational brochure (including application guidelines).
Application information: Applications for the Latin America program will not be accepted. Please contact fund for description of programs, letter of inquiry questions, and upcoming grant cycle. Specific questions need to be addressed in letter of inquiry (questions available on Web site). Application form required.

Initial approach: Letter of inquiry (not to exceed 2 pages)
Copies of proposal: 2
Deadline(s): Check foundation Web site for deadlines
Board meeting date(s): Quarterly
Final notification: Varies

Officers and Directors:* Betsy Fairbanks,* C.E.O. and Pres.; Lynda Marin,* Secy.; Monica Larenas,* Treas.; Ana Maria Enriquez; Robin Levi; Carolina Martinez.

Number of staff: 2 part-time professional; 1 part-time support.

EIN: 770457185

543
Furth Family Foundation ✧

10300 Chalk Hill Rd.
Healdsburg, CA 95448

Established in 1969 in CA.

Donor: Frederick P. Furth.
Foundation type: Independent foundation.
Financial data (yr. ended 12/31/04): Assets, $10,524,620 (M); gifts received, $100; expenditures, $2,941,634; qualifying distributions, $2,441,589; giving activities include $2,327,713 for 146 grants (high: $200,000; low: $75).
Purpose and activities: Giving primarily to Christian churches, and for education and human services.
Fields of interest: Arts; Education; Human services; Public affairs; Christian agencies & churches.
Limitations: Giving primarily in CA. No grants to individuals.
Application information: Application form not required.
Initial approach: Letter
Deadline(s): None

Officers and Trustees:* Peggy J. Furth,* Pres.; Donna W. Furth,* Secy.-Treas.; Frederick P. Furth,* Mgr.; Darby Furth Bonomi.

EIN: 237062014

Selected grants: The following grants were reported in 2004.
$295,204 to Russian Arts Foundation, DC.
$295,204 to Sonoma Academy, Santa Rosa, CA.
$100,000 to Catholic Charities of the Diocese of Santa Rosa, Santa Rosa, CA.
$50,000 to Mayo Foundation, Rochester, MN.
$40,151 to Our Lady of Guadalupe Church, Windsor, CA. 2 grants: $30,151, $10,000
$20,000 to Redwood Empire Food Bank, Santa Rosa, CA.
$5,000 to American Red Cross, Santa Rosa, CA.
$4,070 to Center for Democracy, DC.
$2,000 to Ursuline High School, Santa Rosa, CA.

544
G.T.R. & B. Charitable Foundation ✧

132 S. Rodeo Dr.
Beverly Hills, CA 90212-2415

Established in 1993 in CA.

Donors: Harold A. Brown; Hermione K. Brown; Tom R. Camp; Gregg Harrison; Jeffrey M. Mandell; Kevin S. Marks; Donald S. Passman; Bruce M. Ramer; Lawrence D. Rose; Norman R. Tyre; Nancy L. Boxwell; J. Eugene Solomon; Barbara Silberbusch; Cheryl M. Snow.
Foundation type: Independent foundation.

Financial data (yr. ended 10/31/05): Assets, $353,486 (M); gifts received, $767,576; expenditures, $645,038; qualifying distributions, $642,536; giving activities include $642,536 for 53 grants (high: $171,000; low: $250).
Purpose and activities: Funding primarily for Jewish agencies, human services, education, and the arts and culture.
Fields of interest: Media, film/video; Arts; Higher education; Environment; Animal welfare; Health organizations, association; Human services; Foundations (community); Jewish federated giving programs; Jewish agencies & temples.
Limitations: Applications not accepted. Giving primarily in CA, with emphasis on Los Angeles; some funding nationally. No grants to individuals.
Application information: Contributes only to pre-selected organizations. Unsolicited requests for funds not accepted.

Officers and Directors:* Bruce M. Ramer,* Pres.; Nancy L. Boxwell,* V.P. and C.F.O.; Gregg Harrison,* Secy.

EIN: 954468911

545
Gaia Fund

235 Montgomery St., Ste. 1011
San Francisco, CA 94104 (415) 391-6943
Contact: Mark Schlesinger, Managing Tr.
FAX: (415) 391-6944; *E-mail:* email@gaiaSF.org;
URL: http://www.gaiasf.org

Established in 1994 in CA.

Foundation type: Independent foundation.
Financial data (yr. ended 12/31/05): Assets, $14,341,429 (M); gifts received, $161,941; expenditures, $595,655; qualifying distributions, $583,097; giving activities include $572,000 for 38 grants (high: $200,000; low: $1,000).
Purpose and activities: Support primarily for organizations involved with environmental programs that promote sustainable practices relative to food production, distribution, and consumption. The fund also makes grants to programs serving the Jewish community of San Francisco, CA.
Fields of interest: Environment; Jewish agencies & temples.
Type of support: General/operating support; Continuing support; Program development; Conferences/seminars.
Limitations: Giving primarily in the San Francisco Bay Area, CA. No support for Holocaust related projects, initiatives based in Israel, environmental education programs for children, or social service programs. No grants to individuals.
Application information: Preference given to grant requests for projects with annual budgets of less than $2 million; application procedure on fund Web site. Application form required.
Initial approach: Letter of inquiry
Copies of proposal: 2
Deadline(s): Feb. 15 and Aug. 15
Board meeting date(s): May and Nov.
Final notification: June 30 and Dec. 31

Officers and Directors:* Christine H. Russell,* C.E.O.; Mark L. Schlesinger,* Secy. and C.F.O.

EIN: 943215541

Selected grants: The following grants were reported in 2004.
$25,000 to California Coalition for Food and Farming, Santa Cruz, CA. For campaign for equitable farm policy.

$25,000 to Californians for GE-Free Agriculture, Occidental, CA. For GE Free campaign.
$25,000 to Hebrew Home for Aged Disabled, San Francisco, CA. To rebuild Home's onsite synagogue.
$20,000 to Jewish Community High School of the Bay, San Francisco, CA. For scholarship campaign.
$20,000 to Roots of Change Fund, San Francisco, CA. For endowment.
$5,000 to Center for Agroecology, Santa Cruz, CA. For Apprenticeship program.
$5,000 to Institute for Food and Development Policy, Oakland, CA. For projects affecting California.
$5,000 to Institute for Jewish and Community Research, San Francisco, CA. For Be'Chol Lashon program for Jews of color.
$5,000 to Judah L. Magnes Museum, Berkeley, CA. For general support.
$5,000 to Wild Farm Alliance, Watsonville, CA. For general support.

546
Galil Foundation, Inc. ✧

537 Marina Blvd.
San Francisco, CA 94123
Contact: Jacob Tal, Pres.

Donor: Jacob Tal.
Foundation type: Independent foundation.
Financial data (yr. ended 12/31/04): Assets, $2,110,881 (M); gifts received, $2,000,000; expenditures, $900,020; qualifying distributions, $900,000; giving activities include $900,000 for 1 grant.
Fields of interest: Foundations (public).
Limitations: Giving primarily in CA and NY.
Application information:
Initial approach: Letter

Officer and Trustee:* Jacob Tal,* Pres.
Directors: Rivka Barlev; Izhak Ohel.

EIN: 770440212

Selected grants: The following grants were reported in 2003.
$980,000 to Fidelity Investments Charitable Gift Fund, Boston, MA.

547
The Ernest Gallo Foundation ✧

P.O. Box 1130
Modesto, CA 95353 (209) 341-3203
Contact: Ruby Abel

Incorporated in 1955 in CA.

Donors: Ernest Gallo; Joseph E. Gallo; E & J. Gallo Winery.
Foundation type: Independent foundation.
Financial data (yr. ended 10/31/05): Assets, $24,558,961 (M); expenditures, $1,059,455; qualifying distributions, $1,011,000; giving activities include $1,011,000 for 3 grants (high: $1,000,000; low: $1,000).
Fields of interest: Performing arts centers; Federated giving programs; Roman Catholic agencies & churches.
Limitations: Giving primarily in Modesto, CA. No grants to individuals.
Application information:
Initial approach: Letter
Deadline(s): None

Officers: Ernest Gallo, Pres.; Joseph E. Gallo, V.P.; Mary I. Gallo, V.P.; Richard M. Beal, Secy.
EIN: 946061537
Selected grants: The following grants were reported in 2004.
$850,000 to Central Valley Center for the Arts, Modesto, CA.

548
The Julio R. Gallo Foundation ◇

P.O. Box 1130
Modesto, CA 95353 (209) 341-3375
Contact: Jessie Nelson

Incorporated in 1955 in CA.
Donors: Julio R. Gallo†; Robert J. Gallo; Aileen Gallo; Aileen Gallo Survivor's Trust.
Foundation type: Independent foundation.
Financial data (yr. ended 10/31/05): Assets, $23,932,329 (M); expenditures, $1,851,790; qualifying distributions, $1,740,750; giving activities include $1,079,500 for 61 grants (high: $1,000,500; low: $250).
Purpose and activities: Giving primarily for the arts, education, Roman Catholic churches and organizations, and human services.
Fields of interest: Performing arts, orchestra (symphony); Arts; Higher education; Education; Health organizations; Human services; Children, services; Foundations (community); Federated giving programs; Roman Catholic agencies & churches.
Limitations: Giving primarily in CA. No grants to individuals.
Application information:
Initial approach: Letter
Deadline(s): None
Officers: James E. Coleman, Co-Pres.; Robert J. Gallo, Co-Pres.; Jack B. Owens, Secy.; Anthony L. Youga, Treas.
Directors: Gregory J. Coleman; John R. Gallo.
EIN: 946061539
Selected grants: The following grants were reported in 2003.
$891,500 to Saint Stanislaus Catholic Church, Modesto, CA. For general support.
$55,000 to Oregon State University Foundation, Corvallis, OR. For general support.
$35,000 to ARC of Stanislaus County, Modesto, CA. For general support.
$27,000 to Saint Josephs Catholic Church, Modesto, CA. For general support.
$20,000 to Modesto Symphony Orchestra, Modesto, CA. For general support.
$10,000 to Central Valley Center for the Arts, Modesto, CA. For general support.
$10,000 to Franciscan Friars of the Renewal, Bronx, NY. For general support.
$7,500 to Sonoma Country Day School, Santa Rosa, CA. For general support.
$5,000 to Nature Conservancy, Sacramento, CA. For general support.
$5,000 to Townsend Opera Players, Modesto, CA. For general support.

549
The Gamble Foundation ◇

c/o Pacific Foundation Svcs.
1660 Bush St., Ste. 300
San Francisco, CA 94109 (415) 561-6540, ext. 205
Contact: Eric L. Sloan
FAX: (415) 561-6477; E-mail: esloan@pfs-llc.net;
URL: http://www.pfs-llc.net/gamble/gamble.html

Established in 1968 in CA.
Donors: Launce E. Gamble; Mary S. Gamble†; George F. Gamble; MSG Charitable Trust; Launce L. Gamble; Mark D. Gamble; Aimee Gamble Price; George T. Gamble; Jim Gamble; Joan L. Gamble.
Foundation type: Independent foundation.
Financial data (yr. ended 12/31/05): Assets, $12,069,712 (M); gifts received, $524,063; expenditures, $637,096; qualifying distributions, $631,425; giving activities include $601,425 for 54 grants (high: $88,500; low: $500).
Purpose and activities: The foundation's primary interest is to support organizations that serve disadvantaged children and youth in San Francisco, Marin and Napa counties. Within the field of youth development, the foundation focuses on educational and personal enrichment programs designed to open doors of opportunity for at risk youth in order to help them succeed in school and become productive, self-sufficient members of society. The foundation is particularly interested in agricultural/environmental education, vocational training, and programs that prevent substance abuse and teen violence. To a lesser degree, the foundation supports environmental organizations that focus on land preservation and sustainability, animal welfare and management, and pollution control.
Fields of interest: Environmental education; Public health; Crime/violence prevention, youth; Crime/violence prevention, abuse prevention; Agriculture; Recreation; Youth development, services; Homeless, human services; Human services.
Type of support: Equipment; Program development.
Limitations: Giving primarily in San Francisco and Napa counties, CA. No support for religious organizations. No grants to individuals, or for medical research, endowment funds, capital improvements, or annual appeals.
Publications: Application guidelines; Annual report; Grants list.
Application information: See foundation Web site for application information. Application form not required.
Initial approach: Letter of request
Deadline(s): Jan. 1
Board meeting date(s): 2nd quarter of each year
Officers: Launce E. Gamble, Pres.; Aimee Gamble Price, V.P. and Secy.; Mark D. Gamble, V.P. and Treas.; George F. Gamble, V.P.; Mary Callender, Exec. Dir.
EIN: 941680503
Selected grants: The following grants were reported in 2005.
$25,000 to Aim High for High School, San Francisco, CA. For Headlands Environmental Home providing environmental education for youth.
$25,000 to CyberMill Clubhouse, Napa, CA. For Agriculture in the Valley, multimedia production project serving low income youth.
$25,000 to GirlSource, San Francisco, CA. To provide stipends for at-risk girls participating in Technology and Leadership Program.

$20,000 to Calistoga Friends of the Family Center, Calistoga, CA. Toward salary of Executive Director.
$20,000 to Christian Brothers Ranch, Napa, CA. For ranch/animal care training program for disadvantaged youth.
$20,000 to Level Playing Field Institute, San Francisco, CA. For Summer Math and Science Academy serving talented, low income high school students.
$20,000 to McCormick Sanctuary, Saint Helena, CA. For Kids and Creeks, environmental education and habitat restoration program for youth in Napa and Sonoma counties.
$20,000 to PRBO Conservation Science, Petaluma, CA. Toward PRBO Conservation Science and development and production of Oak and Riparian Woodland Habitat Enhancement Guidebook.
$15,000 to Bay Institute of San Francisco, Novato, CA. For Marin Conservation Corps interns to help lead restoration projects.
$15,000 to Di Rosa Preserve, Napa, CA. For Art and Nature Education Program serving low income youth in Napa Valley.

550
Virginia Lee Gandy & John H. Sandman Charitable Trust ◇ ☆

924 Westwood Blvd., No. 850
Los Angeles, CA 90024-2949

Established in 2005 in CA.
Foundation type: Independent foundation.
Financial data (yr. ended 6/30/05): Assets, $335,461 (M); expenditures, $478,426; qualifying distributions, $476,000; giving activities include $476,000 for 8 grants (high: $118,621; low: $19,318).
Purpose and activities: Giving primarily for human services.
Fields of interest: Elementary/secondary education; Human services.
Limitations: Giving primarily in Los Angeles, CA.
Trustees: Rodolfo Alvarez; Theodore Ihnen; Peter K. More; Don Nelson.
EIN: 201560347

551
The Gap Foundation ▼ ◇

2 Folsom St., 14th Fl.
San Francisco, CA 94105 (415) 427-6473
E-mail: dotti_hatcher@gap.com; URL: http://www.gapinc.com/public/SocialResponsibility/sr_community.shtml

Established in 1977 in CA.
Donor: The Gap, Inc.
Foundation type: Company-sponsored foundation.
Financial data (yr. ended 1/31/06): Assets, $15,270,759 (M); gifts received, $9,968,546; expenditures, $6,229,769; qualifying distributions, $6,229,769; giving activities include $3,557,601 for 241 grants (high: $250,000; low: $500), and $2,672,168 for employee matching gifts.
Purpose and activities: The foundation supports organizations involved with arts and culture, K-12 education, HIV/AIDS, youth development, and human services.
Fields of interest: Arts; Elementary/secondary education; AIDS; Youth development; Human services.

International interests: Canada; Indian Subcontinent & Afghanistan; Southeast Asia; Sub-Saharan Africa; United Kingdom.

Type of support: General/operating support; Program development; Scholarship funds; Employee volunteer services; Sponsorships; Employee matching gifts; Donated equipment; Donated products; In-kind gifts.

Limitations: Applications not accepted. Giving primarily in areas of company operations, with emphasis on San Francisco, CA, and New York, NY; some giving on an international basis. No support for religious, political, or discriminatory organizations. No grants to individuals, or for scholarships, conferences, travel, films, videos, or fundraisers (except for gift card donations).

Publications: Annual report.

Application information: Contributes only to pre-selected organizations.

Board meeting date(s): Quarterly

Officers and Directors:* Donald G. Fisher,* Chair.; Paul Pressler, Pres.; Anne Gust, Secy.-Treas.; Doris F. Fisher; Marka Hansen.

EIN: 942474426

Selected grants: The following grants were reported in 2005.

$750,000 to Boys and Girls Clubs of America, Atlanta, GA. 3 grants: $250,000 each (For CareerLaunch).

$150,000 to Harlem Childrens Zone, New York, NY. For Promise Academy Schools and Community Center.

$150,000 to Lorraine Monroe Leadership Institute, New York, NY. For San Francisco and Harlem School Projects.

$100,000 to Habitat for Humanity International, Americus, GA. For Tsunami Relief.

$50,000 to CARE, Atlanta, GA. For earthquake and Tsunami Relief and rehabilitation.

$20,000 to Boys and Girls Club of Newburgh, Glenn C. Hines Memorial, Newburgh, NY. For Power Hour.

$10,000 to Casa Corazon de la Misericordia, San Pedro Sula, Honduras. For general operating support.

$10,000 to Shadowlawn Elementary School, Miami, FL. For Together We Achieve.

552

The Bertha and John Garabedian Charitable Foundation ✧

P.O. Box 26270
Fresno, CA 93729-6270   (559) 490-7994
Contact: M. Diedre Wilton, Grants Admin.
FAX: (559) 432-1025

Established in 1993 in CA.
Donor: John Garabedian†.
Foundation type: Independent foundation.
Financial data (yr. ended 7/31/04): Assets, $8,544,166 (M); expenditures, $802,104; qualifying distributions, $703,421; giving activities include $592,500 for 89 grants (high: $62,500; low: $1,000).
Purpose and activities: The foundation serves charitable organizations primarily located in central CA, which benefit arts, culture, and humanities, community activities and improvements, education, ethics, religion, and health and human services.
Fields of interest: Arts; Higher education; Education; Health care; Human services; Public policy, research; Religion.
Limitations: Giving primarily in central CA.

Publications: Informational brochure (including application guidelines).
Application information: Application form required.
Initial approach: Letter or telephone
Copies of proposal: 1
Deadline(s): Aug. 1 for letter of inquiry; Sept. 1 for completed application
Board meeting date(s): Monthly
Final notification: Dec.
Trustees: Silvestre Arias; Glenn E. Rose; Malcolm H. Stewart; H. Tookoian, M.D.; Bank of America, N.A.
Number of staff: 1 part-time professional.
EIN: 943188321

553

Silvio and Mary Garaventa Family Foundation ✧ ☆

4080 Mallard Dr.
Concord, CA 94520   (925) 689-8390
Contact: Mary Garaventa, Mgr.

Established in 1986 in CA.
Donors: Silvio Garaventa; Mary Garaventa; SEG Trucking; Contra Costa Waste, Inc.; Garaventa Enterprises, Inc.
Foundation type: Independent foundation.
Financial data (yr. ended 3/31/05): Assets, $2,424,874 (M); gifts received, $222,879; expenditures, $934,145; qualifying distributions, $881,130; giving activities include $881,130 for 13 grants (high: $250,000; low: $2,400).
Fields of interest: Performing arts, orchestra (symphony); Secondary school/education; Higher education; Animals/wildlife, bird preserves; Hospitals (general); Boys clubs; Youth, services; Aging, centers/services; Roman Catholic agencies & churches.
Limitations: Giving primarily in CA, with emphasis on Concord. No grants to individuals.
Application information: Application form not required.
Initial approach: Letter
Deadline(s): None
Officer: Mary Garaventa, Mgr.
Trustees: Marie Adler; Louisa Binswanger; Linda Colvis.
EIN: 680100302

554

The Melvin Garb Foundation ✧

11995 El Camino Real, Ste. 303
San Diego, CA 92103
Contact: Michael Berlin, Dir.; Stephen J. Cohen, Dir.
E-mail: Michael@pamgmt.com

Established in 1991 in CA.
Donor: Melvin Garb†.
Foundation type: Independent foundation.
Financial data (yr. ended 12/31/05): Assets, $22,433,356 (M); expenditures, $1,245,902; qualifying distributions, $900,000; giving activities include $900,000 for 15 grants (high: $150,000; low: $10,000).
Purpose and activities: Support primarily for the arts, human services, education, health care, the environment, and food services.
Fields of interest: Hospitals (general); Salvation Army; Jewish federated giving programs; Jewish agencies & temples.

Type of support: Continuing support; Annual campaigns; Capital campaigns; Building/ renovation; Emergency funds; Professorships.
Limitations: Applications not accepted. Giving primarily in CA. No grants to individuals.
Application information:
Board meeting date(s): Quarterly
Directors: Michael D. Berlin; Peter J. Chortek; Stephen J. Cohen; Nan L. Mannes; David J. Winkler.
EIN: 931067365
Selected grants: The following grants were reported in 2004.
$1,310,298 to Jewish Community Foundation, San Diego, CA.
$75,000 to Whittier Institute for Diabetes and Endocrinology, La Jolla, CA. For research.
$50,000 to Friends of the Jewish Chapel, Annapolis, MD. For construction of chapel.
$50,000 to San Diego Hebrew Homes, Encinitas, CA. For residency and education for Jewish aged.
$50,000 to San Diego Jewish Academy, San Diego, CA. For Jewish education.
$35,000 to Jewish Family Service of San Diego, San Diego, CA. For social services to those in need.
$25,000 to San Diego Food Bank, San Diego, CA.
$25,000 to Simon Wiesenthal Center, Los Angeles, CA. For Jewish tolerance.
$20,000 to Agency for Jewish Education of San Diego County, San Diego, CA.
$10,000 to American Red Magen David for Israel, New York, NY.

555

Garen Family Foundation ✧ ☆

c/o Quintile Wealth Mgmt.
11150 Santa Monica Blvd., Rm. 400
Los Angeles, CA 90025   (310) 475-9505

Established in 1996 in CA.
Donors: Eric R. Garen; Nancy J. Garen.
Foundation type: Independent foundation.
Financial data (yr. ended 12/31/05): Assets, $5,918,479 (M); expenditures, $407,537; qualifying distributions, $404,499; giving activities include $397,855 for 20 grants (high: $200,000; low: $90).
Purpose and activities: Giving primarily to education and social services.
Fields of interest: Media, radio; Museums (art); Performing arts, theater; Elementary/secondary education; Higher education; Engineering school/ education; Environment, natural resources; Environment; Health organizations, association; Human services.
Limitations: Applications not accepted. Giving primarily in CA, with emphasis on Los Angeles. No grants to individuals.
Application information: Contributes only to pre-selected organizations.
Trustees: Eric R. Garen; Nancy J. Garen.
EIN: 954621093

556

John Jewett & Helen Chandler Garland Foundation ▼ ✧

P.O. Box 550
Pasadena, CA 91102-0550
Contact: Lisa M. Hausler, Exec. Dir.

Trust established in 1959 in CA.
Donor: Members of the Garland family.

Foundation type: Independent foundation.
Financial data (yr. ended 12/31/04): Assets, $1,678,372 (M); gifts received, $131,590; expenditures, $3,763,772; qualifying distributions, $3,763,772; giving activities include $3,629,132 for 90 grants (high: $375,000; low: $2,500; average: $10,000–$50,000).
Purpose and activities: Support primarily for cultural and historical programs, secondary and higher education, social services, especially for the elderly, youth agencies, hospitals, and health services.
Fields of interest: Historic preservation/historical societies; Arts; Education; Hospitals (general); Health care; Human services; Youth, services; Aging, centers/services; Homeless, human services; Aging; Homeless.
Type of support: General/operating support; Continuing support; Annual campaigns; Capital campaigns; Building/renovation; Equipment; Endowments; Debt reduction; Emergency funds; Curriculum development; Scholarship funds; Research; Matching/challenge support.
Limitations: Giving primarily in CA, with emphasis on southern CA. No grants to individuals, or for seed money.
Publications: Application guidelines.
Application information: Application form not required.
> *Initial approach:* Letter only; no telephone inquiries
> *Copies of proposal:* 1
> *Deadline(s):* None
> *Board meeting date(s):* 2 times per year
> *Final notification:* After each meeting
Officer: Lisa M. Hausler, Exec. Dir.
Trustees: Ann Kelsey Babcock; Gwendolyn Garland Babcock; John Carlile Babcock; Sarah Garland Babcock; Susan Hinman Babcock; Hillary Duque Garland; William M. Garland II.
EIN: 956023587
Selected grants: The following grants were reported in 2004.
$800,000 to Huntington Library, Friends of the, San Marino, CA. For general support and educational programs at Botanical Center.
$395,000 to Humane Society of Pasadena, Pasadena, CA. For general support and behavior training program.
$150,000 to Kidspace, A Participatory Museum, Pasadena, CA. For general support.
$110,000 to Boys and Girls Clubs of Pasadena, Pasadena, CA. For general support and to make swimming pool accessible year-round.
$110,000 to Polytechnic School, Pasadena, CA. For minority scholarships and for skills enrichment program.
$100,000 to Salvation Army, Southern California Division, Los Angeles, CA. For general support.
$25,000 to Good Shepherd Center for the Homeless, Los Angeles, CA. For general support and capital campaign.
$25,000 to Marlborough School, Los Angeles, CA. For general support and minority scholarships.
$20,000 to K P C C 89.3 Southern California Public Radio, Pasadena, CA. For general support.
$15,000 to Big Brothers and Big Sisters Services, Richmond, VA. For general support.

557
Peter A. & Vernice H. Gasser Foundation ✧
433 Soscol Ave., Ste. A120
Napa, CA 94559-1314
Contact: Joseph G. Peatman, Pres.

Established in 1982 in CA.
Donors: Peter A. Gasser†; Vernice H. Gasser†.
Foundation type: Independent foundation.
Financial data (yr. ended 12/31/05): Assets, $40,777,990 (M); expenditures, $4,213,519; qualifying distributions, $1,410,675; giving activities include $1,221,173 for grants.
Purpose and activities: Giving primarily for education, and health and human services.
Fields of interest: Education; Hospitals (general); Human services; Children/youth, services; Family services.
Type of support: Capital campaigns; Building/renovation; Equipment; Land acquisition; Debt reduction; Program development; Seed money; Curriculum development; Scholarship funds; Matching/challenge support.
Limitations: Applications not accepted. Giving limited to Napa Valley, CA. No grants to individuals.
Application information: Unsolicited requests for funds not accepted.
> *Board meeting date(s):* Quarterly
Officers and Trustees:* Joseph G. Peatman,* Pres.; Julian N. Stern,* Secy.; Amelia Scaruffi,* C.F.O. and Treas.; Ed Barwick; Henry Gundling; Clifford G. Hartle; Alvin Johnson.
Number of staff: 1 full-time professional; 2 full-time support.
EIN: 942816159
Selected grants: The following grants were reported in 2004.
$525,000 to Justin-Siena High School, Napa, CA. 3 grants: $125,000 (For capital improvement), $200,000 (For tuition and curriculum development), $200,000 (For tuition and development).
$255,000 to Aldea, Napa, CA. 2 grants: $205,000, $50,000 (For Wolfe Center Project).
$100,000 to Community Health Clinic Ole, Napa, CA. For organizational structural changes and capacity building.
$100,000 to Queen of the Valley Hospital, Napa, CA. For new CT Scan.
$100,000 to Saint John the Baptist Church. For Community Hall Refurbishing.
$36,800 to Progress Foundation, San Francisco, CA. For Aging Out of Foster Care Program in Napa County.
$25,000 to Napa Valley Symphony Association, Napa, CA. For program support.

558
The David Geffen Foundation
12011 San Vincente Blvd., Ste. 606
Los Angeles, CA 90049-4926 (310) 581-5955
Contact: Richard Sherman, Tr.; J. Dallas Dishman, Prog. Dir.
FAX: (310) 581-5949;
E-mail: ddishman@dreamworks.com

Incorporated in 1986 in CA.
Donor: David Geffen.
Foundation type: Independent foundation.
Financial data (yr. ended 12/31/04): Assets, $612,335 (M); gifts received, $1,000,000;

expenditures, $1,360,472; qualifying distributions, $1,347,776; giving activities include $1,270,904 for 117 grants.
Purpose and activities: The foundation has focused its giving in five major areas: populations affected by HIV/AIDS; civil liberties; the arts; issues of concern to the Jewish community, and health care.
Fields of interest: Arts; Health care; AIDS; Civil rights; Jewish agencies & temples; LGBTQ.
Type of support: General/operating support; Annual campaigns; Capital campaigns; Program development; Program evaluation.
Limitations: Giving primarily in Los Angeles, CA, and New York, NY. Some giving in Israel as well. No grants to individuals or for documentaries or other types of audio-visual programming or media projects, including publication of books or magazines.
Publications: Program policy statement; Program policy statement (including application guidelines).
Application information: Generally does not accept unsolicited requests for funds. Application form not required.
> *Initial approach:* Proposal
> *Copies of proposal:* 1
> *Final notification:* 3-4 months
Trustees: David Geffen; Richard Sherman.
EIN: 954085811
Selected grants: The following grants were reported in 2004.
$100,000 to Human Rights Watch, New York, NY.
$75,000 to Museum of Modern Art, New York, NY.
$52,500 to Lambda Legal Defense and Education Fund, New York, NY.
$50,000 to Lincoln Center for the Performing Arts, New York, NY.
$25,000 to American Society for Yad Vashem, New York, NY.
$10,000 to Jewish Hospice Project Los Angeles, Los Angeles, CA.
$10,000 to Motion Picture and Television Fund, Woodland Hills, CA.
$7,500 to People for the American Way Foundation, Santa Monica, CA.
$5,000 to Los Angeles Jewish Home for the Aging, Reseda, CA.
$4,345 to Los Angeles County Museum of Art, Los Angeles, CA.

559
The Carl Gellert and Celia Berta Gellert Foundation
(formerly The Carl Gellert Foundation)
1169 Market St., Ste. 808
San Francisco, CA 94103 (415) 255-2829
Contact: Jack Fitzpatrick, Secy.
URL: http://www.gellertfoundation.org/

Incorporated in 1958 in CA.
Donors: Carl Gellert†; Gertrude E. Gellert†; Celia Berta Gellert†; Atlas Realty Co.; Pacific Coast Construction Co.
Foundation type: Independent foundation.
Financial data (yr. ended 12/31/05): Assets, $47,455,346 (M); expenditures, $4,970,953; qualifying distributions, $4,573,271; giving activities include $4,427,079 for 170 grants.
Purpose and activities: To promote religious, scientific, library and educational purposes.
Fields of interest: Literature; Elementary school/education; Secondary school/education; Higher education; Engineering school/education; Education; Hospitals (general); Reproductive health,

family planning; Substance abuse, services; Human services; Youth, services; Aging, centers/services; Community development; Engineering.
Type of support: General/operating support; Continuing support; Annual campaigns; Capital campaigns; Building/renovation; Equipment; Endowments; Program development; Publication; Scholarship funds; Research; Technical assistance.
Limitations: Giving limited to the nine counties of the greater San Francisco Bay Area, CA, (Alameda, Contra Costa, Marin, Napa, San Francisco, San Mateo, Santa Clara, Solano and Sonoma). No grants to individuals, or for seed money, emergency funds, land acquisition, matching gifts, conferences, sponsorships, fundraising events sponsorships, dinners, walk-a-thons, tournaments, or fashion shows; no loans.
Publications: Application guidelines; Program policy statement.
Application information: Application form available on Web site. Application form required.
  Initial approach: Proposal with application form
  Copies of proposal: 1
  Deadline(s): Aug. 15 (noon)
  Board meeting date(s): Nov.
  Final notification: Dec. 31
Officers and Directors:* Peter J. Brusati,* Chair.; Andrew A. Cresci,* Vice-Chair.; Jack Fitzpatrick,* Secy. and Exec. Dir.; Marie C. Bentley,* Treas. and Admin. Dir.; Lorraine D'Elia; Robert J. Grassilli; Michael J. King; J. Malcolm Visbal.
Number of staff: 1 full-time professional; 1 full-time support.
EIN: 946062858
Selected grants: The following grants were reported in 2004.
$400,000 to Notre Dame de Namur University, Belmont, CA.
$200,000 to Saint Patricks Seminary, Menlo Park, CA.
$150,000 to Old Saint Marys Cathedral, San Francisco, CA.
$125,000 to Saint Marys Chinese Schools and Center, San Francisco, CA.
$75,000 to Saint Francis Foundation, San Francisco, CA.
$25,000 to YMCA, CA.
$20,000 to Basic Fund, San Francisco, CA.
$10,000 to Sisters of Mercy, Burlingame, CA.
$7,500 to Mills-Peninsula Hospital Foundation, Burlingame, CA.
$5,000 to Saint Vincents Day Home, Oakland, CA.

560
GenCorp Foundation, Incorporated
P.O. Box 15619
Sacramento, CA   95852-0619   (916) 355-3600
Contact: Juanita Garcia, Exec. Dir.
FAX: (916) 355-2515;
E-mail: gencorp.foundation@gencorp.com;
URL: http://www.gencorp.com/pages/gcfound.html

Incorporated in 1999 in CA as successor to the GenCorp Foundation Inc., established in 1961 in OH.
Donor: GenCorp Foundation Inc.
Foundation type: Company-sponsored foundation.
Financial data (yr. ended 11/30/04): Assets, $17,338,419 (M); expenditures, $922,898; qualifying distributions, $832,325; giving activities include $506,007 for 159 grants (high: $100,000;

low: $250; average: $1,000–$20,000), and $255,384 for 315 employee matching gifts.
Purpose and activities: The foundation supports organizations involved with arts and culture, education, human services, science, and minorities.
Fields of interest: Arts; Elementary/secondary education; Higher education; Engineering school/education; Education; Human services; Engineering; Science; Minorities.
Type of support: Equipment; Program development; Curriculum development; Fellowships; Scholarship funds; Employee matching gifts; Employee-related scholarships; Scholarships—to individuals.
Limitations: Giving primarily in areas of company operations, with emphasis on AL, AR, CA, NM, TN, UT, VA, and WA. No support for private foundations, religious organizations, or fraternal, athletic, social, political, or disease-specific organizations. No grants to individuals (except for fellowships and scholarships), or for research, advertising, school trips, or fundraising; no loans.
Publications: Application guidelines; Annual report; Informational brochure (including application guidelines).
Application information: Application form not required.
  Initial approach: Proposal
  Copies of proposal: 1
  Deadline(s): None
  Board meeting date(s): As required
  Final notification: 2 months
Officers and Trustees:* Linda Beech Cutler,* Pres.; Jennifer Goolis,* Secy.; Diane Wallace,* Treas.; Juanita Garcia, Exec. Dir.; Bill Hatch; Ron Samborsky.
Number of staff: 1 full-time professional; 1 part-time support.
EIN: 680441559
Selected grants: The following grants were reported in 2006.
$75,000 to Aerospace Museum of California, McClellan, CA. For learning laboratory.
$75,000 to Crocker Art Museum, Sacramento, CA.
$35,000 to California State University, Sacramento, CA. For mechanical engineering program and community-based math tutoring program.
$30,000 to K V I E, Sacramento, CA. For science programming, including NOVA.
$30,000 to Virginia Polytechnic Institute and State University, Blacksburg, VA. For propulsion fellowship.
$25,000 to Discovery Museum, Challenger Learning Center, Sacramento, CA. For Challenger scholarships and outreach programs.
$25,000 to Explorit Science Center, Davis, CA. For outreach programs.
$25,000 to Resource Area for Teachers, Sacramento Teachers Resource Room, San Jose, CA.
$25,000 to University of California, Davis, CA. For aerospace engineering programs.
$10,000 to Boys and Girls Clubs of Greater Sacramento, Sacramento, CA. For garden and science project.

561
Genentech Access To Care Foundation
1 DNA Way
South San Francisco, CA   94080
URL: http://www.gene.com/gene/about/community/patients/access.jsp

Established in 2002 as a company-sponsored operating foundation.
Donor: Genentech, Inc.
Foundation type: Operating foundation.
Financial data (yr. ended 12/31/05): Assets, $0 (M); gifts received, $191,704,235; expenditures, $194,079,971; qualifying distributions, $194,079,971; giving activities include $194,079,971 for grants to individuals.
Purpose and activities: The foundation provides prescription medication to patients.
Type of support: Grants to individuals; Donated products.
Application information: Application form required.
  Initial approach: Contact foundation for application form
Officers and Trustees:* Michelle Lerandeau,* Pres.; Laura Chavaree, Secy.; John Whiting, C.F.O.; Maria Barajas; Ja Moon; Irene Otten; Mary Stutts; Carol Zigulis.
EIN: 460500266

562
Genentech Foundation ◇
1 DNA Way
South San Francisco, CA   94080
(650) 225-1000

Established in 2002.
Donor: Genentech, Inc.
Foundation type: Company-sponsored foundation.
Financial data (yr. ended 12/31/04): Assets, $3,852,487 (M); gifts received, $4,000,000; expenditures, $350,066; qualifying distributions, $350,000; giving activities include $350,000 for 1 grant.
Purpose and activities: The foundation supports organizations involved with education, health, biomedical research, community development, and biotechnology. Special emphasis is directed toward programs designed to address significant unmet medical needs, foster biomedical sciences, and meet community needs.
Fields of interest: Education; Health care; Biomedicine research; Community development; Biological sciences.
Limitations: No support for political, religious, sectarian, discriminatory organizations, or foundations. No grants to individuals, or for indirect costs, advertising journals or booklets, alumni drives, capital improvements or building projects, chairs or professorships, endowments, memorials, memberships, athletics, or scholarships or yearbooks.
Publications: Application guidelines.
Application information: Executive summaries should be no longer than 1 to 2 pages. Application form not required.
  Initial approach: Proposal
  Copies of proposal: 2
  Deadline(s): None
Officers and Directors:* Myrtle S. Potter,* Chair.; Doug Love, Secy.; David Henderson, C.F.O.; Brian Muma, Exec. Dir.; Audrey Baldwin, Mgr.; Hal Barron; Andrew Chan; Walter Moore; Diane Parks; Todd Pierce; Denise Smith-Hams; Mary Stutts.
EIN: 460500264

563
Genentech Foundation for Biomedical Sciences ◇

(formerly Genentech Research Foundation)
c/o Grant Admin.
1 DNA Way, M.S. 16A
South San Francisco, CA   94080-4990
(650) 225-4219
FAX: (650) 225-5795; E-mail: gfbs-d@gene.com;
URL: http://www.gene.com/gene/about/
community/gfbs/index.jsp

Established in 1988 in CA.
Donors: Genentech, Inc.; Delta Biotechnology, Ltd.
Foundation type: Company-sponsored foundation.
Financial data (yr. ended 3/31/05): Assets,
$3,992,795 (M); gifts received, $452,790;
expenditures, $1,071,396; qualifying distributions,
$1,071,396; giving activities include $1,067,555
for 24 grants (high: $140,000; low: $3,030).
Purpose and activities: The foundation supports
organizations involved with education and research
in the biomedical sciences. Special emphasis is
directed toward programs designed to foster the
participation of underrepresented minorities and
underprivileged groups.
Fields of interest: Museums; Secondary school/
education; Medical school/education; Biomedicine;
Medical research, institute; Biological sciences;
Minorities; Economically disadvantaged.
Type of support: Program development; Curriculum
development; Fellowships; Scholarship funds;
Research.
Limitations: Giving limited to northern CA. No
support for private foundations. No grants to
individuals, or for indirect costs.
Publications: Application guidelines; Program policy
statement.
Application information: Application form not
required.
  Initial approach: Proposal
  Copies of proposal: 2
  Deadline(s): Mar. 16
  Board meeting date(s): Apr.
  Final notification: Following board meeting
Officer and Directors:* Herbert M. Boyer, Ph.D.*,
Chair.; Bruce Alberts, Ph.D.; Goery Delacote, Ph.D.;
Zach W. Hall, Ph.D.; Edward Harris, M.D.
EIN: 943083018
Selected grants: The following grants were reported
in 2004.
$145,606 to San Jose State University, Department
  of Chemistry, San Jose, CA. For Santa Clara
  County Biotechnology Education Partnership.
$75,000 to Exploratorium, San Francisco, CA.
$75,000 to University of California, San Francisco,
  CA.
$72,000 to Stanford University, School of Medicine,
  Stanford, CA.
$50,000 to Bay Area Discovery Museum, Sausalito,
  CA.
$50,000 to Tech Museum of Innovation, San Jose,
  CA.
$38,500 to Berkeley Biotechnology Education,
  Berkeley, CA.
$25,000 to Gateway High School, San Francisco,
  CA.
$20,000 to Chabot Space and Science Center,
  Oakland, CA.
$20,000 to Industry Initiatives for Science and Math
  Education, Santa Clara, CA.

564
Wallace Alexander Gerbode Foundation

111 Pine St., Ste. 1515
San Francisco, CA   94111-5602   (415) 391-0911
Contact: Thomas C. Layton, Pres.
FAX: (415) 391-4587; E-mail: info@gerbode.org;
URL: http://www.foundationcenter.org/
grantmaker/gerbode/

Incorporated in 1953 in CA.
Donor: Members of the Gerbode family.
Foundation type: Independent foundation.
Financial data (yr. ended 12/31/04): Assets,
$72,985,043 (M); gifts received, $2,081;
expenditures, $3,665,760; qualifying distributions,
$3,120,517; giving activities include $2,538,057
for 103 grants (high: $333,333; low: $1,000;
average: $5,000–$25,000), and $24,923 for 3
foundation-administered programs.
Purpose and activities: Support for programs and
projects offering the potential for significant impact
in the areas of arts and culture, the environment,
population, reproductive rights, citizen
participation/building communities/inclusiveness,
the strength of the philanthropic process and the
nonprofit sector, and foundation-initiated special
projects.
Fields of interest: Arts; Environment; Civil liberties,
reproductive rights; Civil rights; Community
development; Philanthropy/voluntarism; Public
policy, research; Public affairs.
Type of support: Program development; Technical
assistance; Consulting services; Program-related
investments/loans.
Limitations: Giving primarily to programs directly
affecting residents of Alameda, Contra Costa,
Marin, San Francisco, and San Mateo counties in
CA, and HI. No support for religious purposes or
private schools. No grants to individuals, or for direct
services, deficit budgets, general operating funds,
building or equipment funds, general fundraising
campaigns, publications, or scholarships.
Publications: Application guidelines; Annual report
(including application guidelines); Financial
statement; Grants list.
Application information: Application form not
required.
  Initial approach: Letter; initial contact should not
    include materials (including videotapes)
    requiring a return
  Copies of proposal: 1
  Deadline(s): None
  Board meeting date(s): 4 times per year
  Final notification: 2 to 3 months
Officers and Trustees:* Maryanna G. Stockholm,*
Chair.; Frank A. Gerbode, M.D.*, Vice-Chair. and
Secy.; Charles M. Stockholm,* Vice-Chair. and
Treas.; Thomas C. Layton,* Pres.; Stacie Ma'a, V.P.
Number of staff: 2 full-time professional; 2 full-time
support; 1 part-time support.
EIN: 946065226
Selected grants: The following grants were reported
in 2005.
$225,000 to Trust for Public Land, Honolulu, HI. For
  Hawaiian Islands Program.
$150,000 to Catholics for a Free Choice, DC. For
  program support, payable over 3 years.
$100,000 to K Q E D, San Francisco, CA. For radio
  series, Truly California: Our State, Our Stories.
$100,000 to Nature Conservancy of Hawaii,
  Honolulu, HI. For land work in Hawaii and
  Asia-Pacific region.

$50,000 to Community Links Hawaii, Honolulu, HI.
  For start-up support to launch management
  support organization in Hawaii.
$45,000 to Heyday Institute, Berkeley, CA. For
  efforts to develop individual donor base.
$40,000 to Commonweal, Bolinas, CA. For Juvenile
  Justice Policy Reform Initiative, payable over 2
  years.
$25,000 to Asian Americans/Pacific Islanders in
  Philanthropy, San Francisco, CA. For program
  support.
$25,000 to Center for Investigative Reporting,
  Berkeley, CA. For Environmental Investigations
  Venture Fund.
$25,000 to Center for Reproductive Rights, New
  York, NY. For International Legal Program.

565
The Gere Foundation ◇

c/o International Business Mgmt.
9696 Culver Blvd., No. 203
Culver City, CA   90232
E-mail: info@gerefoundation.org; URL: http://
www.gerefoundation.org/

Established in 1991 in CA.
Donors: Richard Gere; The Conde Nast
Publications, Inc.; Warner Brothers; Visages RPS,
Inc.; Lakeshore International Corporation.
Foundation type: Independent foundation.
Financial data (yr. ended 12/31/05): Assets,
$3,137,499 (M); gifts received, $1,580,000;
expenditures, $673,653; qualifying distributions,
$673,653; giving activities include $669,620 for 39
grants (high: $375,000; low: $500).
Purpose and activities: The foundation awards
grants to humanitarian organizations supporting
victims of war and natural disasters, providing HIV/
AIDS care and research and addressing human
rights violations occurring around the world. Its
primary mission is to assist the cultural survival of
the Tibetan people through health, technological
and educational projects.
Fields of interest: Arts, cultural/ethnic awareness;
Education; Health care; AIDS; International
development; International human rights.
International interests: Asia.
Limitations: Applications not accepted. Giving on a
national and international basis. No grants to
individuals, or for capital campaigns, for-profit
organizations, or feature film projects.
Publications: Grants list.
Application information: The foundation accepts
letters of inquiry but does not consider unsolicited
proposals. See foundation Web site for guidelines
for submitting letters of inquiry.
Officers: Richard Gere, Pres.; Edgar Gross,
Secy.-Treas.
Director: Jennifer Greenfield.
EIN: 954305828
Selected grants: The following grants were reported
in 2003.
$75,200 to International Campaign for Tibet, DC.
$64,230 to Tibet Fund, New York, NY.
$50,000 to University of Virginia, Charlottesville,
  VA.
$25,000 to Amnesty International USA, DC.
$25,000 to Students for a Free Tibet, New York, NY.
$10,000 to Doctors Without Borders USA, New
  York, NY.
$10,000 to New York Times Neediest Cases Fund,
  New York, NY.
$5,000 to Gods Love We Deliver, New York, NY.

$2,500 to Project Avary, San Rafael, CA.
$1,500 to Seeds of Peace, New York, NY.

566
Cynthia Gershman Foundation ✧ ☆
412 Robert Ln.
Beverly Hills, CA 90210-2632   (213) 386-1773
Contact: Cynthia Palmer Gershman, Tr.

Established in 2000 in CA.
Donors: Cynthia Palmer Gershman; Harold Gershman Char. Annuity Trust; Harold Gershman Char. Lead Unitrust.
Foundation type: Independent foundation.
Financial data (yr. ended 12/31/05): Assets, $129,507 (M); gifts received, $900,000; expenditures, $920,643; qualifying distributions, $901,100; giving activities include $901,100 for grants.
Fields of interest: Health organizations, association; Human services; Children, services; Philanthropy/voluntarism; Religion.
Limitations: Giving primarily in CA.
Application information:
Initial approach: Request on organization letterhead
Deadline(s): None
Trustee: Cynthia Palmer Gershman.
EIN: 957075532
Selected grants: The following grants were reported in 2003.
$75,000 to International Childrens Charity Foundation, Calabasas, CA.
$50,000 to Nancy Davis Foundation for Multiple Sclerosis, Los Angeles, CA.
$21,500 to Larry King Cardiac Foundation, DC.
$15,000 to Tichi Wilkerson Kassel Parkinsons Foundation, Beverly HIlls, CA.
$3,500 to Friends of Sheba Medical Center, Los Angeles, CA.
$3,000 to Colleagues, The, Encino, CA.
$2,000 to SHARE, Beverly Hills, CA.
$600 to Thalians, The, Los Angeles, CA.

567
Ronald and Catherine Gershman Foundation ✧
11633 San Vicente Blvd., Ste. 314
Los Angeles, CA 90049-6514

Established in 1995 in CA.
Donors: Harold Gershman Family Survivors/ Administrative Trust; Charitable Lead Unitrust under Harold Gershman Survivors Trust; Charitable Lead Annuity Trust under H. Gershman Survivors Trust.
Foundation type: Independent foundation.
Financial data (yr. ended 12/31/05): Assets, $9,338,546 (M); gifts received, $1,870,002; expenditures, $624,525; qualifying distributions, $549,043; giving activities include $512,262 for 36 grants (high: $136,800; low: $500).
Purpose and activities: Giving primarily for medical services; funding also for historical preservation and human services.
Fields of interest: Arts; Hospitals (general); Health organizations, association; Cancer; Human services; Children/youth, services.
Limitations: Applications not accepted. Giving on a national basis, with emphasis on CA, NY, and RI. No grants to individuals.

Application information: Contributes only to pre-selected organizations.
Trustees: Catherine Gershman; Ronald A. Gershman.
EIN: 957075530
Selected grants: The following grants were reported in 2004.
$650,000 to Westside Waldorf School, Santa Monica, CA.
$100,000 to Newport Hospital, Newport, RI.

568
Charles M. Geschke and Nancy A. Geschke Foundation ✧
220 University Ave.
Los Altos, CA 94022
Contact: Charles M. Geschke, Pres.

Established in 1987 in CA.
Donors: Charles M. Geschke; Nancy A. Geschke.
Foundation type: Independent foundation.
Financial data (yr. ended 9/30/05): Assets, $12,767,859 (M); expenditures, $600,788; qualifying distributions, $501,128; giving activities include $495,529 for 21 grants (high: $251,629; low: $200).
Purpose and activities: Giving primarily for secondary and higher education, as well as to an atheneaum; funding also for the arts, and children and social services.
Fields of interest: Museums (art); Performing arts, orchestra (symphony); Arts; Secondary school/ education; Higher education; Libraries/library science; Education; American Red Cross; Children, services; Roman Catholic agencies & churches.
Type of support: General/operating support; Capital campaigns; Program development; Scholarship funds.
Limitations: Giving primarily in CA, MA, and OH. No grants to individuals.
Application information: Application form not required.
Initial approach: Letter
Deadline(s): None
Officers: Charles M. Geschke, Pres.; Nancy A. Geschke, Secy.-Treas.
Directors: John M. Geschke; Kathleen A. Geschke.
EIN: 943052556
Selected grants: The following grants were reported in 2005.
$301,629 to Saint Ignatius High School, Cleveland, OH. 2 grants: $50,000, $251,629
$40,000 to Nantucket Atheneum, Nantucket, MA.
$29,000 to San Francisco Symphony, San Francisco, CA.
$25,000 to American Red Cross, Palo Alto, CA.
$25,000 to University of San Francisco, San Francisco, CA.
$6,000 to Exploratorium, San Francisco, CA.
$5,000 to Triton Museum of Art, Santa Clara, CA.
$5,000 to Xavier University, Cincinnati, OH.
$1,000 to Third Street Community Center, San Jose, CA.

569
The Ann and Gordon Getty Foundation ▼ ✧
1 Embarcadero Ctr., Ste. 1050
San Francisco, CA 94111-3600

Established in 1986 in CA.

Donors: Gordon P. Getty; G.P.G. Foundation.
Foundation type: Independent foundation.
Financial data (yr. ended 12/31/04): Assets, $23,601 (M); gifts received, $18,100,000; expenditures, $18,172,841; qualifying distributions, $18,169,578; giving activities include $18,097,609 for 602 grants (high: $1,500,000; low: $350; average: $1,000–$20,000).
Purpose and activities: Support primarily for symphonies, opera companies, and educational institutions.
Fields of interest: Museums; Performing arts; Performing arts, music; Education; Anthropology/ sociology.
Type of support: General/operating support; Continuing support; Annual campaigns; Matching/ challenge support.
Limitations: Applications not accepted. Giving primarily in CA, with emphasis on the San Francisco Bay Area. No grants to individuals.
Application information: Contributes only to pre-selected organizations.
Board meeting date(s): Annually
Officer and Directors:* Gordon P. Getty,* Chair. and Pres.; Lisa DeLan; Matthew A. Hall; William A. Newsom.
EIN: 954078340
Selected grants: The following grants were reported in 2004.
$4,500,000 to Friends of CRAFT (Center for Research into Anthropological Foundations of Technology), Bloomington, IN. 4 grants: $1,125,000 each
$1,750,000 to San Francisco Opera Association, San Francisco, CA. 2 grants: $1,000,000, $750,000
$1,750,000 to San Francisco Symphony, San Francisco, CA. 2 grants: $750,000, $1,000,000
$1,500,000 to San Francisco Conservatory of Music, San Francisco, CA.
$530,808 to Russian Arts Foundation, DC. For Russian National Orchestra.

570
J. Paul Getty Trust ▼ ✧
1200 Getty Ctr. Dr., Ste. 800
Los Angeles, CA 90049-1679   (310) 440-7320
Contact: The Getty Foundation
FAX: (310) 440-7703; E-mail: info@getty.edu.;
URL: http://www.getty.edu

Operating trust established in 1953 in CA as J. Paul Getty Museum; Grant Program established in 1984.
Donor: J. Paul Getty†.
Foundation type: Operating foundation.
Financial data (yr. ended 6/30/05): Assets, $9,618,627,974 (M); gifts received, $2,961,141; expenditures, $344,225,860; qualifying distributions, $340,016,358; giving activities include $18,912,080 for 197+ grants (high: $5,700,000; low: $4,000; average: $500,000), $2,090,939 for 154 grants to individuals (high: $75,000; low: $500; average: $2,500–$40,000), $1,775,338 for 81 employee matching gifts, and $187,680,934 for 4 foundation-administered programs.
Purpose and activities: The J. Paul Getty Trust is a private operating foundation dedicated to the visual arts. The Getty Foundation (formerly the Getty Grants Program), the philanthropic arm of the Trust, fosters work of exceptional merit for which resources are otherwise limited. It supports a wide range of projects that promote research in the

history of art and related fields, advancement of the understanding of art, and conservation of cultural heritage. Grants are awarded to institutions and individuals throughout the world. In addition to the Foundation, the Getty Trust is comprised of the J. Paul Getty Museum, the Getty Research Institute, the Getty Conservation Institute, and the Getty Leadership Institute.

Fields of interest: Arts, cultural/ethnic awareness; Visual arts; Visual arts, architecture; Visual arts, art conservation; Museums; Art history; History/archaeology; Historical activities; Historic preservation/historical societies; Arts; Minorities.

Type of support: Program development; Publication; Fellowships; Internship funds; Research; Employee matching gifts; Grants to individuals; Matching/challenge support.

Limitations: Giving on an international basis. No grants for operating or endowment purposes, start-up, construction or maintenance of buildings, or acquisition of works of art.

Publications: Application guidelines; Annual report; Grants list; Informational brochure.

Application information: Detailed guidelines that outline eligibility requirements, deadlines, application procedures, the review process, and notification dates for most of the grant categories are available online at the foundation's Web site and from the Getty Foundation office. Before submitting an application, potential applicants should review the foundation's funding priorities and application procedure. If applicants are uncertain about how to proceed with their submissions, they should contact the Getty Foundation office for assistance or review the foundation's Web site at URL: http://www.getty.edu/grants. Application form required.

Initial approach: Letter of inquiry
Deadline(s): Varies by grant category. Generally, deadlines for architectural conservation grants, Apr. 10; deadlines for residential and nonresidential research grants are Nov. 1
Board meeting date(s): As necessary
Final notification: Generally 6 months

Officers and Trustees:* Louise H. Bryson,* Chair.; William E.B. Siart,* Vice-Chair.; Jay S. Wintrob,* Vice-Chair.; James N. Wood, C.E.O. and Pres.; Peter C. Erichsen, V.P., Genl. Counsel, and Secy.; Robert Abeles, Interim V.P., Fin. and Admin. and CFO; James M. Williams, V.P., C.I.O. and Treas.; Ron Hartwig, V.P., Comms.; Nancy Ogata, Cont.; Ramon C. Cortines; Joanne Corday Kozberg; Luis G. Nogales; Stewart A. Resnick; Mark S. Siegel; Peter J. Taylor.

Number of staff: 1406
EIN: 951790021

Selected grants: The following grants were reported in 2005.

$3,425,700 to University of California, Los Angeles, CA. 3 grants: $246,000 (For projects), $248,700 (For collaborative research grants), $2,931,000 (For Getty Masters Program at Getty Conservation Institute).

$2,000,000 to Getty Foundation Fund for New Orleans, Fund for New Orleans, Los Angeles, CA. To assist visual arts organizations.

$306,175 to International Centre for the Study of the Preservation and the Restoration of Cultural Property (ICCROM), Rome, Italy. .

$300,000 to National Portrait Gallery, London, England. For cataloguing of collections.

$270,000 to Research Foundation of the State University of New York, Binghamton, NY. For collaborative research grants.

$225,000 to Brown University, Providence, RI. For reference works.

$90,000 to Clark Atlanta University, Atlanta, GA. For campus heritage preservation.

$87,000 to British Empire and Commonwealth Museum, Bristol, England. For Archival Projects.

571
William & Marian Ghidotti Foundation ◇
c/o Wells Fargo Bank, N.A., Trust Tax Dept.
P.O. Box 63954, MAC A0330-011
San Francisco, CA   94163
Application address: c/o William Toms, Tr., 3961 DeSabla Rd., Cameron Park, CA 95682, tel.: (530) 677-3994

Established in 1969 in Nevada City, CA.
Donors: William Ghidotti; Marian Ghidotti†.
Foundation type: Independent foundation.
Financial data (yr. ended 12/31/05): Assets, $11,465,498 (M); expenditures, $647,584; qualifying distributions, $584,678; giving activities include $102,465 for 19 grants (high: $25,000; low: $279), and $477,750 for 144 grants to individuals (high: $35,000; low: $750).
Purpose and activities: Awards student scholarships to graduating seniors residing in and attending Nevada County, CA, high schools; some support also for the arts, education, health care, human services, and community programs.
Fields of interest: Arts; Education; Health care; Human services; Children/youth, services.
Type of support: Equipment; Scholarships—to individuals.
Limitations: Giving limited to Nevada County, CA, residents.
Application information: Scholarship applicants should submit Std. Scholarship APF/Transcript of grades, student and family income, and resume. Application form required.
Deadline(s): Feb. for new scholarships; Aug. for renewals
Trustees: John Bilheimer; Mary Bouma; Erica Erickson; Frank Francis; William Toms; Wells Fargo Bank, N.A.
EIN: 946181833

572
A.P. Giannini Foundation
(formerly Giannini Family Foundation)
57 Post St., Ste. 510
San Francisco, CA   94104   (415) 981-2966
Contact: John S. Blum, Admin.; Kenneth J. Blum, Admin.
FAX: (415) 981-5218;
E-mail: info@gianninifamilyfoundation.org;
URL: http://www.gianninifamilyfoundation.org

Incorporated in 1945 in CA.
Donor: A.P. Giannini†.
Foundation type: Independent foundation.
Financial data (yr. ended 12/31/05): Assets, $18,211,074 (M); gifts received, $52,482; expenditures, $1,019,631; qualifying distributions, $915,720; giving activities include $77,000 for 5 grants (high: $40,000; low: $36,000), and $630,000 for 17 grants to individuals (high: $40,000; low: $5,000).
Purpose and activities: Medical research fellowships for applicants sponsored by accredited medical schools.

Fields of interest: Medical research.
Type of support: Fellowships; Research.
Limitations: Giving limited to CA. No grants to individuals.
Publications: Financial statement.
Application information: Applications accepted for Fellowship Program. See foundation Web site for details. Application form required.
Initial approach: Fellowship application available on foundation Web site
Copies of proposal: 1
Deadline(s): Dec. 1
Board meeting date(s): Feb. and Nov.
Final notification: Mid-Jan.
Officers and Directors:* D.A. Mullane,* Chair.; V. Hammerness,* Vice-Chair.; Caroline O. Boitano,* Pres. and Secy.; Jerry L. Bowman, Treas.; Julius R. Krevans, M.D.; Anne G. McWilliams; Larry McNabb; Daniel P. Riley.
Number of staff: None.
EIN: 946089512

573
Claire Giannini Fund ◇
Gramercy Towers
1177 California St., Ste. 233
San Francisco, CA   94108   (415) 776-8181

Established in 1998 in CA.
Foundation type: Independent foundation.
Financial data (yr. ended 12/31/03): Assets, $32,560,713 (M); expenditures, $2,441,455; qualifying distributions, $2,372,147; giving activities include $2,201,500 for 9 grants.
Purpose and activities: Giving primarily for animals, education, human services, and arts and cultural programs.
Fields of interest: Arts; Education; Animals/wildlife; Children/youth, services.
Limitations: Applications not accepted. Giving primarily in CA. No grants to individuals.
Application information: Contributes only to pre-selected organizations.
Officer: Hilda Yao, Exec. Dir.
Trustee: Dorothy W. Yao.
EIN: 943297004

574
The Gifford Foundation, Inc. ◇
165 Farm Rd.
Woodside, CA   94062

Established in 1998 in CA.
Donor: John F. Gifford.
Foundation type: Independent foundation.
Financial data (yr. ended 5/31/05): Assets, $15,087,117 (M); expenditures, $1,812,364; qualifying distributions, $1,547,398; giving activities include $1,514,677 for 39 grants (high: $275,794; low: $100), and $32,721 for 4 grants to individuals (high: $15,000; low: $721).
Purpose and activities: Giving primarily to university athletic departments, especially for baseball programs, as well as for a tennis program; funding also for social services and health associations.
Fields of interest: Elementary/secondary education; Education; Hospitals (general); Health organizations, association; Athletics/sports, school programs; Athletics/sports, baseball; Athletics/sports, racquet sports; Recreation; Human services; Children/youth, services.

Limitations: Applications not accepted. Giving primarily in CA; some giving in HI.
Application information: Unsolicited requests for funds not accepted.
Officer: John F. Gifford, Pres.
EIN: 943303273

575
The Rosalinde and Arthur Gilbert Foundation ◇ ☆
11400 Olympic Blvd., Rm. 1600
Los Angeles, CA 90064
Contact: Robbie Diamond
Application address: 9454 Wilshire Blvd., Ste. 700, Beverly Hills, CA 90212, tel.: (310) 247-2966

Established in 2002 in CA; funded in 2003 through a merger with another foundation with the same name.
Donor: A & R Gilbert 1982 Trust.
Foundation type: Independent foundation.
Financial data (yr. ended 12/31/04): Assets, $141,079,006 (M); gifts received, $28,655,489; expenditures, $9,540,632; qualifying distributions, $4,994,604; giving activities include $4,397,041 for 108 grants (high: $550,000; low: $500).
Fields of interest: Higher education; Education; Human services; Jewish agencies & temples.
Limitations: Giving primarily in Los Angeles, CA.
Application information:
  Initial approach: Letters of inquiry are accepted by invitation only
Officers: Richard Ziman, C.E.O.; Martin Blank, Jr., Secy.
EIN: 562305694

576
Stephen & Margaret Gill Family Foundation ☆
c/o Margaret G. Gill
32 Flood Cir.
Atherton, CA 94027

Established in 1999 in CA.
Donors: Margaret G. Gill; Stephen P. Gill.
Foundation type: Independent foundation.
Financial data (yr. ended 12/31/05): Assets, $5,938,250 (M); expenditures, $370,583; qualifying distributions, $344,725; giving activities include $343,500 for 14 grants (high: $150,000; low: $1,000).
Fields of interest: Performing arts, ballet; Higher education; Environment, natural resources; Protestant agencies & churches.
Type of support: Program development; General/operating support; Capital campaigns; Annual campaigns.
Limitations: Applications not accepted. Giving in the U.S., primarily in CA. No grants to individuals.
Application information: Contributes only to pre-selected organizations.
  Board meeting date(s): Dec.
Officers: Margaret G. Gill, C.E.O. and Pres.; Stephen P. Gill, V.P. and C.F.O.
Directors: Elizabeth O. Gill; Richard P. Gill.
EIN: 943335952
Selected grants: The following grants were reported in 2005.
$150,000 to San Francisco Ballet, San Francisco, CA.
$50,000 to Episcopal Charities, San Francisco, CA.

$50,000 to Wellesley College, Wellesley, MA.
$25,000 to Yosemite Foundation, San Francisco, CA.
$10,000 to San Francisco Girls Chorus, San Francisco, CA.
$7,500 to ZYZZYVA, San Francisco, CA.
$2,500 to Environmental Defense, DC.
$2,500 to Natural Resources Defense Council, New York, NY.
$1,000 to National Association for Olmsted Parks, DC.

577
The William Gillespie Foundation ◇
610 Newport Ctr., Ste. 950
Newport Beach, CA 92660

Established in 1994 in CA.
Foundation type: Independent foundation.
Financial data (yr. ended 12/31/04): Assets, $5,399,336 (M); expenditures, $490,243; qualifying distributions, $399,700; giving activities include $399,700 for 50 grants (high: $50,000; low: $1,000).
Fields of interest: Performing arts, dance; Performing arts, ballet; Performing arts, theater; Arts; Health organizations; AIDS; Human services.
Limitations: Applications not accepted. Giving primarily in CA. No grants to individuals.
Application information: Contributes only to pre-selected organizations.
Officers: William Gillespie, Pres.; Richard Gadbois III, Secy. and C.F.O.
Director: John M. Gunnin.
EIN: 954480408
Selected grants: The following grants were reported in 2003.
$50,000 to American Ballet Theater, New York, NY.
$25,000 to Ballet Pacifica, Laguna Beach, CA.
$25,000 to Pacific Symphony Orchestra, Santa Ana, CA.
$15,000 to Laguna Art Museum, Laguna Beach, CA.
$15,000 to Pacific Chorale, Santa Ana, CA.
$15,000 to Saint Joseph Ballet Company, Santa Ana, CA.
$10,000 to AIDS Services Foundation Orange County, Irvine, CA.
$10,000 to Casa Youth Shelter, Los Alamitos, CA.
$10,000 to Laguna Playhouse, Laguna Beach, CA.
$7,500 to Someone Cares Soup Kitchen, Irvine, CA.

578
The William G. Gilmore Foundation ◇
120 Montgomery St., Ste. 1880
San Francisco, CA 94104 (415) 546-1400
Contact: Faye Wilson, Exec. Dir.

Incorporated in 1953 in CA.
Donors: William G. Gilmore†; Mrs. William G. Gilmore†.
Foundation type: Independent foundation.
Financial data (yr. ended 12/31/03): Assets, $25,508,263 (M); expenditures, $1,301,276; qualifying distributions, $1,172,855; giving activities include $1,035,025 for 138 grants (high: $50,000; low: $500; average: $500–$5,000).
Purpose and activities: Grants largely for community-based organizations, including development and urban affairs, family and social services, the elderly, child welfare and development,

health services, medical education, AIDS programs, conservation, and the arts.
Fields of interest: Arts; Child development, education; Medical school/education; Education; Environment, natural resources; Health care; Mental health/crisis services; AIDS; Human services; Children/youth, services; Child development, services; Family services; Residential/custodial care, hospices; Aging, centers/services; Homeless, human services; Community development; Public affairs; Aging; Disabilities, people with; AIDS, people with; Economically disadvantaged; Homeless.
Type of support: General/operating support; Continuing support; Annual campaigns; Capital campaigns; Building/renovation; Equipment; Emergency funds; Scholarship funds.
Limitations: Giving primarily in the San Francisco Bay Area, CA and OR. No grants to individuals.
Publications: Application guidelines.
Application information: Application form not required.
  Initial approach: Proposal
  Copies of proposal: 1
  Deadline(s): May 1 and Nov. 1
  Board meeting date(s): June and Dec.
  Final notification: 2 months
Officers and Trustees:* Robert C. Harris,* Pres.; Lee Emerson,* V.P. and Treas.; William R. Mackey,* V.P.; Faye Wilson, Exec. Dir.; Thomas B. Boklund; V. Neil Fulton.
Number of staff: 1 part-time support.
EIN: 946079493
Selected grants: The following grants were reported in 2003.
$50,000 to Queen of the Valley Hospital Foundation, Napa, CA.
$50,000 to YMCA of Pueblo, Community Campus, Pueblo, CO.
$30,000 to Project Open Hand, San Francisco, CA.
$20,000 to San Francisco Opera, San Francisco, CA.
$10,000 to Saint Helena Hospital Foundation, Deer Park, CA.
$7,500 to Napa Valley Symphony Association, Napa, CA.
$5,000 to Boys and Girls Clubs of Oakland, Oakland, CA.
$5,000 to Resource Renewal Institute, San Francisco, CA.
$4,000 to San Francisco Ballet, San Francisco, CA.
$3,500 to Canine Companions for Independence, Santa Rosa, CA.

579
The Gilo Family Foundation ◇
P.O. Box 929
Los Gatos, CA 95030

Established in 1994 in CA.
Donors: Davidi Gilo; Shamaya Gilo.
Foundation type: Independent foundation.
Financial data (yr. ended 8/31/05): Assets, $2,833,563 (M); gifts received, $256,880; expenditures, $1,029,612; qualifying distributions, $972,621; giving activities include $971,450 for 7 grants (high: $733,750; low: $3,700).
Fields of interest: Education; Human services; Jewish agencies & temples.
Limitations: Applications not accepted. Giving on a national and international basis, primarily in New York, NY, as well as in London, England, and Jerusalem, Israel. No grants to individuals.

Application information: Contributes only to pre-selected organizations.

Officer: Davidi Gilo, Pres.

EIN: 943211217

580

Girard Foundation ◇

2223 Avenida de la Playa, Ste. 203
La Jolla, CA 92037
Contact: Susan Wolking, Exec. Dir.
FAX: (858) 551-2723;
E-mail: Swolking@girardfoundation.org; URL: http://www.girardfoundation.org

Established in 1986 in CA.

Donor: R.B. Woolley, Jr.

Foundation type: Independent foundation.

Financial data (yr. ended 12/31/05): Assets, $19,660,122 (M); expenditures, $1,142,912; qualifying distributions, $1,060,203; giving activities include $890,820 for 55 grants (high: $200,000; low: $490).

Purpose and activities: Giving for systemic K-12 reform in San Diego County, CA.

Fields of interest: Education, management/ technical aid; Elementary/secondary education; Education, services.

Type of support: Management development/ capacity building; Continuing support; Program development; Conferences/seminars; Seed money; Curriculum development; Scholarship funds; Research; Technical assistance; Program evaluation; Matching/challenge support.

Limitations: Giving limited to San Diego County, CA. No grants to individuals (directly), or for endowments and capital campaigns.

Publications: Application guidelines.

Application information: Application guidelines, application form, partial grant list, and mission statement are available on foundation Web site only. Application form required.

  Initial approach: Telephone
  Copies of proposal: 1
  Deadline(s): Varies
  Board meeting date(s): 3 to 4 times annually
  Final notification: Within 2 weeks following board meeting

Officers: R.B. Woolley, Jr., Pres.; Scott Woolley, V.P.; Mary Walshok, Secy.; Robert A. Schroeder, Treas.

Number of staff: 1 full-time professional; 1 part-time support.

EIN: 330202832

581

Glenn Foundation for Medical Research, Inc.

(formerly Paul F. Glenn Foundation for Medical Research, Inc.)
6187 Carpinteria Ave., Ste. 300
Carpinteria, CA 93014-5010
Contact: Mark R. Collins, Pres.
E-mail: mrc@glennfoundation.org; URL: http://www.glennfoundation.org

Established in 1965 in NY; reincorporated in 1992 in AZ.

Donor: Paul F. Glenn.

Foundation type: Independent foundation.

Financial data (yr. ended 9/30/05): Assets, $24,673,503 (M); expenditures, $916,633; qualifying distributions, $750,849; giving activities include $644,325 for 9 grants (high: $550,000; low: $325).

Purpose and activities: The purpose of the foundation is to extend the healthy, productive years of life, through research into the mechanisms of biological aging.

Fields of interest: Medical research, institute; Geriatrics research; Biological sciences.

Type of support: Conferences/seminars; Fellowships; Research.

Limitations: Applications not accepted. Giving on a national basis. No support for sociological, as opposed to biological, aging projects.

Publications: Grants list; Informational brochure; Program policy statement.

Application information: Unsolicited requests for funds not accepted.

Officers and Directors:* Paul F. Glenn,* Chair.; Mark R. Collins,* Pres.; K. Leonard Judson,* Secy.-Treas.

Number of staff: None.

EIN: 860710305

Selected grants: The following grants were reported in 2003.

$720,000 to American Federation for Aging Research (AFAR), New York, NY. 3 grants: $675,000, $40,000, $5,000

$231,000 to Buck Institute for Age Research, Novato, CA. 2 grants: $31,000, $200,000

$25,000 to Alliance for Aging Research, DC. 3 grants: $10,000, $5,000, $10,000

$10,000 to International Longevity Center USA, New York, NY.

$3,000 to Oklahoma Medical Research Foundation, Oklahoma City, OK.

582

Morris Glickman Foundation, Inc. ☆

13 Churchill Ln.
Rancho Mirage, CA 92270-3038

Established in NY.

Donors: Marvin S. Glickman; Alma Glickman.

Foundation type: Independent foundation.

Financial data (yr. ended 6/30/06): Assets, $529,378 (M); gifts received, $11,500; expenditures, $510,170; qualifying distributions, $494,975; giving activities include $494,975 for grants.

Purpose and activities: Giving primarily for health, human services, and Jewish organizations.

Fields of interest: Museums; Arts; Hospitals (general); Health organizations, association; Human services; Jewish federated giving programs; Jewish agencies & temples.

Type of support: General/operating support.

Limitations: Applications not accepted. Giving primarily in CA and New York, NY. No grants to individuals.

Application information: Contributes only to pre-selected organizations.

Officers: Marvin S. Glickman, Pres.; Linda Levine, V.P.; Nancy Lipton, V.P.; Joanne Singer, V.P.; Alma Glickman, Secy.

EIN: 116015697

Selected grants: The following grants were reported in 2004.

$101,875 to Eisenhower Medical Center Foundation, Rancho Mirage, CA.

$14,520 to Jewish Community Center of Central Orange County, Costa Mesa, CA.

$10,000 to Israel Relief Fund, Nashville, TN.

$5,100 to Palm Springs Art Museum, Palm Springs, CA.

$5,000 to Jewish Federation of Palm Springs and Desert Area, Palm Springs, CA.

$5,000 to Temple Sinai-Jewish Community Center of Palm Desert, Palm Desert, CA.

$2,575 to Barbara Sinatra Childrens Center at Eisenhower, Rancho Mirage, CA.

$2,500 to Katonah Museum of Art, Katonah, NY.

$1,000 to McCallum Theater, Palm Desert, CA.

$1,000 to Multiple Sclerosis Foundation, Pacific, Los Angeles, CA.

583

Global Environment Project Institute, Inc.

P.O. Box 158
Pacific Palisades, CA 90272-0158
Contact: Rampa R. Hormel, Pres. and Treas.

Established in 1986 in ID.

Donors: Thomas D. Hormel; Philanthropic Collaborative.

Foundation type: Independent foundation.

Financial data (yr. ended 12/31/05): Assets, $1,773,013 (M); gifts received, $634,691; expenditures, $460,670; qualifying distributions, $455,945; giving activities include $400,899 for 6 grants (high: $200,247; low: $10,000).

Purpose and activities: The institute promotes the conservation of biodiversity and the sustainability of life on earth.

Fields of interest: Environment.

Type of support: General/operating support; Continuing support; Program development; Matching/challenge support.

Limitations: Applications not accepted. Giving on a national basis, with emphasis on CA.

Application information: Unsolicited requests for funds not accepted.

Officers: Rampa R. Hormel, Pres. and Treas.; Diane Ives, Secy.

Director: Drummond Pike.

EIN: 820421067

Selected grants: The following grants were reported in 2003.

$80,000 to Ecoventure, Oakland, CA. For global warming campaign.

$80,000 to Tides Foundation, San Francisco, CA. For general support.

$50,000 to Earth Day Network, DC. For general support.

$50,000 to Environmental Working Group, DC. For general support.

$50,000 to Redefining Progress, Oakland, CA. For general support.

$27,500 to Tides Center, San Francisco, CA. For regeneration project.

$20,000 to Consumers Union of United States, DC. For general support.

$20,000 to International Rivers Network, Berkeley, CA. For commission on dams.

$19,200 to Environmental Resource Center, Ketchum, ID. For general support.

$10,000 to Climate Action Network-Australia, Ultimo, Australia. For general support.

584
Maxwell H. Gluck Foundation, Inc. ✧

c/o Camilla Kocol
10375 Wilshire Blvd., Ste. 2
Los Angeles, CA 90024-4728
Contact: Camilla Kocol, Exec. Dir.

Established in 1955 in NY.
Donor: Maxwell H. Gluck‡.
Foundation type: Independent foundation.
Financial data (yr. ended 6/30/05): Assets, $46,474,210 (M); expenditures, $3,105,596; qualifying distributions, $2,535,853; giving activities include $2,436,284 for 13 grants (high: $500,000; low: $500).
Purpose and activities: Support for higher and other education, Jewish welfare, and the arts.
Fields of interest: Arts; Higher education; Education; Human services.
Limitations: Applications not accepted. Giving limited to southern CA. No grants to individuals.
Application information: Contributes only to pre-selected organizations. Unsolicited requests for funds not accepted.
Officers and Directors:* Jon A. Kaswick, M.D.*, Pres.; Richard G. Reinis,* Secy.; Camilla Kocol, Exec. Dir.; Muriel Gluck; Betty S. Shelhamer.
Number of staff: 1 part-time support.
EIN: 953979100

585
God's Gift ▼

P.O. Box 890515
Temecula, CA 92589-0515

Established in 1998 in CA.
Donors: Helen Lovaas; Leeland M. Lovaas.
Foundation type: Independent foundation.
Financial data (yr. ended 12/31/04): Assets, $34,807,730 (M); gifts received, $464,132; expenditures, $4,290,859; qualifying distributions, $3,875,102; giving activities include $3,856,450 for 58 grants (high: $1,000,000; low: $100; average: $2,500–$50,000).
Purpose and activities: Support primarily for human service organizations and religious organizations, including churches.
Fields of interest: Education; Human services; Religion.
Limitations: Applications not accepted. Giving on a national basis primarily in CA, with some giving on an international basis. No grants to individuals.
Application information: Contributes only to pre-selected organizations.
Board meeting date(s): Semiannually
Officers and Board Members:* Helen Lovaas,* Pres. and C.F.O.; Leeland M. Lovaas,* V.P. and Secy.
EIN: 330831475
Selected grants: The following grants were reported in 2004.
$1,000,000 to Alliance Defense Fund, Scottsdale, AZ.
$500,000 to Focus on the Family, Colorado Springs, CO.
$500,000 to Mission Aviation Fellowship, Redlands, CA.
$202,950 to Prison Fellowship Ministries, Lansdowne, VA.
$200,000 to Joni and Friends, Agoura Hills, CA.
$200,000 to World Vision, Federal Way, WA.
$100,000 to Fred Jordan Missions, Covina, CA.

$60,000 to Billy Graham Evangelistic Association, Charlotte, NC.
$22,500 to Operation Homefront, San Diego, CA.
$20,000 to Christar, Reading, PA.

586
Godric Foundation ☆

625 S. Fair Oaks Ave., Ste. 360
South Pasadena, CA 91030
Contact: Elizabeth A. Curtis, Secy.

Established in 1980.
Donor: Marcia W. Constance.
Foundation type: Independent foundation.
Financial data (yr. ended 12/31/05): Assets, $5,978,383 (M); expenditures, $437,809; qualifying distributions, $386,000; giving activities include $386,000 for grants.
Fields of interest: Education; Environment; Youth development.
Type of support: General/operating support; Curriculum development; Building/renovation; Program development.
Limitations: Applications not accepted. Giving primarily in Santa Barbara, CA. No grants to individuals; no loans.
Application information: Unsolicited requests for funds not accepted.
Board meeting date(s): Twice per year and as necessary
Officers and Directors:* Marcia W. Constance,* Pres.; Jamie Constance,* V.P.; Linda J. Blinkenberg,* C.F.O.; Elizabeth A. Curtis, Secy.; Richard E. Llewellyn II.
EIN: 953500486
Selected grants: The following grants were reported in 2003.
$180,000 to University of California at Santa Barbara Foundation, Santa Barbara, CA. For New Dimensions for the Learning: Creating Partnerships to Support Educational Excellence at Gevirtz Research Center.
$25,000 to South Carolina Coastal Conservation League, Charleston, SC. For program support.
$15,000 to Council on Alcoholism and Drug Abuse, Santa Barbara, CA. For John Fisher Sculpture Project.
$10,000 to South Carolina Center for Birds of Prey, Charleston, SC. For program support.
$2,000 to Boys and Girls Clubs of Greater Santa Barbara County, United, Santa Barbara, CA. For program support.
$2,000 to Land Trust for Santa Barbara County, Santa Barbara, CA. For program support.

587
The Goel Foundation ✧ ☆

c/o Prabhu Goel
98 Ridgeview Dr.
Atherton, CA 94027-6464

Established in 1990 in CA.
Donors: Prabhu Goel; Poonam Goel.
Foundation type: Independent foundation.
Financial data (yr. ended 3/31/06): Assets, $7,498,206 (M); expenditures, $414,909; qualifying distributions, $344,354; giving activities include $338,731 for grants.
Purpose and activities: Giving to a charitable gift fund.

Limitations: Applications not accepted. No grants to individuals.
Application information: Unsolicited requests for funds not accepted.
Officers: Poonam Goel, Pres.; Prabhu Goel, Secy.
EIN: 770269072
Selected grants: The following grants were reported in 2003.
$373,500 to Fidelity Investments Charitable Gift Fund, Boston, MA.
$100,000 to Stanford University, Stanford, CA. For general support.
$1,000 to University of California at Santa Cruz Foundation, Santa Cruz, CA. For general support.

588
John Gogian Family Foundation ✧

3305 Fujita St.
Torrance, CA 90505-4016
Contact: Lindsey Stammerjohn, Managing Dir.
URL: http://www.gogianfoundation.org

Established in 1982.
Donors: Rosalia Gogian‡; John Gogian; Pacific Cold Storage, Inc.
Foundation type: Independent foundation.
Financial data (yr. ended 12/31/05): Assets, $11,711,005 (M); expenditures, $763,955; qualifying distributions, $619,104; giving activities include $497,053 for 46 grants (high: $25,000; low: $950).
Purpose and activities: Giving primarily for the developmentally disabled, and abused or neglected youth.
Fields of interest: Down syndrome; Autism; Crime/violence prevention, domestic violence; Children/youth, services; Family services; Developmentally disabled, centers & services.
Type of support: Building/renovation; Equipment; Program development; Matching/challenge support.
Limitations: Giving primarily in Los Angeles County, CA. No support for animal causes, art, cultural programs, or sectarian organizations. No grants to individuals, or for capital campaigns or research.
Publications: Application guidelines; Informational brochure (including application guidelines).
Application information: Application form available on foundation Web site. Grants may be awarded annually for 3 consecutive years. Grants range from $5,000-20,000. Application form required.
Initial approach: Submit application
Copies of proposal: 5
Deadline(s): Jan. 12 and June 28
Board meeting date(s): Quarterly
Final notification: May and Nov.
Officers and Directors:* John J. Gogian, Jr.,* Pres.; Gary Nelson, Secy.; Dan Mueller, Treas.; Robert Ewry; Al Villasenor.
Number of staff: 1 full-time professional; 1 part-time support.
EIN: 953759369

589
Gold Family Foundation ✧

(formerly Gold Family Charitable Foundation)
4444 Lakeside Dr., 2nd Fl.
Burbank, CA 91505 (818) 845-4444
Contact: Ilene C. Gold, Pres.; Stanley P. Gold, V.P.

Established in 1986 in CA.
Donors: Stanley P. Gold; Ilene C. Gold.

Foundation type: Independent foundation.
Financial data (yr. ended 7/31/05): Assets, $2,111 (M); gifts received, $1,076,621; expenditures, $1,079,824; qualifying distributions, $1,078,519; giving activities include $1,078,519 for 73 grants (high: $125,000; low: $75).
Purpose and activities: Support primarily for Jewish organizations, including education, a welfare fund, and temple support; support also for cultural and educational advancement, and for health and social services.
Fields of interest: Arts; Higher education; Theological school/education; Health care; Health organizations, association; Human services; Jewish federated giving programs; Jewish agencies & temples.
Limitations: Giving primarily in CA and NY; some funding nationally. No grants to individuals.
Application information: Application form not required.
　Deadline(s): None
Officers: Ilene C. Gold, Pres.; Stanley P. Gold, V.P. and Treas.
EIN: 954076113
Selected grants: The following grants were reported in 2004.
$150,000 to Israel Policy Forum, New York, NY.
$25,000 to Jewish Television Network, Beverly Hills, CA.
$25,000 to World Union for Progressive Judaism, New York, NY.
$10,000 to Tel Aviv University: American Council, New York, NY.
$5,500 to Westover School, Middlebury, CT.
$2,500 to Congregation Orach Chaim, Brooklyn, NY.
$1,140 to Lawrenceville School, Lawrenceville, NJ.
$1,000 to Denison University, Granville, OH.
$1,000 to Occidental College, Los Angeles, CA.
$250 to Temple Judea, Coral Gables, FL.

590

The David B. Gold Foundation ✧

44 Montgomery St., Ste. 3750
San Francisco, CA　94104　(415) 288-9530
Contact: Steve Pridemore; Elaine Gold, Dir.
FAX: (415) 288-9549;
E-mail: mail@goldfoundation.org; *URL:* http://www.goldfoundation.org/

Established in 1992 in CA.
Donor: David B. Gold‡.
Foundation type: Independent foundation.
Financial data (yr. ended 11/30/03): Assets, $93,225,739 (M); gifts received, $27,962,538; expenditures, $3,374,337; qualifying distributions, $2,873,606; giving activities include $2,311,845 for 39 grants (high: $350,000; low: $500).
Purpose and activities: Giving primarily to early childhood and youth development, social and human services, education, natural resource conservation and protection, democratic society and Jewish culture.
Fields of interest: Education; Environment, natural resources; Reproductive health, family planning; Crime/violence prevention, child abuse; Legal services; Youth development; Human services; Jewish agencies & temples.
Type of support: General/operating support; Continuing support; Capital campaigns; Building/renovation; Land acquisition; Program development.
Limitations: Giving primarily to organizations that have an impact on the San Francisco Bay Area, CA, with emphasis on Alameda and San Francisco

counties and in the Twin Cities of Minneapolis/St. Paul, MN; some funding to national projects that are particularly relevant to the foundation's mission. No support for sectarian organizations, except for those organizations that fall within the foundation's Jewish Culture program area. No grants to individuals.
Publications: Application guidelines.
Application information: Submission of a full proposal is by invitation only. Application form required.
　Initial approach: On-line inquiry
　Copies of proposal: 1
　Deadline(s): None
　Board meeting date(s): Quarterly
　Final notification: Within 6 weeks for on-line inquiry; within 3 months for full proposal
Officers and Directors:* Barbara Gold-Lurie,* Pres.; Diane Gold-Bubier,* Secy.; Steven A. Gold,* Treas.; Elaine Gold; Emily Gold.
EIN: 943169439
Selected grants: The following grants were reported in 2003.
$350,000 to MacPhail Center for Music, Minneapolis, MN. For capital campaign.
$50,000 to Sierra Club, San Francisco, CA. For environmental law program.
$25,000 to Save-the-Redwoods League, San Francisco, CA. For Butano State Park.
$20,000 to Project Open Hand, San Francisco, CA. For general support.
$15,000 to Tides Center, San Francisco, CA. For general support.
$10,000 to Earth Island Institute, San Francisco, CA. For wilderness leadership training.
$10,000 to Family Builders By Adoption, Oakland, CA. For general support.
$5,000 to Gateway High School, San Francisco, CA. For general support.
$1,000 to Sunny Hills Childrens Garden, San Anselmo, CA. For general support.
$500 to Jewish Community Federation of San Francisco, the Peninsula, Marin and Sonoma Counties, San Francisco, CA. For general support.

591

Sheila Gold Foundation ✧

c/o David Gold
4000 Union Pacific Ave.
Los Angeles, CA　90023

Established in 1997 in CA.
Donors: Dave Gold; Sherry Gold.
Foundation type: Independent foundation.
Financial data (yr. ended 12/31/04): Assets, $10,068,993 (M); expenditures, $499,284; qualifying distributions, $499,234; giving activities include $499,199 for 59 grants (high: $50,000; low: $200).
Purpose and activities: Giving primarily for health care and medical purposes, Jewish organizations, and education.
Fields of interest: Medical school/education; Education; Health care; Human services; Jewish agencies & temples.
Limitations: Applications not accepted. Giving primarily in Los Angeles, CA. No grants to individuals.
Application information: Contributes only to pre-selected organizations.
Trustees: David Gold; Howard Gold; Jeff Gold; Sherry Gold; Karen Schiffer.
EIN: 954636060

Selected grants: The following grants were reported in 2004.
$49,999 to Brandeis-Bardin Institute, Brandeis, CA.
$11,999 to Hebrew University of Jerusalem, Jerusalem, Israel. .
$9,999 to American Lung Association, Sacramento, CA.
$9,999 to Camp Max Straus Foundation, Los Angeles, CA.
$9,999 to Muscular Dystrophy Association, New York, NY.
$9,999 to Therapeutic Living Centers for the Blind, Reseda, CA.
$9,999 to Valley Cultural Center, Woodland Hills, CA.
$1,999 to Downtown Womens Center, Los Angeles, CA.
$1,999 to Happy Hats for Kids, Rolling Hills Estates, CA.
$1,999 to Zimmer Jewish Discovery Childrens Museum, Los Angeles, CA.

592

Joseph and Dorothy Goldberg Charitable Trust ✧

530 B St., Ste. 1810
San Diego, CA　92101　(619) 239-1151
Contact: Earl Feldman, Tr.

Established in 1996 in CA.
Donors: Dorothy Goldberg‡; Goldberg Interim Trust.
Foundation type: Independent foundation.
Financial data (yr. ended 12/31/05): Assets, $7,719,862 (M); expenditures, $563,507; qualifying distributions, $529,355; giving activities include $392,750 for 30 grants (high: $110,000; low: $1,000).
Purpose and activities: Giving primarily for Jewish organizations.
Fields of interest: Human services; Aging, centers/services; Foundations (community); Jewish federated giving programs; Jewish agencies & temples.
Type of support: Scholarship funds.
Limitations: Giving primarily in CA, with emphasis on San Diego; some giving in New York, NY, and Israel.
Application information:
　Initial approach: Letter
　Deadline(s): None
Trustees: Earl Feldman; Robert S. Goldberg; Todd Kobernick.
EIN: 336195814
Selected grants: The following grants were reported in 2005.
$80,000 to P.E.F. Israel Endowment Funds, New York, NY.
$25,000 to Friends of Yemin Orde, DC.
$10,000 to Israel Humanitarian Foundation, New York, NY.
$5,000 to University Synagogue, Los Angeles, CA.
$3,000 to Community Campership Council, San Diego, CA.
$2,500 to Project Concern International, San Diego, CA.
$2,000 to Auntie Helens Fluff N Fold, San Diego, CA.
$1,000 to Special Olympics of California, San Francisco, CA.

593
The Frank M. & Lee Goldberg Foundation ◇
1333 Camino del Rio S., Ste. 310
San Diego, CA 92108-3520

Established in 1981 in CA.
Foundation type: Independent foundation.
Financial data (yr. ended 11/30/05): Assets, $2,841,234 (M); expenditures, $573,848; qualifying distributions, $558,820; giving activities include $550,650 for 32 grants (high: $424,500; low: $100).
Fields of interest: Arts; Education; Cancer; Jewish agencies & temples.
Limitations: Applications not accepted. Giving primarily in San Diego, CA. No grants to individuals.
Application information: Contributes only to pre-selected organizations.
Officers: Frank M. Goldberg, Pres.; Lee Goldberg, Secy.
Director: Edward Goldberg.
EIN: 953678549
Selected grants: The following grants were reported in 2004.
$907,000 to United Way of San Diego County, San Diego, CA. 2 grants: $343,500, $563,500
$26,000 to University of California San Diego Cancer Center Foundation, La Jolla, CA. 3 grants: $10,000, $10,000, $6,000
$15,000 to Old Globe Theater, San Diego, CA.
$3,900 to Congregation Beth Israel, San Diego, CA.
$2,000 to Epilepsy Society of San Diego County, San Diego, CA.
$1,500 to University of California at San Diego Foundation, La Jolla, CA.
$1,250 to San Diego Museum of Art, San Diego, CA.

594
Goldman Environmental Foundation ◇
The Presidio, 211 Lincoln Blvd.
P.O. Box 29924
San Francisco, CA 94129 (415) 345-6330
FAX: (415) 345-9686;
E-mail: info@goldmanprize.org; URL: http://www.goldmanprize.org

Established in 1989 in CA.
Donors: Richard N. Goldman; Rhoda H. Goldman†.
Foundation type: Independent foundation.
Financial data (yr. ended 12/31/03): Assets, $31,455,437 (M); expenditures, $3,225,187; qualifying distributions, $2,915,740; giving activities include $73,000 for 26 grants (high: $4,000; low: $1,000), and $750,000 for 7 grants to individuals (high: $125,000; low: $62,500).
Purpose and activities: The foundation's purpose is to annually award one prize to an individual in each of the six inhabited continents in recognition of significant achievement in the field of environmental protection. Grants will not be awarded.
Fields of interest: Environment.
Limitations: Applications not accepted. Giving on an international basis.
Publications: Informational brochure; Newsletter; Occasional report.
Application information: The foundation's grantmaking program has been discontinued. Awards to individuals are by nomination of 30 organizations and a network of environmentalists.

No unsolicited nominations or requests for funds will be considered.
Board meeting date(s): Dec.
Officer and Directors:* Richard N. Goldman,* Pres.; Susan Gelman; Douglas E. Goldman; John D. Goldman.
Number of staff: 4 full-time professional; 2 part-time professional; 1 full-time support.
EIN: 943094857

595
John and Marcia Goldman Foundation ◇
(formerly The John and Marcia Goldman Fund)
10400 Deer Valley Rd
Brentwood, CA 94513 (925) 978-0320
Contact: Janet Lindsay, Exec. Dir.
E-mail: janet-goldmanfound@sbcglobal.net

Established in 1997 in CA.
Donors: John D. Goldman; Marcia L. Goldman.
Foundation type: Independent foundation.
Financial data (yr. ended 12/31/04): Assets, $8,385,123 (M); gifts received, $3,173,005; expenditures, $1,206,721; qualifying distributions, $1,199,570; giving activities include $1,107,890 for 20 grants (high: $300,000; low: $5,340; average: $5,000–$50,000).
Purpose and activities: Giving primarily to underprivileged children and youth.
Fields of interest: Arts; Education; Health care; Recreation; Human services; Children/youth, services; Family services; Jewish federated giving programs.
Type of support: Equipment; Annual campaigns; Capital campaigns; Building/renovation; Program development; Internship funds; Scholarship funds; Research; Technical assistance; Program evaluation.
Limitations: Giving primarily in CA, with emphasis on San Francisco's Mid-Peninsula, specifically San Mateo and Santa Clara counties. No support for sole-denomination religious charities. No grants for salaries, or general operating support.
Publications: Application guidelines.
Application information: Application form not required.
Initial approach: Proposal
Copies of proposal: 1
Deadline(s): None
Board meeting date(s): Quarterly
Final notification: 1 month
Officers: John D. Goldman, Pres.; Marcia L. Goldman, Secy.-Treas.
Number of staff: 1 full-time professional.
EIN: 943274370
Selected grants: The following grants were reported in 2003.
$300,000 to Swarthmore College, Swarthmore, PA. For capital campaign.
$200,000 to Theaterworks, Palo Alto, CA. For general support.
$140,000 to Planned Parenthood Golden Gate, San Francisco, CA. For general support.
$100,000 to Lucile Packard Foundation for Childrens Health, Palo Alto, CA. For general support.
$70,000 to Amazon Conservation Team, Arlington, VA. For general support.
$50,000 to Jewish Community Center of San Francisco, San Francisco, CA. For capital campaign.
$50,000 to Pacific Autism Center of Education (PACE), Sunnyvale, CA. For general support.

$50,000 to Stanford University, Stanford, CA. For general support.
$30,000 to Clara-Mateo Alliance, Menlo Park, CA. For general support.
$20,000 to East Palo Alto Charter School, East Palo Alto, CA. For general support.

596
Lisa and Douglas Goldman Fund
1 Daniel Burnham Ct., Ste. 330C
San Francisco, CA 94109-5460 (415) 771-1717
Contact: Nancy S. Kami, Exec. Dir.
FAX: (415) 771-1797; URL: http://foundationcenter.org/grantmaker/goldman/

Established in 1992 in CA.
Donors: Douglas E. Goldman; Lisa M. Goldman; Douglas E. Goldman 1997 Char. Lead Trust.
Foundation type: Independent foundation.
Financial data (yr. ended 12/31/05): Assets, $20,798,265 (M); gifts received, $3,599,550; expenditures, $1,080,553; qualifying distributions, $1,060,028; giving activities include $956,600 for 70 grants (high: $60,000; low: $500).
Purpose and activities: To provide support for charitable organizations that enhance society, primarily those serving the San Francisco, CA, area.
Fields of interest: Arts; Education, reading; Education; Environment; Health care; Human services; Children/youth, services; Civil rights; Public affairs; Jewish agencies & temples.
Type of support: Continuing support; Capital campaigns; Building/renovation; Program development; Technical assistance.
Limitations: Giving primarily in the San Francisco Bay Area, CA. No grants to individuals; no support for deficit budgets, endowments, conferences, events, documentaries, films, books, or research.
Publications: Annual report (including application guidelines).
Application information: Unsolicited proposals from educational institutions or arts/cultural organizations not accepted. Application guidelines and procedures are available on foundation Web site. Faxes, e-mails, audio/video tapes, not accepted. Applications must also include 3 references familiar with the project. Application form not required.
Initial approach: Brief letter of inquiry (2 pages maximum)
Copies of proposal: 1
Deadline(s): None
Board meeting date(s): 3 times per year
Officers and Directors:* Douglas E. Goldman,* Pres.; Derek T. Knudsen,* Secy.; Lisa M. Goldman,* Treas.; Nancy S. Kami, Exec. Dir.
Number of staff: 1 part-time professional.
EIN: 943167546
Selected grants: The following grants were reported in 2005.
$250,000 to American Jewish World Service, New York, NY. For Asia Tsunami Relief.
$125,000 to Jewish Community Federation of San Francisco, the Peninsula, Marin and Sonoma Counties, San Francisco, CA. For Annual Campaign pledge.
$100,000 to Jewish National and University Library, International Institute for Jewish Genealogy and Paul Jacobi Center, Jerusalem, Israel. For founding grant, payable over 2 years.
$40,000 to San Francisco Planning and Urban Research (SPUR) Association, San Francisco,

CA. For Campaign for Urban Center, payable over 2 years.

$25,000 to Jumpstart for Young Children, Boston, MA. For San Francisco Neighborhood School Success for All initiative, through Western Regional Office.

$21,000 to Redefining Progress, Oakland, CA. For Sustainability Education and Ecological Footprint Teacher Training Program: Four San Francisco Workshops.

$5,000 to New Israel Fund, San Francisco, CA. For general charitable purposes.

$2,500 to Friends of the River Foundation, Sacramento, CA. For general charitable purposes.

$2,500 to Northern California Grantmakers, San Francisco, CA. For Summer Youth Project.

$2,000 to Fine Arts Museums of San Francisco, San Francisco, CA. For general charitable purposes.

597
Richard and Rhoda Goldman Fund ▼
P.O. Box 29924
211 Lincoln Blvd.
San Francisco, CA 94129 (415) 345-6300
Contact: Becky McAllister, Grants Mgr.
FAX: (415) 345-9686; URL: http://www.goldmanfund.org

Incorporated in 1951 in CA.
Donors: Rhoda H. Goldman†; Richard N. Goldman.
Foundation type: Independent foundation.
Financial data (yr. ended 12/31/05): Assets, $439,448,000 (M); expenditures, $43,368,000; qualifying distributions, $36,053,100; giving activities include $36,053,100 for 512+ grants (high: $3,000,000; low: $1,000).
Purpose and activities: Giving primarily to programs that will have a significant positive impact in an array of fields, including: the environment, Jewish affairs, population and quality of life in the San Francisco Bay Area, CA.
Fields of interest: Environment; Population studies; Jewish agencies & temples.
International interests: Israel.
Type of support: General/operating support; Continuing support; Capital campaigns; Land acquisition; Program development; Seed money.
Limitations: Giving primarily in the San Francisco Bay Area, CA, and Israel. Giving nationally and internationally in the areas of population and the environment. No grants to individuals, or for deficit budgets, endowment funds, documentary films, conferences, research, scholarships, fellowships, matching gifts, or general operating budgets of established organizations; no loans.
Publications: Annual report; Financial statement; Grants list.
Application information: Applications sent by fax or e-mail not considered. Application form not required.
  Initial approach: 2-page letter (including a 1-paragraph executive summary)
  Copies of proposal: 1
  Deadline(s): None
  Board meeting date(s): 3 times per year
  Final notification: 6-9 months
Officers and Directors:* Richard N. Goldman,* Pres.; Donald H. Seiler,* V.P. and Secy.; John D. Goldman,* V.P. and Treas.; Mathea Falco,* V.P.; Amy Lyons, Exec. Dir.
Number of staff: 4 full-time professional; 5 full-time support.
EIN: 946064502

Selected grants: The following grants were reported in 2005.
$4,000,000 to Campus for Jewish Life, Los Altos, CA. For capital campaign to build multi-purpose, intergenerational center for Jewish life and culture in South Peninsula.

$2,600,000 to Golden Gate National Parks Conservancy, San Francisco, CA. To restore Lands End Coastal Trail, hiking trail within Golden Gate National Park with views of San Francisco Bay, Golden Gate Bridge and Marin Headlands.

$2,000,000 to California Academy of Sciences, San Francisco, CA. To build state-of-the-art, world class natural history museum, aquarium and planetarium in Golden Gate Park.

$1,750,000 to University of California, School of Journalism, Berkeley, CA. To produce three-part Frontline television series examining structure and evolution of U.S. media and how it has and has not served America's public interest.

$1,000,000 to Nature Conservancy, International Conservation Program, Arlington, VA. For Great Bear Rainforest Campaign, to protect temperate rainforest in coastal British Columbia, one of largest remaining wilderness ecosystems.

$540,000 to Mandel Teacher Educator Institute, Tiburon, CA. To support professional development for teachers at Jewish schools.

$400,000 to Israel Project, DC. For general support of organization that uses strategic communications to strengthen Israel's image in U.S., and reduce anti-Semitism caused by negative images of Israel.

$50,000 to Land Trust Alliance, DC. For Campaign to Defend and Increase Tax Deductions for Land Conservation, to promote national policy favorable to land conservation.

$25,000 to Art Works Downtown, San Rafael, CA. For Burn the Mortgage Campaign, to support operating support for community art gallery in Marin County.

$15,000 to La Casa de las Madres, San Francisco, CA. For general operating support.

598
The Goldrich Family Foundation ◇
5150 Overland Ave.
Culver City, CA 90230 (310) 204-2050
Contact: Jona Goldrich, Pres.

Established in 1987 in CA.
Donors: Jona Goldrich; Ana Hirth; Emanuel Hirth; Goldrich & Kest Industries; Goldrich Trust.
Foundation type: Independent foundation.
Financial data (yr. ended 11/30/05): Assets, $46,696,887 (M); gifts received, $6,575,000; expenditures, $3,129,582; qualifying distributions, $2,995,339; giving activities include $2,993,321 for 99 grants (high: $950,000; low: $25).
Purpose and activities: Support for Jewish education and youth organizations.
Fields of interest: Education; Youth, services; Community development; Jewish agencies & temples.
International interests: Israel.
Limitations: Applications not accepted. Giving primarily in Los Angeles, CA. No grants to individuals.
Application information: Contributes only to pre-selected organizations.
Officers: Jona Goldrich, Pres.; Steve Erdman, Secy.; Evan Roklen, C.F.O.

Directors: Andrea Goldrich; Melinda Goldrich.
EIN: 954155986
Selected grants: The following grants were reported in 2003.
$165,000 to United Jewish Fund, New York, NY.
$115,000 to Cedars-Sinai Medical Center, Los Angeles, CA.
$100,000 to Jewish Federation Council of Greater Los Angeles, Los Angeles, CA.
$100,000 to Tel Aviv University: American Council, New York, NY.
$80,900 to Sinai Temple, Los Angeles, CA.
$55,000 to Brandeis University, Waltham, MA.
$25,000 to Eisenhower Medical Center, Rancho Mirage, CA.
$10,000 to American Youth Symphony, Los Angeles, CA.
$10,000 to Congregation Beth Israel, Los Angeles, CA.
$10,000 to Shalhevet High School, Beverly Hills, CA.

599
Goldsmith Family Foundation ◇
400 N. Roxbury Dr.
Beverly Hills, CA 90210
Contact: Bram Goldsmith, Pres.

Established in 1980 in CA.
Donors: Mrs. Bram Goldsmith; Bram Goldsmith; Karen Goldsmith; Russell Goldsmith.
Foundation type: Independent foundation.
Financial data (yr. ended 9/30/05): Assets, $17,704,843 (M); gifts received, $134,805; expenditures, $841,475; qualifying distributions, $836,540; giving activities include $815,833 for 108 grants (high: $243,175; low: $50).
Fields of interest: Performing arts; Arts; Education; Hospitals (general); Medical research, institute; Human services; Jewish federated giving programs; Jewish agencies & temples.
International interests: Israel.
Type of support: Continuing support; Annual campaigns; Capital campaigns; Building/renovation; Endowments; Professorships; Research; Matching/challenge support.
Limitations: Applications not accepted. Giving primarily in southern CA; some giving also in Israel. No grants to individuals.
Application information: Contributes only to pre-selected organizations.
  Board meeting date(s): As needed
Officers: Bram Goldsmith, Pres.; Elaine Goldsmith, V.P. and Secy.-Treas.
Directors: Bruce L. Goldsmith; Russell Goldsmith.
Number of staff: 1 part-time support.
EIN: 953545880
Selected grants: The following grants were reported in 2005.
$126,000 to Los Angeles Philharmonic Association, Los Angeles, CA.
$75,000 to Habitat for Humanity International.
$62,500 to Alliance for Childrens Rights, Los Angeles, CA.
$23,500 to Music Center, Providence, RI.
$21,500 to Harvard University, Cambridge, MA.
$10,000 to Childrens Museum. 2 grants: $5,000 each
$10,000 to People for the American Way, DC.
$5,000 to Los Angeles County Museum of Art, Los Angeles, CA.
$2,000 to Music Center Unified Fund, Los Angeles, CA.

600

The Samuel Goldwyn Foundation ✧

9570 W. Pico Blvd., Ste. 400
Los Angeles, CA 90035

Established in 1947 in CA.
Donors: Samuel Goldwyn†; Frances H. Goldwyn†.
Foundation type: Independent foundation.
Financial data (yr. ended 12/31/04): Assets, $26,441,305 (M); expenditures, $1,702,529; qualifying distributions, $681,179; giving activities include $494,248 for 59 grants (high: $61,404; low: $250), and $44,766 for 39 employee matching gifts.
Fields of interest: Arts; Elementary/secondary education; Higher education; Libraries (public); Health care; Health organizations, association; Human services; Children/youth, services; Christian agencies & churches; Jewish agencies & temples; Minorities.
Type of support: Annual campaigns; Program development; Seed money; Scholarship funds; Research.
Limitations: Applications not accepted. Giving primarily in CA. No grants to individuals, or for building funds.
Application information: Contributes only to pre-selected organizations.
Board meeting date(s): Quarterly
Officers: Samuel Goldwyn, Jr., Pres.; Peggy Goldwyn, V.P. and Secy.; Meyer Gottlieb, Treas.
Directors: Anthony Goldwyn; Catherine Goldwyn; Francis Goldwyn; John Goldwyn.
Number of staff: 1 full-time professional.
EIN: 956006859
Selected grants: The following grants were reported in 2004.
$72,554 to Sound Art, Los Angeles, CA. 2 grants: $61,404, $11,150
$50,000 to Academy Foundation, Beverly Hills, CA.
$41,500 to Partnership Scholars Program, Little River, CA.
$35,000 to Planned Parenthood of Los Angeles, Los Angeles, CA.
$25,000 to Educating Young Minds, Los Angeles, CA.
$10,000 to Little Star, Aspen, CO.
$10,000 to Teach for America, Los Angeles, CA.
$5,500 to National Public Radio, DC.
$3,500 to Marlborough School, Los Angeles, CA.

601

The Gonda Family Foundation ▼ ✧

(formerly The Gonda Foundation)
c/o Lexington Financial Mgmt., LLC
9350 Wilshire Blvd., 4th Fl.
Beverly Hills, CA 90212
Contact: Cheryl Zoller Simon

Established in 1986 in CA.
Donors: Louis L. Gonda; Kelly S. Gonda.
Foundation type: Independent foundation.
Financial data (yr. ended 11/30/05): Assets, $65,069 (M); gifts received, $8,079,069; expenditures, $7,956,987; qualifying distributions, $7,956,812; giving activities include $7,920,777 for 49 grants (high: $4,239,150; low: $200; average: $1,000–$10,000).
Purpose and activities: Giving primarily for education and health.
Fields of interest: Museums; Performing arts, music; Education; AIDS; Children/youth, services; Jewish agencies & temples.

Type of support: General/operating support; Capital campaigns; Building/renovation.
Limitations: Applications not accepted. Giving primarily in CA. No grants to individuals.
Application information: Contributes only to pre-selected organizations.
Officers: Louis L. Gonda, Pres.; Lawrence H. Heller, Secy.; Harvey S. Gettleson, C.F.O.; Kelly S. Gonda, Treas.
EIN: 954107668
Selected grants: The following grants were reported in 2005.
$4,239,150 to Mayo Foundation, Rochester, MN. For general support.
$2,300,000 to Georgetown University, DC. For general support.
$946,960 to UCLA Foundation, Los Angeles, CA. 2 grants: $17,400 (For general support), $929,560 (For general support).
$93,750 to University of Southern California, Department of Medicine, Los Angeles, CA. For general support.
$51,967 to Cate School, Carpinteria, CA. For general support.
$16,000 to Global Health Access Program, Los Angeles, CA. For general support.

602

Good Hope Medical Foundation ✧

225 S. Lake Ave., No. 271
Pasadena, CA 91101
Contact: Michael J. Connell, Treas.

Established in 1925 in CA.
Donor: Dorothy May Harris†.
Foundation type: Independent foundation.
Financial data (yr. ended 12/31/05): Assets, $25,901,211 (M); gifts received, $367,208; expenditures, $1,652,092; qualifying distributions, $1,511,094; giving activities include $1,498,613 for 5 grants (high: $893,894; low: $76,509).
Purpose and activities: Giving primarily to hospitals.
Fields of interest: Hospitals (general).
Type of support: General/operating support; Equipment.
Limitations: Giving limited to CA. No grants to individuals.
Application information: Application form not required.
Deadline(s): None
Officers: Ernest A. Bryant III, Pres.; J. Patrick Whaley, Secy.; Michael J. Connell, Treas.
EIN: 950782640

603

The Good Works Foundation

2101 Wilshire Blvd., Ste. 225
Santa Monica, CA 90403
Contact: Katherine Hall
URL: http://www.goodworks.org

Established in 1993 in CA.
Foundation type: Independent foundation.
Financial data (yr. ended 6/30/04): Assets, $1,121,816 (M); gifts received, $883,697; expenditures, $940,890; qualifying distributions, $932,017; giving activities include $930,310 for 58 grants (high: $325,000; low: $100).
Purpose and activities: Giving primarily for the arts and education in Santa Monica and West Los

Angeles, CA. Some giving in Chile for environmental purposes, and in Canada, for education.
Fields of interest: Museums (art); Performing arts, opera; Arts; Education; Environment.
International interests: Canada; Chile.
Type of support: General/operating support; Seed money; Matching/challenge support.
Limitations: Giving limited to West Los Angeles and Santa Monica, CA. No support for political causes. No grants to individuals.
Publications: Application guidelines.
Application information: Application guidelines available on foundation Web site. Application form not required.
Initial approach: Personal signed letter
Copies of proposal: 1
Deadline(s): None
Board meeting date(s): Quarterly
Final notification: 3-4 months
Officers: Laura Donnelley, Pres.; John Morton, Secy.-Treas.
Number of staff: 1 part-time support.
EIN: 954471685

604

The Gooding Family Foundation ✧

11455 El Camino Real, Rm. 490
San Diego, CA 92130-3036
Contact: Terence J. Gooding, Tr.

Established in 1997 in CA.
Donor: Terence J. Gooding.
Foundation type: Independent foundation.
Financial data (yr. ended 12/31/05): Assets, $5,784,450 (M); gifts received, $1,663,427; expenditures, $889,947; qualifying distributions, $869,592; giving activities include $691,950 for 17 grants (high: $375,000; low: $200).
Purpose and activities: Giving primarily for medical research, human services, and children and youth services.
Fields of interest: Elementary school/education; Hospitals (general); Cancer research; Heart & circulatory research; Human services; Children/youth, services; Christian agencies & churches.
Limitations: Giving primarily in CA.
Application information:
Initial approach: Letter
Deadline(s): None
Trustee: Terence J. Gooding.
EIN: 336203973

605

The Goodman Family Foundation ✧

c/o Sobul, Primes & Schenkel
12100 Wilshire Blvd., Ste. 1150
Los Angeles, CA 90025

Established in 1977 in CA.
Donor: Lawrence M. Goodman, Jr.
Foundation type: Independent foundation.
Financial data (yr. ended 6/30/05): Assets, $2,139,354 (M); expenditures, $414,865; qualifying distributions, $385,000; giving activities include $385,000 for 4 grants (high: $250,000; low: $10,000).
Purpose and activities: Giving primarily for higher education and health organizations.
Fields of interest: Higher education; Reproductive health, family planning; Health care; Health organizations, association; Human services.

Limitations: Applications not accepted. Giving primarily in Los Angeles, CA. No grants to individuals.
Application information: Contributes only to pre-selected organizations. Unsolicited request for funds not accepted.
Trustees: Meyer Luskin; Christopher Morris; David M. Primes.
EIN: 953169740

606

Google Foundation ✧ ☆
1600 Amphitheatre Pkwy.
Mountain View, CA 94043
URL: http://www.google.org

Established in 2004 in CA.
Donor: Google Inc.
Foundation type: Company-sponsored foundation.
Financial data (yr. ended 12/31/05): Assets, $84,911,196 (M); gifts received, $90,000,000; expenditures, $5,450,223; qualifying distributions, $5,450,223; giving activities include $5,450,000 for 3 grants (high: $5,000,000; low: $200,000).
Purpose and activities: The foundation supports venture philanthropy funds and organizations involved with literacy and entrepreneurism.
Fields of interest: Education, reading; Community development, small businesses; Venture philanthropy.
Type of support: Program development; General/operating support.
Limitations: Applications not accepted. Giving to U.S.-based international organizations.
Application information: Contributes only to pre-selected organizations.
Officers and Directors:* Miriam Rivera, Secy.-Treas.; Larry Brilliant, M.D.*, Exec. Dir.; Sergey Brin; Larry Page; Sheryl Sandberg.
EIN: 201548253

607

The Betsy Gordon Foundation ✧
c/o Elizabeth Gordon
1537 4th St., Box 15
San Rafael, CA 94901

Established in 2001 in DE and NY.
Donor: Elizabeth Gordon.
Foundation type: Independent foundation.
Financial data (yr. ended 10/31/05): Assets, $237,932 (M); gifts received, $1,061,121; expenditures, $875,691; qualifying distributions, $872,436; giving activities include $843,425 for 24 + grants (high: $250,000).
Purpose and activities: Giving primarily for education and spiritual enrichment.
Fields of interest: Education; Foundations (private grantmaking).
Limitations: Applications not accepted. No grants to individuals.
Application information: Contributes only to pre-selected organizations.
Officers: Elizabeth Gordon, Pres.; James Adler, Secy.; Louis Leeburg, Treas.
Trustees: Angeles Arrien; Ricci Coddington; Frances Vaughan, Ph.D.
EIN: 113634807
Selected grants: The following grants were reported in 2005.
$250,000 to Project Self Sufficiency, New York, NY.

$102,327 to Heffter Research Institute, Santa Fe, NM.
$50,000 to Independent Production Fund, New York, NY.
$30,000 to Wellness Community, DC.
$25,000 to Genesis Farm, Blairstown, NJ.
$23,356 to Institute of Noetic Sciences, Petaluma, CA.
$20,000 to American Red Cross.
$20,000 to Foundation for Shamanic Studies, Mill Valley, CA.
$5,000 to Society for the Study of Myth and Tradition, New York, NY.

608

The Gotschall Family Foundation ✧ ☆
6 Fresian
Coto De Caza, CA 92679

Donors: Edward F. Gotschall; Susan K. Gotschall.
Foundation type: Independent foundation.
Financial data (yr. ended 4/30/06): Assets, $861,365 (M); gifts received, $1,831,167; expenditures, $1,000,000; qualifying distributions, $1,000,000; giving activities include $1,000,000 for 1 grant.
Limitations: Applications not accepted.
Application information: Contributes only to pre-selected organizations.
Officers and Directors:* Susan K. Gotschall,* Pres.; Brittany Gotschall,* Secy.; Edward F. Gotschall, C.F.O.
EIN: 710979470

609

The Joseph B. Gould Foundation ✧
5670 Wilshire Blvd., Ste. 1450
Los Angeles, CA 90036 (323) 954-3131
Contact: Carolyn Dirks, Pres.

Established in 1991 in NV.
Donor: Joseph B. Gould.
Foundation type: Independent foundation.
Financial data (yr. ended 12/31/05): Assets, $30,705,160 (M); expenditures, $2,642,918; qualifying distributions, $2,261,238; giving activities include $2,217,071 for 51 grants (high: $412,000; low: $2,000).
Purpose and activities: Giving for health and medical services.
Fields of interest: Higher education; Health care; Human services.
Limitations: Giving primarily in CA, Denver, CO, and Las Vegas, NV. No grants to individuals.
Application information:
Initial approach: Letter
Deadline(s): None
Officers and Directors:* Carolyn Dirks,* Pres.; David Watts, Secy.; Martin Dirks, Treas.; Steven Spector.
EIN: 880232969
Selected grants: The following grants were reported in 2005.
$412,000 to John Wayne Cancer Institute, Santa Monica, CA.
$322,000 to Saint Johns Health Center Foundation, Santa Monica, CA.
$100,000 to John Tracy Clinic, Los Angeles, CA.
$80,931 to Childrens Hospital Los Angeles, Los Angeles, CA.

$62,500 to Elizabeth Taylor AIDS Foundation, Los Angeles, CA.
$60,000 to Stanford University, Stanford, CA.
$50,000 to Music Center Foundation, Los Angeles, CA.
$10,000 to College of Marin, Kentfield, CA.
$10,000 to Elizabeth Center for Cancer Detection, Los Angeles, CA.
$10,000 to Los Angeles Opera Company, Los Angeles, CA.

610

Kelsey Grammer Charitable Foundation ✧
c/o Lucy Bungalow
5555 Melrose Ave.
Los Angeles, CA 90038 (323) 956-5815
Contact: Dalia Leon

Established in 1995 in CA.
Donor: Allen Kelsey Grammer.
Foundation type: Independent foundation.
Financial data (yr. ended 10/31/04): Assets, $600,887 (M); expenditures, $340,140; qualifying distributions, $340,067; giving activities include $339,500 for 15 grants (high: $167,000; low: $1,000).
Purpose and activities: Giving for youth groups, human services, medical research, and reproductive rights.
Fields of interest: Arts; Medical research, institute; Youth development; Human services; Civil liberties, reproductive rights.
Type of support: General/operating support; Building/renovation; Research.
Limitations: Giving limited to CA.
Application information:
Initial approach: Letter and brochure from board of directors of charity describing fundraising event
Officer: Allen Kelsey Grammer, Pres.
EIN: 954557293
Selected grants: The following grants were reported in 2003.
$100,000 to Los Angeles Police Memorial Foundation, Los Angeles, CA. For unrestricted support.
$50,000 to Motion Picture and Television Fund, Woodland Hills, CA. For Cottages & Lodge Campaign.
$25,000 to James J. McBride Special Education Center, Los Angeles, CA. For unrestricted support.
$20,000 to Womens Reproductive Rights Assistance Project, Culver City, CA. For unrestricted support.
$10,000 to Camp Good in the Hood, Los Angeles, CA. For unrestricted support.
$10,000 to Los Angeles Philharmonic, Los Angeles, CA. For unrestricted support.
$5,000 to Mother Cabrini High School, New York, NY. For unrestricted support.
$5,000 to National Breast Cancer Coalition, DC. For unrestricted support.
$5,000 to Puck-Lazaroff Charitable Foundation, Beverly Hills, CA. For unrestricted support.
$5,000 to Save Our Special Schools, Los Angeles, CA. For unrestricted support.

611
Richard Grand Foundation ✧
405 Davis Ct., No. 2504
San Francisco, CA 94111

Established in 1995 in CA.
Donors: Richard Grand; Marcia Grand; Rena Grand†.
Foundation type: Independent foundation.
Financial data (yr. ended 6/30/05): Assets, $10,790,975 (M); expenditures, $702,602; qualifying distributions, $683,025; giving activities include $669,750 for 81 grants (high: $56,000; low: $500).
Purpose and activities: Giving primarily for arts and culture, education, health care, and human services.
Fields of interest: Museums; Performing arts, theater; Arts; Higher education; Law school/education; Education; Environment; Animal welfare; Reproductive health, family planning; Health organizations, association; Food banks; Human services; Children/youth, services; Jewish agencies & temples.
Limitations: Applications not accepted. Giving primarily in Tucson, AZ, San Francisco, CA, and New York, NY. No grants to individuals.
Application information: Contributes only to pre-selected organizations.
Officers: Richard Grand, Chair. and Secy.; Marcia Grand, Pres.; Cindy Grand, V.P. and C.F.O.
EIN: 943221366

612
Leon L. Granoff Foundation ✧
P.O. Box 2148
Gardena, CA 90247

Established in 1978 in CA.
Donors: Leon L. Granoff; Eric Prosser.
Foundation type: Independent foundation.
Financial data (yr. ended 8/31/05): Assets, $0 (M); gifts received, $771,000; expenditures, $709,270; qualifying distributions, $709,270; giving activities include $700,460 for 31 grants (high: $46,862; low: $125).
Purpose and activities: Awards undergraduate scholarships to attend CA colleges and universities.
Type of support: Scholarships—to individuals.
Limitations: Applications not accepted. Giving limited to residents of CA.
Application information: Unsolicited requests for funds not accepted.
Officer: Leon L. Granoff, Pres.
EIN: 953184779

613
George and Reva Graziadio Foundation ✧
16633 Ventura Blvd., Ste. 510
Encino, CA 91436-1807

Established in 1998 in CA.
Donors: George L. Graziadio, Jr.; Reva Graziadio, Jr.
Foundation type: Independent foundation.
Financial data (yr. ended 6/30/05): Assets, $9,316,942 (M); gifts received, $133,117; expenditures, $414,489; qualifying distributions, $406,597; giving activities include $359,498 for 17 + grants (high: $225,000).
Fields of interest: Higher education; Human services; Foundations (community).

Limitations: Applications not accepted. Giving primarily in CA. No grants to individuals.
Application information: Contributes only to pre-selected organizations.
Officers and Directors:* Mary Lou Area,* Pres.; Alida Calvillo,* Secy.; Phillip M. Bardack,* C.F.O.; G. Louis Graziadio III,* Treas.
EIN: 954697062
Selected grants: The following grants were reported in 2003.
$426,000 to Orange County Community Foundation, Irvine, CA.

614
The Green Foundation ✧ ☆
(formerly Leonard I. Green Foundation)
c/o George McCrimlisk
201 S. Lake Ave., Ste. 508
Pasadena, CA 91101

Established in 1994 in CA.
Donors: Leonard I. Green; Emese Green.
Foundation type: Independent foundation.
Financial data (yr. ended 11/30/05): Assets, $9,285,823 (M); gifts received, $10,000,000; expenditures, $1,247,199; qualifying distributions, $1,225,832; giving activities include $1,164,700 for 21 grants (high: $917,000; low: $200).
Purpose and activities: Giving primarily for health, human services, animal welfare, education, and to opera companies.
Fields of interest: Performing arts, opera; Education; Animal welfare; Health organizations, association; Human services; Jewish agencies & temples.
Limitations: Applications not accepted. Giving on a national basis, with emphasis on CA. No grants to individuals.
Application information: Contributes only to pre-selected organizations.
Officers: George H. McCrimlisk, C.E.O. and Pres.; Suzanne Green, Secy.
Board Member: Ron Wilcox.
EIN: 954509163
Selected grants: The following grants were reported in 2005.
$917,000 to Los Angeles Opera Company, Los Angeles, CA.
$50,000 to Metropolitan Opera, New York, NY.
$25,000 to Congregation Beth Israel, Houston, TX.
$25,000 to Woodcraft Rangers, Los Angeles, CA.
$14,000 to American Cancer Society, Los Angeles, CA.
$10,000 to Camino Nuevo Charter Academy, Los Angeles, CA.
$5,000 to Cystic Fibrosis Foundation, Bethesda, MD.
$5,000 to Grand Performances, Los Angeles, CA.
$2,500 to Alzheimers Association, Denville, NJ.
$2,500 to Mayfield Junior School of the Holy Child Jesus, Pasadena, CA.

615
The James R. Greenbaum, Jr. Family Foundation
P.O. Box 9910
Rancho Santa Fe, CA 92067
E-mail: jimgreenbaum@hotmail.com

Established in 1991 in UT.
Donor: James R. Greenbaum, Jr.

Foundation type: Independent foundation.
Financial data (yr. ended 12/31/04): Assets, $30,717,902 (M); expenditures, $1,565,318; qualifying distributions, $1,397,422; giving activities include $1,397,422 for 16 grants (high: $738,000; low: $25).
Fields of interest: Performing arts; Big Brothers/Big Sisters; Human services; Jewish federated giving programs; Jewish agencies & temples.
Limitations: Applications not accepted. Giving primarily in Salt Lake City, UT. No grants to individuals.
Application information: Contributes only to pre-selected organizations.
Trustee: James R. Greenbaum, Jr.
EIN: 876217358
Selected grants: The following grants were reported in 2003.
$860,000 to Kidsave International, DC. For general support.
$94,787 to Forefront, New York, NY. For general support.
$72,120 to Congregation Kol Ami, Salt Lake City, UT. For general support.
$50,000 to Happy Factory, Cedar City, UT. For general support.
$50,000 to Witness, Inc., Brooklyn, NY.
$10,000 to United Jewish Federation of Utah, Salt Lake City, UT. For general support.
$10,000 to Utah Symphony and Opera, Salt Lake City, UT. For general support.
$5,000 to Ballet West, Salt Lake City, UT. For general support.
$5,000 to Rowland Hall-Saint Marks School, Salt Lake City, UT. For general support.
$1,000 to Seattle University, Seattle, WA. For general support.

616
Mary Jo & Hank Greenberg Animal Welfare Foundation ✧
9903 Santa Monica Blvd., PMB 837
Beverly Hills, CA 90212
Contact: Mary Jo Greenberg, Chair.

Established in 1999 in CA.
Donors: Mary Jo Greenberg; Jeffrey Tarola.
Foundation type: Independent foundation.
Financial data (yr. ended 5/31/05): Assets, $153,983 (M); gifts received, $378,325; expenditures, $406,655; qualifying distributions, $405,500; giving activities include $405,500 for 40 grants (high: $27,500; low: $2,500).
Purpose and activities: Giving primarily to organizations that rescue, provide care, housing and services for homeless and neglected animals, especially cats and dogs.
Fields of interest: Animals/wildlife, association; Animal welfare; Animals/wildlife.
Limitations: Giving primarily in CA.
Application information:
Initial approach: Letter
Deadline(s): None
Officers and Board Members:* Mary Jo Greenberg, Chair. and Pres.; Robert Furber,* V.P.; Suzie Levin,* Secy.-Treas.; Marjorie Loeb.
EIN: 954738423
Selected grants: The following grants were reported in 2005.
$27,500 to Friends of Animals, Los Angeles, CA.
$22,500 to CARE, Los Angeles, CA.
$10,000 to Living Free, Mountain Center, CA.
$10,000 to Southland Collie Rescue, Altadena, CA.

$5,000 to Nature of Wildworks, Topanga, CA.

$2,500 to Marine Mammal Center, Sausalito, CA.

617
The Greenberg Foundation ◇
(formerly The Mayer Greenberg Foundation)
6060 Sepulveda Blvd., No. 300
Van Nuys, CA 91411-2501

Established in 1953 in CA.

Donors: Daniel B. Greenberg; Aaron Masowitz Trust; Electro Rent Corp.

Foundation type: Independent foundation.

Financial data (yr. ended 11/30/05): Assets, $8,351,786 (M); expenditures, $475,305; qualifying distributions, $465,328; giving activities include $454,475 for 154 grants (high: $216,250; low: $25).

Purpose and activities: Giving primarily for education, the arts, the environment, and health care.

Fields of interest: Arts education; Media, radio; Museums (art); Museums (specialized); Higher education; Law school/education; Education; Environment; Health organizations, association; Human services.

Limitations: Applications not accepted. Giving on a national basis, with emphasis on CA, Washington, DC, MA, and New York, NY. No grants to individuals.

Application information: Contributes only to pre-selected organizations.

Officers: Daniel B. Greenberg, Pres.; Ben Greenberg, V.P. and Treas.

EIN: 956037502

Selected grants: The following grants were reported in 2005.

$39,500 to NPR Foundation, DC.

$22,300 to Pilchuck Glass School, Seattle, WA.

$20,000 to American Jewish World Service, New York, NY.

$15,820 to Reed College, Portland, OR.

$15,100 to University of Chicago, Chicago, IL.

$4,700 to J. Paul Getty Museum, Malibu, CA.

$500 to University of Washington Foundation, Seattle, WA.

$250 to Global Fund for Women, San Francisco, CA.

$250 to Museum of Contemporary Art San Diego, La Jolla, CA.

$150 to North American Conference on Ethiopian Jewry, New York, NY.

618
The Greer Family Foundation ◇
1 Embarcadero Ctr., Ste. 1060
San Francisco, CA 94111
Contact: Philip Greer, Pres.

Established in 1985 in IL and NY.

Donors: Philip Greer; Nancy Greer.

Foundation type: Independent foundation.

Financial data (yr. ended 12/31/05): Assets, $4,015,608 (M); gifts received, $398,840; expenditures, $724,266; qualifying distributions, $698,561; giving activities include $693,798 for 47 grants (high: $75,000; low: $55).

Purpose and activities: Giving primarily for education; funding also for human services, health organizations, and the arts.

Fields of interest: Arts; Higher education; Health organizations, association; Human services; Children/youth, services.

Type of support: General/operating support; Capital campaigns.

Limitations: Applications not accepted. Giving primarily in CA, CT, and NY. No grants to individuals.

Application information: Unsolicited requests for funds not accepted.

Officers: Philip Greer, Pres.; Norman M. Gold, V.P.; Nancy Greer, V.P.; Stephen Weiss, V.P.

EIN: 133321858

Selected grants: The following grants were reported in 2003.

$156,100 to Tulane Educational Fund, New Orleans, LA. For general support.

$8,591 to Town School for Boys, San Francisco, CA. For general support.

$5,059 to Helpers of the Mentally Retarded, San Francisco, CA. For general support.

$2,700 to Santa Catalina School, Monterey, CA. For general support.

$2,000 to Manhattanville College, Purchase, NY. For annual campaign.

$1,750 to Kids in Crisis, Cos Cob, CT. For general support.

$1,500 to Actors Fund of America, New York, NY. For general support.

$1,000 to Greenwich Hospital, Greenwich, CT. For general support.

$500 to Breast Cancer Alliance, Greenwich, CT. For general support.

$175 to Metropolitan Museum of Art, New York, NY. For general support.

619
Robert A. and Kari L. Grimm Family Foundation ◇
6900 Mountain View Rd.
Bakersfield, CA 93307 (661) 393-3320

Established in 2001 in CA.

Donor: Grimmway Enterprises, Inc.

Foundation type: Independent foundation.

Financial data (yr. ended 12/31/04): Assets, $4,469,343 (M); expenditures, $922,280; qualifying distributions, $919,083; giving activities include $919,083 for 8 grants (high: $625,000; low: $250).

Purpose and activities: Giving primarily for higher education, as well as to Christian organizations, and to a Lutheran church.

Fields of interest: Higher education; Christian agencies & churches; Protestant agencies & churches.

Limitations: Giving primarily in CA.

Application information:
  Initial approach: Letter

Officers: Robert A. Grimm, Pres. and Treas.; Kari L. Grimm, V.P.; Jeffery A. Green, Secy.

EIN: 770554204

620
The Rodney Grimm Family Foundation ◇
7158 Buena Vista Rd.
Bakersfield, CA 93311
Contact: Barbara M. Grimm, Pres.

Established in 2001 in CA.

Donor: Grimmway Enterprises, Inc.

Foundation type: Independent foundation.

Financial data (yr. ended 12/31/04): Assets, $4,018,145 (M); gifts received, $937,500; expenditures, $1,085,672; qualifying distributions,

$1,050,500; giving activities include $1,050,500 for 12 grants (high: $625,000; low: $300).

Fields of interest: Higher education; Education; Christian agencies & churches.

Limitations: Giving primarily in CA; funding also in MN and WI. No grants to individuals.

Application information:
  Initial approach: Letter
  Deadline(s): None

Officers and Director: Barbara M. Grimm, Pres.; Steve Barnes, Secy. and C.F.O.

EIN: 770572545

Selected grants: The following grants were reported in 2003.

$100,000 to Concordia University, Saint Paul, MN. For scholarships.

$60,000 to Concordia University, Portland, OR. For scholarships.

$58,250 to Saint Johns Lutheran Church, Bakersfield, CA.

$37,500 to Pastoral Leadership Institute, Santa Ana, CA. For scholarships.

$15,000 to Cranach Institute, Fort Wayne, IN. For Solomon's Temple book project.

$5,000 to OASIS Ministries, Pasadena, CA.

$2,500 to Concordia University, Mequon, WI. For scholarships.

$2,000 to World Vision, Tacoma, WA.

$1,000 to Garces Memorial High School, Bakersfield, CA. For scholarships.

$1,000 to Samaritans Purse, Boone, NC.

621
Stella B. Gross Charitable Trust ◇
c/o Bank of the West
P.O. Box 1121
San Jose, CA 95108 (408) 947-5160
Contact: Gabe S. Padilla, Trust Admin.; Fatima Mendoza, Trust Assoc.
E-mail: fmendoza@bankofthewest.com; Additional tel.: (800) 232-2430

Trust established in 1966 in CA.

Donor: Stella B. Gross†.

Foundation type: Independent foundation.

Financial data (yr. ended 6/30/05): Assets, $7,525,587 (M); expenditures, $507,367; qualifying distributions, $443,214; giving activities include $410,000 for 62 grants (high: $20,000; low: $1,000).

Fields of interest: Visual arts; Museums; Performing arts; Arts; Child development, education; Elementary school/education; Higher education; Education; Hospitals (general); Health care; Health organizations, association; Cancer; Heart & circulatory diseases; Cancer research; Heart & circulatory research; Human services; Children/youth, services; Child development, services; Residential/custodial care, hospices; Aging, centers/services; Roman Catholic federated giving programs; Government/public administration; Aging; Disabilities, people with.

Type of support: General/operating support; Continuing support; Program development; Seed money.

Limitations: Giving limited to Santa Clara County, CA. No grants to individuals.

Publications: Annual report; Grants list.

Application information: Application form required.
  Copies of proposal: 1
  Deadline(s): May 31 and Nov. 30
  Board meeting date(s): June and Dec.
  Final notification: 6 months

Directors: Hon. Thomas P. Hansen; Arthur K. Lund; Louis O'Neal.
EIN: 237142181

622
The Gross Family Foundation ✧
c/o Ayco
17900 Von Karman Ave., Ste. 200
Irvine, CA 92614

Established around 1994 in CA.
Donors: William Gross; Mrs. William Gross.
Foundation type: Independent foundation.
Financial data (yr. ended 12/31/03): Assets, $32,894,830 (M); gifts received, $6,423,670; expenditures, $963,140; qualifying distributions, $910,042; giving activities include $910,042 for 9 grants (high: $399,042; low: $1,000).
Purpose and activities: Giving primarily for human services.
Fields of interest: Education; Human services; Children, services; Federated giving programs.
Limitations: Applications not accepted. Giving primarily in CA.
Application information: Contributes only to pre-selected organizations.
Officers: William Gross, Pres.; Sue Gross, Secy.
EIN: 330633087
Selected grants: The following grants were reported in 2004.
$303,075 to Sage Hill School, Newport Coast, CA. For building fund.
$24,703 to James Hines Fund. For general support.
$10,000 to Venice Arts: In Neighborhoods, Venice, CA. For general support.
$5,000 to HeArt Project, Los Angeles, CA. For general support.
$2,500 to Center Theater Group of Los Angeles, Los Angeles, CA. For general support.
$1,500 to Free Arts for Abused Children, Los Angeles, CA. For general support.
$1,000 to Saint Joseph Ballet Company, Santa Ana, CA. For general support.

623
Grousbeck Family Foundation ▼ ✧
c/o Stanford University
Graduate School of Business, Rm. L-336
Stanford, CA 94305-5015   (650) 723-0709
Contact: H. Irving Grousbeck, Pres.

Established in 1990 in CA.
Donors: H. Irving Grousbeck; E. Grousbeck†.
Foundation type: Independent foundation.
Financial data (yr. ended 11/30/05): Assets, $120,592,854 (M); gifts received, $10; expenditures, $8,400,605; qualifying distributions, $7,051,516; giving activities include $7,049,946 for 137 grants (high: $450,500; low: $1,000; average: $10,000–$125,000).
Purpose and activities: Grants primarily for higher education, hospitals, eye research and for the environment.
Fields of interest: Higher education; Eye diseases; Eye research.
Limitations: Giving on a national basis. No grants to individuals.
Application information: Application form not required.
Deadline(s): None

Officers: H. Irving Grousbeck, Pres.; Susanne B. Grousbeck, V.P.; Wycliffe K. Grousbeck, Secy.-Treas.; Anne H.G. Matta, C.F.O.
EIN: 770267061
Selected grants: The following grants were reported in 2005.
$450,500 to Eastside College Preparatory School, East Palo Alto, CA. For general support.
$200,000 to Peninsula Open Space Trust, Menlo Park, CA. For general support.
$130,000 to National Braille Press, Boston, MA. For general support.
$100,000 to Childrens Hospital Corporation, Boston, MA. For general support for Child Life Services.
$100,000 to Dexterity Sports and Literacy, San Jose, CA. For general support.
$90,000 to InnVision the Way Home, San Jose, CA. For general support.
$50,000 to Blind Babies Foundation, San Francisco, CA. For general support.
$40,000 to Boys and Girls Clubs of the Peninsula, Menlo Park, CA. For general support.
$40,000 to Circle of Life Foundation, Oakland, CA. For general support.
$30,000 to NewSchools Venture Fund, San Francisco, CA. For general support.

624
Gardner Grout Foundation ✧ ☆
c/o Capital Guardian Trust Co.
333 S. Hope St., 34th Fl.
Los Angeles, CA 90071-1447   (213) 486-9621
Contact: Barbara Brewer, Trust Off., Capital Guardian Trust Co.

Established in 2001 in CA.
Donor: Elizabeth O. Grout.
Foundation type: Independent foundation.
Financial data (yr. ended 12/31/05): Assets, $18,293,935 (M); gifts received, $2,793,532; expenditures, $731,121; qualifying distributions, $627,329; giving activities include $568,500 for 52 grants (high: $60,000; low: $1,000).
Fields of interest: Education; Environment, land resources; Hospitals (general); Health care; Human services.
Type of support: General/operating support.
Limitations: Giving primarily in CA. No grants to individuals.
Application information:
Initial approach: Letter
Deadline(s): None
Trustees: L.G. Brigham; L.B. Hambleton; E.B. Huyck; C.B. Markovich; Capital Guardian Trust Co.
EIN: 957106955
Selected grants: The following grants were reported in 2005.
$60,000 to Pacific Legal Foundation, Sacramento, CA.
$35,000 to Loyola High School, Los Angeles, CA.
$35,000 to Peninsula Open Space Trust, Menlo Park, CA.
$25,000 to Hoag Hospital Foundation, Newport Beach, CA.
$20,000 to American Ballet Theater, New York, NY.
$15,000 to Heritage Foundation, DC.
$15,000 to Huntington Hospital, Pasadena, CA.
$15,000 to San Francisco 49ers Academy, East Palo Alto, CA.
$10,000 to New York Public Library, New York, NY.
$6,000 to Ashland Schools Foundation, Ashland, OR.

625
The Grove Foundation ▼ ✧
P.O. Box 1667
Los Altos, CA 94023-1667

Established in 1986 in CA.
Donors: Andrew S. Grove; Eva K. Grove.
Foundation type: Independent foundation.
Financial data (yr. ended 9/30/05): Assets, $52,968,249 (M); gifts received, $1,699,998; expenditures, $7,839,417; qualifying distributions, $7,648,193; giving activities include $6,568,377 for 136 grants (high: $450,000; low: $1,400; average: $10,000–$100,000), and $312,614 for 2 foundation-administered programs.
Purpose and activities: Giving primarily for family planning and other social services, vocational or professional education, Jewish welfare, international refugee assistance, and the performing arts.
Fields of interest: Performing arts; Higher education; Reproductive health, family planning; Homeless, human services; International relief; Civil rights, advocacy; Civil liberties, reproductive rights; Aging; Women; Immigrants/refugees; Economically disadvantaged; Homeless.
Limitations: Applications not accepted. Giving primarily in CA. No grants to individuals, or for construction.
Application information: Unsolicited requests not considered; funds are fully committed.
Officers and Directors:* Andrew S. Grove,* Pres.; Eva K. Grove,* Secy.-Treas.; Karen Grove; Robie Grove Livingstone.
EIN: 770108124
Selected grants: The following grants were reported in 2005.
$480,462 to Parkinsons Institute, Sunnyvale, CA. 2 grants: $335,887 (For program support), $144,575 (For program support).
$450,000 to Michael J. Fox Foundation for Parkinsons Research, New York, NY. For program support.
$375,000 to Emergency Housing Consortium of Santa Clara County, San Jose, CA. For Raising Income through Scholarship and Education (RISE) Program for homeless parents.
$260,000 to Planned Parenthood Mar Monte, San Jose, CA. For general support and program support.
$200,000 to Center for Reproductive Rights, New York, NY. For general support.
$75,000 to Simon Wiesenthal Center, Los Angeles, CA. For general support.
$70,000 to Harvard University, Cambridge, MA. For medical research.
$60,000 to University of Puget Sound, Tacoma, WA. For occupational therapy program.
$43,000 to Pajaro Valley Unified School District, Watsonville, CA. For scholarship program.

626
Gruber Family Foundation ✧
P.O. Box 214
Ross, CA 94957

Established in 1987 in CA.
Donors: Jon D. Gruber; Linda W. Gruber.
Foundation type: Independent foundation.
Financial data (yr. ended 12/31/05): Assets, $47,435,975 (M); expenditures, $2,808,644; qualifying distributions, $2,739,551; giving

activities include $2,738,650 for 87 grants (high: $400,000; low: $750).

Purpose and activities: Primary areas of interest include education, family planning and women's issues, museums, the homeless, and social services.

Fields of interest: Museums; Arts; Education; Environment; Reproductive health, family planning; Crime/violence prevention, abuse prevention; Human services; Youth, services; Women, centers/ services; Homeless, human services; Civil liberties, reproductive rights; Women; Economically disadvantaged; Homeless.

Type of support: General/operating support; Continuing support; Annual campaigns; Capital campaigns; Building/renovation; Program development; Professorships; Matching/challenge support.

Limitations: Applications not accepted. Giving primarily in CA. No support for religious organizations. No grants to individuals.

Application information: Contributes only to pre-selected organizations.

Officers: Linda W. Gruber, Pres.; Jon D. Gruber, Secy.-Treas.

EIN: 943039716

Selected grants: The following grants were reported in 2005.

$400,000 to Global Fund for Women, San Francisco, CA.

$250,000 to Wellesley College, Wellesley, MA.

$200,000 to NPR Foundation, DC.

$100,000 to Full Circle Fund, San Francisco, CA.

$100,000 to Human Rights Watch, New York, NY.

$100,000 to Media Matters for America, DC.

$100,000 to Summer Search Foundation, San Francisco, CA.

$100,000 to Young Womens Leadership Foundation, New York, NY.

$82,000 to Cate School, Carpinteria, CA.

$5,000 to Silver Eye Center for Photography, Pittsburgh, PA.

627

GSF Foundation ✧ ☆

18301 Von Karman Ave., Ste. 1100
Irvine, CA   92612   (949) 929-1103
E-mail: helpkids@gsffoundation.org; Additional tel.: (877) 473-5437; URL: http://www.gsffoundation.org

Established in 2002 in CA and OR.

Donors: Mark S. Wetterau; Golden State Foods Corp.

Foundation type: Company-sponsored foundation.

Financial data (yr. ended 12/31/04): Assets, $207,279 (M); gifts received, $660,491; expenditures, $634,195; qualifying distributions, $634,195; giving activities include $482,677 for 83 grants (high: $42,000; low: $250).

Purpose and activities: The foundation supports organizations involved with youth development, family services, and children. Special emphasis is directed toward programs designed to serve children with various needs, including food, shelter, clothes, medical treatment, and social activities.

Fields of interest: Youth development; Children, services; Family services.

Type of support: General/operating support; Program development; Employee volunteer services.

Limitations: Giving on a national basis, with emphasis on areas of company operations. No

support for religious, sectarian, political, or lobbying organizations, pass-through organizations, or organizations not associated with an employee of Golden State Foods. No grants for individuals, or for capital campaigns or endowments or debt reduction or budget deficits.

Publications: Application guidelines; Annual report; Newsletter.

Application information: Proposals should be submitted using organization letterhead. Application form required.

Initial approach: Download application form and mail proposal and application form to nearest company facility

Officers and Directors: * Mark Wetterau,* Chair. and C.E.O.; Richard Moretti,* Secy.; Mike Waitukaitis,* Treas.; Chuck Browne,* Exec. Dir.; Steve Becker; Bob Jorge; Frank Listi.

EIN: 460501728

Selected grants: The following grants were reported in 2003.

$30,000 to Ronald McDonald House Charities of Southern California, Los Angeles, CA. For general support.

$24,262 to Atlanta Ronald McDonald House Charities, Atlanta, GA. For general support.

$15,000 to Ronald McDonald House of Orange County, Orange, CA. For general support.

$12,202 to Ronald McDonald House Charities of Western Washington, Seattle, WA. For general support.

$10,000 to Ronald McDonald House Charities of Portland and Southwest Washington, Portland, OR. For general support.

$10,000 to Ronald McDonald House Charities of San Diego, San Diego, CA. For general support.

$5,000 to Big Brothers/Big Sisters of Orange County, Tustin, CA. For general support.

$5,000 to YMCA, San Gabriel Valley Family, Covina, CA. For general support.

$2,000 to Boy Scouts of America, Atlanta Area Council, Atlanta, GA. For general support.

$1,000 to Edmarc Hospice for Children, Norfolk, VA. For general support.

628

Henry L. Guenther Foundation ▼ ✧

2029 Century Park E., Ste. 4392
Los Angeles, CA   90067   (310) 785-0658
Contact: W.D. Milliken, Secy.

Established in 1956.

Donor: Pearl H. Guenther‡.

Foundation type: Independent foundation.

Financial data (yr. ended 12/31/05): Assets, $119,983,025 (M); expenditures, $6,699,861; qualifying distributions, $6,067,862; giving activities include $5,585,000 for 40 grants (high: $1,000,000; low: $5,000; average: $20,000– $100,000).

Purpose and activities: The foundation aims to improve social conditions, promote human welfare, and alleviate pain and suffering.

Fields of interest: Hospitals (general); Medical research, institute; Human services.

Limitations: Giving primarily in southern CA. Generally no support for government agencies, or religious organizations for religious purposes. No grants to individuals, including scholarships; or for operating deficits.

Application information: Application form required.

Initial approach: Letter (no more than 2 pages)
Copies of proposal: 9

Deadline(s): May 31 and Oct. 31
Board meeting date(s): Jan. and July
Final notification: 3 months

Officers and Directors: * W.D. Milliken,* C.O.O. and Secy.; Maurice Koeberle,* Pres.; Joseph P. Battaglia,* V.P.; Otto Heck,* V.P.; D.V. Werderman, C.F.O. and Treas.; Richard Battaglia; Ann Leatherbury; Susanne Sundberg.

EIN: 956026937

Selected grants: The following grants were reported in 2005.

$1,000,000 to Braille Institute of America, Los Angeles, CA. To build new education center in Santa Barbara.

$1,000,000 to Discovery Fund for Eye Research, Los Angeles, CA. To create patient oriented Eye Research Institute.

$700,000 to Loma Linda University Medical Center, Loma Linda, CA. To develop non-invasive proton accelerator treatment for children with epilepsy.

$600,000 to Salk Institute for Biological Studies, San Diego, CA. To build four cell biology labs and to buy confocal microscope.

$500,000 to Huntington Hospital, Pasadena, CA. To build and furnish cardiac catheterization laboratory.

$200,000 to Henry Mayo Newhall Memorial Health Foundation, Valencia, CA. For expansion of Emergency Department.

$100,000 to Childrens Bureau of Southern California, Los Angeles, CA. For building of new family center.

$100,000 to Methodist Hospital of Southern California, Arcadia, CA. For purchase of CT Scanner.

$50,000 to Arroyo Vista Family Health Center, Los Angeles, CA. For renovation and furnishing of new Community Health Center.

$40,000 to TrinityCare Hospice Foundation, Torrance, CA. For discretionary fund which covers expenses not covered by insurance or other public sources.

629

Guess? Foundation ✧

1444 S. Alameda St.
Los Angeles, CA   90021

Established in 1994 in CA.

Donor: Guess ?, Inc.

Foundation type: Company-sponsored foundation.

Financial data (yr. ended 12/31/05): Assets, $68,330 (M); gifts received, $500,000; expenditures, $417,935; qualifying distributions, $417,900; giving activities include $417,900 for 29 grants (high: $120,000; low: $400).

Purpose and activities: The foundation supports organizations involved with education, health, youth development, human services, and Judaism.

Fields of interest: Education; Health care; Youth development; Children/youth, services; Human services; Federated giving programs; Jewish agencies & temples.

Limitations: Giving primarily in CA. No grants to individuals.

Application information: Application form not required.

Initial approach: Proposal
Deadline(s): None

Directors: Armand Marciano; Maurice Marciano; Paul Marciano.

EIN: 954500475

Selected grants: The following grants were reported in 2004.

$57,000 to Childrens Diabetes Foundation, Beverly Hills, CA. 2 grants: $50,000, $7,000

$50,000 to Beit TShuvah, Los Angeles, CA.

$25,000 to Ann Schreiber Ovarian Cancer Research Fund, New York, NY.

$25,000 to Childrens Hospital Los Angeles, Los Angeles, CA.

$25,000 to First Star, Arlington, VA.

$10,000 to Environmental Media Association, Los Angeles, CA.

$10,000 to New York City Outward Bound Center, Long Island City, NY.

$5,000 to Hospital for Special Surgery Fund, New York, NY.

$5,000 to Tourette Syndrome Association, Bayside, NY.

630
Guest House Ministries Foundation ◇ ☆
P.O. Box 8681
Rancho Santa Fe, CA 92067
Contact: Judith A. Jones, Pres.

Donor: Judith A. Jones.
Foundation type: Independent foundation.
Financial data (yr. ended 12/31/05): Assets, $1,571,996 (M); gifts received, $2,000,500; expenditures, $3,726,526; qualifying distributions, $3,687,900; giving activities include $3,687,900 for grants.
Fields of interest: Children, services; Christian agencies & churches.
Officer: Judith A. Jones, Pres.
EIN: 912167994
Selected grants: The following grants were reported in 2003.

$60,000 to Hillview Acres Childrens Home, Chino, CA. For general support.

$25,000 to Gods Kidz in the Hood, Milwaukee, WI. For general support.

$10,000 to Coastline Community Church, Encinitas, CA. For general support.

$10,000 to World Orphans, Colorado Springs, CO. For general support.

$5,000 to Young Life, Colorado Springs, CO. For general support.

$500 to Billy Graham Mission. For general support.

$100 to Gospel for Asia, Carrollton, TX. For general support.

631
Josephine S. Gumbiner Foundation
110 W. Broadway, Ste. 270
Long Beach, CA 90802 (562) 437-2882
Contact: Julie Meenan, Exec. Dir.
FAX: (562) 437-4212; E-mail: jsgf@earthlink.net;
URL: http://jsgf.gumbiner.com/

Established in 1989 in CA.
Donor: Josephine S. Gumbiner‡.
Foundation type: Independent foundation.
Financial data (yr. ended 6/30/05): Assets, $13,530,302 (M); expenditures, $587,601; qualifying distributions, $538,568; giving activities include $440,209 for 42 grants (high: $25,000; low: $1,000).
Purpose and activities: The foundation is dedicated to supporting programs that enrich the women and children in the Long Beach area of southern CA. It

includes programs focusing on day care, education, housing, recreation, the arts, and health care, with a special emphasis on intervention, prevention, and direct service. Previously funded projects by the foundation range from prenatal care to women's shelters to programs for at-risk youth, and participatory cultural programs for children and teens. The foundation's goal is to fund projects that protect and enrich the lives of women and children.
Fields of interest: Crime/violence prevention; domestic violence; Human services; Children/youth, services; Family services; Women, centers/services; Minorities/immigrants, centers/services; Civil liberties, reproductive rights; Minorities; Women; Economically disadvantaged; Homeless.
Type of support: General/operating support; Continuing support; Equipment; Emergency funds; Program development; Technical assistance; Matching/challenge support.
Limitations: Giving limited to Long Beach, CA. No support for political campaigns, pass through organizations, organizations with endowments greater than $5 million, or organizations with Long Beach, CA, client bases of less than 75%. No grants to individuals, or for lobbying efforts, programs that supplant traditional schooling.
Publications: Application guidelines; Grants list; Informational brochure (including application guidelines).
Application information: Application guidelines and procedures available on foundation Web site, but letter of intent questionnaire can be obtained by e-mailing foundation or by letter. Unsolicited requests for funds generally not accepted. Application form required.

  Initial approach: Letter of intent questionnaire
  Copies of proposal: 7
  Deadline(s): Varies
  Board meeting date(s): Generally in Mar., June, Sept., and Nov.
  Final notification: By letter or Web site

Officers and Directors:* Alis Gumbiner,* Pres.; Burke Gumbiner,* V.P.; Julie Meenan,* Secy.; Lee Gumbiner,* C.F.O.; Beth Campbell; Art Gottlieb; Dennis Rockaway.
Number of staff: 1 full-time professional.
EIN: 330345249
Selected grants: The following grants were reported in 2005.

$25,000 to Catholic Charities of the Archdiocese of Los Angeles, Los Angeles, CA. For general operating support.

$20,000 to Long Beach Community Improvement League, Long Beach, CA. For staff development for child care program.

$17,500 to Food Finders Food Bank, Lafayette, IN. For general operating support.

$15,000 to Harbor Interfaith Shelter, San Pedro, CA. For after school program.

$15,000 to Institute for Urban Research and Development, Pasadena, CA. For ACHIEVE LB Emergency Shelter.

$15,000 to Legal Aid Foundation of Long Beach, Long Beach, CA. For Domestic Violence Prevention Clinic.

$15,000 to Long Beach Nonprofit Partnership, Long Beach, CA. For general operating support.

$15,000 to WomenShelter of Long Beach, Long Beach, CA. For Bilingual Domestic Violence Counseling Program.

$12,000 to Long Beach BLAST-Better Learning After School Today, Long Beach, CA. For general operating support for after school tutors.

$11,000 to Cambodian Association of America, Long Beach, CA. For Family Literacy Program.

$10,000 to Boys and Girls Clubs of Long Beach, Long Beach, CA. For general operating support.

$7,000 to Goodwill Industries of Long Beach and South Bay, Long Beach, CA. For Camelitos Nursing Program.

$7,000 to Su Casa Family Crisis and Support Center, Artesia, CA. For staff support.

632
The Guzik Foundation ◇
2443 Wyandotte St.
Mountain View, CA 94043

Established in 1993 in CA.
Donor: Nahum Guzik.
Foundation type: Independent foundation.
Financial data (yr. ended 12/31/04): Assets, $39,120,996 (M); gifts received, $6,000,000; expenditures, $1,541,623; qualifying distributions, $1,356,386; giving activities include $912,050 for 21 grants (high: $500,000; low: $800), and $119,000 for 6 grants to individuals.
Fields of interest: Arts; Higher education; Medical research, institute; Jewish agencies & temples; Buddhism.
Limitations: Applications not accepted. Giving primarily in CA; some funding also in New York, NY.
Application information: Unsolicited requests for funds not accepted.
Trustee: Nahum Guzik; Svetlana Gorzhevskaya.
EIN: 770360079

633
The Chuck & Ellen Haas Foundation ◇
10533 Esquire Pl.
Cupertino, CA 95014-1318

Established in 2000 in CA.
Donors: Charles J. Haas; Ellen Jo Haas.
Foundation type: Independent foundation.
Financial data (yr. ended 3/31/06): Assets, $3,595,600 (M); expenditures, $420,331; qualifying distributions, $419,774; giving activities include $414,614 for 34 grants (high: $76,000; low: $250).
Fields of interest: Hospitals (general); Health care; Health organizations, association; Food services; Housing/shelter, development; Human services; Roman Catholic agencies & churches.
Limitations: Applications not accepted. No grants to individuals.
Application information: Contributes only to pre-selected organizations.
Officers and Directors:* Charles J. Haas,* Pres.; Ellen Jo Haas,* Secy. and C.F.O.
EIN: 770540701
Selected grants: The following grants were reported in 2005.

$105,000 to Napa Valley Wine Auction, Saint Helena, CA. 2 grants: $95,000, $10,000

$100,000 to Alzheimers Association, Chicago, IL.

$30,000 to Salvation Army. 2 grants: $10,000, $20,000

$15,000 to Catholic Charities. 2 grants: $10,000, $5,000

$6,000 to Guardsmen, The, San Francisco, CA.

$5,000 to American Diabetes Association, Alexandria, VA.

$5,000 to American Heart Association, Dallas, TX.

634
Gene Haas Foundation ✧
2800 Sturgis Rd.
Oxnard, CA 93030

Established in 1998 in CA.
Donor: Gene F. Haas.
Foundation type: Independent foundation.
Financial data (yr. ended 12/31/05): Assets, $21,719,253 (M); gifts received, $5,000,000; expenditures, $991,458; qualifying distributions, $927,169; giving activities include $927,169 for 109 grants (high: $200,000; low: $80).
Purpose and activities: Giving primarily for a community foundation, and health and social services; some funding also for education.
Fields of interest: Higher education; Education; Hospitals (general); Medical care, rehabilitation; Health organizations, association; Medical research, institute; Human services; American Red Cross; Salvation Army; Children/youth, services; Family services; Foundations (community); Christian agencies & churches.
Type of support: Matching/challenge support.
Limitations: Applications not accepted. No grants to individuals.
Application information: Contributes only to pre-selected organizations.
Officers: Gene F. Haas, Pres.; Kurt Zierhut, Secy.; Robert Murray, C.F.O.
EIN: 954724825
Selected grants: The following grants were reported in 2005.
$29,584 to American Red Cross.
$25,000 to Best Buy Childrens Foundation, Eden Prairie, MN.
$25,000 to Childrens Hospital Los Angeles, Los Angeles, CA.
$25,000 to Salvation Army.
$19,000 to YMCA. 2 grants: $14,000, $5,000
$12,500 to Boys and Girls Club of Camarillo, Camarillo, CA.
$10,000 to F.O.O.D. Share, Oxnard, CA.
$10,000 to Five Acres, Altadena, CA.
$10,000 to Ventura College Foundation, Ventura, CA.

635
Mimi and Peter Haas Fund ▼
(formerly Miriam and Peter Haas Fund)
201 Filbert St., 5th Fl.
San Francisco, CA 94133-3238 (415) 296-9249
Contact: Gregory Meagher, Financial Mgr.
FAX: (415) 296-8842; E-mail: mphf@mphf.org;
E-mail: gmeagher@mphf.org

Incorporated in 1982 in CA.
Donors: Peter E. Haas†; Miriam L. Haas; Elise S. Haas†.
Foundation type: Independent foundation.
Financial data (yr. ended 12/31/04): Assets, $226,292,353 (M); expenditures, $12,931,388; qualifying distributions, $11,297,230; giving activities include $10,555,572 for 310 grants (high: $1,500,000; low: $50; average: $5,000–$50,000), and $5,898 for 1 foundation-administered program.
Purpose and activities: The fund's primary focus is early childhood development. Support is for activities that provide San Francisco's young (ages 2-5), low-income children and their families with access to high-quality early childhood programs that are part of a comprehensive, coordinated system. The fund recognizes the importance of connecting the work of its direct service grants to the ongoing discussions of public policy and will seek specific opportunities to share and collaborate with organizations to improve early childhood settings. The fund will also continue trustee-initiated grantmaking to arts, education, public affairs, and health and human services organizations.
Fields of interest: Education, early childhood education.
Type of support: General/operating support; Continuing support; Annual campaigns; Capital campaigns; Building/renovation; Equipment; Endowments; Program development; Curriculum development; Matching/challenge support.
Limitations: Giving primarily in San Francisco, CA; early childhood, direct service component is limited to San Francisco. No grants to individuals.
Publications: Application guidelines; Annual report; Financial statement; Grants list.
Application information: Application required for the Program Materials and Equipment grantmaking program only. All other grantmaking is staff or trustee-initiated. Application form not required.
Initial approach: Letter
Copies of proposal: 1
Deadline(s): None
Board meeting date(s): Approximately 4 times per year
Officers and Trustees:* Miriam L. Haas,* Pres.; Cheryl Polk, Exec. Dir.
Number of staff: 5 full-time professional.
EIN: 946064551
Selected grants: The following grants were reported in 2004.
$1,500,000 to University of California at Berkeley Foundation, Berkeley, CA. For campaign.
$500,000 to Stanford University, Stanford, CA. For Haas Center for Public Service Fund.
$266,000 to City College of San Francisco, Child Development and Family Studies, San Francisco, CA. For San Francisco Early Childhood Professional Development Initiative.
$250,000 to Museum of Modern Art, New York, NY. For education programs for elementary school students.
$215,000 to San Francisco State University, San Francisco, CA. For Manan Wright Edelman Institute Early Childhood Professional Development Initiative.
$150,000 to United Way of the Bay Area, San Francisco, CA. For quality early childhood education compensation and retention initiative challenge grant.
$125,000 to Eastside College Preparatory School, East Palo Alto, CA. For capital campaign.
$120,000 to Jumpstart San Francisco, San Francisco, CA. To model center's emergent literacy program.
$115,500 to San Francisco Unified School District, San Francisco, CA. For child development program.
$100,000 to American Friends of the Hebrew University, San Francisco, CA. For Early Childhood Learning and Resource Center's Video-Aided Supervision Program.

636
Walter and Elise Haas Fund ▼ ✧
1 Lombard St., Ste. 305
San Francisco, CA 94111 (415) 398-4474
Contact: Pamela H. David, Exec. Dir.
URL: http://www.haassr.org

Incorporated in 1952 in CA.
Donors: Walter A. Haas†; Elise S. Haas†.
Foundation type: Independent foundation.
Financial data (yr. ended 12/31/05): Assets, $231,132,160 (M); expenditures, $12,923,242; qualifying distributions, $11,094,331; giving activities include $11,094,331 for grants.
Purpose and activities: The mission of the fund is to help build a healthy, just, and vibrant society in which people feel connected to and responsible for their community. The areas of focus are the arts and culture, economic security, Jewish life, and public education. In addition, continuing support is provided to organizations that have long established ties to the fund.
Fields of interest: Arts education; Arts; Education; Economic development; Jewish agencies & temples.
Type of support: General/operating support; Continuing support; Capital campaigns; Building/renovation; Equipment; Program development; Seed money; Technical assistance; Program evaluation; Employee matching gifts; Matching/challenge support.
Limitations: Giving primarily in San Francisco and Alameda County, CA; Jewish Life grants are awarded throughout the Bay Area. No grants to individuals, or for general fundraising, endowment campaigns, scholarships, fellowships, or for video or film production (except through the Creative Work Fund).
Publications: Application guidelines; Annual report; Grants list; Program policy statement.
Application information: Application form not required.
Initial approach: Letter of inquiry, see Web site for required format
Copies of proposal: 1
Deadline(s): None
Board meeting date(s): Four times per year
Final notification: 2-4 months
Officers and Trustees:* John D. Goldman,* Pres.; Pamela H. David, Exec. Dir.; Elizabeth H. Eisenhardt; William S. Goldman; Peter E. Haas, Jr.; Walter J. Haas; Jennifer Haas-Dehejia.
Number of staff: 6 full-time professional; 1 part-time professional; 3 full-time support.
EIN: 946068564
Selected grants: The following grants were reported in 2004.
$1,000,000 to Stern Grove Festival Association, San Francisco, CA. 2 grants: $500,000 each (For capital and endowment campaign).
$625,000 to Jewish Community Federation of the Greater East Bay, Oakland, CA. For Volunteer Action Center's Community Investment Initiative.
$250,000 to Northern California Community Loan Fund, San Francisco, CA. For creation of Capital Fund.
$250,000 to Stanford University, Stanford, CA. To endow and name directorship of Haas Center for Public Service.
$200,000 to Bancroft Library, Friends of the, Berkeley, CA. For capital campaign.
$200,000 to San Francisco Unified School District, San Francisco, CA. For Office of Teacher Affairs and CARE.
$150,000 to San Francisco Foundation, San Francisco, CA. For Bay Area Workforce Funders Collaborative.
$125,000 to KlezCalifornia, Lagunitas, CA.
$110,000 to Joshua Venture Philanthropies, San Francisco, CA. Towards assessment and restructuring and to complete second cohort.

637
Evelyn and Walter Haas, Jr. Fund ▼
1 Market, Landmark, Ste. 400
San Francisco, CA 94105 (415) 856-1400
Contact: Clayton C. Juan, Grants Admin.
FAX: (415) 856-1500;
E-mail: guidelines@haasjr.org; URL: http://www.haasjr.org

Incorporated in 1953 in CA.
Donors: Walter A. Haas, Jr.†; Evelyn D. Haas.
Foundation type: Independent foundation.
Financial data (yr. ended 12/31/05): Assets, $553,365,428 (M); expenditures, $33,708,848; qualifying distributions, $27,224,346; giving activities include $27,224,346 for 432 grants (high: $3,300,000; low: $15,000; average: $25,000–$50,000), and $540,753 for foundation-administered programs.
Purpose and activities: Emphasis on children, youth, families, neighborhoods, equality and justice, and enhancing nonprofit leadership and governance.
Fields of interest: Youth development, services; Family services; Civil rights, immigrants; Civil rights, gays/lesbians; Community development, neighborhood development; Nonprofit management; Financial services; Leadership development; LGBTQ; Immigrants/refugees; Economically disadvantaged.
Type of support: General/operating support; Program development; Seed money; Technical assistance; Consulting services; Program evaluation; Employee matching gifts; Matching/challenge support.
Limitations: Giving primarily in San Francisco and Alameda counties, CA. No support for private foundations, consumer or professional groups, labor or trade associations, research centers, or religious organizations. No grants to individuals, or for deficit or emergency financing, workshops, major equipment, scholarships, direct mail campaigns, fundraising events, annual appeals, conferences, publications, capital or endowment campaigns, films or videos, or basic research.
Publications: Application guidelines; Financial statement; Grants list.
Application information: Application form not required.
　Initial approach: 1- to 2- page letter of inquiry
　Copies of proposal: 1
　Deadline(s): None
　Board meeting date(s): At least 3 times per year
　Final notification: Within 4 months of receipt of full proposal
Officers and Trustees:* Evelyn D. Haas,* Co-Chair.; Walter J. Haas,* Co-Chair.; Ira S. Hirschfield,* Pres.; Michael Blake, V.P., Finance; Jennie Lehua Watson, V.P., Comms.; Sylvia Yee, V.P., Progs.; Elizabeth Haas Eisenhardt,* Secy.; Robert D. Haas,* Treas.; Ramona Rey-Murphy, Cont.
Number of staff: 15 full-time professional; 1 part-time professional; 15 full-time support.
EIN: 946068932

638
Hager Foundation ✧ ☆
8222 Melrose Ave., Ste. 202
Los Angeles, CA 90046

Established in 1997.
Donors: David J. Hager; Judith Hager; Myriam Wohlgelernter; Bina H. Jacobius; Moshe Hager.

Foundation type: Independent foundation.
Financial data (yr. ended 5/31/06): Assets, $10,806,450 (M); gifts received, $950,000; expenditures, $373,277; qualifying distributions, $366,600; giving activities include $366,600 for grants.
Fields of interest: Jewish agencies & temples.
Type of support: General/operating support.
Limitations: Applications not accepted. No grants to individuals.
Application information: Contributes only to pre-selected organizations.
Officers: David Hager, Pres.; Judith Hager, Secy.
EIN: 954592928
Selected grants: The following grants were reported in 2005.
$100,000 to Ezer Mizion, Bnei Brak, Israel. For general support.
$50,000 to Yeshiva University of Los Angeles, Los Angeles, CA. For general support.
$36,000 to Ohr Eliyahu Academy, Culver City, CA. For general support.
$30,000 to Yeshiva Rav Isacsohn Torath Emeth Academy, Los Angeles, CA. For general support.
$18,000 to Peylim/Lev LAchim. For general support.

639
Crescent Porter Hale Foundation
655 Redwood Hwy., Ste. 301
Mill Valley, CA 94941 (415) 388-2333
Contact: Ulla Davis, Exec. Dir.
FAX: (415) 381-4799; URL: http://www.crescentporterhale.org

Incorporated in 1961 in CA.
Donors: Elwyn C. Hale†; M. Eugenie Hale†.
Foundation type: Independent foundation.
Financial data (yr. ended 12/31/04): Assets, $32,800,883 (M); expenditures, $1,607,183; qualifying distributions, $1,519,671; giving activities include $1,308,600 for 105 grants (high: $250,000; low: $1,000).
Purpose and activities: Giving primarily for social services and private, Roman Catholic, education.
Fields of interest: Arts education; Performing arts, music; Elementary/secondary education; Children/youth, services; Family services; Aging, centers/services.
Type of support: Capital campaigns; Building/renovation; General/operating support; Program development; Scholarship funds; Matching/challenge support.
Limitations: Giving limited to the following five Bay Area counties: Alameda, Contra Costa, Marin, San Francisco and San Mateo, CA. No support for health care or public schools. No grants to individuals, or for research.
Publications: Application guidelines; Grants list; Program policy statement.
Application information: See foundation Web site for LOI information. Application form not required.
　Initial approach: Letter of intent (maximum 2 pages) with budget income projections
　Copies of proposal: 1
　Deadline(s): None
　Board meeting date(s): 3 times a year
　Final notification: After board meeting
Officers: Thomas J. Mellon, Jr., Pres.; A.L. Ballard, V.P.; E. William Swanson, Secy.-Treas.; Ulla Davis, Exec. Dir.
Directors: L.E. Alford; Eugene E. Bleck, M.D.; Joan Withers Dinner; Ephraim P. Engleman, M.D.;

Nicholas M. Graves; Robert S. Kelling, Jr.; Sr. Estella Morales.
Number of staff: 1 full-time professional; 1 part-time support.
EIN: 946093385
Selected grants: The following grants were reported in 2004.
$135,000 to Basic Fund, San Francisco, CA.
$15,000 to Boys and Girls Club of the Peninsula, Redwood City, CA.
$15,000 to Dolores Street Community Services, San Francisco, CA.
$10,000 to Girls Club of the Mid-Peninsula, Palo Alto, CA.
$10,000 to Open Heart Kitchen of Livermore, Livermore, CA.
$10,000 to San Francisco Girls Chorus, San Francisco, CA.
$10,000 to Seton Senior Center, Lynwood, CA.
$7,500 to Exploratorium, San Francisco, CA.
$7,500 to Food Bank of Contra Costa and Solano, Concord, CA.
$5,000 to Teach for America, Emeryville, CA.

640
Robert and Ruth Halperin Foundation ✧
P.O. Box 60760
Palo Alto, CA 94306

Established in 1999 in CA.
Donors: Robert Halperin; Ruth Halperin.
Foundation type: Independent foundation.
Financial data (yr. ended 12/31/04): Assets, $62,420,589 (M); expenditures, $3,347,491; qualifying distributions, $2,574,920; giving activities include $2,559,000 for 11 grants (high: $625,000; low: $25,000; average: $50,000–$250,000).
Purpose and activities: Giving primarily for higher education.
Fields of interest: Museums (art); Higher education; Hospitals (general); Jewish federated giving programs.
Limitations: Applications not accepted. Giving primarily in CA; some giving also in IL. No grants to individuals.
Application information: Contributes only to pre-selected organizations.
Officers: Robert Halperin, Pres.; Ruth Halperin, V.P. and Treas.
EIN: 943334424
Selected grants: The following grants were reported in 2003.
$1,296,000 to Stanford University, Stanford, CA. 5 grants: $250,000 to Jewish Life at Stanford (Toward building fund for H. L. Ziff Center for Jewish Life), $250,000 (For Halperin Fund for Professor in Photography), $250,000 (For R. and R. Halperin Scholarship Fund), $500,000 (For Halperin Undergraduate Education and Scholarship Funds), $46,000 to School of Education.
$1,100,000 to University of Chicago, Chicago, IL. 2 grants: $100,000 (For Hanna Gray Professorship), $1,000,000 (For Robert and Ruth Halperin Scholarship).
$500,000 to Fine Arts Museums of San Francisco, San Francisco, CA. For New De Young Museum.
$500,000 to Harvard University, Business School, Cambridge, MA. To establish Halperin Foundation and Fellowship Fund.

$50,000 to Lucile Salter Packard Childrens Hospital at Stanford, Palo Alto, CA. For Returning to School program.

641

O. L. Halsell Foundation ✧
3200 Park Ctr. Dr., No. 1170
Costa Mesa, CA 92626
Application address: c/o Dave Stauffer, Dir., P.O. Box 6300, Santa Ana, CA 92706-0300, tel.: (714) 546-0755

Established in 1948 in CA.
Donor: Oliver L. Halsell†.
Foundation type: Independent foundation.
Financial data (yr. ended 12/31/05): Assets, $17,345,918 (M); gifts received, $5,400; expenditures, $1,010,533; qualifying distributions, $828,014; giving activities include $792,000 for 34 grants (high: $64,000; low: $5,000), and $8,126 for 1 foundation-administered program.
Purpose and activities: Giving primarily for youth-related activities and services. The foundation also maintains a chapel that is used year-round for religious and cultural activities.
Fields of interest: Arts; Hospitals (general); Youth development, centers/clubs; Human services; Children/youth, services; Religion.
Limitations: Giving limited to Orange County, CA. No grants to individuals.
Application information:
Initial approach: Letter on organization letterhead
Deadline(s): 1st Mon. in Nov.
Officers: George Barr, Pres.; Morgan Roach, Secy.
Directors: Royce Johnson; W. David Stauffer.
EIN: 956027266
Selected grants: The following grants were reported in 2004.
$59,000 to Boys and Girls Club of Santa Ana, Santa Ana, CA.
$54,000 to Salvation Army, Redding, CA.
$39,000 to YMCA of Orange County, Irvine, CA.
$24,000 to Boy Scouts of America, Costa Mesa, CA.
$24,000 to Girl Scouts of the U.S.A., Costa Mesa, CA.
$20,000 to Second Harvest Food Bank, San Carlos, CA.
$19,000 to KidSingers, Anaheim, CA.
$18,000 to Human Options, Irvine, CA.
$15,000 to Chapman University, Orange, CA.
$15,000 to THINK Together, Santa Ana, CA.

642

The Hamilton-White Foundation ✧ ☆
P.O. Box 9969
San Diego, CA 92169
URL: http://www.hamiltonwhitefoundation.org

Established in 2003 in CA.
Donor: Hamilton-White Foundation.
Foundation type: Independent foundation.
Financial data (yr. ended 12/31/05): Assets, $3,901,885 (M); expenditures, $12,614,886; qualifying distributions, $12,578,093; giving activities include $12,538,640 for 39 grants (high: $10,692,000; low: $1,890).
Purpose and activities: Giving primarily for philanthropic orgranizations and programs, as well as for higher education, health care, and human services; some funding also for the arts.

Fields of interest: Arts; Higher education; Health care; Human services; Foundations (private grantmaking); Foundations (community); Philanthropy/voluntarism.
Limitations: Applications not accepted. Giving primarily in San Diego, CA. No grants to individuals.
Application information: Contributes only to pre-selected organizations.
Officers: Philip White, Pres.; Frances H. White, V.P.; Harvey P. White, Secy. and C.F.O.
Trustees: Katherine White; Sarah White.
EIN: 200031517

643

Hammer International Foundation ✧ ☆
11111 Santa Monica Blvd., Ste. 1260
Los Angeles, CA 90025
Contact: Michael A. Hammer, C.E.O.

Established in 1998 in CA.
Foundation type: Independent foundation.
Financial data (yr. ended 12/31/05): Assets, $13,217,410 (M); expenditures, $1,431,259; qualifying distributions, $623,439; giving activities include $623,439 for grants.
Purpose and activities: Giving primarily for Christian agencies and churches in the U.S. and the Cayman Islands in the British West Indies.
Fields of interest: Christian agencies & churches.
Limitations: Giving on a national and international basis, with emphasis on CA, and on the Cayman Islands in the British West Indies. No grants to individuals.
Application information: Application form not required.
Deadline(s): None
Officers and Directors:* Michael A. Hammer,* C.E.O. and Pres.; Scott R. Deitrick, V.P.; Dru Hammer,* Secy.
EIN: 980153886
Selected grants: The following grants were reported in 2003.
$102,940 to HTR Vintage Motorsports Foundation, Santa Monica, CA. 2 grants: $2,940 (For endowment), $100,000 (For endowment).
$3,000 to Christian Communications Association, Caribbean. For general support.

644

Bill Hannon Foundation
11611 San Vicente Blvd., Ste. 530
Los Angeles, CA 90049
Contact: Elaine S. Ewen, Chair.
E-mail: elaine@redshift.com

Established in 1999 in NV.
Donor: William H. Hannon†.
Foundation type: Independent foundation.
Financial data (yr. ended 9/30/05): Assets, $57,171,212 (M); expenditures, $6,325,068; qualifying distributions, $5,743,232; giving activities include $5,498,333 for 56 grants (high: $2,300,000; low: $500; average: $25,000–$150,000).
Purpose and activities: Giving primarily for Roman Catholic secondary and higher education, health care and human services.
Fields of interest: Education; Health care; Human services; Religion.

Type of support: Capital campaigns; Building/renovation; Equipment; Program development; Conferences/seminars; Scholarship funds.
Limitations: Applications not accepted. Giving primarily in CA, with emphasis on the Los Angeles area.
Application information: Unsolicited requests for funds not accepted.
Board meeting date(s): Jan., Apr., June, and Oct.
Officers and Directors:* Elaine S. Ewen,* Chair. and Pres.; Fr. Paul L. Locatelli, S.J.*, V.P.; Sr. Kathleen Kelly,* Secy.; A.N. Mosich, Ph.D.*, Treas.; Hon. Jack E. Goertzen.
Number of staff: 1 full-time professional; 1 full-time support.
EIN: 311663038
Selected grants: The following grants were reported in 2004.
$2,000,000 to Santa Clara University, Santa Clara, CA.
$250,000 to Mount Saint Marys College, Los Angeles, CA.
$200,000 to Dominican University of California, San Rafael, CA.
$200,000 to Notre Dame de Namur University, Belmont, CA.
$200,000 to University of San Diego, San Diego, CA.
$200,000 to University of San Francisco, San Francisco, CA.
$100,000 to Saint Marys Academy, Inglewood, CA.
$100,000 to Verbum Dei High School, Los Angeles, CA.
$92,000 to Saint Marys College of California, Moraga, CA.
$50,000 to Don Bosco Technical Institute, Rosemead, CA.

645

William H. Hannon Foundation
729 Montana Ave., Ste. 5
Santa Monica, CA 90403-1369
Contact: Kathleen Hannon Aikenhead, Pres.
FAX: (310) 260-9740; *URL:* http://www.hannonfoundation.org

Established in 1983 in CA.
Donor: William Herbert Hannon†.
Foundation type: Independent foundation.
Financial data (yr. ended 9/30/05): Assets, $57,867,991 (M); expenditures, $4,160,329; qualifying distributions, $3,628,976; giving activities include $3,480,862 for grants.
Purpose and activities: Giving primarily for Roman Catholic education; support also for churches, medical research, hospitals, and social service organizations.
Fields of interest: Elementary/secondary education; Higher education; Education; Hospitals (general); Roman Catholic agencies & churches.
Type of support: General/operating support; Continuing support; Capital campaigns; Building/renovation; Program development; Scholarship funds.
Limitations: Giving primarily in Los Angeles and the southern CA area. No support for private foundations, or for political organizations. No grants to individuals, or for underwriting parties, travel funds, advertisements, or radio or television programming.
Application information: Application information and procedures available on foundation Web site. Application form not required.

Initial approach: Letter
Copies of proposal: 1
Deadline(s): The first of the month prior to the month when a board meeting is held
Board meeting date(s): Sept., Dec., Mar., and June
Final notification: 1 month from receipt
Officers and Directors:* Kathleen Hannon Aikenhead,* Pres.; Nancy B. Cunningham,* V.P. and Secy.; James A. Hannon,* V.P. and C.F.O.; David W. Burcham; David A. Herbst; Robert B. Lawton, S.J.; Msgr. Royale M. Vadakin.
Number of staff: 1 full-time professional; 1 part-time support.
EIN: 953847664
Selected grants: The following grants were reported in 2005.
$500,000 to Loyola High School, Los Angeles, CA.
$215,000 to Cathedral of Our Lady of Angels, Los Angeles, CA. 2 grants: $15,000, $200,000
$100,000 to Mount Saint Marys College, Los Angeles, CA.
$50,000 to Providence Saint Joseph Medical Center, Burbank, CA.
$25,000 to Saint Joseph Center, Venice, CA.
$5,000 to Angel Flight West, Santa Monica, CA.
$2,500 to Saint John Bosco High School, Bellflower, CA.
$2,000 to Mary and Joseph League, Rancho Palos Verdes, CA.
$2,000 to TrinityCare Hospice Foundation, Torrance, CA.

646
Harbison Scholarship Trust ◇
P.O. Box 3262
San Bernardino, CA   92413-3262
Contact: Doreen Thornes, Tr.

Established in 1994 in CA.
Foundation type: Operating foundation.
Financial data (yr. ended 10/31/05): Assets, $5,939,734 (M); expenditures, $428,230; qualifying distributions, $386,475; giving activities include $334,081 for 21 grants to individuals (high: $34,296; low: $2,280).
Purpose and activities: Awards 4-year scholarships to San Bernardino County high school students for college tuition and books. Scholarship awards are based on previous record of scholarship, character, motivation, interests, skills, extracurricular activities, and financial need.
Type of support: Scholarships—to individuals.
Limitations: Applications not accepted. Giving limited to high school students of San Bernardino County, CA.
Application information: Unsolicited requests for funds not accepted.
Trustee: Doreen Thornes.
EIN: 330621341

647
Harden Foundation ◇
P.O. Box 779
Salinas, CA   93902-0779   (831) 442-3005
Contact: Joseph C. Grainger, Exec. Dir.
FAX: (831) 443-1429;
E-mail: maria@hardenfoundation.org; *URL:* http://www.hardenfoundation.org

Established in 1963 in CA.

Donors: Eugene E. Harden†; Ercia E. Harden†.
Foundation type: Independent foundation.
Financial data (yr. ended 2/28/06): Assets, $70,700,304 (M); expenditures, $4,658,315; qualifying distributions, $4,663,251; giving activities include $2,961,192 for grants.
Purpose and activities: The foundation supports projects that improve the well-being of young people; strengthen the family; develop individual self-reliance and health; prevent inappropriate institutionalization of individuals; improve the quality of life through cultural activities; encourage more humane treatment of animals; and eliminate duplication and improve coordination of social and community services.
Fields of interest: Arts; Environment; Animal welfare; Health care; Mental health, treatment; Agriculture/food, formal/general education; Human services; Children/youth, services; Family services; Aging, centers/services.
Type of support: General/operating support; Capital campaigns; Seed money; Matching/challenge support.
Limitations: Giving limited to Monterey County, CA, with emphasis on the Salinas Valley, area. No support for sectarian religious programs, nonagricultural related educational programs, operating foundations, or associations established for the benefit of organizations receiving substantial tax support. No grants for endowments, annual campaigns, conferences, academic or medical research, scholarships to individuals, or fundraising events.
Publications: Application guidelines; Annual report (including application guidelines).
Application information: The foundation does not accept unsolicited proposals from public or private institutions of primary, secondary or higher education. However, grant proposals from public institutions will be considered for special projects which are agriculture related. Application information and guidelines available on foundation Web site. Application form required.
Initial approach: Letter
Copies of proposal: 2
Deadline(s): Mar. 1 and Sept. 1
Board meeting date(s): June and Dec.
Officers and Directors:* Ralph L. Kokjer, Jr.,* Pres.; C. Bill Elliott,* V.P., Investment; Thomas M. Merrill,* V.P.; Patricia Tynan Chapman,* Secy.; Frank E. Ferrasci, Treas.; Joseph C. Grainger, Exec. Dir.
Number of staff: 1 full-time professional; 2 part-time professional; 2 full-time support.
EIN: 946098887

648
The Hargrove Pierce Foundation ◇
c/o Duban
4250 Willshire Blvd.
Los Angeles, CA   90010

Established in 2002.
Foundation type: Independent foundation.
Financial data (yr. ended 12/31/05): Assets, $5,457,731 (M); gifts received, $32,647; expenditures, $339,112; qualifying distributions, $339,112; giving activities include $330,945 for grants.
Limitations: Applications not accepted. Giving primarily in CA. No grants to individuals.
Application information: Unsolicited requests for funds not accepted.

Officers: David Hyde Pierce, C.E.O.; David Brian Hargrove, Secy.
Trustee: Candace Burnett.
EIN: 920183406

649
Harkham Foundation ◇
4890 S. Alameda St.
Vernon, CA   90058   (323) 586-4600
Contact: Naji Harkham, Dir.

Established in 1980 in CA.
Donors: Efrem Harkham; Uri Harkham; Harkham Industries; JM Shoe Group Inc.
Foundation type: Independent foundation.
Financial data (yr. ended 3/31/05): Assets, $3,699 (M); gifts received, $325,100; expenditures, $321,402; qualifying distributions, $321,352; giving activities include $321,352 for grants.
Purpose and activities: Giving for Jewish education and organizations.
Fields of interest: Elementary/secondary education; Higher education; Jewish federated giving programs; Jewish agencies & temples.
International interests: Israel.
Type of support: General/operating support; Grants to individuals.
Limitations: Giving primarily in Tel Aviv, Israel.
Application information: Contributes only to pre-selected organizations and individuals; scholarships awarded through applications submitted to an office in Israel based upon recommendations by school officials.
Initial approach: Letter
Directors: Naji Harkham; Uri Harkham.
EIN: 953532383

650
Harman Family Foundation ◇ ☆
c/o Oak Investment Partners
525 University Ave., Ste. 1300
Palo Alto, CA   94301

Established in 2003 in CA.
Donors: Frederic Harman; Stephanie Curtis Harman.
Foundation type: Independent foundation.
Financial data (yr. ended 12/31/05): Assets, $1,027,379 (M); gifts received, $590,745; expenditures, $597,022; qualifying distributions, $582,167; giving activities include $578,000 for 10 grants (high: $300,000; low: $1,000).
Fields of interest: Arts; Elementary/secondary education; Higher education; Education; Human services; Children/youth, services; Christian agencies & churches.
Limitations: Applications not accepted. Giving primarily in CA and NY; some funding nationally. No grants to individuals.
Application information: Contributes only to pre-selected organizations.
Officers: Stephanie Curtis Harman, Pres.; Frederic Harman, Secy.-Treas.
EIN: 550855839

651
The Reed L. Harman and Nan M. Harman Foundation ◇
1815 Via El Prado, Ste. 403
Redondo Beach, CA 90277

Established in 1987 in CA.
Donors: Nan M. Harman; Reed L. Harman; Hayden K. Harman; Southwest Investment Partners.
Foundation type: Independent foundation.
Financial data (yr. ended 12/31/05): Assets, $5,006,897 (M); expenditures, $565,935; qualifying distributions, $445,949; giving activities include $445,949 for grants.
Fields of interest: Museums; Historic preservation/historical societies; Higher education; Education; Hospitals (general); Reproductive health, family planning; Human services; Residential/custodial care, hospices; Federated giving programs.
Limitations: Applications not accepted. Giving primarily in CA, some funding nationally. No grants to individuals.
Application information: Unsolicited requests for funds will not be considered.
Officers: Reed L. Harman, Pres.; Nan M. Harman, V.P.
Number of staff: 1 part-time professional.
EIN: 330271109
Selected grants: The following grants were reported in 2004.
$30,000 to Weingart Center Association, Los Angeles, CA.
$15,000 to John Wayne Cancer Institute, Santa Monica, CA.
$10,000 to College of Wooster, Wooster, OH.
$10,000 to Loomis Chaffee School, Windsor, CT.
$6,200 to Petersen Automotive Museum, Los Angeles, CA. 2 grants: $1,200, $5,000
$5,000 to Middlebury College, Middlebury, VT.
$1,439 to Adopt-A-Family, Los Angeles, CA. 2 grants: $820, $619
$100 to Richstone Center, Hawthorne, CA.

652
Mark H. & Blanche M. Harrington Foundation ◇
P.O. Box 2549
Rancho Cucamonga, CA 91729-2549
(626) 405-8335

Established in 1956 in CA.
Donors: Mark H. Harrington; Blanche M. Harrington.
Foundation type: Independent foundation.
Financial data (yr. ended 12/31/05): Assets, $22,126,999 (M); expenditures, $1,297,208; qualifying distributions, $1,199,478; giving activities include $1,199,478 for grants.
Fields of interest: Arts; Higher education; Education; Hospitals (general); Medical research, institute; Children/youth, services; Family services; Community development; Federated giving programs; Christian agencies & churches.
Limitations: Giving primarily in CA. No grants to individuals.
Application information:
  Initial approach: Letter
  Deadline(s): None
Trustee: Citizens Business Bank.
EIN: 956025594

653
Fred L. Hartley Family Foundation ◇
19000 MacArthur Blvd., Ste. 610
Irvine, CA 92612-1444 (949) 851-0500
Contact: Margaret A. Hartley, Tr.

Established in 1997 in CA.
Donor: Margaret A. Hartley.
Foundation type: Independent foundation.
Financial data (yr. ended 9/30/05): Assets, $16,092,982 (M); expenditures, $916,019; qualifying distributions, $890,983; giving activities include $890,983 for 28 grants (high: $600,000; low: $1,000).
Purpose and activities: Giving primarily for science, education, health, and social services.
Fields of interest: Education; Hospitals (specialty); Boys & girls clubs; Human services; Science.
Limitations: Giving primarily in CA.
Application information:
  Initial approach: Proposal
  Deadline(s): None
Trustees: Grace M. Brubaker; Daniel F. Gruen; Margaret A. Gruen; Fred L. Hartley, Jr.; Margaret A. Hartley.
EIN: 330783531

654
Brian and Phyllis Harvey Foundation ◇
c/o Brian Harvey
10940 Wilshire Blvd., Ste. 1900
Los Angeles, CA 90024-3930

Established in 2000 in CA.
Donor: Brian L. Harvey.
Foundation type: Independent foundation.
Financial data (yr. ended 12/31/04): Assets, $1,999,817; gifts received, $500,000; expenditures, $470,355; qualifying distributions, $470,000; giving activities include $470,000 for 4 grants (high: $250,000; low: $20,000).
Fields of interest: Medical research; Family services; Jewish federated giving programs.
Type of support: Research.
Limitations: Giving on a national basis.
Officers: Brian L. Harvey, Pres.; Phyllis M. Harvey, V.P.
Director: Larry B. Harvey.
EIN: 954833595

655
J. Samuel Harwit Z"L and Manya Harwit-Aviv Charitable Trust ◇
6310 San Vincente Blvd., Rm. 250
Los Angeles, CA 90048

Established in 1993 in CA.
Donors: Manya Harwit; Manya Harwit Trust.
Foundation type: Independent foundation.
Financial data (yr. ended 6/30/05): Assets, $7,680,259 (M); expenditures, $402,998; qualifying distributions, $394,395; giving activities include $382,500 for 19 grants (high: $60,000; low: $5,000).
Purpose and activities: Support for Jewish organizations, temples, and Hebrew academies.
Fields of interest: Education; Animals/wildlife, special services; Human services; Children/youth, services; Family services; International terrorism; Jewish agencies & temples.

Limitations: Applications not accepted. Giving primarily in CA. No grants to individuals.
Application information: Contributes only to pre-selected organizations.
Trustees: Nora Amrani; Steven Harwit; Frank Lee; Joel A. Levine.
EIN: 956949206

656
The Hatfield Family Foundation ◇
12164 Occidental Rd.
Sebastopol, CA 95472-9649

Established in 2000 in CA.
Donors: Michael Hatfield; Deborah Hatfield.
Foundation type: Independent foundation.
Financial data (yr. ended 12/31/05): Assets, $1,611,768 (M); expenditures, $995,545; qualifying distributions, $969,750; giving activities include $969,750 for 11 grants (high: $800,000; low: $750).
Purpose and activities: Giving primarily for higher education, and for funding of organizations that develop housing and shelter.
Fields of interest: Higher education; College (community/junior); Housing/shelter, development; Human services.
Limitations: Applications not accepted. Giving on a national basis, with some emphasis on CA. No grants to individuals.
Application information: Contributes only to pre-selected organizations.
Officer: Michael Hatfield, C.E.O.
Director: Deborah Hatfield.
EIN: 943347675
Selected grants: The following grants were reported in 2003.
$1,650,000 to Rose-Hulman Institute of Technology, Terre Haute, IN. For operating support.
$650,000 to Indiana Venture Center, Indianapolis, IN. For operating support.
$410,000 to Indiana University, Bloomington, IN. For operating support.
$130,000 to Housing Land Trust of Sonoma County, Petaluma, CA. For operating support.
$109,000 to Committee on the Shelterless (COTS), Petaluma, CA. For operating support.
$82,500 to Sonoma State University Academic Foundation, Rohnert Park, CA. For operating support.
$50,000 to La Luz Center, Boyes Hot Springs, CA. For operating support.
$50,000 to Midwest Entrepreneurial Education Center, Indianapolis, IN. For operating support.
$50,000 to Petaluma Schools, Petaluma, CA. For operating support.
$50,000 to Purdue University, West Lafayette, IN. For operating support.

657
William R. & Virginia Hayden Foundation ◇
(formerly William R. Hayden Foundation)
110 W. Las Tunas Dr., Ste. A
San Gabriel, CA 91776

Established in 1960 in CA.
Donors: William R. Hayden†; Mrs. William R. Hayden†.
Foundation type: Independent foundation.

Financial data (yr. ended 12/31/05): Assets, $10,018,797 (M); gifts received, $811,882; expenditures, $1,395,901; qualifying distributions, $1,278,839; giving activities include $1,273,804 for 54 grants (high: $255,000; low: $500).
Purpose and activities: Emphasis on Roman Catholic religious and social service organizations, including support for churches.
Fields of interest: Human services; Roman Catholic federated giving programs; Roman Catholic agencies & churches.
Type of support: Continuing support; Capital campaigns; Building/renovation.
Limitations: Giving primarily in CA. No grants to individuals.
Application information: Application form not required.
  Initial approach: Letter
  Copies of proposal: 1
  Deadline(s): None
  Board meeting date(s): Annually
Officers and Directors: Stanley D. Hayden,* Pres.; William R. Hayden II,* V.P.; David S. Hayden,* Secy.; Patrick F. Collins,* C.F.O.; David S. Aikenhead; Margaret H. Dietz; Marcia M. Hayden; Catherine H. Marsh; Peter J. Vogelsang.
EIN: 956055676

658
Harold J. & Reta Haynes Family Foundation ◇ ☆
717 Deer Valley Rd.
San Rafael, CA 94903

Established in 1999 in CA.
Donors: Harold J. Haynes; Reta Haynes.
Foundation type: Independent foundation.
Financial data (yr. ended 12/31/05): Assets, $7,923,899 (M); gifts received, $1,204,039; expenditures, $844,059; qualifying distributions, $789,000; giving activities include $789,000 for grants.
Fields of interest: Education; Environment, natural resources; Hospitals (general).
Limitations: Applications not accepted. Giving primarily in CA. No grants to individuals.
Application information: Contributes only to pre-selected organizations.
Officer: Harold J. Haynes, Pres.
EIN: 943332186

659
The John Randolph Haynes and Dora Haynes Foundation
888 W. 6th St., Ste. 1150
Los Angeles, CA 90017-2737 (213) 623-9151
Contact: Diane D. Cornwell, Admin. Dir.
FAX: (213) 623-3951;
E-mail: info@haynesfoundation.org; URL: http://www.haynesfoundation.org

Trust established in 1926 in CA.
Donors: John Randolph Haynes†; Mrs. John Randolph Haynes†.
Foundation type: Independent foundation.
Financial data (yr. ended 8/31/05): Assets, $56,165,085 (M); expenditures, $2,464,579; qualifying distributions, $1,987,182; giving activities include $1,630,127 for grants, and $7,500 for employee matching gifts.

Purpose and activities: Promoting the well-being of mankind by making grants for study and research in the social sciences (economics, history, government, and sociology) with emphasis on education, the environment, immigration and public policy. The foundation also provides undergraduate scholarships, graduate fellowships, and fellowships for faculty members in the social sciences in selected colleges and universities. Grants made only through local colleges and universities or other nonprofit institutions.
Fields of interest: Social sciences; Public policy, research.
Type of support: Fellowships; Research.
Limitations: Giving limited to the greater Los Angeles, CA, area. No support for political or religious organizations. No grants to individuals, or for building or endowment funds, operating budgets, or capital improvements.
Publications: Application guidelines; Annual report; Newsletter; Program policy statement.
Application information: Application for a faculty fellowship, doctoral dissertation fellowship, or research study grant is made directly to the foundation. See foundation Web site for detailed submission guidelines. Application form not required.
  Initial approach: Letter or telephone
  Copies of proposal: 15
  Deadline(s): For Major Research Grants: Mar. 2, May 4, Sept. 7, and Nov. 2
  Board meeting date(s): Quarterly
  Final notification: 1-month from receipt
Officers and Trustees: Jane G. Pisano,* Pres. and Secy.-Treas.; F. Haynes Lindley, Jr.,* V.P.; Gil Garcetti; Philip M. Hawley; Kent Kresa; Daniel A. Mazmanian; Harry P. Pachon; Gilbert T. Ray; Willis B. Wood, Jr.
Number of staff: 1 full-time professional; 1 part-time professional.
EIN: 951644020
Selected grants: The following grants were reported in 2004.
$174,515 to University of Southern California, Los Angeles, CA. 2 grants: $72,807 to Rossier School of Education (For Multiple Measures of Accountability for California Charter Schools: A Pilot Project with Ten Los Angeles Charter Schools), $101,708 to School of Policy, Planning and Development (For Industrial Los Angeles: Social Science Informed Photographic Documentation).
$169,214 to Economic Roundtable, Los Angeles, CA. For The Los Angeles Immigrant Worker Project.
$88,680 to University of California, Edward J. Blakely Center for Sustained Suburban Development, Riverside, CA. For Suburban Sprawl and Housing in the Inland Empire.
$25,000 to K C R W-FM, Santa Monica, CA. For public affairs broadcasting in Southern California.
$25,000 to K P C C 89.3 Southern California Public Radio, Pasadena, CA. For public affairs broadcasting in Southern California.

660
The Morris A. Hazan Family Foundation ◇ ☆
10960 Wilshire Blvd., Ste. 1100
Los Angeles, CA 90024

Established in 1967 in CA.

Donor: Morris A. Hazan†.
Foundation type: Independent foundation.
Financial data (yr. ended 12/31/05): Assets, $10,973,487 (M); gifts received, $8,777,380; expenditures, $424,342; qualifying distributions, $408,428; giving activities include $394,450 for 89 grants (high: $25,800; low: $100).
Purpose and activities: Giving primarily for the arts, education, and to Jewish agencies and temples.
Fields of interest: Arts; Higher education; Health organizations, association; Human services; Foundations (private grantmaking); Jewish federated giving programs; Jewish agencies & temples.
Limitations: Applications not accepted. Giving primarily in CA, with emphasis on Los Angeles. No grants to individuals.
Application information: Contributes only to pre-selected organizations.
Officers and Directors: Morris A. Hazan, Jr.,* Pres.; Judy Carmel,* Secy.; Lovee Arum, C.F.O.
EIN: 956220356

661
The HealthCare Foundation for Orange County ◇
(formerly Westmed Health Foundation)
1450 N. Tustin Ave., Ste. 103
Santa Ana, CA 92705-8641 (714) 245-1650
Contact: Doris Flander, C.E.O.
FAX: (714) 245-1653; E-mail: dflander@hfoc.org;
URL: http://www.hfoc.org

Established 1n 1994 in CA; converted from the sale of United Western Medical Centers and its affiliates.
Donors: United Western Medical Centers; The California Wellness Foundation; Russell Guy and Ruth Louise Morgan Trust.
Foundation type: Independent foundation.
Financial data (yr. ended 3/31/05): Assets, $16,099,898 (M); gifts received, $40,000; expenditures, $1,442,547; qualifying distributions, $719,020; giving activities include $531,214 for 33 grants (high: $85,905; low: $297).
Purpose and activities: To improve the health of the neediest and most underserved residents of Orange County, CA, by advancing access to health promotion, prevention, and basic health care.
Fields of interest: Hospitals (general); Hospitals (specialty); Health care; Mental health/crisis services; Breast cancer; Asthma; Autism; Pediatrics; Obstetrics/gynecology; Human services; Children/youth, services; Family services.
Limitations: Giving primarily in Orange County, CA. No support for biomedical research organizations, disease-specific organizations seeking support for their national programs, or for religious or fraternal organizations. No grants to individuals, or for annual campaigns, social events, telethons, building projects or equipment.
Publications: Annual report; Informational brochure (including application guidelines).
Application information: Application guidelines, procedures, and proposal form available on foundation Web site. Application form required.
  Initial approach: Letter, telephone or Web site
  Deadline(s): None
  Board meeting date(s): Quarterly
Officers and Directors: John O. Strong, M.D.*, Chair.; William B. Stannard,* Vice-Chair. and C.F.O.; Doris Flander, C.E.O.; J. Fernando Niebla, Secy.;

Marven E. Howard; Donald P. Kennedy; Quynh Kieu, M.D.; Timothy P. Mullins; Lilia M. Tanakeyowma.
EIN: 330644620
Selected grants: The following grants were reported in 2004.
$172,625 to University of California Irvine Medical Center, Orange, CA. For treatment of pediatric obesity bridge healthcare.
$101,667 to Childrens Hospital of Orange County, Orange, CA. For mobile asthma outreach.
$15,002 to Camp Fire USA, Tustin, CA. For asset building for teens in Santa Ana and Garden Grove.
$12,000 to YMCA, Anaheim Family, Anaheim, CA. For fitness and nutrition education.
$10,000 to Human Options, Irvine, CA. For Minnie Street Domestic Violence Project.
$10,000 to Laguna Beach Community Clinic, Laguna Beach, CA. For cervical cancer detection in Hispanic women.
$10,000 to Maternal Outreach Management System (MOMS), Santa Ana, CA. For enhancement and expansion of MOMS' health education.
$5,000 to Girls Inc. of Orange County, Costa Mesa, CA. For Santa Ana Healthy Peersuasion.
$5,000 to Olive Crest Abused Childrens Foundation, Santa Ana, CA. For improving mental health and stability in children.
$1,972 to Orange Coast Interfaith Shelter, Costa Mesa, CA. For health incidental assistance.

662
The Heart Foundation ☆
32107 Lindero Canyon Rd., Ste. 235
Westlake Village, CA   91361
FAX: (818) 597-3421;
E-mail: info@theheartfoundation.net; URL: http://www.theheartfoundation.net

Established in 1996 in CA.
Foundation type: Operating foundation.
Financial data (yr. ended 12/31/05): Assets, $131,616 (M); gifts received, $44,460; expenditures, $1,012,709; qualifying distributions, $1,012,107; giving activities include $594,000 for 4 grants (high: $590,000; low: $1,000).
Purpose and activities: The Heart Foundation strives to eradicate heart disease by increasing awareness of heart disease through fundraising activities, special events, and educational programs. The foundation raises funds to improve the prevention, detection, and treatment of heart disease, and support the work of world-renowned cardiologist P.K. Shah, M.D., Director of the Division of Cardiology and Atherosclerosis Research Center at Cedars-Sinai Medical Center in Los Angeles, CA.
Fields of interest: Health care; Heart & circulatory diseases; Heart & circulatory research.
Type of support: Research.
Limitations: Applications not accepted. Giving primarily in Los Angeles, CA, and the surrounding area. No grants to individuals.
Publications: Newsletter.
Application information: Contributes only to pre-selected organizations.
Officers and Trustees:* Mark Litman,* Chair.; Thomas Eisenstadt,* Vice-Chair.; Dana Kates,* Secy.; Howard J. Abrams,* Treas.
Number of staff: 1 full-time professional.
EIN: 450471117

663
Hedco Foundation ✧
1221 Broadway, 21st Fl.
Oakland, CA 94612
Application address: c/o Mary A. Goriup, Fdn. Mgr., P.O. Box 1980, San Ramon, CA 94583, tel.: (925) 242-0257

Incorporated in 1972 in CA.
Donors: Herrick Corp.; Catalina Assocs.; Herrick-Pacific Corp.
Foundation type: Independent foundation.
Financial data (yr. ended 12/31/05): Assets, $37,069,940 (M); gifts received, $2,100,000; expenditures, $1,761,103; qualifying distributions, $1,506,749; giving activities include $1,506,749 for 18 grants (high: $330,750; low: $1,500).
Purpose and activities: Giving predominantly to qualified educational and health institutions; support also for social services.
Fields of interest: Higher education, university; Hospitals (general); Health organizations, association; Human services.
Type of support: Building/renovation; Equipment; Land acquisition; Matching/challenge support.
Limitations: Giving primarily in CA. No grants to individuals, or for general support, operating budgets, endowment funds, scholarships, fellowships, special projects, research, publications, or conferences; no loans.
Application information: Application form not required.
   Initial approach: Proposal
   Copies of proposal: 1
   Deadline(s): None
   Board meeting date(s): Nov.
   Final notification: 3 to 4 months
Officers and Directors:* Dorothy Jernstedt,* Pres.; Rena Brantley,* Secy.; David H. Dornsife,* C.F.O.; Mary A. Goriup, Fdn. Mgr.; Tom Herman; James Appleton; Allen L. Dobbins, Ed.D.; Roger Schwab; Derek Jernstedt.
EIN: 237259742
Selected grants: The following grants were reported in 2004.
$300,000 to California Pacific Medical Center, San Francisco, CA.
$220,000 to Yosemite Foundation, San Francisco, CA.
$200,000 to Options Recovery Services, Berkeley, CA.
$161,650 to House Ear Institute, Los Angeles, CA.
$120,000 to Northwest Housing Alternatives, Milwaukie, OR.
$100,000 to Zephyr Point Presbyterian Conference Center, Zephyr Cove, NV.
$97,000 to San Francisco Food Bank, San Francisco, CA.
$64,280 to Lindsay Wildlife Museum, Walnut Creek, CA.
$37,520 to Lawrence Hall of Science, Berkeley, CA.
$30,000 to Loaves and Fishes.

664
Raymond & Mildred Hegwer
Foundation ✧ ☆
P.O. Box 3099
Ontario, CA   91761

Established in 1996 in CA.
Donors: Mildred Hegwer; Raymond Hegwer.
Foundation type: Independent foundation.

Financial data (yr. ended 12/31/05): Assets, $486,061 (M); expenditures, $811,310; qualifying distributions, $760,052; giving activities include $760,052 for 56 grants (high: $63,600; low: $25).
Fields of interest: Hospitals (general); Human services; Christian agencies & churches; Protestant agencies & churches.
Limitations: Applications not accepted. No grants to individuals.
Application information: Contributes only to pre-selected organizations.
Officer: Mildred Hegwer, Secy. and Mgr.
Director: Raymond Hegwer.
EIN: 330645654

665
Kenneth Heinz Family Foundation ✧
742 Spring Dr.
Walnut Creek, CA   94598-4249

Established in 1997 in CA.
Donor: Kenneth G. Heinz.
Foundation type: Independent foundation.
Financial data (yr. ended 12/31/05): Assets, $2,894,126 (M); gifts received, $25,000; expenditures, $1,241,059; qualifying distributions, $1,221,109; giving activities include $1,215,548 for 25 grants (high: $1,112,000; low: $15).
Fields of interest: Education; Human services; Christian agencies & churches.
Limitations: Applications not accepted. Giving on a national basis. No grants to individuals.
Application information: Contributes only to pre-selected organizations.
Officers and Directors:* Kenneth G. Heinz,* Pres.; Patricia B. Heinz,* V.P.; Scott K. Heinz,* Treas.
EIN: 911803001
Selected grants: The following grants were reported in 2005.
$1,112,000 to Grace Bible Church, Arroyo Grande, CA.
$40,000 to Walk Thru the Bible Ministries, Atlanta, GA.
$9,500 to Haggai Institute for Advanced Leadership Training, Atlanta, GA.
$3,833 to Mount Hermon Association, Mount Hermon, CA.
$500 to Jews for Jesus, San Francisco, CA.
$500 to RBC Ministries, Grand Rapids, MI.

666
Clarence E. Heller Charitable
Foundation ✧
44 Montgomery St., Ste. 1970
San Francisco, CA   94104   (415) 989-9839
Contact: Bruce A. Hirsch, Exec. Dir.
FAX: (415) 989-1909; E-mail: info@cehcf.org;
URL: http://cehcf.org

Established in 1982 in CA.
Donor: Clarence E. Heller‡.
Foundation type: Independent foundation.
Financial data (yr. ended 12/31/04): Assets, $47,339,057 (M); expenditures, $2,673,225; qualifying distributions, $2,157,841; giving activities include $1,499,542 for 59 grants (high: $200,000; low: $5; average: $5,000–$600,000).
Purpose and activities: The mission of the foundation is to protect and improve the quality of life through support of programs in the environment, human health, education and the arts. Giving to

support research, public education, and policy development to reduce health risks from environmental degradation and environmental hazards, innovative educational programs for elementary and secondary students, sustainable natural resource management, and programs that promote the accessibility of symphonic and chamber music.

Fields of interest: Performing arts, music; Education; Environment, research; Environment, public policy; Environment, public education; Environment, natural resources; Agriculture.

Type of support: General/operating support; Continuing support; Equipment; Program development; Publication; Seed money; Curriculum development; Scholarship funds; Research; Technical assistance; Consulting services; Program evaluation.

Limitations: Giving primarily in CA. No grants to individuals.

Publications: Annual report (including application guidelines); Grants list; Program policy statement.

Application information: Telephone for deadline for each funding cycle. Application form not required.

Initial approach: Letter of inquiry
Copies of proposal: 1
Deadline(s): None
Board meeting date(s): 3 times a year, usually Mar., June, and Oct.

Officers and Directors:* Miranda Heller,* Pres.; Alan Mandell,* V.P.; Sarah Coade Mandell,* Secy.-Treas.; Bruce A. Hirsch, Exec. Dir.; Anne Heller Anderson; Janet Harckham; Alfred Heller; Ruth Heller.

Number of staff: 1 full-time professional; 1 full-time support.

EIN: 942814266

Selected grants: The following grants were reported in 2004.

$200,000 to Trust for Conservation Innovation, San Francisco, CA.

$75,000 to Environmental Working Group, DC.

$50,000 to Center for Food Safety, DC.

$50,000 to Urban Education Partnership, Los Angeles, CA.

$40,000 to Harvard University, Cambridge, MA.

$35,000 to San Francisco Symphony, San Francisco, CA.

$30,000 to Center for the Future of Teaching and Learning, Santa Cruz, CA.

$27,000 to American String Teachers Association with National School Orchestra Association, Fairfax, VA.

$25,000 to Friends of the Earth, DC.

$15,000 to Community Music Center, San Francisco, CA.

667
Hellman Family Foundation ✧ ☆
1 Maritime Plz., 12th Fl.
San Francisco, CA 94111 (415) 495-5408

Established in 1983 in CA.
Donor: F. Warren Hellman.
Foundation type: Independent foundation.
Financial data (yr. ended 11/30/05): Assets, $6,939,215 (M); gifts received, $4,809,125; expenditures, $364,580; qualifying distributions, $362,830; giving activities include $360,000 for grants.
Fields of interest: Federated giving programs.
Type of support: General/operating support.

Limitations: Applications not accepted. Giving primarily in CA, with emphasis on San Francisco. No grants to individuals.

Application information: Unsolicited requests for funds not accepted. Funds fully committed for the next few years. No new grantmaking until current commitments have been fulfilled.

Officers and Directors:* Patricia C. Hellman,* Pres.; Marco Hellman,* V.P.; Frances Hellman Dynes; Patricia Hellman Gibbs; Richard D. Gibbs; F. Warren Hellman; Judith Hellman; Sabrina Hellman.
EIN: 942880118

Selected grants: The following grants were reported in 2005.

$200,000 to California Academy of Sciences, San Francisco, CA.

$15,000 to Brandeis-Bardin Institute, Brandeis, CA.

$15,000 to City College of San Francisco, San Francisco, CA.

$10,000 to Jazz Foundation of America, New York, NY.

$10,000 to Jewish Home for the Aged, San Francisco, CA.

$10,000 to Seacology, Berkeley, CA.

$10,000 to Tenderloin Neighborhood Development Corporation, San Francisco, CA.

$10,000 to University of California at Berkeley Foundation, Berkeley, CA.

$5,000 to Coro Northern California, San Francisco, CA.

668
John C. Hench Foundation ☆
556 Sierra Madre Blvd.
San Marino, CA 91108
Contact: Jose Deetjen

Established in 1990 in CA.
Donors: John C. Hench†; Lowry Hench†; Hench Family Living Trust A; Hench Family Living Trust B.
Foundation type: Independent foundation.
Financial data (yr. ended 11/30/05): Assets, $23,614,573 (M); gifts received, $18,235,000; expenditures, $645,335; qualifying distributions, $514,541; giving activities include $425,000 for 14 grants (high: $200,000; low: $5,000).
Purpose and activities: Giving primarily for higher education, including a college of art and design, as well as for health care.
Fields of interest: Arts education; Higher education; Health care; Cancer; Diabetes.
Limitations: Applications not accepted. Giving primarily in CA. No grants to individuals.
Application information: Contributes only to pre-selected organizations.
Board meeting date(s): As required - once a month
Trustees: Jose M. Deetjen; Leonor Deetjen; Sandra L. Huskins.
EIN: 954308746

Selected grants: The following grants were reported in 2005.

$25,000 to American Cancer Society, Atlanta, GA.

$25,000 to American Diabetes Association, Los Angeles, CA.

$5,000 to Braille Institute, Santa Barbara, CA.

$5,000 to Guide Dogs for the Blind, San Rafael, CA.

$5,000 to Sacred Heart High School, Los Angeles, CA.

$5,000 to Special Olympics Southern California, Culver City, CA.

669
The Herbst Foundation, Inc. ✧
30 Van Ness Ave., Ste. 3600
San Francisco, CA 94102 (415) 252-1220
Contact: Dwight L. Merriman, Jr., V.P.

Incorporated in 1961 in CA.
Donors: Herman H. Herbst†; Maurice H. Herbst†.
Foundation type: Independent foundation.
Financial data (yr. ended 7/31/05): Assets, $65,068,861 (M); expenditures, $2,267,664; qualifying distributions, $1,871,171; giving activities include $1,795,819 for 148 grants (high: $550,000; low: $50), and $40,000 for 21 grants to individuals (high: $2,000; low: $1,000).
Purpose and activities: Grants within the city and county of San Francisco for bricks and mortar projects including educational facilities, civic improvement of existing city structures owned by public tax-exempt entities, hospitals, healthcare organizations, and a very small budget per year for broad purposes.
Fields of interest: Elementary school/education; Secondary school/education; Health care; Human services; Community development, neighborhood development.
Type of support: Building/renovation.
Limitations: Applications not accepted. Giving limited to the city and county of San Francisco, CA. No grants to individuals (except for Teaching Excellence Awards), or for endowment funds, scholarships, fellowships, research, or matching gifts; no loans.
Application information: Unsolicited requests for funds not accepted.
Board meeting date(s): Usually in Sept., Nov., Feb., and May
Officers and Directors:* Anthony Cameron, Pres.; William D. Crawford,* V.P.; Melvyn I. Mark,* V.P.; Dwight L. Merriman, Jr.,* V.P.; Bruce W. Hart,* Secy.; Jerrol L. Harris,* Treas.; Robert K. Taylor.
Number of staff: 1 full-time professional.
EIN: 946061680

670
Fannie and John Hertz Foundation
2456 Research Dr.
Livermore, CA 94550-3850 (925) 373-1642
Contact: Linda Kubiak, Fellowship Admin.
FAX: (925) 373-6329;
E-mail: askhertz@hertzfoundation.org; URL: http://www.hertzfoundation.org

Incorporated in 1945 in IL.
Donors: John D. Hertz†; Fannie K. Hertz†; John F. Wakerly; David N. Weise; Daniel W. Weise; Doyne J. Farmer.
Foundation type: Independent foundation.
Financial data (yr. ended 6/30/05): Assets, $23,862,338 (M); gifts received, $1,018,538; expenditures, $4,379,561; qualifying distributions, $4,238,896; giving activities include $2,781,382 for 107 grants to individuals (high: $45,000; low: $3,000).
Purpose and activities: Giving to promote education and the defense of the U.S. through support of fellowships for graduate education for students with outstanding potential in the fields constituting applications of the physical sciences at specified institutions nationwide.
Fields of interest: Physical/earth sciences; Chemistry; Physics; Engineering/technology; Computer science; Engineering; Biological sciences.

Type of support: Fellowships; Grants to individuals.
Publications: Informational brochure.
Application information: No grants for non-Ph.D. aspects of joint Ph.D./professional degree programs; no scholarships or fellowships for classical biological sciences; no undergraduate funding. Application form required.
> *Initial approach:* See foundation Web site for application information
> *Copies of proposal:* 1
> *Deadline(s):* Submit application form in Sept. or Oct.; deadline, late Oct.
> *Board meeting date(s):* Mar. and Oct.
> *Final notification:* By Apr. 1

Officers and Directors:* Gregory H. Canavan,* Chair.; John F. Holzrichter,* Pres.; Peter Strauss,* V.P. and Treas.; Thomas Silk,* Secy.; Wilson K. Talley,* Pres. Emeritus; John W. Boyd; John Brown; Ilene Busch-Vishniac; Ruth David; Jay C. Davis; Gilbert F. Decker; Robert A. Duffy; David J. Galas; W. Daniel Hillis; Arthur R. Kantrowitz; Hans Mark; Thomas McCann; Richard Miles; Harold J. Newman; Maj. Genl. Paul D. Nielsen; Sidney Singer; Thomas A. Weaver; Daniel Weise; Lowell L. Wood.
Number of staff: 4 part-time professional; 1 full-time support; 5 part-time support.
EIN: 362411723
Selected grants: The following grants were reported in 2003.
$200,000 to University of California, Davis, CA. For Edward Teller Professorship.

671

The William and Flora Hewlett Foundation ▼

2121 Sand Hill Rd.
Menlo Park, CA 94025 (650) 234-4500
Contact: Paul Brest, Pres.
FAX: (650) 234-4501; URL: http://www.hewlett.org

Incorporated in 1966 in CA.
Donors: Flora Lamson Hewlett‡; William R. Hewlett‡.
Foundation type: Independent foundation.
Financial data (yr. ended 12/31/05): Assets, $7,336,131,000 (M); expenditures, $355,671,093; qualifying distributions, $319,916,093; giving activities include $319,916,093 for grants, and $3,101,000 for foundation-administered programs.
Purpose and activities: Emphasis on global development, the environment, performing arts, education (K-12 and community college), population studies, community development, and philanthropy.
Fields of interest: Performing arts; Performing arts, dance; Performing arts, theater; Performing arts, music; Arts; Elementary/secondary education; Higher education; Higher education, college (community/junior); Libraries (academic/research); Environment, natural resources; Environment; Reproductive health, family planning; International agricultural development; International economic development; International economics/trade policy; Urban/community development; Community development; Philanthropy/voluntarism; Population studies; International studies; Public policy, research; Minorities.
International interests: Latin America.
Type of support: General/operating support; Continuing support; Land acquisition; Emergency funds; Program development; Seed money;

Program-related investments/loans; Employee matching gifts; Matching/challenge support.
Limitations: Giving limited to the San Francisco Bay Area, CA, for family and community development programs; performing arts primarily limited to the Bay Area. No support for medicine and health-related projects, law, criminal justice, and related fields, juvenile delinquency or drug and alcohol addiction, prevention or treatment programs, problems of the elderly and the handicapped, or television or radio projects. No grants to individuals, or for basic research, equipment, seminars, conferences, festivals, touring costs, fundraising drives, scholarships, or fellowships; no loans (except for program-related investments).
Publications: Application guidelines; Annual report (including application guidelines); Grants list; Informational brochure; Newsletter; Program policy statement.
Application information: The foundation prefers to receive letters of inquiry via its online submission form on their Web site. The foundation is currently not accepting letters of inquiry for the Global Development, Philanthropy, and Population programs. Please do not submit a full proposal until invited to do so. Application form not required.
> *Initial approach:* Letter of inquiry
> *Copies of proposal:* 1
> *Deadline(s):* None
> *Board meeting date(s):* Feb., June, and Oct.
> *Final notification:* 2 to 3 months

Officers and Directors:* Walter B. Hewlett,* Chair.; James C. Gaither,* Vice-Chair.; Paul Brest,* Pres.; Laurance Hoagland, Jr., V.P. and C.I.O.; Susan Bell, V.P.; Nancy Strausser, Corp. Secy.; Susan Ketcham, Treas.; Lucy Ellis, Cont.; Patrick Collins, Chief Info. Off.; Byron Auguste; Steven Chu; Harvey V. Fineberg, M.D.; Eleanor H. Gimon; Juliette Gimon; Mary H. Jaffe; Richard C. Levin; Stephen C. Neal; Jean G. Stromberg.
Number of staff: 55 full-time professional; 7 part-time professional; 23 full-time support; 5 part-time support.
EIN: 941655673
Selected grants: The following grants were reported in 2005.
$3,500,000 to International Projects Assistance Services (IPAS), Chapel Hill, NC. For general operating support, payable over 2 years.
$3,000,000 to American Academy of Arts and Sciences, Cambridge, MA. For capital campaign.
$3,000,000 to Massachusetts Institute of Technology, Cambridge, MA. For continued support of MIT OpenCourseWare - free, open website offering high quality MIT teaching materials to educators, students and self-learners worldwide, payable over 2 years.
$2,400,000 to International Council on Clean Transportation, DC. For general support, payable over 2 years.
$2,050,000 to Guttmacher Institute, New York, NY. For general support, payable over 2 years.
$2,000,000 to Independent Television Service, San Francisco, CA. For launch of public-private International Media Development Fund, documentary and journalistic production initiative to bring international perspectives to American television audiences.
$213,000 to Western Interstate Commission for Higher Education (WICHE), Boulder, CO. For development of business plan and strategy to insure sustainability of EduTools and for support of WCET Director to serve as ambassador for

Open Educational Resources at various meetings throughout world, payable over 2 years.
$200,000 to World Bank, DC. For support for youth reproductive health and demographic change issues in World Bank's World Development Report 2007: Development and the Next Generation, payable over 1.50 years.
$150,000 to Tides Foundation, San Francisco, CA. For campaign to ensure government keeps its commitment to sign off on proposed Great Bear Rainforest agreements.
$120,000 to Chhandam Chitresh Das Dance Company, San Francisco, CA. For general support, payable over 3 years.

672

Hewlett-Packard Company Foundation ◇

3000 Hanover St., M.S. 20AH
Palo Alto, CA 94304-1112
Contact: Bess Stephens, Exec. Dir.
FAX: (650) 857-2982;
E-mail: philanthropy_ed@hp.com; Application address: P.O. Box 10301, Palo Alto, CA 94303; URL: http://www.hp.com/go/grants

Established in 1979 in CA.
Donor: Hewlett-Packard Co.
Foundation type: Company-sponsored foundation.
Financial data (yr. ended 10/31/04): Assets, $5,794,048 (M); expenditures, $1,159,413; qualifying distributions, $1,160,000; giving activities include $1,160,000 for 7 grants (high: $300,000; low: $10,000).
Purpose and activities: The foundation supports organizations involved with arts and culture, education, human services, and science and technology. Special emphasis is directed toward programs designed to build bridges between the sciences and the humanities and enhance the understanding of science, engineering, and technology.
Fields of interest: Arts; Higher education; Engineering school/education; Education; Human services; Engineering/technology; Engineering; Science.
Type of support: Program development.
Limitations: Giving on a national basis, with emphasis on areas of company operations. No support for sectarian, denominational, or political organizations. No grants to individuals, or for conferences, seminars, meetings, or workshops.
Application information:
> *Initial approach:* Proposal
> *Deadline(s):* None

Officers and Directors:* Ann O. Baskins,* Secy.; Bess Stephens,* Exec. Dir.; Debra Dunn; Robert P. Wayman.
EIN: 942618409

673

The Larry L. Hillblom Foundation, Inc. ▼ ◇

755 Baywood Dr., Ste. 180
Petaluma, CA 94954 (707) 762-6691
FAX: (707) 762-6694; E-mail: som@llhf.org;
Additional address: 1458 Draper St., Kingsburg, CA 93631, tel.: (559) 897-7050, FAX: (559) 897-7590, E-mail: dlr@llhf.org; URL: http://www.llhf.org

Established in 1997 in CA.
Donor: Larry L. Hillblom‡.
Foundation type: Independent foundation.

Financial data (yr. ended 12/31/04): Assets,
$163,383,974 (M); expenditures, $7,522,843;
qualifying distributions, $6,159,942; giving
activities include $5,376,006 for 50 grants (high:
$2,673,890; low: $2,000; average: $5,000–
$500,000).
Purpose and activities: The mission of the
foundation is to provide philanthropic support
exclusively for charitable, religious, scientific,
literary and educational purposes. Primarily, the
foundation will support medical research, including
basic scientific research, clinical research and
research related to patient self-care and
management. The foundation supports funding
directed toward efforts to cure, treat, and manage
diabetes mellitus and chronic and degenerative
diseases associated with aging, with the primary
focus on brain and vision disorders.
Fields of interest: Higher education; Health care;
Eye diseases; Brain disorders; Diabetes; Geriatrics;
Medical research, institute.
Type of support: Research.
Limitations: Giving primarily in San Francisco, CA.
No grants to individuals.
Publications: Application guidelines; Grants list.
Application information: See foundation Web site
for guidelines and application form. Grant
applications will be accepted only through online
submission system. Do not file a full application for
funding until you have first filed a Letter of Inquiry
(LOI) and received a letter from the foundation
inviting you to proceed. Application form required.
  Initial approach: Complete Grant Application
    Cover Page and submit Initial Funding Proposal
    as letter of inquiry
  Deadline(s): Jan. 18
Officers and Directors:* Peter J. Donnici,* Chair.,
C.E.O., and Pres.; Lorna Beccaria, Chair., Medical
Advisory Board; Terry C. Hillblom,* Vice-Chair.,
C.O.O., and Exec. V.P.; Grant A. Anderson,* V.P.;
Walter Hillblom,* V.P.; Stephen J. Schwartz,* V.P.;
David R. Jones, Secy. and C.F.O.; Paul Kimoto; Ida
O'Brien; Janice E. Quistad; E. Lewis Reid; William A.
Robinson; Joseph W. Waechter.
EIN: 943241600
Selected grants: The following grants were reported
in 2004.
$2,673,890 to University of California, San
  Francisco, CA. For general support.
$559,705 to Whittier Institute for Diabetes and
  Endocrinology, La Jolla, CA. For general support.
$500,000 to Stanford University, Stanford, CA. For
  general support.
$233,369 to University of California, Irvine, CA. For
  general support.
$196,952 to Kingsburg Joint Union High School,
  Kingsburg, CA. For general support.
$118,800 to Salk Institute for Biological Studies,
  San Diego, CA. For general support.
$97,580 to Hillblom Memorial Fund, Saipan. For
  general support.
$95,000 to Spondylitis Association of America,
  Sherman Oaks, CA. For general support.
$70,000 to University of California, Los Angeles,
  CA. For general support.
$65,000 to Buck Institute for Age Research, Novato,
  CA. For general support.

674
The Edward E. Hills Fund ◇
P.O. Box 471000
San Francisco, CA 94147-1000
Contact: Reuben W. Hills, III, Chair.

Incorporated in 1953 in CA.
Donor: Edward E. Hills†.
Foundation type: Independent foundation.
Financial data (yr. ended 12/31/05): Assets,
$15,441,330 (M); expenditures, $928,769;
qualifying distributions, $495,771; giving activities
include $364,640 for grants.
Purpose and activities: Giving primarily for
museums, performing arts, and education.
Fields of interest: Museums; Performing arts;
Secondary school/education; Higher education.
Limitations: Applications not accepted. Giving
primarily in CA. No grants to individuals.
Application information: Contributes only to
pre-selected organizations.
Officers and Directors:* Reuben W. Hills III,* Chair.;
Ingrid von Mangoldt Hills, Pres.; Donald S. Dodge,
Jr., V.P. and Secy.; William Barksdale, V.P. and
Treas.
EIN: 946062537
Selected grants: The following grants were reported
in 2004.
$200,000 to Asian Art Museum of San Francisco,
  San Francisco, CA.
$150,000 to University of California, School of
  Veterinary, Davis, CA.
$50,500 to Every Child Can Learn Foundation, San
  Francisco, CA.
$50,000 to San Francisco Museum of Modern Art,
  San Francisco, CA.
$35,000 to Berkeley Public Education Foundation,
  Berkeley, CA.
$35,000 to San Francisco Ballet, San Francisco,
  CA.
$30,000 to Stanford University, Stanford, CA.
$29,000 to San Francisco Symphony, San
  Francisco, CA.
$25,000 to Conservation International, DC.
$6,000 to Wolfsong Ranch Foundation, Willcox, AZ.

675
Hinz Family Charitable Foundation ◇
c/o Hi Torque Publications
25233 Anza Dr.
Valencia, CA 91355
Contact: Roland Hinz, Tr.

Established in 1986 in CA.
Donors: Lila Hinz; Roland Hinz.
Foundation type: Operating foundation.
Financial data (yr. ended 6/30/05): Assets,
$1,546,637 (M); gifts received, $2,741,758;
expenditures, $1,047,331; qualifying distributions,
$1,038,576; giving activities include $1,037,811
for 22 grants (high: $495,000; low: $4,000).
Fields of interest: Education, association;
Education; Christian agencies & churches.
Limitations: Giving primarily in CA; some giving
nationally.
Application information: Application form not
required.
  Deadline(s): None
Trustees: Lila Hinz; Roland Hinz.
EIN: 954121438
Selected grants: The following grants were reported
in 2005.
$90,000 to Thornston Educational Fund, Glendora,
  CA.
$78,000 to Motor Racing Outreach, Harrisburg, NC.
$50,000 to Asian Access Life Ministries, San
  Dimas, CA.
$50,000 to Young Life, Colorado Springs, CO.

$25,000 to Lake Avenue Community Foundation,
  Pasadena, CA.
$10,000 to Capitol Ministries, Santa Clarita, CA.

676
The Hitz Foundation ◇
(formerly The XYZZY Foundation)
c/o Frank, Rimerman Co., LLP
1801 Page Mill Rd.
Palo Alto, CA 94304-1211

Established in 2000 in CA.
Donor: David Hitz.
Foundation type: Independent foundation.
Financial data (yr. ended 12/31/05): Assets,
$13,578,429 (M); gifts received, $4,331,618;
expenditures, $711,549; qualifying distributions,
$565,625; giving activities include $562,000 for 62
grants (high: $100,000; low: $1,000).
Fields of interest: Media/communications; Arts;
Education; Human services.
Limitations: Applications not accepted. Giving
primarily in CA, NC, NV, and OR. No grants to
individuals.
Application information: Contributes only to
pre-selected organizations.
Officers: David Hitz, Pres. and C.F.O.; Yen Hitz,
Secy.; Kevin P. McAuliffe, Treas.
EIN: 943379521
Selected grants: The following grants were reported
in 2005.
$100,000 to Deep Springs College, Dyer, NV.
$75,000 to American Civil Liberties Union (ACLU),
  New York, NY.
$30,000 to Institute for OneWorld Health, San
  Francisco, CA.
$30,000 to Worldwatch Institute, DC.
$25,000 to American Heart Association, Dallas, TX.
$25,000 to Oregon Shakespeare Festival, Ashland,
  OR.
$25,000 to Peninsula Open Space Trust, Menlo
  Park, CA.
$10,000 to Montalvo Association, Saratoga, CA.
$5,000 to National Public Radio, DC.
$1,000 to High Tech High Foundation, San Diego,
  CA.

677
Hoag Family Foundation ◇
855 Hamilton Ave.
Palo Alto, CA 94301

Established in 2000 in CA and NV.
Donor: Jay C. Hoag.
Foundation type: Independent foundation.
Financial data (yr. ended 12/31/05): Assets,
$8,517,907 (M); gifts received, $705,507;
expenditures, $523,915; qualifying distributions,
$473,150; giving activities include $459,975 for 15
grants (high: $100,000; low: $25).
Fields of interest: Education; Health organizations,
association; Human services.
Limitations: Applications not accepted. Giving
primarily in CA. No grants to individuals.
Application information: Contributes only to
pre-selected organizations.
Officers: Jay Hoag, Pres.; Michaela Hoag,
Secy.-Treas.
EIN: 943383126

678
George Hoag Family Foundation
(formerly Hoag Foundation)
2665 Main St., Ste. 220
Santa Monica, CA 90405 (310) 664-1358
Contact: Charles W. Smith, Secy. and Exec. Dir.

Incorporated in 1940 in CA.
Donors: George Grant Hoag†; Grace E. Hoag†; George Grant Hoag II†.
Foundation type: Independent foundation.
Financial data (yr. ended 12/31/05): Assets, $75,252,361 (M); expenditures, $4,312,965; qualifying distributions, $3,620,971; giving activities include $3,370,500 for 97 grants (high: $300,000; low: $5,000; average: $10,000–$100,000).
Purpose and activities: To improve social conditions, promote human welfare, and alleviate pain and suffering. Also, to improve and expand medical services, and opportunities for youth in CA.
Fields of interest: Arts; Hospitals (general); Medical research, institute; Youth development, services; Children/youth, services; Human services.
Type of support: Research; Scholarship funds; Program development; General/operating support; Equipment; Building/renovation; Capital campaigns.
Limitations: Giving limited to CA, primarily to southern CA, with emphasis on Los Angeles, and Orange County. No support for government agencies, tax-supported projects, or sectarian or religious organizations for the benefit of their own members. No grants to individuals, or for deficit financing or normal operating expenses.
Publications: Application guidelines; Program policy statement; Program policy statement (including application guidelines).
Application information: Application form required.
   Initial approach: Letter (not exceeding 2 pages)
   Copies of proposal: 9
   Deadline(s): Mar. 31 and Sept. 30
   Board meeting date(s): May and Nov.
   Final notification: Following meeting at which proposal is reviewed
Officers and Directors:* Melinda Hoag Smith,* C.E.O. and Pres.; George Grant Hoag III,* V.P. and Treas.; Charles W. Smith,* Secy. and Exec. Dir.; Gerald E. Boltz; John L. Curci, Jr.; Gwyn P. Parry; Michael D. Stephens.
Number of staff: 1 full-time professional; 1 part-time support.
EIN: 956006885

679
Hoag Foundation ◇
c/o Larry Hoag
7730 4th Pl.
Downey, CA 90241

Established in 1991 in CA.
Donors: C. Larry Hoag; Helen Hoag.
Foundation type: Independent foundation.
Financial data (yr. ended 12/31/05): Assets, $3,925,608 (M); gifts received, $300,000; expenditures, $1,191,772; qualifying distributions, $1,112,000; giving activities include $1,112,000 for 6 grants (high: $750,000; low: $1,000).
Fields of interest: Performing arts, opera; Elementary/secondary education; Higher education, university; Community development, association.
Limitations: Applications not accepted. Giving primarily in Downey, CA. No grants to individuals.

Application information: Contributes only to pre-selected organizations.
Directors: Helen Hoag; Michael Hoag.
EIN: 954315096

680
R. C. Hobbs Foundation ◇ ☆
1110 E. Chapman Ave., Ste. 206
Orange, CA 92866

Established in 2004 in CA.
Donors: Roger C. Hobbs; Kathy Hobbs.
Foundation type: Independent foundation.
Financial data (yr. ended 12/31/05): Assets, $386,614 (M); gifts received, $225,000; expenditures, $345,025; qualifying distributions, $342,500; giving activities include $342,500 for 5 grants (high: $301,000; low: $1,500).
Fields of interest: Education; Foundations (community).
Limitations: Applications not accepted. No grants to individuals.
Application information: Contributes only to pre-selected organizations.
Officers: Roger C. Hobbs, Pres.; Kathy Hobbs, Secy.
EIN: 202037484

681
The Hoehn Family Charitable Trust ◇
9 Rue Fontaine
Newport Beach, CA 92660
Contact: Catheryn E. Hoehn, Tr.

Established in 1998 in IL.
Donor: Dorothy Hoehn.
Foundation type: Independent foundation.
Financial data (yr. ended 12/31/05): Assets, $14,742,919 (M); gifts received, $7,875; expenditures, $765,740; qualifying distributions, $709,771; giving activities include $701,000 for 11 grants (high: $475,000; low: $1,000; average: $10,000–$25,000).
Purpose and activities: Giving primarily for education and health care.
Fields of interest: Higher education, university.
Limitations: Applications not accepted. Giving primarily in CA and WI. No grants to individuals.
Application information: Contributes only to pre-selected organizations.
Trustee: Catheryn Emily Hoehn.
EIN: 364235135

682
The H. Leslie Hoffman and Elaine S. Hoffman Foundation ◇
225 S. Lake Ave., Ste. 1150
Pasadena, CA 91101-3036 (626) 793-0043
Contact: J. Kristoffer Popovich, Tr.

Established in 1952 in CA.
Donors: H. Leslie Hoffman†; Elaine S. Hoffman†.
Foundation type: Independent foundation.
Financial data (yr. ended 12/31/05): Assets, $33,616,456 (M); expenditures, $4,877,958; qualifying distributions, $4,438,428; giving activities include $4,277,291 for 69 grants (high: $3,538,000; low: $1,000).
Purpose and activities: Giving primarily to a children's museum and education.

Fields of interest: Museums (children's); Arts; Education; Human services.
Type of support: General/operating support.
Limitations: Giving primarily in the Los Angeles, CA, area, with emphasis on Pasadena. No grants to individuals.
Application information: Application form not required.
   Initial approach: Letter
   Copies of proposal: 1
   Deadline(s): None
   Board meeting date(s): As required
Trustees: J. Kristoffer Popovich; Jane H. Popovich.
EIN: 956048600
Selected grants: The following grants were reported in 2005.
$151,000 to Childrens Hospital Los Angeles, Los Angeles, CA.
$50,000 to Westridge School for Girls, Pasadena, CA.
$25,000 to Huntington Library, Art Collections and Botanical Gardens, San Marino, CA.
$21,500 to Sun Valley Center for the Arts, Sun Valley, ID.
$21,000 to Polytechnic School, Pasadena, CA.
$21,000 to YMCA of Metropolitan Los Angeles, Los Angeles, CA.
$10,000 to Saint Lukes Wood River Foundation, Ketchum, ID.
$7,800 to YMCA, Wood River Community, Ketchum, ID.
$5,000 to Art Center College of Design, Pasadena, CA.
$5,000 to Los Angeles Opera Company, Los Angeles, CA.

683
K. H. Hofmann Foundation ◇
(formerly The Hofmann Foundation)
P.O. Box 907
Concord, CA 94522
Contact: Dennis Costanza
Application address: 1380 Galaxy Way, Concord, CA 94520, tel.: (925) 687-1826

Established in 1963 in CA.
Donors: The Hofmann Co.; New Discovery, Inc.; Kenneth H. Hofmann; Martha J. Hofmann; The Hofmann 1987 Revocable Trust.
Foundation type: Company-sponsored foundation.
Financial data (yr. ended 12/31/05): Assets, $57,907,885 (M); gifts received, $31,393,952; expenditures, $6,633,488; qualifying distributions, $6,460,752; giving activities include $6,458,616 for 168 grants (high: $1,000,000; low: $50).
Purpose and activities: The foundation supports organizations involved with secondary and higher education, water conservation, animals and wildlife, health, and children.
Fields of interest: Secondary school/education; Higher education; Environment, water resources; Animals/wildlife, preservation/protection; End of life care; Health care; Children, services.
Limitations: Giving primarily in the San Francisco Bay Area, CA, with emphasis on Contra Costa County; some giving for national organizations. No grants to individuals, or for general operating support, capital campaigns, or debt reduction.
Publications: Annual report (including application guidelines).
Application information: Proposals should be no longer than 3 pages. Application form not required.
   Initial approach: Proposal

Copies of proposal: 1
Deadline(s): None
Board meeting date(s): Quarterly
Final notification: 3 to 4 months
Officers: Martha Jean Hofmann, C.E.O.; Lisa Hofmann Seeno, Secy.; Dennis M. Drew, C.F.O.
Number of staff: 4
EIN: 946108897
Selected grants: The following grants were reported in 2003.
$1,000,000 to Mount Diablo Hospital Foundation, Concord, CA.
$500,000 to De La Salle High School, Concord, CA.
$265,000 to Community Youth Center - Concord Campus, Concord, CA. 5 grants: $50,000, $50,000, $20,000, $75,000, $70,000
$200,000 to Ducks Unlimited, Memphis, TN.
$63,000 to Wheelchair Foundation, Danville, CA.
$25,000 to Taylor Family Foundation, Livermore, CA.

684
Homer Family Foundation ◇
c/o Richard Gong, myCFO, Inc.
P.O. Box 10196, Dept. 34
Palo Alto, CA 94303-0972

Established in 1999 in CA.
Donors: Michael J. Homer; Kristina L. Homer.
Foundation type: Independent foundation.
Financial data (yr. ended 2/28/05): Assets, $5,133,193 (M); expenditures, $879,691; qualifying distributions, $800,871; giving activities include $723,366 for 19 grants (high: $200,000; low: $555).
Fields of interest: Museums (specialized); Elementary school/education; Youth development; Human services.
Limitations: Applications not accepted. Giving primarily in CA. No grants to individuals.
Application information: Contributes only to pre-selected organizations.
Trustees: Kristina L. Homer; Michael J. Homer.
EIN: 943346061
Selected grants: The following grants were reported in 2005.
$191,667 to Sacred Heart Schools, Atherton, CA. 2 grants: $166,667, $25,000 (For annual fund).
$128,000 to Cinequest, San Jose, CA.
$55,000 to Tiger Woods Foundation, Los Alamitos, CA.
$33,750 to Ronald McDonald House at Childrens Hospital, Palo Alto, CA. 2 grants: $15,000, $18,750 (For Dance Hall sponsorship).
$15,169 to Cleo Eulau Center for Children and Adolescents, Palo Alto, CA.
$10,000 to Saint Elizabeth Seton School, Palo Alto, CA.

685
Shea Homes Foundation ◇
(formerly Highlands Ranch Foundation)
655 Brea Canyon Rd.
Walnut, CA 91789

Established in 1989 in CA and CO.
Foundation type: Independent foundation.
Financial data (yr. ended 12/31/04): Assets, $2,399,318 (M); expenditures, $452,645; qualifying distributions, $403,617; giving activities

include $403,617 for 85 grants (high: $100,000; low: $100).
Purpose and activities: Giving to higher education and to children and youth services.
Fields of interest: Education; Children/youth, services.
Limitations: Applications not accepted. Giving primarily in CO. No grants to individuals.
Application information: Contributes only to pre-selected organizations.
Officers: John F. Shea, Pres.; Ronald L. Lakey, V.P.; John C. Morrissey, V.P.; Edmund H. Shea, Jr., V.P.; Peter O. Shea, V.P.; James G. Shontere, Secy.; Robert R. O'Dell, Treas.
EIN: 742530267

686
The Horn Foundation ◇
21550 Oxnard St., Ste. 300
Woodland Hills, CA 91367

Established in 1989 in CA.
Donors: Alan F. Horn; Cynthia Horn.
Foundation type: Independent foundation.
Financial data (yr. ended 12/31/05): Assets, $8,390,191 (M); gifts received, $1,750,000; expenditures, $467,084; qualifying distributions, $449,572; giving activities include $441,788 for 63 grants (high: $40,000; low: $100).
Purpose and activities: Giving primarily for arts and culture, education, conservation, health associations, human services, and children and youth services.
Fields of interest: Arts; Elementary/secondary education; Higher education; Medical school/education; Education; Environment; Health organizations, association; Cancer research; Human services; Children/youth, services; Federated giving programs.
Limitations: Applications not accepted. Giving primarily in CA. No grants to individuals.
Application information: Contributes only to pre-selected organizations.
Officers: Alan F. Horn, Mgr.; Cindy Horn, Mgr.
EIN: 954247470

687
House Family Foundation ◇
(formerly Dave House Family Foundation)
1600 Saratoga Ave., No. 403
PMB 269
San Jose, CA 95129

Established in 1999 in CA.
Donor: David House.
Foundation type: Independent foundation.
Financial data (yr. ended 6/30/05): Assets, $23,221,029 (M); expenditures, $2,405,393; qualifying distributions, $1,953,794; giving activities include $1,843,153 for 19 grants (high: $1,050,000; low: $1,000).
Purpose and activities: Giving primarily for higher and other education, children, youth, and social services, and to a museum specializing in computers.
Fields of interest: Museums (specialized); Higher education, university; Education; Boys & girls clubs; Human services; Children/youth, services.
Limitations: Applications not accepted. Giving primarily in CA; funding also in MI. No grants to individuals.

Application information: Contributes only to pre-selected organizations.
Officers: David House, C.E.O. and Pres.; Robert Olsen, V.P.; Shelley Cargill, Secy.; Robert House, Treas.
Director: Karla House.
EIN: 522207366
Selected grants: The following grants were reported in 2003.
$1,100,000 to Computer History Museum, Mountain View, CA. For general support.
$125,530 to San Jose State University Foundation, San Jose, CA. For general support.
$124,280 to Boys and Girls Clubs of the Peninsula, Menlo Park, CA. For general support.
$100,000 to Foothill College, Los Altos Hills, CA. For general support.
$50,000 to Silicon Valley Childrens Fund, San Jose, CA. For general support.
$25,996 to Rock-It Science, Moffett Field, CA. For general support.
$24,160 to Muskegon Public Schools, Muskegon, MI. For general support.
$10,000 to Girls Inc. of Alameda County, San Leandro, CA. For general support.
$6,830 to Girl Scouts of the U.S.A., Michigan Pine and Dunes Council, Muskegon, MI. For general support.
$6,830 to Muskegon Area Intermediate School District, Muskegon, MI. For general support.

688
HRH Foundation ◇
196 Albion Ave.
Woodside, CA 94062-3657

Established in 2000 in CA.
Donors: Harry R. Hagey; Shirley Hagey.
Foundation type: Independent foundation.
Financial data (yr. ended 12/31/05): Assets, $20,892,808 (M); gifts received, $5,480,000; expenditures, $488,905; qualifying distributions, $476,750; giving activities include $476,750 for 35 grants (high: $70,000; low: $1,000; average: $5,000–$35,000).
Fields of interest: Reproductive health, family planning; Health organizations, association; Human services; Family services.
Limitations: Applications not accepted. Giving primarily in CA. No grants to individuals.
Application information: Contributes only to pre-selected organizations.
Officers and Directors:* Harry R. Hagey,* Pres.; Shirley Hagey,* Secy. and C.F.O.
EIN: 943381908
Selected grants: The following grants were reported in 2005.
$40,000 to Community Working Group, Palo Alto, CA.
$35,000 to Nature Conservancy, San Francisco, CA.
$25,000 to Media Projects, Dallas, TX.
$20,000 to Episcopal Community Services, San Diego, CA.
$15,000 to Child and Family Institute, Menlo Park, CA.
$15,000 to Eastside College Preparatory School, East Palo Alto, CA.
$15,000 to YMCA, Wood River Community, Ketchum, ID.
$7,000 to Planned Parenthood Golden Gate, San Francisco, CA.
$7,000 to Planned Parenthood Mar Monte, San Jose, CA.

$5,000 to Peninsula Open Space Trust, Menlo Park, CA.

689
Hsin Hsin Private Foundation ✧
27101 Horseshoe Ln.
Los Altos Hills, CA 94022-1934

Established in 2002 in CA.
Donors: Olivia Hsia; T. Chester Wang.
Foundation type: Independent foundation.
Financial data (yr. ended 12/31/05): Assets, $1,177 (M); gifts received, $237,984; expenditures, $593,001; qualifying distributions, $592,991; giving activities include $592,991 for 2 grants (high: $500,000; low: $92,991).
Fields of interest: Human services; Christian agencies & churches; Religion.
Limitations: Applications not accepted. No grants to individuals.
Application information: Contributes only to pre-selected organizations.
Officers: T. Chester Wang, Pres.; Olivia Hsia, Secy.; Ta-Cheng Wang.
EIN: 010744103

690
Mark Hughes Family Foundation ✧
(formerly Herbalife Family Foundation)
10100 Santa Monica Blvd., Ste. 300
Los Angeles, CA 90067 (310) 772-2216
Contact: Conrad Lee Klein, Secy.

Established in 1994 in CA.
Foundation type: Independent foundation.
Financial data (yr. ended 12/31/04): Assets, $16,802,119 (M); gifts received, $80,297; expenditures, $657,926; qualifying distributions, $619,221; giving activities include $584,423 for 11 grants (high: $200,000; low: $20,000).
Purpose and activities: The foundation contributes to organizations or programs that improve nutrition, support disadvantaged children and families, provide early interventions to life problems, or prevent physical and emotional abuse.
Fields of interest: Mental health, treatment; Mental health/crisis services; Nutrition; Human services; Children/youth, services; Family services.
Type of support: General/operating support; Equipment; Emergency funds; Program development; Curriculum development.
Publications: Informational brochure (including application guidelines).
Application information: Application form required.
Initial approach: Brief letter
Copies of proposal: 1
Deadline(s): None
Officers and Directors:* Jack Reynolds,* Pres.; Carol Hannah,* V.P.; Conrad Lee Klein,* Secy.; William Lowe, Treas.; Joan Kardashian, Exec. Dir.
EIN: 954487544
Selected grants: The following grants were reported in 2004.
$200,000 to Alliance for Childrens Rights, Los Angeles, CA.
$50,000 to CHILD, Warwick, RI.
$50,000 to Heart of Los Angeles Youth, Los Angeles, CA.
$37,423 to Drug Abuse Resistance Education (DARE).

$20,000 to Boys and Girls Club of Hollywood, Hollywood, CA.

691
The Humboldt Area Foundation ✧
373 Indianola Rd.
Bayside, CA 95524 (707) 442-2993
Contact: Peter H. Pennekamp, Exec. Dir.
FAX: (707) 442-3811;
E-mail: irener@hafoundation.org; Additional E-mails: peter@hafoundation.org and laurao@hafoundation.org; URL: http://www.hafoundation.org

Established in 1972 in CA by declaration of trust.
Donors: Vera P. Vietor†; Lynn A. Vietor†.
Foundation type: Community foundation.
Financial data (yr. ended 6/30/05): Assets, $58,614,660 (M); gifts received, $4,321,032; expenditures, $3,793,821; giving activities include $2,296,113 for 535+ grants, and $220,906 for 280 grants to individuals.
Purpose and activities: The foundation seeks to serve as an independent staging ground for residents, individually and in concert, to build social, economic and environmental prosperity to California's North Coast. Primary areas of interest include youth, health, community development, human services, arts and culture and public safety. The foundation also operates a resource center that hosts public workshops covering a range of nonprofit issues.
Fields of interest: Arts; Health care; Safety/disasters; Recreation; Children/youth, services; Family services; Human services; Community development; Disabilities, people with; Economically disadvantaged.
Type of support: Management development/capacity building; Capital campaigns; Building/renovation; Equipment; Emergency funds; Program development; Seed money; Scholarship funds; Technical assistance; Consulting services; Scholarships—to individuals; Matching/challenge support.
Limitations: Giving limited to Del Norte, Humboldt, and Trinity counties, CA. No grants to individuals (except from donor-designated funds); generally no grants for endowment funds, unspecified emergency purposes, deficit financing, or operating budgets.
Publications: Application guidelines; Annual report; Financial statement; Grants list.
Application information: Visit foundation Web site for application forms and additional guidelines per grant type. Application form required.
Initial approach: Application, telephone, or e-mail
Copies of proposal: 1
Deadline(s): June 1 and Dec. 1 for Community Building grants and the 1st of each month for Community Response grants; Mar. 1 for scholarships
Board meeting date(s): Community Response applications reviewed monthly, Community Building applications reviewed near Feb. 15 and Aug. 15
Final notification: Approximately 6 weeks after deadline for Community Building grants and 4 weeks for Community Response grant requests
Officers and Directors:* Kevin Hartwick,* Chair.; James Anderson,* Vice-Chair.; Mary Ann Bansen,* Secy.; Kathleen Moxon, C.A.O. and Prog. Dir., Instit. of the North Coast; Peter H. Pennekamp, Exec. Dir.;

Gary Blatnick; Casey Crabill; Simona Keat; Ken Nakamura; Steve O'Meara; Jon Sapper; Amos Tripp.
Trustees: Wells Fargo Bank, N.A.
Number of staff: 6 full-time professional; 1 part-time professional; 5 full-time support; 2 part-time support.
EIN: 237310660

692
Jaquelin Hume Foundation ▼ ✧
600 Montgomery St., Ste. 2800
San Francisco, CA 94111 (415) 705-5115
Contact: Gisele Huff, Exec. Dir.

Established in 1962 in CA.
Donors: Jaquelin H. Hume†; Caroline H. Hume; William J. Hume.
Foundation type: Independent foundation.
Financial data (yr. ended 12/31/04): Assets, $19,987,134 (M); expenditures, $3,885,225; qualifying distributions, $3,778,733; giving activities include $3,583,043 for 59 grants (high: $500,000; low: $1,000; average: $25,000–$100,000).
Purpose and activities: Giving primarily for K-12 education reform efforts. Giving also for cultural renewal and civility efforts and public affairs organizations.
Fields of interest: Elementary/secondary school reform; Education; Public policy, research.
Type of support: General/operating support; Program development; Research; Program evaluation.
Limitations: Giving to organizations with a national impact. No support for organizations outside the U.S. No grants to individuals.
Publications: Application guidelines.
Application information: Application form not required.
Initial approach: Letter (1-page)
Copies of proposal: 1
Deadline(s): Mar. 15 and Sept. 15
Board meeting date(s): Biannually
Officers and Trustees:* George H. Hume,* Pres. and Secy.; William J. Hume,* V.P. and Treas.; Gisele Huff, Exec. Dir.; Caroline H. Hume; Edward A. Landry.
Number of staff: 1 full-time professional.
EIN: 946080099
Selected grants: The following grants were reported in 2004.
$500,000 to Foundation for Teaching Economics, Davis, CA. For unrestricted support.
$200,000 to Association of American Educators, Mission Viejo, CA. For unrestricted support.
$200,000 to California Academy of Sciences, San Francisco, CA. For unrestricted support.
$200,000 to Music Concourse Community Partnership, San Francisco, CA. For unrestricted support.
$200,000 to San Francisco Symphony, San Francisco, CA. For unrestricted support.
$150,000 to Institute for Justice, DC. For unrestricted support.
$100,000 to Fine Arts Museums of San Francisco, San Francisco, CA. For unrestricted support.
$100,000 to Institute for American Values, New York, NY. For unrestricted support.
$50,000 to Excellent Education for Everyone, Newark, NJ. For unrestricted support.
$25,000 to South Carolina Policy Council, Columbia, SC. For unrestricted support.

693
Hutto-Patterson Charitable Foundation ✧
200 E. Del Mar, Ste. 350
Pasadena, CA 91105 (626) 793-5871
Contact: Glen Leisure

Established in 1988 in CA.
Donor: Clare P. Hutto.
Foundation type: Independent foundation.
Financial data (yr. ended 9/30/05): Assets,
$10,396,052 (M); expenditures, $431,347;
qualifying distributions, $411,560; giving activities
include $407,600 for 9 grants (high: $100,000;
low: $1,000).
Purpose and activities: Funding primarily for higher
and other education as well as for children, and
youth services.
Fields of interest: Arts education; Elementary/
secondary education; Higher education; Social work
school/education; Education; Children/youth,
services.
Limitations: Giving primarily in southern CA.
Application information:
Initial approach: Letter
Deadline(s): Jan. 15, May 15, and Aug. 15
Officer and Trustees:* Clare P. Hutto,* Pres.;
Catherine Hutto Gordon; Harry L. Hathaway; Eileen
Hutto-Powers; Douglas Johnson; Garrett P. Kreditor.
EIN: 954181302
Selected grants: The following grants were reported
in 2003.
$60,000 to Five Acres, Altadena, CA. For school
building conversion.
$60,000 to Hillsides, Pasadena, CA. For Expounds
A Vision capital campaign.
$50,000 to Night Basketball and Books, Pasadena,
CA. For after school intervention program.
$50,000 to Union Station Foundation, Pasadena,
CA. For facilities program.
$31,157 to San Marino Schools Foundation, San
Marino, CA. For computer lab.
$30,000 to University of the Pacific, School of
Dentistry, Stockton, CA. For Oral Healthcare
Center.
$15,000 to University of California, School of Social
Work, Berkeley, CA.
$14,000 to Young and Healthy, Pasadena, CA. For
mobile dental lab.
$6,000 to Boy Scouts of America, Los Angeles Area
Council, Los Angeles, CA. For Club Scouts of Los
Angeles (CSLA) Foundation.

694
Hutton Foundation
26 W. Anapamu, 4th Fl.
Santa Barbara, CA 93101 (805) 957-4740
Contact: Pam Hamlin, Exec. Dir.
FAX: (805) 957-4743;
E-mail: info@huttonfoundation.org; URL: http://
www.huttonfoundation.org

Established in 1980.
Donor: Betty L. Hutton Trust.
Foundation type: Independent foundation.
Financial data (yr. ended 12/31/05): Assets,
$75,840,869 (M); gifts received, $3,070,428;
expenditures, $3,333,928; qualifying distributions,
$3,323,428; giving activities include $2,253,950
for 201 grants (high: $200,000; low: $500), and
$658,849 for 3 loans/program-related
investments.

Purpose and activities: To provide funding to
community-based nonprofit organizations
throughout Santa Barbara County.
Fields of interest: Arts; Education; Health care;
Human services; Children/youth, services; Family
services; Community development.
Type of support: General/operating support; Annual
campaigns; Capital campaigns; Building/
renovation; Equipment; Endowments; Scholarship
funds; Program-related investments/loans.
Limitations: Giving limited to Santa Barbara County,
CA. No support for religious or political
organizations. No grants to individuals.
Publications: Annual report.
Application information: When submitting a request
please use the Foundation Roundtable Common
Grant Application Form. A copy of the Common Grant
Application Form may be found on the Nonprofit
Support Center of Santa Barbara County Web site at
http://www.nscsb.org. Application form required.
Initial approach: Letter (no more than 3 pages).
Faxes will not be accepted
Copies of proposal: 1
Deadline(s): Feb. 15 for health, human services
and education, and Sept. 15 for children, youth
and families, arts and culture, and civic and
community services
Board meeting date(s): Annually
Final notification: 6 to 8 weeks
Officers: Thomas C. Parker, Pres.; Susan Parker,
Exec. V.P.; Arlene R. Craig, V.P. and Secy.-Treas.;
Pam Hamlin, Exec. Dir.
Directors: Thomas Parker; Charles O. Slosser; Sam
Tyler.
Number of staff: 3 full-time professional.
EIN: 330779894
Selected grants: The following grants were reported
in 2004.
$114,260 to Nonprofit Support Center, Santa
Barbara, CA.
$51,985 to Santa Barbara Museum of Natural
History, Santa Barbara, CA.
$47,000 to Recording for the Blind and Dyslexic,
Santa Barbara, CA.
$38,334 to Santa Barbara Maritime Museum,
Santa Barbara, CA.
$29,350 to Chapman University, Orange, CA.
$25,000 to Unity Shoppe, Santa Barbara, CA.
$14,300 to Santa Barbara High School, Santa
Barbara, CA.
$11,000 to Childrens Creative Project, Santa
Barbara, CA.
$10,000 to El Adobe Corporation, Santa Barbara,
CA.
$7,500 to Community Partners in Caring, Santa
Maria, CA.

695
Ingold Family Foundation ✧
c/o Richard F. Levering
P.O. Box 400
Fallbrook, CA 92088-0400

Established in 1991 in CA.
Donors: Randall Ingold; Robert F. Ingold; Arlyne A.
Ingold; Ingold Family 5 Year Charitable Lead Trust.
Foundation type: Independent foundation.
Financial data (yr. ended 4/30/05): Assets,
$1,260,379 (M); gifts received, $224,000;
expenditures, $381,055; qualifying distributions,
$363,772; giving activities include $364,805 for 44
grants (high: $85,000; low: $50).

Purpose and activities: Giving primarily for children
and youth development.
Fields of interest: Secondary school/education;
Hospitals (general); Recreation; Boys & girls clubs;
Human services; Children/youth, services;
Federated giving programs.
Limitations: Applications not accepted. Giving
primarily in Fallbrook, CA, and Colorado Springs, CO.
No grants to individuals.
Application information: Contributes only to
pre-selected organizations.
Trustees: Otis P. Heald; Arlyne A. Ingold; Richard G.
Ingold.
EIN: 954350558
Selected grants: The following grants were reported
in 2005.
$85,000 to Young Life, Colorado Springs, CO.
$32,500 to Fallbrook Music Society, Fallbrook, CA.
$15,000 to California Center for the Arts,
Escondido, CA.
$10,500 to Special Olympics of San Diego, San
Diego, CA.

696
The Intuit Foundation ✧
P.O. Box 7850
Mountain View, CA 94039
E-mail: communityimpact@intuit.com; URL: http://
www.intuit.com/about_intuit/philanthropy

Established in 2002 in CA.
Donor: Intuit Inc.
Foundation type: Company-sponsored foundation.
Financial data (yr. ended 3/31/05): Assets,
$1,027,591 (M); gifts received, $1,822,026;
expenditures, $1,026,989; qualifying distributions,
$790,720; giving activities include $125,441 for
121 grants (high: $6,000; low: $210), and
$665,279 for employee matching gifts.
Purpose and activities: The foundation supports
organizations involved with education, health,
children and youth, human services, community
development, and economically disadvantaged
people. Special emphasis is directed toward
programs designed to foster economic
empowerment.
Fields of interest: Education; Health care; Children/
youth, services; Human services, financial
counseling; Human services; Economic
development; Community development, small
businesses; Community development; Economically
disadvantaged.
International interests: Canada.
Type of support: Employee matching gifts; Employee
volunteer services; Program development.
Limitations: Applications not accepted. Giving
primarily in Tucson, AZ, Mountain View, San Diego,
and Sebastopol, CA, Denver, CO, Stamford, CT,
Boston, MA, Reno, NV, Plano, TX, Fredericksburg,
VA, and Edmonton, Canada. No support for religious
organizations, political or labor organizations,
private foundations, or discriminatory organizations.
No grants to individuals, or for fundraising events or
sponsorships, advertising, souvenir journals, or
dinner programs, or conferences, exhibits, or
academic research.
Application information: Contributes only to
pre-selected organizations.
Directors and Directors: Janelle Wolf, Secy.; Bridget
Smith, Treas.; Susan Mason, Program Mgr.;
Stephen M. Bennett; Scott D. Cook; Robert B.
Henske.
EIN: 470860921

Type of support: General/operating support; Program development; Seed money; Research; Program evaluation; Matching/challenge support.
Limitations: Giving limited to Orange County, CA. No support for religious organizations for religious purposes. No grants to individuals; or to support sporting events or sports-related activities, or to solicit donations or sponsor fund-raising events.
Publications: Informational brochure (including application guidelines); Multi-year report (including application guidelines).
Application information: Foundation prefers to receive funding requests via URL: http://www.grantpartners.net. Application form required.
   Initial approach: Letter or via grantpartners Web site
   Copies of proposal: 1
   Deadline(s): None
   Board meeting date(s): Regularly
Officers and Directors:* David G. Sills,* Chair.; Timothy L. Strader,* Vice-Chair.; Edward B. Kacic, C.E.O. and Pres.; Carol A. Hoffman,* Secy.; John C. Gaffney,* Treas.; Gary H. Hunt, Tr. Emeritus; Jack W. Peltason, Ph.D.; Gerald B. Sinykin, M.D.
Number of staff: 2 full-time professional; 1 full-time support.
EIN: 330141599

700

The William G. Irwin Charity Foundation ◇
711 Russ Bldg.
235 Montgomery St.
San Francisco, CA   94104-2996   (415) 362-6954
Contact: Michael R. Gorman, Exec. Dir.

Trust established in 1919 in CA.
Donors: Fannie M. Irwin†; Helene Irwin Fagan†.
Foundation type: Independent foundation.
Financial data (yr. ended 12/31/04): Assets, $114,410,673 (M); expenditures, $3,353,567; qualifying distributions, $2,904,053; giving activities include $2,668,000 for 21 grants (high: $300,000; low: $5,000; average: $30,000–$300,000).
Purpose and activities: Support for charitable uses, including medical research and other scientific uses designed to promote or improve the physical condition of humankind; support also for hospitals, cultural programs, education, and social service agencies.
Fields of interest: Arts; Higher education; Education; Hospitals (general); Medical research, institute; Human services.
Type of support: General/operating support; Capital campaigns; Building/renovation; Equipment; Land acquisition; Research.
Limitations: Giving limited to CA and HI. No grants to individuals, or for scholarships.
Application information: Applicants must wait twelve months between proposal submissions. Application form not required.
   Initial approach: Letter or proposal
   Copies of proposal: 1
   Deadline(s): Approximately 4-6 weeks prior to board meeting
   Board meeting date(s): Approximately every 2 months
Officers and Trustees:* William Lee Olds, Jr., Pres.; Jane Olds Bogart,* V.P.; Michael R. Gorman, Exec. Dir.; William L. Olds III; Anthony O. Zanze; James F. Zanze.
Number of staff: 2 full-time professional.
EIN: 946069873

Selected grants: The following grants were reported in 2003.
$1,000,000 to Sacred Heart Cathedral Preparatory High School, San Francisco, CA. For capital campaign.
$500,000 to Saint Hilary School, Tiburon, CA. For new gymnasium.
$295,000 to Saint Elizabeth Elementary School, Oakland, CA. For renovations.
$250,000 to Bay Area Discovery Museum, Sausalito, CA. For capital campaign.
$250,000 to Cate School, Carpinteria, CA. For faculty housing.
$250,000 to Dunn School, Los Olivos, CA. For renovations.
$250,000 to Saint Lukes Hospital, San Francisco, CA. For x-ray machine.
$200,000 to French American International School, San Francisco, CA. For capital campaign.
$200,000 to Mid-Pacific Institute, Honolulu, HI. For math/science complex.
$197,000 to Saint Elizabeth High School, Oakland, CA. For electrical upgrade.

701

Isen Family Foundation ◇ ☆
c/o Gordon, Fishburn & Schlossmann
11812 San Vicente Blvd., Ste. 200
Los Angeles, CA   90049

Established in 1999 in IL.
Donor: Stuart Isen.
Foundation type: Independent foundation.
Financial data (yr. ended 12/31/05): Assets, $285,460 (M); expenditures, $316,771; qualifying distributions, $315,650; giving activities include $315,650 for 22 grants (high: $121,000; low: $250).
Fields of interest: Performing arts, music; Arts; Higher education; Health organizations; Jewish agencies & temples.
Limitations: Applications not accepted. Giving primarily in Los Angeles, CA. No grants to individuals.
Application information: Contributes only to pre-selected organizations.
Officers: Stuart Isen, Pres.; Simone Isen, Secy.-Treas.
Director: Theodore Netzky.
EIN: 364291202
Selected grants: The following grants were reported in 2005.
$121,000 to Simon Wiesenthal Center, Los Angeles, CA.
$15,000 to Los Angeles Opera Company, Los Angeles, CA.
$7,500 to Chabad of California, Los Angeles, CA.
$5,500 to Los Angeles Philharmonic Association, Los Angeles, CA.
$2,500 to United States Holocaust Memorial Museum, DC.
$1,500 to American Friends of the Israel Museum, Beverly Hills, CA.

702

The Ishiyama Foundation ◇
465 California St., Ste. 800
San Francisco, CA   94104
Contact: Margaret Raffin, Secy.

Established in 1968 in CA.

Donor: George S. Ishiyama.
Foundation type: Independent foundation.
Financial data (yr. ended 12/31/04): Assets, $44,626,069 (M); expenditures, $2,446,709; qualifying distributions, $2,444,763; giving activities include $2,073,800 for 32 grants (high: $500,000; low: $1,000).
Purpose and activities: Giving primarily to higher and secondary educational institutions, hospitals, and health care, family and social services, and to an environmental foundation.
Fields of interest: Museums (science/technology); Higher education; Education; Environment; Hospitals (general); Human services; Family services; Foundations (private grantmaking).
International interests: Japan.
Limitations: Giving primarily in CA; some giving in Japan. No grants to individuals.
Application information: Application form not required.
   Deadline(s): None
Officers: Setsuko Ishiyama, Pres.; Patsy Ishiyama, V.P.; Margaret Raffin, Secy.; Nelson Ishiyama, Treas.
EIN: 941659373
Selected grants: The following grants were reported in 2004.
$500,000 to International University of Japan, San Francisco, CA.
$350,000 to Maui Arts and Cultural Center, Kahului, HI.
$210,000 to California Academy of Sciences, San Francisco, CA.
$100,000 to Palo Alto Medical Center, Palo Alto, CA.
$100,000 to Trout Unlimited, San Francisco, CA.
$50,000 to National Fish and Wildlife Foundation, Southwest Regional Office, San Francisco, CA.

703

Issa Family Foundation ◇ ☆
P.O. Box 1388
Vista, CA   92083

Established in 1999 in CA.
Donors: Darrell E. Issa; Katharine S. Issa.
Foundation type: Independent foundation.
Financial data (yr. ended 12/31/05): Assets, $15,029,651 (M); expenditures, $570,654; qualifying distributions, $498,660; giving activities include $482,000 for 46 grants (high: $125,000; low: $500).
Purpose and activities: Giving primarily for human services.
Fields of interest: Higher education; Higher education, university; Boys & girls clubs; Human services; Economics; Christian agencies & churches.
Limitations: Applications not accepted. Giving on a national basis. No grants to individuals.
Application information: Contributes only to pre-selected organizations.
Officers: Darrell E. Issa, C.E.O.; Katharine S. Issa, C.F.O.
EIN: 330834068
Selected grants: The following grants were reported in 2003.
$30,300 to Childrens Hospital Los Angeles, Los Angeles, CA.
$15,000 to Boys and Girls Club of Vista, Vista, CA.
$15,000 to San Diego Blood Bank Foundation, San Diego, CA.
$10,000 to ANGELS Foster Family Agency, San Diego, CA.

697
Audrey & Sydney Irmas Charitable Foundation ✧

16830 Ventura Blvd., Ste. 364
Encino, CA 91436-2797 (818) 382-3313
Contact: Robert J. Irmas, Admin.
FAX: (818) 382-3315; E-mail: robirm@aol.com

Established in 1986 in CA.
Donors: Sydney M. Irmas†; Audrey M. Irmas.
Foundation type: Independent foundation.
Financial data (yr. ended 12/31/04): Assets, $24,976,161 (M); expenditures, $2,675,377; qualifying distributions, $2,090,096; giving activities include $2,057,413 for 109 grants (high: $517,500; low: $100).
Purpose and activities: Support primarily for Jewish issues and housing programs; support also for a hospital, higher education, the arts, and inner city issues.
Fields of interest: Arts; Higher education; Hospitals (general); Substance abuse, services; Housing/shelter, development; Human services; Jewish federated giving programs.
Type of support: Emergency funds; Professorships; Program-related investments/loans.
Limitations: Giving primarily in Los Angeles, CA.
Application information: Application form not required.
  Initial approach: Letter
  Copies of proposal: 1
  Deadline(s): None
  Board meeting date(s): Quarterly
Officer and Trustees:* Robert J. Irmas,* Admin.; Audrey M. Irmas.
Number of staff: 1 full-time professional; 1 part-time support.
EIN: 954030813
Selected grants: The following grants were reported in 2004.
$125,833 to Wilshire Boulevard Temple, Los Angeles, CA. 3 grants: $87,500, $5,000, $33,333
$40,000 to Bard College, Annandale on Hudson, NY. 2 grants: $15,000, $25,000
$15,000 to New Israel Fund, DC.
$10,000 to Operation USA, Los Angeles, CA.
$7,500 to Casa Loma College, Van Nuys, CA.
$5,000 to Phoenix Art Museum, Phoenix, AZ.
$1,500 to Santa Monica Museum of Art, Santa Monica, CA.

698
The James Irvine Foundation ▼ ✧

575 Market St., Ste. 3400
San Francisco, CA 94105 (415) 777-2244
Contact: Kelly Martin, Grants Mgr.
FAX: (415) 777-0869; Southern CA office: 865 S. Figueroa St., Ste. 2308, Los Angeles, CA 90017-5430, tel.: (213) 236-0552, FAX: (213) 236-0537; URL: http://www.irvine.org

Incorporated in 1937 in CA.
Donor: James Irvine†.
Foundation type: Independent foundation.
Financial data (yr. ended 12/31/05): Assets, $1,610,480,320 (M); gifts received, $2,000; expenditures, $88,844,858; qualifying distributions, $79,890,545; giving activities include $72,878,220 for grants, $244,836 for employee matching gifts, and $202,935 for foundation-administered programs.

Purpose and activities: The mission of the foundation is to expand opportunity for the people of CA to participate in a vibrant, successful, and inclusive society. Giving primarily for the arts, higher education, workforce development, civic culture, sustainable communities, and children, youth, and families.
Fields of interest: Arts, multipurpose centers/programs; Arts, cultural/ethnic awareness; Arts, folk arts; Arts councils; Performing arts; Performing arts centers; Performing arts, dance; Performing arts, ballet; Performing arts, theater; Performing arts, orchestra (symphony); Performing arts, opera; Higher education; Higher education, college; Higher education, university; Higher education reform; Employment, training; Youth development, centers/clubs; Youth development, services; Civil rights, race/intergroup relations; Community development, management/technical aid; Community development, neighborhood development; Economic development; Nonprofit management; Philanthropy/voluntarism, association; Philanthropy/voluntarism, administration/regulation; Philanthropy/voluntarism, information services; Foundations (public); Foundations (community); Voluntarism promotion; Philanthropy/voluntarism; Public policy, research.
Type of support: General/operating support; Program development; Seed money; Technical assistance; Program evaluation; Employee matching gifts; Matching/challenge support.
Limitations: Giving limited to CA. No support for agencies receiving substantial government support. No grants to individuals.
Publications: Annual report; Newsletter.
Application information: Application form required.
  Initial approach: Online application form
  Copies of proposal: 1
  Deadline(s): Jan. and July 5
  Board meeting date(s): Mar., June, Oct., and Dec.
  Final notification: 8 to 10 weeks
Officers and Directors:* Gary B. Pruitt,* Chair.; Patricia Salas Pineda,* Vice-Chair.; James E. Canales,* C.E.O. and Pres.; Martha S. Campbell, V.P., Progs.; John R. Jenks, Corp. Secy.-Treas. and C.I.O.; Greg Avis; Jane Carney; Paula A. Cordeiro; Frank H. Cruz; David Mas Masumoto; Regina L. Muehlhauser; Molly Munger; Toby Rosenblatt; Steven A. Schroeder; Isaac Stein; Peter J. Taylor; Lydia M. Villarreal.
Number of staff: 21 full-time professional; 12 full-time support.
EIN: 941236937
Selected grants: The following grants were reported in 2005.
$3,500,000 to MDRC, New York, NY. For Student Support Partnership Integrating Resources and Education (SSPIRE), regranting initiative to support efforts to integrate instructional reforms with student support services that improve academic achievement of low-income students, payable over 3 years.
$2,500,000 to New America Foundation, DC. To continue California-based Irvine Fellows Program, which supports public policy writers and thinkers who are addressing California's most pressing issues, payable over 3 years.
$1,750,000 to MPR Associates, Berkeley, CA. For initiative to provide support to innovative and effective career and technical education programs in California high schools, payable over 1.50 years.
$580,000 to Williams Group, Grand Rapids, MI. To create learning community for California

community foundations participating in Communities Advancing the Arts and to create communications products to support local arts donor education and cultivation strategies, payable over 2.75 years.
$575,000 to Community Foundation of the Napa Valley, Napa, CA. To implement plans for growth, payable over 3 years.
$545,000 to California Institute of the Arts, Valencia, CA. To support Community Arts Partnership Pre-College Mentoring Program to improve high school retention and to provide opportunities for training in arts and future educational and professional development, payable over 3 years.
$200,000 to Asian Pacific American Legal Center of Southern California, Los Angeles, CA. To promote voting access for eligible immigrant voters and those with limited-English proficiency through poll monitoring, trainings for community organizations, and analyses of related policies and practices, payable over 2 years.
$195,000 to FSG Social Impact Advisors, San Francisco, CA. To conduct pilot study of three community foundations to help them identify strategic choices for sustainable growth, based on the Interactive Strategy Model, as part of the Community Foundations Initiative II.
$75,000 to San Francisco Art Institute, San Francisco, CA. For improved governance, organizational structure, and communications, as part of Fund for Leadership Advancement.
$31,000 to Alliance for California Traditional Arts, Fresno, CA. For transition of California Traditional Arts Advancement Program, statewide regranting program for folk arts and traditional culture in California, from Fund for Folk Culture to Alliance for California Traditional Arts, payable over 2 years.

699
Irvine Health Foundation

18301 Von Karman Ave., Ste. 440
Irvine, CA 92612-0120
Contact: Edward B. Kacic, Pres.
FAX: (949) 253-2962; E-mail: info@ihf.org; URL: http://www.ihf.org

Established in 1985 in CA; converted from Irvine Medical Center, Inc.
Donor: Irvine Medical Center, Inc.
Foundation type: Independent foundation.
Financial data (yr. ended 6/30/05): Assets, $24,388,471 (M); expenditures, $2,191,956; qualifying distributions, $1,400,355; giving activities include $898,020 for 58 grants (high: $200,000; low: $1,000).
Purpose and activities: The foundation's goal is to improve the health—consisting of the physical, mental, and emotional well-being—of the residents of Orange County, CA. It is focused on promoting health and wellness, insuring the availability of accessible, quality, health-related services, working in the area of health policy, and supporting research designed to develop new knowledge in areas related to health.
Fields of interest: Health care; Substance abuse, services; Mental health/crisis services; Health organizations, association; AIDS; Alcoholism; Biomedicine; Medical research, institute; Nutrition; Residential/custodial care, hospices; Aging, centers/services; Women; Homeless.

$10,000 to Starlight Starbright Childrens Foundation, Los Angeles, CA.

$5,000 to American Foreign Policy Council, DC.

$5,000 to American Task Force for Lebanon, DC.

$5,000 to Horton Walk-San Diegos Walk of Fame, San Diego, CA.

$5,000 to Las Patronas, La Jolla, CA.

$3,000 to Vision of Children, San Diego, CA.

704

It Takes a Family Foundation, Inc. ✧

3912 Calle Ariana
San Clemente, CA   92672

Established in 1997 in CA.

Donors: Kim C. Bengard; Thomas P. Bengard; Tyler T. Bengard.

Foundation type: Independent foundation.

Financial data (yr. ended 12/31/05): Assets, $1,371,654 (M); expenditures, $553,960; qualifying distributions, $553,885; giving activities include $547,977 for 48 grants (high: $140,000; low: $100).

Purpose and activities: Giving primarily for family services, Christian organizations and churches, health associations, as well as for education and human services.

Fields of interest: Education; Health organizations, association; Athletics/sports, school programs; Human services; Children/youth, services; Family services; Social sciences, public policy; Christian agencies & churches.

Limitations: Applications not accepted. Giving primarily in CA; some funding nationally. No grants to individuals.

Application information: Contributes only to pre-selected organizations.

Officers and Directors:* Thomas P. Bengard,* Pres.; Kim C. Bengard,* Secy.-Treas.; Tyler T. Bengard.

EIN: 582276414

Selected grants: The following grants were reported in 2003.

$75,000 to Family Research Council, DC. For general support.

$75,000 to Saddleback Valley Community Church, Mission Viejo, CA. For general support.

$20,000 to University of California, Berkeley, CA. For general support.

$8,000 to Gateways to Better Education, Lake Forest, CA. For general support.

$5,000 to Womens Resource Network, Escondido, CA. For general support.

$2,500 to Orange County Rescue Mission, Tustin, CA. For general support.

$100 to Boys and Girls Club of the South Coast Area, San Clemente, CA. For general support.

$100 to Pittsburg State University, Pittsburg, KS. For general support.

$100 to Wheaton College, Wheaton, IL. For general support.

$50 to UCLA Foundation, Los Angeles, CA. For general support.

705

Jack in the Box Foundation ✧

c/o Tax Dept.
9330 Balboa Ave.
San Diego, CA   92123-1516
URL: http://www.jackinthebox.com/foundation/

Established in 1998 in CA.

Donors: Foodmaker, Inc.; Jack in the Box Inc.

Foundation type: Company-sponsored foundation.

Financial data (yr. ended 10/2/05): Assets, $741,307 (M); gifts received, $1,449,244; expenditures, $930,841; qualifying distributions, $930,841; giving activities include $741,439 for 114 grants (high: $200,000; low: $10), and $75,595 for 105 grants to individuals (high: $1,500; low: $145).

Purpose and activities: The foundation supports organizations involved with education, youth development, human services, children, and economically disadvantaged people. Special emphasis is directed toward programs designed to help children in need.

Fields of interest: Education; Big Brothers/Big Sisters; Youth development; Human services; Federated giving programs; Children; Economically disadvantaged.

Type of support: Matching/challenge support; General/operating support; Program development; Sponsorships; Grants to individuals.

Limitations: Applications not accepted. Giving on a national basis, with some emphasis on San Diego, CA.

Application information: Contributes only through employee-related emergency grants and to pre-selected organizations.

Officers and Directors:* Carlo Cetti,* Pres.; Kathy Kovacevich,* Secy.; Hal Sachs,* Treas.; Mike Bamrick; Gladys DeClouet; Terry Graham; Linda Lang; Brian Luscomb; James Spencer; Eric Tunquist.

EIN: 330776076

Selected grants: The following grants were reported in 2003.

$200,000 to Big Brothers Big Sisters of America, Philadelphia, PA.

$84,074 to Big Brothers and Sisters of San Diego County, San Diego, CA. 3 grants: $46,074, $16,000, $22,000

$50,000 to Monarch School Project, San Diego, CA.

$25,000 to Catholic Big Brothers Big Sisters, Los Angeles, CA.

$20,579 to Big Brothers/Big Sisters of Greater Los Angeles, Los Angeles, CA.

$10,000 to San Diego Hospice and Palliative Care, San Diego, CA.

$9,405 to Big Brothers Big Sisters of Greater Houston, Houston, TX.

$9,086 to United Way of San Diego County, San Diego, CA.

706

The Ann Jackson Family Foundation ✧

P.O. Box 5580
Santa Barbara, CA   93150-5580
(805) 969-2258
Contact: Palmer G. Jackson, Pres.

Established in 1978.

Donors: Ann G. Jackson; The Ann Jackson Family Charitable Trust.

Foundation type: Independent foundation.

Financial data (yr. ended 5/31/05): Assets, $47,674,127 (M); expenditures, $2,578,342; qualifying distributions, $2,292,010; giving activities include $2,290,550 for 184 grants (high: $200,000; low: $1,000).

Purpose and activities: Giving primarily for the arts, education, health care, children, youth and social services, including services for people who are blind, particularly children.

Fields of interest: Museums; Performing arts; Performing arts centers; Historic preservation/ historical societies; Arts; Elementary/secondary education; Higher education; Education; Animals/ wildlife; Hospitals (general); Medical care, rehabilitation; Health care; Health organizations, association; Food banks; Recreation; Boys & girls clubs; Human services; YM/YWCAs & YM/YWHAs; Children/youth, services; Homeless, human services; Community development; Christian agencies & churches; Disabilities, people with; Blind/visually impaired.

Type of support: General/operating support; Capital campaigns; Building/renovation.

Limitations: Giving primarily in Santa Barbara, CA. No grants to individuals.

Application information:

Initial approach: Letter

Deadline(s): None

Officers and Directors:* Palmer G. Jackson,* Pres.; Charles A. Jackson,* V.P.; James H. Jackson,* V.P.; Palmer G. Jackson, Jr.,* Secy.; William L. Jackson,* C.F.O.

EIN: 953367511

Selected grants: The following grants were reported in 2003.

$152,000 to Yale University, New Haven, CT. For general support.

$138,100 to Stanford University, Stanford, CA. For general support.

$132,000 to Santa Barbara Cottage Hospital, Santa Barbara, CA. For general support and for systems technology and equipment.

$114,000 to Santa Barbara Museum of Natural History, Santa Barbara, CA. For general support.

$100,000 to Girls Inc. of Greater Santa Barbara, Santa Barbara, CA. For general support.

$85,000 to Braille Institute, Santa Barbara, CA. For general support.

$66,000 to Laguna Blanca School, Santa Barbara, CA. For general support.

$53,000 to Dunn School, Los Olivos, CA. For general support and building fund.

$45,000 to Endowment for Youth Committee, Santa Barbara, CA. For Yes I Can Program.

$35,000 to Direct Relief International, Santa Barbara, CA. For general support.

707

Jacobs Engineering Foundation ✧

P.O. Box 7084
Pasadena, CA   91109-7084

Established in 1978.

Donor: Jacobs Engineering Group Inc.

Foundation type: Company-sponsored foundation.

Financial data (yr. ended 12/31/03): Assets, $0 (M); gifts received, $402,799; expenditures, $402,799; qualifying distributions, $402,799; giving activities include $402,764 for 153 grants (high: $30,000; low: $50).

Purpose and activities: The foundation supports organizations involved with education, health, human services, children and youth services, and community development.

Fields of interest: Higher education; Education; Hospitals (general); Health organizations, association; Human services; Children/youth, services; Community development; Federated giving programs.

Limitations: Applications not accepted. Giving on a national basis.
Application information: Contributes only to pre-selected organizations.
Officers and Directors:* Joseph J. Jacobs,* Pres.; Noel G. Watson,* V.P.; William C. Markley III,* Secy.; John W. Prosser, Jr.,* Treas.; Nazim G. Thawerbhoy, Cont.
EIN: 953195445

708
Jacobs Family Foundation, Inc. ▼
5160 Federal Blvd.
San Diego, CA 92105-5429 (619) 527-6161
Contact: Jennifer Vanica, C.E.O. and Pres.
FAX: (619) 527-6162; URL: http://www.jacobsfamilyfoundation.org/

Established in 1988 in CA.
Donors: Joseph J. Jacobs, Ph.D.‡; Violet J. Jacobs; Norman Hapke; Valerie Jacobs Hapke.
Foundation type: Independent foundation.
Financial data (yr. ended 6/30/05): Assets, $33,697,371 (M); gifts received, $102,210; expenditures, $7,955,590; qualifying distributions, $7,323,128; giving activities include $3,287,386 for 79 grants (high: $2,000,000; low: $26; average: $1,000–$75,000), $8,773 for 12 employee matching gifts, $15,000 for 4 in-kind gifts, and $229,000 for 2 loans/program-related investments.
Purpose and activities: The foundation invests in and with communities to seed or strengthen projects and programs that build the capacity of under-invested neighborhoods, through neighborhood-based programs, resident-led initiatives, projects that test new ideas, and activities that build community spirit. This is done through five funds: the Partnership Fund, Community-Building Strategies Fund, Spirit of the Diamond Fund, and the Jabara Scholarship Fund.
Fields of interest: Education; Human services; Children/youth, services; Family services; Community development; Economically disadvantaged.
Type of support: General/operating support; Endowments; Program development; Conferences/seminars; Seed money; Scholarship funds; Technical assistance; Consulting services; Employee matching gifts; Matching/challenge support.
Limitations: Giving in CA, with primary emphasis in the southeastern San Diego communities of Valencia Park, Lincoln Park, Webster, Emerald Hills, Chollas View, Mountain View, Mount Hope, North Encanto, Oak Park, and South Encanto. No support for medical services, religious purposes, athletics, or the arts. No grants to individuals, or for medical research.
Publications: Annual report (including application guidelines); Financial statement; Grants list; Informational brochure; Newsletter.
Application information: Applicants are encouraged to contact the foundation before applying. See foundation Web site for full application guidelines and requirements for each grant fund. Application form not required.
Initial approach: Telephone call
Copies of proposal: 1
Deadline(s): None
Board meeting date(s): Quarterly
Final notification: 30 days

Officer and Directors:* Jennifer Vanica,* C.E.O. and Pres.; Norman F. Hapke, Jr.; Valerie Jacobs Hapke; Margaret E. Jacobs; Violet Jabara Jacobs.
Number of staff: 4 full-time professional; 2 full-time support.
EIN: 954187111
Selected grants: The following grants were reported in 2005.
$2,216,500 to Jacobs Center for Nonprofit Innovation, San Diego, CA. 3 grants: $2,000,000 (For outreach, training, and capacity building), $66,500 (For matching grant), $150,000 (For Spirit of Diamond Mini-Grants).
$80,000 to Pazzaz, San Diego, CA. For Tutorial Program.
$75,000 to Diamond Community Development Corporation, San Diego, CA. For general operating support of Diamond Business Improvement District.
$75,000 to Elementary Institute of Science, San Diego, CA. For capital campaign and organizing.
$60,000 to All Congregations Together, San Diego, CA. For general operating support.
$36,000 to Southern Sudanese Community Center of San Diego, San Diego, CA. For after-school tutoring program.
$35,000 to Association of Community Organizations for Reform Now (ACORN), San Diego, CA. For community organizing in Diamond neighborhoods.
$25,000 to Polytechnic University, Brooklyn, NY. For Promise Scholarships.

709
James Family Foundation ◇
(formerly C.M.J. Private Foundation)
410 Jessie St., No. 710
San Francisco, CA 94103
Contact: Laura James, Dir.

Established in 1996 in CA.
Donor: Christopher M. James.
Foundation type: Independent foundation.
Financial data (yr. ended 11/30/04): Assets, $9,233,021 (M); expenditures, $1,825,272; qualifying distributions, $1,757,139; giving activities include $762,500 for 16 grants (high: $250,000; low: $2,000), $327,042 for 10 grants to individuals (high: $45,360; low: $15,597), and $509,000 for 2 employee matching gifts.
Purpose and activities: Scholarships for attending an out of state university, Tulane University, Boston University, New York University, University at Berkeley, Stanford University, University of Virginia, MIT, or any Ivy League school.
Fields of interest: Libraries/library science; Education; Environment, land resources; Hospitals (general); Family services.
Type of support: Continuing support; Scholarships—to individuals.
Limitations: Giving primarily in CA and WY.
Application information: Include high school transcript, 2 teacher recommendations, 1 recommendation from a community member, and a signed scholarship agreement form.
Initial approach: Brief personal statement
Officers and Directors:* Christopher M. James,* Pres.; Nathaniel A. Morrison,* Secy.; Laura Anne James,* Treas.; Bradley G. James.
Number of staff: 1 part-time professional.
EIN: 133864227
Selected grants: The following grants were reported in 2004.

$2,441,030 to Tulane University, New Orleans, LA. 3 grants: $1,911,030, $30,000, $500,000
$250,000 to San Francisco Museum of Modern Art, San Francisco, CA.
$30,000 to Museum of Modern Art, New York, NY. 2 grants: $15,000 each
$25,000 to American University, DC.
$25,000 to Public Art Fund, New York, NY.
$19,957 to Columbia University, New York, NY.
$2,610 to New York University, New York, NY.

710
J. W. and Ida M. Jameson Foundation ◇
P.O. Box 397
Sierra Madre, CA 91025-0397 (626) 355-6973
Contact: Les M. Huhn, Pres.

Incorporated in 1956 in CA.
Donor: Ida M. Jameson†.
Foundation type: Independent foundation.
Financial data (yr. ended 6/30/05): Assets, $14,193,149 (M); expenditures, $1,000,399; qualifying distributions, $700,000; giving activities include $700,000 for 40 grants (high: $50,000; low: $5,000).
Purpose and activities: Emphasis on higher education, including theological seminaries, hospitals and medical research, cultural programs, and youth agencies; grants also for Protestant and Roman Catholic church support.
Fields of interest: Arts; Higher education; Theological school/education; Hospitals (general); Health care; Medical research, institute; Youth, services; Protestant agencies & churches; Roman Catholic agencies & churches.
Type of support: General/operating support; Research.
Limitations: Giving primarily in CA.
Application information: Application form not required.
Initial approach: Proposal
Copies of proposal: 1
Deadline(s): Feb. 1
Board meeting date(s): Mid-March
Final notification: Apr. 30
Officers and Directors:* Les M. Huhn,* Pres.; Bill B. Betz,* V.P. and Secy.; Fred L. Leydorf,* V.P.; Pauline Vetrovec,* Treas.
EIN: 956031465
Selected grants: The following grants were reported in 2005.
$50,000 to Union Station Foundation, Pasadena, CA.
$40,000 to University of Michigan, Ann Arbor, MI.
$25,000 to Reason Foundation, Los Angeles, CA.
$20,000 to Descanso Gardens Guild, La Canada, CA.
$20,000 to House Ear Institute, Los Angeles, CA.
$10,000 to Friends of the Cultural Center, Palm Desert, CA.
$10,000 to Maranatha High School, Sierra Madre, CA.
$10,000 to Maryvale, Rosemead, CA.
$10,000 to Phi Delta Theta Educational Foundation, Oxford, OH.
$5,000 to Assistance League of Pasadena, Pasadena, CA.

711
Jams Foundation ✧ ☆
1920 Main St., Ste. 300
Irvine, CA 92614 (415) 774-2648
Contact: Jay Folberg, Exec. Dir.
E-mail: info@jamsadr.com; Mailing Address: 2
Embarcadero Ctr., Ste. 1500, San Francisco, CA
94111; URL: http://www.jamsadr.com/j_found/
j_foundation.asp

Established in 2001 in CA.
Donor: Daniel Weinstein.
Foundation type: Independent foundation.
Financial data (yr. ended 12/31/05): Assets,
$302,685 (M); gifts received, $395,608;
expenditures, $360,091; qualifying distributions,
$316,669; giving activities include $316,669 for
grants.
Purpose and activities: Provides financial
assistance for conflict resolution initiatives with
national impact; also shares its dispute resolution
experience and judicial expertise for the benefit of
the public interest.
Fields of interest: Courts/judicial administration;
Dispute resolution; Community development, public
policy; Community development, public education;
Law/international law.
Application information: The foundation generally
funds only invited proposals. However, if an
organization believes it has a project or proposal of
interest to the foundation, it may submit a letter of
inquiry of no more than 5 pages, in accordance with
the guidelines detailed on the foundation's Web
site.
Officers and Directors:* Warren Knight,* Chair.; Jay
Welsh, Secy.; Julie Sager, Treas.; Jay Folberg,*
Exec. Dir.; Charles Bakaly; Coleman Fannin; Lester
Levy; Steve Price; James Sullivan; Zara Trowbridge.
EIN: 912147141

712
Elizabeth Bixby Janeway Foundation ✧
c/o Shari Leinwand
2029 Century Park E., Ste. 4000
Los Angeles, CA 90067-3026

Established in 1966 in CA.
Donor: Elizabeth Bixby Janeway‡.
Foundation type: Independent foundation.
Financial data (yr. ended 9/30/05): Assets,
$37,009,693 (M); expenditures, $2,177,222;
qualifying distributions, $1,886,803; giving
activities include $1,885,000 for 49 grants (high:
$250,000; low: $500).
Purpose and activities: Giving primarily for
education as well as for the arts, including the
historical preservation of an adobe building, and a
performing arts center.
Fields of interest: Performing arts; Performing arts,
orchestra (symphony); Arts; Elementary/secondary
education; Higher education; Law school/
education; Libraries/library science; Education;
Recreation, camps; Boys & girls clubs; Family
services; Foundations (community).
Limitations: Applications not accepted. Giving
primarily in southern CA. No grants to individuals.
Application information: Contributes only to
pre-selected organizations.
Officers and Directors:* Preston B. Hotchkis,*
Chair.; John F. Hotchkis,* Pres.; Shari Leinwand,*
Secy.; Sarah H. Ketterer,* C.F.O.
EIN: 952466561

Selected grants: The following grants were reported
in 2005.
$200,000 to Music Center Foundation, Los
Angeles, CA. 2 grants: $100,000 each
$125,000 to Santa Barbara Center for the
Performing Arts, Santa Barbara, CA.
$125,000 to Santa Barbara Cottage Hospital, Santa
Barbara, CA.
$100,000 to Hoover Institution on War, Revolution
and Peace, Stanford, CA.
$90,000 to Laura Bush Foundation for Americas
Libraries, DC.
$50,000 to Teach for America, New York, NY.
$35,000 to Los Angeles County Museum of Art, Los
Angeles, CA.
$30,000 to Planned Parenthood of Los Angeles, Los
Angeles, CA.
$25,000 to Accelerated School, Los Angeles, CA.

713
The Jang Foundation ✧
300 E. State St., Ste. 600
Redlands, CA 92373 (909) 307-9521
Contact: Kathy Shavoley, C.F.O

Established in 2002 in CA.
Donors: G. David Jang, M.D.; Kathy Shavoley.
Foundation type: Independent foundation.
Financial data (yr. ended 12/31/05): Assets,
$3,743,074 (M); gifts received, $432,950;
expenditures, $1,411,650; qualifying distributions,
$1,382,457; giving activities include $1,257,100
for 20 grants (high: $250,000; low: $1,000).
Purpose and activities: Giving primarily for
Seventh-Day Adventist higher education, churches,
and ministries; some giving also for children, family,
and social services.
Fields of interest: Elementary/secondary
education; Higher education; Education; Human
services; Salvation Army; Protestant agencies &
churches.
Limitations: Giving primarily in CA.
Application information: Contact foundation Mgr. to
obtain information form.
  Initial approach: Letter or telephone
  Deadline(s): None
Officers: G. David Jang, M.D., Pres.; Kathy Shavoley,
C.F.O.
Directors: Lawrence T. Geraty, Ph.D.; Myung K.
Hong; Lucy Jung.
EIN: 753080666

714
The JANS Foundation ✧
14357 Horizon Ct.
Poway, CA 92064

Established in 2002 in CA.
Donors: Jan E. Nielsen; J&D Family Foundation.
Foundation type: Independent foundation.
Financial data (yr. ended 12/31/05): Assets,
$19,763,045 (M); gifts received, $8,804;
expenditures, $1,134,916; qualifying distributions,
$974,634; giving activities include $948,241 for 4
grants (high: $400,000; low: $10,000).
Fields of interest: Higher education; Human
services; International relief; Roman Catholic
agencies & churches.
Limitations: Applications not accepted. Giving
primarily in San Diego, CA, Rochester, NY, and
Marietta, OH. No grants to individuals.

Application information: Contributes only to
pre-selected organization.
Trustee: Jan E. Nielsen.
EIN: 306040216

715
**The Janssen/Lagorio Family
  Foundation** ✧ ☆
2771 E. French Camp Rd.
Manteca, CA 95336

Established in 1999 in CA.
Donors: Kathleen Janssen; Dean Janssen; Evelyn
Lagorio.
Foundation type: Independent foundation.
Financial data (yr. ended 2/28/06): Assets,
$1,654,796 (M); gifts received, $11,000;
expenditures, $499,222; qualifying distributions,
$489,774; giving activities include $489,774 for 40
grants (high: $204,600; low: $100).
Fields of interest: Education; Hospitals (general);
Housing/shelter, temporary shelter; Federated
giving programs; Christian agencies & churches.
Limitations: Applications not accepted. Giving
primarily in CA. No grants to individuals.
Application information: Contributes only to
pre-selected organizations.
Trustees: Dean Janssen; Kathleen Janssen.
EIN: 912071872

716
Adalyn Jay Foundation ✧
60 Riordan Pl.
Menlo Park, CA 94025

Established in 1998 in CA.
Donors: William J. Ruehle; Judi A. Ruehle.
Foundation type: Independent foundation.
Financial data (yr. ended 12/31/04): Assets,
$3,839,296 (M); expenditures, $542,655;
qualifying distributions, $541,252; giving activities
include $539,850 for 3 grants (high: $418,500;
low: $41,850).
Purpose and activities: Giving primarily for
children's health services, as well as for higher
education.
Fields of interest: Higher education, college; Health
care; Children/youth, services.
Limitations: Applications not accepted. Giving
primarily in CA; some funding also in Meadville, PA.
No grants to individuals.
Application information: Contributes only to
pre-selected organizations.
Directors: Michelle A. Buck; Judi A. Ruehle; William
J. Ruehle.
EIN: 770487631

717
Jerome Foundation ✧
541 E. Chapman Ave., Ste. B
Orange, CA 92866 (714) 538-2393
Contact: Sherrie Spray

Incorporated in 1956 in CA.
Donors: James M. Andreoli; Frank Jerome;
members of the Jerome family; Baker Commodities,
Inc.
Foundation type: Independent foundation.
Financial data (yr. ended 12/31/05): Assets,
$10,367,656 (M); gifts received, $60,000;

expenditures, $366,531; qualifying distributions, $340,985; giving activities include $340,985 for 50 grants (high: $83,360; low: $1,000).

Purpose and activities: Giving primarily to an affiliated foundation; giving also for hospitals, youth, and education.

Fields of interest: Education; Hospitals (general); Medical research, institute; Human services; YM/YWCAs & YM/YWHAs; Foundations (private grantmaking).

International interests: Philippines.

Limitations: Giving primarily in southern CA. No grants to individuals.

Publications: Annual report.

Application information: Application form not required.

Deadline(s): None

Officers: James M. Andreoli, Pres.; Mitchell Ebright, Secy.-Treas.

Directors: Andrew Andreoli; Anthony Andreoli; James A. Andreoli; Richard Jerome; Maxine Taylor.

EIN: 956039063

Selected grants: The following grants were reported in 2005.

$83,360 to Jerome Foundation, Saint Paul, MN.
$15,000 to YMCA of Greater Whittier, Whittier, CA.
$5,000 to Children of the Night, Van Nuys, CA.
$5,000 to Lilac Blind Foundation, Spokane, WA.
$5,000 to Union Rescue Mission, Los Angeles, CA.
$5,000 to Whittier College, Whittier, CA.
$5,000 to Woodbury University, Burbank, CA.
$2,500 to Bishop Mora Salesian High School, Los Angeles, CA.
$2,500 to Resurrection School, Los Angeles, CA.

718

George Frederick Jewett Foundation ✧

The Russ Bldg.
235 Montgomery St., Ste. 612
San Francisco, CA 94104 (415) 421-1351
Contact: Toni Bermudez, Grants Coord.
FAX: (415) 421-0721; E-mail: tfbjewetttf@aol.com

Trust established in 1957 in MA.

Donor: George Frederick Jewett‡.

Foundation type: Independent foundation.

Financial data (yr. ended 12/31/04): Assets, $44,770,144 (M); expenditures, $1,791,521; qualifying distributions, $1,698,790; giving activities include $1,470,000 for 71 grants (high: $50,000; low: $400).

Purpose and activities: To carry on the charitable interests of the donor to stimulate, encourage, and support activities of established, voluntary, nonprofit organizations which are of importance to human welfare. Interests include arts and culture, music, education, libraries, environment (with particular emphasis on land conservation, oceanographic studies and population), protection of environment, including population issues and scientific research, health and social services.

Fields of interest: Performing arts, music; Arts; Libraries (public); Education; Environment, land resources; Environment, beautification programs; Environmental education; Environment; Health care; Human services; Science, research; Marine science.

Type of support: General/operating support; Building/renovation; Equipment; Land acquisition; Program development; Seed money; Research; Technical assistance; Matching/challenge support.

Limitations: Giving primarily in San Francisco, CA, Spokane, WA, and in geographic areas of which

trustees and family members have knowledge. No support for private or operating foundations or organizations which receive support from public tax funds. No grants to individuals, or for emergency funds (except for disaster relief), purchase of tickets or support of fundraising events; no loans.

Publications: Application guidelines; Annual report (including application guidelines); Program policy statement.

Application information: Formal application by invitation only; unsolicited requests for funds not considered. Application form required.

Initial approach: Letter of inquiry
Copies of proposal: 1
Deadline(s): Quarterly: Mar., June, Sept., and Dec.
Board meeting date(s): No later than mid-Dec.

Officer and Trustees:* George Frederick Jewett, Jr.,* Chair.; Margaret Jewett Greer; William Hershey Greer, Jr.; Lucille McIntyre Jewett.

Number of staff: 1 part-time professional; 1 full-time support.

EIN: 046013832

Selected grants: The following grants were reported in 2003.

$100,000 to Monterey Bay Aquarium, Monterey, CA. For 20th Anniversary Fund for renovations, endowment, and visitor programs.
$40,000 to Inland Northwest Land Trust, Spokane, WA. For general support.
$40,000 to Planned Parenthood of Spokane, Spokane, WA. For communications systems upgrade.
$12,000 to Spokane Art School, Spokane, WA. For general operating support.
$10,000 to San Francisco Free Clinic, San Francisco, CA. For general operating support.
$10,000 to San Francisco Performing Arts Library and Museum, San Francisco, CA. For operating support.
$10,000 to Teach for America, Emeryville, CA. For general support.
$7,500 to Project Open Hand, San Francisco, CA. For general support.
$5,000 to Allegro Baroque and Beyond, Spokane, WA. For general support.
$5,000 to Support for Parents Overcoming Challenges (SPOC) of Spokane, Spokane, WA. For operating support.

719

JG Foundation ▼ ✧

9663 Santa Monica Blvd., Ste. 690
Beverly Hills, CA 90210
Contact: James Gipson, Pres.

Established in 1998 in CA.

Donor: James Gipson.

Foundation type: Independent foundation.

Financial data (yr. ended 5/31/06): Assets, $28,381,389 (M); expenditures, $3,232,540; qualifying distributions, $3,150,000; giving activities include $3,150,000 for 4 grants (high: $2,000,000; low: $50,000).

Purpose and activities: Giving primarily for higher education and to eye institutes.

Fields of interest: Higher education; Eye research.

Limitations: Applications not accepted. Giving primarily in CA. No grants to individuals.

Application information: Contributes only to pre-selected organizations.

Officers: James Gipson, Pres.; Michael Kromm, Secy. and C.F.O.

EIN: 954693758

Selected grants: The following grants were reported in 2005.

$6,000,000 to Harvard University, Cambridge, MA. 2 grants: $1,000,000 (For grant to Business School in Boston), $5,000,000.
$1,000,000 to Johns Hopkins University, Wilmer Ophthalmological Institute, Baltimore, MD. For research.
$150,000 to Doheny Eye Institute, Los Angeles, CA. For research.
$50,000 to Harvard-Westlake School, North Hollywood, CA.
$25,000 to Hoover Institution on War, Revolution and Peace, Stanford, CA.

720

JL Foundation ✧

333 S. Hope St., Ste. 52
Los Angeles, CA 90071-1406 (213) 486-9369

Established in 1988 in CA as a public charity; became a private, independent foundation in 2000.

Donors: Jon B. Lovelace; Lillian P. Lovelace.

Foundation type: Independent foundation.

Financial data (yr. ended 10/31/05): Assets, $21,992,391 (M); expenditures, $8,355,924; qualifying distributions, $8,312,762; giving activities include $8,311,281 for 49 grants (high: $1,385,000; low: $900).

Purpose and activities: Support primarily for the arts, including arts education, public radio, and the fine and performing arts; funding also for education, animals and wildlife, and health and human services.

Fields of interest: Arts education; Media, radio; Performing arts, orchestra (symphony); Arts; Higher education; Teacher school/education; Education; Animals/wildlife; Autism research; Human services; Foundations (community); Philanthropy/voluntarism.

Type of support: General/operating support; Annual campaigns; Capital campaigns; Building/renovation; Program development; Matching/challenge support.

Limitations: Applications not accepted. Giving primarily in states where trustees reside, with emphasis on CA, MN, and VT.

Application information: Contributes only to pre-selected organizations.

Officers and Trustees:* Jon B. Lovelace,* Pres.; Catherine M. Ward,* Secy.-Treas.; Robert J. Denison; Douglas Freeman; William H. Kling; James B. Lovelace; Jeffrey K. Lovelace; Lillian P. Lovelace; Robert W. Lovelace; John D. Maguire; Gail L. Neale; Stefanie Powers.

EIN: 954129163

Selected grants: The following grants were reported in 2005.

$1,455,000 to William Holden Wildlife Foundation, Los Angeles, CA. 2 grants: $1,385,000, $70,000
$1,385,000 to American Public Media Group, Saint Paul, MN.
$1,035,000 to Claremont Graduate University, Claremont, CA.
$475,000 to Claremont University Consortium, Claremont, CA. 2 grants: $125,000, $350,000
$385,000 to Visiting Nurse Association, Burlington, VT.

$70,000 to Colorado Springs School, Colorado Springs, CO.

$70,000 to Idyllwild Arts Foundation, Idyllwild, CA.

$37,500 to Minnesota Public Radio, Saint Paul, MN.

721

J. Stanley and Mary W. Johnson Family Foundation ✧ ☆

2280 University Dr.
Newport Beach, CA   92660-3327

Established in 1998 in CA.
Donor: Mary W. Johnson†.
Foundation type: Independent foundation.
Financial data (yr. ended 12/31/05): Assets, $8,620,710 (M); expenditures, $423,670; qualifying distributions, $364,185; giving activities include $359,450 for 15 grants (high: $250,000; low: $100).
Fields of interest: Education.
Limitations: Applications not accepted. Giving primarily in Orange County, CA. No grants to individuals.
Application information: Contributes only to pre-selected organizations.
Officers: Donald P. Johnson, Pres.; Robert W. Johnson, V.P. and Secy.-Treas.
EIN: 330809657
Selected grants: The following grants were reported in 2004.
$100,000 to California Institute of Technology, Pasadena, CA.
$30,000 to Saint Margarets Episcopal School, San Juan Capistrano, CA.
$6,000 to Scripps College, Claremont, CA.
$5,000 to Claremont McKenna College, Claremont, CA.
$4,000 to Stanford University, Stanford, CA. 2 grants: $1,000 (For Stanford Fund), $3,000 to Graduate School of Business.
$3,000 to Laguna Playhouse, Laguna Beach, CA.
$1,750 to Share Our Selves (SOS) Corporation, Costa Mesa, CA.
$1,000 to Philharmonic Society of Orange County, Irvine, CA.
$250 to Midland School, Los Olivos, CA.

722

Carl W. Johnson Foundation ✧

5750 Wilshire Blvd., Ste. 590
Los Angeles, CA   90036-3697   (323) 634-2400
Contact: Susan J. Ollweiler

Established in 1993 in CA.
Donor: Carl W. Johnson.
Foundation type: Independent foundation.
Financial data (yr. ended 12/31/05): Assets, $7,386,391 (M); expenditures, $485,942; qualifying distributions, $380,000; giving activities include $380,000 for 15 grants (high: $100,000; low: $10,000; average: $10,000–$25,000).
Purpose and activities: Giving primarily for education, health care, and aid to individuals with developmental needs.
Fields of interest: Health care, research; Hospitals (general); Medical research, institute; Disabilities, people with.
Limitations: Giving primarily in southern CA. No grants to individuals.
Application information: Application form not required.

Initial approach: Proposal
Deadline(s): Aug. 1
Officers: Wallace D. Franson, Pres.; David D. Watts, Secy.; Jess S. Morgan, Treas.
Directors: Christopher D. Montan; Kathleen Nelson.
EIN: 954438839
Selected grants: The following grants were reported in 2005.
$100,000 to University of California at Berkeley Foundation, Berkeley, CA.
$40,000 to California State University, Long Beach, CA.
$25,000 to Childrens Hospital Los Angeles, Los Angeles, CA.
$25,000 to Chrysalis Center, Santa Monica, CA.
$25,000 to City of Hope, Los Angeles, CA.
$25,000 to Painted Turtle, Santa Monica, CA.
$25,000 to UNICEF, New York, NY.
$20,000 to Para Los Ninos, Los Angeles, CA.
$12,500 to Canine Companions for Independence, Oceanside, CA.
$10,000 to Junior Blind of America, Los Angeles, CA.

723

Charles and Ann Johnson Foundation ✧

c/o Franklin Resources, Inc.
1 Franklin Pkwy., Bldg. 920, 4th Fl.
San Mateo, CA   94403-1906
Contact: Charles B. Johnson, Tr.

Established in 1986 in CA.
Donors: Ann L. Johnson; Charles B. Johnson.
Foundation type: Independent foundation.
Financial data (yr. ended 12/31/05): Assets, $104,601,310 (M); gifts received, $4,210,260; expenditures, $3,008,850; qualifying distributions, $3,000,179; giving activities include $3,000,144 for 92 grants (high: $1,009,470; low: $500).
Purpose and activities: Giving primarily for arts and culture, higher education, health associations, and human services.
Fields of interest: Museums; Historic preservation/historical societies; Higher education; Education; Botanical gardens; Health organizations, association; Boys & girls clubs; Human services; American Red Cross.
Limitations: Giving primarily in CA. No grants to individuals.
Application information: Application form not required.
Deadline(s): None
Trustees: Ann L. Johnson; Charles B. Johnson.
EIN: 943026398
Selected grants: The following grants were reported in 2004.
$605,091 to California Academy of Sciences, San Francisco, CA.
$208,845 to Ethel Walker School, Simsbury, CT.
$130,020 to Hoover Institution on War, Revolution and Peace, Stanford, CA.
$110,250 to Cornell University, Ithaca, NY.
$33,885 to Yale University, New Haven, CT.
$15,000 to American Museum of Natural History, New York, NY.
$11,000 to Bryn Mawr College, Bryn Mawr, PA.
$10,000 to Herlong Cathedral School, Detroit, MI.
$5,000 to California State Protocol Foundation, Sacramento, CA.
$1,000 to Thunderbird Lodge Preservation Society, Incline Village, NV.

724

The Franklin and Catherine Johnson Foundation ✧

2100 Geng Rd., Ste. 200
Palo Alto, CA   94303
Contact: Tarah Evans, Exec. Dir.

Established in 2001 in CA.
Donors: Catherine Holman Johnson; Franklin Pitcher Johnson, Jr.
Foundation type: Independent foundation.
Financial data (yr. ended 12/31/04): Assets, $541,059 (M); expenditures, $1,018,995; qualifying distributions, $1,018,429; giving activities include $1,011,250 for 26 grants (high: $300,000; low: $5,000).
Fields of interest: Education; Youth, services.
Limitations: Applications not accepted. Giving primarily in Santa Clara, CA. No support for political or religious organizations. No grants to individuals.
Application information: Unsolicited requests for funds not accepted.
Board meeting date(s): Quarterly
Officers: Franklin Pitcher Johnson, Jr., Chair.; Catherine Holman Johnson, C.E.O. and Pres.; William R. Daniels, Secy. and C.F.O.
Directors: Leslie Evers; Franklin L. Johnson.
Number of staff: 1 full-time professional.
EIN: 770573195
Selected grants: The following grants were reported in 2004.
$60,000 to Fresh Lifelines for Youth (FLY), San Jose, CA. For Legal eagle programs at Alta Vista and EPA.
$52,500 to Girls For A Change, San Jose, CA. For new Program Manager position.
$30,000 to Boys and Girls Clubs of the Peninsula, Menlo Park, CA. For new athletic league.
$30,000 to Entrepreneurs Foundation, Sunnyvale, CA. For full-time Community Manager position.
$20,000 to Lenders for Community Development, San Jose, CA. For IDA accounts for EPA families.
$10,000 to Collective Roots Garden Project, Palo Alto, CA. For professional development and strategic planning.
$10,000 to College Track, East Palo Alto, CA. For ASAP program.
$10,000 to Community School of Music and Arts, Mountain View, CA. For general operating support.
$10,000 to East Bay Community Foundation, Future Skills Foundation, Oakland, CA.
$5,000 to A Safe Place, Oakland, CA. For general operating support.

725

Walter S. Johnson Foundation

525 Middlefield Rd., Ste. 160
Menlo Park, CA   94025   (650) 326-0485
Contact: Pancho Chang, Exec. Dir.
FAX: (650) 326-4320; E-mail: info@wsjf.org;
URL: http://www.wsjf.org

Established in 1968 in CA.
Donor: Walter S. Johnson†.
Foundation type: Independent foundation.
Financial data (yr. ended 12/31/04): Assets, $104,475,953 (M); expenditures, $5,172,151; qualifying distributions, $4,592,542; giving activities include $3,892,554 for 120 grants (high: $250,000; low: $400; average: $3,000–$50,000).

Purpose and activities: Giving primarily to help improve youth and educational services in Northern California and Washoe County, Nevada.

Fields of interest: Education, reform; Elementary/secondary education; Graduate/professional education; Youth development, services; Children/youth, services; Family services; Leadership development.

Type of support: General/operating support; Program development; Seed money; Technical assistance; Program-related investments/loans.

Limitations: Giving primarily in northern CA and Washoe County, NV. No support for religious organizations for sectarian purposes or for private schools. No grants to individuals, or for annual campaigns, deficit financing, memorial funds, capital or endowment funds, matching gifts, scholarships, fellowships, publications, or conferences.

Publications: Application guidelines; Financial statement; Grants list; Multi-year report.

Application information: The foundation does not accept capital requests. Application form not required.

Initial approach: Letter of inquiry
Copies of proposal: 1
Deadline(s): None
Board meeting date(s): Feb. May, July and Nov.
Final notification: 20 days

Officers and Trustees:* Gloria Eddie,* Pres.; Sandra Bruckner,* 1st V.P.; Marcus Johnson III, 2nd V.P.; Hathily Winston, Secy.; Scott Shackelton,* Treas.; Pancho Chang, Exec. Dir.; Gloria Jeneal Eddie; Peter Lillevand.

Number of staff: 2 full-time professional; 1 part-time professional; 1 full-time support.

EIN: 237003595

Selected grants: The following grants were reported in 2004.

$346,500 to Youth Law Center, San Francisco, CA.

$225,000 to San Mateo, County of, Human Services Agency, San Mateo, CA.

$200,000 to Santa Clara University, Santa Clara, CA.

$156,000 to Youth Guidance Center Improvement Committee, San Francisco, CA.

$150,000 to People Acting in Community Together, San Jose, CA.

$140,000 to California School-Age Consortium, San Francisco, CA.

$110,000 to On The Move, Walnut Creek, CA.

$100,000 to Court Appointed Special Advocates (CASA) of Sonoma County, Santa Rosa, CA.

$83,500 to San Francisco State University, Bay Area Academy, San Francisco, CA.

$75,000 to Linking Education and Economic Development in Sacramento (LEEDS), Sacramento, CA. For Youth Services Provider Network, promoting positive youth development, learning, networking and resource sharing.

726
Rupert H. Johnson, Jr. Foundation ◇
1 Franklin Pkwy.
Bldg. 920, 4th Fl.
San Mateo, CA 94403
Contact: Rupert H. Johnson, Jr., Tr.

Established in 1992 in CA.
Donor: Rupert H. Johnson, Jr.
Foundation type: Independent foundation.
Financial data (yr. ended 12/31/05): Assets, $74,270,826 (M); gifts received, $38,984,000;

expenditures, $324,386; qualifying distributions, $322,835; giving activities include $322,800 for 32 grants (high: $75,000; low: $300).

Purpose and activities: Giving primarily for higher education; funding also for health, human services, and federated giving programs.

Fields of interest: Museums (specialized); Higher education; Education; Hospitals (general); Health organizations; Human services; Foundations (community); Federated giving programs; Christian agencies & churches.

Limitations: Giving primarily in CA and VA. No grants to individuals.

Application information:
Initial approach: Letter
Trustee: Rupert H. Johnson, Jr.
EIN: 943170047

Selected grants: The following grants were reported in 2004.

$3,029,854 to Washington and Lee University, Lexington, VA.

$5,000 to Lawrenceville School, Lawrenceville, NJ.

727
Jolson Family Foundation ◇ ☆
600 Montgomery St., Ste. 1100
San Francisco, CA 94111

Established in 2003 in CA.
Donor: Joseph A. Jolson.
Foundation type: Independent foundation.
Financial data (yr. ended 12/31/05): Assets, $5,382,580 (M); expenditures, $459,745; qualifying distributions, $371,000; giving activities include $371,000 for 11 grants (high: $100,000; low: $500).

Fields of interest: Human services; American Red Cross; Jewish federated giving programs.

Limitations: Applications not accepted. Giving primarily in CA, with emphasis on Marin County. No grants to individuals.

Application information: Contributes only to pre-selected organizations.

Officers: Joseph A. Jolson, Pres. and Treas.; Kathleen Jolson, Secy.

EIN: 200391079

728
The Fletcher Jones Foundation ▼ ◇
(formerly The Jones Foundation)
523 W. 6th St., Ste. 301
Los Angeles, CA 90014 (213) 943-4646
Contact: Christine Sisley, Treas. and Exec. Dir.
FAX: (213) 943-4648; URL: http://www.fletcherjonesfdn.org

Established in 1969 in CA.
Donor: Fletcher Jones†.
Foundation type: Independent foundation.
Financial data (yr. ended 12/31/05): Assets, $165,421,475 (M); expenditures, $8,559,317; qualifying distributions, $7,117,283; giving activities include $6,886,000 for 88 grants (high: $1,000,000; low: $1,000; average: $5,000–$500,000).

Purpose and activities: Support primarily for private colleges and universities, particularly those in CA (over 96 percent of available funds).

Fields of interest: Higher education.

Type of support: Capital campaigns; Building/renovation; Equipment; Endowments;

Professorships; Fellowships; Scholarship funds; Matching/challenge support.

Limitations: Giving primarily in CA. No support for K-12 schools; political campaigns or organizations. No grants to individuals, or for operating funds, deficit financing, conferences, seminars, workshops, travel exhibits, surveys, or projects supported by government agencies; no loans.

Publications: Annual report (including application guidelines); Financial statement; Grants list.

Application information: Please visit the foundation's Web site for more detailed application procedures. Application form not required.

Initial approach: Prior to any written submission, it is advisable to consult with the foundation's Exec. Dir. in order to discuss a tentative proposal and to determine suitability of the intended request
Copies of proposal: 1
Deadline(s): 6 weeks prior to board meetings
Board meeting date(s): Feb., May, Sept., and Dec.
Final notification: 3 to 6 months

Officers and Trustees:* Peter K. Barker,* Pres.; Samuel P. Bell,* V.P.; Robert F. Erburu,* V.P.; Houston I. Flournoy, V.P.; Parker S. Kennedy,* V.P.; Robert W. Kummer, Jr.,* V.P.; Daniel E. Lungren,* V.P.; Michael D. McKee,* V.P.; Donald E. Nickelson,* V.P.; John P. Pollock,* V.P.; Dickinson C. Ross,* V.P.; John "Jack" D. Pettker, Secy. and Genl. Counsel; Christine Sisley, Treas. and Exec. Dir.

Number of staff: 1 part-time professional; 1 part-time support.

EIN: 237030155

Selected grants: The following grants were reported in 2005.

$1,000,000 to Boy Scouts of America, Los Angeles Area Council, Los Angeles, CA. For renovations and naming of Camp Pollock at Lake Arrowhead.

$500,000 to Chapman University, Orange, CA. To establish The Fletcher Jones Endowed Scholarship Fund.

$500,000 to Loma Linda University, Loma Linda, CA. Toward construction of new North Academic Complex.

$500,000 to Mount Saint Marys College, Los Angeles, CA. To augment The Fletcher Jones Foundation Endowed Scholarship Fund.

$500,000 to Pitzer College, Claremont, CA. Toward Phase I of Residential Life Project.

$500,000 to Thomas Aquinas College, Santa Paula, CA. Toward construction of new building to house faculty offices, student services, and visitor center.

$500,000 to University of San Diego, San Diego, CA. Toward construction of new School of Leadership and Education Sciences building.

$500,000 to Westmont College, Santa Barbara, CA. Toward endowment for Institute of Liberal Arts.

$300,000 to Concordia University, Irvine, CA. Toward construction of education, business, and technology center.

$250,000 to Mills College, Oakland, CA. Toward construction of state-of-the-art Natural Sciences Building.

729
Kenneth Jonsson Family Foundation ◇
2277 Fair Oaks Blvd., No. 290
Sacramento, CA 95825 (916) 921-7000
Contact: Michael Jonsson, Secy.

Donor: The Jonsson Foundation.

Foundation type: Independent foundation.
Financial data (yr. ended 12/31/05): Assets, $3,852,764 (M); expenditures, $473,667; qualifying distributions, $463,645; giving activities include $463,645 for 27 grants (high: $166,311; low: $500).
Purpose and activities: Funding primarily for cancer research, education, arts and culture, and human services.
Fields of interest: Museums (science/technology); Arts; Education; Cancer research; Crime/violence prevention, child abuse; Children/youth, services.
Limitations: Giving primarily in CA. No grants to individuals.
Application information:
Initial approach: Telephone or letter
Deadline(s): None
Officers: Margaret Anne Sedillo, Pres.; Michael Jonsson, Secy.; Kenneth Jonsson, Treas.
Trustees: David Mark Jonsson; Diane Jonsson; Robert Erik Jonsson.
EIN: 953836985

730

The Jim Joseph Foundation
1 Embarcadero Ctr., 30th Fl.
San Francisco, CA 94111 (415) 788-0900
Contact: Chip Edelsberg, Exec. Dir.

Established in 1987 in CA.
Donor: Jim Joseph†.
Foundation type: Independent foundation.
Financial data (yr. ended 12/31/05): Assets, $33,740 (M); expenditures, $529,780; qualifying distributions, $500,000; giving activities include $500,000 for 2 grants (high: $400,000; low: $100,000).
Purpose and activities: To promote excellence in Jewish day school education; funding also for a Jewish theological seminary.
Fields of interest: Theological school/education; Education; Jewish agencies & temples.
Type of support: General/operating support; Program development; Fellowships.
Limitations: Applications not accepted. Giving on a national basis, primarily along the East Coast. No support for capital expansion or development, or for teachers' salaries or benefits. No grants to individuals.
Publications: Newsletter.
Application information: Contributes only to pre-selected organizations.
Directors: Charles "Chip" Edelsberg, Exec. Dir.; Phyllis Cook; Alvin T. Levitt; Jack Slomovic.
EIN: 943057607
Selected grants: The following grants were reported in 2004.
$300,000 to Partnership for Excellence in Jewish Education, Boston, MA. For general support.
$125,000 to Curriculum Initiative, New York, NY.
$100,000 to Rabbi Isaac Elchanan Theological Seminary, New York, NY.
$25,000 to Coalition for the Advancement of Jewish Education, New York, NY. For Early Childhood Department.

731

The Joyard Foundation ◇
2056 Lyans Dr.
La Canada Flintridge, CA 91011-1537

Established in 1997 in CA.
Donor: C. Hilyard Barr.
Foundation type: Independent foundation.
Financial data (yr. ended 12/31/03): Assets, $1,188,195 (M); gifts received, $502,500; expenditures, $411,391; qualifying distributions, $411,300; giving activities include $100,000 for 1 grant, and $305,048 for 10 grants to individuals (high: $55,508).
Fields of interest: Higher education; Hospitals (general).
Limitations: Applications not accepted. Giving primarily in CA.
Application information: Contributes only to pre-selected organizations.
Officers: Hilary Joyce Barr Parker, C.E.O.; Courtland Barr III, Secy.; C. Hilyard Barr, C.F.O.
EIN: 954636168

732

The Don & Maxine Judkins Family Foundation ◇ ☆
6851 McDivitt Dr., Apt. B
Bakersfield, CA 93311-2004
Contact: Don Judkins, Mgr.

Established in 2002 in CA.
Donors: Don Judkins; Donavan Judkins.
Foundation type: Independent foundation.
Financial data (yr. ended 12/31/05): Assets, $4,296,174 (M); gifts received, $1,000,000; expenditures, $568,241; qualifying distributions, $554,480; giving activities include $554,480 for grants.
Fields of interest: Human services; Christian agencies & churches.
Application information:
Initial approach: Letter
Deadline(s): Mar. 31
Officers: Don Judkins, Mgr.; Maxine Judkins, Mgr.
Directors: Donavan Judkins; Greg Judkins.
EIN: 460476311

733

The June Foundation ◇
5150 Overland Ave.
Culver City, CA 90230

Established in 1999 in CA.
Donors: Michael Kest; Susanne Kest; Sol Kest.
Foundation type: Independent foundation.
Financial data (yr. ended 12/31/04): Assets, $8,794,576 (M); gifts received, $1,000,000; expenditures, $425,622; qualifying distributions, $418,042; giving activities include $417,000 for 10 grants (high: $392,000; low: $500).
Fields of interest: Jewish federated giving programs; Jewish agencies & temples.
Limitations: Applications not accepted. Giving primarily in NY. No grants to individuals.
Application information: Contributes only to pre-selected organizations.
Officers: Michael Kest, Pres.; Matthew Kest, Secy.
EIN: 954745292

734

The Juniata Foundation, Inc. ◇ ☆
c/o Pitchfork Mgmt., Inc.
1 Huntington Ct.
Napa, CA 94558

Established in 1997 in WY and UT.
Donor: Robert E. Cook.
Foundation type: Independent foundation.
Financial data (yr. ended 12/31/05): Assets, $249,902 (M); gifts received, $694,505; expenditures, $445,339; qualifying distributions, $378,233; giving activities include $378,233 for grants.
Fields of interest: Education, association; Higher education, university; Economic development; Community development.
Limitations: Applications not accepted. Giving on a national basis. No grants to individuals.
Application information: Contributes only to pre-selected organizations.
Directors: Paula J. Brooks; Camberly G. Cook; Chadwick W. Cook; Robert E. Cook.
EIN: 522018882
Selected grants: The following grants were reported in 2004.
$142,659 to Indiana University of Pennsylvania, Indiana, PA.

735

JWS Foundation, Inc. ◇ ☆
19280 Bainter Ave.
Los Gatos, CA 95030

Established in 1998 in CA and NV.
Donor: John Holton.
Foundation type: Independent foundation.
Financial data (yr. ended 12/31/05): Assets, $1,915,340 (M); gifts received, $10,000; expenditures, $355,168; qualifying distributions, $340,883; giving activities include $325,388 for 21 grants (high: $250,000; low: $50).
Fields of interest: Scholarships/financial aid; Environment, natural resources; Housing/shelter, aging; Housing/shelter, repairs; Foundations (community).
Limitations: Applications not accepted. Giving primarily in CA. No grants to individuals.
Application information: Contributes only to pre-selected organizations.
Officers: John Holton, Chair. and Pres.; Wanda Kownacki, V.P. and Secy.-Treas.
EIN: 680405252

736

K.L. Felicitas Foundation
(formerly Kleissner Family Foundation)
P.O. Box 37
Los Gatos, CA 95031-0037
Contact: Lisa Kleissner, Pres.
E-mail: lisa@kleissner.com

Established in 2000 in CA.
Donors: Karl Kleissner; Lisa Kleissner.
Foundation type: Independent foundation.
Financial data (yr. ended 3/31/06): Assets, $10,477,678 (M); expenditures, $544,617; qualifying distributions, $508,635; giving activities include $474,658 for 6 grants (high: $168,000; low: $470), and $50,000 for 1 loan/program-related investment.
Purpose and activities: The foundation supports social entrepreneurs and economic development in developing countries.
Fields of interest: Environment; Community development.
International interests: Brazil; India; Sri Lanka.

Type of support: Technical assistance; Program-related investments/loans; Income development; Curriculum development; Consulting services; General/operating support; Annual campaigns; Capital campaigns; Building/renovation; Endowments; Program development; Seed money; Research.

Limitations: Applications not accepted. Giving primarily in Big Sur, CA ; funding also in South America, India, and Sri Lanka. No support for religious organizations. No grants to individuals.

Application information: Contributes only to pre-selected organizations.

Board meeting date(s): Jan. 2, June 12-13, and Oct. 30-31

Officers: Lisa Kleissner, Pres.; Karl Kleissner, Secy.-Treas.

EIN: 770539366

737
Kabcenell Family Foundation ◇ ☆
557 Cresta Vista Ln.
Portola Valley, CA 94028

Foundation type: Independent foundation.

Financial data (yr. ended 6/30/05): Assets, $10,270,066 (M); expenditures, $630,052; qualifying distributions, $521,078; giving activities include $520,000 for 1 grant.

Fields of interest: Foundations (private grantmaking).

Application information:

Deadline(s): None

Officers: Charlene C. Kabcenell, Pres.; Dirk A. Kabcenell, Secy. and C.F.O.

EIN: 912198779

738
Kahle/Austin Foundation ◇
c/o B. Kahle
513B Simonds Loop
San Francisco, CA 94129

Established in 1997 in WA.

Donors: Mary K. Austin; Brewster L. Kahle.

Foundation type: Independent foundation.

Financial data (yr. ended 12/31/04): Assets, $44,938,886 (M); expenditures, $3,932,517; qualifying distributions, $3,702,300; giving activities include $3,697,600 for 29 grants (high: $2,928,000; low: $100).

Purpose and activities: Giving primarily for human services and an Internet archive.

Fields of interest: Elementary/secondary education; Human services; Telecommunications, electronic messaging services.

Limitations: Applications not accepted. Giving primarily in San Francisco, CA. No grants to individuals.

Application information: Contributes only to pre-selected organizations.

Officers: Brewster L. Kahle, Pres. and Treas.; Mary K. Austin, V.P. and Secy.

EIN: 911816164

Selected grants: The following grants were reported in 2004.

$2,928,000 to Internet Archive, San Francisco, CA. For general support.

$499,000 to Television Archive, San Francisco, CA. For general support.

$136,500 to San Francisco Center for the Book, San Francisco, CA. For general support.

$40,000 to Stay Free Magazine, Brooklyn, NY. For general support.

$5,000 to Oxbow School, Napa, CA.

$1,000 to Minnesota Center for Book Arts, Minneapolis, MN.

$1,000 to Public Knowledge, DC.

739
The Henry J. Kaiser Family Foundation ◇
2400 Sand Hill Rd.
Menlo Park, CA 94025 (650) 854-9400
Contact: Renee Wells, Grants and Contracts Mgr.
FAX: (650) 854-4800; E-mail: rwells@kff.org;
URL: http://www.kff.org
Additional E-mail: pduckham@kff.org; Washington, DC Office: 1330 G St., N.W., Washington, DC 20005, tel.: (202) 347-5270; FAX: (202) 347-5274

Trust established in 1948 in CA; changed status to operating foundation in 1999.

Donors: Bess F. Kaiser†; Henry J. Kaiser†; Henry J. Kaiser, Jr.†; and others.

Foundation type: Operating foundation.

Financial data (yr. ended 12/31/05): Assets, $555,824,985 (M); gifts received, $558,151; expenditures, $56,406,613; qualifying distributions, $40,070,484; giving activities include $740,735 for grants, $158,565 for employee matching gifts, $19,965,691 for foundation-administered programs and $800,000 for loans/program-related investments.

Purpose and activities: The foundation is a highly specialized health policy research and health communications organization that provides timely information on health issues to policymakers, the media, and the public. The foundation operates most of its own programs, often in partnership with other organizations. Its programs concentrate on three primary areas: Health Policy, Media and Public Education, and South Africa.

Fields of interest: Health care, public policy; Reproductive health; Health care; AIDS; Public policy, research; Minorities; Women; Economically disadvantaged.

International interests: South Africa.

Type of support: Program development; Research; Employee matching gifts.

Limitations: Giving limited to CA for the California Grants Program only; and South Africa for the international grants program; other grants nationwide. No support for political organizations. No grants to individuals (except for Media Fellows and consultants), or for construction, equipment, capital funds, annual appeals, fundraising events, ongoing general operating expenses, or indirect costs; generally no funding for direct service type projects.

Publications: Annual report; Informational brochure (including application guidelines).

Application information: The foundation is an operating foundation. Most grants are initiated by the foundation. Very few unsolicited grants are funded. Application form not required.

Initial approach: 2- to 3-page letter

Deadline(s): None

Board meeting date(s): Mar., June, Sept., and Dec.

Final notification: 3 to 6 months

Officers and Trustees:* Sheila P. Burke,* Chair.; Patricia King,* Vice-Chair.; Drew E. Altman, Ph.D.*, C.E.O. and Pres.; Diane Rowland, Sc.D., Exec. V.P.;

Bruce W. Madding, Sr. V.P. and C.F.O.; Matt James, Sr. V.P. and Exec. Dir.; Michael R. Sinclair, Ph.D., Sr. V.P.; Mollyann Brodie, Ph.D.*, V.P.; Gary Claxton,* V.P.; Tina Hoff,* V.P.; Jackie Judd, V.P. and Sr. Advisor, Comms.; Jennifer Kates, V.P.; Larry Levitt, V.P.; Marsha Lille-Blanton,* V.P.; Barbara Lyons, Ph.D., V.P.; Tricia Neuman, Sc.D.*, V.P.; Vicky Rideout,* V.P.; Alina Salganicoff, Ph.D.*, V.P.; Jennifer Drobac; James Jones; Michael Kaiser; David Kessler, M.D.; Charles J. Ogletree, Jr.; Cokie Roberts; Allan Rosenfield, M.D.; David Satcher, M.D.; Donna E. Shalala, Ph.D.

Number of staff: 41 full-time professional; 34 full-time support.

EIN: 946064808

740
The Kalliopeia Foundation
P.O. Box 151020
San Rafael, CA 94915
Contact: Barbara Cushing, Dir., Grantmaking
E-mail: info@kalliopeia.org; URL: http://www.kalliopeia.org

Established in 1997 in CA.

Donor: Jubilee Group.

Foundation type: Independent foundation.

Financial data (yr. ended 12/31/04): Assets, $37,190,036 (M); gifts received, $3,000,000; expenditures, $2,521,677; qualifying distributions, $2,342,955; giving activities include $2,009,614 for 52 grants (high: $560,000; low: $1,000).

Purpose and activities: Giving to programs that nurture the inner life, fostering inner awareness, responsibility, and creativity programs that increase the well-being of the underserved in our communities, drawing upon and nourishing the dignity and potential of each individual and programs that foster an emerging global consciousness of oneness. Funding also for the revitalization and preservation of Native American cultures, languages, as well as Native American youth.

Fields of interest: Offenders/ex-offenders, rehabilitation; Human services; Children/youth, services; Community development.

Type of support: General/operating support; Program development; Conferences/seminars; Research.

Limitations: Giving on a national basis. No support for international organizations. No grants to individuals.

Publications: Informational brochure.

Application information: The foundation does not accept unsolicited proposals. Letters of intent sent by fax or E-mail are not accepted. Nonprofit organizations that align closely with the foundation's mission and meet their evaluation criteria will be sent a request for proposal. See foundation Web site for application guidelines and procedures. Application form not required.

Initial approach: Letter of inquiry (no more than 5 pages) must be sent via mail only

Deadline(s): Letters of inquiry accepted anytime

Board meeting date(s): Feb., May, Aug., and Nov.

Final notification: Letter of inquiry responded to in 6-8 weeks

Officers: Robert Thomson, Pres.; Barbara Sargent, Secy.

Directors: Barbara Cushing; Lisa Kleger.

Number of staff: 2 full-time professional; 1 part-time professional.

EIN: 943270387

Selected grants: The following grants were reported in 2004.

$560,000 to Tides Foundation, San Francisco, CA. For Bayview Hunters Point Youth Program.

$443,750 to First Nations Development Institute, Fredericksburg, VA. For Native Youth Program.

$53,500 to Hopi Foundation, Hotevilla, AZ. For general support.

$40,000 to Bread for the Journey, Mill Valley, CA. For general support.

$40,000 to Sisters Offering Support, Honolulu, HI. 2 grants: $20,000 each (For general support).

$35,000 to ArtSpring, Inc., Florida City, FL. For general support.

$30,000 to Indigenous Language Institute, Santa Fe, NM. For general support.

$25,000 to Project Renewal, New York, NY. For general support.

$18,000 to Marin Interfaith Homeless Chaplaincy, San Rafael, CA. For general support.

741
Kalmanovitz Charitable Foundation ✧ ☆
c/o Bernard Orsi
100 Shoreline Hwy., B-395
Mill Valley, CA   94941   (415) 332-0550

Established in 2001 in CA.
Donor: Lydia Kalmanovitz.
Foundation type: Independent foundation.
Financial data (yr. ended 6/30/05): Assets, $55,612,585 (M); expenditures, $735,969; qualifying distributions, $700,000; giving activities include $700,000 for grants.
Fields of interest: Higher education; Hospitals (general).
Limitations: Applications not accepted. Giving primarily in Moraga and San Francisco, CA. No grants to individuals.
Application information: Contributes only to pre-selected organizations.
Officer and Trustees:* Rev. John LoSchiavo,* Chair.; Conrad Hewitt; Bernard Orsi.
EIN: 946760317

742
Louis J. & Golda I. Kanitz Scholarship Memorial Fund ✧ ☆
c/o Wells Fargo Bank, N.A.
P.O. Box 63954, MAC 0103-179
San Francisco, CA   94163

Established in 1994 in CA.
Foundation type: Independent foundation.
Financial data (yr. ended 12/31/05): Assets, $5,909,526 (M); expenditures, $438,056; qualifying distributions, $388,067; giving activities include $388,067 for grants.
Purpose and activities: Giving primarily for higher education.
Fields of interest: Higher education; Higher education, college (community/junior); Higher education, college; Higher education, university; Business school/education; Medical school/ education; Scholarships/financial aid; Education; Roman Catholic agencies & churches.
Limitations: Applications not accepted. Giving primarily in CA and MI.
Application information: Unsolicited requests for funds not accepted.

Trustee: Wells Fargo Bank, N.A.
EIN: 946665743

743
The Mitchell Kapor Foundation ✧
543 Howard St., 5th Fl.
San Francisco, CA   94117
Environmental Health Program Address: P.O. Box 29209, San Francisco, CA, 94129; URL: http://www.mkf.org

Established in 1997 in MA.
Donor: Mitchell Kapor.
Foundation type: Independent foundation.
Financial data (yr. ended 12/31/03): Assets, $33,033,028 (M); gifts received, $95,875; expenditures, $2,357,375; qualifying distributions, $2,151,025; giving activities include $1,911,263 for 82 grants (high: $500,000; low: $2,500).
Purpose and activities: The foundation's goals are to improve human well-being and sustain healthy ecosystems that support all life on earth. Two of the programs available for funding are: the Environmental Health Program, focusing primarily on the impact of endocrine disrupting chemicals and other fetal contaminants on human health and on biodiversity; the Level Playing Field Program, focusing on understanding and changing the ways in which attitudes, subcultures, and processes within educational and business environments operate in tandem to create barriers to full participation for disenfranchised groups based on race, ethnicity, culture, gender, sexual orientation, and other factors.
Fields of interest: Education; Environment, pollution control; Environment, toxics; Environment, waste management; Environment; Health care, public policy; Human services; Community development.
Limitations: Applications not accepted. No grants to individuals.
Application information: Unsolicited requests for funds not accepted.
Officers: Mitchell Kapor, Chair.; Amy McDevitt, Treas.
EIN: 943330604
Selected grants: The following grants were reported in 2004.

$150,000 to Mozilla Foundation, San Francisco, CA. For general operating support.

$50,000 to American Civil Liberties Union (ACLU) Foundation of Northern California, San Francisco, CA. For general operating support.

$50,000 to Electronic Frontier Foundation, San Francisco, CA. For general support.

$25,000 to Summer Science Program, Ojai, CA. For general support.

$10,000 to Chemical Weapons Working Group, Berea, KY. For general support.

$10,000 to Environmental Health Coalition, National City, CA. For general support.

$10,000 to Farm Worker Pesticide Project, Seattle, WA. For general support.

$10,000 to Tides Center, San Francisco, CA. For general support.

$5,500 to Advocates for Environmental Human Rights, New Orleans, LA. For general support.

$5,000 to Consultative Group on Biological Diversity, San Francisco, CA. For general support.

744
The Karsh Family Foundation ✧
1201 Tower Grove Dr.
Beverly Hills, CA   90210

Established in 1997 in CA.
Donors: Bruce A. Karsh; Martha L. Karsh.
Foundation type: Independent foundation.
Financial data (yr. ended 6/30/05): Assets, $36,543,004 (M); gifts received, $11,281,000; expenditures, $2,173,580; qualifying distributions, $2,140,076; giving activities include $2,140,076 for 32 grants (high: $1,175,000; low: $450).
Fields of interest: Education; Human services; Jewish agencies & temples.
Limitations: Applications not accepted. Giving primarily in CA. No grants to individuals.
Application information: Contributes only to pre-selected organizations.
Trustees: Bruce A. Karsh; Martha L. Karsh.
EIN: 137147287

745
The Katz Family Foundation ✧
9220 Sunset Blvd., Ste. 315
Los Angeles, CA   90069

Established in 2002 in CA.
Donors: Madelyn Katz; Ronald Katz.
Foundation type: Independent foundation.
Financial data (yr. ended 12/31/05): Assets, $18,781,516 (M); expenditures, $1,011,225; qualifying distributions, $989,054; giving activities include $986,054 for 33 grants (high: $785,000; low: $50).
Fields of interest: Higher education; Foundations (community); Jewish federated giving programs; Jewish agencies & temples.
Limitations: Applications not accepted. Giving primarily in Los Angeles, CA. No grants to individuals.
Application information: Contributes only to pre-selected organizations.
Officers: Ronald Katz, Pres. and C.F.O.; Madelyn Katz, V.P. and Secy.
Directors: Randy Katz; Todd Katz.
EIN: 460493067

746
The Marilyn and Jeffrey Katzenberg Foundation ✧
11400 W. Olympic Blvd., Ste. 550
Los Angeles, CA   90064-1551

Established in 1994 in CA.
Donor: Katzenberg Family Trust.
Foundation type: Independent foundation.
Financial data (yr. ended 12/31/04): Assets, $2,056,330 (M); gifts received, $2,328,000; expenditures, $859,139; qualifying distributions, $859,084; giving activities include $859,084 for 18 grants (high: $200,000; low: $250).
Purpose and activities: Giving primarily for education, the arts, and health and social services.
Fields of interest: Higher education; Hospitals (general); Medical research, institute; Human services.
Limitations: Applications not accepted. Giving primarily in CA. No grants to individuals.
Application information: Contributes only to pre-selected organizations.

Officers: Jeffrey Katzenberg, Pres.; Marilyn Katzenberg, V.P.; Arthur D. Emil, Secy.; David Geffen, Treas.
EIN: 954513461

747
The Glorya Kaufman Charitable Foundation ✧
c/o Schwartz, Kales Accountancy Corp.
6310 San Vincente Blvd., Rm. 250
Los Angeles, CA 90048

Donor: Glorya Kaufman.
Foundation type: Independent foundation.
Financial data (yr. ended 6/30/05): Assets, $9,897,159 (M); expenditures, $689,740; qualifying distributions, $686,427; giving activities include $681,351 for 8 grants (high: $450,000; low: $500).
Fields of interest: Performing arts, theater; Higher education; Hospitals (general).
Limitations: Applications not accepted. Giving primarily in CA. No grants to individuals.
Application information: Contributes only to pre-selected organizations.
Trustees: Julian M. Bieber; Glorya Kaufman; Frank Lee.
EIN: 957098023

748
The Kavli Foundation ▼
1801 Solar Drive, Ste. 250
Oxnard, CA 93030
Contact: David Auston, Pres.
FAX: (805) 988-4800; URL: http://www.kavlifoundation.org/

Established in 2000 in CA.
Donor: Fred Kavli.
Foundation type: Independent foundation.
Financial data (yr. ended 11/30/05): Assets, $108,581,938 (M); gifts received, $1,075,000; expenditures, $8,870,244; qualifying distributions, $8,046,253; giving activities include $7,587,500 for 10 grants (high: $1,250,000; low: $62,500).
Purpose and activities: The foundation is dedicated to the goals of advancing science for the benefit of humanity and promoting increased public understanding of and support for scientists and their work. The foundation has selected three areas in which to focus its activities: astrophysics, neuroscience, and nanoscience. An international program of research institutes, prizes, symposia, and endowed professorships is being established to further these goals.
Fields of interest: Education; Science.
Type of support: Professorships; Research.
Limitations: Applications not accepted. Giving primarily on a national basis; some giving internationally. No grants to individuals.
Publications: Informational brochure.
Application information: Participation in the foundation's programs of fellowships, professorships, symposia and prizes is by invitation only; the foundation does not respond to unsolicited proposals.
Officers and Directors:* Fred Kavli,* Chair.; Rockell N. Hankin,* Vice-Chair.; David Auston, Pres.; Thomas E. Everhart; Douglas K. Freeman; Charles Vest.

Number of staff: 2 full-time professional; 1 part-time professional; 3 full-time support.
EIN: 770560142
Selected grants: The following grants were reported in 2004.
$1,250,000 to Delft University of Technology, Delft, Netherlands. For scientific work.
$1,000,000 to Columbia University, New York, NY. For scientific work.
$750,000 to University of California at San Diego, La Jolla, CA. For scientific work.
$750,000 to University of Chicago, Chicago, IL. For scientific work.
$625,000 to Massachusetts Institute of Technology, Cambridge, MA. For scientific work.
$400,000 to California Institute of Technology, Pasadena, CA. For professorship.

749
Kayne Foundation ✧
1800 Ave. of the Stars, Ste. 200
Los Angeles, CA 90067-4204

Established in 1986 in CA.
Donor: Jerry D. Kayne.
Foundation type: Independent foundation.
Financial data (yr. ended 12/31/04): Assets, $9,146,006 (M); gifts received, $715,982; expenditures, $969,897; qualifying distributions, $832,590; giving activities include $832,590 for grants.
Purpose and activities: Giving primarily for education and human services.
Fields of interest: Education; Health organizations, association; Human services; Aging, centers/services; Jewish federated giving programs.
Limitations: Applications not accepted. Giving on a national basis, with emphasis on CA. No grants to individuals.
Application information: Contributes only to pre-selected organizations.
Officers: Suzanne L. Kayne, Pres.; Jerry D. Kayne, C.F.O.
Director: Richard A. Kayne.
EIN: 954124379

750
W. M. Keck Foundation ▼
550 S. Hope St., Ste. 2500
Los Angeles, CA 90071 (213) 680-3833
Contact: Mercedes Talley, Prog. Dir., Science, Engineering, and Liberal Arts; Dr. Dorothy Fleisher, Prog. Dir., Southern California; Roxanne Ford, Prog. Dir., Medical Research; Matesha Varma, Prog. Dir., Science Engineering and Liberal Arts
FAX: (213) 614-0934; E-mail: info@wmkeck.org; URL: http://www.wmkeck.org

Established in 1954 and incorporated in 1959 in DE.
Donor: William M. Keck‡.
Foundation type: Independent foundation.
Financial data (yr. ended 12/31/05): Assets, $1,333,252,000 (M); expenditures, $78,616,374; qualifying distributions, $70,128,386; giving activities include $62,612,262 for 76 grants (high: $3,300,000; low: $10,000; average: $200,000–$1,000,000), and $2,737,995 for 137 employee matching gifts.
Purpose and activities: The foundation continues to adhere to the directions and guidelines established

by its founder, using an interdisciplinary/cross-program or thematic funding approach. The foundation has designated the following specific areas of funding: Early Learning Program, Science and Engineering Program, Liberal Arts Program, Medical Research Program, and the Southern CA Program. Concentration is placed on strengthening studies and programs in accredited colleges and universities, medical schools, and major independent medical research institutions in the areas of earth science, engineering, medical research, and to some extent, other sciences, and the liberal arts. Some consideration, limited to southern CA, is given to organizations in the categories of arts and culture, civic and community affairs, health care, precollegiate education, and early learning.
Fields of interest: Arts; Elementary school/education; Secondary school/education; Higher education; Engineering school/education; Health care; Medical research, institute; Children/youth, services; Residential/custodial care, hospices; Marine science; Physical/earth sciences; Chemistry; Mathematics; Engineering/technology; Computer science; Engineering; Biological sciences; Science.
Type of support: Capital campaigns; Building/renovation; Equipment; Program development; Curriculum development; Research; Employee matching gifts; Matching/challenge support.
Limitations: Giving nationally to universities, colleges, and major independent medical research institutions. Arts and culture, civic and community, health care, and precollegiate education and early learning are restricted to southern CA, mainly the greater Los Angeles area. No support for conduit organizations or to organizations that have not received permanent tax-exempt ruling determination from the federal government and state of CA (if state exemption is applicable). No grants to individuals, or for routine expenses, general endowments, deficit reduction, fundraising events, dinners, mass mailings, conferences, seminars, publications, films, theatrical productions, or public policy research.
Publications: Annual report (including application guidelines); Grants list; Informational brochure (including application guidelines); Program policy statement (including application guidelines).
Application information: Only those organizations invited upon review may submit proposals. Application form required.
Initial approach: Phase 1: Application
Copies of proposal: 1
Deadline(s): June 1 and Dec. 1 for application; Mar. 5 and Sept. 5 for completed proposals
Board meeting date(s): June and Dec.
Final notification: June and Dec.
Officers and Directors:* Robert A. Day,* Chair., C.E.O., and Pres.; Howard M. Day,* Vice-Chair.; Jonathan D. Jaffrey, V.P., C.O.O. and C.F.O.; Marsh A. Cooper,* V.P.; Walter B. Gerken,* V.P.; W.M. Keck II,* V.P.; Howard B. Keck, Jr.,* V.P; Judith A. Lower, Secy.; Peter K. Barker,* Treas.; James P. Lower,* Genl. Counsel; C. William Verity, Jr., Dir. Emeritus; Lew Allen, Jr.; Norman Barker, Jr.; John E. Bryson; Tammis Day; Theodore J. Day; Joseph Deegan-Day; Richard N. Foster; Lucinda D. Fournier; Stephen M. Keck; Theodore J. Keck; W.M. Keck III; John E. Kolb; Kent Kresa; Michael T. Masin; Kerry K. Mott; Simon Ramo; Nancy Daly Riordan; Stephen J. Ryan, M.D.; Edward C. Stone, Jr.; Hon. David A. Thomas; James R. Ukropina; Julian O. von Kalinowski.

Number of staff: 10 full-time professional; 8 full-time support.
EIN: 956092354

751
William M. Keck, Jr. Foundation
12575 Beatrice St.
Los Angeles, CA 90066-7001
Contact: Hilda Avanesian

Incorporated in 1958 in DE.
Donor: William M. Keck, Jr.
Foundation type: Independent foundation.
Financial data (yr. ended 12/31/05): Assets, $14,546,968 (M); expenditures, $890,523; qualifying distributions, $725,000; giving activities include $725,000 for 6 grants (high: $500,000; low: $5,000).
Purpose and activities: Giving primarily to an institute for international economics, as well as for education.
Fields of interest: Higher education; Health care; Homeless, human services; Economics; Christian agencies & churches.
Limitations: Giving generally limited to southern CA. No grants to individuals.
Application information: Application form not required.
Initial approach: Letter
Copies of proposal: 1
Deadline(s): Nov. 30
Board meeting date(s): Mid-Dec.
Officer and Director:* William M. Keck II,* Pres.
Number of staff: 1 part-time professional; 10 part-time support.
EIN: 136097874

752
The George M. and Adelaide M. Keller Foundation ◇
30 El Cerrito Ave.
San Mateo, CA 94402
Contact: George M. Keller, Pres.

Established in 1990 in CA.
Donors: Adelaide M. Keller; George M. Keller.
Foundation type: Independent foundation.
Financial data (yr. ended 12/31/04): Assets, $6,586,113 (M); gifts received, $157,590; expenditures, $2,095,673; qualifying distributions, $2,085,856; giving activities include $2,080,653 for 37 grants (high: $500,000; low: $500).
Purpose and activities: Giving primarily for higher education, health and human services, youth, and community development.
Fields of interest: Higher education; Hospitals (general); Human services; Children/youth, services; Human services, victim aid; Community development; Religious federated giving programs.
Type of support: General/operating support; Continuing support; Annual campaigns; Capital campaigns; Emergency funds; Program development; Seed money; Scholarship funds.
Limitations: Applications not accepted. Giving primarily in CA, with emphasis on San Mateo and San Francisco counties, and Denver, CO. No grants to individuals.
Application information: Contributes only to pre-selected organizations.

Officers and Directors:* George M. Keller,* Pres.; Adelaide M. Keller,* Secy.-Treas.
EIN: 943128129
Selected grants: The following grants were reported in 2005.
$2,071,326 to San Mateo Medical Center Foundation, San Mateo, CA. 5 grants: $532,326, $518,080, $520,920, $250,000, $250,000
$2,000 to Sequoia Hospital Foundation, Redwood City, CA.

753
Jonathan & Faye Kellerman Foundation ◇
722 N. Sierra Dr.
Beverly Hills, CA 90210 (310) 477-3924
Contact: Jonathan Kellerman, Pres.; Faye Kellerman, Asst. Secy.
Application address: c/o Donald G. Leve, CPA, 10960 Wilshire Blvd., Ste. 1100, Los Angeles, CA 90024

Established in 1996 in CA.
Donors: Faye Kellerman; Jonathan Kellerman.
Foundation type: Independent foundation.
Financial data (yr. ended 8/31/05): Assets, $9,450 (M); gifts received, $653,092; expenditures, $745,337; qualifying distributions, $743,791; giving activities include $742,245 for 27 grants (high: $150,000; low: $150).
Purpose and activities: Giving primarily to Jewish agencies and temples, as well as for Jewish education; funding also for a children's hospital.
Fields of interest: Higher education; Education; Hospitals (specialty); Human services; Jewish federated giving programs; Jewish agencies & temples.
Application information: The foundation generally contributes only to pre-selected organizations.
Officer: Jonathan Kellerman, Pres.
EIN: 954607397

754
Sol and Clara Kest Family Foundation ◇ ☆
5150 Overland Ave.
Culver City, CA 90230

Established in 1987 in CA.
Donors: Clara Kest; Sol Kest; Jona Goldrich; Doretta Goldrich; Michael Kest; Francesca Berkowitz; Ezra Kest; Benjamin Kest; Goldrich & Kest Industries.
Foundation type: Independent foundation.
Financial data (yr. ended 11/30/05): Assets, $13,053,556 (M); expenditures, $819,097; qualifying distributions, $531,035; giving activities include $531,000 for 2 grants (high: $500,000; low: $31,000).
Fields of interest: Jewish agencies & temples.
Limitations: Applications not accepted. No grants to individuals.
Application information: Contributes only to pre-selected organizations.
Officers and Directors:* Sol Kest,* Pres.; Clara Kest,* Secy.; Michael Kest,* Treas.; Francesca Berkowitz; Benjamin Kest; Ezra Kest.
EIN: 954109864

755
Khachaturian Foundation ◇
P.O. Box 513189
Los Angeles, CA 90051-1189
Contact: Rita M. Khachaturian, Secy.-Treas.; Henry Khachaturian, Dir.
Application address: 360 Post St., Ste. 401, San Francisco, CA 94108

Established in 1999 in CA.
Donors: Henry Khachaturian; Rita M. Khachaturian.
Foundation type: Independent foundation.
Financial data (yr. ended 12/31/04): Assets, $7,209,949 (M); gifts received, $1,599,316; expenditures, $433,797; qualifying distributions, $378,875; giving activities include $375,800 for 7 grants (high: $250,000; low: $300).
Fields of interest: Medical research, institute; Christian agencies & churches.
Limitations: Applications not accepted. Giving primarily in San Francisco, CA. No grants to individuals.
Application information: Unsolicited requests for funds not accepted.
Officer and Directors:* Rita M. Khachaturian,* Secy.-Treas.; Daphne Kavich; Henry Khachaturian; Natasha Khachaturian.
EIN: 943337684

756
Kibble Family Foundation ◇
P.O. Box 918
Rancho Santa Fe, CA 92067 (858) 259-0100
Contact: Robert F. Kibble, Pres.

Established in 2001 in CA.
Donor: Robert F. Kibble.
Foundation type: Independent foundation.
Financial data (yr. ended 12/31/04): Assets, $13,024 (M); gifts received, $500,000; expenditures, $500,053; qualifying distributions, $499,999; giving activities include $500,000 for 1 grant.
Purpose and activities: Giving primarily to an amateur athletic association.
Fields of interest: Recreation, association.
Limitations: Giving primarily in Nassau, Bahamas.
Application information: Application form not required.
Deadline(s): None
Officers: Robert F. Kibble, Pres.; Vanessa M. Kibble, Secy. and C.F.O.
EIN: 912169788

757
Kids Care for the Planet Earth ◇
4525 District Blvd.
Vernon, CA 90058 (323) 584-9500
Contact: Mahasti Mashhoon, Dir.

Established in 2000 in CA.
Donors: Diane Cavaricci; James Cavaricci; Bruce J. Molnar; Bon Appetit Danish, Inc.
Foundation type: Independent foundation.
Financial data (yr. ended 12/31/05): Assets, $124,693 (M); gifts received, $687,000; expenditures, $665,819; qualifying distributions, $664,205; giving activities include $664,205 for 13 grants (high: $300,000; low: $25).
Purpose and activities: Giving primarily for children and social services.

Fields of interest: Health organizations, association; Human services; Children/youth, services.

Limitations: Giving primarily in CA; some funding nationally.

Application information: Application form required.

Initial approach: Narrative letter

Deadline(s): None

Directors: Hassan Dolatshahi; Mondana Mashhoon Gordon; Mahasti Mashhoon; Zia Mashhoon; Bruce J. Molnar.

EIN: 330464760

758

Steve and Robin Kim Family Foundation ◇
3530 Wilshire Blvd., Ste. 360
Los Angeles, CA 90010   (213) 351-6880
Contact: Steve Y. Kim, Pres.
FAX: (213) 739-7882;
E-mail: winnie@alcatelventures.com

Established in 1999 in CA.

Donor: Steve Y. Kim.

Foundation type: Independent foundation.

Financial data (yr. ended 12/31/05): Assets, $11,907,023 (M); gifts received, $1,075,000; expenditures, $1,161,550; qualifying distributions, $1,136,694; giving activities include $1,136,694 for 22 grants (high: $298,000; low: $190), and $298,000 for foundation-administered programs.

Fields of interest: Arts; Higher education; Scholarships/financial aid; Christian agencies & churches.

Type of support: Continuing support; Building/renovation; Scholarship funds.

Limitations: Giving primarily in CA and Seoul, Korea.

Application information: Application form not required.

Initial approach: Letter

Deadline(s): None

Officers: Steve Y. Kim, Pres.; Robin H.J. Kim, V.P.

EIN: 954748701

759

The Kimball Foundation
(formerly Sara H. and William R. Kimball Foundation)
1660 Bush St., Ste. 300
San Francisco, CA 94109   (415) 561-6540
Contact: Eric L. Sloan, Sr. Prog. Off.
E-mail: esloan@pfs-llc.net; URL: http://www.pfs-llc.net/kimball/kimball_2005.html

Established in 1997 in CA.

Donors: Sara H. Kimball†; William R. Kimball.

Foundation type: Independent foundation.

Financial data (yr. ended 12/31/04): Assets, $37,913,189 (M); gifts received, $600; expenditures, $1,782,917; qualifying distributions, $1,441,490; giving activities include $1,296,858 for 64 grants (high: $60,000; low: $1,000).

Purpose and activities: Giving primarily to provide opportunities to the disadvantaged and at-risk, including education, youth development, academic enrichment, tutorials, leadership development, vocational training, employment, and sports, recreation and arts activities for low-income youth.

Fields of interest: Historic preservation/historical societies; Environmental education; Children/youth, services.

Type of support: Program development.

Limitations: Giving primarily in San Francisco, San Mateo, Sonoma, and Marin counties, CA. No grants to individuals or for endowment drives, events, annual appeals, videos, medical research, religious organizations, or the environment.

Publications: Application guidelines; Annual report; Grants list.

Application information: Application form not required.

Initial approach: Letter

Copies of proposal: 1

Deadline(s): 12 weeks prior to board meeting

Board meeting date(s): July and Nov.

Final notification: 2 to 3 months

Officers: William R. Kimball, Pres.; Donald J. McCubbin, Secy.-Treas.

Directors: Gerald R. Bush; Andrew W. Edward; Anne Kimball; Gretchen Kimball; Jeffrey Kimball; Stephen Kimball.

EIN: 943263448

Selected grants: The following grants were reported in 2005.

$60,000 to Eastside College Preparatory School, East Palo Alto, CA. For scholarships for four low-income, minority students to attend private high school in East Palo Alto.

$50,000 to Basic Fund, San Francisco, CA. For scholarships for disadvantaged youth to attend private elementary and middle schools.

$50,000 to Homeless Prenatal Program, San Francisco, CA. Toward capital campaign to purchase and renovate building for new Family Resource Center serving homeless and at-risk families and children.

$50,000 to KIPP Bayview Academy, San Francisco, CA. Toward construction of science laboratory at KIPP.

$50,000 to San Francisco Symphony, San Francisco, CA. For operating support for fiscal year 2005.

$40,000 to Making Waves Education Program, Richmond, CA. For Reading and Writing Empowerment Program serving at-risk youth.

$35,000 to Gateway High School, San Francisco, CA. For college counseling program at charter high school serving students with/without learning differences.

$35,000 to Golden Gate Community, San Francisco, CA. For Youth Development Initiative, employment training/personal development program for at-risk youth.

$35,000 to Summer Search Foundation, San Francisco, CA. For scholarships for low income youth to attend summer experiential education programs.

$35,000 to YMCA of San Francisco, Central Branch, San Francisco, CA. For Tenderloin Youth Development Program.

760

The Jena & Michael King Family Foundation ◇
c/o Lexington Financial Management
9350 Wilshire Blvd., Ste. 250
Beverly Hills, CA 90212

Established in 1999 in CA.

Donor: Michael King.

Foundation type: Independent foundation.

Financial data (yr. ended 12/31/04): Assets, $6,058,367 (M); expenditures, $705,132; qualifying distributions, $685,590; giving activities

include $681,220 for 42 grants (high: $100,000; low: $300).

Purpose and activities: Giving primarily for health care and health associations, particularly for children's health, including pediatric AIDS organizations; funding also for family and social services.

Fields of interest: Arts; Environment, natural resources; Health care; Health organizations, association; AIDS; Diabetes; Cancer research; Human services; Children/youth, services; Family services.

Type of support: General/operating support.

Limitations: Applications not accepted. Giving on a national basis, with strong emphasis on CA. No grants to individuals.

Application information: Contributes only to pre-selected organizations.

Officers: Michael King, Pres.; Robert V. Madden, Secy.

Director: Jena Fassett King.

EIN: 954773454

761

Lewis A. Kingsley Foundation ◇
4667 MacArthur Blvd., Ste. 400
Newport Beach, CA 92660

Established in 1963 in CA.

Foundation type: Independent foundation.

Financial data (yr. ended 5/31/05): Assets, $6,588,660 (M); expenditures, $420,212; qualifying distributions, $335,635; giving activities include $320,300 for 55 grants (high: $40,000; low: $250).

Purpose and activities: Support primarily for higher education; funding also for cultural programs and hospitals.

Fields of interest: Arts; Secondary school/education; Higher education; Hospitals (general); Human services.

Type of support: General/operating support; Scholarship funds.

Limitations: Applications not accepted. Giving primarily in the Los Angeles, CA, area. No grants to individuals.

Application information: Contributes only to pre-selected organizations.

Officers: Michael Polito, Pres.; David Streiff, V.P.; Frank Cordon, Secy.

EIN: 956092364

762

The Karl Kirchgessner Foundation
c/o Grants Coord.
1525 Aviation Blvd., No. 168
Redondo Beach, CA 90278
Contact: Christine Tuthill
E-mail: ctuthill@earthlink.net; URL: http://www.kirchgessnerfoundation.org

Established in 1979 in CA and reincorporated in NV due to a merger with The Karl Kirchgessner Foundation (CA) in 2003.

Foundation type: Independent foundation.

Financial data (yr. ended 6/30/05): Assets, $19,890,937 (M); expenditures, $1,209,072; qualifying distributions, $897,856; giving activities include $783,417 for 30+ grants (high: $100,000).

Purpose and activities: The foundation supports institutions actively engaged in the provision of services in the field of vision, primarily to disadvantaged persons, such as the elderly, the young, and the handicapped. While the foundation supports a limited amount of eye research, its emphasis is to support activities in the area of eye care, and helping those with sight problems to become self-sufficient.

Fields of interest: Health care; Eye diseases; Eye research; Blind/visually impaired.

Type of support: General/operating support; Continuing support; Equipment; Endowments; Program development; Professorships; Seed money; Scholarship funds; Research; Technical assistance; Matching/challenge support.

Limitations: Giving primarily in CA, with emphasis on southern CA. No support for private foundations, private operating foundations, supporting organizations, or for lobbying organizations or campaigns. No grants to individuals, or for fundraising campaigns, or for dinners.

Publications: Application guidelines; Informational brochure.

Application information: Letter of intent should not contain any supporting materials. Formal applications will be solicited by the foundation. The foundation strongly encourages applications which incorporate funding through matching grants. Application form required.

> *Initial approach:* Send a brief letter of intent
> *Copies of proposal:* 1
> *Deadline(s):* Nov. 1
> *Board meeting date(s):* May and as required

Officers and Directors:* Martin H. Webster,* Pres.; Karl Kramer,* V.P. and C.F.O.; Darryl W. Cluster, Secy.; Rev. William Cain, S.J.; Robert Huber; Diana Kramer; Kathy Kramer; Michael Kramer.

Number of staff: None.

EIN: 680530356

763
Kissick Family Foundation ◇
922 Napoli Dr.
Pacific Palisades, CA 90272-4036

Established in 1993 in CA.
Donors: John H. Kissick; M. Kathleen Kissick.
Foundation type: Independent foundation.
Financial data (yr. ended 12/31/03): Assets, $13,978,990 (M); gifts received, $1,700,000; expenditures, $905,215; qualifying distributions, $828,071; giving activities include $823,800 for 41 grants (high: $250,000; low: $250).
Purpose and activities: Giving primarily for education; support also for health care.
Fields of interest: Elementary/secondary education; Higher education; Education; Hospitals (general); Health organizations, association.
Limitations: Applications not accepted. Giving primarily in Los Angeles, CA. No grants to individuals.
Application information: Contributes only to pre-selected organizations.
Officers: John H. Kissick, Pres.; M. Kathleen Kissick, Secy.-Treas.
EIN: 954443453

764
Lloyd E. Elisabeth Klein Family Foundation ◇ ☆
101 S. Kraemer Blvd., Ste. 117
Placentia, CA 92870-6109

Established in 2002.
Donors: Elisabeth Klein; Lloyd E. Klein.
Foundation type: Independent foundation.
Financial data (yr. ended 12/31/05): Assets, $17,159,032 (M); gifts received, $12,180,636; expenditures, $373,289; qualifying distributions, $383,200; giving activities include $383,200 for grants.
Fields of interest: Libraries (public); Education; YM/YWCAs & YM/YWHAs.
Limitations: Applications not accepted. No grants to individuals.
Application information: Contributes only to pre-selected organizations.
Officers: Lloyd E. Klein, Chair.; Elisabeth H. Klein, Vice-Chair.; James L. Klein, Pres.; Christine E. Neely, Secy.; Catherine H. Sorensen, Treas.
Directors: Doug Cole; Kenneth Klein.
EIN: 300105588

765
David L. Klein, Jr. Foundation ◇
(formerly David L. Klein, Jr. Memorial Foundation, Inc.)
c/o Boas & Boas
720 Market St., Ste. 900
San Francisco, CA 94102
Contact: Janet E. Traub, V.P.
URL: http://www.blueprintrd.com/kleinfoundation

Incorporated in 1959 in NY.
Donors: David L. Klein†; Miriam Klein†; Endo Laboratories, Inc.
Foundation type: Independent foundation.
Financial data (yr. ended 12/31/05): Assets, $13,660,679 (M); expenditures, $977,098; qualifying distributions, $831,795; giving activities include $757,500 for 67 grants (high: $35,000; low: $1,000).
Purpose and activities: Improving the quality of community life through grants to improve education and preserve natural and historic resources.
Fields of interest: Historic preservation/historical societies; Arts; Education; Environment, natural resources; Health organizations, association; Human services; Science, research; Jewish agencies & temples.
Limitations: Applications not accepted. Giving primarily in the San Francisco Bay Area, CA, and New York, NY. No grants to individuals.
Application information: Contributes only to pre-selected organizations. Grants initiated by trustees.
> *Board meeting date(s):* Annually in Nov.
Officers and Trustees:* Marjorie Traub,* Pres.; Jane Barnet,* V.P.; Janet Traub,* V.P.; Saretta Barnet,* Secy.; Geoff Barnet,* Treas.; Howard Barnet, Jr.; Peter Barnet; Nancy Chirinos; Barry Traub; Jennifer Traub.
Number of staff: 1 part-time professional.
EIN: 136085432

766
The Kling Family Foundation ◇
P.O. Box 1108
Newport Beach, CA 92659

Established in 1999 in CA.
Donors: Donalyn Kling; Griswold Industries, Inc.
Foundation type: Independent foundation.

Financial data (yr. ended 12/31/05): Assets, $1,036,624 (M); gifts received, $600,000; expenditures, $566,181; qualifying distributions, $554,294; giving activities include $553,000 for 55 grants (high: $60,000; low: $50).
Fields of interest: Human services; Federated giving programs.
Limitations: Applications not accepted. Giving primarily in CA. No grants to individuals.
Application information: Contributes only to pre-selected organizations.
Officers: Jackie Glass, Pres.; Allen Kling, Secy.; Darryl Sheetz, Treas.
Directors: Vicki Gumm; Daryl Kling; Donalyn G. Kling; Donalyn Mikles.
EIN: 336272913

767
KLM Foundation ◇
10100 Santa Monica Blvd., Ste. 610
Los Angeles, CA 90067

Established in 1997 in CA.
Donors: Kathleen L. McCarthy; Leavey Charitable Lead Annuity Trust.
Foundation type: Independent foundation.
Financial data (yr. ended 12/31/05): Assets, $25,037,368 (M); gifts received, $2,842,425; expenditures, $895,658; qualifying distributions, $804,055; giving activities include $757,373 for 153 grants (high: $100,000; low: $100).
Fields of interest: Health organizations, association; Human services; Community development; Religion.
Limitations: Applications not accepted. Giving on a national basis. No grants to individuals.
Application information: Contributes only to pre-selected organizations.
Trustee: Kathleen L. McCarthy.
EIN: 954682685
Selected grants: The following grants were reported in 2005.
$100,000 to Marymount High School, Los Angeles, CA.
$50,000 to Loyola Marymount University, Los Angeles, CA.
$10,000 to Paulist Productions, Pacific Palisades, CA.
$10,000 to Saint Paul Church, Kensington, CT.
$5,000 to Catholic Charities.
$5,000 to Childhelp USA, Scottsdale, AZ.
$5,000 to Childrens Institute International, Los Angeles, CA.
$5,000 to Family Service.
$5,000 to Kappa Alpha Theta Foundation, Indianapolis, IN.
$5,000 to Marymount College, Rancho Palos Verdes, CA.

768
The Knight-Ridder, Inc. Fund ◇
(formerly Knight-Ridder Fund, Inc.)
c/o Knight-Ridder, Inc., Tax Dept.
50 W. San Fernando St., Ste. 1500
San Jose, CA 95113
Contact: Polk Laffoon, Secy.
FAX: (408) 938-7755;
E-mail: srosado@knightridder.com

Established in 1985 in FL.
Donor: Knight-Ridder, Inc.

Foundation type: Company-sponsored foundation.
Financial data (yr. ended 12/31/04): Assets, $619,842 (M); gifts received, $1,000,000; expenditures, $2,053,270; qualifying distributions, $2,053,270; giving activities include $2,053,270 for 61 grants (high: $271,194; low: $250).
Purpose and activities: The foundation supports organizations involved with arts and culture, education, housing, disasters, and human services.
Fields of interest: Media/communications; Arts; Higher education; Education; Housing/shelter, development; Disasters, preparedness/services; Youth, services; Human services; Federated giving programs.
Type of support: General/operating support; Annual campaigns; Emergency funds; Employee matching gifts; Employee-related scholarships.
Application information: Application form not required.
  Initial approach: Proposal
  Copies of proposal: 1
  Deadline(s): None
  Board meeting date(s): Quarterly
Officers and Directors:* P. Anthony Ridder,* Pres.; Steven B. Rossi,* V.P. and Treas.; Polk Laffoon, Secy.; Art Brisbane; Jerome Ceppos; Mary Jean Connors; Paula Ellis; Michael Petrak; Hilary A. Schneider; Alice Wang; Gordon Yamate.
EIN: 592610440
Selected grants: The following grants were reported in 2004.
$271,193 to United Way Silicon Valley, San Jose, CA.
$200,000 to Tech Museum of Innovation, San Jose, CA.
$131,500 to San Jose Museum of Art, San Jose, CA. 2 grants: $100,000, $31,500
$100,000 to San Jose Repertory Theater, San Jose, CA.
$57,980 to American Press Institute, Reston, VA.
$55,000 to American Society of Newspaper Editors (ASNE) Foundation, Reston, VA.
$52,443 to United Way of Miami-Dade, Miami, FL. 2 grants: $23,932, $28,511
$50,000 to United Way.

769
Marion Knott Foundation ◇ ☆
41 Royal Saint George Rd.
Newport Beach, CA   92660   (949) 640-2830
Contact: Marion Knott, Pres.

Established in 1998 in CA.
Donor: Marion Knott.
Foundation type: Independent foundation.
Financial data (yr. ended 12/31/05): Assets, $2,530,728 (M); gifts received, $735,750; expenditures, $352,018; qualifying distributions, $352,018; giving activities include $350,000 for 3 grants (high: $250,000; low: $50,000).
Fields of interest: Family services, domestic violence.
Type of support: General/operating support.
Application information: Application form required.
  Deadline(s): None
Officers and Directors:* Marion Knott,* Pres.; Darrel Anderson,* Secy.; Dwight P. Anderson II,* C.F.O.
EIN: 330843154

770
The Bradford & Lauren Koenig Foundation ◇
c/o Goldman Sachs & Co.
555 California St.
San Francisco, CA   94104

Established in 1997 in CA.
Donor: Bradford Koenig.
Foundation type: Independent foundation.
Financial data (yr. ended 12/31/05): Assets, $4,049,650 (M); expenditures, $577,330; qualifying distributions, $577,330; giving activities include $577,330 for 7 grants (high: $250,000; low: $2,500).
Fields of interest: Elementary/secondary education; Higher education; Higher education, university; Boys & girls clubs.
Limitations: Applications not accepted. Giving primarily in CA; with some giving also in NH. No grants to individuals; no loans or scholarships.
Application information: Contributes only to pre-selected organizations.
Trustees: Bradford Koenig; Lauren Koenig; Mark R. Tercek.
EIN: 133993307
Selected grants: The following grants were reported in 2005.
$250,000 to Dartmouth College, Hanover, NH.
$120,000 to Stanford University, Stanford, CA.
$10,000 to Boys and Girls Club of the Olympic Peninsula, Sequim, WA.
$5,000 to Childrens Health Council, Palo Alto, CA.
$2,500 to College Track, East Palo Alto, CA.

771
Allen D. Kohl Charitable Foundation, Inc. ◇
450 N. Roxbury Dr., Ste. 600
Beverly Hills, CA   90210

Incorporated in 1972 in WI.
Donors: Allen D. Kohl; Max Kohl Charitable Trust, No. AK2.
Foundation type: Independent foundation.
Financial data (yr. ended 12/31/04): Assets, $8,691,523 (M); gifts received, $68,307; expenditures, $613,808; qualifying distributions, $442,225; giving activities include $437,250 for 23 grants (high: $150,150; low: $200).
Purpose and activities: Grants for charitable causes of interest to the directors, including support for local Jewish welfare agencies and educational institutions.
Fields of interest: Museums (history); Arts; Education; Jewish federated giving programs; Jewish agencies & temples.
Limitations: Applications not accepted. Giving on a national basis. No grants to individuals.
Application information: Contributes only to pre-selected organizations.
Officers: Allen D. Kohl, Pres.; Jeffrey A. Dinkin, V.P.; Stephanie S. Cohen, Secy.-Treas.
EIN: 237211587
Selected grants: The following grants were reported in 2003.
$150,650 to United Jewish Fund of Greater Los Angeles, Los Angeles, CA. For unrestricted support.
$120,000 to Brentwood School, Los Angeles, CA. For unrestricted support.

$100,000 to Israel, State of, Jerusalem, Israel. For unrestricted support.
$50,000 to Amherst College, Amherst, MA. For unrestricted support.
$50,000 to Wilshire Boulevard Temple, Los Angeles, CA. For unrestricted support.
$10,200 to Milwaukee Jewish Day School, Milwaukee, WI. For unrestricted support.
$10,000 to National Breast Cancer Coalition Fund, DC. For unrestricted support.
$2,700 to Los Angeles Jewish Home for the Aging, Reseda, CA. For unrestricted support.
$2,500 to Jewish Vocational Service. For unrestricted support.
$1,000 to Franklin Educational Foundation, Franklin, WI. For unrestricted support.

772
The Kommerstad Foundation ◇ ☆
218 Deodar Ln.
Bradbury, CA   91010
Contact: Lila M. Kommerstad, Pres.

Established in 1998 in CA.
Donors: Robert M. Kommerstad; Lila M. Kommerstad.
Foundation type: Independent foundation.
Financial data (yr. ended 6/30/06): Assets, $3,545,343 (M); gifts received, $4,684; expenditures, $1,006,944; qualifying distributions, $1,000,000; giving activities include $1,000,000 for grants.
Fields of interest: Big Brothers/Big Sisters.
Limitations: Giving primarily in PA.
Application information:
  Initial approach: Letter
  Deadline(s): None
Officer: Lila M. Kommerstad, Pres. and Secy.
EIN: 954728471

773
Dean & Gerda Koontz Foundation ◇
P.O. Box 9529
Newport Beach, CA   92658-9529

Established in 1994 in CA.
Donors: Dean R. Koontz; Gerda A. Koontz.
Foundation type: Independent foundation.
Financial data (yr. ended 12/31/05): Assets, $177,562 (M); gifts received, $609,000; expenditures, $514,880; qualifying distributions, $514,880; giving activities include $513,000 for 2 grants (high: $509,000; low: $4,000).
Purpose and activities: Giving primarily for animal welfare, as well as to a children's hospital foundation, and a library foundation.
Fields of interest: Libraries/library science; Animal welfare; Hospitals (general).
Limitations: Applications not accepted. Giving in the U.S., primarily in CA. No grants to individuals.
Application information: Contributes only to pre-selected organizations.
Officers: Dean R. Koontz, C.E.O.; Gerda A. Koontz, Secy. and C.F.O.
EIN: 330622423
Selected grants: The following grants were reported in 2004.
$250,000 to Canine Companions for Independence, Oceanside, CA.
$75,000 to Bedford County Federated Library System, Bedford, PA.

$50,000 to Childrens Hospital of Orange County (CHOC) Foundation, Orange, CA.

$25,000 to Northern New Mexico Animal Protection Society, Espanola, NM.

$25,000 to Rescue a Golden of Arizona, Phoenix, AZ.

774
Koret Foundation ▼

33 New Montgomery St., Ste. 1090
San Francisco, CA   94105-4526
Contact: Claudia Hardin, C.F.O.
FAX: (415) 882-7775;
E-mail: koret@koretfoundation.org; URL: http://www.koretfoundation.org

Established in 1966 in CA.
Donors: Joseph Koret‡; Stephanie Koret‡.
Foundation type: Independent foundation.
Financial data (yr. ended 12/31/05): Assets, $247,754,640 (M); gifts received, $236,917; expenditures, $72,184,076; qualifying distributions, $64,209,252; giving activities include $61,608,604 for 386 grants (high: $41,475,292; low: $1,000; average: $5,000–$500,000), and $246,422 for 3 foundation-administered programs.
Purpose and activities: Supports organizations and initiatives that advance economic opportunity, individual freedom, personal initiative and entrepreneurial values in the San Francisco Bay Area, CA and in Israel.
Fields of interest: Arts; Elementary school/education; Secondary school/education; Higher education; Youth development; Community development; Jewish agencies & temples.
International interests: Israel.
Type of support: General/operating support; Continuing support; Annual campaigns; Capital campaigns; Building/renovation; Program development; Professorships; Publication; Seed money; Fellowships; Internship funds; Scholarship funds; Research; Program evaluation; Matching/challenge support.
Limitations: Giving limited to the Bay Area counties of San Francisco, Alameda, Contra Costa, Marin, Santa Clara, and San Mateo, CA; giving also in Israel. No support for private foundations, or veterans', fraternal, military, religious, or sectarian organizations whose principal activity is for the benefit of their own membership. No grants to individuals (except for the Koret Prize), or for general fundraising campaigns, scholarships, endowment funds, equipment funds, deficit financing, or emergency funds; no loans.
Publications: Application guidelines; Annual report; Financial statement; Grants list; Informational brochure; Newsletter.
Application information: The foundation does not accept grant requests via E-mail. Application form not required.
  Initial approach: Letter of inquiry
  Copies of proposal: 1
  Deadline(s): None
  Board meeting date(s): 5 times per year
  Final notification: 2 to 6 months
Officers and Directors:* Susan Koret,* Chair.; Jeffrey A. Farber, C.E.O.; Tad Taube,* Pres.; Claudia J. Hardin, C.F.O.; Richard C. Atkinson; Michael J. Boskin, Ph.D.; William K. Coblentz; Robert Friend; Richard L. Greene; Stanley Herzstein; Abraham D. Sofaer.

Number of staff: 8 full-time professional; 6 full-time support.
EIN: 941624987
Selected grants: The following grants were reported in 2005.
$41,475,292 to Koret Fund, San Francisco, CA.
$1,200,000 to Maybeck Foundation, San Francisco, CA. For restoration of Palace of Fine Arts.
$1,000,000 to San Jose State University, San Jose, CA. For Dr. Martin Luther King Jr. library.
$750,000 to American Friends of the Hebrew University, New York, NY. For capital support for veterinary school.
$550,000 to Jewish Community Federation of San Francisco, the Peninsula, Marin and Sonoma Counties, San Francisco, CA. For annual campaign and Koret-designated community impact projects.
$500,000 to San Francisco Opera Association, San Francisco, CA. For transitional fund campaign.
$240,000 to Jewish Federation of Silicon Valley, Los Gatos, CA. For annual campaign.
$25,000 to Foundation Francisco Marroquin, Stuart, FL. For library campaign at Pontifical Catholic University of Chile (PUCC) in honor of Al Harberger.
$24,500 to Philanthropy Roundtable, DC. For membership and support.
$20,000 to San Jose Museum of Art Association, San Jose, CA. For general operating support.

775
Koret Fund ☆

33 New Montgomery St., Ste. 1090
San Francisco, CA   94105   (415) 882-7740
Contact: Sandra J. Edwards, Dir. of Grants
FAX: (415) 882-7775; URL: http://www.koretfoundation.org

Established in 2004 in CA.
Donor: Koret Foundation.
Foundation type: Independent foundation.
Financial data (yr. ended 12/31/05): Assets, $101,703,856 (M); gifts received, $41,475,292; expenditures, $5,555,828; qualifying distributions, $4,808,510; giving activities include $4,773,000 for 23 grants (high: $1,000,000; low: $8,000).
Purpose and activities: The fund will consider outstanding examples of innovative approaches to community challenges and opportunities in its areas of interest, particularly those that have significant public policy implications. Its areas of funding interest include: San Francisco Bay Area, CA, Jewish community projects, such as strengthening Jewish identity, building capacity in Jewish communal organizations, linking Bay Area Jewry to Israel, and Jewish education/Jewish studies; San Francisco Bay Area community development and support, which includes K-12 education, higher education, community development (including youth development and building self-reliance) and cultural arts; and Israel and international organizations, with emphasis on economic development/free market inititiatives in Israel, and higher education in Israel.
Fields of interest: Arts; Elementary/secondary education; Higher education; Education; Youth development; Community development; Jewish federated giving programs; Jewish agencies & temples.
Limitations: Giving primarily in the San Francisco Bay Area, CA counties of San Francisco, Alameda, Contra Costa, Marin, San Mateo, and Santa Clara. In the area of Jewish funding, grant applications will

be considered from throughout northern CA, and nationally, on a selected basis. No grants for Statement 15.
Application information: See Web site for complete application guidelines and forms. Application form not required.
  Initial approach: 3-page letter of inquiry
Officers and Directors:* Susan Koret,* Chair.; Tad Taube,* Pres.; Claudia J. Hardin, C.F.O.; Jeffrey A. Farber, Exec. Dir.; Sandra J. Edwards, Ph.D., Dir. of Grants; Richard C. Atkinson; Michael J. Boskin; William K. Coblentz; Robert Friend; Richard L. Greene; Stanley Herzstein; Abraham D. Sofaer.
EIN: 201214826

776
Jacob Kornwasser Foundation ◇

336 N. Martel Ave.
Los Angeles, CA   90036

Established in 1991 in CA.
Donors: Jacob Kornwasser; Mila Kornwasser.
Foundation type: Independent foundation.
Financial data (yr. ended 10/31/05): Assets, $9,667,358 (M); gifts received, $1,205,000; expenditures, $426,755; qualifying distributions, $416,000; giving activities include $416,000 for 2 grants (high: $415,000; low: $1,000).
Purpose and activities: Giving primarily for Jewish organizations.
Fields of interest: Elementary/secondary education; Jewish agencies & temples.
Limitations: Applications not accepted. Giving primarily in Los Angeles, CA. No grants to individuals.
Application information: Contributes only to pre-selected organizations.
Officers: Mila Kornwasser, Pres.; Judith Hager, Secy.
EIN: 954337380

777
The Koshland Foundation ◇

P.O. Box 7310
Menlo Park, CA   94026-7310

Established in 1985 in CA.
Donors: Marian E. Koshland‡; James M. Koshland; Daniel E. Koshland, Jr.; Douglas E. Koshland.
Foundation type: Independent foundation.
Financial data (yr. ended 7/31/05): Assets, $26,705,448 (M); gifts received, $255,420; expenditures, $2,986,050; qualifying distributions, $2,859,900; giving activities include $2,859,900 for 12 grants (high: $2,500,000; low: $200).
Fields of interest: Museums (science/technology); Higher education; Human services; Civil rights, voter education; Jewish federated giving programs; Science; Jewish agencies & temples.
Type of support: Endowments; Scholarship funds.
Limitations: Applications not accepted. Giving primarily in CA; some giving nationally. No grants to individuals.
Application information: Contributes only to pre-selected organizations.
Officers and Directors:* Daniel E. Koshland, Jr.,* Pres.; James M. Koshland,* V.P.; James E. Esposto, Secy.-Treas. and C.F.O.; Douglas E. Koshland; Yvonne Koshland; Gail K. Wachtel.
EIN: 680069874

Selected grants: The following grants were reported in 2005.
$2,500,000 to National Academy of Sciences, DC.
$100,000 to Cold Spring Harbor Laboratory, Cold Spring Harbor, NY.
$12,000 to Tides Center, San Francisco, CA.
$1,000 to Planned Parenthood Federation of America, New York, NY.
$200 to Salvation Army Adult Rehabilitation Center, San Francisco, CA.

778
The Trustees of Ivan V. Koulaieff Educational Fund ◇

c/o Stadtler, Rosenblum & Saris
451 Montgomery St., 3rd Fl.
San Francisco, CA 94104-1199

Incorporated in 1930 in CA.
Donor: Ivan V. Koulaieff.
Foundation type: Independent foundation.
Financial data (yr. ended 12/31/05): Assets, $8,710,969 (M); expenditures, $531,627; qualifying distributions, $455,900; giving activities include $300,000 for 38 grants (high: $45,000; low: $500), and $155,900 for 11 grants to individuals (high: $43,800; low: $4,000).
Purpose and activities: Aid to Russian immigrants throughout the world through grants, scholarships, and loans; support also for Russian publications and Russian Orthodox education and churches in the U.S.
Fields of interest: Orthodox Catholic agencies & churches; Immigrants/refugees.
Type of support: Publication; Program-related investments/loans; Grants to individuals; Scholarships—to individuals.
Limitations: Applications not accepted. Giving on a national and international basis.
Application information: Unsolicited requests for funds not accepted.
Officers and Trustees:* Olga P. Hughes, Pres.; Peter A. Yakoubovsky-Lerke,* V.P.; Nikolai A. Kaliakin,* Secy.; Alex D. Psiol,* Treas.; Nicolas A. Hidchenko; Michel Mirkovitch.
Canidate: Anatol Shmelev.
EIN: 946088762

779
Krach Family Foundation ◇

c/o Harris MYCFO, Dept. 26
P.O. Box 10195
Palo Alto, CA 94303

Established in 2000 in CA.
Donors: Keith Krach; Jennifer Krach.
Foundation type: Independent foundation.
Financial data (yr. ended 12/31/04): Assets, $2,052,888 (M); gifts received, $933,000; expenditures, $620,754; qualifying distributions, $592,242; giving activities include $480,600 for 22 grants (high: $100,000; low: $100).
Purpose and activities: Giving primarily for children and youth services and programs; funding also for higher education.
Fields of interest: Higher education; Autism; Children/youth, services.
Limitations: Applications not accepted. Giving primarily in CA. No grants to individuals.
Application information: Contributes only to pre-selected organizations.

Officers: Keith Krach, Chair.; Jennifer Krach, Vice-Chair.; Richard Hester, Pres.; Teresa Holland, Treas.
EIN: 770548505

780
The Krause Foundation ◇

25855 Westwind Way
Los Altos Hills, CA 94022

Established in 1994 in CA.
Donors: L. Gay Krause; William Krause.
Foundation type: Independent foundation.
Financial data (yr. ended 12/31/05): Assets, $8,308,714 (M); expenditures, $441,100; qualifying distributions, $398,373; giving activities include $388,767 for 15 grants (high: $170,000; low: $500).
Fields of interest: Museums; Higher education; Human services.
Limitations: Applications not accepted. Giving primarily in CA. No grants to individuals.
Application information: Contributes only to pre-selected organizations.
Officers: L. Gay Krause, Pres.; L. William Krause, Secy.-Treas.
EIN: 770388463
Selected grants: The following grants were reported in 2005.
$170,000 to Citadel Foundation, Charleston, SC.
$10,000 to Global Heritage Fund, Palo Alto, CA.
$10,000 to Tech Museum of Innovation, San Jose, CA.
$3,000 to Community School of Music and Arts, Mountain View, CA.
$1,000 to Foundation for a College Education, East Palo Alto, CA.
$1,000 to Resource Area for Teachers, San Jose, CA.

781
The Jean & E. Floyd Kvamme Foundation ◇

P.O. Box 2494
Saratoga, CA 95070
Contact: Jean Kvamme, Tr.

Established in 1993 in CA.
Donors: E. Floyd Kvamme; Jean Kvamme.
Foundation type: Independent foundation.
Financial data (yr. ended 6/30/05): Assets, $16,686,642 (M); expenditures, $1,359,082; qualifying distributions, $1,203,592; giving activities include $1,203,592 for 46 grants (high: $348,992; low: $100).
Purpose and activities: Giving primarily to Christian religious organizations, medical grants for Alzheimer's, leukemia, arthritis, and spondylitis research and to the community of northern CA for education and the arts.
Fields of interest: Arts; Engineering school/education; Health organizations, association; Medical research, institute; Federated giving programs; Christian agencies & churches.
International interests: Ecuador.
Type of support: General/operating support; Continuing support; Building/renovation; Equipment; Research; Matching/challenge support.
Limitations: Applications not accepted. Giving primarily in northern CA. No grants to individuals.

Application information: Unsolicited requests for funds not accepted.
Trustees: Damon Kvamme; E. Floyd Kvamme; Jean Kvamme; Todd Kvamme.
Number of staff: 3 part-time support.
EIN: 770359484
Selected grants: The following grants were reported in 2004.
$1,000,000 to Santa Cruz Bible Church, Santa Cruz, CA.
$50,000 to Spondylitis Association of America, Sherman Oaks, CA.
$30,000 to University of California, School of Engineering, Berkeley, CA.
$25,000 to Santa Clara University, Santa Clara, CA.
$20,000 to Partners International, Spokane, WA.
$7,500 to Stanford University Hospital, Stanford, CA.
$5,000 to Oregon Pacific Research Institute, Eugene, OR.
$3,000 to Center for Education Reform, DC.
$2,000 to Hakone Foundation, Saratoga, CA.
$1,000 to Southeastern Legal Foundation, Atlanta, GA.

782
The La Fetra Foundation ◇

1600 E. Euclid Ave.
Berkeley, CA 94709

Established in 1992 in CA.
Donors: Anthony W. La Fetra; Michael W. La Fetra.
Foundation type: Independent foundation.
Financial data (yr. ended 12/31/05): Assets, $10,396,458 (M); gifts received, $236,706; expenditures, $411,061; qualifying distributions, $357,670; giving activities include $350,000 for 20 grants (high: $50,000; low: $3,000).
Purpose and activities: Giving primarily for international relief and the environment.
Fields of interest: Arts, multipurpose centers/programs; Botanical/horticulture/landscape services; International development; Foundations (public).
Limitations: Applications not accepted. Giving primarily in CA. No grants to individuals.
Application information: Contributes only to pre-selected organizations.
Officers: Suzanne La Fetra, Pres.; Anthony W. La Fetra, C.F.O.
Director: Michael W. La Fetra.
EIN: 954380652
Selected grants: The following grants were reported in 2003.
$35,000 to Los Angeles Conservancy, Los Angeles, CA.
$30,000 to TreePeople, Beverly Hills, CA.
$27,000 to Film Arts Foundation, San Francisco, CA.
$20,000 to Habitot Childrens Museum, Berkeley, CA.
$20,000 to Union Station Foundation, Pasadena, CA.
$15,000 to Aid to Artisans, Hartford, CT.
$15,000 to New World Foundation, New York, NY.
$15,000 to Tides Foundation, San Francisco, CA.
$10,000 to Changemakers, San Francisco, CA.
$10,000 to Pacifica Foundation, Berkeley, CA.

783
Lakeside Foundation ▼
3470 Mt. Diablo Blvd., Ste. A-210
Lafayette, CA   94549-7113
Contact: Laura D. Mateo, Pres.

Incorporated in 1953 in CA.
Donor: Paul L. Davies, Jr.
Foundation type: Independent foundation.
Financial data (yr. ended 12/31/05): Assets,
$125,338,359 (M); gifts received, $1,751,059;
expenditures, $7,153,049; qualifying distributions,
$6,842,095; giving activities include $6,798,472
for 132 grants (high: $1,250,000; low: $1,000;
average: $5,000–$100,000).
Purpose and activities: Supports the charitable
interests of the directors.
Limitations: Applications not accepted. Giving
primarily in the San Francisco Bay Area, CA, as well
as the Boston, MA area. No grants to individuals; no
loans.
Application information: Contributes only to
pre-selected organizations; unsolicited contacts are
discouraged.
   Board meeting date(s): Annually, usually in the
       spring
Officers and Directors:* Laura D. Mateo,* Pres.;
Paul L. Davies, Jr.,* V.P.; Bobbie A. Adams, Secy.;
Andrew E. Zeisler, Treas.; Paul Lewis Davies III; Pilar
H. Davies; Segundo Mateo.
EIN: 946066229
Selected grants: The following grants were reported
in 2004.
$1,000,000 to California Academy of Sciences, San
   Francisco, CA. For capital campaign.
$950,000 to Piedmont Community Church,
   Piedmont, CA. For capital campaign.
$500,000 to Childrens Hospital at Stanford, Palo
   Alto, CA. For pediatric emergency work.
$350,000 to University of the Pacific, Stockton, CA.
   For Science Building Fund.
$300,000 to Hoover Institution on War, Revolution
   and Peace, Stanford, CA. For general support.
$250,000 to Monterey Bay Aquarium, Monterey, CA.
   For 20th Anniversary Fund.
$250,000 to Stanford University, Stanford, CA. For
   general support for Campaign for Undergraduate
   Education.
$175,000 to Samuel Merritt College, Oakland, CA.
   For Sharon Clark Diaz Fund.
$10,000 to Menlo School, Atherton, CA. For general
   support.
$2,500 to San Francisco Opera, San Francisco, CA.
   For general support.

784
Hanimireddy Lakireddy Family Foundation ◇
388 E. Yosemite Ave., Ste. 100
Merced, CA   95340

Established in 1999 in CA.
Donor: Hanimireddy Lakireddy.
Foundation type: Independent foundation.
Financial data (yr. ended 12/31/05): Assets,
$1,095,826 (M); gifts received, $600,000;
expenditures, $394,564; qualifying distributions,
$391,600; giving activities include $391,600 for 6
grants (high: $232,000; low: $600).
Purpose and activities: Giving primarily for higher
education, as well as to an association which serves
people of Telugu origin; funding also for medical
school education, and a Hindu temple.

Fields of interest: Higher education; Medical
school/education; Hinduism.
Limitations: Applications not accepted. No grants to
individuals.
Application information: Contributes only to
pre-selected organizations.
Officers: Hanimireddy Lakireddy, Pres.; Vijaya
Lakireddy, Secy.; Sidhardha Lakireddy, C.F.O.
EIN: 770529512

785
Lamond Family Foundation ◇ ☆
167 Isabella Ave.
Atherton, CA   94027-4044   (650) 845-8100
Contact: Pierre Lamond; Christine Lamond

Established in 1994 in CA.
Donors: Pierre Lamond; Christine Lamond.
Foundation type: Independent foundation.
Financial data (yr. ended 12/31/05): Assets,
$1,164,627 (M); gifts received, $965,642;
expenditures, $1,108,542; qualifying distributions,
$1,065,000; giving activities include $1,065,000
for 7 grants (high: $800,000; low: $5,000).
Purpose and activities: Giving primarily for higher
education and the arts.
Fields of interest: Arts; Higher education; Law
school/education; Hospitals (general).
Limitations: Giving primarily in CA. No grants to
individuals.
Application information: Application form not
required.
   Initial approach: Letter
   Deadline(s): None
Officers: Pierre Lamond, Pres.; Christine Lamond,
V.P. and Treas.
EIN: 943204401
Selected grants: The following grants were reported
in 2003.
$65,000 to San Francisco Symphony, San
   Francisco, CA.
$28,850 to San Francisco Museum of Modern Art,
   San Francisco, CA.
$25,000 to Ubuntu, San Leandro, CA.
$5,000 to Massachusetts Institute of Technology,
   Cambridge, MA.

786
Lampert Family Foundation ◇
c/o Mark Lampert
1 Sansome St., 39th Fl.
San Francisco, CA   94104

Established in 2000 in CA.
Donor: Mark Lampert.
Foundation type: Independent foundation.
Financial data (yr. ended 12/31/03): Assets,
$12,639,250 (M); gifts received, $2,900,000;
expenditures, $356,708; qualifying distributions,
$325,350; giving activities include $328,000 for 8
grants (high: $305,000; low: $500).
Fields of interest: Human services; Children/youth,
services; Community development.
Limitations: Applications not accepted. Giving
primarily in CA. No grants to individuals.
Application information: Contributes only to
pre-selected organizations.
Trustees: Susan Byrd; Mark Lampert.
EIN: 367335154
Selected grants: The following grants were reported
in 2004.

$427,000 to San Francisco Foundation, San
   Francisco, CA.

787
Lane Family Charitable Trust ◇
500 Almer Rd., No. 301
Burlingame, CA   94010   (650) 348-4026
Contact: Joan Lane, Tr.; Ralph Lane, Tr.

Established in 1985 in CA.
Donors: Joan Lane; Ralph Lane.
Foundation type: Independent foundation.
Financial data (yr. ended 6/30/05): Assets,
$2,992,641 (M); gifts received, $14,073;
expenditures, $888,954; qualifying distributions,
$865,500; giving activities include $865,500 for 41
grants (high: $250,000; low: $2,000).
Purpose and activities: Giving primarily for higher
education and for community development.
Fields of interest: Secondary school/education;
Higher education; Education; Community
development.
Type of support: General/operating support.
Limitations: Giving primarily in San Francisco, and
San Mateo and Santa Cruz counties, CA. No grants
to individuals.
Application information:
   Initial approach: Letter
Trustees: Joan Lane; Ralph Lane.
EIN: 946585396

788
The Stanley S. Langendorf Foundation ◇
P.O. Box 2509
San Francisco, CA   94126   (415) 217-4919
Contact: Jude P. Damasco

Established in 1982 in CA.
Donor: Stanley S. Langendorf†.
Foundation type: Independent foundation.
Financial data (yr. ended 12/31/05): Assets,
$18,189,147 (M); expenditures, $1,366,253;
qualifying distributions, $1,304,462; giving
activities include $1,252,303 for 108 grants (high:
$250,000; low: $500).
Purpose and activities: Giving primarily for
programs in art, education, community and social
services and youth.
Fields of interest: Arts; Elementary/secondary
education; Youth development; Human services;
Children/youth, services.
Type of support: General/operating support;
Program development; Scholarship funds.
Limitations: Giving primarily in San Francisco, CA.
No grants to individuals.
Publications: Application guidelines.
Application information: Application form required.
   Initial approach: Phone for application guidelines
       before starting process
   Copies of proposal: 6
   Deadline(s): Feb. 1 and Sept. 1 for letter of
       inquiry; Mar. 1 and Oct. 1 for full proposal
   Board meeting date(s): Spring and fall
   Final notification: 3 weeks after meeting dates
Officers and Trustees:* Richard J. Guggenhime,*
Pres.; Ann Langendorf Wagner,* Secy.; Charles H.
Clifford,* C.F.O.; Charles H. Clifford, Jr.; Lisa
Guggenhime Hauswirth.
EIN: 942861512

789

The Lanni Family Charitable Foundation ◇
1585 Orlando Rd.
Pasadena, CA 91106
Contact: J. Terrence Lanni, Secy.-Treas.

Established in 1994 in CA.
Donor: J. Terrence Lanni.
Foundation type: Independent foundation.
Financial data (yr. ended 12/31/05): Assets,
$1,456,954 (M); gifts received, $2,047,500;
expenditures, $1,170,620; qualifying distributions,
$1,170,140; giving activities include $1,170,140
for 20 grants (high: $362,500; low: $400).
Purpose and activities: Giving primarily for health
associations, education, and human services.
Fields of interest: Secondary school/education;
Higher education; Medical school/education;
Education; Hospitals (general); Health
organizations, association; Cancer research;
Human services; Foundations (public).
Limitations: Giving primarily in Los Angeles, CA. No
grants to individuals.
Application information:
Initial approach: Letter
Deadline(s): None
Officers: Deborah M. Lanni, Pres.; J. Terrence Lanni,
Secy.-Treas.
EIN: 954509555
Selected grants: The following grants were reported
in 2003.
$165,000 to Loyola High School, Los Angeles, CA.
   3 grants: $75,000, $80,000, $10,000
$100,000 to Ronald Reagan Presidential
   Foundation, Simi Valley, CA.
$55,000 to Meals on Wheels of Los Angeles, Los
   Angeles, CA. 2 grants: $50,000, $5,000
$50,000 to Mayfield Junior School of the Holy Child
   Jesus, Pasadena, CA.
$2,500 to Childrens Institute International, Los
   Angeles, CA.
$2,250 to University of Southern California, Los
   Angeles, CA.
$2,000 to Nancy Davis Foundation for Multiple
   Sclerosis, Los Angeles, CA.

790

The Walter Lantz Foundation
4444 Lakeside Dr., Ste. 310
Burbank, CA 91505
Contact: Edward A. Landry, Tr.

Established in 1984 in CA.
Donors: Grace T. Lantz†; Walter Lantz†.
Foundation type: Independent foundation.
Financial data (yr. ended 11/30/05): Assets,
$13,752,882 (M); expenditures, $1,055,973;
qualifying distributions, $752,579; giving activities
include $752,579 for 42 grants (high: $137,520;
low: $400).
Purpose and activities: Giving primarily for higher
education and the arts, including art education and
visual arts; support also for health organizations and
social services.
Fields of interest: Arts; Higher education; Botanical
gardens; Health care; Health organizations,
association; Human services; Children/youth,
services.
Limitations: Giving primarily in the Los Angeles, CA,
area. No grants to individuals.
Application information: Application form not
required.
Initial approach: Letter

Copies of proposal: 1
Deadline(s): None
Trustees: Susan J. Hazard; Peggy Jackson; Edward
A. Landry.
Number of staff: 1
EIN: 953994420

791

Lasseter Family Foundation ◇
590 Daniel Young Dr.
Sonoma, CA 95476-7257

Established in 2001 in CA.
Donors: Nancy T. Lasseter; John A. Lasseter.
Foundation type: Independent foundation.
Financial data (yr. ended 12/31/05): Assets,
$128,668 (M); gifts received, $132,119;
expenditures, $325,342; qualifying distributions,
$320,169; giving activities include $320,169 for 15
grants (high: $227,600; low: $1,000; average:
$5,000–$7,500).
Fields of interest: Education; Human services;
Children/youth, services.
Limitations: Applications not accepted. No grants to
individuals.
Application information: Contributes only to
pre-selected organizations.
Trustees: John A. Lasseter; Nancy T. Lasseter.
EIN: 943387076

792

Laurel Resources, Inc. ◇ ☆
1990 N. California Blvd., Ste. 650
Walnut Creek, CA 94596

Established in 1995 in CA.
Foundation type: Independent foundation.
Financial data (yr. ended 12/31/05): Assets,
$1,454,265 (M); expenditures, $1,332,248;
qualifying distributions, $1,257,294; giving
activities include $1,239,163 for 14 grants (high:
$642,523; low: $5,000).
Purpose and activities: Giving primarily for a
charitable gift fund, as well as for services for senior
citizens, and other social services.
Fields of interest: Performing arts, orchestra
(symphony); Food services; Human services;
Residential/custodial care, hospices; Aging,
centers/services; Foundations (public).
Limitations: Applications not accepted. Giving
primarily in Pleasant Hill, CA; some funding also in
Boston, MA. No grants to individuals.
Application information: Contributes only to
pre-selected organizations.
Officers and Directors:* Frank Hesse, M.D.*,
Chair.; Nancy Gibbons,* Secy.; Egon Von
Kaschnitz,* Treas.; Jeffrey Elfont; Eva Glazer, M.D.
EIN: 680044202
Selected grants: The following grants were reported
in 2004.
$25,000 to Sacramento Loaves and Fishes,
   Sacramento, CA.
$13,000 to Futures Explored, Lafayette, CA.
$10,000 to Project Second Chance, Pleasant Hill,
   CA.

793

**Richard and Ruth Lavine Family
Foundation** ◇ ☆
11075 Santa Monica Blvd., Ste. 150
Los Angeles, CA 90025
Application address: c/o Catherine L. Unger, 315
Conway Ave., Los Angeles, CA 90024, tel.: (310)
446-4820

Established in 1990 in CA.
Donors: Richard A. Lavine; Ruth J. Lavine.
Foundation type: Independent foundation.
Financial data (yr. ended 6/30/06): Assets,
$5,133,140 (M); gifts received, $30,058;
expenditures, $618,259; qualifying distributions,
$496,407; giving activities include $496,407 for
grants.
Purpose and activities: Giving primarily for
education and Jewish organizations.
Fields of interest: Performing arts, orchestra
(symphony); Arts; Elementary/secondary education;
Law school/education; Education; Animal welfare;
Reproductive health, family planning; Arthritis;
Crime/violence prevention, child abuse; Human
services; Federated giving programs; Jewish
federated giving programs; Jewish agencies &
temples.
Limitations: Giving primarily in Los Angeles, CA. No
grants to individuals.
Application information: For the foreseeable future,
grant making funds are committed and unsolicited
proposals are not desired by the foundation.
Officers and Directors:* Ruth J. Lavine,* Pres.;
Catherine L. Unger,* V.P.; Leonard Unger,*
Secy.-Treas.
EIN: 954300271
Selected grants: The following grants were reported
in 2005.
$50,000 to K C E T Community Television of
   Southern California, Los Angeles, CA.
$20,000 to American Jewish Committee, New York,
   NY.
$10,000 to City of Hope, Los Angeles, CA.
$10,000 to Los Angeles County Bar Foundation, Los
   Angeles, CA.
$5,000 to Korean American Family Service Center,
   Los Angeles, CA.
$5,000 to Mental Health Advocacy Services, Los
   Angeles, CA.
$2,500 to Los Angeles Free Clinic, Los Angeles, CA.
$2,000 to Union for Reform Judaism, New York, NY.
$1,000 to Levitt and Quinn Family Law Center, Los
   Angeles, CA.
$500 to Western Justice Center Foundation,
   Pasadena, CA.

794

The Lawrence Foundation ◇
530 Wilshire Blvd., Ste. 207
Santa Monica, CA 90401
Contact: Lori Mitchell, Exec. Dir.
FAX: (310) 451-7580;
E-mail: info@thelawrencefoundation.org; Direct Tel.:
(970)870-9456; URL: http://
www.thelawrencefoundation.org

Established in 2000 in CA.
Donors: Jeff Lawrence; Diane Troth.
Foundation type: Independent foundation.
Financial data (yr. ended 12/31/04): Assets,
$4,489,061 (M); expenditures, $664,816;
qualifying distributions, $590,822; giving activities

include $543,729 for 35 grants (high: $99,991; low: $1,000).

Purpose and activities: The mission of The Lawrence Foundation is to make a difference in the world by providing contributions and grants to organizations that are working to solve pressing educational, environmental, health and other issues.

Fields of interest: Education; Environment, pollution control; Environment; Health care; Human services.

Limitations: Giving limited to the U.S. No support for voter registration, music, gardening, recreational, Religious programs, or theater or performance arts programs, hospices or home programs for the elderly, or for international organizations that do not have a qualified domestic 501(c)(3) representative. No grants to individuals or for program related investments, computers or software, audio or video equipment or designing and producing videos, kiosks or promotional material, or dinners, balls or other ticketed events.

Publications: Application guidelines; Grants list.

Application information: Full proposal upon invitation, per review of letter. The most efficient way to currently contact the foundation is via E-mail. Application form not required.

   Initial approach: 2-3-page E-mail or letter
   Copies of proposal: 1
   Deadline(s): Feb. 1 and Aug. 1
   Board meeting date(s): Feb. and Aug.
   Final notification: June and Dec.

Officer: Lori Read Mitchell, Exec. Dir.

Trustees: Jeff Lawrence; Diane Troth.

Number of staff: 1 part-time professional.

EIN: 954804431

795
Lear Family Foundation ◇

100 N. Crescent Dr., Ste. 250
Beverly Hills, CA 90210

Established in 1997 in CA.

Donors: Norman Lear; Lyn Lear.

Foundation type: Independent foundation.

Financial data (yr. ended 12/31/03): Assets, $33,758,447 (M); expenditures, $3,052,807; qualifying distributions, $2,823,160; giving activities include $2,478,845 for 108 grants (high: $500,000; low: $200).

Purpose and activities: Giving for general charitable giving.

Fields of interest: General charitable giving.

Type of support: General/operating support.

Limitations: Applications not accepted. Giving on a national basis. No grants to individuals.

Application information: Contributes only to pre-selected organizations.

Officers and Trustee:* Norman Lear,* Pres.; Tom Asher, Secy.; Julie Dyer, Treas.; Cheryl Snow, Exec. Dir.

EIN: 954661216

Selected grants: The following grants were reported in 2004.

$310,000 to People for the American Way, DC.

$35,000 to Tides Center, San Francisco, CA. 2 grants: $20,000, $15,000

$25,000 to Henry Mancini Institute, Culver City, CA.

$25,000 to University of Chicago, Chicago, IL.

$12,500 to Morehouse College, Atlanta, GA.

$12,500 to Society of Singers, Los Angeles, CA.

$12,000 to Women in Film, Beverly Hills, CA.

$10,000 to K C E T Community Television of Southern California, Los Angeles, CA.

$5,000 to Childrens Defense Fund, DC.

796
Ralph and Eleanor Leatherby Family Foundation ◇

620 Newport Center Dr., 11th Fl.
Newport Beach, CA 92660
Contact: Joann Leatherby, Pres.

Established in 1991 in CA.

Donors: Ralph Leatherby; Eleanor Leatherby.

Foundation type: Independent foundation.

Financial data (yr. ended 12/31/05): Assets, $3,817,156 (M); expenditures, $1,105,501; qualifying distributions, $1,088,508; giving activities include $1,088,473 for 5 grants (high: $1,000,000; low: $10,000).

Fields of interest: Higher education; Health care; Health organizations, association; Cancer; Medical research, institute; Cancer research; Crime/violence prevention, child abuse; Human services.

Type of support: General/operating support; Building/renovation; Program development; Seed money.

Limitations: Applications not accepted. Giving primarily in CA. No grants to individuals.

Application information: Contributes only to pre-selected organizations.

Officers and Directors:* Joann Leatherby,* Pres.; Russell Leatherby,* Secy.-Treas.; Eleanor Leatherby; Kathryn Leatherby.

EIN: 330409041

797
Thomas & Dorothy Leavey Foundation ▼ ◇

10100 Santa Monica Blvd., Ste. 610
Los Angeles, CA 90067 (310) 551-9936
Contact: Kathleen L. McCarthy, Chair.

Established in 1952 in CA.

Donors: Thomas E. Leavey†; Dorothy E. Leavey†.

Foundation type: Independent foundation.

Financial data (yr. ended 12/31/05): Assets, $246,740,827 (M); expenditures, $13,855,136; qualifying distributions, $11,418,948; giving activities include $10,917,500 for 61 grants (high: $2,000,000; low: $1,000; average: $10,000–$250,000), and $275,490 for 75 grants to individuals (high: $37,490; low: $2,000; average: $2,000–$8,000).

Purpose and activities: Giving primarily for hospitals, medical research, higher and secondary education, and Catholic church groups; provides scholarships to children of employees of Farmers Group, Inc.

Fields of interest: Education; Health care; Youth, services; Human services; Community development.

Type of support: Scholarships—to individuals.

Limitations: Giving primarily in southern CA.

Application information:

   Initial approach: Letter
   Copies of proposal: 1
   Deadline(s): None
   Board meeting date(s): As required

Officer and Trustees:* Kathleen L. McCarthy,* Chair.; Louis Castruccio; Leo E. Denlea, Jr.; Michael Enright; J.J. Leavey; Thomas Lemons; John McCarthy; Marie McDonough; Colleen Pennell.

EIN: 956060162

Selected grants: The following grants were reported in 2005.

$2,000,000 to Mount Saint Marys College, Los Angeles, CA. For general operating support.

$2,000,000 to Santa Clara University, Santa Clara, CA. For general operating support.

$1,000,000 to Archdiocese of Los Angeles, Los Angeles, CA. For general operating support.

$1,000,000 to University of California, Jesuit School of Theology, Berkeley, CA. For general operating support.

$1,000,000 to University of Southern California, Los Angeles, CA. For general operating support for Community Center.

$250,000 to Paulist Productions, Pacific Palisades, CA. For general operating support.

$250,000 to University of Puget Sound, Tacoma, WA. For general operating support.

$100,000 to Diocese of Santa Rosa, Santa Rosa, CA. For general operating support.

$50,000 to Para Los Ninos, Los Angeles, CA. For general operating support.

$10,000 to Social Service Auxiliary, Los Angeles, CA. For general operating support.

798
The Iara Lee & George Gund III Foundation ◇ ☆

The Presidio 300
39 Mesa St.
San Francisco, CA 94129
Contact: Thomas Suniville, V.P. and C.F.O.

Established in 2004 in CA, funded in 2005.

Donors: George Gund III; Iara Lee.

Foundation type: Independent foundation.

Financial data (yr. ended 12/31/05): Assets, $253,832 (M); gifts received, $810,495; expenditures, $580,100; qualifying distributions, $579,500; giving activities include $579,500 for 22 grants (high: $50,000; low: $5,000).

Fields of interest: Environment; Animal welfare; International affairs.

International interests: Africa.

Limitations: Applications not accepted. Giving primarily in CA, Washington, DC, and NY.

Application information: Contributes only to pre-selected organziations.

Officers and Directors:* Iara Lee,* Pres.; George Gund III,* Sr. V.P.; Thomas Suniville,* V.P. and C.F.O.; George Gund IV.

EIN: 912146075

799
LEF Foundation

945 Green St., No. 9
San Francisco, CA 94133 (415) 441-9591
Contact: Marina Drummer, Grants Admin. (CA); Lyda Kuth, Dir. (New England)
FAX: (415) 441-2161;
E-mail: marina@lef-foundation.org; New England address: P.O. Box 382066, Cambridge, MA 02238-2866, tel.: (617) 492-5333, FAX: (617) 868-5603; E-mail: lyda@lef-foundation.org;
URL: http://www.lef-foundation.org

Established in 1985 in CA.

Donor: Lyda Ebert†.

Foundation type: Independent foundation.

Financial data (yr. ended 6/30/05): Assets, $13,258,268 (M); gifts received, $810,767;

expenditures, $2,333,522; qualifying distributions, $2,260,751; giving activities include $2,062,522 for 220 grants (high: $250,000; low: $150).

Purpose and activities: The foundation's primary goal is to assist the creation and presentation of contemporary work in the fields of visual arts, architecture, design, media art, literature, and the performing arts.

Fields of interest: Media/communications; Media, film/video; Visual arts, architecture; Performing arts; Arts; Native Americans/American Indians.

Type of support: Program development; Publication; Seed money.

Limitations: Giving primarily in CA and New England; giving in other regions of the U.S. with relevant interests, including Mid-Atlantic, Mountain Plains, the Southeast, and the West. No grants to individuals, or for general/operating support, capital campaigns, building/renovation, land acquisition, endowments, emergency funds, fellowships, research, or matching/challenge support; no program-relating investments or loans.

Publications: Application guidelines; Grants list; Occasional report; Program policy statement.

Application information: Applicants based in New England should contact Cambridge, MA, office. See foundation Web site for application procedures and guidelines. Application form required.

Initial approach: Letter or telephone
Copies of proposal: 1
Deadline(s): Varies; contact foundation or refer to Web site
Board meeting date(s): Varies
Final notification: 2-3 months

Officers and Director:* Marion E. Greene, Pres.; Byron Kuth, V.P.; Lyda Kuth,* Secy.

Number of staff: 2 full-time professional; 2 part-time professional; 1 part-time support.

EIN: 680070194

800
Lehrer Family Foundation ◇ ☆
c/o Robert A. Morin, C.P.A.
116 N. Maryland Ave., Ste. 140
Glendale, CA 91206-4269

Established in 1996 in CA.

Donors: Seymour Lehrer; Shirley Lehrer.

Foundation type: Independent foundation.

Financial data (yr. ended 6/30/06): Assets, $4,510,706 (M); gifts received, $500,000; expenditures, $325,160; qualifying distributions, $321,500; giving activities include $321,500 for 44 grants (high: $50,000; low: $500).

Fields of interest: Museums; Performing arts; Performing arts, education; Humanities; Environment; Zoos/zoological societies; Reproductive health, family planning; Medical research, institute; American Red Cross; Children/youth, services; Jewish federated giving programs; Psychology/behavioral science.

Limitations: Applications not accepted. Giving primarily in CA. No grants to individuals.

Application information: Contributes only to pre-selected organizations.

Officers: Seymour Lehrer, Pres.; Shirley Lehrer, Secy.

Directors: Karen Lehrer; Ellen Lehrer Orlando.

EIN: 770439722

801
The Leichtag Family Foundation
c/o Sheldon Scharlin, C.P.A.
P.O. Box 8901
Rancho Santa Fe, CA 92067

Established in 1991 in CA.

Donors: Max Leichtag; Andre Leichtag.

Foundation type: Independent foundation.

Financial data (yr. ended 12/31/05): Assets, $10,515,152 (M); expenditures, $591,429; qualifying distributions, $578,959; giving activities include $564,125 for 12+ grants (high: $160,000).

Purpose and activities: Giving primarily for federated giving programs and human services.

Fields of interest: Hospitals (general); Human services; Federated giving programs; Jewish federated giving programs; Religion.

Type of support: Equipment; Building/renovation; Capital campaigns; Annual campaigns.

Limitations: Applications not accepted. Giving primarily in CA. No grants to individuals.

Application information: Contributes only to pre-selected organizations. Unsolicited requests for funds not accepted.

Board meeting date(s): May and Nov.

Officers and Directors:* Andre Leichtag,* Pres.; Joli L. Andre,* V.P.; Max Leichtag,* Secy.; Sheldon Scharlin,* C.F.O.; Robert Brunst.

Number of staff: None.

EIN: 330466189

Selected grants: The following grants were reported in 2003.

$210,000 to Jewish Community Foundation, San Diego, CA.

$101,000 to University of California at San Diego Foundation, La Jolla, CA.

$45,000 to Telecare, Uniondale, NY.

$18,775 to Helen Woodward Animal Center, Rancho Santa Fe, CA.

$15,000 to Youth Advocacy Innocent Addict Program, San Diego, CA.

$11,000 to Childrens Hospital and Health Center, San Diego, CA.

$7,500 to Casa de Amparo, Oceanside, CA.

$7,000 to American Friends of the Hebrew University, New York, NY.

$5,000 to Guide Dogs for the Blind, San Diego, CA.

$2,500 to San Diego Repertory Theater, San Diego, CA.

802
Lauren B. Leichtman and Arthur E. Levine Family Foundation ◇
335 N. Maple Dr., Ste. 240
Beverly Hills, CA 90210-3859 (310) 275-5335
Contact: Mila Laparan
URL: http://foundationcenter.org/grantmaker/leichtmanlevine/

Donors: Arthur E. Levine; Lauren B. Leichtman.

Foundation type: Independent foundation.

Financial data (yr. ended 5/31/06): Assets, $587,695 (M); gifts received, $10,000; expenditures, $769,945; qualifying distributions, $754,150; giving activities include $754,150 for 24 grants (high: $125,000; low: $1,000).

Purpose and activities: Giving primarily for higher and other education; funding also for the arts, children services, and Jewish organizations and temples.

Fields of interest: Performing arts, opera; Elementary/secondary education; Higher education; Law school/education; Education; Human services; Children, services; Family services; Jewish agencies & temples.

Type of support: General/operating support.

Limitations: Giving primarily in Los Angeles, CA.

Application information:
Initial approach: Letter
Deadline(s): None

Trustees: Lauren B. Leichtman; Arthur E. Levine.

EIN: 954051968

803
The Frederick P. Lenz Foundation for American Buddhism ◇ ☆
c/o Norman Oberstein
1901 Ave. of the Stars, Ste. 1100
Los Angeles, CA 90067 (310) 470-0416
E-mail: info@fredericklenzfoundation.org;
URL: http://www.fredericklenzfoundation.org/

Established in CA and NY.

Foundation type: Independent foundation.

Financial data (yr. ended 12/31/05): Assets, $13,862,923 (M); gifts received, $1,500; expenditures, $865,077; qualifying distributions, $691,327; giving activities include $570,684 for 12 grants (high: $100,000; low: $4,338).

Purpose and activities: The foundation is dedicated to promoting the benefits of Zen Buddhism, meditation, yoga and related Buddhist practices as a pathway to self-realization and the harmonious blending of the material and spiritual in contemporary American society.

Fields of interest: Buddhism.

Limitations: Giving on a national basis, with some emphasis on CA, CO, OR, and UT. No grants to individuals.

Application information: See Web site for procedures for inquires.

Initial approach: Inquiry letter of no more than 2 pages

Officers and Directors:* Norman Marcus,* Pres.; Norman S. Oberstein,* V.P.; Frederick P. Lenz, Jr.

EIN: 134014022

804
George & Wilma Leonard Charitable Foundation ◇ ☆
145 N. Redwood Dr.
San Rafael, CA 94903

Donors: Wilma F. Leonard†; Mark G. Leonard; Candace H. Leonard; Jon Leonard; William Leonard.

Foundation type: Independent foundation.

Financial data (yr. ended 3/31/06): Assets, $9,450,629 (M); expenditures, $367,846; qualifying distributions, $340,000; giving activities include $340,000 for grants.

Fields of interest: Secondary school/education; Higher education, college; Protestant agencies & churches.

Limitations: Applications not accepted. Giving primarily in CA and MN. No grants to individuals.

Application information: Contributes only to pre-selected organizations.

Officers: Mark G. Leonard, Pres.; Candace H. Leonard, V.P.; William Leonard, Secy.; Jon Leonard, Treas.

Director: Jim Leonard.

EIN: 942598897

Selected grants: The following grants were reported in 2005.

$103,000 to Macalester College, Saint Paul, MN.

$20,000 to Foothills Congregational Church, Los Altos, CA.

$20,000 to Saint Timothys Episcopal Church, Compton, CA.

$5,000 to Foothill College, Los Altos Hills, CA.

$5,000 to Mountain View High School, Mountain View, CA.

$1,000 to Santa Clara University, Santa Clara, CA.

805

Dean & Margaret Lesher Foundation

1333 N. California Blvd., Ste. 330
Walnut Creek, CA 94596 (925) 935-9988
Contact: Kathleen L. Odne, Exec. Dir.
FAX: (925) 935-7459;
E-mail: kodne@lesherfdn.com; URL: http://www.lesherfoundation.org

Established in 1989 in CA.
Donors: Lesher Communications, Inc.; Dean S. Lesher†; Margaret L. Lesher†.
Foundation type: Independent foundation.
Financial data (yr. ended 12/31/05): Assets, $82,337,865 (M); gifts received, $86,757; expenditures, $4,049,486; qualifying distributions, $3,398,979; giving activities include $2,823,715 for 93 grants (high: $500,000; low: $1,000).
Purpose and activities: The foundation is dedicated to improving the quality of life in Contra Costa County, CA, through educational and cultural endeavors and to support children and strengthen families.
Fields of interest: Arts; Education; Children/youth, services; Family services.
Type of support: General/operating support; Continuing support; Capital campaigns; Building/renovation; Equipment; Program development; Technical assistance; Matching/challenge support.
Limitations: Giving limited to Contra Costa County, CA. No support for environmental or open space organizations, health care or for other foundations. No grants to individuals, or for conferences, travel costs, fund drives, annual appeals, endowments or debt retirement; no loans.
Publications: Application guidelines; Annual report; Grants list.
Application information: Application must be accompanied by a detailed proposal. Application and guidelines are available on foundation Web site. Applications sent by fax will not be accepted. Application form required.
 Initial approach: Letter requesting application, refer to Web site for grant guidelines
 Copies of proposal: 1
 Deadline(s): None
 Board meeting date(s): Monthly
 Final notification: Within 90 days
Officers and Directors:* Cynthia A. Lesher,* Pres.; Steve Lesher,* V.P.; Linda L. Tatum,* Secy.-Treas.; Kathleen L. Odne, Exec. Dir.; Kathryn Burns-Jepson; Joseph Lesher; Tim Lesher; Jill Ryan.
Number of staff: 1 full-time professional; 1 full-time support.
EIN: 680208980
Selected grants: The following grants were reported in 2003.

$250,000 to STAND Against Domestic Violence, Concord, CA. For general operating support.

$244,000 to Contra Costa County Office of Education, Pleasant Hill, CA.

$200,000 to Walnut Creek, City of, Walnut Creek, CA. For endowment fund.

$100,000 to Contra Costa College, San Pablo, CA.

$100,000 to Saint Marys College of California, Moraga, CA. For School of Education building.

$75,000 to Diablo Ballet, Walnut Creek, CA.

$57,000 to Food Bank of Contra Costa and Solano, Concord, CA.

$50,000 to California Symphony Orchestra, Walnut Creek, CA.

$50,000 to Community Violence Solutions, San Pablo, CA. For Stepping Stones and Children's Interview Center.

$30,000 to California Shakespeare Theater, Berkeley, CA. For operating support.

806

Leslie Family Foundation ✧ ☆

c/o Mark Leslie
738 Westridge Dr.
Portola Valley, CA 94028-7333

Donor: Leslie Lead Annuity Trust.
Foundation type: Independent foundation.
Financial data (yr. ended 12/31/04): Assets, $11,392,230 (M); gifts received, $1,701,623; expenditures, $557,200; qualifying distributions, $457,009; giving activities include $454,000 for 78 grants (high: $125,000; low: $250).
Fields of interest: Arts; Education; Human services; Jewish agencies & temples.
Limitations: Applications not accepted. Giving primarily in CA; some funding also in NY. No grants to individuals.
Application information: Contributes only to pre-selected organizations.
Officers: Mark Leslie, Pres.; Debra A. Leslie, V.P.; Seth P. Leslie, Secy.; Joshua M. Leslie, Treas.
EIN: 680474709

807

The Lester Family Foundation ✧

3250 Van Ness Ave.
San Francisco, CA 94109
Contact: Kirk Lester, Treas.

Established in 1994 in CA.
Donor: W. Howard Lester.
Foundation type: Independent foundation.
Financial data (yr. ended 12/31/05): Assets, $122,110 (M); expenditures, $1,951,105; qualifying distributions, $1,875,114; giving activities include $1,874,360 for 29 grants (high: $500,000; low: $1,000).
Purpose and activities: Giving primarily to a cancer center, a golf foundation, and other federated giving programs; funding also for education, community development, and human services.
Fields of interest: Business school/education; Education; Health organizations, association; Cancer; Athletics/sports, golf; Human services; Community development; Federated giving programs.
Limitations: Applications not accepted. Giving primarily in San Francisco, CA, St. Augustine, FL, and Houston, TX. No grants to individuals.
Application information: Contributes only to pre-selected organizations.
Officers: W. Howard Lester, Pres.; Mary Lester, V.P.; Kirk Lester, Treas.
EIN: 943205279

Selected grants: The following grants were reported in 2004.

$1,500,000 to University of Oklahoma, Norman, OK.

$150,000 to First Tee of San Francisco, San Francisco, CA.

$140,000 to National Cowgirl Museum and Hall of Fame, Fort Worth, TX.

$20,000 to New York City Opera, New York, NY.

$15,000 to University of California at San Francisco Foundation, San Francisco, CA.

$10,000 to Oklahoma Heritage Association, Oklahoma City, OK.

$10,000 to Sacred Heart Elementary School, Oakland, CA.

$10,000 to San Francisco School Volunteers, San Francisco, CA.

$1,000 to University of Oklahoma Foundation, Norman, OK.

808

Let Love Rule Foundation ✧ ☆

c/o RHF Management Svcs.
10100 Santa Monica Blvd., Ste. 1300
Los Angeles, CA 90067

Established in 2004 in CA.
Donor: Lenny Kravitz.
Foundation type: Independent foundation.
Financial data (yr. ended 12/31/05): Assets, $15,052 (M); gifts received, $642,229; expenditures, $709,508; qualifying distributions, $707,750; giving activities include $707,750 for 3 grants (high: $495,000; low: $93,750).
Fields of interest: Christian agencies & churches.
Limitations: Applications not accepted. Giving primarily in Mission Hills, CA, and Harrisburg, OR. No grants to individuals.
Application information: Contributes only to pre-selected organizations.
Officers: Zoro, C.E.O.; Richard Feldstein, Secy.; Lenny Kravitz, C.F.O.
EIN: 202043926

809

Hyman Levine Family Foundation ✧

9460 Wilshire Blvd., Ste. 300
Beverly Hills, CA 90212
Contact: Dena Schechter, Pres.

Established in 1943 in CA.
Donors: Members of the Levine family; Gayle Trust; Irv Schechter; Dena Schechter; Ronald Trust.
Foundation type: Independent foundation.
Financial data (yr. ended 12/31/05): Assets, $6,640,919 (M); gifts received, $444,571; expenditures, $456,827; qualifying distributions, $445,390; giving activities include $445,360 for 97 grants (high: $100,000; low: $200).
Purpose and activities: Giving primarily for Jewish organizations, including universities for the study of Judaism.
Fields of interest: Higher education; Human services; Jewish federated giving programs; Jewish agencies & temples.
Type of support: Continuing support; Annual campaigns; Capital campaigns; Building/renovation; Endowments; Emergency funds; Conferences/seminars; Professorships.

Limitations: Applications not accepted. Giving primarily in CA. No support for political organizations. No grants to individuals.
Application information: Contributes only to pre-selected organizations.
Officers: Dena Schechter, Pres.; Donald Slate, 1st V.P.; Meldon Levine, 2nd V.P.; Nancy Clavin, Secy.; Jill Levine Stein, Treas.
Number of staff: 1 part-time support.
EIN: 956058255
Selected grants: The following grants were reported in 2005.
$153,000 to University of Judaism, Los Angeles, CA. 4 grants: $25,000, $3,000, $100,000, $25,000
$15,000 to Junior Blind of America, Los Angeles, CA.
$14,500 to Jewish Family Services. 2 grants: $7,500, $7,000
$8,300 to Music Center, Providence, RI.
$5,000 to Pacific Serenades, Los Angeles, CA.
$2,000 to Los Angeles Philharmonic, Los Angeles, CA.

810

Shuki Levy Foundation, Inc. ✧ ☆
(formerly One Light-The Innocent Heart Foundation)
c/o The Walter B. Mandell Group
10960 Wilshire Blvd., Ste. 980
Los Angeles, CA 90024

Established in 1998.
Donors: Shuki Levy; Levy Charitable Trust.
Foundation type: Independent foundation.
Financial data (yr. ended 12/31/05): Assets, $973,969 (M); gifts received, $453,000; expenditures, $447,497; qualifying distributions, $404,126; giving activities include $404,126 for 2 grants (high: $399,126; low: $5,000).
Fields of interest: Federated giving programs; Jewish agencies & temples.
Limitations: Applications not accepted. No grants to individuals.
Application information: Contributes only to pre-selected organizations.
Officers: Shuki Levy, Pres.; Tamara Levy, Secy.
EIN: 954618509

811

Lidow Foundation ✧
233 Kansas St.
El Segundo, CA 90245-4316

Donors: Alexander Lidow; Eric Lidow; Derek Lidow.
Foundation type: Independent foundation.
Financial data (yr. ended 12/31/05): Assets, $2,947,009 (M); gifts received, $17,600; expenditures, $1,198,320; qualifying distributions, $1,197,557; giving activities include $1,195,500 for 14 grants (high: $1,000,000; low: $1,000; average: $5,000–$25,000).
Fields of interest: Medical research, institute; Aging, centers/services; Jewish agencies & temples; Aging.
Type of support: General/operating support.
Limitations: Applications not accepted. Giving primarily in southern CA and NY. No grants to individuals.
Application information: Contributes only to pre-selected organizations.

Officers: Eric Lidow, Pres.; Elizabeth Lidow, V.P.; Verna Kuykendall, Secy.-Treas.
Directors: Alan Lidow; Alexander Lidow; Derek Lidow.
EIN: 952406726
Selected grants: The following grants were reported in 2005.
$25,000 to Harvard-Westlake School, North Hollywood, CA.
$3,000 to United States Holocaust Memorial Museum, DC.
$2,000 to Los Angeles Mission, Los Angeles, CA.

812

The Lincy Foundation ▼ ✧
150 S. Rodeo Dr., Ste. 250
Beverly Hills, CA 90212
Contact: James D. Aljian, Pres.

Established in 1989 in CA.
Donor: Tracinda Corp.
Foundation type: Independent foundation.
Financial data (yr. ended 9/30/05): Assets, $193,767,157 (M); gifts received, $137,290,424; expenditures, $23,895,844; qualifying distributions, $21,060,091; giving activities include $20,369,730 for 128 grants (high: $2,565,151; low: $2,000; average: $10,000–$100,000).
Purpose and activities: Support primarily for Armenian charities, education, and human services.
Fields of interest: Arts; Education; Medical research, institute; Human services; Aging, centers/services; International relief; Religion; Aging.
Type of support: Program-related investments/loans.
Limitations: Giving primarily in CA. No grants to individuals.
Application information: Application form not required.
Initial approach: Letter or proposal
Deadline(s): None
Officers and Directors:* James D. Aljian,* Chair. and Pres.; Harut Sassounian,* Vice-Chair.; Walter C. Hoffer, V.P.; Alex Yemenidjian,* V.P.; Anthony Mandekic,* Secy.-Treas. and C.F.O.; Kirk Kerkorian; Walter M. Sharp.
EIN: 954238697
Selected grants: The following grants were reported in 2005.
$2,565,151 to Armenia, Government of, Yerevan, Armenia. .
$2,270,000 to Nevada Cancer Institute, Las Vegas, NV.
$2,000,000 to American Red Cross, National Headquarters, DC.
$2,000,000 to UCLA Foundation, Los Angeles, CA.
$1,891,314 to United Armenian Fund, Glendale, CA.
$1,000,000 to Cedars-Sinai Medical Center, Department of Psychiatry, Los Angeles, CA.
$700,000 to Motion Picture and Television Fund, Woodland Hills, CA.
$50,000 to Clark County Public Education Foundation, Las Vegas, NV.
$25,000 to Larry King Cardiac Foundation, DC. For program in Valley Glen, CA.
$25,000 to NorCal Armenian Home, Burlingame, CA.

813

Linden Root Dickinson Foundation ✧
3245 Indian Mills Ln.
Jamul, CA 91935

Established in 1990 in CA.
Donor: Dorothy L. Root‡.
Foundation type: Independent foundation.
Financial data (yr. ended 12/31/03): Assets, $34,071,292 (M); expenditures, $1,743,096; qualifying distributions, $1,631,677; giving activities include $1,590,000 for 12 grants (high: $500,000; low: $14,300).
Purpose and activities: Giving primarily to Christian organizations and for Christian education.
Fields of interest: Arts; Higher education; Higher education, university; Christian agencies & churches.
Limitations: Applications not accepted. Giving primarily in CA and CO. No grants to individuals.
Application information: Contributes only to pre-selected organizations.
Officers and Directors:* Robert W. Sanders,* Pres.; Kevin R. Sanders,* V.P. and Secy.; Derek A. Sanders,* V.P.; John R. Henkel,* Treas.
EIN: 330440808
Selected grants: The following grants were reported in 2003.
$500,000 to Oral Roberts University, Tulsa, OK. For general support.
$390,000 to World Vision, Federal Way, WA. For general support.
$135,700 to California Center for the Arts, Escondido, CA. For general support.
$100,000 to Kids and Families Together, Ventura, CA. For general support.
$50,000 to Bayshore Christian Ministries, East Palo Alto, CA. For general support.
$50,000 to Focus on the Family, Colorado Springs, CO. For general support.
$50,000 to Oaks Christian School, Westlake Village, CA. For general support.
$50,000 to Smile Train, New York, NY. For general support.
$50,000 to University of San Diego, San Diego, CA. For general support.
$14,300 to Fraternity House, Escondido, CA. For general support.

814

Bruce Lindorf Memorial Foundation ✧ ☆
412 Aronoso Ln., Unit 401
San Clemente, CA 92672-1651
Contact: Ronald S. Lindorf, Pres.

Donors: Ronald S. Lindorf; David Forsyth; Howard Wahl.
Foundation type: Independent foundation.
Financial data (yr. ended 11/30/05): Assets, $4,408,779 (M); gifts received, $8,000,000; expenditures, $4,581,710; qualifying distributions, $4,568,710; giving activities include $4,568,710 for 8 grants (high: $4,177,000; low: $25).
Purpose and activities: Giving for primarily to the Mormon Church, some giving to education for scholarships.
Fields of interest: Education; Mormon agencies & churches.
Limitations: Giving limited to residents of UT.
Application information:
Initial approach: Letter
Deadline(s): None

Officers: Ronald S. Lindorf, Pres.; Terri Lindorf, Secy.
EIN: 237061702
Selected grants: The following grants were reported in 2003.
$516,025 to Church of Jesus Christ of Latter Day Saints, Salt Lake City, UT.
$70,000 to Called to Serve Foundation, Provo, UT.
$12,002 to Utah Valley State College, Orem, UT.
$9,150 to Brigham Young University, Provo, UT.
$8,119 to California State University, Fullerton, CA.
$2,750 to HELP International, Provo, UT.
$2,500 to Alpine School District Foundation, American Fork, UT.
$2,500 to Weber State University, Ogden, UT.
$1,000 to Choice Humanitarian, West Jordan, UT.

815
The James and Joan Lindsey Family Foundation ◇
36 Hammond Dr.
Santa Barbara, CA 93108

Established in 1994.
Donors: James B. Lindsey, Jr.; Joan Anne Lindsey.
Foundation type: Independent foundation.
Financial data (yr. ended 12/31/05): Assets, $4,450,506 (M); expenditures, $740,059; qualifying distributions, $740,059; giving activities include $740,000 for 12 grants (high: $250,000; low: $5,000).
Purpose and activities: Giving primarily for family and Christian services.
Fields of interest: Family services; Christian agencies & churches.
Limitations: Applications not accepted. Giving primarily in Washington, DC; some giving also in CA and FL. No grants to individuals.
Application information: Contributes only to pre-selected organizations.
Officers: Joan Anne Lindsey, Pres.; James B. Lindsey, Jr., Secy.
EIN: 770390011

816
Lipinsky Family Foundation ◇
(formerly Bernard and Dorris Lipinsky Foundation)
c/o Elaine Lipinsky
977A Lomas Santa Fe Dr.
Solana Beach, CA 92075

Established in 1998 in CA.
Donor: Bernard Lipinsky†.
Foundation type: Independent foundation.
Financial data (yr. ended 12/31/05): Assets, $6,826,141 (M); gifts received, $6,214,284; expenditures, $678,373; qualifying distributions, $659,639; giving activities include $648,377 for 36 grants (high: $130,000; low: $290).
Fields of interest: Arts; Zoos/zoological societies; Health organizations, association; Cancer; Human services; Jewish agencies & temples.
Limitations: Applications not accepted. Giving limited to San Diego, CA. No grants to individuals.
Application information: Contributes only to pre-selected organizations. Unsolicited requests for fund not considered or acknowledged.
Trustees: Elaine Lipinsky; Jeffrey Lipinsky.
EIN: 330818870
Selected grants: The following grants were reported in 2004.

$127,700 to Old Globe Theater, San Diego, CA.
$85,000 to San Diego State University, San Diego, CA.
$25,000 to San Diego Opera Association, San Diego, CA.
$22,000 to Zoological Society of San Diego, San Diego, CA.
$8,500 to La Jolla Playhouse, La Jolla, CA.
$6,500 to San Diego Performing Arts League, San Diego, CA.
$6,000 to University of California at San Diego Foundation, La Jolla, CA.
$1,000 to Friends of County Animal Shelters, La Jolla, CA.

817
The Lipman Family Foundation, Inc. ◇
(formerly Howard and Jean Lipman Foundation, Inc.)
188 Favonio Rd.
Portola Valley, CA 94028
Contact: Beverly S. Lipman, Pres.

Established in 1959 in NY.
Donors: Howard W. Lipman†; Jean Lipman†.
Foundation type: Independent foundation.
Financial data (yr. ended 6/30/05): Assets, $20,771,929 (M); gifts received, $7,204; expenditures, $593,137; qualifying distributions, $486,614; giving activities include $481,311 for 38 grants (high: $120,000; low: $500).
Purpose and activities: Giving primarily for art museums, scientific research, educational institutions, and conservation organizations.
Fields of interest: Arts; Higher education; Environment, natural resources; Health care.
Type of support: Endowments; Seed money; Matching/challenge support.
Limitations: Applications not accepted. Giving primarily in CA and NY. No grants to individuals.
Application information: Contributes only to pre-selected organizations.
Officers and Directors:* Beverly S. Lipman,* Pres.; Roger A. Goldman, V.P. and Treas.; Peter W. Lipman,* V.P.; Timothy E. Lipman,* V.P.; Lester A. Greenberg,* Secy.; Benjamin H. Lipman.
EIN: 136066963
Selected grants: The following grants were reported in 2005.
$50,000 to San Jose Museum of Art, San Jose, CA.
$25,000 to American Geological Institute, Alexandria, VA.
$10,000 to Doctors for Global Health, Atlanta, GA.
$10,000 to Geological Society of America, Boulder, CO.
$1,000 to American Geophysical Union, DC.
$1,000 to Peninsula Open Space Trust, Menlo Park, CA.
$1,000 to Portola Valley, Town of, Portola Valley, CA.
$500 to American Red Cross.
$500 to Di Rosa Preserve, Napa, CA.
$500 to United Way Silicon Valley, San Jose, CA.

818
The Lipp Family Foundation ◇ ☆
1001 B Ave., Ste. 211
Coronado, CA 92118

Established in 2005 in CA.
Donor: David W. Lipp.
Foundation type: Independent foundation.

Financial data (yr. ended 6/30/06): Assets, $5,330,751 (M); gifts received, $5,293,901; expenditures, $442,393; qualifying distributions, $367,500; giving activities include $367,500 for 12 grants (high: $60,000; low: $2,500).
Fields of interest: Higher education.
Limitations: Applications not accepted. No grants to individuals.
Application information: Contributes only to pre-selected organizations.
Officers: William J. Barkhurst, Pres.; Charles W. Hayes, Treas.
EIN: 201985794

819
The Listwin Family Foundation ◇
3480 Woodside Rd.
Woodside, CA 94062

Established in 2000 in CA.
Donors: Donald J. Listwin; Lorene Arey.
Foundation type: Independent foundation.
Financial data (yr. ended 12/31/03): Assets, $12,606,308 (M); gifts received, $113,568; expenditures, $1,777,525; qualifying distributions, $1,550,000; giving activities include $1,550,000 for 6 grants (high: $1,000,000; low: $5,000).
Fields of interest: Cancer research; Human services; Children/youth, services; Women, centers/services; Economically disadvantaged.
Limitations: Applications not accepted. Giving primarily in New York, NY; funding also in Palo Alto, CA, and Seattle, WA. No grants to individuals.
Application information: Contributes only to pre-selected organizations.
Officers and Directors:* Donald J. Listwin,* Pres.; Mary Murillo, Secy.
EIN: 770527982

820
Edmund and Jeannik Littlefield Foundation ◇ ☆
(formerly Edmund Wattis Littlefield Foundation)
3716 San Pablo Dam Rd., No. 5
El Sobrante, CA 94803

Established in 1958 in CA.
Donor: Edmund W. Littlefield†.
Foundation type: Independent foundation.
Financial data (yr. ended 12/31/05): Assets, $42,450,298 (M); expenditures, $2,921,434; qualifying distributions, $2,639,952; giving activities include $2,617,000 for 19 grants (high: $1,000,000; low: $5,000).
Purpose and activities: Giving for higher and secondary education; support also for social service organizations.
Fields of interest: Arts; Secondary school/education; Higher education; Animals/wildlife, preservation/protection; Health organizations, association; Food services; Human services; Children/youth, services.
Limitations: Applications not accepted. Giving primarily in CA. No grants to individuals.
Application information: Contributes only to pre-selected organizations.
Officers: Jeannik M. Littlefield, Pres.; Edmund W. Littlefield, Jr., V.P.; Jacques M. Littlefield, V.P.; Denise Renee Sobel, V.P.; Bonnie Prendy, Secy. and C.F.O.
EIN: 946074780

821
Living Stones Foundation ☆
(formerly Praise The Lord Foundation)
3000 Sand Hill Rd., B1-145
Menlo Park, CA 94025
Contact: Justin A. Eldred, Tr.
FAX: (650) 561-9273;
E-mail: justin@lsfoundation.org; URL: http://www.lsfoundation.org/

Established in 1986 in CA.
Donors: Kenneth A. Eldred; Roberta E. Eldred.
Foundation type: Independent foundation.
Financial data (yr. ended 11/30/05): Assets, $8,002,847 (M); gifts received, $50; expenditures, $418,342; qualifying distributions, $387,125; giving activities include $387,125 for 18 grants (high: $100,000; low: $375).
Purpose and activities: Giving primarily to start-up Christian organizations that have a good track record, women's ministries (especially in the San Francisco Bay Area, CA), and transformation projects in the United States and internationally, and support the propagation of the concepts of Kingdom business.
Fields of interest: Christian agencies & churches; Minorities; Women.
International interests: Central America; Europe; India; Middle East; Oceania; South America.
Type of support: Seed money; Research; Matching/challenge support.
Limitations: Giving on a national and international basis. No grants to individuals.
Publications: Application guidelines; Informational brochure (including application guidelines).
Application information: Complete guidelines available on Web site. Full proposals are accepted by invitation only. Application form required.
> *Initial approach:* E-mail
> *Board meeting date(s):* Varies
> *Final notification:* 4 to 6 weeks after receipt of proposal
Officers and Board Members:* Kenneth A. Eldred, C.E.O. and Treas.; Roberta E. Eldred, Pres.; Kary N. Eldred,* Secy.; Justin A. Eldred; Monica Eldred.
Number of staff: 2 part-time professional; 1 part-time support.
EIN: 770140039
Selected grants: The following grants were reported in 2004.
$51,890 to CityTeam Ministries, San Jose, CA.
$45,000 to Campus Crusade for Christ International, Orlando, FL.
$30,000 to Jesus Institute, Encinitas, CA.
$20,000 to Alliance Defense Fund, Scottsdale, AZ.
$15,000 to Luis Palau Evangelistic Association, Portland, OR.
$7,500 to Praise Chapel Christian Fellowship, Portland, OR.
$7,000 to Origins Community, Boulder, CO.
$5,000 to Christian Services Association (CSA), Sumas, WA.
$5,000 to First Assembly of God Church, San Jose, CA.
$2,000 to Extreme Prophetic, Maricopa, AZ.

822
Livingston Memorial Foundation ◇
c/o Jackson, DeMarco & Peckenpaugh
2801 Townsgate Rd., No. 200
Westlake Village, CA 91361
Contact: Laura K. McAvoy, Asst. Secy.-Treas.

Incorporated about 1974 in CA.
Donor: Ruth Daily Livingston†.
Foundation type: Independent foundation.
Financial data (yr. ended 4/30/06): Assets, $9,544,144 (M); expenditures, $572,317; qualifying distributions, $444,846; giving activities include $375,995 for 31 grants (high: $110,000; low: $1,000).
Purpose and activities: Support for health and health-related activities.
Fields of interest: Hospitals (general); Health care; Health organizations, association.
Type of support: General/operating support; Continuing support; Matching/challenge support.
Limitations: Giving limited to Ventura County, CA. No grants to individuals.
Publications: Application guidelines; Informational brochure (including application guidelines); Program policy statement.
Application information: Application form required.
> *Initial approach:* Letter not exceeding 3 pages
> *Copies of proposal:* 9
> *Deadline(s):* Varies; contact foundation for information
> *Board meeting date(s):* As required
Officers and Directors:* Charles M. Hair, M.D.*, Pres.; W.C. Huff, M.D.*, V.P.; Richard Loft, M.D.*, V.P.; Marcia Donlon,* Secy.; Laura K. McAvoy, C.F.O.; Walter W. Hoffman; John R. Walters, M.D.
EIN: 237364623
Selected grants: The following grants were reported in 2005.
$25,000 to Interface Children Family Services, Camarillo, CA.
$25,000 to Westminster Free Clinic, Oak Park, CA.
$24,000 to Saint Johns Regional Medical Center Foundation, Oxnard, CA.
$20,000 to Salvation Army, Redding, CA.
$15,000 to Free Clinic of Simi Valley, Simi Valley, CA.
$10,000 to Palmer Drug Abuse Program of Ventura County, Camarillo, CA.
$10,000 to YMCA, Southeast Ventura County, Thousand Oaks, CA.
$7,000 to Lutheran Social Services of Southern California, Los Angeles, CA.
$5,000 to American Cancer Society, Oxnard, CA.
$5,000 to Miracle House, Ventura, CA.

823
The John M. Lloyd Foundation
11777 San Vicente Blvd., Ste. 745
Los Angeles, CA 90049 (310) 622-1050
Contact: Melanie Havelin, Exec. Dir.
FAX: (310) 622-1070; E-mail: info@johnmlloyd.org; URL: http://www.johnmlloyd.org/jml_home.html

Established in 1991 in CA.
Foundation type: Independent foundation.
Financial data (yr. ended 12/31/05): Assets, $9,219,126 (M); expenditures, $640,208; qualifying distributions, $526,292; giving activities include $384,175 for grants.
Purpose and activities: Support for innovative programs throughout the world in public policy, education/awareness, and prevention for HIV/AIDS.
Fields of interest: AIDS.
Type of support: Management development/capacity building; Technical assistance; Continuing support; Emergency funds; Program development; Conferences/seminars; Publication; Seed money; Curriculum development.

Limitations: Giving on a worldwide basis. No grants to individuals, or for annual campaigns; generally no grants for operating budgets of established organizations, capital expenditures, health care or service provision, or for indirect costs.
Publications: Application guidelines; Financial statement; Grants list.
Application information: Formal proposals may be submitted by invitation only, unsolicited formal proposals not considered. Preferred submission of concept letters is via e-mail. If e-mail is unavailable, letter may be mailed or faxed. Grant maximum is $20,000. Application guidelines and information available on foundation Web site. Application form required.
> *Initial approach:* Concept letter (no more than 4 pages)
> *Copies of proposal:* 1
> *Deadline(s):* Dec. 15 and Aug. 15 for concept letter
> *Board meeting date(s):* Oct. and Mar.
> *Final notification:* Oct. and Mar.
Officers and Directors:* Robert L. Estrin,* Pres.; Mary Lloyd Estrin,* V.P. and Treas.; Heidi Mage Lloyd,* V.P.; Linda Dorn Klein,* Secy.; Heather Chandler, Cont.; Melanie Havelin, Exec. Dir.; Thomas Coates, Ph.D.; Zoe Lloyd Estrin; Trish Devine Karlin.
Number of staff: 1 full-time professional.
EIN: 363766003
Selected grants: The following grants were reported in 2005.
$20,000 to Advocates for Youth, DC. To promote HIV prevention among at-risk population and build youth leaders through Young Women of Color (YWOC) Leadership Council.
$20,000 to Community and Individual Development (CIDA) Foundation, Fairfield, IA. For broad-based South African HIV/AIDS prevention program for 14-24 year olds entitled, Providing Student Catalysts for Community Behavioral Change.
$20,000 to Community HIV/AIDS Mobilization Project (CHAMP), New York, NY. For Strategy Lab for HIV Prevention Policy formerly known as Prevention Justice Initiative.
$20,000 to Council on Foreign Relations, New York, NY. For Doc-in-a-Box, project to analyze use of shipping containers as durable, easily transportable, and cost-effective health clinics to deliver selected range of infectious disease health services (including HIV treatment and prevention) to under-served communities in resource poor countries.
$20,000 to Global AIDS Alliance, DC. For Global AIDS Activist Leadership Summit.
$20,000 to Human Rights Watch, New York, NY. For HIV/AIDS and Human Rights, which documents human rights abuses and engages in high-level advocacy toward curbing the spread of HIV/AIDS worldwide.
$20,000 to Ms. Foundation for Women, New York, NY. For Women and AIDS Fund, supporting organizations that advocate for policies and services to meet needs of women living with HIV/AIDS in U.S. and to bridge local activists to national policy arena.
$20,000 to Population Action International, DC. To research and document impact of U.S. foreign assistance on sexual and reproductive health services in the developing world, including those pertaining to HIV/AIDS prevention.
$16,710 to Gay Mens Health Crisis (GMHC), New York, NY. For Phase II of implementation advocacy for Medicare Prescription Drug Reform.

$15,000 to International Gay and Lesbian Human Rights Commission, New York, NY. For Global HIV/AIDS Issues and U.S. Policy.

824
LLWW Foundation
625 S. Fair Oaks Ave., Ste. 360
South Pasadena, CA 91030-2630
Contact: Linda J. Blinkenberg, Secy.
FAX: (626) 441-3672

Established in 1980 in CA.
Donor: Laura-Lee Whittier Woods.
Foundation type: Independent foundation.
Financial data (yr. ended 12/31/05): Assets, $19,775,766 (M); expenditures, $887,084; qualifying distributions, $793,491; giving activities include $696,305 for 43 grants (high: $270,000; low: $1,000).
Purpose and activities: Emphasis on the arts, including museums; giving also for education and social services.
Fields of interest: Visual arts; Museums; Performing arts; Arts; Education; Environment; Health care; Human services; Children/youth, services.
Type of support: Program development.
Limitations: Applications not accepted. Giving primarily in southern CA; funding also nationally. No grants to individuals; no loans.
Application information: Due to funding restrictions, the foundation manager prefers to initiate the grants made by the foundation.
Board meeting date(s): As needed
Officers and Directors:* Laura-Lee Whittier Woods,* Pres.; Michael J. Casey,* V.P.; Linda J. Blinkenberg,* Secy.; Michael P. McShane,* C.F.O.
EIN: 953464689

825
The J. M. Long Foundation ◊
(formerly Long Foundation)
P.O. Box 3827
Walnut Creek, CA 94598 (925) 935-4138
Contact: Deborah Bland, Admin.

Established in 1966.
Donors: Joseph M. Long‡; Vera M. Long.
Foundation type: Independent foundation.
Financial data (yr. ended 12/31/04): Assets, $54,608,952 (M); gifts received, $163; expenditures, $2,422,734; qualifying distributions, $2,222,180; giving activities include $2,165,733 for 74 grants (high: $640,740; low: $1,000).
Purpose and activities: Giving to benefit CA and HI located organizations involved with health care, education, and conservation. Preference is given to new initiative projects which will be completed with the foundation's contribution.
Fields of interest: Higher education; Business school/education; Medical school/education; Animals/wildlife, preservation/protection; Pharmacy/prescriptions; Health organizations, association; Youth development, centers/clubs; Youth development; Human services; Children/youth, services.
Limitations: Giving limited to CA and HI. No grants to individuals, or for debt reduction.
Application information: Additional materials and documentation is not to exceed 3 pages. Application form required.

Initial approach: Letter requesting application guidelines
Copies of proposal: 1
Deadline(s): Given out after letter of inquiry received
Board meeting date(s): Varies
Final notification: July or Dec.
Officers and Trustees:* Robert M. Long,* Pres.; W.G. Combs,* V.P.; O.D. Jones,* Secy.; Milton Long; Nick Piediscalzi; M.J. Souyoultzis.
Number of staff: 1 part-time professional.
EIN: 941643626
Selected grants: The following grants were reported in 2004.
$640,740 to University of the Pacific, Stockton, CA.
$410,644 to Claremont McKenna College, Claremont, CA. To construct and operate a health and wellness center.
$98,949 to University of California, Santa Cruz, CA.
$75,000 to California Waterfowl Association, Sacramento, CA. To restore California's nesting grounds for mallards.
$50,000 to California State Parks Foundation, Kentfield, CA. For Park Education Legacy Fund.
$50,000 to Hospice of Marin Foundation, Larkspur, CA.
$50,000 to Muir Heritage Land Trust, Martinez, CA. To acquire 700 acre Ranch in the Franklin Ridge.
$50,000 to Ukiah Valley Cultural and Recreational Center, Ukiah, CA.
$30,000 to East Bay Zoological Society, Oakland, CA. To underwrite construction of the reptile house and discovery room in the new Children's Zoo.
$25,000 to Lupus Foundation of Hawaii, Honolulu, HI.

826
The Thomas J. Long Foundation ▼
2950 Buskirk Ave., Ste. 160
Walnut Creek, CA 94597 (925) 944-3800
Contact: Marcia A. Sander
FAX: (925) 944-3573; *URL:* http://www.thomasjlongfdn.org

Established in 1972.
Donor: Thomas J. Long‡.
Foundation type: Independent foundation.
Financial data (yr. ended 12/31/05): Assets, $91,773,664 (M); expenditures, $4,848,600; qualifying distributions, $4,268,459; giving activities include $3,983,020 for 80 grants (high: $2,400,000; low: $2,500; average: $10,000–$25,000).
Purpose and activities: Giving primarily for education, the arts, health and human services.
Fields of interest: Arts; Education; Health care; Human services.
Limitations: Giving primarily in HI and northern CA with preference given to Alameda County, Contra Costa County, Napa County, Solano County and Sonoma County. No grants to individuals.
Application information: Application form required.
Initial approach: See website for contact information or telephone inquiry
Deadline(s): Based on request for application
Board meeting date(s): Semiannually
Officers and Trustees:* Sidne J. Long,* Pres.; Thomas R. Sweeney,* V.P.; Jill M. Rapier,* Secy.-Treas.; Robert M. Coakley, Exec. Dir.; Howard H. Bell; William G. Combs; Hank Delevati; Catherine M. Fisher; Lolita L. Lowry.

Number of staff: 2 full-time professional.
EIN: 237180712
Selected grants: The following grants were reported in 2004.
$1,900,000 to John Muir Foundation, Walnut Creek, CA. For John Muir Medical Center Capital Campaign.
$559,133 to University of the Pacific, Stockton, CA. For School of Pharmacy and Health Sciences Learning and Health Care Center.
$136,785 to La Clinica de la Raza, Fruitvale Health Project, Oakland, CA. For Pharmacy Enhancement Project.
$100,000 to Philanthropic Ventures Foundation, Oakland, CA. 2 grants: $75,000 (For Immediate Response Special Education Resource Grants), $25,000 (For Special Education Resource Grants Program).
$50,000 to Santa Fe Christian Community School, Solana Beach, CA. For educational and administration building construction.
$25,000 to Planned Parenthood/Shasta-Diablo, Concord, CA. For prenatal program at Richmond Health Center.
$20,000 to Visiting Nurse Association, Central Coast, Monterey, CA. For Telehomecare Patient Units.
$15,000 to Bay Point Family Resource Center, Richmond, CA. For dental equipment.
$15,000 to Childrens Hospital and Research Center at Oakland, Oakland, CA. For FACES for the Future internship program for high school students of color.

827
Vera M. Long Foundation ◊
P.O. Box 3827
Walnut Creek, CA 94598

Established in 1990 in CA.
Donor: Vera M. Long.
Foundation type: Independent foundation.
Financial data (yr. ended 6/30/05): Assets, $17,396,989 (M); expenditures, $1,344,153; qualifying distributions, $558,035; giving activities include $546,094 for 2 grants (high: $273,250; low: $272,844).
Fields of interest: Higher education, college; Theological school/education.
Limitations: Applications not accepted. Giving limited to CA. No grants to individuals.
Application information: Contributes only to pre-selected organizations.
Officers: Robert M. Long, Pres.; Nan Gefen, V.P. and Secy.; Ronald A. Plomgren, V.P. and Treas.
EIN: 943084031
Selected grants: The following grants were reported in 2003.
$503,500 to Mills College, Oakland, CA. 2 grants: $250,000 to Vera M. Long Social Science Research Center, $253,500 to Vera M. Long Social Science Research Center
$100,000 to University of California at San Francisco Foundation, Vera M. Long Gene Therapy Suite Diabetes Center, San Francisco, CA.

828
Los Altos Community Foundation
183 Hillview Ave.
Los Altos, CA 94022 (650) 949-5908
Contact: Roy Lave, Exec. Dir.
FAX: (650) 949-0807; E-mail: lacf@losaltoscf.org;
Additional E-mail: staff@losaltoscf.org; URL: http://
www.losaltoscf.org

Established in 1991 in CA.
Foundation type: Community foundation.
Financial data (yr. ended 6/30/05): Assets,
$4,408,097 (M); gifts received, $2,067,818;
expenditures, $1,079,284; giving activities include
$775,589 for 218 grants (high: $346,615; low:
$25), and $47,989 for 46 grants to individuals
(high: $4,038; low: $28).
Purpose and activities: The foundation supports the
community by making grants for local programs,
building an endowment for the future, and managing
philanthropic funding for other organizations. Giving
primarily for the arts, conflict resolution, community
building, and leadership development.
Fields of interest: Arts; Higher education;
Education; Dispute resolution; Disasters, Hurricane
Katrina; Community development; Philanthropy/
voluntarism, association; Leadership development;
Children/youth.
Type of support: Scholarships—to individuals;
General/operating support; Capital campaigns;
Building/renovation; Program development;
Conferences/seminars; Seed money; Technical
assistance; Program evaluation; Program-related
investments/loans; Matching/challenge support.
Limitations: Giving primarily in Los Altos and Los
Altos Hills, CA, and surrounding unincorporated
areas. No support for governmental, religious, or
profit-making organizations. No grants to individuals
(except for scholarships).
Publications: Application guidelines; Annual report;
Financial statement; Grants list; Informational
brochure; Newsletter; Occasional report; Program
policy statement.
Application information: Visit foundation Web site
for grant application and guidelines. Application
form required.
Initial approach: Submit application and
attachments
Copies of proposal: 1
Deadline(s): None
Board meeting date(s): 3rd Wed. of each month
Final notification: 4 weeks
Officers and Directors:* George Limbach,* Chair.;
Henry Roux,* Secy.; Dennis Young,* C.F.O. and
Treas.; Roy Lave,* Exec. Dir.; Bob Adams; Lois
Adams; Marge Bruno; Mike Bruno; Arthur
Carmichael; Jean Carmichael; Coeta Chambers;
Claudia Coleman; Colette Cranston; Kim Cranston;
Jim Geers; Nan Geschke; Paul Gonella; Mady Kahn;
Mel Kahn; Dave Knudson; Penny Lave; Ginny Lear;
Ann Limbach; Chip Lion; Nancy Lippe; Cindy
Luedtke; Dave Luedtke; Barbara Mordo; Jean
Mordo; Alex Myers; Clyde Noel; Shelly Potvin; Mary
Prochnow; David Reeder; Vicki Reeder; Marge
Sentous; Steve Shepherd; Louise Spangler; Lynn
Szekely-Goode; Emily Thurber; James Thurber; Paul
Van Buren.
Number of staff: 1 full-time support.
EIN: 770273721

829
Ludwick Family Foundation
P.O. Box 1796
Glendora, CA 91740 (626) 852-0092
Contact: Deanna Monaghan, Prog. Off.
FAX: (626) 852-0776;
E-mail: ludwickfndn@ludwick.org; URL: http://
www.ludwick.org

Established in 1990 in CA.
Donors: Arthur J. Ludwick; Sarah Lynne Ludwick.
Foundation type: Independent foundation.
Financial data (yr. ended 12/31/05): Assets,
$36,403,890 (M); expenditures, $1,875,374;
qualifying distributions, $1,645,823; giving
activities include $749,565 for 30 grants (high:
$50,000; low: $100), and $314,562 for 4
foundation-administered programs.
Purpose and activities: The purpose of the
foundation is to assist a broad array of groups
working to make a positive difference.
Fields of interest: Arts; Education; Environment;
Animal welfare; Health care; Housing/shelter,
services; Children/youth, services; Family services;
Community development, neighborhood
development; Science; Disabilities, people with.
Type of support: Building/renovation; Equipment.
Limitations: Giving on a national basis, with
emphasis on CA. No support for voter registration
organizations, or for schools, universities, libraries,
or hospitals (unless invited), or for daycare centers,
fiscal agents, sponsors, or churches. No grants to
individuals, or for salaries, general operating
expenses, scholarships, endowment funds,
fundraising, advertising, or for capital campaigns,
travel or research, or for insurance or maintenance
contacts.
Publications: Application guidelines; Grants list.
Application information: Applicant invitees chosen
from initial requests. See foundation Web site for
application guidelines and online initial request
form.
Initial approach: Must apply via initial request
form on Web site
Deadline(s): Jan. 1, Mar. 1, July 1, Sept. 1
Board meeting date(s): Apr. and Oct.
Officers and Directors:* Sarah Lynne Ludwick,*
Chair.; Sharon L. Warner,* Vice-Chair. and Secy.;
Arthur J. Ludwick,* Vice-Chair., C.F.O. and Treas.;
Patrick Bushman, Exec. V.P. and C.E.O.; Daniel
Hanson; Heidi Ann Hanson; Eileen Ludwick; Erik
Arthur Ludwick; Tom Warner.
Number of staff: 3 full-time professional; 2 full-time
support; 1 part-time support.
EIN: 954296315
Selected grants: The following grants were reported
in 2005.
$50,000 to Childrens Care Hospital and School,
Sioux Falls, SD.
$50,000 to Childrens Home Society of South
Dakota, Sioux Falls, SD.
$50,000 to University of La Verne, La Verne, CA.
$49,545 to Youth and Family Services, Rapid City,
SD.
$49,000 to Grand Vision Foundation, San Pedro,
CA.
$40,000 to Humane Society of the Black Hills,
Rapid City, SD.
$30,000 to Mount San Antonio College Foundation,
Walnut, CA.
$30,000 to World Bird Sanctuary, Valley Park, MO.
$25,000 to Visiting Nurse Association of the Inland
Counties, Riverside, CA.
$20,000 to Casa Pacifica, Camarillo, CA.

830
The Ludwick Family Foundation ✧
491 Santa Rita Ave.
Palo Alto, CA 94301-3944

Established in 1997 in CA.
Donors: Andrew Ludwick; Worth Z. Ludwick; Jocelyn
Ludwick.
Foundation type: Independent foundation.
Financial data (yr. ended 12/31/05): Assets,
$6,726,016 (M); expenditures, $408,185;
qualifying distributions, $387,865; giving activities
include $367,865 for 32 grants (high: $130,000;
low: $50), and $20,000 for 1 employee matching
gift.
Purpose and activities: Support primarily for
education, health, science, medicine, and the
environment in the U.S.
Fields of interest: Education; Environment; Health
care; Science.
Type of support: Matching/challenge support;
Capital campaigns; Endowments.
Limitations: Applications not accepted. Giving on a
national basis. No grants to individuals.
Application information: Contributes only to
pre-selected organizations.
Board meeting date(s): Quarterly
Officers: Worth Z. Ludwick, C.E.O. and Pres.; Jocelyn
Ludwick, Secy.; Andrew Ludwick, C.F.O.
Directors: Christopher Ludwick; Theodore Ludwick.
EIN: 770472486

831
The Sharon D. Lund Foundation ▼ ✧
(formerly The Lund Foundation)
535 N. Brand Blvd., Ste. 504
Glendale, CA 91203
Contact: Patricia Patti, Admin.

Established in 1973 in CA.
Donor: Sharon D. Lund†.
Foundation type: Independent foundation.
Financial data (yr. ended 12/31/04): Assets,
$109,283,389 (M); expenditures, $5,153,692;
qualifying distributions, $4,673,398; giving
activities include $4,488,600 for 36 grants (high:
$1,000,000; low: $500; average: $25,000–
$50,000), and $205 for 1 grant to an individual.
Purpose and activities: Giving primarily for youth,
arts and cultural programs, animal welfare and
health.
Fields of interest: Arts; Animal welfare; Health care;
Learning disorders; Children, services;
Developmentally disabled, centers & services.
Type of support: Grants to individuals; General/
operating support; Capital campaigns; Building/
renovation; Equipment; Seed money; Scholarship
funds; Matching/challenge support.
Limitations: Applications not accepted. Giving
primarily in AZ and CA.
Application information: Contributes only to
pre-selected organizations.
Board meeting date(s): Quarterly
Officers: Michelle A. Lund, Pres.; Bradford D. Lund,
V.P.; Robert L. Wilson, Secy.-Treas.
Director: Gloria Wilson.
Number of staff: 1 full-time professional.
EIN: 237306460
Selected grants: The following grants were reported
in 2004.
$1,000,000 to California Institute of the Arts,
Valencia, CA.

$1,000,000 to Music Center of Los Angeles County, Los Angeles, CA.

$650,000 to Phoenix Childrens Hospital, Phoenix, AZ.

$550,000 to Childrens Hospital Los Angeles, Los Angeles, CA.

$150,000 to Give Kids the World, Kissimmee, FL.

$50,000 to Childrens Burn Foundation, Sherman Oaks, CA.

$50,000 to Ryman Arts, Los Angeles, CA.

$35,000 to John Tracy Clinic, Los Angeles, CA.

$35,000 to Make-A-Wish Foundation of Greater Los Angeles, Los Angeles, CA.

$25,000 to Operation Smile International, Norfolk, VA.

832
Louis R. Lurie Foundation
555 California St., Ste. 5100
San Francisco, CA 94104 (415) 392-2470
Contact: Nancy Terry, Admin.
FAX: (415) 421-8669; URL: http://foundationcenter.org/grantmaker/lurie/

Incorporated in 1948 in CA.
Donors: Louis R. Lurie†; Robert A. Lurie; George S. Lurie†.
Foundation type: Independent foundation.
Financial data (yr. ended 12/31/05): Assets, $16,886,370 (M); expenditures, $2,618,550; qualifying distributions, $2,175,415; giving activities include $2,057,000 for grants, and $29,000 for employee matching gifts.
Purpose and activities: Funding priorities are youth, ages birth through 18 years, with an emphasis on family support, education, health, cultural enrichment, and recreation. The foundation gives priority to youth-serving agencies that have less access to traditional funding sources.
Fields of interest: Arts, multipurpose centers/programs; Arts; Child development, education; Education; Health care; Recreation; Children/youth, services; Family services, counseling.
Type of support: General/operating support; Equipment; Program development; Seed money.
Limitations: Applications not accepted. Giving limited to San Francisco, CA, and Chicago, IL. No support for post secondary schools, conferences, national organizations, local affiliates of national organizations (except programs developed at local level for local need), and religious organizations for religious purposes. No grants to individuals, or for building funds; endowments, operating deficits, underwriting or sponsorships and tables for fundraising or recognition of events.
Application information: Proposals are accepted by invitation only. See foundation Web site for additional information on proposal guidelines and procedures.
  Board meeting date(s): Twice a year
Officers and Directors:* Robert A. Lurie,* Pres.; Eugene L. Valla,* V.P. and Cont.; H. Michael Kurzman,* V.P.; James Hunt, Secy.; Patricia R. Fay; Gary Wood.
EIN: 946065488
Selected grants: The following grants were reported in 2004.
$250,000 to Jewish Community Federation of San Francisco, the Peninsula, Marin and Sonoma Counties, San Francisco, CA.
$104,000 to Salvation Army of San Francisco, San Francisco, CA.
$100,000 to Chicago Youth Programs, Chicago, IL.

$100,000 to DeMarillac Middle School, San Francisco, CA.
$100,000 to Jewish Community Center of San Francisco, San Francisco, CA.
$90,000 to Bay Area Womens and Childrens Center, San Francisco, CA.
$50,000 to Kids Turn, San Francisco, CA.
$35,000 to Edgewood Center for Children and Families, San Francisco, CA.
$25,000 to Center for Young Womens Development, San Francisco, CA.
$25,000 to Chicago Community Trust, Chicago, IL.

833
Lutz Foundation
1251 Grizzly Peak Blvd.
Berkeley, CA 94708
Contact: Elizabeth G. Lutz, Tr.

Established in 1986 in CA.
Donor: Gregory P. Lutz.
Foundation type: Independent foundation.
Financial data (yr. ended 12/31/05): Assets, $1,884,991 (M); gifts received, $3,700; expenditures, $352,993; qualifying distributions, $334,251; giving activities include $332,350 for 12 grants (high: $100,000; low: $850).
Purpose and activities: Giving for local performing arts, human rights, and civil liberties.
Fields of interest: Performing arts; International human rights; Civil rights.
Type of support: Continuing support; General/operating support; Endowments; Emergency funds; Program development.
Limitations: Applications not accepted. Giving primarily in the San Francisco Bay Area, CA. No grants to individuals.
Application information: The foundation prefers to initiate contact with potential donees; unsolicited requests for funds not considered or acknowledged.
Trustees: Elizabeth G. Lutz; Gregory P. Lutz.
EIN: 943033875
Selected grants: The following grants were reported in 2004.
$100,000 to CAL Performances, Berkeley, CA. For centennial campaign.
$50,000 to American Civil Liberties Union Foundation, New York, NY. For immigrants' rights and church/state seperation.
$40,000 to Other Minds, San Francisco, CA.
$35,000 to Doctors Without Borders USA, New York, NY. For general support of relief efforts in Darfur.
$25,000 to Gamelan Sekar Jaya, El Cerrito, CA.
$20,000 to University of California, School of Law, Berkeley, CA. For International Human Rights Law Clinic.
$5,000 to Amrita Performing Arts, Oakland, CA.
$5,000 to Chronicle Season of Sharing Fund, San Francisco, CA.
$5,000 to Foundation for the People of Burma, San Francisco, CA. For human rights projects.
$1,000 to Sonoma Land Trust, Santa Rosa, CA.

834
Miranda Lux Foundation
57 Post St., Ste. 510
San Francisco, CA 94104-5020
Contact: Kenneth J. Blum, Exec. Dir.
E-mail: admin@mirandalux.org; URL: http://www.mirandalux.org

Incorporated in 1908 in CA.
Donor: Miranda W. Lux†.
Foundation type: Independent foundation.
Financial data (yr. ended 6/30/05): Assets, $10,074,369 (M); expenditures, $571,844; qualifying distributions, $516,523; giving activities include $447,800 for 41 grants.
Purpose and activities: Support to promising proposals for preschool through junior college programs in the fields of pre-vocational and vocational education. Also supports innovative academic enrichment, technology training, and performing and visual arts programs to help participants develop core job skills. Grants to organizations and programs are limited to the city and county of San Francisco that serve young people under the age of 18.
Fields of interest: Vocational education; Adult education—literacy, basic skills & GED; Education, reading; Employment, services; Employment, training; Children/youth, services.
Type of support: General/operating support; Continuing support; Equipment; Program development; Seed money; Fellowships; Internship funds; Scholarship funds; Matching/challenge support.
Limitations: Giving limited to San Francisco, CA. No grants to individuals, or for annual campaigns, emergency funds, deficit financing, building or endowment funds, land acquisition, renovations, research, publications, or conferences; no loans.
Publications: Application guidelines; Annual report; Grants list; Informational brochure; Program policy statement.
Application information: See foundation Web site for application guidelines and procedures. Application form not required.
  Initial approach: Telephone
  Copies of proposal: 1
  Deadline(s): None
  Board meeting date(s): Feb., May, Sept., and Nov.
  Final notification: 1 week after board meeting
Officers and Trustees:* David Wisnom, Jr.,* Pres.; Philip F. Spalding,* V.P.; Beatrice Bowles,* Secy.-Treas.; Kenneth J. Blum, Exec. Dir.; Robert J. Cappelloni; Nina Gladish; Betsy Holden Keller.
EIN: 941170404
Selected grants: The following grants were reported in 2004.
$25,000 to Bay Area Video Coalition, San Francisco, CA. For YouthLink Program.
$15,000 to Bernal Heights Neighborhood Center, San Francisco, CA. For Youth Employment Services Program.
$12,500 to Community Learning Center, South San Francisco, CA. For Homework Club.
$11,000 to Math Science Network, Oakland, CA. For Expanding Your Horizons in Science and Mathematics Conference.
$10,000 to A Better Chance, San Francisco, CA. For College Preparatory School Program.
$10,000 to Centerforce, San Rafael, CA. For Leaders in Future Environment Project.
$10,000 to Leadership High School, San Francisco, CA. For Portfolios and Exhibitions Program.
$10,000 to Mission Learning Center, San Francisco, CA. For After-School Education Program.
$10,000 to Richmond District Neighborhood Center, San Francisco, CA. For Community Technology Program.
$10,000 to San Francisco Art and Film Program, San Francisco, CA. For Art and Film for Teenagers Program.

835
The Lynn Foundation ✧ ☆
P.O. Box 494482
Redding, CA 96049

Established in 1989 in CA.
Donor: Don Lynn.
Foundation type: Independent foundation.
Financial data (yr. ended 8/31/06): Assets, $6,464,057 (M); gifts received, $5,700; expenditures, $659,068; qualifying distributions, $620,942; giving activities include $620,942 for grants.
Purpose and activities: Giving to Christian organizations and youth services.
Fields of interest: Children/youth, services; Christian agencies & churches.
Limitations: Applications not accepted. Giving primarily in Redding, CA. No grants to individuals.
Application information: Contributes only to pre-selected organizations.
Officers: Don Lynn, C.E.O. and C.F.O.; Darlene Lynn, V.P.; David Lynn, V.P.
EIN: 680196406
Selected grants: The following grants were reported in 2003.
$135,000 to Youth Alive Church Ministries, Viola, CA.
$19,000 to Cottonwood Bible Baptist Church, Cottonwood, CA.
$18,000 to Shasta Bible College, Redding, CA.
$15,000 to Child Evangelism Fellowship, Pasadena, CA.
$14,000 to North Valley Baptist Church, Redding, CA.
$10,000 to Santiam Christian Schools, Corvallis, OR.
$10,000 to World Vision, Tacoma, WA.
$10,000 to Youth for Christ-Shasta Region, Redding, CA.
$6,000 to KVIP Radio, Redding, CA.
$5,000 to Ripe for Harvest, Mesa, AZ.

836
Bertha Russ Lytel Foundation ✧
P.O. Box 893
Ferndale, CA 95536

Established in 1974 in CA.
Donors: Bertha Russ Lytel†; L.D. O'Rourke†; Rachel H. Hauge†; Margaret McGovern†.
Foundation type: Independent foundation.
Financial data (yr. ended 9/30/05): Assets, $17,334,390 (M); expenditures, $1,002,963; qualifying distributions, $887,214; giving activities include $783,258 for grants, and $50,000 for grants to individuals.
Purpose and activities: Giving primarily to social service agencies for the aged and handicapped, civic and cultural programs, including libraries and museums, elementary and higher education, health associations, including hospitals and hospices, and agricultural funds; also to a scholarship program for Ferndale High School seniors who are planning to attend a four-year university or college in California and major in agriculture. If there are no eligible Ferndale High School students, students from Fortuna High School will be invited to participate.
Fields of interest: Museums; Arts; Elementary school/education; Higher education; Libraries/library science; Education; Hospitals (general); Substance abuse, services; Health organizations, association; Human services; Residential/custodial

care, hospices; Aging, centers/services; Government/public administration; Aging; Disabilities, people with.
Type of support: General/operating support; Continuing support; Building/renovation; Equipment; Seed money; Scholarship funds; Matching/challenge support.
Limitations: Giving limited to Humboldt County, CA. No grants to individuals except for the William Russ Scholarship fund, or for annual campaigns, emergency or endowment funds, deficit financing, land acquisition, renovations, research, demonstration projects, or publications; no loans.
Publications: Application guidelines.
Application information: Full application guidelines and form for the William Russ Scholarship are available by contacting the foundation. Application form required.
> *Initial approach:* Letter
> *Copies of proposal:* 8
> *Deadline(s):* 1st Wed. of each month; April 1 for William Russ Scholarship
> *Board meeting date(s):* Monthly
> *Final notification:* 30 to 60 days
Officers and Directors:* Charles M. Lawrence,* Pres.; Betty Diehl, V.P.; James K. Morrison,* Secy.; Donald Hindley, Mgr.; Charles Lakin; Tom Renner; Jack Russ; Jack Smith.
Number of staff: 1 part-time professional.
EIN: 942271250

837
M & T Foundation
P.O. Box 676370
Rancho Santa Fe, CA 92067-6370
(858) 756-1154
Contact: Frank A. Potenziani, Pres.
E-mail: fpotenziani@mnttrust.com

Established around 1972 in NM.
Donors: Dale J. Bellamah†; A.F. Potenziani; Frank A. Potenziani.
Foundation type: Independent foundation.
Financial data (yr. ended 12/31/05): Assets, $35,484,912 (M); expenditures, $2,083,935; qualifying distributions, $1,650,584; giving activities include $1,155,040 for 21 grants (high: $403,000; low: $1,000).
Purpose and activities: Giving for higher education, including a military academy, hospitals and a diabetes association, social services, youth agencies, and athletics.
Fields of interest: Secondary school/education; Higher education; Hospitals (general); Health care; Health organizations, association; Athletics/sports, training; Athletics/sports, Olympics; Recreation; Big Brothers/Big Sisters; Salvation Army; Children/youth, services; Military/veterans' organizations.
Type of support: General/operating support; Capital campaigns; Equipment; Program development; Scholarship funds; Research.
Limitations: Giving on a national basis. No grants to individuals.
Application information: Application form not required.
> *Initial approach:* Letter
> *Deadline(s):* None
> *Board meeting date(s):* Sept. and Mar.
Officers and Directors:* Frank A. Potenziani,* Pres.; Michael P. Carroll,* V.P. and Secy.; David C. Willson,* V.P. and Treas.; Fred G. Botek,* V.P.; William Potenziani,* V.P.; Kathleen P. Guggino;

Brian McMullen; Cyrena K. Potenziani; Frederich A. Potenziani; Martha M. Potenziani.
Number of staff: 4 full-time professional; 1 full-time support.
EIN: 237177691

838
Hazel I. Maag Foundation ✧
4675 MacArthur Ct., Ste. 700
Newport Beach, CA 92660-1842
(949) 476-2002
Contact: Lloyd G. Copenbarger, Tr.

Donor: Hazel F. Maag Trust.
Foundation type: Independent foundation.
Financial data (yr. ended 12/31/04): Assets, $13,253 (M); gifts received, $504,733; expenditures, $500,546; qualifying distributions, $478,600; giving activities include $478,600 for 27 grants (high: $153,000; low: $25).
Fields of interest: Children, services; Christian agencies & churches.
Type of support: General/operating support.
Limitations: Giving primarily in Whittier, CA.
Application information:
> *Initial approach:* Letter or telephone
> *Deadline(s):* None
Trustee: Lloyd G. Copenbarger.
EIN: 336081632
Selected grants: The following grants were reported in 2004.
$153,000 to California Baptist University, Riverside, CA.
$55,750 to Pacific Justice Institute, Citrus Heights, CA.
$30,000 to Family Community Church, North Highlands, CA.
$4,000 to Mission Aviation Fellowship, Redlands, CA.

839
The William and Inez Mabie Family Foundation ✧
1 Maritime Plz., 18th Fl.
San Francisco, CA 94111
Contact: Ron Malone, Dir.

Established in 1987 in CA.
Donors: William J. Mabie†; Inez Mabie†; Inez Mabie Trust.
Foundation type: Independent foundation.
Financial data (yr. ended 12/31/05): Assets, $14,763,661 (M); expenditures, $916,193; qualifying distributions, $842,000; giving activities include $842,000 for 6 grants (high: $500,000; low: $3,500).
Purpose and activities: Giving primarily for education, public policy research, with emphasis on agriculture, and for health care.
Fields of interest: Education; Hospitals (general); Agriculture/food, public policy; Human services; Public policy, research.
Type of support: Management development/capacity building; Capital campaigns; Building/renovation; Endowments; Conferences/seminars; Professorships; Research; Matching/challenge support.
Limitations: Applications not accepted. Giving primarily in CA. No grants to individuals.
Application information: Contributes only to pre-selected organizations.

Officer: Christine Torres, Secy.-Treas.
Director: Ronald Hayes Malone.
Number of staff: 1 part-time support.
EIN: 943054756

840
The Mac Family Foundation ◇
P.O. Box 91
Igo, CA 96047

Established in 2002 in CA.
Donor: Lara Mac.
Foundation type: Independent foundation.
Financial data (yr. ended 10/31/03): Assets, $0 (M); gifts received, $3,000,000; expenditures, $3,000,000; qualifying distributions, $3,000,000; giving activities include $3,000,000 for 3 grants (high: $1,000,000; low: $1,000,000).
Purpose and activities: Giving to a cancer society, a Baptist church, and to an amateur athletic association.
Fields of interest: Cancer; Athletics/sports, amateur competition; Protestant agencies & churches.
International interests: Bahamas.
Limitations: Applications not accepted. Giving limited to the Bahamas. No grants to individuals.
Application information: Contributes only to pre-selected organizations.
Officer: Lara Mac, C.E.O. and Pres.
EIN: 223885706

841
MacDonald Family Charitable Trust ◇
c/o Mark & Donna MacDonald
1561 Gates Ave.
Manhattan Beach, CA 90266

Established in 2000 in CA.
Donors: Donna Marie MacDonald; Mark MacDonald.
Foundation type: Independent foundation.
Financial data (yr. ended 12/31/05): Assets, $3,198,803 (M); gifts received, $2,115,000; expenditures, $1,117,343; qualifying distributions, $1,095,116; giving activities include $1,095,116 for 15 grants (high: $532,616; low: $500; average: $5,000–$15,000).
Fields of interest: Education; Cerebral palsy; Boys & girls clubs; Religion.
Limitations: Applications not accepted. Giving primarily in CA. No grants to individuals.
Application information: Contributes only to pre-selected organizations.
Trustees: Donna Marie MacDonald; Mark MacDonald.
EIN: 336269762

842
MacDonald Family Foundation
P.O. Box 64788
Los Angeles, CA 90064 (310) 571-2492
Contact: David S. Wang, Tr.
FAX: (310) 571-2496; E-mail: mltglm@aol.com

Established in 1992 in CA.
Foundation type: Independent foundation.
Financial data (yr. ended 2/28/06): Assets, $38,203,225 (M); expenditures, $1,803,880; qualifying distributions, $1,723,482; giving

activities include $1,699,020 for 18 grants (high: $600,000; low: $4,020).
Purpose and activities: Support for elementary/secondary education, and youth development centers and clubs.
Fields of interest: Elementary/secondary education; Youth development, centers/clubs.
Limitations: Applications not accepted. Giving on a national basis. No grants to individuals.
Application information: Contributes only to pre-selected organizations.
Trustees: Roxanne B. Chapman; Peter Hilf; Jane Rodgers; David S. Wang; Marilyn Winthrop.
EIN: 954396044
Selected grants: The following grants were reported in 2005.
$600,000 to Claremont Institute for the Study of Statesmanship and Political Philosophy, Claremont, CA.
$500,000 to Pine Ridge School, Williston, VT.
$75,000 to Volunteers of America, Everett, WA.
$50,000 to AIDS Alliance, Oakland, CA.
$21,000 to Claremont Graduate University, Claremont, CA.

843
The MacKenzie Foundation ◇
c/o Bank of the West
P.O. Box 60078
Los Angeles, CA 90060
Contact: Philip D. Irwin, Tr.

Established about 1978 in CA.
Donor: Sophia MacKenzie‡.
Foundation type: Independent foundation.
Financial data (yr. ended 12/31/05): Assets, $14,974,439 (M); expenditures, $863,128; qualifying distributions, $730,011; giving activities include $690,000 for 10 grants (high: $80,000; low: $25,000).
Purpose and activities: The purpose of the foundation is to make grants for the benefit of pre-medical or medical students enrolled in schools located in the state of CA.
Fields of interest: Medical school/education.
Type of support: Scholarship funds.
Limitations: Giving limited to CA. No grants to individuals; no loans.
Application information:
  Deadline(s): None
Trustees: Verdi S. Boyer; William G. Corey; Philip D. Irwin; Bank of the West.
EIN: 956588350

844
MacNaughton Family Foundation ◇
c/o Genstar Investment Corp.
4 Embarcadero Ctr., Ste. 1900
San Francisco, CA 94111

Established in 1996 in CA.
Donor: Angus A. MacNaughton.
Foundation type: Independent foundation.
Financial data (yr. ended 12/31/04): Assets, $5,346,760 (M); gifts received, $101,148; expenditures, $461,059; qualifying distributions, $416,535; giving activities include $416,500 for 11 grants (high: $140,000; low: $1,000).
Fields of interest: Performing arts, opera; Arts; Education; Boy scouts.

Limitations: Applications not accepted. Giving limited to CA. No grants to individuals.
Application information: Contributes only to pre-selected organizations.
Officers: Cathy C. MacNaughton, Exec. V.P.; Joann Philips, Exec. Dir.
Trustee: Angus A. MacNaughton.
EIN: 946700312
Selected grants: The following grants were reported in 2004.
$140,000 to Boy Scouts of America.
$100,000 to San Francisco Opera Association, San Francisco, CA.
$5,000 to Young Life.
$4,000 to Arthritis Foundation, Atlanta, GA.
$3,000 to American Heart Association, Dallas, TX.

845
Maddie's Fund ◇
(formerly The Duffield Family Foundation)
2223 Santa Clara Ave., Ste. B
Alameda, CA 94501-4416 (510) 337-8989
Contact: Richard Avanzino, Pres.
FAX: (510) 337-8988;
E-mail: info@maddiesfund.org; URL: http://www.maddiesfund.org

Established in 1994 in CA.
Foundation type: Independent foundation.
Financial data (yr. ended 6/30/06): Assets, $281,984,079 (M); gifts received, $1,096; expenditures, $6,375,035; qualifying distributions, $4,487,879; giving activities include $3,236,799 for grants.
Purpose and activities: The fund's mission is to revolutionize the status and well being of companion animals. They are most interested in projects demonstrating the ability to build alliances and develop collaborative community-wide projects. Successful proposals will set forth comprehensive life-saving strategies that involve the participation of cooperating animal shelters, rescue groups, volunteer foster organizations, local animal control agencies, veterinarians, and others.
Fields of interest: Animal welfare.
Limitations: Giving on a national basis. No support for government funded agencies. No grants to individuals, scholarships or for capital building projects, shelter construction, projects for animals other than dogs and cats, land purchase, endowment campaigns, deficit or emergency funding, research, publications, films, videos, or special events.
Publications: Application guidelines; Annual report; Newsletter; Program policy statement.
Application information: Applications are available on foundation Web site. Do not send any additional materials with the initial application unless requested by the fund. One proposal per group per year. Application form required.
  Initial approach: Preliminary application
  Copies of proposal: 2
  Deadline(s): None
  Final notification: Up to 6 months from receipt of proposal
Officers and Directors:* Amy D. Zeifang,* Chair.; Richard Avanzino, Pres.; Laurie E. Peek, Secy.; Cheryl D. Duffield; David A. Duffield; Michael D. Duffield; Margaret L. Taylor.
EIN: 680339626
Selected grants: The following grants were reported in 2005.

$3,500,000 to Cornell University, Ithaca, NY. 2 grants: $1,700,000 (For shelter medicine program), $1,800,000 (For board-directed grant for engineering endowment).

$1,250,000 to Auburn University, College of Veterinary Medicine, Auburn, AL. For shelter medicine program.

$938,800 to Best Friends Animal Society, Kanab, UT. For spay/neuter program and adoptions.

$821,760 to Arizona Animal Welfare League, Phoenix, AZ. For adoptions.

$674,100 to Mayors Alliance for NYCs Animals, New York, NY. For adoptions.

$527,760 to Humane Society, Alachua County, Gainesville, FL. For adoptions.

$500,000 to Tony La Russas Animal Rescue Foundation, Walnut Creek, CA. For capital support.

$330,000 to Tompkins County Society for the Prevention of Cruelty to Animals, Ithaca, NY. For operating support.

$10,000 to Panguitch City Animal Control, Panguitch, UT. For adoptions.

846
The Magali Foundation ◇
8454 El Paseo Grande
La Jolla, CA   92037

Established in CA.
Donors: Maria G. Sulpizio; Richard Sulpizio.
Foundation type: Independent foundation.
Financial data (yr. ended 12/31/05): Assets, $6,241,843 (M); gifts received, $95; expenditures, $937,651; qualifying distributions, $889,692; giving activities include $869,251 for 18 grants (high: $500,000; low: $126; average: $10,000–$40,000).
Purpose and activities: Giving primarily for children and youth services, as well as for higher education; funding also for social services.
Fields of interest: Higher education; Crime/violence prevention, child abuse; Boys & girls clubs; Human services; Children/youth, services.
Limitations: Applications not accepted. Giving primarily in CA.
Application information: Contributes only to pre-selected organizations.
Officers: Maria G. Sulpizio, Pres.; Richard Sulpizio, Secy.
EIN: 912169989

847
Magistro Foundation, Inc. ◇ ☆
3816 Hollins Ave.
Claremont, CA   91711-1442   (909) 982-0207
Contact: Charles M. Magistro, Pres.

Established in 2002 in CA.
Donor: Charles M. Magistro.
Foundation type: Independent foundation.
Financial data (yr. ended 12/31/05): Assets, $691,311 (M); gifts received, $604,200; expenditures, $1,121,461; qualifying distributions, $1,103,252; giving activities include $1,103,252 for 8 grants (high: $1,003,252; low: $2,500).
Purpose and activities: Giving primarily for medical research and education.
Fields of interest: Secondary school/education; Higher education; Education; Physical therapy; End

of life care; Cancer research; Medical research; Human services.
Limitations: Giving primarily in CA, PA, and AK. No grants to individuals.
Application information:
Initial approach: Letter
Deadline(s): None
Officers: Charles M. Magistro, Pres.; Mary N. Magistro, Secy.
Directors: Elise M. Baumgaertner; Andrea M. Nadler; Maria M. Sherry; Paulelle M. Simpson.
EIN: 680527894

848
Majestic Realty Foundation ◇
13191 Crossroads Pkwy. N., 6th Fl.
City of Industry, CA   91746-3497
(562) 654-2725
Contact: Frances L. Inman, Pres.
E-mail: majesticfoundation@majesticrealty.com;
URL: http://www.majesticrealty.com/company/majestic_foundation.asp

Established in 2002 in CA.
Donor: Majestic Realty Co.
Foundation type: Company-sponsored foundation.
Financial data (yr. ended 12/31/03): Assets, $0 (M); gifts received, $991,101; expenditures, $1,073,640; qualifying distributions, $1,072,393; giving activities include $1,072,393 for grants.
Purpose and activities: The foundation supports organizations involved with arts and culture, education, health, violence prevention, employment, youth development, and families.
Fields of interest: Arts; Education; Health care; Crime/violence prevention; Employment; Youth development; Family services.
Type of support: General/operating support; Continuing support; Capital campaigns; Program development; Employee matching gifts; Matching/challenge support.
Limitations: Giving primarily in Los Angeles, CA, Denver, CO, Atlanta, GA, and Las Vegas, NV. No support for federated funds or pass-through organizations, religious or other organizations not of direct benefit to the entire community, or lobbying organizations. No grants to individuals, or for start-up needs.
Application information: Additional information may be requested at a later date. A site visit may be requested. Application form not required.
Initial approach: Letter of inquiry
Copies of proposal: 1
Officers and Directors:* Frances L. Inman,* Pres.; Gail Kiralla,* Secy.; David A. Wheeler,* Treas.
EIN: 043722125
Selected grants: The following grants were reported in 2004.
$25,000 to Boys and Girls Club of Redlands, Redlands, CA.
$25,000 to Cal Poly Pomona Foundation, Pomona, CA.
$25,000 to Childrens Hospital Los Angeles, Los Angeles, CA.
$25,000 to Legal Aid Foundation of Los Angeles, Los Angeles, CA.
$17,982 to Hillview Acres Childrens Home, Chino, CA.
$10,000 to California Science Center Foundation, Los Angeles, CA.
$10,000 to Loma Linda University Childrens Hospital Foundation, Loma Linda, CA.
$10,000 to Trinity School, Atlanta, GA.

$5,000 to Boys and Girls Club, Variety, Los Angeles, CA.
$5,000 to YMCA, Chino Family, Chino, CA.

849
The Ted Mann Family Foundation ◇
c/o BJJSM
9320 Wilshire Blvd., Ste. 300
Beverly Hills, CA   90212

Established in 2002 in DE.
Foundation type: Independent foundation.
Financial data (yr. ended 12/31/03): Assets, $40,902,685 (M); expenditures, $2,451,865; qualifying distributions, $2,066,690; giving activities include $2,066,690 for 17 grants (high: $900,000; low: $500).
Fields of interest: Higher education; Health care; Family services; Philanthropy/voluntarism; Jewish agencies & temples.
Limitations: Applications not accepted. Giving primarily in CA. No grants to individuals.
Application information: Contributes only to pre-selected organizations.
Officers and Directors:* Victoria Mann Simms,* Pres.; Ronald A. Simms,* Secy.-Treas.; Joshua Simms; Julie Simms.
EIN: 311812498
Selected grants: The following grants were reported in 2004.
$973,400 to Ronald A. and Vicki Mann Simms Foundation, Los Angeles, CA.
$740,000 to Vanguard Charitable Endowment Program, Southeastern, PA.
$60,000 to El Nido Family Centers, Los Angeles, CA.
$50,000 to Bnai Brith Hillel Foundation, Los Angeles, CA.
$50,000 to Yale University, New Haven, CT.
$25,000 to University of Texas, Houston, TX.
$24,000 to Entertainment Industry Foundation, Los Angeles, CA.
$20,000 to Beit TShuvah, Los Angeles, CA.
$14,000 to UCLA Foundation, Los Angeles, CA.
$10,000 to Jewish Federation Council of Greater Los Angeles, Los Angeles, CA.

850
The Maurice Marciano Family Foundation ◇
144 S. Beverly Dr., Ste. 600
Beverly Hills, CA   90212

Established in 1995 in CA.
Donor: Maurice Marciano.
Foundation type: Independent foundation.
Financial data (yr. ended 12/31/04): Assets, $8,705,053 (M); gifts received, $5,136,000; expenditures, $921,208; qualifying distributions, $882,500; giving activities include $882,500 for 50 grants (high: $250,000; low: $500).
Purpose and activities: Giving primarily for Sephardic Jewish agencies and temples, as well as for hospitals, and children, youth, and social services.
Fields of interest: Arts; Education; Hospitals (general); Human services; Children/youth, services; Jewish federated giving programs; Jewish agencies & temples.
Limitations: Applications not accepted. Giving primarily in CA. No grants to individuals.

Application information: Contributes only to pre-selected organizations.
Officer and Director:* Maurice Marciano*,* Pres.
EIN: 954554525

851
The Marcled Foundation ✧ ☆
3268 Sacramento St.
San Francisco, CA   94115

Established in 2004 in CA and DE.
Donor: Virginia and Leonard Marx Foundation.
Foundation type: Independent foundation.
Financial data (yr. ended 12/31/05): Assets, $18,370,198 (M); gifts received, $12,767,300; expenditures, $773,665; qualifying distributions, $679,180; giving activities include $546,000 for 41 grants (high: $55,000; low: $2,000).
Purpose and activities: Giving primarily for education, the arts, health care, including equestrian riding therapy, medical services, and hospitals, and children, youth, and social services.
Fields of interest: Arts; Elementary/secondary education; Education; Hospitals (general); Physical therapy; Human services; Jewish agencies & temples.
Limitations: Applications not accepted. Giving primarily in CA, with emphasis on Los Angeles, San Francisco, and San Luis Obispo; some funding nationally. No grants to individuals.
Application information: Contributes only to pre-selected organizations.
Officers and Directors:* Claire Solot,* Pres.; Mary Blanco,* Secy.; Edwin Solot, Jr.,* Treas.
EIN: 200595609

852
The Marcus & Millichap Company Foundation ✧ ☆
777 California Ave.
Palo Alto, CA   94304

Established in 1998 in CA.
Donor: The Marcus & Millichap Co.
Foundation type: Company-sponsored foundation.
Financial data (yr. ended 12/31/05): Assets, $2,145,708 (M); gifts received, $2,000,000; expenditures, $391,705; qualifying distributions, $385,755; giving activities include $385,755 for grants.
Purpose and activities: The foundation supports organizations involved with arts and culture, education, health, medical research, youth development, and human services.
Fields of interest: Performing arts, ballet; Arts; Higher education; Education; Health care; Health organizations, association; Medical research; Youth development; Human services.
Limitations: Applications not accepted. Giving primarily in CA. No grants to individuals.
Application information: Contributes only to pre-selected organizations.
Officers: George M. Marcus, C.E.O.; Marianne Empedocles, Secy.; Donald A. Lorenz, C.F.O.
EIN: 770480868
Selected grants: The following grants were reported in 2004.
$100,000 to Ballet San Jose Silicon Valley, San Jose, CA.
$12,000 to Los Angeles Philharmonic, Friends of the, Los Angeles, CA.

$10,000 to Avenidas, Palo Alto, CA.
$10,000 to California State University at Northridge Foundation, Northridge, CA.
$6,000 to Bay Area Council, San Francisco, CA.
$5,000 to City of Hope, Los Angeles, CA.
$5,000 to Simon Youth Foundation, Indianapolis, IN.
$3,500 to Shelter Partnership, Los Angeles, CA.
$2,100 to University of Judaism, Los Angeles, CA.
$1,000 to Westwood Kehilla, Los Angeles, CA.

853
The George and Judy Marcus Family Foundation ✧ ☆
777 California Ave.
Palo Alto, CA   94304

Established in 1998 in CA.
Donors: George Marcus; Judy Marcus.
Foundation type: Independent foundation.
Financial data (yr. ended 12/31/05): Assets, $5,779,515 (M); gifts received, $3,000,000; expenditures, $2,168,454; qualifying distributions, $2,153,750; giving activities include $2,153,750 for 6 grants (high: $2,000,000; low: $8,750).
Fields of interest: Arts; Animal welfare; Health organizations, association; Human services.
Limitations: Applications not accepted. Giving primarily in CA. No grants to individuals.
Application information: Contributes only to pre-selected organizations.
Officers and Directors:* George Marcus,* Pres.; Marianne Empedocles,* Secy.; Donald Lorenz,* C.F.O.; Judith Marcus.
EIN: 770500373

854
Marin Community Foundation ▼ ✧
5 Hamilton Landing, Ste. 200
Novato, CA   94949   (415) 464-2500
Contact: Fred Silverman, V.P., Mktg. and Comms.
FAX: (415) 464-2555; E-mail: info@marincf.org;
URL: http://www.marincf.org

Incorporated in 1986 in CA; the Leonard and Beryl Buck Foundation, its original donor, was established in 1973 and administered by the San Francisco Foundation through 1986.
Foundation type: Community foundation.
Financial data (yr. ended 6/30/06): Assets, $1,125,930,427 (M); gifts received, $40,303,555; expenditures, $86,100,366; giving activities include $51,649,386 for grants.
Purpose and activities: The Marin Community Foundation is a tax-exempt charity that administers private funds for public purposes. It was established in 1986 to encourage and apply philanthropic contributions to help improve the human condition, embrace diversity, promote a humane and democratic society, and enhance the community's quality of life, now and for future generations. The foundation supports a broad array of programs, projects, and services, including fund development and management for individuals and organizations who place their philanthropic funds in its care. Grants are made in the areas of: Human Needs, Community Development, Education and Training, Religion, Environment, and Arts.
Fields of interest: Arts; Adult education—literacy, basic skills & GED; Education; Environment; AIDS; Legal services; Employment; Housing/shelter,

development; Human services; Community development; Religion; Aging; Disabilities, people with; Homeless.
Type of support: General/operating support; Continuing support; Capital campaigns; Building/renovation; Equipment; Land acquisition; Debt reduction; Emergency funds; Program development; Conferences/seminars; Seed money; Curriculum development; Scholarship funds; Research; Technical assistance; Consulting services; Program evaluation; Program-related investments/loans; Employee matching gifts; Scholarships—to individuals; Matching/challenge support.
Limitations: Giving from Buck Trust limited to Marin County, CA; other giving on a national and international basis with emphasis on the San Francisco Bay Area. No grants to individuals (except for scholarships), or for planning initiatives, or capital projects (except those meeting criteria specified in the funding guidelines). Other limitations specific to each program area are outlined in the funding guidelines.
Publications: Application guidelines; Annual report; Informational brochure (including application guidelines); Newsletter.
Application information: Visit foundation Web site for applications and guidelines. Letters of Intent may be completed online or downloaded and submitted by mail; faxed proposals are not accepted. Application form required.
Initial approach: Contact appropriate Prog. Off.
Copies of proposal: 3
Deadline(s): None
Board meeting date(s): Monthly
Final notification: 3 months minimum
Officers and Trustees:* Sara Barnes,* Chair.; Gary T. Giacomini,* Vice-Chair.; Thomas Peters, Ph.D.*, C.E.O. and Pres.; Marsha E. Bonner, V.P., Progs.; Sid Hartman, V.P., Finance and Admin.; Fred Silverman, V.P., Mktg. and Comms.; Patrick Woods, V.P., Philanthropic Svcs.; Aileen Sweeney, Cont.; George Bull III; Cassandra Flipper, J.D.; Ann Mathieson; Lois Merriweather Moore, Ed.D.; Jay L. Paxton; Carlos Porrata; Margaret Van Camp.
Number of staff: 26 full-time professional; 6 part-time professional; 6 full-time support; 1 part-time support.
EIN: 943007979
Selected grants: The following grants were reported in 2005.
$2,949,000 to Patagonia Land Trust, Conservacion Patagonica, Sausalito, CA. For general operating support.
$1,300,000 to Marin Continuum of Housing and Services, San Rafael, CA. For development of units in Phase II of Hamilton Transitional Housing (HTH) development. Grant made through Buck Trust.
$1,000,000 to Making Waves Education Program, Richmond, CA. For program expansion in Richmond and San Francisco.
$600,000 to Marin Senior Coordinating Council, San Rafael, CA. For programs that serve Marin's elderly and disabled populations. Grant made through Buck Trust.
$474,000 to Marin Arts Council, San Rafael, CA. For Individual Artists Grant and Community Arts Grant Programs. Grant made through Buck Trust.
$460,000 to CaliforniaKids Healthcare Foundation, Woodland Hills, CA. For preventive and primary health care insurance coverage for uninsured Marin children who are not eligible for public insurance programs. Grant made through Buck Trust.

$50,000 to Latino Council of Marin, San Rafael, CA. For programs that work with service providers, County offices, community organizations, businesses and professionals to produce more effective outcomes in Latino community. Grant made through Buck Trust.

$45,000 to Marin Workforce Housing Trust, Tiburon, CA. To encourage development of affordable housing in Marin County. Grant made through Buck Trust.

$33,400 to Strategic Energy Innnovations, San Rafael, CA. For Awareness for Communities about Energy Program. Grant made through Buck Trust.

$25,725 to West Marin Community Services, Point Reyes Station, CA. For Marin School-Linked Services Initiative.

855

The Marisla Foundation ▼
412 N. Coast Hwy., PMB 359
Laguna Beach, CA 92651 (949) 494-0365
Contact: Glenda Menges, Admin.

Established in 1986 in CA.
Foundation type: Independent foundation.
Financial data (yr. ended 12/31/04): Assets, $14,324,696 (M); gifts received, $12,500,000; expenditures, $19,853,506; qualifying distributions, $19,840,416; giving activities include $19,358,600 for 333 grants (high: $1,000,000; low: $1,000; average: $10,000–$125,000).
Purpose and activities: Giving primarily through two programs: an Environmental Program, and a Human Services Program.
Fields of interest: Environment, toxics; Women, centers/services; Marine science.
International interests: Mexico.
Type of support: General/operating support; Program development.
Limitations: Giving primarily on the West Coast of the U.S. (including Baja, CA), HI, and the Western Pacific for the environment; funding for women limited to Los Angeles and Orange County, CA. No support for political campaigns. No grants to individuals, or for scholarships, fellowships, or film or video projects.
Publications: Application guidelines.
Application information: Call to request proposal guidelines. Please do not send letters of inquiry. Application form required.
 Initial approach: Proposal
 Copies of proposal: 1
 Deadline(s): Mar. 1, June 1, Sept. 1, and Dec. 1
 Board meeting date(s): Quarterly
 Final notification: 8 weeks
Officer: Herbert M. Bedolfe, Exec. Dir.
Number of staff: 2 full-time professional; 1 part-time support.
EIN: 330200133
Selected grants: The following grants were reported in 2004.
$1,000,000 to Nature Conservancy, Arlington, VA. 2 grants: $250,000 (For Pacific Islands Marine Conservation), $750,000 (For Palmyra Atoll Project).
$600,000 to Natural Resources Defense Council, New York, NY. For Environmental Campaigns.
$500,000 to Health Care Without Harm, Arlington, VA. For general support to improve medical facilities.
$500,000 to Mono Lake Foundation, Lee Vining, CA. For endowment support.

$500,000 to National Environmental Trust, DC. For Environmental Health Campaign.
$500,000 to Resources Legacy Fund, Sacramento, CA. For Marine Life Protection Act.
$400,000 to Environmental Working Group, DC. For research of environmental health issues.
$300,000 to Nature Conservancy of Hawaii, Honolulu, HI. For Kaiai/Big Island.
$300,000 to Ocean Alliance, Lincoln, MA. For Voyage of the Odyssey.

856

The Markkula Foundation ◇
c/o ACM Investments
P.O. Box 620170
Woodside, CA 94062-0170
Contact: Armas C. Markkula, Jr., C.E.O. and Pres.; Linda K. Markkula, V.P. and Secy.

Established in 1991 in CA.
Donors: Armas C. Markkula, Jr.; Linda K. Markkula.
Foundation type: Independent foundation.
Financial data (yr. ended 6/30/05): Assets, $13,125,074 (M); gifts received, $3,000; expenditures, $655,745; qualifying distributions, $640,970; giving activities include $635,000 for 57 grants (high: $200,000; low: $500).
Purpose and activities: Giving primarily for education, including a children's scholarship fund, human services, community foundations, and to a residence for young men who are being treated for addiction.
Fields of interest: Arts; Higher education, university; Education; Substance abuse, treatment; Boys & girls clubs; Human services; Children, services; Foundations (community).
Limitations: Giving primarily in CA. No grants to individuals.
Application information: Application form not required.
 Deadline(s): None
Officers and Directors:* Armas C. Markkula, Jr.,* C.E.O. and Pres.; Linda K. Markkula,* V.P. and Secy.
EIN: 770272230
Selected grants: The following grants were reported in 2004.
$120,000 to Santa Clara University, Santa Clara, CA.
$25,000 to Boys and Girls Clubs of the Peninsula, Menlo Park, CA.
$5,000 to Habitat for Humanity, Peninsula, Redwood City, CA.
$3,000 to Green Pastures, Mountain View, CA.
$3,000 to Next Door Solutions to Domestic Violence, San Jose, CA.
$3,000 to Saint Vincent de Paul Society, San Francisco, CA.
$1,500 to California Academy of Sciences, San Francisco, CA.
$1,000 to Avenidas, Palo Alto, CA.
$1,000 to San Jose Museum of Art, San Jose, CA.
$1,000 to Woodside School Foundation, Woodside, CA.

857

Michael E. Marks Family Foundation ◇ ☆
c/o Harris myCFO, Inc.
1700 Seaport Blvd., 4th Fl.
Redwood City, CA 94063

Established in 1998 in CA.

Donors: Michael Marks; Carole Marks.
Foundation type: Independent foundation.
Financial data (yr. ended 12/31/05): Assets, $5,876,189 (M); gifts received, $8,000; expenditures, $388,655; qualifying distributions, $367,000; giving activities include $367,000 for grants.
Fields of interest: Education; Health care; Human services.
Limitations: Applications not accepted. No grants to individuals.
Application information: Contributes only to pre-selected organizations.
Officers: Michael Marks, Pres.; Carole Marks, Secy. and C.F.O.
EIN: 770500312
Selected grants: The following grants were reported in 2004.
$60,700 to Juilliard School, New York, NY.
$25,000 to Avenidas, Palo Alto, CA.
$10,000 to Peninsula Community Foundation, San Mateo, CA.
$7,500 to Rebuilding Together, Long Beach, CA.
$5,000 to Project Open Hand, San Francisco, CA.
$2,500 to Oberlin College, Oberlin, OH.

858

Barbara and Garry Marshall Family Foundation ◇
c/o Gelfand, Rennert & Feldman, LLP
1880 Century Park E., Ste. 1600
Los Angeles, CA 90067

Established in 1991 in CA.
Donors: Barbara S. Marshall; Garry K. Marshall.
Foundation type: Independent foundation.
Financial data (yr. ended 12/31/05): Assets, $429,056 (M); gifts received, $300,000; expenditures, $578,049; qualifying distributions, $578,014; giving activities include $578,014 for 67 grants (high: $150,500; low: $50).
Purpose and activities: Giving primarily for the arts and education; support also for health associations and human services.
Fields of interest: Media/communications; Museums; Performing arts, theater; Arts; Education; Health care, association; Health organizations, association; Human services.
Limitations: Applications not accepted. Giving on a national basis with some emphasis on the Los Angeles, CA, area. No grants to individuals.
Application information: Contributes only to pre-selected organizations.
Trustees: Barbara S. Marshall; Garry K. Marshall.
EIN: 954346688

859

The Steve Martin Charitable Foundation ◇ ☆
(formerly Roger's & Betty's Charitable Foundation)
11766 Wilshire Blvd., No. 1610
Los Angeles, CA 90025

Established in 1997 in CA.
Donor: Stephen G. Martin.
Foundation type: Independent foundation.
Financial data (yr. ended 12/31/05): Assets, $857,277 (M); gifts received, $205,000; expenditures, $368,873; qualifying distributions, $368,745; giving activities include $368,745 for 19 grants (high: $200,000; low: $497).

Purpose and activities: Giving primarily for the arts; some funding also for research in hearing.
Fields of interest: Museums; Arts; Ear & throat research.
Limitations: Applications not accepted. Giving primarily in CA and NY. No grants to individuals.
Application information: Contributes only to pre-selected organizations.
Trustee: Stephen G. Martin.
EIN: 954656545

860
The Gilbert J. Martin Foundation ✧ ☆
685 Turquoise St.
La Jolla, CA 92037
Contact: Roger Anderson, Tr.

Established in 1983 in CA.
Donor: Gilbert J. Martin.
Foundation type: Independent foundation.
Financial data (yr. ended 12/31/05): Assets, $7,632,678 (M); gifts received, $1,000,000; expenditures, $416,372; qualifying distributions, $327,500; giving activities include $327,500 for 23 grants (high: $50,000; low: $5,000).
Purpose and activities: Giving primarily for education and Christian churches.
Fields of interest: Performing arts, ballet; Elementary school/education; Secondary school/ education; Higher education; Boy scouts; YM/ YWCAs & YM/YWHAs; Christian agencies & churches.
Limitations: Giving primarily in San Diego County, CA. No grants to individuals.
Application information: Application form not required.
 Deadline(s): None
Trustees: Roger Anderson; Paul Berning; Marc Lanci.
EIN: 330002513
Selected grants: The following grants were reported in 2004.
$50,000 to YMCA of La Jolla, La Jolla, CA.
$20,000 to University of California at San Diego, La Jolla, CA.
$15,000 to La Jolla High School Foundation, La Jolla, CA.
$12,500 to La Jolla Rotary Foundation, La Jolla, CA.
$10,000 to American Red Cross, Imperial Counties Chapter, San Diego, CA.
$10,000 to Salvation Army of San Diego, San Diego, CA.
$10,000 to San Diego Hospice and Palliative Care, San Diego, CA.
$10,000 to United Service Organization of San Diego, San Diego, CA.
$5,000 to Alpha Project for the Homeless, San Diego, CA.
$2,500 to City Ballet, San Diego, CA.

861
Mattel Children's Foundation ▼
(formerly Mattel Foundation)
333 Continental Blvd., M.S. M1-1418
El Segundo, CA 90245 (310) 252-2908
E-mail: foundation@mattel.com; URL: http:// www.mattel.com/about_us/philanthropy/ ci_mcf_philanthropy_mattelFoundation.asp

Established in 1978 in CA.
Donor: Mattel, Inc.

Foundation type: Company-sponsored foundation.
Financial data (yr. ended 12/31/04): Assets, $1,014,431 (M); gifts received, $6,210,300; expenditures, $5,962,050; qualifying distributions, $5,962,015; giving activities include $5,705,150 for 119 grants (high: $5,000,000; low: $300), and $202,156 for employee matching gifts.
Purpose and activities: The foundation supports organizations involved with arts and culture, education, health, youth development, human services, and religion. Special emphasis is directed toward programs designed to improve the lives of children.
Fields of interest: Arts; Elementary/secondary education; Higher education; Education; Hospitals (general); Health care; Youth development; Children/youth, services; Children, services; Human services; Federated giving programs; Religion.
Type of support: General/operating support; Program development; Seed money; Technical assistance; Employee volunteer services; Sponsorships; Employee matching gifts; Employee-related scholarships; Donated products; In-kind gifts.
Limitations: Giving on a national and international basis, with emphasis on Los Angeles, CA, Mount Laurel, NJ, Buffalo, NY, and Madison, WI. No support for religious, fraternal, athletic, social, veterans', or labor organizations. No grants to individuals (except for employee-related scholarships), or for endowments, research, or courtesy advertising; no loans.
Publications: Annual report; Occasional report.
Application information: Application form not required.
 Initial approach: Proposal
 Deadline(s): None
 Board meeting date(s): Feb., May, Aug., and Nov.
Officers: Harold Brown, Chair.; Robert John Normile, Secy.; William Stavro, Treas.
Number of staff: 2 full-time professional; 1 full-time support.
EIN: 953263647
Selected grants: The following grants were reported in 2004.
$5,000,000 to Mattel Childrens Hospital at the University of California at Los Angeles, Los Angeles, CA.
$12,500 to Memorial Sloan-Kettering Cancer Center, New York, NY.
$12,500 to University of Chicago Childrens Hospital, Chicago, IL.
$11,400 to Mercy Hospital Foundation, Buffalo, NY.
$10,000 to Foundation for the Children of the Californias, San Diego, CA.
$10,000 to Women and Childrens Hospital of Buffalo, Buffalo, NY.
$5,000 to Roswell Park Alliance Foundation, Buffalo, NY.

862
The Maxfield Foundation
12930 Saratoga Ave., Ste. B-3
Saratoga, CA 95070
Contact: Robert R. Maxfield, Pres.

Established in 1985 in CA.
Donor: Robert R. Maxfield.
Foundation type: Independent foundation.
Financial data (yr. ended 12/31/05): Assets, $7,599,318 (M); expenditures, $400,641; qualifying distributions, $359,576; giving activities

include $359,521 for 13 grants (high: $69,521; low: $1,000).
Purpose and activities: Support for scientific research in several fields.
Fields of interest: Cancer, leukemia research; Science, research.
Type of support: Seed money; Research.
Publications: Annual report.
Application information: Applicants are encouraged, but not required, to first submit an abbreviated overview of the proposed project to determine if there is any level of interest by the foundation. If so, a detailed proposal would be requested.
Officers: Robert R. Maxfield, Pres.; Melinda Maxfield, V.P.; Clarence J. Ferrari, Jr., Secy.
EIN: 770099366
Selected grants: The following grants were reported in 2005.
$69,521 to Santa Fe Institute, Santa Fe, NM.
$50,000 to Basic Fund, San Francisco, CA.
$35,000 to Foundation for Shamanic Studies, Mill Valley, CA.
$34,000 to Montalvo Association, Saratoga, CA.
$10,000 to Crow Canyon Archaeological Center, Cortez, CO.
$10,000 to San Jose Museum of Art, San Jose, CA.

863
George Henry Mayr Trust ✧
c/o Wells Fargo Bank, N.A.
P.O. Box 63954
San Francisco, CA 94163

Trust established in 1949 in CA.
Donor: George Henry Mayr†.
Foundation type: Independent foundation.
Financial data (yr. ended 12/31/05): Assets, $24,101,874 (M); gifts received, $20,000; expenditures, $1,569,776; qualifying distributions, $1,260,087; giving activities include $1,125,500 for 141 grants (high: $25,000; low: $500).
Purpose and activities: Grants to CA private schools for scholarships to students who have completed the 8th grade and reside in the state.
Fields of interest: Secondary school/education; Higher education; Business school/education; Education; Minorities.
Type of support: Scholarship funds.
Limitations: Applications not accepted. Giving limited to CA. No support for medical education other than dentistry. No grants to individuals.
Application information: Contributes only to pre-selected organizations.
 Board meeting date(s): Quarterly
Directors: Michele McGarry Crahan; Patrick C. Hayden; Catherine Grier Olson.
Trustee: Wells Fargo Bank, N.A.
Number of staff: 1 part-time support.
EIN: 956062009
Selected grants: The following grants were reported in 2003.
$25,000 to Jesuit High School, Sacramento, CA.
$25,000 to University of Southern California, Los Angeles, CA.
$15,000 to Saint Marys Academy, Inglewood, CA.
$15,000 to Verbum Dei High School, Los Angeles, CA.
$10,000 to Alverno High School, Sierra Madre, CA.
$10,000 to Biola University, La Mirada, CA.
$10,000 to Claremont McKenna College, Claremont, CA.

$10,000 to Keck Graduate Institute of Applied Life Sciences, Claremont, CA.

$10,000 to Loyola Marymount University, Los Angeles, CA.

$10,000 to University of Redlands, Redlands, CA.

864

The Harold McAlister Charitable Foundation

4801 Wilshire Blvd., Ste. 232
Los Angeles, CA 90010
Contact: Katrina Bacallao

Incorporated in 1959 in CA.
Donors: Harold McAlister‡; Fern Smith McAlister‡.
Foundation type: Independent foundation.
Financial data (yr. ended 5/31/05): Assets, $32,338,290 (M); expenditures, $1,953,697; qualifying distributions, $1,637,003; giving activities include $1,534,000 for 40 grants (high: $650,000; low: $2,500).
Purpose and activities: Support primarily for human services, health, education, the arts, religion, and animal welfare.
Fields of interest: Higher education; Hospitals (general); Health organizations, association; Heart & circulatory diseases; Heart & circulatory research; Human services; Children/youth, services.
Limitations: Applications not accepted. Giving primarily in the Los Angeles, CA, area. No grants to individuals.
Application information: Unsolicited requests for funds not accepted.
  Board meeting date(s): Monthly
Officer and Trustees: James P. McAlister,* Pres.; David B. Heyler, Jr.; Mari McAlister; Michael H. McAlister.
Number of staff: 1 full-time professional.
EIN: 956050036
Selected grants: The following grants were reported in 2004.
$495,000 to Saint Johns Health Center Foundation, Santa Monica, CA.
$150,000 to Childrens Hospital Los Angeles, Los Angeles, CA.
$150,000 to Stanford University, Stanford, CA.
$50,000 to Los Angeles Heart Institute, Los Angeles, CA.
$25,000 to Assistance League of Southern California, Los Angeles, CA.
$20,000 to Beverly Hills Education Foundation, Beverly Hills, CA.
$10,000 to Sisters of Social Service, Los Angeles, CA.
$5,000 to Humane Society of Park County, Livingston, MT.
$5,000 to University of California, Berkeley, CA.
$2,500 to Los Angeles Master Chorale, Los Angeles, CA.

865

Alletta Morris McBean Charitable Trust

400 S. El Camino Real, Ste. 777
San Mateo, CA 94402 (650) 558-8480
Contact: Charlene Kleiner, Asst. Secy.
FAX: (650) 558-8481;
E-mail: McBeanProperties@worldnet.att.net

Established in 1986 in CA.
Donor: Alletta Morris McBean‡.
Foundation type: Independent foundation.

Financial data (yr. ended 12/31/05): Assets, $54,059,011 (M); expenditures, $3,141,569; qualifying distributions, $2,844,583; giving activities include $2,751,573 for 31 grants (high: $500,000; low: $10,000).
Purpose and activities: To enhance the quality of life in and around Newport and Aquidneck Island, RI.
Fields of interest: Museums; Historic preservation/historical societies; Environment, land resources.
Type of support: Capital campaigns; Building/renovation; Land acquisition; Endowments; Matching/challenge support.
Limitations: Giving primarily in RI. No grants to individuals.
Publications: Application guidelines; Grants list.
Application information: Application form not required.
  Initial approach: Letter with specific project identified
  Copies of proposal: 6
  Deadline(s): Feb. 28 and July 31
  Board meeting date(s): May and Oct.
  Final notification: 30 days from receipt
Officers and Trustees: Noreen Drexel,* Chair.; Donald Christ,* Secy.; John J. Slocum, Jr.; Gladys Szapary; John A. Van Beuren.
Number of staff: 2 part-time support.
EIN: 943019660

866

McBean Family Foundation

(formerly The Atholl McBean Foundation)
400 S. El Camino Real, Ste. 777
San Mateo, CA 94402 (650) 558-8480
Contact: Henry K. Newhall, Pres.; Charlene C. Kleiner, Secy.
FAX: (650) 558-8481;
E-mail: McBeanProperties@worldnet.att.net

Incorporated in 1955 in CA.
Donors: Atholl McBean‡; Peter McBean‡.
Foundation type: Independent foundation.
Financial data (yr. ended 12/31/05): Assets, $16,019,594 (M); expenditures, $1,307,641; qualifying distributions, $1,142,950; giving activities include $1,107,500 for grants.
Purpose and activities: Giving primarily for human services and education organizations that have already been supported by the foundation.
Fields of interest: Arts education; Arts; Animals/wildlife, preservation/protection; Nursing care; Alzheimer's disease research; Children/youth, services; Homeless, human services.
Type of support: General/operating support; Continuing support; Capital campaigns; Research.
Limitations: Applications not accepted. Giving primarily in northern CA, with emphasis on the San Francisco Bay Area. No grants to individuals, or for endowment funds, scholarships, or fellowships; no loans.
Publications: Grants list.
Application information: The foundation only accepts applications from organizations funded in the past or those nominated by a board member.
  Board meeting date(s): Nov. or Dec. and as required
Officers and Directors: Henry Newhall,* Pres.; Judith McBean,* V.P.; Charlene C. Kleiner, Secy.; Clark Nelson, C.F.O. and Treas.; Peter Folger; Deidra S. Head; Sheila McBean Head; Natasha Hunt; Edith McBean; Nancy McBean.
Number of staff: 2 part-time support.
EIN: 946062239

Selected grants: The following grants were reported in 2004.

$125,000 to University of California, San Francisco, CA. For McBean Fellowship in Alzheimer's Disease Research at UCSF Memory and Aging Center and the Gladstone Institute of Neurological Disease.

$25,000 to University of California, Davis, CA. For Equine Reproductive Research.

$25,000 to Wildlife Conservation Society, Bronx, NY. For Community Forest and Concession Management in Uaxactun, Guatemala.

$15,000 to Episcopal Community Services of San Francisco, San Francisco, CA. For Sanctuary operations.

$15,000 to Raphael House, San Francisco, CA. For children's services.

$15,000 to San Francisco Zoological Society, San Francisco, CA. For Wild Places, Wild Things Conservation Lecture Series.

$15,000 to Town School for Boys, San Francisco, CA. For financial aid.

$15,000 to U.S. Sportsmens Alliance Foundation, Columbus, OH. For Trailblazer Adventure Program in California.

$10,000 to Coyote Point Museum Association, San Mateo, CA. For School Services Program.

$10,000 to San Francisco Symphony, San Francisco, CA. For youth orchestra.

867

B. C. McCabe Foundation ▼

8152 Painter Ave., Ste. 201
Whittier, CA 90602 (562) 696-1433
Contact: James D. Shepard, Tr.

Established in 1976 in CA.
Donor: B.C. McCabe Trust‡.
Foundation type: Independent foundation.
Financial data (yr. ended 12/31/05): Assets, $119,230,782 (M); expenditures, $8,616,094; qualifying distributions, $7,969,847; giving activities include $7,741,819 for 108 grants (high: $1,500,000; low: $1,500; average: $10,000–$100,000).
Purpose and activities: Giving primarily for social service organizations, food service associations, and youth development groups.
Fields of interest: Education; Hospitals (general); Youth development; Human services; Youth, services.
Limitations: Giving primarily in CA.
Application information:
  Initial approach: Letter
  Copies of proposal: 2
  Deadline(s): None
Trustees: Roy D. Miller; James D. Shepard.
EIN: 510192036
Selected grants: The following grants were reported in 2005.
$1,500,000 to Presbyterian Intercommunity Hospital Foundation, Whittier, CA. For Emergency Room, Pediatrics, Hospice, and Tower.
$596,000 to Boys and Girls Club of Santa Monica, Santa Monica, CA. For Leaders in Training program.
$175,000 to Los Angeles Regional Foodbank, Los Angeles, CA. For food distribution fund.
$175,000 to Whittier Area First Day Coalition, Whittier, CA. To address homelessness in Whittier community.
$170,900 to Whittier College, Whittier, CA. For Fifth Dimension Tutorial Program.

$150,000 to Long Beach Museum of Art, Long Beach, CA. For educational programming.

$100,000 to Pilgrim Place in Claremont, Claremont, CA. For Health Services Center.

$62,000 to Boys and Girls Club of Whittier, Whittier, CA. For educational, social, and recreational programs for youth.

$25,000 to Southern California Conservatory of Music, Sun Valley, CA. To support blind students in Braille Division of the Conservatory.

$20,000 to Whittier Historical Society, Whittier, CA. For museum operating support.

868
McCarthy Family Foundation

P.O. Box 27389
San Diego, CA 92198-1389
Contact: Rachel McCarthy Bender, Pres.
FAX: (858) 485-0172;
E-mail: mail@mccarthyfamilyfdn.org; Contact for HIV direct service organizations: San Diego HIV Funding Collaborative, c/o Alliance Healthcare Fdn., 9325 Sky Park Ct., Ste. 350, Attn.: Katherine Crow, tel.: (858) 874-3488, E-mail: kcrow@alliancehf.org, URL: http://www.alliancehf.org; URL: http://www.mccarthyfamilyfdn.org/

Established in 1988 in CA.
Donors: James T. McCarthy; Jane D. McCarthy.
Foundation type: Independent foundation.
Financial data (yr. ended 12/31/05): Assets, $9,160,111 (M); gifts received, $295,023; expenditures, $488,624; qualifying distributions, $458,381; giving activities include $437,000 for grants.
Purpose and activities: Primary areas of interest include science education, AIDS, child welfare, and the homeless.
Fields of interest: AIDS; AIDS research; Crime/violence prevention, child abuse; Homeless, human services; Science, formal/general education; Homeless.
Type of support: General/operating support; Capital campaigns; Program development; Publication; Seed money; Research; Matching/challenge support.
Limitations: Giving limited to San Diego County, CA. No support for religious or political activities. No grants to individuals, or for scholarship funds or fundraising drives.
Publications: Application guidelines; Annual report; Financial statement; Grants list; Informational brochure (including application guidelines).
Application information: Formal proposals are by invitation only. Application guidelines available on foundation Web site. Application form not required.
Initial approach: Letter (1-2 pages)
Copies of proposal: 5
Deadline(s): Mar. 15 and Sept. 15
Board meeting date(s): June and Dec.
Final notification: June and Dec.
Officers and Directors:* Rachel McCarthy Bender,* Pres.; Kristin McCarthy Atterbury,* V.P.; Brant R. Bender,* V.P.; Jane D. McCarthy,* Secy; James T. McCarthy,* Treas.
Number of staff: 1 part-time support.
EIN: 954182410

869
Wendy P. McCaw Foundation ✧

P.O. Box 939
Santa Barbara, CA 93102-0939

Established in 1997 in CA.
Donor: Craig O. McCaw.
Foundation type: Independent foundation.
Financial data (yr. ended 12/31/05): Assets, $38,464,181 (M); expenditures, $2,360,355; qualifying distributions, $1,950,955; giving activities include $1,746,000 for 15 grants (high: $1,000,000; low: $1,000).
Purpose and activities: Giving primarily for the enhancement of the environment, and the mitigation of the effect of development and occupancy of land by humans on the environment; funding also for the protection of marine mammals and for general charitable purposes.
Fields of interest: Environment, pollution control; Environment, natural resources; Environment, water resources; Animals/wildlife, preservation/protection.
Limitations: Applications not accepted. Giving primarily in CA. No grants to individuals.
Application information: Contributes only to pre-selected organizations.
Officers and Director:* Wendy P. McCaw,* Pres.; Joseph L. Cole, V.P. and Secy.; Jon Clark, Exec. Dir.
EIN: 770469217
Selected grants: The following grants were reported in 2005.
$1,000,000 to Trust for Public Land, San Francisco, CA.
$500,000 to Santa Barbara Center for the Performing Arts, Santa Barbara, CA.
$100,000 to Humane Society of the United States, DC.
$15,000 to Defenders of Wildlife, DC.
$10,000 to Friends of the Sea Otter, Pacific Grove, CA.
$10,000 to Unity Shoppe, Santa Barbara, CA.
$5,000 to Return to Freedom, Lompoc, CA.
$2,500 to K-9 Placement and Assistance League, Santa Barbara, CA.
$1,000 to In Defense of Animals, San Rafael, CA.

870
The McConnell Foundation ▼

P.O. Box 492050
Redding, CA 96049-2050 (530) 226-6200
Contact: Lee W. Salter, C.E.O. and Pres.
FAX: (530) 226-6210;
E-mail: info@mcconnellfoundation.org; URL: http://www.mcconnellfoundation.org

Established in 1964 in CA.
Donors: Carl R. McConnell†; Leah F. McConnell†; National Parks Service.
Foundation type: Independent foundation.
Financial data (yr. ended 12/31/05): Assets, $376,239,986 (M); expenditures, $13,221,878; qualifying distributions, $17,015,413; giving activities include $4,549,307 for 40 grants (high: $625,000; low: $1,500; average: $2,500–$200,000), $208,987 for 210 employee matching gifts, and $3,543,299 for 4 foundation-administered programs.
Purpose and activities: The foundation is reassessing their priorities. Only outstanding commitments will be paid through 2006. Primary interests include the environment, environmental education, recreation; projects that benefit the working poor; projects that demonstrate broad based community support, and the promotion of voluntarism and philanthropy.
Fields of interest: Museums; Performing arts; Historical activities; Arts; Secondary school/education; Environment; Health care; Recreation; Aging, centers/services; Community development; Voluntarism promotion.
International interests: Nepal.
Type of support: Capital campaigns; Equipment; Scholarship funds; Technical assistance; Employee matching gifts; In-kind gifts; Matching/challenge support.
Limitations: Applications not accepted. Giving limited to Shasta, Trinity, Modoc, Tehema and Siskiyou counties, CA; and Nepal. No support for sectarian religious purposes. No grants to individuals, or for endowment funds, annual fund drives, budget deficits, or purchase or construction of buildings.
Publications: Annual report; Newsletter.
Application information: The foundation's external grant application program has been suspended indefinitely. Current funding commitments will be honored. Check foundation Web site for further details.
Board meeting date(s): Feb., Mar., June, Sept., and Dec.
Officers and Directors:* Doreeta J. Domke,* Chair.; Lee W. Salter,* C.E.O. and Pres.; John A. Mancasola,* Exec. V.P. and Secy.; Gerald C. Gitchell, C.F.O.; Richard J. Stimpel,* Treas.; William B. Nystrom, Dir. Emeritus; Robert P. Blankenship.
Number of staff: 8 full-time professional; 27 full-time support; 2 part-time support.
EIN: 946102700
Selected grants: The following grants were reported in 2005.
$1,153,380 to Turtle Bay Exploration Park, Redding, CA. 3 grants: $375,000 (For general support), $153,380 (For operational software), $625,000 (For general support).
$512,835 to University of California, Berkeley, CA. For College Options Outreach Center in Shasta County.
$470,000 to Shasta Regional Community Foundation, Redding, CA. 2 grants: $200,000 (For community foundation funding), $270,000 (For grant funding for Shasta and Siskiyou Counties).
$273,464 to Mountain Resource Management Group, Nepal. For Sustainable Villages and Rural Income Generation Project.
$213,405 to Asia Foundation, San Francisco, CA. 2 grants: $75,693 (For project to reduce incidence of violence against women in Banke and Doti Districts of Nepal), $137,712 (For community mediation program).
$4,400 to West Valley High School, Anderson, CA. For scholarships.

871
The Bowen H. & Janice Arthur McCoy Charitable Foundation ✧

11400 W. Olympic Blvd., Ste. 243
Los Angeles, CA 90064
Contact: Bowen H. McCoy, Tr.

Established in 1989 in CA.
Donor: Bowen H. McCoy.
Foundation type: Independent foundation.
Financial data (yr. ended 12/31/05): Assets, $8,559,153 (M); expenditures, $480,479;

qualifying distributions, $426,000; giving activities include $426,000 for 37 grants (high: $30,000; low: $3,000).

Purpose and activities: Giving primarily for higher and other education, the arts, and social services; some funding also for churches.

Fields of interest: Arts; Higher education; Education; Human services; Protestant agencies & churches.

Type of support: General/operating support.

Limitations: Giving primarily in CA. No grants to individuals.

Application information: Generally contributes to pre-selected organizations.

Board meeting date(s): Dec.

Trustees: Elizabeth McCoy Chen; Anne McCoy; Bowen H. McCoy; John B. McCoy; Janice McCoy Miller.

EIN: 954247192

872
The McCune Foundation ◇
1187 Coast Village Rd., Ste. 1-408
Montecito, CA 93108 (805) 969-6184
Contact: Pam Maines, Exec. Dir.
FAX: (805) 969-2174;
E-mail: questions@mccunefoundation.org;
URL: http://www.mccunefoundation.org

Established in 1990 in CA.

Donor: Sara Miller McCune.

Foundation type: Operating foundation.

Financial data (yr. ended 2/28/05): Assets, $1,265,464 (M); gifts received, $522,000; expenditures, $530,548; qualifying distributions, $475,150; giving activities include $460,800 for 37 grants (high: $35,000; low: $250).

Purpose and activities: Giving primarily for higher education and emphasis on interdisciplinary social sciences, and for social development.

Fields of interest: Community development; Economics.

Type of support: General/operating support; Income development; Management development/capacity building; Program development; Scholarship funds; Program evaluation.

Limitations: Giving primarily in Santa Barbara and Ventura counties, CA. No support for religious organizations. No grants to individuals; budget deficits, construction or renovation of buildings, general funding drives, or events.

Publications: Application guidelines; Grants list.

Application information: Full proposals are by invitation only, upon review of letter of inquiry. Additional material must not accompany the initial letter. See foundation Web site for application guidelines and procedures. Application form required.

Initial approach: Letter of inquiry (2 pages), from Chair. or Pres. of Board of Dirs.
Copies of proposal: 1
Deadline(s): July 15 (for letters); Sept. 1 (for proposals)
Board meeting date(s): May and Nov.
Final notification: Dec. 1 (for proposals)

Officers: Sara Miller McCune, Chair. and Pres.; David F. McCune, V.P.; Vicki Fisher Magasinn, Secy.; Margaret Sirot, Treas.; Pam Maines, Exec. Dir.; Sandra Ball-Rokeach.

Directors: Marilyn Gittell; Susan McCune Sherman.

EIN: 770242953

Selected grants: The following grants were reported in 2005.

$33,500 to Cares, Inc., Port Richey, FL.
$30,400 to La Casa de la Raza, Santa Barbara, CA.
$30,000 to Future Leaders of America, Ventura, CA.
$23,000 to Peoples Self-Help Housing, San Luis Obispo, CA.
$22,000 to U.S. English Foundation, DC.
$16,000 to Santa Barbara Neighborhood Clinics, Isla Vista, CA.
$5,000 to Wellness Community Valley/Ventura, Westlake Village, CA.
$2,000 to Domus, Westfield, MA.
$1,000 to Little Tokyo Service Center, Los Angeles, CA.

873
The McDonough Foundation ◇
c/o Robert E. McDonough
101 Enterprise
Aliso Viejo, CA 92656

Established in 1997 in CA.

Donor: Robert E. McDonough.

Foundation type: Independent foundation.

Financial data (yr. ended 2/29/04): Assets, $1,201 (M); expenditures, $2,439,640; qualifying distributions, $2,427,581; giving activities include $2,426,985 for 7 grants (high: $2,000,000; low: $130).

Fields of interest: Higher education, university; Christian agencies & churches.

Limitations: Applications not accepted. Giving primarily in CA. No grants to individuals.

Application information: Contributes only to pre-selected organizations.

Officers: Robert E. McDonough, Pres.; Joe Theis, Secy. and C.F.O.

EIN: 330746360

Selected grants: The following grants were reported in 2003.

$100,000 to Mission San Juan Capistrano, San Juan Capistrano, CA. For general support.
$2,686 to Amyotrophic Lateral Sclerosis (ALS) Association, Calabasas, CA. For general support.
$1,800 to Georgetown University, DC. For general support.
$1,000 to Sisters Fund for Youth. For general support.
$500 to American Ireland Fund, San Francisco, CA. For general support.
$200 to Audreys College Fund. For general support.
$200 to Rancho Mission Viejo, San Juan Capistrano, CA. For general support.
$150 to Friends of the Mission, San Juan Capistrano, CA. For general support.
$100 to Saint Josephs. For general support.
$100 to Taller San Jose, Santa Ana, CA. For general support.

874
McFadden Family Foundation ◇
34145 Pacific Coast Hwy., Ste. 195
Dana Point, CA 92629

Established in 2003.

Donors: Global Cornerstone Healthcare Services, Inc.; Guided Alliance Healthcare Services.

Foundation type: Independent foundation.

Financial data (yr. ended 12/31/05): Assets, $559,883 (M); gifts received, $119,194; expenditures, $357,417; qualifying distributions,

$355,600; giving activities include $355,600 for 4 grants (high: $344,500; low: $2,500).

Purpose and activities: Giving primarily for education and human services.

Fields of interest: Elementary/secondary education; Human services; Family services; Roman Catholic agencies & churches.

Limitations: Applications not accepted. Giving primarily in CA. No grants to individuals.

Application information: Contributes only to pre-selected organizations.

Officers: Timothy McFadden, Pres.; Mary McFadden, V.P.

EIN: 200170944

875
Callie D. McGrath Charitable Trust ◇
c/o Bank of America, N.A.
P.O. Box 513189
Los Angeles, CA 90051-1189

Established in 1995 in California.

Foundation type: Independent foundation.

Financial data (yr. ended 12/31/05): Assets, $13,446,388 (M); expenditures, $771,038; qualifying distributions, $712,473; giving activities include $690,524 for 30 grants (high: $75,000; low: $1,000).

Purpose and activities: Giving primarily for hospitals, health organizations, and human services.

Fields of interest: Hospitals (general); Cancer; Alzheimer's disease; Children, foster care.

Limitations: Applications not accepted. Giving primarily in CA. No grants to individuals.

Application information: Contributes only to pre-selected organizations.

Trustee: Bank of America, N.A.

EIN: 956995594

876
The McIntyre Foundation
c/o James A. McIntyre
2425 Olympic Blvd., 3rd Fl. East
Santa Monica, CA 90404
E-mail: JMCINTYRE@FMT.com

Established in 1980 in CA.

Donor: James A. McIntyre.

Foundation type: Independent foundation.

Financial data (yr. ended 11/30/05): Assets, $28,899,446 (M); gifts received, $3,687,376; expenditures, $1,050,061; qualifying distributions, $1,041,081; giving activities include $1,031,710 for 46 grants (high: $500,000; low: $360).

Purpose and activities: Support primarily for local community organizations, particularly those benefiting children and the arts.

Fields of interest: Arts; Education; Children/youth, services; Community development, neighborhood development.

Type of support: Scholarship funds; Scholarships—to individuals.

Limitations: Applications not accepted. Giving primarily in southern CA.

Publications: Informational brochure; Newsletter.

Application information: Unsolicited requests for funds not accepted.

Board meeting date(s): Dec.

Officers and Directors:* James A. McIntyre,* C.E.O.; Alan Faigin, Secy.; Melinda Kopin, C.F.O.; Tracy Fredericks; Amanda McIntyre.
EIN: 953511057
Selected grants: The following grants were reported in 2003.
$25,000 to Carpinteria Unified School District, Carpinteria, CA.
$25,000 to Renaissance Campaign, Fort Wayne, IN.
$25,000 to Westmont High School, Campbell, CA.
$5,000 to Executive Service Corps of Southern California, Los Angeles, CA.
$5,000 to Westerly School of Long Beach, Long Beach, CA.
$2,500 to Music Academy of the West, Santa Barbara, CA.
$1,100 to Calvary Christian School, Pacific Palisades, CA.
$1,000 to Junior League of Los Angeles, Los Angeles, CA.
$1,000 to Juniors of Social Service, Los Angeles, CA.
$1,000 to Santa Barbara Foundation, Santa Barbara, CA.

877

The McKay Foundation ✧
303 Sacramento St., 4th Fl.
San Francisco, CA 94111   (415) 288-1313
FAX: (415) 288-1320; E-mail: fndn@mckayfund.org;
URL: http://www.mckayfund.org

Established in 1992 in CA.
Donors: Robert L. McKay, Sr.; Elaine McKay.
Foundation type: Independent foundation.
Financial data (yr. ended 12/31/04): Assets, $961,124 (M); gifts received, $2,446,672; expenditures, $2,116,634; qualifying distributions, $1,456,500; giving activities include $1,456,500 for 43 grants (high: $75,000; low: $1,000).
Purpose and activities: To strengthen our democracy and promote a more just and equitable American culture, the foundation funds activities that build civil society's energy, leadership, and resources, and utilizes these in the political and policy spheres of civil society. Through grants, capacity building assistance, and other support to allied organizations, the foundation partners with diverse communities in working for long term social, political, and economic progress.
Fields of interest: Environment; Human services; Homeless, human services; Community development; Public policy, research.
Type of support: General/operating support; Income development; Management development/capacity building; Technical assistance.
Limitations: Applications not accepted. Giving primarily in CA.
Publications: Grants list; Occasional report.
Application information: Contributes only to pre-selected organizations. The majority of funding goes to a core set of community organizing groups, located mostly in CA.
Officers: Robert McKay, Pres. and Exec. Dir.; Robert L. McKay, Sr., V.P.; Elaine McKay, Secy.; John P. McKay, Treas.
Number of staff: 3 full-time professional; 1 part-time support.
EIN: 363946926
Selected grants: The following grants were reported in 2003.
$165,000 to Liberty Hill Foundation, Santa Monica, CA.

$80,000 to Coalition on Homelessness, San Francisco, CA.
$60,000 to Working Partnerships USA, San Jose, CA.
$55,000 to Labor Community Strategy Center, Los Angeles, CA.
$50,000 to Hispanics in Philanthropy, San Francisco, CA.
$50,000 to Sacramento Valley Organizing Community, Sacramento, CA.
$40,000 to Santa Cruz Barrios Unidos, Santa Cruz, CA.
$35,000 to Chinatown Community Development Center, San Francisco, CA.
$25,000 to HomeBase, The Center for Common Concerns, San Francisco, CA.
$250 to Just Cause Oakland, Oakland, CA.

878

McKenna Family Foundation ✧
1409 Galloway Ct.
Sunnyvale, CA 94087

Established in 1992 in CA.
Donors: Regis McKenna; Dianne McKenna.
Foundation type: Independent foundation.
Financial data (yr. ended 6/30/05): Assets, $694,978 (M); expenditures, $335,683; qualifying distributions, $326,625; giving activities include $324,850 for 11 grants (high: $130,000; low: $350).
Fields of interest: Higher education; Girl scouts; Human services; Family services, domestic violence.
Limitations: Applications not accepted. Giving primarily in CA. No grants to individuals.
Application information: Contributes only to pre-selected organizations.
Officers: Regis McKenna, Pres. and Treas.; Dianne McKenna, V.P. and Secy.
EIN: 770332016
Selected grants: The following grants were reported in 2004.
$100,000 to National Hispanic University, San Jose, CA.
$25,000 to San Jose State University, San Jose, CA.
$25,000 to Silicon Valley Childrens Fund, San Jose, CA.
$15,000 to Economic Strategy Institute, DC.
$10,000 to Saint Vincent College, Latrobe, PA.
$10,000 to Santa Clara University, Santa Clara, CA.
$10,000 to Trust for Hidden Villa, Los Altos Hills, CA.
$8,500 to Sunnyvale Community Services, Sunnyvale, CA.
$7,500 to California State Parks Foundation, Kentfield, CA.
$5,000 to Pacific Medical Research Foundation, Redwood City, CA.

879

McKesson Foundation, Inc. ▼
(formerly McKesson HBOC Foundation, Inc.)
1 Post St.
San Francisco, CA 94104   (415) 983-9478
Contact: Marcia M. Argyris, Pres.
E-mail: community.relations@mckesson.com;
URL: http://www.mckesson.com/en_us/McKesson.com/Corporate%2BCitizenship/McKesson%2BFoundation/McKesson%2BFoundation.html

Incorporated in 1943 in FL.
Donors: McKesson Corp.; McKesson HBOC, Inc.
Foundation type: Company-sponsored foundation.
Financial data (yr. ended 3/31/05): Assets, $17,528,012 (M); gifts received, $2,055,734; expenditures, $4,630,297; qualifying distributions, $4,493,577; giving activities include $3,965,160 for grants, $64,975 for grants to individuals, and $280,162 for employee matching gifts.
Purpose and activities: The foundation supports programs designed to provide access to quality health care for low-income children and youth and their families and awards college scholarships to pharmacy school students and inner-city high school students.
Fields of interest: Health care, equal rights; Children; Youth; Economically disadvantaged.
Type of support: General/operating support; Continuing support; Equipment; Emergency funds; Program development; Seed money; Employee volunteer services; Employee matching gifts; Employee-related scholarships; Scholarships—to individuals.
Limitations: Giving primarily in areas of major company operations. No support for religious organizations not of direct benefit to the entire community or disease-specific organizations. No grants to individuals (except for scholarships), or for endowments, political causes or campaigns, advertising, or research.
Publications: Application guidelines; Annual report; Grants list.
Application information: Support is limited to 1 contribution per organization during any given year. Application form required.
  Initial approach: Complete online application form
  Deadline(s): None
  Board meeting date(s): Quarterly, beginning in Apr.
  Final notification: 1 month
Officers: Marcia M. Argyris, Pres.; Carrie Varoquiers, Secy. and Prog. Off.; Nicholas A. Loiacono, Treas.
Distribution/Policy Committee: Ann Berkey; Patrick Blake; Ralph de Chabert; John G. Figueroa; John H. Hammergren; Paul Kirincic; Lawrence W. Kurtz; Stephan Lin; Ivan D. Meyerson; Ted Ng; Nigel Rees; Katherine Rohrback; Richard C. Soublet.
Number of staff: 1 full-time professional; 1 part-time professional; 1 full-time support.
EIN: 943140036
Selected grants: The following grants were reported in 2004.
$99,600 to Scholarship America, Saint Peter, MN. For scholarship program.
$50,000 to National Assembly on School-Based Health Care, DC. To develop productivity guidelines for clinics and to evaluate.
$35,000 to La Clinica de la Raza, Fruitvale Health Project, Oakland, CA. For capital support to build clinic.
$25,000 to Ben Massell Dental Clinic, Atlanta, GA. For supplies and operating expenses.
$25,000 to Boys and Girls Clubs of San Francisco, San Francisco, CA. For Club Health.
$25,000 to Ohlhoff Recovery Programs, San Francisco, CA. For Adolescent Treatment Program.
$15,000 to Health Initiatives for Youth, San Francisco, CA. For Peer Health Educator.
$12,500 to Illinois Medical District Guest House Foundation, Chicago, IL. For construction of new guest house.
$12,000 to Texas Scottish Rite Hospital for Children, Dallas, TX. For pulse oximeters.

$10,000 to Homeless Prenatal Program, San Francisco, CA. For general operating support.

$5,000 to Jewish Community Free Clinic, Sebastopol, CA. For general operating support.

880
The Mel and Grace McLean Foundation ◇
1336 Main St.
Fortuna, CA 95540
Contact: Leigh Pierre-Oetker, Exec. Dir.
FAX: (707) 725-1959; E-mail: mclean@foggy.net

Established in 1998 in CA.
Donor: Melvin F. McLean†.
Foundation type: Independent foundation.
Financial data (yr. ended 12/31/05): Assets, $0 (M); gifts received, $651,000; expenditures, $452,695; qualifying distributions, $338,071; giving activities include $338,071 for 125 grants (high: $10,000; low: $119).
Purpose and activities: To enhance the quality of life of the people of Humboldt County, CA.
Fields of interest: Arts; Elementary/secondary education; Education; Human services; Religion.
Type of support: General/operating support; Equipment; Land acquisition; Emergency funds; Program development; Building/renovation; Seed money.
Limitations: Giving limited to Humboldt County, CA. No support for churches. No grants to individuals, or for operating costs, scholarships, travel expenses or conferences.
Publications: Application guidelines.
Application information: Application form required.
Initial approach: Letter requesting eligibility packet
Copies of proposal: 4
Deadline(s): Available upon request
Board meeting date(s): Monthly
Final notification: 60 days after submission date
Officers and Director:* Eugene B. Lucas,* Pres.; Dennis Scott, V.P.; Leslie M. Westfall, Recording Secy.; Leigh Pierre-Oetker, Exec. Dir.
Number of staff: 1 full-time professional.
EIN: 680400603
Selected grants: The following grants were reported in 2003.
$50,000 to Saint Luke Manor.
$10,000 to Heart of the Redwoods Volunteer Hospice, Garberville, CA.
$10,000 to Redwood Discovery Museum, Eureka, CA.
$9,000 to Eureka High School, Eureka, CA.
$9,000 to Southern Humbolt Senior Center, Redway, CA.
$7,140 to Loleta Community evangelical Free Church, Loleta, CA.
$5,000 to Mateel Community Center, Garberville, CA.
$4,063 to North Coast Clinics Network, Eureka, CA.
$3,125 to Humboldt Community Switchboard, Eureka, CA.
$2,500 to Manila Community Services, Arcata, CA.

881
Giles W. and Elise G. Mead Foundation
P.O. Box 2218
Napa, CA 94558 (707) 257-6737
Contact: Directors

FAX: (707) 226-2164;
E-mail: meadfoundation@aol.com; URL: http://www.gileswmeadfoundation.org

Incorporated in 1961 in CA.
Donor: Elise G. Mead†.
Foundation type: Independent foundation.
Financial data (yr. ended 10/31/05): Assets, $21,473,369 (M); expenditures, $1,143,454; qualifying distributions, $1,006,717; giving activities include $942,360 for 28 grants (high: $108,000; low: $1,860).
Purpose and activities: The Mead Foundation supports organizations dedicated to preserving and improving the environment, the advancement of medical science, and other important social needs. Environmental organizations supported by the Mead Foundation generally have as their primary emphasis forestry, fisheries, and the sustainable use of natural resources in western North America. Scientific and medical organizations supported by the Mead Foundation generally have as their primary emphasis the endocrine system, and in particular diabetes and its complications.
Fields of interest: Environment, natural resources; Environment, forests; Environment, Animals/wildlife, fisheries; Health care, research; Diabetes.
Type of support: Equipment; Land acquisition; Program development; Seed money; Research; Matching/challenge support.
Limitations: Giving primarily in the western U.S., with emphasis on AK, northern CA, OR, and WA. No support for local or regional environmental organizations outside the western U.S. No grants to individuals, or for general operating expenses.
Publications: Application guidelines; Annual report (including application guidelines); Biennial report; Grants list.
Application information: Proposals are accepted only after a review of letter of inquiry first. If a proposal is requested, submit the proposal and supporting materials in an environmentally sensitive manner. Please use two-sided copying when possible, and do not use binders or plastic packaging. Funding in other program areas except for the environment, medical science, and social needs, are limited to grant proposals initiated by individual board members. A copy of most recent IRS Determination Letter, a copy of most recent annual report/audited financial statement/990, and a listing of board of directors, trustees, officers and other key people and their affiliations, are to be submitted upon request from the foundation only. Additional copies of the proposal will be upon the request of the foundation. Application form not required.
Initial approach: Inquiry by letter or fax
Deadline(s): None
Board meeting date(s): June and Oct.
Final notification: 2 months
Officers and Directors:* Calder M. Mackay,* Pres.; Jane W. Mead, V.P.; Parry W. Mead,* V.P.; Richard N. Mackay, Secy.-Treas.; Stafford R. Grady; Katherine Cone Keck.
Number of staff: 1 part-time professional.
EIN: 956040921
Selected grants: The following grants were reported in 2004.
$150,000 to Epiphany School, Seattle, WA.
$50,000 to Little Sisters of the Poor, San Pedro, CA.
$50,000 to University of Utah, Salt Lake City, UT.
$30,000 to Amigos Bravos, Taos, NM.
$25,000 to Alaska Conservation Foundation, Anchorage, AK.

$25,000 to YMCA.
$10,000 to Cook Inlet Keeper, Homer, AK.
$10,000 to Rainforest Action Network, San Francisco, CA.
$5,000 to Guide Dogs for the Blind, San Rafael, CA.
$2,000 to Foundation Center, San Francisco, CA.

882
Stanislav Medvedenko Foundation ◇
4824 Gaviota Ave.
Encino, CA 91436

Established in 2002.
Donors: Stanislav Medvedenko; Alexander Krilov; Julia Butler.
Foundation type: Independent foundation.
Financial data (yr. ended 12/31/05): Assets, $0; gifts received, $991,354; expenditures, $331,552; qualifying distributions, $330,000; giving activities include $330,000 for 1 grant.
Purpose and activities: Giving to athletic programs.
Limitations: Applications not accepted. Giving primarily in Kiev, Ukraine. No grants to individuals.
Application information: Contributes only to pre-selected organizations.
Officers: Stanislav Medvedenko, C.E.O.; Alexander Krilov, Secy.
EIN: 710894777

883
Mellam Family Foundation
P.O. Box 610091
Redwood City, CA 94061
FAX: (650) 366-6419; E-mail: info@mellam.org; URL: http://www.mellam.org/

Established in 1987 in NY.
Donor: Laural D. Mellam†.
Foundation type: Independent foundation.
Financial data (yr. ended 12/31/04): Assets, $16,504,612 (M); expenditures, $878,297; qualifying distributions, $801,115; giving activities include $675,660 for 57 grants (high: $25,000; low: $1,000).
Fields of interest: Education; Environment, natural resources; Health care; Medical research, institute; Human services.
Limitations: Applications not accepted. Giving on a national basis, with emphasis on CA, HI, and NY. No grants to individuals.
Publications: Annual report; Financial statement; Grants list.
Application information: Contributes only to pre-selected organizations.
Board meeting date(s): Quarterly
Officers and Directors:* Marilyn Rogers,* Pres.; Tracy Rogers,* Exec. Dir.
Number of staff: 1 full-time professional.
EIN: 136894208
Selected grants: The following grants were reported in 2003.
$55,000 to Stanford University, Stanford, CA. 2 grants: $35,000 to School of Medicine (For Department of Urology), $20,000.
$25,000 to American Heart Association, Dallas, TX.
$25,000 to Surfrider Foundation, San Clemente, CA.
$25,000 to Trust for Public Land, San Francisco, CA.
$20,000 to American Indian College Fund, Denver, CO.
$20,000 to Arthritis Foundation, Atlanta, GA.

$20,000 to Dartmouth College, Hanover, NH.
$20,000 to National Breast Cancer Coalition, DC.
$20,000 to University of Nebraska Foundation, Lincoln, NE.

884
Menard Family Foundation ✧
c/o Lindsay & Brownell, LLP
4225 Executive Sq., Ste. 1150
La Jolla, CA   92037

Established in 1998 in CA.
Donors: Bernard Menard; Mary Menard.
Foundation type: Independent foundation.
Financial data (yr. ended 12/31/05): Assets, $6,105,185 (M); expenditures, $435,986; qualifying distributions, $383,705; giving activities include $366,750 for 27 grants (high: $48,750; low: $3,250).
Purpose and activities: Giving primarily to Roman Catholic organizations, churches, and schools; some funding also for health care, including a children's hospital, the arts, and children, youth, and social services.
Fields of interest: Performing arts; Arts; Animal welfare; Zoos/zoological societies; Hospitals (general); Health organizations, association; Human services; Children/youth, services; Residential/custodial care, hospices; Roman Catholic agencies & churches.
Limitations: Applications not accepted. Giving primarily in CA, with emphasis on San Diego; some funding nationally. No grants to individuals.
Application information: Contributes only to pre-selected organizations.
Officer: Don Harrington, Secy.
Trustees: Barbara J. Menard; Marcel Menard; Marlene Miller.
EIN: 330834790
Selected grants: The following grants were reported in 2005.
$48,750 to Saint Vincent de Paul Village, San Diego, CA.
$48,750 to Zoological Society of San Diego, San Diego, CA.
$32,500 to Catholic Charities, Santa Barbara, CA.
$3,250 to Blessed Sacrament School, Los Angeles, CA.
$3,250 to Childrens Hospital, Rancho Santa Fe, CA.
$3,250 to Helen Woodward Animal Center, Rancho Santa Fe, CA.
$3,250 to Lambs Players Theater, Coronado, CA.
$3,250 to Maryknoll Fathers and Brothers, Maryknoll, NY.
$3,250 to Nativity Prep Academy, San Diego, CA.

885
Menlo Foundation, Inc. ✧
4221 Wilshire Blvd., Ste. 210
Los Angeles, CA   90010-3512   (323) 937-1050
Contact: Sam Menlo, Dir.

Established in 1978.
Donors: Sam Menlo; Vera Menlo; Yesod Fund.
Foundation type: Independent foundation.
Financial data (yr. ended 11/30/04): Assets, $54,914 (M); gifts received, $3,000,000; expenditures, $3,057,015; qualifying distributions, $3,051,678; giving activities include $3,047,385 for grants.

Purpose and activities: Giving primarily for Jewish organizations.
Fields of interest: Theological school/education; Jewish federated giving programs; Jewish agencies & temples.
Limitations: Applications not accepted. Giving primarily in Brooklyn, NY.
Application information: Unsolicited requests for funds not accepted.
Directors: Sam Menlo; Vera Menlo.
EIN: 953388159

886
The Mental Insight Foundation
c/o Virginia Hubbell Assocs., Admin.
283 2nd St. E.
Sonoma, CA   95476   (707) 938-8248

Established in 1996 in CA.
Donor: William D. Kimpton†.
Foundation type: Independent foundation.
Financial data (yr. ended 12/31/05): Assets, $6,783,882 (M); gifts received, $3,304,461; expenditures, $978,067; qualifying distributions, $964,947; giving activities include $803,500 for 56 grants (high: $100,000; low: $1,000).
Purpose and activities: Giving to the 7 following areas: 1) Mental health-specifically traditional and alternative forms of healing depression and other mental illnesses; 2) Impoverished youth-programs targeted to reintegrating children in poverty back into society; 3) Cancer support-programs with an emphasis on reducing the sense of isolation experienced by cancer patients and their families; 4) Animal preservation-focused on spay and neuter programs, shelter for domestic and wild animals, and for programs directed to changing laws that increase the protection of domestic and wild animals and humane treatment of farm animals; 5) Arts-experimental theater, experimental emerging visual arts and new media, and programs that bring art back into the classroom; 6) Environment-direct action programs targeted on global warming and the development of renewable energy; and 7) Indigenous people-preservation of indigenous culture and life.
Fields of interest: Arts; Environment, global warming; Environment; Animals/wildlife, preservation/protection; Mental health/crisis services.
Type of support: General/operating support; Continuing support; Equipment; Program development; Conferences/seminars; Publication; Seed money; Research.
Limitations: Applications not accepted. Giving primarily in the San Francisco Bay Area, CA, and the metropolitan New York, NY, area; giving in some other areas, by board selection. No support for religious organizations. No grants to individuals, or for endowments, operating deficits, fundraising events, capital campaigns, building renovation, or emergency funds; no loans.
Publications: Grants list.
Application information: Unsolicited requests for funds not accepted.
Board meeting date(s): Dec.
Officers: David Herskovits, Pres.; Graham Lawrence Kimpton, V.P.; Isabelle Kimpton, Secy.; Bob Bunje, Treas.
Trustees: Barry Bunshoft; Len Dell'Amico; Jennifer Catherine Egan; Laura Kimpton.

Number of staff: 1 part-time professional; 1 part-time support.
EIN: 943256579
Selected grants: The following grants were reported in 2005.
$100,000 to Midland School, Los Olivos, CA.
$40,500 to Bravewell Collaborative, Minneapolis, MN.
$25,000 to Hoffman Institute Foundation, San Anselmo, CA.
$25,000 to Mind and Life Institute, Louisville, CO.
$25,000 to Rainforest Action Network, San Francisco, CA.
$20,000 to Caduceus Outreach Services, San Francisco, CA.
$20,000 to Coalition for the Homeless, New York, NY.
$15,000 to Big Dance Theater, Brooklyn, NY.
$15,000 to Project Renewal, New York, NY.
$7,500 to Imagine Bus Project, Sausalito, CA.

887
The Paul & Elisabeth Merage Family Foundation ✧ ☆
4350 Von Karman Ave., Ste. 400
Newport Beach, CA   92660

Established in 2002 in NV.
Donors: Paul Merage; Elisabeth Merage.
Foundation type: Independent foundation.
Financial data (yr. ended 12/31/05): Assets, $31,179,940 (M); expenditures, $1,642,093; qualifying distributions, $1,426,564; giving activities include $1,426,564 for grants.
Fields of interest: Performing arts; Higher education, university; Mental health, association; Federated giving programs; Public affairs.
Limitations: Applications not accepted. No grants to individuals.
Application information: Contributes only to pre-selected organizations.
Officers: Paul Merage, Pres.; Elisabeth Merage, Secy.
Directors: Michelle Janavs; Lauren Merage; Richard Merage.
EIN: 680529692

888
Andre & Katherine Merage Foundation of Nevada ✧ ☆
4350 Von Karman Ave., Ste. 400
Newport Beach, CA   92660

Established in 2002 in NV.
Donor: Katherine Merage.
Foundation type: Independent foundation.
Financial data (yr. ended 12/31/05): Assets, $21,551,105 (M); expenditures, $1,097,564; qualifying distributions, $996,225; giving activities include $990,121 for 3 grants (high: $558,621; low: $62,500).
Fields of interest: Jewish agencies & temples.
Limitations: Applications not accepted. No grants to individuals.
Application information: Contributes only to pre-selected organizations.
Officers: Katherine Merage, Pres.; Paul Merage, Secy.
EIN: 020657534

889
Mericos Foundation
625 S. Fair Oaks Ave., Ste. 360
South Pasadena, CA 91030-2630
Contact: Elizabeth Curtis, Asst. V.P., Fdn. Admin.

Established in 1980 in CA.
Donor: Donald W. Whittier Charitable Trust.
Foundation type: Independent foundation.
Financial data (yr. ended 12/31/05): Assets, $34,164,207 (M); expenditures, $2,079,936; qualifying distributions, $1,946,272; giving activities include $1,793,267 for 41 grants (high: $300,000; low: $5,000).
Purpose and activities: Primarily giving for cultural programs, the aged, youth development, community, medicine/health, and education.
Fields of interest: Arts education; Museums (art); Museums (natural history); Arts; Elementary/secondary education; Child development, education; Higher education; Libraries/library science; Education, services; Education; Environment; Animals/wildlife; Hospitals (specialty); Medical care, rehabilitation; Medical research, institute; Housing/shelter, aging; Children/youth, services; Child development, services; Aging, centers/services; Aging; Blind/visually impaired.
Type of support: General/operating support; Building/renovation; Equipment; Program development; Fellowships; Matching/challenge support.
Limitations: Applications not accepted. Giving primarily in CA, with emphasis on Santa Barbara; some giving nationally. No grants to individuals, or for capital support; no loans.
Application information: Due to funding restrictions the foundation manager prefers to initiate the grants made by the foundation.
   Board meeting date(s): As needed, 3 times per year
Officers and Directors:* Joanne W. Blokker,* Pres.; Linda J. Blinkenberg,* V.P.; Elizabeth A. Curtis, Secy.; Michael J. Casey,* C.F.O.; Donja Blokker-Dalquist; Donna S. Coffin; Arlo G. Sorensen; Donald A. Whittier.
EIN: 953500491
Selected grants: The following grants were reported in 2004.
$384,000 to Laguna Cottages for Seniors, Santa Barbara, CA.
$62,500 to Westmont College, Santa Barbara, CA.
$50,000 to Allan Hancock College Foundation, Santa Maria, CA.
$50,000 to Braille Institute, Santa Barbara, CA.
$50,000 to Midland School, Los Olivos, CA.
$50,000 to Rehabilitation Institute at Santa Barbara, Santa Barbara, CA.
$50,000 to Santa Barbara Neighborhood Clinics, Isla Vista, CA.
$50,000 to South Pasadena Educational Foundation, South Pasadena, CA.
$40,000 to Santa Barbara Museum of Art, Santa Barbara, CA.
$35,000 to Wild Swan Theater, Ann Arbor, MI.

890
The Steven L. Merrill Family Foundation ◇
16795 Round Valley Cir.
Grass Valley, CA 95949

Established in 1999 in CA.
Donor: Steven L. Merrill.

Foundation type: Independent foundation.
Financial data (yr. ended 12/31/04): Assets, $14,905,025 (M); expenditures, $922,201; qualifying distributions, $683,510; giving activities include $683,500 for 32 grants (high: $250,000; low: $500).
Purpose and activities: Giving primarily for education; some funding also for the arts.
Fields of interest: Museums (art); Elementary/secondary education; Education; Environment.
Limitations: Applications not accepted. No grants to individuals.
Application information: Contributes only to pre-selected organizations.
Officers: Steven L. Merrill, Pres.; Renate King-O'Neal, Secy.; Dennis Covington, Treas.
EIN: 943333248
Selected grants: The following grants were reported in 2004.
$250,000 to All Kinds of Minds, Chapel Hill, NC.
$60,000 to Drew College Preparatory School, San Francisco, CA.
$30,000 to Global Fund for Women, San Francisco, CA.
$10,000 to Teach for America, New York, NY.
$5,000 to Breakthrough Collaborative, San Francisco, CA.
$5,000 to Lewis and Clark College, Portland, OR.
$2,000 to Town School for Boys, San Francisco, CA.
$1,500 to Avon Old Farms School, Avon, CT.

891
Metabolife Foundation ◇
(formerly The Metabolife International Foundation)
5643 Copley Dr.
San Diego, CA 92111 (858) 490-5222
Contact: Mara Morrison-Lettau

Established in 1997 in CA.
Donors: Michael Blevins; W.R. Bradley; Michael Ellis.
Foundation type: Independent foundation.
Financial data (yr. ended 12/31/03): Assets, $677,261 (M); gifts received, $110,001; expenditures, $624,501; qualifying distributions, $624,501; giving activities include $585,525 for 58 + grants (high: $250,000), and $20,071 for in-kind gifts.
Fields of interest: Children/youth, services.
Type of support: General/operating support; In-kind gifts.
Limitations: Giving primarily in CA and CO. No grants to individuals.
Application information:
   Initial approach: Letter
   Deadline(s): None
Officers and Directors:* Michael Ellis,* Pres.; Michael Blevins,* Secy.; Robert Bradley,* C.F.O.
EIN: 330774588

892
Metta Fund ◇
(formerly The M Health Foundation)
770 Tamalpais Dr., Ste. 309
Corte Madera, CA 94925

Established around 1986; converted in 1992 from Davies Medical Center.
Donor: Franklin Holding Corp.
Foundation type: Independent foundation.

Financial data (yr. ended 12/31/03): Assets, $43,347,369 (M); expenditures, $1,298,297; qualifying distributions, $1,151,752; giving activities include $1,077,500 for 9 grants (high: $960,000; low: $1,500).
Purpose and activities: Giving primarily for health care and medical research; funding also for human services.
Fields of interest: Hospitals (general); Medical research, institute; Cancer research; Orthopedics research; Obstetrics/gynecology research; Crime/violence prevention, abuse prevention.
Limitations: Applications not accepted. Giving primarily in CA; some funding nationally. No grants to individuals.
Application information: Contributes only to pre-selected organizations.
Officers: J. Edward Tippetts, Chair.; Lutz Issleib, Vice-Chair.; James Uyeda, Secy.-Treas.
Director: Gregory G. Monardo.
EIN: 942992640
Selected grants: The following grants were reported in 2003.
$960,000 to California Pacific Medical Center, San Francisco, CA.
$50,000 to Obstetrics and Gynecology Research and Education Foundation, Palo Alto, CA. 2 grants: $25,000 each.
$30,000 to New Orthopaedic Concepts, San Francisco, CA.
$11,000 to American Cancer Society, Atlanta, GA.
$10,000 to Advocates, Saukville, WI.
$10,000 to International Medical Corps, Santa Monica, CA.
$5,000 to American Heart Association, Dallas, TX.
$1,500 to Multiple Sclerosis Society, National, New York, NY.

893
The Barry and Wendy Meyer Charitable Foundation ◇
9460 Wilshire Blvd., Ste. 600
Beverly Hills, CA 90212 (310) 888-3630
Contact: Wendy Meyer, Pres.; Barry Meyer, Secy. and C.F.O

Established in 1999 in CA.
Donors: Wendy Meyer, Ph.D.; Barry Meyer.
Foundation type: Independent foundation.
Financial data (yr. ended 12/31/04): Assets, $1,131,856 (M); expenditures, $767,070; qualifying distributions, $764,293; giving activities include $764,293 for 68 grants (high: $100,000; low: $250).
Fields of interest: Higher education; Education; Reproductive health, family planning; Human services; Children/youth, services; Family services; Jewish agencies & temples.
Limitations: Giving primarily in CA, with some giving in NY.
Application information: Application form required.
   Deadline(s): None
Officers: Wendy Meyer, Ph.D., Pres.; Barry Meyer, Secy. and C.F.O.
EIN: 954754104
Selected grants: The following grants were reported in 2003.
$100,000 to Human Rights Watch, New York, NY. For general support.
$75,000 to United Friends of the Children, Los Angeles, CA. For general support.
$50,000 to Save the Children Federation, Westport, CT. For general support.

$25,000 to Venice Family Clinic, Venice, CA. For general support.

$10,000 to American Red Cross, Los Angeles, CA. For general support.

$10,000 to Childrens Defense Fund, DC. For general support.

$10,000 to Doctors Without Borders USA, New York, NY. For general support.

$10,000 to Grace Center, Pasadena, CA. For general support.

$10,000 to Los Angeles Free Clinic, Friends of, Los Angeles, CA. For general support.

$10,000 to Vocational Instruction Project (VIP) Community Services, Bronx, NY. For general support.

894

MFU Training Plan Trust ✦ ☆

240 2nd St.
San Francisco, CA   94105

Established in 1988 in CA.

Donors: American Ship Management, LLC; Matson Navigation Co., Inc.; Patriot Contract Services, LCC.

Foundation type: Operating foundation.

Financial data (yr. ended 12/31/05): Assets, $255,306 (M); gifts received, $271,190; expenditures, $366,245; qualifying distributions, $359,667; giving activities include $322,384 for 4 grants (high: $156,038; low: $280).

Purpose and activities: Giving to provide training to the approximately 360 Marine Fireman's Union members, CA.

Fields of interest: Education; Disasters, fire prevention/control.

Type of support: Scholarship funds.

Limitations: Applications not accepted. Giving primarily in CA. No grants to individuals.

Application information: Contributes only to pre-selected organizations.

Trustees: Henry Disley; Timothy Gill; Robert Iwata; William O'Brian; Thomas E. Percival; Anthony Poplawski.

EIN: 943058922

895

The Michelson Foundation ✦

1660 Bush St., Ste. 300
San Francisco, CA   94109   (415) 561-6540
Contact: Mary L. Gregory, Sr. Prog. off.
FAX: (415) 561-6477; E-mail: mgregory@pfs-llc.net;
URL: http://www.pfs-llc.net/michelson/michelson.html

Established in 1991 in CA.

Foundation type: Independent foundation.

Financial data (yr. ended 12/31/05): Assets, $4,854,033 (M); expenditures, $1,060,307; qualifying distributions, $1,023,297; giving activities include $950,826 for 41 grants (high: $250,000; low: $75).

Purpose and activities: The foundation's primary interest lies in supporting organizations which benefit children, youth and families through programs which address education, human services and healthcare needs. The board is also interested in organizations which provide mental health services for children and adults, and pregnancy prevention programs.

Fields of interest: Education, early childhood education; Education; Mental health/crisis services; Children/youth, services.

Type of support: Equipment; Program development.

Limitations: Applications not accepted. Giving primarily in San Mateo County, CA, and, to a limited degree, San Francisco.

Publications: Annual report; Grants list.

Application information: Unsolicited requests for funds not accepted.

Board meeting date(s): June and Dec.

Officers: Ellen A. Michelson, Pres.; Michael W. Michelson, V.P.; Susan P. Schoenthaler, C.F.O. and Treas.; Mary S. Callender, Exec. Dir.

EIN: 943131676

Selected grants: The following grants were reported in 2003.

$220,000 to Childrens Program. For Solomon Project, provides pro bono psychiatric consultation services to Juvenile and Family Court judges.

$30,000 to Eastside College Preparatory School, East Palo Alto, CA. For scholarships.

$25,000 to Basic Fund, San Francisco, CA. For scholarships.

$20,000 to AchieveAbility, Philadelphia, PA. For Family Self Sufficiency Program.

$6,000 to Daughters of Charity Ministry Services Corporation, Lynwood, CA. To set up Bring Me A Book Library at Carriage House apartments.

$6,000 to Family Service Agency of San Mateo County, San Mateo, CA. For installation of Bring Me A Book Library.

$5,000 to Child and Family Institute, Sacramento, CA. For capital campaign.

896

Gary Karlin Michelson, M.D. Charitable Foundation, Inc. ✦ ☆

12100 Wilshire Blvd., Ste. 800
Los Angeles, CA   90025
Contact: Gary Karlin Michelson M.D., Pres.

Established in 1995 in CA.

Donor: Gary Karlin Michelson, M.D.

Foundation type: Independent foundation.

Financial data (yr. ended 12/31/05): Assets, $97,808,403 (M); gifts received, $102,674,446; expenditures, $4,197,162; qualifying distributions, $4,136,044; giving activities include $4,126,200 for 9 grants (high: $3,000,000; low: $100).

Fields of interest: Animals/wildlife; Medical research.

Limitations: Applications not accepted. Giving primarily in Los Angeles, CA. No grants to individuals.

Application information: Contributes only to pre-selected organizations.

Officers: Gary Karlin Michelson, M.D., Pres.; Michael Schiffman, M.D., Secy.

EIN: 954551615

897

Lowell Milken Family Foundation ✦

(formerly L.and S. Milken Foundation)
1250 4th St., 3rd Fl.
Santa Monica, CA   90401-1304
Contact: R. Finerman, C.F.O. and Treas.

Established in 1986 in CA.

Donors: L. Milken; S. Milken.

Foundation type: Independent foundation.

Financial data (yr. ended 10/31/05): Assets, $58,323,359 (M); expenditures, $1,853,608; qualifying distributions, $1,595,817; giving activities include $1,506,000 for 64 grants (high: $350,000; low: $500).

Purpose and activities: To build human resources through programs in four major areas: 1) Education: to reward educational innovators, stimulate creativity among students, involve parents and other citizens in the school system, and offer opportunities to the disadvantaged student; 2) Health Care and Medical Research: to make the benefits of both basic and highly advanced health care available to those who need them; 3) Community Services: to support programs and facilities that meet the essential needs at the neighborhood level; and 4) Human Welfare: to meet the compelling needs of the disadvantaged.

Fields of interest: Higher education; Education; Health organizations, association; Cancer; Medical research, institute; Cancer research; Human services; Jewish federated giving programs; Jewish agencies & temples.

Type of support: General/operating support; Building/renovation; Conferences/seminars; Scholarship funds; Research.

Limitations: Applications not accepted. Giving primarily in the Los Angeles, CA, area. No grants to individuals.

Publications: Annual report.

Application information: Contributes only to pre-selected organizations.

Officers and Directors:* L. Milken,* Pres.; S. Milken,* Exec. V.P. and Secy.; R. Finerman,* V.P.; S. Fox, Treas.; D. Milken; J. Milken; R. Milken.

EIN: 954078354

Selected grants: The following grants were reported in 2003.

$550,000 to Cedars-Sinai Medical Center, Los Angeles, CA.

$400,000 to High Tech High, San Diego, CA.

$375,000 to American Friends of Ariel, Coconut Creek, FL.

$161,000 to University of Pennsylvania, Philadelphia, PA.

$100,000 to Jewish Federation Council of Greater Los Angeles, Los Angeles, CA.

$100,000 to Prostate Cancer Research and Education Foundation, La Mesa, CA.

$75,000 to Urban League of Los Angeles, Los Angeles, CA.

$58,500 to University of California, Los Angeles, CA.

$40,000 to American Friends of Aish Hatorah, Los Angeles, CA.

$25,000 to University of California at Berkeley Foundation, Berkeley, CA.

898

The Milken Family Foundation ▼ ✦

1250 4th St., 3rd Fl.
Santa Monica, CA   90401   (310) 570-4800
Contact: Richard Sandler, Exec. V.P.
FAX: (310) 570-4801; E-mail: admin@mff.org;
URL: http://www.mff.org

Established in 1986 in CA.

Donors: Lowell Milken; Michael Milken; Lori A. Milken; Sandra Milken; Department of Education.

Foundation type: Independent foundation.

Financial data (yr. ended 11/30/04): Assets, $238,573,671 (M); gifts received, $1,728,805;

expenditures, $21,053,297; qualifying distributions, $19,485,448; giving activities include $6,680,941 for 305 grants (high: $602,500; low: $500; average: $1,000–$50,000), and $11,103,895 for 7 foundation-administered programs.

Purpose and activities: The purpose of the foundation is to discover and advance inventive and effective ways of helping people help themselves and those around them lead productive and satisfying lives. The foundation advances this mission primarily through its work in education and medical research. In education, the foundation is committed to strengthening the profession by recognizing and rewarding outstanding educators, and by expanding their professional leadership and policy influence; attracting, retaining and motivating the best talent to the teaching profession; stimulating creativity and productivity among educators and students of all ages; fostering the involvement of both family and the community in schools; and helping build vibrant communities, especially by involving young people who have special needs or who live in neighborhoods considered disadvantaged, in school-based programs that contribute to the revitalization of their community and to the well-being of its residents. In medical research, the foundation is committed to advancing and supporting basic and applied medical research, especially in the areas of prostate cancer and epilepsy, and recognizing and rewarding outstanding scientists in these areas; and supporting basic health care programs to assure the well-being of community members of all ages.

Fields of interest: Education, association; Child development, education; Elementary school/education; Secondary school/education; Higher education; Education; Health care; Cancer; Medical research, institute; Cancer research; Human services; Children/youth, services; Child development, services; Community development; Jewish federated giving programs; Jewish agencies & temples; Economically disadvantaged.

Type of support: General/operating support; Building/renovation; Conferences/seminars; Scholarship funds; Research.

Limitations: Giving primarily in the Los Angeles, CA, area.

Publications: Annual report.

Application information:
Initial approach: Letter or proposal
Deadline(s): None

Officers and Directors:* Lowell Milken,* Chair. and Pres.; Lewis C. Solmon,* Exec. V.P., Education, and Dir., Teacher Adv. Prog; Richard Sandler,* Exec. V.P.; Ralph Finerman,* Sr. V.P. and Treas.; Julius Lesner,* Sr. V.P. and Sr. Advisor; Jane Foley, Sr. V.P., Educator Awards; Lawrence Lesser, Sr. V.P., Creative Services; Susan M. Fox, V.P. and C.F.O.; Tamara W. Schiff, V.P., Education, and Assoc. Dir., Teacher Adv. Prog.; Joni Milken-Noah,* V.P., Mike's Math Club; Ian Noah, V.P., Mike's Math Club; Bonnie Somers, V.P., Comms.; Kristan Van Hook, V.P., Public Policy; Rosey Grier,* Prog. Admin., Community Affairs; Thomas C. Boysen; Mariano Guzman; Katherine Nouri Hughes; Thomas J. Kalinske; Ferne Milken; Gregory A. Milken; Lori A. Milken; Michael Milken; Sandra Milken; Lynda Resnick; Ellen Sandler.

EIN: 954073646

Selected grants: The following grants were reported in 2004.

$602,500 to Bureau of Jewish Education of Greater Los Angeles, Los Angeles, CA.

$521,204 to Madison Elementary School District, Phoenix, AZ.

$480,288 to American Epilepsy Society, Hartford, CT.

$361,574 to Beaufort County School District, Beaufort, SC.

$206,500 to Los Angeles Jewish Home for the Aging, Reseda, CA.

$152,500 to Urban League of Los Angeles, Los Angeles, CA.

$15,000 to Elizabeth Glaser Pediatric AIDS Foundation, Santa Monica, CA.

$10,000 to Hebrew Union College-Jewish Institute of Religion, Los Angeles, CA.

$3,000 to Jewish Free Loan Association, Los Angeles, CA.

$1,004 to Amie Karen Cancer Fund for Children, Beverly Hills, CA.

899
The Barbara and Fred Miller Family Foundation ✧ ☆
10580 Wilshire Blvd., Ste. 25NW
Los Angeles, CA 90024

Established in 2001 in CA.
Donors: Barbara Miller; Fred Miller.
Foundation type: Independent foundation.
Financial data (yr. ended 12/31/05): Assets, $460,188 (M); gifts received, $50,000; expenditures, $368,167; qualifying distributions, $367,970; giving activities include $367,915 for 29 grants (high: $93,000; low: $200).
Fields of interest: Higher education; Cystic fibrosis; Cancer; Medical research; Federated giving programs; Jewish federated giving programs; Jewish agencies & temples.
Limitations: Giving primarily in CA and also some giving in NY. No grants to individuals.
Officers: Barbara Miller, C.E.O. and Secy.-Treas.; Fred Miller, Pres.
EIN: 954846488
Selected grants: The following grants were reported in 2004.
$58,250 to Cedars-Sinai Medical Center, Los Angeles, CA.
$46,150 to United Jewish Fund of Greater Los Angeles, Los Angeles, CA.
$15,000 to Jonsson Cancer Center Foundation, Los Angeles, CA.
$10,000 to University of California, Los Angeles, CA.
$8,400 to Crohns and Colitis Foundation of America, New York, NY.
$2,789 to Stop Cancer, Los Angeles, CA.
$2,000 to American Jewish Committee, Los Angeles, CA.
$2,000 to Curtis School, Los Angeles, CA.
$1,500 to Camp Max Straus, Los Angeles, CA.
$1,000 to American ORT Federation, New York, NY.

900
The Alon and Rosana Miller Foundation ✧ ☆
550 S. Hill St., No. 770
Los Angeles, CA 90013-2401 (213) 628-8619

Established in 2003 in CA.
Donors: Alon Miller; Rosana Miller.
Foundation type: Independent foundation.
Financial data (yr. ended 9/30/05): Assets, $672,590 (M); gifts received, $800,000; expenditures, $400,190; qualifying distributions, $399,990; giving activities include $399,990 for grants.
Purpose and activities: Giving primarily to Jewish organizations.
Fields of interest: Education; Jewish agencies & temples.
Limitations: Giving on a national basis. No grants to individuals.
Application information:
Initial approach: Letter
Deadline(s): None
Officers: Alon Miller, Pres.; Rosana Miller, Secy.
EIN: 200515170

901
Earl B. & Loraine H. Miller Foundation
(also known as The Miller Foundation)
192 Marina Dr.
Long Beach, CA 90803 (562) 493-4711
Contact: Walter M. Florie, Jr., C.E.O.
FAX: (562) 493-4719;
E-mail: info@eandlmillerfdn.com

Established in 1967 in CA.
Foundation type: Independent foundation.
Financial data (yr. ended 6/30/05): Assets, $39,253,005 (M); expenditures, $2,609,828; qualifying distributions, $2,232,836; giving activities include $2,081,589 for 54 grants (high: $875,000; low: $1,000).
Purpose and activities: The foundation only awards grants pertaining to children's issues in 5 categories: 1) Health, 2) Education, 3) Child & Family Development, 4) Moral Citizenship, and 5) the arts. Included in this is funding for three children's health clinics, child welfare, a hospital and a hospital building fund, and education; support also for arts and cultural activities, including museums, and symphony education of grade school children. The foundation also funds a health education center, dedicated to promoting a healthy city through culturally and linguistically appropriate health education and health promotion programs, training and leadership development, and collaboration with a diverse community.
Fields of interest: Visual arts; Museums; Performing arts; Arts; Education; Health care; Children/youth, services.
Type of support: General/operating support; Continuing support; Capital campaigns; Building/renovation; Equipment; Program development; Seed money; Curriculum development; Scholarship funds; Technical assistance; Consulting services; Program evaluation; Program-related investments/loans; Matching/challenge support.
Limitations: Applications not accepted. Giving limited to Long Beach, CA. No support for religious or political organizations. No grants to individuals.
Publications: Informational brochure.
Application information: Unsolicited requests for funds not accepted.
Board meeting date(s): Usually Jan., Mar., May, July, Sept. and Nov.
Officers and Trustees:* Walter Florie, Jr.,* C.E.O. and Pres.; Warren Schulten,* V.P.; Jeanne Karatsu,* Secy.; Ron Arias; Warren Iliff; Nancy Kimber; William H. Marmion, Ph.D.
Number of staff: 1 part-time professional; 1 part-time support.
EIN: 952500545

Selected grants: The following grants were reported in 2004.

$200,000 to Childrens Clinic, Long Beach, CA.

$122,120 to Memorial Medical Center Foundation, Long Beach, CA. 2 grants: $61,060 (For children's hospital expansion), $61,060 (For West Pediatric Wing).

$109,000 to Long Beach Symphony Association, Long Beach, CA. For Elementary Ensemble program and family concert.

$100,000 to Boys and Girls Clubs of Long Beach, Long Beach, CA. For general operating support.

$100,000 to Greater Long Beach Child Guidance Center, Long Beach, CA. For MIS System.

$100,000 to YMCA of Greater Long Beach, Long Beach, CA. For S A F E & Renaissance program.

$62,500 to Long Beach Museum of Art, Long Beach, CA. For Education Center.

$40,000 to Childrens Dental Foundation, Long Beach, CA. For specialty care program.

$25,500 to For the Child, Long Beach, CA. For PCI therapy program.

902
The Tony Mistlin and Family Private Foundation ◇
P.O. Box 565
Ripon, CA 95366

Established in 2002 in CA.
Donors: Anthony Mistlin; Joan Mistlin.
Foundation type: Independent foundation.
Financial data (yr. ended 12/31/05): Assets, $1,055,408 (M); expenditures, $500,000; qualifying distributions, $500,000; giving activities include $500,000 for 1 grant.
Fields of interest: Community development.
Limitations: Giving primarily in CA.
Officer: Anthony Mistlin, Pres.
Director: Joan Mistlin.
EIN: 300068588
Selected grants: The following grants were reported in 2003.
$150,000 to Central California Art League, Modesto, CA.
$20,000 to First Congregational Church, Salida, CA.

903
Edward D. and Anna Mitchell Family Foundation ◇
11601 Wilshire Blvd., No. 2400
Los Angeles, CA 90025
Contact: Jonathan E. Mitchell, Pres.

Established in 1953.
Donors: Anna Mitchell‡; Edward D. Mitchell‡; and members of the Mitchell family.
Foundation type: Independent foundation.
Financial data (yr. ended 12/31/04): Assets, $35,229,675 (M); expenditures, $2,834,483; qualifying distributions, $2,402,224; giving activities include $2,402,224 for 42 grants (high: $550,000; low: $227).
Purpose and activities: Giving primarily for Jewish welfare funds, higher education, and social services.
Fields of interest: Higher education; Hospitals (general); Human services; Federated giving programs; Jewish federated giving programs.
Limitations: Applications not accepted. Giving primarily in CA. No grants to individuals.

Application information: Contributes only to pre-selected organizations.
Officers and Directors:* Joseph N. Mitchell,* Chair.; Jonathan E. Mitchell,* Pres.; Kayla Mitchell,* V.P.; Daniel K. Attias,* Secy.-Treas.
Number of staff: 1 part-time professional.
EIN: 954715236
Selected grants: The following grants were reported in 2004.
$550,000 to International Fund for Education and Career Development, Los Angeles, CA.
$80,000 to California Community Foundation, Los Angeles, CA.
$50,000 to United Way, Inc., Region V - Western Region, Los Angeles, CA.
$35,000 to Oxfam America, Boston, MA.
$10,000 to Jewish National Fund, West Hills, CA.
$4,000 to Jewish Fund for Justice, New York, NY.

904
The Modglin Family Foundation ◇
3100 Airway, Ste. 124
Costa Mesa, CA 92626

Established in 1987 in CA.
Donors: Donald L. Modglin; Judy Eastman; Grace Baptist Church; THC Business SVC; Manzanita Baptist Church.
Foundation type: Independent foundation.
Financial data (yr. ended 6/30/04): Assets, $5,465,758 (M); gifts received, $141,570; expenditures, $488,131; qualifying distributions, $457,860; giving activities include $446,372 for 76 grants to individuals (high: $50,000; low: $200).
Purpose and activities: Giving primarily for church growth and renewal through need assessment, resource referral, limited training, and ministry-related grants for local evangelical churches in the Southern California area.
Fields of interest: Christian agencies & churches.
Type of support: Program development; Conferences/seminars; Scholarship funds; Consulting services; Matching/challenge support.
Limitations: Applications not accepted. Giving primarily in southern CA.
Officers: Donald L. Modglin, Pres.; Sharon Marino, V.P.; Steven Modglin, V.P.; Grace M. Modglin, Secy.
Number of staff: 2 full-time professional; 1 part-time professional.
EIN: 330266405
Selected grants: The following grants were reported in 2003.
$30,000 to Western Seminary, Portland, OR.
$11,500 to Grace Church in Glendora, Glendora, CA.
$9,000 to Gods House, Huntington Beach, CA.
$8,000 to Biola University, La Mirada, CA.
$5,000 to Gateways to Better Education, Lake Forest, CA.
$5,000 to Vanguard University, Costa Mesa, CA.
$4,900 to Woodhaven Community Church, Sherwood, OR.
$4,500 to University of California, Davis, CA.
$4,028 to Azusa Pacific University, Azusa, CA.
$2,200 to California Baptist University, Riverside, CA.

905
Mogharebi Family Foundation ◇
15 Rim Ridge
Newport Coast, CA 92657

Established in 2003 in CA.
Donors: Hamed Mogharebi; Kerry Mogharebi.
Foundation type: Independent foundation.
Financial data (yr. ended 12/31/04): Assets, $760,001 (M); gifts received, $750,000; expenditures, $440,125; qualifying distributions, $440,000; giving activities include $440,000 for 1 grant.
Fields of interest: Cancer.
Limitations: Applications not accepted. No grants to individuals.
Application information: Contributes only to pre-selected organizations.
Officers: Hamed Mogharebi, Pres.; Kerry Mogharebi, Secy.
EIN: 200501252

906
The Celia Moh Foundation ◇
23232 Peralta Dr., Ste. 210
Laguna Hills, CA 92653

Established in 2002 in NC.
Donor: Sorgente No. 3 Trust.
Foundation type: Independent foundation.
Financial data (yr. ended 12/31/05): Assets, $8,091,664 (M); gifts received, $3,084,980; expenditures, $576,921; qualifying distributions, $374,705; giving activities include $374,705 for 7 grants (high: $154,300; low: $5,723).
Purpose and activities: Scholarship funds for students provided through the qualified institutions.
Fields of interest: Higher education; Scholarships/financial aid.
Type of support: Scholarship funds.
Limitations: Giving primarily in MI and NC.
Officers: Joe Carroll, Pres.; Lyle T. Lansdell, Treas.
Directors: Celia Moh; Michael Moh; R. Ted Weschler.
EIN: 680492736

907
The Mohn Family Foundation ◇
c/o Lexington Financial Mgmt., LLC
9350 Wilshire Blvd., Ste. 250
Beverly Hills, CA 90212

Established in 2001 in CA.
Donors: Jarl Mohn; Pamela Mohn.
Foundation type: Independent foundation.
Financial data (yr. ended 12/31/04): Assets, $9,932,575 (M); expenditures, $455,612; qualifying distributions, $452,315; giving activities include $449,780 for 36 grants (high: $50,000; low: $180).
Fields of interest: Museums (art); Libraries (public); Education; Environment, natural resources; Human services; Children/youth, services; Civil rights; Philanthropy/voluntarism.
Limitations: Applications not accepted. Giving primarily in CA, KY, and NY; some giving also in Canada. No grants to individuals.
Application information: Contributes only to pre-selected organizations.
Officers: Jarl Mohl, Pres.; Pamela Mohn, Secy.-Treas.
EIN: 954830816

908
Moley Family Foundation ✦
P.O. Box 4316
Carmel, CA 93921

Established in 1999 in CA.
Donors: Elizabeth Moley; Richard Moley.
Foundation type: Independent foundation.
Financial data (yr. ended 10/31/05): Assets, $2,659,847 (M); gifts received, $2,000; expenditures, $628,944; qualifying distributions, $622,500; giving activities include $622,500 for 7 grants (high: $540,000; low: $2,500).
Fields of interest: Performing arts centers; Arts; Elementary/secondary education; Higher education, university; Roman Catholic agencies & churches.
Limitations: Applications not accepted. Giving on a national basis, with emphasis on CA and NY. No grants to individuals.
Application information: Contributes only to pre-selected organizations.
Officers: Elizabeth Moley, Pres.; Richard Moley, Treas.
EIN: 770528059

909
Joy and Jerry Monkarsh Family Foundation ✦
9061 Santa Monica Blvd.
Los Angeles, CA 90069

Established in 2001 in CA.
Donors: Jerry Monkarsh; Joy Monkarsh.
Foundation type: Independent foundation.
Financial data (yr. ended 12/31/05): Assets, $333,293 (M); gifts received, $350,000; expenditures, $438,996; qualifying distributions, $438,500; giving activities include $438,500 for 21 grants (high: $72,000; low: $1,000).
Fields of interest: Museums (art); Arts; Education; Jewish agencies & temples.
Limitations: Applications not accepted. Giving primarily in Los Angeles, CA. No grants to individuals.
Application information: Contributes only to pre-selected organizations.
Trustees: Jerry Monkarsh; Joy Monkarsh.
EIN: 954862874
Selected grants: The following grants were reported in 2004.
$150,500 to University of California, Los Angeles, CA. 2 grants: $95,500, $55,000
$50,000 to Prostate Cancer Foundation, Santa Monica, CA.
$35,000 to United Jewish Fund of Greater Los Angeles, Los Angeles, CA.
$30,000 to University of Judaism, Los Angeles, CA.
$28,900 to Sinai Temple, Los Angeles, CA.
$10,000 to Lynne Cohen Foundation for Ovarian Cancer Research, Los Angeles, CA.
$10,000 to Museum of Contemporary Art (MOCA), Los Angeles, CA.
$5,000 to United States Holocaust Memorial Museum, DC.
$2,500 to National Prostate Cancer Coalition, DC.

910
Monterey Peninsula Foundation ✦
(formerly Monterey Peninsula Golf Foundation)
P.O. Box 869
Monterey, CA 93942 (831) 649-1533
Contact: Laurel Lee-Alexander, Dir., Grant Progs.
FAX: (831) 649-1763;
E-mail: info@montereypeninsulafoundation.org;
Additional contact information (for Laurel Lee-Alexander): tel.: (831) 649-1533, ext. 18; E-mail: lla@attpbgolf.com; URL: http://www.montereypeninsulafoundation.org

Established in 1978 in CA.
Foundation type: Independent foundation.
Financial data (yr. ended 6/30/04): Assets, $16,518,942 (M); gifts received, $971,230; expenditures, $11,779,280; qualifying distributions, $4,477,478; giving activities include $3,631,395 for 125 grants (high: $201,900; low: $500; average: $10,000–$100,000).
Purpose and activities: The foundation, and its giving arm, AT&T Pebble Beach Charities, is exclusively philanthropic and is responsible for the disbursement of funds raised to charitable organizations which enhance the quality of life of the residents of Monterey County, CA and surrounding areas. The foundation hosts the AT&T Pebble Beach National Pro-Am golf tournament and distributes the proceeds to charity.
Fields of interest: Arts; Education; Health care; Health organizations, association; Human services; Youth, services; General charitable giving.
Type of support: General/operating support; Capital campaigns; Building/renovation; Equipment; Technical assistance; Matching/challenge support.
Limitations: Giving limited to Monterey, Santa Cruz, San Benito, and Santa Clara counties, and the San Jose/San Francisco Bay Area, CA. No grants to individuals or for emergency operating funds, deficits, research projects, endowments, development of production of books, films or video projects, organization with a limited constituency, annual meetings, advertising, contests, fundraising, ceremonies, conferences, travel, or memorials.
Publications: Application guidelines; Grants list; Informational brochure; Occasional report.
Application information: Application form and guidelines are available on foundation Web site. E-mailed or faxed applications and videos are not accepted. Please do not bind application or put it in a presentation folder. Application form required.
Initial approach: Completed application form and grant application checklist
Copies of proposal: 2
Deadline(s): None
Final notification: 90-180 days
Officers and Directors:* Clint Eastwood,* Chair.; Peter Ueberroth, Vice-Chair.; John Zoller,* Vice-Chair.; Ollie Nutt, Exec. V.P.; Cindy Zoller Silver, Secy.; Peter Coniglio, Emeritus; Harry Crosby, Emeritus; John Anton; Dave Clark; Bob Ferguson; Paul Leach; Doug Mackenzie; J.B. McIntosh; Dan Tibbitts.
Number of staff: 8 full-time professional; 2 full-time support; 3 part-time support.
EIN: 942541783
Selected grants: The following grants were reported in 2005.
$251,750 to Monterey County Youth Museum, Monterey, CA.
$125,000 to Second Harvest Food Bank.
$123,240 to Boys and Girls Clubs of Monterey County, Seaside, CA.

$106,500 to Action Council of Monterey County, Salinas, CA.
$100,000 to Monterey Bay Aquarium, Monterey, CA.
$100,000 to Salinas Valley Fair Heritage Foundation, King City, CA.
$87,500 to Community Foundation for Monterey County, Monterey, CA. For Rally Salinas, grass-roots campaign to raise funds to prevent Salinas libraries from closing.
$25,000 to Community of Caring Monterey Peninsula, Monterey, CA.
$20,000 to All Saints Episcopal Day School, Carmel, CA.
$10,872 to Youth Arts Collective, Monterey, CA.

911
Silva Watson Moonwalk Fund ✦
175 Via Lerida
Greenbrae, CA 94904
Contact: Vivian L. Schneider, Pres.

Established in 1997 in CA.
Donor: Douglas Watson 1995 Trust.
Foundation type: Independent foundation.
Financial data (yr. ended 9/30/05): Assets, $4,246,949 (M); expenditures, $603,014; qualifying distributions, $424,850; giving activities include $424,850 for 39 grants (high: $80,000; low: $1,300).
Fields of interest: Media, film/video; AIDS; Human services; Women, centers/services; AIDS, people with; LGBTQ.
Limitations: Applications not accepted. Giving primarily in CA, with emphasis on Los Angeles and San Francisco. No grants to individuals.
Application information: Contributes only to pre-selected organizations.
Officer: Vivian L. Schneider, Pres.
EIN: 943286835
Selected grants: The following grants were reported in 2004.
$50,000 to Los Angeles Gay and Lesbian Center, Los Angeles, CA.
$25,000 to Bread and Roses, Corte Madera, CA.
$25,000 to Healing Waters, San Francisco, CA.
$25,000 to Project Angel Food, Los Angeles, CA.
$10,000 to Aid for AIDS, West Hollywood, CA.
$10,000 to National AIDS Memorial Grove, San Francisco, CA.
$10,000 to Stop AIDS Project, San Francisco, CA.
$5,000 to AIDS Assistance Program, Palm Springs, CA.
$5,000 to AIDS Walk, San Francisco, CA.
$5,000 to Dolores Street Community Services, San Francisco, CA.

912
Moore Family Foundation
P.O. Box 3099
Los Altos, CA 94024-0099

Established in 1986.
Donors: Betty I. Moore; Gordon E. Moore.
Foundation type: Independent foundation.
Financial data (yr. ended 9/30/05): Assets, $43,120,633 (M); expenditures, $2,160,427; qualifying distributions, $1,970,133; giving activities include $1,902,001 for 33 grants (high: $406,000; low: $5,000; average: $10,000–$50,000).

Purpose and activities: Giving primarily for higher education, conservation, and science; some giving also for local social services.

Fields of interest: Higher education; Environment, natural resources; Human services; Engineering/technology; Science.

Type of support: General/operating support; Annual campaigns; Capital campaigns; Building/renovation; Equipment; Program development.

Limitations: Applications not accepted. Giving primarily in CA. No grants to individuals.

Application information: Contributes only to pre-selected organizations.

Board meeting date(s): As needed

Trustees: Kathleen E. Justice-Moore; Betty I. Moore; Gordon E. Moore; Kenneth G. Moore; Kristen L. Moore; Steven E. Moore.

Number of staff: 1 full-time professional.

EIN: 943024440

913
Gordon and Betty Moore Foundation ▼

The Presidio of San Francisco
P.O. Box 29910
San Francisco, CA 94129-0910   (415) 561-7700
Contact: Grants Admin. Dept.
FAX: (415) 561-7707; E-mail: info@moore.org;
Additional e-mail: grantprocessing@moore.org;
URL: http://www.moore.org/

Established in 2000 in CA.

Donors: Gordon E. Moore; Betty I. Moore.

Foundation type: Independent foundation.

Financial data (yr. ended 12/31/05): Assets, $5,308,627,945 (M); expenditures, $264,844,807; qualifying distributions, $239,105,590; giving activities include $217,573,897 for 388 grants (high: $36,392,000; low: $500; average: $5,000–$10,000,000), and $1,184,859 for 301 employee matching gifts.

Purpose and activities: Giving primarily to improve the quality of life for future generations, the foundation seeks to develop outcome-based grants that will provide lasting and meaningful benefits to the environment, science and the San Francisco Bay Area community. In doing so, the foundation emphasizes measurable impact and supports programs that clearly identify targeted results and encourage transformative change.

Fields of interest: Environment; Science.

Type of support: Land acquisition; Program development; Research; Program-related investments/loans; Employee matching gifts.

Limitations: Applications not accepted. Giving on a worldwide basis, with some focus on the San Francisco Bay Area, CA, for selected projects. No support for religious or political organizations. No grants to individuals, or for arts, building/renovation, endowments, capital campaigns, labor issues, or for sports programs.

Publications: Financial statement; Grants list.

Application information: Does not accept unsolicited proposals. Instead, the foundation funds foundation-generated initiatives that focus on specific issues, and makes local grants through its San Francisco Bay Area program.

Officers and Trustees:* Gordon E. Moore,* Chair.; Edward E. Penhoet, Ph.D.*, Pres.; William G. Green, Corp. Secy. Genl. Counsel, and Chief Prog. Off., Environment; Alice Ruth, C.I.O.; Kenneth G. Moore,* Dir., Eval. and Inf. Tech.; Bruce Alberts; Lewis W. Coleman; Kathleen Justice-Moore; Betty I. Moore;

Kristen L. Moore; Steven E. Moore; Kenneth F. Siebel.

Number of staff: 72 full-time professional; 56 part-time professional; 6 full-time support; 10 part-time support.

EIN: 943397785

Selected grants: The following grants were reported in 2004.

$37,644,667 to Conservation International, DC. For Global Conservation Fund, Center for Biodiversity Conservation, and Scientific Field Stations.

$21,910,204 to California Institute of Technology, Pasadena, CA. 2 grants: $12,663,458 (For Nanoscale Systems Initiative, which will establish Laboratory for Nanoscale Systems and create new educational opportunities in nanoscale science and engineering), $9,246,746 (For indirect support associated with project grants awarded under Foundation's commitment to CalTech).

$7,932,000 to Sonoma Land Trust, Santa Rosa, CA. For permanent protection and restoration at far northern end of San Pablo Bay.

$4,150,000 to Public Library of Science, San Francisco, CA. To establish online scholarly publisher to make scientific and medical literature a public resource.

$2,961,000 to World Wildlife Fund, DC. For phase II of Amazon Headwaters Initiative, plan to maintain regional terrestrial and freshwater biodiversity.

$1,036,234 to University of California at San Diego, La Jolla, CA. For project, Toward a Distributed Information System for Marine Biology and Limnology.

$268,714 to Nature Conservancy, Arlington, VA. To develop fundraising campaign for protection of Great Bear Rainforest.

$203,100 to Southeast Alaska Conservation Council, Juneau, AK. Toward building local, grassroots support for conservation efforts that protect critical salmon habitat.

$35,000 to Mountain Montessori, Avon, CO. For seed funding for establishment of Mountain Montessori School.

914
Morgan Family Foundation, Inc. ✧

6671 Owens Dr.
Pleasanton, CA 94588

Established in 2000 in CA.

Donor: Kile Morgan, Jr.

Foundation type: Independent foundation.

Financial data (yr. ended 12/31/03): Assets, $596,561 (M); gifts received, $500,000; expenditures, $399,406; qualifying distributions, $399,385; giving activities include $362,800 for 18 grants (high: $112,000; low: $250), and $35,000 for 11 grants to individuals (high: $25,000; low: $1,000).

Fields of interest: Higher education; Boys & girls clubs.

Type of support: Scholarships—to individuals.

Limitations: Applications not accepted. Giving primarily in CA, with emphasis on National City; some giving also in Boulder, CO.

Application information: Unsolicited requests for funds not accepted.

Officers: Linda F. Morasch, C.E.O. and Secy.; Kile Morgan, Jr., Pres.; Judy L. Morgan, V.P.

EIN: 912081052

Selected grants: The following grants were reported in 2004.

$125,000 to Boys and Girls Club of National City, National City, CA. 2 grants: $25,000, $100,000

$5,000 to Pacific Legal Foundation, Sacramento, CA.

$1,500 to Harvard University, Cambridge, MA.

$1,200 to Boys and Girls Club of the Peninsula, Redwood City, CA.

$1,000 to Community Hospital Foundation, Monterey, CA.

$700 to Interplast, Mountain View, CA.

$500 to Angels Gate, Northport, NY.

$500 to YMCA of Santa Clara Valley, San Jose, CA.

$200 to Special Olympics of Northern California, Silicon Valley Region, San Jose, CA.

915
James and Rebecca Morgan Family Foundation

P.O. Box 1742
Los Altos, CA 94023-1742   (650) 941-8802
Contact: Linda Verhulp, Prog. Dir.
FAX: (650) 941-1715;
E-mail: info@morganfamilyfoundation.org;
URL: http://www.morganfamilyfoundation.org

Established in 1993 in CA.

Donors: James C. Morgan; Rebecca Q. Morgan.

Foundation type: Independent foundation.

Financial data (yr. ended 12/31/04): Assets, $52,618,782 (M); expenditures, $2,884,606; qualifying distributions, $2,466,760; giving activities include $2,382,446 for 23 grants (high: $305,107; low: $1,000).

Purpose and activities: The foundation focuses its giving on youth, education, the environment and stewardship. Programs that maximize the potential of an organization and the individuals it serves are of particular interest. The majority of funding is in Santa Clara County and San Mateo County, CA.

Fields of interest: Arts; Education; Environment; Youth development; Foundations (community); Leadership development.

Type of support: General/operating support; Continuing support; Annual campaigns; Capital campaigns; Building/renovation; Land acquisition; Program development; Seed money; Fellowships; Scholarship funds; Research; Technical assistance; Program evaluation; Matching/challenge support.

Limitations: Applications not accepted. Giving primarily in Santa Clara and San Mateo counties, CA. No support for religious organizations. No grants to individuals.

Publications: Grants list.

Application information: Unsolicited applications not accepted. Proposals are by invitation only.

Board meeting date(s): 3 times a year; dates set each year

Officers and Directors:* James C. Morgan,* Chair. and Treas.; Rebecca Q. Morgan,* Pres.; John Finegan,* Secy.

Number of staff: 2 part-time professional; 1 part-time support.

EIN: 943187468

Selected grants: The following grants were reported in 2003.

$1,100,000 to Peninsula Community Foundation, San Mateo, CA. For general support.

$200,000 to Mercersburg Academy, Mercersburg, PA. For general support.

$125,000 to San Jose Childrens Discovery Museum, San Jose, CA. For general support.

$100,000 to Community School of Music and Arts, Mountain View, CA. For general support.

$74,944 to Cultural Initiatives Silicon Valley, San Jose, CA. For general support.

$50,000 to Sustainability Institute, Hartland, VT. For general support.

$40,000 to Adolescent Counseling Services, Palo Alto, CA. For general support.

$40,000 to Dartmouth College, Hanover, NH. For general support.

$40,000 to Friends for Youth, Redwood City, CA. For general support.

$1,780 to Trust for Hidden Villa, Los Altos Hills, CA. For general support.

916
Morris Morgenstern Foundation ◇

c/o Paul Goodnough, CPA
543 Country Club Dr., B-116
Simi Valley, CA 93065

Trust established in 1949 in NY.
Donors: Morris Morgenstern†; Frank N. Morgenstern.
Foundation type: Independent foundation.
Financial data (yr. ended 12/31/03): Assets, $10,617,109 (L); expenditures, $619,729; qualifying distributions, $585,808; giving activities include $585,808 for 62+ grants (high: $175,000).
Purpose and activities: Support for Jewish organizations, including welfare funds, synagogues and other religious institutions, and yeshivas; funding also for hospitals and medical research.
Fields of interest: Elementary/secondary education; Higher education; Hospitals (general); Medical research, institute; Human services; Jewish federated giving programs; Jewish agencies & temples.
Type of support: General/operating support.
Limitations: Applications not accepted. Giving primarily in the metropolitan New York, NY, area. No grants to individuals.
Application information: Contributes only to pre-selected organizations.
Trustee: Frank N. Morgenstern.
EIN: 131635719
Selected grants: The following grants were reported in 2003.

$175,000 to Agudath Israel of America, New York, NY.

$100,000 to Hebrew Academy of Long Beach, Long Beach, NY.

$100,000 to Jewish Communal Fund of New York, New York, NY.

$5,000 to Anti-Defamation League of Bnai Brith, New York, NY.

$2,500 to American Jewish Committee, New York, NY.

$2,500 to World Jewish Congress American Section, New York, NY.

$2,000 to American Committee for Shaare Zedek Hospital in Jerusalem, New York, NY.

$1,500 to Aleph Society, New York, NY.

$1,000 to Jewish National Fund, New York, NY.

$1,000 to Long Beach Medical Center, Long Beach, NY.

917
The Morris Foundation ◇

c/o Dan J. Hall
5000 Hopyard Rd., Ste. 400
Pleasanton, CA 94588

Established in 1993 in CA.
Donors: Kenneth R. Morris; Linda A. Morris.
Foundation type: Independent foundation.
Financial data (yr. ended 12/31/04): Assets, $17,525,414 (M); gifts received, $24,643; expenditures, $917,342; qualifying distributions, $820,000; giving activities include $820,000 for 13 grants (high: $200,000; low: $10,000).
Fields of interest: Elementary/secondary education; Higher education; Education; Housing/shelter, development; Human services; Protestant agencies & churches.
Limitations: Applications not accepted. Giving primarily in CA with emphasis on Modesto; some funding nationally. No grants to individuals.
Application information: Contributes only to pre-selected organizations.
Officers: Kenneth R. Morris, Pres.; Linda A. Morris, V.P.; Carl W. Morris, C.F.O.
EIN: 680313709

918
Morton Foundation ◇

100 Pringle Ave., Ste. 410
Walnut Creek, CA 94596
Contact: Paul F. Morton, Pres.

Established in 1997 in CA.
Donors: Thomas A. Morton; Helen K. Morton.
Foundation type: Independent foundation.
Financial data (yr. ended 12/31/05): Assets, $6,021,285 (M); gifts received, $500,000; expenditures, $484,436; qualifying distributions, $439,500; giving activities include $439,500 for 65 grants (high: $50,000; low: $500).
Fields of interest: Education; Health organizations, association; Human services; Children/youth, services.
Limitations: Giving primarily in CA.
Application information: Application form required.
  Initial approach: Proposal
  Deadline(s): None
  Board meeting date(s): Varies
Officers and Directors:* Paul F. Morton, Pres. and Treas.; Kevin O. Klecka,* V.P.; Brian T. Morton,* V.P.; Helen K. Morton,* V.P.
EIN: 911813416
Selected grants: The following grants were reported in 2005.

$25,000 to Northern California Golf Association Foundation, Pebble Beach, CA.

$20,000 to Basic Fund, San Francisco, CA.

$16,500 to Guide Dogs of America, Sylmar, CA.

$10,000 to Palcare, Burlingame, CA.

$6,000 to American Red Cross, San Francisco, CA.

$5,000 to City of Hope, Los Angeles, CA.

$5,000 to Community Hospital Foundation, Monterey, CA.

$5,000 to Happy Trails Riding Academy, Visalia, CA.

$5,000 to Trips for Kids, Mill Valley, CA.

$2,500 to Oakes Childrens Center, San Francisco, CA.

919
Peter A. Morton Foundation, Inc. ◇

510 N. Robertson Blvd.
Los Angeles, CA 90048

Established in 1999 in DE.
Donor: Peter Morton.
Foundation type: Independent foundation.
Financial data (yr. ended 12/31/04): Assets, $1,960 (M); gifts received, $1,790,684; expenditures, $1,788,907; qualifying distributions, $1,788,907; giving activities include $1,788,845 for 34 grants (high: $1,000,000; low: $50).
Purpose and activities: Giving primarily for environmental conservation, education, and medical research.
Fields of interest: Education; Environment, natural resources; Environment; Health organizations, association; Medical research, institute; Cancer research; Human services; Children, services; Civil rights; Jewish federated giving programs.
Limitations: Applications not accepted. Giving primarily in Los Angeles, CA. No grants to individuals.
Application information: Contributes only to pre-selected organizations.
Officers: Peter Morton, Pres.; Brian Ogaz, Secy.
EIN: 954687071

920
Samuel B. and Margaret C. Mosher Foundation

(also known as The Mosher Foundation)
(formerly Samuel B. Mosher Foundation)
P.O. Box 1079
Santa Barbara, CA 93101 (805) 962-1700
Contact: Edward E. Birch, C.E.O. and Pres.
FAX: (805) 962-1792;
E-mail: info@mosherfoundation.com; Application address: 1114 State St., Ste. 252, Santa Barbara, CA 93101

Incorporated in 1951 in CA.
Donors: Samuel B. Mosher†; Goodwin J. Pelissero†; Deborah S. Pelissero†; Margaret C. Mosher†.
Foundation type: Independent foundation.
Financial data (yr. ended 8/31/05): Assets, $28,552,715 (M); gifts received, $400,000; expenditures, $1,604,565; qualifying distributions, $1,429,757; giving activities include $1,185,200 for 72 grants (high: $500,000; low: $500).
Purpose and activities: Grants mainly for education, health care and the performing arts and some support for agencies or organizations benefiting youth.
Fields of interest: Arts; Secondary school/education; Higher education; Health care.
Type of support: Program evaluation; Program development; Equipment; Endowments; Employee-related scholarships; Consulting services; Capital campaigns; Annual campaigns; General/operating support; Building/renovation; Scholarship funds; Program-related investments/loans.
Limitations: Giving primarily in Santa Barbara County, CA. No grants for capital campaigns or endowments.
Publications: Annual report (including application guidelines); Informational brochure (including application guidelines).
Application information: Application form required.

Initial approach: Proposal
Copies of proposal: 1
Deadline(s): Apr. 27 and Dec. 31
Board meeting date(s): Monthly
Final notification: 2 months
Officer and Trustees:* Edward E. Birch,* C.E.O. and Pres.; Robert J. Emmons; Bruce McFadden; David Winter.
Number of staff: 1 part-time professional; 1 full-time support.
EIN: 956037266

921
Moss Foundation ◇
421 N. Beverly Dr., Ste. 260
Beverly Hills, CA 90210

Established in 1990 in CA.
Donor: Jerome S. Moss.
Foundation type: Independent foundation.
Financial data (yr. ended 12/31/04): Assets, $22,870,430 (M); expenditures, $2,320,414; qualifying distributions, $2,061,125; giving activities include $2,061,125 for 96 grants (high: $500,000; low: $500).
Fields of interest: Higher education; Education; Medical research, institute; Human services; Children/youth, services; Business/industry; Federated giving programs; Jewish agencies & temples.
Limitations: Applications not accepted. Giving primarily in the Los Angeles, CA, area. No grants to individuals.
Application information: Contributes only to pre-selected organizations.
Officers: Jerome S. Moss, Pres.; Ann Holbrook Moss, V.P.; Werner F. Wolfen, Secy.
EIN: 954280605
Selected grants: The following grants were reported in 2003.
$500,000 to Accelerated School, Los Angeles, CA.
$500,000 to Painted Turtle Gang Camp Foundation, Santa Monica, CA.
$500,000 to UCLA Foundation, Los Angeles, CA.
$75,000 to Communities in Schools, Alexandria, VA.
$50,000 to Global Green USA, Santa Monica, CA.
$26,000 to Childrens Diabetes Foundation, Beverly Hills, CA.
$25,000 to Elizabeth Glaser Pediatric AIDS Foundation, Santa Monica, CA.
$25,000 to Musicares Foundation, Santa Monica, CA.
$25,000 to Rainforest Foundation US, New York, NY.
$25,000 to Symphony in the Glen, Los Angeles, CA.

922
Mourier Family Foundation ◇
1430 Blue Oaks Blvd., Ste. 190
Roseville, CA 95747

Established in 2000 in CA.
Donor: John Mourier Construction, Inc.
Foundation type: Independent foundation.
Financial data (yr. ended 12/31/04): Assets, $14,905,992 (L); gifts received, $5,515,000; expenditures, $671,428; qualifying distributions, $666,288; giving activities include $664,500 for 15 grants (high: $150,000; low: $2,000).
Fields of interest: Christian agencies & churches.

Limitations: Applications not accepted. Giving primarily in CA. No grants to individuals.
Application information: Contributes only to pre-selected organizations.
Officers: John Mourier III, Pres.; Laura Mourier, Secy.
EIN: 680463710

923
The Mozilo Family Foundation ◇
2816 Ladbrook Way
Thousand Oaks, CA 91361

Established in 1997 in CA.
Donors: Angelo R. Mozilo; Phyllis G. Mozilo.
Foundation type: Independent foundation.
Financial data (yr. ended 12/31/05): Assets, $12,749,683 (M); gifts received, $1,210,000; expenditures, $912,211; qualifying distributions, $898,422; giving activities include $898,422 for 24 grants (high: $175,000; low: $150).
Fields of interest: Arts; Elementary/secondary education; Higher education; Cancer; Prostate cancer; Roman Catholic agencies & churches.
Limitations: Applications not accepted. Giving primarily in CA. No grants to individuals.
Application information: Contributes only to pre-selected organizations.
Officers: Angelo R. Mozilo, Pres.; Elizabeth A. Fitzpatrick, Secy.; Phyllis G. Mozilo, Treas.
EIN: 954617492

924
Mildred E. & Harvey S. Mudd Foundation ◇
11726 San Vicente Blvd., Ste. 625
Los Angeles, CA 90049

Established in CA.
Foundation type: Independent foundation.
Financial data (yr. ended 5/31/05): Assets, $19,951,038 (M); expenditures, $1,099,988; qualifying distributions, $862,092; giving activities include $816,000 for 9 grants (high: $333,000; low: $9,000).
Purpose and activities: Giving primarily for education, and for health care, particularly a children's hospital.
Fields of interest: Museums; Education; Hospitals (general); Hospitals (specialty); Health care; Diabetes research.
Type of support: General/operating support.
Limitations: Applications not accepted. Giving primarily in CA. No grants to individuals.
Application information: Contributes only to pre-selected organizations.
Trustees: Cynthia Sprague Connolly; Caryll S. Mingst; Norman F. Sprague III; William Stinehart, Jr.
EIN: 956021276
Selected grants: The following grants were reported in 2004.
$420,000 to Childrens Hospital of Los Angeles Foundation, Los Angeles, CA.
$201,000 to Saint Johns Health Center, Santa Monica, CA.
$100,000 to Crane Country Day School, Santa Barbara, CA.
$40,000 to Harvey Mudd College, Claremont, CA.
$10,000 to Juvenile Diabetes Research Foundation International, Culver City, CA.

$5,000 to Bandon Library Development Foundation, Bandon, OR.

925
Muller Family Foundation ◇
(formerly Frank Muller, Sr. Foundation)
2003-168 Bayview Heights Dr.
San Diego, CA 92105

Established in 1965 in CA.
Donor: Frank Muller.
Foundation type: Independent foundation.
Financial data (yr. ended 7/31/05): Assets, $9,208,048 (M); expenditures, $694,799; qualifying distributions, $647,350; giving activities include $540,000 for 279 grants (high: $25,000; low: $100).
Purpose and activities: Funds for education, human services, arts and culture, Roman Catholic agencies, and health organizations.
Fields of interest: Arts; Secondary school/education; Higher education; Hospitals (general); Cerebral palsy; Human services; Children/youth, services; Roman Catholic agencies & churches.
Limitations: Applications not accepted. Giving primarily in CA. No grants to individuals.
Application information: Contributes only to pre-selected organizations.
Officers and Investment Committee:* Richard Vilmure,* Pres.; James Muller,* V.P.; John Muller,* V.P.; Shiela Muller, V.P.; Timothy Muller,* V.P.; Mary Thompson, Secy.-Treas.
EIN: 956121774

926
Alfred C. Munger Foundation ◇
c/o R.D. Esbenshade
355 S. Grand Ave., 35th Fl.
Los Angeles, CA 90071-1560 (213) 683-8790

Established in 1965 in CA.
Donors: Charles T. Munger; Nancy B. Munger; Berkshire Hathaway Inc.
Foundation type: Independent foundation.
Financial data (yr. ended 11/30/04): Assets, $33,156,559 (M); expenditures, $2,682,549; qualifying distributions, $2,589,504; giving activities include $2,589,504 for 65 grants (high: $600,000; low: $132).
Purpose and activities: Grants primarily for higher and secondary education, a hospital, a family planning and population studies institute, and health agencies; giving also for Protestant religious organizations.
Fields of interest: Elementary/secondary education; Higher education; Education; Hospitals (general); Health organizations, association; Protestant agencies & churches.
Limitations: Applications not accepted. Giving primarily in CA. No grants to individuals.
Application information: Contributes only to pre-selected organizations.
Officers and Trustees:* Charles T. Munger,* Pres.; Richard D. Esbenshade,* V.P. and Secy.; Nancy B. Munger,* Treas.
EIN: 952462103
Selected grants: The following grants were reported in 2005.
$350,000 to YMCA. 2 grants: $100,000, $250,000

$300,000 to Hoover Institution on War, Revolution and Peace, Stanford, CA. 2 grants: $250,000, $50,000

$110,000 to Marlborough School, Los Angeles, CA. 2 grants: $100,000, $10,000

$100,000 to Childrens Hospital.

$100,000 to Santa Barbara Maritime Museum, Santa Barbara, CA.

$10,000 to American Museum of Natural History, New York, NY.

$5,000 to Planned Parenthood of Los Angeles, Los Angeles, CA.

927

The Rudolph J. & Daphne A. Munzer Foundation ◇

3450 E. Spring St., Rm. 218
Long Beach, CA 90806

Established in 1995 in CA.
Donors: Rudolph J. Munzer; Daphne A. Munzer.
Foundation type: Independent foundation.
Financial data (yr. ended 12/31/05): Assets, $9,195,551 (M); expenditures, $403,996; qualifying distributions, $348,119; giving activities include $347,500 for 27 grants (high: $45,000; low: $1,000).
Purpose and activities: Giving for education, health associations, including children's health care, and youth development.
Fields of interest: Arts; Elementary/secondary education; Higher education; Hospitals (general); Health organizations, association; Boys & girls clubs; Boy scouts.
Limitations: Applications not accepted. Giving primarily in CA, with emphasis on Long Beach; some funding also in CT. No grants to individuals.
Application information: Contributes only to pre-selected organizations.
Officers and Directors: Daniel W. Munzer, Pres.; Daphne A. Munzer, V.P.; Patcharin Lim, Secy.; Alexandria C. Phillips, Treas.; Anne Bourne Munzer; William J. Munzer.
EIN: 330686779
Selected grants: The following grants were reported in 2003.

$84,000 to Memorial Medical Center Foundation, Long Beach, CA. For general support.

$70,673 to Boy Scouts of America, Long Beach Council, Long Beach, CA. For general support.

$30,500 to Boys and Girls Clubs of Long Beach, Long Beach, CA. For general support.

$30,000 to Saint Joseph Ballet Company, Santa Ana, CA. For general support.

$25,000 to Heart Care International, Greenwich, CT. For general support.

$25,000 to Long Beach Public Library Foundation, Long Beach, CA. For general support.

$15,000 to Long Beach Day Nursery, Long Beach, CA. For general support.

$15,000 to Long Beach Nonprofit Partnership, Long Beach, CA. For general support.

$11,500 to Stanford University, Stanford, CA. For general support.

$10,000 to Marin Academy, San Rafael, CA. For general support.

928

Dan Murphy Foundation ▼ ◇

P.O. Box 711267
Los Angeles, CA 90071 (213) 623-3120
Contact: Daniel J. Donohue, Pres.

Incorporated in 1957 in CA.
Donor: Bernadine Murphy Donohue†.
Foundation type: Independent foundation.
Financial data (yr. ended 12/31/04): Assets, $229,545,436 (M); expenditures, $11,405,311; qualifying distributions, $9,766,526; giving activities include $9,485,250 for 93 grants (high: $2,500,000; low: $1,000; average: $5,000–$100,000).
Purpose and activities: Giving primarily for support of activities and charities of the Roman Catholic Church Archdiocese of Los Angeles, including religious orders, colleges and schools, social service agencies, and medical institutions.
Fields of interest: Elementary/secondary education; Higher education; Hospitals (general); Human services; Roman Catholic federated giving programs; Roman Catholic agencies & churches.
Type of support: General/operating support; Continuing support; Program development.
Limitations: Giving primarily in Los Angeles, CA.
Publications: Informational brochure.
Application information: Grants generally initiated by the trustees.
Initial approach: Letter
Copies of proposal: 1
Deadline(s): None
Board meeting date(s): As needed
Officers and Trustees: Daniel J. Donohue, Pres.; Richard A. Grant, Jr., Secy.-Treas.; Rosemary E. Donohue; James M. Donovan; Maria O. Grant; Edward A. Landry; Julia D. Schwartz.
Number of staff: 1
EIN: 956046963
Selected grants: The following grants were reported in 2004.

$2,710,000 to Roman Catholic Archbishop of Los Angeles, Los Angeles, CA. 2 grants: $1,045,000 (For general support), $1,665,000 (For general support of educational projects).

$2,500,000 to Thomas Aquinas College, Santa Paula, CA. For general support.

$1,000,000 to Vatican, The, Vatican City. For general support.

$275,000 to Sisters of Social Service, Los Angeles, CA. For general support.

$106,000 to Little Sisters of the Poor, San Pedro, CA. For general support.

$76,000 to Loyola Marymount University, Los Angeles, CA. For general support.

$25,000 to Gonzaga University, Spokane, WA. For general support.

$17,500 to Catholic Charities of the Diocese of Stockton, Stockton, CA. For general support.

$5,000 to Prince of Peace Abbey, Oceanside, CA. For general support.

929

The Peter & Mary Muth Foundation ◇

c/o Verlyn Jensen
5100 Campus Dr., Ste. 200
Newport Beach, CA 92660

Established in 1984 in CA.
Donors: Peter Muth; Mary Muth; Orco Block Co., Inc.
Foundation type: Independent foundation.

Financial data (yr. ended 12/31/04): Assets, $1,160,161 (M); gifts received, $800,000; expenditures, $963,248; qualifying distributions, $952,100; giving activities include $952,100 for 31 grants (high: $300,000; low: $100).
Purpose and activities: Giving primarily to the arts and to Roman Catholic federated giving programs.
Fields of interest: Arts; Libraries (special); Federated giving programs; Roman Catholic federated giving programs.
Limitations: Applications not accepted. Giving on a national basis. No grants to individuals.
Application information: Contributes only to pre-selected organizations.
Officers: Verlyn N. Jensen, Pres.; Robert Pralle, V.P.; Richard J. Muth, Secy.; Mary Muth, C.F.O.
Number of staff: 1 part-time professional.
EIN: 330016627

930

My Brother Joey Foundation ◇

155 N. Riverview Dr.
Anaheim Hills, CA 92808-1225

Established in CA.
Donors: Judith Partridge; Roopal Shah; EastWood Insurance Services; Bristol West.
Foundation type: Independent foundation.
Financial data (yr. ended 12/31/05): Assets, $288,409 (M); gifts received, $251,157; expenditures, $413,054; qualifying distributions, $412,386; giving activities include $411,696 for 9 grants (high: $125,000; low: $2,500).
Purpose and activities: Giving primarily to hospitals to support medical research into diseases which afflict children; support also for recreational activities of children with special needs.
Fields of interest: Hospitals (general); Medical research, institute; Children, services.
Type of support: Research.
Limitations: Applications not accepted. Giving primarily in CA. No grants to individuals.
Application information: Contributes only to pre-selected organizations.
Officer: Judith Partridge, Pres.
EIN: 330777548
Selected grants: The following grants were reported in 2004.

$175,000 to Chapman University, Orange, CA.

$25,000 to Goodwill Industries of Orange County, Santa Ana, CA.

$25,000 to United Way, Orange County, Irvine, CA.

$4,000 to YMCA of Orange County, Tustin, CA.

931

Edward M. Nagel Foundation ◇

c/o Melvyn I. Mark
650 California St., 25th Fl.
San Francisco, CA 94108

Established in 1992 in CA.
Donors: Edward M. Nagel; Edward M. Nagel Trust.
Foundation type: Independent foundation.
Financial data (yr. ended 9/30/05): Assets, $4,468,063 (M); expenditures, $470,252; qualifying distributions, $400,000; giving activities include $400,000 for 10 grants (high: $40,000; low: $40,000).
Fields of interest: Higher education; Scholarships/financial aid.
Type of support: Scholarship funds.

Limitations: Applications not accepted. Giving primarily in San Francisco, CA. No grants to individuals.
Application information: Contributes only to pre-selected organizations.
Directors: Frank Brucia; Michael Dotson; Melvyn I. Mark; Daniel Sober.
EIN: 943171093
Selected grants: The following grants were reported in 2005.
$40,000 to Dominican University of California, San Rafael, CA.
$40,000 to Point Loma Nazarene University, San Diego, CA.
$40,000 to San Francisco State University, San Francisco, CA.
$40,000 to University of California at Berkeley Foundation, Berkeley, CA.
$40,000 to University of San Francisco, San Francisco, CA.
$40,000 to University of the Pacific, Stockton, CA.

932
Y. & S. Nazarian Family Foundation ◇
1801 Century Park W., 5th Fl.
Los Angeles, CA   90067

Established in 1999 in CA.
Donors: Younes Nazarian; Soraya J. Nazarian.
Foundation type: Independent foundation.
Financial data (yr. ended 12/31/04): Assets, $34,850,491 (M); expenditures, $1,622,675; qualifying distributions, $1,556,100; giving activities include $1,556,100 for 26 grants (high: $950,000; low: $500).
Fields of interest: Education; Human services; Jewish federated giving programs; Jewish agencies & temples.
Limitations: Applications not accepted. Giving primarily in CA. No grants to individuals.
Application information: Contributes only to pre-selected organizations.
Trustees: Soraya J. Nazarian; Younes Nazarian.
EIN: 954774321

933
NBC Universal Foundation ◇
(formerly Universal Studios Foundation, Ltd.)
100 Universal City Plz.
Universal City, CA   91608
Contact: Jennifer Alwood

Incorporated in 1956 in CA.
Donors: Universal Studios, Inc.; NBC Universal, Inc.
Foundation type: Company-sponsored foundation.
Financial data (yr. ended 12/31/05): Assets, $13,412,370 (M); expenditures, $1,420,140; qualifying distributions, $1,400,000; giving activities include $1,400,000 for grants.
Purpose and activities: The foundation supports programs designed to strengthen secondary education for disadvantaged students.
Fields of interest: Secondary school/education.
Type of support: Program development.
Limitations: Giving primarily in Los Angeles, CA, Washington, DC, Miami, FL, and New York, NY. No support for private foundations or organizations with overhead expenses exceeding 15 percent of the total project budget. No grants for endowments or major equipment purchases, capital campaigns, annual fundraising events or fund drives, partisan lobbying or political campaigns or activities, individual film or television projects, sponsorship of special events, debt reduction, or religious or sectarian purposes.
Publications: Application guidelines.
Application information: Application form required.
Initial approach: Contact foundation for application form
Copies of proposal: 1
Deadline(s): None
Final notification: Following review
Officers and Directors:* Ron Meyer,* Pres.; Maren Christensen,* Exec. V.P. and Secy.; Lynn A. Calpeter, Exec. V.P.; Richard Cotton, Exec. V.P.; Patricia E. Hutton, Exec. V.P.; Kenneth L. Kahrs, Sr. V.P.; Marc Saperstein, Sr. V.P.; Mark Pinkerton, V.P. and Treas.; Todd F. Davis, V.P.; Brian Doerger, V.P.; Sean Gamble, V.P.; H. Stephen Gorden, V.P.; David H. Meyers, V.P.; Brian J. O'Leary, Jr., V.P.; Marc Palotay, V.P.; Cindy Gardner.
Number of staff: 2 full-time professional.
EIN: 136096061
Selected grants: The following grants were reported in 2003.
$100,000 to Saint Joseph Medical Center Foundation, Burbank, CA.
$50,000 to Fulfillment Fund, Los Angeles, CA.
$50,000 to Greater Los Angeles Zoo Association, Los Angeles, CA.
$25,000 to Assistance League of Southern California, Los Angeles, CA.
$25,000 to New York University, Tish School of Arts, New York, NY.
$15,000 to Heart of Los Angeles Youth, Los Angeles, CA.
$10,000 to Geffen Playhouse, Los Angeles, CA.
$10,000 to Interact Theater Company, Universal City, CA.
$10,000 to Museum of Television and Radio, New York, NY.
$10,000 to United States-Japan Bridging Foundation, DC.

934
Craig H. Neilsen Foundation ◇
16633 Ventura Blvd., Ste. 1050
Encino, CA   91316   (818) 762-8533
FAX: (818) 985-4784;
E-mail: info@chnfoundation.org; Tel. for Beth Goldsmith, Fdn. Dir.: (702) 567-7072; e-mail: Beth@chnfoundation.org; URL: http://www.chnfoundation.org

Established in 2002 in ID and NV.
Donor: Craig H. Neilsen.
Foundation type: Independent foundation.
Financial data (yr. ended 12/31/05): Assets, $259,907 (M); gifts received, $2,801,100; expenditures, $2,543,468; qualifying distributions, $2,536,371; giving activities include $2,505,345 for 67 grants (high: $200,000; low: $299).
Purpose and activities: The primary mission of the foundation is to find a cure for spinal cord injury (SCI). In an effort to reach this goal, the foundation supports, 1) cutting edge research that seeks to understand the biological basis for recovery of function after SCI, and to translate these findings to a clinical setting, 2) clinical research that will develop new treatments for people living with SCI, and 3) innovative rehabilitation programs for people living with spinal cord injuries throughout the U.S.

Fields of interest: Education; Medical research; Boys & girls clubs; Roman Catholic agencies & churches.
Limitations: Giving primarily in NV. No grants to individuals.
Publications: Grants list.
Application information: Application information available on foundation Web site, particularly through the foundation's Proposal Central System.
Initial approach: Letter
Deadline(s): Oct. 17
Trustee: Craig H. Neilsen.
Director and Advisory Board Members:* Beth Goldsmith, Fdn. Dir.; Connie Wilson Hill; Gordon R. Kanofsky; Ray H. Neilsen.
EIN: 061695275

935
Nestle USA Foundation ◇
(formerly Carnation Company Foundation)
800 N. Brand Blvd.
Glendale, CA   91203-1289   (818) 549-6000

Incorporated in 1952 in CA.
Donor: Nestle USA, Inc.
Foundation type: Company-sponsored foundation.
Financial data (yr. ended 12/31/05): Assets, $26,968,074 (M); expenditures, $1,517,067; qualifying distributions, $1,402,067; giving activities include $1,402,067 for 15 grants (high: $290,146; low: $3,105).
Purpose and activities: The foundation supports organizations involved with arts and culture, education, youth development, and community development.
Fields of interest: Museums; Arts; Elementary/secondary education; Higher education; Libraries (public); Education, reading; Education; Youth development; American Red Cross; Community development; Federated giving programs.
Type of support: General/operating support.
Limitations: Giving primarily in CA, Washington, DC, and NY. No grants to individuals.
Publications: Annual report.
Application information: Application form not required.
Initial approach: Proposal
Deadline(s): None
Officers: J.M. Weller, Pres.; M.R. Lehmann, V.P. and Treas.; Cam Starrett,* V.P.; J.D. Wyatt, Secy.
EIN: 956027479
Selected grants: The following grants were reported in 2005.
$478,163 to American Red Cross, Los Angeles, CA. 2 grants: $290,146, $188,017
$115,477 to American Red Cross, Lafayette, LA.
$115,466 to American Red Cross, Natchez, MS.
$100,000 to United Negro College Fund, Fairfax, VA.
$12,500 to Library Foundation of Los Angeles, Los Angeles, CA.
$3,105 to Wonder of Reading, Los Angeles, CA.

936
The Henry Mayo Newhall Foundation
57 Post St., Ste. 510
San Francisco, CA   94104   (415) 981-2966
Contact: Kenneth Blum, Admin. Dir.; John S. Blum, Admin. Dir.
FAX: (415) 981-5218;
E-mail: info@newhallfoundation.org; URL: http://www.newhallfoundation.org

Incorporated in 1963 in CA.

Donors: Alice O'Meara†; The Newhall Land and Farming Co.

Foundation type: Independent foundation.

Financial data (yr. ended 12/31/05): Assets, $12,608,137 (M); expenditures, $691,956; qualifying distributions, $586,230; giving activities include $517,500 for 31 grants (high: $85,000; low: $2,500).

Purpose and activities: Giving limited to human services and education in San Francisco, Santa Clarita Valley and Santa Maria Valley, CA.

Fields of interest: Arts; Education; Human services; Children/youth, services; Family services.

Type of support: Seed money; General/operating support; Capital campaigns; Scholarship funds; Matching/challenge support.

Limitations: Giving limited to San Francisco, and the Santa Clarita and Santa Maria Vallies, CA. No grants to individuals.

Publications: Application guidelines; Grants list.

Application information: See foundation Web site for application guidelines and procedures. The foundation encourages telephone calls to inquire as to whether or not a proposed program is eligible. If so, a full proposal can be submitted. Annual grants typically range from $2,000 to $10,000. Application form not required.

Initial approach: Letter or telephone
Copies of proposal: 1
Deadline(s): None
Board meeting date(s): Spring and fall
Final notification: 1 week after board meeting

Officers: Jon Newhall, Pres.; David Newhall, V.P.; Anthony Newhall, Secy.; Roger B. Newhall, Treas.

Directors: Mrs. Robert Chesebrough, Jr.; David Hill; Marion Hill; George Newhall; Jane Newhall; Prudence J. Noon; Edwin Newhall Woods.

EIN: 946073084

Selected grants: The following grants were reported in 2004.

$85,000 to Henry Mayo Newhall Memorial Health Foundation, Valencia, CA. For new Emergency Department and Cardiac Catheterization Lab.

$80,000 to Williams S. Hart Union High School, Santa Clarita, CA. For scholarships.

$25,000 to Samuel Dixon Family Health Center, Val Verde, CA. For construction of Health Care Center administrative office.

$20,000 to Boys and Girls Club of Santa Clarita Valley, Santa Clarita, CA. For expansion of Art Program.

$20,000 to Newhall School District, Valencia, CA. For expansion of instrumental music program.

$16,000 to Santa Maria Joint Union High School District, Santa Maria, CA. For District Scholarship Program.

$15,000 to Domestic Violence Solutions for Santa Barbara County, Santa Barbara, CA. For Transitional Housing Initiative for Women and Children.

$12,000 to Aim High for High School, San Francisco, CA. For program support.

$12,000 to Holy Family Day Home, San Francisco, CA. For Embrace-A-Child Program.

$10,000 to San Francisco State University, San Francisco, CA. For Mission Science Workshop Program.

937

The Nicholas Foundation ✧ ☆
15 Enterprise, Ste. 550
Aliso Viejo, CA 92656-2656

Established in 1998 in CA.

Donors: Henry T. Nicholas; Stacey E. Nicholas; Nicholas Family Trust.

Foundation type: Independent foundation.

Financial data (yr. ended 12/31/05): Assets, $29,461,531 (M); gifts received, $65,700; expenditures, $3,416,905; qualifying distributions, $3,003,405; giving activities include $2,890,000 for 6 grants (high: $2,550,000; low: $5,000).

Fields of interest: Arts; Higher education; Education; Human services; Community development.

Limitations: Applications not accepted. Giving primarily in CA. No grants to individuals.

Application information: Contributes only to pre-selected organizations.

Trustees: Craig Gunther; Henry T. Nicholas III; Stacey E. Nicholas.

EIN: 330810552

Selected grants: The following grants were reported in 2003.

$287,491 to University of California at Irvine Foundation, Irvine, CA.

$50,750 to Saint Margarets Episcopal School, San Juan Capistrano, CA.

$50,000 to Pacific Symphony Association, Santa Ana, CA.

$15,000 to California State University, Fullerton, CA.

$12,500 to South Coast Repertory Theater, Costa Mesa, CA.

$5,000 to Opera Pacific, Santa Ana, CA.

$1,000 to Americas Second Harvest, Chicago, IL.

$1,000 to Childrens Hospital of Orange County, Orange, CA.

$700 to International House of Blues Foundation, Hollywood, CA.

$500 to Samohi Alumni Association, Pacific Palisades, CA.

938

The Nimoy Foundation ✧
501 S. Beverly Dr., 3rd Fl.
Beverly Hills, CA 90212-4514

Established in 2003 in DE.

Donors: Leonard Nimoy; Susan Bay Nimoy; Leonard & Susan Bay Nimoy Family Foundation; Harry and Belle Krupnick Endowment; The Audrey & Sidney Irmas Charitable Foundation; Milken Family Foundation.

Foundation type: Independent foundation.

Financial data (yr. ended 12/31/05): Assets, $0 (M); gifts received, $82,500; expenditures, $640,184; qualifying distributions, $558,463; giving activities include $458,625 for 22 grants (high: $30,000; low: $1,000).

Purpose and activities: Giving primarily for the fine arts. Through performances by the Nimoy Concert Series, funded by contributions to The Nimoy Foundation, contemporary performing and visual artists are able to explore and develop their creativity, and encourage other philanthropists to support the arts and artists.

Fields of interest: Visual arts; Museums; Museums (art).

Limitations: Applications not accepted. Giving on a national basis. No grants to individuals.

Application information: Contributes only to pre-selected organizations.

Officers and Directors:* Leonard Nimoy,* Pres.; Susan Bay Nimoy,* V.P.; Douglas K. Freeman,* Secy.; Richard B. Francis,* Treas.; Bobby Turner.

EIN: 651170235

939

The Nissan Foundation ✧
P.O. Box 191, M.S. N-3-A
Gardena, CA 90248-0191 (310) 771-3300
FAX: (310) 516-7967; URL: http://www.nissanusa.com/about/corporate_info/community_relations.html#TheNissanFoundation

Established in 1993 in CA.

Donors: Nissan Motor Corp. U.S.A.; Nissan North America, Inc.

Foundation type: Company-sponsored foundation.

Financial data (yr. ended 6/30/05): Assets, $8,390,363 (M); gifts received, $1,000,000; expenditures, $402,331; qualifying distributions, $383,000; giving activities include $383,000 for 23 grants (high: $40,000; low: $5,000).

Purpose and activities: The foundation supports organizations involved with automobile industry vocational education and cultural diversity.

Fields of interest: Arts, cultural/ethnic awareness; Vocational education; Employment, services.

Type of support: General/operating support; Program development; Seed money.

Limitations: Giving limited to areas of company operations in southern CA, southeastern MI, south central MS, the New York, NY, metropolitan area, middle TN, and north central TX. No support for disease advocacy, research, or religious organizations. No grants to individuals, or for fundraising events, sponsorships, or political activities or capital campaigns.

Publications: Grants list; Informational brochure (including application guidelines).

Application information: Letters of inquiry should be no longer than 2 double-spaced pages. Application form not required.

Initial approach: Mail or fax letter of inquiry to foundation
Copies of proposal: 3
Deadline(s): Nov. 23
Final notification: Dec.

Officers and Directors:* Jim Morton,* Pres.; Kent Brawner, V.P.; Joy Crose, Secy.; Ralph Porter,* Treas.; John Calandro; Rita Ghosn; Greg Kelly; Lou Knierim; Tony Lucente; Galen Medlin; Michele Mottola; Chris O'Bannion; Mark Perry; Mario Polit; John Spoon; Mark Stout; George Vazquez.

EIN: 954413799

Selected grants: The following grants were reported in 2005.

$35,000 to Accelerated School, Los Angeles, CA.

$25,000 to 100 Black Men of Jackson, Jackson, MS.

$22,500 to Japanese American National Museum, Los Angeles, CA.

$20,000 to Pasadena City College, Pasadena, CA.

$15,000 to Bayside Community Center, San Diego, CA.

$15,000 to Detroit Science Center, Detroit, MI.

$10,000 to Ford Theater Foundation, Los Angeles, CA.

$10,000 to Los Angeles Music and Art School, Los Angeles, CA.

$5,000 to La Jolla Playhouse, La Jolla, CA.

$5,000 to Public Corporation for the Arts, Long Beach, CA.

940
The Kenneth T. and Eileen L. Norris Foundation ▼

11 Golden Shore, Ste. 450
Long Beach, CA 90802 (562) 435-8444
Contact: Ronald R. Barnes, Exec. Dir.
FAX: (562) 436-0584; E-mail: grants@ktn.org;
Additional e-mail: accordino@ktn.org; URL: http://
www.norrisfoundation.org

Trust established in 1963 in CA.
Donors: Kenneth T. Norris†; Eileen L. Norris‡.
Foundation type: Independent foundation.
Financial data (yr. ended 11/30/05): Assets,
$174,171,983 (M); gifts received, $845,833;
expenditures, $8,970,021; qualifying distributions,
$8,170,212; giving activities include $7,627,255
for 309 grants (high: $2,145,000; low: $2,500;
average: $5,000–$100,000).
Purpose and activities: Foundation funding
categories include: medical, education and science,
youth, cultural and community.
Fields of interest: Performing arts; Arts; Secondary
school/education; Higher education; Education;
Hospitals (general); Nursing care; Health care;
Substance abuse, services; Mental health/crisis
services; Cancer; AIDS; Alcoholism; Medical
research, institute; Cancer research; AIDS research;
Crime/law enforcement; Food services; Housing/
shelter, development; Human services; Children/
youth, services; Family services; Women, centers/
services; Homeless, human services; Engineering/
technology; Science; Disabilities, people with;
Women; Economically disadvantaged.
Type of support: General/operating support;
Continuing support; Annual campaigns; Building/
renovation; Equipment; Endowments; Program
development; Professorships; Scholarship funds;
Research; Matching/challenge support.
Limitations: Giving primarily in southern CA. No
support for political organizations or campaigns. No
grants to individuals, or for film or video projects; no
loans.
Publications: Application guidelines; Annual report;
Financial statement.
Application information: Application form is
available on foundation Web site. Qualifying
organizations may submit a request once a year and
receive no more than one grant per year. Application
form required.
> *Initial approach:* Full proposal
> *Copies of proposal:* 1
> *Deadline(s):* Medicine: May 1 - June 30;
> Education/Science: May 1 - June 30; Youth:
> Feb. 15 - Mar. 31; Community/Cultural: Dec.
> 1 - Jan. 31
> *Board meeting date(s):* Mar., May, Aug., and Oct.
> *Final notification:* Within 5 months
Officers and Trustees:* Lisa D. Hansen,* Chair.;
Walter J. Zanino,* Cont.; Ronald R. Barnes,* Exec.
Dir.; William G. Corey, M.D.; James R. Martin;
Bradley K. Norris; Harlyne J. Norris; Kimberley
Presley.
Number of staff: None.
EIN: 956080374
Selected grants: The following grants were reported
in 2005.
$2,170,000 to University of Southern California,
Los Angeles, CA. 2 grants: $25,000 to School of
Pharmacy (For USC Norris Foundation Summer
Research Scholars Program in Alzheimer's
Disease Brain by the Neurosteroid
Allopregnanolone), $2,145,000 (For Harlyne
Norris Cancer Research Tower).

$400,000 to Huntington Library, Art Collections and
Botanical Gardens, San Marino, CA. For
Huntington Art Gallery renovation.
$150,000 to California Institute of Technology,
Pasadena, CA. For Division of Biology Graduate
Fellowships.
$100,000 to Keck Graduate Institute of Applied Life
Sciences, Claremont, CA. For Campus
Establishment Project.
$90,000 to Saint Johns Health Center Foundation,
Santa Monica, CA. To rebuild health center.
$30,000 to Stone Soup Child Care Programs,
Encino, CA. For tuition assistance, staff
development, and program enrichment.
$10,000 to California State University, Long Beach,
CA. For Classroom Connections at Carpenter
Performing Arts Center.
$10,000 to Glendale College Foundation, Glendale,
CA. For Allied Health/Digital Multimedia building.
$10,000 to Skid Row Charity Fund, Los Angeles, CA.
For Father Dollar-Dollars on Skid Row.

941
The Northern California Scholarship Foundation ◇

(formerly The Northern California Scholarship
Foundation and the Scaife Scholarship Foundation)
1547 Lakeside Dr.
Oakland, CA 94612-4520
Contact: Clyde Minar, Secy.-Treas.

Incorporated in 1927 in CA.
Donors: Irene Jones†; Walter B. Scaife†; S. Sidney
Morton; Lois Irene Sweeney†; Mrs. John Gifford; E.
& J. West Trusts; Alumni Association Foundation.
Foundation type: Independent foundation.
Financial data (yr. ended 5/31/05): Assets,
$14,128,855 (M); gifts received, $7,700;
expenditures, $727,063; qualifying distributions,
$685,221; giving activities include $623,725 for
128 grants to individuals (high: $5,000; low:
$1,250).
Purpose and activities: Scholarships for graduates
of northern CA public high schools only.
Fields of interest: Education.
Type of support: Scholarships—to individuals.
Limitations: Giving limited to graduates of northern
CA public high schools.
Publications: Application guidelines; Informational
brochure; Program policy statement.
Application information: Applications sent only to
those students recommended by northern and
central CA public high school administrations.
Applications must be submitted with transcripts of
high school records, college entrance exam scores,
and statement of financial need. Application form
required.
> *Initial approach:* Letter
> *Copies of proposal:* 1
> *Deadline(s):* Mar. 15
> *Board meeting date(s):* Jan., Feb., May, and Aug.
> *Final notification:* Final selections made by May
> 10
Officers: James F. McClung, Jr., Pres.; Norman
Owen, V.P.; Clyde D. Minar, Secy.-Treas.
Trustees: Wade Bingham; Dallas G. Cason; Robert
Crow; Charles DiBari; Thomas D. Eychner; Art
Hughes, Jr.; Julius "Sandy" Kahn III; George
Klopping; Elmer Ross; John Simmons; Hon. Zook
Sutton; George Vukasin; Del Wallis.
Number of staff: 1 part-time professional; 1
part-time support.
EIN: 941540333

942
The Northrop Grumman Foundation ◇

(formerly Foundation of the Litton Industries)
1840 Century Park E., M.S. 122/CC
Los Angeles, CA 90067 (888) 478-5478
Contact: Sandra Evers-Manly, Pres.
Additional tel.: (310) 201-3323; URL: http://
www.northropgrumman.com/com_rel/
foundation.html

Incorporated in 1954 in CA.
Donors: Litton Industries, Inc.; Northrop Grumman
Corp.
Foundation type: Company-sponsored foundation.
Financial data (yr. ended 12/31/04): Assets,
$34,720,683 (M); expenditures, $1,976,235;
qualifying distributions, $1,877,202; giving
activities include $1,869,660 for 2,843 grants
(high: $100,000; low: $50).
Purpose and activities: The foundation supports
organizations involved with arts and culture and
education. Special emphasis is directed toward
programs designed to promote the advancement of
literacy, math, science, and technology in the
pre-college through collegiate levels.
Fields of interest: Humanities; Arts; Elementary/
secondary education; Higher education; Education,
reading; Education; Federated giving programs;
Mathematics; Engineering/technology; Computer
science; Science.
Type of support: Continuing support; Endowments;
Fellowships; Scholarship funds; Employee matching
gifts; Matching/challenge support.
Limitations: Giving primarily in the metropolitan Los
Angeles, CA, area; giving on a national basis for
higher education. No support for campus student
organizations, fraternities, sororities, honor
societies, religious schools or colleges with a
primary focus on religious beliefs, athletic teams or
athletic support organizations, or choirs, bands, or
drill teams. No grants to individuals, or for
fundraising events, advertising or underwriting
expenses, capital campaigns, endowments, or
tuition.
Application information: Proposals should be no
longer than 4 pages. Application form not required.
> *Initial approach:* Proposal
> *Copies of proposal:* 1
> *Deadline(s):* None
> *Board meeting date(s):* As required
Officers and Board Members: Sandra Evers-Manly,
Pres.; Kathy Sauers, Secy.; Silva Saak, Treas.; J.
Michael Hateley; John Mullan; Rosanne O'Brien;
Harris Sperling; Richard Waugh.
EIN: 956095343

943
Peter Norton Family Foundation ▼

225 Arizona, Ste. 350
Santa Monica, CA 90401 (310) 576-7700
Contact: Anne Etheridge, Exec. Dir.; Kelly Barrie, Art
Progs.

Established in 1988 in CA.
Donors: Peter Norton; Eileen Norton.
Foundation type: Independent foundation.
Financial data (yr. ended 12/31/05): Assets,
$27,218,484 (M); expenditures, $3,550,887;
qualifying distributions, $2,994,162.
Purpose and activities: The foundation gives
support in the areas of art, education, and human
services, as well as for exhibitions.

Fields of interest: Visual arts; Museums; Arts; Education, early childhood education; Elementary school/education; AIDS; Human services; Children/youth, services; Family services; Women, centers/services; Minorities; Women.

Type of support: General/operating support; Equipment; Program development; Seed money; Technical assistance.

Limitations: Giving primarily in southern CA for human/social services; giving on a national basis for arts-related grants. No grants to individuals.

Publications: Application guidelines; Grants list.

Application information: Application form not required.

   Initial approach: Telephone call
   Copies of proposal: 1
   Deadline(s): Monthly
   Board meeting date(s): Monthly
   Final notification: 4 weeks after submission

Officers: Peter Norton, Pres.; Eileen Norton, V.P.; Anne Etheridge, Secy.-Treas. and Exec. Dir.

EIN: 954195347

Selected grants: The following grants were reported in 2004.

$1,000,000 to Armand Hammer Museum of Art and Cultural Center, Los Angeles, CA. For building fund.

$1,000,000 to Whitney Museum of American Art, New York, NY. For general operating support.

$500,000 to P.S. 1 Contemporary Art Center, Long Island City, NY. For matching grant for general operating support.

$400,000 to California Institute of the Arts, Valencia, CA. 2 grants: $100,000 (For annual support), $300,000 (For faculty leave initiative).

$250,000 to Jazz at Lincoln Center, New York, NY. For general operating support.

$25,000 to Crossroads School for Arts and Sciences, Santa Monica, CA. For annual campaign.

$25,000 to Wildwood School, Los Angeles, CA. For annual campaign fund.

$10,000 to Museum of Modern Art, New York, NY. For Architecture and Design Committee.

$5,000 to Mar Vista Institute, Mar Vista Family Center, Culver City, CA. To staff pre-school program.

944
The Noyce Foundation ▼

2500 El Camino Real, Ste. 110
Palo Alto, CA 94306-1723 (650) 856-2600
Contact: Ann S. Bowers, Chair.
FAX: (650) 856-2601; E-mail: info@noycefdn.org;
URL: http://www.noycefdn.org

Established in 1990 in CA.

Donor: Robert N. Noyce Residual Trust.

Foundation type: Independent foundation.

Financial data (yr. ended 12/31/05): Assets, $161,866,333 (M); expenditures, $8,180,522; qualifying distributions, $6,522,656; giving activities include $4,851,560 for grants, and $1,671,096 for foundation-administered programs.

Purpose and activities: The foundation is dedicated to stimulating ideas and supporting initiatives designed to produce significant improvement in teaching and learning in mathematics, science and literacy in grades K-12.

Fields of interest: Education, public education; Elementary/secondary education; Education, reading; Mathematics; Science.

Type of support: General/operating support; Continuing support; Program development; Publication; Research; Technical assistance; Program evaluation; Matching/challenge support.

Limitations: Applications not accepted. Giving primarily in Silicon Valley, CA and MA. No grants to individuals.

Publications: Annual report; Financial statement; Grants list.

Application information: Contributes only to pre-selected organizations.

Officer and Trustees:* Ann S. Bowers,* Chair.; Phil Daro; Pendred Noyce, M.D.; John O'Neil; Robert Schwartz.

Number of staff: 14

EIN: 770257009

Selected grants: The following grants were reported in 2005.

$200,000 to New Leaders for New Schools, New York, NY. For external evaluation initiative to formally assess effectiveness and impact of model and to publish results in field.

$190,689 to Policy Analysis for California Education (PACE), Stanford, CA. For two-year project Accountability for California's Public Schools: Sustaining Momentum and Building Consensus for Improvement; and for coordination support for series of legislative seminars aimed at informing policymakers and advocating for policy adjustments for set of high importance education policy issues such as accountability, diversity, school finance, school adequacy, and high school reform, payable over 2 years.

$150,000 to National Public Radio, DC. For Science Friday programming and for Kid's Connection, teacher-friendly companion to Science Friday which provides discussion ideas, activities, selected resources, and related science teaching standards relating to topics discuss on Science Friday.

$80,000 to Massachusetts Institute for a New Commonwealth (MassINC), Boston, MA. For establishment of Rennie Center, non-partisan institute for research and debate on important public policy questions affecting K-12 public education.

$70,000 to Teach for America, New York, NY. For Director of Math and Science Recruitment to increase number of math and science majors joining Teach for America.

$50,000 to Exploratorium, San Francisco, CA. For matching funds for SFUSD-Exploratorium NCLB Teacher Enhancement Program to strengthen science content knowledge and classroom teaching practices of middle school science teachers to improve student learning and engagement, and to help those teachers pass the CSET.

$50,000 to Tech Museum of Innovation, San Jose, CA. For Noyce Center for Learning professional development programs.

$15,000 to Mathematical Sciences Research Institute, Berkeley, CA. For conference regarding critical issues in mathematics education entitled Teachers Knowledge of Mathematics.

945
Dennis and Gloria O'Brien Foundation ◇

950 Tower Ln., Ste. 1250
Foster City, CA 94404

Established in 2002 in CA.

Donors: Dennis C. O'Brien; Gloria A. O'Brien.

Foundation type: Independent foundation.

Financial data (yr. ended 9/30/05): Assets, $7,319,879 (M); gifts received, $5,448,000; expenditures, $378,453; qualifying distributions, $359,769; giving activities include $358,000 for 30 grants (high: $65,000; low: $100).

Purpose and activities: Giving primarily for Roman Catholic agencies and churches; funding also for human services.

Fields of interest: Human services; American Red Cross; Roman Catholic agencies & churches.

Limitations: Applications not accepted. Giving primarily in CA. No grants to individuals.

Application information: Contributes only to pre-selected organizations.

Officers: Dennis C. O'Brien, Pres.; Gloria A. O'Brien, Secy.

Directors: Chris O'Brien; Susan Frimel.

EIN: 522390855

946
Carroll and Nancy O'Connor Foundation ◇

c/o NSBN, LLP
9454 Wilshire Blvd., 4th Fl.
Beverly Hills, CA 90212
Contact: Ken Miles, CPA

Established in 1990 in CA.

Donors: Carroll O'Connor†; Nancy F. O'Connor.

Foundation type: Independent foundation.

Financial data (yr. ended 12/31/03): Assets, $172,313 (M); expenditures, $348,956; qualifying distributions, $343,028; giving activities include $341,403 for 38 grants (high: $160,000; low: $10).

Fields of interest: Cancer; Cancer research.

Limitations: Applications not accepted. Giving primarily in CA. No grants to individuals.

Application information: Contributes only to pre-selected organizations.

Officers: Nancy F. O'Connor, Pres., V.P., and Secy.; Lawrence J. Stern, C.F.O.

EIN: 954299924

Selected grants: The following grants were reported in 2004.

$80,000 to National Museum of the American Indian, DC.

$35,800 to New Roads School, Santa Monica, CA.

$30,150 to University of Montana Foundation, Missoula, MT.

$1,000 to Landmark West, New York, NY.

$500 to Habitat for Humanity International, Americus, GA.

947
The Oak Tree Philanthropic Foundation ◇

330 Oxford St., Ste. 212
Chula Vista, CA 91911

Established in 1992 in CA.

Foundation type: Independent foundation.

Financial data (yr. ended 12/31/05): Assets, $8,182,138 (M); expenditures, $494,751; qualifying distributions, $416,300; giving activities include $409,100 for 45 grants (high: $90,000; low: $1,000).

Purpose and activities: Giving primarily for children and social services, including hurricane relief, as well as for education, including support of U.S.-based Lithuanian education.

Fields of interest: Higher education; Education; Hospitals (general); Safety/disasters; Human

services; Children/youth, services; Roman Catholic agencies & churches.
Limitations: Applications not accepted. Giving on a national basis. No grants to individuals.
Application information: Contributes only to pre-selected organizations.
Officers and Directors:* Algirdas Maciunas,* Chair.; Genevieve Maciunas,* Vice-Chair.; Dana Maciunas-Mockus,* C.E.O. and Pres.; Robert Maciunas, V.P.; Vytautas Mockus, Secy.-Treas.
EIN: 363779795
Selected grants: The following grants were reported in 2003.
$90,000 to Lithuanian Catholic Religious Aid, Brooklyn, NY. For general support.
$40,000 to Society of Franciscan Fathers of Green Maine, Kennebunkport, ME. For general support.
$30,000 to Catholic Relief Services, Baltimore, MD. For general support.
$20,000 to Doctors Without Borders USA, New York, NY. For general support.
$20,000 to Salk Institute for Biological Studies, San Diego, CA. For general support.
$10,000 to Amnesty International USA, New York, NY. For general support.
$10,000 to Shriners Hospitals for Children, Chicago, IL. For general support.
$10,000 to Shriners Hospitals for Children, Tampa, FL. For general support.
$7,500 to Habitat for Humanity, San Diego, San Diego, CA. For general support.
$5,000 to American Lung Association of San Diego and Imperial Counties, San Diego, CA. For general support.

948
The Oakland Athletics Community Fund ✧ ☆
7000 Coliseum Way
Oakland, CA   94621
Contact: Ken Pries
URL: http://oakland.athletics.mlb.com/NASApp/mlb/oak/community/index.jsp

Established in 1981 in CA.
Donors: Athletics Investment Group, LLC; Hofmann Foundation; Citation Homes Central; Teammates for Kids Foundation.
Foundation type: Company-sponsored foundation.
Financial data (yr. ended 12/31/04): Assets, $439,506 (M); gifts received, $1,042,077; expenditures, $1,050,941; qualifying distributions, $1,049,557; giving activities include $604,259 for 119 grants (high: $100,000; low: $65), and $7,000 for 3 grants to individuals (high: $3,000; low: $2,000).
Purpose and activities: The foundation supports organizations involved with education, housing, and recreational activities for children, disabled people, and senior citizens and enables individuals to attend Oakland A's baseball games who might otherwise be unable to afford tickets.
Fields of interest: Education; Housing/shelter; Recreation; Children; Aging; Disabilities, people with.
Type of support: Grants to individuals.
Limitations: Giving primarily in CA.
Publications: Occasional report.
Application information: Application form not required.
Initial approach: Proposal
Copies of proposal: 2

Deadline(s): None
Final notification: 2 to 3 months
Officers: Stephen Schott, C.E.O.; Kenneth H. Hofmann, Pres.; Nick S. Rossi, V.P.; Mike Crowley, C.F.O.
EIN: 942826655
Selected grants: The following grants were reported in 2003.
$75,000 to American Cancer Society, Atlanta, GA.
$3,000 to FamiliesFirst, Davis, CA.
$2,500 to Project Avary, San Rafael, CA.
$1,500 to Danny Foundation, Alamo, CA.
$1,000 to Fred Finch Childrens Home, Oakland, CA.
$1,000 to YMCA of the East Bay, Oakland, CA.
$500 to Adopt A Special Kid, Oakland, CA.
$300 to Silicon Valley Childrens Fund, San Jose, CA.
$250 to Spartan Foundation, San Jose, CA.
$250 to Take Wings Foundation (TWF), Pinole, CA.

949
The Mary Oakley Foundation, Inc. ✧
585 Tree Top Ln.
Thousand Oaks, CA   91360-2455
Application address: Deborah Dunn, c/o Liason, Mary Oakley Foundation, 2969 Glen Albyn Dr., Ste. A, Santa Barbara, CA 93105

Established in 1995 in AZ and CA.
Donor: Oakley Family Trust.
Foundation type: Independent foundation.
Financial data (yr. ended 12/31/05): Assets, $8,283,076 (M); gifts received, $343,288; expenditures, $488,930; qualifying distributions, $468,497; giving activities include $154,450 for 4 grants (high: $70,000; low: $3,000), and $284,594 for 11 grants to individuals.
Purpose and activities: The foundation provides funding for indigent individuals diagnosed with dementia, Alzheimer's Disease, or a related disorder, to stay at residential care facilities.
Fields of interest: Alzheimer's disease.
Type of support: Grants to individuals.
Limitations: Giving limited to long-term residents of the tri-counties of Santa Barbara, San Luis Obispo, and Ventura, CA.
Application information: Application form required.
Initial approach: Letter
Officer: William Stivelman, Pres. and C.F.O.
EIN: 770391113

950
Oberndorf Foundation ✧
591 Redwood Hwy., Ste. 3215
Mill Valley, CA   94941

Established in 1993 in CA.
Donors: William E. Oberndorf; Susan C. Oberndorf.
Foundation type: Independent foundation.
Financial data (yr. ended 12/31/05): Assets, $17,141,745 (M); gifts received, $3,899,750; expenditures, $3,224,585; qualifying distributions, $3,136,929; giving activities include $3,136,929 for 85 grants (high: $567,674; low: $250).
Purpose and activities: Giving primarily for education, health care, and human services.
Fields of interest: Secondary school/education; Higher education; Education; Health organizations, association; Human services; Children/youth, services; Roman Catholic agencies & churches.

Limitations: Applications not accepted. Giving primarily in the San Francisco Bay Area, CA. No grants to individuals.
Application information: Contributes only to pre-selected organizations.
Officers: Susan C. Oberndorf, Pres.; William E. Oberndorf, Secy.
EIN: 680299542
Selected grants: The following grants were reported in 2005.
$567,674 to Williams College, Williamstown, MA.
$406,500 to University of California at San Francisco Foundation, San Francisco, CA.
$300,000 to Thacher School, Ojai, CA.
$209,000 to Stanford University, Stanford, CA.
$125,000 to University School, Hunting Valley, OH.
$100,000 to American Red Cross, San Francisco, CA.
$30,000 to San Francisco School Volunteers, San Francisco, CA.
$11,000 to Edgewood Center for Children and Families, San Francisco, CA.
$1,000 to Episcopal Charities, San Francisco, CA.
$1,000 to Guide Dogs for the Blind, San Rafael, CA.

951
Robert Stewart Odell and Helen Pfeiffer Odell Fund ✧
c/o Wells Fargo Bank, N.A.
P.O. Box 63954
San Francisco, CA   94163
Application address: c/o Eugene Ranghiasci, V.P., Wells Fargo Bank, 420 Montgomery St., 5th Fl., San Francisco, CA 94104, tel.: (415) 396-3215

Established in 1967 in CA.
Donors: Robert Stewart Odell‡; Helen Pfeiffer Odell‡.
Foundation type: Independent foundation.
Financial data (yr. ended 12/31/05): Assets, $38,687,701 (M); expenditures, $2,683,550; qualifying distributions, $2,360,322; giving activities include $2,259,631 for 70 grants (high: $100,000; low: $2,250).
Purpose and activities: Giving primarily to education, the performing arts, human services and Christian agencies.
Fields of interest: Performing arts; Arts; Elementary/secondary education; Higher education; Health organizations, association; Human services; Children/youth, services; Christian agencies & churches; Disabilities, people with.
Limitations: Giving primarily in the San Francisco Bay Area, CA. No grants to individuals.
Application information: Application form not required.
Initial approach: Letter
Copies of proposal: 1
Deadline(s): None
Board meeting date(s): Quarterly
Trustees: James P. Conn; Paul B. Fay, Jr.; Wells Fargo Bank, N.A.
EIN: 946132116
Selected grants: The following grants were reported in 2003.
$100,000 to Basic Fund, San Francisco, CA.
$50,000 to Bellarmine College Preparatory, San Jose, CA. For library and media center endowment fund.
$50,000 to Blind Babies Foundation, San Francisco, CA.
$50,000 to Community Foundation Silicon Valley, San Jose, CA.

$50,000 to Youth Tennis Advantage, Oakland, CA.
$40,000 to Marianist Brothers, Cupertino, CA.
$35,000 to Saint Ignatius High School, Chicago, IL.
$30,000 to Jesuit School of Theology at Berkeley, Berkeley, CA.
$25,000 to Lucile Packard Foundation for Childrens Health, Palo Alto, CA.
$25,000 to San Domenico School, San Anselmo, CA.

952
Omidyar Network Fund, Inc. ▼ ◇ ☆
1991 Broadway St., Ste. 200
Redwood City, CA 94063
URL: http://www.omidyar.net/

Established in 2004 in CA from the transfer of funds from the Omidyar Foundation.
Donors: Pierre M. Omidyar; Omidyar Network, LLC.
Foundation type: Independent foundation.
Financial data (yr. ended 12/31/04): Assets, $49,447,810 (M); gifts received, $57,029,469; expenditures, $9,230,735; qualifying distributions, $8,070,735; giving activities include $8,049,510 for 30 grants (high: $4,000,000; low: $2,680; average: $10,000–$400,000), and $21,225 for employee matching gifts.
Purpose and activities: The fund supports organizations that promote equal access to information, tools and opportunities, as well as encourages a sense of ownership for participants and rich connections around shared interests.
Fields of interest: Media/communications; Higher education; Education; Civil rights; Foundations (community); Public affairs.
Type of support: General/operating support; Employee matching gifts.
Limitations: Applications not accepted. Giving primarily on a national and international basis. No grants to individuals.
Application information: Contributes only to pre-selected organizations.
Officers: Pierre M. Omidyar, Chair.; Iqbal Paroo, Pres.
Trustees: Pamela Omidyar; Michael Mohr.
EIN: 201173866

953
On Shore, Inc. ☆
(formerly Luster Family Foundation, Inc.)
c/o Elizabeth Luster
23768 Malibu Rd.
Malibu, CA 90265
E-mail: nanadogs@verizon.net

Established in 1987 in CA.
Donors: Freda Friedman†; Elizabeth Luster.
Foundation type: Independent foundation.
Financial data (yr. ended 12/31/04): Assets, $8,527,104 (M); gifts received, $40,798; expenditures, $763,468; qualifying distributions, $661,042; giving activities include $568,210 for 138 grants (high: $150,000; low: $250), and $97,265 for 1 foundation-administered program.
Purpose and activities: Giving primarily for animal welfare, wildlife preservation and environmental protection.
Fields of interest: Environment, natural resources; Environment; Animal welfare; Animal population control; Animals/wildlife, preservation/protection; Reproductive health, family planning.

Type of support: General/operating support.
Limitations: Applications not accepted. Giving primarily in the U.S. No support for religious, media or political organizations, or for advocacy and advisory groups. No grants to individuals.
Application information: A brief letter requesting funds once per year only. No mailings accepted after the initial acknowledged letter. Contributes only to pre-selected organizations.
  Board meeting date(s): Fall
Officers: Elizabeth Luster, Pres.; Amy Luster Mueller, Secy. and C.F.O.
Number of staff: None.
EIN: 954100318

954
Open Doors International, Inc. ▼
2953 S. Pullman St.
Santa Ana, CA 92705-5840
URL: http://www.od.org

Established in 1993 in CA.
Foundation type: Operating foundation.
Financial data (yr. ended 12/31/05): Assets, $12,464,605 (M); gifts received, $16,415,494; expenditures, $14,417,486; qualifying distributions, $14,210,580; giving activities include $11,801,222 for 11 grants (high: $5,053,533; low: $594; average: $100,248–$816,973), and $13,030,151 for 4 foundation-administered programs.
Purpose and activities: Support for international Christian missionary programs.
Fields of interest: Christian agencies & churches.
International interests: Africa; Asia; Latin America; Middle East; Southeast Asia.
Limitations: Applications not accepted. Giving on an international basis. No grants to individuals.
Application information: Contributes only to pre-selected organizations.
Officers and Directors:* Sealy Yates,* Chair.; Brian McFarlane,* Vice-Chair.; Johan Companjen, Pres.; Jaap Kamphorst, Exec. V.P.; Evert Schut, V.P., Opers; Jeff Taylor, V.P., Comms.; Robert Martin; Gunnhild Oftedal*; Gabrielle Searle; Deryck Stone.
Number of staff: 19 full-time professional; 6 full-time support.
EIN: 330523832
Selected grants: The following grants were reported in 2005.
$6,206,228 to Open Doors Philippines, Quezon City, Philippines. 2 grants: $5,033,533, $1,172,695.
$2,547,364 to Open Doors South Africa, Johannesburg, South Africa. .
$1,469,634 to Open Doors Gulf, Santa Ana, CA.
$816,973 to Open Doors Latin America, Santa Ana, CA.
$330,922 to Open Doors India, Noida.
$302,292 to Open Doors Central Asia, Santa Ana, CA.
$160,248 to Open Doors Holland, Harderwijk, Netherlands. .
$116,334 to Open Doors Middle East, Santa Ana, CA.

955
Oppenheimer Brothers Foundation ◇ ☆
P. O. Box 30
Beverly Hills, CA 90213-0030 (310) 276-2101

Established in 2001 in CA.
Donor: Doris Jones Stein Charitable Trust.
Foundation type: Independent foundation.
Financial data (yr. ended 12/31/05): Assets, $20,965,625 (M); gifts received, $586,411; expenditures, $1,509,820; qualifying distributions, $1,378,957; giving activities include $1,183,038 for 78 grants (high: $199,828; low: $100), and $2,000 for 1 employee matching gift.
Purpose and activities: Giving generally limited to health care, education, and the arts. Funds are granted at the discretion of the foundation's board of directors.
Fields of interest: Visual arts; Museums; Performing arts; Elementary/secondary education; Higher education; Environment, natural resources; Veterinary medicine, hospital; Health care; Medical research, association; Medical research, institute; Eye research; Human services; Children/youth, services.
Type of support: General/operating support; Annual campaigns; Endowments; Program development; Scholarship funds; Research; Matching/challenge support.
Limitations: Giving primarily in KS, MO, NM, and OK; some giving nationally. No grants to individuals.
Application information: Application form not required.
  Initial approach: Letter
  Deadline(s): None
Officers: Hamilton G. Oppenheimer, Pres. and Secy.; Hal Oppenheimer, V.P.; Reed Oppenheimer, V.P.; Eric Oppenheimer, Treas.
EIN: 954868080

956
Gerald Oppenheimer Family Foundation ◇
(formerly Gerald and Virginia Oppenheimer Family Foundation)
P.O. Box 30
Beverly Hills, CA 90213-0030 (310) 276-2101
Contact: Tracy Boldemann-Tatkin, V.P. and Secy.

Established in 1987 in CA.
Donors: Gerald H. Oppenheimer; Doris Jones Stein Charitable Lead Trust No. 2; Doris Jones Stein Charitable Lead Trust No. 4.
Foundation type: Independent foundation.
Financial data (yr. ended 12/31/05): Assets, $21,267,773 (M); gifts received, $588,211; expenditures, $1,587,804; qualifying distributions, $1,747,781; giving activities include $1,457,944 for 113 grants (high: $400,000; low: $450), and $200,000 for 1 loan/program-related investment.
Purpose and activities: Giving primarily for health care, education, and the arts.
Fields of interest: Arts; Higher education; Health care; Human services.
Limitations: Giving primarily in Los Angeles, CA. No grants to individuals.
Application information: Application form not required.
  Initial approach: Letter
  Deadline(s): None
Officers and Director:* Gerald H. Oppenheimer,* Pres.; Tracy Boldemann-Tatkin, V.P. and Secy.; Patricia Burns, V.P.; Gail Oppenheimer, V.P.; Harold Oppenheimer, V.P.; Mark Oppenheimer, V.P.; Stephen P. Petty, Treas.
EIN: 953957582
Selected grants: The following grants were reported in 2004.

$178,108 to University of California, Los Angeles, CA.

$80,000 to Texas Wesleyan University, Fort Worth, TX.

$34,850 to Los Angeles County Museum of Art, Los Angeles, CA. 4 grants: $13,750, $1,600, $9,500, $10,000

$8,500 to Marymount High School, Los Angeles, CA.

$5,000 to Colonial Williamsburg Foundation, Williamsburg, VA.

$5,000 to Louisville High School, Woodland Hills, CA.

$2,000 to Polytechnic School, Pasadena, CA.

957
Orange County Community Foundation ◇

30 Corporate Park, Ste. 410
Irvine, CA   92606   (949) 553-4202
Contact: Todd Hanson, V.P., Donor Rels. and Community Partnerships
FAX: (949) 553-4211; E-mail: occf@oc-cf.org;
Additional E-mail: thanson@oc-cf.org; URL: http://www.oc-cf.org

Incorporated in 1989 in CA.
Foundation type: Community foundation.
Financial data (yr. ended 6/30/05): Assets, $78,903,041 (M); gifts received, $29,043,919; expenditures, $14,793,336; giving activities include $11,510,270 for 649 grants (high: $699,786; low: $33), and $723,110 for grants to individuals.
Purpose and activities: The foundation seeks to encourage, support and facilitate philanthropy in Orange County through donor services and community partnerships.
Fields of interest: Arts; Education, early childhood education; Education; Environment; Health care; Children/youth, services; Family services; Minorities/immigrants, centers/services; Human services; Civil rights, race/intergroup relations; Aging; Minorities; Economically disadvantaged.
Type of support: General/operating support; Continuing support; Management development/capacity building; Equipment; Program development; Conferences/seminars; Scholarship funds; Technical assistance; Program evaluation; Scholarships—to individuals.
Limitations: Giving limited to Orange County, CA for discretionary grants; donor-advised grants are national in scope. No support for religious organizations for religious purposes. No grants for annual fund drives, capital or endowment campaigns, debt retirement, research, budget deficits, or academic or scientific research projects.
Publications: Annual report; Informational brochure; Newsletter.
Application information: Visit foundation Web site for application information. Application form required.
Initial approach: Telephone
Deadline(s): Varies
Board meeting date(s): 5 times per year
Final notification: 4 to 8 weeks after deadline
Officers and Governors:* David C. Seigle,* Chair.; Paul Frederic Marx,* Vice-Chair. and Treas.; Shelley Hoss, Pres.; Tracy Branson, V.P., Finance and Admin.; Todd Hanson, V.P., Donor Rels. and Community Partnership; Julie Hill, Secy.; Marcia F. Adler; Dick Allen; N. Christian Anderson; K.B. Bala Balkrishna; Jeff Dankberg; Michael Danzi; Paul C. Heeschen; Timothy J. Kay; Donald P. Kennedy; William F. Podlich; Socorro Vasquez.

Number of staff: 8 full-time professional; 3 part-time support.
EIN: 330378778

958
The Orfalea Family Foundation ◇

1283 Coast Village Cir., Ste. A
Santa Barbara, CA   93108   (805) 565-7550
Contact: Solveig Chandler, Grant Dir.
FAX: (805) 565-7554;
E-mail: Schandler@orfalea.org; URL: http://www.orfaleafamilyfoundation.org

Established in 2000 in CA.
Donors: Paul J. Orfalea; Paul Vit; Kinko's Corporation.
Foundation type: Independent foundation.
Financial data (yr. ended 12/31/05): Assets, $34,460,809 (M); gifts received, $6,735,023; expenditures, $4,087,564; qualifying distributions, $2,944,029; giving activities include $2,599,116 for 107 grants (high: $1,000,000; low: $96), $174,500 for 4 employee matching gifts, and $170,413 for 2 foundation-administered programs.
Purpose and activities: The foundation supports organizations and projects which: enhance young people's lives by contributing to quality education, healthy development, and nurturing environments; improve and enrich education and services through community programs; encourage family values; bring together generations; and provide opportunities for those less privileged and those facing learning challenges.
Fields of interest: Education, early childhood education; Children, day care; Developmentally disabled, centers & services.
Type of support: General/operating support; Program development; Scholarship funds; Employee matching gifts; In-kind gifts; Matching/challenge support.
Limitations: Giving primarily in San Luis Obisbo, Santa Barbara, and Ventura County, CA. No grants to individuals.
Application information: See foundation Web site for application guidelines and procedures. If letter of inquiry is approved, then the foundation will request the submission of a detailed proposal and other documented materials. A detailed proposal is by invitation only.
Initial approach: Letter of Inquiry (1-2 pages) via e-mail
Officers: Paul J. Orfalea, Pres. and Treas.; Natalie A. Orfalea, Secy.; Lois Mitchell, Exec. Dir.
Number of staff: 2 full-time professional; 1 part-time professional.
EIN: 770541226
Selected grants: The following grants were reported in 2004.
$500,000 to All Kinds of Minds, Chapel Hill, NC.
$300,000 to Educational Broadcasting Corporation, New York, NY.
$241,214 to Deer Hill Foundation, Mancos, CO.
$166,000 to ONEgeneration, Van Nuys, CA.
$107,200 to Scholarship America, Saint Peter, MN.
$50,000 to Ventura College Foundation, Ventura, CA.
$35,000 to Scholarship Foundation of Santa Barbara, Santa Barbara, CA.
$10,000 to Ocean Futures Society, Santa Barbara, CA.
$5,725 to Unity Shoppe, Santa Barbara, CA.
$3,300 to Santa Barbara High School District, Santa Barbara, CA.

959
Ornest Family Foundation ◇

702 Trenton Dr.
Beverly Hills, CA   90210

Established in 1994 in CA.
Foundation type: Independent foundation.
Financial data (yr. ended 2/28/06): Assets, $10,131,255 (M); expenditures, $537,703; qualifying distributions, $506,599; giving activities include $468,546 for 52 grants (high: $100,000; low: $100).
Purpose and activities: Giving primarily to Jewish organizations and federated giving programs; some giving also to hospitals, and children, youth, and social services including recordings for the blind.
Fields of interest: Arts; Higher education; Education; Hospitals (general); Health care; Mental health/crisis services; Health organizations, association; Heart & circulatory diseases; Diabetes; Human services; Children/youth, services; Child development, services; Jewish federated giving programs; Psychology/behavioral science; Jewish agencies & temples; Blind/visually impaired.
Limitations: Applications not accepted. Giving primarily in CA. No grants to individuals.
Application information: Contributes only to pre-selected organizations.
Officers and Directors:* Ruth Ornest,* Pres.; Laura Ornest,* C.F.O.; Cindy Ornest; Maury Ornest; Michael Ornest.
EIN: 954436139
Selected grants: The following grants were reported in 2006.
$20,000 to Los Angeles Child Development Center, Los Angeles, CA.
$10,000 to American Red Cross.
$10,000 to Vista del Mar Child and Family Services, Los Angeles, CA.
$5,000 to Variety Clubs International, New York, NY.
$200 to Inside Out, Springfield, OH.

960
Mr. & Mrs. Samuel Oschin Family Foundation ◇ ☆

10375 Wilshire Blvd., Rm. 8C
Los Angeles, CA   90024

Established in 2004 in Delaware; established as successor foundation as a result of a merger with foundation of the same name.
Donor: Samuel Oschin Trust.
Foundation type: Independent foundation.
Financial data (yr. ended 9/30/05): Assets, $76,039,450 (M); gifts received, $13,605,037; expenditures, $5,637,483; qualifying distributions, $5,192,548; giving activities include $5,007,800 for 7 grants (high: $3,000,000; low: $100).
Purpose and activities: Giving primarily for hospitals and planetariums.
Fields of interest: Planetarium; Hospitals (general).
Limitations: Applications not accepted. Giving primarily in CA, with emphasis on Los Angeles.
Application information: Does not accept unsolicited applications.
Officers: Lynda Oschin, Chair.; Michael Oschin, C.E.O.; Daniel Oschin, C.F.O. and Secy.
EIN: 200533204

961
Bernard Osher Foundation ▼ ✧
1 Ferry Bldg., Ste. 255
San Francisco, CA 94111 (415) 861-5587
Contact: Patricia T. Nagle, Sr. V.P.
FAX: (415) 677-5868; E-mail (for Patricia T. Nagle): nagle@osherfoundation.com; URL: http://www.osherfoundation.org

Established in 1977 in CA.
Donor: Bernard A. Osher.
Foundation type: Independent foundation.
Financial data (yr. ended 12/31/04): Assets, $50,960,944 (M); expenditures, $32,103,844; qualifying distributions, $31,425,467; giving activities include $30,930,483 for 202 grants (high: $5,000,000; low: $500; average: $2,000–$100,000).
Purpose and activities: The foundation seeks to improve the quality of life for residents of the San Francisco Bay Area and the state of Maine through post-secondary student scholarships and arts and humanities grants. It also supports selected programs in integrative medicine, as well as a national network of lifelong learning institutes for older adults.
Fields of interest: Visual arts; Museums; Performing arts; Performing arts, dance; Performing arts, theater; Performing arts, music; Humanities; Arts; Higher education; Scholarships/financial aid; Education; Environment; Health care.
Type of support: General/operating support; Capital campaigns; Program development.
Limitations: Giving primarily in Alameda and San Francisco counties, CA, and ME. No grants to individuals.
Publications: Application guidelines; Informational brochure.
Application information: Unsolicited proposals are accepted for the local Arts, cultural, and Educational Program. All other program areas are governed by a Request for Proposals (RFP) process. Nonetheless, colleges and universities interested in the four areas of support in the field of higher education may submit letters of inquiry to the foundation along with a concise description of their plans and activities relevant to the given program area. Application form not required.
  Initial approach: Letter
  Copies of proposal: 1
  Deadline(s): None
  Board meeting date(s): 6 times per year
  Final notification: Within 90 days
Officers and Directors:* Barbro Osher,* Chair.; Mary G.F. Bitterman, Pres.; Stephen Mark Dobbs, Exec. V.P.; Patricia T. Nagle, Sr. V.P. and Corp. Secy.; Bernard A. Osher, Treas.; David Agger; Phyllis Cook; Robert Friend; John Gallo; Laura Lauder; John Pritzker.
Number of staff: 1 full-time professional; 1 part-time professional.
EIN: 942506257
Selected grants: The following grants were reported in 2004.
$5,000,000 to University of California, Berkeley, CA. For Incentive Awards San Jose.
$2,500,000 to City College of San Francisco, San Francisco, CA.
$1,900,000 to University of California, Integrative Medicine Building, San Francisco, CA. For Osher Center for Integrative Medicine Building.
$1,500,000 to University of Southern Maine, Portland, ME. For Osher Lifelong Learning Institute.

$1,400,000 to San Francisco Conservatory of Music, San Francisco, CA.
$1,000,000 to Bates College, Lewiston, ME. For endowment.
$1,000,000 to Bowdoin College, Brunswick, ME. For endowment.
$1,000,000 to Brandeis University, Waltham, MA.
$1,000,000 to California College of the Arts, Oakland, CA. For endowment.
$1,000,000 to Colby College, Waterville, ME. For endowment.

962
The Barbro Osher Pro Suecia Foundation ✧
One Ferry Bldg., Rm. 255
San Francisco, CA 94111 (415) 861-5587
Contact: Patricia Nagle, Secy.
FAX: (415) 677-5868;
E-mail: nagle@osherfoundation.com

Established in 1996 in CA.
Donor: Bernard A. Osher.
Foundation type: Independent foundation.
Financial data (yr. ended 12/31/04): Assets, $21,041,036 (M); expenditures, $972,091; qualifying distributions, $901,767; giving activities include $880,485 for 46 grants (high: $150,000; low: $1,450).
Purpose and activities: The foundation's intent is to provide support to nonprofit organizations that benefit Swedish education, culture and arts.
Fields of interest: Museums (art); Higher education; Education.
Limitations: Giving on a national basis. No grants to individuals.
Application information: Application form not required.
Officers: Barbro Osher, Pres.; Bernard Osher, V.P. and C.F.O.; Patricia Nagle, Secy.
Director: Stig Hagstrom.
EIN: 943241225
Selected grants: The following grants were reported in 2004.
$150,000 to American Swedish Institute, Minneapolis, MN. For unrestricted support.
$85,000 to San Francisco Performances, San Francisco, CA. For unrestricted support.
$75,000 to Confidence Learning Center, East Gull Lake, MN. For unrestricted support.
$37,500 to American Swedish Historical Foundation and Museum, Philadelphia, PA. For unrestricted support.
$22,500 to Los Angeles Philharmonic, Los Angeles, CA. For unrestricted support.
$20,000 to International Arts and Artists, DC. For unrestricted support.
$20,000 to Upsala College, East Orange, NJ. For Choral Center.

963
The Oshman Family Foundation ✧
695 Oak Grove Ave., Ste. 210
Menlo Park, CA 94025

Established in 1996 in CA.
Donors: Barbara Oshman; M. Kenneth Oshman.
Foundation type: Independent foundation.
Financial data (yr. ended 12/31/04): Assets, $6,819,212 (M); gifts received, $1,450,006; expenditures, $1,103,513; qualifying distributions,

$1,082,500; giving activities include $1,082,500 for 16 grants (high: $654,000; low: $1,000).
Purpose and activities: Giving activities for the arts, particularly an art museum, higher education, children, youth, and social services, health care, and Jewish organizations.
Fields of interest: Museums (art); Performing arts, opera; Arts; Higher education; Health care; Human services; Children/youth, services; Federated giving programs; Jewish federated giving programs; Jewish agencies & temples.
Limitations: Applications not accepted. Giving primarily in CA. No grants to individuals.
Application information: Contributes only to pre-selected organizations.
Officers and Directors:* Barbara Oshman,* Pres.; Jeff Child, Secy.; M. Kenneth Oshman,* C.F.O.; David R. Oshman; Peter L. Oshman.
EIN: 770443160
Selected grants: The following grants were reported in 2004.
$654,000 to San Jose Museum of Art, San Jose, CA.
$135,000 to Rice University, Houston, TX.
$50,000 to San Francisco Opera, San Francisco, CA.
$25,000 to Stanford Jazz Workshop, Stanford, CA.
$2,500 to Contemporary Jewish Museum, San Francisco, CA.

964
Ostin Family Foundation ✧
c/o Capri Investments
1800 Ave. of the Stars, Ste. 900
Los Angeles, CA 90067
Contact: Werner F. Wolfen

Established in 1999 in CA.
Donors: Michael Ostin; Joyce Ostin; Morris Ostin.
Foundation type: Independent foundation.
Financial data (yr. ended 12/31/04): Assets, $2,877,224 (M); gifts received, $29,030; expenditures, $1,118,430; qualifying distributions, $1,058,166; giving activities include $1,055,480 for 29 grants (high: $500,000; low: $200).
Purpose and activities: Giving primarily for education; funding also for hospitals and health associations, including a children's diabetes foundation, children, youth and social services, and Jewish organizations.
Fields of interest: Arts; Higher education; Education; Hospitals (general); Health organizations, association; Human services; Jewish federated giving programs; Jewish agencies & temples.
Limitations: Giving primarily in Los Angeles, CA. No grants to individuals.
Application information: Application form not required.
  Initial approach: Letter
  Deadline(s): None
Trustees: Morris Ostin; Rachel Ostin.
EIN: 954745068

965
Otter Cove Foundation ✧
316 Mid Valley Ctr., Ste. 123
Carmel, CA 93923-8516
Contact: James P. Read, Jr., Pres.

Established in 1997 in CA.

Donor: James P. Read, Jr.
Foundation type: Independent foundation.
Financial data (yr. ended 12/31/04): Assets, $2,570,025 (M); gifts received, $507,472; expenditures, $894,794; qualifying distributions, $860,000; giving activities include $860,000 for 8 grants (high: $500,000; low: $10,000).
Purpose and activities: Giving to provide a more secure future for the well-being of humans and animals.
Fields of interest: Museums; Animal welfare.
Limitations: Applications not accepted. Giving primarily in CA and WA. No grants to individuals.
Application information: Contributes only to pre-selected organizations.
Officers and Directors:* James P. Read, Jr., Pres.; Mark Plumley, Secy.; Gilan M. Read,* C.F.O.; Megan G. Lindberg.
EIN: 943287969

966
June G. Outhwaite Charitable Trust
c/o Poucher, Englert and Cooney
26 W. Anapamu St., Ste. 103
Santa Barbara, CA 93101-3144
Contact: Jean Volmar
E-mail: jean@outhwaitefoundation.org

Established in 1998 in CA.
Donor: The 1994 June G. Outhwaite Revocable Trust.
Foundation type: Independent foundation.
Financial data (yr. ended 12/31/04): Assets, $24,125,139 (M); expenditures, $1,444,909; qualifying distributions, $1,088,966; giving activities include $1,026,000 for 56 grants (high: $100,000; low: $4,500).
Purpose and activities: Giving primarily for medical care support and research, general assistance to the disabled, elderly and children, support for abused women and children, the prevention of cruelty to animals, for the preservation of wildlife and natural resources, historic preservation, and for educational institutions.
Fields of interest: Museums (marine/maritime); Education; Zoos/zoological societies; Cancer; Medical research; Family services; Physically disabled.
Type of support: Equipment; Capital campaigns; Building/renovation; Annual campaigns; General/operating support.
Limitations: Giving primarily in Santa Barbara County, CA. No support for the arts.
Application information: Application form required.
  Initial approach: Letter
  Copies of proposal: 3
  Deadline(s): July 31
  Final notification: After Dec. 15
Trustees: C. Michael Cooney; Kent L. Englert; John S. Poucher.
Number of staff: 1 part-time support.
EIN: 776154307

967
The Outrageous Foundation, Inc. ◇ ☆
2 6th Ave.
San Francisco, CA 94118

Established around 1978.
Donor: Robert P. McGrath.
Foundation type: Independent foundation.

Financial data (yr. ended 9/30/05): Assets, $7,159,927 (M); expenditures, $462,956; qualifying distributions, $418,838; giving activities include $375,000 for 42 grants (high: $100,000; low: $1,000).
Purpose and activities: Giving primarily for art museums, education, and children's services.
Fields of interest: Museums (art); Performing arts, theater; Secondary school/education; Education; Children/youth, services; Roman Catholic agencies & churches.
Type of support: Capital campaigns.
Limitations: Applications not accepted. Giving primarily in northern CA. No grants to individuals.
Application information: Contributes only to pre-selected organizations.
Officers: R. McGrath, Pres.; J. McGrath, Secy.
EIN: 942474423

968
The Ovitz Family Foundation ◇ ☆
c/o Dreyer, Edmonds, & Assocs.
355 S. Grand Ave., Ste. 2850
Los Angeles, CA 90071-3103

Established in 1986 in CA.
Donor: Michael S. Ovitz.
Foundation type: Independent foundation.
Financial data (yr. ended 12/31/05): Assets, $102,687 (M); expenditures, $330,295; qualifying distributions, $330,250; giving activities include $330,250 for 4 grants (high: $250,000; low: $250).
Fields of interest: Museums (art); Elementary/secondary education; Higher education.
Limitations: Applications not accepted. Giving primarily in Los Angeles, CA, and New York, NY. No grants to individuals.
Application information: Contributes only to pre-selected organizations.
Officers: Michael S. Ovitz, Pres.; Robert F. Goldman, Secy.; Michael S. Dreyer, C.F.O.
EIN: 521354173

969
Oxnard Foundation ◇
4001 MacArthur Blvd., Ste. 102
Newport Beach, CA 92660-2508
(949) 475-0890
Contact: Christopher O. Veitch, Dir.

Established in 1973.
Donor: Thomas Thornton Oxnard‡.
Foundation type: Independent foundation.
Financial data (yr. ended 12/31/05): Assets, $9,639,272 (M); expenditures, $535,657; qualifying distributions, $493,773; giving activities include $457,709 for 6 grants (high: $135,000; low: $50,000).
Purpose and activities: Giving for medical research, particularly cancer and multiple sclerosis research.
Fields of interest: Medical research, institute; Cancer research; Multiple sclerosis research.
Type of support: Research; Matching/challenge support.
Limitations: Giving primarily in CA and NY; some funding also in the Southwest. No grants to individuals, or for general support, capital funds, endowments, scholarships, fellowships, special projects, publications, or conferences; no loans.
Application information: Application form not required.

Initial approach: Letter
Copies of proposal: 1
Deadline(s): None
Board meeting date(s): Quarterly
Final notification: 3 months
Directors: Caroline O. Meade; Gary J. Meade; Thomas Meade; Christopher O. Veitch; Julie Veitch.
Number of staff: 1 part-time support.
EIN: 237323007
Selected grants: The following grants were reported in 2003.
$162,910 to University of Southern California, Keck School of Medicine, Los Angeles, CA. For multiple sclerosis and colorectal cancer.
$151,147 to Stanford University, Stanford, CA. For Prostate Cancer, Fibromyalgia, Antibiotics Research.
$76,095 to University of New Mexico, Albuquerque, NM. For Leukemogenesis, cancer research and treatment center.
$72,580 to University of California San Francisco Medical Center, San Francisco, CA. For brain tumor research.

970
Pacific Life Foundation
(formerly Pacific Mutual Charitable Foundation)
700 Newport Center Dr.
Newport Beach, CA 92660-6397
(949) 219-3787
Contact: Robert G. Haskell, Pres.
FAX: (949) 719-7614; *URL:* http://www.pacificlife.com/About+Pacific+Life/Foundation+or+Community

Established in 1984 in CA.
Donors: Pacific Life Insurance Co.; Pacific Mutual Holding Co.
Foundation type: Company-sponsored foundation.
Financial data (yr. ended 12/31/05): Assets, $52,022,558 (M); gifts received, $6,002,000; expenditures, $4,342,776; qualifying distributions, $4,318,144; giving activities include $4,311,551 for 332 grants (high: $1,000,000; low: $1,000).
Purpose and activities: The foundation supports organizations involved with arts and culture, education, the environment, health, nutrition, shelter for the homeless, human services, community development, and civic affairs.
Fields of interest: Arts; Elementary/secondary education; Education; Environment, natural resources; Environment; Public health; Health care; Nutrition; Housing/shelter, homeless; Human services; Community development; Leadership development; Public affairs.
Type of support: Continuing support; General/operating support; Capital campaigns; Equipment; Program development.
Limitations: Giving primarily in areas of company operations in the greater Orange County, CA, area and Omaha, NE. No support for political parties or candidates or partisan political organizations, labor or fraternal organizations, athletic or social clubs, K-12 schools, school districts, or school foundations (except for 3T's of Education), or sectarian or denominational religious organizations not of direct benefit to the entire community. No grants to individuals, or for fundraising events or advertising sponsorships.
Publications: Application guidelines; Annual report (including application guidelines).
Application information: Support is limited to 1 contribution per organization during any given year

for three years in length. Multi-year funding is not automatic. Audio and video submissions are not encouraged. Application form required.

> Initial approach: Download application form and mail proposal and application form to foundation
> Copies of proposal: 1
> Deadline(s): July 15 to Aug. 31
> Board meeting date(s): Oct.
> Final notification: Early Nov.

Officers and Directors: * Thomas C. Sutton,* Chair.; Robert G. Haskell,* Pres.; Michele Myszka,* V.P.; Audrey L. Milfs, Secy.; Edward R. Byrd, C.F.O.; Michael T. McLaughlin, Genl. Counsel; M. Kathleen McWard; Rex A. Olson; Daragh M. O'Sullivan; Lisa M. Rigdon; Robert F. Stevenson; Richard A. Taube.
Number of staff: 2 full-time professional; 1 full-time support.
EIN: 953433806
Selected grants: The following grants were reported in 2004.
$309,361 to United Way, Orange County, Irvine, CA. For operating support.
$214,000 to County of Orange Health Care Agency, Santa Ana, CA. 2 grants: $114,000, $100,000
$122,471 to Ocean Alliance, Lincoln, MA. For operating support.
$100,000 to South Coast Repertory Theater, Costa Mesa, CA. For capital campaign.
$94,712 to Aquarium of the Pacific, Long Beach, CA. For operating support.
$60,000 to Orange County Department of Education, Costa Mesa, CA. For Advancement via Individual Determination (AVID) Program.
$25,000 to K O C E-TV, Huntington Beach, CA. For capital support.
$22,750 to Community Partners, Los Angeles, CA.
$20,000 to J. F. Shea Therapeutic Riding Center, San Juan Capistrano, CA. For capital campaign.

971
PacifiCare Health Systems Foundation ▼ ✧

5995 Plaza Dr., M.S. CY20-326
Cypress, CA 90630 (714) 825-5233
Contact: Bill Wood, Pres.
Application address: P.O. Box 25186, Santa Ana, CA 92799

Established in 1991.
Donors: PacifiCare Health Systems, Inc.; PacifiCare of California, Inc.; Jeff M. Folick; Alan Hoops; Terry Hartshorn; PacifiCare Health Plan Administrators, Inc.
Foundation type: Company-sponsored foundation.
Financial data (yr. ended 12/31/05): Assets, $491,556 (M); gifts received, $4,355,358; expenditures, $5,486,082; qualifying distributions, $5,485,469; giving activities include $4,317,619 for 467 grants (high: $500,000; low: $75), and $233,960 for 79 grants to individuals (high: $25,000; low: $2,000).
Purpose and activities: The foundation supports organizations involved with education, health, crime prevention, hunger, nutrition, housing, youth development, human services, community development, volunteerism, transportation, and senior citizens and awards college scholarships to Hispanics and Latinos.
Fields of interest: Education, reading; Education; Health care, equal rights; Public health; Health care; Crime/violence prevention; Food services; Nutrition; Housing/shelter; Youth development; Children/

youth, services; Children, day care; Residential/custodial care, special day care; Human services; Community development; Voluntarism promotion; Transportation; Aging; Hispanics/Latinos.
Type of support: Scholarships—to individuals.
Limitations: Giving limited to areas of company operations in AZ, CA, CO, NV, OK, OR, TX, and WA. No support for professional or technical associations or private foundations. No grants to individuals (except for scholarships), or for capital campaigns, annual campaigns, research, endowments, conferences or seminars, programs promoting religious doctrine, sponsorship of special events, or non-education arts and culture programs; no challenge or matching grants.
Publications: Annual report; Informational brochure (including application guidelines).
Application information: Video submissions are not encouraged. Proposals should be no longer than 3 to 5 pages. Application form required.

> Initial approach: Download application form and mail proposal and application form to foundation
> Copies of proposal: 2
> Deadline(s): Jan. 1 and July 1
> Board meeting date(s): June and Dec.
> Final notification: Late June and late Dec.

Officers and Directors: * Terry Hartshorn,* Chair.; Bill Wood,* Pres.; Riva Gebel, Fdn. Dir.; Brad Bowlus; Judy Ehrenreich; Nick Franklin; Alan Hoops; Howard Phanstiel.
EIN: 330473608
Selected grants: The following grants were reported in 2004.
$500,000 to American Heart Association, Dallas, TX.
$310,000 to Painted Turtle, Santa Monica, CA. 2 grants: $300,000, $10,000
$200,000 to American Diabetes Association, National Service Center, Alexandria, VA.
$162,500 to Dream Foundation, Santa Barbara, CA. 2 grants: $150,000, $12,500
$30,000 to Texas Scottish Rite Hospital for Children, Dallas, TX.
$10,000 to AIDS Services Foundation Orange County, Irvine, CA.
$10,000 to Childrens Dental Foundation, Long Beach, CA.
$10,000 to ONEgeneration, Van Nuys, CA.

972
The David and Lucile Packard Foundation ▼

300 2nd St., Ste. 200
Los Altos, CA 94022 (650) 948-7658
Contact: Prog. Off. of area of interest
E-mail: inquiries@packard.org; URL: http://www.packard.org

Incorporated in 1964 in CA.
Donors: David Packard†; Lucile Packard†.
Foundation type: Independent foundation.
Financial data (yr. ended 12/31/05): Assets, $5,788,480,930 (M); expenditures, $185,046,532; qualifying distributions, $196,466,330; giving activities include $148,461,233 for 925 grants (high: $16,569,000; low: $2,500; average: $50,000–$500,000), $1,654,412 for employee matching gifts, $5,026,691 for foundation-administered programs and $25,872,000 for 8 loans/program-related investments.

Purpose and activities: The foundation provides grants to nonprofit organizations in the following program areas: Children, Families, and Communities; Population; and Science and Conservation. National and international grants are provided, with a special focus on the local northern California counties of San Mateo, Santa Clara, Santa Cruz, and Monterey.
Fields of interest: Arts; Education, early childhood education; Environment, natural resources; Environment, energy; Environment; Animals/wildlife, fisheries; Reproductive health, family planning; Health care, insurance; Child development, services; Civil liberties, reproductive rights; Philanthropy/voluntarism; Marine science; Engineering/technology; Science; Population studies.
Type of support: General/operating support; Continuing support; Capital campaigns; Equipment; Land acquisition; Emergency funds; Program development; Fellowships; Research; Technical assistance; Program evaluation; Program-related investments/loans; Employee matching gifts; Matching/challenge support.
Limitations: Giving for the arts and community development primarily in Los Altos and Santa Clara, San Mateo, Santa Cruz, and Monterey counties, CA; Pueblo, CO, and national giving for child health and development; national and international giving for population, conservation, and science. No support for religious purposes. No grants to individuals.
Publications: Application guidelines; Annual report; Financial statement; Grants list; Occasional report.
Application information: Review program guidelines online; foundation does not accept proposals for all of their areas of interest. Application form not required.

> Initial approach: Proposal or 2- to 3-page letter of inquiry
> Copies of proposal: 1
> Deadline(s): None
> Board meeting date(s): Mar., June, Sept., and Dec.
> Final notification: Varies

Officers and Trustees: * Susan Packard Orr,* Chair.; Nancy Packard Burnett,* Vice-Chair.; Julie E. Packard,* Vice-Chair.; Carol S. Larson,* C.E.O. and Pres.; George Vera, V.P. and C.F.O.; Chris DeCardy, V.P. and Dir., Comms.; Barbara P. Wright, Secy. and Genl. Counsel; Edward W. Barnholt; Linda Griego; Donald Kennedy; Franklin M. Orr, Jr.; William K. Reilly; Allan Rosenfield, M.D.; Robert Stephens; Colburn S. Wilbur.
Number of staff: 48 full-time professional; 4 part-time professional; 31 full-time support; 2 part-time support.
EIN: 942278431
Selected grants: The following grants were reported in 2005.
$33,850,000 to Monterey Bay Aquarium Research Institute (MBARI), Moss Landing, CA. For operating and capital support.
$7,000,000 to Energy Foundation, San Francisco, CA. 2 grants: $5,000,000 (For China Sustainable Energy Program), $2,000,000 (For U.S. Climate Program).
$6,000,000 to Resource Legacy Fund Foundation, Sacramento, CA. For California Coastal and Marine Initiative.
$2,159,960 to SeaWeb, DC. For Communications Partnership for Science and the Sea (COMPASS), payable over 2 years.

$2,000,000 to Americas Promise - The Alliance for Youth, Alexandria, VA. For Children's Investment Project, payable over 3 years.

$1,750,000 to Marine Stewardship Council, Seattle, WA. For Accelerating Program.

$1,500,000 to California Polytechnic State University Foundation, San Luis Obispo, CA. For Elucidating Nexus of Science and Society in Morro Bay Ecosystem, payable over 3 years.

$1,300,000 to Audubon California, Sacramento, CA. For Conservation Action Plan, payable over 3 years.

$1,300,000 to Stanford University, Stanford, CA. For Environment Initiative.

973
The Packard Humanities Institute ▼ ✧
300 2nd St.
Los Altos, CA 94022
URL: http://www.packhum.org

Established in 1987 in CA.
Donor: The David and Lucile Packard Foundation.
Foundation type: Operating foundation.
Financial data (yr. ended 12/31/05): Assets, $858,955,029 (M); expenditures, $23,146,427; qualifying distributions, $74,030,045; giving activities include $13,555,364 for 39 grants (high: $2,300,000; low: $11,850; average: $150,000–$1,000,000), and $62,037,125 for 4 foundation-administered programs.
Purpose and activities: Giving primarily for education and the arts.
Fields of interest: Arts; Education; Human services.
Limitations: Applications not accepted. Giving primarily in CA. No grants to individuals.
Application information: Contributes only to pre-selected organizations.
Officers and Directors:* David W. Packard,* Chair. and Pres.; Susan Packard Orr,* V.P.; Barbara P. Wright, Secy.; T.W. Melis, C.F.O.; Edwin E. Van Bronkhorst,* Treas.; G. Gervaise Davis III; Robert J. Glaser, M.D.; Walter B. Hewlett; William A. Johnson; Pamela M. Packard; Christopher J. Wolff.
EIN: 943038401
Selected grants: The following grants were reported in 2004.
$2,500,000 to Stanford Theater Foundation, Palo Alto, CA. 2 grants: $500,000 (For gallery construction, including design and planning), $2,000,000 (For gallery construction).
$2,100,000 to San Jose Redevelopment Agency, San Jose, CA. 4 grants: $600,000 (For San Jose Fox Theater restoration: enhancements and change orders), $500,000 (For San Jose Fox Theater restoration, additional enhancements and changes), $500,000 (For San Jose Fox Theater restoration: revised decorative enhancements), $500,000 (For San Jose Fox Theater restoration: revised enhancements and project close-out costs).
$1,558,270 to University of Texas, Austin, TX. For Chersonnesos and Metaponto archaeological excavations and publication of findings.
$605,000 to Sing-Akademie zu Berlin, Berlin, Germany. For cataloguing, restoration, and preservation work on manuscripts in archive.
$500,000 to Mihai Eminescu Trust, London, England. .
$500,000 to Oakland Unified School District, Oakland, CA. For Reading Lions: purchase of Open Court Reading materials for K-3.

974
Paloheimo Foundation ✧
c/o Wells Fargo Bank, N.A.
P.O. Box 63954
San Francisco, CA 94163

Established in 2000 in CA.
Donor: Leonora Curtin Paloheimo Trust.
Foundation type: Independent foundation.
Financial data (yr. ended 12/31/05): Assets, $26,714,499 (M); expenditures, $1,158,299; qualifying distributions, $831,712; giving activities include $465,844 for 5 grants (high: $199,405; low: $3,839), and $214,000 for 1 employee matching gift.
Purpose and activities: Giving primarily for education, and the arts, including a Finnish-American cultural organization.
Fields of interest: Arts, cultural/ethnic awareness; Museums; Historic preservation/historical societies; Higher education; Education.
Type of support: Continuing support; Program development; Publication; Seed money; Matching/challenge support.
Limitations: Applications not accepted. Giving primarily in CA and NM. No grants to individuals.
Application information: Contributes only to pre-selected organizations.
Trustee: Wells Fargo Bank, N.A.
Board Members: Morgan Halme; Paul Halme; George Paloheimo; Larry Plumer.
EIN: 946752361
Selected grants: The following grants were reported in 2003.
$225,000 to El Rancho de las Golondrinas Museum, Santa Fe, NM. For general support.
$150,000 to Paloheimo Saatio, Finland. For general support.
$131,400 to Pasadena Historical Society, Pasadena, CA.
$90,950 to Finlandia University, Hancock, MI. For general support.
$87,452 to School of American Research, Santa Fe, NM. For general support.
$63,000 to Finlandia Foundation-Boston, Arlington, MA. For general support.

975
The Panda Charitable Foundation ✧
1683 Walnut Grove Ave.
Rosemead, CA 91770-3711
Contact: Kelly Curtis

Changed status to a company-sponsored operating foundation in 1999.
Donors: Panda Management Co., Inc.; Panda Restaurant Group, Inc.
Foundation type: Operating foundation.
Financial data (yr. ended 12/31/04): Assets, $30,419 (M); gifts received, $741,434; expenditures, $715,935; qualifying distributions, $634,150; giving activities include $634,150 for 2 grants (high: $631,650; low: $2,500).
Purpose and activities: The foundation supports organizations involved with education and pediatrics.
Fields of interest: Elementary/secondary education; Education, early childhood education; Child development, education; Pediatrics; Federated giving programs.
International interests: China.
Limitations: Giving primarily in CA, some giving also in China.

Application information: Application form not required.
Initial approach: Letter of inquiry
Deadline(s): None
Trustee: Andrew Cherng.
EIN: 954142346

976
Milan Panic, Jr. Foundation ✧
c/o Milan Panic
15 Morgan Pl.
Irvine, CA 92618

Established 1986 in CA.
Donor: Milan Panic.
Foundation type: Independent foundation.
Financial data (yr. ended 6/30/05): Assets, $607,083 (M); expenditures, $818,145; qualifying distributions, $812,934; giving activities include $812,934 for 18 grants.
Purpose and activities: Giving primarily to the arts.
Fields of interest: Performing arts; Performing arts, opera.
Limitations: Applications not accepted. Giving primarily in CA. No grants to individuals.
Application information: Contributes only to pre-selected organizations.
Officers: Milan Panic, Pres.; Dawn Panic, Secy.
EIN: 954086198
Selected grants: The following grants were reported in 2004.
$887,559 to Los Angeles Opera Company, Los Angeles, CA. For general support.
$176,632 to Opera Pacific, Santa Ana, CA. For general support.
$37,500 to American Youth Symphony, Los Angeles, CA. For general support.
$25,000 to Pasadena POPS Orchestra, Pasadena, CA. For general support.
$25,000 to Philharmonic Society of Orange County, Irvine, CA. For general support.
$10,000 to Advanced Vision Research. For general support.
$10,000 to White Knights Foundation, New York, NY. For general support.
$9,000 to Saint Sava Orthodox School, Milwaukee, WI. For general support.
$6,000 to United Performing Arts Fund, Milwaukee, WI. For general support.
$5,000 to Sundry. For general support.

977
Paramitas Foundation ✧
P.O. Box 700220
San Jose, CA 95170

Established in 1992 in CA.
Donor: Winston H. Chen.
Foundation type: Independent foundation.
Financial data (yr. ended 12/31/05): Assets, $30,492,764 (M); expenditures, $1,092,372; qualifying distributions, $1,092,372; giving activities include $884,200 for grants.
Purpose and activities: Giving primarily to Buddhist temples and societies, and to organizations that aid Taiwanese-Americans.
Fields of interest: Higher education; International affairs, foreign policy; Federated giving programs; Buddhism.
Limitations: Applications not accepted. Giving primarily in CA. No grants to individuals.

Application information: Contributes only to pre-selected organizations.
Officer: Winston H. Chen, Pres.
EIN: 770295773

978
The J. Douglas & Marian R. Pardee Foundation ✧ ☆
6310 San Vicente Blvd., Ste. 255
Los Angeles, CA 90048

Established in 1986 in CA.
Donors: J. Douglas Pardee; Marian R. Pardee.
Foundation type: Independent foundation.
Financial data (yr. ended 11/30/05): Assets, $5,014,174 (M); gifts received, $1,217,505; expenditures, $526,021; qualifying distributions, $514,784; giving activities include $514,784 for grants.
Purpose and activities: Giving primarily for education, health associations, and Episcopal churches; funding also for human services.
Fields of interest: Arts; Higher education; Health organizations, association; Boys & girls clubs; Boy scouts; Human services; Protestant agencies & churches.
Limitations: Applications not accepted. Giving primarily in CA. No grants to individuals.
Application information: Contributes only to pre-selected organizations.
Officers: J. Douglas Pardee, Pres.; Marian R. Pardee, V.P.; Raymond C. Sandler, Secy.-Treas.
EIN: 954070020
Selected grants: The following grants were reported in 2004.
$71,436 to Boys and Girls Clubs of Greater San Diego, San Diego, CA.
$10,100 to Timken Art Gallery, San Diego, CA.
$10,000 to Boy Scouts of America, Western Los Angeles County Council, Van Nuys, CA.
$6,000 to Pepperdine University, Malibu, CA.
$5,000 to University of Southern California, Los Angeles, CA.
$1,500 to McCallum Theater Foundation, Palm Desert, CA.
$1,000 to Eisenhower Medical Center Foundation, Rancho Mirage, CA.
$1,000 to Marlborough School, Los Angeles, CA.
$890 to San Diego Museum of Art, San Diego, CA.
$650 to United Way of the Desert, Palm Springs, CA.

979
The Parker Foundation ✧
4365 Executive Dr., Ste. 1100
San Diego, CA 92121-2133 (858) 677-1431
Contact: Robbin C. Powell, Asst. Secy.
FAX: (858) 677-1401; FAX: (858) 677-1477;
URL: http://www.TheParkerFoundation.org

Trust established in 1971 in CA; incorporated in 1975.
Donors: Gerald T. Parker†; Inez Grant Parker†.
Foundation type: Independent foundation.
Financial data (yr. ended 9/30/05): Assets, $41,519,490 (M); expenditures, $2,007,566; qualifying distributions, $1,826,752; giving activities include $1,736,527 for 83 grants (high: $100,000; low: $2,500).
Purpose and activities: Equal emphasis on cultural programs, health and welfare, including medical support and research, adult services, and youth

agencies; grants also for education and community activities. Giving largely in the form of partial seed money and matching or challenge grants; generally no support that would make an organization dependent on the foundation.
Fields of interest: Arts; Education; Health care; Children/youth, services; Aging, centers/services; Community development.
Type of support: General/operating support; Continuing support; Annual campaigns; Building/renovation; Equipment; Land acquisition; Emergency funds; Program development; Publication; Seed money; Research; Matching/challenge support.
Limitations: Giving limited to San Diego County, CA. No support for sectarian religious purposes. No grants to individuals, or for endowment funds, conferences, symposia, scholarships, or fellowships; no loans.
Publications: Annual report; Informational brochure (including application guidelines).
Application information: For economic reasons, single copies of explanatory or illustrative proposal materials are sufficient; application guidelines available on foundation Web site. Application form not required.
Initial approach: Letter
Copies of proposal: 7
Deadline(s): None
Board meeting date(s): Monthly
Final notification: 2 months
Officers: William E. Beamer, Pres.; Judy McDonald, V.P.; Mary Herron, Secy.; Mark C. Trotter, Treas.
Directors: Ann Davies; Paul Mosher.
EIN: 510141231

980
The Ralph M. Parsons Foundation ▼
1055 Wilshire Blvd., Ste. 1701
Los Angeles, CA 90017-5600 (213) 482-3185
Contact: Wendy G. Hoppe, Exec. Dir.
FAX: (213) 482-8878; URL: http://www.parsonsfoundation.org

Incorporated in 1961 in CA.
Donor: Ralph M. Parsons†.
Foundation type: Independent foundation.
Financial data (yr. ended 12/31/05): Assets, $389,193,588 (M); expenditures, $22,230,129; qualifying distributions, $19,352,423; giving activities include $18,006,924 for 214 grants (high: $666,667; low: $1,500; average: $5,000–$75,000).
Purpose and activities: The foundation strives to support and facilitate the work of the region's best nonprofit organizations, recognizing that many of those in need today will go on to shape the future of southern California, to define it, redefine it, and help it set and achieve new goals. This process will involve the hard work of thousands of organizations, working in widely disparate fields to provide services that, in many respects, people are unable to provide for themselves and that public agencies cannot provide for them.
Fields of interest: Performing arts; Arts; Education, early childhood education; Secondary school/education; Higher education; Engineering school/education; Education; Hospitals (general); Health care; AIDS; Legal services; Housing/shelter, development; Youth development, centers/clubs; Human services; Children/youth, services; Family services; Aging, centers/services; Homeless, human services; Community development;

Engineering; Science; Aging; Economically disadvantaged; Homeless.
Type of support: General/operating support; Capital campaigns; Building/renovation; Equipment; Program development; Seed money; Fellowships; Internship funds; Scholarship funds; Research; Technical assistance; Matching/challenge support.
Limitations: Giving limited to Los Angeles County, CA, with the exception of some grants for higher education. No support for sectarian, religious, or fraternal purposes, or for political organizations. No grants to individuals, or for annual campaigns, fundraising events, dinners, mass mailings, workshops, federated fundraising appeals, seminars, conferences or generally for multi-year funding; no loans.
Publications: Biennial report; Grants list; Informational brochure.
Application information: Unless initiated by a foundation director, personal communication with individual directors by representatives of applicant organizations is not encouraged. If confident that your organization and grant request fits within the foundation's guidelines, you may forego the test letter and submit a full proposal. The foundation does not accept inquiries or requests submitted via fax or E-mail. Application form not required.
Initial approach: Letter
Copies of proposal: 1
Deadline(s): None
Board meeting date(s): Bimonthly beginning in Feb.
Final notification: 9 months
Officers and Directors:* Joseph G. Hurley,* Pres.; Edgar R. Jackson,* V.P.; Wendy G. Hoppe, Secy. and Exec. Dir.; Robert F. Erburu; Elizabeth Lowe; James A. Thomas; Robert E. Tranquada, M.D.; Franklin E. Ulf; Gayle Wilson.
Number of staff: 5 full-time professional; 3 full-time support.
EIN: 956085895
Selected grants: The following grants were reported in 2004.
$2,000,000 to Childrens Hospital Los Angeles, Los Angeles, CA. Toward construction of new patient tower, payable over 3 years.
$1,025,000 to Autry National Center of the American West, Los Angeles, CA. Toward construction of new complex of buildings and for general support.
$1,000,000 to Huntington Hospital, Pasadena, CA. Toward reconfiguration and expansion of emergency department, payable over 2 years.
$750,000 to Childrens Health Initiative of Greater Los Angeles, Los Angeles, CA. For healthcare coverage to uninsured children.
$500,000 to Art Center College of Design, Pasadena, CA. Toward capital campaign for new South Campus in downtown Pasadena, payable over 2 years.
$500,000 to Friends of the Observatory, Los Angeles, CA. Toward renovation and expansion of Griffith Observatory.
$425,000 to Performing Arts Center of Los Angeles County, Education Division, Los Angeles, CA. To bring quality arts education to schools throughout Southern California.
$250,000 to College of the Canyons Foundation, Valencia, CA. For University Center capital campaign, bringing comprehensive higher education programs to Santa Clarita Valley.
$250,000 to Greater Los Angeles Zoo Association, Los Angeles, CA. For Childrens Discovery Center.

$250,000 to Inner-City Arts, Los Angeles, CA. Toward capital campaign for campus expansion.

981

The Albert Parvin Foundation ✧

c/o Lewis, Joffe & Co.
10880 Wilshire Blvd., No. 520
Los Angeles, CA 90024 (310) 475-5676

Incorporated in 1960 in CA.
Donor: Albert B. Parvin†.
Foundation type: Independent foundation.
Financial data (yr. ended 12/31/05): Assets, $8,020,697 (M); expenditures, $483,961; qualifying distributions, $464,349; giving activities include $450,010 for 57 grants (high: $80,000; low: $150).
Purpose and activities: Giving primarily for higher education and human services.
Fields of interest: Arts; Higher education; Health care; Human services; Jewish agencies & temples; Aging.
Type of support: General/operating support; Fellowships.
Limitations: Giving primarily in CA. No grants to individuals.
Application information: Application form not required.
Initial approach: Letter
Deadline(s): None
Officers and Directors:* Phyllis Parvin, Pres.; Harvey G. Joffe,* C.F.O.; Stanley Parvin; Mary C. Rudin; Stephen Silbert.
EIN: 952158989
Selected grants: The following grants were reported in 2004.
$90,000 to University of California, Los Angeles, CA. For Kennamer Fund.
$51,000 to City of Hope, Los Angeles, CA.
$50,000 to University of Hawaii, Honolulu, HI.
$35,000 to One Voice, Los Angeles, CA.
$25,000 to Jewish Free Loan Association, Los Angeles, CA.
$15,000 to Hereditary Disease Foundation, Santa Monica, CA.
$11,250 to Los Angeles Chamber Orchestra Society, Los Angeles, CA.
$10,000 to Southern Poverty Law Center, Montgomery, AL.
$10,000 to Wellness Community-West Los Angeles, Santa Monica, CA.
$5,000 to Berkshire Theater Festival, Stockbridge, MA.

982

Pasadena Community Foundation

(formerly Pasadena Foundation)
260 S. Los Robles Ave., Ste. 119
Pasadena, CA 91101 (626) 796-2097
Contact: Jennifer Fleming DeVoll, Exec. Dir.
FAX: (626) 583-4738;
E-mail: pcfstaff@pasadenacf.org; Additional E-mail: jdevoll@pasadenacf.org; URL: http://www.pasadenacf.org

Established in 1953 in CA by resolution and declaration of trust; in 2003, reorganized as a nonprofit public benefit corporation.
Donors: Louis A. Webb†; Marion L. Webb†; Helen B. Lockett†; Dorothy I. Stewart†; Rebecca R. Anthony†; Lucille Crumb†; Cornelia Eaton†; Ralph Norrington†; Margaret Norrington†; Ella C. Price†; Orrin K. Earl†; Jean Hubbard†.
Foundation type: Community foundation.
Financial data (yr. ended 12/31/05): Assets, $24,135,289 (M); gifts received, $6,509,920; expenditures, $3,496,346; giving activities include $3,007,016 for 1,595 grants (high: $200,000; low: $10).
Purpose and activities: The foundation provides support for nonprofit organizations that provide direct services to people in the Pasadena area in the following four categories: Children, Youth, and Families; Community Development and the Environment; Education, Arts, and Humanities; and Health and People with Special Needs.
Fields of interest: Humanities; Arts; Education; Environment; Health care; Children/youth, services; Family services; Human services; Community development; Youth; Aging; Disabilities, people with.
Type of support: Capital campaigns; Building/renovation; Equipment.
Limitations: Giving limited to the Altadena, Pasadena, and Sierra Madre, CA, areas. No support for private foundations, or for educational institutions or sectarian organizations (except for social service programs sponsored by educational institutions or sectarian organizations). No grants to individuals (except for scholarships), or for continuing support, general or operating support, expenses incurred in performance of program services, or elections.
Publications: Application guidelines; Annual report; Financial statement; Informational brochure; Newsletter.
Application information: Visit foundation Web site for application forms and guidelines. Eligible organizations must be at least 2 years old. Application form required.
Initial approach: Submit grant application and attachments
Copies of proposal: 12
Deadline(s): Mar. 1
Board meeting date(s): Quarterly
Final notification: Late May or June
Officers and Advisory Board:* James D. Gamb,* Chair.; Jennifer Fleming DeVoll, Exec. Dir.; Ann Dobson Barrett; David P. Beringer; Robert E. Carlson; Dave Davis; R-Lene deLang; Raymond Ealy; Betty Chin Ho; G. Arnold Mulder, M.D.; Wendy Munger; Diane Scott.
Number of staff: 2 full-time professional; 2 part-time support.
EIN: 200253310

983

The Patron Saints Foundation

260 S. Los Robles Ave., Ste. 201
Pasadena, CA 91101
Contact: Kathleen T. Shannon, Exec. Dir.
E-mail: patronsaintsfdn@sbcglobal.net; Tel./FAX: (626) 564-0444; URL: http://www.patronsaintsfoundation.org

Established in 1986 in CA.
Donors: Rose Trust; St. Luke Medical Staff; Friends of St. Luke.
Foundation type: Independent foundation.
Financial data (yr. ended 6/30/05): Assets, $10,359,084 (M); expenditures, $571,106; qualifying distributions, $514,073; giving activities include $441,130 for 43 grants (high: $16,725; low: $500).
Purpose and activities: The foundation provides grants to public charities that improve the health of individuals residing in the West San Gabriel Valley through healthcare programs that are consistent with the moral and religious teachings of the Roman Catholic Church.
Fields of interest: Hospitals (general); Medical care, rehabilitation; Health care; Substance abuse, services; Mental health/crisis services; Health organizations, association; Medical research.
Type of support: Continuing support; Capital campaigns; Building/renovation; Equipment; Research.
Limitations: Giving limited to Alhambra, Arcadia, Duarte, El Monte, La Canada Flintridge, Monrovia, Monterey Park, Pasadena, Rosemead, San Gabriel, San Marino, Sierra Madre, South El Monte, South Pasadena, Temple City, and unincorporated areas of LA, known as Altadena and South San Gabriel, CA. No grants to individuals, or for endowment funds, political activities, travel, or surveys.
Publications: Application guidelines; Grants list; Informational brochure.
Application information: Application forms and application guidelines available on foundation Web site. Application form required.
Initial approach: 3-page proposal
Copies of proposal: 2
Deadline(s): 1st Fri. in Mar. and 1st Fri. in Oct.
Board meeting date(s): Mid-May and early Dec.
Final notification: May and mid-Dec.
Officers and Directors:* Sam Sogohomrian,* Pres.; Dorothy Shea, Pres.-Elect; Nathan Lewis, M.D.*, Secy.; Joseph Skeehan,* Treas.; Kathleen Shannon, Exec. Dir.; Gretchen Berger; Thomas M. Collins; J. Benjamin Earl; James W. Graunke; Josephine Buffalino Libaw, M.D.*; Dorothy McVann, M.D.; Sally Sims; Sharon Thralls; Vera Vignes, Ed.D.; Melinda Winston.
Number of staff: 1 part-time professional.
EIN: 953484257
Selected grants: The following grants were reported in 2004.
$20,000 to Childrens Hospital Los Angeles, Los Angeles, CA. For Multidisciplinary Diabetes Outreach program in San Gabriel Valley.
$18,900 to Pasadena Childrens Training Society, The Sycamores, Pasadena, CA. To conduct study to evaluate clinical usefulness of functional brain imaging in improving outcomes for psychiatrically disturbed boys in residential treatment with the use of single-photon-emission computer tomography (SPECT).
$10,000 to Center for Aging Resources, Pasadena, CA. For Clinical Mental Health Outreach to Older Adults Program.
$10,000 to Friends of Foster Children, Arcadia, CA. For basic medical needs not covered by insurance or Medi-Cal.
$10,000 to San Gabriel Unified School District, San Gabriel, CA. For diabetes screening and education program.
$10,000 to Scripps Home, Altadena, CA. For audiology services.
$7,500 to Wellness Community-Foothills, Pasadena, CA. For weekly support groups for cancer patients.
$5,000 to Hospice of Pasadena, Pasadena, CA. For Volunteer Recruitment program.
$5,000 to Rebuilding Together Pasadena, Pasadena, CA. For supplies and materials for home modifications and repairs at no cost to seniors, the disabled and low-income households.

$2,500 to Boys and Girls Club of West San Gabriel Valley, Monterey Park, CA. For SMART (Skills Mastery And Resistance Training) Moves, program designed to help youth develop skills to resist alcohol, tobacco and other drugs.

984

The Edwin W. Pauley Foundation ✧

5670 Wilshire Blvd., Ste. 1450
Los Angeles, CA 90036 (323) 954-3131
Contact: Stephen M. Pauley, Pres.

Established in 1993 in CA as successor to Edwin W. Pauley Foundation.
Donor: Barbara Pauley Pagen†.
Foundation type: Independent foundation.
Financial data (yr. ended 12/31/03): Assets, $6,255,494 (M); expenditures, $677,043; qualifying distributions, $592,729; giving activities include $568,375 for 21 grants (high: $75,000; low: $800).
Purpose and activities: Grants primarily for higher education (in support of marine biology).
Fields of interest: Higher education; Youth development.
Type of support: General/operating support; Continuing support; Annual campaigns; Building/renovation.
Limitations: Giving primarily in CA. No grants to individuals.
Application information: Application form required.
  Initial approach: Proposal
  Copies of proposal: 1
  Deadline(s): None
Officers and Directors:* Stephen M. Pauley,* Pres.; Kevin Hillyer,* V.P.; Tanya Hendrix, Secy.; Matthew V. Pauley, Treas.
EIN: 954332470
Selected grants: The following grants were reported in 2003.
$75,000 to University of Hawaii, Honolulu, HI. For summer Marine Biology program.
$50,000 to Center for a Sustainable Future, Honolulu, HI.
$5,000 to Childrens Bureau Foundation, Los Angeles, CA.
$5,000 to United Cerebral Palsy-Spastic Childrens Foundation of Los Angeles and Ventura Counties, Woodland Hills, CA.
$3,000 to Westridge School for Girls, Pasadena, CA.
$2,500 to Aquarium of the Pacific, Long Beach, CA.
$2,500 to Natural Resources Defense Council, New York, NY.
$1,500 to Idaho Conservation League, Boise, ID.
$1,000 to Community School, Sun Valley, ID.
$1,000 to Pepperdine University, Malibu, CA. For scholarships.

985

Karen & Christopher Payne Family Foundation, Inc. ✧

444 High St., Ste. 300
Palo Alto, CA 94301 (650) 325-3343
Contact: Karen Payne, V.P.; Christopher K. Payne, Pres.

Established in 1996 in CA.
Donors: Christopher K. Payne; Karen Payne.
Foundation type: Independent foundation.
Financial data (yr. ended 12/31/04): Assets, $13,384,101 (M); gifts received, $1,111,734;

expenditures, $781,007; qualifying distributions, $670,720; giving activities include $600,400 for 63 grants (high: $60,000; low: $500).
Purpose and activities: Giving for higher education and health associations.
Fields of interest: Arts; Higher education; Health organizations, association; Human services.
Limitations: Giving on a national basis. No grants to individuals.
Application information:
  Initial approach: Letter
  Deadline(s): None
Officers: Christopher K. Payne, Pres.; Karen Payne, V.P.; Gregory T. Payne, Secy.
Directors: Ann Clark; Steve Hope.
EIN: 770446184
Selected grants: The following grants were reported in 2004.
$60,000 to Foothill College, Krause Center for Innovation, Los Altos Hills, CA. For general support.
$50,000 to University of California, New Teacher Center, Santa Cruz, CA. For general support.
$45,000 to Mountain View High School, Mountain View, CA. For general support.
$41,500 to DonorsChoose, New York, NY. For general support.
$30,000 to Music for Minors, Los Altos, CA. For general support.
$20,000 to East Carolina University, Greenville, NC. For general support.
$15,000 to Catholic Charities of San Jose, San Jose, CA. For general support.
$10,000 to Theaterworks, Palo Alto, CA. For general support.
$10,000 to University of Virginia, Charlottesville, VA. For general support.
$10,000 to Virginia Engineering Foundation, Charlottesville, VA. For general support.

986

Peery Foundation ✧

2560 Mission College Blvd., Ste. 101
Santa Clara, CA 95054
Contact: Richard T. Peery, Pres.

Established in 1977.
Donor: Richard T. Peery.
Foundation type: Independent foundation.
Financial data (yr. ended 9/30/05): Assets, $46,790,754 (M); expenditures, $1,008,342; qualifying distributions, $745,948; giving activities include $741,646 for 55 grants (high: $75,000; low: $300; average: $5,000–$40,000).
Purpose and activities: Grants largely for Mormon religious organizations; some support for youth, education, and civic organizations.
Fields of interest: Education; Youth development, services; Children/youth, services; Foundations (community); Government/public administration; Christian agencies & churches; Mormon agencies & churches.
Type of support: Continuing support; Program development.
Limitations: Applications not accepted. Giving primarily in CA and HI. No grants to individuals.
Application information: Contributes only to pre-selected organizations.
Officers and Directors:* Richard T. Peery, Pres.; Jennifer Peery,* Exec. V.P.; David Peery,* V.P.; Dennis T. Peery, Secy.; Jason Peery, Treas.; Mildred D. Peery.
EIN: 942460894

Selected grants: The following grants were reported in 2005.
$95,000 to ProLiteracy Worldwide, Syracuse, NY. 2 grants: $75,000, $20,000.
$60,000 to California Family Foundation, Palo Alto, CA. 2 grants: $30,000 each
$50,000 to Emergency Housing Consortium, Hollister, CA.
$50,000 to Sister Community Alliances, Salt Lake City, UT.
$40,000 to Utah Valley State College, Orem, UT.
$25,000 to Family and Children Services, Palo Alto, CA.
$25,000 to Trust for Hidden Villa, Los Altos Hills, CA.
$10,000 to YMCA of the Mid-Peninsula, Palo Alto, CA.

987

Pell Family Foundation ✧

100 Smith Ranch Rd., Ste. 325
San Rafael, CA 94903
Contact: Eda Pell, Pres.

Established in 1991.
Donors: Joseph Pell; Eda Pell.
Foundation type: Independent foundation.
Financial data (yr. ended 9/30/04): Assets, $7,969,840 (M); gifts received, $1,001,965; expenditures, $432,127; qualifying distributions, $406,335; giving activities include $406,335 for 51 grants (high: $75,000; low: $25).
Purpose and activities: Funding primarily for education, Jewish agencies, family and community services, and health care.
Fields of interest: Arts; Higher education; Education; Hospitals (general); Human services; Jewish federated giving programs; Jewish agencies & temples.
Type of support: General/operating support.
Limitations: Giving primarily in CA.
Application information:
  Initial approach: Letter on official letterhead
  Deadline(s): None
Officers: Eda Pell, Pres.; Joseph Pell, V.P.
EIN: 680262734

988

Paul & Nancy Pelosi Charitable Foundation ✧ ☆

235 Montgomery St., Ste. 610
San Francisco, CA 94104

Established in 1991 in CA.
Donors: Nancy Pelosi; Paul F. Pelosi.
Foundation type: Independent foundation.
Financial data (yr. ended 12/31/05): Assets, $778,625 (M); expenditures, $318,315; qualifying distributions, $316,550; giving activities include $316,550 for grants.
Fields of interest: Museums (art); Performing arts, opera; Historic preservation/historical societies; Higher education; Higher education, university; Libraries/library science; Education; Health organizations.
Limitations: Applications not accepted. Giving primarily in CA. No grants to individuals.
Application information: Contributes only to pre-selected organizations.
Trustees: Nancy Pelosi; Paul F. Pelosi.
EIN: 943150212

989
Peninsula Community Foundation ▼ ✧
1700 S. El Camino Real, Ste. 300
San Mateo, CA 94402-3049 (650) 358-9369
Contact: For grants: Ellen Clear, V.P., Community
Progs.

Established as a trust in 1964 in CA; incorporated
in 1981; merged with Community Foundation Silicon
Valley in 2006.
Foundation type: Community foundation.
Financial data (yr. ended 12/31/05): Assets,
$614,336,446 (M); gifts received, $63,219,720;
expenditures, $101,727,828; giving activities
include $92,331,777 for 5,409 grants (high:
$9,901,400; low: $50).
Purpose and activities: The foundation supports
local cultural, educational, social service, and
health programs. Primary areas of interest include
homelessness and housing, children and youth,
adult services, social services, and education,
including programs for minorities, the
disadvantaged, and early childhood education; other
interests include the environment, arts and culture,
senior citizens and the needs of the aging, the
disabled, civic concerns, and recreation; provides
counseling services for local fund seekers. Giving
includes grants to individuals as student aid,
emergency assistance, and grants to local artists.
Fields of interest: Arts, services; Arts, artist's
services; Arts; Education, early childhood education;
Child development, education; Education, services;
Education; Environment, natural resources;
Environmental education; Environment; Health care;
Substance abuse, services; Health organizations,
association; Housing/shelter, development;
Disasters, Hurricane Katrina; Recreation; Children/
youth, services; Child development, services; Family
services; Family services, domestic violence; Aging,
centers/services; Homeless, human services;
Human services; Community development,
neighborhood development; Community
development; Philanthropy/voluntarism, single
organization support; Philanthropy/voluntarism,
fund raising/fund distribution; Government/public
administration; Infants/toddlers; Children; Aging;
Disabilities, people with; Minorities; Economically
disadvantaged; Homeless.
Type of support: Continuing support; Emergency
funds; Program development; Conferences/
seminars; Seed money; Curriculum development;
Internship funds; Scholarship funds; Technical
assistance; Consulting services; Program-related
investments/loans; Employee matching gifts;
Scholarships—to individuals; Matching/challenge
support.
Limitations: Giving limited to San Mateo and
northern Santa Clara Counties, CA.
Publications: Application guidelines; Annual report;
Financial statement; Grants list; Informational
brochure; Newsletter.
Application information: The foundation has
merged with Community Foundation Silicon Valley.
Visit www.siliconvalleycf.org for updated application
information and guidelines.
Officers and Directors:* Patricia Bresee,* Chair.;
Vera Bennett, C.F.O.; Marilyn Merz, V.P. and C.O.O.;
Ellen Clear, V.P., Community Progs.; Ash McNeely,
V.P., Philanthropic Svcs.; Kara Coyle, Cont.; Steven
D. Anderson; Gloria Brown; John H. Clinton, Jr.;
Caretha Coleman; Susan Ford Dorsey; Bernadine
Chuck Fong, Ph.D.; Nylda Gemple; Umang Gupta;
Albert J. Horn; Charles "Chip" Huggins; Susan M.
Hyatt; Teri L. Jackson; E. Richard Jones; Betsy

Matteson; Linda R. Meier; Mario Panoringan;
Jennifer M. Raiser; Richard Wilkolaski; Jane H.
Williams.
Number of staff: 37 full-time professional; 3
part-time professional; 18 full-time support; 4
part-time support.
EIN: 942746687

990
Penney Family Fund ✧
c/o Common Counsel Foundation
1221 Preservation Park Way, Ste. 101
Oakland, CA 94612 (510) 834-2995
Contact: Sue Hutchinson
E-mail: ccounsel@igc.org; URL: http://
www.commoncounsel.org/pages/
foundation.html#penney

Established in 1998 in CA.
Foundation type: Independent foundation.
Financial data (yr. ended 12/31/05): Assets,
$9,108,458 (M); expenditures, $810,569;
qualifying distributions, $767,856; giving activities
include $687,500 for 36 grants (high: $50,000;
low: $5,000).
Purpose and activities: Giving primarily for public
affairs centers and for social services.
Fields of interest: Education; Human services;
Children, services; Public affairs.
Type of support: General/operating support;
Program development.
Limitations: Applications not accepted. Giving
primarily in CA, OR, and WA.
Publications: Grants list.
Application information: Contributes only to
pre-selected organizations. Unsolicited requests for
funds not accepted.
Officers: Jeff Malachowsky, Pres.; Alissa
Keny-Guyer, Secy.; Luisa Adrianzen Guyer, Treas.
Trustees: Leigh Guyer; Tom Huntington.
EIN: 943314431

991
The Ann Peppers Foundation
625 S. Fair Oaks Ave., Ste. 360
South Pasadena, CA 91030
Contact: Linda J. Blinkenberg, Asst. Secy.

Established in 1959 in CA.
Donor: Ann Peppers†.
Foundation type: Independent foundation.
Financial data (yr. ended 12/31/05): Assets,
$18,012,797 (M); expenditures, $1,056,004;
qualifying distributions, $970,251; giving activities
include $899,000 for 58 grants (high: $500,000;
low: $1,500).
Purpose and activities: Emphasis on small private
colleges and community organizations with limited
resources for fundraising; support also for activities
that benefit young people and enhance their moral,
educational and social well-being; support also for
activities for senior citizens.
Fields of interest: Arts; Education; Health care;
Human services.
Type of support: General/operating support;
Continuing support; Endowments; Program
development; Scholarship funds.
Limitations: Applications not accepted. Giving
limited to the metropolitan Los Angeles area and
southern CA. No support for government-financed
projects. No grants to individuals.

Application information: Grantseekers may not
re-apply for 15 months, except for scholarships.
Board meeting date(s): Quarterly
Officers and Directors:* Howard O. Wilson,* Pres.;
Philip V. Swan, V.P. and Treas.; H. Ross
MacMichael,* Secy.
EIN: 952114455
Selected grants: The following grants were reported
in 2004.
$50,000 to Braille Institute of America, Los
Angeles, CA. Towards construction of new Braille
Institute in Santa Barbara.
$35,000 to Pepperdine University, Malibu, CA. For
scholarship support.
$35,000 to University of Redlands, Redlands, CA.
For scholarships.
$25,000 to South Pasadena Unified School District,
South Pasadena, CA. For track and field
renovation.
$15,000 to Pasadena Conservatory of Music,
Pasadena, CA. For music education outreach
program.
$10,000 to Art Center College of Design, Pasadena,
CA. For scholarship.
$10,000 to Azusa Pacific University, Azusa, CA. For
Ann Peppers Scholarship Fund.
$10,000 to Boys Republic, Chino Hills, CA. For
aftercare program services.
$10,000 to Claremont Graduate University,
Claremont, CA. For fellowship support for Arts
and Humanities students.
$10,000 to Claremont University Consortium,
Claremont, CA. To equip Treatment Room of the
new Health and Wellness Center.

992
Joseph & Evelyn Pertusati Charitable
Trust ✧
c/o Bank of America, N.A.
P.O. Box 513189, GMF
Los Angeles, CA 90051-1189

Established in 1999 in CA.
Donor: Joseph Pertusati†.
Foundation type: Independent foundation.
Financial data (yr. ended 6/30/05): Assets,
$13,884,866 (M); expenditures, $809,362;
qualifying distributions, $596,539; giving activities
include $560,600 for 14 grants (high: $44,848;
low: $39,242).
Fields of interest: Hospitals (general); Youth
development, adult & child programs; Human
services; Salvation Army.
Limitations: Applications not accepted. Giving
primarily in CA. No grants to individuals.
Application information: Contributes only to
pre-selected organizations.
Trustee: Bank of America, N.A.
EIN: 957088381
Selected grants: The following grants were reported
in 2003.
$42,560 to Childrens Hospital Los Angeles, Los
Angeles, CA. For general support.
$42,560 to Villa Scalabrini Retirement Center, Sun
Valley, CA. For general support.
$37,240 to Braille Institute of America, Los
Angeles, CA. For general support.
$37,240 to Hospitaller Foundation of California, Los
Angeles, CA. For general support.
$37,240 to Huntington Medical Research
Institutes, Pasadena, CA. For general support.
$37,240 to Midnight Mission, Los Angeles, CA. For
general support.

$37,240 to Orthopaedic Hospital, Los Angeles, CA.
For general support.
$37,240 to Providence Saint Joseph Foundation,
Burbank, CA. For general support.
$37,240 to Salvation Army, Southern California
Division, Los Angeles, CA. For general support.
$37,240 to Valley Presbyterian Hospital, Van Nuys,
CA. For general support.

993
Leon S. Peters Foundation, Inc. ◇
4170 S. Fowler Ave.
Fresno, CA 93725-9326
Contact: Alice A. Peters, Pres.

Established in 1959 in CA.
Donor: Leon S. Peters†.
Foundation type: Independent foundation.
Financial data (yr. ended 11/30/04): Assets,
$16,698,754 (M); expenditures, $476,031;
qualifying distributions, $448,599; giving activities
include $443,000 for 52 grants (high: $85,000;
low: $1,000).
Fields of interest: Higher education; Zoos/
zoological societies; Health care, burn centers;
Health care; Human services.
Type of support: General/operating support;
Building/renovation; Scholarship funds.
Limitations: Giving primarily in Fresno, CA. No
grants to individuals.
Application information:
Initial approach: Letter
Deadline(s): None
Board meeting date(s): Feb., May, Aug., and Nov.
Officers: Alice A. Peters, Pres.; Pete P. Peters, V.P.
and Secy.
Directors: Craig Apregan; Janice Chitjian; Darrell
Peters; Kenneth Peters; Ron Peters.
EIN: 946064669

994
Margie & Robert E. Petersen Foundation ◇
6420 Wilshire Blvd., 20th Fl.
Los Angeles, CA 90048-5515 (310) 640-1345
Contact: Alexandria C. Phillips, Treas.

Established in 1997 in CA.
Donors: Margaret M. Petersen; Robert E. Petersen;
Robert E. and Margaret M. Petersen Living Trust.
Foundation type: Independent foundation.
Financial data (yr. ended 12/31/04): Assets,
$47,414,471 (M); gifts received, $495,000;
expenditures, $973,200; qualifying distributions,
$456,145; giving activities include $456,145 for 30
grants (high: $332,360; low: $100).
Fields of interest: Museums (specialized); Animals/
wildlife, preservation/protection; Medical research,
institute; Cancer research; Human services;
Community development; Christian agencies &
churches.
Limitations: Giving primarily in CA. No grants to
individuals.
Application information:
Initial approach: Letter
Deadline(s): None
Officers: Robert E. Petersen, Pres.; Theodore
Calleton, Secy.; Alexandria C. Phillips, Treas.
Director: Margaret M. Petersen.
EIN: 954608757

Selected grants: The following grants were reported
in 2004.
$332,360 to Petersen Automotive Museum, Los
Angeles, CA.
$10,000 to Childrens Hospital Los Angeles, Los
Angeles, CA.
$10,000 to Devil Pups, Los Angeles, CA.
$8,600 to Thalians, The, Los Angeles, CA.
$7,000 to Los Angeles Police Historical Society, Los
Angeles, CA.
$6,000 to Los Angeles Orphanage Guild, Los
Angeles, CA.
$6,000 to Music Center of Los Angeles County, Los
Angeles, CA.
$5,100 to Skid Row Charity Fund, Los Angeles, CA.
$5,000 to Jeffrey Foundation, Los Angeles, CA.
$5,000 to Saint Johns Health Center Foundation,
Santa Monica, CA.

995
The Jeffrey and Karen Peterson Family Foundation ◇
c/o F.T. Andrews and Co.
200 Pringle Ave., Ste. 555
Walnut Creek, CA 94596

Established in 2003 in CA.
Donor: Jeffrey W. Peterson.
Foundation type: Independent foundation.
Financial data (yr. ended 12/31/05): Assets,
$1,758,551 (M); gifts received, $1,004,730;
expenditures, $432,532; qualifying distributions,
$430,370; giving activities include $425,000 for 5
grants (high: $250,000; low: $10,000).
Fields of interest: Performing arts, ballet; Higher
education; Medical research, association; Medical
research, formal/general education; Diabetes
research.
Limitations: Applications not accepted. Giving
primarily in San Francisco, CA. No grants to
individuals.
Application information: Contributes only to
pre-selected organizations.
Officer: Allison Gray, Secy.
Directors: Melinda Ellis Evers; Jeffrey Peterson.
EIN: 721550569

996
The Patricia Price Peterson Foundation ◇
17 Aqua View Dr.
Watsonville, CA 95076-1625
Contact: Stephen W. Bennett, Pres.
E-mail: neyastv@aol.com

Established about 1964.
Donor: Rudolph A. Peterson†.
Foundation type: Independent foundation.
Financial data (yr. ended 12/31/05): Assets,
$10,445,288 (M); expenditures, $337,325;
qualifying distributions, $325,046; giving activities
include $325,046 for grants.
Purpose and activities: Giving primarily for
education and for environmental programs.
Fields of interest: Teacher school/education;
Education; Environment, natural resources;
Agriculture; Physically disabled.
International interests: Central America.
Type of support: General/operating support;
Management development/capacity building;
Equipment; Land acquisition; Emergency funds;

Program development; Professorships; Seed
money; Scholarship funds.
Limitations: Giving in the San Francisco Bay Area,
CA, as well as Central America.
Application information: Application form not
required.
Initial approach: Letter
Copies of proposal: 1
Deadline(s): None
Board meeting date(s): Mid-year
Officers and Directors:* S.W. Bennett,* Pres.; K.S.
Smeby,* Secy.-Treas.; M.K. Bennett; E.P. Peterson;
R. Price Peterson.
EIN: 946109098
Selected grants: The following grants were reported
in 2004.
$60,000 to California Academy of Sciences, San
Francisco, CA. 2 grants: $20,000, $40,000
$55,000 to Lincoln Child Center, Oakland, CA.
$42,350 to Zamorano, DC. 3 grants: $5,350,
$13,000, $24,000
$25,000 to U.S. Foundation of the University of the
Valley of Guatemala, Elmira, NY.
$4,000 to Saint Cornelius School, Richmond, CA.

997
Pfaffinger Foundation ▼
316 W. Second St., Ste. PH-C
Los Angeles, CA 90012 (213) 680-7460
Contact: Mary Tower, Pres.

Incorporated in 1936 in CA.
Donor: Frank X. Pfaffinger†.
Foundation type: Independent foundation.
Financial data (yr. ended 12/31/05): Assets,
$92,300,626 (M); expenditures, $5,183,676;
qualifying distributions, $4,143,468; giving
activities include $1,645,169 for 67 grants (high:
$599,141; low: $1,750; average: $10,000–
$30,000), and $1,876,164 for grants to individuals.
Purpose and activities: Giving to assist former
employees and retirees of the former Times Mirror
Co.; employees and retirees of the Los Angeles
Times; and working poor families in downtown Los
Angeles, CA on the recommendation of partner
agencies. Limited assistance to social service
agencies in Los Angeles and Orange counties in
some years.
Fields of interest: Human services; Economically
disadvantaged.
Type of support: General/operating support.
Limitations: Giving limited to Los Angeles and
Orange counties, CA, for charitable institutions. No
grants to individuals (except company employees);
no scholarships.
Application information: Application form required
for grants to individuals. Application form required.
Initial approach: Letter
Copies of proposal: 1
Deadline(s): July 15 and Oct. 1
Board meeting date(s): May, Sept., and Dec.
Final notification: Sept., and Dec.
Officers and Directors:* Steve Meier,* Chair. and
C.E.O.; Mary Tower, Pres.; William A. Niese,* Secy.;
William R. Isinger,* C.F.O. and Treas.
Number of staff: 6 full-time professional; 2 part-time
professional.
EIN: 951661675
Selected grants: The following grants were reported
in 2004.
$65,000 to Los Angeles Times Family Fund, Los
Angeles, CA. For Holiday Campaign.

$50,000 to Los Angeles Times Summer Camp Fund, Los Angeles, CA.

$30,000 to Consumer Credit Counselors of Los Angeles, Los Angeles, CA.

$25,000 to American Red Cross, CA.

$25,000 to L.A. Family Housing Corporation, North Hollywood, CA.

$20,000 to Norwood Healthy Start, Los Angeles, CA.

$15,000 to Los Angeles Free Clinic, Los Angeles, CA.

$15,000 to Proyecto Pastoral, Los Angeles, CA.

$12,500 to Eisner Pediatric and Family Medical Center, Los Angeles, CA.

$10,000 to Womens Care Cottage, Los Angeles, CA.

998
George T. Pfleger Foundation ◇
c/o Kieckhafer Schiffer & Co, LLP
1920 Main St., Rm. 250
Irvine, CA   92614

Established in 1968 in CA.
Donors: George T. Pfleger; U.S. Motors Foundation.
Foundation type: Independent foundation.
Financial data (yr. ended 12/31/05): Assets, $21,005,753 (M); expenditures, $3,397,144; qualifying distributions, $3,172,623; giving activities include $2,691,800 for 17 grants (high: $1,790,000; low: $2,500).
Purpose and activities: Primarily local giving, with emphasis on the environment, health care, and animal welfare.
Fields of interest: Environment, natural resources; Animal welfare; Hospitals (general); Human services.
Limitations: Applications not accepted. Giving primarily in CA. No grants to individuals.
Application information: Contributes only to pre-selected organizations.
Officers and Trustees:* Thomas G. Pfleger,* Pres.; Victoria L. Cascio, Secy.-Treas.; John P. King, Jr.; Layne Marceau; Shelly Marceau; Sandra B. Pfleger.
EIN: 952561117

999
The Harriet E. Pfleger Foundation ◇
c/o Kieckhafer Schiffer & Co., LLP
1920 Main St., Ste. 250
Irvine, CA   92614

Established in 1999 in CA.
Foundation type: Independent foundation.
Financial data (yr. ended 3/31/05): Assets, $20,939,631 (M); expenditures, $534,071; qualifying distributions, $1,248,009; giving activities include $436,586 for 14 grants (high: $100,000; low: $586).
Purpose and activities: Giving primarily for equestrianism; funding also for human services.
Fields of interest: Ear & throat diseases; Athletics/ sports, equestrianism; Human services.
Limitations: Applications not accepted. Giving primarily in CA and CO; funding also in NJ. No grants to individuals.
Application information: Contributes only to pre-selected organizations.
Officers and Trustees:* Linda Pfleger Edwards,* Pres.; W. Richard Mills, Secy.-Treas.; Marc Edwards.
EIN: 330817673

Selected grants: The following grants were reported in 2004.

$461,061 to Helen Woodward Animal Center, Rancho Santa Fe, CA. For therapeutic riding program.

$250,000 to Little Star, Aspen, CO. For Rancho Milagro Family Center.

$200,000 to United States Equestrian Team, Gladstone, NJ. For developing rider training program.

$200,000 to University of California, Center for Equine Health, Davis, CA. For general support.

$50,000 to United States Navy Memorial Foundation, DC. For Maritime Youth Exchange Program and Top Gun Experience.

$30,000 to SCI Special Fund, Rancho Santa Margarita, CA.

$10,000 to Kids Korps USA, Solana Beach, CA. For general support.

$3,750 to Rancho Santa Fe Community Center, Rancho Santa Fe, CA. For building fund.

$3,000 to California Dressage Society, Carmel Valley, CA. For sponsorship of USET Intermediate Freestyle class.

1000
The PG&E Corporation Foundation ◇
Spear Tower, Tax Dept.
1 Market St., Ste. 400
San Francisco, CA   94105
Application address: 77 Beale St., Ste. B32, San Francisco, CA 94105

Established in 2000 in CA.
Donor: PG&E Gas Transmission, Texas Corp.
Foundation type: Company-sponsored foundation.
Financial data (yr. ended 12/31/04): Assets, $3,092,976 (M); expenditures, $760,035; qualifying distributions, $749,321; giving activities include $470,000 for 10 grants (high: $320,000; low: $5,000), and $279,321 for employee matching gifts.
Purpose and activities: The foundation supports food banks and organizations involved with education, the environment, and human services.
Fields of interest: Education; Environment; Food banks; Disasters, 9/11/01; Human services.
Type of support: Program development; Scholarship funds; Employee matching gifts.
Limitations: Giving primarily in CA and NY. No grants to individuals.
Application information:
 Initial approach: Proposal
 Deadline(s): None
Officers: Leslie H. Everett, C.E.O.; Linda Y.H. Cheng, Secy.; Peter A. Darbee, C.F.O.; Dan C. Quigley, Exec. Dir.
EIN: 943358729

1001
Phelps Family Foundation ◇ ☆
16720 Huerta Rd.
Encino, CA   91436

Established in 2005 in CA.
Donors: Michael E. Phelps; Patricia E. Phelps.
Foundation type: Independent foundation.
Financial data (yr. ended 3/31/06): Assets, $8,010,878 (M); expenditures, $440,913; qualifying distributions, $350,000; giving activities

include $350,000 for 2 grants (high: $325,000; low: $25,000).
Fields of interest: Higher education; Protestant agencies & churches.
Application information: Application form not required.
 Initial approach: Letter
 Deadline(s): None
Officers: Michael E. Phelps,* Pres.; Patricia E. Phelps, V.P. and Secy.; Randy Rich, Treas.
EIN: 201974643

1002
Wilson W. Phelps Foundation ◇
c/o Letwak & Bennett
P.O. Box 10127
Fullerton, CA   92838-9127

Established in 1997 in CA.
Foundation type: Independent foundation.
Financial data (yr. ended 12/31/05): Assets, $7,013,866 (M); gifts received, $5,000; expenditures, $348,077; qualifying distributions, $341,340; giving activities include $341,340 for 17 grants (high: $98,670; low: $1,000).
Fields of interest: Elementary/secondary education; Boys & girls clubs; YM/YWCAs & YM/ YWHAs.
Limitations: Applications not accepted. Giving primarily in Fullerton, CA. No grants to individuals.
Application information: Contributes only to pre-selected organizations.
Officers: John W. Phelps, Pres.; Louise Shamblen, V.P.; Carol B. Phelps, Secy.; James S. Phelps, Treas.
EIN: 330743687
Selected grants: The following grants were reported in 2003.

$114,824 to Fullerton School District Educational Foundation, Fullerton, CA. For computers.

$45,500 to Boys and Girls Clubs of Fullerton, Fullerton, CA. For general operating support.

$30,000 to Fullerton Public Library Foundation, Fullerton, CA.

$30,000 to Gary Center, La Habra, CA. For adolescence substance abuse treatment.

$18,720 to Womens Transitional Living Center, Orange, CA. For database, materials and salary for substance abuse supervisor.

$10,000 to Orange County Bar Foundation, Santa Ana, CA. For Stop Short of Addiction program.

$10,000 to YWCA of North Orange County, Fullerton, CA. For computerization.

$8,000 to California State University, Fullerton, CA. For scholarships.

$1,500 to YMCA, North Orange County, Fullerton, CA.

$1,000 to Recording for the Blind and Dyslexic, Santa Ana, CA. For general operating support.

1003
The Stephen Philibosian Foundation ◇
46-930 W. El Dorado Dr.
Indian Wells, CA   92210-8649
Contact: Joyce Stein, Chair.

Established in 1969 in PA.
Donor: Armenian Missionary Association of America.
Foundation type: Independent foundation.
Financial data (yr. ended 12/31/03): Assets, $11,030,986 (M); expenditures, $844,096;

qualifying distributions, $765,813; giving activities include $765,813 for grants (high: $100,000; low: $100).

Purpose and activities: Grants largely for missionary, educational, and social programs of the Armenian-American Church, including aid for Armenian schools in the Middle East; support also for child welfare.

Fields of interest: Secondary school/education; Higher education; Education; Children/youth, services; Christian agencies & churches.

International interests: Middle East.

Type of support: Continuing support; Annual campaigns; Endowments; Scholarship funds.

Limitations: Applications not accepted. Giving primarily in CA. No grants to individuals, or for operating budgets, seed money, emergency funds, deficit financing, building funds, matching gifts, research, special projects, publications, or conferences; no loans.

Application information: Contributes only to pre-selected organizations.

Board meeting date(s): Spring and fall

Officer and Trustees:* Joyce Stein,* Chair.; Louise Danelian; Stephanie Landes; Albert Momjian; George Phillips.

EIN: 237029751

1004
Picerne Family Foundation ✧ ☆

(formerly Ken and Tonya Picerne Foundation)
30950 Racho Viejo Rd., Ste. 200
San Juan Capistrano, CA 92675
Contact: Kenneth A. Picerne, C.E.O.

Established in 2001 in CA.

Donor: Kenneth A. Picerne.

Foundation type: Independent foundation.

Financial data (yr. ended 12/31/05): Assets, $949 (M); gifts received, $305,500; expenditures, $380,608; qualifying distributions, $356,025; giving activities include $356,025 for grants.

Fields of interest: Education; Youth development.

Limitations: Giving primarily in CA. No grants to individuals.

Application information:

Initial approach: Proposal

Deadline(s): None

Officers: Kenneth A. Picerne, C.E.O.; John Demorest, V.P.; Michael S. Whalen, Secy. and C.F.O.

EIN: 330933243

1005
Mary Pickford Foundation ✧

Ranch Adm. Bldg., 40730 Calle Bandido
Murrieta, CA 92562
Contact: Henry Stotsenberg, Pres.

Established in 1968.

Donor: Mary Pickford Rogers†.

Foundation type: Independent foundation.

Financial data (yr. ended 5/31/05): Assets, $15,224,265 (M); expenditures, $958,304; qualifying distributions, $826,612; giving activities include $725,500 for 77 grants (high: $60,000; low: $500).

Purpose and activities: Grants largely for scholarship funds at colleges and universities, and for well-established medical or community service organizations, including performing arts programs,

museums, and agencies serving the elderly and other disadvantaged groups.

Fields of interest: Media, film/video; Museums; Performing arts, theater; Arts; Higher education; Business school/education; Education; Hospitals (general); Health organizations, association; Human services; Aging, centers/services; Community development; Aging; Economically disadvantaged.

Type of support: General/operating support; Endowments; Scholarship funds.

Limitations: Giving primarily in CA, with emphasis on Los Angeles and Palm Springs. No support for drug rehabilitation programs. No grants to individuals, or for building funds, land acquisition, or medical research.

Application information: Application form not required.

Initial approach: Letter or telephone

Deadline(s): None

Officers and Directors:* Henry Stotsenberg,* Pres.; Gary E. Shoffner,* Secy.; Keith Lawrence, C.F.O.

EIN: 956093487

Selected grants: The following grants were reported in 2005.

$60,000 to Motion Picture and Television Fund, Woodland Hills, CA.

$40,000 to American Film Institute, Los Angeles, CA.

$40,000 to Pepperdine University, Malibu, CA.

$20,000 to Jewish Home for the Aged, San Francisco, CA.

$10,000 to John Tracy Clinic, Los Angeles, CA.

$3,000 to Palm Springs Air Museum, Palm Springs, CA.

$3,000 to Shelter from the Storm, Palm Desert, CA.

$2,500 to Palm Springs International Film Festival, Palm Springs, CA.

$2,350 to Screen Smart Set, Woodland Hills, CA.

$1,000 to Rancho Mirage Public Library, Rancho Mirage, CA.

1006
The Pimco Foundation ✧

840 Newport Center Dr., Ste. 300
Newport Beach, CA 92660 (949) 723-4483
Contact: Mark Porterfield, Secy.

Established in 2001 in CA.

Donors: Bill Benz; Wes Burns; Chris Dialynas; Mohamed El-Erian; Bill Gross; John Hague; Pasi Hamlainen; Brent Harris; Brent Holden; Margaret Isberg; John Loftus; Paul McCulley; Dean Meiling; Jim Muzzy; Bill Podlich; Bill Powers; Ernie Schmider; Lee Thomas; Bill Thompson; Ben Trosky.

Foundation type: Independent foundation.

Financial data (yr. ended 12/31/04): Assets, $13,353,344 (M); gifts received, $83,754; expenditures, $462,409; qualifying distributions, $447,062; giving activities include $439,726 for grants.

Fields of interest: Education; Youth development; Human services; Jewish federated giving programs.

Limitations: Giving primarily in CA and NY. No grants to individuals, political organizations, veterans and labor organizations, fraternal organizations, athletic or social clubs, or sectarian religious organizations.

Application information: Application form required.

Initial approach: Proposal

Deadline(s): Between July 15 and Sept. 15

Officers and Directors:* William H. Gross,* Chair.; William S. Thompson,* Pres.; Mark J. Porterfield,

Secy. and Exec. Dir.; William F. Podlich, Treas.; Wes Burns; Ernie Schmider.

EIN: 330891470

1007
Pitzer Family Foundation ✧

c/o MMA
1999 Harrison St., Ste. 1500
Oakland, CA 94612

Established in 1994 in CA.

Donors: Kenneth S. Pitzer; Jean M. Pitzer; Jean M. Pitzer Survivor's Trust.

Foundation type: Independent foundation.

Financial data (yr. ended 12/31/05): Assets, $12,567,425 (M); expenditures, $1,124,653; qualifying distributions, $1,100,000; giving activities include $1,100,000 for 2 grants (high: $1,000,000; low: $100,000).

Fields of interest: Higher education, college.

Limitations: Applications not accepted. Giving primarily in Berkeley, CA. No grants to individuals.

Application information: Contributes only to pre-selected organizations.

Trustees: Ann E. Pitzer; John S. Pitzer; Russell M. Pitzer.

EIN: 686099475

1008
The PMI Foundation ✧

3003 Oak Rd.
Walnut Creek, CA 94597 (800) 288-1970
Contact: Laura Kinney, Mgr.

Established in 2000 in CA.

Donor: PMI Mortgage Insurance Co.

Foundation type: Company-sponsored foundation.

Financial data (yr. ended 12/31/05): Assets, $495,923 (M); gifts received, $2,415,000; expenditures, $2,454,243; qualifying distributions, $2,454,244; giving activities include $2,193,436 for 95 grants (high: $650,985).

Purpose and activities: The foundation supports organizations involved with higher education, housing, human services, civil rights, community development, and Hispanics.

Fields of interest: Higher education; Housing/shelter, development; American Red Cross; Human services; Civil rights, advocacy; Economic development; Community development; Hispanics/Latinos.

Type of support: Scholarship funds; Program development; General/operating support.

Limitations: Giving on a national basis, with some emphasis on CA. No grants to individuals.

Application information: Application form not required.

Initial approach: Proposal

Deadline(s): None

Officers: Charles Broom, Pres.; David Katkov, V.P.; Victor J. Bacigalupi, Secy.; Diane Giampaoli, C.F.O.; Thomas H. Jeter, Treas.; Laura Kinney, Mgr.

EIN: 943309069

Selected grants: The following grants were reported in 2004.

$405,604 to Habitat for Humanity International, Americus, GA.

$200,000 to National Council of La Raza, DC.

$115,000 to Social Compact, Bethesda, MD.

$20,000 to Neighborhood Reinvestment Corporation, DC.

$5,000 to Downs Community Development Corporation, Oakland, CA.

$2,500 to Chinatown Community Development Center, San Francisco, CA.

$2,500 to Community Housing Partnership, San Francisco, CA.

$2,000 to Avenue Community Development Corporation, Houston, TX.

1009

Vasek and Anna Maria Polak Charitable Foundation ✧

P.O. Box 2932
Torrance, CA 90509-2932

Established in 1994 in CA.
Donors: Vasek Polak; Vasek Polak Enterprises, Inc.; Vasek Polak Revocable Trust.
Foundation type: Independent foundation.
Financial data (yr. ended 12/31/05): Assets, $18,390,717 (M); expenditures, $1,870,831; qualifying distributions, $1,694,692; giving activities include $1,520,449 for 6 grants (high: $600,000; low: $7,770).
Purpose and activities: Giving limited to medical institutions.
Fields of interest: Hospitals (general); Health care.
Limitations: Applications not accepted. Giving primarily in the South Bay Area and Los Angeles County, CA. No grants to individuals.
Application information: Contributes only to pre-selected organizations.
    Board meeting date(s): 4-6 times annually
Officers: Jeffrey M. Bucher, Pres.; Soterios J. Menzelos, V.P. and Secy.
EIN: 330611099
Selected grants: The following grants were reported in 2003.
$400,000 to Little Company of Mary Hospital, Torrance, CA. For general support.
$400,000 to Torrance Memorial Medical Center, Torrance, CA. For general support.
$300,000 to Childrens Clinic, Long Beach, CA. For general support.
$300,000 to Saint Johns Health Center, Santa Monica, CA. For general support.
$50,000 to South Bay Childrens Health Center Association, Redondo Beach, CA. For general support.
$12,463 to Fund for American Studies, DC. For American Institute on Political Systems program at Charles University in Prague, Czech Republic.

1010

Samuel Pollard Foundation ✧

55 S. Lake Ave., Ste. 630
Pasadena, CA 91101-4920
Contact: Rhea C. Yeung

Established in 2003 in CA.
Donor: Dainelo Foundation.
Foundation type: Independent foundation.
Financial data (yr. ended 12/31/03): Assets, $20,445 (M); gifts received, $593,200; expenditures, $572,755; qualifying distributions, $572,700; giving activities include $572,700 for 2 grants (high: $500,000; low: $72,700).
Fields of interest: Education.
Limitations: Applications not accepted. Giving primarily in Washington, DC.

Application information: Contributes only to pre-selected organizations.
Officers: Vincent Sun, C.E.O.; Yung Yeung, C.F.O.
EIN: 200003682

1011

The Lawrence and Sandra Post Family Foundation ✧ ☆

1160 Tower Rd.
Beverly Hills, CA 90210

Established in 1993 in CA.
Donors: Larsand Corp.; Lawrence Post; Sandra Post.
Foundation type: Independent foundation.
Financial data (yr. ended 12/31/05): Assets, $5,900,986 (M); gifts received, $89,812; expenditures, $369,062; qualifying distributions, $356,837; giving activities include $356,837 for 21 + grants (high: $201,000).
Fields of interest: Libraries/library science; Education; Crime/law enforcement, counterterrorism; Jewish federated giving programs.
Type of support: General/operating support.
Limitations: Applications not accepted. Giving primarily in CA. No grants to individuals.
Application information: Contributes only to pre-selected organizations.
Officers: Lawrence A. Post, Pres.; Sandra Post, Secy.
EIN: 954442473
Selected grants: The following grants were reported in 2005.
$30,000 to Milken Institute, Santa Monica, CA.
$25,000 to Hold on to Your Music, Los Angeles, CA.
$10,000 to Childrens Burn Foundation, Sherman Oaks, CA.
$10,000 to Wheels for Humanity, North Hollywood, CA.
$5,000 to Prostate Cancer Foundation, Santa Monica, CA.
$1,000 to Salvation Army, Redding, CA.

1012

Hughes and Sheila Potiker Family Foundation ✧

(formerly Potiker Family Foundation)
3366 N. Torrey Pines Ct., Ste. 210
La Jolla, CA 92037-1025
Contact: Hughes Potiker, Pres.; Sheila Potiker, V.P.

Established in 1992 in MI.
Donor: Members of the Potiker family.
Foundation type: Independent foundation.
Financial data (yr. ended 12/31/03): Assets, $10,509,199 (M); expenditures, $763,784; qualifying distributions, $713,842; giving activities include $661,150 for 27 grants (high: $400,000; low: $250).
Purpose and activities: Giving primarily for the arts, education, health organizations, human services, and Jewish organizations, including federated giving programs.
Fields of interest: Museums; Performing arts; Education; Health organizations; Human services; Jewish federated giving programs; Jewish agencies & temples.
Limitations: Giving primarily in San Diego and La Jolla, CA.
Application information: Application form not required.

Initial approach: Letter
Deadline(s): None
Officers: Sheila Potiker, V.P.; Lowell Potiker, Secy.; Jori Potiker, Treas.
EIN: 383066992
Selected grants: The following grants were reported in 2003.
$400,000 to Theater and Arts Foundation of San Diego County, La Jolla Playhouse, La Jolla, CA.
$50,000 to Childrens Hospital of Michigan, Detroit, MI.
$35,000 to Cleveland Clinic Foundation, Cleveland, OH.
$27,000 to San Diego Opera Association, San Diego, CA.
$25,000 to American Committee for the Weizmann Institute of Science, DC.
$25,000 to Anti-Defamation League of Bnai Brith, San Diego, CA.
$25,000 to San Diego Symphony Orchestra, San Diego, CA.
$10,000 to San Diego Jewish Academy, San Diego, CA.
$6,000 to Museum of Contemporary Art San Diego, La Jolla, CA.
$5,000 to San Diego Museum of Art, San Diego, CA.

1013

The Pottruck Family Foundation

(formerly The Pottruck Scott Family Foundation)
1016 Lincoln Blvd., Ste. 221
San Francisco, CA 94129   (415) 561-6741
Contact: Nancy Wiltsek, Exec. Dir.
FAX: (415) 561-6742;
E-mail: info@pottruckfoundation.org; URL: http://www.pottruckfoundation.org

Established in 1995 in CA.
Donors: David S. Pottruck; Emily Scott Pottruck.
Foundation type: Independent foundation.
Financial data (yr. ended 12/31/04): Assets, $12,494,141 (M); gifts received, $100; expenditures, $650,067; qualifying distributions, $596,007; giving activities include $480,065 for 38 grants (high: $28,500; low: $265).
Purpose and activities: The foundation focuses almost exclusively on foster care, with a particular emphasis on supporting efforts that will improve the ability of foster youth to thrive and to successfully transition from care to adulthood.
Type of support: General/operating support; Continuing support; Program development.
Limitations: Giving primarily in San Francisco, CA. No support for religious or political organizations. No grants to individuals, or for deficit financing, or for benefits.
Publications: Application guidelines; Grants list.
Application information: Proposal submission form available on foundation Web site. Initial letters and proposals should be sent via surface mail, and not by E-mail. Application form required.
    Initial approach: Letter of inquiry or telephone
    Copies of proposal: 1
    Deadline(s): None
    Board meeting date(s): Jun. and Dec.
Officers and Directors:* Emily Scott Pottruck, Pres.; David S. Pottruck, V.P.; Karen Cashen, Secy.; Henry Pilger,* Treas.; Nancy Wiltsek, Exec. Dir.; Terry Pearce.
Number of staff: 1 full-time professional.
EIN: 943193096
Selected grants: The following grants were reported in 2005.

$30,000 to First Place Fund for Youth, Oakland, CA. For supportive housing program.

$30,000 to Larkin Street Youth Services, San Francisco, CA. For Pathways to Independence.

$20,000 to Court Appointed Special Advocates (CASA) Program, San Francisco, San Francisco, CA. For general operating support.

$15,000 to A Home Within, San Francisco, CA. For children's psychotherapy program.

$15,000 to At the Crossroads, San Francisco, CA. For general operating support.

$15,000 to Gateway High School, San Francisco, CA. For College Counseling Program.

$15,000 to GirlSource, San Francisco, CA. For general operating support.

$10,000 to Leadership High School, San Francisco, CA. For advisory program.

$10,000 to Marin Advocates for Children, San Rafael, CA. For Child Abuse Prevention Council.

$5,000 to Summer Search Napa-Sonoma, Petaluma, CA. For general operating support.

1014
The Robert R. and Helga Pralle Family Foundation ◇ ☆
1249A E. Imperial Hwy.
Placentia, CA   92870   (714) 996-9960
Application address: Robert R. Case, 1249a E. Imperial Highway, Placentia, Ca92870, Tel: 714-996-9960

Established in 2002 in CA.
Donors: Robert R. Pralle†; Robert R. and Helga Pralle Family Foundation.
Foundation type: Independent foundation.
Financial data (yr. ended 6/30/05): Assets, $7,603,206 (M); expenditures, $397,822; qualifying distributions, $320,000; giving activities include $320,000 for 15 grants (high: $125,125; low: $2,125).
Fields of interest: Higher education; Animal welfare; Boys & girls clubs; Youth development.
Application information:
   Deadline(s): None
Officers: Helga Pralle, Pres.; Phil Case, Secy.; Kim Pralle Krotta, Treas.; Robert R. Case, Exec. Dir.
EIN: 710888527

1015
The Preuss Family Foundation, Inc. ◇
2223 Avenida De La Playa, Ste. 220
La Jolla, CA   92037

Established in 1985 in CA and DE.
Donors: Peter G. Preuss; Peggy Preuss.
Foundation type: Independent foundation.
Financial data (yr. ended 12/31/05): Assets, $2,180,383 (M); expenditures, $494,615; qualifying distributions, $475,919; giving activities include $474,854 for 2 grants (high: $465,000; low: $9,854).
Purpose and activities: Giving for the opera and to support scientific research, especially related to brain tumors.
Fields of interest: Performing arts, opera; Education; Diabetes; Cancer research; Brain research; YM/YWCAs & YM/YWHAs; Mathematics.
International interests: Germany.
Type of support: General/operating support; Scholarship funds; Research.

Limitations: Applications not accepted. Giving primarily in La Jolla, CA. No grants to individuals.
Application information: Contributes only to pre-selected organizations.
Officers: Peter G. Preuss, Pres.; Peter J. Preuss, V.P.; Peggy Preuss, Secy.
Director: Stephen A. Hurwitz.
EIN: 330229180
Selected grants: The following grants were reported in 2003.
$530,000 to University of California at San Diego Foundation, La Jolla, CA.
$25,000 to San Diego Opera Association, San Diego, CA. For general support.
$10,000 to San Diego Symphony Orchestra, San Diego, CA. For general support.
$10,000 to Taking Control of Your Diabetes, Del Mar, CA.
$9,627 to San Francisco Opera Association, San Francisco, CA. For general support.
$5,000 to University of California at San Diego, La Jolla, CA. For research.
$250 to Oceanographic Teaching Stations, Manhattan Beach, CA.

1016
The Price Family Charitable Fund ◇ ☆
(formerly The Sol & Helen Price Foundation)
7979 Ivanhoe Ave., Ste. 520
La Jolla, CA   92037

Established in 1983 in CA.
Donor: Sol Price.
Foundation type: Independent foundation.
Financial data (yr. ended 12/31/05): Assets, $87,834,011 (M); gifts received, $2,000; expenditures, $2,289,624; qualifying distributions, $1,346,668; giving activities include $751,500 for 1 grant, and $48,607 for grants to individuals.
Purpose and activities: Giving primarily for education and philanthropy.
Fields of interest: Elementary/secondary education; Urban/community development; Economically disadvantaged.
Type of support: Annual campaigns; Fellowships; Scholarship funds; Program evaluation.
Limitations: Applications not accepted. Giving primarily in San Diego, CA.
Application information: Unsolicited requests for funds not accepted.
Officers and Directors:* Sol Price,* Chair.; Robert Price,* Pres.; Joseph R. Satz,* Secy.; Kathy Hillan, Treas.; Murray Galinson; William Gorham; Jack McGrory; Allison Price.
Number of staff: 3 full-time professional; 1 full-time support.
EIN: 953842468
Selected grants: The following grants were reported in 2004.
$15,547,639 to San Diego Foundation, San Diego, CA.
$4,000 to San Diego Mesa College, San Diego, CA.
$500 to Union of Pan Asian Communities, San Diego, CA.

1017
Price Family Foundation ◇
2425 Olympic Blvd., Ste. 650E
Santa Monica, CA   90404
Contact: Christy Stanich, Dir.

Established in 1986 in CA.
Donor: David G. Price.
Foundation type: Independent foundation.
Financial data (yr. ended 12/31/03): Assets, $1,499,229 (M); expenditures, $1,045,893; qualifying distributions, $1,042,631; giving activities include $1,035,149 for 10 grants (high: $784,649; low: $100).
Purpose and activities: Grants through Christian and other organizations to aid disadvantaged groups, including babies, children, and expectant mothers.
Fields of interest: Elementary/secondary education; Human services; Children/youth, services; Family services; Religious federated giving programs.
Limitations: Giving primarily in southern CA. No grants to individuals.
Application information:
   Initial approach: 1-page letter
   Copies of proposal: 1
   Deadline(s): None
   Board meeting date(s): June and Dec.
Officers and Directors:* David G. Price,* Pres.; Dallas P. Price,* V.P.; Sheri L. Price,* Secy.; Jay Bushore, Treas.; Bonnie J. Mattern; David Glyn Price; Jamie B. Price; Richard C. Price; Kevin J. Roberts; Terry A. Roberts; Christy Stanich.
EIN: 954108153
Selected grants: The following grants were reported in 2004.
$465,351 to World Impact, Los Angeles, CA. For Oaks Family Conference Center.
$300,000 to George Fox University, Newberg, OR. For Athletic Complex Project.
$100,000 to Oaks Christian School, Westlake Village, CA. For annual fund.
$12,000 to International Foundation, DC.
$10,000 to Los Angeles Appleseed, Los Angeles, CA.
$10,000 to Pali Community Center Committee, Los Angeles, CA. For Palisades Field of Dreams.
$10,000 to Young Life, Durango, CO.
$1,200 to YMCA, Westside Family, Los Angeles, CA. For general support.
$500 to Young Life, Malibu, CA. For general support.
$250 to Santa Monica Basketball Club, Santa Monica, CA. For general support.

1018
Mary Grant Price Foundation ◇ ☆
2118 Wilshire Blvd., No. 486
Santa Monica, CA   90403

Established in 2003 in CA.
Donor: Mary Grant Price Trust.
Foundation type: Operating foundation.
Financial data (yr. ended 12/31/05): Assets, $256,722 (M); gifts received, $740,000; expenditures, $500,000; qualifying distributions, $500,000; giving activities include $500,000 for 1 grant.
Purpose and activities: Giving primarily for the furtherance of the Christian Science movement.
Fields of interest: Christian agencies & churches.
Limitations: Applications not accepted. Giving primarily in MA and NY.
Application information: Contributes only to pre-selected organizations.
Trustees: Jamie Hammond; Allison Phinney; Jan Phinney.
EIN: 383667390

1019

The William L. Price Foundation ◆ ☆

169 Inner Cir.
Redwood City, CA 94062

Established in 2004 in CA.
Donor: W.L. Price.
Foundation type: Independent foundation.
Financial data (yr. ended 12/31/04): Assets, $5,957,723 (M); gifts received, $243,500; expenditures, $393,293; qualifying distributions, $361,124; giving activities include $359,000 for 93 grants (high: $20,000; low: $500).
Fields of interest: Health organizations, association; Human services; Children/youth, services.
Limitations: Applications not accepted. Giving primarily in CA; funding also in NY and OR. No grants to individuals.
Application information: Contributes only to pre-selected organizations.
Officer: W.L. Price, Pres.
EIN: 200140310

1020

The Priem Family Foundation ▼ ◆

4052 Kettering Terr.
Fremont, CA 94536
URL: http://www.priem.org

Established in 1999 in CA.
Donors: Curtis Priem; Veronica Priem.
Foundation type: Operating foundation.
Financial data (yr. ended 6/30/05): Assets, $231,084,473 (M); expenditures, $14,207,181; qualifying distributions, $12,676,705; giving activities include $12,655,120 for 4 grants (high: $9,600,000; low: $5,000), and $12,705 for foundation-administered programs.
Purpose and activities: The purpose of the foundation is the reduction of non-human induced suffering. The foundation's activities are currently in the area of nature conservancy, education, and the performing arts.
Fields of interest: Performing arts; Education; Environment, natural resources; Environment, land resources.
Limitations: Applications not accepted. No grants to individuals.
Application information: Contributes only to pre-selected organizations.
Officers and Directors: Curtis Priem,* C.E.O. and Pres.; Edward Miles,* V.P.; Veronica Priem,* C.F.O.
EIN: 943340371
Selected grants: The following grants were reported in 2005.
$12,600,000 to Rensselaer Polytechnic Institute, Troy, NY. 2 grants: $3,000,000, $9,600,000
$50,000 to Monterey Bay Aquarium, Monterey, CA. For community outreach program.

1021

The Pritzker Family Foundation ◆

11111 Santa Monica Blvd., Ste. 1650
Los Angeles, CA 90025

Established in 2002 in CA and IL.
Donors: Pritzker Foundation; Pritzker Cousins Foundation.
Foundation type: Independent foundation.

Financial data (yr. ended 12/31/03): Assets, $43,995,979 (M); expenditures, $1,700,939; qualifying distributions, $1,338,782; giving activities include $1,291,485 for 46 grants (high: $277,952; low: $500).
Purpose and activities: Giving primarily to a Holocaust memorial fund.
Fields of interest: Human services; Jewish agencies & temples.
Limitations: Applications not accepted. Giving primarily in CA. No grants to individuals.
Application information: Contributes only to pre-selected organizations.
Officers and Directors: Jay Robert Pritzker,* Pres.; Judy Schroffel, Secy.; Allan Von Halle, Treas.; Anthony N. Pritzker; Mary Kathryn Pritzker.
EIN: 300039820
Selected grants: The following grants were reported in 2003.
$277,952 to Holocaust Memorial Foundation of Illinois, Skokie, IL. For general support.
$260,000 to Milton Academy, Milton, MA. For general support.
$200,000 to Union of American Hebrew Congregations, DC. For general support.
$60,000 to United States Holocaust Memorial Museum, DC. For general support.
$45,000 to Northwestern University, School of Law, Evanston, IL. For general support.
$20,000 to Evanston Northwestern Healthcare, Evanston, IL. For general support.
$20,000 to National Vietnam Veterans Art Museum, Chicago, IL. For general support.
$20,000 to University of North Dakota Foundation, Grand Forks, ND. For general support.
$10,000 to Illinois Council Against Handgun Violence, Chicago, IL. For general support.
$8,333 to Youth Organizations Umbrella (YOU), Evanston, IL. For general support.

1022

The John and Lisa Pritzker Family Fund ◆

c/o Seiler & Co. LLP
1100 Marshall St.
Redwood City, CA 94063

Established in 2002 in CA and IL.
Foundation type: Independent foundation.
Financial data (yr. ended 12/31/03): Assets, $35,827,870 (M); expenditures, $1,012,702; qualifying distributions, $900,000; giving activities include $900,000 for grants.
Fields of interest: Education; Health care; Human services; Jewish agencies & temples.
Limitations: Applications not accepted. Giving primarily in CA. No grants to individuals.
Application information: Contributes only to pre-selected organizations.
Officers: John A. Pritzker, Pres.; Beverly Symonik, Secy.; James G.B. Demartini III, Treas.
Director: Lisa Pritzker.
EIN: 300039815
Selected grants: The following grants were reported in 2004.
$1,700,000 to Jewish Community Federation of San Francisco, the Peninsula, Marin and Sonoma Counties, San Francisco, CA. For general support.
$82,000 to Congregation Emanu-El, San Francisco, CA. For general support.
$35,000 to Museum of Modern Art, New York, NY. For photography program.

$25,000 to Mercy Corps, Portland, OR. For general support.
$15,000 to University of California at San Francisco Foundation, San Francisco, CA. For general support.
$10,000 to Global Peace Congress, Palo Alto, CA. For general support.
$10,000 to Millenium Park Conservancy, Chicago, IL. For general support.
$6,000 to San Francisco Museum of Modern Art, San Francisco, CA. For general support.
$1,500 to Gateway High School, San Francisco, CA. For general support.
$1,000 to El Dorado County Search and Rescue, Placerville, CA. For general support.

1023

Promise Keepers Charitable Foundation ◆ ☆

44 Pinewood
Irvine, CA 92604-3274

Established in 2003 in CA.
Donors: Eric Taylor; Lyn Taylor.
Foundation type: Independent foundation.
Financial data (yr. ended 12/31/05): Assets, $1,587,522 (M); expenditures, $2,120,338; qualifying distributions, $2,111,500; giving activities include $2,111,100 for 1 grant.
Fields of interest: Christian agencies & churches.
Limitations: Applications not accepted. Giving primarily in Irvine, CA. No grants to individuals.
Application information: Contributes only to pre-selected organizations.
Officers: Eric Taylor, Pres.; Lyn Taylor, V.P.
EIN: 200131750

1024

Frank and Denise Quattrone Foundation ◆

c/o Ron Gong, myCFO, Inc.
1700 Seaport Blvd., 4th Fl.
Redwood City, CA 94063

Established in 2002 in CA.
Donors: Denise A. Foderaro; Frank P. Quattrone.
Foundation type: Independent foundation.
Financial data (yr. ended 12/31/04): Assets, $10,077,606 (M); gifts received, $19,111; expenditures, $621,203; qualifying distributions, $579,098; giving activities include $579,098 for 36 grants (high: $150,000; low: $200).
Purpose and activities: Giving primarily to an aquarium, as well as for the arts and education.
Fields of interest: Museums (science/technology); Performing arts, theater; Higher education; Education; Aquariums; Foundations (private grantmaking).
Limitations: Applications not accepted. Giving primarily in CA. No grants to individuals.
Application information: Contributes only to pre-selected organizations.
Trustees: Denise A. Foderaro; Frank P. Quattrone.
EIN: 776220832

1025

Radin Foundation ◆

3142 Willow Ave., Ste. 101
Clovis, CA 93612
Contact: Jason S. Liao, C.F.O.

Established in 1971.
Donor: Leta H. Radin†.
Foundation type: Independent foundation.
Financial data (yr. ended 12/31/05): Assets, $6,972,235 (M); expenditures, $603,027; qualifying distributions, $603,027; giving activities include $580,000 for 13 grants (high: $350,000; low: $2,500).
Purpose and activities: Funding primarily for hospitals and children and youth services.
Fields of interest: Museums; Performing arts, orchestra (symphony); Arts; Higher education; Hospitals (general); Hospitals (specialty); Human services; Children/youth, services.
Limitations: Giving primarily in Fresno, CA. No grants to individuals.
Application information: Application form not required.
Initial approach: Proposal or letter
Deadline(s): None
Officers and Director:* Leslie E. Findley,* Pres.; Jason S. Liao, C.F.O.
EIN: 237155525

1026
Rady Family Foundation ◇ ☆
11455 El Camino Real, Ste. 200
San Diego, CA 92130

Established in 2002 in CA.
Donors: Ernest S. Rady; Evelyn Rady.
Foundation type: Independent foundation.
Financial data (yr. ended 12/31/05): Assets, $4,382,973 (M); gifts received, $3,913,540; expenditures, $5,335,476; qualifying distributions, $5,335,476; giving activities include $5,178,815 for 19 grants (high: $4,998,175; low: $100).
Fields of interest: Higher education; Medical research, institute; Human services; Children/youth, services; Residential/custodial care, hospices; Jewish federated giving programs; Jewish agencies & temples.
Limitations: Applications not accepted. Giving primarily in San Diego, CA. No grants to individuals.
Application information: Contributes only to pre-selected organizations.
Trustee: Ernest S. Rady.
EIN: 760708193

1027
Rahimian Family Foundation ◇
11380 White Rock Rd.
Rancho Cordova, CA 95742

Established in 2000 in CA.
Donors: Majid Rahimian; Javad Rahimian.
Foundation type: Independent foundation.
Financial data (yr. ended 12/31/03): Assets, $942,872 (M); gifts received, $553,046; expenditures, $385,634; qualifying distributions, $381,354; giving activities include $381,700 for 3 grants (high: $344,500; low: $200).
Fields of interest: Arts; Libraries/library science.
Limitations: Applications not accepted. Giving primarily in CA. No grants to individuals.
Application information: Contributes only to pre-selected organizations.
Officers: Majid Rahimian, C.E.O. and Pres.; Ali Rahimian, V.P.; Javad Rahimian, Secy. and C.F.O.

Directors: Ladan Rahimian; Maryam Rahimian; Mehry Rahimian.
EIN: 680460486
Selected grants: The following grants were reported in 2003.
$344,500 to OMead Foundation, Kingston, NY.
$37,000 to Sacramento Area League of Associated Muslims, Sacramento, CA.
$200 to American Cancer Society, Atlanta, GA.

1028
The Raintree Foundation ◇
6054 La Goleta Rd.
Goleta, CA 93117
Contact: Harold R. Frank, Secy.

Established in 1994 in CA.
Donors: Diana D. Frank; Harold R. Frank; H.R. Frank Family Trust.
Foundation type: Independent foundation.
Financial data (yr. ended 12/31/04): Assets, $16,216,854 (M); gifts received, $3,071,861; expenditures, $1,069,883; qualifying distributions, $1,048,226; giving activities include $1,040,480 for 33 grants (high: $600,000; low: $250).
Purpose and activities: Giving primarily for youth services, medical research, and social services.
Fields of interest: Education; Environment, natural resources; Medical research, institute; Youth development, centers/clubs; Human services; Children/youth, services.
Limitations: Giving primarily in Santa Barbara, CA. No grants to individuals.
Application information: Application form not required.
Initial approach: Letter on organization letterhead
Deadline(s): None
Officers: Diana D. Frank, Pres.; Harold R. Frank, Secy. and C.F.O.
Director: James A. Frank.
EIN: 770359291

1029
The Ralphs—Food 4 Less Foundation ◇
(formerly The Food 4 Less Foundation)
c/o Exec. Dir.
P.O. Box 54143
Los Angeles, CA 90054 (310) 884-6205
URL: http://www.thekrogerco.com/corpnews/corpnewsinfo_charitablegiving_ralphs.htm

Established in 1991 in CA.
Donors: Food 4 Less Supermarkets, Inc.; Ralphs Grocery Co.; Ron Burkle.
Foundation type: Company-sponsored foundation.
Financial data (yr. ended 1/30/06): Assets, $3,770,575 (M); gifts received, $1,885,873; expenditures, $3,287,975; qualifying distributions, $3,287,975; giving activities include $3,232,890 for 654 grants (high: $451,772).
Purpose and activities: The foundation supports organizations involved with K-12 education, women's health, hunger, disaster relief, recreation, and other areas.
Fields of interest: Elementary/secondary education; Health care; Food services; Safety/disasters; Recreation; General charitable giving; Women.
Type of support: General/operating support; Program development; Scholarship funds; Sponsorships.

Limitations: Giving primarily in areas of company operations in southern CA. No support for discriminatory organizations. Generally, no grants to individuals, or for memorial campaigns or endowments; no grants for political activities.
Application information: Application form not required.
Initial approach: Proposal
Deadline(s): None
Final notification: Varies
Officers and Trustees: Lynn Marmer, Pres.; Paul Heldman, Secy.; Scot Henderson, Treas.; John Burgon; David Dillon; Jon Flora; Dennis Hackett; Marnette Perry.
EIN: 330492352

1030
Ramsay Family Foundation ◇ ☆
(formerly ABC Foundation)
P.O. Box 193809
San Francisco, CA 94119-3809

Established in 1977 in CA.
Donor: Nonie B. Ramsay.
Foundation type: Independent foundation.
Financial data (yr. ended 12/31/05): Assets, $6,035,727 (M); expenditures, $582,812; qualifying distributions, $564,002; giving activities include $556,400 for 42 grants (high: $50,000; low: $500).
Purpose and activities: Funding primarily for education. Some funding also for arts and culture and human services.
Fields of interest: Arts; Elementary/secondary education; Scholarships/financial aid; Human services; Philanthropy/voluntarism.
Limitations: Applications not accepted. Giving primarily in CA. No grants to individuals.
Application information: Contributes only to pre-selected organizations.
Officers and Directors:* Nonie B. Ramsay,* Pres.; Sheldon C. Ramsay,* V.P.; George T. Argyris, Secy.; Stephen D. Bechtel, Jr.; Stephen A. Ramsay.
EIN: 942415607
Selected grants: The following grants were reported in 2003.
$50,000 to Athenian School, Danville, CA. For capital campaign.
$50,000 to Groton School, Groton, MA. For scholarships.
$50,000 to Santa Catalina School, Monterey, CA. For capital campaign.
$15,000 to Washington International Horse Show, Gaithersburg, MD. For operating support.
$10,000 to California Academy of Sciences, San Francisco, CA. For capital support.
$7,500 to Cate School, Carpinteria, CA.
$5,000 to Achievement Rewards for College Scientists (ARCS) Foundation, San Francisco, CA. For scholarships.
$5,000 to San Francisco Ballet Association, San Francisco, CA. For operating support.
$1,000 to Foundation for Osteoporosis Research and Education, Oakland, CA. For annual suport.
$1,000 to NARAL Pro-Choice America Foundation, San Francisco, CA. For operating support.

1031
Rancho Santa Fe Foundation
(formerly Rancho Santa Fe Community Foundation)
P.O. Box 811
Rancho Santa Fe, CA 92067-0811
(858) 756-6557
Contact: Dan Beals, Finance Mgr.
FAX: (858) 756-6561;
E-mail: christy@rsffoundation.org; URL: http://
www.rsffoundation.org

Established in 1981 in CA.
Foundation type: Community foundation.
Financial data (yr. ended 12/31/05): Assets,
$22,418,463 (M); gifts received, $6,185,770;
expenditures, $3,416,880; giving activities include
$3,110,899 for 605 grants (high: $500,000; low:
$100).
Purpose and activities: The foundation promotes
philanthropy by: 1) assisting donors to build assets
for their chosen charitable purposes; 2) enhancing
the awareness of ways to give purposefully; 3)
exploring and evaluating local and regional
charitable needs; and 4) building endowments for
charitable organizations.
Fields of interest: Community development.
Type of support: Land acquisition; Emergency
funds; Curriculum development; Building/
renovation; Annual campaigns; General/operating
support; Continuing support; Capital campaigns;
Equipment; Program development; Seed money;
Scholarship funds; Technical assistance.
Limitations: Applications not accepted. Giving
primarily in Rancho Santa Fe, CA. No support for
religious organizations (from discretionary funds).
No grants to individuals.
Publications: Annual report; Financial statement;
Informational brochure; Newsletter.
Application information: Unsolicited requests for
funds not accepted.
  Board meeting date(s): Bimonthly
Officers and Directors:* Gregory R. Hillgren,*
Chair.; Daniel E. Pittard,* Chair.-Elect; Robert H.
Goldsmith,* Vice-Chair.; Richard S. Cusac,* Secy.;
James A. Simpson,* Treas.; Christina P. Wilson,
Exec. Dir.; C. Neil Ash; Emily T. Bagnall; James A.
Boyce; Richard E. Carlson; Martin C. Dickinson; Gail
Gillies-Mize; Walter H. Green; William J. Herrick;
Candace A. Humber; Murray H. Hutchinson; Louise
Kasch; Chuck Kendall; Ron Kimura; Connie L.
Matsui; E. Tyler Miller III; Don W. Oliphant; Russell
S. Penniman IV; Mark Pulido; Scott B. Robinson; R.
Roger Rowe; Edward J. Sanderson, Jr.; John M.
Seiber; Charles J. Yash.
Number of staff: 1 full-time professional; 2 part-time
support.
EIN: 953709639

1032
Nancy Buck Ransom Foundation ◇
P.O. Box 749
Monterey, CA 93942-0749 (831) 375-3311
Contact: Nancy Buck Ransom, Pres.

Established in 1979 in CA.
Foundation type: Independent foundation.
Financial data (yr. ended 12/31/05): Assets,
$6,997,529 (M); expenditures, $338,905;
qualifying distributions, $324,653; giving activities
include $323,200 for 11 grants (high: $275,000;
low: $3,000).

Purpose and activities: Support for projects that
provide positive enrichment opportunities for
mainstream youths.
Fields of interest: Arts, public education; Youth
development, centers/clubs.
Type of support: General/operating support.
Limitations: Giving primarily in Monterey County, CA.
No support for governmental or religious programs.
No grants to individuals.
Application information: Application form not
required.
  Initial approach: Proposal
  Deadline(s): Feb. 15
  Board meeting date(s): Apr.
Officers and Directors:* Nancy Buck Ransom,*
Pres.; D. Alan Thompson,* V.P.; Georgiana F.
Shepherd, Secy.; Richard Thorpe,* Treas.; James D.
Devine; Lucinda B. Ewing.
EIN: 942601172
Selected grants: The following grants were reported
in 2003.
$300,000 to Crivitz Youth, Crivitz, WI.
$4,000 to Childrens Experimental Theater, Carmel,
  CA. For general support.
$4,000 to Youth Arts Collective, Monterey, CA. For
  general support.
$3,000 to Community Partnership for Youth,
  Monterey, CA. For general support.
$3,000 to Fridays Child, Monterey, CA. For general
  support.
$3,000 to York School, Monterey, CA. For general
  support.
$3,000 to Youth Music Monterey, Monterey, CA. For
  general support.

1033
The Rav-Noy Family Foundation, Inc. ◇ ☆
c/o KETW
15303 Ventura Blvd., Ste. 1040
Sherman Oaks, CA 91403

Donors: Zeev Rav-Noy; Varda Rav-Noy; Abraham
Bernstein.
Foundation type: Independent foundation.
Financial data (yr. ended 9/30/05): Assets,
$555,011 (M); gifts received, $650,900;
expenditures, $608,521; qualifying distributions,
$607,176; giving activities include $607,176 for
451 grants (high: $75,000; low: $18).
Purpose and activities: Giving primarily to Jewish
agencies, temples, and schools.
Fields of interest: Education; Jewish agencies &
temples.
Limitations: Applications not accepted. No grants to
individuals.
Application information: Contributes only to
pre-selected organizations.
Officers: Zeev Rav-Noy, Pres.; Varda Rav-Noy, Secy.
and C.F.O.
EIN: 954663319
Selected grants: The following grants were reported
in 2005.
$5,000 to Biala Yeshiva, Los Angeles, CA.
$770 to Ezrat Israel, Brooklyn, NY.
$180 to Jews for Judaism, Baltimore, MD.
$90 to Chabad of the Valley, Encino, CA.
$90 to Colel Chabad, Brooklyn, NY. 2 grants: $36,
  $54
$36 to Chamah, New York, NY.

1034
Ray of Light Foundation ◇
c/o RHF Management
10100 Santa Monica Blvd., Ste. 1300
Los Angeles, CA 90067
Contact: Caresse Norman, Tr.

Established in 1998 in CA.
Donor: Madonna Ciccone.
Foundation type: Independent foundation.
Financial data (yr. ended 12/31/05): Assets,
$4,297,778 (M); gifts received, $1,030,557;
expenditures, $647,318; qualifying distributions,
$620,766; giving activities include $620,766 for 13
grants (high: $250,000; low: $1,000).
Purpose and activities: Giving primarily to a
Kabbalah center, as well as for medical research
and health associations, particularly associations
for musicians who are facing health problems;
funding also for human services.
Fields of interest: Hospitals (general); Health care;
Health organizations, association; Medical
research, institute; Human services; Foundations
(private grantmaking); Religion, formal/general
education.
Limitations: Giving primarily in CA, with emphasis on
Los Angeles. No grants to individuals.
Trustees: Madonna Ciccone; Caresse Norman.
EIN: 954716881

1035
Red Husky Foundation ◇
720 University Ave., Ste. 200
Los Gatos, CA 95032

Established in 1997 in NV and CA.
Donors: Jerry Yang; Akiko Yamazaki.
Foundation type: Independent foundation.
Financial data (yr. ended 6/30/05): Assets,
$48,119,471 (M); expenditures, $536,332;
qualifying distributions, $386,487; giving activities
include $386,487 for 8 grants (high: $200,374;
low: $200).
Purpose and activities: Giving primarily for
community foundations and community
development, including a golf foundation to impact
the lives of young people by exposure to the game;
funding also for medical research and human
services, including a center for people who are blind.
Fields of interest: Medical research, institute;
Human services; Youth, services; Community
development; Foundations (private grantmaking);
Foundations (community); Blind/visually impaired.
Limitations: Applications not accepted. Giving
primarily in CA, with some emphasis on San Jose.
No grants to individuals.
Application information: Funds fully committed.
Contributes only to pre-selected organizations.
Unsolicited requests for funds not accepted.
Officers and Director:* Akiko Yamazaki,* Pres.;
Jerry Yang, Secy.; Gregory R. Hardester, Treas.
EIN: 770472127

1036
Will J. Reid Foundation ◇
2801 E. Ocean Blvd.
Long Beach, CA 90803
Contact: E.M. Westbrook, Pres.

Established in 1955 in CA.

Donors: Will J. Reid†; Virginia Reid Moore†; Ella Hancock Reid; Charles Reid Gaylord; Elizabeth Moore Westbrook.
Foundation type: Independent foundation.
Financial data (yr. ended 12/31/05): Assets, $19,992,928 (M); gifts received, $100; expenditures, $999,440; qualifying distributions, $1,034,342; giving activities include $899,166 for 60 grants (high: $100,000; low: $2,000), and $100,000 for 1 loan/program-related investment.
Purpose and activities: Giving for art and cultural institutes, environmental organizations, and for youth and family services.
Fields of interest: Arts; Education; Environment, natural resources; Environment; Human services; Youth, services.
Type of support: General/operating support; Continuing support; Annual campaigns; Land acquisition; Program evaluation.
Limitations: Applications not accepted. Giving primarily in southern CA. No grants to individuals.
Application information: Unsolicited requests for funds not accepted.
  Board meeting date(s): Annual meeting and distribution, usually in May
Officers and Directors:* E.M. Westbrook,* Pres. and Treas.; Charlotte G. Burgess, V.P.; W.J. Hancock, V.P.; C.R. Moore,* Secy.; W.R. Moore.
Number of staff: 1 part-time support.
EIN: 956041915

1037
The Myra Reinhard Family Foundation ◇
c/o Myra Reinhard
15729 Los Gatos Blvd., Ste. 201
Los Gatos, CA 95032-2539 (408) 358-5848
E-mail: MRFfoundation@aol.com

Established in 1999 in CA.
Donor: Myra Reinhard.
Foundation type: Independent foundation.
Financial data (yr. ended 12/31/05): Assets, $1,499,191 (M); gifts received, $1,000,000; expenditures, $1,244,781; qualifying distributions, $1,198,223; giving activities include $1,186,675 for 44 grants (high: $100,000; low: $300).
Fields of interest: Media, film/video; Arts; Education; Hospitals (general); Health organizations, association; Medical research; Children/youth, services; Family services; Jewish agencies & temples.
International interests: Israel.
Type of support: Curriculum development; Continuing support; Program development.
Limitations: Applications not accepted. Giving primarily in CA, Washington, DC, and Israel. No grants for building funds.
Application information: Unsolicited requests for funds not accepted.
  Board meeting date(s): Mar.
Officers and Directors:* Myra Reinhard,* Pres.; Ian Reinhard,* V.P.; Ruth Fletcher,* Secy.; Neil Reinhard,* C.F.O. and Treas.; Erica Krauss.
Number of staff: 1 part-time professional.
EIN: 770514955
Selected grants: The following grants were reported in 2004.
$142,500 to Jewish Federation of Silicon Valley, Los Gatos, CA. 2 grants: $100,000, $42,500
$100,000 to Jewish Community Center. For performing arts audio visual equipment.

$50,000 to American Friends of Mosdot Mesilat of Avot, Brooklyn, NY. For boy's after-school program.
$50,000 to Stanford University, Stanford, CA. For faculty scholars program.
$50,000 to VMC Foundation, San Jose, CA.
$48,000 to Johns Hopkins University, School of Medicine, Baltimore, MD.
$40,000 to National Conference for Community and Justice.
$36,000 to Chabad of the South Bay, Palo Alto, CA. For Friendship Circle.
$30,000 to Habitat for Humanity, Silicon Valley, Milpitas, CA. For two family homes.

1038
Reinhart Foundation ◇ ☆
P.O. Box 5005-85
Rancho Santa Fe, CA 92067

Established in 2002 in CA.
Foundation type: Independent foundation.
Financial data (yr. ended 12/31/05): Assets, $54,370 (M); gifts received, $251,074; expenditures, $571,615; qualifying distributions, $376,127; giving activities include $376,127 for grants.
Fields of interest: Education.
Limitations: Applications not accepted. No grants to individuals.
Application information: Contributes only to pre-selected organizations.
Directors: Leon H. Reinhart; Randyn D. Reinhart.
EIN: 010726374

1039
The Reinhold Foundation ◇
c/o B. Terry Reinhold
624 Harbor Island Dr.
Newport Beach, CA 92660

Established in 1997 in CA.
Donors: Baldwin Reinhold, Jr.; Mary E. Reinhold.
Foundation type: Independent foundation.
Financial data (yr. ended 12/31/05): Assets, $6,434,163 (M); expenditures, $425,771; qualifying distributions, $391,505; giving activities include $388,500 for 10 grants (high: $200,000; low: $1,000).
Purpose and activities: Giving primarily for the performing arts, higher education, health, children and youth services, and federated giving programs.
Fields of interest: Performing arts centers; Elementary/secondary education; Higher education; Hospitals (general); Boys & girls clubs; Children, services.
Limitations: Applications not accepted. Giving primarily in CA. No grants to individuals.
Application information: Contributes only to pre-selected organizations.
Officers: B. Terry Reinhold, Pres.; Mary E. Reinhold, Secy.; Carol A. Reinhold, C.F.O.
EIN: 330756400
Selected grants: The following grants were reported in 2005.
$200,000 to California State Polytechnic University, Pomona, CA.
$50,000 to Boys and Girls Club of the Harbor Area, Costa Mesa, CA.
$50,000 to Hoag Hospital Foundation, Newport Beach, CA.

$6,000 to California State University, Long Beach, CA.
$5,000 to Casa Teresa, Orange, CA.

1040
ResMed Foundation ◇ ☆
14040 Danielson St.
Poway, CA 92064-6857
E-mail: resmedsdbfoundation@resmed.com

Established in 2002 in CA.
Donor: ResMed Inc.
Foundation type: Company-sponsored foundation.
Financial data (yr. ended 12/31/05): Assets, $934,147 (M); gifts received, $250,000; expenditures, $656,464; qualifying distributions, $567,246; giving activities include $567,246 for grants.
Purpose and activities: The foundation supports organizations involved with sleep-disordered breathing research and awareness.
Fields of interest: Public health; Health organizations.
Limitations: Giving on a national basis.
Application information: The foundation may request additional information at a later date. Proposals should be no longer than 5 pages. Organizations receiving support may be asked to provide periodic progress reports and a final report. Application form not required.
  Initial approach: E-mail proposal
  Copies of proposal: 1
  Deadline(s): Feb. 1, May 1, Aug. 1, and Nov. 1
  Final notification: Apr. 30, July 31, Oct. 31, and Jan. 31
Officers: Ronald R. Taylor, Chair.; Peter C. Farrell, Ph.D., Secy.; Mary Berglund, Ph.D., Treas.; Fiona Tudor, Exec. Dir.
Trustees: Edward Blair, Jr.; Terrence M. Davidson, M.D.; Hugh Davies, Ph.D.; Edward A. Dennis, Ph.D.; Ralph Pascualy, M.D.; Jonathan Schwartz, M.D.; Randall E. Williams, M.D.
EIN: 020622126
Selected grants: The following grants were reported in 2004.
$50,000 to K P B S, San Diego, CA.
$50,000 to Mayo Clinic, Rochester, MN.
$37,000 to Yale University, New Haven, CT.
$10,000 to La Jolla Playhouse, La Jolla, CA.
$10,000 to Museum of Photographic Arts, San Diego, CA.
$10,000 to Old Globe Theater, San Diego, CA.
$2,500 to American Heart Association, Dallas, TX.
$500 to Big Brothers.

1041
Resnick Foundation ▼ ◇
(formerly Resnick Family Foundation)
c/o Tax Dept.
11444 W. Olympic Blvd., 10th Fl.
Los Angeles, CA 90064

Established in 1997 in CA.
Donors: Lynda R. Resnick; Stewart A. Resnick; Princess Diana Trust; Resnick Family Foundation, Inc.
Foundation type: Independent foundation.
Financial data (yr. ended 9/30/05): Assets, $800,243 (M); gifts received, $11,279,462; expenditures, $10,859,865; qualifying distributions, $10,859,865; giving activities include

$10,828,608 for 177 grants (high: $4,000,000; low: $100; average: $10,000–$250,000).

Purpose and activities: Giving primarily for museums, education, especially medical schools, 9/11 disaster support, and conservation.

Fields of interest: Museums; Education; Environment, natural resources; Disasters, 9/11/01; Human services; Jewish federated giving programs.

Limitations: Applications not accepted. Giving primarily in Los Angeles, CA and Washington, DC. No grants to individuals.

Application information: Contributes only to pre-selected organizations.

Officers and Directors:* Lynda R. Resnick,* Co-Pres.; Stewart A. Resnick,* Co-Pres.; Kenneth Dinnegan, Treas.

EIN: 954658095

Selected grants: The following grants were reported in 2005.

$4,000,000 to University of California, Geffen School of Medicine, Los Angeles, CA.

$1,000,000 to Aspen Valley Medical Foundation, Aspen, CO.

$1,000,000 to Los Angeles County Museum of Art, Los Angeles, CA.

$575,000 to Aspen Institute, Queenstown, MD. 2 grants: $500,000, $75,000

$250,000 to Prostate Cancer Foundation, Santa Monica, CA.

$249,500 to Natural Resources Defense Council, New York, NY.

$30,000 to Bard College, Graduate Center for Studies in the Decorative Arts, Design, and Culture, Annandale on Hudson, NY.

$25,000 to Hospitaller Foundation of California, Los Angeles, CA.

$10,000 to Aspen Art Museum, Aspen, CO.

1042

The Ressler Family Foundation ✧

6922 Hollywood Blvd., Ste. 900
Los Angeles, CA 90028

Established in 1994 in CA.

Foundation type: Independent foundation.

Financial data (yr. ended 12/31/04): Assets, $5,774,533 (M); expenditures, $876,770; qualifying distributions, $846,335; giving activities include $846,000 for 28 grants (high: $400,000; low: $500).

Purpose and activities: Giving for education, and for health and medical services.

Fields of interest: Higher education; Education; Health care; Jewish federated giving programs.

Limitations: Applications not accepted. Giving primarily in Los Angeles, CA. No grants to individuals.

Application information: Contributes only to pre-selected organizations.

Trustees: Alison Ressler; Richard Ressler.

EIN: 956979496

1043

The Ressler/Gertz Foundation ✧

16130 Ventura Blvd., Ste. 320
Encino, CA 91436

Established in 1997 in CA.

Donors: Jami Gertz; Antony Ressler.

Foundation type: Independent foundation.

Financial data (yr. ended 12/31/05): Assets, $1,125,872 (M); expenditures, $934,430; qualifying distributions, $918,779; giving activities include $917,512 for 62 grants (high: $125,000; low: $500).

Purpose and activities: Giving for early education, Jewish organizations and temples, art and cultural programs, and health and human services.

Fields of interest: Arts; Education, early childhood education; Health organizations, association; Medical research, institute; Children/youth, services; Jewish agencies & temples.

Limitations: Applications not accepted. Giving primarily in Los Angeles, CA. No grants to individuals.

Application information: Contributes only to pre-selected organizations.

Trustees: Jami Gertz; Antony Ressler.

EIN: 311533199

1044

Rest Haven Preventorium for Children, Inc. ✧ ☆

(also known as Children's Health Fund)
P.O. Box 420369
San Diego, CA 92142-0369

Established in 1963 in CA.

Donors: Anna M. Spring Trust; Jessie Castle Roberts Trust.

Foundation type: Operating foundation.

Financial data (yr. ended 12/31/05): Assets, $7,068,956 (M); gifts received, $67,207; expenditures, $686,359; qualifying distributions, $644,840; giving activities include $607,222 for grants.

Purpose and activities: Provides direct monetary assistance to needy children in the San Diego, CA, area only for medical, dental, therapy, hearing, child care, and nutrition expenses. No giving to those outside the target area.

Fields of interest: Health care; Youth development, services; Human services; Economically disadvantaged.

Type of support: Grants to individuals.

Limitations: Applications not accepted. Giving exclusively to residents of San Diego and Imperial County, CA. No grants to individuals residing outside San Diego.

Application information: Unsolicited requests for funds will not be accepted from families outside San Diego or Imperial County, CA.

Officers: Raymond M. Peterson, M.D., Pres.; Jeanne L. Frost, V.P.; David Allsbrook, Secy.; Paul S. Condon, Treas.

EIN: 952128344

1045

The Reveas Foundation ✧

8211 N. Fresno St.
Fresno, CA 93720-2041 (559) 448-8080
Contact: Samuel T. Reeves, Pres.

Established in 1998 in CA and DE.

Donors: Charles Scott Hulme; Elizabeth R. Hulme; Elizabeth W. Reeves; Samuel T. Reeves; Sandra R. Spears.

Foundation type: Independent foundation.

Financial data (yr. ended 12/31/04): Assets, $4,571,326 (M); gifts received, $668,825; expenditures, $694,226; qualifying distributions,

$648,350; giving activities include $648,350 for 28 grants (high: $200,000; low: $250).

Purpose and activities: Giving primarily for higher education, particularly to a medical school, as well as for athletics, and human services; support also for children, youth, and family services, federated giving programs, and Christian organizations, including Presbyterian churches.

Fields of interest: Arts; Higher education; Education; Athletics/sports, football; Human services; Children, services; Youth, services; Family services; Federated giving programs; Christian agencies & churches.

Limitations: Applications not accepted. Giving on a national basis, with some emphasis on Fresno, CA. No grants to individuals.

Application information: Contributes only to pre-selected organizations.

Officers: Samuel T. Reeves, Pres. and Treas.; Charles Scott Hulme, Secy.

Directors: Virginia Reeves Apple; Elizabeth R. Hulme; Annesley R. MacFarlane; Elizabeth W. Reeves; Sandra R. Spears.

EIN: 223621474

Selected grants: The following grants were reported in 2003.

$176,000 to Stanford University, School of Medicine, Stanford, CA. For Pulmonary and Critical Care Medicine programs.

$50,000 to Fresno Pacific University, Fresno, CA. For Paragon Scholarship.

$45,250 to Fellowship of Christian Athletes, Kansas City, MO.

$23,000 to Robin Hood Foundation, New York, NY.

$10,000 to Classroom, Inc., New York, NY.

$10,000 to Fresno Community Food Bank, Fresno, CA.

$5,000 to Valley Public Television, Fresno, CA.

$2,500 to Duke University, Durham, NC.

$1,000 to Fresno Rescue Mission, Fresno, CA.

$1,000 to Navigators, The, Colorado Springs, CO.

1046

The Rey-Vaden Family Foundation ✧

c/o myCFO, Inc.
P.O. Box 10195, Dept. 39
Palo Alto, CA 94303

Established in 1999 in CA.

Donors: Val E. Vaden; Lilli J. Rey.

Foundation type: Independent foundation.

Financial data (yr. ended 2/28/06): Assets, $5,491,461 (M); expenditures, $699,919; qualifying distributions, $683,263; giving activities include $661,013 for 65 grants (high: $320,000; low: $20).

Fields of interest: Education; Cancer.

Limitations: Applications not accepted. No grants to individuals.

Application information: Contributes only to pre-selected organizations.

Officers: Val E. Vaden, Pres.; Lilli J. Rey, Secy.

EIN: 943346004

1047

Reyes Family Foundation ✧

21116 Comer Dr.
Saratoga, CA 95070

Established in 2000 in CA.

Donors: Greg Reyes; Penny Reyes.

Foundation type: Independent foundation.
Financial data (yr. ended 12/31/04): Assets, $7,024,891 (M); gifts received, $35; expenditures, $1,493,085; qualifying distributions, $1,490,575; giving activities include $1,488,050 for 17 grants (high: $350,000; low: $2,500).
Fields of interest: Education; Children/youth, services.
Limitations: Applications not accepted. Giving primarily in CA. No grants to individuals.
Application information: Contributes only to pre-selected organizations.
Officers: Greg Reyes, Pres.; Penny Reyes, V.P.
EIN: 770533938
Selected grants: The following grants were reported in 2003.
$341,000 to Valley Christian Schools, San Jose, CA.
$250,000 to Saratoga High School Foundation, Saratoga, CA.
$100,000 to Fred Finch Childrens Home, Oakland, CA.
$50,000 to California State University at Chico Foundation, Chico, CA.
$10,000 to Boys and Girls Clubs of Silicon Valley, San Jose, CA.
$10,000 to Child Advocates, San Jose, CA.
$10,000 to Second Harvest Food Bank of Santa Clara and San Mateo Counties, San Jose, CA.
$6,000 to All Stars Helping Kids, Redwood City, CA.
$5,000 to HOPE Rehabilitation Services, Santa Clara, CA.
$5,000 to Special Olympics, DC.

1048
The Mabel Wilson Richards Scholarship Fund ◇
4712 Admiralty Way, No. 227
Marina Del Rey, CA 90292
Contact: Joanie C. Freckman, Tr.

Trust established in 1951 in CA.
Donor: Mabel Wilson Richards†.
Foundation type: Independent foundation.
Financial data (yr. ended 6/30/05): Assets, $13,700,425 (M); expenditures, $864,489; qualifying distributions, $626,011; giving activities include $543,119 for 30 grants (high: $100,000; low: $4,950).
Purpose and activities: The fund awards scholarships for worthy and needy residents of the Los Angeles area recommended by financial aid offices of selected CA educational institutions. Trustees select recipients; awards are paid directly to schools.
Type of support: Scholarship funds; Scholarships—to individuals.
Limitations: Giving limited to residents of the greater Los Angeles, CA, area. No grants for building or endowment funds or operating budgets.
Publications: Application guidelines; Program policy statement.
Application information: Application form should be submitted to the financial aid office at the school which the student wishes to attend; direct applications to the fund will not be accepted. Application form required.
  Initial approach: Contact fund for application form
  Copies of proposal: 1
  Deadline(s): Oct. 15 and Feb. 15
  Board meeting date(s): Jan., Apr., July, and Oct.

Trustees: Joanie C. Freckman; Barbara Sandler.
EIN: 956021322
Selected grants: The following grants were reported in 2004.
$160,000 to Stanford University, Stanford, CA. For scholarships.
$48,000 to University of California, Los Angeles, CA. For scholarships.
$46,313 to University of Southern California, Los Angeles, CA. For scholarships.
$20,000 to Loyola Marymount University, Los Angeles, CA. For scholarships.
$10,000 to Compton Community College Development Foundation, Compton, CA. For scholarships.
$8,000 to Harvey Mudd College, Claremont, CA. For scholarships.
$8,000 to Occidental College, Los Angeles, CA. For scholarships.
$8,000 to Pomona College, Claremont, CA. For scholarships.
$5,000 to Pepperdine University, Malibu, CA. For scholarships.
$5,000 to Santa Monica College, Santa Monica, CA. For scholarships.

1049
The Riddle Family Foundation ◇
335 Deodar Ln.
Bradbury, CA 91010

Established in 1997 in CA.
Foundation type: Independent foundation.
Financial data (yr. ended 2/28/05): Assets, $1,088,304 (M); gifts received, $202,000; expenditures, $411,483; qualifying distributions, $389,809; giving activities include $391,968 for 17 grants (high: $98,668; low: $1,000).
Purpose and activities: Giving primarily for education and Christian organizations.
Fields of interest: Higher education; Education; Christian agencies & churches.
Limitations: Applications not accepted. Giving primarily in CA. No grants to individuals.
Application information: Contributes only to pre-selected organizations.
Officers: Richard A. Riddle, Pres.; Lester S. Holstein, V.P.; Nancy L. Riddle, Secy.
Directors: Kim L. Holstein; Scott A. Riddle.
EIN: 954625531
Selected grants: The following grants were reported in 2005.
$98,668 to Masters College, Santa Clarita, CA.
$30,000 to Maranatha High School, Sierra Madre, CA.
$25,000 to Truth for Life, Cleveland, OH.
$15,000 to Alliance for Marriage, Merrifield, VA.
$10,000 to Motor Racing Outreach, Harrisburg, NC.
$10,000 to Pacific Justice Institute, Citrus Heights, CA.
$10,000 to Ronald McDonald House, San Francisco, CA.
$2,500 to Bethany Fellowship, Bloomington, MN.

1050
Righteous Persons Foundation ◇
2800 28th St., Ste. 105
Santa Monica, CA 90405 (310) 314-8393
Contact: Rachel Levin, Prog. Off.
FAX: (310) 314-8396

Established in 1994 in CA.
Donor: Steven Spielberg.
Foundation type: Independent foundation.
Financial data (yr. ended 12/31/04): Assets, $586,684 (M); gifts received, $7,467,600; expenditures, $3,797,278; qualifying distributions, $3,362,600; giving activities include $3,362,600 for 68 grants (high: $400,000; low: $5,000).
Purpose and activities: Giving primarily for Jewish arts and culture, Jewish youth, synagogue revitalization, intergroup relations and social justice.
Fields of interest: Arts; Education; Children/youth, services; Civil rights, advocacy; Jewish agencies & temples.
Type of support: General/operating support; Continuing support; Program development; Seed money; Curriculum development; Fellowships; Technical assistance; Program evaluation; Matching/challenge support.
Limitations: Giving on a national basis. No support for individual schools or synagogues. No grants to individuals or for research, publications, or projects related to the Middle East.
Publications: Application guidelines.
Application information: Application form not required.
  Initial approach: Letter of inquiry
  Copies of proposal: 1
  Deadline(s): Dates change annually
  Board meeting date(s): Twice a year
  Final notification: Usually within six months
Officers and Directors: * Steven Spielberg,* Chair.; Gerald Breslauer,* Pres.; Michael Rutman,* Secy. and C.F.O.; Margery Tabankin, Exec. Dir.; Bruce Ramer.
Number of staff: 1 full-time professional; 1 part-time professional; 1 full-time support; 1 part-time support.
EIN: 954497916
Selected grants: The following grants were reported in 2004.
$400,000 to Birthright Israel North America, New York, NY.
$250,000 to American Society for Yad Vashem, New York, NY.
$100,000 to Center for Jewish History, New York, NY.
$82,500 to Jewish Federation Council of Greater Los Angeles, Los Angeles, CA.
$75,000 to Institute for Jewish and Community Research, San Francisco, CA.
$75,000 to Jewish Television Network, Beverly Hills, CA.
$55,000 to American Jewish World Service, New York, NY.
$50,000 to American Jewish Committee, New York, NY.
$40,000 to Reconstructionist Rabbinical College, Wyncote, PA.
$25,000 to W G B H Educational Foundation, Boston, MA.

1051
Lloyd Rigler Lawrence Deutsch Foundation ▼ ◇
(formerly The Ledler Foundation)
P.O. Box 828
Burbank, CA 91503

Established in 1966 in CA.
Donors: Lawrence E. Deutsch†; Lloyd E. Rigler.
Foundation type: Independent foundation.

Financial data (yr. ended 12/31/05): Assets, $81,850,265 (M); expenditures, $6,617,059; qualifying distributions, $4,444,830; giving activities include $2,616,127 for 43 grants (high: $500,000; low: $90; average: $5,000–$100,000), and $1,361,119 for 1 foundation-administered program.

Purpose and activities: Grants mainly for cultural programs and the performing arts; support also for AIDS and other medical research, health, and environmental conservation organizations.

Fields of interest: Performing arts; Arts; Environment; Health care; AIDS; Health organizations; Medical research, institute; AIDS research.

Limitations: Applications not accepted. Giving primarily in CA. No grants to individuals.

Application information: Contributes only to pre-selected organizations.

Board meeting date(s): As necessary

Officer: Janice A. Crochett, Secy.-Treas.

Trustees: Steven Davis; James Rigler.

EIN: 956155653

Selected grants: The following grants were reported in 2004.

$500,000 to TreePeople, Beverly Hills, CA.

$293,000 to American Society for Technion-Israel Institute of Technology, New York, NY.

$250,000 to North American Conference on Ethiopian Jewry, New York, NY.

$150,000 to K C E T Community Television of Southern California, Los Angeles, CA.

$150,000 to Rutgers, The State University of New Jersey Foundation, New Brunswick, NJ.

$95,779 to New York City Opera, New York, NY.

$76,536 to Northern Plains Ballet, Bismarck, ND.

$55,825 to Lyric Opera of Chicago, Chicago, IL.

$31,375 to American Academy of Dramatic Arts, New York, NY.

$23,390 to Smuin Ballets/SF, San Francisco, CA.

1052
Susan E. Riley Foundation ✧ ☆
200 E. Del Mar Blvd., Ste. 350
Pasadena, CA 91105

Established in 2001 in CA.

Donor: Susan Riley‡.

Foundation type: Independent foundation.

Financial data (yr. ended 12/31/05): Assets, $7,422,332 (M); expenditures, $459,272; qualifying distributions, $359,031; giving activities include $359,031 for grants.

Fields of interest: Medical school/education; Substance abuse, treatment; Organ research.

Type of support: General/operating support.

Limitations: Applications not accepted. Giving primarily in CA. No grants to individuals.

Application information: Contributes only to pre-selected organizations.

Trustees: Harry L. Hathaway; Douglas L. Johnson; Garrett P. Kreditor; Robert M. Newell.

EIN: 954819693

1053
The Harry & Diane Rinker Foundation ✧ ☆
P.O. Box 7250
Newport Beach, CA 92658-7250

Established in 1997 in CA.

Donors: Diane J. Rinker; Harry S. Rinker.

Foundation type: Independent foundation.

Financial data (yr. ended 12/31/05): Assets, $1,015,174 (M); gifts received, $157,000; expenditures, $406,306; qualifying distributions, $405,405; giving activities include $405,405 for grants.

Fields of interest: Higher education; Higher education, university; Eye diseases.

Limitations: Applications not accepted. Giving primarily in CA. No grants to individuals.

Application information: Contributes only to pre-selected organizations.

Officers and Directors:* Harry S. Rinker,* Pres.; Diane J. Rinker,* Secy.

EIN: 330757925

1054
The Riordan Foundation ✧
355 S. Grand Ave., Ste. 4400
Los Angeles, CA 90071 (213) 229-8402
Contact: Ms. Nike Irvin, Pres.
FAX: (213) 229-5061;
E-mail: questions@riordanfoundation.org;
URL: http://www.riordanfoundation.org

Established in 1981 in CA.

Donors: Richard J. Riordan; Jill Riordan.

Foundation type: Independent foundation.

Financial data (yr. ended 12/31/04): Assets, $1,483,083 (M); expenditures, $957,092; qualifying distributions, $888,145; giving activities include $751,042 for 54 grants.

Purpose and activities: The foundation's mission is to ensure that all children become successful readers and writers by the end of second grade. Giving primarily for early childhood education, focusing on the prevention of illiteracy starting from the kindergarten level. Support also for youth programs and leadership programs.

Fields of interest: Education, early childhood education; Youth development, services; Children/youth, services.

Type of support: General/operating support; Program development; Matching/challenge support.

Limitations: Giving limited to Los Angeles, CA. No grants to individuals, or for scholarship aid, endowments, capital campaigns or building funds.

Publications: Application guidelines; Annual report; Informational brochure (including application guidelines); Newsletter.

Application information: Mini-grant offerings for Los Angeles County and their deadlines are announced throughout the year and are geographically restricted. Specific application forms required for technology grants. Application guidelines and forms available on foundation Web site.

Initial approach: Letter of inquiry for agency grants
Copies of proposal: 1
Deadline(s): Varies; refer to Web site for deadlines
Board meeting date(s): Annually
Final notification: Within 3 months

Officers and Directors:* Richard J. Riordan,* Chair.; Nike Irvin, Pres.; Sandy Serna, Secy.; Mary Beth Ferrell; Carl W. McKinzie; Kathy Riordan; Nancy Daly Riordan; Patricia Riordan Torrey.

Number of staff: 2 full-time professional; 1 full-time support.

EIN: 953779967

1055
Rising Family Foundation ✧ ☆
500 N. Brand Blvd., 20th Fl.
Glendale, CA 91203 (818) 547-5117
Contact: Nelson C. Rising, Pres.

Established in 2001 in CA.

Donors: Nelson C. Rising; Sharon L. Rising.

Foundation type: Independent foundation.

Financial data (yr. ended 11/30/05): Assets, $903,571 (M); expenditures, $355,468; qualifying distributions, $348,698; giving activities include $345,750 for 28 grants (high: $60,000; low: $1,000).

Fields of interest: Performing arts centers; Secondary school/education; Higher education; Education; Hospitals (general); Legal services, public interest law; Human services; Roman Catholic agencies & churches.

Limitations: Giving primarily in CA. No grants to individuals.

Officers: Nelson C. Rising, Pres.; Sharon L. Rising, Secy.-Treas.

EIN: 912171961

Selected grants: The following grants were reported in 2004.

$60,000 to Loyola High School, Los Angeles, CA. For program support.

$50,000 to Duke University, Department of Athletics, Durham, NC. For program support.

$25,000 to McLean Hospital, Belmont, MA. For program support.

$15,000 to Armand Hammer Museum of Art and Cultural Center, Los Angeles, CA. For program support.

$10,000 to Homeboy Industries, Los Angeles, CA. For program support.

$10,000 to Music Center of Los Angeles County, Los Angeles, CA. For program support.

1056
Rivendell Stewards' Trust ✧
735 State St., Ste. 632
Santa Barbara, CA 93101
Contact: Amity Wicks, Admin.
FAX: (805) 564-7137; *E-mail:* info@rstrust.org;
URL: http://www.rstrust.org

Established in 1985 in CA.

Donors: K.N. Hansen, Sr.; K.N. Hansen, Jr.; G.W. Hansen.

Foundation type: Independent foundation.

Financial data (yr. ended 12/31/04): Assets, $5,478,957 (M); expenditures, $867,371; qualifying distributions, $855,752; giving activities include $698,947 for 38 grants (high: $50,000; low: $300), and $25,000 for 4 grants to individuals (high: $10,000; low: $5,000).

Purpose and activities: Giving for Christian institutions and missionary efforts in the two-thirds world.

Fields of interest: Theological school/education; Religion.

International interests: Developing countries.

Type of support: General/operating support; Management development/capacity building; Program development; Seed money; Curriculum development; Scholarship funds; Matching/challenge support.

Limitations: Giving internationally, with emphasis on developing countries. No support for Western ministries. No grants to individuals (except for program for retired missionaries).

Publications: Application guidelines.
Application information: Proposals are due Sept. 1 for the following calendar year. At this time, the foundation is only accepting proposals from those ministries it currently supports. However, the foundation is accepting unsolicited synopses of proposed projects. See foundation Web site for full submission guidelines. Application form not required.

Initial approach: Synopsis (1-2 pages)
Copies of proposal: 1
Deadline(s): July 1 for synopsis, and Sept. 1 for proposal
Board meeting date(s): Early Nov.
Final notification: Dec. 15

Officers: G.W. Hansen, Pres.; V.C. Nelson, V.P. and Treas.; D.K. Hansen, Secy.
Trustees: S. Hoke; J. Johnson; C.M. Nelson; D.R. Spurlock; J.M. Spurlock.
Number of staff: 1 part-time support.
EIN: 776016389

1057
Rivkin Family Foundation ◇

(formerly The Polinsky-Rivkin Family Foundation)
836 Prospect St., Ste. 202
La Jolla, CA 92037-4206 (858) 459-2631
Contact: David E. Hunt, Exec. Dir.

Established in 1985 in CA.
Donors: Jessie W. Polinsky†; Jeannie P. Rivkin; Arthur L. Rivkin; Beapol, Inc.; Mike Rivkin; Bob Rivkin; Linda Rivkin.
Foundation type: Independent foundation.
Financial data (yr. ended 12/31/05): Assets, $15,562,751 (M); gifts received, $1,195,561; expenditures, $700,345; qualifying distributions, $648,021; giving activities include $631,293 for 44 grants (high: $234,082; low: $100).
Fields of interest: Arts; Environment; Health care; Children/youth, services; Human services.
Type of support: General/operating support; Capital campaigns; Building/renovation; Emergency funds; Matching/challenge support.
Limitations: Giving primarily in CA. No support for religious organizations. No grants to individuals.
Application information: Application form not required.

Deadline(s): None
Board meeting date(s): Biannually

Officers: Jeannie P. Rivkin, Pres.; Arthur L. Rivkin, V.P.; Robert Rivkin, Secy.; Michael Rivkin, C.F.O.
Directors: Linda Rivkin; Luciene Rivkin.
EIN: 330072770
Selected grants: The following grants were reported in 2003.
$88,000 to Boys and Girls Club.
$50,000 to Childrens Museum of San Diego/Museo de los Ninos, San Diego, CA.
$50,000 to La Jolla Playhouse, La Jolla, CA.
$13,000 to McCallum Theater, Palm Desert, CA.
$11,175 to Variety Club.
$4,125 to Palm Springs Art Museum, Palm Springs, CA.
$3,000 to Shelter from the Storm, Palm Desert, CA.
$2,800 to Living Desert Reserve, Palm Desert, CA.
$600 to YMCA of the Desert Family, Palm Desert, CA.
$250 to Palm Springs International Film Festival, Palm Springs, CA.

1058
The Roberts Foundation ▼ ◇

P.O. Box 29906, Ste. 300
San Francisco, CA 94129-0906 (415) 561-6540
Contact: Lyman H. Casey, V.P.

Established in 1985 in CA.
Donors: George R. Roberts; Leanne B. Roberts; Hewlett Foundation.
Foundation type: Independent foundation.
Financial data (yr. ended 12/31/04): Assets, $74,924,257 (M); gifts received, $15,397,915; expenditures, $8,502,801; qualifying distributions, $8,453,241; giving activities include $8,297,901 for 69 grants (high: $1,305,600; low: $300; average: $5,000–$200,000).
Purpose and activities: Support for the Roberts Enterprise Development Fund (REDF) which creates opportunities for homeless and low-income individuals to move out of poverty. REDF partners with a portfolio of Bay Area nonprofit organizations to create jobs and training opportunities in social purpose enterprises.
Fields of interest: Education, special; Vocational education; Animal welfare; Animals/wildlife, preservation/protection; Health care; Employment; Children/youth, services; Family services; Homeless, human services; Economic development; Economically disadvantaged; Homeless.
Type of support: General/operating support; Continuing support; Program development.
Limitations: Applications not accepted. Giving limited to northern CA, with emphasis on San Francisco, San Mateo, Sonoma, Santa Clara, and San Benito counties. No support for religious organizations. No grants to individuals, or for medical research, endowment funds, or annual or year-end appeals.
Publications: Multi-year report.
Application information: Currently, the foundation has suspended all grantmaking except for that associated with the Roberts Enterprise Development Fund, URL: http://www.redf.org. No proposals are being accepted.

Board meeting date(s): Approximately Jan. and June

Officers and Director:* Leanne B. Roberts,* Pres.; George R. Roberts, V.P., and Secy.-Treas.; Lyman H. Casey, V.P.; Sue Schoenthaler, Treas.
EIN: 942967074
Selected grants: The following grants were reported in 2004.
$2,033,076 to REDF, San Francisco, CA. 2 grants: $1,258,076 (For unrestricted support), $775,000 (For unrestricted support).
$1,800,000 to San Francisco Museum of Modern Art, San Francisco, CA. 2 grants: $1,000,000 (For unrestricted support), $800,000 (For unrestricted support).
$1,620,800 to Culver Educational Foundation, Culver, IN. 2 grants: $820,800 (For unrestricted support for Pledge), $800,000 (For unrestricted support for Pledge).
$1,305,600 to San Francisco Society for the Prevention of Cruelty to Animals, San Francisco, CA. For unrestricted support.
$50,000 to Fine Arts Museums of San Francisco, San Francisco, CA. For unrestricted support.
$25,000 to Claremont McKenna College, Claremont, CA. For unrestricted support for annual fund.
$15,000 to Animali Farm, Santa Maria, CA. For unrestricted support.

1059
Jeanne and Sanford Robertson Fund ◇

825 Francisco St.
San Francisco, CA 94109

Established in 1993 in CA.
Donors: Sanford R. Robertson; Jeanne Robertson.
Foundation type: Independent foundation.
Financial data (yr. ended 3/31/05): Assets, $224,268 (M); expenditures, $618,677; qualifying distributions, $614,979; giving activities include $603,673 for 50 grants (high: $100,000; low: $100).
Purpose and activities: Giving primarily for arts and culture, higher education, hospitals, and human services.
Fields of interest: Museums; Museums (art); Performing arts, orchestra (symphony); Arts; Higher education; Education; Hospitals (general); Mental health/crisis services, formal/general education; Health organizations; Human services; Family services; Federated giving programs.
Limitations: Applications not accepted. Giving primarily in CA, with emphasis on San Francisco; some funding nationally. No grants to individuals.
Application information: Contributes only to pre-selected organizations.
Officers: Sanford R. Robertson, C.E.O. and Pres.; Jeanne Robertson, Secy.-Treas. and C.F.O.
EIN: 943181457

1060
Robinson Foundation for Hearing Disorders, Inc. ◇ ☆

2107 W. Washington Blvd.
Los Angeles, CA 90018-1536
Contact: Joe Adams, Dir.

Incorporated in 1986 in CA.
Donors: Ray Charles Robinson; Alexander Andreadis; Los Angeles Chamber of Commerce; Sun Valley Center; Family Celebration; World Events, LLC; American Ocean Campaign; Cass Productions; Bruce Willis Family Trust; Staples Center Foundation; Goldenvoice, LLC.
Foundation type: Independent foundation.
Financial data (yr. ended 12/31/05): Assets, $0 (M); gifts received, $1,000; expenditures, $500,100; qualifying distributions, $500,100; giving activities include $500,000 for 1 grant.
Purpose and activities: Giving primarily for higher education, human services and medical research, particularly hearing and ear research.
Fields of interest: Higher education; Education; Medical research, institute; Ear & throat research; Human services; Children/youth, services; Human services; Federated giving programs.
Limitations: Giving primarily in Los Angeles, CA and Albany and Atlanta, GA. No grants to individuals.
Application information:

Initial approach: Letter

Director: Joe Adams.
EIN: 954047622

1061
The Rock Foundation ◇

c/o Arthur Rock
1 Maritime Plz., Ste. 1220
San Francisco, CA 94111

Established in 1969.

Donor: Arthur Rock.
Foundation type: Independent foundation.
Financial data (yr. ended 12/31/05): Assets, $32,268,331 (M); gifts received, $5,577; expenditures, $1,727,680; qualifying distributions, $1,597,692; giving activities include $1,561,986 for 108 grants (high: $615,000; low: $40).
Fields of interest: Museums; Performing arts; Arts; Foundations (private grantmaking).
Limitations: Applications not accepted. Giving primarily in CA, with emphasis on the San Francisco Bay Area. No grants to individuals.
Application information: Contributes only to pre-selected organizations.
Officers and Directors:* Arthur Rock,* Pres.; Toni Rembe Rock,* Secy. and C.F.O.
EIN: 941671318
Selected grants: The following grants were reported in 2004.
$100,000 to Boys and Girls Clubs of Oakland, Oakland, CA.
$100,000 to San Francisco Opera Association, San Francisco, CA.
$100,000 to United Way of the Bay Area, San Francisco, CA.
$50,000 to International Rescue Committee, New York, NY.
$23,500 to Aspen Valley Community Foundation, Aspen, CO.
$5,000 to Leadership High School, San Francisco, CA.
$2,500 to Junior Achievement of Silicon Valley and Monterey Bay, Santa Clara, CA.
$1,000 to American Himalayan Foundation, San Francisco, CA.
$1,000 to San Francisco Performances, San Francisco, CA.

1062
Rogers Family Foundation ◇
315 W. Hueneme Rd.
Camarillo, CA 93012

Established in 1992 in CA.
Donor: Elizabeth Lloyd Davis Foundation.
Foundation type: Independent foundation.
Financial data (yr. ended 12/31/04): Assets, $422,097 (M); expenditures, $773,176; qualifying distributions, $771,313; giving activities include $771,313 for 19 grants (high: $726,700; low: $50).
Purpose and activities: Giving for arts and culture, the environment, and education.
Fields of interest: Museums; Arts; Education; Botanical gardens; Medical research, institute; Human services.
Limitations: Applications not accepted. Giving primarily in CA. No grants to individuals.
Application information: Contributes only to pre-selected organizations.
Officers: Richard Rogers, Pres.; Elizabeth Rogers, Secy. and C.F.O.
EIN: 770102429

1063
Mary Stuart Rogers Foundation
1801 H St., Ste. B-1, PMB 306
Modesto, CA 95354
FAX: (209) 572-6090;
E-mail: msroger1@pacbell.net

Established in 1985 in CA.

Donor: Mary Stuart Rogers†.
Foundation type: Independent foundation.
Financial data (yr. ended 12/31/05): Assets, $24,939,860 (M); gifts received, $8,389; expenditures, $2,949,461; qualifying distributions, $2,421,069; giving activities include $2,403,985 for 41 grants (high: $1,000,000; low: $500; average: $10,000–$250,000).
Purpose and activities: Giving primarily for higher education.
Fields of interest: Higher education; Human services; Children/youth, services; Christian agencies & churches.
Limitations: Giving primarily in CA. No grants to individuals.
Application information:
  Initial approach: Standard grant application with details
Officer: John Stuart Rogers, Pres.
EIN: 770099519
Selected grants: The following grants were reported in 2004.
$2,085,000 to Hughson Samaritan Village, Hughson, CA. 5 grants: $250,000 (For general support), $275,000 (For general support), $600,000 (For general support), $630,000 (For general support), $330,000 (For general support).
$1,000,000 to Lewis and Clark College, Portland, OR. For general support.
$750,000 to Notre Dame High School, San Jose, CA. For general support.
$250,000 to Victor Schools Foundation, Victor, MT. For general support.
$200,000 to Our Lady of Fatima Parish, Modesto, CA. For general support.
$200,000 to YMCA of Stanislaus County, Modesto, CA. For general support.

1064
T. Gary and Kathleen Rogers Private Family Foundation ◇ ☆
5929 College Ave., Ste. B2
Oakland, CA 94618

Established in 2003 in CA.
Donors: T. Gary Rogers; Kathleen Rogers.
Foundation type: Independent foundation.
Financial data (yr. ended 12/31/05): Assets, $52,262,576 (M); gifts received, $13,256,498; expenditures, $1,718,016; qualifying distributions, $1,686,272; giving activities include $1,686,247 for 1 grant.
Fields of interest: Foundations (private grantmaking).
Limitations: Applications not accepted. No grants to individuals.
Application information: Contributes only to pre-selected organizations.
Officers: Kathleen Rogers, Pres.; T. Gary Rogers, Secy.; Brian Rogers, Exec. Dir.
EIN: 651202020

1065
Rosenberg Foundation
131 Steuart St., Ste. 650
San Francisco, CA 94105 (415) 644-9777
Contact: Linda Moll, Business and Grants Mgr.
FAX: (415) 357-5016; E-mail: lmoll@rosenfound.org;
URL: http://www.rosenfound.org

Incorporated in 1935 in CA.
Donors: Max L. Rosenberg†; Charlotte S. Mack†.
Foundation type: Independent foundation.
Financial data (yr. ended 12/31/05): Assets, $60,137,166 (M); expenditures, $3,641,440; qualifying distributions, $3,056,232; giving activities include $2,463,600 for 62 grants (high: $150,000; low: $1,000; average: $10,000–$50,000).
Purpose and activities: Priority given to: 1) Families in poverty in rural and urban areas of CA: giving for activities which reduce dependency, promote self-help, create access to the economic mainstream, or which address the causes of poverty; 2) The changing population of CA: giving for activities which promote the full social, economic, and cultural integration of immigrants and other minorities into a pluralistic society; and 3) Child support reform.
Fields of interest: Legal services; Human services, reform; Civil rights, immigrants; Economics; Poverty studies; Public policy, research; Public affairs, reform; Minorities; Economically disadvantaged.
Type of support: Program development.
Limitations: Giving limited to CA, except for national grants. No grants to individuals, or for endowment, building, or capital funds, scholarships, fellowships, continuing support, annual campaigns, emergency funds, deficit financing, matching funds, land acquisition, renovation projects, or conferences and seminars; generally no grants for equipment, films, or publications (except when a necessary part of larger project).
Publications: Application guidelines; Annual report; Grants list.
Application information: The foundation will request additional and specific information if desired after receipt of letter of inquiry. Application form not required.
  Initial approach: Letter of inquiry (1-2 pages) or telephone call to Grants Mgr., no proposals without prior letter of inquiry
  Copies of proposal: 1
  Deadline(s): None
  Board meeting date(s): Varies
  Final notification: Varies
Officers and Directors:* Shauna I. Marshall,* Chair.; Benjamin Todd Jealous,* Pres. and Secy.; Hugo Morales,* Treas.; Phyllis Cook; Robert E. Friedman; Daniel Grossman; Bill Lann Lee; Herma Hill Kay; Leslie L. Luttgens; Albert F. Moreno.
Number of staff: 3 full-time professional; 1 full-time support.
EIN: 941186182

1066
The Louise and Claude Rosenberg, Jr. Family Foundation ◇
2465 Pacific Ave.
San Francisco, CA 94115
Contact: Claude Rosenberg, Jr., Secy.

Established in 1986 in CA.
Donors: Claude N. Rosenberg, Jr.; Louise J. Rosenberg.
Foundation type: Independent foundation.
Financial data (yr. ended 10/31/05): Assets, $33,841,156 (M); expenditures, $2,700,876; qualifying distributions, $2,374,562; giving activities include $2,348,914 for grants.
Purpose and activities: Support primarily for arts and culture, healthcare organizations, and education.

Fields of interest: Arts; Child development, education; Higher education; Health organizations; Human services; Child development, services; Jewish federated giving programs.
Type of support: General/operating support; Program development.
Limitations: Giving primarily in San Francisco, CA. No grants to individuals.
Application information: The foundation generally does not accept unsolicited requests for funds. Application form not required.
  Initial approach: Letter or proposal
  Deadline(s): None
  Board meeting date(s): Monthly
Officers and Directors:* Louise J. Rosenberg,* Pres.; Claude N. Rosenberg, Jr.,* Secy.; John P. Levin.
EIN: 943031132
Selected grants: The following grants were reported in 2004.
$500,000 to Every Child Can Learn Foundation, San Francisco, CA. For facilities renovation project.
$500,000 to University of California, San Francisco, CA. 2 grants: $350,000 (For Neurological Research), $150,000 to Institute for Neurodegenerative Diseases (For research).
$393,719 to Stanford University, Stanford, CA. 2 grants: $202,087 to Graduate School of Business (For Junior Faculty Scholar Fund), $191,632 to Graduate School of Business (For Junior Faculty Scholar Fund).
$200,000 to California Trout, San Francisco, CA. For general support.
$145,981 to K Q E D, San Francisco, CA. For grant made in form or stock.
$75,000 to Gateway High School, San Francisco, CA. For mentoring program.
$50,000 to San Francisco Day School, San Francisco, CA. For Jim Telander endowment for faculty.
$20,000 to San Francisco Ballet, San Francisco, CA. For annual fund.

1067
The Gene and Maxine Rosenfeld Family Foundation ◇ ☆
1100 Glendon Ave., Ste. 1140
Los Angeles, CA   90024

Established in 2004 in CA.
Donors: Eugene S. Rosenfeld; Maxine Rosenfeld.
Foundation type: Independent foundation.
Financial data (yr. ended 12/31/05): Assets, $3,604,989 (M); gifts received, $3,492,100; expenditures, $533,095; qualifying distributions, $533,044; giving activities include $532,834 for 12 grants (high: $369,434; low: $150).
Fields of interest: Media, television; Performing arts; Graduate/professional education; Hospitals (specialty); Human services; Children/youth, services; Disabilities, people with.
Limitations: Applications not accepted. Giving primarily in Los Angeles, CA. No grants to individuals.
Application information: Contributes only to pre-selected organizations.
Officers and Directors:* Eugene S. Rosenfeld,* C.E.O. and Pres.; Maxine Rosenfeld,* Secy. and C.F.O.
EIN: 383710097

1068
Rosengarten Horowitz Fund ◇
134 The Uplands
Berkeley, CA   94705

Established in 1996 in CA.
Donors: Jeffrey Horowitz; Lynn Horowitz.
Foundation type: Independent foundation.
Financial data (yr. ended 12/31/04): Assets, $8,865,724 (M); expenditures, $553,860; qualifying distributions, $426,894; giving activities include $380,000 for 16 grants (high: $50,000; low: $100).
Purpose and activities: Giving primarily for animal welfare, education, human services, federated giving programs, and religious organizations.
Fields of interest: Media/communications; Arts; Higher education; Education; Animal welfare; Health care; Human services; Federated giving programs; Christian agencies & churches; Jewish agencies & temples.
Limitations: Applications not accepted. Giving on a national basis. No grants to individuals.
Application information: Contributes only to pre-selected organizations.
Officers and Directors:* Lynn Horowitz,* Pres.; Jeffrey Horowitz,* Secy.; Jason Briggs,* C.F.O.
EIN: 943257271
Selected grants: The following grants were reported in 2004.
$50,000 to Prospect Sierra School, El Cerrito, CA.
$25,000 to Scripps College, Claremont, CA.
$25,000 to University of Puget Sound, Tacoma, WA.
$25,000 to University of San Diego, San Diego, CA.
$20,000 to Center for International Policy, DC.
$10,000 to Nantucket Historical Association, Nantucket, MA.
$10,000 to Northeast Harbor Library, Northeast Harbor, ME.
$2,000 to Fabric Workshop and Museum, Philadelphia, PA.
$2,000 to Ploughshares Fund, San Francisco, CA.
$1,000 to Global Exchange, San Francisco, CA.

1069
Bob A. Ross Foundation, Inc. ◇ ☆
950 Rockdale Dr.
San Francisco, CA   94127

Established in 1998 in CA.
Donors: Robert A. Ross Revocable Trust; Thomas E. Horn.
Foundation type: Independent foundation.
Financial data (yr. ended 12/31/05): Assets, $162,816 (M); gifts received, $465,000; expenditures, $381,461; qualifying distributions, $375,500; giving activities include $375,500 for grants.
Purpose and activities: Giving primarily for the arts.
Fields of interest: Performing arts, ballet; Arts; Human services.
Limitations: Applications not accepted. Giving primarily in San Francisco, CA. No grants to individuals.
Application information: Contributes only to pre-selected organizations.
Officers: Thomas E. Horn, C.E.O. and Pres.; Paul H. Melbostad, Secy.
EIN: 943254090
Selected grants: The following grants were reported in 2005.
$200,000 to San Francisco Ballet, San Francisco, CA.

$26,000 to AIDS Emergency Fund, San Francisco, CA.
$15,000 to Frameline, San Francisco, CA.
$10,000 to Larkin Street Youth Services, San Francisco, CA.
$5,000 to Episcopal Charities, San Francisco, CA.
$5,000 to Golden Gate Performing Arts, San Francisco, CA.
$5,000 to Lensic Performing Arts Center, Santa Fe, NM.
$2,500 to Theater Rhinoceros, San Francisco, CA.
$1,000 to International Museum of Women, San Francisco, CA.
$1,000 to Maitri Compassionate Care, San Francisco, CA.

1070
Rotasa Foundation ☆
(formerly Webb Roven Foundation)
c/o Joy Martin
775 E. Blithedale Ave., Ste. 309
Mill Valley, CA   94941
FAX: (415) 435-1871; E-mail: info@rotasa.org;
URL: http://www.rotasa.org

Established in 2001 in CA.
Donors: Max Webb; Rose Webb Roven.
Foundation type: Independent foundation.
Financial data (yr. ended 6/30/05): Assets, $152,512 (M); gifts received, $412,618; expenditures, $365,221; qualifying distributions, $351,906; giving activities include $338,578 for 51 grants (high: $75,000; low: $413).
Fields of interest: Media/communications; Visual arts; Performing arts, theater; Education, early childhood education; Environment, natural resources; Health care; Diabetes; Housing/shelter.
Limitations: Applications not accepted. Giving on a national basis, with an emphasis on CA. No grants to individuals.
Application information: Contributes only to pre-selected organizations.
Officers: Rose Webb Roven, Pres.; Susan Cummins, Secy.
EIN: 943412390
Selected grants: The following grants were reported in 2005.
$75,000 to University of California at San Francisco Foundation, San Francisco, CA.
$30,000 to Museum of Fine Arts, Houston, Houston, TX.
$22,000 to Foundation for National Progress, San Francisco, CA.
$21,000 to Marin Country Day School, Corte Madera, CA.
$8,500 to Palo Alto Art Center Foundation, Palo Alto, CA.
$8,360 to Grabhorn Institute, San Francisco, CA.
$6,800 to Headlands Center for the Arts, Sausalito, CA.
$6,000 to Joe Goode Performance Group, San Francisco, CA.
$5,000 to California College of the Arts, San Francisco, CA.
$3,000 to Museum of Craft and Folk Art, San Francisco, CA.

1071
Roth Family Foundation

c/o Rachel Roth
12021 Wilshire Blvd., Ste. 505
Los Angeles, CA   90025
FAX: (310) 264-2570;
E-mail: rachel_rothfamilyfoundation@hotmail.com

Established in 1966 in CA.
Donors: Louis Roth and Co.; Louis Roth†; Fannie Roth†; Harry Roth†.
Foundation type: Independent foundation.
Financial data (yr. ended 10/31/05): Assets, $12,736,495 (M); expenditures, $595,097; qualifying distributions, $570,811; giving activities include $496,003 for 104 grants (high: $30,000; low: $350; average: $1,000–$5,000), and $10,000 for 2 employee matching gifts.
Purpose and activities: The foundation's mission is commitment to progressive social change. The foundation invests in organizations that inspire hope, dignity, and creativity, primarily in the Los Angeles, CA, area. Grounded in a legacy of social justice and civil rights, the foundation helps connect communities to the services, opportunities, and tools for self-empowerment and self-expression.
Fields of interest: Media, television; Media, radio; Humanities; Arts; Environment; Health care; Youth development; Civil rights, equal rights; Civil rights; Economic development.
Type of support: Scholarship funds; Fellowships; Capital campaigns; General/operating support; Matching/challenge support.
Limitations: Giving primarily in Los Angeles, CA. No support for fraternal organizations. No grants to individuals.
Publications: Application guidelines; Grants list.
Application information: Generally, no more than 1 grant per organization per fiscal year; no grants to 1 organization for more than 3 years.
  Initial approach: 1-to 4-page letter
  Deadline(s): None
  Board meeting date(s): Semiannually
Officers and Directors:* Rachel Roth,* C.E.O. and Exec. Dir.; Michael P. Roth,* Pres.; Gil Garcetti,* V.P.; Sukey Garcett,* Secy.-Treas.; Dana Boldt; Eric Garcetti; Sarah Roth; Andrea Roth-Fedida.
Number of staff: 1 part-time professional.
EIN: 880352682
Selected grants: The following grants were reported in 2005.
$25,000 to K C E T Community Television of Southern California, Los Angeles, CA.
$10,000 to Audubon California, Sacramento, CA.
$10,000 to Santa Monica College Foundation, Santa Monica, CA.
$7,500 to Liberty Hill Foundation, Santa Monica, CA.
$7,200 to Taking the Reins, Los Angeles, CA.
$7,000 to International House, Berkeley, CA.
$5,000 to California Institute of the Arts, Valencia, CA.
$5,000 to Center for Nonviolent Education and Parenting, Los Angeles, CA.
$4,000 to Historical Society of Southern California, Los Angeles, CA.
$3,500 to Girls Inc. of Los Angeles, Pasadena, CA.

1072
A. Frank and Dorothy B. Rothschild Fund ✧ ☆

37 Mountain Meadow Dr.
Woodside, CA   94062

Established in 1952 in IL.
Donor: Dorothy B. Rothschild.
Foundation type: Independent foundation.
Financial data (yr. ended 12/31/05): Assets, $724,707 (M); expenditures, $2,151,330; qualifying distributions, $2,126,585; giving activities include $2,126,585 for grants.
Purpose and activities: Giving primarily for health care and various medical disciplines.
Fields of interest: Arts; Education; Environment; Animals/wildlife, preservation/protection; Hospitals (general); Health care; Health organizations, association; Human services; Jewish agencies & temples.
Limitations: Applications not accepted. Giving primarily in IL, MI, and NY. No grants to individuals.
Application information: Contributes only to pre-selected organizations.
Officers: A. Frank Rothschild, Jr., V.P. and Treas.; David N. Rothschild, V.P.; Holly B. Rothschild, V.P.; Lee J. Strauss, Jr., V.P.; Henry DeVos Lawrie, Jr., Secy.
EIN: 366049231

1073
Rudd Family Foundation ✧

3468 Mt. Diablo Blvd., Ste. B-110
Lafayette, CA   94549

Established in 1998 in CA.
Donors: Andrew T. Rudd; Virginia A. Rudd.
Foundation type: Independent foundation.
Financial data (yr. ended 8/31/05): Assets, $18,889,094 (M); expenditures, $2,153,728; qualifying distributions, $1,921,428; giving activities include $1,921,428 for 12 grants (high: $1,100,000; low: $10).
Purpose and activities: Giving primarily for higher education, including youth athletic programs.
Fields of interest: Elementary/secondary education; Higher education; Athletics/sports, school programs; Human services.
Type of support: General/operating support; Equipment; Endowments; Research.
Limitations: Applications not accepted. Giving primarily in MA, NY and NM; some giving also in CA. No grants to individuals.
Application information: Contributes only to pre-selected organizations.
Trustees: Alexandria A. Rudd; Andrew T. Rudd; Christopher A. Rudd; Natalie A. Rudd; Nicholas S. Rudd; Virginia A. Rudd.
EIN: 946715800
Selected grants: The following grants were reported in 2005.
$1,100,000 to University of Massachusetts, Amherst, MA.
$502,260 to Cornell University, Ithaca, NY.
$310,000 to Columbia University, New York, NY.

1074
Arthur N. Rupe Foundation ✧

(formerly Rupe Foundation)
c/o Susan C. Van Aacken
3887 State St., Ste. 22
Santa Barbara, CA   93105   (805) 687-8586

Established in 1991 in CA.
Donor: Arthur N. Rupe.
Foundation type: Independent foundation.
Financial data (yr. ended 6/30/05): Assets, $15,025,746 (M); gifts received, $771,576; expenditures, $703,631; qualifying distributions, $604,096; giving activities include $582,500 for 10 grants (high: $276,500; low: $1,000).
Purpose and activities: Giving to impact and change society by alleviating the trauma that plagues society's struggles over controversial social issues, through such methods as the support of education, objective research, scholarly studies, and the dissemination of the results thereof; to establish and maintain a comprehensive academic discipline or center to deal with human nature as it imparts cultural, political, social and economic behaviors; to educate the public about these issues; to advance the field of medicine such as by assisting in the research, treatment and alleviation of various diseases (including mental health) and their consequences; to contribute or otherwise assist corporations, organizations and institutions carrying on such activities which are consistent with these purposes; to acquire by purchase or gift, such property whether real or personal, to facilitate the foregoing purposes; and to engage in any other lawful activities permitted under the California Nonprofit Public Benefit Corporation Law.
Fields of interest: Higher education; Education; Human services.
Limitations: Applications not accepted. Giving primarily in CA. No support for organizations lacking 501(c)(3) status. No grants to individuals.
Application information: Contributes only to pre-selected organizations.
Officers and Directors:* Arthur N. Rupe,* Pres.; Jerry J. James,* 1st V.P.; Steve Forsell,* 2nd V.P.; Susan C. Van Aacken, Secy.; Richard L. Hunt,* C.F.O.; James S. Huggins; Leonard S. Jarrott; Beverly M. Rupe; Joseph White.
EIN: 770278838
Selected grants: The following grants were reported in 2003.
$645,500 to El Adobe Corporation, Santa Barbara, CA.
$500 to Mon Valley Education Consortium, McKeesport, PA. For general support.

1075
Ryan Family Charitable Foundation ✧ ☆

(formerly David Claude Ryan Foundation)
P.O. Box 6409
San Diego, CA   92166-0409
Contact: Jerome D. Ryan, Pres.

Established in 1959 in CA.
Donors: Jerome D. Ryan; Gladys B. Ryan; Anne E. Ryan; Ryco Assocs.; Gladys B. Ryan Trust.
Foundation type: Independent foundation.
Financial data (yr. ended 12/31/05): Assets, $7,755,654 (M); gifts received, $203,632; expenditures, $560,384; qualifying distributions, $512,159; giving activities include $512,159 for grants.

Purpose and activities: Giving to religious institutions, higher education, and art and cultural institutes; funding also for YMCAs.
Fields of interest: Higher education; Human services; YM/YWCAs & YM/YWHAs; Children/youth, services; Christian agencies & churches; Religion.
Type of support: General/operating support; Continuing support.
Limitations: Giving primarily in CA, with emphasis on San Diego. No grants to individuals.
Application information:
Initial approach: Letter
Deadline(s): None
Officers: Jerome D. Ryan, Pres.; David M. Ryan, V.P. and Secy.-Treas.; Michael F. Ryan, V.P.
EIN: 956051140
Selected grants: The following grants were reported in 2004.
$20,000 to First United Methodist Church, San Diego, CA.
$20,000 to San Diego Rescue Mission, San Diego, CA.
$10,000 to Childrens Hospital Foundation, San Diego, CA.
$8,495 to Salvation Army, Redding, CA.
$8,000 to San Diego Aerospace Museum, San Diego, CA.
$4,500 to Capitol Ministries, Santa Clarita, CA.
$4,000 to Campus Crusade for Christ International, Orlando, FL.
$2,000 to Home of Guiding Hands, Lakeside, CA.
$2,000 to Smile Train, New York, NY.
$1,000 to Kona Historical Society, Captain Cook, HI.

1076
David & Robin Ryan Family Foundation ✧
P.O. Box 7285
Rancho Santa Fe, CA 92067 (858) 259-0100
Contact: David Ryan, Secy.

Established in 2001 in CA.
Donor: David Ryan.
Foundation type: Independent foundation.
Financial data (yr. ended 12/31/05): Assets, $551,601 (M); gifts received, $511,878; expenditures, $525,945; qualifying distributions, $525,755; giving activities include $525,700 for 12 + grants (high: $500,000).
Fields of interest: Education; Cancer research; Protestant agencies & churches.
Limitations: Applications not accepted. Giving primarily in CA. No grants to individuals.
Application information: Unsolicited requests for funds not accepted.
Officers: Robin Ryan, Pres.; David Ryan, Secy. and C.F.O.
EIN: 912169787
Selected grants: The following grants were reported in 2003.
$500,000 to Mission Baptist Church of the Bahamas, Bahamas. .
$5,982 to Childrens Hospital, Rancho Santa Fe, CA.
$3,500 to Rancho Santa Fe Community Center, Rancho Santa Fe, CA.
$2,000 to Rancho Santa Fe School Parent Teacher Organization, Rancho Santa Fe, CA.
$2,000 to Wheeler School, Providence, RI.
$1,000 to Burnham Institute, La Jolla, CA.

1077
Ryzman Foundation, Inc. ✧
c/o Barak
5967 W. 3rd St., Ste. 102
Los Angeles, CA 90036

Established in 1980 in CA.
Donors: Betty Ryzman; Zvi Ryzman.
Foundation type: Independent foundation.
Financial data (yr. ended 11/30/04): Assets, $12,184,581 (M); gifts received, $191,437; expenditures, $874,015; qualifying distributions, $874,010; giving activities include $872,180 for grants.
Fields of interest: Education; Jewish agencies & temples.
Limitations: Applications not accepted. Giving primarily in CA. No grants to individuals.
Application information: Contributes only to pre-selected organizations.
Officers: Zvi Ryzman, Pres.; Betty Ryzman, Secy.-Treas.
EIN: 953653055

1078
S.G. Foundation
P.O. Box 444
Buellton, CA 93427 (805) 688-0088
Contact: Pamela Grattan, Admin.

Established in 1984 in CA.
Donors: Escondido Serenas Develop, Inc.; Lomas La Jolla Financial, Inc.; John M. Perkins Foundation.
Foundation type: Independent foundation.
Financial data (yr. ended 12/31/04): Assets, $13,291,793 (M); gifts received, $25,000; expenditures, $888,944; qualifying distributions, $704,663; giving activities include $634,663 for 31 grants (high: $75,000; low: $750), and $70,000 for 2 employee matching gifts.
Purpose and activities: The foundation's purpose is to encourage and enable individuals and communities to partner together to help people help themselves. The foundation supports projects that are self-help in nature, affirm individual dignity, and create incentives for people to participate in their own self-development. The foundation accepts proposals for program expenses for national and international human service relief and development projects. Projects must demonstrate a specific and focused community-based strategy for economic development in the areas of hunger relief, jobs, and small business start-up. The foundation also accepts proposals for ethnic leadership development programs, senior care, and educational/leadership development programs for youth, child abuse and neglect prevention, and strengthening family values.
Fields of interest: Human services; Family services; Community development; Christian agencies & churches.
Type of support: Program development; General/operating support; Continuing support; Seed money; Program-related investments/loans; Matching/challenge support.
Limitations: Giving primarily in central CA, as well as Central America, Mexico, Haiti, China, Indonesia and Romania. No support for athletics, politics, the arts, music, or museums. No grants for building projects, capital improvement, endowments, research, books, films, or media.
Publications: Application guidelines; Grants list; Occasional report.

Application information: Application form not required.
Initial approach: Letter
Copies of proposal: 1
Deadline(s): None
Officers: William Sauer, Pres.; John Donati, V.P.; Lynn R. Gildred, Secy.; Stuart Gildred, Jr., Treas.
Directors: Russell Fraser; Joseph Lambert.
Number of staff: 1 part-time professional; 1 part-time support.
EIN: 330048410
Selected grants: The following grants were reported in 2003.
$100,000 to Amigos de Honduras, Seattle, WA. For emergency hurricane relief.
$85,000 to International Foundation, DC. For Westmont Bethel Hospital.
$53,500 to Mercy Ships, Garden Valley, TX. For operating support.
$50,000 to Focus on the Family, Colorado Springs, CO. For Alliance Defense Fund.
$50,000 to World Relief, Baltimore, MD. For Nicaraguan Agricultural Expansion.
$47,300 to Direct Relief International, Santa Barbara, CA. 2 grants: $27,300 (For Manos De Auda Clinic in Mexico), $20,000 (For Rio Beni Health Project).
$45,623 to Food for the Hungry, Phoenix, AZ. For housing project.
$40,000 to Opportunity International, Oak Brook, IL. For Latin America Standardizing project.
$20,000 to Young Life, Santa Barbara, CA. For Hispanic and disabled youth program.

1079
Saban Family Foundation ▼ ✧
10100 Santa Monica Blvd., 26th Fl.
Los Angeles, CA 90067 (310) 557-5100
Contact: Shai Waxman-Abramson, Prog. Dir.

Established in 1999 in CA.
Donors: Haim Saban; Cheryl Saban.
Foundation type: Independent foundation.
Financial data (yr. ended 12/31/04): Assets, $3,904,554 (M); expenditures, $5,105,987; qualifying distributions, $5,101,908; giving activities include $4,674,127 for 26 grants (high: $4,100,000; low: $1,000; average: $5,000–$50,000).
Purpose and activities: Support for children's health research and social welfare in Los Angeles, CA, and in Israel.
Fields of interest: Hospitals (specialty); Medical research, institute; Nutrition; Children, services; International affairs; Jewish agencies & temples.
International interests: Israel.
Type of support: General/operating support; Continuing support; Annual campaigns; Building/renovation; Program development; Conferences/seminars; Seed money; Curriculum development; Scholarship funds; Research; Matching/challenge support.
Limitations: Giving primarily in CA and Israel. No grants to individuals.
Publications: Application guidelines.
Application information: Application form required.
Initial approach: Letter on organization letterhead
Copies of proposal: 1
Deadline(s): None
Final notification: Within 6 months
Officers and Directors: * Cheryl Saban,* Pres.; Adam Chesnoff,* V.P.; Niveen Tadros, Secy.; Nancy Schultz, C.F.O.; Haim Saban, Treas.

Number of staff: 1 full-time professional; 1 full-time support.
EIN: 954769273
Selected grants: The following grants were reported in 2004.
$4,100,000 to Childrens Hospital Los Angeles, Los Angeles, CA. For pediatric research and operations.

1080
Sacramento Region Community Foundation

(formerly Sacramento Regional Foundation)
740 University Ave., Ste. 110
Sacramento, CA 95825 (916) 921-7723
Contact: Ruth Blank, C.E.O.; Arlene Wilson-Grant, Prog. Off.
FAX: (916) 921-7725; E-mail: info@sacregcf.org;
Additional E-mail: arlene@sacregcf.org;
Field-of-Interest grant application E-mail:
applications@sacregcf.org; URL: http://
www.sacregcf.org

Incorporated in 1983 in CA.
Foundation type: Community foundation.
Financial data (yr. ended 12/31/05): Assets, $101,767,111 (M); gifts received, $36,431,000; expenditures, $9,370,825; giving activities include $8,032,677 for grants.
Purpose and activities: The mission of the foundation is to serve as a leader and trusted partner in expanding philanthropic activity and enhancing its impact for the betterment of the Sacramento region community.
Fields of interest: Visual arts; Museums; Performing arts; Performing arts, theater; Humanities; Historic preservation/historical societies; Arts; Child development, education; Elementary school/ education; Vocational education; Higher education; Adult education—literacy, basic skills & GED; Education, reading; Education; Environment, natural resources; Environmental education; Environment; Health care; Mental health/crisis services; Health organizations, association; AIDS; Alcoholism; Legal services; Food services; Housing/shelter, development; Youth development, services; Children/youth, services; Child development, services; Family services; Residential/custodial care, hospices; Aging, centers/services; Minorities/ immigrants, centers/services; Homeless, human services; Human services; Urban/community development; Community development; Voluntarism promotion; Social sciences; Public policy, research; Government/public administration; Leadership development; Aging; Disabilities, people with; Minorities; Economically disadvantaged; Homeless.
Type of support: General/operating support; Management development/capacity building; Building/renovation; Emergency funds; Program development; Publication; Seed money; Scholarship funds; Technical assistance; Program evaluation; Employee-related scholarships; Scholarships—to individuals; Matching/challenge support.
Limitations: Giving primarily focused on organizations within or those offering services to El Dorado, Placer, Sacramento, and Yolo counties, CA. No support for sectarian purposes or private foundations. No grants to individuals (except designated fund scholarships and through the Artists in Crisis Fund), or for annual campaigns, operating funds, capital campaigns, endowments, building funds, continuing support, deficit financing,

foundation-managed projects, research, or land acquisition; no loans.
Publications: Annual report; Financial statement; Informational brochure; Newsletter.
Application information: Visit foundation Web site for application forms and guidelines. Applications may be submitted via U.S. mail, e-mail, or fax. Application form required.
Initial approach: Submit application form and attachments
Copies of proposal: 10
Deadline(s): Oct. 18 for Field-of-Interest grants and Oct. 6 for Education mini-grants; varies for scholarships
Board meeting date(s): Jan., Mar., May, July, Sept., and Nov.
Final notification: Nov. 30
Officers and Directors:* Ruth Blank,* C.E.O.; Ralph Andersen,* Pres.; Larry R. Gilzean,* V.P.; Donald C. Poole,* Secy.; Jim McCallum, C.F.O.; William G. Hegg,* Treas.; Nicholas Alexander; Stephen F. Boutin; Stephen A. Brandenburger; Patricia Cochran; Dan Cole; Michael Dunlavey; Robert M. Earl; Scott T. Hanson; Oleta Lambert; Robert L. Lorber; David Lucchetti; Elizabeth Rindskopf Parker; Daniel I. Parrish; Jeanne Reaves; Lillian Sioukas; Fred Teichert; Jesse Vaughan; Frank Whittaker; Mike Ziegler.
Number of staff: 7 full-time professional; 2 full-time support.
EIN: 942891517

1081
Saga Foundation

(formerly W.P. Laughlin Foundation)
1100 Alma St., Ste. 201
Menlo Park, CA 94025 (650) 838-9944
FAX: (650) 838-9990; Mailing address: c/o David S. Kruis, Treas., 136 E. Michigan Ave., Ste. 1201, Kalamazoo, MI 49007-3936; URL: http://
sagafoundation.org/

Established in 1993 in MI as successor to W.P. Laughlin Charitable Foundation Trust.
Donor: Wilbur P. Laughlin.
Foundation type: Operating foundation.
Financial data (yr. ended 12/31/05): Assets, $110,943 (M); gifts received, $1,065,711; expenditures, $1,968,056; qualifying distributions, $1,961,411; giving activities include $615,000 for 3 grants (high: $425,000; low: $30,000).
Purpose and activities: The foundation is dedicated to engaging former heads of state and other world leaders to take action to eliminate weapons of mass destruction - nuclear, chemical, and biological weapons that threaten the safety and very future of our world. The foundation supports attempts to maximize the effectiveness of world leaders and organizations involved in practical, innovative, and ethical solutions to global problems concerning the security and safety of nations and individuals.
Fields of interest: Higher education; International peace/security; International affairs; Public affairs, research; Public policy, research.
Type of support: General/operating support; Program development.
Limitations: Applications not accepted. Giving primarily to national organizations in CA and Washington, DC. No grants to individuals.
Application information: Contributes only to pre-selected organizations.
Officers and Trustees:* Wilbur P. Laughlin,* Chair. and C.E.O.; David J. Bartoshuk,* Pres.; Melissa

Schoeb, Exec. V.P. and Dir. of Comms.; James S. Hilboldt,* V.P.; James C. Melvin,* Secy.; David S. Kruis, Treas.; Julie A. Johnson.
EIN: 383097160

1082
The Sai Ram Foundation ✧

1118 E. Colorado St.
Glendale, CA 91205 (818) 952-9600
Contact: Harshadray Patel, Pres.

Established in 2001 in CA.
Donors: Harshadray Patel; Nilesh Patel.
Foundation type: Independent foundation.
Financial data (yr. ended 12/31/03): Assets, $34,675 (M); gifts received, $114,130; expenditures, $324,740; qualifying distributions, $324,182; giving activities include $323,000 for 2 grants (high: $172,000; low: $151,000).
Fields of interest: Education.
International interests: India.
Limitations: Giving primarily in India.
Application information:
Deadline(s): None
Officers: Harshadray Patel, Pres.; Nilesh Patel, Secy.; Ramila Patel, Treas.
EIN: 954825779

1083
The Lesly & Pat Sajak Foundation ✧

301 N. Lake Ave., Ste. 900
Pasadena, CA 91101

Established in 1995 in CA.
Donors: Pat Sajak; Lesly Sajak.
Foundation type: Independent foundation.
Financial data (yr. ended 12/31/05): Assets, $140,832 (M); gifts received, $260,000; expenditures, $451,685; qualifying distributions, $451,585; giving activities include $451,500 for 14 grants (high: $100,000; low: $1,000).
Purpose and activities: Giving primarily for higher and other education as well as for health and social services.
Fields of interest: Education; Human services; Residential/custodial care, hospices.
Limitations: Applications not accepted. Giving primarily in CA and MD. No grants to individuals.
Application information: Contributes only to pre-selected organizations.
Officers: Pat Sajak, Pres.; Lesly Sajak, Secy.; Gregory B. Stanislawski, Treas.
EIN: 954511126

1084
The Saje Foundation ✧

17291 Irvine Blvd., No. 351
Tustin, CA 92780 (714) 734-7808
FAX: (714) 734-7834;
E-mail: info@sajefoundation.org; URL: http://
www.sajefoundation.org

Established in 1998 in IL.
Donors: Elaine McKay; Robert L. McKay.
Foundation type: Independent foundation.
Financial data (yr. ended 12/31/05): Assets, $18,012 (M); gifts received, $1,962,009; expenditures, $2,077,105; qualifying distributions, $1,961,000; giving activities include $1,961,000 for 28 grants (high: $750,000; low: $1,000).

Purpose and activities: The mission of the foundation is to support Christian organizations in the United States and in the developing world. Focus areas include: 1) HIV/Aids in Africa; 2) Christian Community Development; 3) Spread of Evangelism; 4) Emergency crisis relief and 5) Christian Micro-Enterprise Development.

Fields of interest: Education; AIDS; Youth development; Human services; International economic development; International relief; International affairs; Christian agencies & churches.

International interests: Developing countries.

Limitations: Applications not accepted. Giving on a national and international basis. No grants to individuals.

Application information: Contributes only to pre-selected organizations.

Officer and Trustees:* John McKay,* Pres. and Secy.-Treas.; Elaine McKay; Robert L. McKay, Jr.

EIN: 364309903

Selected grants: The following grants were reported in 2004.

$750,000 to Opportunity International, Oak Brook, IL.

$200,000 to Samaritans Purse, Boone, NC.

$200,000 to World Vision, Federal Way, WA.

$54,000 to Church Resource Ministries, Anaheim, CA.

$50,000 to International Justice Mission, Alexandria, VA.

1085
Sambar Private Foundation ◇

7051 E. Avenida de Santiago
Anaheim, CA 92807

Established in 1998.

Donors: Gerald D. Barnes; Deborah M. Barnes.

Foundation type: Independent foundation.

Financial data (yr. ended 12/31/04): Assets, $1,684,186 (M); gifts received, $1,510; expenditures, $1,500,629; qualifying distributions, $1,500,000; giving activities include $1,500,000 for 2 grants (high: $1,000,000; low: $500,000).

Fields of interest: Secondary school/education; Athletics/sports, academies.

Limitations: Applications not accepted. Giving primarily in CA. No grants to individuals.

Application information: Contributes only to pre-selected organizations.

Trustees: Deborah M. Barnes; Gerald D. Barnes.

EIN: 336231821

1086
The Samueli Foundation ◇

(formerly The Samueli Family Foundation)
537 Newport Center Dr.
P.O. Box 372
Newport Beach, CA 92660 (949) 760-4300
Contact: Mike Lefkowitz, Dir., Spiritual Prog.

Established in 1998 in CA.

Donors: The Samueli 1995 Family Trust; Samueli Charitable Trust No. 00-1.

Foundation type: Independent foundation.

Financial data (yr. ended 12/31/03): Assets, $207,847 (M); expenditures, $2,735,466; qualifying distributions, $2,726,649; giving activities include $2,439,642 for 122 grants (high: $120,000; low: $250).

Purpose and activities: Support for performing arts including opera, ballet, and theater; also education; human services; Christian agencies and churches; and Jewish agencies and temples.

Fields of interest: Performing arts; Performing arts centers; Performing arts, ballet; Performing arts, theater; Performing arts, opera; Education, research; Education; Human services; Family services, parent education; Christian agencies & churches; Jewish agencies & temples.

Limitations: Giving primarily in CA.

Application information: Application form required.
Initial approach: Letter
Deadline(s): None

Officers: Henry Samueli, Pres. and C.F.O.; Susan Samueli, Secy.; Michael Schulman, Exec. Dir.

EIN: 330758237

Selected grants: The following grants were reported in 2004.

$320,943 to Opera Pacific, Santa Ana, CA.

$216,741 to Institute for Jewish and Community Research, San Francisco, CA.

$213,784 to Chapman University, Orange, CA.

$206,000 to Orangewood Childrens Foundation, Santa Ana, CA.

$176,248 to Opportunity International, Oak Brook, IL.

$132,603 to Ocean Institute, Dana Point, CA.

$74,002 to World Impact, Los Angeles, CA.

$70,000 to Josephs Hope, Santa Ana, CA.

$20,090 to Friends of the Observatory, Los Angeles, CA.

$10,000 to University of California, Los Angeles, CA.

1087
The San Diego Foundation ▼

(formerly San Diego Community Foundation)
2508 Historic Decatur Rd., Ste. 200
San Diego, CA 92106 (619) 235-2300
Contact: Robert A. Kelly, C.E.O.
FAX: (619) 239-1710;
E-mail: info@sdfoundation.org; Additional tel.: (858) 385-1595 (for North County); URL: http://www.sdfoundation.org

Established in 1975 in CA.

Foundation type: Community foundation.

Financial data (yr. ended 6/30/06): Assets, $484,163,000 (M); gifts received, $37,005,000; expenditures, $52,251,000; giving activities include $41,231,000 for 2,983 grants (high: $7,800,000; low: $25), and $2,285,000 for 518 grants to individuals (high: $103,000; low: $250).

Purpose and activities: The foundation seeks to improve the quality of life within all local communities by promoting and increasing responsible and effective philanthropy, with giving to nonprofit organizations in the areas of asset building, civil society, education, environment/animal welfare, scholarship, human/social services, health, arts and culture.

Fields of interest: Visual arts; Museums; Performing arts; Performing arts, dance; Performing arts, theater; Performing arts, music; Arts; Education, early childhood education; Child development, education; Elementary school/education; Secondary school/education; Vocational education; Higher education; Adult education—literacy, basic skills & GED; Education, reading; Education; Environment, research; Environment, public policy; Environment, volunteer services; Environment, pollution control; Environment, water resources;

Environment, land resources; Environment; Animal welfare; Reproductive health, family planning; Health care; Substance abuse, services; Mental health/crisis services; Health organizations, association; AIDS; Alcoholism; Medical research, institute; AIDS research; Crime/violence prevention, youth; Housing/shelter, research; Housing/shelter, information services; Housing/shelter, public education; Housing/shelter, development; Recreation; Children/youth, services; Child development, services; Family services; Residential/custodial care, hospices; Aging, centers/services; Women, centers/services; Homeless, human services; Human services; Community development; Voluntarism promotion; Science, research; Science; Aging; Disabilities, people with; Minorities; Women; Economically disadvantaged; Homeless.

International interests: Mexico.

Type of support: General/operating support; Continuing support; Building/renovation; Equipment; Land acquisition; Program development; Publication; Seed money; Curriculum development; Scholarship funds; Technical assistance; Program evaluation; Program-related investments/loans; Employee matching gifts; Scholarships—to individuals; Matching/challenge support.

Limitations: Giving primarily in the greater San Diego, CA, region. No support for religious organizations. No grants to individuals (except for scholarships), or for annual or capital fund campaigns, endowment funds, conferences, travel, or to underwrite fundraising events and performances.

Publications: Annual report; Financial statement; Grants list; Informational brochure; Newsletter.

Application information: Visit foundation Web site for grant application and guidelines. Application form required.
Initial approach: Submit online application and proposal
Deadline(s): Jan. 15
Board meeting date(s): Bimonthly beginning July through May
Final notification: 3 to 5 months

Officers and Board of Governors:* Bruce G. Blakley,* Chair.; John C. Raymond,* Vice-Chair.; Robert A. Kelly, C.E.O. and Pres.; Mariano Diaz, Sr. V.P., Community Partnerships; Deborah Hoffman, Sr. V.P., Fund Svcs.; Paul Thompson, Sr. V.P., Organization Success; Sarah Wilensky, Sr., V.P., Mktg. & Comms.; Sara Slaughter, V.P., Finance & Admin.; Rafael A. Arreola,* Secy.; Duane Drake, C.F.O.; Raymond V. Thomas,* Treas.; Jennifer Adams-Brooks; Fred Applegate; Dennis Arriola; Dr. Roger Cornell; Darcy C. Bingham; James M. Cowley; Martha Dennis, Ph.D.; Nova M. Faine, M.D.; Thomas N. Fat; Bill K. Geppert; Jane Trevor Fetter; Thomas Hall; Jerry Hoffmeister; Gary E. Jacobs; Conny Jamison; Jerome Katzin; Denise Lew, Ph.D.; Paul Meyer; Barry I. Newman; Steven R. Smith; Colette Carson Royston; Eugene L. Step; Daniel Sullivan, Ph.D.; Carisa Wisniewski; John Wylie; Elizabeth Y. Yamada; James Ziegler.

Number of staff: 25 full-time professional; 8 part-time professional; 11 full-time support; 3 part-time support.

EIN: 952942582

Selected grants: The following grants were reported in 2006.

$10,087,366 to San Diego Revitalization Corporation, San Diego, CA. 2 grants: $7,837,366 (For general support), $2,250,000 (For general support).

$1,250,000 to University of California at San Diego Foundation, La Jolla, CA. 2 grants: $750,000 (For Lewis Judd Chair Endowment), $500,000 (For University House Project).

$580,000 to National Cowboy and Western Heritage Museum, Oklahoma City, OK. For general support.

$265,613 to Operation Homefront, San Diego, CA. For general support.

$75,000 to Nonprofit Management Solutions, San Diego, CA. For technology consulting and training for non-profits in San Diego.

$21,500 to Second Chance Youth Program, Salinas, CA. To sponsor STRIVE class.

$20,000 to Campanile Foundation, San Diego, CA. For Reading Recovery program.

$20,000 to Installation Gallery, San Diego, CA. For Make Arts Lively and ongoing aspect of elementary school education, to equip teachers to be effective in incorporating arts into their teaching strategies.

1088
The San Francisco Foundation ▼

225 Bush St., Ste. 500
San Francisco, CA 94104-4224 (415) 733-8500
Contact: Sandra R. Hernandez M.D., C.E.O.
FAX: (415) 477-2783; E-mail: rec@sff.org; Intent to Apply E-mail: apps@sff.org; URL: http://www.sff.org

Established in 1948 in CA by resolution and declaration of trust.
Foundation type: Community foundation.
Financial data (yr. ended 6/30/06): Assets, $883,443,000 (M); gifts received, $70,888,000; expenditures, $73,372,000; giving activities include $67,822,000 for 5,703 grants, and $278,000 for 54 grants to individuals.
Purpose and activities: The foundation mobilizes resources and acts as a catalyst for change to build strong communities, foster civic leadership, and promote philanthropy. Grants principally in six categories: the arts and culture, community health, education, environment, neighborhood and community development, and social justice.
Fields of interest: Arts, cultural/ethnic awareness; Media/communications; Performing arts; Performing arts, dance; Humanities; Arts, artist's services; Arts; Education, early childhood education; Child development, education; Elementary school/education; Higher education; Adult education—literacy, basic skills & GED; Education, reading; Education; Environment, natural resources; Environment; Reproductive health, family planning; Health care; Substance abuse, services; Mental health/crisis services; Health organizations, association; Cancer; AIDS; Alcoholism; Crime/violence prevention, youth; Legal services; Employment; Housing/shelter, development; Youth development, services; Children/youth, services; Child development, services; Family services; Aging, centers/services; Homeless, human services; Human services; International human rights; Civil rights; Urban/community development; Community development; Voluntarism promotion; Public policy, research; Government/public administration; Leadership development; Public affairs; Aging; Disabilities, people with; Minorities; Immigrants/refugees; Economically disadvantaged; Homeless.
Type of support: General/operating support; Program development; Fellowships; Technical assistance; Program-related investments/loans;

Employee matching gifts; Scholarships—to individuals.
Limitations: Giving limited to the San Francisco Bay Area, CA, counties of Alameda, Contra Costa, Marin, San Francisco, and San Mateo. No support for religious purposes, or medical, academic, or scientific research. No grants to individuals (except scholarships and fellowships designated by a donor) or for conferences or one-time events.
Publications: Application guidelines; Annual report; Financial statement; Grants list; Informational brochure (including application guidelines); Newsletter; Program policy statement.
Application information: Submission of an Intent to Apply Form is required for full proposal determination by foundation; only organizations that receive "encouraged" proposal notifications may submit a full proposal. Visit foundation Web site for application forms and additional guidelines. "How to Apply" workshops are held at the foundation each month; visit Web site or call to register. Application form required.
  Initial approach: Mail or e-mail Intent to Apply Form
  Copies of proposal: 1
  Deadline(s): June and Dec. for Intent to Apply; Feb. and Aug. for full proposal
  Board meeting date(s): Monthly except Jan., Apr., and Aug.; applications are reviewed two times each year
  Final notification: Proposal determination letter 8 weeks after Intent to Apply deadline; 3 to 4 months for full proposal
Officers and Trustees: * Tatwina Chinn Lee,* Chair.; Charlene Harvey,* Vice-Chair.; Sandra R. Hernandez, M.D.*, C.E.O. and Secy.; Monica Pressley, C.F.O.; Susan Frohlich, Cont.; Gay Plair Cobb; Stephanie DiMarco; David Friedman; James H. Herbert II; James C. Hormel; Marcela C. Medina; Hugo Morales; John Murray; Gladys Thacher.
Number of staff: 35 full-time professional; 2 part-time professional; 13 full-time support; 3 part-time support.

1089
San Joaquin Foundation, Inc. ✦ ☆

P.O. Box 1607
Stockton, CA 95201 (209) 943-2222
Contact: Rudy Croce, C.F.O.

Donors: Union Bank of California, N.A.; Grupe County Fair; General Mills, Inc.
Foundation type: Independent foundation.
Financial data (yr. ended 12/31/05): Assets, $3,462 (M); gifts received, $597,123; expenditures, $710,021; qualifying distributions, $693,815; giving activities include $693,815 for grants.
Fields of interest: Community development.
Limitations: Giving limited to the San Joaquin County, CA, area. No grants to individuals.
Application information: Application form not required.
  Initial approach: Letter
  Deadline(s): None
Officers: Thomas Shephard, Sr., C.E.O.; Rudy G. Croce, C.F.O.; Douglass Eberhardt, Secy.
EIN: 943140078

1090
San Luis Obispo County Community Foundation

1401 Higuera St.
P.O. Box 1580
San Luis Obispo, CA 93406-1580
(805) 543-2323
Contact: David Edwards, Exec. Dir.; For grants: Janice Fong Wolf, Dir., Grants & Progs.
FAX: (805) 543-2346; E-mail: info@sloccf.org; Additional E-mails: dave@sloccf.org and jwolf@sloccf.org; URL: http://www.sloccf.org

Established in 1998 in CA.
Foundation type: Community foundation.
Financial data (yr. ended 12/31/04): Assets, $17,981,139 (M); gifts received, $2,823,645; expenditures, $2,344,426; giving activities include $1,797,948 for 207 grants (high: $600,000; low: $100).
Purpose and activities: The foundation is a public trust established to assist donors in building an enduring source of charitable funds to meet the changing needs and interests of the community. The foundation offers grants for area nonprofits aimed at helping them increase their organizational capacity.
Fields of interest: Historic preservation/historical societies; Arts; Education; Environment; Health care; Recreation; Human services; Nonprofit management; Community development.
Type of support: General/operating support; Continuing support; Management development/capacity building; Building/renovation; Equipment; Program development; Technical assistance; Consulting services; Scholarships—to individuals; Matching/challenge support.
Limitations: Giving primarily in San Luis Obispo County, CA. No support for religious programs (unless open to the public regardless of religious affiliation), governmental organizations, or fraternal organizations (unless in support of a specific program open to or benefiting the entire community). No grants to individuals (except for scholarships), or for endowments, debt reduction, fundraising events, fellowships, travel, or technical or specialized research.
Publications: Application guidelines; Annual report; Grants list; Informational brochure; Newsletter.
Application information: Visit foundation Web site for application cover sheet and guidelines. The foundation holds an optional applicant workshop in Apr.; visit Web site for more information. Faxed or e-mailed applications are not accepted. Application form required.
  Initial approach: Submit application cover sheet, narrative, and attachments
  Copies of proposal: 6
  Deadline(s): May 15
  Board meeting date(s): Monthly
  Final notification: Sept.
Officers and Directors: * Lyn Baker,* Pres.; John Dunn,* V.P.; Barbara Bell,* Secy.; Wayne Lewis,* C.F.O.; David Edwards, Exec. Dir.; Dave Booker; Wendy Brown; Barbie Butz; Julian Crocker; Nancy DePue; Dee Lacey; Dean Miller; Bill Raver; Warren Sinsheimer; Jane Sinton; Nick Thille.
Number of staff: 1 full-time professional; 3 part-time professional; 1 full-time support.
EIN: 770496500

1091
The San Simeon Fund, Inc. ✧ ☆
c/o William R. Hearst III
765 Market St., No. 34D
San Francisco, CA 94103

Established in 2004 in CA.
Donors: William R. Hearst III; Margaret C. Hearst.
Foundation type: Independent foundation.
Financial data (yr. ended 12/31/05): Assets, $15,979,928 (M); gifts received, $5,340,748; expenditures, $894,571; qualifying distributions, $500,000; giving activities include $500,000 for 13 grants (high: $100,000; low: $10,000).
Fields of interest: Arts; Elementary/secondary education; Environment; Family services.
Limitations: Applications not accepted. Giving primarily in CA. No grants to individuals.
Application information: Contributes only to pre-selected organizations.
Officers: William R. Hearst III, Pres.; Margaret C. Hearst, V.P. and C.F.O.; Cynthia D. Lund, Secy.
EIN: 201986583

1092
George H. Sandy Foundation
P.O. Box 591717
San Francisco, CA 94159-1717
Contact: Chester R. MacPhee, Jr., Tr.

Trust established in 1960 in CA.
Donor: George H. Sandy†.
Foundation type: Independent foundation.
Financial data (yr. ended 12/31/05): Assets, $19,000,848 (M); expenditures, $1,623,029; qualifying distributions, $1,023,797; giving activities include $1,000,000 for 87 grants (high: $30,000; low: $4,000).
Purpose and activities: Giving for charitable purposes, and educational purposes, with emphasis on aid to the handicapped and underprivileged.
Fields of interest: Human services; Disabilities, people with; Economically disadvantaged.
Type of support: General/operating support; Continuing support; Scholarship funds.
Limitations: Giving limited to the San Francisco Bay Area, CA. No support for other private non-operating foundations, or for any particular religious order. No grants to individuals, or for annual campaigns, seed money, emergency funds, deficit financing, capital campaigns, endowment or building funds, matching gifts, scholarships, fellowships, special projects, research, publications, or conferences; no loans.
Application information: Application form not required.
Initial approach: Letter
Copies of proposal: 1
Deadline(s): Sept. 30
Board meeting date(s): Annually, and as needed
Final notification: Varies
Trustees: Thomas J. Feeney; Chester R. MacPhee, Jr.; Union Bank of California, N.A.
EIN: 946054473

1093
Santa Barbara Foundation ▼
15 E. Carrillo St.
Santa Barbara, CA 93101 (805) 963-1873
Contact: Charles O. Slosser, C.E.O.

FAX: (805) 966-2345;
E-mail: cslosser@sbfoundation.org; URL: http://www.sbfoundation.org

Incorporated in 1928 in CA.
Foundation type: Community foundation.
Financial data (yr. ended 12/31/04): Assets, $222,388,000 (M); gifts received, $8,793,250; expenditures, $12,614,067; giving activities include $8,563,387 for 2,888 grants (high: $225,000; low: $425).
Purpose and activities: The foundation's mission is to: 1) serve as a leader, catalyst, and resource for philanthropy; 2) strive for measurable community improvement through strategic funding in such fields as community enhancement, culture, education, environment, health, human services, personal development, and recreation; 3) promote partnerships to address important community issues and leverage resources to meet community needs; 4) build and prudently manage a growing endowment for the community's present and future needs; and 5) provide secure, flexible, and effective opportunities for donors to improve their community.
Fields of interest: Arts; Education; Environment; Animal welfare; Public health; Health care; Substance abuse, services; Housing/shelter; Recreation; Children/youth, services; Children, day care; Human services, personal services; Residential/custodial care, hospices; Aging, centers/services; Human services; Community development; Public affairs, citizen participation.
Type of support: Capital campaigns; Building/renovation; Equipment; Land acquisition; Emergency funds; Program development; Scholarship funds; Scholarships—to individuals; Matching/challenge support; Student loans—to individuals.
Limitations: Giving limited to Santa Barbara County, CA. No support for religious organizations for religious purposes. No grants to individuals (except for scholarships), or for deficit financing, general operating support, seed funding, endowment funds, fundraising drives, conferences, seminars, one-time events, fellowships, or for research.
Publications: Application guidelines; Annual report; Financial statement; Informational brochure; Newsletter; Occasional report.
Application information: Visit foundation Web site for application forms and guidelines. Prior to submitting an application, a representative must attend the appropriate mandatory workshop. Faxed or e-mailed applications are not accepted. Application form required.
Initial approach: Letter or telephone inquiry
Deadline(s): Feb. 21 for Health and Human Services, June 1 for Culture and Recreation, Sept. 5 for Community Enhancement and Environment, and Dec. 6 for Education and Personal Development
Board meeting date(s): Monthly except July; decisions on grant requests made in Mar., June, Sept., and Dec.
Final notification: 3 to 4 months
Officers and Trustees:* Dinah Van Wingerden,* Chair.; Shirley Ann Hurley,* Vice-Chair.; Thomas Parker,* Vice-Chair.; Judith Cosdon Stapelmann,* Vice-Chair.; Charles O. Slosser, C.E.O. and Pres.; Catherine Brozowski, V.P., Progs.; Tanya Gonzales, V.P., Devel.; James S. Rivera, V.P., Admin.; Patricia Dillon Bliss,* Secy.; Karin Svensson, C.F.O.; David R. Alvarado,* Treas.; William J. Cirone,* Chair. Emeritus; David Anderson; Keith Berwick; Robert Emmons; Mason Farrell; Judy Frost; Jane

Haberman; Roberta Heter; Alex Posada; Ken Saxon; Anne Smith; George Thurlow.
Fund Managers: Sanford Bernstein; J.L. Kaplan; Alternative Investment Manager; Capital Research & Management Co.; Canterbury Consulting; Trust Co. of the West; Wells Fargo Bank, N.A.
Number of staff: 12 full-time professional; 4 full-time support.
EIN: 951866094
Selected grants: The following grants were reported in 2004.
$225,000 to Isla Vista Youth Project, Goleta, CA. For Vista Square Capital Campaign, payable over 3 years.
$190,000 to University of California, Santa Barbara, CA. 2 grants: $100,000 (For research at interface of global medicine and neurodegenerative disorders), $90,000 (For Postdoctoral Fellowship).
$120,000 to Goleta Valley Historical Society, Goleta, CA. For three-year grant for capital campaign for Rancho La Patera restoration, payable over 3 years.
$110,000 to Guadalupe-Nipomo Dunes Center, Guadalupe, CA. For capital campaign for new Visitor Center, payable over 2 years.
$110,000 to Santa Barbara Public Education Foundation, Santa Barbara, CA. To build aquatic facility at Dos Pueblos High School, payable over 2 years.
$105,000 to Santa Barbara Trust for Historic Preservation, Santa Barbara, CA. For capital campaign for Presidio Northwest Corner restoration, payable over 3 years.
$100,000 to Nonprofit Support Center, Santa Barbara, CA. For general support for core programs.
$100,000 to Princeton University, Princeton, NJ. For Department of Economics.
$100,000 to Santa Barbara Neighborhood Clinics, Isla Vista, CA. For capital for purchase of new building.

1094
The Sapling Foundation ✧
P.O. Box 620952
Woodside, CA 94062

Established in 1995 in CA.
Donor: Christopher Anderson.
Foundation type: Independent foundation.
Financial data (yr. ended 12/31/04): Assets, $28,238,595 (M); gifts received, $99,474; expenditures, $2,688,267; qualifying distributions, $1,006,915; giving activities include $983,000 for 5 grants (high: $431,000; low: $2,000).
Purpose and activities: Giving primarily to the environment, and to U.S.-based organizations which support global health and poverty issues.
Fields of interest: Environment, natural resources; International affairs.
Limitations: Applications not accepted. Giving primarily in CA, NY, and WA. No grants to individuals.
Application information: Contributes only to pre-selected organizations.
Officers: Susan J. Dawson, Pres.; Christopher Anderson, Secy.
EIN: 943235545
Selected grants: The following grants were reported in 2003.
$245,000 to Environmental Defense, New York, NY. For general support.

$200,000 to Kickstart-International, San Francisco, CA. For general support.

$175,000 to Program for Appropriate Technology in Health (PATH), Seattle, WA. For general support.

$142,000 to Acumen Fund, New York, NY. For general support.

$115,000 to Institute for OneWorld Health, San Francisco, CA. For general support.

$57,350 to WildAid, San Francisco, CA. For general support.

$35,000 to Scripture Union, USA, Wayne, PA. For general support.

1095
Penny and Robert Sarver Charitable Foundation ◇

P.O. Box 675847
Rancho Santa Fe, CA   92067-5847

Donors: Penny Sarver; Robert Sarver.
Foundation type: Independent foundation.
Financial data (yr. ended 12/31/05): Assets, $248,762 (M); expenditures, $511,952; qualifying distributions, $508,627; giving activities include $508,627 for grants.
Fields of interest: Cancer; Jewish federated giving programs; Jewish agencies & temples.
Limitations: Applications not accepted. Giving primarily in AZ and CA. No grants to individuals.
Application information: Contributes only to pre-selected organizations.
Officers: Robert Sarver, Pres.; Penny Sarver, Secy.
Director: Jon R. Young.
EIN: 830320824

1096
Sathya Sai Foundation of America ◇

1220 Oaklawn Rd.
Arcadia, CA   91006

Established in 1997 in CA.
Donors: Rama K.R. Thumati; Narendranath A. Reddy; Choudary D. Voleti; Radha R. Bathina; Ravishankar Kamath; Mahesh Ghayal; Yahish B. Merchant; Venkateswara Reddy Kanubaddi; Rana Bahl; Geetha Kamath; Vijay Chundi; Brahma Sharma.
Foundation type: Independent foundation.
Financial data (yr. ended 12/31/05): Assets, $0 (M); gifts received, $684,908; expenditures, $898,749; qualifying distributions, $879,613; giving activities include $879,613 for 4+ grants (high: $858,348), and $655,400 for 1 foundation-administered program.
Purpose and activities: Giving for medical supplies, for and clothes for the needy, and for rural water development projects.
Fields of interest: Environment, water resources; Medical care, community health systems; Health care; Human services.
Limitations: Applications not accepted. No grants to individuals.
Application information: Contributes only to pre-selected organizations.
Officers: Narendranath A. Reddy, Chair.; Choudary D. Voleti, Pres.; Rama K.R. Thumati, V.P. and Secy.
EIN: 954666929

1097
Saturno Foundation ◇

c/o Wells Fargo Bank, N.A.
P.O. Box 63954, MAC A0330-011
San Francisco, CA   94163
Contact: Eugene Ranghiasci
Application address: c/o Wells Fargo Bank, N.A., 420 Montgomery St., MAC No. 0101-056, San Francisco, CA 94163

Established in 1957 in CA.
Donors: Joseph Saturno†; Victor Saturno.
Foundation type: Independent foundation.
Financial data (yr. ended 10/31/05): Assets, $11,824,226 (M); expenditures, $659,663; qualifying distributions, $572,316; giving activities include $550,000 for 6 grants (high: $147,000; low: $50,000).
Purpose and activities: Grants to United States-based organizations that assist orphaned children in Italy.
Fields of interest: Youth development; YM/YWCAs & YM/YWHAs; Children/youth, services.
International interests: Italy.
Limitations: Giving to national organizations for the benefit of Italy, primarily in Washington DC, and New York, NY. No grants to individuals, or for general support, building or endowment funds, research, scholarships, fellowships, or matching gifts; no loans.
Application information:
   Initial approach: Letter
   Deadline(s): None
Trustee: Wells Fargo Bank, N.A.
EIN: 946073765

1098
Saw Island Foundation, Inc. ◇

(formerly Emil Mosbacher, Jr. Foundation, Inc.)
524 Moore Rd., Ste. A
Woodside, CA   94062
Contact: R. Bruce Mosbacher, Pres.

Incorporated in 1974 in NY.
Donors: Emil Mosbacher, Jr.†; R. Bruce Mosbacher; The Emil Mosbacher Jr. Charitable Annuity Trust.
Foundation type: Independent foundation.
Financial data (yr. ended 11/30/05): Assets, $15,654,968 (M); gifts received, $640,713; expenditures, $664,480; qualifying distributions, $660,000; giving activities include $660,000 for 36 grants (high: $120,150; low: $100).
Fields of interest: Higher education; Higher education, college; Higher education, university; Education; Hospitals (general); Hospitals (specialty); Health organizations, association; Human services.
Type of support: Research; Scholarship funds.
Limitations: Giving primarily in CA, CT, and NY. No grants to individuals.
Application information:
   Initial approach: Letter
   Deadline(s): None
Officers: R. Bruce Mosbacher, Pres.; Patricia R. Mosbacher, V.P.; Nancy J. Ditz, Secy.
EIN: 237454106

1099
The Scaife Scholarship Foundation ◇

1547 Lakeside Dr.
Oakland, CA   94612-4520
Contact: Clyde D. Minar, Secy.-Treas.

Established in fiscal 1992 pursuant to an IRS ruling ending the combined filing of the foundation and the Northern California Scholarship Foundation.
Donors: Clarence Benjamin†; RBC Dain Rauscher Inc.
Foundation type: Independent foundation.
Financial data (yr. ended 5/31/05): Assets, $11,292,343 (M); expenditures, $587,186; qualifying distributions, $545,411; giving activities include $502,500 for 100 grants to individuals (high: $5,000; low: $2,500).
Purpose and activities: Awards scholarships to graduates of northern CA public high schools whose parents were born in the United States.
Type of support: Scholarships—to individuals.
Limitations: Giving limited to northern CA residents.
Application information: Written application on pre-printed forms, including transcripts of high school records, college entrance exam scores, and statement of financial need. Application form required.
   Initial approach: Letter requesting application form
   Deadline(s): Mar. 15
Officers: James F. McKlung, Jr., Pres.; Norman Owen, V.P.; Clyde D. Minar, Secy.-Treas.
Trustees: Wade Bingham; Dallas G. Cason; Robert Crow; Charles DiBari; Thomas D. Eychner; Art Hughes, Jr.; Julius "Sandy" Kahn III; George Klopping; Elmer Ross; John Simmons; Hon. Zook Sutton; George Vukasin; Del Wallis.
EIN: 943161402

1100
Schaeffer Family Foundation ◇

716 N. Maple Dr.
Beverly Hills, CA   90210
Application address: George Schaeffer, Pres., 13034 Saticoy St., North Hollywood, CA 91605; tel.: (818) 759-2400

Established in 2000 in CA.
Donor: Opi Products, Inc.
Foundation type: Independent foundation.
Financial data (yr. ended 12/31/05): Assets, $893,075 (M); gifts received, $1,170,095; expenditures, $988,018; qualifying distributions, $986,504; giving activities include $986,504 for 185 grants (high: $232,800; low: $25).
Purpose and activities: Scholarships awarded to full-time students who maintain a 3.0 GPA or better, attend a U.S.-based school program, are between 14 and 24 years old, are U.S. residents, and dependents of a full-time employee of OPI Products Inc.
Fields of interest: Education; Jewish agencies & temples.
Limitations: Giving primarily in CA and NY.
Application information:
   Deadline(s): June 15
Officers: George Schaeffer, Pres.; Susan Weiss-Fischmann, Secy.; Miriam Schaeffer, Treas.
EIN: 954785084
Selected grants: The following grants were reported in 2004.
$275,000 to Chabad of the Valley, Encino, CA.
$61,100 to Bnai Zion Foundation, New York, NY.

$19,060 to Mesivta of Long Beach, Long Beach, NY.

$2,500 to Sinai Temple, Los Angeles, CA.

$1,200 to Beth Jacob Congregation, Beverly Hills, CA.

$25 to Hebrew Free Burial Association, New York, NY.

$25 to Zionist Organization of America, New York, NY.

$20 to United Synagogue of Conservative Judaism, New York, NY.

1101

The Stephen Harold Schimmel Foundation, Inc. ◇ ☆

8 Archipelago Dr.
Newport Coast, CA   92657

Established in 1995 in DE.

Donors: Stephen Harold Schimmel; Rosalba Schimmel.

Foundation type: Independent foundation.

Financial data (yr. ended 9/30/06): Assets, $4,999,823 (M); expenditures, $396,628; qualifying distributions, $317,500; giving activities include $317,500 for grants.

Purpose and activities: Giving primarily for Christian organizations.

Fields of interest: Botanical gardens; Christian agencies & churches.

Limitations: Applications not accepted. Giving on a national basis. No grants to individuals.

Application information: Contributes only to pre-selected organizations.

Officers: Stephen Harold Schimmel, Pres. and Secy.; Rosalba Schimmel, V.P. and Treas.

EIN: 223386066

1102

Schlinger Foundation

P.O. Box 22257
Santa Barbara, CA   93121-2257
Contact: Leonard Vincent, V.P.

Established in 1986 in CA.

Donor: The William and E.G. Schlinger Trust.

Foundation type: Independent foundation.

Financial data (yr. ended 12/31/04): Assets, $10,149,421 (M); expenditures, $3,019,298; qualifying distributions, $2,885,126; giving activities include $2,335,647 for 44 grants (high: $655,000; low: $20).

Purpose and activities: Giving primarily for natural resources and environmental sciences.

Fields of interest: Museums (specialized); Higher education; Education; Environment, natural resources; Animals/wildlife; Health organizations, association; Agriculture/food; Boys & girls clubs; Human services; Biological sciences; Science.

Type of support: Continuing support; Equipment; Land acquisition; Endowments; Professorships; Fellowships; Scholarship funds; Research.

Limitations: Applications not accepted. Giving on a national basis. No grants to individuals.

Publications: Program policy statement.

Application information: Contributes only to pre-selected organizations.

Board meeting date(s): Varies

Officers and Directors:* Leonard Vincent,* V.P.; Bonnie Irwin,* Secy.-Treas.; Michael E. Irwin.

Number of staff: 3 part-time professional.

EIN: 944065303

Selected grants: The following grants were reported in 2004.

$655,000 to California Academy of Sciences, San Francisco, CA. For general support.

$535,100 to Santa Barbara Museum of Natural History, Santa Barbara, CA. For general support.

$283,520 to University of Illinois at Urbana-Champaign, Urbana, IL. For general support.

$100,000 to Wildlife Conservation Society, Bronx, NY. For general support.

$75,000 to Bishop Museum, Honolulu, HI. For general support.

$65,000 to University of Illinois Foundation, Urbana, IL. For general support.

$60,000 to Seattle Foundation, Seattle, WA. For general support.

$50,000 to Field Museum of Natural History, Chicago, IL. For general support.

$50,000 to Smithsonian Institution, DC. For general support.

$25,000 to University of California at Berkeley Foundation, Berkeley, CA. For general support.

1103

Warren & Katherine Schlinger Foundation

c/o Warren G. Schlinger
3835 Shadow Grove Rd.
Pasadena, CA   91107-2241

Established in 1994 in CA.

Donor: Warren G. Schlinger.

Foundation type: Independent foundation.

Financial data (yr. ended 12/31/05): Assets, $63,343,136 (M); gifts received, $378,403; expenditures, $3,327,639; qualifying distributions, $3,288,885; giving activities include $3,286,150 for 53 grants (high: $2,266,650; low: $1,000).

Purpose and activities: Giving primarily for arts and cultural programs, health associations, Protestant agencies, and education, with emphasis on engineering schools.

Fields of interest: Arts; Engineering school/education; Education; Health organizations, association; Engineering/technology; Protestant agencies & churches.

Type of support: Scholarship funds; Seed money; Professorships; Fellowships; Capital campaigns.

Limitations: Applications not accepted. Giving primarily in CA. No grants to individuals.

Application information: Contributes only to pre-selected organizations.

Board meeting date(s): Nov.

Officers and Directors:* Warren G. Schlinger,* Pres.; Michael S. Schlinger,* V.P.; Norman W. Schlinger,* Secy.; Sarah L. Chrisman,* C.F.O.

EIN: 954494669

Selected grants: The following grants were reported in 2004.

$100,000 to University of California, Berkeley, CA.

$50,000 to Santa Barbara Center for the Performing Arts, Santa Barbara, CA.

$25,000 to Chemical Heritage Foundation, Philadelphia, PA.

$25,000 to Coleman Chamber Music Association, Pasadena, CA.

$25,000 to House Ear Institute, Los Angeles, CA.

$10,000 to Leadership Institute, Arlington, VA.

$10,000 to Los Angeles Opera Company, Los Angeles, CA.

$10,000 to National Academy of Engineering, DC.

$10,000 to Young Americas Foundation, Herndon, VA.

$3,000 to Claremont Institute for the Study of Statesmanship and Political Philosophy, Claremont, CA.

1104

Nancy B. and C. William Schlosser Family Foundation ◇

c/o C. William Schlosser
1255 E. Mountain Dr.
Santa Barbara, CA   93108

Established around 1994.

Donor: C. William Schlosser.

Foundation type: Independent foundation.

Financial data (yr. ended 10/31/04): Assets, $131,984 (M); gifts received, $619,780; expenditures, $532,295; qualifying distributions, $528,750; giving activities include $528,750 for 40 grants (high: $50,250; low: $250).

Fields of interest: Arts; Higher education; Health care; Recreation; Protestant agencies & churches.

Limitations: Applications not accepted. Giving primarily in CA. No grants to individuals.

Application information: Contributes only to pre-selected organizations.

Directors: Mary B. Schaefer; C. William Schlosser; Charles W. Schlosser; Elizabeth Schlosser; Nancy B. Schlosser.

EIN: 841235350

1105

The Schocken Foundation, Inc. ◇ ☆

c/o Miriam Schocken
7758 Boeing Ave.
Los Angeles, CA   90045

Established in 1960.

Donors: Solomon Schocken†; Dora S. Schocken†.

Foundation type: Independent foundation.

Financial data (yr. ended 6/30/05): Assets, $2,720,111 (M); expenditures, $330,980; qualifying distributions, $324,151; giving activities include $322,667 for 9 grants (high: $137,500; low: $15,000).

Purpose and activities: Funding for Jewish agencies and social services.

Fields of interest: Health care, research; Jewish federated giving programs; Jewish agencies & temples.

Limitations: Applications not accepted. Giving on a national basis. No grants to individuals.

Application information: Contributes only to pre-selected organizations.

Officers: Miriam Schocken, Pres.; Shimon Schocken, Secy.; Dan Rome, Treas.

Director: Dora Schocken.

EIN: 136167181

Selected grants: The following grants were reported in 2003.

$50,000 to P.E.F. Israel Endowment Funds, New York, NY.

$45,000 to American Committee for Shenkar College in Israel, New York, NY. For program support.

$27,000 to Hand in Hand, American Friends of the Center for Jewish-Arab Education in Israel, Portland, OR. For program support.

$25,000 to David Yellin College of Education, Jerusalem, Israel. For program support.

$25,000 to V-Day, San Francisco, CA.

$20,000 to Blue Card, New York, NY.

$15,000 to Congregation Beit Ahava. For program support.
$15,000 to Focusing Institute, Spring Valley, NY.
$10,000 to Jewish Reconstructionist Federation, Camp JRF, Elkins Park, PA. For program support.
$6,000 to Natural Area Preservation Association, Dallas, TX.

1106
Stephen C. & Patricia A. Schott Foundation ◇
404 Saratoga Ave., Ste. 100
Santa Clara, CA 95050

Established in CA.
Donors: Patricia A. Schott; Stephen C. Schott; SCS Development.
Foundation type: Independent foundation.
Financial data (yr. ended 12/31/05): Assets, $5,764,165 (M); expenditures, $347,207; qualifying distributions, $319,467; giving activities include $319,467 for 30 grants (high: $279,822; low: $100).
Purpose and activities: Giving for Christian agencies and churches, education, youth services, and for federated giving programs.
Fields of interest: Higher education; Libraries (public); Health organizations, association; Human services; Youth, services; Religion.
Limitations: Applications not accepted. Giving primarily in CA. No grants to individuals.
Application information: Contributes only to pre-selected organizations.
Officers: Stephen C. Schott, Pres. and Treas.; Patricia A. Schott, V.P.; Daniel M. Ikeda, Secy.
EIN: 943192795
Selected grants: The following grants were reported in 2005.
$1,500 to Foundation for Hope, Kansas City, MO.
$1,100 to Loaves and Fishes. 3 grants: $100, $500, $500
$100 to OConnor Hospital Foundation, San Jose, CA.

1107
The Schow Foundation ◇
2975 Huntington Dr., Ste. 200
San Marino, CA 91108

Established in 2000 in CA.
Donors: Howard Schow; Nan Schow.
Foundation type: Independent foundation.
Financial data (yr. ended 12/31/05): Assets, $17,012,792 (M); gifts received, $1,749,000; expenditures, $733,575; qualifying distributions, $621,986; giving activities include $591,500 for 29 grants (high: $200,000; low: $1,500).
Purpose and activities: Giving primarily for a hospital and other health care and for a business school and other educational institutions.
Fields of interest: Elementary/secondary education; Business school/education; Hospitals (general); Health care.
Limitations: Applications not accepted. Giving in the U.S., primarily in CA. No grants to individuals.
Application information: Contributes only to pre-selected organizations.
Officers and Directors:* Howard Schow, Pres.; Melanie J. Schow,* Secy.; Nan Schow,* Treas.; Steven Schow,* C.F.O.; Roger L. Schow.
EIN: 954791558

1108
Ruth Epstein Schuler Foundation
625 S. Fair Oaks Ave., Ste. 360
South Pasadena, CA 91030
Contact: Linda J. Blinkenberg, Secy.

Established in 2000 in CA.
Donors: Barry Schuler; Tracy Schuler; Schuler 1999 CRUT.
Foundation type: Independent foundation.
Financial data (yr. ended 12/31/05): Assets, $3,244,475 (M); expenditures, $475,078; qualifying distributions, $466,002; giving activities include $447,125 for 14 grants (high: $200,000; low: $2,000).
Purpose and activities: Giving primarily for education, including a teacher placement program.
Fields of interest: Elementary/secondary education; Education; Human services; Federated giving programs.
Type of support: Scholarship funds; Program development; General/operating support; Curriculum development.
Limitations: Giving on a national basis, with emphasis on Napa, CA, and Washington, DC.
Application information: Due to funding restrictions, the foundation managers prefer to initiate the grants made by the foundation.
Initial approach: Letter of inquiry
Deadline(s): None
Officers and Directors:* Tracy Schuler,* Pres.; Ari B. Schuler,* V.P.; Linda J. Blinkenberg,* Secy.; Virginia L. Sjoberg,* C.F.O.; Paul Escobosa; Barry Schuler.
EIN: 912036552
Selected grants: The following grants were reported in 2005.
$307,000 to Blue Oak School, Napa, CA. 6 grants: $5,000, $2,000, $200,000, $80,000, $10,000, $10,000

1109
Charles and Helen Schwab Foundation ▼
1650 S. Amphlett Blvd., No. 300
San Mateo, CA 94402-2516 (650) 655-2410
Contact: Ana A. Thompson, Managing Dir. Finance and Admin.
FAX: (650) 655-2411;
E-mail: info@schwabfoundation.org; URL: http://www.schwabfoundation.org

Established in 2001 in DE and CA as a result of the merger of the Schwab Foundation for Learning and The Charles and Helen Schwab Family Foundation.
Foundation type: Independent foundation.
Financial data (yr. ended 6/30/05): Assets, $160,304,016 (M); gifts received, $3,521,474; expenditures, $18,008,701; qualifying distributions, $17,183,099; giving activities include $5,609,571 for 98 grants (high: $450,000; low: $5,000), $15,228 for 51 employee matching gifts, and $9,035,224 for 2 foundation-administered programs.
Purpose and activities: The foundation aspires to help kids with learning and attention problems lead satisfying and productive lives in an environment that recognizes, values, and supports the unique attributes of every child.
Fields of interest: Learning disorders; Human services.
Type of support: Capital campaigns; General/operating support; Continuing support;

Management development/capacity building; Program development; Employee matching gifts.
Limitations: Applications not accepted. Giving primarily in Bay Area, CA.
Application information: Contributes only to pre-selected organizations.
Board meeting date(s): Varies
Officers and Directors:* Charles R. Schwab,* Chair.; Helen O. Schwab,* Pres.; Ana A. Thompson, Treas. and Managing Dir., Finance and Admin.; Nancy Bechtle; Sally Bowles.
Number of staff: 26 full-time professional; 4 full-time support.
EIN: 943374170
Selected grants: The following grants were reported in 2005.
$450,000 to Emergency Housing Consortium of Santa Clara County, San Jose, CA. For Housing First program.
$250,000 to Corporation for Enterprise Development (CFED), West, San Francisco, CA. For Saving for Education, Entrepreneurship, and Downpayment (SEED) program.
$200,000 to Homeless Childrens Network, San Francisco, CA. For Children/Youth Mental Health Collaborative.
$200,000 to Treasure Island Homeless Development Initiative, San Francisco, CA. For Child Youth After-School and School Coordination Project.
$110,000 to San Francisco Foundation Community Initiative Funds, San Francisco, CA. For Foundation Consortium's After-school Initiative.
$100,000 to Earned Assets Resource Network (EARN), San Francisco, CA. For Individual Development Account (IDA) programs.
$75,000 to Center for Community Change, DC. For National Housing Trust Fund Project.
$75,000 to Silicon Valley Childrens Fund, San Jose, CA. For Youth Education Scholarship (YES).
$50,000 to Community Technology Alliance, San Jose, CA. For Regional Homeless Information Network Organization (RHINO) Regional Homeless Management Information System (HMIS) Project.
$50,000 to Free at Last: Community Recovery and Rehabilitation Services, East Palo Alto, CA. For Building Effective Substance Abuse Treatment (BEST) III program support.

1110
The Charles Schwab Foundation ◇
(formerly The Charles Schwab Corporation Foundation)
101 Montgomery St.
San Francisco, CA 94104 (877) 408-5438
Contact: Elinore Robey, Dir.
FAX: (415) 636-3262; E-mail: cis@schwab.com; URL: http://www.aboutschwab.com/schwabcorp/ent_schwab_foundation.html

Established in 1993 in CA.
Donors: The Charles Schwab Corp.; Charles Schwab & Co., Inc.
Foundation type: Company-sponsored foundation.
Financial data (yr. ended 6/30/05): Assets, $4,417,393 (M); gifts received, $1,502,820; expenditures, $2,496,380; qualifying distributions, $2,260,295; giving activities include $1,532,970 for 109 grants (high: $218,750; low: $300), and $727,325 for 1,768 employee matching gifts.

Purpose and activities: The foundation supports organizations involved with financial literacy and other areas.

Fields of interest: Human services, financial counseling; General charitable giving.

Type of support: Continuing support; General/operating support; Employee volunteer services; Sponsorships; Employee matching gifts; In-kind gifts.

Limitations: Giving on a national basis. No support for religious, political, or athletic organizations, disease-specific organizations, member-based organizations, discriminatory organizations, organizations with litigious or divisive public agendas, or private foundations; generally, no support for institutions of higher education or hospitals. No grants to individuals, or for advertising, capital campaigns, challenge support, start-up needs, medical research, cause-related marketing, business development activities, promotional events, travel, or video production.

Publications: Application guidelines; Informational brochure.

Application information: Multi-year funding is not automatic. Application form required.

Initial approach: Contact Charles Schwab employee for application form
Copies of proposal: 1
Deadline(s): None
Final notification: Quarterly

Officers and Directors: Charles R. Schwab,* Chair.; Carrie Schwab Pomerantz, Pres.; Charmel Huffman, Secy.; William L. Atwell, Treas.

Number of staff: 4 full-time professional; 2 part-time professional.

EIN: 943172615

1111
Schwab-Rosenhouse Memorial Foundation ✧
c/o Wells Fargo Bank, N.A.
P.O. Box 63954
San Francisco, CA   94163
Contact: Connie Grueter
Scholarship address: c/o Schwab-Rosenhouse Memorial Scholarships, P.O. Box 4004, Concord, CA 94524-4004, tel.: (925) 808-2034

Established in 1997 in CA.

Donor: Rosenhouse Family Trust.

Foundation type: Independent foundation.

Financial data (yr. ended 12/31/04): Assets, $8,391,365 (M); expenditures, $658,888; qualifying distributions, $573,977; giving activities include $496,832 for grants to individuals.

Purpose and activities: Awards scholarships to high school students who live in the 5 counties in and around the Sacramento, CA, metropolitan area. Students planning to enroll at a college or university, community or an accredited vocational/technical institution located within a 100-mile radius of Sacramento are invited to apply. Variable grants of $1,000 to $5,000 will be awarded. The purpose of the program is to encourage deserving students to pursue their educational career goals by providing funds to continue their studies beyond high school.

Type of support: Scholarships—to individuals.

Limitations: Giving limited to high school seniors residing in the 4 counties in and around Sacramento, CA, and who will enroll at a post secondary institution within a 100-mile radius of Sacramento.

Application information: Application form required.

Initial approach: Completed scholarship questionnaire, with 2 letters of recommendation
Deadline(s): Feb. 1

Trustees: Sandra Felderstein; Candice Fields; Irving Herman, Ph.D.; Marvin Kamras, M.D.; John Lewis; Charles Nadler, Ph.D.; Rabbi Reuvin Taff; Linda Van Rees; Joel Zimmerman.

EIN: 686136241

1112
Geiser Schweers Family Foundation ✧ ☆
627 20th St.
Santa Monica, CA   90402

Established in 2005 in CA.

Foundation type: Independent foundation.

Financial data (yr. ended 11/30/05): Assets, $3,518,435 (M); gifts received, $4,071,600; expenditures, $748,848; qualifying distributions, $685,000; giving activities include $685,000 for 3 grants (high: $625,000; low: $10,000).

Fields of interest: Higher education.

Limitations: Applications not accepted. Giving primarily in CA. No grants to individuals.

Application information: Contributes only to pre-selected organizations.

Officers: Donna Schweers, Chair.; Thomas C. Geiser, Pres. and Secy.-Treas.

EIN: 721589761

1113
Sclavos Family Foundation ✧
c/o Groom and Cave
1570 Z St., Ste. 100
San Jose, CA   95126

Established in 1999 in CA.

Donors: Stratton Sclavos; Jody Sclavos.

Foundation type: Independent foundation.

Financial data (yr. ended 12/31/04): Assets, $1,239,341 (L); gifts received, $3,564; expenditures, $405,755; qualifying distributions, $399,745; giving activities include $393,255 for 7 grants (high: $220,090; low: $500).

Fields of interest: Human services; Religion.

Limitations: Applications not accepted. Giving primarily in CA. No grants to individuals.

Application information: Contributes only to pre-selected organizations.

Officers: Stratton Sclavos, Pres.; Jody Sclavos, V.P.

EIN: 770529807

Selected grants: The following grants were reported in 2004.

$220,090 to Napa Valley Vintners Association, Saint Helena, CA.
$123,756 to Saratoga High School Sports Boosters, Saratoga, CA.
$24,902 to Exploratorium, San Francisco, CA.
$10,000 to Tech Museum of Innovation, San Jose, CA.
$500 to Second Harvest Food Bank, San Carlos, CA.

1114
Virginia Steele Scott Foundation ✧
1151 Oxford Rd.
San Marino, CA   91108   (626) 405-2152
Contact: Maria O. Grant, Pres.

Established in 1974 in CA.

Donors: Virginia Steele Scott†; Grace C. Steele†.

Foundation type: Independent foundation.

Financial data (yr. ended 6/30/05): Assets, $10,152,687 (M); expenditures, $1,274,797; qualifying distributions, $1,237,706; giving activities include $1,202,101 for 14 grants (high: $934,601; low: $4,000).

Purpose and activities: Supports nonprofit, public presentations of the arts in the Pasadena, CA, area. Awards grants and donates works of art to a local art museum and other fine arts organizations.

Fields of interest: Arts; Libraries (public).

Type of support: General/operating support.

Limitations: Giving limited to Pasadena and Los Angeles, CA.

Application information: Application form not required.

Initial approach: Letter
Copies of proposal: 5
Deadline(s): Sept. 30
Final notification: Dec.

Officers and Directors: Maria O. Grant,* Pres.; Paul Karlstrom,* Secy.; Margaret R. Galbraith,* Treas.; John Pettker.

Number of staff: 1 part-time professional; 1 part-time support.

EIN: 237365076

Selected grants: The following grants were reported in 2003.

$170,000 to Huntington Library, Art Collections and Botanical Gardens, San Marino, CA. 2 grants: $30,000 (For public presentation of art), $140,000 (For public presentation of art).
$10,000 to Pasadena Shakespeare Company, Pasadena, CA. For public presentation of art.
$6,000 to Pacific Asia Museum, Pasadena, CA. For public presentation of art.
$5,000 to Armory Center for the Arts, Pasadena, CA. For public presentation of art.
$5,000 to Art Center College of Design, Pasadena, CA. Public presentation of art.
$5,000 to Pasadena Symphony Orchestra, Pasadena, CA. For public presentation of art.
$5,000 to Southwest Chamber Music Society, Pasadena, CA. For public presentation of art.
$4,500 to Pasadena Conservatory of Music, Pasadena, CA. For public presentation of art.
$4,000 to Pasadena Playhouse State Theater of California, Pasadena, CA. For public presentation of art.

1115
The Ellen Browning Scripps Foundation ✧
c/o E. Douglas Dawson
6121 Terryhill Dr.
La Jolla, CA   92037

Established in 1935 in CA.

Donors: Ellen Browning Scripps†; Robert Paine Scripps†.

Foundation type: Independent foundation.

Financial data (yr. ended 6/30/05): Assets, $21,651,433 (M); expenditures, $1,162,943; qualifying distributions, $1,081,985; giving activities include $1,055,000 for 42 grants (high: $100,000; low: $2,000).

Fields of interest: Arts; Education; Animals/wildlife; Health care; Human services; Residential/custodial care, hospices.

Type of support: Equipment; Scholarship funds; Research; Program-related investments/loans.

Limitations: Giving primarily in San Diego County, CA. No grants to individuals.
Application information: Foundation occasionally accepts unsolicited requests for funds. Application form not required.
> *Initial approach:* Letter of proposal (no more than 3 pages)
> *Copies of proposal:* 4
> *Deadline(s):* May 1
> *Board meeting date(s):* June
> *Final notification:* Sept. 1

Trustees: Deborah M. Goddard; Roxanne Davis Greene; Paul K. Scripps.
EIN: 951644633
Selected grants: The following grants were reported in 2004.
$200,000 to Scripps Foundation for Medicine and Science, San Diego, CA. 2 grants: $100,000 each
$200,000 to Zoological Society of San Diego, San Diego, CA. 2 grants: $100,000 each
$50,000 to Bishops School, La Jolla, CA. For scholarships.
$35,000 to Scripps Institution of Oceanography, La Jolla, CA.
$30,000 to Knox College, Galesburg, IL.
$25,000 to Humane Society of San Diego, San Diego, CA.
$25,000 to La Jolla Recreation Council, La Jolla, CA.
$21,000 to Scripps College, Claremont, CA.

1116
Irene S. Scully Family Foundation ◇ ☆
100 Drakes Landing Rd., Ste. 200
Greenbrae, CA 94904 (415) 771-5335
Contact: Irene S. Scully, C.E.O.

Established in 2004 in CA.
Donor: Irene S. Scully.
Foundation type: Independent foundation.
Financial data (yr. ended 12/31/04): Assets, $72,146,630 (M); gifts received, $64,640,000; expenditures, $1,735,549; qualifying distributions, $1,487,708; giving activities include $1,487,708 for 18 grants (high: $500,000; low: $500).
Purpose and activities: Giving primarily for elementary schools; funding also for human services, including a residential community for adults who have developmental disabilities.
Fields of interest: Elementary school/education; Human services; Foundations (private grantmaking); Christian agencies & churches; Mentally disabled.
Limitations: Giving primarily in CA.
Officers and Directors:* Irene S. Scully,* C.E.O. and Pres.; Richard A. Schiller, Secy.
EIN: 200414306

1117
Richard C. Seaver Charitable Trust ◇ ☆
140 S. Lake Ave., Ste. 274
Pasadena, CA 91101
Contact: Myron E. Harpole, Tr.

Established in 1978 in CA.
Foundation type: Independent foundation.
Financial data (yr. ended 12/31/05): Assets, $15,730,143 (M); expenditures, $881,400; qualifying distributions, $880,000; giving activities include $880,000 for 35 grants (high: $100,000; low: $4,000).

Purpose and activities: Giving primarily for education, art and culture.
Fields of interest: Museums; Arts; Elementary/secondary education; Higher education; Hospitals (general); Christian agencies & churches.
Limitations: Giving primarily in CA. No grants to individuals.
Application information:
> *Initial approach:* Letter
> *Deadline(s):* None

Trustee: Myron E. Harpole.
EIN: 953311102
Selected grants: The following grants were reported in 2005.
$80,000 to Opera Pacific, Santa Ana, CA.
$71,000 to Princeton University, Princeton, NJ. 3 grants: $50,000, $11,000, $10,000
$60,000 to Peninsula Youth Theater, Mountain View, CA.
$30,000 to Harvard-Westlake School, North Hollywood, CA.
$25,000 to Center for Hearing and Speech, Houston, TX.
$25,000 to Marlborough School, Los Angeles, CA.
$10,000 to Scripps College, Claremont, CA.
$10,000 to Westerly School of Long Beach, Long Beach, CA.

1118
The Seaver Institute ▼
11611 San Vicente Blvd., Ste. 545
Los Angeles, CA 90049 (310) 979-0298
Contact: Victoria Seaver Dean, Pres.
E-mail: vsd@theseaverinstitute.org

Incorporated in 1955 in CA.
Foundation type: Independent foundation.
Financial data (yr. ended 6/30/06): Assets, $40,868,778 (M); expenditures, $2,669,530; qualifying distributions, $2,314,280; giving activities include $2,314,280 for 52 grants (high: $250,000; low: $400; average: $1,000–$125,000).
Purpose and activities: The Seaver Institute provides seed money to highly regarded organizations for particular projects which offer the potential for significant advancement in their fields.
Fields of interest: Performing arts, music; Arts; Education, research; Science, research.
Type of support: Seed money; Research.
Limitations: Giving on a national basis. No grants to individuals, or for operating budgets, continuing support, annual campaigns, emergency or endowment funds, scholarships, fellowships, deficit financing, capital or building funds, equipment, land acquisition, publications, or conferences; no loans.
Publications: Application guidelines; Informational brochure (including application guidelines).
Application information: Application form not required.
> *Initial approach:* Letter addressed to the president, requesting guidelines
> *Copies of proposal:* 1
> *Deadline(s):* Early Apr. and early Nov.
> *Board meeting date(s):* May

Officers and Directors:* Richard Seaver,* Chair.; Victoria Seaver Dean,* Vice-Chair. and Pres.; Robert Flick,* Secy.; Christopher Seaver,* Treas.; David Alexander; Nancy Bekavac; Richard Call; Myron Harpole; Margaret Keene; Carlton Seaver; Martha Seaver; Patrick Seaver; Roxanne Wilson.
Number of staff: 2 part-time professional.
EIN: 956054764

Selected grants: The following grants were reported in 2005.
$265,000 to Yale University, New Haven, CT.
$222,200 to Carnegie Institution of Washington, DC. For Carnegie Observatory in Pasadena, CA.
$188,350 to Stanford University, Stanford, CA.
$151,000 to Diabetes Research Institute, Miami, FL.
$125,000 to Santa Catalina Island Conservancy, Avalon, CA.
$124,500 to Raincoast Conservation Foundation, Tofino, Canada. .
$100,000 to Jazz at Lincoln Center, New York, NY.
$20,000 to Institute for Systems Biology, Seattle, WA.
$6,000 to Marlborough School, Los Angeles, CA.
$5,000 to Shakespeare on the Sound, Norwalk, CT.

1119
The August Sebastiani Charitable Trust ◇ ☆
135 W. Napa St., 2nd Fl.
Sonoma, CA 95476 (707) 933-1704
Contact: Don Sebastiani, Tr.

Established in 1996 in CA.
Donors: Don Sebastiani; Sebastiani Vineyards, Inc.; Nancy Sebastiani.
Foundation type: Independent foundation.
Financial data (yr. ended 12/31/05): Assets, $18,421 (M); gifts received, $334,000; expenditures, $339,033; qualifying distributions, $339,033; giving activities include $337,774 for 25 grants (high: $158,692; low: $250).
Fields of interest: Museums (art); Education; Cancer; Cancer research; Offenders/ex-offenders, rehabilitation; Human services; Children/youth, services; Roman Catholic agencies & churches.
Limitations: Giving primarily in CA. No grants to individuals.
Application information:
> *Initial approach:* Proposal
> *Deadline(s):* None

Trustees: Don Sebastiani; Sylvia Sebastiani.
EIN: 680386154
Selected grants: The following grants were reported in 2005.
$10,000 to University of San Francisco, San Francisco, CA.
$5,000 to Abbey Foundation of Oregon, Saint Benedict, OR.
$5,000 to Catholic Charities, Arlington, VA.
$3,000 to Ursuline High School, Santa Rosa, CA.
$2,000 to Bellarmine College Preparatory, San Jose, CA.
$1,000 to La Luz Center, Boyes Hot Springs, CA.
$1,000 to Smile Train, New York, NY.

1120
The Albert D. Seeno, Jr. Family Foundation ◇ ☆
4021 Port Chicago Hwy.
Concord, CA 94520

Established in 2000 in CA.
Donors: Sandra L. Seeno; Albert D. Seeno, Jr. Living Trust; Seeno Construction Co.
Foundation type: Independent foundation.
Financial data (yr. ended 12/31/05): Assets, $0 (M); gifts received, $639,500; expenditures, $571,547; qualifying distributions, $571,333;

giving activities include $571,333 for 14 grants (high: $500,000; low: $1,000).

Purpose and activities: Giving primarily for health, education, and human services; funding also for a Roman Catholic cathedral.

Fields of interest: Performing arts; Secondary school/education; Hospitals (specialty); Health organizations, association; Human services; Children/youth, services; Roman Catholic agencies & churches.

Limitations: Applications not accepted. Giving primarily in CA; some funding nationally. No grants to individuals.

Application information: Contributes only to pre-selected organizations.

Officers: Sandra L. Seeno, Pres.; David T. Seeno, V.P.; Jacqueline M. Seeno, Secy.; Albert D. Seeno III, C.F.O.

EIN: 680450314

1121

Barnet Segal Charitable Trust ◇

P.O. Box S-1
Carmel, CA 93921

Established in 1986 in CA.
Foundation type: Independent foundation.
Financial data (yr. ended 3/31/06): Assets, $15,833,708 (M); expenditures, $983,355; qualifying distributions, $833,345; giving activities include $644,500 for 49 grants (high: $100,000; low: $1,000).

Purpose and activities: Giving primarily for conservation, the arts, health care, and human services.

Fields of interest: Arts; Environment, natural resources; Environment, land resources; Animal welfare; Human services; Children/youth, services; Economically disadvantaged.

Type of support: General/operating support; Building/renovation.

Limitations: Applications not accepted. Giving primarily in Carmel, Monterey and Salinas, CA. No grants to individuals.

Application information: Contributes only to pre-selected organizations.

Trustees: Stuart Berman; William Brodsley.
EIN: 776024786
Selected grants: The following grants were reported in 2004.

$170,000 to Natividad Medical Foundation, Salinas, CA.

$150,000 to Monterey County Agricultural and Historic Land Conservancy, Salinas, CA.

$65,000 to Big Sur Land Trust, Carmel, CA. To purchase Notary's Landing.

$50,000 to Action Council of Monterey County, Salinas, CA.

$20,000 to Monterey County Land Watch, Monterey, CA.

$15,000 to Population Services International, Watsonville, CA.

$12,500 to Carmel-By-The-Sea Sunset Center for the Arts, Carmel, CA. For capital campaign to renovate Sunset Center.

$10,000 to Community Hospital Foundation, Monterey, CA.

$10,000 to Planned Parenthood Association of Monterey County, Monterey, CA.

$5,000 to Young at Heart Project, Santa Cruz, CA.

1122

Hal and Jeanette Segerstrom Family Foundation ◇

818 W. Bay Ave.
Newport Beach, CA 92661 (949) 675-3490
Contact: Sally Eileen Segerstrom, C.E.O. and Pres.

Established in 2000 in CA.
Donor: Jeanette E. Segerstrom.
Foundation type: Independent foundation.
Financial data (yr. ended 12/31/04): Assets, $12,369,795 (M); expenditures, $1,244,168; qualifying distributions, $1,102,840; giving activities include $1,100,000 for 4 grants (high: $600,000; low: $100,000).

Purpose and activities: Giving primarily to institutions engaged in providing music and music training, and in the performing arts and training.

Fields of interest: Arts.

Limitations: Giving primarily in CA, with emphasis on Santa Ana. No grants to.

Application information:
  Initial approach: Letter of inquiry
  Deadline(s): None

Officers and Directors:* Sally Eileen Segerstrom,* C.E.O. and Pres.; Sandra Phyllis Segerstrom Daniels,* V.P.; Theodore Walter Segerstrom,* C.F.O.; Susan Jeanette Segerstrom Perry,* Secy.

EIN: 330925151

1123

The Segerstrom Foundation ◇

3315 Fairview Rd.
Costa Mesa, CA 92626 (714) 546-0110
Contact: Mark Heim, Pres.
Application address: c/o Nancy West, 3333 Bristol St., Costa Mesa, CA 92626, tel.: (714) 435-2000

Established in 1987 in CA.
Donors: Henry T. Segerstrom; Jeanette Segerstrom; C. J. Segerstrom & Sons; Nellie R. Segerstrom Trust; Harold T. Segerstrom Residuary Trust.
Foundation type: Independent foundation.
Financial data (yr. ended 12/31/05): Assets, $11,408,508 (M); expenditures, $532,722; qualifying distributions, $465,077; giving activities include $464,500 for 13 grants (high: $150,000; low: $5,000).

Purpose and activities: Giving primarily for the arts including a performing arts center; some giving also for children, youth, and social services.

Fields of interest: Museums (art); Performing arts; Performing arts centers; Performing arts, orchestra (symphony); Performing arts, opera; Secondary school/education; Environment; Athletics/sports, Special Olympics; Human services; Salvation Army; Children/youth, services.

Limitations: Giving primarily in the Orange County, CA, area. No grants to individuals.

Application information: Proposals will be accepted by invitation only following letter of inquiry.
  Initial approach: Letter of inquiry
  Deadline(s): None

Officers: Mark Heim, Pres. and C.F.O.; Nancy West, V.P., Grants; Susan Adams, Secy.

Directors: Sandra Segerstrom Daniels; Anton Segerstrom; Henry T. Segerstrom; Ted Segerstrom.

EIN: 330269599

1124

The Seinfeld Family Foundation ◇

9171 Wilshire Blvd., Ste. 400
Beverly Hills, CA 90210

Established in 1999 in DE.
Donor: Jerome Seinfeld.
Foundation type: Independent foundation.
Financial data (yr. ended 12/31/05): Assets, $3,119,695 (M); gifts received, $3,000,000; expenditures, $1,499,211; qualifying distributions, $1,491,249; giving activities include $1,491,249 for 87 grants (high: $846,049; low: $500).

Purpose and activities: Giving primarily for education, children's services, health associations, and Jewish organizations; funding also for the arts.

Fields of interest: Museums (natural history); Historic preservation/historical societies; Arts; Education; Health organizations, association; Human services; Children/youth, services; Jewish agencies & temples.

Limitations: Applications not accepted. Giving primarily in NY. No grants to individuals.

Application information: Contributes only to pre-selected organizations.

Officers and Directors:* Jerome Seinfeld,* Pres.; Carolyn Liebling,* V.P.; Lawrence Liebling,* Treas.

EIN: 522184487

Selected grants: The following grants were reported in 2004.

$557,494 to Scholarship America, Saint Peter, MN.

$80,000 to International Rescue Committee, New York, NY.

$60,000 to American Museum of Natural History, New York, NY.

$48,800 to Richmond Historic Riverfront Foundation, Richmond, VA.

$15,000 to Sesame Workshop, New York, NY.

$10,000 to National Corporate Theater Fund, New York, NY.

$10,000 to New York Public Library, New York, NY.

$10,000 to University of Judaism, Los Angeles, CA.

$5,000 to American Red Magen David for Israel, New York, NY.

$2,500 to Alliance for the Arts, New York, NY.

1125

The Semel Charitable Foundation ◇

9460 Wilshire Blvd., Ste. 600
Beverly Hills, CA 90212
Contact: Mr. Terry Semel, Chair.

Established in 1998 in CA.
Donors: Terry Semel; Jane Semel.
Foundation type: Independent foundation.
Financial data (yr. ended 12/31/03): Assets, $2,089,006 (M); gifts received, $2,000,000; expenditures, $983,100; qualifying distributions, $983,000; giving activities include $983,000 for 57 grants (high: $90,000; low: $500).

Purpose and activities: Giving primarily for education, health and health associations, particularly children's hospitals, as well as for children's and other social services, and federated giving programs.

Fields of interest: Higher education; Education; Health care; Health organizations, association; Cancer research; Diabetes research; Human services; Children, services; Federated giving programs.

Limitations: Giving on a national basis, primarily in CA and NY.

Application information:

Initial approach: Letter
Deadline(s): None
Officers: Terry Semel, Chair.; Jane Semel, Pres.; Bernard J. Beiser, Secy. and C.F.O.
EIN: 954691748
Selected grants: The following grants were reported in 2003.

$90,000 to John Thomas Dye School, Los Angeles, CA. For general support.

$50,000 to Christopher Reeve Paralysis Foundation, Springfield, NJ. For general support.

$25,000 to UCLA Foundation, Los Angeles, CA. For general support.

$25,000 to United Friends of the Children, Los Angeles, CA. For general support.

$15,000 to Saint Jude Childrens Research Hospital, Memphis, TN. For general support.

$10,000 to Juvenile Diabetes Research Foundation International, Pasadena, CA. For general support.

$10,000 to Volunteers of America of Los Angeles, Los Angeles, CA. For general support.

$5,000 to Rape Treatment Center, Santa Monica, CA. For general support.

$1,500 to Cedars-Sinai Medical Center, Los Angeles, CA. For general support.

$1,000 to Loomis Chaffee School, Windsor, CT. For general support.

1126
The Sence Foundation ✧
1020 E. Mineral King Ave.
Visalia, CA 93292-6916   (559) 625-1588
Contact: Kim A. Oviatt, Pres.

Established in 1958 in CA.
Foundation type: Independent foundation.
Financial data (yr. ended 12/31/05): Assets, $10,530,672 (M); expenditures, $782,668; qualifying distributions, $536,000; giving activities include $536,000 for 74 grants (high: $100,000; low: $1,000).
Purpose and activities: Giving primarily for education and health, including children's health.
Fields of interest: Higher education; Education; Hospitals (general); Health care; Human services; Children/youth, services; Community development.
Limitations: Giving primarily in southern CA.
Application information: Application form not required.
Deadline(s): None
Officers: Kim A. Oviatt, Pres.; Earle C. Blais, V.P.; Stephen I. Chrisman, Secy.; Gary A. Artis, C.F.O.
EIN: 956052236

1127
The Senyei Family Foundation ✧
c/o Andrew E. Senyei
2030 Main St., Ste. 1400
Irvine, CA 92614

Established in 2001 in CA.
Donor: Andrew E. Senyei.
Foundation type: Independent foundation.
Financial data (yr. ended 12/31/05): Assets, $1,537,712 (M); gifts received, $1,000,000; expenditures, $652,665; qualifying distributions, $652,420; giving activities include $607,985 for 10 grants (high: $250,000; low: $500).
Purpose and activities: Giving primarily for higher education; funding also for the performing arts.

Fields of interest: Performing arts, opera; Higher education; Education; Human services.
Limitations: Applications not accepted. Giving primarily in CA.
Application information: Contributes only to pre-selected organizations.
Officers and Directors: * Andrew E. Senyei,* Pres.; Jo Ann C. Senyei,* Secy. and C.F.O.
EIN: 912152440
Selected grants: The following grants were reported in 2004.

$1,025,000 to Northwestern University, Evanston, IL.

$118,706 to San Diego Opera Association, San Diego, CA.

$22,500 to Old Globe Theater, San Diego, CA.

$15,000 to Las Patronas, La Jolla, CA.

$5,000 to Scripps Memorial Hospital, San Diego, CA.

1128
Serenity Fund ✧
P.O. Box 675210
Rancho Santa Fe, CA 92067
Contact: Karen Doshay, C.F.O.

Established in 1998 in CA.
Foundation type: Independent foundation.
Financial data (yr. ended 10/31/05): Assets, $44,823 (M); gifts received, $325,000; expenditures, $329,699; qualifying distributions, $326,544; giving activities include $326,544 for 8 grants (high: $257,995; low: $750).
Purpose and activities: Giving for children's services.
Fields of interest: Children, services.
Type of support: General/operating support; Continuing support; Annual campaigns; Capital campaigns; Building/renovation; Land acquisition; Emergency funds; Program development.
Limitations: Applications not accepted. Giving primarily in San Diego, CA. No grants to individuals.
Application information: Contributes only to pre-selected organizations.
Officer and Directors: * Karen Doshay,* C.F.O.; Glenn Doshay.
EIN: 330784328

1129
The Servants' Charitable Trust ✧
2400 E. Katella Ave., Ste. 1200
Anaheim, CA 92806

Established in 1993 in CA.
Donors: Ann R. Stull; Roger C. Stull.
Foundation type: Independent foundation.
Financial data (yr. ended 12/31/05): Assets, $5,309,219 (M); expenditures, $1,920,923; qualifying distributions, $1,869,834; giving activities include $1,830,900 for 46 grants (high: $185,000; low: $2,500).
Purpose and activities: Giving for Christian service projects and endeavors.
Fields of interest: Christian agencies & churches.
Limitations: Giving primarily in CA, CO, and IN.
Application information: Application form required.
Initial approach: 1-page letter
Copies of proposal: 1
Deadline(s): None
Officers and Trustees: * Roger C. Stull,* Chair.; Ann Stull,* Vice-Chair.

Number of staff: 1
EIN: 330547132
Selected grants: The following grants were reported in 2004.

$200,000 to Desire Street Ministries, New Orleans, LA.

$150,000 to Thornston Educational Fund, Glendora, CA.

$100,000 to CURE International, Harrisburg, PA.

$50,000 to Joni and Friends, Agoura Hills, CA.

$50,000 to World Relief, Baltimore, MD.

$35,000 to Russian-American Christian University, Wheaton, MD.

$34,500 to Servant Group International, Nashville, TN.

$30,000 to Biola University, La Mirada, CA.

$25,000 to Childrens Network International, Bell, CA.

$25,000 to Haggai Institute for Advanced Leadership Training, Atlanta, GA.

1130
The Setzer Foundation ✧
2555 3rd St., Ste. 200
Sacramento, CA 95818
Contact: Hardie C. Setzer, Exec. Tr.

Established in 1965 in CA.
Donor: Members of the Setzer family.
Foundation type: Independent foundation.
Financial data (yr. ended 12/31/05): Assets, $4,979,152 (M); expenditures, $1,120,354; qualifying distributions, $1,037,356; giving activities include $1,037,356 for 318 grants (high: $400,000; low: $12).
Purpose and activities: Giving primarily for education, health, human services, and the arts.
Fields of interest: Museums (specialized); Arts; Education; Hospitals (general); Health organizations, association; Cancer; Human services; Children/youth, services; Christian agencies & churches.
Limitations: Giving on a national basis, with primary emphasis on CA. No grants to individuals.
Application information: Application form not required.
Deadline(s): None
Trustees: G. Cal Setzer; Hardie C. Setzer; Mark Setzer; Scott Setzer.
EIN: 946115578
Selected grants: The following grants were reported in 2005.

$401,750 to Crocker Art Museum, Sacramento, CA. 3 grants: $1,250, $500, $400,000

$10,000 to Salvation Army, Redding, CA.

$5,000 to K V I E, Sacramento, CA.

$5,000 to River Oak Center for Children, Sacramento, CA.

$5,000 to YMCA, CA.

$2,900 to Make-A-Wish Foundation, Mill Valley, CA.

$1,000 to Works in New Directions, Los Angeles, CA.

$1,000 to World Forestry Center, Portland, OR.

1131
Severns Family Foundation ✧
1168 Tangerine Way
Sunnyvale, CA 94087   (408) 203-8982
Contact: David W. Severns, Pres.

FAX: (408) 730-9627;
E-mail: info@severnsfoundation.org; URL: http://www.severnsfoundation.org

Established in 1989 in CA.
Donors: Robert L. Severns†; Helen A. Severns.
Foundation type: Independent foundation.
Financial data (yr. ended 9/30/05): Assets, $9,110,234 (M); gifts received, $9,328; expenditures, $479,372; qualifying distributions, $478,862; giving activities include $469,646 for 21 grants (high: $100,000; low: $1,000).
Purpose and activities: Supporting Northern California community needs in the areas of education, arts/culture, health care, social services and environmental management.
Fields of interest: Education, public policy; Education, reading; Animal welfare; Animals/wildlife.
Type of support: Building/renovation; Equipment; Program development; Curriculum development; Research; Matching/challenge support.
Limitations: Giving primarily in Alameda, Santa Clara, San Francisco, San Benito, and San Mateo counties, CA. No grants to individuals.
Application information: Applications must be submitted via foundation Web site.
  Initial approach: Exploratory letter briefly describing the project prior to a full proposal (E-mail is preferred)
  Deadline(s): See Web site for details
Officers and Board Members:* David W. Severns,* Pres.; Nancy E. Severns,* V.P.; Sharon L. Severns, Treas.
EIN: 770235139
Selected grants: The following grants were reported in 2003.
$150,000 to Lexington Institute, Arlington, VA. For research on education reform.
$50,000 to Beneficent, Inc., Palo Alto, CA. For productization of Internet based reading tool for disabled children.
$50,000 to Minneapolis Heart Institute Foundation, Minneapolis, MN. For Hypertrophic Cardiomyopathy Research.
$46,000 to Grail Family Services, San Jose, CA. For after-school literacy program at San Antonia Elementary School.
$25,000 to Community Association for Rehabilitation, Palo Alto, CA. For new PC learning lab.
$19,170 to OConnor Hospital Foundation, San Jose, CA. For book on Hypertrophic Cardiomyopathy.
$15,000 to Community Foundation Silicon Valley, San Jose, CA. For early literacy program.
$14,661 to California Dictionary Project, Oakland, CA. To purchase dictionaries for third grade students in Oakland and San Jose.

1132
The Gwendolyn Sexton Foundation ✧
260 Maple Ct., Ste. 230
Ventura, CA   93003

Established in 1982 in CA.
Donor: Gwendolyn W. Sexton.
Foundation type: Independent foundation.
Financial data (yr. ended 3/31/05): Assets, $14,065,525 (M); expenditures, $758,308; qualifying distributions, $649,560; giving activities include $614,500 for 13 grants (high: $126,500; low: $2,250).

Purpose and activities: Giving primarily for human services, including YMCAs; funding also for education, and health associations.
Fields of interest: Health care; Health organizations, association; Human services; YM/YWCAs & YM/YWHAs; Children/youth, services.
Limitations: Applications not accepted. Giving primarily in CA. No grants to individuals.
Application information: Contributes only to pre-selected organizations.
Officer: Stanley J. Yates, Secy.
Trustees: David G. Phinney; Michael J. Regan.
EIN: 953783371
Selected grants: The following grants were reported in 2005.
$220,000 to Ventura Unified School District, Ventura, CA. 2 grants: $95,000, $125,000
$186,500 to Glendale Unified School District, Glendale, CA. 2 grants: $126,500, $60,000
$62,000 to Glendale College Foundation, Glendale, CA.
$60,000 to Ventura College Foundation, Ventura, CA.
$25,000 to New Horizons Family Center, Glendale, CA.
$10,000 to YMCA, Channel Islands, Ventura Family Branch, Ventura, CA.
$10,000 to YMCA, Crescenta-Canada, La Canada, CA.
$10,000 to YMCA, Glendale Family, Glendale, CA.

1133
The E. L. and Ruth B. Shannon
Foundation ✧ ☆
c/o E.L. Shannon, Jr.
14081 Summit Dr.
Whittier, CA   90602-1955

Established in 1991 in CA.
Donors: E.L. Shannon, Jr.; Ruth B. Shannon.
Foundation type: Independent foundation.
Financial data (yr. ended 12/31/05): Assets, $2,405,784 (M); gifts received, $25,758; expenditures, $1,721,176; qualifying distributions, $1,704,452; giving activities include $1,704,452 for 21 grants (high: $1,453,475; low: $2,000).
Fields of interest: Arts; Higher education; Libraries/library science; Hospitals (general); Youth development, centers/clubs; Human services; Christian agencies & churches.
Limitations: Applications not accepted. Giving primarily in southern CA. No grants to individuals.
Application information: Contributes only to pre-selected organizations.
Officers and Directors:* Ruth B. Shannon,* Pres.; Michael L. Shannon,* Secy.; E.L. Shannon, Jr.,* Treas.; Kathryn Shannon Johnson; Bruce L. Shannon.
EIN: 954348050
Selected grants: The following grants were reported in 2005.
$50,250 to Morehead State University, Morehead, KY.
$10,100 to Whittier College, Whittier, CA.
$7,140 to Los Angeles Opera Company, Los Angeles, CA.
$6,000 to Hastings College, Hastings, NE.
$5,544 to Boy Scouts of America, Los Angeles, CA.
$4,821 to Los Angeles Philharmonic, Los Angeles, CA.
$2,500 to Boys and Girls Club of Whittier, Whittier, CA.
$2,000 to Library Foundation, Portland, OR.

1134
David and Fela Shapell Foundation ✧
9401 Wilshire Blvd., Ste. 1200
Beverly Hills, CA   90212

Established in 1967.
Donors: David Shapell; Fela Shapell.
Foundation type: Independent foundation.
Financial data (yr. ended 12/31/05): Assets, $14,132,864 (M); gifts received, $1,149,580; expenditures, $2,878,780; qualifying distributions, $2,733,306; giving activities include $2,733,306 for 91 grants (high: $500,000; low: $100).
Purpose and activities: Giving primarily for higher education and Jewish temple support.
Fields of interest: Higher education; Hospitals (general); Health organizations, association; Jewish agencies & temples.
International interests: Israel.
Limitations: Applications not accepted. Giving primarily in CA; some giving also in NY. No grants to individuals.
Application information: Contributes only to pre-selected organizations.
Officers: David Shapell, Pres.; Fela Shapell, V.P. and Treas.
EIN: 956187271
Selected grants: The following grants were reported in 2003.
$1,155,000 to American Committee for the David Shapell College of Jewish Studies, Brooklyn, NY.
$500,000 to American Committee for the Weizmann Institute of Science, Beverly Hills, CA. Grant made in form of bonds.
$400,000 to American Friends of the Hebrew University, Los Angeles, CA. Grant made in form of bonds.
$200,000 to Hadassah Medical Relief Association, New York, NY. 2 grants: $100,000 each.
$150,000 to Jewish Center of the Bay Cities, Santa Monica, CA.
$72,400 to Beth Jacob Congregation, Beverly Hills, CA.
$50,000 to Temple Beth El, Portland, ME.
$30,000 to Temple Beth Haverim, Agoura Hills, CA.
$20,000 to Etta Israel Center, Los Angeles, CA.

1135
Nathan & Lilly Shapell Foundation ✧
8383 Wilshire Blvd., Ste. 724
Beverly Hills, CA   90211

Established in 1959 in CA.
Donors: Nathan Shapell; Shapell Industries.
Foundation type: Independent foundation.
Financial data (yr. ended 5/31/05): Assets, $17,275,555 (M); expenditures, $980,706; qualifying distributions, $837,051; giving activities include $837,051 for 9 grants (high: $300,000; low: $1,000).
Purpose and activities: Giving primarily for higher education, and for Jewish organizations, and federated giving programs for education.
Fields of interest: Higher education; Jewish federated giving programs; Jewish agencies & temples.
Type of support: General/operating support.
Limitations: Applications not accepted. Giving primarily in Los Angeles, CA; funding also in New York, NY. No grants to individuals.
Application information: Contributes only to pre-selected organizations.

Officers and Directors:* Nathan Shapell,* Pres.; Paul Guerin,* V.P.; Gregory Scott,* Secy.; Vera Guerin,* C.F.O. and Treas.; Jeffrey Glassman; Dana Guerin; Lisa Guerin.
EIN: 956047847
Selected grants: The following grants were reported in 2003.
$775,000 to University of Southern California, School of Law, Los Angeles, CA. For general support.
$192,775 to Jewish Community Foundation, Council of Greater Los Angeles, Los Angeles, CA. For general support.

1136
Shapell-Guerin Foundation, Inc. ◇
8383 Wilshire Blvd., Ste. 724
Beverly Hills, CA 90211

Established in 1997 in CA.
Donor: The Nathan Shapell Lead Unitrust.
Foundation type: Independent foundation.
Financial data (yr. ended 9/30/05): Assets, $2,125,579 (M); gifts received, $666,777; expenditures, $545,740; qualifying distributions, $540,500; giving activities include $540,500 for 14 grants (high: $500,000; low: $500).
Purpose and activities: Giving for health, medical and scientific research and services.
Fields of interest: Arts; Higher education; Cancer research.
Limitations: Applications not accepted. Giving primarily in CA. No grants to individuals.
Application information: Contributes only to pre-selected organizations.
Officers and Directors:* Vera Guerin,* Pres.; Jeffrey Glassman, Secy.; D. Gregory Scott,* C.F.O.; Dana Guerin; Lisa Guerin; Michael Guerin; Paul Guerin.
EIN: 954619715
Selected grants: The following grants were reported in 2003.
$200,000 to Hebrew Union College-Jewish Institute of Religion, Skirball Cultural Center, Los Angeles, CA. For general support.
$50,000 to Tufts University, Medford, MA. For general support.
$10,000 to Cedars-Sinai Medical Center, Los Angeles, CA. For general support.
$10,000 to Generation Five, San Francisco, CA. For general support.
$9,200 to Womens Guild Cedars-Sinai Medical Center, Los Angeles, CA. For general support.
$7,200 to Stephen S. Wise Temple, Los Angeles, CA. For general support.
$5,000 to Harvard-Westlake School, North Hollywood, CA. For general support.
$5,000 to Pasadena Childrens Training Society, Pasadena, CA. For general support.
$5,000 to Play for Peace, Chicago, IL. For general support.
$5,000 to Stephen S. Wise Temple Elementary and Milken Community High School, Los Angeles, CA. For general support.

1137
Shapiro Family Charitable Foundation ◇
(formerly The Hanover Foundation)
9401 Wilshire Blvd., No. 1201
Beverly Hills, CA 90212

Established in 1983 in CA.

Donors: Ralph J. Shapiro; Shirley Shapiro; Flavia J. Kavanau; Earl W. Kavanau; Alison Shapiro; Peter W. Shapiro; Kihi Foundation; Knoll International Holdings, Inc.; Raps Industries, LLP; SDI Industries, Inc.; B.D. Fischer; F.K. Fischer.
Foundation type: Independent foundation.
Financial data (yr. ended 1/31/06): Assets, $3,758,061 (M); gifts received, $251,933; expenditures, $1,500,835; qualifying distributions, $1,450,844; giving activities include $1,450,535 for 117 grants (high: $1,000,000; low: $50).
Purpose and activities: Giving primarily for health organizations, human services, national resource conservation, higher education, and children, youth, and social services.
Fields of interest: Arts; Higher education; Theological school/education; Education; Environment, natural resources; Cerebral palsy; Health organizations; Medical research, institute; Human services; Children/youth, services; Foundations (community); Federated giving programs; Jewish agencies & temples.
Type of support: General/operating support.
Limitations: Giving primarily in southern CA. No grants to individuals.
Application information: Application form not required.
 Deadline(s): None
Officers: Ralph J. Shapiro, Chair.; Shirley Shapiro, Pres.; Alison D. Shapiro, V.P.; Peter W. Shapiro, V.P.; Ava Coyne, Secy.; Floyd P. Cook, Jr., C.F.O.
EIN: 953887151

1138
The Shapiro Foundation ◇ ☆
c/o Esmond & Yabuki, Inc.
23901 Calabasas Rd., Ste. 1010
Calabasas, CA 91302-3308

Established in 2000 in MA.
Donors: Barbara J. Shapiro; Edward L. Shapiro.
Foundation type: Independent foundation.
Financial data (yr. ended 12/31/05): Assets, $12,353,533 (M); gifts received, $1,000,000; expenditures, $805,701; qualifying distributions, $460,880; giving activities include $460,880 for 26 grants (high: $290,000; low: $250).
Fields of interest: Education; Hospitals (specialty); Health organizations, association; Cancer; Children/youth, services; Jewish agencies & temples.
Limitations: Applications not accepted. No grants to individuals.
Application information: Contributes only to pre-selected organizations.
Trustees: Barbara J. Shapiro; Edward L. Shapiro.
EIN: 043541595
Selected grants: The following grants were reported in 2004.
$225,000 to Childrens Hospital Corporation, Boston, MA. For research.
$35,000 to Doctors Without Borders USA, New York, NY.
$20,000 to Action Against Hunger - USA, New York, NY.
$10,000 to University of Pennsylvania, Philadelphia, PA. 2 grants: $5,000 each
$8,963 to Childrens Hospital League, Boston, MA. For research.
$7,000 to Horizons for Homeless Children, Dorchester, MA.
$6,500 to Dana-Farber Cancer Institute, Boston, MA.

$5,000 to Cure for Lymphoma Foundation, New York, NY. For research.
$2,000 to Project ALS, Los Angeles, CA.

1139
Shasta Regional Community Foundation
1335-B Arboretum Dr., Ste. B
Redding, CA 96003 (530) 244-1219
Contact: Kathy Ann Anderson, C.E.O.; Beth Freeman, Prog. Off.
FAX: (530) 244-0905; E-mail: info@shastarcf.org;
URL: http://www.shastarcf.org
E-mail for Juliette Read: juliette@shastarcf.org

Established in 2000 in CA.
Foundation type: Community foundation.
Financial data (yr. ended 6/30/05): Assets, $3,693,961 (M); gifts received, $1,552,665; expenditures, $1,060,836; giving activities include $441,851 for 167 grants (high: $30,000; low: $150), $43,000 for 49 grants to individuals (high: $2,500; low: $500), and $162,591 for 3 foundation-administered programs.
Purpose and activities: The mission of the foundation is to build resources to meet needs in Shasta and Siskiyou communities through philanthropy, education, and information.
Fields of interest: Arts; Higher education; Education; Environment; Health care; Safety/disasters; Recreation; Youth development; Human services; Nonprofit management; Community development; Leadership development.
Type of support: General/operating support; Building/renovation; Equipment; Scholarship funds; Scholarships—to individuals.
Limitations: Giving limited to Shasta and Siskiyou counties, CA.
Publications: Application guidelines; Annual report; Grants list; Informational brochure.
Application information: The foundation currently makes grants from individual Scholarship funds and Donor-Advised funds; visit foundation Web site for application information. Application form required.
 Initial approach: Telephone
 Deadline(s): Varies
 Board meeting date(s): Monthly
 Final notification: 1-2 months
Officers and Directors:* Terry Starr,* Chair.; Tracy Edwards,* Vice-Chair.; Kathy Ann Anderson, C.E.O. and Exec. Dir.; Evelyn Jacobs,* Secy.; Larry Dahl,* Treas.; David Collier; Bill Cox; Mark Foster; John Freisen; Ann Kaster; Dan Kupsky; Mark Lascalles; Mike Rodriguez; Mark Vegh.
Number of staff: 3 full-time professional; 2 part-time professional.
EIN: 680242276

1140
Shayne Foundation ◇
2299 Panorama Terr.
Los Angeles, CA 90039

Established in 1993 in TN as partial successor to the Werthan Foundation.
Donors: Herbert M. Shayne†; May W. Shayne†; May W. Shayne Charitable Lead Trust; Herbert M. Shayne Charitable Lead Trust.
Foundation type: Independent foundation.
Financial data (yr. ended 12/31/05): Assets, $5,270,614 (M); gifts received, $640,930; expenditures, $866,115; qualifying distributions,

$813,055; giving activities include $813,055 for 16 grants (high: $434,706; low: $500).

Purpose and activities: Giving primarily for education.

Fields of interest: Higher education; Medical school/education; Human services.

Limitations: Applications not accepted. Giving primarily in TN. No grants to individuals.

Application information: Contributes only to pre-selected organizations.

Trustees: David Shayne; Elizabeth Shayne; Joan Blum Shayne.

EIN: 621540372

1141

Peter and Carolyn Shea Foundation ✧

655 Brea Canyon Rd.
Walnut, CA 91789

Established in 1987 in CA.

Donors: Peter O. Shea; Carolyn H. Shea.

Foundation type: Independent foundation.

Financial data (yr. ended 12/31/04): Assets, $968,106 (M); expenditures, $331,049; qualifying distributions, $330,501; giving activities include $330,620 for 20 grants (high: $196,500; low: $100).

Purpose and activities: Giving to education, medical issues and Christian churches and organizations.

Fields of interest: Arts; Elementary/secondary education; Higher education; Hospitals (general); Health organizations, association; Human services; Women, centers/services; Christian agencies & churches.

Limitations: Applications not accepted. Giving primarily in CA. No grants to individuals.

Application information: Contributes only to pre-selected organizations.

Officers: Peter O. Shea, Pres.; Carolyn H. Shea, Secy.; Catherine Shea Johnson, Treas.

EIN: 954110100

Selected grants: The following grants were reported in 2003.

$103,000 to Orange County Performing Arts Center, Costa Mesa, CA.

$25,000 to Loyola High School, Los Angeles, CA.

$21,400 to Hoag Hospital Foundation, Newport Beach, CA.

$14,279 to Saint Brendan School, Los Angeles, CA.

$11,250 to University of California at Irvine Foundation, Irvine, CA.

$5,170 to Network of Evangelical Women in Ministry, Fountain Valley, CA.

$5,000 to Casa Teresa, Orange, CA.

$5,000 to Cystic Fibrosis Research, Mountain View, CA.

$5,000 to Dennigan Cancer Fund.

$5,000 to Hoover Institution on War, Revolution and Peace, Stanford, CA.

1142

Edmund and Mary Shea Foundation ✧

655 Brea Canyon Rd.
Walnut, CA 91789-3010

Established in 1987 in CA.

Donors: Edmund H. Shea, Jr.; J.F. Shea Co., Inc.

Foundation type: Independent foundation.

Financial data (yr. ended 12/31/04): Assets, $7,218,762 (M); expenditures, $659,444; qualifying distributions, $593,570; giving activities

include $593,570 for 48 grants (high: $100,000; low: $100).

Purpose and activities: Giving primarily to Roman Catholic churches, and for education.

Fields of interest: Elementary/secondary education; Higher education; Hospitals (general); Health organizations, association; Human services; Children, services; Roman Catholic agencies & churches.

Limitations: Applications not accepted. Giving primarily in CA. No grants to individuals.

Application information: Contributes only to pre-selected organizations.

Officers: Edmund H. Shea, Jr., Pres.; Mary S. Shea, Secy.; Colleen Shea Morrissey, Treas.

EIN: 954107214

1143

The John & Dorothy Shea Foundation ✧

655 Brea Canyon Rd.
Walnut, CA 91789

Established in 1986 in CA.

Donors: John F. Shea; Dorothy B. Shea; Matthew Gilbert Shea Trust; Alison Brannen Shea Trust; James William Shea Trust; John F. Shea, Jr. Trust.

Foundation type: Independent foundation.

Financial data (yr. ended 12/31/04): Assets, $36,602,795 (M); gifts received, $803,939; expenditures, $3,836,644; qualifying distributions, $3,401,632; giving activities include $3,401,632 for grants.

Purpose and activities: Giving primarily for Roman Catholic agencies, churches, and schools; funding also for education, health and social services.

Fields of interest: Secondary school/education; Higher education; Education; Health organizations, association; Human services; Roman Catholic agencies & churches.

Limitations: Applications not accepted. Giving primarily in CA. No grants to individuals.

Application information: Contributes only to pre-selected organizations.

Officers: John F. Shea, Pres.; Dorothy B. Shea, Secy.; John F. Shea, Jr., Treas.

EIN: 954084694

1144

Shenandoah Foundation ✧ ☆

P.O. Box 193809
San Francisco, CA 94119-3809

Established in 1968 in CA.

Donor: Shana B. Johnstone.

Foundation type: Independent foundation.

Financial data (yr. ended 12/31/05): Assets, $5,814,319 (M); expenditures, $352,629; qualifying distributions, $347,082; giving activities include $339,500 for 50 grants (high: $62,500; low: $250).

Purpose and activities: Giving primarily for medical, educational, environmental and cultural causes.

Fields of interest: Arts, cultural/ethnic awareness; Arts; Education; Environment; Hospitals (general); Medical research, institute.

Type of support: General/operating support; Annual campaigns.

Limitations: Applications not accepted. Giving primarily in CA and NY. No grants to individuals.

Application information: Contributes only to pre-selected organizations.

Officers and Directors:* Shana B. Johnstone,* Pres.; Elizabeth H. Bechtel,* V.P.; George T. Argyris,* Secy.; Nancy S. Hair, Treas.; R.C. Johnstone, Jr.

EIN: 941675019

Selected grants: The following grants were reported in 2003.

$50,000 to Thacher School, Ojai, CA. For equestrian program.

$25,000 to California Academy of Sciences, San Francisco, CA. For building capital.

$10,000 to Family House, San Francisco, CA. For operating support.

$10,000 to United States Equestrian Team, Gladstone, NJ. For annual and endowment fund.

$10,000 to Vanderbilt University, Nashville, TN. For annual and endowment funds.

$7,500 to John Muir Foundation, Walnut Creek, CA. For operating support.

$7,500 to Pepperdine University, Malibu, CA. For annual and endowment funds.

$5,000 to Fine Arts Museums of San Francisco, San Francisco, CA. For operating support.

$5,000 to Monterey Bay Aquarium, Monterey, CA. For conservation programs.

$5,000 to Orme School, Mayer, AZ. For annual fund.

1145

The Shiley Foundation ✧

P.O. Box 207
Pauma Valley, CA 92061

Donor: Donald P. Shiley.

Foundation type: Independent foundation.

Financial data (yr. ended 12/31/05): Assets, $26,471,429 (M); expenditures, $593,838; qualifying distributions, $579,698; giving activities include $577,500 for 5 grants (high: $500,000; low: $5,000).

Fields of interest: Higher education; Health care; Health organizations, association.

Limitations: Applications not accepted. Giving primarily in CA, with emphasis on San Diego. No grants to individuals.

Application information: Contributes only to pre-selected organizations.

Officers: Donald P. Shiley, Pres.; Darlene V. Shiley, Secy.

EIN: 953466851

1146

Eugene and Daymel Shklar Foundation ☆

P.O. Box 8
Santa Cruz, CA 95063-0008

Contact: Eugene Shklar, Pres.

E-mail: infogrants@shklar.org

Established in 2000 in CA.

Donors: Eugene Shklar; Daymel G. Shklar.

Foundation type: Operating foundation.

Financial data (yr. ended 7/31/05): Assets, $3,873,746 (M); expenditures, $2,276,268; qualifying distributions, $2,049,516; giving activities include $2,026,000 for 4 grants (high: $1,855,000; low: $1,000).

Fields of interest: Performing arts, music; Higher education.

Limitations: Giving primarily in CA.

Application information:

Initial approach: Letter or e-mail

Deadline(s): None

Officers: Eugene Shklar, Pres. and Treas.; Daymel G. Shklar, V.P. and Secy.
EIN: 943373051

1147
Shoresh Foundation ◇
(formerly Wirshup Family Foundation)
132 Hillside Ave.
Piedmont, CA   94611

Established in 1986 in CA.
Donors: David Wirshup; Rochelle Shapell Wirshup; The David and Fela Shapell Lead Unitrust.
Foundation type: Independent foundation.
Financial data (yr. ended 8/31/05): Assets, $2,978,372 (M); gifts received, $820,704; expenditures, $532,440; qualifying distributions, $529,910; giving activities include $529,910 for 24 grants (high: $256,000; low: $250).
Purpose and activities: Giving primarily to Jewish organizations; some funding also for human services.
Fields of interest: Museums (ethnic/folk arts); Education; Human services; Jewish federated giving programs; Jewish agencies & temples.
Limitations: Applications not accepted. Giving primarily in CA. No grants to individuals.
Application information: Contributes only to pre-selected organizations.
Officers: Rochelle Shapell, Pres.; Stan Kubrin, Secy. and C.F.O.
EIN: 943044121
Selected grants: The following grants were reported in 2005.
$256,000 to Jewish Federation of the Greater East Bay, Oakland, CA.
$131,960 to Oakland Hebrew Day School, Oakland, CA.
$30,000 to Chabad of the East Bay, Berkeley, CA.
$24,000 to College Preparatory School, Oakland, CA.
$15,000 to San Francisco Art Institute, San Francisco, CA.
$7,070 to Temple Sinai, Palm Springs, CA.
$2,000 to Associated Parents Club of Piedmont, Piedmont, CA.
$1,800 to Lehrhaus Judaica, Berkeley, CA.
$1,000 to Stanford University, Stanford, CA.
$360 to Jewish Community Foundation, San Diego, CA.

1148
The Tommy E. Short Charitable Foundation ◇ ☆
101 W. Broadway, Ste. 1980
San Diego, CA   92101   (619) 595-0760
FAX: (619) 595-0764; URL: http://www.tescf.org

Established in 2001.
Foundation type: Independent foundation.
Financial data (yr. ended 12/31/05): Assets, $1,285,692 (M); expenditures, $1,661,361; qualifying distributions, $602,005; giving activities include $477,300 for 6+ grants (high: $184,050).
Purpose and activities: Giving to enrich lives through educational and inspirational experiences, and creating, collecting and developing successful concepts through synergetic alliances and associations.
Fields of interest: Disasters, 9/11/01; Boys & girls clubs; Human services; Children/youth, services;

Business/industry; Community development; Federated giving programs.
Limitations: Giving primarily in Fort Collins, CO.
Officers: Tommy E. Short, Pres.; Timothy P. Labeck, V.P.; Darrell Erb, Jr., Secy.-Treas.
EIN: 311678809
Selected grants: The following grants were reported in 2003.
$90,000 to Institute of Noetic Sciences, Petaluma, CA. For Fund for the Future.
$60,000 to New Dimensions Foundation, Ukiah, CA.
$45,397 to Boys and Girls Clubs of Larimer County, Fort Collins, CO.
$25,000 to Lambda Community Center, Fort Collins, CO.
$17,500 to William J. Clinton Presidential Foundation, New York, NY.
$5,000 to Childrens Hospital Association, Denver, CO.
$5,000 to Idea Wild, Fort Collins, CO.
$917 to Artist in Residence.

1149
SHP Foundation ◇ ☆
30 E. 4th Ave.
San Mateo, CA   94401   (650) 344-1500
Contact: Susanna Pau, Secy.

Established in 1999 in CA.
Donors: Susanna Pau; Peter Pau; Sandhill Properties.
Foundation type: Independent foundation.
Financial data (yr. ended 12/31/05): Assets, $58,126 (M); expenditures, $341,083; qualifying distributions, $340,850; giving activities include $340,850 for 28 grants (high: $80,000; low: $850).
Fields of interest: Christian agencies & churches; Children.
Application information:
Initial approach: Letter
Deadline(s): Dec. 31
Officer and Director:* Susanna Pau,* Secy.
EIN: 912017312

1150
The Thomas and Stacey Siebel Foundation ▼ ◇
2207 Bridgepointe Pkwy.
San Mateo, CA   94404   (650) 477-5379
Contact: Thomas M. Siebel, Pres.

Established in 1996 in CA.
Donors: Stacey Siebel; Thomas M. Siebel.
Foundation type: Independent foundation.
Financial data (yr. ended 12/31/04): Assets, $170,951,238 (M); expenditures, $6,831,079; qualifying distributions, $6,776,930; giving activities include $6,729,600 for 24 grants (high: $1,250,000; low: $500; average: $50,000–$500,000).
Purpose and activities: Giving primarily to the Salvation Army for programs for the homeless in San Francisco, CA, as well as for land conservation and children's scholarships and services.
Fields of interest: Education, single organization support; Elementary/secondary education; Environment, land resources; Salvation Army; Children, services; Homeless, human services.
Limitations: Applications not accepted. Giving primarily in CA.

Application information: Contributes only to pre-selected organizations.
Officers: Thomas M. Siebel, Pres.; Stacey Siebel, Secy.
EIN: 943256331
Selected grants: The following grants were reported in 2004.
$1,250,000 to Salvation Army of San Francisco, San Francisco, CA. For general operating support.
$1,250,000 to Salvation Army of Santa Clara County, San Jose, CA. For general operating support.
$1,200,000 to Menlo School, Atherton, CA. For Building Fund.
$500,000 to First Tee of San Francisco, San Francisco, CA. For general operating support.
$500,000 to Salvation Army of Great Falls, Great Falls, MT. For general operating support.
$500,000 to Salvation Army of Helena, Helena, MT. For general operating support.
$500,000 to Salvation Army, Billings, Billings, MT. For general operating support.
$300,000 to Great Falls Soccer Foundation, Great Falls, MT. For general operating support.
$90,000 to Monterey Peninsula College Foundation, Monterey, CA. For general operating support.
$65,000 to Stanford University, Stanford, CA. For general operating support for Golf Team.

1151
Sierra Health Foundation
1321 Garden Hwy.
Sacramento, CA   95833   (916) 922-4755
Contact: Len McCandliss, C.E.O.
FAX: (916) 922-4024; E-mail: info@sierrahealth.org; Applications should be mailed and delivered Attn: Grants Admin.; URL: http://www.sierrahealth.org

Established in 1984 in CA; converted from Foundation Health Plan of Sacramento.
Donor: Foundation Health Plan of Sacramento.
Foundation type: Independent foundation.
Financial data (yr. ended 12/31/04): Assets, $153,872,011 (M); gifts received, $1,700; expenditures, $7,589,803; qualifying distributions, $4,818,005; giving activities include $2,691,242 for 109 grants (high: $259,520; low: $49; average: $1,000–$25,000), $56,679 for 68 employee matching gifts, and $1,096,317 for 3 foundation-administered programs.
Purpose and activities: Giving for health-related programs that 1) will have a long-term impact on the general health of the population; 2) provide a positive change in health care systems; and 3) may cause a positive change in the use of health care resources. Support also for model projects that may be replicated by others.
Fields of interest: Child development, education; Medical care, rehabilitation; Health care; Substance abuse, services; Mental health/crisis services; Health organizations, association; AIDS; Alcoholism; Biomedicine; Crime/violence prevention, youth; Nutrition; Youth development; Human services; Children/youth, services; Child development, services; Family services; Community development; Leadership development; Aging; Minorities; Economically disadvantaged.
Type of support: Program development; Conferences/seminars; Curriculum development; Technical assistance; Program evaluation;

Employee matching gifts; Matching/challenge support.

Limitations: Giving limited to all or a portion of the following CA counties depending on grant program: Alpine, Amador, Butte, Calaveras, Colusa, El Dorado, Glenn, Lassen, Modoc, Mono, Nevada, Placer, Plumas, Sacramento, San Joaquin, Shasta, Sierra, Siskiyou, Solano, Stanislaus, Sutter, Tehama, Trinity, Tuolumne, Yolo, and Yuba. No support for programs, activities, or organizations that are not health-related. No grants to individuals or for endowments.

Publications: Informational brochure; Newsletter; Occasional report.

Application information: Newsletter and funding opportunities are available on foundation Web site.

Board meeting date(s): Quarterly

Officers and Directors:* Robert Petersen, C.P.A.*, Chair.; Manuel Esteban, Ph.D.*, Vice-Chair.; Len McCandliss,* C.E.O. and Pres.; Dorothy Meehan, V.P.; Nancy Lee,* Secy.; Gilbert Alvarado, C.F.O.; George Deubel; Jose Hermocillo; Albert R. Jonsen, Ph.D.; Earl Washburn, M.D.; Carol Whiteside.

Number of staff: 5 full-time professional; 2 part-time professional; 4 full-time support; 5 part-time support.

EIN: 680050036

Selected grants: The following grants were reported in 2003.

$200,000 to Grizzly Creek Ranch, Sacramento, CA. For operating support.

$17,500 to Natomas Unified School District, Sacramento, CA. To support Sacramento START program.

$5,000 to Family Service Agency of the Greater Sacramento Area, Sacramento, CA. For general support.

$5,000 to Grantmakers in Health, DC. For general operating support.

$5,000 to River Oak Center for Children, Sacramento, CA. For general operating support.

$5,000 to Sacramento Area Commerce and Trade Organization, Sacramento, CA. For general operating support.

$5,000 to Sacramento Regional Foundation, Sacramento, CA. For general operating support.

$2,500 to Ronald McDonald House Charities of Northern California, Sacramento, CA. For general support.

$1,500 to American Lung Association, Sacramento, CA. For general operating support.

$1,000 to Capital Unity Council, Sacramento, CA. For general support.

1152
Sierra Pacific Foundation ◇
P.O. Box 496028
Redding, CA 96049-6028 (530) 378-8000
Contact: Carolyn Emmerson Dietz, Pres.
FAX: (530) 378-8109;
E-mail: foundation@spi-ind.com; *URL:* http://www.spi-ind.com/Company/SPFoundation.htm

Established in 1979 in CA.
Donor: Sierra Pacific Industries.
Foundation type: Company-sponsored foundation.
Financial data (yr. ended 6/30/05): Assets, $372,164 (M); gifts received, $1,757,050; expenditures, $1,208,216; qualifying distributions, $1,199,701; giving activities include $931,426 for 337 grants (high: $500,000; low: $13), and $268,275 for 252 grants to individuals (high: $1,750; low: $375).

Purpose and activities: The foundation supports organizations involved with education, the environment, youth development, human services, and community development.

Fields of interest: Education; Environment; Youth development; Human services; Community development.

Type of support: General/operating support; Program development; Employee-related scholarships.

Limitations: Giving primarily in areas of company operations. No support for religious organizations or foundations. No grants to individuals (except for employee-related scholarships), or for salaries, general operating support for schools or public agencies, or religious activities.

Publications: Grants list.

Application information: Telephone calls during the application process are not encouraged. Application form required.

Initial approach: Contact foundation for application form; mail application form to foundation or nearest company facility
Copies of proposal: 1
Board meeting date(s): Mar. 31
Final notification: Approximately 2 months

Officers: Carolyn Emmerson Dietz, Pres.; George Emmerson, V.P.; M.D. Emmerson, Secy.
EIN: 942574178

1153
The Stephen M. Silberstein Foundation ◇
29 Eucalyptus Rd.
Belvedere, CA 94920 (415) 435-1692
Contact: Stephen M. Silberstein, Pres.

Established in 1997 in CA.
Donor: Stephen M. Silberstein.
Foundation type: Independent foundation.
Financial data (yr. ended 12/31/04): Assets, $80,495,360 (M); expenditures, $3,574,186; qualifying distributions, $3,404,850; giving activities include $3,401,850 for 25 grants (high: $1,500,000; low: $350; average: $10,000–$250,000).

Purpose and activities: Giving for arts, higher education, and civil rights.

Fields of interest: Higher education; Education; Health care; Civil rights; Public affairs, equal rights.

Type of support: General/operating support.

Limitations: Applications not accepted. Giving primarily in CA, some funding also in CA and NY. No grants to individuals.

Application information: Contributes only to pre-selected organizations.

Officers: Stephen M. Silberstein, Pres.; Paul Silberstein, Secy. and C.F.O.
EIN: 911852739

Selected grants: The following grants were reported in 2004.

$500,000 to Human Rights Watch, New York, NY.
$200,000 to Sierra Club Foundation, San Francisco, CA.
$100,000 to Project Vote, DC.
$100,000 to Rockridge Institute, Berkeley, CA.
$75,000 to Project Billboard, Berkeley, CA.
$35,000 to Foundation for National Progress, San Francisco, CA.
$15,000 to Berkeley Public Library, Berkeley, CA.
$5,000 to Electronic Frontier Foundation, San Francisco, CA.
$5,000 to Marin County Bicycle Coalition, Fairfax, CA.

$400 to Seva Foundation, Berkeley, CA.

1154
The Silver Giving Foundation ◇
(formerly The Silver Lining Foundation)
c/o Julie Shafer, Exec. Dir.
1 Lombard St., Ste. 305
San Francisco, CA 94111 (415) 834-9934
E-mail: sgiving@pacbell.net

Established in 1997 in CA.
Foundation type: Independent foundation.
Financial data (yr. ended 12/31/03): Assets, $64,720,512 (M); expenditures, $2,503,795; qualifying distributions, $2,397,781; giving activities include $2,233,040 for 54 grants (high: $110,000; low: $1,000).

Purpose and activities: Giving for education, national or international sports competition, and prevention of cruelty to children or animals; giving also for public safety testing.

Fields of interest: Education.

Limitations: Applications not accepted. Giving primarily in the San Francisco Bay Area, CA.

Application information: Unsolicited requests for funds not accepted.

Officers and Directors:* Philip W. Halperin,* Pres.; Peggy Ann Dow,* Secy. and C.F.O.; Julie Shafer, Exec. Dir.
EIN: 943285094

Selected grants: The following grants were reported in 2004.

$117,000 to Stanford University, Stanford, CA.
$100,000 to Compass Community Services, San Francisco, CA.
$100,000 to Jamestown Community Center, San Francisco, CA.
$100,000 to Making Waves Education Program, Richmond, CA.
$65,000 to Raphael House, San Francisco, CA.
$60,000 to Families on Track, South San Francisco, CA.
$50,000 to Exploratorium, San Francisco, CA.
$45,000 to Family Connections, San Carlos, CA.
$40,000 to Richmond District Neighborhood Center, San Francisco, CA.
$35,000 to Imagine Bus Project, Sausalito, CA.

1155
The Ronald A. and Victoria Mann Simms Foundation ◇
1416 6th St.
Santa Monica, CA 90401

Established in 1983 in CA.
Donors: Ronald A. Simms; Victoria Mann Simms; Ted Mann Foundation; Mann Center for Education and Family.
Foundation type: Independent foundation.
Financial data (yr. ended 12/31/04): Assets, $15,577 (M); gifts received, $1,038,400; expenditures, $1,042,320; qualifying distributions, $1,036,473; giving activities include $1,036,473 for 42 grants (high: $250,000; low: $280; average: $1,000–$50,000).

Purpose and activities: Giving primarily for Jewish organizations.

Fields of interest: Performing arts, music; Children, services; Jewish federated giving programs.

Limitations: Applications not accepted. Giving primarily in the Los Angeles, CA, area. No grants to individuals.
Application information: Contributes only to pre-selected organizations.
Officers and Directors:* Ronald A. Simms,* Pres.; Victoria Mann Simms,* Secy.; Stanley Hausner.
EIN: 953806111

1156
The Lucille Ellis Simon Foundation ✧
c/o Avery & Greig, LLP
2811 Wilshire Blvd., Ste. 700
Santa Monica, CA 90403

Incorporated in 1960 in CA.
Donors: Donald Ellis Simon; Lucille Ellis Simon.
Foundation type: Independent foundation.
Financial data (yr. ended 12/31/05): Assets, $9,196,605 (M); expenditures, $531,452; qualifying distributions, $418,863; giving activities include $366,000 for 47 grants (high: $50,000; low: $1,000).
Purpose and activities: Giving for Jewish organizations, education, health services, the environment, and art organizations.
Fields of interest: Museums; Education; Environment; Health care; Health organizations, association; Human services; Civil rights, advocacy; Jewish agencies & temples.
Limitations: Applications not accepted. Giving primarily in CA. No grants to individuals.
Application information: Contributes only to pre-selected organizations.
Officers: Donald Simon, Pres.; Pamela Simon Jensen, V.P.; Douglas Simon, V.P.; Eric Simon, V.P.; Jerome H. Craig, Secy.-Treas.
Trustees: Marie Pascoualle; Lillian Weiner.
EIN: 956035906
Selected grants: The following grants were reported in 2005.
$50,000 to Los Angeles County Museum of Art, Los Angeles, CA.
$48,000 to American Jewish Committee, New York, NY.
$25,000 to RAND Corporation, Santa Monica, CA.
$20,000 to Music Center Unified Fund, Los Angeles, CA.
$15,000 to Braille Institute of America, Los Angeles, CA.
$15,000 to Carlthorp School, Santa Monica, CA.
$12,000 to K C E T Community Television of Southern California, Los Angeles, CA.
$10,000 to Community Counseling Service, Huron, SD.
$6,000 to Vista del Mar Child and Family Services, Los Angeles, CA.
$5,000 to Wonder of Reading, Los Angeles, CA.

1157
Simpson PSB Fund ▼ ✧
P.O. Box 359
Lafayette, CA 94549-0359 (925) 284-7048
Contact: Barclay Simpson, Chair.

Established in 1988 in CA.
Donors: Simpson Manufacturing Co., Inc.; Barclay Simpson.
Foundation type: Company-sponsored foundation.
Financial data (yr. ended 12/31/05): Assets, $66,473,092 (M); expenditures, $16,352,316;

qualifying distributions, $16,075,734; giving activities include $16,075,734 for grants.
Purpose and activities: The foundation supports organizations involved with arts and culture, education, youth development, and human services.
Fields of interest: Museums; Arts; Higher education; Education; Youth development; Human services.
Type of support: General/operating support.
Limitations: Giving primarily in CA. No grants to individuals.
Application information: Application form not required.
Initial approach: Proposal
Deadline(s): None
Officers and Directors:* Barclay Simpson,* Chair.; Sharon Simpson,* V.P.; Charles Lee,* Secy. and C.F.O.; Thomas J. Fitzmyers; Jeffrey P. Gainsborough; Anne K. Gattis; Elizabeth Simpson Murray; Amy C. Simpson; Jean D. Simpson; John B. Simpson; Julie M. Simpson.
EIN: 680168017
Selected grants: The following grants were reported in 2004.
$11,000,000 to University of California, Berkeley, CA. 2 grants: $10,500,000, $500,000 (For Library Fund).
$1,209,780 to Girls Inc., New York, NY.
$1,000,000 to California College of the Arts, Art Center, Oakland, CA.
$1,000,000 to Lafayette Community Foundation, Lafayette, CA. For Lafayette Library and Learning Center.
$500,000 to California Shakespeare Theater, Berkeley, CA.
$100,000 to Boys and Girls Club.
$35,000 to Kala Institute, Berkeley, CA.
$10,000 to Oakland Museum of California, Oakland, CA.
$10,000 to University of Southern California, LMP Foundation, Los Angeles, CA.

1158
The Skoll Foundation ▼ ✧
250 University Ave., Ste. 200
Palo Alto, CA 94301 (650) 331-1031
FAX: (650) 331-1033;
E-mail: grants@skollfoundation.org; URL: http://www.skollfoundation.org/

Established in 2002 in CA. In 2004, the foundation incorporated the Skoll Community Fund into its operations.
Donor: Jeffrey S. Skoll.
Foundation type: Independent foundation.
Financial data (yr. ended 6/30/05): Assets, $275,908,751 (M); gifts received, $53,549,912; expenditures, $10,115,530; qualifying distributions, $9,133,407; giving activities include $6,928,515 for 63 grants (high: $1,607,199; low: $2,500; average: $25,000–$250,000), $1,022,974 for 2 foundation-administered programs and $262,344 for 1 loan/program-related investment.
Purpose and activities: The foundation seeks to advance systemic change to benefit communities around the world by investing in, connecting and celebrating social entrepreneurs.
Limitations: Applications not accepted. No support for organizations with less than a two-year track record, or public sector institutions. No grants to individuals, or for scholarships, endowments or land acquisition.

Publications: Annual report.
Application information: Application procedures for specific programs available on foundation Web site. In general, unsolicited requests for funds are not accepted.
Officers and Directors:* Jeffrey S. Skoll,* Chair.; Sally Osberg, C.E.O. and Pres.; Lauce Henduson, V.P., Prog. and Impact; Sandy Herz, V.P., Marketing and Comms.; Richard Fahey, C.O.O.; James G.B. DeMartini III; Debra L. Dunn; Roger L. Martin.
EIN: 113659133
Selected grants: The following grants were reported in 2005.
$1,607,200 to Americans for Oxford, New York, NY. For Skoll Centre for Social Entrepreneurship.
$310,000 to Citizen Schools, Boston, MA. For core support.
$310,000 to International Development Enterprises - India, New Delhi, India. For core support.
$310,000 to Kickstart-International, San Francisco, CA. For core support.
$310,000 to Transfair USA, Oakland, CA. For core support.
$250,000 to Philanthropic Research, Inc., Williamsburg, VA. For core support.
$100,000 to Bootstrap Fund, Stockton, CA. For core support.
$90,000 to Campaign for Female Education (CAMFED) USA Foundation, San Francisco, CA. For core support.
$25,000 to Acumen Fund, New York, NY. For general operating support.
$25,000 to Global Fund for Children, DC. For general operating support and tsunami relief.

1159
Smidt Family Foundation ✧ ☆
c/o Lisa Peres
3491 Mission Oaks Blvd.
Camarillo, CA 93012-5034

Established in 1999 in CA.
Donors: Allan E. Smidt; Eric L. Smidt.
Foundation type: Independent foundation.
Financial data (yr. ended 12/31/05): Assets, $1,680,438 (M); gifts received, $25,000; expenditures, $328,445; qualifying distributions, $328,420; giving activities include $328,420 for grants.
Purpose and activities: Giving primarily to Jewish charitable organizations.
Fields of interest: Education; Multiple sclerosis; Medical research, institute; Food services; Housing/shelter, temporary shelter; Jewish federated giving programs; Jewish agencies & temples.
Limitations: Giving primarily in CA. No grants to individuals.
Application information: Application form not required.
Initial approach: Letter
Officers and Trustees:* Allan E. Smidt,* Mgr.; Eric Smidt,* Mgr.
EIN: 770507427
Selected grants: The following grants were reported in 2003.
$50,000 to United Jewish Fund of Greater Los Angeles, Los Angeles, CA.
$25,000 to Multiple Sclerosis Society, National, New York, NY.
$2,500 to National Jewish Medical and Research Center, Sherman Oaks, CA.

$2,500 to UCLA Foundation, Los Angeles, CA.
$1,000 to City of Hope, Los Angeles, CA.
$1,000 to Manna Conejo Valley Food Distribution Center, Thousand Oaks, CA.
$1,000 to Union Rescue Mission, Los Angeles, CA.
$500 to Fred Jordan Missions, Covina, CA.
$200 to American Society for Technion-Israel Institute of Technology, Los Angeles, CA.
$200 to Simon Wiesenthal Center, Los Angeles, CA.

1160
Joan Irvine Smith & Athalie R. Clarke Foundation ◇
610 Newport Ctr. Dr., Ste. 1170
Newport Beach, CA 92660
Contact: James I. Swinden, V.P.

Established in 1991 in CA.
Donors: Athalie R. Clarke†; Joan Irvine Smith.
Foundation type: Independent foundation.
Financial data (yr. ended 4/30/05): Assets, $17,422,071 (M); expenditures, $2,469,229; qualifying distributions, $2,171,551; giving activities include $2,171,551 for 26 grants (high: $1,249,550; low: $1,000).
Purpose and activities: Giving for environmental protection and the arts.
Fields of interest: Museums; Arts; Environment, natural resources; Environment; Medical research, institute.
Type of support: Endowments; Research; Matching/challenge support.
Limitations: Applications not accepted. Giving primarily in southern CA. No grants to individuals.
Application information: Contributes only to pre-selected organizations.
Officers and Directors: Joan Irvine Smith,* Pres.; James I. Swinden,* V.P. and Treas.; Russell S. Penniman IV,* V.P.; Brett J. Williamson,* Secy.
EIN: 330461971
Selected grants: The following grants were reported in 2004.
$1,320,500 to Irvine Museum, Irvine, CA.
$650,000 to National Water Research Institute, Fountain Valley, CA.
$88,500 to University of California at Irvine Foundation, Irvine, CA.
$50,000 to University of California, Department of Chemistry, Irvine, CA.
$25,000 to Sage Hill School, Newport Coast, CA.
$20,000 to Scripps Institution of Oceanography, La Jolla, CA.
$13,333 to University of California at San Diego, La Jolla, CA.
$10,000 to Hubbs-Sea World Research Institute, San Diego, CA.
$10,000 to Orangewood Childrens Foundation, Santa Ana, CA.
$10,000 to Pacific Symphony Orchestra, Santa Ana, CA.

1161
May and Stanley Smith Charitable Trust
2320 Marinship Way, Ste. 150
Sausalito, CA 94965 (415) 332-0166
Contact: Ruth Collins, Admin.

Established in 1989.
Foundation type: Independent foundation.
Financial data (yr. ended 12/31/05): Assets, $379,944,057 (M); expenditures, $13,662,478;

qualifying distributions, $12,640,738; giving activities include $8,970,163 for 229 grants (high: $1,050,000; low: $2,500).
Purpose and activities: Giving primarily for education, human services and health care.
Fields of interest: Education; Health care; Human services.
International interests: Australia; Bahamas; Canada; South Africa; United Kingdom.
Type of support: Research; Scholarship funds; Program development; Fellowships; Equipment; Continuing support; General/operating support.
Limitations: Giving on a national basis. No grants to individuals or for endowment funds; capital funding; general support to organizations that enjoy broad popular support, or for organizations receiving significant funding from government sources.
Publications: Application guidelines.
Application information: Application form not required.
  Initial approach: Letter
  Copies of proposal: 1
  Deadline(s): Applications accepted Jan 1. to Sept. 30
  Board meeting date(s): Quarterly
  Final notification: Up to one month
Trustees: Mark J. Avery; John P. Collins, Jr.; N.D. Matheny.
EIN: 946622075

1162
Will and Jada Smith Family Foundation ◇
(formerly Will Smith Foundation)
c/o Gelfand, Rennert & Feldman
1880 Century Park E., Ste. 1600
Los Angeles, CA 90067

Established in 1996 in CA.
Donors: Willard Smith II; Howard J. Saks; WJS Trust.
Foundation type: Independent foundation.
Financial data (yr. ended 12/31/05): Assets, $12,020 (M); gifts received, $1,650,000; expenditures, $1,666,586; qualifying distributions, $1,525,189; giving activities include $1,525,189 for 26 grants (high: $1,000,000; low: $500).
Purpose and activities: Giving primarily for education and youth development; funding also for family and social services.
Fields of interest: Education, public education; Secondary school/education; Higher education; Youth development; Human services; Family services; Community development; Foundations (private grantmaking); Christian agencies & churches.
Limitations: Applications not accepted. Giving primarily in Los Angeles, CA, Baltimore, MD, and Philadelphia, PA. No grants to individuals.
Application information: Contributes only to pre-selected organizations.
Officers: Willard Smith II, Pres.; Jada P. Smith, V.P.; Harry Smith, C.F.O.
Directors: Karen Evans; James Lassiter.
EIN: 954607014
Selected grants: The following grants were reported in 2005.
$75,000 to Glide Memorial United Methodist Church, San Francisco, CA.
$15,000 to GreenMount School, Baltimore, MD.
$15,000 to Magic Johnson Foundation, Los Angeles, CA.
$10,000 to Maryland Committee for Children, Baltimore, MD.
$10,000 to Teach for America, Baltimore, MD.

$5,000 to Hampden Family Center, Baltimore, MD.
$5,000 to Macedonia Baptist Church, Baltimore, MD.

1163
The H. Russell Smith Foundation ◇
150 N. Orange Grove Blvd.
Pasadena, CA 91103

Established in 2002 in CA and DE.
Donors: H. Russell Smith; Jeanne R. Smith.
Foundation type: Independent foundation.
Financial data (yr. ended 12/31/05): Assets, $545,773 (M); expenditures, $1,009,553; qualifying distributions, $1,009,355; giving activities include $1,007,334 for 18 grants (high: $330,000; low: $1,000).
Fields of interest: Performing arts, music; Higher education; Hospitals (general); Hospitals (specialty).
Limitations: Applications not accepted. Giving primarily in CA. No grants to individuals.
Application information: Contributes only to pre-selected organizations.
Officers and Directors: H. Russell Smith,* Chair.; Stewart R. Smith,* Pres.; Jeanne R. Smith,* V.P.; Kate Parker,* Secy.-Treas.
EIN: 562283549

1164
Lon V. Smith Foundation ◇
9440 Santa Monica Blvd., Ste. 300
Beverly Hills, CA 90210-4614

Established in 1952 in CA.
Foundation type: Independent foundation.
Financial data (yr. ended 12/31/05): Assets, $26,169,863 (M); expenditures, $1,660,846; qualifying distributions, $1,488,831; giving activities include $1,359,500 for 140 grants (high: $40,000; low: $1,000).
Purpose and activities: Giving primarily for children's services.
Fields of interest: Arts; Education; Hospitals (general); Health care; Health organizations, association; Housing/shelter, homeless; Human services; Children/youth, services; Family services; Federated giving programs.
Type of support: General/operating support.
Limitations: Applications not accepted. Giving primarily in southern CA. No grants to individuals.
Application information: Contributes only to pre-selected organizations.
Officers: Stefan A. Kantardjieff, Pres.; Lawrence S. Clark, V.P.; John L. Lahn, V.P.; Donald R. Mellert, V.P.; Alexander Rados, V.P.; Marguerite M. Murphy, Secy.-Treas.
EIN: 956045384
Selected grants: The following grants were reported in 2003.
$40,000 to United Way, Inc., Los Angeles, CA. For unrestricted support.
$30,000 to University of California, Irvine, CA. For Cancer Surveillance Program.
$25,000 to Boys Republic, Chino Hills, CA. For unrestricted support.
$25,000 to Childrens Hospital Los Angeles, Los Angeles, CA. For unrestricted support.
$25,000 to Pediatric Cancer Research Foundation, Irvine, CA. For unrestricted support.

$25,000 to University of Southern California Kenneth Norris Jr. Cancer Hospital, Los Angeles, CA. For unrestricted support.

$20,000 to Angel Flight West, Santa Monica, CA. For unrestricted support.

$20,000 to Boy Scouts of America, Orange County Council, Irvine, CA. For unrestricted support.

$20,000 to John Douglas French (JDF) Foundation for Alzheimers Disease Research, Los Angeles, CA. For unrestricted support.

$15,000 to Center for the Partially Sighted, Los Angeles, CA. For unrestricted support.

1165
Barbara Smith Fund ◇
P.O. Box 29209
San Francisco, CA 94129-0209

Established in 2003 in DE.
Donor: Barbara Smith†.
Foundation type: Independent foundation.
Financial data (yr. ended 12/31/04): Assets, $12,591,037 (M); gifts received, $4,267,457; expenditures, $573,110; qualifying distributions, $473,858; giving activities include $360,600 for 2 grants (high: $350,600; low: $10,000).
Fields of interest: Arts; Health care.
Type of support: Continuing support; General/operating support.
Limitations: Applications not accepted. Giving primarily in Washington, DC. No grants to individuals.
Application information: Contributes only to pre-selected organizations.
Officers: Michael Lerner, Pres.; Kathy Sessions, Secy.; Norton Smith, Treas.
Director: Sharyle Patton.
EIN: 680531308

1166
The Stanley Smith Horticultural Trust
2320 Marinship Way, Ste. 150
Sausalito, CA 94965 (415) 321-8358
Contact: Thomas F. Daniel, Grants Dir.
E-mail: tdaniel@calacademy.org; Application address: c/o California Academy of Sciences, Dept. of Botany, 875 Howard St., San Francisco, CA 94103

Established in 1970 in CA.
Donor: May Smith.
Foundation type: Independent foundation.
Financial data (yr. ended 12/31/05): Assets, $16,342,015 (M); expenditures, $824,546; qualifying distributions, $766,241; giving activities include $693,000 for grants (high: $30,000; low: $2,000).
Purpose and activities: Grants to organizations for horticultural programs, including education and research.
Fields of interest: Environment, research.
Type of support: General/operating support; Equipment; Program development; Publication; Research.
Limitations: Giving primarily in North and South America. No grants to individuals, or for endowment funds.
Publications: Application guidelines.
Application information: Proposals should be sent in envelopes no larger than 9 x 12 inches (23 x 30 cm). Proposals sent by a method that requires a signature for delivery, by fax or by e-mail will not be considered. Spiral or plastic bindings should not be used. Application form not required.
  Initial approach: Proposal
  Copies of proposal: 1
  Deadline(s): Jan. 1 to Aug. 15
  Board meeting date(s): As required
  Final notification: Early Dec.
Trustees: John P. Collins, Jr.; Ruth M. Collins; James R. Gibbs; N. Dale Matheny.
EIN: 946209165

1167
The May and Stanley Smith Trust
2320 Marinship Way, Ste. 150
Sausalito, CA 94965 (415) 332-0166
Contact: Ruth Collins, Admin.

Established in 1977 in CA.
Donor: May Smith.
Foundation type: Independent foundation.
Financial data (yr. ended 12/31/05): Assets, $8,763,824 (M); expenditures, $419,562; qualifying distributions, $402,159; giving activities include $390,600 for 89 grants (high: $6,000; low: $2,000).
Purpose and activities: Giving primarily to the disabled, especially the visually impaired, the aged, children, and the disadvantaged; support also for social service agencies.
Fields of interest: Education; Human services; Children/youth, services; Aging, centers/services; Aging; Disabilities, people with; Economically disadvantaged.
International interests: Canada.
Type of support: General/operating support; Equipment; Program development; Scholarship funds.
Limitations: Giving primarily in North America, with emphasis on Canada and the San Francisco Bay Area, CA. No support for organizations that receive a large portion of their funding from government sources. No grants to individuals.
Publications: Application guidelines.
Application information: Application form not required.
  Initial approach: Letter
  Copies of proposal: 1
  Deadline(s): Jan. 1 through Sept. 30
  Board meeting date(s): Late fall
  Final notification: Up to 1 month
Trustees: John P. Collins, Jr.; J.R. Gibbs; N. Dale Matheny.
EIN: 946435244
Selected grants: The following grants were reported in 2004.
$6,000 to Baulines Craft Guild, San Rafael, CA.
$6,000 to Blind Babies Foundation, San Francisco, CA.
$6,000 to Lincoln Center for the Performing Arts, New York, NY.
$6,000 to San Domenico School, San Anselmo, CA.
$6,000 to Santa Barbara Therapeutic Riding Academy, Santa Barbara, CA.
$6,000 to Santa Teresita School, Los Angeles, CA.
$5,000 to Kids Turn, San Francisco, CA.
$5,000 to Young at Heart Project, Santa Cruz, CA.
$4,000 to Special Recreation Services, Reno, NV.
$3,000 to Sproul Ranch, Lancaster, CA.

1168
The Smittcamp Family Foundation ◇
8100 N. Minnewawa Ave.
Clovis, CA 93611

Established in 1996 in CA.
Donors: William Smittcamp; Muriel Smittcamp; Robert Smittcamp; Earl Smittcamp; Summer Prize Fruit Co.; Wawona Frozen Foods; Lyons Magnus, Inc.
Foundation type: Independent foundation.
Financial data (yr. ended 12/31/04): Assets, $6,113,538 (M); expenditures, $1,076,008; qualifying distributions, $1,005,660; giving activities include $1,005,660 for 9 grants (high: $987,945; low: $300).
Purpose and activities: Giving primarily for Christian organizations, education, and human services.
Fields of interest: Higher education; Libraries (public); Education; Hospitals (specialty); Health care; Human services; Children/youth, services; Christian agencies & churches.
Limitations: Giving limited to CA. No grants to individuals, no loans.
Officers: Elizabeth Kimball, Chair.; Carol Copeland, Pres.; Herb Liles, Secy.
Directors: James M. Bell; Albert Peterson; Marie Riggs; Charles Shillito; Robert Smittcamp; William Smittcamp.
EIN: 770343026

1169
Patricia D. and William B. Smullin Foundation
2390 Domingo Ave., No. 163
Berkeley, CA 94705 (510) 704-0194
Contact: Carol Anne Smullin Brown, Pres.
FAX: (510) 704-0295;
E-mail: smullin.foundation@gmail.com

Established in 1990 in OR.
Donors: Patricia D. Smullin†; William B. Smullin†.
Foundation type: Independent foundation.
Financial data (yr. ended 12/31/05): Assets, $11,215,577 (M); expenditures, $1,045,077; qualifying distributions, $943,000; giving activities include $943,000 for 8 grants (high: $620,000; low: $1,000).
Purpose and activities: Giving primarily for higher education, health education, and to Episcopal churches.
Fields of interest: Higher education; Health care, formal/general education; Protestant agencies & churches.
Type of support: Program development; Endowments; General/operating support; Capital campaigns; Scholarship funds.
Limitations: Applications not accepted. Giving limited to northern CA and OR.
Publications: Financial statement; Program policy statement.
Application information: Unsolicited requests for funds not accepted.
  Board meeting date(s): Nov.
Officers and Directors:* Carol Anne Smullin Brown,* Pres. and Exec. Dir.; Nikki C. Hatton,* Secy.; Kevin Smullin Brown; Patsy Smullin.
Number of staff: 1 full-time professional.
EIN: 931055546
Selected grants: The following grants were reported in 2005.

$620,000 to Gales Creek Camp Foundation for Children with Diabetes, Portland, OR. For endowment fund and operating support.

$175,000 to Willamette University, Salem, OR. For scholarship fund.

$65,000 to Humboldt State University, Arcata, CA. For scholarships.

$50,000 to Christ Episcopal Church, Eureka, CA. For general support.

$15,000 to Planned Parenthood, Six Rivers, Eureka, CA. For general support.

$15,000 to Saint Albans Episcopal Church, Arcata, CA. For general support.

$2,000 to No More Hungry Children, CA.

$1,000 to Holiday Funding Partnership, CA.

1170
William D. Smythe Family Foundation ◇
61A Victory Ln.
Los Gatos, CA 95030   (408) 399-5551
Contact: Michael D. Smythe, V.P.

Established in 2000 in CA.
Donors: William D. Smythe; Michael D. Smythe; Linda Smythe; Karen Smythe Cocumelli; William D. Smythe, Jr.; Catherine Smythe Grasso; James J. Smythe; Sally Smythe Godwin; Stephen Godwin.
Foundation type: Independent foundation.
Financial data (yr. ended 12/31/05): Assets, $1,241,158 (M); gifts received, $500,000; expenditures, $353,038; qualifying distributions, $341,300; giving activities include $341,300 for 58 grants (high: $75,000; low: $100).
Fields of interest: Education; Children/youth, services.
Limitations: Giving primarily in San Jose, CA.
Application information:
Initial approach: Letter
Deadline(s): None
Officers: William D. Smythe, C.E.O.; Michael D. Smythe, V.P.; Karen Smythe Cocumelli, Secy.; William D. Smythe, Jr., C.F.O.
Directors: Sally Smythe Godwin; Catherine Smythe Grasso; James J. Smythe.
EIN: 770535273

1171
Phoebe Snow Foundation ◇
591 Redwood Hwy., Ste. 3215
Mill Valley, CA 94941

Established in 1993 in CA.
Donors: John H. Scully; Irene S. Scully; Scully 1994 Family Trust No. 2; The Tyrell Foundation.
Foundation type: Independent foundation.
Financial data (yr. ended 12/31/05): Assets, $64,133,116 (M); gifts received, $16,281,530; expenditures, $2,414,443; qualifying distributions, $2,404,086; giving activities include $2,400,000 for 32 grants (high: $1,607,113; low: $45).
Purpose and activities: Giving primarily for education, and family and social services.
Fields of interest: Higher education; Education; Health organizations; Human services; Roman Catholic agencies & churches; Homeless.
Limitations: Applications not accepted. Giving primarily in CA. No grants to individuals.
Application information: Contributes only to pre-selected organizations.

Officers and Director:* John H. Scully,* Pres. and Treas.; Kim Silva, Secy.
EIN: 680315880

1172
Sobrato Family Foundation ◇
10600 N. De Anza Blvd., Ste. 225
Cupertino, CA 95014-2031   (408) 996-9500
Contact: Lisa S. Sonsini, Pres.
E-mail: grants@sobrato.com; Application address: 10600 N. De Anza Blvd., Ste. 200, Cupertino, CA 95014; FAX: (408) 996-9516; URL: http://www.sobrato.com/foundation

Established in 1996 in CA.
Donors: Sobrato Charitable Capital Trust; John A. Sobrato; Lisa Sobrato; Ann Sobrato Trust Estate; Sobrato Charitable Lead Trust I; Sobrato Charitable Lead Trust II; Sobrato Charitable Lead Trust III; Sobrato Charitable Lead Trust IV.
Foundation type: Independent foundation.
Financial data (yr. ended 12/31/04): Assets, $77,349,852 (M); gifts received, $1,727,989; expenditures, $1,928,460; qualifying distributions, $848,911; giving activities include $643,911 for 20 grants (high: $75,000; low: $75).
Purpose and activities: The foundation is dedicated to helping to create and sustain a strong and vibrant community where all Silicon Valley residents have an equal opportunity to live, work, and be enriched. To accomplish its purpose, the foundation invests in strong community-based organizations that promote self-reliance and economic independence, and positively contribute to the quality of life for economically, physically, and emotionally challenged individuals.
Fields of interest: Education; Health care; Youth development; Human services; Economic development; Community development.
Type of support: General/operating support; Continuing support; Capital campaigns; Building/renovation; Emergency funds; Program development; Seed money; Technical assistance; Program evaluation; Matching/challenge support.
Limitations: Giving limited to Fremont, Hayward, Newark, Santa Clara, San Mateo County, and southern Alameda County, CA. No support for religious organizations for sectarian purposes, or for political or fraternal organizations. No grants to individuals (except through specific scholarship programs), endowment campaigns or annual fund drives, or for fundraising events.
Publications: Application guidelines; Annual report (including application guidelines); Financial statement.
Application information: Pre-application form available on foundation Web site. Full proposal will be requested from successful pre-applicants only. Application form required.
Initial approach: Completed pre-application form
Copies of proposal: 1
Deadline(s): Visit Web site for current deadlines
Board meeting date(s): Quarterly
Final notification: Approximately 2 to 3 months after deadline
Officers and Trustees:* John A. Sobrato,* Chair.; Lisa Sobrato Sonsini,* Pres.; Sheri J. Sobrato,* V.P.; Abby J. Sobrato,* Secy.; Bobbi Mazzone, C.F.O.; Diane Ford, Exec. Dir.; Bryan C. Polster; John M. Sobrato; Susan Sobrato.
Number of staff: 1 full-time professional; 1 full-time support.
EIN: 770348912

Selected grants: The following grants were reported in 2003.

$75,000 to Family Service Agency of San Mateo County, San Mateo, CA. For renovations.

$75,000 to Teach for America, Oakland, CA. For salary support.

$50,000 to City Year, San Jose, CA. For operating support.

$25,000 to Achievekids, Palo Alto, CA. For capital support.

$25,000 to Free at Last: Community Recovery and Rehabilitation Services, East Palo Alto, CA. For salary support.

$25,000 to Loaves and Fishes Family Kitchen, San Jose, CA. For salary support.

$20,000 to Services for Brain Injury, San Jose, CA. For rent support.

$15,000 to Morgan Center, San Jose, CA. For rent support.

$15,000 to Peninsula Conflict Resolution Center, San Mateo, CA. For general operating support.

$4,263 to Northern California Grantmakers, San Francisco, CA. For general operating support.

1173
Y & H Soda Foundation
2 Theater Sq., Ste. 211
Orinda, CA 94563-3346   (925) 253-2630
Contact: Judith Murphy, C.E.O.
FAX: (925) 253-1814;
E-mail: info@yhsodafoundation.org; URL: http://www.yhsodafoundation.org

Established in 1964.
Donors: Y. Charles Soda Trust; Y. Charles Soda†; Helen C. Soda†.
Foundation type: Independent foundation.
Financial data (yr. ended 11/30/05): Assets, $134,990,954 (M); expenditures, $6,685,636; qualifying distributions, $7,254,441; giving activities include $4,678,665 for 375 grants (high: $250,000; low: $500; average: $1,000–$25,000).
Purpose and activities: The foundation, through its charitable activities, seeks to enhance the quality of life for the economically disadvantaged, disabled, elderly and youth; to promote their health and welfare; to provide opportunities for education and to support those organizations whose religious philosophy strengthens the spiritual and temporal well being of those they serve.
Fields of interest: Education, early childhood education; Child development, education; Elementary school/education; Vocational education; Higher education; Food services; Youth development, services; Human services; Children/youth, services; Family services; Aging, centers/services; Women, centers/services; Homeless, human services; Community development; Roman Catholic agencies & churches; Religion; Aging; Disabilities, people with; Minorities; Women; Economically disadvantaged; Homeless.
Type of support: Capital campaigns; General/operating support; Equipment; Program development; Scholarship funds; Matching/challenge support.
Limitations: Giving limited to Alameda and Contra Costa counties, CA. No support for animal welfare, the arts, environmental causes, private foundations, national medical research organizations, or political organizations. No grants to individuals, or for annual fundraising campaigns, faculty chairs, or advocacy grants.
Publications: Application guidelines; Grants list.

Application information: Faxed or E-mailed letters will not be accepted. Application form not required.
Initial approach: Letter
Copies of proposal: 1
Deadline(s): Dec. 1-Jan. 31, Mar. 1-Apr. 30, June 1-July 31, and Sept. 1-Oct. 31
Board meeting date(s): 2nd Thurs. of each month
Final notification: 3 months
Officers and Directors: * Alan Holloway,* Chair.; Judith Murphy,* C.E.O.; Rosemary Soda, V.P.; Alfred Dossa, Secy.; James Dye,* Treas.
Number of staff: 3 full-time professional; 1 part-time professional; 3 full-time support.
EIN: 941611668
Selected grants: The following grants were reported in 2005.
$250,000 to Family Aid-Catholic Education, Oakland, CA.
$125,000 to Dominican Sisters of Mission San Jose, Oakland, CA. For care center and chapel renovation.
$50,000 to Catholic Charities of the East Bay, Oakland, CA. For Family Asset Building Services in East Contra Costa County.
$50,000 to Center for the Education of the Infant Deaf, Berkeley, CA. For Pediatric Audiology Suite Facility Project.
$45,000 to Sacred Heart Church, Palm Desert, CA. For educational project.
$35,000 to A Home Within, San Francisco, CA. For Children's Psychotherapy Project.
$20,000 to Ambulatory Surgery Access Coalition, San Francisco, CA. For Alameda and Contra Costa Program.
$20,000 to Teach for America, New York, NY. To recruit, train, and support professional development for Oakland Corps.
$20,000 to Wellness Community, DC. For support groups for cancer patients.
$15,000 to Center for Independent Living, Berkeley, CA. For training and outreach costs of Moving On Program.

1174
The Sodaro Family Foundation ◇ ☆
4 Corporate Plz., Ste. 102
Newport Beach, CA 92660

Established in 1999 in CA.
Donors: Donald E. Sodaro; Felicity A. Sodaro.
Foundation type: Independent foundation.
Financial data (yr. ended 12/31/05): Assets, $299,057 (M); gifts received, $496,621; expenditures, $563,552; qualifying distributions, $561,278; giving activities include $561,278 for 5 grants (high: $555,000; low: $278).
Purpose and activities: Giving primarily for education and to a hospital foundation; funding also for a performing arts center.
Fields of interest: Performing arts centers; Higher education, university; Hospitals (general).
Limitations: Applications not accepted. Giving primarily in Orange County, CA. No grants to individuals.
Application information: Contributes only to pre-selected organizations.
Officers: Felicity A. Sodaro, Pres.; Faith Sodaro Grimm, Secy.; Martha Sodaro Burke, Treas.
EIN: 330801333

1175
Solano Community Foundation
1261 Travis Blvd., Ste. 320
Fairfield, CA 94533   (707) 399-3846
Contact: Stephanie R. Wolf, C.E.O.
FAX: (707) 399-3849; E-mail: swolf@solanocf.org;
URL: http://www.solanocf.org

Established in 2000 in CA.
Foundation type: Community foundation.
Financial data (yr. ended 12/31/05): Assets, $3,857,358 (M); gifts received, $1,881,425; expenditures, $1,225,521; giving activities include $1,019,219 for 406 grants (high: $100,000; low: $25), and $20,000 for 4 grants to individuals (high: $5,000; low: $2,000).
Purpose and activities: The foundation is dedicated to strengthening the community both now and for future generations. The foundation is a vehicle for private donors to make a lasting contribution to the community.
Fields of interest: Arts; Elementary/secondary education; Higher education; Health care; Children, foster care; Human services; Community development; Youth.
Type of support: General/operating support; Management development/capacity building; Employee matching gifts; Scholarships—to individuals.
Limitations: Applications not accepted. Giving limited to the Solano County, CA area.
Publications: Annual report; Financial statement; Newsletter.
Application information: Unsolicited grants are not being made at this time. All grants are made through Donor-Advised funds.
Board meeting date(s): Each month, except July and Dec.
Officers and Directors: * Mike Conner,* Chair.; Stephanie R. Wolf, C.E.O. and Pres.; Mark Sievers,* V.P.; Brett Johnson,* Secy.-Treas.; Brian Chikowski; Don Erickson; Becky Kendall; Marilyn Manfredi; Mel Orpilla; Margaret Payne.
Number of staff: 1 full-time professional; 1 full-time support; 1 part-time support.
EIN: 680354961

1176
Richard & Mary Solari Charitable Trust ◇
527 St. Andrews Dr.
Aptos, CA 95003-5422

Established in 1984 in CA.
Donors: Richard C. Solari; Mary C. Solari.
Foundation type: Independent foundation.
Financial data (yr. ended 9/30/05): Assets, $10,974,586 (M); expenditures, $596,046; qualifying distributions, $571,713; giving activities include $532,600 for 49 grants (high: $100,000; low: $500).
Purpose and activities: Giving primarily for higher education, health care including medical research, the arts, and youth and social services.
Fields of interest: Arts; Education; Aquariums; Hospitals (general); Diabetes research; Hematology research; Food banks; Human services; Foundations (community); Roman Catholic agencies & churches.
Limitations: Applications not accepted. Giving primarily in CA. No grants to individuals.
Application information: Contributes only to pre-selected organizations.

Trustees: Mary C. Solari; Richard C. Solari.
EIN: 770069120
Selected grants: The following grants were reported in 2005.
$10,000 to Operation USA, Los Angeles, CA.
$5,000 to Catholic Charities.
$5,000 to Pacific Collegiate School, Santa Cruz, CA.
$5,000 to United Way of Santa Cruz County, Capitola, CA.
$4,500 to Pajaro Valley Shelter Services, Watsonville, CA.
$3,600 to Northern California Grantmakers, San Francisco, CA.
$2,000 to Alzheimers Association, Chicago, IL.
$2,000 to Walnut Avenue Womens Center, Santa Cruz, CA.
$1,000 to Cabrillo College Foundation, Aptos, CA.
$1,000 to Cystic Fibrosis Foundation, Bethesda, MD.

1177
Solve, Inc. ◇ ☆
29071 Bauquet Canyon Rd.
Silverado, CA 92676

Foundation type: Independent foundation.
Financial data (yr. ended 12/31/05): Assets, $64,072 (M); gifts received, $664,248; expenditures, $673,700; qualifying distributions, $634,040; giving activities include $634,040 for grants.
Fields of interest: Human services.
Limitations: Applications not accepted.
Application information: Contributes only to pre-selected organizations.
Officers: Florica Hafiz, Pres.; Silvia Hernandez, Secy.; Ana Babii, Treas.
EIN: 311659399

1178
Sonora Area Foundation
20100 Cedar Rd., No. E
P.O. Box 577
Sonora, CA 95370-0577   (209) 533-2596
Contact: Mick Grimes, Exec. Dir.; Lin Freer, Prog. Mgr.
FAX: (209) 533-2412;
E-mail: acorn@sonora-area.org; Grant application E-mail: leaf@sonara-area.org; URL: http://www.sonora-area.org

Established in 1989 in CA.
Foundation type: Community foundation.
Financial data (yr. ended 12/31/05): Assets, $7,068,989 (L); gifts received, $699,619; expenditures, $1,346,879; giving activities include $902,131 for 157 grants (high: $125,000; low: $100), and $70,566 for 75 grants to individuals (high: $3,600; low: $125).
Purpose and activities: The foundation assists donors, makes grants, and provides community leadership. Primary areas of interest include human services, education, arts, culture and humanities, health, public and society benefit, and environment and animals.
Fields of interest: Visual arts; Performing arts; Performing arts, music; Humanities; Arts; Education, early childhood education; Child development, education; Elementary school/education; Libraries/library science; Education; Environment; Animal welfare; Hospitals (general);

Health care; Substance abuse, services; Mental health/crisis services; Health organizations, association; Alcoholism; Food services; Recreation; Children/youth, services; Child development, services; Family services; Residential/custodial care, hospices; Aging, centers/services; Women, centers/services; Human services; Community development; Voluntarism promotion; Aging; Disabilities, people with; Women; Economically disadvantaged.

Type of support: General/operating support; Continuing support; Management development/capacity building; Capital campaigns; Building/renovation; Equipment; Emergency funds; Program development; Conferences/seminars; Publication; Seed money; Curriculum development; Scholarship funds; Technical assistance; Consulting services; Program evaluation; Grants to individuals; Scholarships—to individuals; Matching/challenge support.

Limitations: Giving limited to Tuolumne County, CA. No support for sectarian purposes or private foundations. No grants for annual campaigns, endowment funds, or debt retirement.

Publications: Application guidelines; Annual report; Biennial report; Financial statement; Grants list; Informational brochure; Informational brochure (including application guidelines); Newsletter; Occasional report.

Application information: Visit foundation Web site for application guidelines. The foundation's Board of Directors reviews letters of inquiry at scheduled Board meetings (usually the second Tuesday) in Feb., Apr., June, Aug., Oct., and Dec.; letters of inquiry must be submitted by mid-month preceding these board meetings in order to be considered for the next grant cycle. Application form not required.

Initial approach: Mail, e-mail, or fax letter of inquiry (2-page maximum)
Copies of proposal: 1
Deadline(s): 3rd week of every other month
Board meeting date(s): Monthly
Final notification: 2 months

Officers and Trustees:* Celeste Boyd,* Pres.; Clark Segerstrom,* V.P.; Roger Francis,* Secy.; Jim Gianelli,* Treas.; Mick Grimes, Exec. Dir.; Joan Bergsund; William J. Coffill; Jim Johnson.
Number of staff: 1 full-time professional; 2 full-time support.
EIN: 931023051

1179
Samuel and Helen Soref Foundation ◇
(formerly Samuel M. Soref & Helene K. Soref Foundation)
11530 Dona Dorotea Dr.
Studio City, CA 91604

Established in 1983 in FL.
Foundation type: Independent foundation.
Financial data (yr. ended 12/31/03): Assets, $34,974,831 (M); expenditures, $2,746,176; qualifying distributions, $2,626,176; giving activities include $2,621,840 for 74 grants (high: $1,005,000; low: $500; average: $1,000–$100,000).
Purpose and activities: Giving primarily to Jewish agencies and for education, and federated giving programs.
Fields of interest: Higher education; Human services; Children/youth, services; Family services; Jewish federated giving programs.
Type of support: General/operating support.

Limitations: Applications not accepted. Giving on a national basis. No grants to individuals.
Application information: Contributes only to pre-selected organizations.
Trustee: Benjamin F. Breslauer.
EIN: 592246963
Selected grants: The following grants were reported in 2004.
$350,000 to Hillel: The Foundation for Jewish Campus Life, DC.
$255,000 to American Associates, Ben-Gurion University of the Negev, Los Angeles, CA.
$200,000 to Goldring/Woldenberg Institute of Southern Jewish Life, Jackson, MS.
$163,500 to Washington Institute for Near East Policy, DC.
$100,000 to Jewish Family and Life, Newton, MA.
$100,000 to North American Federation of Temple Brotherhoods, New York, NY.
$75,000 to Jewish Federation Council of Greater Los Angeles, Los Angeles, CA.
$75,000 to Jewish Federation of Greater Houston, Houston, TX.
$60,000 to World Union for Progressive Judaism, Jerusalem, Israel.
$50,000 to Jewish Federation of Greater Long Beach and West Orange County, Long Beach, CA.

1180
Harvey L. & Maud C. Sorensen Foundation ◇
300 Drakes Landing Rd., Ste. 120
Greenbrae, CA 94904

Incorporated in 1960 in CA.
Donors: Harvey L. Sorensen†; Maud C. Sorensen†.
Foundation type: Independent foundation.
Financial data (yr. ended 9/30/05): Assets, $27,825,117 (M); expenditures, $1,405,205; qualifying distributions, $1,309,506; giving activities include $1,283,500 for 48 grants (high: $287,000; low: $1,000).
Fields of interest: Environment, natural resources; Animals/wildlife, preservation/protection; Hospitals (general); Human services.
Type of support: Annual campaigns; Building/renovation; Program development; Matching/challenge support.
Limitations: Applications not accepted. Giving limited to San Francisco, CA. No grants to individuals; no loans.
Application information: Contributes only to pre-selected organizations.
Officers and Directors:* James R. Bancroft,* Pres.; Dean Witter III,* V.P.; George R. Dirkes,* Secy. and C.F.O.; Paul M. Bancroft; Duncan McCormack III; Leslie Tuel.
EIN: 941542559

1181
The W. L. S. Spencer Foundation ◇
1660 Bush St., Ste. 300
San Francisco, CA 94109 (415) 561-6540
Contact: Mary L. Gregory, Admin.
FAX: (415) 561-6477; *E-mail:* mgregory@pfs-llc.net;
URL: http://www.pfs-llc.net/spencer/spencer.html

Established in 1994 in DE.
Donor: John S. Wadsworth, Jr.
Foundation type: Independent foundation.

Financial data (yr. ended 12/31/05): Assets, $15,180,072 (M); gifts received, $51,763; expenditures, $1,268,271; qualifying distributions, $1,187,305; giving activities include $1,105,530 for 44 grants (high: $300,000; low: $500).
Purpose and activities: The mission of the foundation is to fund activities anywhere in the world which foster new ideas in education and encourage creativity. The foundation prefers specific initiatives that conform with this mission. The foundation enjoys the leverage that arises from seed grants, challenge grants, and matching grants.
Fields of interest: Arts; Education.
International interests: Asia.
Type of support: Program development; Seed money; Matching/challenge support.
Limitations: Giving on a worldwide basis. No grants for endowments or ongoing operational expenses.
Publications: Application guidelines; Annual report (including application guidelines); Grants list; Program policy statement.
Application information: Unsolicited grant proposals are not accepted. Application form not required.

Initial approach: Letter
Copies of proposal: 3
Deadline(s): None
Board meeting date(s): Varies
Final notification: Up to 1 month from receipt of application

Officers and Directors:* Bette Sue Wadsworth,* C.E.O.; John S. Wadsworth, Jr.,* C.I.O.; Paul Peppis; Christopher Wadsworth; John Wadsworth; Lela Wadsworth; Libby Wadsworth; Shannon Wadsworth.
EIN: 133799186

1182
Thomas Spiegel Family Foundation ☆
(formerly Columbia Charitable Foundation)
9465 Wilshire Blvd., Ste. 900
Beverly Hills, CA 90212

Established in 2004 in CA as the result of a reorganization of the Columbia Charitable Foundation.
Foundation type: Independent foundation.
Financial data (yr. ended 12/31/04): Assets, $91,826,366 (M); expenditures, $7,200,775; qualifying distributions, $4,365,264; giving activities include $3,788,293 for 32 grants (high: $3,100,000; low: $100).
Fields of interest: Education; Human services; Philanthropy/voluntarism; Jewish agencies & temples.
Limitations: Applications not accepted. Giving primarily in Los Angeles, CA. No grants to individuals.
Application information: Contributes only to pre-selected organizations.
Officers and Directors:* William Elkins,* V.P.; Lisya Mizrahi, C.F.O.; Helene Spiegel; Thomas Spiegel.
EIN: 331050281

1183
Robert R. Sprague Foundation ◇
101 Bayside Pl.
Corona del Mar, CA 92625 (949) 673-7633

Established in 1998 in CA.
Donor: Robert R. Sprague.
Foundation type: Independent foundation.

Financial data (yr. ended 5/31/06): Assets, $11,160,520 (M); gifts received, $51,965; expenditures, $601,682; qualifying distributions, $560,000; giving activities include $560,000 for grants.

Purpose and activities: Giving primarily for higher education.

Fields of interest: Museums; Performing arts; Higher education; Cancer; Human services.

Limitations: Giving primarily in CA.

Officers: Margaret L. Sprague, Mgr.; Robert R. Sprague, Mgr.

EIN: 957052355

Selected grants: The following grants were reported in 2004.

$603,000 to University of California at Irvine Foundation, Irvine, CA.

$25,000 to Orange County Performing Arts Center, Costa Mesa, CA.

$10,000 to Orange County Museum of Art, Newport Beach, CA.

$10,000 to Queen of Hearts Foundation, Newport Beach, CA.

$5,000 to Achievement Rewards for College Scientists (ARCS) Foundation, Newport Beach, CA.

$5,000 to American Red Cross, Orange County Chapter, Santa Ana, CA. For Clara Barton Spectrum Award.

1184

Norman F. Sprague, Jr. Foundation ◇

11726 San Vicente Blvd., No. 625
Los Angeles, CA 90049
Contact: Norman F. Sprague III, Tr.

Established in 1997 in CA.

Foundation type: Independent foundation.

Financial data (yr. ended 2/28/05): Assets, $11,419,409 (M); expenditures, $589,646; qualifying distributions, $490,627; giving activities include $464,000 for 13 grants (high: $300,000; low: $500).

Fields of interest: Museums; Environment, natural resources.

Limitations: Applications not accepted. Giving primarily in CA. No grants to individuals.

Application information: Unsolicited requests for funds not accepted.

Trustees: Cynthia Sprague Connolly; Elizabeth Sprague Day; Caryll Sprague Mingst; Norman F. Sprague III.

EIN: 954621772

Selected grants: The following grants were reported in 2005.

$300,000 to Harvard-Westlake School, North Hollywood, CA.

$32,000 to Los Angeles County Museum of Art, Los Angeles, CA.

$15,000 to Bandon School District, Bandon, OR.

$12,500 to National Museum of Wildlife Art, Jackson, WY.

$11,000 to Childrens Hospital.

$10,000 to Prince of Wales Foundation, DC.

1185

Springcreek Foundation

770 Tamalpais Dr., Ste. 210
Corte Madera, CA 94925 (415) 945-7050
Contact: Tanya Winkley

Established in 1994 in CA.

Donors: T. Dixon Long; Henry H. Corning; Barbara H. Young; Maud-Alison C. Long.

Foundation type: Independent foundation.

Financial data (yr. ended 12/31/04): Assets, $14,160,472 (M); expenditures, $1,597,437; qualifying distributions, $1,448,941; giving activities include $1,447,941 for 180 grants (high: $50,000; low: $200).

Fields of interest: Museums; Performing arts; Performing arts, theater; Performing arts, orchestra (symphony); Literature; Arts; Higher education; Environment, land resources; Environment; Reproductive health, family planning; Human services; Children/youth, services; Community development; Philanthropy/voluntarism.

Type of support: General/operating support.

Limitations: Applications not accepted. Giving primarily in CA. No grants to individuals.

Application information: Contributes only to pre-selected organizations. Unsolicited requests for funds not accepted.

Board meeting date(s): 3rd Mon. in Oct.

Officers and Directors:* Maud-Alison Long, Pres.; Marlis Corning, V.P.; Tanya Winkley,* Secy.-Treas.; Henry H. Corning; T. Dixon Long.

EIN: 680344778

Selected grants: The following grants were reported in 2003.

$500,000 to Friends of CRAFT (Center for Research into Anthropological Foundations of Technology), Bloomington, IN.

$12,500 to Planned Parenthood Golden Gate, San Francisco, CA.

$10,000 to Philanthropy Northwest, Seattle, WA.

$10,000 to San Francisco Opera Association, San Francisco, CA.

$5,000 to Bay Area Discovery Museum, Sausalito, CA.

$5,000 to San Francisco Museum of Modern Art, San Francisco, CA.

$3,000 to Resource Renewal Institute, San Francisco, CA.

$1,500 to Larkin Street Youth Services, San Francisco, CA.

$1,200 to Berkeley Repertory Theater, Berkeley, CA.

$1,000 to Global Fund for Women, San Francisco, CA.

1186

James L. Stamps Foundation, Inc. ◇

2000 E. 4th St., Ste. 230
Santa Ana, CA 92705-3814 (714) 568-9740
Contact: Delores J. Boutault, Mgr.

Incorporated in 1963 in CA.

Donor: James L. Stamps†.

Foundation type: Independent foundation.

Financial data (yr. ended 12/31/04): Assets, $32,970,650 (M); expenditures, $1,932,221; qualifying distributions, $1,787,401; giving activities include $1,696,557 for 60 grants (high: $100,000; low: $1,135; average: $1,000–$50,000).

Purpose and activities: Emphasis on Protestant evangelical churches, seminaries, associations, and programs. Capital fund grants and new equipment grants restricted to Christian organizations; camping grants restricted to Christian camps.

Fields of interest: Elementary/secondary education; Higher education; Christian agencies & churches; Protestant agencies & churches; Religion.

Type of support: General/operating support; Equipment; Program development; Matching/challenge support.

Limitations: Giving primarily in southern CA. No grants to individuals, or for endowment funds, deficit financing, fellowships, publications, or conferences.

Publications: Application guidelines.

Application information: Organizations may be invited to submit further information upon review of letter. Application form required.

Initial approach: Letter

Copies of proposal: 1

Board meeting date(s): Bimonthly beginning in Feb., on the 2nd Tuesday of the month

Officers and Trustees:* Thomas P. Lynch,* Chair.; E.C. Boutault,* Pres.; Richard D. Salyer, V.P.; Richard S. Kredel, Secy.-Treas; Delores J. Boutault, Mgr.; Willis R. Leach.

Number of staff: 2 full-time support; 1 part-time support.

EIN: 956086125

Selected grants: The following grants were reported in 2004.

$100,000 to Azusa Pacific University, Azusa, CA.

$100,000 to Biola University, La Mirada, CA.

$100,000 to Mariners Church, Irvine, CA.

$100,000 to Westmont College, Santa Barbara, CA.

$79,562 to First Baptist Church of Downey, Downey, CA. 2 grants: $64,000, $15,562

$50,000 to California Baptist University, Riverside, CA.

$50,000 to Forest Home Christian Conference Center, Forest Falls, CA.

$30,500 to Church Resource Ministries, Anaheim, CA.

$25,000 to Concordia University, Irvine, CA.

1187

The Roger and Lilah Stangeland Foundation ◇

222 E. Huntington Dr., Ste. 214
Monrovia, CA 91016

Established in 1989 in CA.

Donors: Roger E. Stangeland; Lilah M. Stangeland.

Foundation type: Independent foundation.

Financial data (yr. ended 12/31/05): Assets, $49,813 (M); gifts received, $550,000; expenditures, $584,550; qualifying distributions, $582,000; giving activities include $582,000 for 7 grants (high: $200,000; low: $2,000).

Fields of interest: Performing arts, theater; Education; Protestant agencies & churches.

Limitations: Applications not accepted. Giving on a national basis, with some emphasis on CA; funding also in Bath, England. No grants to individuals.

Application information: Contributes only to pre-selected organizations.

Officers: Mike Henn, Pres.; George H. McCrimlisk, V.P.; Gregory P. Stone, V.P.; Lilah M. Stangeland, Secy.

EIN: 954194768

Selected grants: The following grants were reported in 2004.

$360,000 to Saint Johns Military Academy, Delafield, WI.

$105,000 to Federated Church of Wauconda, Wauconda, IL.

1188
John Stauffer Charitable Trust
301 N. Lake Ave., 10th Fl.
Pasadena, CA 91101-4108 (626) 793-9400
Contact: H. Jess Senecal, Tr.
FAX: (626) 793-5900; E-mail: jesss@lagerlof.com.

Trust established in 1974 in CA.
Donor: John Stauffer‡.
Foundation type: Independent foundation.
Financial data (yr. ended 5/31/06): Assets, $42,062,753 (M); expenditures, $3,170,589; qualifying distributions, $2,488,083; giving activities include $2,250,000 for 5 grants (high: $750,000; low: $500,000).
Purpose and activities: Grants restricted to hospitals, colleges, and universities in California.
Fields of interest: Higher education; Education; Hospitals (general); Chemistry; Biological sciences.
Type of support: Building/renovation; Equipment; Endowments; Professorships; Fellowships; Scholarship funds; Matching/challenge support.
Limitations: Giving limited to CA. No grants to individuals, no loans.
Publications: Application guidelines.
Application information: Application form not required.
Initial approach: Letter
Copies of proposal: 3
Deadline(s): None
Board meeting date(s): Quarterly beginning in Jan.
Final notification: 6 to 9 months
Trustees: John F. Bradley; H. Jess Senecal; Michael S. Whalen.
Number of staff: None.
EIN: 237434707

1189
The Harry and Grace Steele Foundation ◇
441 Old Newport Blvd., Ste. 301
Newport Beach, CA 92663 (949) 631-0418

Incorporated in 1953 in CA.
Donor: Grace C. Steele‡.
Foundation type: Independent foundation.
Financial data (yr. ended 10/31/04): Assets, $18,909,081 (M); expenditures, $689,056; qualifying distributions, $566,992; giving activities include $350,000 for 2 grants (high: $250,000; low: $100,000).
Purpose and activities: Giving primarily for higher education.
Fields of interest: Visual arts; Performing arts; Arts; Secondary school/education; Higher education; Environment; Hospitals (general); Reproductive health, family planning; Children/youth, services.
Type of support: General/operating support; Continuing support; Building/renovation; Equipment; Program development; Scholarship funds.
Limitations: Applications not accepted. Giving primarily in Orange County, CA. No support for tax-supported organizations or private foundations. No grants to individuals; no loans.
Publications: Annual report; Program policy statement.
Application information: Contributes only to pre-selected organizations.
Officers and Trustees:* Audrey Steele Burnand,* Pres.; Elizabeth R. Steele, Secy.; Nolan H. Baird, Jr.
Number of staff: 1 full-time support.
EIN: 956035879

Selected grants: The following grants were reported in 2003.
$1,000,000 to Borrego Community Health Society, Borrego Springs, CA. For general support.

1190
Eugene and Marilyn Stein Family Foundation ◇
333 S. Hope St., 55th Fl.
Los Angeles, CA 90071

Established in 1997 in CA.
Donors: Eugene P. Stein; Marilyn L. Stein.
Foundation type: Independent foundation.
Financial data (yr. ended 12/31/05): Assets, $26,560,994 (M); gifts received, $7,451,023; expenditures, $702,226; qualifying distributions, $671,920; giving activities include $671,350 for grants (high: $300,000; low: $250).
Purpose and activities: Giving for higher education, the arts, and for children's education and health care.
Fields of interest: Arts; Higher education; Education; Health care; Children/youth, services; Foundations (community); Jewish federated giving programs.
Limitations: Applications not accepted. Giving primarily in CA; some giving nationally. No grants to individuals.
Application information: Contributes only to pre-selected organizations.
Officers: Marilyn L. Stein, Chair. and Secy.; Eugene P. Stein, Pres.
EIN: 954659838

1191
Lionel Steiner Trust ◇ ☆
c/o Wells Fargo Bank, N.A., Tax Dept.
P.O. Box 63954, MAC A033-011
San Francisco, CA 94163
Application address: c/o Adrin Cardenas, Acct. Admin., Wells Fargo Bank, N. A., 420 Montgomery St., MAC A010-021, 2nd Fl., San Francisco, CA 94104, tel.: (415) 396-3738

Foundation type: Independent foundation.
Financial data (yr. ended 6/30/05): Assets, $7,004,721 (M); expenditures, $328,382; qualifying distributions, $317,672; giving activities include $320,325 for 6 grants (high: $53,387; low: $53,387).
Fields of interest: Animals/wildlife, special services; Hospitals (general); Human services; Children/youth, services; Family services; Jewish agencies & temples; Disabilities, people with.
Limitations: Giving limited to the San Francisco Bay Area, CA.
Application information:
Initial approach: Letter
Deadline(s): None
Trustee: Wells Fargo Bank, N.A.
EIN: 946445242

1192
Steinmetz Foundation ◇
c/o BCWS
3424 Carson St., Ste. 600
Torrance, CA 90503

Established in 1997 in CA.

Donor: William Steinmetz.
Foundation type: Independent foundation.
Financial data (yr. ended 12/31/04): Assets, $10,094,137 (M); expenditures, $543,050; qualifying distributions, $405,000; giving activities include $405,000 for 19 grants (high: $90,000; low: $500).
Fields of interest: Education, early childhood education; Higher education; Disasters, preparedness/services; Human services; Children/youth, services.
Limitations: Applications not accepted. Giving primarily in CA. No grants to individuals.
Application information: Contributes only to pre-selected organizations.
Officers and Directors:* Charles William Steinmetz,* Pres.; Jean S. Kay, V.P., Admin., and Secy.; Terry Kay, C.F.O.; Mary L. Steinmetz; William A. Steinmetz; Ann Marie Tonkin.
EIN: 954649432
Selected grants: The following grants were reported in 2003.
$78,700 to Saint Lawrence-Watts Youth Center, Friends of, Los Angeles, CA. For literacy center.
$45,000 to Wonder of Reading, Los Angeles, CA.
$35,000 to Ocean Institute, Dana Point, CA. For Adopt-A-Class Program.
$30,035 to Direct Relief International, Santa Barbara, CA. For generic drug program.
$30,000 to Family Reading Partnership, Ithaca, NY. For National Reading Program.
$25,000 to Switzer Learning Center, Torrance, CA. For Sensible Reading and Writing Program.
$12,500 to Descanso Gardens, La Canada, CA. For Discovering Trees Program.
$10,000 to California Literacy, Pasadena, CA. For multigenerational literacy program.
$10,000 to Foothill Family Service, Pasadena, CA. For teen graduation program.
$10,000 to University of California Medical Center, Los Angeles, CA. For pediatric unit playground.

1193
Stephenson Foundation ◇
3000 Sand Hill Rd., Bldg. 4, Ste. 180
Menlo Park, CA 94025 (650) 854-3927
Contact: Barbara Stephenson, Pres.

Established in 1999 in CA.
Donors: Barbara Stephenson; Thomas F. Stephenson.
Foundation type: Independent foundation.
Financial data (yr. ended 12/31/05): Assets, $22,193,372 (M); expenditures, $731,175; qualifying distributions, $606,850; giving activities include $606,850 for 29 grants (high: $250,000; low: $100).
Purpose and activities: Giving primarily for education; funding also for the environment and children's services.
Fields of interest: Higher education; Business school/education; Education; Environment; Children, services.
Limitations: Giving primarily in CA. No grants to individuals.
Application information:
Initial approach: Letter
Deadline(s): None
Officers: Barbara Stephenson, Pres.; Thomas F. Stephenson, V.P.
EIN: 943320092
Selected grants: The following grants were reported in 2004.

$400,000 to Harvard University, School of Business, Cambridge, MA.

$400,000 to San Francisco Zoological Society, San Francisco, CA.

$250,000 to Conservation International, DC.

$100,000 to John F. Kennedy Center for the Performing Arts, DC.

$53,000 to Boys and Girls Clubs of Long Beach, Long Beach, CA.

$35,000 to KIPP Bridge College Preparatory School, Oakland, CA.

$25,000 to Cure Autism Now Foundation, Los Angeles, CA.

$10,000 to All Stars Helping Kids, Redwood City, CA.

$10,000 to Menlo Park-Atherton Education Foundation, Menlo Park, CA.

$10,000 to National Football Foundation and College Hall of Fame, Morristown, NJ.

1194
The Marc and Eva Stern Foundation ✧
(formerly The Stern Family Foundation)
865 S. Figueroa St., Ste. 1800
Los Angeles, CA   90017-2593   (213) 244-0744
Contact: Marc I. Stern, Pres.

Established in 1986 in CA.
Donors: Marc I. Stern; Robert A. Day; Eva Stern; Henley Manufacturing, Inc.; The Henley Group, Inc.; W.K. Day Foundation; The Penates Foundation.
Foundation type: Independent foundation.
Financial data (yr. ended 12/31/04): Assets, $4,879,960 (M); expenditures, $1,830,752; qualifying distributions, $1,785,268; giving activities include $1,780,973 for 58 grants (high: $855,000; low: $250).
Purpose and activities: Giving for the arts, education, and Jewish organizations. The Albert B. Stern Scholarship Awards are limited to graduating seniors at Vineland High School in Vineland, NJ, who plan to continue their education by studying agriculture in college. Preference will be given to a student in agricultural sciences or business and agronomy, but students interested in environmental studies or life sciences may also apply.
Fields of interest: Performing arts, theater; Performing arts, opera; Arts; Higher education; Education; Medical research, institute; Jewish federated giving programs; Jewish agencies & temples.
Limitations: Giving primarily in CA, for non-scholarship grants; some funding also in New York, NY. Giving limited to Vineland, NJ, for scholarships.
Application information: Albert B. Stern Scholarship Award applicants must complete the Vineland High School local scholarship application, as well as submit a transcript, a letter of recommendation from a teacher or counselor, and a 50-word or less statement concerning their interests and career goals, and how their goals relate to agriculture. Scholarship amount is $2,500 per year for up to 4 years.
Initial approach: Letter
Deadline(s): None
Officers: Marc I. Stern, Pres. and C.F.O.; Eva S. Stern, V.P.; Patricia A. Curtis, Secy.
EIN: 330220467

1195
Sidney Stern Memorial Trust ✧
c/o Wells Fargo Bank
P.O. Box 63954
San Francisco, CA   94163
Application address: Board of Advisors, P.O. Box 893, Pacific Palisades, CA 90272

Trust established in 1974 in CA.
Donor: S. Sidney Stern†.
Foundation type: Independent foundation.
Financial data (yr. ended 8/31/05): Assets, $31,967,742 (M); expenditures, $1,716,303; qualifying distributions, $1,462,530; giving activities include $1,360,158 for 486 grants (high: $25,000; low: $250).
Purpose and activities: Giving primarily for higher education, social service agencies, including aid to the handicapped; youth and child welfare agencies; scientific and medical organizations, including health associations; and cultural programs.
Fields of interest: Arts; Higher education; Environment; Hospitals (general); Reproductive health, family planning; Health care; Health organizations, association; Legal services; Human services; Children/youth, services; Civil rights, disabled; Civil rights; Disabilities, people with; Asians/Pacific Islanders; African Americans/ Blacks; Hispanics/Latinos; Native Americans/ American Indians; Immigrants/refugees.
Type of support: General/operating support; Annual campaigns; Building/renovation; Equipment; Land acquisition; Endowments; Emergency funds; Program development; Scholarship funds; Research; Matching/challenge support.
Limitations: Giving primarily in CA; all funds must be used within the U.S. No grants to individuals, or for conferences or redistribution; no loans.
Publications: Application guidelines.
Application information: Application form required.
Initial approach: Letter or proposal (1 1/2 pages describing preferred use of funds)
Copies of proposal: 1
Deadline(s): None
Board meeting date(s): Monthly, except Aug.
Officer and Board of Advisors: * Betty S. Hoffenberg,* Chair.; Peter H. Hoffenberg; Ira E. Bilson; David A. Hoffenberg; Marvin Hoffenberg; Howard O. Wilson.
EIN: 956495222

1196
Georgiana G. Stevens Foundation
c/o Eric L. Sloan
1660 Bush St., Ste. 300
San Francisco, CA   94109
FAX: (415) 561-6477; E-mail: esloan@pfs-llc.net; URL: http://www.pfs-llc.net/ggs/ggs.html

Established in 1992 in CA.
Donor: Georgiana G. Stevens.
Foundation type: Independent foundation.
Financial data (yr. ended 12/31/05): Assets, $7,721,614 (M); gifts received, $3,000,000; expenditures, $339,208; qualifying distributions, $330,000; giving activities include $330,000 for grants.
Fields of interest: Higher education; Education, reading; Education; Nursing care; Medical research, institute.
Type of support: Continuing support; Curriculum development.

Limitations: Applications not accepted. Giving primarily in CA. No grants to individuals.
Application information: Contributes only to pre-selected organizations.
Board meeting date(s): Nov. 1
Officers and Directors: * John H. Kirkwood,* Pres.; Jean K. Casey,* Secy.; Amanda H. Kirkwood.
EIN: 943155521
Selected grants: The following grants were reported in 2003.
$55,000 to Lick-Wilmerding High School, San Francisco, CA. 2 grants: $25,000 (For Aim High program), $30,000 (For capital support).
$40,000 to Ohlhoff Recovery Programs, San Francisco, CA.
$35,000 to Bay School, Santa Cruz, CA.
$25,000 to Marin Education Fund, San Rafael, CA.
$15,000 to San Francisco Public Library, San Francisco, CA. For Project Read.

1197
Stewardship Foundation ✧
1508 W. Mission Rd.
Escondido, CA   92029

Established in 1987 in CA.
Donors: Jacob Brouwer; Joanne Cooper; Theresa Veld Kamp; Garrett Brouwer; Richard Brouwer; Chris Brouwer; Doreen Broek; Jack Brouwer; Escondido Ready Mix Concrete, Inc.; Superior Ready Mix Concrete, LP; JJB Land Company, LP; Brouwer Family Ltd.
Foundation type: Independent foundation.
Financial data (yr. ended 11/30/05): Assets, $27,087,767 (M); gifts received, $4,940,581; expenditures, $1,391,665; qualifying distributions, $1,346,040; giving activities include $1,344,000 for 48 grants (high: $500,000; low: $1,000).
Purpose and activities: Giving primarily to Christian schools, churches and organizations.
Fields of interest: Theological school/education; Youth, services; Christian agencies & churches.
Limitations: Applications not accepted. Giving on a national basis, with some emphasis on CA, especially the Escondido area. No grants to individuals.
Application information: Contributes only to pre-selected organizations.
Directors: Jacob Brouwer; Jeanette Brouwer; Arnold Veldkamp.
EIN: 330273191
Selected grants: The following grants were reported in 2005.
$176,000 to Calvin Christian School, Escondido, CA.
$25,000 to Back to God Hour, Palos Heights, IL.
$10,000 to Bible League, Chicago, IL.
$10,000 to San Diego Rescue Mission, San Diego, CA.
$7,000 to Trinity Christian College, Palos Heights, IL.
$5,000 to Mission 21 India, Grand Rapids, MI.
$5,000 to Reformed Bible College, Grand Rapids, MI.
$3,000 to American Missionary Fellowship, Villanova, PA.
$2,000 to Elizabeth Hospice, Escondido, CA.
$2,000 to Salvation Army, Redding, CA.

1198

Stewart Foundation ✦
c/o Gregory M. Paul
335 N. Maple Dr., Ste. 135
Beverly Hills, CA 90210 (310) 285-2326
Contact: Gregory M. Paul, Tr.

Established in 1997 in CA.
Donor: Stewart Living Trust.
Foundation type: Independent foundation.
Financial data (yr. ended 6/30/05): Assets,
$4,786,637 (M); expenditures, $474,810;
qualifying distributions, $346,500; giving activities
include $346,500 for 11 grants (high: $200,000;
low: $1,500).
Purpose and activities: Giving primarily for health
care, particularly to a health center foundation;
funding also for the arts and human services.
Fields of interest: Museums; Performing arts; Arts;
Hospitals (specialty); Health care; Human services;
Philanthropy/voluntarism.
Limitations: Applications not accepted. Giving on a
national basis, with emphasis on CA. No grants to
individuals.
Application information: Contributes only to
pre-selected organizations.
Trustees: Kelly Stewart Harcourt; Michael H.
McLean; Judy Stewart Merrill; Gregory M. Paul;
Stuart P. Tobisman.
EIN: 954646884
Selected grants: The following grants were reported
in 2004.
$155,000 to Saint Johns Health Center Foundation,
Santa Monica, CA. 2 grants: $5,000, $150,000
$100,000 to Charles Darwin Foundation for the
Galapagos Islands, Falls Church, VA.
$25,000 to James M. Stewart Museum Foundation,
Indiana, PA.
$15,000 to Arizona Institute for Public Life, Phoenix,
AZ.
$10,000 to Heartland Film Festival, Indianapolis, IN.
$5,000 to Lewis and Clark College, Portland, OR.
$5,000 to Pestalozzi United States Childrens
Charity, New York, NY.

1199

Sarah A. Stewart Foundation ✦
212 Yale Ave.
Claremont, CA 91711
Application address: c/o Richard K. Simonds,
19511 Mack Ave., Grosse Point, MI 48236,
tel.: (313) 886-0450

Established in 1980 in CA.
Foundation type: Independent foundation.
Financial data (yr. ended 9/30/05): Assets,
$5,755,309 (M); expenditures, $378,903;
qualifying distributions, $344,730; giving activities
include $330,000 for 24 grants (high: $40,000;
low: $3,000).
Fields of interest: Education; Health care; Medical
research, institute; Human services; Christian
agencies & churches; Protestant agencies &
churches.
Limitations: Giving primarily in CA. No grants to
individuals.
Application information: Generally contributes only
to pre-selected organizations.
Initial approach: Telephone for details
Officers: Daniel M. Gibbs, M.D., Pres.; Nancy
Richard, V.P.; Mary P. Daniel, Secy.
Number of staff: 1 part-time professional.
EIN: 953705192

1200

W. Clement & Jessie V. Stone Foundation
c/o The Presidio
P.O. Box 29255
San Francisco, CA 94129-0255 (415) 561-6691
Contact: Sandra Treacy, Exec. Dir.
FAX: (415) 561-6695; E-mail: info@wcstonefnd.org;
URL: http://www.wcstonefnd.org

Incorporated in 1958 in IL.
Donors: W. Clement Stone†; Jessie V. Stone†.
Foundation type: Independent foundation.
Financial data (yr. ended 12/31/04): Assets,
$29,662,574 (M); gifts received, $13,150,540;
expenditures, $1,201,133; qualifying distributions,
$1,189,433; giving activities include $941,900 for
35 grants (high: $81,900; low: $10,000).
Purpose and activities: Making this world a better
place in which to live through programs in education,
early childhood development and youth
development.
Fields of interest: Education; Youth development.
Type of support: Curriculum development; General/
operating support; Management development/
capacity building; Program development;
Scholarship funds; Program evaluation.
Limitations: Applications not accepted. Giving
limited to Chicago, IL, the San Francisco Bay Area,
CA, New York, NY, and Boston, MA. No grants to
individuals.
Publications: Annual report; Grants list.
Application information: Contributes only to
pre-selected organizations. See foundation Web
site.
Board meeting date(s): May and Oct.
Officers and Directors:* Norman C. Stone,* Pres.;
Steven Stone,* 1st V.P. and Secy.-Treas.; Sandra
Treacy, Exec. Dir.; James T. Rhind; Barbara
Samuels; Amy Stone; Barbara West Stone; David
Stone; Deborah Stone; Jennifer Stone; Michael A.
Stone; Norah Sharpe Stone; Sandra Stone; Sara
Stone; Chad Tingley.
Number of staff: 3 full-time professional.
EIN: 362498125
Selected grants: The following grants were reported
in 2003.
$50,000 to National-Louis University, Center for
Early Childhood Leadership, Evanston, IL. For
test program of administrative leadership scale.
$35,000 to Chicago Public Education Fund,
Chicago, IL. For general support.
$25,000 to Zero to Three: National Center for
Infants, Toddlers and Families, DC. For Center
Program on Excellence.
$20,000 to Civitas Initiative, Chicago, IL. For
general support.
$20,000 to Community Network for Youth
Development, San Francisco, CA.
$20,000 to Jobs for the Future, Boston, MA. For
general support.
$20,000 to Youth Communication/New York
Center, New York, NY. For general support.
$20,000 to Youth Empowerment Center, Oakland,
CA. For general support.
$20,000 to Youth in Focus, Oakland, CA. For general
support.
$20,000 to Youth Leadership Institute, San
Francisco, CA. For Philanthropy Resources
Project.

1201

The Stover Foundation ✦ ☆
220 N. Wiget Ln.
Walnut Creek, CA 94598
Contact: Nancy Ward, Secy.

Established in 1994 in CA.
Donors: Joan C. Stover; W. Robert Stover.
Foundation type: Independent foundation.
Financial data (yr. ended 12/31/05): Assets,
$14,925,415 (M); expenditures, $677,381;
qualifying distributions, $555,208; giving activities
include $545,000 for 8 grants (high: $185,000;
low: $10,000).
Purpose and activities: Giving only to Christian
organizations.
Fields of interest: Human services; Youth, services;
Christian agencies & churches.
Limitations: Giving primarily in CO, NC, and PA. No
grants to individuals.
Application information: Application form not
required.
Initial approach: Letter
Copies of proposal: 1
Deadline(s): Nov. 30
Board meeting date(s): Dec.
Officers: Joan C. Stover, Pres.; W. Robert Stover,
V.P. and Treas.; Nancy Ward, Secy.
Directors: Dave Carlson; Ted Johnson; Susan J.
Stover; Parker Williamson.
EIN: 680392330

1202

Leon Strauss Foundation ✦
5332 Harbor St.
Los Angeles, CA 90040-3943 (323) 728-5440
Contact: Robert P. Vossler, Tr.

Established in 1976.
Donor: Leon Strauss†.
Foundation type: Independent foundation.
Financial data (yr. ended 12/31/04): Assets,
$9,212,270 (M); expenditures, $356,622;
qualifying distributions, $347,867; giving activities
include $338,000 for 59 grants (high: $25,000;
low: $1,000).
Purpose and activities: Giving primarily for
children's camps and hospitals.
Fields of interest: Hospitals (general); Youth
development; Human services; Children/youth,
services.
Type of support: General/operating support;
Continuing support; Annual campaigns; Scholarship
funds; Scholarships—to individuals.
Limitations: Giving primarily in CA.
Application information: Application form not
required.
Initial approach: Letter
Deadline(s): Aug. 1
Board meeting date(s): Oct.
Trustees: Charles Curley; Paul Simon; Ralph Simon;
William Simon; Robert P. Vossler.
EIN: 510205308

1203

Levi Strauss Foundation ▼ ✦
1155 Battery St.
San Francisco, CA 94111 (415) 501-3577
Contact: Theresa Fay-Bustillos, V.P., Secy., and
Exec. Dir.; Stuart C. Burden, Dir., Community Affairs,
The Americas

FAX: (415) 501-6575; E-mail: lsf@levi.com; Application address for Syringe Access Fund: Stuart C. Burden, Dir., Community Affairs, The Americas, 1155 Battery St., San Francisco, CA 94111, E-mail: syringeaccess@levi.com; URL: http://www.levistrauss.com/Citizenship/LeviStraussFoundation.aspx

Incorporated in 1952 in CA.
Donor: Levi Strauss & Co.
Foundation type: Company-sponsored foundation.
Financial data (yr. ended 12/31/04): Assets, $74,186,552 (M); expenditures, $10,842,668; qualifying distributions, $10,246,980; giving activities include $8,867,814 for 317 grants (high: $650,000; low: $50).
Purpose and activities: The foundation supports organizations involved with education, health, HIV/AIDS prevention, disease, HIV/AIDS research, employment, youth development, economic empowerment, economic development, community development, leadership development, and economically disadvantaged people.
Fields of interest: Education; Health care; AIDS; Health organizations; AIDS research; Employment; Youth development; Human services, financial counseling; Economic development; Community development; Leadership development; Economically disadvantaged.
International interests: Asia; Europe; Latin America; South Africa.
Type of support: General/operating support; Continuing support; Management development/capacity building; Equipment; Program development; Publication; Seed money; Scholarship funds; Research; Technical assistance; Employee volunteer services; Program evaluation; Program-related investments/loans; Employee matching gifts; Exchange programs; In-kind gifts.
Limitations: Giving on a national and international basis, with emphasis on areas of company operations. No support for sports teams. No grants to individuals, or for capital campaigns or endowments, athletic competition, advertising, sponsorships, sectarian or religious activities, or political campaigns or causes.
Publications: Grants list.
Application information: Unsolicited requests for non-Syringe Access Fund grants are not accepted.
Initial approach: Contact foundation for application information for Syringe Access Fund
Board meeting date(s): June and Dec.
Officers and Directors:* Robert D. Haas,* Pres.; Theresa Fay-Bustillos,* V.P., Secy., and Exec. Dir.; Jason McBriarty, Cont.; Angela Blackwell; Louis Camarillo; Betsy Haas Eisenhardt; Ted Fox; Gordon T. Geballe; Peter E. Haas, Jr.; Robert Hanson; David Love; Philip Marineau; Bobbi Silten; C.S. Suryanarayanan.
Number of staff: 14
EIN: 946064702
Selected grants: The following grants were reported in 2004.
$650,000 to Tides Foundation, Syringe Access Fund, San Francisco, CA. For HIV/AIDS Prevention Programs.
$430,000 to Charities Aid Foundation (UK), West Malling, England. .
$204,415 to Asia Foundation, San Francisco, CA.
$125,000 to San Francisco Conservation Corps, San Francisco, CA.
$100,000 to Jewish Vocational Service.

$95,750 to Scholarship America, Saint Peter, MN. For scholarships.
$76,250 to Ocean View Development Trust, Cape Town, South Africa. .
$50,000 to United Nations Development Programme, New York, NY.
$35,000 to National AIDS Trust, London, England. For HIV/AIDS Prevention Program.
$25,000 to Hispanics in Philanthropy, San Francisco, CA.

1204
The Streisand Foundation ◇
2800 28th St., Ste. 105
Santa Monica, CA 90405
Contact: Margery Tabankin, Exec. Dir.
FAX: (310) 314-8396; URL: http://www.barbrastreisand.com/bio_streisand_foundation.html

Established in 1986 in NY.
Donors: Barbra Streisand; The Lincy Foundation.
Foundation type: Independent foundation.
Financial data (yr. ended 12/31/05): Assets, $937,882 (M); gifts received, $480; expenditures, $628,710; qualifying distributions, $622,333; giving activities include $507,173 for 98 grants (high: $35,000; low: $366).
Purpose and activities: Giving primarily for civil rights, poverty, the environment, democratic values, and women's issues.
Fields of interest: Education; Environment; Children/youth, services; Civil rights, voter education; Civil liberties, advocacy; Civil rights; Women.
Type of support: General/operating support; Continuing support; Program development.
Limitations: Giving to nationally-based groups; some local giving in Los Angeles, CA for youth organizations. No support for start-up organizations or international organizations. No grants to individuals, or for capital campaigns, documentaries or audio-visual programming, or publication of books or magazines.
Publications: Application guidelines.
Application information: See foundation Web site for full application guidelines and requirements. Application form not required.
Initial approach: 1- to 3-page letter of inquiry
Copies of proposal: 1
Deadline(s): Sept. 2 through Dec. 2
Board meeting date(s): Varies
Final notification: Following summer
Officer and Trustees:* Margery Tabankin,* Exec. Dir.; Richard Baskin; Marilyn Bergman; Jason Gould; Barry Hirsh; Lester Knispel; Barbra Streisand.
Number of staff: 1 part-time professional; 1 full-time support.
EIN: 132620702

1205
Mildred V. Strouss Charitable Testamentary Trust ◇
220 Sansome St., Ste. 700
San Francisco, CA 94104-2722

Established in 1999 in CA.
Donor: Mildred V. Strouss Trust.
Foundation type: Independent foundation.
Financial data (yr. ended 12/31/05): Assets, $760,761 (M); expenditures, $1,394,561;

qualifying distributions, $1,375,000; giving activities include $1,375,000 for 12 grants (high: $500,000; low: $20,000).
Fields of interest: Health care; Jewish agencies & temples.
Limitations: Applications not accepted. Giving primarily in CA. No grants to individuals.
Application information: Contributes only to pre-selected organizations.
Trustees: George I. Hoffman; Paul J. Ruby.
EIN: 680424352
Selected grants: The following grants were reported in 2003.
$250,000 to Jewish Community Federation of the Greater East Bay, Oakland, CA. 2 grants: $100,000 (For community rabbi program), $150,000 (For crisis intervention in Kiryat Malachi).
$50,000 to Pacific Vascular Research Foundation, San Francisco, CA. For research.

1206
Stuart Foundation ▼ ◇
(also known as Elbridge Stuart Foundation)
50 California St., Ste. 3350
San Francisco, CA 94111-4735 (415) 393-1551
FAX: (415) 393-1552;
E-mail: info@stuartfoundation.org; URL: http://www.stuartfoundation.org

Elbridge Stuart Foundation created in 1937 in CA, Elbridge and Mary Stuart Foundation in 1941 in CA, and Mary Horner Stuart Foundation in 1941 in WA; in 1995 and 1996, the two smaller foundations were merged into the Elbridge Stuart Foundation, DBA Stuart Foundation.
Donors: Elbridge A. Stuart†; Elbridge H. Stuart†; Mary H. Stuart†.
Foundation type: Independent foundation.
Financial data (yr. ended 3/17/04): Assets, $339,791,005 (M); expenditures, $12,853,101; qualifying distributions, $12,171,034; giving activities include $11,307,284 for 107 grants (high: $630,000; low: $553; average: $5,000–$250,000), and $1,535 for 11 employee matching gifts.
Purpose and activities: The foundation supports organizations that create opportunities for children and youth; that support and educate them; and that help discover and achieve their full potential. The foundation believes that teachers, social workers and community members who invest their time and unique abilities to help children who need support, guidance and recognition to sustain their valuable work. The foundation partners with organizations in the states of California and Washington that embody the objectives of its three program areas: Public Schools, Child Welfare, and Youth and Communities. The foundation looks for partners that: develop innovative programs and practices that support and expand the potential of young people; promote public policy that improves conditions for children and youth; help build the capacity of public and nonprofit organizations devoted to creating and expanding opportunities for children; and focus on innovative projects that can be broadly replicated or that demonstrate important lessons. The foundation dedicates time, money, expertise and advocacy to each relationship. The foundation sees itself as a partner and convener that can help gather the resources, thought and energy needed to make real change on behalf of children and youth. Many of the

relationships are long-term with some spanning over a decade of successful collaboration.

Fields of interest: Education, public education; Elementary school/education; Secondary school/education; Higher education; Teacher school/education; Education; Youth development; Children/youth, services; Children, foster care; Youth, services; Community development; Public policy, research; Welfare policy/reform.

Type of support: General/operating support; Continuing support; Program development; Seed money; Curriculum development; Research; Technical assistance; Program evaluation; Employee matching gifts.

Limitations: Giving primarily in CA and WA. No support for political or lobbying activities. No grants to individuals, or generally for endowments, building funds, or annual campaigns, capital or operating support to sustain existing service capacity.

Application information: See foundation Web site for application information. Application form required.

> *Initial approach:* Letter of inquiry
> *Copies of proposal:* 1
> *Deadline(s):* None
> *Board meeting date(s):* Mar., Aug. and Nov.
> *Final notification:* Within 8 weeks

Officers and Directors:* Dwight L. Stuart, Jr.,* Chair.; Stuart E. Lucas,* Vice-Chair; E. Hadley Stuart, Jr.,* Vice-Chair.; Christy Pichel, Pres. and Secy.; Elbridge H. Stuart III,* Treas.; Stephanie Titus, Grants Mgr.

Number of staff: 5 full-time professional; 6 full-time support.

EIN: 200882784

Selected grants: The following grants were reported in 2005.

$650,000 to Center for the Future of Teaching and Learning, Santa Cruz, CA. To promote research, policies, and practices to ensure that every California schoolchild has fully qualified and effective teacher.

$600,000 to Center for Strengthening the Teaching Profession (CSTP), Silverdale, WA. To investigate conditions of teaching in Washington and promote policies and practices that support effective teaching needed to help students meet state standards.

$595,404 to University of California, Graduate School of Education and Information Studies, Los Angeles, CA. To increase supply of well-prepared urban teachers by disseminating effective practices for recruiting, preparing, and retaining teachers for urban schools.

$500,000 to Public Health Institute, Oakland, CA. To provide program support for California Permanency for Youth Project (CPYP). CPYP influences development of new public policy, administrative and judicial practice that support and promote better permanency outcomes for older foster youth.

$274,000 to Child and Family Policy Institute, Sacramento, CA. For CalWORKs/Child Welfare Partnership Project, initiative created to promote implementation of practices to improve services for children and families receiving services from both welfare department and child welfare agencies in California, payable over 1.25 years.

$250,000 to Powerful Schools, Seattle, WA. To expand Powerful Schools' ability to effectively partner with Seattle public schools to become centers of learning where students of all backgrounds can achieve their full potential

academically, socially, creatively, and emotionally.

$200,000 to New Futures, Burien, WA. For development of south King County's children and youth by strengthening families and communities through parent support networks, improved school relationships, and building skills for parents to engage in their child's education.

$125,400 to Stanford University, School of Education, Stanford, CA. For development and evaluation of East Palo Alto High School, charter school designed as model of effective schooling for disadvantaged students.

$100,000 to Contra Costa County Employment and Human Services Department, Martinez, CA. For Contra Costa County and Bay Area Training Academy in expansion of Y.O.U.T.H., interactive training focused on changing social worker knowledge, skills and values concerning communicating with foster youth who are preparing for emancipation.

$75,000 to John Gardner Center for Youth and Their Communities at Stanford University, Stanford, CA. For YELL, leadership development program that provides civic engagement, professional skill building, and academic enrichment opportunities for youth at McClymonds Educational Complex in West Oakland.

1207
Hadley and Marion Stuart Foundation ◇
c/o Bogdan & Frasco, LLP
575 Market St., Ste. 2000
San Francisco, CA 94105

Established in 1988 in CA.
Donor: Marion Butler Stuart.
Foundation type: Independent foundation.
Financial data (yr. ended 10/31/05): Assets, $14,115,496 (M); expenditures, $667,388; qualifying distributions, $650,000; giving activities include $650,000 for 18 grants (high: $250,000; low: $10,000).
Purpose and activities: Giving primarily for education and animal welfare.
Fields of interest: Education; Environment, natural resources; Animal welfare.
Limitations: Applications not accepted. Giving on a national basis. No grants to individuals.
Application information: Contributes only to pre-selected organizations.
Trustees: Brett Fullerton Stuart; Nan M. Stuart.
EIN: 946607854
Selected grants: The following grants were reported in 2003.

$125,000 to Cheshire Academy, Cheshire, CT. For general support.

$100,000 to Denver Dumb Friends League-Humane Society of Denver, Denver, CO. For general support.

$100,000 to Humane Society of Boulder Valley, Boulder, CO. For general support.

$50,000 to Code 3 Associates, Erie, CO. For general support.

$30,000 to Overlake School, Redmond, WA. For general support.

$20,000 to Foxcroft School, Middleburg, VA. For general support.

$10,000 to Colorado State University, College of Veterinary Medicine, Fort Collins, CO. For general support.

$10,000 to Colorado Veterinary Medical Foundation, Denver, CO. For general support.

$10,000 to Days End Farm Horse Rescue, Lisbon, MD. For general support.

$5,000 to Alzheimers Association, Chicago, IL. For general support.

1208
Dwight Stuart Youth Foundation ◇
9595 Wilshire Blvd., Ste. 212
Beverly Hills, CA 90212-2502 (310) 777-5050
Contact: Erin Sundell, Grants and Office Admin.
FAX: (310) 777-5060; URL: http://www.dsyf.org

Established in 1998 in CA.
Donor: Dwight L. Stuart†.
Foundation type: Independent foundation.
Financial data (yr. ended 12/31/04): Assets, $73,091,179 (M); expenditures, $4,749,087; qualifying distributions, $4,081,312; giving activities include $3,544,150 for 158 grants (high: $70,000; low: $500; average: $2,000–$25,000).
Purpose and activities: Support for organizations providing direct services and experiences to underserved children and youth to enable them to gain the skills, values and confidence to achieve their potential.
Fields of interest: Arts education; Performing arts; Literature; Education, reading; Education; Employment; Recreation, camps; Youth development, adult & child programs; Youth development, services; Youth development; Children, day care; Leadership development; Youth.
Type of support: General/operating support; Program development; Technical assistance; Program evaluation.
Limitations: Giving primarily in Los Angeles and Orange counties, CA. No support for religious or political organizations, medical or health programs, or private foundations. No grants to individuals, or for buildings, endowments, annual giving campaigns, benefit sponsorship, capital campaigns, deficit reduction, fundraising activities, advertisements, or tables.
Publications: Grants list; Informational brochure.
Application information: Unsolicited full proposals are not accepted. After review of the letter of inquiry, if the foundation determines the request is consistent with its interests, a conference call may be requested. During the conference call, if the foundation decides the request matches its criteria, you will be asked to submit a full proposal and application materials will be mailed to you at that time.

> *Initial approach:* Letter of inquiry (no more than 3 pages)
> *Deadline(s):* None
> *Board meeting date(s):* Feb., June, and Oct.

Officer and Trustees:* Dwight L. Stuart, Jr.,* Chair.; Ann S. Lucas; Bruce F. Stuart; Douglas F. Stuart; William W. Stuart.
Number of staff: 2 full-time professional.
EIN: 957071775

1209
Studenica Foundation ◇
535 4th St., Ste. 203
San Rafael, CA 94901 (415) 451-6900
Contact: Michael D. Djordjevich, Pres.

Established in 1994.
Foundation type: Independent foundation.

Financial data (yr. ended 12/31/05): Assets, $1,710,274 (M); gifts received, $788,500; expenditures, $373,279; qualifying distributions, $329,866; giving activities include $329,866 for 36 grants to individuals (high: $42,150; low: $1,500).
Purpose and activities: Awards scholarships to individuals, with emphasis on students in Yugoslavia.
International interests: Yugoslavia.
Type of support: Scholarships—to individuals.
Limitations: Giving primarily in Yugoslavia.
Application information:
  Deadline(s): None
Officers: Michael D. Djordjevich, Pres.; Dragoslav Georvievich, Secy.; Peter Chelovich, Treas.
Trustee: Alex Djordjevich.
EIN: 943186334

1210
The Morris Stulsaft Foundation
100 Bush St., Ste. 825
San Francisco, CA 94104-3936 (415) 986-7117
FAX: (415) 986-2521; E-mail: Stulsaft@aol.com;
URL: http://www.stulsaft.org

Incorporated in 1953 in CA; sole beneficiary of feeder trust created in 1965.
Donor: The Morris Stulsaft Testamentary Trust.
Foundation type: Independent foundation.
Financial data (yr. ended 6/30/05): Assets, $13,507 (M); gifts received, $1,975,000; expenditures, $1,990,572; qualifying distributions, $1,988,729; giving activities include $1,782,014 for 183 grants (high: $100,000; low: $250; average: $5,000–$15,000).
Purpose and activities: The foundation is dedicated to the well-being of children and youth. Priority areas of funding are: the needs of homeless children and those living in subsidized housing; the needs of children in foster care, especially as they prepare for emancipation; educational assistance for children with disabilities, especially early intervention; and child care for low-income families, along with training for child care providers.
Fields of interest: Arts; Education; Health care; Human services; Children/youth, services; Children, foster care; Children, day care.
Type of support: General/operating support; Continuing support; Capital campaigns; Building/ renovation; Equipment; Program development; Scholarship funds; Technical assistance; Matching/ challenge support.
Limitations: Giving limited to the San Francisco Bay Area, CA: Alameda, Contra Costa, Marin, San Francisco, Santa Clara, and San Mateo counties. No support for sectarian religious projects or ongoing support for private schools. No grants to individuals, or for emergency funding, endowments, annual campaigns, workshops, conferences, or deficit funding.
Publications: Application guidelines; Grants list; Occasional report.
Application information: Application guidelines and form available on foundation Web site. Application form required.
  Initial approach: E-mail or telephone requesting application form. Visit foundation Web site for downloading of application form
  Copies of proposal: 1
  Deadline(s): None
  Board meeting date(s): Jan., Mar., May, July, Sept., and Nov.
  Final notification: Approximately 8 to 10 months

Officers and Directors:* Adele K. Corvin,* Pres.; Isadore Pivnick,* V.P.; Ronald E. Bornstein; Roy L. Bouque; David E. Cassaro; Dana A. Corvin; Judy Shaw.
Number of staff: 1 full-time professional; 1 full-time support.
EIN: 946064379
Selected grants: The following grants were reported in 2005.
$50,000 to California Academy of Sciences, San Francisco, CA. For rebuilding and elevating the oldest scientific institution west of the mississippi into the dynamic 21st century center for natural history, science education, research and discovery.
$50,000 to Jewish Community Center of San Francisco, San Francisco, CA. For scholarships and teacher training in the Claude and Louise Rosenberg Early Childhood Education Program.
$25,000 to Greater Richmond Interfaith Program, Richmond, CA. For capital campaign.
$25,000 to Peninsula Jewish Community Center, Foster City, CA. For scholarships for preschool and summer camp programs for at-risk families.
$25,000 to United Way of the Bay Area, San Francisco, CA. For pre-literacy book bag program offered to low-income families through settings such as childcare centers, family childcare homes, and home-visiting program.
$20,000 to A Home Away from Homelessness, San Francisco, CA. For after-school academic program for homeless middle-school students providing tutoring, education and socialization.
$20,000 to Building Opportunities for Self-Sufficiency (BOSS), Berkeley, CA. For expansion of children's learning center for transform lives of homeless children and youth, specifically for services design and curriculum development and furniture and equipment.
$20,000 to Huckleberry Youth Programs, San Francisco, CA.
$15,000 to A Home Within, San Francisco, CA. For general program support.
$15,000 to Compass Community Services, San Francisco, CA.

1211
Stupski Foundation ◇
(formerly Stupski Family Foundation)
2 Belvedere Pl., Ste. 110
Mill Valley, CA 94941 (415) 384-2400
Contact: Laura Longmire, Chief Learning Off.
FAX: (415) 384-2401; E-mail: info@stupski.org;
URL: http://www.stupski.org

Established in 1996 in CA.
Donor: Lawrence J. Stupski.
Foundation type: Operating foundation.
Financial data (yr. ended 6/30/05): Assets, $58,470,084 (M); gifts received, $4,700,000; expenditures, $19,408,767; qualifying distributions, $19,071,402; giving activities include $3,470,587 for 19 grants (high: $425,615; low: $62), and $13,388,895 for foundation-administered programs.
Purpose and activities: The foundation seeks to help ensure all children in America, regardless of race or income, have access to high quality public education. The foundation believes that its most effective contribution to education reform will be at the district level to support whole systems of excellent schools.

Fields of interest: Education, research; Education, services; Education.
Type of support: Continuing support; Program development; Curriculum development; Technical assistance.
Limitations: Applications not accepted. Giving on a national basis. No grants to individuals.
Application information: Contributes only to pre-selected organizations.
Officers: Lawrence J. Stupski, Chair.; Joyce L. Stupski, Pres.; Kathleen J. Burke, Exec. V.P.; Pamela R. Mantegani, Secy.; Holden Lee, Treas.
Number of staff: 45
EIN: 680397103
Selected grants: The following grants were reported in 2003.
$860,000 to Teach for America, New York, NY. For general support.
$628,659 to University of California, New Teacher Center, Santa Cruz, CA. For general support.
$555,000 to Yakima School District, Yakima, WA.
$375,469 to Gilroy Unified School District, Gilroy, CA.
$273,260 to Oak Grove School District, San Jose, CA.
$260,416 to WestEd, San Francisco, CA.
$250,000 to National Center on Education and the Economy, DC. For general support.
$236,156 to Santa Monica/Malibu Unified School District, Santa Monica, CA.
$140,000 to San Jose State University Foundation, San Jose, CA. For Triple L Collaborative Scholarship.
$73,032 to Pasadena Unified School District, Pasadena, CA.

1212
The Sudikoff Family Foundation ◇
1398 Breckford Ct.
Westlake Village, CA 91361
Application addresses: c/o Joyce Sudikoff, C.E.O., P.O. Box 491669, Los Angeles, CA 90049; c/o Joan Sudikoff, V.P., 23 Karen Rd., Waban, MA 02168

Established in 1992 in CA.
Donors: Jeffrey Sudikoff; Joan Sudikoff; Joyce Sudikoff; Kilhillet Israel; New Moon Trust.
Foundation type: Independent foundation.
Financial data (yr. ended 5/31/05): Assets, $8,011 (M); gifts received, $1,130,000; expenditures, $1,134,328; qualifying distributions, $1,120,832; giving activities include $1,120,832 for 10 grants (high: $500,000; low: $1,326).
Purpose and activities: Giving primarily for higher education; some funding for a television station.
Fields of interest: Arts, alliance; Media, television; Arts; Higher education; Education; Jewish agencies & temples.
Type of support: Building/renovation; Program development.
Limitations: Giving primarily in Los Angeles, CA, and Brooklyn, NY. No grants to individuals.
Application information:
  Initial approach: Typewritten letter
  Deadline(s): None
Officers: Joyce Sudikoff, C.E.O.; Joan Sudikoff, V.P.; Jeffrey Sudikoff, Treas.
Number of staff: 1 part-time support.
EIN: 956941160
Selected grants: The following grants were reported in 2004.
$500,000 to Dartmouth College, Hanover, NH.
$400,000 to UCLA Foundation, Los Angeles, CA.

$17,500 to Hillel Hebrew Academy, Beverly Hills, CA.

$10,000 to Sinai Akiba Academy, Los Angeles, CA.

$5,700 to Upward Bound House of Santa Monica, Santa Monica, CA.

$5,000 to Reconstructionist Rabbinical College, Wyncote, PA.

$4,275 to Archer School for Girls, Los Angeles, CA.

$3,383 to Hollygrove Children and Family Services, Los Angeles, CA.

$1,666 to Independent School Alliance for Minority Affairs, Los Angeles, CA.

$1,576 to Children of the Night, Van Nuys, CA.

1213
The David and Diana Sun Foundation ✧
P.O. Box 8566
Fountain Valley, CA   92728-8566
(714) 435-2640
Contact: Albert Kong

Established in 1999 in CA.
Donors: David Sun; Diana Sun.
Foundation type: Independent foundation.
Financial data (yr. ended 12/31/05): Assets, $160,416 (M); expenditures, $1,008,209; qualifying distributions, $1,008,209; giving activities include $1,003,000 for 2 grants (high: $1,000,000; low: $3,000).
Fields of interest: Asians/Pacific Islanders.
Limitations: Giving primarily in CA, with emphasis on Irvine and Los Angeles. No grants to individuals.
Application information:
   Deadline(s): None
Officers: David Sun, Pres.; Diana Sun, V.P.; Diana Kong, Secy.; Yvonne Curry, Treas.
EIN: 330868088

1214
The Sun Microsystems Foundation, Inc. ✧
901 San Antonio Rd., M.S. PAL-1462
Palo Alto, CA   94303   (650) 336-0545
Contact: Andrea Gooden, Exec. Dir.
FAX: (650) 856-2114; E-mail: corpaffrs@sun.com;
Application address: Global Community Devel., Sun Microsystems, Inc., 4120 Network Circle Dr., M.S. USCA12-310, Santa Clara, CA 95054, tel.: (303) 272-2354; URL: http://www.sun.com/aboutsun/comm_invest/giving/foundation.html

Established as a company-sponsored operating foundation in 1990 in CA.
Donors: Robert F. Sproull; Sun Microsystems, Inc.
Foundation type: Operating foundation.
Financial data (yr. ended 6/30/04): Assets, $3,445,941 (M); gifts received, $3,647,345; expenditures, $2,574,247; qualifying distributions, $2,574,178; giving activities include $1,024,456 for grants, and $1,549,722 for employee matching gifts.
Purpose and activities: The foundation supports organizations involved with education and job training. Special emphasis is directed toward programs designed to increase participation of underrepresented populations in technology courses and careers.
Fields of interest: Elementary/secondary education; Education; Employment, training; Minorities; Economically disadvantaged.
International interests: Scotland.

Type of support: Donated products; Technical assistance; Employee volunteer services; Program development; Employee matching gifts.
Limitations: Giving on a national and international basis in areas of company operations. No support for religious or political organizations or arts and culture organizations. No grants to individuals, or for advertising or fundraising.
Publications: Annual report; Informational brochure (including application guidelines).
Application information: Unsolicited requests for Open Gateways and STEP are not accepted.
   Initial approach: E-mail foundation for application information
   Final notification: 4 to 8 weeks for Community Partnership Program
Officers: Crawford Beveridge, Pres.; Kim Jones, Secy.; Mick Murray, Treas.; Andrea Gooden, Exec. Dir.
Directors: Piper Cole; Andy Lark; Bill McGowan.
EIN: 770244198

1215
Sundean Foundation, Inc. ✧ ☆
35 Penny Ln., Ste. 6
Watsonville, CA   95076
Contact: Michael M. Nelson, Pres.

Established around 1979.
Donors: Harold A. Sundean; Edith P. Sundean.
Foundation type: Independent foundation.
Financial data (yr. ended 1/31/06): Assets, $13,033,021 (M); expenditures, $1,259,430; qualifying distributions, $830,344; giving activities include $830,344 for grants.
Purpose and activities: Giving primarily to S.D.A. Christian organizations and schools.
Fields of interest: Elementary/secondary education; Christian agencies & churches.
Limitations: Giving primarily in Santa Cruz, CA and Silver Springs, MD. No grants to individuals.
Application information:
   Initial approach: Letter
   Deadline(s): None
Officers: Michael M. Nelson, Pres.; Gaelyn K. Betts, V.P.; Christine A. Betts, Secy.
Directors: David R. Dickerson; Marilyn Eggers; John L. Petersen.
EIN: 946050302

1216
Swanson & Thomas Foundation ✧ ☆
1010 Grayson St., Ste. 1
Berkeley, CA   94710

Established in 2002 in CA.
Donors: Susan E. Swanson; Lisa B. Thomas.
Foundation type: Independent foundation.
Financial data (yr. ended 12/31/05): Assets, $1,486,655 (M); expenditures, $412,832; qualifying distributions, $391,010; giving activities include $391,000 for 2 grants (high: $291,000; low: $100,000).
Fields of interest: Media, film/video; Theological school/education.
Limitations: Applications not accepted. No grants to individuals.
Application information: Contributes only to pre-selected organizations.
Agent: Citicorp Trust Co.
EIN: 046991923

Selected grants: The following grants were reported in 2004.
$250,000 to Pacific School of Religion, Berkeley, CA. For general support.

1217
The Swanson Foundation ✧
330 Primrose Rd., Ste. 404
Burlingame, CA   94010

Established in 1994 in CA.
Donor: Swanson Charitable Remainder Unitrust.
Foundation type: Independent foundation.
Financial data (yr. ended 12/31/05): Assets, $14,660,970 (M); expenditures, $908,381; qualifying distributions, $791,000; giving activities include $788,500 for 10 grants (high: $325,000; low: $5,000).
Purpose and activities: Giving primarily for education, as well as for the ballet, family and social services, and health associations.
Fields of interest: Performing arts, ballet; Higher education; Education; Health organizations, association; Human services; Family services.
Limitations: Applications not accepted. Giving primarily in the San Francisco Bay Area, CA and MA. No grants to individuals.
Application information: Contributes only to pre-selected organizations.
Officers: Judy C. Swanson, Pres.; Mary Lynn Bell, Secy.; Christine Sherry, C.F.O. and Treas.
EIN: 943211277

1218
Swenson Family Foundation ✧
34372 St. of the Cove Lantern
Dana Point, CA   92629
Contact: James I. Swenson, Pres.

Established in 1994 in CA.
Donor: James I. Swenson.
Foundation type: Independent foundation.
Financial data (yr. ended 12/31/04): Assets, $58,891,627 (M); expenditures, $3,232,306; qualifying distributions, $3,142,338; giving activities include $3,118,468 for 13 grants (high: $1,091,624; low: $5,000; average: $10,000–$70,000).
Purpose and activities: Giving primarily to arts/cultural programs, education, hospitals, human services, and Christian agencies and churches.
Fields of interest: Arts; Education; Hospitals (general); Human services; Christian agencies & churches.
Type of support: Scholarship funds.
Limitations: Applications not accepted. Giving primarily in CA, Minneapolis, MN, and Superior, WI. No grants to individuals.
Application information: Contributes only to pre-selected organizations.
Officers: James I. Swenson, Pres.; Susan G. Swenson, Secy. and C.F.O.
EIN: 330603766

1219
The Swift Foundation ✧ ☆
1224 Coast Village Cir., Ste. 32
Santa Barbara, CA   93108
Application address: 406 Higuera, Ste. 120, San Luis Obispo, CA 93401, tel.: (805) 544-1557

Established in 2000 in CA.
Foundation type: Independent foundation.
Financial data (yr. ended 9/30/05): Assets, $8,147,440 (M); gifts received, $1,150,000; expenditures, $582,813; qualifying distributions, $542,500; giving activities include $542,500 for 14 grants (high: $180,000; low: $5,000).
Fields of interest: Education; Environment; Community development.
Limitations: Giving primarily in CA.
Application information: Application form not required.
Deadline(s): None
Officers: John Swift, C.E.O.; Kirsten Swift, Secy. and C.F.O.
EIN: 770559600
Selected grants: The following grants were reported in 2004.
$75,000 to World Neighbors, Oklahoma City, OK.
$50,000 to Conservation International, DC.
$25,000 to EngenderHealth, New York, NY.
$13,750 to Idea Wild, Fort Collins, CO.
$5,000 to Charities Aid Foundation (CAF) America, Alexandria, VA.
$5,000 to Rotaplast International, San Francisco, CA.
$5,000 to U.S.-Ukraine Foundation, DC.
$5,000 to William Edelen Ministries, Palm Springs, CA.
$3,000 to Theodore Roosevelt Conservation Partnership, DC.
$1,000 to dZi Foundation, Ridgway, CO.

1220
Swig Foundation ◇
220 Montgomery St., 20th Fl.
San Francisco, CA 94104 (415) 291-1100
Contact: Kent Swig, Tr.

Established in 1957 in CA.
Donors: Benjamin H. Swig†; members of the Swig family.
Foundation type: Independent foundation.
Financial data (yr. ended 12/31/05): Assets, $17,811,406 (M); expenditures, $1,142,951; qualifying distributions, $955,653; giving activities include $929,253 for 213 grants (high: $75,000).
Purpose and activities: Grants for arts and culture, education, community welfare, medical care, and projects for Israel.
Fields of interest: Arts; Higher education; Education; Health care; Health organizations, association; Human services; Jewish federated giving programs.
International interests: Israel.
Limitations: Giving primarily in the San Francisco Bay Area, CA; some giving nationally. No grants to individuals, or for conferences, seminars, or workshops.
Application information: Funds are currently committed; new applications not considered. Application form not required.
Initial approach: Letter
Deadline(s): None
Board meeting date(s): Apr., Aug., and Dec.
Final notification: Immediately following board meeting
Trustees: Carolyn Zecca Ferris; Kent Swig; Susan Watkins.
EIN: 946065205

1221
The Swinerton Foundation ◇ ☆
P.O. Box 77048
San Francisco, CA 94107 (415) 984-1372
FAX: (415) 984-1384;
E-mail: swinertonfoundation@swinerton.com;
URL: http://www.swinerton.com/foundation/index.html

Donor: Swinerton Inc.
Foundation type: Company-sponsored foundation.
Financial data (yr. ended 12/31/05): Assets, $216,893 (M); gifts received, $449,492; expenditures, $376,901; qualifying distributions, $336,443; giving activities include $336,443 for grants.
Purpose and activities: The foundation supports organizations involved with arts and culture, education, health, youth development, human services, and community development.
Fields of interest: Arts; Education; Health organizations, association; Youth development; Human services; Community development.
Limitations: Applications not accepted. No grants to individuals.
Application information: Contributes only to pre-selected organizations.
Officer: Luke Argilla, Chair; Charles P. Kuffner, Pres.; Gary J. Rafferty, Secy.; Michael Re, Treas.; Terrence Bush; James R. Gillette; David H. Grubb, Jr.; Gordon W. Marks; Lucille Morris-Tyndall; Donald E. Sundgren; David K. White.
EIN: 030490864

1222
Synopsys Silicon Valley Science & Technology Outreach Foundation ◇
4 Graceland Dr.
San Rafael, CA 94901-1922 (415) 459-3433
Contact: Gary Robinson, Pres.
FAX: (650) 584-1510;
E-mail: robinson@synopsys.com; Additional E-mail: outreach-foundation@synopsys.com; URL: http://www.outreach-foundation.org

Established as a company-sponsored operating foundation in 1999 in CA.
Donors: Synopsys Technology Education Opportunity Foundation; Industry Initiatives.
Foundation type: Operating foundation.
Financial data (yr. ended 12/31/04): Assets, $131,462 (M); gifts received, $880,752; expenditures, $932,652; qualifying distributions, $885,441; giving activities include $499,794 for grants, and $150,534 for foundation-administered programs.
Purpose and activities: The foundation supports programs designed to promote project-based learning among students and teachers in Silicon Valley, California; and encourage participation in science fairs and awards grants to teachers K-12 teachers and students engaged in project-based learning in select California schools and select schools affiliated with regional offices of Synopsys. emphasis on Silicon Valley.
Fields of interest: Elementary/secondary education; Elementary school/education; Secondary school/education; Higher education; Science.
Type of support: Equipment; Program development; Sponsorships; Grants to individuals.

Limitations: Giving limited to the Silicon Valley, CA, area. No grants for technical papers.
Application information: Science Project Grants for Santa Clara County elementary and middle schools have been allocated for 2006-2007. Support is limited to 20 grants per teacher during any given year for Science Project Grants. Application form required.
Initial approach: Complete online application form for East Side Union High School District teachers
Deadline(s): Oct. 1 for Science Project Grants for Santa Clara County elementary schools; Oct. 15 for Science Project Grants for East Side Union High School and Santa Clara County middle and high schools
Officers and Directors:* Richard Goldman,* Chair.; Gary Robinson, Pres.; Bonnie George,* Secy.; Erin Brennock,* Treas.; Dana Ditmore; Murlin Marks; Roy Okuda; Judy Peterson; Larke Reeber; Lynn Shannon.
EIN: 770520414

1223
Synopsys Technology Education Opportunity Foundation ◇
(formerly Synopsys Technology Opportunity Scholarship Foundation)
700 E. Middlefield Rd.
Mountain View, CA 94043 (650) 584-1772
Contact: Erin Brennock, C.O.O.

Established in 1998 in CA.
Donor: Synopsys, Inc.
Foundation type: Company-sponsored foundation.
Financial data (yr. ended 12/31/05): Assets, $338,350 (M); gifts received, $1,066,273; expenditures, $961,088; qualifying distributions, $960,442; giving activities include $903,894 for 34 + grants (high: $650,000).
Purpose and activities: The foundation supports community foundations and organizations involved with education, hunger, and science.
Fields of interest: Secondary school/education; Education, services; Education; Food banks; American Red Cross; Foundations (community); Science, formal/general education; Mathematics; Science.
Type of support: Scholarship funds; Annual campaigns; Fellowships; Program development; Sponsorships; Employee matching gifts.
Limitations: Giving primarily in CA.
Publications: Application guidelines.
Application information: Organizations receiving support are asked to submit a final report. Application form not required.
Initial approach: Proposal
Deadline(s): June 30 and Dec. 31
Officers: Arte de Geus,* Chair; Erin Brennock, C.O.O.; Steven K. Shevick,* Pres.; Christopher K. Sadeghian, Secy.; Karen Brocher, Treas.
EIN: 770488629
Selected grants: The following grants were reported in 2004.
$253,055 to Synopsys Silicon Valley Science and Technology Outreach Foundation, Mountain View, CA.
$100,000 to World Economic Forum, Geneva, Switzerland. .
$35,000 to Oregon Symphony Association, Portland, OR.
$29,577 to JK Group, Plainsboro, NJ.
$10,000 to Science Service, DC.

$5,000 to San Jose Museum of Art, San Jose, CA.

1224
The Tabasgo Foundation ◇ ☆
3463 State St., Ste. 255
Santa Barbara, CA 93105

Established in 2005 in CA.
Donors: Wayne E. Rosing; Dorothy F. Largay.
Foundation type: Independent foundation.
Financial data (yr. ended 12/31/05): Assets, $89,890,158 (M); gifts received, $95,557,619; expenditures, $8,476,528; qualifying distributions, $8,313,500; giving activities include $8,313,500 for 5 grants (high: $8,000,000; low: $10,000).
Fields of interest: Higher education; Astronomy.
Limitations: Applications not accepted. Giving primarily in CA.
Application information: Contributes only to pre-selected organizations.
Officer: Wayne Rosing, Pres.
EIN: 651251997

1225
Linda Tallen and David Paul Kane Educational & Research Foundation ◇
10100 Santa Monica Blvd., Ste. 2200
Los Angeles, CA 90067

Established in 1994 in CA.
Donor: David Paul Kane†.
Foundation type: Independent foundation.
Financial data (yr. ended 12/31/04): Assets, $13,516,756 (M); expenditures, $1,203,037; qualifying distributions, $701,335; giving activities include $679,243 for 19 grants (high: $100,000; low: $10,000).
Purpose and activities: Giving primarily for medical research, with emphasis on cancer.
Fields of interest: Arts; Education; Hospitals (general); Health organizations, association; Cancer; Medical research.
Limitations: Applications not accepted. Giving primarily in Los Angeles, CA; some giving also in CT and ME. No grants to individuals.
Application information: Contributes only to pre-selected organizations.
Officers: Geraldine Wolf, C.E.O. and Pres.; Stanley Balck, V.P. and Secy.; Andrew S. Garb, C.F.O. and Treas.
EIN: 954477151

1226
S. Mark Taper Foundation ▼
12011 San Vicente Blvd., Ste. 400
Los Angeles, CA 90049 (310) 476-5413
Contact: Raymond F. Reisler, Exec. Dir.
FAX: (310) 471-4993;
E-mail: info@smtfoundation.org; Additional E-mail: rreisler@smtfoundation.org; URL: https://www.smtfoundation.org

Incorporated in 1989 in CA.
Donor: S. Mark Taper†.
Foundation type: Independent foundation.
Financial data (yr. ended 12/31/05): Assets, $125,461,065 (M); expenditures, $6,882,923; qualifying distributions, $5,972,710; giving activities include $5,462,800 for 92 grants (high:

$432,000; low: $5,000; average: $10,000–$100,000).
Purpose and activities: Giving primarily to children and youth, health care, social services, employment, education, and the environment.
Fields of interest: Arts; Education; Environment; Health care; Crime/violence prevention; Employment; Housing/shelter, development; Human services; Children/youth, services; Family services; Civil liberties, reproductive rights; Government/public administration; Aging; Disabilities, people with; Women; AIDS, people with; Economically disadvantaged; Homeless.
Type of support: General/operating support; Annual campaigns; Capital campaigns; Building/renovation; Equipment; Emergency funds; Program development; Conferences/seminars; Publication; Seed money; Curriculum development; Scholarship funds; Research; Program-related investments/loans; Matching/challenge support.
Limitations: Giving primarily in southern CA. No support for religious organizations or specific diseases. No grants to individuals.
Publications: Application guidelines.
Application information: Application form required.
Initial approach: Letter
Copies of proposal: 1
Deadline(s): Dec. 1 to Feb. 28
Board meeting date(s): As required
Final notification: As needed
Officers and Director:* Janice Taper Lazarof,* Pres.; Cynthia Taper Bolker, V.P.; Amelia Taper Bolker, Secy.; Roy Weitz, C.F.O. and C.I.O.; Deborah Taper Ringel, Treas.; Raymond F. Reisler, Exec. Dir.
Number of staff: 3 full-time professional; 2 full-time support.
EIN: 954245076
Selected grants: The following grants were reported in 2004.
$250,000 to Arroyo Vista Family Health Center, Los Angeles, CA.
$230,500 to Los Angeles Free Clinic, Los Angeles, CA.
$210,000 to Exceptional Childrens Foundation, Culver City, CA.
$200,000 to East Valley Community Health Center, West Covina, CA.
$150,000 to Para Los Ninos, Los Angeles, CA.
$100,000 to Families in Schools, Los Angeles, CA.
$80,000 to Vista del Mar Child and Family Services, Los Angeles, CA.
$75,000 to Achievable Foundation, Culver City, CA.
$75,000 to South Bay Youth Project, Friends of, Redondo Beach, CA.
$70,000 to Center for Aging Resources, Pasadena, CA.

1227
The Buddy Taub Foundation ◇
9200 Sunset Blvd., Ste. 525
Los Angeles, CA 90069

Established in 1998 in CA.
Foundation type: Independent foundation.
Financial data (yr. ended 5/31/05): Assets, $11,302,716 (M); expenditures, $567,899; qualifying distributions, $508,158; giving activities include $450,092 for 29 grants (high: $157,573; low: $675).
Purpose and activities: Giving primarily for art museums; funding also for higher education, and children, youth and social services.

Fields of interest: Museums (art); Higher education; Animals/wildlife; Human services; Children/youth, services.
Limitations: Applications not accepted. Giving on a national basis. No grants to individuals.
Application information: Contributes only to pre-selected organizations.
Director: Dennis A. Roach.
EIN: 954588448

1228
Taube Family Foundation ◇
1050 Ralston Ave.
Belmont, CA 94002-2243 (650) 592-3960
Contact: Grants Admin.

Established in 1980 in CA.
Donor: Members of the Taube family.
Foundation type: Independent foundation.
Financial data (yr. ended 12/31/04): Assets, $22,992,621 (M); gifts received, $1,368,847; expenditures, $1,265,213; qualifying distributions, $1,080,077; giving activities include $1,080,077 for 82 grants (high: $300,000; low: $100).
Purpose and activities: Giving primarily to higher education, Jewish organizations and the United Way.
Fields of interest: Arts; Higher education; Children/youth, services; Federated giving programs; Jewish agencies & temples.
Type of support: General/operating support; Continuing support; Building/renovation; Fellowships.
Limitations: Giving primarily in the San Francisco Bay Area, CA.
Application information: Application form not required.
Initial approach: Letter
Copies of proposal: 1
Officers and Directors:* Thaddeus N. Taube,* Chair. and Pres.; Kenneth A. Moline, V.P.; Dianne M. Taube,* V.P.; Beverly Hong, Secy.; Kenneth L. Marciano, C.F.O.
EIN: 942702180
Selected grants: The following grants were reported in 2003.
$316,666 to University of California at San Francisco Foundation, San Francisco, CA. For general support.
$250,000 to United Way of the Bay Area, San Francisco, CA. For general support.
$200,000 to Hoover Institution on War, Revolution and Peace, Stanford, CA. For general support.
$200,000 to Stanford University, Stanford, CA. For Tennis Center.
$50,000 to San Francisco Parks Trust, San Francisco, CA. For general support.
$45,000 to Stanford Center for Economic Policy Research, Stanford, CA. For general support.
$30,000 to San Francisco Opera Association, San Francisco, CA. For general support.
$15,000 to Congregation Beth Am, Los Altos Hills, CA. For general support.
$10,000 to Youth Tennis Advantage, Oakland, CA. For general support.
$2,500 to College Track, East Palo Alto, CA. For general support.

1229
Paul K. Tchang Family Foundation ◇
9171 Wilshire Blvd., Ste. 500
Beverly Hills, CA 90210

Established in 1999 in CA.
Donors: Paul K. Tchang; Techbilt Homes, Inc.
Foundation type: Independent foundation.
Financial data (yr. ended 5/31/05): Assets, $7,298,277 (M); gifts received, $4,477,838; expenditures, $765,356; qualifying distributions, $731,514; giving activities include $730,000 for 4 grants (high: $600,000; low: $10,000).
Purpose and activities: Giving primarily for higher education.
Fields of interest: Museums (history); Higher education; Education.
Limitations: Applications not accepted. Giving on a national and international basis, particularly in San Diego, CA, and Cambridge, MA; funding also in Yunnan, China. No grants to individuals.
Application information: Contributes only to pre-selected organizations.
Officers and Directors:* Paul K. Tchang,* Pres.; Genevieve Tchang Frost,* Secy.; Lorna Tchang Alcala; Rose Tchang; Theodore Tchang.
EIN: 330862430

1230
Jim and Joyce Teel Family Foundation ✧
P.O. Box 15618
Sacramento, CA 95852

Established in 2002 in CA.
Donors: Jim Teel; Joyce Teel.
Foundation type: Independent foundation.
Financial data (yr. ended 12/31/04): Assets, $11,681,052 (M); expenditures, $779,361; qualifying distributions, $668,003; giving activities include $668,003 for 5 grants (high: $593,503; low: $2,000).
Fields of interest: Museums; Human services.
Limitations: Applications not accepted. Giving primarily in CA.
Application information: Unsolicited requests for funds not accepted.
Officers: Joyce Teel, Pres.; Jim Teel, V.P.; Neil Doerhoff, Secy.-Treas.
EIN: 680521463

1231
Teichert Foundation ✧
3500 American River Dr.
Sacramento, CA 95864   (916) 484-3255
URL: http://www.teichert.com/index.cfm?pageid=486

Established in 1990 in CA.
Donors: A. Teichert & Son, Inc.; Teichert, Inc.
Foundation type: Company-sponsored foundation.
Financial data (yr. ended 3/31/06): Assets, $9,750,469 (M); gifts received, $1,722,842; expenditures, $791,800; qualifying distributions, $714,374; giving activities include $714,374 for 109 grants (high: $175,000; low: $25).
Purpose and activities: The foundation supports organizations involved with arts and culture, education, environmental planning and preservation, health, youth development, human services, community development, transportation and planning, civic affairs, and senior citizens. Special emphasis is directed toward programs designed to focus on children and youth.
Fields of interest: Historic preservation/historical societies; Arts; Education; Environment; Medical care, rehabilitation; Health care; Boys & girls clubs;

Youth development; Children/youth, services; Human services; Community development; Federated giving programs; Transportation; Public affairs; Children; Youth; Aging.
Type of support: General/operating support.
Limitations: Giving primarily in Amador, Calaveras, Colusa, El Dorado, Mariposa, Merced, Nevada, North Solano, Placer, Sacramento, San Joaquin, Stanislaus, Sutter, Tuolumne, Yolo, and Yuba counties, CA. No support for religious, political, or fraternal organizations. No grants to individuals, or for courtesy advertising or tickets, telephone solicitations, or national fundraising campaigns.
Publications: Application guidelines; Grants list.
Application information: Proposals should be no longer than 3 pages. Application form not required.
Initial approach: Proposal
Copies of proposal: 2
Deadline(s): Feb. 25 and Aug. 26
Board meeting date(s): Biannually
Final notification: June and Dec.
Officers and Directors:* Anne S. Haslam,* Secy.; Norman Eilert, C.F.O.; Frederick A. Teichert,* Exec. Dir.; Thomas J. Hammer; Judson T. Riggs; Melita M. Teichert.
Number of staff: 1 full-time professional; 1 full-time support.
EIN: 680212355

1232
Bonnie and Marty Tenenbaum Foundation ✧
c/o Jay Martin Tenenbaum
25 Alhambra Ct.
Portola Valley, CA 94028-7722

Established in 2000 in CA.
Donor: Bonnie Tenenbaum.
Foundation type: Independent foundation.
Financial data (yr. ended 12/31/04): Assets, $0 (M); expenditures, $765,375; qualifying distributions, $739,334; giving activities include $735,000 for 10 grants (high: $250,000; low: $5,000).
Purpose and activities: Giving primarily to Jewish organizations, temples, and schools; funding also for health associations.
Fields of interest: Arts; Higher education; Education; Health organizations, association; Federated giving programs; Jewish federated giving programs; Jewish agencies & temples.
Limitations: Applications not accepted. Giving primarily in CA; funding also in New York, NY. No grants to individuals.
Application information: Contributes only to pre-selected organizations.
Officers: Jay M. Tenenbaum, C.E.O. and Pres.; Bonnie Tenenbaum, Secy.
EIN: 943351181
Selected grants: The following grants were reported in 2003.
$144,000 to Bureau of Jewish Education, San Francisco, CA. 2 grants: $134,000, $10,000
$75,000 to Massachusetts Institute of Technology, Cambridge, MA.
$50,000 to Jewish Family and Childrens Services, San Francisco, CA.
$25,000 to Lively Arts at Stanford, Stanford, CA.
$25,000 to San Francisco Jewish Film Festival, San Francisco, CA.
$25,000 to Stanford University, Stanford, CA.
$20,000 to John Wayne Cancer Institute, Santa Monica, CA.

$10,000 to Crystal Springs Uplands School, Hillsborough, CA.
$10,000 to Palo Alto Medical Foundation for Health Care, Research and Education, Palo Alto, CA.

1233
Marilyn Swift Tennity Foundation ✧
74-900 Hwy III, Ste. 127
Indian Wells, CA 92210

Established in 1998 in CA.
Donors: Marilyn Smith Swift Tennity Charitable Trust; Marilyn Swift Tennity.
Foundation type: Independent foundation.
Financial data (yr. ended 12/31/04): Assets, $52,499,030 (M); gifts received, $11,728,249; expenditures, $2,402,758; qualifying distributions, $2,282,000; giving activities include $2,262,533 for 60 grants (high: $530,000; low: $100).
Fields of interest: Museums (marine/maritime); Performing arts, theater; Higher education; Environment; Human services.
Limitations: Applications not accepted. Giving on a national basis. No grants to individuals.
Application information: Contributes only to pre-selected organizations.
Directors: Lantson E. Eldred; Nancy Swift Furlotti; James L. Swift; John F. Swift; Peter D. Swift.
EIN: 330783887
Selected grants: The following grants were reported in 2004.
$530,000 to McCallum Theater, Palm Desert, CA.
$400,000 to World Neighbors, Oklahoma City, OK.
$275,000 to Philemon Foundation, Ardmore, PA.
$200,000 to Environmental Defense, Oakland, CA.
$125,000 to Conservation International, DC.
$100,000 to Davidson College, Davidson, NC.
$100,000 to University of Vermont, Burlington, VT.
$50,000 to Cuesta College, San Luis Obispo, CA.
$50,000 to Lobero Theater, Santa Barbara, CA.
$1,000 to Direct Relief International, Santa Barbara, CA.

1234
The Tesuque Foundation, Inc. ✧
P.O. Box 460639
San Francisco, CA 94146-0639
Contact: David Wilson, V.P.

Established in 1990 in NY.
Donors: Andrea Wilson†; Fred W. Wilson†.
Foundation type: Independent foundation.
Financial data (yr. ended 5/31/05): Assets, $6,475,793 (M); expenditures, $55,000; qualifying distributions, $550,000; giving activities include $550,000 for 10 grants (high: $200,000; low: $2,500).
Purpose and activities: Giving primarily for the arts, libraries, and general charitable giving, with an emphasis on homelessness, and prison rehabilitation programs.
Fields of interest: Arts; Libraries/library science.
Type of support: General/operating support; Capital campaigns; Endowments; Program development.
Limitations: Applications not accepted. Giving primarily in CA.
Application information: Unsolicited requests for funds not considered.
Officers: Pamela Wilson, Pres.; David Wilson, V.P.; Tom Ryckman, Secy.-Treas.

Number of staff: 1 part-time professional.
EIN: 133579598
Selected grants: The following grants were reported in 2003.
$200,000 to Marin County Foundation. For social and community programs in county.
$125,000 to Ounce of Prevention Fund, Chicago, IL. For arts program for early childhood curriculum.
$55,000 to Homeless Prenatal Program, San Francisco, CA. For outreach program for women inmates.
$45,000 to Caduceus Outreach Services, San Francisco, CA.
$35,000 to Hope House. For family relations program for inmates.
$20,000 to Safer Foundation, Chicago, IL. For job training for released inmates.
$20,000 to Saint Leonards Ministries, Chicago, IL. For job training for released inmates.
$10,000 to University of Illinois at Chicago, Chicago, IL. For writing program for underprivileged children.
$7,000 to New York University, ETW/House of Words, New York, NY.

1235

Flora L. Thornton Foundation ✧

c/o Edward A. Landry
1 Wilshire Blvd., Ste. 2000
Los Angeles, CA 90017
Contact: Flora L. Thornton, Tr.

Established in 1983 in CA.
Donor: Flora L. Thornton.
Foundation type: Independent foundation.
Financial data (yr. ended 11/30/05): Assets, $4,526,640 (M); gifts received, $3,166,100; expenditures, $1,552,593; qualifying distributions, $1,518,500; giving activities include $1,518,500 for 50 grants (high: $300,000; low: $1,000).
Purpose and activities: Giving primarily for elementary and higher education, arts and cultural organizations, nutrition and preventive medicine education.
Fields of interest: Performing arts, music; Performing arts, orchestra (symphony); Performing arts, opera; Arts; Elementary school/education; Higher education; Public health; Health organizations, association; Nutrition.
Type of support: General/operating support; Continuing support; Endowments; Conferences/ seminars; Professorships; Scholarship funds; Matching/challenge support.
Limitations: Giving primarily in Los Angeles, CA. No grants to individuals.
Application information: Application form not required.
Initial approach: Letter
Copies of proposal: 1
Deadline(s): None
Board meeting date(s): Quarterly
Trustees: Edward A. Landry; Glen P. McDaniel; Eric L. Small; Flora L. Thornton; William Laney Thornton; Elizabeth Thornton Troy.
Number of staff: 1 part-time support.
EIN: 953855595
Selected grants: The following grants were reported in 2005.
$250,000 to San Francisco Opera, San Francisco, CA.
$60,000 to Los Angeles Opera Company, Los Angeles, CA.

$50,000 to Los Angeles Master Chorale, Los Angeles, CA.
$30,000 to Teach for America, New York, NY.
$25,000 to American Youth Symphony, Los Angeles, CA.
$25,000 to K C E T Community Television of Southern California, Los Angeles, CA.
$20,000 to Music Academy of the West, Santa Barbara, CA.
$17,000 to Saint Matthews Parish School, Pacific Palisades, CA.
$10,000 to Hobart Shakespeareans, Los Angeles, CA.
$10,000 to Santa Fe Opera, Santa Fe, NM.

1236

The Thornton Foundation ✧

523 W. 6th St., Ste. 636
Los Angeles, CA 90014 (213) 629-3867
Contact: Charles B. Thornton, Jr., Pres.

Incorporated in 1958 in CA.
Donors: Charles B. Thornton†; Flora L. Thornton.
Foundation type: Independent foundation.
Financial data (yr. ended 12/31/04): Assets, $25,969,112 (M); expenditures, $1,490,146; qualifying distributions, $1,126,619; giving activities include $1,122,000 for 73 grants (high: $190,000; low: $1,000).
Purpose and activities: Giving primarily for the arts and education.
Fields of interest: Arts; Secondary school/ education; Higher education; Education.
Type of support: General/operating support; Continuing support; Annual campaigns; Building/ renovation; Endowments; Research.
Limitations: Giving primarily in CA. No grants to individuals, or for seed money, emergency funds, deficit financing, equipment, land acquisition, demonstration projects, publications, conferences, scholarships, or fellowships; no loans.
Application information: Application form not required.
Initial approach: Letter
Copies of proposal: 1
Deadline(s): None
Board meeting date(s): As required
Final notification: 1 month
Officers and Trustees:* Charles B. Thornton, Jr.,* Pres.; William Laney Thornton,* V.P.; Terry D. Chapin, Secy.
Number of staff: 2 part-time professional; 2 part-time support.
EIN: 956037178
Selected grants: The following grants were reported in 2004.
$100,000 to Harvard-Westlake School, North Hollywood, CA.
$100,000 to Stanford University, Stanford, CA.
$50,000 to California Academy of Sciences, San Francisco, CA.
$30,000 to Hoover Institution on War, Revolution and Peace, Stanford, CA.
$25,000 to Greenbelt Alliance, San Francisco, CA.
$20,000 to San Francisco Opera, San Francisco, CA.
$18,000 to Crucible, The, Oakland, CA.
$10,000 to San Francisco Museum of Modern Art, San Francisco, CA.
$9,000 to Outward Bound, Garrison, NY.
$6,000 to Art Center College of Design, Pasadena, CA.

1237

The William Hall Tippett and Ruth Rathell Tippett Foundation ✧ ☆

1200 Prospect St., No. 575
La Jolla, CA 92037-3610

Established in 2000 in CA.
Foundation type: Independent foundation.
Financial data (yr. ended 12/31/05): Assets, $4,552,291 (M); expenditures, $377,037; qualifying distributions, $330,000; giving activities include $330,000 for 11 grants (high: $100,000; low: $5,000).
Fields of interest: Arts; Education; Human services; Youth, services.
Limitations: Applications not accepted. No grants to individuals.
Application information: Contributes only to pre-selected organizations.
Officers: Barbara ZoBell, Pres.; Mildred V. Basden, Secy. and C.F.O.
Trustee: Karen Zobell.
EIN: 330903811

1238

Tomlinson Foundation ✧

3652 Monte Real
Escondido, CA 92029-7911

Established in 1989 in CA.
Donors: Thomas W. Tomlinson; Mary A. Tomlinson; Loren Tomlinson†.
Foundation type: Independent foundation.
Financial data (yr. ended 12/31/05): Assets, $1,401,496 (M); gifts received, $15,968; expenditures, $439,203; qualifying distributions, $424,417; giving activities include $423,030 for 22 grants (high: $60,000; low: $250).
Purpose and activities: Giving primarily for higher education, health associations, youth development, human services, a YMCA, and to a Lutheran organization.
Fields of interest: Higher education; Health organizations, association; Boys & girls clubs; Boy scouts; Human services; YM/YWCAs & YM/YWHAs; Protestant agencies & churches.
Limitations: Applications not accepted. Giving primarily in CA. No grants to individuals.
Application information: Contributes only to pre-selected organizations.
Officers: Thomas W. Tomlinson, Pres.; Lynora S. Brown, V.P.; Mary A. Tomlinson, Secy.
EIN: 330383793
Selected grants: The following grants were reported in 2005.
$60,000 to YMCA.
$57,500 to Boy Scouts of America, Anchorage, AK.
$50,000 to Villa Esperanza, Pasadena, CA.
$47,500 to Community Lutheran Church, West Sacramento, CA.
$10,000 to Boys and Girls Club.
$7,000 to Salvation Army.
$2,000 to Multiple Sclerosis Society, Edmonton, Canada.
$1,000 to American Heart Association, Dallas, TX.
$1,000 to Gideons International, Nashville, TN.

1239

Torrey Foundation ✧

2658 Del Mar Heights Rd., No. 424
Del Mar, CA 92014-3100

Established in 1990 in NV.

Donors: Kent R. Wilson; Lana L. Wilson.

Foundation type: Independent foundation.

Financial data (yr. ended 12/31/03): Assets, $13,252,675 (M); expenditures, $691,282; qualifying distributions, $532,750; giving activities include $532,750 for 14 grants (high: $320,297; low: $150).

Purpose and activities: Support primarily for higher education, scientific research, and international organizations.

Fields of interest: Higher education; Science.

Type of support: Research.

Limitations: Applications not accepted. Giving primarily in CA. No grants to individuals.

Publications: Annual report.

Application information: Contributes only to pre-selected organizations.

Officers and Directors: * L. Legallet,* Pres.; T. Wilson, Secy.; M. Wilson, Treas.; M. Chakko.

EIN: 880268986

1240
Tosa Foundation ◇

(formerly Morgridge Family Foundation)
c/o Tashia F. Morgridge
4420 Alpine Rd., Rm. 157
Portola Valley, CA   94028
Contact: Tashia F. Morgridge, Pres.

Established in 1992 in CA.

Donors: Tashia F. Morgridge; John P. Morgridge.

Foundation type: Independent foundation.

Financial data (yr. ended 12/31/04): Assets, $289,325,429 (M); gifts received, $16,884; expenditures, $6,870,597; qualifying distributions, $6,999,635; giving activities include $6,974,185 for 248 grants (high: $618,940; low: $100; average: $1,000–$100,000).

Purpose and activities: Giving support to education, the environment, medical research, the arts, and human services.

Fields of interest: Arts; Higher education; Education; Environment; Animal welfare; Youth development, services; Human services; International development; International affairs.

Limitations: Applications not accepted. Giving on a national basis. No grants to individuals.

Application information: Contributes only to pre-selected organizations.

Officers and Directors: * Tashia F. Morgridge,* Pres.; Kate M. Greswold,* Secy.; John P. Morgridge,* C.F.O.; John D. Morgridge.

EIN: 943165171

Selected grants: The following grants were reported in 2004.

$1,000,000 to Peninsula Community Foundation, San Mateo, CA. 2 grants: $500,000 each

$500,000 to Sparc, Saint Paul, MN.

$350,000 to Oxfam America, Boston, MA.

$156,000 to Squam Lakes Natural Science Center, Holderness, NH.

$100,000 to Global Fund for Women, San Francisco, CA.

$50,000 to United Way Silicon Valley, San Jose, CA.

$25,000 to Business Executives for National Security (BENS), DC.

$5,000 to Student Conservation Association, Charlestown, NH.

$2,500 to Pemi Bridge House, Plymouth, NH.

1241
The Towbes Foundation ◇

P.O. Box 20130
Santa Barbara, CA   93120-0130
(805) 962-2121
Contact: Barbara Ross, Secy.
E-mail: bross@towbes.com; Additional E-mail: MMolina@towbes.com

Established in 1980 in CA.

Donors: Michael Towbes; Gail Towbes†.

Foundation type: Independent foundation.

Financial data (yr. ended 6/30/05): Assets, $412,650 (M); gifts received, $706,000; expenditures, $713,008; qualifying distributions, $699,404; giving activities include $699,000 for 115 grants (high: $35,000; low: $1,000).

Purpose and activities: Primary areas of interest include: education, including scholarships; medical research, especially in the area of neurological disease; promotion of the performing arts; and promotion and preservation of the free enterprise system.

Fields of interest: Performing arts; Higher education; Education; Medical research, institute; Economics.

Type of support: Research; Program development; Capital campaigns; General/operating support; Conferences/seminars; Fellowships; Scholarship funds; Matching/challenge support.

Limitations: Giving primarily in Santa Barbara, CA, and immediate environs. No grants to individuals.

Publications: Application guidelines.

Application information: Foundation generally prefers to initiate grant requests. Application form required.

Initial approach: E-mail, telephone, or letter
Copies of proposal: 5
Deadline(s): Apr. 30, Aug. 31, and Dec. 31
Board meeting date(s): Feb., June, and Oct.
Final notification: Approximately 2 months

Officers and Directors: * Sheridah Gerard,* Pres.; Charles H. Jarvis,* V.P.; Barbara Ross, Secy.; Michael Towbes,* C.F.O.; Robert Skinner.

EIN: 953519577

Selected grants: The following grants were reported in 2004.

$30,000 to Scholarship Foundation of Santa Barbara, Santa Barbara, CA.

$20,000 to Music Academy of the West, Santa Barbara, CA.

$20,000 to Santa Barbara Zoological Gardens, Santa Barbara, CA.

$20,000 to State Street Ballet, Santa Barbara, CA.

$15,000 to Multiple Sclerosis Society, National, Santa Barbara, CA.

$10,000 to Foundation for Teaching Economics, Davis, CA.

$10,000 to Great American Dream Foundation, Lompoc, CA.

$10,000 to Partners in Education, Santa Barbara, CA.

$10,000 to Santa Barbara Bowl Foundation, Santa Barbara, CA.

$10,000 to Womens Economic Ventures, Santa Barbara, CA.

1242
C. E. Towne Scholarship Fund ◇

c/o Wells Fargo Bank, N.A., Trust Tax Dept.
P.O. Box 63954
San Francisco, CA   94163
Contact: Judy Lang
Application address: c/o California Masonic Foundation, 1111 California St., San Francisco, CA 93108, tel.: (415) 292-9196; FAX: (415) 776-7170; URL: http://www.freemason.org

Established in 1996 in CA.

Foundation type: Independent foundation.

Financial data (yr. ended 6/30/03): Assets, $7,252,879 (M); expenditures, $579,498; qualifying distributions, $534,050; giving activities include $514,000 for 44 grants to individuals (high: $16,000; low: $12,000).

Purpose and activities: Giving scholarship awards to children of California Masonic Foundation families.

Fields of interest: Higher education.

Limitations: Giving primarily to children of California Masonic Foundation families in San Francisco, CA.

Application information: Application form to be requested from California Masonic Foundation. Application form required.

Deadline(s): Apr. 15

Trustee: Wells Fargo Bank, N.A.

EIN: 946705897

1243
The Nora Eccles Treadwell Foundation ◇

c/o Nicholas Prepouses
241 Joaquin Ave.
San Leandro, CA   94577
Contact: Patricia Canepa, Chair.

Established in 1962 in UT.

Donors: Nora Eccles Treadwell Harrison†; Nora Eccles Treadwell Charitable Trust.

Foundation type: Independent foundation.

Financial data (yr. ended 12/31/05): Assets, $5,258,610 (M); gifts received, $3,540,405; expenditures, $4,322,015; qualifying distributions, $4,252,691; giving activities include $3,788,320 for grants.

Purpose and activities: Grants primarily for health and cardiovascular, diabetes, and arthritis research.

Fields of interest: Health care; Health organizations, association; Heart & circulatory diseases; Medical research, institute; Heart & circulatory research; Diabetes research.

Type of support: General/operating support; Equipment; Professorships; Research.

Limitations: Giving limited to CA and UT. No grants to individuals, or for research in areas not related to the cardiovascular system, diabetes, or arthritis.

Application information: All applications must be accompanied by a letter from the dean of the medical school or the affiliated institution stating the quality and desirability of the project, and that space, equipment, and personnel are available or can be recruited in a reasonable time. Application form required.

Copies of proposal: 10
Deadline(s): Sept. 15

Officers and Directors: * Patricia Canepa,* Chair.; Kathryn C. Econome, M.D.*, Vice-Chair.; D. William Hilger, M.D.*, Secy.; Nicholas T. Prepouses,* Treas.; Spencer P. Eccles; Lawrence M. Harrison; Alonzo W. Watson, Jr.

Number of staff: 3
EIN: 237425351
Selected grants: The following grants were reported in 2004.
$2,485,100 to University of Utah, Salt Lake City, UT. 8 grants: $355,000, $245,500, $600,000, $180,000, $300,000, $125,000, $350,100, $329,500
$100,000 to University of Southern California, Los Angeles, CA.
$15,000 to Utah State University, Logan, UT.

1244
Truckee Tahoe Community Foundation ◇
P.O. Box 366
Truckee, CA 96160   (530) 587-1776
Contact: Phebe Bell, Prog. Off.
FAX: (530) 550-7985; E-mail: phebe@ttcf.net;
URL: http://www.ttcf.net

Established in 1998 in CA.
Foundation type: Community foundation.
Financial data (yr. ended 6/30/04): Assets, $7,916,603 (L); gifts received, $1,066,282; expenditures, $1,306,108; giving activities include $939,125 for grants.
Purpose and activities: The foundation seeks to enhance the quality of life in the Truckee/Tahoe, CA, area by seeking, accepting, managing, and disbursing funds for the benefit of the community.
Fields of interest: Arts; Education; Environment; Animals/wildlife, preservation/protection; Health care; Recreation; Youth development; Human services; Children/youth, services; Human services; Community development.
Type of support: General/operating support; Continuing support; Income development; Management development/capacity building; Equipment; Program development; Publication; Seed money; Technical assistance; Consulting services.
Limitations: Giving limited to the Truckee/North Tahoe, CA, area. No support for direct religious activities. No grants for capital campaigns, activities that have already occurred, or school-based activities (unless they impact students district wide or impact the broader community).
Publications: Application guidelines; Grants list; Newsletter.
Application information: Visit foundation Web site for application form and guidelines. Application form required.
Initial approach: Telephone
Copies of proposal: 12
Deadline(s): Accepted on an on-going basis, deadlines for review include Jan. 17, May 16, and Sept. 12
Board meeting date(s): 2nd Thurs. of every month
Final notification: 90 days
Officers and Directors:* Scott Ryan,* Chair.; Lisa Dobey, Pres.; Linda Brown; Jim Gaither, Jr.; Richard George; Ernie Grossman; Ed Heneveld; Dr. Fred Ilfeld; Roger Kahn; Rob Kautz; Julie Maurer; Phil McKenney; Jim Porter; Trinkie Watson.
Number of staff: 1 full-time support; 3 part-time support.
EIN: 680416404

1245
True North Foundation
664A Freeman Ln., No. 332
Grass Valley, CA 95949   (530) 274-1620
Contact: Ms. Kerry Anderson, Pres.
E-mail: kka1119@aol.com

Established in 1986 in CO.
Foundation type: Independent foundation.
Financial data (yr. ended 12/31/04): Assets, $25,572,882 (M); expenditures, $2,036,042; qualifying distributions, $1,975,573; giving activities include $1,844,460 for 78 grants (high: $200,000; low: $2,500).
Purpose and activities: Giving primarily for environmental programs such as environmental work in AK, mining reform in the West, and sustainable agriculture in northern CA; also giving to independent living programs for the frail elderly/disabled in the northern CA region.
Fields of interest: Environment, natural resources; Environment; Aging; Disabilities, people with.
Type of support: General/operating support; Equipment; Program development; Conferences/seminars; Seed money; Technical assistance; Consulting services; Matching/challenge support.
Limitations: Giving primarily in AK, and northern CA, with emphasis on the San Francisco Bay Area. No support for religious purposes. No grants to individuals.
Publications: Informational brochure (including application guidelines).
Application information: Application form required.
Initial approach: Letter
Copies of proposal: 1
Deadline(s): None
Board meeting date(s): Generally bimonthly
Final notification: 4-6 weeks
Officer and Directors:* K. Anderson,* Pres.; S. O'Hara; K.F. Stephens.
Number of staff: 1 full-time professional; 1 part-time professional.
EIN: 742421528
Selected grants: The following grants were reported in 2005.
$40,000 to Organic Farming Research Foundation, Santa Cruz, CA. For general support.
$35,000 to Cook Inlet Keeper, Homer, AK. For general support.
$30,000 to San Francisco BayKeeper, San Francisco, CA. For pesticide project.
$30,000 to Trustees for Alaska, Anchorage, AK. For mining program.
$25,000 to Alaska Community Action on Toxics, Anchorage, AK. For general support.
$25,000 to Disability Rights Education and Defense Fund, Berkeley, CA. For accessible health care.
$20,000 to Planning for Elders in the Central City, San Francisco, CA. For general support.
$15,000 to AXIS Dance Company, Oakland, CA. For dance access and community outreach.
$15,000 to Skytruth, Shepherdstown, WV. For mining program.
$10,000 to Meals on Wheels, Alameda, Alameda, CA. For friendly visitors program.

1246
Trust Funds Incorporated
100 Broadway, 3rd Fl.
San Francisco, CA 94111-1404   (415) 434-3323
Contact: James T. Healy, Pres.

Incorporated in 1934 in CA.

Donors: Bartley P. Oliver†; Alfreda S. Cullinan†; Rev. James J. Wynne.
Foundation type: Independent foundation.
Financial data (yr. ended 12/31/05): Assets, $9,441,314 (M); gifts received, $30,000; expenditures, $591,200; qualifying distributions, $494,723; giving activities include $424,503 for 61 grants (high: $30,000; low: $102; average: $2,500–$10,000).
Purpose and activities: Grants for the Roman Catholic religion, education, and social work, primarily through support of institutions and projects related to the Roman Catholic Church.
Fields of interest: Elementary/secondary education; Education; Human services; Roman Catholic agencies & churches; Religion.
Type of support: General/operating support; Equipment; Emergency funds; Program development; Conferences/seminars; Publication; Seed money; Curriculum development; Scholarship funds.
Limitations: Giving limited to the San Francisco Bay Area, CA, or, by exception, to projects of national or global scope which affect the Roman Catholic Church. No support for organizations that draw substantial public support. No grants to individuals directly, or for capital or endowment funds, or annual campaigns; no loans.
Publications: Application guidelines; Informational brochure.
Application information: Application form required.
Initial approach: Letter
Copies of proposal: 5
Deadline(s): Quarterly
Board meeting date(s): Quarterly
Final notification: Within 3 months
Officers and Directors:* James T. Healy,* Pres.; Joan C. O'Rourke,* Secy.; Thomas F. Kubasak,* C.F.O.; Thomas J. Kelley; Robert David Ramsey.
Number of staff: 1 part-time professional.
EIN: 946062952

1247
Alice Tweed Tuohy Foundation
205 E. Carrillo St., Rm. 219
Santa Barbara, CA 93101
FAX: (805) 962-7135; E-mail: atuohyfdn@aol.com;
Mailing address: c/o Harris W. Seed, P.O. Box 1328, Santa Barbara, CA 93102-1328

Incorporated in 1956 in CA.
Donors: Alice Tweed Tuohy†; Kenneth Millar†; Margaret Millar†.
Foundation type: Independent foundation.
Financial data (yr. ended 6/30/05): Assets, $16,446,847 (M); expenditures, $1,035,742; qualifying distributions, $1,394,789; giving activities include $638,870 for 40 grants (high: $83,625; low: $750), and $500,000 for 2 loans/program-related investments (high: $250,000; low: $250,000).
Purpose and activities: Grants to nonprofit organizations within the south coast area of Santa Barbara County, CA, serving young people, educational institutions, selected healthcare and medical organizations, and community projects; substantial support also for the art program at the Duluth Campus of the University of Minnesota.
Fields of interest: Scholarships/financial aid; Human services; Children/youth, services.
Type of support: Capital campaigns; Building/renovation; Equipment; Land acquisition;

Endowments; Scholarship funds; Matching/challenge support.

Limitations: Giving limited to the Santa Barbara, CA, area. No support for private foundations, national campaigns, or private and public grade schools. No grants to individuals, or for operating budgets, research, or unrestricted purposes.

Publications: Biennial report (including application guidelines).

Application information: Proposal must include a list of cash contributions made by board members over prior 3 years. Applicant must also provide FTB determination letter. Application form not required.

   Initial approach: Letter

   Copies of proposal: 6

   Deadline(s): Submit proposal between July 1 and Sept. 15; proposals received after deadline will be deferred for a year

   Board meeting date(s): Apr. or May, and Nov. or Dec.

   Final notification: 3 to 4 months

Officers and Directors:* Harris W. Seed,* C.E.O. and Pres.; Jeanne McKay, Secy.-Treas.; Joseph L. Cole; Paul W. Hartloff; John R. Mackall.

Number of staff: 3 part-time professional.

EIN: 956036471

Selected grants: The following grants were reported in 2004.

$97,125 to Scholarship Foundation of Santa Barbara, Santa Barbara, CA. For general support.

$25,000 to Mental Health Association of Santa Barbara, Santa Barbara, CA. For capital campaign.

$24,730 to Santa Barbara City College, Foundation for, Santa Barbara, CA. For equipment.

$20,000 to Santa Barbara Center for the Performing Arts, Santa Barbara, CA. For capital campaign.

$10,000 to Family Service Agency of Santa Barbara, Santa Barbara, CA. For equipment.

$10,000 to Girls Inc. of Carpinteria, Carpinteria, CA. For scholarships.

$10,000 to YMCA, Channel Islands, Santa Barbara, CA. For summer programs.

$1,200 to Santa Barbara Foundation, Santa Barbara, CA. For Partnership for Excellence conference.

$750 to Bishop Garcia Diego High School, Santa Barbara, CA. For scholarships.

$750 to Santa Barbara High School, Santa Barbara, CA. For scholarships.

1248

Ueberroth Family Foundation ✧

10880 Wilshire Blvd., Ste. 920
Los Angeles, CA   90024
Contact: Virginia Ueberroth, Pres.
Application address: P.O. Box 100, Laguna Beach, CA 92652, tel.: (949) 720-9646

Established in 1984 in CA.

Donors: Peter Ueberroth; Virginia Ueberroth; Kathy Clark; Washington Speakers Bureau; Deutsche Bank; Autry Foundation; William Thompson; Healthcare CEO Summit; KPMG; Redpoint Management LLP; Venture Strategy Group; Ueberroth Family Trust; Building Owners & Mgrs. of O.C.

Foundation type: Independent foundation.

Financial data (yr. ended 11/30/05): Assets, $14,705,621 (M); gifts received, $629,090; expenditures, $640,185; qualifying distributions, $602,500; giving activities include $602,500 for 74 grants (high: $51,000; low: $1,000).

Purpose and activities: Preference given to youth charities and health and human services in CA.

Fields of interest: Arts; Education; Hospitals (general); Health organizations, association; Youth development, centers/clubs; Human services; Children/youth, services; Federated giving programs.

Type of support: General/operating support; Annual campaigns; Capital campaigns; Building/renovation; Equipment; Endowments; Program development; Conferences/seminars; Curriculum development; Research.

Limitations: Giving primarily in southern CA.

Publications: Application guidelines.

Application information: Contributes mainly to groups with donor involvement or connection. Application form required.

   Deadline(s): None

Officers: Virginia Ueberroth, Pres.; Vicki Booth, Secy.; Joseph Ueberroth, C.F.O. and Treas.

EIN: 330078919

Selected grants: The following grants were reported in 2005.

$51,000 to Sage Hill School, Newport Coast, CA.

$36,000 to Hoag Hospital Foundation, Newport Beach, CA.

$20,000 to Human Options, Irvine, CA.

$20,000 to Monterey Peninsula Foundation, Monterey, CA.

$20,000 to Vanderbilt University, Nashville, TN.

$17,000 to Cate School, Carpinteria, CA.

$16,000 to Harbor Day School, Corona del Mar, CA.

$15,000 to Lauras House, San Juan Capistrano, CA.

$6,000 to Dartmouth College, Hanover, NH.

$5,000 to Info Link Orange County, Costa Mesa, CA.

1249

UniHealth Foundation ▼

800 Wilshire Blvd., Ste. 1300
Los Angeles, CA   90017   (213) 630-6500
Contact: Mary Odell, Pres.
FAX: (213) 630-6509;
E-mail: Webadmin@unihealthfoundation.org;
URL: http://www.unihealthfoundation.org/

Established in 1998 in CA.

Foundation type: Independent foundation.

Financial data (yr. ended 9/30/05): Assets, $302,606,349 (M); expenditures, $18,583,153; qualifying distributions, $15,603,789; giving activities include $14,605,670 for 126 grants (high: $558,132; low: $25; average: $50,000–$250,000).

Purpose and activities: To support and facilitate activities that significantly improve the health and well being of individuals and communities within its service area. The majority of funding will be to hospitals in Los Angeles and northern Orange Counties, CA.

Fields of interest: Hospitals (general); Hospitals (specialty); Public health.

Type of support: Management development/capacity building; Program development; Curriculum development; Scholarship funds; Program evaluation; Employee matching gifts.

Limitations: Giving primarily in CA in the following areas: San Fernando and Santa Clarita Valley, Westside and Downtown Los Angeles, San Gabriel Valley, and Long Beach and Orange County. No support for propagandizing and/or influencing legislation, political campaigns, programs that promote religious doctrine, or biomedical/

non-applied research. No grants to individuals, or for endowments, annual drives, or retirement of debt.

Publications: Application guidelines; Annual report (including application guidelines); Financial statement; Grants list; Informational brochure (including application guidelines); Program policy statement.

Application information: Grant application outline available upon request.

   Initial approach: Preliminary letter; those qualified to submit a proposal will be contacted by foundation program staff

   Board meeting date(s): 4 times per year

Officers and Directors:* David R. Carpenter,* Chair. and C.E.O.; Jean Bixby Smith,* Vice-Chair.; Mary Odell, Pres.; Lydia H. Kennard,* Secy.; Kathleen H. Salazar, C.F.O. and Treas.; Bradley C. Call; Charles C. Reed; Keith W. Renken; Frank M. Sanchez, Ph.D.

Number of staff: 5 full-time professional; 3 full-time support.

EIN: 955004033

Selected grants: The following grants were reported in 2005.

$726,650 to National Institute of Transplantation, Los Angeles, CA. For One-on-One Renal Disease Education Project.

$700,000 to California Hospital Medical Center, Los Angeles, CA. 2 grants: $350,000 (For Community Dental Partnership), $350,000 (For Family Medicine Residency Program Strategic Planning and Improvement Project).

$558,132 to Mount Saint Marys College, Los Angeles, CA. For nursing program expansion plan.

$500,000 to California Community Foundation, Los Angeles, CA. For Community Clinic Fund.

$259,169 to Sherman Oaks Hospital and Health Center, Sherman Oaks, CA. For Early Stage Alzheimer's Project.

$199,100 to Saint Francis Medical Center, Lynwood, CA. For Comprehensive Master Plan for Saint Francis Center College.

$165,112 to San Gabriel Valley Medical Center, San Gabriel, CA. For Children's Health Access Program.

$150,825 to University of Southern California, School of Pharmacy, Los Angeles, CA. For Pharmacist Clinical Services to improve health outcomes for asthmatic children in Orange County.

$35,000 to University of California, David Gellen School of Medicine, Los Angeles, CA. For Medical Student Scholarship.

1250

Union Bank of California Foundation ▼ ✧

(formerly Union Bank Foundation)
c/o Union Bank of California, N.A.
445 S. Figueroa St.
Los Angeles, CA   90071
Contact: Laura Johnson
E-mail: laura.johnson@uboc.com; Application addresses: Central CA, Northern CA, and Pacific Northwest: Karen Murakami, Fdn. Off., Union Bank of California, N.A., 400 California St., 8th Fl., M.C. 1-001-08, San Francisco, CA 94101, tel.: (415) 765-3890, E-mail: karen.murakami@uboc.com, Los Angeles, Orange, and Ventura counties, CA: Susana Lopez, Fdn. Off., Union Bank of California, N.A., 445 S. Figueroa St., 4th Fl., M.C. G04-110, Los Angeles, CA 90071, tel.: (213) 236-5540, Imperial, Riverside, San Bernardino, and San Diego counties, CA: Katherine Patoff, V.P., Union Bank of California,

N.A., 530 B St., M.C. S-650, San Diego, CA 92101, tel.: (619) 230-4501, E-mail: kathy.patoff@uboc.com; URL: http://www.uboc.com/about/main/0,,2485_3457,00.html

Trust established in 1953 in CA.

Donors: Union Bank of California, N.A.; UnionBanCal Corp.

Foundation type: Company-sponsored foundation.

Financial data (yr. ended 12/31/05): Assets, $1,066,859 (M); gifts received, $2,769,820; expenditures, $4,142,125; qualifying distributions, $4,142,125; giving activities include $4,142,125 for 507 grants (high: $175,000; low: $400).

Purpose and activities: The foundation supports organizations involved with arts and culture, education, health, employment, housing, public safety, youth development, human services, economic development, community development, and economically disadvantaged people.

Fields of interest: Museums; Arts; Business school/education; Teacher school/education; Adult/continuing education; Libraries/library science; Scholarships/financial aid; Education; Health care; Employment, training; Employment; Housing/shelter; Safety/disasters; Youth development; Human services, financial counseling; Human services; Economic development; Business/industry; Community development; Science; Economically disadvantaged.

Type of support: Continuing support; Income development; Annual campaigns; Building/renovation; Equipment; Emergency funds; Program development; Internship funds; Scholarship funds; Research; Technical assistance; Employee matching gifts.

Limitations: Giving primarily in areas of company operations, with emphasis on Imperial, Los Angeles, Orange, Riverside, San Bernardino, San Diego, and Ventura counties, CA, central and northern CA, and the Pacific Northwest. No support for religious, military, veterans', fraternal, professional, or political organizations or intermediary foundations. No grants to individuals, or for service club activities or general operating support for churches or religious groups, hospitals or other patient care institutions, or educational institutions.

Publications: Application guidelines; Annual report; Grants list.

Application information: Application form not required.

　Initial approach: Proposal to nearest application address or nearest company facility
　Copies of proposal: 1
　Deadline(s): Jan. is preferred
　Board meeting date(s): Bi-monthly
　Final notification: 3 months

Officers and Directors:* Robert A. McNeely,* Chair. and C.E.O.; Carl Ballton, C.O.O. and Pres.; Kathleen Baker; Joe Benoit; Linda Betzer; JoAnn Bourne; Bruce Corbin; Maria Gallo; Jack Knight; Takaaki A. Nakajima; Joe Petitti.

Trustee: Union Bank of California, N.A.

Number of staff: 4 full-time professional; 1 full-time support.

EIN: 956023551

Selected grants: The following grants were reported in 2005.

$175,000 to Operation Hope, Los Angeles, CA.

$85,000 to Habitat for Humanity International, San Francisco, CA. 2 grants: $15,000, $70,000

$80,000 to K C E T Community Television of Southern California, Los Angeles, CA. For Hispanic Heritage Month.

$75,000 to Community HousingWorks, San Diego, CA.

$75,000 to Greenlining Institute, Berkeley, CA.

$33,250 to Independent Colleges of Southern California, Los Angeles, CA.

$25,000 to California Community Economic Development Association, Los Angeles, CA.

$25,000 to K V P T - Channel 18, Fresno, CA. For Hispanic Heritage Month.

$10,000 to Bay Area School Reform Collaborative, San Francisco, CA.

1251
United Cancer Front ◇
(formerly The Cancer Research Foundation, Inc.)
233 Wilshire Blvd., Ste. 400
Santa Monica, CA　90401

Established in 2001 in CA. Classified as a private operating foundation in 2002.

Donors: Henry Yuen; Lilly Tartikoff; Roger Jenkins; Sanela Jenkins; Vivendi Universal Entertainment, LLP; Block Family Foundation.

Foundation type: Operating foundation.

Financial data (yr. ended 12/31/05): Assets, $192,668 (M); gifts received, $61,000; expenditures, $1,027,769; qualifying distributions, $1,025,471; giving activities include $1,005,000 for 8 grants (high: $470,000; low: $20,000).

Fields of interest: Cancer research.

Limitations: Applications not accepted. Giving primarily in CA; funding also nationally, as well as some funding in Edmonton, Alberta, Canada. No grants to individuals.

Application information: Contributes only to pre-selected organizations.

Officer: Lilly Tartikoff, C.E.O. and Pres.

EIN: 954865948

1252
Unocal Foundation ▼ ◇
6001 Bollinger Canyon Rd.
San Ramon, CA　94583
Contact: Laurie Regelbrugge, Mgr.
Application address: 1150 Connecticut Ave. N.W., Ste. 1025, Washington, DC 20036, tel.: (202) 367-2782, FAX: (202) 367-2790, E-mail: laurier@unocal.com

Incorporated in 1962 in CA.

Donors: Unocal Corp.; Union Oil Co. of California.

Foundation type: Company-sponsored foundation.

Financial data (yr. ended 12/31/04): Assets, $2,319,466 (M); expenditures, $3,495,548; qualifying distributions, $3,495,038; giving activities include $2,376,528 for 114 grants (high: $200,000; low: $400), and $1,118,510 for employee matching gifts.

Purpose and activities: The foundation supports organizations involved with arts and culture, education, environmental conservation, health, international affairs, youth development, and community development.

Fields of interest: Arts; Elementary/secondary education; Education; Environment, natural resources; Health care; Youth development; International affairs; Community development; Federated giving programs; Children/youth.

Type of support: Continuing support; Annual campaigns; Equipment; Fellowships; Scholarship funds; Research; Employee matching gifts; Employee-related scholarships.

Limitations: Giving on a national and international basis in areas of company operations. No support for veterans', fraternal, sectarian, social, religious, or athletic organizations, choral, band, or similar groups, trade or business associations, or state agencies or departments. No grants to individuals (except for employee-related scholarships), or for general operating support, capital campaigns for education, elementary or secondary education, endowments, courtesy advertising, conferences, or trips or tours; no loans.

Publications: Annual report.

Application information: Application form not required.

　Initial approach: Contact foundation for application information
　Deadline(s): Varies
　Board meeting date(s): As required
　Final notification: 6 to 8 weeks

Officers and Trustees:* George A. Walker,* Chair.; Gregory F. Huger,* Pres.; Stephen L. Hayes, V.P., Tax; Carl D. McAulay,* V.P.; Roberta E. Kass, Secy.; Darrell D. Chessum, Treas.; Laurie Regelbrugge, Mgr.; Joe D. Cecil; Stephen W. Green; M.L. Luli Heras-De Leon; Christine Lelaurin; Brian W.G. Marcotte; Chaiyasuta Siriporn.

Number of staff: 1 full-time professional; 1 full-time support; 2 part-time support.

EIN: 956071812

Selected grants: The following grants were reported in 2004.

$200,000 to Habitat for Humanity International, Anchorage, AK.

$200,000 to International Youth Foundation, Baltimore, MD. 2 grants: $125,000, $75,000

$200,000 to Pact Institute, DC.

$125,000 to Nature Conservancy, Arlington, VA. 2 grants: $25,000, $100,000

$122,250 to Scholarship America, Saint Peter, MN.

$50,000 to Comdev International, Greenwood Village, CO.

$30,000 to Communities in Schools, Alexandria, VA.

$20,000 to Habitat for Humanity of Midland, Midland, TX.

1253
Ute City Charitable Trust ◇
5484 Shannon Ridge Ln.
San Diego, CA　92130-2757

Established in 1999 in CA.

Donors: Gary B. Davis; Elissa R. Davis.

Foundation type: Independent foundation.

Financial data (yr. ended 12/31/05): Assets, $6,519,974 (M); gifts received, $1,170,000; expenditures, $1,019,320; qualifying distributions, $1,014,600; giving activities include $1,014,600 for 44 grants (high: $350,000; low: $1,000).

Fields of interest: Arts; Education; Jewish agencies & temples.

Limitations: Applications not accepted. Giving primarily in San Diego, CA and New York, NY. No grants to individuals.

Application information: Contributes only to pre-selected organizations.

Trustees: Dawn M. Berson; Elissa R. Davis; Gary B. Davis.

EIN: 330833915

1254

The Vadasz Family Foundation
P.O. Box 1347
Sonoma, CA 95476 (707) 938-3014
Contact: Pamela Winston; Meghan Beynon
FAX: (707) 938-3015;
E-mail: pam@vadaszfoundation.org; Additional
E-mail: meghan@vadaszfoundation.org (for Meghan
Beynon)

Established in 1997 in CA.
Donors: Judy K. Vadasz; Les L. Vadasz.
Foundation type: Independent foundation.
Financial data (yr. ended 11/30/05): Assets,
$27,015,215 (M); expenditures, $1,274,548;
qualifying distributions, $1,259,595; giving
activities include $1,108,022 for grants.
Purpose and activities: Giving primarily for higher
education, as well as for educational foundations;
funding also for health care, including a medical
center, and for the support of social and cultural
community needs.
Fields of interest: Museums (marine/maritime);
Elementary/secondary education; Higher education;
Education; Environment; Hospitals (general); Health
organizations, association; Human services; Aging,
centers/services; Foundations (private
grantmaking).
Limitations: Applications not accepted. Giving
primarily in CA. No grants to individuals.
Application information: Contributes only to
pre-selected organizations.
Officers and Directors:* Les L. Vadasz,* Pres.;
Jeffrey E. Vadasz,* Secy.; Judy K. Vadasz,* Treas.
EIN: 770469457
Selected grants: The following grants were reported
in 2004.
$200,000 to University of California at San
Francisco Foundation, San Francisco, CA.
$131,000 to Sonoma Valley Education Foundation,
Sonoma, CA.
$55,000 to Businesses United in Investing, Lending
and Development (BUILD), Menlo Park, CA.
$50,000 to Sonoma Valley Mentoring Alliance,
Sonoma, CA.
$40,000 to Foundation for a College Education,
East Palo Alto, CA.
$35,000 to Sonoma Valley Museum of Art, Sonoma,
CA.
$25,000 to Community School of Music and Arts,
Mountain View, CA.
$5,000 to Exploratorium, San Francisco, CA.

1255

**The George and Lena Valente
  Foundation** ✧
44465 N. El Macero Dr.
El Macero, CA 95618-1062
Contact: George Valente, Pres.

Established in 1995 in CA.
Donor: George Valente.
Foundation type: Independent foundation.
Financial data (yr. ended 9/30/05): Assets,
$13,683,788 (M); gifts received, $500,000;
expenditures, $922,433; qualifying distributions,
$584,342; giving activities include $584,342 for 10
grants (high: $75,000; low: $25,000).
Purpose and activities: Giving to health
organizations, senior citizens' services, and
education, and medical research.

Fields of interest: Higher education; Health
organizations, association; Medical research,
institute; Human services; Aging.
Limitations: Giving primarily in CA.
Application information:
  Deadline(s): None
Officers: George Valente, Pres.; Gerald Valente,
V.P.; Linda L. Volkerts, Secy.; JoAnn Michaels,
C.F.O.
Directors: Gene Hume; Jared Monez.
EIN: 680370358
Selected grants: The following grants were reported
in 2003.
$110,000 to University of California Medical Center,
Davis, CA.
$51,187 to Senior Legal Hotline, Sacramento, CA.
$50,000 to Woodland Memorial Hospital
Foundation, Woodland, CA.
$25,000 to Big Brothers/Big Sisters of Sacramento,
Sacramento, CA.
$25,000 to Davis Little League, Davis, CA.
$25,000 to Mercy Foundation, Sacramento, CA.
$15,000 to Saint James Catholic School, CA.
$15,000 to Yolo Hospice, Davis, CA.

1256

The Valley Foundation ▼ ✧
16450 Los Gatos Blvd., Ste. 210
Los Gatos, CA 95032-5594 (408) 358-4545
Contact: Ms. Ervie L. Smith, Exec. Dir.
FAX: (408) 358-4548; E-mail: admin@valley.org;
E-mail for Ervie L. Smith, Exec. Dir.: ervie@valley.org;
URL: http://www.valley.org

Established in 1984 in CA.
Foundation type: Independent foundation.
Financial data (yr. ended 9/30/05): Assets,
$66,657,188 (M); expenditures, $4,681,071;
qualifying distributions, $4,109,145; giving
activities include $3,956,844 for 75 grants (high:
$600,000; low: $250; average: $15,000–
$100,000).
Purpose and activities: Support primarily for
medical services and health care for lower-income
households within Santa Clara County and for
research, social services, and education. Support
also for youth, the arts, senior citizens, education,
and general medical areas.
Fields of interest: Arts; Education; Health care;
Medical research, institute; Human services; Youth,
services; Aging, centers/services; Aging;
Economically disadvantaged.
Type of support: General/operating support;
Continuing support; Capital campaigns; Equipment;
Program development; Seed money; Research;
Technical assistance; Matching/challenge support.
Limitations: Giving limited to Santa Clara County,
CA. No support for religious purposes. No grants to
individuals.
Publications: Application guidelines; Annual report;
Grants list; Informational brochure (including
application guidelines).
Application information: Letter of intent should be
submitted online. See foundation Web site for grant
guidelines and application procedures. Application
form required.
  Initial approach: 1-2-page letter of intent due 1
    month prior to submitting application
  Copies of proposal: 1
  Deadline(s): Letter of intent: Oct. 15, Jan. 15, Apr.
    15 and July 15
  Board meeting date(s): Quarterly
  Final notification: Within 2 weeks

Officers and Directors:* Phillip R. Boyce,* Chair.;
Richard Sieve, M.D.*, Vice-Chair.; Herbert Kain,
M.D., Secy.; Edgar G. La Veque, M.D.*, Treas.; Ervie
L. Smith, Exec. Dir.; Ralph Ross, Dir. Emeritus;
Arthur A. Basham; Daniel Doore; Joseph Parisi.
Number of staff: 1 part-time professional; 1
part-time support.
EIN: 941584547
Selected grants: The following grants were reported
in 2005.
$660,000 to San Jose State University Foundation,
San Jose, CA. 2 grants: $300,000, $360,000
$600,000 to YMCA of Santa Clara Valley, San Jose,
CA.
$100,000 to San Jose Conservation Corps and
Charter School, San Jose, CA.
$100,000 to Silicon Valley Childrens Fund, San
Jose, CA.
$100,000 to Stanford University Hospital, Stanford,
CA.
$100,000 to VMC Foundation, San Jose, CA.
$75,000 to San Juan Bautista Child Development
Center, San Jose, CA.
$45,000 to Evergreen Valley College, San Jose, CA.
$40,000 to San Jose Day Nursery, San Jose, CA.

1257

Wayne & Gladys Valley Foundation ▼ ✧
1939 Harrison St., Ste. 510
Oakland, CA 94612-3532 (510) 466-6060
Contact: Michael D. Desler, Exec. Dir.
FAX: (510) 466-6067; E-mail: info@wgvalley.org;
URL: http://foundationcenter.org/grantmaker/
wgvalley/

Established in 1977 in CA.
Donors: F. Wayne Valley‡; Gladys Valley‡.
Foundation type: Independent foundation.
Financial data (yr. ended 9/30/05): Assets,
$623,762,552 (M); gifts received, $172,013;
expenditures, $25,934,036; qualifying
distributions, $23,731,354; giving activities include
$23,117,765 for 92 grants (high: $4,500,000; low:
$45; average: $20,000–$250,000).
Purpose and activities: Primary areas of interest
include higher, secondary, and other education,
medical research, health care, youth, local parks
and recreational facilities and local Catholic
organizations. The foundation seeks to make grants
to organizations having broad based funding
support; specifically defined goals and purposes;
demonstrated effectiveness in its programs;
expectations for continued success in its activities
without future dependence on support from the
foundation; and committed, enthusiastic and
diligent leadership.
Fields of interest: Elementary/secondary
education; Higher education; Health care; Medical
research; Recreation, parks/playgrounds; Human
services; Children/youth, services; Roman Catholic
agencies & churches.
Type of support: General/operating support; Capital
campaigns; Building/renovation; Program
development; Scholarship funds; Research;
Matching/challenge support.
Limitations: Giving primarily in Alameda and Contra
Costa counties, CA. No support for veterans,
fraternal, labor, service club, military, or similar
organizations. No grants to individuals, or for
fundraising events, dinners, advertising, private
operating foundations, or generally for endowments.
Publications: Application guidelines; Annual report.

Application information: More detailed application guidelines may be obtained by contacting the foundation. Application form not required.

   Initial approach: Letter
   Copies of proposal: 1
   Deadline(s): None
   Board meeting date(s): Mar., June, Sept., and Dec.
   Final notification: 3-6 months

Officers and Directors:* Tamara A. Valley,* Pres.; Richard M. Kingsland, V.P., Corp. Secy., and C.F.O.; Michael D. Desler, Exec. Dir.; Robert C. Brown; Stephen M. Chandler; John P. Stock.

Number of staff: 4 full-time professional; 1 full-time support.

EIN: 953203014

Selected grants: The following grants were reported in 2005.

$4,500,000 to Christ the Light Cathedral Corporation, Oakland, CA. For construction.

$3,000,000 to Dominican Sisters of Mission San Jose, Oakland, CA. 2 grants: $1,000,000 (For Circles of Caring project to renovate and retrofit Motherhouse Care Center and Chapel), $2,000,000 (For Circles of Caring project to retrofit and renovate Care Center and Chapel).

$2,500,000 to Cal State Hayward Educational Foundation, Hayward, CA. 2 grants: $1,250,000 each to Wayne and Gladys Valley Business and Technology Center (For construction).

$1,750,000 to Kaiser Foundation Research Institute, Center for Genetic Epidemiology, Oakland, CA. For computerized disease registry to be used as basis for genetic research.

$1,500,000 to Childrens Hospital and Research Center at Oakland, Center for Immunobiology and Vaccine Development, Oakland, CA. For renovations and equipment.

$500,000 to Pacific Vascular Research Foundation, San Francisco, CA. For new Pacific Vascular Research Laboratory.

$100,000 to Project SEED (Special Elementary Education for the Disadvantaged), Berkeley, CA. For program in East Bay schools.

$30,000 to Diabetic Youth Foundation, Concord, CA. For Bearskin Meadow Summer Camp and for Camp Arroyo, weekend camp.

1258
Mike and Linda Van Daele Family Foundation ✧
2900 Adams St., Ste. C-25
Riverside, CA 92504

Established in 1998 in CA.
Donors: Mike Van Daele; Linda Van Daele; Mike and Linda Van Daele Family Trust.
Foundation type: Independent foundation.
Financial data (yr. ended 12/31/05): Assets, $3,179,554 (M); gifts received, $4,000,000; expenditures, $2,269,076; qualifying distributions, $2,268,650; giving activities include $2,221,000 for 25 grants (high: $455,000; low: $500).
Purpose and activities: Giving primarily to Christian organizations.
Fields of interest: Theological school/education; Education; Agriculture; Human services; Family services; Christian agencies & churches.
Limitations: Applications not accepted. Giving primarily in CA, with emphasis on Riverside; some funding nationally. No grants to individuals.
Application information: Contributes only to pre-selected organizations.

Officers: Linda Van Daele, Secy.; Mike Van Daele, Mgr.
EIN: 330833774
Selected grants: The following grants were reported in 2005.
$505,000 to World Impact, Los Angeles, CA. 2 grants: $50,000, $455,000
$350,000 to Focus on the Family, Colorado Springs, CO.
$305,000 to Prison Fellowship Ministries, DC.
$25,000 to Bible Study Fellowship, San Antonio, TX.
$25,000 to Rafiki Foundation, San Antonio, TX.
$1,000 to Point Loma Nazarene University, San Diego, CA.
$500 to Amigos de los Ninos, Santa Ana, CA.

1259
Patrick and Robin Van Daele Family Foundation ✧
2900 Adams St., Ste. C-25
Riverside, CA 92504

Established in 2002 in CA.
Donors: Patrick Van Daele; Robin Van Daele.
Foundation type: Independent foundation.
Financial data (yr. ended 12/31/05): Assets, $2,641,676 (M); gifts received, $2,000,000; expenditures, $436,555; qualifying distributions, $433,010; giving activities include $433,010 for 21 grants (high: $100,000; low: $55).
Purpose and activities: Giving primarily for family and social services, and for Christian and Roman Catholic churches, as well as for Christian education.
Fields of interest: Elementary/secondary education; Human services; Family services; Christian agencies & churches; Roman Catholic agencies & churches.
Limitations: Applications not accepted. Giving primarily in CA. No grants to individuals.
Application information: Contributes only to pre-selected organizations.
Officers: Robin Van Daele, Secy.; Patrick Van Daele, Mgr.
EIN: 050544710

1260
van Loben Sels/RembeRock Foundation ✧
(formerly van Loben Sels Foundation)
131 Steuart St., Ste. 301
San Francisco, CA 94105 (415) 512-0500
Contact: Gail Evans, Prog. Admin.
FAX: (415) 371-0227; *E-mail:* info@vlsrr.org; *Tel. for application information:* Gail Evans, Prog. Admin.
Mail applications to Ms. Toni Rembe; *Additional E-mail:* dcorsello@vlsrr.org; *URL:* http://www.vlsrr.org

Incorporated in 1964 in CA.
Donors: Ernst D. van Loben Sels†; Arthur Rock.
Foundation type: Independent foundation.
Financial data (yr. ended 12/31/04): Assets, $40,001,356 (M); gifts received, $2,000; expenditures, $2,747,057; qualifying distributions, $2,595,400; giving activities include $2,259,000 for 232 grants (high: $38,000; low: $2,000).
Purpose and activities: The foundation's goal is to promote social justice and well-being of the residents and communities of northern California, including project and program start-up funding for new ideas that demonstrate the potential for

improvement and enhancement of life in our communities; projects and programs designed to provide fair treatment and equal access to the law for disadvantaged residents and newcomers; projects and programs targeted toward underserved and at-risk populations; and projects and programs that enhance access to services for underserved populations. Funding for health-related issues for underserved populations is limited.
Fields of interest: Health care; Mental health/crisis services, public policy; Mental health/crisis services, hot-lines; Health organizations, equal rights; AIDS; Crime/violence prevention, youth; Crime/violence prevention, gun control; Crime/law enforcement, correctional facilities; Offenders/ex-offenders, rehabilitation; Crime/violence prevention, domestic violence; Legal services; Legal services, public interest law; Youth development; Human services; Children/youth, services; Children, foster care; Family services; Civil rights, public policy; Civil rights, immigrants; Civil rights, minorities; Civil rights, women; Civil rights, gays/lesbians; Civil liberties, due process; Civil rights; Public affairs; Immigrants/refugees.
Type of support: General/operating support; Management development/capacity building; Emergency funds; Program development; Seed money.
Limitations: Giving limited to northern CA. No support for national organizations unless for a specific local project, or to projects requiring medical, scientific, or other technical knowledge for evaluation. No grants to individuals, or for operating budgets of well-established organizations, deficit financing, capital or endowment funds, scholarships, stipends, or fellowships.
Publications: Application guidelines; Annual report; Annual report (including application guidelines); Grants list; Program policy statement.
Application information: See foundation Web site for application requirements and guidelines. Videotapes, audiotapes, CDs, etc., are not accepted unless requested. Certified or signature-required mail is not accepted. Application form required.
   Initial approach: Proposal
   Copies of proposal: 1
   Deadline(s): Rolling
   Board meeting date(s): Every 4 to 6 weeks
   Final notification: In writing
Officers: Toni Rembe, Pres.; Jewelle Taylor Gibbs, Ph.D., V.P.; Edward A. Nathan, M.S.W., V.P.; Richard Odgers, Secy.-Treas.; Dan Corsello, Exec. Dir.
Number of staff: 1 full-time professional; 1 part-time professional.
EIN: 946109309
Selected grants: The following grants were reported in 2003.
$35,000 to Immigrant Legal Resource Center, San Francisco, CA. For projects, Provider Fraud Prevention and Prosecution Project and Family Adjustment Liaison Groups.
$20,000 to Galt Community Concilio, Galt, CA. For Immigration and Self-Help Law Program.
$20,000 to Jewish Family and Childrens Services of the East Bay, Berkeley, CA. For East Bay Bosnian Family Support Project.
$20,000 to Lawyers Committee for Civil Rights Under Law of the San Francisco Bay Area, San Francisco, CA. For Asylum Program.
$15,000 to Dolores Street Community Services, San Francisco, CA. For Dolores Housing Program.
$10,000 to African Immigrant and Refugee Resource Center, San Francisco, CA. For job

placement and supportive services for African refugees.

$10,000 to Caminos Pathways Learning Center, San Francisco, CA. For workforce development program for immigrant women.

$10,000 to Community Legal Services in East Palo Alto, East Palo Alto, CA. For Tenants' Center, which assists low-income individuals with tenants' rights issues.

$10,000 to San Francisco Lesbian, Gay, Bisexual, Transgender Community Center Project, San Francisco, CA. To establish Youth Recreation Space for lesbian, gay, bisexual, and transgender youth aged 18-23.

$10,000 to Senior Medi-Benefits, Berkeley, CA. For Medi-Cal Eligibility and End-of-Life Project.

1261
J. B. and Emily Van Nuys Charities ◇
P.O. Box 2946
Palos Verdes Peninsula, CA   90274
(310) 544-8045
Contact: For mail and grant information: Franklin F. Moulton, Pres.; For telephone inquiries: Diane Wingerning, Grants Coord.

Incorporated in 1957 in CA.
Donors: Emily Van Nuys†; J. Benton Van Nuys†; J. Benton Van Nuys Trust; Emily Van Nuys Char. Rem. Trust.
Foundation type: Independent foundation.
Financial data (yr. ended 12/31/05): Assets, $637,967 (M); gifts received, $849,782; expenditures, $887,229; qualifying distributions, $874,704; giving activities include $759,000 for 68 grants (high: $30,000; low: $5,000).
Purpose and activities: Preference is given to organizations whose activities are directed toward aid for the needy, providing food and shelter to the poor, disaster relief, child welfare and youth programs for the disadvantaged. Primary areas of interest include health agencies, child welfare, the disadvantaged, and issues of homelessness and hunger.
Fields of interest: Hospitals (general); Health care; Health organizations, association; Crime/violence prevention, domestic violence; Crime/violence prevention, child abuse; Human services; Children/ youth, services; Aging, centers/services; Aging; Disabilities, people with; Economically disadvantaged; Homeless.
Type of support: Continuing support; Capital campaigns; Building/renovation; Equipment; Emergency funds; Program development; Curriculum development; Internship funds; Scholarship funds; Technical assistance.
Limitations: Giving primarily in the Los Angeles, CA, area. No support for religious organizations. No grants to individuals, or for research, fundraising events, or special events.
Publications: Application guidelines.
Application information: Application form not required.
  Initial approach: Full proposal
  Copies of proposal: 1
  Deadline(s): None
  Board meeting date(s): Quarterly to award grants (Feb., May, Aug., and Nov.)
  Final notification: 6 to 9 months
Officers and Trustees:* Franklin F. Moulton,* Pres.; John M. Heidt,* V.P.; Lawrence Chaffin, Jr.,* Secy.; William Schulte,* Treas.

Number of staff: 1 part-time professional.
EIN: 956096134
Selected grants: The following grants were reported in 2005.
$15,000 to A Place Called Home, Los Angeles, CA.
$15,000 to Foodbank of Southern California, Long Beach, CA.
$15,000 to Junior Achievement of Southern California, Los Angeles, CA.
$15,000 to Junior Blind of America, Los Angeles, CA.
$15,000 to Los Angeles Regional Foodbank, Los Angeles, CA.
$15,000 to Saint Annes Maternity Home, Los Angeles, CA.
$15,000 to Teach for America, Los Angeles, CA.
$12,500 to Los Angeles Free Clinic, Los Angeles, CA.
$10,000 to Library Foundation of Los Angeles, Los Angeles, CA.
$10,000 to Salvation Army, Redding, CA.

1262
I. N. & Susanna H. Van Nuys Foundation ◇
444 S. Flower St., Ste. 2340
Los Angeles, CA   90071

Established in 1950 in CA.
Foundation type: Independent foundation.
Financial data (yr. ended 5/31/05): Assets, $17,810,756 (M); expenditures, $848,515; qualifying distributions, $783,608; giving activities include $732,400 for 18 grants (high: $390,473; low: $500).
Purpose and activities: Support primarily in those fields favored by the original grantor, including a private hospital, secondary schools and colleges, and generally related activities.
Fields of interest: Museums; Elementary school/ education; Secondary school/education; Higher education; Education; Hospitals (specialty); Children/youth, services.
Limitations: Applications not accepted. Giving primarily in CA, with emphasis on Los Angeles. No grants to individuals.
Application information: Contributes only to pre-selected organizations.
Trustees: George A. Bender; Maribeth Borthwick; Stuart M. Ketchum.
EIN: 956006019
Selected grants: The following grants were reported in 2005.
$390,473 to Good Samaritan Hospital, Los Angeles, CA. For general support.
$78,092 to Wellesley College, Wellesley, MA. For general support.
$46,859 to Childrens Hospital Los Angeles, Los Angeles, CA. For general support.
$39,049 to California Institute of Technology, Pasadena, CA. For general support.
$25,000 to George Washingtons Mount Vernon Estate and Gardens, Mount Vernon, VA. For general support.
$25,000 to Greater Los Angeles Zoo Association, Los Angeles, CA. For general support.
$15,618 to Huntington Library, Art Collections and Botanical Gardens, San Marino, CA. For general support.
$15,000 to Library Foundation of Los Angeles, Los Angeles, CA. For general support.
$15,000 to Music Center of Los Angeles County, Los Angeles, CA. For general support.

$10,000 to Episcopal Home, Alhambra, CA. For general support.

1263
The Raju Vegesna Foundation ◇ ☆
5808 Trowbridge Way
San Jose, CA   95138

Foundation type: Independent foundation.
Financial data (yr. ended 12/31/05): Assets, $10,353,295 (M); expenditures, $435,923; qualifying distributions, $390,000; giving activities include $390,000 for grants.
Fields of interest: Hinduism.
Limitations: Applications not accepted. Giving primarily in Austin, TX. No grants to individuals.
Application information: Contributes only to pre-selected organizations.
Officers and Directors:* Anatoki Raju Vegesna,* Pres.; Bala Vegesna, Secy.; Richard T. McCoy.
EIN: 061694446

1264
Ventura County Community Foundation
1317 Del Norte Rd., Ste. 150
Camarillo, CA   93010   (805) 988-0196
Contact: Hugh J. Ralston, C.E.O.
FAX: (805) 485-5537; E-mail: vccf@vccf.org;
URL: http://www.vccf.org

Incorporated in 1987 in CA.
Foundation type: Community foundation.
Financial data (yr. ended 9/30/04): Assets, $51,198,402 (M); gifts received, $9,592,055; expenditures, $4,824,871; giving activities include $2,696,739 for grants (high: $2,500; low: $250), $239,040 for 268 grants to individuals, and $650,598 for 2 foundation-administered programs.
Purpose and activities: The foundation seeks to enrich and enhance the quality of life in Ventura County and to provide leadership to residents and nonprofit organizations in building an enduring source of funds and strengthening community participation to meet the changing needs and challenges of the community.
Fields of interest: Arts; Higher education; Education; Environment, natural resources; Environment; Health care; Health organizations, association; Disasters, Hurricane Katrina; Youth, services; Family services; Human services; Nonprofit management; Hispanics/Latinos; Women; Economically disadvantaged.
Type of support: General/operating support; Management development/capacity building; Building/renovation; Equipment; Emergency funds; Program development; Conferences/seminars; Seed money; Curriculum development; Scholarship funds; Technical assistance; Program evaluation; Scholarships—to individuals; Matching/challenge support.
Limitations: Giving primarily in Ventura County, CA. No grants for endowments, annual campaigns, budget deficits, or land acquisition; no program-related investments.
Publications: Application guidelines; Annual report (including application guidelines); Financial statement; Informational brochure; Newsletter.
Application information: Number of requested proposal copies may vary from 1 to 12. Visit foundation Web site for application form and

specific guidelines per grant type. Application form required.

> Initial approach: Send letter or telephone foundation to be added on to mailing list for request for proposals (RFP)
> Deadline(s): Varies (as designated by RFP)
> Board meeting date(s): Bimonthly
> Final notification: June for scholarships; for all other applications, as designated by RFP

Officers and Directors: * Mary Schwabauer,* Chair.; Hugh J. Ralston, C.E.O. and Pres.; Donna Logan, V.P., Finance and Admin.; Sally Yount,* Secy.; Ronald L. Hertel, Sr.,* Treas.; Clare M. Brown, Cont.; William A. Bang; Denis Dupuis; William Hart, M.D.; Robert J. Katch; Henry L. "Hank" Lacayo; Wendy Cole Lascher; Terri E. Lisagor; Timothy J. McCallion; M. Carmen Ramirez; Stacy A. Roscoe; Dr. Richard Rush; Scott B. Samsky; A. Charles Schultz; Pierre Y. Tada; Robin Woodworth.
Number of staff: 4 full-time professional; 1 part-time professional; 5 full-time support; 1 part-time support.
EIN: 770165029

1265
Versacare, Inc. ◈
c/o The VersaFund
702 S. Washburn Ave.
Corona, CA 92882-3354
FAX: (951) 736-3005; E-mail: versacare@aol.com;
URL: http://www.versacare.org

Established in 1996 in CA and FL.
Foundation type: Independent foundation.
Financial data (yr. ended 9/30/05): Assets, $22,289,885 (M); expenditures, $1,435,898; qualifying distributions, $1,027,091; giving activities include $922,594 for 31 grants (high: $76,465; low: $1,000).
Purpose and activities: Giving primarily for innovative ministry ideas, especially in the areas of Seventh-day Adventist Christian education, youth ministry and health care.
Fields of interest: Higher education, university; Health care, association; Hospitals (general); Christian agencies & churches.
Type of support: Equipment; Program development; Curriculum development; Scholarship funds; Matching/challenge support.
Limitations: Giving primarily in North America. No grants for debt reduction, or for salaries or general operations; no grants to individuals.
Publications: Application guidelines; Informational brochure.
Application information: Application form required.
> Initial approach: Submit application
> Copies of proposal: 1
> Deadline(s): Dec. 1
> Final notification: Mar. 1

Officers: Charles C. Sandefur, Chair.; Robert E. Coy, Pres.; Calvin J. Hanson, Secy.; Ellen H. Brodersen, Treas.
Directors: George W. Brown; Deborah Brill; Robert D. Macomber; Ron Wisbey; Derrill E. Yaeger.
EIN: 330052434

1266
The David Vickter Foundation ◈ ☆
865 Via Abajo
Santa Barbara, CA 93110

Established in 1983 in CA.
Donor: David Vickter.
Foundation type: Independent foundation.
Financial data (yr. ended 10/31/05): Assets, $8,421,317 (M); gifts received, $4,670,104; expenditures, $525,914; qualifying distributions, $400,000; giving activities include $400,000 for 15 grants (high: $200,000; low: $1,000).
Fields of interest: Hospitals (general); Arthritis research; Human services; Children/youth, services; Federated giving programs; General charitable giving.
Limitations: Applications not accepted. Giving primarily in CA. No grants to individuals.
Application information: Contributes only to pre-selected organizations.
Officers: Lenore Jacoby, Pres.; Frances Feinman, Secy.
EIN: 953883733
Selected grants: The following grants were reported in 2004.
$7,500 to Direct Relief International, Santa Barbara, CA.
$7,500 to Lowell Alumni Association, San Francisco, CA.
$7,500 to Make-A-Wish Foundation, Mill Valley, CA.
$7,500 to United Pegasus Foundation, El Monte, CA.
$7,500 to Wheels for Humanity, North Hollywood, CA.

1267
Vodafone-US Foundation ◈
(formerly AirTouch Communications Foundation)
2999 Oak Rd., 9th Fl.
Walnut Creek, CA 94597 (925) 210-2777
Contact: June Sugiyama, Grants Mgr.

Established in 1993 as a spin-off of Pacific Telesis Foundation; current name adopted in Jan. 2000.
Donors: AirTouch Communications, Inc.; Vodafone Americas Inc.
Foundation type: Company-sponsored foundation.
Financial data (yr. ended 12/31/04): Assets, $28,269,244 (M); expenditures, $2,300,968; qualifying distributions, $2,250,520; giving activities include $2,077,850 for 64 grants (high: $25,000; low: $1,500).
Purpose and activities: The foundation supports organizations involved with arts and culture, children, families, and citizen participation.
Fields of interest: Arts; Children/youth, services; Family services; Public affairs, citizen participation.
Type of support: General/operating support; Continuing support; Program development.
Limitations: Giving primarily in CA, with emphasis on the San Francisco Bay Area. No support for educational institutions or political organizations or religious organizations not of direct benefit to the entire community, fraternal, veterans', or labor organizations not of direct benefit to the entire community, individual K-12 schools or school districts, or medical clinics or pass-through organizations. No grants to individuals, or for capital campaigns or endowments, sports programs, fundraising events, cause-related marketing, membership emergency appeals, or medical research.
Publications: Informational brochure (including application guidelines).
Application information: Application form not required.
> Initial approach: Proposal

> Copies of proposal: 1
> Board meeting date(s): 2 times per year
> Final notification: Within 60 days

Officers and Directors: * Mark Hickey, Pres.; Dennis Daugherty, Secy.; Jack Lester, Treas.; Patricia Anglin; Sam Ginn; Tomas Isaksson; William Keever; Terry Kramer; Arun Sarin.
Number of staff: 1 part-time professional; 1 full-time support.
EIN: 680315367
Selected grants: The following grants were reported in 2003.
$371,500 to University of Illinois at Urbana-Champaign, College of Engineering, Urbana, IL. For Vodafone Fellows Initiative.
$100,000 to Yosemite Foundation, San Francisco, CA. For Yosemite Falls Campaign.
$25,000 to Berkeley Repertory Theater, Berkeley, CA. For production support of Continental Divide.
$25,000 to Boy Scouts of America, San Francisco Bay Area Council, San Francisco, CA. For capital campaign.
$10,000 to American Red Cross, San Francisco, CA. For annual Bay Area Preparedness training.
$10,000 to Asian Art Museum of San Francisco, San Francisco, CA. For production of interactive videos.
$10,000 to Diablo Regional Arts Association, Walnut Creek, CA. For Center Repertory's Arts X Change Program.
$10,000 to Economic Security 2000, DC. For general operating support.
$10,000 to Habitat for Humanity, Mount Diablo, Concord, CA. For building support for Habitat homes in Oakley.
$10,000 to Napa Valley Museum, Yountville, CA. For general operating support.

1268
Myatt W. Volentine Foundation ◈
19 W. Carrillo St.
Santa Barbara, CA 93101 (805) 962-5719
Contact: Diane K. Hayes, Pres.

Established in 1988 in CA.
Donors: Myatt W. Volentine; Mary G. Volentine.
Foundation type: Independent foundation.
Financial data (yr. ended 12/31/04): Assets, $27,897,844 (M); gifts received, $3,504,870; expenditures, $858,565; qualifying distributions, $549,766; giving activities include $459,815 for 28 grants (high: $61,595; low: $70).
Purpose and activities: Giving for community health services, youth services, and for education.
Fields of interest: Higher education; Medical care, in-patient care; Athletics/sports, water sports; Girls clubs; Human services.
Limitations: Giving limited to Santa Barbara, CA, Loveland, CO and McCook, NE. No grants to individuals.
Application information: Application form required.
> Initial approach: Letter
> Deadline(s): Mar. 31

Officers: Diane K. Hayes, Pres.; John Mackall, V.P.; Claudette Sabiron, Secy.; Richard A. Nightingale, C.F.O.
Director: Nancy K. Popenhagen.
EIN: 770203235

1269
Von der Ahe Foundation
4605 Lankershim Blvd., Ste. 707
North Hollywood, CA 91602
Contact: Thomas Von der Ahe, V.P.
FAX: (818) 980-8721;
E-mail: t.vonderahe@vdaproperty.com

Incorporated in 1951 in CA.
Donors: Members of the Von der Ahe family; Von's Grocery Co.
Foundation type: Independent foundation.
Financial data (yr. ended 12/31/05): Assets, $7,030,045 (M); expenditures, $449,687; qualifying distributions, $379,288; giving activities include $372,150 for 37 grants (high: $50,000; low: $250).
Purpose and activities: To promote scientific and charitable causes; emphasis on Roman Catholic religious institutions and health and welfare services; support also for higher and secondary education and a community foundation.
Fields of interest: Arts; Secondary school/education; Higher education; Education; Health care; Alcoholism; Human services; Government/public administration; Roman Catholic agencies & churches.
Type of support: Capital campaigns; Building/renovation; Emergency funds.
Limitations: Applications not accepted. Giving primarily in CA. No grants to individuals.
Application information: Contributes only to pre-selected organizations.
Board meeting date(s): June and Dec.
Officers: Clyde V. Von der Ahe, M.D., Pres.; Thomas R. Von der Ahe, V.P.; Vincent M. Von der Ahe, Secy.; Frederick T. Von der Ahe, Treas.
Number of staff: 1 part-time professional.
EIN: 956051857
Selected grants: The following grants were reported in 2005.
$83,000 to Archdiocese of Los Angeles, Los Angeles, CA.
$50,000 to Loyola Marymount University, Los Angeles, CA.
$25,000 to Mount Saint Marys College, Los Angeles, CA.
$20,000 to Catholic Relief Services, Baltimore, MD.
$20,000 to Little Sisters of the Poor, San Pedro, CA.
$15,000 to Campbell Hall, North Hollywood, CA.
$15,000 to Loyola High School, Los Angeles, CA.
$5,000 to Notre Dame High School, Belmont, CA.
$2,000 to Nazareth House, Los Angeles, CA.
$1,000 to Saint Thomas the Apostle Church, Los Angeles, CA.

1270
The Vons Charitable Foundation ✧
(formerly The Vons Companies Charitable Foundation, Inc.)
c/o Safeway Inc., Tax Dept.
5918 Stoneridge Mall Rd.
Pleasanton, CA 94588-3229
Application address: c/o Sandra Calderon-Lidskin, P.O. Box 513338, Los Angeles, CA 90051-1338, tel.: (626) 821-7291; URL: http://www.vonsfoundation.org

Established in 1995 in CA.
Foundation type: Operating foundation.
Financial data (yr. ended 4/30/06): Assets, $1,195,264 (M); gifts received, $711,028; expenditures, $849,389; qualifying distributions,
$848,884; giving activities include $665,137 for grants.
Purpose and activities: The foundation supports charitable programs that improve the quality of life in the communities where Vons employees live and work, advocating the philanthropic aims of Vons employees.
Fields of interest: Education; Environment, natural resources; Animal welfare; Health care; Health organizations, association; Crime/law enforcement, police agencies; Disasters, preparedness/services; Human services; Youth, services; Aging, centers/services; Community development, government agencies; Disabilities, people with.
Type of support: Building/renovation; Equipment; Emergency funds; Program development; Consulting services; In-kind gifts.
Limitations: Giving limited to Vons service area within southern CA and NV. No support for sporting venues, expos, other foundations, for-profit organizations, chambers of commerce, or any government-funded group. No grants to individuals, or for conferences or symposiums.
Application information: See foundation Web site for application guidelines and downloading of application form. Application form required.
Initial approach: Letter
Copies of proposal: 1
Deadline(s): None
Board meeting date(s): Third Tues. of each month
Final notification: 8-10 weeks
Officers: Deborah Conrad, Pres.; Bob Erickson, V.P.; Carol Egenias, Treas.
Number of staff: 1 part-time support.
EIN: 954523801
Selected grants: The following grants were reported in 2003.
$377,425 to March of Dimes Birth Defects Foundation, Los Angeles, CA.
$50,000 to Public Counsel, Los Angeles, CA.
$31,000 to College Bound-Dollars for Achievers, Cerritos, CA.
$18,392 to Friends of the Family, Van Nuys, CA.
$17,644 to Special Olympics Southern California, Culver City, CA.
$15,000 to Assistance League of Inland North Country, Escondido, CA.
$15,000 to Beyond Shelter, Los Angeles, CA.
$10,000 to AIDS Project Los Angeles (APLA), Los Angeles, CA.
$10,000 to Long Beach Public Library Foundation, Long Beach, CA.
$10,000 to Women of Color Breast Cancer Survivors Support Project, Inglewood, CA.

1271
Clara Edith Vose Foundation ✧
2665 Buss Dr.
Santa Rosa, CA 95407

Established in 1965.
Foundation type: Independent foundation.
Financial data (yr. ended 12/31/04): Assets, $551,667 (M); expenditures, $438,088; qualifying distributions, $393,062; giving activities include $371,000 for 13 grants (high: $62,500; low: $10,000).
Purpose and activities: Giving to Christian organizations.
Fields of interest: Elementary/secondary education; Protestant agencies & churches.
Limitations: Applications not accepted. Giving primarily in CA and IN. No grants to individuals.

Application information: Unsolicited requests for funds not accepted.
Officers and Trustees:* Stephen M. Todd,* Pres.; Nancy Arnold,* 1st V.P.; George Anderson,* Treas.; Patricia Leeder.
EIN: 956125526

1272
Clara Edith Vose Foundation Trust ✧
c/o Rimel & Nichols
2665 Buss Dr.
Santa Rosa, CA 95407

Established in CA.
Foundation type: Independent foundation.
Financial data (yr. ended 12/31/04): Assets, $582,508 (L); expenditures, $451,967; qualifying distributions, $449,995; giving activities include $448,932 for 12 grants (high: $240,644; low: $5,999).
Fields of interest: Christian agencies & churches.
Limitations: Applications not accepted. Giving primarily in Santa Ana, CA. No grants to individuals.
Application information: Contributes only to pre-selected organizations.
Officers and Trustees:* Stephen M. Todd,* Pres.; Nancy Arnold,* 1st V.P.; George Anderson,* Treas.; Patricia Leeder.
EIN: 237080955

1273
The W.J. Foundation ✧ ☆
4286 Suison Valley Rd.
Fairfield, CA 94535

Established in 1997 in CA.
Donor: Willis J. Johnson.
Foundation type: Independent foundation.
Financial data (yr. ended 12/31/05): Assets, $1,428,573 (M); expenditures, $333,861; qualifying distributions, $329,020; giving activities include $329,020 for grants.
Purpose and activities: Giving primarily to Christian churches and organizations.
Fields of interest: Christian agencies & churches.
Limitations: Applications not accepted. No grants to individuals.
Application information: Contributes only to pre-selected organizations.
Officer: Willis J. Johnson, Pres.
Director: Reba J. Johnson.
EIN: 953287804

1274
The Wagner Family Foundation, Inc. ✧
11766 Wilshire Blvd., Rm. 900
Los Angeles, CA 90025

Established in 1997 in NY.
Donors: Leon Wagner; Marsha Wagner.
Foundation type: Independent foundation.
Financial data (yr. ended 9/30/05): Assets, $5,026,561 (M); gifts received, $1,211,005; expenditures, $780,429; qualifying distributions, $742,985; giving activities include $730,169 for grants.
Fields of interest: Higher education; Hospitals (general); Health organizations, association; Prostate cancer research; Human services;

Federated giving programs; Jewish federated giving programs; Jewish agencies & temples.
Limitations: Applications not accepted. Giving primarily in CA and NY. No grants to individuals.
Application information: Contributes only to pre-selected organizations.
Officers: Leon Wagner, Pres.; Harry Wagner, V.P.; Marsha Wagner, Secy.
Director: Rubin Wagner.
EIN: 133980685
Selected grants: The following grants were reported in 2004.
$187,150 to UJA-Federation of New York, New York, NY. 3 grants: $12,150, $25,000, $150,000
$82,500 to Harvey School, Katonah, NY. 2 grants: $2,500, $80,000
$75,000 to Pups for Peace, Seattle, WA. 2 grants: $50,000, $25,000
$60,000 to University of Chicago, Chicago, IL.
$25,000 to American Friends of Shalva, New York, NY.
$6,000 to Harlem Childrens Zone, New York, NY.

1275
Waitt Family Foundation ▼ ✧
P.O. Box 1948
La Jolla, CA 92038-1948 (858) 551-4839
Contact: Al Panico, C.A.O. and Dir., Grants
FAX: (858) 551-6871;
E-mail: grants@waittfoundation.org; Application address: c/o Siouxland Chapter, P.O. Box 1397, North Sioux City, SD 57049, tel.: (605) 232-9929; FAX: (605) 232-9486; URL: http://www.waittfoundation.org/

Established in 1993 in SD.
Donors: Theodore W. Waitt; Joan Peschel Waitt.
Foundation type: Independent foundation.
Financial data (yr. ended 12/31/04): Assets, $170,479,058 (M); gifts received, $100,130; expenditures, $8,605,953; qualifying distributions, $7,625,802; giving activities include $6,331,986 for 147 grants (high: $1,500,000; low: $80; average: $5,000–$100,000), $310,652 for 332 grants to individuals (high: $5,000; low: $110; average: $250–$1,250), $28,456 for 11 employee matching gifts, $16,751 for 8 in-kind gifts, and $63,982 for foundation-administered programs.
Purpose and activities: The foundation believes that every child and family should have the opportunity to choose their own futures and succeed in fulfilling their dreams. To that end, the foundation seeks to: Empower Communities - enhance the capacity of communities to promote positive social change supportive of families; Leverage Partnerships - partner with projects that show promise and are widely applicable; and Communicate Ideas - help in the dissemination of new ideas to communities and families that will help them plan in the present for a better future.
Fields of interest: Education; Crime/violence prevention, domestic violence; Community development.
Type of support: In-kind gifts; General/operating support; Employee matching gifts; Scholarships—to individuals.
Limitations: Giving primarily in the tri-state Siouxland region of IA, NE, and SD, and San Diego, CA.
Application information: Guidelines can be found on the foundation's Web site. Application form required.
Initial approach: Letter of interest

Deadline(s): Check with foundation
Board meeting date(s): Varies
Officers and Directors:* John D. Heubusch,* Pres.; Joan Peschel Waitt,* V.P.; Stacey Greer, Secy.; Rose Ann Ignell, Treas.; Al Panico, C.A.O. and Dir., Grants; Cindy Waitt; Theodore W. Waitt.
EIN: 460428166
Selected grants: The following grants were reported in 2003.
$525,000 to San Diego Community Foundation, San Diego, CA. For digital divide fund.
$500,000 to All Hallows Academy, La Jolla, CA. For Master Building Plan.
$350,000 to Baystate Medical Center, Springfield, MA. For community building program.
$350,000 to Dudley Street Neighborhood Initiative, Roxbury, MA. 2 grants: $175,000 each (For community building program).
$300,000 to Massachusetts Institute of Technology, Cambridge, MA. For CRCP Community Innovation Lab.
$265,000 to Institute for Community Peace, DC. 2 grants: $90,000 (For violence prevention program), $175,000 (For violence prevention program).
$150,000 to One Economy Corporation, DC. For PC Purchase Program.
$90,000 to Metropolitan Area Advisory Committee on Anti-Poverty of San Diego County, National City, CA. For community building partnership.

1276
Wallis Foundation ▼ ✧
1880 Century Park E., Ste. 950
Los Angeles, CA 90067 (310) 286-9777

Established in 1957 in CA.
Donor: Hal B. Wallis†.
Foundation type: Independent foundation.
Financial data (yr. ended 6/30/05): Assets, $41,926,231 (M); expenditures, $4,836,359; qualifying distributions, $4,550,621; giving activities include $4,436,200 for 197 grants (high: $200,000; low: $1,000; average: $5,000–$50,000).
Purpose and activities: Giving primarily to aid and promote charitable, educational, scientific and religious projects.
Fields of interest: Arts; Environment, natural resources; Environment; Health care; Human services; Children/youth, services; Religious federated giving programs; Science.
Limitations: Applications not accepted. Giving primarily in CA. No grants to individuals.
Application information: Contributes only to pre-selected organizations.
Officers and Directors:* Brent Wallis,* Pres.; Beth Wallis,* V.P.; Jeffrey Glassman,* Secy.; Michael Sack,* C.F.O.; Jack Baker.
EIN: 956027469
Selected grants: The following grants were reported in 2005.
$200,000 to Nature Conservancy, Brunswick, ME.
$150,000 to Cancer Center of Santa Barbara, Santa Barbara, CA.
$145,000 to Humane Society of the United States, DC.
$75,000 to Loyola Marymount University, Los Angeles, CA.
$75,000 to Philharmonia Baroque Orchestra, San Francisco, CA.
$50,000 to Desert AIDS Project, Palm Springs, CA.

$30,000 to Wildlife Conservation Society, Bronx, NY.
$20,000 to Pacific Chamber Symphony, San Leandro, CA.
$20,000 to Santa Barbara ChannelKeeper, Santa Barbara, CA.
$12,500 to Marymount High School, Los Angeles, CA.

1277
Waltmar Foundation ✧
c/o Larry Beltramo
20 Corporate Park, Ste. 160
Irvine, CA 92606

Established in 1980 in CA.
Donors: Don W. Schmid; Richard R. Schmid; Walter R. Schmid†.
Foundation type: Independent foundation.
Financial data (yr. ended 12/31/05): Assets, $7,942,779 (M); expenditures, $471,779; qualifying distributions, $380,000; giving activities include $380,000 for 18 grants (high: $50,000; low: $5,000).
Purpose and activities: Giving primarily for higher education, youth services and human services.
Fields of interest: Higher education; Education; Health care; Cancer research; Boys & girls clubs; Boy scouts; Human services; Salvation Army; Children/youth, services; Children, services; Family services, domestic violence.
Type of support: Capital campaigns; Building/renovation; Program development; Scholarship funds; Research.
Limitations: Applications not accepted. Giving primarily in Orange County, CA. No grants to individuals.
Application information: Contributes only to pre-selected organizations.
Officers: Don W. Schmid, Pres.; Richard R. Schmid, Secy.; Larry Beltramo, Treas.
Directors: Shauna Farley; David W. Schmid.
EIN: 952371506

1278
Ward Family Foundation ✧
P.O. Box 917
Sunset Beach, CA 90742-0917

Established in 1998 in CA.
Donors: Catherine Ward; George Ward.
Foundation type: Independent foundation.
Financial data (yr. ended 12/31/05): Assets, $1,575,911 (M); gifts received, $394,644; expenditures, $752,503; qualifying distributions, $750,100; giving activities include $750,100 for 15 grants (high: $500,000; low: $5,000).
Fields of interest: Secondary school/education.
Limitations: Applications not accepted. Giving primarily in Santa Ana, CA. No grants to individuals.
Application information: Contributes only to pre-selected organizations.
Officers: Catherine Ward, Pres.; George Ward, V.P.; Katherine Watt, Secy.; Brenna Ward, Treas.
EIN: 954659533

1279
Warren Family Foundation ✧
P.O. Box 915
Rancho Santa Fe, CA 92067-0915
(858) 756-3711
Contact: Tracy W. St. Amour, Dir.

Established in 1977 in CA.
Donors: Frank R. Warren; Joanne C. Warren.
Foundation type: Independent foundation.
Financial data (yr. ended 6/30/05): Assets,
$179,086 (M); gifts received, $550,000;
expenditures, $475,071; qualifying distributions,
$475,055; giving activities include $475,020 for 37
grants (high: $251,000; low: $100).
Purpose and activities: Giving primarily to children's
hospitals, and to a center for substance abuse
treatment; funding also for the arts, education,
human services and federated giving programs.
Fields of interest: Arts; Higher education;
Education; Hospitals (specialty); Substance abuse,
services; Human services; Children/youth, services;
Federated giving programs.
Type of support: General/operating support;
Building/renovation; Research.
Limitations: Giving primarily in San Diego County,
CA, with emphasis on San Diego, CA. No grants to
individuals.
Application information:
Initial approach: Letter
Deadline(s): None
Officer: Joanne C. Warren, Pres.
Directors: Richard K. Colbourne; Tracy W. St.
Amour; Frank R. Warren.
EIN: 953201177

1280
Warsh-Mott Legacy
469 Bohemian Hwy.
Freestone, CA 95472-9579 (707) 874-2942
Contact: Roxanne Turnage, Exec. Dir.
FAX: (707) 874-1734; E-mail: inquiries@csfund.org;
URL: http://www.csfund.org

Established in 1985 in CA.
Donors: Maryanne Mott; Herman E. Warsh†.
Foundation type: Independent foundation.
Financial data (yr. ended 9/30/05): Assets,
$22,304,329 (M); gifts received, $535,000;
expenditures, $739,660; qualifying distributions,
$720,071; giving activities include $631,657 for 15
grants (high: $100,000; low: $15,657).
Purpose and activities: Funding in the areas of
biotechnology, economic globalization, food
sovereignty (seed saving, soil building, and
protecting pollinators), and civil liberties.
Type of support: General/operating support;
Continuing support; Conferences/seminars;
Publication; Research; Technical assistance;
Matching/challenge support.
Limitations: Giving on a national basis. No grants
for endowments, capital funds, video or film
production, or emergency requests.
Publications: Application guidelines.
Application information: Application form not
required.
Initial approach: Letter of inquiry preferred over
fax or E-mail
Copies of proposal: 1
Deadline(s): None
Board meeting date(s): May and Nov.
Officers and Board Members:* Michael Warsh,*
Pres.; Marise Meynet Stewart,* V.P.; Maryanne

Mott,* C.F.O.; Roxanne Turnage, Exec. Dir.; Corinne
Meadows Efram; Teresa Robinson.
EIN: 680049658
Selected grants: The following grants were reported
in 2004.
$510,000 to Marin Community Foundation, Novato,
CA.
$90,000 to Funding Exchange, New York, NY.
$88,000 to Tides Center, San Francisco, CA. 2
grants: $13,000, $75,000
$75,000 to Public Citizen Foundation, DC.
$50,000 to Center for Constitutional Rights, New
York, NY.
$50,000 to Political Research Associates,
Somerville, MA.
$40,000 to Center for Environmental Citizenship,
DC.
$35,000 to American Civil Liberties Union
Foundation, New York, NY.
$15,000 to Oregon Environmental Council,
Portland, OR.

1281
Wasserman Foundation ▼ ✧
12100 W. Olympic Blvd., Ste. 400
Los Angeles, CA 90064 (310) 407-0200
FAX: (310) 882-4601; URL: http://
www.wassermanfoundation.org

Incorporated in 1952 in CA.
Donors: Lew R. Wasserman†; Edith B. Wasserman.
Foundation type: Independent foundation.
Financial data (yr. ended 12/31/04): Assets,
$213,191,577 (M); expenditures, $9,204,116;
qualifying distributions, $7,700,066; giving
activities include $7,700,066 for 121 grants (high:
$1,000,000; low: $300; average: $1,000–
$200,000).
Purpose and activities: The mission of the
foundation is to support education, health and
welfare, and Jewish life in order to directly improve
the lives of those who are underserved.
Fields of interest: Performing arts; Higher
education; Hospitals (general); Medical research,
institute; Human services; Jewish federated giving
programs; Public policy, research.
Type of support: Capital campaigns; Endowments;
Scholarship funds; Research; Program-related
investments/loans.
Limitations: Applications not accepted. Giving
primarily in CA. No grants to individuals.
Application information: Contributes only to
pre-selected organizations.
Officers and Directors:* Casey Wasserman,*
C.O.O. and Pres.; Carol A. Leif, V.P.; Lynne
Wasserman, V.P.; Edith B. Wasserman,* Secy. and
C.F.O.
EIN: 956038762
Selected grants: The following grants were reported
in 2004.
$1,000,000 to Birthright Israel Foundation, New
York, NY.
$1,000,000 to Jules and Doris Stein UCLA Support
Group, Beverly Hills, CA.
$1,000,000 to University of California, Jules Stein
Eye Institute, Los Angeles, CA.
$475,000 to Wasserman Institute for Urban School
Leadership.
$406,500 to Motion Picture and Television Fund,
Woodland Hills, CA.
$400,000 to Boston 2004, Boston, MA.

$250,000 to Hebrew Union College-Jewish Institute
of Religion, Skirball Cultural Center, Los Angeles,
CA.
$100,000 to Brentwood School, Los Angeles, CA.
$30,000 to V Foundation for Cancer Research, Cary,
NC.
$25,000 to Leaders Project, DC.

1282
Waterford Foundation ✧
1396 W. Herndon, Ste. 101
Fresno, CA 93711 (559) 436-0900
Contact: Dariush Assemi, C.E.O.

Established in 1997 in CA.
Donors: Darius Assemi; Granville Homes, Inc.
Foundation type: Independent foundation.
Financial data (yr. ended 12/31/05): Assets,
$4,775,407 (M); gifts received, $1,060,050;
expenditures, $1,020,813; qualifying distributions,
$2,216,372; giving activities include $984,800 for
grants, and $24,350 for grants to individuals.
Purpose and activities: Giving primarily to Islamic
organizations and mosques; some funding also for
a Christian church.
Fields of interest: Human services; Christian
agencies & churches; Islam.
Limitations: Giving primarily in Fresno, CA.
Application information:
Initial approach: Letter
Deadline(s): None
Officers: Darius Assemi, C.E.O.; Farshid Assemi,
1st V.P.; Farid Assemi, 2nd V.P.
EIN: 770437521

1283
Phyllis C. Wattis Foundation
369 Pine St., Ste. 720
San Francisco, CA 94104 (415) 986-1571
Contact: Carlie Wilmans
FAX: (415) 986-1547;
E-mail: info@wattisfoundation.org; URL: http://
www.wattisfoundation.org

Established in 2003 in CA.
Donor: Phyllis C. Wattis Trust.
Foundation type: Independent foundation.
Financial data (yr. ended 12/31/05): Assets,
$20,820,840 (M); expenditures, $1,102,741;
qualifying distributions, $975,772; giving activities
include $922,500 for 23 grants (high: $75,000;
low: $2,500).
Purpose and activities: Giving to support the arts in
the San Francisco Bay Area, CA.
Fields of interest: Arts.
Type of support: Program development; Internship
funds; Fellowships.
Limitations: Giving primarily in CA. No grants to
individuals, or for capital campaigns, or general
operating support.
Application information: Application guidelines
available on foundation Web site.
Initial approach: Letter of inquiry
Copies of proposal: 1
Deadline(s): Mar. 1 and Sept. 1
Board meeting date(s): Changes annually
Final notification: 2 to 3 weeks for
acknowledgment
Officers and Directors:* Paul L. Wattis III,* Pres.;
Carol W. Casey,* V.P.; Paul L. Wattis, Jr.,* V.P.;
Carlie W. Hazeltine,* Secy.-Treas.

Number of staff: 1 part-time professional.
EIN: 841624183

1284
Max Webb Foundation ◇
8383 Wilshire Blvd., Ste. 740
Beverly Hills, CA 90211

Incorporated in 1961 in CA.
Donor: Max Webb.
Foundation type: Independent foundation.
Financial data (yr. ended 11/30/05): Assets, $18,858,456 (M); gifts received, $800,000; expenditures, $862,034; qualifying distributions, $731,947; giving activities include $731,947 for grants.
Purpose and activities: Giving primarily to Jewish organizations and education.
Fields of interest: Elementary/secondary education; Higher education; Health organizations, association; Human services; Jewish federated giving programs; Jewish agencies & temples.
Limitations: Applications not accepted. Giving primarily in Beverly Hills and Los Angeles, CA, and New York, NY. No grants to individuals.
Application information: Contributes only to pre-selected organizations.
Officers: Max Webb, Pres.; Rose Webb Roven, V.P.
EIN: 956052391

1285
The Webb Foundation ◇
(formerly The Webb-Berger Foundation)
P.O. Box 13390
Palm Desert, CA 92255-3390

Established in 1992 in CA.
Donor: H.N. and Frances C. Berger Foundation.
Foundation type: Independent foundation.
Financial data (yr. ended 12/31/05): Assets, $25,598,153 (M); expenditures, $1,390,442; qualifying distributions, $1,277,734; giving activities include $785,597 for 70 grants (high: $125,000; low: $500), and $242 for 1 in-kind gift.
Fields of interest: Arts education; Visual arts; Higher education; Education; Hospitals (general); Human services; Youth, services; Protestant agencies & churches.
Type of support: Equipment; Research.
Limitations: Applications not accepted. Giving primarily in CA, with emphasis on southern CA. No grants to individuals.
Application information: Contributes only to pre-selected organizations.
Trustee: Lewis Webb, Jr.
EIN: 954320582
Selected grants: The following grants were reported in 2003.
$125,000 to Childrens Hospital of Los Angeles Foundation, Los Angeles, CA. For basic and clinical research in treatment and cure of Cystic Fibrosis patients.
$44,069 to California State University at San Bernardino Foundation, San Bernardino, CA. For Palm Desert Campus Computer Networking Advancement Study and Training.
$33,000 to Palm Springs Air Museum, Palm Springs, CA. For endowment program.
$25,000 to Fidelity Investments Charitable Gift Fund, Boston, MA. For suspended distribution fund.

$25,000 to I Have A Dream Foundation, Los Angeles, CA. For challenge grant to expand program to adopt more students into program.
$16,395 to Desert Samaritans for the Elderly, Palm Desert, CA. For Chrysler Town and Country Lxi minivan.
$15,425 to College of the Desert Foundation, Palm Desert, CA. For computer and training equipment to be used for Public Safety Academy.
$10,000 to Los Angeles County Office of Education, Downey, CA. For computer equipment to be used by students with developmental delays.
$10,000 to Mesa State College Foundation, Grand Junction, CO. For equipment and supplies to be used by students in Environmental Science and Technology program.
$10,000 to Mount San Antonio College, Walnut, CA. For musical instruments and supplies to be used by Mount San Antonio College Wind Ensemble.

1286
Helen and Will Webster Foundation ◇ ☆
1388 Crest Dr.
Altadena, CA 91001

Established in 1997 in CA.
Foundation type: Independent foundation.
Financial data (yr. ended 12/31/05): Assets, $4,655,545 (M); expenditures, $706,628; qualifying distributions, $649,242; giving activities include $649,242 for grants.
Fields of interest: Performing arts, ballet; Performing arts, opera; Performing arts, music (choral); Arts; Environment, natural resources; Jewish federated giving programs.
Limitations: Applications not accepted. No grants to individuals.
Application information: Contributes only to pre-selected organizations.
Officers and Directors:* Wilton Webster, Jr.,* Pres.; Helen Webster,* V.P.; Alec J. Webster,* Secy.; Richard B. Webster*.
EIN: 954624483
Selected grants: The following grants were reported in 2005.
$12,000 to Second Harvest Food Bank, San Carlos, CA.
$10,000 to Homeless Garden Project, Santa Cruz, CA.
$10,000 to Soquel High School, Soquel, CA.
$5,000 to Scripps Home, Altadena, CA.
$3,000 to K U S P Public Radio, Santa Cruz, CA.

1287
The Joe Weider Foundation ◇
21300 Erwin St.
Woodland Hills, CA 91367

Established in 1993 in CA.
Foundation type: Independent foundation.
Financial data (yr. ended 11/30/05): Assets, $1,731,068 (M); expenditures, $840,570; qualifying distributions, $838,030; giving activities include $815,675 for grants.
Purpose and activities: Giving primarily to education and Jewish organizations.
Fields of interest: Education; Youth, services; Jewish agencies & temples.
International interests: Canada.

Limitations: Applications not accepted. Giving primarily in CA and NY; some giving also in Canada. No grants to individuals.
Application information: Contributes only to pre-selected organizations.
Officers: Joe Weider, C.E.O.; Sidney Machtinger, Secy.; Eric Weider, C.F.O.
EIN: 954349698
Selected grants: The following grants were reported in 2004.
$265,000 to University of Texas Foundation, Austin, TX.
$150,000 to American Friends of Aish Hatorah, Los Angeles, CA.
$100,000 to University of Western Ontario, London, Canada. .
$1,000 to Beth Jacob Congregation, Beverly Hills, CA.
$1,000 to Etz Jacob Hebrew Academy, Los Angeles, CA.
$1,000 to Young Israel of Century City, Los Angeles, CA.

1288
Weingart Foundation ▼
1055 W. 7th St., Ste. 3050
Los Angeles, CA 90017-2305 (213) 688-7799
Contact: Fred J. Ali, C.E.O. and Pres.
FAX: (213) 688-1515; E-mail: info@weingartfnd.org;
URL: http://www.weingartfnd.org

Incorporated in 1951 in CA.
Donors: Ben Weingart†; Stella Weingart†.
Foundation type: Independent foundation.
Financial data (yr. ended 6/30/06): Assets, $839,604,507 (M); expenditures, $50,625,991; qualifying distributions, $40,561,794; giving activities include $40,561,794 for grants.
Purpose and activities: Support for community and social services, education, health care with strong emphasis on programs for children and youth.
Fields of interest: Education, early childhood education; Child development, education; Elementary school/education; Secondary school/education; Higher education; Adult education—literacy, basic skills & GED; Education, reading; Education; Hospitals (general); Medical care, rehabilitation; Nursing care; Health care; Substance abuse, services; AIDS; Crime/violence prevention, youth; Recreation; Youth development, services; Human services; Children/youth, services; Child development, services; Family services; Residential/custodial care, hospices; Minorities/immigrants, centers/services; Homeless, human services; Community development; Leadership development; Disabilities, people with; Minorities; Economically disadvantaged; Homeless.
Type of support: Management development/capacity building; Capital campaigns; Building/renovation; Equipment; Program development; Seed money; Scholarship funds; Employee matching gifts; Matching/challenge support.
Limitations: Giving limited to 7 southern CA counties; Los Angeles, Kern, Orange, Santa Barbara, Riverside, San Bernadino, and Ventura. No support for environmental or religious programs, political refugee or international concerns, federated fundraising groups, or national organizations that do not have chapters operating in Southern California. No grants to individuals, or for endowment funds, normal operating expenses, annual campaigns, emergency funds, deficit financing, fellowships, seminars, conferences,

publications, workshops, travel, surveys, films, medical research, or publishing activities.

Publications: Application guidelines; Annual report (including application guidelines); Grants list; Newsletter.

Application information: The foundation does not accept "test letters" by fax or E-mail. Application form required.

   Initial approach: Brief "test letter" (3 copies)

   Copies of proposal: 20

   Deadline(s): None

   Board meeting date(s): Bimonthly, except July and Aug.

   Final notification: 3 to 4 months

Officers and Directors:* William D. Schulte,* Chair.; Steven D. Broidy, Chair., Exec. Comm.; Fred J. Ali, C.E.O. and Pres.; Laurence A. Wolfe, V.P., Admin. and Real Estate, and Corp. Secy.; Deborah M. Ives, V.P. and Treas.; Andrew E. Bogen; Murray L. Galinson; Monica Lozano; John W. Mack; Steven L. Soboroff.

Number of staff: 7 full-time professional; 4 full-time support.

EIN: 956054814

Selected grants: The following grants were reported in 2005.

$1,160,210 to JWCH Institute, Los Angeles, CA. For Recuperative Care project and Skid Row Homeless Healthcare Initiative, payable over 2 years.

$1,000,000 to White Memorial Medical Center Charitable Foundation, Los Angeles, CA. For reconstruction of buildings to meet State earthquake safety standards.

$900,000 to Painted Turtle Gang Camp Foundation, Santa Monica, CA. For multi-year organizational capacity building challenge grant, payable over 3 years.

$750,000 to Catholic Charities of the Archdiocese of Los Angeles, Los Angeles, CA. For construction of third phase of Women's Village at Good Shepherd Center for Homeless Women.

$750,000 to Henry Mayo Newhall Memorial Health Foundation, Valencia, CA. For construction of new emergency and trauma center.

$750,000 to Hillsides, Pasadena, CA. For purchase, renovation, and start-up of transitional housing program for emancipated youth, payable over 2 years.

$750,000 to New Visions Foundation, Santa Monica, CA. For development of Herb Alpert Educational Village, payable over 1.50 years.

$750,000 to Pueblo Nuevo Development, Los Angeles, CA. For construction of new charter high school.

$650,000 to Meet Each Need with Dignity (MEND), Pacoima, CA. For construction of new facility.

$500,000 to Arroyo Vista Family Health Foundation, Los Angeles, CA. For purchase, renovation and outfitting of community clinic health center.

1289
Frederick R. Weisman Philanthropic Foundation ◇

275 N. Carolwood Dr.
Los Angeles, CA 90077

Established in 1993 in CA and DE.

Donor: Frederick R. Weisman Trust of 1991.

Foundation type: Independent foundation.

Financial data (yr. ended 12/31/04): Assets, $16,243,082 (M); gifts received, $21,990; expenditures, $1,188,140; qualifying distributions,

$1,009,743; giving activities include $690,504 for 33 grants (high: $70,000; low: $3,000).

Purpose and activities: Giving primarily for a Holocaust museum, as well as for a Jewish temple, and higher education.

Fields of interest: Museums (history); Higher education; Health care, clinics/centers; Jewish agencies & temples.

Limitations: Applications not accepted. Giving primarily in Los Angeles, CA. No grants to individuals.

Application information: Contributes only to pre-selected organizations.

Officers and Directors:* Billie Milam Weisman,* Pres.; Ellen Morehead, Secy.; Steven L. Arnold, Treas.; Sidney J. Machtinger; Frederick M. Nicholas.

EIN: 954442308

1290
Mandell Weiss Charitable Trust ◇

P.O. Box 221071
San Diego, CA 92192-1071 (858) 551-2316
Contact: Joseph Satz, Tr.

Established in 1994 in CA.

Foundation type: Independent foundation.

Financial data (yr. ended 12/31/05): Assets, $10,430,282 (M); expenditures, $598,937; qualifying distributions, $491,015; giving activities include $481,000 for 34 grants (high: $50,000; low: $1,000).

Fields of interest: Museums; Performing arts, dance; Performing arts, ballet; Performing arts, theater; Performing arts, orchestra (symphony); Performing arts, opera; Arts; Zoos/zoological societies; Hospitals (general); Children/youth, services.

Limitations: Giving primarily in San Diego, CA. No grants to individuals.

Application information:

   Initial approach: Letter

   Deadline(s): None

Trustees: George Jezek; Joseph Satz.

EIN: 336145298

1291
David and Sylvia Weisz Family Philanthropic Fund ◇

1901 Ave. of the Stars, Ste. 610
Los Angeles, CA 90067-6001 (310) 284-8856

Established in 2001 in CA.

Donor: Sylvia Weisz.

Foundation type: Independent foundation.

Financial data (yr. ended 12/31/05): Assets, $14,258,564 (M); expenditures, $1,122,193; qualifying distributions, $796,730; giving activities include $598,416 for 82 grants (high: $135,000; low: $250).

Fields of interest: Arts; Education; Animal welfare; Human services; Jewish agencies & temples.

Application information: Application form not required.

   Initial approach: Letter

   Deadline(s): None

Officers: Sylvia Weisz, Chair. and Pres.; Jay H. Grodin, V.P. and Treas.; Judith Carroll, V.P.; Catherine Ireland, V.P.; Carey Pearlman, Secy.

Directors: Jennifer Caroll; John Caroll.

EIN: 912172529

1292
WellPoint Foundation ◇

1 WellPoint Way
Thousand Oaks, CA 91362
URL: http://www.wellpoint.com/commitments/charitable_foundations.asp

Established in 2000 in CA.

Donor: WellPoint Health Networks Inc.

Foundation type: Company-sponsored foundation.

Financial data (yr. ended 12/31/05): Assets, $115,282,733 (M); expenditures $20,051,892; qualifying distributions, $19,886,452; giving activities include $17,985,289 for grants.

Purpose and activities: The foundation supports organizations involved with arts and culture, higher education, health, youth development, human services, and public policy. Special emphasis is directed toward programs designed to improve accessibility and affordability of health care and coverage; improve quality of care; support the development of health-related public policy; and help establish best practices in medicine and business management for the health care industry.

Fields of interest: Arts; Higher education; Health care, public policy; Health care, equal rights; Health care, insurance; Health care, cost containment; Health care; Youth development; Human services; Federated giving programs.

Type of support: General/operating support; Equipment; Program development; Scholarship funds; Research; Employee volunteer services; Sponsorships; Employee matching gifts; Scholarships—to individuals.

Limitations: Applications not accepted. Giving on a national basis.

Application information: Contributes only to pre-selected organizations.

Officers and Directors:* Leonard Schaeffer,* Chair.; Caroline Matthews, Pres.; Nancy Purcell, V.P. and Secy.; R. David Kretschmer, V.P. and Treas.; Angela Braly, Secy.; Callen M. Lockett,* Exec. Dir.; David C. Colby; Larry Glasscock.

EIN: 770560867

1293
Wells Family Charitable Foundation ◇

450 Newport Ctr. Dr., Ste. 450
Newport Beach, CA 92660
Contact: Paul C. Heeschen, Secy.

Established in 1985 in CA.

Donors: Frank G. Wells†; Luanne C. Wells.

Foundation type: Independent foundation.

Financial data (yr. ended 12/31/04): Assets, $2,671,380 (M); expenditures, $607,935; qualifying distributions, $576,609; giving activities include $576,609 for 14 grants (high: $280,859; low: $1,000).

Purpose and activities: Giving primarily for the arts and education.

Fields of interest: Arts; Higher education; Health organizations, association; Human services.

Limitations: Applications not accepted. Giving primarily in CA. No grants to individuals.

Application information: Contributes only to pre-selected organizations. Unsolicited requests for funds not accepted.

Officers: Luanne C. Wells, Pres.; Paul C. Heeschen, Secy.

EIN: 953982216

Selected grants: The following grants were reported in 2003.

$200,000 to UCLA Foundation, Law Clinic, Los Angeles, CA.

$51,000 to Stanford University, Stanford, CA.

$25,000 to Beverly Hills Cultural Center Foundation, Beverly Hills, CA.

$25,000 to Music Center of Los Angeles County, Los Angeles, CA.

$5,000 to Los Angeles County Museum of Art, Los Angeles, CA.

$5,000 to University of Southern California, School of Theater, Los Angeles, CA.

$3,000 to Geffen Playhouse, Los Angeles, CA.

$2,500 to Shakespeare Festival of Los Angeles, Los Angeles, CA.

$1,500 to Library Foundation of Los Angeles, Los Angeles, CA.

$1,000 to Henry Mancini Institute, Culver City, CA.

1294

The Wells Fargo Foundation ▼ ◇

(formerly Norwest Foundation)
550 California St., 7th Fl.
San Francisco, CA   94104   (415) 396-5947
Contact: Timothy G. Hanlon, Pres.
Additional address: 333 S. Grand Ave., E2064-200, Los Angeles, CA 90071, tel.: (888) 886-1785; Application address for Wells Fargo Housing Foundation: Kimberly Jackson, Exec. Dir., Wells Fargo Housing Fdn., MAC N9305-192, 90 S. 7th St., Minneapolis, MN 55479, tel.: (612) 667-2146; URL: http://www.wellsfargo.com/donations

Established in 1979 in MN.

Donors: Norwest Corp.; Wells Fargo & Co.; Norwest Ltd.

Foundation type: Company-sponsored foundation.

Financial data (yr. ended 12/31/05): Assets, $554,108,137 (M); gifts received, $24,971,826; expenditures, $66,401,382; qualifying distributions, $65,007,124; giving activities include $58,699,678 for 10,978 grants (high: $500,000; low: $25), and $6,307,446 for employee matching gifts.

Purpose and activities: The foundation supports organizations involved with job creation and job training, housing, human services, and economic development.

Fields of interest: Elementary/secondary education; Education; Employment, services; Housing/shelter; Human services; Economic development; Federated giving programs.

Type of support: General/operating support; Continuing support; Annual campaigns; Program development; Employee matching gifts.

Limitations: Giving primarily in areas of company operations; giving on a national basis for the Wells Fargo Housing Foundation. No support for religious organizations not of direct benefit to the entire community or fraternal organizations. No grants to individuals, or for conferences, tickets, or travel; no loans.

Publications: Application guidelines; Corporate giving report.

Application information:
Initial approach: 2 copies of proposal to application address for Wells Fargo Housing Foundation
Deadline(s): Feb. 1, May 1, Aug. 1, and Nov. 1 for Wells Fargo Housing Foundation
Final notification: 3 months for Wells Fargo Housing Foundation

Officers and Directors:* Timothy G. Hanlon,* Pres.; Richard D. Levy, Sr. V.P. and Treas.; Timothy Chin,

V.P.; James A. Horton, V.P.; Brenda E. Magnuson, V.P.; Mary E. Schaffner, Secy.; Richard M. Kovacevich; Carrie Tolstedt; Robert Worth.

Number of staff: 1 full-time professional; 1 full-time support.

EIN: 411367441

Selected grants: The following grants were reported in 2004.

$1,000,000 to University of Nevada, Reno, NV.

$500,000 to United Way, Inc., Los Angeles, CA.

$250,000 to California Academy of Sciences, San Francisco, CA.

$250,000 to Greenlining Institute, Berkeley, CA.

$200,000 to HomeAid America, Costa Mesa, CA.

$200,000 to Urban League of Los Angeles, Los Angeles, CA.

$25,000 to Southern Minnesota Initiative Foundation, Owatonna, MN.

$20,000 to Alkebu-Lan Cultural Center, Pasadena, CA.

$17,500 to Habitat for Humanity of Council Bluffs, Council Bluffs, IA.

$15,000 to University of Texas System, Austin, TX.

1295

Toby Wells Foundation ◇

17083 Old Coach Rd.
Poway, CA   92064-1417

Established in 2001 in CA.

Donors: Lloyd D. Wells; John Burnham Real Estate; Richardson Pontiac; Business Real Estate.

Foundation type: Independent foundation.

Financial data (yr. ended 12/31/04): Assets, $0 (M); gifts received, $120,336; expenditures, $571,376; qualifying distributions, $556,708; giving activities include $490,510 for 27 grants (high: $400,000; low: $200).

Fields of interest: Animal welfare; Crime/violence prevention, child abuse; Children, services; Developmentally disabled, centers & services.

Limitations: Applications not accepted. Giving primarily in San Diego, CA. No grants to individuals.

Application information: Contributes only to pre-selected organizations.

Officers: Lloyd D. Wells, Chair.; Lynn D. Wells, C.E.O. and Pres.; Adriene A. Castaneda, Secy.

Directors: Brian Filger; Dana Fudurich; Edward Fudurich; Sue Herndon; John Jackson; and 8 additional directors.

EIN: 330946827

1296

The Werner Family Foundation ◇

11601 Wilshire Blvd., Ste. 1840
Los Angeles, CA   90025

Established in 1987 in CA.

Donors: Thomas Werner; Jill Werner.

Foundation type: Independent foundation.

Financial data (yr. ended 9/30/05): Assets, $8,887,001 (M); expenditures, $607,896; qualifying distributions, $443,800; giving activities include $443,800 for 14+ grants (high: $275,000).

Fields of interest: Higher education; Education; Reproductive health, family planning; Health organizations; Human services; Foundations (private grantmaking).

Type of support: General/operating support.

Limitations: Applications not accepted. Giving primarily in CA. No grants to individuals.

Application information: Contributes only to pre-selected organizations.

Officers: Thomas Werner, Pres.; Jill Werner, V.P.

Directors: Carolyn Werner; Edward Werner.

EIN: 954139253

1297

The Steve and Anita Westly Foundation ◇

1 Sansome St., 24th Fl.
San Francisco, CA   94104

Established in 2000 in CA.

Donors: Steve Westly; Anita Westly.

Foundation type: Independent foundation.

Financial data (yr. ended 12/31/04): Assets, $12,092,543 (M); expenditures, $939,998; qualifying distributions, $776,876; giving activities include $730,400 for 53 grants (high: $60,000; low: $2,500).

Fields of interest: Secondary school/education; Higher education; Education; Health organizations, association; Children/youth, services.

Limitations: Applications not accepted. Giving primarily in NY. No grants to individuals.

Application information: Contributes only to pre-selected organizations.

Officers and Directors:* Steve Westly,* Chair.; Nicole Bergeron, Pres.; Anita Yu,* Secy.

EIN: 943368338

1298

Weyrich Family Foundation ◇ ☆

2550 Creston Ridge Ln.
Paso Robles, CA   93446

Established in 1998 in CA.

Donors: David Weyrich; Mary Weyrich.

Foundation type: Independent foundation.

Financial data (yr. ended 12/31/04): Assets, $568,798 (M); expenditures, $845,312; qualifying distributions, $831,800; giving activities include $831,800 for 17 grants (high: $700,000; low: $150).

Purpose and activities: Giving primarily to Roman Catholic organizations and for Roman Catholic education as well as for human services.

Fields of interest: Museums (children's); Arts; Elementary/secondary education; Higher education; Education; Health organizations, association; Human services; Children/youth, services; International peace/security; Civil liberties, right to life; Roman Catholic federated giving programs; Philanthropy/voluntarism; Roman Catholic agencies & churches.

Limitations: Applications not accepted. Giving primarily in CA and NY; some funding nationally. No grants to individuals.

Application information: Contributes only to pre-selected organizations.

Officers: David Weyrich, Pres.; Mary Weyrich, Secy.-Treas.; Therese Corea, C.F.O.

EIN: 770488043

1299

The Whalen Family Foundation ◇

5866 Ostrander Rd.
Oakland, CA   94618-2040

Established in 1999 in CA.

Donors: C. Fesler; Daniel C. Whalen; Katharine C. Whalen.

Foundation type: Independent foundation.

Financial data (yr. ended 12/31/03): Assets, $2,142,309 (M); expenditures, $2,997,313; qualifying distributions, $2,977,818; giving activities include $2,361,410 for 17 grants (high: $607,309; low: $3,000; average: $50,000–$250,000).

Purpose and activities: Grants primarily for youth development; elementary, secondary, and higher education; and catholic churches and religious orders.

Fields of interest: Higher education; Education; Boys & girls clubs; Human services; Protestant agencies & churches; Roman Catholic agencies & churches.

International interests: Bosnia-Herzegovina.

Limitations: Applications not accepted. Giving on a national and international basis, with emphasis on CA and MN, and Sarajevo, Bosnia-Herzegovina. No grants to individuals.

Application information: Contributes only to pre-selected organizations.

Officers: Daniel A. Whalen, Pres.; Katherine C. Whalen, V.P. and Secy.-Treas.

EIN: 943348069

1300
WHH Foundation ✧ ☆
c/o William H. Hurt
333 S. Hope St., 54th Fl.
Los Angeles, CA 90071-1406

Established in 2004 in CA.

Donors: William H. Hurt; Sarah S. Hurt.

Foundation type: Independent foundation.

Financial data (yr. ended 12/31/05): Assets, $9,738,221 (M); gifts received, $1,031,454; expenditures, $583,164; qualifying distributions, $505,891; giving activities include $453,529 for 129 grants (high: $28,515; low: $35).

Fields of interest: Museums; Arts; Libraries (public); Education; Medical research; Human services; Children/youth, services; Community development.

Limitations: Applications not accepted. Giving in the U.S., with emphasis in CA. No grants to individuals.

Application information: Contributes only to pre-selected organizations.

Officers: Mark L. Purnell, Chair.; Bernadette Glenn-Murray, Pres. and C.O.O.; William H. Hurt, V.P.; Katharine J. Purnell, Secy.; Kelley A. Purnell, Treas.

Directors: Kathleen C. Hurt; Sarah S. Hurt; Courtney D. Macmillan; Terrance A. Macmillan; and 8 additional directors.

EIN: 200775264

1301
S T L N White Family Foundation, Inc. ✧
1120 E. Balboa Blvd.
Newport Beach, CA 92661

Established in 1993 in NJ.

Donors: S. Tod White; Linda G. White; BB & TW, Inc.

Foundation type: Independent foundation.

Financial data (yr. ended 12/31/05): Assets, $1,629,128 (M); expenditures, $354,738; qualifying distributions, $329,550; giving activities include $329,550 for 36 grants (high: $250,035; low: $100).

Fields of interest: Arts; Higher education; Human services.

Limitations: Applications not accepted. Giving primarily in CA. No grants to individuals.

Application information: Contributes only to pre-selected organizations.

Trustees: Linda G. White; Nadia D. White; S. Tod White; Stroller B. White.

EIN: 223255009

Selected grants: The following grants were reported in 2005.

$250,035 to Occidental College, Los Angeles, CA.

$2,500 to Bates College, Lewiston, ME.

$2,500 to Missoula Childrens Theater, Missoula, MT.

$750 to Fellows of Contemporary Art, Los Angeles, CA.

$500 to American Diabetes Association, Santa Ana, CA.

$400 to Association of Small Foundations, DC.

$200 to Salvation Army, Redding, CA.

1302
White Horse Christian Ministries Foundation ✧
2911 W. Lomita Blvd.
Torrance, CA 90505

Established in 1997 in CA.

Donor: Medard Cronin.

Foundation type: Independent foundation.

Financial data (yr. ended 12/31/05): Assets, $2,872,474 (M); gifts received, $3,186,648; expenditures, $595,843; qualifying distributions, $436,707; giving activities include $436,707 for 5 grants (high: $201,007; low: $10,000).

Purpose and activities: Giving primarily for food relief programs in Africa, especially to Rwanda, Congo, and Sudan.

Fields of interest: International relief.

International interests: Congo; Rwanda; Sudan.

Limitations: Applications not accepted. Giving primarily in Africa. No grants to individuals.

Application information: Contributes only to pre-selected organizations.

Officers: Medard Cronin,* C.E.O. and Pres.; Lucille Cronin, Secy.

EIN: 330766046

1303
Whitecap Foundation
800 Wilshire Blvd., Ste. 1010
Los Angeles, CA 90017
Contact: Laura Campobasso, Exec. Dir.; Executive Management Academy: Dan Davis
FAX: (213) 624-0529;
E-mail: execdirector@whitecapfdn.org; URL: http://www.whitecapfdn.org

Established in 1986 in CA.

Foundation type: Independent foundation.

Financial data (yr. ended 11/30/05): Assets, $2,879,520 (M); expenditures, $1,678,898; qualifying distributions, $1,661,408; giving activities include $1,454,847 for 55 grants (high: $130,000; low: $4,000).

Purpose and activities: Giving primarily directed to community-based Los Angeles, CA, organizations focusing on children, families, education, and statewide projects in CA for wildlife conservation. The foundation has also developed the Executive

Management Academy (EMA) to provide leadership training and technical assistance for its grantees.

Fields of interest: Adult education—literacy, basic skills & GED; Education, reading; Education; Environment, water resources; Employment; Children/youth, services; Family services; Family services, parent education; Hispanics/Latinos.

Type of support: Continuing support; Program development.

Limitations: Giving primarily in the Los Angeles, CA, area, particularly from Hollywood in the north to the 10 Freeway in the south, and between Western Ave. and the 605 Freeway. No support for religious groups. No grants to individuals, or for building purchase or construction, endowment funds, or tickets for fundraising events.

Publications: Grants list.

Application information:

Initial approach: Letter of inquiry (1-2 pages), either electronically or via regular mail

Deadline(s): None

Final notification: Within 2 months for letter; 3-6 months for proposal

Officers: Elizabeth Duker, Pres.; Brack Duker, Secy. and C.F.O.; Laura Campobasso, Exec. Dir.

Number of staff: 2

EIN: 954111120

Selected grants: The following grants were reported in 2005.

$130,000 to Our Saviour Center, El Monte, CA.

$87,000 to Asian Youth Center, San Gabriel, CA.

$37,600 to Pueblo Nuevo Development, Los Angeles, CA.

$32,542 to Boys and Girls Club of San Gabriel Valley, El Monte, CA.

$27,600 to Las Familias del Pueblo, Los Angeles, CA.

$25,000 to Boys and Girls Club.

$24,000 to Lincoln Heights Tutorial Program, Los Angeles, CA.

$24,000 to Salvation Army.

$22,000 to El Sereno Youth Development Corporation, Alhambra, CA.

$20,000 to Instituto de Educacion Popular del Sur de California, Los Angeles, CA.

1304
L. K. Whittier Foundation ▼
(formerly Whittier Foundation)
625 S. Fair Oaks Ave., Ste. 360
South Pasadena, CA 91030
Contact: Linda J. Blinkenberg, V.P. and Secy.

Incorporated in 1955 in CA.

Donors: Leland K. Whittier†; and members of the Whittier family.

Foundation type: Independent foundation.

Financial data (yr. ended 4/30/05): Assets, $98,810,033 (M); gifts received, $2,553,228; expenditures, $6,246,629; qualifying distributions, $5,890,151; giving activities include $5,594,000 for 7 grants (high: $1,600,000; low: $50,000; average: $400,000–$1,600,000).

Purpose and activities: Emphasis on medical research; support also for youth agencies.

Fields of interest: Higher education; Education; Medical research, institute; Youth, services.

Type of support: Program development; Seed money; Research; Matching/challenge support.

Limitations: Giving limited to southern CA, with emphasis on Los Angeles. No grants to individuals; no loans.

Application information: Foundation manager prefers to initiate grants.

 Initial approach: Letter of inquiry

 Board meeting date(s): Annually and as necessary

Officers and Directors:* Laura-Lee Whittier Woods, Pres.; Linda J. Blinkenberg,* V.P. and Secy.; Michael J. Casey,* V.P.; Michael P. McShane,* C.F.O.; Laure W. Kastanis.

EIN: 956027493

Selected grants: The following grants were reported in 2005.

$1,600,000 to Childrens Hospital of Los Angeles Foundation, Virtual Pediatric Intensive Care Unit, Los Angeles, CA. For expansion.

$1,200,000 to University of Southern California Kenneth Norris Jr. Cancer Hospital, Los Angeles, CA. For Innovative Tailored-Therapies Initiative.

$744,000 to University of Southern California, School of Pharmacy, Los Angeles, CA. For Research Center for the Study of Age Related Diseases.

$400,000 to Keck Graduate Institute of Applied Life Sciences, Claremont, CA. For Doctoral program of Applied Life Science.

1305
Brayton Wilbur Foundation ✧
345 California St., 27th Fl.
San Francisco, CA 94104-2644

Incorporated in 1947 in CA.

Donors: Brayton Wilbur, Jr.†; Wilbur-Ellis Co.

Foundation type: Company-sponsored foundation.

Financial data (yr. ended 12/31/05): Assets, $3,858,213 (M); gifts received, $128,500; expenditures, $487,625; qualifying distributions, $464,000; giving activities include $464,000 for grants.

Purpose and activities: The foundation supports organizations involved with arts and culture, higher education, natural resources, and health.

Fields of interest: Museums (art); Arts; Higher education; Environment, natural resources; Health care.

Type of support: Continuing support; Annual campaigns; Capital campaigns; Building/renovation; Endowments.

Limitations: Applications not accepted. Giving primarily in San Francisco, CA. No grants to individuals.

Application information: Contributes only to pre-selected organizations.

Officers: Carter P. Thacher, V.P.; Herbert B. Tully, Secy.-Treas.

EIN: 946088667

1306
The Wilkes Foundation ✧
13970 Stowe Dr.
Poway, CA 92064

Established in 2000 in CA.

Donors: ADCS, Inc.; David W. Stecher; Brent R. Wilkes; Bill Gowan; Jack McEncroe; Theodore D. Roth; Greg Wilkes; The Community Foundation for the National Capital Region; Douglas E. Barnhar, Inc.; WFI Government Services, Inc.; Cox Communications, Inc.; Sean & Tucker; Unicorn Jewelry & Fine Gifts; Fly W/Best; Custom Putting Green; Diamond Bead Necklace; Steamboat

Springs, Colorado Ski Package; Channel 4/SD Padres Package.

Foundation type: Independent foundation.

Financial data (yr. ended 12/31/05): Assets, $159,981 (M); gifts received, $26,730; expenditures, $520,021; qualifying distributions, $345,129; giving activities include $345,129 for grants.

Fields of interest: Education; Human services; YM/YWCAs & YM/YWHAs; Children/youth, services; Family services; Federated giving programs; Public policy, research.

Limitations: Applications not accepted. Giving primarily in San Diego, CA. No grants to individuals.

Application information: Contributes only to pre-selected organizations.

Officers: Brent R. Wilkes, Pres.; Regina Wilkes, V.P.; Greg Wilkes, Treas.

EIN: 330939613

1307
Williams-Corbett Foundation ✧ ☆
c/o Northern Trust
P.O. Box 22107
Santa Barbara, CA 93121
Contact: Trustees

Established in 1997 in CA.

Donors: Annette W. Corbett; George Corbett.

Foundation type: Independent foundation.

Financial data (yr. ended 12/31/05): Assets, $8,854,400 (M); gifts received, $1,030,377; expenditures, $520,020; qualifying distributions, $447,618; giving activities include $447,618 for 26 grants (high: $47,500; low: $3,000).

Purpose and activities: Giving primarily for the arts, with emphasis on museums, and for health care and human services.

Fields of interest: Museums (marine/maritime); Museums (natural history); Arts; Medical care, rehabilitation; Health care; Human services; Community development; Federated giving programs; Jewish federated giving programs.

Limitations: Giving primarily in Santa Barbara, CA.

Application information: Application form not required.

Trustees: Ann Carneros; Antonio Carneros; Annette W. Corbett.

EIN: 776150330

1308
Wilson Thornhill Foundation ✧
300 Delfern Dr.
Los Angeles, CA 90077-3545

Established in 1992 in CA.

Donor: Gary L. Wilson.

Foundation type: Independent foundation.

Financial data (yr. ended 12/31/05): Assets, $8,362,250 (M); gifts received, $3,187,599; expenditures, $804,185; qualifying distributions, $751,386; giving activities include $751,386 for 15 grants (high: $472,318; low: $100).

Purpose and activities: Giving primarily for higher and other education, including a high school foundation; funding also for children and youth services.

Fields of interest: Secondary school/education; Higher education; Education; Children/youth, services.

Limitations: Applications not accepted. Giving primarily in NC. No grants to individuals.

Application information: Contributes only to pre-selected organizations.

Trustee: Gary L. Wilson.

EIN: 954400754

Selected grants: The following grants were reported in 2004.

$414,722 to Duke University, Durham, NC.

$7,500 to Fight for Children, DC.

$5,000 to Curtis School, Los Angeles, CA.

$5,000 to United Way.

$2,000 to Music Center, Providence, RI.

1309
The Windfall Foundation ✧
c/o Manatt, Phelps, et al.
11355 W. Olympic Blvd.
Los Angeles, CA 90064
Application address: c/o Maryann Wlock, Joel Faden & Co., Inc., 1775 Broadway, New York, NY 10019, tel.: (212) 246-7203

Established in 1992 in CA.

Donors: R. Williams; M. Williams.

Foundation type: Independent foundation.

Financial data (yr. ended 12/31/05): Assets, $52,261 (M); gifts received, $200,000; expenditures, $467,093; qualifying distributions, $467,000; giving activities include $467,000 for 25 grants (high: $100,000; low: $1,000).

Purpose and activities: Giving primarily for education, the arts, and social services.

Fields of interest: Museums; Performing arts, theater; Historic preservation/historical societies; Arts; Education; Environment, natural resources; Health care; Spine disorders; Recreation; Human services; Children/youth, services.

Limitations: Giving primarily in CA; some giving also in New York, NY. No grants to individuals.

Application information:

 Initial approach: Letter

 Deadline(s): None

Officers: Gerald Margolis, Pres.; M. Williams, V.P. and Secy.; Joel Faden, C.F.O.

EIN: 954383183

Selected grants: The following grants were reported in 2004.

$100,000 to Christopher Reeve Paralysis Foundation, Springfield, NJ.

$100,000 to Lance Armstrong Foundation, Austin, TX.

$28,000 to Seacology, Berkeley, CA.

$25,000 to Glide Memorial United Methodist Church, San Francisco, CA.

$25,000 to Juilliard School, New York, NY.

$25,000 to USA Cycling Development Foundation, Colorado Springs, CO.

$15,000 to Nueva School, Hillsborough, CA.

$10,000 to Exploratorium, San Francisco, CA.

$5,000 to Actors Gang, Hollywood, CA.

$5,000 to College of Marin, Kentfield, CA.

1310
The Winnick Family Foundation ▼
(formerly The Gary and Karen Winnick Foundation)
9355 Wilshire Blvd., 4th Floor
Beverly Hills, CA 90210
Contact: Rosalie Zalis, Exec. Dir.

Established in 1983 in MD.

Donors: Gary Winnick; Karen Winnick.
Foundation type: Independent foundation.
Financial data (yr. ended 12/31/04): Assets, $9,804,831 (M); expenditures, $6,967,734; qualifying distributions, $6,920,714; giving activities include $6,599,915 for 184 grants (high: $1,500,000; low: $40; average: $1,000–$200,000).
Purpose and activities: Giving primarily for education, mentoring, medical research, health care and Jewish organizations.
Fields of interest: Arts; Higher education; Adult education—literacy, basic skills & GED; Education; Animals/wildlife; Health organizations, association; Jewish federated giving programs.
International interests: Israel.
Limitations: Giving in the U.S., with strong emphasis on CA and NY. No support for political organizations. No grants to individuals.
Publications: Application guidelines.
Application information: Application form required.
 Initial approach: 3-page proposal
 Copies of proposal: 1
 Deadline(s): None
 Board meeting date(s): Rolling review
 Final notification: Up to 3 months
Officers and Directors:* Gary Winnick,* Chair.; Karen Winnick,* Pres.; Alex Winnick,* V.P.; Rosalie Zalis, Secy. and Exec. Dir.; Gerry Ginsberg, Genl. Counsel; Lod Cook; Adam Winnick.
Number of staff: 1 part-time professional; 1 part-time support.
EIN: 953855792
Selected grants: The following grants were reported in 2004.
 $1,500,000 to Simon Wiesenthal Center, Los Angeles, CA. For unrestricted operating support.
 $1,000,000 to Cedars-Sinai Medical Center, Los Angeles, CA. For unrestricted operating support.
 $1,000,000 to Museum of Modern Art, New York, NY. For unrestricted operating support.
 $500,000 to Birthright Israel North America, New York, NY. For unrestricted operating support.
 $250,000 to William J. Clinton Presidential Center, Little Rock, AR. For unrestricted operating support.
 $5,000 to PEN/Faulkner Foundation, DC. For unrestricted support.
 $2,500 to American Jewish Committee, Los Angeles, CA. For unrestricted operating support.
 $2,500 to UCLA Foundation, Los Angeles, CA. For unrestricted operating support.
 $1,500 to Venice Family Clinic, Venice, CA. For unrestricted operating support.
 $1,000 to Jewish National Fund, New York, NY. For unrestricted operating support.

1311
The Wiskemann Family Foundation ◇
c/o Franklin Resources, Inc.
One Franklin Pkwy., Bldg. 920, 4th Fl.
San Mateo, CA 94403
Contact: Elizabeth Wiskemann, Tr.

Established in 1996 in CA.
Donors: Rico M. Wiskemann; Elizabeth Wiskemann.
Foundation type: Independent foundation.
Financial data (yr. ended 12/31/04): Assets, $20,870,081 (M); gifts received, $2,517,126; expenditures, $518,020; qualifying distributions, $500,000; giving activities include $500,000 for 8 grants (high: $100,000; low: $20,000).

Fields of interest: Museums (history); Elementary/secondary education; Higher education; Hospitals (general); Roman Catholic agencies & churches.
Application information:
 Initial approach: Letter
Trustee: Elizabeth Wiskemann.
EIN: 943256658

1312
Witherbee Foundation ◇
528 Arizona Ave., Ste. 220
Santa Monica, CA 90401

Established in 1996 in CA.
Donor: Victoria Witherbee.
Foundation type: Independent foundation.
Financial data (yr. ended 12/31/05): Assets, $14,247,959 (M); expenditures, $849,315; qualifying distributions, $847,276; giving activities include $808,400 for 25 grants (high: $250,000; low: $4,000).
Purpose and activities: Giving primarily for health care and human services, including organizations for people who are blind and visually impaired, particularly children; funding also for education.
Fields of interest: Museums (specialized); Performing arts, theater; Elementary/secondary education; Secondary school/education; Higher education; Animals/wildlife, preservation/protection; Zoos/zoological societies; Hospitals (general); Children/youth, services; Blind/visually impaired.
Limitations: Applications not accepted. Giving primarily in CA. No grants to individuals.
Application information: Contributes only to pre-selected organizations.
Officers and Director:* Robert Falls,* Pres.; Florita Ruskin, Secy.-Treas.
EIN: 954583560

1313
Bernard E. & Alba Witkin Charitable Foundation ◇ ☆
2740 Shasta Rd.
Berkeley, CA 94708

Established in 2003 in CA.
Donor: Alba Witkin.
Foundation type: Independent foundation.
Financial data (yr. ended 12/31/05): Assets, $46,375 (M); gifts received, $325,000; expenditures, $351,660; qualifying distributions, $336,550; giving activities include $336,550 for 116 grants (high: $25,000; low: $25).
Fields of interest: Education; Food distribution, meals on wheels; Youth, services; Deaf/hearing impaired; Homeless.
Limitations: Applications not accepted. No grants to individuals.
Application information: Contributes only to pre-selected organizations.
Officers: Alba Witkin, Pres.; Kenneth Kuchman, Secy.; Laurence E. Lange, Treas.
EIN: 731661679

1314
Dean Witter Foundation ◇
57 Post St., Ste. 510
San Francisco, CA 94104 (415) 981-2966
Contact: Kenneth J. Blum, Consultant

FAX: (415) 981-5218;
E-mail: admin@deanwitterfoundation.org;
URL: http://www.deanwitterfoundation.org

Incorporated in 1952 in CA.
Donors: Dean Witter‡; Mrs. Dean Witter; Dean Witter & Co.
Foundation type: Independent foundation.
Financial data (yr. ended 6/30/05): Assets, $19,122,243 (M); expenditures, $1,017,509; qualifying distributions, $912,938; giving activities include $770,500 for 30 grants (high: $75,000; low: $2,000), and $50,000 for 5 employee matching gifts.
Purpose and activities: Primary purpose is to support postgraduate research in economics and finance, with a secondary purpose to support conservation.
Fields of interest: Higher education; Environment, natural resources; Economics.
Type of support: Equipment; Program development; Publication; Research.
Limitations: Giving for conservation projects limited to northern CA. No support for religious organizations. No grants to individuals, or for endowment funds, scholarships, capital campaigns, and opportunity deficits; no loans.
Publications: Application guidelines; Annual report (including application guidelines); Grants list.
Application information: Application guidelines available on foundation Web site. Application form not required.
 Initial approach: Letter, telephone, or proposal
 Copies of proposal: 1
 Deadline(s): Submit proposal 6 weeks before board meeting
 Board meeting date(s): Jan., Apr., July, and Oct.
 Final notification: 1 week after board meeting
Officers and Trustees:* Dean Witter III,* Pres.; Roland Tognazzini, Jr., Secy.-Treas.; Stephen Nessier; Deanne Gillette Violich; Malcolm G. Witter; William P. Witter.
EIN: 946065150
Selected grants: The following grants were reported in 2005.
 $75,000 to Hoover Institution on War, Revolution and Peace, Stanford, CA.
 $75,000 to Santa Clara University, Santa Clara, CA.
 $75,000 to Stanford University, Stanford, CA.
 $25,000 to Environmental Defense, Oakland, CA.
 $25,000 to Trout Unlimited, Arlington, VA.
 $20,000 to Ducks Unlimited, Sacramento, CA.
 $20,000 to Smith River Alliance, Crescent City, CA.
 $20,000 to Trust for Public Land, San Francisco, CA.
 $15,000 to Friends of Sausal Creek, Richmond, CA.
 $15,000 to Laguna de Santa Rosa Foundation, Sebastopol, CA.

1315
Mary Wohlford Foundation ◇
c/o Margaretta Kildebeck and Jude Damasco
505 Sansome St., Ste. 1701
San Francisco, CA 94111

Established in 1999 in CA.
Donor: Mary M. Wohlford‡.
Foundation type: Independent foundation.
Financial data (yr. ended 6/30/05): Assets, $19,175,075 (M); gifts received, $133; expenditures, $1,919,809; qualifying distributions, $1,760,618; giving activities include $1,676,653 for 67 grants (high: $147,420; low: $1,000).

Fields of interest: Media, film/video; Arts; Higher education; Education; Environment, natural resources; Environment; Hospitals (general); Reproductive health; Health care; Health organizations, association; Human services; Children/youth, services; Family services; Civil rights; Government/public administration; Christian agencies & churches; Women.

Limitations: Applications not accepted. Giving primarily in CA and New York, NY; some funding nationally, with some emphasis on MA. No grants to individuals.

Application information: Contributes only to pre-selected organizations.

Trustees: Jude Damasco; Margaretta Kildebeck.

EIN: 943318493

Selected grants: The following grants were reported in 2005.

$147,420 to Documentary Educational Resources, Watertown, MA.

$72,000 to Good Samaritan Family Resource Center, San Francisco, CA.

$59,720 to NARAL Pro-Choice America Foundation, DC.

$54,000 to Trauma Foundation, San Francisco, CA.

$50,000 to Ibis Reproductive Health, Cambridge, MA.

$50,000 to International Projects Assistance Services (IPAS), Chapel Hill, NC.

$30,000 to Abortion Access Project, Cambridge, MA.

$30,000 to National Campaign to Prevent Teen Pregnancy, DC.

$29,850 to Johns Hopkins University, Baltimore, MD.

$25,000 to Cine Qua Non, New York, NY.

1316
Wolfen Family Foundation ◇ ☆
c/o Irell & Manella, LLP
1800 Ave. of the Stars, Ste. 900
Los Angeles, CA 90067-4276

Established in 1999 in CA.

Donors: Werner F. Wolfen; Mary G. Wolfen.

Foundation type: Independent foundation.

Financial data (yr. ended 12/31/05): Assets, $4,249,281 (M); gifts received, $645,542; expenditures, $891,856; qualifying distributions, $864,895; giving activities include $864,895 for 69 grants (high: $600,000; low: $50).

Fields of interest: Museums (specialized); Arts; Higher education, university; Health care; Cancer; American Red Cross; Human services; Foundations (public); Federated giving programs; Jewish federated giving programs; Jewish agencies & temples.

Limitations: Applications not accepted. No grants to individuals.

Application information: Contributes only to pre-selected organizations.

Trustees: Mary G. Wolfen; Werner F. Wolfen.

EIN: 954745065

Selected grants: The following grants were reported in 2003.

$52,815 to UCLA Foundation, Los Angeles, CA. For general support.

$50,000 to Jonsson Cancer Center Foundation, Los Angeles, CA. For general support.

$37,500 to Jewish Federation Council of Greater Los Angeles, Los Angeles, CA. For general support.

$30,000 to University of California, Berkeley, CA. For International Human Rights Law Clinic.

$18,050 to GOAL, Culver City, CA. For general support.

$5,500 to Echo Horizon School, Culver City, CA. For general support.

$2,500 to University of California at Berkeley Foundation, Berkeley, CA. For general support.

$1,200 to Leo Baeck Temple, Los Angeles, CA. For general support.

$1,100 to American Red Cross, National Headquarters, DC. For general support.

$1,000 to Entertainment Industry Foundation, Los Angeles, CA. For Revlon Run/Walk for breast and ovarian cancer.

1317
Wollenberg Foundation ◇
800 El Camino Real, Ste. 175
Menlo Park, CA 94025

Trust established in 1952 in CA.

Donor: H.L. Wollenberg†.

Foundation type: Independent foundation.

Financial data (yr. ended 12/31/05): Assets, $34,399,182 (M); expenditures, $1,165,554; qualifying distributions, $1,163,518; giving activities include $1,162,500 for 49 grants (high: $400,000; low: $1,000).

Fields of interest: Higher education; Medical school/education.

Type of support: General/operating support; Endowments; Program development.

Limitations: Applications not accepted. Giving primarily in CA, OR, and WA. No support for sectarian purposes or religious-affiliated institutions. No grants to individuals; no loans.

Application information: Contributes only to pre-selected organizations.

Trustees: Christopher Wollenberg; David A. Wollenberg; Richard P. Wollenberg.

EIN: 946072264

Selected grants: The following grants were reported in 2004.

$400,000 to Reed College, Portland, OR.

$50,000 to Independent Colleges of Washington, Seattle, WA.

$50,000 to United Negro College Fund, San Francisco, CA.

$30,000 to Harvard Business School Fund, Boston, MA.

$15,000 to Oregon Independent College Foundation, Portland, OR.

$15,000 to Oregon Museum of Science and Industry, Portland, OR.

$10,000 to Oregon Symphony Association, Portland, OR.

$10,000 to Smith College, Northampton, MA.

$7,500 to Exploratorium, San Francisco, CA.

$3,000 to Seattle Philharmonic Orchestra, Seattle, WA.

1318
Wood-Claeyssens Foundation ▼ ◇
P.O. Box 30586
Santa Barbara, CA 93130-0586
Contact: Noelle Claeyssens Burkey, Pres.

Established in 1980 in CA.

Donors: Ailene B. Claeyssens†; Pierre P. Claeyssens†; Cynthia Wood†; Claeyssens Charitable Trust.

Foundation type: Independent foundation.

Financial data (yr. ended 3/31/05): Assets, $100,825,510 (M); gifts received, $19,277,648; expenditures, $8,735,288; qualifying distributions, $6,799,003; giving activities include $6,285,300 for 265 grants (high: $500,000; low: $2,000; average: $10,000–$25,000).

Purpose and activities: Grant support primarily for education, housing, and youth; support also for health care and the arts.

Fields of interest: Performing arts, theater; Performing arts, music; Health care; Mental health/crisis services; Health organizations, association; Human services; Children/youth, services; Family services; Aging; Disabilities, people with.

Type of support: General/operating support; Continuing support; Annual campaigns; Capital campaigns; Building/renovation; Equipment.

Limitations: Giving limited to Santa Barbara and Ventura counties, CA. No support for tax-supported educational institutions, government-funded organizations, religious or political organizations, or for medical research. No grants to individuals.

Application information: Application form required.

Initial approach: Letter
Copies of proposal: 1
Deadline(s): June 30
Board meeting date(s): As needed

Officers and Directors:* Noelle Claeyssens Burkey,* Pres. and Genl. Mgr.; Shelby Hughes, Secy.; Charles C. Gray, Treas.; John Broome; Brett L. Burkey; J. Brad Burkey; James Burkey.

Number of staff: 1 full-time professional; 2 full-time support.

EIN: 953514017

Selected grants: The following grants were reported in 2005.

$500,000 to Santa Barbara Cottage Hospital, Santa Barbara, CA. For capital campaign for new state of the art hospital.

$250,000 to Santa Barbara Bowl Foundation, Santa Barbara, CA. For Phase 1B, the pavilion.

$200,000 to Foodbank of Santa Barbara County, Santa Barbara, CA. For capital campaign project.

$100,000 to YMCA, Montecito Family, Santa Barbara, CA. For purchase of land.

$75,000 to Boys and Girls Clubs of Greater Santa Barbara County, United, Santa Barbara, CA. For general program support.

$20,000 to Easy Lift Transportation, Goleta, CA. For general program support.

$20,000 to Planned Parenthood of Santa Barbara, Ventura and San Luis Obispo Counties, Santa Barbara, CA. For general operating support.

$15,000 to Boys and Girls Club of Santa Clara Valley, Santa Paula, CA. For general program support.

$15,000 to Solvang Senior Center, Solvang, CA. For nutrition program.

$15,000 to Ventura County Maritime Museum, Oxnard, CA. For general operating support.

1319
World Children's Fund ◇
5442 Thornwood Dr., Ste. 200
San Jose, CA 95123 (408) 363-8100
FAX: (408) 629-4846; E-mail: info@wcf-intl.org;
URL: http://www.worldchildrensfund.org

Established in 1984 in CA.

Foundation type: Independent foundation.
Financial data (yr. ended 3/31/05): Assets, $1,247,596 (M); gifts received, $6,034,263; expenditures, $5,936,151; qualifying distributions, $5,927,863; giving activities include $339,431 for 10 grants (high: $250,000; low: $700; average: $2,500–$29,500), and $3,642,916 for 1 foundation-administered program.
Purpose and activities: The foundation sends medical equipment and supplies, vegetable seeds, and tents to needy people throughout the world. It also makes donations to charitable organizations to help needy people in foreign countries.
Fields of interest: Children/youth, services; International relief.
Type of support: In-kind gifts.
Limitations: Giving on an international basis. No grants to individuals.
Publications: Annual report; Financial statement.
Application information:
Deadline(s): None
Officers: Joseph Lam, Pres.; Douglas Kendrick, C.F.O.; Ann Chiang, Cont.
Directors: Bruce Barnes; Stanley Chen.
EIN: 770210616

1320

The Wornick Family Foundation, Inc. ✧
c/o Ronald C. Wornick
44 Montgomery St., Ste. 3060
San Francisco, CA 94104-4804
FAX: (415) 438-4859

Established in 1985 in CA.
Donors: Anita L. Wornick; Ronald C. Wornick.
Foundation type: Independent foundation.
Financial data (yr. ended 12/31/04): Assets, $3,017,178 (M); gifts received, $102,739; expenditures, $766,503; qualifying distributions, $759,406; giving activities include $755,938 for 95 grants (high: $139,500; low: $25).
Purpose and activities: Giving primarily for the visual and performing arts, social causes, and Jewish philanthropy.
Fields of interest: Visual arts; Performing arts; Human services; Jewish federated giving programs.
Type of support: Annual campaigns; Capital campaigns.
Limitations: Applications not accepted. Giving primarily in CA. No grants to individuals.
Application information: Contributes only to pre-selected organizations.
Officers: Ronald C. Wornick, Pres.; Anita L. Wornick, V.P.; Jonathan Wornick, V.P.; Kenneth Wornick, V.P.; Michael Wornick, V.P.
EIN: 943001357

1321

Wrather Family Foundation ✧ ☆
(formerly J. D. & Mazie Wrather Foundation)
c/o Ellis, Bristol, Harmon & O'Brien
14310 Ventura Blvd., 2nd Fl.
Sherman Oaks, CA 91423

Established in 1962 as the J. D. & Mazie Wrather Foundation, Inc.
Foundation type: Independent foundation.
Financial data (yr. ended 12/31/05): Assets, $4,202,552 (M); expenditures, $396,607; qualifying distributions, $331,000; giving activities include $331,000 for grants.

Purpose and activities: Giving primarily for health care, including a substance abuse treatment center, as well as for education, medical research, and human services.
Fields of interest: Arts; Higher education; Education; Hospitals (general); Health care; Substance abuse, treatment; Cancer; Human services; Children/youth, services; Family services; Federated giving programs.
Limitations: Applications not accepted. Giving primarily in CA. No grants to individuals.
Application information: Contributes only to pre-selected organizations.
Officers and Directors:* Christopher C. Wrather,* Pres.; Gerald L. Weisberger,* Secy.; Linda W. Finocchiaro,* Treas.; Molly W. Dolle.
EIN: 956100110
Selected grants: The following grants were reported in 2003.
$45,000 to Amnesty International USA, DC.
$40,000 to John Wayne Cancer Institute, Santa Monica, CA.
$10,000 to Santa Barbara City College, Foundation for, Santa Barbara, CA.
$10,000 to UNICEF, New York, NY.
$7,000 to Family Service Agency of Santa Barbara, Santa Barbara, CA.
$5,000 to Larkin Street Youth Services, San Francisco, CA.
$4,000 to Drew College Preparatory School, San Francisco, CA.
$1,000 to Clare Foundation, Santa Monica, CA.
$1,000 to Visiting Nurse and Hospice Care of Santa Barbara, Santa Barbara, CA.
$500 to Choices for Children of Siskiyou County, Yreka, CA.

1322

The Wunderkinder Foundation ✧ ☆
(formerly Max Charitable Foundation)
c/o Breslauer & Rutman, LLC
11400 W. Olympic Blvd., Ste. 550
Los Angeles, CA 90064-1551

Established in 1985 in CA.
Donor: Steven Spielberg.
Foundation type: Independent foundation.
Financial data (yr. ended 11/30/05): Assets, $14,470,492 (M); gifts received, $2,395,640; expenditures, $10,716,619; qualifying distributions, $10,700,123; giving activities include $10,700,123 for 49 grants (high: $6,666,666; low: $500).
Purpose and activities: Giving primarily to the arts, education, war memorials and veterans' organizations, and Jewish organizations; giving also for human services, with an emphasis on children and medical research.
Fields of interest: Historical activities, war memorials; Arts; Education; Environment, natural resources; Health organizations, association; Youth development; Children/youth, services; Military/veterans' organizations; Jewish agencies & temples; Native Americans/American Indians; LGBTQ.
Limitations: Applications not accepted. Giving primarily in CA and NY. No grants to individuals.
Application information: Contributes only to pre-selected organizations.
Officers and Directors:* Gerald Breslauer,* Pres.; Michael Rutman,* Secy.-Treas.; Bruce Ramer.
EIN: 954016320

Selected grants: The following grants were reported in 2004.
$150,000 to United States Holocaust Memorial Museum, DC.
$25,000 to Keep Memory Alive, Las Vegas, NV.
$25,000 to Women in Film, Beverly Hills, CA.
$13,000 to Geffen Playhouse, Los Angeles, CA.
$5,000 to Ellen P. Hermanson Foundation, Great Neck, NY.
$4,500 to American Museum of the Moving Image, Astoria, NY.
$3,264 to Shakespeare Festival of Los Angeles, Los Angeles, CA.
$300 to American Heart Association, San Francisco, CA.

1323

WWW Foundation
625 S. Fair Oaks Ave., Ste. 360
South Pasadena, CA 91030-2630
Contact: Elizabeth A. Curtis, Secy.

Established in 1983 in CA.
Donors: Helen W. Woodward‡; Winifred W. Rhodes; Helen Woodward Charitable Lead Trust.
Foundation type: Independent foundation.
Financial data (yr. ended 12/31/05): Assets, $57,114,877 (M); gifts received, $1,950,685; expenditures, $1,861,193; qualifying distributions, $1,632,146; giving activities include $1,403,003 for 47 grants (high: $450,000; low: $2,500).
Purpose and activities: Giving primarily for an animal care center; support also for boys and girls clubs, hospitals, civic affairs, and the arts.
Fields of interest: Education; Animal welfare; Hospitals (general); Medical research, institute; Boys & girls clubs; Human services; Children/youth, services.
Type of support: Equipment; General/operating support; Building/renovation; Program development; Research; Matching/challenge support.
Limitations: Applications not accepted. Giving primarily in southern CA. No grants to individuals; no loans.
Application information: Unsolicited requests for funds are not accepted. The foundation prefers to initiate grants.
Board meeting date(s): As needed, 2 times a year
Officers and Directors:* Sharon H. Bradford,* Pres.; Bryce W. Rhodes, V.P.; Winifred W. Rhodes,* V.P.; Elizabeth A. Curtis, Secy.; Linda J. Blinkenberg,* C.F.O.; and 6 additional directors.
EIN: 953694741
Selected grants: The following grants were reported in 2004.
$1,300,000 to Helen Woodward Animal Center, Rancho Santa Fe, CA. 4 grants: $20,000, $10,000, $500,000, $770,000
$221,696 to Boys and Girls Club, Variety, Los Angeles, CA. 3 grants: $25,557, $188,000, $8,139
$115,000 to University of California, Davis, CA.
$25,000 to Woodland Park Zoological Society, Seattle, WA.
$7,500 to Cate School, Carpinteria, CA.

1324

Carl E. Wynn Foundation ✧
444 S. Flower St., Ste. 1700
Los Angeles, CA 90071-2901

Established in 1966.
Donors: Bee Wynn†; Carl Wynn†.
Foundation type: Independent foundation.
Financial data (yr. ended 12/31/05): Assets, $28,085,041 (M); expenditures, $892,915; qualifying distributions, $670,001; giving activities include $513,000 for grants.
Purpose and activities: Giving primarily for the welfare of children and for health research.
Fields of interest: Elementary/secondary education; Higher education; Education; Hospitals (general); Medical research, institute; Human services; Children/youth, services; Disabilities, people with; Economically disadvantaged; Homeless.
Limitations: Giving primarily in Los Angeles County, San Gabriel Valley, and Orange County, CA.
Application information: Application form required.
  Initial approach: Letter
  Copies of proposal: 1
  Deadline(s): May 15
  Board meeting date(s): Mar.
  Final notification: Positive responses only
Officers and Trustees:* William R. Christian,* Pres.; Billie A. Fischer,* V.P.; Dorothy L. Frey,* Treas.; Mel Masuda.
EIN: 956136231
Selected grants: The following grants were reported in 2004.
$60,000 to Center for Alaskan Coastal Studies, Homer, AK.
$60,000 to Peppermint Ridge, Corona, CA.
$40,000 to Good Shepherd Shelter, Los Angeles, CA.
$40,000 to Orangewood Childrens Foundation, Santa Ana, CA.
$30,000 to City of Hope, Los Angeles, CA.
$30,000 to Operation Safe House, Riverside, CA.
$30,000 to Saint Mary Medical Center, Apple Valley, CA.
$25,000 to Angel Harvest, Los Angeles, CA.
$20,000 to Los Angeles Regional Foodbank, Los Angeles, CA.
$5,000 to Lutheran Social Services of Southern California, Long Beach, CA.

1325
The Christine Zecca Foundation ◇
51 Santa Rosa Ave.
Sausalito, CA 94965
Contact: Christine Zecca, Pres.

Established in 1997 in CA.
Foundation type: Independent foundation.
Financial data (yr. ended 12/31/04): Assets, $4,783,340 (M); expenditures, $460,231; qualifying distributions, $407,370; giving activities include $370,000 for 8 grants (high: $200,000; low: $5,000), and $37,370 for 8 grants to individuals (high: $25,000; low: $850).
Fields of interest: Education; Human services; Foundations (community); Federated giving programs.
Limitations: Giving primarily in CA and PA.
Application information:
  Initial approach: Letter
  Deadline(s): None
Officers: Christine Zecca, Pres.; Riana Malrigani, Secy.
EIN: 943265224

1326
The Zellerbach Family Foundation ▼
(formerly The Zellerbach Family Fund)
120 Montgomery St., Ste. 1550
San Francisco, CA 94104 (415) 421-2629
Contact: Cindy Rambo, Exec. Dir.
FAX: (415) 421-6713;
E-mail: info@zellerbachfamilyfoundation.org;
URL: http://www.zellerbachfamilyfoundation.org

Incorporated in 1956 in CA.
Donor: Jennie B. Zellerbach†.
Foundation type: Independent foundation.
Financial data (yr. ended 12/31/05): Assets, $118,460,982 (M); gifts received, $255,000; expenditures, $6,268,971; qualifying distributions, $4,806,983; giving activities include $3,800,803 for 334 grants (high: $250,000; low: $1,000).
Purpose and activities: The fund focuses its giving in the San Francisco Bay Area, CA and concentrates on the following program areas: Strengthening communities; Improving the management, practice and accountability of public systems with a focus on child welfare, mental health and education; Improving the quality of life for refugees and immigrants and supporting their participation in society; Youth development through the arts; Major community institutions; and Community Arts.
Fields of interest: Performing arts; Performing arts, dance; Performing arts, theater; Performing arts, music; Arts; Education, public education; Mental health/crisis services, public policy; Youth development; Human services; Community development; Immigrants/refugees.
Type of support: General/operating support; Continuing support; Program development; Technical assistance; Program evaluation.
Limitations: Giving primarily in the San Francisco Bay Area, CA. No grants to individuals, or for capital or endowment funds, research, scholarships, or fellowships; no loans.
Publications: Annual report.
Application information: The foundation accepts proposals only for its Community Arts program. All other programs are initiated by the foundation. Application cover sheet is available on foundation's Web site. Organizations can only receive one grant per calendar year. Application form required.
  Initial approach: Community Arts application with application cover sheet
  Board meeting date(s): Quarterly
Officers and Trustees:* William J. Zellerbach,* Chair.; Thomas H. Zellerbach,* Pres.; Nancy Zellerbach Boschwitz,* V.P. and Secy.; John W. Zellerbach,* V.P. and Treas.; Raymond H. Williams,* V.P.; Cindy Rambo, Exec. Dir.; Jeanette M. Dunckel; Philip S. Ehrlich, Jr.; Mary Ann Milias; Stephen R. Shapiro; Mildred Thompson; Charles R. Zellerbach.
Number of staff: 3 full-time professional; 2 part-time professional; 2 full-time support.
EIN: 946069482
Selected grants: The following grants were reported in 2005.
$500,000 to University of California, Berkeley, CA. For Zellerbach Hall improvements, to replace seating.
$75,000 to California Institute for Mental Health, Sacramento, CA. For Juvenile Justice/Child welfare Mental Health Project, to continue collaboration and training to promote best practices in delivery of mental health services to youth and families involved with the foster care and juvenile justices systems in California and to

evaluate the effectiveness of these training models.
$60,000 to Office of the Public Defender, Tuscaloosa, AL. For Children of Incarcerated Parents Project, to reduce traumas experienced by children when their parents are arrested and improve the way the public service, legal, and corrections systems work together so that families with incarcerated parents have the best opportunities for a better future.
$54,000 to Immigrant Legal Resource Center, San Francisco, CA. For Plan to Lead, Northern California Citizenship Project, for two pilot parent leadership training courses with parents from four community organizations that are involved in efforts to improve local schools.
$50,000 to June Jordan School for Equity, San Francisco, CA. For Parent Leadership and Engagement program, for development and implementation of parent leadership and engagement program at one of two new small high schools that are at the forefront of the San Francisco Unified School District's Secondary School Redesign Initiative.
$40,000 to WAGES International, Miami, FL. To create employment and business ownership opportunities for low-income immigrant women through the formation of environmentally-safe housekeeping cooperatives.
$35,000 to International Institute of the East Bay, Oakland, CA. For immigration Legal Services Program, to provide a variety of immigration legal services to immigrants and refugees residing in Alameda and Contra Costa Counties.
$25,000 to Catholic Charities of the Diocese of Oakland, Oakland, CA. For CARE collaborative.
$25,000 to San Francisco Foundation Community Initiative Funds, San Francisco, CA. For Foster Youth Alliance, for collaboration of agencies serving current and emancipated foster youth promote understanding of mental health needs of youth emancipating from foster care and improve access to mental health services and supports.
$25,000 to United Way of the Bay Area, San Francisco, CA. For Honoring Emancipated Youth.

1327
Ruth/Allen Ziegler Foundation ◇
c/o Gumbiner Savett
1723 Cloverfield Blvd.
Santa Monica, CA 90404

Established in 1986 in CA.
Donors: Allen S. Ziegler; Ruth B. Ziegler.
Foundation type: Independent foundation.
Financial data (yr. ended 11/30/05): Assets, $7,769,246 (M); expenditures, $854,530; qualifying distributions, $836,526; giving activities include $824,000 for 65 grants (high: $30,000; low: $500).
Purpose and activities: Funding primarily for Jewish agencies and human services. Funding also for arts and culture, and education.
Fields of interest: Arts; Education; Human services; Jewish federated giving programs; Jewish agencies & temples.
Limitations: Applications not accepted. Giving primarily in Los Angeles, CA. No grants to individuals.
Application information: Contributes only to pre-selected organizations.

Trustees: Richard Corleto; David Rose; Ronald Ziegler; Ruth B. Ziegler.
EIN: 954113690
Selected grants: The following grants were reported in 2003.
$20,000 to AIDS Project Los Angeles (APLA), Los Angeles, CA. For general support.
$20,000 to American Foundation for AIDS Research (AMFAR), Los Angeles, CA. For general support.
$20,000 to American Friends of the Hebrew University, New York, NY. For general support.
$20,000 to American Society for Technion-Israel Institute of Technology, Los Angeles, CA. For general support.
$20,000 to Fulfillment Fund, Los Angeles, CA. For general support.
$20,000 to Habitat for Humanity International, Los Angeles, CA. For general support.
$20,000 to Independence Center, Los Angeles, CA. For general support.
$20,000 to Jewish Hospice Project Los Angeles, Los Angeles, CA. For general support.
$20,000 to Jewish Television Network, Beverly Hills, CA. For general support.
$10,000 to American Jewish Committee, Los Angeles, CA. For general support.

1328
Max & Pauline Zimmer Family Foundation ✧
4314 Marina City Dr., No. 1016 CTS
Marina del Rey, CA 90292   (310) 305-1393
Contact: Nathan S. Krems, Pres.

Established in 1951 in CA.
Donor: Max Zimmer.
Foundation type: Independent foundation.
Financial data (yr. ended 5/31/05): Assets, $6,183,491 (M); expenditures, $513,116; qualifying distributions, $420,100; giving activities include $420,100 for 19 grants (high: $100,000; low: $500).
Purpose and activities: Giving primarily for higher education and Jewish agencies and temples.
Fields of interest: Performing arts, orchestra (symphony); Higher education; Jewish agencies & temples.
Limitations: Applications not accepted. Giving primarily in CA. No grants to individuals.
Application information: Contributes only to pre-selected organizations.
Officers and Directors:* Nathan S. Krems,* Pres.; Jonathan Flier,* V.P.; Edith Flier,* Secy.; Ruth Lieberman,* Treas.; David Z. Krems; Charles Lieberman; Milton Whitebook.
EIN: 956097374
Selected grants: The following grants were reported in 2004.

$147,300 to Jewish Community Foundation, Council of Greater Los Angeles, Los Angeles, CA.
$100,000 to Zimmer Jewish Discovery Childrens Museum, Los Angeles, CA.
$30,000 to Tel Aviv Sourasky Medical Center, Friends of, New York, NY.
$25,000 to P.E.F. Israel Endowment Funds, New York, NY.
$20,000 to City of Hope, Los Angeles, CA.
$15,000 to Camp Ramah in California, Los Angeles, CA.
$10,000 to University of Judaism, Los Angeles, CA.
$9,000 to American Associates, Ben-Gurion University of the Negev, Los Angeles, CA.
$8,000 to American Friends of Keshet Eilon, New York, NY.
$1,000 to Friends of Sheba Medical Center, Los Angeles, CA.

1329
Myron Zimmerman Foundation ✧ ☆
1330 Broadway, Ste. 1050
Oakland, CA 94612-2509
Contact: Myron Zimmerman, Pres.

Established in 1998 in CA.
Donor: Myron Zimmerman.
Foundation type: Independent foundation.
Financial data (yr. ended 12/31/05): Assets, $7,076,523 (M); gifts received, $750,000; expenditures, $417,901; qualifying distributions, $408,256; giving activities include $408,256 for grants.
Fields of interest: Museums; Arts; Education; Jewish agencies & temples.
Limitations: Giving primarily in CA. No grants to individuals.
Application information:
 Initial approach: Letter
 Deadline(s): None
Officers: Myron Zimmerman, Pres.; Lance Fong, Secy.; Norman Dress, Treas.
EIN: 943316088
Selected grants: The following grants were reported in 2005.
$10,000 to Facts and Logic About the Middle East, San Francisco, CA.
$2,500 to Simon Wiesenthal Center, Los Angeles, CA.
$2,000 to Compass Community Services, San Francisco, CA. 2 grants: $1,000 each
$1,000 to American Jewish Committee, Newark, NJ.
$1,000 to American Red Magen David for Israel, Encino, CA.
$1,000 to Bureau of Jewish Education, San Francisco, CA.
$1,000 to Jewish Family and Childrens Services, San Francisco, CA.

$1,000 to Pathways for Kids, San Francisco, CA.

1330
Morris & Deena Zyskind Charitable Foundation ✧ ☆
c/o Barak, Richter & Dror, CPAs
5967 W. 3rd St., Ste. 102
Los Angeles, CA 90036

Donor: Deena Zyskind Irrevocable Trust.
Foundation type: Independent foundation.
Financial data (yr. ended 5/31/05): Assets, $17,137 (M); gifts received, $258,000; expenditures, $328,150; qualifying distributions, $328,000; giving activities include $327,000 for 10 grants (high: $68,000; low: $300).
Purpose and activities: Giving primarily to Jewish agencies, temples, and schools.
Fields of interest: Elementary/secondary education; Cancer; Children/youth, services; Jewish agencies & temples.
Trustees: Deena Zyskind; Morris Zyskind.
EIN: 912147933

1331
ZZYZX Foundation, Inc. ✧
(formerly Chouinard Family Foundation)
c/o Moss Adams, LLP
11766 Wilshire Blvd., Ste. 900
Los Angeles, CA 90025

Established in 1994 in CA.
Donor: Yvon Chouinard.
Foundation type: Independent foundation.
Financial data (yr. ended 9/30/05): Assets, $3,225,815 (M); gifts received, $1,000,000; expenditures, $1,029,640; qualifying distributions, $1,004,443; giving activities include $1,000,000 for 1 grant.
Purpose and activities: Giving for wildlife protection organizations.
Fields of interest: Environment, natural resources; Animals/wildlife, preservation/protection.
Limitations: Applications not accepted. Giving primarily in Santa Barbara, CA. No grants to individuals.
Application information: Contributes only to pre-selected organizations.
Officers and Directors:* Yvon Chouinard,* Pres.; Jill Zilligin,* Secy.; Robert S. Kelleher,* Treas.; Malinda Pennoyer-Chouinard.
EIN: 770359427

COLORADO

1332

Agur Foundation ✧ ☆

7200 S. Alton Way, Ste. B150
Centennial, CO 80112   (720) 488-6803
FAX: (720) 488-6877;
E-mail: tharvey@agurfoundation.org; URL: http://
www.agurfoundation.org

Established in 2002 in CO.
Donors: Eric S. White; Jane White; Robert Roth.
Foundation type: Independent foundation.
Financial data (yr. ended 12/31/05): Assets,
$6,638,842 (M); gifts received, $3,274,000;
expenditures, $685,202; qualifying distributions,
$558,100; giving activities include $558,100 for 2
grants (high: $550,000; low: $8,100).
Purpose and activities: The foundation's mission is
to build up the body of Christ around the world by
providing properties for new Christian churches to
develop, grow and flourish.
Fields of interest: Christian agencies & churches.
Limitations: Applications not accepted. Giving on a
national and international basis. No grants to
individuals.
Application information: Contributes only to
pre-selected organizations.
Officers: Teena W. Harvey, Secy.; Jane E. White,
Treas.; Eric S. White, Exec. Dir.; Daniel A. White,
Mgr.; Jason R. White, Mgr.
EIN: 550829063

1333

Animal Assistance Foundation

455 Sherman St., Ste. 462
Denver, CO 80203-4405
Contact: David L. Gies, Exec. Dir.
FAX: (303) 744-7065; E-mail: info@aaf-fd.org;
URL: http://www.aaf-fd.org

Established in 1975 in CO.
Donor: Louise C. Harrison‡.
Foundation type: Independent foundation.
Financial data (yr. ended 7/31/05): Assets,
$28,595,778 (M); gifts received, $25;
expenditures, $1,278,096; qualifying distributions,
$1,188,967; giving activities include $821,245 for
52 grants (high: $570,000; low: $89).
Purpose and activities: The foundation's mission is
to provide leadership for the enhancement of animal
welfare through charitable, scientific, and
educational means. Its vision is to transform the
relationship between human beings and all animals,
for the betterment of both. Giving for animal welfare,
especially to prevent cruelty to cats and dogs; also
to promote pet population control, provide for
humane treatment education, and expand scientific
inquiry.
Fields of interest: Animal welfare; Animal population
control.
Type of support: General/operating support;
Building/renovation; Emergency funds; Program
development; Conferences/seminars; Seed money;
Curriculum development; Technical assistance.
Limitations: Giving limited to CO. No grants to
individuals, or for endowment funds, debt
retirement, or long-term funding.

Publications: Annual report; Financial statement;
Multi-year report.
Application information: Programs and application
guidelines will be sent once initial contact has been
made. Application form required.
  Initial approach: Letter or E-mail
  Copies of proposal: 8
  Deadline(s): Generally, last Fri. in Mar. and Sept.
  Board meeting date(s): Bimonthly
  Final notification: Within two weeks
Officers and Directors:* Jon F. Sands,* Pres.;
Elizabeth Holtze, Ph.D*, V.P.; Alison Biggs,* Secy.;
Peter Konrad,* Treas.; Jeff Blomberg; Gina Guy;
George R. Schiel; Apryl Steele, D.V.M.
Number of staff: 2 full-time professional; 1 part-time
support.
EIN: 840715412
Selected grants: The following grants were reported
in 2004.
$700,000 to Harrison Memorial Animal Hospital,
  Denver, CO.
$179,000 to Dumb Friends League, Denver, CO.
$93,598 to Alliance for Contraception in Cats and
  Dogs, Auburn, AL. For veterinary services.
$10,000 to Cat Care Society, Lakewood, CO.
$5,000 to Auburn University, Auburn, AL.

1334

Anschutz Family Foundation

555 17th St., Ste. 2400
Denver, CO 80202
Contact: Sue Anschutz-Rodgers, Pres. and Exec. Dir.
FAX: (303) 299-1235;
E-mail: info@anschutzfamilyfoundation.org;
URL: http://www.anschutzfamilyfoundation.org/

Established in 1982 in CO.
Donors: Fred B. Anschutz‡; Sue Anschutz-Rodgers.
Foundation type: Independent foundation.
Financial data (yr. ended 11/30/05): Assets,
$49,398,699 (M); expenditures, $2,690,188;
qualifying distributions, $2,368,090; giving
activities include $2,091,123 for 374 grants (high:
$25,000; low: $500).
Purpose and activities: The foundation supports
Colorado nonprofit organizations that assist people
to help themselves while nurturing and preserving
their self-respect. The foundation encourages
endeavors that strengthen families and
communities and advance individuals to become
productive and responsible citizens. There is a
special interest in self-sufficiency, community
development, and programs aimed at the
economically disadvantaged, the young, the elderly,
and the disabled. The foundation is dedicated to
funding efforts in rural Colorado.
Fields of interest: Adult education—literacy, basic
skills & GED; Mental health/crisis services; Crime/
violence prevention; Crime/violence prevention,
domestic violence; Food services; Nutrition;
Housing/shelter; Human services; Children/youth,
services; Family services; Homeless, human
services; Economic development; Community
development; Philanthropy/voluntarism; Aging;
Disabilities, people with; Economically
disadvantaged.
Type of support: General/operating support;
Program development; Technical assistance.
Limitations: Giving limited to CO. No support for
religious organizations for religious purposes. No
grants to individuals, or for capital or building funds,
deficit financing, endowment funds, special events

or promotions, conferences, or graduate or
post-graduate research.
Publications: Application guidelines; Annual report
(including application guidelines); Grants list.
Application information: Complete the Colorado
Common Grant Application available at http://
www.coloradononprofits.org. Organizations
receiving successive support for 2 years are
required to take one year off before reapplying. Only
1 proposal per organization per 12-month funding
cycle will be considered. See foundation Web site
for application guidelines and procedures.
Application form required.
  Initial approach: Letter of inquiry, telephone or full
    proposal
  Copies of proposal: 1
  Deadline(s): Submit proposal before Jan. 15 and
    Aug. 1
  Board meeting date(s): Apr. and Nov.
  Final notification: First week of May or Dec.
Officers and Directors:* Sue Anschutz-Rodgers,*
Pres. and Exec. Dir.; Robert S. Rich, V.P. and Secy.;
Susan A. Spindler, Treas.; Melinda Rodgers
Couzens; Susan Rodgers Drumm; Sarah Anschutz
Hunt; Melissa Rodgers Padgett.
Number of staff: 2 full-time professional.
EIN: 742132676
Selected grants: The following grants were reported
in 2003.
$20,000 to Community Resource Center, Denver,
  CO. For scholarships to Colorado Nonprofit
  Leadership and management program.
$10,000 to Care and Share Food Bank, Colorado
  Springs, CO. For general operating support to
  acquire and distribute food to network of partner
  agencies serving poor in Southern Colorado.
$10,000 to Colorado Childrens Campaign, Denver,
  CO. To improve services and outcomes for
  children throughout Colorado.
$10,000 to Hope Center, Denver, CO. For Early
  Childhood Education programs serving inner-city
  children.
$10,000 to Lift-Up/Garfield County, Glenwood
  Springs, CO. For general operating support for
  essential services for poor in Garfield County.
$10,000 to Mercy Housing Southwest, Denver, CO.
  For general operating support to expand
  availability of quality, affordable housing
  projects, ranging from emergency shelters to
  homeownership units.
$10,000 to Project Angel Heart, Denver, CO. For
  general operating support for home-delivered
  meals to people living with HIV/AIDS, cancer, and
  other life-threatening illnesses.
$10,000 to Step 13, Denver, CO. For general
  operating support.
$10,000 to Visiting Nurse Association of Northwest
  Colorado, Steamboat Springs, CO. For general
  operating support to sustain hospice programs
  and community and home health.
$10,000 to Volunteers of America, Denver, CO. For
  Meals on Wheels program serving homebound
  older men and women in metro Denver.

1335

The Anschutz Foundation ▼ ✧

1727 Tremont Pl.
Denver, CO 80202   (303) 308-8220
Contact: M. LaVoy Robison, Exec. Dir.

Established in 1984 in CO.
Donors: Philip F. Anschutz; The Anschutz Corp.
Foundation type: Independent foundation.

Financial data (yr. ended 11/30/04): Assets, $467,692,980 (M); gifts received, $26,791,279; expenditures, $20,706,844; qualifying distributions, $18,969,674; giving activities include $18,909,643 for 199 grants (high: $10,200,000; low: $500; average: $5,000–$100,000).

Purpose and activities: Giving nationally with emphasis on social and cultural organizations which work in areas larger than local communities; support for media projects, projects that support the underprivileged, public policy and traditional family values.

Fields of interest: Arts; Public affairs; Economically disadvantaged.

Type of support: General/operating support.

Limitations: Giving on a national basis. No grants to individuals, or for continuing support.

Publications: Application guidelines.

Application information: Application form not required.

 Initial approach: Letter (no more than 2-3 pages)
 Copies of proposal: 1
 Deadline(s): Feb. 1, June 1, and Sept. 1
 Board meeting date(s): Nov.
 Final notification: Dec.

Officers and Directors:* Philip F. Anschutz,* Chair.; Nancy P. Anschutz,* Pres.; Cannon Y. Harvey,* V.P.; Craig D. Slater,* Secy.-Treas.; M. LaVoy Robison, Exec. Dir.; Christian P. Anschutz; Elizabeth A. Brown; Donald J. Hopkins; Sarah Anschutz Hunt.

Number of staff: 1 full-time support; 1 part-time support.

EIN: 742316617

Selected grants: The following grants were reported in 2004.

$11,460,418 to University of Colorado Hospital Authority, Aurora, CO. 3 grants: $60,418 (For program support), $10,200,000 (For capital support), $1,200,000 (For capital support).

$2,050,000 to Foundation for a Better Life, Denver, CO. For general operating support.

$1,200,000 to Denver Art Museum Foundation, Denver, CO. For capital support.

$300,000 to Denver Foundation, Denver, CO. For program support.

$250,000 to Denver Museum of Nature and Science, Denver, CO. For capital support.

$25,000 to Christian P. Anschutz Foundation, Denver, CO. For general operating support.

$15,000 to Colorado Childrens Immunization Coalition, Denver, CO. For general operating support.

$10,000 to Young Audiences Denver Area Chapter, Denver, CO. For general operating support.

1336

The Arsenault Family Foundation, Inc. ✧ ☆

2400 Industrial Ln., Ste. 2100
Broomfield, CO 80020

Established in 2000.

Donor: Marcel J.C. Arsenault.

Foundation type: Independent foundation.

Financial data (yr. ended 12/31/05): Assets, $7,800,214 (M); expenditures, $378,833; qualifying distributions, $346,000; giving activities include $346,000 for grants.

Fields of interest: Law school/education; Human services; International peace/security.

Limitations: Applications not accepted. Giving primarily in NY. No grants to individuals.

Application information: Contributes only to pre-selected organizations.

Officers: Cynda Collins Arsenault, Pres.; Marcel J.C. Arsenault, V.P.; Sharon K. Eshima, Secy.-Treas.; John F.C. Arsenault, Treas.

EIN: 841569419

Selected grants: The following grants were reported in 2004.

$40,000 to Arts of Peace, Arcata, CA.

$27,650 to New School, New York, NY.

$15,000 to Business Leaders for Sensible Priorities, New York, NY.

$10,000 to Jane Addams Peace Association, New York, NY.

$5,000 to Hague Appeal for Peace, New York, NY.

$5,000 to Search for Common Ground, DC.

$4,600 to Polaris Institute USA, Mill Valley, CA.

$4,000 to University of Colorado Foundation, Boulder, CO.

$3,000 to Council on International and Public Affairs, New York, NY.

$2,661 to World Order Models Project, Newark, NJ.

1337

Aspen Business Center Foundation ✧

(formerly Airport Business Center Foundation)
303 AABC, Ste. E
Aspen, CO 81611-3540

Established in 1986 in CO.

Donors: John P. McBride; John P. McBride, Jr.; Katherine H. McBride; Peter McBride; Lester D. Pedicord; Katherine M. Puckett.

Foundation type: Independent foundation.

Financial data (yr. ended 12/31/05): Assets, $1,198,872 (M); gifts received, $385,000; expenditures, $416,220; qualifying distributions, $416,220; giving activities include $400,350 for 140 grants (high: $20,000; low: $100).

Purpose and activities: To promote the preservation of natural resources, conduct research and educational programs on world over-population and family planning, promote amateur sports, and provide education or medical services for distressed or underprivileged communities.

Fields of interest: Media, radio; Arts; Secondary school/education; Higher education; Education; Environment, natural resources; Environment; Animal welfare; Reproductive health, family planning; Health care, support services; Athletics/sports, amateur competition; Population studies.

Limitations: Applications not accepted. Giving primarily in CO; some funding nationally. No grants to individuals.

Application information: Contributes only to pre-selected organizations.

Trustees: John P. McBride; John P. McBride, Jr.; Laurie M. McBride; Peter M. McBride; Lester D. Pedicord; Kate Puckett.

EIN: 841042661

1338

The Aspen Community Foundation

(formerly Aspen Valley Community Foundation)
110 E. Hallam St., Ste. 126
Aspen, CO 81611 (970) 925-9300
Contact: Tamara Tormohlen, Exec. Dir.; For grants: Sharyn Goodson, Prog. Off.
FAX: (970) 920-2892;
E-mail: info@aspencommunityfoundation.org;
Additional E-mail:

tamara@aspencommunityfoundation.org; Grant information E-mail:
sharyn@aspencommunityfoundation.org;
URL: http://www.aspencommunityfoundation.org/

Established in 1980 in CO.

Foundation type: Community foundation.

Financial data (yr. ended 12/31/04): Assets, $22,985,097 (M); gifts received, $3,138,894; expenditures, $2,430,791; giving activities include $1,864,916 for 468+ grants, and $220,468 for foundation-administered programs.

Purpose and activities: The foundation builds philanthropy and supports nonprofit organizations by connecting donors with community needs, building permanent charitable funds, and bringing people together to solve community problems.

Fields of interest: Education; Health care; Human services; Community development; Aging; Immigrants/refugees.

Type of support: Management development/capacity building; General/operating support; Continuing support; Capital campaigns; Building/renovation; Equipment; Emergency funds; Program development; Seed money; Technical assistance; Program evaluation; Matching/challenge support.

Limitations: Giving primarily from Aspen to Parachute, CO. No support for religious purposes, conduit organizations, or organizations primarily supported by tax-derived funding. No grants to individuals, or for debt retirement, endowments, medical research, scholarships, conferences, seminars, trips, or speaker series.

Publications: Application guidelines; Annual report; Newsletter.

Application information: Visit foundation Web site for grant application information. Application form required.

 Initial approach: Telephone, letter, or e-mail
 Copies of proposal: 2
 Deadline(s): Sept. 6
 Board meeting date(s): Varies
 Final notification: Within 3 months

Officers and Directors:* Michael D. Kaplan,* Chair.; Marcy Edelstein,* Vice-Chair.; Jake Mascotte,* Vice-Chair.; Laurie Michaels,* Secy.; Scott Miller,* Treas.; Tamara Tormohlen, Exec. Dir.; Lawrence Altman; Eric Calderon; Martha Cochran; Susan Crown; Nancy Magoon; Marcie Musser; Brooke Peterson; Arnold Porath; Jay Sandrich; Mary Scanlan; Daniel Shaw; Diano Sirko; Carrie Wells.

Number of staff: 3 full-time professional; 1 part-time professional; 2 part-time support.

EIN: 840829226

1339

Avenir Foundation, Inc. ▼ ✧

3280 Wadsworth Blvd., Ste. 280
Wheat Ridge, CO 80033-4633

Established in 1993 in CO.

Donors: Alice Dodge Wallace; William Dodge Wallace; Margaret Boynton Wallace; Berkshire Hathaway Inc.; Varki Investments, Inc.; Beaumont Investments, Ltd.

Foundation type: Independent foundation.

Financial data (yr. ended 6/30/05): Assets, $506,785 (M); gifts received, $4,570,500; expenditures, $4,683,773; qualifying distributions, $4,683,773; giving activities include $4,633,000 for 11 grants (high: $3,000,000; low: $5,000; average: $25,000–$100,000).

Purpose and activities: Giving primarily for education, with emphasis on an all girls private secondary school; some funding also for the arts, particularly for the opera, as well as to a public research center for music theory in Vienna, Austria, which focuses on the methods of Arnold Schonberg.

Fields of interest: Museums (specialized); Performing arts, opera; Secondary school/education; Libraries (special); Education; Environment, natural resources; Reproductive health; Reproductive health, family planning; Neuroscience research.

International interests: Austria.

Limitations: Applications not accepted. Giving on a national basis with emphasis on CO, as well as in Vienna, Austria. No grants to individuals.

Application information: Contributes only to pre-selected organizations.

Officers and Directors:* Alice Dodge Wallace,* Pres.; William Dodge Wallace,* V.P.; Margaret Boynton Wallace,* Secy.; Norman L. Wilson, Treas.

EIN: 841245939

Selected grants: The following grants were reported in 2005.

$3,000,000 to University of Oklahoma, Norman, OK. For endowment for Physics Department.

$800,000 to American Institute of Physics, College Park, MD. For endowment for oral history project.

$500,000 to Santa Fe Opera, Santa Fe, NM. For production of opera.

$100,000 to Schoenberg Institute, Vienna, Austria. For general operating support.

$58,000 to K G N U Public Radio, Boulder, CO. For Building Fund.

$50,000 to Colorado Symphony Orchestra, Denver, CO. For general operating support.

$25,000 to Opera Colorado, Denver, CO. For general operating support.

$10,000 to Ars Nova Singers, Boulder, CO. For general operating support.

1340

Bacon Family Foundation ✧

c/o Wells Fargo Bank West, N.A.
P.O. Box 4010
Grand Junction, CO   81502-4010

Established in CO.

Foundation type: Independent foundation.

Financial data (yr. ended 6/30/05): Assets, $12,470,782 (M); expenditures, $648,163; qualifying distributions, $608,087; giving activities include $605,270 for 51 grants (high: $50,000; low: $1,000).

Purpose and activities: Giving primarily for social services.

Fields of interest: Arts; Libraries (public); Education; Hospitals (general); Health organizations, association; Human services; Children/youth, services; Federated giving programs; Roman Catholic agencies & churches.

Limitations: Giving primarily in CO, with emphasis on Grand Junction.

Application information: Application form not required.

Deadline(s): None

Officers: Stephen Bacon, Pres.; Andrew Bacon, V.P.; Linda Bacon Reid, Secy.-Treas.

Directors: Herbert Bacon; Laura May Bacon; Pat Gormley; Amy Bacon Hill.

EIN: 841269589

Selected grants: The following grants were reported in 2004.

$58,288 to Mesa State College Foundation, Grand Junction, CO.

$22,000 to United Way of Mesa County, Grand Junction, CO.

$20,000 to Family Health West, Fruita, CO.

$20,000 to Housing Resources of Western Colorado, Grand Junction, CO.

$10,000 to Child and Migrant Services, Palisade, CO.

$10,000 to Family Visitor Program, Glenwood Springs, CO.

$10,000 to Mesa Developmental Services, Grand Junction, CO.

$7,500 to La Puente Home, Alamosa, CO.

$5,000 to C. Henry Kempe National Center for the Prevention and Treatment of Child Abuse, Denver, CO.

$3,000 to Salvation Army of Grand Junction, Grand Junction, CO.

1341

P. Bruce and Virginia C. Benson Foundation ✧

1422 Alamo St.
Colorado Springs, CO   80907-7302
Contact: David Benson, Secy.-Treas.

Established in 1988 in CO.

Donor: P. Bruce Benson†.

Foundation type: Independent foundation.

Financial data (yr. ended 6/30/05): Assets, $6,503,714 (M); expenditures, $457,162; qualifying distributions, $373,000; giving activities include $373,000 for 30 grants (high: $60,000; low: $2,500).

Fields of interest: Higher education; Education; Environment, natural resources; Health care; Human services; YM/YWCAs & YM/YWHAs; Residential/custodial care, hospices.

Limitations: Giving on a national basis. No grants to individuals.

Application information: Application form not required.

Deadline(s): None

Officers: Lucia F. Dhaens, Pres.; Polly Benson-Brown, V.P.; David Benson, Secy.-Treas.

Directors: Bruce D. Benson; Marguerite Benson.

EIN: 841090517

Selected grants: The following grants were reported in 2004.

$25,000 to Childrens Hospital Foundation, Denver, CO.

$20,000 to Capital Partners for Education, DC.

$20,000 to University of Colorado Foundation, Boulder, CO.

$15,000 to North Shore Country Day School, Winnetka, IL.

$13,000 to Hole in the Wall Gang Fund, New Haven, CT.

$12,500 to Darrow School, New Lebanon, NY.

$10,000 to Denver Public Library, Denver, CO.

$10,000 to Hospice of Northeastern Illinois, Barrington, IL.

$5,000 to Pikes Peak Hospice, Colorado Springs, CO.

$4,000 to Mayo Clinic Arizona, Scottsdale, AZ.

1342

Harry H. Beren Trust ✧

c/o Zev Beren
1200 17th St., Ste. 1000
Denver, CO   80202

Established in 1990 in TX.

Donor: Harry H. Beren†.

Foundation type: Independent foundation.

Financial data (yr. ended 12/31/04): Assets, $1,074,294 (M); expenditures, $1,154,900; qualifying distributions, $950,000; giving activities include $950,000 for 36 grants (high: $70,000; low: $5,000).

Purpose and activities: Giving primarily for Jewish education.

Fields of interest: Secondary school/education; Theological school/education; Jewish agencies & temples.

Limitations: Applications not accepted. No grants to individuals.

Application information: Contributes only to pre-selected organizations.

Trustees: David Beren; Zev Beren; Chaskel Feldberger; Isaac Grossman.

EIN: 742584889

1343

Paula & William Bernstein Foundation

16 Polo Club Dr.
Denver, CO   80209
Contact: Paula Bernstein Ph.D., Pres.; William Bernstein M.D., Secy.

Established in 1984.

Donors: Paula Bernstein, Ph.D.; William Bernstein.

Foundation type: Independent foundation.

Financial data (yr. ended 9/30/05): Assets, $10,635,783 (M); expenditures, $776,913; qualifying distributions, $706,046; giving activities include $700,769 for 94 grants (high: $200,100; low: $25).

Purpose and activities: Giving primarily for arts, health and human services.

Fields of interest: Performing arts, music; Health care; Human services; Family services; Jewish federated giving programs; Jewish agencies & temples.

Type of support: General/operating support.

Limitations: Applications not accepted. Giving limited to CO, with emphasis on Denver. No grants to individuals.

Application information: Contributes only to pre-selected organizations. Unsolicited requests for funds not accepted.

Officers: Paula Bernstein, Ph.D., Pres.; William Bernstein, M.D., Secy.

Trustee: Erik Bernstein.

EIN: 742351575

Selected grants: The following grants were reported in 2005.

$200,100 to Wellesley College, Wellesley, MA.

$80,000 to Music Associates of Aspen, Aspen, CO.

$25,000 to Stanford University, Stanford, CA.

$5,500 to Denver Art Museum, Denver, CO.

$1,000 to Denver Center for the Performing Arts, Denver, CO.

$750 to Denver Public Library, Denver, CO.

$500 to Colorado Music Festival, Boulder, CO.

$500 to K B D I Channel 12, Denver, CO.

$500 to Learning Source, Lakewood, CO.

$500 to Up Close and Musical, Englewood, CO.

1344
Boettcher Foundation ▼
600 17th St., Ste. 2210 S.
Denver, CO 80202-5422
Contact: Timothy W. Schultz, Pres. and Exec. Dir.
E-mail: grants@boettcherfoundation.org; Additional
e-mails: scholarships@Boettcherfoundation.org and
info@Boettcherfoundation.org; URL: http://
www.boettcherfoundation.org/

Incorporated in 1937 in CO.
Donors: C.K. Boettcher†; Mrs. C.K. Boettcher†;
Charles Boettcher†; Fannie Boettcher†; Ruth
Boettcher Humphreys†; Mrs. Charles Boettcher II†;
Mae B. Boettcher†.
Foundation type: Independent foundation.
Financial data (yr. ended 12/31/05): Assets,
$244,303,270 (M); expenditures, $13,047,376;
qualifying distributions, $11,985,379; giving
activities include $10,823,926 for 177 grants (high:
$1,099,197; low: $500; average: $10,000–
$100,000).
Purpose and activities: Grants to educational
institutions, with emphasis on the Boettcher
Scholarship Program; community and social
services, including child welfare, women, the
disadvantaged, the homeless, and urban and rural
development; health, including rehabilitation and
drug abuse; and civic and cultural programs,
including support for the fine and performing arts.
Fields of interest: Visual arts; Museums; Performing
arts; Performing arts, music; Historic preservation/
historical societies; Arts; Education, early childhood
education; Higher education; Scholarships/financial
aid; Education; Reproductive health, family
planning; Medical care, rehabilitation; Health care;
Substance abuse, services; Health organizations,
association; Human services; Children/youth,
services; Residential/custodial care, hospices;
Women, centers/services; Homeless, human
services; Rural development; Community
development; Women; Economically disadvantaged;
Homeless.
Type of support: Capital campaigns; Building/
renovation; Land acquisition; Scholarship funds;
Matching/challenge support.
Limitations: Giving limited to CO. No support for
housing, open spaces/parks, organizations that
primarily serve animals, large urban hospitals,
gymnasiums, athletic fields, or religious groups or
organizations for religious purposes. No grants to
individuals, or for endowment funds, pilot programs,
operations, purchase of tables or tickets for
dinners/events, media presentations, small
business start-ups, conferences, seminars,
workshops, debt reduction, or travel.
Publications: Application guidelines; Annual report
(including application guidelines).
Application information: Application form not
required.
  Initial approach: Letter of inquiry
  Copies of proposal: 1
  Deadline(s): Nov. 1 for Boettcher Scholarship
    Program
  Board meeting date(s): Quarterly
  Final notification: 2 to 3 months
Officers and Trustees:* Claudia Boettcher
Merthan,* Chair.; J. William Sorensen,* Vice-Chair.;
Timothy W. Schultz, Pres. and Exec. Dir.; Katie S.
Kramer, V.P.; Harris D. Sherman,* Secy.; Edward D.
White III,* Treas.; Pamela D. Beardsley; Russell
George; M. Ann Penny; Theodore F. Schlegal, M.D.;
Thomas Williams.

Number of staff: 5 full-time professional; 1 part-time
professional; 1 full-time support.
EIN: 840404274

1345
Bohemian Foundation
(formerly The Stryker-Short Foundation)
103 W. Mountain Ave.
Fort Collins, CO 80524   (970) 482-4642
Contact: Merry Hummell, Exec. Dir.
FAX: (970) 482-6139;
E-mail: info@bohemianfoundation.org; URL: http://
www.bohemianfoundation.org

Established in MI in 1995.
Donors: Patricia A. Short; Pat Stryker.
Foundation type: Independent foundation.
Financial data (yr. ended 12/31/05): Assets,
$62,161,420 (M); gifts received, $357;
expenditures, $9,875,680; qualifying distributions,
$9,701,639; giving activities include $9,339,076
for 120 grants (high: $3,913,585; low: $500).
Purpose and activities: The mission of the
foundation is to involve fellow citizens in the care
and improvement of the community.
Fields of interest: Children/youth, services.
Type of support: General/operating support;
Continuing support; Capital campaigns; Building/
renovation; Equipment; Program development;
Publication; Seed money; Research; Technical
assistance; Consulting services; Program
evaluation; Matching/challenge support.
Limitations: Giving limited to the Fort Collins, CO,
area. No support for specific religious programs. No
grants to individuals, or for scholarships, debt
reduction, or for program-related investments.
Publications: Application guidelines.
Application information: Please visit the foundation
Web site for more information as well as grant
guidelines and application form. Application form
required.
  Copies of proposal: 1
  Deadline(s): Feb. and Sept.; specific dates
    available on foundation Web site
  Final notification: May for Feb. deadline; Dec. for
    Sept. deadline; specific dates available on
    foundation Web site
Officers and Director:* Pat Stryker, Pres.; Joe
Zimlich,* Secy.-Treas; Merry Hummell, Exec. Dir.
Number of staff: 1 full-time professional; 1 part-time
professional; 1 full-time support.
EIN: 841605993
Selected grants: The following grants were reported
in 2003.
$356,500 to Community Foundation of Northern
  Colorado, Fort Collins, CO. For Youth Activity
  Center Child Care assistance.
$75,000 to Family Center/La Familia, Fort Collins,
  CO. For services, assistance and information to
  families who desire to improve health and quality
  of their lives.
$70,000 to Firstcall Service Net, Fort Collins, CO. To
  provide community resource information.
$65,000 to Wingshadow, Fort Collins, CO. For
  educational, recreational, housing referrals,
  crisis counseling and other services to
  endangered youth in Northern Colorado.
$61,575 to Respite Care, Fort Collins, CO. For
  short-term quality care for children with
  developmental disabilities.
$28,000 to Project Self-Sufficiency of Loveland-Fort
  Collins, Loveland, CO. To assist low-income
  single parents.

$25,000 to Community Affordable Residences
  Enterprise (CARE) Housing, Fort Collins, CO. For
  Supportive Service program.
$25,000 to Crossroads Safehouse, Fort Collins, CO.
  For Crossroads Children's programs.
$25,000 to Turning Point Center for Youth and
  Family Development, Fort Collins, CO. For general
  community support.
$21,042 to Center for Community Justice
  Partnerships, Fort Collins, CO. for community
  support.

1346
The Bohen Foundation ◇
c/o D. Monte Pascoe
1675 Broadway, Ste. 2600
Denver, CO 80202

Incorporated in 1958 in IA.
Donors: Mildred M. Bohen Charitable Trust; Edna E.
Meredith Charitable Trust.
Foundation type: Independent foundation.
Financial data (yr. ended 6/30/05): Assets,
$8,398,786 (M); expenditures, $2,557,388;
qualifying distributions, $2,172,802; giving
activities include $812,599 for 2 grants (high:
$697,599; low: $115,000), and $371,331 for 4
foundation-administered programs.
Purpose and activities: Giving primarily for arts and
cultural programs with a focus on commissioning
new works of art with particular emphasis on film,
video, new media, and installation of art.
Fields of interest: Museums (art); Arts.
Type of support: General/operating support; Annual
campaigns; Building/renovation; Program
development.
Limitations: Applications not accepted. Giving
primarily in New York, NY. No grants to individuals.
Publications: Grants list.
Application information: Contributes only to
pre-selected organizations.
  Board meeting date(s): As required
Officers and Directors:* Frederick B. Henry,* Pres.;
Linda Cucchiara Behr, Secy.; Frederick B. Henry, Jr.;
Sarah Trundle.
Number of staff: 2 full-time professional; 1 full-time
support; 1 part-time support.
EIN: 426054774

1347
Bonfils-Stanton Foundation
Daniels and Fisher Twr.
1601 Arapahoe St., Ste. 500
Denver, CO 80202   (303) 825-3774
Contact: Dorothy A. Horrell Ph.D., C.E.O.
URL: http://www.bonfils-stanton.org

Established in 1962 in CO.
Donors: Charles E. Stanton†; Robert E. Stanton†.
Foundation type: Independent foundation.
Financial data (yr. ended 6/30/06): Assets,
$79,042,940 (M); expenditures, $3,803,948;
qualifying distributions, $3,384,683; giving
activities include $2,765,650 for 62 grants (high:
$500,000; low: $1,500), and $3,789 for 1 in-kind
gift.
Purpose and activities: The foundation was created
to enhance the quality of life for residents of CO. The
mission of the foundation is to advance excellence
in the areas of arts and culture, community service,
and science and medicine through strategic

investments resulting in significant and unique contributions in these fields. In addition to grantmaking, the foundation annually provides 3 awards to Coloradans who have made significant contributions in the fields of arts and humanities, community service, and science and medicine.

Fields of interest: Humanities; Arts; Human services; Economically disadvantaged.

Type of support: Capital campaigns; Building/renovation; Equipment; Program development; Research; Technical assistance.

Limitations: Giving limited to CO. No support for activities or initiatives that have a religious purpose or objective. Generally no grants to individuals (except for award programs), or for scholarships, fellowships, endowments, seminars, conferences, media productions, fundraising, travel expenses, or to retire debt.

Publications: Annual report (including application guidelines); Grants list.

Application information: Telephone office prior to submitting a request. Application information available on foundation Web site. Application form not required.

  Initial approach: Telephone call
  Copies of proposal: 1
  Deadline(s): Last business day of Jan., Apr., Jul., Oct.
  Board meeting date(s): Jan., Apr., July, and Oct.
  Final notification: Generally 4 months following application deadline

Officers and Trustees:* J. Landis Martin,* Chair.; Dorothy A. Horrell, Ph.D., C.E.O and Pres.; Susan H. France, V.P., Progs.; W. Eileen Greenawalt,* Secy.; Linda Niven, Treas. and Cont.; Johnston R. Livingston,* Chair. Emeritus; Louis J. Duman, M.D.; Flaminia Odescalchi Kelly; Harold R. Logan, Jr.; John E. Repine, M.D.

Number of staff: 2 full-time professional; 1 part-time professional; 1 full-time support.

EIN: 846029014

1348
Bowana Foundation ◇
831 Pearl St.
Boulder, CO 80302   (303) 381-2605
Contact: Bob Brown

Donor: Scott A. Beck.
Foundation type: Independent foundation.
Financial data (yr. ended 11/30/03): Assets, $44,087,606 (M); expenditures, $1,250,594; qualifying distributions, $1,217,299; giving activities include $571,514 for 26 grants (high: $200,000; low: $300), and $580,006 for 1 foundation-administered program.
Purpose and activities: Giving primarily for education and evangelism.
Fields of interest: Higher education; Protestant agencies & churches.
Limitations: Giving primarily in CO.
Application information:
  Initial approach: Letter
  Deadline(s): None
Officer: Scott A. Beck, Pres.
EIN: 363799613
Selected grants: The following grants were reported in 2003.
$200,000 to Global Peace Congress, Palo Alto, CA.
$157,830 to Campus Crusade for Christ International, Orlando, FL.
$25,000 to National Wrestling Hall of Fame, Stillwater, OK.

$24,000 to Tree of Life Presbyterian Church, Boulder, CO.
$20,000 to Family Learning Center, Boulder, CO.
$18,000 to Kids Across America Foundation, Branson, MO.
$10,000 to Rocky Mountain Christian Church, Longmont, CO.
$5,968 to CitiReach International, Colorado Springs, CO.
$5,000 to Emergency Family Assistance Association, Boulder, CO.
$4,500 to Priority Associates, New York, NY.

1349
Brett Family Foundation ◇
1123 Spruce St.
Boulder, CO 80302   (303) 442-1200
FAX: (303) 442-1221;
E-mail: info@brettfoundation.org; URL: http://www.brettfoundation.org

Established in 1999 in CO.
Donors: Stephen M. Brett; Linda J. Shoemaker.
Foundation type: Independent foundation.
Financial data (yr. ended 12/31/05): Assets, $9,402,165 (M); expenditures, $728,265; qualifying distributions, $631,821; giving activities include $521,763 for 67 grants (high: $100,000; low: $100).
Purpose and activities: The foundation supports caring communities by investing in organizations throughout CO which work for social justice, and to Boulder County, CO, nonprofits which address the needs of underserved communities, primarily disadvantaged youth and their families.
Fields of interest: Education; Health care; Youth, services; Community development; Public policy, research.
Type of support: General/operating support; Continuing support; Capital campaigns; Building/renovation; Equipment; Emergency funds; Program development; Seed money; Technical assistance.
Limitations: Giving primarily in Boulder County, CO. No support for religious organizations, or for individual public or private schools (K-12, graduate or post graduate), or for large public charities. No grants to individuals.
Publications: Application guidelines; Annual report.
Application information: Colorado Common Grant Application Form available on Web site. Application form not required.
  Initial approach: Letter
  Copies of proposal: 1
  Deadline(s): Jan. 15 and July 1, for letters of inquiry
  Final notification: 2-3 months
Officers and Trustees:* Stephen M. Brett,* Chair.; Linda J. Shoemaker,* Pres.; Meaghan Jones Collins, Exec. Dir.; Emily Shoemaker Brett; Matthew Stephen Brett; Claudia Brett Goldin.
Number of staff: 1 part-time professional.
EIN: 841525821
Selected grants: The following grants were reported in 2004.
$100,000 to Bell Policy Center, Denver, CO.
$15,000 to Colorado Progressive Coalition, Denver, CO.
$12,500 to Women Donors Network, Palo Alto, CA. 2 grants: $2,500, $10,000
$10,000 to Colorado Childrens Campaign, Denver, CO.
$10,000 to Colorado Consumer Health Initiative, Denver, CO.

$10,000 to Womens Foundation of Colorado, Denver, CO.
$5,000 to Common Cause Education Fund, DC.
$5,000 to Safe Shelter of Saint Vrain Valley, Longmont, CO.
$2,500 to Boulder Valley Womens Health Center, Boulder, CO.

1350
Temple Hoyne Buell Foundation ▼
1666 S. University Blvd., Ste. B
Denver, CO 80210   (303) 744-1688
Contact: Susan J. Steele, Exec. Dir.
FAX: (303) 744-1601;
E-mail: info@buellfoundation.org; URL: http://www.buellfoundation.org

Incorporated in 1962 in CO.
Donor: Temple Hoyne Buell†.
Foundation type: Independent foundation.
Financial data (yr. ended 6/30/06): Assets, $201,643,689 (M); expenditures, $7,999,915; qualifying distributions, $4,940,466; giving activities include $4,940,466 for grants.
Purpose and activities: The foundation is a professional philanthropic organization supporting the positive development of children through grants and partnerships with other sectors of the community.
Fields of interest: Education, early childhood education; Children/youth, services; Children, day care; Youth, pregnancy prevention.
Type of support: General/operating support; Continuing support; Capital campaigns; Building/renovation; Equipment; Technical assistance; Program evaluation.
Limitations: Giving only in CO. No support for political organizations, sectarian programs, or promoting religion. Generally, no support for medical programs. No grants to individuals, or for past operating deficit, or retirement of debt. Generally, no grants for testimonial dinners, multi-year awards, events, annual campaigns, membership drives, emergency needs, conferences, or endowments; no loans.
Publications: Annual report (including application guidelines); Financial statement; Grants list.
Application information: The foundation accepts the Colorado Common Grant Report Format. Proposals sent by fax not considered. Application forms and guidelines are available on the foundation Web site. Organizations are limited to one grant request in any twelve month period. Application form required.
  Initial approach: Proposal or telephone for guidelines
  Copies of proposal: 1
  Deadline(s): 1st business day of Jan., May, and Sept.
  Board meeting date(s): 3 times per year
  Final notification: 4 months after deadline
Officers and Trustees:* Daniel L. Ritchie,* Pres.; Hon. Luis D. Rovira,* Secy.; Thomas J. Curnes,* Treas.; Lisa Ernst, Cont.; Susan J. Steele, Exec. Dir.; Arthur H. Bosworth II; Deedee Gale Mayer; Marguerite Salazar; Reginald L. Washington, M.D.
Number of staff: 3 full-time professional; 1 part-time professional; 1 part-time support.
EIN: 846037604
Selected grants: The following grants were reported in 2005.
$106,641 to Clayton Foundation, Denver, CO. For training on environmental rating scales and

maintenance of inter-rater reliability system in Colorado.

$106,532 to Early Childhood Council of Larimer County, Fort Collins, CO. For Larimer County professional development project.

$100,866 to Durango 4-C Council, Durango, CO. For Early Childhood Professional Development Project.

$80,000 to Boys and Girls Club of Pueblo County, Pueblo, CO. For general operating support.

$62,962 to Colorado State University Foundation, Fort Collins, CO. For Project Secure.

$50,000 to University of Denver, Denver, CO. For Chancellor's Discretionary Fund.

$30,000 to Planned Parenthood of the Rocky Mountains, Denver, CO. For Dollar-A-Day, Growing Up Smart, and Personal Responsibility Education Program.

$15,000 to Park County School District RE-2, Fairplay, CO. For Parents as Teachers program.

$15,000 to Partners in Huerfano-Las Animas Counties, La Veta, CO. For general operating support.

$10,000 to Peak to Peak Healthy Communities Project, Over the Rainbow Community Preschool, Nederland, CO. For general operating support.

1351
Carson Foundation ✧ ☆

(formerly The Leila Carroll Foundation)
1247 S. Vine St.
Denver, CO   80210

Established in 1994 in CO.
Donor: Lelia Carroll.
Foundation type: Independent foundation.
Financial data (yr. ended 12/31/05): Assets, $12,823,716 (M); expenditures, $726,245; qualifying distributions, $648,186; giving activities include $635,934 for 78 grants (high: $170,000; low: $40).
Purpose and activities: Giving primarily for human services, the United Way and other federated giving programs.
Fields of interest: Education; Human services; Federated giving programs.
Limitations: Applications not accepted. Giving primarily in Denver, CO; some funding also in AZ and MA. No grants to individuals.
Application information: Contributes only to pre-selected organizations.
Trustee: Lelia Carroll.
EIN: 846277774
Selected grants: The following grants were reported in 2003.

$74,400 to Carson Residential Alternative Homes, Denver, CO. For program support.

$32,500 to University of Denver, Denver, CO. 3 grants: $2,500 to School of Hotel, Restaurant and Tourism Management (For program support), $5,000 (For lacrosse programs), $25,000 (For scholarships).

$22,000 to Summit Foundation, Breckenridge, CO. For program support.

$10,040 to United Way, Mile High, Denver, CO. For program support.

$4,250 to Denver Academy, Denver, CO. For program support.

$2,000 to Denver Art Museum, Denver, CO. For program support.

$2,000 to Graland Country Day School, Denver, CO. For program support.

$1,500 to Denver Dumb Friends League-Humane Society of Denver, Denver, CO. For program support.

1352
Castle Rock Foundation

4100 E. Mississippi Ave., Ste. 1850
Denver, CO   80246   (303) 388-1636
Contact: Sally W. Rippey, Exec. Dir.; John W. Jackson, National Prog. Advisor
FAX: (303) 388-1684;
E-mail: generalinfo@castlerockfdn.org; URL: http://www.castlerockfoundation.org

Established in 1993 in CO.
Donor: Adolph Coors Foundation.
Foundation type: Independent foundation.
Financial data (yr. ended 11/30/05): Assets, $54,235,113 (M); expenditures, $2,586,987; qualifying distributions, $2,571,922; giving activities include $2,441,285 for 44 grants (high: $200,000; low: $5,000).
Purpose and activities: The mission of the foundation is to: promote a better understanding of the free enterprise system; preserve the principles upon which our democracy was founded to help ensure a limited role for government and the protection of individual rights as provided for in the Constitution; encourage personal responsibility and leadership; and uphold traditional American values.
Fields of interest: Public policy, research; Public affairs.
Type of support: General/operating support.
Limitations: Giving on a national basis. No support for religious organizations. No grants to individuals, or for museums, endowment funds, deficit reduction, publications, films, special events, computer equipment, out of country projects, or scientific or medical research.
Publications: Application guidelines; Annual report; Annual report (including application guidelines).
Application information: Application guidelines available on foundation Web site. Application form not required.

Initial approach: Proposal
Copies of proposal: 1
Deadline(s): Mar. 15
Board meeting date(s): Fall

Officers and Trustees:* Peter H. Coors,* Pres.; Rev. Robert G. Windsor,* V.P.; Jeffrey H. Coors,* Treas.; Sally W. Rippey, Exec. Dir.; Amb. Holland H. Coors; William K. Coors; Cecily Coors Garnsey; Melissa Coors Osborn.
EIN: 841243301
Selected grants: The following grants were reported in 2005.

$250,000 to Air Force Memorial Foundation, Arlington, VA.

$200,000 to Heritage Foundation, DC.

$175,785 to Hillsdale College, Hillsdale, MI.

$125,000 to Childrens Hospital Corporation, Boston, MA.

$75,000 to Intercollegiate Studies Institute, Wilmington, DE.

$75,000 to Pacific Legal Foundation, Sacramento, CA.

$60,000 to Landmark Legal Foundation, Leesburg, VA.

$50,000 to Ethics and Public Policy Center, DC.

$50,000 to Radio America, DC.

$40,000 to National Association of Scholars, Princeton, NJ.

1353
Caulkins Family Foundation ✧

1600 Broadway, Ste. 1400
Denver, CO   80202-4909

Established in 1993 in CO.
Donors: George P. Caulkins, Jr.; John N. Caulkins; Mary I. Caulkins.
Foundation type: Independent foundation.
Financial data (yr. ended 12/31/05): Assets, $5,044,566 (M); expenditures, $383,150; qualifying distributions, $381,989; giving activities include $371,001 for 47 grants (high: $99,500; low: $250).
Fields of interest: Arts; Elementary/secondary education; Environment, natural resources; Food services; Boys & girls clubs; Human services.
Limitations: Applications not accepted. Giving primarily in CO. No grants to individuals.
Application information: Contributes only to pre-selected organizations.
Officers and Directors:* Eleanor N. Caulkins,* Pres.; Maxwell O.B. Caulkins,* V.P. and Secy.; Mary I. Caulkins, V.P. and Treas.; David I. Caulkins,* V.P.; George P. Caulkins III*; John N. Caulkins*.
EIN: 841251441
Selected grants: The following grants were reported in 2003.

$23,000 to Center for Furniture Craftsmanship, Rockport, ME.

$12,000 to Museum of Contemporary Art Denver, Denver, CO.

$12,000 to Opera Colorado, Denver, CO.

$10,000 to Boys and Girls Clubs of Metro Denver, Denver, CO.

$8,000 to Rocky Mountain Institute, Snowmass, CO.

$2,000 to Volunteers for Outdoor Colorado, Denver, CO.

$1,000 to Aspen Music Festival, Aspen, CO.

$1,000 to Colorado Endowment for the Humanities, Denver, CO.

$1,000 to Denver Museum of Nature and Science, Denver, CO.

$1,000 to High Country Foundation, Paonia, CO.

1354
Chambers Family Fund

(formerly Axem Foundation)
1700 Lincoln St., Ste. 3950
Denver, CO   80203-4539   (303) 839-4620
Contact: Letty Bass, Exec. Dir.
FAX: (303) 839-4619;
E-mail: info@chambersfund.org; URL: http://www.chambersfund.org

Established in 1983 in CO.
Donors: Evelyn H. Chambers†; Merle C. Chambers.
Foundation type: Independent foundation.
Financial data (yr. ended 11/30/05): Assets, $60,418,934 (M); gifts received, $170,956; expenditures, $3,459,896; qualifying distributions, $3,197,686; giving activities include $2,568,246 for 86 grants (high: $660,000; low: $25), and $260,431 for 25 employee matching gifts.
Purpose and activities: Giving primarily for women's economic self-sufficiency, early care and education of children, democratic values, and arts and culture.
Fields of interest: Humanities; Arts; Child development, education; Women, centers/services; Civil rights, advocacy.
Type of support: General/operating support; Continuing support; Capital campaigns;

Endowments; Program development; Research; Technical assistance; Program evaluation; Employee matching gifts; Matching/challenge support.

Limitations: Applications not accepted. Giving primarily in CO and the Rocky Mountain region. No grants to individuals.

Publications: Annual report; Grants list.

Application information: All grants are researched and initiated by the foundation. Unsolicited requests for funds not accepted.

  Board meeting date(s): As required

Officers and Directors:* Merle C. Chambers,* Pres.; Letty Bass, Secy. and Exec. Dir.; Joy Hall, Treas.; Hugh A. Grant; Donald J. Hopkins; Marla J. Williams.

Number of staff: 1 full-time professional; 1 full-time support; 1 part-time support.

EIN: 840929410

1355
Colorado Masons Benevolent Fund Association ◇

c/o Scottish Rite Masonic Center
1370 Grant St., Ste. 212
Denver, CO   80203-2347
Contact: Robert L. Bartholic, Exec. Secy.

Established in 1899; incorporated in 1912 in CO.

Foundation type: Operating foundation.

Financial data (yr. ended 10/30/05): Assets, $11,608,765 (M); gifts received, $59,525; expenditures, $737,078; qualifying distributions, $655,073; giving activities include $296,254 for 120 grants (high: $24,079; low: $250), and $323,093 for 68 grants to individuals (high: $7,000; low: $593).

Purpose and activities: A private operating foundation; awards assistance grants to needy, distressed CO Masons and their families through local lodges, and scholarships to CO high school seniors planning to attend college in CO. Masonic affiliation not required for scholarships.

Fields of interest: Economically disadvantaged.

Type of support: Grants to individuals; Scholarships—to individuals; Matching/challenge support; Student loans—to individuals.

Limitations: Applications not accepted. Giving limited to CO.

Application information: Lodge officers seeking assistance on behalf of a member or widow must submit an Application for Assistance to the Fund. Scholarship application forms available in Nov. from CO public high school counselors; individual forms will not be mailed out by the association; letters requesting applications will not be answered. Requests accepted only through Colorado Masonic Lodge. Unsolicited requests for funds not accepted.

Officers and Trustees:* Richard W. Schmidt,* Chair.; Rodney G. Jordan,* Pres.; Ben M. Crossno, V.P.; Robert L. Bartholic, Exec. Secy.; David M. Naiman,* Secy.; Milton Brandwein,* Treas.; Ben H. Bell, Jr.

Number of staff: 1 full-time professional; 1 part-time support.

EIN: 840406813

1356
The Colorado Trust ▼

1600 Sherman St.
Denver, CO   80203-1604   (303) 837-1200
Contact: Carol Breslau, V.P., Initiatives
FAX: (303) 839-9034;
E-mail: Carol@coloradotrust.org; Additional tel.: (888) 847-9140; URL: http://www.coloradotrust.org

Established in 1985 in CO; converted from the proceeds of the sale of Presbyterian/St. Luke's Healthcare Corp. to AM1.

Donor: Presbyterian/St. Luke's Healthcare Corp.

Foundation type: Independent foundation.

Financial data (yr. ended 12/31/05): Assets, $449,283,852 (M); expenditures, $36,436,538; qualifying distributions, $18,841,966; giving activities include $18,729,668 for 302+ grants, and $112,298 for employee matching gifts.

Purpose and activities: To advance the health and well-being of the people of Colorado.

Fields of interest: Health care; Mental health/crisis services; Health organizations, association; Youth development; Family services; Aging.

Type of support: Seed money; Matching/challenge support; General/operating support; Continuing support; Program development; Publication; Fellowships; Research; Technical assistance; Program evaluation; Program-related investments/loans; Employee matching gifts.

Limitations: Giving limited to CO. No support for religious organizations for religious purposes, political organizations, private foundations, or direct subsidization of care to the medically indigent. No grants to individuals, or for endowments, deficit financing or debt retirement, building funds, real estate acquisition, fundraising drives and events, or testimonial dinners.

Publications: Annual report; Informational brochure; Newsletter; Occasional report.

Application information: Application requirements are detailed in specific Requests for Proposals published at intervals throughout the year. Application form not required.

  Initial approach: Applications are accepted following release of Requests for Proposals issued by the trust; to receive a copy, print the RFP directly from the trust Web site or telephone

  Deadline(s): Governed by Requests for Proposals process

  Board meeting date(s): Quarterly

Officers and Trustees:* Jerome M. Buckley, M.D.*, Chair.; William N. Maniatis, M.D.*, Vice-Chair.; Irene M. Ibarra, C.E.O and Pres.; John L. Samuelson, V.P. and C.F.O.; Carol Breslau, V.P., Initiatives; Kathryn A. Paul,* Secy.; Stephen B. Clark,* Treas.; Joanne Johnson, Cont.; Jack D. Henderson, Genl. Counsel; Rev. R. J. Ross, Tr.-Elect; Gail S. Schoettler, Tr.-Elect; Patricia Baca, Ed.D.; Jean C. Jones; Sr. Lillian Murphy, R.S.M.; Judith B. Wagner; Reginald L. Washington, M.D.

Number of staff: 15 full-time professional; 7 full-time support.

EIN: 840994055

Selected grants: The following grants were reported in 2005.

$2,310,000 to Colorado Foundation for Families and Children, Denver, CO.

$1,791,000 to University of Colorado, Denver, CO. 2 grants: $1,425,000 to Center for Public-Private Sector Cooperation, $366,000 to School of Dentistry

$1,448,927 to Colorado Rural Health Resource Center, Denver, CO.

$580,000 to Colorado Springs Assets for Youth, Colorado Springs, CO.

$150,000 to Boys and Girls Club of Pueblo County, Pueblo, CO.

$131,444 to Morgan Community College, Fort Morgan, CO.

$35,000 to Parkview Medical Center, Pueblo, CO.

$20,000 to Lutheran Family Services of Colorado, Denver, CO.

$14,020 to Southern Ute Community Action Program, Ignacio, CO.

1357
Community Foundation of Northern Colorado ◇

(formerly Fort Collins Area Community Foundation)
4745 Wheaton Dr., Ste. 100
Fort Collins, CO   80525   (970) 224-3462
Contact: Ray Caraway, Exec. Dir.; For grants: Roxanne Fry, Dir., Donor Svcs.
FAX: (970) 224-5153; E-mail: info@cfnc.info; Additional E-mail: rcaraway@cfnc.info; Grant inquiry E-mail: Roxanne@cfnc.info; URL: http://www.cfnc.info

Incorporated in 1975 in CO.

Foundation type: Community foundation.

Financial data (yr. ended 6/30/04): Assets, $18,402,095 (M); gifts received, $3,444,091; expenditures, $1,659,501; giving activities include $1,309,071 for 307 grants (high: $250,000; low: $90; average: $90–$250,000).

Purpose and activities: The foundation seeks to build a better community by promoting philanthropy through creative donor services.

Fields of interest: Humanities; Arts; Education; Health care; Disasters, Hurricane Katrina; Human services; Community development.

Type of support: General/operating support; Endowments; Program development; Seed money; Scholarship funds; Matching/challenge support.

Limitations: Giving limited to northern CO, with emphasis on Larimer County.

Publications: Annual report; Newsletter.

Application information: Visit foundation Web site for application forms and guidelines. Application form required.

  Initial approach: Submit application Cover Sheet and attachments

  Copies of proposal: 2

  Deadline(s): Sept. 1 for Community Needs Grant Prog.; varies for others

  Board meeting date(s): Every other month

  Final notification: Late Nov.

Officers and Trustees:* Steve Hagberg,* Chair.; Dave Edwards,* Vice-Chair.; Wynne O'dell,* Secy.-Treas.; Sandra M. Boatman, C.F.O.; Ray Caraway, Exec. Dir.; Donna Beard; Mike Dellenbach; Phil Farley; Bruce Hach; Larry Kendall; Chris Kneeland; Judy Lamy; Lucia Liley; Chris Osborn; Mark Soukup; Steve Todd; Gary Wamsley.

Number of staff: 5 full-time professional; 1 part-time support.

EIN: 840699243

Selected grants: The following grants were reported in 2005.

$626,355 to Fort Collins, City of, Youth Activity Center, Fort Collins, CO.

$87,400 to Serimus Operating Foundation, Fort Collins, CO.

$33,600 to United Way of Larimer County, Fort Collins, CO. 2 grants: $23,600, $10,000
$29,641 to Colorado State University Foundation, Fort Collins, CO.
$25,000 to Poudre School District R-1, Fort Collins, CO. 2 grants: $13,000, $12,000

1358
The Community Foundation Serving Boulder County ◇

(formerly Boulder Area Communities Foundation)
1123 Spruce St.
Boulder, CO   80302-5281   (303) 442-0436
Contact: Josie Heath, Pres.; For grants: Carly Hare, Progs. Dir.
FAX: (303) 442-1221; E-mail: info@commfound.org; Additional tel: (888) 744-7239; Additional E-mail: Carly@commfound.org; Grant application E-mail: grants@commfound.org; URL: http://www.commfound.org

Established in 1991 in CO.
Foundation type: Community foundation.
Financial data (yr. ended 12/31/05): Assets, $30,765,966 (L); gifts received, $7,178,321; expenditures, $5,484,359; giving activities include $4,676,291 for grants.
Purpose and activities: The foundation seeks to improve the quality of life in Boulder County, now and forever, and to encourage an ethic of philanthropy. The foundation provides support primarily for arts and culture, education, the environment, health care, and human services.
Fields of interest: Arts; Education; Environment; Health care; Disasters, Hurricane Katrina; Human services; Public affairs; LGBTQ.
Type of support: General/operating support; Continuing support; Annual campaigns; Capital campaigns; Building/renovation; Equipment; Endowments; Emergency funds; Program development; Conferences/seminars; Seed money; Scholarship funds; Technical assistance; Consulting services; Program-related investments/loans; Employee matching gifts; Scholarships—to individuals; In-kind gifts; Student loans—to individuals.
Limitations: Giving primarily in the Boulder County, CO, area. No support for religious purposes.
Publications: Application guidelines; Annual report; Financial statement; Grants list; Informational brochure (including application guidelines); Newsletter.
Application information: Visit foundation Web site for application form and guidelines. The foundation strongly encourages applicants to submit application via e-mail; faxed applications are not accepted. Application form required.
　Initial approach: Submit application form, concept letter, and attachments
　Copies of proposal: 1
　Deadline(s): Sept. 29
　Board meeting date(s): Monthly
　Final notification: Jan.
Officers and Trustees: * Bob Morehouse,* Chair.; Benita Duran,* Vice-Chair.; Josie Heath,* Pres.; Conrad Lattes,* Secy.; Debbie Gaffney, C.F.O.; Shelly D. Merritt,* Treas.; Janelle Weissman, Exec. Dir., Social Venture Partners - Boulder Co.; Steve Brett; Richard Cross; Brad Field; T.J. Heyman; Robin Luff; Esther Quintana Matheson; Jane McConnell; Mariagnes Medrud; John Neville; Bill Roberts; William S. Rubin; Rick Sterling; Bill Sterner; Jill Stravolemos; Euvaldo Valdez; Kenneth W. Zelie.

Number of staff: 5 full-time professional; 2 part-time professional.
EIN: 841171836

1359
Community Foundation Serving Greeley and Weld County

711 8th Ave.
Greeley, CO   80631-3955   (970) 304-9970
Contact: Judy Knapp, Pres.
FAX: (970) 352-1271;
E-mail: information1@greeleyweldcomfound.org; Additional E-mails: info@greeleyweldcomfound.org and judy@greeleyweldcomfound.org; URL: http://www.greeleyweldcomfound.org

Established in 1972; merged in 1997 in CO.
Donors: Cameron DeCamp; Annette Fulton; Lucile J. Gray; Alpine Gardens; H + H Excavation; BMC West; Siegrist Construction.
Foundation type: Community foundation.
Financial data (yr. ended 12/31/05): Assets, $10,862,011 (M); gifts received, $1,009,502; expenditures, $1,234,843; giving activities include $353,653 for 134 grants (high: $40,000; low: $100), $59,298 for 64 grants to individuals (high: $5,000; low: $63), $3,000 for 3 loans to individuals, and $638,400 for 79 foundation-administered programs.
Purpose and activities: The foundation seeks to facilitate the desires of donors in order to develop growing endowments which will serve to improve the quality of life in the community.
Fields of interest: Arts; Education; Health care; Housing/shelter; Recreation; Youth development; Youth, services; Human services; Community development; Women.
Type of support: General/operating support; Endowments; Emergency funds; Program development; Professorships; Seed money; Curriculum development; Scholarship funds; Consulting services; Matching/challenge support.
Limitations: Giving primarily to residents of Greeley and Weld County, CO. No support for sectarian religious purposes or for-profit organizations. No grants for capital fund drives.
Publications: Application guidelines; Annual report; Financial statement; Informational brochure; Newsletter.
Application information: Visit foundation Web site for application forms and additional guidelines per grant type requested. Application form required.
　Initial approach: Submit application form and attachments
　Deadline(s): Jan. 15 and July 15 for Arts Alive Fund; Jan. 5, Apr. 6, July 6, and Oct. 5 for Littler Youth Fund
　Board meeting date(s): 3rd Mon. of the month
　Final notification: 2 months
Officers and Directors: * Stanley A. Cass,* Chair.; Bill Hertneky,* Vice-Chair.; Judy Knapp, Pres.; Mike Ketterling,* Secy.; Royal Lovell,* Treas.; Nick Berryman; Marsha Biddle; Bonnie B. Dean; Al Dominguez; Betty Hall; Josh Magden; Rhonda Morehead; E.A. "Buck" Moskalski; Tony Pariso; R. Lee Seward; Pat Thomas.
Number of staff: 3 full-time professional.
EIN: 841315296
Selected grants: The following grants were reported in 2005.

$15,000 to North Colorado Medical Center Foundation, Greeley, CO. For First Steps of Weld County.
$12,000 to United Way of Weld County, Greeley, CO. For 211 program.
$10,000 to Weld Food Bank, Greeley, CO. For operating support.
$6,750 to Aims Community College Foundation, Greeley, CO. For scholarships.
$5,000 to Rehabilitation and Visiting Nurse Association, Greeley, CO. For oxygenation assessment and follow-up.
$2,500 to Greeley Philharmonic Orchestra Association, Greeley, CO. For Chamber Music Alive! October outreach.
$2,500 to Greeley Rodarte Dancers, Greeley, CO.
$1,500 to Jefferson Elementary School, Greeley, CO. For literacy program.
$1,000 to Four-H Youth Fund of Colorado, Fort Collins, CO. For scholarships.
$1,000 to Weld Library District Foundation, Greeley, CO. For Twinkle Babies LapSit Story Time.

1360
Adolph Coors Foundation ▼

4100 E. Mississippi Ave., Ste. 1850
Denver, CO   80246   (303) 388-1636
Contact: Sally W. Rippey, Exec. Dir.
E-mail: generalinfo@acoorsfnd.org; URL: http://www.adolphcoors.org

Incorporated in 1975 in CO.
Donors: Adolph Coors, Jr.†; Gertrude S. Coors†; Janet Coors†.
Foundation type: Independent foundation.
Financial data (yr. ended 11/30/05): Assets, $147,826,585 (M); expenditures, $6,689,249; qualifying distributions, $6,600,739; giving activities include $5,891,400 for 147 grants (high: $500,000; low: $1,150; average: $10,000–$100,000).
Purpose and activities: The primary areas of foundation interest are: 1) Health, with emphasis on programs that are preventive in nature, promote wellness and/or can demonstrate a reduction in health-care costs; 2) Education, focusing on institutions and programs that foster excellence in the knowledge of free enterprise, science, technology and ethics; 3) Youth, Community and Human Services, with focus on agencies that assist the disadvantaged in their efforts to be self-sufficient and productive and that nurture the development of integrity and leadership; and 4) Civic and Culture, primarily programs that enhance our culture and heritage, demonstrate our creativity as a people and are likely to be of economic benefit to and broadly used by the communities they serve.
Fields of interest: Education; Health care; Human services; Youth, services; Economically disadvantaged.
Type of support: General/operating support; Capital campaigns; Building/renovation; Program development.
Limitations: Giving primarily in CO. No support for preschools, day care centers, nursing homes or other extended care facilities, museums or museum projects, churches or church projects, animals or animal-related programs, national health organizations, historic renovation, tax-supported organizations or public or private K-12 schools. Generally, no grants to individuals, or for endowment funds, research, production of films or other media-related projects, conduit funding, deficits,

debt retirement, computer equipment, start-up funding, special events, meetings, or seminars.
Publications: Annual report (including application guidelines).
Application information: The foundation does not accept proposals sent by fax or e-mail. Please do not include videos or put proposals into ringed or sealed binders. Only one request is considered for an organization during any 12-month period. Application form not required.

Initial approach: Letter
Copies of proposal: 1
Deadline(s): None
Board meeting date(s): 3 times per year
Final notification: 3 months
Officers and Trustees:* Peter H. Coors,* Chair.; William K. Coors,* V.P.; Robert G. Windsor,* V.P.; Jeffrey H. Coors,* Treas.; Sally W. Rippey, Exec. Dir.; Amb. Holland H. Coors; Cecily Coors Garnsey; Melissa Coors Osborn.
Number of staff: 3 full-time professional; 2 full-time support.
EIN: 510172279
Selected grants: The following grants were reported in 2005.
$2,178,800 to Colorado School of Mines Foundation, Golden, CO. 2 grants: $178,800 (For Herman Coors Professorial Chair in Ceramics), $2,000,000 (For Wellness Center).
$500,000 to National Jewish Medical and Research Center, Denver, CO. For capital support.
$195,000 to Denver Foundation, Denver, CO. For Educational Options for Children.
$50,000 to Jefferson County Childrens Advocacy Center, Lakewood, CO. For capital support.
$40,000 to Colorado UpLIFT, Denver, CO. For general operating support.
$20,000 to Art Students League of Denver, Denver, CO. For capital support.
$20,000 to Young Americans Center for Financial Education, Denver, CO. For general operating support.
$15,000 to Childrens Advocacy Center for the Pikes Peak Region, Colorado Springs, CO. For general operating support.
$15,000 to I Have A Dream Foundation of Boulder County, Boulder, CO. For general operating support.

1361
The Crowell Trust ✧
(also known as Henry P. and Susan C. Crowell Trust)
1880 Office Club Pointe, Ste. 2200
Colorado Springs, CO 80920 (719) 272-8300
Contact: Paul Nelson, Exec. Dir.
FAX: (719) 272-8305; E-mail: info@crowelltrust.org;
URL: http://www.crowelltrust.org

Trust established in 1927 in IL.
Donors: Henry P. Crowell†; Henry P. Crowell Benevolence and Education Trust; Henry P. and Susan C. Crowell Trust.
Foundation type: Independent foundation.
Financial data (yr. ended 12/31/05): Assets, $104,278,712 (M); expenditures, $5,026,670; qualifying distributions, $4,732,256; giving activities include $4,390,000 for 113 grants (high: $380,000; low: $5,000; average: $15,000–$25,000).
Purpose and activities: Created to aid evangelical Christianity by support to organizations having for their purposes its teaching, advancement, and active extension at home and abroad.

Fields of interest: Theological school/education; Christian agencies & churches; Religion.
Type of support: General/operating support; Management development/capacity building; Equipment; Program development; Publication; Curriculum development; Scholarship funds; Technical assistance; Matching/challenge support.
Limitations: No support for churches or schooling from kindergarten through 12th grade. No grants to individuals, or for endowment funds or research; no loans.
Application information: Application form not required.

Initial approach: Preliminary proposal
Copies of proposal: 1
Deadline(s): Considered as received
Board meeting date(s): Spring and fall
Final notification: 1 to 2 months
Officers and Trustees:* Jane Overstreet,* Chair.; John T. Bass,* Vice-Chair.; Lowell L. Kline,* Treas.; Paul Nelson, Exec. Dir.; Edwin L. Frizen, Jr.; John F. Robinson.
Corporate Trustee: Bank of America, N.A.
Number of staff: 1 part-time professional; 2 part-time support.
EIN: 366038028

1362
Daniels Fund ▼
(formerly Daniels Foundation)
101 Monroe St.
Denver, CO 80206 (720) 941-4422
Contact: Peter Droege, V.P., Comms.
FAX: (720) 941-4182;
E-mail: pdroege@danielsfund.org; General tel.: (303) 393-7220; Toll free tel.: (877) 791- 4726; General contact e-mail: contact@danielsfund.org; URL: http://www.danielsfund.org

Established in 1997 in CO.
Donors: R.W. Daniels, Jr.†; Bill Daniels†.
Foundation type: Independent foundation.
Financial data (yr. ended 12/31/05): Assets, $1,090,055,954 (M); gifts received, $1,010,000; expenditures, $53,158,150; qualifying distributions, $51,477,998; giving activities include $37,357,396 for 609 grants (high: $8,159,615; low: $310; average: $25,000–$150,000), $7,570,210 for grants to individuals, and $20,372 for 23 employee matching gifts.
Purpose and activities: Giving primarily for child care and early childhood education, higher education, the elderly, homelessness and self-sufficiency, alcoholism, and substance abuse, amateur athletics, and for people with physical disabilities.
Fields of interest: Education, reform; Education, ethics; Education, early childhood education; Education; Substance abuse, services; Alcoholism; Geriatrics; Housing/shelter, homeless; Athletics/ sports, amateur leagues; Youth development; Developmentally disabled, centers & services; Homeless, human services; Aging; Disabilities, people with; Economically disadvantaged; Homeless.
Type of support: General/operating support; Capital campaigns; Building/renovation; Program development; Program evaluation; Employee matching gifts; Scholarships—to individuals; Matching/challenge support.
Limitations: Giving primarily in CO, with emphasis on Denver; funding also in NM, WY and UT with a limited basis nationally. No support for arts and

cultural programs. No grants to individuals (except for Daniels Fund Scholarship Program or Daniels Rapid Response Fund), or for academic, medical, or scientific research, or conferences, symposia, or workshops, or for debt elimination, endowments, fundraising or special events (purchase of tables or conferences), or for creation, publication or distribution of publications or for video productions.
Publications: Annual report; Financial statement; Grants list; Informational brochure (including application guidelines); IRS Form 990-PF.
Application information: Applicants will be notified in writing of all grant decisions (no phone calls please). Application form available on fund Web site. The fund discourages pre-application meetings, preferring to schedule conference calls or site visits after receiving an application. Application form required.

Initial approach: Application
Deadline(s): None
Board meeting date(s): Quarterly
Final notification: 120 days after receiving a complete proposal
Officers and Directors:* John V. Saeman II,* Chair.; Linda Childears,* C.E.O. and Pres.; Jeb Dickey, Exec. V.P. and C.F.O.; Kristin Donovan, Sr. V.P., Grants and Scholarships; Peter Droege, V.P., Comms.; Gretchen Van Noy, V.P., Finance and Opers.; Hank Brown; Brian Deevy; Diane Daniels Denish; Bruce Dines; Gayle Greer; Leo J. Hindery, Jr.; Tom Marinkovich; Jim Nicholson; Dan Ritchie; Steve Schuck; June Travis.
Number of staff: 33 full-time professional; 6 full-time support; 1 part-time support.
EIN: 841393308
Selected grants: The following grants were reported in 2005.
$8,159,615 to New Mexico Military Institute Foundation, Roswell, NM. For capital campaign.
$1,200,000 to Smithsonian Institution, National Air and Space Museum, DC. For Sea-Air Operations Gallery Exhibit.
$996,600 to Young Americans Education Foundation (YAEF), Denver, CO. For operating support.
$500,000 to Denver Rescue Mission, Denver, CO. For The Crossing.
$500,000 to Gathering Place, Denver, CO. For capital campaign.
$300,000 to Boy Scouts of America, Longs Peak Council, Greeley, CO. For Camp Laramie Peak renovations.
$68,000 to Southeastern Colorado Heritage Center, Pueblo, CO. For general operating support.
$25,000 to American Enterprise Institute for Public Policy Research, DC. For education policy program.
$25,000 to Posada, Pueblo, CO. For general operating support.
$25,000 to Youth Unlimited, Salida, CO. For general operating support.

1363
The Courtenay C. and Lucy Patten Davis Foundation ✧
(formerly The Courtenay C. Davis Foundation)
2595 E. Cedar Ranch
Denver, CO 80209-3204

Established in 1992 in WY.
Donors: Alfred P. Davis; Courtenay C. Davis†; Lucy Davis.
Foundation type: Independent foundation.

Financial data (yr. ended 12/31/05): Assets, $30,338,708 (M); expenditures, $2,565,924; qualifying distributions, $2,462,550; giving activities include $2,405,708 for grants.
Fields of interest: Health care; Diabetes.
Limitations: Applications not accepted. Giving primarily in CO. No grants to individuals.
Application information: Contributes only to pre-selected organizations.
Officer and Directors:* Amy Davis,* Pres.; David S. Cohen; Tyson Dines III.
EIN: 830300897

1364
The Denver Foundation ▼
950 S. Cherry St., Ste. 200
Denver, CO   80246-2662   (303) 300-1790
Contact: David J. Miller, C.E.O.; For grants: Justin Sharp, Grants Mgr.
FAX: (303) 300-6547;
E-mail: information@denverfoundation.org; Grant application E-mail: jsharp@denverfoundation.org;
URL: http://www.denverfoundation.org

Established in 1925 in CO by resolution and declaration of trust.
Foundation type: Community foundation.
Financial data (yr. ended 12/31/05): Assets, $363,533,077 (M); gifts received, $48,755,391; expenditures, $30,083,746; giving activities include $24,791,287 for 3,500 grants, and $87,000 for 3 loans/program-related investments (high: $37,000; low: $25,000).
Purpose and activities: The foundation seeks to improve life in Metro Denver through philanthropy, leadership, and strengthening the community. Grants primarily for education, civic, health, human services, and arts and cultural programs and strengthening neighborhoods with Small Grants Program.
Fields of interest: Arts; Education; Health care; Human services; Community development.
Type of support: General/operating support; Capital campaigns; Building/renovation; Program development; Seed money; Technical assistance; Program-related investments/loans; Matching/challenge support.
Limitations: Giving limited to Adams, Arapahoe, Boulder, Broomfield, Denver, Douglas, and Jefferson counties, CO. No support for government agencies, parochial or religious schools, or organizations that further religious doctrine. No grants to individuals (except for scholarships), or for sponsorships, debt liquidation, debt retirement, endowments or other reserve funds, membership or affiliation campaigns, dinners, or special events, research, publications, films, travel, or conferences, symposiums, workshops, or individual medical procedures, medical, scientific, or academic research, creation or installation of art objects, or multi-year funding requests.
Publications: Application guidelines; Annual report; Annual report (including application guidelines); Informational brochure (including application guidelines); Newsletter.
Application information: Visit foundation Web site for application guidelines. The foundation offers free grant proposal workshops that help organizations learn how to prepare a complete grant proposal. Application form not required.
Initial approach: Submit proposal
Copies of proposal: 1
Deadline(s): Feb. 1, June 1, and Oct. 2

Board meeting date(s): Feb., June, and Oct.
Final notification: Within 5 months
Officers and Trustees:* Mary Sissel,* Chair.; Laura Barton,* Vice-Chair.; Jeff Fard,* Vice-Chair.; David J. Miller, C.E.O. and Pres.; Rebecca Arno, V.P., Comms.; Lauren Casteel, V.P., Philanthropic Partnerships; Daniel Lee, V.P., Finance and Admin.; Betsy Mangone, V.P., Philanthropic Services; Jeff Mirota, V.P., Progs.; Christine Johnson,* Secy.; Fred Taylor,* Treas.; Sami Nakazono, Cont.; Julika Ambrose; Nancy Benson; Mark Berzins; Joe Blake; Jack Fox; Marva Hammons; Anna Jo Haynes; Diana Lee; Rich Lopez; Manuel Martinez; Michael Martinez; Bob Newman; Dean Prina, M.D.; Penfield Tate; Michelle Sie Whitten.
Number of staff: 22 full-time professional; 8 full-time support.
EIN: 846048381
Selected grants: The following grants were reported in 2005.
$1,000,000 to Doctors Without Borders USA, New York, NY. For general operating support.
$525,000 to Church of Jesus Christ of Latter Day Saints, Salt Lake City, UT. For general operating support.
$500,000 to University of Denver, Denver, CO. For creating Institute for Advancement of American Legal System, with purpose to lead national effort to address abuses in legal system.
$425,000 to Denver Art Museum Foundation, Denver, CO. For Bannock Street acquisitions.
$150,000 to Hike Fund, Spring Hill, FL. For purchase of hearing devices for children from birth to age 20.
$10,000 to Bear Creek Evangelical Presbyterian Church, Lakewood, CO. For program support.
$10,000 to Colorado Center on Law and Policy, Denver, CO. For Health Care Program.
$8,080 to Opera Colorado, Denver, CO.
$5,000 to Arrupe Jesuit High School, Denver, CO.
$5,000 to Make-A-Wish Foundation of Colorado, Greenwood Village, CO.

1365
Distinguished Service Foundation ✧ ☆
c/o Reese Henry & Co., Inc.
400 E. Main St.
Aspen, CO   81611

Established in 2001 in CO.
Donor: Richard T. Butera.
Foundation type: Independent foundation.
Financial data (yr. ended 4/30/05): Assets, $503,776 (M); gifts received, $1,136,000; expenditures, $634,699; qualifying distributions, $633,000; giving activities include $633,000 for grants.
Fields of interest: Education.
Type of support: General/operating support.
Limitations: Applications not accepted. Giving primarily in Aspen, CO. No grants to individuals.
Application information: Contributes only to pre-selected organizations.
Trustee: Richard T. Butera.
EIN: 841588998
Selected grants: The following grants were reported in 2004.
$110,500 to Aspen School District, Aspen, CO. For teacher service awards.

1366
Rita & Harold Divine Foundation ✧
1123 Spruce St., No. 303
Boulder, CO   80302
Contact: Janelle Weissman, Exec. Dir.

Established in 1997 in CT.
Donor: Harold S. Divine.
Foundation type: Independent foundation.
Financial data (yr. ended 12/31/05): Assets, $10,788,360 (M); expenditures, $814,225; qualifying distributions, $715,000; giving activities include $715,000 for 78 grants (high: $250,000; low: $500).
Purpose and activities: Giving primarily for Jewish education and continuity, and for peace in Israel.
Fields of interest: Civil rights; Jewish agencies & temples.
International interests: Israel.
Limitations: Applications not accepted. No grants to individuals.
Application information: Contributes only to pre-selected organizations. Unsolicited requests for funds not accepted.
Officer: Janelle Weissman, Exec. Dir.
Trustees: Harold S. Divine; Rita L. Divine.
Number of staff: 1 part-time professional.
EIN: 061501892
Selected grants: The following grants were reported in 2004.
$75,000 to Center for Civic Participation, Minneapolis, MN. 2 grants: $50,000, $25,000
$40,000 to Jewish Community Development Fund, New York, NY.
$35,000 to American Jewish Joint Distribution Committee, New York, NY.
$25,000 to Jewish Funders Network, New York, NY.
$25,000 to Jewish Outreach Institute, New York, NY.
$20,000 to Crested Butte Music Festival, Crested Butte, CO.
$20,000 to Judaism and Democracy Action Alliance of North America, Hasbrouck Heights, NJ.
$10,000 to Family Service.
$10,000 to People for the American Way, DC.

1367
The Donnell Initiative Fund ✧ ☆
c/o Elizabeth Bryant
1866 Vine St.
Denver, CO   80206-1122
Application address: c/o Diana Poole, 1955 Forest St. Pkwy., Denver, CO 80220, tel.: (303) 394-4363

Established in 2000 in CO.
Donors: John D. Donnell; Cathlin Donnell‡.
Foundation type: Independent foundation.
Financial data (yr. ended 6/30/06): Assets, $1,617,491 (M); expenditures, $466,365; qualifying distributions, $436,645; giving activities include $436,645 for grants.
Fields of interest: Education; Environment; Community development.
Limitations: Giving primarily in CO. No grants to individuals.
Application information:
Initial approach: Letter
Deadline(s): None
Officers: Diana Poole, Pres.; Pamela Gagel, Secy.; Elizabeth A. Bryant, Treas.
Director: John Donnell.
EIN: 841553903

1368
Donnell-Kay Foundation, Inc. ✧
730 17th St., No. 950
Denver, CO 80202 (720) 932-1544
Contact: Tony Lewis, Exec. Dir.
FAX: (303) 534-5785;
E-mail: info@dkfoundation.org; URL: http://
www.dkfoundation.org

Established in 1965 in FL.
Donor: Elizabeth D. Kay†.
Foundation type: Independent foundation.
Financial data (yr. ended 1/31/06): Assets,
$30,960,231 (M); gifts received, $25,000;
expenditures, $1,175,136; qualifying distributions,
$1,142,556; giving activities include $577,800 for
37 grants (high: $50,000; low: $800), and
$137,289 for 4 foundation-administered programs.
Purpose and activities: Giving primarily for public
school renewal, higher education, and early
childhood education.
Fields of interest: Secondary school/education;
Higher education; Education; Reproductive health,
family planning; Human services; Economics;
Population studies.
Type of support: General/operating support; Capital
campaigns; Continuing support; Program
development; Conferences/seminars; Publication;
Research.
Limitations: Applications not accepted. Giving
primarily in Denver, CO, and FL. No grants to
individuals.
Application information: Contributes only to
pre-selected organizations; unsolicited applications
not considered.
Officers and Directors:* Allen Dines,* Pres.; Sidney
A. Dines,* V.P. and Treas.; Lucy D. Delsol,* Secy.;
Tony Lewis, Exec. Dir.; Alain Delsol; Connie Dines.
Number of staff: 1 full-time professional; 1 part-time
professional; 1 full-time support.
EIN: 596169704
Selected grants: The following grants were reported
in 2005.
$175,000 to University of Denver, Denver, CO. 3
    grants: $50,000 (For Ritchie Program), $75,000
    (For Principal Program), $50,000 (For capital
    campaign).
$80,000 to Silverton School District No. 1,
    Silverton, CO. For Lake M S Assistant Principal.
$50,000 to Educare Colorado, Denver, CO. For
    general support.
$30,000 to University of Northern Colorado,
    Greeley, CO. For scholarships.
$25,000 to Boys and Girls Clubs of Metro Denver,
    Denver, CO. For general support.
$25,000 to Colorado Academy, Denver, CO. For
    capital campaign.
$25,000 to Public Education and Business
    Coalition, Denver, CO. For Educational Policy
    Journal.
$15,000 to Outward Bound Wilderness, Golden, CO.
    For general support.

1369
Dornick Foundation, Inc. ✧
(formerly Cross Creek Foundation, Inc.)
Box 219
Woody Creek, CO 81656

Established in 1997 in NC.
Donor: William Idema.
Foundation type: Independent foundation.

Financial data (yr. ended 12/31/05): Assets,
$9,108,693 (M); expenditures, $397,007;
qualifying distributions, $344,906; giving activities
include $344,413 for 10 grants (high: $125,000;
low: $10,000).
Purpose and activities: Giving primarily for
education, and for children and family services.
Fields of interest: Higher education; Education;
Family services; Federated giving programs.
Limitations: Applications not accepted. Giving
primarily in NC. No grants to individuals.
Application information: Contributes only to
pre-selected organizations.
Officers: Robert C. Pew III, Pres.; Susan H. Taylor,
Secy.
Board Member: Kate Wolters.
EIN: 562057825

1370
The Dwan Family Foundation ✧
c/o Ronald S. Johnson
6385 Corporate Dr., Ste. 201
Colorado Springs, CO 80919

Established in 1993 in CO.
Donors: Mary Dwan; Mary Clare Dwan; Patricia
Smith; Susan Stockdale; Ann Dwan; Elizabeth
McNamara; John Dwan; Tartan Partners, LP; Charles
J. Vasilius.
Foundation type: Independent foundation.
Financial data (yr. ended 12/31/05): Assets,
$326,837 (M); gifts received, $827,920;
expenditures, $1,107,588; qualifying distributions,
$1,107,588; giving activities include $1,078,581
for 52 grants (high: $513,000; low: $100).
Purpose and activities: Giving primarily to Christian
organizations and for education.
Fields of interest: Education; Health organizations;
Human services; Christian agencies & churches.
Limitations: Applications not accepted. Giving on a
national basis, with emphasis on Colorado Springs,
CO, MN, primarily Duluth, and Jackson, WY. No
grants to individuals.
Application information: Contributes only to
pre-selected organizations.
Trustee: Ronald S. Johnson.
EIN: 846268991
Selected grants: The following grants were reported
in 2005.
$513,000 to Colorado Springs School, Colorado
    Springs, CO.
$30,000 to Community Center for the Arts, Jackson,
    WY.
$30,000 to Dancers Workshop, Jackson, WY.
$10,000 to Pathway School, Norristown, PA.
$10,000 to Teton County Library Foundation,
    Jackson, WY.
$6,000 to Hillsdale College, Hillsdale, MI.
$6,000 to Regis University, Denver, CO.
$1,500 to Marshall School, Duluth, MN.
$1,000 to Colorado Springs Fine Arts Center,
    Colorado Springs, CO.
$500 to Smithsonian Institution, DC.

1371
Ebrahimi Family Foundation ✧ ☆
475 Circle Dr.
Denver, CO 80206
Contact: Mary P. Ebrahimi, Secy.

Established in 1997 in CO.

Donors: F. Fred Ebrahimi; Farhad A. Ebrahimi.
Foundation type: Independent foundation.
Financial data (yr. ended 12/31/05): Assets,
$6,811,694 (M); expenditures, $3,016,679;
qualifying distributions, $3,016,000; giving
activities include $3,016,000 for 3 grants (high:
$3,000,000; low: $1,000).
Fields of interest: Arts; Education; Disasters,
Hurricane Katrina.
Limitations: Applications not accepted. Giving on a
national basis, with emphasis on CO.
Application information: Unsolicited requests for
funds not accepted.
Officers: F. Fred Ebrahimi, Pres.; Mary P. Ebrahimi,
Secy.; Farah A. Ebrahimi, Treas.
Director: Farhad A. Ebrahimi.
EIN: 841441613

1372
ECA Foundation, Inc.
4643 S. Ulster, Ste. 1100
Denver, CO 80237 (303) 694-2667
Contact: Sara DiManna, Prog. Admin.
E-mail: sara@ecadenver.com

Established in 1996 in CO.
Donors: Eastern American Energy Corp.;
Mountaineer Gas Co.; Energy Corp. of America.
Foundation type: Company-sponsored foundation.
Financial data (yr. ended 6/30/06): Assets,
$1,585,720 (M); gifts received, $1,177,495;
expenditures, $1,062,229; qualifying distributions,
$1,045,986; giving activities include $1,045,986
for 96+ grants (high: $300,000).
Purpose and activities: The foundation supports
organizations involved with education, health, and
children and youth.
Fields of interest: Education; Health care; Children/
youth, services.
Type of support: Management development/
capacity building; Program development; Curriculum
development; Scholarship funds; Employee
matching gifts; Matching/challenge support.
Limitations: Giving primarily in the metropolitan
Denver, CO, and Houston, TX, areas and WV. No
grants to individuals, or for publications, films,
media projects, seminars, conferences, events, or
meetings travel, start-up needs, research, general
operating support, capital campaigns or
acquisitions, debt reduction, endowments, or
recruiting or training.
Publications: Grants list; Informational brochure
(including application guidelines).
Application information: Proposals may be
submitted using the Colorado Common Grant
Format. Organizations receiving support are asked
to provide a final report. Application form not
required.
Initial approach: Proposal to foundation or
    telephone foundation
Copies of proposal: 1
Deadline(s): Feb. 1, May 1, Aug. 1, and Nov. 1
Board meeting date(s): Mar., June, Sept., and
    Dec.
Final notification: Approximately 6 weeks
Directors: Joseph E. Casabona; John F. Mork; Julie
M. Mork.
Number of staff: 2 part-time professional.
EIN: 841349588
Selected grants: The following grants were reported
in 2005.
$10,000 to Denver Public Library, Denver, CO. For
    summer reading.

$10,000 to United Cerebral Palsy of Colorado, Denver, CO. For preschool.

$7,200 to Whiz Kids Tutoring, Denver, CO. For tutoring for at-risk elementary students.

$5,000 to Curtis Park Community Center, Denver, CO. For early learning center.

$5,000 to Goodwill Industries of Denver, Denver, CO. For School to Work.

$5,000 to I Have A Dream Foundation, Denver, CO. To follow at-risk students to graduation.

$5,000 to Work Options for Women, Denver, CO.

1373
The Joseph Henry Edmondson Foundation ✧
10 Lake Cir.

Colorado Springs, CO 80906 (719) 471-1241

Contact: Heather L. Carroll, Pres. and Exec. Dir.

E-mail: hcarroll@jhedmondson.org

Established in 1987 in CO.

Foundation type: Independent foundation.

Financial data (yr. ended 7/31/05): Assets, $18,316,509 (M); gifts received, $4,701,115; expenditures, $954,964; qualifying distributions, $859,182; giving activities include $725,280 for 108 grants (high: $250,000; low: $500).

Purpose and activities: Giving limited to the welfare of children, the ill, and the elderly, the preservation and improvement of the environment, and the arts in the Pikes Peak area.

Fields of interest: Arts; Environment; Health care; Children/youth, services; Family services; Homeless, human services.

Type of support: Technical assistance; General/operating support; Continuing support; Capital campaigns; Building/renovation; Equipment; Land acquisition; Emergency funds; Program development; Matching/challenge support.

Limitations: Giving limited to the Colorado Springs, CO, area. No support for evangelical organizations or political organizations. No grants to individuals or for sponsorships or for debt reduction or event funding.

Publications: Application guidelines; Grants list; Informational brochure (including application guidelines).

Application information: Application form not required.

Initial approach: Request guidelines

Copies of proposal: 2

Deadline(s): Dec., Mar., June, and Sept. (Applicant should contact office for exact deadline dates)

Board meeting date(s): Jan., Apr., July, and Oct.

Final notification: Within 7 weeks

Officers and Directors:* Carl Donner,* Chair. and Treas.; Bruce T. Buell,* Vice-Chair. and V.P.; Heather Carroll, Pres. and Exec. Dir.; Sharon Higgins, Secy.; Christopher Bruce Duff; Sean Duff; Mary Kanas; Susie Ramsay.

Number of staff: 1 full-time professional.

EIN: 841090456

Selected grants: The following grants were reported in 2004.

$50,000 to Broadmoor Community Church, Colorado Springs, CO. For capital support.

$25,000 to Pikes Peak Hospice, Colorado Springs, CO. For capital support.

$15,000 to Colorado Conservation Trust, Boulder, CO. For trustee award.

$15,000 to Greccio Housing Unlimited, Colorado Springs, CO. For general operating support.

$15,000 to Pikes Peak Community Action Agency, Colorado Springs, CO. For general operating support.

$10,000 to Colorado Festival of World Theater, Colorado Springs, CO. For capital support.

$10,000 to Educare Colorado, Denver, CO. For general operating support.

$10,000 to El Pueblo Boys and Girls Ranch, Pueblo, CO. For capital support.

$10,000 to United Way, Pikes Peak, Colorado Springs, CO. For program support.

$10,000 to Westside CARES, Colorado Springs, CO. For general operating support.

1374
El Pomar Foundation ▼
10 Lake Cir.

Colorado Springs, CO 80906 (719) 633-7733

Contact: William J. Hybl, Chair.

FAX: (719) 577-5702; *Additional tel.:* (800) 554-7711; *URL:* http://www.elpomar.org

Incorporated in 1937 in CO.

Donors: Spencer Penrose†; Mrs. Spencer Penrose†.

Foundation type: Independent foundation.

Financial data (yr. ended 12/31/05): Assets, $500,113,836 (M); gifts received, $141,365; expenditures, $23,652,278; qualifying distributions, $23,206,867; giving activities include $13,884,260 for 802 grants (high: $2,000,000; low: $113; average: $5,000–$100,000), $277,569 for 103 employee matching gifts, $121,416 for 37 in-kind gifts, and $4,640,879 for 4 foundation-administered programs.

Purpose and activities: Grants only to nonprofit organizations for public, educational, arts and humanities, health, and welfare purposes, including child welfare, the disadvantaged, and housing; municipalities may request funds for specific projects.

Fields of interest: Visual arts; Museums; Performing arts; Performing arts, theater; Performing arts, music; Humanities; Historic preservation/historical societies; Arts; Child development, education; Vocational education; Higher education; Adult/continuing education; Adult education—literacy, basic skills & GED; Libraries/library science; Education, reading; Education; Environment, natural resources; Environment; Hospitals (general); Pharmacy/prescriptions; Health care; Substance abuse, services; Health organizations, association; Employment; Food services; Nutrition; Housing/shelter, development; Recreation; Human services; Children/youth, services; Child development, services; Family services; Residential/custodial care, hospices; Aging, centers/services; Homeless, human services; Community development; Voluntarism promotion; Transportation; Aging; Disabilities, people with; Minorities; Economically disadvantaged; Homeless.

Type of support: General/operating support; Continuing support; Capital campaigns; Building/renovation; Equipment; Land acquisition; Emergency funds; Program development; Scholarship funds; Employee matching gifts; In-kind gifts.

Limitations: Giving limited to CO. No support for organizations that distribute funds to other grantees, religious or political organizations, primary or secondary education, or for camps or seasonal facilities. No grants to individuals, or for travel, film

or other media projects, conferences, seminars, deficit financing, endowment funds, research.

Publications: Application guidelines; Annual report (including application guidelines); Financial statement; Grants list; Informational brochure.

Application information: Application form not required.

Initial approach: Proposal

Copies of proposal: 1

Deadline(s): One month before board meeting

Board meeting date(s): 6 to 8 times a year

Final notification: 90 days

Officers and Trustees:* William J. Hybl,* Chair. and C.E.O.; William R. Ward,* Vice-Chair.; R. Thayer Tutt, Jr.,* Pres. and C.I.O.; Robert J. Hilbert,* Sr. V.P., Admin. and Secy.-Treas.; David J. Palenchar,* Sr. V.P., Opers.; Kyle H. Hybl, Genl. Counsel; Judith M. Bell; Cortlandt S. Dietler; Brenda J. Smith.

Number of staff: 33 full-time professional; 20 full-time support; 7 part-time support.

EIN: 846002373

Selected grants: The following grants were reported in 2005.

$5,000,000 to Colorado Springs Fine Arts Center, Colorado Springs, CO. For expansion and renovation of facilities.

$350,000 to Pikes Peak or Bust Rodeo Foundation, Colorado Springs, CO. For Equestrian Center improvements and operating support.

$300,000 to American Red Cross, Mile High Chapter, Denver, CO. For direct assistance to individuals and families who have moved to Colorado seeking shelter and assistance as a result of Hurricane Katrina, payable over 2 years.

$200,000 to Saint Marys High School, Colorado Springs, CO. For Athletics and Community Center.

$150,000 to Valley-Wide Health Services, Alamosa, CO. For new health and human service complex.

$60,000 to Home Front Cares, Colorado Springs, CO. For support of military families.

$25,000 to Mountain Post Historical Association, Colorado Springs, CO. For Fort Carlson Military Museum.

$15,000 to Foothills Fire Protection District, Golden, CO. For Wildland Fire Fund grant for water tender.

$15,000 to Kent Denver School, Englewood, CO. For Denver Summerbridge Program.

$12,000 to Colorado Springs, City of, Colorado Springs, CO. For El Pomar Seniors in Service program.

1375
The Esther Foundation ✧ ☆
4790 E. Belleview Ave.

Greenwood Village, CO 80121

Established in 1999 in CO.

Donor: R. Scot Sellers.

Foundation type: Independent foundation.

Financial data (yr. ended 12/31/05): Assets, $2,817,391 (M); gifts received, $1,004,440; expenditures, $493,653; qualifying distributions, $441,406; giving activities include $441,345 for 14 grants (high: $250,000; low: $45).

Purpose and activities: Giving for the support of Christian ministries that strengthen or preserve the family.

Fields of interest: Human services; Christian agencies & churches.

Limitations: Applications not accepted. No grants to individuals.

Application information: Contributes only to pre-selected organizations.
Officers and Directors:* R. Scot Sellers,* Pres.; Alanna G. Sellers,* Secy.-Treas.
EIN: 841523209
Selected grants: The following grants were reported in 2004.
$30,000 to Azusa Pacific University, Azusa, CA.
$30,000 to Family Research Council, DC.
$22,500 to Campus Crusade for Christ.
$20,000 to Christian International Scholarship Foundation, Lake Forest, IL.
$20,000 to Focus on the Family, Colorado Springs, CO.
$15,000 to Athletes in Action, Xenia, OH.
$10,000 to Denver Leadership Foundation, Denver, CO.
$3,000 to Operation Good Neighbor Foundation, Bryn Mawr, PA.
$674 to Teammates for Kids, Littleton, CO.

1376

The Falkenberg Foundation ◈ ☆
1501 Wazee St., Unit 4B
Denver, CO 80202-1476

Established in 1995.
Donors: Janis Falkenberg; Ruth Falkenberg; William S. Falkenberg; Charles Falkenberg†; Leslie Whittington†.
Foundation type: Independent foundation.
Financial data (yr. ended 3/31/05): Assets, $2,443,707 (M); gifts received, $2,569,553; expenditures, $2,171,885; qualifying distributions, $2,142,000; giving activities include $2,142,000 for 78 grants (high: $2,000,000; low: $1,000).
Fields of interest: Historical activities; Human services; Federated giving programs.
Type of support: General/operating support.
Limitations: Applications not accepted. Giving primarily in CO. No grants to individuals.
Application information: Contributes only to pre-selected organizations.
Directors: Janis Falkenberg; Ruth Falkenberg; William S. Falkenberg.
EIN: 841232818
Selected grants: The following grants were reported in 2005.
$2,000,000 to Denver Foundation, Denver, CO.

1377

First Data Western Union Foundation ▼ ◈
12500 Belford Ave., M.S. M1I
Englewood, CO 80112 (720) 332-6606
Contact: Luella Chavez D'Angelo, Pres.
FAX: (720) 332-4772;
E-mail: luella.dangelo@westernunion.com;
URL: http://www.westernunion.com/foundation/

Established in 2001 as a company-sponsored operating foundation.
Donors: First Data Corp.; First Data Western Union Corp.
Foundation type: Operating foundation.
Financial data (yr. ended 12/31/05): Assets, $3,117,183 (M); gifts received, $14,463,793; expenditures, $13,643,165; qualifying distributions, $13,623,122; giving activities include $11,043,236 for 365 grants (high: $1,514,319; low: $600), $232,100 for 24 grants to individuals

(high: $3,000; low: $750), and $1,356,537 for 65 employee matching gifts.
Purpose and activities: The foundation supports organizations involved with education, health, hunger, disaster relief, human services, and economically disadvantaged people and awards college scholarships to non-traditional students.
Fields of interest: Education, reading; Education; Health care; Food services; Disasters, preparedness/services; Human services; Economically disadvantaged.
International interests: China; India; Mexico.
Type of support: Continuing support; Emergency funds; Program development; Employee matching gifts; Scholarships—to individuals; Matching/challenge support.
Limitations: Giving on a national and international basis in areas of company operations, with emphasis on the metropolitan Denver, CO, area, Coral Springs and Hollywood, FL, Hagerstown, MD, Omaha, NE, Melville, NY, Houston, TX, and in China, India, and Mexico. No support for pass-through organizations. No grants to individuals (except for scholarships), or for endowments, special events, capital campaigns, scholarship funds, early childhood education, or debt reduction.
Publications: Annual report.
Application information: Support is limited to 1 contribution per organization during any given year for three years in length. Additional information may be requested at a later date. Application form required.
Initial approach: Complete online application form; download application form and express mail or fax to application address for organizations located outside the U.S.
Copies of proposal: 1
Deadline(s): June 1 and Dec. 1; Apr. 1 for scholarships
Board meeting date(s): Quarterly
Final notification: Apr. and Oct.; July for scholarships
Officers and Directors:* Scott T. Scheirman,* Chair.; Luella Chavez D'Angelo,* Pres.; Kelley J. Everetts,* Secy.; Sharon Alexander-Holt; Polly B. Baca; Myron Beard; Rexford G. Brown, Ph.D.; Thomas M. McDermott; William P. Morris; Lisa Olson; David Schlapbach; Constantine Varvias; Thomas Williams.
Number of staff: 6 full-time professional; 2 full-time support.
EIN: 311738614
Selected grants: The following grants were reported in 2005.
$1,514,319 to United Way, Mile High, Denver, CO. For restricted support.
$886,440 to International Federation of Red Cross and Red Crescent Societies at the UN, New York, NY. For unrestricted support.
$500,000 to Americas Second Harvest, Chicago, IL. For unrestricted support.
$500,000 to Education is Freedom Foundation, Dallas, TX. For restricted support.
$500,000 to White Land Foundation, Beirut, Lebanon. For restricted support.
$200,000 to Leukemia Association of North Central Texas, Dallas, TX. For restricted support.
$110,000 to Great Orchestra of Christmas Charity Foundation, Warsaw, Poland. For restricted support.
$25,000 to Shanghai Charity Foundation, Shanghai, China. For unrestricted support.
$20,000 to Asia Foundation, San Francisco, CA. For unrestricted support.

$10,000 to Ronald McDonald House Charities of Baltimore, Baltimore, MD. For unrestricted support.

1378

The Fullerton Family Charitable Trust ◈
510 E. Hyman, Ste. 30
Aspen, CO 81611

Established in 1991 in CA.
Donors: Jessica Fullerton; John B. Fullerton; Baxter Fullerton.
Foundation type: Independent foundation.
Financial data (yr. ended 6/30/05): Assets, $9,831,591 (M); expenditures, $695,116; qualifying distributions, $526,392; giving activities include $526,285 for 20 grants (high: $260,000; low: $500).
Purpose and activities: Giving for the arts, as well as for education, human services, and community development.
Fields of interest: Performing arts; Arts; Elementary/secondary education; Education; Environment; Animal welfare; Cancer research; Big Brothers/Big Sisters; Human services; Federated giving programs.
Limitations: Applications not accepted. Giving in the U.S., primarily in CA and CO. No grants to individuals.
Application information: Contributes only to pre-selected organizations.
Trustees: Jessica Fullerton; John B. Fullerton.
EIN: 680262543

1379

The Gary-Williams Foundation ◈
370 17th St., Ste. 5300
Denver, CO 80202-5653

Established in 2002 in CO.
Donor: Samuel Gary.
Foundation type: Independent foundation.
Financial data (yr. ended 11/30/05): Assets, $17,427,715 (M); gifts received, $5,000,000; expenditures, $5,493,462; qualifying distributions, $5,475,177; giving activities include $5,466,227 for 2 grants (high: $4,466,227; low: $1,000,000).
Purpose and activities: Giving primarily for land conservation.
Fields of interest: Environment, land resources; Foundations (private operating).
Limitations: Applications not accepted. Giving primarily in CO. No grants to individuals.
Application information: Contributes only to pre-selected organizations.
Officers and Directors:* Samuel Gary,* Chair.; Ronald Williams,* Pres.; James E. Bye, Secy.; Dave Younggren,* Treas.
EIN: 810587194

1380

Gates Family Foundation ▼ ◈
(formerly Gates Foundation)
3575 Cherry Creek N. Dr., Ste. 100
Denver, CO 80209 (303) 722-1881
Contact: C. Thomas Kaesemeyer, Exec. Dir.
FAX: (303) 316-3038;
E-mail: info@gatesfamilyfoundation.org;
URL: http://www.gatesfamilyfoundation.org

Incorporated in 1946 in CO.

Donors: Charles C. Gates†; Charles C. Gates, Sr.†; Hazel Gates†; John Gates†; June S. Gates†; Berenice Hopper; Robert Hopper.

Foundation type: Independent foundation.

Financial data (yr. ended 12/31/05): Assets, $345,539,032 (M); expenditures, $13,318,490; qualifying distributions, $10,966,336; giving activities include $10,966,336 for 113 grants (high: $1,000,000; low: $1,000; average: $10,000–$100,000).

Purpose and activities: To promote the health, welfare, and broad education of mankind, whether by means of research, grants, publications, and the foundation's own agencies and activities, or through cooperation with agencies and institutions already in existence. Grants primarily for education and youth services, including leadership development, public policy, historic preservation, humanities, and cultural affairs, health care, including cost reduction, and human services.

Fields of interest: Arts, multipurpose centers/programs; Visual arts; Museums; Performing arts; Performing arts, dance; Performing arts, theater; Performing arts, music; Humanities; Historic preservation/historical societies; Arts; Libraries/library science; Education; Environment, natural resources; Recreation; Youth development, services; Youth development; Human services; Youth, services; Aging, centers/services; Economics; Government/public administration; Leadership development.

Type of support: Capital campaigns; Building/renovation; Land acquisition; Matching/challenge support.

Limitations: Giving limited to CO, with emphasis on the Denver area, except for foundation-initiated grants. No support for private foundations, medical facilities, or individual public schools or public school districts. No grants to individuals, or for operating budgets, medical research, annual campaigns, emergency funds, deficit financing, purchase of tickets for fundraising dinners, parties, balls, or other social fundraising events, purchase of vehicles or office equipment, conferences, meetings, research, or scholarships; no loans.

Publications: Annual report (including application guidelines); Grants list.

Application information: If the summary proposal seems to dovetail with the current interests of the foundation additional information will be required. A Common Grant Application form is provided for this purpose on the foundation's Web site. Application form required.

   Initial approach: Telephone call or short summary proposal
   Copies of proposal: 1
   Deadline(s): Jan. 15, Apr. 1, July 1, and Oct. 1
   Board meeting date(s): Approx. Apr. 1, June 15, Oct. 1, and Dec. 15
   Final notification: 2 weeks following meetings

Officers and Trustees:* Diane Gates Wallach,* Pres.; Charles G. Cannon,* V.P.; C. Thomas Kaesemeyer, Secy. and Exec. Dir.; Thomas C. Stokes,* Treas.; Christina H. Turissini, Compt.; George B. Beardsley; Donald M. Elliman, Jr.; Valerie Gates; Mike Wilfley.

Number of staff: 4 full-time professional; 1 full-time support.

EIN: 840474837

Selected grants: The following grants were reported in 2005.

$1,574,843 to Childrens Hospital Association, Denver, CO. For restricted support to Imagine the Miracles Campaign.

$1,000,000 to Girl Scouts of the U.S.A., Mile High Council, Denver, CO. To expand Magic Sky Ranch.

$500,000 to Museum of Contemporary Art Denver, Denver, CO. Toward construction of Roof Garden in new museum building.

$500,000 to Punahou School, Honolulu, HI. For restricted support to be used for New Middle School.

$210,000 to Conservation Fund, Boulder, CO. Toward purchase of conservation easements on ranches in Navajo River Watershed Project area.

$200,000 to Families First, Denver, CO. For construction of new family center and renovation of existing building.

$200,000 to Regis University, Denver, CO. Toward construction of science building.

$38,542 to Northwest Colorado Dental Coalition, Craig, CO. To renovate and equip new dental clinic.

$34,000 to Kiowa Education Foundation, Kiowa, CO. Toward playground and campus improvement project.

$32,000 to Glenwood Springs Art Council, Glenwood Springs, CO. Toward renovation of historic arts center.

1381
General Service Foundation

557 N. Mill St., Ste. 201
Aspen, CO 81611-1513   (970) 920-6834
FAX: (970) 920-4578;
E-mail: info@generalservice.org; Additional tel. (for William M. Repplinger, Cont.): (970) 920-6834, ext. 5; URL: http://www.generalservice.org

Incorporated in 1946 in IL.

Donors: Clifton R. Musser†; Margaret K. Musser†.

Foundation type: Independent foundation.

Financial data (yr. ended 12/31/05): Assets, $68,142,026 (M); expenditures, $3,505,937; qualifying distributions, $2,807,296; giving activities include $2,130,010 for 103 grants (high: $100,000; low: $2,500).

Purpose and activities: The foundation believes it can make its best contribution at this point in time by addressing some of the world's basic long-term problems in three areas: Human Rights and Democracy, Reproductive Health and Rights, and Resources.

Fields of interest: Reproductive health; Reproductive health, family planning; Youth, pregnancy prevention; International peace/security; International human rights; Civil liberties, reproductive rights.

International interests: Caribbean; Central America; Mexico.

Type of support: General/operating support; Emergency funds; Program development; Conferences/seminars; Seed money; Technical assistance.

Limitations: Giving limited to the U.S., Mexico, Central America, and the Caribbean.

Publications: Application guidelines; Financial statement; Grants list; Informational brochure (including application guidelines).

Application information: Applicants are strongly encouraged to submit letters of inquiry via E-mail or using the online submission form on the foundation Web site. Letters of inquiry are still accepted via regular mail or fax. Application form required.

   Initial approach: Online letter of inquiry (4 pages)
   Copies of proposal: 1
   Deadline(s): Jan. 14 and Sept. 1 for letter of inquiry; Mar. 1 and Oct. 1 for invited proposals; Aug. 1 for 2-5 page letter of inquiry for Colorado Program
   Board meeting date(s): Apr. and Nov.
   Final notification: 6 months

Officers and Directors:* Robert W. Musser,* Pres.; Marcie J. Musser,* V.P. and Treas.; Mary Lloyd Estrin,* V.P.; Robin Halby,* Secy.; William M. Repplinger, Cont.; Lani A. Shaw, Exec. Dir. and Prog. Off., Reproductive Health and Rights; Robert L. Estrin*; Zoe Lloyd Estrin; Peter C. Halby; Susan Halby; Auden Schendler; W. Todd Snidow.

Number of staff: 3 full-time professional; 1 part-time professional; 1 full-time support.

EIN: 366018535

Selected grants: The following grants were reported in 2005.

$80,000 to Washington Office on Latin America, DC. For general support.

$70,000 to Catholics for a Free Choice, DC. For general support.

$70,000 to Center for International Policy, DC. For general support.

$70,000 to Latin America Working Group Education Fund, DC.

$70,000 to National Advocates for Pregnant Women, New York, NY. For general support.

$60,000 to International Labor Rights Fund, DC. For rights of working women in Mexico.

$60,000 to Ms. Foundation for Women, New York, NY. For general support.

$60,000 to National Security Archive Fund, DC. For rights of working women in Mexico.

$50,000 to Hampshire College, Amherst, MA. For general support.

1382
The Gill Foundation ▼ ✧

2215 Market St.
Denver, CO 80205   (303) 292-4455
Contact: Rodger McFarlane, Exec. Dir.
FAX: (303) 292-2155;
E-mail: info@gillfoundation.org; Additional toll free tel.: (888) 530-4455; Additional contact inf. (for Gay & Lesbian Fund for Colorado): 315 E. Costilla St., Colorado Springs, CO 80903, toll free tel.: (800) 964-5643, tel.: (719) 473-4455, FAX: (719) 473-2254, E-mail: info@gayand lesbianfund.org; URL: http://www.gillfoundation.org

Established in 1994 in CO.

Donors: Tim Gill; The Ford Foundation.

Foundation type: Independent foundation.

Financial data (yr. ended 12/31/05): Assets, $178,002,587 (M); gifts received, $11,165; expenditures, $15,170,761; qualifying distributions, $13,370,340; giving activities include $10,926,449 for 735 grants (high: $480,000; low: $100; average: $10,000–$100,000), and $23,621 for 224 employee matching gifts.

Purpose and activities: The mission of the foundation is to secure equal opportunity for all people, regardless of sexual orientation or gender expression. The mission is accomplished by: providing grants to nonprofit organizations, strengthening the leadership and managerial skills of nonprofit leaders, increasing financial resources to nonprofit organizations, strengthening democratic institutions, and building awareness of the contributions people of diverse sexual orientations and gender expressions make to American society.

Fields of interest: AIDS; Civil rights, gays/lesbians; Philanthropy/voluntarism.

Type of support: General/operating support; Continuing support; Annual campaigns; Capital campaigns; Equipment; Emergency funds; Program development; Conferences/seminars; Scholarship funds; Consulting services; Employee matching gifts; Matching/challenge support.

Limitations: Giving primarily to national and state-wide organizations. No support for clinical HIV/AIDS research, direct client services to community based HIV/AIDS organizations outside CO, or art programs for or about HIV. No support to individuals, endowments, scholarships, capital projects, direct care services, pride events, film or media production.

Publications: Application guidelines; Annual report; Biennial report; Program policy statement.

Application information: Organizations requesting funding are required to have a non-discrimination policy including sexual orientation. Grants to national organizations will be by invitation only. Organizations may submit only one application to the foundation every twelve months. Application form required.

  Initial approach: Letter of intent (via mail or Web site)
  Copies of proposal: 1
  Deadline(s): Letter of intent: Mar. 1 and Aug. 1; Application: Apr. 22 and Sept. 23
  Board meeting date(s): Quarterly
  Final notification: Letter of intent: Mar. 29 and Aug. 26; Application: June 30 and Dec. 2

Officers and Board Members:* Tim Gill,* Chair.; Katherine Peck, C.O.O.; David Dechman,* Treas.; Scott Panter, Cont.; Rodger McFarlane, Exec. Dir.; Urvashi Vaid.

Number of staff: 23 full-time professional; 8 full-time support.

EIN: 841264186

Selected grants: The following grants were reported in 2004.

$250,000 to Proteus Fund, Amherst, MA. For program support for Civil Marriage Collaborative.

$150,000 to Astraea Lesbian Foundation for Justice, New York, NY. For program support for Freedom to Marry.

$84,000 to Gay, Lesbian, Bisexual and Transgendered Community Services Center of Colorado, Denver, CO. For general operating support.

$67,500 to Colorado Health Network, Denver, CO. For general operating support.

$60,000 to In the Life Media, New York, NY. For program support for Website enhancement project.

$50,000 to National Lesbian and Gay Journalists Association, DC. For program support for Newsroom Outreach Project.

$10,000 to Funders Concerned About AIDS, New York, NY. For program support for Domestic Philanthropy Summit on HIV/AIDS.

$10,000 to Soulforce in Oklahoma, Stigler, OK. For general operating support.

$3,500 to ARC of Colorado, Greenwood Village, CO. For program support for criminal justice advocacy program.

$3,500 to Littleton Childrens Chorale, Littleton, CO. For general operating support.

1383
M. B. & Shana Glassman Foundation ◇ ☆
1400 Glenarm Pl., Ste. 201
Denver, CO 80202 (303) 534-5005
Contact: M.B. Glassman, Pres.

Established in 1969 in CO.

Donors: M.B. Glassman; Shana Glassman†.

Foundation type: Independent foundation.

Financial data (yr. ended 12/31/05): Assets, $6,963,408 (M); gifts received, $800,000; expenditures, $438,895; qualifying distributions, $399,010; giving activities include $399,010 for grants.

Purpose and activities: Giving primarily for local Jewish organizations.

Fields of interest: Education; Health organizations, association; Jewish agencies & temples.

Limitations: Giving primarily in Denver, CO. No grants to individuals.

Application information:

  Initial approach: Letter
  Copies of proposal: 1
  Deadline(s): None

Officers and Directors:* M.B. Glassman,* Pres.; Evan Makovsky,* Secy.; Philip Mehler, M.D.*, Treas.

EIN: 237038717

Selected grants: The following grants were reported in 2004.

$70,000 to Denver Academy of Torah, Denver, CO.

$5,000 to ALYN/American Society for Crippled Children in Israel, New York, NY.

$5,000 to East Denver Orthodox Synagogue, Denver, CO.

$3,500 to Tomchei Shabbos, Monsey, NY.

$2,500 to Bikur Cholim of Denver, Denver, CO.

$2,500 to Hillel Council of Colorado, Denver, CO.

$2,500 to National Conference of Synagogue Youth, New York, NY.

$1,000 to Arthritis Foundation, Rocky Mountain Chapter, Denver, CO.

$1,000 to Shalom Park, Aurora, CO.

$1,000 to Western Center for Russian Jewry, Denver, CO.

1384
Gooding Family Foundation ◇ ☆
c/o Richard L. Gooding
5445 DTC Pkwy., Ste. 1020
Greenwood Village, CO 80111-3045

Established in 1992 in CO.

Donor: Paragon Ranch, Inc.

Foundation type: Independent foundation.

Financial data (yr. ended 12/31/05): Assets, $1,066,188 (M); gifts received, $676,000; expenditures, $333,339; qualifying distributions, $330,000; giving activities include $330,000 for grants.

Purpose and activities: Giving for youth services and athletic camps.

Fields of interest: Museums (art); Recreation, camps; Girl scouts; Children/youth, services; Community development.

Limitations: Applications not accepted. Giving primarily in Denver, CO. No grants to individuals.

Application information: Contributes only to pre-selected organizations.

Directors: Nancy A. Gooding; Richard L. Gooding.

EIN: 841187150

Selected grants: The following grants were reported in 2003.

$25,000 to Denver Kids, Denver, CO. For general support.

$15,995 to Youth for Christ, Denver, CO. For general support.

$10,000 to Assistance League of Denver, Denver, CO. For general support.

$10,000 to Girl Scouts of the U.S.A., Mile High Council, Denver, CO. For program support.

$10,000 to Rotary Club of Denver, Denver, CO. For general support.

$10,000 to Sense of Security, Broomfield, CO. For general support.

$7,500 to Diana Price Fish Foundation, Denver, CO. For general support.

$5,000 to Advocate Safehouse Project, Glenwood Springs, CO. For general support.

$5,000 to Institute of International Education, Denver, CO. For scholarships.

$5,000 to Pan American Health and Education Foundation, DC. For COMBI Fund.

1385
Green Fund ◇ ☆
c/o Kathryn A. Porter
4155 W. 105th Pl.
Westminster, CO 80031

Established in 1993 in CO.

Donors: Frances M. Green; Alice K. Green.

Foundation type: Independent foundation.

Financial data (yr. ended 12/31/05): Assets, $9,866,661 (M); gifts received, $632,938; expenditures, $353,956; qualifying distributions, $328,139; giving activities include $320,000 for 26 grants (high: $100,000; low: $1,000).

Fields of interest: Higher education; Environment, natural resources; Human services; Federated giving programs.

Limitations: Applications not accepted. Giving primarily in Boulder, CO, and MA. No grants to individuals.

Application information: Contributes only to pre-selected organizations.

Officers and Directors:* Ann C. Wylie,* Pres. and Treas.; Kathryn A. Porter,* V.P. and Secy.; Maggie Fox.

EIN: 841155083

Selected grants: The following grants were reported in 2004.

$50,000 to University of Maryland-College Park, College Park, MD. For scholarships.

$28,000 to Sierra Club, San Francisco, CA. For general support.

$25,000 to Teammates for Kids, Littleton, CO. For general support.

$10,000 to Gathering Place, Denver, CO. For general support.

$6,000 to CollegeBound Foundation, Baltimore, MD. For general support.

$5,000 to Energy Awareness Productions, Boulder, CO. For general support.

$5,000 to Urgent Action Fund for Womens Human Rights, Boulder, CO. For general support.

$5,000 to Western Resource Advocates, Boulder, CO. For general support.

$3,000 to FrontRange Earth Force, Denver, CO. For general support.

$1,000 to Sinapu, Boulder, CO. For general support.

1386
Hach Scientific Foundation ✧
2114 N. Lincoln Ave., Ste. 104
Loveland, CO   80538

Established in 1982 in CO.
Donors: Kathryn C. Hach-Darrow; C & K Enterprises, Ltd.; Hach Co.
Foundation type: Independent foundation.
Financial data (yr. ended 12/31/05): Assets, $39,530,983 (M); gifts received, $204,180; expenditures, $1,722,908; qualifying distributions, $1,511,485; giving activities include $1,217,114 for 49+ grants.
Purpose and activities: Awards scholarships toward bachelor of science degrees in chemistry or chemical engineering for high school graduates in CO and IA.
Fields of interest: Engineering school/education; Chemistry; Engineering.
Limitations: Applications not accepted. Giving primarily in CO and IA.
Application information: Contributes only to pre-selected organizations.
Officer: Kathryn C. Hach-Darrow, Chair.
Trustees: Bill Gunn; Bruce J. Hach; Loel Sirovy; Patricia M. Smith.
Number of staff: 1 part-time professional; 1 part-time support.
EIN: 840900668

1387
The Frederic C. Hamilton Family Foundation ✧
1560 Broadway, Ste. 2200
Denver, CO   80202

Donor: Frederic C. Hamilton.
Foundation type: Independent foundation.
Financial data (yr. ended 12/31/05): Assets, $29,692,449 (M); gifts received, $6,915,300; expenditures, $3,717,818; qualifying distributions, $3,552,312; giving activities include $3,552,312 for 90 grants (high: $540,000; low: $250; average: $1,000–$100,000).
Fields of interest: Arts; Elementary/secondary education; Higher education; Human services; Children/youth, services.
Limitations: Applications not accepted. Giving on a national basis with emphasis on CO. No grants to individuals.
Application information: Contributes only to pre-selected organizations.
Trustees: Frederic C. Hamilton,* Grantor; Crawford M. Hamilton; Frederic C. Hamilton, Jr.; Jane M. Hamilton; Thomas M. Hamilton; Christy Hamilton McGraw.
EIN: 542099318

1388
Zenon C. R. Hansen Foundation ✧
6501 E. Bellview Ave., Ste. 400
Englewood, CO   80111-6020   (303) 694-2190

Established in 1994.
Foundation type: Independent foundation.
Financial data (yr. ended 4/30/05): Assets, $8,331,377 (M); expenditures, $1,467,584; qualifying distributions, $1,337,007; giving activities include $1,322,047 for 30 grants (high: $317,777; low: $1,000).

Purpose and activities: Giving primarily to the Boy Scouts of America and for education.
Fields of interest: Education; Boy scouts.
Limitations: Applications not accepted. Giving on a national basis. No grants to individuals.
Application information: Contributes only to pre-selected organizations.
Officers: Thomas S. Haggai, Pres.; Earl L. Wright, Treas.
EIN: 650428044
Selected grants: The following grants were reported in 2003.
$250,000 to Catholic Inner-City Schools Educational Fund (CISE), Cincinnati, OH.
$150,000 to Boy Scouts of America, Greater Niagara Frontier Council, Buffalo, NY.
$100,000 to High Point University, High Point, NC.
$62,160 to Doane College, Crete, NE.
$60,675 to Boy Scouts of America, Northeast Pennsylvania Council, Moosic, PA.
$60,000 to Boy Scouts of America, Denver Area Council, Denver, CO.
$50,000 to Boy Scouts of America, Istrouma Area Council, Baton Rouge, LA.
$50,000 to Boy Scouts of America, South Florida Council, Miami Lakes, FL.
$50,000 to Horatio Alger Association of Distinguished Americans, Alexandria, VA.
$34,666 to Boy Scouts of America, Katahdin Area Council, Bangor, ME.

1389
Hasan Family Foundation ✧
1607 N. Elizabeth St.
Pueblo, CO   81003-2146

Established in 1994.
Donor: Malik M. Hasan, M.D.
Foundation type: Independent foundation.
Financial data (yr. ended 11/30/05): Assets, $2,940,751 (M); expenditures, $419,855; qualifying distributions, $398,611; giving activities include $398,611 for 35 grants (high: $150,000; low: $100).
Purpose and activities: Giving primarily for education and the arts.
Fields of interest: Arts; Education.
Limitations: Applications not accepted. Giving primarily in CO. No grants to individuals.
Application information: Contributes only to pre-selected organizations.
Directors: Dale Birkbigller, M.D.; Peter Dell; Aliya Gull Khan Hasan; Malika Asma Gull Hasan; Malik M. Hasan, M.D.; Seeme Gull Khan Hasan; Curt Westin.
EIN: 841289731
Selected grants: The following grants were reported in 2005.
$50,000 to Center for the Study of the Presidency, DC.
$41,631 to Bravo Vail Valley Music Festival, Vail, CO. 3 grants: $10,000, $30,000, $1,631
$37,500 to New York University, New York, NY.
$20,000 to Pueblo Community College, Pueblo, CO.
$1,600 to Colorado State University - Pueblo Foundation, Pueblo, CO.
$500 to Pueblo Community College Foundation, Pueblo, CO.
$100 to Center for Science in the Public Interest, DC.

1390
Hawley Family Foundation, Inc. ✧
(formerly RHW Foundation, Inc.)
32065 Castle Ct., Ste. 100
Evergreen, CO   80439
Contact: MacDonald Hawley, Pres.

Established in 1994.
Foundation type: Independent foundation.
Financial data (yr. ended 12/31/04): Assets, $9,662,668 (M); expenditures, $931,899; qualifying distributions, $453,000; giving activities include $453,000 for 28 grants (high: $53,000; low: $1,000).
Purpose and activities: Giving for the arts, education, animal welfare, and hospitals.
Fields of interest: Arts; Education; Environment, natural resources; Animals/wildlife, preservation/protection; Zoos/zoological societies; Hospitals (general).
Limitations: Giving on a national basis. No grants to individuals.
Officers and Directors: MacDonald Hawley,* Pres. and Treas.; James M. Hawley,* V.P. and Secy.
EIN: 841224613

1391
Hewit Family Foundation ✧
621 17th St., Ste. 2555
Denver, CO   80293
Contact: William D. Hewit, Dir.

Established in 1985 in CO.
Donor: members of the Hewit family.
Foundation type: Independent foundation.
Financial data (yr. ended 11/30/05): Assets, $14,438,761 (M); expenditures, $1,021,238; qualifying distributions, $998,333; giving activities include $998,333 for 17 grants (high: $358,333; low: $5,000).
Purpose and activities: Support primarily for health care, youth organizations, and education; funding also for a museum of nature and science.
Fields of interest: Museums; Education; Hospitals (specialty); Health care; Health organizations, association; Children/youth, services.
Limitations: Giving primarily in CO, with emphasis on Denver and Englewood. No support for private foundations or religious organizations. No grants to individuals.
Application information: Application form not required.
   Initial approach: Letter
   Deadline(s): None
Directors: Christie F. Andrews; Richard J. Andrews; Robert S. Brown; Betty Ruth Hewit; William D. Hewit; Jack E. Kennedy.
EIN: 742397040
Selected grants: The following grants were reported in 2005.
$200,000 to Kent Denver School, Englewood, CO.
$100,000 to Denver Museum of Nature and Science, Denver, CO.
$25,000 to Boy Scouts of America, Denver, CO.
$10,000 to Childrens Hospital Foundation, Denver, CO.
$10,000 to Denver Botanic Gardens, Denver, CO.
$10,000 to Denver Zoological Foundation, Denver, CO.
$5,000 to Bonfils Blood Center, Denver, CO.
$5,000 to Colorado UpLIFT, Denver, CO.
$5,000 to Denver Public Library, Denver, CO.
$5,000 to Rainbow Bridge, Denver, CO.

1392
Hill Foundation ✧
c/o Wells Fargo Bank West, N.A.
1740 Broadway, MAC C7300-483
Denver, CO 80274 (720) 947-6820

Established in 1955 in CO.
Donor: Virginia W. Hill‡.
Foundation type: Independent foundation.
Financial data (yr. ended 4/30/05): Assets, $19,117,492 (M); expenditures, $1,486,929; qualifying distributions, $1,204,525; giving activities include $1,165,500 for 121 grants (high: $50,000; low: $1,000).
Purpose and activities: Grants largely for health care for the medically indigent, higher education, services for the elderly, and cultural programs; support also for social service agencies and the disabled.
Fields of interest: Arts; Higher education; Theological school/education; Education; Hospitals (general); Health care, financing; Health organizations, association; Human services; Roman Catholic federated giving programs; Roman Catholic agencies & churches; Homeless.
Type of support: Program development; Scholarship funds; Matching/challenge support.
Limitations: Giving primarily in CO and WY. No grants to individuals, or for capital improvements other than equipment acquisition for health care and related purposes.
Publications: Informational brochure; Program policy statement.
Application information:
  Initial approach: Letter
  Deadline(s): None
  Final notification: Within 5 weeks
Trustees: Francis W. Collopy; John R. Moran; Wells Fargo Bank West, N.A.
EIN: 846081879
Selected grants: The following grants were reported in 2003.
$45,000 to Jesuit Educational Center for Human Development, Silver Spring, MD.
$35,000 to Central City Opera House Association, Denver, CO.
$30,000 to Colorado Coalition for the Homeless, Denver, CO.
$30,000 to Regis University, Denver, CO.
$30,000 to United Way, Mile High, Denver, CO.
$15,000 to Kempe Childrens Foundation, Denver, CO.
$15,000 to La Puente Home, Alamosa, CO.
$15,000 to Learning Source, Lakewood, CO.
$15,000 to University of Denver, Denver, CO.
$12,500 to Sacred Heart House of Denver, Denver, CO.

1393
Mabel Y. Hughes Charitable Trust
c/o Wells Fargo Bank, N.A.
1740 Broadway, MC 7300, No. 483
Denver, CO 80274 (720) 947-6820
Contact: Peggy Toal

Trust established in 1969 in CO.
Donor: Mabel Y. Hughes‡.
Foundation type: Independent foundation.
Financial data (yr. ended 8/31/05): Assets, $12,099,104 (M); expenditures, $841,491; qualifying distributions, $749,912; giving activities include $726,500 for 50 grants (high: $60,000; low: $2,000).

Purpose and activities: Support primarily for the arts, health care and education.
Fields of interest: Museums; Museums (art); Museums (children's); Performing arts centers; Performing arts, opera; Higher education; Education; Reproductive health, family planning; Health care; Human services; Children/youth, services; Family services.
Type of support: General/operating support; Continuing support; Annual campaigns; Equipment; Endowments; Emergency funds; Program development; Seed money; Research.
Limitations: Giving limited to CO, with emphasis on the Denver area. No grants to individuals, or for deficit financing, scholarships, or fellowships; no loans.
Publications: Informational brochure (including application guidelines).
Application information: Application form not required.
  Initial approach: Letter
  Copies of proposal: 1
  Deadline(s): None
Trustees: W. Robert Alexander; Wells Fargo Bank, N.A.
EIN: 846070398

1394
A. V. Hunter Trust, Inc.
650 S. Cherry St., Ste. 535
Glendale, CO 80246-1897 (303) 399-5450
Contact: Sharon Siddons, Exec. Dir
FAX: (303) 399-5499; URL: http://www.avhuntertrust.org
Application address for individuals: P.O. Box 460668, Glendale, CO 80246-0668

Trust established in 1924 in CO.
Donor: A.V. Hunter‡.
Foundation type: Independent foundation.
Financial data (yr. ended 12/31/05): Assets, $65,654,117 (M); expenditures, $2,944,357; qualifying distributions, $2,382,624; giving activities include $1,775,125 for 158 grants (high: $60,000; low: $2,500), and $233,179 for 685 grants to individuals.
Purpose and activities: Distributions to organizations giving aid, comfort, support, or assistance to children, aged persons, indigent adults, or the needy.
Fields of interest: Human services; Children/youth, services; Aging; Disabilities, people with; Economically disadvantaged; Homeless.
Type of support: General/operating support.
Limitations: Giving limited to CO. No support for tax-supported institutions. No grants to individuals directly, or for scholarships, capital improvements, or acquisitions; no loans.
Publications: Application guidelines; Annual report (including application guidelines); Informational brochure (including application guidelines).
Application information: Application form required for grants for individuals; accepts Common Grant Application form for organizations. Application form required.
  Initial approach: Letter
  Copies of proposal: 1
  Deadline(s): Varies; see foundation Web site for more details
  Board meeting date(s): May, Aug., and Nov.
  Final notification: Within 20 days after meeting
Officers and Trustees:* George Gibson,* Pres.; W. Robert Alexander,* V.P.; Sharon Siddons, Secy. and

Exec. Dir.; Bruce K. Alexander,* Treas.; Allan B. Adams; Mary Anstine.
Number of staff: 3 full-time professional; 1 full-time support.
EIN: 840461332

1395
The International Charities, Inc. ✧
(formerly Vickridge Private Foundation, Inc.)
8480 E. Orchard Rd., Ste. 6000
Greenwood Village, CO 80111-5029

Established in 1984 in CO.
Donors: The International; Jene Harper; PGA Tour.
Foundation type: Independent foundation.
Financial data (yr. ended 12/31/05): Assets, $122,605 (M); gifts received, $712,993; expenditures, $684,218; qualifying distributions, $684,211; giving activities include $682,097 for 36 grants.
Purpose and activities: Giving primarily to golf organizations.
Fields of interest: Museums (sports/hobby); Education; Athletics/sports, golf; Boys & girls clubs; Youth development, services.
Limitations: Applications not accepted. Giving primarily in CO. No grants to individuals.
Application information: Contributes only to pre-selected organizations.
Officers and Directors:* Jack A. Vickers,* Pres.; Patricia L. Walker, Secy.; Michael J. MacAdams, Treas.; Keith Schneider, Jr.; Larry O. Thiel; Gregory A. Vickers.
EIN: 840952628
Selected grants: The following grants were reported in 2003.
$50,000 to Colorado State University Foundation, Fort Collins, CO. For general support.
$35,000 to Colorado Professional Golfers Association Foundation, Larkspur, CO. For general support.
$30,000 to Gold Crown Foundation, Greenwood Village, CO. For general support.
$25,000 to Douglas County Educational Foundation, Castle Rock, CO. For general support.
$25,000 to Three Amigos Foundation, Houston, TX. For general support.
$16,000 to Boys and Girls Clubs of Metro Denver, Denver, CO. For general support.
$5,000 to Cherokee Ranch and Castle Foundation, Sedalia, CO. For general operating support.
$5,000 to Childrens Hospital Foundation, Denver, CO. For general support.
$5,000 to Jim Murray Memorial Foundation, Los Angeles, CA. For general support.
$5,000 to Open Fairways, Highlands Ranch, CO. For general support.

1396
The Janus Foundation ✧
151 Detroit St.
Denver, CO 80206 (303) 333-3863
Contact: Karen C. Cortese, V.P.; Kelli Martin, Coord.
FAX: (303) 394-7797;
E-mail: janusfoundation@janus.com; Additional address: 100 Filmore St., Denver, CO 80206-4923; URL: https://ww3.janus.com/Janus/Retail/StaticPage?jsp=jsp/Janushome/JanusFoundation.jsp

Established in 1994 in CO.

Donors: Janus Capital Corp.; Janus Capital Management LLC.

Foundation type: Company-sponsored foundation.

Financial data (yr. ended 12/31/05): Assets, $907,964 (M); gifts received, $2,026,998; expenditures, $3,361,697; qualifying distributions, $3,361,283; giving activities include $2,440,650 for 369 grants (high: $1,200,000; low: $100), and $893,558 for employee matching gifts.

Purpose and activities: The foundation supports organizations involved with arts and culture, youth development, and volunteerism.

Fields of interest: Arts; Youth development; Philanthropy/voluntarism.

Type of support: Employee matching gifts; Continuing support; Program development; Curriculum development; Scholarship funds.

Limitations: Giving on a national basis. No grants to individuals, or for sponsorship events or tables, field trips or tours, recreational activities, conferences, seminars, workshops, annual membership or affiliation campaigns, publication or distribution of books, articles, newsletters, videos, or electronic media, religious or political purposes, health-related programs, or environmental projects.

Publications: Application guidelines.

Application information: Unsolicited requests from cultural institutions located outside the Denver, CO, metropolitan area are not accepted. Application form required.

Initial approach: Download application form and mail proposal and application form to foundation

Copies of proposal: 1

Deadline(s): None

Board meeting date(s): 1st week of each month

Final notification: Within 90 days

Officers and Directors:* Robin C. Beery,* Pres.; Karen C. Cortese,* V.P.; Matthew R. Luoma, V.P. and Treas.; Curt R. Foust, Secy.; Peter Boucher.

Number of staff: 2 part-time professional.

EIN: 841271105

Selected grants: The following grants were reported in 2003.

$58,580 to Denver Center for the Performing Arts, Denver, CO. 2 grants: $20,000 (For Arts in Education), $38,580 (For Denver Center Theater Company).

$20,000 to Metropolitan State College of Denver Foundation, Denver, CO. For scholarships.

$18,000 to Denver Street School, Denver, CO. For comprehensive high school program.

$15,000 to American Red Cross, Mile High Chapter, Denver, CO. For Youth Corps.

$15,000 to Junior Achievement of Metropolitan Denver, Denver, CO. For economic program at Denver Public Schools.

$12,500 to Young Americans Center for Financial Education, Denver, CO. For International Towne.

$12,500 to YouthBiz, Denver, CO. For YouthTech.

$12,000 to Austin Public Education Foundation, Austin, MN. For Victory Program.

$12,000 to University of Denver, Denver, CO. For Bridge Project summer program.

1397
The JFM Foundation ✧

P.O. Box 17965
Denver, CO 80217 (303) 864-2316
Contact: Peter A. Konrad, Fdn. Admin.

Established in 1980 in CO.

Donor: Frederick R. Mayer.

Foundation type: Independent foundation.

Financial data (yr. ended 11/30/05): Assets, $16,844,440 (M); gifts received, $1,276,430; expenditures, $3,965,462; qualifying distributions, $3,648,721; giving activities include $3,516,280 for 50 grants (high: $2,000,000; low: $100).

Purpose and activities: Support for innovative and cooperative projects in the areas of art, education, child development, women's issues and economic development that achieve long lasting and tangible impact.

Fields of interest: Arts; Education; Children/youth, services; Community development; Women.

Type of support: Program development; Seed money; Matching/challenge support.

Limitations: Applications not accepted. Giving limited to CO for community projects and social issues; cultural programs having national or international significance are considered. No support for medical or health-related fields or religious organizations for religious purposes. No grants to individuals, or for endowments, deficit financing, fundraising, testimonials, or basic research.

Publications: Annual report.

Application information: Unsolicited requests for funds are not accepted.

Board meeting date(s): Varies

Officers and Trustees:* Frederick R. Mayer,* Pres.; Jan Perry Mayer,* V.P. and Secy.-Treas.; Barbara Ann Atkeson; Gloria J. Higgins; Harold R. Logan, Jr.; Anthony R. Mayer; Frederick M. Mayer.

Number of staff: 1 part-time professional.

EIN: 840833163

Selected grants: The following grants were reported in 2004.

$1,000,000 to Yale University, New Haven, CT.

$250,000 to Womens Foundation of Colorado, Denver, CO.

$101,699 to Denver Art Museum, Denver, CO.

$40,000 to Denver Zoological Foundation, Denver, CO. For general support.

$25,000 to Eagle Valley Land Trust, Eagle, CO.

$22,000 to Focus Points Family Resource Center, Denver, CO.

$18,000 to Charter Fund, Denver, CO.

$16,000 to Art Students League of Denver, Denver, CO.

$15,000 to Foote School, New Haven, CT.

$10,000 to Summer Scholars, Denver, CO. For general support.

1398
Helen K. and Arthur E. Johnson Foundation ▼ ✧

1700 Broadway, Ste 1100
Denver, CO 80290-2301 (303) 861-4127
Contact: John H. Alexander, Jr., Exec. Dir.; Brigit Ann Davis, V.P. and Prog. Off.
FAX: (303) 861-0607;
E-mail: info@johnsonfoundation.org; Additional tel.: (800) 232-9931; URL: http://www.johnsonfoundation.org

Incorporated in 1948 in CO.

Donors: Arthur E. Johnson†; Helen K. Johnson†.

Foundation type: Independent foundation.

Financial data (yr. ended 12/31/05): Assets, $156,616,536 (M); expenditures, $9,042,901; qualifying distributions, $7,470,885; giving activities include $6,496,934 for 255 grants (high:

$300,000; low: $500; average: $5,000–$25,000), and $9,636 for employee matching gifts.

Purpose and activities: The Helen K. and Arthur E. Johnson Foundation directs its philanthropic resources primarily to tax-exempt Colorado organizations that relieve suffering, meet basic human needs, enrich the quality of life, and promote self-sufficiency.

Fields of interest: Education; Health care; Human services; Children/youth, services; Community development; Aging.

Type of support: General/operating support; Continuing support; Annual campaigns; Capital campaigns; Building/renovation; Equipment; Land acquisition; Program development; Scholarship funds; Matching/challenge support.

Limitations: Giving limited to CO. No support for political organizations. Generally, no grants to individuals, or for scholarships, conferences, endowments; or fundraising dinners or special events; no loans.

Publications: Annual report (including application guidelines).

Application information: The foundation does not accept the Common Grant application or evaluation form. First-time applicants must send a preliminary letter. Previous grant recipients may submit one copy of a full proposal. Postmarks, emails and faxes are not accepted. Application form not required.

Initial approach: Letter (no more than 2 pages)

Copies of proposal: 1

Deadline(s): Jan. 1, Apr. 1, July 1, and Oct. 1

Board meeting date(s): Mar., June, Sept., and Dec.

Final notification: 2 weeks after board meeting

Officers and Trustees:* Lynn H. Campion,* Chair.; Berit K. Campion,* Vice Chair. and Secy.; Ashley C. Campion,* Vice Chair. and Treas.; John H. Alexander, Jr., Pres.; Brigit Ann Davis, V.P. and Prog. Off.; Mrs. James R. Hartley, Chair. Emeritus; Charles R. Hazelrigg, Tr. Emeritus; Roger D. Knight, Jr., Tr. Emeritus; Thomas B. Campion, Jr.; Gerald R. Hillyard, Jr.; Ronald L. Lehr; Stanley D. Neeleman; Matthew D. Semler; Richard G. Wohlgenant.

Number of staff: 2 full-time professional; 1 full-time support; 1 part-time support.

EIN: 846020702

Selected grants: The following grants were reported in 2004.

$200,000 to Saint Joseph Hospital Foundation, Denver, CO. To expand Clinical Scholar Program.

$144,640 to University of Denver, Denver, CO. For Johnson Scholars.

$142,750 to Colorado College, Colorado Springs, CO. For Johnson Scholars.

$127,680 to Planned Parenthood of the Rocky Mountains, Denver, CO. For program expansion.

$125,880 to Regis University, Denver, CO. For Johnson Scholars.

$75,000 to Craig Hospital Foundation, Englewood, CO. For medical equipment.

$75,000 to Little Sisters of the Poor, Denver, CO. To upgrade Intermediate Care Unit.

$75,000 to Red Rocks Community College Foundation, Lakewood, CO. For Johnson Financial Aid.

$75,000 to Western State College of Colorado, Gunnison, CO. For Business School Building.

$65,000 to Visiting Nurse Association of the Denver Area, Denver, CO. For indigent care.

1399

Joy Family Foundation ✧
627 W. Smuggler St.
Aspen, CO 81611

Established in 1996 in CO.
Donors: Sara R. Joy; William N. Joy.
Foundation type: Independent foundation.
Financial data (yr. ended 12/31/05): Assets, $7,998,865 (M); expenditures, $821,975; qualifying distributions, $753,278; giving activities include $746,500 for 5 grants (high: $540,000; low: $2,000).
Purpose and activities: Giving primarily for education and the arts.
Fields of interest: Performing arts, theater; Higher education; Environment, natural resources; Environment, land resources; Health organizations, association; Federated giving programs.
Limitations: Applications not accepted. Giving primarily in CO and CA. No grants to individuals.
Application information: Contributes only to pre-selected organizations.
Officer: William N. Joy, Pres.
Directors: Hayden N. Joy; Madison C. Joy.
EIN: 841361004
Selected grants: The following grants were reported in 2004.
$52,450 to Aspen Institute, Queenstown, MD.
$25,000 to Aspen Education Foundation, Aspen, CO.

1400

The KBK Foundation
(formerly The Kavadas Foundation)
c/o Charles A. Ramunno
1700 Lincoln St., Ste. 4100
Denver, CO 80203-4541

Established in 1991 in CO.
Donor: Kathryn B. Kavadas.
Foundation type: Independent foundation.
Financial data (yr. ended 12/31/05): Assets, $1,021,646 (M); gifts received, $484; expenditures, $629,798; qualifying distributions, $618,000; giving activities include $618,000 for 20 grants (high: $100,000; low: $3,000).
Purpose and activities: Giving primarily for arts and culture, the environment, education, health care, and human services.
Fields of interest: Media, television; Museums; Elementary/secondary education; Higher education; Environment; Reproductive health, family planning; American Red Cross; Residential/custodial care, senior continuing care; Aging.
Type of support: General/operating support; Continuing support; Matching/challenge support.
Limitations: Applications not accepted. Giving primarily in the greater Boston, MA, area. No grants to individuals.
Application information: Contributes only to pre-selected organizations.
Officer and Trustees:* Kathryn B. Kavadas,* Mgr.; Lynn P. Hendrix; Charles A. Ramunno; Stephanie M. Tuthill.
EIN: 841186316

1401

The William C. Kenney Watershed Protection Foundation ✧ ☆
c/o Jay P. Kenney
181 Franklin St.
Denver, CO 80218 (303) 722-0722
FAX: (415) 369-9180;
E-mail: grants@kenneyfdn.org; URL: http://www.kenneyfdn.org

Established in 1994 in CA.
Donors: William C. Kenney Trust; Jay P. Kenney.
Foundation type: Independent foundation.
Financial data (yr. ended 12/31/05): Assets, $2,639,614 (M); gifts received, $100; expenditures, $434,278; qualifying distributions, $405,500; giving activities include $405,500 for 26 grants (high: $40,000; low: $500).
Purpose and activities: The foundation works to protect, preserve, and restore watersheds in the western United States.
Fields of interest: Environment, public policy; Environment, legal rights; Environment, natural resources; Environment, water resources; Environment.
Type of support: General/operating support; Emergency funds; Program development; Technical assistance; Consulting services; Matching/challenge support.
Publications: Annual report.
Application information: The foundation does not accept unsolicited applications for its Leadership Grants. See Web site for application policies regarding its Discretionary and Policy Grants.
Initial approach: E-mail inquiries are accepted. Paper inquiries and e-mail attachments are not accepted
Officers and Directors:* Jay P. Kenney,* Chair.; Thomas J. Barrett, Jr.,* Secy.; Horace S. Kenney; Humphrey Wou.
EIN: 943201589
Selected grants: The following grants were reported in 2003.
$92,000 to Clark Fork Coalition, Missoula, MT. For river protection and restoration.
$40,000 to New Mexico Community Foundation, Santa Fe, NM. For river protection and restoration.
$25,000 to Alaska Wilderness League, DC. For river protection and restoration.
$25,000 to Earthjustice, Oakland, CA. For river protection and restoration.
$20,000 to Colorado Environmental Coalition, Denver, CO. For river protection and restoration.
$12,000 to National Wildlife Federation, Reston, VA. For river protection and restoration.
$5,000 to Equality State Policy Center, Lander, WY. For river protection and restoration.
$5,000 to Friends of the River, Sacramento, CA.
$5,000 to Idaho Conservation League, Boise, ID. For river protection and restoration.
$5,000 to Trout Unlimited, Arlington, VA. For river protection and restoration.

1402

Kern Family Foundation ✧
31 Albion Pl.
Castle Rock, CO 80104

Established in 1999 in CO.
Donors: Jerome Kern; Mary Kern.
Foundation type: Independent foundation.

Financial data (yr. ended 12/31/05): Assets, $4,069,530 (M); expenditures, $1,001,879; qualifying distributions, $995,000; giving activities include $995,000 for 23 grants (high: $500,000; low: $500).
Fields of interest: Performing arts, orchestra (symphony); Education; Health care; Health organizations, association; Human services; Children, services; Science.
Limitations: Giving primarily in Denver, CO.
Officer: Jerome Kern, Pres.
EIN: 841522247
Selected grants: The following grants were reported in 2003.
$75,000 to Saint Marys Academy, Englewood, CO.
$15,000 to Bell Policy Center, Denver, CO.
$10,000 to Volunteers of America, Denver, CO.
$3,500 to Cancer League of Colorado, Englewood, CO.
$2,500 to Rocky Mountain Childrens Law Center, Denver, CO.
$2,000 to Lupus Foundation of Colorado, Denver, CO.
$1,750 to Boy Scouts of America, Denver Area Council, Denver, CO.
$1,000 to Colorado Center for the Book, Denver, CO.
$1,000 to University of Denver, Robert and Judi Newman Center for the Performing Arts, Denver, CO.
$250 to Colorado Symphony Orchestra, Denver, CO.

1403

Kinder Morgan Foundation ✧
(formerly K N Energy Foundation)
370 Van Gordon St.
P.O. Box 281304
Lakewood, CO 80228-8304 (303) 763-3471
Contact: Maureen Bulkley, Community Rels. Coord.
FAX: (303) 984-3306;
E-mail: maureen_bulkley@kindermorgan.com; URL: http://www.kindermorgan.com/community/km_foundation.cfm

Established in 1990 in CO.
Donors: K N Energy, Inc.; Kinder Morgan, Inc.
Foundation type: Company-sponsored foundation.
Financial data (yr. ended 12/31/04): Assets, $2,322,857 (L); expenditures, $729,153; qualifying distributions, $728,923; giving activities include $692,562 for 756 grants (high: $5,445; low: $25), and $35,579 for 140 employee matching gifts.
Purpose and activities: The foundation supports libraries and organizations involved with arts and culture and K-12 education.
Fields of interest: Arts; Elementary/secondary education; Libraries/library science.
Type of support: Program development; Employee matching gifts.
Limitations: Giving primarily in areas of company operations. No support for organizations located outside the U.S. No grants to individuals, or for scholarships, advertising, travel, athletic team sponsorship, general operating support, political causes, or religious projects.
Publications: Informational brochure (including application guidelines).
Application information: Application form required.
Initial approach: Contact foundation for application form
Copies of proposal: 1

Deadline(s): Jan. 10, Mar. 10, May 10, July 10, Sept. 10, and Nov. 10
Final notification: 60 days
Directors: Michael Morgan; Larry S. Pierce; James E. Street; Daniel E. Watson.
EIN: 841148161
Selected grants: The following grants were reported in 2003.
$7,500 to Council of Energy Resource Tribes, Denver, CO. For general support.
$7,500 to Ronald McDonald House of Houston, Houston, TX. For general support.
$7,500 to University of Wyoming Foundation, Laramie, WY. For general support.
$3,000 to Chicago Symphony Orchestra, Chicago, IL. For general support.
$3,000 to DuPage Childrens Museum, Naperville, IL. For general support.
$3,000 to Kilgore College, Kilgore, TX. For general support.
$3,000 to Metropolitan State College of Denver, Denver, CO. For general support.
$2,500 to Artreach, Denver, CO. For general support.
$2,500 to Woodlands Center for the Performing Arts, The Woodlands, TX. For general support.
$2,000 to University of Nebraska, Kearney, NE. For general support.

1404
Kenneth Kendal King Foundation ✧
900 Pennsylvania St.
Denver, CO   80203-3163
Contact: Robert F. Sweeney, Pres.
FAX: (303) 832-4176; *URL:* http://www.KennethKingfoundation.org

Established in 1990 in CO.
Donor: Kenneth Kendal King†.
Foundation type: Independent foundation.
Financial data (yr. ended 12/31/05): Assets, $50,771,954 (M); gifts received, $500; expenditures, $2,672,624; qualifying distributions, $2,098,769; giving activities include $1,495,945 for 346 grants (high: $200,000; low: $250).
Purpose and activities: To fulfill the philosophy of the foundation's founder.
Fields of interest: Higher education; Human services; Christian agencies & churches; Disabilities, people with; Economically disadvantaged; Homeless.
Type of support: Building/renovation; Equipment; Emergency funds; Program development; Scholarship funds; Research; Matching/challenge support.
Limitations: Giving primarily in CO. No grants to individuals.
Publications: Application guidelines; Annual report.
Application information: Application form required.
Initial approach: Letter
Copies of proposal: 2
Deadline(s): 60 days prior to board meeting
Board meeting date(s): To be determined
Final notification: 30 days after board meeting
Officers and Directors:* Robert F. Sweeney,* Pres.; Bernice A. Bettis,* Secy.; Minnie P. Lundberg,* Treas.; Matthew R. "Pete" Banner; Jay Davidson; Joseph Kelly; T.E. "Tim" Welker.
Number of staff: 3 full-time professional; 1 full-time support.
EIN: 841148157

1405
Kitzmiller-Bales Trust
P.O. Box 96
Wray, CO   80758
Contact: Robert U. Hansen, Tr.

Established in 1984 in CO.
Donor: Edna B. Kitzmiller†.
Foundation type: Independent foundation.
Financial data (yr. ended 12/31/05): Assets, $8,198,694 (M); expenditures, $412,516; qualifying distributions, $404,498; giving activities include $402,690 for 7 grants (high: $168,695; low: $3,200).
Purpose and activities: Giving primarily for community development; funding also for education and human services.
Fields of interest: Education; Hospitals (general); Human services; Community development; Government/public administration.
Type of support: Continuing support; Capital campaigns; Building/renovation; Equipment; Program development; Matching/challenge support.
Limitations: Giving limited to projects benefiting the area of East Yuma County School District, RJ-2, CO. No support for religious or political organizations. No grants for scholarships, or endowments.
Publications: Application guidelines.
Application information: Application form not required.
Initial approach: Letter
Copies of proposal: 1
Deadline(s): None
Board meeting date(s): 3rd Mon. of month
Final notification: Following board meetings
Trustees: Duard Fix; Robert U. Hansen; Farmers State Bank.
EIN: 846178085
Selected grants: The following grants were reported in 2005.
$168,695 to Wray School District RD-2, Wray, CO.
$117,795 to Wray Rehabilitation and Activities Center, Wray, CO.
$78,910 to Wray, City of, Wray, CO.
$25,590 to Wray Community Child Care Center, Wray, CO.
$6,500 to Renotta Health Care Systems, Wray, CO.

1406
Lazarus Foundation ✧
511 16th St., Ste. 300
Denver, CO   80202

Established in 2000 in CO.
Donors: Alexis Cranberg; Minnowburn Liquidating Trust; MB Imaging.
Foundation type: Independent foundation.
Financial data (yr. ended 12/31/04): Assets, $620,706 (M); gifts received, $1,494,479; expenditures, $1,370,634; qualifying distributions, $1,369,394; giving activities include $1,062,961 for 26 grants (high: $300,000; low: $500).
Purpose and activities: Giving primarily to provide educational opportunities for low-income children.
Fields of interest: Education; Children, services.
Limitations: Applications not accepted. Giving primarily in Denver, CO. No grants to individuals.
Application information: Contributes only to pre-selected organizations.
Officers: Alex Cranberg, Pres.; Linda Busk, Secy.
Board Member: Susan Morrice.
EIN: 841531063

Selected grants: The following grants were reported in 2004.
$300,000 to Alliance for Choice In Education, Denver, CO.
$100,000 to Denver Center for the Performing Arts, Denver, CO.
$50,000 to Escuela de Guadalupe, Denver, CO.
$42,500 to Independence Institute, Golden, CO.
$16,194 to Public Education and Business Coalition, Denver, CO.
$2,500 to Latin American Educational Foundation, Denver, CO.
$1,000 to Colorado, State of, Denver, CO.

1407
Left Hand Foundation ✧
c/o Matthew McConnell
2350 Linden Ave.
Boulder, CO   80304

Established in 2000 in CO.
Donor: Matthew McConnell.
Foundation type: Independent foundation.
Financial data (yr. ended 5/31/05): Assets, $12,493,857 (M); expenditures, $749,263; qualifying distributions, $617,363; giving activities include $592,000 for 4 grants (high: $490,000; low: $5,000).
Purpose and activities: Emphasis on support for community foundations.
Fields of interest: Foundations (community); Economics.
Limitations: Applications not accepted. Giving primarily in CO. No grants to individuals.
Application information: Contributes only to pre-selected organizations.
Officer: Matthew McConnell, Pres.
EIN: 841550837

1408
The Mike Leprino Family Foundation ✧
1830 W. 38th Ave.
Denver, CO   80211
Contact: Nancy Leprino, Secy.

Established in 1997 in CO.
Donor: Mike Leprino.
Foundation type: Independent foundation.
Financial data (yr. ended 12/31/05): Assets, $7,842,041 (M); expenditures, $565,590; qualifying distributions, $502,700; giving activities include $502,700 for 16 grants (high: $250,000; low: $500).
Purpose and activities: Giving primarily to education, hospitals, human services, and children and youth organizations.
Fields of interest: Higher education, college (community/junior); Hospitals (specialty); Cancer; Youth development, religion; Human services; Children/youth, services.
Limitations: Giving primarily in CO. No grants to individuals, or for lobbying activities.
Application information: Application form not required.
Deadline(s): None
Officers: Mike Leprino, Pres.; Laura Leprino, V.P.; Mary Leprino, V.P.; Nancy Leprino, Secy.
EIN: 311510265
Selected grants: The following grants were reported in 2004.

$130,000 to University of Colorado Foundation, Denver, CO. 2 grants: $100,000 (For Center for Dependency Addiction), $30,000 (For cancer research).

$110,000 to Denver Art Museum, Denver, CO. 2 grants: $10,000, $100,000

$12,500 to Denver Museum of Nature and Science, Denver, CO. For Gates Planetarium.

$6,000 to Anchor Center for Blind Children, Denver, CO.

$5,000 to Boy Scouts of America, Denver Area Council, Denver, CO. For Colorado Child Care.

$5,000 to Challenge Foundation, Englewood, CO. For scholarships.

$5,000 to Kepner Middle School, Denver, CO. For student trip to Washington, DC.

$2,000 to Leadership Program of the Rockies, Denver, CO.

1409
Leptas Foundation Trust ▼ ✧
(formerly Kevin E. & Colleen K. McVaney Family Foundation Trust)
1520 W. Canal Ct., Ste. 220
Littleton, CO 80120

Established in 2000 in CO.
Donors: Kevin E. McVaney; Colleen K. McVaney.
Foundation type: Independent foundation.
Financial data (yr. ended 12/31/04): Assets, $69,214,755 (M); gifts received, $621; expenditures, $3,289,470; qualifying distributions, $3,301,730; giving activities include $3,289,470 for 47 grants (high: $700,000; low: $1,800; average: $10,000–$30,000).
Purpose and activities: Giving primarily for education for religious organizations.
Fields of interest: Education; Christian agencies & churches.
Limitations: Applications not accepted. Giving primarily in CO.
Application information: Contributes only to pre-selected organizations.
Trustee: Kevin E. McVaney.
EIN: 470833530
Selected grants: The following grants were reported in 2004.
$700,000 to Mission Hills Church, Greenwood Village, CO.
$601,500 to Young Life, Colorado Springs, CO.
$510,000 to Christian Medical and Dental Associations, Bristol, TN.
$432,000 to Servant Leadership Foundation, Greenwood Village, CO.
$100,000 to Second Glance Ministries, Aurora, CO.
$92,000 to Mile High Ministries, Denver, CO.
$81,200 to Save Our Youth, Denver, CO.
$70,000 to Focus on the Family, Colorado Springs, CO.
$25,000 to Womens Resource Medical Centers of Southern Nevada, Las Vegas, NV.
$20,000 to Downing House, Englewood, CO.

1410
Richard H. Lewis Family Foundation ✧ ☆
7117 S. Locust Cir.
Englewood, CO 80112

Established in 2000 in CO.
Donor: Richard H. Lewis.
Foundation type: Independent foundation.

Financial data (yr. ended 12/31/05): Assets, $6,029,810 (M); gifts received, $236,385; expenditures, $396,360; qualifying distributions, $352,200; giving activities include $350,220 for 45 grants (high: $231,000; low: $50).
Fields of interest: Higher education; Recreation, parks/playgrounds; Human services; Community development; Federated giving programs; Christian agencies & churches.
Type of support: General/operating support.
Limitations: Applications not accepted. Giving primarily in CO. No grants to individuals.
Application information: Contributes only to pre-selected organizations.
Directors: Bradford H. Lewis; Carol A. Lewis; Richard H. Lewis.
EIN: 841568116
Selected grants: The following grants were reported in 2004.
$10,500 to Young Life, Colorado Springs, CO.
$10,000 to Promise Keepers, Denver, CO.
$3,900 to Youth for Christ, Denver, CO.
$2,000 to Denver Rescue Mission, Denver, CO.
$2,000 to Westmont College, Santa Barbara, CA.
$1,250 to Campus Crusade for Christ, Miami, FL.
$1,000 to First Presbyterian Church, Winston-Salem, NC.
$750 to Focus on the Family, Colorado Springs, CO.
$260 to University of Colorado Foundation, Boulder, CO.
$200 to Alternatives Pregnancy Center, Denver, CO.

1411
The Liniger Family Foundation ✧
c/o David L. Liniger
8390 E. Crescent Pkwy., Ste. 600
Greenwood Village, CO 80111-2800

Established in 2000 in CO.
Donors: David L. Liniger; Mrs. David L. Liniger.
Foundation type: Independent foundation.
Financial data (yr. ended 12/31/04): Assets, $1,092,000 (M); gifts received, $1,500,000; expenditures, $1,197,040; qualifying distributions, $1,196,999; giving activities include $1,196,999 for 27 grants (high: $137,000; low: $1,000).
Fields of interest: Health care; Health organizations, association; Children, services.
Limitations: Applications not accepted. No grants to individuals.
Application information: Contributes only to pre-selected organizations.
Officers and Directors:* David L. Liniger,* Pres.; Gail Liniger,* V.P. and Secy.; Bruce Benham; Bob Fisher; George Graff; Daryl Jesperson; Joe Reynolds; Mike Ryan; Vinnie Tracey.
EIN: 841511731
Selected grants: The following grants were reported in 2003.
$100,000 to Craig Hospital, Englewood, CO.
$100,000 to Gathering Place, Denver, CO.
$6,000 to Alliance for Choice In Education, Denver, CO.
$5,000 to Adoption Options, Charlotte, NC.
$5,000 to Saint Anthony Health Foundation, Denver, CO. For Flight for Life.
$1,000 to Childrens Miracle Network, Salt Lake City, UT.

1412
Ludlow-Griffith Foundation ✧ ☆
P.O. Box 18248
Denver, CO 80218
Contact: William L. Schmidt, Pres,

Established in 1990.
Donors: William G. Griffith; Frances L. Griffith.
Foundation type: Independent foundation.
Financial data (yr. ended 12/31/05): Assets, $1,400,409 (M); gifts received, $131,807; expenditures, $497,564; qualifying distributions, $497,564; giving activities include $497,564 for grants.
Purpose and activities: Giving primarily for the arts, child welfare and health.
Fields of interest: Media, television; Arts; Higher education; Environment; Health organizations, association; Children/youth, services; Christian agencies & churches.
Limitations: Giving primarily in Denver, CO. No grants to individuals.
Application information:
Initial approach: Letter
Deadline(s): May 15 and Nov. 15
Officers: William L. Schmidt, Pres.; Jeff Reder, V.P. and Treas.; Tschudy G. Schmidt, Secy.
EIN: 841157778
Selected grants: The following grants were reported in 2005.
$428,489 to Denver Foundation, Denver, CO.
$34,000 to Nature Conservancy, Arlington, VA.
$23,075 to Boys and Girls Clubs of Metro Denver, Denver, CO.
$10,000 to Ducks Unlimited, Memphis, TN.
$1,000 to Colorado Conservation Trust, Boulder, CO.

1413
M.D.C. Holdings, Inc. Charitable Foundation ✧ ☆
4350 S. Monaco St.
Denver, CO 80237
Contact: Paris G. Reece III, V.P. and Secy.

Established in 1999 in CO.
Donor: M.D.C. Holdings, Inc.
Foundation type: Company-sponsored foundation.
Financial data (yr. ended 12/31/04): Assets, $20,303,010 (M); gifts received, $6,300,000; expenditures, $428,847; qualifying distributions, $404,667; giving activities include $404,667 for 10 grants (high: $166,667; low: $5,000).
Purpose and activities: The foundation supports Jewish agencies and temples, community foundations, and organizations involved with arts and culture, education, health, recreation, youth business, children and youth, and family services.
Fields of interest: Performing arts, ballet; Arts; Higher education; Education; Hospitals (general); Health care; Recreation; Youth development, business; Children/youth, services; Family services; Foundations (community); Jewish agencies & temples.
Type of support: Building/renovation; Program development; Scholarship funds; Research.
Limitations: Giving primarily in CO.
Application information: Application form not required.
Initial approach: Proposal
Deadline(s): None

Officers and Trustees:* Larry A. Mizel,* Pres.; Paris G. Reece III,* V.P. and Secy.; John J. Heaney, V.P. and Treas.; Steven J. Borick; Gilbert Goldstein; David D. Mandanch.
EIN: 841561013

1414
Mallon Family Foundation ◆
c/o Transfinancial Corp.
6359 Snowberry Ln.
Longmont, CO   80503-7146
Contact: Josette P. Mallon, V.P.

Established in 1989 in CO.
Donors: Josette P. Mallon; Theodore J. Mallon.
Foundation type: Independent foundation.
Financial data (yr. ended 12/31/05): Assets, $962,909 (M); gifts received, $795,000; expenditures, $401,738; qualifying distributions, $401,380; giving activities include $398,964 for 23 grants (high: $71,085; low: $150).
Purpose and activities: Giving primarily for higher education, as well as for noetic sciences.
Fields of interest: Higher education; Health organizations, association; Human services; Foundations (private grantmaking).
Limitations: Giving primarily in CO.
Application information:
    Initial approach: Proposal
    Deadline(s): None
Officers: Theodore J. Mallon, Pres.; Josette P. Mallon, V.P.; Heather L. Mallon, Secy.
EIN: 742545904
Selected grants: The following grants were reported in 2003.
$100,000 to Naropa University, Boulder, CO. 2 grants: $80,000 (For Forgiveness Project), $20,000 (For general support).
$25,000 to Center for Psychology and Social Change, Cambridge, MA. For general support.
$25,000 to Childrens Hospital Foundation, Denver, CO. For Children's Circle of Care for the Pediatric Intensive Care Unit.
$10,000 to Changemakers, San Francisco, CA. For general support.
$10,000 to La Puente Home, Alamosa, CO. For general support.
$10,000 to National Jewish Medical and Research Center, Department of Pediatrics, Denver, CO.
$10,000 to Susan G. Komen Breast Cancer Foundation, La Jolla, CA. For general support.
$5,000 to Community Foundation Serving Boulder County, Boulder, CO. For general support.
$5,000 to More than Money, Arlington, MA. For general support.

1415
The Malone Family Foundation ▼
12300 Liberty Blvd.
Englewood, CO   80112
Contact: Cathie Wlaschin, Admin.
E-mail: cathie@malonefamilyfoundation.org;
URL: http://www.malonefamilyfoundation.org

Established in 1997 in CO.
Donor: John C. Malone.
Foundation type: Independent foundation.
Financial data (yr. ended 12/31/05): Assets, $128,742,877 (M); expenditures, $7,479,826; qualifying distributions, $7,244,065; giving activities include $7,240,803 for 8 grants (high:

$2,000,000; low: $43,250; average: $83,926–$2,000,000).
Purpose and activities: The foundation primarily funds endowments to independent secondary schools for scholarships for underfunded, highly capable students. Also, a small discretionary fund supports gifted research.
Fields of interest: Education, gifted students.
Type of support: Endowments; Research.
Limitations: Applications not accepted. Giving on a national basis. No grants to individuals.
Application information: Contributes only to pre-selected organizations.
    Board meeting date(s): May
Officers and Directors:* John C. Malone,* Pres. and Treas.; Leslie A. Malone,* Secy.; Evan D. Malone; Tracy L. Neal.
Number of staff: 1 part-time professional.
EIN: 841408520
Selected grants: The following grants were reported in 2005.
$2,000,000 to Catlin Gabel School, Portland, OR.
$2,000,000 to Trinity Preparatory School of Florida, Orlando, FL.
$2,000,000 to University School of Nashville, Nashville, TN.
$1,000,000 to Saint Andrews Episcopal School, Jackson, MS.
$83,926 to Stanford University, Stanford, CA. For Center for Education for Gifted Youth.
$61,127 to Mary Baldwin College, Staunton, VA.
$52,500 to Northwestern University, Evanston, IL. For Center for Talent Development.
$43,250 to Roper Institute, Bloomfield, MI.

1416
Cydney and Tom Marisco Family Foundation ◆
(formerly CTM Foundation)
5251 DTC Pkwy., Ste 1001
Greenwood Village, CO   80111

Established in 1997 in CO.
Donors: Tom Marsico; Cydney Marsico.
Foundation type: Independent foundation.
Financial data (yr. ended 11/30/05): Assets, $1,361,277 (M); expenditures, $1,845,847; qualifying distributions, $1,820,217; giving activities include $1,558,296 for 39 grants (high: $275,736; low: $952).
Purpose and activities: Giving primarily for health and human services.
Fields of interest: Education, early childhood education; Health care; Human services; Children/youth, services; Women.
Limitations: Applications not accepted. Giving primarily in Denver, CO. No grants to individuals.
Application information: Contributes only to pre-selected organizations.
Officers: Cydney Marsico, Pres.; Tom Marsico, V.P.; Christopher Marsico, Treas.; Cindy Schulz, Exec. Dir.
EIN: 841475920
Selected grants: The following grants were reported in 2005.
$613,500 to Girls Inc. of Metro Denver, Denver, CO. 4 grants: $250,000, $213,000, $23,000, $127,500
$275,736 to Mercy Housing, Denver, CO.
$200,000 to Denver Museum of Nature and Science, Denver, CO. 2 grants: $100,000 each
$62,500 to Warren Village, Denver, CO.
$50,000 to Families First, Denver, CO.
$8,700 to Gathering Place, Denver, CO.

1417
Mater Dei Foundation ◆ ☆
1830 W. 38th Ave.
Denver, CO   80211

Established in 2003 in CO.
Donors: J.G.L. Foundation; Leprino Foods Company.
Foundation type: Independent foundation.
Financial data (yr. ended 12/31/05): Assets, $691 (M); gifts received, $452,000; expenditures, $500,045; qualifying distributions, $500,000; giving activities include $500,000 for 1 grant.
Purpose and activities: The foundation supports programs that encourage, inspire, and direct young people to strengthen their Catholic/Christian faith.
Fields of interest: Secondary school/education.
Limitations: Applications not accepted. Giving primarily in CO. No grants to individuals.
Application information: Contributes only to pre-selected organizations.
Trustees: Richard O. Campbell; James G. Leprino; Daniel A. Vecchiarelli.
EIN: 206073041

1418
Frederick R. Mayer Foundation ◆
P.O. Box 5083
Denver, CO   80217

Established in 1995 in CO.
Donor: Frederick R. Mayer.
Foundation type: Operating foundation.
Financial data (yr. ended 11/30/05): Assets, $4,755,220 (M); gifts received, $145,000; expenditures, $515,910; qualifying distributions, $621,051; giving activities include $500,000 for 1 grant.
Fields of interest: Higher education, university.
Limitations: Applications not accepted.
Application information: Contributes only to pre-selected organizations.
Officers: Frederick R. Mayer, Pres.; Jan Perry Mayer, V.P.; Gloria J. Higgins, Secy.
EIN: 841359652

1419
McCloskey Family Charitable Trust ◆
132 W. Main St.
Aspen, CO   81611-1710

Established in 1997 in CO.
Donor: Thomas D. McCloskey, Jr.
Foundation type: Independent foundation.
Financial data (yr. ended 12/31/04): Assets, $2,028,859 (M); expenditures, $473,246; qualifying distributions, $455,990; giving activities include $454,740 for 9 grants (high: $200,000; low: $100).
Fields of interest: Secondary school/education; Higher education; Education; Health care; Human services; International affairs.
Limitations: Applications not accepted. Giving primarily in Aspen, CO. No grants to individuals.
Application information: Contributes only to pre-selected organizations.
Trustees: Bonnie P. McCloskey; Thomas D. McCloskey, Jr.
EIN: 841428969

1420
McCormick Charitable Trust ◇
3200 Cherry Creek Dr. S., Ste. 230
Denver, CO 80209

Established in 1998 in CO.
Donor: Richard D. McCormick.
Foundation type: Independent foundation.
Financial data (yr. ended 12/31/04): Assets, $3,811,979 (M); expenditures, $581,550; qualifying distributions, $575,050; giving activities include $575,050 for 59 grants (high: $100,000; low: $100).
Purpose and activities: Giving primarily for community, educational, and healthcare purposes, and to Roman Catholic churches.
Fields of interest: Museums (art); Arts; Secondary school/education; Higher education; Education; Health care; Health organizations, association; Human services; Children/youth, services; Roman Catholic agencies & churches.
Limitations: Applications not accepted. Giving primarily in Denver, CO. No grants to individuals.
Application information: Contributes only to pre-selected organizations.
Trustees: Mary Patricia McCormick; Richard D. McCormick.
EIN: 841458182
Selected grants: The following grants were reported in 2004.
$106,000 to Denver Art Museum, Denver, CO. 3 grants: $100,000, $1,000, $5,000
$100,000 to Catholic Foundation for the Archdiocese of Denver, Denver, CO.
$100,000 to Papal Foundation, Philadelphia, PA.
$50,000 to Arrupe Jesuit High School, Denver, CO.
$20,000 to Mercy High School, Omaha, NE.
$20,000 to Third Way Center, Denver, CO.
$10,000 to Opus Spiritus Sancti, Dayton, OH.
$2,500 to Creighton University, Omaha, NE.

1421
J. M. McDonald Foundation, Inc. ◇
P.O. Box 3219
Evergreen, CO 80437-3219 (303) 674-9300
Contact: Donald R. McJunkin, Pres.

Incorporated in 1952 in NE.
Donor: James M. McDonald, Sr.†.
Foundation type: Independent foundation.
Financial data (yr. ended 12/31/04): Assets, $23,127,914 (M); expenditures, $1,162,027; qualifying distributions, $1,038,584; giving activities include $1,020,000 for 19 grants (high: $600,000; low: $5,000).
Purpose and activities: Grants for the aged, orphans, and children who are sick, infirm, blind, or crippled; support for youth and child care in an effort to combat juvenile delinquency and to aid underprivileged, mentally or physically handicapped children. Other interests include health and hospitals and education, especially higher education. The foundation prefers to fund capital projects.
Fields of interest: Higher education; Education; Hospitals (general); Health care; Crime/law enforcement; Human services; Children/youth, services; Aging, centers/services; Aging; Disabilities, people with.
Type of support: General/operating support; Continuing support; Annual campaigns; Capital campaigns; Building/renovation; Equipment.

Limitations: Giving primarily in upstate NY. No grants to individuals, or for seminars, workshops, endowment funds, fellowships, travel, exhibits, or conferences; no loans.
Publications: Application guidelines.
Application information: Application form not required.
    Initial approach: Letter
    Copies of proposal: 1
    Deadline(s): Apr. 15 and Sept. 15
    Board meeting date(s): May and Oct.
    Final notification: May 30 or Oct. 30 for positive responses
Officers and Trustees:* Donald R. McJunkin,* Pres.; Nancy J. Palmer,* V.P.; Janet E. Stanton,* V.P.; Reed L. McJunkin,* Secy.; Donald C. Berry, Jr.,* Treas.
EIN: 471431059

1422
McDonnell Family Foundation ◇
P.O. Box 16909
Golden, CO 80402

Established in 1999 in CO.
Donors: John F. McDonnell; Patricia L. McDonnell.
Foundation type: Independent foundation.
Financial data (yr. ended 12/31/05): Assets, $15,265,787 (M); expenditures, $1,104,837; qualifying distributions, $1,028,465; giving activities include $944,125 for 34 grants (high: $140,000; low: $5,000).
Purpose and activities: Giving primarily for a broad range of social services.
Fields of interest: Education; Health care; Mental health, treatment; Crime/violence prevention, domestic violence; Housing/shelter; Youth development; Human services; Children/youth, services; Family services; Residential/custodial care, group home; Christian agencies & churches.
Limitations: Applications not accepted. Giving primarily in CA and CO; some giving also in OH. No grants to individuals.
Application information: Contributes only to pre-selected organizations, which the foundation's individual board members seek out.
Officers: John F. McDonnell, Pres.; Patricia L. McDonnell, V.P.; Matthew J. McDonnell, Secy.-Treas.
EIN: 841498562

1423
McWhinney Foundation ◇ ☆
2725 Rocky Mountain Ave., Ste. 200
Loveland, CO 80538 (970) 962-9990
Contact: Johnna Bavaso, Exec. Dir.

Established in 2004 in CO.
Donor: McWhinney Holding Comp.
Foundation type: Independent foundation.
Financial data (yr. ended 12/31/05): Assets, $0 (M); gifts received, $362,258; expenditures, $362,483; qualifying distributions, $346,632; giving activities include $346,632 for 45 grants (high: $100,000; low: $100).
Fields of interest: Health organizations; Athletics/sports, training; Human services.
Limitations: Giving primarily in CO.
Application information:
    Deadline(s): None

Officers: Robin McWhinney, Pres.; Lori McWhinney, Secy.; Johnna Bavaso, Exec. Dir.
EIN: 202064195

1424
Andre & Katherine Merage Foundation ◇
6400 Fiddlers Green Cir., Ste. 2050
Englewood, CO 80111

Established in 2002 in CO.
Donor: Katherine Merage.
Foundation type: Independent foundation.
Financial data (yr. ended 11/30/05): Assets, $21,628,264 (M); expenditures, $1,091,109; qualifying distributions, $1,032,248; giving activities include $956,407 for 7 grants (high: $396,533; low: $7,500).
Fields of interest: Jewish federated giving programs; Jewish agencies & temples.
Limitations: Applications not accepted. Giving primarily in CA, CO, FL, and NY. No grants to individuals.
Application information: Contributes only to pre-selected organizations.
Officer: Mary Murphy, Mgr.
Directors: David Merage; Katherine Merage.
EIN: 450493929

1425
David and Laura Merage Foundation ◇
6400 Fiddlers Green Cir., Ste. 2050
Englewood, CO 80111

Established in 2002 in CO.
Donors: David Merage; Laura Merage.
Foundation type: Independent foundation.
Financial data (yr. ended 11/30/05): Assets, $37,642,311 (M); gifts received, $5,006,978; expenditures, $1,657,572; qualifying distributions, $1,555,394; giving activities include $1,439,745 for 46 grants (high: $496,533; low: $28).
Fields of interest: Arts; Education; Jewish federated giving programs; Jewish agencies & temples.
Limitations: Applications not accepted. Giving primarily in CA and CO. No grants to individuals.
Application information: Contributes only to pre-selected organizations.
Officers and Directors:* David Merage,* Pres.; Laura Merage, V.P.; Mary Murphy, Mgr.
EIN: 450493925
Selected grants: The following grants were reported in 2003.
$48,333 to Anti-Defamation League of Bnai Brith, Denver, CO. For operating support.
$12,500 to Allied Jewish Federation of Colorado, Denver, CO. For operating support.
$10,000 to Hebrew Immigrant Aid Society (HIAS), New York, NY. For operating support.
$10,000 to Mizel Center for Arts and Culture, Denver, CO. For operating support.
$10,000 to Saint Marys Academy, Englewood, CO. For operating support.
$10,000 to Survivors of the Shoah Visual History Foundation, Los Angeles, CA. For operating support.
$3,300 to Childrens Hospital Association, Denver, CO. For operating support.
$2,028 to Rocky Mountain Public Broadcasting Network, Denver, CO. For operating support.
$1,500 to Denver Art Museum, Denver, CO. For operating support.

$1,000 to Museum of Contemporary Art Denver, Denver, CO. For operating support.

1426
Mercy and Sharing ✧
(formerly Foundation for Worldwide Mercy & Sharing)
201 N. Mill St., Ste. 201
Aspen, CO   81611-1503   (970) 925-1492
E-mail: haitikids@aol.com; URL: http://www.haitichildren.com

Established in 1995 in CO.
Donors: Joseph Krabacher; Susan Krabacher; Dave Anderson; Robert Brining; Linda Brining; Antony Caine; Terri Caine; Doris Carver; Buck Deane; Natasha Dean; Christopher Hewett; Frances Johnson; Edwin Joseph; Jeffrey Leck; Carolyn McRae; Ginger Reddington; Rotary Foundation of Washington; Fund for the Poor, Inc.; Bridgeway Charitable Foundation; Crystal Foundation; John A. Griffin Foundation, Inc.; Heart to Heart for Kids, Inc.; The Anschutz Foundation.
Foundation type: Independent foundation.
Financial data (yr. ended 12/31/04): Assets, $1,006,608 (M); gifts received, $1,074,197; expenditures, $743,305; qualifying distributions, $579,844; giving activities include $579,844 for 14 grants (high: $204,602; low: $2,714).
Purpose and activities: Giving primarily for health and medical care for children in Haiti.
Fields of interest: Health care; Children, services; Residential/custodial care.
International interests: Haiti.
Type of support: General/operating support; Building/renovation; Program development.
Limitations: Giving primarily in Haiti. No grants to individuals.
Publications: Financial statement; Newsletter.
Application information: Application form not required.
   Deadline(s): None
   Board meeting date(s): Monthly
Officers and Board Members:* Susan Krabacher,* Pres.; B. Joseph Krabacher,* Secy.-Treas.; E.J. Christensen; Steve Gorlin; Ricky Hicks; Jeffrey Leck.
EIN: 841323007

1427
Mizel Global Cultural Fund ✧ ☆
4350 S. Monaco St., 5th Fl.
Denver, CO   80237

Established in 2001 in CO.
Donor: Larry A. Mi Zel.
Foundation type: Independent foundation.
Financial data (yr. ended 12/31/05): Assets, $2,368,451 (M); expenditures, $1,088,578; qualifying distributions, $1,038,270; giving activities include $1,038,270 for 30 grants (high: $236,000; low: $180).
Fields of interest: Performing arts, ballet; Arts; Higher education; Jewish federated giving programs; Jewish agencies & temples.
Limitations: Applications not accepted. Giving on a national basis. No grants to individuals.
Application information: Contributes only to pre-selected organizations.
Officers: Larry A. Mizel, Pres.; Charles G. Hauber, V.P. and Secy.; Carol Mizel, V.P.
EIN: 841588664

1428
Kenneth and Myra Monfort Charitable Foundation, Inc. ✧
134 Oak Ave.
Eaton, CO   80615

Established in 1998 in FL.
Donors: Kenneth Monfort; Myra Monfort.
Foundation type: Independent foundation.
Financial data (yr. ended 12/31/04): Assets, $17,155,278 (M); expenditures, $878,124; qualifying distributions, $807,730; giving activities include $751,337 for 28 grants (high: $231,000; low: $250).
Purpose and activities: Giving primarily for higher education, and to a marine laboratory.
Fields of interest: Performing arts, ballet; Higher education; Boys & girls clubs; Marine science.
Limitations: Applications not accepted. Giving primarily in CO and FL. No grants to individuals.
Application information: Contributes only to pre-selected organizations.
Officers: Myra Monfort, Pres. and Treas.; Brad Ellins, V.P.; Rachel Iozzia, Secy.
EIN: 650881056
Selected grants: The following grants were reported in 2004.
$231,000 to Barnard College, New York, NY.
$102,250 to Mote Marine Laboratory, Sarasota, FL.
$100,000 to University of Colorado Foundation, Boulder, CO.
$73,333 to Boys and Girls Clubs of Weld County, Greeley, CO.
$58,721 to Boys and Girls Club of Sarasota County, Sarasota, FL.
$35,000 to University of Northern Colorado Foundation, Greeley, CO.
$21,760 to Colorado State University Foundation, Fort Collins, CO.
$5,000 to Tabor Academy, Marion, MA.
$2,500 to Girls Inc. of Sarasota, Sarasota, FL.
$1,500 to Boy Scouts of America, Greeley, CO.

1429
Monfort Family Foundation ✧
(formerly Monfort Charitable Foundation)
Box 337300
Greeley, CO   80633   (970) 454-1357
Contact: Dave Evans

Established in 1970 in CO.
Donor: Kenneth W. Monfort†.
Foundation type: Independent foundation.
Financial data (yr. ended 12/31/03): Assets, $46,281,305 (M); gifts received, $349,897; expenditures, $2,502,194; qualifying distributions, $2,308,502; giving activities include $2,141,811 for 51 grants (high: $764,973; low: $1,000; average: $5,000–$100,000).
Purpose and activities: Giving primarily for education, health and medical research, and arts and culture.
Fields of interest: Performing arts; Arts; Education, fund raising/fund distribution; Business school/education; Education; Cancer; Cancer research; Agriculture; Federated giving programs; General charitable giving.
Type of support: General/operating support.
Limitations: Giving primarily in Weld County, CO. No grants to individuals.
Application information: Application form required.
   Copies of proposal: 1

Deadline(s): May 1 and Oct. 1
Board meeting date(s): May and Oct.
Officers and Trustees:* Kaye C. Ward,* Pres.; Kyle Monfort Futo,* V.P.; Charlie Monfort, V.P.; Myra Monfort,* Secy.; Dick Monfort, Treas.
EIN: 237068253
Selected grants: The following grants were reported in 2003.
$764,973 to Colorado State University Foundation, Fort Collins, CO. For student programs.
$370,000 to United Way of Weld County, Greeley, CO. For general operating support.
$152,500 to University of Northern Colorado Foundation, Greeley, CO. For student programs.
$24,000 to Greeley Philharmonic Orchestra, Greeley, CO. For general operating support.
$10,000 to North Colorado Medical Center Foundation, Greeley, CO. For general operating support.
$7,200 to Greeley Childrens Chorale, Greeley, CO. For general operating support.
$5,000 to Mizel Center for Arts and Culture, Denver, CO. For general operating support.
$5,000 to University of Colorado Hospital Authority, Aurora, CO. For general operating support.
$5,000 to University of Denver, Denver, CO. For general operating support.
$1,500 to Greeley Chamber Orchestra, Evans, CO. For general operating support.

1430
Pete Morgan Foundation ✧
(formerly McVaney-Fernalld Family Foundation Trust)
1520 W. Canal Ct., Ste. 220
Littleton, CO   80120
Contact: Scott Sprinkle

Established in 2000 in CO.
Donor: Kylee McVaney Fernalld Trust.
Foundation type: Independent foundation.
Financial data (yr. ended 12/31/04): Assets, $54,252,576 (M); gifts received, $621; expenditures, $2,183,304; qualifying distributions, $2,197,363; giving activities include $2,183,304 for 84 grants (high: $240,200; low: $300).
Purpose and activities: Giving primarily for Christian organizations and human services.
Fields of interest: Education; Human services; Christian agencies & churches.
Limitations: Applications not accepted. Giving primarily in CO and FL.
Application information: Contributes only to pre-selected organizations.
Trustee: Kylee A. Fernalld.
EIN: 470833529
Selected grants: The following grants were reported in 2003.
$210,100 to Campus Crusade for Christ International, Orlando, FL.
$200,000 to Union Baptist Excel Institute, Denver, CO.
$150,000 to Cherry Hills Community Church, Highlands Ranch, CO.
$125,000 to Save Our Youth, Denver, CO.
$120,000 to Servant Leadership Foundation, Greenwood Village, CO.
$100,000 to Alpha USA, New York, NY.
$100,000 to Denver Street School, Denver, CO.
$70,000 to CARE Foundation, Denver, CO.
$61,000 to Compassion International, Colorado Springs, CO.
$50,000 to University of Denver, Denver, CO.

1431
Nagel Foundation ◇
1225 17th St., Ste. 2440
Denver, CO 80202
Contact: Ralph J. Nagel, Pres.

Established in 1994 in CO.
Donors: Ralph J. Nagel; Steven A. Denning; Ciga, LLP; General Atlantic Service Corp.
Foundation type: Independent foundation.
Financial data (yr. ended 12/31/05): Assets, $23,174,996 (M); gifts received, $10,000,250; expenditures, $605,301; qualifying distributions, $584,857; giving activities include $584,857 for 9 grants (high: $282,857; low: $1,000).
Fields of interest: Higher education; Education; Human services.
Limitations: Giving primarily in Denver, CO. No grants to individuals.
Application information:
  Initial approach: Letter
  Deadline(s): Nov. 15
Officer: Ralph J. Nagel, Pres.
EIN: 841285137
Selected grants: The following grants were reported in 2004.
$292,357 to University of Denver, Denver, CO. 2 grants: $192,357, $100,000

1432
Newman Family Foundation ◇ ☆
1873 S. Bellaire St.
Denver, CO 80222

Established in 1993 in CO.
Donors: Robert C. Newman; Judith S. Newman.
Foundation type: Independent foundation.
Financial data (yr. ended 11/30/05): Assets, $8,667,153 (M); expenditures, $671,902; qualifying distributions, $578,357; giving activities include $560,933 for grants.
Fields of interest: Performing arts, orchestra (symphony); Family services; Christian agencies & churches.
Limitations: Applications not accepted. Giving primarily in CO. No grants to individuals.
Application information: Contributes only to pre-selected organizations.
Officers: Robert C. Newman, Pres.; Judith S. Newman, V.P.; Etta M. West, Exec. Dir.
Director: Jennifer A. Newman.
EIN: 841257294

1433
The Norwood Foundation ◇
P.O. Box 792
Manitou Springs, CO 80829
Application address: c/o Christopher S. Jenkins, Secy.-Treas., 111 S. Tejon St., Ste. 222, Colorado Springs, CO 80903, tel.: (719) 593-2600

Established in 2002 in CO.
Donors: Carolyn S. Jenkins; David D. Jenkins; Development Mgmt., Inc.
Foundation type: Independent foundation.
Financial data (yr. ended 2/28/05): Assets, $343,876 (M); gifts received, $557,700; expenditures, $561,465; qualifying distributions, $560,865; giving activities include $540,465 for 42 + grants (high: $250,000), and $20,400 for 1 grant to an individual.

Purpose and activities: Individuals pursuing a college education must be a high school graduate in order to qualify for scholarship awards. Individuals seeking trade or vocational skills need not be a high school graduate but must comply with the admission requirement of the training institution.
Fields of interest: Arts; Environment, natural resources; Human services; Child development, services.
Type of support: General/operating support; Scholarships—to individuals.
Limitations: Giving primarily in CO.
Application information: Application form required.
  Deadline(s): None
Officers: David D. Jenkins, Pres.; Carolyn S. Jenkins, V.P.; Christopher S. Jenkins, Secy.-Treas.
EIN: 010705471
Selected grants: The following grants were reported in 2005.
$25,000 to Ecumenical Social Ministries, Colorado Springs, CO.
$15,000 to YMCA.
$12,700 to American Heart Association, Dallas, TX.
$5,000 to Cystic Fibrosis Foundation, Colorado Springs, CO.
$5,000 to Silver Key Senior Services, Colorado Springs, CO.
$5,000 to ULI Foundation, DC.
$5,000 to Young Life.
$2,500 to Pikes Peak Hospice Foundation, Colorado Springs, CO.
$2,500 to Salvation Army.
$1,500 to Arthritis Foundation, Atlanta, GA.

1434
The Osborn Foundation ◇ ☆
110 Inverness Terr. E., Ste. 200
Englewood, CO 80112 (303) 703-8611
Contact: John E. Osborn, Pres.

Established in 2004 in CO.
Donors: John Osborn; Mary Osborn.
Foundation type: Independent foundation.
Financial data (yr. ended 12/31/05): Assets, $380,928 (M); gifts received, $300,000; expenditures, $328,185; qualifying distributions, $325,800; giving activities include $325,800 for 9 grants (high: $301,800; low: $500).
Purpose and activities: Giving primaily for education, and to a children's hospital.
Fields of interest: Education; Hospitals (specialty); Human services.
Limitations: Giving primarily in Denver, CO.
Application information:
  Initial approach: Letter
  Deadline(s): None
Officers and Directors:* John E. Osborn,* Pres.; Mary E. Osborn,* Secy.; Matthew P. Osborn,* Treas.; Kate O. Lively; Mark M. Osborn.
EIN: 721576920

1435
Terrance and Judith Paul Foundation, Inc. ◇ ☆
2060 Broadway St., No. 200
Boulder, CO 80302

Established in 1997 in WI.
Donors: Judith Paul; Terrance Paul.
Foundation type: Independent foundation.

Financial data (yr. ended 12/31/05): Assets, $4,017,290 (M); expenditures, $1,081,335; qualifying distributions, $1,044,335; giving activities include $1,044,335 for grants.
Purpose and activities: Giving primarily to the arts and social services.
Fields of interest: Arts; Higher education; Health care, clinics/centers; Human services.
Limitations: Applications not accepted. Giving primarily in WI. No grants to individuals.
Application information: Contributes only to pre-selected organizations.
Officers: Judith Paul, Pres. and Treas.; Terrance Paul, V.P. and Secy.
Director: Mia Paul.
EIN: 391914369
Selected grants: The following grants were reported in 2004.
$500,000 to Mayo Foundation, Rochester, MN.
$100,000 to University of Illinois Foundation, Urbana, IL.
$20,000 to University of Wisconsin, Stevens Point, WI.

1436
The Jack Petteys Memorial Foundation ◇
c/o Judy Gunnon
P.O. Box 324
Brush, CO 80723 (970) 842-5101

Established about 1943 in CO.
Foundation type: Independent foundation.
Financial data (yr. ended 12/31/05): Assets, $10,289,520 (M); expenditures, $502,264; qualifying distributions, $497,012; giving activities include $485,125 for 20 grants (high: $200,000; low: $600).
Purpose and activities: Giving primarily to undergraduate scholarship funds; support also for hospitals and civic projects.
Fields of interest: Higher education; Hospitals (general); Government/public administration.
Type of support: Equipment; Scholarship funds.
Limitations: Giving primarily in northeastern CO.
Application information:
  Initial approach: Letter
  Copies of proposal: 1
  Deadline(s): Dec. 1
  Board meeting date(s): Monthly
Directors: Robert Hansen; Robert Petteys; Helen Watrous.
Trustee: Farmers State Bank.
EIN: 846036239

1437
Pikes Peak Community Foundation ◇
P.O. Box 1443
Colorado Springs, CO 80901 (719) 389-1251
Contact: Michael R. Hannigan, Exec. Dir.
FAX: (719) 389-1252; E-mail: info@ppcf.org;
Additional E-mails: jbrown@ppcf.org and mhannigan@ppcf.org; URL: http://www.ppcf.org

Established in 1996 in CO.
Foundation type: Community foundation.
Financial data (yr. ended 12/31/04): Assets, $27,476,056 (M); gifts received, $5,900,450; expenditures, $5,943,920; giving activities include $3,900,974 for 256 grants (high: $359,077; low: $30).

Purpose and activities: The foundation seeks to serve as the leading resource for philanthropy in the Pikes Peak, CO, region, by investing grant funding in the community, helping people create permanent charitable funds, and providing leadership for community issues.

Fields of interest: Arts; Education; Environment; Health care; Housing/shelter; Children/youth, services; Human services; Community development, neighborhood development; Economic development; Community development; Public affairs; Homeless.

Type of support: General/operating support; Continuing support; Income development; Management development/capacity building; Capital campaigns; Building/renovation; Equipment; Emergency funds; Seed money; Curriculum development; Matching/challenge support.

Limitations: Giving primarily in El Paso and Teller counties in CO. No support for religious purposes. No grants to individuals, or for debt retirement, endowment funds, medical, scientific, or academic research, sponsorships or camperships, travel, publications, fees for conferences, symposiums, or workshops, creation or installation of art objects, or annual memberships of affiliation campaigns, dinners, or special events; no loans.

Publications: Annual report (including application guidelines).

Application information: Visit foundation Web site for application form and guidelines. Colorado Common Grant Application Form is also accepted. Application form required.

Initial approach: E-mail, letter, or hand-deliver application form and attachments
Copies of proposal: 1
Deadline(s): Mar. 1, Aug. 1, and Nov. 1
Board meeting date(s): Variable
Final notification: Apr., Sept., and Dec.

Officers and Directors:* Larry R. Gaddis,* Chair.; Katherine H. Loo,* Vice-Chair.; Robert C. McHugh,* Secy.; Michael R. Hannigan, Exec. Dir.; Buck Blessing; Bruce T. Buell; Joe Garcia; Kathleen H. Hybl; Jane Leighty Justis; Paula D. Pollet; Craig Ralston; Jannie Richardson; Annwin B. Sather; Pam Shipp; Gerald G. Tolley; Joseph C. Woodford.
EIN: 841339670

1438
The Pioneer Fund ▼ ✧
1515 Arapahoe St., Ste. 1525
Denver, CO 80202

Established in 1960 in IL.
Donors: Helen M. McLoraine†; Bird Oil Corp.
Foundation type: Independent foundation.
Financial data (yr. ended 12/31/05): Assets, $58,415,228 (M); gifts received, $975,000; expenditures, $11,581,447; qualifying distributions, $11,262,784; giving activities include $11,262,784 for 62 grants (high: $1,500,000; low: $1,000; average: $2,000–$100,000).
Purpose and activities: Giving primarily to a United Methodist church, and for children and youth services; funding also for social services.
Fields of interest: Museums (children's); Medical school/education; Human services; Children/youth, services; Protestant agencies & churches.
Type of support: Endowments.
Limitations: Applications not accepted. Giving primarily in Centennial and Denver, CO. No grants to individuals.

Application information: Contributes only to pre-selected organizations.
Officers: Robert Anderson, Pres. and Treas.; Scott Hamilton, V.P.; James E. Bye, Secy.
EIN: 366108943
Selected grants: The following grants were reported in 2005.
$1,500,000 to Bowling Green State University Foundation, Bowling Green, OH. To endow chair in Entrepreneurial Professorship.
$1,500,000 to Clayton Foundation, Denver, CO. For Early Childhood Education Training Endowment Fund.
$1,000,000 to Summer Scholars, Denver, CO. To endow Youth Reading Program.
$1,000,000 to Urban Peak, Denver, CO. For Homeless Youth Welfare Services Endowment Fund.
$960,000 to Michael J. Fox Foundation for Parkinsons Research, New York, NY. For clinical discovery medical research.
$750,000 to Girl Scouts of the U.S.A., Denver, CO. For Girl's Camp Activity Center Capital Campaign.
$605,559 to Saint Andrew United Methodist Church, Highlands Ranch, CO. For Church Building Capital Campaign Fund.
$500,000 to Multiple Myeloma Research Foundation, Norwalk, CT. For Data Bank/Tissue Bank Project Medical Research.
$30,000 to Teller Elementary School, Denver, CO. For Lindamond-Bell Reading Program.
$20,000 to Safehouse Denver, Denver, CO. For general operating support.

1439
The Piton Foundation ✧
370 17th St., Ste. 5300
Denver, CO 80202-5653 (303) 825-6246
Contact: Carol Bush, Cont.
FAX: (303) 628-3839; E-mail: info@piton.org;
URL: http://www.piton.org

Incorporated in 1976 in CO.
Donors: Samuel Gary; Gary Williams Energy Corp.; The Gary Williams Co.
Foundation type: Operating foundation.
Financial data (yr. ended 11/30/04): Assets, $3,521,789 (M); gifts received, $6,186,442; expenditures, $5,395,115; qualifying distributions, $5,250,715; giving activities include $2,112,472 for grants (high: $237,000), $42,473 for 141 employee matching gifts, $3,443 for 3 in-kind gifts, and $2,616,256 for 15 foundation-administered programs.
Purpose and activities: Highly limited funds to support activities of the foundation in 4 areas: Improving Public Education; Revitalizing Neighborhoods; Promoting Economic Opportunities; and Strengthening Families.
Fields of interest: Education; Employment; Youth development; Family services; Community development; Leadership development.
Type of support: General/operating support; Capital campaigns; Program development; Conferences/seminars; Seed money; Curriculum development; Technical assistance; Program evaluation; Employee matching gifts.
Limitations: Applications not accepted. Giving limited to Denver, CO.
Publications: Biennial report; Informational brochure; Occasional report; Program policy statement.

Application information: Unsolicited requests for funds not considered.
Board meeting date(s): As required
Officers and Directors:* Samuel Gary,* Chair.; Ronald W. Williams,* Vice-Chair.; Mary Gittings Cronin,* Pres.; James E. Bye,* Secy.; Carol Bush, C.F.O.; Dave Younggren,* Treas.; Nancy Gary.
Number of staff: 14 full-time professional; 5 full-time support.
EIN: 840719486
Selected grants: The following grants were reported in 2003.
$195,500 to United Way, Mile High, Denver, CO. For matching funds for individual development accounts of savers who live in Baker, Cole, La Alma/Lincoln Park, and Sun Valley neighborhoods.
$162,000 to Denver Public Schools, Denver, CO. For Early Excellence Program at Harrington Elementary School.
$35,000 to Colorado Nonprofit Development Center, Denver, CO. For general operating support.
$25,000 to Bayaud Industries, Denver, CO. For general operating support.
$25,000 to University of Colorado, Center for Human Investment Policy, Denver, CO. For development of Project ID for Denver Public School students.
$20,000 to Family Resource Center Association, Denver, CO. For general operating support for ALAS coalition.
$10,000 to Colorado Childrens Campaign, Denver, CO. For analysis of fiscal impact of universal preschool for Colorado.
$10,000 to Denver Foundation, Denver, CO. For general operating support for Social Venture Partners.
$10,000 to New Cole Economic Development Corporation, Denver, CO. To support Cole neighborhood community organizing efforts and community economic development planning.
$10,000 to Summer Scholars, Denver, CO. For general operating support.

1440
The June and Craig Ponzio Foundation ✧
34350 Stagecoach Blvd.
Evergreen, CO 80439

Established in CO.
Donors: Craig Ponzio; June Ponzio.
Foundation type: Independent foundation.
Financial data (yr. ended 12/31/05): Assets, $24,504,229 (M); expenditures, $5,671,020; qualifying distributions, $5,405,000; giving activities include $5,405,000 for 6 grants (high: $3,000,000; low: $1,000).
Purpose and activities: Giving primarily to a children's hospital foundation. Support also for a special needs pre-school, and for health care and to Christian organizations.
Fields of interest: Education, special; Hospitals (specialty); Christian agencies & churches.
Limitations: Applications not accepted. No grants to individuals.
Application information: Contributes only to pre-selected organizations.
Officers: June Ponzio, Pres.; Craig Ponzio, Treas.
EIN: 841603731
Selected grants: The following grants were reported in 2004.

$600,000 to Childrens Hospital Foundation. For general support.

$500,000 to Northland College, Ashland, WI. For general support.

$33,000 to Healing Waters, San Francisco, CA. For general support.

$15,000 to Childrens Hospital. For international adoption.

$12,000 to Evergreen High School. For general support.

$5,000 to Chinese Children Charities, Chinese Children Adoption International, Centennial, CO. For general support.

$5,000 to Denver Art Museum, Denver, CO. For general support.

1441
The Precourt Foundation ◇ ☆
328 Mill Creek Cir.
Vail, CO 81657-5168

Established in 1994.
Donor: Jay A. Precourt.
Foundation type: Independent foundation.
Financial data (yr. ended 12/31/05): Assets, $24,002,249 (M); gifts received, $19,979,097; expenditures, $463,757; qualifying distributions, $454,273; giving activities include $454,273 for grants.
Purpose and activities: Giving primarily for art and culture, education, and federated giving programs.
Fields of interest: Arts; Education; Federated giving programs; Philanthropy/voluntarism.
Limitations: Applications not accepted. Giving primarily in CA, CO, MA, and TX. No grants to individuals.
Application information: Contributes only to pre-selected organizations.
Trustee: Jay A. Precourt.
Number of staff: 2 part-time professional; 2 part-time support.
EIN: 760430659
Selected grants: The following grants were reported in 2005.
$200,000 to Phillips Academy, Andover, MA.
$70,000 to Denver Art Museum, Denver, CO.
$37,334 to Stanford University, Stanford, CA.
$34,200 to Vail Valley Foundation, Vail, CO.
$25,000 to Gore Range Natural Science School, Red Cliff, CO.
$13,678 to Eagle Valley Land Trust, Eagle, CO.
$5,000 to Graland Country Day School, Denver, CO.
$2,000 to Bravo Vail Valley Music Festival, Vail, CO.
$833 to Pepperdine University, Malibu, CA.
$500 to National Outdoor Leadership School, Lander, WY.

1442
The Louis and Harold Price Foundation, Inc.
1371 Hecla Dr., Ste. B-1
Louisville, CO 80027 (303) 665-9201
Contact: Timothy A. Jones, Pres.
FAX: (303) 665-1027;
E-mail: grantinquiry@pricefoundation.org; Additional address (in NJ): 20 Wilsey Sq., 2nd Fl., Ridgewood, NJ 07450, tel.: (201) 445-9980, FAX: (201) 445-9982; URL: http://www.pricefoundation.org

Incorporated in 1951 in NY.
Donors: Louis Price†; Harold Price†.

Foundation type: Independent foundation.
Financial data (yr. ended 12/31/05): Assets, $84,916,423 (M); gifts received, $100,000; expenditures, $4,936,825; qualifying distributions, $4,361,381; giving activities include $3,632,486 for 203 grants (high: $300,000; low: $400; average: $1,000–$50,000).
Purpose and activities: The foundation strives to respond to unique challenges, ideas and projects while fulfilling the broad vision of the founders to contribute to social welfare as rooted in the Jewish tradition. The foundation supports innovative programs in the following areas: education, health, human social services, entrepreneurship, arts and the environment.
Fields of interest: Education; Health care; Human services; Community development; Jewish agencies & temples.
Type of support: General/operating support; Continuing support; Annual campaigns; Emergency funds; Program development; Seed money; Matching/challenge support.
Limitations: Giving primarily in southern CA and CO. No grants to individuals, or for building funds, capital campaigns, or endowments.
Publications: Annual report (including application guidelines).
Application information: Receipt of proposals is acknowledged. The foundation grants interviews with applicants when deemed necessary. Application form not required.
  Initial approach: Letter of inquiry (not more than 2 pages)
  Copies of proposal: 1
  Deadline(s): None
  Board meeting date(s): 3 or 4 times per year
  Final notification: 1 to 3 months
Officers and Trustees:* Linda Vitti Herbst,* Chair.; Timothy A. Jones,* Pres.; Rosemary L. Guidone,* Exec. V.P. and Secy.-Treas.; George Asch; Lisa Beshkov; Bonnie Vitti.
Number of staff: 2 full-time professional; 3 part-time support.
EIN: 136121358
Selected grants: The following grants were reported in 2004.
$225,000 to United Jewish Fund of Greater Los Angeles, Los Angeles, CA.
$205,000 to University of Colorado, Boulder, CO. 3 grants: $20,000 (Toward partnership with Aspen Music Festival and School for student outreach, Takacs quartet activities and student involvement with Festival), $125,000 to Entrepreneurship Center for Music, $60,000 to College of Business (For Deming Entrepreneurship Center).
$200,000 to University of California, Los Angeles, CA. For challenge grant in support of Harold Price Center for Entrepreneurial Studies.
$100,000 to National Foundation for Teaching Entrepreneurship, New York, NY.
$65,000 to Net Impact: New Leaders for Better Business, San Francisco, CA. For challenge grant in support of general operations.
$53,900 to Association for Community Living in Boulder County, Longmont, CO. For Beyond Words, parent education program.
$50,000 to Aspen Valley Medical Foundation, Aspen, CO. To lease patient monitoring system for emergency department.
$50,000 to Natural Resources Defense Council, New York, NY.

1443
Qwest Foundation ▼ ◇
(formerly U S WEST Foundation)
1801 California St., 50th Fl.
Denver, CO 80202 (303) 896-1266
Contact: David Bromberg, Mgr.
FAX: (303) 896-4982;
E-mail: qwest.foundation@qwest.com; URL: http://www.qwest.com/about/company/community/foundation/

Established in 1985 in CO.
Donors: U S WEST, Inc.; Qwest Communications International Inc.
Foundation type: Company-sponsored foundation.
Financial data (yr. ended 12/31/05): Assets, $19,023,949 (M); gifts received, $8,550,000; expenditures, $5,395,595; qualifying distributions, $5,356,275; giving activities include $5,267,387 for 1,303 grants (high: $265,000; low: $9).
Purpose and activities: The foundation supports organizations involved with K-12 education, workforce and economic development, and community-based initiatives.
Fields of interest: Arts; Elementary/secondary education; Education; Youth development, services; Minorities/immigrants, centers/services; Rural development; Community development; Voluntarism promotion; Leadership development; Minorities; Native Americans/American Indians; Economically disadvantaged.
Type of support: Continuing support; Program development; Seed money; Technical assistance; Employee matching gifts; Matching/challenge support.
Limitations: Giving limited to areas of company operations. No support for political organizations, national health organizations, private foundations, or United Way-supported organizations (over 3 percent of budget). No grants to individuals, or for capital campaigns, chairs, or endowments, general operating support for disease-specific health organizations, goodwill advertising, or sectarian religious activities.
Publications: Application guidelines; Multi-year report; Newsletter.
Application information: Unsolicited requests for Community grants are not accepted. Application form required.
  Initial approach: Download application form and mail proposal and application form to foundation
  Deadline(s): None
  Final notification: 6 to 8 weeks
Officers and Directors:* Richard Notebaert,* Chair. and C.E.O.; Linda Alvarado,* Pres.; Joan Walker,* Exec. V.P.; Steve Davis,* Sr. V.P.; Jill Sanford,* V.P.; John Lines,* Genl. Counsel.
Number of staff: 2 full-time professional.
EIN: 840978668
Selected grants: The following grants were reported in 2004.
$895,000 to Colorado Institute of Technology, Westminster, CO. For general support.
$350,000 to United Way, Mile High, Denver, CO.
$320,000 to National Lewis and Clark Bicentennial Council, Saint Louis, MO. For signature event support.
$59,000 to Junior Achievement of Metropolitan Denver, Denver, CO. For volunteer programs.
$50,000 to University of Sioux Falls, Augustana College, Sioux Falls, SD. For Business Success Workshops.

$30,000 to American Red Cross, Mile High Chapter, Denver, CO. For disaster preparedness training.

$15,971 to United Way of the National Capital Area, Vienna, VA.

$15,000 to Montana Historical Society, Helena, MT. For Tent of many voices.

$12,000 to Central Arizona College, Coolidge, AZ. For Distance Learning Program.

$10,000 to World Vision, Federal Way, WA. For KidREACH Tutoring Program.

1444

The Blair and Kristin Richardson Foundation, Inc. ✧ ☆

1490 Lafayette St., Ste. 400
Denver, CO 80218

Established in 2002 in CO.
Donor: Blair Richardson.
Foundation type: Independent foundation.
Financial data (yr. ended 12/31/05): Assets, $464,570 (M); expenditures, $995,256; qualifying distributions, $993,000; giving activities include $993,000 for 23 grants (high: $250,000; low: $500).
Fields of interest: Museums (ethnic/folk arts); Education, public education; Education, early childhood education; Scholarships/financial aid; Hospitals (specialty); Multiple sclerosis; Recreation, parks/playgrounds; American Red Cross; Children, services; Christian agencies & churches.
Limitations: Applications not accepted. No grants to individuals.
Application information: Contributes only to pre-selected organizations.
Officers: Kristin M. Genova, Chair.; Blair Richardson, Pres.; Eric B. Wolf, Treas.
Director: Donald Bailey.
EIN: 421556298
Selected grants: The following grants were reported in 2004.
$55,000 to Denver Academy, Denver, CO.
$50,000 to Craig Hospital Foundation, Englewood, CO.
$20,000 to Childrens Hospital Association, Denver, CO. 2 grants: $10,000 each
$20,000 to Saint Annes Episcopal School, Denver, CO.
$17,500 to University of Saskatchewan, Saskatoon, Canada. .
$10,000 to Alliance for Choice In Education, Denver, CO.
$10,000 to Saint Rose of Lima School, Denver, CO.
$4,100 to Leaders Challenge, Denver, CO.
$1,000 to Regis University, Denver, CO.

1445

Rose Community Foundation and Affiliates

600 S. Cherry St., Ste. 1200
Denver, CO 80246-1712 (303) 398-7400
Contact: Sheila R. Bugdanowitz, C.E.O.
FAX: (303) 398-7430; E-mail: rcf@rcfdenver.org;
Grant application E-mail:
grantsmanager@rcfdenver.org; URL: http://
www.rcfdenver.org

Established in 1995; converted with proceeds from the sale of Rose Medical Center.
Foundation type: Community foundation.
Financial data (yr. ended 12/31/05): Assets, $266,973,000 (M); gifts received, $2,457,000;

expenditures, $16,636,000; giving activities include $12,889,000 for 887 grants (high: $771,600; low: $25).
Purpose and activities: The foundation aims to enhance the quality of life in the greater Denver, Colorado, community by identifying and supporting programs in the areas of child and family development, education, aging, health, and Jewish life.
Fields of interest: Elementary/secondary education; Elementary/secondary school reform; Teacher school/education; Education; Health care, public policy; Public health; Health care; Health care, cost containment; End of life care; Health care; Mental health/crisis services; Employment, job counseling; Employment, training; Housing/shelter, services; Children, day care; Children, services; Child development, services; Family services; Family services, parent education; Human services, financial counseling; Residential/custodial care, senior continuing care; Aging, centers/services; Civil rights, race/intergroup relations; Civil rights; Community development; Philanthropy/voluntarism; Jewish agencies & temples; Aging.
Type of support: General/operating support; Income development; Management development/capacity building; Capital campaigns; Building/renovation; Equipment; Program development; Seed money; Technical assistance; Matching/challenge support.
Limitations: Giving primarily in the greater Denver, CO, area of Adams, Arapahoe, Boulder, Broomfield, Denver, Douglas and Jefferson counties. No support for pass-through foundations. No grants to individuals, or for endowments, annual appeals or membership drives, or fundraising events; generally no grants for debt reduction.
Publications: Application guidelines; Annual report; Financial statement; Grants list; Informational brochure (including application guidelines); Newsletter.
Application information: Visit foundation Web site for grant application format and guidelines. Faxed proposals are not accepted. Application form not required.
Initial approach: Telephone or e-mail appropriate Prog. Off.
Copies of proposal: 2
Deadline(s): None
Board meeting date(s): Feb. 21, May 23, Sept. 26, and Dec. 12
Final notification: 4 to 6 months after receipt of complete proposal
Officers and Trustees:* Arlene Hirschfeld,* Chair.; Sheila R. Bugdanowitz, C.E.O. and Pres.; Phil Nash, V.P., Comms.; Carolyn Schaefer Wollard, V.P., Donor Svcs.; Anne M. Garcia, C.F.O.; Ryan Brown, Cont.; Stephanie Foote; Jean Galloway; Marjorie Gart; Debra Herz; Doug Jones; Helayne B. Jones; Donald L. Kortz; Scott Levin; Evan Makovsky; Myron "Micky" Miller; Ronald E. Montoya; Neil Oberfeld; Sr. Lydia M. Pena, Ph.D.; Stephen H. Shogan; Irit Waldbaum.
Number of staff: 21 full-time professional.
EIN: 840418124

1446

Saccomanno Higher Education Foundation ✧

P.O. Box 60353
Grand Junction, CO 81506 (970) 245-5627

Established in 1991 in CO.
Donors: Geno Saccomanno; Virginia Saccomanno.
Foundation type: Independent foundation.

Financial data (yr. ended 12/31/05): Assets, $12,615,550 (M); gifts received, $700; expenditures, $695,582; qualifying distributions, $614,845; giving activities include $575,171 for 91 grants (high: $147,435; low: $372).
Purpose and activities: Awards to educational institutions for academic expenses of Mesa County, CO, and Carbon County, UT, residents; some support also to other charitable organizations.
Fields of interest: Higher education.
Type of support: Scholarship funds; Research; Scholarships—to individuals.
Limitations: Giving limited to Mesa County, CO, and Carbon County, UT.
Publications: Annual report; Financial statement; Program policy statement.
Application information: Application form required.
Copies of proposal: 1
Deadline(s): Apr. 6
Board meeting date(s): Varies
Final notification: July 1
Officers: Virginia Saccomanno, Pres.; Terrance Farina, V.P.; Carol Murphy, Secy.-Treas.
Directors: Gena Cooper; Tim Foster; Robert Ladenburger; J. Timothy Mills; George Orbanek; William Patterson; Linda Siedow; Lenna Watson.
EIN: 841164982
Selected grants: The following grants were reported in 2004.
$136,107 to Mesa State College, Grand Junction, CO.
$61,105 to College of Eastern Utah, Price, UT.
$51,400 to Utah State University, Logan, UT.
$43,100 to Colorado School of Mines, Golden, CO.
$16,350 to Southern Utah University, Cedar City, UT.
$10,200 to University of Northern Colorado, Greeley, CO.
$10,083 to Weber State University, Ogden, UT.
$9,900 to Utah Valley State College, Orem, UT.
$5,500 to Brigham Young University, Provo, UT.
$1,000 to University of Portland, Portland, OR.

1447

Sachs Foundation ✧

90 S. Cascade Ave., Ste. 1410
Colorado Springs, CO 80903 (719) 633-2353
Contact: Morris A. Esmiol, Jr., Pres.
E-mail: info@SachsFoundation.org; URL: http://
www.sachsfoundation.org

Incorporated in 1931 in CO.
Donor: Henry Sachs†.
Foundation type: Independent foundation.
Financial data (yr. ended 12/31/04): Assets, $8,533,070 (M); gifts received, $1,033,878; expenditures, $1,248,403; qualifying distributions, $1,121,730; giving activities include $12,869 for 2 grants (high: $7,869; low: $5,000), and $860,700 for 291 grants to individuals (high: $10,000; low: $66).
Purpose and activities: Giving to provide African American undergraduate scholarships to high school seniors with a 3.5 GPA or better, and who have been CO residents for five or more years; also, limited graduate scholarships only to African Americans who have participated in the undergraduate scholarship program and who have been residents of CO five or more years.
Fields of interest: African Americans/Blacks.
Type of support: Grants to individuals; Scholarships—to individuals.
Limitations: Giving limited to residents of CO.

Publications: Application guidelines; Financial statement.
Application information: Application form, complete application guidelines, and required financial statement are available on foundation Web site. Application form required.
  Initial approach: Letter and E-mail
  Copies of proposal: 2
  Deadline(s): Education Grants, Mar. 15; Community Assistance, no deadline; Judicial Internship, contact foundation for current deadline
  Board meeting date(s): May
  Final notification: 1 month
Officer: Morris A. Esmiol, Jr., Pres.
Directors: Wilton W. Cogswell III; Stewart P. Dodge; John F. Gallagher; Thomas M. James.
Number of staff: 2 full-time professional.
EIN: 840500835

1448
Saeman Family Foundation, Inc. ◇
270 Saint Paul St., Ste. 300
Denver, CO 80206 (303) 722-1600
Contact: Catherine Bortle, Exec. Dir.

Established in 1994 in CO.
Donors: John V. Saeman; Carolyn Saeman.
Foundation type: Independent foundation.
Financial data (yr. ended 12/31/04): Assets, $500,000 (M); expenditures, $1,107,788; qualifying distributions, $1,086,038; giving activities include $1,086,038 for 63 grants (high: $164,180; low: $500).
Purpose and activities: Funding primarily for youth and family services and Catholic agencies and education.
Fields of interest: Education; Hospitals (general); Children/youth, services; Family services; Roman Catholic agencies & churches.
Type of support: General/operating support; Capital campaigns; Program development; Scholarship funds; In-kind gifts.
Limitations: Giving primarily in Denver, CO. No grants to individuals.
Publications: Application guidelines.
Application information: Application form not required.
  Initial approach: Proposal
  Copies of proposal: 1
  Deadline(s): None
  Board meeting date(s): 4th quarter
Officer and Directors:* Catherine Bortle,* Exec. Dir.; Richard O. Campbell; Carolyn Ann Saeman; John V. Saeman; John V. Saeman III.
Number of staff: 1 part-time professional.
EIN: 841264412
Selected grants: The following grants were reported in 2004.
$164,180 to Papal Foundation, Philadelphia, PA.
$140,000 to Loras College, Dubuque, IA.
$100,236 to Seeds of Hope Charitable Trust, Denver, CO.
$65,250 to Archdiocese of Denver, Denver, CO. 3 grants: $50,000, $9,250, $6,000
$50,000 to Samaritans Purse, Boone, NC.
$5,000 to Pontifical North American College, DC.
$1,000 to Christendom College, Front Royal, VA.
$1,000 to University of Wisconsin Foundation, Madison, WI.

1449
The Adler Schermer Foundation ◇
(formerly The Betty A. & Lloyd G. Schermer Foundation)
c/o Lloyd G. Schermer
210 Lake Ave.
Aspen, CO 81611

Established in 1992.
Donors: Betty A. Schermer; Lloyd G. Schermer.
Foundation type: Independent foundation.
Financial data (yr. ended 12/31/05): Assets, $19,115,745 (M); expenditures, $2,233,843; qualifying distributions, $2,067,965; giving activities include $2,067,965 for 67 grants (high: $1,000,000; low: $50).
Fields of interest: Arts, multipurpose centers/programs; Media/communications; Museums; Museums (art); Performing arts, music; Higher education; Health care; Health organizations, association; Jewish federated giving programs; Social sciences; Jewish agencies & temples.
Limitations: Applications not accepted. Giving primarily in CO, with some giving nationally. No grants to individuals.
Application information: Contributes only to pre-selected organizations.
Officer: Betty A. Schermer, Mgr.
EIN: 841210699
Selected grants: The following grants were reported in 2004.
$1,025,000 to University of Montana Foundation, Missoula, MT. 2 grants: $25,000, $1,000,000
$1,001,000 to University of Iowa Foundation, Iowa City, IA. 2 grants: $1,000,000, $1,000
$1,000 to Harvard Business School Fund, Boston, MA.
$1,000 to Saint Ambrose University, Davenport, IA.

1450
Schlessman Family Foundation, Inc.
(formerly Schlessman Foundation, Inc.)
1301 Pennsylvania St., Ste. 800
Denver, CO 80203-5015 (303) 831-5683
Contact: Patricia A. Middendorf, Treas.
FAX: (303) 831-5676;
E-mail: pamiddendorf@qwest.net; *URL:* http://www.schlessmanfoundation.org

Incorporated in 1957 in CO.
Donors: Florence M. Schlessman†; Gerald L. Schlessman†; Lee E. Schlessman.
Foundation type: Independent foundation.
Financial data (yr. ended 3/31/05): Assets, $41,150,601 (M); gifts received, $57,587; expenditures, $2,161,867; qualifying distributions, $1,792,284; giving activities include $1,792,234 for 205 grants (high: $192,650; low: $100).
Purpose and activities: Giving primarily for education, human services, children and youth services, and for the disabled.
Fields of interest: Education; Human services; Children/youth, services; Disabilities, people with.
Type of support: General/operating support; Continuing support; Annual campaigns; Capital campaigns; Equipment; Endowments; Program development; Curriculum development; Scholarship funds; Matching/challenge support.
Limitations: Giving limited to CO, primarily the greater Denver area. No support for charter, private or public school programs. No grants to individuals, or for benefits, conferences or start-up grants.
Publications: Application guidelines.

Application information: Colorado Common Grant Application form accepted, but not required. Application form not required.
  Initial approach: Proposal
  Copies of proposal: 1
  Deadline(s): Dec. 31
  Board meeting date(s): Mar.
  Final notification: Mar. 31
Officers and Board Members:* Lee E. Schlessman,* Pres.; Susan M. Duncan,* V.P.; Dolores J. Schlessman,* V.P.; Gary L. Schlessman,* Secy.; Patricia A. Middendorf, Treas.; Cheryl S. Bennett; Sandra Garnett.
EIN: 846030309

1451
The Schramm Foundation ◇
800 Grant St., Ste. 330
Denver, CO 80203
Contact: Gary S. Kring, Pres.

Established in 1956.
Foundation type: Independent foundation.
Financial data (yr. ended 6/30/05): Assets, $6,637,057 (M); expenditures, $458,850; qualifying distributions, $410,500; giving activities include $407,500 for 99 grants (high: $35,000; low: $1,000).
Purpose and activities: Giving primarily for the arts and higher education.
Fields of interest: Arts; Higher education; Hospitals (general); Cancer; Cancer research; Human services; YM/YWCAs & YM/YWHAs; Children/youth, services.
Type of support: General/operating support; Continuing support; Annual campaigns; Building/renovation; Equipment; Debt reduction; Program development; Matching/challenge support.
Limitations: Giving limited to CO, with emphasis on the Denver area. No support for political, religious organizations or animal welfare rights organizations. No grants to individuals.
Publications: Annual report (including application guidelines).
Application information: Application form required.
  Initial approach: Letter
  Copies of proposal: 1
  Deadline(s): Applications accepted between July 1 and Aug. 31
  Board meeting date(s): Oct. 31
  Final notification: Nov. 15
Officers: Gary S. Kring, Pres.; Mark H. Carson, V.P.; Arnold H. Tietze, Secy.; Mara Marks, Treas.
Number of staff: 1 part-time professional.
EIN: 846032196
Selected grants: The following grants were reported in 2004.
$26,500 to University of Denver, Denver, CO. For scholarships.
$16,000 to University of Northern Colorado, Greeley, CO. For operating support.
$12,500 to University of Colorado Foundation, Boulder, CO. For operating support.
$10,000 to Regis University, Denver, CO. For operating support.
$5,000 to David Taylor Dance Theater, Englewood, CO. For operating support.
$5,000 to Denver Art Museum, Denver, CO. For operating support.
$4,000 to Central City Opera House Association, Denver, CO. For general support.
$4,000 to Opera Colorado, Denver, CO. For operating support.

$2,000 to Colorado Ballet Company, Denver, CO. For operating support.

$2,000 to Mile High Montessori Early Learning Centers, Denver, CO. For operating support.

1452

SEAKR Foundation ✧ ☆

6221 S. Racine Cir.

Centennial, CO   80111-6427   (303) 790-8499

Contact: Raymond E. Anderson, Chair.

URL: http://www.seakr.com/about/foundation.html

Established in 2004 in CO.

Donor: SEAKR Engineering, Inc.

Foundation type: Company-sponsored foundation.

Financial data (yr. ended 12/31/05): Assets, $146 (M); gifts received, $360,250; expenditures, $361,675; qualifying distributions, $361,000; giving activities include $361,000 for 10 grants to individuals (high: $54,000; low: $4,000).

Purpose and activities: The foundation awards grants to the families of soldiers killed in the line of duty.

Type of support: Grants to individuals.

Limitations: Applications not accepted. Giving primarily in CO.

Application information: Contributes only to pre-selected individuals.

Officer and Director: Raymond E. Anderson,* Chair.; Lorraine W. Anderson.

EIN: 200979291

1453

Seay Foundation ✧

c/o American National Bank, Trust Div.

P.O. Box 9250

Colorado Springs, CO   80932

Application address: c/o American National Bank, 102 N. Cascade Ave., Colorado Springs, CO 80903

Foundation type: Independent foundation.

Financial data (yr. ended 12/31/05): Assets, $19,397,778 (M); expenditures, $1,356,832; qualifying distributions, $1,207,161; giving activities include $936,250 for 50 grants (high: $100,000; low: $750), and $265,130 for 39 grants to individuals (high: $15,000; low: $1,000).

Fields of interest: Higher education; Youth development; Human services; Christian agencies & churches.

Type of support: General/operating support; Building/renovation; Scholarships—to individuals.

Limitations: Giving on a national basis.

Application information: Candidates must be nominated by a member of the foundation's Advisory Committee; application forms available upon request by the nominator. Application form required.

  Deadline(s): May 1

Advisory Committee: Nancy Kopper Champion; Elizabeth Kopper Duzan; Susan Kopper Ecklund; Jim Fogle; Carolyn Kopper; W. Bruce Kopper; Catherine Kopper Penshorn.

Trustee: American National Bank.

EIN: 436055549

1454

The Servant Leadership Foundation ✧

950 E. Westglow Ln.

Greenwood Village, CO   80121-1375

(303) 806-0607

Contact: Dan Jessup, Dir.

Donors: Larry LaKamp; Martha LaKamp; TYL Foundation; McVaney Family Foundation.

Foundation type: Independent foundation.

Financial data (yr. ended 12/31/05): Assets, $0 (M); gifts received, $523,950; expenditures, $502,450; qualifying distributions, $455,500; giving activities include $76,500 for 7 grants (high: $20,000; low: $4,000), and $379,000 for 24 grants to individuals (high: $22,000; low: $1,000).

Purpose and activities: Provides scholarships for people in full-time ministry who must raise their own financial support to do so. Funding also to grant men and women who have been in full-time ministry for ten consecutive years or more, and who, due to salary limitations of their ministry, have acquired financial debt. The scholarships will be used strictly for the purpose of paying off, or down, their debt.

Application information:

  Initial approach: Letter

Directors: Dain Domich; Dan Jessup; Jeff Newman; Bob Pourchot; Steven G. Sittko; Don Valencia.

EIN: 841400820

Selected grants: The following grants were reported in 2004.

$68,000 to Young Life, Colorado Springs, CO.

$5,000 to Young Life Foundation, Colorado Springs, CO.

$4,500 to Azusa Pacific University, Azusa, CA.

$4,000 to Young Life, Jefferson County, Arvada, CO.

$2,500 to Colorado Christian University, Lakewood, CO.

$2,000 to Young Life Cambodia, Colorado Springs, CO.

$500 to Campus Crusade for Christ.

1455

The Anna and John J. Sie Foundation ✧ ☆

3300 E. 1st Ave., No. 390

Denver, CO   80206

Established in 2003 in CO.

Donor: John J. Sie.

Foundation type: Independent foundation.

Financial data (yr. ended 12/31/05): Assets, $57,046,882 (M); expenditures, $1,659,580; qualifying distributions, $908,034; giving activities include $801,006 for 20 grants (high: $325,000; low: $200).

Fields of interest: Arts; Higher education; Down syndrome research; Recreation, community facilities; Children/youth, services.

Limitations: Applications not accepted. Giving primarily in CO.

Application information: Contributes only to pre-selected organizations.

Officer: Michelle S. Whitten, Exec. Dir.

Trustees: Anna M. Sie; John J. Sie.

EIN: 836058353

1456

St. John's Foundation ✧ ☆

1419 Pine St.

Boulder, CO   80302-4812   (303) 442-5246

Contact: Robert A. Elmore

Established in 1985 in CO.

Foundation type: Independent foundation.

Financial data (yr. ended 12/31/05): Assets, $0 (M); expenditures, $403,035; qualifying distributions, $378,000; giving activities include $378,000 for grants.

Fields of interest: Health organizations, association; Food services; Children/youth, services; Family services; Minorities/immigrants, centers/services; Homeless, human services; Minorities; Homeless.

Type of support: General/operating support.

Limitations: Giving primarily in Boulder County, CO. No grants to individuals.

Application information: Application form required.

  Deadline(s): Aug. 31

Officers and Directors:* Rev. Rolland W. Hoverstock,* Pres.; Robert A. Elmore,* Secy.-Treas.; Ruth Correll; Phoebe Norton; Jan Snooks; Charles L. Squier; Gail Tate.

EIN: 742363503

1457

The Richard Seth Staley Educational Foundation ✧

(formerly Richard Seth Staley Foundation for Psychological Development)

P.O. Box 4129

Aspen, CO   81612   (970) 920-9003

Contact: Donald H. Keltner, Pres.

Established in 1980 as the Richard Seth Staley Foundation for Psychological Development.

Donor: James Gillett.

Foundation type: Operating foundation.

Financial data (yr. ended 9/30/05): Assets, $13,920,181 (M); gifts received, $55,000; expenditures, $958,428; qualifying distributions, $772,541; giving activities include $670,467 for 61 grants (high: $163,849; low: $100).

Purpose and activities: Giving primarily for education; also giving for social issues, human services, with emphasis on children, the arts, and health organizations.

Fields of interest: Performing arts, music; Arts; Higher education; Education; Health organizations, association; Social sciences; Economics; Public affairs.

Limitations: Giving on a national basis.

Application information: Application form required for educational grants only.

  Deadline(s): None

Officers and Directors:* Donald H. Keltner,* Pres. and Treas.; James F. Beley,* V.P.; Berkeley Johnston; Kathleen Keltner; F. Thomas Meehan.

EIN: 953532336

1458

Stealth Foundation ✧ ☆

P.O. Box 448

Rye, CO   81069

Established in 2003 in CO.

Donors: Jason L. Bulle; Krista J. Bulle; Plasmacam, Inc.

Foundation type: Independent foundation.

Financial data (yr. ended 4/30/05): Assets, $15,426,860 (M); gifts received, $1,500,000; expenditures, $1,105,542; qualifying distributions, $1,100,422; giving activities include $1,100,422 for 4 grants (high: $950,000; low: $2,922).

Fields of interest: Human services; Christian agencies & churches.
Limitations: Applications not accepted. Giving primarily in AZ and CO. No grants to individuals.
Application information: Contributes only to pre-selected organizations.
Officer: Jason L. Bulle, Pres.
Director: Nathan Lutz.
EIN: 200434559

1459
The Steel Partners Foundation ✧ ☆
777 Spruce St.
Aspen, CO 81611 (970) 544-9898
Contact: Warren Lichtenstein, Pres.

Established in 2004 in CO.
Donor: Warren Lichtenstein.
Foundation type: Independent foundation.
Financial data (yr. ended 12/31/05): Assets, $432 (M); gifts received, $1,170,100; expenditures, $1,171,788; qualifying distributions, $1,168,740; giving activities include $1,168,740 for 29 grants (high: $438,750; low: $360).
Fields of interest: Higher education; Education; Health care; Human services.
Limitations: Giving primarily in Aspen, CO. No grants to individuals.
Application information:
  Initial approach: Letter
Officer: Warren G. Lichtenstein, Pres.
Directors: Nicole Beit Halachmy; Diane M. Lichtenstein; Lillian Manderachia.
EIN: 201227557

1460
StorageTek Foundation ✧
1 StorageTek Dr., M.S. 4305
Louisville, CO 80028-4305 (303) 661-2461
Contact: Joe Fuentes, Exec. Dir.
Application address: 1 StorageTek Dr., M.S. 4307, Louisville, CO 80028-4307

Established in 1991 in CO.
Donor: Storage Technology Corp.
Foundation type: Company-sponsored foundation.
Financial data (yr. ended 12/31/05): Assets, $1,261 (M); gifts received, $573,364; expenditures, $573,950; qualifying distributions, $573,529; giving activities include $519,067 for 75 grants (high: $63,000; low: $150), and $54,462 for 170 employee matching gifts.
Purpose and activities: The foundation supports organizations involved with arts and culture, higher education, human services, science and technology, and economically disadvantaged people.
Fields of interest: Arts; Higher education; Human services; Mathematics; Engineering/technology; Science; Economically disadvantaged.
International interests: Mexico.
Type of support: General/operating support; Continuing support; Annual campaigns; Seed money; Employee matching gifts; Matching/challenge support.
Limitations: Giving on a national and international basis in areas of company operations, with emphasis on CO, GA, and NJ, and in Mexico. No support for political or partisan organizations, religious organizations not of direct benefit to the entire community, fraternal organizations, or sports

organizations. No grants to individuals, or for trips or tours or salary expenses.
Publications: Annual report.
Application information: Application form required.
  Initial approach: Contact foundation for application form
  Deadline(s): Sept. 30
  Board meeting date(s): Twice per year
  Final notification: Following review; Dec. and Jan. if not approved
Officers and Directors:* Patrick Martin, Chair.; Mark D. McGregor,* V.P. and Treas.; Joe Fuentes, Exec. Dir.; Eula Adams; Roger Gaston; Robert Kocol.
Number of staff: 1 full-time professional; 1 full-time support.
EIN: 841168359

1461
The Strear Family Foundation, Inc. ✧
6825 E. Tennessee Ave., Ste. 235
Denver, CO 80224

Established in 1987 in CO.
Donors: Leonard Strear; Pluss Poultry; Strear Farms Co., Inc.
Foundation type: Independent foundation.
Financial data (yr. ended 9/30/05): Assets, $8,055,499 (M); gifts received, $247,730; expenditures, $460,101; qualifying distributions, $370,568; giving activities include $347,743 for 101 grants (high: $233,700; low: $6).
Purpose and activities: Giving primarily to Jewish causes.
Fields of interest: Education; Health organizations, association; Human services; Jewish federated giving programs; Jewish agencies & temples.
Limitations: Applications not accepted. Giving primarily in Denver, CO. No grants to individuals.
Application information: Contributes only to pre-selected organizations.
Officers: Leonard Strear, Pres.; Irma Strear, V.P. and Secy.
EIN: 841078190
Selected grants: The following grants were reported in 2004.
$175,000 to Denver Campus for Jewish Education, Denver, CO.
$5,250 to Hillel Council of Colorado, Denver, CO.
$5,100 to Jewish Community Centers of Denver, Denver, CO.
$2,500 to Mizel Museum of Judaica, Denver, CO.
$2,304 to Congregation Emanuel, Denver, CO.
$1,200 to University of Colorado Foundation, Denver, CO.
$500 to Hillel Academy of Denver, Denver, CO.
$500 to Rainbow Bridge, Denver, CO.
$350 to Colorado Coalition for the Homeless, Denver, CO.
$100 to Safehouse Denver, Denver, CO.

1462
Sturm Family Foundation ✧
3033 E. 1st Ave., Ste. 200
Denver, CO 80206
E-mail: foundation@sturmgroup.com

Donors: Donald L. Sturm; Susan M. Sturm.
Foundation type: Independent foundation.
Financial data (yr. ended 12/31/05): Assets, $24,006,641 (M); gifts received, $8,690,712; expenditures, $651,802; qualifying distributions,

$591,731; giving activities include $555,527 for 20 grants (high: $422,237; low: $100).
Fields of interest: Higher education; Education; Children/youth, services; Foundations (community); Jewish federated giving programs; Philanthropy/voluntarism.
Limitations: Applications not accepted. Giving primarily in CO, with emphasis on Denver. No grants to individuals.
Application information: Contributes only to pre-selected organizations.
Officers: Donald L. Sturm, Chair., Pres. and Treas.; Susan M. Sturm, Vice-Chair., V.P. and Secy.; Karen Gerard, Exec. Dir.
EIN: 841483429
Selected grants: The following grants were reported in 2003.
$120,000 to Johns Hopkins Health System, Baltimore, MD.
$100,000 to Denver Art Museum, Denver, CO.
$73,742 to Congregation Kol Halev, Denver, CO.
$15,000 to Jewish Federation of Metropolitan Detroit, Bloomfield Hills, MI.
$12,500 to University of Colorado Foundation, Boulder, CO.
$11,228 to Rocky Mountain Public Broadcasting Network, Denver, CO.
$10,000 to Arapahoe Library Foundation, Englewood, CO.
$5,000 to Anti-Defamation League of Bnai Brith, Denver, CO.
$1,000 to Sewall Child Development Center, Denver, CO.
$500 to Boys and Girls Clubs of Metro Denver, Denver, CO.

1463
The Summit Foundation
108 N. French St.
P.O. Box 4000
Breckenridge, CO 80424 (970) 453-5970
Contact: Lee E. Zimmerman, Exec. Dir.
FAX: (970) 453-1423;
E-mail: sumfound@summitfoundation.org;
Additional E-mail:
TSFADmin@summitfoundation.org; URL: http://www.summitfoundation.org

Established in 1984 in CO.
Foundation type: Community foundation.
Financial data (yr. ended 12/30/05): Assets, $4,041,749 (M); gifts received, $954,237; expenditures, $1,409,992; giving activities include $826,398 for 69 grants (high: $49,810; low: $500), and $103,750 for 33 grants to individuals.
Purpose and activities: The foundation seeks to improve the quality of life for residents and guests of Summit County and neighboring communities. Giving primarily for arts and culture, health and human services, education, environment, sports, scholarships, and all projects with measurable results.
Fields of interest: Media, film/video; Visual arts; Museums; Performing arts; Performing arts, theater; Performing arts, music; Historic preservation/historical societies; Arts; Elementary/secondary education; Education, early childhood education; Elementary school/education; Secondary school/education; Education; Environment, natural resources; Environment; Health care; Mental health/crisis services; Health organizations, association; Recreation; Children/youth, services; Family services; Residential/custodial care,

hospices; Aging, centers/services; Human services; Disabilities, people with.

Type of support: Continuing support; Annual campaigns; Capital campaigns; Building/renovation; Equipment; Land acquisition; Program development; Conferences/seminars; Seed money; Curriculum development; Scholarship funds; Technical assistance; Program evaluation; Exchange programs; Matching/challenge support.

Limitations: Giving limited to Summit County, and the communities of Alma, Buena Vista, Fairplay, Kremmling, and Leadville, CO. No support for religious organizations. No grants to individuals (except for designated scholarship programs), or for operating budgets without specific programs.

Publications: Application guidelines; Annual report; Grants list; Informational brochure; Newsletter; Program policy statement.

Application information: Visit foundation Web site for application form, guidelines, and specific deadlines. Application form required.

Initial approach: Telephone

Deadline(s): Mar. and Aug.

Board meeting date(s): 3rd Wed. of Feb., Mar., May, July, Aug., Sept., Oct., and Nov.; 2nd Wed. of June and Dec.

Final notification: June and Dec.

Officers and Directors:* Larry Beebe,* Pres.; Cary Cooper,* V.P.; Jan Coles,* Secy.; Greg Finch,* Treas.; Lee E. Zimmerman, Exec. Dir.; Brett Barrett; David Barry; Gini Bradley; Theresa Campbell; Dick Carleton; Linda Clem; Bob Craig; Nancy Follett; Tim Gagen; Maggie Hillman; Marilyn Hogan; Peter Janes; Meg Lass; Gary Lindstrom; Win Lockwood; Roger McCarthy; Anne Stonington; Patty Theobald.

Number of staff: 3 full-time professional; 1 full-time support.

EIN: 742341399

Selected grants: The following grants were reported in 2005.

$49,810 to Youth Services Center, Dillon, CO. For Primary Health for children at three schools.

$25,000 to Family and Intercultural Resource Center, Dillon, CO.

$17,120 to Summit Foundation, Breckenridge, CO. For scholarships and equipment.

$17,020 to Carriage House, Breckenridge, CO. For scholarships and training.

$14,700 to Keystone Center, Keystone Science School, Keystone, CO. For Science Camp for Kids.

$7,500 to Smalls Steps, Leadville, CO. For scholarships and educational supplies.

$7,000 to Breckenridge Festival of Film, Breckenridge, CO. For equipment and children's program.

$6,000 to Backstage Theater, Breckenridge, CO. For Children's Theater.

$5,000 to Blue River Watershed Group, Frisco, CO. For developing and operating website.

$4,300 to High Country Conservation, Frisco, CO. For resource guide.

1464

The Ruth and Vernon Taylor Foundation

518 17th St., Ste. 1670

Denver, CO   80202   (303) 893-5284

Contact: Friday A. Green, Tr.

FAX: (303) 893-8263; E-mail: fridayag@aol.com

Trust established in 1950 in PA.

Donor: Members of the Taylor family.

Foundation type: Independent foundation.

Financial data (yr. ended 6/30/05): Assets, $30,209,830 (M); expenditures, $1,269,760; qualifying distributions, $1,189,656; giving activities include $1,136,500 for 149 grants (high: $100,000; low: $250).

Purpose and activities: Giving for education, the arts, health, human services, and environmental conservation.

Fields of interest: Arts; Secondary school/education; Higher education; Environment, natural resources; Environment; Hospitals (general); Medical research, institute; Human services; Youth, services.

Type of support: General/operating support; Building/renovation; Endowments; Research.

Limitations: Applications not accepted. Giving primarily in CO, IL, MT, TX, WY, and the Mid-Atlantic states. No grants to individuals.

Application information: Unsolicited requests for funds not accepted.

Board meeting date(s): May and Sept.

Trustees: Ruth Taylor Campbell; Friday A. Green; Sara Taylor Swift; James C. Taylor; Vernon F. Taylor, Jr.

Number of staff: 1 full-time professional.

EIN: 846021788

Selected grants: The following grants were reported in 2005.

$55,000 to Mills College, Oakland, CA.

$34,000 to Saint Marys Hall, San Antonio, TX.

$29,000 to Madeira School, McLean, VA.

$15,000 to Nature Conservancy, Arlington, VA.

$15,000 to Wilderness Society, DC.

$13,000 to Southwest School of Art and Craft, San Antonio, TX.

$10,000 to Green River Valley Land Trust, Pinedale, WY.

$10,000 to National Baseball Hall of Fame and Museum, Cooperstown, NY.

$5,000 to Helena Presents, Helena, MT.

$2,500 to Colorado Council on Economic Education, Denver, CO.

1465

Telluride Foundation

620 Mountain Village Blvd., Ste. 2B

Telluride, CO   81435   (970) 728-8717

Contact: For grants: April Montgomery, Progs. Dir.

FAX: (970) 728-9007;

E-mail: april@telluridefoundation.org; URL: http://www.telluridefoundation.org

Established in 2000 in CO.

Foundation type: Community foundation.

Financial data (yr. ended 12/31/05): Assets, $5,933,767 (M); gifts received, $3,204,946; expenditures, $2,419,786; giving activities include $1,581,012 for 140 grants (high: $60,000; low: $500; average: $500–$60,000), and $29,028 for grants to individuals.

Purpose and activities: The foundation is committed to preserving and enriching the quality of life of the residents, visitors and workforce of the Telluride, CO, region. It provides year-round support for donors and local community-based organizations by facilitating the charitable intent of donors and grantmaking, technical assistance and education for community groups.

Fields of interest: Arts; Higher education; Education; Environment, land resources; Environment; Animal welfare; Recreation; Children/youth, services; Children, day care; Child development, services; Human services.

Type of support: Scholarships—to individuals; General/operating support; Annual campaigns; Equipment; Program development; Seed money; Scholarship funds; Technical assistance; Consulting services; Matching/challenge support.

Limitations: Giving primarily in Ouray, San Miguel, and West Montrose counties, CO. No support for religious organizations for religious purposes. No grants to individuals (except for designated scholarships), or for capital campaigns, debt reduction, building, renovation, non-educational publications, graduate or post-graduate research, economic development, or endowments; no loans.

Publications: Application guidelines; Annual report (including application guidelines); Financial statement; Grants list; Newsletter; Program policy statement.

Application information: Visit foundation Web site for application form and guidelines. The foundation holds a pre-applications Q&A session; visit Web site for details. Application form required.

Initial approach: Submit application form and attachments

Copies of proposal: 9

Deadline(s): Oct. 21

Board meeting date(s): Dec. and July

Final notification: Dec. 30

Officers and Directors:* Mark Dalton,* Co-Chair.; H. Norman Schwarzkopf, Co-Chair.; Paul Major,* C.E.O. and Pres.; Joanne Corzine,* Secy.; Richard Betts,* Treas.; Ron Allred; Mike Armstrong; Ed Barlow; Harmon Brown; Bill Carstens; Kim Day; Vern Ebert; Davis Fansler; Bunny Freidus; Tully Friedman; Ken Gart; William Gershen; Allan Gerstle; Ron Gilmer; Anne Herrick; Amb. Richard Holbrooke; Chuck Horning; Tricia Maxon; Joan May; Joe Hideo Morita; John Pryor; Marilyn Quayle; Dick Rodgers; Mary Rubadeau; Susan Saint James; Josh Sale; Bob Trenary; Stephen Wald; James Wear.

Number of staff: 2 full-time professional; 2 part-time professional.

EIN: 841530768

Selected grants: The following grants were reported in 2005.

$40,000 to Wright Stuff Community Foundation, Norwood, CO. For general operating support.

$25,000 to San Miguel Open Space Commission, Telluride, CO. For San Miguel Land Heritage Program.

$17,000 to Ah Haa School for the Arts, Telluride, CO. For low-income individuals participating in the children and adult educational programs.

$15,000 to Telluride Ski and Snowboard Club, Telluride, CO. For program support and financial aid to low-income children.

$8,000 to Montrose County Health and Human Services, Montrose, CO. For Homemaker program and licensed childcare for low-income families.

$5,700 to Paradox Valley School, Paradox, CO. For professional development of staff.

$4,000 to Telluride AIDS Benefit, Telluride, CO.

$3,000 to Animal Humane Society of Ouray County, Ridgway, CO. For expansion of programs to reduce pet overpopulation.

$1,000 to Montrose Regional Library, Montrose, CO. For children's books.

1466
The Harry Trueblood Foundation ☆
1720 S. Bellaire, Ste. 908
Denver, CO 80222-4334
FAX: (303) 300-6794;
E-mail: hajtrueblood@yahoo.com

Established in 1969 in CO.
Donor: Harry A. Trueblood, Jr.
Foundation type: Independent foundation.
Financial data (yr. ended 4/30/06): Assets,
$8,469,000 (M); expenditures, $420,000;
qualifying distributions, $350,000; giving activities
include $350,000 for 15 grants (high: $30,000;
low: $7,000).
Purpose and activities: Funding primarily for
fellowships for entrepreneurial and business
programs at undergraduate and graduate levels, and
for general scholarships, based primarily on merit,
for undergraduate and secondary school programs;
funding also for an endowment for partial petroleum
engineering scholarships at University of TX at
Austin.
Fields of interest: Secondary school/education;
Higher education; Business school/education;
Engineering/technology.
Type of support: Fellowships; Scholarship funds.
Limitations: Giving primarily in CO; limited giving
also in TX. No direct grants to individuals for partial
scholarships.
Application information: Application form not
required.
  Initial approach: Letter
  Copies of proposal: 1
  Deadline(s): None
  Board meeting date(s): Biannually
  Final notification: Up to one month
Officers and Directors:* John B. Trueblood,* Pres.;
Harry A. Trueblood, Jr.,* V.P. and Treas.; Julie
Underdahl,* Secy.; Katherine T. Astin; Lucile B.
Trueblood.
EIN: 840593623
Selected grants: The following grants were reported
in 2005.
$30,000 to Colorado State University, Fort Collins,
  CO. For scholarships.
$30,000 to University of Colorado Foundation,
  Boulder, CO. For scholarships.
$30,000 to University of Denver, Denver, CO. For
  scholarships.
$27,000 to Colorado School of Mines, Golden, CO.
  For scholarships.
$27,000 to Regis University, Denver, CO. For
  scholarships.
$27,000 to University of Northern Colorado,
  Greeley, CO. For scholarships.
$25,000 to Colorado Academy, Denver, CO. For
  scholarships.
$25,000 to Kent Denver School, Englewood, CO. For
  scholarships.
$25,000 to Saint Annes Episcopal School, Denver,
  CO. For scholarships.
$25,000 to Saint Marys Academy, Englewood, CO.
  For scholarships.
$14,000 to Colorado Council on Economic
  Education, Denver, CO. For scholarships.

1467
Tuchman Family Foundation ◇ ☆
c/o Mantucket Capital Mgmt. Corp.
5251 DTC Pkwy., Ste. 995
Englewood, CO 80111

Established in 1996.
Donors: Kenneth D. Tuchman; Debra Mautner
Tuchman; Leizor Rosen†.
Foundation type: Independent foundation.
Financial data (yr. ended 12/31/05): Assets,
$3,637,631 (M); gifts received, $397,000;
expenditures, $371,909; qualifying distributions,
$359,808; giving activities include $347,808 for 28
grants (high: $72,390; low: $250).
Fields of interest: Museums (art); Education;
Hospitals (general); Medical research, institute;
Family services, domestic violence; Jewish
federated giving programs; Jewish agencies &
temples.
Limitations: Applications not accepted. Giving
primarily in CO and NY. No grants to individuals.
Application information: Contributes only to
pre-selected organizations.
Officers and Directors:* Kenneth D. Tuchman,*
Pres. and Treas.; Debra Mautner Tuchman,* Secy.
EIN: 841366236
Selected grants: The following grants were reported
in 2004.
$57,000 to Allied Jewish Federation of Colorado,
  Denver, CO. For general support.
$50,000 to CLAL: The National Jewish Center for
  Learning and Leadership, New York, NY. For
  general support.
$20,000 to National Jewish Hospital and Research
  Center, Denver, CO. For Beaux Arts Ball.
$18,750 to Foundation for Sensory Integration
  Research and Therapy, Roxbury, CT. For
  Montessori School Program.
$10,000 to Denver Art Museum, Denver, CO. For
  museum expansion.
$5,000 to Memorial Sloan-Kettering Cancer Center,
  New York, NY. For prostate cancer research.
$5,000 to Silver Lining Foundation, Aspen, CO. For
  general support.
$3,000 to Colorado Academy, Denver, CO. For
  capital campaign.
$1,000 to Lynne Cohen Foundation for Ovarian
  Cancer Research, Los Angeles, CA.
$1,000 to Mizel Museum of Judaica, Denver, CO.
  For general support.

1468
Vail Valley Foundation, Inc. ◇
90 Benchmark Rd., Ste. 300
Avon, CO 81620 (970) 949-1999
FAX: (970) 949-9265; Additional tel.: (888)
VVF-VAIL; Mailing Address: P.O. Box 309, Vail, CO
81658; URL: http://www.vvf.org

Established in 1981 in Colorado.
Foundation type: Community foundation.
Financial data (yr. ended 12/31/04): Assets,
$15,278,173 (M); gifts received, $19,370;
expenditures, $7,995,166; giving activities include
$224,000 for 25 grants (high: $121,000; low:
$500), $114,199 for grants to individuals, and
$2,772,737 for 3 foundation-administered
programs.
Purpose and activities: The foundation seeks to
provide leadership in athletic, cultural, and
educational endeavors to enhance the quality of life
in the Vail Valley, CO, area.
Fields of interest: Arts; Education; Environment;
Athletics/sports, winter sports; Human services.
Limitations: Giving primarily in the Vail Valley, CO,
area. No grants to individuals (except for
scholarships).

Application information:
  Initial approach: Proposal
Officer and Directors:* Cecilia Folz,* Pres.; Terry
Brady, V.P., Opers. and Sales; John Dakin, V.P.,
Comms.; Mark Fernstermacher, C.F.O.; Adam Aron;
Roger Behler; Judith Berkowitz; Marlene Boll; Bjorn
Erik Borgen; Jack Crosby; Andrew Daly; William
Esrey; Johannes Faessler; Tim Finchem; Harry
Frampton III; Stephen Friedman; Gerald Gallegos;
John Galvin; John Garnsey; George Gillett, Jr.; Donna
Giordano; Pepi Gramshammer; Martha Head;
William Hybl; William Jensen; Jack Kemp; Kent
Logan; John Maher; Peter May; Chupa Nelson; Doug
Rippeto; Michael Shannon; Stanley Shuman;
Rodney Slifer; Ann Smead; Oscar Tang; Craig Tuber;
Stewart Turley.
EIN: 742215035

1469
Weaver Family Foundation
P.O. Box 19409
Boulder, CO 80308-9409 (303) 543-8719
Contact: Julie Shaffer, Exec. Dir.
FAX: (303) 545-2414;
E-mail: info@WeaverFoundation.org; URL: http://
weaverfoundation.org

Established in 1999 in CO.
Donors: Lindsey A. Weaver, Jr.; Francine Lavin
Weaver.
Foundation type: Independent foundation.
Financial data (yr. ended 12/31/05): Assets,
$13,644,121 (M); expenditures, $907,560;
qualifying distributions, $891,328; giving activities
include $761,158 for 103 grants (high: $166,170;
low: $18).
Purpose and activities: The foundation funds
Colorado based, non- sectarian charitable programs
that focus on education, community service, and the
preservation of our natural environment. The
foundation also supports programs that enhance
Jewish life and spiritual renewal in the United
States, Israel, and other countries around the world.
Fields of interest: Education; Environment;
Housing/shelter, development; Human services;
Jewish agencies & temples.
International interests: Israel.
Type of support: General/operating support;
Continuing support; Program development;
Conferences/seminars; Curriculum development;
Fellowships; Consulting services; Program-related
investments/loans; Matching/challenge support.
Limitations: Applications not accepted. Giving
primarily in Boulder, CO, and Israel. No grants to
individuals.
Application information: Contributes only to
pre-selected organizations. Requests for proposals
will be solicited by the foundation only.
Officer: Julie Shaffer, Exec. Dir.
Directors: Francine Lavin Weaver; Lindsey A.
Weaver, Jr.
Number of staff: 1 full-time professional.
EIN: 841513850

1470
**Eleanore Mullen Weckbaugh
Foundation** ◇
13691 E. Marina Dr., Apt. 404
Aurora, CO 80014-3724
Contact: Therese A. Polakovic, Pres.

Application address: P.O. Box 34861, Englewood, CO 80155-3486, tel.: (303) 471-1301

Established in 1975 in CO.
Donor: Eleanore Mullen Weckbaugh†.
Foundation type: Independent foundation.
Financial data (yr. ended 3/31/05): Assets, $9,385,290 (M); expenditures, $535,146; qualifying distributions, $469,259; giving activities include $397,964 for 28 grants (high: $49,500; low: $1,800).
Purpose and activities: Emphasis on Roman Catholic church support, grants also for higher and secondary education, libraries, museums and the performing arts, hospitals, health agencies, employment, child welfare and development, and women.
Fields of interest: Performing arts; Language/linguistics; Literature; Arts; Elementary/secondary education; Child development, education; Secondary school/education; Higher education; Adult/continuing education; Education; Hospitals (general); Health organizations, association; Employment; Human services; Children/youth, services; Child development, services; Women, centers/services; Roman Catholic agencies & churches; Religion; Women.
Type of support: General/operating support; Scholarship funds.
Limitations: Giving primarily in CO. No grants to individuals.
Application information: The foundation accepts the Colorado Common Grant Application form. Application form required.
  Initial approach: Letter
  Copies of proposal: 1
  Deadline(s): None
  Board meeting date(s): Mar., June, Sept., and Dec.
Officers and Trustees:* Therese A. Polakovic,* Pres.; Michael J. Polakovic,* V.P. and Secy.; Edward J. Limes,* Treas.; Michael Lascor; Deborah O'Dwyer.
Number of staff: 3 part-time professional; 1 part-time support.
EIN: 237437761

1471
Western Colorado Community Foundation, Inc.

225 North 5th, Ste. 215
P.O. Box 4334
Grand Junction, CO   81502-4334
(970) 243-3767
Contact: Anne Wenzel, Exec. Dir.
FAX: (970) 243-9767; E-mail: ktuinstra@wc-cf.org; URL: http://www.wc-cf.org

Established in 1996 in CO.
Foundation type: Community foundation.
Financial data (yr. ended 12/31/04): Assets, $5,145,796 (M); gifts received, $1,445,853; expenditures, $524,590; giving activities include $295,206 for 97 grants (high: $50,000; low: $48; average: $100–$50,000), and $23,000 for 8 grants to individuals (high: $5,000; low: $1,000).
Purpose and activities: The foundation seeks to promote philanthropy and to build and manage permanent charitable assets to benefit the residents of western CO.
Fields of interest: Arts; Education; Environment; Health care; Human services; Community development.

Type of support: General/operating support; Seed money; Scholarships—to individuals; Matching/challenge support.
Limitations: Giving limited to Delta, Eagle, Garfield, Gunnison, Mesa, Montrose, Ouray and Rio Blanco counties, CO. No grants to individuals (except for scholarships), or for fundraising events.
Publications: Application guidelines; Annual report; Informational brochure; Newsletter.
Application information: Visit foundation Web site for application guidelines. The Colorado Common Grant Application Form is accepted. Application form not required.
  Initial approach: Letter of inquiry or telephone
  Copies of proposal: 1
  Deadline(s): Aug. 15
  Board meeting date(s): Jan., Apr., July, and Oct.
  Final notification: 1-2 months
Officers and Directors:* Anita Cox,* Chair.; Verne Smith,* Vice-Chair.; Bob Johnson,* Secy.; Gary Wade,* Treas.; Anne Wenzel, Exec. Dir.; Kelly Arnold; Rob Bleiberg; Fid Braffett; Bruce Dixson; Shirley Ela; Don Massey; Joseph Prinster; Susan Reed; Linda Bacon Reid; Michael Salogga; Joe Skinner; Richard Tally; Lenna Watson; George Wheeler; Margo Young-Gardney.
Number of staff: 1 full-time professional; 1 part-time professional; 1 part-time support.
EIN: 841354894
Selected grants: The following grants were reported in 2006.
$1,500 to Mesa Developmental Services, Grand Junction, CO. For screening equipment.
$1,000 to Boys and Girls Club, Black Canyon, Montrose, CO. For Olathe Clubhouse Community Greenhouse.
$1,000 to Community Food Bank, Grand Junction, CO. For general support.
$1,000 to Court Appointed Special Advocates (CASA) of Mesa County, Grand Junction, CO. For general support.
$1,000 to Girl Scouts of the U.S.A., Chipeta Council, Grand Junction, CO. For Delta and Montrose programs.
$1,000 to Habitat for Humanity of Montrose County, Montrose, CO. For materials.
$1,000 to HomewardBound of the Grand Valley, Grand Junction, CO. For general support.
$1,000 to Marillac Clinic, Grand Junction, CO. For Williams Sound Pak.
$1,000 to Mesa Land Trust, Grand Junction, CO. For Agricultural Heritage Preservation Project.
$1,000 to Riverside Tutoring Center, Grand Junction, CO. For general support.
$1,000 to Suicide Prevention Foundation of America. For Heart Beat Program in Grand Junction, Colorado.
$1,000 to Surface Creek Community Services, Cedaredge, CO. For general support.
$1,000 to Western Slope Center for Children, Grand Junction, CO. For general support.
$1,000 to Youth Zone, Basalt, CO. For general support.
$500 to Meet the Wilderness, Edwards, CO. For general support.

1472
The Mahlon Thatcher White Foundation ✧
(formerly The Thatcher Foundation)
P.O. Box 2097
Pueblo, CO   81004
Contact: Valeri Hardin

Established in 1924 in CO.
Foundation type: Independent foundation.
Financial data (yr. ended 12/31/05): Assets, $3,866,403 (M); expenditures, $381,193; qualifying distributions, $369,404; giving activities include $317,455 for 24 grants (high: $105,000; low: $225), and $16,691 for 5 grants to individuals (high: $6,350; low: $2,057).
Purpose and activities: Giving for non-profit civic organizations in Pueblo County, CO.
Fields of interest: Arts; Health care; Health organizations, association; Children/youth, services; Federated giving programs.
Limitations: Giving limited to Pueblo County, CO.
Application information: Application form not required.
  Deadline(s): Nov.
  Board meeting date(s): Dec.
Officers and Trustees:* Mahlon T. White,* Pres.; Maylan T. White,* V.P.; Donald J. Banner,* Secy.; M. Andrew White; Mahlon T. White II; Whitney White.
EIN: 840581724
Selected grants: The following grants were reported in 2005.
$105,000 to YMCA of Pueblo, Pueblo, CO.
$40,000 to United Way of Pueblo County, Pueblo, CO.
$20,600 to Sangre de Cristo Arts and Conference Center, Pueblo, CO.
$20,000 to Pueblo Zoological Society, Pueblo, CO.
$20,000 to Rosemount Museum, Pueblo, CO.
$8,000 to Catholic Charities of the Diocese of Pueblo, Pueblo, CO.
$5,000 to Broadway Theater League of Pueblo, Pueblo, CO.
$5,000 to McClelland Center for Child Study, Pueblo, CO.
$1,000 to American Red Cross, Pueblo, CO.

1473
Kate Stamper Wilhite Charitable Foundation ✧ ☆
P.O. Box 463
Englewood, CO   80151-0463
Contact: John H. Stamper, Treas.

Established in 1989 in MO.
Donor: Kate Stamper Wilhite†.
Foundation type: Independent foundation.
Financial data (yr. ended 12/31/05): Assets, $2,114,552 (M); expenditures, $541,884; qualifying distributions, $516,000; giving activities include $516,000 for grants.
Fields of interest: Education; Human services.
Type of support: General/operating support; Annual campaigns; Capital campaigns; Equipment; Scholarship funds; Matching/challenge support.
Limitations: Applications not accepted. Giving primarily in CO, MO, and TX. No grants to individuals.
Application information: Contributes only to pre-selected organizations.
Officers and Directors:* Jane Stamper,* Pres.; Natalie Lake,* V.P.; William D. Stamper,* Secy.; John H. Stamper,* Treas.; Barbara Stamper; Nancy Stamper.
Number of staff: 1 part-time support.
EIN: 431498820
Selected grants: The following grants were reported in 2004.
$50,000 to Colorado Academy, Denver, CO. For capital campaign.
$15,000 to Moberly Area Community College, Moberly, MO.

$10,000 to Community School, Saint Louis, MO.

$10,000 to Saint Louis Art Museum, Saint Louis, MO.

$3,750 to Guiding Eyes for the Blind, Yorktown Heights, NY.

1474

The Williams Family Foundation

626 E. Platte Ave.
Fort Morgan, CO 80701
Contact: Edward L. Zorn, Tr.

Trust established about 1958 in CO.
Donors: A.F. Williams, M.D.†; Mrs. A.F. Williams†.
Foundation type: Independent foundation.
Financial data (yr. ended 12/31/05): Assets, $14,731,357 (M); expenditures, $740,010; qualifying distributions, $723,349; giving activities include $716,573 for grants.
Purpose and activities: Giving for higher and secondary education, limited to graduates of Morgan County high schools for medical-oriented study, hospitals, and civic affairs.
Fields of interest: Secondary school/education; Medical school/education; Hospitals (general); Government/public administration.
Type of support: Scholarship funds; Research.
Limitations: Giving primarily in CO; scholarships limited to Morgan County, CO, high school graduates.
Application information: Scholarship applicants must be graduates of, and be nominated by, Morgan County, CO, high schools. Application form not required.
  Initial approach: Letter
  Copies of proposal: 1
  Deadline(s): None
  Board meeting date(s): 3rd Wed. of each month
  Final notification: 3-6 months
Trustees: Kathleen Thompson; Patrick Thompson; Edward L. Zorn.
EIN: 846023379

1475

Melvin & Elaine Wolf Foundation, Inc. ◇

6825 E. Tennessee Ave., Ste. 235
Denver, CO 80224
Contact: Sandra Wolf, V.P.

Established in 1978 in CO.
Donors: Melvin Wolf; Elaine Wolf.
Foundation type: Independent foundation.
Financial data (yr. ended 6/30/05): Assets, $11,517,443 (M); expenditures, $466,779; qualifying distributions, $344,367; giving activities include $344,367 for grants.
Purpose and activities: Giving primarily for children's services, health care, including a children's hospital, social services, and Jewish organizations.
Fields of interest: Museums (specialized); Arts; Higher education; Zoos/zoological societies; Hospitals (general); Hospitals (specialty); Health care; Health organizations, association; Cancer; Human services; Children/youth, services; Family services; Aging, centers/services; Jewish federated giving programs; Jewish agencies & temples.
Type of support: General/operating support; Equipment; Program development.
Limitations: Giving primarily in Denver, CO. No grants to individuals.

Application information:
  Initial approach: Letter
  Deadline(s): Sept. 30
Officers and Directors:* Elaine Wolf,* Pres.; Ian D. Gardenswartz, V.P. and Treas.; Sandra Wolf,* V.P.
EIN: 840797937
Selected grants: The following grants were reported in 2003.
$26,500 to Childrens Diabetes Foundation at Denver, Denver, CO. For general operating support.
$25,000 to Childrens Hospital Association, Denver, CO. For equipment and operations.
$25,000 to Denver Museum of Nature and Science, Denver, CO. For general operating support.
$25,000 to Jewish Community Centers of Denver, Denver, CO. For general operating support.
$25,000 to Temple Emmanuel, Denver, CO. For general operating support.
$21,000 to Shalom Park, Aurora, CO. For general operating support.
$20,000 to Denver Zoological Foundation, Denver, CO. For general operating support.
$10,000 to Cancer League of Colorado, Englewood, CO. For general operating support.
$10,000 to Colorado Symphony Association, Denver, CO. For general operating support.
$10,000 to National Jewish Medical and Research Center, Denver, CO. For general operating support.

1476

Working Partners Foundation ◇ ☆

2915 Sedona Hills Dr.
Loveland, CO 80537
E-mail: info@wpfintl.org; URL: http://www.wpfint.org

Established in 2005 in CO.
Donor: The New Millennium Trust.
Foundation type: Independent foundation.
Financial data (yr. ended 12/31/05): Assets, $1,333,567 (M); gifts received, $2,313,955; expenditures, $1,008,152; qualifying distributions, $612,340; giving activities include $612,340 for 8 grants (high: $282,300; low: $4,400).
Purpose and activities: The goal of the foundation is to improve basic health and living conditions for people in need through healthcare, micro-economic financing, sanitation and water, education, food, prevention and a magnitude of other community development assistance programs around the globe.
Fields of interest: International agricultural development; International economic development; International relief.
International interests: Africa; Global programs; Middle East; Southeast Asia.
Limitations: Applications not accepted. Giving primarily to U.S-based organizations with international focus.
Application information: Contributes only to pre-selected organizations.
Directors: Yale King; Hollis K. Lundquist.
EIN: 201783302

1477

Yampa Valley Community Foundation

P.O. Box 881869
Steamboat Springs, CO 80488 (970) 879-8632
Contact: Linda C. Haltom, Exec. Dir.

FAX: (970) 871-0431; E-mail: donate@yvcf.org; Additional E-mail: Linda@yvcf.org; URL: http://www.yvcf.org

Established in 1979 in CO.
Foundation type: Community foundation.
Financial data (yr. ended 12/31/05): Assets, $6,069,274 (M); gifts received, $1,298,124; expenditures, $912,644; giving activities include $621,839 for 260 grants (high: $44,397; low: $90), and $72,000 for 48 grants to individuals (high: $2,500; low: $106).
Purpose and activities: The foundation develops annual and growing funds to support organizations and innovative programs that preserve traditions and maintain the character of the community. Giving primarily to arts and culture, education, environment, health organizations, recreation and human services.
Fields of interest: Arts; Education; Environment; Health organizations, association; Recreation; Human services.
Type of support: General/operating support; Continuing support; Annual campaigns; Capital campaigns; Building/renovation; Equipment; Emergency funds; Program development; Conferences/seminars; Seed money; Curriculum development; Scholarships—to individuals; Exchange programs.
Limitations: Giving primarily in Yampa Valley, specifically Moffat and Routt counties, CO. No support for religious purposes. No grants for debt reduction or endowments; generally no grants for team or travel expenses.
Publications: Application guidelines; Annual report; Financial statement; Grants list; Informational brochure; Newsletter.
Application information: Visit foundation Web site for application forms and guidelines. Generally, only one grant for an organization per calendar year. Application form required.
  Initial approach: Submit application forms, 2-page narrative, and attachments
  Copies of proposal: 1
  Deadline(s): Mar. 15 and Sept. 15
  Board meeting date(s): Semi-monthly
  Final notification: Within 12 weeks
Officers and Trustees:* Paula Cooper Black,* Chair.; Rick Dowden,* Vice-Chair.; Donna Howell,* Vice-Chair.; Scott Gordon,* Secy.-Treas.; Linda C. Haltom, Exec. Dir.; J. Edwin Hill,* Chair. Emeritus; Beth Bishop; Jim Bronner; Chris Diamond; Rod Hanna; Malcolm Hawk; John Holloway; Wendy McCreight; C.J. Mucklow; David Nagel; Stu Roberts.
Number of staff: 2 full-time professional; 1 part-time professional; 2 part-time support.
EIN: 840794536
Selected grants: The following grants were reported in 2005.
$5,000 to Boys and Girls Club of Craig, Craig, CO. For general operating support.
$5,000 to Colorado Northwestern Community College, Rangely, CO. For nursing program.
$5,000 to Partners in Routt County, Steamboat Springs, CO. For middle school-based mentoring program.
$4,000 to Strings in the Mountains, Steamboat Springs, CO. For Youth and Family Concert Series.
$2,200 to Tread of Pioneers Museum, Steamboat Springs, CO. For Oral History Initiative.
$2,000 to Community Agriculture Alliance, Steamboat Springs, CO. For annual operating support.

$2,000 to Horizons Specialized Servces, Steamboat Springs, CO. For general operating support.

$1,391 to Yampatika Outdoor Awareness Association, Steamboat Springs, CO. For general operating support.

$1,200 to Hayden, Town of, Hayden, CO. For annual Summerfest.

$1,000 to Maybell Women's Club, Craig, CO. For cemetery improvements.

CONNECTICUT

1478
Abramowitz Family Foundation ✧
P.O. Box 958
Southport, CT 06890

Established in 2002 in NY.
Donors: Kenneth Abramowitz; Nira Abramowitz.
Foundation type: Independent foundation.
Financial data (yr. ended 12/31/04): Assets,
$156,401 (M); gifts received, $126,150;
expenditures, $347,684; qualifying distributions,
$321,628; giving activities include $321,628 for 54
+ grants.
Fields of interest: Education; Human services;
Jewish federated giving programs; Jewish agencies
& temples.
Limitations: Applications not accepted. Giving
primarily in NY. No grants to individuals.
Application information: Contributes only to
pre-selected organizations.
Trustees: Kenneth Abramowitz; Nira Abramowitz.
EIN: 331017742
Selected grants: The following grants were reported
in 2004.
$20,000 to Middle East Forum, Philadelphia, PA.
$10,000 to Jerusalem Fund, DC.
$10,000 to Rabbinical College Academy, Brooklyn,
NY.
$5,000 to Friends of Ir David, Brooklyn, NY.
$3,000 to National Center for Policy Analysis,
Dallas, TX.
$300 to Academy for Jewish Religion, Riverdale, NY.
$180 to Museum of Jewish Heritage, New York, NY.

1479
Aetna Foundation, Inc. ▼ ✧
(formerly Aetna Life & Casualty Foundation, Inc.)
151 Farmington Ave., RE2R
Hartford, CT 06156-3180 (860) 273-6382
FAX: (860) 273-4764;
E-mail: aetnafoundation@aetna.com; Contact for
Quality of Care Grants Prog.: Jessica L. Richard,
E-mail: richardjl@aetna.com; URL: http://
www.aetna.com/foundation

Incorporated in 1972 in CT.
Donor: Aetna Inc.
Foundation type: Company-sponsored foundation.
Financial data (yr. ended 12/31/04): Assets,
$47,211,573 (M); gifts received, $52,284,307;
expenditures, $9,790,750; qualifying distributions,
$9,134,866; giving activities include $3,355,625
for 304 grants (high: $150,000; low: $50; average:
$500–$50,000), and $2,859,984 for employee
matching gifts.
Purpose and activities: The foundation supports
organizations involved with arts and culture,
education, health, mental health, human services,
community development, children, women, and
minorities.
Fields of interest: Arts; Medical school/education;
Education; Dental care; End of life care; Health care,
home services; Health care; Mental health/crisis
services, public education; Mental health,
depression; Mental health/crisis services; Health
organizations, public education; Diabetes; Human

services; Community development; Children;
Minorities; Women.
Type of support: General/operating support;
Continuing support; Emergency funds; Program
development; Conferences/seminars; Research;
Employee volunteer services; Sponsorships;
Employee matching gifts; Matching/challenge
support.
Limitations: Giving on a national basis. No support
for religious organizations not of direct benefit to the
entire community. No grants to individuals, or for
scholarships, capital campaigns, equipment, or
depreciation, advertising, or political causes or
events.
Publications: Corporate giving report; Grants list;
Program policy statement.
Application information: Organizations receiving
support are asked to provide periodic progress
reports. Support is limited to 1 contribution per
organization during any given year. Application form
required.
   Initial approach: Complete online application form
   Deadline(s): June 15 for Voice of Conscience;
      Mar. 31 for the West, Apr. 29 for the
      Mid-Atlantic, North Central, and Southeast,
      and May 31 for the Northeast and Southwest
      for the Regional Community Health Grants
      Program; visit Web site for other deadlines
   Board meeting date(s): Apr. and Dec.
   Final notification: May 16 for the West, July 15 for
      the Mid-Atlantic, North Central, and Southeast,
      and Oct. 17 for the Northeast and Southwest
      for the Regional Community Health Grants
      Program; visit Web site for other dates
Officers and Directors: Marilda L. Gandara, Pres.;
Sharon C. Dalton, V.P.; Christopher A. Montross,
V.P.; Andrew Allocco; Alan M. Bennett; J. Roger
Bolton; Mary Claire Bonner; Troyen A. Brennan,
M.D.; Molly J. Coye, M.D.; Mary C. Fox; Jeffrey E.
Garten; Earl G. Graves, Sr.; Joseph P. Newhouse;
Felicia Norwood; Cheryl B. Pegus, M.D.; John W.
Rowe, M.D.; Ronald A. Williams.
Number of staff: 9 full-time professional.
EIN: 237241940
Selected grants: The following grants were reported
in 2004.
$150,000 to New York Academy of Medicine, New
York, NY. For enhancing palliative and home
hospice care services to minority patients.
$125,000 to Greater New York Hospital Foundation,
New York, NY. For Pilot Funding for Health
Information Tool for Empowerment.
$120,000 to Childrens Defense Fund, DC. For
addressing racial and ethnic disparities in Health
Care.
$56,000 to University of Connecticut Health Center,
Farmington, CT. For Health Professions
Partnership Initiatives.
$50,000 to Baylor College of Medicine, Houston,
TX. For Cultural Competency Training to Improve
Physician-Patient Communication.
$50,000 to Connecticut Childrens Medical Center
Foundation, Hartford, CT. For Reducing Asthma
Morbidity in Urban Children Program.
$50,000 to Horace Bushnell Memorial Hall,
Hartford, CT. For education growth strategy of
PARTNERS program.
$50,000 to National Conference for Community and
Justice, Phoenix, AZ. For Healthcare Integration
Project.
$49,000 to American College of Obstetricians and
Gynecologists, Albany, NY. For advancing quality
health care for diverse female population.

$46,000 to Committee for Hispanic Children and
Families, New York, NY. For Sonnsitas (Little
Smiles) Program for Oral Health.

1480
The ALFA Foundation ✧
240 Greenwich Ave., 3rd Fl.
Greenwich, CT 06830

Established in 2000 in CT.
Donor: Ali Fayed.
Foundation type: Independent foundation.
Financial data (yr. ended 12/31/05): Assets,
$1,927,169 (M); gifts received, $1,000,000;
expenditures, $857,329; qualifying distributions,
$852,000; giving activities include $852,000 for 11
grants (high: $350,000; low: $1,000).
Purpose and activities: Giving primarily for hospitals
and medical research; funding also for education.
Fields of interest: Medical school/education;
Education; Hospitals (general); Medical research,
institute.
Limitations: Applications not accepted. Giving on a
national basis, with emphasis on CT and MD. No
grants to individuals.
Application information: Contributes only to
pre-selected organizations.
Officer: Pier Stiny, Exec. Dir.
Trustees: Ali Fayed; Lee A. Kuntz.
EIN: 137228276
Selected grants: The following grants were reported
in 2004.
$378,336 to Brunswick School, Greenwich, CT.
$150,000 to Greenwich Hospital, Greenwich, CT.
$100,000 to Deer Hill Foundation, Mancos, CO.
$25,000 to American University in Cairo, New York,
NY.
$3,000 to Junior Achievement, National, New York,
NY.
$500 to Byram Volunteer Fire Department,
Greenwich, CT.

1481
Elizabeth Raymond Ambler Trust ✧ ☆
P.O. Box 7266
Wilton, CT 06897-7266

Established in 2000 in CT.
Foundation type: Independent foundation.
Financial data (yr. ended 12/31/05): Assets,
$9,632,221 (M); expenditures, $767,165;
qualifying distributions, $642,528; giving activities
include $357,000 for 23 grants (high: $125,000;
low: $1,000), and $173,135 for 59 grants to
individuals (high: $6,500; low: $1,000).
Fields of interest: Arts; Libraries (public);
Scholarships/financial aid; AIDS; Human services;
Residential/custodial care, senior continuing care;
Christian agencies & churches.
Type of support: Scholarships—to individuals.
Limitations: Giving primarily in the town of Wilton,
CT, and surrounding towns.
Application information: Preference for
scholarships is given to students who reside in the
Town of Wilton, CT and surrounding towns; for
charitable distributions preference is given to
entities servicing the Town of Wilton and its
surrounding communities. Application form
required.

Initial approach: Letter; for scholarships, must submit application form with required attachments

Deadline(s): None; scholarship awards are usually made in the spring for the following academic year, and charitable distributions are generally determined and made in the fall.

Trustees: Thomas T. Adams; Dr. David F. Clune; Rev. William L. Sachs.

EIN: 066473263

Selected grants: The following grants were reported in 2004.

$25,000 to Wilton Library Association, Wilton, CT.

$6,000 to Wilton, Town of, Wilton, CT.

$5,000 to Housatonic Community College, Bridgeport, CT.

$5,000 to Norwalk Community College, Norwalk, CT.

$5,000 to Norwalk Emergency Shelter, South Norwalk, CT.

$3,000 to Interfaith, Atlanta, GA.

1482
American Savings Foundation ✧

(formerly American Savings Charitable Foundation, Inc.)

185 Main St.

New Britain, CT   06051   (860) 827-2556

Contact: David Davison, Pres.

E-mail: info@asfdn.org; URL: http://www.asfdn.org

Established in 1995 in CT.

Donor: American Financial Holdings, Inc.

Foundation type: Independent foundation.

Financial data (yr. ended 12/31/05): Assets, $82,679,249 (M); expenditures, $4,258,561; qualifying distributions, $3,692,067; giving activities include $2,737,609 for 141 grants (high: $200,000; low: $50; average: $5,000–$100,000), $545,665 for 674 grants to individuals (high: $7,500; low: $250; average: $500–$2,250), and $40,287 for 3 foundation-administered programs.

Purpose and activities: The foundation is dedicated to strengthening the community by supporting education, human services, and the arts, with a special emphasis on the needs of children, youth, and families, through grants to community organizations and college scholarships.

Fields of interest: Arts; Education; Youth development; Human services; Family services.

Type of support: Capital campaigns; Program development; Internship funds; Scholarship funds; Scholarships—to individuals.

Limitations: Giving only within 64-CT town service area.

Publications: Application guidelines; Annual report; Financial statement; Grants list; Informational brochure; Informational brochure (including application guidelines); Occasional report.

Application information: See foundation Web site for guidelines for scholarships, program grants and capital grants. Application form not required.

Initial approach: Proposals for Program Grants, Letter of Intent for Capital Grants, visit Web site for scholarships

Copies of proposal: 1

Deadline(s): Mar. 31 for scholarships; June 30 for renewal applications

Board meeting date(s): Quarterly

Officers and Directors:* Robert T. Kenney,* Chair.; David Davison,* C.E.O. and Pres.; Sheri C. Pasqualoni,* V.P. and Secy.; Charles J. Boulier III,* Treas.; Charles S. Beach; Donald Davidson; Norman E.W. Erickson; Marie S. Gustin; Gregory B. Howey;

Joseph T. Hughes; Mark E. Karp; Harry N. Mazadoorian; John J. Patrick, Jr.; Stanley W. Shepard; Laurence A. Tanner; Jeffery T. Witherwax.

Number of staff: 3 full-time professional; 1 full-time support.

EIN: 061563163

1483
Andor Capital Management Foundation ✧

c/o Andor Capital Mgmt., LLC

107 Elm St., 7th Fl.

Stamford, CT   06902

Established in 2001 in CT.

Donors: Daniel C. Benton; Douglas Mueller; Aimee Mueller; Peter Streinger; Kevin O'Brien; Jeanine O'Brien; Charlie Hannigan; Katherine Bailon; Julia Daily; John Levinson; Ellen Levinson; Cheryl Warren; Moshe Metzger; Jose Fernandez; Nancy Fernandez.

Foundation type: Independent foundation.

Financial data (yr. ended 8/31/05): Assets, $18,487,227 (M); gifts received, $1,196,903; expenditures, $2,180,487; qualifying distributions, $2,178,087; giving activities include $2,176,037 for 20 grants (high: $414,000; low: $2,500).

Purpose and activities: Giving primarily for human services organizations, including youth services.

Fields of interest: Health care; Human services; Children/youth, services.

Limitations: Applications not accepted. Giving primarily in NY. No grants to individuals.

Application information: Contributes only to pre-selected organizations.

Officers: Peter Streinger, Pres.; Julia Dailey, V.P. and Secy.; Kevin O'Brien, Treas.

EIN: 061631047

Selected grants: The following grants were reported in 2005.

$414,000 to World Cares Center, September Space, New York, NY.

$250,000 to Special Operations Fund, Arlington, VA.

$188,850 to Child Guidance Center of Southern Connecticut, Stamford, CT.

$182,840 to Asociacion Tepeyac de New York, New York, NY.

$150,000 to Tanenbaum Center for Interreligious Understanding, New York, NY.

$115,000 to Exchange Club Center for the Prevention of Child Abuse of Southern Connecticut, Stamford, CT.

$100,000 to Larkin Street Youth Services, San Francisco, CA.

$100,000 to Pegasus Therapeutic Riding, Stamford, CT.

$100,000 to Person-to-Person, Darien, CT.

$99,540 to Partnership with Children, New York, NY.

1484
The Applera Charitable Foundation, Inc. ✧ ☆

(formerly PE Charitable Foundation)

301 Merritt 7

P.O. Box 5435

Norwalk, CT   06856-5435

Contact: Ugo D. DeBlasi, Pres. and Exec. Dir.

URL: http://www.applera.com/applera/ applerahome.nsf/sectionhome/ 0CAA5C55AD38D1FC85256D9B0068B98D

Established in 1999 in CT and DE.

Donors: PE Corp.; Applera Corp.

Foundation type: Company-sponsored foundation.

Financial data (yr. ended 6/30/06): Assets, $2,291,167 (M); expenditures, $617,208; qualifying distributions, $556,106; giving activities include $556,106 for grants.

Purpose and activities: The foundation supports programs designed to promote genomics education and help educate individuals regarding new genomics and related scientific technologies and their implications for society.

Fields of interest: Medical research, public education; Science; Biological sciences.

Type of support: Program development; Employee matching gifts.

Limitations: Giving on a national basis, with emphasis on areas of company operations. No support for religious, fraternal, political, athletic, social, or veterans' organizations, organizations with a financial deficit, or private foundations. No grants to individuals, or for capital campaigns, endowments, contingency needs, memorials, or general operating support.

Application information: Letters of intent should be no longer than 2 pages. Application form not required.

Initial approach: Letter of intent

Deadline(s): None

Board meeting date(s): Semi-annual

Officers and Directors:* Ugo DeBlasi,* Pres. and Exec. Dir.; Thomas P. Livingston,* Secy.; John S. Ostaszewski,* Treas.; William B. Sawch; Tony White; Dennis L. Winger.

EIN: 061553291

Selected grants: The following grants were reported in 2004.

$115,000 to Bay Area Biotechnology Education Consortium, Morgan Hill, CA. To provide PCR based lab activities.

$66,180 to Stanford University, School of Medicine, Stanford, CA. For development and design of graduate courses and website and electronic courseware package in bioscience, bioengineering and bioinformatics.

1485
The Aronson Family Foundation ✧

15 Westfair Dr.

Westport, CT   06880

Contact: Dennis B. Poster, Tr.

Established in 1992 in NY.

Foundation type: Independent foundation.

Financial data (yr. ended 12/31/03): Assets, $11,903,004 (M); expenditures, $979,546; qualifying distributions, $816,350; giving activities include $748,500 for 37 grants (high: $200,000; low: $500).

Purpose and activities: Giving primarily for health organizations and hospitals, including a camp for children with cancer or other life threatening illnesses.

Fields of interest: Museums (art); Hospitals (general); Health organizations, association; Jewish agencies & temples.

Limitations: Applications not accepted. Giving primarily in New York, NY. No grants to individuals.

Application information: Contributes only to pre-selected organizations.

Trustees: Henry W. Berinstein; Roger A. Goldman; Dennis B. Poster.

EIN: 133693381

1486
The Elinor Patterson Baker Foundation ✧
c/o R.A. Beer, Cummings & Lockwood
P.O. Box 120
Stamford, CT 06904
Application address: c/o Putnam Trust Co., 10
Mason St., Greenwich, CT 06830, tel.: (203)
869-3000

Established in 1984 in CT.
Donor: Elinor Patterson Baker‡.
Foundation type: Independent foundation.
Financial data (yr. ended 5/31/05): Assets,
$43,329,341 (M); expenditures, $1,994,890;
qualifying distributions, $1,740,387; giving
activities include $1,455,500 for 109 grants (high:
$300,000; low: $1,000).
Purpose and activities: Grants are usually made for
the general purposes of the entities which are public
charities that help to care for dogs, cats, and other
animals.
Fields of interest: Animal welfare; Animals/wildlife,
preservation/protection.
Limitations: Giving primarily in CT to organizations
exempt from the state succession tax. In the case
of organizations incorporated outside of CT,
reciprocity must exist between CT and the state of
incorporation in order for the organization to qualify
for a grant.
Application information: Application form required.
Initial approach: Letter
Deadline(s): None
Trustee: Putnam Trust Co.
EIN: 066276403
Selected grants: The following grants were reported
in 2005.
$750,000 to Humane Society of the United States,
DC. 3 grants: $300,000, $150,000 (For
Immunocontraception program), $300,000.
$75,000 to Marine Mammal Center, Sausalito, CA.
$35,000 to Greater Yellowstone Coalition,
Bozeman, MT.
$35,000 to Wildlife Center of Virginia, Waynesboro,
VA.
$10,000 to Audubon Society of Connecticut, CT.
$10,000 to Environmental Alliance-US-China
Environmental Fund, Mount Horeb, WI.
$10,000 to SoundWaters, Stamford, CT.
$3,000 to Cheyenne Animal Shelter Services,
Cheyenne, WY.

1487
The Baldwin Foundation
c/o D. Brandrup
57 Old Post Rd., No. 2
Greenwich, CT 06830

Established in 1980 in DE and NY.
Donor: Winifred B. Baldwin‡.
Foundation type: Independent foundation.
Financial data (yr. ended 12/31/05): Assets,
$7,446,725 (M); expenditures, $430,653;
qualifying distributions, $396,673; giving activities
include $330,000 for 7 grants (high: $100,000;
low: $10,000).
Purpose and activities: Giving primarily for
education; some support also for environmental
conservation and animal welfare.
Fields of interest: Elementary/secondary
education; Environment, natural resources;
Animals/wildlife, preservation/protection;
Hospitals (general).

Type of support: General/operating support; Annual
campaigns; Capital campaigns; Building/
renovation; Land acquisition; Emergency funds;
Matching/challenge support.
Limitations: Applications not accepted. Giving
primarily in southern ME. No grants to individuals, or
for scholarships.
Publications: Annual report.
Application information: Contributes only to
pre-selected organizations.
Board meeting date(s): July and Aug.
Officers and Directors:* Diana B. Dunnan,* Pres.;
Rev. D. Stuart Dunnan,* V.P.; Winifred D. Faust,*
V.P.; Joan W. Trimble,* V.P.; Douglas W. Brandrup,
Secy.-Treas.
EIN: 133039728
Selected grants: The following grants were reported
in 2004.
$100,000 to Nature Conservancy, Brunswick, ME.
$100,000 to Saint James School, Saint James, MD.
$75,000 to York Hospital, York, ME.
$15,000 to Animal Welfare Society, West
Kennebunk, ME.
$10,000 to Laudholm Trust, Wells, ME.
$10,000 to Old York Historical Society, York, ME.

1488
Barnes Group Foundation, Inc. ✧
123 Main St.
Bristol, CT 06010

Incorporated in 1973 in CT.
Donor: Barnes Group Inc.
Foundation type: Company-sponsored foundation.
Financial data (yr. ended 12/31/05): Assets,
$37,549 (M); gifts received, $756,034;
expenditures, $1,094,740; qualifying distributions,
$1,093,819; giving activities include $1,063,163
for 599 grants (high: $160,225; low: $30).
Purpose and activities: The foundation supports
organizations involved with arts and culture,
education, health, and cancer.
Fields of interest: Media, television; Performing
arts; Arts; Higher education; Business school/
education; Education; Hospitals (general); Health
care; Cancer; American Red Cross; Federated giving
programs.
Type of support: General/operating support; Annual
campaigns; Endowments; Employee-related
scholarships.
Limitations: Giving primarily in areas of company
operations, with emphasis on CT. No grants to
individuals (except for employee-related
scholarships).
Application information:
Initial approach: Contact foundation for
application information
Deadline(s): None
Officers and Directors: Edmund M. Carpenter,
Pres.; William C. Denninger, V.P.; Thomas O.
Barnes, Secy.; John R. Arrington; Signe S. Gates.
Trustee: Bank of America, N.A.
EIN: 237339727
Selected grants: The following grants were reported
in 2004.
$311,000 to Scholarship America, Saint Peter, MN.
2 grants: $155,500 each
$144,962 to United Way. 2 grants: $60,339,
$84,623
$12,000 to Greater Hartford Arts Center, Hartford,
CT.
$10,000 to Connecticut Public Broadcasting,
Hartford, CT.

$5,000 to Farmington Village Green and Library
Association, Farmington, CT.
$500 to Huntington House Museum, Windsor, CT.
$500 to Vermont Community Foundation,
Middlebury, VT.
$400 to Saint Catherines High School, Racine, WI.

1489
The Bauer Foundation ✧
128 Dunning Rd.
New Canaan, CT 06840-4010

Established in 1989 in CT and GA.
Donor: George P. Bauer.
Foundation type: Independent foundation.
Financial data (yr. ended 12/31/05): Assets,
$19,824,316 (M); gifts received, $2,070,000;
expenditures, $998,810; qualifying distributions,
$998,010; giving activities include $935,500 for 11
grants (high: $750,000; low: $2,000).
Purpose and activities: Giving primarily for health
care, including nursing and home care.
Fields of interest: Theological school/education;
Health care; Federated giving programs.
Limitations: Applications not accepted. Giving
primarily in CT. No grants to individuals.
Application information: Contributes only to
pre-selected organizations.
Officers: George P. Bauer, Pres.; Carol Bauer, Secy.
Board Members: Brad Bauer; Jocelyn Bauer;
Jennifer Bauer Toll.
EIN: 581861919
Selected grants: The following grants were reported
in 2003.
$500,000 to AmeriCares, Stamford, CT.
$50,000 to I Have A Dream Foundation, Norwalk,
CT. For after-school program.
$33,000 to Yale University, New Haven, CT. For
Center for Faith and Culture.
$25,000 to Luther Seminary, Saint Paul, MN. For
Center for Lifelong Learning.
$16,200 to Norwalk Hospital Association, Norwalk,
CT. For scholarship programs for nurses.
$10,000 to Canaan United Methodist Church,
Canaan, CT. For Cape Town, South Africa
homeless program.
$10,000 to Norwalk Community College, Norwalk,
CT. For scholarship program.
$10,000 to Norwalk River Rowing Association,
Norwalk, CT. For Reach Out and Row program.
$10,000 to United Way of New Canaan, New
Canaan, CT.
$5,000 to Boy Scouts of America, Connecticut
Yankee Council, Milford, CT. For scouting
program.

1490
Carl and Dorothy Bennett Foundation ✧
c/o Carl Bennett
28 Windrose Way
Greenwich, CT 06830-7232

Established in 1963.
Donors: Carl Bennett; Dorothy Bennett; Caldor, Inc.;
and members of the Bennett family.
Foundation type: Independent foundation.
Financial data (yr. ended 6/30/05): Assets,
$7,356,581 (M); gifts received, $6,000,000;
expenditures, $746,267; qualifying distributions,
$744,758; giving activities include $729,672 for 1
grant.

Fields of interest: Hospitals (general).
Limitations: Applications not accepted. Giving primarily in CT. No grants to individuals.
Application information: Contributes only to pre-selected organizations.
Officers and Directors:* Carl Bennett,* Pres.; Bruce Bennett,* V.P.; Marc Bennett,* V.P.; Robin B. Kanarek,* V.P.; Dorothy Bennett,* Treas.; Harold Karun; Malcolm Martin; Bruce Shapiro; Grace Tully.
EIN: 066051371
Selected grants: The following grants were reported in 2005.
$729,672 to Stamford Health Foundation, Stamford, CT. For improvements to hospital.

1491
Walter J. Berbecker and Lille A. Berbecker Scholarship Fund ◇
(formerly Walter J. Berbecker and Lille A. Webb Scholarship Fund)
c/o Cummings & Lockwood
P.O. Box 120
Stamford, CT 06904 (203) 351-4294
Contact: Robert A. Beer, Tr.

Established in 1988 in NY.
Foundation type: Independent foundation.
Financial data (yr. ended 2/28/05): Assets, $5,021,064 (M); gifts received, $16,023; expenditures, $815,939; qualifying distributions, $765,398; giving activities include $750,000 for 5 grants (high: $250,000; low: $50,000).
Purpose and activities: Giving primarily for higher education scholarships; funding also for medical research at universities.
Fields of interest: Higher education; Medical school/education; Scholarships/financial aid.
Limitations: Giving primarily in CT, FL, MA and NC. No grants to individuals.
Application information: Application form not required.
Initial approach: Letter
Deadline(s): None
Trustees: Robert A. Beer; F. Brower Moffitt.
EIN: 222801843
Selected grants: The following grants were reported in 2005.
$250,000 to Duke University, Durham, NC. For scholarships.
$250,000 to Wesleyan University, Middletown, CT. For scholarships.
$125,000 to Cystic Fibrosis Foundation, Bethesda, MD. For medical research.
$75,000 to Hazelden Foundation, Center City, MN. For scholarships.
$50,000 to Massachusetts General Hospital, Harvard Medical School, Boston, MA. For research on lyme disease.

1492
The Berkley Foundation, Inc. ◇
475 Steamboat Rd.
Greenwich, CT 06830
Contact: William R. Berkley, Pres.

Established in 1997 in NY.
Donors: William R. Berkley; W.R. Berkley Corp.
Foundation type: Operating foundation.
Financial data (yr. ended 12/31/04): Assets, $14,897,150 (M); expenditures, $1,731,911; qualifying distributions, $1,686,308; giving

activities include $1,683,889 for 48 grants (high: $500,000; low: $75).
Purpose and activities: Giving primarily for higher education, including to a school of business; funding also for a research library of American history, as well as for medical research, family and social services, and Jewish organizations.
Fields of interest: Museums (ethnic/folk arts); Higher education; Business school/education; Libraries (special); Education; Medical research, institute; Human services; Family services; Jewish federated giving programs.
Limitations: Giving primarily in New York, NY, as well as some funding in Lake Placid; some funding nationally, particularly in CT, Washington, DC, and MA. No grants to individuals.
Application information:
Initial approach: Letter
Officers and Directors:* William R. Berkley,* Pres.; Jack H. Nusbaum,* Secy.; Peter W. Schmidt.
EIN: 133947554
Selected grants: The following grants were reported in 2003.
$525,000 to Mercy College, Dobbs Ferry, NY.
$50,000 to Library of American Landscape History, Amherst, MA.
$50,000 to University of Connecticut Foundation, Storrs, CT.
$25,000 to Georgetown University, DC.
$25,000 to New York University, New York, NY.
$15,000 to Family Centers, Greenwich, CT.
$10,000 to American Antiquarian Society, Worcester, MA.
$5,000 to Jewish Theological Seminary of America, New York, NY.
$5,000 to New York Public Library, New York, NY.
$2,000 to Young Peoples Leadership Foundation, New York, NY.

1493
The Bingham Trust ◇
(formerly Mr. Bingham's Trust for Charity)
c/o Patricia F. Davidson
65 Parker Hill Rd. Ext.
Killingworth, CT 06419-2311

Trust established in 1935 in NY.
Donor: William Bingham II†.
Foundation type: Independent foundation.
Financial data (yr. ended 12/31/04): Assets, $54,466,644 (M); expenditures, $3,002,165; qualifying distributions, $2,689,530; giving activities include $2,538,450 for 9 grants (high: $750,000; low: $100,000).
Purpose and activities: Since its inception, the trust has confined its grants to a small group of institutions to achieve maximum philanthropic effect. Every five years it reviews its focus and may choose new fields of interest. Because its grant criteria are extremely narrow, all grantees are selected by invitation only after research by the trustees.
Fields of interest: Performing arts, music; Education, early childhood education; Environment; Crime/violence prevention, domestic violence; Economically disadvantaged.
Type of support: Land acquisition; Program development; Curriculum development; Research.
Limitations: Applications not accepted. No support for religious organizations. No grants to individuals, or for scholarships or fellowships.
Publications: Multi-year report.

Application information: Contributes only to pre-selected organizations.
Board meeting date(s): Quarterly
Trustees: Donald M. Barr; Patricia F. Davidson; U.S. Trust.
EIN: 136069740

1494
The Biondi Family Foundation ◇
555 Lake Ave.
Greenwich, CT 06830

Established in 2000 in CT.
Donors: Cynthia G. Biondi; Michael J. Biondi.
Foundation type: Independent foundation.
Financial data (yr. ended 5/31/05): Assets, $1,551,607 (M); gifts received, $1,000; expenditures, $547,800; qualifying distributions, $529,500; giving activities include $529,500 for 23 grants (high: $267,000; low: $500).
Purpose and activities: Giving primarily for education, children and youth services, and to a Presbyterian church; funding also for social services.
Fields of interest: Education; Human services; Children/youth, services; Protestant agencies & churches.
Limitations: Applications not accepted. Giving primarily in CT; funding also in NH and NY. No grants to individuals.
Application information: Contributes only to pre-selected organizations.
Trustees: Cynthia G. Biondi; Michael J. Biondi.
EIN: 061621058
Selected grants: The following grants were reported in 2005.
$267,000 to Brunswick School, Greenwich, CT.
$102,000 to Dartmouth College, Hanover, NH.
$20,000 to Greenwich Hospital, Greenwich, CT.
$10,000 to American Red Cross, Stamford, CT.
$6,000 to Breast Cancer Alliance, Greenwich, CT.
$3,000 to Homeboy Industries, Los Angeles, CA.
$2,500 to Legal Aid Society, New York, NY.
$1,000 to Childrens Day School, Riverside, CT.
$1,000 to Rape Foundation, North Hollywood, CA.
$500 to Amigos de las Americas, Mill Valley, CA.

1495
J. Walton Bissell Foundation, Inc. ◇
P.O. Box 370067
West Hartford, CT 06137 (860) 586-8201
Contact: J. Danford Anthony, Jr., C.E.O. and Pres.

Established in 1989 in CT as successor to J. Walton Bissell Foundation.
Donor: J. Walton Bissell†.
Foundation type: Independent foundation.
Financial data (yr. ended 12/31/05): Assets, $21,455,107 (M); expenditures, $1,253,523; qualifying distributions, $1,164,210; giving activities include $1,071,500 for 106 grants (high: $30,000; low: $4,000).
Purpose and activities: Giving primarily for the arts, and social services, including child welfare and programs for the blind; some support also for community affairs projects.
Fields of interest: Performing arts; Arts; Elementary/secondary education; Higher education; Education; Human services; Children/youth, services; Family services; Community development;

Christian agencies & churches; Disabilities, people with.

Type of support: General/operating support; Program development; Seed money.

Limitations: Giving primarily in the Connecticut River Valley area, with emphasis on the greater Hartford, CT, area. No grants to individuals, or for endowments.

Publications: Application guidelines.

Application information:

Initial approach: Letter

Copies of proposal: 1

Deadline(s): No set deadline; requests should be submitted 4 months before funding is needed

Officers and Trustees:* J. Danford Anthony, Jr., C.E.O. and Pres.; Philip Reynolds,* Secy.-Treas.; Hyacinth Douglas-Bailey; Grace S. Webb.

EIN: 061245402

Selected grants: The following grants were reported in 2004.

$30,000 to New England Kurn Hattin Homes, Westminster, VT.

$20,000 to Hartford Symphony Orchestra, Hartford, CT.

$16,000 to National Braille Press, Boston, MA.

$15,000 to American School for the Deaf, West Hartford, CT.

$12,500 to Community Renewal Team, Hartford, CT.

$12,000 to Trust House, Hartford, CT.

$10,000 to Hartford School of Music, Hartford, CT.

$10,000 to Junior League of Hartford, Hartford, CT.

$10,000 to Mercy Housing and Shelter Corporation, Hartford, CT.

$10,000 to Shelter for Women, Hartford, CT.

1496

The Bluebell Foundation ✧

c/o Judith L. Biggs, Tr.
390 Riversville Rd.
Greenwich, CT 06831

Established in 2003 in CT.

Donor: Judith L. Biggs.

Foundation type: Independent foundation.

Financial data (yr. ended 12/31/05): Assets, $8,684,648 (M); gifts received, $2,012,474; expenditures, $471,596; qualifying distributions, $420,100; giving activities include $420,100 for 14 grants (high: $120,100; low: $2,000).

Fields of interest: Performing arts, orchestra (symphony); Higher education; Education; Children/ youth, services; International affairs, foreign policy; Christian agencies & churches.

Limitations: Applications not accepted. Giving primarily in Greenwich, CT, Sun Valley, ID, and NY. No grants to individuals.

Application information: Contributes only to pre-selected organizations.

Trustee: Judith L. Biggs.

EIN: 364527728

1497

Bodenwein Public Benevolent Foundation

c/o Bank of America, N.A., Fdns. and Philanthropic Svcs.
777 Main St., CT2-102-22-02
Hartford, CT 06115

Contact: Amy R. Lynch, V.P., Bank of America, N.A.

Established in 1938 in CT.

Donors: The Day Trust; Theodore Bodenwein†.

Foundation type: Independent foundation.

Financial data (yr. ended 12/31/05): Assets, $514,351 (M); gifts received, $386,998; expenditures, $362,274; qualifying distributions, $358,305; giving activities include $350,958 for 65 grants (high: $14,000; low: $1,000).

Purpose and activities: Giving to social service and health agencies, including AIDS support, the fine and performing arts and other cultural programs, youth and child welfare agencies, civic affairs and community development groups, education, and minority programs.

Fields of interest: Visual arts; Museums; Performing arts; Performing arts, theater; Language/linguistics; Literature; Arts; Education, early childhood education; Child development, education; Adult/ continuing education; Adult education—literacy, basic skills & GED; Libraries/library science; Education, reading; Education; Environment; Animal welfare; Hospitals (general); Reproductive health, family planning; Medical care, rehabilitation; Health care; Substance abuse, services; Mental health/ crisis services; Health organizations, association; Alcoholism; Cancer research; AIDS research; Legal services; Youth development, services; Human services; Children/youth, services; Child development, services; Family services; Aging, centers/services; Women, centers/services; Minorities/immigrants, centers/services; Community development; Voluntarism promotion; Jewish federated giving programs; Engineering/ technology; Science; Government/public administration; Transportation; Leadership development; Religion; Aging; Minorities; Women.

Type of support: Capital campaigns; Equipment; Program development; Publication; Seed money; Scholarship funds; Matching/challenge support.

Limitations: Giving limited to Lyme, Old Lyme, East Lyme, Waterford, New London, Montville, Groton, Ledyard, Stonington, and North Stonington, CT.

Publications: Informational brochure (including application guidelines).

Application information: Each applicant may submit only 1 grant application per calendar year. Application form required.

Copies of proposal: 5

Deadline(s): May 15 and Nov. 15

Board meeting date(s): Jan. and July

Final notification: Jan. and July

Trustee: Bank of America, N.A.

EIN: 066030548

1498

Boehringer Ingelheim Cares Foundation, Inc. ▼

900 Ridgebury Rd.
Ridgefield, CT 06877

Contact: Amy Fry, Pres.

URL: http://us.boehringer-ingelheim.com/ about-us/philanthropy.html

Established as a company-sponsored operating foundation in 2001 in CT.

Donor: Boehringer Ingelheim Pharmaceuticals, Inc.

Foundation type: Operating foundation.

Financial data (yr. ended 12/31/05): Assets, $18,549,163 (M); gifts received, $162,576,935; expenditures, $152,981,275; qualifying distributions, $152,981,275; giving activities include $2,456,824 for 122 grants (high: $233,000; low: $480), and $145,539,730 for grants to individuals.

Purpose and activities: The foundation supports organizations involved with arts and culture, education, health, disaster relief, and human services and provides Boehringer Ingelheim pharmaceuticals to patients in need. Special emphasis is directed toward programs designed to provide access to medical care and improve math and scientific skills.

Fields of interest: Arts; Education; Health care, equal rights; Health care; Disasters, preparedness/ services; Human services; Science, formal/general education; Mathematics; Economically disadvantaged.

Type of support: General/operating support; Program development; Research; Employee volunteer services; Grants to individuals; Donated products.

Limitations: Giving primarily in northern Fairfield County, CT. No support for political or religious organizations.

Application information: Application form required.

Initial approach: Download application form and mail to foundation

Copies of proposal: 1

Deadline(s): None

Final notification: 1 month

Officers: Amy Fry, Pres.; Frank Pomer, Secy.-Treas.

Directors: J. Martin Carroll; Franz Josef Goergen; Hermann Tetzner.

EIN: 311810072

Selected grants: The following grants were reported in 2004.

$300,000 to University of Connecticut Foundation, School of Pharmacy, Storrs, CT.

$206,712 to United Way of Northern Fairfield County, Danbury, CT. For annual campaign and programs.

$126,132 to Yale University, Office of Development, New Haven, CT. For STARS (Science, Technology and Research Scholars) Program, supporting racial/ethnic minorities, women and physically challenged students in science and engineering majors.

$115,000 to Connecticut United for Research Excellence, New Haven, CT. For research programs and Connecticut BioBus.

$109,186 to Pharmaceutical Research and Manufacturers of America Foundation, DC. For annual support.

$68,935 to United Way of Central Ohio, Columbus, OH. For annual campaign and programs.

$50,000 to National AIDS Treatment Advocacy Project, New York, NY. For HIV Treatment Education Programs.

$50,000 to Science Horizons, Danbury, CT. For Science Fairs.

$50,000 to Stony Brook Foundation, Stony Brook, NY. For program support.

$45,000 to Ability Beyond Disability, Bethel, CT. For annual support.

1499

The Bondi Foundation ✧ ☆

c/o Wagga Enterprises
1 E. Putnam Ave.
Greenwich, CT 06830

Contact: Kim Margaret Bible, Pres.

Established in 1998 in DE.

Donor: Geoffrey Cyril Maitland Bible.

Foundation type: Independent foundation.

Financial data (yr. ended 12/31/05): Assets, $8,562,442 (M); expenditures, $335,082;

qualifying distributions, $330,000; giving activities include $330,000 for grants.
Fields of interest: Arts; Health care; Children, services; Family services, counseling; Aging; Economically disadvantaged.
Limitations: Giving primarily in AZ, CT, and NY.
Application information:
   Initial approach: Letter
   Deadline(s): None
Officers: Kim Margaret Bible, Pres.; Sara Curtis McDonald Bible, V.P.; Geoffrey Cyril Maitland Bible, Secy.
EIN: 134015931

1500
The Lawrence A. Bossidy Foundation ◇ ☆
452 W. Mountain Rd.
Ridgefield, CT   06877

Established in 1986 in CT.
Donor: Lawrence A. Bossidy.
Foundation type: Independent foundation.
Financial data (yr. ended 12/31/05): Assets, $4,908,559 (M); gifts received, $1,002,794; expenditures, $445,789; qualifying distributions, $440,897; giving activities include $440,897 for 23 grants (high: $123,347; low: $100).
Purpose and activities: Giving primarily to health associations and to Christian agencies and churches.
Fields of interest: Performing arts, theater; Health organizations, association; Cancer research; Federated giving programs; Christian agencies & churches; Roman Catholic agencies & churches.
Type of support: General/operating support.
Limitations: Applications not accepted. Giving primarily in the northeastern U.S., with emphasis on CT. No grants to individuals.
Application information: Contributes only to pre-selected organizations.
Trustee: Lawrence A. Bossidy.
EIN: 061188527
Selected grants: The following grants were reported in 2004.
  $92,000 to Saint Marys Roman Catholic Church, Ridgefield, CT.
  $28,750 to Westport Country Playhouse, Westport, CT.
  $25,000 to Damon Runyon Cancer Research Foundation, New York, NY.
  $10,000 to National Center for Learning Disabilities, New York, NY.
  $10,000 to Ridgefield Library and Historical Association, Ridgefield, CT.
  $2,000 to Boys and Girls Club of Ridgefield, Ridgefield, CT.
  $1,150 to Visiting Nurse Association of Ridgefield, Ridgefield, CT.
  $1,000 to Colgate University, Hamilton, NY.
  $1,000 to Regis College, Weston, MA.
  $100 to Ridgefield Volunteer Fire Department, Ridgefield, CT.

1501
Donald C. Brace Foundation ◇
30 Maltbie Rd.
Newtown, CT   06470
Contact: Robert A. Beer, Tr.

Established in 1987 in CT.
Donor: Donna Brace Ogilvie.

Foundation type: Independent foundation.
Financial data (yr. ended 12/31/05): Assets, $6,446,206 (M); expenditures, $694,638; qualifying distributions, $610,100; giving activities include $587,600 for 14 grants (high: $150,000; low: $5,000).
Fields of interest: Arts; Education; Hospitals (general); Children/youth, services; Federated giving programs.
Limitations: Giving primarily in Stamford, CT, and Westhampton, NY; some giving nationally.
Application information:
   Initial approach: Letter
   Deadline(s): None
Trustees: Robert A. Beer; Katharine Butler; John Brace Latham; Donna Brace Ogilvie; Karen Scheid.
EIN: 133442680
Selected grants: The following grants were reported in 2004.
  $250,000 to Phillips Academy, Andover, MA. 2 grants: $150,000 (For Richard L. Gelb Science Center), $100,000 (For restoration of Bell Tower).
  $150,000 to Girls Inc. of Stamford, Stamford, CT. For endowments.
  $150,000 to Stamford Health Foundation, Stamford, CT. For Brace Community Conference Center.
  $90,950 to Girls Inc. of Sarasota, Sarasota, FL. For restoration of kitchen.
  $20,000 to Academy at Charlemont, Charlemont, MA. For scholarships.
  $16,500 to Friends of the Teton River, Driggs, ID. For education and outreach director.
  $15,000 to Westhampton Cultural Consortium, Westhampton Beach, NY. For concerts on Village Green in Westhampton Beach.
  $10,000 to Cooper Union for the Advancement of Science and Art, New York, NY. For endowments and funds for art school.
  $5,000 to Transitional Living Center, Lancaster, PA.

1502
The Lyman B. Brainerd Family Foundation, Inc. ◇ ☆
16 Kenmore Rd.
Bloomfield, CT   06002

Established in 1993 in CT.
Donor: Judith B. Brainerd.
Foundation type: Independent foundation.
Financial data (yr. ended 12/31/05): Assets, $2,692,228 (M); expenditures, $537,015; qualifying distributions, $518,507; giving activities include $500,000 for 18 grants (high: $156,000; low: $250).
Purpose and activities: Giving primarily for education and athletics.
Fields of interest: Arts; Education; Athletics/sports, amateur leagues; Children/youth, services.
Type of support: Scholarship funds.
Limitations: Applications not accepted. Giving on a national basis. No grants to individuals.
Application information: Contributes only to pre-selected organizations.
Officers: Richard P. Brainerd, Pres.; Lyman B. Brainerd, Jr., Secy.
EIN: 061387773

1503
Bridgemill Foundation ◇
c/o John H. T. Wilson
9 Sawmill Ln.
Greenwich, CT   06830

Established in 1992 in DE and CT.
Donor: John H.T. Wilson.
Foundation type: Independent foundation.
Financial data (yr. ended 12/31/04): Assets, $7,475,266 (M); expenditures, $432,960; qualifying distributions, $403,753; giving activities include $400,500 for 70 grants (high: $40,000; low: $250).
Purpose and activities: Giving primarily for higher education, health associations, and children's and social services.
Fields of interest: Performing arts; Higher education; Education; Animals/wildlife; Hospitals (general); Health organizations, association; Human services; Children, services; International affairs; Foundations (community); Federated giving programs.
Limitations: Applications not accepted. Giving primarily in CT and NY. No grants to individuals.
Application information: Contributes only to pre-selected organizations.
Officers: John H.T. Wilson, Pres.; Sandra W. Wilson, V.P.
EIN: 133671059

1504
The Greater Bridgeport Area Foundation, Inc.
211 State St., 3rd Fl.
Bridgeport, CT   06604   (203) 334-7511
Contact: Cindy S. Kissin, C.E.O.; For grants: Anne Watkins, Dir., Progs.
FAX: (203) 333-4652;
E-mail: info@gbafoundation.org; Grant information E-mail: awatkins@gbafoundation.org; URL: http://www.gbafoundation.org

Incorporated in 1967 in CT.
Foundation type: Community foundation.
Financial data (yr. ended 12/31/05): Assets, $39,936,927 (M); gifts received, $825,359; expenditures, $1,939,641; giving activities include $857,780 for 281 grants (high: $26,000; low: $50), $172,433 for 132 grants to individuals (high: $15,000; low: $250), and $101,760 for 1 foundation-administered program.
Purpose and activities: The foundation's mission is to participate actively in shaping the well-being of the region. Giving in the form of grants and scholarships to organizations and students in the foundation's community. The foundation also runs a non-profit resource center to support the organizational development of the non-profit community.
Fields of interest: Arts education; Performing arts, dance; Performing arts, theater; Performing arts, music; Arts; Higher education; Education; Environment, public education; Environment; Health care; Mental health/crisis services; Legal services; Employment; Housing/shelter; Recreation; Youth development; Human services; Economic development; Nonprofit management; Community development.
Type of support: General/operating support; Continuing support; Management development/capacity building; Program development; Conferences/seminars; Seed money; Technical

assistance; Consulting services; Program evaluation; Scholarships—to individuals.

Limitations: Giving through competitive process for programs in Bridgeport, Easton, Fairfield, Milford, Monroe, Shelton, Stratford, Southbury, Trumbull, and Westport, CT. No support for religious purposes or for-profit organizations. No grants to individuals (except for scholarships), or for annual appeals, major capital campaigns, deficit financing, endowments, or memorials; no loans.

Publications: Application guidelines; Annual report; Financial statement.

Application information: Visit foundation Web site for application form and guidelines. Letter of Inquiry approval is required before application submission. Application form required.

   Initial approach: Letter of Inquiry form
   Copies of proposal: 1
   Deadline(s): Jan. 15 and July 15 for Letter of Inquiry form; Mar. 1 and Sept. 1 for full proposal; June 1 for scholarships
   Board meeting date(s): Mar., June, and Nov.; distribution committee meets in June and Nov.
   Final notification: June 15 and Dec. 15

Officers and Directors:* Peter F. Hurst, Jr.,* Chair.; Ron Noren,* Vice-Chair.; Cindy S. Kissin, C.E.O. and Pres.; Julie Mauri, V.P., Comms. and Devel.; Margaret M. "Peg" Sheahan,* Secy.; David Sullivan III,* Treas.; Octavio G. Choy, M.D.; Marshal D. Gibson; Mickey Herbert; Joseph Hoffman; Richard M. Hoyt; John A. Klein; Jim Kreitler; Robert H. Laska; Thomas D. Lenci; George B. Longstreth III; Fred McKinney, Ph.D.; Janice Park.

Number of staff: 7 full-time professional; 1 full-time support; 1 part-time support.

EIN: 066103832

1505
Broadcasters Foundation, Inc. ✧ ☆
7 Lincoln Ave.
Greenwich, CT 06830
Contact: Gordon Hastings, C.E.O. and Pres.

Established in 1942.

Foundation type: Independent foundation.

Financial data (yr. ended 12/31/05): Assets, $1,928,329 (M); gifts received, $1,268,192; expenditures, $1,478,602; qualifying distributions, $520,033; giving activities include $520,033 for grants to individuals.

Purpose and activities: Giving primarily to indigent persons; support for educational scholarships.

Type of support: Grants to individuals; Scholarships—to individuals.

Publications: Newsletter.

Application information: Contributes only to members of the broadcast industry and their families. Application form required.

   Initial approach: Letter
   Deadline(s): None

Officers: Philip J. Lombardo, Co-Chair.; Edward McLaughlin, Co-Chair.; Gordon H. Hastings, C.E.O. and Pres.; Philip R. Beuth, V.P.; Richard A. Foreman, V.P.; Lucille F. Luongo, V.P.; Diane Linen Powell, Secy.; Arthur M. Angstreich, Treas.

Directors: David Abramson; David Barrett; Martin Beck; Arthur Carlson; James E. Champlin; Peggy Conlon; Vincent Curtis; Aaron Daniels; Erica Farber; Gary Fries; Edward O. Fritts; Ragan Henry; Catherine Hughes; John A. Knebel; M. Scott Knight; Jerry Lee; Anthony Malara; Stanley M. Moger; Dawson Nail; Deborah Noville; William O'Shaughnessy; Frances

Preston; Edward T. Reilly; Joseph Reiley; Dennis Swanson; Sherril Taylor; Nick Verbitsky.

Number of staff: 2 full-time professional; 1 part-time professional.

EIN: 131975618

1506
The Louis Calder Foundation ▼
175 Elm St.
New Canaan, CT 06840   (203) 966-8925
Contact: Holly Nuechterlein, Grant Prog. Mgr.
FAX: (203) 966-5785; E-mail: admin@calderfdn.org;
URL: http://www.louiscalderfdn.org

Trust established in 1951 in NY.

Donor: Louis Calder‡.

Foundation type: Independent foundation.

Financial data (yr. ended 10/31/05): Assets, $147,799,970 (M); expenditures, $8,463,684; qualifying distributions, $7,287,111; giving activities include $6,572,550 for 120 grants (high: $600,000; low: $1,000; average: $10,000–$100,000).

Purpose and activities: Giving primarily in the area of K-12 education to promote the educational and scholastic development of children and youth by improving academic content at charter and parochial schools and at community based organizations.

Fields of interest: Elementary/secondary education.

Type of support: Capital campaigns; Building/renovation; Program development; Curriculum development; Matching/challenge support.

Limitations: Giving primarily in the greater New York, NY, metropolitan area and surrounding areas. No support for political organizations, private foundations, or governmental organizations. No grants to individuals.

Publications: Annual report (including application guidelines); Financial statement; Grants list.

Application information: Full proposals may only be submitted if requested by the foundation. The foundation accepts the NYRAG application form.

   Initial approach: Letter of inquiry
   Copies of proposal: 1
   Deadline(s): See foundation's Web site for deadlines
   Board meeting date(s): Monthly

Trustees: Paul R. Brenner; Peter D. Calder; JPMorgan Chase Bank, N.A.

Number of staff: 1 full-time professional; 2 full-time support.

EIN: 136015562

Selected grants: The following grants were reported in 2004.

$955,500 to Patrons Program, New York, NY. 2 grants: $855,500 (To enhance out-of-school-time educational activities at archdiocese schools), $100,000 (For Library Connections program, revitalizing inner-city elementary school libraries).

$300,000 to American Museum of Natural History, New York, NY. For education website.

$217,020 to College of Saint Rose, Albany, NY. To develop, design, implement and evaluate model program based on replicable curriculum to allow middle school students to explore mathematics, science, technology, history, drama and literature through College-sponsored summer camp.

$200,000 to New Visions for Public Schools, New York, NY. For Small High Schools Library Initiative.

$150,000 to Cristo Rey High School, New York, NY. For building renovations for new high school.

$100,000 to Brooklyn Jesuit Prep, Brooklyn, NY. For renovations to electrical system.

$100,000 to Gilder Lehrman Institute of American History, New York, NY. For expansion of middle school program and related Saturday Academy and Summer Seminar.

$75,000 to Explore Charter School, Friends of, New York, NY. For Saturday Academy, instructional technology services, technology consultants, art, music, physical education and classroom supplies, and computer-related capital needs.

$75,000 to Legal Outreach, New York, NY. To support expansion goals and objectives.

1507
Marjorie Sells Carter Boy Scout Scholarship Fund ✧
c/o Cummings & Lockwood (RAB)
P.O. Box 120
Stamford, CT 06904   (203) 351-4294
Application address: c/o Joan Shaffer, P.O. Box 527, Chatham, MA 02269

Established in 1974.

Donor: Marjorie Sells Carter‡.

Foundation type: Independent foundation.

Financial data (yr. ended 8/31/03): Assets, $25,408 (M); expenditures, $1,262,867; qualifying distributions, $1,261,524; giving activities include $1,260,948 for 3 grants (high: $420,316; low: $420,316).

Purpose and activities: Awards undergraduate scholarships only to New England high school seniors demonstrating achievement and leadership in the Boy Scouts.

Limitations: Giving limited to New England.

Application information: Application form required.

   Deadline(s): Apr. 1

Trustees: Robert A. Beer; John P. Hammond; Wachovia Bank, N.A.

Number of staff: 1 part-time support.

EIN: 066174937

1508
Cheryl Chase & Stuart Bear Family Foundation, Inc. ✧
c/o Chase Enterprises
225 Asylum St., 29th Fl.
Hartford, CT 06103   (860) 549-1674
Contact: John P. Redding, V.P.

Established in 2000 in CT.

Donor: Cheryl A. Chase.

Foundation type: Independent foundation.

Financial data (yr. ended 9/30/05): Assets, $2,248,469 (M); gifts received, $1,128,633; expenditures, $1,284,832; qualifying distributions, $1,192,631; giving activities include $1,190,519 for 69 grants (high: $582,900; low: $45).

Fields of interest: Media, television; Museums (art); Performing arts; Performing arts centers; Performing arts, theater; Performing arts, orchestra (symphony); Performing arts, opera; Arts; Education; Hospitals (general); Human services; Federated giving programs.

Limitations: Giving primarily in CT, with some emphasis on Hartford. No grants to individuals.

Application information: Application form not required.

Initial approach: Letter
Deadline(s): None
Officers and Directors: * Cheryl A. Chase, Chair. and Pres.; Stuart Bear,* Exec. V.P.; John P. Redding, V.P.; Arnold L. Chase; David T. Chase.
EIN: 061562154

1509

The Rhoda & David Chase Family Foundation, Inc. ✧

(formerly The Chase Family Foundation, Inc.)
c/o Chase Enterprises, Inc.
Goodwin Sq., 225 Asylum St.
Hartford, CT 06103 (860) 549-1674
Contact: John P. Redding, V.P.

Established in 1997 in CT.
Donor: Rhoda L. Chase.
Foundation type: Independent foundation.
Financial data (yr. ended 9/30/05): Assets, $7,403,988 (L); gifts received, $27,079; expenditures, $3,256,226; qualifying distributions, $3,226,112; giving activities include $3,224,107 for 135 grants (high: $1,000,000; low: $18).
Fields of interest: Health care; Health organizations, association; Foundations (community); Jewish agencies & temples.
Limitations: Giving primarily in Hartford, CT.
Application information: Application form not required.
Deadline(s): None
Officers: Rhoda L. Chase, V.P.; John P. Redding, V.P.; Theresa Kasuga, Secy.
Director: David T. Chase.
EIN: 061499922
Selected grants: The following grants were reported in 2004.
$863,000 to Rabbinical College of America, Morristown, NJ.
$30,100 to University of Hartford, West Hartford, CT.
$1,000 to Womens American ORT, New York, NY.
$300 to New England Cognitive Center, Hartford, CT.
$180 to Hebrew High School of New England, West Hartford, CT.
$100 to Greater Hartford Academy of the Arts, Hartford, CT.

1510

The Jane Coffin Childs Memorial Fund for Medical Research ✧

333 Cedar St., SHM L300 MC 0191
P.O. Box 20800
New Haven, CT 06520-8000 (203) 785-4612
Contact: Kim Roberts, Admin. Dir.
FAX: (203) 785-3301; E-mail: jccFund@yale.edu

Trust established in 1937 in CT.
Donors: Alice S. Coffin†; Starling W. Childs†; John W. Childs; Merck & Co., Inc.; Agouron Institute; Torrington Area Foundation; Heiman/Fidelity Foundation.
Foundation type: Independent foundation.
Financial data (yr. ended 6/30/05): Assets, $40,112,466 (M); gifts received, $552,822; expenditures, $3,539,118; qualifying distributions, $3,447,342; giving activities include $77,852 for 2 grants (high: $56,873; low: $20,979), and $3,136,039 for 77 grants to individuals (high: $44,917; low: $7,167).

Purpose and activities: Giving primarily for medical research into the causes, origins and treatment of cancer. Grants to institutions only for support of cancer research fellowships.
Fields of interest: Medical research, institute; Cancer research.
Type of support: Fellowships; Research.
Limitations: Giving primarily in CA, MA, and NY; some funding nationally. No grants to individuals (except for fellowships), or for building or endowment funds, matching gifts, or general purposes; no loans.
Publications: Application guidelines; Annual report; Program policy statement.
Application information: Applicants for fellowships in general should not be more than 2 years post-doctoral. They must hold either an M.D. or a Ph.D. in the field in which they propose to study. Applicants may be citizens of any country, but foreign nationals awards will be made only for study in the U.S. American citizens may hold a fellowship either in the U.S. or in a foreign country. The initial appointment may be for 2 or 3 years. Application form required.
Initial approach: Letter or telephone
Copies of proposal: 5
Deadline(s): Jan. 1
Board meeting date(s): Oct. or Nov. and Apr. or May
Final notification: May
Officers and Managers: * William G. Gridley, Jr.,* Chair.; James E. Childs,* Vice-Chair.; John W. Childs, Secy.; Hendon C. Pingeon,* Treas.; Robert N. Schmalz, Legal Counsel; John W. Barclay; Richard S. Childs, Jr., M.D.; Charles H. Collins; Elizabeth Childs Gill; Starling R. Lawrence; Adair P. Mali; Frederic M. Richards.
Number of staff: 1 full-time professional; 1 full-time support.
EIN: 066034840

1511

The Chilton Foundation ✧

(formerly The Chilton Family Foundation)
1266 E. Main St., 7th Fl.
Stamford, CT 06902 (203) 352-4080
Contact: Jenny Goldstock Wright
E-mail: jgoldstockwright@chiltonfoundation.com

Established in 1995 in NY.
Donors: Richard Lockwood Chilton, Jr.; Mrs. Richard Lockwood Chilton, Jr.
Foundation type: Independent foundation.
Financial data (yr. ended 12/31/03): Assets, $19,409,453 (M); gifts received, $10,000,000; expenditures, $1,902,267; qualifying distributions, $1,874,027; giving activities include $1,839,283 for 53 grants (high: $500,000; low: $500).
Fields of interest: Museums (art); Historic preservation/historical societies; Arts; Education; Human services.
Type of support: Scholarship funds; Matching/challenge support; General/operating support; Emergency funds; Capital campaigns; Annual campaigns.
Limitations: Giving primarily in CT, MA, and NY. No grants to individuals.
Application information: 1 copy of initial proposal and 5 of final proposal required. Application form not required.
Initial approach: E-mail or letter of inquiry
Deadline(s): Varies

Board meeting date(s): Four times a year (changes annually)
Final notification: Varies
Trustees: Maureen K. Chilton; Richard Lockwood Chilton, Jr.; Patricia Mallon.
EIN: 137077903
Selected grants: The following grants were reported in 2003.
$500,000 to Robin Hood Foundation, New York, NY. For general support.
$375,000 to Winterthur Museum, Garden and Library, Winterthur, DE. For general support.
$50,000 to Groton School, Groton, MA. For annual fund.
$25,000 to New-York Historical Society, New York, NY. For general support.
$20,000 to New Life of New York City, New York, NY. For general support.
$16,000 to Harlem Childrens Zone, New York, NY. For general support.
$10,000 to New York City Opera, New York, NY. For general support.
$5,000 to Darien Library, Darien, CT. For general support.
$1,000 to East Harlem Tutorial Program, New York, NY. For general support.
$1,000 to Historic House Trust of New York City, New York, NY. For general support.

1512

Steven A. and Alexandra M. Cohen Foundation ▼ ✧

c/o Stephen Canna, SAC Capital Advisors, LLC
72 Cummings Point Rd.
Stamford, CT 06902

Established in 2001 in CT.
Donors: Stephen Canna; Alexandra M. Cohen; Steven A. Cohen; Sac Capital Advisors, LLC.
Foundation type: Independent foundation.
Financial data (yr. ended 12/31/05): Assets, $6,059,330 (M); gifts received, $13,465,560; expenditures, $8,044,794; qualifying distributions, $8,037,545; giving activities include $8,030,670 for 174 grants (high: $1,000,000; low: $35; average: $2,000–$100,000).
Purpose and activities: Giving primarily to a foundation concerned with people who are economically disadvantaged; funding also for health as well as to a hospital, youth services, and social services, including a YWCA.
Fields of interest: Hospitals (general); Autism; Human services; YM/YWCAs & YM/YWHAs; Youth, services; Philanthropy/voluntarism; Economically disadvantaged.
Limitations: Applications not accepted. Giving primarily in CT and NY.
Application information: Contributes only to pre-selected organizations.
Officers: Alexandra M. Cohen, Pres. and Secy.; Steven A. Cohen, V.P. and Treas.
EIN: 061627638
Selected grants: The following grants were reported in 2004.
$1,090,000 to Convent of the Sacred Heart, Greenwich, CT. 3 grants: $40,000 (For youth services), $50,000 (For youth services), $1,000,000 (For school-linked services for children and youth).
$550,000 to Robin Hood Foundation, New York, NY. 2 grants: $300,000, $250,000
$100,000 to Make-A-Wish Foundation of Connecticut, Trumbull, CT.

$50,000 to Harlem Childrens Zone, New York, NY.

$50,000 to Joe Torre Safe at Home Foundation, Harrison, NY.

$25,000 to Foundation Fighting Blindness, New York, NY.

$20,000 to Coalition for Hispanic Family Services, Brooklyn, NY.

1513
The Collis Foundation
24 Calhoun Dr.
Greenwich, CT 06831
Contact: Astrid C. Womble, Pres.

Established in 1997 in RI.
Donor: Charles A. Collis.
Foundation type: Independent foundation.
Financial data (yr. ended 2/28/06): Assets, $8,062,669 (M); expenditures, $431,492; qualifying distributions, $431,492; giving activities include $342,000 for 24 grants (high: $50,000; low: $2,500).
Purpose and activities: The primary focus is on children's education, scholarships and literacy programs, and basic human needs.
Fields of interest: Education, reading; Education; Food services; Human services.
Type of support: General/operating support; Continuing support; Annual campaigns; Capital campaigns; Building/renovation; Endowments; Emergency funds; Program development; Scholarship funds; Matching/challenge support.
Limitations: Giving limited to the greater RI area. No support for environmental, rehabilitation, addiction or adoption programs.
Application information: Current grantees should contact the Executive Director before submitting a new proposal. Application form not required.
 Initial approach: Letter of inquiry
 Copies of proposal: 1
 Deadline(s): None
 Board meeting date(s): Spring and winter
 Final notification: Spring and winter
Officer and Directors:* Astrid C. Womble,* Pres.; Frohman Anderson; Charles A. Collis; Elfriede A. Collis.
Number of staff: 1 full-time professional.
EIN: 061472006
Selected grants: The following grants were reported in 2006.
$50,000 to San Miguel Education Center, Providence, RI.
$37,000 to Rhode Island Community Food Bank Association, Providence, RI.
$32,000 to Providence Public Library, Providence, RI.
$17,500 to Greenwich Academy, Greenwich, CT.
$17,500 to Moses Brown School, Providence, RI.
$10,500 to Save Blithewold, Bristol, RI.
$10,000 to Providence Childrens Museum, Providence, RI.
$5,000 to Old Colony Historical Society, Taunton, MA.
$2,500 to Gordon School, East Providence, RI.

1514
The Community Foundation for Greater New Haven ▼ ✧
(formerly The New Haven Foundation)
70 Audubon St.
New Haven, CT 06510-9755 (203) 777-2386
Contact: William W. Ginsberg, C.E.O.
FAX: (203) 787-6584; E-mail: contactus@cfgnh.org;
URL: http://www.cfgnh.org

Established in 1928 in CT by resolution and declaration of trust.
Foundation type: Community foundation.
Financial data (yr. ended 12/31/05): Assets, $245,930,290 (M); gifts received, $7,961,736; expenditures, $15,695,554; giving activities include $12,847,458 for grants, and $1,219,593 for foundation-administered programs.
Purpose and activities: The foundation seeks to create positive and sustainable change in Greater New Haven, CT by increasing the amount of and enhancing the impact of community philanthropy.
Fields of interest: Arts, multipurpose centers/programs; Arts, cultural/ethnic awareness; Arts; Education; Environment, beautification programs; Environment; Health care; Housing/shelter, development; Housing/shelter; Disasters, Hurricane Katrina; Recreation; Youth development; Community development, neighborhood development; Economic development; Business/industry; Community development.
Type of support: General/operating support; Continuing support; Capital campaigns; Building/renovation; Equipment; Emergency funds; Program development; Conferences/seminars; Seed money; Scholarship funds; Technical assistance; Consulting services; Program evaluation; Program-related investments/loans; Matching/challenge support.
Limitations: Giving primarily in greater New Haven, CT, and the lower Naugatuck River Valley. No support for religious activities. No grants to individuals (including direct scholarships), or for annual campaigns, deficit financing, endowment funds, research, fellowships, travel, or generally for capital projects.
Publications: Application guidelines; Annual report (including application guidelines); Financial statement; Informational brochure (including application guidelines); Newsletter.
Application information: Visit foundation Web site for application forms, guidelines, and specific deadlines. Application form required.
 Initial approach: Telephone
 Copies of proposal: 1
 Deadline(s): Varies
 Board meeting date(s): Varies
 Final notification: Within 10 days of board meeting
Officers and Directors:* Barbara L. Pearce,* Chair.; Frederick P. Leaf,* Vice-Chair.; William W. Ginsberg, C.E.O. and Pres.; A.F. Drew Alden, Sr. V.P., Finance, Investments, and Admin.; Laura A. Berry, Sr. V.P., Philanthropic Svcs.; Leon Bailey, V.P., Human Resources; Bruce D. Alexander; Theodore L. Brooks, Sr.; Mary Jane Burt; James E. Cohen; John J. Crawford; Annie Garcia Kaplan; David R. Schaefer; Alan J. Tyma; Susan Whetstone.
Trustees: BankBoston Connecticut; Bank of America, N.A.; New Alliance Bank; Wachovia Bank, N.A.; Webster Trust Co., N.A.
Number of staff: 18 full-time professional; 8 full-time support.
EIN: 066032106

Selected grants: The following grants were reported in 2005.
$350,000 to New Haven International Festival of Arts and Ideas, New Haven, CT. 2 grants: $250,000 (For general operating support), $100,000 (For festival).
$150,000 to Long Wharf Theater, New Haven, CT. For general operating support.
$100,000 to Neighborhood Music School, New Haven, CT. For capital project providing building upgrades and addressing space needs.
$65,000 to High Hopes Therapeutic Riding, Old Lyme, CT. For programs to improve balance, posture, and emotional function.
$60,000 to Columbus House, New Haven, CT. For new shelter building.
$60,000 to Corporation for Supportive Housing, New Haven, CT. For Next Step Initiative, payable over 3 years.
$60,000 to Fellowship Place, New Haven, CT. For Therapeutic Riding and Equine Management Program.
$50,000 to Leeway, New Haven, CT. For full-time nurse practitioner and administrative costs, payable over 2 years.
$50,000 to New Haven Colony Historical Society, New Haven, CT. For general operating support.

1515
Community Foundation of Greater New Britain ✧
(formerly New Britain Foundation for Public Giving)
74A Vine St.
New Britain, CT 06052-1431 (860) 229-6018
Contact: James G. Williamson, Pres.
FAX: (860) 225-2666; E-mail: cfgnb@cfgnb.org;
Grant application E-mail: jwruck@cfgnb.org;
URL: http://www.cfgnb.org

Established in 1941 in CT.
Foundation type: Community foundation.
Financial data (yr. ended 12/31/04): Assets, $29,606,244 (M); gifts received, $457,144; expenditures, $1,557,254; giving activities include $722,444 for grants.
Purpose and activities: The foundation seeks to meet the needs of the greater New Britain, CT, community through support of programs dedicated to health and human services, education, community and economic development, the environment, arts and humanities, and civic affairs.
Fields of interest: Humanities; Arts; Child development, education; Secondary school/education; Libraries/library science; Education; Environment; Hospitals (general); Reproductive health, family planning; Health care; Substance abuse, services; Mental health/crisis services; Health organizations, association; Crime/violence prevention, domestic violence; Youth development, services; Children/youth, services; Child development, services; Family services; Aging, centers/services; Homeless, human services; Human services; Economic development; Community development; Leadership development; General charitable giving; Aging; Disabilities, people with; African Americans/Blacks; Hispanics/Latinos; AIDS, people with; Economically disadvantaged; Homeless.
Type of support: General/operating support; Continuing support; Capital campaigns; Building/renovation; Equipment; Emergency funds; Program development; Conferences/seminars; Seed money; Curriculum development; Technical assistance;

Consulting services; Scholarships—to individuals; Matching/challenge support.

Limitations: Giving limited to Berlin, New Britain, Plainville, and Southington, CT. No support for religious activities. No grants to individuals (except through scholarships), or for annual or endowment campaigns, budget deficits, or sponsorships.

Publications: Application guidelines; Annual report (including application guidelines); Financial statement; Grants list; Informational brochure; Newsletter.

Application information: Visit foundation Web site for application guidelines per grant type. Proposals should be no longer than 5 pages in length and contain a cover sheet. Application form not required.

   Initial approach: Letter or telephone
   Copies of proposal: 15
   Deadline(s): Jan. 15, Apr. 15, July 15, and Oct. 15
   Board meeting date(s): Mar., June, Sept., and Dec.
   Final notification: Following quarterly meeting

Officers and Directors:* Robert A. Scalise, Jr.,* Chair; Donna C. Lasher,* Vice-Chair. and Chair.-Elect; James G. Williamson, Pres. and Secy.; Charles Leach, Jr., M.D.*, Treas.; Louis G. "Gerry" Amodio; Charles W. Bauer; Rosemary Conway Beaupre; Geraldine Brown-Springer; Manon-Lu Christ; Rev. Leonard G. Clough; Charles "C.J." Jones; Andrew Meade; Gail E. Millerick; Rev. Hugh B. Penney.

Number of staff: 4 full-time professional; 1 part-time professional; 1 full-time support.

EIN: 066036461

1516
The Community Foundation of Northwest Connecticut, Inc.

(formerly Torrington Area Foundation for Public Giving)
32 City Hall Ave.
P.O. Box 1144
Torrington, CT   06790   (860) 626-1245
Contact: Guy Rovezzi, Pres.
FAX: (860) 489-7517; E-mail: info@cfnwct.org; Grant application E-mail: jobrien@cfnwct.org; URL: http://www.cfnwct.org

Established in 1969; Incorporated in 1999 in CT under Northwest Connecticut Community Foundation, Inc.

Donors: Carlton D. Fyler‡; Jenny R. Fyler‡; Robert Venn Carr; John H. Brooks‡; Margaret C. Tupper‡; Eva Coty‡; Vincent Stanulis‡; BankBoston, N.A. Fund; B.O.A.T. Fund; Brooks Bank Fund; First National Bank of Litchfield Fund; Torrington Savings Bank; Marion Wm. Edwards‡; Alice Edwards‡.

Foundation type: Community foundation.

Financial data (yr. ended 12/31/05): Assets, $12,402,278 (M); gifts received, $921,172; expenditures, $967,719; giving activities include $525,369 for 125 grants, and $105,275 for 163 grants to individuals.

Purpose and activities: The foundation seeks to enhance the quality of life for the citizens of its service area by: 1) identifying community needs and opportunities with a focus on the arts, education, the environment, health and social services; 2) responding to those needs and opportunities with grants to nonprofit 501(c)(3) organizations in an informed and responsible way; 3) providing financial assistance for higher education in the form of scholarships; 4) providing donors with a permanent

endowment for philanthropic giving; and 5) prudently investing those funds entrusted to it.

Fields of interest: Museums; Performing arts; Historic preservation/historical societies; Arts; Higher education; Libraries/library science; Education; Environment; Animal welfare; Hospitals (general); Health care; Mental health/crisis services; Housing/shelter; Recreation, parks/playgrounds; Recreation; Children/youth, services; Human services, emergency aid; Aging, centers/services; Human services; Community development.

Type of support: General/operating support; Continuing support; Equipment; Endowments; Emergency funds; Program development; Publication; Seed money; Scholarship funds; Technical assistance; Scholarships—to individuals; Matching/challenge support.

Limitations: Giving limited to the Barkhamsted, Bethlehem, Colebrook, Cornwall, Falls Village, Goshen, Hartland, Harwinton, Kent, Litchfield, Morris, New Hartford, Norfolk, North Canaan, Salisbury, Sharon, Torrington, Warren, Washington, and Winsted, CT, areas. No grants for operating deficits, debt liquidation, or membership or affiliation campaigns.

Publications: Application guidelines; Annual report; Financial statement; Informational brochure; Informational brochure (including application guidelines); Newsletter; Occasional report.

Application information: Visit foundation Web site for application form, guidelines, and specific deadlines. Application form required.

   Initial approach: Letter, telephone, or e-mail
   Copies of proposal: 19
   Deadline(s): Varies for grants; Apr. 1 for scholarships
   Board meeting date(s): Monthly
   Final notification: Varies

Officers and Directors:* Ann Auburn,* Chair.; Brian McCormick,* Vice-Chair.; Guy Rovezzi, Pres.; Margaret Roraback,* Secy.; John R. Ursone,* Treas.; James C. Allen; Alan Colavecchio; William G. Harding; John Janco; Carol Lugar; Roberta Ohotnicky, Ph.D.; James O'Leary; E. Frederick Petersen; Rose Ponte; Jan Rathbun; JoAnn Ryan.

Trustee Banks: First National Bank of Litchfield; Bank of America, N.A.; Torrington Savings Bank.

Number of staff: 2 full-time professional; 1 part-time professional.

EIN: 066114199

1517
The Community Foundation of Southeastern Connecticut

(formerly The Pequot Community Foundation, Inc.)
147 State St.
P.O. Box 769
New London, CT   06320   (860) 442-3572
Contact: Alice F. Fitzpatrick, Pres.; Edward J. Wozniak, C.F.O.
FAX: (860) 442-0584; E-mail: ewozniak@cfsect.org; URL: http://www.cfsect.org

Established in 1982 in CT.

Donors: J. Martin Leatherman‡; Beatrice G. McEwen‡; Dorothy Morgan‡; Jim Smith; members of the White Family.

Foundation type: Community foundation.

Financial data (yr. ended 12/31/05): Assets, $26,212,193 (L); gifts received, $1,805,037; expenditures, $1,710,094; giving activities include $877,400 for 184 grants (high: $15,000; low:

$250), and $213,300 for 127 grants to individuals (high: $16,000; low: $1,000).

Purpose and activities: The foundation permanently strengthens shared community through the promotion of local philanthropy and the responsible stewardship of endowed funds.

Fields of interest: Arts; Libraries/library science; Education; Environment, natural resources; Environment; Health care; Substance abuse, services; Mental health/crisis services; Children/youth, services; Family services; Aging, centers/services; Women, centers/services; Human services; Community development; Voluntarism promotion; Aging; Disabilities, people with; Women; Economically disadvantaged.

Type of support: General/operating support; Management development/capacity building; Building/renovation; Equipment; Emergency funds; Program development; Seed money; Scholarship funds; Technical assistance; Consulting services; Scholarships—to individuals.

Limitations: Giving limited to southeastern CT, including East Lyme, Groton, Ledyard, Lyme, Montville, New London, North Stonington, Old Lyme, Salem, Stonington, and Waterford. No support for sectarian or religious programs. No grants to individuals (except for scholarships), or for fundraising events, or endowment, memorial, or building funds, deficit financing, annual campaigns, or debt retirement; no loans.

Publications: Application guidelines; Annual report (including application guidelines); Financial statement; Grants list; Informational brochure; Newsletter.

Application information: Visit foundation Web site for application form and guidelines. The Connecticut Common Grant Application Form may be submitted in lieu of the foundation's application form. Application form required.

   Initial approach: Telephone or e-mail
   Copies of proposal: 2
   Deadline(s): Nov. 15 for grants; Apr. 1 for scholarship applications; Aug. 1 for women and girls grant applications; Mar. 15 for Let's Read grant applications
   Board meeting date(s): Jan., Mar., June, Sept., and Nov.
   Final notification: Grants are distributed by Apr. 1; scholarships awarded in June; women and girls grants awarded in Oct.

Officers and Trustees:* Bridget Baird,* Chair.; Granville R. Morris,* Vice-Chair.; Alice F. Fitzpatrick,* Pres.; Merrylyn Weaver,* Secy.; Ed Wozniak, C.F.O.; David Zuckerbraun,* Treas.; Laurel A. Butler; Anne A. Clement; Mary Dangremond; Anthony T. Enders; James P. English, Jr.; Royden A. Grimm; Rosetta E. Jones; Saking King; William A. Lieber; Ellen H. McGuire; Dyanne Rafal; Kate Robins; Ruth Saunders; Doreen Thomas.

Number of staff: 5 full-time professional.

EIN: 061080097

1518
The Connecticut Community Foundation ◇

(formerly The Waterbury Foundation)
43 Field St.
Waterbury, CT   06702   (203) 753-1315
FAX: (203) 756-3054; E-mail: info@conncf.org; Additional Address: 3413 Main St., New Milford, CT 06776, tel.: (860) 355-2834; URL: http://conncf.org

Incorporated in 1923 by special Act of the CT Legislature.

Donors: Katherine Pomeroy†; Edith Chase†.

Foundation type: Community foundation.

Financial data (yr. ended 12/31/04): Assets, $45,044,484 (M); gifts received, $5,474,354; expenditures, $2,555,025; giving activities include $1,383,599 for 652+ grants (high: $50,000; low: $100), and $283,824 for 217 grants to individuals (high: $5,200; low: $75).

Purpose and activities: The foundation serves the people of Central Naugatuck Valley and Litchfield Hills to improve the quality of life by: 1) giving grants, scholarships, and organizational support to address the changing needs of the community; 2) helping donors create a legacy for the future through a permanent endowment fund; 3) promoting informed philanthropy and volunteerism to increase charitable resources for the region; and 4) providing leadership and building partnerships to identify and solve community concerns.

Fields of interest: Humanities; Historic preservation/historical societies; Arts; Education, early childhood education; Child development, education; Secondary school/education; Vocational education; Higher education; Adult/continuing education; Education; Health care; Substance abuse, services; Mental health/crisis services; Health organizations, association; Heart & circulatory diseases; AIDS; Employment; Housing/shelter, development; Recreation; Children/youth, services; Child development, services; Family services; Residential/custodial care, hospices; Aging, centers/services; Homeless, human services; Human services; Economic development; Community development; Aging; Disabilities, people with; Minorities; Economically disadvantaged; Homeless.

Type of support: Management development/capacity building; Capital campaigns; Building/renovation; Equipment; Program development; Conferences/seminars; Publication; Seed money; Curriculum development; Scholarship funds; Research; Technical assistance; Consulting services; Scholarships—to individuals; Matching/challenge support.

Limitations: Giving limited to Beacon Falls, Bethlehem, Bridgewater, Cheshire, Goshen, Litchfield, Middlebury, Morris, Naugatuck, New Milford, Oxford, Prospect, Roxbury, Southbury, Thomaston, Warren, Washington, Waterbury, Watertown, Wolcott, or Woodbury, CT. No support for sectarian or religious purposes. No grants to individuals (except for college scholarships), or for general operating support, capital campaigns for endowments, deficit financing, continuing support, annual campaigns, previously incurred expenses, audio/visual equipment or vans, or fundraising by one agency on behalf of another; no loans.

Publications: Application guidelines; Annual report; Newsletter.

Application information: The foundation will send a complete grant application packet to agencies whose requests are deemed appropriate based on their letters of inquiry. Interested applicants should contact the foundation prior to submitting a letter of inquiry. Visit Foundation Web site for application guidelines. Application form required.

Initial approach: Mail, fax or e-mail letter of inquiry (no more than 2 pages)

Copies of proposal: 17

Deadline(s): Jan. 13, Apr. 7, and Sept. 8 for letter of inquiry; Jan. 27, Apr. 21, and Sept. 22 for full grant application; Mar. 1 for scholarships

Board meeting date(s): Mar., June, and Nov.; grants committee meets twice, 6 weeks and 1 week prior to each board meeting

Final notification: Within 1 week for full proposal determination; 10 weeks for grant determination

Officers and Trustees:* Ingrid Manning, C.E.O.; Fred L. Baker,* Pres.; Ann M. Burton, Ph.D.*, V.P.; Peter J. Jacoby, M.D.*, Secy.; Stedman G. Sweet,* Treas.; Katherine Berman; Sam S.F. Caligiuri; Isabelle V. Curtiss; Judith Eslami; Harold Gootrad; Betsy Manning; Molly Parker; Edwin R. Rodriquez; Marvin Schwartz; Annie M. Scott; Arri B. Sendzimir; Daniel Sherr; Richard J. Ulbrich; Mark C. Yanarella.

Number of staff: 7 full-time professional; 1 part-time professional; 2 full-time support; 1 part-time support.

EIN: 066038074

Selected grants: The following grants were reported in 2005.

$133,378 to LitLinks. For consultant to research early childhood literacy programs and for Connecticut Humanities Council to provide training and technical support to Motheread/Fatheread sites.

$50,000 to Mattatuck Museum, Waterbury, CT. For capital campaign to redesign and update exhibit on Waterbury-area museum.

$44,000 to Greater Waterbury Interfaith Ministries, Waterbury, CT. To expand Resource Center providing information and referral services to needy residents, payable over 3 years.

$32,119 to Childrens Center of New Milford, New Milford, CT. To improve program quality to increase students' kindergarten readiness, payable over 3 years.

$31,047 to Stay Well Health Center, Waterbury, CT. For Pediatric Access to Care Program, payable over 3 years.

$30,000 to Susan B. Anthony Project, Torrington, CT. For education and prevention workshops in schools in Northwest Connecticut on bullying, domestic violence, and other issues, payable over 3 years.

$21,112 to Cheshire, Town of, Cheshire, CT. To pilot and implement Adaptive Community Programming (ACP) for special needs youth, payable over 3 years.

$20,000 to Aspira of Connecticut, Bridgeport, CT. For after school programs at Kennedy High School and West Side Middle School in Waterbury with goal of reducing dropout rate among Latino students, payable over 3 years.

$10,667 to Brass City Ballet, Waterbury, CT. For Reading in Motion program with Driggs School in Waterbury.

$8,000 to Housatonic Valley Association, Kent, CT. To develop and expand volunteer stream teams and to test water quality in specific sites.

$5,200 to Naugatuck Valley Housing Development Corporation, Waterbury, CT. To train co-op owners to improve governance and operation at their co-op.

1519

Connecticut Health Foundation, Inc. ▼

74B Vine St.
New Britain, CT 06052 (860) 224-2200
Contact: Patricia Baker, C.E.O. and Pres.
FAX: (860) 224-2230; *E-mail:* info@cthealth.org;
URL: http://www.cthealth.org/matriarch/default.asp

Established in 2000 in CT; converted in 1999 from Connecticare Health Plan.

Foundation type: Independent foundation.

Financial data (yr. ended 12/31/05): Assets, $140,473,764 (M); expenditures, $7,443,804; qualifying distributions, $6,720,285; giving activities include $4,534,070 for 111 grants (high: $180,000; low: $1,500; average: $50,000–$125,000).

Purpose and activities: The foundation focuses on three main areas: 1) Improving access and utilization of mental health services by children and their families; 2) Reducing racial and ethnic health disparities; 3) Expanding access to and utilization of oral health services by children.

Fields of interest: Health care, equal rights; Dental care; Health care; Mental health, treatment; Children/youth, services.

Type of support: Research; Management development/capacity building; General/operating support; Equipment; Conferences/seminars; Scholarship funds; Technical assistance; Consulting services; Program evaluation.

Limitations: Giving limited to CT. No grants to individuals, or for construction of buildings, capital projects, endowments, or chairs associated with universities and medical schools, or conferences (unless part of a greater project or program).

Publications: Application guidelines; Annual report; Financial statement; Grants list; Informational brochure; Newsletter; Occasional report.

Application information: The foundation will announce requests for proposals (RFP). Application form for unsolicited grant proposals available on foundation Web site. Application form required.

Initial approach: Concept paper

Copies of proposal: 10

Deadline(s): As announced

Board meeting date(s): Quarterly

Final notification: Within 2 weeks following the board meeting

Officers and Directors:* Leo C. Canty,* Chair.; Susan S. Addiss,* Vice-Chair.; Patricia Baker, C.E.O. and Pres.; William F. Crimi, V.P., Progs. and Eval.; Monette Goodrich, V.P., Comms. and Public Affairs; Carol Pollack, V.P., Finance and Opers.; Michael Williams,* Secy.; Corine T. Norgaard,* Treas.; Jean Adnopoz; Marilyn Alverio; Raymond S. Andrews, Jr.; Sanford Cloud, Jr.; Laura Green; Katherine C. III, M.D.; Henry E. Parker; Jean L. Rexford; Arthur L. Sperling, P.M.D.; Lynelle Thomas, M.D.; Margarita V. Torres.

Number of staff: 7 full-time professional; 2 part-time support.

EIN: 061057387

Selected grants: The following grants were reported in 2005.

$180,000 to Community Foundation for Greater New Haven, New Haven, CT. For project evaluation for Healthy Start Program.

$160,000 to New Haven Family Alliance, New Haven, CT. For We Walk/WeWIN program to continue work to improve physical activity of selected New Haven residents initiated under Multicultural Initiative.

$150,000 to Bridgeport Child Advocacy Coalition, Bridgeport, CT. For general operating support.

$150,000 to LEARN, Old Lyme, CT. To increase maternal and early childhood oral health and utilization of nutrition and exercise programs for children through proven, evidence-based practices.

$113,127 to FAVOR, Rocky Hill, CT. For general operating support.

$100,000 to Bridgeport Hospital, Bridgeport, CT. For matching grant for Child FIRST program for identifying and treating emotional and behavioral problems among very young children through family-based approach, payable over 4 years.

$75,000 to Mashantucket Pequot Tribal Council, Mashantucket, CT. For Strengthening Pequot Families.

$70,000 to Operation Fuel, Bloomfield, CT. For general support.

$50,000 to Northwest Caring Connection, Torrington, CT. To evaluate current process and structure of CST and allow each community, based on data, to develop and implement corrective measures to improve planning process.

$49,131 to Visiting Nurse Association of Connecticut, New Britain, CT. For full-time Care Caller case manager to meet increased demand for services in community and facilitate prenatal, postpartum, and child immunization services.

1520
Carle C. Conway Scholarship Foundation, Inc. ✧

c/o M.L. Colten
95 Alexandra Dr.
Stamford, CT   06903-1731

Established in 1950.
Donors: Continental Can Co., Inc.; Franklin Holdings, Inc.
Foundation type: Company-sponsored foundation.
Financial data (yr. ended 6/30/05): Assets, $6,059,814 (M); expenditures, $694,014; qualifying distributions, $688,853; giving activities include $60,000 for 2 grants (high: $50,000; low: $10,000), and $592,051 for 69 grants to individuals (high: $10,000; low: $164).
Purpose and activities: The foundation supports organizations involved with higher education.
Fields of interest: Higher education.
Type of support: General/operating support; Employee-related scholarships.
Limitations: Applications not accepted. Giving on a national basis.
Application information: Contributes only through employee-related scholarships and to pre-selected organizations.
  Board meeting date(s): Usually May
Officers and Director: S. Bermas, Pres.; M.L. Colten, V.P. and Secy.-Treas.; R.S. Cohen.
EIN: 136088936

1521
The Daphne Seybolt Culpeper Memorial Foundation, Inc.

129 Musket Ridge Rd.
Norwalk, CT   06850-1315   (203) 762-3984
Contact: Nicholas J. Nardi, Secy.-Treas.
Application address: P.O. Box 206, Norwalk, CT 06852-0206

Established in 1983 in DE.
Donor: Daphne Seybolt Culpeper†.
Foundation type: Independent foundation.
Financial data (yr. ended 12/31/05): Assets, $17,389,563 (M); expenditures, $910,346; qualifying distributions, $866,569; giving activities include $838,900 for 191 grants (high: $100,000; low: $100).

Purpose and activities: Giving primarily for education, health care and human services.
Fields of interest: Higher education; Medical school/education; Nursing school/education; Education; Hospitals (general); Health care; Health organizations, association; Crime/violence prevention, domestic violence; Food services; Human services; Children/youth, services; Residential/custodial care, hospices; Aging; Disabilities, people with; Minorities; Native Americans/American Indians; Women; Economically disadvantaged; Homeless.
Type of support: General/operating support; Annual campaigns; Capital campaigns; Building/renovation; Equipment; Program development; Scholarship funds; Matching/challenge support.
Limitations: Giving limited to Fairfield County, CT and Palm Beach County, FL. No grants to individuals, or for endowments, forums, conferences, seminars, gratuities, honorariums, travel, meals or lodging.
Publications: Application guidelines.
Application information: Application form not required.
  Initial approach: Letter
  Copies of proposal: 1
  Deadline(s): None
  Board meeting date(s): Varies
Officers and Trustees: Rodney S. Eielson,* Pres.; Nicholas J. Nardi,* Secy.-Treas.
Number of staff: 1 full-time professional.
EIN: 222478755
Selected grants: The following grants were reported in 2004.

$100,000 to Bethesda Hospital Foundation, Boynton Beach, FL. For capital campaign.

$60,000 to Advent Lutheran Church, Boca Raton, FL. To purchase land.

$50,000 to Florida Atlantic University, Charles E. Schmidt College of Science, Boca Raton, FL. To research on Multiple Myeloma.

$50,000 to Norwalk Hospital Foundation, Norwalk, CT. To purchase Nitric Oxide Analyzer.

$50,000 to Saint Thomas of Villanova Church, Rosemont, PA. To install sprinkler system.

$35,000 to AIDS Project New Haven, New Haven, CT. For Meal Delivery and Pantry program.

$25,000 to AmeriCares Free Clinic, New Canaan, CT. For Free Clinic in Norwalk.

$25,000 to Habitat for Humanity of South Palm Beach County, Delray Beach, FL. For general support.

$15,000 to University of Connecticut, School of Law, West Hartford, CT. To publish Connecticut Journal of International Law.

$10,000 to Connecticut Association for Children and Adults with Learning Disabilities, East Norwalk, CT. For publishing newsletters.

1522
Dalio Family Foundation, Inc. ✧

1 Glendinning Pl.
Westport, CT   06880

Established in 2003 in CT.
Donor: Raymond T. Dalio.
Foundation type: Independent foundation.
Financial data (yr. ended 12/31/05): Assets, $25,633,846 (M); gifts received, $1,189,572; expenditures, $3,911,343; qualifying distributions, $3,861,731; giving activities include $3,861,518 for 305 grants (high: $1,000,000; low: $125; average: $1,000–$10,000).

Fields of interest: Health organizations, association; Human services.
Limitations: Applications not accepted. Giving primarily in CT; some funding nationally. No grants to individuals.
Application information: Contributes only to pre-selected organizations.
Officer and Directors: Raymond T. Dalio,* Pres.; Matthew Dalio; Paul Dalio.
EIN: 431965846

1523
The Daniell Family Foundation, Inc. ✧

c/o C. Jacques-Soto, Capital Strategies
2 Barnard Ln.
Bloomfield, CT   06002

Established in 1992 in CT.
Donors: Barbara E. Daniell; Robert F. Daniell.
Foundation type: Independent foundation.
Financial data (yr. ended 12/31/05): Assets, $14,634,134 (M); gifts received, $86,364; expenditures, $706,614; qualifying distributions, $620,250; giving activities include $620,250 for 69 grants (high: $104,000; low: $100).
Fields of interest: Performing arts, music; Higher education; Education; Hospitals (general); Health organizations, association; Children/youth, services; Human services; Christian agencies & churches.
Limitations: Applications not accepted. Giving primarily in CT and NH. No grants to individuals.
Application information: Contributes only to pre-selected organizations.
Officers and Directors: Barbara E. Daniell,* Pres.; Robert F. Daniell,* Secy.; Holly D. Miller.
EIN: 061356015
Selected grants: The following grants were reported in 2004.

$78,000 to Gilford Community Church, Gilford, NH. For unrestricted support.

$70,000 to Catholic Medical Center, Manchester, NH. For unrestricted support.

$65,000 to Lakes Region General Hospital Association, Laconia, NH. For unrestricted support.

$30,000 to New Hampshire Music Festival, Gilford, NH. For unrestricted support.

$15,000 to Circle Program, Plymouth, NH. For unrestricted support.

$15,000 to Mayhew, Bristol, NH. For unrestricted support.

$15,000 to Ramapo College Foundation, Mahwah, NJ. For unrestricted support.

$10,000 to Bergen Catholic High School, Oradell, NJ. For unrestricted support.

$10,000 to Boys and Girls Club of Lodi, Lodi, NJ. For unrestricted support.

$10,000 to Perlman Music Program, New York, NY. For unrestricted support.

1524
The Peter Dartley Charitable Trust ✧

c/o Pequot Capital Mgmt.
500 Nyala Farms Rd., Ste. 2
Westport, CT   06880

Established in 1986 in CT and NY.
Donor: Peter Dartley.
Foundation type: Independent foundation.
Financial data (yr. ended 12/31/04): Assets, $7,612,729 (M); expenditures, $679,552;

qualifying distributions, $667,052; giving activities include $664,572 for 16 grants (high: $500,000; low: $250).

Purpose and activities: Giving primarily for education; funding also for health, and human services.

Fields of interest: Education; Health organizations, association; Cancer; Food services; Human services; Children, services; Federated giving programs; Roman Catholic agencies & churches.

Limitations: Applications not accepted. Giving primarily in CT, MA, and NY. No grants to individuals.

Application information: Contributes only to pre-selected organizations.

Trustees: Karen Dartley; Peter Dartley.

EIN: 133405097

1525

The Ellen and Gary Davis Foundation ◇

45 Pecksland Rd.
Greenwich, CT 06831

Established in 1992 in CT.

Donors: Gary S. Davis; Ellen Davis; Brad Klein.

Foundation type: Independent foundation.

Financial data (yr. ended 12/31/04): Assets, $5,824,851 (M); gifts received, $651,500; expenditures, $837,143; qualifying distributions, $819,632; giving activities include $817,647 for 75 grants (high: $250,000; low: $20).

Purpose and activities: Giving primarily for higher education, Jewish agencies, cultural institutions, health care and human services.

Fields of interest: Museums (art); Higher education; Education; Hospitals (general); Health organizations, association; Medical research, institute; Human services; Jewish federated giving programs; Jewish agencies & temples.

Limitations: Applications not accepted. Giving primarily in CT. No grants to individuals.

Application information: Contributes only to pre-selected organizations.

Trustees: Richard J. Bronstein; Ellen Davis; Gary S. Davis.

EIN: 061357318

1526

The Hilda and Preston Davis Foundation ◇

c/o Foundation Services LLC
640 W. Putman Ave., 3rd Fl.
Greenwich, CT 06830
E-mail: davis@fsllc.net; Additional e-mail: info@fsllc.net; URL: http://www.hpdavis.org

Established in 1998 in PA.

Donors: Hilda J. Davis†; Preston Davis†.

Foundation type: Independent foundation.

Financial data (yr. ended 12/31/05): Assets, $7,690,609 (M); expenditures, $574,333; qualifying distributions, $470,682; giving activities include $361,498 for 16 grants (high: $50,299; low: $600).

Fields of interest: Education; Mental health, eating disorders; Children, services.

Limitations: Giving on a national basis, with some emphasis on CT. No support for organizations lacking 501(c)(3) status, government agencies, or organizations that subsist mainly on third party funding and have demonstrated no ability or expended little effort to attract private funding. No

grants to individuals, or for general fundraising drives or endowments.

Application information: Application form available on foundation Web site. Application form required.

Initial approach: Fill out on-line application form
Deadline(s): None

Trustees: John D. Iskrant; Geoffrey M. Parkinson.

EIN: 237966458

Selected grants: The following grants were reported in 2003.

$25,000 to Greenwich Chaplaincy Services, Greenwich, CT. For general support.

$25,000 to Horace Mann School, Riverdale, NY. For general support.

$25,000 to Medical Missions for Children, Paterson, NJ. For general support.

$25,000 to National Eating Disorders Association, Seattle, WA. For general support.

$20,000 to Marshall Legacy Institute, Alexandria, VA. For general support.

$15,000 to Greenwich Rotary Club, Greenwich, CT. For general support.

$10,000 to ECRI, Plymouth Meeting, PA. For general support.

$10,000 to Friends of Bosnia, Boston, MA. For general support.

$10,000 to Kids with A PromiseDevelopment Fund, New York, NY. For general support.

$10,000 to Theater by the Blind Corporation, New York, NY. For general support.

1527

Deloitte Foundation ◇

(formerly Deloitte & Touche Foundation)
10 Westport Rd.
P.O. Box 820
Wilton, CT 06897-0820 (203) 761-3474
Contact: Janet Butchko, Mgr., Academic Devel.
URL: http://www.deloitte.com/dtt/section_node/0,1042,sid%253D2257,00.html

Incorporated in 1928 in NY.

Donors: Deloitte Haskins & Sells; Deloitte & Touche LLP; Charles Stewart Ludlam†; Charles C. Croggon†; Weldon Powell†; Deloitte & Touche USA LLP.

Foundation type: Company-sponsored foundation.

Financial data (yr. ended 5/28/05): Assets, $6,970,259 (M); gifts received, $4,209,112; expenditures, $3,943,507; qualifying distributions, $3,941,055; giving activities include $1,202,375 for 19 grants (high: $270,000; low: $4,000), and $2,700,119 for 309 employee matching gifts.

Purpose and activities: The foundation supports organizations involved with education and awards fellowships to doctoral accounting students.

Fields of interest: Higher education; Business school/education; Education.

Type of support: Conferences/seminars; Professorships; Curriculum development; Fellowships; Research; Sponsorships; Employee matching gifts.

Limitations: Giving on a national basis. No grants for general operating support, capital campaigns, special programs, or publications; no loans; no matching support.

Publications: Informational brochure.

Application information: An application form is required for Doctoral Fellowships.

Initial approach: Letter of inquiry; contact accounting department head at educational institution for application form for Doctoral Fellowships

Copies of proposal: 1
Deadline(s): None; Oct. 15 for Doctoral Fellowships
Board meeting date(s): 3 times per year
Final notification: Dec. 15 for Doctoral Fellowships

Officers and Directors:* Sharon L. Allen,* Chair.; Mark M. Chain, Pres.; Allen S. Thomas, Secy.-Treas.; Catherine A. Benko; Kimberly P. Ellis; Howard S. Engle; David A. Foley; Lawrence A. Hilsheimer; Brent W. Loebig; Gerald Pietroforte.

EIN: 136400341

Selected grants: The following grants were reported in 2005.

$158,483 to Federation of Schools of Accountancy, Charlottesville, VA. 2 grants: $58,483 (For faculty consortium), $100,000 (For faculty consortium).

$90,000 to University of Kansas, Lawrence, KS. For auditing symposium.

$75,000 to Howard University, Center for Accounting Education, School of Business, DC.

$25,000 to Consortium for Graduate Study in Management, Saint Louis, MO.

$10,000 to Council for Aid to Education (CAE), New York, NY.

$5,000 to Boston University, Boston, MA. For Women's Leadership Forum.

$4,000 to Council for Advancement and Support of Education, DC.

$2,500 to Kent State University, Kent, OH. For education in accounting.

1528

The Diebold Foundation, Inc. ◇

102 Painter Hill Rd.
Roxbury, CT 06783

Established in 2000 in CT.

Foundation type: Independent foundation.

Financial data (yr. ended 12/31/05): Assets, $29,966,252 (M); expenditures, $1,599,397; qualifying distributions, $1,370,051; giving activities include $1,309,100 for 16 grants (high: $400,000; low: $5,000; average: $20,000–$150,000).

Fields of interest: Education; Hospitals (general); Hospitals (specialty).

Limitations: Applications not accepted. Giving primarily in CT, with emphasis on Roxbury and Waterford; some giving in New York, NY. Generally, no support for Christian organizations. No grants to individuals.

Application information: Contributes only to pre-selected organizations.

Directors: Caitlin Diebold; Dudley Diebold; Honoria Diebold; Daphne Stoughton.

EIN: 311681649

1529

The Patrick and Catherine Weldon Donaghue Medical Research Foundation ▼ ◇

18 N. Main St.
West Hartford, CT 06107-1919
Contact: Lynne Garner, Exec. Dir.
FAX: (860) 521-9018; E-mail: office@donaghue.org;
URL: http://www.donaghue.org

Established in 1989 in CT.

Donor: Ethel F. Donaghue†.

Foundation type: Independent foundation.
Financial data (yr. ended 12/31/05): Assets, $69,164,215 (M); expenditures, $5,562,068; qualifying distributions, $4,677,418; giving activities include $4,677,418 for 41 grants.
Purpose and activities: Support for clinical, pre-clinical and basic biomedical research as well as epidemiological, community health, and health services research in cancer, cardiovascular disease, mental health, and neurodegenerative diseases at medical, academic, and other health-related institutions in CT. The foundation provides support to the careers of scientific researchers through two programs: 1) Donaghue Investigator Grants; and 2) Research in Clinical and Community Health Issues.
Fields of interest: Medical research, institute.
Type of support: Fellowships; Research; Grants to individuals.
Limitations: Giving limited to CT.
Publications: Application guidelines; Annual report; Financial statement; Newsletter.
Application information: See foundation's Web site for more application information. Application form required.
   Initial approach: Proposal
   Deadline(s): Varies
Officers: Lynne Garner, Ph.D., Exec. Dir.
Trustees: Raymond S. Andrews, Jr.; Bank of America, N.A.
Scientific Advisory Committee: T.V. Rajan, M.D., Ph.D., Chair, Danaghie Investigation Advisory Comm.; Hon. Alvin W. Thompson, Chair., Policy Advisory Comm.; William White, M.D., Chair., Clinical and Community Health Issues Review Comm.; Nancy Angoff, M.D.; Howard L. Bailit, DMD, Ph.D.; Cheryl Tatano Beck, DNSc; Adam Borgida, M.D.; Lawrence Brass, M.D.; Ernesto Canalis, M.D.; Linda Frisman, Ph.D.; Michael Gaffney, Ph.D.; Tony George, MD; George C. Hastings; George Heninger, M.D.; Katherine C. III, M.D.; Beth A. Janes, Ph.D, MD; Stanislav V. Kasl, Ph.D.; David Knecht, Ph.D.; Harlan Krumholz, M.D., FACC; Mark Litt, Ph.D.; Mark Metersky, M.D.; Patricia Neafsey, RD, Ph.D.; Godfrey Pearlson, M.D.; Martha Radford, M.D.; Susan Ratzan, M.D.; Michael Rion; Lawrence Scahill, Ph.D.; Jonathan G. Seidman, Ph.D.; Jonathan Sporn, M.D.; Howard Tennen, Ph.D.; Wilma Wasco, Ph.D.
Number of staff: 2 full-time professional.
EIN: 066348275
Selected grants: The following grants were reported in 2004.
$1,366,088 to Yale University, New Haven, CT. 5 grants: $502,500 to School of Medicine (For Connecticut Collaborative Fall Prevention Project), $250,000 to School of Nursing (For Program for Study of Health Care Relationships), $118,973 to School of Medicine (For quality improvement efforts in care of older adults), $80,810 to School of Medicine (For research project, potential predictor to response to Cognitive Behavioral Therapy (CBT)), $413,805 (For Ethel Donaghue Women's Health Investigator Program).
$243,084 to Wesleyan University, Middletown, CT. 2 grants: $128,684 (For research project, Structural studies of sickle cell hemoglobin fibers), $114,400 (For research project, Impact of child psychopathology and intervention on later substance use).
$238,684 to University of Connecticut Health Center, Farmington, CT. 2 grants: $128,684 (For research project, Mechanisms of inflammatory central nervous system injury), $110,000 (For

research project, Strategy to optimize vaccine efficacy in older adults).
$160,700 to Saint Francis Hospital and Medical Center, Hartford, CT. For project, Hospitals and Churches: Partnership to Improve Health.

1530
Alma Gibbs Donchian Charitable Foundation, Inc. ◇
(formerly Alma Gibbs Donchian Foundation)
c/o Foundation Services, LLC
640 W. Putman Ave., 3rd Fl.
Greenwich, CT   06830
Contact: Geoffrey M. Parkinson, Dir.
FAX: (203) 629-0806; E-mail: agd@fsllc.net; Additional e-mail: info@fsllc.net; URL: http://www.agdonchian.org

Established in 1991 in CT; reincorporated in 1998.
Donor: Alma G. Donchian†.
Foundation type: Independent foundation.
Financial data (yr. ended 12/31/05): Assets, $6,551,437 (M); expenditures, $477,562; qualifying distributions, $404,968; giving activities include $325,493 for 22 grants (high: $50,000; low: $2,730).
Purpose and activities: It is the primary mission of the Alma Gibbs Donchian Foundation to provide assistance to various specified institutions in Castleton, VT and the immediate environs to address the following areas of concern: issues affecting the elderly, education (especially as pertaining to those with disabilities) and programs that further fundamental values such as self-reliance and respect for tradition.
Fields of interest: Education; Environment; Human services.
Limitations: Giving primarily in VT. No grants to individuals.
Application information: Application form available on foundation Web site. Online application form is preferred. Application form required.
   Initial approach: Complete application form online
   Deadline(s): None
Directors: Holly Hitchcock; Geoffrey M. Parkinson; Leland C. Selby.
EIN: 061514400
Selected grants: The following grants were reported in 2003.
$50,000 to Castleton State College, Woodruff Institute for School Leadership, Castleton, VT.
$35,000 to Clarke School for the Deaf, Northampton, MA. For Alma Gibbs Donchian Future Directions Initiative and program support.
$15,000 to Camp Thorpe, Goshen, VT. For accessibility project.
$10,000 to Greenwich Adult Day Care, Greenwich, CT. For general support.
$10,000 to Mars Hill Graduate School, Bothell, WA. For general support.
$10,000 to Tuberous Sclerosis Alliance, Silver Spring, MD. For general support.
$10,000 to Vermont Achievement Center, Rutland, VT. For general support.
$5,000 to Boy Scouts of America, Greenwich Council, Greenwich, CT. For general support.
$5,000 to Greenwich Country Day School, Greenwich, CT. For general support.
$5,000 to Montana Land Reliance, Helena, MT. For general support.

1531
Richard Davoud Donchian Foundation ◇
(formerly Richard D. Donchian Charitable Foundation, Inc.)
c/o Foundation Svcs., LLC
640 W. Putnam Ave., 3rd Fl.
Greenwich, CT   06830   (203) 629-8552
Contact: Geoffrey M. Parkinson, Dir.
FAX: (928) 396-6975; E-mail: rdd@fsllc.net; URL: http://www.rddonchian.org

Established in 1991 in CT; reincorporated in 1998.
Donor: Richard D. Donchian†.
Foundation type: Independent foundation.
Financial data (yr. ended 12/31/05): Assets, $10,158,193 (M); expenditures, $641,609; qualifying distributions, $548,475; giving activities include $463,050 for 27 grants (high: $60,000; low: $5,000).
Purpose and activities: The foundation focuses its grantmaking in three key areas: 1) Business Integrity and Leadership; 2) Literary and Education; and 3) Ethics and Personal Development.
Fields of interest: Libraries/library science; Education; Health care, support services; Human services; Urban/community development; Public affairs, ethics.
Limitations: Giving primarily in CT and NY.
Application information: Application form required.
   Initial approach: See Web site for guidelines
   Deadline(s): None
Directors: Geoffrey M. Parkinson; Leland C. Selby; Clark M. Whittemore, Jr.
EIN: 061514402

1532
Doty Family Foundation
1359 Fairfield Beach Rd.
Fairfield, CT   06824
Contact: Anne Marie Paine, Secy.

Established in 1977 in NY.
Donor: George E. Doty.
Foundation type: Independent foundation.
Financial data (yr. ended 2/28/06): Assets, $8,028,770 (M); gifts received, $100,020; expenditures, $657,825; qualifying distributions, $583,401; giving activities include $576,430 for 103 grants (high: $200,000; low: $150).
Purpose and activities: Grants only for churches and charitable organizations with which members of the family are involved.
Fields of interest: Christian agencies & churches.
Limitations: Applications not accepted. Giving on a national basis. No grants to individuals.
Application information: Only charities in which Doty family members are actively involved are considered. Unsolicited requests for funds not considered.
Officers and Trustees: * William W. Doty, Pres. and Treas.; Anne Marie Paine,* Secy.; Barbara E. Doty; George E. Doty; George E. Doty, Jr.; Marie J. Doty; Virginia M. Doty.
EIN: 132921496
Selected grants: The following grants were reported in 2005.
$250,000 to Sisters of Mary, Manila, Philippines. For general support.
$101,250 to University of Pennsylvania, Philadelphia, PA. 2 grants: $26,250, $75,000 (For general support).
$100,000 to New York Foundling Hospital, New York, NY. For general support.

$37,500 to Boston College, Chestnut Hill, MA. For general support.
$18,750 to Harvard University, Business School, Cambridge, MA. For general support.
$15,000 to Dalton Schools, New York, NY. For general support.
$7,500 to University of Chicago, Business School, Chicago, IL. For general support.
$4,770 to Saint Pauls Roman Catholic Church, Princeton, NJ. For general support.
$1,875 to Church of the Resurrection, Rye, NY. For general support.

1533
The Educational Foundation of America ▼ ✧
35 Church Ln.
Westport, CT 06880-3515 (203) 226-6498
Contact: Diane M. Allison, Exec. Dir.
E-mail: efa@efaw.org; Letter of inquiry E-mail: loi@efaw.org; URL: http://www.efaw.org

Trust established in 1959 in NY.
Donors: Richard P. Ettinger†; Elsie Ettinger†; Richard P. Ettinger, Jr.†; Elaine P. Hapgood; Paul R. Andrews†; Virgil P. Ettinger†.
Foundation type: Independent foundation.
Financial data (yr. ended 12/31/04): Assets, $225,558,331 (M); expenditures, $15,439,834; qualifying distributions, $13,065,815; giving activities include $12,406,169 for 271 grants (high: $250,000; low: $1,000; average: $10,000–$75,000), and $24,300 for employee matching gifts.
Purpose and activities: Grants primarily for arts, education, energy and the environment, reproductive health and rights, population, and education programs benefiting Native Americans.
Fields of interest: Arts; Education; Environment, natural resources; Environment, energy; Environment; Reproductive health, family planning; Civil liberties, reproductive rights; Native Americans/American Indians.
Type of support: Employee matching gifts; Program development; Seed money; Matching/challenge support.
Limitations: Giving limited to the U.S. No grants to individuals, annual fundraising campaigns, or for capital or endowment funds; no loans.
Publications: Application guidelines; Annual report; Grants list.
Application information: Letter of inquiry form is available on foundation Web site. Application form required.
 Initial approach: Letter of inquiry sent via E-mail only
 Copies of proposal: 2
 Deadline(s): None
 Board meeting date(s): Varies
 Final notification: Usually within 2 weeks
Officers and Board Members: Elaine P. Hapgood,* Pres.; Diane M. Allison, Exec. Dir.; David L. Godfrey, Fin. Dir.; Matthew Hapgood,* Member, Adjunct Comm.; Jerry Babicka; Lynn P. Babicka; Barbara P. Ettinger; Christian P. Ettinger; Heidi P. Ettinger; Wendy W.P. Ettinger; Barbara Hapgood; Sven Huseby; Nancy Keenan; Derek McLane; John Powers; Trevor Renner; Frances Stott.
Adjunct Committee Members: Ronene E. Anderson; Clarice Annegers; Jonathan Babicka; James Bohart, Jr.; Leland P. Ettinger; Matthew Ettinger; Nash Landesman; North Landesman;

Christopher Renner; Austin Schumacher; Lauren Zuskin; Morey Zuskin.
Number of staff: 3 full-time professional; 2 part-time professional; 1 full-time support.
EIN: 133424750
Selected grants: The following grants were reported in 2005.
$400,000 to Wilderness Society, Denver, CO. For Southern Rockies Conservation Alliance Coalition.
$240,000 to Religious Coalition for Reproductive Choice Educational Fund, DC. For Spiritual Youth for Reproductive Freedom.
$220,000 to Demos: A Network for Ideas and Action, New York, NY. For Election Reform and Voting Rights Project.
$160,000 to National Priorities Project, Northampton, MA. For Abroad and at Home: Exploring Alternative Policies for a Misguided Superpower.
$155,050 to Norwalk Public Schools, Norwalk, CT. For Ettinger Scholarship Awards.
$150,000 to National Dance Institute New Mexico, Santa Fe, NM. For Albuquerque Program.
$140,000 to University of California, San Francisco, CA. For Expanding Pregnancy Care by Advanced Practice Nurses (EPC-APN).
$100,000 to Fund for Constitutional Government, DC. For OpenTheGovernment.org.
$75,000 to Container Recycling Institute, Alexandria, VA. For 2020 Vision: Setting One's Sights on Zero Beverage Container Waste.
$50,000 to Cornerstones Community Partnerships, Santa Fe, NM. For Preservation Studies and Applied Learning Program.

1534
The Ellis Fund ✧
55 Highland St.
New Haven, CT 06511
Contact: Charles D. Ellis, Tr.

Established in 1983 in CT.
Donor: Charles D. Ellis.
Foundation type: Independent foundation.
Financial data (yr. ended 12/31/04): Assets, $11,775,796 (M); expenditures, $1,026,089; qualifying distributions, $991,983; giving activities include $991,983 for 68 grants (high: $350,000; low: $100).
Purpose and activities: Support primarily for education.
Fields of interest: Education; Human services; Christian agencies & churches.
Limitations: Giving primarily in CT and MA. No grants to individuals.
Trustees: Charles D. Ellis.
EIN: 222505228

1535
The Ensworth Charitable Foundation
c/o Bank of America, N.A., Fdn. and Philanthropic Svcs.
777 Main St., CT2-102-22-02
Hartford, CT 06115
Contact: Amy R. Lynch, V.P., Bank of America, N.A.

Trust established in 1948 in CT.
Donor: Antoinette L. Ensworth†.
Foundation type: Independent foundation.

Financial data (yr. ended 5/31/06): Assets, $19,498,921 (M); expenditures, $1,070,925; qualifying distributions, $991,832; giving activities include $909,022 for 130 grants (high: $25,000; low: $1,500).
Purpose and activities: Primary areas of interest include health and welfare programs, youth activities, enjoyment of the natural environment, relief of human suffering, education, religion, and the arts, particularly music.
Fields of interest: Arts; Education; Environment; Health care; Health organizations, association; AIDS research; Housing/shelter, development; Human services; Youth, services; Family services; Homeless, human services; Community development.
Type of support: Program development; Seed money; Technical assistance; Matching/challenge support.
Limitations: Giving limited to Hartford, CT, and contiguous surrounding areas. No grants to individuals, or for operating budgets, annual campaigns, deficit financing, building or endowment funds, equipment and materials, land acquisition, scholarships, fellowships, research, or publications; no loans.
Publications: Program policy statement.
Application information:
 Initial approach: Letter
 Copies of proposal: 5
 Deadline(s): Jan. 15 and July 15
 Board meeting date(s): Feb., May, Aug., and Nov.
 Final notification: 10 weeks after deadline
Trustee: Bank of America, N.A.
Number of staff: 1 full-time professional.
EIN: 066026018
Selected grants: The following grants were reported in 2005.
$25,000 to Community Health Services, Hartford, CT. For renovation.
$20,000 to Capital Community College, Hartford, CT. For pre-nursing program.
$20,000 to Trinity College, Hartford, CT. For Dream Camp.
$15,000 to Artists Collective, Hartford, CT. For training program for arts component.
$15,000 to Connecticut Forum, Hartford, CT. For youth forums.
$15,000 to Gifts of Love, Avon, CT. For food pantry, clothing, and household items.
$10,000 to Compass Youth Collaborative, Hartford, CT. For program at Bellizzi Middle School.
$7,000 to Everybody Wins Connecticut, Hartford, CT. For Readers as Leaders Project.
$6,000 to Center City Churches, Hartford, CT. For Center for Youth after-school programs.
$5,500 to Hartford Jazz Society, Bloomfield, CT. For education program.

1536
The Ettinger Foundation, Inc. ✧
c/o Allison & Godfrey, attn.: Diane M. Allison
35 Church Ln.
Westport, CT 06880-3515

Incorporated in 1949 in DE.
Donor: Members of the Ettinger family.
Foundation type: Independent foundation.
Financial data (yr. ended 12/31/04): Assets, $28,410,252 (M); gifts received, $12,928; expenditures, $1,657,224; qualifying distributions, $1,412,052; giving activities include $1,404,647 for 286 grants (high: $45,000; low: $100).

Purpose and activities: Giving primarily for education, the arts, environmental conservation, health care, and children, youth, and women's services, as well as family and social services.

Fields of interest: Performing arts; Performing arts, theater; Historic preservation/historical societies; Arts; Elementary/secondary education; Higher education; Education; Environment, natural resources; Environment; Animals/wildlife, preservation/protection; Hospitals (general); Reproductive health, family planning; Health care; Health organizations, association; Recreation; Human services; Children/youth, services; Family services; Residential/custodial care, hospices; Civil liberties, reproductive rights; Community development; Population studies; Christian agencies & churches; Women.

Type of support: General/operating support; Program development; Seed money; Matching/challenge support.

Limitations: Applications not accepted. Giving on a national basis. No grants to individuals, or for building or endowment funds; no loans.

Application information: Contributes only to pre-selected organizations.

Board meeting date(s): Varies

Officers and Directors:* Elaine P. Hapgood,* Pres.; Barbara P. Ettinger, V.P.; John P. Powers,* V.P.; Diane M. Allison, Secy.; David L. Godfrey, Treas.; Lynn P. Babicka*; Heidi P. Ettinger; Wendy P. Ettinger.

EIN: 066038938

1537
Fairfield County Community Foundation, Inc.

(also known as FCCF)
523 Danbury Rd.
Wilton, CT 06897 (203) 834-9393
Contact: For grants and scholarships: Jeanette Allam, Grants Asst.
FAX: (203) 834-9996;
E-mail: info@fccfoundation.org; E-mail for guidelines: jallam@fccfoundation.org; URL: http://www.fccfoundation.org

Established in 1992 in CT as a result of the merger of the Five Town Foundation, Danbury Community Endowment, Fairfield County Cooperative Foundation, Greenwich Foundation for Public Giving, and Stamford Foundation.

Foundation type: Community foundation.

Financial data (yr. ended 6/30/06): Assets, $82,600,227 (M); gifts received, $20,092,362; expenditures, $8,956,687; giving activities include $7,538,908 for 88+ grants.

Purpose and activities: The foundation promotes the growth of philanthropy by helping donors achieve their philanthropic goals. Grants from discretionary funds primarily support program areas of children, youth and families (with a special emphasis on early childhood education and youth development), economic opportunity (including affordable housing, neighborhood and workforce development), and the environment, health, nonprofit organizational effectiveness, and arts and culture.

Fields of interest: Arts; Education, early childhood education; Higher education; Education; Environment; Health care; Employment; Housing/shelter; Youth development; Children/youth, services; Human services; Economic development; Urban/community development; Nonprofit management; Economically disadvantaged.

Type of support: General/operating support; Management development/capacity building; Equipment; Program development; Scholarship funds; Technical assistance; Scholarships—to individuals; Matching/challenge support.

Limitations: Giving limited to the Fairfield County, CT, area from discretionary funds; giving throughout the U.S. from grants made from Donor-Advised funds. No support for religious purposes, or for start-up or new nonprofit organizations, or for parochial, charter, or private schools. No grants for endowments, building campaigns, deficit financing, fellowships, annual campaigns, or fundraising events.

Publications: Application guidelines; Annual report; Financial statement; Grants list; Informational brochure; Newsletter; Occasional report.

Application information: Visit foundation Web site for application information. The foundation's staff will respond to letter of inquiry with a preliminary assessment of the project's fit with foundation program priorities; if letter of inquiry is a good fit, applicants will receive a full grant application. Contact Prog. Asst. for letter of inquiry guidelines. Application form required.

Initial approach: Fax or e-mail letter of inquiry (no more than 3 pages)
Copies of proposal: 1
Deadline(s): Rolling basis for letter of inquiry; 3 times annually for full applications
Board meeting date(s): Quarterly
Final notification: 2 weeks after board meeting

Officers and Directors:* Wilmot L. Harris, Jr.,* Chair.; W. Michael Funck, Vice-Chair. and Devel. Chair.; Susan M. Ross,* C.E.O. and Pres.; Durham J. Monsma, Secy.; Mark J. Gabrielson,* Treas.; Sheila Perrin,* Chair., Program; Susan Sweitzer,* Chair., Governance; Edgar W. Barksdale, Jr.; Barbara P. Bellinger; Edwin A. Bescherer, Jr.; Daniel L. Daniels; Deborah Elam; Juan A. Figueroa; Peter P. Hanson; Barry C. Hawkins; Andrea Jabara; Mary Lee Kiernan; Anne S. Leonhardt; Barbara Leonhardt; Susan Mandel; James S. Martin; Joseph J. McGee; Lindsay J.H. Reimers; Edgar T. See; Ann E. Sheffer.

Number of staff: 3 full-time professional; 2 part-time professional; 3 full-time support; 2 part-time support.

EIN: 061083893

1538
The Kurt A. and Anne Pelletier Feuerman Foundation ✧

1 Rocky Point Rd.
Rowayton, CT 06853

Established in 1999 in CT.

Donor: Kurt Feuerman.

Foundation type: Independent foundation.

Financial data (yr. ended 12/31/05): Assets, $9,334,190 (M); gifts received, $546,934; expenditures, $476,746; qualifying distributions, $452,440; giving activities include $447,600 for 25 grants (high: $260,000; low: $100).

Purpose and activities: Giving for education and human services.

Fields of interest: Business school/education; Human services; Christian agencies & churches.

Limitations: Applications not accepted. Giving primarily in CT. No grants to individuals.

Application information: Contributes only to pre-selected organizations.

Officer and Trustees:* Kurt Feuerman,* Treas.; Anne Pelletier Feuerman.

EIN: 061555350

Selected grants: The following grants were reported in 2004.

$200,000 to Harvey School, Katonah, NY.

1539
Betsy and Jesse Fink Foundation ✧

20 Marshall St., Ste. 300
Norwalk, CT 06854-2204

Established in 1999 in CT.

Donors: Jesse Fink; Betsy Fink.

Foundation type: Independent foundation.

Financial data (yr. ended 12/31/04): Assets, $9,022,624 (M); expenditures, $1,164,449; qualifying distributions, $1,143,297; giving activities include $1,143,297 for 15 grants.

Purpose and activities: Giving primarily for environmental conservation; funding also for a library association and for farm lands.

Fields of interest: Education; Environment; Agriculture, farmlands.

Limitations: Applications not accepted. Giving on a national basis. No grants to individuals.

Application information: Contributes only to pre-selected organizations.

Trustees: Betsy Fink; Jesse Fink.

EIN: 137219308

Selected grants: The following grants were reported in 2004.

$275,000 to Wilton Library Association, Wilton, CT.
$250,000 to American Farmland Trust, DC.
$205,197 to Student Conservation Association, Charlestown, NH. 2 grants: $200,000, $5,197
$100,000 to Environmental Defense, New York, NY.
$100,000 to Nature Conservancy, Arlington, VA.
$75,000 to Fairfield County Community Foundation, Wilton, CT.
$65,000 to Trust for Public Land, New Haven, CT. 2 grants: $40,000, $25,000
$5,000 to Solar Youth, New Haven, CT.

1540
Grace J. Fippinger Foundation, Inc. ✧

c/o Hynes, Himmelreich, Glennon & Co.
30 Old Kings Hwy. S., P.O. Box 4004
Darien, CT 06820 (203) 656-5501
Contact: Thomas W. Hynes, Pres.
FAX: (203) 656-5500

Established in 1989 in CT.

Donor: Grace J. Fippinger†.

Foundation type: Independent foundation.

Financial data (yr. ended 12/31/05): Assets, $7,995,598 (M); expenditures, $489,606; qualifying distributions, $389,815; giving activities include $354,030 for 16 grants (high: $100,000; low: $500; average: $1,000–$50,000).

Fields of interest: Arts; Higher education; Education; Cancer.

Type of support: Seed money; Fellowships; Scholarship funds; Research.

Limitations: Applications not accepted. Giving primarily in NY. No grants to individuals.

Application information: Contributes only to pre-selected organizations.

Board meeting date(s): Quarterly

Officers and Directors:* Thomas W. Hynes,* Pres.; David Himmelreich,* Treas.; Lorraine C. Pennoyer; Ann Works.
Number of staff: 1 full-time professional.
EIN: 223019876
Selected grants: The following grants were reported in 2005.
$100,000 to Saint Lawrence University, Canton, NY.
$51,179 to Memorial Sloan-Kettering Cancer Center, New York, NY.
$40,000 to Red Cloud Indian School, Pine Ridge, SD.
$35,250 to Hicksville High School, Hicksville, NY.
$12,000 to Shelter for the Homeless, Stamford, CT.
$2,500 to Senior Services of Stamford, Stamford, CT.
$1,000 to Sacred Heart Academy, Hamden, CT.
$1,000 to Xavier High School, New York, NY.
$500 to Stamford Center for the Arts, Stamford, CT.

1541
First County Bank Foundation, Inc. ◇ ☆
117 Prospect St.
Stamford, CT 06901 (203) 462-4492
Contact: Katherine Harris, V.P.

Established in 2000 in CT.
Foundation type: Independent foundation.
Financial data (yr. ended 12/31/05): Assets, $6,423,535 (M); gifts received, $1,386,502; expenditures, $492,548; qualifying distributions, $440,584; giving activities include $440,584 for grants.
Fields of interest: Arts; Health care; Human services; Children/youth, services.
Limitations: Giving primarily in Darien, Greenwich, New Canaan, Norwalk, Stamford, and Westport, CT.
Application information: Application form required.
   Deadline(s): Mar. 1- Apr. 30
Officers and Directors:* Richard E. Taber,* Pres.; Katherine Harris, V.P.; Ronald Holbert, Treas.; Thomas Bartram; Robert Beer; Marcia Bull; Francis DeLuca; Nicholas Dubiago; Robert Emslie; Mark Lapine; James Mcardle, Jr.; Alphonse Palmer.
EIN: 061604469
Selected grants: The following grants were reported in 2004.
$25,000 to Childcare Learning Centers, Stamford, CT.
$25,000 to Kids in Crisis, Cos Cob, CT.
$25,000 to Rebuilding Together, Stamford, CT.
$17,526 to CTE, Inc., Stamford, CT.
$15,000 to New Neighborhoods, Stamford, CT.
$15,000 to Yerwood Center, Stamford, CT.
$10,000 to Family Centers, Greenwich, CT.
$10,000 to Malta House, Norwalk, CT.
$10,000 to Salvation Army, Meriden, CT.
$9,000 to YMCA of Norwalk, Norwalk, CT.

1542
Fisher Foundation, Inc. ◇
36 Brookside Blvd.
West Hartford, CT 06107 (860) 570-0221
Contact: Hinda Fisher, Pres.
FAX: (860) 570-0225; E-mail: bboyle@fisherfdn.org; Contact for information regarding application form or the foundation's requirements: Beverly Boyle, Pres.; URL: http://www.fisherfdn.org

Established in 1959.
Donors: Stanley D. Fisher Trust; FIP Corp.

Foundation type: Independent foundation.
Financial data (yr. ended 12/31/05): Assets, $10,549,249 (M); expenditures, $630,714; qualifying distributions, $537,282; giving activities include $485,930 for 93 grants (high: $10,000; low: $500).
Purpose and activities: Giving primarily for education, arts and culture, health, and human services.
Fields of interest: Arts; Education, early childhood education; Elementary school/education; Adult education—literacy, basic skills & GED; Education, reading; Health care; Employment; Housing/shelter, development; Human services; Children/youth, services; Aging, centers/services; Homeless, human services; Community development; Jewish federated giving programs; Aging; Minorities; Economically disadvantaged.
Type of support: General/operating support; Program development.
Limitations: Giving primarily in the greater Hartford, CT, area, (Avon, Bloomfield, East Hartford, Enfield, Farmington, Glastonbury, Hartford, Manchester, Newington, Rocky Hill, Simsbury, South Windsor, Vernon, West Hartford, Wethersfield, and Windsor). No grants for conferences, retreats, performances or events, or for capital campaigns.
Publications: Application guidelines; Annual report (including application guidelines); Grants list; Informational brochure.
Application information: Application information and form available on foundation Web site. Audio or videotapes are not accepted, nor are applications submitted via fax or email. Application form required.
   Initial approach: Letter or telephone
   Copies of proposal: 2
   Deadline(s): Jan. 15, Apr. 15, and Sept. 15
   Board meeting date(s): Mar., June, and Nov.
Officers and Directors:* Hinda N. Fisher,* Pres. and Treas.; Diane Fisher Bell,* V.P.; Lois Fisher Dietzel,* V.P.; Beverly Boyle, Secy. and Exec. Dir.; Michael Finkelstein.
Number of staff: 1 part-time professional.
EIN: 066039415
Selected grants: The following grants were reported in 2004.
$80,000 to Jewish Federation of Greater Hartford, West Hartford, CT.
$17,500 to Center for Childrens Advocacy, Hartford, CT. 2 grants: $7,500, $10,000
$10,000 to Big Brothers.
$8,000 to Greater Hartford Arts Council, Hartford, CT.
$7,500 to Habitat for Humanity International.
$7,500 to Literacy Volunteers of Greater Hartford, Hartford, CT.
$5,000 to Artists Collective, Hartford, CT.
$5,000 to Bridge Family Center, West Hartford, CT.
$2,500 to Williams College, Williamstown, MA.

1543
The Lawrence Flinn, Jr. Charitable Trust ◇
3 Greenwich Office Park
Greenwich, CT 06831

Established in 1995 in CT.
Donor: Lawrence Flinn, Jr.
Foundation type: Independent foundation.
Financial data (yr. ended 12/31/04): Assets, $19,842,645 (M); expenditures, $1,077,934; qualifying distributions, $953,551; giving activities

include $953,551 for 95 grants (high: $200,000; low: $25).
Purpose and activities: Giving primarily for the arts, education, the environment, health, youth development, community development, and federated giving programs.
Fields of interest: Arts; Education; Environment, natural resources; Hospitals (general); Health care; Health organizations, association; Cancer; Youth development; Human services; Community development; Federated giving programs.
Limitations: Applications not accepted. Giving primarily in CT, FL, and NY. No grants to individuals.
Application information: Contributes only to pre-selected organizations.
Trustees: Lawrence Flinn, Jr.; Stephanie Flinn.
EIN: 137044737

1544
Lawrence & Megan Foley Family Foundation, Inc. ◇
44 Morehouse Ln.
Southport, CT 06890

Established in 2001 in CT.
Donors: Lawrence G. Foley; Megan M. Foley.
Foundation type: Independent foundation.
Financial data (yr. ended 11/30/04): Assets, $1,028,943 (M); expenditures, $402,423; qualifying distributions, $400,166; giving activities include $400,569 for 42 grants (high: $45,000; low: $25).
Fields of interest: Museums; Performing arts centers; Performing arts, theater; Education; Health care; Parkinson's disease; Youth development; Human services; Community development; Christian agencies & churches.
Limitations: Applications not accepted. Giving primarily in CT. No grants to individuals.
Application information: Contributes only to pre-selected organizations.
Directors: Lawrence G. Foley; Megan M. Foley; David J. McCabe.
EIN: 421528874

1545
Maud Glover Folsom Foundation, Inc.
1228 King St., House #5
Greenwich, CT 06830
E-mail: sarahdouglas.burdett@snet.net
Application address: 7 Beldenwood Rd., Simsbury, CT 06070-2130, tel.: (860) 729-7498

Incorporated in 1957 in NY.
Donor: Charles Stuart Folsom†.
Foundation type: Independent foundation.
Financial data (yr. ended 7/31/05): Assets, $8,039,636 (M); gifts received, $1,000; expenditures, $436,985; qualifying distributions, $404,387; giving activities include $361,250 for 85 grants to individuals (high: $7,500; low: $1,250).
Purpose and activities: To provide education for selected male students of American ancestry, and of Anglo-Saxon or German descent between the ages of 14 and 20, subject to certain conditions; ineligible to apply upon reaching age 20. Annual grants of $5,000 will continue, providing grantee maintains a C-plus average while pursuing his education, which could continue through a doctorate.
Type of support: Scholarships—to individuals.

Limitations: Giving on a national basis.
Publications: Informational brochure (including application guidelines).
Application information: Application form required.
Initial approach: Letter
Deadline(s): None
Board meeting date(s): As required
Final notification: After individual interviews
Officers and Trustees: Douglas M. Burdett,* Pres.; John L. Raye,* Secy.; William F. Austin,* Treas.
EIN: 111965890

1546
Foster-Davis Foundation, Inc. ◇
P.O. Box 1669
Greenwich, CT   06836-1669

Established about 1966 in CT.
Donor: Alma F. Davis Charitable Lead Trust.
Foundation type: Independent foundation.
Financial data (yr. ended 12/31/05): Assets, $11,047,246 (M); expenditures, $649,087; qualifying distributions, $563,500; giving activities include $563,500 for 61 grants (high: $100,000; low: $250).
Purpose and activities: Giving primarily to higher education; grants also for research in mental health and biology, recreational facilities, fisheries and wildlife preservation, and health associations.
Fields of interest: Higher education; Animals/wildlife, preservation/protection; Hospitals (general); Mental health/crisis services; Health organizations, association; Recreation; Biological sciences.
Limitations: Applications not accepted. Giving primarily in CT and NY. No grants to individuals.
Application information: Contributes only to pre-selected organizations.
Board meeting date(s): 3rd week in July
Officers and Directors: Foster Bam, Pres.; Edward F. Rodenbach,* V.P. and Secy.; Patricia S. Bam, Treas.; Howard S. Tuthill.
EIN: 060811599

1547
Fox Family Foundation ◇ ☆
304 Wahackme Rd.
New Canaan, CT   06840

Established in CT.
Donor: Rodman Fox.
Foundation type: Independent foundation.
Financial data (yr. ended 12/31/05): Assets, $371,918 (M); gifts received, $263,472; expenditures, $829,140; qualifying distributions, $829,140; giving activities include $827,350 for 8 grants (high: $800,000; low: $50).
Fields of interest: Higher education; Human services.
Limitations: Applications not accepted. Giving primarily in New Canaan, CT. No grants to individuals.
Application information: Contributes only to pre-selected organizations.
Officers: Rodman Fox, Pres.; Darby Fox, Secy.-Treas.
EIN: 201789061

1548
Freas Foundation, Inc.
11 Halstead Ln.
Branford, CT   06405
Contact: David M. Trout, Mgr.

Established in 1951.
Foundation type: Independent foundation.
Financial data (yr. ended 12/31/05): Assets, $7,909,193 (M); expenditures, $440,969; qualifying distributions, $372,598; giving activities include $372,598 for grants.
Purpose and activities: Giving primarily for the arts, education, and human services.
Fields of interest: Arts; Higher education; Human services; Children/youth, services.
Type of support: General/operating support; Annual campaigns; Capital campaigns; Program development; Scholarship funds; Matching/challenge support.
Limitations: Applications not accepted. Giving primarily in PA. No grants to individuals.
Application information: Contributes only to pre-selected organizations.
Managers: Arthur K. Freas; Margery H. Freas; David M. Trout; Rebecca F. Trout.
EIN: 221714810
Selected grants: The following grants were reported in 2005.
$148,000 to Bucknell University, Lewisburg, PA.
$17,240 to York County Heritage Trust, York, PA.
$7,000 to Harrisburg Area Community College, Harrisburg, PA.
$6,000 to York Catholic High School, York, PA.
$5,000 to Goodspeed Opera House Foundation, East Haddam, CT.
$5,000 to York College of Pennsylvania, York, PA.
$5,000 to York Union Rescue Mission, York, PA.
$4,500 to Childrens Home of York, York, PA.
$3,250 to Holy Family School Inner-City Youth Foundation, Des Moines, IA.
$2,000 to Childrens Center, Hamden, CT.

1549
FSB Foundation, Inc. ◇ ☆
c/o Farmington Savings Bank
32 Main St.
Farmington, CT   06032   (860) 677-4541
Contact: John Hangen, Treas.

Established in 1998 in CT.
Donor: Farmington Savings Bank.
Foundation type: Company-sponsored foundation.
Financial data (yr. ended 12/31/05): Assets, $2,599,305 (M); gifts received, $282,503; expenditures, $365,466; qualifying distributions, $363,212; giving activities include $363,212 for grants.
Fields of interest: Child development, education; Education; Environment; Family services.
Limitations: Giving limited to the Farmington Valley, CT.
Application information: Application form not required.
Initial approach: Proposal
Deadline(s): None
Officers and Directors: Bryan P. Bowerman,* Chair. and Pres.; Brenda O. Kowalski,* Secy.; John H. Hangen,* Treas.; David M. Drew; Robert F. Edmunds, Jr.
EIN: 061523804

1550
The Fuscone Family Foundation ◇
14 Cowdray Park Dr.
Greenwich, CT   06831

Established in 2000 in NY.
Donors: Richard M. Fuscone; Marjorie M. Fuscone.
Foundation type: Independent foundation.
Financial data (yr. ended 12/31/03): Assets, $0 (M); gifts received, $672,223; expenditures, $687,969; qualifying distributions, $682,807; giving activities include $329,137 for 75 grants (high: $30,000; low: $20).
Fields of interest: Education.
Limitations: Giving primarily in Greenwich, CT. No grants to individuals.
Officers: Richard M. Fuscone, Pres.; Marjorie M. Fuscone, V.P.
EIN: 256729848
Selected grants: The following grants were reported in 2003.
$30,000 to Memorial Sloan-Kettering Cancer Center, New York, NY.
$25,000 to Brunswick School, Greenwich, CT.
$25,000 to Greenwich Country Day School, Greenwich, CT.
$25,000 to Greenwich Hospital, Greenwich, CT.
$20,500 to Kids in Crisis, Cos Cob, CT. 2 grants: $10,500, $10,000
$20,000 to Juvenile Diabetes Research Foundation International, New York, NY.
$18,033 to United Way of Greenwich, Greenwich, CT.
$15,000 to Historical Society of the Town of Greenwich, Cos Cob, CT.
$10,000 to Transportation Association of Greenwich, Riverside, CT.

1551
The Catherine and Henry J. Gaisman Foundation ◇
44 N. Stanwich Rd.
Greenwich, CT   06831

Incorporated in 1934 in DE.
Donor: Henry J. Gaisman†.
Foundation type: Independent foundation.
Financial data (yr. ended 12/31/05): Assets, $49,183,333 (M); expenditures, $1,017,599; qualifying distributions, $1,014,164; giving activities include $1,013,870 for 11 grants (high: $401,250; low: $350).
Purpose and activities: Giving for hospitals and medical research, including ophthalmologic research, and Roman Catholic church support.
Fields of interest: Higher education; Hospitals (general); Medical research, institute; Eye research; Lung research; Roman Catholic agencies & churches.
Limitations: Applications not accepted. Giving primarily in NY. No grants to individuals.
Application information: Contributes only to pre-selected organizations.
Officer and Directors: Catherine V. Gaisman,* Mgr.; Robert Arias; Eric W. Waldman.
EIN: 136129464

1552
Garden Homes Fund
29 Knapp St.
P.O. Box 4401
Stamford, CT 06907-1799
Contact: Joel E. Freedman, Tr.

Established in 1981 in CT.
Donor: Members of the Joel Freedman family.
Foundation type: Independent foundation.
Financial data (yr. ended 12/31/05): Assets, $8,032,751 (M); gifts received, $178,232; expenditures, $900,667; qualifying distributions, $405,645; giving activities include $405,645 for 108 grants (high: $20,000; low: $85).
Purpose and activities: Giving primarily for conservation, education, and social services.
Fields of interest: Education; Environment, natural resources; Human services.
Type of support: Endowments; Annual campaigns; Capital campaigns; Building/renovation; Employee-related scholarships.
Limitations: Applications not accepted. Giving primarily in CT, NJ, and NY. No support for religious organizations.
Application information: Contributes only to pre-selected organizations. Unsolicited requests for funds not accepted.
Trustees: Deborah Freedman; Jane Freedman; Joel E. Freedman; Naomi K. Freedman; Richard Freedman.
Number of staff: None.
EIN: 061043730

1553
GE Foundation ▼ ✧
(formerly GE Fund)
3135 Easton Tpke.
Fairfield, CT 06828-0001 (203) 373-3216
Contact: Robert L. Corcoran, Pres.
FAX: (203) 373-3029;
E-mail: gefoundation@ge.com; URL: http://www.gefoundation.com

Trust established in 1952 in NY.
Donor: General Electric Co.
Foundation type: Company-sponsored foundation.
Financial data (yr. ended 12/31/05): Assets, $3,677,622 (M); gifts received, $62,100,000; expenditures, $72,580,973; qualifying distributions, $71,382,322; giving activities include $70,635,496 for grants.
Purpose and activities: The foundation supports organizations involved with education, diversity, minorities, and economically disadvantaged people.
Fields of interest: Elementary/secondary education; Higher education; Business school/education; Engineering school/education; Scholarships/financial aid; Civil rights, equal rights; Mathematics; Science; Minorities; Economically disadvantaged.
International interests: China; India; Mexico.
Type of support: Continuing support; Program development; Publication; Curriculum development; Fellowships; Scholarship funds; Research; Employee matching gifts; Employee-related scholarships.
Limitations: Applications not accepted. Giving on a national and international basis, with emphasis on areas of company operations. No support for religious or political organizations. No grants to individuals (except for employee-related scholarships and fellowships), or for capital

campaigns, endowments, or other special purpose campaigns; no loans; no equipment donations.
Publications: Grants list.
Application information: Contributes only to pre-selected organizations.
Board meeting date(s): Quarterly
Officers and Directors: William J. Conaty,* Chair.; Robert L. Corcoran,* Pres.; Marie Hurd, Secy. and Compt.; Michael J. Cosgrove, Treas.; Ferdinando Beccalli; Pamela Daley; Nancy Dorn; Henry A. Hubschman; Marc Saperstein; Keith S. Sherin; Lloyd G. Trotter.
Number of staff: 6 full-time professional; 1 part-time professional; 4 full-time support.
EIN: 222621967
Selected grants: The following grants were reported in 2004.
$2,453,417 to United Way of Tri-State, New York, NY. 2 grants: $1,961,087, $492,330
$1,796,100 to Institute of International Education, New York, NY. 2 grants: $811,000, $985,100
$1,000,000 to American Red Cross.
$750,000 to United Way of America, Alexandria, VA.
$700,000 to United Way of Greater Cincinnati, Cincinnati, OH.
$697,600 to United States Fund for UNICEF, New York, NY.
$425,000 to International Youth Foundation, Baltimore, MD.
$375,000 to Junior Achievement International, Atlanta, GA.

1554
The Georgescu Family Foundation ✧ ☆
P.O. Box 2630
Westport, CT 06880
Application address: c/o Barbara and Peter Georgescu, 435 E. 52nd St., New York, NY 10022, tel.: (203) 226-8997

Donors: Peter Georgescu; Barbara Georgescu.
Foundation type: Independent foundation.
Financial data (yr. ended 12/31/05): Assets, $239,449 (M); expenditures, $377,212; qualifying distributions, $371,426; giving activities include $371,426 for 70 grants (high: $105,000; low: $50).
Purpose and activities: Giving primarily for the arts and health care.
Fields of interest: Performing arts, theater; Performing arts, orchestra (symphony); Arts; Education; Hospitals (general); Health care; Human services; Protestant agencies & churches.
Limitations: Giving primarily in NY.
Application information: Application form not required.
Initial approach: Letter
Deadline(s): None
Officers: Peter Georgescu, Pres.; Andrew Georgescu, V.P.; Barbara Georgescu, Secy.-Treas.
EIN: 134111095

1555
Marsha Lilien Gladstein Foundation ✧
c/o Gary S. Gladstein
15 Wyckham Hill Ln.
Greenwich, CT 06831-3049

Foundation type: Independent foundation.
Financial data (yr. ended 12/31/05): Assets, $9,273,035 (M); expenditures, $1,120,470; qualifying distributions, $1,086,410; giving

activities include $1,086,402 for 47 grants (high: $1,000,000; low: $15).
Purpose and activities: Giving primarily for education, and to Jewish agencies; funding also for social services.
Fields of interest: Higher education; Education; Cancer research; Human services; Jewish federated giving programs; Jewish agencies & temples; Economically disadvantaged.
Limitations: Applications not accepted. Giving primarily in CT and New York, NY.
Application information: Contributes only to pre-selected organizations.
Trustees: Gary Gladstein; Jeff Gladstein; Mindy A. Grafstein.
EIN: 061581875

1556
The Goergen Foundation, Inc. ✧
c/o Thomas E. Finn
35 Mason St.
Greenwich, CT 06830-5420

Established in 1986 in CT.
Donor: Robert B. Goergen.
Foundation type: Independent foundation.
Financial data (yr. ended 12/31/05): Assets, $13,859,747 (M); expenditures, $912,034; qualifying distributions, $700,574; giving activities include $700,574 for grants.
Purpose and activities: Giving primarily for higher education and educational institutions. Support also for human services, the arts, particularly museums, animals and wildlife, and the environment.
Fields of interest: Museums (art); Arts; Higher education; Environment; Animals/wildlife; Hospitals (general); Human services.
Type of support: General/operating support.
Limitations: Applications not accepted. Giving primarily in CT, NY, and PA. No grants to individuals.
Application information: Contributes only to pre-selected organizations.
Officers and Trustees: Robert B. Goergen,* Pres.; Robert B. Goergen, Jr.,* V.P.; Todd A. Goergen,* V.P.; Pamela M. Goergen,* Secy.-Treas.
EIN: 061180035
Selected grants: The following grants were reported in 2003.
$100,757 to YMCA of Greenwich, Greenwich, CT. For general support.
$100,520 to Boys and Girls Club of Greenwich, Greenwich, CT. For general support.
$25,000 to Cato Institute, DC. For general support.
$13,561 to University of Rochester, Rochester, NY. For general support.
$10,000 to Greenwich School Age Child Care, Riverside, CT. For general support.
$5,000 to Immaculata University, Immaculata, PA. For general support.
$3,000 to Historical Society of the Town of Greenwich, Cos Cob, CT. For general support.
$1,000 to Bruce Museum, Greenwich, CT. For general support.
$1,000 to Room to Grow, New York, NY. For general support.
$1,000 to Wake Forest University, Winston-Salem, NC. For general support.

1557
The Goldhirsh Foundation, Inc. ✧
(formerly The Bernard A. and Wendy J. Goldhirsh Foundation, Inc.)
c/o Rita D. Berkson, Exec. Dir.
113 Linden Ave.
Branford, CT 06405
E-mail: rdberkson@goldhirshfoundation.org;
Application address: c/o Sally E. McNagny, M.D., M.P.H., Dir., Brain Tumor Research Awards Program, 95 Berkeley St., Ste. 201, Boston, MA 02116; tel.: (617) 279-2254, FAX: (617) 423-4619; E-mail: smcnagny@goldhirshfoundation.org; tel./FAX for Rita D. Berkson in Branford, CT: (203) 488-2697; URL: http://www.goldhirshfoundation.org

Established in 2000 in MA.
Donor: Bernard A. Goldhirsh†.
Foundation type: Independent foundation.
Financial data (yr. ended 12/31/04): Assets, $60,755,511 (M); gifts received, $2,000,000; expenditures, $3,181,772; qualifying distributions, $2,587,258; giving activities include $2,110,000 for 2 grants (high: $2,100,000; low: $10,000), and $180,000 for 31 employee matching gifts.
Purpose and activities: The foundation is interested in providing strategic investment in both pediatric and adult brain tumor research to accelerate progress toward more effective treatment for malignant diffuse glioma tumors. The foundation seeks responses from investigators working in the continuum between basic research and clinical application, integrating and translating knowledge in various disciplines into meaningful progress for patients. Examples of funding areas include, but are not limited to, oncogenomics and proteomics, genetically engineered models, the discovery and testing of small molecule therapies, unusual drug delivery systems, or improved brain imaging techniques. The foundation also encourages submission of research projects at the interface of developmental biology and cancer along the stem cell to glial axis.
Fields of interest: Cancer research.
Limitations: Giving primarily in MA. No grants to individuals.
Publications: Grants list.
Application information: Refer to the foundation Web site for details on the application process.
Officers and Directors:* Philip D. Cutter, M.D.*, Chair.; Richard N. Thielen, Treas.; Rita D. Berkson,* Exec. Dir.; Richard E. Cavanagh; Benjamin Goldhirsh; Elizabeth Goldhirsh; Robert F. Higgins.
EIN: 043540874
Selected grants: The following grants were reported in 2004.
$2,100,000 to Medical Foundation, Boston, MA.

1558
The Goodnow Fund ✧
9 Old Kings Hwy. S.
Darien, CT 06820-4523 (203) 655-6272
Contact: Edward B. Goodnow, Tr.

Established in 1993 in CT.
Donor: Edward B. Goodnow.
Foundation type: Independent foundation.
Financial data (yr. ended 12/31/04): Assets, $17,871,647 (M); expenditures, $741,528; qualifying distributions, $677,891; giving activities include $675,300 for 121 grants (high: $100,000; low: $100).

Fields of interest: Education; Animals/wildlife, fisheries; Health care; Human services; Salvation Army; Children/youth, services; Federated giving programs.
Limitations: Giving primarily in CT. No grants to individuals.
Application information: Application form not required.
Initial approach: Letter
Deadline(s): None
Trustee: Edward B. Goodnow.
EIN: 066395384

1559
William Caspar Graustein Memorial Fund ▼
1 Hamden Ctr.
2319 Whitney Ave., Ste. 2B
Hamden, CT 06518 (203) 230-3330
Contact: David M. Nee, Exec. Dir.
FAX: (203) 230-3331; E-mail: gmfmail@wcgmf.org; URL: http://www.wcgmf.org

Established in 1964 in NY.
Donors: Archibald R. Graustein†; Hallie H. Graustein†; William C. Graustein; D.W. Rich & Co., Inc.; Jean Graustein; Thelma Ewig.
Foundation type: Independent foundation.
Financial data (yr. ended 12/31/05): Assets, $106,393,064 (M); gifts received, $1,708,549; expenditures, $5,502,774; qualifying distributions, $5,136,157; giving activities include $4,888,631 for 35 grants (high: $100,000; low: $10,000; average: $10,000–$100,000), and $820,167 for 1 loan/program-related investment.
Purpose and activities: The mission of the fund is to improve the effectiveness of education in fostering both personal development and leadership. To accomplish this mission, the fund has set three goals: 1) to engage young children more deeply in their own education; 2) to support Connecticut communities in improving education for their elementary and pre-school children; and 3) to develop both statewide and local leadership dedicated to improving and advocating for education.
Fields of interest: Education, early childhood education; Elementary school/education.
Type of support: General/operating support; Program development; Conferences/seminars; Seed money; Curriculum development; Research; Technical assistance; Consulting services; Program evaluation; Program-related investments/loans.
Limitations: Giving primarily in CT. No support for religious organizations for sectarian purposes or political causes and activities. No grants to individuals or for capital campaigns or scholarships.
Publications: Annual report.
Application information: Contact foundation or see foundation Web site for program specific application guidelines. Application form required.
Initial approach: Telephone
Copies of proposal: 12
Deadline(s): 6 weeks prior
Board meeting date(s): Apr., June, and Dec.
Final notification: 6 weeks
Officer: David M. Nee, Exec. Dir.
Trustees: Lisa Graustein; William C. Graustein; P. Ranganath Nayak; David C. Oxman; Benjamin R. Shute, Jr.; Barbara Tinney.

Number of staff: 4 full-time professional; 3 full-time support.
EIN: 046037391
Selected grants: The following grants were reported in 2003.
$800,000 to Connecticut Center for School Change, Hartford, CT. 2 grants: $500,000, $300,000
$130,500 to Connecticut Voices for Children, New Haven, CT. 2 grants: $64,250 (For Early Care and Education in Connecticut), $66,250 (For Capitalizing on Progress: Early Care and Education in Connecticut).
$100,000 to League of Women Voters of Connecticut Education Fund, Hamden, CT. For Community Conversations About Education.
$95,000 to Womens Center of Northeastern Connecticut, Willimantic, CT. For Killingly, Plainfield, and Putnam Discovery Grant.
$65,000 to Bridgeport Child Advocacy Coalition, Bridgeport, CT. For Parent Information, Advocacy, and Empowerment: Assessment of Parent Engagement in Bridgeport Schools.
$60,000 to Meriden Children First Initiative, Meriden, CT. For Meriden Discovery Grant.
$45,000 to Bridgeport Public Education Fund, Bridgeport, CT. For Bridgeport Discovery Grant.
$45,000 to United Way of Northern Fairfield County, Danbury, CT. For Danbury Discovery Grant.

1560
Sanford J. Grossman Charitable Trust ✧
c/o QFS, Inc.
10 Glenville St.
Greenwich, CT 06831

Established in 2002 in CT.
Donor: Sanford J. Grossman.
Foundation type: Independent foundation.
Financial data (yr. ended 12/31/05): Assets, $2,618,038 (M); gifts received, $2,124; expenditures, $492,632; qualifying distributions, $491,571; giving activities include $489,474 for 14 grants (high: $245,000; low: $100; average: $2,000–$75,000).
Purpose and activities: Giving primarily for education, the arts, and health associations.
Fields of interest: Performing arts; Performing arts, opera; Arts; Higher education; Hospitals (general); Health organizations, association; Human services; International terrorism.
Limitations: Applications not accepted. Giving to national organizations, primarily in CT, Washington, DC, and New York, NY. No grants to individuals.
Application information: Contributes only to pre-selected organizations.
Officers: Bruce Wilson, Exec. V.P. and Secy.-Treas.
Trustee: Sanford J. Grossman.
EIN: 336316059

1561
The GW Foundation ✧ ☆
39 Wilshire Rd.
Greenwich, CT 06831
Contact: Gary C. Wendt, Tr.

Established in 1998 in CT.
Donor: Gary C. Wendt.
Foundation type: Independent foundation.
Financial data (yr. ended 12/31/05): Assets, $3,526,733 (M); expenditures, $646,359; qualifying distributions, $612,000; giving activities

include $612,000 for 5 grants (high: $540,000; low: $2,000).

Fields of interest: Boys & girls clubs; Family services.

Limitations: Applications not accepted. Giving primarily in CT, GA, and NY. No grants to individuals.

Application information: Contributes only to pre-selected organizations.

Trustees: Gary C. Wendt; Rosemarie Wendt.

EIN: 066469925

1562

The Hampshire Foundation ✧

P.O. Box 370-326
West Hartford, CT   06137
E-mail: info@hampshirefoundation.org; Tel./FAX: (860) 236-5751; e-mail for application inquiries: sshelby@hampshirefoundation.org; URL: http://www.hampshirefoundation.org

Established in 2000 in CT.

Donor: The Hadley Trust.

Foundation type: Independent foundation.

Financial data (yr. ended 12/31/05): Assets, $14,816,076 (M); expenditures, $620,195; qualifying distributions, $564,444; giving activities include $538,250 for 21 grants (high: $131,250; low: $1,000).

Purpose and activities: In Hartford, CT, prepare and engage the youth and provide training in business skills and income generation. In Peru, provide training in business skills and income generation through vocational training, micro-lending, and the promotion of sustainable agriculture.

Fields of interest: Education; Human services.

International interests: Peru.

Limitations: Giving primarily in Hartford, CT and Peru. No grants to individuals.

Application information: Application guidelines available on foundation Web site.

   Initial approach: Letter of inquiry
   Deadline(s): Apr. 1 for the spring; Sept. 1 for the fall

Trustees: Nicholas N. Cournoyer; Sabina E. Cournoyer; Sabina G. Cournoyer.

EIN: 061584535

Selected grants: The following grants were reported in 2005.

$135,000 to Pro Mujer, New York, NY. 3 grants: $10,000, $100,000, $25,000

$75,000 to Aid to Artisans, Hartford, CT.

$44,000 to American Jewish World Service, New York, NY.

$29,450 to CARE, New York, NY.

$10,000 to Capital Workforce Partners, Hartford, CT.

$8,500 to Hispanic Health Council, Hartford, CT.

$5,500 to Family Life Education, Hartford, CT.

$5,000 to Riverfront Recapture, Hartford, CT.

1563

The Hartford Courant Foundation, Inc.

285 Broad St.
Hartford, CT   06115-3719   (860) 241-6472
Contact: Kate Miller, Exec. Dir.
FAX: (860) 520-6988; E-mail: kmiller@hcfdn.org; URL: http://www.hcfdn.org

Established in 1950 in CT as a corporate foundation; restructured in 1980 as a private, independent foundation.

Donor: The Hartford Courant Co.

Foundation type: Independent foundation.

Financial data (yr. ended 12/31/05): Assets, $17,063,393 (M); gifts received, $5,805; expenditures, $913,968; qualifying distributions, $837,316; giving activities include $614,125 for 87 + grants (high: $15,000), and $70,000 for 1 employee matching gift.

Purpose and activities: Giving primarily for arts and cultural programs, education, health, social services, and community development, with a strong focus on programs that benefit youth, children, and families.

Fields of interest: Museums; Arts; Education, early childhood education; Child development, education; Education; Health care; Crime/violence prevention, domestic violence; Housing/shelter, development; Human services; Children/youth, services; Child development, services; Family services; Homeless, human services; Community development; Minorities; Economically disadvantaged; Homeless.

Type of support: General/operating support; Capital campaigns; Building/renovation; Equipment; Land acquisition; Program development; Seed money; Matching/challenge support.

Limitations: Giving limited to New Britain, Middletown and the capital region of CT. No support for religious organizations for sectarian purposes, veterans', fraternal, professional, or business associations, or private schools. No grants to individuals, or for continuing support, endowment or emergency funds, conferences, performances, or other short-term, one-time events; no loans.

Publications: Application guidelines; Annual report; Financial statement; Grants list; Informational brochure; Program policy statement (including application guidelines).

Application information: Grant guidelines, application forms, and all reports available on foundation Web site. Application form required.

   Initial approach: Telephone. (Faxed or e-mailed application will not be accepted)
   Copies of proposal: 1
   Deadline(s): Mar. 15, June 15, Sept. 15, and Dec. 15
   Board meeting date(s): Feb., May, Sept., and Nov.
   Final notification: 3 months

Officers and Trustees:* Richard N. Palmer,* Pres.; Toni Smith-Rosario,* V.P.; Kate Miller, Secy. and Exec. Dir.; David Carson,* Treas.; Christel Ford Berry; Steve Carver; Sanford Cloud, Jr.; Anita Ford-Saunders; Rick Graziano; Estela Lopez; David McDonald; Christopher Morrill; Christopher Skomorowski.

Number of staff: 1 full-time professional.

EIN: 060759107

Selected grants: The following grants were reported in 2003.

$70,000 to Greater Hartford Arts Council, Hartford, CT. For challenge grant.

$20,000 to Northwest Catholic High School, West Hartford, CT. For Hispanic program.

$15,000 to Boys and Girls Clubs of Hartford, Hartford, CT. For gang prevention and outreach program.

$15,000 to Shelter for Women, Hartford, CT. For renovation of facility.

$15,000 to Tri-Town Shelter Services, Vernon, CT. For renovation of Vernon shelter.

$12,000 to Center for Childrens Advocacy, Hartford, CT. For Medical-Legal Partnership Project.

$10,000 to Community Partners in Action, Hartford, CT. For Resettlement Program.

$10,000 to Families in Crisis, Hartford, CT. For youth enrichment services.

$10,000 to Trust House, Hartford, CT. For operating support.

$8,000 to Organized Parents Make a Difference, Hartford, CT. For operating support.

1564

Hartford Foundation for Public Giving ▼

10 Columbus Blvd., 8th Fl.
Hartford, CT   06106   (860) 548-1888
Contact: Richard Porth, V.P., Grantmaking
FAX: (860) 524-8346; E-mail: hfpg2@hfpg.org; Additional E-mail: RPorth@hfpg.org; URL: http://www.hfpg.org

Established in 1925 in CT by resolution and declaration of trust.

Foundation type: Community foundation.

Financial data (yr. ended 12/31/05): Assets, $664,546,568 (M); gifts received, $8,845,952; expenditures, $31,477,083; giving activities include $24,763,885 for grants, and $3,399,185 for 5 foundation-administered programs.

Purpose and activities: As Greater Hartford's community-wide charitable endowment, the foundation is permanently committed to improving the quality of life for residents throughout the region. Giving for demonstration programs and capital purposes, with emphasis on community advancement, educational institutions, youth groups, hospitals, social services, including the aged, and cultural and civic endeavors.

Fields of interest: Arts; Education; Health care; AIDS; Children/youth, services; Aging, centers/services; Human services; Economic development; Community development; Aging.

Type of support: Continuing support; Management development/capacity building; Annual campaigns; Capital campaigns; Building/renovation; Equipment; Land acquisition; Emergency funds; Program development; Publication; Seed money; Curriculum development; Scholarship funds; Technical assistance; Consulting services; Program evaluation; Program-related investments/loans; Matching/challenge support.

Limitations: Giving limited to the Greater Hartford, CT, area. No support for sectarian purposes, private foundations, tax-supported agencies, or activities primarily national or international in perspective. No grants to individuals (except for scholarships), or for operating budgets, deficit financing, endowment funds, research, or conferences.

Publications: Application guidelines; Annual report; Grants list; Informational brochure; Newsletter; Occasional report; Program policy statement.

Application information: Visit foundation Web site for application information. Once an applicant has confirmed with a Prog. Officer that the agency is eligible for a foundation grant, a complete grant application packet will be sent. Application form required.

   Initial approach: Telephone
   Copies of proposal: 3
   Deadline(s): None
   Board meeting date(s): Monthly except Jan., Apr., Aug., and Oct.
   Final notification: 60 to 90 days

Officers and Directors:* Mark F. Korber, Chair.; Lewis J. Robinson, Jr.,* Vice-Chair.; Linda J. Kelly, Pres.; Virgil Blondet, Jr., V.P., Finance and Admin.; Christopher H. Hall, V.P., Progs. and Special Projects; Richard Porth, V.P., Grantmaking; Sandra

B. Wood, V.P., Philanthropic Svcs.; Francisco L. Borges, Treas.; Blanche S. Goldenberg,* Chair., Emeritus; Edward J. Forand, Jr.; Beverly P. Greenberg; Bonnie J. Malley; Thomas M. Malloy; Stephen B. Middlebrook; Yvette Melendez Thiesfield.

Trustee Banks: Bank of America, N.A.; U.S. Trust Company, N.A.

Number of staff: 29 full-time professional; 5 part-time professional; 10 full-time support; 3 part-time support.

EIN: 060699252

Selected grants: The following grants were reported in 2005.

$800,000 to Greater Hartford Arts Council, Hartford, CT. For general support.

$500,000 to Connecticut Center for Science and Exploration, Hartford, CT. For capital campaign.

$400,000 to Hartford Area Child Care Collaborative, Hartford, CT. For Brighter Futures Initiative.

$375,000 to Local Initiatives Support Corporation (LISC), Hartford, CT. For program support.

$355,000 to Hartford Symphony Orchestra, Hartford, CT. For program support.

$350,000 to Hartford Economic Development Corporation (HEDCO), Hartford, CT. For operating support.

$350,000 to MetroHartford Alliance, Hartford, CT. For program support.

$275,000 to Connecticut Historical Society, Hartford, CT. For capital campaign.

$250,000 to American School for the Deaf, West Hartford, CT. For program support.

$240,000 to Catholic Charities, Hartford, CT. For after-school initiative.

1565

The Hartwell Foundation ✧

164 Belden Rd.
Falls Village, CT   06031

Established in 1996 in CT.

Donors: Laurence H. Smead; Transnetyx.

Foundation type: Independent foundation.

Financial data (yr. ended 6/30/05): Assets, $51,444,258 (M); expenditures, $2,648,521; qualifying distributions, $2,408,603; giving activities include $2,400,000 for 3 grants (high: $1,520,000; low: $80,000).

Purpose and activities: Giving primarily for philanthropy management, as well as to a children's hospital.

Fields of interest: Higher education; Hospitals (specialty); Philanthropy/voluntarism.

Limitations: Applications not accepted. Giving primarily in Memphis, TN. No grants to individuals.

Application information: Contributes only to pre-selected organizations.

Officers and Directors: Laurence H. Smead,* Pres.; Preston J. Smead,* Secy.-Treas.; Milton Greene, C.F.O.

EIN: 061468749

Selected grants: The following grants were reported in 2005.

$1,520,000 to Fidelity Investments Charitable Gift Fund, Boston, MA. For general support.

$800,000 to Washington University, Saint Louis, MO. For general support.

$80,000 to Saint Jude Childrens Research Hospital, Memphis, TN. For general support.

1566

The Heimbold Foundation ✧

c/o HHG
30 Old Kings Hwy. S.
Darien, CT   06820-4004   (203) 656-5500

Established in 1986 in CT.

Donors: Charles A. Heimbold, Jr.; Monika A. Heimbold.

Foundation type: Independent foundation.

Financial data (yr. ended 12/31/05): Assets, $6,345,398 (M); expenditures, $606,173; qualifying distributions, $557,003; giving activities include $537,003 for 90 grants (high: $100,000; low: $100).

Fields of interest: Arts; Higher education; Medical care, in-patient care; Children/youth, services; Federated giving programs.

Limitations: Applications not accepted. Giving on a national basis. No grants to individuals.

Application information: Contributes only to pre-selected organizations.

Directors: Eric C. Heimbold; Joanna M. Heimbold; Leif C. Heimbold; Monika A. Heimbold; Peter Heimbold.

EIN: 061188361

1567

Annette Heyman Foundation, Inc. ▼ ✧

P.O. Box 7002
Westport, CT   06881-7002
Contact: James R. Mazzeo, Treas.

Established in 1960.

Donors: Annette Heyman; Samuel J. Heyman.

Foundation type: Independent foundation.

Financial data (yr. ended 9/30/05): Assets, $12,461,963 (M); gifts received, $5,165,301; expenditures, $2,234,472; qualifying distributions, $2,195,475; giving activities include $2,195,475 for 123 grants (high: $416,667; low: $100; average: $5,000–$100,000).

Fields of interest: Museums (art); Higher education; Education; Hospitals (general); Health organizations, association; Human services; Jewish federated giving programs; Jewish agencies & temples.

Type of support: Annual campaigns; Capital campaigns; Endowments; Professorships; Research.

Limitations: Applications not accepted. Giving primarily in CT and NY. No grants to individuals.

Application information: Contributes only to pre-selected organizations.

Officers: Annette Heyman, Pres.; Ronnie F. Heyman, Secy.; James R. Mazzeo, Treas.

Director: Samuel J. Heyman.

EIN: 066035519

Selected grants: The following grants were reported in 2004.

$3,750,002 to Partnership for Public Service, DC. 8 grants: $416,667 (For unrestricted support), $150,000 (For unrestricted support), $416,667 (For unrestricted support), $416,667 (For unrestricted support), $1,100,000 (For unrestricted support), $416,667 (For unrestricted support), $416,667 (For unrestricted support), $416,667 (For unrestricted support).

$250,000 to Yale University, New Haven, CT. For unrestricted support.

$100,000 to American Friends of the Israel Museum, New York, NY. For unrestricted support.

1568

The Maximilian E. & Marion O. Hoffman Foundation, Inc. ✧

970 Farmington Ave., Ste. 203
West Hartford, CT   06107   (860) 521-2949
Contact: Marion Barrak, Pres.

Established in 1986 in CT as a successor foundation of the Maximilian E. & Marion O. Hoffman Foundation.

Foundation type: Independent foundation.

Financial data (yr. ended 6/30/05): Assets, $60,085,984 (M); expenditures, $3,408,483; qualifying distributions, $2,632,776; giving activities include $2,589,084 for 74 grants (high: $250,000; low: $1,000).

Purpose and activities: Support for a hospital, as well as secondary and higher education.

Fields of interest: Medical school/education; Education; Hospitals (general).

Type of support: General/operating support; Program development.

Limitations: Giving primarily in the Northeast with emphasis on CT. No grants to individuals.

Application information: Application form required.
Initial approach: Letter
Copies of proposal: 1
Deadline(s): 2 months prior to board meeting
Board meeting date(s): Mid-Oct., Jan., Apr., and June
Final notification: Few weeks after board meeting

Officers and Directors: Marion Barrak,* Pres.; Michael Chaho, M.D., Treas.; Doris C. Chaho; Joseph J. Fauliso; Marie Gustin, Ph.D.; Robert M. Jeresaty, M.D.

Number of staff: 3 full-time professional.

EIN: 222648036

Selected grants: The following grants were reported in 2005.

$250,000 to Saint Francis Hospital and Medical Center, Hartford, CT. For continuing support for Hoffman Heart Institute.

$250,000 to Saint Joseph College, West Hartford, CT. For continuing support for athletic center.

$200,000 to Connecticut Center for Science and Exploration, Hartford, CT. For capital campaign.

$200,000 to Yale University, Women's Health Research at Yale, New Haven, CT. Toward endowment.

$150,000 to Saint Peter Church, Hartford, CT. For acculturation programs.

$125,000 to New Britain General Hospital, New Britain, CT. For continuing support of capital campaign.

$100,000 to American University of Beirut, New York, NY. For scholarship for medical student from Zahle, Lebanon.

$75,000 to YMCA of New Britain-Berlin, New Britain, CT. For capital improvements.

$20,000 to Holy Apostles College and Seminary, Cromwell, CT. For liturgical organ and renovations to chapel.

$10,000 to National Society of the Colonial Dames of America, Wethersfield, CT. For stabilization and refurbishment of Webb House at Webb-Deane-Stevens Museum.

1569

The Harvey Hubbell Foundation ✧ ☆

584 Derby Milford Rd.
P.O. Box 549
Orange, CT   06477

Trust established in 1959 in CT.
Donor: Hubbell Inc.
Foundation type: Company-sponsored foundation.
Financial data (yr. ended 12/31/05): Assets,
$5,756,340 (M); gifts received, $150,000;
expenditures, $485,584; qualifying distributions,
$485,584; giving activities include $405,129 for
150 grants (high: $100,000; low: $100), and
$72,906 for 97 employee matching gifts.
Purpose and activities: The foundation supports
organizations involved with education, health,
cancer, fire prevention, human services, and
community development.
Fields of interest: Higher education; Education;
Hospitals (general); Health care; Cancer; Disasters,
fire prevention/control; Human services;
Community development; Federated giving
programs.
Type of support: Annual campaigns; Capital
campaigns; Building/renovation; Employee
matching gifts.
Limitations: Applications not accepted. Giving
primarily in areas of company operations in CT. No
grants to individuals.
Application information: Contributes only to
pre-selected organizations.
Trustees: Gregory F. Covino; Richard W. Davies;
Timothy H. Powers.
EIN: 066078177

1570
The Huisking Foundation, Inc. ✧
291 Peddlers Rd.
Guilford, CT 06437-2324
Contact: Frank R. Huisking, Secy.-Treas.

Incorporated in 1946 in NY.
Donors: Claire F. Hanavan; Richard V. Huisking;
Jean M. Steinschneider; and members of the
Huisking family and family-related corps.
Foundation type: Independent foundation.
Financial data (yr. ended 12/31/05): Assets,
$22,371,951 (M); expenditures, $1,170,294;
qualifying distributions, $1,057,120; giving
activities include $1,040,000 for 333 grants (high:
$25,000; low: $500).
Purpose and activities: Giving primarily for arts and
culture, education, the environment, animal
protection, health and hospitals, human services,
federated giving programs, and religious purposes.
Fields of interest: Media/communications;
Museums; Performing arts; Historic preservation/
historical societies; Higher education; Education;
Environment, natural resources; Animal welfare;
Hospitals (general); Health organizations,
association; Medical research, institute; Human
services; Federated giving programs; Roman
Catholic agencies & churches.
Type of support: General/operating support;
Continuing support; Building/renovation;
Endowments; Program development; Scholarship
funds; Research.
Limitations: Giving on a national basis. No grants to
individuals.
Application information: Application form not
required.
  Initial approach: Letter
  Copies of proposal: 1
  Deadline(s): Submit proposal in Feb. and Aug.
  Board meeting date(s): Apr. and Nov.
Officers and Directors: William W. Huisking,*
Chair. and Pres.; Robert P. Daly,* V.P.; Claire-Marie
Field,* V.P.; Claire F. Hanavan,* V.P.; Jean M.

Steinschneider,* V.P.; Frank R. Huisking,*
Secy.-Treas.; Laura S. Colebank; Helen H. Crawford;
Charles L. Huisking III; Paul Huisking; Richard V.
Huisking; Richard V. Huisking, Jr.; Sarah F. Huisking;
Margaret McCrary; Anne Roome.
EIN: 136117501

1571
International Paper Company
Foundation ▼ ✧
400 Atlantic St.
Stamford, CT 06921
Contact: Kimberly Wirth, Exec. Dir.
FAX: (203) 541-8261; URL: http://
www.internationalpaper.com/OurCompany/
IPGiving/index.html

Incorporated in 1952 in NY.
Donor: International Paper Co.
Foundation type: Company-sponsored foundation.
Financial data (yr. ended 12/31/04): Assets,
$42,337,864 (M); gifts received, $1,364,044;
expenditures, $5,551,270; qualifying distributions,
$5,371,322; giving activities include $4,904,312
for 889 grants (high: $583,992; low: $150),
$219,663 for 628 employee matching gifts, and
$247,347 for in-kind gifts.
Purpose and activities: The foundation supports
organizations involved with K-12 education, literacy,
environmental education, career development for
women and minorities in manufacturing,
engineering, and forestry, and other areas.
Fields of interest: Elementary/secondary
education; Education, reading; Environmental
education; Employment, training; General charitable
giving; Minorities; Women.
Type of support: General/operating support;
Continuing support; Program development; Seed
money; Curriculum development; Employee
volunteer services; Employee matching gifts; In-kind
gifts.
Limitations: Giving primarily in areas of company
operations. No support for athletic, veterans', labor,
or political organizations or religious organizations.
No grants to individuals, or for sponsorships or
advertising, travel expenses, or national
conferences or other one-time events; no loans.
Publications: Application guidelines.
Application information: Application form required.
  Initial approach: Download application form and
    mail proposal and application form to nearest
    company facility
  Copies of proposal: 1
  Deadline(s): Varies
  Board meeting date(s): Sept.
Officers and Directors: Mark Sullivan, Pres.;
Deborah Haraldson, Secy.; Carol Tusch, Treas.;
Kimberly Wirth, Exec. Dir.; Marianne Parrs; Darial
Sneed; W. Dennis Thomas.
Trustee: U.S. Trust Co., N.A.
Number of staff: 3 full-time professional; 2 part-time
professional; 1 part-time support.
EIN: 136155080
Selected grants: The following grants were reported
in 2004.
$35,000 to Environmental Education Fund, Raleigh,
  NC. For Love-A-Tree program.
$32,525 to Armstrong Atlantic State University,
  Savannah, GA. For teacher's environment
  program.
$30,000 to Professional Logging Contractors of
  Maine, Fort Kent, ME. For Master Logger
  Certification.

$30,000 to West Virginia University Extension
  Service, Lewis County, Weston, WV. For program
  support for National 4-H Forestry Invitational.
$27,325 to Earths Birthday Project, Santa Fe, NM.
$27,247 to Texas Forestry Association Educational
  Fund, Lufkin, TX. For forestry bookcover
  distribution.
$25,000 to Childrens Museum of Memphis,
  Memphis, TN. For Pollution Detectives.
$25,000 to Conservation International, DC.
$25,000 to Nature Conservancy, Arlington, VA. For
  International Leadership Council.
$25,000 to Resources for the Future, DC. For
  program support.

1572
The Robert A. & Elizabeth R. Jeffe
Foundation ✧ ☆
19 Hawkwood Ln.
Greenwich, CT 06830

Established in 1997 in CT.
Donors: Robert A. Jeffe; Elizabeth R. Jeffe.
Foundation type: Independent foundation.
Financial data (yr. ended 12/31/05): Assets,
$9,840,169 (M); gifts received, $552,791;
expenditures, $507,566; qualifying distributions,
$500,000; giving activities include $500,000 for 2
grants (high: $300,000; low: $200,000).
Fields of interest: Higher education; Roman
Catholic agencies & churches.
Limitations: Applications not accepted. Giving
primarily in CA and NY. No grants to individuals.
Application information: Contributes only to
pre-selected organizations.
Trustees: Elizabeth R. Jeffe; Robert A. Jeffe.
EIN: 066455294
Selected grants: The following grants were reported
in 2004.
$200,000 to Maryknoll Fathers and Brothers,
  Maryknoll, NY.
$200,000 to Stanford University, Stanford, CA.
$8,450 to Saint Vincent Ferrer High School, New
  York, NY.

1573
Paul L. Jones Fund ✧
c/o Webster Trust Co., N.A.
80 Elm St.
New Haven, CT 06510

Established in 1979 in CT.
Foundation type: Independent foundation.
Financial data (yr. ended 10/31/05): Assets,
$6,667,413 (M); expenditures, $400,691;
qualifying distributions, $347,655; giving activities
include $345,000 for 11 grants (high: $75,000;
low: $10,000; average: $15,000–$50,000).
Purpose and activities: Giving only for scholarship
programs to assist students in medical and
health-related fields.
Fields of interest: Higher education.
Type of support: Scholarship funds.
Limitations: Applications not accepted. Giving
limited to CT. No grants to individuals.
Application information: Contributes only to
pre-selected organizations. Unsolicited requests for
funds not accepted.
Trustee: Webster Trust Co., N.A.
EIN: 066222118

Selected grants: The following grants were reported in 2003.

$50,000 to Fairfield University, Fairfield, CT. For scholarships.

$50,000 to Quinnipiac University, Hamden, CT. For scholarships.

$50,000 to Saint Joseph College, West Hartford, CT. For scholarships.

$50,000 to University of Connecticut Foundation, Storrs, CT. For scholarships.

$40,000 to Manchester Community College, Manchester, CT. For scholarships.

$15,000 to Southern Connecticut State University, New Haven, CT. For scholarships.

$15,000 to Three Rivers Community College, Norwich, CT. For scholarships.

$10,000 to Central Connecticut State University, New Britain, CT. For scholarships.

$10,000 to Gateway Community College, New Haven, CT. For scholarships.

$10,000 to Western Connecticut State University, Danbury, CT. For scholarships.

1574
The Chester W. Kitchings Foundation
c/o Coca-Cola Bottling Co. of Sene, Inc.
951 Bank St.
P.O. Box 1310
New London, CT   06320

Established in 1961 in CT.
Donors: Chester W. Kitchings, Sr.; Margaret Howe Kitchings.
Foundation type: Independent foundation.
Financial data (yr. ended 12/31/05): Assets, $21,096,674 (M); gifts received, $2,000,544; expenditures, $1,258,124; qualifying distributions, $1,217,224; giving activities include $1,167,586 for 113 grants (high: $25,000; low: $1,000).
Purpose and activities: Giving primarily for cultural programs, human service agencies and youth groups; support also for education and health.
Fields of interest: Arts; Education; Health care; Health organizations, association; Human services; Children/youth, services; Foundations (community); Federated giving programs.
Limitations: Applications not accepted. Giving limited to southeastern CT. No grants to individuals.
Application information: Contributes only to pre-selected organizations. Unsolicited requests for funds not accepted.
Manager: Chester W. Kitchings, Jr.
EIN: 066044228

1575
Kohn-Joseloff Foundation, Inc. ✧
(formerly Morris Joseloff Foundation, Inc.)
125 LaSalle Rd., Rm. 200
West Hartford, CT   06107   (860) 521-7010
Contact: Bernhard L. Kohn, Sr., Pres.

Incorporated in 1936 in CT.
Donors: Lillian L. Joseloff†; Morris Joseloff†; Morris Joseloff Foundation Trust.
Foundation type: Independent foundation.
Financial data (yr. ended 12/31/04): Assets, $10,642,504 (M); expenditures, $674,596; qualifying distributions, $601,765; giving activities include $562,945 for 89 grants (high: $175,000; low: $25).

Fields of interest: Arts; Education; Hospitals (general); Health organizations, association; Cancer research; Boys & girls clubs; Human services; Federated giving programs; Jewish federated giving programs.
Limitations: Giving primarily in CT, with emphasis on Hartford. No grants to individuals; no loans.
Application information: Application form not required.
Deadline(s): None
Board meeting date(s): 2nd Mon. in Jan.
Officers: Bernhard L. Kohn, Sr., Pres.; Bernhard L. Kohn, Jr., V.P.; Kathryn K. Rieger, V.P.; Joan J. Kohn, Secy.
Number of staff: 2
EIN: 136062846
Selected grants: The following grants were reported in 2003.
$200,000 to Wadsworth Atheneum, Hartford, CT.
$50,000 to Renbrook School, West Hartford, CT.
$33,300 to Kingswood-Oxford School, West Hartford, CT.
$20,000 to Connecticut Golf Foundation, Rocky Hill, CT. For HGC Marathon.
$20,000 to Connecticut Institute for the Blind, Hartford, CT.
$20,000 to Jewish Federation of Greater Hartford, West Hartford, CT.
$10,000 to Equistrides Therapeutic Riding Center, North Granby, CT.
$10,000 to United Way of the Capital Area, Hartford, CT.
$7,000 to Gray Lodge, Hartford, CT.
$3,000 to Smith College, Northampton, MA.

1576
John & Evelyn Kossak Foundation, Inc. ✧
68 Cross Hwy.
Westport, CT   06880-2147
Contact: Evelyn K. Kossak, Pres.

Established in 1969 in CT.
Donors: Evelyn K. Kossak; Jeffrey Kossak; Steven M. Kossak.
Foundation type: Independent foundation.
Financial data (yr. ended 12/31/05): Assets, $8,749,033 (M); gifts received, $425,000; expenditures, $549,093; qualifying distributions, $543,910; giving activities include $543,910 for 68 grants (high: $200,000; low: $200).
Purpose and activities: Support primarily for higher education, health organizations, music, and the fine arts.
Fields of interest: Visual arts; Museums; Performing arts; Performing arts, music; Higher education; Health care; Health organizations, association.
Limitations: Applications not accepted. No grants to individuals.
Application information: Contributes only to pre-selected organizations.
Officers: Evelyn K. Kossak, Pres.; Jeffrey Kossak, V.P.; Steven M. Kossak, Treas.
EIN: 237045906

1577
The Arthur B. and Alice Kramer Charitable Foundation ✧ ☆
688 Westover Rd.
Stamford, CT   06902

Established in 1993 in CT.

Donor: Arthur B. Kramer.
Foundation type: Independent foundation.
Financial data (yr. ended 3/31/06): Assets, $642,814 (M); expenditures, $363,184; qualifying distributions, $331,949; giving activities include $331,949 for grants.
Purpose and activities: Giving for higher education, art and cultural institutes, and Jewish organizations.
Fields of interest: Arts; Higher education; Higher education, college; Youth development, services; Human services; Children/youth, services; Jewish agencies & temples.
Limitations: Applications not accepted. Giving primarily in New York, NY. No grants to individuals.
Application information: Contributes only to pre-selected organizations.
Trustees: Alice Kramer; Arthur B. Kramer.
EIN: 223232820
Selected grants: The following grants were reported in 2005.
$145,500 to Yale University, New Haven, CT. 4 grants: $50,000, $10,000, $5,000, $80,500
$5,000 to National Alliance for the Mentally Ill (NAMI), Arlington, VA.
$1,000 to Jewish Fund for Justice, New York, NY.
$500 to Sanctuary for Families, New York, NY.
$500 to Working Theater, Cleveland, OH.
$250 to Columbia University, New York, NY.

1578
Larrabee Fund Association ✧
c/o Bank of America, N.A.
777 Main St., CT2-102-22-04
Hartford, CT   06115

Established in 1941.
Donors: Larrabee Fund; Willie O. Burr†; Charles G. Woodward†; Camilla Jillson Potter†; Francis Wells†.
Foundation type: Independent foundation.
Financial data (yr. ended 10/31/05): Assets, $4,472,243 (M); gifts received, $277,256; expenditures, $426,520; qualifying distributions, $392,931; giving activities include $391,457 for grants to individuals.
Purpose and activities: Giving to the aid of elderly, sick, indigent and needy women in the Hartford, CT, area.
Fields of interest: Women, centers/services; Women; Economically disadvantaged.
Type of support: Grants to individuals.
Limitations: Giving limited to female residents of the greater Hartford, CT, area.
Application information: Applications available at churches in the Hartford, CT, area. Requests must come from the individual's social worker.
Deadline(s): Twice a month; within a week before the 1st and last Thursdays
Officers: Gladys Hernandez, Pres.; Cynthia Lawler, Pres.; Pauline Barrows, 1st V.P.; C.J. Hauss, 1st V.P.; Beth Bush, 2nd V.P; Jane Charette, Secy.; Olivette Thomas, Secy.; Connie Bain, Treas.
EIN: 066038638

1579
Larsen Fund ✧
P.O. Box 271677
West Hartford, CT   06127-0677   (860) 231-9722
Contact: Jeanne Dubosar

Incorporated in 1941 in NY.
Donor: Roy E. Larsen†.

Foundation type: Independent foundation.
Financial data (yr. ended 12/31/03): Assets, $11,837,488 (M); expenditures, $785,278; qualifying distributions, $633,313; giving activities include $543,750 for 97 grants (high: $50,000; low: $250).
Purpose and activities: Support for: 1) education, including medical and secondary schools, educational research, computer sciences, and social sciences; 2) human services, including youth, family services, and family planning; 3) hospitals; 4) population studies; 5) law, justice and urban affairs; 6) intercultural relations; 7) conservation, ecology, and wildlife preservation; and 8) the arts.
Fields of interest: Museums; Education, research; Secondary school/education; Higher education; Medical school/education; Libraries/library science; Environment, natural resources; Environment; Animals/wildlife, preservation/protection; Hospitals (general); Children/youth, services; Family services; Civil rights, race/intergroup relations; Community development; Computer science; Social sciences; Public affairs.
Type of support: Annual campaigns; Capital campaigns; Land acquisition; Program development; Professorships; Curriculum development; Fellowships; Internship funds; Scholarship funds; Research.
Limitations: Applications not accepted. Giving primarily in CT, MA, the Minneapolis, MN, area, and the New York, NY, area. No grants to individuals.
Publications: Annual report.
Application information: Unsolicited requests for funds not accepted.
  Board meeting date(s): Beginning of Nov.
Officers and Directors:* Christopher Larsen,* Pres.; Jonathan Z. Larsen,* V.P.; Susan Z. Ritz,* V.P.; Ann Larsen Simonson,* V.P.; Chad M. Larsen, Secy.; Gordon H. Ritz,* Treas.
Number of staff: 1 part-time support.
EIN: 136104430
Selected grants: The following grants were reported in 2003.
$50,000 to Wadsworth Atheneum, Hartford, CT. For capital campaign.
$12,000 to Nantucket Cottage Hospital, Nantucket, MA. For capital campaign.
$10,000 to Defenders of Wildlife, DC. Toward building purchase.
$10,000 to Hartford Symphony Orchestra, Hartford, CT. For annual campaign.
$3,000 to Hartford Hospital, Hartford, CT. For annual campaign.
$2,000 to EARTH University Foundation, Atlanta, GA. For scholarships.
$2,000 to Wellesley College, Wellesley, MA. For annual campaign.
$1,500 to Cambridge College, Cambridge, MA. For annual campaign.
$1,500 to Planned Parenthood of Minnesota, North Dakota, South Dakota, Saint Paul, MN. For annual campaign.
$1,000 to Nature Conservancy, Minnesota Chapter, Minneapolis, MN. For annual campaign.

1580
The William and Cordelia Laverack Foundation ◇ ☆
c/o Nancy Blair
P.O. Box 1214
Stamford, CT   06904
Application address: c/o William Laverack, 141 Briscoe Rd., New Canaan, CT 06840, tel.: (203) 973-1400

Established in 2002.
Donors: Cordelia Laverack; William Laverack.
Foundation type: Independent foundation.
Financial data (yr. ended 11/30/05): Assets, $3,699,192 (M); gifts received, $18,163; expenditures, $415,023; qualifying distributions, $391,667; giving activities include $391,667 for 7 grants (high: $125,000; low: $5,000).
Fields of interest: Higher education; Education; Christian agencies & churches.
Application information:
  Initial approach: Letter or telephone
  Deadline(s): None
Trustees: Cordelia Laverack; William Laverack.
EIN: 562307477

1581
Raymond P. Lavietes Foundation, Inc. ◇ ☆
c/o Achille A. Apicella
680 Bridgeport Ave.
Shelton, CT   06484

Established in 1989 in CT.
Donor: Raymond P. Lavietes.
Foundation type: Independent foundation.
Financial data (yr. ended 12/31/04): Assets, $4,656,618 (M); gifts received, $2,826,229; expenditures, $354,932; qualifying distributions, $320,000; giving activities include $320,000 for grants.
Fields of interest: Arts; Higher education; Hospitals (general); Health organizations, association; Boys & girls clubs; Children/youth, services.
Limitations: Applications not accepted. Giving primarily in CT and MA. No grants to individuals.
Application information: Contributes only to pre-selected organizations.
Officers and Directors:* Achille A. Apicella,* Pres.; Donald Anderson,* V.P.; Estelle Lavietes.
EIN: 061276735

1582
The Lee Family Foundation, Inc. ◇ ☆
c/o Day, Berry & Howard, LLP
1 Canterbury Green
Stamford, CT   06901

Established in 1999 in CT.
Donor: Charles R. Lee.
Foundation type: Independent foundation.
Financial data (yr. ended 10/31/05): Assets, $5,981,920 (M); gifts received, $816,500; expenditures, $401,297; qualifying distributions, $329,500; giving activities include $329,500 for 21 grants (high: $150,000; low: $1,000).
Fields of interest: Museums (art); Performing arts, ballet; Higher education; Hospitals (general); Cancer; Youth development; Federated giving programs; Christian agencies & churches.

Limitations: Applications not accepted. Giving primarily in CT. No grants to individuals.
Application information: Contributes only to pre-selected organizations.
Officers and Directors:* Charles R. Lee,* Pres.; Ilda G. Lee,* V.P.; Bruce Carswell,* Secy.; Robert J. Miller,* Treas.
EIN: 061563501
Selected grants: The following grants were reported in 2003.
$50,000 to Second Congregational Church, Greenwich, CT.
$25,000 to Breast Cancer Alliance, Greenwich, CT.
$20,000 to University of Pittsburgh Medical Center, Melanoma Center, Pittsburgh, PA.
$15,000 to Ronald McDonald House of Dallas, Dallas, TX.
$10,000 to Heart Care International, Greenwich, CT.
$7,500 to Ballet Theater Foundation, New York, NY.
$5,000 to Womens Auxiliary to the Childrens Medical Center, Dallas, TX. For fashion show.

1583
The Leever Foundation, Inc.
c/o Connecticut Community Foundation
43 Field St.
Waterbury, CT   06702-1906   (203) 753-1315
Contact: C. O'Donnell
FAX: (203) 756-3054; E-mail: Codonnell@conncf.org

Established in 1991 in CT.
Donors: Harold Leever†; Ruth Ann Leever.
Foundation type: Independent foundation.
Financial data (yr. ended 12/31/05): Assets, $6,800,257 (M); gifts received, $350,000; expenditures, $482,811; qualifying distributions, $464,774; giving activities include $418,874 for 41 grants (high: $78,000; low: $100).
Fields of interest: Scholarships/financial aid; Health care; Human services; Federated giving programs; Youth.
Type of support: Annual campaigns; Capital campaigns; Seed money; Scholarship funds.
Limitations: Giving primarily in greater Waterbury, CT. No grants for endowments.
Publications: Application guidelines; Program policy statement.
Application information: Must be pre-approved to submit an application. Unsolicited requests for funds not accepted. Application form required.
  Initial approach: Letter or telephone
  Copies of proposal: 8
  Deadline(s): Generally in Feb., May and Oct.
  Board meeting date(s): Feb., May, and Oct.
  Final notification: Feb., May, and Oct.
Officer: Ruth Ann Leever, Chair.
Directors: Suzanne Leever Hart; Andrew Leever; Daniel Leever; Thomas Leever; David L. Sfara.
EIN: 223115036

1584
The Lehrman Institute ◇
1 Fawcett Pl., Ste. 130
Greenwich, CT   06830   (203) 661-6100
Contact: Richard J. Behn, Dir.

Donors: Lewis E. Lehrman; Five Way Partners, LLP; F.P. Trotta.
Foundation type: Operating foundation.
Financial data (yr. ended 7/31/05): Assets, $13,024,359 (L); expenditures, $2,278,483;

qualifying distributions, $2,010,650; giving activities include $2,010,650 for 55 grants (high: $400,000; low: $750).

Purpose and activities: Giving primarily for human services, education, and Roman Catholic organizations; a limited number of research fellowships are awarded each year to writers who will be completing book-length projects in areas broadly complementary to the institute's overall studies program. Academics (who will have completed their graduate studies), journalists, and other freelance authors are invited to apply.

Fields of interest: Historical activities; Higher education; Education; Botanical gardens; Medical research, institute; Human services; Social sciences, public policy; Christian agencies & churches.

Type of support: General/operating support; Fellowships; Research; Grants to individuals.

Limitations: Giving primarily in CT and NY.

Publications: Application guidelines.

Application information: Contact foundation for complete guidelines.

> *Initial approach:* Proposal, not to exceed 5-10 pages
> *Copies of proposal:* 4
> *Deadline(s):* Nov. 15
> *Final notification:* Apr. 1

Directors: Richard J. Behn; D. Gilbert Lehrman; Lewis E. Lehrman; Louise Lehrman.

EIN: 237218534

Selected grants: The following grants were reported in 2005.

$400,000 to Saint Thomas More Catholic Chapel and Center at Yale University, New Haven, CT.

$130,000 to Hill School, Pottstown, PA.

$100,000 to Heritage Foundation, DC.

$50,000 to Cold Spring Harbor Laboratory, Cold Spring Harbor, NY.

$45,000 to New-York Historical Society, New York, NY.

$38,000 to University of Virginia Fund, Charlottesville, VA.

$29,000 to Claremont Institute for the Study of Statesmanship and Political Philosophy, Claremont, CA.

$25,000 to Project for the New American Century, DC.

$10,000 to Tandem Friends School, Charlottesville, VA.

$8,400 to Tredegar National Civil War Center Foundation, Richmond, VA.

1585
Marvin Lender Family Foundation, Inc. ✧

1764 Litchfield Tpke.
Woodbridge, CT 06525

Established in 1994.

Donors: Marvin Lender; Heidi Lender; Keith Lender; Sondra Lender.

Foundation type: Independent foundation.

Financial data (yr. ended 12/31/04): Assets, $1,716,959 (M); gifts received, $223,860; expenditures, $407,671; qualifying distributions, $385,514; giving activities include $386,582 for 34 grants (high: $157,755; low: $250).

Purpose and activities: Giving primarily to Jewish causes and education.

Fields of interest: Arts; Higher education; Human services; Jewish federated giving programs; Jewish agencies & temples.

Limitations: Applications not accepted. Giving primarily in CT. No grants to individuals.

Application information: Contributes only to pre-selected organizations.

Officers: Marvin Lender, Pres. and Treas.; Helaine Lender, Secy.

EIN: 061395243

Selected grants: The following grants were reported in 2004.

$157,754 to Jewish Federation.

$1,000 to United Way.

1586
Liberty Bank Foundation, Inc. ✧

P.O. Box 1212
55 High St.
Middletown, CT 06457 (860) 704-2181
Contact: Betty Weintraub; Susan Murphy, V.P. and Secy.
Additional tel.: (860) 638-2959; URL: http://www.liberty-bank.com/liberty_foundation.asp

Established in 1997 in CT.

Donor: Liberty Bank.

Foundation type: Company-sponsored foundation.

Financial data (yr. ended 12/31/03): Assets, $7,704,180 (M); gifts received, $910,889; expenditures, $505,312; qualifying distributions, $471,777; giving activities include $436,814 for 75 grants (high: $35,000; low: $278).

Purpose and activities: The foundation supports organizations involved with arts and culture, education, health, housing, human services, and community development.

Fields of interest: Arts; Education; Health care; Housing/shelter; Human services; Economic development; Community development.

Type of support: General/operating support; Capital campaigns; Building/renovation; Equipment; Program development; Technical assistance; Program-related investments/loans; Matching/challenge support.

Limitations: Giving limited to Cheshire, Madison, Mansfield, Marlborough, North Haven, Wallingford, and Windham and areas of bank operations in Middlesex and New London counties, CT. No support for fraternal organizations or organizations not of direct benefit to the entire community. No grants to individuals, or for college, university, or hospital annual campaigns, endowments, debt reduction, scientific or medical research, or trips, tours, or conferences.

Publications: Application guidelines; Corporate giving report; Grants list.

Application information: Application form required.

> *Initial approach:* Telephone for preliminary discussion
> *Copies of proposal:* 1
> *Deadline(s):* Last day of Mar., June, Sept., and Dec.
> *Board meeting date(s):* 3rd Wed. of Mar., June, Sept., and Dec.
> *Final notification:* Within 3 months

Officers: Michael Helfgott, Chair.; Paul R. McConnell, Pres.; Susan Murphy, V.P. and Secy.; Thomas J. Pastorello, Treas.

Directors: Mark Gingras; Willard McRae; Calvin Price; Richard Tomc.

Number of staff: 2 part-time professional.

EIN: 061479957

1587
Lingnan Foundation ✧

(formerly Trustees of Lingnan University)
P.O. Box 208340
New Haven, CT 06520-8340 (203) 432-1063
Contact: Mary Chang, Prog. Off.
FAX: (203) 432-7246;
E-mail: leslie.stone@yale.edu; Application tel.: (203) 432-1066; Application E-mail: lignan@yale.edu; URL: http://www.lingnanfoundation.org

Established in 1893 in NY.

Donors: Anna Luk Liu; Huey Wong; Pausang Wong.

Foundation type: Independent foundation.

Financial data (yr. ended 6/30/05): Assets, $19,906,594 (M); gifts received, $335,231; expenditures, $1,194,960; qualifying distributions, $1,044,152; giving activities include $859,567 for 10 grants (high: $262,167; low: $3,000).

Purpose and activities: Grants only for support of higher education at specific institutions in Guangzhou (Canton) and Hong Kong.

Fields of interest: Higher education; Social sciences; International studies.

International interests: China; Hong Kong.

Type of support: General/operating support; Continuing support; Management development/capacity building; Building/renovation; Program development; Conferences/seminars; Professorships; Publication; Seed money; Curriculum development; Internship funds; Research; Exchange programs.

Limitations: Giving primarily in Hong Kong and in the People's Republic of China. No grants to individuals, or for annual campaigns or emergency, capital, or endowment funds; no loans.

Publications: Application guidelines; Annual report; Program policy statement.

Application information: See foundation Web site for application guidelines and procedures. Application form not required.

> *Initial approach:* Proposal or letter
> *Copies of proposal:* 1
> *Deadline(s):* Inquire with foundation
> *Board meeting date(s):* May and Nov.
> *Final notification:* 2 months after meetings

Officers and Trustees:* Shirley Mow,* Chair.; Ralph Lerner,* Secy.; Alex Banker,* Treas.; Leslie B. Stone,* Exec. Dir.; and 12 additional trustees.

Number of staff: 2 part-time professional.

EIN: 136400470

Selected grants: The following grants were reported in 2005.

$287,500 to Lingnan College, Hong Kong. 2 grants: $181,000, $106,500.

$262,167 to Sun Yat-Sen University of Medical Sciences, Guangzhou, China. .

$100,000 to University of Hong Kong, Hong Kong. .

$65,650 to University of California, Los Angeles, CA. For BruinCorps, public service and leadership development program for students.

$48,250 to Institute of International Education, New York, NY.

$47,500 to University of California, Berkeley, CA. For Cal Corps, public service and leadership development program for students.

$28,500 to Yale-China Association, New Haven, CT.

$17,000 to Chinese University of Hong Kong, Hong Kong. .

$3,000 to Vermont Law School, South Royalton, VT.

1588

The LittleJohn Family Foundation ◇
648 Smith Ridge Rd.
New Canaan, CT 06840

Donor: Angus C. LittleJohn, Jr.
Foundation type: Independent foundation.
Financial data (yr. ended 12/31/03): Assets, $2,128,689 (M); gifts received, $1,000,000; expenditures, $406,760; qualifying distributions, $406,760; giving activities include $406,750 for 8 grants (high: $250,000; low: $2,000).
Fields of interest: Museums (children's); Elementary/secondary education; Higher education; Education.
Limitations: Applications not accepted. Giving primarily in CT and PA. No grants to individuals.
Application information: Contributes only to pre-selected organizations.
Officer: Angus C. LittleJohn, Jr., Mgr.
EIN: 133948281
Selected grants: The following grants were reported in 2004.
$50,000 to Middlesex School, Concord, MA.
$50,000 to Taft School, Watertown, CT.
$45,000 to University of Pennsylvania, Philadelphia, PA.
$25,000 to Vanderbilt University, Nashville, TN.
$10,000 to Stepping Stones Museum for Children, Norwalk, CT.
$5,000 to Horizons Student Enrichment Program, New Canaan, CT.
$5,000 to YMCA, New Canaan Community, New Canaan, CT.
$2,000 to New Canaan Community Foundation, New Canaan, CT.
$2,000 to New Canaan Country School, New Canaan, CT.

1589

Lone Pine Foundation, Inc. ◇
c/o Lone Pine Capital, LLC
2 Greenwich Plz., 2nd Fl.
Greenwich, CT 06830
Contact: Lucy Ball, Exec. Dir.

Established in 2001 in CT.
Donors: Stephen F. Mandel, Jr.; Kerry Tyler; Lone Pine Capital, LLC.
Foundation type: Independent foundation.
Financial data (yr. ended 12/31/05): Assets, $14,319,353 (M); gifts received, $5,551,916; expenditures, $2,680,314; qualifying distributions, $2,531,104; giving activities include $2,531,056 for 167 grants (high: $150,000; low: $100).
Purpose and activities: Support primarily for educational programs, especially for the under-resourced, and to family and children's organizations.
Fields of interest: Education; Children/youth, services; Family services.
Type of support: General/operating support; Program development.
Limitations: Giving limited to New York, NY, Westchester County, NY, and Fairfield County, CT.
Application information: Accepts NY/NJ Common Application Form provided by NYRAG. The foundation generally does not accept unsolicited applications. Application form required.
Initial approach: Letter of inquiry
Officers and Directors:* Stephen F. Mandel, Jr.,* Chair. and Pres.; Kerry A. Tyler,* V.P. and Treas.;

Christeen Bernard,* Secy.; Lucy Ball,* Exec. Dir.; John B. Sommi.
Number of staff: 1 full-time professional; 1 part-time professional.
EIN: 061637040
Selected grants: The following grants were reported in 2005.
$150,000 to Building Educated Leaders for Life (BELL) Foundation, Bronx, NY. For general operating support.
$150,000 to Childrens Village, Dobbs Ferry, NY. For WAY Program.
$150,000 to Domus Foundation, Stamford, CT. For After-School Program.
$150,000 to Family Centers, Greenwich, CT. For Head Start Programs.
$150,000 to Good Shepherd Services, New York, NY. For South Brooklyn Community High School.
$150,000 to Harlem Childrens Zone, New York, NY. For Baby College and Harlem Gems.
$125,300 to Prep for Prep, New York, NY. For general operating support.
$125,000 to FSW, Inc., Bridgeport, CT. For asset building division.
$5,000 to Boston College, Chestnut Hill, MA. For general operating support.
$2,500 to Bridgeport Child Advocacy Coalition, Bridgeport, CT. For general operating support.

1590

George A. and Grace L. Long Foundation
c/o Bank of America, N.A., Fdn. and Philanthropic Svcs.
777 Main St., CT2-102-22-02
Hartford, CT 06115 (860) 952-7392
Contact: Carmen Britt, Prog. Off., Bank of America

Trust established in 1960 in CT.
Donors: George A. Long†; Grace L. Long†.
Foundation type: Independent foundation.
Financial data (yr. ended 12/31/05): Assets, $10,632,887 (M); expenditures, $557,543; qualifying distributions, $523,025; giving activities include $460,236 for 168 grants (high: $10,000; low: $1,500).
Purpose and activities: Primary areas of interest include the arts, education, health services, community development, and family services.
Fields of interest: Arts; Education, early childhood education; Child development, education; Adult/continuing education; Education; Environment; Hospitals (general); Health care; Health organizations, association; AIDS; AIDS research; Human services; Children/youth, services; Child development, services; Family services; Aging, centers/services; Community development; Aging; Disabilities, people with; Minorities.
Type of support: General/operating support; Continuing support; Program development; Technical assistance.
Limitations: Giving limited to CT. No grants to individuals, or for operating budgets or endowment funds; no loans.
Publications: Informational brochure (including application guidelines).
Application information: Unsolicited requests for funds are generally not accepted. Application form required.
Initial approach: Letter or telephone
Copies of proposal: 2
Deadline(s): Mar. 15 and Sept. 15
Board meeting date(s): May and Nov.

Trustee: Alan S. Parker.
EIN: 066030953
Selected grants: The following grants were reported in 2004.
$10,000 to Almada Lodge-Times Farm Camp Corporation, Andover, CT.
$10,000 to Trinity College, Hartford, CT. For Dream Camp.
$6,000 to Hartford Interval House, Hartford, CT. For Shelter and Children's Program.
$5,000 to Mercy Housing and Shelter Corporation, Hartford, CT. For Family Services Program.
$5,000 to Plainville Community Food Pantry, Plainville, CT. For critical staffing needs.
$5,000 to Salvation Army of Hartford, Hartford, CT. For Housing First Program for Homeless Families.
$4,000 to Chamber Music Plus, Hartford, CT. For Music Speak to Me.
$4,000 to Habitat for Humanity, Hartford Area, Hartford, CT. For building project, Houe of Faith.
$4,000 to Science EpiCenter and DNA Learning Center, New London, CT. For YouthAlive Program.
$4,000 to Urban League of Greater Hartford, Hartford, CT. For employment service for students.

1591

The Ronald P. and Susan E. Lynch Foundation ◇
8 Bayberry Ln.
Greenwich, CT 06831

Established in 1985 in NY.
Donors: Ronald P. Lynch†; Susan E. Lynch.
Foundation type: Independent foundation.
Financial data (yr. ended 12/31/05): Assets, $15,081,470 (M); expenditures, $693,264; qualifying distributions, $649,629; giving activities include $646,463 for 36 grants (high: $75,000; low: $1,000).
Fields of interest: Museums; Higher education; Medical school/education; Education; Cancer research; Roman Catholic agencies & churches.
Limitations: Applications not accepted. Giving primarily in NY. No grants to individuals.
Application information: Contributes only to pre-selected organizations.
Trustees: Charles R. Lynch; Susan E. Lynch.
EIN: 136863977

1592

The Macauley Foundation, Inc. ◇
88 Hamilton Ave.
Stamford, CT 06902
Contact: Annie Yates, Exec. Dir.
FAX: (203) 263-3816;
E-mail: info@themacauleyfoundation.org

Established in 1995 in CT.
Donor: Robert C. Macauley.
Foundation type: Independent foundation.
Financial data (yr. ended 6/30/05): Assets, $2,519,898 (M); expenditures, $1,441,061; qualifying distributions, $1,364,900; giving activities include $1,364,900 for 23+ grants (high: $480,000).
Purpose and activities: Funding for various human service agencies.

Fields of interest: Cancer research; Food services; Housing/shelter, homeless; Human services; Children, services; Foundations (public).
Publications: Financial statement.
Application information: Once received, applications in Spanish will need to be translated, therefore, response time may be longer.
  Initial approach: Telephone or written request for application
  Copies of proposal: 3
  Deadline(s): None
  Board meeting date(s): Nov. and June
  Final notification: Up to 6 months
Officers and Directors:* Robert C. Macauley,* Pres.; Alma Jane Macauley,* Exec. V.P.; Annie Yates, Exec. Dir.; Melinda Rice Macauley; Robert C. Macauley, Jr.; Anne Marie Weirether.
Number of staff: 1 part-time professional.
EIN: 061439255
Selected grants: The following grants were reported in 2005.
$580,000 to AmeriCares, Stamford, CT. 2 grants: $480,000 (To provide food, clothing, and medical supplies to the needy), $100,000 (For HomeFront, community-based volunteer home repair program helping homeowners physically or financially unable to maintain their properties).
$200,000 to Liberty Community Services, New Haven, CT. For housing for individuals with HIV.
$160,000 to Heart of America Foundation, DC. To identify elementary school children, teens, amateur athletes, and community leaders who work to better the lives of others through selfless acts of kindness.
$100,000 to Camp AmeriKids, New Canaan, CT. To provide food, clothing, and medical supplies to the needy.
$100,000 to George Bush Presidential Library Foundation, College Station, TX. For George Bush Forty-One Endowment Fund for research for treatment of breast and prostate cancer.
$100,000 to Mayo Foundation, Rochester, MN. For medical care, medical education, and scientific research.
$20,000 to Grace Childrens Foundation, New York, NY.
$20,000 to Haitian Health Foundation, Norwich, CT. For outpatient medical, dental, and eye care.
$10,100 to Saint Jude Childrens Research Hospital, Memphis, TN. For treatment for children with deadly diseases.

1593
Arthur & Myra Mahon Charitable Foundation ✧ ☆
(also known as The Trarym Foundation)
16 Cambridge Dr.
Madison, CT   06443

Donor: Arthur Mahon.
Foundation type: Independent foundation.
Financial data (yr. ended 11/30/05): Assets, $654,758 (M); gifts received, $520,000; expenditures, $460,000; qualifying distributions, $460,000; giving activities include $460,000 for 4 grants (high: $400,000; low: $10,000).
Fields of interest: Higher education; Scholarships/financial aid.
Limitations: Applications not accepted. No grants to individuals.
Application information: Contributes only to pre-selected organizations.

Trustees: Arthur Mahon; Myra Mahon.
EIN: 061527656

1594
Main Street Community Foundation
200 Main St.
P.O. Box 2702
Bristol, CT   06011-2702   (860) 583-6363
Contact: Cheryl Dumont-Smith, C.E.O.; For grants: Jarre B. Betts, Prog. Dir.
FAX: (860) 589-1252;
E-mail: office@mainstreetfoundation.org; Additional E-mail: cheryl@mainstreetfoundation.org; Grant questions E-mail: jarre@mainstreetfoundation.org; URL: http://www.mainstreetfoundation.org

Established in 1995 in CT.
Foundation type: Community foundation.
Financial data (yr. ended 12/31/05): Assets, $24,329,025 (M); gifts received, $1,216,909; expenditures, $634,581; giving activities include $278,866 for 47 grants, and $79,092 for 124 grants to individuals.
Purpose and activities: The foundation is committed to assisting donors who wish to build charitable endowments to support the communities of Bristol, Burlington, Plainville, Plymouth, Southington, and Wolcott, CT, helping to make each town a better community in which to live and work.
Fields of interest: Arts; Higher education; Education; Environment; Health care; Youth development; Human services; Community development.
Type of support: General/operating support; Building/renovation; Equipment; Emergency funds; Program development; Conferences/seminars; Seed money; Curriculum development; Scholarship funds; Technical assistance; Grants to individuals; Scholarships—to individuals; Matching/challenge support.
Limitations: Giving primarily in Bristol, Burlington, Plainville, Plymouth, Southington, and Wolcott, CT. No support for governmental agencies unless it is determined that overriding special circumstances exist, or religious activities. No grants to individuals (except through the scholarship program, immediate response funds), or for operating or budget deficits, previously incurred obligations, fundraising events, endowments, research, property repairs and maintenance, or memorials; no loans.
Publications: Application guidelines; Annual report; Financial statement; Informational brochure; Newsletter.
Application information: Visit foundation Web site for application form and guidelines. Application form required.
  Initial approach: Telephone
  Copies of proposal: 16
  Deadline(s): Mar. 31 and Sept. 30 for general grants; Mar. 30 for scholarships
  Board meeting date(s): 2nd Fri. of each month
  Final notification: Late June and late Dec.
Officers and Directors:* Thomas O. Barnes,* Chair.; Bryan P. Bowerman,* Vice-Chair.; Cheryl Dumont-Smith,* C.E.O. and Pres.; Mark J. Blum,* Secy.; William J. Tracy, Jr.,* Treas.; Robert M. Caiaze; Dolly Chamberlin; Dennis Cleary; Bruce Daigle; Dwight Harris; Mary Ellen Hobson; Richard Larkin; John Letizia; Diane L. Macklosky; Jacqueline M. Merchant; Janis G. Neri; Bonnie Pina; John E. Smith; Barry Thompson; Tracey Yarde-Smith.

Number of staff: 1 full-time professional; 3 part-time support.
EIN: 061433299

1595
Andrew J. & Joyce D. Mandell Family Foundation, Inc. ✧
(formerly The Mandell Family Foundation, Inc.)
240 Hartford Ave.
Newington, CT   06111

Established in 1984 in CT.
Donors: Andrew J. Mandell; Joyce D. Mandell; Bruce A. Mandell; Mark N. Mandell; Meryl L. Mandell Braunstein.
Foundation type: Independent foundation.
Financial data (yr. ended 4/30/05): Assets, $10,928,677 (M); gifts received, $1,225,950; expenditures, $679,832; qualifying distributions, $679,832; giving activities include $678,320 for 36 grants (high: $375,125; low: $250).
Fields of interest: Hospitals (general); Health organizations, association; Boys & girls clubs; Jewish federated giving programs; Jewish agencies & temples.
Limitations: Applications not accepted. Giving primarily in CT, with some emphasis on Hartford; some funding also in New York, NY. No grants to individuals.
Application information: Contributes only to pre-selected organizations.
Officers: Joyce D. Mandell, Pres.; Andrew J. Mandell, V.P.; Bruce A. Mandell, Secy.
Directors: Meryl L. Mandell Braunstein; Mark N. Mandell.
EIN: 222536600
Selected grants: The following grants were reported in 2005.
$375,125 to Jewish Federation of Greater Hartford, West Hartford, CT. For general support.
$50,000 to Middlesex Hospital, Middletown, CT. For general support of Family Advocacy program.
$30,000 to Childrens Tumor Foundation, New York, NY. For general support.
$25,000 to Horace Bushnell Memorial Hall, Hartford, CT. For general support.
$25,000 to Koby Mandell Foundation, Bethesda, MD. For general support.
$22,000 to Greater Hartford Arts Council, Hartford, CT. For general support.
$10,000 to American Friends of the Ghetto Fighters House, Teaneck, NJ. For general support.
$10,000 to CJ Foundation for SIDS (Sudden Infant Death Syndrome), Hackensack, NJ. For general support.
$6,525 to Arthritis Foundation, Southern New England Chapter, Rocky Hill, CT. For general support.
$3,000 to Cancer Care of Connecticut, Norwalk, CT. For general support.

1596
Mandeville Foundation, Inc. ✧
P.O. Box 395
Sherman, CT   06784
Contact: Hubert T. Mandeville, Pres.

Incorporated in 1963 in CT.
Donor: Ernest W. Mandeville.
Foundation type: Independent foundation.

Financial data (yr. ended 12/31/03): Assets, $433 (M); expenditures, $656,567; qualifying distributions, $611,706; giving activities include $593,213 for 32 grants (high: $54,760; low: $1,000).
Purpose and activities: Giving for education and youth services.
Fields of interest: Secondary school/education; Higher education; Libraries/library science; Education; Hospitals (general); Health organizations, association; Youth development, citizenship; Children/youth, services.
Limitations: Giving primarily in CT and NY.
Application information: Application form not required.
Deadline(s): None
Final notification: 90 days
Officers and Directors:* P. Kempton Mandeville,* Pres.; Meredith H. Hollis,* V.P.; Maurice C. Greenbaum,* Secy.; Jonathan Mandeville; Matthew T. Mandeville.
Number of staff: 2
EIN: 066043343

1597
B. L. Manger Foundation, Inc. ✧
c/o Zone & Bernstein
123 Prospect St.
Stamford, CT 06901 (203) 324-4131
Contact: Harold Bernstein, V.P.

Established in 1974 in CT.
Foundation type: Independent foundation.
Financial data (yr. ended 4/30/06): Assets, $8,522,637 (M); expenditures, $491,083; qualifying distributions, $416,500; giving activities include $416,500 for 43 grants (high: $60,000; low: $100).
Purpose and activities: Giving primarily for Jewish organizations.
Fields of interest: Education; Human services; Jewish federated giving programs; Jewish agencies & temples.
Limitations: Giving primarily in CT. No grants to individuals.
Application information:
Initial approach: Letter
Deadline(s): None
Officers: Joseph Lieberman, Pres. and Treas.; Harold Bernstein, V.P.
EIN: 237405994
Selected grants: The following grants were reported in 2005.
$86,000 to Chabad of Stamford, Stamford, CT. For general support.
$60,000 to Stamford Health System, Stamford, CT. For general support.
$50,000 to Dandelion Productions, Bethany, CT. For general support.
$50,000 to Jewish Home for the Elderly of Fairfield County Foundation, Fairfield, CT. For general support.
$25,000 to Aish HaTorah. For general support.
$25,000 to Bar-Ilan University in Israel, Beverly Hills, CA. For general support.
$18,000 to Bi-Cultural Day School, Stamford, CT. For general support.
$18,000 to Gateways Organization, Monsey, NY. For general support.
$13,000 to Hebrew Academy for Special Children, Brooklyn, NY. For general support.
$5,000 to Chai Center, Los Angeles, CA. For general support.

1598
The John G. Martin Foundation ✧
2 Batterson Park Rd.
Farmington, CT 06032 (860) 677-4574
Contact: Frank M. Loehmann, Jr., Pres.
FAX: (860) 674-1490;
E-mail: frank@resmgtcorp.com

Established about 1958 as the Jane & John Martin Foundation.
Donor: John G. Martin†.
Foundation type: Independent foundation.
Financial data (yr. ended 12/31/04): Assets, $8,398,029 (M); expenditures, $576,741; qualifying distributions, $496,133; giving activities include $438,993 for 30 grants (high: $151,072; low: $25).
Purpose and activities: Primary areas of interest include the elderly, the homeless, higher education, and the performing arts.
Fields of interest: Visual arts; Performing arts; Arts; Education, fund raising/fund distribution; Education, early childhood education; Elementary school/education; Secondary school/education; Higher education; Education; Health care; Health organizations, association; Human services; Children/youth, services; Aging, centers/services; Homeless, human services; Community development; General charitable giving; Aging; Economically disadvantaged; Homeless.
Type of support: Capital campaigns; Building/renovation; Matching/challenge support.
Limitations: Giving primarily in the Hartford, CT, area.
Application information: Application form not required.
Initial approach: Letter
Copies of proposal: 1
Deadline(s): None
Board meeting date(s): Quarterly, and as needed
Officers: Frank M. Loehmann, Jr., Pres.; Sandra Johnson, V.P.; Patricia O'Sullivan, Secy.
Trustee: Garrett S. Flynn.
EIN: 066042495
Selected grants: The following grants were reported in 2004.
$151,072 to University of Connecticut Law School Foundation, Hartford, CT.
$20,000 to Farmington Village Green and Library Association, Farmington, CT.
$20,000 to Hartford Public Library, Hartford, CT.
$10,000 to Fidelco Guide Dog Foundation, Bloomfield, CT.
$10,000 to Urban League of Greater Hartford, Hartford, CT.
$6,750 to Saint Joseph College, West Hartford, CT.
$1,500 to Colgate University, Hamilton, NY.
$100 to Gifts of Love, Avon, CT.
$100 to Ronald McDonald House of Connecticut, New Haven, CT.
$100 to Salvation Army, Meriden, CT.

1599
The MassMutual Foundation for Hartford, Inc. ✧
(formerly The Connecticut Mutual Life Foundation)
100 Bright Meadow Blvd.
Enfield, CT 06082
Contact: Ronald A. Copes, Exec. Dir.

Established in 1976.
Donor: Massachusetts Mutual Life Insurance Co.

Foundation type: Company-sponsored foundation.
Financial data (yr. ended 12/31/05): Assets, $1,276,740 (M); expenditures, $1,178,173; qualifying distributions, $1,167,273; giving activities include $1,156,350 for 65 grants (high: $220,000; low: $600).
Purpose and activities: The foundation supports organizations involved with arts and culture and education.
Fields of interest: Arts; Education; Federated giving programs.
Type of support: Capital campaigns; Program development.
Limitations: Giving primarily in the greater Hartford, CT, area. No support for sectarian organizations or political, fraternal, labor, or veterans' organizations. No grants to individuals, or for endowments, debt reduction, emergency needs, publications, land acquisition, fellowships, or advertising.
Publications: Corporate giving report; Informational brochure (including application guidelines).
Application information: An interview or site visit may be requested. The Connecticut Common Grant Form is accepted. Application form required.
Initial approach: Contact foundation for application form
Copies of proposal: 1
Deadline(s): 1 month prior to board meetings
Board meeting date(s): Mar., June, Sept., and Nov.
Final notification: 2 months
Officers and Directors:* Constance Clayton,* Pres.; Eustis Walcott,* V.P.; James Puhala, Secy.; James M. Lynch, Treas.; Ronald A. Copes,* Exec. Dir.; John L. Abbott; Suzanne M. Bergin; Michael A. Chong; William B. Ellis; Frances Emerson; Beverly Holmes; James E. Miller; Kevin M. Sweeney.
Number of staff: 2 full-time professional; 1 part-time professional.
EIN: 510192500
Selected grants: The following grants were reported in 2005.
$220,000 to University of Connecticut Foundation, Storrs, CT.
$177,620 to United Way of the Capital Area, Hartford, CT. 2 grants: $50,000, $127,620
$100,000 to Community Health Services, Hartford, CT.
$90,000 to Hartford Symphony Orchestra, Hartford, CT.
$60,000 to Greater Hartford Arts Council, Hartford, CT.
$50,000 to Foodshare Commission of Greater Hartford, Windsor, CT.
$50,000 to Hispanic Health Council, Hartford, CT.
$20,000 to University of Hartford, West Hartford, CT.
$10,000 to Ravinia Festival Association, Highland Park, IL.

1600
The Katharine Matthies Foundation
c/o Bank of America, N.A.
777 Main St., CT2-102-22-02
Hartford, CT 06115
Contact: Amy R. Lynch, V.P., Bank of America, N.A.

Established in 1987 in CT.
Donor: Katharine Matthies†.
Foundation type: Independent foundation.
Financial data (yr. ended 12/31/05): Assets, $16,847,226 (M); expenditures, $945,204; qualifying distributions, $903,034; giving activities

include $815,650 for 57 grants (high: $30,000; low: $250).

Purpose and activities: Giving primarily for educational, religious, charitable, scientific, and literacy purposes, and for the prevention of cruelty to children and animals.

Fields of interest: Arts; Animals/wildlife; Recreation; Human services; Youth, services; Family services; Community development.

Type of support: General/operating support; Capital campaigns; Building/renovation; Equipment; Program development; Publication; Seed money; Matching/challenge support.

Limitations: Giving limited to Seymour, Ansonia, Derby, Oxford, and Beacon Falls, CT; special consideration is given to programs that benefit Seymour, CT, residents.

Publications: Application guidelines; Grants list.

Application information: Application form required.

  Initial approach: Letter
  Copies of proposal: 6
  Deadline(s): May 1
  Board meeting date(s): June
  Final notification: June

Trustee: Bank of America, N.A.

EIN: 066261860

1601

The McKenzie Foundation, Inc. ✧

114 John St.
Greenwich, CT 06831
Contact: Kathryn H. Smith, Dir.
FAX: (203) 861-7526; *URL:* http://www.mckenziefoundation.us

Established in 1998 in CT.

Foundation type: Independent foundation.

Financial data (yr. ended 9/30/05): Assets, $13,720,259 (M); gifts received, $2,000,000; expenditures, $786,004; qualifying distributions, $731,033; giving activities include $660,192 for 44 grants (high: $50,000; low: $2,500).

Purpose and activities: Giving for education, health, human services, and cultural and environmental concerns.

Fields of interest: Elementary/secondary education; Scholarships/financial aid; Education; Environment.

Type of support: General/operating support; Equipment; Program development; Scholarship funds.

Limitations: Applications not accepted. Giving on a national basis. No grants to individuals, or for endowments, scholarships, fellowships, capital construction, fundraisers or deficit financing.

Application information: Unsolicited requests for funds not accepted.

  Board meeting date(s): Aug.

Officers and Directors:* Richard C. McKenzie, Jr.,* Pres.; Margaret Byrne McKenzie,* Secy.-Treas.; Eileen Grace McKenzie Baylis; James Richard McKenzie; Jennifer Kathleen McKenzie; Maria Prawdzik; Kathryn H. Smith.

Number of staff: 2 part-time professional.

EIN: 061508410

Selected grants: The following grants were reported in 2004.

$50,101 to Safe Space, New York, NY. For scholarships.

$30,000 to Catholic Big Brothers Big Sisters, Los Angeles, CA. For general support.

$25,000 to Family Centers, Greenwich, CT.

$25,000 to Hubbard Museum of the American West, Ruidoso Downs, NM. For operating support.

$25,000 to Institute for Advanced Study, Princeton, NJ.

$25,000 to Make-A-Wish Foundation of New Jersey, Union, NJ.

$25,000 to March of Dimes Birth Defects Foundation, San Francisco, CA.

$25,000 to Prostate Cancer Foundation, Santa Monica, CA. For general support.

$22,539 to Memorial Sloan-Kettering Cancer Center, New York, NY.

$20,000 to Babson College, Babson Park, MA.

1602

The Melville Foundation ✧ ☆

c/o Harry Burn, III
P.O. Box 1810, 8 Sound Shore Dr.
Greenwich, CT 06836

Established in 1986 in CT.

Donor: Harry Burn III.

Foundation type: Independent foundation.

Financial data (yr. ended 12/31/05): Assets, $8,058,115 (M); gifts received, $966,885; expenditures, $390,251; qualifying distributions, $387,500; giving activities include $387,500 for grants.

Purpose and activities: Giving for historical and environmental conservation, higher education, boys and girls clubs and Christian organizations.

Fields of interest: Higher education; Education; Environment; Children/youth, services; Christian agencies & churches.

Limitations: Applications not accepted. Giving primarily in CT and VA. No grants to individuals.

Application information: Contributes only to pre-selected organizations.

Trustees: Harry Burn III; Jean Burn.

EIN: 222777140

Selected grants: The following grants were reported in 2004.

$75,000 to Jefferson Scholars Foundation, Charlottesville, VA.

$25,000 to Trinity College, Hartford, CT.

$10,000 to Boys and Girls Club of Greenwich, Greenwich, CT.

$5,000 to Thomas Jefferson Memorial Foundation, Charlottesville, VA.

$5,000 to University of Virginia, Charlottesville, VA.

$1,000 to Old Westbury Gardens, Old Westbury, NY.

$750 to Robert E. Lee Memorial Association, Stratford Hall Plantation, Stratford, VA.

$500 to Museum of the Confederacy, Richmond, VA.

$500 to National Arboretum, Friends of the, DC.

$500 to University of the South, Sewanee, TN.

1603

The Meriden Foundation ✧

c/o Webster Trust Co., N.A.
The Michaels Bldg.
Webster Plz.
Waterbury, CT 06702 (203) 782-4531
Contact: Jeffrey Otis, Dir.

Established in 1983.

Donors: A. Leo Ricci‡; I. Margaret Mesite; Rose Mesite; Jessie Wilcox Clark‡; Warren Gardner‡; Charles Hasburg‡.

Foundation type: Independent foundation.

Financial data (yr. ended 12/31/03): Assets, $21,809,932 (M); gifts received, $366,570; expenditures, $1,324,143; qualifying distributions, $1,116,232; giving activities include $901,201 for 66+ grants (high: $64,231), and $200,350 for 87 grants to individuals (high: $10,000; low: $175).

Purpose and activities: Giving to organizations that benefit the greater Meriden, CT, area.

Fields of interest: Arts; Higher education; Law school/education; Libraries (public); Education; Hospitals (general); Hospitals (specialty); Health organizations, association; Boys & girls clubs; Human services; Federated giving programs; Christian agencies & churches.

Type of support: General/operating support; Annual campaigns; Scholarships—to individuals.

Limitations: Giving limited to the Meriden-Wallingford, CT, area.

Application information: Application form required.

  Initial approach: Letter, on organizational letterhead, for grants; application form for scholarship requests
  Deadline(s): None

Director: Jeffrey Otis.

Trustees: Walter G. Alwang; Elisa Bradford; Thomas Griglun; Maureen Kane; Peter Vouras, Jr.; Webster Trust Co., N.A.

EIN: 066037849

Selected grants: The following grants were reported in 2004.

$29,480 to Meriden Public Library, Meriden, CT. 2 grants: $20,185, $9,295

$29,023 to First Baptist Church.

$25,347 to Salvation Army.

$18,928 to Boys and Girls Club.

$18,928 to YMCA.

$18,155 to American Heart Association, Dallas, TX.

$18,155 to American Red Cross.

$18,155 to Gaylord Hospital, Wallingford, CT.

$18,155 to United Way.

1604

Marion Moore Foundation, Inc. ✧ ☆

30 Lismore Ln.
Greenwich, CT 06831

Established in 2004 in CT.

Foundation type: Independent foundation.

Financial data (yr. ended 12/31/04): Assets, $18,820,863 (M); gifts received, $12,175,424; expenditures, $880,205; qualifying distributions, $705,941; giving activities include $717,750 for grants.

Fields of interest: Museums; Performing arts, music; Education; Health care; Human services.

Limitations: Giving primarily in CT and NY.

Officers and Directors:* John W. Cross III,* Pres.; John F. Baron, Secy.; John W. Cross IV; Jane Gilbert; Jeffery Z. Gilbert; Louisa Gilbert; Marion Moore Gilbert; Cynthia Cross Lawrence; Katrina Gilbert Millard; Lois Cross Willis.

EIN: 200249695

1605

The William & Alice Mortensen Foundation

94 Pheasant Hill Dr.
West Hartford, CT 06107 (860) 521-4740
Contact: Robert S. Carter, Jr., Pres.
E-mail: bob58car@comcast.net

Established in 1982 in DE.

Donors: William Mortensen†; Trice Mortenson†.
Foundation type: Independent foundation.
Financial data (yr. ended 12/31/05): Assets, $16,026,419 (M); gifts received, $148,253; expenditures, $691,545; qualifying distributions, $646,823; giving activities include $608,816 for 53 grants (high: $200,000; low: $458).
Fields of interest: Historic preservation/historical societies; Arts; Elementary/secondary education; Higher education; Education; Hospitals (general); Human services; Religion; Children.
Type of support: Equipment; Program development; Seed money; Research; Technical assistance.
Limitations: Giving primarily in CT, with emphasis on Hartford.
Publications: Application guidelines; Program policy statement (including application guidelines).
Application information: Applicants should submit one original plus 3 copies of the proposal. Application form required.
  Initial approach: Letter or telephone
  Copies of proposal: 4
  Deadline(s): May 15 and Nov. 15
  Board meeting date(s): May 25 and Nov. 25
Officer: Robert S. Carter, Jr., Pres. and Treas.
Directors: Hon. Alfred V. Covello; Robert M. Hadley, C.P.A.; Ellen Coote Solek, Ph.D.
EIN: 061064150
Selected grants: The following grants were reported in 2003.
$150,000 to Bushnell Fund for the First Century, Hartford, CT. For program support.
$30,000 to Riverfront Recapture, Hartford, CT. For general support.
$20,000 to Hill-Stead Museum, Farmington, CT. For general support.
$20,000 to Northwest Catholic High School, West Hartford, CT. For program support.
$15,000 to Hartford Public Library, Hartford, CT. For program support.
$14,405 to Asylum Hill Boys and Girls Club Development Association, West Hartford, CT. For program support.
$5,000 to Hartford Symphony Orchestra, Hartford, CT. For program support.
$5,000 to Noah Webster House Foundation and Historical Society of West Hartford, West Hartford, CT. For program support.
$5,000 to Trinity College, Hartford, CT. For program support.
$2,500 to Operation Fuel, Bloomfield, CT. For program support.

1606
Alex G. Nason Foundation, Inc.
1177 High Ridge Rd.
Stamford, CT   06905

Established in 1992 in OH as partial successor to the Nason Foundation.
Donors: Alexander G. Nason; The Nason Foundation.
Foundation type: Independent foundation.
Financial data (yr. ended 12/31/05): Assets, $12,068,174 (M); expenditures, $962,331; qualifying distributions, $743,100; giving activities include $743,100 for 65 grants (high: $100,000; low: $100).
Purpose and activities: Giving primarily for the arts, education and human services.
Fields of interest: Arts; Elementary/secondary education; Higher education; Hospitals (general); Marine science.

Limitations: Applications not accepted. Giving primarily in CT, FL, and NY. No grants to individuals.
Application information: Contributes only to pre-selected organizations.
Officers and Directors:* Sofia Blanchard,* Chair.; Alexander G. Nason,* Pres. and Treas.; Vincent Burke,* V.P.; Lucie Burke,* Secy.
EIN: 341757149
Selected grants: The following grants were reported in 2004.
$60,000 to Syracuse University, Syracuse, NY.
$50,000 to University of Miami, Miami, FL.
$45,000 to New Canaan Country School, New Canaan, CT.
$40,000 to Choate Rosemary Hall, Wallingford, CT.
$40,000 to Maritime Aquarium at Norwalk, Norwalk, CT.
$20,000 to Arts for Healing, New Canaan, CT.
$20,000 to Institute of Nautical Archaeology, College Station, TX.
$15,000 to Silvermine Guild Arts Center, New Canaan, CT.
$5,000 to Museum of Modern Art, New York, NY.
$1,000 to Smile Train, New York, NY.

1607
Edward and Barbara Netter Foundation, Inc. ✧
96 Cummings Point Rd.
Stamford, CT   06902-7912

Established in 1986 in NY.
Donor: Edward Netter.
Foundation type: Independent foundation.
Financial data (yr. ended 10/31/05): Assets, $7,302,751 (M); expenditures, $462,341; qualifying distributions, $458,380; giving activities include $458,120 for 32 grants (high: $200,000; low: $100).
Purpose and activities: Giving primarily for higher education and to Jewish organizations.
Fields of interest: Arts; Education; Human services; Children/youth, services; Jewish agencies & temples.
Limitations: Applications not accepted. Giving primarily in CT and NY. No grants to individuals.
Application information: Contributes only to pre-selected organizations.
Officers: Edward Netter, Pres.; Barbara Netter, V.P. and Treas.; Richard Netter, Secy.
Directors: Vicki Netter Fitzgerald; Donald Netter.
EIN: 133350070
Selected grants: The following grants were reported in 2004.
$170,000 to Jewish Communal Fund of New York, New York, NY.
$137,600 to University of Pennsylvania, Philadelphia, PA.
$30,000 to National Alliance for Research on Schizophrenia and Depression (NARSAD), Great Neck, NY.
$15,000 to American Friends of Israel.
$15,000 to Family Centers, Greenwich, CT.
$15,000 to Westport Country Playhouse, Westport, CT.
$9,000 to Alvin Ailey Dance Foundation, New York, NY.
$5,000 to American Classical Orchestra, Norwalk, CT.
$4,500 to Greenwich Library, Greenwich, CT.
$3,000 to Connecticut Ballet Theater, Stamford, CT.

1608
Leo Nevas Family Foundation, Inc. ✧
(formerly Leo & Libby Nevas Family Foundation, Inc.)
P.O. Box 299
Chester, CT   06412
Contact: Jo-Ann Price, V.P.

Established in 1961 in CT.
Donor: Leo Nevas.
Foundation type: Independent foundation.
Financial data (yr. ended 11/30/05): Assets, $6,894,392 (M); gifts received, $262; expenditures, $422,122; qualifying distributions, $402,448; giving activities include $402,448 for grants (high: $60,000; low: $15).
Fields of interest: Arts; Student services/organizations; Jewish agencies & temples.
Type of support: General/operating support.
Limitations: Giving primarily in CT and NY. No grants to individuals.
Application information: Application form not required.
  Deadline(s): None
Officers: Leo Nevas, Pres.; Jo-Ann Price, V.P.
EIN: 066068842
Selected grants: The following grants were reported in 2003.
$400,000 to Fairfield County Foundation, Lancaster, OH.
$85,000 to Temple Israel Westport, Westport, CT. 2 grants: $60,000, $25,000
$25,000 to Conservative Synagogue of Westport, Westport, CT.
$20,000 to Yale University, Medical School, New Haven, CT.
$17,500 to American Jewish Committee, New York, NY.
$13,500 to New Israel Fund, DC.
$10,000 to American Jewish World Service, New York, NY. To help alleviate poverty, hunger, and disease among world population.
$10,000 to Interns for Peace, New York, NY. To promote Jewish-Arab relations by community service.
$10,000 to Israel Policy Forum, New York, NY.

1609
Newman's Own Foundation, Inc. ✧
c/o Joan Williams
246 Post Rd. E.
Westport, CT   06880

Established in 1989 in CT.
Donors: Paul L. Newman; Meadowlea Foods.
Foundation type: Independent foundation.
Financial data (yr. ended 8/31/05): Assets, $153,551 (M); gifts received, $551,796; expenditures, $840,753; qualifying distributions, $840,724; giving activities include $839,674 for 94 grants (high: $20,000; low: $1,087).
Purpose and activities: Giving primarily for children's health and human services.
Fields of interest: Education; Hospitals (general); Health care; Cancer; Nerve, muscle & bone diseases; Asthma; Health organizations; Children/youth, services; Homeless, human services; Disabilities, people with; Economically disadvantaged.
Limitations: Giving limited to Australia and New Zealand. No grants to individuals.
Publications: Grants list.
Application information: Application form required.

Initial approach: Proposal
Deadline(s): None
Officers and Directors:* Paul Newman,* Pres.;
Jamie Gerard, Secy.; Joanne Woodward.
EIN: 061247230

1610

The Niblack Foundation ◇

c/o Day, Berry & Howard, LLP
1 Canterbury Green
Stamford, CT 06901

Established in 2003 in CT.
Donors: John F. Niblack; Heidi G. Niblack.
Foundation type: Independent foundation.
Financial data (yr. ended 12/31/05): Assets,
$2,174,966 (M); expenditures, $2,367,549;
qualifying distributions, $2,366,450; giving
activities include $2,366,450 for 12 grants (high:
$2,050,000; low: $200).
Fields of interest: Museums; Higher education;
Education; Human services.
Limitations: Applications not accepted. Giving
primarily in CT. No grants to individuals.
Application information: Contributes only to
pre-selected organizations.
Trustees: Elwood B. Davis; Robert J. Miller; Heidi G.
Niblack; John F. Niblack.
EIN: 527323778

1611

Henry E. Niles Foundation ◇

c/o Fogarty, Cohen, Selby, & Nemiroff LLC
88 Field Point Rd.
Greenwich, CT 06830 (203) 629-7314
Contact: Rose Anna Miller
FAX: (203) 629-7350; E-mail: rmiller@fcsn.com;
URL: http://www.heniles.org

Established in 1990 in CT.
Foundation type: Independent foundation.
Financial data (yr. ended 12/31/05): Assets,
$29,679,951 (M); expenditures, $1,909,746;
qualifying distributions, $1,742,507; giving
activities include $1,591,207 for 36 grants.
Purpose and activities: The foundation strives to
support humanitarian efforts, including faith-based
endeavors, that: 1) strengthen education, including
special education, literacy, and others; 2) fight
economic hardships through self-help opportunities;
and 3) enhance public health and sanitation on a
global basis. The foundation also has particular
interest in organizations that promote partnerships
and collaborative efforts among multiple groups and
organizations, and it encourages pilot initiatives that
test new program models.
Fields of interest: Higher education; Education;
Reproductive health, family planning; Disasters,
9/11/01; Human services.
Limitations: Giving primarily in the Northeast, with
emphasis on CT and NY; some funding nationally.
No support for government agencies or for
organizations that subsist mainly on third-party
funding, and that have demonstrated no ability or
have exerted little effort to attract public funding. No
grants to individuals or for general fundraising
drives.
Application information: Application form on
foundation Web site. Application form required.
Initial approach: Fill out on-line application form
Copies of proposal: 5

Deadline(s): 2nd Fri. of each month
Board meeting date(s): Monthly
Officers and Directors:* Geoffrey M. Parkinson,*
Pres.; Leland C. Selby,* V.P. and Secy.; James R.
Lamb,* Treas.
EIN: 061252486
Selected grants: The following grants were reported
in 2004.
$150,000 to World Vision, New York, NY.
$100,000 to Wheelchair Foundation, Danville, CA.
$5,000 to University of Pennsylvania, Philadelphia,
PA.

1612

Laura J. Niles Foundation ◇

c/o Fogerty, Cohen, Selby, & Nemiroff LLC
88 Field Point Rd.
Greenwich, CT 06830-2508 (203) 629-7315
Contact: Anne M. Piedade, Admin.
FAX: (203) 629-0806; E-mail: rmiller@fcsn.com;
E-mail to Anne Piedade: apiedade@fcsn.com;
URL: http://www.ljniles.org

Established in 1997 in CT.
Donors: Laura Janet Niles†; Laura J. Niles
Revocable Trust.
Foundation type: Independent foundation.
Financial data (yr. ended 12/31/05): Assets,
$23,963,276 (M); gifts received, $322,004;
expenditures, $1,653,487; qualifying distributions,
$1,497,790; giving activities include $1,353,790
for 49 grants (high: $150,000; low: $5,000).
Purpose and activities: The foundation encourages
and supports efforts to improve the lives of both
people and animals. The foundation seeks to
benefit animals, primarily dogs, through research,
training, and adoption, especially where people and
animals benefit simultaneously. Additionally, the
foundation strives to nurture and assist individuals
in leading responsible and productive lives by
enabling them to help themselves.
Fields of interest: Education; Animals/wildlife;
Employment; Children/youth, services; Disabilities,
people with; Economically disadvantaged.
Limitations: Giving primarily in the northeastern U.S.
No grants to individuals.
Publications: Application guidelines.
Application information: Application information
available on foundation Web site. Application form
required.
Initial approach: Telephone or e-mail for grant
application
Officers and Directors:* Geoffrey M. Parkinson,*
Pres.; A. Daniel D'Ambrosio,* V.P.; Leland C.
Selby,* Secy.; James R. Lamb,* Treas.
EIN: 223188304
Selected grants: The following grants were reported
in 2004.
$125,000 to North Shore Animal League, Port
Washington, NY.
$30,000 to Best Friends Animal Society, Kanab, UT.
$10,000 to University of Richmond, Richmond, VA.

1613

Nirenberg Foundation, Inc. ◇

(formerly Nirenberg Family Charitable Foundation,
Inc.)
1 Hartfield Blvd., Ste. 102
East Windsor, CT 06088
Application address: c/o Charles Nirenberg, Pres.,
24 Deep Brook Harbor, Suffield, CT 06078,
tel.: (860) 623-5252

Established in 1989 in CT.
Donors: Charles Nirenberg; Janet Nirenberg.
Foundation type: Independent foundation.
Financial data (yr. ended 4/30/06): Assets,
$4,402,593 (L); gifts received, $1,000,000;
expenditures, $620,550; qualifying distributions,
$526,200; giving activities include $526,200 for 37
grants (high: $110,000; low: $200).
Purpose and activities: Support primarily for Jewish
organizations and schools.
Fields of interest: Elementary/secondary
education; Higher education; Theological school/
education; Education; Hospitals (general); Breast
cancer research; Human services; Jewish federated
giving programs; Jewish agencies & temples.
Limitations: Giving primarily in MA. No grants to
individuals.
Application information: Application information
available upon request.
Initial approach: Letter
Deadline(s): None
Officers and Directors:* Charles Nirenberg,* Pres.;
Jonathan K. Bernstein,* Secy.; Janet Nirenberg,*
Treas.
EIN: 223059287
Selected grants: The following grants were reported
in 2004.
$75,000 to Jewish Federation of Greater
Springfield, Springfield, MA. 2 grants: $65,000,
$10,000
$63,000 to Jewish Theological Seminary of
America, New York, NY. 2 grants: $45,000,
$18,000
$45,000 to Dana-Farber Cancer Institute, Boston,
MA.
$45,000 to University of Massachusetts, Amherst,
MA.
$20,000 to Hebrew High School of New England,
West Hartford, CT.
$20,000 to Jewish Education Service of North
America, New York, NY.
$10,000 to Washington State Holocaust Education
Resource Center, Seattle, WA.
$7,500 to Camp Ramah of New England, Needham,
MA.

1614

Northeast Utilities Foundation, Inc. ◇

P.O. Box 5563
Hartford, CT 06102-5563 (860) 721-4063
Contact: Theresa Hopkins-Staten, Chair. and Pres.
FAX: (860) 721-4331; Contact in MA: Edgar
Alejandro, Mgr., Economic and Community Devel.,
tel.: (413) 787-9333, FAX: (413) 787-9082, E-mail:
alejae@nu.com; Application address in MA: P.O. Box
2010, West Springfield, MA 01090; Contact in NH:
Nury Marquez, Mgr., Community Rels., tel.: (603)
634-2777, FAX: (603) 634-2367, E-mail:
marquns@nu.com; Application address in NH:
Public Service Co. of New Hampshire, P.O. Box 330,
Manchester, NH 03105; URL: http://www.nu.com/
aboutnu/foundation.asp

Additional URL: http://www.cl-p.com/community/partners/grants/nufoundation.asp

Established in 1998 in CT.

Donors: The Connecticut Light and Power Co.; Northeast Nuclear Energy Co.; Northeast Utilities; Public Service Co. of New Hampshire; Western Massachusetts Electric Co.

Foundation type: Company-sponsored foundation.

Financial data (yr. ended 12/31/03): Assets, $3,346,379 (M); gifts received, $3,005,621; expenditures, $1,408,296; qualifying distributions, $1,386,830; giving activities include $1,241,692 for 31 grants (high: $110,000; low: $15,000), $57,108 for grants to individuals, and $88,030 for employee matching gifts.

Purpose and activities: The foundation supports organizations involved with arts and culture, education, the environment, human services, and community development.

Fields of interest: Arts; Higher education; Education; Environment; Employment, training; Housing/shelter; Human services; Economic development; Community development.

Limitations: Giving primarily in areas of company operations. No support for private foundations, health care organizations, religious, political, fraternal, or veterans' organizations not of direct benefit to the entire community, or bands. No grants for fundraising, athletics, debt reduction, endowments, advertising, scouting, or charitable events.

Application information: Application form required.
Initial approach: Download application form and mail or fax to nearest application address or contact
Deadline(s): Jan. 10, Mar. 14, June 13, and Sept. 12
Board meeting date(s): Feb., May, Aug., and Nov.

Officers and Directors:* Theresa Hopkins-Staten,* Chair., Pres., and Exec. Dir.; David R. McHale, Treas.; Gregory B. Butler; John H. Forsgren; Cheryl W. Grise; Michael G. Morris; Mary Jo Keating.

EIN: 061527290

Selected grants: The following grants were reported in 2003.

$110,000 to University of Connecticut, NEAG School of Education, Storrs, CT.

$70,036 to Greater Hartford Arts Council, Hartford, CT.

$50,000 to Dance Connecticut, Hartford, CT.

$41,000 to Oxford Economic Development Corporation, Oxford, CT.

$36,123 to Mystic Seaport Museum, Mystic, CT.

$25,000 to Audubon Society of New Hampshire, Concord, NH.

$25,000 to Capitol Center for the Arts, Concord, NH.

$25,000 to Mashantucket Pequot Museum and Research Center, Mashantucket, CT.

$17,500 to Leadership Teacher, Bow, NH.

$15,963 to United Way of the Capital Area, Hartford, CT.

1615
Grace Swift Nye & Alfred Gibbs Nye Scholarship Trust

c/o Elaine H. LeLaurin, Admin.
P.O. Box 271369
West Hartford, CT 06127-1369

Established in 1995 in MA.

Donor: Grace S. Nye†.

Foundation type: Independent foundation.

Financial data (yr. ended 12/31/04): Assets, $5,321,751 (M); expenditures, $407,363; qualifying distributions, $342,949; giving activities include $320,497 for grants to individuals.

Purpose and activities: Giving to provide undergraduate financial assistance with renewable scholarships.

Fields of interest: Human services.

Type of support: Scholarships—to individuals.

Limitations: Giving limited to graduating high school seniors of Plymouth, Wareham, Bourne and Sandwich, MA.

Publications: Application guidelines.

Application information: Application form required.
Deadline(s): Early Apr.
Final notification: June

Trustees: Elaine H. LeLaurin; David E. Nye; Fiduciary Trust Co.

Number of staff: 1 part-time support.

EIN: 066421534

1616
The Oaklawn Foundation ◇

c/o Ann K. Arnold
1 Old Church Rd., Unit 8
Greenwich, CT 06830 (203) 629-1911
Contact: Ann Kies Arnold, Pres.

Incorporated in 1948 in NY.

Donors: Mabel B. Kies†; W.S. Kies†; Margaret K. Gibb†.

Foundation type: Independent foundation.

Financial data (yr. ended 12/31/05): Assets, $16,201,589 (M); expenditures, $928,407; qualifying distributions, $824,223; giving activities include $696,500 for 60 grants (high: $60,000; low: $500).

Purpose and activities: Giving primarily for education, with emphasis on higher and private secondary education.

Fields of interest: Secondary school/education; Higher education; Human services; Christian agencies & churches; Protestant agencies & churches.

Type of support: Endowments; Scholarship funds.

Limitations: Giving primarily in CT. No grants to individuals, or for operating budgets, deficit financing, emergency funds, capital funds, research, special projects, publications, or conferences; no loans.

Application information: Application form not required.
Initial approach: Proposal
Copies of proposal: 1
Deadline(s): None
Board meeting date(s): Mar., June, and Oct.
Final notification: 2 to 3 months

Officers and Directors:* Ann Kies Arnold,* Pres.; Audrey S. Paight,* Treas.; William A. Arnold IV; Stephen K. Grimm; Cameron F. Hopper; William S. Kies III; Joseph Paight; Betsy K. Raftery.

Number of staff: 2 part-time professional; 2 part-time support.

EIN: 136127896

Selected grants: The following grants were reported in 2005.

$60,000 to Southern Methodist University, Dallas, TX.

$40,000 to Greenwich Academy, Greenwich, CT.

$25,000 to Sacred Heart University, Fairfield, CT.

$25,000 to Susan Fund, Westport, CT.

$20,000 to American Red Cross.

$20,000 to AmeriCares, Stamford, CT.

$17,500 to Sweet Briar College, Sweet Briar, VA.

$15,000 to Mercy Housing and Shelter Corporation, Hartford, CT.

$14,000 to Kids in Crisis, Cos Cob, CT. 2 grants: $10,000, $4,000

1617
The October Hill Foundation ◇

17 Taunton Ridge Rd.
Newtown, CT 06470

Established in 1994 in DE.

Donor: Gretchen A. Bauta.

Foundation type: Independent foundation.

Financial data (yr. ended 12/31/05): Assets, $11,082,345 (M); expenditures, $578,637; qualifying distributions, $571,232; giving activities include $567,500 for 32 grants (high: $160,000; low: $1,000).

Purpose and activities: Giving primarily for animal welfare and environmental conservation.

Fields of interest: Environment, natural resources; Animal welfare; Human services.

Type of support: General/operating support.

Limitations: Applications not accepted. Giving primarily in the U.S. and Canada. No grants to individuals.

Application information: Contributes only to pre-selected organizations.

Officers: Gretchen A. Bauta, Pres.; Christian Bauta, V.P. and Secy.; Humberto P. Bauta, V.P. and Treas.; Nicholas Bauta, V.P.; Pilar Bauta, V.P.

EIN: 137049883

Selected grants: The following grants were reported in 2004.

$130,000 to Ecology Action Centre, Halifax, Canada. .

$77,000 to Michoacan Reforestation Fund, Alameda, CA. For program support.

$30,000 to Woonasquatucket Valley Community Build, Providence, RI. For general support.

$25,000 to Wilderness Society, DC. For reforestation of land.

$20,000 to Charities Aid Foundation (CAF) America, Alexandria, VA. For organic farming.

$15,000 to Aid to Artisans, Hartford, CT. For program support.

$15,000 to World Wildlife Fund, DC.

$15,000 to YMCA, Western Connecticut Regional, Brookfield, CT. To purchase exercise equipment.

$10,000 to American Forests, DC. For Artisans Program.

$10,000 to Danbury Hospital, Department of Pediatrics, Danbury, CT.

1618
The Olson Foundation ◇

c/o Cummings & Lockwood
P.O. Box 2505
Greenwich, CT 06836-2505

Established in 2000 in NY.

Donors: Brian T. Olson; Jill J. Olson.

Foundation type: Independent foundation.

Financial data (yr. ended 12/31/05): Assets, $8,280,695 (M); gifts received, $5,000,000; expenditures, $878,195; qualifying distributions, $867,000; giving activities include $867,000 for 12 grants (high: $400,000; low: $2,000).

Fields of interest: Elementary/secondary education; Health care; Human services.

Limitations: Applications not accepted. Giving primarily in New York, NY and CT. No grants to individuals.
Application information: Contributes only to pre-selected organizations; unsolicited requests for funds not accepted.
Trustees: Brian T. Olson; Jill J. Olson.
EIN: 223769020
Selected grants: The following grants were reported in 2004.
$100,000 to Mayo Foundation, Rochester, MN.
$25,000 to Greenwich Country Day School, Greenwich, CT.
$25,000 to TEAK Fellowship, New York, NY.
$10,000 to National Down Syndrome Society, New York, NY.
$5,000 to Greenwich Hospital, Greenwich, CT.

1619
The Orchard Farm Foundation ✧
c/o Graham Capital Management, LP
40 Highland Ave.
Norwalk, CT   06853-1510

Established in 1998 in CT.
Donors: Kenneth G. Tropin; Paul Jones; Nicholas Maounis.
Foundation type: Independent foundation.
Financial data (yr. ended 12/31/04): Assets, $482,070 (M); gifts received, $1,325,000; expenditures, $1,164,122; qualifying distributions, $1,162,622; giving activities include $1,162,622 for 47 grants (high: $300,000; low: $500).
Purpose and activities: Giving primarily for children and youth services, an arts foundation, health associations, and human services.
Fields of interest: Arts; Education; Animals/wildlife, preservation/protection; Health organizations, association; Food banks; Housing/shelter, homeless; Human services; Children/youth, services; Homeless, human services; Economically disadvantaged.
Limitations: Applications not accepted. Giving on a national basis. No grants to individuals.
Application information: Contributes only to pre-selected organizations.
Officer: Kenneth G. Tropin, Pres.
EIN: 223626152
Selected grants: The following grants were reported in 2003.
$300,000 to Robin Hood Foundation, New York, NY.
$200,000 to Norwalk Emergency Shelter, South Norwalk, CT.
$100,000 to Connecticut Food Bank, New Haven, CT.
$100,000 to Kids in Crisis, Cos Cob, CT.
$100,000 to Sheridan Arts Foundation, Telluride, CO.
$75,000 to Interfaith Housing Association of Westport and Weston, Westport, CT.
$37,500 to Buoniconti Fund to Cure Paralysis, New York, NY.
$35,000 to ABC (A Better Chance) of New Canaan, New Canaan, CT.
$25,000 to Joe Torre Safe at Home Foundation, Harrison, NY.
$12,500 to Leukemia & Lymphoma Society, New York, NY.

1620
The Owenoke Foundation ✧
100 Allyn St., Ste. 300
Hartford, CT   06103-1418

Established in 1999 in DE.
Donors: Underhill Charitable Trust; A.M. Rockefeller Trust; Rockefeller Charitable Trust.
Foundation type: Independent foundation.
Financial data (yr. ended 11/30/05): Assets, $10,615,777 (M); gifts received, $318,460; expenditures, $558,399; qualifying distributions, $455,100; giving activities include $450,000 for 27 grants (high: $50,000; low: $2,000).
Fields of interest: Education; Human services; Christian agencies & churches.
Limitations: Applications not accepted. Giving primarily in CT; some funding nationally. No grants to individuals.
Application information: Contributes only to pre-selected organizations.
Officers and Directors:* Avery Rockefeller III,* Pres.; Mary Runestad,* Secy.; Monica Rockefeller; Rodney Runestad.
EIN: 223483048
Selected grants: The following grants were reported in 2005.
$50,000 to Kingswood-Oxford School, West Hartford, CT.
$40,000 to AmeriCares, Stamford, CT.
$30,000 to Adirondack Council, Elizabethtown, NY.
$25,000 to Literacy Volunteers of Greater Hartford, Hartford, CT.
$20,000 to Center City Churches, Hartford, CT.
$20,000 to Connecticut Childrens Medical Center, Hartford, CT.
$20,000 to V Foundation for Cancer Research, Cary, NC.
$10,000 to Duke University, Durham, NC.
$10,000 to Hartford Hospital, Hartford, CT.
$10,000 to Saint Lukes LifeWorks, Stamford, CT.

1621
The Frank Loomis Palmer Fund
c/o Bank of America, N.A.
777 Main St., CT2-102-22-02
Hartford, CT   06115
Contact: Amy R. Lynch, V.P., Bank of America, N.A.

Trust established in 1936 in CT.
Donor: Virginia Palmer†.
Foundation type: Independent foundation.
Financial data (yr. ended 7/31/05): Assets, $33,121,545 (M); expenditures, $1,380,265; qualifying distributions, $1,309,831; giving activities include $1,176,770 for 64 grants (high: $75,000; low: $500).
Purpose and activities: Grants to encourage new projects and to provide seed money, with emphasis on child welfare and family services and youth agencies; support also for civic groups, cultural programs, social services, and educational programs.
Fields of interest: Performing arts; Arts; Elementary school/education; Secondary school/education; Higher education; Adult/continuing education; Libraries/library science; Education; Environment, natural resources; Environment; Hospitals (general); Reproductive health, family planning; Health care; Health organizations, association; AIDS; Alcoholism; AIDS research; Legal services; Safety/disasters; Children/youth, services; Family services; Residential/custodial care, hospices;

Aging, centers/services; Minorities/immigrants, centers/services; Community development; Engineering/technology; Science; Government/public administration; Transportation; Religion; Aging; Minorities.
Type of support: Equipment; Program development; Conferences/seminars; Publication; Seed money; Scholarship funds; Research; Consulting services; Matching/challenge support.
Limitations: Giving limited to New London, CT. No grants to individuals, or for endowment funds.
Publications: Informational brochure (including application guidelines).
Application information: Application form required.
  Initial approach: Telephone
  Copies of proposal: 1
  Deadline(s): May 15 and Nov. 15
  Board meeting date(s): Jan. and July
  Final notification: Feb. 1 and Aug. 1
Trustee: Bank of America, N.A.
EIN: 066026043
Selected grants: The following grants were reported in 2005.
$75,000 to New London Development Corporation, New London, CT. For House New London program.
$60,000 to Mitchell College, New London, CT. For financial aid for New London students.
$50,000 to Garde Arts Center, New London, CT.
$50,000 to Williams School, New London, CT. To provide scholarships to disadvantaged students.
$48,000 to Child and Family Agency of Southeastern Connecticut, New London, CT. For transportation cost and project expansion.
$29,227 to New London Rotary Foundation, New London, CT. For public site/boundless playground.
$20,000 to Eugene ONeill Memorial Theater Center, Waterford, CT. For annual O'Neill celebration.
$20,000 to Literacy Volunteers, Southeastern Connecticut, New London, CT. For ESOL program.
$15,000 to United Way of Southeastern Connecticut, Gales Ferry, CT. For fuel and electricity support to families.
$12,800 to New London Community Boating, New London, CT. For scholarships for students.

1622
Panwy Foundation, Inc. ✧
4 Greenwich Office Park
10 Valley Dr.
Greenwich, CT   06831   (203) 661-6616
Contact: Ralph M. Wyman, Pres.

Established in 1943 in NY; incorporated in 1951 in NJ; reincorporated in 1988 in CT.
Donors: Olga Resseguier†; Henry W. Wyman†; Maria Wyman†; Ralph M. Wyman; Ruth L. Russell; Carla Benka; Alexis Dorf.
Foundation type: Independent foundation.
Financial data (yr. ended 12/31/04): Assets, $5,311,832 (M); gifts received, $45,000; expenditures, $522,020; qualifying distributions, $456,089; giving activities include $454,270 for 244 grants (high: $94,967; low: $100).
Purpose and activities: Current interests involve strengthening of the family.
Fields of interest: Employment, job counseling; Youth, services; Family services, parent education; Family services, counseling.
Type of support: Program development; Seed money.

Limitations: Applications not accepted. Giving primarily in southern CT, and the Boston, MA, area. No grants to individuals, or for matching gifts, scholarship funds, capital campaigns, or operating deficit funding.

Application information: Unsolicited requests for funds not accepted. Foundation initiates contact.

Board meeting date(s): As required

Officers and Trustees:* Ralph M. Wyman,* Pres.; Ruth L. Russell,* V.P.; Marguerite A. Wyman,* V.P.; Virginia A.W. Meyer,* Secy.-Treas.

EIN: 136130759

Selected grants: The following grants were reported in 2003.

$71,933 to First Presbyterian Church, New Canaan, CT.

$55,000 to Metropolitan Opera Association, New York, NY.

$33,250 to Fairfield County Community Foundation, Wilton, CT.

$15,000 to Families First, Cambridge, MA.

$12,000 to United Way of Greenwich, Greenwich, CT.

$10,000 to Boston Lyric Opera Company, Boston, MA.

$7,500 to Brookline Community Fund, Brookline, MA.

$5,000 to Sherrill House, Jamaica Plain, MA.

$3,100 to Kids in Crisis, Cos Cob, CT.

$1,500 to Rosies Place, Boston, MA.

1623
The Robert & Margaret Patricelli Family Foundation ◇ ☆
77 Hartford Rd.
Simsbury, CT 06070
Contact: Robert E. Patricelli, Chair.

Established in 1996 in CT.

Donors: Robert E. Patricelli; Margaret S. Patricelli.

Foundation type: Independent foundation.

Financial data (yr. ended 6/30/05): Assets, $3,289,695 (M); gifts received, $1,000; expenditures, $445,338; qualifying distributions, $413,722; giving activities include $383,890 for 108 grants (high: $100,000; low: $50).

Fields of interest: Arts; Education, formal/general education; Higher education; Education; Environment, natural resources; Health care; Human services; Federated giving programs.

Type of support: General/operating support; Annual campaigns; Program development; Research.

Limitations: Giving primarily in CT. No grants to individuals, or for capital campaigns.

Publications: Application guidelines.

Application information: Application form not required.

Deadline(s): None

Officers: Robert E. Patricelli, Chair.; Margaret S. Patricelli, Pres.

Directors: Alison J. Patricelli; Thomas R. Patricelli.

Number of staff: 1 part-time professional.

EIN: 061487230

Selected grants: The following grants were reported in 2003.

$275,000 to Wesleyan University, Middletown, CT. 2 grants: $25,000, $250,000

$100,000 to Loomis Chaffee School, Windsor, CT. F.

$33,333 to Planned Parenthood League of Connecticut, Hartford, CT.

$30,000 to Horace Bushnell Memorial Hall, Hartford, CT.

$20,000 to Dance Connecticut, Hartford, CT. 2 grants: $10,000 each

$10,150 to Haitian Health Foundation, Norwich, CT.

$10,000 to United Way of the Capital Area, Hartford, CT.

$5,000 to Cystic Fibrosis Foundation, Wethersfield, CT.

1624
Robert Leet Patterson & Clara Guthrie Patterson Trust
c/o Bank of America, N.A., Fdns. and Philanthropic Svcs.
777 Main St., CT2-102-22-02
Hartford, CT 06115
Contact: Carmen Britt, Prog. Off.

Established in 1981 in CT.

Donors: Robert Leet Patterson†; Clara Guthrie Patterson†; Robert Patterson Trust No. 2.

Foundation type: Independent foundation.

Financial data (yr. ended 1/30/06): Assets, $19,675,303 (M); expenditures, $1,078,420; qualifying distributions, $1,025,509; giving activities include $950,000 for 16 grants (high: $62,500; low: $50,000).

Purpose and activities: Giving to organizations which are devoted to the advancement of medical science and are engaged in research relating to human diseases, their causes and relief thereof, and to such organizations as are engaged in the treatment of such diseases.

Fields of interest: Medical research, institute.

Type of support: Research.

Limitations: Giving limited to the continental U.S. No grants to individuals, or for operating budgets, continuing support, annual campaigns, emergency funds, deficit financing, endowment funds, consulting services, technical assistance, demonstration projects, publications, conferences and seminars, or for medical equipment; no loans.

Application information: Recommendations subject to trust committee approval. Application form required.

Initial approach: Letter or proposal

Copies of proposal: 6

Deadline(s): May 1 for June meeting and Nov. 15 for Dec. meeting

Board meeting date(s): June and Dec.

Final notification: 3 months

Trustee: Bank of America, N.A.

EIN: 066236358

Selected grants: The following grants were reported in 2005.

$400,000 to Yale University, New Haven, CT. 6 grants: $60,000 (For medical research), $55,000 (For medical research), $60,000, $75,000, $75,000, $75,000.

$175,000 to Childrens Hospital Trust, Boston, MA. 3 grants: $60,000 (For medical research), $60,000 (For medical research), $55,000 (For medical research).

$75,000 to University of Connecticut Health Center, Farmington, CT.

1625
The Pequot Capital Foundation, Inc. ◇
500 Nyala Farm Rd.
Westport, CT 06880

Established in 2000 in CT.

Donors: Pequot Capital Management, Inc.; Sheila Clancy.

Foundation type: Company-sponsored foundation.

Financial data (yr. ended 9/30/04): Assets, $4,384,276 (M); gifts received, $4,500; expenditures, $743,885; qualifying distributions, $742,580; giving activities include $742,200 for 187 grants (high: $200,000; low: $50).

Purpose and activities: The foundation supports food banks and organizations involved with arts and culture, education, health, youth development, human services, religion, and economically disadvantaged people.

Fields of interest: Museums (art); Arts; Education; Health care; Eye diseases; Food banks; Youth development; Human services; Philanthropy/voluntarism; Religion; Economically disadvantaged.

Type of support: General/operating support.

Limitations: Applications not accepted. Giving primarily in CT and NY.

Application information: Contributes only to pre-selected organizations.

Officers: Arthur J. Samberg,* Chair.; Sheila Clancy, Pres.

EIN: 061601746

Selected grants: The following grants were reported in 2003.

$46,000 to Robin Hood Foundation, New York, NY.

$45,000 to ARC of Greenwich, Greenwich, CT.

$25,250 to Foundation Fighting Blindness, New York, NY.

$25,000 to Cystic Fibrosis Association of Greater New York, New York, NY.

$25,000 to Westport Country Playhouse, Westport, CT.

$25,000 to Young Israel of Riverdale, Bronx, NY.

$15,000 to Brooklyn Arts Council, Brooklyn, NY.

$15,000 to Caroline House, Bridgeport, CT.

$10,000 to Autism Coalition for Research and Education, Port Chester, NY.

$10,000 to Yale University, New Haven, CT.

1626
The Perrin Family Foundation
4 Prospect St.
Ridgefield, CT 06877-4510 (203) 438-7349
Contact: Nancy Holland, Grants Mgr.
FAX: (203) 438-5062;
E-mail: info@perrinfamilyfoundation.org;
URL: http://www.perrinfamilyfoundation.org

Established in 1994 in CT.

Donors: Charles Perrin; Sheila Perrin.

Foundation type: Independent foundation.

Financial data (yr. ended 12/31/04): Assets, $17,044,389 (M); gifts received, $496,382; expenditures, $946,520; qualifying distributions, $811,421; giving activities include $763,666 for 61 grants (high: $30,000; low: $2,500).

Purpose and activities: The foundation's mission is to provide equal opportunities for children and young adults to lead safe, productive, and creative lives. Giving for education, health and cultural services for children, including after-school programs.

Fields of interest: Arts; Education; Health care; Children, services; Family services.

Type of support: General/operating support; Continuing support; Program development.

Limitations: Giving primarily in Fairfield County, CT. No support for public or private schools. No grants to individuals.

Publications: Application guidelines; Grants list.

Application information: Proposals accepted from organizations providing direct services to children. See foundation Web site for application guidelines and procedures. Accepts Connecticut Council for Philanthropy application form. Application form required.
Initial approach: Letter of intent
Copies of proposal: 1
Deadline(s): Apr. 1, Sept. 1, and Dec. 1
Board meeting date(s): Three times a year
Final notification: Within 3 months of receiving application
Officer and Trustees:* Sheila A. Perrin,* Pres.; Anne Kenan; Charles R. Perrin; David B. Perrin; Jeffrey L. Perrin.
Number of staff: 1 part-time professional.
EIN: 223309886
Selected grants: The following grants were reported in 2006.
$40,000 to Human Services Council, Norwalk, CT. For expansion of service hours at Dr. Robert Appleby School Based Health Center.
$30,000 to Norwalk Education Foundation, Norwalk, CT. For after-school program.
$25,000 to Carver Foundation of Norwalk, Norwalk, CT. For Youth Leadership program.
$25,000 to Center for Women and Families of Eastern Fairfield County, Bridgeport, CT. For child advocate staff.
$25,000 to Prevent Blindness Tri-State, Middlebury, CT. For sight screening for preschoolers.
$25,000 to SoundWaters, Stamford, CT. For Outdoor Ecology program.
$20,000 to Person-to-Person, Darien, CT. For Summer Camp scholarships.
$16,762 to Bridgeport Public Education Fund, Bridgeport, CT. For Mentoring for Academic Achievement and College Success staff.
$15,000 to Hord Foundation, Danbury, CT.
$12,750 to Mercy Learning Center of Bridgeport, Bridgeport, CT. For educational materials.
$10,000 to Child Guidance Center of Southern Connecticut, Stamford, CT. For Crime Victims-Community Policing program.

1627
The Phoenix Foundation, Inc. ✧
1 American Row
Hartford, CT 06102-5056 (860) 403-7831
Contact: Tina Muzzy, Grants Off.

Established in 1997 in CT.
Donors: Phoenix Home Life Mutual Insurance Co.; The Phoenix Cos., Inc.
Foundation type: Company-sponsored foundation.
Financial data (yr. ended 12/31/04): Assets, $7,011,380 (M); gifts received, $253,875; expenditures, $1,206,250; qualifying distributions, $1,196,088; giving activities include $1,125,899 for grants.
Purpose and activities: The foundation supports organizations involved with secondary and higher education, human services, and economic development.
Fields of interest: Secondary school/education; Higher education; Youth, services; Human services; Economic development.
Type of support: Capital campaigns; Employee matching gifts.
Limitations: Giving primarily in Enfield and Hartford, CT, and Albany, NY. No support for school athletic teams. No grants to individuals, or for debt

reduction, fundraising events, religious programs, or sponsorships.
Publications: Application guidelines.
Application information: Application form required.
Initial approach: Contact foundation for application form
Copies of proposal: 1
Deadline(s): Sept. 15
Board meeting date(s): Nov.
Final notification: Jan. 1
Officers and Directors:* Charles Olson,* Chair. and Pres.; Jane L. Driscoll, V.P.; Brian A. Giantonio, Secy.; Carl T. Chadburn; Robert W. Fiondella; Maura L. Melley; David W. Searfoss; Dona D. Young.
Trustee: Phoenix National Trust Co.
Number of staff: 2 part-time professional; 1 part-time support.
EIN: 061493188
Selected grants: The following grants were reported in 2005.
$145,000 to United Way of the Capital Area, Hartford, CT.
$100,000 to Neighborhoods of Hartford, Hartford, CT.
$30,000 to Corporation for Supportive Housing, New Haven, CT.
$30,000 to Greater Hartford Arts Council, Hartford, CT.
$15,000 to Fred D. Wish School, Hartford, CT.
$10,000 to Community Economic Development Fund Foundation, Hartford, CT.
$1,500 to Habitat for Humanity International, Americus, GA.
$1,000 to Main Street Community Foundation, Bristol, CT.
$500 to Goodspeed Opera House Foundation, East Haddam, CT.
$200 to East Catholic High School, Manchester, CT.

1628
The William H. Pitt Foundation, Inc.
(formerly The William H. Pitt III Foundation, Inc.)
1177 High Ridge Rd.
Stamford, CT 06905 (203) 321-2170
Contact: Debra Hertz, Exec. Dir.
FAX: (203) 321-1277; E-mail: dhertz@williampitt.com

Established in 1984.
Donor: William H. Pitt†.
Foundation type: Independent foundation.
Financial data (yr. ended 9/30/05): Assets, $73,654,232 (M); gifts received, $474,388; expenditures, $6,226,984; qualifying distributions, $3,375,780; giving activities include $3,149,830 for 99 grants (high: $400,000; low: $100; average: $10,000–$100,000).
Fields of interest: Elementary/secondary education; Higher education; Boys & girls clubs; Human services; Christian agencies & churches.
Type of support: General/operating support; Scholarship funds.
Limitations: Giving primarily in Fairfield County, CT and Palm Beach County, FL. No grants to individuals.
Publications: Application guidelines.
Application information: Application form not required.
Initial approach: Letter
Copies of proposal: 1
Deadline(s): None
Board meeting date(s): Mar. and Oct.
Officers: Robert Scinto, Chair. and C.E.O.; Robert G. Simses, C.O.O. and Pres.; Debra Hertz, Exec. Dir.

Directors: Alphonsus J. Donahue, Jr.; Charles Mallory; Pauline Baker Pitt; Lesly Smith.
Number of staff: 1 full-time professional.
EIN: 222570737
Selected grants: The following grants were reported in 2004.
$618,154 to Sacred Heart University, Fairfield, CT.
$130,000 to Academy of the Palm Beaches, West Palm Beach, FL.
$40,000 to Brunswick School, Greenwich, CT.
$40,000 to Domus Foundation, Stamford, CT.
$40,000 to Saint Lukes School, New York, NY.
$30,000 to Norwalk Community College, Norwalk, CT.
$25,000 to McGivney Community Center, Bridgeport, CT.
$25,000 to Turtle Nest Village, West Palm Beach, FL.
$25,000 to YMCA of Stamford, Stamford, CT.
$15,000 to Childrens Storefront, New York, NY.

1629
Praxair Foundation, Inc. ✧
39 Old Ridgebury Rd.
Danbury, CT 06810-5113
URL: http://www.praxair.com/praxair.nsf/AllContent/1E607B9456292F1185256BF800779733?OpenDocument

Established in 1994.
Donor: Praxair, Inc.
Foundation type: Company-sponsored foundation.
Financial data (yr. ended 11/30/05): Assets, $297,632 (M); gifts received, $2,889,400; expenditures, $2,795,300; qualifying distributions, $2,795,300; giving activities include $2,795,300 for grants.
Purpose and activities: The foundation supports public libraries and organizations involved with higher education, the environment, health, community development, and minorities.
Fields of interest: Higher education; Engineering school/education; Libraries (public); Environmental education; Environment; Health care; Community development; Federated giving programs; Science; Minorities.
Type of support: General/operating support; Equipment; Program development; Scholarship funds; Employee volunteer services; Employee matching gifts.
Limitations: Giving on a national and international basis in areas of company operations, including in Asia. No grants to individuals.
Application information: Application form required.
Initial approach: Complete online application form
Officers and Directors:* Nigel D. Muir,* Pres.; Robert Bassett, Secy.; S. Mark Seymour, Treas.
EIN: 061413665

1630
The Prentice Foundation, Inc. ✧
35 Church Ln.
Westport, CT 06880
Contact: Diane H. Allison, Exec. Dir.

Established in 1994 in CT.
Donor: Elaine P. Hapgood.
Foundation type: Independent foundation.
Financial data (yr. ended 12/31/04): Assets, $22,771,032 (M); gifts received, $242,343;

expenditures, $1,297,974; qualifying distributions, $1,083,466; giving activities include $1,079,000 for 159 grants (high: $20,000; low: $250).

Purpose and activities: Giving primarily for environmental programs.

Fields of interest: Education; Environment; Population studies; Government/public administration.

Type of support: Program development; Seed money; Matching/challenge support.

Limitations: Applications not accepted. Giving on a national basis. No grants to individuals, or for capital campaigns or endowments; no loans.

Application information: Contributes only to pre-selected organizations.

Board meeting date(s): Varies

Officers: Elaine Hopgood, Pres.; Jerry Babicka, V.P.; Lynn P. Babicka, V.P.; John P. Powers, V.P.; Diane M. Allison, Secy.; David L. Godfrey, Treas.

EIN: 061386173

1631
William H. Prusoff Foundation ✧
880 Old Post Rd.
Fairfield, CT 06824

Established in 2000 in CT.

Donor: William H. Prusoff Charitable Lead Annuity Trust.

Foundation type: Independent foundation.

Financial data (yr. ended 12/31/05): Assets, $4,840,043 (M); gifts received, $1,471,304; expenditures, $1,149,346; qualifying distributions, $1,147,000; giving activities include $1,141,000 for 38 grants (high: $250,000; low: $2,500).

Fields of interest: Higher education; Health care; Health organizations, association; Cancer; Human services.

Limitations: Applications not accepted. Giving primarily in CT and NY; funding also nationally. No grants to individuals.

Application information: Contributes only to pre-selected organizations.

Trustees: Alvin Prusoff; Laura Prusoff.

EIN: 061601597

Selected grants: The following grants were reported in 2004.

$200,000 to University of Texas M. D. Anderson Cancer Center, Houston, TX.

$165,000 to Committee Against Anti-Asian Violence, Bronx, NY.

$50,000 to New Haven Free Public Library, New Haven, CT.

$50,000 to Yale University, School of Medicine, New Haven, CT.

$30,000 to Fairfield Theater Company, Fairfield, CT.

$10,000 to Connecticut Food Bank, New Haven, CT.

$10,000 to InterVarsity Christian Fellowship/USA, Madison, WI.

$10,000 to National Geographic Society, DC.

$10,000 to Simons Rock College of Bard, Great Barrington, MA.

$5,000 to Easter Seals Goodwill Industries Rehabilitation Center, New Haven, CT.

1632
Smith Richardson Foundation, Inc. ▼
60 Jesup Rd.
Westport, CT 06880   (203) 222-6222
Contact: Marin J. Strmecki, Sr. V.P. and Dir., Progs.
FAX: (203) 222-6282; URL: http://www.srf.org

Incorporated in 1935 in NC.

Donors: H.S. Richardson, Sr.†; Grace Jones Richardson†.

Foundation type: Independent foundation.

Financial data (yr. ended 12/31/05): Assets, $498,683,646 (M); gifts received, $2,333,044; expenditures, $21,475,474; qualifying distributions, $22,782,308; giving activities include $16,781,745 for 227 grants (high: $369,781; low: $500; average: $10,000–$200,000).

Purpose and activities: The mission of the foundation is to contribute to important public debates and to help address serious public policy challenges facing the United States. The foundation seeks to help ensure the vitality of social, economic, and governmental institutions. It also seeks to assist with the development of effective policies to compete internationally and advance U.S. interests and values abroad. This mission is embodied in their domestic and international grant programs.

Fields of interest: Education; Youth, pregnancy prevention; International affairs, foreign policy; International affairs; Social sciences; Economics; Political science; International studies; Public policy, research; Government/public administration.

International interests: Asia; Europe; Middle East; Soviet Union (Former).

Type of support: Conferences/seminars; Publication; Research.

Limitations: Giving limited to U.S.-based organizations only. No support for programs in the arts and humanities, direct service programs, or historic restoration projects. No grants to individuals, or for deficit financing, building or construction projects, or research in the physical sciences; no loans.

Publications: Annual report (including application guidelines).

Application information: Most projects funded are initiated by the foundation. The staff does not meet with applicants. Application form not required.

Initial approach: Concept paper (no longer than 5 pages)
Copies of proposal: 1
Deadline(s): None
Final notification: 45 to 60 days

Officers and Trustees:* Peter L. Richardson,* Chair., Pres. and Gov.; Marin J. Strmecki, Sr. V.P. and Dir., Progs.; Arvid R. Nelson,* Secy. and Gov.; Ross F. Hemphill, Treas.; W. Winburne King III.

Board of Governors: Hon. Zbigniew Brzezinski; Christopher DeMuth; Martin Feldstein; Stephen Goldsmith; Fred C. Ikle; Roderick MacFarquhar; Genl. Edward C. Meyer; June E. O'Neill; Jane B. Preyer; Adele Richardson Ray; Lunsford Richardson, Jr.; Stuart S. Richardson; E. William Stetson III; R. James Woolsey; Edward F. Zigler.

Number of staff: 6 full-time professional; 7 full-time support.

EIN: 560611550

1633
Ritter Family Foundation ✧ ☆
38 Peaceable St.
Ridgefield, CT 06877

Donors: Bruce Ritter; Diane Ritter.

Foundation type: Independent foundation.

Financial data (yr. ended 12/31/05): Assets, $1,078,116 (M); gifts received, $100,000; expenditures, $431,324; qualifying distributions, $431,299; giving activities include $431,299 for 12 grants (high: $350,000; low: $719).

Fields of interest: Higher education; Safety/disasters; Children/youth, services.

Type of support: Research.

Limitations: Applications not accepted. No grants to individuals.

Application information: Contributes only to pre-selected organizations.

Officers: Diane Ritter, Pres.; Kathryn Ritter, V.P.; Bruce Ritter, Secy.

EIN: 061468578

1634
The Robbins Family Foundation, Inc. ✧
(formerly Robbins Foundation, Inc.)
c/o Clifton S. Robbins
32 Calhoun Dr.
Greenwich, CT 06831-4437

Established in 1993 in NY.

Donors: Clifton S. Robbins; Edwin Robbins; Beverly Robbins; General Atlantic Service Corp.

Foundation type: Independent foundation.

Financial data (yr. ended 12/31/05): Assets, $1,293,162 (M); gifts received, $1,557,433; expenditures, $739,613; qualifying distributions, $738,513; giving activities include $738,513 for 121 grants (high: $200,000; low: $25).

Fields of interest: Museums (art); Museums (history); Arts; Higher education, college; Law school/education; Education; Hospitals (general); Health organizations, association; Cerebral palsy; Cancer research; Human services; Children/youth, services; Jewish federated giving programs; Jewish agencies & temples.

Limitations: Applications not accepted. Giving primarily in NY. No grants to individuals.

Application information: Contributes only to pre-selected organizations.

Officers: Clifton S. Robbins, Pres.; Edwin Robbins, V.P.

EIN: 133745914

Selected grants: The following grants were reported in 2004.

$37,500 to Memorial Sloan-Kettering Cancer Center, Society of, New York, NY. 2 grants: $25,000, $12,500

$23,000 to Central Park Conservancy, New York, NY. 2 grants: $8,000, $15,000

$10,000 to Math for America, New York, NY. 2 grants: $5,000 each

$10,000 to United States Holocaust Memorial Museum, DC.

$5,000 to Columbia University, School of Law, New York, NY.

$5,000 to Montefiore Medical Center, Bronx, NY.

$2,500 to Arthur J. Meyer Jewish Academy, West Palm Beach, FL.

1635
Clinton S. Roberts Foundation, Inc. ✧
201 West St.
Bristol, CT 06011-1399
Application address: c/o Christopher Ziogas, P.O. Box 1399, Bristol, CT 06010

Established in 1987.

Foundation type: Independent foundation.

Financial data (yr. ended 12/31/04): Assets, $8,162,523 (M); gifts received, $5,626; expenditures, $411,552; qualifying distributions,

$345,500; giving activities include $345,500 for 33 grants (high: $20,000; low: $1,000).
Purpose and activities: Giving primarily for family and social services, YMCAs, and to a Methodist church.
Fields of interest: Health organizations, association; Human services; YM/YWCAs & YM/YWHAs; Youth, services; Family services; Community development, neighborhood development; Protestant agencies & churches.
Limitations: Giving primarily in the greater Bristol, CT, area.
Application information:
Initial approach: Letter
Trustees: Linda Roberts Arbesman; Ellen Roberts Ferrier; Leonard Roberts; Christopher Ziogas.
EIN: 222867088
Selected grants: The following grants were reported in 2003.
$30,300 to Family Center, Bristol, CT. For new building.
$25,000 to Bristol Hospital Development Foundation, Bristol, CT. For operating support.
$25,000 to Fidelco Guide Dog Foundation, Bloomfield, CT. For operating support.
$15,000 to Tunxis Community College Foundation, Farmington, CT. For operating support.
$15,000 to University of Connecticut, Storrs, CT. For operating support.
$15,000 to University of Massachusetts, Stockbridge School, Amherst, MA. For operating support.
$10,000 to Prospect United Methodist Church, Bristol, CT. For operating support.
$10,000 to Salvation Army of Bristol, Bristol, CT. For operating support.
$10,000 to YMCA, Wheeler Regional Branch, Plainville, CT. For capital support.
$6,500 to Four-H Development Fund, Storrs, CT. For operating support.

1636
The Rogow Greenberg Foundation, Inc. ✧
(formerly The Rogow Birken Foundation, Inc.)
c/o Birken Manufacturing Co.
3 Old Windsor Rd.
Bloomfield, CT   06002
Contact: Gary Greenberg, V.P.

Established in 1981 in CT.
Donors: Louis B. Rogow†; Glen Greenberg; Sidney Greenberg; Helen Rogow†; Bruce Rogow.
Foundation type: Independent foundation.
Financial data (yr. ended 12/31/05): Assets, $8,386,330 (M); expenditures, $603,814; qualifying distributions, $508,345; giving activities include $377,390 for 63 grants (high: $101,000; low: $100), and $75,940 for 18 grants to individuals (high: $15,000; low: $470).
Purpose and activities: Giving primarily for higher education and Jewish organizations.
Fields of interest: Higher education; Scholarships/financial aid; Health organizations; Human services; Children/youth, services; Federated giving programs; Jewish federated giving programs; Jewish agencies & temples.
Type of support: General/operating support; Annual campaigns; Capital campaigns; Scholarship funds; Scholarships—to individuals.
Limitations: Giving primarily in CT, FL, MA, and NY.
Application information:
Initial approach: Letter
Deadline(s): None

Officers: Sidney Greenberg, Pres.; Bruce Rogow, Exec. V.P.; Gary Greenberg, V.P.; Paul Bourdeau, Secy.
EIN: 061051591
Selected grants: The following grants were reported in 2005.
$31,250 to Transylvania County Library Foundation, Brevard, NC.
$25,000 to Miami City Ballet, Miami Beach, FL.
$7,500 to Connecticut Childrens Medical Center, Hartford, CT.
$5,000 to Broward Public Library Foundation, Fort Lauderdale, FL.
$5,000 to Community Foundation of Broward, Fort Lauderdale, FL.
$5,000 to Loomis Chaffee School, Windsor, CT.
$5,000 to United Way.
$2,500 to Renbrook School, West Hartford, CT.
$2,500 to Sewanee Fund, Sewanee, TN.
$1,000 to Museum of Discovery and Science, Fort Lauderdale, FL.

1637
The Clare Rose Foundation, Inc. ✧
211 Otter Rock Dr.
Greenwich, CT   06830

Established in 1997 in CT.
Donor: Valerie Vincent.
Foundation type: Independent foundation.
Financial data (yr. ended 12/31/05): Assets, $12,015,863 (M); gifts received, $4,467,000; expenditures, $567,530; qualifying distributions, $525,000; giving activities include $525,000 for 30 grants (high: $65,000; low: $5,000).
Purpose and activities: Giving primarily for children and youth services, and Roman Catholic education and organizations.
Fields of interest: Elementary/secondary education; Higher education; Education; Health care; Health organizations, association; Human services; YM/YWCAs & YM/YWHAs; Children/youth, services; Roman Catholic agencies & churches.
Limitations: Applications not accepted. Giving primarily in CT and NY. No grants to individuals.
Application information: Contributes only to pre-selected organizations.
Officers and Directors:* Valerie Vincent,* Chair. and Pres.; Elizabeth Layton, Secy.; John J. Ferguson; Anne B. Vincent; William Vincent.
EIN: 061480029

1638
The Richard and Hinda Rosenthal Foundation ✧
5 High Ridge Park
Stamford, CT   06905   (203) 322-9900
Contact: Hinda Gould Rosenthal, Pres.

Established in 1948 in NY.
Donors: The Richard L. Rosenthal family; and associated interests.
Foundation type: Independent foundation.
Financial data (yr. ended 12/31/05): Assets, $19,051,221 (M); gifts received, $184,150; expenditures, $1,126,845; qualifying distributions, $920,572; giving activities include $725,001 for 206 grants (high: $88,500; low: $100).
Purpose and activities: To encourage achievement and excellence in the arts, social sciences, medical

and scientific research, and clinical medicine. Conceived and annually sponsors the Rosenthal Awards for Fiction and for Painting through the American Academy and National Institute of Arts and Letters; also conceived and sponsors five national awards in clinical medicine through the American College of Physicians, American Heart Association, American Association for Cancer Research, and others. Has sponsored similar "discovery" awards for film.
Fields of interest: Media/communications; Media, film/video; Media, journalism/publishing; Museums; Performing arts, theater; Language/linguistics; Literature; Child development, education; Higher education; Business school/education; Education; Biomedicine; Medical research, institute; Human services; Child development, services; Residential/custodial care, hospices; Jewish federated giving programs; Social sciences; Economics; Public affairs.
Type of support: General/operating support; Continuing support; Program development; Conferences/seminars; Fellowships; Research; Matching/challenge support.
Limitations: Giving primarily in CT and NY. No grants to individuals.
Publications: Program policy statement.
Application information: Application form not required.
Initial approach: Letter
Copies of proposal: 1
Deadline(s): None
Board meeting date(s): As required
Officers and Trustees:* Hinda Gould Rosenthal,* Pres.; Jamie R. Wolf,* Secy.; Rick Rosenthal,* Treas.; Joni M. Cherbo; Nancy Stephens Rosenthal; David M. Wolf; Kate Wolf; Noah Rosenthal.
Number of staff: 2 part-time professional; 2 part-time support.
EIN: 136104817

1639
Royce Family Fund, Inc. ✧
c/o Royce & Associates
8 Sound Shore Dr., Ste. 140
Greenwich, CT   06830

Established in 1985 in DE.
Donor: Charles M. Royce.
Foundation type: Independent foundation.
Financial data (yr. ended 12/31/04): Assets, $64,885,165 (M); gifts received, $20,222,138; expenditures, $4,613,726; qualifying distributions, $6,735,648; giving activities include $4,112,264 for 158 grants (high: $1,000,000; low: $1,000).
Purpose and activities: Giving primarily for higher education and the arts and to Christian agencies and churches.
Fields of interest: Museums; Historic preservation/historical societies; Arts; Business school/education; Education; Religion.
Limitations: Applications not accepted. Giving primarily in CT and NY. No grants to individuals.
Application information: Contributes only to pre-selected organizations.
Officers and Directors:* Charles M. Royce,* Pres.; Adrianne K. Boynton,* Secy.-Treas.; Karen P. Free.
EIN: 133318620
Selected grants: The following grants were reported in 2003.
$100,000 to Boys and Girls Club of Greenwich, Greenwich, CT.
$50,000 to Columbia University, New York, NY.

$50,000 to Westerly Hospital, Westerly, RI.

$20,000 to Greenwich Academy, Greenwich, CT.

$20,000 to YWCA of Greenwich, Greenwich, CT.

$10,000 to Choate Rosemary Hall Foundation, Wallingford, CT.

$10,000 to Group One Acting Company, New York, NY. For The Acting Company.

$10,000 to Jazz at Lincoln Center, New York, NY.

$10,000 to New-York Historical Society, New York, NY.

$10,000 to United Way of Greenwich, Greenwich, CT.

1640

The Sage Foundation, Inc. ✧

16 Khakum Dr.

Greenwich, CT 06831

Contact: Steven A. Denning, Secy.

Established in 1997 in CT.

Donor: Steven A. Denning.

Foundation type: Independent foundation.

Financial data (yr. ended 12/31/04): Assets, $2,242,608 (M); gifts received, $3,513,747; expenditures, $2,686,748; qualifying distributions, $2,653,226; giving activities include $2,653,226 for 29 grants (high: $740,533; low: $500).

Purpose and activities: Giving primarily for the arts and education.

Fields of interest: Museums (natural history); Higher education; American Red Cross.

Limitations: Applications not accepted. Giving primarily in CA, CT, NY, and WY. No grants to individuals.

Application information: Contributes only to pre-selected organizations.

Officers: Roberta D. Bowman, Chair.; Steven A. Denning, Secy.

Director: Alan H. Rappaport.

EIN: 061478711

Selected grants: The following grants were reported in 2005.

$725,000 to Stanford University, Stanford, CA.

$688,333 to American Museum of Natural History, New York, NY.

$100,000 to American Red Cross, Greenwich, CT.

$50,000 to International Center of Photography, New York, NY.

$50,000 to Natural History Museum of the Adirondacks, Tupper Lake, NY.

$25,000 to Classroom, Inc., New York, NY.

$5,000 to Grand Teton Music Festival, Teton Village, WY.

$2,500 to Greenwich Country Day School, Greenwich, CT.

$1,000 to Exit Art, New York, NY.

1641

The Ruth F. Savage and Harlow D. Savage, Jr. Foundation ✧

c/o Shipman & Goodwin, LLP

1 American Row

Hartford, CT 06103-2819

Established in 1999 in CT.

Donor: Harlow D. Savage, Jr.

Foundation type: Independent foundation.

Financial data (yr. ended 12/31/03): Assets, $177,718 (M); expenditures, $505,284; qualifying distributions, $500,000; giving activities include $500,000 for 1 grant.

Fields of interest: Human services.

Limitations: Applications not accepted. Giving primarily in CT. No grants to individuals.

Application information: Contributes only to pre-selected organizations.

Trustees: Foster M. Fargo, Jr.; Seddon R. Savage.

EIN: 066477882

1642

Say Yes to Education, Inc. ▼ ✧

c/o George Weiss Assocs.

1 State St.

Hartford, CT 06103

URL: http://www.sayyestoeducation.org

Established in 1992 in CT.

Donors: George A. Weiss; Winson Ho; CIBC World Markets Corp.; The Jesse & Caryl Philips Foundation.

Foundation type: Independent foundation.

Financial data (yr. ended 12/31/04): Assets, $19,543,793 (M); gifts received, $317,276; expenditures, $7,607,856; qualifying distributions, $7,413,746; giving activities include $7,168,572 for 11 grants (high: $4,275,000; low: $5,000; average: $25,000–$655,651).

Purpose and activities: Giving primarily for education.

Fields of interest: Higher education; Children/youth, services.

Type of support: Scholarship funds.

Limitations: Applications not accepted. Giving primarily in Philadelphia, PA. No grants to individuals.

Application information: Contributes only to pre-selected organizations.

Officers and Directors:* George A. Weiss,* Pres. and Treas.; Norman Newberg,* Secy.; Jerell Baynes; Joseph Burke; Michael Glazer; Irma Handel; Sophie Hayward; Peg Heer; Rhonda Laver; Deborah Miller; Harold Shields; Janine Spruill; Jane Toll; Joseph A. Watkins; Alison B. Weiss.

EIN: 223139858

Selected grants: The following grants were reported in 2004.

$5,371,517 to University of Pennsylvania, Philadelphia, PA. 2 grants: $4,275,000 (For undergraduate endowed financial aid and professorship programs and collegiate athletic programs), $1,096,517 (For operating support for Say Yes to Education, minority leadership grants, and undergraduate educational and athletic programs).

$742,764 to Lesley University, Cambridge, MA. For Project Promise operating support for Massachusetts program.

$655,651 to Teachers College Columbia University, New York, NY. For Say Yes to Education commitment for program expansion into school in Harlem area of New York.

$253,640 to University of Hartford, West Hartford, CT. For Say Yes to Education operating support for Hartford program.

$20,000 to Minds Matter, New York, NY. For mentoring services and financial aid to inner city high school students seeking to gain entrance into full-time college programs.

$5,000 to Athletic Resources, Trenton, NJ. For comprehensive and meaningful academic, athletic and social resources to students participating in athletics in City of Trenton.

1643

Saybrook Charitable Trust ✧

33 Brook St.

West Hartford, CT 06110-2350   (860) 232-6853

Contact: Thomas E. Cross, Mgr.

Donor: Robert A. Foisie.

Foundation type: Independent foundation.

Financial data (yr. ended 12/31/05): Assets, $11,789,974 (M); expenditures, $742,516; qualifying distributions, $688,500; giving activities include $688,500 for 12 grants (high: $485,000; low: $500).

Purpose and activities: Giving primarily for education, and hospitals and health associations; funding also for human services.

Fields of interest: Elementary/secondary education; Hospitals (general); Health organizations; Human services.

Type of support: General/operating support.

Limitations: Giving primarily in CT. No grants to individuals.

Application information:

Initial approach: Letter

Deadline(s): None

Officer: Thomas E. Cross, Mgr.

Trustees: Michael R. Foisie; Lauren F. Glennon; Lisa B. Salvio.

EIN: 222501925

Selected grants: The following grants were reported in 2004.

$25,000 to Watkinson School, Hartford, CT.

$5,000 to March of Dimes Birth Defects Foundation, White Plains, NY.

$500 to Salvation Army.

1644

SBM Charitable Foundation, Inc. ✧

935 Main St., Unit B-101

Manchester, CT 06040   (860) 533-0355

Contact: Sheila B. Flanagan, Exec. Dir.

FAX: (860) 533-0241; *URL:* http://www.sbmfoundation.org

Established as a company-sponsored foundation in 2000 in CT; status changed to independent foundation in 2004.

Donor: Savings Bank of Manchester Foundation, Inc.

Foundation type: Independent foundation.

Financial data (yr. ended 12/31/04): Assets, $42,288,754 (M); expenditures, $2,011,897; qualifying distributions, $1,621,324; giving activities include $1,410,600 for 125 grants (high: $200,000; low: $500), and $95,500 for grants to individuals.

Purpose and activities: The foundation supports organizations involved with arts and culture, education, health, housing, human services, and children and youth.

Fields of interest: Arts; Education; Hospitals (general); Health care; Housing/shelter; Children/youth, services; Human services; Federated giving programs.

Type of support: In-kind gifts; Grants to individuals.

Limitations: Giving primarily in CT.

Application information: Application form required.

Initial approach: Download application form and mail to foundation

Copies of proposal: 1

Deadline(s): Jan. 1 through Sept. 15

Officers and Trustees:* Laurence P. Rubinow, Chair.; Richard P. Meduski, Pres.; Douglas

Anderson,* V.P.; Charles L. Pike,* V.P.; Sheila B. Flanagan, Exec. Dir.; A. Paul Berte; Timothy J. Devanney; Michael J. Hartl; Linda Klein; John D. La Belle, Jr.; Eric A. Marziali; Timothy J. Moyniham; Jon L. Norris; William D. O'Neill; Brian A. Orenstein; John G. Sommers; Richard Suski; Thomas E. Toomey; Gregory S. Wolff.
Number of staff: 2 full-time support; 1 part-time support.
EIN: 061574365
Selected grants: The following grants were reported in 2004.
$200,000 to Eastern Connecticut Health Network (ECHN), Manchester, CT.
$50,000 to Eastern Connecticut State University Foundation, Willimantic, CT.
$48,000 to Manchester, Town of, Manchester, CT.
$30,000 to Community Child Guidance Clinic, Manchester, CT.
$25,000 to Connecticut Childrens Medical Center, Hartford, CT.
$25,000 to Habitat for Humanity International.
$23,500 to Riverfront Recapture, Hartford, CT.
$12,500 to YMCA.
$10,000 to Lutz Childrens Museum, Manchester, CT.
$4,000 to Connecticut College, New London, CT.

1645
Seedlings Foundation ◇ ☆
984 Main St.
Branford, CT 06405

Established in 2002 in IL.
Donors: Pritzker Foundation; Pritzker Cousins Foundation; Karen Pritzker.
Foundation type: Independent foundation.
Financial data (yr. ended 12/31/05): Assets, $48,656,251 (M); gifts received, $7,449,519; expenditures, $3,906,378; qualifying distributions, $3,558,516; giving activities include $3,558,516 for 69 grants (high: $325,000; low: $2,000).
Purpose and activities: Support for housing, education, and the arts.
Fields of interest: Arts, multipurpose centers/programs; Performing arts, theater; Secondary school/education; Education, reading; Education; Housing/shelter, development.
Type of support: General/operating support.
Limitations: Applications not accepted. Giving on a national basis. No grants to individuals.
Application information: Contributes only to pre-selected organizations.
Officers and Directors:* Karen Pritzker-Vlock,* Pres.; Michael Vlock,* Secy.-Treas.; Linda Pritzker; Audrey Ratner.
EIN: 043600502

1646
The Ivan Seidenberg Foundation ◇
c/o HHG
P.O. Box 4004
Darien, CT 06820-4004

Established in 1993 in CT.
Donors: Ivan Seidenberg; Phyllis Seidenberg.
Foundation type: Independent foundation.
Financial data (yr. ended 12/31/05): Assets, $561,788 (M); gifts received, $457,072; expenditures, $927,697; qualifying distributions,

$925,702; giving activities include $925,702 for 56 grants (high: $500,000; low: $17).
Purpose and activities: Giving for higher and other education, Jewish organizations, federated giving programs and for health services.
Fields of interest: Higher education; Hospitals (general); Jewish agencies & temples.
Limitations: Applications not accepted. Giving primarily in the New York, NY, area. No grants to individuals.
Application information: Contributes only to pre-selected organizations.
Directors: Douglas Seidenberg; Ivan Seidenberg; Lisa Seidenberg; Phyllis Seidenberg.
EIN: 061386525
Selected grants: The following grants were reported in 2003.
$120,000 to Temple Beth Shalom, New York, NY. 3 grants: $50,000 (For general support), $20,000 (For general support), $50,000 (For general support).
$105,000 to New York Hall of Science, Corona, NY. 2 grants: $5,000 (For general support), $100,000 (For general support).
$100,000 to United Jewish Communities, New York, NY. For general support.
$30,000 to United Way of New York City, New York, NY. For general support.
$15,000 to New York-Presbyterian Hospital, New York, NY. For general support.
$10,000 to Pace University, New York, NY. For general support.
$5,000 to Teach for America, New York, NY. For general support.

1647
Senior Services of Stamford, Inc. ◇
945 Summer St.
Stamford, CT 06905-5519
Contact: John Atkinson, Treas.

Established in 1908 in CT.
Donors: Katherine D. Uehling†; Katharine J. Adamson; The Advocate and Greenwich Times Holiday Fund; First County Bank; Interfaith Council; Saugatuck Capital; Wachovia Bank, N.A.; St. John's Community Foundation; Friendship House, Inc.
Foundation type: Independent foundation.
Financial data (yr. ended 2/28/05): Assets, $13,097,056 (M); gifts received, $122,931; expenditures, $868,634; qualifying distributions, $764,158; giving activities include $9,535 for 2 grants (high: $8,000; low: $1,535), and $441,700 for grants to individuals.
Purpose and activities: Support for: 1) social service organizations serving the elderly; 2) organizations that provide information, referral, counseling, advocacy, and emergency financial assistance to needy elderly; and 3) operation of a senior center. Focus on programs offering innovative solutions to problems of older persons, particularly in access to health care, housing, transportation, and isolation.
Fields of interest: Health care, home services; Aging, centers/services; Aging.
Type of support: Annual campaigns; Endowments; Grants to individuals.
Limitations: Giving limited to Stamford, CT.
Publications: Annual report; Informational brochure.
Application information: Application form required.
Initial approach: Letter requesting application form

Copies of proposal: 1
Deadline(s): None
Officers and Directors:* Susan Greenberg,* Chair.; Ernest Abate,* Vice-Chair.; Beverly Shafter,* Vice-Chair.; Pamela Vass,* Secy.; John Atkinson,* Treas.; Roberta Ratcliff, Exec. Dir.; and 19 additional directors.
Number of staff: 1 full-time professional; 2 part-time professional; 1 full-time support; 1 part-time support.
EIN: 060646916

1648
Elmina B. Sewall Foundation ◇
234 Church St., Rm. 1003
New Haven, CT 06510
Contact: William E. Curran, Treas.

Established in 1983 in ME.
Donor: Elmina B. Sewall.
Foundation type: Independent foundation.
Financial data (yr. ended 9/30/05): Assets, $16,919,474 (M); expenditures, $1,418,982; qualifying distributions, $1,366,500; giving activities include $1,366,500 for 99 grants (high: $50,000; low: $3,000).
Purpose and activities: Giving for animal welfare, youth and social services, conservation, arts, historical preservation and land preservation in ME.
Fields of interest: Historic preservation/historical societies; Arts; Higher education; Environment, plant conservation; Environment; Animal welfare; Animals/wildlife, preservation/protection; Human services; Children/youth, services.
Type of support: Continuing support; Annual campaigns; Land acquisition; Scholarship funds.
Limitations: Applications not accepted. Giving primarily in New England. No grants to individuals.
Application information: Contributes only to pre-selected organizations.
Board meeting date(s): 2nd Thurs. in May and Sept.
Officers and Directors:* Margaret Sewall Barbour,* Pres.; Harold E. Woodsum, Jr.,* Secy.; William E. Curran,* Treas.; Helen Brewster; Pamela Brewster Duffy; David E. Norris; James S. Zoldy, Jr.
EIN: 010387404
Selected grants: The following grants were reported in 2005.
$60,000 to Animal Welfare Society, West Kennebunk, ME.
$50,000 to University of New England, Biddeford, ME.
$25,000 to American Red Cross, Portland, ME.
$25,000 to Laudholm Trust, Wells, ME.
$20,000 to National Trust for Scotland, Edinburgh, Scotland. .
$15,000 to Kennebunk Free Library, Kennebunk, ME.
$15,000 to Portland Symphony Orchestra, Portland, ME.
$15,000 to Wilderness Society, New York, NY.
$10,000 to New England Wildlife Center, Hingham, MA.
$7,500 to Preble Street Resource Center, Portland, ME.

1649
The Shei'rah Foundation, Inc. ◇
10 Town Hill Rd.
Warren, CT 06754

Established in 2000 in CT and NY.
Donor: Sheryl S. Leach.
Foundation type: Independent foundation.
Financial data (yr. ended 5/31/04): Assets, $2,487,850 (M); expenditures, $2,327,865; qualifying distributions, $2,171,484; giving activities include $1,885,100 for 17 grants (high: $1,460,000; low: $50).
Purpose and activities: Giving primarily for television and media.
Fields of interest: Media/communications; Media, television; Education; Human services; Human services, mind/body enrichment.
Limitations: Applications not accepted. Giving primarily in NY and CA, with emphasis on San Francisco. No grants to individuals.
Application information: Contributes only to pre-selected organizations.
Officers: Sheryl S. Leach, Co-Pres.; Howard Rosenfeld, Co-Pres.
EIN: 311727614
Selected grants: The following grants were reported in 2004.
$1,460,000 to Link Media, San Francisco, CA. For general support.
$115,000 to Foundation for Conscious Evolution, San Rafael, CA. For general support.
$100,000 to Internews Interactive, San Anselmo, CA. For general support.
$51,250 to Global Youth Action Network, New York, NY. For general support.
$30,000 to Black United Fund, National, Newark, NJ. For general support.
$30,000 to Tides Center, San Francisco, CA. For general support.
$12,950 to Connecticut Public Broadcasting, Hartford, CT. For general support.
$2,500 to Rudolf Steiner Foundation, San Francisco, CA. For general support.
$2,000 to National Alliance for the Mentally Ill (NAMI) of New York City, New York, NY. For general support.
$500 to Sesame Workshop, New York, NY. For general support.

1650
The Cindy and John Sites Charitable Foundation ✧
79 Harbor Dr.
Greenwich, CT   06830

Established in 1994 in NY.
Donor: John C. Sites, Jr.
Foundation type: Independent foundation.
Financial data (yr. ended 12/31/05): Assets, $2,285,164 (M); gifts received, $2,779,471; expenditures, $507,926; qualifying distributions, $507,006; giving activities include $505,867 for 43 grants (high: $100,000; low: $500).
Fields of interest: Performing arts, ballet; Arts; Elementary/secondary education; Higher education; Hospitals (general); Food services; Human services; Christian agencies & churches.
Limitations: Applications not accepted. Giving primarily in CT and NY. No grants to individuals.
Application information: Contributes only to pre-selected organizations.
Trustees: Cindy Sites; John C. Sites, Jr.
EIN: 133802846

1651
The Smart Family Foundation ▼ ✧
74 Pin Oak Ln.
Wilton, CT   06897-1329   (203) 834-0400
Contact: Raymond L. Smart, Pres.

Trust established in 1951 in IL.
Donors: David A. Smart†; A.D. Elden†; Vera Elden†; John Smart†; Edgar G. Richards†; Florence Richards†.
Foundation type: Independent foundation.
Financial data (yr. ended 12/31/04): Assets, $175,253,011 (M); expenditures, $10,661,710; qualifying distributions, $8,716,361; giving activities include $8,365,687 for 114 grants (high: $893,571; low: $1,000; average: $10,000–$100,000).
Purpose and activities: The foundation is primarily interested in education projects and has, in particular, been focusing on projects that affect primary and secondary school children.
Fields of interest: Elementary school/education; Secondary school/education; Education.
Type of support: Seed money; Research; Program-related investments/loans.
Limitations: Giving on a national basis. No grants to individuals.
Application information: Unsolicited applications are discouraged. Application form not required.
Initial approach: 1-page letter fully describing project and cost
Copies of proposal: 1
Deadline(s): Jan. 1 and June 1
Board meeting date(s): Fall and spring
Final notification: Within 6 weeks after board meetings
Officers and Directors:* Robert Feitler,* Chair.; Raymond L. Smart,* Pres.; Mary Smart,* Secy.; William Oswald,* Treas.; Joan Feitler; Ellen Smart Oswald; David Stone.
Number of staff: 1 full-time professional; 1 part-time support.
EIN: 061232323
Selected grants: The following grants were reported in 2005.
$1,292,922 to University of Chicago, Chicago, IL. For operating support.
$1,253,045 to Achievement First, New Haven, CT. For operating support.
$850,000 to Francis W. Parker School, Chicago, IL. For operating support.
$800,000 to Amistad Academy, New Haven, CT. For operating support.
$195,000 to Yeshiva University Museum, New York, NY. For operating support.
$125,000 to David and Alfred Smart Museum of Art, Chicago, IL. For operating support.
$100,000 to Eli Whitney Museum, Hamden, CT. For operating support.
$100,000 to New Jersey Performing Arts Center, Newark, NJ. For operating support.
$99,990 to Connecticut Academy for Education in Mathematics, Science and Technology, Middletown, CT. For operating support.
$25,000 to Friends of the Old Croton Aqueduct, Dobbs Ferry, NY. For operating support.

1652
Theodore & Vada Stanley Foundation ✧
47 Richards Ave.
Norwalk, CT   06857-1915
Contact: Theodore R. Stanley, Tr.

Established in 1985 in CT.
Donor: Theodore R. Stanley.
Foundation type: Independent foundation.
Financial data (yr. ended 12/31/05): Assets, $4,630,902 (M); gifts received, $4,000,000; expenditures, $5,251,038; qualifying distributions, $5,203,000; giving activities include $5,203,000 for 31 grants (high: $3,250,000; low: $1,000).
Purpose and activities: Support primarily to a mental health organization, as well as for education and human services; funding also for the arts.
Fields of interest: Arts; Education; Mental health/crisis services; Human services.
Limitations: Applications not accepted. No grants to individuals.
Application information: Contributes only to pre-selected organizations.
Trustees: Theodore R. Stanley; Vada Stanley.
EIN: 061157888

1653
William & Lynda Steere Foundation ✧
P.O. Box 2630
Westport, CT   06880-0630

Established in 1999.
Donors: William Steere, Jr.; Lynda Steere.
Foundation type: Independent foundation.
Financial data (yr. ended 12/31/05): Assets, $6,058,789 (M); expenditures, $2,844,711; qualifying distributions, $2,791,233; giving activities include $2,791,233 for 39 grants (high: $1,000,000; low: $400).
Purpose and activities: Giving primarily for health care, particularly to a cancer hospital, as well as for the arts, and to botanical gardens.
Fields of interest: Arts; Botanical gardens; Hospitals (specialty); Health care.
Limitations: Applications not accepted. Giving primarily in NY. No grants to individuals.
Application information: Contributes only to pre-selected organizations.
Trustees: Catherine Davis; Elwood B. Davis.
EIN: 656286705
Selected grants: The following grants were reported in 2005.
$250,000 to Stanford University, Stanford, CA.
$50,000 to Naples Christian Academy, Naples, FL.
$50,000 to YMCA. 2 grants: $25,000 each
$25,000 to Chess in the Schools, New York, NY.
$20,000 to HOPE of Southwest Florida, Fort Myers, FL.
$11,000 to Harpeth Hall School, Nashville, TN. 2 grants: $10,000, $1,000
$11,000 to Inwood House, New York, NY. 2 grants: $5,000, $6,000

1654
The Stone Foundation, Inc. ✧
c/o HHG Foundation Svcs.
30 Old Kings Hwy. S.
Darien, CT   06820   (203) 656-5500

Incorporated in 1964 in OH; reincorporated in 1972 in CT.
Donors: Marion H. Stone†; Charles Lynn Stone†.
Foundation type: Independent foundation.
Financial data (yr. ended 12/31/05): Assets, $16,896,667 (M); expenditures, $640,138; qualifying distributions, $518,080; giving activities

include $363,197 for 12 grants (high: $50,325; low: $12,500).

Purpose and activities: Primary interest in seed money for unique programs in medicine, education, science, and related areas.

Fields of interest: Nursing school/education; Education; Community development; Science, research.

Type of support: General/operating support; Continuing support; Capital campaigns; Building/renovation; Endowments; Program development; Professorships; Seed money; Research.

Limitations: Applications not accepted. Giving on a national basis, primarily in CT. No grants to individuals, or for matching gifts, scholarships, fellowships, or special projects; no loans.

Application information: Unsolicited requests for funds not accepted.

Board meeting date(s): Dec.

Officers and Trustees:* Charles Lynn Stone, Jr.,* Pres.; Edward E. Stone,* V.P.; Amy Wilfert, Secy.; Thomas W. Hynes, Treas.

Number of staff: 2 part-time professional.

EIN: 237148468

Selected grants: The following grants were reported in 2003.

$100,000 to Columbia University, School of Nursing, New York, NY. For general support.

$83,500 to Bank Street School for Children, New York, NY. For general support.

$70,000 to Fairfield Country Day School, Fairfield, CT. For general support.

$50,000 to Huntington Hospital, Huntington, NY. For general support.

$25,000 to Cold Spring Harbor Laboratory, Cold Spring Harbor, NY. For general support.

$25,000 to Court Appointed Special Advocates (CASA), New York, NY. For general support.

$25,000 to Family and Childrens Agency, Norwalk, CT. For general support.

$21,270 to Hastings College, Hastings, NE. For general support.

$18,750 to Hastings College Foundation, Hastings, NE. For general support.

$12,500 to Fairfield County Community Foundation, Wilton, CT. For general support.

1655
Ray & Pauline Sullivan Foundation

c/o Bank of America, N.A.
777 Main St. CT2-102-22-02
Hartford, CT 06115
Contact: Amy R. Lynch, V.P.

Established in 1972 in CT.

Donor: Ray H. Sullivan†.

Foundation type: Independent foundation.

Financial data (yr. ended 1/31/06): Assets, $13,961,924 (M); expenditures, $685,632; qualifying distributions, $669,124; giving activities include $529,670 for 39 grants (high: $100,000; low: $1,000), $52,500 for 24 grants to individuals (high: $3,500; low: $2,000), and $10,000 for 5 loans to individuals (high: $2,000; low: $2,000).

Purpose and activities: Giving primarily to Roman Catholic charities and educational institutions located in the Diocese of Norwich, CT only; also awards scholarships and student loans to graduates of St. Bernard's High School in Uncasville, CT.

Fields of interest: Elementary/secondary education; Human services; Roman Catholic agencies & churches.

Type of support: Scholarship funds; Scholarships—to individuals; Student loans—to individuals.

Limitations: Giving limited to the Diocese of Norwich, CT.

Application information: Application form required for scholarships and loans. Application form required.

Initial approach: Letter
Deadline(s): May 1 for scholarships and loans
Final notification: 8 weeks

Trustees: Fr. Joseph Castaldi; Jeremiah J. Lowney, Jr.; James C. McGuire; Therese Sprecace; Bank of America, N.A.

EIN: 066141242

Selected grants: The following grants were reported in 2005.

$135,000 to Saint Bernard High School, Uncasville, CT. 2 grants: $35,000, $100,000

$50,000 to Saint Joseph School, Rockville, CT.

$35,000 to Haitian Health Foundation, Norwich, CT.

$27,000 to Lawrence and Memorial Hospital, New London, CT.

$20,000 to Mercy High School, Middletown, CT.

$17,000 to Diocese of Norwich, Norwich, CT. 3 grants: $5,000, $5,000, $7,000

$2,000 to Mitchell College, New London, CT.

1656
Sun Hill Foundation ✧

c/o Fred F. French Investing, LLC
1 Station Pl.
Stamford, CT 06902 (203) 353-5320
Contact: Donald R. Milligan

Established in 1992 in CT as partial successor to the Tudor Foundation.

Donor: Edwin A. Malloy†.

Foundation type: Independent foundation.

Financial data (yr. ended 12/31/04): Assets, $7,673,668 (M); expenditures, $541,627; qualifying distributions, $482,614; giving activities include $482,614 for 35 grants.

Fields of interest: Historic preservation/historical societies; Arts; Education; Environment, natural resources; Human services; Jewish agencies & temples.

Limitations: Giving primarily in the Northeast. No grants to individuals.

Publications: Annual report.

Application information: Funds are currently awarded based on recommendations and approval of board members. Application form not required.

Deadline(s): None

Officers: Susan R. Malloy, Pres.; Timon J. Malloy, Secy.; Jennifer Malloy Combs, Treas.

EIN: 061326091

Selected grants: The following grants were reported in 2004.

$76,668 to Vermont Law School, South Royalton, VT.

$40,000 to New Israel Fund, DC.

$27,096 to Harvard University, Cambridge, MA.

$25,000 to Waterkeeper Alliance, Tarrytown, NY.

$24,056 to Natural Resources Defense Council, New York, NY.

$20,000 to Domestic Violence Crisis Center, Norwalk, CT.

$20,000 to Educational Alliance, New York, NY.

$20,000 to Fruitlands Museums, Harvard, MA.

$15,000 to High 5 Tickets to the Arts, New York, NY.

$10,000 to Rocky Mountain Institute, Snowmass, CO.

1657
The Tauck Foundation ✧

(formerly The Arthur C. and Lee Anne Tauck Foundation)
P.O. Box 5020
Norwalk, CT 06856
Contact: Kendra St. John, Assoc. Dir.
FAX: (203) 286-1340;
E-mail: kendra@tauckfoundation.org; Contact for Destination Grants and Special Community Grants: Liz Walters, Fdn. Mgr. at fdn., toll-free tel.: (866) 838-2536 or E-mail: info@tauckfoundation.org; URL: http://www.tauckfoundation.org

Established in 1994 in CT.

Donor: Arthur C. Tauck.

Foundation type: Independent foundation.

Financial data (yr. ended 12/31/03): Assets, $15,697,054 (M); expenditures, $948,524; qualifying distributions, $938,042; giving activities include $899,716 for 117 grants (high: $250,000; low: $250).

Purpose and activities: The foundation provides charitable grants to non-profit organizations. The Tauck Foundation currently focuses its giving in three areas: Destination Grants fund historical, cultural and environmental preservation projects in specific geographic locales. Community Giving supports community organizations in southwestern Connecticut. Special Community grants support one-time project needs of local (CT) organizations that have received past funding from the Tauck Foundation.

Fields of interest: Museums; Historic preservation/historical societies; Arts; Education, drop-out prevention; Environment; Employment, training; Youth development, volunteer services; Youth development, centers/clubs; Youth development, adult & child programs; Youth development, community service clubs; Youth development; Human services; Philanthropy/voluntarism.

Type of support: General/operating support; Continuing support; Capital campaigns; Building/renovation; Equipment; Land acquisition; Program development; Conferences/seminars; Scholarship funds; Technical assistance; Matching/challenge support.

Limitations: Giving primarily in Fairfield County, CT, the other New England states, NY, and WA.

Publications: Grants list; Informational brochure (including application guidelines).

Application information: There is no application for Community Giving requests; the initial letter serves as the application. Special Community Grant requests must be invited by the foundation board. See Web site for application guidelines and policies. Application form not required.

Initial approach: Letter of inquiry (no more than 2 pages)
Copies of proposal: 1
Deadline(s): See foundation Web site for deadlines
Board meeting date(s): Oct.
Final notification: 30 days

Trustee: Arthur C. Tauck, Jr.

Number of staff: 1

EIN: 061396951

1658
The Wade F. B. Thompson Charitable Foundation, Inc. ✧
261 Old Black Point Rd.
Niantic, CT 06357
Contact: Wade F.B. Thompson, V.P.

Established in 1986 in CT.
Donor: Wade F.B. Thompson.
Foundation type: Independent foundation.
Financial data (yr. ended 5/31/05): Assets, $8,035,664 (M); expenditures, $613,220; qualifying distributions, $551,504; giving activities include $551,504 for 47 grants (high: $65,000; low: $500).
Purpose and activities: Giving for historic preservation, arts and culture, education, the environment and medical research, specifically research devoted to finding a cure for prostate cancer.
Fields of interest: Historic preservation/historical societies; Arts; Education; Environment; General charitable giving.
Type of support: General/operating support; Annual campaigns; Building/renovation; Land acquisition; Seed money.
Limitations: Applications not accepted. Giving primarily in CT and the greater New York, NY, area. No grants to individuals.
Application information: Contributes only to pre-selected organizations.
Officers and Directors:* Angela E. Thompson,* Pres.; Wade F.B. Thompson,* V.P.; Alan Siegel, Secy.; Amanda J.T. Riegel; Charles A.Y. Thompson.
EIN: 061194385
Selected grants: The following grants were reported in 2005.
$220,000 to Seventh Regiment Armory Conservancy, New York, NY. 5 grants: $36,000 (For general operating support), $32,000 (For general operating support), $45,000 (For general operating support), $65,000 (For general operating support), $42,000 (For general operating support).
$103,690 to Brady Center to Prevent Gun Violence, DC. 2 grants: $50,000 (For general operating support), $53,690 (For general operating support).
$50,000 to University of Victoria, Victoria, Canada. 2 grants: $25,000 each (For general operating support).
$2,500 to National Trust for Historic Preservation, DC. For general operating support.

1659
The Tombros Foundation ✧
159 Lambert Rd.
New Canaan, CT 06840

Established in 2000 in DE.
Donor: Peter G. Tombros.
Foundation type: Independent foundation.
Financial data (yr. ended 12/31/05): Assets, $13,565,974 (M); expenditures, $763,094; qualifying distributions, $591,500; giving activities include $591,500 for 14 grants (high: $490,000; low: $500).
Fields of interest: Higher education; Health organizations, association; Human services.
Limitations: Applications not accepted. Giving on a national basis. No grants to individuals.
Application information: Contributes only to pre-selected organizations.

Officers: Peter G. Tombros, Pres.; Ann C. Tombros, V.P.; Robert L. Campbell, Secy.-Treas.
EIN: 522284151

1660
The Leonard & Claire Tow Charitable Trust, Inc. ✧
c/o Citizens Communications
3 High Ridge Park
Stamford, CT 06905

Established in 1999 in CT.
Donors: Claire Tow; Leonard Tow.
Foundation type: Independent foundation.
Financial data (yr. ended 12/31/03): Assets, $3,280,515 (M); expenditures, $694,493; qualifying distributions, $694,345; giving activities include $691,250 for 8 grants (high: $650,000; low: $250; average: $2,000–$10,000).
Purpose and activities: Giving primarily for a cancer hospital; support also for higher education, Jewish centers, botanical gardens and performing arts theaters.
Fields of interest: Performing arts, theater; Arts; Higher education; Botanical gardens; Environment; Hospitals (specialty); Cancer; Health organizations; Human services; Children, services; Federated giving programs.
Limitations: Applications not accepted. Giving primarily in the New York, NY, metropolitan area including CT and NJ. No grants to individuals.
Application information: Contributes only to pre-selected organizations.
Officers: Leonard Tow, Chair.; Claire Tow, Pres.; David Rosensweig, Secy.; Scott N. Schneider, Treas.; Emily Tow Jackson, Exec. Dir.
Director: Frank Tow.
EIN: 066484045

1661
The Tow Foundation, Inc.
43 Danbury Rd., 2nd Fl.
Wilton, CT 06897 (203) 761-6604
Contact: Emily Tow Jackson, Exec. Dir.
FAX: (203) 761-6605; URL: http://www.towfoundation.org

Established in 1988 in CT.
Donors: Leonard Tow; Claire Tow.
Foundation type: Independent foundation.
Financial data (yr. ended 12/31/05): Assets, $56,833,607 (M); expenditures, $1,887,548; qualifying distributions, $1,674,043; giving activities include $1,310,142 for 72 grants (high: $50,000; low: $1,000).
Purpose and activities: The foundation's mission is to promote and support effective nonprofit programs and to encourage the development of initiatives that are based on sound research. The foundation seeks to leverage funding from various sources to ensure the long-term quality of services and is committed to finding ways to fill some of the gaps left by other funders. The foundation currently is committed to supporting programs and services designed to improve outcomes for vulnerable families and children and advancing public policy reform in the areas of juvenile justice, youth development, child welfare and education. Other funding interests include breakthrough medical research, particularly in the areas of cancer and neuro-muscular diseases;

the performing arts, and post-secondary public service internships and professorships.
Fields of interest: Education; Cancer; Nerve, muscle & bone diseases; Medical research; Crime/violence prevention, youth; Courts/judicial administration; Youth development; Children/youth, services; Youth.
Type of support: General/operating support; Program development; Seed money; Program evaluation.
Limitations: Applications not accepted. Giving primarily in Fairfield and New Haven counties, CT, and Westchester County, NY. No support for political causes, campaigns, government or for organizations lacking tax-exempt status. No grants to individuals, or for capital campaigns.
Publications: Annual report; Grants list.
Application information: The Tow Foundation primarily does not accept unsolicited proposals. If an organization fits the foundation's very specific criteria they may send a letter of inquiry. The foundation staff will contact applicants.
Board meeting date(s): Mar., June, Sept., and Dec.
Officers and Directors:* Leonard Tow,* Chair.; Claire Tow,* Pres.; Frank Tow,* V.P.; David Rosensweig,* Secy.; Scott Schneider,* Treas.; Emily Tow Jackson,* Exec. Dir.
Number of staff: 4 full-time professional.
EIN: 061255825
Selected grants: The following grants were reported in 2003.
$50,000 to Mid-Fairfield Child Guidance Center, Norwalk, CT. For enhanced intensive outpatient program for children and youth.
$50,000 to Music and Arts Center for Humanity, Bridgeport, CT. For ArtWorks, Youth Entrepreneurial Program, Court and Agency Referred Program and Detention Center Program.
$49,500 to Child Health and Development Institute of Connecticut, Center for Effective Practice, Farmington, CT. For education services on Multi-Systemic Therapy.
$40,500 to FSW, Inc., Bridgeport, CT. For Juvenile Case Management Collaborative Program.
$40,000 to Builders for the Family and Youth of the Diocese of Brooklyn, Brooklyn, NY. For Pre-Teen/Teen Time Program at the Children's Center of Bedford Hills Correctional Facility in Bedford Hills, NY.
$40,000 to Center for Childrens Advocacy, Hartford, CT. For TeamChild Project and Juvenile Justice Initiatives.
$40,000 to Connecticut Renaissance, Norwalk, CT. For Outpatient Adolescent Program Services.
$40,000 to Consultation Center, New Haven, CT. For Relationship Violence Prevention Program and curriculum development.
$35,000 to Family ReEntry, Norwalk, CT. For New Directions Youthful Offender Services.
$31,000 to EPIC (Every Person Influences Children), Buffalo, NY. For Juvenile Justice Program in Connecticut.

1662
Emily Hall Tremaine Foundation, Inc. ▼
290 Pratt St.
Meriden, CT 06450
Contact: Stewart J. Hudson, Pres.
FAX: (203) 639-5545;
E-mail: info@tremainefoundation.org; URL: http://www.tremainefoundation.org

Established in 1987 in CT.

Donors: Emily Hall Tremaine†; Burton G. Tremaine, Sr.†; Burton G. Tremaine, Jr.†.

Foundation type: Independent foundation.

Financial data (yr. ended 12/31/05): Assets, $90,781,935 (M); expenditures, $4,878,883; qualifying distributions, $4,223,256; giving activities include $3,613,005 for 184 grants (high: $180,000; low: $500; average: $1,000–$50,000).

Purpose and activities: The foundation seeks to fund innovative projects that advance practical solutions to basic problems in our society. With an overall emphasis on education principally in the United States, it takes an active role in the arts, the environment, and in learning disabilities.

Fields of interest: Arts; Environment; Learning disorders.

Type of support: General/operating support; Continuing support; Program development; Conferences/seminars; Publication; Seed money; Curriculum development; Technical assistance; Matching/challenge support.

Publications: Biennial report.

Application information: Unsolicited proposals and letters of inquiry are not encouraged.

  Initial approach: 2-page letter of inquiry
  Deadline(s): None
  Board meeting date(s): 2 times a year

Officers and Directors:* Janet Tremaine Stanley, Chair.; Stewart J. Hudson,* Pres.; Burton G. Tremaine III,* Secy.; Atwood Collins III,* Treas.; Peter Stanley, Assoc. Dir.; Susan Tremaine, At-Large Dir.; Barbara S. Tremaine, Assoc. Dir.; Dorothy Tremaine Hildt; John M. Tremaine; Sarah C. Tremaine; K. Bryant Wick, Jr.

Number of staff: 3 full-time professional; 1 part-time support.

EIN: 222533743

1663
Tsunami Foundation ✧

c/o Anson M. Beard, Jr.
241 Bedford Rd.
Greenwich, CT   06831

Established in 1993 in CT.

Donor: Anson McCook Beard, Jr.

Foundation type: Independent foundation.

Financial data (yr. ended 12/31/05): Assets, $10,964,913 (M); gifts received, $88,691; expenditures, $681,448; qualifying distributions, $571,702; giving activities include $564,712 for 30 grants (high: $47,500; low: $2).

Fields of interest: Arts; Education; Environment; natural resources; Hospitals (general); Recreation, parks/playgrounds; Human services.

Limitations: Applications not accepted. Giving primarily in CT, MA, NY, and PA; some funding in ID.

Application information: Unsolicited requests for funds not accepted.

Trustees: Anson McCook Beard, Jr.; Jean Jones Beard.

EIN: 137019761

1664
The Tudor Foundation, Inc. ▼ ✧

1275 King St.
Greenwich, CT   06831

Established in 1997 in CT.

Donors: Tudor Arbitrage Partners; Tudor Group Holdings, LLC; Tudor Proprietary Trading, LLC; Tudor Investment Corp.

Foundation type: Independent foundation.

Financial data (yr. ended 12/31/05): Assets, $4,319,392 (M); gifts received, $5,108,597; expenditures, $5,946,072; qualifying distributions, $5,847,824; giving activities include $5,828,000 for 101 grants (high: $510,000; low: $2,500; average: $5,000–$250,000).

Purpose and activities: Giving primarily for education and human services, with emphasis on children and youth services.

Fields of interest: Education; Human services; Children/youth, services.

International interests: Australia; England.

Limitations: Applications not accepted. Giving on a national and international basis. No grants to individuals.

Application information: Contributes only to pre-selected organizations.

Officers and Directors:* James J. Pallotta,* Chair.; Andrew S. Paul,* Pres. and Secy.-Treas.; Thomas Bannatyne; William T. Flaherty; Paul T. Jones II.

EIN: 061502288

Selected grants: The following grants were reported in 2005.

$510,000 to Nashoba Learning Group, Westford, MA.

$374,590 to SHINE (Support and Help In Education), Ewell, England. .

$250,000 to Lovelane Special Needs Horseback Riding Program, Lincoln, MA.

$218,387 to Childrens Trust, Tadworth, England. .

$218,325 to CHASE Childrens Hospice Service, Guildford, England. .

$218,262 to Queen Elizabeths Foundation for Disabled People, Leatherhead, England. .

$210,000 to Childrens Hospital Corporation, Boston, MA.

$50,000 to Campagna Center, Alexandria, VA.

$35,000 to Early Steps, New York, NY.

$30,000 to Greenwich Hospital, Greenwich, CT.

1665
Daniel P. and Grace I. Tully Charitable Trust ✧

280 Tokeneke Rd.
P.O. Box 4080
Darien, CT   06820   (203) 655-2800
Contact: Eileen Ceglarski, Dir.

Established in 1986 in CT.

Donor: Daniel P. Tully.

Foundation type: Independent foundation.

Financial data (yr. ended 11/30/05): Assets, $5,861,145 (M); gifts received, $38,681; expenditures, $1,382,723; qualifying distributions, $1,297,600; giving activities include $1,297,600 for 22 grants (high: $1,000,000; low: $400).

Purpose and activities: Giving primarily to hospitals, schools, and educational facilities.

Fields of interest: Elementary/secondary education; Higher education; Hospitals (general); Health organizations, association.

Type of support: General/operating support; Program development; Curriculum development; Research.

Limitations: Giving primarily in CT and NY. No grants to individuals.

Application information: Application form not required.

  Initial approach: Letter

Copies of proposal: 2

Deadline(s): None

Trustees: Daniel P. Tully; Grace I. Tully.

Directors: Elizabeth Berry; Eileen Ceglarski; Alex Holland; Mark Ricca; Daniel G. Tully.

EIN: 222804896

Selected grants: The following grants were reported in 2005.

$1,011,000 to Stamford Health Foundation, Stamford, CT. 2 grants: $11,000, $1,000,000

$60,000 to United Way.

$50,000 to Bascom Palmer Eye Institute, Miami, FL.

$17,200 to Cystic Fibrosis Foundation, Bethesda, MD.

$10,000 to Lupus Research Institute, New York, NY.

$5,000 to Childrens Heart Foundation, Chicago, IL.

$1,000 to Martin Memorial Foundation, Stuart, FL.

$500 to Belmont Child Care Association, Elmont, NY.

$400 to Irish American Partnership, Boston, MA.

1666
The TWS Foundation ✧

323 Railroad Ave.
Greenwich, CT   06830-6306
Contact: Thomas W. Smith, Tr.

Established in 1984 in CT.

Donor: Thomas W. Smith.

Foundation type: Independent foundation.

Financial data (yr. ended 12/31/05): Assets, $6,675,390 (L); expenditures, $1,136,953; qualifying distributions, $1,126,929; giving activities include $1,126,929 for 121 grants (high: $200,000; low: $25).

Fields of interest: Arts; Education; Health care; Health organizations, association; Human services; Community development; Public policy, research.

Type of support: General/operating support; Scholarship funds.

Limitations: Giving primarily in CT, NY, RI, and TX. No grants to individuals.

Application information:

  Initial approach: Letter
  Deadline(s): None

Trustee: Thomas W. Smith.

EIN: 133258067

1667
The Tyrrell Foundation, Inc. ✧

c/o Dawson-Herman Capital Mgmt., Inc.
354 Pequot Ave.
Southport, CT   06890

Established in 1996 in CT.

Donor: Jonathan T. Dawson.

Foundation type: Independent foundation.

Financial data (yr. ended 12/31/05): Assets, $16,024,198 (M); expenditures, $2,903,612; qualifying distributions, $2,788,134; giving activities include $2,775,780 for 13 grants (high: $1,188,554; low: $2).

Fields of interest: Education; Environment, forests; Environment; Animals/wildlife, association.

Limitations: Applications not accepted. Giving on a national basis, with some emphasis on NH. No grants to individuals.

Application information: Contributes only to pre-selected organizations.

Officers and Directors:* Jonathan T. Dawson,* Pres. and Treas.; Judith A. Mack,* V.P. and Secy.

Number of staff: 1 part-time professional.
EIN: 061469527

1668
The United Illuminating Foundation ◇
P.O. Box 1564, Tax Section 1-15A
New Haven, CT   06506-0901

Established in 1990 in CT.
Donor: The United Illuminating Co.
Foundation type: Company-sponsored foundation.
Financial data (yr. ended 12/31/03): Assets, $204,495 (M); expenditures, $496,901; qualifying distributions, $496,864; giving activities include $496,813 for grants (high: $175,704).
Purpose and activities: The foundation supports hospitals and organizations involved with arts and culture, human services, children and youth services, and community development.
Fields of interest: Museums; Performing arts, orchestra (symphony); Arts; Higher education; Hospitals (general); Human services; Children/youth, services; Community development; Federated giving programs.
Type of support: General/operating support.
Limitations: Applications not accepted. Giving limited to CT. No grants to individuals.
Application information: Contributes only to pre-selected organizations.
Trustees: Mary Ellen Cody; Anthony J. Vallillo; Nathaniel Woodson.
EIN: 061310455

1669
Lawson Valentine Foundation ◇
1000 Farmington Ave.
West Hartford, CT   06107
Contact: Valentine Doyle, Prog. Off.
E-mail: valentinedoyle@sbcglobal.net

Established in 1989 in CT.
Donor: Alice P. Doyle†.
Foundation type: Independent foundation.
Financial data (yr. ended 12/31/05): Assets, $14,604,771 (M); expenditures, $855,629; qualifying distributions, $775,181; giving activities include $665,550 for 72 grants (high: $27,500; low: $300).
Purpose and activities: Primary areas of interest include human rights, environmental and economic justice, and food systems, including sustainable agriculture.
Fields of interest: Environment, legal rights; Agriculture, soil/water issues; Agriculture/food; International human rights; Civil rights, advocacy.
Type of support: General/operating support; Continuing support; Program development; Seed money; Technical assistance.
Limitations: Giving mostly in the northeastern U.S. No support for religious activities, schools, or land trusts. No grants to individuals.
Publications: Annual report (including application guidelines).
Application information: Certified mail and express mail applications not accepted. Application form not required.
  Initial approach: Letter
  Deadline(s): None
  Board meeting date(s): Spring and fall
  Final notification: Following board meetings

Trustees: Allen Doyle; Valentine Doyle; Mark Lindeman; Lucy Miller; Paul E. Vawter; William D. Zabel.
Number of staff: 2 part-time professional.
EIN: 136920044
Selected grants: The following grants were reported in 2004.
$4,000 to Northeast Action, Hartford, CT.
$3,000 to Conception Coast Project, Santa Barbara, CA.

1670
The Vasey Foundation ◇ ☆
c/o Thomas E. Finn, P.C.
35 Mason St.
Greenwich, CT   06830

Established in 1993 in CT.
Donor: Roger M. Vasey.
Foundation type: Independent foundation.
Financial data (yr. ended 12/31/05): Assets, $776,432 (M); gifts received, $2,374; expenditures, $555,123; qualifying distributions, $546,485; giving activities include $546,485 for 24 grants (high: $170,500; low: $500).
Purpose and activities: Giving primarily for education and human services.
Fields of interest: Higher education; Education; Hospitals (general); Diabetes research; YM/YWCAs & YM/YWHAs; Federated giving programs.
Limitations: Applications not accepted. Giving on a national basis. No grants to individuals.
Application information: Contributes only to pre-selected organizations.
Trustee: Roger M. Vasey.
EIN: 061360683
Selected grants: The following grants were reported in 2005.
$134,675 to YMCA. 2 grants: $98,775, $35,900
$25,000 to Gunnery, Washington, CT.
$25,000 to YMCA Camping Services, Seattle, WA.
$5,000 to Partnership with Children, New York, NY.
$3,000 to Childrens Heart Foundation, Chicago, IL.
$2,000 to National Alliance for the Mentally Ill (NAMI), Arlington, VA.
$1,000 to Childrens Hospital.
$1,000 to Yerwood Center, Stamford, CT.
$950 to Cystic Fibrosis Foundation, Bethesda, MD.

1671
Vervane, Inc. ◇
c/o Josephine Merick
171 Cat Rock Rd.
Cos Cob, CT   06807

Established in 1993 in CT.
Donor: Josephine Merck.
Foundation type: Independent foundation.
Financial data (yr. ended 12/31/05): Assets, $9,200,590 (M); expenditures, $633,424; qualifying distributions, $555,634; giving activities include $525,000 for 26 grants (high: $100,000; low: $5,000).
Fields of interest: Media, television; Media, journalism/publishing; Media, radio; Historic preservation/historical societies; Arts; Higher education; Education; Environment; Agriculture/food.
Type of support: General/operating support; Land acquisition.

Limitations: Applications not accepted. Giving primarily in CT and NY; some giving nationally. No grants to individuals.
Application information: Contributes only to pre-selected organizations.
  Board meeting date(s): Dec.
Officers: Josephine Merck, Pres.; Tom Passios, Secy.-Treas.
Director: Oona Coy.
EIN: 223256829

1672
The Vik Brothers Foundation ◇ ☆
(formerly Northwestern National Insurance Foundation)
10 Ashton Dr.
Greenwich, CT   06831

Established in 1967 in WI.
Donor: Armco Insurance Group, Inc.
Foundation type: Company-sponsored foundation.
Financial data (yr. ended 12/31/04): Assets, $942,161 (M); expenditures, $1,114,078; qualifying distributions, $1,114,078; giving activities include $1,113,513 for 20 grants (high: $600,000; low: $100).
Purpose and activities: The foundation supports hospitals and organizations involved with arts and culture, education, and youth development.
Fields of interest: Arts; Secondary school/education; Higher education; Hospitals (general); Youth development; Federated giving programs.
Type of support: General/operating support; Capital campaigns; Employee matching gifts.
Limitations: Applications not accepted. Giving primarily in CT, MA, NJ, NY, and PA. No grants to individuals.
Application information: Contributes only to pre-selected organizations.
Trustees: Alexander M. Vik; G.M. Vik.
EIN: 396102416
Selected grants: The following grants were reported in 2004.
$600,000 to Greenwich Academy, Greenwich, CT.
$500,000 to Harvard University, Cambridge, MA.
$2,000 to Princeton Day School, Princeton, NJ.
$250 to Eagle Hill School, Greenwich, CT.

1673
The Vranos Family Foundation ◇
c/o Ellington Mgmt. Group
53 Forest Ave., 2nd Fl.
Old Greenwich, CT   06870

Established in 1997 in DE.
Donor: Michael Vranos.
Foundation type: Independent foundation.
Financial data (yr. ended 12/31/05): Assets, $714,908 (M); gifts received, $515,740; expenditures, $1,152,629; qualifying distributions, $1,144,589; giving activities include $1,134,154 for 120 grants (high: $250,000; low: $100).
Purpose and activities: Giving primarily for health care, education, human services, children's services, and international relief.
Fields of interest: Education; Health care; Cancer research; Human services; Children, services; International development; International relief.
Limitations: Applications not accepted. Giving on a national basis, with some emphasis on NY. No grants to individuals.
Application information:

Application information: Contributes only to pre-selected organizations.
Trustees: James Ledley; Michael Vranos.
EIN: 133948273
Selected grants: The following grants were reported in 2004.
$10,000 to Wave Hill, Bronx, NY.

1674

The Jean and David W. Wallace Foundation, Inc. ▼
P.O. Box 1423
Greenwich, CT   06836-1423
Contact: David W. Wallace, Pres.
E-mail: steamboatdww@aol.com

Established in 2001 in CT and DE.
Donors: David W. Wallace; Jean M. Wallace; Robert R. Young Foundation.
Foundation type: Independent foundation.
Financial data (yr. ended 12/31/05): Assets, $9,627,523 (M); gifts received, $3,913,937; expenditures, $4,145,431; qualifying distributions, $4,135,021; giving activities include $4,133,950 for 35 grants (high: $2,000,000; low: $100).
Purpose and activities: Giving primarily for education and to hospitals.
Fields of interest: Higher education; Hospitals (general); YM/YWCAs & YM/YWHAs; Protestant agencies & churches.
Type of support: Scholarship funds; Professorships; Capital campaigns; Building/renovation.
Limitations: Applications not accepted. Giving primarily in CT, NY, and RI. No support for political organizations. No grants to individuals.
Application information: Contributes only to pre-selected organizations.
Board meeting date(s): Varies
Officers and Director: * David W. Wallace,* Pres.; Jean M. Wallace, V.P. and Secy.; Anne S. Wallace Juge, V.P. and Treas.
Number of staff: 4
EIN: 061626691
Selected grants: The following grants were reported in 2005.
$2,000,000 to Yale University, School of Medicine, New Haven, CT. For unrestricted support.
$1,000,000 to Weill Medical College of Cornell University, New York, NY. To endow Wallace-Starr Professorship in Pediatric Cardiology.
$710,250 to Salve Regina University, Newport, RI. For general support. Grant made in form of stock.
$200,000 to Christ Church Tashua, Trumbull, CT. 4 grants: $50,000 each (For building fund).
$20,000 to Brick Presbyterian Church, Greenwich, CT. For general support.
$10,000 to Greenwich Academy, Greenwich, CT. For annual fund.
$5,000 to REACH (Responsibility, Excellence, Achievement, Character, Honor) Prep, Stamford, CT. For general support.

1675

The Stephen & Sandra Waters Foundation ✧
7 Larkspur Ln.
Greenwich, CT   06831

Established in 1986 in CT.
Donors: Sandra Waters; Stephen M. Waters.
Foundation type: Independent foundation.

Financial data (yr. ended 8/31/05): Assets, $1,437,106 (M); expenditures, $1,236,609; qualifying distributions, $1,179,000; giving activities include $1,179,000 for 21 grants (high: $510,000; low: $200).
Purpose and activities: Giving primarily for education; some giving also for religion.
Fields of interest: Education; Health care; Human services; YM/YWCAs & YM/YWHAs; Children/youth, services; Protestant agencies & churches.
Limitations: Applications not accepted. No grants to individuals.
Application information: Contributes only to pre-selected organizations.
Officers: Stephen M. Waters, Pres. and Treas.; Sandra Waters, V.P. and Secy.
EIN: 222642703
Selected grants: The following grants were reported in 2004.
$640,000 to YWCA of Greenwich, Greenwich, CT.
$1,000 to Joseph Kushner Hebrew Academy, Livingston, NJ.
$100 to Phi Beta Kappa Society, DC.

1676

The Whittingham Family Foundation, Inc. ✧
700 Canal St.
Stamford, CT   06902-5921

Established in 1997 in CT.
Donors: Cecil A. Whittingham; C. Anthony Whittingham.
Foundation type: Independent foundation.
Financial data (yr. ended 12/31/05): Assets, $157,713 (M); expenditures, $477,896; qualifying distributions, $475,000; giving activities include $475,000 for 2 grants (high: $375,000; low: $100,000).
Fields of interest: Hospitals (general); Health care.
Type of support: General/operating support.
Limitations: Applications not accepted. Giving primarily in CT. No grants to individuals.
Application information: Contributes only to pre-selected organizations.
Officer: C. Anthony Whittingham, Pres.
EIN: 061476873

1677

Malcolm Hewitt Wiener Foundation, Inc. ▼ ✧
c/o The Millburn Corporation
66 Vista Dr.
Greenwich, CT   06830
Contact: Christina Padgett

Incorporated in 1984 in NY.
Donor: Malcolm H. Wiener.
Foundation type: Independent foundation.
Financial data (yr. ended 12/31/04): Assets, $65,278,986 (M); expenditures, $8,169,708; qualifying distributions, $7,713,133; giving activities include $7,713,133 for 116 grants (high: $4,000,000; low: $35; average: $5,000–$250,000).
Purpose and activities: Giving primarily for international affairs, arts and cultural programs, and higher education. Support also for public affairs.
Fields of interest: Museums (art); Humanities; Higher education; International affairs, goodwill

promotion; International peace/security; International affairs, foreign policy.
Limitations: Applications not accepted. No grants to individuals.
Application information: Contributes only to pre-selected organizations.
Officers and Directors: * Malcolm H. Wiener,* Pres. and Treas.; Harvey Beker,* V.P.; George E. Crapple,* V.P.; Martin J. Whitman; Carolyn S. Wiener.
EIN: 133250321
Selected grants: The following grants were reported in 2004.
$4,000,000 to Institute for Aegean Prehistory Study Center for East Crete, New York, NY.
$600,000 to Weill Medical College of Cornell University, New York, NY.
$284,804 to American School of Classical Studies at Athens, Princeton, NJ.
$250,000 to Cornell University, Department of the History of Art and Archaeology, Ithaca, NY.
$157,000 to Greenwich Academy, Greenwich, CT.
$133,640 to Metropolitan Museum of Art, New York, NY.
$92,930 to American Associates of the Royal Academy Trust, New York, NY.
$75,000 to Council on Foreign Relations, New York, NY.
$55,100 to Temple University, Philadelphia, PA.
$50,000 to Doctors of the World USA, New York, NY.

1678

The David, Helen, and Marian Woodward Fund-Watertown ✧
(also known as Marian W. Ottley Trust-Watertown)
Box 817
Watertown, CT   06795-0817
Contact: M. Heminway Merriman, Member, Selection Comm.

Established in 1975 in GA.
Donor: Marian W. Ottley†.
Foundation type: Independent foundation.
Financial data (yr. ended 5/31/05): Assets, $16,584,055 (M); expenditures, $920,580; qualifying distributions, $782,843; giving activities include $782,350 for 36 grants (high: $100,000; low: $700).
Purpose and activities: Giving primarily for secondary, elementary, and early childhood education, social services, health services, and libraries. Support for building funds for education and hospitals.
Fields of interest: Museums; Education, fund raising/fund distribution; Education, early childhood education; Elementary school/education; Secondary school/education; Libraries/library science; Education; Environment; Hospitals (general); Medical care, rehabilitation; Health care; Health organizations, association; Human services; Youth, services; Residential/custodial care, hospices; Christian agencies & churches; Native Americans/American Indians.
Type of support: Capital campaigns; Building/renovation; Equipment; Endowments; Scholarship funds.
Limitations: Giving limited to local organizations in New England and NY. No support for institutions of higher education, or organizations lacking 501(c)(3) tax-exempt status. No grants to individuals, or for general operating funds; generally no multi-year grants.
Publications: Application guidelines.

Application information: Education awards limited to the pre-collegiate level. Application form not required.

Initial approach: 2-page letter
Copies of proposal: 3
Deadline(s): May 15
Board meeting date(s): May

Selection Committee: Anne Fitzgerald; M. Heminway Merriman; William J. Zito, M.D.

Trustee: First National Bank of Atlanta.

EIN: 586222005

Selected grants: The following grants were reported in 2005.

$100,000 to Chase Collegiate School, Waterbury, CT.

$100,000 to Taft School, Watertown, CT.

$86,250 to Waterbury Hospital, Waterbury, CT.

$75,000 to Gunnery, Washington, CT.

$60,000 to Harold Leever Regional Cancer Center, Waterbury, CT.

$50,000 to Greater Waterbury Interfaith Ministries, Waterbury, CT.

$40,000 to VNA Health at Home, Watertown, CT.

$30,000 to Saint Mary Magdalen School, Oakville, CT.

$15,000 to Clockwork Productions, Oakville, CT.

$10,000 to National Society, Daughters of the American Revolution (DAR), DC.

1679
The Worthington Family Foundation, Inc. ✦

P.O. Box 196
Greens Farms, CT 06838 (203) 227-1281
Contact: Worthington Johnson, Jr., Treas.

Established in 1991 in CT.

Donor: Worthington Johnson†.

Foundation type: Independent foundation.

Financial data (yr. ended 12/31/05): Assets, $9,245,225 (M); expenditures, $541,716; qualifying distributions, $475,540; giving activities include $475,540 for 38 grants (high: $35,000; low: $500).

Fields of interest: Historic preservation/historical societies; Arts; Education; Environment, natural resources; Animal welfare; Children/youth, services.

Type of support: Capital campaigns; Building/renovation; Equipment.

Limitations: Giving primarily in the Northeast, with emphasis on CT and MA. No grants to individuals, or for travel, meals, or lodging for conferences or symposia.

Application information: Application form not required.

Initial approach: Proposal
Deadline(s): Oct. 1

Officers and Directors:* Marina Johnson Sutro,* Pres.; Joan Johnson Stott,* Secy.; Worthington Johnson, Jr.,* Treas.

EIN: 223100891

1680
The Xerox Foundation

800 Long Ridge Rd.
P.O. Box 1600
Stamford, CT 06904 (203) 968-3445
Contact: Joseph M. Cahalan, V.P.
FAX: (203) 968-3330; Additional tel.: (203) 968-4416; URL: http://www.xerox.com/foundation

Incorporated in 1979 in DE as successor to the Xerox Fund.

Donor: Xerox Corp.

Foundation type: Company-sponsored foundation.

Financial data (yr. ended 12/31/05): Assets, $24,198 (M); gifts received, $2,605,500; expenditures, $2,587,150; qualifying distributions, $2,587,150; giving activities include $2,430,150 for 25+ grants, and $157,000 for 119 grants to individuals (high: $10,000; low: $1,000).

Purpose and activities: The foundation supports organizations involved with arts and culture, education, including the application of information technology, employment, human services, increased business quality and productivity, community development, science and technology, civic affairs, minorities, women, and economically disadvantaged people.

Fields of interest: Performing arts, theater; Arts; Higher education; Adult education—literacy, basic skills & GED; Education; Employment; Children/youth, services; Family services; Human services; Business/industry; Community development; Engineering/technology; Science; Public policy, research; Public affairs; Minorities; Women; Economically disadvantaged.

Type of support: General/operating support; Continuing support; Program development; Seed money; Scholarship funds; Research; Technical assistance; Employee volunteer services; Sponsorships; Employee matching gifts; Scholarships—to individuals.

Limitations: Giving on a national basis. No support for political organizations or candidates, religious or sectarian organizations, or government agencies. No grants to individuals (except for scholarships), or for endowments; no product donations.

Publications: Application guidelines; Corporate giving report (including application guidelines); Informational brochure (including application guidelines); Program policy statement (including application guidelines).

Application information: Proposals should be brief. Multi-year funding is not automatic. Application form not required.

Initial approach: Proposal
Copies of proposal: 1
Deadline(s): None
Board meeting date(s): Quarterly
Final notification: 30 to 60 days

Officers and Directors: Anne M. Mulcahy, C.E.O.; Joseph M. Cahalan, V.P.; Emerson Fullwood; Patricia M. Nazemetz.

Number of staff: 2 full-time professional; 1 full-time support.

EIN: 060996443

1681
Robert R. Young Foundation ✦

c/o David W. Wallace
680 Steamboat Rd.
Greenwich, CT 06830-7147 (203) 661-4247

Established about 1959.

Donor: Anita O'Keefe Young†.

Foundation type: Independent foundation.

Financial data (yr. ended 12/31/05): Assets, $41,524,903 (M); expenditures, $3,983,188; qualifying distributions, $3,931,785; giving activities include $3,931,785 for 2 grants (high: $3,930,785; low: $1,000).

Fields of interest: Higher education; Education; Hospitals (general); Protestant agencies & churches.

Type of support: General/operating support; Research.

Limitations: Applications not accepted. Giving primarily in CT, NY, and RI. No grants to individuals.

Application information: Contributes only to pre-selected organizations.

Officers: David W. Wallace, Pres.; Jean W. Wallace, Secy.

EIN: 136131394

Selected grants: The following grants were reported in 2003.

$1,500,000 to Salve Regina University, Newport, RI.

$1,277,516 to Greenwich Hospital, Greenwich, CT.

$1,000,000 to Yale University, New Haven, CT.

1682
The Zachs Family Foundation, Inc. ☆

(formerly The Henry M. Zachs & Judith M. Zachs Foundation, Inc.)
c/o Henry M. Zachs
40 Woodland St.
Hartford, CT 06105
FAX: (860) 727-5702;
E-mail: HZachs@mcmgmt.com

Established in 1985 in CT.

Donors: Henry M. Zachs; William Zachs; Eric Zachs; Judith M. Zachs; Jessica P. Zachs; Louise Zachs.

Foundation type: Independent foundation.

Financial data (yr. ended 6/30/06): Assets, $2,784,710 (M); gifts received, $96,000; expenditures, $862,237; qualifying distributions, $856,990; giving activities include $856,990 for grants.

Purpose and activities: Funding primarily for Jewish agencies and temples and higher education. Also some general charitable giving.

Fields of interest: Education, fund raising/fund distribution; Secondary school/education; Higher education; Education; Hospitals (general); Federated giving programs; Jewish agencies & temples.

Type of support: Annual campaigns; Capital campaigns; Building/renovation; Endowments; Scholarship funds.

Limitations: Applications not accepted. Giving primarily in the northeastern U.S., with emphasis on CT. No grants to individuals.

Publications: Financial statement.

Application information: Contributes only to pre-selected organizations.

Officers and Directors:* Henry M. Zachs,* Pres. and Treas.; Judith M. Zachs,* V.P. and Secy.; Newton D. Brenner; Eric Zachs; William Zachs.

Number of staff: None.

EIN: 061157320

1683
The E. Matilda Ziegler Foundation for the Blind, Inc. ✦

c/o Swisher Intl.
20 Thorndal Cir., 1st Fl.
Darien, CT 06820 (203) 656-8000
Contact: Beatrice H. Page, Treas.

Incorporated in 1928 in NY.

Donor: Mrs. William Ziegler†.

Foundation type: Independent foundation.

Financial data (yr. ended 12/31/04): Assets, $20,032,063 (M); expenditures, $2,074,286; qualifying distributions, $1,856,079; giving activities include $1,833,400 for 23 grants (high: $420,000; low: $2,000).

Purpose and activities: Giving for charitable and educational work to ameliorate the condition of the blind; support largely for the monthly publication and free distribution of the Matilda Ziegler Magazine for the Blind.

Fields of interest: Eye diseases; Eye research; Disabilities, people with.

Type of support: General/operating support; Continuing support; Annual campaigns; Research.

Limitations: Giving on a national basis. No grants to individuals, or for endowment funds, scholarships, or matching gifts; no loans.

Application information: Application form not required.

Initial approach: Proposal
Copies of proposal: 1
Deadline(s): June 29
Board meeting date(s): Dec.
Final notification: Dec. 31

Officers and Directors:* William Ziegler III,* Pres.; Helen Z. Steinkraus,* V.P. and Secy.; Beatrice H. Page, Treas.; Cynthia Z. Brighton; Charles C. Cook; C. Michael Mellor; Marvin L. Sears; Eric M. Steinkraus; Philip Steinkraus; Karl Ziegler.

Number of staff: 2 full-time professional; 1 part-time professional; 1 part-time support.

EIN: 136086195

1684
Sarah L. Boles and Joseph R. Zimmel Foundation

(formerly Sarah B. and Joseph R. Zimmel Foundation)
c/o Kolbrenner & Alex
15 Valley Dr., 3rd. Fl.
Greenwich, CT   06831

Established in 1990 in NJ.

Donor: Joseph R. Zimmel.

Foundation type: Independent foundation.

Financial data (yr. ended 7/31/05): Assets, $8,719,373 (M); gifts received, $5,000; expenditures, $355,000; qualifying distributions, $350,000; giving activities include $350,000 for 9 grants (high: $125,000; low: $5,000).

Purpose and activities: Giving primarily to a Congregational church as well as to a hospital, and for education and human services.

Fields of interest: Education; Hospitals (general); Human services; Protestant agencies & churches.

Limitations: Applications not accepted. Giving primarily in Greenwich, CT; some funding also in New York, NY. No grants to individuals; no loans.

Application information: Contributes only to pre-selected organizations.

Trustees: David R. Boles; Sarah L. Boles; Joseph R. Zimmel.

EIN: 133596015

Selected grants: The following grants were reported in 2004.

$100,000 to Second Congregational Church, Greenwich, CT.

$50,000 to Student Sponsor Partners, New York, NY.

$30,000 to Greenwich Country Day School, Greenwich, CT.

$25,000 to Greenwich Emergency Medical Service, Riverside, CT.

$25,000 to River Foundation, Roanoke, VA.

$15,000 to Boys and Girls Club of Greenwich, Greenwich, CT.

$10,000 to Greenwich Library, Greenwich, CT.

$6,125 to Georgetown University, DC.

$5,000 to Family Centers, Greenwich, CT.

$5,000 to Small World Foundation, Fort Lauderdale, FL.

1685
The ZOOM Foundation ▼ ✧
c/o Cummings and Lockwood
2 Greenwich Plz.
Greenwich, CT   06830

Established in 2000 in CT.

Donors: Stephen F. Mandel, Jr.; Susan Z. Mandel.

Foundation type: Independent foundation.

Financial data (yr. ended 6/30/05): Assets, $115,871,942 (M); gifts received, $3,003,783; expenditures, $4,003,783; qualifying distributions, $4,000,000; giving activities include $4,000,000 for 2 grants (high: $2,500,000; low: $1,500,000).

Purpose and activities: Giving primarily to education.

Fields of interest: Elementary/secondary education; Higher education; Education.

Limitations: Applications not accepted. Giving primarily in CT. No grants to individuals.

Application information: Contributes only to pre-selected organizations.

Trustees: Stephen F. Mandel, Jr.; Susan Z. Mandel.

EIN: 061600601

Selected grants: The following grants were reported in 2005.

$2,500,000 to Fidelity Investments Charitable Gift Fund, Boston, MA.

$1,500,000 to Environmental Defense, New York, NY.

DELAWARE

1686
The ABE Charitable Foundation, Inc. ✧ ☆
c/o Foundation Source
501 Silverside Rd., Ste. 123
Wilmington, DE   19809-1377

Established in 2004 in DE.
Donors: Jeffrey R. Serra; Deanna Serra.
Foundation type: Independent foundation.
Financial data (yr. ended 12/31/05): Assets,
$2,834,336 (M); expenditures, $343,724;
qualifying distributions, $320,500; giving activities
include $320,500 for 27 grants (high: $125,000;
low: $1,000).
Limitations: Applications not accepted. Giving
primarily in TX. No grants to individuals.
Application information: Contributes only to
pre-selected organizations.
Officers and Directors:* Deanna L. Serra,* Pres.;
Amanda Serra, V.P.; Benjamin Serra, V.P.; Jeffrey R.
Serra,* V.P.
EIN: 201650254

1687
Arguild Foundation ✧
P.O. Box 2207
Wilmington, DE   19899-2207
Application address: c/o Arthur G. Connolly, Jr.,
1007 N. Orange St., Wilmington, DE 19801

Established in 1959 in DE.
Donor: Arthur G. Connolly, Sr.
Foundation type: Independent foundation.
Financial data (yr. ended 12/31/05): Assets,
$7,342,576 (M); expenditures, $367,490;
qualifying distributions, $332,300; giving activities
include $332,300 for 50 grants (high: $110,000;
low: $300).
Purpose and activities: Giving primarily for
education, social services, and for children and
youth services, including a children's hospital.
Fields of interest: Elementary/secondary
education; Higher education; Hospitals (specialty);
Human services; Children/youth, services;
Federated giving programs.
Limitations: Giving primarily in Wilmington, DE. No
grants to individuals.
Application information:
  Initial approach: Letter
  Deadline(s): None
Officers: Mary Connolly Braun, Pres.; Arthur G.
Connolly, Jr., Secy.
EIN: 516016487
Selected grants: The following grants were reported
in 2004.
$50,000 to Princeton University, Princeton, NJ.
$5,000 to United Way.
$2,500 to Archmere Academy, Claymont, DE.
$2,000 to Georgetown University, DC.

1688
Bartsch Memorial Trust ✧
(formerly Ruth Bartsch Memorial Bank Trust)
c/o JPMorgan Services Inc.
P.O. Box 6089
Newark, DE   19714-6089
Application address: c/o Peggy Swarzman, V.P.,
JPMorgan Chase Bank, 345 Park Ave., 4th Fl., New
York NY 10154; tel.: (212) 464-2342

Established in 1983 in NY.
Donor: Ruth Bartsch†.
Foundation type: Independent foundation.
Financial data (yr. ended 11/30/05): Assets,
$9,543,782 (M); expenditures, $521,306;
qualifying distributions, $451,681; giving activities
include $420,000 for 8 grants (high: $168,000;
low: $21,000).
Fields of interest: Secondary school/education;
Hospitals (general); Health organizations,
association; Human services.
Limitations: Giving on a national basis, with
emphasis on CT, FL, IL, and MI. No grants to
individuals.
Application information: Application form not
required.
  Initial approach: Letter
  Deadline(s): None
Trustees: Vincent William Richards, Jr.; JPMorgan
Chase Bank, N.A.
EIN: 133188775
Selected grants: The following grants were reported
in 2004.
$140,000 to Vanguard School, Lake Wales, FL. 2
  grants: $70,000 each
$35,000 to Coast Guard Foundation, Stonington,
  CT. 2 grants: $17,500 each
$35,000 to Salvation Army. 2 grants: $17,500 each
$17,500 to Boy Scouts of America, Pontiac, MI.
$17,500 to Lighthouse of Oakland County, Pontiac,
  MI.

1689
Beckwith Family Foundation ✧
c/o J.P. Morgan Svcs., Inc.
P.O. Box 6089
Newark, DE   19714-6089
Application address: c/o John E. Trabucco, Arch
Street Mgmt., LLC, 2790 Mosside Blvd., Ste. 610,
Monroeville, PA 15146

Established in 1999 in PA.
Donor: Virginia P. Beckwith†.
Foundation type: Independent foundation.
Financial data (yr. ended 9/30/05): Assets,
$8,626,691 (M); expenditures, $445,444;
qualifying distributions, $406,223; giving activities
include $402,012 for 25 grants (high: $115,000;
low: $12).
Fields of interest: Medical school/education;
Education; Botanical gardens; Reproductive health,
family planning; Human services; YM/YWCAs & YM/
YWHAs; Children, services.
Limitations: Giving primarily in CT, FL, PA, and RI.
No grants to individuals.
Application information:
  Initial approach: Proposal
  Deadline(s): None
Officers and Trustee:* G. Nicholas Beckwith III,
Pres.; John E. Trabucco, Secy.; James S. Beckwith
III,* Treas.
EIN: 311607888

Selected grants: The following grants were reported
in 2005.
$50,000 to Chatham College, Pittsburgh, PA.
$50,000 to Naples Botanical Garden, Naples, FL.
$30,000 to Allegheny Conference on Community
  Development, Pittsburgh, PA.
$25,000 to Andy Warhol Museum, Pittsburgh, PA.
$15,000 to Family Guidance, Sewickley, PA.
$10,000 to Homewood Cemetery Historical Fund,
  Pittsburgh, PA.
$10,000 to Western Pennsylvania Conservancy,
  Pittsburgh, PA.
$10,000 to Womens Center and Shelter of Greater
  Pittsburgh, Pittsburgh, PA.
$7,500 to North Hills Community Outreach, Allison
  Park, PA.
$4,000 to Hill School, Pottstown, PA.

1690
C. E. Bennett Foundation ✧
Little Falls Two
2751 Centerville Rd., Ste. 300
Wilmington, DE   19808

Established in 1964 in DE.
Donor: C. Eugene Bennett†.
Foundation type: Independent foundation.
Financial data (yr. ended 12/31/05): Assets,
$7,763,937 (M); expenditures, $437,788;
qualifying distributions, $394,950; giving activities
include $393,175 for 10 grants (high: $100,000;
low: $225).
Fields of interest: Museums (natural history);
Performing arts; Arts; Education; Human services;
Christian agencies & churches.
Type of support: Annual campaigns;
Professorships; Scholarship funds; Program-related
investments/loans.
Limitations: Applications not accepted. Giving
primarily in DE. No grants to individuals.
Application information: Contributes only to
pre-selected organizations.
Officers: Edna B. Pierce, Pres.; Karl E. Bennett, V.P.
EIN: 510102289

1691
W. R. Berkley Corporation Charitable
Foundation ✧ ☆
c/o Foundation Source
501 Silverside Rd., Ste. 123
Wilmington, DE   19809-1377

Established in 2002 in DE.
Donor: W.R. Berkley Corp.
Foundation type: Company-sponsored foundation.
Financial data (yr. ended 12/31/05): Assets,
$151,864 (M); gifts received, $649,840;
expenditures, $687,292; qualifying distributions,
$685,393; giving activities include $685,393 for
grants.
Purpose and activities: The foundation supports
organizations involved with arts and culture,
education, health, youth development, and human
services.
Fields of interest: Arts; Higher education;
Education; Health organizations, association; Youth
development; Human services; Jewish federated
giving programs.
Limitations: Applications not accepted. No grants to
individuals.

Application information: Contributes only to pre-selected organizations.
Officers and Directors:* William R. Berkley,* Pres.; Josephine Ralmondi,* V.P. and Secy.; William R. Berkley, Jr.,* V.P. and Treas.
Trustee: W.R. Berkley Corp.
EIN: 364516560
Selected grants: The following grants were reported in 2003.
$10,000 to Metropolitan Museum of Art, New York, NY. For general support.
$7,500 to Boy Scouts of America, Greater New York Councils, New York, NY. For general support.
$5,000 to Brooklyn Academy of Music, Brooklyn, NY. For general support.
$5,000 to Institute of International Education, New York, NY. For general support.
$5,000 to Jacksonville University, Jacksonville, FL. For general support.
$5,000 to Multiple Sclerosis Society, National, Gateway Chapter, Saint Louis, MO. For general support.
$2,500 to Historical Society of the Town of Greenwich, Cos Cob, CT. For general support.
$2,000 to Community Hospice of Northeast Florida, Jacksonville, FL. For general support.
$2,000 to Saint Augustine Youth Services, Saint Augustine, FL. For general support.
$1,000 to Greenwich Emergency Medical Service, Riverside, CT. For general support.

1692

Stephen and Mary Birch Foundation, Inc. ▼

103 Foulk Rd., Ste. 200
Wilmington, DE 19803
Contact: Rose B. Patek, Secy.-Treas.

Incorporated in 1938 in DE.
Donor: Stephen Birch†.
Foundation type: Independent foundation.
Financial data (yr. ended 12/31/04): Assets, $136,347,421 (M); expenditures, $10,711,678; qualifying distributions, $7,261,003; giving activities include $7,022,350 for 211 grants (high: $600,000; low: $500).
Purpose and activities: The foundation provides funding in support of other nonprofit institutions, communities, and organizations that are or that have been instrumental in strengthening and heightening both culturally and educationally, the impact of research, medical, health, educational, sports, social service, and artistic programs in communities across the nation, from coast to coast.
Fields of interest: Arts education; Museums (sports/hobby); Arts; Education; Health care; Human services; Youth, services; International relief; Government/public administration; Christian agencies & churches.
Limitations: Giving on a national basis. No support for political organizations.
Application information: Application form not required.
Initial approach: Letter only
Copies of proposal: 1
Deadline(s): None
Board meeting date(s): Quarterly
Officers: Patrick J. Patek, Pres.; Christopher Patek, V.P.; Rose B. Patek, Secy-Treas.
EIN: 221713022
Selected grants: The following grants were reported in 2004.

$600,000 to Roundabout Theater Company, New York, NY.
$583,000 to Saint Pius X Catholic Church, Chula Vista, CA.
$350,000 to Kick Start, Houston, TX.
$333,000 to Jewels of Charity, Wilmington, DE.
$100,000 to Saint James School, Seguin, TX.
$40,000 to Guadalupe County Childrens Advocacy Center, Seguin, TX.
$33,000 to United Cerebral Palsy of Metropolitan Dallas, Dallas, TX.
$25,000 to San Felipe de Jesus Catholic Church, Brownsville, TX.
$25,000 to Special Olympics Southern California, Culver City, CA.
$10,000 to Arizona Memorial Museum Association, Honolulu, HI.

1693

Edward E. and Lillian H. Bishop Foundation ◇ ☆

c/o Wilmington Trust Co.
1100 N. Market St.
Wilmington, DE 19890-0001
Application address: c/o Richard Pratt, P.O. Box 699, Bradenton, FL 34206

Trust established in 1953 in DE.
Donor: Lillian H. Bishop.
Foundation type: Independent foundation.
Financial data (yr. ended 12/31/05): Assets, $8,291,924 (M); expenditures, $379,489; qualifying distributions, $340,935; giving activities include $340,935 for grants.
Fields of interest: Museums; Animal welfare; Human services; Children/youth, services; Federated giving programs; Astronomy.
Type of support: General/operating support.
Limitations: Giving primarily in Manatee County, FL.
Publications: Informational brochure (including application guidelines).
Application information: Application form required.
Initial approach: Letter
Deadline(s): Apr. 30
Board meeting date(s): Dec.
Final notification: Positive responses only
Trustees: Robert Blalock; Mary Parker; Richard Pratt; Willett E. Wentzell, M.D.; P. Woodrow Young; Wilmington Trust Co.
EIN: 516017762

1694

Lillian H. Bishop Trust A for the SPCA of Manatee County, Florida ◇

c/o Wilmington Trust Co.
1100 N. Market St.
Wilmington, DE 19890-0001

Established in 1973 in DE.
Foundation type: Independent foundation.
Financial data (yr. ended 12/31/05): Assets, $19,683,917 (M); expenditures, $932,710; qualifying distributions, $831,646; giving activities include $736,094 for 9 grants (high: $374,386; low: $25,000).
Purpose and activities: Grants primarily for animal welfare associations and a museum; support also for human services and youth groups.
Fields of interest: Museums; Animal welfare; Girls clubs; YM/YWCAs & YM/YWHAs; Community development, service clubs.

Limitations: Applications not accepted. Giving primarily in Manatee County, FL. No grants to individuals.
Application information: Contributes only to pre-selected organizations.
Trustee: Wilmington Trust Co.
EIN: 237334266

1695

H. W. Buckner Charitable Residuary Trust ◇

c/o JPMorgan Chase Bank, N.A., Services, Inc.
P.O. Box 6089
Newark, DE 19714-6089

Established in 1991 in DE.
Donor: Helen W. Buckner†.
Foundation type: Independent foundation.
Financial data (yr. ended 12/31/05): Assets, $2,838,435 (M); expenditures, $1,453,605; qualifying distributions, $1,439,287; giving activities include $1,437,579 for 31 grants (high: $200,000; low: $1,000).
Purpose and activities: Support primarily for education and cultural organizations; some funding also for the environment.
Fields of interest: Performing arts, music; Higher education; Education; Environment, natural resources; Human services; Youth, services; Foundations (public).
Limitations: Giving primarily in MA, NY, and RI. No grants to individuals.
Application information:
Initial approach: Letter
Deadline(s): None
Trustee: JPMorgan Chase Bank, N.A.
Advisory Committee: Elizabeth Buckner; Thomas W. Buckner; Walker G. Buckner, Jr.; Mary B. Shea.
EIN: 516179860
Selected grants: The following grants were reported in 2003.
$200,177 to Lotus Fine Arts Productions, New York, NY. 2 grants: $75,000 (For general support), $125,177 (For general support).
$165,000 to World Music Institute, New York, NY. 2 grants: $75,000 (For general support), $90,000 (For general support).
$107,000 to Camphill Soltane, Glenmoore, PA. For general support.
$55,000 to Youth Communication/New York Center, New York, NY. For general support.
$35,000 to New School, New York, NY. For general support.
$15,000 to Brotherhood/Sister Sol, New York, NY. For general support.
$10,000 to Harvard University, Cambridge, MA. For general support.
$10,000 to Recorded Anthology of American Music, New World Records, New York, NY. For general support.

1696

The Cawley Family Foundation ◇

c/o Charles M. Cawley
1111 Berkeley Rd.
Wilmington, DE 19807-2815

Established in 1997 in DE.
Donors: Charles M. Cawley; Julie P. Cawley.
Foundation type: Independent foundation.

Financial data (yr. ended 12/31/04): Assets, $2,226,717 (M); gifts received, $3,500,000; expenditures, $3,454,355; qualifying distributions, $3,454,330; giving activities include $3,454,330 for 197 grants (high: $500,000; low: $150).
Purpose and activities: Support for the arts, education, health associations, particularly a heart association, the environment, youth, human services, and Roman Catholic agencies & churches.
Fields of interest: Museums; Performing arts; Secondary school/education; Higher education; Environment, natural resources; Health care; Health organizations, association; Youth development; Human services; Roman Catholic agencies & churches.
Type of support: General/operating support; Continuing support; Annual campaigns; Building/renovation; Debt reduction; Program development; Scholarship funds.
Limitations: Applications not accepted. Giving on a national basis, with emphasis on Washington, DC, DE, ME, MD, NJ, and PA. No grants to individuals.
Application information: Contributes only to pre-selected organizations.
Officers and Directors: * Charles M. Cawley,* Pres. and Treas.; Julie P. Cawley,* V.P. and Secy.; Charles M. Cawley III; Maureen Rhodes.
EIN: 510379108

1697
Cedar Hill Foundation ◇
c/o JPMorgan Chase Bank, N.A.
P.O. Box 6089
Newark, DE   19714-6089
Application address: c/o JPMorgan Chase Bank, N.A., attn.: Shannon Hennessey, 345 Park Ave., New York, NY 10154-0101

Established in 1997 in DE and NY.
Foundation type: Independent foundation.
Financial data (yr. ended 12/31/05): Assets, $17,193,437 (M); gifts received, $190; expenditures, $908,679; qualifying distributions, $818,618; giving activities include $815,000 for 12 grants (high: $250,000; low: $10,000).
Purpose and activities: Giving for education, animal welfare, and human services.
Fields of interest: Education; Animals/wildlife; Hospitals (general); Human services.
Limitations: Giving on a national basis, with some emphasis on national organizations in NY.
Application information: Application form not required.
Deadline(s): None
Officers and Directors: * Clare P. Potter,* V.P.; William Parsons, Jr.,* Secy.
EIN: 133948444

1698
Chichester duPont Foundation, Inc. ◇
3120 Kennett Pike
Wilmington, DE   19807-3052   (302) 658-5244
Contact: Gregory F. Fields, Secy.

Incorporated in 1946 in DE.
Donors: Lydia Chichester duPont†; Mary Chichester duPont Clark†; A. Felix duPont, Jr.; Alice duPont Mills.
Foundation type: Independent foundation.
Financial data (yr. ended 12/31/03): Assets, $51,983,186 (M); expenditures, $2,918,627;

qualifying distributions, $2,662,577; giving activities include $2,600,000 for 49 grants (high: $410,500; low: $500).
Purpose and activities: Emphasis on child welfare, including support for a camp for handicapped children, education, health, and cultural programs; some support for conservation.
Fields of interest: Elementary/secondary education; Education; Environment, natural resources; Health care; Human services; Children/youth, services.
Type of support: General/operating support; Building/renovation.
Limitations: Giving primarily in DE and MD. No grants to individuals.
Application information: Application form not required.
Deadline(s): Oct. 1
Board meeting date(s): Dec.
Final notification: 2 weeks after meeting
Officers and Trustees: * Katharine Gahagan,* Pres.; Caroline Prickett,* V.P.; Gregory F. Fields, Secy.; Christopher T. Dupont,* Treas.; Mary Mills Abel-Smith; Lynne L. Dorsey; Allaire duPont, Sr.; Alexis Gahagan; Sophie Mills; Phyllis Mills Wyeth.
EIN: 516011641
Selected grants: The following grants were reported in 2004.
$375,000 to Childrens Beach House, Wilmington, DE. For annual operating support and campaign development.
$200,000 to Saint Andrews School of Delaware, Middletown, DE. For O'Briens Arts Center project.
$150,000 to Easter Seal Society of Del-Mar, New Castle, DE. For early intervention program.
$100,000 to Fauquier Hospital Foundation, Warrenton, VA. For hospital improvements.
$93,500 to Ronald McDonald House of Delaware, Wilmington, DE. For capital campaign.
$75,000 to Christiana Care Health System, Wilmington, DE. For endowment campaign.
$75,000 to Community School, Sun Valley, ID. To add science room to Middle School.
$75,000 to Ministry of Caring, Wilmington, DE. For Caring Child Care operating support and Guardian Angel.
$75,000 to Union Hospital, Elkton, MD. For computer equipment.
$70,000 to Three Bays Preservation, Osterville, MA. For freshwater mitigation programs.

1699
The Choptank Foundation ◇
c/o Morris, Nichols, Arsht & Tunnell
P.O. Box 1347
Wilmington, DE   19899-1347
Contact: Johannes R. Krahmer, Pres.

Established in 1965 in DE.
Donors: Sewell C. Biggs†; Franklin B. Biggs†.
Foundation type: Independent foundation.
Financial data (yr. ended 12/31/05): Assets, $8,792,173 (M); gifts received, $500,000; expenditures, $1,032,505; qualifying distributions, $926,448; giving activities include $902,000 for 3 grants (high: $552,000; low: $100,000).
Fields of interest: Museums (art).
Limitations: Giving limited to DE. No grants to individuals.
Application information: Application form not required.
Deadline(s): None

Officers and Trustees: * Johannes R. Krahmer,* Pres.; Pierre duP. Hayward,* V.P.; Thomas R. Pulsifer,* Secy.-Treas.
EIN: 516019601
Selected grants: The following grants were reported in 2004.
$279,000 to Sewell C. Biggs Trust, Dover, DE.

1700
The Common Wealth Trust ◇
c/o PNC Bank, N.A.-Delaware
222 Delaware Ave.
Wilmington, DE   19899

Established in 1978.
Donor: Ralph W. Hayes†.
Foundation type: Independent foundation.
Financial data (yr. ended 12/31/05): Assets, $9,464,881 (M); expenditures, $663,804; qualifying distributions, $577,156; giving activities include $264,000 for 4 grants (high: $250,000; low: $1,000), and $250,000 for 5 grants to individuals (high: $50,000; low: $50,000).
Purpose and activities: Support for a historical society and for educational purposes; also gives distinguished service awards to prominent individuals in the fields of literature, science and invention, public service, sociology, government and mass communication.
Fields of interest: Performing arts; Literature; Historic preservation/historical societies; Higher education, university; Human services; Community development; Science.
Type of support: General/operating support; Grants to individuals.
Limitations: Applications not accepted. Giving on a national basis, with emphasis on Cleveland, OH.
Application information: Recipients must be nominated by specific professional associations and selection committees on a pro-bono basis.
Officer: Connie Bond Stuart, Chair.
Members: Eleanor D. Craig; George W. Forbes; Joshua W. Martin III; William H. Willis, Jr.
Trustee: PNC Bank, N.A.
EIN: 510232187
Selected grants: The following grants were reported in 2003.
$250,000 to Western Reserve Historical Society, Cleveland, OH.
$7,000 to Crestline, City of, Crestline, OH.
$6,000 to Case Western Reserve University, Cleveland, OH.
$1,000 to City Club of Cleveland, Cleveland, OH.

1701
Crestlea Foundation, Inc. ◇
100 W. 10th St., Ste. 1109
Wilmington, DE   19801-1694   (302) 654-2477
Contact: Stephen A. Martinenza, Secy.-Treas.

Incorporated in 1955 in DE.
Donor: Henry B. duPont†.
Foundation type: Independent foundation.
Financial data (yr. ended 12/31/05): Assets, $35,269,636 (M); gifts received, $424,424; expenditures, $777,320; qualifying distributions, $671,726; giving activities include $614,871 for 63 grants (high: $40,000; low: $500).
Purpose and activities: Giving primarily for secondary education; some giving also for the arts, and health, community, and social services.

Fields of interest: Museums; Secondary school/education; Higher education; Environment, natural resources; Health care; Housing/shelter, development; Human services; Community development; Federated giving programs; Public affairs.

Type of support: Annual campaigns; Capital campaigns; Building/renovation; Equipment.

Limitations: Giving primarily in the Wilmington, DE area, and Pomfret, CT; some giving also in PA. No grants to individuals.

Application information: Solicitations for grants are only considered from organizations that are located within 50 miles of Wilmington, DE. Application form not required.

Initial approach: 2-page letter
Copies of proposal: 1
Deadline(s): Nov. 1
Board meeting date(s): As required
Final notification: Dec. 31

Officers: Otto C. Fad, Pres.; Stephen A. Martinenza, Secy.-Treas.

Number of staff: 1

EIN: 516015638

Selected grants: The following grants were reported in 2004.

$1,082,333 to Pomfret School, Pomfret, CT.

$50,000 to Episcopal Academy, Merion, PA.

$30,000 to Philadelphia Orchestra Association, Philadelphia, PA.

$25,000 to Philadelphia Museum of Art, Philadelphia, PA.

$20,000 to Delaware Hospice, Wilmington, DE.

$20,000 to Northeast Harbor Library, Northeast Harbor, ME.

$10,000 to Episcopal Community Services, Wyndmoor, PA.

$10,000 to Exceptional Care for Children, Newark, DE.

$10,000 to Independence School, Newark, DE.

$10,000 to Pennsylvania Academy of the Fine Arts, Philadelphia, PA.

1702
Crystal Trust ▼
P.O. Box 39
Montchanin, DE   19710-0039   (302) 651-0533
Contact: Stephen C. Doberstein, Dir.

Trust established in 1947 in DE.

Donor: Irenee duPont‡.

Foundation type: Independent foundation.

Financial data (yr. ended 12/31/05): Assets, $137,719,714 (M); expenditures, $6,852,247; qualifying distributions, $6,824,415; giving activities include $6,618,570 for 62 grants (high: $750,000; low: $2,100; average: $10,000–$100,000).

Purpose and activities: Giving mainly for higher and secondary education and social and family services, including youth and child welfare agencies, family planning, and programs for the aged, the disadvantaged, and the homeless; support also for the arts and cultural programs, health and hospitals, conservation programs, and historical preservation. Needs of the State of Delaware have priority.

Fields of interest: Museums; Performing arts, music; Arts; Secondary school/education; Higher education; Libraries/library science; Education; Environment, natural resources; Hospitals (general); Reproductive health, family planning; Health care; Health organizations, association; Food services; Housing/shelter, development; Human services;

Children/youth, services; Family services; Residential/custodial care, hospices; Aging, centers/services; Homeless, human services; Aging; Economically disadvantaged; Homeless.

Type of support: Capital campaigns; Building/renovation; Equipment; Land acquisition.

Limitations: Giving primarily in DE, with emphasis on Wilmington. No grants to individuals, or for endowment funds, research, scholarships, fellowships, or matching gifts.

Publications: Informational brochure (including application guidelines).

Application information: Application form not required.

Initial approach: Proposal
Copies of proposal: 1
Deadline(s): Sept. 30
Board meeting date(s): Nov.
Final notification: Dec. 15

Director: Stephen C. Doberstein.

Trustees: Eleanor S. Maroney, Advisory Tr.; Ernest N. May, Jr., Advisory Tr.; Irenee duPont, Jr.

Number of staff: 1 part-time professional; 1 part-time support.

EIN: 516015063

Selected grants: The following grants were reported in 2005.

$750,000 to Mount Cuba Astronomical Observatory, Wilmington, DE. For equipment.

$750,000 to William Penn Charter School, Philadelphia, PA. For capital campaign.

$670,000 to Chemical Heritage Foundation, Philadelphia, PA. For capital support.

$615,870 to University of Delaware, Newark, DE. For capital campaign.

$500,000 to Hagley Museum and Library, Wilmington, DE. For capital campaign.

$500,000 to Teton Valley Ranch Camp (TVRC) Education Foundation, Jackson, WY. For capital campaign.

$100,000 to Salvation Army of Wilmington, Wilmington, DE. For capital campaign.

$50,000 to Nativity Preparatory School of Wilmington, Wilmington, DE. For capital campaign.

$35,000 to Howard J. Weston Community and Senior Center, New Castle, DE. For building repairs.

$25,000 to Delaware Architecture Foundation, Wilmington, DE. For restoration.

1703
CTW Foundation, Inc. ◇
(formerly Beneficial Foundation, Inc.)
c/o Finn M.W. Casperson, V.P.
P.O. Box 911
Wilmington, DE   19899-0911   (302) 429-9425
Contact: Robert A. Tucker, Pres.
Application address: P.O. Box 2205, Wilmington, DE 19899; NJ tel.: (908) 781-3010

Incorporated in 1951 in DE.

Donors: Beneficial Corp.; Beneficial New Jersey.

Foundation type: Company-sponsored foundation.

Financial data (yr. ended 12/31/04): Assets, $13,526,721 (M); expenditures, $1,021,884; qualifying distributions, $837,637; giving activities include $803,525 for 15 grants (high: $250,000; low: $5,000), and $14,000 for 3 grants to individuals (high: $7,000; low: $3,000).

Purpose and activities: The foundation supports organizations involved with arts and culture,

secondary and higher education, and medical research.

Fields of interest: Arts; Secondary school/education; Higher education; Higher education, university; Scholarships/financial aid; Hospitals (general); Medical research.

Type of support: Continuing support; Annual campaigns; Building/renovation; Equipment; Program development; Seed money; Research; Employee-related scholarships.

Limitations: Giving on a national basis. No grants for endowments; no loans.

Application information:

Initial approach: Proposal
Deadline(s): Oct. 1
Board meeting date(s): Usually in May and Dec.

Officers and Directors:* Robert A. Tucker,* Pres.; Finn M.W. Caspersen,* V.P.; Eileen D. Dickey, Secy.; Charles W. Bower, Treas.; Finn M.W. Caspersen, Jr.; James H. Gilliam, Jr.; John O. Williams.

Number of staff: 2 part-time support.

EIN: 516011637

Selected grants: The following grants were reported in 2003.

$250,000 to Brown University, John Carter Brown Library, Providence, RI.

$250,000 to Westerly Hospital Foundation, Westerly, RI.

$150,000 to Princeton International Regatta Association, Princeton Junction, NJ.

$25,000 to Morgan State University, Baltimore, MD.

$25,000 to New Jersey Museum of Agriculture, North Brunswick, NJ.

$15,000 to Drew University, Madison, NJ.

$15,000 to Shakespeare Theater of New Jersey, Madison, NJ.

$15,000 to Wesleyan University, Middletown, CT.

$10,000 to Cardigan Mountain School, Canaan, NH.

$10,000 to Harness Racing Museum and Hall of Fame, Goshen, NY.

1704
Nancy Sayles Day Foundation ◇
c/o Wilmington Trust Co.
1100 N. Market St.
Wilmington, DE   19890-0001

Trust established in 1964 in CT.

Donors: Nancy Sayles Day‡; Mrs. Lee Day Gillespie.

Foundation type: Independent foundation.

Financial data (yr. ended 9/30/05): Assets, $14,576,578 (M); expenditures, $1,376,031; qualifying distributions, $1,242,540; giving activities include $1,228,994 for 6 grants (high: $1,000,000; low: $5,000).

Fields of interest: Arts; Higher education; Education; Environment, natural resources; Hospitals (general).

Type of support: General/operating support; Continuing support.

Limitations: Applications not accepted. Giving primarily in MA. No grants to individuals, or for building or endowment funds, research, or matching gifts; no loans.

Application information: Contributes only to pre-selected organizations.

Trustees: Susan Nickel; Mary West; Wilmington Trust Co.

EIN: 066071254

1705
Beatrice P. Delany Charitable Trust ▼ ✧
c/o JPMorgan Chase Bank, N.A.
P.O. Box 6089
Newark, DE   19714-6089
Contact: Ronald Lelen
Application address: c/o JPMorgan Chase Bank, N.A., 345 Park Ave., 8th Fl., New York, NY 10154

Trust established about 1977 in NY.
Donor: Beatrice P. Delany†.
Foundation type: Independent foundation.
Financial data (yr. ended 10/31/05): Assets, $100,968,192 (M); expenditures, $20,519,985; qualifying distributions, $20,322,750; giving activities include $20,215,000 for grants.
Purpose and activities: Giving largely for education, especially higher education, hospitals, health organizations, religion, and cultural programs.
Fields of interest: Arts; Higher education; Education; Hospitals (general); Health care; Health organizations, association; Religion.
Type of support: General/operating support.
Limitations: Giving primarily in the metropolitan Chicago, IL, area. No grants to individuals.
Application information: Application form not required.
Initial approach: Proposal
Deadline(s): None
Trustee: JPMorgan Chase Bank, N.A.
EIN: 136748171
Selected grants: The following grants were reported in 2004.
$3,000,000 to Devereux Foundation, Villanova, PA. For general support.
$1,027,500 to Rush University Medical Center, Chicago, IL. For general support.
$1,000,000 to Illinois Institute of Technology, Chicago, IL. For general support.
$1,000,000 to Night Ministry, Chicago, IL. For general support.
$500,000 to Trinity Church, Boston, MA. For general support.
$350,000 to Lyric Opera of Chicago, Chicago, IL. For general support.
$50,000 to Saint Jude Childrens Research Hospital, Memphis, TN. For general support.
$27,500 to Evans Scholars Foundation, Golf, IL. For general support.
$25,000 to Lawrence Hall Youth Services, Chicago, IL. For general support.
$10,000 to Salvation Army of Chicago, Chicago, IL. For general support.

1706
Delaware Community Foundation ✧
P.O. Box 1636
Wilmington, DE   19899   (302) 571-8004
Contact: Elizabeth M. Bouchelle, Dir., Grants Admin.
FAX: (302) 571-1553; E-mail: info@delcf.org; Tel. for grant application inquiries: (302) 504-5239; E-mail for grant application inquiries: bbouchelle@delcf.org; Tel. for administered scholarships: (302) 504-5222; E-mail for administered scholarships: rgentsch@delcf.org; URL: http://www.delcf.org

Incorporated in 1986 in DE.
Foundation type: Community foundation.
Financial data (yr. ended 6/30/05): Assets, $188,911,440 (M); gifts received, $18,396,211; expenditures, $9,952,597; giving activities include $6,194,390 for 911 grants (high: $690,000; low: $15).
Purpose and activities: The foundation is a nonprofit, philanthropic community organization created by and for the people of Delaware to build community. The DCF is dedicated to inspiring and helping people of all backgrounds and means create lasting legacies to benefit the people of Delaware. It enables people with philanthropic interests to easily and effectively support the issues they care about by establishing a charitable fund at the foundation and recommending grants to nonprofit groups they want to support. The foundation offers personalized service, local expertise and community leadership. The foundation itself awards grants to qualified nonprofit organizations that serve Delawareans for selected programs and capital projects.
Fields of interest: Arts; Education; Environment; Animals/wildlife; Health care; Substance abuse, prevention; Health organizations, association; Crime/violence prevention, child abuse; Nutrition; Housing/shelter, development; Children/youth, services; Human services; Community development; Aging.
Type of support: Continuing support; Capital campaigns; Building/renovation; Equipment; Program development; Seed money; Technical assistance.
Limitations: Giving limited to DE. No support for religious organizations for sectarian purposes or educational institutions for capital projects. No grants to individuals (except for scholarships), or for annual fundraising campaigns, operating costs, endowments, debt reduction, or sports clubs or leagues.
Publications: Application guidelines; Annual report; Informational brochure; Newsletter.
Application information: Visit foundation Web site for application form and guidelines. Handwritten or faxed application forms are not accepted. Application form required.
Initial approach: Submit application form and attachments
Copies of proposal: 1
Deadline(s): Jan. 31 for Capital grants, and Sept. 30 for Program grants
Board meeting date(s): Quarterly
Final notification: Approx. 60 days
Officers and Directors:* Donald R. Kirtley,* Chair.; Thomas R. Pulsifer, Vice-Chair.; Fred C. Sears II, C.E.O. and Pres.; Richard A. Gentsch, Exec. V.P. and Dir., Admin. Svcs.; Hugh D. Leahy, Jr., Sr. V.P., S. Delaware Office; Gregory E. Johnson, M.P.A., Sr. V.P., Devel.; Kathleen F. McDonough, Secy.; Thomas D. Croft, Treas.; David G. Burton, Chair., Southern Delaware Advisory Comm.; William L. Allen, Jr.; Lisa Blunt-Bradley; James C. Borel; Linda L. Chick; William F. D'Alonzo; Linda G.J. Gilliam; Martha S. Gilman; Cecil C. Gordon, Jr.; Marc A. Ham; Paul H. Harrell, Jr.; Mary B. Hickok; D. Wayne Holden; Stephen P. Lamb; John A. "Drew" Langloh; Howard R. Layton; Caroline M. Lunger; Maria M. Matos; Geoffrey M. Rogers; Thomas J. Shopa; Julie Topkis-Scanlan; Mark A. Turner; Katherine K. Wilkinson; Thomas D. Wren.
Number of staff: 10 full-time professional; 2 part-time professional.
EIN: 222804785
Selected grants: The following grants were reported in 2005.
$25,000 to Canine Partners for Life, Cochranville, PA. For grant made through Lane McAlister Fund.
$25,000 to Faithful Friends, Wilmington, DE. For grant made through Lane McAlister Fund.
$25,000 to Tri-State Bird Rescue and Research, Newark, DE. For grant made through Lane McAlister Fund.
$20,000 to Boys and Girls Clubs of Delaware, Wilmington, DE. For Beating the Streets.
$20,000 to Slaughter Neck Community Action Agency, Lincoln, DE. For capital support.
$20,000 to Southern Delaware Horse Retirement Association, Georgetown, DE. For grant made through Lane McAlister Fund.
$20,000 to University of Delaware, Cooperative Extension, Newark, DE. For Hickory Tree Family Program.
$15,000 to Bayhealth Foundation, Dover, DE. For High School Wellness Centers.
$15,000 to Christmas in April, Wilmington, Wilmington, DE. For capital support.
$15,000 to New Knollwood Civic Association, Claymont, DE. For capital support.

1707
Devonwood Foundation ✧
c/o Wilmington Trust Co.
1100 N. Market St.
Wilmington, DE   19801-1243   (302) 651-1940

Established in 1968 in DE.
Donors: E.H. Brodie; L.S. Brodie.
Foundation type: Independent foundation.
Financial data (yr. ended 12/31/05): Assets, $13,053,706 (M); gifts received, $514,978; expenditures, $349,949; qualifying distributions, $324,343; giving activities include $320,180 for 21 grants (high: $100,000; low: $500).
Purpose and activities: Giving primarily for higher education and arts/cultural programs.
Fields of interest: Arts; Higher education.
Type of support: General/operating support; Endowments.
Limitations: Applications not accepted. Giving primarily in New York, NY and Durham, NC, with some giving in ME and NJ. No grants to individuals.
Application information: Contributes only to pre-selected organizations.
Trustees: Brenda B. Brodie; Bryson B. Brodie; Cameron K. Brodie; H. Keith H. Brodie; Tyler H. Brodie; Melissa B. Hanenberger; Wilmington Trust Co.
EIN: 516024607
Selected grants: The following grants were reported in 2005.
$80,000 to South Eastern Efforts Developing Sustainable Spaces (SEEDS), Durham, NC.
$74,680 to Duke University, Durham, NC.
$41,000 to Durham Academy, Durham, NC.
$5,000 to Columbia University, New York, NY.
$3,000 to Shady Hill School, Cambridge, MA.
$2,000 to Princeton University, Princeton, NJ.
$1,000 to Bowdoin College, Brunswick, ME.
$1,000 to Triangle Land Conservancy, Raleigh, NC.

1708
The Harriet Ford Dickenson Foundation ✧
c/o JPMorgan Chase Bank, N.A.
P.O. Box 6089
Newark, DE   19714-6089
Contact: James Largey, V.P. and Trust Off., JPMorgan Chase Bank, N.A.

Application address: c/o JPMorgan Chase Bank, N.A., 345 Park Ave., New York, NY 10154

Established about 1958 in NY.
Donor: Harriet Ford Dickenson†.
Foundation type: Independent foundation.
Financial data (yr. ended 12/31/05): Assets, $28,226,466 (M); expenditures, $5,333,460; qualifying distributions, $5,160,407; giving activities include $5,147,000 for 67 grants (high: $2,200,000; low: $750).
Purpose and activities: Giving primarily for the arts, botanical gardens, hospitals, a community foundation, and human services.
Fields of interest: Museums; Performing arts; Arts; Botanical gardens; Hospitals (general); Human services.
Limitations: Giving primarily in Broome County, and the New York, NY, area. No grants to individuals.
Application information:
Initial approach: Letter
Deadline(s): None
Advisory Committee: Gillian Attfield; Anne A. Hubbard; David J. Hubbard; Thomas J. Hubbard.
Trustee: JPMorgan Chase Bank, N.A.
EIN: 136047225
Selected grants: The following grants were reported in 2003.
$1,200,000 to New York City Ballet, New York, NY. For general support.
$1,050,000 to New York Botanical Garden, Bronx, NY. For general support.
$130,000 to Metropolitan Opera Association, New York, NY. For general support.
$25,000 to Adirondack Council, Elizabethtown, NY. For general support.
$25,000 to Audubon Society of New York State, Selkirk, NY. For general support.
$25,000 to Nature Conservancy, New York, NY. For general support.
$25,000 to New York Parks and Conservation Association, Albany, NY. For general support.
$25,000 to Peconic Land Trust, Southampton, NY. For general support.
$25,000 to Preservation League of New York State, Albany, NY. For general support.
$15,000 to Scenic Hudson, Poughkeepsie, NY. For general support.

1709
Eisenberg Family Charitable Trust ◇ ☆
c/o JPMorgan Chase Bank, N.A.
P.O. Box 6089
Newark, DE 19714-6089

Established in 1996 in NY.
Donor: Estelle Eisenberg†.
Foundation type: Independent foundation.
Financial data (yr. ended 4/30/05): Assets, $7,405,571 (M); gifts received, $3,485; expenditures, $480,852; qualifying distributions, $412,685; giving activities include $400,000 for 2 grants (high: $200,000; low: $200,000).
Fields of interest: Alzheimer's disease.
Limitations: Applications not accepted. No grants to individuals.
Publications: Grants list.
Application information: Contributes only to pre-selected organizations.
Board meeting date(s): Apr.
Trustee: JPMorgan Chase Bank, N.A.
EIN: 527091392

Selected grants: The following grants were reported in 2004.
$125,000 to Alzheimers Disease and Related Disorders Association, Easthampton, MA. 2 grants: $50,000, $75,000

1710
The Esperance Family Foundation ◇ ☆
c/o Foundation Source
501 Silverside Rd., Ste. 123
Wilmington, DE 19809

Donors: Roger S. Newton; Coco Newton.
Foundation type: Independent foundation.
Financial data (yr. ended 12/31/05): Assets, $10,390,720 (M); expenditures, $787,708; qualifying distributions, $743,493; giving activities include $743,493 for grants.
Fields of interest: Performing arts, music; Performing arts, education; YM/YWCAs & YM/YWHAs.
Limitations: Applications not accepted. Giving primarily in CT and MI. No grants to individuals.
Application information: Contributes only to pre-selected organizations.
Officers and Directors:* Roger S. Newton, Pres.; Alex Newton,* V.P.; Coco Newton,* V.P.; Keri Newton, V.P.; Russell Newton,* V.P.
EIN: 200494459

1711
Oliver Etnier Charitable Trust ◇
c/o Wilmington Trust Co.
1100 N. Market St.
Wilmington, DE 19890-0001
Contact: Elizabeth Fallon, Trust Off.

Established in 1989 in DE.
Donor: Oliver L. Etnier.
Foundation type: Independent foundation.
Financial data (yr. ended 4/30/05): Assets, $16,693,968 (M); expenditures, $842,426; qualifying distributions, $688,596; giving activities include $602,099 for 5 grants (high: $233,857; low: $19,969).
Purpose and activities: Scholarships awarded to local area high school graduates majoring in engineering, physics, or computer science at one of six qualifying universities.
Fields of interest: Higher education; Scholarships/financial aid.
Type of support: Scholarships—to individuals; Scholarship funds.
Limitations: Giving primarily in NJ, NY, and PA.
Application information: Grants selected by trustees.
Trustee: Wilmington Trust Co.
EIN: 516170516
Selected grants: The following grants were reported in 2003.
$208,380 to Carnegie Mellon University, Pittsburgh, PA.
$184,970 to Cornell University, Ithaca, NY.
$152,878 to Mount Union Area School District, Mount Union, PA.
$131,523 to Stevens Institute of Technology, Hoboken, NJ.
$74,244 to Rensselaer Polytechnic Institute, Troy, NY.

1712
The Evelyn Foundation ◇ ☆
c/o Foundation Source
501 Silverside Rd., Ste. 123
Wilmington, DE 19809-1377

Established in 2004 in DE.
Donors: Evelyn Freed; Frank Freed.
Foundation type: Independent foundation.
Financial data (yr. ended 12/31/05): Assets, $51,131 (M); gifts received, $3,832,680; expenditures, $3,658,035; qualifying distributions, $3,631,935; giving activities include $3,624,666 for 9 grants (high: $1,300,000; low: $5,000).
Fields of interest: Performing arts; Theological school/education; Christian agencies & churches.
Limitations: Applications not accepted. Giving primarily in CA. No grants to individuals.
Application information: Contributes only to pre-selected organizations.
Officers and Directors:* Evelyn Freed,* Pres. and Secy.; Robert Hutchins,* V.P.; Alan Tuck III, V.P.; Barry Tuck,* V.P.; Brett Tuck, V.P.; Richard Watts,* V.P.
EIN: 201296329

1713
Fair Play Foundation ◇
100 W. 10th St., Ste. 1010
Wilmington, DE 19801
Contact: Blaine T. Phillips, Pres.

Established about 1961 in DE.
Foundation type: Independent foundation.
Financial data (yr. ended 12/31/05): Assets, $13,125,476 (M); expenditures, $833,029; qualifying distributions, $668,901; giving activities include $560,000 for 47 grants (high: $50,000; low: $5,000).
Fields of interest: Museums; Arts; Higher education; Environment, water resources; Animals/wildlife, preservation/protection.
Type of support: Building/renovation; Equipment; Land acquisition.
Limitations: Giving on a national basis. No support for business-oriented organizations.
Application information: Application form not required.
Initial approach: 1-page Letter
Copies of proposal: 1
Deadline(s): Oct. 1
Board meeting date(s): Dec.
Final notification: Positive responses only
Officer and Trustees:* Blaine T. Phillips,* Pres. and Exec. Dir.; James F. Burnett; Thomas H. Fooks V; Milbrey R. Jacobs; Blaine T. Phillips, Jr.; W. Halsey Spruance, Jr.
Number of staff: 1 full-time professional.
EIN: 516017779
Selected grants: The following grants were reported in 2004.
$50,000 to University of Virginia, Charlottesville, VA. 2 grants: $25,000 to School of Law (For Environmental Law professorship), $25,000 to Virginia Center for Digital History (For Digitizing History of Eastern Shore of Delaware, Maryland, Virginia, and Chesapeake Bay).
$45,000 to Chesapeake Bay Foundation, Annapolis, MD. For Oyster and Crab restoration program.
$45,000 to Conservation Fund, Arlington, VA.

$25,000 to Hagley Museum and Library, Wilmington, DE. For restorations and enhancement of security.

$25,000 to Winterthur Museum, Garden and Library, Winterthur, DE. For restoration of Garden Statuary and Ornaments.

$20,000 to African Elephant Conservation Trust, Newburyport, MA. For Elephant research.

$20,000 to Delaware Wild Lands, Odessa, DE.

$20,000 to National Fish and Wildlife Foundation, DC.

$15,000 to Brandywine Conservancy, Chadds Ford, PA. For replacement of landscaping equipment that had been stolen.

1714
Glencoe Foundation, Inc. ✧
Greenville Ctr., Bldg. C, Ste. 300
3801 Kennett Pike, Ste. C-300
Greenville, DE 19807-2377 (302) 654-9933
Contact: Ellice McDonald, Jr., Pres.

Established in 1975 in DE.
Donors: Ellice McDonald, Jr.; Rosa H. McDonald.
Foundation type: Independent foundation.
Financial data (yr. ended 12/31/04): Assets, $6,079,764 (M); gifts received, $51,000; expenditures, $471,678; qualifying distributions, $462,082; giving activities include $462,082 for 2 grants (high: $431,932; low: $30,000).
Purpose and activities: Gives exclusively to Scottish and American charitable organizations, such as museums, hospitals, educational institutions, and other publicly-oriented organizations that promote and preserve Scottish-American traditions and culture located in the Highlands and the islands of Scotland.
International interests: Scotland.
Type of support: General/operating support; Continuing support; Building/renovation; Equipment; Emergency funds; Program development.
Limitations: Giving limited to the Highlands and islands of Scotland. No grants to individuals, or for scholarships, fellowships, or matching gifts; no loans.
Publications: Application guidelines.
Application information: Application form required.
Initial approach: Proposal
Copies of proposal: 1
Deadline(s): None
Board meeting date(s): Annually and as required
Final notification: 2 to 3 months
Officers and Directors:* Ellice McDonald, Jr.,* Pres.; Rosa H. McDonald,* V.P.; John C. Milner, Secy.-Treas.; Gregory A. Inskip; John P. Sinclair.
EIN: 510164761

1715
Good Samaritan, Inc. ✧
600 Ctr. Mill Rd.
Wilmington, DE 19807-1502 (302) 654-7558
Contact: Ed N. Carpenter II, Pres.

Incorporated in 1938 in DE.
Donor: Elias Ahuja‡.
Foundation type: Independent foundation.
Financial data (yr. ended 12/31/05): Assets, $37,406,776 (M); expenditures, $2,397,848; qualifying distributions, $1,997,493; giving activities include $1,989,000 for 25 grants (high:

$250,000; low: $10,000; average: $25,000–$50,000).
Purpose and activities: Giving primarily for higher education; funding also for hospitals, particularly a cancer center, and human services.
Fields of interest: Secondary school/education; Higher education; Education; Hospitals (general); Cancer research; Human services; Economically disadvantaged.
International interests: Italy.
Type of support: General/operating support; Endowments; Program development; Conferences/seminars; Professorships.
Limitations: Giving primarily in the U.S., with some emphasis on DE. No grants to individuals, or for building funds, or other capital assets.
Publications: Application guidelines.
Application information: Application form not required.
Initial approach: Proposal
Copies of proposal: 1
Deadline(s): 4 weeks before 1st Thurs. in June and Nov.
Board meeting date(s): As required
Officers and Directors:* Ed N. Carpenter II,* Pres.; Carroll M. Carpenter, V.P.; Lea C. duPont,* V.P.; Jeffrey M. Nielsen, Secy.-Treas.; Rev. Edmund K. Sherrill II; H. Sinclair Sherrill.
Number of staff: 1 part-time support.
EIN: 516000401
Selected grants: The following grants were reported in 2004.
$178,700 to Massachusetts General Hospital, Boston, MA.
$125,874 to Childrens Hospital Corporation, Boston, MA.
$125,000 to Big Sister Association of Greater Boston, Boston, MA.
$100,000 to Episcopal Theological Seminary of the Southwest, Austin, TX.
$75,000 to Lesley University, Cambridge, MA.
$70,000 to Linden Hill School, Northfield, MA.
$55,042 to Delaware Technical and Community College, Dover, DE.
$50,000 to Stand Up for Whats Right and Just, Wilmington, DE.
$50,000 to Urban League, Metropolitan Wilmington, Wilmington, DE.
$15,000 to Delaware Adolescent Program, Wilmington, DE.

1716
The Jai N. Gupta Family Foundation, Inc. ✧ ☆
c/o Foundation Source
501 Silverside Rd., Ste. 123
Wilmington, DE 19809-1377

Established in 2004 in DE.
Donors: Jai Gupta; Shashi Gupta; RSSJ Associates, LLC.
Foundation type: Independent foundation.
Financial data (yr. ended 12/31/05): Assets, $1,019,499 (M); gifts received, $576,890; expenditures, $340,468; qualifying distributions, $334,516; giving activities include $325,000 for 2 grants (high: $250,000; low: $75,000).
Purpose and activities: Giving primarily to a university; support also for a Hindu temple.
Fields of interest: Higher education; Hinduism.
Limitations: Applications not accepted. Giving primarily in IN and VA. No grants to individuals.

Application information: Contributes only to pre-selected organizations.
Officer and Director:* Jai N. Gupta,* Pres.
EIN: 202029865

1717
Gynesis Women's International Foundation ✧ ☆
(formerly Des Femmes International Foundation)
c/o Wilmington Trust Co.
1100 N. Market St.
Wilmington, DE 19890-0900

Established in 2002 in DE.
Donor: Scaler Foundation, Inc.
Foundation type: Independent foundation.
Financial data (yr. ended 7/31/05): Assets, $7,170,961 (M); expenditures, $650,752; qualifying distributions, $516,007; giving activities include $465,070 for 7 grants (high: $130,510; low: $6,553).
Fields of interest: Education; Health care; Women; Young adults, female.
Limitations: Applications not accepted. Giving primarily in France. No grants to individuals.
Application information: Contributes only to pre-selected organizations.
Officer and Directors:* Antoinette Fougue,* Pres.; Sylvinia Boissonnas; Michele Idels; Elisabeth Nicoli; Florence Prudhomme.
EIN: 510412529

1718
Evelyn A. J. Hall Charitable Trust ✧
c/o JPMorgan Chase Bank, N.A., Svcs. Dept.
P.O. Box 6089
Newark, DE 19714-6089

Established in 1952 in NY.
Donor: Evelyn A. Hall.
Foundation type: Independent foundation.
Financial data (yr. ended 12/31/05): Assets, $5,965,132 (M); expenditures, $593,865; qualifying distributions, $560,095; giving activities include $557,250 for grants.
Purpose and activities: Primary areas of interest include cultural programs, hospitals, and medical research.
Fields of interest: Museums; Historic preservation/historical societies; Arts; Higher education; Environment, natural resources; Hospitals (general); Medical research, institute; Human services; Children/youth, services; Community development.
Type of support: General/operating support.
Limitations: Applications not accepted. Giving primarily in FL and New York, NY. No grants to individuals.
Application information:
Board meeting date(s): Varies
Trustee: JPMorgan Chase Bank, N.A.
EIN: 236286760

1719
D.A. Hamel Family Charitable Trust ✧
c/o JPMorgan Chase Bank, N.A.
P.O. Box 6089
Newark, DE 19714-6089

Established in 1986 in NY.
Foundation type: Independent foundation.

Financial data (yr. ended 11/30/05): Assets, $11,594,110 (M); expenditures, $486,335; qualifying distributions, $403,509; giving activities include $387,500 for 27 grants (high: $135,000; low: $500).
Purpose and activities: Giving primarily for health care and to historical societies; funding also for education and human services.
Fields of interest: Historic preservation/historical societies; Arts; Higher education; Libraries (public); Education; Hospitals (general); Recreation, centers; Human services; Children, services.
Type of support: General/operating support; Building/renovation.
Limitations: Applications not accepted. Giving primarily in FL, MA and NH; some funding nationally. No grants to individuals.
Application information: Contributes only to pre-selected organizations.
Trustees: Dana A. Hamel; Kathryn P. Hamel; JPMorgan Chase Bank, N.A.
EIN: 136873334

1720

The Russell P. & Elizabeth Crimian Heuer Foundation ✧ ☆
(formerly The Heuer Foundation)
c/o Wilmington Trust Co.
1100 N. Market St.
Rodney Sq. N.
Wilmington, DE   19890-1243

Established about 1980 as the Russell Pearce & Elizabeth Crimian Heuer Foundation.
Donors: Charlotte H. de Serio; Russell P. Heuer, Jr.‡.
Foundation type: Independent foundation.
Financial data (yr. ended 11/30/05): Assets, $4,128,409 (M); expenditures, $635,599; qualifying distributions, $609,991; giving activities include $572,500 for 14 grants (high: $375,000; low: $2,500).
Fields of interest: Higher education, college; Higher education, university; Hospitals (general).
Type of support: General/operating support.
Limitations: Applications not accepted. Giving primarily in PA. No grants to individuals.
Application information: Contributes only to pre-selected organizations.
 Board meeting date(s): April
Trustees: Charlotte H. de Serio; James Johnston; William R. Watson; Wilmington Trust Co.
EIN: 510255378
Selected grants: The following grants were reported in 2003.
$50,000 to Baldwin School, Bryn Mawr, PA.
$50,000 to Hereditary Neurological Disease Center, Wichita, KS. For general support.
$30,500 to Center for the Blind and Visually Impaired, Chester, PA. For general support.
$30,000 to Bryn Mawr Hospital Foundation, Bryn Mawr, PA. For general support.
$25,000 to Council of Independent Colleges, DC. For general support.
$20,000 to Bowdoin Summer Music Festival, Brunswick, ME. For general support.
$18,000 to Villanova University, Villanova, PA. For general support for Criminal Justice Admin Scholarship Program.
$15,000 to Saint Lawrence University, Canton, NY. For general support.
$10,000 to Delaware Valley Science Fairs, Philadelphia, PA. For general support.

$10,000 to Moore College of Art and Design, Philadelphia, PA. For general support.

1721

Irma T. Hirschl Trust for Charitable Purposes ✧
c/o JPMorgan Chase Bank, N.A., Svcs. Dept.
P.O. Box 6089
Newark, DE   19714-6089

Trust established in 1973 in NY.
Donor: Irma T. Hirschl‡.
Foundation type: Independent foundation.
Financial data (yr. ended 10/31/05): Assets, $57,466,806 (M); expenditures, $3,159,736; qualifying distributions, $3,085,038; giving activities include $2,946,000 for 20 grants (high: $510,000; low: $5,000).
Purpose and activities: Grants primarily to 6 medical schools for partial funding of selected medical research projects; annual medical scholarships to 6 designated medical schools; support also for 14 designated social service and health agencies.
Fields of interest: Higher education; Medical school/education; Health care; Medical research, institute; Human services; Federated giving programs; Jewish federated giving programs.
Type of support: Scholarship funds; Research.
Limitations: Applications not accepted. Giving primarily in New York, NY. No support for private foundations. No grants to individuals (except for Medical Scholar Program).
Application information: Unsolicited requests for funds not accepted.
Trustees: Robert Todd Lang; Leo Schmolka; JPMorgan Chase Bank, N.A.
EIN: 136356381
Selected grants: The following grants were reported in 2005.
$510,000 to Weill Medical College of Cornell University, New York, NY.
$460,000 to Albert Einstein College of Medicine of Yeshiva University, Bronx, NY.
$460,000 to Columbia University, New York, NY.
$435,000 to New York University, School of Medicine, New York, NY.
$310,000 to Mount Sinai School of Medicine of New York University, New York, NY.
$230,000 to Rockefeller University, New York, NY.
$104,000 to New York Foundling Hospital, New York, NY.
$62,000 to Visiting Nurse Service of New York, New York, NY.
$47,000 to Jewish Guild for the Blind, New York, NY.
$43,000 to Hebrew Home for the Aged at Riverdale, Riverdale, NY.

1722

Renate, Hans & Maria Hofmann Trust ✧
(formerly Hofmann Article 5 Charitable Trust)
c/o JPMorgan Chase Bank, N.A., Svcs. Dept.
P.O. Box 6089
Newark, DE   19714-6089

Established in 1996 in NY.
Foundation type: Independent foundation.
Financial data (yr. ended 6/30/05): Assets, $38,627,476 (M); expenditures, $1,027,181; qualifying distributions, $778,965; giving activities

include $467,940 for 5 grants (high: $400,000; low: $7,000).
Purpose and activities: Giving primarily to a Roman Catholic Church in Germany; funding also for the arts.
Fields of interest: Arts, association; Roman Catholic agencies & churches.
International interests: Germany.
Limitations: Applications not accepted. Giving on a national and international basis, primarily in New York, NY and Germany. No grants to individuals.
Application information: Contributes only to pre-selected organizations.
Trustees: Patricia A. Gallagher; Robert S. Warshaw; JPMorgan Chase Bank, N.A.
EIN: 137102172

1723

The Ada Howe Kent Foundation, Inc. ✧
1209 Orange St.
Wilmington, DE   19801

Incorporated in 1962 in DE.
Donor: Marjorie K. Kilpatrick‡.
Foundation type: Independent foundation.
Financial data (yr. ended 9/30/05): Assets, $12,200,829 (M); expenditures, $717,229; qualifying distributions, $654,444; giving activities include $534,000 for grants.
Purpose and activities: Giving for higher education and religious organizations carrying out studies and practical work in comparative religion; grants also for social service agencies.
Fields of interest: Higher education; Education; Religion.
Limitations: Applications not accepted. Giving primarily in MA and NY. No grants to individuals.
Application information: Contributes only to pre-selected organizations.
Officers and Directors:* John P. Campbell,* Pres.; Henry P. Renard,* V.P.; Edward Ortiz,* Secy.
EIN: 136066978
Selected grants: The following grants were reported in 2005.
$105,000 to Cornell University, Ithaca, NY. 2 grants: $30,000, $75,000
$75,000 to Harvard University, Cambridge, MA.
$75,000 to Smith College, Northampton, MA.
$50,000 to Clarkson University, Potsdam, NY.
$30,000 to Middlesex School, Concord, MA.
$5,000 to Juilliard School, New York, NY.

1724

The Kingsley Foundation ✧
c/o Wilmington Trust Co.
1100 N. Market St.
Wilmington, DE   19890-0900

Established in 1961 in CT.
Donors: F.G. Kingsley; Ora K. Smith.
Foundation type: Independent foundation.
Financial data (yr. ended 12/31/05): Assets, $7,119,181 (M); expenditures, $327,152; qualifying distributions, $320,975; giving activities include $320,250 for 35 grants (high: $65,000; low: $1,000).
Fields of interest: Museums; Performing arts; Performing arts, opera; Arts; Education; Environment; Hospitals (general).
Type of support: General/operating support.

Limitations: Applications not accepted. Giving primarily in NY; some giving also in CA, CT, Washington, DC, and ME. No grants to individuals.
Application information: Contributes only to pre-selected organizations.
Advisors: Catherine S. Cuthell; Elizabeth S. Reed; Margaret J. Smith; Ora K. Smith; Roger K. Smith.
Trustee: Wilmington Trust Co.
EIN: 516163698

1725
Laffey-McHugh Foundation ✧
P.O. Box 2286
Wilmington, DE 19899 (302) 654-1680
Contact: David Sysko
FAX: (302) 654-1681

Incorporated in 1959 in DE.
Donors: Alice L. McHugh†; Frank A. McHugh, Jr.†.
Foundation type: Independent foundation.
Financial data (yr. ended 12/31/03): Assets, $66,213,669 (M); expenditures, $3,912,093; qualifying distributions, $3,488,763; giving activities include $3,414,040 for 141 grants (high: $200,000; low: $1,500).
Purpose and activities: Grants for Roman Catholic church support and church-related institutions, including schools, welfare agencies, religious associations, child welfare agencies, and a school for the handicapped; support also for a community fund, higher education, and hospitals.
Fields of interest: Elementary/secondary education; Secondary school/education; Higher education; Hospitals (general); Human services; Children/youth, services; Federated giving programs; Roman Catholic federated giving programs; Roman Catholic agencies & churches; Religion; Disabilities, people with.
Type of support: Annual campaigns; Building/renovation; Equipment; Land acquisition; Emergency funds; Seed money; Matching/challenge support.
Limitations: Giving primarily in DE, with emphasis on Wilmington. No grants to individuals, or for operating budgets, endowment funds, research, demonstration projects, publications, conferences, professorships, internships, consulting services, technical assistance, scholarships, or fellowships; no loans or program-related investments.
Application information: Application form not required.
Initial approach: Letter
Copies of proposal: 1
Deadline(s): Apr. and Oct.
Board meeting date(s): May and Nov.
Final notification: Shortly after board meeting
Officers and Directors:* Arthur G. Connolly, Jr.,* Pres.; Arthur G. Connolly III,* V.P.; Collins J. Seitz, Jr.,* V.P.; Mary C. Braun,* Secy.; Thomas A. Connolly,* Treas.; Arthur G. Connolly, Sr.; Marie Louise McHugh.
EIN: 516015095

1726
Lennox Foundation
c/o Foundation Source
501 Silverside Rd., Ste 123
Wilmington, DE 19809
Application address: c/o David H. Anderson, Treas., 1114 State St., Ste. 200, Santa Barbara, CA 93101-2767, tel.: (805) 963-6503

Incorporated in 1951 in IA.
Donor: Lennox Industries, Inc.
Foundation type: Independent foundation.
Financial data (yr. ended 12/31/05): Assets, $31,443,318 (M); expenditures, $1,387,909; qualifying distributions, $1,278,399; giving activities include $1,202,460 for 24 grants (high: $100,000; low: $5,460).
Purpose and activities: Grants primarily for land conservation, human services, education, health, and arts and culture.
Fields of interest: Arts; Education; Environment, land resources; Health care; Human services.
Type of support: General/operating support; Continuing support; Annual campaigns; Capital campaigns; Building/renovation; Equipment; Land acquisition; Program development; Matching/challenge support.
Limitations: Applications not accepted. Giving limited to areas of family involvement in CA, IA, ID, MA, and ME. No grants to individuals.
Application information: Unsolicited requests for funds not accepted.
Board meeting date(s): Mar. and Sept.
Officers and Trustees:* Betsy L. Booth,* Chair.; Frank Zink,* Vice-Chair.; Lynn B. Storey,* Secy.; David H. Anderson,* Treas.; Beth A. Booth; Cathy Houlihan; Meg James; Laura Newman; Stefan Norris; Andrew Rattner; John Zink.
EIN: 426053380
Selected grants: The following grants were reported in 2004.
$100,000 to Nature Conservancy of Texas, San Antonio, TX.
$100,000 to Preble Street Resource Center, Portland, ME.
$74,966 to Iowa State University Foundation, Ames, IA.
$70,000 to Planned Parenthood Mar Monte, San Jose, CA.
$60,000 to Land Trust Alliance, DC.
$50,000 to Nature Conservancy, Arlington, VA.
$37,500 to Portland Trails, Portland, ME.
$31,828 to World Wildlife Fund, DC.
$25,000 to Center for Cultural Exchange, Portland, ME.
$20,000 to Sunbridge College, Spring Valley, NY.

1727
Longwood Foundation, Inc. ▼ ✧
100 W. 10th St., Ste. 1109
Wilmington, DE 19801
Contact: Peter C. Morrow, Exec. Dir.

Incorporated in 1937 in DE.
Donor: Pierre S. duPont†.
Foundation type: Independent foundation.
Financial data (yr. ended 9/30/05): Assets, $785,221,853 (M); expenditures, $36,370,014; qualifying distributions, $30,961,384; giving activities include $30,528,172 for 79 grants (high: $14,000,000; low: $4,500; average: $50,000–$1,000,000).
Purpose and activities: Primary obligation is the support, operation, and development of Longwood Gardens, which is open to the public; limited grants generally to educational institutions, to local hospitals for construction purposes, and to social service and youth agencies, and cultural programs.
Fields of interest: Arts; Education, fund raising/fund distribution; Education; Hospitals (general); Human services; Youth, services.

Type of support: Capital campaigns; Building/renovation; Equipment; Land acquisition.
Limitations: Giving primarily in DE and southern Chester County, PA. No grants to individuals, or for special projects or events. Generally no grants for endowments or operating support.
Application information: Application form not required.
Initial approach: Letter (2 pages) and proposal
Copies of proposal: 1
Deadline(s): Mar. 15 and Sept. 15
Board meeting date(s): May and Nov.
Final notification: The following board meeting (approximately 60 days)
Officers and Trustees:* H. Rodney Sharp III,* Pres.; Edward B. duPont,* V.P.; Irenee duPont May,* Secy.; Henry H. Silliman, Jr.,* Treas.; Peter C. Morrow, Exec. Dir.; Charles T.L. Copeland; Gerret van S. Copeland; David L. Craven; Eleuthere I. duPont; Pierre S. duPont IV.
Number of staff: 4 full-time professional; 1 part-time professional.
EIN: 510066734
Selected grants: The following grants were reported in 2005.
$2,000,000 to Tatnall School, Wilmington, DE.
$1,000,000 to Archmere Academy, Claymont, DE.
$1,000,000 to Delaware Art Museum, Wilmington, DE.
$1,000,000 to W H Y Y, Wilmington, DE.
$1,000,000 to Wilmington College, New Castle, DE.
$1,000,000 to YMCA of Delaware, Wilmington, DE.
$850,000 to Wilmington Music School, Wilmington, DE.
$500,000 to Layton Preparatory School, New Castle, DE.
$500,000 to Modern Maturity Center, Dover, DE.
$500,000 to Saint Edmunds Academy, Pittsburgh, PA.

1728
The Marmot Foundation ✧
100 W. 10th St., Ste. 1109
Wilmington, DE 19801-1694
Contact: Charles F. Gummey, Jr., Secy. (for DE organizations)
Application address for FL organizations: P.O. Box 2468, Palm Beach, FL 33480

Established in 1968 in DE.
Donor: Margaret F. duPont Trust.
Foundation type: Independent foundation.
Financial data (yr. ended 12/31/03): Assets, $31,691,697 (M); expenditures, $1,658,487; qualifying distributions, $1,516,891; giving activities include $1,500,000 for 108 grants (high: $60,000; low: $2,250).
Purpose and activities: Support for hospitals, health, higher and secondary education, (including libraries), community funds, cultural programs, (including museums), youth agencies, social services, literacy programs, and environmental and ecological organizations.
Fields of interest: Museums; Arts; Secondary school/education; Higher education; Adult education—literacy, basic skills & GED; Libraries/library science; Education, reading; Environment, natural resources; Environment; Hospitals (general); Reproductive health, family planning; Health care; Health organizations, association; Housing/shelter, development; Human services; Children/youth, services; Residential/custodial care, hospices; Homeless.

Type of support: Capital campaigns; Building/ renovation; Equipment; Land acquisition; Research; Matching/challenge support.

Limitations: Giving primarily in DE and FL. No support for political or religious organizations. No grants to individuals, or for operating budgets, endowments or scholarships; no loans.

Publications: Application guidelines.

Application information: Application form not required.

Initial approach: Letter
Copies of proposal: 1
Deadline(s): Apr. 30 and Oct. 31 for DE and Oct. 31 for FL.
Board meeting date(s): Late May and late Nov. in DE and late Nov. in FL.
Final notification: 2 weeks after board meeting

Officers and Trustees:* Willis H. duPont,* Chair.; Charles F. Gummey, Secy.; Lammot Joseph duPont; Miren duPont; Miren duPont Sanchez.

Number of staff: 1 part-time professional; 1 part-time support.

EIN: 516022487

Selected grants: The following grants were reported in 2004.

$60,000 to United Way of Delaware, Wilmington, DE. For general support.

$50,000 to Bascom Palmer Eye Institute, Miami, FL. For general support.

$50,000 to Rollins College, Winter Park, FL. For general support.

$50,000 to Tatnall School, Wilmington, DE. For general support.

$40,000 to Christiana Care Health System, Wilmington, DE. For general support.

$40,000 to University of Delaware, Newark, DE. For general support.

$35,000 to Brandywine Conservancy, Chadds Ford, PA. For general support.

$35,000 to Memorial Sloan-Kettering Cancer Center, New York, NY. For general support.

$30,000 to Delaware State University, Dover, DE. For general support.

$30,000 to Easter Seal Society of Del-Mar, New Castle, DE. For general support.

1729

The Charles A. Mastronardi Foundation ✧

(formerly The Charles A. Mastronardi Charitable Foundation)
c/o Wilmington Trust Co.
1100 N. Market St., Ste. 612230
Wilmington, DE 19890-0001 (212) 415-0526
Contact: Adrienne Iglehart

Established in 1964 in NY.

Donor: Charles A. Mastronardi‡.

Foundation type: Independent foundation.

Financial data (yr. ended 12/31/05): Assets, $21,004,307 (M); expenditures, $1,122,221; qualifying distributions, $1,017,853; giving activities include $961,000 for 85 grants (high: $105,000; low: $1,000).

Purpose and activities: Giving primarily for hospitals and children's services; funding also for higher education and human services.

Fields of interest: Secondary school/education; Higher education; Hospitals (general); Health organizations, association; Human services; Children, services; Child development, services; Civil liberties, right to life; Roman Catholic agencies & churches.

Type of support: General/operating support; Continuing support; Capital campaigns; Equipment; Seed money; Research.

Limitations: Giving primarily in NY; some funding nationally. No grants to individuals.

Application information: Application form not required.

Deadline(s): None
Board meeting date(s): May and Nov.

Officers: Olga DeFelippo, Exec. V.P.; Margaret Mastronardi, V.P.; Nicholas D. Mastronardi, V.P.; Bernadette Traub, V.P.; Mary Turino, V.P.

EIN: 136167916

1730

The MBNA Foundation ▼ ✧

1100 N. King St.
Wilmington, DE 19884-0723
Tel. for Cleveland Excellence in Education Grants: (216) 545-8000, (800) 410-6262, ext. 58000; Tel. for Cleveland Scholars Prog.: (216) 545-4178, (800) 410-6262, ext. 54178; Tel. for Community Donations: (302) 432-5205, (800) 205-8877, option 3; Tel. for Delaware Excellence in Education Grants and Helen F. Graham Grants: (302) 432-5288, (800) 205-8877, option 1; Tel. for Delaware Scholars Prog. and HBCU Scholarship Prog.: (302) 432-4800, option 2, (800) 205-8877, option 2; Tel. for Maine Excellence in Education Grants: (800) 386-6262, ext. 65886; Tel. for Maine Scholars Prog.: (800) 386-6262, ext. 65878; E-mail for Helen F. Graham Grants: grahamgrants@mbna.com; E-mail for Maine Excellence in Education Grants: mainegrants@mbna.com; URL: http://www.mbnafoundation.org

Established in 2000 in DE and ME.

Donors: MBNA America Bank, N.A.; The Cawley Family Foundation.

Foundation type: Company-sponsored foundation.

Financial data (yr. ended 12/31/05): Assets, $66,263,356 (M); gifts received, $30,841,779; expenditures, $36,766,565; qualifying distributions, $36,554,434; giving activities include $30,204,089 for 1,838 grants (high: $1,800,000; low: $57), and $5,779,216 for 227 grants to individuals (high: $7,100; low: $240).

Purpose and activities: The foundation supports organizations involved with arts and culture, education, health, human services, mentally disabled people, and economically disadvantaged people. Special emphasis is directed toward programs designed to improve the quality and availability of education; assist the less fortunate in communities; and promote the arts.

Fields of interest: Arts; Education, special; Education; Health care; Human services; Mentally disabled; Economically disadvantaged.

Type of support: General/operating support; Continuing support; Program development; Curriculum development; Employee volunteer services; Employee-related scholarships; Grants to individuals; Scholarships—to individuals.

Limitations: Giving primarily in areas of company operations, with emphasis on DE, ME, and OH. No support for religious organizations not of direct benefit to the entire community or political organizations or candidates. No grants for salaries or benefits, capital campaigns, large equipment purchases, school supplies customarily included in school budgets, private employer work programs, research, travel, or sponsorships or fundraising.

Application information: An application form is required for Excellence in Education Grants and scholarships. Proposals should be no longer than 1 to 2 pages.

Initial approach: Download application form and mail to foundation for Excellence in Education Grants; mail proposal to foundation for Community Donations; telephone foundation for application form for scholarships
Deadline(s): Sept. 30 for Community Donations; Dec. for scholarships
Final notification: Early Apr. for scholarships

Officers and Trustees:* Lance L. Weaver,* Chair.; Victor P. Manning,* Pres. and Exec. Dir.; John W. Scheflen,* Secy.; Vernon H.C. Wright,* Treas.; David B. Kedash, C.F.O.; Kenneth F. Boehl; John R. Cochran III; Stuart L. Markowitz; David W. Spartin; Penelope J. Taylor.

EIN: 522191136

Selected grants: The following grants were reported in 2004.

$1,800,000 to Cleveland Clinic Foundation, Cleveland, OH. For general support.

$1,400,000 to Christiana Care Health System, Wilmington, DE. For general support.

$1,100,000 to Saint Benedicts Preparatory School, Newark, NJ. For general support.

$1,000,000 to University of Delaware, Newark, DE. For general support.

$300,000 to Brandywine Conservancy, Chadds Ford, PA. For general support.

$200,000 to YMCA, Waldo County, Belfast, ME. For general support.

$50,000 to Greater Baltimore Medical Center, Towson, MD. For general support.

$25,000 to ARC of Howard County, Columbia, MD. For general support.

$20,000 to Wilma Theater, Philadelphia, PA. For general support.

$18,000 to Collinwood High School, Cleveland, OH.

1731

The John & Tammy Miller Private Foundation, Inc. ✧

(formerly The Foundation Source 9 Inc.)
c/o Foundation Source Phil. Svcs., Inc.
501 Silverside Rd., Ste. 123
Wilmington, DE 19809-1377

Established in 2002 in DE.

Donors: John Miller; Tammy Lee Miller.

Foundation type: Independent foundation.

Financial data (yr. ended 12/31/04): Assets, $2,388 (M); expenditures, $380,839; qualifying distributions, $377,307; giving activities include $375,000 for 2 grants (high: $325,000; low: $50,000).

Fields of interest: Food services; Human services.

Limitations: Applications not accepted. No grants to individuals.

Application information: Contributes only to pre-selected organizations.

Officer and Directors:* John Miller,* Pres. and Secy.; Tammy Lee Miller.

EIN: 010548653

1732

The Gerrish H. Milliken Foundation ✧

c/o Wilmington Trust Co.
1100 N. Market St.
Wilmington, DE 19890

Established in 1962 in CT and DE.
Donor: Gerrish H. Milliken, Jr.
Foundation type: Independent foundation.
Financial data (yr. ended 12/31/05): Assets, $5,918,667 (M); gifts received, $1,300,000; expenditures, $1,087,605; qualifying distributions, $1,083,975; giving activities include $1,083,250 for 119 grants (high: $252,500; low: $50).
Purpose and activities: Giving for education, environmental conservation, art and cultural programs, historical preservation and research, and health and human services.
Fields of interest: Historic preservation/historical societies; Higher education; Education; Environment; Health care; Human services; Government/public administration; Protestant agencies & churches.
Type of support: General/operating support.
Limitations: Applications not accepted. Giving primarily in the northeastern U.S. No grants to individuals.
Application information: Contributes only to pre-selected organizations.
Officer and Trustees:* James F. Zahrn,* Treas.; Peter Milliken; Phoebe Milliken; Roger Milliken.
EIN: 066037106
Selected grants: The following grants were reported in 2003.
$100,000 to Beatrix Farrand Society, Mount Desert, ME. For general support.
$25,000 to Friends of Acadia, Bar Harbor, ME. For general support.
$20,000 to Saint Mary of Providence, Chicago, IL. For general support.
$11,000 to Heritage Foundation, DC. For general support.
$10,000 to Audubon Society of Greenwich, Greenwich, CT. For general support.
$10,000 to Eagle Forum Education and Legal Defense Fund, Alton, IL. For general support.
$10,000 to Mount Desert Island Hospital, Bar Harbor, ME. For general support.
$5,000 to Greenwich Hospital, Greenwich, CT. For general support.
$5,000 to Greenwich Police Department, Greenwich, CT. For general support.
$5,000 to Maine Coast Heritage Trust, Topsham, ME. For general support.

1733
Morania Foundation, Inc. ◇
c/o JPMorgan Chase Bank, N.A.
P.O. Box 6089
Newark, DE   19714-6089   (302) 634-3820
Contact: William J. McCormack, Pres.

Incorporated in 1960 in NY.
Donor: William J. McCormack.
Foundation type: Independent foundation.
Financial data (yr. ended 10/31/05): Assets, $9,823,564 (M); expenditures, $1,111,744; qualifying distributions, $1,092,629; giving activities include $1,088,000 for 33 grants (high: $250,000; low: $1,000).
Purpose and activities: Grants largely for Roman Catholic church-related institutions, foreign missions, and welfare funds.
Fields of interest: Human services; Roman Catholic federated giving programs; Roman Catholic agencies & churches.
Limitations: Giving primarily in NY. No grants to individuals.

Application information: Application form not required.
Initial approach: Proposal
Deadline(s): None
Officers and Directors:* William J. McCormack,* Pres.; Julia M. Greenough,* V.P.; William M. Waterman,* Secy.
EIN: 136141577
Selected grants: The following grants were reported in 2004.
$140,000 to Catholic Relief Services, Baltimore, MD. 2 grants: $40,000, $100,000
$100,000 to Society for the Propagation of the Faith, New York, NY.
$50,000 to Catholic Near East Welfare Association, New York, NY.
$25,000 to Franciscan Sisters of the Poor, New York, NY.
$25,000 to Little Sisters of the Poor, Queens Village, NY.
$20,000 to Carmelite Sisters for the Aged and Infirm of Marion Manor, Germantown, NY.
$20,000 to Dominican Sisters Family Health Service, Ossining, NY.
$20,000 to Tropical Diseases Research Center, Ndola, Zambia. .
$10,000 to Student Sponsorship Programme Umfundaze, New York, NY.

1734
Mt. Cuba Center, Inc. ◇ ☆
100 W. 10th St., Ste. 1109
Wilmington, DE   19801
URL: http://www.mtcubacenter.org/index.htm

Incorporated in 1953 in DE.
Donor: Lammot duPont Copeland.
Foundation type: Independent foundation.
Financial data (yr. ended 12/31/05): Assets, $309,949,273 (M); expenditures, $9,532,742; qualifying distributions, $9,607,418; giving activities include $3,605,000 for 4 grants (high: $2,000,000; low: $500).
Purpose and activities: Giving primarily to foster an appreciation for plants of the Appalachian Piedmont and the conservation of their environment through garden display, education, and research.
Limitations: Applications not accepted. Giving limited to Wilmington, DE, and its 50-mile radius. No grants to individuals.
Application information: Contributes only to pre-selected organizations.
Officers: Blaine T. Phillips, Pres.; Charles L. Copeland, V.P.; Ann C. Rose, Secy.; David D. Shields, Treas.
Directors: Mrs. James C. Biddle; Gerret van S. Copeland; Lammot duPont Copeland; Louisa C. Duemling; Mrs. Nathan Hayward III; Mrs. William M.W. Sharp.
EIN: 516001265

1735
The Neuberger Berman Foundation ◇
c/o Neuberger Berman Trust Co. of Delaware
919 Market St., Ste. 506
Wilmington, DE   19801-3065

Established in 1999 in DE.
Donors: Neuberger Berman Inc.; Dietrich Weismann.
Foundation type: Company-sponsored foundation.

Financial data (yr. ended 12/31/04): Assets, $6,307,462 (M); expenditures, $531,611; qualifying distributions, $460,537; giving activities include $452,700 for 28 grants (high: $75,000; low: $2,000).
Purpose and activities: The foundation supports organizations involved with arts and culture, education, health, youth development, and human services.
Fields of interest: Museums; Performing arts; Arts; Higher education; Education; Health care; Disasters, fire prevention/control; Disasters, 9/11/01; Youth development; American Red Cross; Human services, emergency aid; Human services; Federated giving programs.
Type of support: General/operating support.
Limitations: Giving on a national basis in areas of company operations, with some emphasis on New York, NY. No grants to individuals.
Application information: Application form not required.
Initial approach: Proposal
Deadline(s): None
Advisory Committee: Jeffrey B. Lane; Robert Matza.
Trustee: Lehman Brothers Trust Co. of Delaware.
EIN: 527000306

1736
The Barnett and Annalee Newman Foundation ◇ ☆
c/o JPMorgan Chase Bank, N.A.
P.O. Box 6089
Newark, DE   19714-6089

Established in 1996 in NY.
Donor: Annalee Newman†.
Foundation type: Independent foundation.
Financial data (yr. ended 12/31/05): Assets, $32,539,036 (M); expenditures, $1,038,086; qualifying distributions, $938,000; giving activities include $938,000 for grants.
Purpose and activities: Giving primarily to the arts.
Fields of interest: Museums (art).
Limitations: Applications not accepted. Giving primarily in Philadelphia, PA. No grants to individuals.
Application information: Contributes only to pre-selected organizations.
Trustee: Frank Stella.
EIN: 137105549
Selected grants: The following grants were reported in 2003.
$200,000 to Philadelphia Museum of Art, Philadelphia, PA. For operating support.

1737
The Orange Tree Foundation ◇
P.O. Box 730
Wilmington, DE   19899-0730

Established in 1987 in VA.
Donors: Alletta DuPont Bredin-Bell; Octavia DuPont Bredin.
Foundation type: Independent foundation.
Financial data (yr. ended 6/30/05): Assets, $2,427,110 (M); gifts received, $300,000; expenditures, $575,982; qualifying distributions, $542,857; giving activities include $542,857 for 18 grants (high: $100,671; low: $1,000).
Fields of interest: Arts; Education; Environment; Human services.

Limitations: Applications not accepted. Giving primarily in VA; some funding nationally. No grants to individuals.
Application information: Contributes only to pre-selected organizations.
Officers and Directors:* Alletta DuPont Bredin-Bell,* Pres.; Thomas C.T. Brokaw,* Secy.; J. Bruce Bell; Mariana Bell.
EIN: 541394716
Selected grants: The following grants were reported in 2004.
$100,514 to World Healing Institute in Hawaii, Keswick, VA. For general support.
$99,775 to Operation Smile International, Norfolk, VA. For general support.
$9,925 to Nature Conservancy of Hawaii, Honolulu, HI. For general support.
$4,962 to Brady Center to Prevent Gun Violence, DC.
$4,962 to Davidson College, Davidson, NC. For general support.
$4,962 to Foxcroft School, Middleburg, VA. For general support.
$3,000 to Live Arts, Charlottesville, VA. For general support.
$3,000 to Piedmont Environmental Council, Warrenton, VA. For general support.
$3,000 to Rails to Trails Conservancy, DC. For general support.
$1,000 to RARE Center for Tropical Conservation, Arlington, VA. For general support.

1738
The Mary E. Parker Foundation ✧
c/o Wilmington Trust Co.
1100 N. Market St.
Wilmington, DE 19890-0900
Contact: Richard W. Pratt, Tr.
Application address: c/o C.P.A. Associates, 1301 6th Ave. W., Ste. 600, Bradenton, FL 34205

Established in 1986 in FL.
Donor: Mary E. Parker.
Foundation type: Independent foundation.
Financial data (yr. ended 12/31/05): Assets, $18,577,776 (M); expenditures, $925,918; qualifying distributions, $828,273; giving activities include $828,273 for 65 grants (high: $411,000; low: $1,000).
Purpose and activities: Giving for the arts, nursing, higher education, youth and social services, community funds, animal welfare, and guide dog training for the visually impaired.
Fields of interest: Museums; Arts; Higher education; Animal welfare; Nursing care; Human services; Children/youth, services; Federated giving programs.
Type of support: General/operating support; Endowments.
Limitations: Giving primarily in FL.
Publications: Informational brochure (including application guidelines).
Application information: Application form required.
Initial approach: Letter
Deadline(s): Nov. 15
Board meeting date(s): Dec.
Final notification: Positive responses only
Trustees: Robert G. Blalock; Mary E. Parker; Richard W. Pratt; Willett E. Wentzell; Wilmington Trust Co.
EIN: 592708325

1739
The L. E. Phillips Family Foundation, Inc. ▼ ✧
P.O. Box 4669
Wilmington, DE 19807
Contact: Melvin S. Cohen, Pres.
Application address: 3925 N. Hastings Way, Eau Claire, WI 54703, tel.: (715) 839-2139

Incorporated in 1943 in WI.
Donor: Members of the Phillips family and a family-related company.
Foundation type: Independent foundation.
Financial data (yr. ended 2/28/06): Assets, $74,312,067 (M); expenditures, $3,297,908; qualifying distributions, $3,331,136; giving activities include $3,168,171 for 107 grants (high: $2,421,081; low: $25; average: $100–$1,000).
Purpose and activities: Support primarily for a Jewish welfare fund; giving also for higher education, and human services.
Fields of interest: Arts; Higher education; Health organizations, association; Human services; Jewish federated giving programs; Jewish agencies & temples.
Type of support: General/operating support; Building/renovation; Endowments; Program development; Scholarship funds; Research.
Limitations: Giving primarily in northwestern WI, with emphasis on Eau Claire and Chippewa County. No grants to individuals.
Application information: Application form not required.
Initial approach: Letter
Deadline(s): None
Board meeting date(s): As required
Final notification: 1 month
Officers and Directors:* Melvin S. Cohen,* Pres.; Maryjo R. Cohen,* V.P. and Treas.; Edith Phillips,* V.P.; James F. Bartl,* Secy.; Eileen Cohen.
Number of staff: 1 full-time professional; 2 part-time support.
EIN: 396046126
Selected grants: The following grants were reported in 2006.
$2,421,081 to Melvin S. Cohen Trust, Eau Claire, WI. For Minneapolis Federation for Jewish Service.
$400,000 to W Y E S Greater New Orleans Educational Television, New Orleans, LA. For operating support.
$116,600 to University of Wisconsin Foundation, Eau Claire, WI. 2 grants: $61,000 (For internship program), $55,600 (For professorship).
$25,000 to Milwaukee Institute of Art and Design, Milwaukee, WI. For operating support.
$25,000 to Robey Charitable Trust, Clearwater, FL. For operating support.
$15,000 to Literacy Volunteers of America, Chippewa Valley Chapter, Eau Claire, WI. For operating support.
$15,000 to United Way of Greater Eau Claire, Eau Claire, WI. For operating support.

1740
The Presto Foundation ✧
1011 Centre Rd.
Wilmington, DE 19805
Contact: Norma Jaenke
Application address: 3925 N. Hastings Way, Eau Claire, WI 54703, tel.: (715) 839-2119

Incorporated in 1952 in WI.
Donor: National Presto Industries, Inc.
Foundation type: Company-sponsored foundation.
Financial data (yr. ended 5/31/05): Assets, $15,420,915 (M); expenditures, $743,024; qualifying distributions, $690,198; giving activities include $372,250 for 73 grants (high: $132,000; low: $50), and $310,208 for 31 grants to individuals (high: $11,000; low: $522).
Purpose and activities: The foundation supports organizations involved with arts and culture, education, the environment, health, recreation, youth development, human services, and religion.
Fields of interest: Media/communications; Arts; Higher education; Education; Environment; Hospitals (general); Health care; Recreation; Youth development; Human services; Federated giving programs; Religion.
Type of support: General/operating support; Employee-related scholarships.
Limitations: Giving primarily in northwestern WI, with emphasis on Chippewa and Eau Claire counties.
Application information:
Initial approach: Letter of inquiry
Deadline(s): None
Officers and Trustees:* Melvin S. Cohen,* Chair. and Pres.; Maryjo R. Cohen,* V.P. and Treas.; James F. Barti,* V.P.; John Frank,* V.P.; Randy F. Lieble,* V.P.; Arthur Petzold,* V.P.; Geraldine Eaton,* Secy.; Dean Boehne; Eileen Phillips Cohen; Richard Myhers.
EIN: 396045769

1741
Raskob Foundation for Catholic Activities, Inc. ▼ ✧
P.O. Box 4019
Wilmington, DE 19807-0019 (302) 655-4440
Contact: Frederick J. Perella, Jr., Exec. V.P.
FAX: (302) 655-3223; *URL:* http://www.rfca.org

Incorporated in 1945 in DE.
Donors: John J. Raskob†; Helena Raskob†.
Foundation type: Independent foundation.
Financial data (yr. ended 12/31/05): Assets, $142,454,356 (M); expenditures, $7,083,778; qualifying distributions, $6,178,370; giving activities include $4,844,350 for 421 grants (high: $637,112; low: $350; average: $1,000–$25,000).
Purpose and activities: To support Roman Catholic church organizations and activities worldwide by providing funds to official Catholic organizations for education, training, social services, health, emergency relief, as well as a wide variety of charitable needs.
Fields of interest: Education; Health care; Health organizations, association; Human services; Children/youth, services; International relief; Roman Catholic federated giving programs; Roman Catholic agencies & churches; Religion; Native Americans/American Indians; Economically disadvantaged.
Type of support: General/operating support; Management development/capacity building; Building/renovation; Equipment; Emergency funds; Program development; Conferences/seminars; Publication; Seed money; Curriculum development; Technical assistance; Consulting services; Program evaluation; Program-related investments/loans; Matching/challenge support.
Limitations: Giving to domestic and international programs affiliated with the Roman Catholic church. No grants to individuals, or for continuing support,

annual campaigns, deficit financing (except missions), endowment funds, tuition, scholarships, fellowships, individual research, capital campaigns, building projects prior to the start or after the completion of construction, continuing subsidies, or requests that are after-the-fact by the time of the spring and fall trustee meetings.

Publications: Application guidelines; Grants list.

Application information: The foundation does not accept applications via E-mail. Application form required.

> *Initial approach:* Request application package via mail or fax on organization letter head
> *Copies of proposal:* 1
> *Deadline(s):* Applications accepted for spring meeting from Dec. 8 to Feb. 8, for fall meeting from June 8 to Aug. 8
> *Board meeting date(s):* Early-May and mid-Nov.
> *Final notification:* 4 months

Officers and Trustees:* William F. Raskob III,* Chair.; Helen R. Doordan,* Pres.; Frederick J. Perella, Jr., Exec. V.P.; Anthony W. Raskob, Jr.,* 1st V.P.; Daniel M. Villalon, 2nd. V.P.; Patricia M. Garey, V.P., Grants Mgmt.; Kathleen D. Smith,* Secy.; Russell Raskob,* Treas.; Ann R. Borden; Noelle M. Fracyon; Sr. Patricia Geuting; Patrick W. McGrory; Richard G. Raskob; Timothy T. Raskob; Lucia I. Robinson; Margaret Y. Robinson.

Number of staff: 4 full-time professional; 6 full-time support; 1 part-time support.

EIN: 510070060

Selected grants: The following grants were reported in 2004.

$335,081 to PICO National Network, Oakland, CA. To implement Skipper Initiative by congregation-based community organizations in PICO Network.

$90,000 to Archdiocese of Santa Fe, Albuquerque, NM. Toward Interfaith LEAP, to develop one-stop Family Resource Center in Chimayo, to respond to issues of substance abuse, domestic violence, poverty, and mental health concerns of families and children in poor rural communities of northern New Mexico.

$80,204 to Kamwokya Christian Caring Community, Kampala, Uganda. To improve existing community structures and networks in Kamwokya II Parish HIV/AIDS Psychosocial Support Program and surrounding villages in order to mitigate medical, psychosocial, economic and physical effects of HIV/AIDS.

$50,000 to Holy Family Hospital, Bethlehem, West Bank/Gaza. Toward equipment, personnel, supplies, and overhead to run outpatient maternal and child health clinic.

$38,748 to Catholic Relief Services, Kumbo, Cameroon. To reduce impact of HIV/AIDS pandemic on orphans and vulnerable children in Kumbo Diocese, North West Province, Cameroon, through multi-faceted community-based approach through counseling, educational support, and financing of vocational training/apprenticeship program.

$35,000 to Brothers of the Sacred Heart, India. Toward purchase of furniture and equipment for technical school to empower and provide alternative livelihood skills to unemployed and young tribal drop-outs through non-formal education in the fields of tailoring and embroidery, computer education, cooking, and making of notebooks, hollow blocks, pickles, detergents, and disinfectants.

$12,500 to Diocese of Lubbock, Lubbock, TX. Toward salary/benefits, mileage, educational

literature, supplies of Legalization Outreach Coordinator to assist immigrants seeking legalization.

$10,000 to Mercy Outreach Center, Rochester, NY. For program support (personnel, supplies, equipment) of No Falling Thru the Cracks Mammography Program and Saving Lives Health Care Program, providing neighborhood comprehensive health care, dental and other human service and free prescriptions and onsite mammography.

$5,800 to Presentation College, Aberdeen, SD. For computer equipment for library on Lakota Campus located on Cheyenne River Sioux Reservation.

$4,700 to Seva Missionary Sisters of Mary, India. For labor, materials, transport to dig bore well, install pump, lay pipeline, and construct overhead water tank to provide clean drinking water for novices at Arul Jyothi Novitiate and surrounding community of Dalit families and repair toilets and lay bathroom tiles at Novitiate.

1742
The Repass-Rodgers Family Foundation, Inc. ☆

c/o Foundation Source
501 Silverside Rd., Ste. 123
Wilmington, DE 19809-1377

Established in 2002 in DE.
Donor: Randy Repass.
Foundation type: Independent foundation.
Financial data (yr. ended 12/31/05): Assets, $4,729,958 (M); expenditures, $696,222; qualifying distributions, $674,333; giving activities include $674,333 for grants.
Fields of interest: Secondary school/education; Higher education; Children/youth, services.
Limitations: Applications not accepted. No grants to individuals.
Application information: Contributes only to pre-selected organizations.
Officers and Directors:* Randy Repass,* Pres.; Sally-Christine Rodgers,* V.P.
EIN: 050545292

1743
Marshall Reynolds Foundation ◇

c/o Wilmington Trust Co.
1100 N. Market St.
Wilmington, DE 19801-1281

Established in DE.
Foundation type: Independent foundation.
Financial data (yr. ended 6/30/05): Assets, $27,443,116 (M); expenditures, $1,294,363; qualifying distributions, $1,189,928; giving activities include $1,115,170 for 46 grants (high: $100,000; low: $1,000).
Purpose and activities: Giving primarily for environmental conservation, health care, including hospitals, and to Quaker and Lutheran ministries and organizations; some giving also for education, and social services.
Fields of interest: Museums (natural history); Arts; Higher education; Libraries/library science; Education; Environment, natural resources; Hospitals (general); Reproductive health, family planning; Health care; Human services; YM/YWCAs & YM/YWHAs; Aging, centers/services;

International relief; Community development, neighborhood development; Protestant agencies & churches; Economically disadvantaged.
Limitations: Applications not accepted. Giving primarily in DE and PA, with emphasis on Philadelphia. No grants to individuals.
Application information: Contributes only to pre-selected organizations.
Trustees: Jacklen E. Powell, Exec. Tr.; Dorothea Morse; Richard A. Newman, M.D.; Minturn T. Wright III.
EIN: 233053828
Selected grants: The following grants were reported in 2004.

$80,000 to Academy of Natural Sciences of Philadelphia, Philadelphia, PA. For general support.

$30,000 to Chester County Library, Exton, PA. For Family Place Workshops.

$30,000 to Community Volunteers in Medicine, West Chester, PA. For general operating support.

$30,000 to YMCA of the Brandywine Valley, Coatesville, PA. For annual campaign.

$15,000 to Chester Springs Studio, Chester Springs, PA. For Art Partners studio program.

$10,000 to Metropolitan AIDS Neighborhood Nutrition Alliance (MANNA), Philadelphia, PA. For general support.

$10,000 to Natural Lands Trust, Media, PA. For general operating support.

$5,000 to Educating Children for Parenting, Philadelphia, PA. For general support.

$1,000 to Community Gardens of Chester County, Embreeville, PA. For general support.

$1,000 to Elderhostel, Boston, MA. For general support.

1744
Richard Robinson & Helen Benham Charitable Fund ◇

c/o JPMorgan Chase Bank, N.A.
P.O. Box 6089
Newark, DE 19714

Established in 1992 in NY.
Donor: Richard Robinson.
Foundation type: Independent foundation.
Financial data (yr. ended 11/30/05): Assets, $3,020,772 (M); expenditures, $549,447; qualifying distributions, $524,106; giving activities include $517,583 for 27 grants (high: $300,000; low: $250).
Purpose and activities: Giving primarily for children's services, and higher and other education.
Fields of interest: Higher education; Teacher school/education; Education; Hospitals (general); Human services; Children/youth, services.
Limitations: Applications not accepted. Giving primarily in NY; some funding also nationally. No grants to individuals.
Application information: Contributes only to pre-selected organizations.
Trustees: Helen Benham; Richard Robinson; JPMorgan Chase Bank, N.A.
EIN: 137005989
Selected grants: The following grants were reported in 2004.

$300,000 to Teachers College Columbia University, New York, NY. For general support.

$100,000 to Polytechnic Preparatory Country Day School, Brooklyn, NY. For general support.

$63,333 to Corlears School, New York, NY. For general support.

$60,000 to Harvard University, Graduate School of Education, Cambridge, MA. For general support.

$10,000 to Stand for Children Leadership Center, Portland, OR. For general support.

$5,000 to American Museum of Natural History, New York, NY. For general support.

$5,000 to Childrens Defense Fund, DC. For general support.

$5,000 to Childrens Foundation, DC. For general support.

$5,000 to Erikson Institute, Chicago, IL. For general support.

$5,000 to National Black Child Development Institute, DC. For general support.

1745
Maurice R. Robinson Fund, Inc. ◇
c/o JPMorgan Chase Bank, N.A.
P.O. Box 6089
Newark, DE 19714-6089
Application address: c/o Marian Steffens, Secy., Scholastic Corp., 100 Plz. Dr., Secaucus, NJ 07094

Established in 1960 in NY.
Donors: Maurice R. Robinson†; Florence L. Robinson†; Scholastic Inc.
Foundation type: Independent foundation.
Financial data (yr. ended 6/30/05): Assets, $11,429,753 (M); expenditures, $589,006; qualifying distributions, $533,648; giving activities include $530,000 for 4 grants (high: $505,000; low: $5,000).
Purpose and activities: Giving primarily for the arts and education.
Fields of interest: Arts, alliance; Museums; Arts; Higher education; Human services; Children/youth, services.
Type of support: Program development; Seed money; Curriculum development; Internship funds; Scholarship funds; Program-related investments/ loans.
Limitations: Giving primarily on the East Coast, with emphasis on the metropolitan New York, NY, area. No grants to individuals.
Application information:
Initial approach: Letter
Deadline(s): None
Board meeting date(s): Varies
Officers: Ernest Fleishman, Pres.; Marian Steffens, Secy.; John Quinn, Treas.
Trustee: JPMorgan Chase Bank, N.A.
Number of staff: 3 part-time professional.
EIN: 136161094
Selected grants: The following grants were reported in 2004.
$505,000 to Alliance for Young Artists and Writers, New York, NY. For general support.
$20,000 to Constitutional Rights Foundation, Los Angeles, CA. For general support.
$17,000 to Learning Leaders, New York, NY. For general support.
$10,000 to Bronx Charter School for Children, Bronx, NY. For general support.
$10,000 to Trinity College, DC. For general support.
$5,000 to Catamount Film and Arts Company, Saint Johnsbury, VT. For general support.
$5,000 to Fairbanks Museum and Planetarium, Saint Johnsbury, VT. For general support.

1746
The Roby Foundation ◇
c/o JPMorgan Services, Inc.
P.O. Box 6089
Newark, DE 19714-6089
Contact: Joe L. Roby, Comm. Member

Established in 1996 in NY.
Donor: Joe L. Roby.
Foundation type: Independent foundation.
Financial data (yr. ended 12/31/05): Assets, $2,428,035 (M); expenditures, $739,145; qualifying distributions, $703,992; giving activities include $697,100 for grants.
Purpose and activities: Giving primarily for education, the arts, and human services.
Fields of interest: Arts; Education; Health organizations, association; Human services.
Limitations: Giving primarily in New York, NY.
Application information: Application form not required.
Deadline(s): None
Distribution Committee: Hilppa A. Roby; Joe L. Roby.
Trustee: JPMorgan Chase Bank, N.A.
EIN: 133932915
Selected grants: The following grants were reported in 2004.
$511,000 to Vanderbilt University, Nashville, TN.
$25,000 to Central Park Conservancy, New York, NY.
$10,000 to American-Scandinavian Foundation, New York, NY.
$10,000 to Harvard Business School Fund, Boston, MA.
$6,000 to Allen-Stevenson School, New York, NY.
$1,000 to Gildas Club Worldwide, New York, NY.
$1,000 to Southampton Hospital Foundation, Southampton, NY.
$1,000 to Thomas G. Labrecque Foundation, New York, NY.
$500 to American Society for the Prevention of Cruelty to Animals, New York, NY.

1747
Romill Foundation ◇
c/o Wilmington Trust Co.
1100 N. Market St.
Wilmington, DE 19890-0900

Trust established in 1960 in SC.
Donors: Roger Milliken; Gerrish H. Milliken, Sr.; Justine V. Milliken.
Foundation type: Independent foundation.
Financial data (yr. ended 12/31/05): Assets, $7,216,417 (M); gifts received, $126,902; expenditures, $688,146; qualifying distributions, $675,534; giving activities include $674,809 for 20 grants (high: $255,000; low: $1,000).
Purpose and activities: Giving primarily for the arts and education.
Fields of interest: Arts councils; Historic preservation/historical societies; Arts; Higher education; Education; Boy scouts; Federated giving programs; Public affairs; Roman Catholic agencies & churches.
Type of support: General/operating support.
Limitations: Applications not accepted. Giving primarily in Spartanburg County, SC. No grants to individuals.
Application information: Contributes only to pre-selected organizations.
Board meeting date(s): As required

Officer: James F. Zahrn, Treas.
Trustees: Gerrish H. Milliken; Nancy Milliken; Roger Milliken; Justine V.R. Russell.
EIN: 136102069
Selected grants: The following grants were reported in 2004.
$455,000 to Arts Council of Spartanburg County, Spartanburg, SC. For general support.
$300,000 to Converse College, Spartanburg, SC. For general support.
$162,246 to Spartanburg Day School, Spartanburg, SC. For general support.
$50,000 to Eagle Forum Education and Legal Defense Fund, Alton, IL. For general support.
$30,000 to Southeastern Legal Foundation, Atlanta, GA. For general support.
$25,000 to Boy Scouts of America, Spartanburg, SC. For general support.
$25,000 to Yale University, New Haven, CT. For general support.
$20,000 to Freedom Alliance, Dulles, VA. For general support.
$13,750 to United Way of the Piedmont, Spartanburg, SC. For general support.
$10,000 to Northeast Harbor Library, Northeast Harbor, ME. For general support.

1748
Rowe Family Foundation ◇
c/o Foundation Source
501 Silverside Rd., Ste. 123
Wilmington, DE 19809

Established in 2004 in DE.
Donors: John Rowe; Valeria Rowe.
Foundation type: Independent foundation.
Financial data (yr. ended 12/31/05): Assets, $4,094,906 (M); gifts received, $4,114,650; expenditures, $3,190,252; qualifying distributions, $3,122,572; giving activities include $3,105,000 for 21 grants (high: $450,000; low: $5,000).
Fields of interest: Higher education; Education; Health care.
Limitations: Applications not accepted. Giving primarily in NY. No grants to individuals.
Application information: Contributes only to pre-selected organizations.
Officers: John W. Rowe, Pres.; Abigail M. Rowe, V.P.; Meredith L. Rowe, V.P.; Rebecca J. Rowe, V.P.; Valerie A. Rowe, Secy.-Treas.
EIN: 200721105

1749
Rowland Foundation, Inc. ◇
c/o JPMorgan Chase Bank, N.A.
P.O. Box 6089
Newark, DE 19714-6089 (302) 634-2931
Contact: Valerie Smallwood, Pres.

Incorporated in 1960 in DE.
Donors: Edwin H. Land†; Helen M. Land.
Foundation type: Independent foundation.
Financial data (yr. ended 11/30/05): Assets, $30,078,286 (M); expenditures, $934,895; qualifying distributions, $866,527; giving activities include $836,560 for 22 grants (high: $150,000; low: $5,000).
Purpose and activities: Grants primarily for a science institute, as well as for education, including colleges and universities, social services, health, medical research, conservation, and cultural

programs, including museums and historical associations.

Fields of interest: Museums; History/archaeology; Arts; Elementary/secondary education; Higher education; Environment, natural resources; Hospitals (general); Health organizations, association; Medical research, institute; Human services; Science.

Type of support: General/operating support; Professorships; Research.

Limitations: Giving primarily in the Boston-Cambridge, MA, area. No grants to individuals, or for capital or endowment funds, or matching gifts; no loans.

Application information: Application form not required.

Initial approach: Letter
Deadline(s): None
Board meeting date(s): As required

Officers and Trustees:* Valerie Smallwood,* Pres.; Philip DuBois,* V.P.; Joseph Haley, Secy.; Guy Smallwood,* Treas.; Daniel Drake; Edward Smallwood.

EIN: 046046756

Selected grants: The following grants were reported in 2004.

$150,000 to Crotched Mountain Foundation, Greenfield, NH. For unrestricted support.

$100,000 to Cambridge College, Cambridge, MA. For unrestricted support.

$100,000 to Year Up, Boston, MA. For unrestricted support.

$34,080 to Young Audiences of Massachusetts, Somerville, MA. For unrestricted support.

$30,000 to East End House, Cambridge, MA. For unrestricted support.

$30,000 to From the Top, Boston, MA. For unrestricted support.

$30,000 to Greater Boston Youth Symphony Orchestra, Boston, MA. For unrestricted support.

$27,250 to Boston Arts Academy, Boston, MA. For unrestricted support.

$20,000 to Center for Teen Empowerment, Boston, MA. For unrestricted support.

$20,000 to Outdoor Explorations, Medford, MA. For unrestricted support.

1750

The Dorothy Schiff Foundation ✧

c/o JPMorgan Chase Bank, N.A.
P.O. Box 6089
Newark, DE 19714-6089
Contact: Adele Hall Sweet, Pres.
Application address: 53 E. 66th St., New York, NY 10021, tel.: (212) 789-5042

Incorporated in 1951 in NY.

Donors: Dorothy Schiff‡; New York Post Corp.

Foundation type: Independent foundation.

Financial data (yr. ended 12/31/05): Assets, $2,312,356 (M); expenditures, $1,055,570; qualifying distributions, $1,021,350; giving activities include $1,020,000 for 10 grants (high: $425,000; low: $10,000).

Purpose and activities: Giving primarily for education and hospitals.

Fields of interest: Media/communications; Elementary/secondary education; Higher education; Medical school/education; Education; Hospitals (general); Health organizations, association; Crime/ violence prevention, youth; Human services; Children/youth, services; Family services; Community development.

Limitations: Giving primarily in NY. No grants to individuals, or for endowments, capital funds, or matching gifts; no loans.

Application information:

Initial approach: Letter
Deadline(s): None
Board meeting date(s): Monthly except Aug.

Officers: Adele Hall Sweet, Pres.; Sarah Ann Kramarsky, Secy.; Mortimer W. Hall, Treas.

Trustee: JPMorgan Chase Bank, N.A.

EIN: 136018311

1751

The Bernard Lee Schwartz Foundation, Inc. ✧

c/o Wilmington Trust SP Svcs., Inc.
1105 N. Market St., Ste. 1300
Wilmington, DE 19801-1241

Incorporated in 1951 in NY.

Donors: Tilda R. Orr; Bernard L. Schwartz‡; Eric A. Schwartz; Michael L. Schwartz; Rosalyn R. Schwartz.

Foundation type: Independent foundation.

Financial data (yr. ended 9/30/05): Assets, $18,690,771 (M); expenditures, $1,017,169; qualifying distributions, $901,853; giving activities include $853,978 for 40 grants (high: $175,000; low: $25).

Purpose and activities: Support largely for higher, elementary, and secondary education, including a scholarship program for children who are economically disadvantaged; funding also for cultural programs, and medical tax-exempt institutions, including hospitals and research facilities.

Fields of interest: Arts; Elementary/secondary education; Higher education; Health organizations, association; Medical research, institute; Cancer research; Human services.

Type of support: Continuing support; Building/ renovation; Equipment; Endowments; Fellowships; Internship funds; Research.

Limitations: Applications not accepted. Giving on a national basis, with some emphasis on CA. No grants to individuals, or for annual campaigns, seed money, emergency funds, deficit financing, land acquisition, demonstration projects, publications, or conferences; no loans.

Application information: Contributes only to pre-selected organizations.

Officers: Michael L. Schwartz, Pres.; Eric A. Schwartz, V.P. and Treas.; Tilda R. Orr, Secy.

EIN: 136096198

Selected grants: The following grants were reported in 2005.

$90,000 to Bryn Mawr College, Bryn Mawr, PA.

$75,000 to Alliance for School Choice, Phoenix, AZ.

$75,000 to American Gastroenterological Association, Bethesda, MD.

$30,000 to National Stroke Association, Englewood, CO.

$25,000 to Hyde Foundation, Bath, ME.

$25,000 to Pacific Research Institute for Public Policy, San Francisco, CA.

$20,000 to International Center of Photography, New York, NY.

$20,000 to Thomas B. Fordham Institute, DC.

$10,000 to National Dance Institute, New York, NY.

$50 to Susan G. Komen Breast Cancer Foundation, Dallas, TX.

1752

Seevak Family Foundation ✧

c/o JPMorgan Chase Bank, N.A.
P.O. Box 6089
Newark, DE 19714-6089

Established in 1981 in NY.

Donors: Sheldon Seevak; Elinor A. Seevak.

Foundation type: Independent foundation.

Financial data (yr. ended 3/31/06): Assets, $2,727,017 (M); gifts received, $104,953; expenditures, $419,708; qualifying distributions, $391,866; giving activities include $391,866 for grants.

Purpose and activities: Giving primarily for the arts, education, health services, and Jewish agencies and temples.

Fields of interest: Performing arts, theater; Historical activities; Arts; Higher education; Education; Heart & circulatory research; Federated giving programs; Jewish agencies & temples; Women.

Limitations: Applications not accepted. Giving primarily in MA, NJ, and New York, NY. No grants to individuals.

Application information: Contributes only to pre-selected organizations.

Trustees: Elinor A. Seevak; Sheldon Seevak; JPMorgan Chase Bank, N.A.

EIN: 133102898

Selected grants: The following grants were reported in 2005.

$100,000 to Trigeminal Neuralgia Association, Gainesville, FL.

$50,000 to Boston Latin School Association, Boston, MA.

$25,000 to Brookings Institution, DC.

$25,000 to Metropolitan Opera Association, New York, NY.

$8,681 to University of Pennsylvania, Philadelphia, PA.

$2,500 to Childrens Book Project, San Francisco, CA.

$1,000 to Associated Parents Club of Piedmont, Piedmont, CA.

$1,000 to Meritus College Fund, San Francisco, CA.

$1,000 to Piedmont Educational Foundation, Piedmont, CA.

$500 to Alzheimers Services of the East Bay, Berkeley, CA.

1753

The Paul Singer Family Foundation ✧

(formerly The Paul & Linda Singer Foundation)
1105 N. Market St., Ste. 1300
Wilmington, DE 19801

Established in 1986 in DE.

Donors: Linda Singer; Paul E. Singer.

Foundation type: Independent foundation.

Financial data (yr. ended 11/30/04): Assets, $16,330,424 (M); expenditures, $3,788,079; qualifying distributions, $3,763,895; giving activities include $3,761,417 for 90 grants (high: $500,000; low: $50).

Purpose and activities: Giving primarily to Jewish federated giving programs and organizations, education, the arts, particularly museums, human services, and medical organizations.

Fields of interest: Museums; Arts; Higher education; Environment, natural resources; Health organizations; Disasters, 9/11/01; Human services; Civil rights; Jewish federated giving programs; Philanthropy/voluntarism; Jewish agencies & temples.

Limitations: Applications not accepted. Giving primarily in the metropolitan New York, NY, area. No grants to individuals.

Application information: Contributes only to pre-selected organizations.

Officers and Directors:* Paul E. Singer,* Pres.; Andrew Singer,* V.P.; Gordon Singer,* V.P.

EIN: 222664654

1754

The Alexandrine and Alexander L. Sinsheimer Fund ✧

c/o JPMorgan Chase Bank, N.A.
P.O. Box 6089
Newark, DE   19714-6089

Established in 1959 in NY.

Donors: Alexander L. Sinsheimer†; Alexandrine Sinsheimer†.

Foundation type: Independent foundation.

Financial data (yr. ended 4/30/05): Assets, $11,592,428 (M); expenditures, $675,709; qualifying distributions, $586,178; giving activities include $576,500 for 9 grants (high: $100,000; low: $40,000).

Purpose and activities: Grants to medical schools to support scientific research relating to the prevention and cure of human diseases.

Fields of interest: Medical school/education; Medical research, institute.

Type of support: Research.

Limitations: Giving primarily in the metropolitan New York, NY, area; some funding also in Rochester, and Syracuse, NY.

Application information: Application form required.
Deadline(s): Feb. 15

Trustee: JPMorgan Chase Bank, N.A.

EIN: 136047421

Selected grants: The following grants were reported in 2003.

$93,632 to Columbia University, College of Physicians and Surgeons, New York, NY. For general support.

$93,632 to New York University, School of Medicine, New York, NY. For general support.

$93,632 to Weill Medical College of Cornell University, New York, NY. For general support.

$80,000 to Albert Einstein College of Medicine of Yeshiva University, Bronx, NY. For general support.

$80,000 to Rockefeller University, New York, NY. For general support.

$80,000 to State University of New York Health Science Center at Brooklyn, Brooklyn, NY. For general support.

$40,000 to New Jersey Medical School, Newark, NJ. For general support.

$40,000 to University of Rochester, School of Medicine, Rochester, NY. For general support.

1755

The Spilka Family Foundation, Inc.

c/o Foundation Source
501 Silverside Rd., Ste. 123
Wilmington, DE   19809-1377

Established in 2003 in DE.

Donor: Robert E. Spilka.

Foundation type: Independent foundation.

Financial data (yr. ended 12/31/05): Assets, $1,509,628 (M); gifts received, $734,132; expenditures, $353,788; qualifying distributions, $353,788; giving activities include $349,788 for 46 grants (high: $150,000; low: $180).

Fields of interest: Elementary/secondary education; Human services; Jewish agencies & temples.

Limitations: Applications not accepted. Giving primarily in CT and NY. No grants to individuals.

Application information: Contributes only to pre-selected organizations.

Officer and Director:* Edward Spilka,* Pres. and Secy.

EIN: 542133110

1756

The Sternlicht Family Foundation, Inc.

c/o Foundation Source
501 Silverside Rd., Ste. 123
Wilmington, DE   19809-1377

Donor: Barry Sternlicht.

Foundation type: Independent foundation.

Financial data (yr. ended 12/31/05): Assets, $20,864,935 (M); gifts received, $1,613,025; expenditures, $1,197,688; qualifying distributions, $1,192,588; giving activities include $1,131,568 for 77 grants (high: $250,000; low: $250).

Purpose and activities: Giving primarily to Jewish and other local organizations.

Fields of interest: Boys & girls clubs; Human services; Children/youth, services; Jewish federated giving programs; Jewish agencies & temples; Religion, interfaith issues.

Limitations: Applications not accepted. Giving primarily in CT and NY. No grants to individuals.

Application information: Contributes only to pre-selected organizations.

Officers and Directors:* Barry Sternlicht,* Pres.; David Lewis Dubrow,* V.P.; Miriam Klein Sternlicht,* V.P.; Russell Sternlicht.

EIN: 260039094

1757

Stroud Foundation ✧ ☆

c/o Wilmington Trust Co.
1100 N. Market St., Ste. 094000
Wilmington, DE   19890-0001

Trust established in 1961 in PA.

Donor: Joan M. Stroud†.

Foundation type: Independent foundation.

Financial data (yr. ended 12/31/05): Assets, $3,788 (M); expenditures, $2,085,964; qualifying distributions, $2,029,617; giving activities include $2,029,249 for 19 grants (high: $1,063,471; low: $2,000).

Purpose and activities: Giving primarily to an academy of nature science and social science.

Fields of interest: Higher education; Environment, natural resources; Environment, water resources; Hospitals (general); Human services; Science; Social sciences.

Type of support: Research.

Limitations: Applications not accepted. No grants to individuals, or for matching gifts; no loans.

Application information: Contributes only to pre-selected organizations.
Board meeting date(s): Annually

Trustees: Joan S. Blaine; John Fisher; Rod Moorhead; Morris W. Stroud; Stephen Stroud; W.B. Dixon Stroud.

EIN: 236255701

Selected grants: The following grants were reported in 2004.

$2,056,000 to Stroud Water Research Center, Avondale, PA. For general support.

$150,000 to Marine Environmental Research Institute, Blue Hill, ME. For general support.

$140,000 to Guanacaste Dry Forest Conservation Fund, Philadelphia, PA. For general support.

$40,000 to Millbrook School, Millbrook, NY. For general support.

$35,000 to Brandywine Conservancy, Chadds Ford, PA. For general support.

$35,000 to Nature Conservancy, Maine Chapter, Brunswick, ME. For general support.

$25,000 to Cheshire Hunt Conservation Land Preservation Fund, Kennett Square, PA. For general support.

$25,000 to Hill School, Pottstown, PA. For general support.

$25,000 to Kingswood-Oxford School, West Hartford, CT. For general support.

$20,000 to Mosaic Multicultural Foundation, Seattle, WA. For general support.

1758

The Struthers Family Foundation ✧ ☆

900 Old Kennett Rd.
Greenville, DE   19807-1520

Established in 1999 in DE.

Donors: Richard K. Struthers; Sharon M. Struthers.

Foundation type: Independent foundation.

Financial data (yr. ended 12/31/05): Assets, $1,112,928 (M); expenditures, $581,920; qualifying distributions, $529,119; giving activities include $529,119 for 14 grants (high: $200,000; low: $1,000).

Fields of interest: Higher education; Education; Safety/disasters; Girl scouts; American Red Cross; Federated giving programs; Christian agencies & churches.

International interests: Ireland.

Type of support: General/operating support.

Limitations: Applications not accepted. Giving primarily in DE and PA. No grants to individuals.

Application information: Contributes only to pre-selected organizations.

Officers: Richard K. Struthers, Pres. and Treas.; Sharon M. Struthers, V.P. and Secy.

EIN: 510392526

Selected grants: The following grants were reported in 2004.

$248,819 to Pennsylvania State University, University Park, PA. For general support.

$15,000 to University of Maryland-Baltimore, Baltimore, MD. For general support.

$2,500 to Episcopal Relief and Development, New York, NY. For general support for Tsunami Relief Fund.

$500 to Reno Memorial Fund. For general support.

1759

The Vitale Family Foundation, Inc. ✧

c/o Foundation Source
501 Silverside Rd., Ste. 123
Wilmington, DE   19809-1377

Established in 2002 in DE.

Donors: David Vitale; Marilyn Vitale.

Foundation type: Independent foundation.

Financial data (yr. ended 12/31/05): Assets, $3,493,956 (M); gifts received, $200,000; expenditures, $579,844; qualifying distributions, $557,311; giving activities include $540,400 for 59 grants (high: $20,000; low: $100).

Fields of interest: Arts; Higher education; Education; Human services; Children/youth, services.

Limitations: Applications not accepted. Giving primarily in Chicago, IL. No grants to individuals.

Application information: Contributes only to pre-selected organizations.

Officers and Directors:* David Vitale,* Pres.; Marilyn Vitale,* V.P.

EIN: 510414438

1760

The Wasily Family Foundation, Inc. ✧

c/o JPMorgan Chase Bank, N.A.
P.O. Box 6089
Newark, DE 19714-6089
Contact: Patrick N. Moloney, V.P.
Application address: c/o Independent Investors, Inc., 181 Smithtown Blvd., Nesconset, NY 11767, tel.: (631) 979-2142

Established in 1988 in NY.

Donors: Anne V. Wasily; H. Vira Kolisch‡.

Foundation type: Independent foundation.

Financial data (yr. ended 6/30/05): Assets, $38,785,159 (M); gifts received, $1,425,000; expenditures, $2,039,545; qualifying distributions, $1,724,942; giving activities include $1,640,000 for 56 grants (high: $50,000; low: $20,000).

Purpose and activities: Giving primarily for health and human services.

Fields of interest: Arts education; Arts; Hospitals (general); Health organizations; Cancer research; Human services; Children/youth, services; Family services; Federated giving programs; Roman Catholic agencies & churches.

Type of support: General/operating support; Research.

Limitations: Giving primarily in New York, NY.

Application information: Application form not required.

  Initial approach: Letter
  Deadline(s): None
  Board meeting date(s): June

Officers: Anne V. Wasily, Pres.; Patrick Moloney, V.P.; Margaret Moloney, Secy.; Frank Suchomel, Jr., Treas.

EIN: 133503227

Selected grants: The following grants were reported in 2005.

$90,000 to Doctors Without Borders USA, New York, NY. 2 grants: $50,000, $40,000

$40,000 to American Heart Association, New York, NY.

$40,000 to Lighthouse International, New York, NY.

$40,000 to National Childrens Leukemia Foundation, Brooklyn, NY.

$40,000 to New York Foundling Hospital, New York, NY.

$40,000 to New York University Medical Center, New York, NY.

$40,000 to Parkinsons Disease Foundation, New York, NY.

$40,000 to Servants of Relief for Incurable Cancer, Hawthorne, NY.

$30,000 to Covenant House, New York, NY.

1761

Arthur K. Watson Charitable Trust ✧

c/o JPMorgan Chase Bank, N.A.
P.O. Box 6089
Newark, DE 19714-6089

Donor: Thomas J. Watson Foundation.

Foundation type: Independent foundation.

Financial data (yr. ended 5/31/05): Assets, $16,526,914 (M); expenditures, $1,198,075; qualifying distributions, $1,069,593; giving activities include $1,060,281 for 14 grants (high: $200,000; low: $20,000).

Fields of interest: Museums (children's); Education; Medical research, institute.

Limitations: Applications not accepted. Giving limited to CT, MA, ME, NH, NY, and VT. No grants to individuals.

Application information: Contributes only to pre-selected organizations.

Advisory Committee: Ann W. Bresnahan; Caroline W. Morong; Jane W. Stetson; Arthur K. Watson, Jr.; David J. Watson; Stuart H. Watson.

Trustees: Ann H. Symington; JPMorgan Chase Bank, N.A.

EIN: 132989468

Selected grants: The following grants were reported in 2004.

$100,000 to Boston Biomedical Research Institute, Boston, MA. For general operating support.

$100,000 to Rainforest Alliance, New York, NY. For general operating support.

$70,000 to Stepping Stones Museum for Children, Norwalk, CT.

$50,000 to Kieve Affective Education, Nobleboro, ME. For general operating support.

$45,000 to Atlantic Challenge Foundation, Rockland, ME. For general operating support.

$30,000 to Crossroads Academy, Lyme, NH. For general operating support.

$25,000 to Community School, Camden, ME. For general operating support.

$25,000 to Northern Stage Company, White River Junction, VT.

$25,000 to Youthlinks, Rockland, ME. For general operating support.

$20,000 to Island Institute, Rockland, ME. For general operating support.

1762

Welfare Foundation, Inc. ▼ ✧

100 W. 10th St., Ste. 1109
Wilmington, DE 19801
Contact: Peter C. Morrow, Exec. Dir.

Incorporated in 1930 in DE.

Donor: Pierre S. duPont‡.

Foundation type: Independent foundation.

Financial data (yr. ended 12/31/05): Assets, $133,447,457 (M); expenditures, $5,615,408; qualifying distributions, $4,897,523; giving activities include $4,649,506 for 67 grants (high: $250,000; low: $300).

Purpose and activities: Emphasis on education, hospitals, and social service agencies.

Fields of interest: Humanities; Arts; Education; Environment; Hospitals (general); Human services; Government/public administration.

Type of support: Capital campaigns; Building/renovation; Equipment; Matching/challenge support.

Limitations: Giving limited to DE and southern Chester County, PA. No grants to individuals, endowments, or for operating support.

Application information: Application form not required.

  Initial approach: Letter (2 pages) and proposal
  Copies of proposal: 1
  Deadline(s): Apr. 15 and Oct. 15
  Board meeting date(s): May and Dec.
  Final notification: 60 days

Officers and Trustees:* Edward B. duPont,* Pres.; Robert H. Bolling, Jr.,* V.P.; J. Simpson Dean, Jr.,* V.P.; Robert C. McCoy, V.P., Real Estate; Leatrice D. Elliman,* Secy.; W. Laird Stabler III,* Treas.; Peter C. Morrow, Exec. Dir.; Robert H. Bolling III; E. Bradford duPont, Jr.; Mrs. W. Laird Stabler, Jr.

Number of staff: 4 part-time professional.

EIN: 516015916

Selected grants: The following grants were reported in 2004.

$1,661,100 to New Castle County Vocational Technical School District, Wilmington, DE. For construction of school.

$400,000 to Christiana Care Home Health and Community Services, New Castle, DE. For capital campaign.

$400,000 to YMCA of Delaware, Wilmington, DE. To construct new facility and renovate facility.

$350,000 to Nature Conservancy, Wilmington, DE. For land acquisition.

$250,000 to Wilmington Music School, Wilmington, DE. For facility expansion and renovation.

$150,000 to Stroud Water Research Center, Avondale, PA. For program support and equipment.

$100,000 to Delaware Adolescent Program, Wilmington, DE. To acquire and renovate facility.

$100,000 to Modern Maturity Center, Dover, DE. For construction of medical facility.

$100,000 to Saint Edmonds Academy, Wilmington, DE. For facility expansion.

$50,000 to Center for the Creative Arts, Yorklyn, DE. For facility renovation.

1763

The Winky Foundation ✧ ☆

c/o Wilmington Trust Co.
1100 N. Market St.
Wilmington, DE 19890-0900

Established in 1998 in DE.

Donor: Gerrish H. Milliken III.

Foundation type: Independent foundation.

Financial data (yr. ended 12/31/05): Assets, $4,173,949 (M); expenditures, $319,489; qualifying distributions, $317,000; giving activities include $317,000 for grants.

Fields of interest: Higher education; Education; International peace/security; General charitable giving.

Limitations: Applications not accepted. Giving on a national basis. No grants to individuals.

Application information: Contributes only to pre-selected organizations.

Trustee: Wilmington Trust Co.

Advisors: Gerrish H. Milliken III; Stephen G. Milliken.

EIN: 516508170

Selected grants: The following grants were reported in 2004.

$6,000 to Grassroots International, Boston, MA. For general support.

$6,000 to Seventh Generation Fund for Indian Development, Arcata, CA. For general support.

$5,000 to Doctors Without Borders USA, New York, NY. For general support.

$5,000 to Resist, Inc., Somerville, MA. For general support.

$4,000 to Funding Exchange, New York, NY. For general support.

$2,000 to American Civil Liberties Union (ACLU), New York, NY. For general support.

$2,000 to American Rivers, DC. For general support.

$2,000 to Amnesty International USA, DC. For general support.

$2,000 to Coalition for the Homeless, New York, NY. For general support.

$2,000 to Friends of the Earth, DC. For general support.

DISTRICT OF COLUMBIA

1764

Agua Fund, Inc. ✧
2715 M St. N.W., Ste. 300
Washington, DC 20007-3732 (202) 944-9622
E-mail: info@aguafundinc.org; *URL:* http://
foundationcenter.org/grantmaker/aguafund/

Established in 2002 in DC.
Donor: Catherine M. Conover.
Foundation type: Independent foundation.
Financial data (yr. ended 12/31/04): Assets,
$5,664,878 (M); expenditures, $2,107,000;
qualifying distributions, $2,014,444; giving
activities include $1,790,250 for 101 grants (high:
$250,000; low: $2,500).
Purpose and activities: The mission of the fund is
to improve the quality of life through support of work
to protect the natural environment and to help the
poor, disadvantaged, and underserved.
Discretionary grants are also made by individual
Board members, largely to social, cultural, and
educational institutions of special interest. In
addition, the fund seeks to help musicians who need
social services and to ensure that K-12 school
children have access to music programs as part of
their education.
Fields of interest: Environment, natural resources;
Human services; Economically disadvantaged.
Limitations: Applications not accepted. Giving
primarily in specific parts of the U.S. where the
family has ties, including the greater metropolitan
Washington, DC, area, MD, VA, southwest FL,
western CO, and Cape Cod, MA. No grants to
individuals.
Publications: Grants list.
Application information: The foundation considers
invited proposals only.
   Board meeting date(s): 4 times annually
Officers and Directors:* Catherine M. Conover,*
Pres.; Richard J. Cicero,* V.P.; Cecily Kihn, Secy.;
Michael Hunter, Treas.
EIN: 113659697

1765

**Aid Association for the Blind of the District
of Columbia** ✧
5008 44th St. N.W.
Washington, DC 20016
Contact: Betsy Paull O'Connell, Pres.
FAX: (202) 244-0649; *E-mail:* bpoc@starpower.net

Established in 1989 in DC.
Foundation type: Independent foundation.
Financial data (yr. ended 6/30/05): Assets,
$6,715,571 (M); expenditures, $509,701;
qualifying distributions, $457,000; giving activities
include $457,000 for 18 grants (high: $70,000;
low: $9,000).
Purpose and activities: Giving to hospitals, clinics,
social service agencies, and issue-oriented projects
serving the blind/visually impaired people in the
Washington, DC, metropolitan area.
Fields of interest: Medical school/education;
Hospitals (general); Optometry/vision screening;

Eye diseases; Eye research; Disabilities, people
with; Blind/visually impaired.
Type of support: General/operating support; Annual
campaigns; Capital campaigns; Building/
renovation; Equipment; Emergency funds; Program
development; Publication; Seed money;
Fellowships; Internship funds; Research.
Limitations: Giving primarily in the Washington, DC
metropolitan area. No grants to individuals.
Publications: Informational brochure (including
application guidelines).
Application information: Send one of the three
proposals via E-mail or disk. Application form
required.
   Initial approach: Request guidelines and
      application form; submit form and proposal
   Copies of proposal: 3
   Deadline(s): Dec. 31
   Board meeting date(s): Mid-Oct., mid-Jan.,
      mid-Apr., and mid-June
   Final notification: June
Officers and Directors:* Betsy Paull O'Connell,*
Pres.; Anne Norman,* Secy.; William Glew,* Treas.;
Pat Beattie; James Dickson; Betsy Feinberg; Wendy
Gasch; Mary Louise Howe; John O'Neill; Carolyn
Post; Ulysses Rice; Beth Rocks; Denise Rozell.
EIN: 530196564
Selected grants: The following grants were reported
in 2004.
$70,000 to Childrens National Medical Center,
   Department of Ophthalmology, DC.
$60,000 to Washington Hospital Center,
   Washington National Eye Center, DC.
$58,000 to Services for the Visually Impaired,
   Dallas, TX.
$25,000 to American Association of People with
   Disabilities, DC.
$25,000 to American Council of the Blind, DC.
$22,000 to Prevention of Blindness Society of
   Metropolitan Washington, DC.
$20,000 to So Others Might Eat (SOME), DC.
$20,000 to Transcen, Rockville, MD.
$12,000 to University Ophthalmic Consultants
   Research and Educational Foundation, Chevy
   Chase, MD.
$10,000 to Low Vision Information Center,
   Bethesda, MD.

1766

The Antonovych Foundation, Inc. ✧
5143 Cathedral Ave. N.W.
Washington, DC 20016
Application address: P.O. Box 40818, Washington,
DC 20011

Established in MD.
Donors: Omelan Antonovych; Tatiana Antonovych.
Foundation type: Independent foundation.
Financial data (yr. ended 11/30/04): Assets,
$1,683,870 (M); gifts received, $771,000;
expenditures, $869,657; qualifying distributions,
$868,105; giving activities include $865,000 for 5
grants (high: $400,000; low: $10,000).
Purpose and activities: Awards for achievements in
Ukrainian literature and science or teaching.
International interests: Ukraine.
Limitations: Giving primarily in the Ukraine.
Application information:
   Initial approach: Letter with published material
   Deadline(s): Oct.
Director: Omelan Antonovych.
EIN: 521224032

1767

The Arca Foundation
1308 19th St. N.W.
Washington, DC 20036
Contact: Donna F. Edwards, Exec. Dir.
FAX: (202) 785-1446;
E-mail: grants@arcafoundation.org; *URL:* http://
www.arcafoundation.org

Incorporated in 1952 in NY.
Donor: Nancy S. Reynolds†.
Foundation type: Independent foundation.
Financial data (yr. ended 12/31/05): Assets,
$59,135,492 (M); expenditures, $3,725,115;
qualifying distributions, $3,700,103; giving
activities include $2,990,713 for 71 grants (high:
$100,000; low: $500).
Purpose and activities: To help citizens shape
public policy, particularly on social and economic
justice issues. Domestically, emphasis is on
projects related to media reform policy and
alternative content, geared towards creation of a
more diverse, democratic media system.
Fields of interest: International affairs, foreign
policy; International human rights; Public policy,
research.
Type of support: General/operating support;
Continuing support; Program development;
Conferences/seminars; Seed money; Matching/
challenge support.
Limitations: Giving to U.S.-based groups in the
Western Hemisphere for national and international
programs. No support for direct social services,
government programs, or groups outside the U.S.
No grants to individuals, or for annual campaigns,
emergency funds, capital or endowment funds,
scholarly research, deficit financing, scholarships,
or fellowships; no loans.
Publications: Annual report; Annual report (including
application guidelines); Grants list.
Application information: Proposals received via fax
or e-mail will not be considered; preliminary letters
of inquiry are discouraged; the foundation no longer
accepts unsolicited proposals in the area of
campaign finance reform. Application form not
required.
   Initial approach: Proposal (maximum 10 pages)
   Copies of proposal: 1
   Deadline(s): Mar. 1 and Sept. 1
   Board meeting date(s): June and Dec.
   Final notification: 2 weeks after board's decision
Officers and Directors:* Smith W. Bagley,* Pres.;
Nancy R. Bagley,* V.P.; Mary E. King,* Secy.; Eric
Sklar,* Treas.; Donna F. Edwards, Exec. Dir.; Nicole
Bagley; Ellsworth Culver; Michael Lux; William
Maines; Janet Shenk; Margery A. Tabankin;
DeWayne Wickham.
Number of staff: 2 full-time professional.
EIN: 132751798

1768

The Arcana Foundation, Inc. ✧
1156 15th St. N.W., Ste. 605
Washington, DC 20005 (202) 789-7280

Incorporated in 1986 in DE.
Donors: Ladislaus von Hoffmann; Beatrix von
Hoffmann.
Foundation type: Independent foundation.
Financial data (yr. ended 9/30/05): Assets,
$1,075,205 (M); gifts received, $500,000;
expenditures, $627,772; qualifying distributions,

$627,289; giving activities include $582,000 for 11 grants (high: $100,000; low: $20,000).

Purpose and activities: Giving primarily for social services, and arts and cultural institutions.

Fields of interest: Human services; Children/youth, services; Family services; Economically disadvantaged.

Type of support: General/operating support.

Limitations: Applications not accepted. Giving primarily in Washington, DC. No grants to individuals.

Application information: The foundation is reviewing its policies and, therefore, will not be accepting applications at this time.

Officers and Directors: * Ladislaus von Hoffmann,* Pres. and Treas.; Beatrix von Hoffmann,* V.P.; Holly Kennedy,* Secy.; George A. Didden III.

Number of staff: 1 part-time professional.

EIN: 521515952

1769
Banyan Tree Foundation ▼

1919 Pennsylvania Ave. N.W., Ste. 725
Washington, DC 20006
Contact: Carolyn Stremlau, Exec. Dir.

Established in 1986 in CA.

Donors: Peter Ackerman; Joanne Leedom Ackerman.

Foundation type: Independent foundation.

Financial data (yr. ended 12/31/04): Assets, $6,223 (M); gifts received, $5,580,000; expenditures, $5,653,706; qualifying distributions, $5,111,449; giving activities include $5,111,449 for 70 grants (high: $346,947; low: $10,000; average: $20,000–$160,000).

Purpose and activities: Giving primarily to international education and childrens' rights programs; support also for education programs in Washington, DC.

Fields of interest: Education.

International interests: Africa; Southeast Asia.

Type of support: General/operating support; Continuing support; Program development; Matching/challenge support.

Limitations: Applications not accepted. Giving on an international basis to select countries in Africa and Southeast Asia and on a limited basis in Washington, DC. No support for organizations with religious affiliations and/or medical or environmental focus or for individual schools; no grants outside listed geographic focus. No grants to individuals.

Application information: Unsolicited requests for funds not accepted.

Officers: Joanne Leedom-Ackerman, Pres.; Peter Ackerman, Secy.-Treas.; Carolyn Stremlau, Exec. Dir.

Number of staff: 2 full-time professional; 2 part-time professional.

EIN: 954088915

Selected grants: The following grants were reported in 2004.

$291,000 to Campaign for Female Education (CAMFED) International, Cambridge, England. .

$200,000 to World University Service - United Kingdom, London, England. .

$179,702 to Molteno Project, Braamfontein, South Africa. .

$111,631 to Management of Schools Training Programme (MSTP), Auckland Park, South Africa. .

$93,976 to Institute of Training and Education for Capacity Building, East London, South Africa. .

$91,855 to Saint Marys Interactive Learning Experience (SMILE), Kloof, South Africa. .

$90,000 to Associates in Research and Education for Development, Dakar, Senegal. .

$85,000 to Childrens Book Project, Dar es Salaam, Tanzania. .

$75,455 to Curriculum Development Project (CDP), Johannesburg, South Africa. .

$75,000 to In2Books, DC.

1770
Bauman Family Foundation, Inc. ▼ ◇

c/o Jewett House
2040 S St. N.W.
Washington, DC 20009-1110 (202) 328-2040
Contact: Patricia Bauman, Pres.; John L. Bryant, Jr., Dir.

Established in 1982 in NY.

Donor: Lionel R. Bauman†.

Foundation type: Independent foundation.

Financial data (yr. ended 6/30/05): Assets, $61,552,121 (M); expenditures, $7,238,468; qualifying distributions, $5,958,444; giving activities include $5,604,500 for 46 grants (high: $550,000; low: $2,500; average: $10,000–$100,000).

Purpose and activities: Grants to local, state, or national organizations with a clear strategy for translating their projects into nationally applicable ideas, including support for issues at the intersection of the economy and the environment, e.g., reconciliation of worker and community interests in sustainable economic development, trade and the environment, and jobs and the environment; support also for fostering citizens' access to information, increasing awareness of civic rights and responsibilities, and encouraging a central role for interdisciplinary education in achieving the goals of education reform.

Fields of interest: Arts; Education; Environment; Economic development; Public policy, research.

Type of support: General/operating support; Continuing support; Program development; Conferences/seminars; Publication; Seed money; Curriculum development; Research; Technical assistance; Matching/challenge support.

Limitations: Applications not accepted. Giving on a national basis. No grants to individuals.

Application information: Only applications solicited by the foundation are accepted.

Board meeting date(s): Quarterly

Officer and Directors: * Patricia Bauman,* Pres.; John Bryant, Jr.; Irene Crowe; Diane Ives.

Number of staff: 2 full-time professional; 1 full-time support.

EIN: 133119290

Selected grants: The following grants were reported in 2005.

$550,000 to Earth Day Network, DC. For general support.

$500,000 to Center for Civic Participation, Minneapolis, MN. For general support.

$275,000 to People for the American Way Foundation, DC. For general support.

$250,000 to Corcoran Gallery of Art, DC. For general support.

$250,000 to USAction Education Fund, DC. For general support.

$200,000 to American Institute for Social Justice, DC. For general support.

$200,000 to Montefiore Medical Center, Bronx, NY. For clinical information system.

$150,000 to Tides Center, San Francisco, CA. For Women's Voices Women's Vote.

$35,000 to Fund for Constitutional Government, DC. For Right-to-Know work.

$25,000 to Center for Health, Environment and Justice, Falls Church, VA. For general support.

1771
The Beech Street Foundation ◇

3125 Beech St. N.W.
Washington, DC 20015 (202) 966-9159
Contact: Jeffrey Bauman, Tr.

Established in 1987 in DC.

Donors: Jeffrey Bauman; Linda Fienberg.

Foundation type: Independent foundation.

Financial data (yr. ended 12/31/03): Assets, $2,775,599 (M); gifts received, $294,773; expenditures, $341,131; qualifying distributions, $341,002; giving activities include $340,347 for 39 grants (high: $50,000; low: $67).

Purpose and activities: Giving primarily for the performing arts, and legal services, including advocacy groups, public interest law, and women's rights; funding also for social services.

Fields of interest: Performing arts; Performing arts, theater; Performing arts, music; Education; Health organizations, association; Crime/violence prevention, domestic violence; Legal services; Legal services, public interest law; Human services; Children/youth, services; Civil rights, women; Women; Homeless.

Limitations: Giving primarily in Washington, DC. No grants to individuals.

Application information:

Initial approach: Proposal

Deadline(s): None

Trustees: Jeffrey Bauman; Linda Fienberg.

EIN: 526415627

Selected grants: The following grants were reported in 2003.

$50,000 to Shakespeare Theater, DC.

$35,000 to National Womens Law Center, DC.

$30,000 to National Partnership for Women and Families, DC.

$30,000 to Washington Legal Clinic for the Homeless, DC.

$25,000 to Frederick B. Abramson Memorial Foundation, DC.

$25,000 to Levine School of Music, DC.

$20,000 to Arena Stage, DC.

$20,000 to Theater Lab, DC.

$2,500 to National Child Research Center, DC.

$2,000 to Chicago Classical Recording Foundation, Chicago, IL.

1772
Bender Foundation, Inc.

1120 Connecticut Ave. N.W., Ste. 1200
Washington, DC 20036 (202) 828-9000
Contact: Julie Bender Silver, Pres.

Incorporated in 1958 in DC.

Donors: Jack I. Bender†; Howard M. Bender; Julie B. Silver; Stanley S. Bender.

Foundation type: Independent foundation.

Financial data (yr. ended 12/31/05): Assets, $15,657,700 (M); gifts received, $927,775; expenditures, $1,228,459; qualifying distributions,

$797,898; giving activities include $797,898 for 96 grants (high: $100,000; low: $75).

Fields of interest: Performing arts; Higher education; Health care; Health organizations, association; Human services; Jewish federated giving programs; Jewish agencies & temples.

Type of support: General/operating support; Annual campaigns; Capital campaigns; Building/ renovation; Endowments; Program development; Seed money; Curriculum development; Scholarship funds; Research; Matching/challenge support.

Limitations: Giving primarily in Washington, DC, and MD. No grants to individuals.

Publications: Annual report.

Application information: Application form not required.

> *Initial approach:* Letter
> *Copies of proposal:* 1
> *Deadline(s):* Nov. 30
> *Board meeting date(s):* Quarterly

Officers and Directors:* Sondra D. Bender,* Chair.; Julie Bender Silver,* Pres.; Howard M. Bender,* Exec. V.P.; David S. Bender,* V.P.; Eileen Bender Greenberg,* V.P.; Barbara Bender Laskow,* V.P.; Nan Bender; Richard Greenberg; David Silver.

Number of staff: 1 full-time professional.

EIN: 526054193

1773
Benton Foundation

1625 K. St. N.W., 11th Fl.
Washington, DC   20006   (202) 638-5770
Contact: Gloria Tristani, Pres.
FAX: (202) 638-5771; *E-mail:* info@benton.org;
URL: http://www.benton.org

Incorporated in 1948 in NY.

Donor: William Benton†.

Foundation type: Independent foundation.

Financial data (yr. ended 12/31/04): Assets, $12,842,249 (M); gifts received, $3,386,801; expenditures, $4,853,694; qualifying distributions, $4,759,928; giving activities include $1,648,697 for 75 grants (high: $168,000; low: $100; average: $500–$5,000), and $2,843,801 for 4 foundation-administered programs.

Purpose and activities: The Benton Foundation's mission is to realize the social benefits made possible by the public interest use of communications, because the foundation believes that communications in the public interest is essential to a strong democracy. The foundation bridges the worlds of philanthropy, community practice, and public policy. It develops and provides effective information and communication tools and strategies to equip and engage individuals and organizations in the emerging digital and communications environment.

Fields of interest: Media/communications; Health care; Public policy, research; Telecommunications.

Type of support: Conferences/seminars; Internship funds; Research; Technical assistance.

Limitations: Applications not accepted.

Publications: Annual report; Financial statement; Informational brochure; Newsletter; Occasional report; Program policy statement.

Application information: Disbursements primarily through operating projects initiated by the board of directors; few direct grants awarded. The foundation does not accept unsolicited grant applications or offer general grants.

> *Board meeting date(s):* May and Nov.

Officers and Directors:* Charles Benton,* Chair. and C.E.O.; Gloria Tristani, Pres.; Karen Menichelli, Exec. V.P. and Secy.; Michael Smith,* Treas.; Henry Rivera, Genl. Counsel; Elizabeth Daley; Adrianne Benton Furniss; Terry Goddard; Lee Lynch; Leonard Schrager; Woodward Wickham.

Number of staff: 4 full-time professional.

EIN: 136075750

Selected grants: The following grants were reported in 2004.

$218,000 to Education Development Center, Newton, MA. 2 grants: $168,000, $50,000

$54,000 to Rocky Mountain Public Broadcasting Network, Denver, CO.

$54,000 to University of New Hampshire, Durham, NH.

$54,000 to W H Y Y, Philadelphia, PA.

$31,500 to Hawaii Public Radio, Honolulu, HI.

$31,500 to Hopi Foundation, Hotevilla, AZ.

$31,500 to W N C U-FM, Durham, NC.

$31,458 to University of Alabama, Birmingham, AL.

$30,735 to Radio Bilingue, Fresno, CA.

1774
Irving & Betty Berman Family Foundation ◇ ☆

c/o Allen J. Berman
5100 Lowell Ln. N.W.
Washington, DC   20016-2608

Established in 1997 in DC and VA.

Donors: Betty Berman; Irving Berman.

Foundation type: Independent foundation.

Financial data (yr. ended 12/31/05): Assets, $426,735 (M); gifts received, $84,908; expenditures, $520,713; qualifying distributions, $515,476; giving activities include $515,476 for 54 grants (high: $224,294; low: $100).

Fields of interest: Arts; Libraries (public); Recreation, parks/playgrounds; Jewish agencies & temples.

Limitations: Applications not accepted. Giving on a national basis. No grants to individuals.

Application information: Contributes only to pre-selected organizations.

Directors: Allen J. Berman; Gregory Andrew Berman; M.J. Berman; Michele G. Berman.

EIN: 522057768

1775
Diane & Norman Bernstein Foundation, Inc. ◇

1400 16th St. N.W., Ste. 500
Washington, DC   20036   (202) 797-5472
Contact: Katherine Krug, Asst.

Established in 1965 in DC.

Donors: Diane Bernstein; Norman Bernstein.

Foundation type: Independent foundation.

Financial data (yr. ended 12/31/05): Assets, $7,431,246 (M); gifts received, $133,334; expenditures, $1,215,096; qualifying distributions, $1,104,176; giving activities include $1,103,334 for 32 grants (high: $260,000; low: $5,000).

Purpose and activities: Primary areas of interest include the arts, health, social services, Jewish welfare, and Israel. Support for those institutions and organizations, identified by the foundation's donors and their family members, which perpetuate and nurture the educational, religious,

humanitarian, health, cultural and social aspects of society, including support for the Jewish community.

Fields of interest: Performing arts; Performing arts, music; Arts; Elementary/secondary education; Health care; Health organizations, association; AIDS; AIDS research; Human services; Child development, services; Jewish federated giving programs; Biological sciences; Religion.

International interests: Israel.

Type of support: General/operating support; Continuing support; Annual campaigns; Capital campaigns; Program development.

Limitations: Applications not accepted. Giving primarily in Washington, DC; support for the Jewish community on a local, national, and international basis. No grants to individuals.

Publications: Annual report.

Application information: Contributes only to pre-selected organizations.

> *Board meeting date(s):* Oct. and Aug.

Officers and Directors:* Norman Bernstein,* Pres. and Secy.; Diane Bernstein,* V.P.; Joshua Benjamin Bernstein,* Treas.; Celia Ellen Bernstein; Lisa Bernstein; Susan Amy Bernstein; Marianne Bernstein Kalb; Robert Kalb; Elizabeth B. Norton; Robert Norton; Nancy Bernstein Schoen; Robert Schoen; Jodie Siegel.

Number of staff: 1 part-time professional.

EIN: 526047356

Selected grants: The following grants were reported in 2004.

$200,000 to Sidwell Friends School, DC.

$100,000 to United Jewish Appeal Federation, DC.

$25,000 to Jewish Community Center of the District of Columbia, DC.

$15,000 to Jewish Social Service Agency of Metropolitan Washington, Rockville, MD.

$15,000 to Jewish Theological Seminary of America, New York, NY.

$10,000 to Arena Stage, DC.

$10,000 to CentroNia, DC.

$10,000 to Childrens National Medical Center, DC.

$10,000 to New Israel Fund, DC.

$10,000 to Project Vote, Columbus, OH.

1776
Herb Block Foundation

1730 M St. N.W., Ste. 901
Washington, DC   20036   (202) 223-8801
FAX: (202) 223-8804; *E-mail:* info@herbblock.org;
URL: http://www.herbblockfoundation.org/
Scholarship information contact: Scholarship and Recognition Programs office, (609) 771-7878 (Princeton, NJ)

Established in 2001 in DC and VA.

Donor: Herbert L. Block†.

Foundation type: Independent foundation.

Financial data (yr. ended 9/30/05): Assets, $57,978,156 (M); gifts received, $93,422; expenditures, $2,266,737; qualifying distributions, $2,012,426; giving activities include $1,163,000 for 59 grants (high: $150,000; low: $2,500).

Purpose and activities: The foundation is committed to defending the basic freedoms guaranteed to all Americans, combating all forms of discrimination and prejudice, and improving the conditions of the poor and underprivileged through the creation or support of charitable and educational programs with the same goals. It is also committed to providing educational opportunity to deserving students through post-secondary education scholarships, and to promoting editorial cartooning through continued research.

Fields of interest: Adult education—literacy, basic skills & GED; Scholarships/financial aid; Education; Employment, services; Youth development; Civil liberties, advocacy; Civil liberties, first amendment; Civil rights; Public affairs, citizen participation; Economically disadvantaged.

Type of support: General/operating support; Emergency funds; Program development; Curriculum development; Program evaluation; Matching/challenge support.

Limitations: Giving limited for the benefit of the greater metropolitan Washington, DC, region, including Montgomery and Prince George's counties, MD, and the counties of Arlington, Fairfax, and the city of Alexandria, VA. Applicants for the Defending Basic Freedoms Program may be located in or provide services in areas outside the District of Columbia region. No support for sectarian religious purposes. No grants for capital or endowment programs.

Publications: Grants list; Informational brochure; Program policy statement.

Application information: The foundation uses Washington Grantmakers' Common Grant Application Form. See foundation Web site for full application information, including grant program cycles, application timelines, and eligibility requirements. Application form required.

Initial approach: Letter of inquiry; submit proposals upon foundation invitation only
Copies of proposal: 1
Deadline(s): Check foundation Web site for application deadlines
Board meeting date(s): Jan., May, and late Sept.
Final notification: Approximately 4 weeks

Officers and Executive Committee:* Frank Swoboda,* Pres.; Sarah Armstrong,* Secy.; Robin Meszoly,* Treas.; Jean J. Rickard,* Exec. Dir.; Marcela Brane; Athelia Knight; Clarence Page.

Directors: Jane Asher; Robert Asher; Lynda Bonieskie; Raymond Bonieskie; Laura Hutchison; Haynes Johnson; Donna McNulty; Jill Stanley; Laurie Strayer; Roger Wilkins.

Number of staff: 4 full-time professional; 1 part-time professional.

EIN: 260008276

Selected grants: The following grants were reported in 2004.
$100,000 to Library of Congress, DC.
$25,000 to Center for Democracy and Technology, DC.
$25,000 to Center for Multicultural Human Services, Falls Church, VA.
$25,000 to Class Acts Arts, Silver Spring, MD.
$25,000 to Georgetown University, DC.
$25,000 to Legal Momentum, New York, NY.
$25,000 to Public Citizen Foundation, DC.
$25,000 to Urban Alliance Foundation, DC.
$20,000 to Patricia M. Sitar Center for the Arts, DC.
$5,000 to Resurrection Childrens Center, Alexandria, VA.

1777
Carolyn & Kenneth D. Brody Foundation, Inc. ✧
c/o Winslow Partners, LLC
1300 Connecticut Ave. N.W., Ste. 850
Washington, DC 20036

Established in 1999 in Washington, DC.
Donors: Carolyn Brody; Kenneth D. Brody.

Foundation type: Independent foundation.
Financial data (yr. ended 9/30/05): Assets, $47,367 (M); gifts received, $430,000; expenditures, $463,177; qualifying distributions, $461,977; giving activities include $460,288 for 68 grants (high: $100,000; low: $100).
Purpose and activities: Giving to a business school and other educational institutions; funding also for the arts, with emphasis on the performing arts and art museums, as well as for health associations.
Fields of interest: Museums; Museums (art); Performing arts; Historic preservation/historical societies; Arts; Higher education; Business school/education; Education; Health organizations, association; Human services.
Limitations: Applications not accepted. Giving primarily in Washington, DC, MD, and NY. No grants to individuals.
Application information: Contributes only to pre-selected organizations.
Officers and Directors:* Kenneth D. Brody,* Chair.; Carolyn Brody,* Pres.; Robin S. Rothstein,* Secy.-Treas.; Arnold T. Cattani, Jr.
EIN: 522140128

1778
Building Hope...A Charter School Facilities Fund ✧ ☆
910 17th St. N.W., Ste. 1100
Washington, DC 20006

Established in 2003 in VA.
Foundation type: Operating foundation.
Financial data (yr. ended 12/31/04): Assets, $51,297,347 (M); gifts received, $28,563,218; expenditures, $777,538; qualifying distributions, $8,945,536; giving activities include $379,115 for 11 grants (high: $180,055; low: $500).
Purpose and activities: The fund exists to support charter schools.
Fields of interest: Elementary/secondary education.
Limitations: Applications not accepted.
Application information: Contributes only to pre-selected organizations.
Officers: Marianne M. Keler, Chair.; S. Joseph Bruno, Pres. and Treas.; Kathleen DeLaski, Vice-Chair.; Carol R. Rakatansky, Secy.
Directors: Fern Barrueta; Albert A. D'Alessandro; Sheila Ryan; Bill Quinby.
EIN: 200367954

1779
The Butler Family Fund ✧
1301 Connecticut Ave. N.W., Ste. 500
Washington, DC 20036 (202) 463-8288
Contact: Martha A. Toll, Exec. Dir.
FAX: (202) 463-8294;
E-mail: info@butlerfamilyfund.org; URL: http://www.butlerfamilyfund.org

Established in 1992 in DC.
Donor: J.E. and Z.B. Butler Foundation.
Foundation type: Independent foundation.
Financial data (yr. ended 12/31/05): Assets, $11,628,505 (M); expenditures, $1,370,807; qualifying distributions, $1,264,365; giving activities include $1,084,292 for 106 grants (high: $94,000; low: $250; average: $1,000–$15,000).
Purpose and activities: Support for homeless families and criminal justice reform (death penalty,

juvenile justice, and drug policy); also global warming.
Fields of interest: Environment, global warming; Crime/law enforcement, reform; Housing/shelter; Civil liberties, death penalty issues; Homeless.
International interests: United Kingdom.
Type of support: General/operating support; Program development; Seed money; Program-related investments/loans.
Limitations: Applications not accepted. Giving primarily in Los Angeles, San Diego and the San Francisco Bay Area, CA, Washington, DC, Chicago, IL, NY, Philadelphia, PA, WI, and London, England. No grants to individuals.
Publications: Grants list; Multi-year report; Program policy statement.
Application information: Unsolicited proposals or letters of inquiry are not accepted. No grants for more than 3 consecutive years.
Board meeting date(s): Biannually
Officers and Directors:* Alan B. Morrison,* Pres.; Anne S. Morrison, Secy.; Martha A. Toll, Exec. Dir.; Suzanne H. Binswanger; Lowell A. Blankfort; Laurence A. Gravin; Alexandra Hirsh; Georgina Hirsh; John B. Hirsch; Steven R. Hirsch; Peggy A. Horan; Rebecca Morrison; Jody Binswager Snider; Eve B. Wildrick.
Number of staff: 1 part-time professional; 1 part-time support.
EIN: 521786778
Selected grants: The following grants were reported in 2003.
$100,000 to Sierra Club Foundation, San Francisco, CA. For fuel economy campaign.
$45,000 to Chicago Coalition for the Homeless, Chicago, IL. To prevent homelessness stemming from incarcerating mothers, in collaboration with Chicago Legal Advocacy for Incarcerated Mothers.
$40,000 to Drug Policy Alliance, New York, NY. For Internet Expansion Campaign.
$35,000 to National Low Income Housing Coalition and Low Income Housing Information Service, DC. For campaign for federal housing trust fund.
$25,000 to Center for Community Change, DC. To support planning process for national campaign on affordable housing.
$25,000 to Center on Budget and Policy Priorities, DC. For work on intersection of housing and welfare policy.
$25,000 to Center on Policy Initiatives, San Diego, CA. For campaign on affordable housing.
$25,000 to Corporation for Supportive Housing, New York, NY. For national advocacy program.
$25,000 to Juvenile Death Penalty Initiative, DC. For general support.
$25,000 to Non-Profit Housing Association of Northern California, San Francisco, CA. For advocacy, public policy, and education on affordable housing.

1780
The Morris and Gwendolyn Cafritz Foundation ▼
1825 K St. N.W., Ste. 1400
Washington, DC 20006 (202) 223-3100
FAX: (202) 296-7567;
E-mail: info@cafritzfoundation.org; URL: http://www.cafritzfoundation.org

Incorporated in 1948 in DC.
Donors: Morris Cafritz†; Gwendolyn D. Cafritz†.
Foundation type: Independent foundation.

Financial data (yr. ended 4/30/05): Assets, $470,394,214 (M); expenditures, $32,320,920; qualifying distributions, $13,819,935; giving activities include $11,067,642 for 478 grants (high: $250,000; low: $100; average: $5,000–$100,000), and $518,634 for employee matching gifts.

Purpose and activities: The foundation is committed to building a stronger community for residents of the Washington, D.C. area through support of programs in arts and humanities, community services, education, and health.

Fields of interest: Museums; Performing arts; Performing arts, dance; Performing arts, theater; Performing arts, music; Arts; Education, association; Education, early childhood education; Child development, education; Elementary school/education; Secondary school/education; Higher education; Medical school/education; Adult/continuing education; Adult education—literacy, basic skills & GED; Environment, natural resources; Environment; Reproductive health, family planning; Medical care, rehabilitation; Health care; Substance abuse, services; Mental health/crisis services; AIDS; Health organizations; AIDS research; Crime/law enforcement; Housing/shelter, development; Human services; Children/youth, services; Child development, services; Family services; Residential/custodial care, hospices; Aging, centers/services; Women, centers/services; Homeless, human services; Civil rights, immigrants; Civil rights, minorities; Civil rights, women; Civil rights, aging; Civil liberties, reproductive rights; Civil rights; Community development; Voluntarism promotion; Aging; Disabilities, people with; Minorities; Asians/Pacific Islanders; African Americans/Blacks; Hispanics/Latinos; Women; AIDS, people with; Immigrants/refugees; Economically disadvantaged; Homeless.

Type of support: General/operating support; Continuing support; Management development/capacity building; Equipment; Program development; Seed money; Fellowships; Scholarship funds; Technical assistance; Employee matching gifts; Matching/challenge support.

Limitations: Giving limited to the Washington, DC, area and the immediate surrounding counties in MD and VA, specifically Prince George and Montgomery counties, MD, and Arlington and Fairfax counties, and the city of Alexandria, VA. No grants to individuals, or for emergency funds, deficit financing, capital, endowment, or building funds, demonstration projects, or conferences; no loans.

Publications: Application guidelines; Annual report; Grants list.

Application information: The foundation requires that all organizations use the Washington Grantmakers' Common Grant Application. Proposals may not be submitted via fax or e-mail. Application form required.

　Initial approach: Proposal
　Copies of proposal: 1
　Deadline(s): Mar. 1, July 1, and Nov. 1
　Board meeting date(s): Generally 3 to 9 months after deadline dates
　Final notification: 6 to 9 months

Officers and Directors:* Calvin Cafritz,* Chair., C.E.O. and Pres.; Daniel J. Callahan III,* Vice-Chair. and Treas.; John H.C. Barron, Jr., Secy.; Rose Ann Cleveland, Exec. Dir.; Terence C. Golden; Earl A. Powell III; Alice M. Rivlin; Guy T. Steuart II.

Advisory Board: Anne Allen; Anthony W. Cafritz; Elliot S. Cafritz; Jane Lipton Cafritz; Kate D. Clark; Carolyn J. Deaver; Hon. Robert W. Cumling; Hon.

Constance A. Morella; Elizabeth M. Peltekian; Julia Sparkman Shepard.

Number of staff: 6 full-time professional; 6 full-time support.

EIN: 526036989

Selected grants: The following grants were reported in 2005.

$500,000 to Multicultural Career Intern Program, Bell Multicultural High School, DC. For Bell Multicultural High School and Lincoln Middle School in Columbia Heights.

$500,000 to Washington Opera, DC. For Domingo-Cafritz Young Artists Program.

$450,000 to John F. Kennedy Center for the Performing Arts, DC. For month-long Prelude Festival.

$300,000 to Planned Parenthood Association of Metropolitan Washington, DC. For general support.

$119,000 to George Washington University, DC. For Morris and Gwendolyn Cafritz Foundation Awards.

$75,000 to DC Campaign to Prevent Teen Pregnancy, DC. For general support.

$40,000 to La Clinica del Pueblo, DC. For general support.

$25,000 to W E T A-Greater Washington Educational Telecommunications Association, Arlington, VA. For Ready to Learn and Between the Lions Instructional Program.

$20,000 to KidSafe, DC. For general support for Job Training Programs and KidSafe Center.

$20,000 to U Street Theater Foundation, Lincoln Theater, DC. For general support.

1781
Capital Athletic Foundation ✧
(formerly National Institute of Torah Foundation)
c/o Jack Abramoff
1700 Pennsylvania Ave. N.W., Rm. 400
Washington, DC 20006

Established in 1999 in DC and MD.

Donors: Jack Abramoff; Alan J. Broder; Debra Frenkel; Jacob Frenkel; Alabama-Coushatta Entertainment Center; Chevy Chase Bank; Mississippi Band of Choctaw Indians; National Center for Public Policy Research; S.P.I. Spirits (Cyprus) Limited; Saginaw Chippewa Indian Tribe; Atlantic Research & Analysis.

Foundation type: Independent foundation.

Financial data (yr. ended 12/31/03): Assets, $214,009 (M); gifts received, $2,158,941; expenditures, $3,016,103; qualifying distributions, $2,721,474; giving activities include $2,721,474 for 6+ grants (high: $2,366,512).

Fields of interest: Education; Athletics/sports, school programs; Youth development; Jewish agencies & temples.

International interests: Israel.

Limitations: Applications not accepted. Giving primarily in Washington, DC, MD, and NY; some giving also in Israel. No grants to individuals.

Application information: Unsolicited requests for funds not considered.

Trustees: Jack Abramoff; Pamela Abramoff; Capital Athletic Foundation, LLC.

EIN: 522181892

1782
The Case Foundation ▼ ✧
(formerly The Stephen Case Foundation)
c/o Ben Binswanger, Sr. V.P.
1720 N St. N.W.
Washington, DC 20036   (202) 467-5788
Contact: Ben Binswanger, Sr. V.P.
FAX: (202) 775-9161;
E-mail: info@casefoundation.org; URL: http://www.casefoundation.org

Established in 1997 in VA.

Donors: Stephen M. Case; Jean N. Case.

Foundation type: Independent foundation.

Financial data (yr. ended 12/31/04): Assets, $31,236,640 (M); expenditures, $10,622,556; qualifying distributions, $10,248,692; giving activities include $8,571,906 for 77 grants (high: $1,631,867; low: $109; average: $1,000–$150,000).

Purpose and activities: Giving to achieve sustainable solutions to complex social problems by investing in collaboration, leadership, and entrepreneurship. Supports individuals and organizations that have the strategy, leadership, and commitment to make positive, widespread social change. The foundation seeks to meet the needs of families and children in poverty; create thriving and sustainable economic development for communities; bridge cultural and religious divides; expand civic engagement and volunteerism; and accelerate innovative approaches to health care.

Fields of interest: Education; Health care; Youth development, services; Community development; Engineering/technology.

Limitations: Applications not accepted. Giving in the U.S. and abroad. No grants to individuals.

Application information: Contributes only to pre-selected organizations.

Officers and Directors:* Stephen M. Case,* Chair.; Jean N. Case,* C.E.O.; John Agee, V.P.; Shannon Rosser, Secy.-Treas.

Number of staff: 2 full-time professional; 1 part-time professional; 3 full-time support; 1 part-time support.

EIN: 541848791

Selected grants: The following grants were reported in 2004.

$635,000 to City Year DC, DC.

$500,000 to Americas Promise - The Alliance for Youth, Alexandria, VA.

$250,000 to Boys and Girls Clubs of America, Rockville, MD.

$125,000 to Best Friends Foundation, DC.

$125,000 to Hawaii Alliance for Community-Based Economic Development, Honolulu, HI.

$125,000 to Social Enterprise Alliance, Columbus, OH. For Perfect Balance Project.

$120,000 to Share Our Strength (SOS), DC. For domestic community development programs.

$100,000 to In2Books, DC.

$100,000 to Kickstart-International, San Francisco, CA.

$100,000 to King Abdullah II Fund for Development, Amman, Jordan. .

1783
The CityBridge Foundation, Inc.
(formerly The Advisory Board Foundation, Inc.)
600 New Hampshire Ave. N.W., Ste. 800
Washington, DC 20037   (202) 266-7249

Established in 1993 in DC.

Donors: David G. Bradley; Katherine B. Bradley.
Foundation type: Independent foundation.
Financial data (yr. ended 12/31/04): Assets, $6,915,899 (M); gifts received, $2,515,396; expenditures, $2,705,331; qualifying distributions, $1,825,549; giving activities include $1,243,234 for 253 grants (high: $168,000; low: $20), and $1,424,506 for 4 foundation-administered programs.
Purpose and activities: Giving primarily for youth, voluntarism promotion, and international development and relief.
Fields of interest: Public health; Health care; Health organizations, association; Medical research; Employment; Housing/shelter; Youth development; Children/youth, services; International development; International relief; Voluntarism promotion.
International interests: Philippines; South Africa.
Limitations: Applications not accepted. Giving in the U.S. (primarily in the greater metropolitan Washington, DC, area) and internationally, with emphasis on South Africa and the Philippines. No grants to individuals.
Application information: Contributes only to pre-selected organizations.
Officers and Directors:* Katherine B. Bradley,* Pres.; David G. Bradley,* V.P. and Secy.-Treas.; Andrew W. Lee, Exec. Dir.; James C. Snipes.
Number of staff: 6 full-time professional.
EIN: 521870074
Selected grants: The following grants were reported in 2003.
$168,000 to Foundation for Professional Development, Lynwood Ridge, South Africa. .
$75,000 to Urban Alliance Foundation, DC.
$50,000 to Harvard University, AIDS Institute, Cambridge, MA.
$5,000 to Greater DC Cares, DC.
$5,000 to Urban Institute, DC.
$1,250 to Healthy Babies Project, DC.
$1,100 to Kids, DC.
$500 to Multiple Sclerosis Society, National, DC.
$350 to Elizabeth Glaser Pediatric AIDS Foundation, Santa Monica, CA.
$250 to Leukemia & Lymphoma Society, Alexandria, VA.

1784
George E. Coleman, Jr. Foundation ✧
c/o Alan Dye
1747 Pennsylvania Ave.
Washington, DC 20006
Contact: Daniel Oliver, Tr.
Application address: 3105 Woodley Rd. N.W., Washington, DC 20008, tel.: (202) 986-2888

Established in DC.
Foundation type: Independent foundation.
Financial data (yr. ended 12/31/04): Assets, $6,931,746 (M); expenditures, $804,393; qualifying distributions, $729,750; giving activities include $729,750 for 40 grants (high: $183,400; low: $200).
Fields of interest: History/archaeology; Historic preservation/historical societies; Arts; Higher education; Philanthropy/voluntarism; Economics; Public policy, research; Christian agencies & churches.
Limitations: Giving on a national basis. No grants to individuals.
Application information:

Initial approach: Letter
Deadline(s): None
Trustees: Andrew Oliver, Jr.; Daniel Oliver; Louise Oliver.
EIN: 527044220

1785
The Community Foundation for the National Capital Region ▼ ✧
(formerly The Foundation for the National Capital Region)
1201 15th St. N.W., Ste. 420
Washington, DC 20005 (202) 955-5890
Contact: Terri Lee Freeman, Pres.; For grant applications: Alicia Reid, Grants Coord.
FAX: (202) 955-8084; E-mail: tfreeman@cfncr.org; Tel. for grant applications: (202) 955-5890, ext. 119; E-mail for grant applications: areid@cfncr.org; URL: http://www.cfncr.org

Incorporated in 1973 in DC.
Foundation type: Community foundation.
Financial data (yr. ended 3/31/06): Assets, $346,982,198 (M); gifts received, $80,688,350; expenditures, $95,370,948; giving activities include $91,235,382 for grants.
Purpose and activities: The foundation exists to foster a culture of giving in the diverse and dynamic community comprising Washington, DC, and nearby MD and VA. Through its programs and discretionary grants, the foundation works to build philanthropic capital dedicated to improving the region's quality of life, to strengthen the region's nonprofit organizations and improve their financial stability, and to fund projects and experiments offering new solutions to community needs.
Fields of interest: Arts; Elementary/secondary education; Education; Environment; Health care; Health organizations, association; Housing/shelter; Youth development, services; Children/youth, services; Human services; Civil rights, advocacy; Nonprofit management; Community development; Aging.
Type of support: General/operating support; Program development; Technical assistance; Program evaluation.
Limitations: Giving limited to the Washington, DC, Prince George's and Montgomery counties, MD, and northern VA. No grants to individuals, or from discretionary funds for annual campaigns, endowment funds, equipment, land acquisition, renovation projects, operating budgets, or matching gifts.
Publications: Application guidelines; Annual report; Financial statement; Program policy statement.
Application information: Visit foundation Web site for application forms, deadlines, and guidelines. Application form required.
Initial approach: Contact foundation
Copies of proposal: 1
Deadline(s): Varies
Board meeting date(s): Quarterly
Officers and Trustees:* Charito Kruvant,* Chair.; James F. Lafond,* Vice-Chair.; Terri Lee Freeman,* Pres.; Kathy A. Whelpley, Sr. V.P., Governance, Strategic Planning and Special Projects; Kenny Emson, Sr. V.P. and C.F.O.; Vicki Kirkbride, V.P., Devel. & Donor Svcs.; Thomas Kam, Interim V.P., Community Investment; Douglas M. Bibby,* Secy.; David M. Bradt, Jr.,* Treas.; R. Robert Linowes, Emeritus; Victoria P. Sant, Emeritus; Larry Bailey; Wayne K. Curry; Jack Davies; Allison Cryor DiNardo;

Nancy "Bitsey" Folger; Michele Hagans; Gary F. Jonas; Daniel K. Mayers; Mark D. Rothman; Jonathan Silver; Neal Simon; Rodney E. Slater; Richard W. Snowdon; Eugene Steuerle; George Vradenburg; Clarice Dibble Walker; Ann Wexler.
Number of staff: 20 full-time professional; 2 part-time professional; 2 full-time support; 1 part-time support.
EIN: 237343119
Selected grants: The following grants were reported in 2006.
$1,548,750 to Northern Virginia Family Service, Oakton, VA.
$1,000,000 to Laura Bush Foundation for Americas Libraries, DC. For Gulf Coast Recovery.
$997,000 to Rockefeller Philanthropy Advisors, Philanthropic Collaborative, New York, NY. For general support.
$600,000 to Fort Ticonderoga Association, Ticonderoga, NY.
$202,251 to N Street Village, DC.
$60,000 to Habitat for Humanity of Orange County, Chapel Hill, NC.
$35,146 to United Way of the National Capital Area, Vienna, VA.
$30,000 to Teaching for Change, DC.
$25,380 to Christian Communities Group Homes, DC.
$25,000 to W E T A-Greater Washington Educational Telecommunications Association, Arlington, VA.

1786
Consumer Health Foundation ✧
1400 16th St. N.W., Ste. 710
Washington, DC 20036-2224 (202) 939-3390
Contact: Margaret K. O'Bryon, C.E.O. and Pres.
FAX: (202) 939-3391;
E-mail: chf@consumerhealthfdn.org; URL: http://www.consumerhealthfdn.org

Established in 1994 in DC; converted from the proceeds of the sale of Group Health Association to Humana, Inc.
Donor: Group Health Assn., Inc.
Foundation type: Independent foundation.
Financial data (yr. ended 12/31/04): Assets, $43,800,593 (M); gifts received, $37,010; expenditures, $2,849,490; qualifying distributions, $2,328,063; giving activities include $1,591,390 for 66 grants (high: $50,000; low: $500).
Purpose and activities: The foundation's strategic grantmaking program focuses on improving access to health care and emphasizes consumer empowerment and education, provider education and training, and health system change. It also invests in communities through unsolicited grantmaking, enabling it to respond to pressing needs in the community that cannot be anticipated. These grants are used to support and develop the organizational capabilities of nonprofit partners, helping to make them more effective organizations so that they are better equipped to manage their work in the community. Current work in this area includes program design, evaluation, technology, and communications assistance. Finally, unsolicited grantmaking enables the foundation to support valuable health-related coalitions and partnerships, particularly those working toward health system change to benefit the most vulnerable consumers.
Fields of interest: Public health; Health care.
Type of support: Continuing support; Program development; Conferences/seminars; Publication;

Seed money; Technical assistance; Program evaluation.

Limitations: Giving limited to organizations within the metropolitan Washington, DC, area, including Prince George's and Montgomery counties, MD, and northern VA. National, regional or statewide organizations providing services in metropolitan Washington, DC, and working in full partnership with local, community-based organizations will also be considered. No support for organizations lacking 501(c)(3) status. No grants to individuals, or for general operating support, capital campaigns, or for building/renovation activities.

Publications: Application guidelines; Annual report; Financial statement; Grants list; Newsletter.

Application information: See foundation Web site for further application information, application guidelines and procedures. Application form required.

   Initial approach: Letter of intent
   Copies of proposal: 1
   Deadline(s): Annually for strategic grantmaking program; unsolicited grants on a rolling basis. Contact foundation for dates
   Board meeting date(s): Quarterly; committees meet in the interim
   Final notification: Annually for strategic grantmaking program; quarterly for unsolicited grants

Officers and Trustees:* Jonca C. Bull-Humphries,* Chair.; Eleanor A. Walker,* Vice-Chair.; Margaret K. O'Bryon,* C.E.O. and Pres.; David M. Vladeck,* Secy.-Treas.; Deborah L. Chang; Thomas W. Chapman; Stephen P. Gorman; Karyne Jones; Robin Kelley; Diane Lewis; Ruth Ruttenburg; Mary B. Tierney; Monica Villalta; Eleanor A. Walker; Matthew S. Watson.

Number of staff: 2 full-time professional; 1 part-time professional.

EIN: 530078064

Selected grants: The following grants were reported in 2004.

$50,000 to Latin American Youth Center, DC. For Teen Health Promoters Program, which trains Latino high school students to provide health information and counseling to their peers at Mary's Center for Maternal and Child Care's Teen Clinic and Unity Health Care's Upper Cardozo Clinic.

$45,000 to DC Action for Children, DC. For DC Covering Kids and Families Initiative aimed at identifying and enrolling children and their parents in a health coverage program, particularly government-run programs that are currently underutilized.

$45,000 to La Clinica del Pueblo, DC.

$40,000 to Childrens Hospital Foundation, DC. For Mobile Clinic's Referral Management Initiative (RMI) designed to improve compliance with the specialty and wrap-around services that primary care providers may recommend for their patients through education and case management. Funding also for Clinic's Parent Educator program that compliments the RMI by sending a parent educator for home visits to the Clinic's most at-risk patients with chronic health issues.

$40,000 to Families USA Foundation, DC. For D.C. Consumer Health Technical Assistance and Support Project, which works with local organizations, consumers, and government agencies on a variety of issues including strengthening existing DC-based consumer assistance programs and working to improve access to health insurance in the District.

$40,000 to Tenants and Workers Support Committee, Alexandria, VA. For Healthy Community Program which mobilizes and educates immigrant health consumers to advocate for greater public and private resources for uninsured health care, including community based primary care.

$38,000 to Mobile Medical Care, Bethesda, MD. For overweight and obesity management program for homeless and low-income adults on its second mobile clinic, which focuses primarily on chronic diseases, especially diabetes and hypertension. Patients will receive physical examinations, and education materials, case management, coaching sessions, and on-going weekly support.

$38,000 to New York Avenue Presbyterian Church, DC. For BestHealth project that provides hands-on, intensive advocacy, education and communication training by and for consumers of mental health services.

$35,000 to Alliance for Fairness in Reforms to Medicaid (AFFIRM), DC.

$25,000 to Young Womens Project, DC. For Body Project, a program that arms teen women and men with information and skills to develop sound nutrition and food preparation habits, develop and implement exercise programs, and develop healthy ways to respond to stress in order to decrease obesity and nutrition-related illnesses and build healthy lifestyles.

1787
Dallas Morse Coors Foundation for the Performing Arts

c/o Covington & Burling LLP
1201 Pennsylvania Ave. N.W.
Washington, DC 20004-2401
Contact: Doris D. Blazek-White, Tr.
E-mail: dmcfoundation@cov.com

Established in 1990 in DC.

Donor: Dallas M. Coors‡.

Foundation type: Independent foundation.

Financial data (yr. ended 12/31/05): Assets, $10,908,410 (M); expenditures, $608,745; qualifying distributions, $498,307; giving activities include $450,000 for 47 grants (high: $80,000; low: $1,500; average: $2,000–$10,000).

Purpose and activities: Awards given to general organizations or entities involved in the performing arts in the metropolitan District of Columbia area.

Fields of interest: Performing arts.

Type of support: General/operating support; Continuing support.

Limitations: Giving limited to the greater metropolitan Washington, DC, area, including portions of MD and VA. No support for organizations which are not directly involved in the performing arts.

Application information: Application form required.

   Initial approach: Request application form
   Copies of proposal: 1
   Deadline(s): Sept. 15
   Board meeting date(s): Apr. and Oct.
   Final notification: 2 months

Trustee: Doris D. Blazek-White.

Number of staff: 1 part-time support.

EIN: 526436554

1788
Marshall B. Coyne Foundation, Inc. ✧

c/o Madison Mgmt.
1156 15th St. N.W., Ste. 300
Washington, DC 20005-1704

Established in 1952.

Donor: Marshall B. Coyne‡.

Foundation type: Independent foundation.

Financial data (yr. ended 8/31/05): Assets, $17,391,573 (M); gifts received, $3,692,050; expenditures, $872,144; qualifying distributions, $814,700; giving activities include $814,700 for 70 grants (high: $100,000; low: $100).

Purpose and activities: Giving primarily for education, health associations, including a children's hospital, human services, including services for people who are blind, the arts, and Jewish organizations.

Fields of interest: Museums (art); Historic preservation/historical societies; Elementary/secondary education; Higher education; Hospitals (specialty); Health organizations; Food services; Human services; Children, services; Jewish agencies & temples.

Type of support: General/operating support; Conferences/seminars; Research; Employee matching gifts.

Limitations: Giving on a national basis, with some emphasis on Washington, DC.

Application information: Application form not required.

   Deadline(s): None

Trustees: C. Richard Beyda; Sheldon Cohen; Amelia McCarthy; Bennett Stichman.

EIN: 526054965

1789
The Dimick Foundation

2001 L St. N.W., Ste. 400
Washington, DC 20036 (202) 822-8888
Contact: John M. Lynham, Jr., Tr.
E-mail: cbelinky@rossmarshfoster.com

Established in 1957 in DC.

Donors: John Dimick‡; Marion T. Dimick‡.

Foundation type: Independent foundation.

Financial data (yr. ended 12/31/05): Assets, $7,745,702 (M); expenditures, $495,989; qualifying distributions, $478,744; giving activities include $383,500 for 79 grants (high: $30,000; low: $1,000).

Purpose and activities: Emphasis on cultural programs, especially music and other performing arts groups; support also for social services and youth clubs.

Fields of interest: Performing arts; Performing arts, music; Arts; Youth development; Human services; Children/youth, services.

Type of support: General/operating support; Continuing support; Annual campaigns.

Limitations: Giving primarily in the Washington, DC, metropolitan area, including portions of MD and VA. No support for propaganda or lobbying organizations. No grants to individuals.

Publications: Application guidelines; Financial statement; Grants list.

Application information: Application form not required.

   Initial approach: Letter
   Copies of proposal: 1
   Deadline(s): About 8 weeks prior to meetings

Board meeting date(s): May and Nov.
Final notification: Shortly after board meetings
Trustees: Nancy Johnson; Michelle Riley Levenson; John M. Lynham, Jr.
EIN: 526038149
Selected grants: The following grants were reported in 2004.
$35,000 to Christmas Pageant of Peace, DC.
$20,000 to Washington Performing Arts Society, DC.
$7,500 to Everybody Wins! DC, DC.
$7,500 to Iona Senior Services, DC.
$5,000 to Foundation Schools, Rockville, MD.
$5,000 to Mary House, DC.
$5,000 to Washington Chorus, DC.
$3,000 to Calvary Womens Services, DC.
$3,000 to Recording for the Blind and Dyslexic, DC.
$2,500 to Black Student Fund, DC.

1790

The Samuel R. Dweck Foundation ◇
1730 M St. N.W., Ste. 408
Washington, DC   20036   (202) 296-0360

Established in 1971 in DC.
Donors: Samuel R. Dweck; Morris Dweck; Ralph Dweck; Rena Dweck; Aboud Dweck; Susan Dweck; and members of the Dweck family.
Foundation type: Independent foundation.
Financial data (yr. ended 12/31/05): Assets, $11,295,937 (L); gifts received, $250,000; expenditures, $952,937; qualifying distributions, $821,903; giving activities include $821,903 for 73 grants (high: $194,000; low: $100).
Purpose and activities: Giving primarily to Jewish organizations, including federated giving programs, congregations, yeshivas, and other community groups.
Fields of interest: Secondary school/education; Higher education; Health organizations, association; Human services; Children/youth, services; Jewish federated giving programs; Jewish agencies & temples.
Limitations: Giving primarily in Washington, DC, MD, and NY.
Application information: Application form not required.
Deadline(s): None
Directors: Morris Dweck; Ralph Dweck; Rena Dweck.
EIN: 526060826

1791

El-Hibri Charitable Foundation ◇
1420 16th St. N.W.
Washington, DC   20036-0000
Application address: Robert L. Smith Jr., c/o East West Resources Corp., 1684 East Gude Dr., 3rd Fl., Rockville, MD 20850, tel.: (301) 217-9929

Established in 2001 in DC.
Donor: Fuad El-Hibri.
Foundation type: Independent foundation.
Financial data (yr. ended 12/31/04): Assets, $3,678,476 (M); gifts received, $6,293,000; expenditures, $4,783,549; qualifying distributions, $4,784,402; giving activities include $4,592,500 for 3 grants (high: $4,500,000; low: $7,500).
Fields of interest: Education; Islam.
Limitations: Giving primarily in the Washington, DC area, and Lebanon.

Application information:
Initial approach: Letter
Deadline(s): None
Officers and Directors: * Robert L. Smith, Jr.,* Pres.; Azizah Al-Hibri,* V.P. and Secy.; Fuad El-Hibri,* Treas.; Karim El-Hibri; Samir El-Hibri; Yasmine Gibellini.
EIN: 522306995

1792

The Enfranchisement Foundation ◇
P.O. Box 32224
Washington, DC   20007

Established in 1999 in NY.
Donors: Daniel H. Leeds; Sunita G. Leeds.
Foundation type: Independent foundation.
Financial data (yr. ended 3/31/06): Assets, $15,474,986 (M); expenditures, $765,195; qualifying distributions, $679,556; giving activities include $669,661 for 28 grants (high: $135,000; low: $100).
Purpose and activities: Giving primarily to public policy organizations, education, and human services.
Fields of interest: Higher education; Education; Reproductive health, family planning; Human services; Public policy, research.
Limitations: Applications not accepted. Giving primarily in Washington, DC, and NY. No grants to individuals.
Application information: Contributes only to pre-selected organizations.
Trustees: Daniel H. Leeds; Sunita G. Leeds.
EIN: 134055747
Selected grants: The following grants were reported in 2005.
$262,500 to University of Colorado Foundation, Boulder, CO.
$122,000 to Alliance for Excellent Education, DC.
$60,000 to Maret School, DC.
$50,000 to Institute for Student Achievement, Lake Success, NY.
$50,000 to People for the American Way Foundation, DC.
$25,000 to Massachusetts Institute of Technology, Cambridge, MA.
$2,500 to Rock the Vote Education Fund, Los Angeles, CA.
$2,000 to Multicultural Career Intern Program, DC.

1793

Fannie Mae Foundation ▼ ◇
4000 Wisconsin Ave., N.W.
N. Tower, Ste. 1
Washington, DC   20016-2804   (202) 274-8057
FAX: (202) 274-8100;
E-mail: grants@fanniemaefoundation.org;
Application addresses: James A. Johnson Community Fellowship Prog.: Wendy New, Dir., Policy and Leadership Devel., 4000 Wisconsin Ave., N.W., N. Tower, Ste. 1, Washington, DC 20016-2804, tel.: (202) 274-8043, FAX: (202) 274-8101, E-mail: wnew@fanniemaefoundation.org, Maxwell Awards of Excellence Prog.: Maxwell Awards of Excellence, c/o Christine Tucker, Mgr., Policy and Leadership Devel., 4000 Wisconsin Ave., N.W., N. Tower, Ste. 1, Washington, DC 20016-2804, tel.: (202) 274-8044, E-mail: ctucker@fanniemaefoundation.org; Contact for

Fannie Mae Foundation Fellowship Program at the Kennedy School of Government: Wendy New, Dir., Policy and Leadership Devel., tel.: (202) 274-8043, FAX: (202) 274-8101, E-mail: wnew@fanniemaefoundation.org; Tel. for Fannie Mae Foundation Innovations in American Government Award in Affordable Housing: (800) 722-0074; E-mail for Fannie Mae Foundation Innovations in American Government Award in Affordable Housing: webmaster@innovationsaward.harvard.edu; URL: http://www.fanniemaefoundation.org

Established in 1979 in DC.
Donor: Federal National Mortgage Assn.
Foundation type: Company-sponsored foundation.
Financial data (yr. ended 12/31/05): Assets, $95,163,874 (M); expenditures, $70,682,430; qualifying distributions, $71,183,024; giving activities include $38,722,905 for grants.
Purpose and activities: The foundation supports organizations involved with education reform, affordable housing, and homelessness and awards fellowships to affordable housing and community development professionals and senior state and local government officials and nonprofit leaders committed to advancing the field of affordable housing in the U.S.
Fields of interest: Education, reform; Housing/shelter, alliance; Housing/shelter, development; Housing/shelter; Homeless, human services; Government/public administration.
Type of support: General/operating support; Program development; Fellowships; Research; Employee volunteer services; Program-related investments/loans; Employee matching gifts; Donated equipment.
Limitations: Giving on a national basis, with emphasis on Washington, DC. No support for discriminatory organizations. No grants to individuals (except for fellowships); no mortgage loans.
Publications: Annual report; Financial statement.
Application information: Application form required.
Initial approach: Download application form and mail to application address for James A. Johnson Fellowships; download application form and mail 4 copies to application address for Maxwell Awards; complete online application form for Innovations Award
Deadline(s): Sept. 12 for Innovations Award; Mar. 31 for Kennedy School Fellowships; postmarked by May 31 for James A. Johnson Fellowships; postmarked by June 30 for Maxwell Awards
Final notification: Oct. 30 for Maxwell Awards
Officers and Directors: * Daniel H. Mudd,* Chair.; Kenneth J. Bacon,* Vice-Chair.; Stacey Davis Stewart,* C.E.O. and Pres.; Kevin P. Smith,* Sr. V.P., Secy., and C.A.O.; Peter Beard, Sr. V.P., Comms., Strategy, and Inf.; James H. Carr, Sr. V.P., Research; Ellen Lazar, Sr. V.P., Housing and Community Initiatives; Lisa Mallory-Hodge, Sr. V.P., Policy and Consulting; Anne Kelso,* Treas.; Rev. Floyd Flake; Stephen Goldsmith; Charles V. "Chuck" Greener; Colleen Hernandez; Louis W. Hoyes; Stewart Kwoh; Rebecca Senhauser; Karen Hastie Williams; Barry Zigas*.
Number of staff: 65 full-time professional; 1 part-time professional; 9 full-time support.
EIN: 521172718
Selected grants: The following grants were reported in 2004.

$4,000,000 to Enterprise Community Partners, Columbia, MD. For general operating support to preserve and expand supply of affordable rental housing and increase homeownership opportunities in low-income communities around country, payable over 4 years.

$2,000,000 to Living Cities: The National Community Development Initiative, New York, NY. For national funders partnership working to increase scale and breadth of community development activities to build, promote, and sustain healthy communities in major urban centers of United States, payable over 3 years.

$1,226,347 to Urban Institute, DC. For research affiliation to develop and refine inter-related research and policy analysis initiatives focusing on housing and neighborhood conditions in D.C. and Washington, D.C., metropolitan area, and nationally, payable over 3.25 years.

$1,200,000 to National Council of La Raza, DC. For general operating support for nonprofit financing, homeownership network, and policy initiatives, payable over 3 years.

$1,050,000 to Housing Partnership Network, Boston, MA. For general operating support to promote regional nonprofit housing partnerships, payable over 3 years.

$1,050,000 to National Church Residences, Columbus, OH. For general operating support to produce, preserve, and manage affordable rental housing across country, with special expertise in elderly housing, payable over 3 years.

$950,000 to BRIDGE Housing Corporation, San Francisco, CA. For general operating support, payable over 3 years.

$900,000 to Consumer Federation of America, DC. For housing and homeownership work, payable over 2.75 years.

$825,000 to East of the River Community Development Corporation, DC. For general operating support to generate community and economic development, commercial revitalization activities, and human services initiatives in Ward 8, Washington, D.C, payable over 3 years.

$690,000 to Harvard University, Joint Center for Housing Studies, Cambridge, MA. For Foundation Innovations in American Government Award to recognize programs in affordable housing development, payable over 3 years.

1794

The Fernandez Foundation, Inc. ✧
c/o The Fernandez Group
2401 Pennsylvania Ave. N.W., Ste. 475
Washington, DC   20037

Established in 1998 in VA.
Donors: Raul J. Fernandez; Richard Kay; Internosis; Jill Eber; Jill Hertzberg; Kjets, LLC.
Foundation type: Independent foundation.
Financial data (yr. ended 12/31/04): Assets, $1,141,778 (M); gifts received, $311,727; expenditures, $423,401; qualifying distributions, $374,676; giving activities include $374,680 for 9 grants (high: $150,000; low: $4,000).
Fields of interest: Arts; Education; Health care; Human services; Children/youth, services; Federated giving programs.
Type of support: General/operating support.
Limitations: Applications not accepted. Giving primarily in Washington, DC, FL, and VA. No grants to individuals.

Application information: Contributes only to pre-selected organizations.
Officers: Raul J. Fernandez, Chair., C.E.O. and Treas.; Jean-Marie Fernandez, Pres.
EIN: 541928658
Selected grants: The following grants were reported in 2004.
$150,000 to Center City Consortium, DC. For unrestricted support.
$99,680 to Our Lady of Mercy Catholic Church, Potomac, MD. For unrestricted support.
$42,000 to Best Buddies International, Miami, FL. For unrestricted support.
$36,500 to Fight for Children, DC. For unrestricted support.
$15,000 to Manhattan Theater Club, New York, NY. For unrestricted support.
$10,000 to Community Foundation for the National Capital Region, DC. For unrestricted support.
$10,000 to National Gallery of Art, DC. For unrestricted support.
$7,500 to Choral Arts Society of Washington, DC. For unrestricted support.
$4,000 to Knock Out Abuse, McLean, VA. For unrestricted support.

1795

Thomas B. Fordham Foundation ✧
1701 K St. N.W., Ste. 1000
Washington, DC   20006   (202) 223-5452
Contact: Chester E. Finn, Jr., Pres.
FAX: (202) 223-9226;
E-mail: backtalk@edexcellence.net; URL: http://www.edexcellence.net

Established in 1959 in OH.
Donor: Thelma Fordham Pruett‡.
Foundation type: Independent foundation.
Financial data (yr. ended 12/31/04): Assets, $43,989,468 (M); expenditures, $2,284,808; qualifying distributions, $2,061,136; giving activities include $820,500 for 46 grants (high: $200,000; low: $100), $30,000 for 1 employee matching gift, and $1,474,897 for 4 foundation-administered programs.
Purpose and activities: The foundation's work in education seeks to advance understanding and acceptance of effective reform strategies that incorporate these principles: the need for dramatically higher standards; an education system designed for and responsive to the needs of its users; verifiable outcomes and accountability; equality of opportunity; a solid core curriculum taught by knowledgeable, expert instructors; and educational diversity, competition, and choice.
Fields of interest: Elementary/secondary school reform; Education.
Type of support: Seed money; Research; Technical assistance; Program evaluation.
Limitations: Giving on a national basis, primarily in the Dayton, OH, area. No grants to individuals (expect for education excellence awards), or for capital or construction campaigns or ongoing or routine operating support.
Publications: Informational brochure.
Application information: The foundation will consider proposals for start-up, development, and emergency grants for community (charter) schools in the Dayton, OH, area only.
Initial approach: Letter
Board meeting date(s): Varies
Officers and Trustees:* Chester E. Finn, Jr.,* Pres.; Eric Osberg, V.P. and Treas.; Michael J. Petrilli, V.P.,

National Progs.; Terry Ryan, V.P., Ohio Progs.; Chester E. Finn; Thomas A. Holton; Michael W. Kelly; Craig Kennedy; Bruno V. Manno; Rod Paige; David H. Ponitz; Diane Ravitch.
Number of staff: 4 full-time professional; 1 full-time support; 1 part-time support.
EIN: 316032844
Selected grants: The following grants were reported in 2004.
$300,000 to Parents Advancing Choice in Education (PACE), Dayton, OH. 2 grants: $200,000 (For scholarship program), $100,000 (For scholarship program).
$50,000 to Harvard University, Cambridge, MA. For operating support and publication of EducationNext.
$33,000 to Arts Center Foundation, Dayton, OH.
$30,000 to National Council on Teacher Quality, DC. For general operating support.
$25,000 to Accountability Works, DC. For program support.
$15,000 to Black Alliance for Educational Options, DC. For general support.
$10,000 to Council of the Great City Schools, DC.
$10,000 to Greatschools.net, San Francisco, CA. For operating support CharterSchoolsRatings.org.
$10,000 to University of Washington, Seattle, WA. For operating support for Center for Reinventing Public Education.

1796

Foundation for Middle East Peace ✧
1761 N. St. N.W.
Washington, DC   20036   (202) 835-3650
Contact: Philip C. Wilcox, Jr., Pres.
FAX: (202) 835-3651; E-mail: info@fmep.org;
Additional E-mail: pcwilcox@fmep.org (Philip C. Wilcox, Jr., Pres.) or jeff@fmep.org (Geoffrey Aronson, Dir. for Publications and Research);
URL: http://www.fmep.org

Incorporated in 1979 in DC.
Donors: Merle Thorpe, Jr.‡; Stephen Hartwell; Nelson B. Delavan Foundation; W.H. Rosenwald Family Fund.
Foundation type: Independent foundation.
Financial data (yr. ended 9/30/05): Assets, $12,459,519 (M); gifts received, $39,174; expenditures, $836,890; qualifying distributions, $770,532; giving activities include $318,475 for 29 grants (high: $44,150; low: $425).
Purpose and activities: To promote an understanding of the Israeli-Palestinian conflict, including the identification of U.S. interests, and to contribute to a just and peaceful resolution of the conflict with security for both peoples. Support directed to elements within the Arab and Jewish communities working for a peaceful resolution of the conflict. Publication of bimonthly Report on Israeli Settlement in the Occupied Territories.
Fields of interest: International peace/security.
International interests: Israel.
Type of support: General/operating support; Conferences/seminars; Publication; Research; Matching/challenge support.
Limitations: Giving primarily in Washington, DC, Israel, and Palestine for programs concerning conflict resolution in the Middle East.
Publications: Application guidelines; Informational brochure; Newsletter; Program policy statement.
Application information: Application form not required.

Initial approach: Letter
Deadline(s): None
Board meeting date(s): As required
Final notification: 30 days
Officers and Trustees:* Calvin H. Cobb, Jr.,* Chair.; Amb. Philip C. Wilcox, Jr.,* Pres.; Amb. Lucius D. Battle; Landrum R. Bolling; James J. Cromwell; Peter Gubser; Stephen Hartwell; Richard S.T. Marsh; Amb. Richard Murphy; Jean Newsom; Gail Pressberg; William B. Quandt; Nicholas A. Veliotes.
Number of staff: 2 full-time professional; 1 full-time support.
EIN: 526055574
Selected grants: The following grants were reported in 2005.
$36,300 to Americans for Peace Now, DC.
$20,000 to Middle East Institute, DC.
$15,000 to Partners for Peace, DC.
$7,500 to Ir Amim, West Bank/Gaza. .
$5,000 to Mercy Corps, Portland, OR.
$5,000 to Search for Common Ground, DC.
$4,000 to Columbia University Press, New York, NY.
$3,000 to Seeds of Peace, DC.
$2,500 to New Israel Fund, DC.
$2,500 to New Jersey Scholars Program, Lawrenceville, NJ.

1797
John Edward Fowler Memorial Foundation
1725 K St., N.W., Ste. 1201
Washington, DC 20006 (202) 728-9080
Contact: Richard H. Lee, Pres.
URL: http://foundationcenter.org/grantmaker/fowler/

Incorporated in 1964 in DE.
Donor: Pearl Gunn Fowler‡.
Foundation type: Independent foundation.
Financial data (yr. ended 12/31/04): Assets, $23,078,595 (M); expenditures, $2,015,195; qualifying distributions, $1,897,706; giving activities include $1,744,500 for 57 grants (high: $1,500,000; low: $2,000).
Purpose and activities: Primary areas of interest include the disadvantaged, with emphasis on the homeless and housing. Giving primarily to small community service organizations without public funding, especially for programs that benefit children and youth; support also for social service agencies, literacy programs, and programs that help the elderly maintain their independence.
Fields of interest: Child development, education; Adult education—literacy, basic skills & GED; Education, reading; Food services; Housing/shelter, development; Human services; Children/youth, services; Child development, services; Aging, centers/services; Homeless, human services; Aging; African Americans/Blacks; Hispanics/Latinos; Immigrants/refugees; Economically disadvantaged; Homeless.
Type of support: General/operating support; Capital campaigns; Building/renovation; Equipment; Consulting services; Matching/challenge support.
Limitations: Giving limited to the Washington, DC, Beltway area, including nearby suburbs in MD and VA. No support for agencies principally funded by local, state or federal government sources or national health organizations. No grants to individuals or for medical research programs; no loans.
Publications: Application guidelines; Grants list.
Application information: WG Common Grant Application Form accepted, but not required.

Application form and application guidelines available on foundation Web site. Application form required.
Initial approach: Telephone call requesting application form and guidelines. Do not send letters of inquiry
Copies of proposal: 1
Deadline(s): None
Board meeting date(s): Periodically
Final notification: Approximately 6 months
Officers and Trustees:* Richard H. Lee,* Pres.; Michael P. Bentzen,* Secy.; Jeffery P. Capron,* Treas.
Number of staff: 1 part-time professional.
EIN: 516019469
Selected grants: The following grants were reported in 2004.
$1,000,000 to Building Bridges Across the River, DC.
$75,000 to Boys and Girls Clubs of Greater Washington, Silver Spring, MD.
$30,000 to House of Ruth, DC.
$25,000 to For Love of Children (FLOC), DC.
$15,000 to Downtown Clusters Geriatric Day Care Center, DC.
$15,000 to Washington Jesuit Academy, DC.
$15,000 to Washington Middle School for Girls, DC.
$10,000 to Gift Family Resource Center, DC.
$10,000 to Good Shepherd Ministries, DC.
$10,000 to Rachaels Womens Center, DC.

1798
The Freed Foundation
1025 Thomas Jefferson St., Ste. 308 E.
Washington, DC 20007 (202) 337-5487
Contact: Grants Comm.

Incorporated in 1954 in DC.
Donors: Frances W. Freed‡; Gerald A. Freed‡.
Foundation type: Independent foundation.
Financial data (yr. ended 12/31/05): Assets, $24,925,979 (M); expenditures, $1,388,838; qualifying distributions, $1,303,886; giving activities include $1,099,320 for 23 grants (high: $200,000; low: $2,000).
Purpose and activities: Support for programs for vulnerable elderly and children populations, and animal welfare organizations.
Fields of interest: Animals/wildlife.
Type of support: General/operating support; Continuing support; Annual campaigns; Equipment; Program development; Publication.
Limitations: Giving primarily in the metropolitan Washington, DC, area. No support for foreign organizations or international projects. No grants to individuals, or for scholarships, endowment funds, research, or conferences and meetings.
Publications: Annual report (including application guidelines).
Application information: Application form not required.
Initial approach: Proposal
Copies of proposal: 1
Deadline(s): Dec. 31st
Board meeting date(s): Varies
Final notification: Within 3 months
Officers and Directors:* Elizabeth Ann Freed,* Pres. and Treas.; Lorraine Barnhart,* V.P.; Lloyd J. Derrickson,* Secy.; Jane M. Freed.
Number of staff: 2 full-time professional.
EIN: 526047591
Selected grants: The following grants were reported in 2004.

$200,000 to Lenox Hill Hospital, New York, NY. For Emergency Department fund.
$100,000 to Friends of the National Zoo, DC. For Asia Trail Exhibit.
$70,000 to CPC Behavioral Healthcare, Red Bank, NJ. 2 grants: $35,000 each (For general support).
$50,000 to Discovery Creek Childrens Museum of Washington, DC. For general support.
$50,000 to Smithsonian Institution, DC. For National Museum of the American Indian.
$47,000 to Family Support Center, Bethesda, MD. For SISTERS Coordinator.
$25,000 to Center for Science in the Public Interest, DC. For Eating Green Campaign.
$25,000 to Rutgers, The State University of New Jersey Foundation, New Brunswick, NJ. For Network for Family Life Education Substance Abuse Education.
$20,000 to American Kidney Fund, Rockville, MD. For Summer Enrichment Program.

1799
Friedman-French Foundation, Inc. ◇
2330 California St. N.W.
Washington, DC 20008-1637

Established in 1993 in DC.
Donors: Emanuel Friedman; Kindy French.
Foundation type: Independent foundation.
Financial data (yr. ended 6/30/05): Assets, $7,990,695 (M); gifts received, $3,928,000; expenditures, $489,556; qualifying distributions, $472,303; giving activities include $470,050 for 10 grants (high: $180,000; low: $5,000).
Fields of interest: Museums (history); Arts; Education; Environment, natural resources; Hospitals (specialty); Health organizations, association; Human services; Children, services; Jewish agencies & temples.
Limitations: Applications not accepted. Giving primarily in CA, Washington, DC, MD, and NY. No grants to individuals.
Application information: Contributes only to pre-selected organizations.
Directors: Kindy French; Emanuel Friedman.
EIN: 521853718
Selected grants: The following grants were reported in 2005.
$100,000 to Childrens Hospital Foundation, DC.
$10,000 to Capital Partners for Education, DC.
$5,000 to Urban League, Greater Washington, DC.

1800
Future of Russia ◇ ☆
1250 24th St. N.W. 350
Washington, DC 20037

Donor: Thomas J. Murray.
Foundation type: Operating foundation.
Financial data (yr. ended 12/31/05): Assets, $104,886 (M); gifts received, $519,241; expenditures, $1,898,930; qualifying distributions, $1,911,646; giving activities include $1,239,604 for 1 grant, and $1,911,646 for 1 foundation-administered program.
Purpose and activities: Giving primarily for medical supplies and technology in Russia.
Fields of interest: Health care.
Limitations: Giving primarily in Russia. No grants to individuals.

Officers: John C. Straub, C.E.O.; Thomas J. Murray, Pres.; Harvey L. Frutkin, Secy.
EIN: 300014318

1801
Bernard & Sarah Gewirz Foundation, Inc. ◇ ☆
1666 K St. N.W., Ste. 430
Washington, DC 20006
Contact: Bernard S. Gewirz, Treas.

Established in 1984 in DC.
Donors: Bernard S. Gewirz; Sarah M. Gewirz.
Foundation type: Independent foundation.
Financial data (yr. ended 11/30/04): Assets, $4,624,751 (M); expenditures, $381,703; qualifying distributions, $373,480; giving activities include $373,480 for 55 grants (high: $124,100; low: $52).
Purpose and activities: Support primarily for education and Jewish giving.
Fields of interest: Arts; Education; Human services; Jewish federated giving programs; Jewish agencies & temples.
Limitations: Giving primarily in the metropolitan Washington, DC, area.
Application information: Application form not required.
   Initial approach: Letter
   Deadline(s): None
Officers and Directors:* Michael K. Gewirz,* V.P.; Sarah M. Gewirz,* Secy.; Bernard S. Gewirz,* Treas.; Jonathan K. Gewirz; Steven B. Gewirz.
EIN: 521381689
Selected grants: The following grants were reported in 2004.
$124,100 to United Way of Rhode Island, Providence, RI.
$51,000 to Georgetown University, DC.
$27,500 to Ballet Florida, West Palm Beach, FL.
$25,000 to Jewish Federation of Greater Washington, Rockville, MD.
$12,000 to National Gallery of Art, DC.
$10,000 to Historical Society of Washington, DC, DC.
$6,000 to Washington Ballet, DC.
$4,000 to Corcoran Gallery of Art, DC.
$2,000 to American Friends of the Hebrew University, New York, NY.
$1,000 to Latino Student Fund, DC.

1802
Stephen A. and Diana L. Goldberg Foundation ◇
1615 M St. N.W., Ste. 850
Washington, DC 20036
Contact: Mark Spisak

Established in 1994 in DE.
Donors: Stephen Goldberg; Diana Goldberg; Rae Goldberg‡; Shadyside Assocs. Limited Partnership.
Foundation type: Independent foundation.
Financial data (yr. ended 12/31/05): Assets, $177,929 (M); gifts received, $1,910,709; expenditures, $1,811,292; qualifying distributions, $1,810,798; giving activities include $1,810,798 for 149+ grants (high: $250,000; average: $10,000–$50,000).
Purpose and activities: Support primarily for children's health care and development; giving also

for the arts, the environment, civil rights, and public affairs.
Fields of interest: Arts, association; Museums; Education; Hospitals (specialty); Health organizations, association; Pediatrics; Youth development; Human services; Children/youth, services; Civil rights; Jewish federated giving programs; Public affairs, research.
Type of support: General/operating support.
Limitations: Giving on a national basis, with some emphasis on NY, CA, MA, MI, MT, and Washington, DC.
Application information: Application form not required.
   Deadline(s): None
Officers: Stephen A. Goldberg, Pres.; Diana L. Goldberg, V.P.; Martin J. Kirsch, Secy.
Directors: Brian L. Goldberg; Lauren B. Goldberg; Stuart W. Goldberg.
EIN: 510326473
Selected grants: The following grants were reported in 2004.
$839,800 to Childrens Hospital.
$100,000 to Rhode Island School of Design, Providence, RI.
$50,000 to Black Student Fund, DC.
$30,000 to National Kidney Foundation of the National Capital Area, DC.
$30,000 to Washington AIDS Partnership, DC.
$10,000 to Brown University, Providence, RI.
$10,000 to Christopher Reeve Paralysis Foundation, Springfield, NJ.
$2,000 to Saint Albans School, DC.
$1,000 to Childrens Hearing and Speech Center, DC.
$1,000 to Doctors Without Borders USA, New York, NY.

1803
The Gottesman Fund ▼ ◇
1818 N St. N.W., Ste. 700
Washington, DC 20036 (202) 785-2727

Established in 1965 in DC.
Donors: Merchant's National Properties, Inc.; Members of the Gottesman family.
Foundation type: Independent foundation.
Financial data (yr. ended 8/31/05): Assets, $249,367,988 (M); gifts received, $7,845,679; expenditures, $9,161,974; qualifying distributions, $8,620,415; giving activities include $8,594,590 for 138 grants (high: $1,080,000; low: $250; average: $1,000–$10,000).
Purpose and activities: Support primarily for higher educational institutions, hospitals, and cultural organizations, particularly museums.
Fields of interest: Museums (ethnic/folk arts); Arts; Higher education; Hospitals (general); Human services; Jewish federated giving programs; Jewish agencies & temples.
Type of support: General/operating support.
Limitations: Applications not accepted. Giving primarily in NY. No grants to individuals.
Application information: Contributes only to pre-selected organizations.
Officers: David S. Gottesman, Pres.; Alice R. Gottesman, V.P.; Ruth L. Gottesman, V.P.; William L. Gottesman, V.P.; Robert W. Gottesman, Treas.
EIN: 526061469
Selected grants: The following grants were reported in 2005.
$1,080,000 to Mount Sinai Hospital, New York, NY. For general support.

$1,013,740 to Yeshiva University, New York, NY. For general support.
$1,000,000 to Hadassah, The Womens Zionist Organization of America, New York, NY. For general support.
$951,900 to American Museum of Natural History, New York, NY. For general support.
$865,000 to P.E.F. Israel Endowment Funds, New York, NY. For general support.
$300,000 to Partnership for Excellence in Jewish Education, Boston, MA. For general support.
$75,000 to Shalem Foundation, New York, NY. For general support.
$10,000 to Alexander Muss Institute for Israel Education, North Miami, FL. For general support.
$5,000 to Greenwich Hospital, Greenwich, CT. For general support.
$5,000 to High 5 Tickets to the Arts, New York, NY. For general support.

1804
Philip L. Graham Fund ▼
c/o The Washington Post Co.
1150 15th St. N.W.
Washington, DC 20071 (202) 334-6640
Contact: Candice C. Bryant, Pres.
FAX: (202) 334-4498;
E-mail: plgfund@washpost.com

Trust established in 1963 in DC.
Donors: Katharine Graham‡; Frederick S. Beebe‡; The Washington Post Co.; Newsweek, Inc.; Post-Newsweek Stations.
Foundation type: Independent foundation.
Financial data (yr. ended 12/31/05): Assets, $96,816,282 (M); expenditures, $5,701,419; qualifying distributions, $5,589,045; giving activities include $5,315,635 for grants.
Purpose and activities: Support for one-time infrastructure investments in health and human services, for children, youth, and families, pre-collegiate education, arts and humanities, and community needs. Grants for journalism, media and communications are extremely limited, and generally awarded only to those who have received media grants in the past.
Fields of interest: Arts; Education, early childhood education; Education; Human services; Youth, services.
Type of support: Capital campaigns; Building/renovation; Equipment; Program development; Seed money; Matching/challenge support.
Limitations: Giving primarily in the metropolitan Washington, DC, area. No support for national or international organizations, membership organizations, lobbying or political activities, or for religious purposes. No grants to individuals, or for medical services, research, annual campaigns, fundraising events, endowments, seminars, conferences, publications, tickets, films, travel expenses, courtesy advertising, advocacy, or litigation.
Publications: Application guidelines; Grants list; Program policy statement.
Application information: Application form not required.
   Initial approach: Request guidelines by letter or telephone
   Copies of proposal: 3
   Deadline(s): Feb. 1, May 1, Aug. 1, and Oct. 15
   Board meeting date(s): 120 days from application deadline
   Final notification: 6 months

Officers and Trustees: Candice C. Bryant, Pres.; Mary M. Bellor,* Secy.; Martin Cohen,* Treas.; Donald E. Graham; Theodore M. Lutz; Lionel W. Neptune.

Number of staff: 1 full-time professional; 1 full-time support.

EIN: 526051781

Selected grants: The following grants were reported in 2004.

$300,000 to District of Columbia College Access Program, DC. To encourage and enable more DC public high school students to enroll in and graduate from college.

$200,000 to Signature Theater, Arlington, VA. For capital campaign for newly constructed theater.

$175,000 to Shakespeare Theater, DC. To build new second performance space in downtown Washington, DC.

$150,000 to National Gallery of Art, DC. For creation of permanent multi-purpose education room.

$150,000 to Washington Drama Society, Arena Stage, DC. For The Next Stage Campaign.

$100,000 to Atlas Performing Arts Center, DC. Toward renovation of Atlas Theater Complex on H Street, as community-based performing arts space.

$100,000 to Center City Consortium, DC. For capital improvements to inner-city Catholic schools.

$100,000 to Foundation for the National Archives, DC. For The Learning Center component of National Archives Experience.

$100,000 to GALA Hispanic Theater, DC. To build state of the art performing arts facility in renovated Tivoli Theater.

$80,000 to Higher Achievement Program, DC. To purchase and renovate rowhouse for administrative headquarters.

1805

The Isadore and Bertha Gudelsky Family Foundation, Inc.

3000 Connecticut Ave. N.W., Ste. B
Washington, DC 20008
Contact: Philip N. Margolius, Secy.-Treas.
FAX: (202) 332-1800;
E-mail: jennifer@themargoliusfirm.com

Incorporated in 1955 in MD.

Donor: Members of the Gudelsky family.

Foundation type: Independent foundation.

Financial data (yr. ended 4/30/05): Assets, $14,137,012 (M); expenditures, $783,437; qualifying distributions, $1,217,009; giving activities include $618,605 for 15 grants (high: $400,000; low: $5,000).

Purpose and activities: Giving primarily to Jewish organizations, and for the arts.

Fields of interest: Performing arts centers; Arts; Education; Human services; Jewish federated giving programs; Jewish agencies & temples.

International interests: Israel.

Type of support: Scholarship funds; Program development; Professorships; General/operating support; Fellowships; Emergency funds; Continuing support; Capital campaigns; Conferences/seminars; Building/renovation.

Limitations: Giving primarily in the Washington, DC, area, as well as in Rockville, MD. No grants to individuals.

Application information: Application form not required.

Initial approach: Letter
Copies of proposal: 1

Deadline(s): None
Board meeting date(s): May or June

Officers: Arlene G. Kaufman, Pres.; Shelley G. Mulitz, V.P.; Philip N. Margolius, Secy.-Treas.

Board Members: Paul S. Berger; Michael Friedman; Laura Bryna Gudelsky Mulitz.

Number of staff: 1 part-time professional.

EIN: 526036621

Selected grants: The following grants were reported in 2004.

$450,000 to Jewish Federation of Greater Washington, Rockville, MD. For general support.

$77,605 to Charles E. Smith Jewish Day School of Greater Washington, Rockville, MD. For general support.

$45,000 to Jewish Community Center of Greater Washington, Rockville, MD. For general support.

$30,000 to Bnai Israel Congregation, Rockville, MD. For general support.

$25,000 to Hillel: The Foundation for Jewish Campus Life, DC. For general support.

$25,000 to Israel Education Fund, New York, NY. For general support.

$20,000 to Hebrew Home of Greater Washington, Rockville, MD. For general support.

$20,000 to John F. Kennedy Center for the Performing Arts, Friends of the, DC. For general support.

$10,000 to Girls and Boys Town, Boys Town, NE. For general support.

1806

The Hanley Foundation ✧

1101 30th St. NW, Ste. 500
Washington, DC 20007

Established in 1999 in DC.

Donor: Michael J. Hanley.

Foundation type: Independent foundation.

Financial data (yr. ended 12/31/05): Assets, $7,670,531 (M); gifts received, $4,000,000; expenditures, $632,401; qualifying distributions, $621,350; giving activities include $621,350 for 32 grants (high: $150,000; low: $500; average: $5,000–$10,000).

Purpose and activities: Giving primarily for water resource conservation, as well as for education and social services, including services for people who are blind.

Fields of interest: Education; Environment, water resources; Human services; Homeless, human services; Blind/visually impaired.

Limitations: Applications not accepted. Giving in the U.S., primarily in Washington, DC, and MD. No grants to individuals.

Application information: Contributes only to pre-selected organizations.

Officers: Michael J. Hanley, Pres.; Kathryn J. Hanley, V.P.; Ellen McMacken, Secy.

EIN: 522204367

Selected grants: The following grants were reported in 2004.

$100,000 to Chesapeake Bay Foundation, Annapolis, MD.

$25,000 to Recording for the Blind and Dyslexic, Princeton, NJ.

$10,000 to Capital Partners for Education, DC.

$10,000 to Uganda Childrens Charity Foundation, Dallas, TX.

$10,000 to Washington Tennis and Education Foundation, DC.

$5,000 to Marthas Table, DC.

$1,000 to American University, DC.

$500 to Bay Ridge Trust, Annapolis, MD.

1807

Harman Family Foundation ▼ ✧

1101 Pennsylvania Ave. N.W.
Washington, DC 20004

Established in 1985 in DC.

Donors: Sidney Harman; Hon. Jane Harman.

Foundation type: Independent foundation.

Financial data (yr. ended 2/28/05): Assets, $1,603,481 (M); gifts received, $5,850,000; expenditures, $4,446,717; qualifying distributions, $4,212,841; giving activities include $4,212,841 for 94 grants (high: $2,800,000; low: $500; average: $5,000–$50,000).

Purpose and activities: Giving primarily for the performing arts, international affairs, education, and human services.

Fields of interest: Performing arts; Performing arts centers; Performing arts, ballet; Performing arts, theater (musical); Performing arts, opera; Arts; Higher education; Boys & girls clubs; Human services; Children/youth, services; International affairs; Jewish federated giving programs; Jewish agencies & temples.

Type of support: General/operating support.

Limitations: Applications not accepted. Giving primarily in Los Angeles, CA, Washington, DC, MD, and New York, NY. No grants to individuals.

Application information: Contributes only to pre-selected organizations.

Officers: Sidney Harman, Pres.; Hon. Jane Harman, V.P.

Director: Barbara Harman.

EIN: 521437943

Selected grants: The following grants were reported in 2005.

$2,800,000 to Shakespeare Theater, DC. To produce and preserve classical theater in the United States.

$200,000 to Oxfam America, Boston, MA. For Tsunami Disaster Relief.

$200,000 to Save the Children Federation, Westport, CT. For Tsunami Disaster Relief.

$50,000 to University of Pennsylvania, Philadelphia, PA. For Student Performing Arts House.

$40,000 to American Jewish World Service, New York, NY. For Tsunami Disaster Relief.

$36,400 to Aspen Institute, DC. For arts programs.

$25,000 to Business Executives for National Security (BENS), DC. To conduct non-partisan public educational functions concerning national security.

$25,000 to United States Association for United Nations High Commissioner for Refugees, DC. For education program in Africa.

$10,000 to Film Arts Foundation, San Francisco, CA. For Save Our Schools.

$5,000 to Theater Downtown, Washington Stage Guild, DC. For performance support.

1808

The Henry Foundation, Inc. ✧

1990 M St. N.W., Ste. 250
Washington, DC 20036 (202) 887-8992
Contact: C. Wolcott Henry III, Pres.

Established in 1986 in FL.

Foundation type: Independent foundation.

Financial data (yr. ended 12/31/05): Assets, $11,722,565 (M); expenditures, $732,491; qualifying distributions, $644,576; giving activities include $578,150 for 89 grants (high: $75,000; low: $125).

Purpose and activities: Giving primarily for education, coral reef conservation and for animal welfare.

Fields of interest: Secondary school/education; Higher education; Environment, water resources; Animals/wildlife, preservation/protection; Mental health/crisis services.

International interests: Caribbean.

Type of support: Program development; Conferences/seminars; Publication; Seed money; Matching/challenge support.

Limitations: Giving primarily in FL and Washington, DC. No grants to individuals, or for capital campaigns or endowments.

Publications: Application guidelines; Grants list.

Application information: Applications are accepted only for the Coral Reef Conservation Program. No other applications will be considered.

> *Initial approach:* Letter of inquiry (for Coral Reef Program only)
> *Copies of proposal:* 1
> *Deadline(s):* July 31
> *Board meeting date(s):* Dec.
> *Final notification:* 4-6 months

Officers and Directors:* Nancy Cummings Henry,* Chair.; C. Wolcott Henry III,* Pres.; Nancy H. McKelvy,* Secy.; H. Alexander Henry,* Treas.

Number of staff: 2 part-time professional.

EIN: 592827461

1809
Hill-Snowdon Foundation

1301 Connecticut Ave. N.W., Ste. 500
Washington, DC 20036 (202) 833-8600
FAX: (202) 833-8606; E-mail: info@hillsnowdon.org;
URL: http://www.hillsnowdon.org/

Established in 1959 in NJ.

Donor: Arthur B. Hill†.

Foundation type: Independent foundation.

Financial data (yr. ended 12/31/05): Assets, $36,000,204 (M); gifts received, $172,997; expenditures, $2,509,423; qualifying distributions, $2,277,089; giving activities include $1,886,000 for 130 grants (high: $50,000; low: $500), and $2,650 for 7 employee matching gifts.

Purpose and activities: The foundation's mission is to work with low-income families and communities to create a fair and just society by helping them develop the capacity and leadership skills necessary to influence the decisions that shape their lives. HSF seeks to accomplish this mission by providing grants to organizations that work directly to build the power of low-income families; leveraging our and others' resources; and promoting opportunities for learning and growth.

Fields of interest: Employment, services; Youth development; Human services; Children/youth, services; Family services; Civil rights, advocacy; Economic development; Community development; Leadership development; Youth; Minorities; Women; Economically disadvantaged; Homeless.

Type of support: General/operating support.

Limitations: Applications not accepted. Giving in the U.S., primarily in Washington, DC, New York, NY, CA, and with a special focus on the South. No grants to individuals.

Publications: Grants list; Program policy statement.

Application information: While unsolicited proposals are not considered, the foundation will accept initial inquiry contacts from nonprofits whose work intersects with its areas of interest.

> *Board meeting date(s):* Nov.

Officers and Trustees:* Ashley Snowdon,* Pres.; Marguerite H. Snowdon,* V.P.; Richard Snowdon III,* Secy.-Treas.; Andrew Snowdon; Edward W. Snowdon, Jr.; Elizabeth Snowdon.

Number of staff: 3 full-time professional; 1 part-time professional.

EIN: 226081122

Selected grants: The following grants were reported in 2003.

$110,000 to National Childrens Museum, DC. For general support.

$40,000 to Youth Ministries for Peace and Justice, Bronx, NY. For general support.

$40,000 to YouthAction, Albuquerque, NM. For general support.

$30,000 to Concerned Citizens for a Better Tunica County, Tunica, MS. For general support.

$30,000 to Saint Thomas Health Services, New Orleans, LA. For general support.

$25,000 to North Carolina Lambda Youth Network, Durham, NC. For general support.

$20,000 to Action Communication and Education Reform, Duck Hill, MS. For general support.

$15,000 to Georgia Citizens Coalition on Hunger, Atlanta, GA. For general support.

$5,000 to Institute for Food and Development Policy, Oakland, CA. For general support.

$1,000 to Duke University, Durham, NC. For general support.

1810
The Hitachi Foundation

1215 17th St. N.W., 3rd Fl.
Washington, DC 20036 (202) 457-0588
Contact: Barbara Dyer, C.E.O. and Pres.; Mark Popovich, Sr. Prog. Off.
FAX: (202) 298-1098; URL: http://www.hitachifoundation.org

Established in 1985 in DC.

Donor: Hitachi, Ltd.

Foundation type: Independent foundation.

Financial data (yr. ended 12/31/04): Assets, $22,731,308 (M); gifts received, $2,268,244; expenditures, $2,579,322; qualifying distributions, $3,090,474; giving activities include $1,007,654 for 283 grants (high: $300,000; low: $250).

Purpose and activities: The foundation supports organizations involved with education, employment, and economically disadvantaged people and awards grants to high school seniors.

Fields of interest: Employment; Economically disadvantaged.

Type of support: Program development; Employee volunteer services; Matching/challenge support.

Limitations: Giving on a national basis. No grants to individuals (except for Yoshiyama Awards), or for capital campaigns or fundraising.

Publications: Application guidelines; Annual report; Financial statement; Grants list; Informational brochure; Occasional report.

Application information: Application forms are available online. Application form required.

> *Initial approach:* Complete online letter of inquiry form for Business and Communities Grants; complete online narration form for Yoshiyama Awards
> *Copies of proposal:* 1

> *Deadline(s):* Apr. 1 for Yoshiyama Awards
> *Board meeting date(s):* Spring, summer, and fall
> *Final notification:* Aug. or Sept. for Yoshiyama Awards

Officers and Directors:* Bruce MacLaury, Ph.D., Chair.; Barbara Dyer,* C.E.O. and Pres.; Nalin Liyanamara, C.F.O.; Sherry Salway Black; David Dodson; Frances Garcia; Patrick W. Gross; Trish Karter; Herman B. "Dutch" Leonard, Ph.D.

Number of staff: 4 full-time professional; 3 full-time support.

EIN: 521429292

1811
HRH Foundation ◇

3100 R St. N.W.
Washington, DC 20007-2937
Contact: Helen Lee Henderson, Exec. Dir.

Established in 1997 in PA.

Donors: Helen Ruth Henderson†; Helen Lee Henderson; Benson G. Henderson†.

Foundation type: Independent foundation.

Financial data (yr. ended 12/31/05): Assets, $17,760,738 (M); gifts received, $353,174; expenditures, $2,256,486; qualifying distributions, $2,247,515; giving activities include $2,091,686 for 5 grants (high: $870,390; low: $100,000).

Purpose and activities: Giving primarily for the visual and performing arts, and education.

Fields of interest: Museums (art); Performing arts centers; Historic preservation/historical societies; Higher education, university.

Limitations: Applications not accepted. Giving limited to Washington, DC, PA, and VA. No grants to individuals.

Application information: Contributes only to pre-selected organizations.

Officer: Helen Lee Henderson, Exec. Dir.

EIN: 522048784

Selected grants: The following grants were reported in 2003.

$401,500 to John F. Kennedy Center for the Performing Arts, DC.

$175,000 to National Gallery of Art, Department of Exhibitions Video Productions, DC.

$150,000 to Colonial Williamsburg Foundation, Williamsburg, VA. For Hallam-Douglas Theater.

$125,000 to Pennsylvania State University, University Park, PA. For George H. Deike Memorial Scholarship.

1812
The Johnson Family Fund ◇

2099 Pennsylvania Ave. N.W., Ste. 900
Washington, DC 20006

Established in 1999 in DC.

Donor: James A. Johnson.

Foundation type: Independent foundation.

Financial data (yr. ended 8/31/05): Assets, $3,063,033 (M); gifts received, $583,520; expenditures, $896,850; qualifying distributions, $891,250; giving activities include $891,250 for 43 grants (high: $211,500; low: $150).

Fields of interest: Performing arts centers; Arts; Elementary/secondary education; Human services.

Limitations: Applications not accepted. Giving primarily in Washington, DC, MN, and NY. No grants to individuals.

Application information: Contributes only to pre-selected organizations.
Officer: James A. Johnson, Pres.
EIN: 311677317
Selected grants: The following grants were reported in 2005.
$110,000 to Augsburg College, Minneapolis, MN. 2 grants: $100,000, $10,000
$50,000 to Minneapolis Institute of Arts, Minneapolis, MN.
$50,000 to Sidwell Friends School, DC.
$15,000 to National Campaign to Prevent Teen Pregnancy, DC.
$10,000 to Folger Shakespeare Library, DC.
$7,500 to YMCA.
$5,000 to A Better Chance, New York, NY.
$5,000 to International Womens Media Foundation, DC.
$5,000 to Project Children, Greenwood Lake, NY.

1813
The Joseph E. & Marjorie B. Jones Foundation ◇

1666 Connecticut Ave. N.W., Ste. 200
Washington, DC 20009-1039 (202) 797-6720
Contact: Joyce Havard, Dir.

Established in 1989 in DC.
Donors: Marjorie B. Jones; Joseph E. Jones Charitable Remainder Annuity Trust; Marjorie B. Jones Charitable Remainder Annuity Trust.
Foundation type: Independent foundation.
Financial data (yr. ended 12/31/05): Assets, $18,408,975 (M); gifts received, $161,112; expenditures, $3,114,187; qualifying distributions, $746,225; giving activities include $735,000 for 19 grants (high: $145,000; low: $10,000).
Purpose and activities: Support for human services, including youth groups, family programs, and the homeless; health organizations, including pediatrics, eye research, mental health, and medical research; and conservation education.
Fields of interest: Higher education; Health care; Pediatrics; Medical research, institute; Human services; Children/youth, services.
Type of support: Program development; Research.
Limitations: Giving primarily in the Washington, DC, area.
Application information: Application form required.
  Initial approach: Letter requesting application
  Deadline(s): June 30
Officer: Harris W. Havard, Pres.
Directors: John Curtin; Donald Havard; Joyce Havard; Mary J. Havard; Stephanie Havard; Irving Kator.
EIN: 521628951

1814
Jovid Foundation ◇

5335 Wisconsin Ave. N.W., Ste. 440
Washington, DC 20015-2003 (202) 686-2616
Contact: Bob Wittig, Exec. Dir.
FAX: (202) 686-2621;
E-mail: jovidfoundation@yahoo.com; URL: http://www.jovid.org

Established in 1990 in DC; funded in 1991.
Donors: David O. Maxwell; Joan P. Maxwell.
Foundation type: Independent foundation.
Financial data (yr. ended 12/31/05): Assets, $5,709,034 (M); expenditures, $604,705;

qualifying distributions, $569,860; giving activities include $496,911 for grants.
Purpose and activities: The foundation's primary interest is in supporting nonprofit organizations in the District of Columbia whose work is aimed at helping people in or at risk of long-term poverty to become more self-sufficient. Because the foundation is small and seeks to make a real difference to the projects it funds, it is particularly interested in neighborhood-based efforts that provide programs and services to adults, including its funding for vocational education and job counseling. The foundation also has a modest budget for support of the arts.
Fields of interest: Vocational education; Employment, job counseling.
Type of support: General/operating support; Continuing support; Program development; Seed money; Research; Program evaluation.
Limitations: Giving primarily in Washington, DC. No support for sectarian projects. No grants to individuals.
Publications: Annual report (including application guidelines).
Application information: WG Common Grant Letter of Intent Format is preferred. Will not accept unsolicited proposals. Application form not required.
  Initial approach: Letter of inquiry
  Copies of proposal: 1
  Deadline(s): 2006 deadlines: Jan. 10, Apr. 4, July 11 and Oct. 3
  Board meeting date(s): Mar., June, Sept., and Dec.
  Final notification: After board meeting
Officers and Directors:* Joan P. Maxwell,* Pres.; David O. Maxwell,* V.P. and Treas.; Doris D. Blazek-White,* Secy.; Bob Wittig, Exec. Dir.
Number of staff: 1 part-time professional.
EIN: 521694387

1815
Danny Kaye and Sylvia Fine Kaye Foundation ◇

c/o The Weidenfeld Law Firm
888 17th St. N.W., Rm. 900
Washington, DC 20006

Established in 1995 in CO.
Donors: Danny Kaye†; Sylvia Fine Kaye†.
Foundation type: Independent foundation.
Financial data (yr. ended 12/31/05): Assets, $15,128,998 (M); expenditures, $932,732; qualifying distributions, $699,638; giving activities include $659,150 for 19 grants (high: $190,000; low: $450; average: $2,500–$25,000).
Purpose and activities: Giving primarily for the performing arts, health, human services, and a center of reproductive law and policy.
Fields of interest: Performing arts, dance; Performing arts, music; Arts; Hospitals (general); Health care; Human services; Civil liberties, reproductive rights.
Type of support: General/operating support; Building/renovation; Endowments.
Limitations: Applications not accepted. Giving primarily in CA, CO, and New York, NY. No grants to individuals.
Application information: Contributes only to pre-selected organizations.
Directors: Dena Kaye; William Stinehart, Jr.; Edward L. Weidenfeld.
EIN: 841283914

Selected grants: The following grants were reported in 2003.
$478,000 to Center for Reproductive Rights, New York, NY. 4 grants: $25,000, $82,500, $82,500, $288,000 (For India Project).
$200,000 to Jazz at Aspen-Snowmass, Aspen, CO. 2 grants: $100,000 each
$37,500 to Jazz at Lincoln Center, New York, NY.
$13,500 to Aspen Film Festival, Aspen, CO.
$10,000 to Aspen Valley Community Foundation, Aspen, CO.
$10,000 to Natural Resources Defense Council, New York, NY.

1816
The Joseph P. Kennedy, Jr. Foundation

1133 19th St. N.W., 12th Fl.
Washington, DC 20036 (202) 393-1250
Contact: Steven M. Eidelman
FAX: (202) 824-0351; E-mail: info@jpkf.org;
URL: http://www.jpkf.org

Incorporated in 1946 in DC.
Donors: Joseph P. Kennedy†; Mrs. Joseph P. Kennedy†.
Foundation type: Independent foundation.
Financial data (yr. ended 6/30/04): Assets, $16,071,728 (M); gifts received, $38,513; expenditures, $1,344,029; qualifying distributions, $1,213,323; giving activities include $600,000 for 8 grants (high: $190,000; low: $5,000).
Purpose and activities: The foundation's main objectives are the prevention of mental retardation by identifying its causes and improving means by which society deals with its mentally retarded citizens. Emphasis on the use of funds in areas where a multiplier effect is possible. Fellowships limited to four one-year Washington, DC-based Kennedy Foundation Public Policy Leadership Fellows.
Fields of interest: Learning disorders research; Developmentally disabled, centers & services.
International interests: Central America; Nicaragua.
Type of support: Program development; Seed money; Fellowships; Technical assistance; Consulting services.
Limitations: Giving on a national basis. No grants to individuals, or for building or endowment funds, equipment, or operating budgets of schools or service organizations.
Publications: Application guidelines.
Application information: The foundation will not invite unsolicited full proposals for the remainder of 2007. Funds are substantially committed to grants initiated by the foundation; only proposals in the field of intellectual disability are funded. Application packet and information available on foundation Web site. Application form not required.
  Initial approach: 2-page letter of intent/concept paper
  Copies of proposal: 1
  Deadline(s): Concept papers accepted year-round. Full proposals are solicited from concept papers and are typically accepted between July 1 and Dec. 1
  Board meeting date(s): Usually spring
  Final notification: 2 weeks to 1 month
Officers and Trustees:* Sen. Edward M. Kennedy,* Pres.; Caroline Kennedy; Christopher Kennedy; Edward M. Kennedy, Jr.; Rory E. Kennedy; Sydney McKelvy; Eunice Kennedy Shriver; Robert S. Shriver III; Jean Kennedy Smith; Stephen E. Smith, Jr.

Number of staff: 1 full-time professional; 1 part-time professional; 1 full-time support; 1 part-time support.
EIN: 136083407

1817
Kimsey Foundation ◇
c/o Lydia Miles, V.P., Progs.
1700 Pennsylvania Ave. N.W., Ste. 850
Washington, DC 20006
FAX: (202) 638-7272; E-mail: kimseyfdn@aol.com;
URL: http://www.kimseyfoundation.org

Established in 1997 in VA.
Donor: James V. Kimsey.
Foundation type: Independent foundation.
Financial data (yr. ended 12/31/04): Assets, $25,940,598 (M); expenditures, $3,019,632; qualifying distributions, $2,866,730; giving activities include $2,128,028 for 39 grants (high: $1,001,500; low: $310; average: $5,000–$25,000).
Purpose and activities: The foundation focuses on educational and cultural initiatives; supporting thriving communities that offer hope and opportunity to youth. The foundation gives preference to organizations using a proactive collaborative approach. The foundation participates in funding partnerships. It also serves the international community through policy research and humanitarian outreach. The foundation has narrowed its focus to include a few specific projects that leverage systemic change in public education and community development. The majority of new grants will be related to existing partnerships and initiatives.
Fields of interest: Arts; Education; Children/youth, services; International affairs, public policy; International human rights; Community development; Public affairs, political organizations; Immigrants/refugees.
Type of support: General/operating support; Program development; Technical assistance; Matching/challenge support.
Limitations: Applications not accepted. Giving primarily in Washington, DC. No grants to individuals, or for building or renovations, endowments, capital campaigns, conferences, or for competition expenses.
Application information: The foundation does not accept unsolicited proposals. A few focused projects are chosen each year based on research in the field.
Officers: James V. Kimsey, Chair.; Michael P. Kimsey, Pres. and Exec. Dir.; Lydia Miles, V.P., Progs.; Daniel F. Katz, Secy.; Michael Fox, Treas.
Directors: Mark J. Kimsey; Ray Kimsey.
Board Member: James Gibson.
Number of staff: 2 full-time professional; 1 part-time professional.
EIN: 522007895
Selected grants: The following grants were reported in 2003.
$1,037,000 to John F. Kennedy Center for the Performing Arts, DC. For theater program for fifth grade students.
$500,000 to Georgetown University, DC. For general operating support.
$464,750 to Childrens Scholarship Fund, New York, NY. For general operating support.
$250,000 to Refugees International, DC. For general operating support.

$200,000 to District of Columbia College Access Program, DC. For college advising.
$125,000 to Washington Opera, DC. For general operating support.
$66,000 to Trinity College, DC. For Education Technology Leadership Institute (ETLI) Program.
$55,000 to Fight for Children, DC. For School Night and Fight Night.
$50,000 to New Leaders for New Schools, New York, NY. For general operating support.
$40,000 to Carnegie Endowment for International Peace, DC. For general operating support.

1818
The Kiplinger Foundation
1729 H St. N.W.
Washington, DC 20006 (202) 887-6559
Contact: Andrea B. Wilkes, Secy.
E-mail: foundation@kiplinger.com

Incorporated in 1948 in MD.
Donor: Willard M. Kiplinger‡.
Foundation type: Independent foundation.
Financial data (yr. ended 12/31/05): Assets, $15,842,278 (M); gifts received, $8,420; expenditures, $1,922,775; qualifying distributions, $1,807,686; giving activities include $1,718,816 for 29 grants (high: $500,000; low: $50), and $59,250 for 71 employee matching gifts.
Purpose and activities: Support primarily for educational, health, welfare, civic, and cultural organizations.
Fields of interest: Arts; Education; Human services.
Type of support: General/operating support; Continuing support; Annual campaigns; Capital campaigns; Building/renovation; Endowments; Employee matching gifts.
Limitations: Giving primarily in the greater Washington, DC, area. No grants to individuals, or for seed money, emergency funds, deficit financing, equipment and materials, medical research, land acquisition, or scholarship funds.
Publications: Application guidelines.
Application information: Washington Regional Association of Grantmakers applications are acceptable. Application form not required.
Initial approach: Letter
Copies of proposal: 1
Deadline(s): None
Board meeting date(s): 4 times per year
Final notification: 3 to 6 months
Officers and Trustees:* Austin H. Kiplinger,* Pres.; Andrea B. Wilkes,* Secy.; David M. Daugherty, Treas.; Knight A. Kiplinger; Todd L. Kiplinger; Janet Bodnar Linnehan.
Number of staff: 1 part-time professional.
EIN: 520792570
Selected grants: The following grants were reported in 2004.
$110,000 to Cornell University, Ithaca, NY.
$100,000 to Atlas Performing Arts Center, DC.
$75,500 to National Press Foundation, DC.
$75,000 to Oldfields School, Glencoe, MD.
$35,000 to National Symphony Orchestra, DC.
$30,130 to Independent College Fund of Maryland, Baltimore, MD.
$25,000 to Historical Society of Washington, DC, DC.
$15,000 to Black Student Fund, DC.
$10,000 to Washington Performing Arts Society, DC.
$500 to Mount Saint Michael Academy, Bronx, NY.

1819
Charles G. Koch Charitable Foundation ◇
655 15th St. N.W., Ste. 445
Washington, DC 20005 (202) 393-2354
Contact: Admin.
FAX: (202) 393-2355;
E-mail: email@cgkfoundation.org; URL: http://www.cgkfoundation.org

Established in 1981 in KS.
Donors: Charles G. Koch; Fred C. Koch Foundation; Fred C. Koch Trusts for Charity.
Foundation type: Independent foundation.
Financial data (yr. ended 12/31/04): Assets, $49,176,396 (M); gifts received, $16,019,933; expenditures, $3,200,630; qualifying distributions, $2,985,334; giving activities include $2,103,027 for 22 grants (high: $777,500; low: $975).
Purpose and activities: Funding for academic and public policy research directed at solving significant social problems through voluntary action and free enterprise. Support for projects that find market-based solutions to problematic social issues. For research, the foundation primarily funds institutions working with doctorate-level investigators in disciplines such as economics, history, philosophy, political science, and organizational behavior.
Fields of interest: Environment; Legal services; Economics; Public policy, research.
Type of support: General/operating support; Program development; Conferences/seminars; Seed money; Research; Program evaluation.
Limitations: Giving on a national basis, with some emphasis on Washington, DC. No support for lobbying activities or candidates for political office. No grants to individuals (except through summer fellows program).
Publications: Application guidelines.
Application information: See foundation Web site for application guidelines and procedures. Application form not required.
Initial approach: Letter (no more than 3 pages)
Copies of proposal: 1
Deadline(s): None
Officers and Directors:* Richard Fink,* Pres.; Kevin L. Gentry, V.P.; Andrew Woodlief, V.P.; Kelly Young, V.P.; Mark Humphrey, Secy.; Vonda Holliman, Treas.; Charles Chase Koch; Charles G. Koch; Elizabeth B. Koch; Elizabeth Robinson Koch.
EIN: 480918408
Selected grants: The following grants were reported in 2003.
$90,000 to Pacific Research Institute for Public Policy, San Francisco, CA. For general operating support.
$71,200 to Federalist Society for Law and Public Policy Studies, DC. For general operating support.
$57,516 to Environmental Literacy Council, DC. For general operating support.
$46,750 to Sand County Foundation, Madison, WI. For general operating support.
$27,000 to Mercatus Center, Arlington, VA. For general operating support.
$15,000 to Wildlife Habitat Council, Silver Spring, MD. For general operating support.
$14,500 to Property and Environment Research Center, Bozeman, MT. For general operating support.
$10,000 to Institute for Responsible Citizenship, DC. For general operating support.

1820
Claude R. Lambe Charitable Foundation ✧
655 15th St. N.W., Ste. 445
Washington, DC 20005 (202) 393-2354
Contact: Grants Admin.

Established in 1982 in DC and KS.
Donors: Claude R. Lambe†; Fred C. and Mary R. Koch Foundation.
Foundation type: Independent foundation.
Financial data (yr. ended 12/31/04): Assets, $21,829,353 (M); gifts received, $440,000; expenditures, $3,187,110; qualifying distributions, $3,110,086; giving activities include $2,615,640 for 34 grants (high: $465,000; low: $2,500).
Fields of interest: Public affairs, research.
Type of support: General/operating support; Research.
Limitations: Giving on a national basis, with some emphasis on the greater metropolitan Washington, DC, area. No grants to individuals.
Application information:
 Initial approach: Letter
 Deadline(s): None
Officers and Directors:* Richard H. Fink,* Pres.; Kevin Gentry, V.P.; Anthony Woodlief, V.P.; Kelly Young, V.P.; Mark Humphrey, Secy.; Vonda Holliman, Treas.; Charles Chase Koch; Charles G. Koch; Elizabeth B. Koch; Elizabeth Robinson Koch.
EIN: 480935563
Selected grants: The following grants were reported in 2004.
$465,000 to Heritage Foundation, DC.
$423,000 to Brookings Institution, DC.
$250,000 to Cato Institute, DC.
$200,000 to Manhattan Institute for Policy Research, New York, NY.
$150,000 to Washington Legal Foundation, DC.
$50,000 to Competitive Enterprise Institute, DC.
$50,000 to John Locke Foundation, Raleigh, NC.
$50,000 to Leadership Institute, Arlington, VA.
$50,000 to Tax Foundation, DC.
$50,000 to Texas Public Policy Foundation, Austin, TX.

1821
Jacob and Charlotte Lehrman Foundation, Inc.
1027 33rd St. N.W., 2nd Fl.
Washington, DC 20007 (202) 338-8400
FAX: (202) 338-8405;
E-mail: info@lehrmanfoundation.org; URL: http://www.lehrmanfoundation.org

Incorporated in 1953 in DC.
Donors: Jacob J. Lehrman†; Charlotte F. Lehrman†.
Foundation type: Independent foundation.
Financial data (yr. ended 10/31/05): Assets, $11,528,147 (M); expenditures, $590,622; qualifying distributions, $512,086; giving activities include $473,750 for 37 grants (high: $150,000; low: $1,000).
Purpose and activities: Giving to establish scholarships and fellowships at institutions of learning, and to foster research in medicine and science; grants also for Jewish welfare funds, care of the aged and sick, cancer research, the establishment of trade schools, the fostering of religious observance, and museums.
Fields of interest: Museums; Vocational education; Education; Health care; Health organizations, association; Cancer; Medical research, institute;

Cancer research; Human services; Aging, centers/services; Community development; Jewish federated giving programs; Jewish agencies & temples; Aging.
Type of support: General/operating support; Scholarship funds; Research.
Limitations: Applications not accepted. Giving primarily in metropolitan Washington, DC. No grants to individuals; no loans.
Publications: Grants list.
Application information: Unsolicited requests for funds will not be accepted. All proposals will be by invitation only.
 Board meeting date(s): Apr. and Oct.
Officers and Trustees:* Heidi Berry,* Pres.; Robert Lehrman,* V.P. and Admin.; Samuel Lehrman,* V.P.; Scott Rosenberg,* V.P.; Elizabeth Berry,* Secy.; Barry Wertlieb,* Treas.
EIN: 526035666

1822
The Leonsis Foundation ✧
401 9th St. N.W., Ste. 750
Washington, DC 20004
Contact: Ellen Kennedy Folts
FAX: (202) 347-5580; E-mail: leonsisfdn@aol.com; URL: http://www.leonsisfoundation.org

Established in 2000 in DC.
Donors: Theodore J. Leonsis; Lynn M. Leonsis.
Foundation type: Independent foundation.
Financial data (yr. ended 12/31/05): Assets, $956,311 (M); gifts received, $704,914; expenditures, $444,912; qualifying distributions, $413,040; giving activities include $409,553 for 10 grants (high: $125,000; low: $3,000).
Purpose and activities: The Leonsis Foundation primarily focuses on innovative programs that expand horizons and create opportunity for children under the age of eighteen. The foundation is particularly interested in educational and mentoring programs which incorporate computer internet technology. The foundation also has a strong interest in the health and well-being of all children.
Fields of interest: Education; Children, services.
Type of support: General/operating support; Continuing support; Program development; Scholarship funds.
Limitations: Applications not accepted. Giving primarily in Washington, DC, MD, and VA.
Application information: Unsolicited requests for funds not accepted. Letters of inquiry are accepted, but not every letter will get a response.
Officers and Directors:* Lynn M. Leonsis,* Pres.; Theodore J. Leonsis,* V.P. and Treas.; George P. Stamas,* Secy.
EIN: 522206647

1823
Mary and Daniel Loughran Foundation, Inc.
4910 Mass Ave. N.W., Ste. 215
Washington, DC 20016-4300 (202) 362-7986
Contact: F. William Burke, Exec. Dir.

Incorporated in 1967 in DC.
Donor: John Loughran†.
Foundation type: Independent foundation.
Financial data (yr. ended 7/31/05): Assets, $15,438,159 (M); expenditures, $903,817; qualifying distributions, $659,000; giving activities

include $659,000 for 85 grants (high: $25,000; low: $4,000).
Purpose and activities: Giving for education, arts and culture, and human services.
Fields of interest: Performing arts, theater; Arts; Higher education; Business school/education; Human services; Children/youth, services; Disabilities, people with.
Type of support: General/operating support; Continuing support; Annual campaigns; Scholarship funds; Matching/challenge support.
Limitations: Giving limited to Washington, DC, MD, and VA. No grants to individuals, or for capital or endowment funds; no loans.
Publications: Annual report.
Application information: Letter up to two pages. Application form not required.
 Initial approach: Letter
 Copies of proposal: 1
 Deadline(s): May 1
 Board meeting date(s): Apr., July, Aug., and Dec.
 Final notification: Aug. or Sept.
Officers and Directors:* Richard J.M. Poulson,* Pres.; Walter R. Fatzinger, Jr.,* V.P.; F. William Burke, Secy. and Exec. Dir.; Stephen D. Harlan,* Treas.; William Couper; Carl L. Gell; John T. Hazel; A. Linwood Holton, Jr.; R. Robert Linowes; John P. McDaniel; C. James Pailthorp; Howard M. Weiss.
Trustee: Bank of America, N.A.
Number of staff: 1 full-time professional; 1 part-time support.
EIN: 521095883
Selected grants: The following grants were reported in 2003.
$30,000 to Corcoran Gallery of Art, DC.
$30,000 to University of Maryland Foundation, Adelphi, MD.
$25,000 to George Mason University Foundation, Fairfax, VA. For scholarship endowment fund.
$20,000 to Childrens National Medical Center, DC.
$20,000 to Community Foundation for the National Capital Region, DC.
$20,000 to Phillips Collection, DC. For operating support.
$20,000 to Washington and Lee University, Lexington, VA.
$15,000 to Catholic University of America, DC. For scholarship endowment fund.
$15,000 to Keswick Equestrian Foundation, Keswick, VA.
$15,000 to Randolph-Macon Academy, Front Royal, VA.

1824
Richard Lounsbery Foundation, Inc. ✧
1020 19th St. N.W., Ste. LL60
Washington, DC 20036 (202) 872-8080
Contact: Maxmillian Angerholzer III, Secy.
FAX: (202) 872-9292;
E-mail: foundation@rlounsbery.org; URL: http://www.rlounsbery.org/

Incorporated in 1959 in NY.
Donors: Richard Lounsbery†; Richard Lounsbery Foundation Trust, Inc.
Foundation type: Independent foundation.
Financial data (yr. ended 12/31/04): Assets, $24,227,873 (M); gifts received, $2,228,834; expenditures, $3,487,202; qualifying distributions, $3,190,825; giving activities include $2,617,108 for 66 grants (high: $167,925; low: $1,000).
Purpose and activities: The Richard Lounsbery Foundation aims to enhance national strengths in

science and technology through support of programs in the following areas: science and technology components of key U.S. policy issues; elementary and secondary science and math education; historical studies and contemporary assessments of key trends in the physical and biomedical sciences; and start-up assistance for establishing the infrastructure of research projects.

Fields of interest: Elementary/secondary education; Health care; Biomedicine research; Science, public policy; Science.

Type of support: Seed money; Matching/challenge support.

Limitations: Giving nationally and internationally. No grants to individuals, or for endowments, capital or building funds; no loans.

Publications: Annual report.

Application information: Funds mainly committed to projects developed by the director. The foundation does not print any material and has no mailing list. Application form not required.

Initial approach: E-mail 2-page inquiry
Board meeting date(s): Jan., Apr., July and Oct.

Officers and Directors:* David M. Abshire,* Pres.; William Happer,* V.P.; Maxmillian Angerholzer III, Secy. and Exec. Dir.; Florence F. Arwade, Treas.; Jesse Ausubel; Richard J. McHenry; Homer A. Neal; David D. Sabatini; Frederick Seitz, Ph.D.

Number of staff: 2 full-time professional; 1 part-time professional; 1 full-time support.

EIN: 136081860

Selected grants: The following grants were reported in 2003.

$500,000 to Rockefeller University, New York, NY. For Frederick and Elizabeth Seitz Postdoctoral Fellowship Fund, payable over 4 years.

$142,477 to Consortium for Oceanographic Research and Education, DC. For Census of Marine Life project.

$85,134 to George Washington University, DC. For community mental health education program.

$80,000 to Woodrow Wilson International Center for Scholars, DC. For Serious Games Initiative.

$70,000 to American Association for the Advancement of Science, Center for Science, Techology, and Progress, DC.

$50,000 to Institut des Hautes Etudes Scientifiques (IHES), Bures-sur-Yvette, France. For Lounsbery Fellowship.

$50,000 to University of California, Oakland, CA. For Emerging Matter Project.

$25,000 to Chemical Heritage Foundation, Philadelphia, PA. For Joseph Priestly exhibit.

$25,000 to Manhattan Institute for Policy Research, Center for Medical Progress, New York, NY.

$10,000 to Clarke School for the Deaf, Northampton, MA. For Millennium Mathematics Curriculum Project.

1825
The Loyola Foundation, Inc.

308 C St. N.E.
Washington, DC   20002-5710   (202) 546-9400
Contact: Albert G. McCarthy III

Incorporated in 1957 in DC.

Donor: Members of the Albert Gregory McCarthy, Jr. family.

Foundation type: Independent foundation.

Financial data (yr. ended 10/31/05): Assets, $37,968,620 (M); gifts received, $3,905; expenditures, $1,775,823; qualifying distributions,

$1,560,940; giving activities include $1,359,063 for 238 grants (high: $74,599; low: $250).

Purpose and activities: Grants primarily for basic overseas Roman Catholic missionary work and other Catholic activities of special interest to the trustees. Primary interest in nonrecurring requests for capital improvements in the missionary area, which are self-sustaining after completion; special consideration given to requests where there are matching contributions from the missionary area, itself.

Fields of interest: Roman Catholic agencies & churches.

International interests: Africa; Asia; Developing countries; Latin America.

Type of support: Building/renovation; Equipment; Matching/challenge support.

Limitations: Giving primarily in Third World developing nations. Grants made in the U.S. only to institutions or organizations of special interest to the trustees. No support for minor seminaries. No grants to individuals, or for annual budgets, endowment funds, research, continuing support, operating expenses, emergency funds, deficit financing, publications, conferences, scholarships, fellowships, travel and meetings, or for used or reconditioned vehicles; no loans.

Publications: Application guidelines; Multi-year report.

Application information: All requests must be in English. If the initial request meets the foundation guidelines, an application form will be sent. For requests for projects whose cost is in excess of $50,000, applications cannot be accepted until at least 75 percent of the total funds needed for the project have been secured from other sources. Application form required.

Initial approach: Letter
Copies of proposal: 1
Deadline(s): Apr. 30 and Oct. 31
Board meeting date(s): June and Dec.
Final notification: Jan. and July

Officers and Trustees:* Denise M. Hattler,* Pres. and Treas.; John N. Malyska,* V.P.; A. Gregory McCarthy IV,* Exec. Dir.; Daniel J. Altobello; Rev. William J. Byron, S.J.; Kathleen D.H. Carr; Paul R. Dean; Ann M. Farrell; Hilary A. Hattler; Andrea M. Hattler-Bramson; Cardinal Theodore E. McCarrick; Albert G. McCarthy III; Raymond W. Merritt; Amy Hattler Page.

Number of staff: 1 full-time professional; 1 part-time professional.

EIN: 520781255

1826
The Ludwig Family Foundation, Inc. ✧ ☆

c/o Eugene A. Ludwig
1201 Pennsylvania Ave., Ste. 617
Washington, DC   20004

Established in 2002 in DC.

Donor: Eugene A. Ludwig.

Foundation type: Independent foundation.

Financial data (yr. ended 12/31/05): Assets, $907,203 (M); gifts received, $500,000; expenditures, $930,447; qualifying distributions, $928,550; giving activities include $927,350 for 55 grants (high: $525,000; low: $150).

Fields of interest: Higher education; Health care; Human services.

Limitations: Applications not accepted. Giving primarily in Washington, DC. No grants to individuals.

Application information: Unsolicited requests for funds not accepted.

Officers: Eugene A. Ludwig, Pres. and Treas.; Carol Ludwig, Secy.

Director: Robert B. Barnett.

EIN: 562305290

Selected grants: The following grants were reported in 2004.

$63,500 to National Academy Foundation, New York, NY.

$20,000 to National Cathedral School, DC.

$10,000 to Corporate Angel Network, White Plains, NY.

$10,000 to National Building Museum, DC.

1827
The J. Willard and Alice S. Marriott Foundation ▼ ✧

(formerly The J. Willard Marriott Foundation)
Marriott Dr.
Washington, DC   20058
Contact: Anne Gunsteens, Exec. Dir.

Established in 1966 in DC.

Donors: J. Willard Marriott‡; Alice S. Marriott‡; J. Willard Marriott Charitable Annuity Trust.

Foundation type: Independent foundation.

Financial data (yr. ended 12/31/04): Assets, $463,842,794 (M); gifts received, $7,706,796; expenditures, $14,302,383; qualifying distributions, $14,047,398; giving activities include $13,881,181 for 237 grants (high: $1,000,000; low: $500; average: $5,000–$150,000).

Purpose and activities: Grants primarily to local, previously supported charities, and a few general scholarship funds.

Fields of interest: Arts; Education; Health care; Human services.

Limitations: Applications not accepted. Giving primarily in Washington, DC. No grants to individuals.

Application information: Contributes only to pre-selected organizations.

Officers: Anne Gunsteens, Exec. Dir.; Melanie Winters, Grants and Fin. Mgr.

Trustees: J. Willard Marriott, Jr.; Richard E. Marriott.

Number of staff: 1 full-time professional; 1 full-time support.

EIN: 526068678

Selected grants: The following grants were reported in 2004.

$1,000,000 to Southern Virginia College, Buena Vista, VA. For capital campaign.

$500,000 to Mayo Foundation, Rochester, MN. For Marriott Program for Heart Disease Research.

$475,000 to Boys and Girls Clubs of Greater Washington, Silver Spring, MD. For high school clubs.

$330,000 to Marriott Foundation for People with Disabilities, DC. For technology infrastructure, training and development, and external communications materials.

$250,000 to Washington DC Convention and Tourism Foundation, DC. For America Celebrates the Greatest Generation program.

$125,000 to This is the Place Heritage Park, Salt Lake City, UT. For general operating support.

$25,000 to College Summit, DC. For college access program.

$20,000 to University of Maryland Medical System Foundation, Baltimore, MD. For Jarvik 2000 Research Project.

$18,000 to John F. Kennedy Center for the Performing Arts, DC. For program support of Honors Gala.

$10,000 to Mentors, DC. For program support.

1828

The Mazda Foundation (USA), Inc. ✧
1025 Connecticut Ave. N.W., Ste. 910
Washington, DC 20036
FAX: (202) 223-6490; URL: http://www.mazdafoundation.org

Established in 1990 in MI.

Donors: Mazda North American Opers.; Mazda Motor of America; Mazda Research & Development of North America.

Foundation type: Company-sponsored foundation.

Financial data (yr. ended 9/30/05): Assets, $8,720,320 (M); expenditures, $490,010; qualifying distributions, $445,946; giving activities include $425,893 for 12 grants (high: $85,000; low: $5,000).

Purpose and activities: The foundation supports organizations involved with education, the environment, human services, cross-cultural understanding, and scientific research.

Fields of interest: Education, reading; Education; Environment; Human services; Civil rights, race/intergroup relations; Science, research.

Type of support: General/operating support; Curriculum development; Scholarship funds; Research; Exchange programs.

Limitations: Giving to national organizations located in CA, Washington, DC, LA, NH, NC, and TX. No support for political or religious organizations. No grants to individuals, or for fundraising dinners or events or capital campaigns, endowments, or debt reduction.

Publications: Application guidelines; Annual report.

Application information: Application form required.
Initial approach: Download application form and mail or fax to foundation
Copies of proposal: 1
Deadline(s): Between May 1 and July 1
Board meeting date(s): Aug.
Final notification: By the end of Sept.

Officers and Trustees:* James J. O'Sullivan,* Chair.; Jay Amestoy,* Pres.; Renee Lewis, Secy.; Shusuke Koreeda,* Treas.

EIN: 382952236

Selected grants: The following grants were reported in 2005.

$85,000 to Dillard University, New Orleans, LA.

$62,055 to Hispanic Scholarship Fund, San Francisco, CA.

$25,000 to Orangewood Childrens Foundation, Santa Ana, CA.

$25,000 to THINK Together, Santa Ana, CA.

$20,000 to American Red Cross, National Headquarters, DC.

$5,000 to Information Center, Taylor, MI.

1829

The Patrick H. McGettigan Foundation ✧ ☆
c/o Joan Holtz
3327 N St. N.W.
Washington, DC 20007-2808

Established in 1998 in VA.

Donor: Patrick H. McGettigan.

Foundation type: Independent foundation.

Financial data (yr. ended 12/31/05): Assets, $33,919 (M); gifts received, $480,571; expenditures, $461,096; qualifying distributions, $451,916; giving activities include $451,916 for grants.

Fields of interest: Secondary school/education; Scholarships/financial aid.

Limitations: Applications not accepted. No grants to individuals.

Application information: Contributes only to pre-selected organizations.

Officers: Patrick H. McGettigan, Pres. and Treas.; Michael P. McGettigan, V.P.; Kristen McGettigan, Secy.

EIN: 541875819

1830

William G. McGowan Charitable Fund ▼
P.O. Box 40515
Washington, DC 20016-0515 (301) 320-8570
Contact: Bernard A. Goodrich, Exec. Dir.
FAX: (301) 320-8627; E-mail (for Bernard A. Goodrich): goodric@aol.com; URL: http://www.mcgowanfund.org

Established in 1992 in DC.

Donor: William G. McGowan†.

Foundation type: Independent foundation.

Financial data (yr. ended 6/30/05): Assets, $143,488,788 (M); expenditures, $5,120,471; qualifying distributions, $4,250,987; giving activities include $3,852,558 for 129 grants (high: $1,206,000; low: $2,000; average: $15,000–$100,000), and $175,000 for 24 employee matching gifts.

Purpose and activities: Giving primarily to inner-city educational organizations, advanced college business scholarships, and medical research.

Fields of interest: Education; Medical research; Youth development.

Type of support: General/operating support; Continuing support; Equipment; Program development; Scholarship funds; Research; Technical assistance; Matching/challenge support.

Limitations: Giving limited to the Washington, DC, area, Chicago, IL, the metropolitan Kansas City, KS, area, western NY, northeastern PA, and northern VA (but does not apply to colleges and universities seeking McGowan Scholar grants). No support for political organizations.

Publications: Application guidelines; Informational brochure (including application guidelines); Program policy statement.

Application information: Application form required.
Initial approach: Letter requesting application or download application from Web site
Copies of proposal: 2
Deadline(s): Jan. 2, May 1, and Sept. 1
Board meeting date(s): Mar., July, and Nov.
Final notification: Following board meeting

Officers and Trustees:* Msgr. Andrew J. McGowan,* Chair.; Sue Gin McGowan,* Pres.; A. Joseph Rosica,* Secy.; Bernard A. Goodrich, Exec. Dir.; Orville Wright, Emeritus; Michael M. Cachine, Sr.; Kenneth Cox; Calvin Gin; Sherilyn Kingsbury; Gertrude McGowan; Leo McGowan; Thomas McGowan; Daniel Rosica; Kathryn Rosica; Lenore Rosica; Mark Rosica; MaryPat Swartz.

Number of staff: 1 full-time professional; 1 part-time support.

EIN: 521829785

Selected grants: The following grants were reported in 2005.

$1,200,000 to Capitol College, Laurel, MD. For construction of William G. McGowan Learning Center.

$500,000 to Georgetown University, DC. To establish William G. McGowan Chair in Chemistry.

$100,000 to Big Shoulders Fund, Chicago, IL. For Chairman's Scholarship Fund to help inner-city students and their families with tuition assistance.

$75,000 to Catholic Education Foundation of Northeast Kansas, Kansas City, KS. For program to increase reading skills of inner city non-public school children.

$50,000 to Bishop Timon - Saint Jude High School, Buffalo, NY. For matching grant for structural equipment and training needs.

$35,000 to Rush University Medical Center, Chicago, IL. For scholarships for medical students.

$25,000 to Bishop Hafey Junior/Senior High School, Hazleton, PA. To establish endowment/scholarship fund for disenfranchised students.

$25,000 to Building Educated Leaders for Life (BELL) Foundation, Baltimore, MD. For summer academic and social enrichment programs.

$18,000 to La Salle University, Philadelphia, PA. For McGowan Scholars.

$10,000 to Retired Scientists, Engineers and Technicians, DC. For ReSET program.

1831

The McIntosh Foundation
1200 18th St. N.W., Ste. 801
Washington, DC 20036-2542 (202) 338-8055

Incorporated in 1949 in NY.

Donors: Josephine H. McIntosh†; Karen McIntosh†; Peter McIntosh†; Marie Joy McIntosh†.

Foundation type: Independent foundation.

Financial data (yr. ended 12/31/05): Assets, $38,149,705 (M); expenditures, $1,110,861; qualifying distributions, $846,704; giving activities include $560,850 for 38 grants (high: $120,000; low: $1,000).

Purpose and activities: Giving primarily for environmental conservation.

Fields of interest: Environment, natural resources.

Type of support: General/operating support.

Limitations: Applications not accepted. Giving limited primarily to southeastern AK.

Application information: Due to the number of ongoing and/or permanent projects, the foundation is accepting grant applications by invitation only.
Board meeting date(s): Every 4 months

Officers and Directors:* Michael A. McIntosh,* Pres. and C.I.O.; Joan H. McIntosh,* V.P.; Winsome D. McIntosh,* V.P.; Frederick A. Terry, Jr.,* Secy.; Colin H. McIntosh; Hunter H. McIntosh; Michael A. McIntosh, Jr.

Number of staff: 1 full-time professional; 1 part-time professional; 1 full-time support.

EIN: 136096459

Selected grants: The following grants were reported in 2005.

$90,000 to Rachels Network, DC.

$50,000 to Defenders of Wildlife, DC.

$27,500 to Florida State University, Tallahassee, FL.

$25,000 to Rockefeller University, New York, NY.

$15,000 to Vermont Law School, South Royalton, VT.

$11,800 to Philanthropy Roundtable, DC.

$10,000 to Childrens Cancer Foundation, Baltimore, MD.

$10,000 to League of Conservation Voters Education Fund, DC.

$7,500 to Muscular Dystrophy Association, Tucson, AZ.

$5,000 to Center for Health, Environment and Justice, Falls Church, VA.

1832
Mead Family Foundation
(formerly Gilbert and Jaylee Mead Family Foundation)
2700 Virginia Ave. N.W., No. 701
Washington, DC   20037   (202) 338-0398
Contact: Linda Smith, Exec. Dir.
FAX: (202) 388-4407;
E-mail: meadfoundation@earthlink.net; Additional address: 16300 Spring Water Ct., Rockville, MD 20853; URL: http://foundationcenter.org/grantmaker/mead/

Established in 1989 in MD.
Donors: Gilbert D. Mead; Jaylee M. Mead; Betsy Mead; Diana Mead-Siohan; Marilyn K. Mead.
Foundation type: Independent foundation.
Financial data (yr. ended 12/31/05): Assets, $20,162,983 (M); gifts received, $49,875; expenditures, $1,168,509; qualifying distributions, $1,111,508; giving activities include $975,000 for 95 grants (high: $30,000; low: $5,000).
Purpose and activities: Giving primarily for education (K through 12), performing arts education and outreach, crisis prevention for children and youth, and strengthening families.
Fields of interest: Performing arts; Elementary/secondary education; Family services.
Type of support: Continuing support; Equipment; Program development; Curriculum development.
Limitations: Giving limited to Washington, DC, and Montgomery County, MD. No grants to individuals or for capital campaigns.
Publications: Application guidelines; Grants list; Informational brochure.
Application information: Letters of inquiry or proposals received by fax or E-mail will not be considered. Proposal requirements are distributed upon approval of letter of inquiry. See foundation Web site for full application guidelines and requirements. Application form required.
  Initial approach: First-time grantseekers must submit a brief letter of inquiry. Organizations not funded by the foundation in the past 2 years must also send a letter of inquiry
  Copies of proposal: 1
  Deadline(s): June 15 and Dec. 15 for organizations required to submit a letter of inquiry. Sept.1 and Mar. 1 proposal deadlines
  Board meeting date(s): Nov. and May
  Final notification: Nov. 15 and May. 15
Officers and Directors:* Gilbert D. Mead,* Chair.; Betsy A. Mead,* Pres. and Treas.; Diana C. Mead-Siohan,* V.P., International and Corp. Secy.; Jaylee M. Mead,* V.P.; Linda Smith, Exec. Dir.; Marilyn K. Mead.
Number of staff: 3 part-time professional.
EIN: 521646030
Selected grants: The following grants were reported in 2005.
$12,000 to Center for Inspired Teaching, DC.

$12,000 to CentroNia, DC.

$12,000 to Choral Arts Society of Washington, DC.

$12,000 to Class Acts Arts, Silver Spring, MD.

$12,000 to Community Bridges, Silver Spring, MD.

$12,000 to Dance Institute of Washington, DC.

$12,000 to DC Arts and Humanities Education Collaborative, DC.

$12,000 to DC SCORES, DC.

$12,000 to Family Place, DC.

$12,000 to Family Services Agency, Gaithersburg, MD.

1833
Merriman Foundation ◇ ☆ ☆
1747 Pennsylvania Ave., Ste. 1000
Washington, DC   20006-4604

Foundation type: Independent foundation.
Financial data (yr. ended 12/31/05): Assets, $8,012,732 (M); gifts received, $1,096,460; expenditures, $365,379; qualifying distributions, $347,102; giving activities include $347,102 for grants.
Fields of interest: Arts; Education; Medical research, institute; Boys & girls clubs; Boy scouts; Human services; Federated giving programs; Religion.
International interests: Bahamas.
Limitations: Applications not accepted. Giving primarily in Palm Beach, FL, and Kansas City, MO; funding also in Nassau, Bahamas. No grants to individuals.
Application information: Contributes only to pre-selected organizations.
Officers: Joe Jack Merriman, Pres.; Elaine A. Merriman, V.P.; Michael A. Merriman, Secy.-Treas.
EIN: 237113720
Selected grants: The following grants were reported in 2004.
$10,000 to Pembroke Hill School, Kansas City, MO.

$5,000 to Royal Poinciana Chapel, Palm Beach, FL.

$5,000 to Saint Andrews Episcopal Church, Kansas City, MO.

$5,000 to Southern Methodist University, Dallas, TX.

$500 to Palm Beach Civic Association, Palm Beach, FL.

$150 to Henry Morrison Flagler Museum, Palm Beach, FL.

$107 to Boy Scouts of America, Kansas City, MO.

1834
Eugene and Agnes E. Meyer Foundation ▼
1400 16th St. N.W., Ste. 360
Washington, DC   20036   (202) 483-8294
Contact: Julie L. Rogers, Pres.
FAX: (202) 328-6850; E-mail: meyer@meyerfdn.org; URL: http://www.meyerfoundation.org

Incorporated in 1944 in NY.
Donors: Eugene Meyer‡; Agnes E. Meyer‡; Marpat Foundation.
Foundation type: Independent foundation.
Financial data (yr. ended 12/31/05): Assets, $193,092,698 (M); gifts received, $5,000; expenditures, $10,050,190; qualifying distributions, $9,668,548; giving activities include $7,156,264 for 258 grants, and $222,500 for 9 loans/program-related investments (high: $75,000; low: $11,000).

Purpose and activities: The foundation works to develop Greater Washington, DC as a community by supporting capable, community-based nonprofit organizations that foster the well-being of all people in the region. The foundation is especially concerned about low-income people and creating healthy neighborhoods. It values and seeks to promote the region's diversity. The foundation accomplishes its work by: 1) finding visionary and talented nonprofit leaders; making early and strategic investments in nonprofit organizations; 2) strengthening the organizational capacity of nonprofits in the region; 3) promoting a strong and influential nonprofit sector; building partnerships to foster the sector's work; and 4) serving as a resource to other donors who want to make effective charitable investments in the region. Grants principally for arts, heritage and culture, children, youth and families; civic engagement; education; employment and skills training; health and mental health; homelessness and hunger; housing and community development; immigrant communities; law and justice; nonprofit sector strengthening and management assistance.
Fields of interest: Performing arts, theater; Humanities; Arts; Education, early childhood education; Child development, education; Elementary school/education; Secondary school/education; Vocational education; Adult education—literacy, basic skills & GED; Education, reading; Education; Dental care; Health care; Substance abuse, services; Mental health/crisis services; Health organizations; Legal services; Crime/law enforcement; Employment; Housing/shelter, development; Youth development, services; Human services; Children/youth, services; Child development, services; Women, centers/services; Minorities/immigrants, centers/services; Homeless, human services; Civil rights, race/intergroup relations; Civil rights; Urban/community development; Community development; Voluntarism promotion; Leadership development; Minorities; Women; Immigrants/refugees; Economically disadvantaged; Homeless.
Type of support: General/operating support; Management development/capacity building; Capital campaigns; Building/renovation; Program development; Seed money; Technical assistance; Consulting services; Program-related investments/loans; Matching/challenge support.
Limitations: Giving limited to the metropolitan Washington, DC, area, including Montgomery, Prince George's, Calvert, Charles, and St. Mary's counties in suburban MD and Arlington, Fairfax, Loudoun, Prince William and Stafford counties, and the cities of Alexandria, Falls Church, Manassas, and Manassas Park in northern VA. No support for sectarian purposes, or for programs that are national or international in scope. No grants to individuals, or for annual campaigns, deficit financing, endowment funds, equipment, scholarships, fellowships, scientific or medical research, publications, special events or conferences.
Publications: Application guidelines; Annual report (including application guidelines); Grants list; Newsletter.
Application information: For a thorough understanding of application procedures, interested parties are strongly urged to read the foundation's annual report and guidelines, which are available on the Web site. Letters of inquiry must be received before 5 p.m. on the day of the deadline. The foundation will acknowledge receipt of all letters within two weeks. If further information is needed,

the applicant will be contacted by a foundation staff member. The foundation may or may not invite a full proposal. Accepts WG Common Grant Application Form. Letter of inquiry application coversheet required. Application form required.

Initial approach: 2-page letter of inquiry with coversheet and requested documents (original and 1 copy)

Copies of proposal: 2

Deadline(s): Consult Web site or call foundation office for letter of inquiry deadlines

Board meeting date(s): Applications considered at Feb., June, and Oct. meetings; board meets also in Apr. and Dec.

Final notification: Within 1 month after board meeting

Officers and Directors:* Edward H. Bersoff, Ph.D.*, Chair.; Barbara J. Krumsiek,* Vice-Chair.; Julie L. Rogers, Pres.; Kristen Conte, V.P., Finance and Admin.; Albert Ruesga, V.P., Progs. and Comms.; Thomas W. Chapman,* Secy.-Treas.; Joshua B. Bernstein; Maria S. Gomez; Newman T. Halvorson, Jr.; Eric H. Holder, Jr.; Boisfeuillet Jones, Jr.; Patricia A. McGuire; Robert G. Templin, Jr.; Gloria WilderBrathwaite; Francey Lim Youngberg.

Number of staff: 8 full-time professional; 2 part-time professional; 5 full-time support; 1 part-time support.

EIN: 530241716

Selected grants: The following grants were reported in 2005.

$250,000 to District of Columbia Primary Care Association, DC. For public policy work and Medical Homes DC project, payable over 3 years.

$250,000 to Signature Theater, Arlington, VA. For capital campaign for new facility.

$200,000 to Jubilee Housing, DC. For Campaign for a New Jubilee.

$150,000 to Higher Achievement Program, DC. For capital campaign.

$100,000 to Carlos Rosario International Career Center, DC. For capital campaign.

$100,000 to Dance/USA, DC. For Dance/MetroDC.

$100,000 to HSC Foundation, DC. For Medical Home for Children with Special Needs, payable over 3 years.

$100,000 to Patricia M. Sitar Center for the Arts, DC. For capital campaign.

$75,000 to Wolf Trap Foundation for the Performing Arts, Vienna, VA. For values-based fundraising campaign targeting individual donors, payable over 3 years.

$60,000 to CentroNia, DC. To develop and implement child care program at Carlos Rosario International Public Charter School, payable over 2 years.

1835
Moriah Fund ▼

1 Farragut Sq. S.
1634 I St. N.W., Ste. 1000
Washington, DC 20006 (202) 783-8488
Contact: Mary Ann Stein, Pres.
FAX: (202) 783-8499; E-mail: info@moriahfund.org;
Additional E-mail: proposals@moriahfund.org;
Requests in Israel: Don Futterman, Beilenson St., No. 3, Apt. 1, Kfar Saba, Israel 44350; URL: http://www.moriahfund.org/index.htm

Established in 1985 in IN.

Donors: Clarence W. Efroymson†; Robert A. Efroymson†; Ben-Ephraim Gershon Fund; Gustave Aaron Efroymson Fund.

Foundation type: Independent foundation.

Financial data (yr. ended 12/31/04): Assets, $163,804,749 (M); expenditures, $10,653,881; qualifying distributions, $9,341,636; giving activities include $8,039,916 for 205 grants (high: $1,401,000; low: $1,500; average: $10,000–$30,000), and $200,000 for 1 loan/program-related investment.

Purpose and activities: Support primarily for pluralism, democracy, and community development in Israel; human rights, civic participation and leadership of indigenous people, rural development, and social justice in Guatemala; for reproductive health and women's rights; and for community-based development and programs to help families overcome poverty and gain self-sufficiency in Washington, DC, only.

Fields of interest: Reproductive health; Reproductive health, family planning; Family services, single parents; International human rights; Civil rights; Rural development; Community development; Leadership development.

International interests: Guatemala; Israel; Latin America; Russia; Ukraine.

Type of support: General/operating support; Continuing support; Income development; Management development/capacity building; Endowments; Emergency funds; Program development; Conferences/seminars; Seed money; Technical assistance; Program evaluation; Program-related investments/loans; In-kind gifts; Matching/challenge support.

Limitations: Giving nationally and internationally, including Israel and Latin America, specifically Guatemala; giving primarily in Washington, DC for poverty program. No support for lobbying or political campaigns, private foundations, or arts organizations. No grants to individuals, or for medical research.

Publications: Application guidelines; Grants list; Program policy statement.

Application information: All inquiries should be directed to the Washington, DC office except for Israel inquiries. Application must include proposal checklist which can be downloaded from the foundation Web site. Application form not required.

Initial approach: Letter of inquiry (not exceeding 2 to 3 pages) which must be received at least 1 month prior to application deadline. Letters are reviewed throughout the year

Copies of proposal: 1

Deadline(s): Mar. 1 and Aug. 1; Feb. 1 and July 1 for Israel program

Board meeting date(s): May and Nov.

Final notification: 1-2 weeks

Officers and Program Board:* Mary Ann Stein,* Pres.; Judith Lichtman,* 1st V.P. and Treas.; Shira Saperstein, 2nd V.P. and Prog. Dir., Women's Rights/Reprod.; Karl Mathiasen,* Secy.; Barbara Schrirfer, C.F.O.; Melody Charisse Barnes; Bonnie R. Cohen; Geeta Rao Gupta; Norman Rosenberg; Noah Stein.

Number of staff: 8 full-time professional; 1 part-time professional; 3 full-time support.

EIN: 311129589

Selected grants: The following grants were reported in 2005.

$440,000 to New Israel Fund, DC. 2 grants: $290,000 (For capacity building program, SHATIL, to provide technical assistance through projects: Assistance to Ethiopian Immigrants Project; Conflict Transformation and Management Center; Social and Economic Justice Initiative (formerly the Low-Income

Neighborhoods Project); and Palestinian Initiative), $150,000 (For Fidel-Association for Education and Social Integration for Ethiopian Jews, which empowers the Ethiopian community in Israel through training educational mediators, establishment of a model school and centers for youth at-risk).

$100,000 to Leadership Conference on Civil Rights Education Fund, DC. For general support.

$85,000 to Environmental Leadership Program, DC. For Jack Venderryn Fellowship Program, which supports young environmental leaders working in the Southeastern United States.

$60,000 to Center for Health and Gender Equity (CHANGE), Takoma Park, MD. For general support.

$30,000 to Center for Economic and Policy Research, DC. For global economic policy project, which seeks to change debate over trade, development, and global economic integration on issues that are pivotal to economic and social progress of developing countries, especially Latin America.

$30,000 to International Womens Health Coalition, New York, NY. For general support.

$25,000 to Ecologic Development Fund, Cambridge, MA. For Tropico Verde.

$25,000 to Legal Momentum, DC. For Immigrant Women's Program.

$25,000 to Nations Capital Child and Family Development, DC. For Child Care Advocacy Project.

1836
Stewart R. Mott Charitable Trust ✧

(formerly Stewart R. Mott Charitable Trust/Spectemur Agendo)
122 Maryland Ave. N.E.
Washington, DC 20002 (202) 546-3732
Contact: Bonnie Bacon, Prog. Asst.
FAX: (202) 543-3156;
E-mail: BaconBonnie@aol.com; Additional E-mail: bethannchapman@aol.com; URL: http://www.srmtrust.org

Trust established in 1968 in NY; reorganized in 1989 in NY.

Donors: Stewart R. Mott; Ruth R. Mott†.

Foundation type: Independent foundation.

Financial data (yr. ended 12/31/05): Assets, $15,885,291 (M); expenditures, $1,554,647; qualifying distributions, $1,426,284; giving activities include $1,063,961 for 216 grants (high: $350,000; low: $25; average: $1,000–$10,000).

Purpose and activities: The foundation funds organizations with small general operating grants. Areas of interest are those shared by Stewart Mott and the trustees. These include: population issues, family planning, peace and security, government reform, civil rights, and civil liberties.

Fields of interest: Reproductive health, family planning; International peace/security; International affairs, arms control; International affairs, foreign policy; International human rights; Civil rights; Government/public administration; Public affairs.

Type of support: General/operating support.

Limitations: Giving on a national and international basis. Generally, no support for local, regional, grassroots efforts, or ethnic-specific organizations. No grants to individuals, or for emergency support, conferences, media/arts projects or exchange programs.

Publications: Application guidelines.

Application information: The trust accepts the Common Grant Application of the National Network of Grantmakers. See foundation Web site for application guidelines and procedures.

   Initial approach: Letter of inquiry or proposal (no more than 3-6 pages). More detailed proposals are by invitation only

   Deadline(s): None

   Board meeting date(s): 4 to 6 meetings per year

Officer: Conrad Martin, Exec. Dir.

Trustees: Julie Burton; Stewart R. Mott; Kappy J. Wells.

Number of staff: 2 full-time professional; 1 part-time professional.

EIN: 237002554

Selected grants: The following grants were reported in 2003.

$75,000 to Fund for Constitutional Government, DC.

$15,000 to Consumers Choice Council, DC.

$12,500 to Grupo de Informacion en Reproduccion Elegida (GIRE), Mexico City, Mexico. .

$12,500 to Population Action International, DC.

$12,000 to Womens Action for New Directions (WAND) Education Fund, Arlington, MA.

$10,000 to National Security Archive Fund, DC.

$2,000 to Rainforest Action Network, San Francisco, CA.

$1,500 to Nation Institute, New York, NY.

$1,000 to City at Peace, DC.

$1,000 to Immigrant Workers Citizenship Project, Las Vegas, NV.

1837
Curtis & Edith Munson Foundation

1990 M St. N.W., Ste. 250
Washington, DC 20036 (202) 887-8992
Contact: Angel Braestrup, Exec. Dir.
FAX: (202) 887-8987; *E-mail:* info@munsonfdn.org;
URL: http://www.munsonfdn.org

Incorporated in 1982 in FL.

Foundation type: Independent foundation.

Financial data (yr. ended 12/31/05): Assets, $32,140,746 (M); expenditures, $2,299,231; qualifying distributions, $2,215,665; giving activities include $1,987,850 for 139 grants (high: $50,000; low: $1,000; average: $10,000–$25,000).

Purpose and activities: Support for conservation of marine wildlife and natural resources in North America, and U.S. population and immigration issues.

Fields of interest: Environment, natural resources; Environment, water resources; Environment; Animals/wildlife, fisheries.

Type of support: General/operating support; Program development; Conferences/seminars; Seed money; Matching/challenge support.

Limitations: Giving primarily in AL and FL; some giving also in the Chesapeake Bay watershed. No grants to individuals, or for endowment funds, capital campaigns, or for building or renovation; no loans.

Publications: Application guidelines; Grants list.

Application information: Contributes primarily to pre-selected organizations. Full proposals will not be accepted unless invited by the foundation. Application form required.

   Initial approach: 1-2 page letter of inquiry, along with separate project summary whose form must follow guidelines on foundation Web site. E-mail inquires are accepted

   Copies of proposal: 1

   Deadline(s): Apr. 6 and Aug. 31 for letters of inquiry and project summary

   Board meeting date(s): July, Nov., and as required

   Final notification: 3 weeks after meetings

Officers and Directors:* C. Wolcott Henry III,* Pres.; Bruce Reid,* Secy.; H. Alexander Henry, Treas.; Angel Braestrup, Exec. Dir.; Truman M. Hobbs, Jr.

Number of staff: None.

EIN: 592235907

1838
The National Academy of Education

500 5th St. N.W., No. 307
Washington, DC 20001
Contact: Gregory White, Exec. Dir.
FAX: (202) 334-2350; *E-mail:* info@naeducation.org;
URL: http://www.naeducation.org/

Established in 1965 in NY; classified as a private operating foundation in 1973.

Donors: The Ford Foundation; Spencer Foundation.

Foundation type: Operating foundation.

Financial data (yr. ended 12/31/04): Assets, $5,795,778 (M); gifts received, $4,435,388; expenditures, $2,153,920; qualifying distributions, $2,153,788; giving activities include $1,464,292 for 61 grants to individuals (high: $50,000; low: $2,692; average: $12,500–$25,000), and $1,622,495 for 2 foundation-administered programs.

Purpose and activities: Awards fellowships to recent recipients of Ph.D., Ed.D., or equivalent degrees planning to study matters relevant to the improvement of education.

Fields of interest: Education, research; Education.

Type of support: Fellowships.

Limitations: Giving on an international basis. No support for organizations.

Publications: Application guidelines; Informational brochure.

Application information: Request application before Nov. 1. Applications must be in English. Application guidelines are available on foundation Web site. Application form required.

   Initial approach: Letter, telephone, E-mail, or download application from Web site

   Copies of proposal: 6

   Deadline(s): Contact foundation for deadlines

   Board meeting date(s): Apr. and Oct.

   Final notification: Mid-May

Officers: Lorrie A. Shepard, Pres.; Andrew Porter, V.P.; Susan H. Fuhrman, Secy.-Treas.; Gregory White, Exec. Dir.

Number of staff: 2 full-time professional; 1 part-time professional.

EIN: 770415802

1839
Evelyn Stefansson Nef Foundation ✧

2726 N St. N.W.
Washington, DC 20007

Established around 1993 in DC.

Donor: Evelyn S. Nef.

Foundation type: Independent foundation.

Financial data (yr. ended 12/31/05): Assets, $4,693,741 (M); expenditures, $386,805; qualifying distributions, $347,500; giving activities include $347,500 for 20 grants (high: $25,000; low: $5,000).

Fields of interest: Museums (art); Arts; Education; Hospitals (general); Children/youth, services.

Limitations: Applications not accepted. Giving primarily in MA, New York, NY, and Washington, DC. No grants to individuals.

Application information: Contributes only to pre-selected organizations.

Officers: Evelyn S. Nef, Pres.; Mary Carswell, V.P.; Linda C. Yahn, Secy.

Director: Sheila Platt.

EIN: 521803459

1840
The Cissy Patterson Foundation ✧

c/o Ruth S. Flynn, Esq. PLLC
1666 Connecticut Ave., N.W.
Washington, DC 20009

Established in 1993 in DC.

Donor: The Cissy Patterson Trust.

Foundation type: Independent foundation.

Financial data (yr. ended 12/31/05): Assets, $4,949,690 (M); expenditures, $585,689; qualifying distributions, $567,986; giving activities include $561,030 for 17 grants (high: $93,000; low: $1,500).

Fields of interest: Arts, formal/general education; Performing arts, theater; Historic preservation/historical societies; Arts; Environment, natural resources; Environment; Human services; Civil rights, women; Foundations (private grantmaking); Foundations (community).

Limitations: Applications not accepted. Giving on a national basis. No grants to individuals.

Application information: Contributes only to pre-selected organizations.

Officers: Alice Arlen, Pres.; Joseph P. Albright, V.P.; Blandina A. Rojek, Secy.; Adam Albright, Treas.

EIN: 521795554

1841
Phillips Foundation, Inc.

1 Massachusetts Ave. N.W., Ste. 620
Washington, DC 20001 (202) 842-2002
Contact: John W. Farley, Secy.
FAX: (202) 216-9188; *E-mail:* jfarley@phillips.com;
Contact for scholarships: D. Jeffrey Hollingsworth, tel. (202) 250-3887, ext. 628, E-mail: jhollingsworth@phillips.com; *URL:* http://www.thephillipsfoundation.org

Established in 1990 in MD.

Donors: Phillips Publishing International, Inc.; Phillips International, Inc.; The Lynde and Harry Bradley Foundation, Inc.

Foundation type: Company-sponsored foundation.

Financial data (yr. ended 9/30/04): Assets, $11,205,349 (M); gifts received, $278,420; expenditures, $661,734; qualifying distributions, $568,997; giving activities include $372,500 for 60 grants to individuals (high: $35,000; low: $1,000).

Purpose and activities: The foundation awards college scholarships to college undergraduates and fellowships to working print journalists.

Type of support: Fellowships; Scholarships—to individuals.

Limitations: Giving on a national basis.

Application information: Application form required.

   Initial approach: Download application form

Deadline(s): Jan. 15 for scholarships; Mar. 1 for fellowships
Final notification: Late Mar. to early Apr. for scholarships
Officers and Trustees:* Thomas L. Phillips,* Chair.; John W. Farley, Secy.; Peter De Angelo, Treas.; Becky Norton Dunlop; Thomas A. Fuentes; Robert D. Novak; Alfred S. Regnery; Ron Robinson.
EIN: 521707001

1842
The Marjorie Merriweather Post Foundation

c/o U.S. Trust Co., N.A.
600 14th St. N.W., Ste. 400
Washington, DC 20005 (202) 585-4100
Contact: Bernard K. Jarvis
FAX: (202) 783-7161;
E-mail: bernard_jarvis@ustrust.com

Established in 1956 in DC.
Donor: Marjorie Merriweather Post†.
Foundation type: Independent foundation.
Financial data (yr. ended 12/31/04): Assets, $6,845,182 (M); expenditures, $452,880; qualifying distributions, $348,000; giving activities include $348,000 for 60 grants (high: $20,000; low: $1,000).
Fields of interest: Museums (natural history); Performing arts centers; Performing arts, orchestra (symphony); Historical activities; Arts; Elementary school/education; Higher education; Environment, natural resources; Environment, forests; Hospitals (general); Human services; Roman Catholic agencies & churches.
Limitations: Giving primarily on the East Coast, with emphasis on Washington, DC. No grants to individuals.
Publications: Application guidelines.
Application information: All grant monies must be used within the territorial U.S. Application form not required.
Initial approach: Proposal
Copies of proposal: 1
Deadline(s): Mar. 1 and Sept. 1
Board meeting date(s): Spring and fall
Final notification: Notification sent only to those organizations which are approved for grants
Officers: John A. Logan, Jr., Chair.; Spottswood P. Dudley, Vice-Chair.; Nina Craig Rumbough, Vice-Chair.; L.L. Silverstein, Treas.
Trustees: Henry A. Dudley, Jr.; George B. Hartzog, Jr.
EIN: 526054705

1843
Professional Athletes Foundation ✧

2021 L St. N.W., 6th Fl.
Washington, DC 20036

Established around 1981 in Washington, DC.
Donors: The National Football League; The National Football League Players Association.
Foundation type: Independent foundation.
Financial data (yr. ended 12/31/04): Assets, $11,868,935 (M); gifts received, $2,157,142; expenditures, $989,391; qualifying distributions, $873,170; giving activities include $301,200 for 28 + grants, and $571,970 for 115 grants to individuals (high: $15,000; low: $154).

Purpose and activities: Giving primarily to support former professional and amateur athletes and their families in times of financial crisis.
Type of support: Grants to individuals.
Limitations: Applications not accepted. Giving on a national basis.
Application information: Contributes only to pre-selected organizations.
Officers: Eugene Ushaw, Pres.; Beverly Pitts, V.P.; Frank Woschitz, V.P.; Delinda Rauch-Becker, Secy.; William Garner, Treas.
Directors: Ron Actis; Irv Cross; Brig Owens; Charles Swisher; Leen Teeuws.
EIN: 521205920

1844
Public Welfare Foundation, Inc. ▼

1200 U St. N.W.
Washington, DC 20009-4443 (202) 965-1800
Contact: Review Comm.
FAX: (202) 265-8851;
E-mail: reviewcommittee@publicwelfare.org;
URL: http://www.publicwelfare.org

Incorporated in 1947 in TX; reincorporated in 1951 in DE.
Donor: Charles Edward Marsh†.
Foundation type: Independent foundation.
Financial data (yr. ended 10/31/05): Assets, $473,653,127 (M); expenditures, $25,562,311; qualifying distributions, $23,006,938; giving activities include $19,974,450 for 515 grants (high: $500,000; low: $750), and $18,000 for 1 in-kind gift.
Purpose and activities: Support primarily for organizations that address human needs in disadvantaged communities, with strong emphasis on organizations that include service, advocacy and empowerment in their approach: service that remedies specific problems; advocacy that addresses those problems in a systemic way through changes in public policy; and strategies to empower people in need to play leading roles in achieving those policy changes and in remedying specific problems. Also grants for organizations that link their community and local work to other efforts to effect broader public policy change.
Fields of interest: Environment; Reproductive health; Reproductive health, family planning; Health care; Health organizations, association; AIDS; Crime/violence prevention, gun control; Offenders/ex-offenders, rehabilitation; Offenders/ex-offenders, prison alternatives; Legal services; Nutrition; Housing/shelter, development; Youth development, services; Children/youth, services; Minorities/immigrants, centers/services; Homeless, human services; International affairs, arms control; International human rights; Civil rights, race/intergroup relations; Civil rights; Community development; Minorities; Immigrants/refugees; Economically disadvantaged; Homeless.
International interests: El Salvador; Haiti; Mexico; South Africa.
Type of support: General/operating support; Continuing support; Program development; Seed money; Matching/challenge support.
Limitations: Giving is generally limited to the U.S. (more than 90 percent). No grants to individuals, or for building funds, capital improvements, endowments, government projects, scholarships, graduate work, foreign study, conferences, seminars, publications, research, workshops, or annual campaigns; no loans.

Publications: Annual report (including application guidelines); Financial statement; Grants list.
Application information: All renewal applicants must use the downloadable full proposal format on the foundation Web site. Application form not required.
Initial approach: Online letter of inquiry (must be completed by all first time applicants)
Copies of proposal: 1
Deadline(s): None
Board meeting date(s): Board (or a committee of the board) meets 7 times annually
Final notification: 3 to 4 months
Officers and Directors:* Thomas J. Scanlon,* Chair.; Robert H. Haskell,* Vice-Chair.; Deborah Leff, Pres.; C. Elizabeth Warner,* Secy.-Treas.; Phillipa P. Taylor, C.F.O. and C.A.O.; Peter Edelman; Thomas Ehrlich; Juliet Villarreal Garcia; Brent L. Henry; Myrtis H. Powell; Thomas W. Scoville; Jerome W.D. Stokes; Michael C. Williams.
Number of staff: 13 full-time professional; 5 full-time support.
EIN: 540597601

1845
Henry S. and Anne S. Reich Family Foundation ✧

1156 15th St. N.W., Ste. 329
Washington, DC 20005 (202) 785-8887
Contact: Stephen A. Bodzin, V.P.

Established in 1983 in DC.
Donors: Anne S. Reich; Hilary Reich; Amy Rubenstein; Barton Rubenstein; Anne S. Reich 1983 Charitable Lead Trust No. 1; Anne S. Reich 1983 Charitable Lead Trust No. 2.
Foundation type: Independent foundation.
Financial data (yr. ended 5/31/04): Assets, $1,254,055 (M); gifts received, $688,000; expenditures, $716,724; qualifying distributions, $691,353; giving activities include $672,674 for 108 grants.
Purpose and activities: Giving for Jewish welfare, temple support, and yeshivas; support also for the performing arts and education.
Fields of interest: Performing arts; Arts; Higher education; Health organizations, association; Human services; Children, services; Jewish federated giving programs; Jewish agencies & temples.
Type of support: General/operating support; Continuing support; Capital campaigns; Emergency funds; Program development; Seed money; Curriculum development; Scholarship funds; Research; Program-related investments/loans; Matching/challenge support.
Limitations: Giving primarily in Washington, DC, MD, and VA. No grants to individuals.
Application information: Application form not required.
Initial approach: Letter
Deadline(s): None
Board meeting date(s): May 31
Officers and Directors:* Beth Dana Rubenstein,* Pres.; Stephen A. Bodzin,* V.P.; Lisa R. Kopkin,* Secy.-Treas.; Hilary Reich; Amy Sara Rubenstein; Barton S. Rubenstein.
EIN: 521308578

1846
Luther I. Replogle Foundation
1900 L St. N.W., Ste. 205
Washington, DC 20036-5002 (202) 679-0677
Contact: Gwenn Gebhard, Exec. Dir.
FAX: (202) 293-7554; E-mail: info@lirf.org;
URL: http://www.lirf.org/

Established in 1966.
Foundation type: Independent foundation.
Financial data (yr. ended 12/31/05): Assets,
$12,536,244 (M); expenditures, $609,090;
qualifying distributions, $552,208; giving activities
include $425,745 for 92 grants (high: $45,000;
low: $250).
Purpose and activities: The foundation focuses its
giving on the following areas: 1) Programs
addressing the needs of youth and children living in,
or at risk for long term poverty. These include teen
pregnancy prevention and a broad spectrum of
social services; 2) Programs that improve
educational opportunities for inner-city children,
including enrichment programs in the arts and
sciences, mentoring, and alternative schools; 3)
Programs for affordable housing that reach
under-served groups, with emphasis on programs
that enable individuals to become self-sufficient;
and 4) Programs that encourage classical
archaeology, as well as programs that work for the
conservation of maps and globes.
Fields of interest: Arts; Elementary/secondary
education; Education; Reproductive health, family
planning; Human services; Children/youth,
services; Family services.
Type of support: General/operating support;
Continuing support; Program development;
Fellowships; Scholarship funds; Matching/
challenge support.
Limitations: Giving primarily in Washington, DC,
Chicago, IL, and Minneapolis, MN. Generally no
support for nationally-affiliated organizations. No
grants to individuals (except for the Luther I.
Replogle Award for Management).
Publications: Application guidelines; Annual report;
Grants list; Program policy statement.
Application information: Applicants must go
through the web-based eligibility quiz, letter of
inquiry form, and grant application form on the
foundation Web site. Paper applications are NOT
accepted. Luther I. Replogle Award for Management
Improvement recipients selected by the U.S.
Department of State. Application form required.
  Initial approach: Refer to foundation Web site
  Copies of proposal: 1
  Deadline(s): Mar. 15 for Apr. meeting, Sept. 15
  for Nov. meeting
  Board meeting date(s): Apr. and Nov.
  Final notification: 2 weeks
Officers and Directors:* Paul R.S. Gebhard,* Pres.;
William O. Petersen,* Secy.; Elizabeth R. Dickie,
Treas.; Gwenn H.S. Gebhard, Exec. Dir.; Sophia
Gebhard Anema; David Replogle; Anne Witkowsky.
Number of staff: 1 part-time professional.
EIN: 366141697
Selected grants: The following grants were reported
in 2006.
$25,000 to Holy Family Lutheran School, Chicago,
  IL.
$15,000 to Merit School of Music, Chicago, IL.
$7,500 to Banyan Foundation, Minneapolis, MN.
$7,500 to Chicago Child Care Society, Chicago, IL.
$7,000 to Homeless on the Move for Equality
  (HOME), Chicago, IL.
$7,000 to Hull House Association, Chicago, IL.

$5,000 to Bright Beginnings, DC.
$5,000 to Hope and a Home, DC.
$5,000 to Metropolitan Interfaith Council on
  Affordable Housing, Minneapolis, MN.
$5,000 to Minnesota Housing Partnership, Saint
  Paul, MN.
$4,000 to Chicago Youth Rowing Club, Chicago, IL.
$3,000 to Fort Dupont Ice Arena, Friends of, DC.
$2,500 to N Street Village, DC.
$2,000 to Emergency Fund for Needy People,
  Chicago, IL.
$1,000 to Girl Scouts of the U.S.A., Council of the
  National Capital, DC.

1847
Roshan Cultural Heritage Institute ✧
1050 Connecticut Ave. N.W., Ste. 1000
Washington, DC 20036 (202) 772-4271
Contact: Magda Hirsch, Exec. Asst.
FAX: (703) 997-4875; URL: http://
www.roshan-institute.org

Established in 2000 in TN.
Donor: Pierre Omidyar.
Foundation type: Independent foundation.
Financial data (yr. ended 6/30/05): Assets,
$8,595,835 (M); expenditures, $591,860;
qualifying distributions, $529,381; giving activities
include $394,079 for 11 grants (high: $130,000;
low: $3,000).
Purpose and activities: The institute sponsors
activities and programs whose primary focus is the
preservation, transmission, and instruction of
Persian culture. To execute its mission, the Institute
develops initiatives that provide support for
partnerships with other nonprofit organizations and
institutions such as schools, universities, libraries,
museums, and private sector donors. It also offers
a limited number of individual fellowships to
qualified graduate students engaged in writing their
doctoral dissertation in the field of Persian Studies.
Fields of interest: Language/linguistics; Arts;
Education.
Type of support: Program development;
Conferences/seminars; Professorships; Curriculum
development; Fellowships; Scholarship funds;
Research; Program evaluation.
Limitations: No support for political organizations.
Application information: Application guidelines
available on the institute's Web site. Application
form required.
  Initial approach: Letter
  Copies of proposal: 4
  Deadline(s): None for grants; Mar. 1 for
  fellowships
  Board meeting date(s): May
  Final notification: June 30
Officers and Directors:* Elah'e Mir-Djalali
Omidyar,* C.E.O. and Pres.; Kimberley A. Williams,*
Secy.; James E. Alatis, Ph.D.; Dorn McGrath, Jr.,
Ph.D.; Pierre Omidyar*; Jan Schneider.
Trustee: SunTrust Bank.
EIN: 770560800
Selected grants: The following grants were reported
in 2004.
$150,000 to University of Washington, Seattle, WA.
  For general support.
$25,000 to American Friends. For general support.
$15,000 to Persian Heritage Foundation, New York,
  NY. For general support.

1848
The Sprenger-Lang Foundation
1614 20th St. N.W.
Washington, DC 20009 (202) 386-7980
Contact: Paul Sprenger, Tr.; Jane Lang, Tr.
FAX: (202) 386-7985;
E-mail: lvandruff@sprengerandlang.com

Established in 1997 in Washington, DC.
Donors: Jane Lang; Paul Sprenger.
Foundation type: Independent foundation.
Financial data (yr. ended 12/31/05): Assets,
$12,320,906 (M); gifts received, $240,743;
expenditures, $1,321,448; qualifying distributions,
$1,130,795; giving activities include $987,450 for
40 grants (high: $825,540; low: $500), and
$279,764 for foundation-administered programs.
Purpose and activities: Giving primarily to fund
programs and organizations that are associated with
the Atlas Performing Arts Center, in Near-Northeast
Washington, DC.
Fields of interest: Arts education; Performing arts,
theater; Performing arts, music; Education.
Type of support: General/operating support;
Scholarship funds.
Limitations: Giving primarily in Washington, DC, and
MD. No grants to individuals.
Application information: Application form not
required.
  Initial approach: Letter
  Copies of proposal: 1
  Deadline(s): None
  Board meeting date(s): Bimonthly
  Final notification: 60 days
Trustees: Jane Lang; Paul Sprenger.
Number of staff: 1 full-time professional.
EIN: 522067636
Selected grants: The following grants were reported
in 2004.
$951,093 to Atlas Performing Arts Center, DC. For
  capital campaign.
$50,000 to Studio Theater, DC. For capital
  campaign.
$43,400 to Garrett Lakes Arts Festival, Mc Henry,
  MD.
$15,000 to Impact Fund, Berkeley, CA. 2 grants:
  $5,000 (For general support), $10,000 (For
  Tim's Anniversary Reception).
$15,000 to Levine School of Music, DC. For gala.
$10,000 to National Partnership for Women and
  Families, DC. For general support.
$6,000 to Theater J, DC. For general support.
$5,000 to Peninsula Community Foundation, San
  Mateo, CA. For Alana Dupont Rine Arts Education
  Fund.
$5,000 to Swarthmore College, Swarthmore, PA. For
  general support.

1849
The Spring Creek Foundation ✧
2201 P. St. N.W.
Washington, DC 20037 (202) 547-8762
Contact: Kelley Ellsworth, Pres.
FAX: (202) 547-8952;
E-mail: springcreekfndtn@aol.com

Established in 1996 in DC.
Foundation type: Independent foundation.
Financial data (yr. ended 12/31/05): Assets,
$7,412,115 (M); expenditures, $877,910;
qualifying distributions, $843,096; giving activities
include $783,500 for 92 grants (high: $30,000;
low: $1,000).

Purpose and activities: The purpose of the foundation is to fund organizations in the metropolitan Washington, DC, area, whose goals and programs benefit the human environment by providing assistance to low-income individuals and families in housing, employment, education, and emergency services, as well as organizations whose goals are the protection and enhancement of the natural environment.

Fields of interest: Education, services; Environment, natural resources; Employment, services; Housing/shelter, services; Human services; Family services.

Type of support: General/operating support; Continuing support; Management development/ capacity building; Emergency funds; Program development; Publication; Seed money; Curriculum development; Scholarship funds; Research; Matching/challenge support.

Limitations: Giving limited to the metropolitan Washington, DC, area. No grants to individuals, or for capital campaigns, real property acquisition, or construction.

Publications: Application guidelines; Grants list; Informational brochure.

Application information: Application form not required.

Initial approach: Telephone
Copies of proposal: 1
Deadline(s): Apr. 15 and Oct. 15
Board meeting date(s): Jan. and June
Final notification: 60-90 days

Officers and Directors:* Kelley Ellsworth,* Pres. and Exec. Dir.; Lawrence E. Molumby, V.P.; Mary M. Dwan,* Secy.; Richard Halberstein,* Treas.; James M. Didden; Ralph H. Dwan, Jr.; Maryann "Molly" Ellsworth*; Clyde B. Richardson; Kathryn "Kathy" Smith.

Number of staff: 2 part-time professional.

EIN: 521963479

Selected grants: The following grants were reported in 2004.

$30,000 to American Chestnut Land Trust, Port Republic, MD.

$25,000 to Perry School Community Services Center, DC.

$15,000 to Bright Beginnings, DC.

$15,000 to Foundation Schools, Rockville, MD.

$10,000 to Chesapeake Bay Foundation, Annapolis, MD.

$10,000 to Earth Conservation Corps, DC.

$10,000 to Housing Unlimited, Rockville, MD.

$10,000 to Potomac Riverkeeper, Rockville, MD.

$8,000 to Father McKenna Center, DC.

$7,500 to Black Student Fund, DC.

1850
Alexander and Margaret Stewart Trust ▼ ✧

888 17th St. N.W., Ste. 610
Washington, DC 20006-3321 (202) 785-9892
Contact: Doris E. Lustine, Exec. Secy.
FAX: (202) 785-0918; URL: http://www.stewart-trust.org

Trust established in 1947 in DC; in 1997 combined with the Helen S. Devore Trust that was established in 1960.

Donors: Helen S. Devore†; Mary E. Stewart†.

Foundation type: Independent foundation.

Financial data (yr. ended 12/31/04): Assets, $98,795,061 (M); expenditures, $4,547,931;

qualifying distributions, $4,222,268; giving activities include $4,105,036 for 52 grants (high: $500,000; low: $5,000; average: $50,000–$150,000).

Purpose and activities: Giving for the care, prevention, and treatment of cancer; the care of children who are physically or mentally ill or handicapped; and research, education, or prevention of diseases common to childhood, including societal behavioral patterns having a negative impact on the welfare of children.

Fields of interest: Health care, infants; Health care; Cancer; Children/youth, services; Economically disadvantaged.

Type of support: General/operating support; Continuing support; Equipment; Program development; Research.

Limitations: Giving primarily in the Washington, DC, area. No grants to individuals, or for endowment funds, annual campaigns, building funds, land acquisition, renovation projects, scholarships, or fellowships.

Publications: Application guidelines; Grants list.

Application information: Application form required.

Initial approach: Online application form
Copies of proposal: 1
Deadline(s): Sept. 15
Board meeting date(s): Monthly
Final notification: Usually by late Dec.

Trustees: William J. Bierbower; Howard H. Williams III; The Washington Trust Co.

Number of staff: 1 part-time support.

EIN: 526020260

Selected grants: The following grants were reported in 2004.

$950,000 to Childrens National Medical Center, DC. 3 grants: $100,000 (For Community Pediatric Health Centers in Southeast Washington), $500,000 (For rehabilitation of operating rooms), $350,000 (For hematology and oncology programs).

$275,000 to Washington Hospital Center Foundation, DC. 2 grants: $150,000 (For Teen Alliance for Prepared Parenting (TAPP) Program), $125,000 (For cancer patient care).

$130,000 to Washington Home, DC. For hospice and palliative care.

$100,000 to Christ House, Alexandria, VA. For care of homeless persons with cancer.

$75,000 to Saint Anns Infant and Maternity Home, Hyattsville, MD. For nurse care and therapy for high-risk and disabled children.

$70,000 to Providence Health Foundation, DC. For Neonatal Charity Fund.

$70,000 to Rosemount Center, DC. For Special Needs Intervention Team Program.

1851
Hattie M. Strong Foundation

1620 Eye St. N.W., Ste. 700
Washington, DC 20006-2402 (202) 331-1619
Contact: Judith B. Cyphers, Secy. and Dir. of Grants
FAX: (202) 466-2894;
E-mail: hmsf@hmstrongfoundation.org; URL: http://www.hmstrongfoundation.org/

Incorporated in 1928 in DC.

Donors: Hattie M. Strong†; L. Corrin Strong†.

Foundation type: Independent foundation.

Financial data (yr. ended 8/31/05): Assets, $30,773,552 (M); gifts received, $2,256; expenditures, $1,668,627; qualifying distributions, $1,481,252; giving activities include $325,050 for

62 grants (high: $8,000; low: $2,500), and $486,650 for 110 loans to individuals (high: $5,000; low: $1,250).

Purpose and activities: The foundation administers two distinct programs: 1) non-interest-bearing loans to students who are within one year of their degree in college or graduate school; maximum loan to college students is $5,000; and 2) a grant program focused primarily on educational programs for the disadvantaged in the Washington, DC, area, including remedial and enrichment programs, literacy for at-risk youth and adults, tutoring, basic vocational and occupational skills training, and academic mentoring.

Fields of interest: Elementary/secondary education; Adult education—literacy, basic skills & GED; Education, reading; Education.

Type of support: General/operating support; Program development; Curriculum development; Student loans—to individuals.

Limitations: Giving limited to the Washington, DC, area for grant program; loan program is national in scope. No support for programs of national or international scope. No grants to individuals (except for loans), or for building or endowment funds, research, scholarships, fellowships, equipment, conferences, special events or benefits, or projects designed to educate the general public.

Publications: Application guidelines; Annual report; Grants list; Informational brochure.

Application information: Application form required for loan program. Maximum student loan is $5,000. Foreign students temporarily in the U.S. do not qualify for loans. See foundation Web site for guidelines on both grant and loan programs. Application form required.

Initial approach: Contact foundation for grant guidelines, proposal requirements, and format for grant program
Copies of proposal: 2
Deadline(s): 5 pm on Jan. 15, Apr. 15, July 15, and Oct. 15 for organizations; between Jan. 1 and Mar. 31 prior to final year of degree program for student loans
Board meeting date(s): Mar., June, Sept., and Dec.
Final notification: July for loan program; within 2 weeks after board meetings for grant program

Officers and Directors:* Henry Strong,* Chair. and Pres.; Henry L. Strong,* V.P.; Judith B. Cyphers, Secy. and Dir. of Grants; Robin C. Tanner, Treas. and Dir. of Loans; Barbara B. Cantrell; Mary D. Janney; Gay P. Lord; John M. Lynham, Jr.; Richard S.T. Marsh; Sigrid S. Reynolds; Carol L. Schwartz; Bente Strong; Michael O. Suddath; Togo D. West, Jr.

Number of staff: 2 full-time professional; 3 full-time support.

EIN: 530237223

1852
The Summit Foundation ✧

(formerly The Summit Charitable Foundation, Inc.)
2100 Pennsylvania Ave. N.W., Ste. 525
Washington, DC 20037 (202) 912-2900
Contact: Victoria P. Sant, Pres.
FAX: (202) 912-2901; *E-mail:* info@summitfdn.org; URL: http://www.summitfdn.org/foundation/index.html

Established in 1991 in DE.

Donors: Roger W. Sant; Victoria P. Sant; AES Corp.; Aspen Charitable Remainder Unitrust No. 3.

Foundation type: Independent foundation.

Financial data (yr. ended 12/31/04): Assets, $31,787,558 (M); gifts received, $75,000; expenditures, $3,382,030; qualifying distributions, $3,159,616; giving activities include $2,424,067 for 46 grants (high: $340,000; low: $1,049).
Purpose and activities: Funding currently for two program areas: Conservation of the Mesoamerican Reef and Global Population and Youth Leadership. The foundation's message is to promote the health and well being of the planet, its people and its natural environment by achieving a sustainable population, empowering young people, and protecting the earth's biodiversity.
Fields of interest: Environment, research; Environment, water pollution; Environment, natural resources; Environment; Reproductive health; Reproductive health, family planning; Reproductive health, fertility; Reproductive health, sexuality education; Health care; Youth development, adult & child programs; Youth development; International human rights.
International interests: Caribbean; Latin America.
Type of support: General/operating support; Continuing support; Program development; Seed money; Technical assistance; Program evaluation; Matching/challenge support.
Limitations: Applications not accepted. Giving through Biodiversity Program focuses on Mesoamerican Reef countries only; Population Advocacy Program focuses on Europe and the United States; and Population Youth Leadership Program focuses on Central America. No grants to individuals, or for freestanding conferences, film and video projects or basic research.
Publications: Grants list; Informational brochure; Program policy statement.
Application information: Unsolicited requests for funds not considered.
Board meeting date(s): 2 times a year
Officers and Trustees:* Roger Sant,* Chair.; Victoria P. Sant,* Pres.; Shari Sant Plummer,* Secy.; Alexis Sant,* Treas.; Carlos Saavedra, Exec. Dir. and Sr. Prog. Off., Conservation of the Mesoamerican Reef Program; J. Martin Goebel; Peter A. Nadosy; Dan Plummer; Michael Sant; Shira Saperstein.
Number of staff: 2 full-time professional.
EIN: 521743817
Selected grants: The following grants were reported in 2003.
$1,429,505 to Public Health Institute, Oakland, CA. 2 grants: $69,505 (For program planning activity for Emerging Reproductive Health Leaders Program), $1,360,000 (For Emerging Leaders in Reproductive Health (PLESR) Program, leadership development program for young professionals involved in adolescent reproductive health in Belize, Guatemala, Honduras and Quintana Roo, Mexico).
$450,765 to Nature Conservancy, Arlington, VA. For project, Conservation of Fish Spawning Aggregations in Mesoamerican Reef.
$150,000 to World Wildlife Fund, DC. For research project, Reducing Agricultural Effluent Threats in the Mesoamerican Reef Ecoregion.
$51,788 to Mexican Nature Conservation Fund, Mexico City, Mexico. To establish endowed private ecoregional financial mechanism for Mesoamerican Reef Ecoregion.
$50,000 to Advocates for Youth, DC. For project, Improving Adolescent Reproductive and Sexual Health Programs and Policies through Youth Activism and Youth-Adult Partnerships.

$50,000 to Population Action International, DC. For general support.
$40,000 to Conservation International, DC. For planning grant for efforts to engage travel industry to achieve conservation results.
$40,000 to Planned Parenthood Federation of America, New York, NY. For general support of Planned Parenthood Global Partners Program.
$40,000 to Planned Parenthood Federation, International, European Network Office, Brussels, Belgium. To establish Young European Leader's Steering Committee on International Conference on Population and Development (ICPD) Plus 10 and Beyond.

1853
Trellis Fund
1400 16th St. N.W., Ste. 710
Washington, DC 20036 (202) 939-3399
FAX: (202) 939-3392; E-mail: trellis@trellisfund.org;
URL: http://www.trellisfund.org

Established in 1998 in DC.
Donors: Betsy Karel; The Helen and Milton Kimmelman Foundation.
Foundation type: Independent foundation.
Financial data (yr. ended 12/31/05): Assets, $19,516,235 (M); gifts received, $2,754,467; expenditures, $1,311,701; qualifying distributions, $1,257,029; giving activities include $1,036,548 for 26 grants (high: $100,000; low: $2,000), and $5,811 for 3 employee matching gifts.
Purpose and activities: To encourage both the public and the nonprofit sectors to be more responsive to the needs of the Greater Washington, DC, area community through systemic change in public and private institutions.
Type of support: General/operating support; Continuing support; Program development; Seed money; Employee matching gifts; Matching/challenge support.
Limitations: Applications not accepted. Giving primarily in the greater Washington, DC, area. No support for sectarian religious activities or direct social service delivery programs. No grants to individuals, or for scholarship funds, deficit or debt reduction, or for conferences, special events, education, housing, community development or the environment.
Publications: Annual report; Grants list.
Application information: Unsolicited requests for funds not accepted.
Officer: Betsy Karel, Chair.
Trustees: Frank Karel III; Helen Kimmel; Christine Russell.
Number of staff: 1 part-time professional; 1 part-time support.
EIN: 521451828
Selected grants: The following grants were reported in 2004.
$110,000 to National Gallery of Art, DC. For inaugural series of exhibitions in the new photography galleries in West Building.
$60,000 to District of Columbia Employment Justice Center, DC. For general operating support to secure and enforce the rights of low-income workers in D.C.
$50,000 to Fiscal Policy Institute, Latham, NY. For operating support to support analysis of budget and tax issues that affect low and moderate-income residents of the District.
$50,000 to Nonprofit Roundtable of Greater Washington, DC. For start-up costs.

$50,000 to Yale University, New Haven, CT. For general operating support for Art Gallery's acquisition of photographs created by the American photographer Robert Adams.
$40,000 to Council for Court Excellence, DC. For Child Abuse and Neglect System Reform Project, which facilitates and monitors improvements in D.C. child welfare system.
$40,000 to Tahirih Justice Center, Falls Church, VA. For general operating support for advocacy and public policy efforts to secure legal and social justice for immigrant women fleeing gender-based violence and other human rights violations.
$40,000 to Washington AIDS Partnership, DC. For Syringe Access Working Group(SAWG, a new collaborative project of Washington AIDS Partnership, D.C. Appleseed, Whitman-Walker Clinic and Prevention Works, to plan and advocate for syringe access in D.C.
$30,000 to Brookings Institution, DC. For analysis of proposed new federal infrastructure payment to the District.
$25,000 to DC Appleseed Center for Law and Justice, DC. For efforts to address the city's structural deficit.

1854
Alice and Russell True Foundation ✧
c/o Alice T. Gasch, Pres.
4100 Cathedral Ave. N.W., Ste. 510
Washington, DC 20016

Established in 1997 in Washington, DC.
Foundation type: Independent foundation.
Financial data (yr. ended 12/31/05): Assets, $14,802,965 (M); gifts received, $868; expenditures, $768,448; qualifying distributions, $689,169; giving activities include $683,500 for 8 grants (high: $500,000; low: $4,000).
Purpose and activities: Giving primarily for biomedical research and education, as well as for the attainment of social justice for women and children, with a focus on education, health and economic well being.
Fields of interest: Biomedicine research; Human services; Children, services; Women.
Type of support: Equipment; Program development; Research.
Limitations: Applications not accepted. Giving primarily in Washington, DC. No grants to individuals.
Application information: Contributes only to pre-selected organizations.
Board meeting date(s): Varies
Officers and Directors:* Alice True Gasch, M.D., Pres. and Treas.; Linda Brown,* Secy.; Adele West, M.D.
EIN: 522048715
Selected grants: The following grants were reported in 2004.
$300,000 to Kingsbury Center, DC.
$148,295 to Washington National Eye Center, DC.
$100,000 to Family and Child Services of Washington, DC, DC.
$25,000 to Recording for the Blind and Dyslexic, Princeton, NJ.
$18,000 to Holton-Arms School, Bethesda, MD.
$10,000 to Washington Tennis and Education Foundation, DC.

1855
Vaterstetten Foundation ✧

c/o Moore & Bruce, LLP
1072 Thomas Jefferson St. N.W.
Washington, DC   20007-3835

Established in 1999 in DC.
Foundation type: Independent foundation.
Financial data (yr. ended 12/31/04): Assets,
$5,832,368 (M); expenditures, $829,763;
qualifying distributions, $790,002; giving activities
include $728,011 for 16 grants (high: $83,000;
low: $10).
Fields of interest: Performing arts; Arts; Education;
Human services; Children/youth, services;
Community development; Foundations (community).
Limitations: Applications not accepted. Giving
primarily in Santa Fe, NM. No grants to individuals.
Application information: Contributes only to
pre-selected organizations.
Trustees: Charles M. Bruce; Vaterstetten
Foundation Management, Ltd.
Director: James M. De May, Managing Dir.
EIN: 980215093
Selected grants: The following grants were reported
in 2004.
$308,200 to Santa Fe Community Foundation,
   Santa Fe, NM.
$83,000 to Santa Fe Pro Musica, Santa Fe, NM. For
   capital campaign.
$75,000 to National Renewal Energy Laboratory -
   Junior Solar Spirit, Golden, CO.
$71,400 to Life Link, Santa Fe, NM.
$62,220 to Boy Scouts of America, Great Southwest
   Council, Albuquerque, NM.
$60,000 to Santa Fe Opera, Santa Fe, NM.
$25,500 to Santa Fe Preparatory School, Santa Fe,
   NM.
$10,000 to Duke of Edinburghs Award Scheme,
   London, England. .
$5,000 to Habitat for Humanity International, Santa
   Fe, NM.
$4,000 to Aspen Santa Fe Ballet, Santa Fe, NM.

1856
Vradenburg Foundation ✧

c/o George A. Vradenburg III, Pres.
1720 N. St. N.W.
Washington, DC   20008

Established in 1999 in DE and DC.
Donors: George A. Vradenburg III; Trish Vradenburg.
Foundation type: Independent foundation.
Financial data (yr. ended 6/30/05): Assets,
$8,389,510 (M); gifts received, $922,220;
expenditures, $1,103,463; qualifying distributions,
$1,064,168; giving activities include $922,110 for
38 grants (high: $275,500; low: $100).
Fields of interest: Arts; Heart & circulatory
diseases; Alzheimer's disease; Community
development.
Type of support: General/operating support; Income
development; Management development/capacity
building; Program development.
Limitations: Applications not accepted. Giving
primarily in the greater Washington, DC, region. No
grants to individuals.
Application information: Contributes only to
pre-selected organizations.
Officers: George A. Vradenburg III, Pres.; Patricia L.
Vradenburg, Secy.-Treas.
Directors: Alissa Vradenburg; Tyler Vradenburg.
EIN: 770529620

1857
Wallace Genetic Foundation, Inc. ▼

4910 Massachusetts Ave., Ste. 221
Washington, DC   20016   (202) 966-2932
Contact: Patricia Lee, Co-Exec. Dir.; Carolyn Sand,
Co-Exec. Dir.
FAX: (202) 966-3370;
E-mail: president@wallacegenetic.org; URL: http://
www.wallacegenetic.org

Incorporated in 1959 in NY.
Donor: Henry A. Wallace†.
Foundation type: Independent foundation.
Financial data (yr. ended 12/31/05): Assets,
$99,645,806 (M); gifts received, $1,003,644;
expenditures, $5,120,704; qualifying distributions,
$4,887,410; giving activities include $4,708,681
for 112 grants (high: $1,000,000; low: $5,000;
average: $25,000–$50,000).
Purpose and activities: Areas of interest are
sustainable agriculture, protection of farmland near
cities, plant genetic research, biodiversity
protection, and environmental education.
Fields of interest: Environment, natural resources;
Environmental education; Agriculture; Public policy,
research.
International interests: Latin America; Soviet Union
(Former).
Type of support: General/operating support;
Continuing support; Land acquisition; Program
development; Seed money; Research; Matching/
challenge support.
Publications: Grants list.
Application information: Faxed or E-mailed
proposals will not be accepted. Application form not
required.
   Initial approach: 1- or 2-page letter and proposal
   Copies of proposal: 1
   Deadline(s): None
   Board meeting date(s): Six times a year
   Final notification: None
Officers and Directors:* Jean W. Douglas,* Pres.;
Ann D. Cornell,* V.P. and Secy.; Joan D. Murray,*
V.P. and Treas.; David W. Douglas,* V.P., Research;
Patricia Lee, Co-Exec. Dir.; Carolyn Sand, Co-Exec.
Dir.
Number of staff: 2 part-time professional.
EIN: 136162575
Selected grants: The following grants were reported
in 2004.
$1,200,000 to Conservation Fund, Arlington, VA. 2
   grants: $200,000 (For Chesapeake Bay
   Initiative), $1,000,000 (For Chesapeake Bay
   Initiative).
$150,000 to American Fund for Charities, DC. 2
   grants: $75,000 each (For Soil Association's
   campaign to build a more sustainable food and
   agriculture policy worldwide).
$100,000 to Seed Savers Exchange, Decorah, IA.
   For Producing Certified Organic Seeds at Heritage
   Farm and Capital Campaign for Twin Valleys.
$80,000 to Beyond Pesticides/NCAMP, DC. For
   Children's Environment Program.
$50,000 to K C T S/Channel 9, Seattle, WA. For
   Warner Hanson Television's Chefs A'Field.
$50,000 to Land Institute, Salina, KS. For general
   support.
$30,000 to Accokeek Foundation, Accokeek, MD.
   For general support.
$30,000 to Forest Trends Association, DC. For
   establishment of ecoagriculture field projects.

1858
Wallace Global Fund ▼

1990 M St. N.W., Ste. 250
Washington, DC   20036   (202) 452-1530
Contact: Melissa S. Dann, Exec. Dir.
FAX: (202) 452-0922; E-mail: (for Tina Kroll-Guerch):
tkroll@wgf.org; URL: http://www.wgf.org

Established in 1995.
Donors: Robert B. Wallace†; Gordon G. Wallace†;
Henry A. Wallace†; Ilo B. Wallace†.
Foundation type: Independent foundation.
Financial data (yr. ended 12/31/04): Assets,
$226,019,435 (M); gifts received, $86,495,483;
expenditures, $10,022,869; qualifying
distributions, $9,307,990; giving activities include
$8,053,713 for 118 grants (high: $200,000; low:
$1,000; average: $25,000–$100,000).
Purpose and activities: To promote an informed and
engaged citizenry, to fight injustice, and to protect
the diversity of nature and the natural systems upon
which all life depends. The fund seeks to further its
mission generally through fundamental public policy
and systemic change.
Fields of interest: Media/communications;
Environment, global warming; Environment, energy;
Environment, forests; Reproductive health, family
planning; Reproductive health, abortion clinics/
services; Reproductive health, sexuality education;
Youth, pregnancy prevention; International
economic development; International economics/
trade policy; International human rights; Civil rights,
women; Civil liberties, advocacy; Civil liberties,
reproductive rights; Civil liberties, due process; Civil
liberties, death penalty issues.
International interests: Europe.
Type of support: General/operating support;
Continuing support; Program development;
Matching/challenge support.
Limitations: Giving on an international basis. No
grants to individuals, or for scholarships, purchase
of land, capital construction, profit-making
businesses, debt reduction, endowment
campaigns, fundraising drives/events, or tuition,
assistance or other forms of personal financial aid.
Publications: Application guidelines; Financial
statement; Grants list; Occasional report.
Application information: Application form not
required.
   Initial approach: Letter of inquiry with 3 page
   concept paper (E-mail preferred) prior to
   submission of full proposal
   Copies of proposal: 1
   Deadline(s): None
   Board meeting date(s): 3 times a year
Officers and Trustees:* R. Bruce Wallace,* Pres.;
Randall C. Wallace,* V.P.; H. Scott Wallace,* Secy.;
Christy A. Wallace,* Treas.; Melissa S. Dann, Exec.
Dir.; Scott Fitzmorris; Jonathan Lash; Jackie
Wallace; Susan Wallace.
Number of staff: 2 full-time professional; 1 part-time
professional; 1 full-time support.
EIN: 521918002
Selected grants: The following grants were reported
in 2005.
$200,000 to Democracy Now Productions, New
   York, NY. For core support for independent,
   progressive, daily international and national
   news programming.
$125,000 to Advocates for Youth, DC. For work
   demonstrating how US goverment has used
   religious ideology rather than science to shape
   international reproductive health and HIV/AIDS
   policies, denying world's youth access to

reproductive health services when they most need it.

$100,000 to International Projects Assistance Services (IPAS), Chapel Hill, NC. To increase women's access to safe abortion, by increasing support for policy reforms at global and national levels and by portraying abortion as only one aspect of women's sexual and reproductive health and clear part of women's reproductive rights.

$100,000 to National Environmental Trust, DC. For Global Warming Public Education Campaign.

$100,000 to Rainforest Action Network, San Francisco, CA. For Jumpstart Ford, Global Finance, and Old-Growth Campaign.

$92,000 to Corner House Foundation, Princeton, NJ. For Human Rights, Trade, Investment and the Environment Project.

$50,000 to Citizens for Responsibility and Ethics in Washington, DC. For general support.

$50,000 to Families Against Mandatory Minimums Foundation, DC. For work against mandatory minimum prison sentences and in favor of individualized sentencing, through public education, media advocacy, policy briefings, policy books, grassroots mobilization, and appellate litigation.

$50,000 to Institute for Americas Future, DC. For general support.

$40,000 to Corporate Ethics International, Portland, OR. For Business Ethics Network's work improving effetiveness of corporate campaigns involving collaboration among diferse organizations by improving strategic planning, exchange of knowledge among organizations, and organization's skills, abilities, and resources.

1859
Washington Management Corporation Foundation ◇
1101 Vermont Ave. N.W., Ste. 800
Washington, DC 20005 (202) 842-5559
Contact: James H. Lemon, Jr., Pres.

Established in 1997 in DC.
Foundation type: Independent foundation.
Financial data (yr. ended 12/31/05): Assets, $382,723 (M); expenditures $390,231; qualifying distributions, $390,231; giving activities include $390,081 for grants.
Purpose and activities: Giving primarily for education, health care, and human services.
Fields of interest: Elementary/secondary education; Higher education; Education; Health care; Human services; Christian agencies & churches; Protestant agencies & churches.
Limitations: Applications not accepted. Giving primarily in the greater Washington, DC, area. No grants to individuals.
Application information: The foundation prefers to initiate grant programs and does not seek grant applications.
Officers and Directors:* James H. Lemon, Jr.,* Pres.; Stephen Hartwell,* V.P.; Harry J. Lister,* V.P.; Howard L. Kitzmiller, Secy.-Treas.
EIN: 522014122
Selected grants: The following grants were reported in 2005.
$114,000 to Mount Vernon Ladies Association, Mount Vernon, VA. 3 grants: $2,500, $100,000, $11,500
$10,000 to International Womens Forum, DC.

$6,000 to Saint Marks Episcopal Church, Richmond, VA.
$5,000 to Connelly School of the Holy Child, Potomac, MD.
$5,000 to Hollins University, Roanoke, VA.
$2,500 to Loyola Retreat House, Faulkner, MD.
$1,000 to Concord Coalition, Arlington, VA.
$1,000 to Princeton University, Princeton, NJ.

1860
The Washington Times Foundation, Inc. ◇
3600 New York Ave. N.E.
Washington, DC 20002

Established in 2002.
Donor: International Peace Foundation.
Foundation type: Company-sponsored foundation.
Financial data (yr. ended 3/31/05): Assets, $38,279 (M); gifts received, $1,646,000; expenditures, $1,568,677; qualifying distributions, $1,564,879; giving activities include $823,000 for 5 grants (high: $786,300; low: $200), and $741,879 for 1 foundation-administered program.
Purpose and activities: The foundation supports organizations involved with community development, philanthropy and volunteerism, and religion.
Fields of interest: Community development; Philanthropy/voluntarism; Religion.
Limitations: Applications not accepted. Giving primarily in Washington, DC. No grants to individuals.
Application information: Contributes only to pre-selected organizations.
Officers: Dong Moon Joo, Pres.; Larry Moffitt, V.P.; Thomas McDevitt, Secy.; Keith Cooperrider, Treas.
EIN: 521832151
Selected grants: The following grants were reported in 2005.
$786,300 to American Family Coalition, DC.
$25,000 to American Conservative Union Foundation, Alexandria, VA.

1861
Helen Parker Willard Foundation ◇ ☆
P.O. Box 3596
Washington, DC 20007
Contact: Vera A. Graham, Secy.

Established in 1961 in DC.
Donor: Helen Parker Willard‡.
Foundation type: Independent foundation.
Financial data (yr. ended 12/31/05): Assets, $2,601,413 (M); expenditures, $852,060; qualifying distributions, $825,000; giving activities include $825,000 for grants.
Fields of interest: Education; Health care; Human services; Protestant agencies & churches; Disabilities, people with.
Type of support: Building/renovation; Endowments; Scholarship funds; Research.
Limitations: Giving primarily in Washington, DC. No grants to individuals.
Publications: Annual report.
Application information: Telephone inquiries are not accepted. Application form not required.
Initial approach: Letter or proposal
Copies of proposal: 1
Deadline(s): Mar. 31
Board meeting date(s): Annually
Final notification: Sept. 30

Officers and Directors:* Amie Willard Block, Pres.; Vera A. Graham, Secy.; Sarah Taylor Stephenson,* Treas.; Henry K. Willard II; William B. Willard, Jr.
EIN: 526036750
Selected grants: The following grants were reported in 2004.
$135,000 to Nantucket Land Council, Nantucket, MA.
$50,000 to Nantucket Conservation Foundation, Nantucket, MA.
$25,000 to United Way of Jefferson County, Charles Town, WV.
$25,000 to Yale University, New Haven, CT.
$15,000 to Sconset Trust, Siasconset, MA.
$15,000 to Tudor Place Foundation, DC.
$10,000 to Ethel Walker School, Simsbury, CT.
$10,000 to Mount Vernon Ladies Association, Mount Vernon, VA.
$10,000 to Nature Conservancy, Charleston, WV.
$5,000 to Saint Albans School, DC.

1862
Ruth S. Willoughby Foundation ☆
c/o J. Bruce Whelihan
4720 Quebec St. N.W.
Washington, DC 20016

Established in 2002 in VA.
Donor: Ruth S. Willoughby‡.
Foundation type: Independent foundation.
Financial data (yr. ended 12/31/05): Assets, $2,666,777; expenditures, $350,805; qualifying distributions, $349,955; giving activities include $349,105 for 6 grants (high: $250,000; low: $1,500).
Purpose and activities: Support primarily for education and children's sports and health activities.
Fields of interest: Elementary/secondary education; Children/youth, services; Protestant agencies & churches.
Type of support: Capital campaigns; Building/ renovation; Equipment; Program development; Seed money; Curriculum development.
Limitations: Applications not accepted. Giving primarily in the Washington, DC, area. No grants to individuals.
Application information: Contributes only to pre-selected organizations.
Board meeting date(s): No less than annually, upon preference of the Chair.
Trustees: J. Daniel McNamara; J. Bruce Whelihan.
Number of staff: 1 part-time professional; 1 part-time support.
EIN: 043617275
Selected grants: The following grants were reported in 2004.
$100,000 to Saint Patricks Episcopal Day School, DC. For general support.
$50,000 to Concord Hill School, Chevy Chase, MD. For general support.
$41,000 to Bethesda Community School, Bethesda, MD. For general support.
$32,430 to Saint Davids Episcopal Church, DC. For general support.
$5,000 to Palisades Sports Association, DC. For general support.
$1,000 to Washington Tennis and Education Foundation, DC. For general support.

1863
The Winslow Foundation

(formerly Windie Foundation)
1225 Connecticut Ave. N.W., 4th Fl.
Washington, DC 20036 (202) 833-4714
Contact: Betty Ann Ottinger, Dir.

Established in 1987 in NJ.
Donor: Julia D. Winslow†.
Foundation type: Independent foundation.
Financial data (yr. ended 12/31/05): Assets, $33,079,254 (M); expenditures, $1,836,551; qualifying distributions, $1,380,948; giving activities include $1,219,800 for 63 grants (high: $50,000; low: $500).
Purpose and activities: Giving primarily for the environment and population studies.
Fields of interest: Environment, natural resources; Population studies.
Type of support: General/operating support; Continuing support; Program development; Conferences/seminars; Seed money; Research; Matching/challenge support.
Limitations: Giving on a national basis. No grants to individuals.
Application information: Unsolicited requests for funds are generally not accepted. Application form not required.
> *Initial approach:* 2-page letter of inquiry
> *Copies of proposal:* 1
> *Deadline(s):* None
> *Board meeting date(s):* Varies

Officers and Directors: * Wren Winslow Wirth,* Pres.; Samuel W. Lambert III,* V.P. and Treas.; Betty Ann Ottinger,* Secy.; Christopher Wirth; Kelsey Wirth.
Number of staff: 1 part-time professional; 1 part-time support.
EIN: 222778703
Selected grants: The following grants were reported in 2005.
$100,000 to Stanford University, Stanford, CA.
$55,000 to Worldwatch Institute, DC. 2 grants:
   $50,000, $5,000
$50,000 to Center for Resource Economics, DC.

$50,000 to International Forum on Globalization, San Francisco, CA.
$50,000 to Marine Conservation Biology Institute, Redmond, WA.
$50,000 to Population Action International, DC.
$30,000 to Health Care Without Harm, Arlington, VA.
$15,000 to American Wildlands, Bozeman, MT.
$10,000 to University of Toronto, Toronto, Canada. .

1864
The Wyss Foundation ▼

1601 Connecticut Ave., N.W., Ste. 802
Washington, DC 20009
Contact: Francesca DiSilvio
FAX: (301) 654-5091;
E-mail: email@wyssfoundation.org; URL: http://www.wyssfoundation.org

Established in 1990 in PA.
Donor: Hansjoerg Wyss.
Foundation type: Independent foundation.
Financial data (yr. ended 12/31/04): Assets, $57,603,329 (M); expenditures, $9,716,885; qualifying distributions, $8,964,410; giving activities include $8,143,571 for 112 grants (high: $518,500; low: $250; average: $5,000–$200,000).
Purpose and activities: The purpose of the foundation is to preserve, protect, and restore public lands, waters, and open spaces of the American west to achieve ecological health across the landscape.
Fields of interest: Environment, natural resources.
Type of support: General/operating support; Program development; Seed money; Research.
Limitations: Applications not accepted. Giving primarily in the western U.S. (AZ, CO, ID, MT, NV, NM, UT, WY). No grants to individuals.
Application information: Unsolicited requests for funds not accepted. Proposals by requests only.
> *Board meeting date(s):* Varies

Officers: Hansjoerg Wyss, Chair.; Joseph M. Fisher, Mgr.
Number of staff: 5 full-time professional; 1 part-time professional.
EIN: 251823874
Selected grants: The following grants were reported in 2004.
$518,500 to Wilderness Society, DC.
$394,443 to Sonoran Institute, Tucson, AZ.
$385,000 to Trout Unlimited, Arlington, VA.
$345,000 to Western Resource Advocates, Boulder, CO.
$325,000 to Earthjustice, Denver, CO.
$268,000 to Sierra Club Foundation, San Francisco, CA.
$185,800 to Montana Wildlife Federation, Helena, MT.
$80,000 to National Wildlife Federation, Reston, VA.
$60,000 to World Wildlife Fund, DC.
$50,000 to Western Colorado Congress, Grand Junction, CO.

1865
The Zients Family Foundation, Inc. ✧

600 New Hampshire Ave. N.W., 8th Fl.
Washington, DC 20037

Established in 2003 in DC.
Donor: Jeffery Zients.
Foundation type: Independent foundation.
Financial data (yr. ended 12/31/05): Assets, $2,487,396 (M); gifts received, $1,089,706; expenditures, $634,132; qualifying distributions, $633,856; giving activities include $621,818 for 142 grants (high: $100,000; low: $250; average: $1,000–$50,000).
Fields of interest: Youth development.
Limitations: Applications not accepted.
Application information: Contributes only to pre-selected organizations.
Trustees: Michael D'Amato; Jeffery Zients; Mary Zients.
EIN: 546520936

FLORIDA

1866
A Friends' Foundation Trust
9000 Hubbard Pl.
Orlando, FL 32819 (407) 876-3122
Contact: L. Evans Hubbard, Chair.
E-mail: ehubbard@cfl.rr.com

Established in 1959 in FL as the Hubbard Foundation; merged in 1985 with A Friends' Fund, Inc., into A Friends' Foundation Trust.
Donors: Frank M. Hubbard; A Friends' Fund, Inc.
Foundation type: Independent foundation.
Financial data (yr. ended 12/31/05): Assets, $9,678,658 (M); gifts received, $4,500; expenditures, $493,443; qualifying distributions, $466,345; giving activities include $386,500 for 65 grants (high: $33,000; low: $1,000).
Purpose and activities: Support for private higher education, civic affairs, the arts, youth activities, religion, and health in central FL.
Fields of interest: Arts; Higher education; Health care; Health organizations, association; Disasters, preparedness/services; Human services; Children/youth, services; Religion.
Type of support: General/operating support; Continuing support; Annual campaigns; Capital campaigns; Building/renovation; Equipment; Land acquisition; Emergency funds; Program development; Matching/challenge support.
Limitations: Applications not accepted. Giving primarily in central FL.
Publications: Grants list; Informational brochure.
Application information: Unsolicited requests for funds not considered or acknowledged.
Board meeting date(s): Oct.
Officer: L. Evans Hubbard, Chair.
Board Members: Frank M. Hubbard; Michael E. Hubbard; Ruth Hubbard; Ruth C.H. Miller.
Trustee: Merrill Lynch.
Number of staff: 2 part-time professional.
EIN: 596125247
Selected grants: The following grants were reported in 2003.
$43,000 to YMCA, Central Florida, Cocoa, FL. 2 grants: $33,000, $10,000
$33,000 to University of Central Florida Foundation, Orlando, FL.
$25,000 to Church of the Good Shepherd, Jacksonville, FL. For capital support.
$25,000 to United Arts of Central Florida, Orlando, FL.
$10,000 to Boys and Girls Clubs of Central Florida, Orlando, FL.
$10,000 to Junior Achievement of Central Florida, Orlando, FL.
$10,000 to Orlando Science Center, Orlando, FL.
$8,500 to Canine Companions for Independence, Orlando, FL.
$6,000 to Saint Michaels Episcopal Church, FL.

1867
Anthony R. Abraham Foundation, Inc. ✧
6600 S.W. 57th Ave.
Miami, FL 33143 (305) 665-2222
Contact: Anthony R. Abraham, Chair.

Established in 1978 in FL.

Donor: Anthony R. Abraham.
Foundation type: Independent foundation.
Financial data (yr. ended 12/31/05): Assets, $38,931,942 (M); expenditures, $1,822,832; qualifying distributions, $1,822,832; giving activities include $1,532,180 for 203 grants (high: $850,000; low: $50; average: $100–$1,000).
Fields of interest: Education; Hospitals (general); Health organizations, association; Medical research, institute; Human services; Children/youth, services; Roman Catholic federated giving programs; Roman Catholic agencies & churches.
International interests: Lebanon.
Limitations: Giving primarily in Miami, FL. No grants to individuals.
Application information: Application form not required.
Initial approach: Letter
Copies of proposal: 1
Deadline(s): None
Board meeting date(s): Various
Officers and Directors:* Anthony R. Abraham,* Chair. and Pres.; Thomas G. Abraham,* Secy.-Treas.; Norma Jean Abraham; William Haddad; Thomas H. Malouf; Anthony Shaker.
EIN: 591837290
Selected grants: The following grants were reported in 2005.
$505,000 to Catholic Near East Welfare Association, New York, NY.
$40,000 to Ransom Everglades School, Miami, FL.
$250 to CRUDEM Foundation, Saint Louis, MO.
$250 to National Association of Private Catholic Independent Schools (NAPCIS), Sacramento, CA.
$200 to International Rescue Committee, New York, NY.
$200 to Saint Lawrence Seminary High School, Mount Calvary, WI.
$100 to Catholic Relief Services, Baltimore, MD.
$100 to Communities in Schools, Alexandria, VA.
$100 to Somerset Academy, Pembroke Pines, FL.

1868
The Abramson Family Foundation ▼ ✧
376 Regatta Dr.
Jupiter, FL 33477
Contact: Judith Abramson Felgoise, Tr.

Established in 1996 in FL.
Donor: Judith Abramson Felgoise.
Foundation type: Independent foundation.
Financial data (yr. ended 6/30/05): Assets, $60,342,817 (M); gifts received, $346,650; expenditures, $16,343,717; qualifying distributions, $16,025,097; giving activities include $15,763,070 for 127 grants (high: $4,100,000; low: $50; average: $1,000–$100,000), and $1,000 for 1 grant to an individual.
Purpose and activities: Giving primarily to Jewish organizations, educational institutions, and health associations.
Fields of interest: Arts; Higher education; Education; Hospitals (general); Human services; Jewish federated giving programs; Jewish agencies & temples.
International interests: Israel.
Type of support: Scholarships—to individuals.
Limitations: Giving on a national basis.
Application information: Contact foundation for scholarship application guidelines. Application form required.
Initial approach: Proposal
Deadline(s): None

Trustees: Leonard Abramson; Madlyn Abramson; Judith Abramson Felgoise; Jerome S. Goodman; Marcy Abramson Shoemaker; Nancy Abramson Wolfson; Joseph M. Yohlin.
EIN: 311482888
Selected grants: The following grants were reported in 2005.
$1,500,000 to Madlyn and Leonard Abramson Center for Jewish Life, North Wales, PA. 2 grants: $500,000 (For general support), $1,000,000 (For general support).
$500,000 to Johns Hopkins University, Baltimore, MD. For general support.
$411,025 to Congregation Beth Or, Springhouse, PA. For general support.
$400,000 to Montgomery Hospital, Norristown, PA. For general support.
$100,000 to Chabad of Argentina Relief Appeal, New York, NY. For general support.
$100,000 to Partnership for Excellence in Jewish Education, Boston, MA. For general support.
$100,000 to Philadelphia Orchestra Association, Philadelphia, PA. For endowment.
$100,000 to United States Holocaust Memorial Museum, DC. For general support.
$66,850 to Raymond and Ruth Perelman Jewish Day School, Wynnewood, PA. For general support.

1869
Adam Foundation, Inc. ✧ ☆
121 Alhambra Plz., PH1, Ste. 1600
Coral Gables, FL 33134

Established in 2002 in FL.
Donor: ODM, Ltd.
Foundation type: Independent foundation.
Financial data (yr. ended 9/30/05): Assets, $231,211 (M); gifts received, $63,765; expenditures, $817,793; qualifying distributions, $817,617; giving activities include $813,389 for 4 grants (high: $787,000; low: $1,800).
Fields of interest: Christian agencies & churches.
Limitations: Applications not accepted. Giving on a national basis, with some emphasis on FL. No grants to individuals.
Application information: Contributes only to pre-selected organizations.
Officers and Directors:* W. Allen Morris,* Pres.; Diane Y. Morris,* V.P.; Dale I. Graham, V.P.; Gil Yazmin, Treas.; Kathryn Bell Mauldin.
EIN: 431988647

1870
ADFAM Charities, Inc.
(formerly A. Darius Davis Family - W.D. Charities, Inc.)
4310 Pablo Oaks Ct.
Jacksonville, FL 32224-9631

Established in 1950 in FL.
Donor: A. Darius Davis.
Foundation type: Independent foundation.
Financial data (yr. ended 12/31/05): Assets, $17,178,401 (M); expenditures, $1,071,425; qualifying distributions, $1,037,581; giving activities include $1,037,500 for 46 grants (high: $600,000; low: $1,000).
Fields of interest: Arts; Higher education; Medical research, institute; Children/youth, services; Christian agencies & churches.

Limitations: Applications not accepted. Giving primarily in Jacksonville, FL. No grants to individuals.
Application information: Contributes only to pre-selected organizations.
Officers and Directors:* Robert D. Davis,* Pres.; H.J. Skelton, V.P. and Treas.; David C. Clowe, V.P.; H.D. Francis, V.P.; Susan C. Thorne, V.P.; Judy B. Morgan, Secy.; Lee W. Davis; Caroline D. Fitzgerald.
EIN: 596128575

1871

Adler Family Foundation, Inc. ✧

(formerly Frederick R. Adler Foundation, Inc.)
1520 S. Ocean Blvd.
Palm Beach, FL 33480

Established in 1983 in NY.
Donor: Frederick R. Adler.
Foundation type: Independent foundation.
Financial data (yr. ended 11/30/05): Assets, $2,731,312 (M); expenditures, $719,593; qualifying distributions, $711,460; giving activities include $707,875 for 74 grants (high: $175,000; low: $50; average: $1,000–$25,000).
Purpose and activities: Giving primarily for the arts, health care, and education.
Fields of interest: Museums; Arts; Elementary/secondary education; Higher education; Law school/education; Education; Veterinary medicine, hospital; Hospitals (general); Health care; Health organizations, association; Cancer; Medical research, institute; Cancer research; Human services; Community development; Jewish federated giving programs; Jewish agencies & temples.
Limitations: Applications not accepted. Giving primarily in FL and NY; some giving nationally. No grants to individuals.
Application information: Contributes only to pre-selected organizations.
Trustees: Catherine Adler; Frederick R. Adler; William Bush.
EIN: 133157738
Selected grants: The following grants were reported in 2003.
$200,000 to Harvard University, Cambridge, MA.
$150,000 to Memorial Sloan-Kettering Cancer Center, Society of, New York, NY.
$50,000 to Horace Mann School, Riverdale, NY.
$50,000 to Memorial Sloan-Kettering Cancer Center, New York, NY.
$50,000 to Palm Beach Day School, Palm Beach, FL.
$25,000 to American Society for Technion-Israel Institute of Technology, New York, NY.
$25,000 to Jewish Federation of Palm Beach County, West Palm Beach, FL. For general support.
$25,000 to National Alliance for Research on Schizophrenia and Depression (NARSAD), Great Neck, NY.
$25,000 to Raymond F. Kravis Center for the Performing Arts, West Palm Beach, FL. For Sally George Program for Senior Citizens.
$10,000 to Washington Institute, DC. For general support.

1872

Albrecht Foundation ✧ ☆

794 N. E. Harbour Dr.
Boca Raton, FL 33431

Established in 2003 in NV.
Donor: Ralph W. Albrecht.
Foundation type: Operating foundation.
Financial data (yr. ended 12/31/05): Assets, $1,169,073 (M); gifts received, $1,550,000; expenditures, $521,884; qualifying distributions, $521,559; giving activities include $521,559 for 27 grants (high: $116,200; low: $20).
Fields of interest: Human services; Salvation Army; Christian agencies & churches.
Limitations: Giving primarily in CA.
Officers: Ralph W. Albrecht, Sr., Pres.; Philip D. Bogetto, Secy.
EIN: 870694527

1873

The Amaturo Family Foundation, Inc. ✧

3101 N. Federal Hwy., Ste. 601
Fort Lauderdale, FL 33306-1042
(954) 565-1411
Contact: Jeanette E. Nickel, Mgr.
FAX: (954) 565-1311;
E-mail: jan@amaturogroups.com

Established in 1986 in FL.
Donors: Joseph C. Amaturo; Winifred J. Amaturo.
Foundation type: Independent foundation.
Financial data (yr. ended 6/30/05): Assets, $20,484,963 (M); gifts received, $2,400; expenditures, $1,326,583; qualifying distributions, $1,312,507; giving activities include $1,312,507 for 149 grants (high: $300,000; low: $50).
Purpose and activities: Giving primarily for education, child welfare, and medical research, with emphasis on Roman Catholic organizations.
Fields of interest: Education; Medical research, institute; Human services; Children/youth, services; Roman Catholic federated giving programs; Roman Catholic agencies & churches.
Type of support: Continuing support; Building/renovation; Scholarship funds; Research; Matching/challenge support.
Limitations: Giving primarily in FL. No grants to individuals, or for fellowships.
Publications: Application guidelines.
Application information: Application form not required.
Initial approach: Letter
Copies of proposal: 1
Deadline(s): None
Officers and Directors:* Winifred J. Amaturo,* Pres.; Jeanette E. Nickel,* Mgr.; Douglas Q. Amaturo; Joseph C. Amaturo; Lawrence V. Amaturo; Winifred L. Amaturo; Cara E. Cameron; Elizabeth A. Eisenstein; William J. Ruane; Lorna J. Walsh.
EIN: 592718130
Selected grants: The following grants were reported in 2004.
$208,000 to Catholic Medical Mission Board, New York, NY. For preventing HIV transmission to newborns.
$200,000 to Georgetown University, DC. For research.
$60,000 to Boston College, Chestnut Hill, MA. For theological education.
$50,000 to Nova Southeastern University, Fort Lauderdale, FL. For entrepreneurship program.
$35,000 to Memorial Sloan-Kettering Cancer Center, New York, NY. For research.
$15,000 to University of Florida, Department of Neurological Surgery, Gainesville, FL.
$2,000 to Florida Center for Theological Studies, Miami, FL. For scholarships.

$1,000 to Broward Public Library Foundation, Fort Lauderdale, FL. For literacy programs.
$1,000 to Cystic Fibrosis Foundation, DC. For research.
$1,000 to Kids in Distress (KID), Fort Lauderdale, FL. For general support.

1874

The Walter & Louise Schmid and Ida Thomas & Walter Schmid Jr. Foundation, Inc. ✧ ☆

7045 N. Tamiami Trail
Sarasota, FL 34234

Foundation type: Independent foundation.
Financial data (yr. ended 12/31/04): Assets, $3,094 (M); gifts received, $71,000; expenditures, $1,069,897; qualifying distributions, $1,064,440; giving activities include $1,064,440 for 15 grants (high: $975,000; low: $270).
Purpose and activities: Giving primarily to a Presbyterian foundation for assistance to members in financial crises; funding also for assistance to families, single parents and displaced homemakers in financial times of crises.
Fields of interest: Family services; Protestant agencies & churches; Economically disadvantaged.
Limitations: Giving primarily in Sarasota FL; funding also in Jeffersonville, IN.
Application information:
Initial approach: Letter
Deadline(s): None
Officers: Ida Thomas, Pres.; Walter Schmid, Jr., V.P.; Barbara Bogan, Secy.; Walter Conover, Treas.
Director: Jack Nethery.
EIN: 590867199

1875

Martin Andersen and Gracia Andersen Foundation, Inc. ✧

P.O. Box 547918
Orlando, FL 32854-7918
Contact: Thomas P. Warlow III, Pres.

Established in 1953 in FL.
Donor: Gracia B. Andersen†.
Foundation type: Independent foundation.
Financial data (yr. ended 10/31/05): Assets, $59,649,788 (M); gifts received, $8,970; expenditures, $3,580,373; qualifying distributions, $2,613,677; giving activities include $2,114,976 for 1+ grant.
Purpose and activities: Giving primarily to a hospital foundation.
Fields of interest: Hospitals (general).
Limitations: Giving primarily in Orlando, FL. No grants to individuals.
Application information:
Initial approach: Letter
Deadline(s): None
Officers: Thomas P. Warlow III, Pres.; L. Graham Barr, Jr., V.P.; Richard F. Trismen, Secy.; Marina C. Nice, Treas.
Director: T. Picton Warlow IV.
EIN: 596166589

1876
Lee R. Anderson Family Foundation ▼ ✧
3054 Gordon Dr.
Naples, FL 34102 (763) 545-1004

Established in 1997 in FL.
Donors: Katherine M. Anderson; Lee R. Anderson, Sr.
Foundation type: Independent foundation.
Financial data (yr. ended 6/30/06): Assets, $14,136 (M); gifts received, $1,372,615; expenditures, $1,594,676; qualifying distributions, $1,452,475; giving activities include $1,452,475 for 18 grants (high: $430,430; low: $500; average: $1,000–$50,000).
Purpose and activities: Giving primarily for education, health associations, social services, children's services, and religion.
Fields of interest: Elementary/secondary education; Education; Animals/wildlife, preservation/protection; Health organizations, association; Medical research; Athletics/sports, school programs; Human services; Children, services; Religion.
Limitations: Applications not accepted. Giving on a national basis. No grants to individuals.
Application information: Contributes only to pre-selected organizations.
Officers and Directors:* Lee R. Anderson, Sr.,* Co-Pres.; Lee R. "Andy" Anderson, Jr.,* Co-Pres.; Katherine M. Anderson,* Secy. and Treas.; Katherine E. Anderson,* Treas.; Vickie J. Bates; Charles R. Gehrke.
EIN: 656254123
Selected grants: The following grants were reported in 2005.
$6,200,000 to Association of Graduates of the United States Military Academy, West Point, NY. For general support.
$174,869 to Breck School, Minneapolis, MN. For general support.
$100,000 to Pine Manor College, Chestnut Hill, MA. For general support.
$5,000 to University of Saint Thomas, Law School, Minneapolis, MN. For general support.
$2,500 to Dunwoody College of Technology, Minneapolis, MN. For general support.
$2,500 to Minnesota Council on Economic Education, Saint Paul, MN. For general support.
$250 to West Point Fund, West Point, NY. For general support.

1877
Ansin Foundation ✧
P.O. Box 610727
Miami, FL 33261-0727

Established in 1957.
Donors: Sunbeam Television Corp.; WHDH-TV, Inc.; Sunbeam Development Corp.; Sunbeam Properties, Inc.
Foundation type: Company-sponsored foundation.
Financial data (yr. ended 12/31/04): Assets, $8,001,182 (M); gifts received, $1,065,000; expenditures, $652,196; qualifying distributions, $643,498; giving activities include $643,498 for 33 grants (high: $230,000; low: $100).
Purpose and activities: The foundation supports Jewish agencies and temples and organizations involved with arts and culture, education, health, and human services.

Fields of interest: Arts; Education; Health care; Human services; Federated giving programs; Jewish agencies & temples.
Type of support: General/operating support; Scholarship funds.
Limitations: Applications not accepted. Giving primarily in FL and MA. No grants to individuals.
Application information: Contributes only to pre-selected organizations.
Trustee: Edmund N. Ansin.
EIN: 046046113

1878
The Applebaum Foundation, Inc. ✧
11111 Biscayne Blvd., Twr. 3, Apt. 853
North Miami, FL 33181

Incorporated in 1949 in NY.
Donors: Joseph Applebaum†; Leila Applebaum.
Foundation type: Independent foundation.
Financial data (yr. ended 2/28/06): Assets, $41,330,866 (M); gifts received, $492,313; expenditures, $2,135,689; qualifying distributions, $2,004,895; giving activities include $2,001,500 for 136 grants (high: $300,000; low: $100; average: $1,000–$25,000).
Purpose and activities: Emphasis on higher education, hospitals and medical research, and Jewish organizations, including welfare agencies, schools, and temple support.
Fields of interest: Elementary/secondary education; Higher education; Hospitals (general); Medical research, institute; Human services; Federated giving programs; Jewish federated giving programs; Jewish agencies & temples.
Limitations: Applications not accepted. Giving primarily in Miami, FL, and New York, NY. No grants to individuals.
Application information: Contributes only to pre-selected organizations.
Officers: Leila Applebaum, Pres.; Warren Weiss, V.P.
EIN: 591002714
Selected grants: The following grants were reported in 2006.
$100,000 to College of William and Mary, Williamsburg, VA.
$100,000 to United Way.
$50,000 to Fund for Medicine, New York, NY.
$50,000 to Jewish Museum, New York, NY. 2 grants: $30,000, $20,000
$25,000 to EDAH, New York, NY.
$10,000 to Kolel Pesora Daba, Brooklyn, NY.
$5,000 to Childrens Hospital.
$2,000 to Barrington Stage Company, Sheffield, MA.
$2,000 to Georgetown University, DC.

1879
The Appleby Foundation ✧
c/o SunTrust Bank
P.O. Box 2018
Sarasota, FL 34230 (941) 951-3324

Established in 1958 in DC.
Donor: Scott B. Appleby‡.
Foundation type: Independent foundation.
Financial data (yr. ended 12/31/05): Assets, $12,763,323 (M); gifts received, $67,672; expenditures, $789,963; qualifying distributions,

$651,071; giving activities include $639,157 for 53 grants (high: $110,000; low: $1,000).
Purpose and activities: Grants primarily for higher education; giving also for youth agencies, music, Protestant church support, cultural programs, hospitals, and hospices.
Fields of interest: Performing arts, music; Arts; Higher education; Hospitals (general); Children/youth, services; Residential/custodial care, hospices; Protestant agencies & churches.
Type of support: General/operating support; Scholarship funds.
Limitations: Giving primarily in FL and GA.
Application information:
  Initial approach: Letter
  Deadline(s): None
  Board meeting date(s): July or Aug.
Trustees: Benjamin N. Colby; F. Jordan Colby; Sarah Rob Colby Pierce; SunTrust Bank.
Number of staff: 1 part-time support.
EIN: 526026971

1880
Ted Arison Charitable Trust ▼ ✧
c/o JPMorgan Chase Bank, N.A.
10800 Biscayne Blvd., Ste. 950
Miami, FL 33161

Established in 2001.
Donors: The Ted Arison 1992 Trust No. 2; Ted Arison Family Foundation USA, Inc.
Foundation type: Independent foundation.
Financial data (yr. ended 12/31/04): Assets, $195,684,557 (M); gifts received, $22,622; expenditures, $5,891,308; qualifying distributions, $4,883,623; giving activities include $4,883,623 for 6 grants (high: $2,900,000; low: $100,000).
Purpose and activities: Giving primarily for human services and arts and cultural programs.
Fields of interest: Arts; Human services; Jewish agencies & temples.
Limitations: Applications not accepted. Giving primarily in FL and in Israel. No grants to individuals.
Application information: Contributes only to pre-selected organizations.
Trustee: JPMorgan Chase Bank, N.A.
EIN: 522303418
Selected grants: The following grants were reported in 2004.
$2,900,000 to Essence of Life, Tel Aviv, Israel. For operating support.
$800,000 to Arison Israel Foundation, Tel Aviv, Israel. For operating support.
$500,000 to Jewish Federation of Greater Miami, Miami, FL. For operating support.
$170,000 to Interdisciplinary Center (IDC) Herzliya, Israel. For construction of Arison School of Business.
$100,000 to University of Miami, Coral Gables, FL. For operating support.

1881
Ted Arison Family Foundation USA, Inc. ▼ ✧
(formerly Arison Foundation, Inc.)
c/o Safo, LLC
10800 Biscayne Blvd., Rm. 950
Miami, FL 33161 (305) 891-0017
Contact: Madelon Rosenberg

Incorporated in 1981 in FL.

Donors: Carnival Cruise Lines, Inc.; Festivale Maritime, Inc.; Intercon Overseas, Inc.
Foundation type: Independent foundation.
Financial data (yr. ended 12/31/04): Assets, $310,056,805 (M); expenditures, $5,538,316; qualifying distributions, $3,387,687; giving activities include $3,330,687 for 13 grants (high: $1,100,000; low: $22,622).
Purpose and activities: Emphasis on arts and cultural programs; support also for Jewish welfare funds.
Fields of interest: Arts; Human services; Jewish federated giving programs.
Limitations: Giving primarily in NY.
Application information:
  Deadline(s): None
Officers: Shari Arison Glazer, Pres.; Arnaldo Perez, V.P.
Trustees: Cassie Arison; David Arison; Jason Arison; Marilyn Arison.
EIN: 592128429
Selected grants: The following grants were reported in 2004.
$1,850,000 to Tel Aviv Sourasky Medical Center, Friends of, New York, NY. 2 grants: $750,000 (For building of living quarters over nursing school), $1,100,000 (For development of hospital entrance).
$500,000 to MATAN - Your Way to Give, Tel Aviv, Israel. For operating support.
$300,000 to Or Media, Tel Aviv, Israel. For Israeli TV Channel.
$250,000 to Entertainment Industry Foundation, Los Angeles, CA. For national colorectal cancer research alliance.
$100,000 to Meir Hospital Sapir Medical Center, Israel. For research.
$77,065 to Essence of Life-International, Miami, FL. 2 grants: $40,000 (For operating support), $37,065.
$51,000 to Orange Private Aircraft, Israel. For transportation for organ transplant.
$22,622 to Jersey Charitable Trust, Jersey. For operating support.

1882
The Aurora Foundation ✧
(also known as The Aurora Ministries)
P.O. Box 1848
Bradenton, FL   34206
Contact: Joseph A. Aleppo, Exec. Dir.
FAX: (941) 748-2625;
E-mail: aurora@auroraministries.org; URL: http://www.auroraministries.org

Established in 1969.
Donor: Anthony T. Rossi.
Foundation type: Independent foundation.
Financial data (yr. ended 12/31/05): Assets, $43,862,328 (M); expenditures, $4,176,835; qualifying distributions, $3,711,311; giving activities include $2,919,974 for 3 grants (high: $1,383,091; low: $153,954).
Purpose and activities: Support largely for missionary work; grants also for Christian church support, religious associations, education, and social services; also administers and operates the Bradenton Missionary Village, a rent-free housing complex for retired missionaries.
Fields of interest: Christian agencies & churches.
Type of support: General/operating support; Continuing support.

Limitations: Applications not accepted. Giving on a national basis. No grants for professorships or building funds of schools and colleges.
Application information: Unsolicited requests for funds not considered.
  Board meeting date(s): Usually mid-Oct.
Officers: Ezio Aleppo, C.O.O.; Mark Stingley, Sr., Cont.; Joseph A. Aleppo, Exec. Dir.
Board Members: Mike Hamrick; Sanna B. Rossi.
Number of staff: 38 full-time support; 2 part-time support.
EIN: 237044641

1883
Aurora Ministries, Inc. ✧
(formerly Bible Alliance, Inc.)
P.O. Box 1848
Bradenton, FL   34206   (941) 748-4100
FAX: (941) 748-2625;
E-mail: aurora@auroraministries.org; URL: http://www.auroraministries.org

Established in 1972 in FL.
Donors: Anthony T. Rossi; The Aurora Foundation; Jon MacArthur.
Foundation type: Operating foundation.
Financial data (yr. ended 12/31/05): Assets, $6,899,656 (M); gifts received, $1,572,221; expenditures, $3,249,532; qualifying distributions, $2,148,309; giving activities include $12,000 for 1 grant, $1,808,552 for grants to individuals, and $2,075,406 for 3 foundation-administered programs.
Purpose and activities: Production and distribution of recorded portions of the Bible on cassette tape for use primarily by people who are visually and physically handicapped, or who are unable to read or write. The ministries also minister to and train prison chaplains.
Fields of interest: Christian agencies & churches.
Type of support: In-kind gifts.
Limitations: Applications not accepted. Giving on a national basis.
Application information: Unsolicited requests for funds will no longer be accepted.
Officers and Directors:* Joseph A. Aleppo,* Pres.; Phillip R. Johnson,* V.P.; James Pike,* Secy.; Ron Pierre,* Treas.; Georgia Aleppo; Carey Hardy; Steve Kreloff; Larry McCall; Sanna Rossi.
Number of staff: 18 full-time support.
EIN: 237178299

1884
Avrum Gray Family Fund ✧ ☆
13353 Provence Dr.
Palm Beach Gardens, FL   33410
Contact: Avrum Gray, V.P.

Established in 2004 in IL.
Donors: Joseph J. Gray Fund; G-Bar Ltd. Partnership; Mae K. Gray Revocable Trust.
Foundation type: Independent foundation.
Financial data (yr. ended 12/31/05): Assets, $3,446,182 (M); gifts received, $1,738,407; expenditures, $692,918; qualifying distributions, $692,918; giving activities include $673,480 for 40 grants (high: $557,500; low: $50).
Fields of interest: Education; Medical research, institute; Human services; Jewish agencies & temples.
Limitations: Giving primarily in Chicago, IL.

Application information:
  Initial approach: Letter
  Deadline(s): None
Officers: Lori Gray Faversham, Pres.; Avrum Gray, V.P. and Treas.; James Gray, V.P.; Joyce Gray, V.P.; Mathew Gray, V.P.
EIN: 201533159

1885
The Azeez Foundation ✧ ☆
(formerly The Michael and Kathleen Azeez Foundation)
2187 Marseille Dr.
Palm Beach Gardens, FL   33410

Established in 1998 in NJ.
Donors: Michael Azeez; Kathleen Azeez.
Foundation type: Independent foundation.
Financial data (yr. ended 12/31/05): Assets, $15,944,769 (M); expenditures, $870,265; qualifying distributions, $836,320; giving activities include $836,320 for grants.
Fields of interest: Human services; Jewish agencies & temples.
Limitations: Applications not accepted. Giving on a national basis. No grants to individuals.
Application information: Contributes only to pre-selected organizations.
Directors: Anne Azeez; Kathleen Azeez; Michael Azeez.
EIN: 232967146
Selected grants: The following grants were reported in 2004.
$30,000 to National Institute of Transplantation, Los Angeles, CA.
$20,000 to Shore Memorial Hospital, Somers Point, NJ.
$10,000 to Aleph Society, New York, NY.
$10,000 to Chabad of Santa Barbara, Santa Barbara, CA.
$2,000 to University of Denver, Denver, CO.
$500 to Atlanticare Foundation, Egg Harbor Township, NJ.
$500 to Saint Joseph Regional School, Port Vue, PA.

1886
Bacardi Foundation ✧
SunTrust Bldg.
515 E. Las Olas Blvd., Ste. 860
Fort Lauderdale, FL   33301
Contact: Roger Haagenson, Tr.

Established in 1994 in FL.
Donor: Hilda Bacardi†.
Foundation type: Independent foundation.
Financial data (yr. ended 12/31/04): Assets, $10,062,702 (M); expenditures, $793,090; qualifying distributions, $645,000; giving activities include $645,000 for 1 grant.
Fields of interest: Animals/wildlife, research.
Limitations: Giving primarily in FL.
Application information:
  Initial approach: Letter
  Deadline(s): None
Trustees: Facundo Bacardi; Roger Haagenson; Sherry Haagenson.
EIN: 650342998
Selected grants: The following grants were reported in 2003.
$688,037 to Lubee Foundation, Gainesville, FL. For animal research.

1887
The Bailey Family Foundation, Inc. ✧
550 Reo St., Ste. 300
Tampa, FL 33609-1065 (813) 261-2741
FAX: (813) 261-5194;
E-mail: bailey@bailey-family.org; URL: http://
www.bailey-family.org/

Established in 1997 in VA.
Donors: Beverly W. Bailey; Ron K. Bailey; Greg
Manocherian; Florida Coastal School of Law; Strayer
University Educational Foundation.
Foundation type: Operating foundation.
Financial data (yr. ended 12/31/05): Assets,
$58,684,297 (M); gifts received, $34,793;
expenditures, $3,524,688; qualifying distributions,
$3,126,102; giving activities include $702,340 for
50 grants (high: $500,000; low: $250), and
$1,511,930 for 460 grants to individuals (high:
$20,000; low: $48).
Purpose and activities: The primary mission of the
foundation is to expand the availability and enhance
the quality of post secondary education by providing
financial assistance to students based on their
academic record, financial need and level of
community involvement. The foundation also
conducts research directed toward improving the
state of higher education.
Fields of interest: Education; Human services.
Type of support: Research; Scholarships—to
individuals.
Limitations: Giving primarily, but not limited to,
students attending educational institutions in FL
and VA.
Application information: See foundation Web site
for application guidelines and requirements.
Application form required.
   Initial approach: Letter
   Deadline(s): See foundation Web site for
      deadlines
Officer and Directors:* Ron K. Bailey,* Pres.;
Beverly W. Bailey; Ronnie Kyle Bailey; Ryan Kent
Bailey.
EIN: 541850780
Selected grants: The following grants were reported
in 2004.
$51,000 to Academy of the Holy Names, Albany, NY.
$50,000 to Florida Aquarium, Tampa, FL.
$40,000 to Computer Mentors Group, Tampa, FL.
$15,000 to Salvation Army.
$7,000 to University of Tampa, Tampa, FL.
$1,000 to Citadel, The, Charleston, SC.
$1,000 to Karen Academy Foundation for African
   Education, DC.
$1,000 to Metropolitan Ministries, Tampa, FL.
$1,000 to Phi Delta Theta Educational Foundation,
   Oxford, OH.
$1,000 to Salvation Army World Service Office,
   Alexandria, VA.

1888
George M. Baldwin Foundation ✧ ☆
50 N. Laura St., No. 2150
Jacksonville, FL 32202

Established in 2004 in FL.
Donor: George M. Baldwin†.
Foundation type: Independent foundation.
Financial data (yr. ended 12/31/05): Assets,
$16,871,525 (M); gifts received, $2,695,309;
expenditures, $612,167; qualifying distributions,
$603,150; giving activities include $601,000 for 12
grants (high: $306,000; low: $10,000).

Fields of interest: Scholarships/financial aid;
Education; Salvation Army; Children/youth,
services; Human services; Federated giving
programs.
Limitations: Applications not accepted. No grants to
individuals.
Application information: Contributes only to
pre-selected organizations.
Trustee: John G. Grimsley.
EIN: 201377117

1889
Banbury Fund, Inc. ✧
501 Goodlette Rd. N., Ste. D100
Naples, FL 34102
Contact: William S. Robertson, Pres.

Incorporated in 1946 in NY.
Donors: Marie H. Robertson†; Charles S.
Robertson†.
Foundation type: Independent foundation.
Financial data (yr. ended 12/31/04): Assets,
$36,522,808 (M); expenditures, $7,352,166;
qualifying distributions, $7,083,504; giving
activities include $1,591,350 for 52 grants (high:
$275,000; low: $500).
Purpose and activities: Primary areas of interest
include higher and other education, and health,
including cancer and other medical research.
Fields of interest: Secondary school/education;
Higher education; Education; Environment; Health
care; Health organizations, association; Cancer;
Alcoholism; Medical research, institute; Cancer
research; Crime/law enforcement; Human services;
Marine science; Engineering/technology; Biological
sciences; Science; Economically disadvantaged.
Type of support: General/operating support;
Continuing support; Annual campaigns; Capital
campaigns; Building/renovation; Equipment;
Endowments; Debt reduction; Emergency funds;
Seed money; Research.
Limitations: Applications not accepted. Giving
primarily in NY. No grants to individuals.
Application information: Contributes only to
pre-selected organizations.
Officers and Directors:* William S. Robertson,*
Pres.; Walter C. Meier,* V.P.; Katherine R. Ernst,*
Secy.; Anne E. Meier,* Treas.; Robert Ernst.
Number of staff: 4 part-time professional.
EIN: 136062463
Selected grants: The following grants were reported
in 2004.
$275,000 to Harbor Branch Oceanographic
   Institution, Fort Pierce, FL.
$260,000 to Cold Spring Harbor Laboratory, Cold
   Spring Harbor, NY.
$200,000 to University of Colorado Foundation,
   Denver, CO.
$80,000 to Owl Research Institute, Missoula, MT.
$55,000 to Claremont Institute for the Study of
   Statesmanship and Political Philosophy,
   Claremont, CA.
$50,000 to Memorial Sloan-Kettering Cancer
   Center, New York, NY.
$22,000 to Oldfields School, Glencoe, MD.
$20,000 to Pacific Research Institute for Public
   Policy, San Francisco, CA.
$10,000 to Planned Parenthood Hudson Peconic,
   Hawthorne, NY.
$5,000 to Robert Louis Stevenson School, New
   York, NY.

1890
Bank of America, N.A. Client
Foundation ✧
(formerly Bank of America Community Foundation)
1800 2nd St., Ste. 750
Sarasota, FL 34236 (941) 957-0442
Contact: Debra Jacobs, Admin.
FAX: (941) 957-3135; URL: http://
www.selbyfdn.org/bankOfAmerica.html

Established in 1961 in FL as the Sarasota Bank and
Trust Company Community Foundation.
Donors: Eileen Kroeger; Julius Brandenburg†.
Foundation type: Independent foundation.
Financial data (yr. ended 12/31/05): Assets,
$9,344,213 (M); gifts received, $3,767,122;
expenditures, $874,864; qualifying distributions,
$798,747; giving activities include $771,747 for 25
grants (high: $167,000; low: $100).
Purpose and activities: Giving primarily for the arts,
education, human services, natural science, youth
and family organizations, and historic preservation.
Fields of interest: Media, film/video; Visual arts;
Museums; Performing arts; Performing arts, dance;
Performing arts, theater; Humanities; Historic
preservation/historical societies; Arts; Education,
early childhood education; Child development,
education; Elementary school/education;
Secondary school/education; Vocational education;
Higher education; Adult education—literacy, basic
skills & GED; Education, reading; Education;
Environment, natural resources; Environment;
Reproductive health, family planning; Health care;
Mental health/crisis services; Health organizations,
association; AIDS; Crime/violence prevention,
youth; Recreation; Human services; Children/youth,
services; Child development, services; Family
services; Residential/custodial care, hospices;
Aging, centers/services; Women, centers/services;
Minorities/immigrants, centers/services;
Homeless, human services; Urban/community
development; Community development; Marine
science; Aging; Disabilities, people with; Minorities;
Women; Economically disadvantaged; Homeless.
Type of support: Building/renovation; Equipment;
Program development; Matching/challenge support.
Limitations: Giving limited to organizations
operating in or providing services to residents of
Sarasota County, FL. No grants to individuals, or for
deficit financing, debt reduction, conferences,
seminars, workshops, travel, surveys, fund-raising,
annual campaigns, endowments or general
operating support.
Publications: Application guidelines.
Application information: See Web site for
application guidelines. Application form required.
   Initial approach: Proposal
   Copies of proposal: 7
   Deadline(s): May 1 and Oct. 15
   Board meeting date(s): End of June and Nov.
   Final notification: Feb. 1 and Aug. 15
Trustee: Bank of America, N.A.
EIN: 596142753

1891
BankAtlantic Foundation, Inc.
2100 W. Cypress Creek Rd.
Fort Lauderdale, FL 33309 (954) 940-5058
Contact: Shelley Levan Margolis, Exec. Dir.
FAX: (954) 940-5030; URL: http://
www.bankatlantic.com/bafoundation

Established in 1994 in FL.

Donors: BankAtlantic, F.S.B.; The Annenberg Foundation; BankAtlantic.

Foundation type: Company-sponsored foundation.

Financial data (yr. ended 12/31/05): Assets, $2,109,703 (M); expenditures, $626,952; qualifying distributions, $617,470; giving activities include $617,470 for grants.

Purpose and activities: The foundation supports organizations involved with arts and culture, education, human services, and commuity development.

Fields of interest: Arts; Higher education; Education; Children/youth, services; Human services; Community development.

Limitations: Giving primarily in FL.

Application information:
  Deadline(s): None

Officers: Alan Levan, Pres.; Lewis Sarrica, Secy.; Shelley Levan Margolis, Exec. Dir.

EIN: 650499150

Selected grants: The following grants were reported in 2004.

$25,000 to Broward Community College Foundation, Fort Lauderdale, FL.

$15,000 to Greater Miami Opera, Miami, FL.

$10,000 to Junior Achievement of the Palm Beaches, West Palm Beach, FL.

$7,500 to Leadership Broward Foundation, Fort Lauderdale, FL. 2 grants: $2,500, $5,000

$3,500 to Community Partnership for Homeless, Miami, FL.

$3,500 to Florida Council on Economic Education, Tampa, FL.

$2,500 to Boy Scouts of America, Tampa, FL.

$2,500 to Concert Association of Florida, Miami Beach, FL.

$2,500 to Florida Resource Center for Women and Children, West Palm Beach, FL.

1892
John E. and Nellie J. Bastien Memorial Foundation

440 E. Sample Rd., Ste. 209
Pompano Beach, FL 33064
Contact: The Trustees

Trust established in 1965 in FL.

Donor: Nellie J. Bastien†.

Foundation type: Independent foundation.

Financial data (yr. ended 12/31/05): Assets, $9,524,474 (M); expenditures, $539,574; qualifying distributions, $470,772; giving activities include $360,000 for 114 grants (high: $25,000; low: $500).

Fields of interest: Performing arts; Child development, education; Higher education; Environment; Animal welfare; Hospitals (general); Health care; Substance abuse, services; Health organizations, association; Cancer; Heart & circulatory diseases; AIDS; Alcoholism; Biomedicine; Medical research, institute; Cancer research; Heart & circulatory research; AIDS research; Human services; Youth, services; Child development, services; Family services; Residential/custodial care, hospices; Aging, centers/services; Roman Catholic federated giving programs; Marine science; Religion; Aging; Economically disadvantaged.

Type of support: General/operating support; Scholarship funds.

Limitations: Giving primarily in FL.

Application information: Application form not required.
  Initial approach: Letter
  Copies of proposal: 1
  Deadline(s): None
  Final notification: 3 weeks

Trustees: Carol R. Kearns; Jill T. Lawson; Carolyn E. Schneider.

EIN: 596160694

1893
The Batchelor Foundation, Inc. ▼ ✧

111 N.E. 1st St., 8th Fl.
Miami, FL 33132
Contact: Anne O. Batchelor, Tr.

Established in 1990 in FL.

Donors: International Air Leases, Inc.; Batchelor Enterprises; George E. Batchelor†.

Foundation type: Company-sponsored foundation.

Financial data (yr. ended 6/30/05): Assets, $123,698,086 (M); expenditures, $11,777,195; qualifying distributions, $11,041,726; giving activities include $10,934,802 for 93 grants (high: $2,500,000; low: $250).

Purpose and activities: The foundation supports community foundations and organizations involved with education, the environment, animals and wildlife, health, housing, and human services. Special emphasis is directed toward programs designed to engage in medical research and provide care for childhood diseases; and promote study, preservation, and public awareness of the natural environment.

Fields of interest: Higher education; Education; Environment, research; Environment, public education; Environment, natural resources; Environment; Animals/wildlife; Hospitals (general); Health care; Health organizations; Medical research; Housing/shelter; Children/youth, services; Human services; Foundations (community); Children.

Type of support: General/operating support.

Limitations: Giving primarily in Miami, FL. No grants to individuals.

Application information: Application form required.
  Initial approach: Contact foundation for application form

Officers and Trustees: Nancy Ansley, V.P. and C.F.O.; Caridad Velasco, V.P. and Cont.; Anne O. Batchelor; Jack Falk; Daniel J. Ferraresi.

EIN: 650188171

Selected grants: The following grants were reported in 2005.

$2,500,000 to Zoological Society of Florida, Miami MetroZoo, Miami, FL. For general support.

$1,600,000 to Audubon Society of Florida, Miami, FL. 2 grants: $100,000 (For general support), $1,500,000 (For general support).

$815,350 to Community Partnership for Homeless, Miami, FL. For general support.

$300,000 to Catholic University of America, DC. For general support.

$200,000 to American Cancer Society, Miami, FL. For general support.

$100,000 to McCarthys Wildlife Sanctuary, West Palm Beach, FL. For general support.

$100,000 to Muscular Dystrophy Association, Tucson, AZ. For general support.

$25,000 to Cushman School, Miami, FL. For general support.

$11,000 to CHARLEE of Dade County, Miami, FL. For general support.

1894
Robert & Patricia Bauman Family Foundation, Inc. ✧

c/o Robert P. Bauman
6720 S.E. Harbor Cir.
Stuart, FL 34996-1963

Established in 1997 in FL.

Donors: Patricia Bauman; Robert Bauman; Patricia McVey.

Foundation type: Independent foundation.

Financial data (yr. ended 12/31/05): Assets, $10,999,053 (M); gifts received, $900,000; expenditures, $632,788; qualifying distributions, $527,000; giving activities include $527,000 for 57 grants (high: $140,000; low: $500).

Purpose and activities: Giving primarily for education.

Fields of interest: Higher education; Hospitals (general); Federated giving programs.

Limitations: Applications not accepted. Giving on a national basis, with some emphasis on OH. No grants to individuals.

Application information: Contributes only to pre-selected organizations.

Directors: Elizabeth Bauman; John Bauman; Robert Bauman; John McVey.

EIN: 311535223

1895
The C. Kenneth and Laura Baxter Foundation, Inc. ✧

c/o Caler, Donten & Levine, et al., P.A.
505 S. Flagler Dr., Ste. 900
West Palm Beach, FL 33401

Incorporated in 1986 in FL.

Donors: C. Kenneth Baxter; Laura Baxter.

Foundation type: Independent foundation.

Financial data (yr. ended 12/31/05): Assets, $5,775,417 (M); expenditures, $792,683; qualifying distributions, $634,028; giving activities include $460,500 for 33 grants (high: $100,000; low: $1,500).

Purpose and activities: Giving primarily to health associations, particularly for Alzheimer's disease, as well as to youth agencies and services; some giving also to Christian organizations, and for education.

Fields of interest: Elementary/secondary education; Higher education; Animal welfare; Health organizations, association; Alzheimer's disease; Boys & girls clubs; Boy scouts; Human services; Children/youth, services; Christian agencies & churches.

Limitations: Applications not accepted. Giving primarily in FL. No grants to individuals.

Application information: Contributes only to pre-selected organizations.

Directors: Laura Baxter; David S. Donten; Pamela A. Markley.

EIN: 592706460

1896
The Bay Branch Foundation ✧

1515 S. Federal Hwy., Ste. 201
Boca Raton, FL 33432-7404

Trust established in 1963 in NJ.

Donors: Keith C. Wold, Jr.; Mary Lea Johnson Richards Charitable Trust.

Foundation type: Independent foundation.
Financial data (yr. ended 12/31/05): Assets, $20,947,530 (M); gifts received, $150,972; expenditures, $893,931; qualifying distributions, $862,694; giving activities include $862,694 for 72 grants (high: $160,000; low: $100).
Purpose and activities: Giving primarily for health care, education, and the arts.
Fields of interest: Arts; Education; Hospitals (general); Health organizations, association; Marine science; Protestant agencies & churches.
Limitations: Applications not accepted. Giving primarily in CA, FL, and NY. No grants to individuals.
Application information: Contributes only to pre-selected organizations.
Directors: Diana J. Wold; Elaine J. Wold; Keith C. Wold, Jr.
Trustees: Donald Baker; Andrea P. Westergom.
EIN: 226054888
Selected grants: The following grants were reported in 2004.
$1,011,123 to Lynn University, Boca Raton, FL.
$220,240 to Calhoun School, New York, NY.
$140,000 to Harbor Branch Oceanographic Institution, Fort Pierce, FL.
$5,000 to Saint Andrews School, Boca Raton, FL.
$2,000 to Ethel Walker School, Simsbury, CT.
$1,000 to George Washington University, DC.
$1,000 to Gulf Stream School, Gulf Stream, FL.
$1,000 to Nova Southeastern University, Fort Lauderdale, FL.
$1,000 to Saint Paul Academy and Summit School, Saint Paul, MN.
$1,000 to Southern Scholarship Foundation, Tallahassee, FL.

1897
Beaver Street Foundation, Inc. ✧
P.O. Box 41430
Jacksonville, FL 32203-1430

Established in 1986 in FL.
Donor: Beaver Street Fisheries, Inc.
Foundation type: Company-sponsored foundation.
Financial data (yr. ended 12/31/04): Assets, $6,944,155 (M); gifts received, $500,000; expenditures, $347,863; qualifying distributions, $342,663; giving activities include $342,499 for grants.
Purpose and activities: The foundation supports organizations involved with education, health, human services, and Judaism.
Fields of interest: Education; Health care; Human services; Salvation Army; Jewish federated giving programs; Jewish agencies & temples.
Limitations: Applications not accepted. Giving primarily in Jacksonville, FL. No grants to individuals.
Application information: Contributes only to pre-selected organizations.
Directors: Alfred Frisch; Benjamin Frisch; Hans Frisch; Karl Frisch.
EIN: 592714980

1898
The Henry E. Becker and Pauline S. Becker Charitable Foundation ✧ ☆
4700 Bay Shore Rd.
Sarasota, FL 34234

Established in 2004 in FL.
Donor: Pauline S. Becker.

Foundation type: Independent foundation.
Financial data (yr. ended 12/31/05): Assets, $4,451,644 (M); gifts received, $1,600,000; expenditures, $476,171; qualifying distributions, $475,600; giving activities include $475,600 for 30 grants (high: $90,000; low: $3,000).
Fields of interest: Arts; Education; Health organizations; Youth development; Human services.
Limitations: Applications not accepted. Giving primarily in FL.
Application information: Contributes only to pre-selected organizations.
Trustee: Pauline S. Becker.
EIN: 206297485

1899
Behring Foundation ▼ ✧
c/o Elliot D. Stein
2131 Hollywood Blvd., Ste. 505
Hollywood, FL 33020 (954) 920-5300
Contact: Elliot D. Stein, Tr.

Established in 1993 in CA.
Donor: Kenneth E. Behring.
Foundation type: Independent foundation.
Financial data (yr. ended 12/31/05): Assets, $29,211 (M); gifts received, $5,629,725; expenditures, $1,971,953; qualifying distributions, $1,844,400; giving activities include $1,844,400 for 11 grants (high: $1,500,000; low: $500).
Purpose and activities: Giving primarily for animal and wildlife associations, including a large grant to the Smithsonian Institute.
Fields of interest: Museums; Animals/wildlife.
Limitations: Giving primarily in CA and Washington, DC.
Application information: Resume, transcripts, short statement of career options, 3 letters of reference, and an essay required for fellowships.
Initial approach: Letter
Deadline(s): None
Trustees: David E. Behring; Kenneth E. Behring; Joel S. Ehrenkranz; Elliot D. Stein.
EIN: 680306096
Selected grants: The following grants were reported in 2004.
$10,723,585 to Smithsonian Institution, DC. 2 grants: $8,707,092 (For renovation of Museum of American History), $2,016,493 (For renovation of Museum of American History).
$10,470 to All Wars Memorial Foundation, Danville, CA. For completion of memorial.

1900
The Believers Foundation, Inc.
P.O. Box 428
Mango, FL 33550-0428
Contact: Kenneth Fuller, Exec. Dir.

Established in 1987 in GA.
Donors: Robert Jaeb†; Lorena Jaeb; Stephen Jaeb.
Foundation type: Independent foundation.
Financial data (yr. ended 8/31/05): Assets, $3,941,708 (M); expenditures, $2,884,199; qualifying distributions, $2,671,360; giving activities include $2,599,344 for 26 grants (high: $1,032,000; low: $2,000), and $59,530 for foundation-administered programs.
Purpose and activities: Giving to religious organizations to proclaim the gospel of Christ, and

for training of pastors and disciples to preach the Word.
Fields of interest: Christian agencies & churches; Protestant agencies & churches.
Type of support: General/operating support; Continuing support; Program development; Conferences/seminars; Publication; Curriculum development; Technical assistance.
Limitations: Giving on a national and international basis. No support for political organizations.
Publications: Annual report.
Application information: Application form not required.
Initial approach: Letter
Copies of proposal: 1
Deadline(s): None
Board meeting date(s): Varies
Officers and Directors:* Stephen Jaeb,* Pres.; Lorena Jaeb,* V.P. and Treas.; Kenneth Fuller,* Secy. and Exec. Dir.; Dave Wismer.
Number of staff: 2 full-time professional.
EIN: 592851282
Selected grants: The following grants were reported in 2003.
$1,131,990 to Grace Community Church, Sun Valley, CA.
$350,000 to Masters College, Santa Clarita, CA. 2 grants: $300,000, $50,000
$180,000 to Slavic Gospel Association, Loves Park, IL.
$170,000 to Christ Baptist Church, South Africa. .
$152,000 to Grace to You, Valencia, CA.
$130,000 to Community Bible Church of the Foothills, La Crescenta, CA.
$85,800 to Calvary Baptist Church, Burbank, CA.
$50,000 to Bethel Baptist Church, Lancaster, CA.
$46,198 to Believers Fellowship of San Antonio, San Antonio, TX.

1901
Bell Family Foundation ✧ ☆
100 Casuarina Concourse
Coral Gables, FL 33143-6504

Established in 1987 in FL.
Donor: Daniel M. Bell.
Foundation type: Independent foundation.
Financial data (yr. ended 12/31/05): Assets, $4,862,871 (M); gifts received, $2,160,000; expenditures, $488,487; qualifying distributions, $473,500; giving activities include $473,500 for 2 grants (high: $425,500; low: $48,000).
Purpose and activities: Giving for religion.
Fields of interest: Protestant agencies & churches.
Limitations: Applications not accepted. Giving primarily in Miami, FL. No grants to individuals.
Application information: Contributes only to pre-selected organizations.
Officers: Daniel M. Bell, Pres.; Patricia B. Bell, V.P. and Secy.
Trustees: Daniel M. Bell, Jr.; Rodney H. Bell.
EIN: 650016516

1902
Robert R. Bellamy Memorial Foundation, Inc. ✧ ☆
4649 Ponce de Leon Blvd., Ste. 403
Coral Gables, FL 33146-2121 (305) 666-5770
Contact: Robert R. Bellamy, Pres.

Established in 1947 in NC.

Foundation type: Independent foundation.
Financial data (yr. ended 12/31/05): Assets, $7,022,153 (M); expenditures, $363,206; qualifying distributions, $318,500; giving activities include $318,500 for grants.
Purpose and activities: Giving primarily for higher education, and hospitals and health associations.
Fields of interest: Historic preservation/historical societies; Higher education; Education; Hospitals (general); Health organizations, association; Human services.
Type of support: General/operating support.
Limitations: Giving primarily in FL and NC. No grants to individuals.
Application information: Application form not required.
   Initial approach: Letter
   Deadline(s): None
Officers and Trustees:* Robert R. Bellamy,* Pres. and Treas.; Cyrus D. Hogue, Jr.,* Secy.; Hugh MacRae II; Sarah Bellamy McMerty; Kathryn R. Posten; P.R. Smith, Jr.
EIN: 566040601
Selected grants: The following grants were reported in 2004.
$110,000 to Florida International University, Miami, FL. For general support.
$50,000 to Historic Preservation Foundation of North Carolina, Raleigh, NC. For general support.
$37,000 to University of Miami, Coral Gables, FL. For general support.
$20,000 to Mercy Hospital Foundation, Miami, FL. For general support.
$10,000 to Cape Fear Academy, Wilmington, NC. For general support.
$10,000 to Mississippi State University Foundation, Mississippi State, MS. For general support.
$5,000 to North Carolina Coastal Land Trust, Wilmington, NC. For general support.
$5,000 to University of North Carolina, Chapel Hill, NC. For general support.
$1,000 to Mount Sinai Medical Center, Miami Beach, FL. For general support.
$1,000 to Saint James Episcopal Church, Hendersonville, NC. For general support.

1903
Berg Family Charitable Foundation ◇
225 Water St., Ste. 1987
Jacksonville, FL   32202

Established in 1986 in FL.
Donors: Gilchrist B. Berg; Berkshire Hathaway Inc.
Foundation type: Independent foundation.
Financial data (yr. ended 12/31/05): Assets, $5,890,485 (M); expenditures, $631,291; qualifying distributions, $630,970; giving activities include $628,102 for 32 grants (high: $220,084; low: $25).
Purpose and activities: Giving for the arts, higher education, Christian organizations, and human services.
Fields of interest: Arts; Secondary school/education; Higher education; Hospitals (general); Health organizations, association; Human services; Salvation Army; Protestant agencies & churches.
Limitations: Applications not accepted. Giving on a national basis. No grants to individuals.
Application information: Contributes only to pre-selected organizations.
Trustee: Gilchrist B. Berg.
EIN: 592803980

1904
The Bernstein Family Charitable Foundation ◇
P.O. Box 810664
Boca Raton, FL   33481-0664

Established in 1999 in FL.
Donor: Steven E. Bernstein.
Foundation type: Independent foundation.
Financial data (yr. ended 6/30/05): Assets, $3,419,559 (M); expenditures, $542,863; qualifying distributions, $520,400; giving activities include $520,400 for 7 grants (high: $409,900; low: $500).
Purpose and activities: Giving primarily for children's services.
Fields of interest: Elementary/secondary education; Human services; Children, services.
Limitations: Applications not accepted. Giving primarily in FL, with emphasis on Boca Raton and West Palm Beach. No grants to individuals.
Application information: Contributes only to pre-selected organizations.
Officer: Steven E. Bernstein, Pres.
EIN: 656317066
Selected grants: The following grants were reported in 2004.
$400,000 to Childrens Place at Home Safe, West Palm Beach, FL. For general support.
$8,500 to Jewish Community Center of Greater Pittsburgh, Pittsburgh, PA. For general support.
$250 to American Cancer Society, Boca Raton, FL. For general support.
$225 to Bob Beamon Golf & Tennis Classic, Fort Lauderdale, FL. For general support.

1905
Better Way Foundation, Inc. ◇
(formerly Alpha Omega Foundation, Inc.)
c/o Adler Mgmt.
1167 3rd St. S., Ste. 102
Naples, FL   34102

Established around 1994.
Donors: North Star Ventures; Arbeit Investment, LP; Arbeit & Co.
Foundation type: Independent foundation.
Financial data (yr. ended 12/31/05): Assets, $29,365,027 (M); expenditures, $893,286; qualifying distributions, $855,773; giving activities include $758,491 for 17 grants (high: $245,000; low: $1,611).
Purpose and activities: Giving primarily for higher education and to Roman Catholic churches and organizations.
Fields of interest: Higher education; Health organizations, association; Federated giving programs; Roman Catholic agencies & churches.
Limitations: Applications not accepted. Giving primarily in IL, MD, and MN; some funding also in NY. No grants to individuals.
Application information: Contributes only to pre-selected organizations.
Officers and Directors:* A.R. Goldman,* Pres.; Luz Campa, V.P.; Matthew G. Rauenhorst,* Treas.; J.R. Mahoney; Gia Rauenhorst; Margaret Rauenhorst; Rebecca Elizabeth Rauenhorst.
EIN: 411795984
Selected grants: The following grants were reported in 2003.
$425,000 to Catholic Community Foundation, Saint Paul, MN. For general operating support.

$15,000 to Habitat for Humanity, Twin Cities, Minneapolis, MN. For general operating support.
$15,000 to International Rescue Committee, New York, NY. For general operating support.
$15,000 to Saint Marys College, Notre Dame, IN. For general operating support.
$10,000 to Academy of the Holy Names School, Tampa, FL. For general operating support.
$10,000 to Alzheimers Association of Minnesota-North Dakota, Minneapolis, MN. For general operating support.
$10,000 to Alzheimers Support Network, Naples, FL. For general operating support.
$7,500 to Iona Senior Services, DC. For general operating support.
$7,500 to Saint Patricks Episcopal Day School, DC. For general operating support.
$5,000 to Saint Paul Catholic School, Saint Petersburg, FL. For general operating support.

1906
The Beveridge Family Foundation, Inc. ◇
1340 U.S. Highway 1, Rm. 102
Jupiter, FL   33469

Established in 2000 in MA.
Foundation type: Independent foundation.
Financial data (yr. ended 12/31/04): Assets, $14,240,143 (M); gifts received, $55,435; expenditures, $788,150; qualifying distributions, $700,798; giving activities include $646,155 for 1 grant.
Fields of interest: Recreation, parks/playgrounds.
Limitations: Applications not accepted. Giving primarily in MA. No grants to individuals.
Application information: Contributes only to pre-selected organizations.
Officers: Philip Caswell, Pres.; Ward S. Caswell, Clerk; Carole S. Lenhart, Treas.
EIN: 311698286
Selected grants: The following grants were reported in 2003.
$607,000 to Stanley Park of Westfield, Westfield, MA.

1907
The Frank Stanley Beveridge Foundation, Inc. ◇
1340 U.S. Hwy. 1, Ste. 102
Jupiter, FL   33469   (800) 600-3723
Contact: Philip Caswell, Pres.
E-mail: administrator@beveridge.org; *Fax:* (888) 726-8631eFax; *URL:* http://www.beveridge.org

Trust established in 1947 in MA; incorporated in 1956.
Donor: Frank Stanley Beveridge†.
Foundation type: Independent foundation.
Financial data (yr. ended 12/31/04): Assets, $39,442,203 (M); expenditures, $2,142,531; qualifying distributions, $1,887,587; giving activities include $1,552,548 for 102 grants (high: $400,000; low: $252).
Purpose and activities: Giving primarily for higher and secondary educational institutions attended by the Beveridge family, social service and youth agencies, community development, culture, health, minorities, ecological programs, and religious organizations attended by the Beveridge family.
Fields of interest: Historic preservation/historical societies; Education, early childhood education;

Child development, education; Adult/continuing education; Education; Animal welfare; Hospitals (general); Health care; Mental health/crisis services; Health organizations; Nutrition; Housing/shelter, development; Human services; Youth, services; Child development, services; Family services; Residential/custodial care, hospices; Aging, centers/services; Minorities/immigrants, centers/services; Voluntarism promotion; Christian agencies & churches; Protestant agencies & churches; Religion; Aging; Disabilities, people with; Minorities.

Type of support: Management development/capacity building; Income development; Annual campaigns; Capital campaigns; Building/renovation; Equipment; Land acquisition; Emergency funds; Program development; Seed money; Research; Technical assistance; In-kind gifts; Matching/challenge support.

Limitations: Giving limited to Hampden and Hampshire counties, MA. No support for governmental agencies, private foundations or federated giving programs, or for private educational institutions not attended by members of the Beveridge family. No grants to individuals, or for general operating support, income development, internships, endowment or operating funds, awards or competitions, commissioning of new works, conferences and seminars, curriculum development, debt reduction, matching gifts, multi-year payments, exhibitions, film or radio production, scholarships, fellowships, foreign organizations or for foreign expenditure; no loans.

Publications: Grants list.

Application information: Application information available on foundation Web site. Application form required.

Initial approach: Web site application only
Copies of proposal: 1
Deadline(s): Feb. 1 and Aug. 1
Board meeting date(s): Apr. and Oct.
Final notification: May 1 and Nov. 1

Officers and Directors:* Philip Caswell,* Pres.; Carole S. Lenhart, V.P. and Treas.; Ward S. Caswell, Clerk; Christa P. Bigue; Latimer B. Eddy; Alfred L. Griggs; Carol A. Leary, Ph.D.; Ian C. Palmer; Joseph Beveridge Palmer; Frederick W. Stecher; Patsy Palmer Stecher.

Number of staff: 1 full-time professional; 1 part-time professional.

EIN: 046032164

1908
BJ's Foundation, Inc. ◆
521 E. Las Olas Blvd.
Fort Lauderdale, FL 33301

Established in 1998.
Donor: Elizabeth H. Buntrock.
Foundation type: Operating foundation.
Financial data (yr. ended 12/31/04): Assets, $5,799,395 (M); gifts received, $263,767; expenditures, $550,777; qualifying distributions, $483,413; giving activities include $895,116 for 105 grants (high: $409,533; low: $25; average: $100–$5,000).
Purpose and activities: Giving for Christian services, and for human services.
Fields of interest: Arts; Education; Human services; Foundations (private operating); Christian agencies & churches.
Limitations: Applications not accepted. Giving primarily in FL. No grants to individuals.

Application information: Contributes only to pre-selected organizations.
Officer and Directors:* Elizabeth H. Buntrock,* Pres.; Cecily Buntrock; Dana L. Buntrock.
EIN: 650745280

1909
The Blank Family Foundation, Inc. ◆ ☆
(formerly The New Blank Family Foundation, Inc.)
3455 N.W. 54th St.
Miami, FL 33142 (305) 633-8587
Contact: Andrew S. Blank, V.P.

Established in 2002 in FL.
Foundation type: Independent foundation.
Financial data (yr. ended 12/31/04): Assets, $22,990,973 (M); gifts received, $5,542,787; expenditures, $1,041,753; qualifying distributions, $849,950; giving activities include $849,950 for 53 grants (high: $300,000; low: $200).
Purpose and activities: Giving primarily for Jewish causes, including federated giving programs; support also for human services, education, the environment, and the arts.
Fields of interest: Arts; Higher education; Education; Environment, natural resources; Goodwill Industries; Human services; Jewish federated giving programs; Jewish agencies & temples.
Type of support: General/operating support.
Limitations: Giving primarily in FL, ID, and UT; some funding nationally. No grants to individuals.
Application information:
Initial approach: Letter
Deadline(s): None
Officers and Directors:* Jerome Blank,* Pres.; Andrew S. Blank,* V.P.; Martin Gallant,* V.P.
EIN: 920185953

1910
David Strouse Blount Educational Foundation ◆ ☆
c/o SunTrust Bank
P.O. Box 1908
Orlando, FL 32802-1908
Application address: c/o SunTrust Bank, Attn.: Carolyn McCoy, 510 S. Jefferson St., Roanoke, VA 24038, tel.: (540) 982-3014

Established in 1973 in VA.
Foundation type: Independent foundation.
Financial data (yr. ended 3/31/06): Assets, $3,053,508 (M); expenditures, $372,470; qualifying distributions, $347,013; giving activities include $335,500 for 134 grants to individuals (high: $10,000; low: $2,500).
Purpose and activities: Scholarship awards to residents of VA, attending local colleges and universities.
Type of support: Scholarships—to individuals.
Limitations: Giving limited to residents of VA.
Application information: Application form required.
Deadline(s): None
Trustee: SunTrust Bank.
EIN: 546111717

1911
The Blue Foundation for a Healthy Florida, Inc. ◆
4800 Deerwood Campus Pkwy., Ste. DC3-4
Jacksonville, FL 32246 (800) 477-3736, ext. 63215
Contact: Susan B. Towler, Exec. Dir.
E-mail: bluefoundationfl@bcbsfl.com; Application address for Sapphire Award: The Sapphire Award, 4800 Deerwood Campus Pkwy., Bldg. 300, 4th Fl., Jacksonville, FL 32246-8273, E-mail: thesapphireaward@bcbsfl.com; URL: http://www.bluefoundationfl.org

Established in 2001 in FL.
Donors: Blue Cross and Blue Shield of Florida, Inc.; Health Options, Inc.
Foundation type: Company-sponsored foundation.
Financial data (yr. ended 12/31/05): Assets, $44,412,323 (M); gifts received, $9,054,545; expenditures, $2,026,105; qualifying distributions, $1,468,908; giving activities include $1,468,908 for grants.
Purpose and activities: The foundation supports organizations involved with health and human services. Special emphasis is directed toward programs designed to address the health and well-being of the uninsured and underserved.
Fields of interest: Health care, financing; Health care; Family services; Human services; Economically disadvantaged.
Limitations: Giving limited to FL. No support for religious organizations not of direct benefit to the entire community. No grants to individuals.
Publications: Application guidelines; Corporate giving report.
Application information: Application form required.
Initial approach: Download application form; download application form and mail to application address for Sapphire Award
Copies of proposal: 4
Deadline(s): Summer and winter; May for Sapphire Award
Board meeting date(s): Every 2 months
Final notification: Fall for Sapphire Award
Officers and Directors:* Randy M. Kammer,* Pres.; Tony Jenkins, V.P.; Varnum "Chip" Kenyon, Secy.; Deanna McDonald,* Treas.; Susan B. Towler,* Exec. Dir.; Anthony Benevento; Michael Cascone, Jr.; Melvyn Fletcher, M.D.; Rebecca Gay; Cyrus M. Jollivette; Robert Mirsky, M.D.; Mark Swink.
Number of staff: 2 full-time professional; 1 part-time professional.
EIN: 593707820

1912
The Walter and Adi Blum Foundation, Inc. ◆
c/o Murphy, Reid, Pilotte, Ord & Austin
340 Royal Palm Way, Ste. 100
Palm Beach, FL 33480-4307

Established in 1987 in FL.
Donor: Adi Blum Revocable Trust.
Foundation type: Independent foundation.
Financial data (yr. ended 12/31/05): Assets, $12,952,087 (M); expenditures, $695,378; qualifying distributions, $558,468; giving activities include $472,815 for 41 grants (high: $25,000; low: $500; average: $5,000–$10,000).
Purpose and activities: Giving primarily for community development, arts and culture,

education, health and human services, and youth organizations.

Fields of interest: Arts; Education; Hospitals (general); Health organizations, association; Recreation; Human services; Children/youth, services; Community development; Foundations (community).

Limitations: Applications not accepted. Giving primarily in Palm Beach, FL. No grants to individuals.

Application information: Contributes only to pre-selected organizations.

Officers and Directors:* Norman Shaw,* Pres.; Eugene W. Murphy, Jr.,* V.P. and Treas.; Sandra E. Gambill,* Secy.

EIN: 650008826

1913

The Bond Foundation, Inc. ✧ ☆

800 S. Dillard St.
Winter Garden, FL   34787

Established in 1997 in FL.

Donor: Walter Bond‡.

Foundation type: Independent foundation.

Financial data (yr. ended 6/30/05): Assets, $7,247,560 (M); expenditures, $460,306; qualifying distributions, $361,958; giving activities include $338,180 for 46 grants (high: $127,680; low: $1,000).

Fields of interest: Higher education; Health organizations, association; Human services; YM/YWCAs & YM/YWHAs; Christian agencies & churches.

Limitations: Applications not accepted. Giving primarily in FL. No grants to individuals.

Application information: Contributes only to pre-selected organizations.

Officers: Derek J. Blakeslee, Pres.; Ann G. Blakeslee, Secy.-Treas.

Directors: Mark Griffith; Carole Wingate; Don Wingate.

EIN: 593468830

Selected grants: The following grants were reported in 2005.

$6,000 to MicheLee Puppets, Orlando, FL.

$5,000 to American Diabetes Association, Alexandria, VA.

$5,000 to Boy Scouts of America, Apopka, FL.

$5,000 to Montreat Conference Center, Montreat, NC.

$5,000 to United Cerebral Palsy of Central Florida, Orlando, FL.

$3,500 to American Cancer Society, Tampa, FL.

$2,500 to Duvall Presbyterian Home, Glenwood, FL.

$2,500 to Freedom Ride, Winter Park, FL.

$2,500 to Junior Achievement of Central Florida, Orlando, FL.

$1,000 to Ronald McDonald House Charities of Central Florida, Orlando, FL.

1914

Alex and Roxanna Booth Foundation, Inc. ✧ ☆

2001 Sailfish Point Blvd., Apt. 316
Stuart, FL   34996
E-mail: seasideweiss@cs.com
Application address for individuals: c/o Christa Weiss, 940 N.W. Fresco Way, Apt. 202, Jensen Beach, FL 34957

Established in 2002 in FL.

Donor: Alex Booth, Jr.

Foundation type: Independent foundation.

Financial data (yr. ended 12/31/05): Assets, $69,497 (M); gifts received, $765,260; expenditures, $717,012; qualifying distributions, $671,012; giving activities include $616,837 for 2 grants (high: $523,791; low: $93,045), and $54,175 for 21 grants to individuals (high: $9,000; low: $375).

Fields of interest: Education.

Type of support: Scholarships—to individuals.

Limitations: Giving limited to residents of Martin, St. Lucie, Okeechobee, and Indian River counties, FL.

Application information:

Deadline(s): None

Officers and Directors:* Alex Booth, Jr.,* Pres.; Christa Weiss,* Secy.-Treas.; Teena Jones.

EIN: 134230772

1915

Norman and Irma Braman Foundation, Inc. ✧

2060 Biscayne Blvd., 2nd Fl.
Miami, FL   33137

Established in 1995 in FL.

Donors: Irma Braman; Dacra Development Corp.

Foundation type: Independent foundation.

Financial data (yr. ended 12/31/04): Assets, $33,098,914 (M); gifts received, $1,144,146; expenditures, $2,852,072; qualifying distributions, $2,763,633; giving activities include $2,745,311 for 104 grants (high: $1,025,000; low: $100).

Fields of interest: Museums (art); Higher education; Human services; Federated giving programs; Jewish federated giving programs; Jewish agencies & temples.

International interests: Israel.

Limitations: Applications not accepted. Giving on a national basis, with some emphasis on FL; giving also to a high school in Israel. No grants to individuals.

Application information: Unsolicited requests for funds not accepted.

Officers and Directors:* Norman Braman, Pres. and Treas.; Susan B. Lustgarten,* V.P.; Debra B. Wechsler,* V.P.; Irma Braman,* Secy.

EIN: 650542566

Selected grants: The following grants were reported in 2004.

$50,000 to Jewish Community Services, Flint, MI.

$38,500 to I Have A Dream Foundation, New York, NY.

$36,000 to Ransom Everglades School, Miami, FL.

$25,000 to Israel, State of, Jerusalem, Israel. .

$25,000 to Miami Childrens Museum, Miami, FL.

$25,000 to United Way of Miami-Dade, Miami, FL.

$25,000 to Yeshiva University, New York, NY.

$15,000 to Community Partnership, Macon, GA.

$15,000 to Jewish Museum of Florida, Miami Beach, FL.

$14,700 to Shipley School, Bryn Mawr, PA.

1916

The Shepard Broad Foundation, Inc. ✧

801 Brickell Ave., Ste. 2350
Miami, FL   33131   (305) 358-5941
Contact: John Bussel, Pres.

Incorporated in 1956 in FL.

Donors: Shepard Broad; Ruth K. Broad; Morris N. Broad.

Foundation type: Independent foundation.

Financial data (yr. ended 12/31/04): Assets, $9,433,000 (M); gifts received, $1,344,571; expenditures, $577,003; qualifying distributions, $474,956; giving activities include $474,956 for 112 grants (high: $50,000; low: $36).

Fields of interest: Higher education; Education; Hospitals (general); Health care; Jewish agencies & temples.

Limitations: Giving primarily in FL. No grants to individuals.

Application information: Application form not required.

Initial approach: Proposal

Deadline(s): None

Officers and Directors:* Morris N. Broad,* Chair.; John M. Bussel,* Pres.; Ann B. Bussel,* V.P.; Deborah Bussel,* Treas.; Karen A.B. Berman; Daniel J. Bussel.

EIN: 590998866

1917

Ann L. Bronfman Foundation ✧

c/o Marilyn Silver
7700 Wexford Way
Port St. Lucie, FL   34986-3007

Established in 1958.

Donor: Ann L. Bronfman.

Foundation type: Independent foundation.

Financial data (yr. ended 7/31/05): Assets, $21,203,085 (M); expenditures, $1,701,041; qualifying distributions, $1,579,090; giving activities include $1,576,750 for 47 grants (high: $125,000; low: $200).

Purpose and activities: Giving primarily for higher education and health institutions; also funding the arts.

Fields of interest: Arts; Higher education; Education; Hospitals (specialty); Crime/violence prevention; Human services; Children/youth, services; Jewish federated giving programs; Population studies; Jewish agencies & temples.

Type of support: General/operating support.

Limitations: Applications not accepted. Giving primarily in Washington, DC, and New York, NY; some funding nationally. No grants to individuals.

Application information: Contributes only to pre-selected organizations.

Officers: Ann L. Bronfman, Pres.; Ron Stein, Secy.; Jerome Manning, Treas.

EIN: 136085595

Selected grants: The following grants were reported in 2005.

$125,000 to Children of Bellevue, New York, NY.

$125,000 to Multicultural Career Intern Program, DC.

$125,000 to Population Action International, DC.

$77,500 to Teamwork Foundation, Bronx, NY.

$50,000 to Hazelden Foundation, Center City, MN.

$50,000 to Watkinson School, Hartford, CT.

$30,000 to National Trust for Historic Preservation, DC.

$25,000 to Childrens Hospital Foundation, DC.

$20,000 to Opera Orchestra of New York, New York, NY.

$2,000 to Saint Josephs Indian School, Chamberlain, SD.

1918
Bryson Foundation ☆
719 Grove Pl.
Vero Beach, FL 32963-9560

Established in 1991 in IN.
Donor: Vaughn D. Bryson.
Foundation type: Independent foundation.
Financial data (yr. ended 12/31/05): Assets, $11,878,522 (M); gifts received, $1,635,710; expenditures, $1,013,205; qualifying distributions, $985,450; giving activities include $985,450 for grants.
Fields of interest: Arts; Higher education.
Type of support: General/operating support.
Limitations: Applications not accepted. Giving in the U.S., with some emphasis on FL and NC. No support for religious or political organizations. No grants to individuals.
Application information: Unsolicited requests for funds not accepted.
Officers: Vaughn D. Bryson, Pres. and Treas.; Nancy F. Bryson, Secy.
Directors: William D. Bryson; Catherine Bryson Moore; Jeffrey Thomasson.
EIN: 351854017
Selected grants: The following grants were reported in 2004.
$50,000 to ORBIS International, New York, NY.
$10,000 to Berry College, Mount Berry, GA.
$5,000 to Nature Conservancy, Altamonte Springs, FL.
$500 to Brebeuf Preparatory School, Indianapolis, IN.
$500 to Environmental Learning Center, Vero Beach, FL.
$200 to Little Traverse Conservancy, Harbor Springs, MI.
$100 to Indian River Community College, Fort Pierce, FL.

1919
Al and Nancy Burnett Charitable Foundation, Inc. ◇ ☆
(formerly Al Burnett Charitable Foundation, Inc.)
1025 Anchorage Ct.
Winter Park, FL 32789-2671

Established in 1985 in FL.
Donor: J. Albert Burnett.
Foundation type: Independent foundation.
Financial data (yr. ended 11/30/05): Assets, $2,506,919 (M); expenditures, $1,839,943; qualifying distributions, $1,830,000; giving activities include $1,830,000 for 7 grants (high: $1,800,000; low: $500).
Fields of interest: Higher education; Federated giving programs; Protestant agencies & churches.
Limitations: Applications not accepted. Giving primarily in Winter Park, FL. No grants to individuals.
Application information: Contributes only to pre-selected organizations.
Officer and Directors:* J. Albert Burnett,* Pres. and Secy.-Treas.; Bruce K. Burnett; Nancy Burnett; Becky Ellrich; Amy Gravina; Mindy Steele.
EIN: 592620060

1920
Donald A. Burns Foundation, Inc. ◇
450 Royal Palm Way, Ste. 450
Palm Beach, FL 33480
Contact: Carol Cottone
E-mail: jmurphy@dabfoundation.org

Established in 1998 in FL.
Donor: Donald A. Burns.
Foundation type: Independent foundation.
Financial data (yr. ended 12/31/05): Assets, $10,706,628 (M); expenditures, $1,301,804; qualifying distributions, $825,893; giving activities include $713,572 for grants.
Fields of interest: Arts, formal/general education; Museums; Elementary/secondary education; Reproductive health, prenatal care; Human services; Children/youth, services; Family services.
Type of support: Technical assistance; Curriculum development; Program development; Equipment; Annual campaigns.
Limitations: Giving primarily in FL. No grants for capital campaigns or for salaries.
Application information:
Initial approach: E-mail letter requesting guidelines
Copies of proposal: 1
Deadline(s): Varies
Final notification: Varies
Officers: Donald A. Burns, Pres.; Leslie T. Merrick, V.P.; Nicholas A. Merrick, Treas.
Director: Ruth Burns.
Number of staff: 3 full-time professional.
EIN: 650870379
Selected grants: The following grants were reported in 2005.
$40,922 to Glades Day School, Belle Glade, FL.
$28,625 to Gods Love We Deliver, New York, NY.
$25,000 to Parrish Art Museum, Southampton, NY.
$25,000 to Salvation Army, Lutz, FL.
$15,335 to Childrens Place at Home Safe, West Palm Beach, FL.
$10,001 to Barton Elementary School, West Palm Beach, FL.
$10,000 to Childrens Hunger Fund, Mission Hills, CA.
$10,000 to Friends of the High Line, New York, NY.
$10,000 to Union Settlement Association, New York, NY.
$9,000 to South Florida Science Museum, West Palm Beach, FL.

1921
Burton Foundation, Inc. ◇
1899 Sycamore Ln.
Fernandina Beach, FL 32034

Established in 2001 in FL.
Donor: Barry A. Gray.
Foundation type: Independent foundation.
Financial data (yr. ended 12/31/05): Assets, $17,507,141 (M); expenditures, $889,087; qualifying distributions, $769,290; giving activities include $670,269 for 12 grants (high: $646,327; low: $1,000).
Fields of interest: Higher education; Education; Environment, natural resources; Animals/wildlife, preservation/protection; Foundations (community); Christian agencies & churches.
Limitations: Applications not accepted. Giving primarily in OK; some funding nationally. No grants to individuals.

Application information: Contributes only to pre-selected organizations.
Directors: B.A. Gray; D.A. Gray; G.S. Gray; J.M. Gray; R.C. Gray; E.D. Wall.
Trustee: D. Brown.
EIN: 731584983

1922
Edyth Bush Charitable Foundation, Inc.
199 E. Welbourne Ave.
P.O. Box 1967
Winter Park, FL 32790-1967 (407) 647-4322
Contact: David A. Odahowski, C.E.O.
FAX: (407) 647-7716;
E-mail: dhessler@edythbush.org; Deborah Hessler direct tel.: x17; Additional tel.: (888) 647-4322;
URL: http://www.edythbush.org

Originally incorporated in 1966 in MN; reincorporated in 1973 in FL.
Donor: Edyth Bassler Bush†.
Foundation type: Independent foundation.
Financial data (yr. ended 8/31/05): Assets, $78,748,750 (M); expenditures, $3,877,618; qualifying distributions, $2,178,953; giving activities include $2,121,366 for 92 grants (high: $750,000; low: $100), $57,587 for employee matching gifts, and $87,790 for foundation-administered programs.
Purpose and activities: Support for charitable, educational, and health service organizations, with emphasis on human services, the elderly, youth services, the handicapped, and nationally recognized quality arts or cultural programs. Provides limited number of program-related investment loans for construction, land purchase, emergency or similar purposes to organizations otherwise qualified to receive grants. Active programs directly managed and/or financed for management/volunteer development of nonprofits.
Fields of interest: Arts education; Arts; Education; Health care; Crime/violence prevention, domestic violence; Human services; Children/youth, services; Aging, centers/services; Nonprofit management; Philanthropy/voluntarism, association; Aging; Disabilities, people with; Women; Economically disadvantaged; Homeless.
Type of support: Management development/capacity building; Capital campaigns; Building/renovation; Equipment; Land acquisition; Emergency funds; Program development; Technical assistance; Consulting services; Program-related investments/loans; Employee matching gifts; Matching/challenge support.
Limitations: Giving primarily within Orange, Seminole, and Osceola counties, FL. No support for alcohol or drug abuse prevention/treatment projects or organizations, religious facilities or functions, primarily (50 percent or more) tax-supported institutions, advocacy organizations, foreign organizations, or, generally, for cultural programs. No grants to individuals, or for scholarships or individual research projects, endowments, fellowships, travel, routine operating expenses, annual campaigns, or deficit financing.
Publications: Application guidelines; Financial statement; Grants list; Informational brochure; Program policy statement.
Application information: See Policy Statement and call foundation office before applying. Application guidelines available upon request. Application form not required.
Initial approach: Telephone

Copies of proposal: 2
Deadline(s): None
Board meeting date(s): Quarterly
Final notification: 3 weeks after board meetings
Officers and Directors:* Mary Gretchen Belloff,* Vice-Chair.; David A. Odahowski,* C.E.O. and Pres.; Michael R. Cross, V.P., Fin. and C.I.O.; Deborah J. Hessler, Corp. Secy. and Prog. Off.; Mary Ellen Hutcheson, Treas. and C.F.O.; Matthew Certo; Gerald F. Hilbrich; Herbert W. Holm; John S. Lord; Joan Ruffier.
Number of staff: 3 full-time professional; 3 full-time support.
EIN: 237318041
Selected grants: The following grants were reported in 2004.
$330,913 to Rollins College, Winter Park, FL. For Philanthropy and Non-profit Leadership Center.
$120,000 to Ounce of Prevention Fund of Florida, Tallahassee, FL. For Jump Start Program.
$98,160 to American Red Cross, Winter Park, FL. To expand fundraising infrastructure.
$95,740 to Community Service Center of South Orange County, Orlando, FL. For Development Department.
$85,404 to Civic Theater of Central Florida, Orlando, FL. For Edyth Bush Theater renovation.
$66,386 to Shepherds Hope, Orlando, FL. For Development Director.
$66,200 to Second Harvest Food Bank of Central Florida, Orlando, FL. For capacity building.
$63,295 to Justice and Peace Office, Apopka, FL. For Development Director.
$60,700 to Coalition for the Homeless of Central Florida, Orlando, FL. To implement Development Office.
$50,430 to Federation of Congregations United to Serve (FOCUS), Orlando, FL. For Executive Assistant and office equipment.

1923
The Campbell Foundation
5975 N. Federal Hwy., No. 126
Fort Lauderdale, FL 33308 (954) 493-8822
Contact: Ken Rapkin, Prog. Off.
FAX: (954) 493-8801; E-mail: campfound@aol.com; URL: http://members.aol.com/campfound

Established in 1986 in FL.
Donor: Richard Campbell Zahn†.
Foundation type: Independent foundation.
Financial data (yr. ended 12/31/05): Assets, $10,303,604 (M); gifts received, $135; expenditures, $861,107; qualifying distributions, $733,512; giving activities include $603,400 for 23 grants (high: $160,000; low: $4,000).
Purpose and activities: The foundation supports other nonprofit organizations conducting clinical research into the prevention and treatment of HIV/AIDS, and related conditions and illnesses. The focus of the Campbell Foundation's funding lies in alternative, nontraditional avenues of research.
Fields of interest: AIDS research.
Type of support: Research.
Limitations: Giving primarily on a national basis; some consideration also for foreign nonprofit entities. No grants to individuals, or for discretionary grants, or equipment.
Publications: Application guidelines; Grants list; Program policy statement; Program policy statement (including application guidelines).
Application information: A 1-page lay-language Letter of Intent is requested prior to submission of full grant proposals. All grant requests should be as detailed and concise as possible; preferably, no more than 10 to 12 pages of text. The policy of the foundation is to entertain budget requests for first-year funding only, and it will consider funding no more than 10 percent for indirect costs. See foundation Web site for application guidelines and procedures. 15 copies of any color charts/graphs are required. Application form not required.
Initial approach: Letter of intent
Copies of proposal: 1
Deadline(s): None
Board meeting date(s): Varies
Final notification: 1-year from receipt
Trustee: Thomas P. Todd.
Number of staff: 2 full-time professional.
EIN: 586205065

1924
Capital City Group Foundation, Inc. ✧
217 N. Monroe St.
Tallahassee, FL 32301-7690
Application address: P.O. Box 11248, Tallahassee, FL 32302, tel.: (904) 224-1171

Established in 1983.
Donors: Capital City First National Bank; Capital City Bank.
Foundation type: Company-sponsored foundation.
Financial data (yr. ended 12/31/03): Assets, $2,051,336 (M); gifts received, $403,705; expenditures, $489,335; qualifying distributions, $487,204; giving activities include $479,355 for 118 grants (high: $112,500; low: $100).
Purpose and activities: The foundation supports organizations involved with arts and culture, education, health, youth development, human services, and community development.
Fields of interest: Arts; Higher education; Education; Hospitals (general); Health organizations, association; Youth development; Human services; Community development; Federated giving programs.
Type of support: General/operating support.
Limitations: Giving primarily in FL. No support for political or religious organizations or athletic teams. No grants for advertising, association memberships, fundraising events, or athletic event sponsorships.
Application information: Application form required.
Initial approach: Write to foundation for application form
Board meeting date(s): Annually
Final notification: 30 days following board meeting
Officers: William G. Smith, Jr., Chair.; Robert H. Smith, Pres.; Flecia Braswell, Secy.-Treas.
EIN: 592276367

1925
The Wayne L. Carse & Jimmie L. Carse Charitable Family Foundation ✧ ☆
1700 S. Bumby St.
Orlando, FL 32808

Established in 1999 in FL.
Donors: Jimmie L. Carse; Wayne L. Carse.
Foundation type: Independent foundation.
Financial data (yr. ended 12/31/05): Assets, $93 (M); gifts received, $316,950; expenditures, $317,018; qualifying distributions, $316,638; giving activities include $316,638 for grants.
Fields of interest: Higher education; Community development; Christian agencies & churches.
Limitations: Applications not accepted. No grants to individuals.
Application information: Contributes only to pre-selected organizations.
Advisory Committee and Trustee:* Jimmie L. Carse; Wayne L. Carse; Phyllis Kirby*; Robert H. Ragans, Jr.
EIN: 597169093
Selected grants: The following grants were reported in 2004.
$67,000 to Simpson College, Indianola, IA.
$5,000 to Community Foundation of Western North Carolina, Highlands Community Foundation, Asheville, NC.
$5,000 to Seminole Community College Foundation, Sanford, FL.
$3,500 to University of Florida Foundation, Gainesville, FL.
$2,500 to Bach Festival Society of Winter Park, Winter Park, FL.
$2,500 to Easter Seal Society.
$1,000 to Childrens Miracle Network, Salt Lake City, UT.
$500 to Windermere Knights.
$100 to Martin-Lipscomb Performing Arts Center, Highlands, NC.
$100 to Performing Arts Center, Highlands, NC.

1926
The Michael Cascone Jr. and Elizabeth Belyea Cascone Family Foundation ✧ ☆
2111 Corporate Sq. Blvd.
Jacksonville, FL 32216

Established in 2004 in FL.
Donors: Elizabeth Cascone; Michael Cascone, Jr.
Foundation type: Independent foundation.
Financial data (yr. ended 12/31/05): Assets, $8,413,307 (M); gifts received, $300,000; expenditures, $530,948; qualifying distributions, $526,090; giving activities include $526,090 for 40 grants (high: $111,000; low: $240).
Purpose and activities: Giving primarily to a federated giving program and to Roman Catholic agencies, churches, and schools.
Fields of interest: Elementary/secondary education; Higher education; Boys & girls clubs; Youth development; Human services; Federated giving programs; Roman Catholic federated giving programs; Roman Catholic agencies & churches.
Limitations: Applications not accepted. Giving primarily in Jacksonville, FL. No grants to individuals.
Application information: Contributes only to pre-selected organizations.
Directors: Brian J. Cascone; Elizabeth B. Cascone; Kathleen D. Cascone; Michael J. Cascone; Michael Cascone, Jr.; Steven D. Cascone; Juliette C. Gredenhag; Elizabeth C. Higgs.
EIN: 597246237

1927
O. W. Caspersen Foundation for Aid to Health and Education, Inc.
c/o Westby Mgmt., Inc.
11450 S.E. Dixie Hwy., Ste. 203
Hobe Sound, FL 33455 (772) 545-9000
Contact: Finn M.W. Caspersen, Pres.

Incorporated in 1964 in DE.

Donor: O.W. Caspersen†.
Foundation type: Independent foundation.
Financial data (yr. ended 12/31/04): Assets, $14,652,546 (M); gifts received, $536,934; expenditures, $823,610; qualifying distributions, $688,000; giving activities include $688,000 for 32 grants (high: $157,500; low: $250).
Purpose and activities: Support for education, including higher and secondary education, as well as health and hospitals. Present policy is to make grants only to those educational and health-oriented institutions with which the foundation has had extensive previous experience.
Fields of interest: Arts; Secondary school/education; Higher education; Education; Hospitals (general); Health care; Health organizations, association; Cancer; Cancer research.
Type of support: General/operating support; Continuing support; Annual campaigns; Capital campaigns; Building/renovation; Equipment; Emergency funds; Research.
Limitations: Applications not accepted. Giving primarily in the eastern coastal states, with emphasis on MA and NJ. No grants to individuals, or for seed money, scholarships, fellowships, or matching gifts; no loans.
Application information: Unsolicited requests for funds not accepted.
  Board meeting date(s): June and Dec.
Officers and Directors:* Finn M.W. Caspersen,* Pres.; Barbara M. Caspersen,* V.P. and Treas.; Andrew W.W. Caspersen,* V.P.; Erik M.W. Caspersen,* V.P.; Finn M.W. Caspersen, Jr.,* V.P.; Samuel M.W. Caspersen,* V.P.; Lucille Keegan, Secy.-Treas.
Number of staff: None.
EIN: 510101350
Selected grants: The following grants were reported in 2004.
$157,500 to Peddie School, Hightstown, NJ.
$120,700 to Cardigan Mountain School, Canaan, NH.
$50,000 to Princeton International Regatta Association, Princeton Junction, NJ.
$50,000 to University of Rhode Island Foundation, Kingston, RI.
$26,000 to Peck School, Morristown, NJ.
$7,500 to Princeton University, Princeton, NJ.
$6,000 to Groton School, Groton, MA.
$5,000 to Harvard University, Cambridge, MA.
$5,000 to Saint Bernards School, New York, NY.
$4,000 to Brick Church School, New York, NY.

1928
Lawrence P. Castellani Family Foundation ✧ ☆
3030 Grand Bay Blvd., No. 394
Longboat Key, FL 34228

Established in 1993 in NY.
Donors: Lawrence P. Castellani; Joan J. Castellani.
Foundation type: Independent foundation.
Financial data (yr. ended 12/31/05): Assets, $2,946,452 (M); expenditures, $644,300; qualifying distributions, $644,000; giving activities include $644,000 for grants.
Fields of interest: Museums (art); Education; Recreation, fund raising/fund distribution; Christian agencies & churches.
Type of support: General/operating support.
Limitations: Applications not accepted. Giving primarily in NY, with some giving in VA. No grants to individuals.

Application information: Contributes only to pre-selected organizations.
Trustees: Joan J. Castellani; Lawrence P. Castellani.
EIN: 166399132
Selected grants: The following grants were reported in 2005.
$200,000 to Art Museum of Western Virginia, Roanoke, VA.
$151,000 to Roswell Park Alliance Foundation, Buffalo, NY.
$50,000 to Virginia Tech Foundation, Blacksburg, VA.
$30,000 to United Way of Roanoke Valley, Roanoke, VA.
$15,000 to Boy Scouts of America, Roanoke, VA.
$5,000 to University of Buffalo Foundation, Buffalo, NY.

1929
Catlin Foundation, Inc. ✧
c/o Bessemer Trust Co. of Florida
801 Brickell Ave.
Miami, FL 33131   (305) 372-5005

Established in 1996.
Donor: Nancy Wainwright.
Foundation type: Independent foundation.
Financial data (yr. ended 12/31/05): Assets, $1,921 (M); gifts received, $22,000; expenditures, $860,932; qualifying distributions, $858,825; giving activities include $850,000 for 14 grants (high: $150,000; low: $20,000).
Fields of interest: Elementary/secondary education; Higher education; Theological school/education; Human services; International affairs; Christian agencies & churches.
International interests: Middle East.
Limitations: Giving primarily in CA.
Application information:
  Initial approach: Letter
  Deadline(s): None
Officer: Nancy Wainwright, Pres.
Directors: Clara Pascal; Robin C. Wainwright.
EIN: 650646287

1930
The Cejas Family Foundation, Inc. ✧ ☆
420 Lincoln Rd., Ste. 330
Miami, FL 33119-1768
Contact: Hilda Montero, Secy.

Established in 1994 in FL.
Donor: Paul L. Cejas.
Foundation type: Independent foundation.
Financial data (yr. ended 10/31/05): Assets, $369,339 (M); gifts received, $863,683; expenditures, $1,306,086; qualifying distributions, $1,273,000; giving activities include $1,273,000 for 9 grants (high: $1,000,000; low: $5,000).
Fields of interest: Museums (art); Higher education; Breast cancer; Foundations (private grantmaking).
Limitations: Giving primarily in Miami, FL. No grants to individuals.
Application information:
  Deadline(s): None
Officers: Paul L. Cejas, Pres.; Gertrude Cejas, V.P.; Hilda C. Montero, Secy.; Pablo L. Cejas, Treas.
EIN: 650534149
Selected grants: The following grants were reported in 2005.
$15,000 to New World Symphony, Miami Beach, FL.

$10,000 to Smithsonian Institution, DC.
$5,000 to James E. Scott Community Association, Miami, FL.
$5,000 to Mount Sinai Medical Center Foundation, Miami Beach, FL.

1931
The Charitable and Research Foundation, Inc. ✧
c/o H.P. Headley
3321 Sunset Key Cir., Ste. 704
Punta Gorda, FL 33955   (941) 661-0499
Contact: Harry P. Headley, Exec. Dir.

Established in 1996 in NJ.
Donor: Harry P. Headley.
Foundation type: Independent foundation.
Financial data (yr. ended 11/30/05): Assets, $2,952,763 (M); gifts received, $1,000,000; expenditures, $1,122,753; qualifying distributions, $1,103,500; giving activities include $1,103,500 for 12 grants (high: $400,000; low: $500).
Purpose and activities: Scientific research grants are limited to the medical fields of cancer and osteogenesis imperfecta.
Fields of interest: Cancer; Nerve, muscle & bone diseases; Pediatrics; Roman Catholic agencies & churches.
Limitations: Giving primarily in MD and VA; some funding nationally.
Application information:
  Initial approach: Letter or telephone to Exec. Dir. to obtain specific instructions regarding the form of application and required materials
  Deadline(s): None
Officers: Dorothy Headley, Recording Secy.; Harry P. Headley, Exec. Dir.; Kathleen Kowis, Mgr.
EIN: 522006338
Selected grants: The following grants were reported in 2004.
$270,000 to Kennedy Krieger Institute, Baltimore, MD.
$161,000 to Osteogenesis Imperfecta Foundation, Gaithersburg, MD. For general support.
$10,000 to Felician Sisters, Lodi, NJ. For general support.
$10,000 to University of Maryland-Baltimore, Baltimore, MD. For cancer research.
$3,500 to Food for the Poor, Deerfield Beach, FL. For general support.
$2,000 to Memorial Sloan-Kettering Cancer Center, New York, NY.
$1,000 to University of the Cumberlands, Williamsburg, KY. For general support.

1932
The Chatlos Foundation, Inc. ▼
P.O. Box 915048
Longwood, FL 32791-5048   (407) 862-5077
Contact: William J. Chatlos, C.E.O. and Pres.
E-mail: info@chatlos.org; URL: http://www.chatlos.org

Incorporated in 1953 in NY.
Donors: Bristol Door and Lumber Co., Inc.; William F. Chatlos†.
Foundation type: Independent foundation.
Financial data (yr. ended 12/30/05): Assets, $90,311,574 (M); expenditures, $6,823,601; qualifying distributions, $5,991,748; giving

activities include $4,074,695 for 257 grants (high: $500,000; low: $250; average: $1,000–$25,000).

Purpose and activities: Grants for higher education and religious causes; giving also for hospitals, health agencies, social services, and child welfare.

Fields of interest: Higher education; Nursing school/education; Theological school/education; Education; Hospitals (general); Health care; Health organizations, association; Human services; Children/youth, services; Homeless.

Type of support: Scholarship funds; Curriculum development; Debt reduction; General/operating support; Building/renovation; Equipment; Land acquisition; Program development; Publication; Technical assistance; Matching/challenge support.

Limitations: No support for individual church congregations, primary or secondary schools or for the arts, or for organizations in existence for less than two years. No grants to individuals, or for seed money, deficit financing, endowment funds, medical research, conferences, bricks and mortar, or multi-year grants; no loans.

Publications: Application guidelines; Informational brochure (including application guidelines).

Application information: See foundation Web site for proposal instructions. Application form may be requested in writing or printed from the foundation Web site. Only 1 grant to an organization within a 12-month period. Application form required.

Initial approach: Proposal (no more than 5 pages)
Copies of proposal: 1
Deadline(s): None
Board meeting date(s): Quarterly
Final notification: Immediately

Officers and Trustees:* Kathryn A. Randle,* Chair.; William J. Chatlos,* C.E.O. and Pres.; Michele C. Roach, V.P. and Secy.; Cindee L. Random, Treas.; Carol J. Chatlos; Janet Chatlos; Charles O. Morgan.

Number of staff: 5 full-time professional; 1 part-time professional.

EIN: 136161425

Selected grants: The following grants were reported in 2005.

$500,000 to Foundation Fighting Blindness, Owings Mills, MD. For Health Education Program.

$200,000 to Moody Bible Institute of Chicago, Chicago, IL. For second year of ministry for Division of Broadcasting Stewardship.

$100,000 to Reformed Theological Seminary, Maitland, FL. Toward making up difference between student tuition and actual costs of educating students.

$75,000 to Asbury Theological Seminary, Wilmore, KY. For scholarships to help students attending E. Stanley Jones School of World Mission and Evangelism.

$55,000 to Scheie Eye Institute, Philadelphia, PA. To explore treatment of hereditary retinal degenerations by determining if visual brain of candidate patients is ready for retinal therapy.

$50,000 to Campus Crusade for Christ International, Orlando, FL. Toward Here's Life Inner City warehouse and outreach to New York City.

$50,000 to Dallas Theological Seminary, Dallas, TX. For Emergency Student Aid program.

$50,000 to Florida Southern College, Lakeland, FL. For purchase of essential computer, software and broadcast equipment.

$50,000 to Samaritans Purse, Boone, NC. For construction of dining room and chapel of Calcutta Seminary.

$50,000 to Tyndale Theological Seminary, Amsterdam, Netherlands. For scholarships for needy students.

1933
Chia Family Foundation, Inc. ✧

7801 Blue Heron Way
West Palm Beach, FL   33412

Established in 1996 in NY.

Donors: Pei-Yuan Chia; Frances T.C. Chia; Kitty S.H. Chia.

Foundation type: Independent foundation.

Financial data (yr. ended 3/31/05): Assets, $13,453,192 (M); gifts received, $74,080; expenditures, $852,533; qualifying distributions, $716,000; giving activities include $716,000 for 8 grants (high: $400,000; low: $1,000).

Purpose and activities: Giving primarily for business education, as well as to Asian culture organizations.

Fields of interest: Higher education; Business school/education; Education; Medical research, institute; Cancer research; Human services; Asians/Pacific Islanders.

Limitations: Applications not accepted. Giving primarily in NY and PA. No grants to individuals.

Application information: Contributes only to pre-selected organizations.

Directors: Candice Chia; Douglas Chia; Katherine Chia; Pei-Yuan Chia.

EIN: 133904882

Selected grants: The following grants were reported in 2004.

$400,000 to University of Pennsylvania, Wharton School of Business, Philadelphia, PA.

$50,000 to Yale-China Association, New Haven, CT.

$40,000 to Amherst College, Amherst, MA.

$25,000 to Nathaniel Wharton Fund for Research in Brain, Body and Behavior, New York, NY.

$10,000 to Asia Society, New York, NY.

1934
Cisneros Fontanals Foundation for the Arts ✧

5960 S.W. 57th Ave.
Miami, FL   33143

Established in 2002 in DE.

Donor: EFC Holdings, Inc.

Foundation type: Company-sponsored foundation.

Financial data (yr. ended 12/31/04): Assets, $12,280 (M); gifts received, $640,000; expenditures, $1,576,950; qualifying distributions, $1,571,652; giving activities include $1,375,270 for 11 grants (high: $1,180,000; low: $200).

Purpose and activities: The foundation supports art museums and organizations involved with performing arts and higher education.

Fields of interest: Museums (art); Performing arts; Higher education.

Type of support: Annual campaigns; Program development; Scholarship funds.

Limitations: Applications not accepted. Giving primarily in Miami, FL, and New York, NY. No grants to individuals.

Application information: Contributes only to pre-selected organizations.

Officers: Ella Fontanals De Cisneros,* Chair.; Maria Ela Cisneros Fontanals, Pres.; Claudia Cisneros Macaya, V.P.; Javier Macaya, Treas.

EIN: 542081286

1935
Cobb Family Foundation, Inc. ✧

255 Aragon Ave., Ste. 333
Coral Gables, FL   33134   (305) 441-1700
Contact: Charles E. Cobb, Jr., Pres.

Established in 1984 in FL.

Donor: Charles E. Cobb, Jr.

Foundation type: Independent foundation.

Financial data (yr. ended 9/30/05): Assets, $13,175,786 (M); gifts received, $624,300; expenditures, $516,652; qualifying distributions, $489,375; giving activities include $483,375 for 129 grants (high: $25,000; low: $25).

Purpose and activities: Support primarily for higher and secondary education and a Protestant church; some support for community development and sports facilities.

Fields of interest: Secondary school/education; Higher education; Recreation; Community development; Protestant agencies & churches.

Type of support: General/operating support.

Limitations: Giving primarily in the Dade County, FL, area.

Application information: Application form not required.

Deadline(s): None
Board meeting date(s): Aug.

Officers: Charles E. Cobb, Jr., Pres.; Christian M. Cobb, V.P.; Sue M. Cobb, V.P.; Tobin T. Cobb, V.P.

Directors: Colleen O. Cobb; Luisa S Cobb.

EIN: 592477459

Selected grants: The following grants were reported in 2003.

$190,000 to University of Miami, Coral Gables, FL. 5 grants: $25,000 (For Cobb Stadium), $20,000 to Miller School of Judaic Studies (For endowed chair), $20,000 (For Sue and Leonard Center for contemporary Judaic Studies), $25,000 (For Presidents Fund), $100,000 (For Ambassador Sue M. Cobb Scholarship Fund for Jamaican Students).

$25,000 to Stanford University, Stanford, CA. For Cobb Track and Angell Field.

$18,500 to United Way of Jamaica, Kingston, Jamaica. .

$15,000 to United Way of Miami-Dade, Miami, FL.

$10,000 to Goodwill Industries of South Florida, Miami, FL.

$5,000 to American Red Cross, Miami, FL.

1936
Cobb Foundation ✧

336 Coconut Palm Rd.
Boca Raton, FL   33432

Established in 1996 in FL.

Foundation type: Independent foundation.

Financial data (yr. ended 12/31/05): Assets, $20,128,904 (M); expenditures, $1,547,775; qualifying distributions, $1,241,619; giving activities include $1,194,450 for 28 grants (high: $867,450; low: $1,000).

Purpose and activities: Giving primarily for education and human services, including a home for children.

Fields of interest: Museums; Elementary/secondary education; Higher education; Medical care, in-patient care; Boy scouts; Girl scouts; American Red Cross; Residential/custodial care; Christian agencies & churches; Protestant agencies & churches.

Limitations: Giving on a national basis.

Application information: Telephone inquiries not accepted. Application form required.

Initial approach: Letter

Deadline(s): None

Officers and Directors:* Rhoda W. Cobb,* Pres.; William R. Cobb,* V.P. and Treas.; Bradley Cobb; Rhoda Juckett; Jennifer Little.

EIN: 650593216

Selected grants: The following grants were reported in 2003.

$100,000 to Water for People, Denver, CO. For general support.

$88,000 to Baptist Home for Children, Jacksonville, FL. For general support.

$75,000 to Sayre School, Lexington, KY. For general support.

$50,000 to Baptist Health System, Jacksonville, FL. For general support.

$50,000 to Junior League of Boca Raton, Boca Raton, FL. For general support.

$50,000 to University of Pennsylvania, Philadelphia, PA. For general support.

$30,000 to Saint Andrews School. For general support.

$20,000 to Salem College, Winston-Salem, NC. For general support.

$10,000 to Mint Museum of Art, Charlotte, NC. For general support.

$10,000 to Myers Park Presbyterian Church, Charlotte, NC. For general support.

1937
Ruth and Baron Coleman Charitable Foundation, Inc. ✧ ☆

7383 Orangewood Ln., Ste. 402
Boca Raton, FL 33433-7470
Contact: Ruth Coleman, Pres.

Established in 1996 in FL.

Donors: Baron Coleman; Ruth Coleman.

Foundation type: Independent foundation.

Financial data (yr. ended 3/31/05): Assets, $514 (M); gifts received, $271,858; expenditures, $407,227; qualifying distributions, $407,139; giving activities include $406,225 for 21 grants (high: $100,000; low: $25).

Purpose and activities: Giving primarily to health and human service organizations.

Fields of interest: Higher education, university; Hospitals (specialty); Health organizations; Children/youth, services; Aging, centers/services; Jewish federated giving programs; Jewish agencies & temples.

Limitations: Giving on a national basis. No grants to individuals.

Application information: Application form not required.

Initial approach: Letter

Deadline(s): None

Officers: Ruth Coleman, Pres.; Nancy Swart, V.P.; Royce Fischel, Secy.-Treas.

EIN: 650711225

1938
The Colen Foundation, Inc.

(formerly The On Top of the World Foundation, Inc.)
8447 S.W. 99th St.
Ocala, FL 34481-4547

Established in 1984 in FL.

Donors: Kenneth D. Colen; Sidney Colen.

Foundation type: Independent foundation.

Financial data (yr. ended 11/30/05): Assets, $11,121,029 (M); gifts received, $32,462; expenditures, $581,048; qualifying distributions, $561,859; giving activities include $515,100 for 40 grants (high: $125,000; low: $500), and $3,600 for loans/program-related investments.

Purpose and activities: The foundation makes grants to qualified charities and provides assistance to the charitable class of the aged to enable members of the class to maintain a modest standard of living in their communities during their declining years.

Fields of interest: Museums (history); Performing arts, music; Elementary school/education; Higher education; Education; Horticulture/garden clubs; Developmentally disabled, centers & services; Federated giving programs; Jewish agencies & temples.

Limitations: Giving primarily in FL.

Application information: Application form required.

Initial approach: Letter

Copies of proposal: 2

Deadline(s): None

Board meeting date(s): Three times annually

Final notification: Up to 6 months

Officers and Directors:* Sidney Colen,* Pres.; Kenneth D. Colen,* V.P. and Treas.; Ina A. Colen,* Secy.; Gerald R. Colen; Leslee R. Colen; Robert Colen.

Number of staff: None.

EIN: 592474711

Selected grants: The following grants were reported in 2004.

$285,000 to Horticultural Arts and Park Design Institute, Ocala, FL. 2 grants: $100,000, $185,000

$56,000 to Community Foundation of Tampa Bay, Tampa, FL.

$27,000 to Florida Orchestra, Tampa, FL. 2 grants: $7,000, $20,000

$20,000 to University of Florida, Gainesville, FL. For Hillel Foundation.

$15,000 to Morton Plant Mease Health Care Foundation, Clearwater, FL.

$10,000 to COTA-Childrens Organ Transplant Association, Bloomington, IN.

$5,000 to Central Florida Symphony, Ocala, FL.

$4,000 to P.E.F. Israel Endowment Funds, New York, NY.

1939
Community Foundation for Palm Beach and Martin Counties, Inc. ▼

(formerly Palm Beach County Community Foundation)
700 S. Dixie Hwy., Ste. 200
West Palm Beach, FL 33401   (561) 659-6800
Contact: For grants: Linda Raybin, V.P., Progs.
FAX: (561) 832-6542; *E-mail:* info@cfpbmc.org;
Additional tel.: (888) 853-4438; Grant application
E-mail: lraybin@cfpbmc.org; URL: http://
www.yourcommunityfoundation.org
Additional URL: http://www.cfpbmc.org

Incorporated in 1972 in FL.

Foundation type: Community foundation.

Financial data (yr. ended 6/30/05): Assets, $111,772,572 (M); gifts received, $26,873,864; expenditures, $8,111,292; giving activities include $5,226,021 for grants.

Purpose and activities: The mission of the foundation is to enhance the quality of life for all residents, build permanent endowment, address needs through grantmaking, and provide community leadership. Primary areas of interest include health, social services, youth, race relations, education, arts and culture, conservation and preservation, and community development.

Fields of interest: Historic preservation/historical societies; Arts; Education, early childhood education; Elementary school/education; Adult education—literacy, basic skills & GED; Education, reading; Education; Environment, natural resources; Environment; Health care; Health organizations, association; AIDS; Youth development, intergenerational programs; Children/youth, services; Human services; Civil rights, race/intergroup relations; Economic development; Community development; Children/youth; Aging.

Type of support: Management development/capacity building; Equipment; Program development; Conferences/seminars; Seed money; Scholarship funds; Technical assistance; Consulting services; Employee-related scholarships; Scholarships—to individuals; Matching/challenge support.

Limitations: Giving primarily in Palm Beach and Martin counties, FL. No support for religious organizations for religious purposes. No grants to individuals (except for scholarships and the Dwight Allison Fellows Program), or for operating funds, building campaigns, computers, endowments, annual campaigns, fundraising events, fundraising feasibility studies, celebration functions, or deficit financing.

Publications: Application guidelines; Annual report (including application guidelines); Grants list; Informational brochure; Newsletter.

Application information: Visit foundation Web site for proposal summary forms and guidelines. Faxed or e-mailed proposals are not accepted. Grant Seekers Seminars are offered periodically to introduce new grant seekers to the application process; call the foundation to reserve a seat. Application form required.

Initial approach: Telephone

Copies of proposal: 1

Deadline(s): None

Board meeting date(s): Feb., Apr., May, Sept., Oct., and Dec.

Final notification: Within weeks of proposal

Officers and Directors:* Eliot I. Snider,* Chair.; Deborah Dale Pucillo,* Vice-Chair.; Allyson Dupree Smith,* Vice-Chair., Progs.; Patricia Toppel,* Vice-Chair., Devel.; Shannon Sadler Hull, C.E.O. and Pres.; Danielle Cameron, V.P., Donor Svcs.; Linda Raybin, V.P., Progs.; Gloria Ortega Rex, V.P., Finance; Barbara Bishop Chapin,* Secy.; William Matthews,* Treas.; Ronald Alvarez; Carol Ohmer Collins; Elaine Bennett Darwin; Pedro D. del Sol; John B. Dodge; Rebecca Walter Dunn; Joy Crockett Funston; Sally Gringras; Louis B. Green; Reuben B. Johnson III; Kenn Karakul; Peter Matwiczyk; S. Bruce McDonald; Lisa N. Mulhall; James F. Orr III; Edward Rodgers; John E. Shuff; Royall Victor III.

Number of staff: 9 full-time professional; 5 full-time support.

EIN: 237181875

Selected grants: The following grants were reported in 2005.

$150,000 to Crown Financial Ministries, Gainesville, GA.

$126,590 to Wesleyan University, Middletown, CT.

$111,000 to American Red Cross, National Headquarters, DC.

$100,000 to Childrens National Medical Center, DC.

$50,000 to South County Foundation for Mental Health, Delray Beach, FL.

$30,000 to Solomon R. Guggenheim Foundation, New York, NY.

$25,000 to Center for Technology Enterprise and Development, Delray Beach, FL. For Youth Entrepreneur Program.

$25,000 to Palm Beach County Education Commission, West Palm Beach, FL. For contracted facilitator for Career Development in Child Development (CD2) initiative to develop systemic approach to training early childhood instructional staff in Palm Beach.

$20,040 to National Parkinson Foundation, Miami, FL. To launch therapeutic exercise program for persons with Parkinson's disease at diverse sites in Palm Beach and Martin Counties.

$20,000 to Adopt-A-Family of the Palm Beaches, West Palm Beach, FL. To expand project GROW, after-school program serving homeless and other low-income children.

1940

The Community Foundation in Jacksonville ▼ ✧

(also known as The Community Foundation)
121 W. Forsyth St., Ste. 900
Jacksonville, FL 32202 (904) 356-4483
Contact: Judy Herrin, V.P., Professional Svcs.; For grants: Cheryl Riddick, V.P., Grantmaking Svcs.
FAX: (904) 356-7910; E-mail: jherrin@jaxcf.org; Additional E-mails: jzell@jaxcf.org and nwaters@jaxcf.org; Grant application E-mail: applications@jaxcf.org; URL: http://www.jaxcf.org

Established in 1979 in FL.
Foundation type: Community foundation.
Financial data (yr. ended 12/31/04): Assets, $105,025,898 (M); gifts received, $36,135,575; expenditures, $11,213,095; giving activities include $9,376,331 for 1,604 grants (high: $1,025,000; low: $13), and $170,606 for grants to individuals.
Purpose and activities: The foundation's goal is to be the most effective vehicle for gathering and employing assets to build a better community for all to share.
Fields of interest: Performing arts, theater; Arts; Children/youth, services; Aging, centers/services; Infants/toddlers; Children/youth; Aging.
Type of support: Endowments; Emergency funds; Program development; Seed money; Internship funds; Scholarship funds; Technical assistance; Consulting services; Program-related investments/loans; Grants to individuals; Matching/challenge support.
Limitations: Giving primarily in northeastern FL, including Baker, Clay, Duval, Nassau and St. Johns counties. No support for food programs or religious instruction. No grants for general operating support, construction or renovation, equipment, or tickets for fundraising activities.
Publications: Application guidelines; Annual report; Informational brochure; Newsletter.
Application information: Visit foundation Web site for preliminary application form and guidelines. If preliminary application is selected for further consideration, the foundation will provide a full grant application and related information to the organization's contact person (full applications are available only to organizations which are invited to apply based on preliminary applications).
Application form required.
Initial approach: Submit preliminary application
Copies of proposal: 1
Deadline(s): Mar. 1 for preliminary application; June 1 for final application
Board meeting date(s): Mar., June, Sept., and Nov.
Final notification: Aug.
Officers and Trustees: Hon. Harvey E. Schlesinger,* Chair.; Nina M. Waters, Pres.; Judy Herrin, V.P., Professional Svcs.; Cheryl Riddick, V.P., Grantmaking Svcs.; Grace Sacerdote, V.P., Finance; John Zell, V.P., Donor Svcs.; Jackie Werner, Cont.; L. Andrew Bell III, Pres. Emeritus; Rev. Frank S. Cerveny; Cynthia Edelman; Michael W. Fisher; Eleanor J. Gay; Delores Kesler; Helen M. Lane; Wilford C. Lyon, Jr.; C.B. McIntosh, M.D.; Joan Wellhouse Newton; Duane L. Ottenstroer; C. Daniel Rice; William E. Scheu; Richard G. Skinner, Jr., M.D.; James Van Vleck; Tracey Westbrook.
Number of staff: 6 full-time professional; 2 part-time professional; 4 full-time support.
EIN: 596150746
Selected grants: The following grants were reported in 2004.

$49,963 to Jacksonville Marine Institute, Jacksonville, FL. To use reflective practice to learn if they are employing best practices for youth and families and determine if resources are being utilized as effectively as possible.

$20,580 to Barnabas Center, Fernandina Beach, FL. 2 grants: $10,000 (To institute Girl Power, intervention program designed to support, enhance and teach middle-school-aged girls to improve school participation/results, enhance self-confidence and lower at-risk behaviors), $10,580 (To increase literacy and life skills among women in Nassau County).

$20,000 to Womens Center of Jacksonville, Jacksonville, FL. For continuation of Expanded Horizons: A Woman Positive Learning and Literacy Training Program.

$10,000 to Cathedral Arts Project (CAP), Jacksonville, FL. To provide after-school dance instruction in elementary schools where little or no arts instruction is provided.

$10,000 to Girls Inc. of Jacksonville, Jacksonville, FL. To combine PhotoVoice curriculum with photography exhibit, Game Face: What Does a Female Athlete Look Like?

$10,000 to National Council of Negro Women, Child Watch Partnership of Jacksonville, Jacksonville, FL. To provide comprehensive educational center designed for girls at-risk at Reed Educational Campus.

$10,000 to Shoshannah Arts, Jacksonville, FL. To provide after-school arts programs in dance, drama and visual arts for students at West Jacksonville Elementary School.

1941

Community Foundation of Broward

(formerly Broward Community Foundation, Inc.)
1401 E. Broward Blvd., Ste. 100
Fort Lauderdale, FL 33301 (954) 761-9503
Contact: Linda B. Carter, C.E.O.; For grant applications: Sheri Brown, V.P., Grants and Initiatives
FAX: (954) 761-7102; E-mail: lcarter@cfbroward.org; Tel. for Sheri Brown: (954) 761-9503, ext. 103; Grant application E-mail: sbrown@cfbroward.org; URL: http://www.cfbroward.org

Incorporated in 1984 in FL.
Foundation type: Community foundation.
Financial data (yr. ended 6/30/05): Assets, $60,675,519 (M); gifts received, $13,747,014; expenditures, $3,644,515; giving activities include $2,545,558 for 248 grants (high: $137,763; low: $100), and $237,298 for 80 grants to individuals.
Purpose and activities: The foundation seeks to help people become philanthropists by connecting them to the causes they care about, so they can make a difference through strategic giving. Gives priority to programs which: address emerging needs not being met by existing government or private charitable agencies or by existing revenue sources, strengthen internal management capabilities of existing organizations, reach a broad segment of the community or serve those not being adequately served by the community's resources, promote collaboration and avoid duplication of service among charitable agencies, test or demonstrate new approaches and techniques for solving problems, generate matching funds or attract contributions from other donors to the community or agency, and promote volunteer participation and citizen involvement in community affairs.
Fields of interest: Arts; Education; Environment; Animal welfare; Health care; Cancer; Arthritis; AIDS; Children/youth, services; Children, foster care; Youth, services; Family services; Human services; Engineering/technology; Public affairs; Young adults.
Type of support: Management development/capacity building; Program development; Seed money; Research; Technical assistance; Scholarships—to individuals; Matching/challenge support.
Limitations: Giving limited to Broward County, FL. No support for religious purposes. No grants to individuals (except for designated scholarship funds), or for capital campaigns, annual campaigns, fundraising events, building funds, deficit financing, endowment funds, or operating budgets; no loans.
Publications: Application guidelines; Annual report; Financial statement; Informational brochure (including application guidelines); Newsletter.
Application information: Visit foundation Web site for application form and guidelines. The Grant Application Cover Sheet must be mailed to the foundation with proposal as well as e-mailed (solely) the same day proposal is mailed. Application form required.
Initial approach: Submit Grant Application Cover Sheet, proposal, and attachments
Copies of proposal: 1
Deadline(s): Mar. 17, June 17, Aug. 15, and Dec. 17
Board meeting date(s): Various, 6-7 times per year
Final notification: Mar. 25, June 24, Sept. 30, and Nov. 28
Officers and Directors: Carlos J. Reyes, Jr.,* Chair.; Frank E. Helsom,* Vice-Chair.; Linda B. Carter, C.E.O. and Pres.; Sheri Brown, V.P., Grants and Initiatives; Barbara Whitte, V.P., Philanthropic Svcs.; Christine L. Lambertus,* Secy.; Carol Dorko, C.F.O.; Steve Hyatt,* Treas.; Ann Bartram, Cont.; Holly Bodenweber; Rita Case; Barbara R. Castell; Jan R. Cummings; Richard L. Engberg; Linda L. Gill; Frederick L. Hicks; David Horvitz; Edwin A. Huston; Robert B. Judd; Raymond Leightman; Albert Miniaci; Charles L. Palmer; Myrtle Potter; J. Kenneth Tate; Judith Thiel; Leslie C. Tworoger; Elaine Vasquez.

Number of staff: 9 full-time professional.
EIN: 592477112

1942
Community Foundation of Central Florida, Inc.

1411 Edgewater Dr., Ste. 203
Orlando, FL 32804 (407) 872-3050
Contact: Mark Brewer, C.E.O.
FAX: (407) 425-2990; E-mail: info@cfcflorida.org;
Additional Address: P.O. Box 2071, Orlando, FL
32802; URL: http://www.cfcflorida.org

Established in 1993 in FL.
Foundation type: Community foundation.
Financial data (yr. ended 4/30/05): Assets,
$32,761,755 (M); gifts received, $3,973,442;
expenditures, $2,992,935; giving activities include
$1,843,053 for 147 grants (high: $189,845; low:
$100), and $66,202 for 40 grants to individuals
(high: $3,000; low: $240).
Purpose and activities: The mission of the
foundation is "Building Community by Building
Philanthropy." The foundation works to fulfill this
mission by carefully investing and managing donor's
funds, informing and connecting donors with
projects and issues they feel passionate about, and
providing resources for local nonprofits.
Fields of interest: Arts; Elementary/secondary
education; Higher education; Health care; Children/
youth, services; Youth, services; Human services;
Community development; Aging.
Type of support: Scholarships—to individuals;
Management development/capacity building;
Program development; Seed money; Scholarship
funds.
Limitations: Giving limited to central FL, with
emphasis on Orange, Osceola, and Seminole
counties. No grants to individuals (except for
scholarships).
Publications: Application guidelines; Annual report;
Financial statement; Grants list; Informational
brochure; Informational brochure (including
application guidelines); Newsletter.
Application information: Visit foundation Web site
for application guidelines. Application form required.
Initial approach: Complete online eligibility quiz
Copies of proposal: 1
Deadline(s): July 15
Board meeting date(s): Monthly
Final notification: Aug. 31
Officers and Board Members:* Suzie Allen,* Chair.;
Braham Aggarwal,* Vice-Chair.; Mark Brewer,*
C.E.O. and Pres.; Jeffrey R. Pickering, V.P.,
Philanthropic Svcs.; Ed Timberlake,* Secy.; Meghan
Warrick, C.F.O.; Jonathan Baety,* Treas.; Jeff Adler;
J. Gordon Arkin; Richard Bogue; Sydney Green;
Michael Harbison; Gregory L. Hess; Richard T.
"Rick" Hurt; Steve Kirby; Rita Lowdnes; John
Saboor.
Number of staff: 4 full-time professional; 2 full-time
support.
EIN: 593182886

1943
Community Foundation of Collier County ◇

c/o Mary George
2400 Tamiami Trail N., Ste. 300
Naples, FL 34103 (239) 649-5000
Contact: Mary Ellen Barrett, V.P., Progs.; For grants:
Kay Jasso, Prog. Coord.
FAX: (239) 649-5337;
E-mail: mgeorge@cfcollier.org; Additional tel.: (877)
907-1449; Additional E-mail: Kjasso@cfcollier.org;
URL: http://www.cfcollier.org

Incorporated in 1983 in FL.
Foundation type: Community foundation.
Financial data (yr. ended 5/31/05): Assets,
$45,323,440 (M); gifts received, $3,582,285;
expenditures, $3,526,476; giving activities include
$2,431,399 for 576+ grants.
Purpose and activities: The foundation provides
support for organizations dedicated to solving
community problems in the areas of health and
human services, youth, education, civic affairs, the
environment, and arts and culture.
Fields of interest: Arts, cultural/ethnic awareness;
Arts; Education, early childhood education; Adult
education—literacy, basic skills & GED; Education,
services; Education; Environment, natural
resources; Environment; Health care; Food services;
Housing/shelter, homeless; Children/youth,
services; Family services, domestic violence;
Human services; Philanthropy/voluntarism;
Disabilities, people with.
Type of support: Building/renovation; Equipment;
Emergency funds; Program development; Seed
money; Internship funds; Scholarship funds;
Technical assistance; Program evaluation;
Matching/challenge support.
Limitations: Giving limited to Collier County, FL. No
support for religious purposes or private schools. No
grants to individuals (except for scholarships), or for
operating budgets, deficit financing, scholarly
research, school-day activities, curriculum, and
materials, annual campaigns, capital campaigns,
conferences, or endowment funds.
Publications: Application guidelines; Annual report
(including application guidelines); Newsletter.
Application information: Organizations must
complete a profile on www.guidestar.org and E-mail
the foundation about registration before submitting
an application. Visit foundation Web site for
application forms and guidelines per grant type.
Application form required.
Initial approach: Submit an Agency Profile by
registering on GuideStar
Deadline(s): Jan. 19, Apr. 13, Aug., and Oct. for
Community Proj. grants; Sept. 15 for Capital
grant letters of intent
Board meeting date(s): Monthly from Oct. to May
Final notification: Within 6 weeks for Community
Proj.
Officers and Trustees:* Dorothy A. "Dottie"
Gerrity,* Chair.; Thomas G. Schneider,* Vice-Chair.;
Mary George, C.E.O. and Pres.; William Franz, Exec.
V.P. and C.O.O.; Mary Ellen Barrett, V.P., Progs.;
Jane Billings, V.P., Devel. and Mktg.; Deborah L.
Russell,* Secy.; Ned R. Sachs,* Treas.; Scott E.
Alexander; Jeffrey R. Erickson; Lynne Groth; Frank L.
Klapperich, Jr.; William Laimbeer, Sr.; James B.
Lancaster, Jr.; Phyllis M. Landes; Linda R. Malone;
James T. Rideoutte; Dolly Bodick Roberts; Michael
J. Schroeder; Duane Stranahan, Jr.; William E.
Thomas; Gordon R. Watson.

Number of staff: 5 full-time professional; 3 full-time
support; 1 part-time support.
EIN: 592396243

1944
The Community Foundation of Greater Lakeland, Inc. ◇

4720 Cleveland Heights Blvd.
Lakeland, FL 33813 (863) 607-9800
Contact: Kimberly Grady Brock, Pres.
FAX: (863) 607-9855; E-mail: kgbrock@cfgl.org;
URL: http://www.cfgl.org

Established in 1997 in FL.
Foundation type: Community foundation.
Financial data (yr. ended 6/30/05): Assets,
$42,696,508 (M); gifts received, $5,667,999;
expenditures, $8,264,157; giving activities include
$7,984,432 for 214 grants (high: $2,467,424; low:
$250).
Purpose and activities: The foundation seeks to
improve the quality of life in all areas of greater
Lakeland, Fl. It does this by serving donors, local
nonprofit charities, and the community at large.
Fields of interest: Historic preservation/historical
societies; Arts; Education; Environment; Health
care; Housing/shelter; Family services; Aging,
centers/services; Human services; Community
development; Youth.
Type of support: Capital campaigns; Equipment;
Seed money; Matching/challenge support.
Limitations: Giving primarily in the greater Lakeland,
FL, area. No support for sectarian religious projects
that are not open to all. No grants for to individuals
(except for scholarships and emergency grants), or
for tickets, annual or building campaigns,
endowments, operating expense, membership
dues, or fundraising events or celebrations.
Application information: Visit foundation Web site
for application form and guidelines. The foundation
offers one grant orientation each fiscal year;
attendance is mandatory. Application form required.
Initial approach: Attend grant orientation
Copies of proposal: 12
Deadline(s): Sept. 15
Final notification: Oct. for initial qualification
determination
Board Members: Kelly Norton,* Chair.; Ihla
Sloman,* Vice-Chair.; Kimberly Grady Brock, Pres.;
Becky Murphy, V.P., Devel.; Joy Proctor, V.P., Donor
Rels.; Charles McPherson,* Secy.-Treas.; Bruce
Abels; Ralph Allen; Lew Belcourt; John Cannon;
Brenda Craft; John Fitzwater; Sam Hart; Kevin
Hennessey; A.L. "Judge" Holmes; Anne Kerr; Lynn
Fischer Kryger; Martha Linder; Steve Moore; John W.
Scheck; Rick Stevens; David Touchton; John
Vreeland; Jeff Walker; Terry Worthington.
EIN: 593649871

1945
The Community Foundation of North Florida, Inc. ☆

1621 Metropolitan Blvd., Ste. A
Tallahassee, FL 32308 (850) 222-2899
Contact: Joy Watkins, Pres.
FAX: (850) 222-3624; E-mail: jwatkins@cfnf.org;
URL: http://www.cfnf.org

Established in 1997 in FL.
Foundation type: Community foundation.

Financial data (yr. ended 12/31/05): Assets, $9,979,180 (M); gifts received, $1,710,435; expenditures, $726,346; giving activities include $457,707 for 132+ grants (high: $45,000; low: $25).

Purpose and activities: The foundation's primary purpose is to receive and raise charitable giving from third parties and to distribute property and extend financial aid and support through grants, gifts, and assistance to qualified charitable organizations.

Fields of interest: Arts; Education; Environment; Housing/shelter; Youth, services; Family services; Human services; Economic development; Community development.

Limitations: Giving limited to the North Florida counties of Franklin, Gadsden, Gulf, Jackson, Jefferson, Leon, Liberty, Madison, Taylor and Wakulla. No grants to individuals.

Publications: Application guidelines; Annual report; Financial statement; Grants list; Informational brochure.

Application information: Visit foundation Web site for application guidelines. Faxed or e-mailed proposals are not accepted. Application form not required.

 Initial approach: Submit proposal
 Copies of proposal: 1
 Deadline(s): On-going
 Board meeting date(s): 2nd Thurs. of Jan., Mar., May, July, Sept., and Nov.
 Final notification: Within 60 days

Officers and Directors:* Palmer Proctor,* Chair.; Paul Sullivan,* Vice-Chair. and Treas.; Joy Watkins,* Pres.; Stan Barnes,* Secy.; Louise Humphrey, Emeritus; Ruth Ruggles Akers; Thomas W. Allen; Martha Barnett; Ken Boutwell; Cliff Butler; Ray Bye; Bud Carlson; Benjamin Crump; Carrol Dadisman; Wayne Edwards; Steve Evans; Sheriff David Harvey; Calynne Hill; Janet Hinkle; Wilson Hinson; Harold Knowles; Chuck Mitchell; Mike Pate; J. Vereen Smith; Marcia Thornberry.

Number of staff: 2 full-time professional; 1 part-time support.

EIN: 593473384

1946
The Community Foundation of Sarasota County, Inc.

(formerly The Sarasota County Community Foundation, Inc.)
P.O. Box 49587
Sarasota, FL 34230-6587 (941) 955-3000
Contact: Stewart W. Stearns, C.E.O.; For grant applications: Wendy Hopkins, V.P., Grant & Prog. Svcs.
FAX: (941) 952-1951;
E-mail: info@sarasota-foundation.org; Office address: 2635 Fruitville Rd., Sarasota, FL 34237; Grant application tel.: (941) 556-7152; Grant inquiry E-mail: wendy@sarasota-foundation.org; URL: http://www.sarasota-foundation.org

Incorporated in 1979 in FL.
Foundation type: Community foundation.
Financial data (yr. ended 5/31/05): Assets, $78,417,606 (M); gifts received, $8,314,685; expenditures, $5,997,822; giving activities include $2,781,502 for 288 grants (high: $356,937; low: $100), and $241,358 for 154 grants to individuals (high: $12,500; low: $150).

Purpose and activities: The foundation brings together citizens and organizations who care deeply

about their community and who believe that people can act locally to improve quality of life. The foundation supports organizations involved with the arts, education, environment, animal protection, health care, human services, and community development.

Fields of interest: Humanities; Arts; Child development, education; Higher education; Education; Environment; Animals/wildlife; Health care; Mental health/crisis services; Health organizations, association; Youth development, centers/clubs; Children/youth, services; Family services; Residential/custodial care, hospices; Human services; Community development; Youth; Aging; Disabilities, people with; Economically disadvantaged.

Type of support: Equipment; Emergency funds; Program development; Seed money; Scholarship funds; Scholarships—to individuals.

Limitations: Giving primarily in Sarasota County, FL, and surrounding communities. No support for fraternal organizations, societies or orders, or religious organizations for sectarian purposes. No grants to individuals (except for selected scholarships), or for annual campaigns, building campaigns, endowment funds, deficit financing, debt retirement, publications, operating expenses, travel, fundraising events, scientific research, or conferences.

Publications: Application guidelines; Annual report; Grants list; Informational brochure; Newsletter; Occasional report (including application guidelines); Program policy statement.

Application information: Visit foundation Web site for application guidelines. Application form required.

 Initial approach: Contact V.P., Grants & Prog. Svcs. by telephone and/or meeting prior to submitting proposal
 Copies of proposal: 1
 Deadline(s): None
 Board meeting date(s): Jan., Mar., May, July, Sept., and Nov.
 Final notification: Within 4 months

Officers and Directors:* Sophia LaRusso,* Chair.; Lee Wetherington,* 1st Vice-Chair.; James Shedivy,* 2nd Vice-Chair. and Treas.; Stewart W. Stearns, C.E.O. and Pres.; Wendy Hopkins, V.P., Grant and Prog. Svcs.; Christie Lewis, V.P., Nonprofit Capacity Building; Mark Rehder, V.P., Finance and Admin.; Tom Waters, V.P., Charitable Planning; Gina Mascio,* Secy. and Comm. Chair., Mktg.; Gloria Manzenberger, Cont.; Charla M. Burchett,* Chair., Grants Comm. & Charitable Planning Comm.; Steven N. Dahlquist,* Co-Chair., Investment Comm.; Ervin Sande,* Co-Chair., Investment Comm.; Motaz Agabani; Hank Battie; Vern Buchanan; Mary Fran Carroll; Jimmy Dean; Philip A. Delaney, Jr.; Barbara Ford-Coates; Donald E. Griffith; J. Garrett Heard IV; Larry Holland; Martha Honey; Ronald Koepsel; Frederick D. Lugar; Helen McBean; Diane McFarlin; J. Ronald Skipper; Barry F. Spivey; Richard Swier; James Taylor; William Young.

Number of staff: 6 full-time professional; 2 part-time professional; 2 full-time support.

EIN: 591956886

Selected grants: The following grants were reported in 2005.

$356,937 to Hospice of Southwest Florida, Sarasota, FL.
$172,000 to Wellesley College, Wellesley, MA.
$117,000 to Museum of Asian Art, Sarasota, FL.
$103,432 to Senior Friendship Centers, Sarasota, FL.
$90,000 to Loras College, Dubuque, IA.

$81,601 to United Way of Charlotte County, Port Charlotte, FL.
$48,377 to United Way of Sarasota County, Sarasota, FL.
$36,381 to Glasser-Schoenbaum Human Services Center, Sarasota, FL.
$29,027 to School Readiness Coalition of Sarasota, Sarasota, FL.
$25,000 to NPR Foundation, DC.

1947
Community Foundation of South Lake County, Inc.

(formerly South Lake County Community Foundation, Inc.)
P.O. Box 121543
Clermont, FL 34712-1543 (352) 394-3818
Contact: Bruce Greer, Exec. Dir.; For grants: Cheryl Fishel, Prog. Mgr.
FAX: (352) 394-7739; E-mail: info@cfslc.org; Additional E-mail: bruce@cfslc.org; Grant inquiry E-mail: slcfishel@earthlink.net; URL: http://www.cfslc.org

Established in 1995 in FL; converted from endowment resulting from the joint partnership between South Lake Hospital and Orlando Regional Healthcare System.
Foundation type: Community foundation.
Financial data (yr. ended 9/30/05): Assets, $9,381,091 (M); gifts received, $11,688; expenditures, $571,144; giving activities include $289,305 for grants, and $45,200 for grants to individuals.

Purpose and activities: The mission of the foundation is to provide leadership to enhance the quality of life in South Lake County by identifying community needs and seeking philanthropic support as permanent funding to meet those needs.

Fields of interest: Arts; Higher education; Education; Health care; Youth, services; Family services; Community development, association; Community development.

Type of support: General/operating support; Building/renovation; Equipment; Endowments; Program development; Conferences/seminars; Scholarship funds; Scholarships—to individuals; Matching/challenge support.

Limitations: Giving primarily in South Lake County, FL. No support for religious organizations for religious purposes. No grants to individuals (except for scholarships), or for salaries.

Publications: Application guidelines; Annual report; Financial statement; Grants list; Informational brochure; Newsletter.

Application information: Visit foundation Web site for application form and guidelines. Application form required.

 Initial approach: Telephone
 Copies of proposal: 6
 Deadline(s): Mar. 30
 Board meeting date(s): Last Thurs. of every other month
 Final notification: June 30

Officers and Directors:* Sally Hessberg,* Pres.; Kelly Cartier,* V.P.; Julia Law,* Secy.; Jeffery Rice,* Treas.; Bruce Greer, Exec. Dir.; Oakley Seaver,* Chair. Emeritus; Ron MacFarlane, Honorary Member; Ed Augustine; Gary Clark; Shannon Elswick; Tom English; Anita Geraci; JoAnn Jones; Stephen Lee; Leslie Longacre; Mike Mowdy; Paul Rountree; J.M. Vander Meer; Denise Wallace.

Number of staff: 1 full-time professional; 1 full-time support; 1 part-time support.
EIN: 593343026

1948
Community Foundation of Tampa Bay, Inc.
(formerly The Community Foundation of Greater Tampa, Inc.)
4950 W. Kennedy Blvd., Ste. 250
Tampa, FL 33609-1837 (813) 282-1975
Contact: David J. Fischer, C.E.O.; Ann Berg, Asst. to the Pres.; For grants: Paula Fraher, Dir., Grants
FAX: (813) 282-3119;
E-mail: aberg@cftampabay.org; Grant application E-mail: pfraher@cftampabay.org; Additional E-mail: dfischer@cftampabay.org; URL: http://www.cftampabay.org

Established in 1990 in FL.
Foundation type: Community foundation.
Financial data (yr. ended 6/30/05): Assets, $95,987,167 (M); gifts received, $10,390,962; expenditures, $9,535,919; giving activities include $8,803,267 for 473 grants (high: $614,000; low: $75).
Purpose and activities: The mission of the foundation and its Board is to encourage the residents and nonprofits of the Tampa Bay area to take advantage of the foundation's flexibility in developing and implementing their charitable giving through programs that will make the Tampa Bay area a better place for all its citizens.
Fields of interest: Visual arts; Performing arts; Historic preservation/historical societies; Arts; Elementary school/education; Higher education; Education; Environment; Animals/wildlife; Health care; Medical research, institute; Housing/shelter, development; Children/youth, services; Family services; Aging, centers/services; Human services; Community development, neighborhood development; Community development; Government/public administration; Public affairs; Aging; Homeless.
Type of support: Equipment; Emergency funds; Program development; Seed money; Curriculum development; Scholarship funds; Technical assistance; Consulting services; Matching/challenge support.
Limitations: Giving generally limited to Hillsborough, Pasco, and Pinellas counties, FL. No support for religious or sectarian purposes. No grants to individuals (except for scholarships), or for operating costs of established programs, capital campaigns, experimental medical research, start-up organization funding, advertising, or tickets to sponsor events; no loans.
Publications: Application guidelines; Annual report; Annual report (including application guidelines); Financial statement; Informational brochure; Newsletter.
Application information: Visit foundation Web site for application guidelines. Application form required.
Initial approach: Contact foundation
Copies of proposal: 1
Deadline(s): Mar. 1 and Sept. 1
Board meeting date(s): Jan., Mar., May, Sept., and Nov.
Final notification: Apr. 15 and Oct. 15
Officers and Trustees:* Frank J. Rief III,* Chair.; William E. Starkey,* Vice-Chair.; David J. Fischer,* C.E.O. and Pres.; Martin Silbiger,* Secy.; Louis Mock, C.F.O.; Martin B. Solomon,* Treas.; George J. Baxter,* Pres. Emeritus; Diana Baker; Keith Dunn;

Joseph Garcia; Dick A. Greco; Arthur H. Haedike; Paul J. Hanna II; H. William Heller; Michael L. Jamieson; Gene Marshall; Alfred T. May; Roy J. McCraw, Jr.; Robert H. Mohr; Roger Robson; Barbara Romano; Franci Golman Rudolph; Jerome Ryans; Catherine Lowry Straz; Robert S. Trinkle.
Number of staff: 4 full-time professional; 1 part-time professional; 3 full-time support; 1 part-time support.
EIN: 593001853

1949
Community Foundation of the Florida Keys, Inc.
P.O. Box 162
Key West, FL 33041 (305) 292-1502
Contact: Dianna Sutton, C.E.O.
FAX: (305) 292-1598; E-mail: cffk@bellsouth.net; URL: http://www.cffk.org

Established in 1996 in FL.
Foundation type: Community foundation.
Financial data (yr. ended 6/30/06): Assets, $9,102,319 (M); gifts received, $6,850,662; expenditures, $2,669,000; giving activities include $2,404,466 for 151 grants (high: $250,000; low: $250).
Purpose and activities: The foundation seeks to help support quality of life in the community by providing a way for donors to give financial support to charitable organizations that meet the community's varied needs.
Fields of interest: Historic preservation/historical societies; Arts; Education; Environment; Health care; Recreation; Human services; Public affairs.
Type of support: Management development/capacity building; General/operating support; Emergency funds; Curriculum development; Continuing support; Capital campaigns; Building/renovation; Annual campaigns; Program development; Conferences/seminars; Scholarship funds; Scholarships—to individuals; Matching/challenge support.
Limitations: Giving primarily in Monroe County, FL. No support for religious purposes.
Publications: Application guidelines; Annual report; Financial statement; Informational brochure; Newsletter; Quarterly report.
Application information: Application form required.
Initial approach: Contact foundation
Copies of proposal: 5
Deadline(s): Dec. 31
Board meeting date(s): 3rd Tues. monthly
Final notification: 1 month
Officers and Board Members:* Jeff Overby,* Chair.; John Kent Cooke, Jr.,* Vice-Chair. and Secy.; Kerry Shelby,* Vice-Chair. and Treas.; Ken Domanski,* Vice-Chair.; Matthew Helmerich,* Vice-Chair.; Philip Miani,* Vice-Chair.; Jim Smith,* Vice-Chair.; Dianna Sutton, C.E.O. and Pres.; Jon Allen; William Andersen; John Behmke; Chris Bellard; Thomas Clements; John Dolan-Heitlinger; Shirley Freeman; Holly Merrill; Doug Morgan; Karen Sharp.
Number of staff: 2 full-time professional.
EIN: 650648968

1950
The Conese Foundation, Inc. ✧
2200 N.W. 84th Ave.
Miami, FL 33122 (305) 774-3536
Contact: Martha de Leon, Secy.

Established in 1986 in CT and FL.
Donors: Eugene P. Conese, Sr.; Eugene P. Conese, Jr.; The Greenwich Co., Ltd.; Greenwich Air Svcs., Inc.; GE Engine Serives, Inc.; General Electric, Inc.
Foundation type: Independent foundation.
Financial data (yr. ended 12/31/03): Assets, $3,682,448 (M); expenditures, $353,840; qualifying distributions, $352,925; giving activities include $352,925 for 18 grants (high: $150,000; low: $75).
Purpose and activities: Giving primarily for education, health, and human services.
Fields of interest: Museums (art); Historic preservation/historical societies; Higher education; Education; Hospitals (general); Health care; Health organizations, association; Human services; Children/youth, services; Foundations (private grantmaking).
Limitations: Giving primarily in Miami, FL; funding also in New Rochelle, NY, and Newport, RI. No grants to individuals.
Application information:
Initial approach: Typewritten letter
Deadline(s): None
Officers and Directors:* Eugene P. Conese, Sr.,* Chair. and Pres.; Anna May Conese,* V.P.; Martha de Leon, Secy.; Deborah Conese Eagan; Susan Conese Metzger.
EIN: 222776289
Selected grants: The following grants were reported in 2003.
$150,000 to Iona College, New Rochelle, NY. For capital campaign.
$110,100 to Jackson Memorial Foundation, Miami, FL.
$11,000 to American Cancer Society, Miami, FL.
$10,800 to Preservation Society of Newport County, Newport, RI.
$5,000 to Newport Hospital Foundation, Newport, RI.
$4,750 to American Red Cross, Miami, FL.
$3,650 to Make-A-Wish Foundation of South Florida, Fort Lauderdale, FL.
$2,000 to University of Florida, Levin College of Law, Gainesville, FL.
$1,450 to Nova Southeastern University, Fort Lauderdale, FL.
$75 to Buoniconti Fund to Cure Paralysis, Miami, FL.

1951
Conn Memorial Foundation, Inc.
2910 W. Bay to Bay Blvd., Ste. 200
Tampa, FL 33629
Contact: Maggie Osborn, Dir., Grants

Incorporated in 1954 in FL.
Donors: Fred K. Conn†; Edith F. Conn†.
Foundation type: Independent foundation.
Financial data (yr. ended 7/31/05): Assets, $22,550,138 (M); expenditures, $1,282,598; qualifying distributions, $1,017,627; giving activities include $889,905 for 52 grants (high: $50,000; low: $2,460; average: $5,000–$50,000).
Purpose and activities: Giving primarily for programs that support at-risk children and families in Hillsborough County, FL; funding also for inner-city youth outreach, scholarships, and capacity grants.
Fields of interest: Education; Crime/violence prevention, child abuse; Human services; Children/youth, services; Family services; Human services, emergency aid.
Type of support: General/operating support; Continuing support; Management development/

capacity building; Capital campaigns; Building/renovation; Equipment; Emergency funds; Program development; Conferences/seminars; Seed money; Scholarship funds; Technical assistance; Consulting services; Program evaluation; Matching/challenge support.

Limitations: Giving limited to Hillsborough County, FL. No grants for individual scholarships, no loans.

Publications: Informational brochure (including application guidelines).

Application information: Applications are by invitation only following acceptance of letter of intent. Application form required.

Initial approach: 1-page letter of intent
Copies of proposal: 1
Deadline(s): Nov. 15 (for Dec. meeting) and Mar. 15 (for May meeting)
Board meeting date(s): Monthly
Final notification: Following board meetings

Officers and Director:* Sheffield Crowder,* Pres.; Donna Jenkins, Cont.

Number of staff: 2 part-time professional; 1 part-time support.

EIN: 590978713

Selected grants: The following grants were reported in 2005.

$50,000 to Boys and Girls Clubs of Tampa Bay, Tampa, FL.
$40,000 to Metropolitan Ministries, Tampa, FL.
$30,000 to Boys and Girls Club.
$25,000 to Media Access Project, DC.
$25,000 to Tampa Bay History Center, Tampa, FL.
$25,000 to Young Life.
$20,000 to All Sports Community Service, Tampa, FL.
$20,000 to Americas Second Harvest, Chicago, IL.
$20,000 to Tampa United Methodist Centers, Tampa, FL.
$10,000 to American Red Cross.

1952
Consolidated Anti-Aging Foundation ✧

c/o Charles M. Kelly, Jr.
2640 Golden Gate Pkwy., No. 305
Naples, FL 34105-3203

Established in 1996 in FL.

Donors: R. Ross†; F. Ross†.

Foundation type: Independent foundation.

Financial data (yr. ended 12/31/04): Assets, $10,900,079 (M); expenditures, $997,903; qualifying distributions, $752,632; giving activities include $546,000 for 9 grants (high: $180,000; low: $5,000).

Fields of interest: Hospitals (general); Medical research, institute.

Limitations: Applications not accepted. Giving on a national basis. No grants to individuals.

Application information: Contributes only to pre-selected organizations.

Trustees: Cheryl L. Ross; Robin S. Ross.

EIN: 656222748

1953
Couch Family Foundation, Inc. ✧

1717 E. Fowler Ave.
Tampa, FL 33612

Established in 1989 in FL.

Donor: Theodore J. Couch, Sr.

Foundation type: Independent foundation.

Financial data (yr. ended 12/31/04): Assets, $3,866,071 (M); gifts received, $400,000; expenditures, $390,907; qualifying distributions, $344,999; giving activities include $345,675 for 18 grants (high: $250,000; low: $500).

Fields of interest: Higher education; Health care, fund raising/fund distribution; Protestant agencies & churches.

Limitations: Applications not accepted. Giving primarily in Tampa, FL. No grants to individuals.

Application information: Contributes only to pre-selected organizations.

Officers and Directors:* Martha K. Couch,* Pres.; Theodore J. Couch, Sr.,* V.P. and Treas.; William C. Crowder,* Secy.; Theodore J. Couch, Jr.

EIN: 592926563

Selected grants: The following grants were reported in 2003.

$75,000 to Academy of the Holy Names School, Tampa, FL. For general support.
$50,000 to Appalachian State University Foundation, Boone, NC. For general support.
$25,000 to Tampa Bay Performing Arts Center, Tampa, FL. For general support.
$10,000 to Sacred Heart Church, Tampa, FL. For general support.
$6,000 to Hillsborough Educational Partnership Foundation, Tampa, FL. For general support.
$5,000 to Jesuit High School Foundation, Tampa, FL. For general support.
$5,000 to University of South Florida Foundation, Tampa, FL. For general support.
$2,500 to Abe Brown Ministries, Tampa, FL. For general support.
$2,500 to MacDonald Training Center, Tampa, FL. For general support.
$1,000 to Life Enrichment Senior Center, Tampa, FL. For general support.

1954
Wallace H. Coulter Foundation ▼ ✧

790 N.W. 107th Ave., Ste. 215
Miami, FL 33172-3158 (305) 559-2991
Contact: Wayne A. Barlin, V.P. and Genl. Counsel
FAX: (305) 559-5490; *URL:* http://www.whcf.org

Established in 2000 in DE and FL.

Donors: Wallace H. Coulter Charitable Remainder Unitrust; Wallace H. Coulter Trust.

Foundation type: Independent foundation.

Financial data (yr. ended 9/30/05): Assets, $418,327,787 (M); expenditures, $23,581,718; qualifying distributions, $19,769,022; giving activities include $18,381,525 for 37 grants (high: $9,000,000; low: $2,500; average: $100,000–$1,000,000).

Purpose and activities: The foundation is dedicated to improving human health care by supporting translational research in biomedical engineering-research directed at the transfer of promising technologies within the university research laboratory that are progressing towards commercial development and clinical practice.

Fields of interest: Health care; Biomedicine; Medical research, institute; Federated giving programs; Science.

Type of support: Research.

Limitations: No support for religious organizations. No grants to individuals.

Application information: See foundation Web site for more application information. Application forms are available on the foundation Web site. Application form required.

Initial approach: Preliminary application

Officers: Sue Van, C.E.O. and Pres.; Susan Racher, V.P. and C.F.O.; Wayne A. Barlin, V.P. and Genl. Counsel; Robert Morff, V.P. and Chief Scientific Off.; James Wilcox, Cont.

EIN: 311546126

Selected grants: The following grants were reported in 2004.

$7,615,000 to Clarkson University, Potsdam, NY. 2 grants: $7,500,000 (For research and education in colloidal science; program in rehabilitation engineering; engineering faculty supplements and research funding; endowment of graduate and undergraduate engineering fellowships and scholarships; developing new engineering programs and initiatives; providing funding for laboratory equipment; and support for program enhancements), $115,000 (For educational and commemorative exhibition about engineering and the life of Wallace Coulter, in The Wallace H. Coulter College of Engineering).
$2,765,318 to Westminster College, Fulton, MO. For renovation and expansion of Wallace H. Coulter Science Center.
$577,660 to Smith College, Northampton, MA. For scholarships for women who are citizens of developing countries and who pursue a degree in engineering or science.
$300,000 to American Society of Hematology, DC. 2 grants: $200,000 (For second annual Clinical Research Training Institute for hematology fellows-in-training and junior faculty physicians), $100,000 (For ASH Scholar in Translational Medical Research, for research on hematopoietic stem cell transplantation and graft versus host disease).
$250,000 to Georgia Tech Foundation, Atlanta, GA. 2 grants: $200,000 (For educational exhibit about biomedical engineering and Wallace Coulter's life), $50,000 (For translational research in biomedical engineering, Display Enhanced Testing for Concussions and mTBI (DETECT)).
$100,000 to American Association for Clinical Chemistry, DC. For sponsorship of Oakridge conference, international conference dedicated to advancing technology that has potential for future applications in hospital laboratories.
$100,000 to Biomedical Engineering Society, Landover, MD. To implement accreditation process for biomedical engineering departments in universities in the U.S.

1955
Wallace H. Coulter Trust ✧

790 N.W. 107th Ave., Ste. 215
Miami, FL 33172 (305) 559-2991
Contact: Wayne A. Barlin, Genl. Counsel

Established in 1999 in FL.

Donors: Wallace H. Coulter; Wallace H. Coulter Irrevocable Trust.

Foundation type: Independent foundation.

Financial data (yr. ended 9/30/04): Assets, $55,318,250 (M); gifts received, $7,675,797; expenditures, $1,654,603; qualifying distributions, $1,315,911; giving activities include $1,315,911 for 3 grants (high: $675,000; low: $15,911).

Purpose and activities: The foundation's grantmaking will focus on the scientific, educational, and humanitarian interests of the donor, primarily with institutions and organizations that the donor had a relationship during his life.

Fields of interest: Higher education; Medical school/education; Medical research; Philanthropy/voluntarism.

Limitations: Giving on a national basis.

Application information:

Deadline(s): None

Officer: Susan Racher, C.F.O.

Trustee: Sue Van.

EIN: 656310670

Selected grants: The following grants were reported in 2004.

$675,000 to City College 21st Century Foundation, New York, NY.

$625,000 to University of Miami, School of Medicine, Coral Gables, FL.

$15,911 to Clarkson University, Potsdam, NY.

1956
Crawford Family Foundation, Inc. ✦ ☆
9995 Gate Pkwy. N., Ste. 200
Jacksonville, FL   32246

Established in FL.

Donor: Felix A. Crawford.

Foundation type: Independent foundation.

Financial data (yr. ended 12/31/05): Assets, $26,191 (M); gifts received, $352,814; expenditures, $323,071; qualifying distributions, $322,261; giving activities include $322,261 for 10 grants (high: $150,203; low: $1,910).

Fields of interest: Education; Hospitals (specialty); Human services; Children/youth, services; Federated giving programs; Christian agencies & churches.

Limitations: Applications not accepted. Giving primarily in Jacksonville, FL. No grants to individuals.

Application information: Contributes only to pre-selected organizations.

Officers and Directors: * Antonio Crawford, * Pres.; Patricia Cannan, * V.P.; Mary Catherine McCrimon, * V.P.; Douglas R. Aiosa, Secy.-Treas.; Felix A. Crawford.

EIN: 593725418

1957
Dade Community Foundation, Inc. ▼ ✦
(formerly Dade Foundation)
200 S. Biscayne Blvd., Ste. 505
Miami, FL   33131-2343   (305) 371-2711
Contact: Ruth Shack, Pres.; For grant applications: Charisse L. Grant, Dir., Progs.; For grant applications: Betty Alonso, Sr. Prog. Off.
FAX: (305) 371-5342;
E-mail: ruth.shack@dadecommunityfoundation.org;
Additional E-mails:
Charisse.grant@dadecommunityfoundation.org,
Betty.alonso@dadecommunityfoundation.org, and
Todd.weeks@dadecommunityfoundation.org;
URL: http://www.dadecommunityfoundation.org

Established in 1967 in FL.

Foundation type: Community foundation.

Financial data (yr. ended 12/31/05): Assets, $127,078,828 (M); gifts received, $7,268,486; expenditures, $10,554,011; giving activities include $6,543,368 for 446+ grants, and $139,000 for 106 grants to individuals (high: $2,500; low: $500).

Purpose and activities: The foundation seeks to encourage philanthropy and charitable giving by developing a permanent endowment to meet current and future emerging charitable needs. Grants are made in broad program areas including education, health, human services, arts and culture, the environment, and community and economic development. In addition, field of interest and special funding initiatives have enabled significant grantmaking addressing the issues of abused and neglected children, immigrants and refugees, AIDS, homelessness, social justice, black affairs, care of animals, and heart disease.

Fields of interest: Arts, multipurpose centers/programs; Visual arts; Arts; Education; Environment; Animal welfare; Health care; Health organizations, association; Heart & circulatory diseases; AIDS; Alzheimer's disease; Crime/violence prevention; child abuse; Housing/shelter; Disasters, 9/11/01; Youth development; Children/youth, services; Homeless, human services; Human services; Civil rights, minorities; Civil rights, gays/lesbians; Civil rights; Community development, neighborhood development; Economic development; Community development; Aging; African Americans/Blacks; AIDS, people with; LGBTQ; Immigrants/refugees; Economically disadvantaged; Homeless.

Type of support: General/operating support; Building/renovation; Equipment; Land acquisition; Endowments; Emergency funds; Program development; Publication; Seed money; Scholarship funds; Research; Technical assistance; Consulting services; Program-related investments/loans; Scholarships—to individuals; Matching/challenge support.

Limitations: Giving limited to Miami-Dade County, FL. No grants to individuals (except through scholarship funds), or for memberships, fundraising, memorials, deficit financing, or conferences.

Publications: Application guidelines; Annual report; Newsletter; Occasional report.

Application information: Visit foundation Web site for application Cover form, Budget form, and guidelines. E-mailed or faxed proposals are not accepted. New applicants are encouraged to contact the Program Department staff prior to submitting an application. The foundation conducts a free information workshop about the Community Grants Program; call foundation to register. Application form required.

Initial approach: Mail application Cover form, Budget form, and proposal

Copies of proposal: 2

Deadline(s): Oct. 1 through Nov. 15

Board meeting date(s): Feb., May, Sept., and Nov.

Final notification: Feb.

Officers and Governors: * Teresa Valdes-Fauli Weintraub, * Chair.; Keith T. Ward, * Vice-Chair.; Ruth Shack, Pres.; John J. Grundhauser, * Secy.; Maricarmen Martinez, * Treas.; Juan C. Antunez; John R. Anzivino; Marsha B. Elser; George W. Foyo; Elizabeth "Liebe" Gadinsky; Sandra P. Greenblatt; Hank Klein; Richard Lavina; Jorge Luis Lopez; Marsha G. Madorsky; Cristina Mendoza; Theodore J. Pappas; Damian J. Pardo; Beverly A. Parker; C. Carl Randolph; Joseph H. Serota; Roger Soman.

Number of staff: 5 full-time professional; 4 full-time support; 1 part-time support.

EIN: 650350357

Selected grants: The following grants were reported in 2005.

$291,000 to Saint Thomas University, Miami Gardens, FL.

$285,025 to Jackson Memorial Foundation, Miami, FL.

$250,000 to Haggai Institute for Advanced Leadership Training, Atlanta, GA.

$185,000 to Miami Childrens Museum, Miami, FL.

$122,000 to Mothers Voices South Florida, Miami, FL. For Community AIDS Partnership and Johnson and Johnson/National AIDS Fund's Women and Families Initiative. Grant made through Community AIDS Partnership.

$116,940 to United Way of Miami-Dade, Miami, FL.

$102,500 to Childrens Resource Fund, Miami, FL.

$20,000 to Miami Country Day School Foundation, Miami, FL.

$15,250 to Tigertail Productions, Miami, FL.

$13,100 to Broward Partnership for the Homeless, Fort Lauderdale, FL.

1958
The Dahan Family Foundation, Inc. ✦ ☆
20155 N.E. 38th Ct., Apt. 2801
Aventura, FL   33180

Established in 2004 in FL.

Donors: Rene Dahan; Elisabeth Dahan.

Foundation type: Independent foundation.

Financial data (yr. ended 12/31/05): Assets, $3,733,126 (M); expenditures, $858,993; qualifying distributions, $850,000; giving activities include $850,000 for 2 grants (high: $800,000; low: $50,000).

Fields of interest: Animal welfare; Health care.

Limitations: Applications not accepted. No grants to individuals.

Application information: Contributes only to pre-selected organizations.

Officers and Directors: * Rene Dahan, * Pres. and Treas.; Elisabeth Dahan, * V.P. and Secy.

EIN: 201959792

1959
Dahl Family Foundation, Inc. ✦ ☆
1200 Riverplace Blvd., Ste. 902
Jacksonville, FL   32207-1806

Donors: James H. Dahl; William Dahl.

Foundation type: Independent foundation.

Financial data (yr. ended 12/31/05): Assets, $3,270,103 (M); gifts received, $732,460; expenditures, $434,263; qualifying distributions, $429,140; giving activities include $429,140 for 8 grants (high: $250,000; low: $40).

Fields of interest: Education, research; Higher education; Education; Athletics/sports, amateur leagues; Human services.

Limitations: Applications not accepted. Giving primarily in FL. No grants to individuals.

Application information: Contributes only to pre-selected organizations.

Officers and Directors: * James H. Dahl, * Pres.; William L. Dahl, * V.P. and Secy.-Treas.; Trina Dahl Miller.

EIN: 562360547

1960
Darden Restaurants, Inc. Foundation ▼
5900 Lake Ellenor Dr.
P.O. Box 593330
Orlando, FL   32859-3330   (407) 245-5213
Contact: Patty DeYoung, Exec. Admin.

FAX: (407) 245-4462;
E-mail: pdeyoung@darden.com; URL: http://
www.dardenrestaurants.com/
com_overview_foundation.asp

Established in 1995 in FL.
Donor: Darden Restaurants, Inc.
Foundation type: Company-sponsored foundation.
Financial data (yr. ended 5/31/05): Assets,
$4,818,243 (M); gifts received, $7,231,000;
expenditures, $5,127,894; qualifying distributions,
$5,121,894; giving activities include $5,121,894
for 99+ grants (high: $1,000,000).
Purpose and activities: The foundation supports
organizations involved with arts and culture,
education, the environment, employment training,
nutrition, human services, and diversity.
Fields of interest: Arts, cultural/ethnic awareness;
Visual arts; Performing arts; Arts; Education,
reading; Education; Environment, public education;
Environment, natural resources; Environment;
Employment, training; Nutrition; Children, services;
Human services; Civil rights, equal rights.
Type of support: General/operating support; Capital
campaigns; Program development; Employee
volunteer services; Employee matching gifts; In-kind
gifts; Matching/challenge support.
Limitations: Giving primarily in the central FL area.
No support for religious organizations not of direct
benefit to the entire community or international or
disease-specific organizations. No grants to
individuals, or for one-time, short-term events,
advertising, team sponsorships, athletic
scholarships, or national conferences.
Publications: Application guidelines; Corporate
giving report.
Application information: Application form required.
Initial approach: Download application form and
mail proposal and application form to
foundation
Copies of proposal: 2
Deadline(s): 6 weeks prior to board meetings
Board meeting date(s): Feb., May, Aug., and Nov.
Final notification: 2 weeks following board
meetings
Officers and Trustees:* Clarence Otis, Jr.,* Chair.;
Richard J. Walsh,* V.P.; Paula J. Shives,* Secy.;
Linda J. Dimopoulas, Treas.; Stoddard Crane; Mary
Darden; Joe R. Lee; Blaine Sweatt III; Robert
Waggoner.
Number of staff: 1 full-time professional.
EIN: 593332929
Selected grants: The following grants were reported
in 2005.
$1,000,000 to Volunteer Florida Foundation,
Tallahassee, FL. For unrestricted support.
$310,000 to United Way, Heart of Florida, Orlando,
FL. For unrestricted support.
$150,000 to Central Florida Zoological Society,
Lake Monroe, FL. For unrestricted support.
$139,113 to YMCA, Central Florida, Cocoa, FL. For
unrestricted support.
$125,000 to United Arts of Central Florida, Orlando,
FL. For unrestricted support.
$97,561 to University of Florida, Gainesville, FL. For
unrestricted support.
$40,000 to Lobster Conservancy, Friendship, ME.
For unrestricted support.
$30,000 to Smithsonian American Art Museum, DC.
For unrestricted support.
$20,000 to Foundation for Osceola Education,
Kissimmee, FL. For unrestricted support.
$20,000 to House of Hope, Orlando, FL. For
unrestricted support.

1961
Vera Davis - W.D. Charities, Inc.
(formerly Vera Davis Parsons - W.D. Charities, Inc.)
4310 Pablo Oaks Ct.
Jacksonville, FL   32224

Established in 1967 in FL.
Donors: Vera Davis Parsons; DFS Trust 2003; DFS
Trust 2004.
Foundation type: Independent foundation.
Financial data (yr. ended 12/31/05): Assets,
$1,666,484 (M); expenditures, $3,821,861;
qualifying distributions, $3,818,783; giving
activities include $3,817,033 for grants.
Purpose and activities: Giving primarily for youth
activities and medical research and health; support
also for education, welfare relief, and social service
agencies.
Fields of interest: Education; Health care; Health
organizations, association; Medical research,
institute; Human services; Children/youth, services.
Limitations: Applications not accepted. Giving
primarily in Jacksonville, FL and NC. No grants to
individuals.
Application information: Contributes only to
pre-selected organizations.
Officers: H.J. Skelton, Pres.; Robert D. Davis, V.P.
and Treas.; David C. Clowe, V.P.; H.D. Francis, V.P.;
Susan C. Thorne, V.P.; Judy B. Morgan, Secy.
Directors: A. Dano Davis; T. Wayne Davis; Charles
P. Stephens.
EIN: 596180346

1962
Austin Davis Family - W.D. Charities, Inc.
4310 Pablo Oaks Ct.
Jacksonville, FL   32224-9631

Incorporated in 1950 in FL.
Donor: Milton Austin Davis.
Foundation type: Independent foundation.
Financial data (yr. ended 12/31/05): Assets,
$16,605,132 (M); expenditures, $477,313;
qualifying distributions, $451,925; giving activities
include $447,000 for 19 grants (high: $110,000;
low: $5,000).
Fields of interest: Elementary/secondary
education; Higher education; Health care; Human
services; Children/youth, services.
Type of support: General/operating support.
Limitations: Applications not accepted. Giving
primarily in the southeastern U.S. No grants to
individuals.
Application information: Contributes only to
pre-selected organizations.
Officers and Directors:* Charles P. Stephens,*
Pres.; H.J. Skelton,* V.P. and Treas.; David C.
Clowe, V.P.; H.D. Francis,* V.P.; Sandra D.
Stephens,* V.P.; Susan C. Thorne, V.P.; Judy B.
Morgan, Secy.; Alice K. Davis.
EIN: 596128871

1963
The Tine W. Davis Family - W.D. Charities, Inc. ✧
1910 San Marco Blvd.
Jacksonville, FL   32207-3204   (904) 398-3986
Contact: Charitable Grants Comm.

Incorporated in 1950 in FL.
Donor: Tine W. Davis.

Foundation type: Independent foundation.
Financial data (yr. ended 12/31/03): Assets,
$15,136,082 (M); expenditures, $1,681,768;
qualifying distributions, $1,197,380; giving
activities include $838,032 for 39 grants (high:
$250,000; low: $100).
Fields of interest: Higher education; Health care;
Medical research, institute; Human services;
Children/youth, services; Federated giving
programs; Christian agencies & churches.
Limitations: Giving limited to the southeastern U.S.
No grants to individuals.
Publications: Application guidelines.
Application information: Application form required.
Initial approach: Letter requesting grant
application
Copies of proposal: 1
Deadline(s): None
Board meeting date(s): 2nd Tues. in Apr.
Officer: Tine Wayne Davis, Jr., Pres. and
Secy.-Treas.
Directors: Margaret M. Riley; Paul K. Saffell.
Number of staff: 3
EIN: 590995388

1964
The Arthur Vining Davis Foundations ▼
225 Water St., Ste. 1510
Jacksonville, FL   32202-5185   (904) 359-0670
Contact: Dr. Jonathan T. Howe, Exec. Dir.
FAX: (904) 359-0675;
E-mail: arthurvining@bellsouth.net; URL: http://
www.avdfdn.org/

The Foundations are comprised of three separate
foundations established in 1952 and 1965 in PA;
and in 1965 in FL. In early 2001, Foundation No. 1
merged with Foundation No. 2.
Donor: Arthur Vining Davis†.
Foundation type: Independent foundation.
Financial data (yr. ended 12/31/05): Assets,
$232,665,000 (M); expenditures, $11,972,904;
qualifying distributions, $11,157,738; giving
activities include $10,164,097 for 57 grants (high:
$700,000; average: $50,000–$200,000), and
$3,762 for 22 employee matching gifts.
Purpose and activities: Support largely for private
higher education; secondary education, to
strengthen teachers and their teaching in high
schools, health care with emphasis on caring
attitudes, public television, and graduate
theological education.
Fields of interest: Media, film/video; Secondary
school/education; Higher education; Medical
school/education; Theological school/education.
Type of support: Employee matching gifts; General/
operating support; Continuing support; Capital
campaigns; Building/renovation; Equipment;
Endowments; Program development;
Professorships; Publication; Curriculum
development; Fellowships; Internship funds;
Scholarship funds; Research; Technical assistance;
Consulting services; Program evaluation; Matching/
challenge support.
Limitations: Giving limited to the U.S. and its
possessions and territories. No support for
community chests, publicly governed colleges and
universities, and institutions primarily supported by
government funds (except in secondary education
and health care programs), voter education, voter
registration drives, or projects incurring obligations
extending over many years. No grants to individuals;
no loans.

Publications: Annual report (including application guidelines); Grants list; Informational brochure.
Application information: Proposals are not accepted via fax or E-mail. Application form not required.
  Initial approach: Letter
  Copies of proposal: 1
  Deadline(s): None
  Board meeting date(s): Spring, fall, and winter
  Final notification: 10 to 15 months for approvals
Officers and Trustees:* J.H. Dow Davis,* Chair.; Doreen Flippin, V.P., Admin.; Jane M. Estes, C.F.O.; Jonathan T. Howe, Exec. Dir.; W.R. Wright, Emeritus; Haley Davis Melanson, Tr.; Holbrook R. Davis; Joel P. Davis; Sarah H. Davis; Rev. Davis Given; Mrs. John L. Kee, Jr.; William G. Kee; Margaret Davis Maiden; Dr. Max K. Morris; Mellon Bank, N.A.; SunTrust Bank.
Number of staff: 5 full-time professional; 1 full-time support.
Selected grants: The following grants were reported in 2005.
$400,000 to W E T A-Greater Washington Educational Telecommunications Association, Arlington, VA. For Ken Burns' documentary film projects for first decade of new century.
$300,000 to W N E T Channel 13, New York, NY. For programs on Willa Cather and Ernest Hemingway.
$250,000 to W Q E D Metropolitan Pittsburgh Educational Television, Pittsburgh, PA. For completion funding for War that Made America.
$200,000 to College of the Atlantic, Bar Harbor, ME. For Endowed Chair in Human Ecology.
$200,000 to Hendrix College, Conway, AR. For Award for Excellence.
$200,000 to Heritage University, Toppenish, WA. For Scholarship Program.
$200,000 to McDaniel College, Westminster, MD. For construction of academic building.
$200,000 to Reed College, Portland, OR. For Quantitative Skills Center, supporting the academic program with tutoring and seminars.
$200,000 to W G B H Educational Foundation, Boston, MA. For completion funding and outreach for Postcards from Busters.
$200,000 to Yale University, New Haven, CT. For Grand Strategy Project.

1965
Marion Park Deaver and Harry Gilbert Deaver Foundation ✧
c/o Wachovia Bank, N.A.
975 S. Federal Hwy.
Boca Raton, FL 33432-6129

Established in 1991 in FL.
Donor: Marion Park Deaver†.
Foundation type: Independent foundation.
Financial data (yr. ended 12/31/03): Assets, $18,253,971 (M); expenditures, $874,345; qualifying distributions, $768,410; giving activities include $700,410 for 36 grants (high: $90,000; low: $500), and $68,000 for 66 grants to individuals.
Purpose and activities: Giving primarily for private schools (K-12).
Fields of interest: Elementary/secondary education; Higher education; Human services; Roman Catholic agencies & churches.
Limitations: Giving primarily in FL, MN, and WI.
Publications: IRS Form 990-PF.

Application information: Application form not required.
  Deadline(s): None
Trustee: Wachovia Bank, N.A.
EIN: 656066225

1966
The Jon Holden DeHaan Foundation ✧ ☆
975 6th Ave. S., Ste. 103
Naples, FL 34102
Contact: Jon Holden DeHaan, Tr.

Established in 1990 in IN.
Donor: J. Holden DeHaan.
Foundation type: Independent foundation.
Financial data (yr. ended 12/31/05): Assets, $12,472,675 (M); expenditures, $548,174; qualifying distributions, $317,400; giving activities include $317,400 for grants.
Purpose and activities: Giving primarily for education and medicine.
Fields of interest: Elementary/secondary education; Education; Health care; Health organizations, association; Foundations (private grantmaking).
Limitations: Giving primarily in Naples, FL. No grants to individuals.
Application information:
  Initial approach: Letter
  Deadline(s): None
Officer: Thomas H. DeHaan, Mgr.
Trustee: Jon Holden DeHaan.
EIN: 346924212
Selected grants: The following grants were reported in 2004.
$65,000 to American Heart Association, Dallas, TX.
$50,000 to Park Tudor School, Indianapolis, IN.
$10,000 to Special Olympics, DC.
$5,500 to Boys and Girls Club.
$5,000 to Seacrest Country Day School, Naples, FL.
$5,000 to YMCA.
$1,000 to Alzheimers Association, Chicago, IL.

1967
Demetree Family Foundation ✧
3740 Beach Blvd., Ste. 300
Jacksonville, FL 32207

Established in 1996 in FL.
Donors: Elisa A. Demetree; Jack C. Demetree.
Foundation type: Independent foundation.
Financial data (yr. ended 12/31/05): Assets, $5,832,269 (M); gifts received, $2,209,583; expenditures, $402,821; qualifying distributions, $371,366; giving activities include $371,085 for 67 grants (high: $50,000; low: $400).
Purpose and activities: Giving primarily to Christian and Roman Catholic agencies and churches. Support also for children, youth, and social services, health care, and the United Way.
Fields of interest: Hospitals (general); Health care; Human services; Children/youth, services; Federated giving programs; Christian agencies & churches; Roman Catholic agencies & churches.
Limitations: Applications not accepted. Giving primarily in FL, with emphasis on Jacksonville. No grants to individuals.
Application information: Contributes only to pre-selected organizations.
Officers and Directors:* Jack C. Demetree,* Pres.; Jack C. Demetree, Jr.,* V.P.; Elisa A. Demetree,*

Secy.-Treas.; Betty A. Demetree; Christopher C. Demetree; Mark C. Demetree; Leslie A. Demetree-Doherty.
EIN: 593407379
Selected grants: The following grants were reported in 2004.
$100,000 to Diocese of Saint Augustine, Jacksonville, FL.
$33,000 to Saint Vincents Foundation, Jacksonville, FL.
$20,000 to Holy Family Hospital Foundation, DC.
$10,000 to Ronald McDonald House of Jacksonville, Jacksonville, FL.
$5,000 to Guardian of Dreams, Jacksonville, FL.
$5,000 to University of North Florida, Jacksonville, FL.
$3,000 to Florida School for the Deaf and Blind, Saint Augustine, FL.
$1,500 to City Rescue Mission, Jacksonville, FL.
$1,000 to Franciscan Friars of the Renewal, Bronx, NY.
$1,000 to Saint Marys Catholic Church, Macclenny, FL.

1968
Arthur S. DeMoss Foundation ▼ ✧
Phillips Point-W. Twr.
777 S. Flagler Dr., Ste. 1600W
West Palm Beach, FL 33401
Contact: Nancy S. DeMoss, Chair.

Incorporated in PA in 1955 as the National Liberty Foundation of Valley Forge, Inc.
Donor: Arthur S. DeMoss†.
Foundation type: Independent foundation.
Financial data (yr. ended 12/31/04): Assets, $404,839,028 (M); expenditures, $37,141,293; qualifying distributions, $34,728,855; giving activities include $23,542,949 for 87 grants, and $5,265,904 for 3 foundation-administered programs.
Purpose and activities: Support primarily for operating programs initiated and managed by the foundation itself that are evangelistic and disciplined in nature in the U.S. and other countries, primarily the Third World. To a limited extent, a few grants are made to organizations both in the U.S. and overseas that have these same goals.
Fields of interest: Christian agencies & churches.
International interests: Kenya; Tanzania; Uganda.
Type of support: Program development.
Limitations: Giving on an international basis. No support for local churches, denominational agencies and/or schools or colleges. No grants to individuals, or for scholarships or endowments; no loans.
Publications: Informational brochure (including application guidelines).
Application information: Application form not required.
  Initial approach: Brief proposal of not more than 2 pages
  Copies of proposal: 1
  Deadline(s): None
  Board meeting date(s): Quarterly
  Final notification: 90 to 120 days
Officers and Directors:* Nancy S. DeMoss,* Chair., C.E.O., and Treas.; Robert G. DeMoss,* Pres.; Charlotte DeMoss, Secy.; Elizabeth J. DeMoss.
Number of staff: 9 full-time professional; 8 full-time support.
EIN: 236404136
Selected grants: The following grants were reported in 2004.

$6,470,173 to Confederation of Independent States Ministries, Moscow, Russia. .
$3,300,000 to Prison Fellowship Ministries, DC.
$2,353,898 to Campus Crusade for Christ International, Orlando, FL. For programs in Eastern Europe.
$1,680,271 to East Africa Ministries, Nairobi, Kenya. .
$1,255,600 to Moody Bible Institute of Chicago, Chicago, IL.
$1,134,333 to Life Action Ministries, Buchanan, MI.
$200,000 to Delaware County Christian School, Newtown Square, PA.
$143,215 to Tennessee Temple University, Chattanooga, TN.
$75,000 to Fellowship of Christian Athletes, Kansas City, MO.
$10,000 to Morality in Media, New York, NY.

1969
The Overton and Katherine Dennis Fund ◇
c/o SunTrust Bank
P.O. Box 1908
Orlando, FL   32802
Application address: c/o SunTrust Bank, Attn.: Mgr., P.O. Box 26548, Richmond, VA 23261, tel.: (804) 782-5230

Established in 1987 in VA as successor trust to Dennis Fund.
Foundation type: Independent foundation.
Financial data (yr. ended 5/31/05): Assets, $7,375,355 (M); expenditures, $433,081; qualifying distributions, $392,960; giving activities include $380,500 for 51 grants (high: $25,000; low: $2,500).
Purpose and activities: Giving primarily for education, children and social services, Episcopal churches, and federated giving programs.
Fields of interest: Higher education; Education; Environment; Human services; Children, services; Federated giving programs; Protestant agencies & churches.
Type of support: Scholarship funds.
Limitations: Giving primarily in VA, with emphasis on Richmond. No grants to individuals.
Application information:
   Initial approach: Letter or proposal
   Deadline(s): None
   Board meeting date(s): Apr.
Officers and Directors:* Overton D. Dennis, Jr.,* Pres.; Janet D. Branch; Elizabeth O. Dennis; Janet Jackson Dennis.
Agent: SunTrust Bank.
EIN: 541418161
Selected grants: The following grants were reported in 2004.
$15,000 to Virginia College Fund, Richmond, VA.
$12,500 to Saint James Episcopal Church, Richmond, VA.
$10,000 to New Community School, Richmond, VA.
$10,000 to Virginia Union University, Richmond, VA.
$7,500 to Episcopal Diocese of Virginia, Richmond, VA.
$7,500 to Saint Catherines School, Richmond, VA.
$6,000 to William Byrd Community House, Richmond, VA.
$5,000 to Hampton University, Hampton, VA.
$2,500 to Christchurch School, Christchurch, VA.
$1,500 to Episcopal High School, Alexandria, VA.

1970
Wayne M. Densch Charitable Trust ◇
1603 E. Marks St.
Orlando, FL   32803
Contact: Leonard E. Williams, Pres.

Established in 1997 in FL.
Foundation type: Independent foundation.
Financial data (yr. ended 12/31/05): Assets, $27,483,224 (M); gifts received, $50,000; expenditures, $1,444,895; qualifying distributions, $1,340,196; giving activities include $1,334,846 for 23 grants (high: $400,000; low: $500).
Purpose and activities: Giving primarily for disadvantaged populations; support also for education.
Fields of interest: Education; Human services.
Limitations: Giving primarily in FL and NC. No grants to individuals.
Application information:
   Initial approach: Proposal
   Deadline(s): None
Officers: Leonard E. Williams, Pres. and Secy.-Treas.; John A. Williams, V.P.
EIN: 597033503

1971
The Dharma Foundation III, Inc. ◇
(formerly Worrell Foundation, Inc.)
14 S. Swinton Ave.
Delray Beach, FL   33444

Established in 1990 in DE and FL.
Donors: Thomas E. Worrell, Jr.; Odette A. Worrell; The Shaffer Worrell Charitable Lead Trust; First Union National Bank; Dharma Holdings, Ltd.
Foundation type: Operating foundation.
Financial data (yr. ended 11/30/04): Assets, $2,613,505 (M); gifts received, $280,386; expenditures, $726,072; qualifying distributions, $703,740; giving activities include $588,344 for 5 grants (high: $268,050; low: $15,000).
Purpose and activities: Giving primarily for education and human services.
Fields of interest: Education; Environmental education; Human services.
Limitations: Applications not accepted. Giving primarily in Delray Beach, FL, and Taos, NM; some funding also in New York, NY. No grants to individuals.
Application information: Contributes only to pre-selected organizations.
Officers and Director:* Thomas E. Worrell,* Chair.; Kimberly A. Goodyear, Pres. and Treas.; William Wintzer, Secy.
EIN: 650239353

1972
Margaret E. Dickins Foundation, Inc. ◇
1010 Monterey Blvd. N.E.
St. Petersburg, FL   33704
Contact: Laura Jenkins, Pres.

Established in 2001 in FL.
Donor: Margaret E. Dickens.
Foundation type: Independent foundation.
Financial data (yr. ended 12/31/03): Assets, $7,665,980 (M); gifts received, $283,800; expenditures, $413,095; qualifying distributions, $344,301; giving activities include $344,276 for 22 grants (high: $50,000; low: $1,000).

Purpose and activities: Giving primarily for the arts, health associations, and animal welfare; funding also for social services and children services, including an association for retarded children.
Fields of interest: Arts; Animal welfare; Health organizations, association; Crime/violence prevention, abuse prevention; Human services; Children, services.
Limitations: Giving primarily in FL. No grants to individuals.
Application information:
   Initial approach: Letter
   Deadline(s): None
Officers: Laura Jenkins, Pres.; Margaret Decker, Secy.; Norma Hanley, Treas.
EIN: 651082411
Selected grants: The following grants were reported in 2004.
$50,000 to Breast Cancer Research Foundation, New York, NY. For unrestricted support.
$50,000 to Society for the Prevention of Cruelty to Animals of Pinellas County, Largo, FL. For Cat room.
$30,000 to Christmas Toy Shop Project, Saint Petersburg, FL. 2 grants: $15,000 each (For unrestricted support).
$25,000 to Association for Retarded Children, Pinellas, Saint Petersburg, FL. For Toddler Computer Lab.
$20,000 to American Heart Association, Saint Petersburg, FL. For CPR program for high school students.
$20,000 to Great Explorations, Saint Petersburg, FL.
$20,000 to Science Center of Pinellas County, Saint Petersburg, FL. For Marine Life Room.
$15,000 to American Lung Association, Saint Petersburg, FL. For resource library.
$15,000 to Southeastern Guide Dogs, Palmetto, FL. For puppy raising program.

1973
The Dickinson Foundation, Inc. ◇ ☆
c/o Robert H. Dickinson
3655 N.W. 87th Ave.
Miami, FL   33178

Established in 2004 in FL.
Donor: Robert H. Dickinson.
Foundation type: Independent foundation.
Financial data (yr. ended 12/31/05): Assets, $3,214,907 (M); gifts received, $649,166; expenditures, $383,166; qualifying distributions, $365,125; giving activities include $365,125 for 7 grants (high: $310,000; low: $2,000).
Officers: Robert H. Dickinson, Pres.; Jolynn Dickinson, V.P.; Kristin M. Hogue, Treas.
EIN: 223901478

1974
The Paul J. DiMare Foundation ◇
c/o Paul J. DiMare
P.O. Box 900460
Homestead, FL   33090-0460

Established in 1995 in FL.
Donor: Paul J. DiMare.
Foundation type: Independent foundation.
Financial data (yr. ended 12/31/05): Assets, $21,485,330 (M); gifts received, $2,000,000; expenditures, $1,140,388; qualifying distributions,

$1,068,031; giving activities include $1,068,031 for 32 grants (high: $400,001; low: $500).

Purpose and activities: Giving primarily for education; support also for Roman Catholic churches.

Fields of interest: Secondary school/education; Higher education; Higher education, college; Homeless, human services; Roman Catholic agencies & churches.

Limitations: Applications not accepted. Giving primarily in FL. No grants to individuals.

Application information: Contributes only to pre-selected organizations.

Trustee: Paul J. DiMare.

EIN: 650537843

1975
Walter S. and Lucienne B. Driskill Charitable Foundation ◇

4333 N. Ocean Blvd.
Delray Beach, FL   33483

Established in 1986 in FL.

Donor: Walter S. Driskill.

Foundation type: Independent foundation.

Financial data (yr. ended 12/31/05): Assets, $4,633,834 (M); expenditures, $397,939; qualifying distributions, $389,692; giving activities include $355,000 for 7 grants (high: $100,000; low: $1,500).

Purpose and activities: Giving primarily to hospitals including a cancer center; some funding also for youth, and social services including services for people who are blind or partially sighted.

Fields of interest: Hospitals (general); Hospitals (specialty); Children/youth, services; Protestant agencies & churches; Blind/visually impaired; Migrant workers.

Limitations: Applications not accepted. Giving primarily in Boynton Beach, FL; some funding also in New York, NY and CT. No grants to individuals.

Application information: Contributes only to pre-selected organizations.

Directors: Ronald L. Barnard; Carmine Figlilio; Edward A. Kennedy.

EIN: 061190296

1976
The Ds Foundation ◇ ☆

7446 Fisher Island Dr.
Fisher Island, FL   33109

Foundation type: Independent foundation.

Financial data (yr. ended 12/31/04): Assets, $3,088,686 (M); expenditures, $792,608; qualifying distributions, $792,250; giving activities include $744,250 for 5 grants (high: $600,000; low: $1,000).

Purpose and activities: Giving to organizations that are interested in social and economic changes in India through education, employment, and public health projects.

Fields of interest: Elementary school/education; Higher education; Women; Economically disadvantaged.

Limitations: Applications not accepted.

Application information: Unsolicited requests for funds not accepted.

Directors: Bharat Desai; Neerja Sethi.

EIN: 412115627

1977
DuBow Family Foundation, Inc. ◇

P.O. Box 57759
Jacksonville, FL   32241-7759

Established in 1989.

Donor: Lawrence J. DuBow.

Foundation type: Independent foundation.

Financial data (yr. ended 8/31/05): Assets, $9,322,790 (M); gifts received, $477,749; expenditures, $435,048; qualifying distributions, $419,346; giving activities include $419,308 for 74 grants (high: $143,000; low: $50).

Purpose and activities: Giving to Jewish organizations and for Jewish education, including a theological seminary, as well for the arts, education, children and family services, and social services for the homeless and the needy.

Fields of interest: Arts; Elementary/secondary education; Higher education; Education; Health organizations, association; Human services; Children/youth, services; Family services; Jewish federated giving programs; Jewish agencies & temples.

Limitations: Applications not accepted. Giving primarily in Jacksonville, FL; some funding nationally. No grants to individuals.

Application information: Unsolicited requests for funds not accepted.

Officers and Trustees:* Lawrence J. DuBow,* Pres.; Helen A. DuBow, V.P.; Michael DuBow,* V.P.; Susan E. DuBow,* V.P.; Linda J. DuBow,* Treas.

EIN: 592981682

1978
Frank E. Duckwall Foundation, Inc. ◇

P.O. Box 3351
Tampa, FL   33601-3351   (813) 258-6660
Contact: Frank J. Rief, III, Tr.

Established in 1983 in FL.

Donor: Frank E. Duckwall†.

Foundation type: Independent foundation.

Financial data (yr. ended 12/31/05): Assets, $9,828,101 (M); expenditures, $582,299; qualifying distributions, $492,946; giving activities include $464,285 for 34 grants (high: $100,000; low: $1,000), and $7,776 for 1 employee matching gift.

Fields of interest: Museums; Higher education; Environment; Human services.

Type of support: Capital campaigns; Building/ renovation; Equipment; Endowments; Professorships; Scholarship funds; Research; Matching/challenge support.

Limitations: Giving limited to the Tampa Bay, FL, area.

Publications: Financial statement; Informational brochure (including application guidelines); Occasional report.

Application information: Application form required.

  Initial approach: Letter
  Copies of proposal: 3
  Deadline(s): 2 weeks before meeting
  Board meeting date(s): Mar., June, Sept., and Dec.
  Final notification: 2 weeks after board meeting

Officer and Trustees:* James M. Kelly,* Pres.; G. Lowe Morrison; Frank J. Rief III.

EIN: 596773462

1979
Elizabeth Ordway Dunn Foundation, Inc. ◇

P.O. Box 016309
Miami, FL   33101-6309   (305) 445-5521
Contact: Robert W. Jensen, Dir.
E-mail: rwjensen@eodunn.org; Additional application address: c/o E. Rodman Titcomb, Jr., Dir., P.O. Box 3267, Palm Beach, FL, 33480-3267, tel.: (561) 832-5826; E-mail: eodf@worldnet.att.net; URL: http://www.eodunn.org/

Incorporated in 1984 in FL.

Donor: Elizabeth Ordway Dunn Charitable Lead Trust.

Foundation type: Independent foundation.

Financial data (yr. ended 12/31/04): Assets, $916,479 (M); gifts received, $661,772; expenditures, $689,800; qualifying distributions, $677,111; giving activities include $532,000 for 32 grants (high: $40,000; low: $5,000).

Purpose and activities: Giving for conservation, ecology, wildlife, and other environmental concerns in the state of FL.

Fields of interest: Environment, natural resources; Environment.

Type of support: Program development; Seed money; Matching/challenge support.

Limitations: Giving primarily in FL. No support for sectarian religious activities. No grants to individuals, or for capital purposes, operating budgets, endowments, or deficit financing.

Publications: Annual report; Informational brochure (including application guidelines).

Application information: Applicants are urged to submit concept papers; if the paper is reviewed favorably, a full proposal will be requested. One copy should be sent to the main address, and one to the additional application address. Applications sent by fax not accepted. Application form not required.

  Initial approach: Telephone calls to Program Staff encouraged
  Copies of proposal: 2
  Deadline(s): Mar. 15 and Sept. 15
  Board meeting date(s): May and Nov.
  Final notification: Following board meetings

Directors: Robert W. Jensen; Donna McKinney Lummus; E. Rodman Titcomb, Jr.

Number of staff: 2 part-time professional; 1 part-time support.

EIN: 592393843

Selected grants: The following grants were reported in 2003.

$30,000 to Florida Wildlife Federation, Tallahassee, FL.

$25,000 to Apalachicola Bay and Riverkeeper, Apalachicola, FL.

$25,000 to Conservancy of Southwest Florida, Naples, FL.

$25,000 to Conservation Fund, Arlington, VA.

$25,000 to Defenders of Wildlife, DC.

$25,000 to Environmental Law Institute, DC.

$20,000 to Legal Environmental Assistance Foundation, Tallahassee, FL.

$20,000 to Tall Timbers Research Stations, Tallahassee, FL.

$15,000 to University of Florida Foundation, Gainesville, FL.

$10,000 to Reef Relief, Key West, FL.

1980
Dunn's Foundation for the Advancement of Right Thinking ✧
309 S.E. Osceola St., Ste. 208
Stuart, FL 34994
Contact: William A. Dunn, Tr.

Established in 1993 in FL.
Donors: William A. Dunn; William A. Dunn Trust.
Foundation type: Independent foundation.
Financial data (yr. ended 3/31/06): Assets, $64,996,983 (M); gifts received, $600,000; expenditures, $3,274,471; qualifying distributions, $3,215,009; giving activities include $3,185,000 for 25 grants (high: $480,000; low: $5,000).
Purpose and activities: Giving primarily to organizations that are concerned with public affairs issues.
Fields of interest: Public affairs, research; Public policy, research; Public affairs.
Limitations: Applications not accepted. Giving primarily in GA. No grants to individuals.
Application information: Contributes only to pre-selected organizations.
Trustee: William A. Dunn.
EIN: 650415977
Selected grants: The following grants were reported in 2005.
$500,000 to Competitive Enterprise Institute, DC.
$450,000 to Reason Foundation, Los Angeles, CA.
$350,000 to Institute for Justice, DC.
$350,000 to Landmark Legal Foundation, Leesburg, VA.
$200,000 to Pacific Legal Foundation, Sacramento, CA.
$170,000 to National Tax Research Committee, Houston, TX.
$126,000 to Mackinac Center for Public Policy, Midland, MI.
$100,000 to Cato Institute, DC.
$75,000 to Institute for Humane Studies, Arlington, VA.
$60,000 to Objectivist Center, Poughkeepsie, NY.

1981
The Dunspaugh-Dalton Foundation, Inc. ✧
1500 San Remo Ave., Ste. 103
Coral Gables, FL 33146-3054
Contact: William A. Lane, Jr., Pres.
Application address: 1533 Sunset Dr., Ste. 150, Coral Gables, FL 33143

Incorporated in 1963 in FL.
Donor: Ann V. Dalton†.
Foundation type: Independent foundation.
Financial data (yr. ended 12/31/04): Assets, $36,348,192 (M); expenditures, $2,014,759; qualifying distributions, $1,617,626; giving activities include $1,290,065 for 60 grants (high: $200,000; low: $500).
Purpose and activities: Giving primarily for the arts, education, health, social services, and youth activities.
Fields of interest: Performing arts; Arts; Elementary/secondary education; Higher education; Education; Hospitals (general); Health organizations, association; Boys & girls clubs; Youth development, services; Human services; Children/youth, services; Protestant agencies & churches.
Type of support: General/operating support; Continuing support; Capital campaigns; Endowments; Program development; Professorships; Matching/challenge support.

Limitations: Giving primarily in San Francisco and Monterey, CA, Dade County, FL, and NC. No grants to individuals; no loans.
Publications: Application guidelines.
Application information: Application form required.
Initial approach: Letter
Copies of proposal: 1
Deadline(s): None
Board meeting date(s): Monthly
Officers and Trustees:* William A. Lane, Jr.,* Pres.; Sarah H. Bonner,* V.P.; Leslie Buchanan, Secy.-Treas.; Thomas H. Wakefield, Secy.-Treas.
Number of staff: 3 part-time professional; 2 part-time support.
EIN: 591055300
Selected grants: The following grants were reported in 2003.
$162,000 to Palmer Trinity School, Miami, FL. For general support.
$30,000 to Coconut Grove Playhouse State Theater of Florida Corporation, Miami, FL. For general support.
$25,000 to Boys and Girls Clubs of Monterey County, Seaside, CA. For general support.
$20,000 to Hearing Research Institute, South Miami, FL. For general support.
$10,000 to Hope Center, Miami, FL. For general support.
$10,000 to Monterey Jazz Festival, Monterey, CA. For general support.
$5,500 to Barry University, Miami, FL. For general support.
$5,000 to Forest Theater Guild, Carmel, CA. For general support.
$5,000 to Miami Rescue Mission, Miami, FL. For general support.
$2,000 to Chartwell School, Seaside, CA. For general support.

1982
Alfred I. duPont Foundation, Inc.
4600 Touchton Rd. E., Bldg. 200, Ste. 120
Jacksonville, FL 32246 (904) 232-4123
Contact: Rosemary C. Wills, Secy.

Incorporated in 1936 in FL.
Donor: Jessie Ball duPont†.
Foundation type: Independent foundation.
Financial data (yr. ended 12/31/05): Assets, $35,165,662 (M); expenditures, $1,740,235; qualifying distributions, $1,600,454; giving activities include $1,031,450 for 106 grants, and $460,575 for 350 grants to individuals.
Purpose and activities: Giving primarily to the elderly in distressed situations requiring health, economic, or educational assistance; support also for higher education and medical research.
Fields of interest: Higher education; Medical research, institute; Aging, centers/services; Christian agencies & churches; Protestant agencies & churches; Roman Catholic agencies & churches; Aging; Economically disadvantaged.
Type of support: General/operating support; Grants to individuals.
Limitations: Giving primarily in the southeastern U.S., with emphasis on FL.
Application information: Application forms are mailed upon request. Application form required.
Initial approach: Letter
Copies of proposal: 1
Deadline(s): None
Board meeting date(s): 2nd Tues. in Feb.

Officers and Directors:* R.E. Nedley,* Pres. and Treas.; E.C. Brownlie,* V.P.; W.W. Carlson,* V.P.; Rosemary C. Wills,* Secy.; Braden Ball, Jr.; Fred Kent, Jr.; Rush Loving; John Vaughn.
EIN: 591297267

1983
Jessie Ball duPont Fund ▼
(formerly Jessie Ball duPont Religious, Charitable and Educational Fund)
1 Independent Dr., Ste. 1400
Jacksonville, FL 32202-5011 (800) 252-3452
Contact: Sherry P. Magill Ph.D., Pres.
FAX: (904) 353-3870;
E-mail: contactus@dupontfund.org; Additional tel.: (800) 252-3452; Additional e-mails: smagill@dupontfund.org (for Sherry P. Magill), jbennett@dupontfund.org (for Jo Ann P. Bennett), sdouglass@dupontfund.org (for Sally Douglass), ekingjr.@dupontfund.org (for Edward King), sgreene@dupontfund.org (for Sharon Greene) and DSawyer@dupontfund.org (for Davena Sawyer); URL: http://www.dupontfund.org/

Trust established in 1976 in FL.
Donor: Jessie Ball duPont†.
Foundation type: Independent foundation.
Financial data (yr. ended 12/31/05): Assets, $293,833,036 (M); gifts received, $78,477; expenditures, $16,528,013; qualifying distributions, $15,266,503; giving activities include $12,732,685 for 504 grants (high: $500,000; low: $1,240; average: $5,000–$100,000), $45,000 for 2 loans to individuals, and $525,147 for 6 foundation-administered programs.
Purpose and activities: The Jessie Ball duPont Fund invests in organizations and communities that were important to Jessie Ball duPont.
Fields of interest: Historic preservation/historical societies; Arts; Secondary school/education; Higher education; Education; Health care; Crime/violence prevention; Human services; Children, day care; Youth, services; Economic development; Community development; Religion; AIDS, people with; Economically disadvantaged; Homeless.
Type of support: General/operating support; Management development/capacity building; Equipment; Program development; Conferences/seminars; Professorships; Publication; Seed money; Curriculum development; Research; Technical assistance; Consulting services; Program evaluation; Program-related investments/loans; Matching/challenge support.
Limitations: Giving primarily in the South, especially DE, FL, and VA. No support for organizations other than those awarded gifts by the donor from 1960-1964. No grants to individuals, or generally for capital campaigns or endowments.
Publications: Annual report (including application guidelines); Financial statement; Grants list; Informational brochure; Occasional report.
Application information: First-time applicants must submit proof with initial application that a contribution was received from the donor between 1960 and 1964. Application form required.
Initial approach: Brief proposal or telephone call to program staff
Copies of proposal: 1
Deadline(s): None
Board meeting date(s): Quarterly, beginning in Feb.
Final notification: Approximately 1 month

Officers and Trustees:* Mary K. Phillips,* Chair.; Leroy Davis,* Vice-Chair.; Sherry P. Magill, Ph.D., Pres.; Rt. Rev. Stephen H. Jecko, Clerical Tr.; Thomas Jeavons; Audrey McKibbin Moran; Robert M. Franklin.

Corporate Trustees: Stephen A. Lynch III; Northern Trust Bank of Florida, N.A.

Number of staff: 4 full-time professional; 3 full-time support.

EIN: 596368632

Selected grants: The following grants were reported in 2005.

$500,000 to American Red Cross, Delmarva Peninsula Chapter, Wilmington, DE. For relief effort for Hurricane Katrina, to be handled through National Headquarters.

$363,675 to Georgetown University, DC. To design and deliver annual executive institutes, and initiate professional development programs for institute alumni, building capacity of Fund eligible nonprofits, payable over 3 years.

$300,000 to Alfred I. duPont Awards Foundation, Jacksonville, FL. For Alfred I. duPont - Columbia University Awards in Broadcast Journalism.

$284,000 to Irvington Baptist Church, Irvington, VA. For partnership with Northern Neck Free Health Clinic to expand community pharmacy program for poor and elderly, payable over 3 years.

$280,000 to Epiphany Episcopal Church, Timonium, MD. For partnership with Episcopal Housing Corporation for core operating and capital support, payable over 4 years.

$200,000 to United Way of Northeast Florida, Jacksonville, FL. To provide saving match dollars for Jacksonville IDA partnerships, payable over 2 years.

$193,000 to Bluefield College, Bluefield, VA. To implement Noel-Levitz enrollment and revenue management system and undertake market research toward enrollment.

$50,000 to Catholic Charities Bureau, Jacksonville, FL. For partnership with Interchurch Coalition for Action, Reconciliation and Empowerment (ICARE).

$12,132 to Milligan College, Milligan College, TN. For faculty member participation in duPont Fund - National Humanities Center Summer Seminar.

$10,000 to Stetson University, DeLand, FL. For President's Discretionary Fund.

1984
David and Harriet Dyer Family Foundation ✧
100 Beach Dr. N.E., Ste. 1802
St. Petersburg, FL 33701-3969

Established in 2002 in WI.

Donors: David F. Dyer; Harriet Dyer.

Foundation type: Independent foundation.

Financial data (yr. ended 12/31/04): Assets, $2,700,178 (M); expenditures, $402,106; qualifying distributions, $366,219; giving activities include $370,000 for 5 grants (high: $250,000; low: $5,000).

Fields of interest: Higher education, college; Protestant agencies & churches.

Limitations: Applications not accepted. Giving primarily in MO and TX. No grants to individuals.

Application information: Contributes only to pre-selected organizations.

Trustees: David F. Dyer; Harriet Dyer.

EIN: 716193877

1985
Eagle's Wing Foundation, Inc. ✧ ☆
520 4th St. N.
Saint Petersburg, FL 33701 (727) 892-4688

Established in 1997 in FL.

Donor: William D. Morean.

Foundation type: Independent foundation.

Financial data (yr. ended 12/31/05): Assets, $12,505,316 (M); expenditures, $615,124; qualifying distributions, $607,500; giving activities include $607,500 for 6 grants (high: $500,000; low: $500).

Fields of interest: Human services; American Red Cross; Salvation Army.

Limitations: Applications not accepted. Giving limited to St. Petersburg, FL. No grants to individuals.

Application information: Contributes only to pre-selected organizations.

Officers and Directors:* Kelly D. Morean,* Pres. and Secy.; William D. Morean,* Treas.; Audrey Peterson.

EIN: 593437684

1986
Eckerd Family Foundation, Inc. ▼ ✧
P.O. Box 5165
Clearwater, FL 33758-5165 (727) 446-2996
E-mail: info@eckerdfamilyfoundation.org; E-mail concerning projects: grants@eckerdfamilyfoundation.org; URL: http://www.eckerdfamilyfoundation.org

Established in 1998 in FL.

Donor: Jack Eckerd‡.

Foundation type: Independent foundation.

Financial data (yr. ended 6/30/05): Assets, $33,682,023 (M); gifts received, $36,725,000; expenditures, $4,386,659; qualifying distributions, $4,383,175; giving activities include $3,782,517 for 64 grants (high: $242,194; low: $1,000; average: $10,000–$125,000).

Purpose and activities: The foundation is committed to promoting meaningful and lasting change to transform the lives of vulnerable youth and their families. The Eckerd Family Foundation's mission is to award grants to nonprofit organizations that provide and support innovative educational, preventative, therapeutic and rehabilitative programs for youth and their families.

Fields of interest: Elementary/secondary education; Housing/shelter; Boys & girls clubs; Human services; YM/YWCAs & YM/YWHAs; Children/youth, services; Family services; Women, centers/services; Homeless, human services; Community development; Foundations (community).

Type of support: Research.

Limitations: Giving primarily in FL. No grants to individuals, or for event tickets, advertising, or legislative lobbying.

Publications: Grants list.

Application information: Proposals are by invitation only. See foundation Web site for guidelines.

Initial approach: Concept paper (no more than 3 pages)

Deadline(s): None for concept paper; proposal deadlines will be assigned upon invitation

Officer: Joseph W. Clark, Pres.

Directors: Kathleen Swann Brooks; Terrell S. Clark; K. Richard Eckerd; Ruth B. Eckerd; William K.

Eckerd; Nancy E. Hart; Rosemary E. Lassiter; James T. Swann.

EIN: 592803659

Selected grants: The following grants were reported in 2005.

$242,194 to University of Miami, Center for Family Studies, Miami, FL. To train family therapists.

$230,346 to YMCA of the Suncoast, Clearwater, FL. To meet challenge grant from capital campaign.

$200,000 to Highlands Community Child Development Center, Highlands, NC. For capital construction project.

$198,209 to Eckerd Youth Alternatives, Clearwater, FL. For Hi-Five Early Intervention Program and scholarships.

$125,000 to Space Coast Marine Institute, Titusville, FL. For construction on Student Services and Administrative Building.

$101,500 to Computer Mentors Group, Tampa, FL. For computer training program and scholarships.

$68,500 to Young Life in Tampa, Tampa, FL. For Bridging the Achievement GAP Program.

$61,500 to Nativity Preparatory School of Wilmington, Wilmington, DE. For summer program and scholarships.

$49,000 to YMCA, Sarasota Family, Sarasota, FL. For emergency shelter and scholarships.

$40,000 to Childrens Campaign, Tallahassee, FL. For quantitative research on juvenile justice.

1987
The Cynthia G. Edelman Family Foundation ✧
6622 Southpoint Dr. S., Ste. 495
Jacksonville, FL 32216

Established in FL.

Donor: Cynthia G. Edelman.

Foundation type: Independent foundation.

Financial data (yr. ended 6/30/05): Assets, $15,862,419 (M); gifts received, $296,300; expenditures, $725,323; qualifying distributions, $708,900; giving activities include $708,900 for 21 grants (high: $101,300; low: $500).

Purpose and activities: Giving primarily to Jewish organizations and cultural educational organizations.

Fields of interest: Museums; Arts; Higher education; Theological school/education; Federated giving programs; Jewish federated giving programs; Jewish agencies & temples.

Limitations: Applications not accepted. Giving primarily in Jacksonville, FL; some funding also in New York, NY. No grants to individuals.

Application information: Contributes only to pre-selected organizations.

Trustee: Cynthia G. Edelman.

EIN: 597109743

Selected grants: The following grants were reported in 2004.

$300,500 to Hebrew Union College-Jewish Institute of Religion, New York, NY.

$100,000 to Cummer Museum of Art and Gardens, Jacksonville, FL.

$100,000 to Vanderbilt University, Nashville, TN. 2 grants: $50,000 each

$30,000 to Florida State University, Holocaust Institute, Tallahassee, FL.

$30,000 to Guardian of Dreams, Jacksonville, FL.

$15,000 to Hope Haven Childrens Clinic and Family Center, Jacksonville, FL.

$15,000 to United Way of Northeast Florida, Jacksonville, FL.

$9,150 to Bolles School, Jacksonville, FL.
$5,000 to Leadership Jacksonville, Jacksonville, FL.

1988
Emanuel and Klara Edelstein Foundation, Inc. ✧ ☆

c/o M. Beame
2425 Hollywood Blvd.
Hollywood, FL 33020
Contact: Emanuel Edelstein, Pres.

Established in 1979 in FL.
Donor: Emanuel Edelstein.
Foundation type: Independent foundation.
Financial data (yr. ended 8/31/05): Assets, $1,032,889 (M); expenditures, $551,927; qualifying distributions, $551,127; giving activities include $551,127 for 122 grants (high: $150,000; low: $18).
Purpose and activities: Grants for Jewish organizations, with emphasis on religious education and temple support.
Fields of interest: Elementary/secondary education; Human services; Jewish federated giving programs; Jewish agencies & temples.
International interests: Israel.
Limitations: Giving on a national and international basis, with emphasis on Israel.
Application information: Application form not required.
    Initial approach: Letter
    Deadline(s): None
Officer: Emanuel Edelstein, Pres.
EIN: 591932960

1989
The Edgemer Foundation, Inc. ✧

401 E. Las Olas Blvd., Ste. 2200
Fort Lauderdale, FL 33301

Established in 2000 in FL.
Donors: WLD Trust; DL Trust.
Foundation type: Independent foundation.
Financial data (yr. ended 12/31/05): Assets, $8,711,508 (M); gifts received, $3,000,000; expenditures, $2,625,823; qualifying distributions, $2,602,250; giving activities include $2,602,250 for 17 grants (high: $1,015,000; low: $10,000).
Fields of interest: Museums (art); Performing arts, orchestra (symphony); Higher education; Hospitals (general).
Limitations: Applications not accepted. No grants to individuals.
Application information: Contributes only to pre-selected organizations.
Directors: David W. Horvitz; David M. Roth; Linda H. Roth.
EIN: 650976539
Selected grants: The following grants were reported in 2005.
$1,015,000 to Bowdoin College, Brunswick, ME.
$435,000 to Wadsworth Atheneum, Hartford, CT.
$250,000 to Hartford Symphony Orchestra, Hartford, CT.
$100,000 to Connecticut Opera Association, Hartford, CT.
$75,000 to Mark Twain House, Hartford, CT.
$70,000 to Jewish Federation of Greater Hartford, West Hartford, CT.
$50,000 to Third Way Foundation, DC.

$20,000 to American Friends of the Wallace Collection, New York, NY.
$20,000 to Hartford Hospital, Hartford, CT.

1990
Edwards Family Foundation, Inc. ✧ ☆

(formerly William Edwards Foundation, Inc.)
6090 Central Ave.
St. Petersburg, FL 33707

Donor: William Edwards.
Foundation type: Independent foundation.
Financial data (yr. ended 6/30/05): Assets, $86,678 (M); gifts received, $1,627,460; expenditures, $1,585,099; qualifying distributions, $1,521,976; giving activities include $1,521,976 for 9 grants (high: $114,000; low: $2,499).
Fields of interest: Hospitals (general); Human services; Family services.
Limitations: Applications not accepted. Giving primarily in St. Petersburg, FL. No grants to individuals.
Application information: Contributes only to pre-selected organizations.
Directors: William L. Edwards; Michelle Sylvia; Derek Van Hoose.
EIN: 200198747

1991
Albert E. & Birdie W. Einstein Fund ✧

P.O. Box 246
Islamorada, FL 33036 (305) 664-5436
Contact: Joyce Boyer, Pres.

Established about 1967 in FL.
Donors: Albert E. Einstein†; Birdie W. Einstein†.
Foundation type: Independent foundation.
Financial data (yr. ended 6/30/05): Assets, $11,666,659 (M); expenditures, $1,116,862; qualifying distributions, $956,698; giving activities include $956,698 for 38 grants (high: $200,000; low: $350).
Purpose and activities: Giving primarily for the arts, education, and human services.
Fields of interest: Arts; Education; Boy scouts; Human services; Children/youth, services; Family services; Jewish federated giving programs; Christian agencies & churches; Jewish agencies & temples.
Limitations: Giving primarily in FL. No grants to individuals.
Application information: Application form required.
    Deadline(s): None
Officers: Joyce Boyer, Pres.; R.M. Gardner, V.P.; Harold Satchell, Secy.-Treas.
EIN: 596127412

1992
Ellis Foundation, Inc. ✧

P.O. Box 1879
Tarpon Springs, FL 34688-1879
(727) 938-0160
Contact: Peter J. Ristorcelli

Established in 1984 in FL.
Donor: A.L. Ellis†.
Foundation type: Independent foundation.
Financial data (yr. ended 12/31/05): Assets, $10,499,566 (M); expenditures, $525,229; qualifying distributions, $439,065; giving activities

include $414,100 for 14 grants (high: $280,000; low: $100).
Fields of interest: Higher education; Education; Hospitals (general); Human services; Children/youth, services; Christian agencies & churches.
Limitations: Giving primarily in FL. No grants to individuals.
Application information: Unsolicited requests for funds are generally not accepted. Most contributions are pre-selected.
    Initial approach: Letter
    Deadline(s): None
Officers and Directors:* Carol E. Martin,* Chair.; Stanley G. Gibson, Jr.,* Pres.; Stella Himonetos, Secy.
Directors: Helen J. Cahalin; Christine L. Gagnon; Paul Martin; Lynn A. Sharpe; John G. Thompson.
EIN: 592471638
Selected grants: The following grants were reported in 2003.
$100,000 to Saint Petersburg Junior College Development Foundation, Saint Petersburg, FL.
$80,000 to Pinellas County Education Foundation, Helen Ellis Memorial Scholarship Program, Largo, FL.
$50,000 to Tarpon Springs Shepherd Center, Tarpon Springs, FL.
$40,000 to Childrens Home Society of Florida, Tampa, FL.
$25,000 to University of South Florida Foundation, Tampa, FL.
$10,000 to Metropolitan Ministries, Tampa, FL.
$2,000 to University of South Florida, Center for Cardiovascular Research, Tampa, FL.
$1,000 to Make-A-Wish Foundation of Sarasota/Tampa Bay, Sarasota, FL.
$1,000 to Special Olympics Florida, Clermont, FL.
$500 to American Heart Association, Saint Petersburg, FL.

1993
Elster Foundation

35 Watergate Dr., Apt. 1504
Sarasota, FL 34236
Contact: Sydney E. Goldstein, Tr.

Established in 1964 in NY.
Donor: Robert S. Elster†.
Foundation type: Independent foundation.
Financial data (yr. ended 12/31/05): Assets, $6,762,581 (M); expenditures, $479,055; qualifying distributions, $365,750; giving activities include $365,750 for 43 grants (high: $85,500; low: $250).
Purpose and activities: Giving for the arts, education, the environment, health, and Jewish organizations.
Fields of interest: Arts; Higher education; Education; Cancer research; Housing/shelter, development; Federated giving programs; Jewish agencies & temples.
Type of support: Continuing support; Annual campaigns; Capital campaigns; Building/renovation.
Limitations: Applications not accepted. Giving primarily in FL, Atlanta, GA, Buffalo, NY, and Martinsville, VA. No support for political organizations or religious education. No grants to individuals.
Application information: Contributes only to pre-selected organizations.

Trustees: Amy Gerome-Acuff; Douglas R. Goldstein; Elizabeth Geer Goldstein; Jerome E. Goldstein; Sydney E. Goldstein.
EIN: 166054742
Selected grants: The following grants were reported in 2004.
$53,000 to Sarasota Ballet of Florida, Sarasota, FL.
$25,000 to Carlisle School, Martinsville, VA.
$16,000 to Florida West Coast Symphony, Sarasota, FL.
$15,000 to Buffalo Philharmonic Orchestra, Buffalo, NY.
$7,500 to Salvation Army.
$2,500 to Alliance Theater, New Haven, CT.
$2,500 to Museum of Asian Art, Sarasota, FL.
$1,500 to Charity League, Corpus Christi, TX.
$1,000 to Sigma Alpha Mu Foundation, Carmel, IN.
$1,000 to Wake Forest University, Winston-Salem, NC.

1994
The Engelberg Foundation
1050 N. Lake Way
Palm Beach, FL 33480
Contact: Alfred B. Engelberg, Tr.
E-mail: aengelberg@nglbrg.com

Established in 1990 in CT.
Donor: Alfred Engelberg.
Foundation type: Independent foundation.
Financial data (yr. ended 1/31/06): Assets, $30,418,709 (M); expenditures, $2,712,242; qualifying distributions, $2,594,111; giving activities include $2,535,877 for 98 grants (high: $270,000; low: $250).
Purpose and activities: Primary areas of interest include primary healthcare coverage and serving the disadvantaged; some support also for issues concerning intellectual property law, Jewish organizations, and arts education.
Fields of interest: Arts, formal/general education; Arts education; Health care; Human services; Children/youth, services; Child development, services; Jewish agencies & temples; Economically disadvantaged.
International interests: Israel.
Type of support: General/operating support; Continuing support; Annual campaigns; Capital campaigns; Building/renovation; Emergency funds; Program development; Conferences/seminars; Professorships; Seed money; Curriculum development; Fellowships; Program evaluation; Program-related investments/loans.
Limitations: Applications not accepted. Giving primarily in FL and NY. No grants to individuals.
Application information:
Board meeting date(s): None
Trustees: Alfred Engelberg; Gail Engelberg.
Number of staff: None.
EIN: 061309603
Selected grants: The following grants were reported in 2004.
$2,000,000 to UJA-Federation of New York, New York, NY. For Engelberg Center for Children and Youth at Myers-JDC-Brookdale Institute in Jerusalem, devoted to promoting well-being of Israel's children and youth (Jewish and Arab-Israeli), with special commitment to the disadvantaged.
$167,000 to Congregation Beth Israel, Northfield, NJ. To pay off mortgage.
$100,000 to Jazz at Lincoln Center, New York, NY. For Essentially Ellington, high school music

program, and for construction of new education, performance, and broadcast facility.
$100,000 to National Museum of American Jewish History, Philadelphia, PA. For capital support.
$100,000 to Solomon R. Guggenheim Foundation, New York, NY. For unrestricted support.
$100,000 to United Hospital Fund of New York, New York, NY. To evaluate managed care programs in New York City.
$50,000 to Columbia University, New York, NY. To endow chair at Mailman School of Public Health and for fellowships for minority students.
$50,000 to Interactive Aging Network (IANet), New York, NY.
$50,000 to Jewish Community Center in Manhattan, New York, NY. For capital support.
$40,000 to Institute for Jewish and Community Research, San Francisco, CA. For unrestricted support.

1995
Epilepsy Research Foundation of Florida, Inc. ◇
10530 N.W. 15th Pl.
Gainesville, FL 32606
Contact: B.J. Wilder M.D., Pres.

Donors: Pfizer Pharmaceutical Co., Inc.; McNeil Pharmaceuticals; Ortho-McNeil Pharmaceutical, Inc.; Warner-Lambert Co.; Rose Wichtenstein†; Abbott/Wendermere; Cybelonics; E.I. du Pont de Nemours and Co.; Parke, Davis & Co.; Novartis Corp., Inc.
Foundation type: Independent foundation.
Financial data (yr. ended 8/31/05): Assets, $7,643,092 (M); gifts received, $53,900; expenditures, $772,376; qualifying distributions, $740,704; giving activities include $555,150 for 2 grants (high: $550,150; low: $5,000).
Purpose and activities: Giving only for the study of the nature and treatment of epileptic disorders.
Fields of interest: Medical research, institute.
Limitations: Giving limited to northern FL.
Application information:
Initial approach: Proposal
Deadline(s): None
Officers: B.J. Wilder, M.D., Pres.
Director: B.J. Wilder, Jr.
EIN: 237290166

1996
Faigen Family Foundation, Inc. ◇
P.O. Box 42
Palm Beach, FL 33480

Established in 1997 in FL.
Donor: George Faigen.
Foundation type: Independent foundation.
Financial data (yr. ended 12/31/05): Assets, $10,651,244 (M); expenditures, $707,725; qualifying distributions, $644,617; giving activities include $643,000 for 3 grants (high: $300,000; low: $135,000).
Fields of interest: Elementary/secondary education; Dental care; Protestant agencies & churches.
Type of support: General/operating support.
Limitations: Applications not accepted. Giving primarily in Washington, DC, Tallahassee and West Palm Beach, FL, and Baltimore, MD. No grants to individuals.

Application information: Contributes only to pre-selected organizations.
Officers: Greta Faigen, Pres.; Lisa Seigel, V.P.; Brenda McGowan, Secy.; Andrew Faigen, Treas.
Directors: Amanda Faigen; Warren Miller.
EIN: 311509512

1997
Miguel B. Fernandez Family Foundation ◇ ☆
121 Alhambra Plz., Ste. 1100
Coral Gables, FL 33134

Established in 2002.
Donor: Miguel B. Fernandez.
Foundation type: Independent foundation.
Financial data (yr. ended 12/31/05): Assets, $292,196 (M); gifts received, $195,000; expenditures, $356,058; qualifying distributions, $327,950; giving activities include $327,950 for 11 grants (high: $219,000; low: $200).
Limitations: Applications not accepted. No grants to individuals.
Application information: Contributes only to pre-selected organizations.
Trustee: Miguel B. Fernandez.
EIN: 597228125

1998
Ferraro Family Foundation, Inc. ◇
4000 Ponce De Leon Blvd., Ste. 700
Coral Gables, FL 33146

Established in 1999 in FL.
Donor: James L. Ferraro.
Foundation type: Independent foundation.
Financial data (yr. ended 6/30/05): Assets, $1,855,650 (M); gifts received, $1,341,000; expenditures, $660,632; qualifying distributions, $594,404; giving activities include $594,404 for 15 grants (high: $200,000; low: $500).
Fields of interest: Education; Health organizations, association; Cancer research; Human services; Children/youth, services.
Limitations: Applications not accepted. Giving primarily in Miami, FL. No grants to individuals.
Application information: Contributes only to pre-selected organizations.
Officers and Directors:* James L. Ferraro,* Pres.; Louis Ferraro; Luella S. Ferraro.
EIN: 650953780
Selected grants: The following grants were reported in 2003.
$48,000 to Make-A-Wish Foundation of South Florida, West Coast Office, Fort Lauderdale, FL. For general operating support.
$30,250 to Childrens Home Society of Florida, Miami, FL. For general operating support.
$29,300 to Buoniconti Fund to Cure Paralysis, Miami, FL. For general operating support.
$25,000 to Jackson Memorial Foundation, Miami, FL. For general operating support.
$24,500 to ICARE Bay Point Schools, Miami, FL. 2 grants: $14,300 (For general operating support), $10,200 (For general operating support).
$22,000 to American Cancer Society, Miami, FL. For general operating support.
$12,500 to Archdiocese of Miami, Miami Shores, FL. For general operating support.
$500 to Elway Foundation, Englewood, CO. For general operating support.

$500 to University of Miami, Womens Cancer Association, Coral Gables, FL. For general operating support.

1999
Jerome & Anne C. Fisher Charitable Foundation ✧
c/o Caler, Donten & Levine, et al.
505 S. Flagler Dr., Ste. 900
West Palm Beach, FL   33401-5923

Established in 1996 in CT and FL.
Foundation type: Independent foundation.
Financial data (yr. ended 12/31/04): Assets, $16,184,358 (M); expenditures, $1,662,826; qualifying distributions, $1,437,066; giving activities include $1,330,958 for 40 grants (high: $500,000; low: $20).
Purpose and activities: Giving primarily for health associations, the arts, education, social services, federated giving programs, Roman Catholic churches, and Jewish organizations.
Fields of interest: Museums (art); Museums (ethnic/folk arts); Arts; Higher education; Cancer research; Biomedicine research; Human services; Jewish federated giving programs; Roman Catholic agencies & churches; Jewish agencies & temples.
Limitations: Applications not accepted. Giving primarily in FL, and New York, NY. No grants to individuals.
Application information: Contributes only to pre-selected organizations.
Officer: Jodi Fisher, Mgr.
Trustees: Joel Kozol; John Zampino.
EIN: 650533147
Selected grants: The following grants were reported in 2004.
$53,000 to Greenwich Country Day School, Greenwich, CT.
$26,000 to Norton Museum of Art, West Palm Beach, FL.
$12,025 to Saint Edwards Catholic Church, Palm Beach, FL.
$7,000 to Womens International Zionist Organization, New York, NY.
$5,550 to Childrens Place at Home Safe, West Palm Beach, FL.
$3,000 to Special Operations Warrior Foundation, Tampa, FL.
$2,500 to Breast Cancer Alliance, Greenwich, CT.
$2,250 to Elizabeth Glaser Pediatric AIDS Foundation, New York, NY.
$1,000 to Diocese of Palm Beach, Palm Beach Gardens, FL.
$900 to Childrens Home Society of Florida, West Palm Beach, FL.

2000
Miles and Shirley Fiterman Charitable Foundation ✧
229 Via Las Brisas
Palm Beach, FL   33480

Established in 1986 in FL.
Donors: Miles Q. Fiterman; Shirley L. Fiterman.
Foundation type: Independent foundation.
Financial data (yr. ended 12/31/05): Assets, $54,371,459 (M); expenditures, $2,848,876; qualifying distributions, $2,795,697; giving activities include $2,793,792 for 44 grants (high: $255,000; low: $50).

Purpose and activities: Giving primarily for the arts, and Jewish welfare; support also for medical research culture, and higher education.
Fields of interest: Arts; Higher education; Health organizations, association; Medical research, institute; Jewish federated giving programs; Jewish agencies & temples.
Limitations: Applications not accepted. Giving on a national basis. No grants to individuals.
Application information: Contributes only to pre-selected organizations.
Trustees: Miles Q. Fiterman; Shirley L. Fiterman; Valerie Hershmann.
EIN: 411582224
Selected grants: The following grants were reported in 2005.
$325,000 to Jewish Federation of Palm Beach County, West Palm Beach, FL.
$255,000 to Norton Museum of Art, West Palm Beach, FL.
$50,200 to Gastro-Intestinal Research Foundation, Chicago, IL.
$40,000 to American Friends of the Israel Museum, New York, NY.
$25,000 to Palm Beach County Cultural Council, West Palm Beach, FL.
$21,000 to American Friends of the Tel Aviv Museum, New York, NY.
$11,000 to Rochester Art Center, Rochester, MN.
$5,900 to Society of the Four Arts, Palm Beach, FL.
$5,450 to Minneapolis Institute of Arts, Minneapolis, MN.
$5,000 to Center for Creative Education, West Palm Beach, FL.

2001
Five Millers Family Foundation, Inc. ✧
c/o Paul Steinberg & Neil Mangot
767 Arthur Godfrey Rd.
Miami Beach, FL   33140-3413
Contact: Paul Steinberg, Pres.

Established in 1997 in FL.
Donors: Dora Miller Irrevocable Trust; Sadye Miller Irrevocable Trust.
Foundation type: Independent foundation.
Financial data (yr. ended 12/31/04): Assets, $6,768,454 (M); gifts received, $145,944; expenditures, $538,215; qualifying distributions, $538,215; giving activities include $359,471 for 40 grants (high: $51,025; low: $250).
Purpose and activities: Giving primarily to hospitals, and Jewish agencies and temples. Organizations to which Sadye or Dora Miller or members of their families contributed during their lifetimes will be given greater consideration.
Fields of interest: Museums (children's); Hospitals (general); Hospitals (specialty); Health organizations, association; Human services; Federated giving programs; Jewish federated giving programs; Jewish agencies & temples.
Limitations: Giving primarily in Miami, FL, and NY; some funding nationally. No grants to individuals.
Application information:
  Initial approach: Letter
  Deadline(s): None
Officers and Directors:* Paul Steinberg,* Pres.; Neil Mangot,* V.P. and Secy.
EIN: 650715711
Selected grants: The following grants were reported in 2003.
$61,000 to Miami Childrens Museum, Miami, FL. For general support.

$33,000 to Diabetes Research Institute, Miami, FL. For general support.
$25,000 to Nova Southeastern University, School of Dental Medicine, Fort Lauderdale, FL. For general support.
$24,000 to Coalition Against Domestic Violence, Superior, WI. For general support.
$15,000 to Coconut Grove Playhouse State Theater of Florida Corporation, Miami, FL. For general support.
$12,000 to Daughters of Sarah Jewish Foundation, Albany, NY. For general support.
$10,000 to Yeshiva University, New York, NY. For general support.
$5,000 to Miami Childrens Hospital, Miami, FL. For general support.
$5,000 to YMCA of Greater New York, New York, NY. For general support.
$1,200 to Temple Beth Sholom, Miami Beach, FL. For general support.

2002
Flight Attendant Medical Research Institute, Inc. ☆
201 S. Biscayne Blvd., Ste. 1310
Miami, FL   33131   (305) 379-7007
Contact: Elizabeth A. Kress, Exec. Dir.
FAX: (305) 577-0005; E-mail: ekress@famri.org;
URL: http://www.famri.org

Established in 2000 in FL.
Foundation type: Independent foundation.
Financial data (yr. ended 9/30/05): Assets, $299,116,348 (M); expenditures, $34,324,238; qualifying distributions, $23,171,341; giving activities include $21,339,401 for 159 grants (high: $1,627,494; low: $20,000; average: $108,500–$217,000).
Purpose and activities: FAMRI's mission is to sponsor scientific and medical research for the early detection, prevention, treatment and cure of diseases and medical conditions caused from exposure to tobacco smoke and to ensure that health care providers ask the right questions of their patients about second hand tobacco smoke exposure.
Fields of interest: Cancer; Medical research, institute; Cancer research; Medical research; Science.
Limitations: Giving on a national basis. No grants to individuals who are currently receiving money from tobacco companies.
Publications: Application guidelines.
Application information: Each proposal must be accompanied by an institutional Tobacco Disclosure statement and an individual Disclosure statement. NOTE: Submissions for clinical Innovator awards and Young clinical scientist awards for the 2006-2007 funding cycle are no longer being accepted. Application form required.
  Initial approach: Download application forms provided for applicant's proposal on foundation Web site
  Deadline(s): Sept. 15
  Final notification: Mar. 1
Officers and Trustees:* Stanley Rosenblatt,* Chair. and C.E.O.; Elizabeth A. Kress, Exec. Dir.; Lani Blissard; Bland Lane; John B. Ostrow; Susan Rosenblatt; Leisa Sudderth; Patricia L. Young.
EIN: 651057724

2003
Florida Rock Industries Foundation, Inc. ◇
155 E. 21st St.
Jacksonville, FL 32206-2136 (904) 355-1781
Contact: John D. Milton, Jr., Secy.-Treas.
Application address: P.O. Box 4667, Jacksonville, FL 32201

Established in 1981 in FL.
Donor: Florida Rock Industries, Inc.
Foundation type: Company-sponsored foundation.
Financial data (yr. ended 9/30/05): Assets, $3,065,118 (L); gifts received, $600,000; expenditures, $536,610; qualifying distributions, $517,706; giving activities include $517,706 for 50 grants (high: $25,000; low: $300).
Purpose and activities: The foundation supports organizations involved with arts and culture, education, health, human services, and Christianity.
Fields of interest: Museums; Arts; Higher education; Education; Health care; Children/youth, services; Human services; Federated giving programs; Christian agencies & churches.
Type of support: Scholarship funds.
Limitations: Giving primarily in FL. No grants to individuals.
Application information: Application form not required.
 Initial approach: Proposal
 Deadline(s): None
Officers: Edward L. Baker, Pres.; John D. Baker II, V.P.; John D. Milton, Jr., Secy.-Treas.
Director: Thompson S. Baker II.
EIN: 592143326
Selected grants: The following grants were reported in 2003.
$40,000 to Saint Vincents Foundation, Jacksonville, FL.
$25,000 to Jacksonville Symphony Association, Jacksonville, FL.
$22,000 to United Way of Northeast Florida, Jacksonville, FL. 2 grants: $17,000, $5,000
$20,000 to First Coast Educational Leadership Center, Jacksonville, FL.
$20,000 to Jacksonville Zoological Society, Jacksonville, FL.
$20,000 to Kesler Mentoring Connection, Jacksonville, FL.
$10,000 to Edward Waters College, Jacksonville, FL.
$10,000 to Seamark Ranch, Jacksonville, FL.
$5,000 to Junior Achievement of Floridas First Coast, Jacksonville, FL.

2004
The Florman Family Foundation, Inc. ◇
401 E. Las Olas Blvd., Ste. 2200
Fort Lauderdale, FL 33301
Contact: Robert J. Puck, Pres.

Established in 1996 in FL.
Donor: Betty E. Florman†.
Foundation type: Independent foundation.
Financial data (yr. ended 12/31/03): Assets, $9,028,307 (M); gifts received, $120; expenditures, $546,339; qualifying distributions, $423,108; giving activities include $409,000 for 25 grants (high: $50,000; low: $1,000).
Purpose and activities: Giving for international higher education.
Fields of interest: Higher education; Human services.
Limitations: Giving primarily in FL.

Application information:
 Initial approach: Letter
 Deadline(s): None
Officers: Robert J. Puck, Pres.; Shelley Marciano, Secy.-Treas.
Directors: Mark Blank; Neil Florman.
EIN: 650662182
Selected grants: The following grants were reported in 2004.
$70,000 to Miami Childrens Hospital Foundation, Miami, FL.
$30,000 to Miami Childrens Museum, Miami, FL.
$30,000 to Miami Jewish Home and Hospital for the Aged, Miami, FL.
$25,000 to Big Brothers Big Sisters of Greater Miami, Miami, FL.
$25,000 to Farm Share, Florida City, FL.
$25,000 to Miami City Ballet, Miami Beach, FL.
$12,000 to Childrens Bereavement Center, South Miami, FL.
$10,000 to American Red Cross, Miami, FL.
$10,000 to Voices for Children Foundation, Miami, FL.
$5,000 to Best Buddies International, Miami, FL.

2005
The Foley Family Charitable Foundation ◇
601 Riverside Ave., 12th Fl.
Jacksonville, FL 32204-2950

Established in 1997 in CA.
Donor: William P. Foley II.
Foundation type: Independent foundation.
Financial data (yr. ended 12/31/05): Assets, $35,017,030 (M); gifts received, $7,015,000; expenditures, $5,385,628; qualifying distributions, $5,297,354; giving activities include $5,276,273 for 11 grants (high: $5,000,000; low: $1,000).
Purpose and activities: Giving primarily for education.
Fields of interest: Elementary school/education; Higher education; Education.
Limitations: Applications not accepted. Giving primarily in CA. No grants to individuals.
Application information: Contributes only to pre-selected organizations.
Officers: Lindsay E. Foley, Pres.; Carol J. Foley, Secy.
Directors: Ed Dewey; William P. Foley; Frank Willey.
EIN: 770472642
Selected grants: The following grants were reported in 2004.
$381,563 to Chapman University, Orange, CA. For general support.
$100,000 to Bolles School, Jacksonville, FL. For general support.
$100,000 to West Point Fund, West Point, NY. For general support.
$25,000 to First Tee of Monterey, Monterey, CA. For general support.
$25,000 to United States Central Command Memorial Foundation, Saint Petersburg, FL. For general support.
$13,500 to Montana Land Reliance, Helena, MT. For general support.
$10,000 to University of California at Santa Barbara Foundation, Santa Barbara, CA. For general support.
$10,000 to University of Washington, Seattle, WA. For general support.
$10,000 to Whitman College, Walla Walla, WA. For general support.
$1,000 to Disabled Sports USA, Alpine Meadows, CA. For general support.

2006
Mary C. Forbes Charitable Foundation ◇
c/o D'Arcy R. Clarie
1101 Pasadena Ave. S., Ste. 3
South Pasadena, FL 33707-2815

Established in 1998.
Donor: Mary C. Forbes.
Foundation type: Independent foundation.
Financial data (yr. ended 6/30/05): Assets, $6,648,806 (M); expenditures, $566,774; qualifying distributions, $456,675; giving activities include $369,628 for grants.
Purpose and activities: Giving to schools on behalf of students who are active practitioners of the Roman Catholic faith for the purpose of financing their Catholic education.
Fields of interest: Elementary/secondary education; Higher education; Theological school/education; Education.
Limitations: Applications not accepted. Giving primarily in FL. No grants to individuals.
Application information: Unsolicited requests for funds not accepted.
Trustee: D'Arcy R. Clarie.
EIN: 597112797
Selected grants: The following grants were reported in 2004.
$80,250 to Saint Petersburg Catholic High School, Saint Petersburg, FL. For scholarships.
$38,377 to Transfiguration Parish School, Saint Petersburg, FL. For scholarships.
$6,750 to Saint Peter Claver School, Tampa, FL. For scholarships.
$4,750 to Tampa Catholic High School, Tampa, FL. For scholarships.
$4,300 to Saint Anthony School, San Antonio, FL. For scholarships.
$4,000 to Clearwater Central Catholic High School, Clearwater, FL. For scholarships.
$3,000 to Villa Madonna School, Tampa, FL. For scholarships.
$2,900 to Guardian Angels Catholic School, Clearwater, FL. For scholarships.
$1,500 to Academy of the Holy Names School, Tampa, FL. For scholarships.
$1,250 to Mary Help of Christians School, Tampa, FL. For scholarships.

2007
The Fortin Foundation of Florida, Inc. ◇
125 Worth Ave., Ste. 318
Palm Beach, FL 33480
Contact: Lesly Stockard Smith, Pres.

Established in 1986 in FL.
Donor: Mary Alice Fortin.
Foundation type: Independent foundation.
Financial data (yr. ended 12/31/05): Assets, $47,767,701 (M); gifts received, $1,610,000; expenditures, $2,482,924; qualifying distributions, $2,204,358; giving activities include $2,168,218 for 150 grants (high: $500,000; low: $100).
Purpose and activities: Giving primarily for children's and other health care associations, a day care center, children, youth and social services, federated giving programs, and Roman Catholic churches.
Fields of interest: Higher education; Education; Health care; Health organizations; Disasters, preparedness/services; Human services; Children/youth, services; Children, day care; Federated giving programs; Roman Catholic agencies & churches.

Limitations: Giving primarily in FL and MT. No grants to individuals.
Application information: Application form not required.
> *Deadline(s):* None

Officers and Directors:* Lesly Stockard Smith,* Pres.; Susan Stockard Channing,* V.P.; Danielle Hickox.
EIN: 592707197

2008
Foundation for Cardiovascular Research ✧ ☆
100 Worth Ave., Ste. 609
Palm Beach, FL 33480-6710 (561) 655-4747
Contact: Jean Bellet Green, Pres.

Established in 1954 in FL and DE.
Foundation type: Independent foundation.
Financial data (yr. ended 7/31/05): Assets, $656,378 (M); expenditures, $357,405; qualifying distributions, $347,221; giving activities include $336,300 for 10 grants (high: $100,000; low: $300).
Purpose and activities: Giving primarily for medical research and health services.
Fields of interest: Higher education; Health care; Health organizations, association; Heart & circulatory diseases; Alzheimer's disease; Geriatrics; Residential/custodial care, hospices.
Type of support: General/operating support; Research.
Limitations: Giving in the U.S., with some emphasis on FL. No grants to individuals.
Application information:
> *Initial approach:* Letter
> *Deadline(s):* None

Officer: Jean Bellet Green, Pres.
EIN: 231476325

2009
Foundation in Christ Ministries: 1 Cor. 3:11, Inc. ✧ ☆
411 Spring Valley Ln.
Altamonte Springs, FL 32714

Established in 1995.
Donor: Kelly E. Curry.
Foundation type: Independent foundation.
Financial data (yr. ended 9/30/05): Assets, $359,187 (M); gifts received, $750,000; expenditures, $1,028,902; qualifying distributions, $1,021,492; giving activities include $1,021,492 for grants.
Fields of interest: Christian agencies & churches.
Limitations: Applications not accepted. Giving primarily in Galway, Ireland. No grants to individuals.
Application information: Contributes only to pre-selected organizations.
Officers: Kelly E. Curry, Pres.; Raymond L. Johnson, Secy.
Director: Susan M. Curry.
EIN: 593271100
Selected grants: The following grants were reported in 2003.
$101,966 to Foundation in Christ Ministries I Cor 3 11, Galway, Ireland. .
$10,000 to Gabriel House Foundation, Fort Myers, FL.
$10,000 to Only A Servant Ministries, San Antonio, TX.

$5,000 to Caring for China, Santa Ana, CA. For Teachers for China program.
$5,000 to Cornerstone Ministries, Jacksonville, FL.

2010
FPL Group Foundation, Inc. ✧
(formerly FPL Foundation, Inc.)
700 Universe Blvd.
Juno Beach, FL 33408-2683
Contact: John L. Kitchens, Mgr., Community Rels.
E-mail: john_kitchens@fpl.com; Application address: P.O. Box 029100, Miami, FL 33102

Established in 1987 in FL.
Donor: Florida Power & Light Co.
Foundation type: Company-sponsored foundation.
Financial data (yr. ended 12/31/05): Assets, $8,919,869 (M); gifts received, $1,870,763; expenditures, $2,444,477; qualifying distributions, $2,439,651; giving activities include $2,409,890 for 209 grants (high: $241,900).
Purpose and activities: The foundation supports organizations involved with arts and culture, education, the environment, health, human services, intergroup and race relations, community development, senior citizens, disabled people, minorities, economically disadvantaged people, and homeless people.
Fields of interest: Visual arts; Performing arts; Arts; Higher education; Education; Environment, energy; Environment; Health care; Human services; Civil rights, race/intergroup relations; Community development; Voluntarism promotion; Aging; Disabilities, people with; Minorities; African Americans/Blacks; Hispanics/Latinos; Economically disadvantaged; Homeless.
Type of support: Capital campaigns; Endowments; Employee matching gifts.
Limitations: Giving primarily in areas of company operations, with emphasis on the east coast of FL and the west coast from Bradenton to Naples. No support for religious or political organizations or United Way-affiliated agencies. No grants to individuals, or for endowments, travel, or conferences.
Publications: Application guidelines.
Application information: Application form required.
> *Initial approach:* Contact foundation for application form
> *Copies of proposal:* 1
> *Deadline(s):* Aug.
> *Final notification:* 4 to 6 weeks

Officers and Directors:* Lewis Hay III,* Chair.; Armando J. Olivera,* Pres. and Treas.; Dennis P. Coyle,* Secy.
Number of staff: 2 part-time support.
EIN: 650031452
Selected grants: The following grants were reported in 2004.
$277,000 to Volunteer Florida Foundation, Tallahassee, FL.
$266,875 to United Way. 2 grants: $254,000, $12,875
$75,000 to World Wildlife Fund, DC.
$50,000 to Salvation Army.
$17,500 to Benjamin School, North Palm Beach, FL.
$11,560 to National Merit Scholarship Corporation, Evanston, IL.
$10,941 to American Red Cross.
$3,500 to Save the Manatee Club, Maitland, FL.
$597 to Wake Forest University, Winston-Salem, NC.

2011
The Frazier Foundation ✧ ☆
201 Beachside Dr.
Vero Beach, FL 32963

Established in 2000.
Donor: Gary W. Frazier.
Foundation type: Independent foundation.
Financial data (yr. ended 6/30/06): Assets, $1,524,754 (M); gifts received, $1,200; expenditures, $426,786; qualifying distributions, $405,000; giving activities include $405,000 for grants.
Fields of interest: Cancer; Medical research; Human services; Economically disadvantaged; Homeless.
Limitations: Applications not accepted. Giving primarily in FL. No grants to individuals.
Application information: Contributes only to pre-selected organizations.
Officer: Gary W. Frazier, Pres.
EIN: 541993898
Selected grants: The following grants were reported in 2005.
$100,000 to Buoniconti Fund to Cure Paralysis, Miami, FL.
$75,000 to Cancer Institute of Florida, FL.
$10,000 to Source, The, Vero Beach, FL.
$5,000 to City Light Ministry Center, FL.
$2,000 to Council on Aging of Martin County, Stuart, FL.
$1,000 to Sneaker Exchange of Indian River County, Vero Beach, FL.

2012
Free Family Foundation Corp. ✧
P.O. Box 2036
Clearwater, FL 33757-2036

Established in 1999 in FL.
Donors: Harry J. Free; Carole J. Free.
Foundation type: Independent foundation.
Financial data (yr. ended 12/31/05): Assets, $1,622,201 (M); gifts received, $2,000,000; expenditures, $1,191,739; qualifying distributions, $1,190,195; giving activities include $1,182,000 for 22 grants (high: $500,000; low: $5,000).
Purpose and activities: Giving primarily for youth organizations, family and human service associations, environmental causes and Christian agencies.
Fields of interest: Education, ESL programs; Environment; Aquariums; Hospitals (general); Health care; Youth development, services; Human services; Aging, centers/services.
Limitations: Applications not accepted. Giving primarily in FL. No grants to individuals.
Application information: Contributes only to pre-selected organizations.
Officers: Harry J. Free, Pres.; Carole J. Free, V.P.; Diane E Hanlon, Secy.; Douglas J. Free, Treas.
Director: Thomas E. Free.
EIN: 593611945
Selected grants: The following grants were reported in 2004.
$100,000 to International Justice Mission, Alexandria, VA. For general support.
$100,000 to Lifelink Legacy Fund, Tampa, FL. For general support.
$100,000 to Missionary Flights International, West Palm Beach, FL. For general support.
$100,000 to UPARC Foundation. For general support.

$50,000 to Samaritans Purse, Boone, NC. For general support.

$50,000 to Teen Challenge International, USA, Springfield, MO. For general support.

$20,000 to Clearwater Marine Aquarium, Clearwater, FL. For general support.

$20,000 to Florida Oceanographic Society, Stuart, FL. For general support.

$20,000 to George T. Harrell History Center, FL. For general support.

$20,000 to Mercy Ships, Garden Valley, TX. For general support.

2013
The Fricks Private Foundation Trust ◇
2641 Bulrush Ln.
Naples, FL 34105-3049

Established in 2001 in FL.
Donor: William P. Fricks.
Foundation type: Independent foundation.
Financial data (yr. ended 12/31/05): Assets, $4,950,383 (M); gifts received, $30,126; expenditures, $418,868; qualifying distributions, $395,470; giving activities include $379,000 for 10 grants (high: $200,000; low: $5,000).
Purpose and activities: Giving primarily to Christian organizations and churches.
Fields of interest: Higher education; Christian agencies & churches.
Limitations: Applications not accepted. Giving on a national basis, with some emphasis on VA. No grants to individuals.
Application information: Contributes only to pre-selected organizations.
Officer: William P. Fricks, Pres.
Trustee: Deanie D. Fricks.
EIN: 656387910
Selected grants: The following grants were reported in 2005.
$106,000 to Regent University, Virginia Beach, VA.
$10,000 to Benny Hinn Ministries, Irving, TX.
$10,000 to International Fellowship of Christians and Jews, Chicago, IL.
$10,000 to Youth With A Mission, Lakeside, MT.

2014
Robert G. Friedman Foundation ◇
76 Isla Bahia Dr.
Fort Lauderdale, FL 33316-2331

Established in 1977.
Donors: Robert G. Friedman; Eugenie S. Friedman.
Foundation type: Independent foundation.
Financial data (yr. ended 12/31/05): Assets, $6,737,884 (M); expenditures, $435,377; qualifying distributions, $327,208; giving activities include $327,208 for 68 grants (high: $35,000; low: $25; average: $1,000–$5,000).
Purpose and activities: Giving primarily for the arts, education, health, and human services.
Fields of interest: Arts; Elementary/secondary education; Higher education; Medical care, in-patient care; Human services; Children/youth, services; Federated giving programs; Roman Catholic agencies & churches.
Type of support: General/operating support; Grants to individuals.
Limitations: Applications not accepted. Giving primarily in FL, MA, MI, OH, and WI.

Application information: Contributes only to pre-selected organizations.
Officers: Robert G. Friedman, Pres.; Eugenie S. Friedman, V.P.
Directors: Jane F. Anspach; Mary Friedman Baske; Jennifer Friedman Hillis; Elizabeth F. O'Connor.
EIN: 591726262

2015
Gainesville Community Foundation, Inc. ◇
2622 N.W. 43rd St., Ste. B3
Gainesville, FL 32606 (352) 367-0060
FAX: (352) 378-1718; E-mail: info@gnvcf.org;
URL: http://www.gnvcf.org

Established in 1998 in FL.
Foundation type: Community foundation.
Financial data (yr. ended 12/31/05): Assets, $2,045,000 (M); gifts received, $235,880; expenditures, $611,300; giving activities include $563,739 for 35 grants (high: $238,000; low: $16), and $3,000 for 2 grants to individuals (high: $1,500; low: $1,500).
Purpose and activities: The foundation seeks to promote and sustain philanthropy among the citizens of Gainesville and the surrounding areas.
Fields of interest: Arts; Higher education; Libraries/library science; Education; Environment; Animal welfare; Hospitals (general); Health care; Substance abuse, prevention; Medical research; Housing/shelter; Athletics/sports, water sports; Recreation; Family services; Human services; Philanthropy/voluntarism; Religion; Children/youth; Aging; Economically disadvantaged; Homeless.
Type of support: Grants to individuals.
Limitations: Giving limited to Gainesville and the surrounding areas in north central FL.
Officers and Directors:* Marilyn Tubb,* Chair.; Barzella Papa, C.E.O. and Pres.; Dink Henderson,* V.P.; Tony Kendzior,* Secy.; Michael Tillman,* Treas.; Jan Hughley,* Exec. Dir.; Jimmy Carnes; Ginny Cauthen; Phil Emmer; Howard Hall; Joan Jones; John Kirkpatrick; Wes Marston; Perry McGriff; Susan Parrish; Howard W. Patrick; Susannah Peddie; Mike Ryals; Stephen Shey; Melanie Shore; Thomas Spain; Portia Taylor; Ester Tibbs; Terry Van Nortwick; Stuart Wegener; Richard White; Vam York.
EIN: 593532330

2016
Joseph and Rae Gann Charitable Foundation ◇
10185 Collins Ave., Apt. 317
Bal Harbour, FL 33154

Established in 1990 in FL.
Donors: Joseph Gann†; Rae Gann†.
Foundation type: Independent foundation.
Financial data (yr. ended 12/31/05): Assets, $66,790,424 (M); expenditures, $3,178,665; qualifying distributions, $3,104,774; giving activities include $3,104,774 for 166 grants (high: $933,334; low: $100).
Purpose and activities: Giving primarily to Jewish agencies, schools, and temples.
Fields of interest: Elementary/secondary education; Jewish federated giving programs; Jewish agencies & temples.
Limitations: Applications not accepted. Giving primarily in the Boston, MA, area. No grants to individuals.

Application information: Contributes only to pre-selected organizations.
Trustees: Beverly G. Bavly; Herbert M. Gann; Shirley R. Saunders.
EIN: 656043241
Selected grants: The following grants were reported in 2005.
$934,334 to Hebrew College, Newton Centre, MA. 2 grants: $933,334, $1,000
$802,000 to Gann Academy New Jewish High School, Waltham, MA.
$203,600 to Hebrew Rehabilitation Center for Aged, Boston, MA.
$11,000 to Newton-Wellesley Hospital Charitable Foundation, Newton, MA.
$11,000 to Yeshiva Torah Vodaath, Brooklyn, NY.
$10,500 to New England Hebrew Academy, Brookline, MA.
$10,000 to Chelsea Jewish Nursing Home Foundation, Chelsea, MA.
$500 to Childrens Hospital.
$500 to Lahey Clinic Foundation, Burlington, MA.

2017
Garfinkle-Minard Foundation, Inc. ◇ ☆
(formerly Norton Garfinkle Foundation, Inc.)
2800 S. Ocean Blvd., Ste. 16-G
Boca Raton, FL 33432
Contact: Norton Garfinkle, Chair.
Application address: c/o Rita Buttolph, 133 E. 62nd St., New York, NY 10021, tel.: (212) 486-0194

Established in 1989 in FL.
Donor: Norton Garfinkle.
Foundation type: Independent foundation.
Financial data (yr. ended 12/31/05): Assets, $31,010 (M); gifts received, $261,244; expenditures, $347,765; qualifying distributions, $335,257; giving activities include $335,257 for grants.
Fields of interest: Historic preservation/historical societies; Arts; Higher education; Health organizations, association; Human services; Federated giving programs.
Type of support: General/operating support.
Limitations: Giving primarily in New York, NY. No grants to individuals.
Application information:
Initial approach: Letter
Deadline(s): None
Officers and Directors:* Norton Garfinkle,* Chair.; Sally Minard,* Pres.; Gillian Garfinkle; Nicholas Garfinkle.
EIN: 650104540
Selected grants: The following grants were reported in 2004.
$25,000 to Smith College, Northampton, MA.
$20,000 to Boston 2004, Boston, MA.
$20,000 to Communitarian Network, DC.
$3,900 to Metropolitan Museum of Art, New York, NY.
$1,500 to Battery Conservancy, New York, NY.
$1,250 to Montclair Art Museum, Montclair, NJ.
$1,200 to New York Public Library, New York, NY.
$1,000 to Museum of the City of New York, New York, NY.
$1,000 to Prep for Prep, New York, NY.
$1,000 to Womens Campaign International, Bala Cynwyd, PA.

2018
The Garner Foundation, Inc.
333 N.E. 23rd St.
Miami, FL 33137
Contact: Gerald W. Moore; John M. Garner

Established in 1987 in FL as a family foundation.
Foundation type: Independent foundation.
Financial data (yr. ended 3/31/06): Assets,
$11,128,942 (M); expenditures, $620,180;
qualifying distributions, $572,817; giving activities
include $570,267 for 49 grants (high: $100,000;
low: $500).
Purpose and activities: Giving primarily for
educational, religious, and medical organizations;
support also for community and cultural
organizations in FL and NC.
Fields of interest: Education; Health organizations,
association; Human services; Community
development.
Limitations: Giving primarily in FL and NC. No
support for political organizations. No grants to
individuals.
Application information: Application form not
required.
  Initial approach: Letter
  Deadline(s): None
  Board meeting date(s): Apr. and Dec.
Officers and Directors:* Beverly Garner Graves,*
Pres.; John Michael Garner,* V.P.; James W.
Moore,* Secy.; Kathryn Anne Paulk,* Treas.; Gerald
W. Moore; Janice Gayle Topping; Mary Garner
Wright.
Number of staff: 1 part-time professional.
EIN: 311471961
Selected grants: The following grants were reported
in 2005.
$100,000 to Miami Country Day School, Miami, FL.
$51,334 to Barry University, Miami, FL. 2 grants:
  $50,000, $1,334
$25,000 to Jackson Memorial Hospital, Miami, FL.
$10,000 to Players by the Sea, Jacksonville, FL.
$5,000 to Daily Bread Food Bank, Miami, FL.
$3,500 to American Red Cross, Miami, FL.
$2,500 to Miami Light Project, Miami, FL.
$1,060 to Fairchild Tropical Garden, Coral Gables,
  FL.
$1,000 to Women of Tomorrow, Miramar, FL.

2019
Gemcon Family Foundation ✧
231 Bradley Pl., Rm. 201
Palm Beach, FL 33480

Established in 2004 in FL.
Foundation type: Independent foundation.
Financial data (yr. ended 12/31/05): Assets,
$7,924,976 (M); gifts received, $2,349,178;
expenditures, $575,136; qualifying distributions,
$566,871; giving activities include $509,087 for 11
grants (high: $105,000; low: $1,087).
Purpose and activities: Giving primarily for the
educational purposes and betterment of at risk
youth; children with disabilities, and the promotion
of literacy.
Fields of interest: Adult education—literacy, basic
skills & GED; Education; Autism; Medical research;
Disasters, floods; Human services; Child
development, services; Family services.
Limitations: Applications not accepted. Giving
primarily in FL. No grants to individuals.
Application information: Unsolicited requests for
funds not accepted.

Trustees: Norma J. Bach; Judith Ann Jokiel; Charles
H. Warick III.
EIN: 576199853

2020
Louis V. Gerstner, Jr. Foundation, Inc. ✧
c/o Bessemer Trust Co. of Florida
222 Royal Palm Way
Palm Beach, FL 33480

Established in 1989 in NY.
Donor: Louis V. Gerstner, Jr.
Foundation type: Independent foundation.
Financial data (yr. ended 12/31/03): Assets,
$57,009,412 (M); gifts received, $6,285,413;
expenditures, $2,589,410; qualifying distributions,
$2,279,978; giving activities include $2,245,958
for 40 grants.
Purpose and activities: Giving primarily to a
university's department of ophthalmology, as well
as to a Roman Catholic church and a diocese;
funding also for the arts, hospitals, and human
services.
Fields of interest: Arts; Higher education; Medical
school/education; Hospitals (general); Eye
research; Human services; Roman Catholic
agencies & churches.
Limitations: Applications not accepted. Giving
primarily in Bridgeport and Greenwich, CT, and New
York, NY. No grants to individuals.
Application information: Contributes only to
pre-selected organizations.
Officers and Directors:* Louis V. Gerstner, Jr.,*
Chair.; Elizabeth R. Gerstner,* V.P.; Louis V.
Gerstner III,* V.P.; Darlene Jeris,* Secy.; Preston
Koster; Stan Litow.
EIN: 223045721
Selected grants: The following grants were reported
in 2003.
$1,021,900 to Memorial Sloan-Kettering Cancer
  Center, New York, NY.
$50,000 to Mayo Foundation, Rochester, MN.
$4,520 to Lincoln Center for the Performing Arts,
  New York, NY.
$2,773 to Columbia University, New York, NY. 2
  grants: $773, $2,000 to Department of
  Opthalmology
$1,000 to American Academy of Arts and Sciences,
  Cambridge, MA.
$1,000 to Hospital for Special Surgery, New York,
  NY.
$500 to Family Centers, Greenwich, CT.
$300 to Emory University, Atlanta, GA.
$100 to Greenwich Emergency Medical Service,
  Riverside, CT.

2021
The Gibney Family Foundation, Inc.
c/o Kerkering & Barberio
1858 Ringling Blvd.
Sarasota, FL 34236
Contact: Frank A. Gibney, C.E.O. and Pres.
E-mail: info@tgff.org; URL: http://www.tgff.org

Established in 1991 in FL.
Donor: Albert L. Gibney.
Foundation type: Independent foundation.
Financial data (yr. ended 12/31/05): Assets,
$24,474,247 (M); expenditures, $1,300,613;
qualifying distributions, $1,158,655; giving
activities include $1,012,068 for 57 grants.

Purpose and activities: Support primarily for
organizations that benefit the blind and visually
impaired.
Fields of interest: Eye diseases.
Type of support: Technical assistance; Scholarship
funds; Publication; Program development;
Matching/challenge support; Management
development/capacity building.
Limitations: Applications not accepted. Giving on a
national basis. Current states are AZ, CA, CT, FL, ID,
MA, ME, NH and upstate areas of NY, OR, VT, UT,
WA. No support for research projects or religious or
political organizations. No grants to individuals.
Application information: Contributes only to
pre-selected organizations.
Officers: Frank A. Gibney, C.E.O. and Pres.; Sue
Gibney Young, V.P. and Secy.; Joan Gibney
Whittaker, V.P. and Treas.
Number of staff: 1 full-time professional; 2 part-time
professional; 1 part-time support.
EIN: 650286170

2022
Ginsburg Family Foundation, Inc. ✧ ☆
(formerly Alan and Harriet Ginsburg Family
Foundation, Inc.)
875 Concourse Pkwy. S., Ste. 150
Maitland, FL 32751
Contact: Sharon Ginsberg, Pres.
Application address: 1551 Sandspur Rd., Maitland,
FL 32751, tel.: (407) 741-8500

Established in 2002 in FL.
Donor: Alan H. Ginsburg.
Foundation type: Independent foundation.
Financial data (yr. ended 12/31/05): Assets,
$625,632 (M); gifts received, $1,080,000;
expenditures, $860,733; qualifying distributions,
$856,150; giving activities include $824,804 for 31
grants (high: $231,500; low: $500).
Fields of interest: Arts; Education; Jewish federated
giving programs; Jewish agencies & temples.
Limitations: Giving primarily in FL. No grants to
individuals.
Application information:
  Initial approach: Letter
  Deadline(s): Nov. 1
Officers: Sharon L. Ginsburg, Pres.; Alan H.
Ginsburg, Secy.
Director: Ronald M. Ginsburg.
EIN: 043624306
Selected grants: The following grants were reported
in 2004.
$338,000 to Jewish Federation of Greater Orlando,
  Maitland, FL.
$230,100 to La Amistad Foundation, Fern Park, FL.
$100,000 to Orlando Performing Arts Center,
  Orlando, FL.
$100,000 to Rollins College, Winter Park, FL.
$98,354 to Seeds of Peace, New York, NY.
$10,000 to BETA Center, Orlando, FL.
$10,000 to United Arts of Central Florida, Orlando,
  FL.
$7,000 to American Red Magen David for Israel,
  Miami, FL.
$2,000 to Parsons Dance Company, New York, NY.
$1,200 to American Heart Association, Orlando, FL.

2023
The Glaubinger Foundation ◇
c/o Sterling House
6307 S. Highway A1A, Ste. 253
Melbourne Beach, FL 32951

Established in 1988 in FL.
Donor: Lawrence D. Glaubinger.
Foundation type: Independent foundation.
Financial data (yr. ended 12/31/05): Assets,
$3,798,442 (M); gifts received, $300,000;
expenditures, $2,130,113; qualifying distributions,
$2,126,956; giving activities include $2,125,366
for 6 grants (high: $1,880,863; low: $3,902).
Fields of interest: Education, fund raising/fund
distribution; Higher education, university.
International interests: Canada.
Type of support: Scholarship funds.
Limitations: Applications not accepted. Giving
primarily in IN and NY. No grants to individuals.
Application information: Contributes only to
pre-selected organizations.
Trustees: Jane Glaubinger; Lawrence D. Glaubinger;
Lucienne M. Glaubinger; James E. Jordon.
EIN: 592862615
Selected grants: The following grants were reported
in 2003.
$146,418 to Indiana University Foundation,
Bloomington, IN.
$103,212 to Columbia University, School of
Business, New York, NY.
$25,000 to University of Pennsylvania, Philadelphia,
PA.
$18,828 to Pennsylvania State University, State
College, PA.
$13,806 to University of Notre Dame, Notre Dame,
IN.
$4,202 to State University of New York at Albany,
Albany, NY.
$3,828 to McGill University, Montreal, Canada. .
$630 to John Jay College of Criminal Justice of the
City University of New York, New York, NY.

2024
Glazer Family Foundation, Inc. ◇
c/o Coord.
1 Buccaneer Pl.
Tampa, FL 33607
URL: http://www.glazerfamilyfoundation.com/

Established in 1999 in FL.
Donors: Buccaneer L.P.; Florida Sports Foundation.
Foundation type: Company-sponsored foundation.
Financial data (yr. ended 12/31/03): Assets,
$56,273 (M); gifts received, $247,218;
expenditures, $469,622; qualifying distributions,
$448,704; giving activities include $448,704 for
107+ grants (high: $100,000).
Purpose and activities: The foundation supports
organizations involved with education, health,
recreation, human services, and community
development.
Fields of interest: Education; Health care;
Recreation; Human services; Community
development; Jewish federated giving programs.
Limitations: Giving primarily in Tampa Bay and the
west central FL area, with emphasis on
Hillsborough, Manatee, Orange, Osceola, Pasco,
Pinellas, Polk, and Sarasota counties. No support
for political organizations. No grants to individuals,
or for fundraising, celebrations, administrative/
training costs, capital campaigns, sponsorships,
scholarships, basic research/conferences, or
political campaigns.
Application information: Application form required.
Initial approach: Download application form
Copies of proposal: 3
Deadline(s): May 1 through July 1 and Sept. 1
through Nov. 1
Final notification: Within 1 month following
deadlines
Officers: Malcolm Glazer, Pres.; Bryan Glazer, Exec.
V.P.; Edward Glazer, Exec. V.P.; Joel Glazer, Exec.
V.P.; Veronica Costello, Exec. Dir.
EIN: 593578188

2025
Global Village Charitable Trust ◇
3505 S. Mooring Way
Coconut Grove, FL 33133-6519

Established in 1993 in OH.
Donor: Daniel R. Lewis.
Foundation type: Independent foundation.
Financial data (yr. ended 12/31/05): Assets,
$14,072,003 (M); gifts received, $4,248,902;
expenditures, $2,192,852; qualifying distributions,
$2,189,627; giving activities include $2,189,627
for 18 grants (high: $1,331,862; low: $5,000).
Purpose and activities: Giving primarily for Jewish
giving programs, the arts and human services.
Fields of interest: Arts; Hospitals (general); Human
services; Jewish federated giving programs.
Limitations: Applications not accepted. Giving
primarily in CA, FL, and NY. No grants to individuals.
Application information: Contributes only to
pre-selected organizations.
Trustee: Daniel R. Lewis.
EIN: 341757652
Selected grants: The following grants were reported
in 2003.
$3,995,028 to Cleveland Orchestra, Cleveland, OH.
$1,002,497 to American Civil Liberties Union
Foundation, New York, NY.
$497,820 to Temple Beth Am, Miami, FL.
$280,000 to Corporate Accountability International,
Boston, MA.
$74,716 to Barnard College, New York, NY. For
development.
$67,098 to Florida Philharmonic Orchestra, Fort
Lauderdale, FL.
$33,434 to Early Childhood Foundation, Miami, FL.
$25,063 to American Symphony Orchestra League,
New York, NY.
$25,000 to New World Symphony, Miami Beach, FL.
$24,955 to Solomon R. Guggenheim Museum, New
York, NY.

2026
Goldhammer Family Foundation ◇
c/o Robert F. Goldhammer
284 Locha Dr.
Jupiter, FL 33458

Incorporated in 1986 in MA.
Donor: Robert F. Goldhammer.
Foundation type: Independent foundation.
Financial data (yr. ended 5/31/05): Assets,
$804,967 (M); gifts received, $986,492;
expenditures, $1,042,669; qualifying distributions,
$1,037,315; giving activities include $1,037,315
for 15 grants (high: $1,000,000; low: $240).
Purpose and activities: Giving primarily education,
especially a university endowment; support also for
the arts and hospitals.
Fields of interest: Arts; Higher education; Higher
education, college; Medical school/education;
Hospitals (general); Christian agencies & churches.
Type of support: Research; Matching/challenge
support; Scholarship funds; Program development;
Endowments; Building/renovation; Annual
campaigns; General/operating support.
Limitations: Applications not accepted. Giving on a
national basis. No grants to individuals.
Application information: Contributes only to
pre-selected organizations.
Officers and Trustees: * Robert F. Goldhammer,*
Pres.; Richard Goldhammer,* Secy.; Gina
Goldhammer,* Treas.
EIN: 046549241

2027
Alfred & Ann Goldstein Foundation, Inc. ◇
c/o Alfred R. Goldstein, Pres.
682 Mourning Dove Dr.
Sarasota, FL 34236-1926

Established in 1955 in NY.
Donors: Alfred R. Goldstein; Ann L. Goldstein;
Joseph I. Lubin†.
Foundation type: Independent foundation.
Financial data (yr. ended 12/31/05): Assets,
$14,324,266 (M); expenditures, $746,608;
qualifying distributions, $718,193; giving activities
include $715,805 for 124 grants (high: $150,000;
low: $25).
Purpose and activities: Grants primarily for the arts
and education; support also for health associations,
Jewish organizations, and marine science.
Fields of interest: Arts; Education; Health
organizations, association; Human services; Jewish
federated giving programs; Marine science; Jewish
agencies & temples.
Limitations: Applications not accepted. Giving
primarily in FL and NY. No grants to individuals.
Application information: Contributes only to
pre-selected organizations.
Officers: Alfred R. Goldstein, Pres.; Ann L.
Goldstein, V.P.
Directors: Wendy H. Cohen; Cynthia Goldstein;
Richard Goldstein; Steven R. Goldstein; Dana
Yaphe.
EIN: 136033997
Selected grants: The following grants were reported
in 2004.
$485,000 to Ringling School of Art and Design,
Sarasota, FL. For general support.
$28,000 to Mote Marine Laboratory, Sarasota, FL.
For general support.
$25,000 to Cleveland Clinic Foundation, Cleveland,
OH. For general support.
$25,000 to Sarasota Manatee Jewish Housing
Council, Sarasota, FL. For general support.
$25,000 to Sarasota Memorial Healthcare
Foundation, Sarasota, FL. For general support.
$10,000 to Cornell University, Ithaca, NY. For
general support.
$7,500 to Womens American ORT of Sarasota,
Sarasota, FL. For general support.
$7,000 to Chautauqua Foundation, Chautauqua,
NY. For general support.
$5,000 to Asolo Theater Company, Sarasota, FL.
For general support.
$5,000 to Players Theater of Columbus, Columbus,
OH. For general support.

2028
The Lucy Gooding Charitable Foundation Trust ▼ ✧

P.O. Box 37349
Jacksonville, FL 32236-7349 (904) 786-4796
Contact: Bonnie H. Smith, Tr.
FAX: (904) 786-4796;
E-mail: bhsmith@bellsouth.net

Established in 1988 in FL.
Donor: Lucy B. Gooding‡.
Foundation type: Independent foundation.
Financial data (yr. ended 12/31/05): Assets, $93,428,175 (M); gifts received, $72,250,565; expenditures, $4,818,636; qualifying distributions, $3,992,523; giving activities include $3,844,757 for 43 grants (high: $1,000,000; low: $4,000; average: $10,000–$50,000).
Purpose and activities: Funding preference is for organizations in the coast counties of Florida with projects helping children.
Fields of interest: Education; Human services; Children/youth, services; Residential/custodial care, hospices; Children; Disabilities, people with; Economically disadvantaged; Homeless.
Type of support: General/operating support; Continuing support; Annual campaigns; Capital campaigns; Building/renovation; Equipment; Land acquisition; Endowments; Program development.
Limitations: Giving limited to the Jacksonville, FL, area. No support for private foundations. No grants to individuals.
Publications: Annual report; Informational brochure (including application guidelines).
Application information: Application form required.
 Copies of proposal: 1
 Deadline(s): Sept. 30
 Final notification: By Dec. 1
Trustees: Wilford C. Lyon, Jr.; Robert A. Mills; Bonnie H. Smith.
Number of staff: 1 full-time professional; 2 part-time professional.
EIN: 592891582
Selected grants: The following grants were reported in 2005.
$1,000,000 to Baptist Medical Center, Wolfson Children's Hospital, Jacksonville, FL. For Pediatric Neurosurgical Center.
$1,000,000 to Community Foundation, Jacksonville, FL. To establish Endowment Fund.
$450,000 to United Way of Northeast Florida, Jacksonville, FL. To establish full service site in local school.
$305,000 to Saint Vincents Foundation, Jacksonville, FL. For mobile health outreach program for children.
$100,000 to American Red Cross, Delmarva Peninsula Chapter, Wilmington, DE. For hurricane relief.
$50,000 to Malivai Washington Kids Foundation, Jacksonville Beach, FL. For capital campaign.
$35,000 to Catholic Charities Bureau, Jacksonville, FL. For Emergency Assistance Fund for people in need.
$30,000 to Hope Haven Childrens Clinic and Family Center, Jacksonville, FL. To operate LBG Learning Center.
$26,657 to Cerebral Palsy Foundation of Florida, Jacksonville, FL. To construct bathroom for special needs clients.
$5,000 to Association of Small Foundations, DC. For general operating support for work in Florida.

2029
Leo Goodwin Foundation, Inc. ✧

800 Corporate Dr., Ste. 510
Fort Lauderdale, FL 33334-3621
Contact: Helen M. Furia, Pres.

Established in 1977 in FL.
Donor: Leo Goodwin, Jr.‡.
Foundation type: Independent foundation.
Financial data (yr. ended 10/31/05): Assets, $14,760,572 (M); gifts received, $940; expenditures, $1,006,085; qualifying distributions, $713,188; giving activities include $579,300 for 49 grants (high: $115,000; low: $1,000).
Purpose and activities: Support primarily for child welfare and cancer research; some support also for youth groups and education.
Fields of interest: Arts; Education; Cancer; Cancer research; Children/youth, services.
Type of support: General/operating support; Scholarship funds.
Limitations: Giving primarily in FL. No grants to individuals.
Application information: Application form not required.
 Initial approach: Letter
 Deadline(s): Allow sufficient time for review before end of fiscal year, Oct. 31
Officers: Helen M. Furia, Pres.; Elliot P. Borkson, V.P.; Alan J. Goldberg, Treas.
EIN: 526054098

2030
Mark J. Gordon Foundation ✧

(formerly Gail and Mark Gordon Foundation)
2875 N.E. 191st St., Ste. 400
Aventura, FL 33180

Established in 1999 in DE and FL.
Donor: Mark J. Gordon.
Foundation type: Independent foundation.
Financial data (yr. ended 12/31/05): Assets, $6,683,967 (M); expenditures, $972,810; qualifying distributions, $693,441; giving activities include $653,441 for 29 grants (high: $255,000; low: $50; average: $1,000–$25,000).
Fields of interest: Cancer; Breast cancer; Cancer research; Jewish agencies & temples.
Limitations: Applications not accepted. Giving primarily in FL. No grants to individuals.
Application information: Contributes only to pre-selected organizations.
Officer: Mark J. Gordon, Pres. and Secy.
Directors: Dorothy Dedario; Nancy Platt.
EIN: 650995291

2031
Gore Family Memorial Foundation ✧

c/o SunTrust Bank
P.O. Box 14728
Fort Lauderdale, FL 33302
Application address: 4747 N. Ocean Dr., Ste. 204, Fort Lauderdale, FL 33308

Trust established in 1973 in FL.
Donor: R.H. Gore Trust.
Foundation type: Independent foundation.
Financial data (yr. ended 1/31/06): Assets, $20,326,450 (M); expenditures, $1,146,782; qualifying distributions, $810,542; giving activities include $271,273 for 34 grants (high: $20,000; low: $2,625), and $379,799 for 74 grants to individuals (high: $35,000; low: $387).
Purpose and activities: Aid to the needy and handicapped; aid to the needy restricted to Broward County, FL; scholarships restricted to Broward County residents, except for severely handicapped applicants.
Fields of interest: Higher education; Disabilities, people with; Economically disadvantaged.
Type of support: General/operating support; Grants to individuals; Scholarships—to individuals.
Limitations: Giving primarily in FL, particularly in Broward County. No grants for general programs, capital expenditures, or scholarships for graduate studies (except for the handicapped); no loans.
Application information:
 Initial approach: Letter
 Deadline(s): None
Trustees: George Gore; Peter Gore; Theodore T. Gore; Nancy Saravia; SunTrust Bank.
Number of staff: 2 full-time support.
EIN: 596497544

2032
Nehemias Gorin Foundation ✧

7028 Leopardi Ct.
Naples, FL 34114-2650
Contact: Stephen Goldenberg, Tr.
Additional address: 37 Carlson Ln., Unit 7, Falmouth, MA 02540-2529

Established in 1964 in MA.
Donors: Nehemias Gorin‡; William Gorin‡.
Foundation type: Independent foundation.
Financial data (yr. ended 11/30/04): Assets, $2,227,804 (M); expenditures, $492,415; qualifying distributions, $436,353; giving activities include $425,000 for 74 grants (high: $50,000; low: $1,000).
Purpose and activities: Support for health, including hospitals and cancer research; Jewish welfare funds, other Jewish organizations and Israel; higher education; museums and other cultural programs; community funds; and Roman Catholic organizations.
Fields of interest: Museums; Arts; Higher education; Education; Hospitals (general); Health care; Health organizations, association; Cancer; Cancer research; Human services; Aging, centers/services; Federated giving programs; Jewish federated giving programs; Roman Catholic agencies & churches; Jewish agencies & temples; Aging; Disabilities, people with.
International interests: Israel.
Limitations: Giving primarily in MA. No grants to individuals.
Application information: Application form not required.
 Initial approach: Letter. Phone calls will not be accepted
 Copies of proposal: 1
 Deadline(s): None
 Board meeting date(s): Varies
Trustees: Stephen Goldenberg; Howard Gorin; Ralph Gorin.
EIN: 046119939
Selected grants: The following grants were reported in 2003.
$50,000 to Combined Jewish Philanthropies of Greater Boston, Boston, MA.
$10,000 to Beth Israel Deaconess Medical Center, Boston, MA.

$10,000 to Boston Symphony Orchestra, Boston, MA.

$10,000 to Boys and Girls Club of Allston-Brighton, West End House, Allston, MA.

$10,000 to Hebrew Rehabilitation Center for Aged, Boston, MA.

$10,000 to Massachusetts General Hospital, Boston, MA.

$6,250 to Rensselaer Polytechnic Institute, Troy, NY.

$5,000 to Memorial Sloan-Kettering Cancer Center, New York, NY.

$2,500 to Lifelong AIDS Alliance, Seattle, WA.

$2,500 to New England School of Law, Boston, MA.

2033
Green Family Foundation, Inc. ✧
2601 S. Bayshore Dr., Ste. 800
Coconut Grove, FL 33133

Established in 1991 in FL.
Donor: Steven J. Green.
Foundation type: Independent foundation.
Financial data (yr. ended 12/31/04): Assets, $7,645,845 (M); gifts received, $541,701; expenditures, $1,188,362; qualifying distributions, $905,852; giving activities include $905,852 for 31 + grants (high: $541,000).
Purpose and activities: Giving primarily for arts and culture, education and human services.
Fields of interest: Museums (art); Arts; Higher education; Libraries/library science; Education; Hospitals (general); Human services; American Red Cross; Federated giving programs.
Limitations: Applications not accepted. Giving primarily in FL. No grants to individuals.
Application information: Contributes only to pre-selected organizations.
Officer: Jeffrey A. Safchik, Pres.
Director: Kimberly Green.
EIN: 650284913

2034
The Greenburg-May Foundation, Inc.
P.O. Box 54-5816
Miami, FL 33154
Contact: Isabel May, Pres.
Application address: 9999 Collins Ave., Apt. 15A, Bal Harbour, FL 33154

Incorporated in 1947 in DE.
Donors: Harry Greenburg†; Samuel D. May†.
Foundation type: Independent foundation.
Financial data (yr. ended 12/31/05): Assets, $14,938,465 (M); expenditures, $719,240; qualifying distributions, $558,430; giving activities include $557,486 for 115 grants (high: $125,000; low: $50; average: $1,000–$10,000).
Purpose and activities: Grants almost entirely for medical research, primarily cancer, heart, diabetes, Parkinson's, and neurological research; support also for the aged, hospitals, Jewish welfare funds, and temples.
Fields of interest: Hospitals (general); Cancer; Heart & circulatory diseases; Neuroscience; Medical research, institute; Cancer research; Human services; Aging, centers/services; Jewish federated giving programs; Jewish agencies & temples; Aging.
International interests: Israel.
Type of support: General/operating support; Continuing support; Annual campaigns;

Endowments; Emergency funds; Program development; Internship funds; Scholarship funds; Research; Consulting services.
Limitations: Giving primarily in southern FL and NY. No grants to individuals, or for conferences; generally no grants for scholarships or fellowships; no loans.
Application information: Application form required.
Initial approach: Letter
Copies of proposal: 1
Deadline(s): None
Board meeting date(s): Jan., Apr., July, and Oct.
Final notification: 1 to 2 months
Officers and Directors:* Isabel May,* Pres.; Peter May,* V.P. and Treas.; Jonathan May, V.P.; Linda Sklar,* V.P.
Number of staff: 2 part-time support.
EIN: 136162935
Selected grants: The following grants were reported in 2004.
$11,000 to National Parkinson Foundation, Miami, FL.
$8,100 to Greater Miami Opera, Miami, FL.
$5,500 to Coconut Grove Playhouse State Theater of Florida Corporation, Miami, FL.
$4,363 to United Way.
$2,600 to American Jewish Committee, New York, NY.
$1,250 to United Jewish Appeal, New York, NY.
$1,000 to Childrens Home Society.
$900 to New World Symphony, Miami Beach, FL.
$300 to American Jewish Congress, New York, NY.
$200 to Kesher - Information, Guidance and Counseling Center for Parents, Jerusalem, Israel. .

2035
Greenfield Foundation
(formerly The Goldsmith-Greenfield Foundation, Inc.)
1800 2nd St., Ste. 750
Sarasota, FL 34236   (941) 957-0442
Contact: Debra Jacobs, Secy. and Admin.
FAX: (941) 957-3135; URL: http://www.selbyfdn.org/greenfield.htm

Established in 1991 in FL; merged with The Alexis Rosenberg Foundation in 2005.
Foundation type: Independent foundation.
Financial data (yr. ended 5/31/06): Assets, $14,620,936 (M); expenditures, $796,858; qualifying distributions, $675,014; giving activities include $654,764 for 38 grants (high: $195,000; low: $1,100).
Purpose and activities: Giving primarily for education, the arts, and human services.
Fields of interest: Arts; Education; Human services.
Limitations: Applications not accepted. Giving on a national basis. No grants to individuals, endowments, deficit financing, debt reduction, operating expenses, conferences/seminars, workshops, travel, surveys, advertising, fundraising, research, or for annual campaigns.
Publications: Informational brochure.
Application information: Proposals must be sponsored by a trustee. Unsolicited requests for funds not accepted.
Board meeting date(s): Varies
Officer: Debra Jacobs, Secy. and Admin.
EIN: 650301946

2036
The Griffin Foundation, Inc. ✧
1601 Gulf Shore Blvd. N., Unit 16
Naples, FL 34102

Established in 2000 in FL.
Donor: John F. Griffin.
Foundation type: Independent foundation.
Financial data (yr. ended 12/31/05): Assets, $1,501,753 (M); gifts received, $6,000; expenditures, $382,278; qualifying distributions, $380,782; giving activities include $379,333 for 13 grants (high: $50,000; low: $2,000).
Fields of interest: Human services; Roman Catholic federated giving programs; Roman Catholic agencies & churches.
Limitations: Applications not accepted. Giving primarily in Washington, DC and MD; some funding nationally. No grants to individuals.
Application information: Contributes only to pre-selected organizations.
Officer and Directors:* D. Clay Lovett,* Treas.; John F. Griffin; Martin P. Griffin; Nancy M. Griffin.
EIN: 311730661
Selected grants: The following grants were reported in 2004.
$215,000 to Center City Consortium, DC.
$50,000 to Hope for Haiti, Naples, FL.
$7,500 to Archbishop Carroll High School, DC.

2037
Alice Busch Gronewaldt Foundation, Inc. ✧
c/o Caldwell & Pacetti
324 Royal Palm Way, Ste. 300
Palm Beach, FL 33480

Established in 1990 in FL.
Donor: Alice Busch Gronewaldt†.
Foundation type: Independent foundation.
Financial data (yr. ended 12/31/04): Assets, $11,368,767 (M); expenditures, $648,305; qualifying distributions, $575,610; giving activities include $575,610 for 71 grants (high: $70,000; low: $500).
Purpose and activities: Support primarily for education, the arts, animal welfare, and health care.
Fields of interest: Arts; Elementary/secondary education; Education; Animal welfare; Hospitals (general); Health care.
Type of support: General/operating support.
Limitations: Applications not accepted. Giving primarily in Palm Beach, FL, and Cooperstown, NY. No grants to individuals.
Application information: Contributes only to pre-selected organizations.
Officers and Directors:* Louis Busch Hager, Jr., Pres.; Alice Hager Holbrook,* V.P.; Mary Hager Thomas,* V.P.; Andrew W. Regan,* Secy.
EIN: 650212289
Selected grants: The following grants were reported in 2003.
$100,000 to Mary Imogene Bassett Hospital and Clinics, Cooperstown, NY. 2 grants: $30,000, $70,000
$50,000 to Millbrook School, Millbrook, NY.
$43,323 to Rosarian Academy, West Palm Beach, FL. 2 grants: $21,500 (For annual fund), $21,823 (For scholarships).
$30,000 to Glimmerglass Opera, Cooperstown, NY. 2 grants: $10,000 (For general operating support), $20,000 (For general operating support).

$30,000 to Hyde Hall, Friends of, East Springfield, NY. For general operating support.

$28,475 to Duke University, Durham, NC. For scholarships.

$15,000 to Greenwich Country Day School, Greenwich, CT.

2038
Audrey and Martin Gruss Foundation ✧

(formerly Martin D. Gruss Foundation)
1574 S. Ocean Blvd.
Palm Beach, FL   33480-5119

Established in 1982 in NY.
Donor: Martin D. Gruss.
Foundation type: Independent foundation.
Financial data (yr. ended 8/31/05): Assets, $66,941,697 (M); gifts received, $5,940,362; expenditures, $4,151,314; qualifying distributions, $2,599,514; giving activities include $2,599,514 for 111 grants (high: $500,000; low: $400).
Purpose and activities: Giving primarily for secondary education, museums, and welfare funds; some support also for hospitals.
Fields of interest: Arts; Education; Hospitals (general); Health care; Jewish federated giving programs.
Limitations: Applications not accepted. Giving primarily in FL and NY. No grants to individuals.
Application information: Contributes only to pre-selected organizations.
Trustees: Audrey Butay Gruss; Martin D. Gruss.
EIN: 133132987
Selected grants: The following grants were reported in 2005.

$246,697 to Trinity College, Hartford, CT.

$200,000 to University of Pennsylvania, Philadelphia, PA.

$55,000 to Lawrenceville School, Lawrenceville, NJ.

$50,000 to Metropole Film Board, New York, NY.

$50,000 to Weill Medical College of Cornell University, New York, NY.

$25,000 to American Friends of the Israel Museum, New York, NY.

$25,000 to Tufts University, Medford, MA.

$23,000 to Lincoln Center for the Performing Arts, New York, NY.

$8,833 to Metropolitan Museum of Art, New York, NY.

$4,598 to Museum of Modern Art, New York, NY.

2039
GSB Family Foundation, Inc. ✧

301 W. Camino Gardens Blvd., Ste. 101
Boca Raton, FL   33432

Established in 1996 in FL.
Donor: Gary S. Bailey.
Foundation type: Independent foundation.
Financial data (yr. ended 12/31/05): Assets, $391,494 (M); gifts received, $248,671; expenditures, $344,975; qualifying distributions, $343,350; giving activities include $343,350 for grants.
Fields of interest: Higher education, university; Environment, natural resources; Hospitals (general); Christian agencies & churches.
Limitations: Applications not accepted. Giving primarily in FL. No grants to individuals.
Application information: Contributes only to pre-selected organizations.

Officers: Gary S. Bailey, Pres. and Treas.; Brenda M. Bailey, V.P. and Secy.
EIN: 650714038
Selected grants: The following grants were reported in 2004.

$25,000 to Vail Mountain School, Vail, CO.

$7,000 to Loxahatchee Historical Society, Jupiter, FL. 2 grants: $2,000, $5,000

$4,000 to Safe Harbor Animal Rescue, Jupiter, FL. 2 grants: $1,500, $2,500

$3,500 to Genesis Womens Shelter, Dallas, TX.

$3,000 to American Red Cross.

$2,500 to Dallas Childrens Advocacy Center, Dallas, TX.

$2,500 to Ronald McDonald House.

$1,500 to Historical Society of Palm Beach County, Palm Beach, FL.

2040
GTE Federal Credit Union Charitable Trust ✧ ☆

P.O. Box 172599
Tampa, FL   33679-0550

Established in 2002 in FL.
Donors: GTE Federal Credit Union; Member Gateways, LLC; PSCU.
Foundation type: Independent foundation.
Financial data (yr. ended 12/31/05): Assets, $718,127 (M); gifts received, $635,835; expenditures, $473,040; qualifying distributions, $457,129; giving activities include $389,799 for 26 grants (high: $223,976; low: $575), and $67,330 for 27 grants to individuals (high: $4,400; low: $1,000).
Purpose and activities: Giving disaster-relief aid to individuals as well as grants to organizations.
Fields of interest: Museums (art); Education; Boys & girls clubs; Youth development; Human services; American Red Cross; Federated giving programs.
Type of support: Grants to individuals.
Limitations: Applications not accepted. Giving primarily in FL and LA.
Application information: Unsolicited requests for funds not accepted.
Officers: Rose Bass, Chair.; Paula Jurgenson, Secy.; Richard Helber, Treas.
Trustees: Charlie Beauchamp; Neil Timson.
EIN: 826104767
Selected grants: The following grants were reported in 2004.

$5,000 to Alpha House of Tampa, Tampa, FL.

$5,000 to Hillsborough Educational Partnership Foundation, Tampa, FL.

$5,000 to Junior Achievement of Greater Tampa, Tampa, FL.

$5,000 to Spring of Tampa Bay, Tampa, FL.

$3,000 to Seniors in Service of Tampa Bay, Tampa, FL.

$3,000 to Tampa Bay Academy of Hope, Tampa, FL.

$2,500 to Child Abuse Council, Tampa, FL.

$2,500 to Juvenile Bipolar Research Foundation, Maplewood, NJ.

$1,000 to Tampa Heights Junior Civic Association, Tampa, FL.

2041
Gulf Coast Community Foundation of Venice ✧

(formerly The Gulf Coast Community Foundation)
601 Tamiami Trail S.
Venice, FL   34285-3237   (941) 486-4600
Contact: Teri A. Hansen, C.E.O.
FAX: (941) 486-4699; E-mail: info@gulfcoastcf.org;
Additional E-mail: thansen@gulfcoastcf.org;
URL: http://www.gulfcoastcf.org

Established in 1995 in FL; converted from sale of Venice Hospital.
Foundation type: Community foundation.
Financial data (yr. ended 6/30/05): Assets, $205,836,350 (M); gifts received, $3,068,156; expenditures, $7,175,975; giving activities include $5,892,225 for 178+ grants, and $315,725 for grants to individuals.
Purpose and activities: The foundation is a nonprofit community foundation that provides funding for programs in the areas of health and human services, arts and culture, education, and civic affairs. As a community foundation, it supports projects and organizations that serve the residents of Venice, FL and its surrounding communities.
Fields of interest: Media, film/video; Arts; Higher education; Education; Environmental education; Environment; Health care; Mental health/crisis services; Disasters, preparedness/services; Youth development; Youth, services; Aging, centers/services; Human services; Community development, neighborhood development; Community development, citizen coalitions; Public affairs, citizen participation; Public affairs.
Type of support: Management development/capacity building; Capital campaigns; Building/renovation; Equipment; Land acquisition; Program development; Publication; Curriculum development; Scholarship funds; Technical assistance; Program evaluation; Scholarships—to individuals.
Limitations: Giving limited to the city of Venice, FL, and the surrounding communities. No support for religious purposes. No grants to individuals (except for scholarships), or for endowments, debt reduction, basic scientific research, events, or travel; no loans.
Publications: Annual report; Grants list; Informational brochure (including application guidelines); Newsletter.
Application information: Visit foundation Web site for application forms, specific deadlines, and additional guidelines per grant type; number of copies vary per grant type. Requests over $20,001 require an invitation from the foundation to submit a formal application based on the organization's Letter of Intent. Application form required.

Initial approach: Submit Letter of Intent
Copies of proposal: 20
Deadline(s): Varies
Board meeting date(s): Bimonthly
Final notification: Varies

Officers and Directors:* Joseph Thro,* Chair.; Jean Trammell,* Vice-Chair.; Teri A. Hansen,* C.E.O. and Pres.; W. Michael Bigner, V.P., Prog. Svcs.; Marjorie A. Floyd, V.P., Mktg. and Comms.; Beth Harrison, V.P., Donor Svcs.; Wendy Deming, Chief of Staff and Corp. Secy.; Diane Leger, C.F.O.; Sydney Young, Cont.; Richard Conroy, M.D.; Rev. Chris Gray; James Hanks; Michael Hartley; Donald Hay; Susan Hines; Martha Jarrett; Karl Kokomoor; Dorothy Korszen; Gratia Schroeder; Tiffany Taylor; Nelda Thompson; Carol Tilley.

Number of staff: 7 full-time professional; 5 full-time support; 2 part-time support.
EIN: 591052433
Selected grants: The following grants were reported in 2004.
$881,143 to YMCA, Sarasota Family, Sarasota, FL. For Gold Seal Project, expansion/extension (early childhood education).
$526,170 to Venice, City of, Venice, FL. To complete funding for expansion and renovation of Venice Community Center.
$476,137 to University of South Florida, Sarasota, FL. For Southern Sarasota County Higher Education Initiative.
$476,000 to Venice Presbyterian Church, Venice, FL. To provide critically needed spaces for infant care and other classroom improvements.
$395,000 to Venice Area Beautification, Venice, FL. For Segment 8 of Venetian Waterway Park.
$196,950 to Englewood Art Center, Englewood, FL. For Expand the Reach of Art facility expansion.
$178,014 to Florida West Coast Public Broadcasting, WEDU-TV, Tampa, FL. For A Gulf Coast Journal with Jack Perkins, magazine program for public television.
$150,000 to Senior Friendship Centers, Sarasota, FL. For Friendship at Home: North Port and Englewood Expansion.
$63,650 to Forty Carrots of Sarasota, Sarasota, FL. For Forty Carrots Parenting Program on Wheels: Target South County Libraries.
$54,116 to First Step of Sarasota, Sarasota, FL. To create presence in North Port with clinical position and office and enhance technology in Venice.

2042
Gulf Power Foundation, Inc. ☆
1 Energy Pl.
Pensacola, FL 32520-0786 (850) 444-6806
Contact: Candace Klinglesmith, Admin.
FAX: (850) 444-6026;
E-mail: chklingl@southernco.com; URL: http://www.southerncompany.com/gulfpower/community/charity.asp

Established in 1987 in FL.
Donor: Gulf Power Co.
Foundation type: Company-sponsored foundation.
Financial data (yr. ended 12/31/04): Assets, $3,683,913 (M); expenditures, $333,394; qualifying distributions, $330,983; giving activities include $283,883 for 64 grants (high: $100,000; low: $250; average: $250–$5,000), and $6,595 for 36 employee matching gifts.
Purpose and activities: The foundation supports organizations involved with education, health, community development, and other areas.
Fields of interest: Higher education; Education; Health care; Community development; General charitable giving.
Type of support: Employee matching gifts; General/operating support; Continuing support; Annual campaigns; Capital campaigns; Building/renovation; Equipment; Emergency funds; Program development; Scholarship funds.
Limitations: Giving primarily in areas of company operations in northwestern FL. No support for political or lobbying organizations or arts councils (except for capital campaigns). No grants to individuals.
Publications: Annual report; Informational brochure (including application guidelines).

Application information: Requests should include a copy of the organization's Florida Solicitation Letter. Application form required.
Initial approach: Contact foundation for application form
Copies of proposal: 1
Deadline(s): Feb. 15, May 15, Aug. 15, and Nov. 15
Board meeting date(s): Quarterly
Final notification: 1 month
Officers and Trustees:* P. Bernard Jacob, Chair.; Susan D. Ritenour, Secy.-Treas.; Francis M. Fisher, Jr.; Ronnie R. Labrato; Penny M. Manuel.
EIN: 592817740
Selected grants: The following grants were reported in 2004.
$100,000 to University of West Florida, Pensacola, FL.
$33,128 to United Way of Escambia County, Pensacola, FL.
$15,891 to United Way of Northwest Florida, Panama City, FL.
$12,266 to United Way of Santa Rosa County, Milton, FL.
$10,000 to Mary Brogan Museum of Art and Science, Tallahassee, FL.
$10,000 to YMCA of Metropolitan Pensacola, Pensacola, FL.
$5,000 to Arts Council of Northwest Florida, Pensacola, FL.
$5,000 to Pensacola Junior College, Pensacola, FL.
$2,000 to University of Florida, Gainesville, FL.
$1,000 to Salvation Army, Saint Petersburg, FL.

2043
The John R. and Ruth W. Gurtler Foundation, Inc. ◇
P.O. Box 880
Winter Park, FL 32790-0880
Application address: c/o Mary W. Christian, 61 Oakleigh Dr., Maitland, FL 32751

Established in 1999 in FL.
Foundation type: Independent foundation.
Financial data (yr. ended 12/31/05): Assets, $7,428,996 (M); expenditures, $396,141; qualifying distributions, $345,296; giving activities include $316,147 for 10 grants (high: $100,000; low: $4,470).
Fields of interest: Higher education; Youth development; Religion.
Limitations: Giving primarily in central FL. No grants to individuals.
Application information: Application form not required.
Initial approach: Proposal
Copies of proposal: 3
Deadline(s): None
Officers and Directors:* Harold A. Ward III,* Pres.; Mary W. Christian,* V.P., Secy.-Treas., and Exec. Dir.; W. Graham White.
EIN: 593437461
Selected grants: The following grants were reported in 2003.
$125,000 to Rollins College, Winter Park, FL. To purchase nuclear magnetic resonance spectrometer.
$110,960 to First Congregational Church, Winter Park, FL. 2 grants: $97,280 (For positions, equipment and programs for the youth and children), $13,680 (For conferences, enrichment programs and materials).

$53,700 to Johns Hopkins University, School of Nursing, Baltimore, MD. For scholarships for Peace Corps Volunteers for accelerated undergraduate nursing program.
$23,900 to Christian Service Center for Central Florida, Orlando, FL. For Kidsfocus and Operation Home Fires programs.
$18,000 to Mental Health Association of Central Florida, FL. For Youth Court Diversion program.
$16,040 to Winter Park Public Library, Winter Park, FL. For Summer Reading Program and for new computers and software for children and youth rooms.
$10,000 to Boggy Creek Gang-A Hole in the Wall Gang Camp, Eustis, FL. To provide nurses for ill children and their families.
$9,001 to Interfaith Hospitality Network of Orange and Seminole Counties, Orlando, FL. To provide payment for transport van.
$5,000 to Winter Park High School Foundation, Winter Park, FL. For new computer equipment.

2044
Hahn Family Foundation, Inc. ◇
c/o D. Tescher
2101 Corporate Blvd., Ste. 107
Boca Raton, FL 33431-7319
Application address: c/o Barry Hahn, 1313 Hastings St., Teaneck, NJ 07666, NY tel.: (718) 252-2319

Established in 1997 in FL.
Donors: Elliot Hahn; Lillian Hahn.
Foundation type: Independent foundation.
Financial data (yr. ended 12/31/05): Assets, $6,740,184 (M); gifts received, $975,240; expenditures, $409,130; qualifying distributions, $353,423; giving activities include $353,423 for 69 grants (high: $160,036; low: $18).
Fields of interest: Human services; Jewish agencies & temples.
Application information:
Deadline(s): None
Directors: Barry Hahn; Helen Helfman; Max Helfman.
EIN: 650757808
Selected grants: The following grants were reported in 2005.
$40,000 to Yeshiva University, New York, NY.
$7,950 to Yeshiva of North Jersey, River Edge, NJ.
$5,000 to American Friends of Beit Issie Shapiro, New York, NY.
$2,000 to Torah Schools for Israel, New York, NY.
$1,800 to Kesher - Information, Guidance and Counseling Center for Parents, Jerusalem, Israel. .
$280 to Hebrew Academy for Special Children, Brooklyn, NY.
$180 to Jewish Center for Special Education, Brooklyn, NY.
$100 to Bais Medrash Elyon, Monsey, NY.
$72 to PTACH, Brooklyn, NY.

2045
D. Ray and Sibyl Hall Charitable Foundation ◇
P.O. Box 863
Williston, FL 32696

Established in 2000 in FL.
Donor: Sibyl Hall.
Foundation type: Independent foundation.

Financial data (yr. ended 12/31/05): Assets, $9,552,881 (M); expenditures, $762,372; qualifying distributions, $554,000; giving activities include $500,000 for 9 grants (high: $150,000; low: $10,000).
Purpose and activities: Giving primarily for social services for aid to senior citizens.
Fields of interest: Food services; Housing/shelter, development; Human services; Christian agencies & churches; Aging; Economically disadvantaged.
Limitations: Applications not accepted. Giving primarily in WV. No grants to individuals.
Application information: Contributes only to pre-selected organizations.
Trustees: James Cornelius; Sandra Raye Hall; James D. Stonestreet.
EIN: 597190426

2046
Ruth A. Hamilton-Forbes Charitable Trust ✧ ☆
P.O. Box 1908
Orlando, FL   32802-1908

Established in 2003 in FL.
Donor: Ruth Hamilton-Forbes‡.
Foundation type: Independent foundation.
Financial data (yr. ended 12/31/05): Assets, $8,915,119 (M); expenditures, $995,315; qualifying distributions, $933,733; giving activities include $933,733 for grants.
Fields of interest: Higher education, university; Human services; Salvation Army; Roman Catholic agencies & churches.
Limitations: Applications not accepted. No grants to individuals.
Application information: Contributes only to pre-selected organizations.
Trustee: SunTrust Bank.
EIN: 597228592

2047
Hard Rock Cafe Foundation, Inc. ✧
6100 Old Park Ln.
Orlando, FL   32835

Established in 2000 in FL.
Donor: Hard Rock Cafe International (USA) Inc.
Foundation type: Company-sponsored foundation.
Financial data (yr. ended 12/31/04): Assets, $16 (M); gifts received, $550,415; expenditures, $550,599; qualifying distributions, $550,112; giving activities include $550,112 for 16 grants (high: $309,492; low: $1,328).
Purpose and activities: The foundation supports organizations involved with arts and culture, breast cancer, and human services.
Fields of interest: Arts; Breast cancer; Cancer research; Breast cancer research; Disasters, 9/11/01; Children, services; Family services; Human services.
Limitations: Applications not accepted.
Application information: Contributes only to pre-selected organizations.
Officers and Directors:* Hamish Dodds,* Pres.; Jay Wolszczak,* Secy.; Michael Salter,* Treas.
EIN: 593686985

2048
The Hardison Family Foundation ✧
1682 Edith Esplanade
Cape Coral, FL   33904

Established in 1996 in FL.
Donor: Leslie Hardison.
Foundation type: Independent foundation.
Financial data (yr. ended 12/31/05): Assets, $7,385,537 (M); expenditures, $431,430; qualifying distributions, $426,750; giving activities include $425,000 for 15 grants (high: $50,000; low: $7,500).
Purpose and activities: Giving primarily for social services.
Fields of interest: Higher education; Engineering school/education; Hospitals (specialty); Food banks; Human services; Children, services; Federated giving programs.
Limitations: Giving on a national basis. No grants to individuals.
Trustees: Susan Black; Dolores E. Hardison; James Hardison; Janet Hardison; Jill Hardison; John Hardison; Leslie C. Hardison; Paul Hardison; Patricia Jackson.
EIN: 650700303
Selected grants: The following grants were reported in 2005.
$50,000 to Childrens Hospital.
$50,000 to Greater Chicago Food Depository, Chicago, IL.
$50,000 to Illinois Institute of Technology, Chicago, IL.
$50,000 to Salvation Army.
$15,000 to Americas Second Harvest, Chicago, IL.
$15,000 to March of Dimes Birth Defects Foundation, White Plains, NY.
$7,500 to Old McDonalds Farm, Corbett, OR.

2049
The Harrington Family Foundation ✧ ☆
c/o Ronald G. Harrington
13 Sail Point Rd.
Key Largo, FL   33037

Established in 2002 in OH.
Donor: Ronald G. Harrington.
Foundation type: Independent foundation.
Financial data (yr. ended 12/31/04): Assets, $3,415,312 (M); expenditures, $583,512; qualifying distributions, $569,724; giving activities include $569,724 for 20 grants (high: $333,719; low: $30).
Fields of interest: Education; Human services; Christian agencies & churches.
Limitations: Applications not accepted. No grants to individuals.
Application information: Contributes only to pre-selected organizations.
Trustees: Nancy A. Harrington; Ronald G. Harrington; Ronald M. Harrington; Jill A. McLaughlin; Stephen M. McLaughlin.
EIN: 830343509

2050
Harris Foundation
1025 W. NASA Blvd., A12A
Melbourne, FL   32919

Incorporated in 1958 in OH.
Donor: Harris Corp.

Foundation type: Company-sponsored foundation.
Financial data (yr. ended 6/30/05): Assets, $4,551,200 (M); gifts received, $2,161,486; expenditures, $1,997,257; qualifying distributions, $1,996,898; giving activities include $1,766,833 for 98 grants (high: $610,000; low: $120), and $215,304 for employee matching gifts.
Purpose and activities: The foundation supports organizations involved with arts and culture, education, health, and human services.
Fields of interest: Arts; Higher education; Education; Health care; Children/youth, services; Human services; Federated giving programs.
Type of support: Employee matching gifts.
Limitations: Applications not accepted. Giving limited to areas of company operations. No grants to individuals, or for endowments; no loans.
Application information: Contributes only to pre-selected organizations.
Officers and Trustee: Howard L. Lance, Pres.; Gary L. McArthur, Treas.; Jeffrey Shuman, V.P.; Scott Mituen, Secy.; Brenda Morrish.
EIN: 346520425

2051
Hayden Foundation ✧
3240 N.E. Sugar Hill
Jensen Beach, FL   34957

Established in 1964 in MI.
Donor: Donald C. Hayden.
Foundation type: Independent foundation.
Financial data (yr. ended 12/31/04): Assets, $4,077,190 (M); expenditures, $322,788; qualifying distributions, $321,580; giving activities include $321,446 for 230 grants (high: $100,000; low: $10).
Purpose and activities: Giving for education and Protestant organizations.
Fields of interest: Education; Protestant agencies & churches.
Limitations: Applications not accepted. Giving on a national basis. No grants to individuals.
Application information: Contributes only to pre-selected organizations.
Officers: Donald C. Hayden, Pres.; A.R. Hayden, V.P.; R.H. Barrie, Secy.-Treas.
EIN: 386118718
Selected grants: The following grants were reported in 2004.
$5,000 to American Red Cross.
$1,355 to Prison Fellowship Ministries, Lansdowne, VA. 2 grants: $380, $975
$1,000 to Lyric Theater, Minneapolis, MN.
$1,000 to Media Research Center, Alexandria, VA. 2 grants: $200, $800
$500 to Cato Institute, DC.
$500 to Salvation Army.
$200 to Bethel Mission, Des Moines, IA.
$100 to U.S. English, DC.

2052
The Hayes Family Charitable Foundation ✧ ☆
917 S. 1st St., No. 601
Jacksonville Beach, FL   32250   (904) 246-4447
Contact: Cris Hayes
Application address: c/o Traci VanPelt, Admin., 922 S. 1st St., No. 401, Jacksonville Beach, FL 32250, tel.: (904) 247-0062, E-mail: traci@hayesone.com; URL: http://www.hayesfamilyfoundation.org

Established in 1997 in FL.
Donors: Christine P. Hayes; Jerome A. Hayes.
Foundation type: Independent foundation.
Financial data (yr. ended 12/31/05): Assets, $1,989,492 (M); gifts received, $492,352; expenditures, $473,153; qualifying distributions, $457,929; giving activities include $457,929 for 26 grants (high: $382,000; low: $50).
Purpose and activities: Giving to Catholic programs and human service organizations.
Fields of interest: Reproductive health, sexuality education; Substance abuse, prevention; Housing/shelter, temporary shelter; Family services, adolescent parents; Roman Catholic agencies & churches.
Type of support: Emergency funds; Scholarship funds; Matching/challenge support.
Limitations: Giving primarily in St. Johns and Duval counties, FL. No grants to individuals.
Application information: Application guidelines available on foundation Web site. Application form not required.
   Initial approach: Letter
   Copies of proposal: 1
   Deadline(s): None
   Board meeting date(s): Nov.
   Final notification: 60 days
Trustees: Christine P. Hayes; Jerome A. Hayes.
EIN: 311504028

2053
The John T. and Winifred Hayward Foundation Charitable Trust ◆
c/o AmSouth Bank
P.O. Box 2918
Clearwater, FL 33757-2918 (727) 592-6907
Contact: Laura Papasergi, AmSouth Bank

Trust established in 1973 in FL.
Donors: John T. Hayward‡; Winifred M. Hayward‡.
Foundation type: Independent foundation.
Financial data (yr. ended 12/31/05): Assets, $9,458,451 (M); expenditures, $612,635; qualifying distributions, $562,285; giving activities include $460,000 for 4 grants (high: $285,000; low: $35,000).
Purpose and activities: Support for medical research organizations and schools involved in the field of genetics, with emphasis on birth defects and inheritable diseases.
Fields of interest: Medical research, institute.
Type of support: Research.
Limitations: Applications not accepted. Giving on a national basis. No grants to individuals, or for building or endowment funds or operating budgets.
Application information: Contributes only to pre-selected organizations.
Trustees: William R. LaRosa, M.D.; Browder Rives; Howard P. Rives; AmSouth Bank.
EIN: 237363201

2054
Heartbeat International Worldwide, Inc. ◆
(formerly Heartbeat International of West Central Florida)
6800 N. Dale Mabry Hwy., No. 124
Tampa, FL 33614 (813) 243-8769
Contact: Liz Campos, Admin. Coord.
FAX: (813) 496-1319;
E-mail: info@heartbeatintl.org; URL: http://www.heartbeatintl.org

Established in 1984.
Donors: Medtronic, Inc.; Pacesetter Systems, Inc.; Intermedics, Inc.; St. Joseph's Hospital; Watson Clinic Foundation; St. Jude Medical, CRM Div.; George Lorton.
Foundation type: Operating foundation.
Financial data (yr. ended 12/31/05): Assets, $11,597,711 (M); gifts received, $14,268,433; expenditures, $9,703,440; qualifying distributions, $9,703,440; giving activities include $9,195,500 for grants.
Purpose and activities: Giving primarily for cardiac pacemakers.
Fields of interest: Heart & circulatory diseases.
Type of support: Equipment; Matching/challenge support.
Publications: Informational brochure; Newsletter.
Application information:
   Board meeting date(s): Mar. and Nov.
Officers: Benedict Maniscalco, M.D., C.E.O.; Will Mick, Pres.; George H. Lorton, Treas.
Number of staff: 1 full-time professional; 2 full-time support; 1 part-time support.
EIN: 593236060

2055
George A. Helow Family Foundation, Inc. ◆
8118 Summit Ridge Ln.
Jacksonville, FL 32256-7149

Established in 1988 in FL.
Foundation type: Independent foundation.
Financial data (yr. ended 12/31/05): Assets, $6,671,114 (M); gifts received, $2,700; expenditures, $408,571; qualifying distributions, $387,800; giving activities include $387,800 for 26 grants (high: $114,800; low: $1,000).
Purpose and activities: Giving primarily to Roman Catholic organizations.
Fields of interest: Education; Human services; Residential/custodial care, hospices; Roman Catholic agencies & churches.
Limitations: Applications not accepted. Giving primarily in Jacksonville, FL. No grants to individuals.
Application information: Contributes only to pre-selected organizations.
Officers and Directors:* George A. Helow,* Chair.; Joseph P. Helow,* Pres.; Margaret O. Helow,* Secy.-Treas.; Anne Helow Darling; Katherine Helow Gilligan; Diane Helow Parker; Mary Helow Pritchard; Theresa Helow Ryan.
EIN: 592904267
Selected grants: The following grants were reported in 2004.
$79,400 to Holy Family Catholic Church, Jacksonville, FL.
$50,000 to Diocese of Saint Augustine, Jacksonville, FL.
$20,000 to Catholic Relief Services, Baltimore, MD.
$10,000 to Catholic Charities Bureau, Jacksonville, FL.
$10,000 to Catholic Charities of the Diocese of Venice, Venice, FL.
$10,000 to Eternal Word Television Network, Birmingham, AL.
$10,000 to Food for the Poor, Deerfield Beach, FL.
$6,000 to Sisters of Saint Joseph, Saint Augustine, FL.
$5,000 to Franciscan Friars of the Renewal, Bronx, NY.
$5,000 to Hospice of Northeast Florida, Jacksonville, FL.

2056
The A. D. Henderson Foundation, Inc.
P.O. Box 14096
Fort Lauderdale, FL 33302 (954) 764-2819
Contact: Karen Pfeiffer
E-mail: staff@hendersonfdn.org; URL: http://www.hendersonfdn.org

Established in 1969.
Foundation type: Independent foundation.
Financial data (yr. ended 9/30/05): Assets, $58,602,216 (M); expenditures, $3,287,055; qualifying distributions, $2,811,930; giving activities include $2,253,449 for 89 grants (high: $86,250; low: $6,250).
Purpose and activities: Giving limited to programs involving the preparation of children to learn once they enter school, and to create and sustain affordable and effective childcare, and to strengthen the bond between communities, families, and children.
Fields of interest: Child development, education; Reproductive health, family planning; Children/youth, services; Child development, services.
Type of support: Continuing support; Management development/capacity building; Program development; Seed money; Curriculum development; Technical assistance; Matching/challenge support.
Limitations: Giving primarily in Broward and Marion Counties, FL and VT. No grants to individuals; loans; annual campaigns; building/renovation; capital campaigns; debt reduction; general/operating support or research.
Publications: Application guidelines; Program policy statement; Program policy statement (including application guidelines).
Application information: Application guidelines available on foundation Web site.
   Initial approach: Telephone
   Deadline(s): Quarterly
   Board meeting date(s): Quarterly
Officers and Trustees:* Allen Douglas Henderson,* Pres.; Barbara K. Henderson,* V.P.; Lucia Henderson,* V.P.; James M. Lyon,* V.P.; Bruce D. Oberfest,* Secy.-Treas.
Number of staff: 1 full-time professional; 1 part-time professional; 1 full-time support; 1 part-time support.
EIN: 237047045

2057
The Henriksen Charitable Trust ◆
9218 Cypress Green Dr., Ste. 2
Jacksonville, FL 32256

Established in 2000 in CT.
Foundation type: Independent foundation.
Financial data (yr. ended 12/31/05): Assets, $11,129,793 (M); expenditures, $661,567; qualifying distributions, $523,371; giving activities include $405,200 for 7 grants (high: $125,000; low: $200).
Fields of interest: Secondary school/education; Higher education; Health care, ethics; Christian agencies & churches.
Limitations: Applications not accepted. Giving primarily in CT and FL. No grants to individuals.
Application information: Contributes only to pre-selected organizations.
Trustee: Bradley S. Anderson.
EIN: 066460490

2058
Dorothy B. Hersh Foundation, Inc.
1299 N. Tamiami Trail, Ste. 423
Sarasota, FL 34236-2466 (941) 951-0531
Contact: Robert W. Donnelly, Sr., Secy. and Admin.
FAX: (941) 951-0532;
E-mail: rwdonnelly@comcast.net

Established in 1982 in NJ.
Donor: Dorothy B. Hersh†.
Foundation type: Independent foundation.
Financial data (yr. ended 5/31/06): Assets,
$12,033,423 (M); expenditures, $755,717;
qualifying distributions, $687,882; giving activities
include $527,456 for 10 grants (high: $141,000;
low: $200), and $103,333 for 1 employee matching
gift.
Purpose and activities: Giving limited to agencies
that represent handicapped children.
Fields of interest: Hospitals (general); Health
organizations, association; Human services;
Children/youth, services.
Type of support: Capital campaigns; Building/
renovation; Equipment; Land acquisition; Matching/
challenge support.
Limitations: Giving limited to NJ. No grants to
individuals, or for programs, or operating budgets.
Publications: Application guidelines; Annual report.
Application information: Grant requests must be for
capital purposes for handicapped children only.
Application form required.
  Initial approach: Letter requesting application
    requirements
  Copies of proposal: 6
  Deadline(s): None
  Board meeting date(s): Varies
  Final notification: After board meetings
Officers and Directors:* Robert Donnelly, Jr.,*
Pres.; Robert W. Donnelly, Sr., Secy. and Admin.;
William Johnson; Paul Schack.
Number of staff: 1 part-time professional.
EIN: 222280011
Selected grants: The following grants were reported
in 2004.
$150,000 to Saint Peters University Hospital, New
  Brunswick, NJ. For Children's Hospital.
$130,000 to Midland School, North Branch, NJ. For
  capital campaign.
$125,000 to Cerebral Palsy Association of
  Middlesex County, Edison, NJ. For challenge
  grant.
$79,000 to CPC Behavioral Healthcare, Red Bank,
  NJ.
$75,000 to Delbarton School, Morristown, NJ. To
  endow scholarship fund for city students.
$20,000 to Phoenix Center, Little Falls, NJ.
$15,000 to Occupational Center of Union County,
  Roselle, NJ. To upgrade and replace old kitchen
  equipment.

2059
The Hicks Charitable Foundation ✧
1725 Memorial Park Dr.
Jacksonville, FL 32204

Established in 1979.
Donors: David M. Hicks; Wendell C. Webster;
Jacksonville Housing Authority; United Way of
Northeast Florida.
Foundation type: Independent foundation.
Financial data (yr. ended 3/31/05): Assets,
$93,144 (M); gifts received, $620,045;
expenditures, $597,260; qualifying distributions,

$55,198; giving activities include $541,904 for 56
grants (high: $250,000; low: $30).
Purpose and activities: Giving primarily for
education, human services, community
development, and Episcopal churches.
Fields of interest: Museums (art); Higher education;
Education; Housing/shelter, development; Human
services; Community development; Protestant
agencies & churches.
Limitations: Applications not accepted. Giving
primarily in Jacksonville, FL. No grants to individuals.
Application information: Contributes only to
pre-selected organizations.
Trustees: W. Robinson Frazier; Ann C. Hicks; David
M. Hicks.
EIN: 591947616

2060
Roch & Carol Hillenbrand Foundation ✧ ☆
c/o Michael R. Hillenbrand
149 10th Ave. S.
Naples, FL 34102

Established in 1999 in NJ.
Donor: Michael R. Hillenbrand.
Foundation type: Independent foundation.
Financial data (yr. ended 9/30/05): Assets,
$5,357,565 (M); gifts received, $1,353,874;
expenditures, $424,613; qualifying distributions,
$404,000; giving activities include $404,000 for
grants.
Fields of interest: Education; Human services.
Limitations: Applications not accepted. Giving
primarily in NJ and NY. No grants to individuals.
Application information: Contributes only to
pre-selected organizations.
Trustees: Carol Hillenbrand; Justin Hillenbrand;
Michael R. Hillenbrand; Molly Vernon.
EIN: 134050660

2061
Hilton Family Foundation ✧ ☆
P.O. Box 59462
Panama City, FL 32412-0462

Established in 2002 in FL.
Donor: Charles and Lela Hilton Foundation.
Foundation type: Independent foundation.
Financial data (yr. ended 12/31/05): Assets,
$3,712,370 (M); gifts received, $1,360,000;
expenditures, $403,882; qualifying distributions,
$387,269; giving activities include $387,269 for 29
grants (high: $86,250; low: $400).
Fields of interest: Education; Health care; Mental
health, schizophrenia; Alzheimer's disease
research; Boy scouts.
Limitations: Applications not accepted. No grants to
individuals.
Application information: Contributes only to
pre-selected organizations.
Directors: Charles Hilton; Lela Hilton.
EIN: 593748610
Selected grants: The following grants were reported
in 2004.
$150,000 to Holy Nativity Episcopal Church, Plano,
  TX.
$15,000 to Boy Scouts of America.
$3,000 to Tax Foundation, DC.
$600 to American Civil Rights Institute,
  Sacramento, CA.

$500 to American Institute for Cancer Research,
  DC.
$500 to Arthritis Foundation, Atlanta, GA.
$500 to Media Research Center, Alexandria, VA.

2062
Count and Countess de Hoernle Foundation, Inc. ✧
c/o Donald C. Sider & Assocs.
6751 N. Federal Hwy., Ste. 200
Boca Raton, FL 33487

Established in 1991 in FL.
Donors: A.W. Hoernle Foundation; Countess
Henrietta de Hoernle.
Foundation type: Independent foundation.
Financial data (yr. ended 12/31/05): Assets,
$2,846,667 (M); expenditures, $2,579,007;
qualifying distributions, $2,574,000; giving
activities include $2,574,000 for 1 grant.
Fields of interest: Foundations (public).
Limitations: Applications not accepted. Giving
primarily in Boca Raton, FL. No grants to individuals.
Application information: Contributes only to
pre-selected organizations.
Officer and Directors:* Countess Henrietta de
Hoernle,* Pres.; James J. Oussani.
EIN: 650221652

2063
The Ralph and Nancy Holden Charitable Foundation, Inc. ✧
969 A1A
Hillsboro Beach, FL 33062 (954) 785-8424
Contact: Nancy Holden Secy.; Ralph Holden, Pres.

Established in 1998 in FL.
Donors: Nancy Holden; Ralph Holden.
Foundation type: Independent foundation.
Financial data (yr. ended 12/31/03): Assets,
$829,769 (M); expenditures, $407,620; qualifying
distributions, $396,487; giving activities include
$396,707 for 9 grants (high: $302,107; low:
$2,500).
Purpose and activities: Giving primarily to multiple
sclerosis organizations as well as for cancer
research, and for human services.
Fields of interest: Higher education; Multiple
sclerosis; Cancer research; Human services;
Christian agencies & churches.
Limitations: Giving on a national basis.
Application information:
  Initial approach: Letter
  Deadline(s): None
Officers: Ralph Holden, Pres.; Nancy Holden, Secy.;
Robert Dungan, Treas.
EIN: 650819397

2064
Pick Hollinger Charitable Trust ✧ ☆
c/o CB&T
P.O. Box 12966
Pensacola, FL 32591

Established in 1994 in FL.
Foundation type: Independent foundation.
Financial data (yr. ended 5/31/05): Assets,
$6,218,191 (M); expenditures, $373,848;
qualifying distributions, $315,604; giving activities

include $318,045 for 7 grants (high: $118,479; low: $5,000).

Purpose and activities: Giving primarily to Baptist organizations and churches.

Fields of interest: Protestant agencies & churches.

Limitations: Applications not accepted. Giving primarily in FL. No grants to individuals.

Application information: Contributes only to pre-selected organizations.

    Board meeting date(s): July

Trustee: CB&T.

EIN: 597045666

Selected grants: The following grants were reported in 2003.

$71,725 to Florida Baptist Convention, Jacksonville, FL. 2 grants: $51,232, $20,493

$36,887 to Florida Baptist Theological College, Graceville, FL.

$34,838 to First Church in Blountstown, Blountstown, FL.

$22,542 to Baptist Health Care Foundation, Pensacola, FL.

$20,493 to Southern Baptist Convention, Nashville, TN.

$8,000 to Cove Baptist Church, Panama City, FL.

$5,000 to First Baptist Church, Panama City, FL.

$5,000 to First Baptist Church of Marianna, Marianna, FL.

$3,000 to Westview Baptist Church, Panama City, FL.

2065
David & Francie Horvitz Family Foundation, Inc. ✧
401 E. Las Olas Blvd., Ste. 2200
Fort Lauderdale, FL 33301

Established in 2000 in FL.

Foundation type: Independent foundation.

Financial data (yr. ended 12/31/05): Assets, $3,108,306 (M); gifts received, $3,000,000; expenditures, $1,725,611; qualifying distributions, $1,725,550; giving activities include $1,725,550 for 36 grants (high: $700,000; low: $250).

Purpose and activities: Giving primarily for the arts, education, and youth programs.

Fields of interest: Arts; Higher education; Youth development, services; Jewish agencies & temples.

Limitations: Applications not accepted. Giving primarily in FL. No grants to individuals.

Application information: Contributes only to pre-selected organizations.

Officers: David W. Horvitz, Pres.; Francie Horvitz, Secy.; Robert J. Puck, Treas.

EIN: 650974291

Selected grants: The following grants were reported in 2005.

$200,000 to Young at Art Childrens Museum, Davie, FL.

$155,000 to Museum of Art, Fort Lauderdale, FL.

$50,750 to Gildas Club of South Florida, Fort Lauderdale, FL.

$50,000 to Jack and Jill Childrens Center, Fort Lauderdale, FL.

$20,000 to Broward Education Foundation, Fort Lauderdale, FL.

$20,000 to Urban League.

$15,000 to Gold Coast Jazz Society, Fort Lauderdale, FL.

$12,500 to Jewish Museum of Florida, Miami Beach, FL.

$12,000 to Kenyon College, Gambier, OH.

$10,000 to Fort Lauderdale Historical Society, Fort Lauderdale, FL.

2066
The Hough Family Foundation, Inc.
5700 Mariner St., No. 201 E
Tampa, FL 33609
Contact: Susan Hough Henry Ph.D., Pres.
E-mail: susanhenry@tampabay.rr.com

Established in 1996 in FL.

Donor: William R. Hough.

Foundation type: Independent foundation.

Financial data (yr. ended 12/31/05): Assets, $15,350,675 (M); gifts received, $800,000; expenditures, $1,635,782; qualifying distributions, $1,599,001; giving activities include $1,599,001 for 24 grants (high: $250,000; low: $1,001).

Purpose and activities: Giving primarily for the arts and education.

Fields of interest: Arts, multipurpose centers/programs; Performing arts, theater; Higher education; Health care.

Type of support: Capital campaigns; Building/renovation.

Limitations: Applications not accepted. Giving primarily in FL. No grants to individuals.

Application information: Unsolicited requests for funds not accepted.

    Board meeting date(s): June 30

Officers and Directors:* Susan Hough Henry, Ph.D.,*, Pres.; Hazel C. Hough,* V.P.; William R. Hough,* V.P.; W. Robb Hough,* Secy.; Helen H. Feinberg,* Treas.

EIN: 593395491

Selected grants: The following grants were reported in 2004.

$700,000 to University of Florida Foundation, Gainesville, FL.

$375,000 to Canterbury School, Fort Myers, FL. 3 grants: $300,000, $25,000, $50,000

$50,000 to Eckerd College, Saint Petersburg, FL. 2 grants: $25,000 each

$25,000 to Florida Orchestra, Tampa, FL.

$25,000 to Mahaffey Theater Foundation, Saint Petersburg, FL.

$25,000 to Palladium Theater, Saint Petersburg, FL.

$5,000 to Tampa Museum of Art, Tampa, FL.

2067
HTR Foundation, Inc. ✧
100 2nd Ave. S., Ste. 600
St. Petersburg, FL 33701-4336 (727) 821-6161
Contact: Jeffrey P. McClanathan, Pres.
E-mail: jmcclanathan@gsscpa.com

Established in 1997 in FL.

Donor: A. Copeland Hill Trust.

Foundation type: Independent foundation.

Financial data (yr. ended 6/30/05): Assets, $15,107,778 (M); gifts received, $98,078; expenditures, $791,457; qualifying distributions, $699,274; giving activities include $650,000 for 1 grant.

Purpose and activities: Giving for the education of Civil War history, and preservation of Civil War battlefields.

Fields of interest: Historic preservation/historical societies.

Application information:

    Initial approach: Letter (no more than 3 pages)

    Deadline(s): None

    Board meeting date(s): Winter, spring, and fall

    Final notification: 1 month

Officers: Jeffrey P. McClanathan, Pres.; James A. Wesley, Treas.

EIN: 593496606

Selected grants: The following grants were reported in 2005.

$650,000 to Civil War Preservation Trust, Hagerstown, MD. To purchase battlefield.

2068
Huizenga Family Foundation ✧
450 E. Las Olas Blvd., Ste. 1500
Fort Lauderdale, FL 33301
Contact: H. Wayne Huizenga, Jr., Pres.

Established in 1987 in FL.

Donor: H. Wayne Huizenga.

Foundation type: Independent foundation.

Financial data (yr. ended 12/31/04): Assets, $25,335,780 (M); gifts received, $29,635,775; expenditures, $6,700,387; qualifying distributions, $6,419,725; giving activities include $6,417,104 for 192 grants (high: $1,000,000; low: $50).

Purpose and activities: Giving primarily for social services.

Fields of interest: Education; Animal welfare; Hospitals (general); Health care; Cancer; Recreation; Boys & girls clubs; Human services; Philanthropy/voluntarism.

Limitations: Applications not accepted. Giving primarily in FL.

Application information: Contributes only to pre-selected organizations.

Officers and Directors:* H. Wayne Huizenga, Jr.,* Pres.; Martha Jean Huizenga,* V.P.; Cris V. Branden,* Treas.; Harris W. Hudson; H. Wayne Huizenga.

EIN: 650018158

2069
Emily S. and Coleman A. Hunter Trust ✧
c/o SunTrust Bank
P.O. Box 1908
Orlando, FL 32802

Established in 1985 in VA.

Donors: Coleman A. Hunter†; Emily S. Hunter†.

Foundation type: Independent foundation.

Financial data (yr. ended 2/28/06): Assets, $6,688,053 (M); expenditures, $353,472; qualifying distributions, $338,192; giving activities include $323,850 for 24 grants (high: $25,000; low: $3,750; average: $5,000–$10,000).

Purpose and activities: Funding primarily for education.

Fields of interest: Museums; Arts; Education; Hospitals (general); Health organizations, association; Human services; Children/youth, services; Roman Catholic agencies & churches.

Limitations: Applications not accepted. Giving limited to VA, with emphasis on Richmond. No grants to individuals.

Application information: Contributes only to pre-selected organizations.

Trustee: SunTrust Bank.

EIN: 546219496

Selected grants: The following grants were reported in 2003.

$20,000 to Hospital Hospitality House of Richmond, Richmond, VA. For general support.

$20,000 to Special Olympics Virginia, Richmond, VA. For general support.

$20,000 to Westminster-Canterbury Foundation, Richmond, VA. For general support.

$17,500 to Virginia Historical Society, Richmond, VA. For general support.

$15,000 to American Heart Association, Richmond, VA.

$10,000 to Childrens Museum of Richmond, Richmond, VA. For general support.

$10,000 to Greater Richmond SCAN (Stop Child Abuse Now), Richmond, VA. For general support.

$10,000 to Saint Gertrude High School, Richmond, VA. For general support.

$10,000 to Virginia College Fund, Richmond, VA. For general support.

$10,000 to Virginia Home for Boys and Girls, Richmond, VA. For general support.

2070
The Isenberg Family Charitable Trust ✧
c/o PricewaterhouseCoopers, LLP
222 Lakeview Ave., Ste. 360
West Palm Beach, FL 33401
Contact: W. Fong

Established in 1987 in FL.
Donors: Eugene M. Isenberg; Salmon Atlas, LP.
Foundation type: Independent foundation.
Financial data (yr. ended 12/31/03): Assets, $10,997,160 (M); expenditures, $696,597; qualifying distributions, $612,775; giving activities include $612,775 for 58 grants (high: $85,000; low: $40).
Purpose and activities: Support primarily for arts and culture, education, health care, and Jewish organizations.
Fields of interest: Performing arts, opera; Arts; Higher education; Education; Hospitals (general); Health care; Health organizations, association; Human services; Youth, services; Civil rights; Jewish agencies & temples.
Limitations: Applications not accepted. Giving on a national basis, with some emphasis on FL, MA, and NY. Generally no grants to individuals.
Application information: Generally contributes only to pre-selected organizations.
Trustees: Diane S. Isenberg; Christopher Papouras.
EIN: 596874814
Selected grants: The following grants were reported in 2003.
$200,000 to Massachusetts General Hospital, Boston, MA.
$61,170 to Metropolitan Opera Association, New York, NY.
$29,050 to Palm Beach Opera, Palm Beach, FL.
$15,380 to Brigham and Womens Hospital, Boston, MA.
$5,000 to Florida Philharmonic Orchestra, Fort Lauderdale, FL.
$500 to Dana-Farber Cancer Institute, Boston, MA.
$500 to New York University, School of Medicine, New York, NY.
$300 to Philharmonic-Symphony Society of New York, New York Philharmonic, New York, NY.
$200 to Leukemia & Lymphoma Society, West Palm Beach, FL.
$100 to Multiple Sclerosis Society, National, Fort Lauderdale, FL.

2071
Jacksonville Jaguars Foundation ✧
1 ALLTEL Stadium Pl.
Jacksonville, FL 32202-1917 (904) 633-5437
Contact: Peter M. Racine, Exec. Dir.
FAX: (904) 633-5683; URL: http://www.jaguars.com/Foundation

Established in 1994 in FL.
Donor: Jacksonville Jaguars, Ltd.
Foundation type: Company-sponsored foundation.
Financial data (yr. ended 12/31/04): Assets, $4,940,427 (L); gifts received, $1,872,428; expenditures, $2,000,030; qualifying distributions, $1,416,275; giving activities include $1,145,661 for 69 grants (high: $100,000; low: $840).
Purpose and activities: The foundation supports organizations involved with arts and culture, higher education, recreation, youth development, and families.
Fields of interest: Arts; Higher education; Recreation; Youth development; Family services.
Type of support: General/operating support; Continuing support; Capital campaigns; Building/renovation; Equipment; Program development; Technical assistance; Program evaluation; In-kind gifts; Matching/challenge support.
Limitations: Giving limited to the greater Jacksonville, FL, area, including Baker, Clay, Duval, Nassau, and St. Johns counties. No support for schools, religious organizations not of direct benefit to the entire community, or disease-specific organizations. No grants to individuals, or for fundraising or sponsorships.
Publications: Application guidelines; Grants list; Informational brochure (including application guidelines).
Application information: Application form required.
Initial approach: Download application form and mail to foundation
Copies of proposal: 4
Deadline(s): Generally, Feb. and July
Board meeting date(s): Generally, summer and winter
Final notification: Within 4 months
Officers and Directors:* Delores Barr Weaver,* Chair. and C.E.O.; Lawrence Dubow,* Secy.-Treas.; Peter M. Racine, Exec. Dir.; Elizabeth Petway; J. Wayne Weaver.
Number of staff: 3 full-time professional; 1 full-time support; 1 part-time support.
EIN: 593249687
Selected grants: The following grants were reported in 2003.
$45,000 to Planned Parenthood of Northeast Florida, Jacksonville, FL.
$35,000 to Jacksonville Museum of Modern Art, Jacksonville, FL.
$25,000 to Boys and Girls Club of Nassau County Foundation, Fernandina Beach, FL.
$19,149 to University of Florida, Health Science Center, Jacksonville, FL.
$13,389 to PACE Center for Girls of Jacksonville, Jacksonville, FL.
$12,500 to Junior Achievement of Floridas First Coast, Jacksonville, FL.
$12,000 to Theaterworks, Jacksonville, FL.
$9,000 to Limelight Theater, Saint Augustine, FL.
$8,985 to Family Nurturing Center of Florida, Jacksonville, FL.
$2,000 to Jacksonville Public Library Foundation, Jacksonville, FL.

2072
Irving and Eleanor Jaffe Foundation, Inc. ✧
20290 Fairway Oaks Dr., Ste. 284
Boca Raton, FL 33434
Contact: Eleanor Jaffe, Secy.-Treas.

Established in 1987 in GA.
Donors: Eleanor Jaffe; Irving Jaffe; Jack Jaffe.
Foundation type: Independent foundation.
Financial data (yr. ended 6/30/04): Assets, $1,904,177 (M); expenditures, $1,581,578; qualifying distributions, $1,567,650; giving activities include $1,567,650 for 9 grants (high: $1,500,000; low: $100).
Purpose and activities: Giving primarily for social services and to Jewish agencies and temples.
Fields of interest: Education; Health care; Human services; Jewish federated giving programs; Jewish agencies & temples.
Type of support: Scholarship funds.
Limitations: Giving primarily in CA, FL, and NY. No grants to individuals.
Application information: Application form not required.
Initial approach: Letter
Deadline(s): None
Officers: Irving Jaffe, Pres.; Jack Jaffe, V.P.; Eleanor Jaffe, Secy.-Treas.
EIN: 592751352

2073
The Jaharis Family Foundation, Inc. ✧
2200 N. Commerce Pkwy., 3rd Fl.
Weston, FL 33326-3258 (954) 331-3811
Contact: Kathryn Jaharis, Pres.

Established in 1986 in FL.
Donors: Michael Jaharis, Jr.; Mary Jaharis; The 1998 Katina Charitable Trust; The 1998 MJ Trust; The 1998 Katina Charitable Trust No. 2.
Foundation type: Independent foundation.
Financial data (yr. ended 9/30/05): Assets, $35,198,080 (M); gifts received, $713,864; expenditures, $4,436,559; qualifying distributions, $4,303,588; giving activities include $4,303,588 for 38 grants (high: $1,500,000; low: $2,000).
Fields of interest: Museums; Arts; Higher education; Medical school/education; Education; Hospitals (general); Human services; Residential/custodial care, senior continuing care; Orthodox Catholic agencies & churches.
Type of support: Building/renovation.
Limitations: Giving primarily in FL and NY; some giving also in Greece. No grants to individuals.
Application information: Application form not required.
Deadline(s): None
Officer and Directors:* Kathryn Jaharis,* Pres. and Secy.-Treas.; Steven K. Aronoff; Michael Jaharis; Steven Jaharis.
EIN: 592751110

2074
Jasam Foundation, Inc. ✧
c/o Samuel B. Davis
15923 Roseto Way
Naples, FL 34110

Established in 1953 in OH.
Donor: Samuel S. Davis†.
Foundation type: Independent foundation.

Financial data (yr. ended 12/31/03): Assets, $7,911,471 (M); expenditures, $698,393; qualifying distributions, $544,875; giving activities include $544,875 for 4 grants (high: $335,624; low: $50,000).

Purpose and activities: Giving primarily to institutions of higher learning. Support also for human services and health care.

Fields of interest: Higher education; Health care; Human services; YM/YWCAs & YM/YWHAs; Children, services; Foundations (community).

Type of support: Program development; Seed money.

Limitations: Applications not accepted. Giving primarily in Franklin County, OH. No grants to individuals.

Application information: Contributes only to pre-selected organizations.

Officer and Trustee:* Samuel B. Davis,* Pres. and Secy.

EIN: 316036574

2075
Jehovah-Jireh Foundation, Inc. ◇
P.O. Box 1571
Oneco, FL 34264 (941) 755-4235
E-mail: jjirfdn@aol.com; *URL:* http://www.jehovahjirehministries.org

Established in 2001 in FL.
Donor: James F. Bosse.
Foundation type: Operating foundation.
Financial data (yr. ended 11/30/05): Assets, $596,732 (M); gifts received, $54,550; expenditures, $585,313; qualifying distributions, $475,000; giving activities include $475,000 for 14 grants (high: $60,000; low: $5,000).
Purpose and activities: Provides financial assistance to new Baptist churches.
Fields of interest: Protestant agencies & churches.
Limitations: Giving on a national and international basis. No grants to individuals.
Application information: Application form required.
   Deadline(s): Dec. 15
Officers and Board Members:* James F. Bosse,* Pres.; Bob Vallier,* V.P.; Lois Bosse, Secy.-Treas.; Steve Davis; Jeff Fugate; Daniel Hicks; Rev. Ron Jarvis; Rev. Dan McAvoy; Kevin Schaal; Rev. Jeff Sizemore; Rev. Bob Warnick.
EIN: 651104291
Selected grants: The following grants were reported in 2003.
$80,000 to Grace Baptist Church, Buford, GA.
$40,200 to Calvary Baptist Church, Lansdale, PA.
$30,000 to Highlands Baptist Church At Castle Rock, Castle Rock, CO.
$15,000 to Pioneer Baptist Church, North Pole, AK.

2076
The Jelks Family Foundation, Inc. ◇ ☆
516 McKenzie Ave.
Panama City, FL 32401

Established in 1995 in FL.
Foundation type: Independent foundation.
Financial data (yr. ended 12/31/05): Assets, $5,293,689 (M); expenditures, $454,191; qualifying distributions, $410,709; giving activities include $410,709 for grants.
Fields of interest: Arts; Higher education, university; Environment, natural resources; Animal welfare;

Health organizations, association; Children/youth, services; Federated giving programs.
Limitations: Applications not accepted. Giving primarily in FL. No grants to individuals.
Application information: Contributes only to pre-selected organizations.
Directors: Allen Jelks; Allen N. Jelks, Jr.; Deborah Stephens Jelks; Howard L. Jelks; Lisa Grace Jelks; Mary Jelks; Benjamin A. King; Bryan King; Christopher B. King; Helen J. King; Alice J. Lezcano; Edgar Lezcano.
EIN: 593270436
Selected grants: The following grants were reported in 2004.
$61,000 to Nature Conservancy, Tallahassee, FL.
$15,000 to Florida Wildlife Federation, Tallahassee, FL.
$5,000 to Legal Environmental Assistance Foundation, Tallahassee, FL.
$1,250 to Asolo Theater Company, Sarasota, FL.
$1,200 to United Way of Northwest Florida, Panama City, FL.
$1,000 to American Red Cross, Orlando, FL.
$1,000 to Boy Scouts of America, Southwest Florida Council, Fort Myers, FL.
$1,000 to Education Foundation for Sarasota County, Sarasota, FL.
$1,000 to Florida Studio Theater, Sarasota, FL.
$1,000 to Sarasota Ballet of Florida, Sarasota, FL.

2077
Theodore R. & Vivian M. Johnson Scholarship Foundation, Inc. ▼ ◇
700 S. Dixie Hwy., Ste. 100
West Palm Beach, FL 33401 (561) 659-2005
Contact: Sharon Wood, Grants Admin.
FAX: (561) 659-1054; *E-mail:* wood@jsf.bz;
Additional tel.: (888) 523-7797; *URL:* http://www.jsf.bz

Established in 1991 in FL.
Donors: Theodore R. Johnson†; Vivian M. Johnson†.
Foundation type: Independent foundation.
Financial data (yr. ended 12/31/04): Assets, $139,817,836 (M); expenditures, $6,801,317; qualifying distributions, $5,820,134; giving activities include $5,138,186 for 36+ grants (high: $1,215,000; low: $1,000; average: $10,000–$400,000).
Purpose and activities: Scholarship grants are made to a variety of institutions and programs specified by the founders and the Board of Directors. The foundation seeks to enable qualified individuals, who might not be able to otherwise do so, to acquire skills and develop strengths which enable them to realize their potential. The foundation believes that by doing so, they can became positive contributing members of their community and its economy.
Fields of interest: Higher education.
Type of support: Curriculum development; Scholarship funds; Employee matching gifts; Matching/challenge support.
Limitations: Giving on a national basis. No grants to individuals directly.
Publications: Annual report; Financial statement.
Application information: See foundation's Web site for application forms and more information.
Applicants must apply directly to one of the following organizations: 1) Palm Beach Atlantic University, 2) Scholarship America (for UPS scholarships), 3) Florida School for the Deaf and the Blind, 4) State

University System of Florida, 5) American Indian Tribal Colleges, 6) Gallaudet University, and 7) Gonzaga University. Application form required.
   Board meeting date(s): Spring and fall
Officers and Directors:* R. Malcolm Macleod, Q.C.*, C.E.O. and Pres.; Diane N. Johnson,* V.P.; Hugh M. Brown,* Secy.; Richard A. Krause,* C.F.O. and Treas.; David L. Blaikie; Samuel D. Isaly; David B. Rinker; Lois G. Steele, M.D.
Number of staff: 1 full-time professional; 2 part-time professional.
EIN: 311613890
Selected grants: The following grants were reported in 2005.
$1,215,000 to Palm Beach Atlantic University, West Palm Beach, FL. For scholarships.
$975,000 to UPS Foundation, Atlanta, GA. For scholarships for children of Florida-based UPS employees and retirees to attend post-secondary schools in Florida.
$500,000 to Florida School for the Deaf and Blind, Saint Augustine, FL. For special projects support.
$500,000 to Gallaudet University, DC. For scholarships.
$450,000 to Berklee College of Music, Boston, MA. For program for teenagers living in and around Boston, full scholarships to City Music program graduates, and matching grants to establish endowment.
$239,370 to Gonzaga University, Spokane, WA. For on-site and distance learning program leading to Master's Degree in American Indian Entrepreneurship.
$150,000 to Guide Dogs for the Blind, San Rafael, CA. For training disabled to work with personal service dog.
$150,000 to National Education for Assistance Dog Services (NEADS), West Boylston, MA. To train disabled to work with personal service dog.
$40,000 to Turtle Mountain Community College, Belcourt, ND. For scholarships for business and entrepreneurship students.
$39,375 to Sinte Gleska University, Mission, SD. For scholarships for business and entrepreneurship students.

2078
1996 M. M. Kaplan Family Foundation, Inc. ◇ ☆
c/o Alan Stark
3876 Sheridan St.
Hollywood, FL 33021

Established in 1996 in NJ.
Donor: Myron M. Kaplan.
Foundation type: Independent foundation.
Financial data (yr. ended 7/31/05): Assets, $16,547,250 (M); expenditures, $583,447; qualifying distributions, $687,258; giving activities include $429,814 for 97 grants (high: $250,000; low: $50).
Purpose and activities: Giving primarily for the arts, education and Jewish organizations.
Fields of interest: Arts education; Higher education; Education; Human services; Jewish agencies & temples.
Limitations: Applications not accepted. Giving on a national basis. No grants to individuals.
Application information: Contributes only to pre-selected organizations.

Officers and Trustees:* Myron M. Kaplan,* Pres. and Treas.; Annette Hollander, M.D.*, V.P. and Secy.; Amelia H. Kaplan; Eve F. Kaplan.
EIN: 223461156
Selected grants: The following grants were reported in 2004.
$50,000 to Long Island Community Foundation, Jericho, NY. 2 grants: $25,000 each (For general support).
$26,000 to Chicagoland Conservative Jewish High School Foundation, Morton Grove, IL. For general support.
$20,000 to Seeds of Peace, New York, NY. For general support.
$15,000 to Alexander Technique International, Cambridge, MA. For general support.
$10,000 to Alzheimers Disease Alliance of Western Pennsylvania, Pittsburgh, PA. For general support.
$10,000 to Mount Sinai Medical Center, Miami Beach, FL. For general support.
$10,000 to National Student Parent Mock Elections, Tucson, AZ. For general support.
$10,000 to Whitney Museum of American Art, New York, NY. For general support.
$8,500 to Metropolitan Museum of Art, New York, NY. For general support.

2079

The Lillian Jean Kaplan Foundation, Inc. ✧

802 N.E. 20th Ave.
Fort Lauderdale, FL 33304 (954) 525-5656
Contact: Guma Aguiar, Dir.
FAX: (954) 525-5556;
E-mail: guma@ljkfoundation.org; URL: http://www.ljkfoundation.org

Donors: Thomas Kaplan; Consolidated Commodities Ltd.
Foundation type: Independent foundation.
Financial data (yr. ended 12/31/04): Assets, $322,841 (M); gifts received, $1,140,000; expenditures, $660,876; qualifying distributions, $499,510; giving activities include $489,160 for 22 grants (high: $154,500; low: $1,000).
Purpose and activities: Giving primarily to support and recognize outstanding achievement in clinical research and excellence in kidney and pancreas-related programs, and to improving the overall quality of life; funding also for Jewish organizations.
Fields of interest: Kidney research; Jewish agencies & temples.
Limitations: Giving on a national basis, with emphasis on FL and NY.
Application information:
Initial approach: Letter
Deadline(s): None
Directors: Guma Aguiar; Robert Denison; Scott Mager.
EIN: 300127083

2080

The Katcher Family Foundation, Inc. ✧ ☆

1111 Brickell Ave., Rm. 2920
Miami, FL 33131 (305) 358-4222
Contact: Gerald Katcher, Dir.

Established in 1996 in DE and FL.
Donor: Gerald Katcher.
Foundation type: Independent foundation.

Financial data (yr. ended 11/30/05): Assets, $8,591,549 (M); gifts received, $2,185,700; expenditures, $945,694; qualifying distributions, $930,039; giving activities include $930,039 for 47 grants (high: $333,553; low: $75).
Purpose and activities: Giving primarily for the arts, particularly to museums, as well as for higher education, and children and youth services.
Fields of interest: Museums (art); Museums (ethnic/folk arts); Performing arts, music; Arts; Higher education; Education; Environment, research; Children/youth, services.
Limitations: Giving primarily in CO, FL and NY.
Application information:
Initial approach: Letter or telephone
Deadline(s): None
Directors: Lesley Heller; Gerald Katcher; Jane Katcher.
EIN: 650715498

2081

The Eleanor M. and Herbert D. Katz Family Foundation, Inc. ✧

c/o Thomas O. Katz, Secy.-Treas.
P.O. Box 1900
Fort Lauderdale, FL 33302

Established in 1983 in FL.
Donors: Eleanor M. Katz; Herbert D. Katz.
Foundation type: Independent foundation.
Financial data (yr. ended 12/31/04): Assets, $14,639,791 (M); expenditures, $557,051; qualifying distributions, $435,435; giving activities include $435,435 for 44+ grants (high: $62,500).
Purpose and activities: Primary areas of interest include higher education, and Jewish organizations.
Fields of interest: Higher education; Education; Health organizations, association; Human services; Jewish federated giving programs; Leadership development; Jewish agencies & temples.
International interests: Israel.
Type of support: Continuing support; Annual campaigns; Capital campaigns; Program development.
Limitations: Applications not accepted. Giving primarily in FL, Philadelphia, PA, and New York, NY. No grants to individuals.
Application information: Contributes only to pre-selected organizations.
Officers and Directors:* Eleanor M. Katz,* Pres.; Herbert D. Katz,* V.P.; Thomas O. Katz,* Secy.-Treas.; Laura Katz Cutler; Daniel Katz; Sally Katz; Walter Katz.
EIN: 592320940
Selected grants: The following grants were reported in 2003.
$103,150 to United Jewish Community of Broward County, Davie, FL. For annual fund.
$30,000 to University of Pennsylvania, Philadelphia, PA. For annual fund.
$11,000 to Jewish Federation of Greater Washington, Rockville, MD. For annual fund.
$11,000 to Jewish Federation of South Palm Beach County, Boca Raton, FL. For annual fund.
$6,000 to Pine Crest School, Fort Lauderdale, FL. For annual fund.
$3,750 to Jewish Primary Day School of the Nations Capital, Silver Spring, MD. For annual fund.
$1,000 to Harvard Law School Association, Cambridge, MA. For annual fund.
$1,000 to Holocaust Documentation and Education Center, North Miami, FL. For annual fund.

$600 to National Foundation for Jewish Culture, New York, NY. For annual fund.
$500 to Florida International University, Miami, FL. For annual fund.

2082

Henry & Elaine Kaufman Foundation, Inc. ▼ ✧

c/o Edward I. Speer, CPA
4400 N. Federal Hwy., Ste. 210
Boca Raton, FL 33431
Application address: c/o Henry Kaufman, Pres., and Elaine Kaufman, V.P., 660 Madison Ave., New York, NY 10021

Established in 1969.
Donors: Elaine Kaufman; Henry Kaufman; Henry Kaufman Charitable Lead Trust.
Foundation type: Independent foundation.
Financial data (yr. ended 12/31/04): Assets, $32,180,208 (M); expenditures, $9,015,062; qualifying distributions, $8,425,305; giving activities include $8,423,805 for 180 grants (high: $1,000,000; low: $25; average: $500–$100,000).
Purpose and activities: Support primarily for Jewish organizations, museums and other cultural institutions, and education; funding also for human services and hospitals.
Fields of interest: Arts, multipurpose centers/programs; Museums; Arts; Higher education; Business school/education; Education; Animal welfare; Hospitals (general); Human services; Jewish federated giving programs; Jewish agencies & temples.
Type of support: General/operating support; Annual campaigns.
Limitations: Giving primarily in the metropolitan New York, NY, area, including portions of NJ; some funding also in Atlanta, GA.
Application information:
Initial approach: Letter
Deadline(s): None
Officers and Directors:* Henry Kaufman,* Pres. and Treas.; Elaine Kaufman,* V.P.; Daniel S. Kaufman,* Secy.; Craig S. Kaufman; Glenn D. Kaufman.
EIN: 237045903
Selected grants: The following grants were reported in 2004.
$1,000,000 to New York University, Stern School of Business, New York, NY.
$989,734 to Comcast, Philadelphia, PA. For grant made in form of stock.
$945,000 to Institute of International Education, New York, NY.
$883,856 to Laboratory Corporation of America Holdings (LabCorp), Burlington, NC. For grant made in form of stock.
$722,808 to UnitedHealth Group, Minneapolis, MN. For grant made in form of stock.
$597,621 to Iron Mountain, Boston, MA. For grant made in form of stock.
$391,471 to Shaw Communications, Canada. For grant made in form of stock.
$200,000 to Elaine Kaufman Cultural Center, New York, NY.
$25,000 to Bretton Woods Committee, DC.
$5,000 to Hospital for Special Surgery, New York, NY.

2083
The Kaul Foundation ✧
c/o Victor Holcomb
201 N. Armenia Ave.
Tampa, FL 33609

Established in 1986 in FL.
Donor: Ralph Kaul†.
Foundation type: Independent foundation.
Financial data (yr. ended 11/30/05): Assets, $9,070,945 (M); expenditures, $479,007; qualifying distributions, $401,250; giving activities include $391,250 for 13 grants (high: $100,000; low: $5,000).
Purpose and activities: Provides awards for excellence on both a national and local level to individuals. The foundation's board of directors requests nominations from anonymous groups and selects recipients after review.
Fields of interest: Education.
Type of support: Grants to individuals.
Limitations: Applications not accepted. Giving on a national basis, with some emphasis on FL.
Application information: Unsolicited requests for funds not accepted.
Trustees: John Holcomb; Victor Holcomb; William F. Poe, Jr.; William Smalley.
EIN: 546244744
Selected grants: The following grants were reported in 2004.
$252,000 to H. Lee Moffitt Cancer Center and Research Institute, Tampa, FL.
$20,000 to Academy of the Holy Names School, Tampa, FL.
$20,000 to Boys and Girls Clubs of Tampa Bay, Tampa, FL.
$20,000 to ChairScholars Foundation, Odessa, FL.
$20,000 to LifePath Hospice and Palliative Care, Tampa, FL.
$10,000 to American Red Cross, Tampa, FL.
$10,000 to Davidson College, Davidson, NC.
$10,000 to Florida School Choice Fund, Tampa, FL.
$10,000 to Japan American Conference, Carmichael, CA.
$10,000 to Jesuit High School, Tampa, FL.

2084
Keating Family Foundation ✧
5824 Bee Ridge Rd., PMB 420
Sarasota, FL 34233-5065 (941) 343-9919
Contact: Deborah J. Gilliland, Admin.

Incorporated in 1967 in IL.
Donor: Edward Keating.
Foundation type: Independent foundation.
Financial data (yr. ended 12/31/05): Assets, $3,312,956 (M); gifts received, $49; expenditures, $406,905; qualifying distributions, $393,795; giving activities include $393,795 for 78 grants (high: $100,000; low: $43; average: $1,000–$5,000).
Purpose and activities: Giving primarily for the arts, education and human services.
Fields of interest: Performing arts; Arts; Higher education; Health organizations, association; Human services; Children/youth, services; Federated giving programs; Biological sciences.
Type of support: Continuing support; Annual campaigns; Capital campaigns; Building/renovation; Endowments; Research; Matching/challenge support.

Limitations: Applications not accepted. Giving primarily in Sarasota, FL, and Chicago, IL. No grants to individuals.
Application information: Contributes only to pre-selected organizations.
Officers and Directors:* Edward Keating,* Pres.; Arthur E. Keating,* V.P.; Elaine Keating,* V.P.; Lee B. Keating,* V.P.; Lucie S. Keating,* V.P.; Patricia Brosterhous,* Secy.; Deborah Gilliland,* Treas. and Admin.; Joel Mogy.
Trustee: The Northern Trust Co.
EIN: 366198002

2085
Kelco Foundation, Inc. ✧
c/o G. Spencer
4595 Bayview Dr.
Fort Lauderdale, FL 33308

Established in 1988 in FL.
Foundation type: Independent foundation.
Financial data (yr. ended 12/31/05): Assets, $1,751,974 (M); gifts received, $1,053,577; expenditures, $961,499; qualifying distributions, $910,000; giving activities include $910,000 for 1 grant.
Purpose and activities: Grants to Roman Catholic churches, education and evangelical efforts.
Fields of interest: Roman Catholic agencies & churches.
Limitations: Applications not accepted. Giving primarily in Broward County, FL. No grants to individuals.
Application information: Contributes only to pre-selected organizations. Unsolicited requests for funds not accepted.
Directors: V. Kelly; Janet Molchan; Susan M. Shaheen.
EIN: 650019085
Selected grants: The following grants were reported in 2003.
$600,000 to Saint Thomas Aquinas High School, Fort Lauderdale, FL. For scholarships.
$25,000 to Saint Senans Scholarship, Fort Lauderdale, FL. For scholarships.

2086
Kelly Foundation, Inc. ✧
801 E. Sugarland Hwy.
Clewiston, FL 33440-2621 (941) 983-8177
Contact: Alden M. Wyse, Secy.-Treas.

Established in 1956 in FL.
Donor: Kelly Tractor Co.
Foundation type: Company-sponsored foundation.
Financial data (yr. ended 12/31/05): Assets, $10,644,926 (M); gifts received, $1,200; expenditures, $459,281; qualifying distributions, $451,193; giving activities include $256,327 for 43 grants (high: $100,000; low: $100), and $191,150 for 103 grants to individuals (high: $10,000; low: $500).
Purpose and activities: The foundation supports hospitals and organizations involved with Protestantism and awards college scholarships.
Fields of interest: Hospitals (general); Protestant agencies & churches.
Type of support: General/operating support; Scholarships—to individuals.
Limitations: Giving primarily in FL.

Application information: Generally, unsolicited requests for general operating support are not accepted. Application form required.
Initial approach: Contact foundation for application form
Deadline(s): None for scholarships
Officers: Loyd G. Kelly, Pres.; Robert W. Kelly, V.P.; Alden M. Wyse, Secy.-Treas.
Directors: Eileen I. Kelly; Louisa Kelly; Loyd Patrick Kelly; Marjorie H. Kelly; Nicholas D. Kelly; Robert W. Kelly, Jr.
EIN: 596153269

2087
The Ethel & W. George Kennedy Family Foundation, Inc.
1550 Madruga Ave., Ste. 225
Coral Gables, FL 33146 (305) 666-6226
Contact: Kathleen Kennedy-Olsen, Managing Dir.
FAX: (305) 666-2441;
E-mail: admin@kennedyfamilyfdn.org; URL: http://www.kennedyfamilyfdn.org

Established in 1968 in FL.
Donor: W. George Kennedy†.
Foundation type: Independent foundation.
Financial data (yr. ended 12/31/05): Assets, $26,731,127 (M); expenditures, $1,233,186; qualifying distributions, $1,003,032; giving activities include $876,056 for 78 grants (high: $40,500; low: $250).
Purpose and activities: Giving primarily to organizations that directly support children and families by means of education, health care, technological assistance, rehabilitation and welfare.
Fields of interest: Education; Human services; Children/youth, services; Child development, services; Family services; Economically disadvantaged.
Type of support: General/operating support; Capital campaigns; Building/renovation; Equipment; Endowments; Program development; Seed money; Scholarship funds; Technical assistance; Matching/challenge support.
Limitations: Giving limited to Miami-Dade County, FL. No grants to individuals.
Publications: Application guidelines.
Application information: Criteria, guidelines, and application procedural details will be provided upon receipt of a letter of introduction. Application form required.
Initial approach: Letter
Copies of proposal: 8
Deadline(s): Feb. 15 and Sept. 15
Board meeting date(s): Mar. and Oct.
Final notification: Two weeks after board meetings, via letter
Officers and Directors:* Karyn Kennedy Herterich,* Pres.; Kendel Kennedy,* V.P.; Kimberly Kennedy,* V.P.; Kathleen Kennedy-Olsen,* Secy.-Treas. and Managing Dir.; Forrest Mulcahy; Martin Nash; Guy Rizzo.
Number of staff: 2 full-time professional.
EIN: 596204880
Selected grants: The following grants were reported in 2003.
$300,000 to University of Miami, Coral Gables, FL. 2 grants: $200,000 to Center for Family Studies, $100,000 to Center for Research
$57,100 to Miami Childrens Museum, Miami, FL.
$53,500 to Fairchild Tropical Garden, Coral Gables, FL.

$52,500 to Childrens Home Society of Florida, Miami, FL.
$35,000 to Overtown Youth Center, Miami, FL.
$32,286 to KidVentures, Coral Gables, FL.
$22,000 to House of Hope, Orlando, FL.
$21,307 to American Red Cross, Miami, FL.
$11,000 to Womens Fund of Miami-Dade County, Miami, FL.

2088
Ethel Kennedy Foundation ◇
271 Johns Island Dr.
Vero Beach, FL   32963
Contact: Ethel K. Marran, Pres.

Established in 1986 in DE and NY.
Foundation type: Independent foundation.
Financial data (yr. ended 12/31/05): Assets, $9,960,429 (M); expenditures, $644,112; qualifying distributions, $610,169; giving activities include $602,250 for 70 grants (high: $100,500; low: $500).
Purpose and activities: Giving primarily to religious, educational, medical, or welfare organizations.
Fields of interest: Arts; Secondary school/education; Higher education; Environment; Reproductive health, family planning; Health organizations, association; Medical research, institute; Eye research; Human services; Family services; Residential/custodial care, hospices; Women.
Limitations: Giving primarily in NY. No grants to individuals.
Application information: Application form required.
Initial approach: Proposal
Deadline(s): None
Officers: Ethel K. Marran, Pres. and Treas.; Elizabeth Marran, V.P.; Laura Marran, Secy.
EIN: 112768682

2089
The John R. Kennedy Foundation, Inc. ◇ ☆
201 Terrapin Point
Vero Beach, FL   32963

Incorporated in 1951 in DE.
Donors: John R. Kennedy, Sr.†; Luke A. Mulligan†.
Foundation type: Independent foundation.
Financial data (yr. ended 12/31/05): Assets, $10,182,342 (M); expenditures, $553,578; qualifying distributions, $380,145; giving activities include $340,145 for 29 grants (high: $100,000; low: $100).
Fields of interest: Performing arts; Arts; Higher education; Medical school/education; Education; Hospitals (general); Health care; Health organizations, association; Human services; Foundations (private grantmaking).
Limitations: Applications not accepted. Giving primarily in New York, NY, and East Hampton, NY; funding also in FL, particularly Vero Beach. No grants to individuals.
Application information: Contributes only to pre-selected organizations.
Officers: John R. Kennedy, Pres. and Treas.; James W. Kennedy, V.P. and Secy.; John R. Kennedy III, V.P.
Trustees: Elizabeth C. Kennedy; Paula Kennedy.
EIN: 221714822
Selected grants: The following grants were reported in 2004.

$88,078 to Weill Medical College of Cornell University, New York, NY.
$50,000 to East Hampton Healthcare Foundation, East Hampton, NY.
$40,000 to Riverside Theater, Vero Beach, FL.
$35,000 to Weston Jesuit School of Theology, Cambridge, MA.
$25,000 to Homeless Family Center, Vero Beach, FL.
$2,000 to AIDS Research and Treatment Center of the Treasure Coast, Fort Pierce, FL. 2 grants: $1,000 each
$2,000 to Lincoln Center for the Performing Arts, New York, NY.
$1,500 to Boys and Girls Harbor, New York, NY.
$500 to Childrens Home Society of Florida, Fort Pierce, FL.

2090
The Delores Pass Kesler Foundation, Inc. ◇
9700 Philips Hwy., Ste. 101
Jacksonville, FL   32256   (904) 996-7082
Contact: Delores Kesler, Pres.

Established in 1997 in FL.
Donor: Delores Kesler.
Foundation type: Independent foundation.
Financial data (yr. ended 6/30/05): Assets, $1,492,555 (M); gifts received, $300,000; expenditures, $467,312; qualifying distributions, $404,283; giving activities include $330,783 for 73 grants (high: $50,000; low: $50).
Purpose and activities: Giving primarily for human services, children and youth services, and to Jewish organizations and temples.
Fields of interest: Arts; Higher education; Education; Environment; Health organizations, association; Human services; Children/youth, services; Jewish agencies & temples.
Limitations: Giving primarily in FL. No grants to individuals.
Application information: Background material on the organization is accepted with the application, but cannot exceed 5 pages.
Initial approach: Proposal, maximum of 5 pages
Deadline(s): None
Officers: Delores Kesler, Pres.; Deborah Pass, Secy.; Mark Pass, Treas.
EIN: 593391143

2091
The Edward & Lucille Kimmel Foundation, Inc. ◇
625 N. Flagler Dr.
West Palm Beach, FL   33401

Established in 1983 in FL.
Donors: Joan K. Eigen; Edward A. Kimmel†.
Foundation type: Independent foundation.
Financial data (yr. ended 12/31/04): Assets, $8,362,697 (M); expenditures, $532,301; qualifying distributions, $395,494; giving activities include $360,950 for 60 grants (high: $73,600; low: $295).
Purpose and activities: Giving primarily for education, health care, and to Jewish federated giving programs.
Fields of interest: Arts; Medical school/education; Education; Health organizations; Medical research,

institute; Human services; Jewish federated giving programs.
Limitations: Applications not accepted. Giving primarily in FL, with emphasis on West Palm Beach, and in New York, NY. No grants to individuals.
Application information: Contributes only to pre-selected organizations.
Officers and Directors:* Joan K. Eigen,* Pres. and Secy.; Lucille Kimmel,* V.P. and Treas.; Deborah Barth; David L. Eigen; David Kimmel.
EIN: 592380662

2092
The Thomas M. and Irene B. Kirbo Charitable Trust ◇
550 Water St., Ste. 1327
Jacksonville, FL   32202   (904) 354-7212
Contact: R. Murray Jenks, Pres.

Established in 1959 in GA.
Donors: Thomas M. Kirbo†; Irene B. Kirbo.
Foundation type: Independent foundation.
Financial data (yr. ended 9/30/05): Assets, $34,262,865 (M); expenditures, $2,164,843; qualifying distributions, $2,002,146; giving activities include $1,940,800 for 100 grants (high: $150,000; low: $1,000).
Purpose and activities: Giving primarily for religion, hospitals, universities, and youth.
Fields of interest: Higher education; Libraries/library science; Hospitals (general); Human services; Youth, services; Christian agencies & churches; Protestant agencies & churches.
Limitations: Giving primarily in FL and GA. No grants to individuals.
Application information: Application form required.
Initial approach: Application form
Deadline(s): None
Officers: Bruce W. Kirbo, Chair.; R. Murray Jenks, Pres.
Trustees: John T. Jenks; Charles H. Kirbo, Jr.
EIN: 592151720
Selected grants: The following grants were reported in 2004.

$400,000 to University of Georgia Foundation, Athens, GA. 2 grants: $150,000, $250,000
$72,500 to Decatur County Board of Education, Bainbridge, GA. 2 grants: $50,000, $22,500
$50,000 to University of Florida Foundation, Gainesville, FL.
$42,000 to YMCA. 2 grants: $21,000 each
$25,000 to Community Hospice of Northeast Florida, Jacksonville, FL.
$20,000 to Atlanta Union Mission, Atlanta, GA.
$15,000 to North Fulton Community Charities, Roswell, GA.

2093
Jay I. Kislak Foundation, Inc. ◇
7900 Miami Lakes Dr., W.
Miami Lakes, FL   33016-5897
URL: http://www.kislakfoundation.org/

Established in 1984 in FL.
Donors: J.I. Kislak, Inc.; Foundation of Jewish Philanthropies; Kislak Family Fund, Inc.; The Miami Jewish Federation.
Foundation type: Operating foundation.
Financial data (yr. ended 12/31/04): Assets, $8,553,558 (M); gifts received, $50; expenditures,

$7,179,745; qualifying distributions, $7,167,794; giving activities include $6,886,892 for 1 grant.

Purpose and activities: The foundation is engaged in the collection, conservation, research and interpretation of rare books, manuscripts, maps and indigenous art and cultural artifacts of the Americas.

Fields of interest: Humanities; Historic preservation/historical societies.

Limitations: Applications not accepted. Giving on a national basis. No grants to individuals.

Application information: Contributes only to pre-selected organizations.

Officers and Trustees:* Jay I. Kislak,* Pres.; Jonathan I. Kislak,* V.P.; Thomas Bartelmo,* Secy.-Treas.; Jean H. Kislak.

EIN: 592438331

2094
Kiwanis Club of Bradenton Foundation, Inc. ✧

P.O. Box 1032
Bradenton, FL   34206-1032

Established in 1990 in FL.

Donors: Dozier Hilliard; Kiwanis Club of Bradenton, Inc.; Stanley Nieby Revocable Trust; Revocable Living Trust of Elmer J. Trulaske.

Foundation type: Independent foundation.

Financial data (yr. ended 9/30/05): Assets, $9,872,831 (M); gifts received, $426,497; expenditures, $528,454; qualifying distributions, $414,428; giving activities include $404,148 for 17 grants (high: $125,000; low: $1,000).

Fields of interest: Higher education; Education; Youth development, business; YM/YWCAs & YM/YWHAs; Children/youth, services; Federated giving programs.

Limitations: Giving primarily in FL.

Application information: Application form not required.

   Deadline(s): None

Officers: John Vita, Pres.; David Bassett, V.P.; Bill Blalock, Secy.; Greg Bustle, Treas.; Mary Beth Bustle, Exec. Dir.

Directors: Larry Coleman; David Cruikshank; Steve Dye; Robert Farrance; Kay Rowlett; Connie Schingledecker; David Wilcox.

EIN: 650221660

Selected grants: The following grants were reported in 2004.

$141,000 to Manatee Community College Foundation, Bradenton, FL. For operating support.

$75,000 to South Florida Museum, Bradenton, FL. For operating support.

$60,000 to YMCA, Manatee County Family, Bradenton, FL. For operating support.

$12,250 to University of Florida, Gainesville, FL. For scholarships.

$12,000 to United Way of Manatee County, Bradenton, FL. For operating support.

$10,000 to University of South Florida, Tampa, FL. For scholarships.

$9,457 to Childrens Haven and Adult Community Services, Sarasota, FL. For operating support.

$7,000 to Manatee County Agricultural Museum, Palmetto, FL. For operating support.

$3,750 to University of Central Florida, Orlando, FL. For scholarships.

$1,250 to Florida State University, Tallahassee, FL. For scholarships.

2095
The Peter D. & Eleanore A. Kleist Foundation, Inc. ✧

12734 Kenwood Ln., Ste. 89
Fort Myers, FL   33907
Contact: Peter D. Kleist, Pres.

Established in 1983 in OH.

Foundation type: Independent foundation.

Financial data (yr. ended 12/31/05): Assets, $764,167 (M); expenditures, $756,440; qualifying distributions, $746,265; giving activities include $744,211 for 19 grants (high: $250,000; low: $250).

Purpose and activities: Giving primarily for higher education and to Methodist churches.

Fields of interest: Secondary school/education; Higher education; Education; Human services; Christian agencies & churches.

Type of support: Capital campaigns; Scholarship funds; Matching/challenge support.

Limitations: Applications not accepted. Giving primarily in Fort Myers, FL, and OH, with some emphasis on Cleveland. No grants to individuals.

Application information: Applications by invitation only.

Officers and Directors:* Peter D. Kleist,* Pres.; Kathryn Derheimer,* 2nd V.P.

EIN: 341437974

Selected grants: The following grants were reported in 2003.

$200,000 to Union College, Barbourville, KY.

$50,000 to Boy Scouts of America, Southwest Florida Council, Fort Myers, FL.

$50,000 to Kentucky Wesleyan College, Owensboro, KY.

$20,000 to Edison Community College Foundation, Fort Myers, FL.

$20,000 to University of the Cumberlands, Williamsburg, KY. For scholarships.

$15,000 to Cypress Lake United Methodist Church.

$15,000 to United Way of Lee County, Fort Myers, FL.

$6,500 to Foundation for Lee County Public Schools, Fort Myers, FL.

$5,000 to Canterbury School, Fort Myers, FL.

$5,000 to Southwest Florida Community Foundation, Fort Myers, FL.

2096
KMD Foundation ✧ ☆

980 N. Federal Hwy., Ste. 307
Boca Raton, FL   33432

Established in 1981 in MI.

Donors: Irving A. Smokler; Toba Smokler Trust.

Foundation type: Independent foundation.

Financial data (yr. ended 12/31/05): Assets, $1,093,900 (M); gifts received, $45,612; expenditures, $698,440; qualifying distributions, $649,801; giving activities include $645,136 for 32 grants (high: $100,000; low: $100).

Purpose and activities: Giving primarily to Jewish agencies, temples, schools, and federated giving programs.

Fields of interest: Higher education; Education; Human services; Jewish federated giving programs; Jewish agencies & temples.

Limitations: Applications not accepted. Giving on a national basis. No grants to individuals; no loans or program-related investments.

Application information: Contributes only to pre-selected organizations.

Trustees: Carol S. Smokler; Irving A. Smokler.

EIN: 382378958

2097
John S. and James L. Knight Foundation ▼
(formerly Knight Foundation)
Wachovia Financial Ctr., Ste. 3300
200 S. Biscayne Blvd.
Miami, FL   33131-2349   (305) 908-2600
Contact: Attn: Grant Request
FAX: (305) 908-2698; Additional tel. for publication requests: (305) 908-2629; E-mail: publications@knightfdn.org, or web@knightfdn.org
URL: http://www.knightfdn.org

Incorporated in 1950 in OH.

Donors: John S. Knight†; James L. Knight†; and their families.

Foundation type: Independent foundation.

Financial data (yr. ended 12/31/05): Assets, $2,071,507,291 (M); gifts received, $1,364,567; expenditures, $110,000,000; qualifying distributions, $103,000,000; giving activities include $89,692,091 for grants, $205,374 for employee matching gifts, and $2,679,697 for foundation-administered programs.

Purpose and activities: The foundation promotes excellence in journalism worldwide and invests in the vitality of 26 U.S. communities. Focus is on two signature programs, Journalism and Knight Community Partners, which includes education, well-being of children and families, housing and community development, economic development, civic engagement/positive human relations, and vitality of cultural life, each area with its own eligibility requirements. A third program, the National Venture Fund, supports innovative opportunities and initiatives at the national level that relate directly or indirectly to Knight's work in its 26 communities.

Fields of interest: Media, journalism/publishing; Arts; Education; Housing/shelter, development; Housing/shelter; Children, services; Family services; Civil rights, race/intergroup relations; Community development, neighborhood development; Economic development; Public affairs, citizen participation.

Type of support: General/operating support; Capital campaigns; Building/renovation; Endowments; Emergency funds; Seed money; Curriculum development; Program-related investments/loans; Employee matching gifts.

Limitations: Giving limited to projects serving the 26 communities where the Knight brothers published newspapers for Community Initiatives Program and local grants: Long Beach and San Jose, CA, Boulder, CO, Boca Raton, Bradenton, Miami, and Tallahassee, FL, Columbus, Macon, and Milledgeville, GA, Fort Wayne and Gary, IN, Wichita, KS, Lexington, KY, Detroit, MI, Duluth and St. Paul, MN, Biloxi, MS, Charlotte, NC, Grand Forks, ND, Akron, OH, Philadelphia and State College, PA, Columbia and Myrtle Beach, SC, and Aberdeen, SD; international for Journalism. No support for organizations whose mission is to prevent, eradicate and/or alleviate the effects of a specific disease; hospitals, unless for community-wide capital campaigns; activities to propagate a religious faith or restricted to one religion or denomination; political candidates; international programs, except U.S.-based organizations supporting free press around the world; charities operated by service clubs; or activities that are the responsibility of government (the foundation will in selective cases, join with units of government in supporting special projects). No grants to individuals, or generally for fundraising events; second requests for previously funded capital campaigns; operating deficits; general operating support; films, videos, or television programs; honoraria for distinguished guests-except in initiatives of the foundation in all three cases; group travel; memorials; medical research; or conferences.

Publications: Annual report (including application guidelines); Informational brochure; Newsletter; Occasional report.

Application information: Please do not submit an application until you have been invited to do so by the Grants Admin. or a Prog. Off. Application form required.

Initial approach: Online inquiry

Copies of proposal: 2

Deadline(s): None, except for special initiatives (approximately 6-month grant cycle)

Board meeting date(s): Mar., June, Sept., and Dec.

Final notification: 2 weeks after meeting dates

Officers and Trustees:* W. Gerald Austen, M.D.*, Chair.; Robert W. Briggs,* Vice-Chair.; Paula Ellis, V.P., National and New Initiatives; Alberto Ibarguen,* C.E.O. and Pres.; Larry Meyer, V.P., Comms. and Secy.; Juan J. Martinez, V.P. and C.F.O.; Belinda Turner Lawrence, V.P. and C.A.O.; Michael Maidenberg,* V.P. and Chief Prog. Off.; Eric Newton, V.P., Knight Journalism Prog.; Cesar L. Alvarez; Mary Sue Coleman; Marjorie Knight Crane; James N. Crutchfield; Paul S. Grogan; Rolfe Neill; Mariam C. Noland; Beverly Knight Olson; Earl W. Powell; John W. Rogers, Jr.; E. Roe Stamps IV; Paul Steiger.

Number of staff: 34 full-time professional; 18 full-time support; 1 part-time support.

EIN: 650464177

Selected grants: The following grants were reported in 2005.

$4,405,000 to International Center for Journalists, DC. To expand and improve Knight International Press Fellowships, payable over 2 years.

$2,280,000 to University of Missouri, Columbia, MO. To establish home for Committee of Concerned Journalists and move toward self-sufficiency, payable over 3 years.

$2,023,300 to Local Initiatives Support Corporation (LISC), New York, NY. To establish Housing Equity Partnership to increase affordability of home ownership in Overtown for at least fifty households, and to expand homebuyer training programs, payable over 4 years.

$1,050,000 to Akron Community Service Center and Urban League, Akron, OH. 2 grants: $800,000 (To increase job opportunities by boosting participation of women and minorities in construction industry as workers, contractors, and suppliers, payable over 4 years), $250,000 (To support construction of new Community Learning Center with matching funds toward a one million dollar challenge grant from the GAR Foundation).

$1,000,000 to Detroit Youth Foundation, Detroit, MI. To renovate facility for use as YouthVille Detroit, a neighborhood-based, comprehensive youth development center, payable over 2 years.

$130,000 to Catawba Riverkeeper Foundation, Charlotte, NC. To expand education component of Riverkeeper programs along Catawba River and to educate regional opinion leaders about

value of preserving open space, payable over 3 years.

$60,000 to Court Appointed Special Advocates (CASA) of Aberdeen, Fifth Judicial Circuit, Aberdeen, SD. To create team of professionals to develop protocols, provide training and serve drug-endangered children whose lives are jeopardized by their families' illegal manufacturing, sale, possession and use of methamphetamine in the home, payable over 2 years.

$20,000 to Mental Health Association of South Mississippi, Gulfport, MS. For general operating support and to provide outreach to families in Harrison County needing mental health services.

$10,000 to United Way, Centre County, State College, PA. To continue to increase awareness of early childhood mental health issues and build capacity among professions that intersect with lives of young children.

2098
Koch Foundation, Inc. ▼
4421 N.W. 39th Ave., Bldg. 1, Ste. 1
Gainesville, FL 32606 (352) 373-7491
Contact: Michael A. Marconi, Exec. Dir.

Incorporated in 1979 in FL.

Donors: Carl E. Koch†; Paula Koch†.

Foundation type: Independent foundation.

Financial data (yr. ended 3/31/06): Assets, $160,818,656 (M); expenditures, $10,351,291; qualifying distributions, $9,844,443; giving activities include $9,465,754 for 698 grants (high: $500,000; low: $1,875).

Purpose and activities: Grants only for Roman Catholic organizations that propagate the faith. Grants are made for direct evangelization programs, preparation of evangelists, Roman Catholic schools in resource-poor areas, and where the schools are the principal means of evangelization, a Roman Catholic presence in the media, and capital expenditures, such as construction and repair of churches or formation centers. In capital expenditures, priority is given to situations involving financially distressed, underdeveloped areas.

Fields of interest: Roman Catholic agencies & churches.

Type of support: Building/renovation; Equipment; Program development; Conferences/seminars; Publication; Seed money; Curriculum development; Matching/challenge support.

Limitations: Giving on a national and international basis. No grants to individuals, or for endowment funds, deficit financing, emergency funds, or for scholarships or fellowships; no loans.

Publications: Application guidelines; Annual report (including application guidelines).

Application information: All applicants outside the U.S. must list a diocese or religious congregation in the U.S. to act as Fiscal Agent through which funds may be distributed. The fiscal agent must be an organization listed in the Official Catholic Directory (OCD). Application form required.

Initial approach: Letter of request for an application that briefly describes the project; submit between Jan. 1 and May 1. All requests must be made in English. Fax, telephone, or E-mail requests will not be accepted

Copies of proposal: 1

Deadline(s): 90 days after receipt of application

Board meeting date(s): Feb.

Final notification: 1 month after Feb. board meeting

Officers and Directors:* Carolyn L. Bomberger,* Pres.; Inge L. Vraney,* V.P.; Rachel A. Bomberger,* Secy.; Lawrence E. Vraney, Jr.,* Treas.; Michael A. Marconi, Exec. Dir.; Dorothy C. Bomberger; Matthew A. Bomberger; Michelle H. Bomberger; William A. Bomberger; Charlotte L. Spacinsky; Maura J. Vraney.

Number of staff: 1 full-time professional; 4 full-time support.

EIN: 591885997

Selected grants: The following grants were reported in 2005.

$300,000 to Society for the Propagation of the Faith, New York, NY. For preparation of evangelists.

$75,000 to Paulist National Catholic Evangelization Association, DC. For direct evangelization.

$50,000 to Diocese of Pensacola-Tallahassee, Pensacola, FL. For capital support.

$25,000 to Province of Saint Augustine of the Capuchin Order, Pittsburgh, PA. For capital support.

$25,000 to Saint Cecilia School, Dallas, TX.

$25,000 to Saint James Catholic School, Miami, FL.

$20,000 to Franciscan School of Theology, Berkeley, CA. For preparation of evangelists.

$20,000 to Washington Theological Union, DC. For preparation of evangelists.

$15,000 to Fraternita San Francesco, Italy. For direct evangelization.

$15,000 to University of Saint Mary of the Lake-Mundelein Seminary, Mundelein, IL. For preparation of evangelists.

2099
Sidney Kohl Foundation, Inc. ✧
340 Royal Poinciana Way, Ste. 305
Palm Beach, FL 33480 (561) 833-4211
Contact: Sidney Kohl, Pres.

Incorporated in 1972 in WI.

Donors: Sidney Kohl; Max Kohl Charitable Trust; Glendale, Inc.

Foundation type: Independent foundation.

Financial data (yr. ended 6/30/05): Assets, $7,284,483 (M); expenditures, $535,938; qualifying distributions, $508,825; giving activities include $506,039 for 47 grants (high: $101,100; low: $2).

Purpose and activities: Grants primarily for Jewish welfare funds; some support for other charitable and educational organizations.

Fields of interest: Performing arts centers; Education; Human services; Jewish federated giving programs; Jewish agencies & temples.

Limitations: Giving primarily in Palm Beach and West Palm Beach, FL; some giving also in New York, NY. No grants to individuals.

Application information:

Initial approach: Letter or telephone

Officers: Sidney Kohl, Pres.; James C. Jenkins, Treas.

Director: Dorothy Kohl.

EIN: 237206459

Selected grants: The following grants were reported in 2005.

$80,200 to Alexis de Tocqueville Society, Alexandria, VA.

$58,179 to Jewish Federation of Palm Beach County, West Palm Beach, FL.

$20,000 to West Side Montessori School, New York, NY.

$15,350 to Temple Emanuel of Palm Beach, Palm Beach, FL.

$15,248 to Solomon R. Guggenheim Foundation, New York, NY.

$6,000 to Norton Museum of Art, West Palm Beach, FL.

$5,000 to Zimmer Jewish Discovery Childrens Museum, Los Angeles, CA.

$4,000 to South Florida Science Museum, West Palm Beach, FL.

$2,000 to University of Chicago, Chicago, IL.

$1,400 to Society of the Four Arts, Palm Beach, FL.

2100
C. L. C. Kramer Foundation, Inc. ✧
3840 Prairie Dunes Dr.
Sarasota, FL 34238
E-mail: Clckramerfoundation@dellhost.net;
URL: http://www.clckramerfoundation.org

Established in 1966.
Donor: Catherine Kramer†.
Foundation type: Independent foundation.
Financial data (yr. ended 9/30/05): Assets, $7,673,193 (M); expenditures, $481,691; qualifying distributions, $409,611; giving activities include $401,000 for 24 grants (high: $60,000; low: $1,000).
Purpose and activities: Giving primarily for hospitals, as well as to an organization for people who are blind; funding also for the performing arts and Jewish organizations.
Fields of interest: Performing arts; Hospitals (general); Medical research, institute; Human services; Jewish federated giving programs.
Type of support: General/operating support; Continuing support.
Limitations: Applications not accepted. Giving primarily in New York, NY. No grants to individuals.
Application information: Contributes only to pre-selected organizations.
Officers: Robert Zabelle, Pres.; Lawrence Rothenberg, Secy.; David Marks, Treas.
EIN: 136226513
Selected grants: The following grants were reported in 2005.
$25,000 to Mount Sinai Medical Center, New York, NY.
$25,000 to Saint Francis Hospital, Roslyn, NY.
$10,000 to Chamber Music Society of Lincoln Center, New York, NY.
$10,000 to Manhattan Theater Club, New York, NY.
$10,000 to Philharmonic-Symphony Society of New York, New York, NY.
$10,000 to Sarasota Ballet of Florida, Sarasota, FL.
$5,000 to Carnegie Hall Society, New York, NY.
$5,000 to Musicians Foundation, New York, NY.
$5,000 to New York City Ballet, New York, NY.
$5,000 to New York City Opera, New York, NY.

2101
Krauss, Miller, Lutz Charitable Trust Foundation, Inc. ✧ ☆
P.O. Box 23493
Tampa, FL 33623

Established in 2003 in FL.
Donor: Elmer J. Krauss†.
Foundation type: Independent foundation.

Financial data (yr. ended 12/31/05): Assets, $42,949,948 (M); expenditures, $4,713,384; qualifying distributions, $3,940,000; giving activities include $3,940,000 for 4 grants.
Fields of interest: Higher education; Youth development; Philanthropy/voluntarism; Protestant agencies & churches.
Type of support: General/operating support.
Limitations: Applications not accepted. Giving primarily in FL and WI. No grants to individuals.
Application information: Contributes only to pre-selected organizations.
Officers: John E. Kearney, Sr., Pres.; Andrew Siriani, V.P.; Kim Miller, Secy.-Treas.
Directors: Virginia Miller; Walt Weinlander.
EIN: 201727663

2102
Frances Langford Foundation ✧ ☆
P.O. Box 96
Jensen Beach, FL 34958
Contact: Evans Crary, Jr., Tr.; John B. Turner, Tr.

Established in 1989 in FL.
Donor: Frances Langford Stuart.
Foundation type: Independent foundation.
Financial data (yr. ended 12/31/05): Assets, $1,548,001 (M); expenditures, $414,597; qualifying distributions, $414,597; giving activities include $410,000 for 5 grants (high: $100,000; low: $10,000).
Purpose and activities: Giving primarily for the health care, including hospital services, for children and families, as well as for child abuse services.
Fields of interest: Hospitals (general); Nursing care; Human services; Children/youth, services; Family services; Crime/abuse victims.
Limitations: Giving primarily in Stuart, FL. No grants to individuals.
Application information: Application form not required.
   Initial approach: Letter
   Copies of proposal: 1
   Deadline(s): None
Trustees: Evans Crary, Jr.; John B. Turner.
EIN: 656041900

2103
The Lanie Foundation ✧
794 N.E. Harbour Dr.
Boca Raton, FL 33431

Established in 2001 in NV.
Donor: Ralph W. Albrecht.
Foundation type: Independent foundation.
Financial data (yr. ended 12/31/05): Assets, $757,900 (M); gifts received, $450,000; expenditures, $384,808; qualifying distributions, $384,700; giving activities include $384,700 for 23 grants (high: $125,000; low: $100).
Fields of interest: Elementary/secondary education; Prostate cancer research; Human services.
Limitations: Applications not accepted. Giving primarily in Sacramento, CA. No grants to individuals.
Application information: Contributes only to pre-selected organizations.
Officers: Ralph W. Albrecht, Pres.; Erick Castillo, Secy.; Margaret J. Hershey, Treas.
EIN: 880431967

2104
Forrest C. Lattner Foundation, Inc. ▼ ✧
777 E. Atlantic Ave., Ste. 317
Delray Beach, FL 33483-5352 (561) 278-3781
Contact: Susan L. Lloyd, Pres.; Martha L. Walker, Chair.
FAX: (561) 278-3167; E-mail: lattner@bellsouth.net;
URL: http://www.lattnerfoundation.org

Incorporated in 1981 in FL.
Donors: Mrs. Forrest C. Lattner†; Forrest C. Lattner†; Frances H. Lattner†.
Foundation type: Independent foundation.
Financial data (yr. ended 12/31/04): Assets, $171,019,460 (M); expenditures, $9,442,227; qualifying distributions, $7,865,855; giving activities include $7,865,855 for 276 grants (high: $200,000; low: $1,000; average: $5,000–$100,000).
Purpose and activities: The foundation's primary areas of giving are research, education, conservation, health and social services, arts and humanities, and the preservation of historical, cultural, and environmental resources.
Fields of interest: Arts; Education; Environment, natural resources; Environment; Health organizations, association.
Type of support: General/operating support; Building/renovation; Capital campaigns; Equipment; Endowments; Program development; Curriculum development; Scholarship funds; Research; Matching/challenge support.
Limitations: Giving primarily in San Francisco, CA, Palm Beach County, FL, Atlanta, GA, Wichita, KS, Philadelphia, PA, Westerly, RI, and Dallas, TX.
Publications: Application guidelines.
Application information: Application form not required.
   Initial approach: Letter stating grant request
   Copies of proposal: 1
   Deadline(s): Mar. 1 and Sept. 1
   Board meeting date(s): June and Dec.
   Final notification: 3 months after board meetings
Officers and Directors:* Martha L. Walker,* Chair.; Susan L. Lloyd,* Pres.; Forrest C. Brown, M.D.; Susan B. Funke; Andrew Harris; Richard M. Harris; David W. Hollenbeck; Douglas W. Hollenbeck; Drew Hollenbeck.
Number of staff: 1 part-time professional; 2 part-time support.
EIN: 592147657
Selected grants: The following grants were reported in 2004.
$250,000 to San Antonio Museum of Art, San Antonio, TX.
$200,000 to Atlanta Youth Academy, Atlanta, GA.
$200,000 to Childrens Healthcare of Atlanta, Atlanta, GA.
$130,000 to Surfrider Foundation, San Clemente, CA.
$125,000 to Boys and Girls Club of Delray Beach, Delray Beach, FL.
$75,000 to Adopt-A-Family, Los Angeles, CA.
$50,000 to Marine Corps Law Enforcement Foundation, Denville, NJ.
$25,000 to Center for Resource Economics, Island Press, DC.
$25,000 to Earthjustice, Oakland, CA.
$20,000 to Family First, Tampa, FL.

2105
Gasper & Irene Lazzara Charitable Foundation ✧
5000 Sawgrass Village Cir., Rm. 28
Ponte Vedra Beach, FL 32082
Contact: Irene Lazzara, Pres.

Established in 1996 in FL.
Donors: Gasper Lazzara; Irene Lazzara.
Foundation type: Independent foundation.
Financial data (yr. ended 4/30/05): Assets, $8,886,545 (M); expenditures, $958,311; qualifying distributions, $916,290; giving activities include $916,290 for 49 grants (high: $234,517; low: $100).
Purpose and activities: Grants are awarded to non-profit institutions that engage in research relevant to developing strategies for the prevention and treatment of cancer.
Fields of interest: Cancer; Human services; Community development.
Limitations: Giving primarily in Jacksonville, FL.
Application information: Unsolicited requests for research grants not accepted. Application form not required.
Initial approach: Letter
Deadline(s): None
Officers: Irene Lazzara, Pres.; Gasper Lazzara, V.P.
EIN: 597079426
Selected grants: The following grants were reported in 2004.
$1,743,753 to Jacksonville University, Jacksonville, FL.
$297,000 to University of Colorado, Boulder, CO.
$260,500 to University of North Florida, Jacksonville, FL.
$202,500 to Museum of Science and History, Jacksonville, FL.
$60,000 to Bolles School, Jacksonville, FL.
$32,500 to Baptist Medical Center, Wolfson Children's Hospital, Jacksonville, FL. For medical research.
$26,475 to Saint Vincents Foundation, Jacksonville, FL. For medical research.
$25,250 to Jacksonville Museum of Modern Art, Jacksonville, FL.
$25,000 to Greenwood School, Jacksonville, FL.
$25,000 to Jacksonville Country Day School, Jacksonville, FL.

2106
The Bennett and Geraldine LeBow Foundation, Inc. ✧
1200 Brickell, Ste. 700
Miami, FL 33131
Contact: Stephanie Don, Dir.
Application address: 5203 Fisher Island Dr., Fisher Island, FL 33109

Established in 1997 in FL.
Foundation type: Independent foundation.
Financial data (yr. ended 12/31/04): Assets, $2,068,683 (M); expenditures, $2,989,762; qualifying distributions, $2,970,198; giving activities include $2,970,198 for 8 grants (high: $1,939,229; low: $33,000).
Purpose and activities: Giving primarily for higher education, as well for programs children with life-threatening illnesses.
Fields of interest: Higher education; Higher education, university; Recreation, camps.

Limitations: Giving primarily in PA; funding also nationally.
Application information:
Initial approach: Letter
Deadline(s): None
Officers: Bennett S. LeBow, Pres.; Geraldine C. LeBow, Secy.
Director: Stephanie Don.
EIN: 650755022
Selected grants: The following grants were reported in 2003.
$1,600,000 to Dana-Farber Cancer Institute, Boston, MA.
$425,000 to Weill Medical College of Cornell University, New York, NY.
$375,000 to University of California, San Francisco, CA.
$250,000 to Arkansas Cancer Research Center, Little Rock, AR.
$250,000 to Mayo Clinic, Rochester, MN.
$207,045 to University of Miami, School of Medicine, Coral Gables, FL.
$175,000 to Rockefeller University, New York, NY.
$100,000 to Mount Sinai Medical Center, Miami Beach, FL.
$100,000 to University of Minnesota, Minneapolis, MN.
$50,000 to Florida International University, Miami, FL.

2107
Mildred S. Lee Charitable Foundation ✧
44 Cocoanut Row, Ste. 221A
Palm Beach, FL 33480-4040

Established in 1985 in MA.
Donor: Mildred S. Lee.
Foundation type: Independent foundation.
Financial data (yr. ended 12/31/04): Assets, $1,027,283 (M); gifts received, $1,475; expenditures, $365,219; qualifying distributions, $356,786; giving activities include $357,025 for 12 grants (high: $300,000; low: $25).
Fields of interest: Museums (art); Arts; Federated giving programs; Jewish federated giving programs.
Type of support: General/operating support; Continuing support; Annual campaigns; Capital campaigns.
Limitations: Applications not accepted. Giving primarily in FL and MA. No grants to individuals.
Application information: Contributes only to pre-selected organizations.
Trustees: Herbert Lee; Mildred S. Lee.
EIN: 061141211
Selected grants: The following grants were reported in 2004.
$300,000 to Norton Museum of Art, West Palm Beach, FL.
$10,000 to Society of the Four Arts, Palm Beach, FL.
$5,000 to American Heart Association, Dallas, TX.
$3,000 to Provincetown Art Association and Museum, Provincetown, MA.
$2,500 to Wang Center for the Performing Arts, Boston, MA.
$1,000 to Massachusetts Eye and Ear Infirmary, Boston, MA.

2108
Josephine S. Leiser Foundation, Inc. ✧ ☆
c/o James Ridley
1401 E. Broward Blvd., Ste. 200
Fort Lauderdale, FL 33301

Established in 1992 in FL.
Donor: Josephine S. Leiser†.
Foundation type: Independent foundation.
Financial data (yr. ended 5/31/06): Assets, $8,878,638 (M); expenditures, $601,992; qualifying distributions, $340,480; giving activities include $340,480 for grants.
Purpose and activities: Giving primarily for the Florida Grand Opera, FL.
Fields of interest: Performing arts, opera; Arts; Education, early childhood education; Human services; Children, services.
Type of support: General/operating support.
Limitations: Applications not accepted. Giving limited to FL. No grants to individuals.
Application information: Unsolicited requests for funds not accepted.
Officers: Robert Judd, Pres.; Theodore Friedt, V.P.; James Turner, Secy.; Joan Beard, Treas.
EIN: 650347903
Selected grants: The following grants were reported in 2005.
$75,000 to Bascom Palmer Eye Institute, Miami, FL.
$65,000 to W P B T Channel 2, Miami, FL.
$24,770 to Lighthouse of Broward County, Fort Lauderdale, FL.
$11,000 to Greater Miami Opera, Miami, FL.
$6,500 to United Way of Broward County, Fort Lauderdale, FL.
$4,000 to Salvation Army, Saint Petersburg, FL.
$3,000 to Museum of Art, Fort Lauderdale, FL.
$2,500 to Humane Society of Broward County, Fort Lauderdale, FL.
$1,000 to Fort Lauderdale Historical Society, Fort Lauderdale, FL.

2109
The Lennar Foundation, Inc. ▼ ✧
c/o Lennar Corp.
700 N.W. 107th Ave., Ste. 400
Miami, FL 33172 (305) 229-6400
Contact: Marshall Ames, V.P.

Established in 1989 in FL.
Donor: Lennar Corp.
Foundation type: Company-sponsored foundation.
Financial data (yr. ended 11/30/05): Assets, $28,017,002 (M); gifts received, $17,590,668; expenditures, $7,905,108; qualifying distributions, $7,520,893; giving activities include $7,512,225 for 75 grants (high: $3,025,000; low: $1,000).
Purpose and activities: The foundation supports organizations involved with education, health, cancer, cancer research, and homeless people.
Fields of interest: Higher education; Education; Health care; Cancer; Cancer research; American Red Cross; Homeless, human services; Federated giving programs; Homeless.
Type of support: General/operating support.
Limitations: Giving primarily in Miami, FL. No grants to individuals.
Application information: Application form not required.
Initial approach: Proposal
Deadline(s): None
Officers and Trustees:* Stuart A. Miller,* Pres.; Marshall Ames, V.P.; Waynewright Malcolm,* V.P.;

Allan Pekor,* Exec. Dir.; Jim Carr; Samantha Fels; Ezra Katz; Shelley Rubin.

EIN: 650171539

Selected grants: The following grants were reported in 2004.

$500,000 to City of Hope, Los Angeles, CA.

$500,000 to Volunteer Florida, Tallahassee, FL. For Florida Hurricane Relief Fund.

$350,000 to United Way of Miami-Dade, Miami, FL.

$250,000 to Nevada Cancer Institute, Las Vegas, NV.

$125,000 to Council for Educational Change, Davie, FL.

$100,000 to Community Partnership for Homeless, Miami, FL.

$100,000 to Founders Academy, Los Angeles, CA.

$100,000 to Jackson Memorial Foundation, Miami, FL. For Schiff Liver Clinic.

$50,000 to Maricopa Medical Center, Phoenix, AZ. For Arizona Burn Center.

$25,000 to Family Violence Prevention Center, Raleigh, NC.

2110
Levin & Papantonio Family Foundation, Inc. ◇

316 S. Baylen St., Ste. 600
Pensacola, FL 32502 (850) 944-5437
Contact: Suzie Page, Secy.-Treas.

Established in 1998 in FL.

Donors: Frederic G. Levin; J. Michael Papantonio; Martin H. Levin; R. Larry Morris.

Foundation type: Independent foundation.

Financial data (yr. ended 12/31/05): Assets, $716,445 (M); gifts received, $228,158; expenditures, $380,925; qualifying distributions, $375,909; giving activities include $367,602 for 76 grants (high: $62,500; low: $50), and $5,700 for 4 grants to individuals (high: $5,000; low: $250).

Purpose and activities: Giving primarily for education and human services for children in the Pensacola, FL, area; also awards those considered to be outstanding teachers and volunteers making a difference in the Escambia County, FL, community.

Fields of interest: Education; Health care; Health organizations, association; Youth development; Human services; Christian agencies & churches.

Type of support: Emergency funds; Grants to individuals.

Limitations: Giving primarily in Pensacola, FL.

Application information: Application form required.

Copies of proposal: 1

Deadline(s): None

Officers: Martin H. Levin, Pres.; Suzie Page, Secy.-Treas.

Director: Michael Papantonio.

Board Members: Virginia Buchanan; Terri Levin; Terri Papantonio; Sheila Reed; Sue Straughn; Randy Williams.

EIN: 593107428

Selected grants: The following grants were reported in 2005.

$62,500 to United Way of Escambia County, Pensacola, FL. For local Hurricane Katrina refugee funds.

$50,000 to Rebuild Northwest Florida, Pensacola, FL. For Hurricane Ivan rebuilding efforts.

$20,000 to Olive Baptist Church, Pensacola, FL. For local Hurricane Katrina refugee funds.

$20,000 to Salvation Army of Pensacola, Pensacola, FL. For social services evacuees.

$20,000 to United Way of Santa Rosa County, Milton, FL. For local Hurricane Katrina refugee funds.

$10,000 to Loaves and Fishes Soup Kitchen, Pensacola, FL.

$3,500 to Foundation for Excellence in Education, Pensacola, FL. 2 grants: $2,500 (For local Hurricane Katrina refugee funds), $1,000.

$3,000 to Big Brothers/Big Sisters of Northwest Florida, Pensacola, FL. For Bowl for Kids Sake.

$1,000 to PACE Center for Girls of Escambia-Santa Rosa, Pensacola, FL.

2111
Laurence Levine Charitable Fund, Inc. ◇ ☆

1801 N. Flagler Dr., No. 902
West Palm Beach, FL 33401
Contact: S.C. Langham, Exec. Dir.

Established in 2003 in FL.

Donor: Laurence W. Levine Foundation, Inc.

Foundation type: Independent foundation.

Financial data (yr. ended 12/31/05): Assets, $5,336,818 (M); gifts received, $150,000; expenditures, $1,229,317; qualifying distributions, $817,504; giving activities include $617,450 for 65 grants (high: $103,000; low: $100).

Purpose and activities: Giving primarily for the arts, particularly museums, as well as for education, and human services.

Fields of interest: Museums (art); Performing arts; Higher education; Law school/education; Education; Health organizations, association; Human services; Protestant agencies & churches.

Limitations: Giving on a national basis, with some emphasis on New York, NY.

Application information:

Initial approach: Letter

Deadline(s): None

Officers: T.R. Moore, Pres.; S.J. Kimble, V.P.; W.B. Warren, Treas.; S.C. Langham, Exec. Dir.

EIN: 020704231

2112
Mildred & Abner Levine Family Foundation ◇

16858 River Birch Cir.
Delray Beach, FL 33445-7055

Established in 1965.

Foundation type: Independent foundation.

Financial data (yr. ended 12/31/05): Assets, $3,956,355 (M); expenditures, $502,862; qualifying distributions, $502,537; giving activities include $502,537 for grants.

Purpose and activities: Giving primarily to Jewish agencies and associations.

Fields of interest: Human services; Jewish federated giving programs; Jewish agencies & temples.

Limitations: Applications not accepted. No grants to individuals.

Application information: Contributes only to pre-selected organizations.

Directors: Abner Levine; Lawrence I. Levine; Michael F. Levine; Mildred Levine; Ellen K. Miller.

EIN: 136172502

2113
The A. L. Levine Foundation, Inc. ◇

(formerly Blanche & A. L. Levine Foundation, Inc.)
c/o The Coates Law Firm
Chancellor Corporate Ctr., Ste 107
12012 South Shore Blvd.
Wellington, FL 33414
Application address: 1 Wayne Hills Mall, Wayne, NJ 07470, FAX: (973) 696-4499; tel.: (973) 696-4400

Established in 1996 in FL.

Donor: A.L. Levine.

Foundation type: Independent foundation.

Financial data (yr. ended 9/30/05): Assets, $10,203,371 (M); expenditures, $485,053; qualifying distributions, $437,024; giving activities include $429,296 for grants.

Purpose and activities: Giving primarily for the arts, health care, Jewish organizations and human services.

Fields of interest: Visual arts, painting; Arts; Hospitals (general); Human services; Jewish agencies & temples.

Application information: Application form required.

Copies of proposal: 1

Board meeting date(s): Yearly

Officers and Directors:* Carole Ann Steiger,* Pres.; Adam J. Steiger,* V.P.; David L. Steiger,* V.P.; Andrew R. Steiger,* Secy.; Joel J. Steiger,* Treas.; Arthur L. Levine; Peter L. Levine.

EIN: 650554692

Selected grants: The following grants were reported in 2003.

$1,400,000 to Community Health Center of Branch County, Coldwater, MI. For unrestricted support.

$128,000 to Daughters of Miriam Center, Clifton, NJ. For unrestricted support.

$112,000 to Valley Hospital Foundation, Ridgewood, NJ. For unrestricted support.

$31,000 to Barnert Temple, Franklin Lakes, NJ. For unrestricted support.

$25,000 to Metropolitan Museum of Art, New York, NY. For unrestricted support.

$25,000 to Parkinsons Disease Foundation, New York, NY. For unrestricted support.

$25,000 to Raymond F. Kravis Center for the Performing Arts, West Palm Beach, FL. For unrestricted support.

$25,000 to UJA Federation of Northern New Jersey, Wayne, NJ. For unrestricted support.

$20,000 to Our Lady of Mercy Medical Center, Comprehensive Cancer Center, Bronx, NY.

$15,000 to YM-YWHA of North Jersey, Wayne, NJ. For unrestricted support.

2114
Frank J. Lewis Foundation, Inc. ◇

P.O. Box 9726
Riviera Beach, FL 33419

Established in 1996 in FL.

Foundation type: Independent foundation.

Financial data (yr. ended 12/31/05): Assets, $18,428,168 (M); expenditures, $2,550,485; qualifying distributions, $2,380,386; giving activities include $2,369,595 for 167 grants (high: $100,000; low: $1,000).

Purpose and activities: Giving primarily for education, human services, and Roman Catholic churches and agencies.

Fields of interest: Higher education; Education; Health care; Human services; Roman Catholic agencies & churches.

Type of support: General/operating support.
Limitations: Giving on a national basis, with some emphasis on FL.
Trustees: Megan Lewis Lesko; Diana Lewis; Edward Lewis; Philip D. Lewis; Timothy P. Lewis; Patricia Lewis Navarro.
EIN: 650652107
Selected grants: The following grants were reported in 2005.
$200,000 to Catholic Relief Services, Baltimore, MD. 2 grants: $100,000 each
$50,000 to Diocese of Helena, Helena, MT.
$50,000 to Lewis University, Romeoville, IL.
$30,000 to Gratitude House, West Palm Beach, FL.
$25,000 to Catholic Charities of the Archdiocese of Chicago, Chicago, IL.
$25,000 to Hanley Center, West Palm Beach, FL.
$10,000 to Cristo Rey Jesuit High School, Chicago, IL.
$10,000 to School Sisters of Notre Dame, Wilton, CT.
$5,000 to Mercy Home for Boys and Girls, Chicago, IL.

2115
Libra Foundation, Inc. ◇
96 N.E. 4th Ave.
Delray Beach, FL 33483-4597

Established in 1994 in FL.
Donors: Jane E. Werly; Charles M. Werly‡.
Foundation type: Independent foundation.
Financial data (yr. ended 12/31/05): Assets, $16,156,987 (M); gifts received, $17,324; expenditures, $647,951; qualifying distributions, $566,026; giving activities include $566,026 for 24 grants (high: $75,000; low: $4,995).
Fields of interest: Food services; Boys & girls clubs; Human services; Children, services; Family services.
Limitations: Applications not accepted. Giving limited to FL. No grants to individuals.
Application information: Contributes only to pre-selected organizations.
Officer and Directors:* Jane E. Werly,* Pres.; Horace S. Nichols; Thomas A. Smith.
EIN: 650469849
Selected grants: The following grants were reported in 2004.
$57,000 to Habitat for Humanity of South Palm Beach County, Delray Beach, FL.
$50,000 to Friends of Abused Children, West Palm Beach, FL.
$50,000 to Palm Beach County Literacy Coalition, Delray Beach, FL.
$46,000 to Lords Place, West Palm Beach, FL.
$43,635 to Salvation Army, Saint Petersburg, FL.
$30,000 to Rosies Place, Boston, MA.
$26,000 to Daily Bread Food Bank, Miami, FL.
$12,425 to Pine Street Inn, Boston, MA.
$10,000 to Soup Kitchen, Boynton Beach, FL.

2116
Life's Requite, Inc. ◇
15900 Gulf Blvd.
Redington Beach, FL 33708

Established in 1997 in FL.
Donor: Thomas A. Sansone.
Foundation type: Independent foundation.

Financial data (yr. ended 12/31/05): Assets, $20,107,617 (M); expenditures, $915,607; qualifying distributions, $898,000; giving activities include $898,000 for 20 grants (high: $400,000; low: $3,000).
Fields of interest: Arts; Higher education; Hospitals (specialty); Human services; YM/YWCAs & YM/YWHAs; Federated giving programs; Religion.
Limitations: Applications not accepted. Giving primarily in St. Petersburg and Tampa, FL. No grants to individuals.
Application information: Contributes only to pre-selected organizations.
Officer and Directors:* Thomas A. Sansone,* Pres. and Secy.-Treas.; Jeffery T. Sansone; Laura A. Sansone; Cathy L. Unruh.
EIN: 593446719
Selected grants: The following grants were reported in 2004.
$400,000 to Academy Prep Foundation, Saint Petersburg, FL.
$100,000 to Church by the Sea, Miami Beach, FL.
$10,000 to Arts Center Association, Saint Petersburg, FL.
$10,000 to Florida Resurrection House, Saint Petersburg, FL.
$10,000 to Mayors Beautification Program, Tampa, FL.
$10,000 to Metropolitan Ministries, Tampa, FL.
$10,000 to Spring of Tampa Bay, Tampa, FL.
$10,000 to Tampa Museum of Art, Tampa, FL.
$10,000 to YMCA of Greater Saint Petersburg, Saint Petersburg, FL.
$5,000 to All Childrens Hospital, Saint Petersburg, FL.

2117
The Light Foundation, Inc. ◇
c/o John Garthwaite
15310 Amberly Dr., Ste. 220
Tampa, FL 33647

Established in 1997 in FL.
Foundation type: Independent foundation.
Financial data (yr. ended 12/31/04): Assets, $5,600,289 (M); expenditures, $559,234; qualifying distributions, $554,583; giving activities include $554,583 for 30 grants (high: $204,000; low: $72).
Purpose and activities: Giving primarily for Christian ministries, including United Methodist churches and organizations; some funding also for children, youth, and social services.
Fields of interest: Education; Cancer research; Human services; YM/YWCAs & YM/YWHAs; Children/youth, services; Family services; Christian agencies & churches.
Limitations: Applications not accepted. Giving primarily in Tampa, FL. No grants to individuals.
Application information: Contributes only to pre-selected organizations.
Officers and Directors:* Scott Luttrell,* Pres.; Jason Wolfe, Secy.-Treas.; Michael Bissonnette; Laura Luttrell.
EIN: 593489135

2118
The Alan S. Lorberbaum Family Foundation ◇
c/o C. Gerak, Bessemer Trust
801 Brickell Ave.
Miami, FL 33131
Application address: c/o Suzanne L. Helen, Tr., 701 Osprey Point Cir., Boca Raton, FL 33431, tel. (561) 362-7024

Established in 1998 in FL.
Donor: Alan S. Lorberbaum.
Foundation type: Independent foundation.
Financial data (yr. ended 12/31/05): Assets, $18,993,656 (M); expenditures, $1,131,003; qualifying distributions, $1,104,748; giving activities include $1,103,301 for 16 grants (high: $505,126; low: $5,048).
Purpose and activities: Giving primarily for education.
Fields of interest: Museums (art); Higher education; Education; Children/youth, services; Jewish federated giving programs.
Limitations: Giving primarily in GA, NJ, and TN.
Application information:
  Initial approach: Written summary (not more than 2 pages)
  Deadline(s): None
Trustees: Suzanne L. Helen; Alan S. Lorberbaum; Jeffrey Lorberbaum; Mark Lorberbaum.
EIN: 586368036

2119
Audrey Love Charitable Foundation
290 Sunrise Dr., Ste. 204
Key Biscayne, FL 33149

Established in 1994 in DE.
Donor: Audrey B. Love Trust.
Foundation type: Independent foundation.
Financial data (yr. ended 12/31/05): Assets, $33,995,499 (M); gifts received, $14,042,500; expenditures, $1,098,743; qualifying distributions, $990,860; giving activities include $728,500 for 88 grants (high: $100,000; low: $500).
Purpose and activities: Giving for the arts including performing arts, medical research, elder care, and animal welfare.
Fields of interest: Performing arts; Arts; Medical school/education; Animals/wildlife; Human services.
Limitations: Applications not accepted. Giving on a national basis with emphasis on Miami, FL. No grants to individuals.
Application information: Contributes only to pre-selected organizations.
Officers: Ralph Lutrin, Pres.; Paul W. Doll, Jr., V.P. and Secy.-Treas.
Directors: Gerard B. Bajek; Alfred Allan Lewis.
EIN: 222766994
Selected grants: The following grants were reported in 2005.
$100,000 to Greater Miami Opera, Miami, FL.
$29,500 to Carnegie Hall Society, New York, NY.
$25,000 to Georgia Museum of Art, Athens, GA.
$25,000 to Metropolitan Museum of Art, New York, NY.
$10,000 to Mount Sinai Medical Center, Miami Beach, FL.
$6,000 to Doctors Without Borders USA, New York, NY.
$5,000 to PAWS Chicago, Chicago, IL.
$5,000 to Tigertail Productions, Miami, FL.

$2,500 to Animal Medical Center, New York, NY.

$2,500 to Best Friends Animal Society, Kanab, UT.

2120

E. M. Lynn Foundation ✦

2501 N. Military Trail
Boca Raton, FL   33431-6398

Established in 1977.

Donors: E.M. Lynn†; Mrs. E.M. Lynn; The Christopher E. and Krista Mary DaSilva Charitable Lead Annuity Trust.

Foundation type: Independent foundation.

Financial data (yr. ended 10/31/05): Assets, $174,983,489 (M); gifts received, $3,111; expenditures, $5,964,167; qualifying distributions, $5,547,200; giving activities include $5,547,200 for 28 grants (high: $5,000,000; low: $200).

Purpose and activities: Giving primarily for education, the arts, and health care.

Fields of interest: Arts; Higher education; Hospitals (general); Health care; Medical research, institute; Human services.

Type of support: General/operating support.

Limitations: Applications not accepted. Giving primarily in FL. No grants to individuals.

Application information: Contributes only to pre-selected organizations.

Trustee: C.E. Lynn.

EIN: 591788859

Selected grants: The following grants were reported in 2003.

$5,000,000 to Florida Atlantic University Foundation, Boca Raton, FL. To build College of Nursing.

$45,000 to Lynn University, Boca Raton, FL. 2 grants: $25,000 (For general support), $20,000 (For general support).

$38,406 to Boca Raton Historical Society, Boca Raton, FL. For general support.

$25,000 to Stetson University, DeLand, FL. For general support.

$20,000 to Boca Raton Community Hospital Foundation, Boca Raton, FL. 2 grants: $10,000 each (For general support).

$20,000 to Mae Volen Senior Center, Boca Raton, FL. For general support.

$10,000 to Debbie-Rand Memorial Service League, Boca Raton, FL. For general support.

$10,000 to Florence Fuller Child Development Center, Boca Raton, FL. For general support.

2121

Dr. John T. MacDonald Foundation, Inc.

1550 Madruga Ave., Ste. 215
Coral Gables, FL   33146-3017   (305) 667-6017
Contact: Kim Greene, Exec. Dir.
FAX: (305) 667-9135;
E-mail: info@jtmacdonaldfdn.org; URL: http://www.jtmacdonaldfdn.org

Established in 1992 in FL; converted from sale of Doctors' Hospital to HEALTHSOUTH Rehabilitation Corporation; became a private foundation in 1992.

Donors: Adele H. Goddard Trust; Ramona K. Inglis Trust.

Foundation type: Independent foundation.

Financial data (yr. ended 12/31/04): Assets, $35,525,514 (M); gifts received, $450,686; expenditures, $3,274,259; qualifying distributions,

$3,022,215; giving activities include $2,739,251 for 18 grants (high: $1,344,372; low: $8,775).

Purpose and activities: To provide funding for programs and projects designed to improve, preserve or restore the health and health care of the people in Miami-Dade County, FL.

Fields of interest: Medical school/education; Health care; Mental health/crisis services; Human services.

Type of support: General/operating support; Continuing support; Equipment; Program development; Seed money; Scholarship funds; Technical assistance; Program evaluation.

Limitations: Giving limited to Miami-Dade County, FL. No support for projects that promote religious faith. No grants to individuals directly, or for fundraising campaigns, for-profit organizations, other grantmaking foundations, or national projects where funding would leave Miami-Dade County, FL.

Publications: Application guidelines; Annual report; Grants list.

Application information: Application form and deadlines available on request. Application procedures and form are also available on foundation Web site. Application form required.

> *Initial approach:* Letters of inquiry (no more than 2 pages) submitted first. Selected applicants are then invited to fill out application
> *Copies of proposal:* 1
> *Deadline(s):* Apr.
> *Board meeting date(s):* Quarterly
> *Final notification:* June

Officers and Directors:* Karl Smiley, M.D.*, Chair.; Dean H. Roller, M.D.*, Vice Chair.; Margaret C. Starner,* Secy.; Kim Greene, Exec. Dir.; Robert G. Breier; Aldo C. Busot, M.D.; George M. Corrigan; Gary W. Dix; Charles A. Dunn, M.D.; R. Rodney Howell, M.D.; Thomas M. Mark, M.D.; George D. Mekras, M.D.; John C. Nordt III, M.D.; Steven S. Pabalan, M.D.; Latanae R. Parker, Jr., M.D.; Stuart H. Savedoff, D.D.S.; Dazelle D. Simpson, M.D.; David A. Wolfberg.

Number of staff: 1 full-time professional; 1 part-time professional.

EIN: 590818918

2122

The MacDougald Foundation, Inc. ✦ ☆

260 1st Ave. S., Ste. 110
St. Petersburg, FL   33701

Established in 1997 in FL.

Donors: MacDougald Family Limited Partnership; James E. MacDougald; Suzanne M. MacDougald.

Foundation type: Independent foundation.

Financial data (yr. ended 7/31/05): Assets, $244,777 (M); gifts received, $6,750; expenditures, $519,930; qualifying distributions, $512,930; giving activities include $511,000 for 4 grants (high: $250,000; low: $1,000).

Purpose and activities: Giving primarily for a museum, and to a scholarship and financial aid fund for the children of special operations personnel who were killed in an operational mission or training accident; funding also for human services.

Fields of interest: Museums (art); Scholarships/financial aid; Human services.

Limitations: Applications not accepted. Giving primarily in FL. No grants to individuals.

Application information: Contributes only to pre-selected organizations.

Officers: James E. MacDougald, Pres.; Suzanne M. MacDougald, Secy.-Treas.

Director: Joseph J. MacDougald.

EIN: 593468929

2123

John J. & Lucille C. Madigan Charitable Foundation, Inc. ✦

c/o Robert F. Drabik
1313 S. Lakeshore Dr.
Sarasota, FL   34231-3403

Established in 1992 in FL.

Foundation type: Independent foundation.

Financial data (yr. ended 12/31/04): Assets, $4,527,192 (M); expenditures, $460,414; qualifying distributions, $419,991; giving activities include $332,047 for 24 grants (high: $60,200; low: $700).

Purpose and activities: Giving primarily to Christian agencies and churches, education, human services, and to a camp.

Fields of interest: Higher education; Education; Recreation, camps; Human services; Christian agencies & churches.

Type of support: General/operating support; Scholarship funds.

Limitations: Applications not accepted. Giving primarily in FL, IL, MA, MO, NY, and OH. No grants to individuals.

Application information: Contributes only to pre-selected organizations.

Officers and Directors:* Robert F. Drabik, Pres.; Patricia Drabik,* Mgr.; Mark Tousey.

EIN: 650352871

Selected grants: The following grants were reported in 2004.

$60,000 to First Church of Christ Scientist, Boston, MA.

$46,000 to Cedars Camps, Manchester, MO.

$17,000 to Broward Community College, Fort Lauderdale, FL.

$13,500 to Principle Foundation, Kansas City, MO.

$10,000 to High Ridge House, Riverdale, NY.

$10,000 to Peace Haven Association, Saint Louis, MO.

$8,000 to Columbia Theological Seminary, Decatur, GA.

2124

Arthur and Holly Magill Foundation ✦

c/o Nixon Peabody, LLP
4400 PGA Blvd., Ste. 900
Palm Beach Gardens, FL   33410
Contact: Stephen Newman

Established in 1981 in SC.

Donors: Arthur F. Magill†; Alice H. Magill.

Foundation type: Operating foundation.

Financial data (yr. ended 12/31/05): Assets, $12,562,164 (M); expenditures, $1,024,192; qualifying distributions, $621,506; giving activities include $621,506 for 7 grants (high: $279,506; low: $5,000).

Fields of interest: Performing arts, music; Arts; Eye diseases; Christian agencies & churches.

Type of support: General/operating support.

Limitations: Giving primarily in Greenville, SC. No grants to individuals.

Application information: Application form not required.

> *Initial approach:* Letter of request
> *Deadline(s):* None

Director and Trustees:* Arturo Melosi*; Bette Bush; Gianfranco D'Augustino; Holly Melosi; Stephen M. Newman; William Woodson.
EIN: 570713587

2125
Chesley G. Magruder Foundation, Inc. ✧
c/o SunTrust Bank
P.O. Box 620005
Orlando, FL 32862-0005 (407) 237-5907

Established in 1979 in FL.
Donors: Chesley G. Magruder Trust; Trustco Capital Mgmt.
Foundation type: Independent foundation.
Financial data (yr. ended 6/30/05): Assets, $14,984,698 (M); expenditures, $613,997; qualifying distributions, $550,856; giving activities include $507,048 for 48 grants (high: $25,000; low: $2,500).
Purpose and activities: Giving primarily for education and human services, and to Christian agencies and churches.
Fields of interest: Arts; Higher education; Education; Housing/shelter, development; Human services; Residential/custodial care; Christian agencies & churches.
Limitations: Giving limited to central FL, including Orange, Osceola, and Seminole counties. No grants to individuals.
Application information: Applicants must complete the foundation's synopsis sheet. Additional information may be requested by the foundation after a proposal is received. Application form required.
  Initial approach: Proposal
  Copies of proposal: 6
  Deadline(s): 4 weeks prior to trustee meeting
  Board meeting date(s): 3rd Fri. of Feb., Apr., June, Aug., Oct. and the 2nd Fri. of Dec.
  Final notification: Within 1 month
Trustee: SunTrust Bank.
EIN: 591920736
Selected grants: The following grants were reported in 2004.
$25,000 to Lake Highland Preparatory School, Orlando, FL.
$25,000 to Orlando Museum of Art, Orlando, FL.
$25,000 to Rollins College, Winter Park, FL.
$25,000 to YMCA, Central Florida, Cocoa, FL.
$20,000 to Trinity Preparatory School of Florida, Orlando, FL.
$10,000 to Christian Service Center for Central Florida, Orlando, FL.
$10,000 to Justice and Peace Office, Apopka, FL.
$6,750 to Adult Literacy League, Orlando, FL.
$6,000 to A Gift for Teaching, Orlando, FL.
$5,000 to Orlando Opera Company, Orlando, FL.

2126
The Milton and Tamar Maltz Family Foundation
5500 Military Trail, Ste. 22-367
Jupiter, FL 33458
E-mail: maltzfoundation@aol.com

Established in 1989 in FL.
Donors: Milton S. Maltz; Tamar Maltz; Daniel Maltz; David Maltz; Julie Konigsberg.
Foundation type: Independent foundation.

Financial data (yr. ended 6/30/05): Assets, $14,590,279 (M); gifts received, $2,235,000; expenditures, $470,546; qualifying distributions, $430,000; giving activities include $430,000 for 15 grants (high: $198,500; low: $1,000).
Purpose and activities: Giving primarily for the arts, medical research, and human services.
Fields of interest: Arts; Environment, natural resources; Medical research, institute; Human services; Aging, centers/services; Jewish federated giving programs.
Type of support: General/operating support; Annual campaigns; Building/renovation; Research.
Limitations: Applications not accepted. Giving on a national basis, with emphasis on FL and Cleveland, OH. No grants to individuals.
Application information: Contributes only to pre-selected organizations.
Officers: Milton S. Maltz, Pres.; Julie E. Konigsberg, V.P.; Daniel Maltz, V.P.; Tamar Maltz, Secy.; David Maltz, Treas.
Number of staff: None.
EIN: 650164300
Selected grants: The following grants were reported in 2005.
$198,500 to NARSAD Research Institute, Great Neck, NY. For research.
$100,000 to Conservation Fund, Arlington, VA.
$50,000 to Hadassah, The Womens Zionist Organization of America, New York, NY. For Stem Cell research.
$25,000 to United Community Health Center, Sahuarita, AZ. For Integrated Behavioral Health Program.
$12,000 to Jewish Federation of Palm Beach County, West Palm Beach, FL.
$12,000 to Laura and Alvin Siegal College of Judaic Studies, Cleveland, OH.
$7,500 to Cleveland Orchestra, Cleveland, OH. For general operating support.
$1,800 to Anti-Defamation League of Bnai Brith, New York, NY. For general operating support.
$1,000 to Cleveland Baseball Federation, Cleveland, OH. For amateau baseball program.
$1,000 to Memorial Sloan-Kettering Cancer Center, New York, NY. For research.

2127
Bernard A. & Chris Marden Foundation ✧ ☆
2 North Breakers Row
Palm Beach, FL 33480

Established in 1993 in DE and FL.
Foundation type: Independent foundation.
Financial data (yr. ended 12/31/05): Assets, $954,660 (M); expenditures, $343,630; qualifying distributions, $343,630; giving activities include $339,200 for 20 grants (high: $148,000; low: $100).
Fields of interest: Performing arts, opera; Arts; Environment, natural resources; Health care, clinics/centers; Jewish federated giving programs.
Limitations: Applications not accepted. Giving primarily in FL and NY. No grants to individuals.
Application information: Contributes only to pre-selected organizations.
Officers: Bernard A. Marden, Pres.; Chris Marden, V.P.
Directors: Patrice Marden Auld; James Marden.
EIN: 650409920
Selected grants: The following grants were reported in 2005.

$100,000 to Jewish Federation of Palm Beach County, West Palm Beach, FL.
$12,500 to Palm Beach Opera, Palm Beach, FL.
$10,000 to Bruce and Marsha Moskowitz Foundation, Palm Beach, FL.
$2,000 to Actors Fund of America, New York, NY.
$1,000 to Patrons of the Arts in the Vatican Museums, Palm Beach, FL.
$1,000 to Society of the Four Arts, Palm Beach, FL.

2128
Thomas H. Maren Foundation ✧
c/o Emily Maren
621 S.W. 26th Pl.
Gainesville, FL 32601-9014

Established in 1999 in FL.
Donor: Maren Royalty Trust.
Foundation type: Independent foundation.
Financial data (yr. ended 12/31/04): Assets, $13,412,103 (M); gifts received, $3,875,599; expenditures, $2,818,303; qualifying distributions, $2,793,431; giving activities include $2,786,421 for 106 grants (high: $200,000; low: $2,000).
Purpose and activities: Giving primarily for education, health care and human services; funding also for Roman Catholic and Protestant organizations and ministries.
Fields of interest: Elementary/secondary education; Higher education; Education; Health care; Human services; Protestant agencies & churches; Roman Catholic agencies & churches.
Limitations: Giving primarily in FL; some funding nationally, particularly in AZ and ME. No grants to individuals.
Application information:
  Initial approach: Letter
  Deadline(s): None
Trustees: Susan Fellner; David K. Maren; Emily Maren; Erik Swenson.
EIN: 133855243
Selected grants: The following grants were reported in 2004.
$200,000 to Northwest Center, Seattle, WA.
$164,000 to Alachua County Public Schools Foundation, Gainesville, FL. 2 grants: $64,000, $100,000
$110,000 to Aquinas High School, Bronx, NY. 2 grants: $50,000, $60,000
$85,250 to Mount Desert Island Biological Laboratory, Salsbury Cove, ME. 2 grants: $20,750, $64,500
$50,000 to Mount Desert Island Hospital, Bar Harbor, ME.
$40,060 to Mathewson Street United Methodist Church, Providence, RI.
$25,000 to Seattles Union Gospel Mission, Seattle, WA.

2129
Maroone Family Foundation ✧ ☆
2494 S. Ocean Blvd., No. A7
Boca Raton, FL 33432

Established in 1997 in FL.
Donor: Albert Maroone.
Foundation type: Independent foundation.
Financial data (yr. ended 12/31/05): Assets, $163,178 (M); expenditures, $625,424; qualifying distributions, $623,000; giving activities include

$623,000 for 5 grants (high: $500,000; low: $1,000).

Purpose and activities: Giving primarily to health and human service organizations.

Fields of interest: Health organizations, association; Human services; Children/youth, services.

Limitations: Applications not accepted. Giving primarily in FL. No grants to individuals.

Application information: Contributes only to pre-selected organizations.

Trustees: Albert Maroone; Katherine Maroone; Michael Maroone; Donald J. Reese.

EIN: 166466934

2130
The Martin Foundation, Inc. ✧
5051 Castello Sq., Ste. 204
Naples, FL 34103-8982
Contact: Geraldine F. Martin, Pres.
URL: http://www.nibco.com/cms.do?id=545

Incorporated in 1953 in IN.

Donors: Ross Martin†; Esther Martin†; Lee Martin; Geraldine F. Martin.

Foundation type: Independent foundation.

Financial data (yr. ended 6/30/05): Assets, $29,303,605 (M); expenditures, $1,821,850; qualifying distributions, $1,572,650; giving activities include $1,548,650 for 50 grants (high: $250,000; low: $1,000).

Purpose and activities: Emphasis on education and social services, including programs for women and youth, environmental and conservation organizations; support also for cultural programs, public interest programs, and international development.

Fields of interest: Media/communications; Museums; Arts; Education, early childhood education; Higher education; Adult/continuing education; Libraries/library science; Education, reading; Education; Environment, natural resources; Environment; Animal welfare; Animals/wildlife, preservation/protection; Health care, clinics/centers; Reproductive health, family planning; Medical care, rehabilitation; Mental health/crisis services; Housing/shelter, development; Boys & girls clubs; Human services; Youth, services; Family services; Women, centers/services; Minorities/immigrants, centers/services; International economic development; International peace/security; Community development; Federated giving programs; Population studies; Public affairs; Minorities; Women; Economically disadvantaged.

Limitations: Giving primarily in FL and IN; some funding also in MA and WA. No grants to individuals.

Publications: Annual report (including application guidelines).

Application information: Write to the foundation for guidelines and annual report. Application form not required.
   Initial approach: Letter
   Copies of proposal: 1
   Deadline(s): None
   Board meeting date(s): As required
   Final notification: 4 to 8 weeks

Officers: Geraldine F. Martin, Pres.; Casper Martin, Secy.-Treas.

Directors: Jennifer L. Martin; Lisa Martin.

EIN: 351070929

2131
The Masters Foundation, Inc. ✧ ☆
1900 Summit Tower Blvd., Ste. 260
Orlando, FL 32810

Established in 1986 in FL.

Donors: Jamie Hershiser; Orel Hershiser.

Foundation type: Independent foundation.

Financial data (yr. ended 5/31/06): Assets, $20,657 (M); expenditures, $714,346; qualifying distributions, $694,989; giving activities include $694,989 for 8 grants (high: $344,252; low: $1,500).

Purpose and activities: Giving primarily for Christian ministry.

Fields of interest: Human services; Religious federated giving programs; Christian agencies & churches; Protestant agencies & churches.

Type of support: General/operating support.

Limitations: Applications not accepted. Giving primarily in Orlando, FL.

Application information: Unsolicited requests for funds not accepted.

Officers and Director:* Orel Hershiser,* Pres.; Jamie Hershiser, Secy.; Paul Kraus, Treas.

EIN: 592700563

2132
Joy McCann Foundation, Inc. ✧
(formerly Culverhouse Family Foundation, Inc.)
1700 S. Macdill Ave., Ste. 360
Tampa, FL 33629
E-mail: administration@joymccannfoundation.org

Established in 1996 in FL.

Foundation type: Independent foundation.

Financial data (yr. ended 12/31/04): Assets, $17,711,170 (M); expenditures, $4,121,739; qualifying distributions, $3,992,943; giving activities include $3,877,666 for 23 grants (high: $525,000; low: $1,000; average: $2,500–$25,000).

Purpose and activities: Giving primarily to medical research and higher education.

Fields of interest: Arts; Higher education; Medical research, institute; Youth development.

Limitations: Applications not accepted. No grants to individuals.

Application information: Contributes only to pre-selected organizations.

Officers and Directors:* Thomas Purcell,* Pres.; Scott Lynch, V.P.; Mark J. Bryn,* Secy.; Andres Bolano, Jr.,* Treas.; Joy M. Culverhouse; Robert M. Daughtery, Jr.

EIN: 593166283

Selected grants: The following grants were reported in 2004.

$525,000 to Meharry Medical College, Nashville, TN. For Women in Science and Medicine Professorship.

$525,000 to Mercer University, Macon, GA.

$525,000 to University of Massachusetts, Boston, MA.

$500,000 to Stetson University, College of Law, DeLand, FL.

$500,000 to University of Kansas, Lawrence, KS. For Women in Science and Medicine professorship.

$500,000 to University of Nevada, Las Vegas, NV.

$250,000 to Tampa Bay Performing Arts Center, Tampa, FL. For Multimedia Center and Library.

$166,666 to Physicians for Reproductive Choice and Health, New York, NY.

$35,000 to Association of American Medical Colleges, DC.

$20,000 to College of William and Mary, Marshall-Wythe School of Law, Williamsburg, VA. For general operating support.

2133
McKeen Fund ✧
c/o Bessemer Trust Co. of FL
222 Royal Palm Way
Palm Beach, FL 33480 (561) 655-4030
Contact: James J. Daly, Tr.

Established in 1993 in FL.

Foundation type: Independent foundation.

Financial data (yr. ended 12/31/05): Assets, $15,956,927 (M); expenditures, $1,023,529; qualifying distributions, $806,196; giving activities include $610,379 for 49 grants (high: $100,000; low: $500).

Purpose and activities: Giving primarily to hospitals, universities, social welfare organizations, and cultural institutions; of particular interest is providing for the maintenance and care of the aged and infirm, retarded and mentally disabled, and for the education of persons studying for the priesthood.

Fields of interest: Higher education; Hospitals (general); American Red Cross; Roman Catholic agencies & churches.

Limitations: Giving primarily in FL and NY. No grants to individuals.

Application information:
   Initial approach: Letter
   Deadline(s): None

Trustees: Beth A. Daly; James J. Daly.

EIN: 137002920

2134
McKnight Brain Research Foundation ✧
P.O. Box 1908
Orlando, FL 32802-1908
Contact: Teresa Borcheck
Application address: c/o SunTrust Bank, P.O. Box 3838, Orlando, FL 32802, tel.: (407) 237-5907

Established in 1998 in FL.

Donor: Evelyn Franks McKnight†.

Foundation type: Independent foundation.

Financial data (yr. ended 6/30/05): Assets, $51,898,266 (M); gifts received, $250; expenditures, $3,227,882; qualifying distributions, $3,026,049; giving activities include $2,875,000 for 2 grants (high: $2,000,000; low: $875,000).

Purpose and activities: Provides support for medical research of the brain, to accomplish alleviation of memory loss of the aging, including making grants to charities involved in such research.

Fields of interest: Brain research.

Limitations: Giving primarily in FL.

Application information: Application form not required.
   Deadline(s): None

Trustees: J. Lee Dockery; Michael L. Dockery, M.D.; Nina Ellenbogen Raim; SunTrust Bank.

EIN: 656301255

2135
McNamara Family Foundation, Inc. ◇
1095 Mariner Dr.
Key Biscayne, FL 33149

Established in 2002 in FL.
Donor: James M. McNamara.
Foundation type: Independent foundation.
Financial data (yr. ended 12/31/03): Assets,
$10,611,202 (M); expenditures, $532,955;
qualifying distributions, $500,000; giving activities
include $500,000 for 1 grant.
Fields of interest: Education.
Limitations: Applications not accepted. Giving on a
national basis. No grants to individuals.
Application information: Contributes only to
pre-selected organizations.
Directors: Christine McNamara; Elizabeth
McNamara; James M. McNamara; Lana McNamara.
EIN: 141861856
Selected grants: The following grants were reported
in 2004.
$500,000 to Hispanic Scholarship Fund, San
 Francisco, CA.

2136
Julia & Gilbert Merrill Foundation, Inc. ◇ ☆
4709 Banyan Ln.
Tamarac, FL 33319

Established in 1990 in NY.
Donors: Gilbert Merrill; Julia Merrill.
Foundation type: Independent foundation.
Financial data (yr. ended 12/31/05): Assets,
$3,039,656 (M); expenditures, $449,124;
qualifying distributions, $373,255; giving activities
include $373,255 for grants.
Purpose and activities: Giving primarily for Jewish
organizations.
Fields of interest: Education; Health care; Health
organizations, association; Civil rights; Jewish
federated giving programs; Jewish agencies &
temples.
Limitations: Applications not accepted. Giving
primarily in FL and NY. No grants to individuals.
Application information: Contributes only to
pre-selected organizations.
Officers: Julia Merrill, Pres.; Abby Merrill, V.P.
EIN: 521711329

2137
The Arthur I. and Sydelle F. Meyer Private Charitable Foundation ◇
1601 Belvedere Rd., Ste. 407S
West Palm Beach, FL 33406-1518
Contact: Sydelle F. Meyer, Dir.

Established in 1995 in FL.
Donors: Arthur I. Meyer; Sydelle F. Meyer; Meyer
Mutual Foundation; Meyer Mutual Fund.
Foundation type: Independent foundation.
Financial data (yr. ended 12/31/05): Assets,
$3,826,740 (M); gifts received, $290,000;
expenditures, $923,675; qualifying distributions,
$923,148; giving activities include $923,148 for 18
+ grants (high: $258,679).
Purpose and activities: Giving primarily for higher
education, the performing arts, and to Jewish
organizations, schools, and temples.

Fields of interest: Arts education; Museums;
Museums (art); Performing arts, ballet; Performing
arts, opera; Higher education; Medical school/
education; Jewish federated giving programs;
Jewish agencies & temples.
Limitations: Giving primarily in FL, with emphasis on
West Palm Beach; some funding also in New York,
NY. No grants to individuals.
Application information:
 Initial approach: Letter
 Deadline(s): None
Directors: Arthur I. Meyer; Sydelle F. Meyer.
EIN: 650498422
Selected grants: The following grants were reported
in 2005.
$258,679 to Norton Museum of Art, West Palm
 Beach, FL.
$249,416 to Jewish Federation of Palm Beach
 County, West Palm Beach, FL.
$105,700 to Temple Judea, Coral Gables, FL.
$11,940 to Ballet Florida, West Palm Beach, FL.
$10,000 to South Florida Science Museum, West
 Palm Beach, FL.
$7,500 to Palm Beach Opera, Palm Beach, FL.
$5,000 to Florida Stage, Manalapan, FL.
$2,500 to Armory Art Center, West Palm Beach, FL.
$1,000 to American Friends of Livnot Ulehibanot,
 New York, NY.
$500 to Barry Telecommunications, Boynton Beach,
 FL.

2138
The J. S. & S. Michaan Foundation ◇ ☆
220 Sunrise Ave.
Palm Beach, FL 33480

Established in 1995 in FL.
Donors: Joseph Michaan; Suzanne Michaan.
Foundation type: Operating foundation.
Financial data (yr. ended 6/30/05): Assets,
$4,270,741 (M); expenditures, $366,926;
qualifying distributions, $365,951; giving activities
include $364,736 for 95 grants (high: $100,000;
low: $50).
Purpose and activities: Giving primarily to Jewish
organizations, as well as to health associations.
Fields of interest: Health care; Health
organizations, association; Human services;
Federated giving programs; Jewish federated giving
programs; Military/veterans' organizations; Jewish
agencies & temples.
Limitations: Applications not accepted. Giving
primarily in FL and NY. No grants to individuals.
Application information: Contributes only to
pre-selected organizations.
Trustees: Joseph Michaan; Suzanne Michaan.
EIN: 650635890
Selected grants: The following grants were reported
in 2004.
$52,000 to Torch Federation. For unrestricted
 support.
$25,000 to Alliance Israelite Universelle, Paris,
 France. For unrestricted support.
$20,000 to Jewish Federation of Palm Beach
 County, West Palm Beach, FL. For unrestricted
 support.
$10,000 to Friends of the Israel Defense Forces,
 New York, NY. For unrestricted support.
$5,000 to Anti-Defamation League of Bnai Brith,
 West Palm Beach, FL. For unrestricted support.
$5,000 to Tel Aviv University, Tel Aviv, Israel. For
 unrestricted support.

$3,000 to Biomotion Foundation, West Palm Beach,
 FL. For unrestricted support.
$2,500 to Bikur Cholim Hospital, Jerusalem, Israel.
 For unrestricted support.
$2,500 to Palm Beach Orthodox Synagogue, Palm
 Beach, FL. For unrestricted support.
$1,000 to Jewish National Fund, New York, NY. For
 unrestricted support.

2139
The MIDA Foundation ◇
c/o Isaac Arguetty
617 N. 21st Ave.
Hollywood, FL 33020

Established in 1988 in FL.
Donor: Isaac Arguetty.
Foundation type: Independent foundation.
Financial data (yr. ended 12/31/05): Assets,
$4,599,507 (M); expenditures, $486,983;
qualifying distributions, $445,648; giving activities
include $348,844 for 8 grants (high: $150,000;
low: $1,080).
Fields of interest: Human services; Foundations
(community); Jewish federated giving programs;
Jewish agencies & temples.
Limitations: Applications not accepted. Giving
primarily in FL. No grants to individuals.
Application information: Contributes only to
pre-selected organizations.
Trustees: Isaac Arguetty; Tim Richards; Vincent
Tubito.
Number of staff: 1 part-time professional.
EIN: 650098919
Selected grants: The following grants were reported
in 2003.
$235,000 to Lear Foundation, Davie, FL.
$60,000 to Leonies Light, Miami, FL.
$26,200 to United Jewish Communities, New York,
 NY.
$23,096 to Chabad Lubavitch of Wellington,
 Wellington, FL.
$20,000 to Temple Beth Torah of Palm Beach
 County, Wellington, FL.
$5,000 to Moody Manor, Southwest Ranches, FL.
$1,800 to Chabad Lubavitch of Venetian Causeway
 and Surrounding Islands, The Shul, Miami Beach,
 FL.
$1,080 to Beccas Closet, Plantation, FL.
$360 to Leukemia & Lymphoma Society, Hollywood,
 FL.
$250 to Hadassah, Miami Beach, FL.

2140
Stuart A. Miller Family Foundation, Inc. ◇
700 N.W. 107th Ave., Ste. 400
Miami, FL 33172

Established in 2002 in FL.
Donor: Stuart A. Miller.
Foundation type: Independent foundation.
Financial data (yr. ended 6/30/05): Assets,
$2,698,751 (M); gifts received, $200;
expenditures, $2,626,678; qualifying distributions,
$2,616,514; giving activities include $2,616,514
for 10 grants (high: $1,500,000; low: $1,000).
Fields of interest: Arts; Elementary/secondary
education; Higher education.
Limitations: Applications not accepted. Giving
primarily in FL. No grants to individuals.

Application information: Contributes only to pre-selected organizations.
Officer: Stuart A. Miller, Pres.
Directors: Marshall Ames; Brian L. Bilzin.
EIN: 371452682

2141

Miller Foundation, Inc. ✧
(formerly Miller Family Foundation, Inc.)
700 N.W. 107th Ave., 4th Fl.
Miami, FL 33172

Established in 1984 in FL.
Donors: Leonard Miller; Susan Miller; Miller Charitable Fund LLLP.
Foundation type: Independent foundation.
Financial data (yr. ended 11/30/05): Assets, $41,933,084 (M); expenditures, $4,382,349; qualifying distributions, $4,375,706; giving activities include $4,375,706 for 34 grants (high: $1,000,000; low: $1,000).
Purpose and activities: Giving primarily for higher education as well as to Jewish organizations; some giving also for the arts including a performing arts center, and health and social services.
Fields of interest: Museums (art); Education; Human services; Children/youth, services; Federated giving programs; Jewish federated giving programs; Jewish agencies & temples.
Limitations: Applications not accepted. Giving primarily in FL, with emphasis on Miami and Miami Beach. No grants to individuals.
Application information: Contributes only to pre-selected organizations.
Officers: Susan Miller, Pres.; Brian Bilzin, V.P.
Directors: Jeffrey Miller; Stuart Miller; Leslie Saiontz; Steven Saiontz.
EIN: 592474323
Selected grants: The following grants were reported in 2005.
$200,000 to Cleveland Orchestra, Cleveland, OH.
$200,000 to Council for Educational Change, Davie, FL.
$115,000 to Harvard University, Cambridge, MA.
$50,000 to Performing Arts Center Foundation, Clearwater, FL.
$35,000 to University of Miami, Coral Gables, FL.
$25,000 to Bass Museum of Art, Miami Beach, FL.
$25,000 to Museum of the City of New York, New York, NY.
$10,000 to W P B T Channel 2, Miami, FL.
$5,000 to New World Symphony, Miami Beach, FL.

2142

Martha G. Moore Foundation, Inc. ✧
2020 N.E. 55th Ct.
Fort Lauderdale, FL 33308

Established in 1976 in FL.
Donor: Martha G. Moore†.
Foundation type: Independent foundation.
Financial data (yr. ended 6/30/05): Assets, $8,164,860 (M); expenditures, $498,667; qualifying distributions, $385,081; giving activities include $362,000 for 36 grants (high: $30,000; low: $2,000).
Purpose and activities: Giving primarily for health care and for Christian agencies and causes.
Fields of interest: Hospitals (general); Medical research, institute; Food banks; Human services;

Women, centers/services; Christian agencies & churches.
Limitations: Applications not accepted. Giving primarily in FL. No grants to individuals.
Application information: Contributes only to pre-selected organizations.
Officers: Dean R. Bailey,* Chair.; Calvin M. Johnson, Vice-Chair.
Trustee: Donald J. O'Malley.
EIN: 510201970
Selected grants: The following grants were reported in 2004.
$40,000 to Food for the Poor, Deerfield Beach, FL.
$20,000 to Salk Institute for Biological Studies, San Diego, CA.
$12,500 to Caridad Health Clinic, Boynton Beach, FL.
$10,000 to Cleveland Clinic Florida Naples, Naples, FL.
$10,000 to Gateway Community Outreach, Deerfield Beach, FL.
$10,000 to Holy Cross Hospital Foundation, Fort Lauderdale, FL.
$10,000 to Our Fathers House Soup Kitchen, Pompano Beach, FL.
$5,000 to Boys and Girls Clubs of Broward County, Fort Lauderdale, FL.
$5,000 to Light of the World Clinic, Fort Lauderdale, FL.
$5,000 to Poverello Center, Wilton Manors, FL.

2143

The Jim Moran Foundation, Inc. ✧ ☆
c/o Janice M. Moran
P.O. Box 4007
Deerfield Beach, FL 33442-4007
(954) 429-2122
FAX: (954) 429-2699;
E-mail: information@jimmoranfoundation.org;
URL: http://www.jimmoranfoundation.org/

Established in 2000 in FL.
Donors: James M. Moran; Janice M. Moran; JM Family Enterprises, Inc.
Foundation type: Company-sponsored foundation.
Financial data (yr. ended 12/31/04): Assets, $25,565,850 (M); gifts received, $9,397,948; expenditures, $1,060,636; qualifying distributions, $1,056,330; giving activities include $1,056,330 for grants.
Purpose and activities: The foundation supports organizations involved with arts and culture, education, domestic violence and child abuse prevention, human services, and community development.
Fields of interest: Arts; Education, reading; Education; Crime/violence prevention, domestic violence; Crime/violence prevention, child abuse; Human services; Children, foster care; Children, day care; Community development.
Limitations: Giving primarily in FL. No grants to individuals, or for administrative or overhead costs, capital campaigns, capacity building, or events.
Publications: Application guidelines; Grants list.
Application information: Application form required.
Initial approach: Complete online application form
Deadline(s): Varies
Final notification: 90 days
Officers and Directors:* Janice M. Moran,* Chair. and Pres.; Larry D. McGinnes,* V.P.; Melanie A. Burgess, Secy. and Exec. Dir.; Thomas K. Blanton,*

Treas.; Francis B. Brogan, Jr., Legal Counsel; James M. Moran; Rick Noland; Melvin T. Stith.
EIN: 651058044

2144

Morcom Foundation, Inc. ✧
339 Coral Way W.
Indialantic, FL 32903

Established in 2001 in FL.
Donor: Russell Morcom.
Foundation type: Independent foundation.
Financial data (yr. ended 12/31/05): Assets, $1,194,528 (M); gifts received, $98,559; expenditures, $465,894; qualifying distributions, $456,500; giving activities include $456,500 for 9 grants (high: $200,000; low: $1,500).
Purpose and activities: Giving primarily for higher education and human services.
Fields of interest: Higher education; Housing/shelter, development; Human services.
Limitations: Applications not accepted. Giving primarily in Tallahassee, FL. No grants to individuals.
Application information: Contributes only to pre-selected organizations.
Officers: W. Russell Morcom, Pres. and Treas.; Brad A. Morcom, V.P.; Todd R. Morcom, V.P.; Eugenia M. Morcom, Secy.
EIN: 593759718
Selected grants: The following grants were reported in 2003.
$200,000 to Florida State University, Tallahassee, FL.
$110,000 to Seminole Boosters, Tallahassee, FL.
$5,000 to Americas Second Harvest of the Big Bend, Tallahassee, FL.
$5,000 to Habitat for Humanity of Tallahassee, Tallahassee, FL.
$5,000 to Habitat for Humanity, South Brevard, West Melbourne, FL.
$5,000 to Second Harvest Food Bank of Central Florida, Brevard Branch, Orlando, FL.
$5,000 to Space Coast Early Intervention Center, Melbourne, FL.

2145

The Allen Morris Foundation
121 Alhambra Plz., PH 1
Coral Gables, FL 33134
Contact: Diane Collins, Exec. Dir.

Established in 1962 in FL.
Donors: Ida Akers Morris; W. Allen Morris; Ida Morris Bell; Morris Family Business; The Allen Morris Co.; Morris Investments; Kathryn M. Rupp.
Foundation type: Independent foundation.
Financial data (yr. ended 2/28/06): Assets, $3,331,542 (M); expenditures, $643,374; qualifying distributions, $565,638; giving activities include $537,488 for 58 grants (high: $70,000; low: $75).
Purpose and activities: Giving primarily for Christian organizations and churches, as well as for education, human services, and federated giving programs.
Fields of interest: Theological school/education; Education; Human services; Youth, services; International affairs; Federated giving programs; Christian agencies & churches.

Type of support: General/operating support; Continuing support; Annual campaigns; Equipment; Program development; Conferences/seminars; Seed money; Matching/challenge support.
Limitations: Giving on a national basis. No grants to individuals.
Application information: Application form not required.
Initial approach: Letter
Copies of proposal: 1
Deadline(s): None
Board meeting date(s): As necessary
Final notification: Positive responses only
Officers and Directors:* W. Allen Morris,* Chair. and Pres.; Ida M. Bell,* V.P.; Kathryn M. Rupp,* V.P.; James F. Bell, Jr.,* Secy.-Treas.; Diane Collins, Exec. Dir.; Diane Y. Morris; Ida Akers Morris; Gary L. Rupp.
Number of staff: 1 part-time professional; 1 part-time support.
EIN: 596152420
Selected grants: The following grants were reported in 2004.
$205,580 to World Sports, Bonita Springs, FL.
$56,150 to Campus Crusade for Christ International, Orlando, FL.
$51,000 to Evangelical Alliance Mission (TEAM), Wheaton, IL.
$50,000 to Psychological Studies Institute, Atlanta, GA.
$41,000 to Boy Scouts of America, South Florida Council, Miami, FL.
$20,900 to Fellowship of Christian Athletes, Kansas City, MO.
$13,500 to Wesleyan School, Norcross, GA.
$10,000 to United Way of Miami-Dade, Miami, FL.
$10,000 to Young Life, Athens, GA.
$7,000 to Westminster Christian School, Miami, FL.

2146
Morrison Family Foundation ◇
c/o Wollman, Gehrke & Assocs.
5129 Castello Dr., Ste. 1
Naples, FL 34103-1903

Established in 1997 in FL.
Donors: John M. Morrison; Susan M. Morrison; Fosta-Tek Optics.
Foundation type: Independent foundation.
Financial data (yr. ended 6/30/05): Assets, $3,283,975 (M); gifts received, $27,800; expenditures, $659,639; qualifying distributions, $597,191; giving activities include $593,717 for 28 grants (high: $150,000; low: $350).
Fields of interest: Higher education; Health organizations, association; Roman Catholic agencies & churches.
Limitations: Applications not accepted. Giving primarily in Minneapolis-St. Paul, MN. No grants to individuals.
Application information: Contributes only to pre-selected organizations.
Officer: Robert L. Harley, V.P.
Trustees: Jeanne M. Cook; John M. Morrison; John M. Morrison, Jr.; Julie Morrison; Mary Sue Morrison; Susan M. Morrison.
EIN: 656254131

2147
Frank and Carol Morsani Foundation, Inc. ◇
16007 N. Florida Ave.
Lutz, FL 33549 (813) 963-6757

Established in FL.
Donors: Frank L. Morsani; Carol D. Morsani.
Foundation type: Independent foundation.
Financial data (yr. ended 8/31/05): Assets, $13,130,628 (M); gifts received, $250,000; expenditures, $400,755; qualifying distributions, $337,500; giving activities include $337,500 for 5 grants (high: $200,000; low: $2,500).
Purpose and activities: Giving primarily to a cancer center, and for higher education.
Fields of interest: Higher education; Health care, clinics/centers; Cancer; Human services.
Limitations: Applications not accepted. Giving primarily in FL. No grants to individuals.
Application information: Contributes only to pre-selected organizations.
Directors: Alan Higbee; Carol D. Morsani; Frank L. Morsani.
EIN: 593543872
Selected grants: The following grants were reported in 2004.
$330,000 to Tampa Museum of Art, Tampa, FL. 2 grants: $30,000, $300,000
$150,000 to University of South Florida, Tampa, FL.

2148
Mote Scientific Foundation, Inc. ▼ ◇
1600 Ken Thompson Pkwy.
Sarasota, FL 34236
Contact: Helen Pratt, Secy.

Incorporated in 1950 in NY.
Donors: William R. Mote†; T.R. Bartels†; Theodore R. Bartels†.
Foundation type: Independent foundation.
Financial data (yr. ended 11/30/05): Assets, $25,217,452 (M); expenditures, $3,750,700; qualifying distributions, $3,161,399; giving activities include $3,097,250 for 4 grants (high: $3,090,750; low: $500; average: $1,000–$5,000).
Purpose and activities: Giving mainly for oceanography; support primarily for the Mote Marine Laboratory; support also for social services.
Fields of interest: Education; Environment; Marine science.
Type of support: General/operating support; Research.
Limitations: Applications not accepted. Giving primarily in FL. No grants to individuals.
Publications: Annual report.
Application information: Contributes only to pre-selected organizations.
Board meeting date(s): Quarterly
Officers and Trustees:* Peter Hull,* Pres.; Helen Pratt,* Secy.; Bill Galvano,* Treas.; Kumar Mahadevan; Bill Ritchie.
Number of staff: 1 part-time support.
EIN: 136117615
Selected grants: The following grants were reported in 2005.
$3,090,750 to Mote Marine Laboratory, Sarasota, FL. For general support.
$5,000 to Manatee County Schools Foundation, Bradenton, FL. For general support.
$1,000 to Clearwater Christian College, Clearwater, FL. For general support.

$500 to Oak Park School, Sarasota, FL. For general support of Parent-Teacher-Student Organization.

2149
The Stephen Muss Foundation, Inc. ◇
1691 Michigan Ave., Ste. 250
Miami Beach, FL 33139

Donor: Stephen Muss.
Foundation type: Independent foundation.
Financial data (yr. ended 10/31/05): Assets, $1,794,123 (M); gifts received, $650,000; expenditures, $600,569; qualifying distributions, $583,200; giving activities include $583,200 for 11 grants (high: $250,000; low: $1,200).
Fields of interest: Jewish federated giving programs; Jewish agencies & temples.
Limitations: Applications not accepted. Giving primarily in FL. No grants to individuals.
Application information: Contributes only to pre-selected organizations.
Directors: Brian Bilzin; Stephen Muss; Alan Rosenbloom.
EIN: 237424763

2150
Nanci's Animal Rights Foundation, Inc. ◇ ☆
7809 Afton Villa Ct.
Boca Raton, FL 33433

Donor: Nanci Alexander.
Foundation type: Independent foundation.
Financial data (yr. ended 6/30/05): Assets, $55,487,486 (M); gifts received, $25,002,000; expenditures, $10,002,000; qualifying distributions, $10,000,000; giving activities include $10,000,000 for 2 grants (high: $5,000,000; low: $5,000,000).
Fields of interest: Animals/wildlife, equal rights; Animal welfare.
Limitations: Applications not accepted. Giving on a national basis. No grants to individuals.
Application information: Unsolicited requests for funds not accepted.
Trustees: Nanci Alexander.
EIN: 651174489

2151
Naples Children and Education Foundation, Inc. ▼ ◇
6200 Shirley St., Ste. 206
Naples, FL 34109 (239) 514-2239
Contact: Dawn Montecalvo, Exec. Dir.

Established in 2000 in FL.
Donor: Dwight D. Opperman.
Foundation type: Independent foundation.
Financial data (yr. ended 6/30/05): Assets, $12,464,807 (M); gifts received, $2,284,991; expenditures, $7,107,053; qualifying distributions, $5,261,154; giving activities include $4,990,390 for 18 grants (high: $850,000; low: $15,000; average: $100,000–$300,000).
Fields of interest: Elementary/secondary education; Education; Youth development, adult & child programs; Human services; Children/youth, services.
Limitations: Giving primarily in FL. No grants to individuals.

Application information: Application form required.
Initial approach: Preformatted application
Deadline(s): Oct. 3
Officers: Scott Lutgert, Co-Chair.; Simone Lutgert, Co-Chair.; Dawn Monteca, Exec. Dir.
Trustees: J.D. Clinton; Mary Susan Clinton; Arlene D'Alessandro; Michael D'Alessandro; and 57additional trustees.
EIN: 651001650
Selected grants: The following grants were reported in 2005.
$850,000 to Boys and Girls Club of Collier County, Naples, FL. To assist underprivileged children.
$800,000 to Guadalupe Center, Immokalee, FL. To assist underprivileged children.
$750,000 to University of North Florida, Jacksonville, FL. For Early Language Literacy Model (ELLM) program at Florida Institute of Education, and to assist underprivileged children.
$300,000 to Collier County Child Advocates, Naples, FL. To assist underprivileged children.
$300,000 to Collier Health Services, Immokalee, FL. To assist underprivileged children.
$300,000 to Foster Care Council of Southwest Florida, Naples, FL. To assist underprivileged children.
$280,000 to PACE Center for Girls of Collier, Immokalee, FL. To assist underprivileged children.
$160,000 to Shelter for Abused Women of Collier County, Naples, FL. To assist underprivileged children.

2152
The Melvin B. Nessel Charitable Foundation ◇
200 Bradley Pl.
Palm Beach, FL   33480

Established in 1990 in FL.
Donor: Melvin B. Nessel.
Foundation type: Independent foundation.
Financial data (yr. ended 12/31/04): Assets, $6,034,003 (M); gifts received, $495,000; expenditures, $922,460; qualifying distributions, $917,554; giving activities include $917,554 for 41 grants (high: $446,282; low: $50).
Purpose and activities: Giving for health associations, community services, and Jewish organizations.
Fields of interest: Arts; Education; Hospitals (general); Health organizations, association; Human services; Children/youth, services; Community development; Jewish federated giving programs; Jewish agencies & temples.
Limitations: Applications not accepted. Giving primarily in the West Palm Beach, FL, area, and MA. No grants to individuals.
Application information: Contributes only to pre-selected organizations.
Trustee: Melvin B. Nessel.
EIN: 650206833
Selected grants: The following grants were reported in 2004.
$446,282 to Massachusetts General Hospital, Boston, MA.
$200,000 to Community Chest-United Way of Palm Beach, Palm Beach, FL.
$135,250 to Norton Gallery and School of Art, West Palm Beach, FL.
$50,500 to Jewish Federation of Palm Beach County, West Palm Beach, FL.

$15,000 to Brandeis University, Waltham, MA.
$15,000 to Combined Jewish Philanthropies of Greater Boston, Boston, MA.
$10,000 to Washington Institute, DC.
$6,000 to American Jewish Committee, New York, NY.
$5,000 to Raymond F. Kravis Center for the Performing Arts, West Palm Beach, FL.
$2,500 to American Cancer Society, Hartford, CT.

2153
North Dade Medical Foundation, Inc. ◇ ☆
c/o Sandra Giblin, C.E.O.
1175 N.E. 125th St., Ste. 417
North Miami, FL   33161

Established in 1997 in FL; converted from North Shore Medical Center.
Foundation type: Independent foundation.
Financial data (yr. ended 9/30/05): Assets, $24,342,983 (M); gifts received, $533,194; expenditures, $13,552,682; qualifying distributions, $12,964,941; giving activities include $12,964,941 for grants.
Purpose and activities: The foundation provides support to organizations and groups that improve the life of residents in northern Miami Dade County, FL.
Fields of interest: Education; Health care; Human services.
Type of support: General/operating support; Continuing support; Income development; Management development/capacity building; Endowments; Conferences/seminars; Scholarship funds; Technical assistance; Program evaluation; Matching/challenge support.
Limitations: Applications not accepted. Giving primarily in North Miami, FL.
Application information: Contributes only to pre-selected organizations.
Officers and Trustees:* Chester H. Morris, M.D.*, Chair.; Sandra R. Giblin,* C.E.O.; John H. Kathe, M.D.*, Secy.; William J. Heffernan,* Treas.; George P. Daviglus, M.D.; Jorge L. Garcia; Allan M. Greenberg, M.D.; Herta D. Holly; Cesar J. Sastre, M.D.; Harold C. Spear, M.D.
Number of staff: 1 full-time professional; 1 part-time professional; 1 full-time support.
EIN: 590694393

2154
Esther B. O'Keeffe Charitable Foundation ◇
505 S. Flagler Dr., Ste. 900
West Palm Beach, FL   33401-5948
Contact: Arthur O'Keeffe, Exec. Tr.

Established in 1990 in FL.
Donor: Esther B. O'Keeffe.
Foundation type: Independent foundation.
Financial data (yr. ended 12/31/04): Assets, $37,670,594 (M); expenditures, $1,612,765; qualifying distributions, $800,000; giving activities include $800,000 for 3 grants.
Purpose and activities: Giving primarily to a cultural arts center, as well as to a hospital and a heart association.
Fields of interest: Arts, multipurpose centers/programs; Hospitals (general); Health organizations, association; Heart & circulatory research.

Limitations: Applications not accepted. Giving primarily in FL and MA. No grants to individuals.
Application information: Contributes only to pre-selected organizations.
Trustees: Ruth O'Keeffe, Exec. Tr.; Arthur O'Keeffe, M.D.; Brian O'Keeffe; Clare O'Keeffe; Daniel O'Keeffe.
EIN: 650244287
Selected grants: The following grants were reported in 2004.
$500,000 to Society of the Four Arts, Palm Beach, FL. For capital campaign.
$200,000 to Massachusetts General Hospital, Boston, MA. For capital campaign.
$100,000 to American Heart Association, West Palm Beach, FL. For capital campaign.

2155
The M. G. O'Neil Foundation ◇
104 Banyan Isle Dr.
Palm Beach Gardens, FL   33418
(561) 691-4962
Contact: M.G. O'Neil, Pres.

Incorporated in 1953 in OH.
Donor: M.G. O'Neil.
Foundation type: Independent foundation.
Financial data (yr. ended 12/31/05): Assets, $1,438,182 (M); expenditures, $366,685; qualifying distributions, $364,120; giving activities include $362,400 for 69 grants.
Purpose and activities: Giving primarily for Roman Catholic organizations; support also for community funds and social service agencies.
Fields of interest: Education; Youth development, centers/clubs; Human services; Federated giving programs; Roman Catholic agencies & churches.
Type of support: General/operating support.
Limitations: Giving primarily in OH. No grants for conferences, seminars, or special projects.
Application information: Application form not required.
Initial approach: Letter
Copies of proposal: 1
Deadline(s): None
Officers: M.G. O'Neil, Pres. and Treas.; T.M. Haidnick, V.P.; E.R. Dye, Secy.
Trustees: Joe Leydon; Jean O'Neil.
EIN: 346516968
Selected grants: The following grants were reported in 2003.
$36,000 to Saint Vincent de Paul Society, Akron, OH. 2 grants: $18,000 each
$30,000 to Saint Marys Church, Akron, OH.
$24,000 to Spring Lake Ranch, Cuttingsville, VT.
$20,000 to First Step Cleaning Company, Milford, OH.
$20,000 to Sisters, Servants of the Immaculate Heart of Mary, Bloomfield Hills, MI.
$10,000 to Hospitality House of Charlotte, Charlotte, NC.
$10,000 to Kevin Guest House, Buffalo, NY.
$10,000 to Regina Health Center, Richfield, OH.
$10,000 to Sisters of Charity of Saint Elizabeth, Convent Station, NJ.

2156
Ocean Reef Foundation, Inc.
(formerly Ocean Reef Community Foundation)
200 Anchor Dr., Ste. B
Key Largo, FL 33037 (305) 367-4707
Contact: Rose Michno, Secy.
FAX: (305) 367-6327;
E-mail: rmichno@oceanreef.com; URL: http://www.orfound.org

Established in 1994 in FL.
Foundation type: Community foundation.
Financial data (yr. ended 10/31/05): Assets, $8,333,893 (M); gifts received, $1,689,071; expenditures, $1,914,066; giving activities include $1,863,182 for grants.
Purpose and activities: The foundation is an independent, charitable, nonprofit organization, established for the members of the Ocean Reef community to promote and enhance responsible and effective philanthropy.
Fields of interest: Historic preservation/historical societies; Arts; Education; Environment; Hospitals (general); Health care; Human services; Community development; Aging.
Limitations: Giving primarily in Ocean Reef, FL. No grants to individuals.
Application information: Visit foundation Web site for application information. The foundation's Grants Committee reviews all proposals summary and budget form applications. If a program is deemed consistent with foundation criteria, values, and priorities, a full proposal will be invited. Application form required.
   Initial approach: Contact foundation
   Deadline(s): None
Officers and Directors:* Alan J. Goldstein,* Chair.; John N. Taylor, Jr.,* Pres.; Tom Davidson,* V.P.; Rose Michno,* Secy. and Admin.; Shirley Shipley,* Treas.; George Aronoff; Paul Astbury; Richard T. Farmer; James Gardner; Edmund Hajim; Jean Hunt; John Lee; Rich Miller; Louis A. Mitchell; Albert Monk; Denny Morgan; Emery G. Olcott; J. Gregory Poole, Jr.; David Ritz; Frank Shumway; Janie Sims; Richard Skelly; Adelaide Skoglund; James A. Williams.
EIN: 650509255

2157
The Isaac Olemberg and Nieves Olemberg Private Foundation ◇
800 N.W. 21st St.
Miami, FL 33127

Established in 1992 in FL.
Donors: Isaac Olemberg; Nieves Olemberg; Michael A. Kirsh; Michael Furst; Olem Shoe Corp.
Foundation type: Independent foundation.
Financial data (yr. ended 12/31/05): Assets, $3,837,043 (M); gifts received, $1,000,000; expenditures, $504,079; qualifying distributions, $502,650; giving activities include $502,650 for 43 grants (high: $145,000; low: $500).
Purpose and activities: Giving primarily to Jewish organizations.
Fields of interest: Human services; Jewish federated giving programs; Jewish agencies & temples.
Limitations: Applications not accepted. Giving primarily in FL and NY. No grants to individuals.
Application information: Contributes only to pre-selected organizations.

Directors: Isaac Olemberg; Nieves Olemberg; Roberto Olemberg.
EIN: 650375570

2158
Scott Opler Foundation ◇
c/o James N. Peebles
1300 North Shore Dr. N.E.
St. Petersburg, FL 33701-1426

Established in 1993 in MA.
Donor: Scott Opler‡.
Foundation type: Independent foundation.
Financial data (yr. ended 6/30/05): Assets, $0 (M); expenditures, $1,249,340; qualifying distributions, $1,130,300; giving activities include $1,130,300 for 24 grants (high: $250,000; low: $500).
Purpose and activities: Primary fields of interest are: 1) scholarly study and preservation of art and architecture; 2) nature conservation and wildlife preservation; and 3) AIDS-related services and education.
Fields of interest: Arts education; History/archaeology; Environment, natural resources; Animals/wildlife, preservation/protection; AIDS.
International interests: Italy.
Type of support: General/operating support; Capital campaigns; Building/renovation; Equipment; Land acquisition; Endowments; Emergency funds; Conferences/seminars; Professorships; Publication; Seed money; Fellowships; Scholarship funds; Matching/challenge support.
Limitations: Applications not accepted. Giving primarily in St. Petersburg, FL, Boston, MA, and Jackson, WY.
Publications: Financial statement.
Application information: Contributes only to pre-selected organizations.
Officers and Directors:* Cathe Henry,* Pres.; C. Cabell Chinnis, Jr.,* Clerk; James N. Peebles,* Treas.
EIN: 043201088

2159
Overstreet Foundation ◇ ☆
P.O. Box 111
Orlando, FL 32802-0111

Established in 1965 in FL.
Donors: Overstreet Investment Co.; M. Overstreet Charitable Trust.
Foundation type: Independent foundation.
Financial data (yr. ended 12/31/05): Assets, $2,691,515 (M); expenditures, $2,547,942; qualifying distributions, $2,533,463; giving activities include $2,533,463 for grants.
Purpose and activities: The foundation supports Christian agencies and churches and organizations involved with health and human services, particularly the homeless.
Fields of interest: Higher education; Health organizations, association; Athletics/sports, Special Olympics; Human services; Federated giving programs; Christian agencies & churches; Homeless.
Limitations: Applications not accepted. Giving primarily in FL. No grants to individuals.
Application information: Contributes only to pre-selected organizations.
Trustees: Robin O. Sheldon; Anne E. Tolleson.
EIN: 596164658

2160
P & M Charities, Inc. ◇
3001 Tamiani Trail N., Ste. 207
Naples, FL 34103

Established in 2002 in FL.
Donor: Miles C. Collier.
Foundation type: Independent foundation.
Financial data (yr. ended 12/31/04): Assets, $1,425,735 (M); expenditures, $910,771; qualifying distributions, $875,360; giving activities include $874,850 for 29 grants (high: $250,000; low: $100).
Purpose and activities: Giving primarily for education, health associations, including a neurobehavioral center, human services, and federated giving programs.
Fields of interest: Higher education; Education; Health care; Health organizations, association; Human services; Foundations (private grantmaking).
Limitations: Applications not accepted. Giving primarily in FL. No grants to individuals.
Application information: Contributes only to pre-selected organizations.
Officers and Directors:* Miles C. Collier,* C.E.O.; Parker J. Collier,* Pres.; Joseph I. Perkovich,* V.P. and Secy.; Sandra D. Walker, Treas.
EIN: 010644503

2161
Palm Beach Community Trust Fund ◇
c/o First National Bank of Palm Beach
255 S. County Rd.
Palm Beach, FL 33480
Contact: James Y. Arnold, Mgr.

Established in 1955 in FL.
Donors: William Regan‡; Fisher Charitable Trust.
Foundation type: Independent foundation.
Financial data (yr. ended 12/31/03): Assets, $20,288,889 (M); expenditures, $1,363,680; qualifying distributions, $1,182,266; giving activities include $1,180,000 for 29 grants (high: $100,000; low: $5,000).
Purpose and activities: Giving primarily for human services, health care, and the arts.
Fields of interest: Museums; Higher education; Hospitals (general); Health organizations, association; Human services; Children/youth, services; Family services.
Limitations: Giving primarily in Palm Beach, FL. No grants to individuals.
Application information: Application form not required.
   Deadline(s): None
Officer: Wyckoff Myers, Mgr.
EIN: 510144921
Selected grants: The following grants were reported in 2004.
$100,000 to Florida Southern College, Lakeland, FL.
$100,000 to Stetson University, DeLand, FL.
$90,000 to Colby-Sawyer College, New London, NH.
$85,000 to Flagler College, Saint Augustine, FL.
$85,000 to Kenyon College, Gambier, OH.
$85,000 to Oberlin College, Oberlin, OH.
$65,000 to Rollins College, Winter Park, FL.
$60,000 to Lighthouse for the Blind, West Palm Beach, FL.
$60,000 to Rehabilitation Center for Children and Adults, Palm Beach, FL.
$20,000 to Cafe Joshua, West Palm Beach, FL.

2162
Pamphalon Foundation, Inc. ◇ ☆
P.O. 13826
Gainesville, FL   32604

Established in 2003 in FL.
Foundation type: Operating foundation.
Financial data (yr. ended 12/31/05): Assets,
$11,201,450 (M); expenditures, $413,830;
qualifying distributions, $408,976; giving activities
include $408,976 for 50 grants (high: $38,846;
low: $21).
Fields of interest: Education; Human services;
Federated giving programs; Christian agencies &
churches.
Limitations: Applications not accepted. Giving
primarily in FL. No grants to individuals.
Application information: Contributes only to
pre-selected organizations.
Officers and Directors:* Rolf E. Hummel,* Pres.;
Daniel Maico,* V.P.; Waltrude E. Hummel,* Secy.
EIN: 141876459

2163
Pascal International, Inc. ◇
c/o Bessemer Trust
801 Brickell Ave.
Miami, FL   33131   (305) 372-5005
Contact: Clara Pascal, Pres.

Foundation type: Independent foundation.
Financial data (yr. ended 12/31/04): Assets,
$6,015,189 (M); expenditures, $462,504;
qualifying distributions, $430,981; giving activities
include $365,700 for 12 grants (high: $190,000;
low: $1,700).
Fields of interest: Human services; Children/youth,
services; Christian agencies & churches; Protestant
agencies & churches.
Limitations: Giving primarily in FL. No grants to
individuals.
Application information:
 Initial approach: Letter
 Deadline(s): None
Officers and Directors:* Clara Pascal,* Pres.;
Nancy Wainwright,* V.P.; Robin Pascal.
EIN: 651066949

2164
**The Jeno & Lois Paulucci Family
 Foundation** ◇ ☆
(formerly The Paulucci Family Foundation)
201 W. 1st St.
Sanford, FL   32771-1273   (407) 321-7004
Contact: Larry W. Nelson, V.P. and Treas.

Incorporated in 1966 in MN.
Donor: Jeno F. Paulucci.
Foundation type: Independent foundation.
Financial data (yr. ended 12/31/05): Assets,
$1,723,160 (M); expenditures, $606,693;
qualifying distributions, $567,646; giving activities
include $567,646 for grants.
Purpose and activities: Giving primarily for
education and human services.
Fields of interest: Historic preservation/historical
societies; Education; Environment, beautification
programs; Cancer, leukemia; Medical research,
institute; Cancer, leukemia research; Human
services; Christian agencies & churches.

Limitations: Giving primarily in FL and MN. No grants
to individuals.
Application information:
 Initial approach: Letter
 Copies of proposal: 1
 Deadline(s): Oct.
 Board meeting date(s): Annually
Officers and Directors:* Jeno F. Paulucci,* Pres.;
Larry W. Nelson,* V.P. and Treas.; David Gaddie;
Laurence C. Hames; Lois M. Paulucci.
EIN: 416054004
Selected grants: The following grants were reported
in 2004.
$215,000 to Duluth, City of, Duluth, MN. 2 grants:
   $180,000, $35,000
$100,000 to Mayo Foundation, Rochester, MN.
$10,000 to Pine Manor College, Chestnut Hill, MA.
$5,000 to Hibbing Community College, Hibbing, MN.
$3,500 to All Saints Academy, Winter Haven, FL.

2165
Peacock Foundation, Inc.
100 S.E. 2nd St., Ste. 2370
Miami, FL   33131-2127   (305) 373-1386
Contact: Joelle Allen, Exec. Dir.

Incorporated in 1947 in FL.
Donor: Henry B. Peacock, Jr.†.
Foundation type: Independent foundation.
Financial data (yr. ended 11/30/05): Assets,
$48,015,167 (M); expenditures, $2,690,869;
qualifying distributions, $2,242,508; giving
activities include $2,040,190 for 64 grants (high:
$350,000; low: $2,250).
Purpose and activities: The foundation's priorities
include: supporting educational programs in the arts
and the environment, as well as special education
for disabled persons; contributing to medical
research, healthcare organizations, and hospitals;
and making grants to human services providers that
promote youth development, assist abused or
neglected children, women, and the elderly, and
seek to reduce abuse, prevent homelessness, and
end hunger.
Fields of interest: Arts education; Education;
Environmental education; Hospitals (general);
Mental health/crisis services; Health organizations,
association; Medical research, institute; Human
services; Youth, services; Aging.
Type of support: General/operating support;
Continuing support; Program development;
Research; Matching/challenge support.
Limitations: Giving primarily in the southeast FL
communities located in Broward, Miami-Dade, and
Monroe counties. No support for political lobbying or
religious organizations unless project benefits entire
community. No grants to individuals or for
construction campaigns, deficit financing or debt
reduction, conferences, or fundraising/special/
athletic events.
Application information: Application form not
required.
 Initial approach: 2-page letter of inquiry
 Copies of proposal: 1
 Deadline(s): None
 Board meeting date(s): Quarterly
Officers and Directors:* Barbara A. Rickard,* Pres.;
Thomas R. Post,* V.P.; Robin Reiter-Faragalli,*
Secy.; Joelle Allen, Exec. Dir.
Number of staff: 3 full-time professional.
EIN: 590999759
Selected grants: The following grants were reported
in 2003.

$350,000 to Buoniconti Fund to Cure Paralysis,
  Miami, FL. For regeneration, neuroprotection,
  and rehabilitation research.
$130,000 to Miami Childrens Hospital Foundation,
  Miami, FL. For Overtown Kids.
$75,000 to Community Partnership for Homeless,
  Miami, FL. For Healthy Families Project.
$75,000 to Kristi House, Miami, FL. For Play
  Therapy Expansion.
$65,600 to Dr. Bruce Heiken Memorial Fund, Miami,
  FL. For expansion project.
$55,000 to Boys and Girls Clubs of Miami, Miami,
  FL. For program support.
$50,000 to Baptist Health Systems of South Florida
  Foundation, Miami, FL. For Child Development
  Center.
$50,000 to Shake-A-Leg Miami, Coconut Grove, FL.
  For Comprehensive Community Youth Center.
$40,000 to CHARLEE of Dade County, Miami, FL.
  For Foster Care program.
$35,500 to Guardianship Program of Dade County,
  Miami, FL. For case management.

2166
The Dr. M. Lee Pearce Foundation, Inc. ◇
11880 Bird Rd., Ste. 203
Miami, FL   33175

Established in 1984 in DE and FL.
Donor: M. Lee Pearce, M.D.
Foundation type: Independent foundation.
Financial data (yr. ended 12/31/04): Assets,
$15,367,039 (M); expenditures, $1,227,295;
qualifying distributions, $784,985; giving activities
include $760,800 for 48 grants (high: $250,000;
low: $1,000).
Purpose and activities: Giving primarily for arts and
culture, education, and health.
Fields of interest: Performing arts; Historic
preservation/historical societies; Arts; Higher
education; Medical school/education; Health care;
Human services; Federated giving programs; Jewish
agencies & temples.
Limitations: Applications not accepted. Giving on a
national basis. No grants to individuals.
Application information: Contributes only to
pre-selected organizations.
Officers and Directors:* M. Lee Pearce, M.D.,
Chair.; Robert Tancredi,* Pres.; Robert L. Achor;
Richard Colvin; Charles Douglas; Michael E.
Gallagher; Robert Potts; Dale Rustad; Muneer
Satter; Jose Valle.
EIN: 592424272
Selected grants: The following grants were reported
in 2004.
$250,000 to Metropolitan Opera Association, New
  York, NY.
$25,000 to Carnegie Hall Society, New York, NY.
$10,000 to International Festival Society, Santa
  Monica, CA.
$10,000 to Students Today Aren't Ready for Sex
  (STARS), Portland, OR.
$5,000 to Infant Welfare Society of Chicago,
  Chicago, IL.
$5,000 to Los Angeles Philharmonic, Los Angeles,
  CA.
$2,500 to Highland Hospital Foundation,
  Rochester, NY.
$2,500 to New World Symphony, Miami Beach, FL.
$1,000 to Cleveland Clinic Foundation, Cleveland,
  OH.
$1,000 to Metropolitan Museum of Art, New York,
  NY.

2167
The Petway Family Foundation, Inc. ✧
(formerly The Universal Foundation, Inc.)
5011 Gate Pkwy.
Jacksonville, FL 32256

Donor: Thomas F. Petway III.
Foundation type: Independent foundation.
Financial data (yr. ended 6/30/05): Assets,
$26,950 (M); gifts received, $582,500;
expenditures, $573,533; qualifying distributions,
$572,500; giving activities include $572,500 for 9
grants (high: $165,000; low: $5,000).
Purpose and activities: Giving primarily for
education as well as to a Baptist church, an
Episcopal church, and an Episcopal summer camp
for children and youth; some funding also for health
care including a hospice and a children's hospital,
and for animal protection and preservation.
Fields of interest: Higher education; Zoos/
zoological societies; Human services; Children/
youth, services; Residential/custodial care,
hospices; Federated giving programs; Protestant
agencies & churches.
Limitations: Applications not accepted. Giving
primarily in Jacksonville, FL. No grants to individuals.
Application information: Contributes only to
pre-selected organizations.
Officers: Thomas F. Petway III, Chair. and Treas.;
Elizabeth P. Petway, Vice-Chair.; Brette E. Petway,
Pres.; Thomas F. Petway IV, Secy.
EIN: 592735054

2168
The Dr. P. Phillips Foundation
60 W. Robinson St.
P.O. Box 3753
Orlando, FL 32802 (407) 422-6105
Contact: J.A. Hinson, Chair. and Pres.

Incorporated in 1953 in FL.
Donors: Della Phillips†; Howard Phillips†; Dr.
Phillips, Inc.
Foundation type: Independent foundation.
Financial data (yr. ended 5/31/06): Assets,
$39,397,592 (M); expenditures, $1,675,160;
qualifying distributions, $1,387,928; giving
activities include $891,201 for 51 grants (high:
$180,000; low: $300), and $48,454 for 1
foundation-administered program.
Purpose and activities: Emphasis on education,
child development and welfare, youth, the elderly,
and community development, including arts and
culture, museums, recreation, and social and family
services.
Fields of interest: Arts; Child development,
education; Education; Human services; Children/
youth, services; Child development, services; Family
services; Aging, centers/services; Community
development; Aging.
Type of support: Capital campaigns; Building/
renovation; Equipment; Program development;
Program-related investments/loans; Matching/
challenge support.
Limitations: Giving generally limited to Orange and
Osceola counties, FL. No support for social,
religious, fraternal or veterans groups that primarily
benefit their own members or adherents, or for
legislative lobbying. No support to Type III support
organizations. No grants to individuals, or for
endowment funds, or to retire accumulated debt.
Publications: Application guidelines.
Application information: Application form required.

Initial approach: Grant application form
Copies of proposal: 1
Deadline(s): 45 days prior to board meetings
Board meeting date(s): Annual meeting: summer;
to review grant requests: Apr., Aug. and Nov.
Final notification: Varies
Officers and Directors:* J.A. Hinson,* Chair. and
Pres.; E.F. Furey,* V.P. and Treas.; Ann F. Manley,
Secy. and Exec. Dir.; H.L. Burnett; L. Evans Hubbard;
David F. Scott, Jr.
Number of staff: None.
EIN: 596135403
Selected grants: The following grants were reported
in 2005.
$136,815 to Central Florida Zoological Society,
Lake Monroe, FL.
$50,000 to Orlando Ballet, Orlando, FL.
$41,000 to Community Vision, Kissimmee, FL.
$25,000 to Lisa Merlin House, Orlando, FL.
$10,000 to Davidson College, Davidson, NC.
$10,000 to Orlando Opera Company, Orlando, FL.
$10,000 to University of Georgia Foundation,
Athens, GA.
$5,000 to Florida United Methodist Childrens
Home, Deltona, FL.
$4,800 to Edgewood Ranch Endowment,
Windermere, FL.
$1,500 to Columbia Theological Seminary, Decatur,
GA.

2169
The Picower Foundation ▼ ✧
(formerly The Jeffry M. & Barbara Picower
Foundation)
1410 S. Ocean Blvd.
Palm Beach, FL 33480 (212) 935-9860
Contact: Barbara Picower, Pres.

Established in 1989 in FL.
Donor: Jeffry M. Picower.
Foundation type: Independent foundation.
Financial data (yr. ended 12/31/05): Assets,
$604,882,964 (M); expenditures, $31,473,604;
qualifying distributions, $30,534,426; giving
activities include $27,662,893 for 138 grants (high:
$10,000,000; low: $100; average: $25,000–
$250,000).
Purpose and activities: To improve the quality of life
and increase opportunities to ensure that
individuals, families and communities, particularly
the underserved, may achieve their full potential.
Fields of interest: Arts education; Education, early
childhood education; Health care, infants;
Biomedicine research; Youth development; Civil
rights, public education; Civil rights; Engineering/
technology; Jewish agencies & temples.
Type of support: General/operating support;
Continuing support; Program development;
Fellowships; Internship funds; Research.
Limitations: Applications not accepted. Giving on a
national basis, primarily in southeast FL and the
Northeast. No grants to individuals.
Publications: Informational brochure.
Application information: Contributes only to
pre-selected organizations.
Board meeting date(s): 6 times per year
Officer and Trustees:* Barbara Picower,* Pres. and
Exec. Dir.; Norman B. Leventhal; Gerald C.
McNamara; Jeffry M. Picower; Martin R. Post, M.D.;
William D. Zabel.
Number of staff: 5 full-time professional; 3 full-time
support.
EIN: 136927043

Selected grants: The following grants were reported
in 2005.
$10,000,000 to Massachusetts Institute of
Technology, Cambridge, MA. For Picower Institute
for Learning and Memory.
$750,000 to University of Pittsburgh, Pittsburgh,
PA. For pathogenic mechanisms as therapeutic
targets in Parkinson's Disease.
$726,525 to Northwestern University, Department
of Physiology, Ward 5-315, Evanston, IL. For
Molecular and Cellular Mechanisms of
Parkinson's disease.
$690,000 to New York Public Library, New York, NY.
For Fort Washington Children's Library.
$578,000 to Southern Poverty Law Center,
Montgomery, AL. For special project.
$512,209 to Palm Beach County School District,
West Palm Beach, FL. For Single School Culture
for Academics.
$425,000 to Center for Reproductive Rights, New
York, NY. For Domestic Program.
$270,000 to Columbia University, Medical Center,
New York, NY. For VMAT2 expression as a
therapy for Parkinson's disease.
$250,000 to Planned Parenthood Federation of
America, New York, NY. For Mobilizing to Win
Initiative.
$50,000 to De La Salle Academy, New York, NY. For
scholarship support.

2170
Pinellas County Community Foundation ✧
P.O. Box 205
Clearwater, FL 33757-0205 (727) 446-0058
Contact: Julie Scales, Secy.
FAX: (727) 446-0948; E-mail: info@pinellasccf.org;
URL: http://www.pinellasccf.org

Established in 1969 in FL by trust agreement.
Foundation type: Community foundation.
Financial data (yr. ended 12/31/05): Assets,
$63,239,600 (M); gifts received, $2,230,142;
expenditures, $2,081,143; giving activities include
$1,783,815 for 149+ grants, and $96,130 for 65
grants to individuals.
Purpose and activities: The purpose of the
foundation is to receive donations from people and
organizations interested in helping their community
and to oversee the investment of those funds by
monitoring the work of the Trustees and then to
distribute the income to sound charitable
organizations that meet community needs. Primary
areas of interest include family services, the
disadvantaged, low income, handicapped, and other
social services.
Fields of interest: Arts; Education; Environment;
Animal welfare; Health care; Substance abuse,
services; Mental health/crisis services; Crime/
violence prevention, abuse prevention; Housing/
shelter; Children/youth, services; Family services;
Aging, centers/services; Developmentally disabled,
centers & services; Women, centers/services;
Human services; Religion; Disabilities, people with;
Economically disadvantaged; Homeless.
Type of support: General/operating support;
Continuing support; Building/renovation;
Equipment; Scholarship funds; Scholarships—to
individuals.
Limitations: Giving limited to Pinellas County, FL. No
grants for endowment funds, or for research,
fellowships, or matching gifts; no loans.

Publications: Application guidelines; Annual report (including application guidelines); Informational brochure; Newsletter; Occasional report.
Application information: Application form required.
  Initial approach: Telephone
  Copies of proposal: 1
  Deadline(s): Oct. 1
  Board meeting date(s): Feb., Sept., and Dec.
  Final notification: 2 months
Officers and Governors:* Harry S. Wilks, M.D.*, Chair.; J. Marvin Guthrie,* Vice-Chair.; Julie Scales, Secy. and Exec. Dir.; Dr. Herman Allen; Sandra Diamond; Tamara Felton Dudley; Virginia G. England; John R. Kessinger; Jack T. Lee; Janice L. Starling; Jay H. Tiffin; Joseph L. Wells.
Trustee Banks: AmSouth Bank; Bank of America, N.A.; CB&T; Fifth Third Bank; Merrill Lynch Trust Co.; Northern Trust Bank of Florida, N.A.; Raymond James Trust Co.; Sabal Co.; SunTrust Bank; Wachovia Bank, N.A.
Number of staff: 1 full-time professional; 1 part-time support.
EIN: 237113194

2171
Plan for Social Excellence, Inc. ✧
2502 Rocky Point Dr., Ste. 880
Tampa, FL 33607   (813) 282-1966
Contact: Hloy C Pena, Sr. Prog. Off.
FAX: (813) 282-9359; E-mail: info@pfse.org; E-mail address for Hloy C. Pena: pfscehcp@pfse.org; Application address for Chance to Succeed Proposals: Susan Boiko, 375 Parkside Dr., Palo Alto, CA 94306; URL: http://www.pfse.org

Established in 1989 in NY.
Donors: James A. Kohlberg; Nancy S. Kohlberg.
Foundation type: Operating foundation.
Financial data (yr. ended 7/31/04): Assets, $556,320 (M); gifts received, $1,001,325; expenditures, $1,660,278; qualifying distributions, $1,611,805; giving activities include $977,208 for 35 grants (high: $100,000; low: $78).
Purpose and activities: Giving primarily for education to introduce innovative practices, including parent involvement, college interns and tutors, early childhood programs, and outward bound programs, and for technologically-driven educational reforms.
Fields of interest: Education, reform; Elementary/secondary education; Higher education; Education, PTA groups; Youth development, services; Children/youth, services.
Publications: Newsletter.
Application information: The Plan does not make operating grants. Projects desiring consideration must be for either the replication of Plan's projects or new initiatives.
  Initial approach: Proposal (hard copy and either by E-mail or on a disc)
Officers: James A. Kohlberg, Pres.; Mario J. Pena, V.P. and Exec. Dir.; Walter W. Farley, Secy.; Eileen M. Capone, Treas.
Directors: James P. Honan; Suzanne Kohlberg; Hloy Pena.
Trustee: Kisco Management Corp.
EIN: 066082681

2172
Plangere Foundation, Inc. ✧
3829 Partridge Pl.
S. Quail Ridge
Boynton Beach, FL 33436

Established in 1997 in FL.
Donors: Jules L. Plangere, Jr.; The Plangere KCA Charitable Trust; The Plangere KRDJ Charitable Trust.
Foundation type: Independent foundation.
Financial data (yr. ended 4/30/05): Assets, $2,147,789 (M); gifts received, $1,279,060; expenditures, $1,310,775; qualifying distributions, $1,258,030; giving activities include $1,236,500 for 9 grants (high: $710,000; low: $500).
Purpose and activities: Giving primarily for higher education and human services.
Fields of interest: Higher education; Hospitals (general); Human services; Children, services.
Limitations: Applications not accepted. Giving primarily in FL and NJ. No grants to individuals.
Application information: Contributes only to pre-selected organizations.
Officers: Jules Plangere, Jr., Chair.; Jules L. Plangere III, Treas.
Board Members: Wendy Bickart; Jeffrey Conover; John C. Conover III.
EIN: 650747053
Selected grants: The following grants were reported in 2004.
$610,000 to Monmouth University, West Long Branch, NJ. For general support.
$550,000 to Rutgers, The State University of New Jersey, New Brunswick, NJ. For general support.
$50,000 to Bethesda Memorial Hospital, Boynton Beach, FL. For general support.
$50,000 to YMCA, Community, Red Bank, NJ. For general support.
$6,500 to CRC Recovery Foundation, Delray Beach, FL. For general support.
$2,000 to Community Child Care Center of Delray Beach, Delray Beach, FL. For general support.
$1,500 to Monmouth Day Care Center, Red Bank, NJ. For general support.
$1,000 to Palm Beach Post Season to Share Fund, West Palm Beach, FL. For general support.
$500 to Interfaith Neighbors, Asbury Park, NJ. For general support.
$200 to Mercy Center Corporation, Asbury Park, NJ. For general support.

2173
William F. Poe Foundation ✧
2 Harbour Pl.
302 Knights Run Ave., Ste. 700
Tampa, FL 33602   (813) 259-4000
Contact: William F. Poe, Sr., Tr.

Established in 1978 in FL.
Donors: William F. Poe, Sr.; Charles E. Poe; Keren P. Smith; Janice P. Mitchell; Marilyn Lunskis.
Foundation type: Independent foundation.
Financial data (yr. ended 8/31/04): Assets, $1,236,644 (M); gifts received, $895,000; expenditures, $1,153,207; qualifying distributions, $1,149,830; giving activities include $1,149,830 for 131 grants (high: $100,000; low: $10).
Purpose and activities: Giving primarily for education, health associations, human services, federated giving programs, and to Baptist churches.
Fields of interest: Secondary school/education; Higher education; Scholarships/financial aid;

Education; Health organizations, association; Human services; Federated giving programs; Protestant agencies & churches.
Limitations: Giving primarily in FL. No grants to individuals.
Application information: Applicant should submit a letter indicating that it qualifies under 501(c)(3), not 509, and is not controlled by the William F. Poe Foundation.
  Initial approach: Letter
  Deadline(s): None
Trustees: Charles W. Poe; Elizabeth B. Poe; William F. Poe, Sr.
EIN: 591957094

2174
The Lois Pope Life Foundation ✧
6274 Linton Blvd., Ste. 103
Delray Beach, FL 33484   (561) 865-0955
FAX: (561) 865-0938; E-mail: life@life-edu.org; URL: http://www.life-edu.org

Established in 1996 in FL.
Donors: Lois B. Pope; The Cessna Aircraft Co.
Foundation type: Independent foundation.
Financial data (yr. ended 12/31/05): Assets, $636,714 (M); gifts received, $1,025,000; expenditures, $1,212,735; qualifying distributions, $1,163,011; giving activities include $710,030 for 18 grants (high: $250,000; low: $450).
Purpose and activities: Giving primarily for higher education, health associations, social services, federated giving programs, Jewish agencies and temples, disabled veterans' organizations, and for national public radio.
Fields of interest: Media, radio; Higher education; Health organizations, association; Human services; Federated giving programs; Military/veterans' organizations; Jewish agencies & temples.
Limitations: Applications not accepted. Giving on a national basis.
Application information: Unsolicited requests for funds not accepted.
Trustees: Robert C. Miller; Lois B. Pope.
EIN: 137086087

2175
Posnack Family Foundation of Hollywood ✧
c/o Bank of America, N.A.
P.O. Box 40200, MC FL9-100-10-19
Jacksonville, FL 32203-0200
Application address: c/o Bank of America, N.A., attn.: Beverly Rogers, 1 Financial Plz., 8th Fl., Fort Lauderdale, FL 33394-0002

Established in 1984 in FL.
Foundation type: Independent foundation.
Financial data (yr. ended 1/31/05): Assets, $3,954,499 (M); expenditures, $556,892; qualifying distributions, $525,214; giving activities include $516,500 for 20 grants (high: $100,000; low: $500).
Purpose and activities: Support for Jewish organizations, including welfare funds and educational institutions.
Fields of interest: Elementary/secondary education; Human services; Jewish federated giving programs; Jewish agencies & temples.
International interests: Israel.

Limitations: Giving primarily in FL and NY. No grants to individuals.
Application information: Application form not required.

Deadline(s): None
Trustee: Bank of America, N.A.
EIN: 592484512
Selected grants: The following grants were reported in 2003.

$152,500 to Jewish Adoption and Foster Care Options, Fort Lauderdale, FL.
$101,000 to Jewish Federation of Greater Fort Lauderdale, Fort Lauderdale, FL.
$55,000 to Jewish Community Center of Greater Fort Lauderdale, Fort Lauderdale, FL.
$25,000 to ALYN Orthopedic Hospital of the Society for Handicapped Children, Jerusalem, Israel. .
$25,000 to American Associates, Ben-Gurion University of the Negev, Hollywood, FL.
$10,000 to Center for the Advancement of Jewish Education (CAJE), Miami, FL.
$10,000 to World Union for Progressive Judaism, Jerusalem, Israel. .
$8,000 to Boggy Creek Gang-A Hole in the Wall Gang Camp, Eustis, FL.
$5,000 to Alexander Muss Institute for Israel Education, North Miami, FL.
$5,000 to Israel Education Fund, New York, NY.

2176
Potamkin Family Foundation I, Inc. ✦ ☆
2333 Ponce de Leon Blvd., Ste. 550
Coral Gables, FL 33134

Foundation type: Independent foundation.
Financial data (yr. ended 5/31/05): Assets, $9,370,228 (M); expenditures, $956,828; qualifying distributions, $805,227; giving activities include $805,227 for 65 grants (high: $359,000; low: $100).
Fields of interest: Arts; Health organizations, association; Human services; Children/youth, services; Federated giving programs.
Limitations: Applications not accepted. Giving primarily in FL; some funding also nationally. No grants to individuals.
Application information: Contributes only to pre-selected organizations.
Trustees: Peter Paris; Alan Potamkin; Robert Potamkin.
EIN: 030387456

2177
The John E. & Aliese Price Foundation, Inc.
1279 Lavin Ln.
Fort Myers, FL 33917 (239) 656-0196
Contact: T. Wainwright Miller, Jr., Pres.

Incorporated in 1961 in FL.
Donors: John E. Price†; Aliese Price†.
Foundation type: Independent foundation.
Financial data (yr. ended 8/31/05): Assets, $15,609,949 (M); expenditures, $941,521; qualifying distributions, $665,842; giving activities include $456,842 for 53 grants (high: $77,700; low: $500).
Purpose and activities: Grants primarily for church support and religious associations; some support also for youth agencies, health agencies, and education associations in the Fort Myers, FL, area.

Fields of interest: Performing arts; Education, association; Elementary/secondary education; Education, early childhood education; Engineering school/education; Adult education—literacy, basic skills & GED; Education, reading; Education; Nursing care; Health care; AIDS; Biomedicine; Medical research, institute; AIDS research; Youth development, citizenship; Youth, services; Residential/custodial care, hospices; Mathematics; Engineering; Public affairs, citizen participation; Christian agencies & churches; Religion.
Type of support: Continuing support; Research; Matching/challenge support.
Limitations: Giving primarily in southwest FL, with emphasis on the Fort Myers area. No grants to individuals.
Application information: Application form not required.

Initial approach: Telephone
Deadline(s): None
Board meeting date(s): Jan. and Sept.
Officers and Trustees:* John E. Price, Jr.,* Chair. and V.P.; T. Wainwright Miller, Jr.,* Pres. and Treas.; Dennis G. Small,* Secy.; Daniel F. Adams; Mavis S. Miller; Russell Priddy; Mary Jo Sanders Walker.
Number of staff: 3 full-time support.
EIN: 591056841
Selected grants: The following grants were reported in 2005.

$25,000 to University of Florida Foundation, Gainesville, FL.
$20,000 to Georgia Tech Foundation, Atlanta, GA.
$15,000 to Florida Gulf Coast University Foundation, Fort Myers, FL.
$12,740 to Habitat for Humanity of Lee County, North Fort Myers, FL.
$10,000 to United Way of Lee County, Fort Myers, FL.
$10,000 to University of South Carolina, Columbia, SC.
$9,000 to Edison Community College Foundation, Fort Myers, FL.
$6,000 to First United Methodist Church, Tampa, FL.
$5,000 to American Heart Association, Bonita Springs, FL.
$5,000 to Stetson University, DeLand, FL.

2178
Priority Healthcare Foundation, Inc. ✦
250 Technology Park, Ste. 124
Lake Mary, FL 32746-6232

Established in 1999 in FL.
Foundation type: Independent foundation.
Financial data (yr. ended 12/31/04): Assets, $18,662 (L); gifts received, $606,584; expenditures, $726,805; qualifying distributions, $396,764; giving activities include $396,764 for 192 grants (high: $40,000; low: $150).
Purpose and activities: Giving for programs that seek to educate the public about disease management.
Fields of interest: Health care.
Limitations: Giving on a national basis.
Directors: Steven D. Cosler; Stephen M. Saft; Rebecca M. Shanahan.
EIN: 593573517
Selected grants: The following grants were reported in 2004.

$40,000 to Presbyterian Hospital of Dallas, Dallas, TX.

$5,825 to Pulmonary Hypertension Association, Silver Spring, MD.
$3,750 to Cleveland Clinic Foundation, Cleveland, OH.
$2,692 to George Washington University, DC.
$1,500 to Carolinas Medical Center, Charlotte, NC.
$1,000 to Community Education Foundation, Council Bluffs, IA.
$1,000 to East Carolina University, Greenville, NC.
$1,000 to Emory Clinic, Atlanta, GA.
$1,000 to Long Island College Hospital, Brooklyn, NY.
$500 to American Lung Association, New York, NY.

2179
J. Crayton Pruitt Foundation, Inc.
100 1st Ave. S.
St. Petersburg, FL 33701

Established in 1989 in FL; funded in 1990.
Donor: J. Crayton Pruitt.
Foundation type: Independent foundation.
Financial data (yr. ended 12/31/04): Assets, $2,493,477 (M); gifts received, $916,902; expenditures, $409,871; qualifying distributions, $407,749; giving activities include $407,650 for 11 grants (high: $400,000; low: $30).
Fields of interest: Higher education.
Limitations: Applications not accepted. Giving primarily in FL. No grants to individuals.
Application information: Unsolicited requests for funds not accepted.
Directors: Natalie Pruitt Judge; Frances M. Pruitt; J. Crayton Pruitt; Helen G. Pruitt Wallace.
EIN: 592876499
Selected grants: The following grants were reported in 2004.

$400,000 to University of Florida Foundation, Gainesville, FL.
$3,000 to Pinellas County Education Foundation, Largo, FL.
$1,100 to American Cancer Society, Miami, FL.
$1,000 to Lance Armstrong Foundation, Austin, TX.
$350 to Wake Forest University, Winston-Salem, NC. 2 grants: $100, $250
$70 to Salvation Army, Saint Petersburg, FL.

2180
Publix Super Markets Charities ▼ ✦
(formerly George W. Jenkins Foundation, Inc.)
3300 Publix Corporate Pkwy.
Lakeland, FL 33811 (863) 680-5250
Contact: Sharon Miller, Exec. Dir.
Application address: P.O. Box 407, Lakeland, FL 33802-0407

Incorporated in 1967 in FL.
Donor: George W. Jenkins†.
Foundation type: Independent foundation.
Financial data (yr. ended 12/31/05): Assets, $561,304,225 (M); expenditures, $26,862,048; qualifying distributions, $25,393,972; giving activities include $25,367,240 for 3,443 grants (high: $1,467,300; low: $25; average: $1,000–$25,000).
Purpose and activities: Giving primarily for education, children and youth, and the United Way and its agencies.
Fields of interest: Education; Children/youth, services; Children, services; Youth, services; Federated giving programs.

Type of support: General/operating support; Capital campaigns; Building/renovation; Equipment; Program development; Employee matching gifts.

Limitations: Giving primarily in AL, FL, GA, SC, and TN. No grants to individuals.

Application information:

Initial approach: Letter of request

Copies of proposal: 1

Deadline(s): None

Board meeting date(s): Monthly

Final notification: 6 to 8 weeks

Officers and Directors:* Carol Barnett,* Chair. and C.E.O.; Hoyt Barnett,* V.P.; John Attaway, Secy.; Tina Johnson, Treas.; Sharon Miller,* Exec. Dir.; Barbara Hart.

Number of staff: 3 full-time professional.

EIN: 596194119

Selected grants: The following grants were reported in 2004.

$1,693,700 to United Way of Central Florida, Highland City, FL.

$1,298,100 to United Way of Metropolitan Atlanta, Atlanta, GA.

$1,001,500 to United Way of Tampa Bay, Tampa, FL.

$789,600 to United Way of Broward County, Fort Lauderdale, FL.

$639,600 to United Way, Heart of Florida, Orlando, FL.

$575,400 to United Way of Miami-Dade, Miami, FL.

$554,500 to United Way of Palm Beach County, Boynton Beach, FL.

$400,000 to Florida Southern College, Lakeland, FL.

$330,900 to United Way of Lee County, Fort Myers, FL.

$312,900 to United Way of Northeast Florida, Jacksonville, FL.

2181

Quantum Foundation ▼ ✧

505 S. Flagler Dr., Ste. 220
West Palm Beach, FL   33401-5923
(561) 832-7497
Contact: Timothy J. Henderson, V.P., Prog.
URL: http://www.quantumfnd.org

Established in 1995 in FL; converted from sale of John F. Kennedy Hospital to Columbia/HCA.

Foundation type: Independent foundation.

Financial data (yr. ended 12/31/04): Assets, $158,328,477 (M); gifts received, $197,500; expenditures, $7,881,004; qualifying distributions, $6,816,435; giving activities include $5,677,315 for 99 grants (high: $362,500; low: $2,500; average: $2,500–$100,000), and $350,138 for 108 employee matching gifts.

Purpose and activities: The foundation seeks to advance the health, education, and community betterment for the residents of Palm Beach County, FL.

Fields of interest: Education; Health care; Community development; Aging.

Type of support: Technical assistance; Program evaluation; Program development; Management development/capacity building; General/operating support; Emergency funds; Employee matching gifts; Matching/challenge support.

Limitations: Giving limited to Palm Beach County, FL. No support for projects of a partisan or religious nature. No grants to individuals, or for fundraising.

Publications: Application guidelines; Annual report; Grants list.

Application information: Applicants are encouraged to contact the foundation's program staff prior to any submission of a concept paper. Concept paper can be submitted online on the foundation's Web site. Application form required.

Initial approach: Letter for application packet and concept paper (no more than 6 pages)

Copies of proposal: 1

Deadline(s): Year-round

Board meeting date(s): Year-round

Final notification: 4 - 6 weeks

Officers and Trustees:* Stephen C. Moore,* Chair.; Anthony J. McNicholas III,* 1st Vice-Chair.; Stephen A. Levin,* 2nd Vice-Chair.; Paul Gionfriddo, Pres.; Christine Koehn, V.P., Prog.; Trudy McConnell, V.P., Community Rels.; Michele Gurto DeLong, C.F.O.; Jeanette M. Corbett,* Pres. Emeritus; Frank Brogan; Marshall A. Falk, M.D.; Keith Alan James; James P. Kintz; William A. Meyer; Richard Sussman; Lucy Valencia; Maria Vallejo, Ph.D.

Number of staff: 5 full-time professional; 2 full-time support.

EIN: 590812783

Selected grants: The following grants were reported in 2005.

$800,000 to Florida Atlantic University, Boca Raton, FL. For School Based Community Wellness Centers.

$550,000 to Palm Beach County Community Health Alliance, West Palm Beach, FL. For regional shared health record system.

$390,000 to Joe DiMaggio Childrens Hospital Foundation, Hollywood, FL. For Florida Partnership for Access to Sickle Cell Services.

$350,000 to Childrens Services Council of Palm Beach County, West Palm Beach, FL. For Project Connect.

$320,000 to Palm Beach County Medical Society, Palm Beach, FL. For Project Access.

$207,000 to YMCA of South Palm Beach County, Boca Raton, FL. For Safe Water Instruction Program.

$200,000 to Sun Sentinel Childrens Fund, Fort Lauderdale, FL. For Hurricane Wilma recovery effort.

$135,000 to Urban League of Palm Beach County, West Palm Beach, FL. For Each One, Reach One.

$50,000 to HOPE Project, West Palm Beach, FL. For HOPE Mobile Mammography Project.

$15,000 to Beacon School, Riviera Beach, FL. For emergency relief in the aftermath of Hurricane Wilma.

2182

The Thomas C. Quick Charitable Trust dated December 29, 1986 ✧

291 El Vedado
Palm Beach, FL   33480

Established in 1986 in FL.

Donor: Thomas C. Quick.

Foundation type: Independent foundation.

Financial data (yr. ended 11/30/04): Assets, $14,724,481 (M); expenditures, $1,222,314; qualifying distributions, $1,202,791; giving activities include $1,178,675 for 85 grants (high: $500,000; low: $50).

Purpose and activities: Giving primarily for education, health care, and human services.

Fields of interest: Higher education; Education; Hospitals (general); Health care; Down syndrome; Health organizations; Human services; Christian agencies & churches.

Limitations: Applications not accepted. Giving primarily in FL and New York, NY. No grants to individuals.

Application information: Contributes only to pre-selected organizations.

Trustee: Thomas C. Quick.

EIN: 592819786

Selected grants: The following grants were reported in 2004.

$500,000 to Fairfield University, Fairfield, CT.

$51,000 to American Ireland Fund, Boston, MA. 2 grants: $50,000, $1,000

$50,000 to Breast Cancer Research Foundation, New York, NY.

$21,000 to American Cancer Society, New York, NY. 2 grants: $1,000, $20,000

$10,000 to American Heart Association, New York, NY. 2 grants: $5,000 each

$10,000 to Arthritis Foundation, Jacksonville, FL.

$5,000 to Inner-City Scholarship Fund, New York, NY.

2183

Quimby Family Foundation ✧ ☆

P.O. Box 802
Palm Beach, FL   33480

Established in 2003 in ME.

Donor: Roxanne Quimby.

Foundation type: Independent foundation.

Financial data (yr. ended 12/31/05): Assets, $11,962,830 (M); expenditures, $560,209; qualifying distributions, $537,748; giving activities include $508,500 for 17 grants (high: $50,000; low: $10,000).

Fields of interest: Environmental education; Animals/wildlife, preservation/protection; Animals/wildlife.

Limitations: Applications not accepted. Giving primarily in ME. No grants to individuals.

Application information: Contributes only to pre-selected organizations.

Officers and Directors:* Roxanne Quimby,* Pres.; Renee Quimby,* Treas.

EIN: 200041017

2184

The Norman R. Rales and Ruth Rales Foundation ✧

998 S. Federal Hwy., Ste. 200
Boca Raton, FL   33432

Established in 1986 in FL.

Donors: Norman R. Rales; Paul Pearl.

Foundation type: Independent foundation.

Financial data (yr. ended 11/30/05): Assets, $18,306,352 (M); gifts received, $10,350; expenditures, $1,089,932; qualifying distributions, $1,070,098; giving activities include $939,279 for 84+ grants (high: $125,000), and $13,500 for 7 grants to individuals (high: $5,000; low: $500).

Purpose and activities: Giving primarily for hospitals and health associations; funding also for Jewish organizations and temples, as well as for Roman Catholic churches and organizations, higher and other education, children, youth, and social services, and federated giving programs.

Fields of interest: Performing arts centers; Elementary/secondary education; Higher education; Education; Hospitals (general); Health organizations, association; Human services;

Children/youth, services; Community development; Foundations (private grantmaking); Federated giving programs; Jewish federated giving programs; Roman Catholic agencies & churches; Jewish agencies & temples.

Limitations: Applications not accepted. Giving on a national basis, with emphasis on Washington, DC, FL, MD, NY, and VA.

Application information: Unsolicited requests for funds not accepted.

Trustees: Morris Edelstein; Roberta Kaplan; Norman R. Rales; Morris E. Sampson; Leonard Weiner.

EIN: 596874589

Selected grants: The following grants were reported in 2004.

$271,000 to Boca Raton Community Hospital, Boca Raton, FL.

$100,000 to Norwood School, Bethesda, MD.

$20,000 to Fight for Children, DC.

$10,000 to Jewish Social Service Agency of Metropolitan Washington, Rockville, MD.

$5,000 to Jewish Outreach Institute, New York, NY.

$5,000 to Miami Childrens Hospital, Miami, FL.

$5,000 to United Way of Greater Boca Raton, Boca Raton, FL.

$5,000 to University of Maryland-College Park, College Park, MD.

$3,000 to Suburban Hospital, Bethesda, MD.

$2,430 to Lynn University, Boca Raton, FL.

2185
Gerald and Henrietta Rauenhorst Foundation, Inc. ✧ ☆

c/o Adler Management, LLC
1167 3rd St., Ste. 102
Naples, FL 34102

Established in 2004 in FL.

Donor: Gerald Rauenhorst Family Foundation.

Foundation type: Independent foundation.

Financial data (yr. ended 12/31/05): Assets, $43,444,838 (M); gifts received, $11,954,577; expenditures, $1,381,334; qualifying distributions, $986,574; giving activities include $863,840 for 17 grants.

Fields of interest: Higher education; Health care; Human services.

Limitations: Applications not accepted. Giving on a national basis. No grants to individuals.

Application information: Contributes only to pre-selected organizations.

Officers and Directors:* Gerald Rauenhorst,* Chair.; Amy R. Goldman,* Vice-Chair.; Luz Campa, Secy.; Mark Rauenhorst, Treas.; Don Neureuther, Exec. Dir.; Peter Karoff; Joseph J. Rauenhorst.

EIN: 030547519

2186
The Rawlings Foundation, Inc. ✧

2554 Players Ct.
Wellington, FL 33414

Established in 2001 in FL.

Donors: George R. Rawlings; The Rawlings Co., LLC.

Foundation type: Operating foundation.

Financial data (yr. ended 12/31/05): Assets, $14,502,948 (M); gifts received, $8,456,054; expenditures, $4,861,255; qualifying distributions, $5,592,707; giving activities include $1,239,836 for 43 grants (high: $210,000; low: $256),

$3,568,398 for 4 foundation-administered programs and $736,561 for 3 loans/program-related investments.

Fields of interest: Education; Cancer; Human services; Christian agencies & churches.

Limitations: Applications not accepted. Giving on a national basis.

Application information: Unsolicited requests for funds not accepted.

Officers and Directors:* George R. Rawlings,* Pres.; Beverly S. Rawlings,* V.P. and Secy.; Herbert M. Rawlings, Treas.

EIN: 651051638

2187
Raygar Foundation ✧

c/o Annie M. Sloan
430 Tivoli Ave.
Coral Gables, FL 33143-6345

Established in 1993 in FL.

Donors: Annie M. Sloan; Garrett Sloan; Raygar Realty Group.

Foundation type: Independent foundation.

Financial data (yr. ended 8/31/05): Assets, $6,651,873 (M); gifts received, $70,000; expenditures, $377,244; qualifying distributions, $375,000; giving activities include $375,000 for 17 grants (high: $65,000; low: $1,000).

Purpose and activities: Giving primarily to Christian ministries and organizations, as well as for social services.

Fields of interest: Media/communications; Education; Salvation Army; Christian agencies & churches.

Limitations: Applications not accepted. No grants to individuals.

Application information: Contributes only to pre-selected organizations.

Trustee: Annie M. Sloan.

EIN: 656128544

Selected grants: The following grants were reported in 2004.

$75,000 to Dutch Sheets Ministries, Colorado Springs, CO. For general support.

$59,000 to Trinity Broadcasting Network, Tustin, CA. For general support.

$41,000 to Benny Hinn Ministries, Irving, TX. For general support.

$35,000 to Reasons to Believe, Pasadena, CA. For general support.

$20,000 to Touching Lives Campaign, Sioux Falls, SD. For general support.

$11,000 to Focus on the Family, Colorado Springs, CO. For general support.

$2,000 to Intercessors for America, Reston, VA. For general support.

$2,000 to Love Worth Finding Ministries, Memphis, TN. For general support.

$1,000 to Guideposts, Carmel, NY. For general support.

$1,000 to Miami Rescue Mission, Miami, FL. For general support.

2188
Raymund Foundation, Inc. ✧ ☆

5350 Tech Data Dr.
Clearwater, FL 33760
Contact: Steven A. Raymund, Pres.

Established in 1997 in FL.

Donors: Sonia V. Raymund; Steven A. Raymund.

Foundation type: Independent foundation.

Financial data (yr. ended 12/31/05): Assets, $8,434,075 (M); gifts received, $328,810; expenditures, $516,602; qualifying distributions, $489,957; giving activities include $489,957 for grants.

Purpose and activities: Giving primarily for education, social services, and religious purposes.

Fields of interest: Higher education; Education; Children/youth, services; Community development; Jewish agencies & temples.

Limitations: Giving primarily in FL.

Application information: Application form not required.

Initial approach: Letter
Deadline(s): None

Officer: Steven A. Raymund, Pres.

EIN: 593447494

2189
The Rayonier Foundation ✧

(formerly The ITT Rayonier Foundation)
50 N. Laura St., Ste. 1900
Jacksonville, FL 32202 (904) 357-9100
Contact: Jay A. Fredericksen, V.P.

Incorporated in 1952 in NY.

Donors: ITT Rayonier Inc.; Rayonier Inc.

Foundation type: Company-sponsored foundation.

Financial data (yr. ended 12/31/04): Assets, $5,931,175 (M); gifts received, $11,300; expenditures, $454,755; qualifying distributions, $450,376; giving activities include $450,376 for 239 grants (high: $100,154; low: $50).

Purpose and activities: The foundation supports organizations involved with performing arts, education, natural resources, health, substance abuse, mental health, alcoholism, recreation, human services, community development, disabled people, minorities, women, and economically disadvantaged people.

Fields of interest: Performing arts; Libraries/library science; Education; Environment, natural resources; Hospitals (general); Medical care, rehabilitation; Health care; Substance abuse, services; Mental health/crisis services; Alcoholism; Recreation; Children/youth, services; Family services; Human services; Community development; Voluntarism promotion; Federated giving programs; Science, formal/general education; Engineering/technology; Disabilities, people with; Minorities; Women; Economically disadvantaged.

Type of support: General/operating support; Continuing support; Annual campaigns; Capital campaigns; Building/renovation; Equipment; Land acquisition; Endowments; Debt reduction; Emergency funds; Program development; Seed money; Scholarship funds; Research; Employee matching gifts; Employee-related scholarships; In-kind gifts; Matching/challenge support.

Limitations: Giving primarily in areas of company operations in Nassau County, FL, Wayne County, GA, and the Olympic Peninsula, WA, area.

Application information: Application form not required.

Initial approach: Proposal
Copies of proposal: 1
Board meeting date(s): Feb.

Officers and Directors:* W. Lee Nutter,* Chair. and Pres.; Jay A. Fredericksen,* V.P.; Ed Frazier III,

Secy.; Macdonald Auguste, Treas.; Hans E. Vanden Noort, Cont.; Paul G. Boynton; Timothy H. Brannon.
EIN: 136064462

2190
Carmen Rebozo Foundation, Inc. ✧
6274 S.W. 35th St.
Miami, FL 33155
Contact: Olga Guilarte, Secy.-Treas.

Established in 1985 in FL.
Donors: Charles G. Rebozo†; Mary Bouterse†.
Foundation type: Independent foundation.
Financial data (yr. ended 6/30/05): Assets, $18,883,625 (M); expenditures, $956,357; qualifying distributions, $889,483; giving activities include $887,900 for 17 grants (high: $397,780; low: $500).
Purpose and activities: Giving primarily to benefit a private library, and for a Boys and Girls club of Miami.
Fields of interest: Libraries/library science; Boys & girls clubs.
Limitations: Applications not accepted. Giving primarily in FL.
Officers and Directors:* Charles F. Rebozo,* Pres.; Tricia Nixon Cox,* V.P.; Julie Nixon Eisenhower,* V.P.; Christina Gilbert,* V.P.; Thomas H. Wakefield,* V.P.; Olga Guilarte,* Secy.-Treas.
EIN: 592667397

2191
The John M. Regan, Jr. & Prudence S. Regan Foundation, Inc. ✧ ☆
c/o R. Chapin
1201 George Bush Blvd.
Delray Beach, FL 33483-7203

Established in 1993 in FL.
Donors: John M. Regan, Jr.; Prudence S. Regan.
Foundation type: Independent foundation.
Financial data (yr. ended 12/31/05): Assets, $1,122,367 (M); expenditures, $1,098,073; qualifying distributions, $1,066,261; giving activities include $1,066,261 for grants.
Purpose and activities: Giving primarily for higher education, and to Roman Catholic churches and organizations.
Fields of interest: Higher education; Education; Environment, natural resources; Hospitals (general); Human services; Roman Catholic agencies & churches.
Limitations: Applications not accepted. Giving on a national basis. No grants to individuals.
Application information: Contributes only to pre-selected organizations.
Officers and Directors:* John M. Regan, Jr.,* Pres. and Treas.; Prudence S. Regan,* V.P.; Robert D. Chapin, Secy.; Deborah Regan Edwards; Prudence R. Hallarman; John M. Regan III; Peter M. Regan; R. Christopher Regan.
EIN: 650374592
Selected grants: The following grants were reported in 2005.
$7,500 to Lawrence Hospital, Bronxville, NY.
$7,000 to Connecticut College, New London, CT.
$7,000 to Riverside Foundation, Lincolnshire, IL.
$5,000 to Westerly Hospital Foundation, Westerly, RI.
$1,500 to Garden Conservancy, Cold Spring, NY.
$1,000 to Habitat for Humanity International.

$1,000 to Watch Hill Chapel Society, Watch Hill, RI.

2192
Rehm Family Foundation ✧
(formerly Cynthia & Jack Rehm Private Foundation)
7116 S.E. Greenview Pl.
Hobe Sound, FL 33455

Established in 1996 in IA.
Donors: Cynthia Rehm; Jack Rehm.
Foundation type: Independent foundation.
Financial data (yr. ended 6/30/05): Assets, $1,649,521 (M); gifts received, $17,111; expenditures, $344,807; qualifying distributions, $328,535; giving activities include $328,535 for 35 grants (high: $221,000; low: $100).
Purpose and activities: Giving primarily to higher education, civic and culture, health associations, and Roman Catholic churches.
Fields of interest: Arts; Higher education; Health organizations, association; Roman Catholic agencies & churches.
Type of support: Continuing support; Annual campaigns; Capital campaigns; Building/renovation.
Limitations: Applications not accepted. Giving on a national basis. No grants to individuals.
Application information: Contributes only to pre-selected organizations.
Trustees: Cynthia Rehm; Jack Rehm.
EIN: 421464826

2193
Reis-Wein Family Charitable Foundation ✧
c/o Mermelstein Hidalgo, LLP
3211 Ponce de Leon Blvd., Ste. 305
Coral Gables, FL 33134

Established in 1993 in NY.
Donors: David Reis; Dina Wein-Reis.
Foundation type: Independent foundation.
Financial data (yr. ended 12/31/04): Assets, $0 (M); gifts received, $580,000; expenditures, $684,512; qualifying distributions, $683,951; giving activities include $683,951 for 48 grants (high: $323,528; low: $150).
Purpose and activities: Giving primarily to Jewish temples, agencies, and schools.
Fields of interest: Education; Health organizations, association; Jewish federated giving programs; Jewish agencies & temples.
Limitations: Applications not accepted. Giving primarily in NY. No grants to individuals.
Application information: Contributes only to pre-selected organizations.
Officers: Dina Wein-Reis, Pres.; David Reis, Mgr.
EIN: 521807458
Selected grants: The following grants were reported in 2004.
$32,664 to Yeshiva Ketana of Manhattan, New York, NY.
$3,600 to Shalom Task Force, New York, NY.
$3,000 to Zion Orphanage, Fresh Meadows, NY.
$2,500 to American Friends of Yad Yemin, Brooklyn, NY.
$1,000 to Cystic Fibrosis Foundation, Bethesda, MD.
$1,000 to Hebron Yeshiva, Jerusalem, Israel. .
$428 to Aish HaTorah.

2194
Resler Foundation ✧ ☆
c/o John B. Resler
P.O. Box 310008
Miami, FL 33231

Established in 1946 in OH.
Foundation type: Independent foundation.
Financial data (yr. ended 12/31/05): Assets, $1,673,978 (M); expenditures, $332,848; qualifying distributions, $330,323; giving activities include $330,000 for 4 grants (high: $100,000; low: $20,000).
Purpose and activities: Support primarily for social services, with emphasis on shelters and programs for the homeless.
Fields of interest: Food banks; Human services; Homeless.
Limitations: Applications not accepted. Giving primarily in Columbus, OH. No grants to individuals.
Application information: Contributes only to pre-selected organizations.
Officer: John B. Resler, Pres. and Secy.-Treas.
EIN: 316042069

2195
The Rinker Companies Foundation, Inc. ✧
(formerly CSR America Companies Foundation, Inc.)
c/o Jim Barontini, Pres.
1501 Belvedere Rd.
West Palm Beach, FL 33406-1517
(561) 833-5555

Incorporated in 1957 in FL.
Donors: Rinker Materials Inc.; CSR Companies Foundation, Inc.
Foundation type: Independent foundation.
Financial data (yr. ended 3/31/05): Assets, $6,877,535 (M); gifts received, $100; expenditures, $570,105; qualifying distributions, $519,500; giving activities include $519,500 for 15 grants (high: $100,000; low: $5,000).
Purpose and activities: Grants primarily for higher education, including scholarships to FL residents with business or construction industry-related majors; support also for arts organizations and the United Way.
Fields of interest: Arts; Higher education; Federated giving programs.
Type of support: General/operating support; Continuing support.
Limitations: Applications not accepted. Giving primarily in FL. No grants to individuals.
Application information: Unsolicited requests for funds not accepted.
Officers and Directors:* Jim Barontini,* Pres.; Thomas G. Burmeister,* V.P.; Michael F. Egan,* Secy.; Ira Fialkow,* Treas.; David Clarke.
EIN: 596139266
Selected grants: The following grants were reported in 2004.
$125,000 to Florida Masonry Apprentice and Education Foundation, Boca Raton, FL. For program support.
$110,000 to University of Florida, Gainesville, FL. 2 grants: $100,000 (For program support), $10,000 to M.E. Rinker, Sr. School of Building Construction Homepage (For scholarships).
$50,000 to Enterprise Florida, Orlando, FL.
$50,000 to RMC Research Corporation, Portland, OR.
$40,000 to Palm Beach Atlantic University, West Palm Beach, FL. For program support.

$21,840 to Front Porch Florida Governors Commission Revitalization Council, Tallahassee, FL.

$10,000 to Raymond F. Kravis Center for the Performing Arts, West Palm Beach, FL. For Corporate Partner Program.

$10,000 to University of Missouri, Rolla, MO. For scholarships.

$5,000 to University of Nevada, Reno, NV. For scholarships.

2196

Marshall and Vera Lea Rinker Foundation, Inc. ✧

380 Columbia Dr., Ste. 110
West Palm Beach, FL   33409

Reincorporated in 1998 in FL.
Foundation type: Independent foundation.
Financial data (yr. ended 12/31/05): Assets, $31,489,450 (M); expenditures, $1,720,184; qualifying distributions, $1,512,761; giving activities include $1,436,500 for 9 grants (high: $400,000; low: $1,500).
Purpose and activities: Giving primarily for higher education, Christian churches and social services.
Fields of interest: Arts; Higher education; Hospitals (general); Human services; Christian agencies & churches.
Type of support: Capital campaigns; Building/renovation; Land acquisition.
Limitations: Applications not accepted. Giving limited to FL, with emphasis on south and central FL. No grants to individuals.
Application information: Contributes only to pre-selected organizations.
  Board meeting date(s): March, June, Sept., and Dec.
Officers and Directors:* John J. Rinker,* Pres.; Sheila A. Rinker,* V.P.; Michael J. Stevens,* Secy.-Treas.; R. Hagan Kohler; R. Michael Strickland.
EIN: 311610196
Selected grants: The following grants were reported in 2005.
$535,000 to Palm Beach Atlantic University, West Palm Beach, FL. 2 grants: $135,000, $400,000
$400,000 to Boy Scouts of America, Palm Beach Gardens, FL.
$400,000 to Stetson University, DeLand, FL.
$50,000 to Raymond F. Kravis Center for the Performing Arts, West Palm Beach, FL.
$30,000 to Habitat for Humanity of Palm Beach County, West Palm Beach, FL.
$10,000 to Rollins College, Winter Park, FL.
$10,000 to Urban Youth Impact, West Palm Beach, FL.

2197

Marshall E. Rinker, Sr. Foundation, Inc.

310 Okeechobee Blvd.
West Palm Beach, FL   33401
Contact: Fdn. Admin.

Established in 1998 in FL.
Donor: M.E. Rinker, Sr.
Foundation type: Independent foundation.
Financial data (yr. ended 12/31/05): Assets, $30,563,119 (M); expenditures, $1,747,471; qualifying distributions, $1,556,920; giving

activities include $1,444,800 for 21 grants (high: $310,000; low: $1,500).
Purpose and activities: Giving primarily for higher education.
Fields of interest: Education; Health care; Community development; Religion.
Type of support: Capital campaigns; Endowments.
Limitations: Applications not accepted. Giving primarily in FL. No grants to individuals.
Application information:
  Board meeting date(s): Quarterly
Officers and Directors:* David B. Rinker,* Pres.; Leighan R. Rinker,* 1st V.P.; Paul C. Bremer,* Secy.-Treas.; Marshall M. Criser; Richard S. Johnson.
EIN: 650871532
Selected grants: The following grants were reported in 2004.
$275,000 to Furman University, Greenville, SC. For capital campaign.
$260,000 to Palm Beach Atlantic University, West Palm Beach, FL. For capital campaign.
$150,000 to University of Florida, ME Rinker, Sr. School of Building Construction, Gainesville, FL.
$114,000 to Stetson University, DeLand, FL. For scholarship endowment.
$80,000 to Boy Scouts of America, Palm Beach Gardens, FL. For capital campaign.
$50,000 to Ball State University, Muncie, IN. For capital campaign.
$50,000 to Habitat for Humanity International, FL. For capital campaign.
$50,000 to Raymond F. Kravis Center for the Performing Arts, West Palm Beach, FL. For capital campaign.
$50,000 to Roberts Wesleyan College, Rochester, NY. For capital campaign.
$45,000 to Boggy Creek Gang-A Hole in the Wall Gang Camp, Eustis, FL. For capital campaign and camperships.

2198

River Branch Foundation ✧

1514 Nira St.
Jacksonville, FL   32207
Contact: Judith Leroux, Tr.

Trust established in 1963 in NJ.
Donors: J. Seward Johnson 1951 and 1961 Charitable Trusts; The Atlantic Foundation.
Foundation type: Independent foundation.
Financial data (yr. ended 12/31/04): Assets, $27,514,293 (M); expenditures, $713,813; qualifying distributions, $516,482; giving activities include $514,000 for 20 grants (high: $125,000; low: $2,000).
Purpose and activities: Giving primarily for human services, children's services, education, the arts and the environment.
Fields of interest: Arts; Environment; Children/youth, services.
Limitations: Giving primarily in the Jacksonville, FL, area. No grants to individuals.
Publications: Informational brochure.
Application information: Application form not required.
  Initial approach: Letter; do not telephone
  Copies of proposal: 1
  Deadline(s): None
Director: Jennifer Johnson Duke.
Trustees: Jason Gregg; Simon Gregg; Judith Leroux.
EIN: 226054887

Selected grants: The following grants were reported in 2003.
$150,000 to Communities in Schools of Jacksonville, Jacksonville, FL.
$125,000 to Bolles School, Jacksonville, FL.
$100,000 to I.M. Sulzbacher Center for the Homeless, Jacksonville, FL.
$100,000 to Nature Conservancy, Tallahassee, FL.
$50,000 to Jacksonville Housing Partnership, Jacksonville, FL.
$25,000 to Theater Jacksonville, Jacksonville, FL.
$20,000 to 1000 Friends of Florida, Tallahassee, FL.
$20,000 to Hubbard House, Jacksonville, FL.
$2,000 to Greenscape of Jacksonville, Jacksonville, FL.
$1,750 to Cultural Council of Greater Jacksonville, Jacksonville, FL.

2199

River Oaks Foundation, Inc. ✧

(formerly William & Norma Horvitz Family Foundation, Inc.)
401 E. Las Olas Blvd., Ste. 2200
Fort Lauderdale, FL   33301   (954) 523-7771

Established in 1986 in FL.
Donors: William D. Horvitz; Norma Horvitz.
Foundation type: Independent foundation.
Financial data (yr. ended 12/31/05): Assets, $5,619,817 (M); expenditures, $360,595; qualifying distributions, $337,950; giving activities include $337,950 for 26 grants (high: $250,000; low: $100).
Purpose and activities: Giving primarily for the arts, education and human services.
Fields of interest: Museums (art); Arts; Higher education; Hospitals (specialty); Medical care, rehabilitation; Eye diseases; Neighborhood centers; Jewish federated giving programs; Jewish agencies & temples.
Limitations: Applications not accepted. Giving primarily in FL. No grants to individuals.
Application information: Contributes only to pre-selected organizations.
Directors: Alicia Gregory; Wayne A. Gregory, Jr.; Norma Horvitz.
EIN: 592722308
Selected grants: The following grants were reported in 2004.
$250,000 to Nova Southeastern University, Fort Lauderdale, FL.
$96,193 to Bascom Palmer Eye Institute, Miami, FL.
$29,989 to Ayn Rand Institute, Irvine, CA.
$2,500 to Spoleto Festival USA, Charleston, SC.
$2,000 to Berea College, Berea, KY.
$1,000 to Andy Warhol Museum, Pittsburgh, PA.
$1,000 to KidsCommons Columbus Community Childrens Museum, Columbus, IN.

2200

Riverside Foundation, Inc. ✧

9090 Barrister Ct.
Jacksonville, FL   32257   (904) 982-3676
Contact: Helen Werking, Secy.
Application address: P.O. Box 2982, Jacksonville, FL 32203; tel.: (904) 308-8941

Established in 1992 in FL.
Foundation type: Independent foundation.

Financial data (yr. ended 12/31/05): Assets, $11,397,178 (M); gifts received, $1,128; expenditures, $573,156; qualifying distributions, $523,768; giving activities include $523,768 for grants.
Purpose and activities: Giving primarily to healthcare organizations.
Fields of interest: Health care; Health organizations, association; Foundations (community).
Limitations: Giving limited to the five-county area of northeast FL. No grants to individuals.
Application information: Application form required.
  Initial approach: Letter requesting application guidelines
  Deadline(s): None
  Board meeting date(s): Quarterly
Officers: Julian Hickory Fant, Pres.; Sylvia F. Sinclair, V.P.; Helen Werking, Secy.; W. Lester Varn, Jr., Treas.
Directors: George A. Anderson, M.D.; A. Leland Burpee; Arch W. Cassidy; Fred M. Cone, Jr.; M. Harlan Johnston, M.D.; Katy Towers, Jr.; George E. Utsey, Jr.; William Walton III; Charles J. Williams III.
EIN: 593057267

2201
Roberts Charitable Foundation ☆
P.O. Box 3439
Ponte Vedra Beach, FL 32004-3439
Contact: Janet L. Drake
FAX: (904) 708-3804;
E-mail: janet@drakelawoffice.com

Established in 2003 in FL.
Donor: Alfred M. Roberts, Jr.
Foundation type: Independent foundation.
Financial data (yr. ended 12/31/04): Assets, $11,250,550 (M); expenditures, $710,678; qualifying distributions, $505,000; giving activities include $375,000 for grants.
Purpose and activities: The foundation's primary mission is to benefit charitable organizations in the two communities in which Cmdr. Roberts made his home— Jacksonville and northern Florida and Watch Hill, Westerly, Rhode Island. A particular focus is to identify unmet community needs and to develop innovative strategies to address them.
Fields of interest: Historic preservation/historical societies; Education; Environment, plant conservation; Animal welfare.
Type of support: Continuing support; Capital campaigns; Seed money.
Limitations: Applications not accepted.
Application information: Unsolicited requests for funds not accepted.
  Board meeting date(s): Semi-annual as needed
Trustees: Dorothy H. Roberts; Chaplin B. Barnes; Citigroup Trust.
EIN: 226948512

2202
Robinson Family Charitable Trust ◈
6208 N.W. 43rd St.
Gainesville, FL 32653

Established in 2002 in FL.
Donor: G.W. Robinson.
Foundation type: Independent foundation.
Financial data (yr. ended 12/31/04): Assets, $734,354 (M); gifts received, $675,822;

expenditures, $333,145; qualifying distributions, $333,145; giving activities include $333,145 for 43 + grants (high: $141,500).
Fields of interest: Christian agencies & churches.
Trustees: G.W. Robinson; Kate Robinson.
EIN: 597227324
Selected grants: The following grants were reported in 2004.
$90,000 to American Bible Society, New York, NY.
$22,500 to Christian Aid Mission, Charlottesville, VA.
$5,000 to League of A Prayer, Montgomery, AL.
$2,076 to Campus Crusade for Christ, Miami, FL.
$2,000 to Life Outreach International, Fort Worth, TX.
$1,450 to World Impact, Los Angeles, CA.
$1,350 to Jews for Jesus, San Francisco, CA.
$1,000 to Christ for the Nations, Dallas, TX.
$900 to World Missionary Press, New Paris, IN.
$600 to Every Home for Christ, Colorado Springs, CO.

2203
William D. Rollnick and Nancy Ellison Rollnick Foundation ◈
(formerly William D. and Nancy Ellison Rollnick Foundation)
1 N. Breakers Row, Ste. 351
Palm Beach, FL 33480

Established in 1992 in FL.
Donor: William D. Rollnick.
Foundation type: Independent foundation.
Financial data (yr. ended 9/30/05): Assets, $74,057 (M); gifts received, $410,000; expenditures, $423,349; qualifying distributions, $421,175; giving activities include $419,650 for 16 grants (high: $200,000; low: $1,000).
Purpose and activities: Giving primarily to the arts; funding also for children, youth and social services.
Fields of interest: Performing arts centers; Performing arts, ballet; Performing arts, opera; Arts; Human services; Children/youth, services.
Limitations: Applications not accepted. Giving on a national basis, with emphasis on New York, NY, and Washington, DC. No grants to individuals.
Application information: Contributes only to pre-selected organizations.
Director: William D. Rollnick.
EIN: 954394898

2204
Rooms to Go Children's Fund ◈
11540 Hwy. 92 E.
Seffner, FL 33584   (813) 623-5400
Contact: Lewis Stein, V.P.

Established in 1998 in FL.
Donor: Rooms To Go, Inc.
Foundation type: Independent foundation.
Financial data (yr. ended 12/31/04): Assets, $3,188,648 (M); gifts received, $1,500,000; expenditures, $650,425; qualifying distributions, $630,327; giving activities include $623,440 for grants.
Fields of interest: Zoos/zoological societies; Hospitals (general); Health care; Health organizations, association; Disasters, 9/11/01; Human services; YM/YWCAs & YM/YWHAs; Children/youth, services; Federated giving programs; Jewish agencies & temples.

Type of support: General/operating support.
Limitations: Giving primarily in FL.
Officers and Directors:* Jeffrey Seaman,* Pres.; Lewis Stein, V.P. and Secy.-Treas.; J. Michael Kettle.
EIN: 650878894
Selected grants: The following grants were reported in 2003.
$100,000 to Lowry Park Zoo Endowment Foundation, Tampa, FL.
$31,500 to H. Lee Moffitt Cancer Center and Research Institute Foundation, Tampa, FL.
$25,000 to Muscular Dystrophy Association, Phoenix, AZ.
$25,000 to YMCA, Tampa Metropolitan Area, Tampa, FL.
$7,500 to Saint Josephs Hospital of Tampa Foundation, Cancer Institute, Tampa, FL.
$5,000 to Childrens Cancer Center, Tampa, FL.
$2,500 to Cystic Fibrosis Foundation, Bethesda, MD.
$2,500 to Tampa General Hospital Foundation, Tampa, FL.
$1,500 to Coastal Conservation Association-Florida, Winter Park, FL.
$1,000 to Prevent Child Abuse Georgia, Atlanta, GA.

2205
The Harris Rosen Foundation, Inc. ◈
9840 International Dr.
Orlando, FL 32819-8293

Established in 1987 in FL.
Donors: Harris Rosen; Daytona International Speedway; Florida Hospital Medical Center; Southern Area of The Links, Inc.; Wayne M. Densch Charitable Trust; National Council of Negro Women; The Procter & Gamble Co.; The Links, Inc.
Foundation type: Independent foundation.
Financial data (yr. ended 12/31/05): Assets, $2,608,031 (M); gifts received, $475,059; expenditures, $1,013,963; qualifying distributions, $1,013,963; giving activities include $906,971 for 15 grants (high: $500,000; low: $200).
Fields of interest: Higher education; Education.
Type of support: Scholarship funds.
Limitations: Applications not accepted. Giving primarily in FL. No grants to individuals.
Application information: Contributes only to four pre-selected organizations specified in the governing instrument.
Officers and Directors:* Harris Rosen,* Pres.; Garritt Toohey,* V.P.; Frank Santos,* Secy.-Treas.
EIN: 592890420

2206
William Rosenberg Family Foundation, Inc. ◈
2424 No. Federal Hwy., Ste. 455
Boca Raton, FL 33431
Contact: Ann Rosenberg, Pres.

Established in 1986 in FL.
Donors: Ann Rosenberg; William Rosenberg‡.
Foundation type: Independent foundation.
Financial data (yr. ended 12/31/05): Assets, $21,285,145 (M); gifts received, $3,197,788; expenditures, $1,248,568; qualifying distributions, $1,157,710; giving activities include $1,120,000 for 73 grants (high: $75,000; low: $1,000).

Purpose and activities: Support for child development and welfare, social services, Jewish giving, and health.

Fields of interest: Education, association; Child development, education; Business school/education; Health care; Health organizations, association; Cancer; Medical research, institute; Cancer research; Human services; Child development, services; Residential/custodial care, hospices; Jewish agencies & temples.

Type of support: General/operating support; Continuing support; Capital campaigns; Building/renovation; Equipment; Endowments; Program development; Professorships; Research.

Limitations: Applications not accepted. Giving primarily in New England and FL. No grants to individuals.

Application information: Contributes only to pre-selected organizations.

Board meeting date(s): 1st week in Dec.

Officers and Trustees: * Ann Rosenberg,* Pres.; Jill Gottlieb,* V.P.; Carolyn Ryan,* Secy.; Donald Rosenberg,* Co-Treas.; James Rosenberg,* Co-Treas.; Jennifer Rosenberg; John Rosenberg; Linda Rosenberg; Robert Rosenberg; Michael Ryan.

Number of staff: 1 part-time professional.

EIN: 592675613

2207
Richard M. and Elizabeth M. Ross Family Foundation ◇

(formerly Elizabeth M. Ross Family Foundation)
P.O. Box 2180
Vero Beach, FL 32961-2180 (772) 978-9686
Contact: Marcia R. Blackburn, Secy.-Treas.
FAX: (561) 978-9685;
E-mail: rossfund@earthlink.net

Established in 1996 in OH.

Donor: Elizabeth M. Ross.

Foundation type: Independent foundation.

Financial data (yr. ended 12/31/05): Assets, $13,108,577 (M); expenditures, $642,770; qualifying distributions, $594,001; giving activities include $585,000 for 64 grants (high: $40,000; low: $500).

Purpose and activities: Giving primarily for medical research and for children's health and welfare.

Fields of interest: Museums; Medical research, institute; Children/youth, services; Christian agencies & churches.

Limitations: Applications not accepted. Giving on a national basis.

Application information: Unsolicited requests for funds not accepted.

Board meeting date(s): Mar., Aug., and Dec.

Officers and Trustees: * Elizabeth M. Ross,* Pres.; Marcia Ross Blackburn,* Secy.-Treas.; Elizabeth L. Blackburn; William R. Blackburn; Katherine Blackburn Reay; Alison G. Ross; Elizabeth Manbeck Ross; George A. Ross; Margaret M. Ross; Rachael E. Ross; Richard M. Ross, Jr.; Sarah Ross Soter; Sarah W. Ziegler.

Agent: The Huntington National Bank.

Number of staff: 1

EIN: 311480761

2208
Rosser Charitable Trust ◇

1424 Nighthawk Pointe
Naples, FL 34105

Established in 1997 in CT.

Foundation type: Independent foundation.

Financial data (yr. ended 12/31/05): Assets, $1,871,266 (M); gifts received, $5,878; expenditures, $397,378; qualifying distributions, $388,305; giving activities include $386,667 for 8 grants (high: $166,667; low: $10,000).

Fields of interest: Higher education, university; Human services; Christian agencies & churches; Protestant agencies & churches.

Limitations: Giving on a national basis.

Trustees: Harold O. Rosser II; Rita Elaine Rosser.

EIN: 226717205

Selected grants: The following grants were reported in 2004.

$110,000 to Wake Forest University, Winston-Salem, NC.

$100,000 to Integrity Worship Ministries, Mobile, AL.

$20,000 to Greens Farms Academy, Greens Farms, CT.

$10,000 to In Touch Ministries, Atlanta, GA.

$10,000 to New Canaan Society, New York, NY.

2209
Rothberg Family Charitable Foundation for Children's Diseases ◇

c/o Michael J. Rothberg
7551 Isla Verde Way
Delray Beach, FL 33446

Established in CT.

Donors: Jonathan M. Rothberg; Henry M. Rothberg; Lilliam R. Rothberg.

Foundation type: Independent foundation.

Financial data (yr. ended 12/31/04): Assets, $32,665,714 (M); expenditures, $3,225,718; qualifying distributions, $3,200,000; giving activities include $3,200,000 for 8 grants (high: $500,000; low: $200,000; average: $400,000–$500,000).

Purpose and activities: Giving primarily for the support of research relating to, and the development of medications for the treatment and cure of Tuberous Sclerosis Complex (TSC).

Fields of interest: Genetics/birth defects; Pediatrics research.

Type of support: Research.

Limitations: Applications not accepted. Giving primarily in Guilford, CT. No grants to individuals.

Application information: Contributes only to pre-selected organizations.

Trustees: Jonathan M. Rothberg; Michael J. Rothberg.

EIN: 061519674

2210
The Rothman Foundation ◇

c/o Robert Rothman
1 Tampa City Ctr., Ste. 2880
Tampa, FL 33602-5102

Established in NY 1997.

Donor: Robert Rothman.

Foundation type: Independent foundation.

Financial data (yr. ended 12/31/04): Assets, $2,403,238 (M); expenditures, $2,603,140; qualifying distributions, $2,580,000; giving activities include $2,580,000 for 7 grants (high: $1,000,000; low: $20,000).

Fields of interest: Elementary/secondary education; Higher education, university; Hospitals (general); Cancer; Roman Catholic agencies & churches.

Limitations: Applications not accepted. No grants to individuals.

Application information: Contributes only to pre-selected organizations.

Trustees: Margaret Rothman; Robert Rothman.

EIN: 137115394

Selected grants: The following grants were reported in 2003.

$1,000,000 to University of Chicago, Chicago, IL.

$700,000 to H. Lee Moffitt Cancer Center and Research Institute, Tampa, FL.

$250,000 to University of Florida, Gainesville, FL.

$75,000 to Academy of the Holy Names School, Tampa, FL.

$30,000 to YMCA, Tampa Metropolitan Area, Tampa, FL.

$20,000 to University of Pennsylvania, Wharton School of Business, Philadelphia, PA. For annual fund.

$5,000 to Berkeley Preparatory School, Tampa, FL.

$5,000 to Tampa Preparatory School, Tampa, FL.

2211
J. M. Rubin Foundation, Inc. ◇

505 S. Flagler Dr., Ste. 1320
West Palm Beach, FL 33401 (561) 833-3309
FAX: (561) 833-2258; E-mail: info@jmrf.org;
URL: http://www.jmrf.org

Established in 1973 in FL.

Donor: Jacob M. Rubin‡.

Foundation type: Independent foundation.

Financial data (yr. ended 11/30/05): Assets, $52,255,549 (M); gifts received, $22,826,891; expenditures, $2,217,473; qualifying distributions, $1,405,066; giving activities include $557,500 for 49 grants (high: $150,000; low: $100), and $579,730 for 173 grants to individuals (high: $6,250; low: $250).

Purpose and activities: Giving primarily for higher education.

Fields of interest: Higher education; Health organizations, association; Human services; Youth, services; Family services; Residential/custodial care, hospices.

Type of support: Scholarship funds.

Limitations: Giving primarily in Palm Beach, FL; scholarships limited to U.S. citizens who are residents of Palm Beach County, FL.

Publications: Application guidelines.

Application information: Application information available on the foundation Web site. Application form required.

Initial approach: Complete online application
Deadline(s): June 1 for renewal applications
Final notification: May

Officers: Robert T. Owens, C.E.O. and Pres.; Mary S. Harper, V.P. and Secy.; Kimberly L. Harris, Treas.

EIN: 591958240

Selected grants: The following grants were reported in 2005.

$150,000 to Palm Beach Atlantic University, West Palm Beach, FL.

$25,000 to Rosarian Academy, West Palm Beach, FL.

$15,000 to Adopt-A-Family of the Palm Beaches, West Palm Beach, FL.

$12,500 to New York University, New York, NY. 2 grants: $6,250 each

$6,250 to Samford University, Birmingham, AL.
$5,000 to Friends of Abused Children, West Palm Beach, FL.
$4,200 to Emory University, Atlanta, GA.
$2,000 to Salvation Army.
$1,000 to Covenant House Florida, Fort Lauderdale, FL.

2212
Robert Russell Memorial Foundation

c/o Greenberg Traurig
1221 Brickell Ave., 17th Fl.
Miami, FL 33131-2804
Contact: Norman H. Lipoff, Chair.
FAX: (305) 961-5503; E-mail: Lipoffn@Gtlaw.com

Established in 1984 in FL.
Foundation type: Independent foundation.
Financial data (yr. ended 8/31/05): Assets, $18,953,539 (M); expenditures, $1,502,563; qualifying distributions, $1,411,299; giving activities include $1,315,500 for 67 grants (high: $210,000; low: $1,000; average: $5,000–$50,000).
Purpose and activities: Support primarily for Jewish and Israeli programs and agencies, including education, social or research programs, capital projects, religious tolerance, Middle East studies, Jewish leadership development, and interfaith activity.
Fields of interest: Jewish federated giving programs.
International interests: Israel.
Type of support: General/operating support; Continuing support; Annual campaigns; Capital campaigns; Building/renovation; Program development; Fellowships; Scholarship funds; Matching/challenge support.
Limitations: Giving primarily in the Miami Dade County, FL, area; giving also in Israel. No grants to individuals.
Publications: Application guidelines.
Application information: Application form required.
 Initial approach: Letter
 Copies of proposal: 5
 Deadline(s): Mar. 31
 Board meeting date(s): May
 Final notification: Following board meeting
Trustees: Norman H. Lipoff, Chair.; Northern Trust Bank of Florida, N.A.
EIN: 592486579
Selected grants: The following grants were reported in 2004.
$210,000 to United Jewish Communities, New York, NY.
$150,000 to Alexander Muss High School in Israel, Israel. .
$100,000 to Dave and Mary Alper Jewish Community Center, Miami, FL.
$100,000 to Michael-Ann Russell Jewish Community Center, North Miami Beach, FL.
$25,000 to American Friends of Shalom Hartman Institute, New York, NY.
$25,000 to American Friends of the Jaffa Institute, Flushing, NY.
$5,000 to Education Fund, Miami, FL.
$5,000 to Gesher Foundation, New York, NY.
$5,000 to Jewish Education Service of North America, New York, NY.
$1,000 to Donors Forum of South Florida, Miami, FL.

2213
The Ryder System Charitable Foundation, Inc. ✧

c/o Corp. Tax
11690 N.W. 105th St.
Miami, FL 33178 (305) 500-3031

Established in 1984 in FL.
Donor: Ryder System, Inc.
Foundation type: Company-sponsored foundation.
Financial data (yr. ended 12/31/04): Assets, $133,383 (M); gifts received, $1,167,962; expenditures, $1,287,089; qualifying distributions, $1,287,089; giving activities include $1,261,714 for 130 grants (high: $100,000; low: $25), $25,275 for 44 grants to individuals (high: $1,850; low: $150), and $100 for 1 employee matching gift.
Purpose and activities: The foundation supports organizations involved with arts and culture, education, health, human services, community development, civic affairs, minorities, and economically disadvantaged people.
Fields of interest: Arts; Elementary school/education; Secondary school/education; Higher education; Education; Health care; Minorities/immigrants, centers/services; Human services; Community development; Federated giving programs; Government/public administration; Minorities; Economically disadvantaged.
Type of support: General/operating support; Annual campaigns; Employee matching gifts; Grants to individuals; In-kind gifts.
Limitations: Giving limited to Los Angeles, CA, southern FL, Atlanta, GA, Detroit, MI, St. Louis, MO, Cincinnati, OH, and Dallas, TX.
Publications: Corporate giving report.
Application information: Application form not required.
 Initial approach: Proposal
 Copies of proposal: 1
 Deadline(s): None
 Board meeting date(s): Annually and as needed
 Final notification: Within 60 days
Officers and Directors:* Gregory T. Swienton,* Pres.; Robert D. Fatovic,* V.P. and Secy.; W. Daniel Susik, V.P. and Treas.; Tracy A. Leinbach,* V.P.; Vicki A. O'Meara, V.P. and Secy.; Richard H. Siegel, V.P.; R. Ray Goode,* C.A.O. and Exec. Dir.
Number of staff: 1 full-time professional; 1 full-time support.
EIN: 592462315

2214
Gordon Samstag Fine Arts Trust ✧

c/o Bank of America, N.A.
P.O. Box 40200, FL9-100-10-19
Jacksonville, FL 32203-0200
E-mail: samstag@unisa.edu.au; Application address: c/o Ross Wolfe, Dir., Samstag Scholarship Program, University of South Australia, GPO Box 2471, Adelaide, South Australia 5001, tel.: (08) 8302-0865; FAX: (08) 8302-0866; International Code for Australia is 618; URL: http://www.unisa.edu.au/samstag

Established in 1991 in FL.
Donor: Gordon Samstag†.
Foundation type: Independent foundation.
Financial data (yr. ended 12/31/05): Assets, $10,159,349 (M); expenditures, $663,101; qualifying distributions, $606,259; giving activities include $382,545 for 21 grants to individuals (high:

$55,073; low: $156), and $606,259 for foundation-administered programs.
Purpose and activities: Scholarship funds awarded to residents of Australia to further studies in the visual arts in NY or overseas.
Fields of interest: Visual arts; Performing arts.
International interests: Australia.
Type of support: Scholarship funds.
Limitations: Giving limited to residents of Australia. No grants to individuals directly.
Publications: Application guidelines.
Application information: Application guidelines and application form can be downloaded on trust Web site. Application forms must be sent by mail. No faxed application forms will be accepted. Application form required.
 Initial approach: Letter, e-mail, telephone, or see Web site
 Deadline(s): June 30
 Final notification: Sept.
Director: Ross Wolfe.
Trustee: Bank of America, N.A.
EIN: 656064217

2215
Lawrence A. Sanders Foundation, Inc.

c/o J. Daniel Brede
1900 Corporate Blvd. N.W.
E. Bldg., Ste. 201E
Boca Raton, FL 33431-7320

Established in 1991 in FL.
Donors: Lawrence Sanders Enterprises; Lawrence A. Sanders Rev. Trust; Lawrence A. Sanders CRUT.
Foundation type: Independent foundation.
Financial data (yr. ended 12/31/05): Assets, $19,916,658 (M); expenditures, $998,126; qualifying distributions, $878,228; giving activities include $850,400 for 43 grants (high: $125,000; low: $400).
Purpose and activities: The foundation supports organizations involved with arts and culture, education, housing/shelter development, and human services.
Fields of interest: Arts; Education; Food services; Housing/shelter, development; Boys clubs; Human services; American Red Cross; Salvation Army; Foundations (private grantmaking); Foundations (community); Federated giving programs; Roman Catholic agencies & churches.
Limitations: Applications not accepted. Giving primarily in FL. No grants to individuals.
Application information: Contributes only to pre-selected organizations.
Directors: Helen Brede; J. Daniel Brede; James E. Roberts.
EIN: 650270066
Selected grants: The following grants were reported in 2005.
$100,000 to Florida Atlantic University Foundation, Boca Raton, FL.
$50,000 to American Red Cross, Fort Lauderdale, FL.
$45,000 to Martin County Council for the Arts, Stuart, FL.
$30,000 to Catholic Charities, Gainesville, FL.
$30,000 to Palm Beach County Cultural Council, West Palm Beach, FL.
$25,000 to Boca Helping Hands, Boca Raton, FL.
$10,000 to Cooperative Feeding Program, Fort Lauderdale, FL.
$10,000 to Daily Bread Food Bank, Miami, FL.
$10,000 to YMCA, FL.

$400 to Maryland Institute College of Art, Baltimore, MD.

2216
Harvey and Phyllis Sandler Foundation, Inc. ✧

21170 N.E. 22nd Ct.
Miami, FL   33180

Established in 1993 in FL.
Donor: Harvey Sandler.
Foundation type: Independent foundation.
Financial data (yr. ended 12/31/05): Assets, $13,217,366 (M); expenditures, $2,623,489; qualifying distributions, $2,608,413; giving activities include $2,398,586 for 103 grants (high: $1,500,000; low: $20).
Purpose and activities: Funding primarily for Jewish agencies and temples. Funding also for medical research, human services, and arts and culture.
Fields of interest: Arts; Education; Medical research, institute; Human services; Jewish federated giving programs; Jewish agencies & temples.
Limitations: Applications not accepted. Giving primarily in FL and New York, NY. No grants to individuals.
Application information: Contributes only to pre-selected organizations.
Officers and Directors:* Harvey Sandler,* Pres.; Jeffrey Levine,* V.P.; Phyllis Sandler,* Secy.
EIN: 650452582

2217
Sansing Foundation, Inc. ✧

6200 Pensacola Blvd.
Pensacola, FL   32505-2214

Established in 1995 in FL.
Donors: Robert C. Sansing; Peggy L. Sansing.
Foundation type: Independent foundation.
Financial data (yr. ended 12/31/05): Assets, $444,182 (M); gifts received, $850,000; expenditures, $808,948; qualifying distributions, $808,948; giving activities include $807,700 for 35 grants (high: $241,000; low: $100).
Fields of interest: Higher education; Education; Health organizations, association; Human services; Salvation Army; Children/youth, services; Federated giving programs; Christian agencies & churches.
Limitations: Applications not accepted. Giving primarily in FL; some funding nationally. No grants to individuals.
Application information: Contributes only to pre-selected organizations.
Officers and Trustees:* Robert C. Sansing,* Pres.; Peggy L. Sansing,* V.P.; Thomas M. Bizzell.
EIN: 593284550
Selected grants: The following grants were reported in 2004.
$130,000 to World Help, Forest, VA.
$117,405 to Big Oak Ranch, Springville, AL. 2 grants: $1,405, $116,000
$60,500 to Fellowship of Christian Athletes, Kansas City, MO.
$30,000 to Salvation Army, Saint Petersburg, FL.
$28,150 to Campus Crusade for Christ International, Orlando, FL.
$27,500 to Pensacola Junior College Foundation, Pensacola, FL. 2 grants: $2,500, $25,000
$5,000 to Make-A-Wish Foundation, Maitland, FL.

$4,200 to Gulf Coast Kids House, Pensacola, FL.

2218
Sansom Foundation, Inc. ✧

P.O. Box 14274, 6th Fl.
Fort Lauderdale, FL   33302

Established in 1958 in NY.
Donor: Ira D. Glackens†.
Foundation type: Independent foundation.
Financial data (yr. ended 12/31/04): Assets, $20,740,058 (L); expenditures, $799,893; qualifying distributions, $714,498; giving activities include $440,566 for 6 grants (high: $321,676; low: $3,890), and $145,000 for 1 loan/program-related investment.
Purpose and activities: Donates and loans works of art to museums and galleries.
Fields of interest: Museums (art); Higher education, university.
Limitations: Applications not accepted. Giving primarily in FL. No grants to individuals.
Application information: Contributes only to pre-selected organizations.
Officers: Donald G. Hilker, Pres.; Frank Buscaglia, V.P. and Treas.; Rev. Edward M. DePaoli, Secy.
Director: Jorge H. Santis.
EIN: 136136127
Selected grants: The following grants were reported in 2003.
$90,000 to Ball State University, Muncie, IN. For the arts.
$45,200 to Museum of Art, Fort Lauderdale, FL. For general support.
$20,000 to Saint Georges School, Spokane, WA. For Governor's Fund.
$15,000 to Chimp Haven, Shreveport, LA. For general support.
$10,000 to American Museum of Asmat Art, Saint Paul, MN. For general support.

2219
The Saunders Foundation ✧

c/o Bank of America, N.A.
P.O. Box 31813
Tampa, FL   33631-3813   (813) 225-8588
Contact: Kathleen J. Belmonte, Dir.

Established in 1970 in FL.
Donors: William N. Saunders†; Ruby Lee Saunders†.
Foundation type: Independent foundation.
Financial data (yr. ended 12/31/05): Assets, $14,686,780 (M); expenditures, $841,609; qualifying distributions, $786,885; giving activities include $699,400 for 34 grants (high: $250,000; low: $1,000).
Fields of interest: Performing arts centers; Performing arts, theater; Arts; Higher education; Hospitals (general); Health organizations, association; Human services.
Type of support: Building/renovation; Program development; Scholarship funds; Matching/challenge support.
Limitations: Giving primarily in the Tampa Bay, FL, area. No support for organizations that promote sports or athletic competition. No grants to individuals, or for fellowships, travel projects, or operating funds.
Publications: Application guidelines.
Application information: Application form required.

Copies of proposal: 2
Deadline(s): None
Board meeting date(s): 1st Wed. of each month
Officers and Directors:* Solon F. O'Neal, Jr.,* Pres.; James M. Kelly,* V.P. and Treas.; George B. Howell III,* Secy.; Kathleen J. Belmonte.
EIN: 596152326
Selected grants: The following grants were reported in 2004.
$250,000 to University of Tampa, Tampa, FL.
$75,000 to Tampa Bay Performing Arts Center, Tampa, FL. 2 grants: $25,000, $50,000
$25,000 to H. Lee Moffitt Cancer Center and Research Institute Foundation, Tampa, FL.
$25,000 to Tampa General Hospital Foundation, Tampa, FL.
$15,000 to ChairScholars Foundation, Odessa, FL.
$5,000 to A Gift for Teaching, Orlando, FL.
$5,000 to Florida Humanities Council, Saint Petersburg, FL.
$5,000 to More Health, Tampa, FL.
$3,700 to Tampa Bay History Center, Tampa, FL.

2220
Scaife Family Foundation ▼ ✧

West Tower, Ste. 903
777 So. Flagler Dr.
West Palm Beach, FL   33401   (561) 659-1188
Contact: Barbara M. Sloan, Exec. Dir.
URL: http://www.scaifefamily.org

Established in 1983 in PA.
Donor: Sarah Mellon Scaife†.
Foundation type: Independent foundation.
Financial data (yr. ended 12/31/05): Assets, $84,016,540 (M); expenditures, $5,097,502; qualifying distributions, $4,806,033; giving activities include $4,406,377 for 73 grants (high: $1,200,000; low: $2,000; average: $10,000–$125,000).
Purpose and activities: Grants to support and develop programs that strengthen families, address issues surrounding the health and welfare of women and children, promote animal welfare, and that demonstrate the beneficial interaction between humans and animals; Support also for conservation, and early intervention and prevention efforts in the area of drug and alcohol addiction.
Fields of interest: Animal welfare; Health care; Substance abuse, prevention.
Type of support: General/operating support; Program development.
Limitations: Giving on a national basis. No grants to individuals; no loans.
Publications: Annual report; Grants list.
Application information: Application form not required.
   Initial approach: Letter
   Copies of proposal: 1
   Deadline(s): Grant applications are normally considered quarterly; no set deadline
   Board meeting date(s): Quarterly
   Final notification: Following board meetings
Officers and Trustees:* Jennie K. Scaife,* Chair.; Barbara M. Sloan, Pres., Secy.-Treas., and Exec. Dir.; Beth H. Genter,* V.P.; Mary T. Walton,* V.P.
Number of staff: 1 full-time professional; 1 full-time support.
EIN: 251427015
Selected grants: The following grants were reported in 2004.
$300,000 to Children of Alcoholics Foundation, New York, NY. For program support.

$250,000 to Edvocacy Research Corporation, Concord, MA. For program support.

$200,000 to Allegheny Council to Improve Our Neighborhoods (ACTION)-Housing, Pittsburgh, PA. For Development Fund.

$150,000 to Richard J. Caron Foundation, Wernersville, PA. 2 grants: $100,000 (For Campaign for Recovery), $50,000 (For Medical Student Program in Alcohol and Other Drug Dependencies).

$125,000 to All Creatures Sanctuary, Palm Beach Gardens, FL. For operating support.

$100,000 to Allegheny Cemetery Historical Association, Pittsburgh, PA. For capital support.

$100,000 to Puppies Behind Bars, New York, NY. For program support.

$62,437 to Saint Lukes-Roosevelt Hospital Center, New York, NY. For Crime Victims Treatment Center.

$30,000 to Assistance Dogs of America, Swanton, OH. For program support.

2221
The John F. Scarpa Foundation ◇
c/o John F. Scarpa
1676 S. Ocean Blvd.
Palm Beach, FL   33480-5117

Established in 1997 in FL.
Donor: John F. Scarpa.
Foundation type: Independent foundation.
Financial data (yr. ended 12/31/04): Assets, $4,523,824 (M); expenditures, $1,581,831; qualifying distributions, $1,552,379; giving activities include $1,552,379 for 45 grants (high: $1,000,000; low: $250).
Fields of interest: Higher education; Education; Health organizations, association; Cystic fibrosis research; Human services; Children/youth, services; Residential/custodial care, hospices; Foundations (community); Federated giving programs; Roman Catholic agencies & churches.
Limitations: Applications not accepted. Giving on a national basis, with emphasis on NJ, FL, and CA.
Application information: Contributes only to pre-selected organizations.
Officers and Directors:* John F. Scarpa,* Pres.; Michael P. Haney, Secy.; Michael B. Azeez,* Treas.
EIN: 232939489
Selected grants: The following grants were reported in 2004.
$1,000,000 to Villanova University, School of Law, Villanova, PA.
$150,000 to South Jersey Healthcare Foundation, Vineland, NJ.
$60,000 to United Way of Palm Beach County, Boynton Beach, FL. 2 grants: $50,000, $10,000
$25,000 to Police Athletic League, New York, NY.
$15,000 to Palm Beach Fellowship of Christians and Jews, Palm Beach, FL.
$15,000 to Prostate Cancer Foundation, Santa Monica, CA.
$10,000 to Community Chest-United Way of Palm Beach, Palm Beach, FL.
$10,000 to Easter Seal Society, West Palm Beach, FL.
$10,000 to Rosarian Academy, West Palm Beach, FL. For capital campaign.

2222
Rowland & Sylvia Schaefer Family Foundation, Inc. ◇
P.O. Box 9312
Miami, FL   33014-9861   (954) 433-3900
Contact: Rowland Schaefer, Pres.

Established in 1996 in FL.
Donor: Rowland Schaefer.
Foundation type: Independent foundation.
Financial data (yr. ended 8/31/06): Assets, $10,248,623 (M); expenditures, $707,856; qualifying distributions, $660,100; giving activities include $660,100 for grants.
Fields of interest: Arts; Elementary/secondary education; Hospitals (general); Health care; Health organizations, association; Diabetes research; Human services; Jewish agencies & temples.
Limitations: Giving primarily in Miami, FL, and New York, NY.
Application information: Application form not required.
Deadline(s): None
Officer and Directors:* Rowland Schaefer,* Pres.; Eileen Bonnie Schaefer; Sylvia Schaefer; Roberta Schaefer Waller; Marla Schaefer Weishoff.
EIN: 650757807
Selected grants: The following grants were reported in 2003.
$175,000 to Mount Sinai Medical Center, Miami Beach, FL. 3 grants: $50,000 to Wein Center, $25,000 to Wein Center, $100,000 to Wein Center
$75,000 to Concert Association of Florida, Miami Beach, FL. 2 grants: $25,000, $50,000
$25,000 to American Friends of Beit Issie Shapiro, New York, NY.
$25,000 to Aventura Turnberry Jewish Center Beth Jacob, Miami, FL.
$20,000 to Central Synagogue, New York, NY.
$20,000 to New York University Medical Center, New York, NY.
$10,000 to National Ovarian Cancer Coalition, Boca Raton, FL.

2223
The Scharlin Family Foundation, Inc. ◇
1111 Brickell Ave., Ste. 2920
Miami, FL   33130   (305) 358-4333
Contact: Gloria Scharlin, Pres.

Established in 2000 in FL.
Donors: Gloria G. Scharlin; Howard R. Scharlin†.
Foundation type: Independent foundation.
Financial data (yr. ended 11/30/05): Assets, $756,110 (M); gifts received, $100,000; expenditures, $871,556; qualifying distributions, $871,139; giving activities include $871,139 for 46 grants (high: $486,023; low: $25).
Purpose and activities: Giving primarily for the arts and education.
Fields of interest: Arts; Education; Human services; Jewish agencies & temples.
Limitations: Giving primarily in Aspen, CO, and Miami, FL.
Application information:
Initial approach: Letter
Officers: Gloria Scharlin, Pres.; Peggy Ann Scharlin, V.P.; David Michael Scharlin, Secy.; Kerri Sue Scharlin, Treas.
EIN: 651063194

Selected grants: The following grants were reported in 2005.
$42,000 to I Have A Dream Foundation, New York, NY.
$15,086 to Music Associates of Aspen, Aspen, CO.
$15,000 to Coconut Grove Playhouse State Theater of Florida Corporation, Miami, FL.
$5,000 to Spence School, New York, NY.
$3,000 to Theater for a New Audience, New York, NY.
$600 to Anderson Ranch Arts Center, Snowmass Village, CO.
$250 to Lowe Art Museum, Coral Gables, FL.

2224
J. W. Schippmann Foundation ◇ ☆
1515 Riverside Ave., Ste. A
Jacksonville, FL   32204

Established in FL.
Donor: Bernice S. Crawley.
Foundation type: Independent foundation.
Financial data (yr. ended 12/31/04): Assets, $1,155,034 (M); gifts received, $310,383; expenditures, $343,413; qualifying distributions, $343,413; giving activities include $340,383 for 16 grants.
Fields of interest: Health organizations; Salvation Army.
Limitations: Applications not accepted. Giving primarily in FL. No grants to individuals.
Application information: Contributes only to pre-selected organizations.
Officers and Directors:* William R. Frazier,* Pres.; W. Rob Frazier,* V.P.; J.C. Schmidt,* V.P.
EIN: 591004904
Selected grants: The following grants were reported in 2005.
$10,000 to City Rescue Mission, Jacksonville, FL.
$10,000 to Salvation Army, Saint Petersburg, FL.
$5,000 to Episcopal High School, Jacksonville, FL.
$4,000 to YMCA, FL.
$2,500 to University of North Florida, Jacksonville, FL.

2225
Schmidt Family Foundation ◇
399 N.W. Boca Raton Blvd.
Boca Raton, FL   33432
Contact: Maria Levix

Established in 1982 in FL.
Donor: Charles E. Schmidt†.
Foundation type: Independent foundation.
Financial data (yr. ended 12/31/05): Assets, $43,671,967 (M); expenditures, $2,490,573; qualifying distributions, $2,353,566; giving activities include $2,198,568 for 45 grants (high: $565,568; low: $2,500).
Purpose and activities: Giving primarily for educational programs in south FL.
Fields of interest: Education.
Type of support: General/operating support; Scholarship funds; Matching/challenge support.
Limitations: Giving primarily in southern FL. No grants to individuals.
Application information: Application form not required.
Initial approach: Letter
Copies of proposal: 1

Deadline(s): None
Board meeting date(s): Apr., Sept., and Jan.
Trustees: Barbara M. Schmidt; Catherine B. Schmidt; Richard L. Schmidt; Raymond Webb; JPMorgan Chase Bank, N.A.
Number of staff: 1 part-time professional.
EIN: 136808881
Selected grants: The following grants were reported in 2004.
$500,000 to Community Television Foundation of South Florida, Miami, FL.
$200,000 to University of Chicago, Chicago, IL.
$25,000 to Chris Evert Charities, Boca Raton, FL.
$25,000 to Florence Fuller Child Development Center, Boca Raton, FL.
$25,000 to Lynn University, Boca Raton, FL.
$10,000 to Boca Raton Historical Society, Boca Raton, FL.
$10,000 to Make-A-Wish Foundation, Maitland, FL.
$5,000 to Boca Helping Hands, Boca Raton, FL.
$5,000 to Kind Program, Boca Raton, FL.
$2,500 to Christians Reaching Out To Society, West Palm Beach, FL.

2226
Schoen Foundation ✧
5801 Pelican Bay Blvd., Ste. 502
Naples, FL 34108 (239) 598-2900
Contact: Jodi Bailey

Established in 1993 in FL.
Donors: Sharon A. Schoen; William J. Schoen.
Foundation type: Independent foundation.
Financial data (yr. ended 12/31/05): Assets, $24,613,955 (M); expenditures, $2,105,258; qualifying distributions, $2,030,666; giving activities include $2,026,636 for 35 grants (high: $1,031,200; low: $100).
Fields of interest: Arts; Elementary/secondary education; Education; Christian agencies & churches; Protestant agencies & churches.
Application information: Application form not required.
Deadline(s): Sept. 30
Trustees: Joe B. Cox; Alan Hilfiker; Kristine L. Pollard; Kathryn L. Schoen; Sharon A. Schoen; William J. Schoen; Karen A. Sutton.
EIN: 650379356

2227
The Schoenbaum Family Foundation, Inc. ✧
P.O. Box 580
Sarasota, FL 34230-0580
Contact: Raydel R. Walston, Exec. Asst. to Pres.

Established in 1988 in FL.
Donor: Alex Schoenbaum‡.
Foundation type: Independent foundation.
Financial data (yr. ended 12/31/04): Assets, $23,931,794 (L); expenditures, $1,318,415; qualifying distributions, $1,208,685; giving activities include $1,197,468 for 81 grants (high: $200,000; low: $750).
Purpose and activities: Grants for health, education and welfare.
Fields of interest: Human services; Jewish federated giving programs.
Type of support: Program development; Scholarship funds.

Limitations: Applications not accepted. Giving on a national basis, with emphasis on FL and WV.
Application information:
Board meeting date(s): Varies
Officers and Trustees:* Betty Frank Schoenbaum,* Pres. and Secy.-Treas.; Joann Schoenbaum Miller,* V.P.; Emily Schoenbaum,* V.P.; Jeffry F. Schoenbaum,* V.P.; Raymond D. Schoenbaum,* V.P.
Number of staff: 1 part-time support.
EIN: 650043921
Selected grants: The following grants were reported in 2004.
$200,000 to Ohio State University Foundation, Columbus, OH.
$35,000 to Womens Health Center of West Virginia, Charleston, WV.
$17,500 to Pinellas County Education Foundation, Largo, FL.
$15,000 to Mountaineer Food Bank, Gassaway, WV.
$15,000 to YMCA of Kanawha Valley, Charleston, WV.
$10,000 to Bread for the City, DC.
$7,500 to Direct Action Welfare Group, Charleston, WV.
$7,000 to Marys Center for Maternal and Child Care, DC.
$5,000 to Atlanta Community Food Bank, Atlanta, GA.
$5,000 to Covenant House, Charleston, WV.

2228
Schumann Foundation, Inc. ✧
c/o Harry C. Offutt, Treas.
3003 Cardinal Dr., Ste. C
Vero Beach, FL 32963

Established in 1992 in FL.
Donor: Ruth D. Schumann.
Foundation type: Independent foundation.
Financial data (yr. ended 9/30/05): Assets, $1,407,773 (M); expenditures, $797,912; qualifying distributions, $795,217; giving activities include $789,025 for 39 grants (high: $120,000; low: $1,000).
Fields of interest: Historical activities; Education; Human services; Children/youth, services; Space/aviation.
Limitations: Applications not accepted. Giving primarily in Vero Beach, FL. No grants to individuals.
Application information: Contributes only to pre-selected organizations.
Officers and Directors:* John J. Schumann, Jr.,* Pres.; Katherine G. Schumann,* V.P.; Byron T. Cooksey,* Secy.; Harry C. Offutt III,* Treas.; Mark K. Schumann.
EIN: 650298172
Selected grants: The following grants were reported in 2005.
$100,000 to Environmental Learning Center, Vero Beach, FL.
$100,000 to Habitat for Humanity of Indian River County, Vero Beach, FL.
$50,000 to Humane Society.
$12,000 to Indian River Community College Foundation, Fort Pierce, FL.
$10,000 to American Red Cross, Vero Beach, FL.
$5,000 to Association for Retarded Citizens of Indian River County, Vero Beach, FL.
$5,000 to Eckerd College, Saint Petersburg, FL.
$5,000 to Education Foundation of Indian River County, Vero Beach, FL.

$3,000 to Wheelchair Foundation, Danville, CA.
$1,000 to Ronald Reagan Presidential Foundation, Simi Valley, CA.

2229
The Seaman Family Foundation, Inc. ✧
11540 Highway 92 E.
Seffner, FL 33584 (813) 623-5400
Contact: Lewis Stein, Treas.

Established in 1999 in FL.
Donor: Jeffrey Seaman.
Foundation type: Independent foundation.
Financial data (yr. ended 12/31/04): Assets, $2,517,069 (M); gifts received, $1,500,000; expenditures, $1,387,499; qualifying distributions, $1,386,190; giving activities include $1,385,000 for 7 grants (high: $600,000; low: $10,000).
Fields of interest: Higher education, university; Jewish federated giving programs; Jewish agencies & temples.
Limitations: Giving primarily in FL, GA, and PA.
Officers and Directors:* Jeffrey Seaman, Pres.; Julie Seaman,* Secy.; Lewis Stein,* Treas.
EIN: 593631102
Selected grants: The following grants were reported in 2004.
$600,000 to Jewish Federation of Greater Atlanta, Atlanta, GA.
$500,000 to Piedmont Hospital Foundation, Atlanta, GA.
$75,000 to Emory University, Atlanta, GA.
$10,000 to Pace Academy, Atlanta, GA.

2230
William G. Selby and Marie Selby Foundation ✧
1800 2nd St., Ste. 750
Sarasota, FL 34236 (941) 957-0442
Contact: Debra M. Jacobs, Pres.
FAX: (941) 957-3135; URL: http:// www.selbyfdn.org/selby.html

Trust established in 1955 in FL.
Donors: William G. Selby†; Marie Selby†.
Foundation type: Independent foundation.
Financial data (yr. ended 5/31/05): Assets, $71,198,434 (M); expenditures, $4,668,051; qualifying distributions, $4,218,011; giving activities include $3,388,616 for 66 grants (high: $250,000; low: $1,000), and $454,000 for grants to individuals.
Purpose and activities: The foundation seeks to make grants that will improve the quality of life in Sarasota County, FL, and its bordering counties. Scholarships are given annually to students from the local area for undergraduate study.
Fields of interest: Visual arts; Performing arts; Historic preservation/historical societies; Arts; Child development, education; Elementary school/education; Secondary school/education; Higher education; Education; Housing/shelter, development; Recreation, parks/playgrounds; Human services; Youth, services; Child development, services; Aging, centers/services; Community development; Physical/earth sciences; Aging.
Type of support: Capital campaigns; Building/renovation; Equipment; Land acquisition; Scholarships—to individuals.

Limitations: Giving limited to Charlotte, DeSoto, Manatee, and Sarasota counties, FL. No support for private K-12 schools, public schools, or childcare facilities. No grants to individuals (except through Selby Scholars Program), or for debt reduction, annual campaigns, deficit financing, operating budgets, endowment funds, surveys, program advertising, research, seminars, workshops, travel, fundraising, or conferences; no loans.

Publications: Informational brochure (including application guidelines).

Application information: Application must be submitted using the foundation's guidelines. No applications for amounts under $10,000. Application form for Selby Scholars available on foundation Web site. Application form required.

Initial approach: Letter
Copies of proposal: 10
Deadline(s): Feb. 1 and Aug. 1 for grants; Apr. 1 for Selby Scholars Program; Dec. 1 for Innovative Partnership program
Board meeting date(s): Apr. and Nov.
Final notification: May 15 and Dec. 15

Officer: Debra M. Jacobs, C.E.O. and Pres.
Trustee: Wachovia Bank, N.A.
Number of staff: 1 full-time professional; 2 full-time support.
EIN: 596121242
Selected grants: The following grants were reported in 2003.

$1,600,000 to John and Mable Ringling Museum of Art Foundation, Sarasota, FL.

$716,777 to YMCA, Sarasota Family, Sarasota, FL.

$300,000 to Southeastern Guide Dogs, Palmetto, FL.

$158,740 to Florida Studio Theater, Sarasota, FL.

$100,500 to Education Foundation for Sarasota County, Sarasota, FL.

$80,719 to Sarasota Opera Association, Sarasota, FL.

$65,000 to Childrens Haven and Adult Community Services, Sarasota, FL.

$50,000 to Florida West Coast Public Broadcasting, Tampa, FL.

$50,000 to Longboat Key Art Center, Sarasota, FL.

$45,000 to Cultural Center of Charlotte County, Port Charlotte, FL.

2231

Seneff Family Foundation, Inc. ✧

P.O. Box 4920
Orlando, FL 32802-4920 (407) 650-1000
Contact: Mark Amerman

Established in 1999 in FL.
Donors: James M. Seneff; CNL Financial Group, Inc.
Foundation type: Independent foundation.
Financial data (yr. ended 12/31/04): Assets, $259,948 (M); gifts received, $2,815,700; expenditures, $2,565,872; qualifying distributions, $2,565,856; giving activities include $2,509,050 for 14 grants (high: $1,000,000; low: $5,000).
Purpose and activities: Giving primarily to churches and to religious schools which offer secondary and higher education.
Fields of interest: Education; Christian agencies & churches; Protestant agencies & churches.
Limitations: Giving primarily in FL and GA.
Application information: Application form required.
Initial approach: Letter
Deadline(s): None

Officers: Dayle L. Seneff, Chair.; James M. Seneff, Jr., Vice-Chair.; Timothy J. Seneff, Pres.; Rebecca L. Sandberg, Secy.-Treas.
EIN: 593613338
Selected grants: The following grants were reported in 2003.

$1,000,000 to Foundation for Reformation, Orlando, FL.

$100,000 to Reformed Theological Seminary, Maitland, FL.

$40,000 to Trinity Forum, Orlando, FL.

$26,000 to Asian Access Life Ministries, San Dimas, CA.

$25,000 to Prison Fellowship Ministries, Lansdowne, VA.

$20,000 to Harbor Presbyterian Church, San Diego, CA.

$20,000 to In Medias Res Educational Foundation, Ivy, VA.

$18,200 to Haggai Institute for Advanced Leadership Training, Atlanta, GA. For evangelistic training.

$10,000 to Crown Financial Ministries, Gainesville, GA.

$10,000 to Mission to North America, Atlanta, GA.

2232

Margaret F. Shackelford Charitable Trust ✧

P.O. Box 1908
Orlando, FL 32802-1908
Contact: Paul A. Calame, Jr.
Application address: 326 S. Goodlett St., Memphis, TN 38117, tel.: (901) 458-6654

Established in 1999 in TN.
Foundation type: Independent foundation.
Financial data (yr. ended 12/31/05): Assets, $9,807,028 (M); expenditures, $667,203; qualifying distributions, $618,446; giving activities include $570,205 for grants (high: $381,727; low: $54,855).
Purpose and activities: Giving primarily for natural resource and wildlife conservation and protection, with particular interest in hardwood trees, (reforestation and management).
Fields of interest: Environment, natural resources; Animals/wildlife, preservation/protection.
Limitations: Giving primarily in MS. No grants to individuals.
Application information: Application form not required.
Initial approach: Letter
Copies of proposal: 3
Deadline(s): None
Board meeting date(s): Quarterly
Trustee: SunTrust Bank.
EIN: 626363101

2233

Sherman Family Foundation ✧

(formerly The Betsy R. and George M. Sherman Private Foundation)
7292 Fisher Island Dr.
Miami Beach, FL 33109

Established in 1994 in MD.
Donor: George M. Sherman.
Foundation type: Independent foundation.
Financial data (yr. ended 12/31/03): Assets, $23,094,264 (M); expenditures, $1,096,097;

qualifying distributions, $799,078; giving activities include $799,078 for 28 grants (high: $300,000; low: $23).
Purpose and activities: Giving primarily for the arts, including an art museum, and a center which offers youth education through media arts; funding also for family services, higher education, health associations, including a medical foundation, social services, and federated giving programs.
Fields of interest: Arts education; Media/ communications; Media, radio; Museums (art); Arts; Higher education; Health organizations, association; Crime/law enforcement, police agencies; Human services; Family services; Federated giving programs.
Type of support: General/operating support.
Limitations: Applications not accepted. Giving primarily in Miami, FL, and Baltimore, MD. No grants to individuals.
Application information: Contributes only to pre-selected organizations.
Trustee: George M. Sherman.
EIN: 526723302
Selected grants: The following grants were reported in 2004.

$210,000 to University of Maryland-Baltimore Foundation, Baltimore, MD.

$140,000 to Walters Art Museum, Baltimore, MD.

$125,000 to United Way of Miami-Dade, Miami, FL.

$43,000 to Family Tree, Baltimore, MD.

$20,000 to YMCA, Sussex Family, Rehoboth Beach, DE.

$15,000 to Center Stage Associates, Baltimore, MD.

$10,000 to Johns Hopkins University, Baltimore, MD.

$8,500 to Florence Crittenton Services of Baltimore, Baltimore, MD.

$5,000 to Maryland Food Bank, Baltimore, MD.

$5,000 to National Aquarium in Baltimore, Baltimore, MD.

2234

Barry & Judy Silverman Foundation, Inc. ✧

(formerly Silverman Family Foundation, Inc.)
2801 N.E. 208th Terr., Ste. 102
Aventura, FL 33180
Contact: Ronni Silverman Bianco, Treas.

Established in 1995.
Donors: Barry Silverman; Judy Silverman.
Foundation type: Independent foundation.
Financial data (yr. ended 9/30/05): Assets, $5,784,112 (M); expenditures, $781,166; qualifying distributions, $709,257; giving activities include $676,762 for 54 grants (high: $201,667; low: $25).
Purpose and activities: Funding primarily for Jewish agencies and federated giving programs. Some funding also for higher education and human services.
Fields of interest: Higher education; Human services; Jewish federated giving programs; Jewish agencies & temples.
Type of support: Continuing support; Annual campaigns; Capital campaigns; Building/ renovation; Equipment; Emergency funds; Research; Matching/challenge support.
Limitations: Applications not accepted. Giving primarily in southern FL.
Application information: Unsolicited requests for funds not accepted.
Board meeting date(s): Varies

Officers: Barry J. Silverman, Chair. and Pres.; Paul Bianco, V.P.; Laurie Karen Silverman, V.P.; Judy Silverman, Secy.; Ronni Silverman Bianco, Treas.
Number of staff: 1 full-time professional.
EIN: 650526279
Selected grants: The following grants were reported in 2005.
$81,000 to Nova Southeastern University, Fort Lauderdale, FL.
$50,000 to Jewish Federation of Greater Baton Rouge, Baton Rouge, LA.
$25,000 to Hebrew College, Newton Centre, MA.
$11,800 to Hillel: The Foundation for Jewish Campus Life, DC.
$11,075 to University of Pennsylvania, Philadelphia, PA.
$6,600 to Victory School, Aventura, FL.
$1,000 to Hillel Community Day School, North Miami Beach, FL.

2235
The Sidney, Milton and Leoma Simon Foundation-Florida ✧
101 Plz. Real S., Ste. 405
Boca Raton, FL 33432 (561) 241-9298
Contact: Joseph Warner, Tr.

Donor: Sidney, Milton & Leoma Simon Foundation.
Foundation type: Independent foundation.
Financial data (yr. ended 5/31/05): Assets, $17,073,166 (M); expenditures, $1,010,219; qualifying distributions, $824,510; giving activities include $650,000 for 64 grants (high: $15,000; low: $3,000).
Purpose and activities: Giving primarily for hospitals and health associations, including services for people who are blind; funding also for the arts, and Jewish organizations.
Fields of interest: Museums (art); Performing arts centers; Arts; Hospitals (general); Health organizations; Human services; Jewish agencies & temples.
Limitations: Giving primarily in NY.
Application information:
Initial approach: Letter on organization's letterhead
Deadline(s): None
Trustees: Burt Bergenfield; Joseph Warner; Meryll Warner.
EIN: 656282105
Selected grants: The following grants were reported in 2005.
$15,000 to Alzheimers Association and Related Disease Disorders Assoc.
$14,000 to American Foundation for the Blind, New York, NY.
$12,000 to Broward Performing Arts Foundation, Fort Lauderdale, FL.
$12,000 to Kennedy Krieger Institute, Baltimore, MD.
$12,000 to New York Public Library, New York, NY.
$12,000 to Saint Vincents Services, Brooklyn, NY.
$12,000 to United Cerebral Palsy, DC.
$11,000 to Boys Club of New York, New York, NY.
$11,000 to Saint Lukes-Roosevelt Hospital Center, New York, NY.
$10,000 to Lincoln Center Theater, New York, NY.

2236
The Six Pillar Foundation, Inc.
P.O. Box 6
Melbourne, FL 32902-0006

Established in 1999 in FL.
Donor: James W. Toy.
Foundation type: Independent foundation.
Financial data (yr. ended 10/31/05): Assets, $14,731,938 (M); expenditures, $697,264; qualifying distributions, $667,654; giving activities include $663,107 for 16 grants (high: $100,000; low: $3,000).
Purpose and activities: Giving primarily for children and family activities offering Christian spiritual content; funding also for the construction and renovation of educational and human service buildings, and the rehabilitation of teen drug addicts.
Fields of interest: Education; Substance abuse, treatment; Boys & girls clubs; Youth, services.
Limitations: Giving primarily in central FL, particularly Brevard County.
Application information: Formal application will be furnished after initial screening. Application form required.
Initial approach: Proposal (5 pages or less)
Deadline(s): None
Officers and Directors:* James W. Toy, Pres. and Treas.; Clare C. Toy,* V.P. and Secy.; Brian D. Toy; Steven C. Toy.
EIN: 593573979

2237
The Gertrude E. Skelly Charitable Foundation
4600 N. Ocean Blvd., Ste. 206
Boynton Beach, FL 33435-7365
(561) 276-1008
Contact: Erik Edward Joh, Tr.
E-mail: skelly@erikjoh.com

Established in 1991 in FL.
Donor: Gertrude E. Skelly†.
Foundation type: Independent foundation.
Financial data (yr. ended 12/31/05): Assets, $19,021,078 (M); expenditures, $1,520,679; qualifying distributions, $1,373,290; giving activities include $1,248,700 for 63 grants (high: $50,000; low: $1,000).
Purpose and activities: The foundation's primary mission is to provide educational opportunities, mainly at colleges and universities, and needed medical care for those who are unable to afford them. All grants must affect multiple individuals and meet some educational, medical or emergency need.
Fields of interest: Scholarships/financial aid; Education; Hospitals (general).
Type of support: Emergency funds; Fellowships; Internship funds; Scholarship funds; Research; Matching/challenge support.
Limitations: Giving on a national basis. No grants to individuals.
Publications: Application guidelines.
Application information: 7 copies of current board members and 2 copies of exemption letter and financial statements. Application form not required.
Initial approach: Letter
Copies of proposal: 7
Deadline(s): July 31

Board meeting date(s): Oct.
Final notification: Oct.
Trustees: Erik Edward Joh; SunTrust Bank.
Number of staff: 1 part-time professional; 1 part-time support.
EIN: 656085406
Selected grants: The following grants were reported in 2005.
$1,005,000 to South Florida Science Museum, West Palm Beach, FL. 2 grants: $5,000, $1,000,000
$80,000 to Florida International University, Miami, FL. 2 grants: $40,000 each
$30,000 to University of North Dakota Foundation, Grand Forks, ND.
$25,000 to American Red Cross, National Headquarters, DC.
$25,000 to Broward Community College Foundation, Fort Lauderdale, FL.
$25,000 to Polk Community College Foundation, Winter Haven, FL.
$20,000 to Childrens Aid and Family Services, Paramus, NJ.
$10,000 to Brookwood Community, Brookshire, TX.

2238
Buckingham Smith Benevolent Association ✧
17 Pacific St., Ste. A
St. Augustine, FL 32084-2753

Established in 1873 in FL.
Foundation type: Independent foundation.
Financial data (yr. ended 12/31/05): Assets, $7,145,857 (M); expenditures, $439,661; qualifying distributions, $368,236; giving activities include $361,718 for 11 grants (high: $99,939; low: $3,750; average: $15,000–$55,000).
Purpose and activities: Giving limited to organizations aiding indigent African Americans of St. Augustine, FL; aid includes medical care, emergency food, and utilities.
Fields of interest: Education; Housing/shelter, repairs; Human services; Children/youth, services; Family services, domestic violence; Residential/custodial care; Minorities/immigrants, centers/services; Christian agencies & churches; African Americans/Blacks.
Type of support: Scholarship funds; Continuing support.
Limitations: Applications not accepted. Giving limited to St. Augustine, FL.
Application information: Unsolicited requests for funds not accepted.
Board meeting date(s): Quarterly
Officers and Trustees:* Reuben J. Plant,* Pres.; Darrell Poli,* V.P.; Bradley K. Davis,* Secy.-Treas.; Joseph L. Boles, Jr.; Lauren Brown; Otis Mason; Michael Sanders.
Number of staff: 1 part-time professional.
EIN: 596137514
Selected grants: The following grants were reported in 2005.
$42,137 to Saint Joseph Academy, Saint Augustine, FL. 2 grants: $35,065, $7,072
$23,542 to Saint Johns County Council on Aging, Saint Augustine, FL.
$15,000 to Safety Shelter of Saint Johns County, Saint Augustine, FL.
$3,750 to Flagler College, Saint Augustine, FL.

2239
Sontag Foundation, Inc. ✧
822 A1A North, Ste. 300
Ponte Vedra Beach, FL 32082
E-mail: kverble@sontagfoundation.com;
URL: http://www.sontagfoundation.com

Established in 2000 in FL.
Donor: Frederick B. Sontag.
Foundation type: Independent foundation.
Financial data (yr. ended 12/31/04): Assets,
$60,323,983 (M); expenditures, $5,855,881;
qualifying distributions, $5,274,567; giving
activities include $5,135,436 for 10 grants (high:
$4,150,000; low: $37,480).
Purpose and activities: Giving primarily for brain
cancer and brain tumor research, rheumatoid
arthritis research, and grants to support programs
in northeast FL.
Fields of interest: Brain research; Arthritis research;
Human services.
Type of support: General/operating support.
Limitations: Applications not accepted. Giving on a
national basis, with some emphasis on northeast
FL. No grants to individuals.
Application information: See foundation Web site
for the application guidelines and procedures which
must be followed.
Officers and Directors: Frederick B. Sontag,*
Pres.; Cindy L. Sontag Hudgins,* V.P.; Bradley D.
Mottier, V.P.; Daniel M. Ryan, V.P.; Frederick T.
Sontag,* V.P.; Susan T. Sontag,* V.P.; Charles R.
Gregory, Jr.,* Secy.-Treas.; Kay W. Verble, Exec. Dir.
EIN: 593634325

2240
**The Southwest Florida Community
Foundation, Inc.**
8260 College Pkwy., Ste. 101
Fort Myers, FL 33919 (239) 274-5900
Contact: For grants: Carol McLaughlin, Chief Prog.
Off.
FAX: (239) 274-5930;
E-mail: info@floridacommunity.com; URL: http://
www.floridacommunity.com

Incorporated in 1976 in FL.
Donors: Dorothy M. Beall†; Beryl Berry†; Marguerite
Covington†; Herbert E. Hussey†; Isabel
Kirkpatrick†; Leonard Santini†; Earl Riggs†; Mrs.
Earl Riggs†.
Foundation type: Community foundation.
Financial data (yr. ended 6/30/05): Assets,
$45,698,864 (M); gifts received, $5,768,153;
expenditures, $5,069,795; giving activities include
$4,034,657 for 521 grants (high: $100,000; low:
$225), and $397,190 for 165 grants to individuals
(high: $20,000; low: $1,000).
Purpose and activities: The goals of the foundation
are to significantly strengthen the ability of existing
institutions to reach a broader segment of the
community; to provide innovative responses to
community needs which do not unnecessarily
duplicate other efforts; and to create a sense of
community through neighborhood involvement and
outreach. Emphasis also on organizational
capacity-building for area nonprofit organizations.
Fields of interest: Historic preservation/historical
societies; Arts; Higher education; Education;
Environment; Animal welfare; Animals/wildlife;
Health care; Mental health/crisis services; Safety/
disasters; Children/youth, services; Human

services; Community development; Economically
disadvantaged.
Type of support: Management development/
capacity building; Capital campaigns; Building/
renovation; Equipment; Endowments; Emergency
funds; Program development; Scholarship funds;
Consulting services; Scholarships—to individuals;
Matching/challenge support.
Limitations: Giving limited to Charlotte, Collier,
Glades, Hendry and Lee counties, FL. No support for
fraternal organizations, societies, or orders, or
religious organizations for sectarian purposes
(except where designated by a fund donor). No
grants to individuals (except for scholarships), or for
operating budgets, continuing support, start-up
costs, research, annual funds, debt retirement,
professional conferences, sports team travel, class
trips, or fundraising events; no loans.
Publications: Application guidelines; Annual report
(including application guidelines); Financial
statement; Grants list; Informational brochure;
Newsletter; Occasional report; Program policy
statement; Program policy statement (including
application guidelines); Quarterly report.
Application information: Visit foundation Web site
for application form, guidelines and specific
deadlines. Faxed or e-mailed applications are not
accepted. Application form required.
Initial approach: Contact Prog. Off.
Copies of proposal: 3
Deadline(s): Mar. and Sept.
Board meeting date(s): Varies
Final notification: Several days after board
meetings
Officers and Trustees: Chris Gair,* Chair.; Melvin
Morgan,* Vice-Chair.; Paul B. Flynn, C.E.O. and
Pres.; Julia East, V.P.; Donna Kaye,* Secy.-Treas.;
Dale Cable, C.F.O.; Luci Nigro, Cont.; Audrea
Anderson; Gary Aubuchon; Susan Bennett; Frank
Bireley; Jay Brett; Joseph Catti; Robert Da Frota;
Dawn-Marie Driscoll; Guy Emerich; Susan Fersner;
Virginia Fleming; Jane Goble; Francis L. Howington,
M.D.; Charles Idelson; David Lucas; Joe
Mazurkiewicz; James R. Nathan; John Pollock; Will
Prather; Carolyn Rogers; Arnold L. Sarlo; David
Shellenbarger; John W. Sheppard; J. Thomas
Smoot, Jr.; Gene Solomon; J. Thomas Uhler; A. Scott
White.
Number of staff: 5 full-time professional; 1 part-time
professional; 3 full-time support; 1 part-time
support.
EIN: 596580974
Selected grants: The following grants were reported
in 2006.
$100,000 to Harry Chapin Food Bank of Southwest
Florida, Fort Myers, FL.
$100,000 to Southwest Florida Addiction Services,
Fort Myers, FL.
$25,000 to Educational Concerns for Hunger
Organization (ECHO), North Fort Myers, FL.
$20,000 to Agape Home, Moore Haven, FL.
$20,000 to Bonita Springs Lions Club, Bonita
Springs, FL.
$20,000 to Community Cooperative Ministries, Fort
Myers, FL.
$20,000 to Hendry-Glades Mental Health Clinic,
LaBelle, FL.
$16,000 to Down Syndrome Supported Living, Cape
Coral, FL.
$15,000 to Animal Refuge Center, Fort Myers, FL.
$15,000 to Communities Reaching Out, Fort Myers,
FL.

2241
Roy M. Speer Foundation ✧
2535 Success Dr.
Odessa, FL 33556 (727) 372-8808
Contact: Richard W. Baker, Tr.

Established in 1986 in FL.
Donor: Richard W. Baker.
Foundation type: Independent foundation.
Financial data (yr. ended 6/30/05): Assets,
$15,780,103 (M); expenditures, $871,176;
qualifying distributions, $748,891; giving activities
include $748,000 for 6 grants (high: $632,000;
low: $5,000).
Purpose and activities: Giving primarily to a
Christian federated giving program, as well as for
medical education and research, and to a Baptist
church.
Fields of interest: Medical school/education;
Hospitals (general); Cancer research; Religious
federated giving programs; Protestant agencies &
churches.
Limitations: Giving primarily in FL. No grants to
individuals.
Application information:
Initial approach: Letter
Deadline(s): None
Trustee: Richard W. Baker.
EIN: 592785945
Selected grants: The following grants were reported
in 2005.
$632,000 to Practical Christianity Foundation,
Odessa, FL.
$50,000 to University of Florida, Gainesville, FL. 2
grants: $25,000 each to College of Medicine
$36,000 to First Baptist Church, Elfers, FL.
$25,000 to Memorial Sloan-Kettering Cancer
Center, New York, NY.
$5,000 to Salvation Army, Lutz, FL.

2242
The Spurlino Foundation ✧ ☆
4809 Ehrlich Rd., Ste. 203
Tampa, FL 33624
Application address: c/o Cyrus W. Spurlino, 7214 N.
Mobley Rd., Odessa, FL 33556

Established in 1986 in FL.
Donor: Cyrus W. Spurlino.
Foundation type: Independent foundation.
Financial data (yr. ended 12/31/05): Assets,
$10,420,012 (M); gifts received, $4,299,979;
expenditures, $374,061; qualifying distributions,
$374,061; giving activities include $350,000 for 26
grants (high: $25,000; low: $5,000).
Purpose and activities: Giving for children's
services, higher education, and federated giving
programs.
Fields of interest: Higher education, university;
Libraries/library science; Animals/wildlife,
preservation/protection; Health organizations,
association; YM/YWCAs & YM/YWHAs; Children/
youth, services; Federated giving programs.
Limitations: Giving primarily in Tampa, FL. No grants
to individuals.
Application information: Application form not
required.
Deadline(s): None
Trustee: Cyrus W. Spurlino.
EIN: 596875441
Selected grants: The following grants were reported
in 2005.
$25,000 to Reef Ball Foundation, Woodstock, GA.

$25,000 to Smile Train, New York, NY.
$15,000 to Childhood League Center, Columbus, OH.
$12,500 to Canine Companions for Independence, Delaware, OH.
$10,000 to Boys and Girls Clubs of Las Vegas, Las Vegas, NV.
$10,000 to Childrens Cancer Center, Tampa, FL.
$10,000 to Parkinsons Disease Foundation, New York, NY.
$10,000 to Saint Leo University, Saint Leo, FL.
$10,000 to Silver Lining Foundation, Aspen, CO.
$10,000 to Spring of Tampa Bay, Tampa, FL.

2243
Sragowicz Foundation, inc. ✧ ☆
166 Bal Bay Dr.
Bal Harbour, FL   33154-1311

Established in 1994 in FL.
Donor: Leon Sragowicz.
Foundation type: Independent foundation.
Financial data (yr. ended 12/31/05): Assets, $8,715,767 (M); gifts received, $225,000; expenditures, $750,820; qualifying distributions, $748,261; giving activities include $747,481 for 18 grants (high: $483,000).
Purpose and activities: Giving primarily for Jewish organizations and for Jewish education.
Fields of interest: Education; Jewish agencies & temples.
Limitations: Applications not accepted. Giving primarily in FL. No grants to individuals.
Application information: Contributes only to pre-selected organizations.
Officers: Leon Sragowicz, Pres.; Moises Sragowicz, Secy.; Azriel Sragowicz, Treas.
EIN: 650444814

2244
St. Joe Community Foundation, Inc.
(formerly Northwest Florida Improvement Foundation, Inc.)
120 Bechrich Rd., Ste. 225
Panama City Beach, FL   32407   (850) 636-6500
Contact: Jane McNabb, Exec. Dir.
FAX: (850) 636-6501; E-mail: jmcnabb@stjcf.com;
URL: http://www.stjcf.com

Established in 1999 in FL.
Foundation type: Community foundation.
Financial data (yr. ended 12/31/05): Assets, $1,900,523 (M); expenditures, $2,588,134; giving activities include $2,482,199 for 62 grants (high: $500,000; low: $200).
Purpose and activities: The foundation seeks to enrich the quality of life of the people who live, work, and play in northwest FL.
Fields of interest: Arts; Education; Environment; Health care; Human services; Community development.
Type of support: Capital campaigns; Building/renovation; Equipment; Endowments; Professorships; Publication; Seed money; Curriculum development; Fellowships; Scholarship funds; Research.
Limitations: Giving limited to Bay, Calhoun, Franklin, Gadsden, Gulf, Jefferson, Leon, Liberty, Wakulla, Walton counties, FL. No support for sectarian or religious activities. No grants to individuals, or for fundraising events, health initiatives other than

regional health care delivery, or individual sports teams.
Publications: Annual report; Annual report (including application guidelines); Financial statement; Grants list; Informational brochure; Occasional report.
Application information: Visit foundation Web site for application form, application guidelines, and specific deadlines. Application form required.
Initial approach: Complete online application form
Copies of proposal: 1
Deadline(s): Varies
Board meeting date(s): Quarterly
Final notification: Within 4 to 6 months
Officers and Directors:* Lewis Howell,* Pres.; Billy Buzzet,* V.P.; Rod Wilson,* Secy.; Clay Smallwood,* Treas.; Jane McNabb, Exec. Dir.; Chris Corr; Everett Drew; W.M. Britton Greene.
Number of staff: 2 full-time professional.
EIN: 593576402
Selected grants: The following grants were reported in 2004.
$200,000 to Sacred Heart Foundation, Pensacola, FL.
$100,000 to American Heart Association, Saint Petersburg, FL.
$77,950 to Bay Education Foundation, Panama City, FL.
$52,500 to Gulf Coast Community College Foundation, Panama City, FL.
$30,000 to Salvation Army, Saint Petersburg, FL.
$30,000 to Taunton Family Childrens Home, Wewahitchka, FL.
$28,350 to Saint Andrew Bay Center, Lynn Haven, FL.
$25,000 to Covenant Hospice, Panama City, FL.
$17,000 to Muscular Dystrophy Association, Miami, FL.
$15,000 to American Cancer Society, Miami, FL.

2245
St. Petersburg Times Scholarship Fund ✧
(formerly The Poynter Fund)
P.O. Box 1121
St. Petersburg, FL   33731-1121
Application address: c/o Andrew Corty, 490 First Ave. S., St. Petersburg, FL 33701

Incorporated in 1953 in DC.
Donors: Henrietta M. Poynter†; Nelson Poynter†; Congressional Quarterly; Times Publishing Co.
Foundation type: Independent foundation.
Financial data (yr. ended 12/31/03): Assets, $13,511,660 (M); gifts received, $13,023,896; expenditures, $1,017,879; qualifying distributions, $1,013,324; giving activities include $452,293 for grants, and $320,800 for grants to individuals.
Purpose and activities: Scholarships to train, assist, and inspire journalists of all media, with emphasis on print journalism.
Fields of interest: Media/communications; Media, journalism/publishing; Education; Minorities.
Type of support: Fellowships; Scholarship funds; Scholarships—to individuals.
Limitations: Giving limited to FL.
Application information: Application form not required.
Deadline(s): July 1 for scholarships
Board meeting date(s): Jan.
Officers and Trustees:* Andrew E. Barnes,* Pres.; Andrew P. Corty,* Secy.; Michael Carroll,* Treas.; Stephen Buckley; Sebastian Dortch; Marty Petty; David Rapp; Paul Tash; Nancy Waclawek.
EIN: 596142547

2246
Festus and Helen Stacy Foundation, Inc. ✧
5110 N. Federal Hwy., Ste. 100
Fort Lauderdale, FL   33308   (954) 776-3386
Contact: Sharon Bizzell

Established in 1980 in FL.
Donor: Festus Stacy.
Foundation type: Independent foundation.
Financial data (yr. ended 10/31/05): Assets, $89,339,272 (M); gifts received, $609,308; expenditures, $4,887,757; qualifying distributions, $3,689,402; giving activities include $2,730,346 for 40 grants (high: $1,704,000; low: $25).
Purpose and activities: Support of charitable works that are consistent with making a genuine Christian impact benefiting mankind.
Fields of interest: Human services; Christian agencies & churches.
International interests: Africa; Asia; Europe.
Type of support: Seed money; In-kind gifts; Matching/challenge support.
Limitations: Giving on a local, national, and international basis. No grants to individuals, or for endowments; no grants for general operating budgets and/or capital expenditures to churches.
Publications: Application guidelines.
Application information: Application form required.
Initial approach: Letter (no more than 2 pages) or request application
Copies of proposal: 3
Deadline(s): Nov. 1 and Apr. 1
Board meeting date(s): Jan. and June
Officers and Directors:* Douglas A. Stepelton,* Pres.; Virlee Stacy Stepelton,* Secy.-Treas.; Brett Stepelton; Sean Stepelton.
EIN: 311706311
Selected grants: The following grants were reported in 2003.
$250,000 to Salvation Army, Saint Petersburg, FL.
$166,667 to CURE International, Harrisburg, PA.
$120,000 to ELAM Foundation, Fairfax, VA.
$50,000 to Operation Mobilization, Tyrone, GA.
$36,400 to Haggai Institute for Advanced Leadership Training, Atlanta, GA.
$35,300 to Galcom International USA, Tampa, FL.
$30,000 to Joni and Friends, Agoura Hills, CA.
$10,000 to American Tract Society, Garland, TX.
$10,000 to Gathering, The, Tyler, TX.
$5,000 to Champions for Life, Dallas, TX.

2247
The John R. and Inge P. Stafford Foundation ✧
16682 Captiva Dr.
P.O. Box 355
Captiva, FL   33924
Contact: John R. Stafford, Tr.

Established in 1996 in NJ.
Donors: John R. Stafford; Inge P. Stafford.
Foundation type: Independent foundation.
Financial data (yr. ended 6/30/05): Assets, $3,003,715 (M); expenditures, $2,346,954; qualifying distributions, $2,321,125; giving activities include $2,321,125 for 71 grants (high: $2,050,000; low: $50).
Purpose and activities: Giving primarily for higher education.
Fields of interest: Arts; Higher education; Health care.

Limitations: Giving on a national basis. No grants to individuals.
Application information: Application form not required.
Initial approach: Letter
Deadline(s): None
Trustees: Christina Stafford Chaplin; Jennifer Stafford Farrow; Charlotte Stafford; Inge P. Stafford; John R. Stafford; Carolyn Stafford Stein.
EIN: 226710521
Selected grants: The following grants were reported in 2005.
$2,050,000 to Dickinson College, Carlisle, PA.
$20,000 to Cornell University, Ithaca, NY.
$20,000 to Viewpoint Educational Foundation, Calabasas, CA.
$5,000 to Albany College of Pharmacy, Albany, NY.
$5,000 to Clarkson University, Potsdam, NY.
$5,000 to Iowa State University, Ames, IA.
$5,000 to Messiah College, Grantham, PA.
$5,000 to Swarthmore College, Swarthmore, PA.
$5,000 to University of New Hampshire, Durham, NH.
$5,000 to Washington University, Saint Louis, MO.

2248
The Star Family Foundation ☆
(formerly Stanley A. Star Foundation)
400 5th Ave. S., Ste. 201
Naples, FL 34102
Contact: Stanley A. Star, Tr.

Established in 1996 in FL.
Donors: Stanley A. Star; CliffStar Corp.
Foundation type: Independent foundation.
Financial data (yr. ended 12/31/05): Assets, $6,820 (M); gifts received, $321,000; expenditures, $316,044; qualifying distributions, $316,000; giving activities include $316,000 for 3 grants (high: $300,000; low: $6,000).
Purpose and activities: Giving for education, legal education, and medical centers.
Fields of interest: Higher education; Jewish agencies & temples.
Type of support: Scholarship funds.
Application information: Application form not required.
Deadline(s): None
Trustees: Elizabeth A. Star; Richard Star; Stanley A. Star; Elizabeth Star Winer.
EIN: 650712086

2249
Jay Stein Foundation Trust ◇
1200 Riverplace Blvd., 10th Fl.
Jacksonville, FL 32207

Donor: Jay Stein.
Foundation type: Independent foundation.
Financial data (yr. ended 6/30/06): Assets, $26,715,333 (M); expenditures, $1,874,520; qualifying distributions, $1,855,363; giving activities include $1,852,816 for 33 grants (high: $748,040; low: $200).
Purpose and activities: Giving primarily to the arts, and for educational and religious purposes.
Fields of interest: Performing arts, orchestra (symphony); Arts; Education; Jewish federated giving programs; Jewish agencies & temples.

Limitations: Applications not accepted. Giving primarily in FL and NY; some funding nationally. No grants to individuals.
Application information: Contributes only to pre-selected organizations.
Trustee: Jay Stein.
EIN: 311585141
Selected grants: The following grants were reported in 2004.
$78,000 to John F. Kennedy Center for the Performing Arts, DC.
$12,500 to University of North Florida, Jacksonville, FL.
$10,000 to Police Athletic League, Jacksonville, FL.
$10,000 to United Way.
$4,000 to Appeal of Conscience Foundation, New York, NY.
$4,000 to Episcopal High School, Jacksonville, FL.
$1,920 to Congregation Ahavath Chesed, Jacksonville, FL.
$1,200 to Jacksonville Jewish Center, Jacksonville, FL.
$912 to Jewish Community Alliance, Jacksonville, FL.
$200 to Fund for Park Avenue, New York, NY.

2250
Louis & Bessie Stein Foundation ◇
4201 N. Ocean Blvd., Ste. 1606C
Boca Raton, FL 33431-5304
Contact: Ruth Leventhal Nathanson, Pres. and Treas.

Established in 1953 in NJ.
Donors: Louis Stein†; Walter Leventhal; Stanley Merves; Bessie Stein; Stein, Stein & Engel.
Foundation type: Independent foundation.
Financial data (yr. ended 12/31/05): Assets, $28,959,172 (M); expenditures, $1,470,882; qualifying distributions, $1,385,041; giving activities include $1,323,593 for 30 grants (high: $532,183; low: $50).
Fields of interest: Higher education; Cancer; Health organizations; Human services; Jewish federated giving programs; Jewish agencies & temples.
Limitations: Applications not accepted. Giving primarily in NY and PA; funding also in SC. No grants to individuals.
Application information: Contributes only to pre-selected organizations.
Officer: Ruth Leventhal Nathanson, Pres. and Treas.
EIN: 236395253
Selected grants: The following grants were reported in 2003.
$162,500 to American Friends of Israel Elwyn, Philadelphia, PA. For general support.
$144,200 to Hadassah, Philadelphia, PA. For general support.
$101,100 to American Society for Technion-Israel Institute of Technology, Philadelphia, PA. For general support.
$67,198 to Jewish Family and Childrens Service of Greater Philadelphia, Philadelphia, PA. For general support.
$50,000 to Fordham University, School of Law, Bronx, NY. For general support.
$25,000 to Lautenberg Center for General and Tumor Immunology, Jerusalem, Israel. For general support.
$25,000 to Philadelphia Jewish Archives Center, Philadelphia, PA. For general support.
$25,000 to University of Pennsylvania, Philadelphia, PA. For general support.

$20,500 to Sinai Academy of the Berkshires, Pittsfield, MA. For general support.
$10,000 to Israel Guide Dog Center for the Blind, Warrington, PA. For general support.

2251
Ida Mae Stevens Foundation, Inc. ◇
4595 Lexington Ave., Ste.100
Jacksonville, FL 32210-2058 (904) 387-5400
Contact: Douglas J. Milne, Tr.

Established in 1967 in FL.
Donor: Virgil A. Stevens†.
Foundation type: Operating foundation.
Financial data (yr. ended 12/31/03): Assets, $14,770,574 (M); expenditures, $1,414,411; qualifying distributions, $697,891; giving activities include $490,009 for 43+ grants (high: $50,000), and $393,048 for 3 foundation-administered programs.
Purpose and activities: A private operating foundation; giving for programs benefiting the elderly.
Fields of interest: Health care; Health organizations, association; Housing/shelter, development; Aging, centers/services; Aging.
Type of support: General/operating support; Land acquisition; Conferences/seminars; Technical assistance; Program-related investments/loans.
Limitations: Giving limited to Jacksonville, FL.
Publications: Financial statement.
Application information: Application form required.
Initial approach: Written proposal
Copies of proposal: 1
Deadline(s): None
Trustees: G.L. Garnett Ashby; Ben W. Hightower; David Lemmel; Douglas J. Milne.
Number of staff: 2 full-time support; 2 part-time support.
EIN: 591746148
Selected grants: The following grants were reported in 2003.
$50,000 to Jacksonville Community Council, Jacksonville, FL. For program support.
$46,200 to Hospice of Northeast Florida, Jacksonville, FL.
$38,396 to Volunteer Jacksonville, Jacksonville, FL. To encourage and train volunteers to work with elderly service providers.
$23,000 to Episcopal Diocese of Florida, Jacksonville, FL. For program support.
$20,429 to Grove House of Jacksonville, Jacksonville, FL.
$20,000 to Ronald McDonald House of Jacksonville, Jacksonville, FL. For program support.
$14,758 to Womens Center of Jacksonville, Jacksonville, FL. For program support.
$12,000 to PACE Center for Girls of Jacksonville, Jacksonville, FL. To promote elderly interaction between ideas, emphasizing needs of seniors.
$10,000 to YMCA, Floridas First Coast Metropolitan, Jacksonville, FL. For program support.
$5,000 to American Red Cross, Jacksonville, FL. For program support.

2252
George B. Storer Foundation, Inc. ▼ ✧
c/o Thomas R. McDonald
P.O. Box 1040
Tavernier, FL 33070
Contact: Peter Storer, Pres.

Incorporated in 1955 in FL.
Foundation type: Independent foundation.
Financial data (yr. ended 12/31/05): Assets, $87,749,853 (M); expenditures, $4,961,077; qualifying distributions, $4,300,000; giving activities include $4,300,000 for 130 grants (high: $600,000; low: $2,000; average: $10,000–$100,000).
Purpose and activities: Giving primarily for educational, environmental and medical purposes.
Fields of interest: Arts; Higher education; Environment, natural resources; Hospitals (general); Human services; Children/youth, services; Disabilities, people with.
Type of support: General/operating support; Building/renovation; Endowments; Research; Matching/challenge support.
Limitations: Giving primarily in FL. No grants for scholarships or fellowships; no loans.
Publications: Grants list.
Application information: Application form not required.
 Initial approach: Letter and proposal
 Copies of proposal: 1
 Deadline(s): Send proposal between Oct. 15 and Nov. 15
 Board meeting date(s): Dec.
Officers and Directors:* Peter Storer,* Pres. and Treas.; James P. Storer,* Secy.; William Michaels.
EIN: 596136392
Selected grants: The following grants were reported in 2005.
$600,000 to Nature Conservancy, Arlington, VA.
$333,000 to Saratoga Community Building Project.
$235,000 to Dade Community Foundation, Miami, FL.
$100,000 to American Red Cross, National Headquarters, DC. For Tsunami Relief Fund.
$100,000 to College of Wooster, Wooster, OH.
$50,000 to Cleveland Clinic Foundation, Cleveland, OH.
$50,000 to Trout Unlimited, Arlington, VA. For CCF Board Fund.
$50,000 to Wells College, Aurora, NY.
$16,000 to Seeing Eye, Morristown, NJ.
$15,000 to Gates Mills Garden Club, Gates Mills, OH.

2253
Robert J. Stransky Foundation ✧
c/o Norman E. Benz
3475 Shady Run Rd.
Melbourne, FL 32934-8569

Established in 1987 in NY.
Donors: Robert J. Stransky‡; Stransky, Inc.
Foundation type: Independent foundation.
Financial data (yr. ended 6/30/05): Assets, $8,983,289 (M); expenditures, $762,740; qualifying distributions, $662,282; giving activities include $662,282 for 22 grants (high: $176,516; low: $1,000).
Purpose and activities: Giving primarily for education, human services, and Christian agencies and churches.

Fields of interest: Arts; Education; Human services; Christian agencies & churches.
Type of support: General/operating support.
Limitations: Applications not accepted. Giving primarily in Buffalo, NY, and FL; some funding nationally, particularly in AZ. No grants to individuals.
Application information: Contributes only to pre-selected organizations.
Trustees: Norman E. Benz; Michael C. Trimboli.
EIN: 222849600
Selected grants: The following grants were reported in 2004.
$300,000 to Holos Institutes of Health, Fair Grove, MO.
$155,884 to College of the Holy Cross, Worcester, MA.
$65,000 to Arizona State University Foundation, Tempe, AZ.
$20,000 to Saint Lukes Mission of Mercy, Buffalo, NY.
$15,000 to Catholic Relief Services, Baltimore, MD.
$15,000 to Food for the Poor, Deerfield Beach, FL.
$10,000 to Canisius High School, Buffalo, NY.
$10,000 to Harvest House of South Buffalo, Buffalo, NY.
$9,500 to Spiritus Sanctus Academy, Ann Arbor, MI.
$8,500 to Diocese of Montego Bay, Montego Bay, Jamaica. .

2254
David A. Straz, Jr. Foundation ✧
4401 W. Kennedy Blvd., Ste 150
Tampa, FL 33609 (813) 639-0155
Contact: David A. Straz, Jr., Tr.

Established in 1983 in WI.
Donor: David A. Straz, Jr.
Foundation type: Independent foundation.
Financial data (yr. ended 12/31/05): Assets, $38,766,037 (M); gifts received, $1,417,800; expenditures, $2,025,614; qualifying distributions, $1,845,079; giving activities include $1,792,950 for 22 grants (high: $1,010,000; low: $100).
Purpose and activities: Giving for the arts, education, hospitals, and human services.
Fields of interest: Performing arts; Arts; Higher education; Hospitals (general); Human services.
Type of support: Annual campaigns; Capital campaigns; Building/renovation.
Limitations: Giving primarily in Tampa, FL, and Milwaukee, WI.
Application information: Application form not required.
 Initial approach: Proposal
 Deadline(s): None
Trustee: David A. Straz, Jr.
Number of staff: 1 full-time professional.
EIN: 391776211
Selected grants: The following grants were reported in 2004.
$244,400 to Lowry Park Zoological Society of Tampa, Tampa, FL. For annual support.
$213,500 to Marquette University, Milwaukee, WI. For Blue and Gold Fund and for operating support.
$210,000 to Metropolitan Opera, New York, NY. For endowment.
$210,000 to University of Tampa, Tampa, FL. For capital campaign and annual fund.
$15,630 to Tampa General Hospital Foundation, Tampa, FL. For operating support.

$15,000 to Tampa Bay Performing Arts Center, Tampa, FL. For performing arts center annual fund campaign.
$10,000 to ChairScholars Foundation, Odessa, FL. For scholarships.
$10,000 to Metropolitan Ministries, Tampa, FL. For Family Care Center.
$9,950 to Berkeley Preparatory School, Tampa, FL. For annual fund.
$5,000 to Tampa Museum of Art, Tampa, FL. For operating support.

2255
The Harry Sudakoff Foundation, Inc. ✧ ☆
1800 2nd St., Ste. 750
Sarasota, FL 34236-6802 (941) 957-0442
Contact: Debra M. Jacobs
FAX: (941) 957-3135; URL: http://www.selbyfdn.org/Sudakoff_Harry.html

Incorporated in 1956 in NY.
Donors: The Harry and Ruth Sudakoff Trust; Ruth Sudakoff‡; Harry Sudakoff.
Foundation type: Independent foundation.
Financial data (yr. ended 12/31/05): Assets, $6,839,492 (M); expenditures, $445,330; qualifying distributions, $445,330; giving activities include $342,208 for 10 grants (high: $100,000; low: $10,000).
Fields of interest: Higher education; Human services; Federated giving programs.
Limitations: Giving primarily in Sarasota County, FL. No grants to individuals, or for endowments, deficit financing, debt reduction, operating expenses, conferences, seminars, workshops, travel, surveys, advertising, fund raising, research, or for annual campaigns.
Application information:
 Initial approach: Call or see Web site for application guidelines
 Deadline(s): Aug. 15
 Final notification: Nov. 1
Officers: Bertram Axelrad, Pres.; Gary A. Bucholtz, V.P. and Treas.; William T. Harrison, Jr., Secy.
EIN: 650439722
Selected grants: The following grants were reported in 2004.
$50,000 to Habitat for Humanity International.
$45,000 to Sarasota Memorial Healthcare Foundation, Sarasota, FL.
$25,000 to Boy Scouts of America.
$25,000 to Girl Scouts of the U.S.A..
$25,000 to United Way of Sarasota County, Sarasota, FL.
$20,000 to Ringling School of Art and Design, Sarasota, FL.
$10,000 to Childrens Haven and Adult Community Services, Sarasota, FL.
$5,000 to Circus Sarasota, Sarasota, FL.
$5,000 to Naples Public Library, Naples, ME.

2256
Roberta Leventhal Sudakoff Foundation, Inc. ✧
1800 2nd St., Ste. 750
Sarasota, FL 34236 (941) 957-0442
Contact: Debra M. Jacobs
FAX: (941) 957-3135; URL: http://www.selbyfdn.org/sudakoff_Roberta.html

Established in 1997 in FL.

Donor: Roberta L. Sudakoff‡.
Foundation type: Independent foundation.
Financial data (yr. ended 12/31/05): Assets, $20,075,361 (M); gifts received, $283,457; expenditures, $1,263,659; qualifying distributions, $1,263,659; giving activities include $1,004,320 for 23 grants (high: $125,000; low: $7,500).
Fields of interest: Performing arts, theater; Higher education; YM/YWCAs & YM/YWHAs; Community development.
Limitations: Giving primarily in Sarasota County, FL. No grants to individuals, endowments, debt reduction, operating support, conferences/ seminars, annual campaigns, and research.
Application information: See Web site for application guidelines.
  Initial approach: Letter
  Deadline(s): July 1
  Final notification: By Sept. 30
Officers: Gary A. Bucholtz, Pres. and Treas.; Larry Hietbrink, V.P.; William T. Harrison, Jr., Secy.
EIN: 311483381
Selected grants: The following grants were reported in 2004.
$100,000 to Florida Studio Theater, Sarasota, FL. For general support.
$100,000 to Habitat for Humanity, Manasota, Sarasota, FL. For general support.
$100,000 to Sarasota Memorial Healthcare Foundation, Sarasota, FL. For general support.
$75,000 to Mote Marine Laboratory, Sarasota, FL. For general support.
$58,333 to YMCA, Sarasota Family, Sarasota, FL. For general support.
$57,890 to Sarasota Ballet of Florida, Sarasota, FL. For general support.
$55,000 to American Red Cross, Sarasota, FL. For general support.
$50,000 to Girl Scouts of the U.S.A., Gulfcoast Council, Sarasota, FL. For general support.
$46,689 to Girls Inc. of Sarasota, Sarasota, FL. For general support.
$35,650 to Marie Selby Botanical Gardens, Sarasota, FL. For general support.

2257

Tom & Glory Sullivan Foundation, Inc. ◇
905 Ponte Vedra Blvd.
Ponte Vedra Beach, FL 32082-3524

Established in 1994.
Donors: Thomas F.P. Sullivan; Glory L. Sullivan.
Foundation type: Independent foundation.
Financial data (yr. ended 6/30/05): Assets, $5,075,493 (M); gifts received, $222,195; expenditures, $942,699; qualifying distributions, $933,348; giving activities include $933,348 for 26 grants (high: $300,000; low: $167).
Purpose and activities: Giving primarily to Roman Catholic organizations, education and churches.
Fields of interest: Roman Catholic agencies & churches.
Type of support: Building/renovation.
Limitations: Giving on a national and international basis, particularly in the Philippines, Belize, Boliva, and Mexico. No grants to individuals or for endowments.
Publications: Application guidelines.
Application information: Application form required.
  Initial approach: Letter
  Copies of proposal: 1
  Deadline(s): May 1

Officers and Directors:* Thomas F.P. Sullivan,* Pres.; Glory L. Sullivan,* Secy.-Treas.; Rev. William Finch; Kathleen A. Keener; Rev. Mark Knestout; Colleen M. Opack; Thomas F. Sullivan, Jr.
Number of staff: 1 part-time professional.
EIN: 521905859
Selected grants: The following grants were reported in 2003.
$367,184 to Asian Relief, Greenbelt, MD.
$50,000 to Redemptorists-Denver Province, Denver, CO.
$45,000 to Archdiocese of Washington, DC.
$36,005 to Saint Anns Infant and Maternity Home, Hyattsville, MD.
$20,905 to Good Shepherd School for Children, Saint Louis, MO.
$15,000 to Archdiocese of Denver, Denver, CO.
$11,340 to Missionaries of the Poor, Jamaica. .
$10,000 to Franciscan University of Steubenville, Steubenville, OH.
$10,000 to Saint Johns Missions, Saint Louis, MO.
$5,000 to Christ Child Society of Washington, DC, DC.

2258

Sunshine Natural Wellbeing Foundation ◇
(formerly Sunshine Foundation)
6547 Midnight Pass Rd., Ste. 63
Sarasota, FL 34242   (941) 346-5297
Contact: D. Clark Swalm, Jr.

Established in 1996 in FL.
Donors: D. Clarke Swalm; Nicole B. Swalm.
Foundation type: Independent foundation.
Financial data (yr. ended 6/30/05): Assets, $12,000,109 (M); expenditures, $720,796; qualifying distributions, $599,997; giving activities include $585,027 for 1+ grant (high: $585,000).
Purpose and activities: Giving primarily for alternative health, particularly to a therapeutic riding center.
Type of support: Endowments.
Limitations: Giving primarily in FL. No grants to individuals.
Application information:
  Initial approach: Letter form with exemption certificate attached
  Deadline(s): None
  Board meeting date(s): Nov. and Dec.
  Final notification: Dec. 31
Officers: D. Clark Swalm, Jr., Pres. and Treas.; Nicole B. Swalm, V.P. and Secy.
Trustee: Joe Cox.
Number of staff: 1 part-time support.
EIN: 656220389
Selected grants: The following grants were reported in 2003.
$606,000 to Smith Center for Therapeutic Riding, Nokomis, FL.

2259

SunTrust Bank Memphis Foundation ◇
(formerly National Bank of Commerce Foundation Inc.)
P.O. Box 1908
Orlando, FL 32802-1908
Contact: Charles A. Neale
Application address: SunTrust Bank, 850 Ridgelake Blvd., Ste. 101, Memphis, TN 38120, tel.: (901) 415-6463

Established in 2001 in TN.
Donors: National Bank of Commerce; SunTrust Bank.
Foundation type: Company-sponsored foundation.
Financial data (yr. ended 12/31/05): Assets, $560,099 (M); gifts received, $766,932; expenditures, $745,144; qualifying distributions, $742,083; giving activities include $738,222 for 75 grants (high: $150,000; low: $20).
Purpose and activities: The foundation supports organizations involved with arts and culture, education, economic development, and Christianity.
Fields of interest: Museums; Performing arts, orchestra (symphony); Arts; Higher education; Education; Economic development; Federated giving programs; Christian agencies & churches.
Limitations: Giving primarily in TN, with emphasis on Memphis. No grants to individuals.
Application information: Application form not required.
  Initial approach: Proposal
  Deadline(s): None
  Board meeting date(s): Bi-monthly
Officers and Directors:* John Frazer,* Chair.; Keith Turbett, Secy.; Mark Papachristou, Treas.; Bo Allen; Billy Frank; Mary Kim Hamner; Jonathan B. Moore; Tracy Oakley; Jeanie Rittenberry; Ray Skinner.
EIN: 621837568

2260

SWS Charitable Foundation, Inc.
1600 N.W. 163rd St.
Miami, FL 33169
Contact: Robert M. Hersh

Established in 2000 in FL.
Donor: Southern Wine & Spirits of America, Inc.
Foundation type: Company-sponsored foundation.
Financial data (yr. ended 12/31/05): Assets, $4,378,337 (M); gifts received, $256,092; expenditures, $2,554,471; qualifying distributions, $2,552,061; giving activities include $2,549,061 for 350 grants (high: $372,000; low: $100), and $3,000 for 1 grant to an individual.
Purpose and activities: The foundation supports organizations involved with arts and culture, education, health, medical research, and human services.
Fields of interest: Arts; Education; Health care; Medical research; Human services.
Type of support: Employee matching gifts; Emergency funds; General/operating support; Grants to individuals.
Limitations: Applications not accepted. Giving on a national basis, with some emphasis on FL. No grants to individuals (except for employee-related disaster relief grants).
Application information: Contributes only to pre-selected organizations.
Officers: Harvey R. Chaplin, Chair.; Wayne E. Chaplin, Pres.; Steven R. Becker, Exec. V.P. and Treas.; Melvin A. Dick, Sr. V.P.; Lee Hager, Secy.
Director: Paul B. Chaplin.
EIN: 651054944

2261

John H. Sykes Foundation, Inc. ☆
(formerly John H. Sykes Charitable Foundation, Inc.)
c/o Susan Sykes
P.O. Box 2044
Tampa, FL 33601-2044

Established in 1997 in FL.
Donors: John H. Sykes; Susan Sykes.
Foundation type: Independent foundation.
Financial data (yr. ended 8/31/05): Assets, $6,106,225 (M); gifts received, $100,000; expenditures, $390,577; qualifying distributions, $376,476; giving activities include $377,900 for 16 grants (high: $210,500; low: $300).
Purpose and activities: Giving primarily for education and disadvantaged children.
Fields of interest: Museums (children's); Performing arts centers; Education; Hospitals (general); Pediatrics; Human services; YM/YWCAs & YM/YWHAs; Children, services.
Type of support: Equipment; Matching/challenge support.
Limitations: Applications not accepted. Giving primarily in Tampa, FL. No support for religious and political organizations. No grants to individuals.
Application information: Contributes only to pre-selected organizations.
Board meeting date(s): Sept.
Officer and Directors:* Susan W. Sykes,* Pres. and Secy.-Treas.; Kathy S. Stroker; Karen Taylor.
Trustee: SunTrust Bank.
Number of staff: None.
EIN: 656218520
Selected grants: The following grants were reported in 2005.
$210,500 to Tampa General Hospital Foundation, Tampa, FL.
$50,000 to Tampa Bay Performing Arts Center, Tampa, FL.
$26,000 to United Way of Tampa Bay, Tampa, FL.
$25,000 to YMCA.
$21,000 to Florida Orchestra, Tampa, FL.
$5,000 to Judeo Christian Health Clinic, Tampa, FL.
$1,600 to Spring of Tampa Bay, Tampa, FL.

2262
The Taishoff Family Foundation ✧
c/o Kelly
2390 N. Tamiami Trail, No. 204
Naples, FL 34103

Established in 1995.
Foundation type: Independent foundation.
Financial data (yr. ended 12/31/05): Assets, $7,295,947 (M); expenditures, $393,571; qualifying distributions, $376,579; giving activities include $359,586 for 59 grants (high: $50,000; low: $100).
Purpose and activities: Giving primarily for education and help for the needy, and for medical research.
Fields of interest: Education; Medical research, institute; Human services.
Type of support: General/operating support; Continuing support; Annual campaigns; Scholarship funds; Research.
Limitations: Applications not accepted. Giving on a national basis, with emphasis on FL and the greater metropolitan Washington, DC, area, including MD and VA. No grants to individuals.
Application information: Unsolicited requests for funds not accepted.
Trustees: Joel Miller; Lawrence B. Taishoff; Randall P. Taishoff; Robert P. Taishoff.
EIN: 656162787
Selected grants: The following grants were reported in 2005.
$100,000 to Kennedy Krieger Institute, Baltimore, MD. 2 grants: $50,000 each

$9,050 to National Press Foundation, DC.
$5,000 to American Diabetes Association, Alexandria, VA.
$5,000 to Childrens Hospital Foundation, DC.
$5,000 to Hebrew Home of Greater Washington, Rockville, MD.
$2,500 to American Cancer Society, Naples, FL.
$2,500 to American Heart Association, Dallas, TX.
$2,500 to American Heart Association, Bonita Springs, FL.
$1,000 to Santa Fe Childrens Museum, Santa Fe, NM.

2263
Tangelo Park Pilot Program, Inc. ✧
9840 International Dr.
Orlando, FL 32819

Established in 2004 in FL.
Donors: Harris Rosen; The Harris Rosen Foundation, Inc.; Rosen Family Charitable Trust.
Foundation type: Independent foundation.
Financial data (yr. ended 12/31/05): Assets, $66,374 (M); gifts received, $550,000; expenditures, $512,960; qualifying distributions, $512,960; giving activities include $502,141 for grants.
Purpose and activities: Giving to programs that improve the quality of life for residents of Tangelo Park Elementary School, in FL.
Fields of interest: Elementary/secondary education.
Type of support: General/operating support.
Limitations: Applications not accepted. Giving limited to Tangelo Park, FL.
Application information: Contributes only to pre-selected organizations.
Officers and Directors:* Charles Holiday,* Chair.; Robert Allen,* Pres.; Juanita Reed,* Secy.; Malvin Anthon; Samuel Butler; Harris Rosen; John Stover; Eugene Trochinski.
EIN: 593224659

2264
Sol Taplin Charitable Foundation ✧
c/o Barbara Ingalls
8350 N.W. 52nd Terr., Ste. 200
Miami, FL 33166-7708

Established in 1998 in FL.
Donors: Jack G. Taplin; Martin W. Taplin; Sheila Elias Taplin.
Foundation type: Independent foundation.
Financial data (yr. ended 6/30/05): Assets, $8,222,759 (M); expenditures, $469,159; qualifying distributions, $402,506; giving activities include $385,000 for 12 grants (high: $150,000; low: $5,000).
Fields of interest: Museums (art); Theological school/education; Homeless, human services; Federated giving programs; Jewish federated giving programs; Jewish agencies & temples.
Limitations: Giving primarily in FL. No grants to individuals.
Application information:
Initial approach: Letter
Deadline(s): None
Trustees: Aaron S. Podhurst; Jack G. Taplin; Martin W. Taplin; Sheila Elias Taplin.
EIN: 656272903

Selected grants: The following grants were reported in 2005.
$150,000 to Miami Childrens Museum, Miami, FL.
$75,000 to Jewish Federation of Greater Miami, Miami, FL.
$50,000 to Michael-Ann Russell Jewish Community Center, North Miami Beach, FL.
$10,000 to Bass Museum of Art, Miami Beach, FL.
$10,000 to Mount Sinai Medical Center Foundation, Miami Beach, FL.
$5,000 to Operation USA, Los Angeles, CA.

2265
Amy E. Tarrant Foundation, Inc. ✧ ☆
12750 W. Hwy. 40
Ocala, FL 34481
Application address: c/o Ron Roberts, 360 Rt. 201, Ste. 3A, Bedford, NH 03110, tel. (603) 471-9909

Established in 2000 in VT.
Donor: Amy E. Tarrant.
Foundation type: Independent foundation.
Financial data (yr. ended 12/31/05): Assets, $14,427,195 (M); gifts received, $10,283,626; expenditures, $378,445; qualifying distributions, $332,000; giving activities include $332,000 for 28 grants (high: $50,000; low: $2,000).
Purpose and activities: Supports the activities of educational organizations that provide care and assistance for the needy, the indigent and those who cannot help themselves.
Fields of interest: Humanities; Education; Environment, recycling; Animal welfare; Food services; Housing/shelter, temporary shelter; Family services; Human services, victim aid; Aging, centers/services.
Limitations: Giving primarily in VT.
Application information: Application form not required.
Initial approach: Letter
Deadline(s): None
Directors: Amy E. Tarrant; Brian Tarrant; Jeremiah Tarrant; Richard E. Tarrant, Jr.
EIN: 020514457
Selected grants: The following grants were reported in 2004.
$50,000 to Mater Christi School, Burlington, VT.
$25,000 to Humane Society of Chittenden County, South Burlington, VT.
$25,000 to University of Vermont, Burlington, VT.
$10,000 to Chittenden Emergency Food Shelf, Burlington, VT.
$10,000 to Dismas House, Burlington, VT.
$10,000 to King Street Youth Center, Burlington, VT.
$10,000 to Vermont Campaign to End Childhood Hunger, South Burlington, VT.
$10,000 to Vermont Foodbank, South Barre, VT.
$5,000 to Vermont Humanities Council, Morrisville, VT.
$5,000 to Vermont Respite House, Burlington, VT.

2266
The Jean and Farris Tatum Charitable Foundation, Inc. ✧
c/o SunTrust Bank
P.O. Box 1908
Orlando, FL 32802-1908
Contact: Charles P. Gordon

Established in 2001 in GA.

Donor: Alan J.W. Tatum†.
Foundation type: Independent foundation.
Financial data (yr. ended 12/31/04): Assets, $241,450 (M); gifts received, $22,491; expenditures, $464,822; qualifying distributions, $454,911; giving activities include $450,000 for 3 grants (high: $200,000; low: $50,000).
Fields of interest: Protestant agencies & churches.
Limitations: Giving primarily in GA. No grants to individuals.
Application information:
  Initial approach: Letter
  Deadline(s): None
Officers: Wilton D. Looney, Chair. and Treas.; Robert G. Edge, Vice Chair. and Secy.
Trustees: J.J. Hollifield; SunTrust Bank.
EIN: 311764605

2267
Jerry Taylor and Nancy Bryant Foundation ✧
1 Las Olas Cir., No. 1003
Fort Lauderdale, FL 33316

Established in 1999 in FL.
Donor: Galen D. Taylor Charitable Lead Trust.
Foundation type: Independent foundation.
Financial data (yr. ended 12/31/05): Assets, $9,739,083 (M); gifts received, $168,000; expenditures, $484,266; qualifying distributions, $431,133; giving activities include $423,550 for 33 grants (high: $75,000; low: $250).
Purpose and activities: Giving primarily for human services.
Fields of interest: Education; Environment; Human services; Children, services; Foundations (community); Women.
International interests: Bahamas.
Type of support: General/operating support; Emergency funds; Program development.
Limitations: Applications not accepted. Giving primarily in Washington DC and Fort Lauderdale/Broward County, FL; some funding also in Nassau, Bahamas. No grants to individuals.
Application information: Contributes only to pre-selected organizations.
  Board meeting date(s): Nov.
Trustees: Nancy Bryant; Galen D. Taylor; Gerald Taylor.
EIN: 522134053
Selected grants: The following grants were reported in 2003.
$75,000 to Community Foundation of Broward, Fort Lauderdale, FL.
$40,000 to Latin American Youth Center, DC. For program support.
$35,000 to Higher Achievement Program, DC. For general operating support.
$25,350 to John F. Kennedy Center for the Performing Arts, DC.
$15,000 to Kids in Distress (KID), Fort Lauderdale, FL.
$12,000 to Emmaus Services for the Aging, DC.
$10,000 to Academy of Hope, DC.
$10,000 to Environmentors Project, DC.
$7,500 to Sun Sentinel Childrens Fund, Fort Lauderdale, FL. For program support.
$5,000 to Reef Ball Foundation, Woodstock, GA.

2268
Taylor Family Foundation, Inc. ✧
516 Sanderling Cir.
Bradenton, FL 34209

Established in 1996 in WI and FL.
Foundation type: Independent foundation.
Financial data (yr. ended 12/31/04): Assets, $15,218,205 (M); gifts received, $2,100; expenditures, $1,482,172; qualifying distributions, $1,026,761; giving activities include $1,026,761 for 42 grants (high: $471,583; low: $126).
Purpose and activities: Giving primarily for children, youth and social services, and for medical research.
Fields of interest: Animal welfare; Medical research, institute; Human services; Children/youth, services; Christian agencies & churches.
Limitations: Applications not accepted. Giving primarily in FL; some funding nationally; some funding also in Scotland. No grants to individuals.
Application information: Contributes only to pre-selected organizations.
Directors: Edward Huetig; Ilona Kenrick; Katherine Kittsmiller; Ritchey Nelson Taylor.
EIN: 396058301

2269
Jack Taylor Family Foundation, Inc. ✧
1111 Kane Concourse, Ste. 619
Bay Harbor Islands, FL 33154

Established in 1968.
Donors: Taylor Development Corp.; Jack Taylor; Mitchell Taylor; and other members of the Taylor family.
Foundation type: Independent foundation.
Financial data (yr. ended 12/31/05): Assets, $7,705,990 (M); expenditures, $1,112,727; qualifying distributions, $1,068,500; giving activities include $1,068,500 for 10 grants (high: $1,000,000; low: $1,000).
Purpose and activities: Giving primarily for health organizations, as well as for the arts, education, and human services.
Fields of interest: Arts; Higher education; Health organizations; Medical research, institute; Human services; American Red Cross; Foundations (private grantmaking).
Limitations: Applications not accepted. No grants to individuals.
Application information: Contributes only to pre-selected organizations.
Officers and Directors:* Elizabeth Taylor,* Pres.; Mitchell Taylor,* V.P.; Ilene Eefting, Secy.-Treas.; Victor D. Dembrow, M.D.; Seth D. Rosen, M.D.
EIN: 596205187

2270
TECO Energy Foundation, Inc. ✧
702 N. Franklin St.
Tampa, FL 33602 (813) 228-4273
Contact: Jack Amor, Dir.
Application address: P.O. Box 111, Plz. 8, Tampa, FL 33601-0111

Established as a company-sponsored operating foundation.
Donor: TECO Energy, Inc.
Foundation type: Operating foundation.
Financial data (yr. ended 12/31/04): Assets, $81,715 (M); gifts received, $520,497;

expenditures, $517,397; qualifying distributions, $467,900; giving activities include $467,900 for 14 grants (high: $200,000; low: $1,000).
Purpose and activities: The foundation supports organizations involved with arts and culture, education, health, recreation, children and youth, human services, and community development.
Fields of interest: Arts; Education; Health care; Recreation; Children/youth, services; Human services; Community development; Federated giving programs.
Type of support: Program development; Capital campaigns.
Limitations: Giving primarily in FL.
Application information: Application form required.
  Initial approach: Contact foundation for application form
  Deadline(s): Dec. 1
Officers and Directors: Shirley Payne, V.P. and Treas.; David Schwartz, Secy.; Jack Amor; Gordon Gillette; Sheila McDevitt; Johnny Page.
EIN: 010598444
Selected grants: The following grants were reported in 2003.
$166,672 to University of South Florida Foundation, Tampa, FL. For capital campaign.
$125,000 to University of Tampa, Tampa, FL. For Center for Leadership campaign.
$53,350 to United Way of Tampa Bay, Tampa, FL.
$50,000 to Lowry Park Zoological Society of Tampa, Tampa, FL.
$37,500 to American Cancer Society, Tampa, FL. For Campaign for the Hope Lodge.
$20,000 to Urban League of Greater Tampa, Tampa, FL. To restore the West Tampa Centro Espanola Building.
$16,200 to United Way of Central Florida, Highland City, FL.
$15,000 to University Area Community Development Corporation, Tampa, FL.
$11,202 to Center for Women, Tampa, FL. For Senior Home Improvements Program.
$10,000 to YMCA, West Central Florida, Lakeland, FL. For capital campaign.

2271
C. Herman & Mary Virginia Terry Foundation ✧
(formerly C. Herman Terry Foundation)
1301 Riverplace Blvd., Ste. 2109
Jacksonville, FL 32207-9027

Established in 1982 in FL.
Donor: C. Herman Terry.
Foundation type: Independent foundation.
Financial data (yr. ended 12/31/05): Assets, $5,874,073 (M); expenditures, $554,895; qualifying distributions, $519,009; giving activities include $513,300 for 5 grants (high: $500,000; low: $1,500).
Purpose and activities: Giving primarily for health organizations, including a children's hospital.
Fields of interest: Hospitals (specialty); Health care; Cancer research; Children/youth, services.
Limitations: Applications not accepted. Giving primarily in Jacksonville, FL. No grants to individuals.
Application information: Contributes only to pre-selected organizations.
Trustees: Kenneth A. Barneby; Sandra M. Corbett; Betsy Cox; Mary Virginia Terry; James H. Winston.
EIN: 592241642
Selected grants: The following grants were reported in 2004.

$105,000 to Jacksonville University, Jacksonville, FL.

$100,000 to Jericho School, Jacksonville, FL.

$10,000 to Boy Scouts of America, Jacksonville, FL.

$10,000 to Seamark Ranch, Jacksonville, FL.

$10,000 to United Way, FL.

$5,000 to American Cancer Society, Jacksonville, FL.

$5,000 to Childrens Home Society of Florida, Jacksonville, FL.

$2,500 to Salvation Army, Saint Petersburg, FL.

2272
The Thanksgiving Fund ◇
(formerly The STB Family Foundation)
1700 S. MacDill Ave., Ste. 200
Tampa, FL 33629-5218 (813) 258-1177
Contact: Brett Hendee, Dir.

Established in 2000 in FL.
Donors: Stewart T. Bertron; Tammy B. Bertron.
Foundation type: Independent foundation.
Financial data (yr. ended 12/31/05): Assets, $8,123,915 (M); expenditures, $336,704; qualifying distributions, $322,581; giving activities include $320,600 for 2 grants (high: $320,000; low: $600).
Purpose and activities: Giving primarily to a community foundation.
Fields of interest: Foundations (community); Christian agencies & churches.
Limitations: Applications not accepted. Giving primarily in CA and FL. No grants to individuals.
Application information: Contributes only to pre-selected organizations.
Officer and Directors: * Stewart T. Bertron,* Pres. and Secy.-Treas.; Tammy B. Bertron; Brett Hendee.
EIN: 593627428
Selected grants: The following grants were reported in 2003.
$100,000 to Saint Marys Episcopal Day School, Tampa, FL.
$100,000 to Tampa Bay Performing Arts Center, Tampa, FL.
$87,000 to Palma Ceia Presbyterian Church, Tampa, FL.
$37,056 to Young Life, Colorado Springs, CO.
$11,500 to United Way of Tampa Bay, Tampa, FL.
$10,000 to University of Tampa, Tampa, FL.
$10,000 to University of Virginia, Charlottesville, VA.
$5,000 to Children First America, Bentonville, AR. For scholarships.
$3,500 to Family First, Tampa, FL. For geneal program support.
$2,250 to University of North Carolina, Chapel Hill, NC.

2273
Samuel E. & Mary W. Thatcher Foundation, Inc. ◇
P.O. Box 37-0129
Miami, FL 33137
Contact: John W. Thatcher, Pres.

Established in 1982 in FL.
Donors: John W. Thatcher; Mary W. Thatcher‡; Mary Thatcher Irrevocable Trust.
Foundation type: Independent foundation.
Financial data (yr. ended 12/31/05): Assets, $7,977,725 (M); gifts received, $31,860;

expenditures, $2,794,178; qualifying distributions, $2,606,550; giving activities include $2,606,550 for 252 grants (high: $550,000; low: $100).
Purpose and activities: Support primarily for religious ministries, particularly for youth; giving also for higher education.
Fields of interest: Higher education; Education; Youth, services; Christian agencies & churches.
Limitations: Applications not accepted. Giving primarily in FL. No grants to individuals.
Application information: Contributes only to pre-selected organizations.
Officers: John W. Thatcher, Pres. and Treas.; William R. Jordan, V.P.; Paul M. Stokes, Secy.
EIN: 592230243
Selected grants: The following grants were reported in 2004.
$500,000 to Darlington School, Rome, GA.
$250,000 to Davidson College, Davidson, NC.
$85,000 to Youth for Christ. 2 grants: $10,000, $75,000
$60,000 to Youth for Christ/USA, Wheaton, IL.
$26,200 to Christian Enterprises, Kent, WA.
$25,000 to Man in the Mirror, Casselberry, FL.
$25,000 to Whitworth College, Spokane, WA.
$10,800 to Good News Ministries, Austin, IN.
$10,000 to King College, Bristol, TN.

2274
The Toppel Family Foundation, Inc. ☆
(formerly Harold & Patricia Toppel Foundation)
c/o Betsi Kassebaum
7900 Glades Rd., Ste. 600
Boca Raton, FL 33434

Established in 1970.
Donors: Harold Toppel; Patricia Toppel.
Foundation type: Independent foundation.
Financial data (yr. ended 12/31/04): Assets, $2,800,356 (M); gifts received, $1,000,000; expenditures, $1,098,582; qualifying distributions, $1,068,896; giving activities include $962,918 for 56 grants (high: $600,000; low: $50).
Purpose and activities: The foundation focuses its philanthropy in the areas of youth, education (early childhood and higher education), the arts and community betterment programs.
Fields of interest: Arts; Education; Children/youth, services.
Type of support: Annual campaigns; Equipment; Endowments; Program development; Curriculum development; Program evaluation; In-kind gifts; Matching/challenge support.
Limitations: Applications not accepted. Giving primarily in southeastern FL. No grants to individuals.
Application information: Unsolicited requests for funds not accepted.
  Board meeting date(s): Quarterly
Officers and Directors: * Patricia Toppel,* Pres.; Jonathan Toppel,* V.P. and Treas.; Brooke Toppel,* V.P.; Jeffrey Toppel,* V.P.; Jennifer Toppel-Sawyer,* V.P.; Sheri Sauer,* Secy.; Harold Toppel, Chair. Emeritus.
EIN: 237050394
Selected grants: The following grants were reported in 2004.
$600,000 to University of Miami, Miami, FL.
$80,000 to Florida Atlantic University, Boca Raton, FL.
$70,000 to Kind Program, Boca Raton, FL.
$8,500 to Lynn University, Boca Raton, FL. 3 grants: $2,500, $1,000, $5,000

$5,000 to Adolph and Rose Levis Jewish Community Center, Boca Raton, FL.
$5,000 to Kids at Home, Boca Raton, FL.
$1,200 to American Red Cross, National Headquarters, DC.

2275
Tupperware Children's Foundation ◇ ☆
c/o Tupperware Corp.
14901 S. Orange Blossom Trail
Orlando, FL 32837
URL: http://order.tupperware.com/pls/htprod_www/tup_company.child

Established in 2003 in FL.
Donor: Tupperware U.S., Inc.
Foundation type: Company-sponsored foundation.
Financial data (yr. ended 12/31/05): Assets, $289,772 (M); gifts received, $867,679; expenditures, $581,828; qualifying distributions, $581,735; giving activities include $581,735 for grants.
Purpose and activities: The foundation supports programs designed to protect, support, teach, and empower children.
Fields of interest: Boys & girls clubs; Children, services.
Limitations: Giving on a national and international basis.
Officers and Directors: * Thomas M. Roehlk,* Pres.; Michael Poteshman,* V.P.; Josef Hajek,* Treas.; Mark W. Shamley, Exec. Dir.
EIN: 550824285

2276
United States Sugar Corporation Charitable Trust ◇
c/o United States Sugar Corp.
111 Ponce de Leon Ave.
Clewiston, FL 33440 (863) 983-8121
Contact: Robert E. Coker, Tr.

Trust established in 1952 in FL.
Donor: United States Sugar Corp.
Foundation type: Company-sponsored foundation.
Financial data (yr. ended 10/31/04): Assets, $1,090,145 (M); expenditures, $348,700; qualifying distributions, $348,700; giving activities include $348,700 for 79 grants (high: $25,000; low: $500).
Purpose and activities: The trust supports organizations involved with arts and culture, education, health, children and youth services, and community development.
Fields of interest: Museums; Arts; Education; Hospitals (general); Health organizations, association; Children/youth, services; Human services; Community development; Federated giving programs.
Limitations: Giving primarily in FL. No grants to individuals, or for scholarships or fellowships; no loans.
Application information: Application form not required.
  Initial approach: Proposal
  Deadline(s): None
  Board meeting date(s): Jan., Apr., July, and Oct.
Trustees: Robert H. Buker, Jr.; Robert E. Coker; Malcolm S. Wade, Jr.
EIN: 596142825

Selected grants: The following grants were reported in 2004.

$25,000 to Congressional Black Caucus Foundation, DC.

$25,000 to Glades Day School, Belle Glade, FL.

$10,000 to Cystic Fibrosis Foundation, Miami, FL.

$6,000 to Junior Achievement of the Palm Beaches, West Palm Beach, FL.

$5,000 to Boy Scouts of America, Palm Beach Gardens, FL.

$5,000 to Utah Families Foundation, Salt Lake City, UT.

$2,500 to American Red Cross, West Palm Beach, FL.

$2,500 to Girl Scouts of the U.S.A., Lake Worth, FL.

$2,500 to March of Dimes Birth Defects Foundation, Arlington, VA.

$2,000 to Florida Education Foundation, Tallahassee, FL.

2277
Van Vleet Foundation ✧
P.O. Box 1908
Orlando, FL   32802

Established in 1962 in TN.

Donor: Harriet Smith Van Vleet†.

Foundation type: Independent foundation.

Financial data (yr. ended 12/31/05): Assets, $11,257,473 (M); expenditures, $737,932; qualifying distributions, $668,656; giving activities include $611,732 for 4 grants (high: $292,300; low: $19,432).

Purpose and activities: Grants to local area universities, as well as to a children's hospital.

Fields of interest: Higher education; Hospitals (general).

Type of support: Equipment; Endowments; Fellowships; Scholarship funds.

Limitations: Applications not accepted. Giving limited to Memphis, TN. No grants to individuals.

Application information: Contributes only to pre-selected organizations.

Advisors: B. Snowden Boyle, Jr.; William L. Richmond.

Trustee: SunTrust Bank.

EIN: 626034067

Selected grants: The following grants were reported in 2003.

$243,688 to University of Tennessee, Memphis, TN. For endowed chair and scholarships.

$120,000 to University of Memphis, Memphis, TN. For fellowship scholarships.

$100,000 to Saint Jude Childrens Research Hospital, Memphis, TN. For endowment fund.

$40,000 to Childrens Museum of Memphis, Memphis, TN.

$19,627 to Rhodes College, Memphis, TN. For endowment fund.

2278
The Vanneck-Bailey Foundation ✧
c/o William P. Vanneck
217 West Indies Dr.
Palm Beach, FL   33480
Contact: William P. Vanneck, Treas.

Established in 1971 in NY through the consolidation of The Vanneck Foundation, incorporated in 1949 in NY, and The Frank and Marie Bailey Foundation.

Donors: John Vanneck†; Barbara Bailey Vanneck.

Foundation type: Independent foundation.

Financial data (yr. ended 12/31/05): Assets, $6,403,007 (M); expenditures, $331,452; qualifying distributions, $327,926; giving activities include $322,000 for 70 grants (high: $25,000; low: $500).

Fields of interest: Higher education; Environment, natural resources; Hospitals (general); Community development; Protestant agencies & churches.

Type of support: Continuing support; Research.

Limitations: Applications not accepted. Giving primarily on the East Coast. No grants to individuals.

Application information: Contributes only to pre-selected organizations.

Officers: Barbara V. May, Pres.; Jeanne M. Wiedenman, Secy.; William P. Vanneck, Treas.

EIN: 237165285

2279
Vaughn-Jordan Foundation, Inc. ✧ ☆
c/o Suntrust Bank
P.O. Box 1908
Orlando, FL   32802-1908
Application address: c/o Katherine Hetzel, Exec. Dir., P.O. Box 4642, West Palm Beach, FL 33402

Established in 1988 in FL.

Foundation type: Independent foundation.

Financial data (yr. ended 12/31/05): Assets, $3,793,138 (M); expenditures, $400,372; qualifying distributions, $373,502; giving activities include $332,425 for 10 grants (high: $84,000; low: $5,000).

Purpose and activities: Giving for the furtherance of botanical science.

Fields of interest: Higher education; Botany.

Type of support: Capital campaigns; Program development; Scholarship funds; Research.

Limitations: Giving primarily in FL and GA. No grants to individuals.

Publications: Annual report.

Application information: Application form not required.

Initial approach: Letter
Copies of proposal: 6
Deadline(s): Oct. 1

Officer and Trustees: * Katherine Hetzel, * Exec. Dir.; C. Roland Vaughn III; Clarence Vaughn, Jr.; James A. Vaughn, Jr.; James P. Vaughn; James L. Watt.

Agent: Suntrust Bank.

EIN: 650362992

Selected grants: The following grants were reported in 2004.

$50,000 to Fairchild Tropical Garden, Coral Gables, FL.

$41,200 to University of Georgia Foundation, Athens, GA.

$40,000 to Wake Forest University, Winston-Salem, NC.

$20,000 to Ida Cason Callaway Foundation, Pine Mountain, GA.

$15,000 to Florida Institute of Technology, Melbourne, FL.

$15,000 to Palm Beach Atlantic University, West Palm Beach, FL.

$15,000 to Stetson University, DeLand, FL.

$5,000 to Earlham College, Richmond, IN.

2280
Victory Foundation, Inc. ✧
c/o Robert M. Franzblau
5401 Hangar Ct.
Tampa, FL   33634-5341

Established in 1998 in FL.

Donor: Robert M. Franzblau.

Foundation type: Independent foundation.

Financial data (yr. ended 12/31/05): Assets, $1,203,549 (M); gifts received, $25,000; expenditures, $361,004; qualifying distributions, $360,708; giving activities include $357,800 for 40 grants (high: $60,000; low: $100).

Fields of interest: Museums (art); Performing arts, orchestra (symphony); Higher education; Education; Health organizations, association; Human services; Foundations (community); Jewish agencies & temples.

Type of support: General/operating support.

Limitations: Applications not accepted. Giving primarily in FL. No grants to individuals.

Application information: Contributes only to pre-selected organizations.

Directors: Alix F. Dorr; Charles A. Franzblau; Jo Franzblau; Robert M. Franzblau.

EIN: 593536437

Selected grants: The following grants were reported in 2005.

$85,000 to Southeastern Guide Dogs, Palmetto, FL. 2 grants: $25,000; $60,000

$40,000 to State University of New York Maritime College Foundation, Bronx, NY.

$23,000 to Tampa Museum of Art, Tampa, FL.

$20,000 to Berkeley Preparatory School, Tampa, FL.

$20,000 to Salvador Dali Museum, Saint Petersburg, FL.

$12,500 to Wayne State University, Detroit, MI.

$12,000 to Florida Orchestra, Tampa, FL.

$10,000 to University of South Florida, Tampa, FL.

$5,000 to Music Educators National Conference, Reston, VA.

2281
The Clifford and Jill Viner Family Foundation ✧
5052 Sanctuary Ln.
Boca Raton, FL   33431

Established in 1995 in FL.

Donors: Jill Viner; Warren Mosler; Clifford Viner.

Foundation type: Independent foundation.

Financial data (yr. ended 12/31/05): Assets, $2,455,305 (M); gifts received, $1,350,000; expenditures, $1,161,280; qualifying distributions, $1,160,980; giving activities include $1,160,919 for 52 grants (high: $435,614; low: $500).

Purpose and activities: Giving for education, family services, community and social services.

Fields of interest: Higher education; Jewish agencies & temples; Religion.

Limitations: Applications not accepted. Giving primarily in FL. No grants to individuals.

Application information: Contributes only to pre-selected organizations.

Officer: Clifford A. Viner, Pres.

Director: Jeffrey A. Deutch.

Trustee: Jill Viner.

EIN: 650633896

2282
Alberto Vollmer Foundation, Inc.
1101 Brickell Ave., Ste. 1004, S. Twr.
Miami, FL 33131
FAX: (305) 377-2711; *E-mail:* info@vollmer.com

Established in 1988 in NJ.
Donor: Vollmer Foundation, Inc.
Foundation type: Independent foundation.
Financial data (yr. ended 12/31/05): Assets, $5,616,078 (M); expenditures, $1,209,082; qualifying distributions, $1,166,222; giving activities include $792,856 for grants, and $62,613 for foundation-administered programs.
Purpose and activities: The foundation gives assistance to scientific, cultural, and educational activities in Venezuela.
Fields of interest: Higher education; Education; Biomedicine; Medical research, institute; Family services; Roman Catholic agencies & churches.
International interests: Venezuela.
Type of support: General/operating support.
Limitations: Giving primarily in Venezuela. No grants to individuals.
Application information: Contributes mostly to pre-selected organizations. Application form not required.
Initial approach: Letter
Copies of proposal: 1
Deadline(s): None
Board meeting date(s): As necessary
Officers: Alberto J. Vollmer, Pres.; Christine de Vollmer, V.P.; Cristina Burelli, Secy.
Number of staff: 1 full-time professional.
EIN: 222872241

2283
The William J. von Liebig Foundation, Inc. ✧
P.O. Box 620005, MC 2105
Orlando, FL 32862-0005
Contact: Teresa W. Borcheck
FAX: (407) 237-5604;
E-mail: teresa.borcheck@suntrust.com;
URL: http://www.vonliebigfoundation.com

Established in 1997 in FL.
Donor: William J. von Liebig‡.
Foundation type: Operating foundation.
Financial data (yr. ended 12/31/04): Assets, $16,403,818 (M); expenditures, $2,672,485; qualifying distributions, $2,395,548; giving activities include $2,352,579 for 12 grants (high: $400,000; low: $2,500; average: $10,000–$300,000).
Purpose and activities: Giving primarily to vascular research programs and medical research.
Fields of interest: Medical research, institute.
Type of support: Fellowships; Research; Employee matching gifts; Grants to individuals.
Limitations: Applications not accepted. Giving limited to the U.S.
Publications: Informational brochure.
Application information: Does not accept unsolicited requests.
Board meeting date(s): Varies
Officers and Directors:* Suzanne von Liebig,* Chair.; Linda Hamilton,* Pres. and Secy.-Treas.; Jean A. Goggins, Ph.D.
Number of staff: 1 part-time professional; 1 part-time support.
EIN: 311470886

Selected grants: The following grants were reported in 2003.
$711,720 to Lifeline Foundation, Beverly, MA. For research training program for vascular surgeons.
$538,556 to Harvard University, Cambridge, MA. For research of vascular devices and technologies at Medical School in Boston.
$200,000 to Thoracic Surgery Foundation for Research and Education, Beverly, MA. For Mentored Clinical Scientist Development Award Program.
$100,000 to University of California, Office of Research Affairs, San Francisco, CA. For Endovascular and Basic Science Fellowships.
$72,504 to University of Washington, School of Medicine, Seattle, WA. For Vascular Surgery Residency Fellowship.
$67,492 to Mayo Foundation for Medical Education and Research, Jacksonville, FL. For research.

2284
Wahlert Foundation ✧
P.O. Box 61477
Fort Myers, FL 33906-1477
Contact: R.H. Wahlert, Pres.
E-mail: Bob16307@aol.com; Summer address: P.O. Box 736, Dubuque, IA 52004-0736

Incorporated in 1948 in IA.
Donors: Dubuque Packing Co.; FDL Foods, Inc.; H.W. Wahlert‡; and officers of the foundation.
Foundation type: Independent foundation.
Financial data (yr. ended 8/31/05): Assets, $7,133,269 (M); gifts received, $23,439; expenditures, $565,724; qualifying distributions, $464,137; giving activities include $464,137 for 38 grants (high: $125,000; low: $500).
Purpose and activities: Support primarily for higher, secondary, and medical education; grants also for health services and hospitals, including medical and cancer research, social service agencies, including drug abuse prevention programs and services for families, the homeless and the handicapped, child welfare programs for minorities, cultural activities, including the arts and museums, and Catholic welfare organizations and schools.
Fields of interest: Secondary school/education; Higher education; Health care; Human services; Aging, centers/services; Roman Catholic agencies & churches.
International interests: Honduras.
Type of support: General/operating support; Capital campaigns; Annual campaigns; Building/renovation; Equipment; Emergency funds; Program development; Scholarship funds.
Limitations: Giving primarily in the metropolitan Dubuque, IA, area. No grants to individuals, or for publications, conferences, or matching gifts; no loans.
Application information: Application form not required.
Initial approach: 1-page letter
Copies of proposal: 1
Deadline(s): Aug. 25
Board meeting date(s): 2nd Sat. of Sept.
Final notification: 1 month after board meeting
Officers and Trustees:* Robert H. Wahlert,* Pres. and Treas.; David Wahlert,* V.P.; Alfred E. Hughes,* Secy.; Kathy Wahlert Chameli; Marni Wahlert Peck; Amy Wahlert Principi; Alan Wahlert; Celeste Wahlert; Donna Wahlert; James Wahlert; Mark Wahlert; Nancy Wahlert; R.C. Wahlert II; Susan Wahlert.

Number of staff: 1 part-time professional.
EIN: 426051124
Selected grants: The following grants were reported in 2004.
$50,000 to Wahlert High School, Dubuque, IA. For scholarships.
$25,000 to New Mellerary Abbey. For infirmary construction.
$21,000 to Catholic Charities.
$15,000 to Shalom Retreat Center.
$10,000 to Dubuque Rescue Mission, Dubuque, IA.
$10,000 to Finley Health Foundation, Dubuque, IA.
$10,000 to Stonehill Care Center, Dubuque, IA.
$6,000 to Salvation Army.
$5,000 to Divine Word College Seminary, Epworth, IA.
$5,000 to Dubuque Food Pantry, Dubuque, IA.

2285
I. Waldbaum Family Foundation, Inc. ✧
16519 Ironwood Dr.
Delray Beach, FL 33445 (561) 499-6519
Contact: Bernice Waldbaum, Pres.

Incorporated in 1961 in NY.
Donors: Bernice Waldbaum; Ira Waldbaum; Waldbaum, Inc.
Foundation type: Independent foundation.
Financial data (yr. ended 12/31/05): Assets, $14,665,532 (M); expenditures, $919,625; qualifying distributions, $704,525; giving activities include $653,775 for 55 grants (high: $150,000; low: $100).
Purpose and activities: Giving primarily to Jewish organizations, including welfare funds, religious schools, temple support, and to cultural programs, and hospitals.
Fields of interest: Child development, education; Parkinson's disease; Human services; Child development, services; Jewish federated giving programs; Jewish agencies & temples.
Type of support: Capital campaigns; Building/renovation; Endowments; Seed money.
Limitations: Giving primarily in NY.
Application information: Application form not required.
Initial approach: Proposal
Copies of proposal: 1
Deadline(s): Oct. 31
Officers: Bernice Waldbaum, Pres.; Randie Malinsky, V.P. and Secy.; Nancy Waldbaum Nimkoff, V.P. and Treas.
Number of staff: 1 full-time professional.
EIN: 136145916
Selected grants: The following grants were reported in 2005.
$20,000 to JARC, Farmington Hills, MI.
$12,500 to Island Harvest, Mineola, NY. 2 grants: $7,500, $5,000
$10,000 to Yeshiva of the South Shore, Hewlett, NY. 2 grants: $5,000 each
$5,100 to Hospice by the Sea, Boca Raton, FL. 2 grants: $100, $5,000
$5,000 to Jewish Family Service Associates, Long Beach, CA.
$5,000 to New York University Medical Center, New York, NY.
$500 to Belmont Child Care Association, Elmont, NY.

2286
The Walter Foundation ✧
(formerly Jim Walter Corporation Foundation)
13623 N. Florida Ave.
Tampa, FL 33613 (813) 961-0530
Contact: W.K. Baker, Tr.

Established in 1966 in FL.
Donor: Walter Industries, Inc.
Foundation type: Company-sponsored foundation.
Financial data (yr. ended 8/31/05): Assets, $17,022,722 (M); expenditures, $758,575; qualifying distributions, $587,782; giving activities include $537,800 for 30 grants (high: $125,000; low: $500).
Purpose and activities: The foundation supports Christian agencies and churches and organizations involved with arts and culture, education, health, and youth development.
Fields of interest: Arts; Elementary/secondary education; Higher education; Health care; Youth development; Christian agencies & churches.
Type of support: General/operating support.
Limitations: Giving primarily in FL. No grants to individuals.
Application information: Application form not required.
  Initial approach: Proposal
  Deadline(s): None
Trustees: W.K. Baker; S.L. Myers; R.A. Walter.
EIN: 596205802
Selected grants: The following grants were reported in 2004.
$125,000 to Tampa Preparatory School, Tampa, FL.
$20,000 to Boys and Girls Clubs of Tampa Bay, Tampa, FL.
$10,000 to YMCA, Tampa Metropolitan Area, Tampa, FL.
$5,000 to LifePath Hospice and Palliative Care, Tampa, FL.
$5,000 to Tall Timbers Research Stations, Tallahassee, FL.
$5,000 to Tampa Lighthouse for the Blind, Tampa, FL.
$2,500 to Florida Orchestra, Tampa, FL.
$2,000 to Alpha House of Tampa, Tampa, FL.
$1,000 to Childrens Home Society of Florida, Tampa, FL.
$1,000 to Morning Star School, Orlando, FL.

2287
The Ware Foundation ✧
6858 Granada Blvd.
Coral Gables, FL 33146

Trust established in 1950 in PA.
Donor: John H. Ware, Jr.†
Foundation type: Independent foundation.
Financial data (yr. ended 12/31/04): Assets, $24,700,025 (M); expenditures, $1,469,122; qualifying distributions, $1,232,269; giving activities include $1,058,168 for 27 grants (high: $167,000; low: $5,000).
Purpose and activities: Giving primarily for higher education and Christian organizations, including schools; support also for youth agencies and social services.
Fields of interest: Elementary/secondary education; Higher education; Hospitals (general); Human services; Children/youth, services; Protestant agencies & churches; Roman Catholic agencies & churches.

Limitations: Giving primarily in FL. No support for private foundations. No grants to individuals.
Application information: Telephone inquiries are not accepted. Application form required.
  Initial approach: Letter or proposal
  Deadline(s): Sept. 1
  Final notification: Positive responses only
Officer: Mark Edwards, Secy.-Treas.
Trustees: Elizabeth E. Kuiper; Morgan Ware Soumah; Martha Ware.
EIN: 237286585
Selected grants: The following grants were reported in 2004.
$167,000 to Jackson Memorial Foundation, Miami, FL.
$125,000 to Baptist Hospital Foundation, Nashville, TN.
$100,000 to Community Partnership, Macon, GA. 2 grants: $50,000 each
$25,000 to Ebenezer Foundation, Minneapolis, MN.
$25,000 to Mercersburg Academy, Mercersburg, PA.
$5,000 to American Heart Association, Dallas, TX.

2288
The William R. Watts Foundation, Inc.
(formerly The Watts Foundation, Inc.)
P.O. Box 39238
Fort Lauderdale, FL 33339
Contact: Wilson B. Greaton, Jr., Pres.

Established in 1992 in FL.
Donor: William R. Watts, Sr.†
Foundation type: Independent foundation.
Financial data (yr. ended 10/31/05): Assets, $19,411,583 (M); expenditures, $1,152,287; qualifying distributions, $966,331; giving activities include $900,000 for 30 grants (high: $90,000; low: $5,000).
Fields of interest: Higher education, university; Boys & girls clubs; Salvation Army; Federated giving programs; Protestant agencies & churches.
Type of support: General/operating support; Continuing support; Annual campaigns; Capital campaigns; Building/renovation; Endowments; Debt reduction; Scholarship funds.
Limitations: Giving limited to Miami-Dade and Broward counties, FL.
Publications: Application guidelines; Annual report.
Application information: Application form not required.
  Initial approach: Letter
  Copies of proposal: 1
  Deadline(s): Aug. 1
  Board meeting date(s): Sept.
  Final notification: Oct. 31
Officers and Directors:* Wilson B. Greaton, Jr.,* Pres.; Elizabeth G. Stephany, V.P.; Alan Loehr,* Secy.; Jose Mesa,* Treas.; Hugh Chapell; Richard G. Coker; Paul E. Daly; Ruth Shack; Louis W. Witt, Jr.
Number of staff: 1 part-time professional; 1 part-time support.
EIN: 591971220
Selected grants: The following grants were reported in 2003.
$60,000 to Boys and Girls Clubs of Broward County, Fort Lauderdale, FL. For general support.
$60,000 to Community Foundation of Broward, Fort Lauderdale, FL. For general support.
$60,000 to Dade Community Foundation, Miami, FL. For general support.

$60,000 to First Presbyterian Church of Fort Lauderdale, Fort Lauderdale, FL. For general support.
$60,000 to Salvation Army of Broward County, Fort Lauderdale, FL. For general support.
$60,000 to United Way of Broward County, Fort Lauderdale, FL. For general support.
$60,000 to United Way of Miami County, Peru, IN. For general support.
$25,000 to Washington University, Saint Louis, MO. For general support.
$15,000 to Habitat for Humanity of Broward, Fort Lauderdale, FL. For general support.
$15,000 to Stranahan House, Fort Lauderdale, FL. For general support.

2289
The Weaver Family Foundation ✧
1 ALLTEL Stadium Pl.
Jacksonville, FL 32202 (904) 633-6000
Contact: Delores Barr Weaver, Tr.

Established in 1990 in CT.
Donors: J. Wayne Weaver; Delores B. Weaver.
Foundation type: Independent foundation.
Financial data (yr. ended 12/31/04): Assets, $17,846,840 (M); gifts received, $325,000; expenditures, $2,692,811; qualifying distributions, $2,670,000; giving activities include $2,670,000 for 57 grants (high: $1,500,000; low: $100).
Purpose and activities: Giving primarily for health, children's services, and the arts.
Fields of interest: Performing arts, dance; Hospitals (specialty).
Type of support: Annual campaigns; Capital campaigns; Building/renovation; Endowments; Scholarship funds; Technical assistance.
Limitations: Applications not accepted. Giving primarily in FL. No grants to individuals.
Application information: Contributes only to pre-selected organizations. Unsolicited requests for funds not considered.
Trustees: Delores B. Weaver; J. Wayne Weaver.
EIN: 223087387
Selected grants: The following grants were reported in 2004.
$1,500,000 to Jacksonville Zoological Society, Jacksonville, FL.
$321,300 to Jacksonville Museum of Modern Art, Jacksonville, FL.
$202,000 to United Way of Northeast Florida, Jacksonville, FL.
$102,000 to Saint Vincents Foundation, Jacksonville, FL.
$100,000 to Boston Medical Center, Boston, MA.
$1,000 to Riverside Fine Arts Association, Jacksonville, FL.
$500 to Association of Fundraising Professionals, Alexandria, VA.

2290
The Weiler Foundation, Inc. ✧
231 Bradley Pl., Ste. 204
Palm Beach, FL 33480 (561) 659-2212
Contact: Bartlett Burnap, Pres.

Established in 1961 in CA.
Donor: Ralph J. Weiler†
Foundation type: Independent foundation.
Financial data (yr. ended 4/30/05): Assets, $10,540,818 (M); expenditures, $645,405;

qualifying distributions, $522,453; giving activities include $420,400 for 26 grants (high: $50,000; low: $400).

Purpose and activities: Giving primarily for education; funding also for wildlife preservation, and children's and social services.

Fields of interest: Arts, public education; Media, television; Higher education; Education; Animals/ wildlife, preservation/protection; Human services; Children, services; Social sciences, public policy.

Limitations: Giving primarily in CA and FL; funding also in NY. No support for individual churches or religious organizations. No grants to individuals, or for capital campaigns, capital improvements, start-up funds for new organizations, or to institutions supported by state or federal funds.

Publications: Application guidelines.

Application information: Application form required.

> *Initial approach:* Proposal
> *Copies of proposal:* 3
> *Deadline(s):* Mar.
> *Board meeting date(s):* Monthly

Officers: Bartlett Burnap, Pres.; William Bullis, V.P.

Directors: Christiane Burnap; Ian Burnap.

EIN: 311475728

2291

Ted and Jean Weiller Foundation, Inc. ✧ ☆

663 Mourning Dove Dr.
Sarasota, FL   34236
Contact: Edwin A. Weiller, III, Pres.

Established in 1995 in FL.

Donor: Edwin A. Weiller III.

Foundation type: Independent foundation.

Financial data (yr. ended 12/31/05): Assets, $1,590,314 (M); expenditures, $396,156; qualifying distributions, $375,205; giving activities include $372,735 for 25 grants (high: $249,500; low: $100).

Purpose and activities: Giving primarily for the arts and Jewish organizations.

Fields of interest: Performing arts, orchestra (symphony); Arts; Boys & girls clubs; YM/YWCAs & YM/YWHAs; Foundations (community); Jewish federated giving programs; Jewish agencies & temples.

Limitations: Giving limited to Manatee and Sarasota counties, FL and Berkshire County, MA. No grants to individuals.

Application information:

> *Initial approach:* Letter
> *Deadline(s):* July 31

Officers: Edwin A. Weiller III, Pres.; Jean A. Weiller, V.P.

EIN: 650538553

Selected grants: The following grants were reported in 2004.

$37,500 to Boys and Girls Club.

$5,100 to National Alliance for Research on Schizophrenia and Depression (NARSAD), Great Neck, NY.

$2,500 to Boston Symphony Orchestra, Boston, MA.

$2,000 to Van Wezel Foundation, Sarasota, FL.

$1,000 to Video Archives, Sarasota, FL.

$250 to Museum of Asian Art, Sarasota, FL.

$100 to American Folk Art Museum, New York, NY.

$100 to Berkshire Museum, Pittsfield, MA.

2292

Joseph Weintraub Family Foundation, Inc. ✧

(formerly Weintraub-Landfield Charity Foundation, Inc.)
801 Brickell Ave., Ste. 2470
Miami, FL   33131   (305) 377-6942
Contact: Michael Weintraub, Pres.

Established in 1949 in FL.

Donor: Joseph Weintraub.

Foundation type: Independent foundation.

Financial data (yr. ended 10/31/05): Assets, $9,652,423 (M); expenditures, $527,273; qualifying distributions, $489,150; giving activities include $489,150 for 19 grants (high: $250,000; low: $100).

Purpose and activities: Support primarily for higher education, social services, health associations, and hospitals, including cancer research.

Fields of interest: Higher education; Law school/ education; Medical school/education; Animal welfare; Hospitals (general); Health organizations, association; Cancer; Cancer research; Heart & circulatory research; Human services; Children/ youth, services; Jewish federated giving programs; Jewish agencies & temples.

Limitations: Giving primarily in FL. No grants to individuals.

Application information: Application form not required.

> *Initial approach:* Letter
> *Deadline(s):* None

Officers and Trustees:* Michael Weintraub,* Pres.; Sandra S. Spooner, V.P. and Secy.-Treas.; Miles Gauntt; Barbara A. Weintraub.

EIN: 590975815

Selected grants: The following grants were reported in 2004.

$120,000 to University of Miami, Coral Gables, FL. For unrestricted support.

$100,000 to University of Virginia, School of Law, Charlottesville, VA. For unrestricted support.

$50,500 to Barry University, Miami, FL.

$50,000 to Mayo Foundation, Rochester, MN. For unrestricted support.

$35,000 to United Way of Miami-Dade, Miami, FL. For unrestricted support.

$22,600 to Temple Israel of Greater Miami, Miami, FL. For unrestricted support.

$10,000 to Humane Society of Greater Miami, Miami, FL. For unrestricted support.

$10,000 to University of Miami, Sylvester Cancer Center, Miami, FL. For unrestricted support.

$10,000 to Watauga Medical Center, Boone, NC. For unrestricted support.

$5,000 to Broward House, Fort Lauderdale, FL. For unrestricted support.

2293

The Wellman Family Foundation ✧

1326 Noble Heron Way
Naples, FL   34105

Established in 2000 in NC.

Donor: F. Selby Wellman, Jr.

Foundation type: Independent foundation.

Financial data (yr. ended 12/31/05): Assets, $592,006 (M); gifts received, $2,337; expenditures, $828,401; qualifying distributions, $818,984; giving activities include $818,984 for 7 grants (high: $369,000; low: $4,782).

Purpose and activities: Giving primarily for education.

Fields of interest: Education, administration/ regulation; Elementary/secondary education; Higher education; Human services; American Red Cross.

Limitations: Applications not accepted. No grants to individuals.

Application information: Contributes only to pre-selected organizations.

Officers: F. Selby Wellman, Jr., Pres.; Donna Bias Wellman, V.P. and Secy.; Brent Alan Wellman, V.P.; Brian Ashley Wellman, V.P.

EIN: 562210377

Selected grants: The following grants were reported in 2004.

$305,000 to Marshall University Foundation, Huntington, WV.

$107,000 to SAS in-School.

$15,000 to Gods Net Childrens Center.

$2,826 to Kiwanis Day Care Center, Huntington, WV.

$2,000 to Victory Junction Gang Camp, Randleman, NC.

$1,240 to East Bank Middle School, East Bank, WV.

2294

Lillian S. Wells Foundation, Inc. ✧

600 Sagamore Rd.
Fort Lauderdale, FL   33301-2215
(954) 462-8639
Contact: Barbara W. Van Fleet, Pres.

Established around 1975 in FL.

Donors: Barbara W. Van Fleet; Preston A. Wells, Jr.

Foundation type: Independent foundation.

Financial data (yr. ended 12/31/05): Assets, $46,328,300 (M); gifts received, $17,931,566; expenditures, $1,941,461; qualifying distributions, $1,906,000; giving activities include $1,906,000 for 9 grants (high: $700,000; low: $5,000).

Fields of interest: Higher education; Education; Hospitals (general); Medical research, institute; Philanthropy/voluntarism, research.

Type of support: General/operating support; Endowments; Scholarship funds; Research.

Limitations: Giving primarily in Washington, DC, Fort Lauderdale, FL, and Chicago, IL.

Application information: Application form not required.

> *Deadline(s):* None

Officers: Barbara W. Van Fleet, Pres.; James I. Ulmer, V.P.; Barbara W. Kenney, Secy.; Joseph Malacek, Treas.

Director: G. Greeley Wells.

EIN: 237433827

2295

The Welsh Family Foundation, Inc. ✧

7 Sea Ct.
Vero Beach, FL   32963
Contact: Patrick J. Welsh, Tr.

Established in 1994 in NJ.

Donors: Patrick J. Welsh; Carol A. Welsh.

Foundation type: Independent foundation.

Financial data (yr. ended 12/31/05): Assets, $5,838,237 (M); expenditures, $652,584; qualifying distributions, $597,000; giving activities include $597,000 for 13 grants (high: $400,000; low: $1,000).

Purpose and activities: Giving primarily for health and human services.

Fields of interest: Education; Hospitals (general); Health care; Human services; Protestant agencies & churches.

Limitations: Applications not accepted. Giving primarily in NJ. No grants to individuals.

Application information: Unsolicited requests for funds not accepted.

Trustees: Carol A. Welsh; Eric A. Welsh; Patrick J. Welsh.

EIN: 223331136

2296
Westgate Resorts Foundation, Inc. ✧

(formerly Westgate Foundation, Inc.)
5601 Windhover Dr.
Orlando, FL 32819

Established in 2001 in FL.

Donors: Central Florida Investments, Inc.; David Siegel.

Foundation type: Independent foundation.

Financial data (yr. ended 12/31/05): Assets, $776,261 (M); gifts received, $1,513,584; expenditures, $1,256,293; qualifying distributions, $904,744; giving activities include $904,744 for 137 grants (high: $100,000; low: $25).

Purpose and activities: The foundation supports organizations involved with education, health, human services, and other areas.

Fields of interest: Education; Health care; Children/youth, services; Human services; General charitable giving.

Type of support: General/operating support; Scholarship funds.

Limitations: Giving limited to areas of company operations in Miami and central, FL, Las Vegas, NV, Gatlinburg, TN, and Park City, UT. No grants to individuals.

Application information: Contact foundation for application guidelines and policies.

Officers and Directors: David Siegel, Pres.; Mark Waltrip, V.P.; Hon. David Crabtree; Tom Dugan; Jim Gissy; Jean McNeal; Barry Siegel; Jacqueline Siegel; Richard Siegel; Steve Siegel; Karen Waltrip.

EIN: 593725617

2297
Whitehall Foundation, Inc. ▼

P.O. Box 3423
Palm Beach, FL 33480
Contact: George M. Moffett II, Pres.
E-mail: email@whitehall.org; Express mail address: 125 Worth Ave., Ste. 220, Palm Beach, FL 33480; URL: http://www.whitehall.org

Incorporated in 1937 in NJ.

Donor: George M. Moffett†.

Foundation type: Independent foundation.

Financial data (yr. ended 9/30/05): Assets, $96,650,120 (M); expenditures, $4,571,797; qualifying distributions, $4,356,882; giving activities include $4,109,755 for 23 grants (high: $75,000; low: $500; average: $5,000–$75,000).

Purpose and activities: Support for scholarly research in the life sciences, with emphasis on behavioral neuroscience and invertebrate neurophysiology; innovative and imaginative projects preferred. Research grants are paid to

sponsoring institutions, rather than directly to individuals.

Fields of interest: Biological sciences.

Type of support: Equipment; Program development; Research.

Limitations: Giving limited to the U.S. No support for investigators who already have, or expect to receive, substantial support from other quarters. No grants for salary support for principal investigator, travel to conferences or for consultation, secretarial or office expenses, construction projects or laboratory renovations, or tuition or fellowships.

Publications: Grants list.

Application information: See foundation Web site for specific application guidelines. The letter of intent must be submitted in hard copy on institutional letterhead.

Initial approach: Letter of intent
Deadline(s): Letter of intent: Jan. 15, Apr. 15, and Oct. 1; Application: Feb. 15, June 1, and Sept. 1
Board meeting date(s): 3 grant review sessions per year
Final notification: May 1, Aug. 15, and Dec. 1

Officers and Trustees:* George M. Moffett II,* Pres.; J. Wright Rumbough, Jr.,* V.P.; Peter Gibbons Neff,* Assoc. V.P.; Catherine M. Thomas, Corp. Secy.; Kenneth S. Beall, Jr.; Helen M. Brooks; Michael Dawes; E. Anthony Newton.

Number of staff: 1 full-time professional; 1 part-time professional.

EIN: 135637595

Selected grants: The following grants were reported in 2005.

$450,000 to Johns Hopkins University, Baltimore, MD. 2 grants: $225,000 (For research, The Role of Non-Protein Coding, mRNA-like Transcripts in Mouse Retinal Development, payable over 3 years), $225,000 (For research, Molecular and Genetic Studies of Pain Sensing Neurons, payable over 3 years).

$450,000 to Stanford University, Stanford, CA. 2 grants: $225,000 (For research, Circuit Mechanisms Linking Brain Activity to Adult Neurogenesis, payable over 3 years), $225,000 (For research, The Neural Basis of Object Recognition in Humans: Features, Objects, or Categories, payable over 3 years).

$225,000 to Beckman Research Institute of the City of Hope, Duarte, CA. For research, Regulation of Neural Stem Cell Self-Renewal by TLX Signaling, payable over 3 years.

$225,000 to Columbia University, New York, NY. For research, Neural Substrates of 5-HT2A Receptor-Mediated Hallucinogenesis, payable over 3 years.

$225,000 to Duke University, Durham, NC. For research, Molecular Mechanisms of Evolutionary Conserved Nociception, payable over 3 years.

$225,000 to Mount Sinai School of Medicine of New York University, New York, NY. For research, Morphological Plasticity of Corticostriatal Connections and its Regulation by Dopamine, payable over 3 years.

$225,000 to University of California, Davis, CA. For research, Characterization of Novel Membrane Proteins in Synapse Formation, payable over 3 years.

$225,000 to University of California, Irvine, CA. For research, Roof Plate Signaling in Dorsal Telencephalic Development, payable over 3 years.

2298
Wilkes-Desmond Educational
Foundation ✧

2211 S. Flagler Dr.
West Palm Beach, FL 33401-8007
Contact: J. Cole

Donor: William C. Desmond†.

Foundation type: Operating foundation.

Financial data (yr. ended 5/31/05): Assets, $8,416,280 (M); expenditures, $554,520; qualifying distributions, $442,157; giving activities include $345,357 for 60 grants (high: $73,592; low: $100).

Fields of interest: Higher education; Education.

Limitations: Applications not accepted. Giving primarily in NY. No grants to individuals.

Application information: Contributes only to pre-selected organizations.

Trustee: David Beuttenmuller.

EIN: 650961676

Selected grants: The following grants were reported in 2005.

$67,411 to Monroe Community College, Rochester, NY.

$20,000 to Nazareth College of Rochester, Rochester, NY.

$9,780 to Saint John Fisher College, Rochester, NY.

$8,100 to Cazenovia College, Cazenovia, NY.

$7,128 to Syracuse University, Syracuse, NY.

$5,850 to Ithaca College, Ithaca, NY.

$4,250 to Canisius College, Buffalo, NY.

$4,250 to University of Dayton, Dayton, OH.

$3,970 to Rochester Institute of Technology, Rochester, NY.

$2,350 to Mohawk Valley Community College, Utica, NY.

2299
Edna Sproull Williams Foundation ✧

c/o James W. Burke
2046 Eventide Rd.
Switzerland, FL 32259

Established in 1976.

Donor: Edna Sproull Williams†.

Foundation type: Independent foundation.

Financial data (yr. ended 12/31/05): Assets, $19,644,531 (M); expenditures, $1,233,524; qualifying distributions, $1,101,006; giving activities include $1,014,916 for 51 grants (high: $100,000; low: $1,000).

Purpose and activities: Giving primarily to Christian causes.

Fields of interest: Arts; Higher education; Theological school/education; Hospitals (general); Health organizations, association; Youth development, centers/clubs; Youth, services; Christian agencies & churches.

Limitations: Applications not accepted. Giving primarily in FL. No grants to individuals.

Application information: Contributes only to pre-selected organizations.

Trustees: Susan W. Brodeur; James W. Burke; Edward McCarthy, Jr.; Charles Williams III; David F. Williams; Patrick M. Williams.

EIN: 510198606

Selected grants: The following grants were reported in 2005.

$100,000 to American Red Cross.

$50,000 to YMCA.

$45,000 to Young Life.

$35,000 to Salvation Army.

$30,000 to Davidson College, Davidson, NC.
$25,000 to Mercy Ships, Garden Valley, TX.
$25,000 to United Way.
$20,000 to Presbyterian Social Ministries, Jacksonville, FL.
$20,000 to University of Florida Foundation, Gainesville, FL.
$10,000 to Angelwood, Jacksonville, FL.

2300
Wilson-Wood Foundation, Inc.
(formerly Hugh & Mary Wilson Foundation, Inc.)
930 Scherer Way
Osprey, FL   34229   (941) 966-3635
Contact: Susan Wood, Treas. and Exec. Dir.

Established in 1983 in FL.
Donors: Hugh H. Wilson†; Mary P. Wilson†; John R. Wood.
Foundation type: Independent foundation.
Financial data (yr. ended 12/31/05): Assets, $9,740,857 (M); expenditures, $539,840; qualifying distributions, $469,484; giving activities include $409,905 for 22 grants (high: $30,000; low: $5,000).
Purpose and activities: Giving primarily for the underprivileged and the less fortunate in the local community.
Fields of interest: Adult education—literacy, basic skills & GED; Education, reading; Education; Health care; Nutrition; Housing/shelter, development; Human services; Children/youth, services; Aging, centers/services; Women, centers/services; Aging; Minorities; Women; Economically disadvantaged.
Type of support: General/operating support; Capital campaigns; Building/renovation; Equipment.
Limitations: Giving limited to the Manatee-Sarasota, FL, area. No support for foreign organizations or private foundations. No grants to individuals, or for endowment funds, deficit financing, travel projects, research, fundraising costs, multi-year projects, conferences, emergency funding or start up costs.
Publications: Annual report (including application guidelines).
Application information: Application form not required.
   Initial approach: Letter of inquiry
   Copies of proposal: 2
   Deadline(s): Initial letter of inquiry must be received by June 1
   Board meeting date(s): Mar., June, and Sept.
   Final notification: July
Officers and Directors:* John R. Wood,* Pres.; George Fraley,* V.P.; Sadie L. Wood,* Secy.; Susan Wood,* Treas. and Exec. Dir.; Thomas A. Faessler.
Number of staff: 1 full-time professional.
EIN: 592243926

2301
Winn-Dixie Stores Foundation ✧
c/o A. Baragona
5050 Edgewood Ct.
Jacksonville, FL   32254   (904) 783-5000
Contact: Susan Tubman

Incorporated in 1943 in FL.
Donor: Winn-Dixie Stores, Inc.
Foundation type: Company-sponsored foundation.
Financial data (yr. ended 12/31/05): Assets, $504,448 (M); gifts received, $135,350; expenditures, $1,029,858; qualifying distributions,

$1,028,659; giving activities include $575,756 for 17 grants (high: $357,143; low: $500), and $239,566 for 129 employee matching gifts.
Purpose and activities: The foundation supports zoological societies and organizations involved with education, health, cancer, youth development, and community development.
Fields of interest: Education; Zoos/zoological societies; Health care; Cancer; Youth development; Community development; Federated giving programs.
Type of support: Continuing support; Annual campaigns; Building/renovation; Equipment; Program development; Conferences/seminars; Scholarship funds; Research; Employee matching gifts; Matching/challenge support.
Limitations: Giving on a national basis in areas of company operations. No support for religious or political organizations. No grants to individuals.
Publications: Annual report.
Application information: Proposals should be submitted using organization letterhead. Application form not required.
   Initial approach: Proposal
   Deadline(s): None
   Board meeting date(s): As required
   Final notification: 30 days
Officers and Directors:* D.F. Henry,* Pres.; L.B. Appel, V.P. and Secy.; K.D. Hardee,* V.P. and Treas.; D.M. Byrum,* V.P.; C.A. Forehand, V.P.; M.J. Istre, V.P.; D.G. Lafever, V.P.; L.R. Rodriquez, V.P.; M.A. Sellers, V.P.
EIN: 590995428

2302
Winston Family Foundation ✧ ☆
(formerly James H. Winston Charitable Foundation)
601 Riverside Ave., Ste. 619
Jacksonville, FL   32204

Established in 1986 in FL.
Donor: James H. Winston.
Foundation type: Independent foundation.
Financial data (yr. ended 12/31/05): Assets, $2,224,124 (M); expenditures, $558,259; qualifying distributions, $558,037; giving activities include $554,594 for 86 grants (high: $400,000; low: $35).
Fields of interest: Performing arts, music; Secondary school/education; Christian agencies & churches.
Limitations: Applications not accepted. Giving primarily in FL. No grants to individuals.
Application information: Contributes only to pre-selected organizations.
Trustees: James H. Winston; James H. Winston, Jr.; Mary Winston-Mason.
EIN: 592678732
Selected grants: The following grants were reported in 2005.
$20,293 to Saint Vincents Foundation, Jacksonville, FL.
$13,981 to United Way of Northeast Florida, Jacksonville, FL.
$9,206 to YMCA, Floridas First Coast Metropolitan, Jacksonville, FL. 3 grants: $3,093, $5,113, $1,000
$5,158 to University of Florida Foundation, Gainesville, FL.
$2,042 to Episcopal High School, Jacksonville, FL. 2 grants: $1,042, $1,000
$1,500 to Cummer Museum of Art and Gardens, Jacksonville, FL. 2 grants: $1,000, $500

2303
Winter Park Health Foundation ✧
(formerly Winter Park Memorial Hospital Association, Inc.)
220 Edinburgh Dr.
Winter Park, FL   32792   (407) 644-2300
FAX: (407) 644-0174; E-mail: contact@wphf.org;
Mailing address: P.O. Box 2647, Winter Park, FL 32790; URL: http://www.wphf.org

Donor: Lola E. Nowers Fund.
Foundation type: Independent foundation.
Financial data (yr. ended 12/31/05): Assets, $129,677,900 (M); gifts received, $5,980; expenditures, $8,070,904; qualifying distributions, $7,899,478; giving activities include $4,219,909 for 127 grants (high: $1,500,000; low: $500), and $1,597,421 for 3 foundation-administered programs.
Purpose and activities: Giving primarily for health associations and hospitals, education, children, youth and social services, services for the elderly, YMCAs, and federated giving programs; funding also for the arts and religious purposes.
Fields of interest: Museums; Arts; Secondary school/education; Education; Hospitals (general); Health organizations, association; Human services; YM/YWCAs & YM/YWHAs; Children/youth, services; Aging, centers/services; Federated giving programs; Religion.
Limitations: Giving primarily in the greater Winter Park, FL, area; some giving also in central FL. No support for private organizations. No grants to individuals, political purposes, lobbying, and electioneering, social events, or funding, endowment, or routine operating expenses.
Application information: Application form available on foundation Web Site. Application form required.
Officers and Trustees:* Allan E. Keen,* Chair.; Ivan J. Castro, M.D.*, Vice-Chair., Older Adults; Barbara DeVane,* Vice-Chair., Children and Youth; Anne K. Fray,* Vice-Chair., Winter Park Memorial Hospital; Jay Hughes,* Vice-Chair., Access to Health Care; Patricia Maddox,* Pres.; Ron Pecora,* Secy.; John C. Hitt,* Treas.; Suzanne M. Ackley; Rebecca Guillory Gilmer; John D. Guameri, M.D.; M. Scott Hillman; Thomas Holley; Brenda Holson, M.D.; Charles F. Pierce; Michael W. Poole; Joan Ruffier; Debra A. St. Louis; Thaddeus Seymour; Judith G. Thames.
EIN: 590669460
Selected grants: The following grants were reported in 2005.
$324,937 to Orange County Public Schools, Orlando, FL. 2 grants: $185,783, $139,154
$102,500 to Winter Park Public Library, Winter Park, FL. 2 grants: $100,000, $2,500
$100,000 to American Red Cross, Orlando, FL. 2 grants: $50,000 each (For relief efforts for Hurricane Katrina victims who have been displaced to Central Florida).
$92,500 to Seniors First, Orlando, FL. 3 grants: $2,500, $40,000, $50,000
$10,000 to Hospice of the Comforter, Altamonte Springs, FL.

2304
The Wolfson Family Foundation, Inc. ✧
P.O. Box 4
Jacksonville, FL   32201

Incorporated in 1951 in FL.

Donors: Louis E. Wolfson; Sam W. Wolfson†; Saul Wolfson; Florence M. Wolfson†; Cecil Wolfson.
Foundation type: Independent foundation.
Financial data (yr. ended 9/30/05): Assets, $434,004 (M); gifts received, $1,950; expenditures, $579,286; qualifying distributions, $555,805; giving activities include $522,408 for 23 grants (high: $500,000; low: $100).
Purpose and activities: Giving for medical care and health associations.
Fields of interest: Hospitals (general); Health organizations, association; Human services; Jewish agencies & temples; Disabilities, people with.
Type of support: Building/renovation; Equipment.
Limitations: Applications not accepted. Giving primarily in FL. No grants to individuals.
Application information: Contributes only to pre-selected organizations.
Officers and Directors:* Cecil Wolfson,* Chair.; Nathan Wolfson,* Vice-Chair.; M.C. Tomberlin,* Secy.; Robert O. Johnson, Treas.
Trustees: Joe I. Degen; Michael S. Wolfson; Morris D. Wolfson; Richard J. Wolfson; Saul Wolfson; Stephen P. Wolfson.
Number of staff: 5 part-time support.
EIN: 590995431

2305
Lynn and Louis Wolfson II Family Foundation, Inc. ✧

(formerly Loulyfran Wolfson Foundation, Inc.)
1110 Brickell Ave., Ste. 202
Miami, FL 33131

Established in 1967 in FL.
Donor: Lynn Wolfson.
Foundation type: Independent foundation.
Financial data (yr. ended 12/31/05): Assets, $2,954,227 (M); gifts received, $309,620; expenditures, $337,854; qualifying distributions, $321,300; giving activities include $321,300 for 11 grants (high: $200,000; low: $200).
Purpose and activities: Giving primarily for the arts, especially performing arts centers; funding also for federated giving programs, and human services.
Fields of interest: Museums (art); Performing arts centers; Performing arts, ballet; Performing arts, opera; Arts; Education; Human services; Federated giving programs; Homeless.
Type of support: General/operating support.
Limitations: Applications not accepted. Giving primarily in Miami, FL; some funding also in Washington, DC. No grants to individuals.
Application information: Contributes only to pre-selected organizations.
Officers and Trustees:* Lynn Wolfson,* Pres.; J. Bruce Irving, Secy.; Harold Auerbach, Treas.; Louis Wolfson III.
EIN: 596196403
Selected grants: The following grants were reported in 2004.
$200,000 to United Way of Miami-Dade, Miami, FL.

$30,000 to United Way. 2 grants: $25,000, $5,000
$2,500 to Temple Israel, West Palm Beach, FL.
$2,300 to Greater Miami Opera, Miami, FL. 2 grants: $1,760, $540
$1,296 to Concert Association of Florida, Miami Beach, FL.
$1,000 to American Red Cross, Washington, NC.

2306
Rubin and Gladys Wollowick Foundation, Inc. ✧

c/o Mellon Trust of Florida
1111 Brickell Ave., 30th Fl.
Miami, FL 33131
Contact: Tamara Chaskes

Established in 1984 in FL.
Donor: Gladys Wollowick†.
Foundation type: Independent foundation.
Financial data (yr. ended 1/31/05): Assets, $6,988,092 (M); expenditures, $822,330; qualifying distributions, $657,000; giving activities include $657,000 for 68 grants (high: $100,000; low: $2,000).
Fields of interest: Education; Hospitals (general); Eye diseases; Medical research, institute; Eye research; Multiple sclerosis research; Human services; Jewish federated giving programs; Jewish agencies & temples.
International interests: Israel.
Type of support: General/operating support; Annual campaigns; Equipment; Emergency funds; Research; Matching/challenge support.
Limitations: Giving primarily in Miami, FL. No grants to individuals.
Application information: Application form not required.
  Initial approach: Letter
  Deadline(s): None
  Board meeting date(s): Varies
Officers: Patricia Wollowick, Pres. and Secy.; Edward Levinson, V.P. and Treas.
Directors: Richard Lowe; Sandra Lowe; Rhoda Samuels; Robert Tesher; Janet Amy Wollowick; Patricia Wollowick.
EIN: 592469452
Selected grants: The following grants were reported in 2004.
$100,000 to Yeshiva University, New York, NY. For general support.
$50,000 to Bar-Ilan University in Israel, Miami, FL. For general support.
$50,000 to Multiple Sclerosis Society, National, Miami, FL. For general support.
$29,400 to Bascom Palmer Eye Institute, Miami, FL. For general support.
$25,000 to United Way of Miami-Dade, Miami, FL. For general support.
$25,000 to University of Miami, Coral Gables, FL. For Wollowick Scholarship Fund.
$25,000 to Weizmann Institute of Science, Rehovot, Israel. For general support.

$20,000 to Coconut Grove Playhouse State Theater of Florida Corporation, Miami, FL. For general support.
$15,000 to American Red Magen David for Israel, New York, NY. For general support.
$15,000 to Jewish Federation of Greater Miami, Miami, FL. For general support.

2307
Norman E. & Harriet S. Wymbs Foundation ✧

7050 Skyline Dr.
Delray Beach, FL 33446-2212

Established in 1993 in FL.
Donors: Harriet S. Wymbs; Norman E. Wymbs.
Foundation type: Independent foundation.
Financial data (yr. ended 12/31/05): Assets, $7,801,679 (M); gifts received, $5,013,492; expenditures, $779,652; qualifying distributions, $755,561; giving activities include $616,542 for 2 grants (high: $606,542; low: $10,000).
Fields of interest: Museums; Foundations (private operating); Protestant agencies & churches.
Limitations: Applications not accepted. Giving primarily in IL. No grants to individuals.
Application information: Contributes only to pre-selected organizations.
Officers: Norman E. Wymbs, Pres.; Harriet S. Wymbs, V.P.
Directors: Charles Beckman; Ellen Wymbs Crouse; William E. Jones; James Ness.
EIN: 650352321

2308
The Bryan J. and June B. Zwan Foundation, Inc. ✧

3000 Bayport Dr., Ste. 800
Tampa, FL 33607   (813) 287-6337
Contact: Paul Ragaini, Dir.

Established in 1999 in FL.
Donors: Bryan J. Zwan; June B. Zwan.
Foundation type: Independent foundation.
Financial data (yr. ended 12/31/04): Assets, $159,334 (M); gifts received, $3,000,000; expenditures, $3,230,398; qualifying distributions, $3,228,397; giving activities include $3,226,396 for 12 grants (high: $1,639,696; low: $500).
Fields of interest: Education; Civil liberties, advocacy; Religion.
Limitations: Giving primarily in FL. No grants to individuals.
Application information:
  Initial approach: Letter
  Deadline(s): None
Officers and Directors:* Bryan J. Zwan,* Pres.; June B. Zwan,* Secy.-Treas.; Paul Ragaini.
EIN: 593611266

GEORGIA

2309

Howell E. Adams, Jr. Charitable Trust ✧
290 W. Wesley Rd. N.W.
Atlanta, GA   30305

Established in GA.
Donors: Madeline R. Adams; Howell E. Adams, Jr.
Foundation type: Independent foundation.
Financial data (yr. ended 12/31/05): Assets, $1,047,605 (M); gifts received, $501,716; expenditures, $1,247,246; qualifying distributions, $1,149,596; giving activities include $1,149,596 for 189 grants (high: $200,000; low: $15).
Fields of interest: Performing arts, orchestra (symphony); Arts; Higher education; Education; Health organizations, association; Human services; Christian agencies & churches.
Limitations: Applications not accepted. Giving primarily in GA and TN. No grants to individuals.
Application information: Contributes only to pre-selected organizations.
Trustee: Madeline R. Adams.
EIN: 586157758
Selected grants: The following grants were reported in 2004.
$250,000 to Community Foundation for Greater Atlanta, Atlanta, GA.
$240,000 to United Way of Metropolitan Atlanta, Atlanta, GA. 2 grants: $35,000, $205,000
$150,000 to FCS Urban Ministries, Atlanta, GA.
$103,000 to Trinity Presbyterian Church of Atlanta, Atlanta, GA.
$32,000 to Altamont First Baptist Church, Altamont, TN.
$25,000 to Boy Scouts of America, Atlanta Area Council, Atlanta, GA.
$25,000 to Girl Scouts of the U.S.A., Northwest Georgia Council, Atlanta, GA.
$20,000 to Atlanta Union Mission, Atlanta, GA.
$15,000 to YMCA of Metropolitan Atlanta, Atlanta, GA.

2310

The AEC Trust
c/o Atlantic Trust Co., N.A.
1170 Peachtree St., Ste. 2300
Atlanta, GA   30309
Contact: Julia Beisel, Trust Off., Atlantic Trust Co.
URL: http://www.fsrequests.com/aec

Established in 1980 in IL.
Donor: Members of the Cofrin family.
Foundation type: Independent foundation.
Financial data (yr. ended 12/31/05): Assets, $30,430,139 (M); expenditures, $1,626,242; qualifying distributions, $1,466,150; giving activities include $1,430,000 for 14 grants (high: $1,150,000; low: $5,000).
Purpose and activities: Giving primarily for the arts, educational support for pre-selected schools, environment, women's issues, and AIDS related services.
Fields of interest: Museums; Arts; Education; Environment; Women; AIDS, people with.
Type of support: General/operating support; Capital campaigns; Building/renovation; Equipment; Land acquisition; Debt reduction; Conferences/seminars;

Professorships; Publication; Research; Technical assistance; Matching/challenge support.
Limitations: Giving primarily in Boulder, CO, Gainesville, FL, western MA, Green Bay, WI, and Atlanta, GA; support in Atlanta limited to organizations with offices inside the perimeter. No support for religious organizations, government agencies, affiliates of large public charities, sponsorships, or special events. No grants to individuals or for organizations with budgets over $1 million; endowments generally not funded.
Application information: All proposals must be submitted electronically via foundation Web site. Paper documents will not be reviewed or accepted. Application form required.
Initial approach: Take eligibility quiz on foundation Web site
Deadline(s): Apr. 1 and Sept. 1
Board meeting date(s): May and Oct.
Final notification: On a rolling basis
Advisory Committee: Edith D. Cofrin, Chair.; David A. Cofrin; David H. Cofrin; Gladys G. Cofrin; Mary Ann H. Cofrin; Mary Ann P. Cofrin; Paige W. Cofrin.
Corporate Trustee: Atlantic Trust Co., N.A.
EIN: 366725987

2311

The Aflac Foundation, Inc. ▼
1932 Wynnton Rd.
Columbus, GA   31999
Contact: Francine Medley, Admin.
FAX: (706) 320-2288; *E-mail:* fmedley@aflac.com

Established in 1999 in GA.
Donor: American Family Life Assurance Co. of Columbus.
Foundation type: Company-sponsored foundation.
Financial data (yr. ended 12/31/05): Assets, $1,766,335 (M); gifts received, $3,408,150; expenditures, $6,858,432; qualifying distributions, $6,858,150; giving activities include $6,858,150 for 47 grants (high: $2,183,122; low: $5,000).
Purpose and activities: The foundation supports community health systems and community foundations and organizations involved with education, pediatric cancer, disease, cancer research, public safety, and human services.
Fields of interest: Education; Medical care, community health systems; Cancer; Health organizations; Cancer research; Safety/disasters; Children/youth, services; Human services; Foundations (community); Federated giving programs; Children.
Type of support: Fellowships; Endowments; Employee volunteer services; Cause-related marketing; General/operating support; Annual campaigns; Capital campaigns; Program development; Research.
Limitations: Giving primarily in areas of company operations, with emphasis on the greater Atlanta, GA, area. No support for religious or political organizations. No grants to individuals.
Application information: Application form not required.
Initial approach: Proposal
Copies of proposal: 1
Board meeting date(s): Bi-monthly
Officers: Kathelen V. Amos, Pres.; Sharon H. Douglas, V.P.; Alfred O. Blackmar, Secy.; Rebecca K. Davis, Treas.
EIN: 582509396
Selected grants: The following grants were reported in 2005.

$2,000,000 to Childrens Healthcare of Atlanta, Atlanta, GA. For capital campaign.
$1,005,000 to American Red Cross, West Central Georgia Chapter, Columbus, GA. For National Disaster Relief Fund.
$1,000,000 to Washington DC Martin Luther King, Jr. National Memorial Project Foundation, DC. For general support.
$500,000 to Smithsonian Institution, National Museum of African American History, DC.
$458,528 to United Way of the Chattahoochee Valley, Columbus, GA. For annual campaign.
$250,000 to Chattahoochee Valley Regional Library System, Columbus, GA. For capital campaign.
$250,000 to Columbus Regional Healthcare System, Columbus, GA. For John B. Amos Cancer Center.
$25,000 to RiverCenter for the Performing Arts, Columbus, GA. For general support.
$25,000 to Saint Francis Hospital Foundation, Columbus, GA. For capital campaign.
$15,000 to University of Nebraska Foundation, Omaha, NE. For general support.

2312

AGL Resources Private Foundation, Inc. ✧
c/o Wachovia Bank, N.A.
P.O. Box 4569, Location 1601
Atlanta, GA   30302-4569
Contact: Staci Bush, Asst. Secy.
URL: http://www.aglresources.com/community/guidelines.aspx

Established in 1998 in GA.
Donors: Georgia Gas Co.; AGL Foundation; AGL Resources Inc.
Foundation type: Company-sponsored foundation.
Financial data (yr. ended 12/31/05): Assets, $12,413,616 (M); expenditures, $1,895,111; qualifying distributions, $1,843,675; giving activities include $1,779,895 for 189 grants (high: $75,000; low: $25).
Purpose and activities: The foundation supports organizations involved with arts and culture, literacy, K-12 and higher math and science education, the environment, senior citizens, minority and women leadership development, economically disadvantaged people, and energy assistance for low-income households.
Fields of interest: Arts; Elementary/secondary education; Higher education; Education, reading; Environment, air pollution; Environment, natural resources; Environment, beautification programs; Leadership development; Aging; Minorities; Women; Economically disadvantaged.
Type of support: Annual campaigns; Capital campaigns; Building/renovation; Endowments; Program development; Seed money; Scholarship funds; Sponsorships.
Limitations: Giving primarily in Brevard County and Miami, FL, GA, NJ, Chattanooga, TN, Houston, TX, and VA. No support for religious organizations or private K-12 schools. No grants to individuals.
Publications: Annual report.
Application information: Application form not required.
Initial approach: Proposal
Copies of proposal: 1
Deadline(s): Sept. 1
Board meeting date(s): Nov.
Final notification: 4 to 6 weeks
Officer: Melanie Platt, Pres.

Trustee: Wachovia Bank, N.A.
EIN: 582399946

2313

The Jeffrey & Jennifer Allred Family Foundation, Inc. ✧ ☆
3399 Peachtree Rd., Ste. 700
Atlanta, GA 30326

Established in 2003.
Donor: Jeffrey Allred.
Foundation type: Independent foundation.
Financial data (yr. ended 12/31/05): Assets, $38,695 (M); gifts received, $413,542; expenditures, $1,486,429; qualifying distributions, $1,483,014; giving activities include $1,483,014 for 9 grants (high: $850,000; low: $5,000).
Fields of interest: Higher education, university; Education.
Limitations: Applications not accepted. Giving with a strong emphasis in GA.
Application information: Unsolicited requests for funds not accepted.
Officers: Jeffery C. Allred, Pres.; Jennifer Allred, Secy.
EIN: 201052873

2314

Paul S. Amos Educational Foundation, Inc.
c/o Selection Comm.
P.O. Box 5605
Columbus, GA 31906-0605

Established in 1990 in GA.
Donors: American Family Life Assurance Co. of Columbus; Paul S. Amos; Daniel P. Amos.
Foundation type: Independent foundation.
Financial data (yr. ended 12/31/04): Assets, $7,128,738 (L); gifts received, $300,000; expenditures, $1,289,848; qualifying distributions, $1,263,740; giving activities include $1,263,740 for 51 grants (high: $250,000; low: $100).
Purpose and activities: The foundation supports organizations involved with higher education, cancer, and housing.
Fields of interest: Higher education; Cancer; Housing/shelter.
Type of support: Program development; Scholarship funds; Employee-related scholarships.
Limitations: Giving primarily in AL, FL, and GA.
Application information: Application form not required.
   Initial approach: Contact foundation for application information
   Copies of proposal: 1
   Deadline(s): None
Officers and Trustees:* Paul S. Amos,* Pres.; Daniel P. Amos, Secy.-Treas.; Jean R. Amos; Lauren A. Amos; Paul S. Amos II.
EIN: 581949673
Selected grants: The following grants were reported in 2003.
$198,000 to University of the Cumberlands, Williamsburg, KY. For program support.
$120,000 to Asbury Theological Seminary, Atlanta, GA. For program support.
$50,000 to Samaritans Purse, Boone, NC. For general support.
$18,081 to Auburn University, Auburn, AL. For scholarships.

$18,067 to Columbus State University, Columbus, GA. For program support.
$16,345 to Troy University, Phenix City, AL. For scholarships.
$5,000 to New Horizons Community Education Board, Columbus, GA. For program support.
$3,647 to Samford University, Birmingham, AL. For scholarships.
$3,000 to Campus Crusade for Christ, Atlanta, GA. For program support.
$2,000 to Furman University, Greenville, SC. For scholarships.

2315

Daniel P. Amos Family Foundation ✧
(formerly Daniel P. and Shannon L. Amos Foundation, Inc.)
c/o Selection Comm.
P.O. Box 5346
Columbus, GA 31906   (706) 324-0251

Established in 1992 in GA.
Donors: Daniel P. Amos; Shannon L. Amos; Paul Amos Trust; Jean Amos Trust.
Foundation type: Independent foundation.
Financial data (yr. ended 12/31/04): Assets, $58,533,394 (M); gifts received, $4,818,795; expenditures, $2,090,711; qualifying distributions, $1,992,500; giving activities include $1,992,500 for 28 grants (high: $325,000; low: $250).
Purpose and activities: Giving primarily for human services, health associations, United Methodist churches and Christian organizations, as well as to an interdenominational theological seminary; funding also for a television foundation.
Fields of interest: Media, television; Higher education; Theological school/education; Health organizations, association; Cancer research; Human services; Christian agencies & churches; Protestant agencies & churches.
Type of support: Building/renovation.
Limitations: Giving primarily in Columbus and Atlanta, GA. No grants to individuals.
Application information: Application form not required.
   Deadline(s): None
Officers and Trustees:* Daniel P. Amos,* Pres.; David B. Plyler, Secy.; Lauren A. Amos; Paul S. Amos.
EIN: 582005391
Selected grants: The following grants were reported in 2003.
$499,000 to Johns Hopkins Bayview Medical Center, Baltimore, MD. For grant made in honor of Dr. Hellmann.
$300,000 to Asbury Theological Seminary, Wilmore, KY.
$260,000 to Wynnbrook Baptist Church, Columbus, GA. For underprivileged children.
$250,000 to Saint Luke United Methodist Church, Columbus, GA. For capital building support.
$50,000 to Habitat for Humanity International, Americus, GA.
$25,000 to English Language Institute in China, San Dimas, CA.
$20,000 to Teen Challenge of Georgia, Atlanta, GA. For Yucchi Project.
$16,667 to Teen Advisors, Columbus, GA.
$10,000 to Columbus Community Center, Columbus, GA. For capital building fund.
$10,000 to United Way of the Chattahoochee Valley, Columbus, GA.

2316

John and Elena Amos Foundation, Inc. ✧ ☆
(formerly John and Elena Diaz-Verson Amos Foundation, Inc.)
6751 Macon Rd., Ste. 4
Columbus, GA 31907
Contact: Eva Brown

Established in 1992 in GA.
Donor: Elena Diaz-Verson Amos†.
Foundation type: Independent foundation.
Financial data (yr. ended 12/31/05): Assets, $5,770,597 (M); expenditures, $930,872; qualifying distributions, $930,872; giving activities include $925,857 for 10 grants (high: $285,714; low: $2,000).
Fields of interest: Education; Health organizations, association; Human services; Roman Catholic federated giving programs.
Type of support: Grants to individuals; Scholarships—to individuals.
Limitations: Giving primarily in GA.
Application information: Application form not required.
   Initial approach: Letter
   Deadline(s): None
Officers: Salvador Diaz-Verson, Chair.; Maria Teresa Amos Frith, Secy.; John Shelby Amos II, Treas.
EIN: 582006020
Selected grants: The following grants were reported in 2003.
$70,000 to Saint Anne Elementary School, Columbus, GA. For capital campaign.
$36,000 to Faith In Action La Ermita De La Caridad, Miami, FL. For general support.
$6,000 to Steeplechase, Columbus, GA.
$1,989 to Goodwill Industries of Chattachoochee Valley, Columbus, GA. For general support.
$1,000 to Fellowship of Christians and Churches United in Service, Columbus, GA. For general support.
$1,000 to Habitat for Humanity, Harris County, Pine Mountain, GA. For general support.
$1,000 to Holy Transfiguration Greek Orthodox Church, Columbus, GA. For general support.

2317

The Peyton Anderson Foundation, Inc. ✧
577 Mulberry St., Ste. 1111
Macon, GA 31201   (478) 743-5359
Contact: Juanita T. Jordan, Exec. Dir.
FAX: (478) 742-5201; E-mail (for Juanita T. Jordan, Exec. Dir.): jtjordan@peytonanderson.org

Incorporated in 1988 in GA; funded in 1989.
Donor: Peyton Tooke Anderson, Jr.†.
Foundation type: Independent foundation.
Financial data (yr. ended 12/31/05): Assets, $93,761,275 (M); expenditures, $5,866,589; qualifying distributions, $4,971,756; giving activities include $4,500,000 for 47 grants (high: $750,000; low: $400; average: $10,000–$200,000).
Purpose and activities: Giving primarily for the arts, education, housing development, and human services.
Fields of interest: Performing arts, theater; Arts; Elementary school/education; Higher education; Adult education—literacy, basic skills & GED; Education, reading; Education; Housing/shelter,

development; Human services; Children/youth, services.
Type of support: Program development; Seed money; Matching/challenge support.
Limitations: Giving limited to Bibb County and Macon, GA. No support for private foundations, private schools, or churches. No grants to individuals, or for endowments or special events.
Publications: Informational brochure (including application guidelines).
Application information: Contact foundation for application. Please do not bind application attachments. Application form required.
Initial approach: Letter or telephone
Copies of proposal: 6
Deadline(s): Apr. 1 and Aug. 1
Board meeting date(s): 3 times per year
Final notification: Grants awarded twice a year
Officers: E.S. Sell, Jr., Pres.; John D. Comer, 1st V.P.; Ed S. Sell III, 2nd V.P.; R. Reid Hanson, Secy.; Juanita T. Jordan, Treas. and Exec. Dir.
Number of staff: 1 full-time professional; 2 full-time support.
EIN: 581803562
Selected grants: The following grants were reported in 2005.
$750,000 to Georgia Trust for Historic Preservation, Atlanta, GA. To restore Hay House.
$600,000 to Mid-State Childrens Challenge Projects, Macon, GA. For Georgia Children's Museum and Educational Annex.
$510,000 to Newtown Macon, Macon, GA. For trail construction and creation of mixed-use development.
$505,000 to Medcen Foundation, Macon, GA. For Sylvia Bond Leadership Institute, and construction of heart hospital.
$334,000 to Macon College Foundation, Macon, GA. For Invest in Success capital campaign.
$300,000 to Macon-Bibb County Convention and Visitors Bureau, Macon, GA. To revitalize bus station into new visitors' center and headquarters.
$250,000 to Mercer University, Macon, GA. For renovations and upgrades at Grand Opera House.
$200,000 to Community Foundation of Central Georgia, Macon Economic Development Commission, Macon, GA. For Macon Now initiative.
$174,290 to Georgia Sports Hall of Fame Foundation, Macon, GA. To replace computers and repair exhibits and theater.
$10,000 to First Presbyterian Day School, Macon, GA. For capital campaign.

2318
Anncox Foundation, Inc. ◇
c/o Dow, Lohnes & Albertson
1 Ravinia Dr., Ste. 1600
Atlanta, GA   30346

Incorporated in 1960 in GA.
Donor: Anne Cox Chambers.
Foundation type: Independent foundation.
Financial data (yr. ended 12/31/05): Assets, $253,047 (M); gifts received, $912,329; expenditures, $1,203,231; qualifying distributions, $1,166,675; giving activities include $1,166,675 for 55 grants (high: $333,333; low: $100).
Purpose and activities: Giving primarily for museums and education, animal welfare, health, and human services.

Fields of interest: Museums; Education; Animal welfare; Animals/wildlife, preservation/protection; Health organizations, association; Human services; Federated giving programs.
Limitations: Applications not accepted. Giving primarily in GA, and the greater metropolitan New York, NY, area. No grants to individuals.
Application information: Contributes only to pre-selected organizations.
Officers and Trustee:* Anne Cox Chambers, Pres. and Treas.; James Cox Chambers,* V.P. and Treas.
EIN: 586033966

2319
Arnold Fund
1201 W. Peachtree St.
Atlanta, GA   30309-3400   (404) 881-7886
Contact: John C. Sawyer, Exec. Dir.

Established in 1952 in GA.
Donors: Florence Arnold†; Robert O. Arnold†.
Foundation type: Independent foundation.
Financial data (yr. ended 12/31/05): Assets, $18,204,052 (M); expenditures, $982,031; qualifying distributions, $881,448; giving activities include $881,448 for grants.
Fields of interest: Performing arts; Performing arts, music; Higher education; Libraries/library science; Education; Biomedicine; Medical research, institute; YM/YWCAs & YM/YWHAs; Federated giving programs.
Limitations: Applications not accepted. Giving limited to Covington, GA. No grants to individuals.
Application information: Unsolicited requests for funds not accepted.
Board meeting date(s): Spring and fall
Officer: John C. Sawyer, Exec. Dir.
Trustees: Robert F. Fowler III; David A. Newman; Frank B. Turner.
EIN: 586032079

2320
Atlanta Foundation ◇
c/o Wachovia Bank, N.A.
3414 Peachtree Rd., 5th Fl., MC GA8023
Atlanta, GA   30326
Contact: Alice Sheets; Lydia Whitman
E-mail: grantinquiries@wachovia.com; URL: http://www.wachovia.com/corp_inst/charitable_services

Established in 1921 in GA by bank resolution and declaration of trust.
Foundation type: Independent foundation.
Financial data (yr. ended 12/31/05): Assets, $28,138,823 (M); expenditures, $1,219,011; qualifying distributions, $1,059,601; giving activities include $1,044,100 for 42 grants (high: $30,000; low: $4,000).
Purpose and activities: Assistance to charitable and educational institutions to promote education and improve local living conditions. Primary areas of interest include education, cultural programs, housing, and other general charitable activities in Fulton and DeKalb counties, GA.
Fields of interest: Arts; Adult education—literacy, basic skills & GED; Education, reading; Education; Hospitals (general); Health care; Housing/shelter, development; Recreation; Human services; Youth, services; Community development; Federated giving programs.

Type of support: General/operating support; Capital campaigns; Building/renovation; Equipment; Program development.
Limitations: Giving limited to Fulton and DeKalb counties, GA. No grants to individuals, or for scholarships or fellowships; no loans.
Publications: Application guidelines; Grants list.
Application information: Guidelines available on foundation Web site. Application form required.
Initial approach: Letter, no longer than 2 pages
Copies of proposal: 1
Deadline(s): Mar. 1 and Sept. 1
Board meeting date(s): July/Aug.
Final notification: Sept.1
Officers: Randy Karesh, Secy.
Directors: Juanita Eber; Scott Fisher; Linda Selig; Dom H. Wyant.
Trustee: Wachovia Bank, N.A.
EIN: 586026879

2321
Atlanta Law School ◇
880 W. Peachtree St. N.E., Ste. B
Atlanta, GA   30309

Established in 1996 in GA.
Foundation type: Independent foundation.
Financial data (yr. ended 12/31/05): Assets, $3,254,125 (M); expenditures, $624,961; qualifying distributions, $537,068; giving activities include $495,873 for 2 grants (high: $312,300; low: $183,573).
Fields of interest: Higher education.
Type of support: Scholarship funds.
Limitations: Applications not accepted. Giving limited to Atlanta, GA. No grants to individuals directly.
Application information: Contributes only to pre-selected organizations.
Trustees: David H. Flint; E. Lewis Hansen; Harvey W. Moskowitz.
EIN: 586000080

2322
The Azalea Foundation ◇
(formerly JVM & JKM Foundation)
P.O. Box 20567
St. Simons Island, GA   31522-0167
Contact: Jeanne K. Manning, Pres.

Established in 1993.
Donor: James V. Manning.
Foundation type: Independent foundation.
Financial data (yr. ended 11/30/04): Assets, $8,314,634 (M); gifts received, $389,469; expenditures, $523,660; qualifying distributions, $485,757; giving activities include $461,814 for 41 grants.
Purpose and activities: Giving primarily for education, children, youth and social services, health care, and federated giving programs.
Fields of interest: Higher education; Libraries/library science; Education; Health care; Human services; Children/youth, services; Family services; Foundations (community); Federated giving programs.
Type of support: General/operating support; Annual campaigns; Capital campaigns.
Limitations: Giving primarily in Glynn County, GA, and Santa Fe County, NM. No grants to individuals.

Application information: Contributes mostly to pre-selected organizations. Applications accepted only from Glynn County, GA, and Santa Fe County, NM, areas, and for projects serving children and families at risk. Application form not required.

Initial approach: Letter
Deadline(s): None
Board meeting date(s): Varies

Officers and Trustees: Jeanne K. Manning,* Pres.; James V. Manning,* V.P.

EIN: 226617071

Selected grants: The following grants were reported in 2003.

$70,000 to Georgia, State of, Coastal Medical Access Project, Atlanta, GA. For medical care for families at risk.

$60,000 to Agnes Scott College, Decatur, GA. For capital campaign.

$30,000 to United Way of Santa Fe County, Santa Fe, NM.

$20,000 to Planned Parenthood of Georgia, Atlanta, GA.

$15,000 to YWCA of Brunswick, Brunswick, GA.

$12,500 to Santa Fe Opera, Santa Fe, NM.

$12,000 to Harwood Museum Alliance, Taos, NM.

$10,000 to Frederica Academy, Saint Simons Island, GA. For capital campaign.

$10,000 to University of Michigan, Ann Arbor, MI.

$6,000 to Boys and Girls Clubs of Southeast Georgia, Brunswick, GA.

2323
BellSouth Foundation ◇

c/o BellSouth Corp.
1155 Peachtree St., N.E., Rm. 7H08
Atlanta, GA 30309-3610 (404) 249-2396
FAX: (404) 249-5696;
E-mail: grants.manager@bellsouth.com; Additional tel.: (404) 249-2429, (404) 249-2428; URL: http://www.bellsouthfoundation.org

Established in 1986 in GA.

Donor: BellSouth Corp.

Foundation type: Company-sponsored foundation.

Financial data (yr. ended 12/31/04): Assets, $60,611,229 (M); expenditures, $3,003,387; qualifying distributions, $2,704,316; giving activities include $2,408,242 for 199 grants (high: $160,000; low: $16).

Purpose and activities: The foundation supports organizations involved with education, minorities, and economically disadvantaged students. Special emphasis is directed toward programs designed to improve teaching quality; impact state and national education policy; strengthen educational leadership; and integrate technology effectively.

Fields of interest: Education, reform; Elementary/secondary education; Higher education; Engineering/technology; Minorities; Economically disadvantaged.

Type of support: Employee-related scholarships; Employee volunteer services; Program development; Seed money.

Limitations: Applications not accepted. Giving limited to areas of company local telephone operations in AL, FL, GA, KY, LA, MS, NC, SC, and TN. No support for single K-12 schools that are not part of a larger district reform effort or discriminatory organizations. No grants to individuals (except for employee-related scholarships), or for capital campaigns, endowments, general operating support, educational product development, equipment, individual study, research or travel,

fundraising events, programs with limited impact or non-education-related programs, or single discipline curricula unrelated to a broader reform effort.

Publications: Annual report; Grants list.

Application information: Contributes only to pre-selected organizations.

Board meeting date(s): Apr. and Nov.

Officers and Trustees: Richard Anderson,* Chair.; Mary Boehm, Pres.; Tom Harvey, Treas.; Daniel Bradley, Genl. Counsel; Valencia I. Adams; Francis A. Dramis, Jr.; Rebecca M. Dunn; Mark Feidler; Margaret Greene; Isaiah Harris, Jr.; John M. McCullouch; Roderick D. Odom; William C. Pate; Krista Tillman.

Number of staff: 3 full-time professional; 1 full-time support.

EIN: 581708046

2324
Beloco Foundation, Inc. ◇

P.O. Box 140
Columbus, GA 31902-0140 (706) 571-6040
Contact: Lovick P. Corn, Pres.
Application address: P.O. Box 23024, Columbus, GA 31902; tel.: (706) 571-6040

Established in 1967 in GA.

Donors: Lovick P. Corn; Elizabeth T. Corn.

Foundation type: Independent foundation.

Financial data (yr. ended 6/30/05): Assets, $16,481,613 (M); gifts received, $300,000; expenditures, $958,636; qualifying distributions, $880,662; giving activities include $875,603 for 29 grants (high: $200,813; low: $1,000).

Purpose and activities: Giving primarily for education, health, human services, and religion.

Fields of interest: Higher education, college; Higher education, university; Education; Health organizations; Human services; Christian agencies & churches; Religion.

Type of support: General/operating support; Continuing support; Capital campaigns.

Limitations: Giving primarily in GA, with some emphasis on Columbus; some giving also in New York, NY. No grants to individuals.

Application information:

Initial approach: Proposal
Deadline(s): None

Officers: Lovick P. Corn, Pres.; Elizabeth T. Corn, V.P.; Elizabeth C. Ogie, V.P.; Polly C. Miller, Secy.; Katherine C. Foster, Treas.

Trustees: Abby C. Irby; Gilbert B. Miller; Susan C. Wainwright.

EIN: 586065378

Selected grants: The following grants were reported in 2004.

$105,344 to Columbus Regional Medical Foundation, Columbus, GA. For general support.

$73,267 to National Childhood Cancer Foundation, Arcadia, CA. For general support.

$50,000 to LaGrange College, La Grange, GA. For general support.

$50,000 to University of North Carolina, Chapel Hill, NC. For general support.

$25,000 to Shepherd Center, Atlanta, GA. For general support.

$15,000 to Campus Crusade for Christ International, Orlando, FL. For general support.

$10,000 to Childrens Healthcare of Atlanta, Atlanta, GA. For general support.

$10,000 to Cotton Foundation, Memphis, TN. For general support.

$10,000 to Mayo Clinic Jacksonville, Jacksonville, FL. For general support.

$10,000 to Springer Opera House Arts Association, Columbus, GA. For general support.

2325
The Arthur M. Blank Family Foundation ▼ ◇

c/o Elise Eplan
3223 Howell Mill Rd. N.W.
Atlanta, GA 30327 (404) 367-2100
FAX: (404) 367-2059; E-mail: kday@ambfo.com; URL: http://www.blankfoundation.org

Established in 1995 in GA.

Donor: Arthur M. Blank.

Foundation type: Independent foundation.

Financial data (yr. ended 12/31/05): Assets, $54,947,112 (M); gifts received, $12,437,590; expenditures, $18,558,642; qualifying distributions, $18,208,051; giving activities include $15,935,684 for grants.

Purpose and activities: The mission going forward is to promote positive change in people's lives and to build and enhance the communities in which they live. The foundation has an especially strong interest in supporting innovative endeavors leading to better circumstances for low-income youth and their families. The foundation seeks to learn from their investments, share what they have learned, and inspire others in the public and private sectors to make similar commitments. The foundation has established two primary initiatives: 1) Fostering Opportunity - to support efforts that help create access to opportunity and improve life chances for low-income young people and their families; and 2) Enhancing Quality of Life - to preserve green space and parks, and sustain a vibrant arts community.

Fields of interest: Performing arts, theater; Education; Environment; Youth development, services.

Type of support: Research; Employee matching gifts.

Limitations: Applications not accepted. Giving primarily in Maricopa County, AZ, Atlanta, GA, and Beaufort County, SC. No support for government agencies, municipalities, parochial or private schools, or therapeutic programs. No grants to individuals, or for events.

Publications: Annual report.

Application information: Within the scope of its strategic plan, the Blank Family Foundation will identify and invite potential partners to apply for grants around its specific initiatives. The foundation will seek partners from all sectors - public, private and nonprofit. The foundation will no longer accept unsolicited grant requests.

Board meeting date(s): Aug. and Dec.

Officers and Trustees: Arthur M. Blank,* Chair.; Penelope "Penny" McPhee,* C.E.O. and Pres.; John Bare, V.P., Strategic Planning and Eval.; Elise Eplan, V.P., Special Initiatives; Janine E. Lee, V.P., Fostering Opportunity Prog.; Danielle Blank; Dena Blank; Kenny Blank; Michael Blank; Nancy Blank; Stephanie Blank.

Number of staff: 8 full-time professional; 1 part-time professional; 3 full-time support.

EIN: 586292769

Selected grants: The following grants were reported in 2004.

$1,000,000 to Pace Academy, Atlanta, GA.

$875,000 to PATH Foundation, Atlanta, GA.

$584,000 to Babson College, Babson Park, MA.

$378,061 to Trust for Public Land, Atlanta, GA.

$280,000 to Atlanta History Center, Atlanta, GA.

$225,000 to Park Pride Atlanta, Atlanta, GA.

$200,000 to Project GRAD Atlanta, Atlanta, GA.

$187,500 to Appalachian State University, Boone, NC.

$170,000 to Boys and Girls Clubs of Hall County, Gainesville, GA. For grant made through Atlanta Falcons Youth Foundation.

$150,000 to Boys and Girls Clubs of Metro Atlanta, Atlanta, GA.

2326
Bradley-Turner Foundation, Inc. ▼ ✧
P.O. Box 140
Columbus, GA 31902 (706) 571-6040
Contact: Tom B. Black, Admin.

Incorporated in 1943 in GA as W.C. and Sarah H. Bradley Foundation; in 1982 absorbed the D.A. and Elizabeth Turner Foundation, Inc., also of GA.

Donors: W.C. Bradley†; D.A. Turner†; Elizabeth B. Turner†; Elizabeth T. Corn.

Foundation type: Independent foundation.

Financial data (yr. ended 12/31/04): Assets, $153,881,202 (M); gifts received, $4,848,014; expenditures, $19,886,749; qualifying distributions, $19,208,703; giving activities include $19,208,703 for 169 grants (high: $5,003,225; low: $400; average: $10,000–$250,000).

Purpose and activities: Giving primarily for higher education, religious associations, community funds, and youth and social service agencies; support also for cultural and health-related programs.

Fields of interest: Arts; Higher education; Education; Health care; Health organizations, association; Human services; Youth, services; Religion.

Type of support: General/operating support.

Limitations: Giving primarily in GA, with emphasis on Columbus. No grants to individuals.

Application information: Application form not required.

Initial approach: Letter
Copies of proposal: 2
Deadline(s): None
Board meeting date(s): Quarterly
Final notification: Varies

Officers: Stephen T. Butler, Chair.; Lovick P. Corn, Vice-Chair.; William B. Turner, Treas.

EIN: 586032142

Selected grants: The following grants were reported in 2004.

$5,403,873 to Columbus State University, Columbus, GA. 2 grants: $5,003,225 (For capital and operating support. Grant made in form of stock), $400,648 (For capital and operating support. Grant made in form of stock).

$1,003,761 to Brookstone School, Columbus, GA. For capital and operating support. Grant made in form of stock.

$525,444 to United Way. 2 grants: $250,000 (For capital and operating support), $275,444 (For capital and operating support. Grant made in form of stock).

$401,455 to Wesleyan College, Macon, GA. For capital and operating support. Grant made in form of stock.

$335,773 to Wesley United Methodist Church. For capital and operating support. Grant made in form of stock.

$251,447 to Haggai Institute for Advanced Leadership Training, Atlanta, GA. For capital and operating support. Grant made in form of stock.

$203,153 to Community Foundation, Jacksonville, FL. For capital and operating support. Grant made in form of stock.

$201,719 to Epworth By The Sea, Saint Simons Island, GA. For capital and operating support. Grant made in form of stock.

2327
The Benjamin F. Brady Charitable Foundation ✧ ☆
P.O. Box 1200
Cumming, GA 30028-1200

Foundation type: Independent foundation.

Financial data (yr. ended 12/31/05): Assets, $13,804,041 (M); expenditures, $819,503; qualifying distributions, $690,000; giving activities include $690,000 for 6 grants (high: $500,000; low: $10,000).

Fields of interest: Health care; Human services; Christian agencies & churches.

Limitations: Applications not accepted. Giving primarily in GA. No grants to individuals.

Application information: Contributes only to pre-selected organizations.

Trustees: Phillip Bettis; Benjamin F. Brady; Eric S. Chofnas; James J. Myers; Ronald M. Pilcher.

EIN: 582413726

2328
Frances Hollis Brain Foundation, Inc.
1219 Clifton Rd.
Atlanta, GA 30307 (404) 371-9389
Contact: Diane B. Bryant, Secy.
FAX: (404) 377-1754;
E-mail: diane@fhbfoundation.org; Additional address: c/o Nancy Brain, 32 Orchard St., Portland, ME 04102, tel.: (207) 774-3968; FAX: (207) 774-4326; E-mail: nancy@fhbfoundation.org; URL: http://www.fhbfoundation.org

Established in 1992 in KY.

Donors: David L. Brain; Frances H. Brain.

Foundation type: Independent foundation.

Financial data (yr. ended 8/31/05): Assets, $10,879,047 (M); expenditures, $556,463; qualifying distributions, $504,829; giving activities include $437,076 for 58 grants (high: $90,000; low: $926).

Purpose and activities: Giving primarily for education and health and human services.

Fields of interest: Education; Health care; Human services.

Type of support: General/operating support; Continuing support; Capital campaigns; Emergency funds; Matching/challenge support.

Limitations: Giving primarily in GA, KY and ME. No grants to individuals, or for conferences, seminars, tickets to charitable events or dinners, or to sponsor special events, productions or performances.

Publications: Application guidelines; Grants list; Program policy statement; Program policy statement (including application guidelines).

Application information: Application form not required.

Initial approach: Letter or telephone
Copies of proposal: 1
Deadline(s): May 1 and Oct. 1

Board meeting date(s): Aug. and Nov.
Final notification: 3 weeks after board meeting

Officers: David L. Brain, Pres.; Frances H. Brain, V.P.; Diane B. Bryant, Secy.; Nancy R. Brain, Treas.

Number of staff: 2 part-time professional.

EIN: 611227049

Selected grants: The following grants were reported in 2004.

$15,000 to Maine Medical Center, Portland, ME.

$10,000 to Center for Grieving Children, Portland, ME.

$10,000 to Waynflete School, Portland, ME.

$5,000 to Community School, Camden, ME.

$5,000 to Maine Breast Cancer Coalition, Old Town, ME.

$5,000 to Maine Equal Justice Partners, Augusta, ME.

$5,000 to Sheltering Arms Early Education and Family Centers, Atlanta, GA.

$5,000 to Youthlinks, Rockland, ME.

$3,700 to Gods Pantry Food Bank, Lexington, KY.

$3,000 to Atlanta Community Food Bank, Atlanta, GA.

2329
Ron and Lisa Brill Charitable Trust ✧
225 N. Chambord Dr.
Atlanta, GA 30327

Established in 1992 in GA.

Donors: Lisa S. Brill; Ronald M. Brill.

Foundation type: Independent foundation.

Financial data (yr. ended 6/30/05): Assets, $5,050,032 (M); gifts received, $1,000,034; expenditures, $604,165; qualifying distributions, $489,142; giving activities include $488,585 for 59 grants (high: $154,850; low: $100).

Purpose and activities: Support primarily for a Jewish federation and to a Jewish temple; some giving also to the arts with emphasis on an art museum, and to Jewish organizations including a community center.

Fields of interest: Museums (art); Arts; Education; Health organizations, association; Recreation, community facilities; Human services; Foundations (public); Jewish federated giving programs; Jewish agencies & temples.

Limitations: Applications not accepted. Giving primarily in Atlanta, GA. No grants to individuals.

Application information: Contributes only to pre-selected organizations.

Trustees: Lisa S. Brill; Ronald M. Brill.

EIN: 586275452

Selected grants: The following grants were reported in 2004.

$172,122 to Jewish Federation of Greater Atlanta, Atlanta, GA.

$40,000 to High Museum of Art, Atlanta, GA.

$21,330 to Marcus Jewish Community Center of Atlanta, Dunwoody, GA.

$6,000 to William Breman Jewish Heritage Museum, Atlanta, GA.

$1,468 to Alliance Theater Company, Atlanta, GA.

$1,000 to Robert W. Woodruff Arts Center, Atlanta, GA.

$500 to Atlanta Symphony Orchestra, Atlanta, GA.

$200 to Steadman Hawkins Sports Medicine Foundation, Vail, CO.

$180 to Torah Day School of Atlanta, Tucker, GA.

$100 to Vail Valley Medical Center Foundation, Vail, CO.

2330
The Broadfield Foundation ◇
P.O. Box 30351
Sea Island, GA 31561

Established in 2003 in GA.
Donor: Alfred W. Jones III.
Foundation type: Independent foundation.
Financial data (yr. ended 12/31/05): Assets, $4,681,366 (M); expenditures, $505,985; qualifying distributions, $477,273; giving activities include $477,273 for 21 grants (high: $200,000; low: $500).
Purpose and activities: Giving primarily for education, environmental conservation, and animals/wildlife, including a sea turtle center.
Fields of interest: Historic preservation/historical societies; Elementary/secondary education; Higher education; Environment, natural resources; Animals/wildlife, preservation/protection; Human services; Children/youth, services; Federated giving programs; Protestant agencies & churches.
Limitations: Applications not accepted. Giving primarily in GA. No grants to individuals.
Application information: Contributes only to pre-selected organizations.
Distribution Committee: Sarah Hopper Jones; Davis Love III.
Trustee: Alfred W. Jones III.
EIN: 586462442

2331
Mary L. M. Brown Charitable Trust ◇
c/o SunTrust Bank
P.O. Box 4655
Atlanta, GA 30302
Contact: Robert Mays

Established in 1994 in GA.
Foundation type: Independent foundation.
Financial data (yr. ended 12/31/05): Assets, $12,287,791 (M); expenditures, $671,748; qualifying distributions, $607,246; giving activities include $556,500 for grants.
Purpose and activities: Giving primarily for those who are poor, disabled and needy; funding also for smaller charities, and helping handicapped children and adults.
Fields of interest: Housing/shelter, development; Human services; Children, services; Religion; Women; Homeless.
Type of support: General/operating support; Capital campaigns; Building/renovation; Scholarship funds.
Limitations: Giving primarily in Atlanta, GA. No grants to individuals.
Application information: Application form not required.
Initial approach: 1-page letter
Copies of proposal: 1
Deadline(s): Feb. 28 and Sept. 1
Board meeting date(s): Fall and spring
Trustees: Betsy Dixon; Nancy Markham; Mary Louise Morris Brown Jewell; SunTrust Bank.
EIN: 586289241

2332
Warren Brown Family Foundation ◇
2095 Hwy. 211 N.W., Ste. 2-F, No. 355
Braselton, GA 30517
Contact: Jan Brown, Pres.

Established in 1996 in OH.
Donor: D. Warren Brown†.
Foundation type: Independent foundation.
Financial data (yr. ended 12/31/04): Assets, $5,311,711 (M); expenditures, $420,521; qualifying distributions, $334,200; giving activities include $334,200 for 24 grants (high: $150,000; low: $1,000).
Purpose and activities: Giving primarily for youth, education, church/ministry, health, and the Marion, OH, community.
Fields of interest: Arts; Education; Children/youth, services; Federated giving programs.
Type of support: General/operating support; Continuing support; Annual campaigns; Capital campaigns; Building/renovation; Equipment; Endowments; Emergency funds; Professorships; Scholarship funds; Research.
Limitations: Giving primarily in Marion, OH. No grants to individuals.
Application information: Application form not required.
Initial approach: Letter (no more than 3 pages)
Copies of proposal: 5
Deadline(s): Sept. 1
Board meeting date(s): Quarterly
Final notification: Dec. 31
Officers: Janice J. Brown, Pres.; Douglas W. Brown, Secy.; Joe D. Donithen, Treas.
Trustees: Katherine B. Shepherd; James H. Wyland.
EIN: 341811779
Selected grants: The following grants were reported in 2004.
$150,000 to Ohio State University, Columbus, OH.
$58,000 to Fellowship of Christian Athletes, Kansas City, MO.
$22,000 to Lakeview Academy, Gainesville, GA.
$18,000 to Saint Brigid of Kildaire School.
$12,500 to Turning Point.
$11,000 to YMCA, Marion Family, Marion, OH.
$10,000 to Childrens Center for Developmental Enrichment, Columbus, OH.
$10,000 to Opportunity International, Oak Brook, IL.
$5,000 to Ohio Business Week Foundation, Columbus, OH.
$5,000 to United Way of Marion County, Marion, OH.

2333
The Buisson Foundation, Inc. ◇
6354 J.F. Jay Rd.
Gainesville, GA 30506-3420 (770) 535-0784
Contact: Robert T. Buisson, Dir.

Established in 1997 in GA.
Donor: Robert T. Buisson.
Foundation type: Independent foundation.
Financial data (yr. ended 12/31/04): Assets, $12,791,059 (M); gifts received, $100,583; expenditures, $666,541; qualifying distributions, $640,800; giving activities include $640,800 for 28 grants (high: $250,000; low: $100).
Purpose and activities: Giving primarily to a Roman Catholic church; support also for the arts, with emphasis on the performing arts; some giving for community and social services.
Fields of interest: Higher education; Housing/shelter; Human services; Youth, services; Family services; Protestant agencies & churches; Roman Catholic agencies & churches.
Type of support: General/operating support.
Limitations: Giving primarily in GA, with emphasis on Cleveland and Dahlonega; funding also in LA.
Application information:

Initial approach: Letter
Final notification: None
Officers: Marion B. Velis, Pres.; Elizabeth M. Buisson, V.P.; Robert T. Buisson, Jr., Secy.; Beau T. Buisson, Treas.
Directors: Marion R. Buisson; Robert T. Buisson.
EIN: 582297642

2334
Walter & Frances Bunzl Foundation, Inc. ◇ ☆
750 Park Ave. N.E., Apt. 34N
Atlanta, GA 30326-3269

Established in 1981 GA.
Donors: Walter Y. Bunzl†; Frances B. Bunzl.
Foundation type: Independent foundation.
Financial data (yr. ended 11/30/05): Assets, $2,384,453 (M); expenditures, $343,488; qualifying distributions, $335,274; giving activities include $335,274 for grants.
Fields of interest: Performing arts centers.
Limitations: Applications not accepted. Giving primarily in Atlanta, GA. No grants to individuals.
Application information: Contributes only to pre-selected organizations.
Officers: Frances B. Bunzl, Pres.; Richard Bunzl, V.P.; Suzanne B. Wilner, V.P.; Bennett Kight, Secy.
EIN: 581458440

2335
Susan C. and James E. Butler, Jr. Family Foundation, Inc. ◇ ☆
P.O. Box 2766
Columbus, GA 31902

Established in 2000 in GA.
Donors: Susan C. Butler; James E. Butler, Jr.
Foundation type: Independent foundation.
Financial data (yr. ended 12/31/05): Assets, $840,021 (M); expenditures, $621,563; qualifying distributions, $620,000; giving activities include $620,000 for 3 grants (high: $600,000; low: $10,000).
Fields of interest: Higher education.
Type of support: Annual campaigns.
Limitations: Applications not accepted. Giving primarily in GA. No grants to individuals.
Application information: Contributes only to pre-selected organizations.
Officers: James E. Butler, Jr., Pres.; Susan C. Butler, Secy.-Treas.
Trustee: James E. Butler III.
EIN: 582585886

2336
Fuller E. Callaway Foundation ◇
P.O. Box 790
LaGrange, GA 30241 (706) 884-7348
Contact: H. Speer Burdette III, Genl. Mgr.
FAX: (706) 884-0201; E-mail: hsburdette@callaway-foundation.org

Incorporated in 1917 in GA.
Donors: Fuller E. Callaway, Sr.†; and family.
Foundation type: Independent foundation.
Financial data (yr. ended 12/31/04): Assets, $50,574,972 (M); gifts received, $427,613; expenditures, $6,979,463; qualifying distributions, $6,304,316; giving activities include $453,920 for

13 grants (high: $375,000; low: $500; average: $1,500–$15,000), $321,570 for 97 grants to individuals (low: $500; average: $500–$10,000), and $417,613 for in-kind gifts.

Purpose and activities: Grants to religious, charitable, and educational organizations; scholarships for worthy students; modest gifts toward operating expenses of community welfare agencies, including youth programs, and health organizations.

Fields of interest: Education; Hospitals (general); Health care; Health organizations, association; Human services; Youth, services.

Type of support: Capital campaigns; Building/renovation; Equipment; Scholarships—to individuals; Matching/challenge support.

Limitations: Giving primarily in the city of LaGrange and Troup County, GA. No grants for endowment funds; no loans.

Publications: Informational brochure.

Application information: Application form required only for scholarship program. Application form not required.

   Initial approach: Letter
   Copies of proposal: 1
   Deadline(s): End of the month preceding board meeting for grants; Feb. 15 for college scholarships; June 30 for graduate school scholarships
   Board meeting date(s): Jan., Apr., July, and Oct.
   Final notification: 60 to 90 days

Officers: H. Speer Burdette III, Pres. and Genl. Mgr.; D. Ray McKenzie, Jr., V.P.; Esther S. Rainey, Secy.-Treas.

Trustees: Jane Alice Craig; Ellen H. Harris; Charles D. Hudson, Jr.; Ida H. Russell.

EIN: 580566148

2337
Callaway Foundation, Inc. ▼

P.O. Box 790
LaGrange, GA 30241 (706) 884-7348
Contact: H. Speer Burdette, III, Pres.
FAX: (706) 884-0201; E-mail: hsburdette@callaway-foundation.org

Incorporated in 1943 in GA.

Donors: Textile Benefit Assn.; Callaway Mills; Callaway Institute, Inc.

Foundation type: Independent foundation.

Financial data (yr. ended 9/30/04): Assets, $190,429,216 (M); expenditures, $15,804,653; qualifying distributions, $16,444,526; giving activities include $14,214,885 for 65 grants (high: $3,000,000; low: $879; average: $1,000–$200,000), and $1,750,000 for 1 loan/program-related investment.

Purpose and activities: Giving for elementary, higher, and secondary education, including libraries and buildings, and equipment; health and hospitals; community funds; care for the aged; community development; historic preservation; and church support.

Fields of interest: Historic preservation/historical societies; Elementary school/education; Secondary school/education; Higher education; Libraries/library science; Education; Hospitals (general); Health care; Health organizations, association; Aging, centers/services; Community development; Christian agencies & churches; General charitable giving; Aging.

Type of support: Program-related investments/loans; General/operating support; Continuing

support; Annual campaigns; Capital campaigns; Building/renovation; Equipment; Land acquisition; In-kind gifts; Matching/challenge support.

Limitations: Giving primarily in GA, with emphasis on the City of La Grange and Troup County. No grants to individuals, or for endowment funds, deficit financing, scholarships, or fellowships; no loans.

Publications: Annual report (including application guidelines).

Application information: Application form not required.

   Initial approach: Letter
   Copies of proposal: 1
   Deadline(s): End of month preceding board meetings
   Board meeting date(s): Jan., Apr., July, and Oct.
   Final notification: 2 months

Officers: H. Speer Burdette III, Pres. and Genl. Mgr.; D. Ray McKenzie, Jr., V.P.; Esther S. Rainey, Secy.-Treas.

Trustees: Jane Alice Craig; Ellen H. Harris; Charles D. Hudson, Jr.; Ida H. Russell.

EIN: 580566147

Selected grants: The following grants were reported in 2005.

$6,500,000 to La Grange, City of, La Grange, GA. For Parking Deck Project.

$2,000,000 to West Georgia Health Foundation, La Grange, GA. For new emergency care facility.

$1,000,000 to LaGrange College, La Grange, GA. For auditorium renovation.

$784,033 to LaFayette Society for Performing Arts, La Grange, GA. 2 grants: $109,033 (For operating support), $675,000 (For renovations).

$500,000 to World of the Bible Center (WBC) Foundation, La Grange, GA. For Explorations in Antiquity Center construction project.

$300,000 to West Georgia Technical College, La Grange, GA. To purchase property.

$250,000 to Auburn University Foundation, Auburn, AL. For renovation project.

$240,000 to Chattahoochee Valley Art Museum, La Grange, GA. For Plaza Construction Project.

$50,000 to Leadership Georgia Foundation, Atlanta, GA. For endowment campaign.

2338
Camp Younts Foundation

c/o SunTrust Bank
P.O. Box 4655, MC 221
Atlanta, GA 30302-4655
Contact: Robert Mays

Established in 1955 in GA.

Donors: Charles Younts†; Willie Camp Younts†.

Foundation type: Independent foundation.

Financial data (yr. ended 12/31/05): Assets, $41,896,913 (M); expenditures, $2,239,593; qualifying distributions, $2,212,249; giving activities include $2,165,101 for 401 grants (high: $125,000; low: $450).

Purpose and activities: Giving primarily for education, with emphasis on higher and secondary educational institutions (including colleges and universities), and social services; support also for youth, Protestant giving, and health associations and hospitals with focus on helping poor and needy people.

Fields of interest: Secondary school/education; Higher education; Education; Hospitals (general); Health organizations, association; Human services; Youth, services; Protestant agencies & churches.

Limitations: Giving primarily in GA (only for operating and capital grants) and VA. No grants to individuals.

Application information: Application form not required.

   Initial approach: Letter
   Deadline(s): Aug. 31
   Board meeting date(s): Dec.

Trustees: Harold S. Atkinson; John M. Camp, Jr.; Paul Camp Marks; Harry W. Walker; SunTrust Bank.

EIN: 586026001

2339
J. Bulow Campbell Foundation ▼

The Hurt Building, Ste. 850
50 Hurt Plz.
Atlanta, GA 30303 (404) 658-9066
Contact: John W. Stephenson, Exec. Dir.
FAX: (404) 659-4802; URL: http://www.jbcf.org

Trust established in 1940 in GA.

Donors: J. Bulow Campbell†; Virginia Campbell Courts†.

Foundation type: Independent foundation.

Financial data (yr. ended 12/31/05): Assets, $561,671,985 (M); expenditures, $30,324,939; qualifying distributions, $29,667,510; giving activities include $28,891,099 for 43 grants (high: $5,061,312; low: $6,000; average: $100,000–$600,000).

Purpose and activities: Broad purposes include, but are not limited to, privately-supported education, human welfare, youth development, the arts, Christian church-related agencies and agencies of the Presbyterian Church (not congregations) operating within the foundation's giving area. Concern for improving quality of spiritual and intellectual life, preferably projects of permanent nature or for capital funds. Gives anonymously and requests no publicity.

Fields of interest: Arts; Secondary school/education; Higher education; Education; Youth development; Human services; Children/youth, services; Family services; Christian agencies & churches; Protestant agencies & churches; Religion.

Type of support: Capital campaigns; Building/renovation; Land acquisition; Endowments; Matching/challenge support.

Limitations: Giving primarily in GA; very limited giving in AL, FL, NC, SC, and TN. No support for local church congregations. No grants to individuals, or for current scholarships, fellowships, operating budgets, or recurring items; no loans.

Publications: Application guidelines; Informational brochure (including application guidelines).

Application information: Submit 1-page proposal, 1 copy of tax information. Application form not required.

   Initial approach: Letter or telephone
   Copies of proposal: 1
   Deadline(s): 1st of Jan., Apr., July, and Oct.
   Board meeting date(s): Jan., Apr., July, and Oct.
   Final notification: Within 1 week of board meetings

Officers and Trustees:* Joseph T. Spence, Chair.; Larry L. Prince,* Vice-Chair.; John W. Stephenson, Exec. Dir.; David E. Boyd; Peter M. Candler; Bickerton W. Cardwell, Jr.; L. Barry Teague; SunTrust Bank.

Number of staff: 2 full-time professional; 2 full-time support.

EIN: 580566149

Selected grants: The following grants were reported in 2005.

$2,000,000 to Boys and Girls Clubs of Metro Atlanta, Atlanta, GA. Toward Growing Stronger Together campaign.

$2,000,000 to Mercer University, Macon, GA. Toward Phase III of campaign to fund new science and engineering building.

$2,000,000 to Morehouse College, Atlanta, GA. Toward capital campaign.

$1,500,000 to Center for Family Resources, Marietta, GA. Toward development of new Center.

$1,000,000 to American Red Cross, Metropolitan Atlanta Chapter, Atlanta, GA. Toward regional blood processing facility.

$1,000,000 to Fernbank Museum of Natural History, Atlanta, GA. Toward capital improvements.

$1,000,000 to McCallie School, Chattanooga, TN. Toward new freshmen dormitory.

$1,000,000 to Wesleyan College, Macon, GA. Toward capital campaign.

$750,000 to Reinhardt College, Waleska, GA. Toward new Student Life Center.

$700,000 to Childrens School, Atlanta, GA. Toward Future is Here capital campaign.

2340
Andrew & Eula Carlos Foundation, Inc. ✧
750 Park Ave., Ste. 15 SE
Atlanta, GA   30326   (404) 812-3811
Contact: Eula Carlos, Pres.

Established around 1981 in GA.
Donors: Andrew C. Carlos; Eula Carlos.
Foundation type: Independent foundation.
Financial data (yr. ended 12/31/05): Assets, $69,857 (M); gifts received, $800,000; expenditures, $1,353,690; qualifying distributions, $1,353,588; giving activities include $1,353,588 for 16 grants (high: $800,000; low: $50).
Purpose and activities: Giving for Greek Orthodox religious institutes and other religious institutes, and for public medical and educational institutes.
Fields of interest: Education, public education; Medical school/education; Education; Health care; Spine disorders; Recreation, camps; Human services; Religion.
Limitations: Giving primarily in Atlanta, GA. No grants to individuals.
Application information:
  Initial approach: Letter
  Deadline(s): None
Officer: Eula Carlos, Pres.
EIN: 581486620

2341
Thalia & Michael C. Carlos Foundation ✧
1 National Dr.
Atlanta, GA   30336
Contact: Thalia N. Carlos, Pres.

Established in 1980 in GA.
Donors: Michael C. Carlos; Eula Carlos; National Distributing Co., Inc.; Bay Distributors, Inc.; NDC Distributors, Inc.
Foundation type: Independent foundation.
Financial data (yr. ended 12/31/05): Assets, $4,091,743 (M); gifts received, $1,739,358; expenditures, $2,300,519; qualifying distributions, $2,280,600; giving activities include $2,280,600 for 4 grants (high: $1,103,400; low: $77,200).

Fields of interest: Museums; Higher education; Hospitals (general); Orthodox Catholic agencies & churches.
Limitations: Giving primarily in Atlanta, GA. No grants to individuals.
Application information: Application form not required.
  Initial approach: Letter
  Deadline(s): None
Officer: Thalia N. Carlos, Pres.
EIN: 581410420

2342
The Cawood Foundation, Inc. ✧
103 Clover Green
Peachtree City, GA   30269
Contact: Gayle Cawood, Secy.-Treas.

Established in 1977 in GA.
Donor: Frank Cawood.
Foundation type: Independent foundation.
Financial data (yr. ended 12/31/05): Assets, $22,387,095 (M); gifts received, $2,027,557; expenditures, $1,354,417; qualifying distributions, $1,276,408; giving activities include $1,276,408 for 46 grants (high: $495,015; low: $2,500).
Purpose and activities: Giving for education and Christian organizations.
Fields of interest: Higher education, college; Residential/custodial care; Christian agencies & churches.
Type of support: General/operating support; Building/renovation; Equipment; Program development; Scholarship funds; Grants to individuals.
Limitations: Applications not accepted. Giving primarily in GA.
Application information: Unsolicited requests for funds not accepted.
Officers and Trustees: * Frank Cawood,* Pres.; Gayle Cawood,* Secy.-Treas.
EIN: 581295620

2343
Cay Foundation, Inc. ✧ ☆
25 Bull St.
Savannah, GA   31401

Established in 2005 in GA.
Foundation type: Independent foundation.
Financial data (yr. ended 12/31/05): Assets, $2,286,267 (M); gifts received, $2,734,591; expenditures, $597,627; qualifying distributions, $585,000; giving activities include $585,000 for 6 grants (high: $200,000; low: $10,000).
Fields of interest: Elementary/secondary education; Higher education; Medical care, in-patient care.
Limitations: Applications not accepted. Giving primarily in Savannah, GA. No grants to individuals.
Application information: Contributes only to pre-selected organizations.
Trustees: Christopher W. Cay; John E. Cay III; John E. Cay IV; Catherine C. Dreese.
EIN: 202768500

2344
The Challenge Foundation ✧
1155 Perimeter Ctr. W., Ste. 600
Atlanta, GA   30338
Contact: William J. Steinbrook, Jr., Exec. Dir.
E-mail: information@challengefoundation.org;
URL: http://www.challengefoundation.org

Established in 1989 in GA.
Donor: John D. Bryan.
Foundation type: Independent foundation.
Financial data (yr. ended 12/30/05): Assets, $24,928,622 (M); gifts received, $333,975; expenditures, $2,173,154; qualifying distributions, $2,021,493; giving activities include $1,533,700 for 27 grants (high: $200,000; low: $5,000; average: $10,000–$50,000).
Purpose and activities: The foundation's mission is to support model educational initiatives that make it possible for every American child to attain a high school education that produces literate, factually aware, and thinking graduates second to none in the world. To do this the foundation provides start-up grants and support for charter schools.
Fields of interest: Education, association; Elementary/secondary education; Education, early childhood education; Elementary school/education; Secondary school/education; Education.
Type of support: Equipment; Program development; Conferences/seminars; Seed money; Curriculum development; Scholarship funds; Technical assistance; Consulting services; Program evaluation; Matching/challenge support.
Limitations: Applications not accepted. Giving on a national basis. No grants to individuals, or for general operating funds, fundraising, debt reduction, endowments, construction, land purchases or renovations.
Application information: Unsolicited requests for funds not accepted. Grant proposals are received only at the foundation's request.
  Board meeting date(s): Apr. and Nov.
Officer: William J. Steinbrook, Jr., Exec. Dir.
Trustees: John D. Bryan; Martha Bryan.
Number of staff: 3 full-time professional; 1 part-time professional.
EIN: 581817816
Selected grants: The following grants were reported in 2003.
$85,500 to 21st Century Charter School, Indianapolis, IN. For A+ Orchard and CEI Educational Software.
$50,000 to Rapoport Academy, Waco, TX. For state-of-the-art science lab developed in collaboration with Texas State Technical College.
$48,409 to Moreno Valley High School, Moreno Valley, CA. To establish a science lab including furnishings and equipment.
$45,000 to Self Enhancement, Portland, OR. For curriculum design consultants and new lead teacher to develop the schools curricula.
$41,300 to ANSER of Idaho, Boise, ID. For staff training in the Expeditionary Learning model.
$38,280 to TEAM Academy Charter School, Newark, NJ. For end of year trip to Washington, D.C. to match student or parent contributions for students.
$34,000 to Seed Academy, Harvest Preparatory School, Minneapolis, MN. To purchase used passenger bus to provide transportation for families who cannot otherwise get their children to school.

$27,100 to Neighborhood Charter School, Atlanta, GA. For curriculum development of fourth grade program.

$26,583 to Austin College, Sherman, TX. For classroom furnishings, equipment, and supplies including maps, science and math manipulatives, textbooks, library and media center materials, reference books, and instructional software.

$25,000 to Hyde Leadership Public Charter School, DC. For Rising Stars Program and after school and Saturday tutoring program to include all students.

2345
The Charter Foundation, Inc. ✧
P.O. Box 472
West Point, GA 31833 (706) 645-3210
Contact: Bonnie F. Bonner, Dir.

Established in 1995 in AL.
Foundation type: Independent foundation.
Financial data (yr. ended 12/31/05): Assets, $7,182,114 (M); expenditures, $407,284; qualifying distributions, $441,630; giving activities include $353,200 for 35 grants (high: $50,000; low: $1,000).
Purpose and activities: Giving primarily for education, youth development, and community development.
Fields of interest: Historic preservation/historical societies; Arts; Education; Youth development; Human services; Children/youth, services; Community development.
Limitations: Giving limited to Chambers and Lee counties, AL, and Harris and Troup counties, GA. No grants for operations.
Application information: Application form not required.
Initial approach: Letter
Copies of proposal: 1
Deadline(s): Apr. 1 for May cycle, Oct. 1 for Nov. cycle
Board meeting date(s): 2nd Tues. of Feb., May, Aug., and Nov.
Final notification: Within 1 week of May and Nov. board meetings
Officers and Directors:* Robert L. Johnson,* Pres.; William C. Gladden,* V.P.; Bonnie F. Bonner,* Secy.; Joe H. Wooley,* Treas.; Doris Mote; Joel Phillips; Monroe Smith; Michael Stiggers; Peggy Taunton; Donny Turner; Rob Upchurch; Jane Walker.
EIN: 582144961
Selected grants: The following grants were reported in 2003.
$50,000 to Chattahoochee Valley Educational Foundation, Lanett, AL. For legacy endowment campaign.
$32,022 to Valley, City of, Valley, AL. For Girl Scout House.
$20,000 to Hillcrest Elementary School, La Grange, GA. For Fine Arts.
$20,000 to Rosemont Baptist Church, La Grange, GA. To renovate gym.
$17,500 to Junior Service League of La Grange, La Grange, GA. To sponsor Habitat House.
$15,000 to Harvest Evangelism, Lanett, AL. For repair work.
$12,000 to Pastoral Institute, Columbus, GA. For operating support.
$10,000 to Child Advocacy Center of East Alabama, Opelika, AL. For operating support.

$10,000 to East Alabama Water District, Valley, AL. For firemen testing equipment.
$10,000 to Ebenezer Baptist Church, Lanett, AL. To replace roof.

2346
The Chatham Foundation ✧
(formerly Savannah Foods Foundation)
P.O. Box 1313
Savannah, GA 31402-1313
Contact: Odilo Blanco, Secy.

Trust established in 1953 in GA.
Foundation type: Independent foundation.
Financial data (yr. ended 12/31/04): Assets, $7,868,836 (M); expenditures, $461,573; qualifying distributions, $389,975; giving activities include $356,000 for 67 grants (high: $40,000; low: $100).
Purpose and activities: Giving primarily for education and human services.
Fields of interest: Arts; Education; Health care; Health organizations, association; Children/youth, services; Family services.
Type of support: General/operating support; Annual campaigns; Building/renovation; Endowments.
Limitations: Applications not accepted. Giving primarily in Savannah, GA. No grants to individuals.
Application information:
Board meeting date(s): 1st Tues. in June and Dec.
Officers and Trustees:* Ben Oxnard III, Chair.; Odilo Blanco,* Secy. and Fdn. Mgr.; Courtney Flexon; Marion McKenna; Ben Oxnard, Jr.; William W. Sprague, Jr.; William W. Sprague III.
Corporate Trustee: Bank of America, N.A.
EIN: 586033047

2347
The Chatham Valley Foundation, Inc. ✧
c/o Wachovia Charitable Svcs.
191 Peachtree St., GA 8023
Atlanta, GA 30303
Contact: Susanna Adams

Incorporated in 1962 in GA.
Donors: A.J. Weinberg‡; Eliot Goldstein.
Foundation type: Independent foundation.
Financial data (yr. ended 7/31/05): Assets, $9,166,592 (M); gifts received, $5,000; expenditures, $673,104; qualifying distributions, $606,805; giving activities include $603,753 for 191 grants (high: $230,000; low: $25).
Purpose and activities: Giving primarily for a local Jewish welfare federation and other Jewish organizations; broad support for local charitable, educational, cultural, and civic activities.
Fields of interest: Museums; Performing arts; Arts; Higher education; Education; Health care; Health organizations, association; Cancer; Biomedicine; Medical research, institute; Cancer research; Crime/law enforcement; Human services; Homeless, human services; Jewish federated giving programs; Jewish agencies & temples; Economically disadvantaged; Homeless.
Type of support: General/operating support; Annual campaigns; Capital campaigns; Building/renovation; Endowments; Program development.
Limitations: Applications not accepted. Giving primarily in the metropolitan Atlanta, GA, area. No grants to individuals.

Application information: Contributes only to pre-selected organizations.
Board meeting date(s): Aug.
Officers and Trustees:* Elliott Goldstein,* Co-Chair.; W.B. Schwartz, Jr.,* Co-Chair.; Harriet Goldstein,* Vice-Chair.; Sonia Schwartz,* Vice-Chair.; Arthur Jay Schwartz,* Secy.; William B. Schwartz III,* Treas.; Lillian Friedlander; Ellen Goldstein; Robert C. Schwartz.
EIN: 586039344
Selected grants: The following grants were reported in 2003.
$272,500 to Jewish Federation of Greater Atlanta, Atlanta, GA. 2 grants: $210,000 (For general support), $62,500 (For general support).
$250,000 to Temple, The, Atlanta, GA. 2 grants: $50,000 (For general support), $200,000 (For general support).
$25,000 to Atlanta History Center, Atlanta, GA.
$20,000 to Camp Sunshine, Decatur, GA. For general support.
$20,000 to Davis Academy, Atlanta, GA. For general support.
$18,000 to United Way of Metropolitan Atlanta, Atlanta, GA. For general support.
$10,000 to Anti-Defamation League of Bnai Brith, Atlanta, GA. For general support.
$10,000 to Feminist Womens Health Center, Atlanta, GA.

2348
Chesed, Inc. ✧
c/o Marcus Family Office, LLC
1266 W. Paces Ferry Rd., Ste. 615
Atlanta, GA 30327-2306

Established in 1993 in GA.
Donor: Fredrick R. Marcus.
Foundation type: Independent foundation.
Financial data (yr. ended 12/31/03): Assets, $9,552,141 (M); expenditures, $616,316; qualifying distributions, $603,232; giving activities include $583,985 for 13+ grants (high: $260,000).
Purpose and activities: Giving primarily for Jewish education and organizations.
Fields of interest: Secondary school/education; Higher education; Jewish agencies & temples.
International interests: Canada.
Limitations: Applications not accepted. Giving primarily in the U.S., with some emphasis on GA and WI; some funding also in Quebec, Canada. No grants to individuals.
Application information: Contributes only to pre-selected organizations.
Officers: Fredrick R. Marcus, Pres.; Nancy Dubois Marcus, Secy.; Douglas Dinapoli, Treas.
EIN: 580231691
Selected grants: The following grants were reported in 2004.
$181,252 to Yeshiva Elementary School, Milwaukee, WI. 2 grants: $81,252, $100,000
$5,000 to Marcus Institute for Development and Learning, Atlanta, GA.
$2,500 to Canine Assistants, Alpharetta, GA.
$500 to Temple Kol Emeth, Marietta, GA.

2349
Ty Cobb Educational Fund ✧
P.O. Box 937
Sharpsburg, GA 30277
Contact: Cathy Scott, Secy.

E-mail: tycobb@mindspring.com; *URL:* http://www.tycobbfoundation.com

Trust established in 1953 in GA.
Donor: Tyrus R. Cobb‡.
Foundation type: Independent foundation.
Financial data (yr. ended 12/31/05): Assets, $11,951,617 (M); expenditures, $535,785; qualifying distributions, $499,807; giving activities include $420,000 for 80 grants to individuals (high: $87,000; low: $1,000; average: $1,500–$5,000).
Purpose and activities: The foundation was established by the late Tyrus R. Cobb for the purpose of assisting capable and deserving residents of GA who need financial assistance in completing their college education. Foundation scholarships are granted to qualified students for the purpose of attending an accredited college or university full time.
Fields of interest: Higher education; Medical school/education; Dental care.
Type of support: Scholarships—to individuals.
Limitations: Giving limited to GA residents. No grants for building or endowment funds, operating budgets, special projects, or matching gifts; no loans.
Publications: Application guidelines; Informational brochure.
Application information: Application must include a letter of recommendation from student's academic dean or advisor and transcripts of all college studies; transcripts must be received by June 15th. Application form required.
  Initial approach: Letter or e-mail for guidelines
  Copies of proposal: 1
  Deadline(s): June 15
  Board meeting date(s): Jan. and July
  Final notification: Within 5 business days
Officers and Scholarship Board:* Harry S. Downs,* Chair.; Cathy Scott,* Secy.; Edward D. Jackson, Jr.; Walter Y. Murphy; Francis J. Tedesco.
Trustee: SunTrust Bank.
Number of staff: 1 part-time support.
EIN: 586026003

2350
The Coca-Cola Bottlers Foundation, Inc. ◇
3282 Northside Pkwy.
Atlanta, GA 30327 (678) 539-2302

Donor: Coca-Cola Bottlers' Assn.
Foundation type: Independent foundation.
Financial data (yr. ended 12/31/05): Assets, $279,437 (M); gifts received, $3,242,360; expenditures, $3,344,198; qualifying distributions, $3,320,998; giving activities include $3,320,998 for 533 grants (high: $350,000; low: $500; average: $1,000–$10,000).
Fields of interest: Secondary school/education; Higher education; Education; Hospitals (general); Health organizations, association; Boys & girls clubs; Human services; YM/YWCAs & YM/YWHAs; Children/youth, services; Federated giving programs.
Limitations: Applications not accepted.
Application information: Contributes only to pre-selected organizations.
Officers: Wesley Elmer, Pres.; W. Thomas Haynes, V.P.; Mark Cannon, Secy.
Board Members: Neil Barry; J. Frank Harrison.
EIN: 582627567
Selected grants: The following grants were reported in 2004.

$450,000 to YMCA of Greater Charlotte, Charlotte, NC.
$50,000 to YMCA, Saint Cloud Area Family, Saint Cloud, MN.
$35,000 to Boys and Girls Villages Foundation, Lake Charles, LA.
$33,333 to Baton Rouge Area Foundation, Baton Rouge, LA.
$30,000 to Kimmel Center for the Performing Arts, Philadelphia, PA.
$30,000 to Welcome America, Philadelphia, PA.
$25,000 to Project Strive, Albany, NY.
$25,000 to YMCA of Metropolitan Birmingham, Birmingham, AL.
$20,000 to Decatur General Hospital Foundation, Decatur, AL.
$20,000 to Sixteenth Street Foundation, Birmingham, AL.

2351
The Coca-Cola Enterprises Charitable Foundation ◇ ☆
2500 Windy Ridge Pkwy., Ste. 1500
Atlanta, GA 30339

Established in 2002.
Donor: Coca-Cola Enterprises Inc.
Foundation type: Company-sponsored foundation.
Financial data (yr. ended 12/31/04): Assets, $459,212 (M); gifts received, $750,000; expenditures, $680,526; qualifying distributions, $680,526; giving activities include $613,078 for 129 grants to individuals (high: $7,500; low: $1,844).
Purpose and activities: The foundation awards college scholarships to children of employees of Coca-Cola Enterprises and its subsidiaries.
Type of support: Employee-related scholarships.
Limitations: Applications not accepted. Giving primarily in areas of company operations.
Application information: Contributes only through employee-related scholarships.
Directors: John R. Alm; Laura Asman; E. Liston Bishop III; Dan Bowling; John H. Downs, Jr.; Lowry F. Kline; Joyce King Lavinder; Vicki R. Palmer; Terri L. Purcell; Cyril Turner.
EIN: 582660344

2352
The Coca-Cola Foundation, Inc. ▼ ◇
c/o Grants Admin.
P.O. Box 1734
Atlanta, GA 30301 (404) 676-2568
Contact: Helen Smith Price, Exec. Dir.
FAX: (404) 676-8804; *URL:* http://www2.coca-cola.com/citizenship/foundation_coke.html

Incorporated in 1984 in GA.
Donor: The Coca-Cola Co.
Foundation type: Company-sponsored foundation.
Financial data (yr. ended 12/31/05): Assets, $63,988,882 (M); gifts received, $75,000,000; expenditures, $24,040,111; qualifying distributions, $23,912,780; giving activities include $23,912,780 for 126 grants (high: $2,000,000; low: $5,000).
Purpose and activities: The foundation supports organizations involved with education, international exchange, and minorities.

Fields of interest: Elementary/secondary education; Higher education; Graduate/professional education; Scholarships/financial aid; Education; International exchange, students; Minorities.
Type of support: General/operating support; Program development; Curriculum development; Fellowships; Scholarship funds; Matching/challenge support.
Limitations: Giving on a national and international basis. No support for religious organizations, political, legislative, lobbying, or fraternal organizations, hospitals, or local chapters of national organizations. No grants to individuals, or for workshops, travel, conferences, seminars, or related advertising publications, equipment, or religious endeavors; no loans.
Publications: Application guidelines; Annual report; Grants list; Program policy statement.
Application information: Proposals should be no longer than 5 pages. Application form required.
  Initial approach: Download application form and mail proposal and application form to foundation
  Copies of proposal: 1
  Deadline(s): None
  Board meeting date(s): Quarterly
  Final notification: 2 months
Officers and Directors:* Ingrid Saunders Jones,* Chair.; John H. Downs, Jr.,* Secy.; Gary P. Fayard,* Treas.; David C. Bucey, Genl. Counsel; Helen Smith Price,* Exec. Dir.; William Hawkins; Joseph W. Jones; Melody C. Justice; Mary E. Minnick; Deval L. Patrick; Clyde C. Tuggle.
Number of staff: 6 full-time professional; 5 full-time support.
EIN: 581574705
Selected grants: The following grants were reported in 2005.

$10,000,000 to Colombian Foundation for Education and Opportunity, Bogota, Colombia. For start-up support.
$2,000,000 to American University of Beirut, New York, NY. For endowed chair in marketing at Olayan School of Business.
$1,260,000 to United Negro College Fund, Fairfax, VA. For infrastructure support and for scholarships.
$1,250,000 to Hispanic Scholarship Fund, San Francisco, CA. For expansion of Coca-Cola's Advancing to Universities Program.
$1,000,000 to American Indian College Fund, Denver, CO. For Coca-Cola Foundation First Generation Scholars Program, payable over 4 years.
$1,000,000 to American Red Cross, National Headquarters, DC. For Hurricane Katrina relief efforts.
$1,000,000 to National Infantry Foundation, Columbus, GA. For Robert Woodruff and General Dwight Eisenhower Coca-Cola IMAX Theater in National Infantry Museum.
$50,000 to Holy Innocents Episcopal School, Atlanta, GA. For private school strategy.
$25,000 to Hispanic Chamber of Commerce Foundation of the U.S., DC. For Community Entrepreneurship Program.
$25,000 to National Hispanic Cultural Center Foundation, Albuquerque, NM. For education programs.

2353
Colonial Foundation, Inc. ✧

P.O. Box 576
Savannah, GA 31402-0576 (912) 236-1331
Contact: Frances A. Brown, V.P. and Treas.

Established in 1986 in GA.
Donor: Colonial Oil Industries, Inc.
Foundation type: Company-sponsored foundation.
Financial data (yr. ended 12/31/05): Assets,
$5,450,553 (L); gifts received, $1,000,122;
expenditures, $782,066; qualifying distributions,
$745,835; giving activities include $745,835 for
122 grants (high: $100,000; low: $91).
Purpose and activities: The foundation supports
organizations involved with arts and culture,
education, and human services.
Fields of interest: Museums (art); Arts; Higher
education; Education; Boy scouts; Salvation Army;
YM/YWCAs & YM/YWHAs; Children/youth,
services; Human services.
Limitations: Giving primarily in GA. No grants to
individuals.
Application information:
Initial approach: Proposal
Deadline(s): None
Officers: R.H. Demere, Jr., Pres. and Secy.; Frances
A. Brown, V.P. and Treas.; W.A. Baker, Jr., V.P.
EIN: 581693323
Selected grants: The following grants were reported
in 2003.
$51,000 to United Way of the Coastal Empire,
Savannah, GA.
$50,000 to Savannah Country Day School,
Savannah, GA.
$50,000 to Telfair Academy of Arts and Sciences,
Savannah, GA.
$50,000 to YMCA of Savannah, Savannah, GA.
$30,000 to Saint Andrews on the Marsh, Savannah,
GA.
$20,000 to Benedictine Military School, Savannah,
GA.
$20,000 to Hospice of Savannah, Savannah, GA.
For Spirit of Living campaign.
$20,000 to Mercy Housing SouthEast, Atlanta, GA.
$20,000 to Mighty Eighth Air Force Heritage
Museum, Savannah, GA.
$20,000 to Second Harvest Food Bank of Coastal
Georgia, Savannah, GA.

2354
Community Enterprises, Inc. ✧

P.O. Box 1089
Thomaston, GA 30286
Contact: Neil H. Hightower, Pres.

Incorporated in 1944 in GA.
Donors: Julian T. Hightower‡; Thomaston Cotton
Mills.
Foundation type: Independent foundation.
Financial data (yr. ended 6/30/05): Assets,
$10,851,615 (M); expenditures, $562,118;
qualifying distributions, $502,037; giving activities
include $490,372 for 29 grants (high: $200,000;
low: $340).
Purpose and activities: Giving primarily for higher
education and to a United Methodist church.
Fields of interest: Higher education; Human
services; Government/public administration;
Protestant agencies & churches.
Limitations: Giving primarily in Thomaston and
Upson counties, GA. No grants to individuals.
Application information:

Initial approach: Letter
Deadline(s): Dec. 31
Officers and Trustees:* Neil H. Hightower,* Pres.;
George H. Hightower, Jr.,* V.P.; H. Stewart Davis,*
Secy.-Treas.; Neil H. Hightower, Jr.; William H.
Hightower IV.
EIN: 586043415
Selected grants: The following grants were reported
in 2004.
$200,000 to First United Methodist Church. For
unrestricted support.
$30,450 to Georgia Tech Foundation, Atlanta, GA.
2 grants: $30,000 (For unrestricted support),
$450 (For unrestricted support).
$25,000 to Emory University, Atlanta, GA. For
unrestricted support.
$20,000 to Alexander-Tharpe Fund, Atlanta, GA. For
unrestricted support.
$15,750 to Georgia Institute of Technology, Atlanta,
GA. For unrestricted support.
$10,000 to Gordon College Foundation, Wenham,
MA. For unrestricted support.
$10,000 to United Way of Upson County,
Thomaston, GA. For unrestricted support.
$6,000 to Boy Scouts of America, Flint River
Council, Griffin, GA. For unrestricted support.
$1,500 to University of Georgia, Athens, GA. For
unrestricted support.

2355
Community Foundation for Greater Atlanta, Inc. ▼

(formerly Metropolitan Atlanta Community
Foundation, Inc.)
50 Hurt Plz., Ste. 449
Atlanta, GA 30303 (404) 688-5525
Contact: Alicia Philipp, Pres.
FAX: (404) 688-3060; E-mail: info@atlcf.org;
Additional E-mail: grants@atlcf.org (for grant
guidelines and grant orientation session
registration); URL: http://www.atlcf.org
Additional E-mail: karanas@atlcf.org (for scholarship
opportunities)

Incorporated in 1977 as successor to Metropolitan
Foundation of Atlanta established in 1951 in GA by
bank resolution and declaration of trust.
Foundation type: Community foundation.
Financial data (yr. ended 6/30/06): Assets,
$638,817,268 (M); gifts received, $105,617,249;
expenditures, $100,393,076; giving activities
include $71,641,368 for 4,628 grants.
Purpose and activities: Organized for the
permanent administration of funds placed in trust by
various donors for charitable purposes. Grants,
unless designated by the donor, are confined to a
23-county metropolitan area of Atlanta, with
emphasis on human services, arts and culture,
education, health, and community development.
Fields of interest: Arts education; Arts; Education;
Environment, natural resources; Health care; AIDS;
Housing/shelter, development; Housing/shelter;
Youth development; Youth, services; Family
services; Family services, parent education;
Women, centers/services; Homeless, human
services; Human services; Community
development, neighborhood development;
Community development; Women; AIDS, people
with; Homeless.
Type of support: General/operating support;
Program development; Scholarship funds; Technical
assistance.

Limitations: Giving limited to the 23-county
metropolitan area of Atlanta, GA. No support for
religious organizations (except through
donor-advised funds). No grants to individuals
(except for scholarships), or for endowment funds,
continuing support, annual campaigns, special
fundraising events, deficit financing, long-term
research, films, equipment, vehicles, conferences,
or fellowships; a limited number of grants for
operating budgets.
Publications: Application guidelines; Annual report;
Informational brochure; Newsletter; Program policy
statement.
Application information: The foundation
encourages all potential applicants to attend a grant
orientation session before submitting an
application. Visit foundation Web site for application
form, guidelines, and specific deadlines. Faxed
applications are not accepted. Application form
required.
Initial approach: Mail or e-mail application form
and attachments to foundation
Copies of proposal: 7
Deadline(s): Jan. and July
Board meeting date(s): Jan., Mar., May, and Sept.
Final notification: May and Nov.
Officers and Directors:* Ray Christman,* Chair.;
Alicia Philipp, Pres.; Lesley Grady, V.P., Community
Partnerships; Lauren Norton, V.P., Comms. and
Mktg.; Rob Smulian, V.P., Philanthropic Svcs.; Lisa
Williams, V.P., Finance and Opers.; Antoinette
Dowdy, Cont.; Benjamin T. White, Legal Counsel;
Jeff Giglio; D.R. Grimes; Jack Guynn; Joia M.
Johnson; Michael Kay; Bertram Levy; Steve Linowes;
Sunny K. Park; Margaret C. Reiser; Vicki J. Riedel;
Frank Ros; David Satcher, M.D.; Lynn Wentworth;
Karen Wibell.
Number of staff: 29 full-time professional; 3
part-time professional; 4 full-time support; 3
part-time support.
EIN: 581344646
Selected grants: The following grants were reported
in 2005.
$2,719,000 to Atlanta Shakespeare Company,
Atlanta, GA. For Shakespeare Tavern.
$2,090,550 to Atlanta Speech School, Atlanta, GA.
$1,610,850 to East Tennessee Foundation,
Knoxville, TN.
$1,010,494 to CHRIS Kids, Atlanta, GA. For CHRIS
kid's campaign and advance program of healing
children and families.
$400,000 to University of the Cumberlands,
Williamsburg, KY.
$263,800 to Peachtree Presbyterian Church,
Atlanta, GA.
$27,250 to Friends of the Mansion, Oklahoma City,
OK.
$22,500 to Hands On Atlanta, Atlanta, GA. For
unrestricted support.
$20,000 to Woodberry Forest School, Woodberry
Forest, VA.
$18,000 to Cherokee Child Advocacy Council,
Woodstock, GA. For unrestricted support.

2356
Community Foundation for Northeast Georgia ✧

6500 Sugarloaf Pkwy., Ste. 220
Duluth, GA 30097 (770) 813-3380
Contact: Beverly Shackelford, Dir., Finance
FAX: (770) 813-3375; E-mail: beverly@cfneg.org;
URL: http://www.cfneg.org

Incorporated in 1985 in GA.

Foundation type: Community foundation.

Financial data (yr. ended 12/31/04): Assets, $14,138,366 (M); gifts received, $1,338,425; expenditures, $2,481,728; giving activities include $2,011,765 for 276 grants (high: $200,000; low: $50).

Purpose and activities: The foundation strengthens the community by assisting donors with their charitable giving, attracting and managing charitable funds, making effective grants and providing leadership to address community needs.

Fields of interest: Performing arts; Arts; Education; Health care; Human services; Community development; Children/youth; Youth; Aging.

Type of support: Capital campaigns; Building/renovation; Equipment; Emergency funds; Program development; Seed money.

Limitations: Giving limited to organizations or services directly benefiting citizens of northeast GA. No support for religious purposes, or commonly accepted community services. No grants to individuals, or for endowment support, debt reduction, fundraising or annual campaigns, membership contributions, research, travel, or ongoing operating support.

Publications: Annual report (including application guidelines); Grants list; Newsletter.

Application information: Visit foundation Web site for application form and guidelines. Faxed applications are not accepted. Application form required.

 Initial approach: Submit grant proposal cover sheet and attachments

 Copies of proposal: 15

 Deadline(s): Mar. 1

 Board meeting date(s): 5 times annually

 Final notification: June

Officers and Directors:* Bartow Morgan, Jr.,* Pres.; Joe McCart,* V.P.; Steven W. Williams,* Secy.; Tracey Mason Blasi,* Treas.; Judy Waters, Exec. Dir.; Julie Keeton Arnold; Bennie Boswell, Jr.; Stacie Britt; Renee Byrd-Lewis; Richard B. Chandler, Jr.; Duane Davenport; James F. Fleming; Steven K. Hill; Thomas P. Hughes; Hon. Chung H. Lee; James J. Maran; Wayne H. Mason; William E. McLendon; Judy Fowler Ottley; Maxie Price, Jr.; Louise Radloff; Thomas H. Rogers III; William "Bill" Russell, Ph.D.; David M. Seago; William R. Short; Mary Louise Stark; T. Michael Tennant; Richard L. Tucker.

Trustees: American Funds; Crawford Investment; SunTrust Bank; UBS Wealth Management.

Number of staff: 2 full-time professional; 2 part-time support.

EIN: 581557995

2357
Community Foundation for the Central Savannah River Area

(formerly CSRA Community Foundation, Inc.)
1450 Greene St., Ste. 228
Augusta, GA 30901 (706) 724-1314
Contact: R. Lee Smith, Jr., C.E.O.
FAX: (706) 724-1315; E-mail: info@cfcsra.org;
Mailing address: P.O. Box 31358, Augusta, GA 30903; URL: http://www.cfcsra.org

Established in 1995 in GA.

Donors: Norman Shapiro; Mrs. Norman Shapiro.

Foundation type: Community foundation.

Financial data (yr. ended 12/31/04): Assets, $20,915,501 (M); gifts received, $3,726,125;

expenditures, $1,775,697; giving activities include $1,467,543 for 346 grants (high: $72,500; low: $100).

Purpose and activities: The mission of the foundation is to encourage and promote philanthropy through education, responsible management of charitable contributions and the distribution of these funds, and to provide the structure for this to be accomplished by individuals, companies and organizations.

Fields of interest: Arts; Higher education; Education; Environment; Health care; Children, services; Youth, services; Family services; Human services; Community development, neighborhood development; Economic development; Community development; Government/public administration; Religion.

Type of support: Annual campaigns; Capital campaigns; Seed money; Scholarship funds; Matching/challenge support.

Limitations: Giving limited to the greater Augusta, GA, area, including Burke, Columbia, McDuffie, and Richmond counties, GA, and Aiken and Edgefield counties, SC. No support for fraternal organizations or professional associations. No grants to individuals (except for scholarships), or for building campaigns, deficit financing, debt reduction, endowments, fundraisers, surveys, travel, or for film and video production.

Publications: Application guidelines; Grants list; Informational brochure; Newsletter; Occasional report (including application guidelines).

Application information: Visit foundation Web site for downloadable application form and instructions. Applications submitted by fax are not accepted or considered. The foundation holds a free grantmaker session/seminar for organizations that wish to apply for funding; reservations are limited, please call or e-mail foundation. Application form required.

 Initial approach: Submit application form and attachments

 Copies of proposal: 8

 Deadline(s): July 31

 Board meeting date(s): Quarterly

 Final notification: Dec.

Officers and Directors:* Thomas M. Blanchard, Jr.,* Chair.; H.M. Osteen, Jr.,* Chair.-Elect; R. Lee Smith, Jr.,* C.E.O. and Pres.; C.P. Boardman II,* V.P., Investment Comm.; Abram Serotta,* V.P., Grants Comm.; Braye C. Boardman,* Secy.-Treas.; D. Douglas Barnard, Jr.,* Honorary Member; William P. Copenhaver,* Honorary Dir.; William S. Morris III,* Honorary Dir.; Bettis Rainsford,* Honorary Dir.; Charles H. Bellmann; David S. Copenhaver; Nick W. Evans, Jr.; Joseph D. Greene, Ph.D.; C. LaFay Hargrove, Ph.D.; Mrs. Jerry W. Howington; James M. Hull; Robert E. Knox, Jr.; Brian J. Marks; Mrs. Wyck A. Knox, Jr.; John W. Lee*; William S. Morris IV; Julian W. Osbon; Aubrey C. Rhodes, Jr.; Barry L. Storey; William H. Tucker.

Number of staff: 2 full-time professional; 1 full-time support.

EIN: 582184345

2358
Community Foundation of Central Georgia, Inc.

(also known as Community Foundation, Inc.)
277 Martin Luther King, Jr. Blvd., Ste. 303
Macon, GA 31201-3489 (478) 750-9338
Contact: Kathryn H. Dennis, Pres.

FAX: (478) 738-9214; E-mail: info@cfcgga.org;
Additional tel.: (866) 750-9338; URL: http://www.cfcgga.org

Established in 1993 in GA.

Foundation type: Community foundation.

Financial data (yr. ended 6/30/05): Assets, $33,170,807 (M); gifts received, $7,106,036; expenditures, $3,883,088; giving activities include $3,276,396 for 603+ grants (high: $350,000).

Purpose and activities: The foundation seeks to enhance the quality of life for the people of Central Georgia. To accomplish its mission, the foundation has five primary goals: 1) to be a catalyst for the establishment of endowments to benefit the community now and for all time; 2) to provide leadership and resources in identifying and meeting local needs; 3) to serve donors' varied interests and needs; 4) to promote local philanthropy; and 5) to serve as stewards of funds.

Fields of interest: Historic preservation/historical societies; Arts; Education; Environment; Health care; Human services; Economic development; Community development; Children; Youth.

Type of support: General/operating support; Equipment; Scholarship funds; Matching/challenge support.

Limitations: Giving limited to central GA. No support for sectarian religious purposes.

Publications: Annual report; Financial statement; Informational brochure; Newsletter.

Application information: Visit foundation Web site for application form and guidelines. Applications must be mailed or hand delivered. Faxed, e-mailed, and/or incomplete applications will not be considered. Application form required.

 Initial approach: Submit application form and attachments

 Copies of proposal: 14

 Deadline(s): Apr. 15 and Oct. 1

Officers and Directors:* Joe E. Timberlake III,* Chair.; Kathryn H. Dennis, Pres.; Starr H. Purdue,* Secy.; Hazle W. Hamilton, C.F.O.; Bertram Maxwell III,* Treas.; Nancy B. Anderson; W. Carter Bates III; Albert Billingslea; Malcolm S. Burgess, Jr.; Mary A. Comer; Mardie R. Herndon, Jr.; Frank C. Jones; Juanita T. Jordan; Melvin I. Kruger; William M. Matthews; Sidney E. Middlebrooks; W.J. O'Shaughnessy, Jr., M.D.; Billy Pitts; Herbert M. Ponder, Jr.; Albert P. Reichert, Jr.; Monty W. Rogers; Dr. Alvin D. Sewell, M.D.; Chris R. Sheridan, Jr.; F. Tredway Shurling; G. Boone Smith III; Rett Walker; D.T. Walton, Jr., D.D.S.

Number of staff: 4 full-time professional; 1 part-time support.

EIN: 582053465

2359
Community Foundation of Northwest Georgia, Inc.

742 S. Thorton Ave.
P.O. Box 942
Dalton, GA 30722-0942 (706) 275-9117
Contact: David Aft, Pres.
FAX: (706) 275-9118;
E-mail: thefoundation@communityfoundationnwga.org; URL: http://www.communityfoundationnwga.org

Established in 1998 in GA.

Foundation type: Community foundation.

Financial data (yr. ended 12/31/04): Assets, $18,416,059 (M); gifts received, $8,784,273; expenditures, $3,889,771; giving activities include

$3,455,811 for 123 grants (high: $1,079,179; low: $200).

Purpose and activities: The foundation seeks to enhance the quality of life in the northwest GA region for both present and future generations by promoting philanthropy; building and maintaining permanent endowment funds to be used for the broad charitable needs of the region; serving as a leader in identifying and prioritizing needs in the community; serving as a catalyst in developing effective responses to community issues; encouraging collaboration between organizations and agencies to shape solutions; and serving as a steward of the funds in the endowment.

Fields of interest: Historic preservation/historical societies; Arts; Education; Environment; Animal welfare; Health care; Youth development; Children/ youth, services; Human services; Community development; Religion.

Type of support: Program development; Seed money; Matching/challenge support.

Limitations: Giving limited to Bartow, Catoosa, Chattooga, Dade, Fannin, Floyd, Gilmer, Gordon, Murray, Pickens, Walker, and Whitfield, GA.

Publications: Application guidelines; Annual report; Informational brochure.

Application information: Visit foundation Web site for application form and guidelines; faxed or e-mailed applications are not accepted. Application form required.

Initial approach: Call or visit the foundation
Copies of proposal: 10
Deadline(s): Mar. 31 and Oct. 1

Officers and Directors:* Jim Bethel,* Chair.; Norris Little,* Vice-Chair.; David Aft, Pres.; John P. Neal III,* Secy.; Gordon C. Morehouse,* Treas.; Norman D. Burkett, Sr.,* Prog. Chair.; Charles D. Miller,* Investment Chair.; Vance D. Bell; Linda Blackman; James E. Brown; Sis Brown; Carl L. Griggs; Bryan Hair; James Jarrett; Walter M. Jones; David Lance; John D. Tice; Larry Winter.

Number of staff: 1 full-time professional; 1 full-time support.

EIN: 582360356

2360
Community Foundation of Southwest Georgia, Inc. ✧
135 N. Broad St., Ste. 202
P.O. Box 2654
Thomasville, GA   31799-2654   (229) 228-5088
Contact: Wade Miller, Pres.
FAX: (229) 228-0848; Additional tel.: (888) 544-2317; URL: http://www.cfsga.org

Established in 1995 in GA.
Foundation type: Community foundation.
Financial data (yr. ended 12/31/04): Assets, $18,837,621 (M); gifts received, $3,257,310; expenditures, $1,931,485; giving activities include $1,420,283 for 308 grants (high: $262,053; low: $50), and $32,747 for 56 grants to individuals (high: $5,500; low: $44).

Purpose and activities: The organization raises funds from local individuals and businesses to benefit local charities and needy individuals by establishing Designated funds, Donor-Advised funds, and Scholarship funds.

Type of support: Scholarships—to individuals.

Limitations: Applications not accepted. Giving limited to southwest GA.

Application information: Unsolicited requests for funds not accepted.

Officers and Board Members:* Karen S. Leabo,* Chair.; James M. Jeter,* Vice-Chair.; Wade Miller,* Pres. and Exec. Dir.; Thomas H. Vann, Jr.,* Secy.; Malcolm M. Palmer,* Treas.; John M. Carlton, Jr.; William Eager; Gene Hill; Charles Jenkins, Sr.; Harry T. Jones III; John McTier; W. Ralph Rodgers, Jr.; E.J. "Jud" Vann IV.

EIN: 582210876

2361
Community Foundation of the Chattahoochee Valley ✧
(formerly Chattahoochee Valley Community Foundation, Inc.)
11 10th St.
P.O. Box 1620
Columbus, GA   31902-1620   (706) 320-0027
Contact: Betsy W. Covington, Exec. Dir.
FAX: (706) 320-9331; E-mail: info@cfcv.com;
Additional E-mail: bcovington@cfcv.com;
URL: http://www.cfcv.com

Established in 1998 in GA.
Foundation type: Community foundation.
Financial data (yr. ended 9/30/04): Assets, $18,560,499 (M); gifts received, $1,347,853; expenditures, $2,470,007; giving activities include $2,142,901 for 408 grants (high: $235,500).

Purpose and activities: The foundation is a nonprofit charitable organization dedicated to strengthening the Chattahoochee Valley's diverse community for both present and future generations. It promotes philanthropy, builds and maintains a permanent collection of endowment funds, and serves as a trustworthy partner and leader in shaping effective responses to community needs and opportunities.

Fields of interest: Arts; Education; Environment, natural resources; Youth development; Children/ youth, services; Human services; Community development.

Type of support: Program evaluation.

Limitations: Applications not accepted. Giving limited to the Chattahoochee Valley Region in west central GA and east central AL. No support for religious activities, or international programs. No grants to individuals, or for general operating support, annual fundraising campaigns or fundraising events, operating deficits, endowments, medical research, memorials, conferences, group travel, or honoraria for distinguished guests.

Application information: The foundation is not currently accepting grant applications.

Officers and Trustees:* D. Raines Jordan,* Pres.; J. Mike Venable,* V.P.; Susan C. Lawhorne,* Secy.; Gardiner W. Garrard, Jr.,* Treas.; Betsy W. Covington, Exec. Dir.; Martha B. Smith, Cont.; Thomas B. Black; Otis B. Burnham; Charles E. Clark, Sr.; F. Karl Douglass; Frank S. Etheridge III; J.H. Flakes, Jr.; Linda U. Hadley; Angela S. Hart; Christopher D. Hohlstein; Lula Huff*; C. Dexter Jordan, Jr.; Elizabeth C. Ogie; Virginia T. Peebles; Alan F. Rothschild, Jr.; Mary W. Schley, M.D.; Todd A. Schuster; W. David Varner, Jr., M.D.

Number of staff: 2 full-time professional.

EIN: 582381589

2362
Community Foundation of West Georgia ☆
200 Northside Dr.
Carrollton, GA   30117   (770) 832-1462
Contact: Kim B. Jones, Pres.
FAX: (770) 832-1300; E-mail: info@cfwg.net;
URL: http://www.cfwg.net

Established in 2003 in GA.
Foundation type: Community foundation.
Financial data (yr. ended 12/31/05): Assets, $10,837,871 (M); gifts received, $2,803,264; expenditures, $879,954; giving activities include $778,122 for 45 grants.

Purpose and activities: The foundation seeks to enhance the quality of life for the people of the West Georgia area.

Fields of interest: Arts; Education; Botanical/ horticulture/landscape services; Environment; Health care; Residential/custodial care, hospices; Human services; Economic development; Community development.

Type of support: General/operating support; Building/renovation; Equipment; Program development; Seed money; Technical assistance; Matching/challenge support.

Limitations: Giving primarily in Carroll, Haralson, and Heard counties, GA. No support for religious organizations (unless there are no religious requirements), for-profit organizations, or charities operated by service clubs or organizations that in turn make grants to others. No grants to individuals, or for annual fundraising campaigns, fundraising events, operating deficits, endowments, or memorials.

Publications: Application guidelines; Annual report; Financial statement; Grants list; Informational brochure; Newsletter.

Application information: Visit foundation Web site for application information. Application form required.

Initial approach: Contact foundation
Copies of proposal: 8
Deadline(s): Spring and fall
Board meeting date(s): Bi-monthly
Final notification: 60 days

Officers and Directors:* P.J. Younglove Hovey,* Chair.; Tom Upchurch,* Vice-Chair.; Kim B. Jones, Pres.; Gelon Wasdin,* Secy.-Treas.; Patricia Barr; Mary Covington; Dr. Jorge Gaytan; Tee Green; Edie Haney; Andy Horton; Fred O'Neal; Artie Richards; Tom Richards; Zachary Steed.

Number of staff: 1 full-time professional; 1 full-time support.

EIN: 030472714

2363
Frederick E. Cooper and Helen Dykes Cooper Charitable Foundation, Inc. ✧
170 W. Paces Ferry Rd. N.E.
Atlanta, GA   30305

Established in 1998 in FL.
Donors: Frederick E. Cooper; Helen D. Cooper.
Foundation type: Independent foundation.
Financial data (yr. ended 9/30/05): Assets, $7,064,437 (M); expenditures, $353,350; qualifying distributions, $334,175; giving activities include $334,175 for 46 grants (high: $50,000; low: $100).

Purpose and activities: Giving primarily for educational and environmental purposes as well as for purposes which involve poverty; funding also for historical preservation, medical research, particularly cancer research, and to Presbyterian churches.

Fields of interest: Historic preservation/historical societies; Higher education; Environment; Animals/wildlife, preservation/protection; Hospitals (general); Medical research, institute; Cancer research; Human services; Protestant agencies & churches; Economically disadvantaged.

Limitations: Giving primarily in GA and VA.

Application information:
Initial approach: Proposal
Deadline(s): None

Directors: Beckwith Archer Cooper; Frederick E. Cooper; Frederick E. Cooper, Jr.; Helen D. Cooper; Johnson Joseph Cooper; Bernard Lanigan, Jr.

EIN: 582433546

2364
Courts Foundation, Inc. ✧

50 Hurt Plz., Ste. 850
Atlanta, GA 30303 (404) 658-9066
Contact: John W. Stephenson, Exec. Dir.

Incorporated in 1950 in GA.

Donors: Richard W. Courts†; Virginia Campbell Courts†; Malon C. Courts†; Richard W. Courts II; Atlantic Realty Co.

Foundation type: Independent foundation.

Financial data (yr. ended 12/31/04): Assets, $119,649,756 (M); gifts received, $29,369; expenditures, $5,638,349; qualifying distributions, $5,182,517; giving activities include $5,139,513 for 45 grants (high: $2,500,000; low: $1,000).

Purpose and activities: Support primarily for education, religion, health care, human services, and arts and culture.

Fields of interest: Arts; Higher education; Education; Children/youth, services; Christian agencies & churches.

Type of support: Capital campaigns; Building/renovation; Land acquisition; Endowments; Program development; Professorships.

Limitations: Giving primarily in Atlanta, GA, with a secondary emphasis on Georgia-based organizations. No grants to individuals.

Publications: Informational brochure (including application guidelines).

Application information: Application form not required.
Initial approach: Letter
Copies of proposal: 1
Deadline(s): First day of the month in which board meeting takes place
Board meeting date(s): Mar., June, Sept., and Dec.
Final notification: 1 month

Officers and Trustees:* Richard W. Courts II,* Pres.; John B. Ellis,* V.P.; Malon W. Courts,* Secy.-Treas.; John W. Stephenson, Exec. Dir.; Clay L. Courts; Richard W. Courts IV; T. Bradbury Courts; William A. Parker, Jr.

Number of staff: 2 part-time professional; 2 part-time support.

EIN: 586036859

Selected grants: The following grants were reported in 2004.
$2,500,000 to Community Foundation for Greater Atlanta, Atlanta, GA.
$500,000 to Emory University, Atlanta, GA.
$350,000 to Atlanta Speech School, Atlanta, GA.

$260,000 to Robert W. Woodruff Arts Center, Atlanta, GA. 2 grants: $250,000, $10,000
$255,000 to Piedmont Hospital, Atlanta, GA. 2 grants: $250,000, $5,000
$119,000 to Roanoke College, Salem, VA.
$100,000 to Atlanta International School, Atlanta, GA.
$100,000 to Shepherd Center, Atlanta, GA.

2365
The Cousins Foundation, Inc. ✧

3445 Peachtree Rd., Ste. 175
Atlanta, GA 30326 (404) 233-4339
Contact: Laura Rust, Secy.-Treas.
FAX: (404) 233-8852; E-mail: lrust@cffdn.org

Incorporated in 1963 in GA.

Donor: Thomas G. Cousins.

Foundation type: Independent foundation.

Financial data (yr. ended 12/31/03): Assets, $38,852,790 (M); gifts received, $9,522,164; expenditures, $1,150,268; qualifying distributions, $1,120,187; giving activities include $1,084,189 for 54 grants (high: $200,000; low: $250).

Purpose and activities: The foundation supports organizations that strengthen the spiritual, mental and moral fiber of a community. There is a special focus on children, and an emphasis on programs that seek to break the cycle of poverty.

Fields of interest: Arts; Education; Human services; Children/youth, services; Community development; Christian agencies & churches.

Type of support: Program evaluation; Program development; Endowments; Building/renovation; Capital campaigns; General/operating support; Annual campaigns.

Limitations: Applications not accepted. Giving primarily in the metropolitan Atlanta, GA, area. No grants to individuals; or for scholarships.

Application information: Unsolicited requests for funds not accepted.
Board meeting date(s): May and Dec.

Officers and Trustees:* Lillian C. Giornelli,* Chair. and Pres.; Ann D. Cousins,* Vice-Chair.; Laura Rust,* Secy.-Treas.

EIN: 586043765

Selected grants: The following grants were reported in 2003.
$200,000 to High Museum of Art, Atlanta, GA.
$100,000 to Georgia State University, School of Music, Atlanta, GA.
$25,000 to Atlanta Resource Foundation, Atlanta, GA.
$10,000 to Atlanta Ballet, Atlanta, GA.
$5,000 to Auburn University, Auburn, AL.
$2,500 to Midtown Assistance Center, Atlanta, GA.
$2,000 to Atlanta Preservation Center, Atlanta, GA.
$1,000 to Boys and Girls Clubs of America, Atlanta, GA.
$650 to Georgia Trust for Historic Preservation, Atlanta, GA.
$500 to Emory University, Atlanta, GA.

2366
The Covenant Foundation, Inc. ✧

(formerly The Davis Foundation)
1 National Dr.
Atlanta, GA 30336 (404) 696-9440
Contact: Jay M. Davis, Pres.

Established in 1960.

Donors: Alfred M. Davis; Jay M. Davis; Ann Davis; ADP Rental Co.; Raleigh Linen Svc., Inc.; Servitex, Inc.; Truck Rental Co.; National Distributing Co., Inc.; and subsidiaries.

Foundation type: Independent foundation.

Financial data (yr. ended 7/31/05): Assets, $5,971,175 (M); gifts received, $495,045; expenditures, $961,455; qualifying distributions, $961,305; giving activities include $955,172 for grants.

Purpose and activities: Grants primarily for Jewish welfare funds and temple support and for higher education; support also for cultural programs.

Fields of interest: Museums; Performing arts, orchestra (symphony); Arts; Education; Health care; Human services; Federated giving programs; Jewish federated giving programs; Jewish agencies & temples.

Limitations: Giving primarily in Atlanta, GA.

Application information:
Initial approach: Proposal
Deadline(s): None

Officers: Jay M. Davis, Pres.; Ann Davis, V.P.

EIN: 586035088

Selected grants: The following grants were reported in 2004.
$366,200 to Jewish Federation of Greater Atlanta, Atlanta, GA.
$305,850 to Davis Academy, Atlanta, GA.
$12,750 to Crohns and Colitis Foundation of America, Atlanta, GA.
$10,000 to United Way of Metropolitan Atlanta, Atlanta, GA.
$5,000 to American Jewish Committee, Atlanta, GA.
$5,000 to Anti-Defamation League of Bnai Brith, Atlanta, GA.
$1,200 to Emory University, Michael C. Carlos Museum, Atlanta, GA.
$500 to Multiple Sclerosis Society, National, Atlanta, GA.
$250 to Epstein School, Atlanta, GA.
$50 to Hospice Atlanta, Atlanta, GA.

2367
The James M. Cox Foundation of Georgia, Inc. ▼ ✧

c/o Cox Enterprises, Inc.
P.O. Box 105357
Atlanta, GA 30348-5720 (678) 645-0000
Contact: Leigh Ann Launius, Asst. Secy.
FAX: (678) 645-1708

Incorporated in 1957 in GA.

Donor: Cox Enterprises, Inc.

Foundation type: Company-sponsored foundation.

Financial data (yr. ended 12/31/04): Assets, $6,185,319 (M); gifts received, $3,250,000; expenditures, $3,484,908; qualifying distributions, $3,455,000; giving activities include $3,455,000 for 65 grants (high: $600,000; low: $5,000).

Purpose and activities: The foundation supports organizations involved with the environment, human services, arts and culture, health, and education.

Fields of interest: Media, journalism/publishing; Visual arts; Museums; Performing arts; Arts; Child development, education; Education; Hospitals (general); Health care; Child development, services; Family services; Residential/custodial care, hospices; Human services; Engineering/technology; Science.

Type of support: Capital campaigns; Building/renovation; Equipment; Land acquisition;

Endowments; Emergency funds; Program development.

Limitations: Giving limited to areas of company operations. No grants to individuals.

Publications: Application guidelines.

Application information: Application form not required.

   Initial approach: Proposal

   Copies of proposal: 3

   Deadline(s): 1 month prior to board meetings

   Board meeting date(s): Quarterly; usually 3rd week of Apr., July, and Oct. and 2nd week of Dec.

   Final notification: Within 3 months

Officers and Trustees:* Anne Cox Chambers,* Chair.; Barbara Cox Anthony,* Pres.; Timothy W. Hughes,* V.P.; Andrew A. Merdek, Secy.; John G. Boyette, Treas.; James C. Kennedy.

EIN: 586032469

Selected grants: The following grants were reported in 2004.

$850,000 to High Museum of Art, Atlanta, GA. 2 grants: $600,000 (For capital support for Louvre-Atlanta Project), $250,000 (For capital support).

$300,000 to Kennesaw State University, Cox Family Enterprise Center, Kennesaw, GA. For general support.

$200,000 to PATH Foundation, Atlanta, GA. For capital support.

$100,000 to Shepherd Center, Atlanta, GA. For capital support.

$90,000 to Communities in Schools of Georgia, Atlanta, GA. For capital support.

$50,000 to Atlanta History Center, Atlanta, GA. For capital support for Olympic Museum.

$50,000 to Childrens Healthcare of Atlanta Foundation, Atlanta, GA. For capital support.

$40,000 to Chattahoochee Nature Center, Roswell, GA. For general operating support.

$40,000 to Communities in Schools of Atlanta, Atlanta, GA. For general operating support.

2368
Jim Cox, Jr. Foundation
3414 Peachtree Rd., Ste. 722
Atlanta, GA   30326   (404) 842-1870
Contact: Larry B. Hooks, Tr.

Established in 1995 in GA.

Foundation type: Independent foundation.

Financial data (yr. ended 12/31/05): Assets, $22,027,360 (M); expenditures, $1,237,149; qualifying distributions, $1,068,677; giving activities include $1,031,426 for 21 grants (high: $200,000; low: $1,000).

Fields of interest: Museums; Performing arts, orchestra (symphony); Arts; Higher education; Education.

Type of support: Program development; General/operating support; Curriculum development; Continuing support; Capital campaigns; Building/renovation; Annual campaigns.

Limitations: Giving primarily in metropolitan Atlanta, GA. No grants for endowments.

Publications: Application guidelines.

Application information: Application form not required.

   Initial approach: Letter

   Copies of proposal: 1

   Deadline(s): Mar. 31

Board meeting date(s): Annually, generally in May or June

   Final notification: 1 week after board meeting

Trustee: Larry B. Hooks.

EIN: 586285853

Selected grants: The following grants were reported in 2003.

$300,000 to University of Georgia Foundation, Athens, GA. 2 grants: $150,000 (For international mass communications studies), $150,000 (For Newspaper Management Studies).

$212,565 to Emory University, Atlanta, GA. 2 grants: $100,000 to School of Medicine, $112,565.

$200,000 to Atlanta Symphony Orchestra, Atlanta, GA.

$200,000 to High Museum of Art, Atlanta, GA.

$75,000 to Piedmont College, Demorest, GA.

2369
The Creel Foundation ◇ ☆
P.O. Box 1467
Augusta, GA   30903-1467   (706) 724-3550
Contact: Robbie T. White, Dir.

Established in 1989 in TX.

Foundation type: Independent foundation.

Financial data (yr. ended 12/31/04): Assets, $16,197,584 (M); expenditures, $992,063; qualifying distributions, $758,891; giving activities include $743,227 for 67 grants (high: $55,000; low: $1,200).

Fields of interest: Historic preservation/historical societies; Education; Hospitals (specialty); Athletics/sports, golf; Boys clubs; American Red Cross; Family services; Protestant agencies & churches.

Type of support: Equipment; Program development; Curriculum development; Matching/challenge support.

Limitations: Giving limited to CO, the Augusta, GA, area, and TX. No grants to individuals.

Publications: Application guidelines.

Application information: Application form required.

   Copies of proposal: 4

   Deadline(s): None

   Board meeting date(s): Feb., May, Aug., and Nov.

   Final notification: Dec.

Director: Robbie T. White.

Trustees: W.A. Copenhaver; William P. Copenhaver; Phil S. Harison; Phil S. Harison, Jr.; SunTrust Bank of Augusta, N.A.

Number of staff: 1 part-time professional.

EIN: 760297535

2370
The Daft Family Foundation ◇ ☆
c/o Kay Goff
177 Sandra Dr.
Lilburn, GA   30047

Established in 1998 in GA.

Donors: Delphine H. Daft; Douglas N. Daft.

Foundation type: Independent foundation.

Financial data (yr. ended 12/31/05): Assets, $3,063,438 (M); gifts received, $1,239; expenditures, $373,873; qualifying distributions, $372,634; giving activities include $372,634 for grants.

Fields of interest: Performing arts, theater; Arts; Higher education; Boys & girls clubs; Federated giving programs.

Limitations: Applications not accepted. Giving primarily in GA and MA. No grants to individuals.

Application information: Contributes only to pre-selected organizations.

Trustee and Distribution Committee:* Alexandra L. Bonner; Delphine H. Daft*; Douglas N. Daft; Nicholas Daft.

EIN: 586379765

Selected grants: The following grants were reported in 2005.

$101,496 to Cambridge in America, New York, NY.

$78,320 to Williamstown Theater Festival, Williamstown, MA.

$76,320 to Sterling and Francine Clark Art Institute, Williamstown, MA.

$25,620 to Williams College, Williamstown, MA.

$20,000 to Brandeis University, Waltham, MA.

$10,878 to American Australian Association, New York, NY.

$10,000 to North Adams Regional Hospital, North Adams, MA.

$10,000 to Westminster Schools, Atlanta, GA.

$5,000 to Appeal of Conscience Foundation, New York, NY.

2371
Cecil B. Day Foundation, Inc.
4725 Peachtree Corners Cir., Ste. 300
Norcross, GA   30092   (770) 446-1500
Contact: Edward L. White, Jr., Pres.

Incorporated in 1968 in GA.

Donors: Cecil B. Day†; Deen Day Sanders.

Foundation type: Independent foundation.

Financial data (yr. ended 12/31/05): Assets, $27,076,430 (M); expenditures, $2,125,837; qualifying distributions, $1,973,269; giving activities include $1,901,255 for grants.

Purpose and activities: Grants to Christian churches, especially Baptist churches, for evangelism, missions, and disciplineships, and for Pastor's Leadership Training.

Fields of interest: Christian agencies & churches; Protestant agencies & churches.

Type of support: General/operating support; Continuing support; Capital campaigns; Building/renovation; Equipment; Emergency funds; Seed money; Matching/challenge support.

Limitations: Giving primarily in the New England states; special consideration for GA, primarily in the metropolitan Atlanta area. No grants to individuals, or for deficit financing, endowment funds, scholarships, or fellowships.

Publications: Informational brochure.

Application information: Application form not required.

   Initial approach: Letter requesting program brochure

   Copies of proposal: 1

   Deadline(s): None

   Board meeting date(s): Annually

Officers and Trustees:* Deen Day Sanders,* Vice-Chair.; Edward L. White, Jr.,* Pres.; R.D. Spear,* V.P.; Joann F. Dollar, Secy.; Charles A. Sanders,* Treas.; C. Burke Day; C. Parke Day; C. Peyton Day; Clinton M. Day; Kathie Day; Lon L. Day, Jr.

EIN: 581030351

Selected grants: The following grants were reported in 2004.

$125,000 to Haggai Institute for Advanced Leadership Training, Atlanta, GA.

$40,000 to Big Creek Church, Alpharetta, GA.

$30,000 to Christian and Missionary Alliance, Colorado Springs, CO.

$30,000 to Ravi Zacharias International Ministries, Norcross, GA.

$25,000 to Blood N Fire Ministries, Atlanta, GA.

$15,000 to Georgia Family Council, Norcross, GA.

$10,000 to Emmanuel Gospel Center, Boston, MA.

$10,000 to FCS Urban Ministries, Atlanta, GA.

$5,000 to Vision New England, Acton, MA.

$3,000 to Georgia Baptist Childrens Homes and Family Ministries, Palmetto, GA.

2372
The Delta Air Lines Foundation ✧
Dept. 983
P.O. Box 20706
Atlanta, GA 30320-6001 (404) 715-5487
Contact: Jerome Miller, Pres.
FAX: (404) 715-3267;
E-mail: foundation.delta@delta.com; URL: http://www.delta.com/about_delta/community_involvement/delta_foundation/index.jsp

Established in 1968 in DE.
Donor: Delta Air Lines, Inc.
Foundation type: Company-sponsored foundation.
Financial data (yr. ended 12/31/04): Assets, $29,050,587 (M); expenditures, $3,077,052; qualifying distributions, $2,812,936; giving activities include $2,597,250 for 41 grants (high: $680,000; low: $2,250), and $194,864 for employee matching gifts.
Purpose and activities: The foundation supports organizations involved with arts and culture, health and wellness, youth, economic development, and community enrichment.
Fields of interest: Arts; Health care; Youth, services; Economic development; Community development.
Type of support: Continuing support; General/operating support; Program development; Research; Employee matching gifts.
Limitations: Giving primarily in areas of company operations. No support for fraternal organizations, professional associations, or membership groups. No grants to individuals, or for endowments, non-community building capital campaigns, fundraising events, or religious activities.
Publications: Annual report.
Application information: Multi-year funding is not automatic. Application form required.
  Initial approach: Download application form and mail to foundation
  Copies of proposal: 1
  Deadline(s): Apr. 1, June 1, Sept. 1, and Nov. 1
  Board meeting date(s): Mar., June, Sept., and Nov.
  Final notification: Within 2 weeks of board meetings
Officers and Trustees:* Jerome Miller, Pres.; Todd Helvie, V.P.; Sheba A. Rourk, Secy.; James B. Taylor, Treas.; Gerald Grinstein; Michael J. Palumbo; Greg L. Riggs.
EIN: 586073119
Selected grants: The following grants were reported in 2003.
$700,000 to United Way of Metropolitan Atlanta, Atlanta, GA.
$100,000 to Robert W. Woodruff Arts Center, Atlanta, GA.

$75,000 to Atlanta Symphony Orchestra, Atlanta, GA.

$50,000 to CARE, Atlanta, GA.

$31,000 to Literacy Action, Atlanta, GA.

$20,000 to High Museum of Art, Atlanta, GA.

$5,000 to Atlanta Legal Aid Endowment Fund, Atlanta, GA.

$5,000 to Camp Kudzu, Atlanta, GA.

$5,000 to Lupus Foundation of America, Atlanta, GA.

$2,000 to Americans for the Arts, DC.

2373
R. Howard Dobbs, Jr. Foundation, Inc.
(formerly Helen and Howard Dobbs Foundation, Inc.)
50 Hurt Plz., Ste. 1212
Atlanta, GA 30303 (404) 221-0005
FAX: (404) 221-1101;
E-mail: foundation@rhdobbs.net; URL: http://www.dobbsfoundation.org

Established in 1959.
Donor: R. Howard Dobbs, Jr.‡.
Foundation type: Independent foundation.
Financial data (yr. ended 10/31/05): Assets, $14,917,378 (M); expenditures, $975,721; qualifying distributions, $945,934; giving activities include $834,822 for 22 grants (high: $100,000; low: $1,500).
Purpose and activities: The purpose of the foundation is to improve the quality of life for individuals, families and communities by supporting educational opportunities, improving access to health services and promoting environmental stewardship.
Fields of interest: Education; Environment; Health care; Human services; Community development.
Type of support: Capital campaigns; Building/renovation.
Limitations: Giving primarily in the southeastern U.S. No grants to individuals.
Publications: Grants list; Informational brochure (including application guidelines).
Application information: Application form not required.
  Initial approach: Telephone
  Copies of proposal: 1
  Deadline(s): July 1 and Dec. 1
  Board meeting date(s): Jan., Apr., July, and Oct.
Officers and Director:* E. Cody Laird, Jr.,* Chair.; Nancy C. Crosswell, Secy.; Dameron Black III, Treas.; Lisa B. Williams, Exec. Dir.
Trustee: Dorothy L. Williams.
Number of staff: 2 full-time professional.
EIN: 586033186
Selected grants: The following grants were reported in 2004.
$75,000 to Inner Harbour, Douglasville, GA. For construction of new residence facility.
$75,000 to Nature Conservancy, Atlanta, GA. For land acquisition.
$50,000 to Georgia Conservancy, Atlanta, GA. For development and production of water education.
$40,000 to Fernbank, Inc., Atlanta, GA. For operating support.
$35,000 to Southface Energy Institute, Atlanta, GA. For construction of office and demonstration.
$30,000 to American Rivers, DC. For database integration project.
$30,000 to Atlanta Community Food Bank, Atlanta, GA. For construction of new warehouse and distribution.

$30,000 to Sheltering Arms Early Education and Family Centers, Atlanta, GA. For construction of Head Start center in Fulton County.
$30,000 to Southern Environmental Law Center, Charlottesville, VA. To furnish and equip new Atlanta office expansion.
$25,000 to Childhood Autism Diagnostic and Educational Foundation, Atlanta, GA. For operating support.

2374
The Frances and Beverly DuBose Foundation, Inc. ✧
N.W. Bldg. 11
4200 Northside Pkwy. Sq., Ste. 200
Atlanta, GA 30327

Established in 1990 in GA.
Donors: Frances W. DuBose; DuBose Family Charitable Annuity Trust.
Foundation type: Independent foundation.
Financial data (yr. ended 6/30/05): Assets, $16,002,402 (M); gifts received, $340,250; expenditures, $1,005,363; qualifying distributions, $713,750; giving activities include $713,750 for 20 grants (high: $250,000; low: $250; average: $5,000–$75,000).
Fields of interest: Historic preservation/historical societies; Higher education; Education.
Type of support: Annual campaigns; Capital campaigns; Building/renovation; Land acquisition; Endowments; Conferences/seminars; Seed money; Internship funds; Research.
Limitations: Applications not accepted. Giving primarily in GA; some funding also in VA. No grants to individuals.
Publications: Annual report.
Application information: Contributes only to pre-selected organizations.
Officers and Trustees:* Frances W. DuBose,* Chair.; Dean DuBose Smith,* Secy.; Beverly M. DuBose III,* Treas.; Eileen Erickson DuBose; Elizabeth Egleston DuBose; Thomas Edward Lewis; H. Bronson Smith.
EIN: 581901090

2375
Robert and Polly Dunn Foundation, Inc.
P.O. Box 723194
Atlanta, GA 31139 (404) 816-2883
Contact: Karen C. Wilbanks, Exec. Dir.
FAX: (404) 237-5120; E-mail: kwilbanks@lawnet.org

Established in 1986 in GA.
Foundation type: Independent foundation.
Financial data (yr. ended 12/31/05): Assets, $15,987,151 (M); expenditures, $865,478; qualifying distributions, $760,288; giving activities include $706,399 for 50 grants (high: $89,290; low: $100).
Fields of interest: Children/youth, services; Child development, services.
Type of support: General/operating support; Annual campaigns; Scholarship funds.
Limitations: Giving limited to the southeast, with emphasis on the metropolitan Atlanta, GA, area. No support for private schools. No grants to individuals, or for endowment funds, capital campaigns, buildings, or day care; no loans or program-related investments.
Publications: Application guidelines.

Application information: Application form not required.

   Initial approach: Letter
   Copies of proposal: 1
   Deadline(s): Apr. 30, for June meeting; Sept. 30, for Dec. meeting
   Board meeting date(s): June and Dec.
   Final notification: July for June meeting; Late Dec. for December meeting.

Officers and Trustees:* Preston Hays, Chair.; Karen C. Wilbanks,* Exec. Dir.; Richard B. Freeman; Andy Perry.

Number of staff: 1 part-time professional.

EIN: 581671255

Selected grants: The following grants were reported in 2005.

$50,000 to CHRIS Kids, Atlanta, GA.

$50,000 to Eagle Ranch, Chestnut Mountain, GA.

$50,000 to Paul Anderson Youth Home, Vidalia, GA.

$50,000 to Tommy Nobis Center, Marietta, GA. For summer program.

$15,000 to Georgia Association of Homes and Services for Children Foundation, Atlanta, GA. For scholarships.

2376
The Jim Ellis Foundation, Inc. ✧

5901 Peachtree Industrial Blvd.
Atlanta, GA 30341-1630

Established in 1999 in GA.

Donors: James W. Ellis, Jr.; Jim Ellis.

Foundation type: Independent foundation.

Financial data (yr. ended 6/30/06): Assets, $5,728,312 (M); gifts received, $700,000; expenditures, $346,355; qualifying distributions, $342,500; giving activities include $342,500 for grants.

Fields of interest: Hospitals (general); Christian agencies & churches.

Limitations: Applications not accepted. No grants to individuals.

Application information: Contributes only to pre-selected organizations.

Trustees: Billie S. Ellis; James E. Ellis; James W. Ellis, Jr.

EIN: 582500810

Selected grants: The following grants were reported in 2005.

$25,000 to International Mission Board, Johnson City, NY.

$25,000 to Salvation Army.

$2,000 to Campus Crusade for Christ.

2377
The Endover Foundation, Inc. ✧

4401 Northside Pkwy., Ste. 200
Atlanta, GA 30327
Contact: George D. Overend, Pres.

Established in 1997 in GA.

Donors: The Coca-Cola Co.; George D. Overend.

Foundation type: Independent foundation.

Financial data (yr. ended 12/31/03): Assets, $1,035,450 (M); expenditures, $386,334; qualifying distributions, $381,623; giving activities include $382,500 for 5 grants (high: $300,000; low: $5,000).

Fields of interest: Higher education, college; Education.

Type of support: General/operating support.

Limitations: Giving primarily in GA. No grants to individuals.

Application information:

   Initial approach: Letter
   Deadline(s): None

Officers and Directors:* George D. Overend,* Pres. and Treas.; Carol C. Overend,* Secy.; G. David Overend; William M. Overend; Clarence H. Ridley.

EIN: 582439787

Selected grants: The following grants were reported in 2004.

$32,500 to Rhodes College, Memphis, TN.

$30,000 to Washington and Lee University, Lexington, VA.

$5,000 to Peabody Essex Museum, Salem, MA.

$5,000 to Presbyterian Homes of Georgia, Atlanta, GA.

$5,000 to University of Georgia Foundation, Athens, GA.

$2,500 to Emory University, Atlanta, GA.

2378
The Florence C. and Harry L. English Memorial Fund ✧

c/o SunTrust Bank
P.O. Box 4655
Atlanta, GA 30302
Contact: Raymond B. King, Secy.
FAX: (404) 724-3082; *URL:* http://www.suntrustatlantafoundation.org/funds.html

Established in 1964 in GA.

Donor: Florence Cruft English‡.

Foundation type: Independent foundation.

Financial data (yr. ended 12/31/05): Assets, $14,984,262 (M); expenditures, $686,563; qualifying distributions, $651,817; giving activities include $630,820 for 79 grants (high: $33,000; low: $1,400).

Purpose and activities: Grants only for education, health, general welfare, and culture, with emphasis on assisting the aged and chronically ill, the blind, and those persons generally designated as being underprivileged.

Fields of interest: Arts; Higher education; Education; Community development.

Type of support: Capital campaigns; Building/renovation; Equipment.

Limitations: Giving limited to the metropolitan Atlanta, GA, area. No support for veterans' organizations or organizations which have not been operating without a deficit for at least a year. No grants to individuals, or for general operating support, maintenance, or for debt service; no loans.

Publications: Application guidelines; Program policy statement.

Application information: Application form available on fund Web site. Application form required.

   Initial approach: Letter
   Copies of proposal: 1
   Deadline(s): Mar. 31, Aug. 31, and Dec. 1
   Board meeting date(s): Jan., Apr., July, and Oct.

Officers and Distribution Committee:* E. Jenner Wood III,* Chair.; Raymond B. King, Secy.; L.P. Humann; Gary Peacock; James M. Wells.

Trustee: SunTrust Bank.

Number of staff: 1 full-time professional.

EIN: 586045781

2379
Equifax Foundation ✧

1550 Peachtree St. N.W.
Atlanta, GA 30309
Contact: Kirby Thompson
E-mail: kirby.thompson@equifax.com

Trust established in 1978 in GA.

Donors: Retail Credit Co.; Equifax Inc.

Foundation type: Company-sponsored foundation.

Financial data (yr. ended 12/31/04): Assets, $1,804,313 (M); gifts received, $725,000; expenditures, $782,667; qualifying distributions, $780,002; giving activities include $780,002 for grants.

Purpose and activities: The foundation supports organizations involved with arts and culture, higher education, health, and human services.

Fields of interest: Arts; Higher education; Health care; Human services; Federated giving programs.

Type of support: Capital campaigns; Building/renovation; Land acquisition; Seed money; Research.

Limitations: Giving primarily in Atlanta, GA. No grants to individuals, or for debt reduction, fellowships, publications, or travel; no matching or challenge grants.

Publications: Informational brochure (including application guidelines).

Application information: Application form not required.

   Initial approach: Proposal
   Copies of proposal: 1
   Deadline(s): None
   Board meeting date(s): June and Dec.
   Final notification: 60 days

Trustees: John Chandler; Tom Chapman; Karen H. Gasten; Phillip J. Mazzilli.

Number of staff: 1 part-time professional.

EIN: 581296807

2380
Exposition Foundation, Inc. ✧

520 E. Paces Ferry Rd. N.E.
Atlanta, GA 30305 (404) 233-6404
Contact: Jane C. Black, Pres.

Incorporated in 1950 in GA.

Foundation type: Independent foundation.

Financial data (yr. ended 8/31/05): Assets, $0 (M); expenditures, $1,064,553; qualifying distributions, $1,046,993; giving activities include $1,046,993 for 29 grants (high: $239,650; low: $1,500).

Purpose and activities: Primary areas of interest include the fine arts and higher and secondary education; support also for social services, housing, and health.

Fields of interest: Visual arts; Museums; Performing arts; Performing arts, music; Historic preservation/historical societies; Arts; Secondary school/education; Higher education; Education; Health care; Health organizations, association; AIDS; Housing/shelter, development; Human services.

International interests: Latin America.

Type of support: General/operating support; Annual campaigns; Capital campaigns; Building/renovation; Equipment; Endowments; Program development; Scholarship funds.

Limitations: Giving primarily in Atlanta, GA; some giving in Latin America.

Publications: Annual report.

Application information: Application form not required.

Initial approach: Letter
Copies of proposal: 1
Board meeting date(s): Varies
Officers and Trustees: Jane C. Black,* Pres. and Treas.; James Floyd Black, Secy.; Dameron Black IV.
EIN: 586043273
Selected grants: The following grants were reported in 2004.
$242,256 to High Museum of Art, Atlanta, GA.
$115,000 to EARTH University Foundation, Atlanta, GA.
$50,000 to Benjamin Franklin Academy, Atlanta, GA.
$50,000 to University of Georgia Foundation, Athens, GA.
$10,000 to Atlanta Speech School, Atlanta, GA.
$10,000 to Good Samaritan Health Center, Atlanta, GA.
$10,000 to Metro Atlanta Task Force for the Homeless, Atlanta, GA.
$5,000 to Atlanta History Center, Atlanta, GA.
$3,000 to Creating Pride - Atlanta, Atlanta, GA.
$2,500 to Georgia Foundation for Independent Colleges, Atlanta, GA.

2381

Faith Ventures Foundation, Inc. ✧
748 Iron Mountain Rd.
Canton, GA 30115

Established in 2002 in GA.
Donor: The William M. and Phyllis B. Johnson Foundation, Inc.
Foundation type: Independent foundation.
Financial data (yr. ended 12/31/05): Assets, $7,722,126 (M); gifts received, $2,400; expenditures, $409,685; qualifying distributions, $349,904; giving activities include $349,904 for 24 grants (high: $150,000; low: $100).
Purpose and activities: Giving primarily to Christian and Methodist organizations and churches.
Fields of interest: Human services; Christian agencies & churches.
Limitations: Applications not accepted. Giving primarily in GA. No grants to individuals.
Application information: Contributes only to pre-selected organizations.
Officers: William M. Johnson, Pres. and Treas.; Phyllis B. Johnson, V.P. and Secy.
EIN: 820554456

2382

The Farris Foundation, Inc. ✧
P.O. Box 304
Lawrenceville, GA 30046

Established in 1995 in GA.
Donor: Timothy J. Farris.
Foundation type: Operating foundation.
Financial data (yr. ended 12/31/05): Assets, $2,389,333 (M); gifts received, $302; expenditures, $577,667; qualifying distributions, $568,065; giving activities include $372,892 for 29 grants (high: $54,391; low: $260), and $231,251 for 4 foundation-administered programs.
Purpose and activities: Giving primarily for children's services and education.
Fields of interest: Education; Children/youth, services; Christian agencies & churches.

Limitations: Applications not accepted. Giving in the southern U.S., with emphasis on GA, KY, NC, TN, and TX. No grants to individuals.
Application information: Contributes only to pre-selected organizations.
Officers and Directors: Timothy J. Farris,* Chair.; Otis P. Jones,* Pres.; Sandra I. Jones,* V.P.
EIN: 582204830

2383

Five Smith's Foundation, Inc. ✧ ☆
(formerly Atlanta Falcons Foundation, Inc.)
4355J Cobb Pkwy., No. 310
Atlanta, GA 30339
Contact: John O. Knox, Jr., Pres.

Established about 1970 in GA as the Falcons Foundation, Inc. of Atlanta.
Donors: Rankin M. Smith, Sr.‡; Taylor W. Smith.
Foundation type: Independent foundation.
Financial data (yr. ended 12/31/05): Assets, $0 (M); expenditures, $560,222; qualifying distributions, $559,347; giving activities include $559,347 for grants.
Fields of interest: Museums (history); Education; Children/youth, services.
Limitations: Giving primarily in GA. No grants to individuals.
Application information: Application form not required.
Initial approach: Letter
Deadline(s): None
Officers: Taylor W. Smith, Chair.; John O. Knox, Jr., Pres.; James I. Hay, Secy.
EIN: 237075113
Selected grants: The following grants were reported in 2003.
$55,000 to Schenck School, Atlanta, GA. For unrestricted support.
$35,000 to Fernbank Museum of Natural History, Atlanta, GA. For unrestricted support.
$7,500 to Murphy-Harpst Childrens Centers, Cedartown, GA. For unrestricted support.
$5,000 to Reinhardt College, Waleska, GA. For unrestricted support.
$2,500 to Whitey Zimmerman Scholarship Fund. For unrestricted support.
$1,600 to Tommy Nobis Center, Marietta, GA. For unrestricted support.
$1,400 to Lovett School, Atlanta, GA. For unrestricted support.
$1,000 to Alice Hay Memorial Fund. For unrestricted support.
$1,000 to Susan G. Komen Breast Cancer Foundation, Atlanta, GA. For unrestricted support.
$500 to Childrens Healthcare of Atlanta, Atlanta, GA. For unrestricted support.

2384

William Howard Flowers, Jr. Foundation, Inc. ✧
P.O. Box 6100
Thomasville, GA 31758-6100

Established in 1991 in GA.
Donors: William H. Flowers, Jr.‡; Maury Flowers Shields; McFadden Trust; Parker Trust.
Foundation type: Independent foundation.
Financial data (yr. ended 12/31/05): Assets, $50,779,505 (M); gifts received, $257,547;

expenditures, $2,435,873; qualifying distributions, $2,344,164; giving activities include $2,230,000 for 109 grants (high: $505,000; low: $1,000).
Purpose and activities: Giving primarily for the arts. Also giving to Christian organizations and the YMCA.
Fields of interest: Performing arts, music; Arts; Human services; YM/YWCAs & YM/YWHAs; Children/youth, services; Christian agencies & churches.
Type of support: General/operating support.
Limitations: Applications not accepted. Giving primarily in GA. No grants to individuals.
Application information: Contributes only to pre-selected organizations.
Board meeting date(s): Twice yearly
Trustees: Taliaferro F. Crozer; Maury Flowers Shields; Daphne F. Wood.
Number of staff: 1 full-time professional; 1 part-time professional.
EIN: 581399036
Selected grants: The following grants were reported in 2004.
$435,000 to Brookwood School, Thomasville, GA.
$195,000 to Prison Fellowship Ministries, Lansdowne, VA.
$50,000 to Focus on the Family, Colorado Springs, CO.
$35,000 to Thomasville Community Resource Center, Thomasville, GA.
$35,000 to University of Virginia, Charlottesville, VA.
$30,000 to Thomasville Landmarks, Thomasville, GA.
$10,000 to American Red Cross.
$10,000 to Thomas Jefferson Memorial Foundation, Charlottesville, VA.
$10,000 to Thomasville Antiques Show Foundation, Thomasville, GA.
$7,500 to Madeira School, McLean, VA.

2385

The Fonda Family Foundation, Inc. ✧
P.O. Box 5840
Atlanta, GA 31107-5840
Contact: Austin Stephens, Treas.
E-mail: info@fffinc.org

Established in 1998 in GA.
Donor: Jane S. Fonda.
Foundation type: Independent foundation.
Financial data (yr. ended 12/31/05): Assets, $9,395,610 (M); gifts received, $121,130; expenditures, $604,999; qualifying distributions, $568,635; giving activities include $451,725 for 35 grants (high: $80,000; low: $75).
Purpose and activities: Giving primarily for human rights and social services.
Fields of interest: Media/communications; Human services; Civil rights.
Limitations: Applications not accepted. Giving on a national basis.
Application information: Unsolicited requests for funds not accepted.
Board meeting date(s): July and Dec.
Officers and Directors: Jane S. Fonda,* Chair. and Pres.; Patricia Durrett, Secy.; Austin Stephens, Treas.; Troy Garity; Nathalie Vadim; Vanessa Vadim; Mary Williams.
EIN: 582365665

2386
Jane Fonda Foundation, Inc. ✧
P.O. Box 5840
Atlanta, GA 31107-0840

Established in 2004 in GA.
Donors: Avery Pix; Fischer Ross Group.
Foundation type: Independent foundation.
Financial data (yr. ended 12/31/05): Assets, $231,631 (M); gifts received, $79,011; expenditures, $500,430; qualifying distributions, $500,030; giving activities include $500,000 for 1 grant.
Fields of interest: Higher education; Medical school/education.
Limitations: Applications not accepted. Giving primarily in Atlanta, GA.
Application information: Contributes only to pre-selected organizations.
Officers and Director:* Jane S. Fonda,* Chair. and Pres.; C. Austin Stephens, Secy.; Steven E. Bennett, Treas.
EIN: 141890432

2387
Mildred Miller Fort Foundation, Inc.
P.O. Box 2665
Columbus, GA 31902-2665 (706) 341-6662
Contact: Susan Cochran, Fdn. Admin.
FAX: (706) 320-3828;
E-mail: fortfoundation@bellsouth.net

Established in 1992 in GA.
Donor: Mildred Miller Fort.
Foundation type: Independent foundation.
Financial data (yr. ended 12/31/05): Assets, $29,055,290 (M); gifts received, $21,263,288; expenditures, $555,984; qualifying distributions, $526,751; giving activities include $507,000 for 25 grants (high: $201,000; low: $1,000).
Purpose and activities: Giving primarily for education, the arts, health care, environmental protection and beautification, and relief of the underserved.
Fields of interest: Arts; Education; Environment; Health care.
Limitations: Applications not accepted. Giving primarily in Columbus, GA.
Application information: Unsolicited requests for funds not accepted.
Officer and Trustees:* Alan F. Rothschild, Jr.,* Pres.; Sally B. Hatcher; Edward W. Neal; J. Kyle Spencer; William C. Woolfolf III.
Number of staff: 1 part-time professional.
EIN: 581991612

2388
Foundation for Agronomic Research, Inc. ✧
655 Engineering Dr., Ste. 110
Norcross, GA 30092-2843
Contact: T.L. Roberts, V.P.
URL: http://www.ppi-far.org

Established in 1980 in DE.
Donors: U.S. Borax Inc.; DowElanco; Gold Kist Inc.; United Soybean Board.
Foundation type: Independent foundation.
Financial data (yr. ended 12/31/04): Assets, $834,684 (M); gifts received, $670,052; expenditures, $818,159; qualifying distributions,

$790,616; giving activities include $374,630 for 53 grants (high: $31,163; low: $150).
Purpose and activities: To improve the economic vigor and sustainability of agriculture in North America and around the world, while protecting and enhancing the environment. Grants primarily to North American universities and research organizations for studies of soil management and improved crop yields.
Fields of interest: Environment, plant conservation; Agriculture.
International interests: Canada.
Type of support: Research.
Limitations: Applications not accepted. Giving primarily in the U.S. and Canada. No support for profit-making organizations. No grants to individuals.
Publications: Annual report.
Application information: Unsolicited requests for funds not accepted.
  Board meeting date(s): Oct.
Officers: William J. Doyle, Chair.; Frederic Corrigan, Vice-Chair.; Harold R. Reetz, Jr., Pres.; Paul E. Fixen, V.P.; Terry L. Roberts, V.P.
Directors: Charles Adams; Dennis J. Addis; S. Eugene Allred; Dan Froelich; Ray A. Hoyum; Kenneth D. Kunz; Larry S. Murphy.
EIN: 581406074
Selected grants: The following grants were reported in 2003.
$44,349 to Virginia Polytechnic Institute and State University, Blacksburg, VA. For cropping system evaluation.
$37,500 to Mississippi State University, Mississippi State, MS. For soybean research verification program.
$27,837 to University of Arkansas, Fayetteville, AR. For evaluation of precision agriculture technology incorporated into an ongoing statewide technology transfer program.
$23,980 to Iowa State University, Ames, IA. For Iowa component of Coordination of Management Practices Enhancing Total Efficiency (COMPETE) project.
$22,986 to North Carolina State University, Raleigh, NC. For management systems in a precision agriculture environment.
$16,954 to Purdue Research Foundation, West Lafayette, IN. For evaluation of site specific soybean management systems.
$16,000 to University of Wisconsin, Madison, WI. For evaluation of precision farming systems for soybeans.
$12,501 to University of Nebraska, Lincoln, NE. For ecological intensifications of irrigated corn and soybean systems.
$11,050 to University of Georgia, Athens, GA. For Agricultural and Environmental Studies in Costa Rica.
$4,800 to Kansas State University, Manhattan, KS. For maximizing irrigated corn yields in the Great Plains.

2389
John and Mary Franklin Foundation, Inc.
3282 Northside Pkwy. N.W., Ste. 100
Atlanta, GA 30327 (404) 279-5244
Contact: Marilu H. McCarty, Exec. Secy.

Incorporated in 1955 in GA.
Donors: John Franklin†; Mary O. Franklin†.
Foundation type: Independent foundation.

Financial data (yr. ended 12/31/03): Assets, $33,790,662 (M); expenditures, $1,281,146; qualifying distributions, $1,134,820; giving activities include $987,600 for 108 grants (high: $50,000; low: $100), and $69,500 for 39 employee matching gifts.
Purpose and activities: Giving primarily for education, health, youth services, and the arts.
Fields of interest: Historical activities; Arts; Higher education; Education; Health care; Health organizations, association; Boys clubs; Children/youth, services; Federated giving programs.
Type of support: General/operating support; Continuing support; Annual campaigns; Capital campaigns; Building/renovation; Scholarship funds; Research.
Limitations: Giving primarily in GA, with emphasis on the metropolitan Atlanta area. No support for religious organizations, political organizations or private schools (except under specific conditions). No grants to individuals.
Application information: Application form not required.
  Initial approach: Varies
  Copies of proposal: 1
  Deadline(s): Dec. 31
  Board meeting date(s): Apr. and Dec., and as needed
  Final notification: Jan. and Dec.
Officers: Marilu H. McCarty, Exec. Secy.
Trustees: Richard W. Courts II; John B. Ellis; Marion B. Glover; Frank M. Malone, Jr.; Jerry W. Nix; Alexander W. Smith, Jr.; E. Kendrick Smith.
Number of staff: 1 part-time professional; 1 part-time support.
EIN: 586036131
Selected grants: The following grants were reported in 2004.
$90,000 to University of Georgia Foundation, Athens, GA. For clinics and programs.
$60,000 to Georgia Institute of Technology, Atlanta, GA. For John McCarty chair for Electrical Engineering.
$52,000 to Atlanta Speech School, Atlanta, GA. For general support.
$50,000 to Fernbank Museum of Natural History, Atlanta, GA. For general support.
$50,000 to George West Mental Health Foundation, Atlanta, GA. For general support.
$50,000 to Georgia State University Foundation, Atlanta, GA. For Science building.
$32,000 to Auburn University, Auburn, AL. For Franklin-Littleton lecture series.
$30,000 to Robert W. Woodruff Arts Center, Atlanta, GA. For general support.
$25,000 to Brenau University, Gainesville, GA. For general support.
$20,000 to Community Advanced Practice Nurses, Atlanta, GA. For general support.

2390
The Fraser-Parker Foundation
The Hurt Bldg.
50 Hurt Plz., Ste. 850
Atlanta, GA 30303 (404) 658-9066
Contact: John Stephenson, Exec. Dir.

Established in 1987 in GA.
Donors: William A. Parker, Jr.; Nancy F. Parker†.
Foundation type: Independent foundation.
Financial data (yr. ended 12/31/05): Assets, $16,610,608 (M); expenditures, $840,024; qualifying distributions, $797,176; giving activities

include $725,000 for 39 grants (high: $122,000; low: $1,000; average: $10,000–$20,000).

Purpose and activities: Support primarily for organizations that are traditionally supported by the family, including the arts and education.

Fields of interest: Museums; Secondary school/education; Education; Medical research, institute; Youth, services; Religion.

Type of support: General/operating support; Continuing support; Capital campaigns.

Limitations: Giving primarily in the metropolitan Atlanta, GA, area. No grants to individuals, or for emergency funds, deficit financing, or deficit operating budgets; no loans.

Publications: Informational brochure (including application guidelines).

Application information: Application form not required.

  Initial approach: Letter

  Copies of proposal: 1

  Deadline(s): Apr. 15 and Oct. 15

  Board meeting date(s): May and Nov.

  Final notification: June 1 and Dec. 1

Officers and Trustees: * William A. Parker, Jr.,* Chair.; Richard Carlyle Parker,* Vice-Chair.; Richard W. Courts II; Katharine G. Farnham; Isobel P. Mills; William A. Parker III.

Number of staff: 2 part-time professional; 2 part-time support.

EIN: 586212344

2391
J. B. Fuqua Foundation, Inc. ✧

1201 W. Peachtree St. N.E., Ste. 5000
Atlanta, GA 30309
Contact: J.B. Fuqua, Pres.
Application address: 1 Atlantic Ctr., Ste. 5000, Atlanta, GA 30309

Incorporated in 1970 in GA.

Donors: J.B. Fuqua; J.B. Fuqua Family Charitable Lead Unitrust.

Foundation type: Independent foundation.

Financial data (yr. ended 12/31/05): Assets, $19,602,017 (M); gifts received, $2,185,644; expenditures, $867,617; qualifying distributions, $793,475; giving activities include $581,200 for 25 grants (high: $200,000; low: $200).

Purpose and activities: Grants primarily for education; support also for health, hospitals, and social services.

Fields of interest: Higher education; Medical school/education; Education; Hospitals (general); Health care; Human services.

Limitations: Giving primarily in GA, NC, and VA. No support for partisan political programs. No grants to individuals.

Application information: Application form not required.

  Deadline(s): None

Officers: J.B. Fuqua, Pres.; Dorothy C. Fuqua, Secy.; J. Rex Fuqua, Treas.

Number of staff: 3 part-time support.

EIN: 237122039

Selected grants: The following grants were reported in 2003.

$869,069 to Emory University, Atlanta, GA. 2 grants: $500,000 to School of Medicine, $369,069

$666,667 to Trinity School, Atlanta, GA.

$300,000 to Atlanta Union Mission, Atlanta, GA. 2 grants: $150,000 each

$250,000 to Fuqua School, Farmville, VA. 2 grants: $150,000, $100,000

$200,000 to Pace Academy, Development Office, Atlanta, GA.

$100,000 to Piedmont Hospital, Atlanta, GA.

$100,000 to Womens Auxiliary of Piedmont Hospital, Atlanta, GA.

2392
Philip and Irene Toll Gage Foundation

3414 Peachtree Rd., Ste. 722
Atlanta, GA 30326 (404) 842-1870
Contact: Larry B. Hooks, Tr.
FAX: (404) 842-1869; *Application address:* 3414 Peachtree Rd., Ste. 722, Atlanta, GA 30326

Established in 1985 in GA.

Donor: Betty G. Holland†.

Foundation type: Independent foundation.

Financial data (yr. ended 11/30/05): Assets, $9,041,717 (M); gifts received, $19,390; expenditures, $511,914; qualifying distributions, $441,409; giving activities include $420,890 for 8 grants (high: $300,000; low: $500).

Purpose and activities: Support for education, culture, including the arts and theater, and hospitals and health services; some funding also for Protestant agencies and churches.

Fields of interest: Museums; Performing arts, theater; Arts; Education, fund raising/fund distribution; Education; Environment; Animal welfare; Hospitals (general); Health care; Health organizations, association; Children/youth, services; Community development; Protestant agencies & churches.

Type of support: General/operating support; Annual campaigns; Building/renovation.

Limitations: Giving primarily outside of the U.S. No grants to individuals, or for endowment programs.

Publications: Application guidelines.

Application information: Application form not required.

  Initial approach: Letter

  Copies of proposal: 1

  Deadline(s): Mar. 31

  Board meeting date(s): Annually in May or June

  Final notification: Within 1 week of board meeting

Trustee: Larry Hooks.

EIN: 581727394

2393
Courtney Knight Gaines Foundation ✧

70 Shipwatch Rd.
Savannah, GA 31410

Established in 1998 in GA.

Donor: Courtney Knight Gaines.

Foundation type: Independent foundation.

Financial data (yr. ended 12/31/05): Assets, $9,987,139 (M); expenditures, $537,736; qualifying distributions, $487,978; giving activities include $454,500 for 39 grants (high: $120,000; low: $1,000).

Purpose and activities: Giving primarily for education, conservation and wildlife, and for health and human services.

Fields of interest: Arts; Education; Environment, natural resources; Animals/wildlife, preservation/protection; Health organizations, association; Human services; Religion.

Limitations: Applications not accepted. Giving primarily in GA. No grants to individuals.

Application information: Contributes only to pre-selected organizations.

Officers: Courtney Knight Gaines, Pres.; Christopher E. Klein, Secy.

Directors: Courtney Gaines Fetz; Ezekiel Baldwin Gaines III; Grace Gaines Gattis.

Agent: Citibank, N.A.

EIN: 582398209

Selected grants: The following grants were reported in 2003.

$111,000 to Wesley Monumental United Methodist Church, Savannah, GA.

$4,000 to Meharry Medical College, Nashville, TN.

$3,000 to Berea College, Berea, KY.

$2,000 to National Parks Conservation Association, DC.

$2,000 to Savannah Area Family Emergency Shelter, Savannah, GA.

$2,000 to World Wildlife Fund, DC.

$1,500 to Mercy Housing SouthEast, Atlanta, GA.

$1,000 to Gorilla Foundation, Woodside, CA.

$1,000 to Savannah State University, Savannah, GA.

$1,000 to Trust for Public Land, San Francisco, CA.

2394
Georgia Health Foundation, Inc. ✧

4 Executive Park Dr., Ste. 1210
Atlanta, GA 30329 (404) 636-2525
Contact: Robert L. Zwald, Secy.
FAX: (404) 636-9072;
E-mail: gahealthfdn@bellsouth.net; *URL:* http://www.gahealthfdn.org

Established in 1985 in GA; converted from Georgia Medical Plan, Inc.

Donor: Georgia Medical Plan, Inc.

Foundation type: Independent foundation.

Financial data (yr. ended 12/31/05): Assets, $10,006,140 (M); expenditures, $517,786; qualifying distributions, $477,785; giving activities include $385,500 for 23+ grants (high: $25,000).

Purpose and activities: Giving for public health education, as well as for health-related projects and programs in GA.

Fields of interest: Medical school/education; Public health school/education; Public health; Health care; Health organizations, association; Medical research, institute.

Type of support: General/operating support; Building/renovation; Equipment; Program development; Conferences/seminars; Publication; Seed money; Research; Matching/challenge support.

Limitations: Giving limited to GA.

Publications: Application guidelines; Annual report; Informational brochure (including application guidelines).

Application information: Fax or e-mail transmittals will not be accepted. See foundation Web site for application guidelines. Application form not required.

  Initial approach: Proposal

  Copies of proposal: 1

  Deadline(s): Preferably before May 1; final deadline, Aug. 1

  Board meeting date(s): 1st Tues. of Feb., May, Sept., and Nov.

  Final notification: Dec. 1. Grant awards are normally paid on the 2nd Fri. of Dec.

Officers and Directors:* S. Jarvin Levison, J.D.*, Chair.; Nancy M. Paris,* Vice-Chair.; Robert L. Zwald,* Secy.; Henry D. Cornelius,* Treas.; John M. Borek, Jr., Ph.D.; Richard Elmer, M.D.; Jaquelin Gotlieb, M.D.; J. Rhodes Haverty, M.D.
Number of staff: 1 part-time support.
EIN: 581352076

2395
Georgia Power Foundation, Inc. ▼
241 Ralph McGill Blvd., N.E., Bin 10131
Atlanta, GA 30308-3374 (404) 506-6784
Contact: Susan M. Carter, Secy. and Exec. Dir.
FAX: (404) 506-1485;
E-mail: gpfoundation@southernco.com; URL: http://www.southerncompany.com/gapower/charitable/home.asp

Established in 1986 in GA.
Donor: Georgia Power Co.
Foundation type: Company-sponsored foundation.
Financial data (yr. ended 12/31/05): Assets, $126,494,362 (M); gifts received, $3,327,533; expenditures, $7,007,166; qualifying distributions, $6,330,757; giving activities include $4,450,678 for 331 grants (high: $300,000; low: $325), and $98,379 for employee matching gifts.
Purpose and activities: The foundation supports organizations involved with education, the environment, and workforce planning.
Fields of interest: Education; Environment; Salvation Army; Federated giving programs.
Type of support: General/operating support; Continuing support; Annual campaigns; Capital campaigns; Equipment; Emergency funds; Program development; Conferences/seminars; Scholarship funds; Employee volunteer services; Sponsorships; Employee matching gifts; Donated equipment; Donated land; In-kind gifts.
Limitations: Giving primarily in GA. No support for private foundations, political or religious organizations, private elementary or secondary schools, or non-public charities. No grants to individuals, or for political campaigns or causes.
Publications: Application guidelines; Informational brochure (including application guidelines).
Application information: Multi-year funding is not automatic. Application form not required.
Initial approach: Mail proposal to foundation or complete online application form
Copies of proposal: 1
Deadline(s): 1 month prior to board meetings for requests of over $10,000
Board meeting date(s): Mar., June, Sept., and Dec.
Final notification: 1 month following board meetings for requests of over $10,000
Officers and Directors:* Judy M. Anderson,* Pres.; Susan M. Carter,* Secy. and Exec. Dir.; Cliff S. Thrasher,* C.F.O.; Mickey Brown; O. Ben Harris; Richard Holmes; Christopher Womack.
EIN: 581709417
Selected grants: The following grants were reported in 2005.
$150,000 to American Red Cross, Metropolitan Atlanta Chapter, Atlanta, GA. For project support.
$100,000 to Communities in Schools of Georgia, Atlanta, GA. For project support.
$100,000 to Georgia Partnership for Excellence in Education, Atlanta, GA. For operating support.
$100,000 to Piedmont Park Conservancy, Atlanta, GA. For capital support.

$100,000 to United Negro College Fund, Atlanta, GA. For operating support.
$75,000 to Medical College of Georgia Foundation, Augusta, GA. For capital support.
$60,000 to Nature Conservancy, Atlanta, GA. For project support.
$50,000 to Atlanta Workforce Development Agency, Atlanta, GA. For project support.
$50,000 to Georgia State University, Atlanta, GA. For operating support.
$50,000 to Georgia Wildlife Federation, Covington, GA. For capital support.

2396
Georgia Youth Foundation, Inc. ✦ ☆
2539 Lafayette Plaza Dr.
Albany, GA 31707

Foundation type: Independent foundation.
Financial data (yr. ended 11/30/05): Assets, $57,694 (M); expenditures, $350,600; qualifying distributions, $350,000; giving activities include $350,000 for 4 grants (high: $100,000; low: $75,000).
Fields of interest: Higher education.
Limitations: Applications not accepted. Giving on a national basis. No grants to individuals.
Application information: Contributes only to pre-selected organizations.
Officers: Robert F. McKinney, Pres.; James H. Daniel, Jr., Secy.-Treas.
EIN: 580966704

2397
Georgia-Pacific Foundation, Inc. ▼ ✦
133 Peachtree St. N.E.
Atlanta, GA 30303 (404) 652-4182
Contact: Curley M. Dossman, Jr., Pres.
FAX: (404) 749-2754; URL: http://www.gp.com/center/community/index.html

Incorporated in 1958 in OR.
Donor: Georgia-Pacific Corp.
Foundation type: Company-sponsored foundation.
Financial data (yr. ended 12/31/05): Assets, $515,201 (M); gifts received, $4,388,500; expenditures, $4,046,002; qualifying distributions, $4,046,002; giving activities include $3,867,180 for 582 grants (high: $100,000; low: $20), and $178,000 for 90 grants to individuals (high: $2,000; low: $1,000).
Purpose and activities: The foundation supports organizations involved with arts and culture, education, the environment, animals and wildlife, health education, crime and law enforcement, employment, housing, safety, parks, youth development, intergroup and race relations, and community development.
Fields of interest: Historic preservation/historical societies; Arts; Vocational education; Scholarships/financial aid; Education, reading; Education; Environment, recycling; Environment, natural resources; Environmental education; Environment; Animals/wildlife, preservation/protection; Public health; Crime/violence prevention; Crime/law enforcement; Employment, training; Employment; Housing/shelter; Safety, education; Recreation, parks/playgrounds; Youth development; Civil rights, race/intergroup relations; Community development, equal rights; Economic development; Community development; Federated giving programs.

Type of support: General/operating support; Continuing support; Annual campaigns; Capital campaigns; Building/renovation; Program development; Conferences/seminars; Seed money; Scholarship funds; Employee volunteer services; Sponsorships; Employee matching gifts; Employee-related scholarships; Scholarships—to individuals.
Limitations: Giving limited to areas of company operations. No support for discriminatory organizations, political candidates, churches or religious denominations, religious or theological schools, social, labor, veterans', alumni, or fraternal organizations not of direct benefit to the entire community, athletic associations, national organizations with local chapters already receiving support, medical or nursing schools, or pass-through organizations. No grants to individuals (except for scholarships), or for emergency needs for general operating support, political causes, legislative lobbying, or advocacy efforts, goodwill advertising, sporting events, general operating support for United Way member agencies, tickets or tables for testimonials or similar benefit events, named academic chairs, social sciences or health science programs, fundraising events, or trips or tours.
Publications: Application guidelines; Biennial report; Corporate giving report; Informational brochure (including application guidelines); Program policy statement.
Application information: Extraneous proposal materials are not encouraged. Application form not required.
Initial approach: Proposal
Copies of proposal: 1
Deadline(s): Between Jan. 1 and Oct. 31
Board meeting date(s): As required
Final notification: Within 45 days
Officers: Danny W. Huff, Jr., Chair.; Curley M. Dossman, Jr., Pres.; Kenneth F. Khoury, V.P. and Genl. Counsel; Phillip M. Johnson, Treas.
Number of staff: 5 full-time professional; 1 full-time support.
EIN: 936023726
Selected grants: The following grants were reported in 2004.
$395,706 to National Merit Scholarship Corporation, Evanston, IL.
$75,000 to Marcus Institute for Development and Learning, Atlanta, GA.
$60,000 to Rebuilding Together.
$57,728 to United Way of Ashley County, Hamburg, AR.
$50,000 to Junior Achievement of Georgia, Atlanta, GA.
$50,000 to Robert W. Woodruff Arts Center, Atlanta, GA.
$40,000 to Keep America Beautiful, Stamford, CT.
$20,000 to Georgia Trust for Historic Preservation, Atlanta, GA.
$16,666 to National Action Council for Minorities in Engineering (NACME), White Plains, NY.
$16,000 to United Way of Eastern Maine, Bangor, ME.

2398
GKW Foundation, Inc. ✦ ☆
c/o Alston & Bird
1201 W. Peachtree St.
Atlanta, GA 30309-3424
Contact: Benjamin T. White, Asst. Secy.

Established in 1994 in GA.
Donor: Gerry Hull.
Foundation type: Independent foundation.
Financial data (yr. ended 12/31/05): Assets, $181,117 (M); expenditures, $685,171; qualifying distributions, $680,789; giving activities include $680,789 for grants.
Purpose and activities: Giving primarily for education.
Fields of interest: Elementary/secondary education; Higher education; Education; Foundations (community).
Limitations: Giving primarily in GA. No grants to individuals.
Application information:
Initial approach: Letter
Deadline(s): None
Officer: Gerry Hull, Chair. and Secy.-Treas.
EIN: 582115483
Selected grants: The following grants were reported in 2005.
$515,515 to Atlanta International School, Atlanta, GA.
$20,000 to Atlanta Youth Academy, Atlanta, GA.
$2,500 to Nature Conservancy, Arlington, VA.
$1,500 to Chastain Horse Park, Atlanta, GA.

2399
The Wilbur and Hilda Glenn Family Foundation ▼
(formerly Cust Bluegrass Foundation)
1201 W. Peachtree St., Ste. 5000
Atlanta, GA 30309
Contact: Thomas K. Glenn II, Tr.

Established in 1996 in GA.
Donors: Thomas K. Glenn II; Wilbur Glenn Irrevocable Trust.
Foundation type: Independent foundation.
Financial data (yr. ended 12/31/04): Assets, $128,311,105 (M); gifts received, $17,831,699; expenditures, $5,115,364; qualifying distributions, $4,600,263; giving activities include $4,600,263 for 11 grants (high: $2,500,000; low: $5,000; average: $100,000–$500,000).
Purpose and activities: To fund fields of interest about which the trustees are most passionate.
Fields of interest: Education; Health care; Human services.
Type of support: Equipment; Management development/capacity building; Emergency funds; Debt reduction; Continuing support; Capital campaigns; Income development; Endowments; Program development; Film/video/radio; Research; Matching/challenge support.
Limitations: Applications not accepted. Giving primarily in Atlanta, GA. No grants to individuals.
Application information: Unsolicited requests for funds not accepted.
Officers and Trustees:* Thomas K. Glenn II,* Pres.; Henry Bowden, Jr.,* Secy.; Louisa Glenn D'Antignac; Louise R. Glenn; Rand Glenn Hagen.
Number of staff: 1 part-time support.
EIN: 586328896
Selected grants: The following grants were reported in 2004.
$2,510,000 to Westminster Schools, Atlanta, GA. 2 grants: $2,500,000 (For Glenn Institute for Philanthropy and Service Learning), $10,000 (For The Ellen Bowden Art Fund).

$500,000 to Community Foundation for Greater Atlanta, Atlanta, GA. For National Monuments Foundation.
$500,000 to Emory University, Winship Cancer Institute, Atlanta, GA. To acquire MALDI TOF mass spectrometer for cancer research.
$500,000 to Whitefoord Community Program, Atlanta, GA. To expand services and for continuing operating support.
$400,000 to East Lake Community Foundation, Atlanta, GA. For after-school and summer program, and building construction.
$100,000 to Boys and Girls Clubs of Metro Atlanta, Atlanta, GA. For Helping Teens Succeed.
$70,263 to Center for the Visually Impaired, Atlanta, GA. For challenge grant to diversify funding sources.
$10,000 to Marcus Institute for Development and Learning, Atlanta, GA. For general support.

2400
The Goizueta Foundation ▼
4401 Northside Pkwy., Ste. 520
Atlanta, GA 30327-3057 (404) 239-0390
Contact: Amanda Smith, Assoc. Dir.
FAX: (404) 239-0018;
E-mail: info@goizuetafoundation.org; URL: http://www.goizuetafoundation.org

Established in 1992 in GA.
Donor: Roberto C. Goizueta†.
Foundation type: Independent foundation.
Financial data (yr. ended 12/31/05): Assets, $387,886,712 (M); expenditures, $23,528,185; qualifying distributions, $22,717,035; giving activities include $21,913,734 for 28 grants (high: $1,820,000; low: $4,000; average: $500,000–$1,000,000), and $20,000 for 2 employee matching gifts.
Purpose and activities: The primary focus of the foundation is to assist organizations that empower individuals and families through educational opportunities to improve the quality of their lives.
Fields of interest: Education, early childhood education; Elementary school/education; Secondary school/education; Higher education; Education; Legal services; Employment, services; Youth development; Youth, services; Family services, parent education; Residential/custodial care; Developmentally disabled, centers & services; Minorities/immigrants, centers/services; Disabilities, people with; Immigrants/refugees.
Type of support: Program development; Scholarship funds; Employee matching gifts.
Limitations: Giving primarily in GA. No support for political organizations, government agencies, or public schools. No grants to individuals, or for general operating expenses, capital investment, construction/renovation, equipment purchase, retirement of debt, annual appeals, special events, conferences, or awards, prizes, or competitions; no loans.
Publications: Informational brochure (including application guidelines).
Application information: See Web site for educational and human service organizational overview forms. The foundation does not accept blind proposals and requires all grantees to submit interim and final reports. Organizations may submit only one organizational overview form each year. Application form not required.

Initial approach: Submit completed organizational overview form. The form is available on the foundation Web site
Copies of proposal: 1
Deadline(s): None
Board meeting date(s): May and Nov.
Final notification: Within 30 days of exec. committee meeting
Officers and Distribution Committee:* Olga C. de Goizueta,* Chair.; Maria Elena Retter, Exec. Dir.; Eduardo M. Carreras; Javier C. Goizueta; Olga Goizueta Rawls.
Number of staff: 6 full-time professional.
EIN: 586269421
Selected grants: The following grants were reported in 2005.
$4,000,000 to Hispanic Scholarship Fund, San Francisco, CA. For program development.
$2,363,546 to Junior Achievement Worldwide, Colorado Springs, CO. For program development.
$1,820,000 to Big Brothers Big Sisters of America, Philadelphia, PA. For program development.
$1,676,864 to Dalton State College, Dalton, GA. For program development and endowment fund.
$1,126,317 to Refugee Family Services, Clarkston, GA. For program development and endowment fund.
$1,005,000 to Goldey-Beacom College, Wilmington, DE. For matching gift and endowment fund.
$1,000,000 to Boston College, Chestnut Hill, MA. For endowment fund.
$534,325 to Gwinnett County Association for Retarded Citizens, Lawrenceville, GA. For program development.
$500,000 to Walker School, Marietta, GA. For endowment fund.
$300,000 to Wesley Community Centers of Savannah, Savannah, GA. For program development and endowment fund.

2401
The Good Shepherds Trust Foundation ◇
P.O. Box 835
Edison, GA 39846

Established in 1986 in GA.
Donors: Desmond J. Toal; Scott R. Toal; Leona Toal; DL Capital, LLC.
Foundation type: Independent foundation.
Financial data (yr. ended 12/31/04): Assets, $4,176,161 (M); gifts received, $18,100; expenditures, $689,281; qualifying distributions, $663,027; giving activities include $662,120 for 14 grants (high: $200,000; low: $3,000).
Purpose and activities: Giving primarily for Christian agencies and churches.
Fields of interest: Human services; Christian agencies & churches.
Limitations: Applications not accepted. Giving on a national basis, with emphasis on GA. No grants to individuals.
Application information: Contributes only to pre-selected organizations.
Directors: Leona Toal; Scott R. Toal.
EIN: 311243905
Selected grants: The following grants were reported in 2003.
$300,000 to Mailbox Club, Valdosta, GA. For general support.
$145,000 to Child Evangelism Fellowship, Warrenton, MO. For general support.
$100,000 to Teen Mania Ministries, Garden Valley, TX. For general support.

$93,040 to Agape Christian Fellowship, Saint Marys, GA. For general support.

$25,000 to SAT-7 North American, Easton, MD. For general support.

$25,000 to YWAM, Garden Valley, TX. For general support.

$23,000 to Lifeline Ministries, Thomasville, GA. For general support.

$10,000 to Americas Second Harvest of South Georgia, Valdosta, GA. For general support.

$4,000 to Christian Fellowship International, Amelia City, FL. For general support.

$3,000 to Heart for the World Ministries, El Paso, TX. For general support.

2402
The Evelyn and Frank Gordy Foundation ◇ ☆
2641 Mabry Rd.
Atlanta, GA   30319
Contact: Nancy Gordy Simms, Distrib. Comm.

Established in 1997 in GA.
Donor: Evelyn Gordy Rankin.
Foundation type: Independent foundation.
Financial data (yr. ended 4/30/05): Assets, $6,883,094 (M); expenditures, $376,650; qualifying distributions, $348,484; giving activities include $350,000 for 10 grants (high: $100,000; low: $1,000).
Fields of interest: Health care; Health organizations, association; Human services; Children/youth, services; Christian agencies & churches.
Limitations: Giving primarily in GA. No grants to individuals.
Application information:
Initial approach: Letter
Deadline(s): 180 days from date of published notice
Distribution Committee: Caroline Muir Browne; Douglas Gordon Muir III.
Trustees: Evelyn Gordy Rankin; Nancy Gordy Simms.
EIN: 586343707
Selected grants: The following grants were reported in 2004.
$50,000 to Feed My Lambs, Marietta, GA. For general support.
$30,000 to Childrens Healthcare of Atlanta Foundation, Atlanta, GA. For general support.
$30,000 to Vision Atlanta, Marietta, GA. For general support.
$15,000 to Atlanta Union Mission, Atlanta, GA. For general support.
$5,000 to Foundation of Wesley Woods, Atlanta, GA. For general support.
$5,000 to Youth for Christ, Atlanta, GA. For general support.

2403
The Graves Foundation, Inc. ◇
P.O. Box 53015
Atlanta, GA   30305

Established in 1989 in GA.
Donor: William M. Graves.
Foundation type: Independent foundation.
Financial data (yr. ended 12/31/04): Assets, $5,782,153 (M); expenditures, $704,643; qualifying distributions, $638,983; giving activities

include $638,983 for 55 grants (high: $184,200; low: $100).
Purpose and activities: Giving primarily for education, and to Presbyterian churches and agencies; funding also for the performing arts, juvenile diabetes research, and federated giving programs.
Fields of interest: Performing arts; Performing arts, orchestra (symphony); Arts; Higher education; Education; Health care; Diabetes research; Federated giving programs; Protestant agencies & churches.
Limitations: Applications not accepted. Giving primarily in the greater Atlanta, GA, area. No grants to individuals.
Application information: Contributes only to pre-selected organizations.
Officers: William M. Graves, Pres. and Treas.; Frances B. Graves, V.P. and Secy.
Trustees: John Hill Bailey, Jr.; William M. Graves, Jr.; Robert E. Hicks; Martha Graves Marriott.
EIN: 581876906
Selected grants: The following grants were reported in 2003.
$100,000 to Trinity Presbyterian Church of Atlanta, Atlanta, GA. For Generation to Generation campaign.
$10,000 to Trinity School, Atlanta, GA.
$5,000 to United Way of Metropolitan Atlanta, Atlanta, GA.
$1,500 to Bridge Family Center of Atlanta, Atlanta, GA.
$1,100 to Visiting Nurse Health System of Metropolitan Atlanta, Norcross, GA.
$1,000 to Presbyterian College, Demorest, GA.
$1,000 to W P B A-TV 30, Atlanta, GA.
$500 to PATH Foundation, Atlanta, GA.
$500 to Westminster Schools, Atlanta, GA.
$500 to Young Audiences of Atlanta, Atlanta, GA.

2404
The Greene-Sawtell Foundation
c/o SunTrust Bank, Atlanta
P.O. Box 4418, MC041
Atlanta, GA   30302-4655   (404) 827-6902
Contact: Raymond King, Sr. V.P., SunTrust Bank
URL: http://www.greenesawtellfoundation.org

Established in 1963 in GA.
Donor: Alice Greene-Sawtell‡.
Foundation type: Independent foundation.
Financial data (yr. ended 12/31/05): Assets, $9,407,484 (M); expenditures, $470,849; qualifying distributions, $440,694; giving activities include $418,000 for 39 grants (high: $50,000; low: $2,500).
Fields of interest: Higher education; Hospitals (general); Medical research; Human services.
Type of support: Capital campaigns; Building/renovation; Equipment.
Limitations: Giving primarily in Atlanta, GA. No grants to individuals.
Publications: Application guidelines.
Application information: Application form and guidelines are available on foundation Web site. Application form required.
Initial approach: Completed application
Copies of proposal: 1
Deadline(s): Mar. 31, Aug. 31, and Nov. 30
Board meeting date(s): Jan., May, and Oct.
Trustee: SunTrust Bank.
EIN: 586037828

2405
The Hanley Family Foundation, Inc.
2029 Rivermeade Way
Atlanta, GA   30327
Contact: Michael J. Hanley, Pres.
E-mail: info@hanleyfamilyfoundation.org;
URL: http://www.hanleyfamilyfoundation.org

Established in 1986 in FL.
Donors: John W. Hanley, Sr.; John W. Hanley, Jr.; Michael J. Hanley; Susan Hanley Myers; Mary Reel Hanley.
Foundation type: Independent foundation.
Financial data (yr. ended 5/31/06): Assets, $19,425,452 (M); gifts received, $663,261; expenditures, $1,102,225; qualifying distributions, $928,201; giving activities include $856,207 for 14 grants (high: $410,000; low: $1,000).
Purpose and activities: Giving limited strictly to non-profit organizations whose primary mission is the treatment or prevention of alcoholism or chemical dependency.
Fields of interest: Substance abuse, prevention; Substance abuse, treatment; Alcoholism.
Type of support: Seed money; Capital campaigns; Program development; Matching/challenge support.
Publications: Multi-year report (including application guidelines).
Application information: Online submission of proposal is strongly preferred. Application form required.
Initial approach: See foundation Web site for application guidelines
Copies of proposal: 1
Deadline(s): None
Board meeting date(s): As required
Officers and Directors: * John W. Hanley, Jr.,* Chair.; Michael J. Hanley,* Pres.; Linda H. Hanley, Secy.; Amy L. Hanley; John W. Hanley, Sr.; Kristen Hanley; Mary Jane Hanley; Mimi Hanley; Sondra Hanley; Susan H. Myers; Stephen Roegiers; Lara J. Stickney; Douglas Tieman.
EIN: 592745187

2406
The Sally and Frank Hanna Family Foundation ◇
245 Perimeter Ctr. Pkwy., Ste. 610
Atlanta, GA   30346
Contact: James P. Kelly III

Established in 1999 in GA.
Donor: Frank J. Hanna III.
Foundation type: Independent foundation.
Financial data (yr. ended 12/31/03): Assets, $164,084 (M); gifts received, $500,000; expenditures, $428,665; qualifying distributions, $401,375; giving activities include $401,400 for 10 grants (high: $200,000; low: $1,000).
Fields of interest: Arts; Education; Health care; Roman Catholic agencies & churches.
Application information: Application form not required.
Deadline(s): None
Trustee: James P. Kelly III.
Advisory Committee: Elizabeth Hanna; Frank J. Hanna III; Sally R. Hanna.
EIN: 586406309
Selected grants: The following grants were reported in 2003.
$200,000 to Pinecrest Academy, Cumming, GA.
$125,000 to Morley Publishing Group, DC.

$40,000 to Saint Francis Fund.

$10,000 to Archdiocese of Atlanta, Atlanta, GA. For annual appeal.

$10,000 to Ida Cason Callaway Foundation, Pine Mountain, GA.

$5,000 to American Association of the Sovereign Military Order of Malta, New York, NY.

$5,000 to Georgia Conservative Coalition Education Fund, GA.

$4,400 to Georgia Community Foundation, Alpharetta, GA.

$1,000 to Childrens Miracle Network, Salt Lake City, UT.

$1,000 to Institute for American Values, New York, NY.

2407
John H. and Wilhelmina D. Harland Charitable Foundation, Inc.
2 Piedmont Ctr., Ste. 106
Atlanta, GA   30305   (404) 264-9912
Contact: Jane G. Hardesty

Incorporated in 1972 in GA.
Donors: John H. Harland†; Miriam H. Conant†; John A. Conant†.
Foundation type: Independent foundation.
Financial data (yr. ended 12/31/04): Assets, $32,867,472 (M); gifts received, $2,491,989; expenditures, $2,171,069; qualifying distributions, $1,916,518; giving activities include $1,708,783 for 77 grants (high: $201,548; low: $2,500).
Purpose and activities: Support for youth services, community services, cultural programs, education, and health. The focus is local rather than regional or national, and priority is given to institutions in metropolitan Atlanta, GA.
Fields of interest: Museums; Arts; Elementary/secondary education; Adult education—literacy, basic skills & GED; Education; Health care; Children/youth, services; Child development, services; Community development; Religion; Disabilities, people with.
Type of support: General/operating support; Capital campaigns; Building/renovation; Equipment; Scholarship funds; Matching/challenge support.
Limitations: Giving limited to GA, with emphasis on metropolitan Atlanta. No support for private, primary, or secondary schools, except for those serving the handicapped. No grants to individuals, or for annual campaigns or special events; no loans.
Publications: Annual report (including application guidelines).
Application information: 21-month waiting period for new grant proposals from previously considered applicants. Application form required.
  Initial approach: Telephone call preferred
  Copies of proposal: 1
  Deadline(s): Mar. 1 and Sept. 1
  Board meeting date(s): Apr. 1 and Oct. 1
  Final notification: 3 to 4 weeks after board meeting
Officers and Trustees:* Margaret C. Reiser,* Pres.; Winifred Davis,* V.P. and Treas.; Robert E. Reiser, Jr., Secy.; James M. Sibley; Allison F. Williams.
Number of staff: 1 full-time professional; 1 full-time support.
EIN: 237225012
Selected grants: The following grants were reported in 2003.
$201,510 to Atlanta Symphony Orchestra, Atlanta, GA. For capital campaign.

$26,301 to Atlanta Community Food Bank, Atlanta, GA. For capital campaign.

$25,784 to Berry College, Mount Berry, GA. For scientific equipment in new science center.

$20,000 to Boys and Girls Clubs of Metro Atlanta, Atlanta, GA. For Teen Pilot Initiative.

$12,500 to Bobby Dodd Institute, Atlanta, GA. For Work and Progress program.

$10,000 to Georgia Center for Children, Atlanta, GA. For operating support.

$10,000 to Johnson C. Smith Theological Seminary, Atlanta, GA. For scholarships.

$10,000 to Kids In Need of Dreams, Atlanta, GA. For early intervention program.

$10,000 to Progressive Redevelopment, Decatur, GA. For Learning Link after-school program.

$10,000 to Southwest Christian Hospice, Union City, GA. For computer equipment upgrades.

2408
Clarence E. Harris Foundation, Inc. ✧
c/o George W. Hillegass
1200 Ashwood Pkwy., Ste. 300
Atlanta, GA   30338

Established in 1985 in GA.
Foundation type: Independent foundation.
Financial data (yr. ended 2/28/05): Assets, $14,424,228 (M); expenditures, $817,361; qualifying distributions, $631,105; giving activities include $591,000 for 14 grants (high: $120,000; low: $10,000).
Purpose and activities: Giving primarily for education, the arts, health care, and human services.
Fields of interest: Arts councils; Museums; Arts; Business school/education; Education; Hospitals (general); Housing/shelter, development; Human services; YM/YWCAs & YM/YWHAs; Children/youth, services; Family services; Family services, domestic violence; Developmentally disabled, centers & services; Foundations (private independent).
Type of support: General/operating support; Continuing support; Endowments; Program development; Matching/challenge support.
Limitations: Applications not accepted. Giving limited to Calhoun, GA, and Chattanooga, TN. No grants to individuals.
Application information: Contributes only to pre-selected organizations. Unsolicited requests for funds not accepted.
  Board meeting date(s): Apr. and Oct.
Officers: Bobbye F. Harris,* Pres.; George W. Hillegass, V.P.; Joel B. Piassick,* V.P.
Director: Stephen R. Dickinson.
EIN: 581674685
Selected grants: The following grants were reported in 2004.
$200,000 to Calhoun Gordon Arts Council, Calhoun, GA.

$100,000 to University of Tennessee, Chattanooga, TN.

$65,000 to YMCA of Chattanooga, Chattanooga, TN.

$50,000 to Creative Discovery Museum, Chattanooga, TN.

$43,000 to Habitat for Humanity of Greater Chattanooga, Chattanooga, TN.

$15,000 to Northwest Georgia Family Crisis Center, Dalton, GA.

$10,000 to Big Brothers/Big Sisters of Chattanooga, Chattanooga, TN.

$10,000 to Chattanooga Room in the Inn, Chattanooga, TN.

$10,000 to Hospice of Chattanooga, Chattanooga, TN.

$10,000 to National Conference for Community and Justice, New York, NY.

2409
The Albert E. Harrison Foundation ✧
224 Dalton St.
Ellijay, GA   30540
Contact: John M. Harrison, Pres.

Established in 2000 in GA.
Donor: Albert E. Harrison.
Foundation type: Independent foundation.
Financial data (yr. ended 12/31/05): Assets, $7,222,329 (M); expenditures, $376,531; qualifying distributions, $364,000; giving activities include $364,000 for 18 grants (high: $100,000; low: $1,000).
Purpose and activities: Giving primarily for education, human services, arts associations, Christian organizations, and to a United Methodist church.
Fields of interest: Arts, association; Elementary/secondary education; Education; Food banks; Human services; Children/youth, services; Pregnancy centers; Christian agencies & churches; Protestant agencies & churches.
Limitations: Giving primarily in Gilmer County, GA. No grants to individuals.
Application information: Application form required.
  Deadline(s): None
Officers and Trustees:* John M. Harrison,* Pres.; Marianne H. Bowman,* V.P.; Douglas P. Harrison,* Secy.-Treas.
EIN: 582501770

2410
The Luther & Susie Harrison Foundation, Inc.
3414 Peachtree Rd., Ste. 722
Atlanta, GA   30326   (404) 842-1870
Contact: Larry B. Hooks

Established in 1994 in GA.
Donor: R. Harold Harrison†.
Foundation type: Independent foundation.
Financial data (yr. ended 12/31/05): Assets, $15,781,999 (M); gifts received, $1,640,486; expenditures, $1,919,769; qualifying distributions, $1,777,804; giving activities include $1,759,822 for 21 grants (high: $400,000; low: $5,000).
Purpose and activities: Giving to enhance lives through education, faith, and health, primarily in north GA.
Fields of interest: Education; Health care; Mental health/crisis services; Health organizations, association; Medical research, institute; Protestant agencies & churches.
Type of support: Scholarship funds; Program development; Professorships; Equipment; Curriculum development; Capital campaigns; Building/renovation; Annual campaigns.
Limitations: Giving primarily in northern GA.
Publications: Application guidelines.
Application information: No more than 1 grant request per grantee per year. Application form required.
  Initial approach: Narrative letter

Copies of proposal: 4
Deadline(s): Feb. 15 and Aug. 15
Board meeting date(s): Apr. and Oct.
Final notification: Following board meetings
Directors: J. Curtis Pruett; Virginia S. Pruett; Bobbie Ann Reynolds; Kelly B. Tison.
EIN: 582169694

2411
Healthcare Georgia Foundation, Inc. ▼
50 Hurt Plz., Ste. 1100
Atlanta, GA 30303 (404) 653-0990
Contact: Gary D. Nelson Ph.D., Pres.
FAX: (404) 577-8386;
E-mail: info@healthcaregeorgia.org; URL: http://www.healthcaregeorgia.org/

Established in 1999 in GA; converted from the merger of Blue Cross Blue Shield of Georgia with Wellpoint Health Networks.
Donor: Blue Cross and Blue Shield of Georgia, Inc.
Foundation type: Independent foundation.
Financial data (yr. ended 12/31/05): Assets, $125,273,023 (M); gifts received, $27,847; expenditures, $6,875,426; qualifying distributions, $5,646,849; giving activities include $4,269,300 for 53 grants (high: $420,000; low: $1,500; average: $10,000–$125,000).
Purpose and activities: The foundation's mission is to advance the health of all Georgians and to expand access to affordable, quality health care for underserved individuals and communities. Specific goals include protecting and promoting the health of individuals, families and communities; improving the availability, quality, appropriateness and financing of health care services; and integrating and coordinating efforts to improve health and health care services. The foundation has also established the following grantmaking priorities: 1) addressing health disparities; 2) strengthening nonprofit health organizations; and 3) expanding access to primary health care.
Fields of interest: Public health; Health care.
Type of support: General/operating support; Income development; Management development/capacity building; Program development; Conferences/seminars; Research; Technical assistance; Program evaluation.
Limitations: Giving limited to GA. No support for sectarian programs (benefiting only one religious organization). No grants to individuals, or for capital campaigns, or major equipment.
Publications: Application guidelines; Annual report; Grants list; Informational brochure (including application guidelines); Occasional report; Program policy statement.
Application information: The foundation engages in both proactive (solicited) and responsive (unsolicited) grantmaking. Proactive grantmaking will be carried out through an RFP process that addresses specific areas within the foundation's funding priorities. Responsive grantmaking will allow the foundation to support unsolicited proposals that fit our mission and fall within our funding priorities. See foundation Web site for full application requirements and guidelines. Application form required.
Initial approach: Letter of inquiry (no more than 2 pages)
Copies of proposal: 2
Deadline(s): None

Board meeting date(s): Quarterly
Final notification: Within 3 months for letters of inquiry; within 8 to 9 months for proposals; declinations are announced quarterly
Officers and Directors:* Richard D. Shirk,* Chair.; Gary D. Nelson, Ph.D., Pres.; Michael F. Kemp,* Treas.; Rich D'Amaro; Dewey Hickman; Ted Holloway, M.D.; Andrea Hinojosa; Linda Lowe; Ecleamus Ricks.
Number of staff: 6 full-time professional; 2 full-time support.
EIN: 582418091
Selected grants: The following grants were reported in 2006.
$360,000 to Georgia Budget and Policy Institute (GBPI), Atlanta, GA. To analyze Georgia's budget and tax policies affecting health and access to health care, and to conduct retreat for health policy analysis in Georgia.
$200,000 to Georgia Free Clinic Network, Smyrna, GA. To establish organizational home for free clinics providing access to quality and affordable health care for Georgia's medically underserved.
$190,000 to Georgia State University, Atlanta, GA. To develop and test efficiency and cost-effectiveness of community-based participatory research strategy designed to reduce inappropriate use of emergency medical services (EMS) and emergency department (ED) services.
$185,000 to National Academy of Sciences, DC. For health disparities roundtable, series of national and regional convenings on health disparities, including Atlanta symposium on measuring programs that address them.
$175,000 to Reece & Associates, Atlanta, GA. To educate policymakers on need for enhanced trauma care and value of comprehensive statewide trauma network.
$150,000 to Albany Area Primary Health Care, Albany, GA. To provide comprehensive geriatric medical services to residents of Baker, Calhoun, Dougherty, Lee and Terrell counties.
$150,000 to HealthMPowers, Atlanta, GA. For school-based health education physical activity and nutrition program for elementary and middle school youth in Walton and Greene counties.
$145,000 to Health Care Central Georgia, Forsyth, GA. Toward planning for implementation of multi-share healthcare coverage program in seven central Georgia counties.
$78,500 to Georgia Legal Services Program, Atlanta, GA. For health advocacy outreach program for individuals with physical and developmental disabilities in Northwest Georgia.
$25,000 to University of Georgia, Athens, GA. To conduct economic impact analysis of Georgia nonprofit organizations engaged in health and health care.

2412
Hertz Family Foundation, Inc. ✧
(formerly Jennings Hertz Foundation, Inc.)
5500 United Dr.
Smyrna, GA 30082

Established in 1981 in GA.
Donors: Douglas J. Hertz; Jennings M. Hertz, Jr.; Standard Distributing Co., Inc.; United Distributors, Inc.
Foundation type: Independent foundation.
Financial data (yr. ended 12/31/04): Assets, $4,791,735 (M); gifts received, $600,000;

expenditures, $523,477; qualifying distributions, $492,357; giving activities include $492,357 for 51 grants (high: $57,402; low: $205).
Purpose and activities: Giving primarily to cultural institutions, Jewish agencies, temples, and federated giving programs, health associations, and human services.
Fields of interest: Arts; Higher education; Health organizations, association; Human services; Children/youth, services; Federated giving programs; Jewish federated giving programs; Jewish agencies & temples.
Limitations: Applications not accepted. Giving primarily in GA. No grants to individuals.
Application information: Contributes only to pre-selected organizations.
Officers: Jennings M. Hertz, Jr., Pres.; Douglas J. Hertz, V.P.; Patricia H. Reid, Secy.
EIN: 581423564
Selected grants: The following grants were reported in 2003.
$100,000 to Jewish Federation of Greater Atlanta, Atlanta, GA.
$20,000 to Childrens Healthcare of Atlanta, Atlanta, GA.
$10,000 to Atlanta Symphony Orchestra, Atlanta, GA.
$5,000 to Genesis Shelter, Atlanta, GA.
$5,000 to High Museum of Art, Atlanta, GA.
$1,500 to Families First, Atlanta, GA.
$1,500 to Prevent Child Abuse Georgia, Atlanta, GA.
$1,000 to Georgia Shakespeare Festival, Atlanta, GA.
$376 to Marcus Jewish Community Center of Atlanta, Dunwoody, GA.
$250 to Jewish Family and Career Services, Atlanta, GA.

2413
The Holder Construction Foundation ✧
3333 Riverwood Pkwy., Ste. 400
Atlanta, GA 30339 (770) 988-3280
Contact: J.C. Pendrey, Jr., Tr.

Donor: Holder Construction Co.
Foundation type: Company-sponsored foundation.
Financial data (yr. ended 12/31/04): Assets, $905,197 (M); gifts received, $405,000; expenditures, $461,154; qualifying distributions, $460,795; giving activities include $459,520 for grants.
Purpose and activities: The foundation supports organizations involved with arts and culture, education, and human services.
Fields of interest: Performing arts, ballet; Arts; Higher education; Business school/education; Nursing school/education; Education; Human services; Federated giving programs.
Limitations: Giving on a national basis, with emphasis on the greater metropolitan Atlanta, GA, area.
Application information:
Initial approach: Proposal or telephone
Deadline(s): None
Distribution Committee: Elizabeth D. Holder; Thomas M. Holder.
Trustee: J.C. Pendrey, Jr.
EIN: 586412965
Selected grants: The following grants were reported in 2005.
$63,000 to American Red Cross. 2 grants: $45,000, $18,000
$50,000 to Lovett School, Atlanta, GA.

$36,000 to United Way.
$30,000 to Albany Tomorrow, Albany, GA.
$25,000 to Trust for Public Land, San Francisco, CA.
$20,000 to Robert W. Woodruff Arts Center, Atlanta, GA.
$10,000 to University of Florida Foundation, Gainesville, FL.
$6,000 to Atlanta Ballet, Atlanta, GA.
$1,000 to United Way of McLean County, Bloomington, IL.

2414
Hooters Community Endowment Fund, Inc. ✧
1815 The Exchange
Atlanta, GA 30339-2027

Established in 1992.
Donor: Hooters of America, Inc.
Foundation type: Company-sponsored foundation.
Financial data (yr. ended 12/31/05): Assets, $170,552 (M); gifts received, $569,647; expenditures, $604,275; qualifying distributions, $604,275; giving activities include $437,255 for grants.
Purpose and activities: The foundation supports organizations involved with higher education, health, medical research, recreation, human services, and Christianity.
Fields of interest: Higher education; Health care; Medical research; Recreation; Children/youth, services; Human services; Christian agencies & churches.
Limitations: Applications not accepted. Giving on a national basis. No grants to individuals.
Application information: Contributes only to pre-selected organizations.
Officers: Richard W. Aram, C.E.O.; Ken L. Abbott, Secy.
EIN: 582006561
Selected grants: The following grants were reported in 2004.
$250,000 to Clemson University Foundation, Clemson, SC.
$50,250 to V Foundation for Cancer Research, Cary, NC. 2 grants: $250, $50,000
$10,250 to American Diabetes Association, Alexandria, VA.
$3,000 to Happy Days and Special Times, Charleston, SC.
$2,000 to American Cancer Society, Atlanta, GA.
$1,380 to Epilepsy Association, Cleveland, OH.
$1,000 to Spina Bifida Association of Jacksonville, Jacksonville, FL.
$500 to Alzheimers Association, Chicago, IL.
$500 to March of Dimes Birth Defects Foundation, White Plains, NY.

2415
Horowitz Family Foundation, Inc. ✧ ☆
(formerly Gerald D. Horowitz Foundation, Inc.)
c/o Gerald D.Horowitz
3860 Northside Dr.
Atlanta, GA 30305-1033

Established in 1974.
Donor: Gerald D. Horowitz.
Foundation type: Independent foundation.
Financial data (yr. ended 12/31/05): Assets, $1,327,651 (M); gifts received, $43,070; expenditures, $332,329; qualifying distributions,

$329,583; giving activities include $329,583 for grants.
Purpose and activities: Giving primarily for Jewish agencies, health and medicine, and community programs.
Fields of interest: Arts; Education; Health organizations, association; Developmentally disabled, centers & services; Jewish federated giving programs; Jewish agencies & temples.
Type of support: Annual campaigns; Capital campaigns; Building/renovation; Emergency funds; Program development; Seed money.
Limitations: Applications not accepted. No grants to individuals.
Application information: Contributes only to pre-selected organizations.
Officers: Gerald D. Horowitz, Pres.; Pearlann Horowitz, V.P.; Scott Horowitz, Treas.
EIN: 586066393
Selected grants: The following grants were reported in 2004.
$25,000 to High Museum of Art, Atlanta, GA.
$15,000 to American Friends of Hatzalah Yehuda and Shomron, Brooklyn, NY.
$14,077 to Congregation Shearith Israel.
$9,000 to American Cancer Society, Atlanta, GA.
$8,150 to William Breman Jewish Home, Atlanta, GA.
$3,800 to Jewish Family and Career Services, Atlanta, GA.
$3,000 to American Jewish Committee, Atlanta, GA.
$2,500 to Fulton County CASA.
$2,500 to United Way.
$2,325 to Marcus Jewish Community Center of Atlanta, Dunwoody, GA.

2416
John P. and Dorothy S. Illges Foundation, Inc. ✧
P.O. Box 1673
Columbus, GA 31902
Contact: John P. Illges III, Pres.

Incorporated in 1947 in GA.
Donor: John P. Illges†.
Foundation type: Independent foundation.
Financial data (yr. ended 9/30/05): Assets, $7,060,902 (M); expenditures, $431,506; qualifying distributions, $343,060; giving activities include $328,900 for 10 grants (high: $75,000; low: $11,600).
Purpose and activities: Primary areas of interest include education, youth, social services, health, the environment, and local community concerns in the Columbus, GA, area.
Fields of interest: Museums (specialized); Education; Health care; Children/youth, services; Community development, neighborhood development.
Type of support: Annual campaigns; Capital campaigns; Building/renovation; Equipment; Program development.
Limitations: Giving primarily in the Columbus, GA, area. No grants to individuals, or for seed money.
Application information: Application form not required.
Initial approach: Letter
Copies of proposal: 1
Deadline(s): None
Board meeting date(s): 3rd Thurs. of Jan., May, and Sept.
Final notification: Following board meeting review

Officers and Directors:* John P. Illges III,* Pres.; Philip A. Badcock,* V.P.; Mary S. Boyd, Secy.; Richard B. Illges,* Treas.; Susan I. Lanier; John W. Mayher, Jr.
Number of staff: 1 part-time professional.
EIN: 580691476
Selected grants: The following grants were reported in 2003.
$100,000 to Columbus Regional Medical Foundation, Columbus, GA. For general support.
$50,000 to Our House, Decatur, GA. For general support.
$33,334 to Pine Eden Christian Retreat Center, Hamilton, GA. For general support.
$25,000 to Make-A-Wish Foundation of Greater Atlanta and North Georgia, Atlanta, GA. For general support.
$22,597 to Valley Rescue Mission, Columbus, GA. For general support.
$10,000 to Shepherd Center, Atlanta, GA. For general support.
$10,000 to Young Life, Columbus, GA. For general support.
$9,000 to Presbyterian Homes of Georgia, Atlanta, GA. For general support.
$8,000 to Muscogee County School District, Columbus, GA. For general support.
$5,000 to New Horizon Theater, Pittsburgh, PA. For general support.

2417
The Imlay Foundation, Inc. ✧
945 E. Paces Ferry Rd., Ste. 2450
Atlanta, GA 30326-1125
Contact: Mary Ellen Imlay, Exec. Dir.

Established in 1989 in GA.
Donor: John P. Imlay, Jr.
Foundation type: Independent foundation.
Financial data (yr. ended 12/31/04): Assets, $19,787,541 (M); expenditures, $803,486; qualifying distributions, $704,000; giving activities include $704,000 for 74 grants (high: $30,000; low: $2,500).
Purpose and activities: Giving primarily for the arts, education, health associations, children, youth, family, and social services including a book service for the blind.
Fields of interest: Museums; Performing arts; Historic preservation/historical societies; Arts; Higher education; Education; Botanical gardens; Hospitals (specialty); Health care; Health organizations, association; Human services; Children, services; Family services; Residential/custodial care, hospices; Federated giving programs; Protestant agencies & churches.
Type of support: General/operating support; Annual campaigns; Capital campaigns; Building/renovation; Program development; Curriculum development; Scholarship funds; Research.
Limitations: Giving primarily in Atlanta, GA. No grants to individuals.
Application information: Application form not required.
Initial approach: Letter
Copies of proposal: 2
Deadline(s): None
Board meeting date(s): Apr., Aug., and Dec.
Officers: John P. Imlay, Jr., Pres.; I. Sigmund Mosley, Jr., V.P. and Secy.; Gerard G. Imlay, V.P.; Mary Ellen Imlay, Exec. Dir.

Directors: Donald Hardie; John P. Imlay III; Melanie Bialko Leeth; John Dayton; Kimberly Charlotte Dayton; Lucinda Imlay; Paula Imlay; Alan Zubay, Jr.
Number of staff: 1 part-time professional; 1 part-time support.
EIN: 581868936

2418
ING Foundation ✧
(formerly ReliaStar Foundation)
5780 Powers Ferry Rd., N.W.
Atlanta, GA 30327-4390 (770) 980-6580
Contact: Maria Balais, Mgr., Community Rels.
E-mail: ingfoundation@us.ing.com; URL: http://www.ing-usa.com/us/aboutING/communityconnections/index.htm

Established in 1990 in MN.
Donors: ReliaStar Financial Corp.; Northern Life Insurance Co.; ReliaStar Bankers Security Life Insurance Co.; ReliaStar United Services Life Insurance Co.; ReliaStar Life Insurance Co.
Foundation type: Company-sponsored foundation.
Financial data (yr. ended 12/31/04): Assets, $3,012,326 (M); gifts received, $3,315,448; expenditures, $2,537,980; qualifying distributions, $2,454,093; giving activities include $2,278,581 for 2,398+ grants (high: $125,000).
Purpose and activities: The foundation supports organizations involved with arts and culture, education, health, employment, housing, youth development, children, human services, economic development, minorities, women, and economically disadvantaged people. Special emphasis is directed toward programs designed to motivate individuals to assume personal responsibility for their financial well-being.
Fields of interest: Arts; Education; Health care; Employment, services; Housing/shelter; Youth development; Children/youth, services; Family services; Human services, financial counseling; Human services; Economic development; Minorities; Women; Economically disadvantaged.
Type of support: General/operating support; Program development; Employee volunteer services; Employee matching gifts.
Limitations: Giving primarily in areas of company operations. No support for religious organizations not of direct benefit to the entire community, fraternal organizations, social clubs, labor organizations, lobbying or political organizations, or discriminatory organizations. No grants to individuals, or for institutional, civic, or commemorative advertising, conferences, workshops, or other meetings, or travel, benefits, testimonial dinners, or other fundraising activities.
Publications: Annual report (including application guidelines); Corporate giving report; Newsletter.
Application information: Application form required.
  Initial approach: Complete online application form
  Deadline(s): Feb. 15, May 23, and Sept. 15
  Board meeting date(s): Quarterly
  Final notification: 3 to 4 weeks
Officers and Directors:* Thomas J. McInerney,* Chair.; Rhoda Mims Simpson,* Pres.; David S. Pendergrass, V.P. and Treas.; B. Scott Burton, Secy.; Kevin P. Brown; Robert Crispin; Kathleen Murphy.
Number of staff: 1 full-time professional; 1 full-time support.
EIN: 411682766

Selected grants: The following grants were reported in 2003.
$555,667 to University of Connecticut Foundation, Storrs, CT.
$75,032 to United Way, Greater Twin Cities, Minneapolis, MN.
$1,000 to Carleton College, Northfield, MN.
$1,000 to Childrens Health Care Foundation, Minneapolis, MN.
$680 to American Cancer Society, Minneapolis, MN.
$250 to Humane Society for Companion Animals, Saint Paul, MN.
$125 to Childrens Home Society and Family Services, Saint Paul, MN.
$100 to Childrens Theater Company and School, Minneapolis, MN.
$100 to Clare Housing, Minneapolis, MN.
$60 to Canine Companions for Independence, Santa Rosa, CA.

2419
The Irving Foundation, Inc. ✧ ☆
P.O. Box 1983
Athens, GA 30603

Established in 1991 in GA.
Donor: Joe D. Irving.
Foundation type: Independent foundation.
Financial data (yr. ended 12/31/05): Assets, $245 (M); gifts received, $337,870; expenditures, $337,889; qualifying distributions, $332,850; giving activities include $332,850 for 19 grants (high: $263,000; low: $100).
Fields of interest: Health organizations, association; Aging, centers/services; Aging.
Limitations: Applications not accepted. Giving primarily in GA. No grants to individuals.
Application information: Contributes only to pre-selected organizations.
Officers and Directors:* Joe D. Irving,* Pres. and Treas.; Tony G. Mills,* Secy.; James L. Newland.
EIN: 581943208
Selected grants: The following grants were reported in 2005.
$263,000 to Athens Community Council on Aging, Athens, GA.
$4,000 to Eagle Ranch, Chestnut Mountain, GA.
$4,000 to Mission House, Jacksonville Beach, FL.
$100 to YMCA.

2420
JBS Foundation
(formerly Jocelyn Botterell Staton Foundation)
c/o Mark Drake, SunTrust Bank
P.O. Box 4655
Atlanta, GA 30302-4655

Established in 1995 in GA.
Foundation type: Independent foundation.
Financial data (yr. ended 12/31/05): Assets, $5,748,345 (M); expenditures, $402,322; qualifying distributions, $385,062; giving activities include $367,500 for 15 grants (high: $175,000; low: $5,000).
Fields of interest: Arts; Education; Botanical gardens; Spine disorders; Youth development, scouting agencies (general); Human services; Federated giving programs.
Limitations: Applications not accepted. Giving primarily in GA, with emphasis on Atlanta. No grants to individuals.

Application information:
  Board meeting date(s): Dec.
Committee Members: Louise Staton Gunn; John C. Staton, Jr.; Margaret A. Staton; Mary Staton.
Trustee: SunTrust Bank.
EIN: 586301523
Selected grants: The following grants were reported in 2005.
$17,500 to Lovett School, Atlanta, GA.
$15,000 to Atlanta History Center, Atlanta, GA.
$15,000 to VSA Arts of Georgia, Atlanta, GA.
$10,000 to Atlanta Opera, Atlanta, GA.
$10,000 to Atlanta Symphony Orchestra, Atlanta, GA.
$10,000 to United Way.
$7,500 to Girl Scouts of the U.S.A..
$5,000 to Atlanta Ballet, Atlanta, GA.

2421
JCK Foundation, Inc.
6205 Peachtree Dunwoody Rd.
Atlanta, GA 30328
Contact: Leigh Ann Launius

Established in 2003 in GA.
Donor: James C. Kennedy.
Foundation type: Independent foundation.
Financial data (yr. ended 12/31/05): Assets, $10,899,858 (M); gifts received, $168,408; expenditures, $479,326; qualifying distributions, $387,300; giving activities include $387,300 for 36 grants (high: $50,000; low: $200; average: $1,000–$25,000).
Fields of interest: Environment.
Limitations: Applications not accepted. Giving on a national basis, with some emphasis on GA. No grants to individuals.
Application information: Contributes only to pre-selected organizations.
Officers and Directors:* James C. Kennedy,* Pres.; Barbara C. Kennedy,* V.P.; James C. Kennedy, Jr.,* Secy.-Treas.; Macon Cherp; Clay K. Kennedy.
EIN: 200424251

2422
Ruth T. Jinks Foundation
P.O. Box 375
Colquitt, GA 39837
Contact: G.C. Jinks, Jr., Pres.

Established in 1955.
Donor: Members of the Jinks family.
Foundation type: Independent foundation.
Financial data (yr. ended 11/30/05): Assets, $30,147,229 (M); gifts received, $1,000; expenditures, $1,654,027; qualifying distributions, $1,627,705; giving activities include $1,588,221 for 62 grants (high: $512,019; low: $500).
Purpose and activities: Giving primarily for community development, religion, and higher education.
Fields of interest: Arts, multipurpose centers/programs; Arts; Elementary/secondary education; Education; Youth development; Human services; Urban/community development; Rural development; Community development; Christian agencies & churches.
Type of support: General/operating support; Annual campaigns; Building/renovation; Program development; Matching/challenge support.

Limitations: Applications not accepted. Giving primarily in GA.
Application information: Unsolicited requests for funds not considered or acknowledged.
Board meeting date(s): Annually
Officers and Board Members:* G.C. Jinks, Jr.,* Pres. and Treas.; G.C. Jinks III,* V.P.; Peggy J. Jinks,* V.P.
Number of staff: 1 part-time support.
EIN: 586043856
Selected grants: The following grants were reported in 2004.
$827,550 to Colquitt-Miller County Historic and Economic Revitalization Organization, Colquitt, GA. 2 grants: $783,372, $44,178
$779,784 to Colquitt, City of, Colquitt, GA.
$136,700 to Hospital Authority of Miller County, Colquitt, GA.
$100,000 to Florida State University Foundation, Tallahassee, FL.
$68,593 to Miller, County of, Colquitt, GA.
$41,140 to Colquitt United Methodist Church, Colquitt, GA.
$35,000 to Saint Luke United Methodist Church, Columbus, GA.
$25,000 to LaGrange College, La Grange, GA.
$15,000 to Emory University, Atlanta, GA.

2423

Leodelle Lassiter Jolley Foundation ✧ ☆
c/o Malinda J. Mortin
P.O. Box 152
Marietta, GA   30061-0152

Established in 2002 in GA.
Foundation type: Independent foundation.
Financial data (yr. ended 12/31/05): Assets, $3,634,193 (M); expenditures, $507,088; qualifying distributions, $500,000; giving activities include $500,000 for grants.
Fields of interest: Residential/custodial care, hospices; Christian agencies & churches.
Limitations: Applications not accepted. No grants to individuals.
Application information: Contributes only to pre-selected organizations.
Trustees: Ruthanna Jolley Bost; Malinda J. Mortin; Catherine Peters.
EIN: 586454877
Selected grants: The following grants were reported in 2004.
$150,000 to Saint Annes Episcopal Church, Atlanta, GA.
$125,000 to Lassiter Band Booster Association, Marietta, GA.

2424

Charles H. Jones Family Foundation, Inc. ✧
P.O. Box 7345
Macon, GA   31209
Application address: c/o Charles H. Jones, Chair., P.O. Box 7564, Macon, GA 31209, tel.: (478) 471-2520

Established in 1985 in GA.
Donors: Charles H. Jones; Dwight C. Jones; Ocmulgee Fields, Inc.; Landmark Developers of Macon.
Foundation type: Independent foundation.

Financial data (yr. ended 5/31/05): Assets, $11,525,681 (M); gifts received, $1,720,000; expenditures, $393,460; qualifying distributions, $366,550; giving activities include $366,550 for 19 grants (high: $150,000; low: $100).
Purpose and activities: Giving primarily for the arts, education, and to a Presbyterian church and school.
Fields of interest: Museums (specialized); Performing arts, orchestra (symphony); Arts; Elementary/secondary education; Higher education; Medical school/education; Libraries/library science; Education; Athletics/sports, racquet sports; Human services; Community development, neighborhood development; Federated giving programs; Military/veterans' organizations; Protestant agencies & churches.
Limitations: Giving primarily in Macon, GA. No grants to individuals.
Application information:
  Initial approach: Letter
  Deadline(s): None
Officer and Directors:* Charles H. Jones,* Chair.; Dwight C. Jones; Ves Jones; Stella Patterson.
EIN: 581678452
Selected grants: The following grants were reported in 2003.
$150,250 to Tubman African-American Museum, Macon, GA.
$50,000 to Newtown Macon, Macon, GA.
$25,500 to Medcen Foundation, Macon, GA.
$20,000 to Macon Symphony Orchestra, Macon, GA.
$20,000 to South Georgia Methodist Home for the Aging, Magnolia Manor, Americus, GA.
$15,500 to Mercer University, Macon, GA.
$15,000 to Georgia State University, Atlanta, GA.
$15,000 to United Way of Central Georgia, Macon, GA.
$5,000 to Reformed Theological Seminary, Charlotte, NC.
$2,500 to Adopt-A-Role Model, Macon, GA.

2425

The Jordan Foundation, Inc. ✧ ☆
6001 River Rd., Ste. 100
Columbus, GA   31904-2949   (706) 327-4962
Contact: A.J. Allen, Secy.-Treas.

Foundation type: Independent foundation.
Financial data (yr. ended 7/31/06): Assets, $109,050 (M); gifts received, $457,032; expenditures, $394,575; qualifying distributions, $384,000; giving activities include $384,000 for grants.
Fields of interest: Education; Foundations (community); Christian agencies & churches.
Limitations: Giving primarily in GA.
Application information:
  Initial approach: Letter
  Deadline(s): None
Officers: Helen S. Jordan, Pres.; Helen J. Olnich, V.P.; A.J. Allen, Secy.-Treas.
Trustees: Gardiner W. Garrard; Katherine J. Waddell.
EIN: 586039423
Selected grants: The following grants were reported in 2005.
$75,000 to Columbus State University Foundation, Columbus, GA. For general support.
$50,000 to Trinity Episcopal Church, Columbus, GA. For general support.
$20,000 to Stewart Community Home, Columbus, GA. For general support.

$10,000 to Brookstone School, Columbus, GA. For general support.
$10,000 to Columbus Symphony Orchestra, Columbus, GA. For general support.
$10,000 to Historic Linwood Foundation, Columbus, GA. For general support.
$10,000 to New Horizons Community Service Board, Columbus, GA. For general support.
$3,000 to Chattahoochee Valley Sports Hall of Fame, Columbus, GA. For general support.
$1,000 to Carpenters Way Ranch, Fortson, GA. For general support.

2426

Donald and Marilyn Keough Foundation
(formerly Donald R. Keough Foundation)
c/o Michael Keough
200 Galleria Pkwy., Ste. 970
Atlanta, GA   30339

Established in 1986 in GA.
Donor: Donald R. Keough.
Foundation type: Independent foundation.
Financial data (yr. ended 12/31/05): Assets, $5,677,145 (M); gifts received, $2,000; expenditures, $333,247; qualifying distributions, $327,000; giving activities include $325,000 for 48 grants (high: $50,000; low: $1,000).
Purpose and activities: Support primarily for Irish-American associations and Roman Catholic organizations; giving also for higher education.
Fields of interest: Higher education; International affairs, goodwill promotion; Civil rights, race/intergroup relations; Roman Catholic agencies & churches.
Type of support: General/operating support; Continuing support.
Limitations: Applications not accepted. Giving on a national basis. No grants to individuals.
Application information: Contributes only to pre-selected organizations.
Officers and Trustees:* Donald R. Keough,* Chair.; Marilyn M. Keough,* Pres.
EIN: 581709967
Selected grants: The following grants were reported in 2005.
$50,000 to Atlanta Opera, Atlanta, GA.
$20,000 to Special Olympics, DC.
$13,000 to Convent of the Sacred Heart, New York, NY.
$12,500 to Creighton University, Omaha, NE.
$10,000 to Marcus Institute for Development and Learning, Atlanta, GA.
$10,000 to Saint Josephs Mercy Foundation, Atlanta, GA.
$10,000 to Society of the Sacred Heart, Saint Louis, MO.
$7,500 to Lovett School, Atlanta, GA.
$5,000 to Smithsonian American Art Museum, DC.
$3,000 to Saint Anthony Catholic Church, Harlingen, TX.

2427

The Knox Foundation ✧
3133 Washington Rd. N.W.
Thomson, GA   30824   (706) 595-1907
Contact: Boone A. Knox, Tr.

Established in 1981.
Donors: Boone A. Knox; Knox, Ltd.; Folkstone Ltd.; Julia P. R. Knox.

Foundation type: Independent foundation.
Financial data (yr. ended 12/31/05): Assets, $66,263,983 (M); gifts received, $1,241,292; expenditures, $2,884,287; qualifying distributions, $2,369,283; giving activities include $2,231,725 for 78 grants (high: $485,000; low: $250).
Fields of interest: Arts; Higher education; Human services.
Type of support: General/operating support; Continuing support; Annual campaigns; Capital campaigns; Building/renovation; Endowments; Program development; Matching/challenge support.
Limitations: Giving generally limited to Augusta and Thomson, GA. No grants to individuals.
Application information: Application form required.
  Initial approach: Letter requesting application form
  Copies of proposal: 2
  Deadline(s): None
  Board meeting date(s): Apr. and Oct.
  Final notification: Feb. 15 and Aug. 15
Director: Jefferson B.A. Knox.
Trustee: Boone A. Knox.
EIN: 586163728

2428
The Sartain Lanier Family Foundation, Inc. ◇

(formerly Oxford Foundation, Inc.)
25 Puritan Mill
950 Lowery Blvd.
Atlanta, GA 30318 (404) 564-1259
Contact: Mark B. Riley, Dir.
FAX: (404) 564-1251;
E-mail: info@lanierfamilyfoundation.org; Additional E-mail: plummus@lanierfamilyfoundation.org;
URL: http://www.lanierfamilyfoundation.org

Established in 1963 in GA.
Donor: Sartain Lanier†.
Foundation type: Independent foundation.
Financial data (yr. ended 12/31/04): Assets, $94,842,567 (M); expenditures, $3,716,273; qualifying distributions, $3,029,214; giving activities include $2,885,572 for 64 grants (high: $1,258,520; low: $500; average: $7,000–$50,000).
Purpose and activities: The foundation targets its grants to the following areas with priority in the order listed. Special consideration is given to institutions that were supported by Mr. Lanier during his lifetime. The target areas are: 1) education, 2) health and human services, 3) arts, and 4) environment and community development.
Fields of interest: Arts; Elementary/secondary education; Education; Human services; Community development.
Type of support: General/operating support; Capital campaigns; Building/renovation; Endowments; Program development; Program-related investments/loans.
Limitations: Giving primarily in the southeastern U.S., with primary emphasis on Atlanta, GA. No support for churches or religious organizations (for projects that primarily benefit their own members), or for political purposes. No grants to individuals, or for tickets to charitable events or dinners, or to sponsor special events or fundraisers.
Publications: Application guidelines.
Application information: Application guidelines available on foundation Web site. Application form not required.

  Initial approach: Letter (not exceeding 2 pages)
  Deadline(s): Apr. 1 and Oct. 1
  Board meeting date(s): May and Nov.
Officers and Trustees:* J. Hicks Lanier,* Chair.; George H. Lanier,* Secy.-Treas.; Cecil D. Conlee; John B. Ellis; Julie W. Lanier; Wilton D. Looney.
Director: Mark B. Riley.
Number of staff: 1 part-time professional; 1 part-time support.
EIN: 586045056
Selected grants: The following grants were reported in 2003.
$1,250,706 to Vanderbilt University, Nashville, TN. For general support.
$299,957 to Emory University, Atlanta, GA. For general support.
$75,000 to Robert W. Woodruff Arts Center, Atlanta, GA. For general support.
$50,000 to American Cancer Society, Atlanta, GA. For general support.
$30,000 to Canine Assistants, Alpharetta, GA. For general support.
$10,000 to Atlanta Symphony Orchestra, Atlanta, GA. For general support.
$8,333 to Genesis Shelter, Atlanta, GA. For general support.
$5,000 to Literacy Action, Atlanta, GA. For general support.
$5,000 to National Kidney Foundation of Georgia, Atlanta, GA. For general support.
$5,000 to Nature Conservancy, Atlanta, GA. For general support.

2429
The Lanier Family Foundation ◇
P.O. Box 510
West Point, GA 31833

Established in 1990 in GA.
Donors: Campbell B. Lanier III; Jane Z. Lanier; J. Smith Lanier II; Elizabeth W. Lanier; Anthony L. Collins; Mary E. Collins; Edith C. Hodges; David Gaines Lanier; Capstone Funding, LLC.
Foundation type: Independent foundation.
Financial data (yr. ended 12/31/05): Assets, $4,054,476 (M); gifts received, $137,301; expenditures, $1,717,628; qualifying distributions, $1,681,599; giving activities include $1,680,385 for 27 grants (high: $1,005,000; low: $500).
Purpose and activities: Giving primarily for education.
Fields of interest: Higher education, college; Education; Christian agencies & churches.
Limitations: Applications not accepted. Giving in the South, primarily in AL and GA. No grants to individuals.
Application information: Contributes only to pre-selected organizations.
Trustees: Campbell B. Lanier III; J. Smith Lanier II.
EIN: 586247169
Selected grants: The following grants were reported in 2003.
$7,422,328 to Chattahoochee Valley Educational Foundation, Lanett, AL.
$251,100 to LaGrange College, La Grange, GA.
$160,000 to Spring Road Christian Church, Lanett, AL.
$100,000 to Chambers County Education Foundation.
$100,000 to Marion Military Institute, Marion, AL.
$100,000 to McDonough Christian Church, McDonough, GA.
$40,000 to Lee County Education Foundation.

$25,000 to Focus on the Family, Colorado Springs, CO.
$25,000 to Marannook, Lafayette, AL.
$25,000 to Prison Fellowship Ministries, Lansdowne, VA.

2430
The Thomas H. Lanier Foundation ◇ ☆
c/o Yancey L. McCollum, Tr.
2655 Battle Overlook N.W.
Atlanta, GA 30327-1202

Established in 1994 in GA.
Foundation type: Independent foundation.
Financial data (yr. ended 3/31/05): Assets, $6,990,085 (M); gifts received, $299,801; expenditures, $353,385; qualifying distributions, $328,298; giving activities include $330,500 for 65 grants (high: $62,500; low: $500).
Purpose and activities: Giving primarily for arts and culture, education, health, children and youth services, and social services.
Fields of interest: Arts; Higher education; Education; Health care; Health organizations, association; Human services; American Red Cross; Children/youth, services; Federated giving programs.
Limitations: Applications not accepted. Giving primarily in Atlanta, GA. No grants to individuals.
Application information: Contributes only to pre-selected organizations.
Trustees: J. Reese Lanier; Yancey L. McCollum.
EIN: 586266735
Selected grants: The following grants were reported in 2005.
$62,500 to Westminster Schools, Atlanta, GA.
$27,500 to Atlanta Speech School, Atlanta, GA.
$22,500 to Lovett School, Atlanta, GA.
$15,000 to Robert W. Woodruff Arts Center, Atlanta, GA.
$12,500 to McCallie School, Chattanooga, TN.
$10,000 to Shepherd Center, Atlanta, GA.
$8,500 to University of Georgia Foundation, Athens, GA.
$7,500 to Salvation Army, Norcross, GA.
$2,500 to Community Childrens Home, Carrollton, GA.
$1,500 to Atlanta History Center, Atlanta, GA.

2431
Lanier Goodman Foundation
c/o SunTrust Bank
P.O. Box 4655
Atlanta, GA 30302
Contact: J. Allen Mast, Jr.

Established in 1995 in GA.
Donor: Helen S. Lanier Foundation, Inc.
Foundation type: Independent foundation.
Financial data (yr. ended 12/31/05): Assets, $7,796,480 (M); expenditures, $556,959; qualifying distributions, $535,732; giving activities include $517,285 for grants.
Purpose and activities: Giving primarily for the arts, particularly museums, and a center for puppetry arts; funding also for education, including an Episcopal high school.
Fields of interest: Museums (art); Museums (natural history); Arts; Secondary school/education; Education; Hospitals (general); Health organizations, association; Spine disorders; Human

services; Children, services; Federated giving programs.
Limitations: Giving primarily in Palm Beach, FL, and Atlanta, GA.
Application information: Application form not required.
  Initial approach: Letter
  Deadline(s): Sept. 30
  Final notification: 90 days
Trustees: Carol Doty; Carol Lanier Goodman; Scott Goodman; SunTrust Bank.
EIN: 586396903

2432
The Ray M. and Mary Elizabeth Lee Foundation, Inc.
3414 Peachtree Rd., Ste. 722
Atlanta, GA   30326   (404) 842-1870
Contact: Larry B. Hooks, Admin. Mgr.

Incorporated in 1966 in GA.
Donors: Ray M. Lee†; Mary Elizabeth Lee†.
Foundation type: Independent foundation.
Financial data (yr. ended 9/30/05): Assets, $11,188,769 (M); expenditures, $634,899; qualifying distributions, $553,995; giving activities include $473,500 for 80 grants (high: $50,000; low: $1,000).
Fields of interest: Arts, multipurpose centers/programs; Performing arts; Performing arts, theater; Arts; Elementary/secondary education; Higher education; Education; Hospitals (general); Health care; Health organizations, association; Human services; YM/YWCAs & YM/YWHAs; Children/youth, services; Family services; Christian agencies & churches; Religion.
Type of support: Scholarship funds; General/operating support; Continuing support; Annual campaigns; Capital campaigns; Building/renovation; Equipment; Land acquisition; Debt reduction; Emergency funds; Program development; Conferences/seminars; Professorships; Publication; Curriculum development; Fellowships; Internship funds; Research; Technical assistance; Consulting services; Program-related investments/loans; Exchange programs; Matching/challenge support.
Limitations: Giving limited to the metropolitan Atlanta, GA, area. No grants to individuals or for endowments.
Publications: Application guidelines.
Application information: Application form not required.
  Initial approach: Letter
  Copies of proposal: 1
  Deadline(s): Jan. 31, Apr. 30, July 31, and Oct. 31
  Board meeting date(s): Feb., May, Aug., and Nov.
  Final notification: Following board meeting
Officer: William B. Stark, Pres.
Trustees: Ronald Gann; Donald D. Smith.
EIN: 586049441
Selected grants: The following grants were reported in 2005.
$50,000 to Robert W. Woodruff Arts Center, Atlanta, GA.
$25,000 to Eagle Ranch, Chestnut Mountain, GA.
$20,000 to Good Samaritan Health Center, Atlanta, GA.
$10,000 to Angel Flight of Georgia, Chamblee, GA.
$10,000 to United Negro College Fund, Fairfax, VA.
$7,500 to Boy Scouts of America, Atlanta, GA.
$5,000 to American Red Cross, Atlanta, GA.

$5,000 to Camp Highland, Alpharetta, GA.
$5,000 to Fernbank Museum of Natural History, Atlanta, GA.
$5,000 to Teach for America, Atlanta, GA.

2433
Dorothy V. & Logan Lewis Foundation, Inc. ✧
(formerly Dorothy V. & N. Logan Lewis Foundation, Inc.)
c/o Edward J. Harrell
240 3rd St.
Macon, GA   31201   (478) 749-1727
Contact: Cubbedge Snow, Jr., Secy.

Established in 1979.
Donor: Dorothy V. Lewis†.
Foundation type: Independent foundation.
Financial data (yr. ended 1/31/06): Assets, $77,229,381 (M); gifts received, $27,591,715; expenditures, $3,376,165; qualifying distributions, $2,729,929; giving activities include $2,729,929 for 6 grants (high: $1,167,929; low: $20,000).
Purpose and activities: Giving primarily for Roman Catholic elementary and secondary schools.
Fields of interest: Elementary/secondary education; Education; Roman Catholic agencies & churches.
Type of support: General/operating support.
Limitations: Giving primarily in Macon and Savannah, GA. No support for private foundations.
Application information: No more than 3 supplemental pages may be attached to proposal. Application form required.
  Initial approach: Proposal
  Copies of proposal: 7
  Deadline(s): Nov. 15 for Dec. meeting
  Board meeting date(s): Apr. and Dec.
Officers and Directors:* David G. Jeffords III,* Pres.; Cubbedge Snow, Jr.,* Secy.; Edward J. Harrell,* Invest. Off.; Fr. John Cuddy; Chris R. Sheridan.
EIN: 581365128

2434
J. C. Lewis Foundation, Inc.
P.O. Box 13666
Savannah, GA   31416-0666
Contact: Charles E. Izlar, Treas.
Application address: P.O. Box 60759, Savannah, GA 31420-0759

Established in 1951 in GA.
Donors: Lewis Broadcasting Corp.; J.C. Lewis Motor Co.
Foundation type: Independent foundation.
Financial data (yr. ended 12/31/05): Assets, $2,011,562 (M); gifts received, $1,000; expenditures, $3,270,985; qualifying distributions, $3,260,009; giving activities include $3,253,784 for 102 grants (high: $3,000,000; low: $50; average: $1,000–$10,000).
Purpose and activities: Giving primarily to evangelical Christian agencies and churches; some giving for health and human services.
Fields of interest: Health organizations, association; Human services; Residential/custodial care, hospices; Federated giving programs; Christian agencies & churches; Protestant agencies & churches; Jewish agencies & temples; General charitable giving.

Limitations: Giving primarily in Savannah, GA.
Application information: Application form not required.
  Initial approach: Letter
  Deadline(s): None
Officers and Board Members:* Nancy N. Lewis,* Pres.; J.C. Lewis III,* Secy.; Charles E. Izlar, Treas.
EIN: 586043785

2435
Livingston Foundation, Inc. ✧
171 17th St. N.W., Ste. 2100
Atlanta, GA   30363   (404) 873-8500
Contact: Milton W. Brannon, Pres.

Incorporated in 1964 in GA.
Donors: Roy N. Livingston†; Leslie Livingston Kellar†; Bess B. Livingston†.
Foundation type: Independent foundation.
Financial data (yr. ended 9/30/05): Assets, $8,021,937 (M); expenditures, $830,973; qualifying distributions, $739,558; giving activities include $692,921 for 25 grants (high: $115,000; low: $5,000).
Purpose and activities: Giving primarily for education, the fine arts, and health care.
Fields of interest: Visual arts; Museums; Performing arts; Historic preservation/historical societies; Arts; Education; Hospitals (general); Medical research, institute; Community development; International studies.
Type of support: General/operating support; Continuing support; Annual campaigns; Capital campaigns; Building/renovation; Endowments; Conferences/seminars; Seed money; Curriculum development; Matching/challenge support.
Limitations: Giving primarily in the metropolitan Atlanta, GA, area. No grants to individuals, or for scholarships, fellowships, or matching gifts; no loans.
Application information: Application form not required.
  Initial approach: Letter
  Copies of proposal: 1
  Deadline(s): None
  Board meeting date(s): Quarterly
  Final notification: 4 months
Officers and Trustees:* Jonathan Golden,* Chair.; Milton W. Brannon,* Pres. and Treas.; C.E. Gregory III,* Secy.; Greer Brannon; Michael Golden; Charles Gregory; Bill Jacobs.
Number of staff: 1 part-time support.
EIN: 586044858
Selected grants: The following grants were reported in 2005.
$61,000 to Boys and Girls Club, Warren Memorial, Atlanta, GA.
$30,000 to Camp Sunshine, Decatur, GA.
$30,000 to Center for the Visually Impaired, Atlanta, GA.
$20,000 to Schenck School, Atlanta, GA.
$16,821 to Atlanta History Center, Atlanta, GA.
$15,600 to High Museum of Art, Atlanta, GA.
$15,000 to Atlanta Speech School, Atlanta, GA.
$15,000 to Atlanta Symphony Orchestra, Atlanta, GA.
$10,000 to Atlanta Union Mission, Atlanta, GA.
$10,000 to Quality Care for Children, Atlanta, GA.

2436
The Martha and Wilton Looney Foundation, Inc. ✧ ☆
4470 Sentinel Post Rd. N.W.
Atlanta, GA 30327 (404) 760-0246
Contact: Bruce L. Dick, Secy.-Treas.

Established in 1992 in GA.
Donors: Wilton D. Looney; Martha W. Looney.
Foundation type: Independent foundation.
Financial data (yr. ended 12/31/05): Assets, $5,814,688 (M); gifts received, $602,720; expenditures, $325,356; qualifying distributions, $320,689; giving activities include $319,500 for 32 grants (high: $75,000; low: $1,000).
Fields of interest: Education; Animal welfare; Health care; Health organizations, association; Human services; Protestant agencies & churches.
Limitations: Giving primarily in GA. No grants to individuals.
Application information: Application form not required.
Initial approach: Letter
Deadline(s): None
Officers: Sylvia L. Dick, Chair.; Wilton D. Looney, Vice-Chair.; Bruce L. Dick, Secy.-Treas.
Trustee: Martha W. Looney.
EIN: 582022885
Selected grants: The following grants were reported in 2005.
$75,000 to American Red Cross, Atlanta, GA.
$50,000 to Salvation Army, Norcross, GA.
$25,000 to Emory University, Atlanta, GA.
$12,000 to Canine Assistants, Alpharetta, GA.
$10,000 to Lovett School, Atlanta, GA.
$10,000 to University of Georgia Foundation, Athens, GA.
$10,000 to Wake Forest University, Winston-Salem, NC.
$7,500 to Atlanta Speech School, Atlanta, GA.
$7,000 to University of South Carolina, Columbia, SC.
$6,000 to Good Samaritan Health Center, Atlanta, GA.

2437
Gay and Erskine Love Foundation, Inc. ✧
4335 Wendell Dr. S.W.
P.O. Box 43687
Atlanta, GA 30336-0687 (404) 691-5830
Contact: Linda Burdett, Asst.
E-mail: info@printpack.com; URL: http://www.printpack.com/PPcust/Menu/com.asp

Established in 1976 in GA.
Donors: Printpack Inc.; Love Family Charitable Lead Trust.
Foundation type: Company-sponsored foundation.
Financial data (yr. ended 12/31/05): Assets, $9,039,705 (M); gifts received, $862,819; expenditures, $2,071,593; qualifying distributions, $2,026,493; giving activities include $2,026,493 for 99 grants (high: $325,000; low: $100).
Purpose and activities: The foundation supports organizations involved with arts and culture, education, human services, and Christianity.
Fields of interest: Arts; Education, special; Higher education; Education; Boy scouts; Children/youth, services; Residential/custodial care, half-way house; Homeless, human services; Human services; Federated giving programs; Christian agencies & churches.

Type of support: General/operating support; Scholarship funds.
Limitations: Applications not accepted. Giving limited to Atlanta, GA. No grants to individuals.
Application information: Contributes only to pre-selected organizations.
Trustees: R. Michael Hembree; Dennis M. Love; Gay M. Love.
EIN: 510198585
Selected grants: The following grants were reported in 2004.
$342,650 to Boy Scouts of America, Anchorage, AK.
$334,118 to Duke University, Durham, NC.
$202,000 to Atlanta Union Mission, Atlanta, GA.
$141,206 to United Way.
$110,000 to Atlanta Speech School, Atlanta, GA.
$50,000 to Saint Christophers School Foundation, Richmond, VA.
$35,000 to Fulton Industrial Boys Association, Atlanta, GA.
$26,000 to Atlanta Symphony Orchestra, Atlanta, GA.
$8,000 to Columbia Theological Seminary, Decatur, GA.
$1,000 to Four Seasons Hospice, Hendersonville, NC.

2438
Lubo Fund, Inc. ✧
c/o Robert L. Bunnen
147 15th St. N.E., No. 9-B
Atlanta, GA 30309
Contact: Lucinda W. Bunnen, Pres.

Incorporated in 1958 in GA.
Donors: Belinda Reusch; members of the Bunnen family.
Foundation type: Independent foundation.
Financial data (yr. ended 12/31/04): Assets, $8,344,028 (M); gifts received, $90,258; expenditures, $416,752; qualifying distributions, $370,854; giving activities include $365,333 for 270 grants (high: $98,600; low: $50).
Purpose and activities: Giving primarily for cultural programs, including museums, performing and visual arts, with an emphasis on photography; support also for education.
Fields of interest: Visual arts, photography; Performing arts; Arts; Education; Environment; Health organizations, association; Civil liberties, advocacy; Jewish agencies & temples.
Type of support: General/operating support; Continuing support; Annual campaigns; Emergency funds; Program development; Publication; Seed money; Matching/challenge support.
Limitations: Giving primarily in GA, with emphasis on Atlanta. No grants to individuals, or for land acquisition, renovation projects, endowment funds, scholarships, fellowships, research, or conferences; no loans.
Application information: Application form not required.
Initial approach: Letter or proposal
Copies of proposal: 1
Deadline(s): None
Board meeting date(s): July
Final notification: 1 to 3 months
Officers: Lucinda W. Bunnen, Pres.; Robert L. Bunnen, Sr., V.P. and Secy.-Treas.
EIN: 586043631

2439
Ma-Ran Foundation ✧
(formerly R. Randall and Margaret H. Rollins Foundation)
c/o RFA Mgmt. Co., LLC
P.O. Box 647
Atlanta, GA 30301-0647

Established in 1991 in GA.
Donor: R. Randall Rollins.
Foundation type: Independent foundation.
Financial data (yr. ended 12/31/04): Assets, $29,170,794 (M); expenditures, $1,224,129; qualifying distributions, $1,105,340; giving activities include $1,105,340 for 22 grants (high: $445,300; low: $1,000).
Purpose and activities: Giving primarily to a donor-advised fund, as well as to a Methodist church; some giving for education, and children, youth, and social services.
Fields of interest: Elementary/secondary education; Higher education; Libraries (public); Education; Animals/wildlife, preservation/protection; Hospitals (general); Speech/hearing centers; Health organizations, association; Learning disorders; Recreation, parks/playgrounds; Human services; Children/youth, services; Community development; Protestant agencies & churches.
Limitations: Applications not accepted. Giving primarily in Atlanta, GA. No grants to individuals.
Application information: Contributes only to pre-selected organizations.
Trustees: Gary W. Rollins; Margaret H. Rollins; R. Randall Rollins.
EIN: 586263945
Selected grants: The following grants were reported in 2003.
$746,735 to Community Foundation for Greater Atlanta, Atlanta, GA.
$60,000 to Emory University Hospital, Atlanta, GA.
$30,000 to Texas A & M University Development Foundation, College Station, TX.
$25,000 to Chastain Horse Park, Atlanta, GA.
$25,000 to Greater Lewes Foundation, Lewes, DE.
$15,000 to Peachtree Road United Methodist Church, Atlanta, GA.
$5,000 to Childrens Healthcare of Atlanta, Atlanta, GA.
$5,000 to Westminster Schools, Atlanta, GA.
$4,500 to Northside Youth Organization, Atlanta, GA.
$1,000 to Lovett School, Atlanta, GA.

2440
The Billi Marcus Foundation, Inc. ✧
1266 W. Paces Ferry Rd.
Atlanta, GA 30327

Established in 1998 in GA.
Foundation type: Independent foundation.
Financial data (yr. ended 12/31/04): Assets, $11,144,138 (M); expenditures, $420,633; qualifying distributions, $416,100; giving activities include $416,100 for 40 grants (high: $26,000; low: $500).
Purpose and activities: Giving primarily for human services; giving also for theater and Jewish organizations.
Fields of interest: Performing arts, theater; Athletics/sports, golf; Human services; Residential/custodial care, hospices; Jewish federated giving programs; Jewish agencies & temples.

Limitations: Applications not accepted. Giving primarily in GA. No grants to individuals.
Application information: Contributes only to pre-selected organizations.
Officers: Billi Marcus, Chair.; Frederick S. Slagle, Secy.-Treas.
Director: Carolyn Paller.
EIN: 582396542

2441
The Marcus Foundation, Inc. ▼ ✧
1266 W. Paces Ferry Rd., No. 615
Atlanta, GA 30327-2306 (404) 240-7700
Contact: Frederick Slagle, Exec. Dir.

Established in 1989 in GA.
Donor: Bernard Marcus.
Foundation type: Independent foundation.
Financial data (yr. ended 12/31/04): Assets, $75,163,578 (M); gifts received, $64,392,418; expenditures, $24,729,177; qualifying distributions, $24,883,068; giving activities include $20,288,893 for 148 grants (high: $5,363,900; low: $500), $1,103,174 for 1 foundation-administered program and $703,207 for 2 loans/program-related investments.
Purpose and activities: Support primarily for human services, mental health, Jewish federated giving programs, education, and public affairs.
Fields of interest: Education; Health care; Mental health, treatment; Jewish agencies & temples.
Type of support: Program-related investments/loans.
Limitations: Applications not accepted. Giving primarily in Atlanta, GA. No grants to individuals.
Application information: Contributes only to pre-selected organizations.
Officers and Directors:* Bernard Marcus,* Chair.; Billi Marcus,* Vice-Chair.; Frederick Slagle, Secy.-Treas. and Exec. Dir.; Lisa Brill; Susanne Collins; Dennis Cooper; James Grien; Jeffrey Koplan; Ken Langone; Michael Leven; Frederick Marcus; Michael Morris; Larry Smith.
EIN: 581815651
Selected grants: The following grants were reported in 2004.
$5,363,900 to American Friends of the Israel Democracy Institute, Atlanta, GA. For general operating support.
$1,604,999 to City of Hope National Medical Center, Duarte, CA. For research on non-myeloablative cancers.
$1,125,000 to Shepherd Center, Atlanta, GA. For Bridge Program.
$1,033,000 to Jewish Federation of Greater Atlanta, Atlanta, GA. For general operating support.
$1,010,000 to Marcus Institute for Development and Learning, Atlanta, GA. 2 grants: $1,000,000 (For President's Fund), $10,000 (For Big Splash project).
$1,000,000 to Birthright Israel Foundation, New York, NY. For general operating support.
$883,062 to National Center for Neighborhood Enterprise, DC. For general operating support.
$500,000 to Friends of Yemin Orde, DC. For general operating support.
$50,000 to Federalist Society for Law and Public Policy Studies, DC. For general operating support.

2442
Harriet McDaniel Marshall Trust in Memory of Sanders McDaniel ✧
c/o SunTrust Bank Atlanta, Community Affairs Fdn. Prog.
P.O. Box 4655
Atlanta, GA 30302
Contact: Raymond B. King, Secy.
URL: http://www.suntrustatlantafoundation.org

Trust established in 1962 in GA.
Donor: Harriet McDaniel Marshall†.
Foundation type: Independent foundation.
Financial data (yr. ended 11/30/05): Assets, $7,920,819 (M); expenditures, $428,895; qualifying distributions, $408,497; giving activities include $379,817 for 93 grants (high: $20,000; low: $600).
Purpose and activities: Giving primarily for education and building funds for educational institutions, health, and the handicapped; support also for welfare, including organizations assisting the disadvantaged, the homeless, and the elderly, community funds and development, and arts and culture.
Fields of interest: Arts; Elementary/secondary education; Higher education; Education; Community development.
Type of support: Capital campaigns; Building/renovation; Equipment.
Limitations: Giving primarily in the metropolitan Atlanta, GA, area. No grants to individuals, or for scholarships or fellowships; no loans.
Publications: Application guidelines; Program policy statement.
Application information: Application form and guidelines available on foundation Web site. Application form required.
Initial approach: Letter
Copies of proposal: 1
Deadline(s): Mar. 31, Aug. 31, and Dec. 1
Board meeting date(s): Jan., Apr., July, and Oct.
Officers and Distribution Committee:* E. Jenner Wood,* Chair.; Raymond B. King,* Secy.; J. Scott Wilfong; L.P. Humann; James M. Willis.
Trustee: SunTrust Bank.
Number of staff: None.
EIN: 586089937

2443
MARTA Charity Club ✧
2424 Piedmont Rd.
Atlanta, GA 30324

Foundation type: Independent foundation.
Financial data (yr. ended 12/31/04): Assets, $552,480 (M); gifts received, $585,443; expenditures, $604,718; qualifying distributions, $561,185; giving activities include $561,185 for grants.
Fields of interest: Health organizations, association.
Limitations: Giving primarily in the greater metropolitan Atlanta, GA, area. No grants to individuals.
Application information:
Initial approach: Letter
Deadline(s): None
Officers: Warren McMichael, C.E.O.; Gloria James, Secy.; Darlene West, C.F.O.
EIN: 581576346

2444
The Carlos and Marguerite Mason Fund ▼ ✧
c/o Wachovia Bank of Georgia, N.A.
191 Peachtree St. N.E.
Atlanta, GA 30303
Contact: Alice Sheets; Lydia Whitman
E-mail: grantinquiriesga@wachovia.com; Application address: c/o Wachovia Bank, N.A., 3414 Peachtree Rd., 5th Fl., MC GA8023, Atlanta, GA 30326;
URL: http://www.wachovia.com/privatefoundations

Established in 1991 in GA.
Donor: Marguerite F. Mason†.
Foundation type: Independent foundation.
Financial data (yr. ended 12/31/05): Assets, $104,273,313 (M); expenditures, $5,370,386; qualifying distributions, $4,973,313; giving activities include $4,419,240 for 13 grants (high: $1,100,000; low: $20,000; average: $45,000–$550,000).
Purpose and activities: Support only for Georgia organizations involved with organ transplantation and related research.
Fields of interest: Health care, organ/tissue banks; Organ research.
Type of support: Equipment; Program development; Professorships; Research.
Limitations: Giving limited to GA. No grants to individuals or for general goodwill advertising.
Publications: Application guidelines.
Application information: See guidelines on Web site. Application form required.
Initial approach: Telephone
Copies of proposal: 5
Deadline(s): June 1
Board meeting date(s): Sept.
Final notification: Sept. 30
Officer and Advisory Committee:* George W.P. Atkins,* Chair.; Carol Hoffman; Randy M. Karesh.
Trustee: Wachovia Bank, N.A.
EIN: 581996431
Selected grants: The following grants were reported in 2004.
$1,132,824 to Medical College of Georgia Foundation, Augusta, GA. For comprehensive transplant program.
$1,089,568 to University of Georgia Research Foundation, Athens, GA. 2 grants: $789,568 (For Medication Access Program - MAP), $300,000 (For Sharing Immunosuppressive Therapy program).
$1,024,850 to Georgia Transplant Foundation, Atlanta, GA. 3 grants: $55,000 (For statewide communication plan), $920,000 (For Mason Patient Services Fund), $49,850 (For salary support for Director of Development).
$900,000 to Childrens Healthcare of Atlanta Foundation, Atlanta, GA. 2 grants: $650,000 (To endow chair in liver transplantation), $250,000 (For liver resection clinical research).
$400,000 to Emory University, Atlanta, GA. For Mason Transplant Outpatient Clinic.
$112,350 to Childrens Healthcare of Atlanta, Atlanta, GA. For Sonosite Titan portable ultrasound.

2445
James T. McAfee, Jr. and Carolyn T. McAfee Foundation ✧
10580 Big Canoe
Big Canoe, GA 30143

Established in 1988 in GA.
Donors: James T. McAfee, Jr.; Raymond C. Townsend; Carolyn T. McAfee.
Foundation type: Independent foundation.
Financial data (yr. ended 12/31/05): Assets, $7,486,060 (M); gifts received, $755,000; expenditures, $662,172; qualifying distributions, $620,074; giving activities include $515,000 for 2 grants (high: $500,000; low: $15,000).
Fields of interest: Higher education.
Limitations: Applications not accepted. Giving primarily in GA. No grants to individuals.
Application information: Contributes only to pre-selected organizations.
Advisory Committee: James T. McAfee III.
Trustees: Carolyn T. McAfee; James T. McAfee, Jr.
EIN: 586219512

2446
Bert & Mary Meyer Foundation, Inc. ✧
1237 Ralph David Abernathy Blvd. S.W.
Atlanta, GA 30310 (404) 758-1007
Contact: Laverne Robinson, Admin. Coord.
E-mail: bammf@aol.com

Established in 1984 in GA.
Donors: Barbara C. Meyer; Mary C. Meyer†.
Foundation type: Independent foundation.
Financial data (yr. ended 12/31/05): Assets, $16,457,446 (M); gifts received, $179,358; expenditures, $1,841,318; qualifying distributions, $1,630,623; giving activities include $1,062,950 for 5 grants (high: $1,020,200; low: $1,000).
Purpose and activities: Support for rural people's organizations and coalitions that are: 1) educating and organizing communities to initiate, build and sustain progressive movements; 2) aimed at establishing political, economic, and social institutions which value democracy, equity, and human dignity; and 3) working to create a non-racial, non-sexist society in which human beings and communities can reach their full potential.
Type of support: General/operating support; Continuing support; Program development; Seed money; Technical assistance.
Limitations: Applications not accepted. Giving limited to the southeastern U.S. No support for schools, hospitals, single-disease organizations, government-related institutions, or organizations that are not self-governed. No grants to individuals.
Application information: Unsolicited requests for funds not accepted.
Officers: Barbara Meyer, Chair. and Treas.; Ron White, Vice-Chair.; Mary Levy, Secy.; Hubert Sapp, Exec. Dir.
Trustees: Tirso Moreno; Karen Watson.
Number of staff: 1 full-time support.
EIN: 592348082

2447
Ginny Millner Foundation, Inc. ✧
3640 Tuxedo Rd. N.W.
Atlanta, GA 30305 (404) 240-0054
Contact: Ginny Millner

Established in 1994 in GA.
Foundation type: Independent foundation.
Financial data (yr. ended 12/31/05): Assets, $4,520,512 (M); gifts received, $4,888,493; expenditures, $797,049; qualifying distributions,

$748,156; giving activities include $748,156 for grants.
Purpose and activities: Giving primarily to Christian ministries and services.
Fields of interest: Human services; Christian agencies & churches.
Limitations: Giving primarily in FL, and Atlanta, GA. No grants to individuals.
Application information: Application form not required.
Initial approach: Letter of request
Officers and Directors:* Virginia Wright Millner,* Pres.; Karen A. Finley,* V.P.; Sally B. Perley, Secy.; Betsy Akers,* Treas.; Judy Riddle; Mimi Stickley.
EIN: 582121970
Selected grants: The following grants were reported in 2004.
$35,000 to Big Dream Ministries, Alpharetta, GA.
$21,000 to Christ Church, Savannah, GA.
$4,000 to Reflections Ministries, Atlanta, GA.
$3,000 to Feed My Lambs, Marietta, GA.
$1,000 to Pioneers, Inc., Orlando, FL.
$500 to Atlanta Union Mission, Atlanta, GA.
$300 to Henry W. Grady Foundation, Atlanta, GA.
$200 to CARE, Atlanta, GA.
$150 to World Vision, Tacoma, WA.
$100 to March of Dimes Birth Defects Foundation, Atlanta, GA.

2448
Charles L. Mix Memorial Fund, Inc. ✧
P.O. Box 704
Americus, GA 31709

Incorporated in 1957 in GA.
Donor: Jeannette C. Mix†.
Foundation type: Independent foundation.
Financial data (yr. ended 12/31/05): Assets, $9,201,438 (M); expenditures, $503,577; qualifying distributions, $457,334; giving activities include $421,039 for 14 grants (high: $166,000; low: $2,000).
Purpose and activities: Giving primarily for higher education, particularly for research into the causes and cures of mental and emotional disorders; funding also for a theater and cultural center.
Fields of interest: Performing arts, theater; Historical activities; Higher education; Human services; American Red Cross.
Limitations: Applications not accepted. Giving limited to Americus, GA. No grants to individuals.
Application information: Contributes only to pre-selected organizations.
Officers: Charles R. Crisp, Chair.; Russell Thomas, Jr., Vice-Chair.; James C. Gatewood, Secy.-Treas.
Directors: Gatewood Dudley; Wade Halstead; Michael Haynes; Rickey Whaley.
EIN: 580699008

2449
Joe and Mary Moeller Foundation ✧ ☆
c/o Joe Moeller
4720 Jett Rd.
Atlanta, GA 30327

Established in 2004 in KS.
Donor: Joseph W. Moeller.
Foundation type: Independent foundation.
Financial data (yr. ended 12/31/05): Assets, $4,464,387 (M); gifts received, $2,500,153; expenditures, $341,417; qualifying distributions,

$321,120; giving activities include $321,120 for 42 grants (high: $80,000; low: $250).
Fields of interest: Education; Human services; Roman Catholic agencies & churches.
Limitations: Applications not accepted. No grants to individuals.
Application information: Contributes only to pre-selected organizations.
Officers: Joseph W. Moeller, Pres. and Secy.; Mary F. Moeller, Treas.
Director: Margaret Sharon Walker.
EIN: 830411709

2450
Money-Arenz Foundation, Inc. ✧
c/o Wachovia Bank
191 Peachtree St., 24th Fl.
Atlanta, GA 30303
Contact: Lydia Clements Whitman, Advisor

Established in 1993 in GA.
Foundation type: Independent foundation.
Financial data (yr. ended 12/31/04): Assets, $1,142,355 (M); gifts received, $464,670; expenditures, $510,537; qualifying distributions, $487,275; giving activities include $475,800 for 80 grants (high: $60,000; low: $300).
Fields of interest: Elementary/secondary education; Higher education; Environment, research; Environment, natural resources; Animal welfare; Human services; Children/youth, services.
Limitations: Applications not accepted. Giving on a national basis. No grants to individuals.
Application information: Contributes only to pre-selected organizations. Unsolicited requests for funds not accepted.
Officers: Betty M. Arenz, Pres.; Ronnie L. Bridges, Secy.
EIN: 582049998
Selected grants: The following grants were reported in 2004.
$60,000 to Hearts and Minds Foundation. For general support.
$43,000 to Wild Earth Society, Richmond, VT. For general support.
$34,000 to Scripps Research Institute, La Jolla, CA. For general support.
$31,000 to University of California, Berkeley, CA. For general support.
$20,000 to Whittier Institute for Diabetes and Endocrinology, La Jolla, CA. For general support.
$12,000 to Salvation Army National Headquarters, Alexandria, VA. For general support.
$10,500 to San Diego Center for Children, San Diego, CA. For general support.
$10,000 to John Marshall High School, Los Angeles, CA. For general support.
$10,000 to University of Georgia, Athens, GA. For general support.
$9,000 to Voices for Children, San Diego, CA. For general suppport.

2451
Sara Giles Moore Foundation ✧ ☆
c/o Sara Hehir
2870 Peachtree Rd., Ste. 413
Atlanta, GA 30305
Contact: Starr Moore, Chair.

Established in 1997 in GA.
Donor: Sara Giles Moore†.

Foundation type: Independent foundation.
Financial data (yr. ended 12/31/05): Assets, $40,960,262 (M); gifts received, $31,494,356; expenditures, $1,549,409; qualifying distributions, $1,423,719; giving activities include $1,400,000 for 36 grants (high: $250,000; low: $1,000).
Purpose and activities: Giving to art and cultural institutes.
Fields of interest: Visual arts; Museums; Hospitals (general).
Type of support: General/operating support; Annual campaigns; Capital campaigns; Building/renovation; Endowments.
Limitations: Giving primarily in West Palm Beach, FL and Atlanta, GA.
Application information: Application form not required.
  Initial approach: Letter
  Copies of proposal: 1
  Deadline(s): None
  Board meeting date(s): Oct.
  Final notification: 3 to 6 months
Officers and Trustees:* Starr Moore,* Chair.; Frank McGaughey, Vice-Chair.; Frank Butterfield, Secy.-Treas.; Sara A. Hehir; Orin Woodall.
EIN: 586343477

2452
James Starr Moore Memorial Foundation, Inc. ✧
3290 Northside Pkwy., Ste. 390
Atlanta, GA 30327

Incorporated in 1953 in GA.
Donors: Sara Giles Moore†; Starr Moore.
Foundation type: Independent foundation.
Financial data (yr. ended 12/31/05): Assets, $13,119,674 (M); expenditures, $713,153; qualifying distributions, $633,148; giving activities include $600,000 for 68 grants (high: $100,000; low: $100).
Fields of interest: Performing arts; Historic preservation/historical societies; Arts; Education, research; Higher education; Hospitals (general); Reproductive health, family planning; Nursing care; Health care; AIDS; AIDS research; Human services; Residential/custodial care, hospices; Federated giving programs; Protestant agencies & churches; Economically disadvantaged.
Type of support: General/operating support; Endowments; Capital campaigns; Building/renovation; Annual campaigns.
Limitations: Giving primarily in GA. No grants to individuals.
Application information: Application form not required.
  Initial approach: Letter
  Copies of proposal: 1
  Deadline(s): None
  Board meeting date(s): Dec.
  Final notification: 3 to 6 months
Officer and Trustees:* Starr Moore,* Chair.; Sara Armour Hehir; Emily Redwine.
EIN: 586033190

2453
Morgens West Foundation ✧
3562 Knollwood Dr.
Atlanta, GA 30305-1022

Established around 1968.

Donor: Morgens West Charitable Lead Annuity Trust.
Foundation type: Independent foundation.
Financial data (yr. ended 12/31/04): Assets, $8,064,999 (M); gifts received, $996,477; expenditures, $613,993; qualifying distributions, $526,163; giving activities include $499,750 for 39 grants (high: $100,000; low: $100).
Fields of interest: Museums; Higher education; Environment, natural resources; Environment, land resources; Human services; Federated giving programs; Protestant agencies & churches.
Limitations: Applications not accepted. Giving primarily in Atlanta, GA. No grants to individuals.
Application information: Contributes only to pre-selected organizations.
Trustees: E.H. Morgens; J.H. Morgens; S.F. Morgens.
EIN: 316090957
Selected grants: The following grants were reported in 2003.
$96,200 to High Museum of Art, Atlanta, GA.
$77,500 to Emory University, Michael C. Carlos Museum, Atlanta, GA.
$75,000 to Trust for Public Land, Atlanta, GA.
$60,000 to Atlanta Enterprise Center, Atlanta, GA.
$25,500 to First Presbyterian Church of Atlanta, Atlanta, GA.
$25,000 to Salvation Army of Atlanta, Atlanta, GA.
$20,000 to Saving Places for Atlantas Community Environments (SPACE), Atlanta, GA.
$10,000 to United Way of Metropolitan Atlanta, Atlanta, GA.
$7,175 to Atlanta Botanical Garden, Atlanta, GA.
$5,000 to Trees Atlanta, Atlanta, GA.

2454
Morris Communications Foundation, Inc. ✧
(formerly Stauffer Communications Foundation)
P.O. Box 936
Augusta, GA 30903-0936
Contact: William S. Morris IV, Tr.

Established in 1976 in KS.
Donors: Stauffer Communications, Inc.; Morris Communications Corp.; Morris Communications Co., LLC.
Foundation type: Company-sponsored foundation.
Financial data (yr. ended 12/31/03): Assets, $1,075,864 (M); gifts received, $2,113,167; expenditures, $2,177,294; qualifying distributions, $2,175,957; giving activities include $2,172,191 for 55 grants (high: $400,000; low: $100).
Purpose and activities: The foundation supports hospitals and organizations involved with the arts and culture, education, natural resources, housing, and community development.
Fields of interest: Arts; Education, fund raising/fund distribution; Higher education; Education; Environment, natural resources; Hospitals (general); Health care; Children/youth, services; Community development; Federated giving programs.
Type of support: Capital campaigns; Building/renovation.
Limitations: Giving limited to areas of company operations. Generally, no grants to individuals.
Application information: Application form not required.
  Initial approach: Proposal
  Deadline(s): None
  Board meeting date(s): 3rd week of Mar., June, Sept., and Dec.

Trustees: John Fish; Gregg A. Ireland; William S. Morris IV; John H. Stauffer; Stanley H. Stauffer.
EIN: 486212412

2455
The Morris Family Foundation, Inc. ✧
(formerly The Michael A. Morris Foundation, Inc.)
1266 W. Paces Ferry Rd., Ste. 615
Atlanta, GA 30327

Established in 1998 in GA.
Donor: Bernard Marcus.
Foundation type: Independent foundation.
Financial data (yr. ended 12/31/04): Assets, $10,247,438 (M); expenditures, $626,619; qualifying distributions, $608,816; giving activities include $510,141 for grants.
Purpose and activities: Giving primarily for Jewish organizations.
Fields of interest: Museums (art); Museums (children's); Secondary school/education; Higher education; Zoos/zoological societies; Civil rights; Federated giving programs; Christian agencies & churches; Jewish agencies & temples.
Limitations: Applications not accepted. Giving on a national basis. No grants to individuals.
Application information: Contributes only to pre-selected organizations.
Officers: Michael Morris, Chair.; Frederick Slagle, Secy.-Treas.
Director: Belinda Morris.
Trustee: Donna Goldberg.
EIN: 582396544
Selected grants: The following grants were reported in 2003.
$123,065 to Jewish Federation of Greater Atlanta, Atlanta, GA. For general operating support.
$72,795 to Woodward Academy, College Park, GA. For general operating support.
$32,000 to Los Angeles Contemporary Exhibitions, Los Angeles, CA. For general operating support.
$17,757 to Temple Emanu-El of Greater Atlanta, Atlanta, GA. For general operating support.
$15,050 to Marcus Jewish Community Center of Atlanta, Dunwoody, GA. For general operating support.
$15,000 to Friends of Common Denominator, Flushing, NY. For general operating support.
$12,704 to Childrens Museum of Atlanta, Atlanta, GA. For general operating support.
$12,500 to American Friends of the Israel Philharmonic Orchestra, New York, NY. For general operating support.
$12,500 to American Jewish Committee, New York, NY. For general operating support.
$10,000 to Saint Judes Recovery Center, Atlanta, GA. For general operating support.

2456
Katherine John Murphy Foundation
50 Hurt Plz., Ste. 1210
Atlanta, GA 30303 (404) 589-8090
Contact: Brenda Rambeau, Dir.; Martin Gatins, Chair.
E-mail: info@murphyfoundation.org; *URL:* http://www.kjmurphyfoundation.org

Trust established in 1954 in GA.
Donor: Katherine Murphy Riley†.
Foundation type: Independent foundation.

Financial data (yr. ended 12/31/05): Assets, $20,740,553 (M); expenditures, $1,486,607; qualifying distributions, $1,388,954; giving activities include $1,081,000 for 90 grants (high: $50,000; low: $1,000), and $31,867 for 15 employee matching gifts.

Purpose and activities: Giving primarily for the arts, higher education, the environment, hospitals, and youth services.

Fields of interest: Arts; Higher education; Environment; Health care; Children/youth, services.

International interests: Latin America.

Type of support: Capital campaigns; Building/renovation; Equipment; Scholarship funds.

Limitations: Giving primarily in Atlanta, GA. No grants to individuals, or for research, or matching gifts; no loans.

Publications: Application guidelines.

Application information: The foundation accepts unsolicited applications only in metro Atlanta, GA. Application form not required.

 Initial approach: Letter
 Copies of proposal: 1
 Deadline(s): Mar. 30, June 30, Sept. 30, and Dec. 15
 Board meeting date(s): Jan., Apr., July, and Sept.
 Final notification: 6 months

Officer and Trustees:* Martin Gatins,* Chair.; Dameron Black III; Phillip Gatins; SunTrust Bank.

Number of staff: 1 full-time professional.

EIN: 586026045

Selected grants: The following grants were reported in 2003.

$105,378 to EARTH University Foundation, Atlanta, GA. 2 grants: $50,000 (For general support), $55,378 (For Emory Cocke Black Scholarship).

$50,189 to High Museum of Art, Atlanta, GA. For general support.

$50,000 to Zoo Atlanta, Atlanta, GA. For Save the Panda campaign and capital campaign.

$40,000 to Nature Conservancy, Atlanta, GA. For Altamaha Project.

$35,000 to Marist School, Atlanta, GA. For Harnett Scholarship Fund.

$35,000 to University of Georgia Foundation, Athens, GA. For renovation of Moore College.

$28,250 to Latin American Association, Atlanta, GA. For capital campaign and youth internship.

$25,000 to Trinity School, Atlanta, GA. For capital campaign.

$15,000 to Piedmont Hospital Foundation, Atlanta, GA. For Sixty Plus program.

2457
Stuart and Eulene Murray Foundation ✧

c/o Joel Reed
2970 Clairmont Rd., Ste. 725
Atlanta, GA 30329-4440

Established in 1991 in GA.

Donor: Eulene H. Murray.

Foundation type: Independent foundation.

Financial data (yr. ended 6/30/05): Assets, $27,748,566 (M); gifts received, $21,320,932; expenditures, $1,369,134; qualifying distributions, $456,100; giving activities include $447,000 for 6 grants (high: $350,000; low: $2,000).

Purpose and activities: Giving primarily for education, including to a Christian school.

Fields of interest: Elementary/secondary education; Recreation, camps; Christian agencies & churches.

Limitations: Applications not accepted. Giving primarily in GA. No grants to individuals.

Application information: Contributes only to pre-selected organizations.

Trustees: Joel Reed; Marilyn Rowland; Wachovia Bank, N.A.

EIN: 581936483

Selected grants: The following grants were reported in 2003.

$500,000 to Reinhardt College, Waleska, GA. For music school.

$350,000 to Lovett School, Atlanta, GA. For building fund.

$50,000 to Hopewell Baptist Church, Canton, GA. For unrestricted support.

$50,000 to Mount Paran Christian School, Kennesaw, GA. For unrestricted support.

$5,000 to Good Samaritan Health Center, Atlanta, GA. For unrestricted support.

2458
North Georgia Community Foundation

(formerly Gainesville Community Foundation)
615F Oak St., Ste. 1300
Gainesville, GA 30501 (770) 535-7880
Contact: James E. Mathis, Jr., C.E.O.
FAX: (770) 503-0439; E-mail: info@ngcf.org;
Additional E-mail: jmathis@ngcf.org; URL: http://www.ngcf.org

Established in 1985 in GA.

Foundation type: Community foundation.

Financial data (yr. ended 6/30/05): Assets, $23,408,741 (M); gifts received, $5,093,125; expenditures, $3,504,112; giving activities include $2,911,632 for grants.

Purpose and activities: The foundation exists to be the primary vehicle for building and managing the community's permanent charitable resources.

Fields of interest: Arts; Education; Environment; Health care; Human services; Economic development; Community development; Philanthropy/voluntarism; Religion.

Type of support: General/operating support; Management development/capacity building; Equipment; Program development; Seed money; Technical assistance; Program evaluation; Matching/challenge support.

Limitations: Giving limited to the 15-county area of northeast GA. No grants to individuals (except for scholarships), or for annual fund campaigns.

Publications: Application guidelines; Financial statement; Occasional report.

Application information: Visit foundation Web site for application information. Application form required.

 Initial approach: Telephone
 Copies of proposal: 1
 Deadline(s): Mar. 31
 Board meeting date(s): 2nd Wed. monthly
 Final notification: 8-10 weeks

Officers and Directors:* Douglas A. Carter,* Chair.; Lindsay B. Robertson,* Vice-Chair.; James E. Mathis, Jr., C.E.O. and Pres.; Janice P. Ward, V.P., Progs. & Donor Svcs.; Lynda D. Askew,* Secy.; Lawrence B. Schrage,* Treas.; Catherine M. Amos; Margaret Ballard; Tom Calkins; Alan C. Crumley; Anthony W. Dye; Anderson Flen; Phillip Hester; Brent W. Hoffman; J. Russell Ivie; Carol C. Jackson; Deborah K. Mack; Kayanne S. Massey; James H. Moore; John M. Nix; Eula G. Pearce; L. Gordon Sawyer; LeTrell Simpson; Dean C. Swanson; George Thomas; Dick Valentine; Gus Whalen.

Number of staff: 5 full-time professional.

EIN: 581610318

2459
The Carl & Frances Patrick Foundation, Inc. ✧ ☆

2701 Lynda Ln.
Columbus, GA 31906
Contact: Carl L. Patrick, Pres.

Established in 1985 in GA.

Donor: Carl L. Patrick.

Foundation type: Independent foundation.

Financial data (yr. ended 11/30/05): Assets, $599,873 (M); expenditures, $374,733; qualifying distributions, $354,678; giving activities include $354,678 for 19+ grants (high: $250,000).

Fields of interest: Arts; Higher education, college; Higher education, university; Education; Federated giving programs; Christian agencies & churches.

Limitations: Applications not accepted. Giving primarily in GA. No grants to individuals.

Application information: Contributes only to pre-selected organizations.

Officers: Carl L. Patrick, Pres.; Frances E. Patrick, Secy.

Directors: Carl L. Patrick, Jr.; Michael W. Patrick.

EIN: 581653421

Selected grants: The following grants were reported in 2003.

$150,000 to Columbus Technical College Foundation, Columbus, GA. For general support.

$15,000 to Saint Luke United Methodist Church, Columbus, GA. For general support.

$4,500 to University of the Cumberlands, Williamsburg, KY. For general support.

$4,000 to Georgia Southwestern State University Foundation, Americus, GA. For general support.

$3,000 to Columbus Museum, Columbus, GA. For general support.

$2,500 to Boys Club of Columbus and Phenix City, Columbus, GA. For general support.

$1,500 to Columbus Symphony Orchestra, Columbus, GA. For general support.

$1,200 to United Way of the Chattahoochee Valley, Columbus, GA. For general support.

$1,000 to Eisenhower Medical Center, Rancho Mirage, CA. For general support.

$1,000 to Will Rogers Institute, Toluca Lake, CA. For general support.

2460
Patterson-Barclay Memorial Foundation, Inc.

5555 Triangle Pkwy., Ste. 120
Norcross, GA 30092 (770) 300-0906
Contact: Hugh R. Powell, Jr., Secy.

Incorporated in 1953 in GA.

Donor: Frederick W. Patterson†.

Foundation type: Independent foundation.

Financial data (yr. ended 12/31/05): Assets, $11,128,045 (M); expenditures, $776,105; qualifying distributions, $592,800; giving activities include $592,800 for 90 grants (high: $40,000; low: $800; average: $5,000–$10,000).

Purpose and activities: Giving for Christian organizations, hospitals, and higher secondary, and other education; grants also for health, social service and youth agencies, arts and culture, and the environment.

Fields of interest: Museums; Performing arts; Performing arts, theater; Arts; Education, association; Child development, education; Secondary school/education; Higher education; Environment, natural resources; Environment; Animals/wildlife, preservation/protection; Hospitals (general); Medical care, rehabilitation; Health care; Substance abuse, services; Human services; Children/youth, services; Child development, services; Residential/custodial care, hospices; Aging, centers/services; Women, centers/services; Homeless, human services; Community development; Christian agencies & churches; Religion; Economically disadvantaged.

Type of support: General/operating support; Continuing support; Annual campaigns; Capital campaigns; Building/renovation; Endowments; Scholarship funds.

Limitations: Giving primarily in the metropolitan Atlanta, GA, area. No grants to individuals.

Publications: Application guidelines.

Application information: Guidelines will be faxed. Application form not required.

   Copies of proposal: 1
   Deadline(s): Oct. 1
   Board meeting date(s): 3rd Wed. in May and Oct.
   Final notification: Positive responses only

Officers and Trustees:* Mrs. Lee Barclay Patterson Allen,* Pres. and Treas.; Jack W. Allen,* V.P.; Hugh R. Powell, Jr., Secy.; Hugh B. Allen; Laurell Allen.

EIN: 580904580

Selected grants: The following grants were reported in 2004.

$40,000 to Davidson College, Davidson, NC.
$20,000 to American Red Cross.
$20,000 to Appalachian State University, Boone, NC.
$10,000 to Feed the Hungry Foundation, Marietta, GA.
$10,000 to Haitian Project, Providence, RI.
$6,500 to Boys and Girls Club.
$5,500 to Alzheimers Association, Chicago, IL.
$5,000 to Girl Scouts of the U.S.A..
$5,000 to Hemophilia of Georgia, Atlanta, GA.
$5,000 to Place of Forsyth County, Cumming, GA.

2461
The Pechter Foundation ◆ ☆
1266 Bellaire Dr.
Atlanta, GA 30319

Established in 1993 in NJ and DE.
Donor: Richard S. Pechter.
Foundation type: Independent foundation.
Financial data (yr. ended 12/31/05): Assets, $2,744,055 (M); expenditures, $466,869; qualifying distributions, $466,540; giving activities include $466,540 for 97 grants (high: $100,000; low: $100).
Fields of interest: Arts; Higher education; Education; Health organizations, association; Human services.
Limitations: Applications not accepted. Giving primarily in NJ and NY. No grants to individuals.
Application information: Contributes only to pre-selected organizations.
Officer: Richard S. Pechter, Pres. and Secy.-Treas.
EIN: 133711334

2462
Pickett & Hatcher Educational Fund, Inc.
P.O. Box 8169
Columbus, GA 31908-8169 (706) 327-6586
FAX: (706) 324-6788; E-mail: info@phef.org; E-mail for Scholarships: kenowens@phef.org; Additional tel.: (800) 864-8308; URL: http://www.phef.org

Incorporated in 1938 in GA.
Donor: Claud A. Hatcher†.
Foundation type: Independent foundation.
Financial data (yr. ended 9/30/05): Assets, $34,893,636 (M); gifts received, $10,000; expenditures, $2,972,618; qualifying distributions, $2,780,018; giving activities include $2,301,356 for 643 loans to individuals.
Purpose and activities: Giving in the U.S. to encourage worthy students to secure a broad liberal education by providing student loans.
Type of support: Student loans—to individuals.
Limitations: Giving limited to the U.S. No support for students planning to enter career fields of medicine, law, or the ministry. No grants for any purpose other than educational loans.
Publications: Informational brochure (including application guidelines).
Application information: Applications are no longer being distributed to first-time borrowers for the 2006-2007 academic year. Distribution of applications to first-time borrowers will resume January 2007, for the 2007-2008 academic year. See foundation Web site for current application guidelines and procedures. Application form required.
   Initial approach: Letter or telephone
   Copies of proposal: 1
   Deadline(s): Varies based on availability of funds
   Board meeting date(s): May and Nov.
   Final notification: 2 months
Officers and Directors:* William K. Hatcher,* Chair.; Kenneth R. Owens, Pres.; Margaret G. Zollo,* Secy.; James W. Key,* Treas.; Donna S. Hand; William B. Hardegree; Jerry M. Smith.
Number of staff: 1 full-time professional; 4 full-time support; 1 part-time support.
EIN: 580566216

2463
William I. H. and Lula E. Pitts Foundation ▼
c/o SunTrust Bank
P.O. Box 4655, MC221
Atlanta, GA 30302 (404) 813-9105
Contact: Allen Mast, Secy.
URL: http://www.pittsfoundation.org

Trust established in 1941 in GA.
Donors: William I.H. Pitts†; Margaret A. Pitts.
Foundation type: Independent foundation.
Financial data (yr. ended 12/31/05): Assets, $70,087,069 (M); expenditures, $3,688,032; qualifying distributions, $3,570,650; giving activities include $3,465,007 for 49 grants (high: $486,003; low: $959; average: $5,000–$51,798).
Purpose and activities: Giving exclusively to organizations affiliated with the United Methodist Conference; emphasis on higher education and care of the aged.
Fields of interest: Higher education; Human services; Aging, centers/services; Protestant agencies & churches; Aging.

Type of support: General/operating support; Continuing support; Building/renovation; Equipment; Conferences/seminars; Professorships; Scholarship funds.
Limitations: Giving limited to GA. No grants to individuals, or for endowment funds, research, scholarships, fellowships, or matching gifts; no loans.
Publications: Application guidelines.
Application information: Application form available on foundation's Web site. Application form required.
   Initial approach: Letter
   Copies of proposal: 1
   Deadline(s): Mar. 1
   Board meeting date(s): Apr.
Officers and Directors:* Bishop L. Bevel Jones III,* Chair.; Allen Mast, Secy.; John B. Floyd; Columbus Gilmore; F. Stuart Gulley; Ralph Morrison; Elizabeth C. Ogie; David A. Palmer; E. Jenner Wood III.
Trustee: SunTrust Bank.
EIN: 586026047
Selected grants: The following grants were reported in 2004.

$887,693 to Andrew College, Cuthbert, GA. 2 grants: $433,537 (For grant made in form of stock), $454,156 (For grant made in form of stock).
$887,693 to LaGrange College, La Grange, GA. 2 grants: $433,537 (For grant made in form of stock), $454,156 (For grant made in form of stock).
$314,934 to South Georgia Methodist Home for the Aging, Americus, GA. 2 grants: $156,760 to Magnolia Manor (For grant made in form of stock), $158,174 to Magnolia Manor (For grant made in form of stock).
$198,423 to Epworth By The Sea, Saint Simons Island, GA. 2 grants: $89,976 (For grant made in form of stock), $108,447 (For grant made in form of stock).
$67,795 to Reinhardt College, Waleska, GA. For grant made in form of stock.
$67,795 to Wesleyan College, Macon, GA. For grant made in form of stock.

2464
The Pittulloch Foundation, Inc. ◆
5830 E. Ponce de Leon Ave.
Stone Mountain, GA 30083

Established in 1985 in GA.
Donors: Stone Mountain Industrial Park, Inc.; Pattillo Split Interest Trust; Rockdale Industries, Inc.; Genuine Parts Company; Peter Winters.
Foundation type: Independent foundation.
Financial data (yr. ended 12/31/05): Assets, $30,995,885 (M); gifts received, $521,500; expenditures, $1,659,482; qualifying distributions, $1,568,085; giving activities include $1,558,000 for 25 grants (high: $650,000; low: $500).
Purpose and activities: Support primarily for education, youth development, leadership development and social services.
Fields of interest: Performing arts; Education, fund raising/fund distribution; Education, early childhood education; Elementary school/education; Higher education; Theological school/education; Adult education—literacy, basic skills & GED; Education, reading; Youth development, services; Human services; Youth, services; Leadership development.
Type of support: General/operating support.
Limitations: Applications not accepted. Giving primarily in GA. No grants to individuals.

Application information: Contributes only to pre-selected organizations.
Officers and Directors:* Lynn L. Pattillo-Cohen, Chair.; Michael G. Kerman, Secy.; Robert C. Goddard; Anita Kern; Peter Winter.
EIN: 581651352
Selected grants: The following grants were reported in 2005.
$650,000 to Early Learning Property Management, Tucker, GA.
$250,000 to Georgia State University, Atlanta, GA.
$100,000 to Dalton Public Schools, Dalton, GA.
$100,000 to Georgia Center for Children, Atlanta, GA.
$25,000 to Georgia Council on Economic Education, Atlanta, GA.
$18,000 to Premier Academy, Atlanta, GA.
$15,000 to Georgia Partnership for Excellence in Education, Atlanta, GA.
$500 to Georgia Foundation for Independent Colleges, Atlanta, GA.

2465
Parker Poe Charitable Trust ◇
P.O. Box 1395
Thomasville, GA 31799

Established in 1991 in GA.
Donor: Parker Poe†.
Foundation type: Independent foundation.
Financial data (yr. ended 3/31/05): Assets, $12,179,697 (M); expenditures, $873,881; qualifying distributions, $650,939; giving activities include $649,500 for 22 grants (high: $138,000; low: $1,000).
Purpose and activities: Giving primarily for education, the arts, particularly to an opera association, and a cultural center; funding also for land preservation, education, health associations, and human services.
Fields of interest: Arts, multipurpose centers/programs; Performing arts; Performing arts, opera; Arts; Elementary/secondary education; Higher education; Education; Environment, land resources; Health organizations, association; Human services; YM/YWCAs & YM/YWHAs; Federated giving programs.
Limitations: Applications not accepted. Giving primarily in GA; funding also in FL and NY. No grants to individuals.
Application information: Contributes only to pre-selected organizations.
Trustees: M.H. Allen; Kate Ireland.
EIN: 596968647

2466
The Poole Family Charitable Trust ◇
c/o James P. Poole
3549 Paces Ferry Rd. N.W.
Atlanta, GA 30327-2931

Established in 1997 in GA.
Donors: Dorothy Gay Poole; James P. Poole.
Foundation type: Independent foundation.
Financial data (yr. ended 12/31/04): Assets, $774,080 (M); gifts received, $1,205,700; expenditures, $607,890; qualifying distributions, $606,875; giving activities include $606,875 for 15 grants (high: $150,000; low: $1,875).

Purpose and activities: Giving primarily for education, community development, and religious purposes.
Fields of interest: Higher education; Community development; Religion, research.
Limitations: Applications not accepted. Giving primarily in GA. No grants to individuals.
Application information: Contributes only to pre-selected organizations.
Trustees: Dorothy Gay Poole; James P. Poole.
EIN: 586335604

2467
The Pope Foundation ◇
655A Lambert Dr. N.E.
Atlanta, GA 30324-4125

Established in 1997 in GA.
Donor: Mark C. Pope III.
Foundation type: Independent foundation.
Financial data (yr. ended 12/31/05): Assets, $5,400,314 (M); expenditures, $777,992; qualifying distributions, $773,436; giving activities include $761,044 for 75 grants (high: $200,000; low: $50).
Purpose and activities: Giving primarily for health organizations.
Fields of interest: Historic preservation/historical societies; Education; Health organizations, association; Digestive diseases.
Type of support: General/operating support.
Limitations: Applications not accepted. No grants to individuals.
Application information: Contributes only to pre-selected organizations.
Trustee: Mark C. Pope III.
EIN: 586353574
Selected grants: The following grants were reported in 2004.
$225,000 to Lovett School, Atlanta, GA.

2468
James Hyde Porter Testamentary Trust ◇
c/o SunTrust Bank
P.O. Box 4248
Macon, GA 31208 (478) 741-2265

Established in 1949 in GA.
Donor: James Hyde Porter†.
Foundation type: Independent foundation.
Financial data (yr. ended 12/31/05): Assets, $11,510,902 (M); expenditures, $478,711; qualifying distributions, $447,235; giving activities include $447,235 for 41 grants (high: $45,000; low: $500).
Purpose and activities: Giving for higher education, health and social services, cultural programs, and civic affairs.
Fields of interest: Museums; Literature; Historic preservation/historical societies; Arts; Secondary school/education; Higher education; Libraries/library science; Youth development; Human services; Developmentally disabled, centers & services; Protestant agencies & churches.
Type of support: Building/renovation; Seed money; Matching/challenge support.
Limitations: Giving strictly limited to Bibb and Newton counties, GA. No grants to individuals, or for endowment funds, research programs, scholarships, or fellowships; no loans.
Publications: Application guidelines.

Application information: Application form required.
Initial approach: Telephone
Copies of proposal: 7
Deadline(s): Submit proposal preferably in Mar.; deadline Apr. 20
Board meeting date(s): June
Managers: Rodney M. Browne; Mayor Jack Ellis; Ben F. Hendricks; Katherine M. Kalish; Steve Krueger; Tommy Olmstead; Henry Patton; Ed Sell III; Aaron Varner; Rev. William Wade.
Trustee: SunTrust Bank.
EIN: 586034882
Selected grants: The following grants were reported in 2004.
$50,000 to Museum of Arts and Sciences, Macon, GA. For operating support.
$41,733 to Wesleyan College, Macon, GA. For operating support.
$30,000 to Bibb County Department of Family and Childrens Services, Macon, GA. For operating support.
$30,000 to Macon Rescue Mission, Macon, GA. For operating support.
$30,000 to Theater Macon, Macon, GA. For operating support.
$25,000 to Boys and Girls Clubs of Central Georgia, Macon, GA. For operating support.
$25,000 to Newton County Library System, Covington, GA. For operating support.
$25,000 to Progressive Christian Academy, Macon, GA. For operating support.
$25,000 to Tubman African-American Museum, Macon, GA. For operating support.
$15,000 to South Georgia Methodist Home for the Aging, Americus, GA. For operating support.

2469
Forrest & Helen Ramser Charitable Foundation, Inc.
c/o SunTrust Bank
MC GA-Athens-8216
P.O. Box 4418
Atlanta, GA 30302
Contact: Elaine Buck

Established in 1998 in GA.
Donors: Forrest L. Ramser; Helen M. Ramser.
Foundation type: Independent foundation.
Financial data (yr. ended 12/31/05): Assets, $140,419 (M); gifts received, $150,000; expenditures, $357,699; qualifying distributions, $353,004; giving activities include $353,004 for 19 grants (high: $200,000; low: $1,000).
Fields of interest: Higher education, college; Human services; Youth, services; Federated giving programs; Christian agencies & churches.
Limitations: Giving primarily in GA.
Application information: Application form not required.
Deadline(s): None
Officers: Forrest L. Ramser, Pres.; Helen M. Ramser, V.P.; Janet L. Burd, Secy.-Treas.
EIN: 582433100
Selected grants: The following grants were reported in 2004.
$200,000 to Atlanta Christian College, East Point, GA.
$26,000 to TCM International, Indianapolis, IN.
$25,000 to Fellowship of Associates of Medical Evangelism (FAME), Indianapolis, IN.
$23,181 to Athens Christian Church, Athens, GA.
$16,667 to Milligan College, Milligan College, TN.

$7,500 to United Way of Northeast Georgia, Athens, GA.

$7,000 to Emmanuel School of Religion, Johnson City, TN.

$5,000 to Christian Campus Fellowship, Athens, GA.

$5,000 to Christian City Home for Children, Union City, GA.

$2,000 to Southwest Christian Hospice, Union City, GA.

2470
Realan Foundation, Inc. ✧
1201 W. Peachtree St. N.W., Ste. 5000
Atlanta, GA 30309

Established in 1985 in GA.
Donor: J. Rex Fuqua.
Foundation type: Independent foundation.
Financial data (yr. ended 12/31/05): Assets, $10,623,851 (M); gifts received, $1,687,526; expenditures, $696,321; qualifying distributions, $622,228; giving activities include $615,972 for grants.
Purpose and activities: Giving primarily for education, children and youth, and human services.
Fields of interest: Education; Mental health/crisis services, single organization support; Human services; Children/youth, services.
Limitations: Applications not accepted. Giving primarily in Atlanta, GA. No grants to individuals.
Application information: Contributes only to pre-selected organizations.
Officers and Directors:* J. Rex Fuqua,* Pres.; Duvall S. Fuqua,* V.P.; John G. Wright, Secy.-Treas.
EIN: 581648407
Selected grants: The following grants were reported in 2004.
$220,924 to Duke University, Durham, NC.
$125,000 to Cathedral of Saint Philip, Atlanta, GA.
$25,000 to Inner Harbour, Douglasville, GA.
$22,000 to Camp Sunshine, Decatur, GA.
$15,000 to United Way of Metropolitan Atlanta, Atlanta, GA.
$10,000 to Sheridan Arts Foundation, Telluride, CO.
$10,000 to Trinity School, Atlanta, GA.
$9,200 to Atlanta Botanical Garden, Atlanta, GA.
$9,000 to George West Mental Health Foundation, Atlanta, GA.
$8,000 to Robert W. Woodruff Arts Center, Atlanta, GA.

2471
Charles & Catherine B. Rice Foundation ✧ ☆
c/o Harris MYCFO, Inc.
3348 Peachtree Rd. N.E., Ste 500
Atlanta, GA 30326

Established in 2004 in GA.
Donor: Charles B. Rice, Sr.
Foundation type: Independent foundation.
Financial data (yr. ended 12/31/05): Assets, $10,229,347 (M); expenditures, $556,898; qualifying distributions, $502,586; giving activities include $502,586 for grants.
Fields of interest: Historic preservation/historical societies; Higher education; Environment; Human services.

Limitations: Applications not accepted. Giving primarily in GA, with some emphasis on Atlanta. No grants to individuals.
Application information: Contributes only to pre-selected organizations.
Officer: Allan J. Zachariah, Secy.
Trustees: Catherine B. Rice; Charles B. Rice, Sr.
EIN: 201957591

2472
The Rich Foundation, Inc.
11 Piedmont Ctr., Ste. 204
Atlanta, GA 30305 (404) 262-2266
Contact: Anne Poland Berg, Grant Consultant

Incorporated in 1943 in GA.
Donor: Rich's, Inc.
Foundation type: Independent foundation.
Financial data (yr. ended 1/31/06): Assets, $49,702,816 (M); expenditures, $2,401,780; qualifying distributions, $2,239,143; giving activities include $2,134,500 for 72 grants (high: $200,000; low: $2,500).
Purpose and activities: Giving primarily for the performing arts and other cultural programs, higher education, and social services, including programs for the homeless and people with AIDS. Support also for youth agencies, hospitals, and for research in heart disease.
Fields of interest: Performing arts, theater; Arts; Higher education; Environment; Hospitals (general); Health care; Health organizations, association; Heart & circulatory research; Human services; Children/youth, services; Homeless, human services; Aging; Disabilities, people with; AIDS, people with; Economically disadvantaged; Homeless.
Type of support: General/operating support; Annual campaigns; Capital campaigns; Building/renovation; Equipment; Endowments; Research; Technical assistance.
Limitations: Giving limited to the Atlanta, GA, area. No support for religious, political or fraternal organizations. No grants to individuals, or for matching gifts, conferences and seminars, fundraising luncheons or dinners, sporting events, and accumulated debt; no loans.
Publications: Application guidelines.
Application information: Only 1 copy of IRS determination letter and audited financial statement is needed. Application form required.
  Initial approach: Letter
  Copies of proposal: 5
  Deadline(s): Dec. 15, Mar. 15, June 15, and Sept. 15
  Board meeting date(s): Feb., May, Aug., and Nov.
  Final notification: 2 weeks after quarterly meeting
Officers and Trustees:* Joel Goldberg,* Pres.; Thomas J. Asher,* V.P. and Secy.; Margaret S. Weiller, Treas.; David S. Baker.
EIN: 586038037
Selected grants: The following grants were reported in 2005.
$200,000 to Robert W. Woodruff Arts Center, Atlanta, GA.
$150,000 to High Museum of Art, Atlanta, GA.
$125,000 to Emory University, Atlanta, GA.
$100,000 to United Way.
$50,000 to Alliance Theater Company, Atlanta, GA.
$50,000 to Teach for America, New York, NY.
$40,000 to Hands On Atlanta, Atlanta, GA.
$25,000 to American Red Cross.
$10,000 to Atlanta Urban Ministry, Atlanta, GA.

$10,000 to Theatrical Outfit, Atlanta, GA.

2473
J. Mack Robinson Foundation ✧
c/o Peachtree Insurance Ctr.
4370 Peachtree Rd. N.E.
Atlanta, GA 30319-3023 (404) 231-2111
Contact: J. Mack Robinson, Tr.

Established in 1987 in GA.
Donors: J. Mack Robinson; Jill Robinson; Robin Robinson.
Foundation type: Independent foundation.
Financial data (yr. ended 12/31/05): Assets, $20,610,587 (M); gifts received, $200,000; expenditures, $1,116,585; qualifying distributions, $1,089,168; giving activities include $1,089,168 for 9+ grants (high: $600,000).
Purpose and activities: Giving primarily for education.
Fields of interest: Arts; Secondary school/education; Higher education; Christian agencies & churches.
Limitations: Giving limited to GA, with emphasis on Atlanta. No grants to individuals.
Application information:
  Initial approach: Letter
  Deadline(s): None
Trustee: J. Mack Robinson.
Number of staff: 1 part-time professional.
EIN: 581758256
Selected grants: The following grants were reported in 2004.
$1,100,000 to Georgia State University Foundation, Atlanta, GA. For unrestricted support.
$525,200 to Second Ponce de Leon Baptist Church, Atlanta, GA. For unrestricted support.
$250,000 to A New High for Atlanta, Atlanta, GA. For unrestricted support.
$100,000 to Oglethorpe University, Atlanta, GA. For unrestricted support.
$50,000 to United Way of Metropolitan Atlanta, Atlanta, GA. For unrestricted support.
$20,000 to Buckhead Christian Ministry, Atlanta, GA. For unrestricted support.
$20,000 to University System of Georgia Foundation, Atlanta, GA. For unrestricted support.
$19,500 to High Museum of Art, Atlanta, GA. For unrestricted support.
$12,500 to Westminster Schools, Atlanta, GA. For unrestricted support.
$10,000 to Metropolitan Atlanta Arts Fund, Atlanta, GA. For unrestricted support.

2474
The Rockdale Foundation, Inc. ✧
c/o David D. Weitnauer
2200 Century Pkwy., Ste. 100
Atlanta, GA 30345 (678) 365-4750
FAX: (678) 365-4752; E-mail: info@rockdalefdn.org; Additional tel.: (678) 365-4757; URL: http://www.rockdalefdn.org

Established in 1995 in GA.
Donor: Robert Pattillo Properties, Inc.
Foundation type: Independent foundation.
Financial data (yr. ended 12/31/05): Assets, $2,508,882 (M); gifts received, $452,305; expenditures, $1,689,604; qualifying distributions,

$1,544,622; giving activities include $1,035,999 for 121 grants (high: $356,570; low: $35).
Purpose and activities: The foundation primarily supports organizations involved with education and microfinance.
Fields of interest: Elementary/secondary school reform; Education.
International interests: Cuba; Middle East.
Type of support: Program development; Conferences/seminars; Technical assistance; Program evaluation; Employee matching gifts; Matching/challenge support.
Limitations: Applications not accepted. Giving on a national and international basis, with emphasis on the metropolitan Atlanta, GA, area, North Africa, Cuba, and the Middle East. No grants to individuals.
Publications: Annual report.
Application information: Contributes only to pre-selected organizations.
Officers and Directors:* Robert A. Pattillo,* Pres.; James H. Topple,* Secy.; Rev. Joanna Adams; Ricardo Carvalho; Winsome Hawkins; Bob Lupton; Kathleen Barksdale Pattillo.
Number of staff: 2 full-time professional; 2 full-time support.
EIN: 582147850
Selected grants: The following grants were reported in 2004.
$225,000 to ACCION International, Boston, MA. 2 grants: $200,000, $25,000
$104,585 to Catholic Relief Services, Baltimore, MD.
$25,000 to Teach for America, Atlanta, GA.
$24,000 to Evangelical Theological Seminary, Osijek, Croatia. 2 grants: $9,000, $15,000.
$21,500 to EARTH University Foundation, Atlanta, GA.
$20,000 to Tech High Foundation, Atlanta, GA.
$5,000 to Atlanta Committee for Public Education, Atlanta, GA.
$2,500 to Southern Center for International Studies, Atlanta, GA.

2475
O. Wayne Rollins Foundation ✧
c/o RFA Mgmt. Co., Inc.
P.O. Box 647
Atlanta, GA 30301-0647
Contact: Amy Rollins Kreisler, Exec. Dir.
E-mail: akreisler@lor.com

Established in 1967 in GA.
Donors: O. Wayne Rollins†; Grace C. Rollins.
Foundation type: Independent foundation.
Financial data (yr. ended 12/31/04): Assets, $66,001,706 (M); gifts received, $625,000; expenditures, $4,065,442; qualifying distributions, $3,272,005; giving activities include $3,240,000 for 40 grants (high: $1,000,000; low: $1,000).
Purpose and activities: Giving primarily for higher education, as well as for health care, children and youth services, and to a United Methodist church.
Fields of interest: Arts; Elementary school/ education; Higher education; Education; Speech/ hearing centers; Public health; Health care; Learning disorders; Medical research, institute; Children/ youth, services; Community development; Foundations (community); Protestant agencies & churches.
Type of support: Building/renovation; Scholarship funds.
Limitations: Applications not accepted. Giving primarily in GA. No grants to individuals.

Application information: Contributes only to pre-selected organizations.
Board meeting date(s): Nov.
Officer: Amy Rollins Kreisler, Exec. Dir.
Trustees: Gary W. Rollins; R. Randall Rollins; H.B. Tippie.
EIN: 586066677
Selected grants: The following grants were reported in 2003.
$1,015,000 to Emory University, Atlanta, GA.
$549,414 to Atlanta Speech School, Atlanta, GA.
$100,000 to Foundation of Wesley Woods, Atlanta, GA.
$30,000 to Young Harris College, Young Harris, GA.
$14,000 to Trinity School, Atlanta, GA.
$7,500 to Berry College, Mount Berry, GA.
$5,000 to University of Georgia, Athens, GA.
$2,500 to Dalton State College, Dalton, GA.
$2,500 to LaGrange College, La Grange, GA.
$2,500 to Shorter College, Rome, GA.

2476
Rosenberg Family Foundation, Inc. ✧
1 National Dr.
Atlanta, GA 30336-1631 (404) 696-9440
Contact: H. Jerome Rosenberg III, Tr.

Established in 1995 in GA.
Donors: H. Jerome Rosenberg III; Dulcy D. Rosenberg; National Distributing Co., Inc.
Foundation type: Independent foundation.
Financial data (yr. ended 12/31/05): Assets, $948,548 (M); gifts received, $540,000; expenditures, $693,842; qualifying distributions, $693,842; giving activities include $684,713 for 30 grants (high: $206,625; low: $18).
Purpose and activities: Giving primarily for Jewish organizations; funding also for health associations, human services, and the arts.
Fields of interest: Museums (art); Arts; Higher education; Health organizations, association; Medical research, institute; Cancer research; Human services; Children/youth, services; Jewish federated giving programs; Jewish agencies & temples.
Limitations: Giving primarily in Atlanta, GA.
Application information: Application form not required.
Initial approach: Letter
Deadline(s): None
Trustees: Dulcy D. Rosenberg; H. Jerome Rosenberg III.
EIN: 582166389

2477
The RTM Foundation, Inc. ✧
5995 Barfield Rd. N.E.
Atlanta, GA 30328 (404) 705-1398

Established in 1986 in GA.
Donors: RTM, Inc.; RTM Restaurant Group.
Foundation type: Company-sponsored foundation.
Financial data (yr. ended 12/31/04): Assets, $7,269 (M); gifts received, $375,000; expenditures, $374,755; qualifying distributions, $374,617; giving activities include $374,607 for 16 grants (high: $101,649; low: $250).
Purpose and activities: The foundation supports camps, community foundations, and organizations involved with arts and culture, education, health, youth baseball, and human services.

Fields of interest: Performing arts; Arts; Elementary/secondary education; Higher education; Education; Health care; Recreation, camps; Athletics/sports, baseball; Human services; Youth, services; Foundations (community).
Type of support: General/operating support.
Limitations: Applications not accepted. Giving primarily in Atlanta, GA. No grants to individuals.
Application information: Contributes only to pre-selected organizations.
Officers and Directors:* Dennis E. Cooper,* Chair. and Exec. Dir.; Russell V. Umphenour, Jr.,* C.E.O.; Sharon S. Umphenour; J. Russell Welch.
EIN: 581662253
Selected grants: The following grants were reported in 2004.
$101,649 to Woodward Academy, College Park, GA. For general support.
$100,000 to Kennesaw State University Foundation, Kennesaw, GA. For general support.
$50,000 to East Lake Community Foundation, Atlanta, GA. For general support.
$40,000 to Royal Family Kids Camp, Santa Ana, CA. For general support.
$35,000 to East Cobb Baseball, Marietta, GA. For general support.

2478
Russell Charitable Trust ✧ ☆
P.O. Box 1064
Decatur, GA 30031
Application address: c/o Judy A. Moore, 394 Holly Hill Dr., Columbus, NC 28722, tel.: (828) 894-8293

Established in 1960 in ME.
Donor: H.M. Russell.
Foundation type: Independent foundation.
Financial data (yr. ended 7/31/05): Assets, $729,665 (M); expenditures, $445,436; qualifying distributions, $421,896; giving activities include $368,500 for 11 grants (high: $100,000; low: $8,500).
Purpose and activities: Giving to religious-related institutions in the fields of higher education, medical and health-related human and animal services, media and communication which seek to promote quality human and animal services, and to institutions serving youth and the elderly.
Fields of interest: Higher education; Animals/ wildlife; Health care; Human services; Community development; Protestant agencies & churches; Disabilities, people with.
Type of support: General/operating support; Capital campaigns; Endowments; Seed money.
Limitations: Giving primarily in AZ, GA, ME, NC, and SC. No grants to individuals or churches operating budgets.
Application information:
Initial approach: 1 page letter
Deadline(s): None. Applications not accepted in July and Dec.
Board meeting date(s): Quarterly
Final notification: Grants are made at the beginning of each calendar quarter
Trustees: Ernest J. Arnold; Frances P. Arnold.
Director: Judy A. Moore.
EIN: 016009882
Selected grants: The following grants were reported in 2004.
$10,000 to Saint Lukes Hospital, Columbus, NC.
$5,000 to Childrens Literature for Children, Atlanta, GA. For operating support.

2479
The Sapelo Foundation, Inc. ✧

(formerly Sapelo Island Research Foundation, Inc.)
1712 Ellis St., 2nd Fl.
Brunswick, GA 31520 (912) 265-0520
Contact: Phyllis Bowen, Exec. Dir.
FAX: (912) 265-1888;
E-mail: sapelofoundation@mindspring.com;
URL: http://www.sapelofoundation.org

Incorporated in 1949 in GA.
Donor: Richard J. Reynolds, Jr.†.
Foundation type: Independent foundation.
Financial data (yr. ended 6/30/05): Assets,
$33,354,403 (M); expenditures, $2,002,290;
qualifying distributions, $1,877,519; giving
activities include $1,611,519 for 51 grants (high:
$125,000; low: $4,000).
Purpose and activities: The foundation promotes
progressive social change affecting, in particular,
vulnerable populations, rural communities and the
natural environment.
Fields of interest: Environment, public policy;
Environment, air pollution; Environment, toxics;
Environment, water resources; Environment,
forests; Animals/wildlife, preservation/protection;
Legal services, public interest law; Civil liberties,
due process; Civil liberties, death penalty issues;
Civil rights.
Type of support: General/operating support;
Continuing support; Annual campaigns; Program
development; Matching/challenge support.
Limitations: Giving limited to rural and statewide
GA; no support for metro Atlanta projects. No grants
for capital, emergency, or endowment funds, deficit
financing, or publications; no loans.
Publications: Application guidelines; Annual report;
Grants list.
Application information: Visit foundation Web site
for complete application guidelines and procedures;
proposals not accepted by fax or e-mail. Incomplete
proposals are not accepted. Application form
required.
Initial approach: Phone inquiry or visit Web site
Copies of proposal: 1
Deadline(s): Mar. 1 and Sept. 1
Board meeting date(s): May and Nov.
Final notification: Within two weeks following
board meeting
Officers and Trustees:* Susan Lehman
Carmichael,* Pres.; Henry H. Carey,* V.P.; William
K. Broker,* Secy.; Irene Reynolds, Treas.; Phyllis
Bowen, Exec. Dir.; Nicole Bagley; Katherine R. Grant;
Bettieanne Hart; Russell Long; Nan Grogan Orrock;
Annemarie Reynolds.
Number of staff: 2 full-time professional.
EIN: 580827472
Selected grants: The following grants were reported
in 2005.
$80,000 to Georgia Wildlife Federation, Covington,
GA. 2 grants: $40,000 each
$40,000 to Georgia Center for Law in the Public
Interest, Atlanta, GA.
$40,000 to Georgia Conservancy, Atlanta, GA.
$40,000 to Southern Environmental Law Center,
Charlottesville, VA.
$40,000 to Upper Chattahoochee Riverkeeper
Fund, Atlanta, GA.
$20,000 to Carolina Peace Resource Center,
Columbia, SC.
$20,000 to Center for Policy Alternatives, DC.
$20,000 to Glynn Environmental Coalition,
Brunswick, GA.

$20,000 to League of Women Voters of Georgia,
Atlanta, GA.

2480
The Savannah Community Foundation

(formerly The Savannah Foundation)
7393 Hodgson Memorial Dr., Ste. 204
Savannah, GA 31406 (912) 921-7700
Contact: K. Russell Simpson, Pres.
FAX: (912) 921-3230;
E-mail: russ@savfoundation.org

Established in 1953 in GA; re-incorporated as a
community foundation in 1986.
Foundation type: Community foundation.
Financial data (yr. ended 6/30/06): Assets,
$16,225,605 (M); gifts received, $1,925,014;
expenditures, $2,563,722; giving activities include
$2,257,918 for 859 grants (high: $125,000; low:
$100).
Purpose and activities: The foundation supports
organizations involved with arts, education, health,
human services, and religion.
Fields of interest: Arts; Education; Health care;
Health organizations, association; Medical
research, institute; Human services; Religion.
Type of support: General/operating support; Annual
campaigns; Building/renovation; Equipment; Land
acquisition; Endowments; Emergency funds;
Program development; Conferences/seminars;
Publication; Seed money; Scholarship funds; In-kind
gifts.
Limitations: Giving limited to southeastern GA. No
grants to individuals (except for scholarships), or for
continuing support, deficit financing,
foundation-managed projects, or matching or
challenge grants; no program-related investments.
Publications: Application guidelines; Financial
statement; Grants list; Informational brochure
(including application guidelines).
Application information: Only one copy of
application is required if e-mailed to the foundation.
Application form required.
Initial approach: Letter or telephone
Copies of proposal: 4
Deadline(s): None
Board meeting date(s): Jan., Apr., July, and Oct.
Final notification: Varies
Officers and Directors:* Bert M. Tenenbaum,*
Chair.; K. Russell Simpson, Pres.; Al Kennickell,
Jr.,* V.P.; Dolly Chisholm,* Secy.; S. Stewart
Bromley,* Treas.; Dale C. Critz, Jr.; Helen Downing;
Linda Evans; Verne Hartson; John C. Helmken II;
Russell C. Jacobs III; Michael F. Kemp; Melanie L.
Marks; Charles McMillan, Sr.; Paul D. Meyer;
Howard J. Morrison, Jr.; David Paddison.
Number of staff: 1 part-time professional; 1
part-time support.
EIN: 586033468

2481
Sawnee Mountain Foundation, Inc. ✧ ☆

725 Pilgrim Mill Rd.
Cumming, GA 30040

Established in 2001 in GA.
Donor: Forsyth County, GA.
Foundation type: Independent foundation.
Financial data (yr. ended 2/28/05): Assets, $0 (M);
expenditures, $318,352; qualifying distributions,

$316,838; giving activities include $316,838 for 2
grants (high: $314,413; low: $2,425).
Purpose and activities: The foundation was
established for the sole purpose of managing,
maintaining, repairing and improving conserved
lands in Forsyth County, GA.
Fields of interest: Environment.
Limitations: Applications not accepted. Giving
limited to Forsyth County, GA. No grants to
individuals.
Application information: Contributes only to
pre-selected organizations.
Officer: Mary Helen McGruder, Chair.
Directors: John Cromartie, Jr.; Chris Deming; John
McGruder.
EIN: 582631867

2482
Scientific-Atlanta Foundation, Inc. ✧

5030 Sugarloaf Pkwy.
P.O. Box 465447
Lawrenceville, GA 30042-5447
Contact: William F. McCargo, V.P.
E-mail: safoundation@sciatl.com; URL: http://
www.sciatl.com/aboutus/SAFoundation.htm

Established in 1998 in GA.
Donor: Scientific-Atlanta, Inc.
Foundation type: Company-sponsored foundation.
Financial data (yr. ended 6/30/05): Assets,
$17,449,175 (M); gifts received, $3,700,000;
expenditures, $1,647,668; qualifying distributions,
$1,486,721; giving activities include $1,083,318
for 105 grants (high: $189,000; low: $50), and
$212,095 for employee matching gifts.
Purpose and activities: The foundation supports
organizations involved with arts and culture,
education, health, human services, economic
development, and civic affairs.
Fields of interest: Arts, cultural/ethnic awareness;
Arts; Education; Health care; Human services;
Economic development; Science, formal/general
education; Mathematics; Public affairs.
International interests: Canada; Mexico.
Type of support: General/operating support;
Continuing support; Annual campaigns; Capital
campaigns; Building/renovation; Equipment; Land
acquisition; Endowments; Debt reduction;
Emergency funds; Program development;
Conferences/seminars; Curriculum development;
Internship funds; Scholarship funds; Technical
assistance; Employee-related scholarships; In-kind
gifts; Matching/challenge support.
Limitations: Giving primarily in Cupertino, CA,
Orlando, FL, Atlanta, GA, and Chicago, IL; some
giving also in Toronto and Vancouver, Canada, and
Juarez, Mexico. No support for religious
organizations, athletic organizations, or
discriminatory organizations. No grants to
individuals (except for employee-related
scholarships), or for political causes, theological
functions or church-sponsored programs,
conferences, seminars, trips, or tours, or
fundraising activities related to individual
sponsorship.
Application information: Application form not
required.
Initial approach: Proposal
Deadline(s): Mar. through May
Board meeting date(s): As necessary
Final notification: July 31
Officers and Trustees:* J. Lawrence Bradner,*
Pres.; William F. McCargo, V.P. and Secy.; George A.

Steiner, V.P. and Treas.; Julian W. Eidson,* V.P.; Dwight B. Duke; H. Allen Ecker; Wallace G. Haislip; Brian C. Koenig; Gregory Taylor; Michael C. Veysey.
EIN: 582452986
Selected grants: The following grants were reported in 2005.
$189,000 to United Way.
$65,000 to Gwinnett Hospital System Foundation, Lawrenceville, GA.
$51,000 to American Red Cross.
$50,000 to Robert W. Woodruff Arts Center, Atlanta, GA.
$35,000 to American Cancer Society, Atlanta, GA.
$32,500 to Habitat for Humanity International.
$25,300 to National Merit Scholarship Corporation, Evanston, IL.
$25,000 to High Museum of Art, Atlanta, GA.
$25,000 to Junior Achievement.
$20,000 to Community Foundation for Northeast Georgia, Duluth, GA.

2483
Scott Foundation, Inc. ✧
1594 Rainier Falls Dr.
Atlanta, GA   30329

Established in 1980 in GA.
Donor: Milton C. Scott.
Foundation type: Independent foundation.
Financial data (yr. ended 5/31/06): Assets, $1,165,767 (M); expenditures, $510,146; qualifying distributions, $499,704; giving activities include $499,704 for grants.
Fields of interest: Human services; Religion.
Limitations: Giving primarily in the southern U.S.
Officers: David W. Scott, Pres.; Hansford Sams, Jr., Treas.
EIN: 581378681

2484
The Selig Foundation ✧
1100 Spring St. N.W., Ste. 550
Atlanta, GA   30309
Contact: S. Stephen Selig, III, Pres.

Established in 1968.
Donors: Cathy Selig; S. Stephen Selig III; Selig Enterprises, Inc.
Foundation type: Independent foundation.
Financial data (yr. ended 12/31/05): Assets, $111,704 (M); gifts received, $700,000; expenditures, $666,077; qualifying distributions, $665,460; giving activities include $665,460 for 68 grants (high: $374,908; low: $36).
Purpose and activities: Giving primarily for Jewish organizations and federated giving programs; funding also for the arts, education and health associations.
Fields of interest: Museums (art); Arts; Higher education; Education; Health organizations, association; Recreation, camps; Jewish federated giving programs; Jewish agencies & temples.
Limitations: Giving primarily in Atlanta, GA. No grants to individuals.
Application information:
Initial approach: Proposal
Deadline(s): None
Officers: S. Stephen Selig III, Pres.; Cathy Selig, Treas.
EIN: 586074209

Selected grants: The following grants were reported in 2003.
$586,595 to Jewish Federation of Greater Atlanta, Atlanta, GA. For general support.
$114,945 to Temple, The, Atlanta, GA. For general support.
$30,000 to High Museum of Art, Atlanta, GA. For general support.
$22,840 to Davis Academy, Atlanta, GA. For general support.
$22,600 to American Jewish Committee, Atlanta, GA. For general support.
$10,600 to Shepherd Center, Atlanta, GA. For general support.
$10,500 to Camp Sunshine, Decatur, GA. For general support.
$10,000 to Robert W. Woodruff Arts Center, Atlanta, GA. For general support.
$5,100 to United Jewish Communities, New York, NY. For general support.
$3,150 to Atlanta History Center, Atlanta, GA. For general support.

2485
Servant's Heart Foundation, Inc. ✧
(formerly For HIS Adopted Children, Inc.)
3414 Peachtree Rd. N.E., Ste. 1144
Atlanta, GA   30326

Established in 1995 in GA.
Donors: Paul A. Neff; Verne Murray.
Foundation type: Independent foundation.
Financial data (yr. ended 12/31/04): Assets, $12,291,545 (M); expenditures, $1,043,641; qualifying distributions, $887,942; giving activities include $764,372 for 36+ grants (high: $230,600).
Purpose and activities: Giving primarily for religion.
Fields of interest: Higher education; Christian agencies & churches.
Limitations: Applications not accepted. Giving primarily in CA. No grants to individuals.
Application information: Contributes only to pre-selected organizations.
Officer: Patricia A. Rothenberger, Secy.
Directors: Richard Haugen; Kathy A. Neff; Paul A. Neff.
EIN: 582218044
Selected grants: The following grants were reported in 2004.
$230,600 to Mariners Church, Irvine, CA.
$55,291 to Every Generation Ministries, Orange, CA.
$33,333 to Prison Fellowship Ministries, Lansdowne, VA.
$25,000 to YouthBuilders, San Juan Capistrano, CA.
$5,000 to Gathering, The, Tyler, TX.
$4,000 to World Impact, Los Angeles, CA.
$2,500 to Boy Scouts of America, Santa Ana, CA.
$1,000 to Priority Living, Orange, CA.

2486
The SF Foundation II ✧
c/o Phillip E. Sadler
7000 Central Pkwy., Ste. 650
Atlanta, GA   30328

Established in 1996 in GA.
Donors: Dorothy C. Sadler; Phillip E. Sadler.
Foundation type: Independent foundation.

Financial data (yr. ended 12/31/05): Assets, $5,861,499 (M); expenditures, $504,334; qualifying distributions, $501,066; giving activities include $501,066 for 33 grants (high: $110,000; low: $500).
Purpose and activities: Giving primarily to education, animal welfare, health care, federated giving programs, and religious organizations.
Fields of interest: Higher education, university; Animal welfare; Health care; Federated giving programs; Protestant agencies & churches.
Limitations: Applications not accepted. Giving primarily in GA. No grants to individuals.
Application information: Contributes only to pre-selected organizations.
Trustees: Dorothy C. Sadler; Phillip E. Sadler.
EIN: 582277136

2487
William F. Shallenberger Trust Fund ✧
1201 W. Peachtree St. N.W., Ste. 4200
Atlanta, GA   30309-3424   (404) 881-7000
Contact: Benjamin T. White, Mgr.

Established in 1980 in GA.
Foundation type: Independent foundation.
Financial data (yr. ended 12/31/05): Assets, $9,275,563 (M); expenditures, $476,736; qualifying distributions, $409,000; giving activities include $405,000 for 25 grants (high: $50,000; low: $5,000).
Purpose and activities: Giving primarily for health, children, youth, and social services.
Fields of interest: Education; Hospitals (general); Health care; Food banks; Human services; Children/youth, services; Aging, centers/services; Aging.
Limitations: Giving primarily in Atlanta, GA. No grants to individuals.
Application information:
Initial approach: Letter
Deadline(s): None
Manager: Benjamin T. White.
Trustees: Mark P. Pentecost, Jr., M.D.; Frank Wilson, M.D.; Charles K. Wright, M.D.
EIN: 581403009
Selected grants: The following grants were reported in 2005.
$50,000 to Atlanta Community Food Bank, Atlanta, GA.
$50,000 to Atlanta Union Mission, Atlanta, GA.
$50,000 to Midtown Assistance Center, Atlanta, GA.
$30,000 to Piedmont Hospital, Atlanta, GA.
$15,000 to A. G. Rhodes Home, Atlanta, GA.
$10,000 to Genesis Shelter, Atlanta, GA.
$5,000 to Atlanta Alliance on Developmental Disabilities, Atlanta, GA.
$5,000 to Kids Health, Atlanta, GA.
$5,000 to Samaritan House of Atlanta, Atlanta, GA.

2488
Sheffield-Harrold Charitable Trust ✧
61 Brighton Rd. N.E.
Atlanta, GA   30309
Contact: Bradley Hale, Tr.

Established in 1984 in GA.
Donors: Frank Sheffield; Anne S. Hale; Bradley Hale.
Foundation type: Independent foundation.

Financial data (yr. ended 12/31/05): Assets, $2,447,113 (M); expenditures, $431,829; qualifying distributions, $363,232; giving activities include $347,873 for 23 grants (high: $70,500; low: $50).

Purpose and activities: Giving primarily to the arts, particularly for historical preservation and institutions, as well as for education, and human services.

Fields of interest: Historic preservation/historical societies; Arts; Higher education; Human services; Foundations (community); Christian agencies & churches.

Limitations: Applications not accepted. Giving primarily in Atlanta, GA. No grants to individuals.

Application information: Contributes only to pre-selected organizations.

Trustee: Bradley Hale.

EIN: 586185174

Selected grants: The following grants were reported in 2004.

$141,675 to Alabama Archives and History Foundation, Montgomery, AL.

$29,000 to National Trust for Historic Preservation, DC.

$20,100 to Sweet Briar College, Sweet Briar, VA.

$15,255 to Atlanta History Center, Atlanta, GA.

$12,905 to Marengo County Historical Society, Demopolis, AL.

$11,050 to Georgia Trust for Historic Preservation, Atlanta, GA.

$10,325 to Alabama Shakespeare Festival, Montgomery, AL.

$625 to Society of the Cincinnati, DC.

$500 to Schenck School, Atlanta, GA.

$250 to Westminster Schools, Atlanta, GA.

2489
The M. L. Simpson Foundation Trust ▼ ✧ ☆
300 W. Third St.
Jackson, GA 30233

Donor: L. Simpson Charitable Remainder Trust.
Foundation type: Independent foundation.
Financial data (yr. ended 12/31/05): Assets, $10,897,914 (M); gifts received, $16,037,451; expenditures, $8,410,998; qualifying distributions, $8,126,000; giving activities include $8,126,000 for 7 grants (high: $5,000,000; low: $1,000).

Purpose and activities: Giving primarily for Baptist ministries, including a church and a seminary; funding also for medical research and an eye center.

Fields of interest: Medical research, institute; Eye research; Athletics/sports, football; Human services; Protestant agencies & churches.

Limitations: Applications not accepted. Giving primarily in Jacksonville, FL and Atlanta, GA.

Application information: Unsolicited requests for funds not accepted.

Trustees: Thomas M. Aaberg; Martha Almond; William Foege; Frederick W. Owens; Alicia Philipp; Charles F. Stanley.

EIN: 586418299

2490
Lewis Hall & Mildred Sasser Singletary Foundation, Inc.
P.O. Box 1095
Thomasville, GA 31799
Contact: Nina Jones

FAX: (229) 226-2474;
E-mail: njones@broadstreetoffices.com

Established in 1990.
Donor: Lewis Hall Singletary†.
Foundation type: Independent foundation.
Financial data (yr. ended 12/31/05): Assets, $34,643,096 (M); expenditures, $1,808,856; qualifying distributions, $1,647,890; giving activities include $1,647,890 for 53 grants (high: $404,090; low: $500; average: $10,000–$50,000).

Purpose and activities: Giving primarily for kids at risk mainly in the Southeast and primarily in southwest GA.

Fields of interest: Libraries (public); Libraries (special); Environmental education; YM/YWCAs & YM/YWHAs; Children, adoption.

Type of support: Capital campaigns; Seed money; Matching/challenge support.

Limitations: Giving primarily in the southeastern U.S., with emphasis on Thomas County, GA. No grants to individuals.

Publications: Application guidelines.

Application information: Application form required.
Initial approach: Letter requesting application guidelines
Copies of proposal: 1
Deadline(s): Aug. 31
Board meeting date(s): Nov.
Final notification: Dec.

Officers: Karen L. Singletary, Pres.; Lewis Hall Singletary II, V.P.; Jeanne Hamil, Secy.; Richard L. Singletary, Jr., Treas.

Directors: Greg Hamil; Jeanne S. Hamil; J. Philip Leabo; J. Philip Leabo, Jr.; Karen S. Leabo; Julia Singletary; Rebecca Singletary; Richard L. Singletary; Tim Singletary.

Number of staff: 1 part-time professional.

EIN: 581906094

Selected grants: The following grants were reported in 2004.

$60,000 to Perimeter Church, Duluth, GA.

$60,000 to Vashti Center for Children and Families, Thomasville, GA.

$50,000 to Greater Atlanta Christian Schools, Norcross, GA.

$39,000 to Brookwood School, Thomasville, GA.

$20,000 to Fellowship of Christian Athletes, Atlanta, GA.

$17,000 to Thomasville Landmarks, Thomasville, GA.

$15,000 to Thomasville Cultural Center, Thomasville, GA.

$15,000 to Wellspring of Living Water, Peachtree City, GA.

$10,000 to Presbyterian Homes of Georgia, Atlanta, GA.

$7,500 to Thomasville Community Resource Center, Thomasville, GA.

2491
Hal & John Smith Family Foundation ✧
(formerly Hal L. & Julia T. Smith Foundation)
c/o Bank of America, N.A.
600 Peachtree St., Ste. 1100
Atlanta, GA 30308
Contact: Susan Tante, Trust Off., Bank of America, N.A.

Established about 1962 in GA.
Donors: Hal L. Smith†; Julia T. Smith†.
Foundation type: Independent foundation.

Financial data (yr. ended 12/31/04): Assets, $5,898,244 (M); expenditures, $646,450; qualifying distributions, $620,669; giving activities include $610,000 for 9 grants (high: $400,000; low: $1,000; average: $1,000–$125,000).

Purpose and activities: Giving primarily for higher education; some funding also to health organizations, human services, and Christian organizations, particularly to a Presbyterian church.

Fields of interest: Higher education; Education; Health care, clinics/centers; Human services; Christian agencies & churches.

Type of support: Scholarship funds; Matching/challenge support; Fellowships; Endowments; Capital campaigns.

Limitations: Giving primarily in Atlanta, GA. No support for art organizations. No grants to individuals.

Application information: Application form not required.
Initial approach: Letter
Deadline(s): None

Officers and Trustees:* John E. Smith II,* Chair.; Bessie Bonister, Secy.; Robert G. Edge; Claiborne S. Jones; Hayden P. Smith; Bank of America, N.A.

EIN: 586025759

2492
The Snodgrass Foundation, Inc. ✧ ☆
3074 Slaton Dr.
Atlanta, GA 30305 (770) 638-0722
Contact: John D. Snodgrass, Tr.

Established in 1997 in GA.
Donor: John D. Snodgrass.
Foundation type: Independent foundation.
Financial data (yr. ended 12/31/04): Assets, $4,828,352 (M); expenditures, $517,370; qualifying distributions, $415,607; giving activities include $414,200 for 22 grants (high: $250,000; low: $500).

Purpose and activities: Giving primarily for Protestant organizations in Atlanta, GA; funding also for historical societies, education, and human services.

Fields of interest: Historical activities; Elementary school/education; Secondary school/education; Human services; Aging, centers/services; Civil rights, advocacy; Community development, service clubs; Protestant agencies & churches.

Limitations: Giving primarily in GA, with emphasis on Atlanta.

Trustee: John D. Snodgrass.
EIN: 582311474

2493
South Family Foundation, Inc. ✧ ☆
c/o John T. South, III
12 Water Witch Crossing
Savannah, GA 31411

Donor: John T. South III.
Foundation type: Operating foundation.
Financial data (yr. ended 12/31/05): Assets, $345,972 (M); expenditures, $338,777; qualifying distributions, $333,000; giving activities include $333,000 for 1 grant.

Purpose and activities: Giving primarily to a Presbyterian church.

Fields of interest: Protestant agencies & churches.

Limitations: Applications not accepted. Giving primarily in GA.
Application information: Contributes only to pre-selected organizations.
Officers: John T. South III, Pres.; Donna M. South, Secy.-Treas.
EIN: 200528181

2494
Southern Company Charitable Foundation, Inc. ☆
241 Ralph McGill Blvd., N.E., BIN 10131
Atlanta, GA 30308-3374
Contact: Susan M. Carter, Secy.

Established in 1999 in GA.
Donor: The Southern Co.
Foundation type: Company-sponsored foundation.
Financial data (yr. ended 12/31/05): Assets, $5,960,061 (M); gifts received, $853,628; expenditures, $1,169,877; qualifying distributions, $1,158,492; giving activities include $670,000 for 15 grants (high: $100,000; low: $1,000), $422,000 for 180 grants to individuals (high: $2,500; low: $500), and $61,361 for employee matching gifts.
Purpose and activities: The foundation supports organizations involved with education, the environment, and disaster relief.
Fields of interest: Education; Environment; Disasters, preparedness/services.
Type of support: Grants to individuals; General/operating support; Continuing support; Annual campaigns; Capital campaigns; Building/renovation; Endowments; Emergency funds; Program development.
Limitations: Giving primarily in AL, FL, GA, and MS. No support for religious organizations or private or secondary schools or non-public foundations. No grants to individuals (except for employee-related emergency assistance grants).
Application information: Multi-year funding is not automatic. Application form not required.
  Initial approach: Proposal
  Copies of proposal: 1
  Deadline(s): None
  Final notification: 1 month
Officers and Directors:* Judy M. Anderson,* Pres.; David R. Altman,* V.P.; Susan M. Carter, Secy.; Roger S. Steffens, Treas.; Dwight Evans.
EIN: 582514027

2495
The Spray Foundation, Inc. ◈
(formerly ACK Foundation, Inc.)
1 Buckhead Plz., Ste. 1005
3060 Peachtree Rd.
Atlanta, GA 30305

Established in 1995 in GA.
Donors: James G. Kenan; Anne R. Kenan; Brutus C. Kenan.
Foundation type: Independent foundation.
Financial data (yr. ended 12/31/05): Assets, $46,789,161 (M); gifts received, $562,182; expenditures, $2,481,145; qualifying distributions, $2,383,581; giving activities include $2,295,000 for 29 grants (high: $425,000; low: $10,000).
Fields of interest: Museums (art); Performing arts, ballet; Arts; Elementary/secondary education; Child development, education; Education, special; Higher

education; Environment, natural resources; Environment; Hospitals (specialty); Speech/hearing centers; End of life care; Alzheimer's disease; Legal services; Housing/shelter, repairs; Human services; Children, services.
Limitations: Applications not accepted. Giving primarily in Atlanta, GA; some giving nationally. No grants to individuals.
Application information: Contributes only to pre-selected organizations.
Officers and Directors:* James G. Kenan III, Pres. and Treas.; Hazel Nystrom,* Secy.; George Branch; Sarah K. Kennedy; Clay Kenan Kirk.
EIN: 582219018
Selected grants: The following grants were reported in 2005.
$235,000 to Atlanta Alliance on Developmental Disabilities, Atlanta, GA.
$200,000 to Atlanta Speech School, Atlanta, GA.
$100,000 to Marcus Institute for Development and Learning, Atlanta, GA.
$100,000 to Metropolitan Atlanta Arts Fund, Atlanta, GA.
$97,500 to HealthCare Chaplaincy, New York, NY.
$90,000 to Lenox Hill Neighborhood House, New York, NY.
$87,500 to Rainforest Alliance, New York, NY.
$50,000 to Lexington School, Lexington, KY.
$30,000 to Bluegrass Conservancy, Lexington, KY.
$25,000 to Salisbury School, Salisbury, CT.

2496
SunTrust Bank, Atlanta Foundation
(formerly Trust Company of Georgia Foundation)
c/o SunTrust Banks, Inc.
P.O. Box 4418, M.C. 041
Atlanta, GA 30302-4418 (404) 588-8250
Contact: Raymond B. King, Secy.
FAX: (404) 724-3082; URL: http://www.suntrustatlantafoundation.org

Trust established in 1959 in GA.
Donors: SunTrust Bank, Atlanta; SunTrust Banks, Inc.; SunTrust Bank.
Foundation type: Company-sponsored foundation.
Financial data (yr. ended 12/31/04): Assets, $13,848,475 (M); gifts received, $301,038; expenditures, $1,416,884; qualifying distributions, $1,401,545; giving activities include $615,175 for 148 grants (high: $50,000; low: $30), and $764,378 for 531 employee matching gifts.
Purpose and activities: The foundation supports organizations involved with arts and culture, education, youth, and community development.
Fields of interest: Visual arts; Performing arts; Arts; Education, fund raising/fund distribution; Higher education; Education; Youth, services; Community development.
Type of support: Capital campaigns; Building/renovation; Equipment; Employee matching gifts.
Limitations: Giving primarily in Clayton, Cobb, DeKalb, Douglas, Fayette, Fulton, Gwinnett, Henry, and Rockdale counties and the metropolitan Atlanta, GA, area. No support for churches or political organizations. No grants to individuals, or for scholarships, fellowships, salaries, maintenance, or debt reduction; no loans.
Publications: Application guidelines; Program policy statement.
Application information: Application form required.
  Initial approach: Download application form and mail to foundation
  Copies of proposal: 1

Deadline(s): Mar. 31, Aug. 31, and Nov. 30
Board meeting date(s): Jan., May, and Oct.
Final notification: Following review
Officers and Distribution Committee:* E. Jenner Wood III,* Chair.; Raymond B. King,* Secy.; L. Phillip Humann; Gary Peacock; James M. Wells.
Trustee: SunTrust Banks, Inc.
Number of staff: 1 full-time professional; 1 full-time support.
EIN: 586026063

2497
The Synovus Foundation ◈
(formerly CB&T Charitable Trust)
c/o Synovus Trust Co.
P.O. Box 23024
Columbus, GA 31902 (706) 644-3496
Contact: Fray McCormick, Dir.

Established in 1969.
Donors: Columbus Bank and Trust Co.; Synovus Financial Corp.; Total System Services, Inc.
Foundation type: Company-sponsored foundation.
Financial data (yr. ended 12/31/04): Assets, $1,010,166 (M); gifts received, $2,779,280; expenditures, $1,777,527; qualifying distributions, $1,777,500; giving activities include $1,777,500 for 31 grants (high: $525,000; low: $5,000).
Purpose and activities: The foundation supports museums and organizations involved with arts and culture, education, human services, and community development.
Fields of interest: Museums; Historic preservation/historical societies; Arts; Elementary/secondary education; Higher education; Education; Children/youth, services; Human services; Community development; Federated giving programs.
Type of support: General/operating support; Annual campaigns; Capital campaigns; Building/renovation; Endowments.
Limitations: Giving primarily in the Columbus, GA, area. No support for religious organizations. No grants to individuals.
Application information: Application form not required.
  Initial approach: Proposal
  Deadline(s): None
  Board meeting date(s): Monthly
Officers and Directors:* Calvin Smyre,* Chair.; Richard W. Ussery,* Vice-Chair.; Steve Melton,* Secy.; Billy Blanchard; Fray McCormick; Teddie Ussery.
Number of staff: 7
EIN: 237024198
Selected grants: The following grants were reported in 2004.
$525,000 to Columbus State University, Columbus, GA.
$300,000 to United Way.
$50,000 to Boys and Girls Club.
$50,000 to Columbus Community Center, Columbus, GA.
$50,000 to Mother Mary School, Phenix City, AL.
$50,000 to Our House.
$50,000 to Salvation Army.
$40,000 to LaGrange College, La Grange, GA.
$20,000 to Florida State University, Tallahassee, FL.
$10,000 to Young Life.

2498
The Terwilliger Family Foundation Charitable Trust ✧

6020 Winterthur Sr.
Atlanta, GA 30328
Contact: Patricia B. Terwilliger, Tr.

Established in 1990 in GA.
Donor: J. Ronald Terwilliger.
Foundation type: Independent foundation.
Financial data (yr. ended 12/31/05): Assets, $11,526,045 (M); expenditures, $658,512; qualifying distributions, $531,932; giving activities include $530,350 for 28 grants (high: $250,000; low: $200).
Purpose and activities: Giving primarily for education, health associations, children and youth services, including a children's healthcare foundation, and to Presbyterian churches.
Fields of interest: Education; Health organizations, association; Human services; Children/youth, services; Residential/custodial care; Protestant agencies & churches.
Limitations: Applications not accepted. Giving primarily in Atlanta, GA. No grants to individuals.
Application information: Contributes only to pre-selected organizations.
Trustees: Margaret Bowman; Tracy T. Dean; Bonnie T. Leadbetter; Patricia B. Terwilliger.
EIN: 586218070
Selected grants: The following grants were reported in 2003.
$100,000 to Link Counseling Center, Atlanta, GA. For capital campaign.
$60,000 to United States Naval Academy Foundation, Annapolis, MD. For capital campaign.
$60,000 to Young Life, Atlanta, GA. For annual fund.
$23,500 to Trinity School, Atlanta, GA. For capital campaign.
$10,000 to Eagle Ranch, Chestnut Mountain, GA. For annual fund.
$10,000 to United Way of Metropolitan Atlanta, Atlanta, GA. For annual campaign.
$5,000 to Forward Atlanta, Atlanta, GA. For capital campaign.
$5,000 to Wellspring of Living Water, Peachtree City, GA. For annual fund.
$2,500 to United Negro College Fund, Fairfax, VA. For annual fund.
$1,000 to Sandy Springs Historic Community Foundation, Atlanta, GA. For annual fund.

2499
The Thoresen Foundation

2725 Woodridge Chase
Canton, GA 30114
Contact: Michael W. Thoresen, Tr.

Established in 1952 in IL.
Donors: William E. Thoresen†; Catherine E. Thoresen†.
Foundation type: Independent foundation.
Financial data (yr. ended 12/31/05): Assets, $47,661,744 (M); expenditures, $3,276,679; qualifying distributions, $2,850,000; giving activities include $2,850,000 for 51 grants (high: $310,000; low: $5,000).
Purpose and activities: Giving primarily for higher education, the environment and wildlife conservation, and to health associations.
Fields of interest: Performing arts, theater; Higher education; Education; Environment; Animals/

wildlife, preservation/protection; Health organizations, association; Cancer research.
Limitations: Applications not accepted. Giving on a national basis. No grants to individuals, or for scholarships.
Application information: Unsolicited requests for funds not accepted.
Board meeting date(s): As required
Trustees: Paul V. O'Connell; Michael W. Thoresen.
EIN: 366102493
Selected grants: The following grants were reported in 2005.
$310,000 to Rocky Mountain Elk Foundation, Missoula, MT.
$174,000 to Theater in the Square, Marietta, GA.
$105,000 to Lees-McRae College, Banner Elk, NC.
$100,000 to Duke University, Durham, NC.
$100,000 to Explorers Club, New York, NY.
$100,000 to Ward Burton Wildlife Foundation, Halifax, VA.
$75,000 to Stagebridge, Oakland, CA.
$50,000 to College of the Ozarks, Point Lookout, MO.
$25,000 to Bring Me A Book Foundation, Mountain View, CA.
$25,000 to Performing Arts Workshop, San Francisco, CA.

2500
The Tull Charitable Foundation ▼

50 Hurt Plz., Ste. 1245
Atlanta, GA 30303 (404) 659-7079
Contact: Barbara Cleveland, Secy.-Treas and Exec. Dir.
URL: http://www.tullfoundation.org

Trust established in 1952 in GA as The J.M. Tull Foundation; reorganized under current name in 1984 with the Tull Charitable Foundation.
Donors: J.M. Tull‡; J.M. Tull Metal and Supply Co., Inc.
Foundation type: Independent foundation.
Financial data (yr. ended 12/31/05): Assets, $85,014,827 (M); expenditures, $4,649,177; qualifying distributions, $4,075,486; giving activities include $3,477,495 for 75 grants (high: $500,000; low: $1,000; average: $25,000–$100,000), and $252,350 for 172 employee matching gifts.
Purpose and activities: To assist Georgia nonprofit organizations with one-time capital costs associated with the implementation of strategic growth initiatives.
Fields of interest: Arts; Secondary school/education; Higher education; Education; Environment; Health care; Health organizations, association; Housing/shelter, development; Youth development, services; Human services; Children/youth, services; Homeless, human services; Homeless.
Type of support: Capital campaigns; Building/renovation; Endowments; Employee matching gifts.
Limitations: Giving limited to GA. No support for projects of religious organizations that primarily benefit their own adherents. No grants to individuals, or for conferences or seminars, scientific research, purchase of tickets to benefit events, sponsorship of performances, operating support, or scholarships (except for scholarship endowments); no loans.
Publications: Informational brochure (including application guidelines).

Application information: The foundation does not accept grant proposals via E-mail. Application form not required.
Initial approach: Letter
Copies of proposal: 1
Deadline(s): 1st day of month of meeting
Board meeting date(s): Jan., Apr., July, and Oct.
Final notification: 1 week after board meeting, in writing
Officers and Trustees:* John McIntyre,* Chair.; Barbara Cleveland, Secy.-Treas. and Exec. Dir.; Sylvia L. Dick; Harald R. Hansen; Warren Jobe; Solon Patterson; Larry Prince; Franklin Skinner.
Agent: SunTrust Bank.
Number of staff: 1 full-time professional; 1 part-time professional.
EIN: 581687028
Selected grants: The following grants were reported in 2004.
$580,379 to Community Foundation for Greater Atlanta, Atlanta, GA. For grants to be awarded by Donor Advised Fund.
$500,000 to Childrens Healthcare of Atlanta, Atlanta, GA. For construction and renovation of Scottish Rite and Egelston Childrens hospitals.
$300,000 to United Way of Metropolitan Atlanta, Atlanta, GA. For renovation of building to serve as new 24-7 Homeless Service Center.
$250,000 to Fernbank Museum of Natural History, Atlanta, GA. For improvements to facilities and exhibitions.
$200,000 to High Museum of Art, Atlanta, GA. For Louvre-Atlanta project.
$150,000 to Early Learning Property Management, Tucker, GA. For construction and renovation of facilities for child development programs for low-income families.
$150,000 to Inner Harbour, Douglasville, GA. For construction of new facility for pre-adolescent boys.
$50,000 to Callanwolde Foundation, Atlanta, GA. For facility and landscaping improvements.
$50,000 to Saint Pius X High School, Atlanta, GA. For expansion of facilities and endowment fund.
$1,000 to Midtown Assistance Center, Atlanta, GA. For emergency assistance fund.

2501
Turner Foundation, Inc. ▼ ✧

c/o Michael Finley
133 Luckie St. N.W., 2nd Fl.
Atlanta, GA 30303 (404) 681-9900
FAX: (404) 681-0172;
E-mail: turnerfi@turnerfoundation.org; URL: http://www.turnerfoundation.org

Established in 1990 in GA.
Donor: R.E. Turner III.
Foundation type: Independent foundation.
Financial data (yr. ended 12/31/04): Assets, $10,302,070 (M); gifts received, $6,000,000; expenditures, $15,005,741; qualifying distributions, $14,891,677; giving activities include $13,905,363 for 147 grants (high: $1,250,000; low: $2,000; average: $10,000–$50,000).
Purpose and activities: The foundation is committed to preventing damage to the natural systems - water, air, and land - on which all life depends.
Fields of interest: Environment, pollution control; Environment, water pollution; Environment, toxics; Environment, natural resources; Environment, energy; Environment; Animals/wildlife,

preservation/protection; Animals/wildlife; Population studies.

Type of support: General/operating support; Continuing support; Capital campaigns; Research; Technical assistance; Matching/challenge support.

Limitations: Applications not accepted. Giving primarily on a national basis; priority consideration to programs in CO, FL, GA, MT, NE, NM, and SC. No grants to individuals, or for buildings, land acquisition, endowments, start-up funds, films, books, magazines, and other specific media projects.

Publications: Annual report.

Application information: The foundation has implemented an invitation-only grantmaking process. Letters of inquiry and unsolicited proposals are not accepted.

> *Board meeting date(s):* Mar./Apr., July, Sept., and Dec.

Officers and Trustees:* Robert E. "Ted" Turner III,* Chair.; Michael Finley,* Pres. and Treas.; J. Rutherford Seydel II, Secy.; Jennie Turner Garlington; Laura Turner Seydel; Reed Beauregard Turner; Rhett Lee Turner; Teddy Turner.

Number of staff: 6 full-time professional; 1 part-time professional; 5 full-time support.

EIN: 581924590

Selected grants: The following grants were reported in 2004.

$1,250,000 to League of Conservation Voters Education Fund, DC. To strengthen and deploy state partnership projects on key issues throughout the country, and upgrade capacity of environmental feeders and organizers on front lines of shaping environmental policy at state and local levels.

$400,000 to Turner Endangered Species Fund, Atlanta, GA. For general support to conserve biodiversity, with special focus on carnivores, grasslands, plant-pollinator complexes, and species that historically ranged onto properties owned by Ted Turner.

$375,000 to Upper Chattahoochee Riverkeeper Fund, Atlanta, GA. For general support of work to advocate for and secure protection and stewardship of Upper Chattahoochee River and its tributaries and watershed, with particular focus on monitoring, evaluating and impacting time-critical opportunities for establishing regional and statewide water policy and water-related funding priorities.

$350,000 to Georgia Campaign for Adolescent Pregnancy Prevention, Atlanta, GA. For general support.

$200,000 to NARAL Pro-Choice America Foundation, DC. For continuation of Pro-Choice Organizing Project in partnership with Planned Parenthood Federation of America. For investments in technology, both e-advocacy and technological infrastructure, which have been key elements of POP; training and technical assistance for affiliates; list maintenance and national office staffing administration.

$200,000 to Pew Charitable Trusts, Philadelphia, PA. For Partnership Project coalition of US-based environmental groups.

$100,000 to Wild Salmon Center, Portland, OR. For rapid assessments and start-up of new site-based salmon conservation programs in Russian Far East and Oregon.

$50,000 to National Campaign to Prevent Teen Pregnancy, DC. To compile research-based set of ideas, tips and strategies for working with Hispanic youth regarding teen pregnancy and related issues.

$40,000 to National Wildlife Federation, Anchorage, AK. For general support.

$35,000 to Amigos Bravos, Taos, NM. For priorities and programs including; holding polluters accountable, restoring watershed health, and building sustainable rivers movement.

2502

The University Financing Foundation, Inc. ✧

(formerly Georgia Scientific and Technical Research Foundation)
3333 Busbee Dr., Ste. 150
Kennesaw, GA 30144 (770) 420-4300
Contact: Thomas H. Hall III, Pres.
E-mail: tuff@tuff.org; *URL:* http://www.tuff.org

Classified as a private operating foundation in 1989.

Foundation type: Operating foundation.

Financial data (yr. ended 12/31/05): Assets, $406,290,289 (M); expenditures, $30,597,313; qualifying distributions, $12,303,681; giving activities include $507,184 for grants, $9,999,497 for foundation-administered programs and $2,304,184 for 2 loans/program-related investments.

Purpose and activities: Giving primarily for education or research to public or private non-profit colleges or universities only.

Fields of interest: Higher education; Public policy, research.

Type of support: Building/renovation; Equipment.

Limitations: Giving primarily in Atlanta, GA.

Application information: Very limited outright grants or gifts awarded. Application form not required.

> *Initial approach:* Letter or telephone
> *Deadline(s):* None

Officers and Directors:* Thomas H. Hall III,* Pres.; J. Frank Smith, Jr.,* V.P. and Secy.; John E. Aderhold,* V.P. and Treas.; James M. Sibley, Dir. Emeritus.

EIN: 581505902

2503

The UPS Foundation ▼ ✧

55 Glenlake Pkwy., N.E.
Atlanta, GA 30328 (404) 828-6374
Contact: Evern D. Cooper Epps, Pres.
FAX: (404) 828-7435; *URL:* http://www.community.ups.com/philanthropy/main.html

Incorporated in 1951 in DE.

Donor: United Parcel Service of America, Inc.

Foundation type: Company-sponsored foundation.

Financial data (yr. ended 12/31/05): Assets, $36,752,899 (M); gifts received, $39,093,519; expenditures, $41,683,483; qualifying distributions, $39,751,375; giving activities include $37,702,661 for 2,442 grants (high: $1,731,290; low: $25), and $1,992,081 for employee matching gifts.

Purpose and activities: The foundation supports organizations involved with education, obesity, hunger, nutrition, human services, community development, volunteerism, youth, senior citizens, disabled people, mentally disabled people, economically disadvantaged people, and homeless people. Special emphasis is directed toward programs designed to address hunger, literacy, and volunteerism.

Fields of interest: Education, research; Education, reading; Education; Mental health, eating disorders; Food services; Nutrition; Children, services; Family services; Human services; Community development; Voluntarism promotion; Youth; Aging; Disabilities, people with; Mentally disabled; Economically disadvantaged; Homeless.

International interests: Canada; Mexico.

Type of support: Management development/capacity building; Research; Technical assistance; Employee matching gifts.

Limitations: Giving on a national basis and in Canada and Mexico; giving also to statewide, regional, national, and international organizations. No support for religious organizations not of direct benefit to the entire community. No grants to individuals; generally, no grants for capital campaigns, endowments, or general operating support.

Publications: Application guidelines; Annual report; Informational brochure (including application guidelines).

Application information: Proposals should be no longer than 2 pages. Application form not required.

> *Initial approach:* Proposal
> *Copies of proposal:* 1
> *Deadline(s):* Sept. 1
> *Board meeting date(s):* Oct. and Nov.

Officers and Trustees:* Allen E. Hill,* Chair.; Evern D. Cooper Epps,* Pres.; John J. Beystehner,* Secy.; D. Scott Davis,* Treas.; David P. Abney; Michael L. Eskew; Teri McClure; Christine M. Owens.

Number of staff: 7 full-time professional; 4 full-time support.

EIN: 136099176

Selected grants: The following grants were reported in 2005.

$9,584,445 to United Way of America, Alexandria, VA.

$1,731,290 to National Merit Scholarship Corporation, Evanston, IL.

$1,000,000 to Committee to Encourage Corporate Philanthropy, New York, NY.

$675,000 to Urban League, National, New York, NY.

$500,000 to Atlanta Symphony Orchestra, Atlanta, GA.

$250,000 to United Negro College Fund, Fairfax, VA.

$60,000 to Foundation for American Communications, Pasadena, CA.

$40,000 to BoardSource, DC.

$33,475 to Scholarship America, Saint Peter, MN.

$25,000 to Happy Factory, Cedar City, UT.

2504

Vogel Family Foundation, Inc. ✧ ☆

c/o William A. Vogel
2410 Spalding Dr.
Atlanta, GA 30350
Contact: William A. Vogel

Established in 2004 in GA.

Foundation type: Independent foundation.

Financial data (yr. ended 12/31/05): Assets, $5,497,699 (M); expenditures, $692,019; qualifying distributions, $665,052; giving activities include $665,052 for 42 grants (high: $299,207; low: $20).

Fields of interest: Performing arts, music; Higher education; Human services; Protestant agencies & churches.

Limitations: Giving primarily in Atlanta, GA.

Application information: Application form not required.

Initial approach: Letter

Deadline(s): None

Directors: Judith M. Vogel; William A. Vogel.

EIN: 202015587

2505
Stanley D. and Kay B. Walker Foundation, Inc. ◇

4080 McGinnis Ferry Rd., Ste. 1003
Alpharetta, GA   30005

Established in 1999 in GA.

Donors: Stanley D. Walker; Kay B. Walker.

Foundation type: Independent foundation.

Financial data (yr. ended 12/31/05): Assets, $8,333,592 (M); expenditures, $1,922,341; qualifying distributions, $1,840,000; giving activities include $1,840,000 for grants.

Fields of interest: Christian agencies & churches.

Limitations: Applications not accepted. No grants to individuals.

Application information: Contributes only to pre-selected organizations.

Officers: Stanley D. Walker, Jr., Chair.; Kay B. Walker, Vice-Chair.

Trustees: Victor Logan; Ronald D. Morris, Jr.; S. Benton Walker III.

EIN: 582491026

Selected grants: The following grants were reported in 2004.

$230,000 to Luis Palau Evangelistic Association, Portland, OR.

$110,000 to Camp Highland, Alpharetta, GA.

$75,000 to Salvation Army.

$50,000 to Young Life.

2506
The Edna Wardlaw Charitable Trust

c/o SunTrust Bank
P.O. Box 4655
Atlanta, GA   30302-4655   (404) 813-9105
Contact: Allen Mast

Established in 1992 in GA.

Donor: Edna Wardlaw.

Foundation type: Independent foundation.

Financial data (yr. ended 12/31/05): Assets, $20,361,110 (M); expenditures, $1,311,103; qualifying distributions, $1,253,949; giving activities include $1,214,801 for 170 grants (high: $30,000; low: $33).

Purpose and activities: Giving primarily for children's services and environmental conservation.

Fields of interest: Environment, natural resources; Reproductive health, family planning; Children/ youth, services; Homeless, human services; International affairs, goodwill promotion; International peace/security; International human rights.

Limitations: Giving on a national basis.

Application information: Application form not required.

Initial approach: Letter

Deadline(s): None

Distribution Committee: Edna Raine Coker; Elizabeth H. Coker; Charlotte S. Hoffman; Trudie Olavarrieta-Coker; Julia Milner Wardlaw; William C. Wardlaw III.

Trustee: SunTrust Bank.

EIN: 586278167

2507
Gertrude and William C. Wardlaw Fund, Inc.

c/o SunTrust Bank
P.O. Box 4655
Atlanta, GA   30302
Contact: Allen Mast, Secy.

Established in 1936 in GA; incorporated in 1951.

Donors: Gertrude Wardlaw; William C. Wardlaw, Jr.†.

Foundation type: Independent foundation.

Financial data (yr. ended 12/31/05): Assets, $18,330,076 (M); expenditures, $1,117,239; qualifying distributions, $1,029,443; giving activities include $994,496 for 112 grants (high: $100,000; low: $57).

Purpose and activities: Emphasis on education, including higher education, youth agencies, cultural programs, a community fund, and health and hospitals.

Fields of interest: Higher education; Hospitals (general); Health organizations, association; Human services; Homeless.

Type of support: General/operating support.

Limitations: Giving primarily in Atlanta, GA. No grants to individuals.

Application information: Application form not required.

Initial approach: Letter

Deadline(s): Feb. 15

Board meeting date(s): Mar.

Officer: Allen Mast, Secy.

Trustees: Charlotte Hoffman; William C. Wardlaw III; SunTrust Bank.

EIN: 586026065

2508
Watkins Christian Foundation, Inc. ◇

1958 Monroe Dr., N.E.
Atlanta, GA   30324-4887

Established in 1983 in GA.

Donors: Bill Watkins†; Watkins Associated Industries, Inc.

Foundation type: Independent foundation.

Financial data (yr. ended 12/31/05): Assets, $46,623,236 (M); gifts received, $2,251,369; expenditures, $4,830,151; qualifying distributions, $4,522,730; giving activities include $4,522,700 for 64 grants (high: $730,000; low: $2,000; average: $10,000–$250,000).

Purpose and activities: Grants for evangelism, churches, ministries, and a variety of religious organizations, including support for human welfare and feeding the hungry.

Fields of interest: Food services; Human services; Religious federated giving programs; Christian agencies & churches.

Limitations: Applications not accepted. Giving primarily in FL and GA. No grants to individuals.

Application information: Contributes only to pre-selected organizations.

Officers and Trustees:* George C. Watkins,* Chair.; John F. Watkins,* Pres.; W. Neal Freeman,* V.P.; Michael L. Watkins,* V.P.; George W. Ready, Jr.,*

Secy.-Treas.; Ruth Anne Smith; Kimberly Watkins; W.B. Watkins IV.

EIN: 581494832

Selected grants: The following grants were reported in 2005.

$730,000 to Young Life in Tampa, Tampa, FL.

$550,000 to First United Methodist Church, Tampa, FL.

$250,000 to All Saints Academy, Winter Haven, FL.

$250,000 to Palma Ceia Presbyterian Church, Tampa, FL.

$150,000 to Young Life, Wyldlife, Singapore. .

$100,000 to Youth for Christ, Atlanta, GA.

$75,000 to Central Baptist Church.

$50,000 to Lionheart School, Alpharetta, GA.

$50,000 to Norcross Cooperative Ministry, Norcross, GA.

$25,000 to Florida Sheriffs Youth Ranches, Live Oak, FL.

2509
Watson-Brown Foundation, Inc.

310 Tom Watson Way
Thomson, GA   30824-0037   (706) 595-8886
Contact: Thomas W. Brown, Jr.
FAX: (706) 595-3948; E-mail: twbjr@bellsouth.net;
URL: http://www.watson-brown.org/

Established in 1970 in GA.

Donor: Walter J. Brown†.

Foundation type: Independent foundation.

Financial data (yr. ended 12/31/04): Assets, $128,358,577 (M); gifts received, $905,700; expenditures, $4,693,670; qualifying distributions, $3,578,998; giving activities include $1,581,420 for grants, and $1,073,500 for grants to individuals.

Purpose and activities: The foundation focuses its giving within the Southeast by funding nonprofit organizations and institutions that advance education. Most grants to colleges and universities are to fund programs in the areas of history, literature, law, agricultural education, and historic preservation. The foundation also provides college scholarships for students from the Central Savannah River Area (CSRA) of Georgia and South Carolina.

Fields of interest: History/archaeology; Literature; Historic preservation/historical societies; Higher education; Law school/education; Agriculture.

Type of support: General/operating support; Capital campaigns; Building/renovation; Program development; Conferences/seminars; Publication; Fellowships; Scholarship funds; Research; Scholarships—to individuals; Matching/challenge support.

Limitations: Giving limited to the Southeast, primarily in GA and SC. No support for religious programs. No grants for debt reduction, advertising or marketing efforts, or for social events such as sports tournaments or galas.

Publications: Application guidelines; Newsletter.

Application information: Scholarship awards paid directly to the individual recipient's educational institution. See foundation Web site for full scholarship application guidelines. Application form required.

Initial approach: Letter

Copies of proposal: 7

Deadline(s): Apr. 15

Board meeting date(s): Quarterly

Final notification: Within 1 month of board's 3rd quarter meeting

Officers and Trustees:* Tom Watson Brown,* Chair.; Thomas W. Brown, Jr.,* Pres.; R. Byron Attridge; Joab Lesesne; John Woodham.
Number of staff: 4 full-time professional; 9 full-time support; 1 part-time support.
EIN: 237097393

2510
The Joseph and Felicia Weber Family Foundation, Inc. ◇
3406 Old Plantation Rd. N.W.
Atlanta, GA   30327

Established in 2003 in GA.
Donor: Joseph F. Weber.
Foundation type: Independent foundation.
Financial data (yr. ended 6/30/05): Assets, $16,642,329 (M); gifts received, $1,000,000; expenditures, $1,174,740; qualifying distributions, $1,084,785; giving activities include $1,084,785 for 22 grants (high: $515,000; low: $1,000).
Fields of interest: Media/communications; Elementary/secondary education; Higher education; International human rights; Civil liberties, first amendment; Jewish agencies & temples.
Limitations: Applications not accepted. Giving on a national basis, with emphasis on the Atlanta, GA, area. No grants to individuals.
Application information: Contributes only to pre-selected organizations.
Officers and Trustees:* Joseph F. Weber,* Chair.; Felicia P. Weber,* Secy.-Treas.
EIN: 200510704

2511
Wehadkee Foundation, Inc. ◇ ☆
P.O. Box 150
West Point, GA   31833

Incorporated in 1952 in AL.
Donor: D.A. Turner.
Foundation type: Independent foundation.
Financial data (yr. ended 12/31/05): Assets, $2,475,898 (M); gifts received, $3,208; expenditures, $1,128,212; qualifying distributions, $1,106,488; giving activities include $1,106,488 for grants.
Purpose and activities: Giving primarily for education.
Fields of interest: Higher education; Education; Health care; Human services; Youth, services.
Limitations: Applications not accepted. Giving primarily in GA. No grants to individuals.
Application information: Contributes only to pre-selected organizations.
Officers: Bruce N. Lanier, Jr., Pres.; George H. Lanier II, V.P.; Jim Floyd, Secy.-Treas.
EIN: 636049784
Selected grants: The following grants were reported in 2003.
$35,000 to Chattahoochee Valley Educational Foundation, Lanett, AL.
$10,000 to Darlington School, Rome, GA. For annual fund.
$10,000 to Talladega College, Talladega, AL.
$7,500 to Valley United Fund, West Point, GA.
$7,000 to Boy Scouts of America, Chattahoochee Council, Columbus, GA.
$5,000 to United Way of North Talladega, Talladega, AL.

$4,500 to Alabama Foundation for Independent Colleges and Universities, Birmingham, AL.
$4,000 to Boy Scouts of America, Greater Alabama Council, Birmingham, AL.
$4,000 to Georgia Foundation for Independent Colleges, Atlanta, GA.
$2,500 to United Way of East Central Alabama, Anniston, AL.

2512
The April & Jerry Weiner Family Foundation, Inc. ◇
8200 Jett Ferry Rd.
Atlanta, GA   30350

Established in 1998 in GA.
Donor: Jerold G. Weiner.
Foundation type: Independent foundation.
Financial data (yr. ended 3/31/06): Assets, $1,408,046 (M); expenditures, $339,829; qualifying distributions, $327,169; giving activities include $327,169 for grants.
Purpose and activities: Giving primarily for Jewish organizations.
Fields of interest: Education; Jewish agencies & temples.
Limitations: Applications not accepted. No grants to individuals.
Application information: Contributes only to pre-selected organizations.
Officers and Directors:* Jerold G. Weiner,* Pres.; April A. Weiner, Secy.-Treas.; Larry S. Urbach.
EIN: 582325523
Selected grants: The following grants were reported in 2005.
$50,000 to Epstein School Foundation, Atlanta, GA.
$29,040 to Jewish Family and Career Services, Atlanta, GA.
$28,135 to Jewish Federation of Greater Atlanta, Atlanta, GA.
$13,216 to Epstein School, Atlanta, GA.
$13,000 to William Breman Jewish Home, Atlanta, GA.
$10,000 to Hillels of Georgia, Atlanta, GA.
$6,540 to Weber School, Dunwoody, GA.
$6,205 to Marcus Jewish Community Center of Atlanta, Dunwoody, GA.
$500 to Jewish Healthcare International, Atlanta, GA.
$118 to Davis Academy, Atlanta, GA.

2513
WestPoint Stevens Foundation, Inc. ◇
(formerly West Point-Pepperell Foundation)
P.O. Box 71
West Point, GA   31833
Contact: Toni Cauble

Incorporated in 1953 in GA as West Point Foundation, Inc.; merged with Sanford Dunson Foundation, Inc. in 1965.
Donors: West Point-Pepperell, Inc.; WestPoint Stevens Inc.
Foundation type: Company-sponsored foundation.
Financial data (yr. ended 12/31/03): Assets, $3,706,954 (M); expenditures, $625,180; qualifying distributions, $617,054; giving activities include $557,500 for 79 grants (high: $100,000; low: $500), and $54,000 for 54 grants to individuals (high: $1,000; low: $1,000).

Purpose and activities: The foundation supports organizations involved with arts and culture, education, health, and government and public administration.
Fields of interest: Arts; Secondary school/education; Higher education; Education; Health organizations, association; Youth, services; Federated giving programs; Government/public administration.
Type of support: General/operating support; Employee matching gifts.
Limitations: Giving primarily in areas of company operations in AL, FL, ME, NC, SC, and TX.
Application information: Application form not required.
Initial approach: Proposal
Copies of proposal: 1
Deadline(s): None
Board meeting date(s): Varies
Officers and Directors:* M.L. Fontenot,* Pres.; Christopher N. Zodrow, V.P. and Secy.; Lester D. Sears,* V.P. and Treas.; Toni M. Cauble, V.P.; Thomas M. Lane, V.P.; Hugh M. Chapman; Holcombe Green.
Number of staff: 2 full-time professional; 2 part-time support.
EIN: 580801512

2514
Williams Family Foundation of Georgia, Inc.
P.O. Box 1011
Thomasville, GA   31799
Contact: Alston P. Watt, Exec. Dir.

Established in 1980 in GA.
Donors: Diane W. Parker; Marguerite N. Williams†; Thomas L. Williams III; Bennie G. Williams†.
Foundation type: Independent foundation.
Financial data (yr. ended 11/30/05): Assets, $60,382,095 (M); expenditures, $2,957,788; qualifying distributions, $2,744,213; giving activities include $2,633,501 for 64 grants (high: $271,500; low: $1,000).
Purpose and activities: The foundation gives to religious, educational, and public charities in the GA area.
Fields of interest: Visual arts; Museums; Performing arts; Historic preservation/historical societies; Arts; Secondary school/education; Higher education; Libraries/library science; Education; Environment, natural resources; Environment; Animals/wildlife, preservation/protection; Family services; Community development; Government/public administration.
Type of support: General/operating support; Building/renovation; Program development; Matching/challenge support.
Limitations: Giving primarily in GA, with emphasis on Thomasville and Thomas County. No grants to individuals.
Publications: Application guidelines; Corporate giving report; Informational brochure (including application guidelines).
Application information: New contributions limited due to numerous commitments. Application form required.
Initial approach: Letter
Copies of proposal: 1
Deadline(s): Feb. 15 and Aug. 15
Board meeting date(s): May and Nov.
Final notification: June 10 and Nov. 10

Officers and Directors:* Thomas L. Williams III,* Pres.; Stephen T. Parker, V.P.; Diane W. Parker,* Secy.; Bernard Lanigan, Jr.,* Treas.; Alston P. Watt, Exec. Dir.; Joseph E. Beverly; Frederick E. Cooper; Lawrence A. Harmon; Thomas W. Parker; Thomas H. Vann, Jr.

Number of staff: 1 part-time support.

EIN: 581414850

Selected grants: The following grants were reported in 2004.

$506,000 to YMCA and Youth Center of Thomasville, Thomasville, GA. For general operating support.

$260,000 to Boys and Girls Clubs of Thomas County, Thomasville, GA. For general operating support.

$260,000 to Brookwood School, Thomasville, GA. For general operating support.

$250,000 to Washington and Lee University, Lexington, VA. For general operating support.

$50,000 to Coastal Georgia Historical Society, Saint Simons Island, GA. For general operating support.

2515
Jesse Parker Williams Foundation, Inc. ◈

50 Hurt Plz. S.E., Ste. 850
Atlanta, GA 30303-2945 (404) 658-1112
Contact: Joan F. Nakutis, Secy.

Established in 1956.

Foundation type: Independent foundation.

Financial data (yr. ended 12/31/03): Assets, $37,616,314 (M); expenditures, $2,115,945; qualifying distributions, $1,912,339; giving activities include $1,760,224 for 20 grants (high: $450,000; low: $500).

Purpose and activities: Contributions are limited to the medical and charitable care of women and children under 12.

Fields of interest: Hospitals (general); Health organizations, association; Children; Women.

Limitations: Giving limited to GA. No grants to individuals.

Application information:

Initial approach: Letter

Deadline(s): None

Officers and Directors:* Joseph B. Haynes,* Chair.; Lucy C. Vance,* Vice-Chair.; Joan F. Nakutis, Secy.; Larry L. Gellerstedt III; Robert A. Pattillo; E. Jenner Wood III.

EIN: 580601653

Selected grants: The following grants were reported in 2003.

$450,000 to A. G. Rhodes Home, Atlanta, GA. For care of women and children.

$250,000 to Childrens Healthcare of Atlanta Foundation, Atlanta, GA. For care of women and children.

$150,000 to Presbyterian Village, Atlanta, GA. For care of women and children.

$112,500 to Foundation of Wesley Woods, Atlanta, GA. For care of women and children.

$100,000 to Good Samaritan Health Center, Atlanta, GA. For care of women and children.

$100,000 to Hospice Atlanta, Atlanta, GA. For care of women and children.

$50,000 to Gatchell Home, Atlanta, GA. For care of women and children.

$30,000 to Georgia Center for Children, Atlanta, GA. For care of women and children.

$10,000 to Link Counseling Center, Atlanta, GA. For care of women and children.

$500 to Visiting Nurse Association of Metropolitan Atlanta, Atlanta, GA. For care of women and children.

2516
Betty A. and James B. Williams Foundation, Inc.

c/o SunTrust Bank
P.O. Box 4655, MC 221
Atlanta, GA 30302
Contact: Robert Mays, Off.

Established in 1996 in GA.

Donor: James B. Williams.

Foundation type: Independent foundation.

Financial data (yr. ended 12/31/05): Assets, $8,067,334 (M); expenditures, $449,888; qualifying distributions, $368,300; giving activities include $368,270 for 13 grants (high: $100,000; low: $1,000).

Purpose and activities: Giving primarily for education, and to a Presbyterian church.

Fields of interest: Arts; Elementary/secondary education; Education; Environment, natural resources; Health organizations, association; Boys & girls clubs; Boy scouts; Federated giving programs; Protestant agencies & churches.

Limitations: Applications not accepted. No grants to individuals.

Application information: Unsolicited requests for funds not accepted.

Officers: Betty A. Williams, Chair.; James B. Williams, Secy.

EIN: 582302288

Selected grants: The following grants were reported in 2005.

$75,000 to Emory University, Atlanta, GA.

$50,000 to Boy Scouts of America, Anchorage, AK.

$50,000 to Peachtree Presbyterian Church, Atlanta, GA.

$50,000 to United Way.

$10,000 to American Red Cross.

$10,000 to Robert W. Woodruff Arts Center, Atlanta, GA.

$1,000 to Nature Conservancy, Arlington, VA.

2517
A. L. Williams, Jr. Family Foundation, Inc. ◈

3473 Satellite Blvd., Ste. 211
Duluth, GA 30096
Contact: James E. Kelly, Exec. V.P.

Incorporated 1985 in GA.

Donors: Arthur L. Williams, Jr.; Angela H. Williams; Boe Adams.

Foundation type: Independent foundation.

Financial data (yr. ended 12/31/04): Assets, $68,265,986 (M); expenditures, $3,822,190; qualifying distributions, $3,505,561; giving activities include $3,505,561 for 38 grants (high: $1,000,000; low: $500).

Purpose and activities: Giving primarily for Protestant ministries and organizations, as well as for education, social services, and to a hospital foundation.

Fields of interest: Higher education; Education; Hospitals (general); Human services; Christian agencies & churches; Protestant agencies & churches.

Limitations: Giving primarily in FL and GA.

Application information: Application form not required.

Initial approach: Letter

Deadline(s): None

Officers and Trustees:* Angela H. Williams, Pres. and Treas.; James E. Kelly,* Exec. V.P.; April Williams Demoss,* V.P.; Paula J. Weed, V.P.; Arthur R. Williams III,* V.P.; Gloice Y. Crim, Secy.

EIN: 581650389

Selected grants: The following grants were reported in 2004.

$1,000,000 to Highlands-Cashiers Hospital Foundation, Highlands, NC.

$819,892 to George Walton Academy, Monroe, GA.

$458,977 to Liberty University, Lynchburg, VA.

$60,000 to Tom Atkins Evangelistic Association, Monroe, GA.

$48,000 to Community Bible Church, Highlands, NC.

$33,000 to Cooperative Baptist Fellowship, Atlanta, GA.

$20,000 to Evangelism Explosion International, Fort Lauderdale, FL.

$18,000 to International Interns, Pasadena, CA.

$18,000 to Pathway of Life Fellowship, West Palm Beach, FL.

$10,000 to Furman University, Greenville, SC.

2518
James M. Williams, Jr. Family Foundation, Inc. ◈

2076 W. Park Pl.
Stone Mountain, GA 30087-3533

Established in 1996 in GA.

Donor: James M. Williams, Jr.

Foundation type: Operating foundation.

Financial data (yr. ended 12/31/05): Assets, $12,095,032 (M); expenditures, $552,346; qualifying distributions, $458,550; giving activities include $458,550 for 20 grants (high: $185,000; low: $100).

Purpose and activities: Giving primarily to Baptist churches.

Fields of interest: Human services; Protestant agencies & churches.

Limitations: Applications not accepted. No grants to individuals.

Application information: Contributes only to pre-selected organizations.

Officers: James M. Williams, Jr., Pres.; Barbara Williams Bowling, Secy.-Treas.

Directors: Dondi Anne Bosson; Candace Cheri O'Neal; Linda Sue Williams.

EIN: 582275806

2519
The Frances Wood Wilson Foundation, Inc.

250 E. Ponce de Leon Ave., Ste. 702
Decatur, GA 30030 (404) 370-0035
Contact: W.T. Wingfield, Pres.
E-mail: fwwf@bellsouth.net

Incorporated in 1954 in GA.

Donors: Fred B. Wilson†; Mrs. Frances W. Wilson†; St. Louis-San Francisco Railroad.

Foundation type: Independent foundation.

Financial data (yr. ended 5/31/05): Assets, $41,463,069 (M); expenditures, $2,242,129; qualifying distributions, $2,006,114; giving

activities include $1,823,800 for 120 grants (high: $100,000; low: $1,000).

Purpose and activities: Grants largely for child welfare, and religious, civic, health, and higher educational organizations; support also for college scholarship funds.

Fields of interest: Higher education; Health care; Health organizations, association; Children/youth, services; Religion.

Type of support: General/operating support; Continuing support; Annual campaigns; Capital campaigns; Building/renovation; Equipment; Land acquisition; Scholarship funds.

Limitations: Giving limited to GA, except for programs carried on by Chestnut Hill Benevolent Assn. in Boston, MA. No grants to individuals, or for endowment funds; no loans.

Publications: Application guidelines.

Application information: Application form not required.

> *Initial approach:* Proposal
> *Copies of proposal:* 1
> *Deadline(s):* Mar. 1 and Sept. 1
> *Board meeting date(s):* Apr. and Oct.

Officers and Trustees:* W.T. Wingfield,* Pres.; B.A. Bird,* Exec. V.P. and Secy.-Treas.; J.B. Edmunds, Jr.; G.B. Haley; D.G. Loggins; J.M. Pate; J.H. Terrell, Jr.

Number of staff: 1 part-time support.

EIN: 586035441

Selected grants: The following grants were reported in 2004.

$100,000 to Eagle Ranch, Chestnut Mountain, GA.

$55,000 to Wesleyan College, Macon, GA.

$50,000 to Chestnut Hill Benevolent Association, Brookline, MA.

$50,000 to Childrens Healthcare of Atlanta, Atlanta, GA.

$50,000 to Young Harris College, Young Harris, GA.

$25,000 to Robert W. Woodruff Arts Center, Atlanta, GA.

$12,000 to Mercer University, Macon, GA.

$11,400 to Morning Light Foundation, Atlanta, GA.

$10,000 to Saint Josephs Mercy Foundation, Atlanta, GA.

$10,000 to Theatrical Outfit, Atlanta, GA.

2520
WinShape Centre, Inc. ✧

5200 Buffington Rd.
Atlanta, GA 30349-2998 (800) 448-6955, ext. 1121
FAX: (706) 238-7742;
E-mail: dvance@winshape.com; URL: http://www.winshape.com
Scholarship application address: Winshape Centre, Berry College, P.O. Box 490009, Mount Berry, GA 30149-0009, tel.: (706) 238-7718

Established as a company-sponsored operating foundation in 1984 in GA.

Donors: Chick-fil-A, Inc.; S. Truett Cathy; CFA Properties, Inc.

Foundation type: Operating foundation.

Financial data (yr. ended 12/31/04): Assets, $37,659,572 (M); gifts received, $10,790,785; expenditures, $10,685,319; qualifying distributions, $13,686,153; giving activities include $770,651 for 6 grants (high: $512,119; low: $1,500), and $8,288,789 for 4 foundation-administered programs.

Purpose and activities: The foundation supports Christian agencies and churches and organizations involved with education, children and youth, and religion and awards college scholarships to undergraduate students attending Berry College.

Fields of interest: Child development, education; Secondary school/education; Education; Youth development; Children/youth, services; Child development, services; Christian agencies & churches; Religion.

Type of support: Continuing support; Scholarships —to individuals.

Limitations: Giving primarily in Rome, GA.

Publications: Application guidelines; Informational brochure (including application guidelines).

Application information: Unsolicited requests from organizations are not accepted. Application form required.

> *Initial approach:* Complete online application form or contact foundation for application form
> *Deadline(s):* Feb. 1; Nov. 30 is preferred
> *Board meeting date(s):* Varies
> *Final notification:* Apr. 1

Officers: S. Truett Cathy, Pres.; Donald M. Cathy, V.P.; James B. McCabe, Secy.-Treas.

Number of staff: 33 full-time professional.

EIN: 581595471

Selected grants: The following were reported in 2003.

$421,849 to Berry College, Mount Berry, GA. For scholarships.

$165,480 to Lar WinShape, Brasilia, Brazil. For general support.

$5,000 to American Rights Coalition, Grand Rapids, MI. For general support.

$1,000 to Family Research Council, DC. For general support.

2521
Robert W. Woodruff Foundation, Inc. ▼ ✧

(formerly Trebor Foundation, Inc.)
50 Hurt Plz., Ste. 1200
Atlanta, GA 30303 (404) 522-6755
FAX: (404) 522-7026; E-mail: fdns@woodruff.org;
URL: http://www.woodruff.org

Incorporated in 1937 in DE.

Donors: Robert W. Woodruff†; The Acmaro Securities Corp.; and others.

Foundation type: Independent foundation.

Financial data (yr. ended 12/31/05): Assets, $1,950,691,385 (M); expenditures, $103,819,883; qualifying distributions, $101,944,982; giving activities include $101,030,268 for 94 grants (high: $6,248,742; low: $13,480).

Purpose and activities: Principal giving interests are focused on the following program areas: elementary, secondary, and higher education; health care and education; human services, particularly for children and youth; economic development and civic affairs; art and cultural activities; and conservation of natural resources and environmental protection. Preference is given to one-time capital projects of established private charitable organizations.

Fields of interest: Arts; Elementary/secondary education; Higher education; Education; Environment, natural resources; Environment; Health care; Health organizations, association; Human services; Children/youth, services; Aging, centers/services; Economic development; Government/public administration; Public affairs; Aging.

Type of support: Capital campaigns; Building/renovation; Equipment; Land acquisition; Program development.

Limitations: Giving primarily in GA, with emphasis on the metropolitan Atlanta area. No support for churches, denominational programs, or youth services outside Atlanta, GA. No grants to individuals, or for annual operating support, festivals or performances, films and documentaries, or seed money; no loans.

Publications: Application guidelines; Grants list; Informational brochure.

Application information: The foundation shares offices and administrative staff with the Joseph B. Whitehead Foundation, Lettie Pate Whitehead Foundation, Inc., Lettie Pate Evans Foundation, Inc., Ichauway, Inc., and the Robert W. Woodruff Health Sciences Center Fund, Inc. Grant inquiries or proposals submitted to the Robert W. Woodruff Foundation, Inc. may also be considered by one or more of the foundations sharing this common administrative arrangement. It is not necessary to communicate separately with more than one of these foundations in seeking information or requesting grant support. Application form not required.

> *Initial approach:* Letter
> *Copies of proposal:* 1
> *Deadline(s):* Feb. 1 and Sept. 1
> *Board meeting date(s):* Apr. and Nov.
> *Final notification:* Within 30 days of trustee meeting

Officers and Trustees:* James B. Williams,* Chair.; James M. Sibley,* Vice-Chair.; P. Russell Hardin, Pres.; J. Lee Tribble, Treas.; Charles B. Ginden; Wilton D. Looney.

EIN: 581695425

Selected grants: The following grants were reported in 2005.

$6,248,742 to Robert W. Woodruff Arts Center, Atlanta, GA. For construction of addition to High Museum of Art.

$6,150,000 to Georgia Department of Natural Resources, Atlanta, GA. For acquisition and conservation of natural areas in Georgia.

$5,118,000 to Robert W. Woodruff Health Sciences Center Fund, Atlanta, GA. For general support and Winship Cancer Center.

$5,000,000 to Georgia Institute of Technology, Atlanta, GA. For design and construction of Nanotechnology Research Center.

$4,000,016 to Childrens Healthcare of Atlanta, Atlanta, GA. For capital improvements to Hughes Spalding Children's Hospital.

$2,600,000 to Chamber Foundation of Greater Atlanta, Atlanta, GA. For Forward Atlanta initiatives.

$2,000,000 to American Red Cross, National Headquarters, DC. For Hurricane Katrina disaster relief: half applied to relief efforts in affected Gulf Coast areas, and remainder directed to relief efforts in metropolitan Atlanta area.

$2,000,000 to Atlanta Ronald McDonald House Charities, Atlanta, GA. For capital campaign to expand Houston Mill Road facility.

$1,956,250 to Ichauway, Newton, GA. For capital support and operating support.

$395,000 to Association of Governing Boards of Universities and Colleges, DC. For national initiative on college costs.

2522
J. W. & Ethel I. Woodruff Foundation ✧
c/o J. Barnett Woodruff
P.O. Box 750
Columbus, GA 31902-0750

Established in 1960 in GA.
Donors: Ethel I. Woodruff; James W. Woodruff; J. Barnett Woodruff; members of the Woodruff family.
Foundation type: Independent foundation.
Financial data (yr. ended 7/31/05): Assets, $19,870,682 (M); expenditures, $1,131,531; qualifying distributions, $1,115,729; giving activities include $1,113,300 for 55 grants (high: $155,000; low: $3,000).
Purpose and activities: Giving primarily for education, and youth development programs and organizations; funding also for environmental conservation, the arts, and health and social services.
Fields of interest: Museums (specialized); Performing arts; Historic preservation/historical societies; Arts; Elementary/secondary education; Higher education; Education; Environment, natural resources; Hospitals (general); Physical therapy; Speech/hearing centers; Health care; Health organizations, association; Boys & girls clubs; Human services; Children/youth, services; Family services; Christian agencies & churches.
Limitations: Applications not accepted. Giving primarily in GA, with emphasis on Columbus. No grants to individuals; no loans.
Application information: Contributes only to pre-selected organizations.
Officers and Directors:* J. Barnett Woodruff,* Chair.; Steve B. Woodruff,* Secy.; Stephen E. Draper; Sherri D. Ferry; Chevin Woodruff; James W. Woodruff III.
EIN: 586049589
Selected grants: The following grants were reported in 2005.
$155,000 to Columbus State University, Columbus, GA.
$85,000 to Brookstone School, Columbus, GA.
$55,000 to Westville Historic Handicrafts, Lumpkin, GA.
$28,000 to Georgia Conservancy, Atlanta, GA.
$20,000 to Presbyterian Home, Quitman, GA.
$11,000 to Rabun Gap-Nacoochee School, Rabun Gap, GA.
$10,000 to Columbus Museum, Columbus, GA.
$10,000 to Valley Rescue Mission, Columbus, GA.
$6,000 to Chattahoochee Riverkeeper, Columbus, GA.
$5,000 to Stewart Community Home, Columbus, GA.

2523
David, Helen, and Marian Woodward Fund ✧
c/o Wachovia Bank, N.A.
3414 Peachtree Rd., 5th Fl., MC GA8023
Atlanta, GA 30326 (404) 332-4152
Contact: Lydia Whitman; Alice Sheets
E-mail: grantinquiriesga@wachovia.com;
URL: http://www.wachovia.com/corp_inst/charitable_services/0,,4267_4268_4306,00.html

Established in 1975 in GA.
Donor: Marian W. Ottley†.
Foundation type: Independent foundation.
Financial data (yr. ended 5/31/06): Assets, $55,616,499 (M); expenditures, $2,928,075;

qualifying distributions, $2,590,800; giving activities include $2,590,000 for grants.
Purpose and activities: Giving primarily for the arts, civic affairs, education, hospitals, social services, and youth.
Fields of interest: Arts; Education; Hospitals (general); Human services; Children/youth, services.
Type of support: Capital campaigns; Building/renovation; Equipment; Program development.
Limitations: Giving primarily in the metropolitan Atlanta, GA, area. No grants to individuals, or for scholarships or student loans.
Application information: Grant guidelines can be found on the foundation's Web site. Application form not required.
Initial approach: Letter (no more than 2 pages)
Copies of proposal: 1
Deadline(s): May 1 and Nov. 1
Board meeting date(s): June and Dec.
Final notification: Jan. 1 and Aug. 1
Distribution Committee: Crawford Barnett, M.D.; William D. Ellis, Jr.; Robert L. Foreman, Jr.; Horace Sibley; D. Gary Thompson.
Trustee: Wachovia Bank, N.A.
Number of staff: 1 full-time professional; 1 full-time support.
EIN: 586222004

2524
T. G. Woolford, Jr. and F. T. Woolford, Jr. Trust
c/o SunTrust Bank
P.O. Box 4418
Atlanta, GA 30302-4418
Application address: c/o Raymond B. King, Sr. V.P., SunTrust Bank, Atlanta, Community Affairs Foundation Program, P.O. Box 4418, MC 041, Atlanta, GA 30302, tel.: Kay Miller (404) 588-8250

Donor: T. Guy Woolford†.
Foundation type: Independent foundation.
Financial data (yr. ended 12/31/05): Assets, $13,508,038 (M); expenditures, $653,297; qualifying distributions, $611,280; giving activities include $575,796 for 67 grants (high: $33,000; low: $1,000).
Fields of interest: Arts; Higher education; Education; Community development.
Type of support: Capital campaigns; Building/renovation.
Limitations: Giving primarily in the Atlanta, GA metro area. No grants to individuals.
Application information: Application form required.
Deadline(s): Committee considerations: Sept., Oct., Nov. for Jan.; Dec., Jan., Feb., and Mar. for May; Apr., May, June, and July for Oct.
Final notification: Jan., May, and Oct.
Officers: E. Jenner Wood III, Chair.; Raymond B. King, Secy.
Committee Members: L. Phillip Humann; Gary Peacock; Jim Wells.
Trustee: SunTrust Bank.
EIN: 586026070

2525
The Vasser Woolley Foundation, Inc. ✧
c/o Gerald V. Thomas II, Secy.-Treas.
1 Atlantic Ctr., 1201 W. Peachtree St., Ste. 4200
Atlanta, GA 30309-3424 (404) 881-7993

Incorporated in 1961 in GA.
Donor: Vasser Woolley†.
Foundation type: Independent foundation.
Financial data (yr. ended 12/31/03): Assets, $8,781,939 (M); expenditures, $450,097; qualifying distributions, $376,501; giving activities include $370,000 for 14 grants (high: $40,000; low: $15,000).
Purpose and activities: Emphasis on higher education; support also for the arts, youth agencies, community funds, crime prevention, and aid to the handicapped.
Fields of interest: Arts; Higher education; Education; Crime/law enforcement; Youth, services; Federated giving programs; Disabilities, people with.
Type of support: Building/renovation; Equipment; Land acquisition; Emergency funds; Professorships; Seed money; Scholarship funds; Matching/challenge support.
Limitations: Applications not accepted. Giving primarily in the metropolitan Atlanta, GA, area. No grants to individuals, or for operating budgets, continuing support, annual campaigns, deficit financing, special projects, research, publications, or conferences; no loans.
Application information: Contributes only to pre-selected organizations.
Officers and Trustees:* L. Neil Williams, Jr.,* Chair.; Gerald V. Thomas II, Secy.-Treas.; R. Neal Batson; Susan Seydel Cofer; M. Hill Jeffries, Jr.; Oscar N. Persons; Michael T. Petrik; John R. Seydel; Paul V. Seydel.
EIN: 586034197
Selected grants: The following grants were reported in 2003.
$40,000 to Georgia Tech Foundation, Atlanta, GA. For Vasser Woolley Chair in Chemistry.
$30,000 to Atlanta Enterprise Center, Atlanta, GA.
$25,000 to Atlanta Speech School, Atlanta, GA.
$25,000 to Atlanta Union Mission, Atlanta, GA.
$25,000 to Genesis Shelter, Atlanta, GA.
$25,000 to Georgia Institute of Technology, Atlanta, GA. For research.
$25,000 to Howard Schools, Atlanta, GA.
$25,000 to Shepherd Center, Atlanta, GA. For capital campaign.
$25,000 to Stepping Stones Educational Therapy Center, Griffin, GA.
$15,000 to Theatrical Outfit, Atlanta, GA. For capital campaign.

2526
Worwin Foundation ✧ ☆
c/o Long Aldridge & Norman, LLP
303 Peachtree St., Ste. 5300
Atlanta, GA 30308

Donor: David R. Graham.
Foundation type: Independent foundation.
Financial data (yr. ended 12/31/04): Assets, $4,100,138 (M); gifts received, $125,000; expenditures, $666,222; qualifying distributions, $542,591; giving activities include $542,591 for grants.
Fields of interest: Foundations (community).
International interests: Canada.
Limitations: Applications not accepted. Giving primarily in Ontario, Canada. No grants to individuals.
Application information: Contributes only to pre-selected organizations.
Officer: Clay Long, Pres.

Director: David R. Graham.
EIN: 582094975

2527
Jane H. and William D. Young Foundation ✦ ☆

1271-A Tacoma Dr. N.W.
Atlanta, GA 30318

Established in 1992 in GA.
Donors: Jane H. Young; William D. Young, Sr.
Foundation type: Independent foundation.
Financial data (yr. ended 6/30/06): Assets, $3,858,690 (M); gifts received, $1,000,000; expenditures, $618,764; qualifying distributions, $615,949; giving activities include $615,949 for grants.
Purpose and activities: Giving for religion, education, and human services.
Fields of interest: Museums; Arts; Education; Youth development, services; Human services; Protestant agencies & churches.
Limitations: Applications not accepted. Giving primarily in Atlanta, GA. No grants to individuals.
Application information: Contributes only to pre-selected organizations.
Trustees: Jane H. Young; William D. Young, Sr.
EIN: 582021302
Selected grants: The following grants were reported in 2005.
$70,000 to Peachtree Presbyterian Church, Atlanta, GA.
$50,000 to Translational Genomics Research Institute (TGen), Phoenix, AZ.
$11,000 to Community Bible Church, Highlands, NC.
$3,500 to Thornwell Home and School for Children, Clinton, SC.
$2,000 to Christ School, Arden, NC.
$2,000 to Marist School, Atlanta, GA.
$1,000 to Atlanta History Center, Atlanta, GA.
$1,000 to Georgia Council on Economic Education, Atlanta, GA.
$1,000 to Shepherd Center, Atlanta, GA.
$1,000 to Southeastern Flower Show, Atlanta, GA.

2528
Zaban Foundation, Inc. ✦

3475 Lenox Rd. N.E., Ste. 950
Atlanta, GA 30326

Established in 1960 in GA.
Donors: Erwin Zaban; Zaban Investments, L.P.
Foundation type: Independent foundation.
Financial data (yr. ended 6/30/05): Assets, $5,633,227 (M); gifts received, $501,363; expenditures, $375,228; qualifying distributions, $367,509; giving activities include $366,184 for 21 grants (high: $154,234; low: $1,000).
Purpose and activities: Giving primarily to Jewish agencies and temples; funding also for human services and education.
Fields of interest: Education; Human services; Federated giving programs; Jewish federated giving programs; Jewish agencies & temples.
Limitations: Applications not accepted. Giving primarily in Atlanta, GA. No grants to individuals.
Application information: Contributes only to pre-selected organizations.
Officers: Erwin Zaban, Pres. and Treas.; Stephen M. Berman, Secy.
EIN: 586034590
Selected grants: The following grants were reported in 2005.
$154,233 to Jewish Federation of Greater Atlanta, Atlanta, GA.
$5,000 to East Lake Community Foundation, Atlanta, GA.

2529
Zeist Foundation, Inc. ✦

3715 Northside Pkwy. N.W., Ste. 3-195
Atlanta, GA 30327-2812 (404) 949-3162

Established in 1989 in GA.
Donors: George W. Brumley, Jr.†; Jean S. Brumley†; Elizabeth Stanback†.
Foundation type: Independent foundation.
Financial data (yr. ended 12/31/03): Assets, $58,709,376 (M); gifts received, $50,547,257; expenditures, $3,196,670; qualifying distributions, $3,100,422; giving activities include $2,801,178 for 59 grants (high: $510,336; low: $50; average: $500–$25,000).
Purpose and activities: Primarily supports education, children and youth services, community building, health and the arts, the environment, and wildlife conservation.
Fields of interest: Arts; Education; Environment, natural resources; Health organizations, association; Human services; Children/youth, services; Community development; Federated giving programs.
Type of support: General/operating support; Annual campaigns; Capital campaigns; Building/ renovation; Land acquisition; Debt reduction; Conferences/seminars; Curriculum development; Internship funds; Research; Technical assistance; Consulting services; Program evaluation; Matching/ challenge support.
Limitations: Applications not accepted. Giving primarily in the metropolitan Atlanta, GA, and Research Triangle, NC, areas. No grants to individuals.
Publications: Informational brochure.
Application information: Contributes only to pre-selected organizations.
Board meeting date(s): Quarterly
Officers and Directors:* Nancy J. Brumley,* Pres.; R. Brad Foster,* V.P.; Marie B. Foster, Secy.-Treas.
Number of staff: 1 full-time professional; 1 full-time support.
EIN: 581890927
Selected grants: The following grants were reported in 2004.
$1,100,000 to Emory University, Atlanta, GA.
$979,261 to Whiteford Community Program, Atlanta, GA.
$500,000 to Atlanta Symphony Orchestra, Atlanta, GA.
$390,000 to Durham Academy, Durham, NC.
$250,000 to Morehouse College, Atlanta, GA.
$200,000 to Community Foundation for Greater Atlanta, Atlanta, GA.
$30,000 to Hill Center, Durham, NC.
$25,000 to Georgia Partnership for Excellence in Education, Atlanta, GA.

HAWAII

2530

Alexander & Baldwin Foundation

P.O. Box 3440
Honolulu, HI 96801-3440 (808) 525-6642
Contact: Meredith J. Ching, V.P.
FAX: (808) 525-6677; E-mail: lhowe@abinc.com;
Application address: c/o Matson Navigation Co.,
555 12th St., Oakland, CA 94607, tel.: (707)
421-8121, FAX: (707) 421-1835, E-mail:
plmifm@aol.com; URL: http://
www.alexanderbaldwin.com/abf/index.htm

Established in 1991 in HI.
Donors: Alexander & Baldwin, Inc.; A&B Properties,
Inc.; East Maui Irrigation Co., Ltd.; Hawaiian
Commercial and Sugar Co.; Kahului Trucking and
Storage; Kauai Coffee Co.; Kauai Commerical Co.,
Inc.; Matson Navigation Co., Inc.
Foundation type: Company-sponsored foundation.
Financial data (yr. ended 12/31/05): Assets,
$3,042,093 (M); gifts received, $2,117,500;
expenditures, $2,172,132; qualifying distributions,
$2,162,132; giving activities include $2,090,335
for 772 grants (high: $125,000).
Purpose and activities: The foundation supports
organizations involved with arts and culture,
education, the environment, health, human
services, and community development.
Fields of interest: Museums (marine/maritime);
Arts; Education; Environment; Health care; Human
services; Community development; Federated giving
programs.
Type of support: Employee-related scholarships;
Employee volunteer services; General/operating
support; Annual campaigns; Capital campaigns;
Building/renovation; Equipment; Program
development; Seed money; Employee matching
gifts.
Limitations: Giving primarily in areas of company
operations in CA and HI. No support for religious
organizations or veterans', fraternal, or labor
organizations. No grants to individuals (except for
employee-related scholarships), or for travel or
endowments, secondary giving, religious activities
not of direct benefit to the entire community,
advertising, sponsorship of events, or general
operating support for United Way agencies; no
product or service donations.
Publications: Application guidelines; Annual report;
Grants list; Program policy statement.
Application information: Faxed or E-mailed
applications are accepted but an original copy must
be provided. Support is limited to 1 contribution per
organization during any given year. Proposals with a
request of $2000 or less should be no longer than
3 pages in length. Organizations requesting an
amount greater than $2000 should include an
executive summary of no more than 250 words.
Application form required.
  Initial approach: Download application form and
    mail proposal and application form to
    foundation for organizations located in Hawaii
    and the Pacific Islands; mail to Oakland, CA
    facility for organizations located in the U.S.
  Copies of proposal: 1
  Deadline(s): Feb. 1, Apr. 1, June 1, Aug. 1, Oct. 1,
    and Dec. 1 for Hawaii Committee; first of the
    month for Mainland Committee

Board meeting date(s): Bimonthly for Hawaii
  Committee; monthly for Mainland Committee
Final notification: Within one week of committee
  meeting
Officers and Directors:* W. Allen Doane,* Pres.;
Christopher J. Benjamin,* V.P. and Treas.; Meredith
J. Ching,* V.P.; Linda M. Howe, V.P.; Paul K. Ito,
V.P.; Alyson J. Nakamura, Secy.; James S.
Andrasick; Michael P. Choo; Grant Y.M. Chun; G.
Stephen Holaday; Gary J. North; Robert K. Sasaki.
Number of staff: 2 part-time professional; 1
part-time support.
EIN: 990291942
Selected grants: The following grants were reported
in 2004.
$131,000 to United Way. 2 grants: $125,000,
  $6,000
$40,000 to Pacific Arts Foundation, Honolulu, HI.
$35,000 to Punahou School, Honolulu, HI.
$25,000 to Blood Bank of Hawaii, Honolulu, HI.
$15,000 to YMCA.
$2,500 to Alta Bates Summit Foundation, Berkeley,
  CA.
$2,000 to Kauai Hospice, Lihue, HI.
$400 to Ohio Wesleyan University, Delaware, OH.
$250 to Maui Arts and Cultural Center, Kahului, HI.

2531

The Barbara Cox Anthony Foundation ✧

1132 Bishop St., Ste. 1200
Honolulu, HI 96813-2870
Contact: Garner Anthony, V.P.
Application address: P.O. Box 4316, Honolulu, HI
96812, tel.: (808) 536-1877

Incorporated in 1960 in HI.
Donors: Barbara Cox Anthony; James M. Cox†.
Foundation type: Independent foundation.
Financial data (yr. ended 12/31/04): Assets,
$250,544 (M); gifts received, $581,913;
expenditures, $378,034; qualifying distributions,
$378,034; giving activities include $378,029 for 53
grants.
Purpose and activities: Giving primarily for
education, as well as for health associations and
human services.
Fields of interest: Performing arts, orchestra
(symphony); Arts; Higher education; Education;
Environment, natural resources; Animals/wildlife,
preservation/protection; Health organizations,
association; Medical research, institute; Human
services; Federated giving programs.
Type of support: General/operating support;
Scholarship funds; Scholarships—to individuals.
Limitations: Giving primarily in HI, with emphasis on
Honolulu.
Application information: Application form not
required.
  Deadline(s): None
Officers and Directors:* Barbara Cox Anthony,*
Pres.; Garner Anthony,* V.P. and Secy.-Treas.;
James Cox Kennedy; Blair Perry-Okeden.
EIN: 996005049
Selected grants: The following grants were reported
in 2003.
$275,000 to La Pietra-Hawaii School for Girls,
  Honolulu, HI. For operating support.
$46,200 to Punahou School, Honolulu, HI. For
  scholarships.
$14,980 to Assets School, Honolulu, HI. For
  scholarships.
$5,000 to Hawaii Preparatory Academy, Kamuela,
  HI. For scholarships.

$1,674 to University of Hawaii, Honolulu, HI. For
  scholarships.
$1,500 to Habitat for Humanity of Hawaii, Honolulu,
  HI. For operating support.
$1,250 to Honolulu Academy of Arts, Honolulu, HI.
  For operating support.
$1,000 to Breakthroughs for Youth at Risk, Pearl
  City, HI. For operating support.
$1,000 to Easter Seal Society of Hawaii, Honolulu,
  HI. For operating support.
$1,000 to United Care USA Hawaii, Honolulu, HI. For
  operating support.

2532

Atherton Family Foundation ▼ ✧

c/o Hawaii Community Foundation
1164 Bishop St., Ste. 800
Honolulu, HI 96813 (808) 566-5524
Contact: Lissa Schiff, Private Fdn. Svcs. Off.
FAX: (808) 521-6286;
E-mail: Foundations@hcf-hawaii.org; Additional tel.:
(888) 731-3863 (Hawaii and neighbor islands only);
URL: http://
atherton.hawaiicommunityfoundation.org/

Incorporated in 1975 in HI as successor to Juliette
M. Atherton Trust established in 1915; F. C.
Atherton Trust merged into the foundation in 1976.
Donors: Juliette M. Atherton†; Frank C. Atherton†.
Foundation type: Independent foundation.
Financial data (yr. ended 12/31/05): Assets,
$96,627,129 (M); expenditures, $5,151,560;
qualifying distributions, $4,139,108; giving
activities include $3,721,271 for grants, and
$133,700 for grants to individuals.
Purpose and activities: The foundation is concerned
with education, human services, culture and the
arts, health, religion, and the environment. Focus
also on programs that benefit the people of Hawaii.
Scholarships for the postgraduate education of
Protestant ministers, Protestant ministers' children
for undergraduate study, and for graduate
theological education at a Protestant seminary.
Fields of interest: Humanities; Arts; Theological
school/education; Education; Environment; Health
care; Health organizations, association; Human
services; Protestant agencies & churches.
Type of support: Management development/
capacity building; Annual campaigns; Capital
campaigns; Building/renovation; Equipment;
Program development; Seed money; Curriculum
development; Research; Technical assistance;
Program evaluation; Scholarships—to individuals;
Matching/challenge support.
Limitations: Giving limited to HI; student aid for HI
residents only. Generally, no support for private
foundations, or for lobbying, individual Department
of Education schools, or for organizations engaged
in fundraising for the purpose of distributing grants
to recipients of their own choosing. No grants to
individuals (except for scholarships), generally no
giving for endowment funds, or for annual operating
support; no conferences, festivals or one-time
events; no loans.
Publications: Annual report; Financial statement;
Grants list.
Application information: Application form required
for scholarships and automation grants. See
foundation Web site for application details.
Application form not required.
  Initial approach: Proposal with coversheet
  Copies of proposal: 1

Deadline(s): Feb. 1, Apr. 1, Aug. 1, Oct. 1, and Dec. 1 for organizations; Mar. 1 for scholarships

Board meeting date(s): Feb., Apr., June, Oct., and Dec.

Final notification: 2 to 3 months

Officers and Directors:* Robert R. Midkiff,* Pres.; Judith M. Dawson,* V.P. and Secy.; Frank C. Atherton,* V.P. and Treas.; Patricia R. Giles,* V.P.; Paul F. Morgan,* V.P.; Joan H. Rohlfing,* V.P.

Agent: Bank of Hawaii.

EIN: 510175971

Selected grants: The following grants were reported in 2004.

$250,000 to United Way, Aloha, Honolulu, HI. For annual campaign for challenge match grant.

$200,000 to Mid-Pacific Institute, Honolulu, HI. For capital campaign for Technology Learning Complex.

$200,000 to Punahou School, Honolulu, HI. For middle school project.

$200,000 to YMCA of Honolulu, Metropolitan Office, Honolulu, HI. For Reaching for Tomorrow Capital Campaign.

$100,000 to Bishop Museum, Honolulu, HI. For Science Learning Center.

$100,000 to Hawaii Theater Center, Honolulu, HI. For Light Up the Hawaii Capital Campaign.

$30,000 to Honolulu Symphony, Honolulu, HI. For annual grant.

$25,000 to Parker School, Kamuela, HI. For Phase II Middle School construction.

$15,000 to Women Helping Women, Wailuku, HI. For Hale Lokomaikai Project Manager.

$12,500 to Hawaii Community Foundation, Honolulu, HI. For Family Foundation Conference.

2533
Leburta Atherton Foundation ◇

c/o Bank of Hawaii
P.O. Box 3170
Honolulu, HI 96802-3170

Established in 1997 in HI.

Foundation type: Independent foundation.

Financial data (yr. ended 12/31/04): Assets, $9,620,892 (M); expenditures, $357,250; qualifying distributions, $342,566; giving activities include $337,000 for 11 grants (high: $100,000; low: $1,000).

Purpose and activities: Giving for education and the environment.

Fields of interest: Education; Environment.

Limitations: Applications not accepted. Giving primarily in Honolulu, HI.

Application information: Unsolicited requests for funds not accepted.

Officers and Directors:* Leburta G. Atherton,* Pres.; Marjory A. Newell,* V.P.; Frank C. Atherton,* Secy.; Balbi A. Brooks,* Treas.

Trustee: Bank of Hawaii.

EIN: 943260209

Selected grants: The following grants were reported in 2004.

$75,000 to North Hawaii Community Hospital, Kamuela, HI.

$50,000 to Island School, Lihue, HI.

$20,000 to American Red Cross, Honolulu, HI.

$10,000 to Rancho Los Cerritos Foundation, Long Beach, CA.

$10,000 to Waimea Outdoor Circle, Waimea, HI.

$1,000 to Hawaii Preparatory Academy, Kamuela, HI.

2534
The Earl & Doris Bakken Foundation

Hale Ku'e Plz., No. 207
73-5619 Kauhola St.
Kailua Kona, HI 96740 (808) 326-9171
Contact: Georgine L. Busch, Treas.
FAX: (808) 326-9173; E-mail: buschg@hawaii.rr.com

Established in 1999 in HI.

Donors: Doris J. Bakken; Earl E. Bakken.

Foundation type: Independent foundation.

Financial data (yr. ended 12/31/05): Assets, $1,295,305 (M); gifts received, $4,467,372; expenditures, $4,065,239; qualifying distributions, $4,046,397; giving activities include $3,107,847 for grants, and $938,550 for 3 foundation-administered programs.

Purpose and activities: Giving primarily for education and health care; some support also for medical research.

Fields of interest: Education; Hospitals (general); Health care; Medical research, institute; Cancer research; Athletics/sports, water sports; Human services; Children/youth, services.

Limitations: Applications not accepted. Giving primarily in HI, with some emphasis on Kamuela. No grants to individuals.

Application information: Contributes only to pre-selected organizations. Unsolicited requests for funds not accepted.

Officers: Earl E. Bakken, Pres.; Doris J. Bakken, V.P.; John L. Powers, Secy.; Georgine L. Busch, Treas.

Number of staff: 4 full-time professional; 1 part-time support.

EIN: 990339501

Selected grants: The following grants were reported in 2005.

$700,000 to Minnesota Medical Foundation, Minneapolis, MN. For research.

$500,000 to University of Minnesota Foundation, Minneapolis, MN. 2 grants: $300,000 (For Center for Spirituality and Healing), $200,000 (For medical instruction in Mind and Development).

$200,000 to Courage Center, Golden Valley, MN. For general support.

$200,000 to Friends of the Future Fund, Kailua, HI. For grants management position.

$100,000 to North Hawaii Community Hospital, Kamuela, HI. For research.

$72,304 to Pavek Museum of Broadcasting, Saint Louis Park, MN. For mortgage payoff.

$41,250 to Kohala Center, Kamuela, HI. For general support.

$34,000 to Bravewell Collaborative, Minneapolis, MN. For general support.

$10,000 to Waikoloa Community Church, Waikoloa, HI. For general support.

2535
Bank of Hawaii Charitable Foundation ◇

(formerly Bancorp Hawaii Charitable Foundation)
c/o Foundation Admin. #758
P.O. Box 3170
Honolulu, HI 96802-3170 (808) 538-4944
Contact: Elaine Moniz, Trust Specialist
FAX: (808) 538-4006; E-mail: emoniz@boh.com;
Additional tel.: (808) 538-4945; Additional E-mail: pboyce@boh.com; URL: https://www.boh.com/about/community/471_504.asp

Established in 1981 in HI.

Donor: Bank of Hawaii.

Foundation type: Company-sponsored foundation.

Financial data (yr. ended 12/31/04): Assets, $8,486,984 (M); gifts received, $2,200,000; expenditures, $2,796,411; qualifying distributions, $2,738,320; giving activities include $1,895,300 for 131 grants (high: $112,175; low: $500), and $755,392 for 80 grants to individuals (high: $15,000; low: $1,098).

Purpose and activities: The foundation supports organizations involved with arts and culture, education, health, human services, and community development.

Fields of interest: Arts; Education; Health care; Human services; Community development.

Type of support: General/operating support; Continuing support; Annual campaigns; Capital campaigns; Building/renovation; Equipment; Endowments; Emergency funds; Program development; Scholarship funds; Technical assistance; Matching/challenge support.

Limitations: Giving primarily in areas of company operations in HI, the South Pacific, and the West Pacific.

Publications: Application guidelines; Grants list.

Application information: Proposals should be no longer than 5 pages. Executive summaries should be no longer than 1 page. Application form required.

Initial approach: Download application form and mail proposal, application form, and executive summary to foundation

Copies of proposal: 1

Deadline(s): Feb. 1, May 1, Aug. 1, and Nov. 1

Final notification: 60 days

Officers and Directors:* Michael E. O'Neill,* Pres.; Allan R. Landon,* V.P.; Cori Weston, Secy.; Richard Keene, Treas.; S. Haunani Apoliona; Peter D. Baldwin; Mary G.F. Bitterman; Michael Chun; Clinton R. Churchill; David A. Heenan; Robert Huret; Alton Kuioka; William C. Nelson; Martin A. Stein; Donald M. Takaki; Barbara J. Tanabe; Donna A. Tanoue; David W. Thomas; Robert W. Wo, Jr.

EIN: 990210467

Selected grants: The following grants were reported in 2004.

$50,000 to Iolani School, Honolulu, HI. For capital campaign.

$50,000 to Pacific Aviation Museum Pearl Harbor, Honolulu, HI. For capital campaign for Pacific Aviation Museum on Ford Island.

$50,000 to Punahou School, Honolulu, HI. For Case Middle School capital campaign.

$40,000 to Maryknoll Schools, Honolulu, HI. For capital campaign for Maryknoll School Community Center.

$25,000 to Foundation for Excellent Schools, Cornwall, VT. For participation by Oahu public school in Century Program.

$25,000 to Hawaii State Junior Golf Association, Honolulu, HI. For programs to serve youth statewide.

$25,000 to Honolulu Symphony Society, Honolulu, HI. For program support.

$25,000 to Seabury Hall, Makawao, HI. For construction and expansion capital campaign.

$25,000 to University of Hawaii Foundation, Honolulu, HI. For University of Hawaii at Manoa football program.

$20,000 to Chaminade University of Honolulu, Honolulu, HI. For Hogan Entrepreneurs business plan competition.

2536
James & Abigail Campbell Family Foundation ◇
(formerly James & Abigail Campbell Foundation)
1001 Kamokila Blvd.
Kapolei, HI 96707 (808) 674-6674
Contact: D. Keola Lloyd, Grants Mgr.
FAX: (808) 674-3349;
E-mail: keolal@campbellestate.com; URL: http://www.campbellestate.com/guidelines_fdn.htm

Established in 1980 in HI.
Donor: Members of the Campbell family.
Foundation type: Independent foundation.
Financial data (yr. ended 12/31/04): Assets, $19,011,833 (M); gifts received, $977,362; expenditures, $994,482; qualifying distributions, $834,288; giving activities include $779,680 for 48 grants (high: $125,000; low: $780).
Purpose and activities: The foundation presently emphasizes the following areas of need: 1) Youth services - programs that address the problems of youth such as truancy, low self-esteem, vandalism, violence, youth gangs, and substance abuse; 2) Education - support for public schools and educational programs; and 3) Hawaiian - programs that promote the social welfare of Hawaiians.
Fields of interest: Education; Human services; Children/youth, services.
Type of support: Curriculum development; Continuing support; Building/renovation; Equipment; Program development; Seed money; Scholarship funds.
Limitations: Giving limited to HI, with emphasis on West Oahu (Ewa/Ewa Beach, Kapolei, Makakilo and the Waianae Coast), Kahuku, Lahaina on Maui, and Pahoa on the island of Hawaii. No support for sectarian or religious programs. No grants to individuals, or for endowments, or highly technical research projects; no loans.
Publications: Annual report.
Application information: The foundation considers 1 request per organization per calendar year. Application guidelines available on foundation Web site. Application form not required.
Initial approach: Letter
Copies of proposal: 1
Deadline(s): Feb. 1 and Aug. 1
Board meeting date(s): Last working day of Apr. and Oct.
Final notification: 2 weeks after board meeting
Officers and Directors:* James Shingle,* Pres.; Clint Churchill,* V.P.; Dorna Del Zotto,* V.P.; Kapiolani Marignoli, V.P.; Jonathan Staub,* V.P.; James Growney,* Secy.; Wendy Crabb,* Treas.; D. Keola Lloyd, Grants Mgr.
Number of staff: 2 part-time professional; 1 part-time support.
EIN: 990203078

2537
Harold K. L. Castle Foundation ▼
146 Hekili St., Ste. 203
Kailua, HI 96734 (808) 263-7073
Contact: Jana Fry, Grants Mgr.
FAX: (808) 262-6918;
E-mail: jfry@castlefoundation.org; URL: http://www.castlefoundation.org

Incorporated in 1962 in HI.
Donors: Harold K.L. Castle†; Mrs. Harold K.L. Castle†.

Foundation type: Independent foundation.
Financial data (yr. ended 12/31/04): Assets, $158,444,901 (M); expenditures, $9,425,692; qualifying distributions, $7,077,177; giving activities include $6,651,958 for 77 grants (high: $1,200,000; low: $2,500; average: $25,000–$100,000).
Purpose and activities: As the largest private foundation in the state of Hawaii, the foundation grants approximately $7,000,000 per year to organizations that serve Hawaii. The foundation is currently focusing on three strategic program areas: 1) Public Education Redesign and Enhancement; 2) Near-Shore Marine Resource Conservation; and 3) Windward Oahu.
Fields of interest: Education, management/technical aid; Education, public policy; Education, reform; Education, public education; Elementary school/education; Elementary/secondary school reform; Education; Environment, public policy; Environment, water resources; Environment; Youth development; Community development.
Type of support: Management development/capacity building; Program development; Seed money; Technical assistance; Program evaluation.
Limitations: Giving limited to HI with priority given to Windward Oahu. No grants to individuals, or for ongoing operating expenses, endowments, annual fund drives, vehicles, or sponsorships or special events.
Application information: Within one month of receipt of inquiry, the foundation will write either to invite a full proposal or to inform applicant that the foundation will be unable to consider the request due to a mismatch with current foundation priorities. If applicant does not receive notification within a month after submitting online application, please contact Jana Fry, Grants Mgr., at tel.: (808) 263-7073 or E-mail: jfry@castlefoundation.org. Additionally, all prospective applicants must submit information explaining the extent to which the proposed project will help the foundation achieve its strategic goals. Application form required.
Initial approach: Submit online inquiry in foundation's Website
Copies of proposal: 1
Deadline(s): None
Board meeting date(s): Bimonthly
Final notification: Within 1 month of scheduled meeting; The foundation has deferred all decisions on requests for capital grants until Dec. 2006
Officers and Directors:* James C. McIntosh,* Chair.; H. Mitchell D'Olier,* C.E.O. and Pres.; John C. Baldwin,* V.P. and Secy.; Terrence R. George, V.P. and Exec. Dir.; Carlton K.C. Au, C.F.O. and Treas.; William E. Aull; Randolph G. Moore.
Number of staff: 2 full-time professional; 2 part-time professional; 2 full-time support.
EIN: 996005445
Selected grants: The following grants were reported in 2005.
$2,000,000 to Boys and Girls Club of Hawaii, Honolulu, HI. For challenge grant to establish club in Kailua.
$1,000,000 to Mid-Pacific Institute, Honolulu, HI. For construction of elementary school.
$900,000 to Nature Conservancy of Hawaii, Honolulu, HI. To build community capacity for effective marine conservation and to build network of Marine Managed Areas in Hawaii.
$750,000 to Hui Noeau Visual Arts Center, Makawao, HI. To purchase and renovate property.

$500,000 to Arizona-Sonora Desert Museum, Tucson, AZ. For construction of education building.
$500,000 to Contemporary Museum, Honolulu, HI. To build gallery spaces.
$500,000 to Hawaii Baptist Academy, Honolulu, HI. For construction of middle school campus.
$100,000 to Arizona Memorial Museum Association, Honolulu, HI. To replace and upgrade Visitor Center at U.S.S. Arizona Memorial.
$51,305 to University of Hawaii Foundation, School of Ocean and Earth Science and Technology, Honolulu, HI. For West Hawaii near shore marine resource conservation.
$50,000 to Good Beginnings Alliance, Honolulu, HI. For statewide communications campaign to promote importance of Universal Pre-Kindergarten.

2538
Samuel N. and Mary Castle Foundation
Pacific Guardian Ctr., Makai Twr.
733 Bishop St., Ste. 1275
Honolulu, HI 96813 (808) 522-1101
Contact: Alfred L. Castle, Exec. Dir.
FAX: (802) 522-1103; E-mail: acastle@aloha.net; URL: http://foundationcenter.org/grantmaker/castle/

Founded as S.N. Castle Memorial Trust in 1894; incorporated as a foundation in 1925 in HI.
Donors: Mary Castle†; Samuel N. Castle†.
Foundation type: Independent foundation.
Financial data (yr. ended 12/31/05): Assets, $46,958,791 (M); expenditures, $2,495,199; qualifying distributions, $2,008,520; giving activities include $2,008,520 for 59 grants (high: $200,000; low: $3,000).
Purpose and activities: Emphasis on private education, K through 12, early education teacher training, arts and culture, and human services for children birth to age 5; special fund for early childhood education programs. Most grants for direct service activities, small capital improvements or technical assistance.
Fields of interest: Historical activities; Arts; Education, early childhood education; Elementary school/education; Secondary school/education; Teacher school/education; Child development, services.
Type of support: Capital campaigns; Building/renovation; Equipment; Program development; Seed money; Curriculum development; Scholarship funds; Technical assistance; Program evaluation; Matching/challenge support.
Limitations: Giving generally limited to HI. Generally, no support for publicly funded organizations or lobbying organizations. No grants to individuals, or for continuing support; generally, no support for general operating budgets, endowment funds, more than 30 to 40 percent of total project cost, projects in which parents and community have not been properly involved in planning and funding, annual campaigns, scholarships, or research; no loans.
Publications: Annual report (including application guidelines); Financial statement; Grants list; Informational brochure; Informational brochure (including application guidelines); Program policy statement.
Application information: Major capital requests of $25,000 or more considered at Dec. meeting only, with preferences given to organizations with which

trustees are involved or that trustees have invited to apply. Application form not required.

Initial approach: Telephone or in-person visit is required prior to submitting a proposal
Copies of proposal: 2
Deadline(s): Feb. 1, June 1, and Oct. 1
Board meeting date(s): Apr., Aug., and Dec.
Final notification: 2 months

Officers and Trustees:* John C. Baldwin,* Pres.; James C. McIntosh,* V.P.; Randolph Moore, V.P.; Cynthia Quisenberry,* Secy.; Alfred L. Castle,* Treas. and Exec. Dir.

Number of staff: 1 full-time professional; 1 part-time support.

EIN: 996003321

Selected grants: The following grants were reported in 2005.

$200,000 to Kindergarten and Childrens Aid Association (KCAA) Preschools of Hawaii, Honolulu, HI. For preschools capital improvements.

$149,000 to Chaminade University of Honolulu, Honolulu, HI. 2 grants: $79,000 (For Castle Education Resource Center), $70,000 (For training for pre-school directors program).

$100,000 to Child and Family Service, Ewa Beach, HI. For construction of outdoor play area and drop-off and pick-up area.

$100,000 to Mid-Pacific Institute, Honolulu, HI. For fundraising campaign for preschool construction.

$100,000 to Sacred Hearts Academy, Honolulu, HI. For construction of Performing Arts Center.

$75,000 to Christian Liberty School, Keaau, HI. For capital improvement of new building.

$75,000 to Mililani Baptist Church, Mililani, HI. For preschool renovation.

$75,000 to Montessori School of Maui, Makawao, HI. For capital campaign for school construction.

$75,000 to YWCA of Oahu, Honolulu, HI. For renovation of facility.

2539
Change Happens Foundation ◇ ☆

P.O. Box 415
Holualoa, HI 96725
Contact: Douglas D. Troxel, Pres.
FAX: (808) 443-0067;
E-mail: admin@changehappens.us; *URL:* http://www.changehappens.us

Established in 2001 in CA.
Donor: Douglas D. Troxel.
Foundation type: Independent foundation.
Financial data (yr. ended 12/31/05): Assets, $23,445,042 (M); gifts received, $4,690,000; expenditures, $962,910; qualifying distributions, $723,700; giving activities include $723,700 for grants.
Purpose and activities: The goal of the foundation is to act as a meaningful catalyst toward positive change in our global community. The foundation's mission is to fund the development and implementation of innovative technology and progressive ideas to generate a positive force for change in our world.
Fields of interest: Education; Environment; Hospitals (general); Community development; Foundations (private grantmaking).
Limitations: Giving primarily in CA, HI, and IA. No support for religious activities. No grants to individuals, or for graduate or undergraduate scholarships.

Application information: If letter of inquiry is accepted for further consideration, the foundation will invite the applicant to submit a formal grant proposal. Unsolicited proposals not accepted.
Initial approach: Letter of inquiry (available on Web site)
Officers: Douglas D. Troxel, Pres.; Sergei George Troxel, Secy.; Michael Douglas Troxel, C.F.O.
EIN: 990355027

2540
Hung Wo & Elizabeth Lau Ching
Foundation ◇ ☆

841 Bishop St., Ste. 940
Honolulu, HI 96813-3910 (808) 521-4961
Contact: Han Hsin Ching, V.P.; Han Ping Ching, V.P.

Established around 1963.
Donors: Hung Wo Ching; Elizabeth Lau Ching.
Foundation type: Independent foundation.
Financial data (yr. ended 1/31/06): Assets, $7,628,322 (M); expenditures, $610,600; qualifying distributions, $562,900; giving activities include $552,900 for 37 grants (high: $150,000; low: $400), and $10,000 for 4 grants to individuals (high: $2,500; low: $2,500).
Purpose and activities: Giving primarily for education, human services, and child and family welfare.
Fields of interest: Museums; Education; Hospitals (specialty); Health organizations, association; Human services; Children/youth, services; Christian agencies & churches.
Type of support: Grants to individuals.
Limitations: Giving primarily in HI.
Application information:
Initial approach: Proposal
Deadline(s): None
Officers and Directors:* Han Hsin Ching,* V.P.; Han Ping Ching,* V.P.; Edric M. Ching, Secy.; Marie Kanno, Treas.; Shelli Mei Li Ching.
EIN: 996008990
Selected grants: The following grants were reported in 2006.
$150,000 to Iolani School, Honolulu, HI.
$150,000 to Punahou School, Honolulu, HI.
$10,000 to McKinley High School, Honolulu, HI.
$3,500 to American Red Cross.
$3,500 to Hospice Hawaii, Honolulu, HI.
$3,500 to Palama Settlement, Honolulu, HI.
$3,500 to Palolo Chinese Home, Honolulu, HI.
$3,500 to Ronald McDonald House.
$3,500 to Salvation Army.
$3,500 to YMCA of Honolulu, Waipahu, HI.

2541
Cooke Foundation, Ltd. ◇

c/o Hawaii Community Foundation
1164 Bishop St., Ste. 800
Honolulu, HI 96813 (808) 566-5524
Contact: Lissa Schiff
E-mail: foundations@hcf-hawaii.org; *Toll free tel.:* (888) 731-3863; *URL:* http://www.cookefdn.org

Trust established in 1920 in HI; incorporated in 1971.
Donor: Anna C. Cooke†.
Foundation type: Independent foundation.
Financial data (yr. ended 6/30/05): Assets, $24,945,152 (M); expenditures, $1,338,934; qualifying distributions, $1,198,191; giving

activities include $1,058,200 for 65 grants (high: $100,000; low: $2,500).
Purpose and activities: Giving to assure the continuance of, as well as to expand and extend all worthy endeavors for the betterment and welfare of the people of Hawaii.
Fields of interest: Humanities; Education; Environment; Health care; Health organizations, association; Human services.
Type of support: Management development/capacity building; Capital campaigns; Building/renovation; Equipment; Program development; Seed money; Technical assistance; Consulting services; Program evaluation; Matching/challenge support.
Limitations: Giving limited to HI and organizations serving the people of HI. No support for religious organizations, unless the forebears were involved with them. No grants to individuals, or for scholarships, fellowships, general operations, or endowment funds; no loans.
Publications: Annual report (including application guidelines); Grants list.
Application information: The required funding request coversheet is available on foundation Web site. Application guidelines, requirements, and procedures are also available on foundation Web site. Application form not required.
Initial approach: 3- to 5- page proposal with coversheet
Copies of proposal: 1
Deadline(s): First business day of Sept. for Nov. meeting; first business day of Mar. for May meeting
Board meeting date(s): 3rd Wed. in Sept., Jan., and May
Final notification: 3 weeks after board meeting
Officers and Trustees:* Samuel A. Cooke,* Pres.; Dale S. Bachman, V.P.; Lynne Johnson,* V.P.; Charles C. Spalding, Jr.,* V.P.; Anna D. Blackwell,* Secy.; Lissa Dunford,* Treas.
EIN: 237120804
Selected grants: The following grants were reported in 2004.
$100,000 to Honolulu Academy of Arts, Honolulu, HI. For annual grant.
$50,000 to Daughters of Hawaii, Honolulu, HI. For Hulihe's Palace Kuakini Building renovation and expansion.
$50,000 to Hanahauoli School, Honolulu, HI. For capital campaign.
$50,000 to La Pietra-Hawaii School for Girls, Honolulu, HI. For capital campaign.
$42,000 to Kona Historical Society, Captain Cook, HI. For Kona Heritage Ranch and Stores project planning.
$25,000 to Assistance League of Hawaii, Honolulu, HI. For remodeling of community service center.
$25,000 to Chaminade University of Honolulu, Honolulu, HI. For curriculum restructuring and enrichment in the humanities.
$25,000 to Hawaii Opera Theater, Honolulu, HI. For summer programming pilot project.
$25,000 to Hawaii Theater Center, Honolulu, HI. For capital campaign to complete restoration of theater exterior.
$25,000 to Historic Hawaii Foundation, Honolulu, HI. For Argonauta project.

2542
First Hawaiian Foundation ◇

P.O. Box 3200
Honolulu, HI 96847 (808) 525-7777
Contact: Sharon Shiroma Brown, Pres.

Established in 1975 in HI.
Donor: First Hawaiian Bank.
Foundation type: Company-sponsored foundation.
Financial data (yr. ended 12/31/05): Assets, $14,405,308 (M); gifts received, $2,002,004; expenditures, $1,975,335; qualifying distributions, $1,957,332; giving activities include $1,957,332 for 111 grants (high: $300,000; low: $1,000).
Purpose and activities: The foundation supports organizations involved with arts and culture, education, health, human services, civic affairs, and religion.
Fields of interest: Arts; Education; Health care, equal rights; Medical care, in-patient care; Health care; Children/youth, services; Human services; Public affairs; Religion.
Type of support: Annual campaigns; Capital campaigns; Building/renovation; Program development.
Limitations: Giving primarily in areas of company operations.
Publications: Annual report (including application guidelines).
Application information: Application form not required.
   Initial approach: Proposal
   Deadline(s): None
   Board meeting date(s): Quarterly
Officers and Directors:* Donald G. Horner,* Chair.; Sharon Shiroma Brown,* Pres.; William E. Atwater; Gary L. Caulfield; Walter A. Dods, Jr.; Brandt G. Farias; Mark H. Felmet; Robert T. Fujioka; Anthony R. Guerrero, Jr.; Robert S. Harrison; Corbert A K. Kalama; Howard H. Karr; Robin S. Midkiff; Raymond S. Ono; Edward Y.W. Pei; Frederick J. Shine III; Sheila M. Sumida; Albert M. Yamada*; Lily K. Yao.
EIN: 237437822
Selected grants: The following grants were reported in 2004.
$100,000 to Hawaii Maritime Center, Honolulu, HI. For corporate pledge.
$50,000 to Contemporary Museum, Honolulu, HI. For corporate pledge.
$40,000 to Iolani School, Honolulu, HI. For financial aid program.
$40,000 to Punahou School, Honolulu, HI. For capital campaign for new middle school.
$33,333 to Blood Bank of Hawaii, Honolulu, HI. To establish blood testing facility on Oahu.
$25,000 to Chaminade University of Honolulu, Honolulu, HI. For scholarships.
$25,000 to Foundation for Excellent Schools, Cornwall, VT. For Century Program.
$25,000 to Honolulu Festival Foundation, Honolulu, HI. For staging and marketing of festival.
$25,000 to Kapiolani Health Foundation, Honolulu, HI. For Children's Specialty Center.
$25,000 to Seabury Hall, Makawao, HI. For capital campaign.

2543

Mary D. and Walter F. Frear Eleemosynary Trust ◈
c/o Bank of Hawaii
P.O. Box 3170
Honolulu, HI 96802-3170 (808) 538-4944
Contact: Paula Boyce, Asst. V.P., Bank of Hawaii

Trust established in 1936 in HI.
Donors: Mary D. Frear‡; Walter F. Frear‡.
Foundation type: Independent foundation.
Financial data (yr. ended 12/31/03): Assets, $14,148,957 (M); expenditures, $1,326,790;

qualifying distributions, $1,323,669; giving activities include $1,320,397 for 116 grants (high: $150,000; low: $1,000; average: $5,000–$25,000).
Purpose and activities: Giving primarily for child welfare and youth; support also for education, social services, music and the arts.
Fields of interest: Performing arts, music; Arts; Education; Health care; Human services; Children/youth, services.
Type of support: Building/renovation; Equipment; Program development; Seed money; Matching/challenge support.
Limitations: Giving limited to HI. No grants to individuals, or for endowment funds, reserve funds, travel, or deficit financing; no loans.
Publications: Annual report (including application guidelines).
Application information: Schools' scholarship requests considered at Mar. meeting; no major capital campaign requests considered. Foundation cover memo obtained from foundation office must accompany all proposals. Application form not required.
   Initial approach: Telephone or proposal
   Copies of proposal: 4
   Deadline(s): Jan. 1, July 1, and Oct. 1
   Board meeting date(s): Apr., Aug. and Dec.
   Final notification: 3 to 6 months
Distribution Committee: Sharon McPhee, Chair.; Bruce J. Glor; Howard Hamamoto.
Trustee: Bank of Hawaii.
EIN: 996002270

2544

Victoria S. & Bradley L. Geist Foundation ◈
c/o Hawaii Community Foundation
1164 Bishop St., Ste. 800
Honolulu, HI 96813 (808) 566-5524
Contact: Robin Johnson, Prog. Off., Private Foundations
E-mail: foundations@hcf-hawaii.org; Tel. for Robin Johnson: (808) 537-6333; URL: http://www.hawaiicommunityfoundation.org/grants/pfGrants.php

Established in 1975 in HI.
Donor: Bradley L. Geist Trust.
Foundation type: Independent foundation.
Financial data (yr. ended 12/31/04): Assets, $42,292,428 (M); expenditures, $2,143,001; qualifying distributions, $1,954,074; giving activities include $1,537,411 for 52 grants (high: $1,000,000; low: $85; average: $250,000), and $283,000 for 120 grants to individuals (high: $4,000; low: $500).
Purpose and activities: The foundation has particular interest in programs involving the recruitment, initial and follow-up training, or retention of foster parents, sibling connectivity projects and supporting transitioning foster youth. The foundation also provides grants for medical research, and to support researchers to investigate key health issues within the context of both national research trends, and the reality of conducting studies in today's high-cost environment.
Fields of interest: Higher education; Education; Human services; Children/youth, services.
Type of support: Program development; Seed money; Research; Consulting services; Program evaluation; Scholarships—to individuals.

Limitations: Giving limited to HI residents and organizations. No grants for capital projects, endowment funds, or for on-going or general operating costs.
Publications: Application guidelines.
Application information: The required funding request cover sheet is available on the foundation Web site.
   Initial approach: Proposal with coversheet
   Copies of proposal: 1
   Deadline(s): Jan. 1, May 1, and Sept. 1 for Transitioning Foster Youth and Foster Parent funds; and the 1st business days of Mar. and Sept. for Medical Research funds
   Board meeting date(s): Mar., July, and Nov. for Transitioning Foster Youth and Foster Parent funds; and May and Nov. for Medical Research
   Final notification: Three weeks following board meeting
Trustees: Charman J. Akina; Gary S. Morimoto; Bank of Hawaii.
EIN: 990163400
Selected grants: The following grants were reported in 2003.
$104,350 to Foster Family Programs of Hawaii, Honolulu, HI. 2 grants: $70,000 (For PIN block grant to assist children in foster care system), $34,350 (For Hawaii Foster Youth Coalition).
$100,000 to Hawaii Community Foundation, Honolulu, HI. For organizational capacity building grantmaking.
$70,000 to Childrens Alliance of Hawaii, Honolulu, HI. For PIN block grant to assist children in foster care system.
$48,000 to Hale Kipa, Honolulu, HI. For salary for full-time family development specialist.
$40,000 to Catholic Charities of Honolulu, Honolulu, HI. For foster parent retention program, through Catholic Charities Family Services.
$40,000 to Child and Family Service, Ewa Beach, HI. For foster parent recruitment, training, and support network for therapeutic homes.
$35,000 to Hui Malama Learning Center, Wailuku, HI. For phase-out funding for Help your Kids Succeed.
$32,000 to Read Aloud America, Honolulu, HI. For Read Aloud Program (RAP).
$30,000 to Bishop Museum, Honolulu, HI. For Family Sundays, Family Passport to Learning and Fun.

2545

Hawaii Community Foundation ▼ ◈
(formerly The Hawaiian Foundation)
1164 Bishop St., Ste. 800
Honolulu, HI 96813 (808) 537-6333
Contact: Kelvin H. Taketa, C.E.O.
FAX: (808) 521-6286; E-mail: info@hcf-hawaii.org; Additional tel.: (888) 731-3863; Scholarship inquiry E-mail: scholarships@hcf-hawaii.org; URL: http://www.hawaiicommunityfoundation.org

Established in 1916 in HI by trust resolution; incorporated in 1987; reorganized in 1988.
Foundation type: Community foundation.
Financial data (yr. ended 12/31/04): Assets, $263,717,137 (M); gifts received, $17,012,993; expenditures, $23,951,706; giving activities include $15,502,239 for 1,740 grants (high: $502,079; low: $17), and $2,627,817 for grants to individuals.
Purpose and activities: The foundation helps people make a difference by inspiring the spirit of

giving and by investing in people and solutions to benefit every island community.

Fields of interest: Historic preservation/historical societies; Arts; Adult/continuing education; Education, reading; Education; Environment, natural resources; Environmental education; Environment; Health care; Mental health, treatment; Medical research, institute; Residential/custodial care; Aging, centers/services; Human services; Nonprofit management; Community development; Leadership development; Aging; Economically disadvantaged.

Type of support: Management development/capacity building; Equipment; Program development; Conferences/seminars; Seed money; Scholarship funds; Research; Technical assistance; Consulting services; Scholarships—to individuals.

Limitations: Giving limited to HI. No support for government agencies or large nonprofit organizations. No grants to individuals (except for scholarships), or for annual campaigns, emergency support, endowments, major capital projects, ongoing operating support, tuition aid programs, or deficit financing; no loans.

Publications: Application guidelines; Annual report; Informational brochure; Newsletter; Program policy statement.

Application information: Application procedures vary with foundation's different grantmaking programs. Visit foundation Web site for application instructions, application forms, and specific deadlines. Application form required.

Initial approach: Contact foundation
Copies of proposal: 1
Deadline(s): Varies
Board meeting date(s): Varies
Final notification: Within 3 months of proposal deadline

Officers and Board Members:* Robert R. Bean,* Chair.; Barry K. Taniguchi,* Vice-Chair.; Kelvin H. Taketa, C.E.O. and Pres.; Lori Abe, V.P., Public Rels. and Comms.; Kate Lloyd, V.P., Opers. and Genl. Counsel; Mariko Miho, V.P., Mktg. and Donor Svcs.; Chris van Bergeijk, V.P., Progs.; Margaret B. Cole,* Treas.; Terry Conlan, Cont.; Laurie Ainslie; Claire L. Asam, Ph.D.; Eugene Bal III; Gary Caulfield; Samuel A. Cooke; Jean F. Cornuelle; Anthony R. Guerrero, Jr.; Peter Ho; Lawrence M. Johnson; Mervina Cash Kaeo; Charlie King; Paul Kosaso; Cathy Luke; David Nakada; Jennifer Sabas; Jeffrey N. Watanabe; Eric Yeaman.

Trustees: Central Pacific Bank; First Hawaiian Bank; Pacific Century Trust.

Number of staff: 24 full-time professional; 3 part-time professional; 12 full-time support; 1 part-time support.

EIN: 990261283

Selected grants: The following grants were reported in 2004.

$1,336,346 to University of Hawaii, Office of Research Services, Honolulu, HI.
$260,650 to Punahou School, Honolulu, HI.
$253,800 to University of Hawaii Foundation, Honolulu, HI.
$250,000 to Kalihi-Palama Health Center, Honolulu, HI.
$240,000 to Kauai Rural Health Association, Lihue, HI.
$180,000 to Hawaii Legacy Foundation, Honolulu, HI.
$179,250 to Hawaii Theater Center, Honolulu, HI.
$152,500 to Collaborative Action for Public Education, Wahiawa, HI.
$152,500 to Hawaii Literacy, Honolulu, HI.
$142,316 to Bishop Museum, Honolulu, HI.

2546
Hawaiian Electric Industries Charitable Foundation ◇
(also known as H.E.I. Charitable Foundation)
P.O. Box 730
Honolulu, HI 96808-0730 (808) 532-5862
Contact: Alan T. Yamamoto, Dir., Community Rels.
FAX: (808) 532-5869; URL: http://www.hei.com/heicf/heicf.html

Established in 1984 in HI.

Donor: Hawaiian Electric Industries, Inc.

Foundation type: Company-sponsored foundation.

Financial data (yr. ended 12/31/04): Assets, $5,904,094 (M); gifts received, $3,545,000; expenditures, $1,438,407; qualifying distributions, $1,413,721; giving activities include $1,385,440 for 64 grants (high: $407,000; low: $500), and $28,275 for employee matching gifts.

Purpose and activities: The foundation supports organizations involved with education, the environment, family services, and community development.

Fields of interest: Education; Environment; Family services; Community development.

Type of support: Land acquisition; General/operating support; Capital campaigns; Program development; Employee matching gifts; Employee-related scholarships.

Limitations: Applications not accepted. Giving limited to HI. No support for political, religious, veterans', or fraternal organizations. No grants to individuals (except for employee-related scholarships), or for advertising, dinners, or tournaments.

Publications: Annual report.

Application information: Contributes only through employee-related scholarships and to pre-selected organizations.

Board meeting date(s): Quarterly

Officers and Directors:* Robert F. Clarke,* Pres.; Constance H. Lau,* V.P.; T. Michael May,* V.P.; Patricia U. Wong, Secy.; Curtis Y. Harada, Treas.; Victor H. Li; Oswald K. Stender; Jeffrey N. Watanabe.

Number of staff: 1 full-time professional; 1 full-time support.

EIN: 990230697

Selected grants: The following grants were reported in 2004.

$407,000 to United Way Statewide Association of Hawaii, Honolulu, HI.
$100,000 to Enterprise Honolulu, Honolulu, HI.
$68,000 to Pacific Gateway Center, Honolulu, HI.
$50,000 to Hawaii Homeownership Center, Honolulu, HI.
$50,000 to Punahou School, Honolulu, HI.
$35,000 to Iolani School, Honolulu, HI.
$30,000 to YMCA of Honolulu, Metropolitan Office, Honolulu, HI.
$29,250 to Hawaii Public Radio, Honolulu, HI.
$28,800 to Scholarship America, Saint Peter, MN.
$25,000 to Hawaii Theater Center, Honolulu, HI.

2547
HMSA Foundation ◇
(also known as Hawaii Medical Service Association Foundation)
P.O. Box 860
818 Ke'eaumoku St.
Honolulu, HI 96808-0860 (808) 948-5585
Contact: Cliff K. Cisco, V.P.

FAX: (808) 948-6860; URL: http://www.hmsafoundation.org

Established in 1997 in HI.

Donors: Pacific Century Trust; American Healthways; Hawaii Community Services Council; Hawaii Institute for Integrative Healthcare Research; University of California, San Francisco; Health Plan Hawaii Foundation.

Foundation type: Independent foundation.

Financial data (yr. ended 12/31/04): Assets, $28,885,148 (M); gifts received, $18,470; expenditures, $1,391,468; qualifying distributions, $1,105,568; giving activities include $1,105,568 for 36 grants (high: $98,724; low: $1,000).

Purpose and activities: The purpose of the foundation is to provide access to cost-effective health care services; health promotion, education, and research; and the promotion of social welfare.

Fields of interest: Higher education; Medical care, outpatient care; Pharmacy/prescriptions; Health care; Health organizations, association; Medical research, institute; Children, services; Residential/custodial care, hospices; Community development.

Type of support: General/operating support; Scholarship funds.

Limitations: Giving primarily in Honolulu, HI. No grants to individuals; or for scholarship funds, lobbying, voter registration, capital projects, endowments, development campaigns or multi-year commitments.

Application information: Application information available on foundation Web site.

Initial approach: Letter and telephone
Copies of proposal: 1
Deadline(s): Jan 1 for Mar. review, Apr. 1 for June review, July 1 for Sept. review, and Oct. 1 for Dec. review

Officers and Directors:* Robert P. Hiam,* Pres.; Cliff K. Cisco, V.P.; Alfred J. Fortin, Ph.D., Secy.; Steve Van Ribbink, Treas.; Harriet Aoki; Robin Campaniano; Andrew I.T. Chang; Michael J. Chun, Ph.D.; Julia Frolich, M.D.; Marvin B. Hall; Gary Kajiwara.

EIN: 990250429

Selected grants: The following grants were reported in 2004.

$98,724 to Hawaii Health Information Corporation, Honolulu, HI. To develop a statewide patient safety data repository and reporting system.
$51,000 to Salvation Army of Hawaiian Islands, Honolulu, HI. For substance abuse treatment and counseling for homeless women living at Institute for Human Services.
$50,000 to Hawaii Foodbank, Honolulu, HI. For Ohana Produce Program to improve nutrition and health of working families, seniors, homeless and handicapped.
$40,000 to University of Hawaii, Pacific Basin Rehabilitation Research and Training Center, Honolulu, HI. To evaluate programs serving persons with traumatic brain injury.
$39,092 to March of Dimes Birth Defects Foundation, Honolulu, HI. For NICU family support program.
$20,400 to Queens Medical Center, Honolulu, HI. For managing and treating substance abuse in primary care settings.

2548
Teresa F. Hughes Trust ✧
P.O. Box 3170
Honolulu, HI 96802-3170
Application address: c/o Grants Admin., Hawaii
Community Foundation, 1164 Bishop St., Ste. 800,
Honolulu, HI 96813, tel.: (808) 537-6333

Established in 1991 in HI.
Donor: Teresa F. Hughes†.
Foundation type: Independent foundation.
Financial data (yr. ended 3/31/05): Assets,
$9,150,666 (M); expenditures, $537,683;
qualifying distributions, $483,530; giving activities
include $436,550 for 44 grants (high: $25,000;
low: $3,000).
Purpose and activities: Grants restricted to
orphans, half-orphans, social orphans (neglected or
abused), children born out-of-wedlock to teen
mothers, and indigent and infirm adults over age 50.
Fields of interest: Human services; Children/youth,
services; Family services; Aging, centers/services;
Aging; Economically disadvantaged.
Type of support: General/operating support; Grants
to individuals.
Limitations: Giving limited to HI.
Application information: Social summary must
accompany application. Application form required.
 Initial approach: 2-3 page proposal for grants
 Copies of proposal: 2
 Deadline(s): Oct. 1 for grants
 Board meeting date(s): Every other month
Trustees: Suzanne Smith Churchill; Bank of Hawaii.
EIN: 990042494
Selected grants: The following grants were reported
in 2005.
$50,000 to Childrens Alliance of Hawaii, Honolulu,
 HI. 2 grants: $25,000 each
$35,000 to Hawaii Island Adult Care, Hilo, HI. 2
 grants: $15,000, $20,000
$20,000 to Kokua Kalihi Valley Comprehensive
 Family Services, Honolulu, HI.
$10,000 to Foster Family Programs of Hawaii,
 Honolulu, HI.
$7,500 to Bay Clinic, Hilo, HI.
$6,000 to Molokai General Hospital, Kaunakakai,
 HI. 2 grants: $3,000 each
$3,750 to Hui No Ke Ola Pono, Wailuku, HI.

2549
The Kosasa Foundation ✧
766 Pohukaina St.
Honolulu, HI 96813
Contact: Paul J. Kosasa, Pres.

Established in 1994 in HI.
Donors: Minnie Kosasa; Sidney S. Kosasa; Paul J.
Kosasa.
Foundation type: Independent foundation.
Financial data (yr. ended 7/31/05): Assets,
$10,950,654 (M); gifts received, $751,458;
expenditures, $667,491; qualifying distributions,
$571,000; giving activities include $571,000 for 50
grants (high: $120,000; low: $1,000).
Purpose and activities: Giving primarily for
education, religion, and youth services.
Fields of interest: Arts; Education; Health care; Boy
scouts; Human services; Children/youth, services;
Science; Religion.
Limitations: Giving primarily in Honolulu, HI.
Application information: Application form not
required.

Initial approach: Letter
Deadline(s): None
Officers and Directors:* Sidney S. Kosasa,* Chair.;
Minnie Kosasa,* Vice-Chair.; Paul J. Kosasa,* Pres.
and Treas.; Gloria Gainsley,* V.P.; Susan M.
Kosasa,* Secy.; Thomas S. Kosasa.
EIN: 990313279
Selected grants: The following grants were reported
in 2003.
$120,000 to Punahou School, Honolulu, HI. To build
 new Case Middle School.
$55,000 to Iolani School, Honolulu, HI. For capital
 improvements.
$50,000 to YMCA of Honolulu, Waipahu, HI. For
 capital campaign.
$30,000 to Boy Scouts of America, Aloha Council,
 Honolulu, HI. For capital campaign for New
 Service Center.
$20,000 to Palolo Chinese Home, Honolulu, HI. For
 capital campaign.
$15,000 to Honolulu Symphony, Honolulu, HI. For
 concert sponsorship.
$15,000 to Saint Francis Health Care Foundation of
 Hawaii, Honolulu, HI. For Renal Institute Home
 Dialysis Center.
$10,000 to Goodwill Industries of Honolulu,
 Honolulu, HI. For job training and employment
 services programs.
$10,000 to Moiliili Community Center, Honolulu, HI.
$10,000 to Palama Settlement, Honolulu, HI. For
 Leland Blackfield Scholarship.

2550
Robert F. Lange Foundation ✧
c/o Bank of Hawaii
P.O. Box 3170, Dept. 715
Honolulu, HI 96802-3170

Established in 1972 in HI.
Donors: Anna Lange†; Nora E. Lange†.
Foundation type: Independent foundation.
Financial data (yr. ended 12/31/05): Assets,
$9,748,075 (M); gifts received, $500;
expenditures, $544,068; qualifying distributions,
$423,449; giving activities include $410,000 for 2
grants (high: $205,000; low: $205,000).
Purpose and activities: Giving primarily for Asian art
and services for children.
Fields of interest: Arts, cultural/ethnic awareness;
Museums; Children/youth, services; Family
services.
Type of support: Program development.
Limitations: Applications not accepted. Giving
limited to Honolulu, HI. No grants to individuals.
Application information: Contributes only to
pre-selected organizations.
 Board meeting date(s): Mar.
Officers and Directors:* John Lockwood,* Pres.;
Ruedi Thoeni,* V.P.; H. Dan Williamson,* V.P.;
Marilynn Matsumoto,* Secy.-Treas.; David Franklin;
Patti Lyons; Mary F. Williamson.
Agent: Bank of Hawaii.
EIN: 237241511

2551
McInerny Foundation ✧
c/o Bank of Hawaii
P.O. Box 3170
Honolulu, HI 96802-3170 (808) 538-4944
Contact: Paula Boyce, Asst. V.P.

FAX: (808) 538-4006; E-mail: pboyce@boh.com or
emoniz@boh.com

Trust established in 1937 in HI.
Donors: William H. McInerny†; James D. McInerny†;
Ella McInerny†.
Foundation type: Independent foundation.
Financial data (yr. ended 9/30/05): Assets,
$58,777,872 (M); expenditures, $2,968,234;
qualifying distributions, $2,028,128; giving
activities include $1,865,367 for grants.
Purpose and activities: Emphasis on education,
youth rehabilitation, and social services. Giving also
for health, environment, and culture and the arts.
Fields of interest: Arts; Education; Health care;
Health organizations, association; AIDS; Human
services; Youth, services; Homeless.
Type of support: General/operating support;
Continuing support; Capital campaigns; Building/
renovation; Equipment; Program development; Seed
money; Scholarship funds; Matching/challenge
support.
Limitations: Giving limited to HI. No support for
religious institutions. No grants to individuals, or for
endowment funds, deficit financing, or research; no
loans.
Publications: Annual report (including application
guidelines).
Application information: Application form required
for major capital projects and school scholarship
programs. Foundation cover memo must accompany
all proposals and can be obtained from foundation
office. Application form required.
 Initial approach: Telephone or 3-page proposal
 Copies of proposal: 7
 Deadline(s): Nov. 15 for scholarship funds to
  schools; July 1 for major capital fund drives;
  none for others
 Board meeting date(s): Distribution Committee
  generally meets monthly
 Final notification: 3 months
Officers and Distribution Committee:* George
Fillion,* Chair.; Henry B. Clark, Jr.,* Vice-Chair.;
Paula Boyce, Grants Admin. Off.; Mrs. Gerry Ching.
Trustee: Bank of Hawaii.
EIN: 996002356
Selected grants: The following grants were reported
in 2004.
$250,000 to Palolo Chinese Home, Honolulu, HI.
 For Continue the Legacy Capital Campaign for
 renovation and construction expansion.
$131,000 to Punahou School, Honolulu, HI. 2
 grants: $70,000 (For middle school capital
 campaign), $61,000 (For tuition aid program).
$75,000 to Ronald McDonald House Charities of
 Hawaii, Honolulu, HI. For renovations for Judd
 Hillside House.
$70,000 to Nisei Veterans Memorial Center,
 Wailuku, HI. For capital campaign.
$53,000 to Mental Health Kokua, Honolulu, HI. For
 capital campaign to provide additional facilities
 for community-based programs in Hilo, Maui and
 Oahu.
$50,000 to Boys and Girls Club of Hawaii, Honolulu,
 HI. For RALLY Project at Central Middle School.
$50,000 to University of Hawaii Foundation,
 Honolulu, HI. For matching challenge grant for
 alumni giving.
$50,000 to YMCA of Honolulu, Central Branch,
 Honolulu, HI. For Reaching for Tomorrow Capital
 Campaign for new facilities and improvements.
$43,000 to Mid-Pacific Institute, Honolulu, HI. For
 tuition aid program.

2552
The James and Patricia Schuler Foundation ✧
P.O. Box 3708
Honolulu, HI 96811
Application address: c/o James K. Schuler, 828 Fort St. Mall, 4th Fl., Honolulu, HI 96813

Established in 1995 in HI.
Donors: James K. Schuler; Patricia T. Schuler.
Foundation type: Independent foundation.
Financial data (yr. ended 12/31/04): Assets, $23,334,073 (M); gifts received, $1,755,000; expenditures, $622,700; qualifying distributions, $572,686; giving activities include $572,686 for 70 grants (high: $50,000; low: $1,000).
Purpose and activities: Giving primarily for youth, family and social services, as well as for education, the arts, and cancer research.
Fields of interest: Performing arts; Education; Health organizations; Cancer research; Youth development; Human services; Children/youth, services; Family services; Federated giving programs.
Type of support: General/operating support; Research.
Limitations: Giving primarily in Honolulu, HI.
Application information: Application form not required.
  Initial approach: Letter
  Deadline(s): None
Officers: James K. Schuler, Pres.; Pamela S. Jones, V.P. and Treas.
Directors: Christopher T. Schuler; Mark J. Schuler; Jeffrey S. Whiteman.
EIN: 990316347

2553
M. M. Scott Scholarship Fund - Gertrude S. Straub Trust Estate ✧
c/o Bank of Hawaii
P.O. Box 3170
Honolulu, HI 96802-3170
Contact: Meleen P. Corenevsky, Asst. V.P., Bank of Hawaii
Scholarship address: c/o Hawaii Community Fdn., 1164 Bishop St., Ste. 800, Honolulu, HI 96813, tel.: (808) 537-6333

Established in 1966.
Donor: Gertrude S. Straub†.
Foundation type: Independent foundation.
Financial data (yr. ended 3/31/04): Assets, $8,466,901 (M); expenditures, $431,814; qualifying distributions, $414,675; giving activities include $379,350 for 247 grants to individuals (high: $2,800; low: $450).
Purpose and activities: Scholarship grants to HI public high school graduates to attend mainland colleges and major in a subject relating to the better understanding of peace and the promotion of international peace.
Fields of interest: International peace/security; International affairs; International studies.
Type of support: Scholarships—to individuals.
Limitations: Giving limited to residents of HI.
Publications: Informational brochure (including application guidelines).
Application information: Applicants must be graduates of public high schools in HI. Application form required.
  Initial approach: Telephone or letter of inquiry

Copies of proposal: 1
Deadline(s): Submit application preferably between Jan. 1 and Mar. 1; deadline Mar. 1
Board meeting date(s): Apr.
Trustee: Bank of Hawaii.
EIN: 996003243

2554
The Shaw (U.S.) Foundation ✧
c/o Deloitte & Touche, LLP
1132 Bishop St., Ste. 1200
Honolulu, HI 96813-2870

Established in 1995 in DE and HI.
Donor: Sir Run Run Shaw.
Foundation type: Independent foundation.
Financial data (yr. ended 12/31/05): Assets, $27,177,380 (M); expenditures, $1,360,424; qualifying distributions, $1,353,877; giving activities include $1,348,748 for 3 grants (high: $513,809; low: $321,130).
Purpose and activities: Giving primarily for higher education in China.
Fields of interest: Higher education.
International interests: China.
Limitations: Applications not accepted. Giving on an international basis. No grants to individuals.
Application information: Contributes only to pre-selected organizations.
Officers and Directors:* Mona Fong,* Pres.; Louis Page,* V.P.; Roger Epstein, Secy.; Jerry Rajakulendran, Treas.; Julie Ng; Choy Venus.
EIN: 990291105

2555
The Strong Foundation ✧
c/o Bank of Hawaii
P.O. Box 3170
Honolulu, HI 96802

Established in 1995 in HI.
Foundation type: Independent foundation.
Financial data (yr. ended 8/31/05): Assets, $29,806,917 (M); expenditures, $1,605,468; qualifying distributions, $1,465,349; giving activities include $1,452,000 for 19 grants (high: $150,000; low: $25,000).
Purpose and activities: Giving primarily for nature conservation and for the arts. Some giving for education and human services.
Fields of interest: Performing arts, theater; Performing arts, opera; Higher education; Education; Environment; Human services; Federated giving programs.
Limitations: Applications not accepted. Giving limited to HI. No grants to individuals.
Application information: Contributes only to pre-selected organizations.
Officers and Trustees:* William E. Aull,* Pres.; Samuel A. Cooke,* V.P.; Marilynn Matsumoto, Secy.; Douglas Philpotts,* Treas.; S.J. Beardmore; Anne Strong Carter; Charles M. Holland; Robert H. Rath, Sr.; Henry F. Rice.
EIN: 990090807
Selected grants: The following grants were reported in 2004.
$125,000 to Doris Todd Memorial Christian Day School, Paia, HI. For capital campaign.
$125,000 to Punahou School, Honolulu, HI. For Case Middle School capital campaign.

$100,000 to Ballet Hawaii, Honolulu, HI. For renovations to office and dance studio at Dole Cannery.
$100,000 to Honolulu Waldorf School, Honolulu, HI. For roof repairs and room addition.
$100,000 to Island School, Lihue, HI. For Phase I of campus expansion project.
$100,000 to YMCA of Honolulu, Metropolitan Office, Honolulu, HI. For Capital Campaign for expansion and/or improvements to various YMCA branches across Oahu.
$75,000 to Hawaii Opera Theater, Honolulu, HI. For performance of The Mikado, and support of additional education and outreach coordinator.
$75,000 to Hawaii Youth Symphony Association, Honolulu, HI. For expansion of office, music library and musical instrument storage space, and operating support for music program.
$25,000 to Hawaii Architectural Foundation, Honolulu, HI. For creation and publication of book, Honolulu's Chinatown Today.
$25,000 to Honolulu Community Media Council, Honolulu, HI. For Youth Speakers Bureau's community outreach project, start-up and operating support.

2556
The Trimble Foundation ✧ ☆
1350 Ala Moana Blvd., Ste. 1811
Honolulu, HI 96814

Established in 1994 in HI.
Donor: Robert A. Trimble.
Foundation type: Independent foundation.
Financial data (yr. ended 12/31/05): Assets, $7,437,872 (M); gifts received, $54,803; expenditures, $367,578; qualifying distributions, $365,000; giving activities include $365,000 for 3 grants (high: $350,000; low: $5,000).
Purpose and activities: Giving for higher education.
Fields of interest: Education; Human services.
Limitations: Applications not accepted. Giving primarily in WA. No grants to individuals.
Application information: Contributes only to pre-selected organizations.
Officers: Gordon M. Trimble, Pres.; Robert A. Trimble, 1st V.P.; Charles R. Trimble, 2nd V.P.; Sonia U. Trimble, Treas.
EIN: 990316453
Selected grants: The following grants were reported in 2004.
$160,000 to University of Puget Sound, Tacoma, WA. For Asian Studies.
$32,000 to National Federation of the Blind of Hawaii, Honolulu, HI. For general support.
$19,700 to Grassroot Institute of Hawaii, Honolulu, HI. For general support.

2557
A. & E. Vidinha Charitable Trust ✧
c/o Bank of Hawaii, Fdn. Admin. No. 758
P.O. Box 3170
Honolulu, HI 96802-3170
Contact: Paula Boyce, Asst. V.P.

Established in 1989 in HI.
Donors: Antone Vidinha†; Edene Vidinha†.
Foundation type: Independent foundation.
Financial data (yr. ended 6/30/05): Assets, $7,487,212 (M); expenditures, $382,127; qualifying distributions, $356,846; giving activities

include $330,800 for 12 grants (high: $88,750; low: $7,500).
Fields of interest: Scholarships/financial aid; Health care; Health organizations; Religion.
Type of support: General/operating support; Building/renovation; Equipment; Program development; Scholarship funds.
Limitations: Giving limited to Kauai Island, HI, only. No grants to individuals.
Publications: Annual report (including application guidelines).
Application information: Foundation cover memo must accompany all proposals and can be obtained from foundation officer. Application form required.
   Initial approach: Proposal (no more than 3 pages)
   Copies of proposal: 4
   Deadline(s): Mar. 1
   Board meeting date(s): May or June
   Final notification: 2 to 3 months
Trustee: Bank of Hawaii.
EIN: 990273993
Selected grants: The following grants were reported in 2003.
$70,000 to University of Hawaii Foundation, Honolulu, HI. For scholarships.
$60,000 to Saint Francis Health Care Foundation of Hawaii, Honolulu, HI. To replace Medical Waste Sterilizer at Lihue Dialysis Facility.
$52,350 to Lihue Baptist Church, Lihue, HI. For renovation project.
$30,675 to Wilcox Hospital Foundation, Lihue, HI. For Diagnostic Center equipment.
$30,000 to American Cancer Society, Honolulu, HI.
$20,000 to Lihue Christian Church, Lihue, HI. To develop a parking lot.
$10,000 to American Lung Association of Hawaii, Honolulu, HI. For Asthma Sports Day Camp.
$10,000 to Chaminade University of Honolulu, Honolulu, HI. For scholarships.
$10,000 to Easter Seal Society of Hawaii, Honolulu, HI.
$10,000 to Hawaii Pacific University, Honolulu, HI. For scholarship program.

2558
J. Watumull Fund ✧
(formerly J. Watumull Estate, Inc.)
c/o Watumull Bros., Ltd.
P.O. Box 88296
Honolulu, HI 96830-8296 (808) 971-8800
Contact: Gulab Watumull, Pres.
Application address: Watumull Bldg., 307 Lewers St., 6th Fl., Honolulu, HI 96815; FAX: (808) 971-8824

Established in 1980 in HI.
Donors: Jhamandos Watumull‡; Watumull Bros., Ltd.
Foundation type: Independent foundation.
Financial data (yr. ended 12/31/04): Assets, $10,561,098 (M); gifts received, $200,000; expenditures, $602,894; qualifying distributions, $485,141; giving activities include $414,750 for 138 grants (high: $40,000; low: $1,000), and $50,000 for 50 grants to individuals (high: $6,000; low: $1,000).
Purpose and activities: Support for community development, education, including higher education, social services, and culture; foundation is interested in programs in HI, and India.
Fields of interest: Museums; Arts; Higher education; Hospitals (general); Human services; Family services.

International interests: India.
Type of support: General/operating support; Capital campaigns; Building/renovation; Endowments; Program development; Fellowships; Scholarship funds; Scholarships—to individuals.
Limitations: Giving primarily in HI, and nationally to organizations interested in India.
Application information: Application form not required.
   Initial approach: Letter
   Copies of proposal: 1
   Deadline(s): None
   Board meeting date(s): Apr., June and Nov.
   Final notification: 4 months or less
Officers and Directors:* Gulab Watumull,* Pres.; Jaidev Watumull,* V.P. and Treas.; Khubchand Watumull,* V.P.; Vik Watumull, V.P.; Jyoti Watumull,* Secy.
EIN: 510205431

2559
G. N. Wilcox Trust ✧
c/o Bank of Hawaii
P.O. Box 3170
Honolulu, HI 96802-3170
Contact: Paula Boyce, Asst. V.P., Bank of Hawaii
E-mail: pboyce@boh.com, or emoniz@boh.com

Trust established in 1916 in HI.
Donor: George N. Wilcox‡.
Foundation type: Independent foundation.
Financial data (yr. ended 12/31/04): Assets, $23,800,141 (M); expenditures, $1,022,476; qualifying distributions, $999,336; giving activities include $936,253 for 112 grants (high: $50,000; low: $1,500).
Purpose and activities: Primary areas of interest include social services, child welfare, family services, education, and health. Support also for literacy programs, the elderly, arts and culture, hospices, AIDS services and education, community funds, delinquency and crime prevention, and Protestant church support. No multi-year pledges.
Fields of interest: Arts; Adult education—literacy, basic skills & GED; Education, reading; Education; Health care; Health organizations, association; AIDS; Crime/violence prevention, youth; Crime/law enforcement; Human services; Children/youth, services; Family services; Residential/custodial care, hospices; Aging, centers/services; Protestant agencies & churches; Religion.
Type of support: General/operating support; Building/renovation; Equipment; Program development; Seed money; Scholarship funds; Matching/challenge support.
Limitations: Giving limited to HI, with emphasis on the Island of Kauai. No support for government agencies or organizations substantially supported by government funds. No grants to individuals, or for endowment funds, reserve funds, research, or deficit financing; no direct student aid or scholarships; no loans.
Publications: Annual report (including application guidelines).
Application information: Schools' scholarship requests considered at Mar. meeting; The trust accepts unsolicited applications from Hawaii only. Application form required.
   Initial approach: Letter (no more than 3 pages)
   Copies of proposal: 4
   Deadline(s): Jan 1, Apr. 1, July 1, and Oct. 1

   Board meeting date(s): Mar., June, Sept., and Dec.
   Final notification: 3 months
Committee on Beneficiaries: Marilynn Matsumoto, Chair.; Gale Fisher Carswell; Aletha Kaohi.
Trustee: Bank of Hawaii.
EIN: 996002445
Selected grants: The following grants were reported in 2004.
$50,000 to Wilcox Hospital Foundation, Lihue, HI. For Zeiss OPMI Microscope Surgical Equipment.
$25,000 to ARC of Kauai, Lihue, HI. For renovation and restoration to the Ford Coffman Center.
$25,000 to Kauai Food Bank, Lihue, HI. For program support.
$25,000 to YMCA of Honolulu, Waipahu, HI. For ADA renovations for Camp Erdman.
$20,000 to Hawaii Conference of the United Church of Christ, Honolulu, HI. For pilot program for KAUCC Community Integration Center.
$20,000 to Kauai Childrens Discovery Museum, Kapaa, HI. For operating support.
$15,000 to Adult Friends for Youth, Honolulu, HI. For Clinical and Competency based Alternative Education Program.
$15,000 to National Tropical Botanical Garden, Kalaheo, HI. To purchase service building equipment.
$15,000 to Seabury Hall, Makawao, HI. For equipment for Technology Center.
$10,000 to Meals on Wheels of Hawaii, Honolulu, HI. For expansion of home delivery.

2560
Harry Chow & Nee-Chang Chock Wong Foundation ✧ ☆
1164 Bishop St., Ste. 530
Honolulu, HI 96813 (808) 523-1621
Contact: Robert H.Y. Leong, Pres.

Established about 1970 in HI.
Donors: Harry C. Wong‡; Nee-Chang Chock Wong‡.
Foundation type: Independent foundation.
Financial data (yr. ended 12/31/05): Assets, $13,013,809 (M); expenditures, $536,963; qualifying distributions, $386,000; giving activities include $386,000 for 8 grants (high: $100,000; low: $5,000).
Purpose and activities: Giving primarily for educational, scientific and charitable purposes primarily for the benefit of 501(c)(3) organizations in Hawaii.
Fields of interest: Secondary school/education; Higher education; Higher education, college; Libraries/library science; Health organizations, association.
Type of support: General/operating support; Continuing support; Curriculum development; Scholarship funds.
Limitations: Giving limited to HI. No grants to individuals.
Application information:
   Deadline(s): None
Officers and Directors:* Robert H.Y. Leong,* Pres. and Secy.-Treas.; Robin L. Leong,* V.P.; Toni L. Leong,* V.P.; Maxine W. Leong, V.P.
EIN: 996012585
Selected grants: The following grants were reported in 2004.
$115,000 to Hawaii Foodbank, Honolulu, HI. For general support.
$15,000 to First Chinese Church of Christ in Hawaii, Honolulu, HI. For general support.

$11,500 to ARC in Hawaii, Honolulu, HI. For general support.

2561
Hans and Clara Davis Zimmerman Foundation ◇
c/o Bank of Hawaii
1164 Bishop St., Ste. 800
Honolulu, HI 96802-3170 (808) 537-6333

Established in 1963 in HI.

Donors: Hans Zimmerman†; Clara Zimmerman†.
Foundation type: Independent foundation.
Financial data (yr. ended 12/31/04): Assets, $13,983,711 (M); expenditures, $778,307; qualifying distributions, $703,825; giving activities include $653,025 for 327 grants to individuals (high: $6,000; low: $500).
Purpose and activities: Giving for scholarships, with preference given to students majoring in medicine, nursing, related health fields and majoring in education.

Fields of interest: Medical school/education; Pharmacy/prescriptions; Nursing care; Health care; Health organizations, association.
Type of support: Scholarships—to individuals.
Limitations: Giving limited to residents of HI.
Publications: Informational brochure (including application guidelines).
Application information: Request application forms by Feb. 1. Application form required.
  Deadline(s): Mar. 1
  Board meeting date(s): May
Trustee: Bank of Hawaii.
EIN: 996006669

IDAHO

2562
J. A. & Kathryn Albertson Foundation, Inc. ▼
501 Baybrook Ct.
P.O. Box 70002
Boise, ID 83707-0102 (208) 424-2600
Contact: Lori Fisher, Exec. Dir.
FAX: (208) 424-2626; E-mail: fdn@jkaf.org;
URL: http://www.jkaf.org

Established in 1966 in ID.
Donors: J.A. Albertson†; Kathryn Albertson†.
Foundation type: Independent foundation.
Financial data (yr. ended 12/31/04): Assets,
$522,008,821 (M); expenditures $26,383,550;
qualifying distributions, $25,191,107; giving
activities include $23,851,024 for 323 grants (high:
$8,765,181; low: $19; average: $1,000–
$200,000).
Purpose and activities: To improve education in
Idaho.
Fields of interest: Elementary/secondary
education; Education, early childhood education;
Higher education, college (community/junior).
Type of support: Program development;
Conferences/seminars; Curriculum development.
Limitations: Applications not accepted. Giving
limited to ID. No grants to individuals.
Publications: Annual report; Informational brochure;
Newsletter.
Application information: Unsolicited requests not
accepted. All giving done through RFP or invitations
to apply. Check Web site for current initiatives and
programs.
Board meeting date(s): Quarterly
Officers and Directors:* Joseph B. Scott,* Chair.;
Thomas J. Wilford,* C.E.O.; Jamie J. Scott,*
Secy.-Treas. and Prog. Off., Community Grants; Rex
Butler, Cont.; Lori Fisher, Exec. Dir.; Everett L. Doty;
Gary Michael; Barbara J. Newman; J.L. Scott.
Number of staff: 6 full-time professional; 1 part-time
support.
EIN: 826012000
Selected grants: The following grants were reported
in 2004.
$8,765,181 to Idaho State Department of
Education, Boise, ID. For Idaho Student
Information Management System (ISIMS)
Operations.
$716,600 to Boise City Independent School
District, Boise, ID. 2 grants: $360,000 (For
implementation of strategic plan of district),
$356,600 (For educational model being
implemented for Mountain View and McKinley
Schools specifically).
$315,000 to Pocatello-Chubbuck School District
No. 25, Pocatello, ID. For implementation of
strategic plan of district.
$270,000 to Nampa School District No. 131,
Nampa, ID. For implementation of strategic plan
of district.
$225,000 to Jerome Joint School District No. 261,
Jerome, ID. For implementation of strategic plan
of district.
$216,000 to Coeur d Alene School District No. 271,
Coeur d Alene, ID. For implementation of
strategic plan of district.
$200,000 to Albertson College of Idaho, Caldwell,
ID.

$195,750 to Middleton School District No. 134,
Middleton, ID. For implementation of strategic
plan of district.
$28,889 to Bonneville School District, Idaho Falls,
ID. For The Open Book Initiative (TOBI) Fellow
Salary Buyouts.

2563
Albertson's Stores Charitable Foundation, Inc. ◇
(formerly Albertson's Charitable Foundation, Inc.)
P.O. Box 20
Boise, ID 83726
Contact: Dee M.K. Mooney, V.P.
Application address: 250 Parkcenter Blvd., Boise, ID
83726, tel.: (208) 395-5610

Established in 2003 in ID.
Donor: General Mills, Inc.
Foundation type: Company-sponsored foundation.
Financial data (yr. ended 1/31/05): Assets,
$1,058,254 (M); gifts received, $2,069,554;
expenditures, $2,312,886; qualifying distributions,
$2,312,223; giving activities include $2,312,223
for 55 grants (high: $339,000; low: $1,000).
Purpose and activities: The foundation supports
organizations involved with education, health,
hunger, nutrition, and youth.
Fields of interest: Education; Health care; Food
services; Food banks; Nutrition; Youth, services.
Limitations: Giving primarily in areas of company
operations.
Application information: Application form required.
Initial approach: Contact foundation for
application form
Deadline(s): Dec. and May
Officers and Directors:* Susan M. Neumann,*
Pres.; Dee M.K. Mooney, V.P.; Joel H. Guth, Secy.;
John F. Boyd,* Treas.; Paul G. Rowan.
EIN: 200051735

2564
Boswell Family Foundation ▼ ◇
c/o James G. Boswell, II
P.O. Box 413
Ketchum, ID 83340

Donor: J.G. Boswell II.
Foundation type: Independent foundation.
Financial data (yr. ended 12/31/05): Assets,
$6,601,144 (M); expenditures, $619,274;
qualifying distributions, $572,422; giving activities
include $534,802 for 3 grants (high: $500,000;
low: $10,000).
Fields of interest: Education; Children/youth,
services.
Limitations: Applications not accepted. Giving
primarily in CA and Hailey, ID. No grants to
individuals.
Application information: Contributes only to
pre-selected organizations.
Officers and Trustees:* Lorraine Wilcox,* Pres.;
Barbara Wallace,* V.P.; Theresa E. Williams,*
Secy.-Treas.; J.G. Boswell II.
EIN: 820514966
Selected grants: The following grants were reported
in 2004.
$3,000,000 to Corcoran Community Foundation,
Corcoran, CA. For capital campaign for
endowment fund.

$2,500,000 to Stanford University, Stanford, CA.
For capital campaign for Medical Center.
$50,000 to Blaine County School District No. 61,
Hailey, ID. For capital campaign.
$31,561 to Four-H Club of Blaine County, Hailey, ID.
For operating support.

2565
The John H. and Orah I. Brandt Foundation ◇ ☆
c/o Don K. Brandt
203 11th Ave. S.
Nampa, ID 83651-3920

Established in 1990 in ID.
Donor: John H. Brandt.
Foundation type: Independent foundation.
Financial data (yr. ended 12/31/05): Assets,
$16,187,453 (M); gifts received, $35,207;
expenditures, $815,821; qualifying distributions,
$532,138; giving activities include $532,138 for
grants.
Fields of interest: Higher education, college; Higher
education, university; Salvation Army.
Limitations: Applications not accepted. Giving
primarily in Nampa, ID.
Application information: Unsolicited requests for
funds not accepted.
Trustees: Don K. Brandt; Lawrence V. Gray; Jerry
Hess; Vic Sachtjen; J.R. Schiller.
EIN: 943124992

2566
CHC Foundation ◇
245 N. Placer Ave.
P.O. Box 1644
Idaho Falls, ID 83403 (208) 522-2368
Contact: Ralph Isom, Pres.
E-mail: info@chcfoundation.net; URL: http://
www.chcfoundation.net

Established in 1985 in ID.
Foundation type: Independent foundation.
Financial data (yr. ended 12/31/05): Assets,
$13,312,260 (M); expenditures, $837,148;
qualifying distributions, $662,861; giving activities
include $591,330 for grants.
Fields of interest: Arts; Elementary/secondary
education; Education; Environment, natural
resources; Human services; Children/youth,
services; Aging, centers/services; Community
development.
Type of support: Capital campaigns; Building/
renovation; Equipment; Matching/challenge
support.
Limitations: Giving limited to southeastern ID. No
support for religious organizations, or for lobbying
groups, interstate organizations or other charitable
foundations. No grants to individuals or for operating
expenses, trips, workshops, competitions,
scholarships, or for advertising.
Publications: Informational brochure (including
application guidelines).
Application information: Application coversheet
available on foundation Web site. Application form
required.
Initial approach: Check of foundation Web site
Copies of proposal: 13
Deadline(s): Mar. 15 and Sept. 1
Board meeting date(s): 1st Wed. of the month
Final notification: 10 weeks

Officers: Donald R. Bjornson, M.D., Pres.; Peggy Sharp, V.P.; Milton F. Adam, Secy.; Margaret A. Leverett, Treas.

Directors: Ralph Isom; Forde Johnson; Carole Lentz; Leslee Martin; Charles M. Rice; John I. Sackett; Anne S. Voilleque.

Number of staff: 1 part-time support.

EIN: 820211282

Selected grants: The following grants were reported in 2005.

$100,000 to YMCA of Idaho Falls, Idaho Falls, ID.

$70,000 to Hospice of Eastern Idaho, Idaho Falls, ID.

$40,000 to Bonneville County Historical Society, Idaho Falls, ID.

$33,111 to Eastern Idaho Special Services Agency, Idaho Falls, ID.

$30,000 to Family Safety Network, Driggs, ID.

$28,385 to Club, Inc., Idaho Falls, ID.

$25,000 to Help Inc., Idaho Falls, ID.

$21,600 to Community and Rural Transportation (CART), Idaho Falls, ID.

$20,000 to Clark County District Library, Dubois, ID.

$16,025 to Actors Repertory Theater of Idaho, Idaho Falls, ID.

2567
Laura Moore Cunningham Foundation, Inc. ▼

P.O. Box 1157
Boise, ID   83701
Contact: Laura Bettis, Secy.
E-mail: lmbettis@hotmail.com

Incorporated in 1964 in ID.

Donors: Harry Bettis; Laura Moore Cunningham†.

Foundation type: Independent foundation.

Financial data (yr. ended 8/31/05): Assets, $94,247,028 (M); expenditures, $4,340,529; qualifying distributions, $4,179,028; giving activities include $4,164,900 for 36 grants (high: $1,600,000; low: $1,200; average: $20,000–$250,000).

Purpose and activities: Emphasis on higher and other education, particularly for scholarship funds; support also for hospitals, child welfare, and educational programs.

Fields of interest: Arts; Higher education; Health care; Human services; Children/youth, services.

Type of support: Seed money; General/operating support; Building/renovation; Equipment; Endowments; Program development; Scholarship funds.

Limitations: Giving limited to ID. No grants to individuals.

Publications: Informational brochure (including application guidelines).

Application information: Application form required.

Initial approach: Request application
Copies of proposal: 3
Deadline(s): Mar. 31
Board meeting date(s): Spring
Final notification: Approx. 2-4 months

Officers: Harry Bettis, Pres.; Janelle Wise, V.P.; Laura Bettis, Secy.-Treas.

EIN: 826008294

Selected grants: The following grants were reported in 2005.

$1,780,000 to University of Idaho, Moscow, ID. 2 grants: $1,600,000 (For capital campaign), $180,000 (For scholarships).

$435,000 to Albertson College of Idaho, Caldwell, ID. For scholarships.

$280,000 to Northwest Nazarene University, Nampa, ID. For scholarships.

$250,000 to Idaho Public Television, Boise, ID. For local production.

$240,000 to Boise State University, Boise, ID. 2 grants: $180,000 (For scholarships), $60,000 to School of Nursing (For scholarships).

$100,000 to Peregrine Fund, Boise, ID. For Raptor Biology Educational Programs.

$100,000 to Wildlife Conservation Society, Bronx, NY. For educational programs in Bellevue, Idaho.

$50,000 to Discovery Center of Idaho, Boise, ID. For regional outreach program.

2568
Robert M. Golden Foundation ✧

c/o Morley Golden
P.O. Box 286
Sun Valley, ID   83353-0286

Established in 1960.

Foundation type: Independent foundation.

Financial data (yr. ended 12/31/05): Assets, $7,199,614 (M); expenditures, $460,244; qualifying distributions, $409,721; giving activities include $404,761 for 121 grants (high: $15,000; low: $50).

Fields of interest: Arts; Higher education; Environment.

Limitations: Applications not accepted. Giving limited to CA and ID. No grants to individuals.

Application information: Contributes only to pre-selected organizations.

Officers: Connie Golden, Pres.; Marilyn Golden Kelley, V.P.; Morley Golden, Secy.-Treas.

EIN: 956099985

Selected grants: The following grants were reported in 2005.

$15,000 to YMCA of La Jolla, La Jolla, CA.

$15,000 to Young Life. 2 grants: $5,000, $10,000

$10,000 to Childrens Hospital.

$10,000 to YMCA.

$5,000 to Oregon Dental Foundation, Portland, OR.

$5,000 to San Diego Natural History Museum, San Diego, CA.

$5,000 to San Diego Public Library, San Diego, CA.

$5,000 to Special Olympics, DC.

$5,000 to Zoological Society of San Diego, San Diego, CA.

2569
The Good Works Institute, Inc. ✧

P.O. Box 1811
Sun Valley, ID   83353   (208) 726-4421
Contact: Ann M. Down, Pres.

Established in 1999 in ID.

Donor: Ann M. Down.

Foundation type: Independent foundation.

Financial data (yr. ended 9/30/05): Assets, $66,761 (M); gifts received, $384,942; expenditures, $502,124; qualifying distributions, $499,362; giving activities include $496,920 for 11 grants (high: $125,000; low: $2,000).

Fields of interest: Arts; Education; Health care; Children/youth, services.

Application information: Application form not required.

Deadline(s): None

Officers: Ann M. Down, Pres.; Douglas I. Aanestad, Secy.; Michael Gene Brown, Treas.

EIN: 820518035

Selected grants: The following grants were reported in 2005.

$125,000 to Two Cultures/One Heart, Los Angeles, CA. For general support.

$116,508 to Advocates for the West, Boise, ID. For general support.

$69,902 to Western Watersheds Project, Hailey, ID. For general support.

$40,000 to Solar Cookers International, Sacramento, CA. For general support.

$35,000 to Sechen Monastery, Nepal. For general support.

$17,954 to Little Sisters Fund, Ketchum, ID. For general support.

$10,000 to Clear Light Sangha, Santa Barbara, CA. For general support.

2570
Idaho Community Foundation

c/o Cathy Silak
210 W. State St.
Boise, ID   83702   (208) 342-3535
Contact: Holly Motes, Cont.; For grants: Kay Harper, Grant Specialist
FAX: (208) 342-3577; *E-mail:* info@idcomfdn.org; Mailing address: P.O. Box 8143, Boise, ID 83707; Additional tel.: (800) 657-5357; Additional E-mail: hmotes@idcomfdn.org; Grant inquiry E-mail: grants@idcomfdn.org; URL: http://www.idcomfdn.org

Incorporated in 1988 in ID.

Foundation type: Community foundation.

Financial data (yr. ended 12/31/05): Assets, $58,186,000 (M); gifts received, $5,746,000; expenditures, $5,070,000; giving activities include $4,140,400 for 1,000+ grants (high: $140,000; low: $250), and $185,000 for 80 grants to individuals (high: $5,000; low: $500).

Purpose and activities: The mission of the foundation is to enrich the quality of life throughout ID.

Fields of interest: Arts; Libraries/library science; Education; Health care; Human services; Community development, neighborhood development.

Type of support: General/operating support; Continuing support; Management development/capacity building; Building/renovation; Equipment; Seed money; Curriculum development; Scholarship funds; Matching/challenge support.

Limitations: Giving primarily in ID. No support for religious purposes, or organizations typically funded by the government, or national organizations, unless monies expended are for sole benefit of ID citizens. No grants to individuals (except for scholarships), or for debt reduction, fundraising projects, travel, conferences or seminars, or endowments.

Publications: Application guidelines; Annual report; Financial statement; Grants list; Informational brochure (including application guidelines); Newsletter; Program policy statement.

Application information: Visit foundation Web site for application and guidelines. Application form required.

Initial approach: Complete online grant application
Copies of proposal: 1

Deadline(s): Jan. 15 for northern region, Apr. 1 for eastern region, and July 1 for southwestern region

Board meeting date(s): Feb., May, Aug., and Nov.

Final notification: June for northern region; Sept. for eastern region; Jan. for southwestern region

Officers and Directors:* Duane Jacklin,* Chair.; Brad Little,* Vice-Chair.; Douglas R. Nelson,* Vice-Chair.; Cathy Silak, C.E.O. and Pres.; John Rosholt,* Secy.; Irv Littman,* Treas.; Holly Motes, Cont.; John Bennett; Carol Burnett; Doug Chadderdon; Sandra Fery; Ralph M. Hartwell; Sus Helpenstell; Richard F. Hutter; Dan Keller; Todd Maddock; Joe Marshall; Michael A. McBride; Diane Plastino-Graves; Ron Sali; Jordan P. Smith; Kiki Tidwell; Nancy Sue Wallace; Paul Yochum.

Number of staff: 4 full-time professional; 3 full-time support; 1 part-time support.

EIN: 820425063

Selected grants: The following grants were reported in 2005.

$10,000 to Girl Scouts of the U.S.A., Silver Sage Council, Boise, ID.

$3,800 to Boise Rescue Mission, Boise, ID.

$2,500 to Sun Valley Opera Company, Ketchum, ID.

$2,000 to Garden City Public Library, Garden City, ID.

$1,000 to Blaine County Recreation District, Hailey, ID.

$1,000 to Richfield Senior Center, Richfield, ID.

$1,000 to Warhawk Air Museum, Nampa, ID.

$500 to Idaho Youth Ranch, Boise, ID.

$500 to MCPAWS, McCall, ID.

2571

Micron Technology Foundation, Inc. ▼ ✧

8000 S. Federal Way
P.O. Box 6
Boise, ID 83707-0006 (208) 363-3675
Contact: Kami Faylor
E-mail: mtf@micron.com; URL: http://www.micron.com/foundation

Established in 1999 in ID.

Donors: Micron Technology, Inc.; Micron Semiconductor Products, Inc.; Blue Cross of Idaho Health Service, Inc.

Foundation type: Company-sponsored foundation.

Financial data (yr. ended 12/31/05): Assets, $110,078,436 (M); gifts received, $30,425; expenditures, $5,410,103; qualifying distributions, $4,798,789; giving activities include $4,043,167 for 182 grants (high: $722,080; low: $25), and $315,166 for 66 grants to individuals (high: $27,500; low: $2,500).

Purpose and activities: The foundation supports organizations involved with K-12 and higher education. Special emphasis is directed toward programs designed to promote education in the areas of engineering, science, chemistry, mathematics, and computer science.

Fields of interest: Education, research; Elementary/secondary education; Secondary school/education; Higher education; Engineering school/education; Science, formal/general education; Chemistry; Mathematics; Engineering/technology; Computer science.

International interests: Italy; Japan; Singapore.

Type of support: General/operating support; Program development; Curriculum development; Scholarship funds; Research; Scholarships—to individuals.

Limitations: Giving limited to areas of company operations in Boise, ID, Avezzano, Italy, Nishiwaki, Japan, Singapore, Lehi, UT, and Manassas, VA; giving in CO, ID, TX, UT, and VA for scholarships. No support for religious, fraternal, veterans', or political organizations, discriminatory organizations, or pass-through organizations or private foundations. No grants to individuals (except for scholarships), or for luncheons, dinners, auctions, or events, travel or related expenses, courtesy advertisements, endowments, annual campaigns, or lobbying activities.

Publications: Application guidelines; IRS Form 990-PF.

Application information: Unsolicited requests for University Relations are not accepted. Application form required.

Initial approach: Download application form and mail proposal and application form to foundation for Community and K-12 Relations; download application form for Micron Science and Technology Scholars Program; contact university financial aid office for University Scholars

Deadline(s): None; Jan. 19 for Micron Science and Technology Scholars Program

Officers and Directors:* Steven R. Appleton,* Chair.; Kipp A. Bedard,* Pres.; Roderick W. Lewis,* Secy.; Wilbur G. Stover,* Treas.; Mark Duncan.

EIN: 820516178

Selected grants: The following grants were reported in 2004.

$971,840 to Boise State University, Boise, ID.

$499,910 to Boise Public Schools Education Foundation, Boise, ID.

$362,050 to Saint Lukes Health Foundation, Boise, ID.

$252,000 to Saint Alphonsus Foundation, Boise, ID.

$175,600 to University of Illinois at Urbana-Champaign, Urbana, IL.

$132,700 to Iowa State University, Ames, IA.

$131,800 to Utah State University, Logan, UT.

$100,000 to Oklahoma State University, Stillwater, OK.

$80,699 to Virginia Tech Foundation, Blacksburg, VA.

$75,000 to University of Texas, Austin, TX.

2572

Harry W. Morrison Foundation, Inc. ✧

3505 Crescent Rim Dr.
Boise, ID 83706-2722
Contact: Velma V. Morrison, Chair.

Incorporated in 1952 in ID.

Donors: Harry W. Morrison‡; Velma V. Morrison.

Foundation type: Independent foundation.

Financial data (yr. ended 12/31/05): Assets, $11,364,118 (M); expenditures, $1,064,870; qualifying distributions, $765,863; giving activities include $647,748 for 27 grants (high: $200,000; low: $100).

Purpose and activities: Giving primarily for education, and children and youth services.

Fields of interest: Arts; Higher education; Hospitals (general); Human services; Children/youth, services; Protestant agencies & churches.

Type of support: General/operating support; Building/renovation; Conferences/seminars; Scholarship funds.

Limitations: Giving primarily in Boise, ID. No grants to individuals.

Application information: Application form required.

Initial approach: Proposal

Deadline(s): Mar. 1

Board meeting date(s): Annually in May

Officers: Velma V. Morrison, Chair.; Justin Wilkerson, C.E.O. and Pres.; Judith V. Roberts, V.P.; Linda L. Klingner, Secy.-Treas.

Directors: John J. Hockberger; Michael E. Thomas; Frank Winsor.

Number of staff: 1 part-time professional; 1 part-time support.

EIN: 826008111

Selected grants: The following grants were reported in 2004.

$200,000 to Boise State University Foundation, Boise, ID.

$50,000 to Idaho Elks Rehabilitation Hospital, Boise, ID.

$50,000 to Saint Lukes Regional Medical Center, Boise, ID.

$25,000 to University of Idaho, Moscow, ID.

$3,750 to Syringa General Hospital Foundation, Grangeville, ID.

$500 to Capital High School, Olympia, WA.

2573

The John F. Nagel Foundation ✧

P.O. Box 1157
Boise, ID 83701 (208) 344-2666
E-mail: foundation@nagelbev.com; Application address: c/o William E. Morris, 350 N. 9th St., Ste. 500, Boise, ID 83702; URL: http://www.nagelbev.com/johnf

Established in 1989 in ID.

Donors: Mildred E. Nagel; Nagel Beverage Co., Inc.

Foundation type: Independent foundation.

Financial data (yr. ended 12/31/05): Assets, $6,060,116 (M); expenditures, $709,910; qualifying distributions, $702,835; giving activities include $702,835 for 34 grants (high: $123,904; low: $1,500).

Purpose and activities: Giving to organizations in the southwestern counties of ID, particularly to assist, equip or provide for the maintenance of institutions for the advancement of learning, hospitals and rehabilitation centers, and for the moral, intellectual and physical development of young men and women. Giving also to scholarship programs at universities in ID.

Fields of interest: Higher education; Education; Hospitals (general); Health care; Human services; Children/youth, services; Family services.

Type of support: General/operating support; Scholarship funds.

Limitations: Giving primarily in southwestern ID, with emphasis on Boise. No grants to individuals.

Application information: Application guidelines available on Web site. Application form required.

Initial approach: Write or E-mail for application form

Copies of proposal: 2

Deadline(s): Oct. 31

Board meeting date(s): Fall

Officers and Directors:* Anne Matthews,* Pres.; Vance Miller,* V.P.; Robert J. Ennis, Secy.; William E. Morris, Treas.

EIN: 820431505

Selected grants: The following grants were reported in 2003.

$124,928 to Boise State University, Boise, ID. For scholarship fund.

$55,000 to Northwest Nazarene University, Nampa, ID. For scholarship fund.

$50,000 to Boise Rescue Mission, Boise, ID. For operating support.

$50,000 to Community Christian Center of Boise, Boise, ID.

$50,000 to Special Olympics Idaho, Boise, ID. For housing and transportation.

$40,000 to Albertson College of Idaho, Caldwell, ID. For scholarship fund.

$40,000 to Salvation Army of Boise, Boise, ID. For building fund.

$20,000 to Childrens Home Society of Idaho, Boise, ID. For operating support.

$20,000 to Idaho Youth Ranch, Boise, ID. For weatherization of Emancipation Home.

$15,000 to Learning Lab, Boise, ID. For scholarship fund.

2574
J. R. Simplot Company Foundation, Inc. ✧
P.O. Box 27
Boise, ID 83707

Established in 2000 in ID.
Donor: J.R. Simplot Co.
Foundation type: Company-sponsored foundation.
Financial data (yr. ended 3/31/05): Assets, $4,237,739 (M); expenditures, $524,318; qualifying distributions, $498,508; giving activities include $395,699 for 52+ grants (high: $100,000).
Purpose and activities: The foundation supports organizations involved with arts and culture, higher education, health, youth development, human services, Christianity, and Hispanics and Latinos.
Fields of interest: Arts; Higher education; Hospitals (general); Health care; Youth development; Human services; Federated giving programs; Christian agencies & churches; Hispanics/Latinos.
Limitations: Applications not accepted. Giving primarily in ID. No grants to individuals.
Application information: Contributes only to pre-selected organizations.
Officers and Directors: * Gay C. Simplot, * Pres.; John Edward Simplot, * V.P.; Ronald N. Graves, Secy.; Annette Elg, Treas.; Don J. Simplot; Scott R. Simplot.
EIN: 820522113
Selected grants: The following grants were reported in 2005.
$100,000 to Hispanic Cultural Center of Idaho, Nampa, ID.
$36,205 to United Way of Treasure Valley, Boise, ID.
$25,000 to Aberdeen School District 6-1, Aberdeen, SD.
$10,000 to Terry Reilly Health Services, Nampa, ID.
$7,000 to Ballet Idaho, Boise, ID.
$7,000 to Idaho State University Foundation, Pocatello, ID.
$5,000 to Boise Philharmonic Association, Boise, ID.
$3,250 to Albertson College of Idaho, Caldwell, ID.
$2,000 to Utah State University, Logan, UT.
$1,200 to Saint Lukes Regional Medical Center, Boise, ID.

2575
J. R. Simplot Foundation, Inc. ✧
P.O. Box 27
Boise, ID 83707-0027
Contact: Fred Zerza

Established in 1953 in ID.
Foundation type: Independent foundation.
Financial data (yr. ended 9/30/05): Assets, $69,282,383 (M); gifts received, $6,706; expenditures, $1,100,741; qualifying distributions, $953,255; giving activities include $800,206 for 27 + grants (high: $400,000; average: $5,000–$25,000).
Fields of interest: Arts; Libraries/library science; Education; Human services; Community development, neighborhood development; Public affairs, government agencies.
Type of support: General/operating support; Continuing support; Capital campaigns; Building/renovation; Endowments; Scholarship funds; In-kind gifts; Matching/challenge support.
Limitations: Applications not accepted. Giving limited to ID headquarters and company locations of the J.R. Simplot Co. No grants to individuals.
Publications: Informational brochure.
Application information: Contributes only to pre-selected organizations.
Officers and Directors: * Lawrence Hlobik, * Pres.; Annette Elg, Sr. V.P. and C.F.O.; Terry Uhling, V.P. and Genl. Counsel.
EIN: 826003437
Selected grants: The following grants were reported in 2004.
$1,000,030 to Boise, City of, Boise, ID.
$200,000 to YMCA, Caldwell Family, Caldwell, ID.
$50,000 to Ballet Idaho, Boise, ID.
$50,000 to Saint Lukes Health Foundation, Boise, ID.
$40,000 to Esther Simplot Performing Arts Academy, Boise, ID.
$32,500 to Boise Philharmonic Association, Boise, ID.
$25,000 to Big Bend Community College, Moses Lake, WA.
$25,000 to Idaho Elks Rehabilitation Hospital, Boise, ID.
$25,000 to Opera Idaho, Boise, ID.

2576
Robert W. and Bernice Ingalls Staton Foundation ✧
455 Gustafson Dr.
Idaho Falls, ID 83402

Established in 2001 in ID.
Donor: Bernice Ingalls Staton.
Foundation type: Independent foundation.
Financial data (yr. ended 12/31/05): Assets, $5,622,048 (M); gifts received, $2,135,124; expenditures, $3,530,413; qualifying distributions, $3,520,888; giving activities include $3,520,888 for 5 grants (high: $2,313,060; low: $2,000).
Purpose and activities: Giving primarily for higher education.
Fields of interest: Higher education; Scholarships/financial aid.
Limitations: Applications not accepted. Giving primarily in Eugene, OR. No grants to individuals.
Application information: Contributes only to pre-selected organizations.

Trustees: Bernice Ingalls Staton; Colin M. Staton; Richard Christopher Staton; Robert Dennis Staton; Anne Voilleque.
EIN: 820533021
Selected grants: The following grants were reported in 2005.
$2,897,700 to University of Oregon Foundation, Eugene, OR. 2 grants: $584,640 (For scholarships), $2,313,060 (For scholarships).
$621,188 to Lane Community College Development Foundation, Eugene, OR. 2 grants: $109,880 (For scholarships), $511,308 (For scholarships).

2577
Harold E. & Phyllis S. Thomas Foundation ✧
12549 W. Bowmont Ct.
Boise, ID 83713 (208) 377-3005
Contact: Judy Rasmussen, Dir.

Established in 1995 in ID.
Donors: Harold Thomas; Phyllis Thomas.
Foundation type: Independent foundation.
Financial data (yr. ended 12/31/05): Assets, $0 (M); expenditures, $841,570; qualifying distributions, $714,359; giving activities include $664,359 for 36 grants (high: $50,000; low: $500), and $50,000 for 1 employee matching gift.
Purpose and activities: Grants are awarded for Christian evangelical work with particular consideration for missions and organizations engaged in missionary teachings and work. Some giving also for other religious philanthropic organizations.
Fields of interest: Christian agencies & churches.
Limitations: Giving on a national basis, with emphasis on ID and WA.
Application information: Application form required.
    Initial approach: Proposal
    Deadline(s): None
Trustees: Dave Hills; James Mitchell; Robert Renfro; Harold E. Thomas; Phyllis S. Thomas; Rick Thomas.
Director: Judy Rasmussen.
EIN: 820477243
Selected grants: The following grants were reported in 2005.
$100,000 to Young Life, Boise, ID. 2 grants: $50,000 (For general ministry support), $50,000 (For matching grant).
$50,000 to Heritage Christian Fellowship Church, San Clemente, CA. For DVD distribution.
$50,000 to Luis Palau Evangelistic Association, Portland, OR. For Washington DC crusade.
$50,000 to Young Life, Santa Barbara, CA. For Young Life Russia.
$40,000 to Cole Community Church, Boise, ID.
$35,000 to Phoenix Rescue Mission, Phoenix, AZ. For women and children's center.
$25,000 to Campus Crusade for Christ International, Orlando, FL. For University of Idaho campus funding and for personal ministry support.
$25,000 to Idaho Mountain Ministries, Boise, ID. For personal ministry support.
$20,000 to Fellowship of Christian Athletes, Kansas City, MO. For general ministry support.

2578
Washington Group Foundation ◇ ☆
(formerly Morrison Knudsen Corporation
Foundation)
P.O. Box 73
Boise, ID 83729
Contact: Marlene M. Puckett, Secy.
Application address: 1 Morrison Knudsen Plz.,
Boise, ID 83729

Established in 1947 in ID as a company-sponsored
operating foundation.
Donors: Morrison Knudsen Corp.; Washington
Group International, Inc.; WGI Holdings England.
Foundation type: Operating foundation.
Financial data (yr. ended 12/31/04): Assets,
$6,236,847 (M); expenditures, $373,914;
qualifying distributions, $359,326; giving activities

include $103,205 for 137+ grants, and $255,361
for 241 grants to individuals (high: $9,500; low:
$23).
Purpose and activities: The foundation awards
grants to needy individuals.
Fields of interest: Economically disadvantaged.
Type of support: Employee matching gifts; Grants to
individuals.
Limitations: Giving on a national basis in areas of
company operations.
Application information: Application form required.
Initial approach: Contact foundation for
application form
Copies of proposal: 1
Deadline(s): None
Board meeting date(s): Quarterly

Officers and Directors:* Stephen G. Hanks,* Pres.;
Marlene M. Puckett,* Secy. and Admin.; Matt
Reece,* Treas.;* Frank Finlayson; Betty Hurd; Dawn
Yantek.
Number of staff: 1 full-time professional.
EIN: 826005410
Selected grants: The following grants were reported
in 2004.
$6,250 to Idaho Shakespeare Festival, Boise, ID.
$5,175 to Learning Lab, Boise, ID.
$2,400 to University of Idaho, Moscow, ID.
$2,000 to Idaho Community Foundation, Boise, ID.
$1,500 to Lakewood Christian Service Center,
Lakewood, OH.
$1,258 to Idaho Public Television, Boise, ID.
$1,000 to Marquette University, Milwaukee, WI.
$1,000 to YMCA.
$925 to Rensselaer Polytechnic Institute, Troy, NY.
$65 to University of Dayton, Dayton, OH.

ILLINOIS

2579
The Clara Abbott Foundation ▼ ✧
1505 White Oak Dr.
Waukegan, IL   60085   (800) 972-3859
Contact: Glenn S. Warner, V.P. and Exec. Dir.
URL: http://clara.abbott.com

Established in 1940 in IL.
Donors: Clara Abbott†; Louis B. Kyle; Mr. Joseph Miller, Jr.; Mrs. Joseph Miller, Jr.; Marie Wilkinson; Jack Moss Trust for Euluos Moss; Rieker Rieker Charitable Remainder Trust; Mr. Charles S. Brown; Mrs. Charles S. Brown; Marcia Thomas; John C. Kane; Bernard Semler; Gary P. Coughlan; W. Thomas Brady; Lucilee Heine.
Foundation type: Independent foundation.
Financial data (yr. ended 12/31/04): Assets, $274,447,766 (M); gifts received, $282,564; expenditures, $22,380,946; qualifying distributions, $20,282,877; giving activities include $13,613,681 for grants to individuals, $417,000 for loans to individuals, and $17,612,763 for foundation-administered programs.
Purpose and activities: The mission of the foundation is to efficiently and responsibly provide needed assistance to Abbott families worldwide. Grants, loans, financial education and counseling services are made to Abbott Laboratories employees and retirees for financial aid due to financial hardships. Educational grants are made only to dependents of Abbott Laboratories employees (of at least one year) and retirees based on a financial need criteria.
Fields of interest: Education; Human services; Aging; Economically disadvantaged.
Type of support: Continuing support; Emergency funds; Consulting services; Program-related investments/loans; Employee-related scholarships; Grants to individuals; Scholarships—to individuals.
Limitations: Giving primarily to Abbott Laboratories employees (of at least one year) and retirees worldwide.
Publications: Annual report (including application guidelines); Financial statement; Informational brochure.
Application information: Application form required.
  Initial approach: Contact consultant contracted with foundation for complete application
  Deadline(s): Varies
  Board meeting date(s): Apr. and Oct.
  Final notification: Varies
Officers and Directors:* Philip J. Tobin,* Pres.; Heather Lowe, V.P. and Exec. Dir.; Sheila Rivera-Fathallah, Cont.; Jack S. Aten; Catherine V. Babington; William Thomas Brady; Thomas F. Chen; Jaime Contreras; Stanley R. Flood; Stephen R. Fussell; Terrence C. Kearney; Nancy A. Kravcisin-Mclain; John C. Landgraf; Elaine R. Leavenworth; Greg W. Linder; Richard H. Morehead; David W. Olson; Theodore A. Olson; William H. Preece, Jr.; Laura J. Schumacher; Marcia A. Thomas; Anthony T. Thompson; James D. Walton; Michael J. Warmuth; Thomas M. Wascoe; Susan M. Widner; Guy R. Wiebking; Diane Winnard.
Number of staff: 25 full-time professional; 4 part-time professional; 12 full-time support; 1 part-time support.
EIN: 366069632

2580
Abbott Laboratories Fund ▼ ✧
100 Abbott Park Rd., D379/AP6D
Abbott Park, IL   60064-3500   (847) 937-7075
Contact: Cindy Schwab, V.P.
URL: http://www.abbott.com/global/url/content/en_US/40.80:80/general_content/General_Content_00070.htm

Incorporated in 1951 in IL.
Donor: Abbott Laboratories.
Foundation type: Company-sponsored foundation.
Financial data (yr. ended 12/31/05): Assets, $121,826,609 (M); gifts received, $741,400; expenditures, $28,785,618; qualifying distributions, $28,544,915; giving activities include $22,478,588 for 247 grants (high: $10,298,747; low: $250), and $3,737,956 for 2,541 employee matching gifts.
Purpose and activities: The fund supports organizations involved with arts and culture, education, the environment, health, HIV/AIDS, human services, community development, civic affairs, and children.
Fields of interest: Arts; Elementary/secondary education; Education; Environment; Health care; AIDS; Human services, public policy; Human services; Community development; Science, formal/general education; Public affairs; Children.
Type of support: General/operating support; Continuing support; Scholarship funds; Research; Employee matching gifts.
Limitations: Giving primarily in areas of company operations. No support for social organizations, political parties or candidates, or sectarian religious organizations. No grants to individuals, or for advertising journals or booklets, ticket purchases, travel expenses, sporting events, continuing medical education, capital campaigns, memorials, or special events; no employee volunteer services.
Application information: Application form not required.
  Initial approach: Proposal
  Board meeting date(s): Ongoing
Officers and Directors:* Catherine V. Babington,* Pres.; Cindy Schwab, V.P.; Brian J. Smith, Secy.; Carol Sebesta, Treas.; Thomas M. Wascoe; Miles D. White.
Number of staff: 1 full-time professional; 1 part-time professional; 1 full-time support; 1 part-time support.
EIN: 366069793
Selected grants: The following grants were reported in 2004.
$1,744,810 to Baylor College of Medicine, Houston, TX.
$1,300,000 to International HIV/AIDS Alliance, Brighton, England. .
$300,000 to Stanford University, Stanford, CA.
$200,000 to Northwestern University, Evanston, IL.
$100,000 to AIDS Foundation of Chicago, Chicago, IL. For National AIDS Marathon Training Program.
$100,000 to Barat College, Lake Forest, IL.
$70,950 to National Merit Scholarship Corporation, Evanston, IL.
$70,000 to HealthReach Clinic, Waukegan, IL.
$69,500 to University of Illinois at Chicago, Chicago, IL.
$65,000 to Elizabeth Glaser Pediatric AIDS Foundation, Santa Monica, CA.

2581
Lester S. Abelson Foundation ✧
55 E. Monroe St.
Chicago, IL   60603

Established in 1966 in IL.
Donors: Lester S. Abelson†; and members of the Abelson family.
Foundation type: Independent foundation.
Financial data (yr. ended 12/31/05): Assets, $690,266 (M); expenditures, $446,309; qualifying distributions, $438,750; giving activities include $438,750 for 52 grants (high: $200,000; low: $50).
Purpose and activities: Support primarily for cultural programs, including music, dance, theater, museums and the fine arts; support also for environmental organizations.
Fields of interest: Visual arts; Museums; Performing arts; Performing arts, dance; Performing arts, theater; Performing arts, music; Arts; Environment.
Limitations: Applications not accepted. Giving primarily in IL. No grants to individuals.
Application information: Contributes only to pre-selected organizations.
Officers and Directors:* Hope A. Abelson,* Pres.; Katherine A. Abelson,* Secy.-Treas.; Claude Kahn.
EIN: 366153888
Selected grants: The following grants were reported in 2005.
$25,000 to Lyric Opera of Chicago, Chicago, IL.
$15,000 to Ravinia Festival Association, Highland Park, IL.
$10,000 to Goodman Theater, Chicago, IL.
$5,000 to Sun Valley Center for the Arts, Sun Valley, ID.
$2,000 to Court Theater, Chicago, IL.
$2,000 to Museum of Contemporary Art, Chicago, IL.
$500 to League of Chicago Theaters, Chicago, IL.
$500 to Victory Gardens Theater, Chicago, IL.
$500 to Writers Theater, Glencoe, IL.
$250 to Facets Multimedia, Chicago, IL.

2582
Ace Hardware Foundation ✧
2200 Kensington Ct.
Oak Brook, IL   60523   (630) 990-6600
Contact: Rita D. Kahle, Treas.
URL: http://www.acehardware.com/corp/index.jsp?page=community

Donor: Ace Hardware Corp.
Foundation type: Company-sponsored foundation.
Financial data (yr. ended 1/1/05): Assets, $1,788,774 (M); gifts received, $2,780,914; expenditures, $2,025,816; qualifying distributions, $2,025,816; giving activities include $1,760,661 for 4 grants (high: $1,621,958; low: $18,703).
Purpose and activities: The foundation supports organizations involved with human services and pediatrics.
Fields of interest: Health care; Pediatrics; Human services.
Limitations: Giving on a national basis. No grants to individuals.
Application information: Application form not required.
  Initial approach: Proposal
  Deadline(s): Dec. 31
Officers and Directors:* Jimmy Alexander,* Pres.; Lori L. Bossmann, V.P.; David F. Hodnik,* V.P.; David W. League,* Secy.; Rita D. Kahle,* Treas.;

Richard F. Baalmann, Jr.; Eric R. Bibens; J. Thomas Glenn; Kenneth L. Nichols; Lori J. Terpstra.
EIN: 363820478
Selected grants: The following grants were reported in 2004.
$1,385,839 to Childrens Miracle Network, Salt Lake City, UT.
$50,000 to City of Hope National Medical Center, Duarte, CA.
$15,000 to Kapiolani Womens and Childrens Medical Center, Honolulu, HI.
$15,000 to Our Lady of the Lake Foundation, Baton Rouge, LA.
$15,000 to Riley Hospital for Children, Indianapolis, IN.
$10,000 to Childrens Hospital of Illinois, Peoria, IL.
$10,000 to East Tennessee Childrens Hospital, Knoxville, TN.
$10,000 to Miami Childrens Hospital, Miami, FL.
$2,633 to American Red Cross, Chester, VA.

2583
The Acorn Foundation ✧
c/o Cottle
120 S. LaSalle St., Ste. 1955
Chicago, IL 60603

Established around 1995 in IL.
Donors: Ralph Wanger; Leah Zell Wanger.
Foundation type: Independent foundation.
Financial data (yr. ended 12/31/05): Assets, $5,586,819 (M); gifts received, $2,860,517; expenditures, $1,681,375; qualifying distributions, $1,670,636; giving activities include $1,668,500 for 40 grants (high: $300,000; low: $200; average: $1,000–$100,000).
Fields of interest: Arts; Education; Health organizations, association; Children/youth, services; Jewish federated giving programs.
Limitations: Applications not accepted. Giving primarily in Chicago, IL. No grants to individuals.
Application information: Contributes only to pre-selected organizations.
Officers and Directors:* Ralph Wanger,* Pres. and Treas.; Leah Zell Wanger,* V.P.; Eric David Wanger; Leonard Ralph Wanger; Debra Wanger Yaruss.
EIN: 363991208

2584
The Adjuvant Foundation ✧
(formerly Irving Harris Foundation B)
191 N. Wacker Dr., Ste. 1500
Chicago, IL 60606-1899
Contact: Virginia H. Polsky, Pres.

Established in 1993 in IL.
Donor: Virginia H. Polsky.
Foundation type: Independent foundation.
Financial data (yr. ended 12/31/04): Assets, $14,594,356 (M); gifts received, $3,008; expenditures, $1,604,440; qualifying distributions, $1,298,512; giving activities include $1,296,460 for 20+ grants (high: $420,000).
Fields of interest: Higher education; Higher education, university; Education; Hospitals (general).
Limitations: Applications not accepted. Giving primarily in MA and NY. No grants to individuals.
Application information: Contributes only to pre-selected organizations.

Officers and Directors:* Virginia H. Polsky,* Pres. and Secy.; Charles Polsky,* V.P.; George Polsky,* V.P.; Jack Polsky,* V.P.; James Polsky,* V.P.; Jean Polsky, V.P.; Richard Polsky,* V.P.; Michael Resnick, Treas.
EIN: 363866528
Selected grants: The following grants were reported in 2004.
$420,000 to StreetSquash, New York, NY.
$400,000 to Massachusetts General Hospital, Boston, MA.
$300,000 to Rhode Island Hospital Foundation, Providence, RI.
$50,000 to Lafayette College, Easton, PA.
$10,000 to Ethical Culture Fieldston Schools, New York, NY.
$5,000 to Mary Meyer School, Chicago, IL.
$5,000 to Planned Parenthood Federation of America, New York, NY.
$5,000 to Prep for Prep, New York, NY.
$2,500 to Perspectives Charter School, Chicago, IL.
$1,000 to Research Foundation of the State University of New York, Brooklyn, NY.

2585
Adreani Foundation ✧ ☆
7458 N. Harlem Ave.
Chicago, IL 60631

Established in 1978 in IL.
Donor: Raymond J. Adreani.
Foundation type: Independent foundation.
Financial data (yr. ended 11/30/05): Assets, $5,453,167 (M); gifts received, $265,570; expenditures, $1,217,635; qualifying distributions, $1,207,110; giving activities include $1,206,100 for 45 grants (high: $1,160,000; low: $100).
Purpose and activities: Giving primarily for hospitals and social services; support also for education, health associations, and Christian churches.
Fields of interest: Education; Hospitals (general); Health organizations, association; Human services; YM/YWCAs & YM/YWHAs; Community development; Foundations (community); Christian agencies & churches.
Limitations: Applications not accepted. Giving primarily in IL. No grants to individuals.
Application information: Contributes only to pre-selected organizations.
Director: Raymond J. Adreani.
EIN: 363059439
Selected grants: The following grants were reported in 2004.
$26,500 to YMCA of Metropolitan Chicago, Lattof International Branch, Des Plaines, IL.
$15,000 to Childrens Memorial Foundation, Chicago, IL.
$10,000 to Holy Family Medical Center, Des Plaines, IL.
$10,000 to Roosevelt University, Chicago, IL.
$5,500 to Multiple Sclerosis Society, National, Chicago, IL.
$5,000 to Triton College Foundation, River Grove, IL.
$1,500 to American Heart Association, Midwest Affiliate, Chicago, IL.
$1,500 to Northwestern Memorial Foundation, Chicago, IL.
$1,500 to Shriners Hospitals for Children, Chicago, IL.
$1,000 to March of Dimes Birth Defects Foundation, Chicago, IL.

2586
Fred & Jean Allegretti Foundation, Inc. ✧
5069 Shoreline Rd.
Barrington, IL 60010
Contact: Jean Allegretti, Pres.
Application address: 158 Algonquin St., Barrington, IL 60010

Established in 1997 in IL.
Donor: Jean Allegretti.
Foundation type: Operating foundation.
Financial data (yr. ended 10/31/05): Assets, $12,116,941 (L); expenditures, $624,792; qualifying distributions, $606,090; giving activities include $606,090 for 23 grants (high: $100,000; low: $5,000).
Fields of interest: Education; Hospitals (specialty); Health care; Health organizations, association; Human services; Children/youth, services; Roman Catholic agencies & churches.
Limitations: Giving primarily in IL. No grants to individuals.
Application information:
Initial approach: Proposal
Deadline(s): None
Officers: Jean Allegretti, Pres.; James Allegretti, V.P.; Carol Allegretti, Secy.; Fred Allegretti, Treas.
Directors: Antoniette Allegretti; Elizabeth Allegretti; Sharon Barson; Joseph Nolfi.
EIN: 364110761

2587
Allen-Heath Memorial Foundation ✧
222 N. LaSalle St., Ste. 300
Chicago, IL 60601-1081

Incorporated in 1947 in CA.
Donors: Harriet A. Heath†; John E.S. Heath†.
Foundation type: Independent foundation.
Financial data (yr. ended 12/31/05): Assets, $5,879,212 (M); expenditures, $419,106; qualifying distributions, $369,000; giving activities include $365,000 for 30 grants (high: $25,000; low: $2,000).
Fields of interest: Media, radio; Performing arts, theater; Arts; Higher education; Libraries (public); Health care; Crime/violence prevention, abuse prevention; Food services; Human services; Children, services; Women, centers/services.
Type of support: General/operating support; Program development.
Limitations: Applications not accepted. Giving on a national basis. No support for religious or foreign organizations, private foundations, or conduit organizations. No grants to individuals; no loans.
Application information: Contributes only to pre-selected organizations.
Officers and Directors:* Charles K. Heath,* Pres.; Ruth R. Hooper,* V.P.; James Harbert, Secy.-Treas.; Nolan H. Baird, Jr.; Deborah J. Burditt; Elizabeth K. Phillips.
EIN: 363056910
Selected grants: The following grants were reported in 2005.
$25,000 to CALSTAR, Hayward, CA.
$15,000 to Chicago Abused Women Coalition, Chicago, IL.
$15,000 to Greater Chicago Food Depository, Chicago, IL.
$15,000 to New England Historic Genealogical Society, Boston, MA.
$15,000 to Peoples Resource Center, Wheaton, IL.

$15,000 to Rocky Mountain Institute, Snowmass, CO.

$15,000 to Solar Energy International, Carbondale, CO.

$15,000 to Ukiah Players Theater, Ukiah, CA.

$10,000 to Family Shelter Service, Wheaton, IL.

$10,000 to National Center for Missing and Exploited Children, Alexandria, VA.

2588
The Allstate Foundation ▼ ✧
2775 Sanders Rd., Ste. F4
Northbrook, IL 60062-6127   (847) 402-5502
Contact: Jan Epstein, Exec. Dir.
FAX: (847) 326-7517;
E-mail: allfound@allstate.com; URL: http://www.allstate.com/foundation

Incorporated in 1952 in IL.
Donors: The Allstate Corp.; Allstate Insurance Co.
Foundation type: Company-sponsored foundation.
Financial data (yr. ended 12/31/05): Assets, $44,911,191 (M); gifts received, $17,556,835; expenditures, $16,448,852; qualifying distributions, $16,148,852; giving activities include $15,983,966 for 3,234 grants (high: $1,000,000; low: $25).
Purpose and activities: The foundation supports organizations involved with insurance education, youth violence prevention, automotive safety, disaster relief, domestic violence, financial and economic literacy, tolerance, and neighborhood development.
Fields of interest: Business school/education; Crime/violence prevention, youth; Safety, automotive safety; Safety/disasters; Family services, domestic violence; Human services, financial counseling; Civil rights, race/intergroup relations; Community development, neighborhood development.
Type of support: General/operating support; Program development; Employee volunteer services; Employee matching gifts; Employee-related scholarships.
Limitations: Giving on a national basis; giving also to regional and national organizations. No support for athletic teams, bands or choirs, religious organizations not of direct benefit to the entire community, pass-through organizations, scouting groups, or private secondary schools. No grants to individuals (except for employee-related scholarships), or for fundraising events or sponsorships, capital campaigns or endowments, equipment not part of a community outreach program, athletic events, memorials, travel, audio, film, or video production, or continuing support.
Publications: Application guidelines; Informational brochure (including application guidelines).
Application information: Application form not required.
  Initial approach: Complete online questionnaire for application information
  Deadline(s): None
  Board meeting date(s): Mar., June, Sept., and Dec.
Officers and Trustees: * Edward M. Liddy,* Pres.; Robert W. Pike,* V.P. and Secy.; Eric A. Simonson,* V.P. and C.I.O.; Peter Debreceny, V.P.; James P. Zils, Treas.; Jan Epstein,* Exec. Dir.; Dan L. Hale; Casey J. Sylia; Thomas J. Wilson.
Number of staff: 2 full-time professional.
EIN: 366116535

Selected grants: The following grants were reported in 2005.
$1,000,000 to Boys and Girls Clubs of America, Atlanta, GA.
$1,000,000 to Mississippi Hurricane Recovery Fund, Jackson, MS. To help Hurricane Katrina victims rebuild and restore their lives.
$700,000 to Greater New Orleans Foundation, New Orleans, LA.
$425,000 to Facing History and Ourselves National Foundation, Brookline, MA.
$400,000 to National Network to End Domestic Violence, DC.
$400,000 to Scholarship America, Saint Peter, MN.
$200,000 to Chicago, City of, Chicago, IL. For Chicago Alternative Policing Strategy (CAPS).
$154,000 to Insurance Industry Charitable Foundation, Moraga, CA.
$30,100 to Florida Alliance for Safe Homes (FLASH), Tallahassee, FL.
$15,000 to Junior Achievement of Akron, Akron, OH.

2589
Alphawood Foundation ▼
(formerly WPWR-TV Channel 50 Foundation)
2451 N. Lincoln Ave., Ste. 205
Chicago, IL 60614   (773) 477-8984
Contact: Agnes Meneses, Prog. Off. and Grants Mgr.
FAX: (773) 477-9019;
E-mail: info@alphawoodfoundation.org

Established in 1991 in IL.
Donors: Fred Eychaner; Newsweb Corp.
Foundation type: Independent foundation.
Financial data (yr. ended 2/28/06): Assets, $136,084,139 (M); expenditures, $7,402,725; qualifying distributions, $6,937,852; giving activities include $6,859,400 for 260 grants (high: $1,000,000; low: $360; average: $5,000–$100,000).
Purpose and activities: The foundation provides general operating support to non-profit organizations whose primary mission involves the arts, arts education for children, institutional advocacy for social change, domestic violence intervention/prevention programs, and architecture and preservation.
Fields of interest: Arts education; Visual arts; Visual arts, architecture; Performing arts, dance; Performing arts, theater; Performing arts, music; Performing arts (multimedia); Literature; Historic preservation/historical societies; Arts; Crime/violence prevention, domestic violence.
Type of support: General/operating support.
Limitations: Applications not accepted. Giving primarily in the metropolitan Chicago, IL, area and northwestern IN. No support for religious or fraternal purposes, or for political campaigns. No grants to individuals, or for scholarships, underwriting or tables for events, capital campaigns, or special projects, programs, or productions.
Publications: Program policy statement.
Application information: Unsolicited requests for funds not accepted. New proposals from organizations not currently being funded are by invitation only.
  Board meeting date(s): Varies
Officers and Directors: * Fred Eychaner,* Pres. and Treas.; Don Hilliker,* Secy.; Laura Samson, Exec. Dir.; Barbara Richardson.
Number of staff: 2 full-time professional.
EIN: 363805338

Selected grants: The following grants were reported in 2006.
$35,000 to Landmarks Preservation Council of Illinois, Chicago, IL. For general operating support.
$10,000 to Shanti Foundation for Peace, Evanston, IL. For general operating support.
$10,000 to Timeline Theater Company, Chicago, IL. For general operating support.
$7,500 to Family Rescue, Chicago, IL. For general operating support.

2590
Alsdorf Foundation ✧
c/o Marilynn B. Alsdorf
209 E. Lake Shore Dr., No. 15W
Chicago, IL 60611-1307

Incorporated in 1944 in IL.
Donor: James W. Alsdorf†.
Foundation type: Independent foundation.
Financial data (yr. ended 12/31/04): Assets, $7,886,141 (M); expenditures, $589,165; qualifying distributions, $504,731; giving activities include $458,006 for 27+ grants (high: $181,430).
Purpose and activities: Giving primarily for the arts, particularly art museums, and for education.
Fields of interest: Museums; Museums (art); Arts; Higher education; Education; Zoos/zoological societies; Community development.
Type of support: Annual campaigns; Capital campaigns; Endowments.
Limitations: Applications not accepted. Giving primarily in Chicago, IL. No grants to individuals, or for scholarships, fellowships, or prizes; no loans.
Application information: Contributes only to pre-selected organizations.
  Board meeting date(s): Dec. and as required
Officers: Marilynn B. Alsdorf, Pres. and Treas.; Robert N. Grant, V.P. and Secy.; Jeffrey A. Alsdorf, V.P.; Robert Gluth, V.P.
Number of staff: 1 full-time professional; 1 full-time support.
EIN: 366065388

2591
AMCORE Bank Foundation ✧
501 7th St.
P.O. Box 1537
Rockford, IL 61110-0037
Contact: James S. Waddell, Pres.

Established in 1957 in IL.
Donors: AMCORE Financial, Inc.; AMCORE Bank, N.A.
Foundation type: Company-sponsored foundation.
Financial data (yr. ended 11/30/04): Assets, $722,702 (M); gifts received, $401,415; expenditures, $355,614; qualifying distributions, $355,450; giving activities include $355,450 for 42 grants (high: $100,000; low: $300).
Purpose and activities: The foundation supports organizations involved with arts and culture, education, youth development, human services, community development, and civic affairs and awards college scholarships.
Fields of interest: Arts; Education; Youth development; Human services; Community development; Government/public administration.
Type of support: General/operating support; Scholarships—to individuals.

Limitations: Giving primarily in Rockford, IL. No grants to individuals (except for scholarships).
Publications: Application guidelines; Annual report (including application guidelines); Informational brochure.
Application information: An application form is required for scholarships.
  Initial approach: Proposal; contact foundation for application form for scholarships
  Board meeting date(s): Quarterly
Officers and Directors: James S. Waddell, Pres.; Bruce Lammers,* Secy.; Patricia Bonavia; Robert A. Doyle; Kenneth Edge; Joseph McGougan; Richard D. Nordlof; Michael Tulley.
EIN: 366042947

2592
Amicus Foundation ◇ ☆
98 E. Naperville Rd., Ste., 200
Westmont, IL   60559-1559

Established in 1985 in IL.
Donors: Joan C. Erickson; Peter E. Erickson; Hubbard H. Erickson, Jr.; Peggy Bigelow; Peter H. Erickson; Michael Beemer.
Foundation type: Independent foundation.
Financial data (yr. ended 12/31/05): Assets, $13,074,442 (M); gifts received, $875,246; expenditures, $603,318; qualifying distributions, $549,800; giving activities include $548,000 for 12 grants (high: $200,000; low: $5,000; average: $25,000–$50,000).
Purpose and activities: Giving primarily for health and human services, particularly services for people who are blind.
Fields of interest: Health care; Housing/shelter, development; Human services.
Limitations: Applications not accepted. Giving primarily in IL, with emphasis on Chicago. No grants to individuals.
Application information: Contributes only to pre-selected organizations.
Officers and Directors:* John H. Erickson,* Pres.; Joan C. Erickson,* V.P.; Peter Erickson,* V.P.; Mary Christine Flannery,* Secy.; Hubbard H. Erickson, Jr.,* Treas.; Michael G. Beemer; Karen E. Cronin; Ernest A. Janus; Joanne E. Smith.
EIN: 363378462
Selected grants: The following grants were reported in 2005.
$200,000 to Bridge Communities, Glen Ellyn, IL.
$50,000 to Inspiration Corporation, Chicago, IL.
$50,000 to Recording for the Blind and Dyslexic, Chicago, IL.
$25,000 to Christopher House, Chicago, IL.
$25,000 to New Moms, Chicago, IL.
$15,000 to Cabrini Green Legal Aid Clinic, Chicago, IL.
$5,000 to Giant Steps Illinois, Westmont, IL.

2593
Amsted Industries Foundation ◇
205 N. Michigan Ave., 44th Fl.
Chicago, IL   60601-5927   (312) 645-1700
Contact: Shirley Whitsell

Established in 1953 in IL.
Donor: Amsted Industries Inc.
Foundation type: Company-sponsored foundation.
Financial data (yr. ended 9/30/03): Assets, $1,620,457 (M); expenditures, $352,323;

qualifying distributions, $348,788; giving activities include $348,788 for 412 grants (high: $20,000; low: $50).
Purpose and activities: The foundation supports organizations involved with arts and culture, education, health, and human services.
Fields of interest: Arts; Education; Health care; Health organizations, association; Human services; Federated giving programs; Government/public administration.
Type of support: General/operating support; Continuing support; Building/renovation; Employee matching gifts.
Limitations: Giving limited to areas of company operations, with some emphasis on Chicago, IL. No support for religious organizations or veterans' organizations. No grants to individuals, or for endowments, scholarships, fellowships, or advertising; no loans.
Application information:
  Initial approach: Proposal
  Deadline(s): None
Trustees: T.C. Berg; M.J. Hower; W.R. Reum.
Number of staff: 1 part-time professional; 1 part-time support.
EIN: 366050609
Selected grants: The following grants were reported in 2005.
$17,000 to United Way of Metropolitan Chicago, Chicago, IL.
$15,000 to Morton Arboretum, Lisle, IL. 2 grants: $10,000, $5,000
$5,000 to Chicago Chamber Musicians, Chicago, IL.
$5,000 to Johns Hopkins University, Baltimore, MD.
$3,500 to Teen Ranch, Marlette, MI.
$3,000 to United Way of Central Indiana, Indianapolis, IN.
$1,000 to Museum of Science and Industry, Chicago, IL.
$450 to Butler University, Indianapolis, IN.
$250 to Rose Brooks Center, Kansas City, MO.

2594
Anderson Family Gardens Foundation ◇ ☆
(formerly John R. and Linda L. Anderson Charitable Trust)
330 Spring Creek Rd.
Rockford, IL   61107-1035

Established in 1986 in IL.
Donors: David J. Anderson; Kristin L. Pecora; Tracy E. Fitzgerald; Jeffrey R. Anderson; John R. Anderson; Ralph Anderson.
Foundation type: Independent foundation.
Financial data (yr. ended 12/31/05): Assets, $7,000,903 (M); gifts received, $2,229,396; expenditures, $1,055,728; qualifying distributions, $995,207; giving activities include $995,207 for 2 grants (high: $995,000; low: $207).
Fields of interest: Environment, natural resources; Recreation, single organization support; Recreation, parks/playgrounds.
Limitations: Applications not accepted. Giving primarily in Rockford, IL. No grants to individuals.
Application information: Contributes only to pre-selected organizations.
Officers and Directors:* John R. Anderson,* Pres.; Linda L. Anderson,* V.P.; David J. Anderson,* Secy.; Duane R. Bach,* Treas.; Jeffrey R. Anderson; Kristin L. Anderson; Tracy E. Anderson.
EIN: 363480352
Selected grants: The following grants were reported in 2003.

$216,000 to Anderson Gardens, Rockford, IL.

2595
The Andrew Family Foundation ◇
14628 John Humphrey Dr.
Orland Park, IL   60462
Contact: Kim Llumiquinga

Established in 1993 in IL.
Donors: Edward J. Andrew; Edward J. Andrew, Jr.; Laurel J. Andrew; Edith G. Andrew; Richard G. Andrew; William V. Andrew; Kathryn A. Willett; Whitecap Investments G.P.
Foundation type: Independent foundation.
Financial data (yr. ended 10/31/05): Assets, $13,308,194 (L); expenditures, $482,298; qualifying distributions, $418,974; giving activities include $314,833 for 5 grants (high: $92,500; low: $25,000), and $91,084 for 8 grants to individuals (high: $18,250; low: $3,250).
Purpose and activities: Giving primarily for education including scholarships as well as for the arts particularly to museums; some giving also for health care, and children and social services.
Fields of interest: Museums; Museums (children's); Museums (natural history); Museums (science/technology); Performing arts, theater; Arts; Elementary/secondary education; Higher education; Libraries/library science; Education; Hospitals (specialty); Human services; Children/youth, services; Christian agencies & churches; Orthodox Catholic agencies & churches.
Type of support: General/operating support; Annual campaigns; Capital campaigns; Building/renovation; Scholarship funds.
Limitations: Giving on a national basis, with some emphasis on IL. No support for religious programs.
Application information: Application form not required.
  Initial approach: Letter
  Copies of proposal: 2
  Deadline(s): None
  Board meeting date(s): 4 times per year
Officers and Directors:* Edward J. Andrew,* Pres.; Edward J. Andrew, Jr.,* V.P.; Edith G. Andrew,* Secy.; Laurel J. Andrew,* Treas.; Richard G. Andrew; William V. Andrew; Kathryn A. Willett.
EIN: 363926511

2596
Aileen S. Andrew Foundation ◇
10701 Winterset Dr.
Orland Park, IL   60467   (708) 349-4445
Contact: Robert E. Hord, Jr., Pres.

Incorporated in 1946 in IL.
Donors: Andrew Corp.; Edward J. Andrew; Richard G. Andrew; Juanita A. Hord.
Foundation type: Independent foundation.
Financial data (yr. ended 11/30/05): Assets, $52,477,867 (M); gifts received, $720,000; expenditures, $2,965,983; qualifying distributions, $2,660,450; giving activities include $2,150,086 for 762 grants (high: $125,000; low: $50; average: $1,000–$15,000), and $331,971 for 57 grants to individuals (high: $14,000; low: $235; average: $2,000–$6,000).
Purpose and activities: Giving for higher education, including scholarships for children of Andrew Corp. employees and graduates of a local high school;

support also for civic affairs and general charitable giving locally.

Fields of interest: Arts; Higher education; Education; Animal welfare; Health organizations, association; Human services; American Red Cross; Children/youth, services; Family services; Government/public administration; Christian agencies & churches.

Type of support: General/operating support; Employee-related scholarships.

Limitations: Giving primarily in Orland Park, IL. No support for taxable corporations, political organizations or private foundations. No grants to individuals (except scholarships); no loans.

Application information: Application forms are available for scholarship program.

Initial approach: Letter of intent
Deadline(s): Apr. 1 for scholarships
Board meeting date(s): Several times per year
Final notification: May 1 for scholarships

Officers and Directors:* Robert E. Hord, Jr.,* Pres.; Joyce Smith, V.P.; Aileen H. Daly,* Secy.; Richard L. Dybala, Treas.; Edward J. Andrew, Jr.; Laurel J. Andrew; Richard G. Andrew; Juanita A. Hord; Robert E. Hord, Sr.

EIN: 366049910

Selected grants: The following grants were reported in 2005.

$125,000 to IMSA Fund for Advancement of Education, Aurora, IL.

$100,000 to Sertoma Centre, Alsip, IL.

$83,000 to Trinity Christian College, Palos Heights, IL.

$50,000 to Saint Colettas of Illinois, Palos Park, IL.

$50,000 to University of Illinois at Chicago, Chicago, IL.

$40,000 to University of Chicago, Chicago, IL.

$20,000 to Parents Association for Cerebral Palsy Children, Chicago, IL.

$1,000 to March of Dimes Birth Defects Foundation, White Plains, NY.

$1,000 to Phillips Exeter Academy, Exeter, NH.

$200 to American Red Cross.

2597
L. & R. Anixter Foundation ◇
c/o Northern Trust Co.
P.O. Box 803878
Chicago, IL 60680-3878

Established in 1985 in IL.
Donor: Lester J. Anixter Trust.
Foundation type: Independent foundation.
Financial data (yr. ended 7/31/05): Assets, $14,785,208 (M); gifts received, $282,184; expenditures, $809,814; qualifying distributions, $748,318; giving activities include $641,921 for 19 grants (high: $431,921; low: $1,000).
Fields of interest: Museums (art); Arts; Scholarships/financial aid; Civil rights, minorities; Jewish federated giving programs; Jewish agencies & temples.
Limitations: Applications not accepted. Giving primarily in Chicago, IL. No grants to individuals.
Application information: Contributes only to pre-selected organizations.
Officers and Trustee:* Edward Anixter, Pres.; Jack Ehrlich,* V.P. and Secy.; Steven Anixter, V.P.; Joann Anixter Silva, V.P.; Charles H. Wiggins, Jr., Secy.-Treas.
EIN: 363458779
Selected grants: The following grants were reported in 2005.

$40,000 to Medical Development for Israel, New York, NY.

$35,000 to Anixter Center, Chicago, IL.

$30,000 to United States Holocaust Memorial Museum, DC. 2 grants: $20,000, $10,000

$20,000 to Childrens Memorial Hospital, Chicago, IL.

$10,000 to Illinois Institute of Technology, Chicago, IL.

$10,000 to National Equal Justice Association, San Francisco, CA.

$7,500 to Jesus Guadalupe Foundation, Warrenville, IL.

$5,000 to Ravinia Festival Association, Highland Park, IL.

$3,000 to Hebrew Seminary of the Deaf, Skokie, IL.

2598
Aon Foundation ◇
(formerly Combined International Foundation)
P.O. Box 8264
Chicago, IL 60680 (312) 381-3549
Contact: Carolyn E. Labutka, V.P. and Exec. Dir.
Application address: 200 E. Randolph St., Chicago, IL 60601

Established in 1984 in IL.
Donor: Aon Corp.
Foundation type: Company-sponsored foundation.
Financial data (yr. ended 12/31/05): Assets, $861,849 (M); gifts received, $7,212,121; expenditures, $7,786,777; qualifying distributions, $7,786,777; giving activities include $7,243,287 for 3,318 grants (high: $50,000).
Purpose and activities: The foundation supports organizations involved with education, health, parks and playgrounds, baseball, youth development, children and youth, and economic development.
Fields of interest: Elementary/secondary education; Higher education; Education; Hospitals (general); Health care; Recreation, parks/playgrounds; Athletics/sports, baseball; Boys & girls clubs; American Red Cross; Children/youth, services; Economic development; Federated giving programs.
Type of support: General/operating support; Endowments; Program development; Employee matching gifts.
Limitations: Giving on a national basis. No grants for general operating support for secondary or vocational schools.
Publications: Application guidelines.
Application information: Application form not required.
Initial approach: Proposal
Deadline(s): None
Board meeting date(s): 3 times per year
Final notification: Varies
Officers and Directors:* R. Eden Martin,* Chair.; Patrick G. Ryan,* Pres.; Carolyn E. Labutka,* V.P. and Exec. Dir.; Kevann M. Cooke, Secy.; Harvey N. Medvin, Treas.; Gregory C. Chase; Andrew J. McKenna.
Number of staff: 4
EIN: 363337340
Selected grants: The following grants were reported in 2004.

$450,000 to United Way of Metropolitan Chicago, Chicago, IL.

$161,000 to Chicago Symphony Orchestra, Chicago, IL. 2 grants: $150,000, $11,000

$125,000 to Northwestern University, Evanston, IL.

$100,000 to Commercial Club Foundation, Chicago, IL.

$25,000 to Maryville Academy, Des Plaines, IL.

$20,000 to Chicago United, Chicago, IL.

$15,500 to UJA-Federation of New York, New York, NY.

$10,000 to Saint Vincents Services, Brooklyn, NY.

$10,000 to University of Notre Dame, Notre Dame, IN.

2599
Edith Marie Appleton Foundation ◇
460 Winnetka Ave., Ste. 22
Winnetka, IL 60093

Established in 1999 in IL.
Donor: Edith Marie Appleton†.
Foundation type: Independent foundation.
Financial data (yr. ended 12/31/05): Assets, $13,528,890 (M); expenditures, $1,894,902; qualifying distributions, $1,876,956; giving activities include $1,867,000 for 22 grants (high: $500,000; low: $5,000).
Purpose and activities: Giving primarily for women's issues and for the performing arts in the Chicago, IL area.
Fields of interest: Arts; Human services; Women.
Limitations: Applications not accepted. Giving primarily in Chicago, IL. No grants to individuals.
Application information: Contributes only to pre-selected organizations.
Board meeting date(s): Annually
Officers and Directors:* Albert I. Goodman,* Pres. and Treas.; Cathy Smerch,* V.P.; Jane Hannon,* Secy.; Terry Dickenson; Robert Dunagan; Maria Goodman.
EIN: 364329167

2600
ARIA Foundation, Inc. ◇
c/o Elliott M. Friedman
1313 W. 175th St.
Homewood, IL 60430

Established in 1991 in VT.
Donors: Adam Albright; Rachel Albright.
Foundation type: Independent foundation.
Financial data (yr. ended 10/31/05): Assets, $32,205,224 (M); gifts received, $1,848,221; expenditures, $1,556,526; qualifying distributions, $1,256,184; giving activities include $1,244,960 for 35 grants (high: $559,960; low: $1,000).
Purpose and activities: Giving primarily for the protection and preservation of our natural resources and the global environment.
Fields of interest: Elementary/secondary education; Higher education; Education; Environment, natural resources; Environment; Children/youth, services; Family services; International affairs; Public affairs, research; Native Americans/American Indians; Women.
Limitations: Applications not accepted. Giving on a national basis. No grants to individuals.
Application information: Contributes only to pre-selected organizations.
Officers: Adam Albright, Pres.; Rachel Albright, V.P.; Ruth S. Flynn, Secy.; Elliott M. Friedman, Treas.
EIN: 133603275
Selected grants: The following grants were reported in 2005.

$559,960 to Natural Resources Defense Council, New York, NY.

$90,000 to Global Fund for Women, San Francisco, CA.

$80,000 to Amazon Conservation Team, Arlington, VA.

$75,000 to Rocky Mountain Institute, Snowmass, CO.

$65,000 to Kripalu Yoga Fellowship, Lenox, MA.

$35,000 to Futures for Children, Albuquerque, NM.

$25,000 to Worldwatch Institute, DC.

$20,000 to Dine College, Tsaile, AZ.

$15,000 to Stone Child College, Box Elder, MT.

$10,000 to Woods Hole Research Center, Woods Hole, MA.

2601
The Arthur Foundation ▼
(formerly MacNeal Health Foundation)
3322 S. Oak Park Ave.
Berwyn, IL 60402-3407   (708) 749-1678
Contact: Thomas A. Hett, Dir., Progs.
FAX: (708) 749-2318; E-mail: thett@arthurfdn.org;
Additional tel.: (708) 749-3270; URL: http://
www.arthurfdn.org

Established in 2000 in IL; converted from MacNeal Memorial Hospital; changed its name to The Arthur Foundation in 2006.
Foundation type: Independent foundation.
Financial data (yr. ended 12/31/04): Assets, $88,527,621 (M); expenditures, $4,670,086; qualifying distributions, $4,058,749; giving activities include $3,671,038 for 22 grants (high: $1,195,050; low: $2,000; average: $10,000–$150,000).
Purpose and activities: The foundation aims to improve the health of the community by supporting accessible, affordable and appropriate health services to vulnerable populations. The foundation recognizes that actual health care or health related service is only one of the factors determining the health status of individuals and families of these same communities. The health of the people is also determined by the educational status of its people, especially its youth. Therefore, the foundation will also consider grant requests that foster and improve education and educational opportunities for the citizens of the area it seeks to serve.
Fields of interest: Medical school/education; Nursing school/education; Education, ESL programs; Education; Health care; Medical research.
Type of support: Program evaluation; Fellowships; General/operating support; Continuing support; Income development; Management development/capacity building; Building/renovation; Equipment; Program development; Professorships; Curriculum development; Internship funds; Scholarship funds; Research; Matching/challenge support.
Limitations: Giving primarily in Berwyn and Cicero, IL for education grants. Medical research and health care grants for western Cook County, IL. No support for organizations without charitable status, political parties or candidates, sponsorship of service clubs, sport teams, fraternal organizations, advocacy or lobby groups, or for foreign organizations. No grants to individuals, or for endowments or matching funds, operating budgets for pre-existing programs, organization overhead expenses not directly applicable to a grant project, salaries for participants with faculty appointments at institutions of higher learning, programs normally

funded by governmental agencies, fundraising events (including advertising, tickets, raffles and dinners), debt reduction, stand-alone research, individual scholarship support, conferences/seminars, books/periodicals, memberships, travel expenses, any attempt to influence legislation, sectarian religious activities, foreign expenditures, telephone solicitations; no loans.
Publications: Application guidelines.
Application information: Please do not telephone or fax with LOIs. Shortly after receipt of LOI the foundation will send letter of acknowledgement. Applicants meeting foundation criteria for funding will be asked to submit additional information within six weeks of date of letter requesting information. The foundation will also notify those if it is unable to consider funding. Application form not required.
Initial approach: Letter of inquiry including cover page (no more than 3 pages)
Copies of proposal: 2
Deadline(s): LOI deadlines: Apr. 1 and Sept.1
Board meeting date(s): Quarterly
Officers and Board Members:* Luke McGuiness,* Chair.; William J. Hank,* Vice-Chair. and V.P.; Michael P. Kenahan,* Pres.; Raymond Nootens, M.D., Secy.; Gerald J. Sebesta,* Treas.
Directors: Rolf Gunnar, M.D.; Allen B. Hank; Jeffrey P. Huml, M.D.; Roxanne Martino; Carmen Velasquez.
Number of staff: 2 full-time professional.
EIN: 364324067
Selected grants: The following grants were reported in 2004.
$1,195,051 to University of Chicago, Chicago, IL. For creation of Department of Family and Community Medicine with research on best practices of Family and Community Medicine to occur in Berwyn/Cicero area, and educational aspect of campus.
$1,105,358 to University of Notre Dame, Institute for Latino Studies, Notre Dame, IN. For Needs Assessment of Berwyn/Cicero communities, as well as base line data accumulation, leadership identification and capacity education and building.
$499,505 to Loyola University of Chicago, Chicago, IL. 2 grants: $349,505 (For Hispanic Nursing Initiative to give scholarships to men and women interested in nursing profession), $150,000 to Marcella Niehoff School of Nursing (For successful Hispanic Nurse Initiative that provides scholarships to men and women interested in nursing profession).
$150,000 to Alivio Medical Center, Chicago, IL. Toward establishing new model of service.
$125,000 to Northeastern Illinois University, College of Education, Chicago, IL. For planning grant for Chicago Teachers Center to develop plans for and to executive Foundation's Initiative for Educational Excellence, in cooperation with Cicero Education Forum and Interfaith Leadership Project, including writing additional grants to assist in funding Initiative, as well as setting up model of family cooperation and information center in Cicero Public Schools.
$100,000 to Robert R. McCormick Tribune Foundation, Chicago, IL. For grant for Chicago Tribune Charities to participate in program that provides matching funds, which on foundation's recommendation was paid to Loyola's Marcella Niehoff School of Nursing.
$80,000 to Saint Xavier University, Chicago, IL. Toward program that seeks to assist former nurses in Mexico to upgrade linguistic and

clinical skills to meet Illinois licensure requirements; collaboration with Mercy Hospital, Alivio Medical Center, and City Colleges of Chicago.
$50,000 to Fenwick High School, Oak Park, IL. For tuition abatement and scholarships for Hispanic students.
$9,500 to Holy Cross Hospital, Chicago, IL. Toward study to assess feasibility of acquiring certification as Federally Qualified Health Center.

2602
Astellas USA Foundation ◇
(formerly Yamanouchi USA Foundation)
3 Parkway N.
Deerfield, IL 60015

Established in 1993 in DC.
Foundation type: Independent foundation.
Financial data (yr. ended 12/31/05): Assets, $32,246,743 (M); expenditures, $2,510,720; qualifying distributions, $2,494,477; giving activities include $2,418,000 for 98 grants.
Purpose and activities: Giving primarily to higher education, medical schools, and health organizations.
Fields of interest: Higher education, university; Health sciences school/education; Medical care, community health systems.
Limitations: Applications not accepted. Giving on a national basis. No grants to individuals.
Application information: Contributes only to pre-selected organizations.
Officers and Directors:* Hatsuo Aoki,* Chair.; Akihito Matsubara,* Pres.; Michio Yamashita,* Secy.; Kazumasa Saito,* Treas.; Makoto Nishimura; Masafumo Nogimori; Toshinari Tamura; Touichi Takenaka.
EIN: 521820099
Selected grants: The following grants were reported in 2004.
$65,000 to American Historical Association, DC.
$65,000 to University of Pennsylvania, Philadelphia, PA.
$50,000 to Institute of Cultural Affairs, DC.
$50,000 to Louisiana State University Health Sciences Center, New Orleans, LA.
$33,000 to Duke University Medical Center, Durham, NC.
$30,000 to California Institute of Technology, Pasadena, CA.
$30,000 to Cincinnati Childrens Hospital Medical Center, Cincinnati, OH.
$30,000 to Thomas Jefferson University, Philadelphia, PA.
$30,000 to Yale University, New Haven, CT.
$25,000 to Childrens Specialized Hospital, Mountainside, NJ.

2603
The Atlas Heritage Foundation ◇
c/o The Northern Trust Co.
P.O. Box 803878
Chicago, IL 60680

Established in 2000 in DE.
Donor: James M. Kilts.
Foundation type: Independent foundation.
Financial data (yr. ended 12/31/05): Assets, $9,453,975 (M); expenditures, $356,778; qualifying distributions, $323,815; giving activities

include $322,415 for 13 grants (high: $200,000; low: $100).

Fields of interest: Elementary/secondary education; Higher education; Business school/education; Human services; Protestant agencies & churches.

Limitations: Applications not accepted. Giving primarily in IL; some funding also in NY. No grants to individuals.

Application information: Contributes only to pre-selected organizations.

Officers: James M. Kilts, Pres.; Sandra M. Kilts, V.P. and Secy.

Director: James M. Kilts, Jr.

EIN: 134147482

Selected grants: The following grants were reported in 2005.

$205,000 to University of Chicago, Chicago, IL. 2 grants: $200,000, $5,000

$20,000 to Knox College, Galesburg, IL.

$5,000 to Cato Institute, DC.

$2,500 to Westchester Land Trust, Bedford Hills, NY.

$2,000 to Skidmore College, Saratoga Springs, NY. 2 grants: $1,000 each

2604
G. Carl Ball Family Foundation ✧ ☆
800 Roosevelt Rd., Ste. E216
Glen Ellyn, IL 60137

Established in 2003 in IL.
Donor: G. Carl Ball†.
Foundation type: Independent foundation.
Financial data (yr. ended 12/31/05): Assets, $4,320,193 (M); expenditures, $1,011,220; qualifying distributions, $1,011,220; giving activities include $1,009,400 for 3 grants (high: $1,000,000; low: $4,400).
Fields of interest: Education; Foundations (community).
Limitations: Applications not accepted. Giving primarily in MO.
Application information: Contributes only to pre-selected organizations.
Officers and Directors:* Anna C. Ball,* Pres. and Secy.; Susannah P. Ball,* V.P. and Treas.; Jane Mann.
EIN: 830366015

2605
Charles and Margery Barancik Foundation ✧ ☆
c/o Northbrook Mgmt. Corp.
555 Skokie Blvd., Ste. 366
Northbrook, IL 60062-2854

Established in 1986 in IL.
Donors: Charles L. Barancik; Margery L. Barancik.
Foundation type: Independent foundation.
Financial data (yr. ended 4/30/06): Assets, $811,577 (M); gifts received, $711,508; expenditures, $348,008; qualifying distributions, $347,988; giving activities include $347,988 for grants.
Fields of interest: Arts; Multiple sclerosis research; YM/YWCAs & YM/YWHAs; Jewish federated giving programs.
Limitations: Applications not accepted. Giving primarily in FL and IL. No grants to individuals.

Application information: Contributes only to pre-selected organizations.
Officers and Directors:* Charles L. Barancik,* Pres.; Margery L. Barancik,* V.P.; Deborah K. Hanson, Secy.; Michael E. Gronli,* Treas.
EIN: 363442474
Selected grants: The following grants were reported in 2003.
$86,500 to Multiple Sclerosis Society, National, New York, NY.
$20,748 to Ravinia Festival Association, Highland Park, IL.
$5,000 to Jewish Federation, Sarasota-Manatee, Sarasota, FL.
$5,000 to Jewish United Fund.
$3,000 to YMCA.
$2,000 to Sarasota Ballet of Florida, Sarasota, FL.
$2,000 to Van Wezel Foundation, Sarasota, FL.
$1,495 to Temple Beth Israel.
$1,000 to Anti-Defamation League of Bnai Brith, New York, NY.
$1,000 to Memorial Sloan-Kettering Cancer Center, New York, NY.

2606
Gertrude A. Barnett Foundation ✧
c/o The Northern Trust Bank of Florida, N.A.
P.O. Box 803878
Chicago, IL 60680

Established in 1997 in FL.
Foundation type: Independent foundation.
Financial data (yr. ended 12/31/05): Assets, $10,619,850 (M); expenditures, $548,338; qualifying distributions, $506,411; giving activities include $502,734 for 10 grants (high: $70,308; low: $39,978).
Purpose and activities: Giving primarily for children and youth services.
Fields of interest: Education; Medical research; Human services; Children/youth, services; Protestant agencies & churches.
Limitations: Applications not accepted. Giving primarily in FL. No grants to individuals.
Application information: Contributes only to pre-selected organizations.
Trustee: The Northern Trust Co.
EIN: 656245681

2607
Baskes Family Foundation ✧ ☆
980 N. Michigan Ave., No. 1380
Chicago, IL 60611-4528

Established in 2004 in IL.
Foundation type: Independent foundation.
Financial data (yr. ended 7/31/05): Assets, $13,889,816 (M); expenditures, $813,712; qualifying distributions, $813,712; giving activities include $741,260 for 61 grants (high: $273,810; low: $150).
Purpose and activities: Giving primarily for the arts, particularly the performing arts, as well as for higher education and libraries, including the Library of Congress; funding also to Jewish organizations, and children, youth, and social services.
Fields of interest: Museums (art); Performing arts; Performing arts, opera; Higher education; Libraries (special); Education; Reproductive health, family planning; Human services; Children/youth,

services; Family services; Jewish federated giving programs; Jewish agencies & temples.
Limitations: Giving primarily in Chicago, IL, and New York, NY; some giving nationally.
Officers and Directors:* Julie Z. Baskes,* Pres.; Daniel L. Baskes,* V.P.; Jeremy A. Baskes,* V.P.; Laura Baskes Litwin,* V.P.; Roger S. Baskes,* Secy.-Treas.
EIN: 300257951

2608
Alben F. & Clara G. Bates Foundation ✧ ☆
159 Cottage Hill Rd., Apt. 113
Elmhurst, IL 60126

Established in 1952 in IL.
Donor: Henry G. Bates.
Foundation type: Independent foundation.
Financial data (yr. ended 12/31/05): Assets, $5,331,366 (M); expenditures, $468,577; qualifying distributions, $450,998; giving activities include $450,998 for grants.
Fields of interest: Arts; Higher education; Education; Hospitals (general); Health care; Human services; Children/youth, services.
Limitations: Applications not accepted. Giving primarily in IL. No grants to individuals.
Application information: Contributes only to pre-selected organizations.
Officers: Alben F. Bates, Jr., Pres.; Henry G. Bates, V.P. and Treas.
EIN: 366081072
Selected grants: The following grants were reported in 2005.
$200,000 to DuPage Community Foundation, Wheaton, IL.
$17,000 to Elmhurst College, Elmhurst, IL.
$15,000 to Elgin Academy, Elgin, IL.
$10,100 to YMCA.
$8,000 to American Red Cross. 2 grants: $5,000, $3,000
$1,500 to United Way.
$1,000 to Fox Valley Hospice, Geneva, IL.
$1,000 to Pine Manor College, Chestnut Hill, MA.
$1,000 to Salvation Army.

2609
M. R. Bauer Foundation
208 S. LaSalle St., Ste. 1750
Chicago, IL 60604-1170 (312) 372-1947
Contact: Kent Lawrence, Pres. and Exec. Dir.
FAX: (312) 372-2389; E-mail: klawrence@lksu.com

Established in 1995 in IL.
Donors: Modestus R. Bauer†; Evalyn M. Bauer†.
Foundation type: Independent foundation.
Financial data (yr. ended 12/31/05): Assets, $14,884,335 (M); expenditures, $736,452; qualifying distributions, $685,515; giving activities include $639,150 for 41 grants (high: $256,150; low: $500).
Fields of interest: Reproductive health, family planning; Medical research, institute; Courts/judicial administration.
Type of support: General/operating support; Continuing support; Endowments; Conferences/seminars; Research; Program evaluation.
Limitations: Applications not accepted. Giving primarily in IL. No grants to individuals.

Application information: Unsolicited requests for funds not accepted.

Board meeting date(s): Quarterly

Officers and Directors:* Kent Lawrence,* Pres. and Exec. Dir.; Kathleen A. Lawrence,* Secy.-Treas.; Inger Lawrence.

EIN: 363980782

2610
Modestus Bauer Foundation ◇

c/o Robert J. Lawrence
208 S. LaSalle St., Ste. 1750
Chicago, IL 60604

Established in 2001 in IL.

Foundation type: Independent foundation.

Financial data (yr. ended 12/31/05): Assets, $15,648,864 (M); expenditures, $773,421; qualifying distributions, $709,820; giving activities include $673,800 for 104 grants (high: $35,000; low: $250).

Fields of interest: Education; Health organizations, association; Human services; Jewish agencies & temples.

Limitations: Applications not accepted. No grants to individuals.

Application information: Contributes only to pre-selected organizations.

Officers and Directors:* Robert J. Lawrence,* Pres.; Lawrence A. Reich,* V.P.; David Reich,* Secy.; Linda Lawrence.

EIN: 364473692

2611
The Baxter International Foundation

(formerly The Baxter Allegiance Foundation)
1 Baxter Pkwy.
Deerfield, IL 60015 (847) 948-4605
Contact: Celene Peurye, Secy. and Exec. Dir.
FAX: (847) 948-4559; E-mail: fdninfo@baxter.com;
URL: http://www.baxter.com/about_baxter/foundation/index.html

Established in 1982 in IL.

Donors: Baxter International Inc.; American Hospital Supply Corp.; Allegiance Corp.

Foundation type: Company-sponsored foundation.

Financial data (yr. ended 12/31/05): Assets, $37,877,732 (M); expenditures, $3,916,010; qualifying distributions, $3,590,007; giving activities include $2,943,266 for 152 grants (high: $285,495; low: $250), and $646,741 for 126 employee matching gifts.

Purpose and activities: The foundation supports organizations involved with health.

Fields of interest: Health care.

International interests: Asia; Canada; Europe; Latin America; Mexico; Oceania.

Type of support: Program development; Employee volunteer services; Employee matching gifts; Employee-related scholarships.

Limitations: Giving on a national and international basis in areas of company operations, including in Asia-Pacific, Canada, Europe, Latin America, and Mexico. No support for religious organizations, hospitals, or disease-specific organizations. No grants to individuals (except for employee-related scholarships), or for dinners, special fundraising events, capital campaigns or endowments, or non-health care activities at educational institutions.

Publications: Annual report (including application guidelines).

Application information: Application form not required.

Initial approach: Fax or E-mail foundation; mail proposal to foundation
Copies of proposal: 1
Deadline(s): 2 months prior to board meetings
Board meeting date(s): Quarterly

Officers and Directors: John J. Greisch, Pres.; Celene Peurye, Secy. and Exec. Dir.; Charles W. Thurman, Treas.; Alice J. Campbell; Susan Lichtenstein; Shaun Newlon; Pablo Toledo.

Number of staff: 1 full-time professional; 1 full-time support.

EIN: 363159396

2612
BCS Charitable Fund ◇

c/o Shepard, Schwartz & Harris LLP
123 N. Wacker Dr., Ste. 1400
Chicago, IL 60606
Application address: c/o Myron Szold, 1 N. Franklin St., Ste. 450, Chicago, IL 60606-3423

Established in 1997 in IL.

Donor: Myron Szold.

Foundation type: Independent foundation.

Financial data (yr. ended 6/30/05): Assets, $110,748 (M); gifts received, $250,000; expenditures, $339,736; qualifying distributions, $332,360; giving activities include $332,360 for 49 grants (high: $150,000; low: $100).

Purpose and activities: Giving primarily for the arts.

Fields of interest: Arts education; Performing arts; Performing arts, dance; Performing arts, theater; Performing arts, music; Arts; Higher education.

Limitations: Giving primarily in Chicago, IL. No grants to individuals.

Application information: Application form not required.

Deadline(s): None

Trustees: Jennifer Bohnert; Pamela Crutchfield; Myron Szold.

EIN: 367191434

Selected grants: The following grants were reported in 2005.

$10,000 to Chicago Childrens Choir, Chicago, IL.
$10,000 to United Way, IL.
$7,000 to Chicago Historical Society, Chicago, IL.
$6,000 to Chicago Shakespeare Theater, Chicago, IL.
$5,000 to Chicago Symphony Orchestra, Chicago, IL.
$5,000 to Old Town School of Folk Music, Chicago, IL.
$5,000 to Weizmann Institute of Science, Rehovot, Israel. .
$2,500 to Chicago Foundation for Women, Chicago, IL.
$2,500 to Free Street Programs, Chicago, IL.
$1,000 to Victory Gardens Theater, Chicago, IL.

2613
Francis Beidler Foundation ◇

53 W. Jackson Blvd., Ste. 530
Chicago, IL 60604 (312) 922-3792
Contact: Thomas B. Dorris, Tr.

Established in 1999 in IL.

Foundation type: Independent foundation.

Financial data (yr. ended 12/31/05): Assets, $15,007,137 (M); expenditures, $595,408; qualifying distributions, $508,208; giving activities include $499,450 for 128 grants (high: $40,000; low: $300).

Fields of interest: Higher education; Animals/wildlife, preservation/protection; Reproductive health, family planning; Crime/violence prevention; Human services; Neighborhood centers; Children/youth, services; Community development, business promotion; Federated giving programs.

Limitations: Giving primarily in Chicago, IL. No grants to individuals.

Application information:

Initial approach: Letter
Deadline(s): None

Trustees: Francis Beidler III; Thomas B. Dorris; Elizabeth Tisdahl.

EIN: 364260449

Selected grants: The following grants were reported in 2004.

$39,000 to Better Government Association, Chicago, IL.
$35,000 to Hull House Association, Chicago, IL.
$34,000 to Chicago Youth Centers, Chicago, IL.
$29,500 to Chapin Hall Center for Children, Chicago, IL.
$22,000 to Audubon Society, National, Harleyville, SC.
$22,000 to Chicago Childrens Museum, Chicago, IL.
$20,250 to Public Interest Law Initiative, Chicago, IL.
$12,500 to Project on Government Oversight, DC.
$7,000 to Brown University, Providence, RI.
$3,000 to Family Focus, Chicago, IL.

2614
Bell Family Foundation, Inc. ◇

445 S. Frontage Rd.
Burr Ridge, IL 60527 (630) 325-9800

Established in 1990 in IL.

Donor: William J. Bell.

Foundation type: Independent foundation.

Financial data (yr. ended 9/30/05): Assets, $10,660,292 (M); expenditures, $1,085,089; qualifying distributions, $1,039,440; giving activities include $1,026,375 for 78 grants (high: $110,000; low: $200).

Purpose and activities: Giving primarily for the arts; funding also for medical research, education, and the environment.

Fields of interest: Performing arts; Arts; Higher education; Environment; Health organizations, association; Human services; Children/youth, services.

Limitations: Applications not accepted. Giving primarily in CA; funding also in CO and Washington, DC.

Application information: Contributes only to pre-selected organizations.

Officers: Lee Phillip Bell, Pres.; Burton A. Bowen, Secy.; William James Bell, Treas.

Directors: Bradley P. Bell; Lauralee K. Bell; William Joseph Bell.

EIN: 363773191

Selected grants: The following grants were reported in 2005.

$76,500 to Aspen Art Museum, Aspen, CO.
$31,000 to John Thomas Dye School, Los Angeles, CA.
$29,000 to Heal The Bay, Santa Monica, CA.

$25,000 to Alzheimers Association, San Diego, CA.
$25,000 to Los Angeles Police Foundation, Los Angeles, CA.
$20,000 to Shake-A-Leg, Newport, RI.
$13,500 to City of Hope, Los Angeles, CA.
$10,000 to Childrens Institute International, Los Angeles, CA.
$9,875 to Estelle Doheny Eye Foundation, Los Angeles, CA.
$5,000 to Aspen Music Festival, Aspen, CO.

2615
Bellebyron Foundation ✧
c/o D.B. Smith
88 Hawley Woods Rd.
Barrington, IL   60010-5108

Established in 1983 in IL.
Donor: Harold Byron Smith.
Foundation type: Independent foundation.
Financial data (yr. ended 12/31/05): Assets, $7,510,286 (M); expenditures, $753,366; qualifying distributions, $750,195; giving activities include $750,195 for 9 grants (high: $230,002; low: $20,000).
Fields of interest: Arts, formal/general education; Performing arts, theater; Botanical gardens; Aquariums; Substance abuse, treatment.
Limitations: Applications not accepted. Giving primarily in IL. No grants to Individuals.
Application information: Contributes only to pre-selected organizations.
Officers: Stephen B. Smith, Chair. and Pres.; Christopher B. Smith, V.P.; David B. Smith, Secy.-Treas.
EIN: 366058056

2616
Bere Foundation, Inc. ✧
641 S. Elm St.
Hinsdale, IL   60521-4623
Contact: Barbara Van Dellen Bere, Pres.

Incorporated in 1983 in IL.
Donors: Barbara L. Bere; James F. Bere†.
Foundation type: Independent foundation.
Financial data (yr. ended 12/31/05): Assets, $6,352,593 (M); expenditures, $702,560; qualifying distributions, $656,166; giving activities include $638,500 for 38 grants (high: $200,000; low: $200).
Fields of interest: Performing arts centers; Arts; Higher education; Theological school/education; Education; Health organizations, association; Human services; Christian agencies & churches.
Type of support: General/operating support; Continuing support; Annual campaigns; Capital campaigns.
Limitations: Applications not accepted. Giving primarily in the greater Chicago, IL, area. No grants to individuals.
Application information: Contributes only to pre-selected organizations.
Officers and Directors: Barbara Van Dellen Bere,* Pres.; James F. Bere, Jr.,* V.P.; Robert P. Bere,* V.P.; Becky B. Sigfusson,* V.P.; Lynn B. Stine,* V.P.; David L. Bere,* Secy.-Treas.
EIN: 363272779

2617
The Berner Charitable and Scholarship Foundation ✧
P.O. Box 06560
Chicago, IL   60606-6560   (312) 782-5885

Established in 1994 in IL.
Foundation type: Independent foundation.
Financial data (yr. ended 12/31/05): Assets, $10,507,626 (M); expenditures, $690,477; qualifying distributions, $633,137; giving activities include $369,031 for grants, and $198,602 for 15 grants to individuals (high: $30,000; low: $5,000).
Purpose and activities: Giving primarily for education and health associations. Scholarship awards to residents of the U.S. who are attending, or who are planning to attend, any U.S. college or university. Selection shall be based on scholastic achievements, or the potential to make scholastic achievements, financial need, and demonstrated quality of leadership. Applicants who are seeking a scholarship for undergraduate degree must have graduated from high school with a "C" average or better. Applicants who are seeking a scholarship for a graduate degree, must have graduated from college with a "C" average or better. Applicants must enroll as full-time students and carry a full-time course load.
Fields of interest: Higher education; Education; Animal welfare; Health care; Health organizations, association; Medical research, institute; Cancer research; Crime/violence prevention, child abuse; Human services; Children/youth, services.
Type of support: General/operating support; Scholarships—to individuals.
Limitations: Giving primarily in Chicago, IL.
Trustees: Norman N. Schwartz; Ruben R. Vernof.
EIN: 363923844

2618
Grace A. Bersted Foundation ✧
c/o Bank of America, N.A.
231 S. LaSalle St.
Chicago, IL   60697   (312) 828-1785
Contact: M. Catherine Ryan

Established in 1986 in IL.
Donor: Grace A. Bersted†.
Foundation type: Independent foundation.
Financial data (yr. ended 12/31/05): Assets, $9,475,867 (M); expenditures, $467,596; qualifying distributions, $408,797; giving activities include $396,000 for 17 grants (high: $100,000; low: $500).
Purpose and activities: Giving primarily for human services; funding also for secondary and higher education, a conservation unit, YM/YWCAs, family services, and an independent foundation.
Fields of interest: Secondary school/education; Higher education; Environment, natural resources; Human services; YM/YWCAs & YM/YWHAs; Family services; Foundations (private independent).
Limitations: Giving limited to DuPage, Kane, Lake, and McHenry counties, IL. No grants to individuals.
Application information: Application form not required.
  Initial approach: Proposal
  Deadline(s): None
Trustee: Bank of America, N.A.
EIN: 366841348
Selected grants: The following grants were reported in 2005.

$100,000 to Saint Martin de Porres High School, Waukegan, IL.
$75,000 to Wheaton College, Wheaton, IL.
$54,000 to Morton Arboretum, Lisle, IL.
$20,000 to Catholic Charities of the Archdiocese of Chicago, Chicago, IL.
$20,000 to YMCA of Elgin, Elgin, IL. 2 grants: $10,000 each
$15,000 to Liberty Prairie Conservancy, Grayslake, IL.
$10,000 to Chicago Botanic Garden, Glencoe, IL.
$10,000 to Salvation Army of Elgin, Elgin, IL.

2619
The Bersted Foundation ✧
c/o Bank of America, N.A.
231 S. LaSalle St.
Chicago, IL   60697   (312) 828-1785
Contact: M. Catherine Ryan

Established in 1972 in IL.
Donor: Alfred Bersted†.
Foundation type: Independent foundation.
Financial data (yr. ended 12/31/05): Assets, $22,060,513 (M); expenditures, $1,040,968; qualifying distributions, $964,440; giving activities include $931,000 for 49 grants (high: $50,000; low: $5,000).
Purpose and activities: Giving primarily for children, youth, and families and social services.
Fields of interest: Human services; Children/youth, services; Family services; Christian agencies & churches.
Type of support: General/operating support; Continuing support; Building/renovation; Technical assistance.
Limitations: Giving limited to DeKalb, DuPage, Kane, and McHenry counties, in IL. No support for religious houses of worship, degree-conferring institutions of higher learning or for organizations that are testing for public safety. No grants to individuals; or for endowment funds exclusively, deficit financing or political campaigns.
Publications: Multi-year report (including application guidelines).
Application information: Send 2 copies of cover letter containing a brief summary of the purpose request, the specific amount requested, and the name, address, and phone number of the person submitting the request. Application form not required.
  Initial approach: Proposal along with a cover letter
  Copies of proposal: 2
  Deadline(s): To allow adequate time for review, mail proposals 2 months prior to board meetings
  Board meeting date(s): Generally in Jan., Apr., July, and Oct.
  Final notification: Up to 90 days
Trustee: Bank of America, N.A.
EIN: 366493609

2620
The Bielfeldt Foundation ✧
(formerly The Gary K. and Carlotta J. Bielfeldt Foundation)
4700 N. Prospect Rd., SPC 10
Peoria Heights, IL   61616-6469
Contact: Carlotta J. Bielfeldt, Pres.

Established in 1985 in IL.

Donor: Gary K. Bielfeldt.
Foundation type: Independent foundation.
Financial data (yr. ended 12/31/05): Assets, $14,017,102 (M); expenditures, $936,117; qualifying distributions, $794,569; giving activities include $628,400 for 41 grants (high: $400,000; low: $100).
Purpose and activities: Giving primarily for the arts, education, health associations, children, youth and social services, and to Lutheran churches and organizations, as well as to a Methodist medical center foundation.
Fields of interest: Arts, multipurpose centers/programs; Museums; Performing arts, opera; Higher education; Education; Cancer; Alzheimer's disease research; Crime/violence prevention, abuse prevention; Human services; Salvation Army; Children/youth, services; Protestant agencies & churches.
Limitations: Giving primarily in Peoria, IL. No grants to individuals.
Publications: Application guidelines.
Application information: Application form required.
  Initial approach: Letter requesting application form
  Deadline(s): None
  Board meeting date(s): End of Mar., June, Oct., and Dec.
  Final notification: 1 week after board meetings
Officers and Directors:* Douglas G. Stewart,* Pres.; Jane B. Converse, V.P.; Gary Anna, Secy.-Treas.; Carlotta Biefeldt, Exec. Dir.; William R. Barick.
Number of staff: 1
EIN: 371188243

2621
William Blair & Company Foundation ◇
222 W. Adams St., 28th Fl.
Chicago, IL 60606-5307   (312) 236-1600
Contact: E. David Coolidge III, V.P.

Established in 1980 in IL.
Donor: William Blair & Co., L.L.C.
Foundation type: Company-sponsored foundation.
Financial data (yr. ended 8/31/05): Assets, $3,281,382 (M); gifts received, $1,200,000; expenditures, $1,250,029; qualifying distributions, $1,247,872; giving activities include $1,247,872 for 353 grants (high: $50,000; low: $200).
Purpose and activities: The foundation supports organizations involved with arts and culture, higher education, health, cancer, human services, civic affairs, Christianity, and Judaism.
Fields of interest: Arts; Higher education; Hospitals (general); Health care; Cancer; Cancer research; Children/youth, services; Human services; Government/public administration; Public affairs; Roman Catholic agencies & churches; Jewish agencies & temples.
Type of support: General/operating support; Continuing support; Annual campaigns; Capital campaigns; Building/renovation; Endowments; Fellowships; Internship funds.
Limitations: Giving primarily in the metropolitan Chicago, IL, area. No grants to individuals.
Application information: Application form not required.
  Initial approach: Proposal
  Copies of proposal: 1
  Deadline(s): None

Officers: Edgar D. Jannotta, Pres.; E. David Coolidge III, V.P.; Michelle S. Musolino, V.P.; John R. Ettelson, Secy.; Stephen Campbell, Treas.
EIN: 363092291
Selected grants: The following grants were reported in 2005.
$50,000 to After School Matters, Chicago, IL.
$12,500 to Hull House Association, Chicago, IL.
$10,000 to Cystic Fibrosis Foundation, Bethesda, MD.
$10,000 to Northwestern University, Evanston, IL.
$10,000 to Pathways Awareness Foundation, Chicago, IL.
$3,500 to Adler Planetarium, Chicago, IL.
$3,000 to Golden Apple Foundation, Chicago, IL.
$2,750 to Boy Scouts of America, Anchorage, AK.
$2,500 to American Heart Association, Dallas, TX.
$2,500 to North Shore Senior Center, Northfield, IL.

2622
Blair Foundation ◇
c/o The Northern Trust Co.
P.O. Box 803878
Chicago, IL 60680
Application address: Dorothy Blair, c/o The Northern Trust Co., 4001 Tamiami Trail N., Naples, FL 34103, tel.: (239) 262-8800

Established in FL.
Donor: Dorothy Blair.
Foundation type: Independent foundation.
Financial data (yr. ended 12/31/05): Assets, $9,166,560 (M); expenditures, $456,241; qualifying distributions, $421,931; giving activities include $389,130 for 84 grants (high: $25,000; low: $500; average: $2,500–$8,000).
Purpose and activities: Giving primarily for higher education; some giving for conservation, animals and wildlife, as well as for health, human services, children and youth services, family services, and community development.
Fields of interest: Education; Environment, natural resources; Animals/wildlife; Health care; Human services; Children/youth, services; Family services; Community development.
Limitations: Giving primarily in FL, with emphasis on Naples; some giving also in Washington, DC, and NC. No grants to individuals.
Application information: Application form not required.
  Deadline(s): None
Advisors: Dorothy Blair; John Graham; Robert Rieman, M.D.
Trustee: Northern Trust Bank, N.A.
EIN: 656072965

2623
The Blowitz-Ridgeway Foundation ◇
1701 E. Woodfield Rd., Ste. 201
Schaumburg, IL 60173   (847) 330-1020
Contact: Megan C. Wilson, Admin.
FAX: (847) 330-1028;
E-mail: laura@blowitzridgeway.org; URL: http://www.blowitzridgeway.org/

Status changed from public charity to private foundation in 1984; converted from Ridgeway Hospital.
Foundation type: Independent foundation.
Financial data (yr. ended 9/30/05): Assets, $26,278,891 (M); expenditures, $1,687,149;

qualifying distributions, $1,575,646; giving activities include $1,134,800 for 107 grants (high: $50,000; low: $1,000).
Purpose and activities: Giving through program, general operating capital, and research grants primarily in the areas of health, mental and physical disability, and social services, with emphasis on children and youth.
Fields of interest: Health care; Mental health/crisis services; Medical research, institute; Human services; Children/youth, services; Disabilities, people with.
Type of support: General/operating support; Continuing support; Capital campaigns; Program development; Research; Program-related investments/loans.
Limitations: Giving generally limited to IL, except for medical research grants. No support for government agencies, religious purposes, or organizations that subsist mainly on third-party funding. No grants to individuals, or for production or writing of audio-visual materials.
Publications: Annual report; Annual report (including application guidelines); Grants list; Informational brochure (including application guidelines).
Application information: See foundation Web site for application guidelines and forms. Return applicants are required to submit their final report for the previous grant, before the new grant request can be reviewed. Application form required.
  Initial approach: Letter or telephone requesting guidelines
  Copies of proposal: 5
  Deadline(s): Ongoing
  Board meeting date(s): Monthly
  Final notification: 3-6 months
Officers and Trustees:* Max Pastin,* Pres.; Daniel L. Kline,* V.P.; Rev. James W. Jackson,* Secy.; Anthony M. Dean,* Treas.; Arthur R. Collison; Pierre LeBreton, Ph.D.; Patricia A. MacAlister; Marvin J. Pitluk, Ph.D.; Sandra Swantek, M.D.; Samuel G. Winston.
Number of staff: 1 full-time professional; 1 full-time support.
EIN: 362488355

2624
The Nathan and Emily S. Blum Foundation ◇
P.O. Box 755
Chicago, IL 60690
Contact: Thaddeus S. Plis

Established in 1980.
Donor: Nathan Blum†.
Foundation type: Independent foundation.
Financial data (yr. ended 12/31/05): Assets, $12,089,148 (M); expenditures, $634,365; qualifying distributions, $570,015; giving activities include $570,000 for 7 grants (high: $171,000; low: $7,100).
Fields of interest: Law school/education; Human services; Federated giving programs; Jewish federated giving programs.
Limitations: Giving primarily in Chicago, IL. No grants to individuals.
Application information:
  Initial approach: Letter
Trustee: Harris Bank, N.A.
EIN: 366706638

2625
Blum-Kovler Foundation ▼ ✧
875 N. Michigan Ave., Ste. 3400
Chicago, IL 60611-1958 (312) 664-5050
Contact: Hymen Bregar, Secy.

Incorporated in 1953 in IL.
Donors: Harry Blum‡; Everett Kovler.
Foundation type: Independent foundation.
Financial data (yr. ended 12/31/04): Assets,
$92,630,380 (M); expenditures, $4,280,077;
qualifying distributions, $3,757,900; giving
activities include $3,594,330 for 223 grants (high:
$250,000; low: $100; average: $1,000–$50,000).
Purpose and activities: Emphasis on social
services, Jewish welfare funds, higher education,
hospitals, health services, medical research, and
cultural programs; support also for youth and child
welfare agencies and public interest and civic affairs
groups.
Fields of interest: Arts; Higher education; Hospitals
(general); Health care; Medical research, institute;
Human services; Children/youth, services; Jewish
federated giving programs; Public policy, research;
Government/public administration.
Type of support: General/operating support.
Limitations: Giving primarily in the Chicago, IL, area.
Application information: Application form not
required.
   Initial approach: Written proposal (1-2 pages)
   Copies of proposal: 1
   Deadline(s): Nov.
   Board meeting date(s): As required
   Final notification: Varies
Officers: H. Jonathan Kovler, Pres.; Peter Kovler,
V.P.; Hymen Bregar, Secy.
Number of staff: 4 full-time professional; 1 part-time
professional; 3 part-time support.
EIN: 362476143
Selected grants: The following grants were reported
in 2003.
$504,350 to Museum of Contemporary Art,
   Chicago, IL.
$130,000 to Barbara Davis Center for Childhood
   Diabetes, Denver, CO.
$125,000 to Northwestern Memorial Hospital,
   Chicago, IL.
$100,000 to Evanston Northwestern Healthcare,
   Evanston, IL.
$100,000 to Family Institute, Evanston, IL.
$100,000 to Survivors of the Shoah Visual History
   Foundation, Los Angeles, CA.
$75,000 to University of Chicago, Chicago, IL. For
   Brendler Research Program in Urology.
$50,000 to John F. Kennedy Center for the
   Performing Arts, DC.
$40,190 to Rehabilitation Institute of Chicago,
   Chicago, IL.
$40,000 to Dartmouth College, Hanover, NH.

2626
The Alec Borden Foundation ✧
c/o The Northern Trust Co.
P.O. Box 803878
Chicago, IL 60680

Established in 2001 in CA.
Foundation type: Independent foundation.
Financial data (yr. ended 9/30/05): Assets,
$271,556 (M); expenditures, $457,185; qualifying
distributions, $456,311; giving activities include
$456,000 for 3 grants (high: $250,000; low:
$5,000).

Fields of interest: Hospitals (general); Aging,
centers/services.
Limitations: Applications not accepted. Giving
primarily in Los Angeles and Reseda, CA. No grants
to individuals.
Application information: Contributes only to
pre-selected organizations.
Trustee: The Northern Trust Co.
EIN: 527242859
Selected grants: The following grants were reported
in 2005.
$250,000 to City of Hope, Los Angeles, CA.
$201,000 to Cedars-Sinai Medical Center, Los
   Angeles, CA.
$5,000 to Los Angeles Jewish Home for the Aging,
   Reseda, CA.

2627
Borwell Charitable Foundation ✧
c/o Naomi T. Borwell
1040 N. Lake Shore Dr.
Chicago, IL 60611

Established in 1981 in IL.
Donors: Naomi T. Borwell; Robert C. Borwell, Sr.;
Mrs. Robert C. Borwell, Sr.
Foundation type: Independent foundation.
Financial data (yr. ended 10/31/05): Assets,
$96,860 (M); gifts received, $827,943;
expenditures, $1,112,889; qualifying distributions,
$1,100,571; giving activities include $1,096,300
for 34 grants (high: $220,000; low: $100).
Purpose and activities: Giving primarily for arts and
culture, including a music education program for
disadvantaged youth; funding also for hospitals and
health associations, social services, and to
Episcopal and Presbyterian churches.
Fields of interest: Arts education; Performing arts,
orchestra (symphony); Arts; Environment, land
resources; Health organizations, association;
Human services; Urban/community development;
Protestant agencies & churches.
Limitations: Applications not accepted. Giving
primarily in IL, with emphasis on Chicago; some
giving also in MI. No grants to individuals.
Application information: Contributes only to
pre-selected organizations.
Officers and Directors:* Naomi T. Borwell,* Pres.;
Robert C. Borwell, Jr.,* V.P.; Herbert T. Knight,*
V.P.; Elsie B. Revenaugh,* V.P.; Gail Carpenter Van
Goethem,* Secy.-Treas.
EIN: 363155489

2628
BP Foundation, Inc. ▼ ✧
(formerly BP Amoco Foundation, Inc.)
4101 Winfield Rd., M.C. 1W
Warrenville, IL 60555-3521
URL: http://www.bp.com/subsection.do?
categoryId=9004440&contentId=7009902

Incorporated in 1952 in IN.
Donors: Amoco Corp.; BP Amoco Corp.; BP Corp.
North America Inc.; BP America Inc.; Amoco
Production Co.; Atlantic Richfield Co.
Foundation type: Company-sponsored foundation.
Financial data (yr. ended 12/31/05): Assets,
$49,879,908 (M); gifts received, $36,000,000;
expenditures, $36,368,040; qualifying
distributions, $36,228,300; giving activities include

$35,500,792 for 269 grants (high: $3,273,570;
low: $1,000).
Purpose and activities: The foundation supports
organizations involved with disaster relief.
Fields of interest: Disasters, preparedness/
services.
Type of support: General/operating support;
Emergency funds; Employee volunteer services;
Employee matching gifts.
Limitations: Applications not accepted. Giving on a
national and international basis. No support for
religious, fraternal, political, social, or athletic
organizations; generally, no support for
organizations already receiving general operating
support through the United Way. No grants to
individuals, or for endowments, medical research,
publications, or conferences.
Publications: Financial statement.
Application information: Contributes only to
pre-selected organizations.
   Board meeting date(s): Apr., July, and Nov.
Officers and Directors:* Ross J. Pillari, Chair.;
Patricia D. Wright, Pres.; Yvonne Queen, Secy.; Mark
E. Thompson, Treas.; Brian K. Dinges,* Exec. Dir.;
Polly Flinn; J.C. Hughes; Dan B. Pinkert.
Number of staff: 4 full-time professional; 1 full-time
support.
EIN: 366046879
Selected grants: The following grants were reported
in 2004.
$3,000,000 to K C E T Community Television of
   Southern California, Los Angeles, CA. For
   unrestricted support.
$2,899,944 to Charities Aid Foundation (UK), West
   Malling, England. For unrestricted support.
$2,057,387 to JK Group, Plainsboro, NJ. For
   unrestricted support.
$1,905,600 to University of Alaska Foundation,
   Fairbanks, AK. For unrestricted support.
$1,000,000 to International Federation of Red
   Cross and Red Crescent Societies, Geneva,
   Switzerland. For unrestricted support for disaster
   relief in Asia.
$1,000,000 to National Energy Education
   Development (NEED) Project, Manassas, VA. For
   unrestricted support.
$31,726 to United Way of Greater Toledo, Toledo,
   OH. For unrestricted support.
$30,000 to Green Star, Anchorage, AK. For
   unrestricted support.
$25,000 to Prairie Crossing Charter School,
   Grayslake, IL. For unrestricted support.
$21,500 to Chicago Symphony Orchestra, Chicago,
   IL. For unrestricted support.

2629
Edwin J. Brach Foundation ✧
c/o CBIZ
1 S. Wacker Dr., Ste. 1800
Chicago, IL 60606

Incorporated in 1962 in IL.
Foundation type: Independent foundation.
Financial data (yr. ended 10/31/05): Assets,
$8,766,839 (M); expenditures, $361,298;
qualifying distributions, $338,724; giving activities
include $335,000 for 14 grants (high: $110,000;
low: $1,500).
Fields of interest: Higher education; Hospitals
(general); Reproductive health, family planning;
Health organizations, association; Medical
research, institute; Food services; Housing/shelter;

Human services; Aging, centers/services; Jewish agencies & temples.

Limitations: Applications not accepted. Giving primarily in Chicago IL, and Tucson, AZ; some funding also in Denver, CO. No grants to individuals.

Application information: Contributes only to pre-selected organizations.

Officers and Directors:* Bertram Z. Brodie,* Pres. and Treas.; Sharon King,* Secy.; Holly McDonald.

EIN: 366073506

Selected grants: The following grants were reported in 2003.

$150,000 to University of Arizona Health Sciences Center, Tucson, AZ. For general support.

$75,000 to American Red Cross, Chicago, IL. For general support.

$50,000 to Lawyers Committee for Better Housing, Chicago, IL. For general support.

$40,000 to Mobile Meals of Tucson, Tucson, AZ. For general support.

$25,000 to University of Arizona, Cancer Center, Tucson, AZ. For general support.

$20,000 to Planned Parenthood of Southern Arizona, Tucson, AZ. For general support.

$15,000 to Tucson Shalom House, Tucson, AZ. For general support.

$10,000 to National Jewish Medical and Research Center, Denver, CO. For general support.

$6,000 to Hadley School for the Blind, Winnetka, IL. For general support.

$5,000 to Childrens Home and Aid Society of Illinois, Chicago, IL. For general support.

2630
Helen Brach Foundation ▼ ✧

55 W. Wacker Dr., Ste. 701
Chicago, IL 60601-1609
Contact: John P. Hagnell, Assoc. Dir.

Established in 1974 in IL.

Donor: Helen Brach‡.

Foundation type: Independent foundation.

Financial data (yr. ended 3/31/06): Assets, $122,361,458 (M); gifts received, $10,000,000; expenditures, $6,200,954; qualifying distributions, $5,718,444; giving activities include $5,084,925 for 510 grants (high: $150,000; low: $175; average: $10,000–$50,000).

Purpose and activities: The foundation's charter provides that it should operate for the following purposes: charitable, educational, literary, prevention of cruelty to animals, prevention of cruelty to children, promotion of music, arts and theater, religious and scientific.

Fields of interest: Arts; Secondary school/education; Higher education; Education; Environment; Animal welfare; Housing/shelter; Youth development, services; Human services; Children/youth, services; Homeless, human services; Disabilities, people with; Economically disadvantaged.

Type of support: General/operating support; Annual campaigns; Building/renovation; Equipment; Program development; Conferences/seminars; Publication; Scholarship funds.

Limitations: Giving primarily in the Midwest, and CA, MA, OH, PA and SC. No grants outside continental U.S. No support for political organizations. No grants to individuals, or to organizations with less than one year of budget history.

Publications: Application guidelines; Biennial report (including application guidelines).

Application information: No grants under $5,000. Application form required.

Initial approach: Letter or fax
Copies of proposal: 7
Deadline(s): Dec. 31 (earlier preferred)
Board meeting date(s): Quarterly; grants considered at Mar. meeting
Final notification: Mar. and Apr.

Officers and Directors:* R. Matthew Simon,* Chair.; Raymond F. Simon,* Pres.; James J. O'Connor,* V.P.; John J. Sheridan,* Secy.-Treas.; Charles A. Vorhees.

Number of staff: 3 full-time professional.

EIN: 237376427

Selected grants: The following grants were reported in 2004.

$100,000 to Chicago Zoological Society, Brookfield Zoo, Brookfield, IL. For operating support and pioneer research in animal behavior.

$100,000 to Lincoln Park Zoo, Chicago, IL. For continued support for The Malott Family Zoo Intern program and for the Lester E. Fisher Center for the study and conservation of apes.

$50,000 to Cristo Rey Jesuit High School, Chicago, IL. For continued support of the Science program to enable expansion and refinement of college preparatory science curriculum.

$50,000 to DePaul University, Chicago, IL. For support for Egan Hope Scholars Program providing scholarships and services for low-income students.

$50,000 to Jesuit Seminary Association, Chicago, IL. For support of training and formation of men for priestly service to the Society of Jesus.

$50,000 to Josephinum High School, Chicago, IL. For general operating support and scholarships.

$50,000 to Orphans of the Storm, Deerfield, IL. For operating support.

$40,000 to De La Salle Institute, Chicago, IL. For new lighting system providing better cost- and energy-efficiency.

$40,000 to Loyola Academy, Wilmette, IL. For support of development of Glenview Campus.

$40,000 to Regina Dominican High School, Wilmette, IL. For scholarship assistance for students from Chicago metropolitan area.

2631
The Braeside Foundation ✧

c/o Sherwin J. Stone
174 Indian Tree Dr.
Highland Park, IL 60035

Established in 1992 in IL.

Foundation type: Independent foundation.

Financial data (yr. ended 12/31/05): Assets, $7,760,084 (M); expenditures, $439,856; qualifying distributions, $392,406; giving activities include $349,300 for 83 grants (high: $40,000; low: $500).

Purpose and activities: Giving primarily for health care; some giving also for children's services, and for Jewish agencies.

Fields of interest: Arts; Elementary/secondary education; Higher education; Graduate/professional education; Hospitals (general); Medical care, rehabilitation; Health organizations, association; Human services; Children/youth, services; Jewish federated giving programs; Jewish agencies & temples.

Limitations: Applications not accepted. Giving primarily in IL. No grants to individuals.

Application information: Contributes only to pre-selected organizations.

Officer: Sherwin J. Stone, Pres.

Trustees: Jeffrey Stone; Marjorie Stone; Susan A. Stone.

EIN: 363779797

Selected grants: The following grants were reported in 2005.

$20,000 to Childrens Hospital.

$10,000 to National Parkinson Foundation, Miami, FL.

$8,000 to Lambs Farm, Libertyville, IL.

$7,500 to Chicago Symphony Orchestra, Chicago, IL.

$7,500 to City of Hope National Medical Center, Duarte, CA.

$7,000 to Nature Conservancy, Arlington, VA.

$5,000 to American Indian College Fund, Denver, CO.

$4,000 to American Jewish Congress, New York, NY.

$3,000 to Great Books Foundation, Chicago, IL.

$2,500 to Jewish Community Centers, Boston, MA.

2632
Robert N. Brewer Family Foundation ✧ ☆

115 W. Jefferson St., Ste. 200
Bloomington, IL 61702-3217
Application address: 2 North Park Ave., Herrin, IL 62948

Established in 1997 in IL.

Donor: Robert N. Brewer‡.

Foundation type: Independent foundation.

Financial data (yr. ended 12/31/05): Assets, $12,672,264 (M); gifts received, $600,000; expenditures, $1,198,794; qualifying distributions, $1,070,859; giving activities include $650,100 for 2 grants (high: $650,000; low: $100), and $367,500 for 137 grants to individuals (high: $3,000; low: $1,500).

Purpose and activities: Giving primarily for scholarships for post-secondary education; some giving to community organizations.

Fields of interest: Secondary school/education; Education; Substance abuse, prevention.

Type of support: Scholarships—to individuals.

Limitations: Giving primarily in IL, with emphasis on Herrin and Marion.

Application information: Application form required.

Initial approach: Letter or telephone requesting scholarship application

Directors: R. Denver Brewer; David L. Gename; L. Eugene Striegel.

EIN: 364129119

Selected grants: The following grants were reported in 2004.

$650,000 to Mayo Foundation, Rochester, MN.

2633
The Brinson Foundation

737 N. Michigan Ave., Ste. 1850
Chicago, IL 60611   (312) 799-4500
FAX: (312) 799-4310;
E-mail: mail@brinsonfoundation.org; URL: http://www.brinsonfoundation.org

Established in 2000 in IL.

Foundation type: Independent foundation.

Financial data (yr. ended 12/31/04): Assets, $97,370,571 (M); expenditures, $3,942,483;

qualifying distributions, $3,146,480; giving activities include $2,724,713 for 73 grants (high: $115,000; low: $2,713).

Purpose and activities: The Brinson Foundation is a philanthropic, nonprofit organization whose purpose is to support educational, public health and scientific research programs that engage, inform and inspire committed citizens to confront the challenges that face humanity.

Fields of interest: Elementary/secondary education; Adult/continuing education; Libraries/library science; Medicine/medical care, public education; Medical research; Science, research.

Type of support: General/operating support; Continuing support; Program development; Fellowships; Scholarship funds; Research.

Limitations: Applications not accepted. Giving primarily in the Chicago, IL, area. No support for promotion of religion, voter registration, political lobbying activity, or for human cloning. No grants for capital improvements, endowments, or fundraising events.

Publications: Annual report.

Application information: Preliminary information form available on foundation Web site. Unsolicited grant applications are not accepted. Full applications accepted by invitation only.

Board meeting date(s): May and Oct.

Officer: James D. Parsons, Pres.

Trustees: Gary P. Brinson; Monique Brinson; Suzann Boaz Brinson; Tally Sue Mclone.

Number of staff: 3 full-time professional; 1 full-time support.

EIN: 367331362

Selected grants: The following grants were reported in 2003.

$100,000 to University of Chicago, Division of Biological Sciences, Chicago, IL. To continue scientific research into possible causes and treatments of osteosarconia cancers.

$50,000 to Art Institute of Chicago, Chicago, IL. For ongoing efforts to educate community about exceptional art collections and exhibitions.

$50,000 to Jackson Hole Land Trust, Jackson, WY. For Campaign for Our Valley to protect Jackson Hole's most critical remaining habitats.

$42,000 to Daniel Murphy Scholarship Foundation, Chicago, IL. For scholarships for low-income, inner-city students to attend exceptional private high schools.

$25,000 to Access Community Health Network, Chicago, IL. For case manager at Servicios Medicos La Villita Health Center.

$25,000 to Center for Collaborative Education-Metro Boston, Boston, MA. To implement plan to transform Boston High School into new Boston Community Leadership Academy.

$25,000 to Loyola University Medical Center, Maywood, IL. For Loyola Mobile Medical Unit, which expands and enhances existing asthma and other health screening tests for school children in distressed Chicago neighborhoods.

$25,000 to Wildlife of the American West, National Museum of Wildlife Art, Jackson, WY. For gallery display and exhibit that will educate visitors on life and habitats of elk and other wildlife in Jackson Hole.

$17,000 to Cabrini-Green Tutoring Program, Chicago, IL. For tutoring program and to purchase software packages to quantify progress students make in reading, writing, and arithmetic.

$10,000 to Lake Forest Academy, Lake Forest, IL. To establish Class of '93 Scholarship Fund as operating scholarship to support financial aid students for four years at Academy.

2634
Julia Harrison Bruce Foundation ◇

c/o The Bank of Herrin
101 S. Park Ave.
Herrin, IL   62948-3609   (618) 942-6666

Established in 1969.

Donors: Carl Bruce; Julia H. Bruce; Julia Bruce Living Trust; Tony Galines Foundation.

Foundation type: Independent foundation.

Financial data (yr. ended 12/31/05): Assets, $11,649,697 (M); gifts received, $7,406; expenditures, $589,945; qualifying distributions, $507,800; giving activities include $489,019 for 20 grants (high: $100,000; low: $500).

Purpose and activities: Giving primarily to the city of Herrin, IL, as well as for education and social services.

Fields of interest: Education; Human services; Community development.

Type of support: Scholarship funds.

Limitations: Giving primarily in Herrin, IL.

Application information:

Initial approach: Letter or telephone

Deadline(s): None

Advisors: Carl Goodwin; Ed Goodwin; Barbara Jacobs; Dorothy Mercer.

Trustee: The Bank of Herrin.

EIN: 376085206

Selected grants: The following grants were reported in 2004.

$116,348 to Herrin, City of, Herrin, IL.

$62,939 to Herrin Community Unit School District No. 4, Herrin, IL.

$44,325 to Hurst, City of, Hurst, TX.

$35,000 to First Baptist Church, Herrin, IL.

$26,073 to Herrin Teen Town, Herrin, IL.

$22,950 to John A. Logan College, Carterville, IL.

$15,997 to Williamson County Sheriffs Department, Marion, IL.

$10,907 to Herrin Civic Center, Herrin, IL.

$5,000 to Samaritans Purse, Boone, NC.

$1,000 to Herrin Junior Ball League, Herrin, IL.

2635
The Bruning Foundation ◇

c/o Larry J. Brooks
787 Berkshire Ln.
Des Plaines, IL   60016-7545

Established in 1960.

Donors: Herbert F. Bruning; Paul J. Bruning.

Foundation type: Independent foundation.

Financial data (yr. ended 12/31/05): Assets, $18,909,369 (M); expenditures, $1,050,050; qualifying distributions, $891,350; giving activities include $891,350 for 94 grants (high: $73,050; low: $500).

Purpose and activities: Giving primarily to Roman Catholic, Episcopal, Lutheran and United Methodist churches, and organizations as well as for education and the arts; giving also for the environment and prevention of cruelty to children and animals.

Fields of interest: Elementary/secondary education; Higher education; Animals/wildlife; Health organizations, association; Health organizations; Human services; Protestant agencies & churches; Roman Catholic agencies & churches.

Type of support: General/operating support.

Limitations: Applications not accepted. Giving primarily in IL. No grants to individuals.

Application information: Contributes only to pre-selected organizations.

Officers and Directors:* Charles Bruning III,* Pres.; Kathleen Bruning, Secy.; Edwin C. Bruning,* Treas.; Larry J. Brooks, Mgr.; Charles Bruning III; John Bruning.

EIN: 366068626

Selected grants: The following grants were reported in 2004.

$63,500 to Northwest Community Healthcare Foundation, Arlington Heights, IL.

$60,000 to Converse College, Spartanburg, SC.

$60,000 to Sanibel-Captiva Conservation Foundation, Sanibel, FL.

$50,000 to Beloit College, Beloit, WI.

$50,000 to Ducks Unlimited, Memphis, TN.

$50,000 to Monmouth College, Monmouth, IL.

$50,000 to Shattuck-Saint Marys School, Faribault, MN.

$35,500 to Max McGraw Wildlife Foundation, Dundee, IL.

$30,000 to Ravinia Festival Association, Highland Park, IL. For annual fund.

$15,000 to Amherst College, Amherst, MA.

2636
The Brunswick Foundation, Inc. ◇

1 N. Field Ct.
Lake Forest, IL   60045-4811   (847) 735-4467

Contact: B. Russell Lockridge

Incorporated in 1957 in IL.

Donors: Brunswick Corp.; Peter N. Larson.

Foundation type: Company-sponsored foundation.

Financial data (yr. ended 12/31/05): Assets, $4,485,827 (M); expenditures, $489,493; qualifying distributions, $466,130; giving activities include $91,630 for 104 grants (high: $7,500; low: $150), and $374,500 for 208 grants to individuals (high: $2,000; low: $500).

Purpose and activities: The foundation supports organizations involved with arts and culture, education, the environment, health, and human services.

Fields of interest: Arts, multipurpose centers/programs; Arts; Higher education; Education; Environment; Health organizations, association; Human services.

Type of support: Employee volunteer services; General/operating support; Continuing support; Capital campaigns; Building/renovation; Program development; Scholarship funds; Employee matching gifts; Employee-related scholarships.

Limitations: Giving primarily in areas of company operations. No support for religious organizations, preschools, primary or secondary schools, fraternal orders, or veterans' or labor organizations. No grants to individuals (except for employee-related scholarships), or for endowments or capital campaigns, trips, tours, tickets, or advertising; no in-kind gifts; no program-related investments; no loans.

Publications: Application guidelines.

Application information: Application form required.

Initial approach: Write to foundation for application form

Copies of proposal: 2

Deadline(s): Mar. 22

Board meeting date(s): Quarterly

Final notification: 5 to 12 months

Officers and Directors:* B. Russell Lockridge,*
Pres.; Marschall I. Smith,* V.P. and Secy.; Kathryn
J. Chieger, V.P.; William L. Metzger, V.P. and Treas.;
George W. Buckley; Victoria J. Reich.
Number of staff: 1 full-time professional.
EIN: 366033576

2637

The Buchanan Family Foundation ✧

222 E. Wisconsin Ave.
Lake Forest, IL 60045-1701

Established in 1967 in IL.
Donors: D.W. Buchanan, Sr.‡; D.W. Buchanan, Jr.
Foundation type: Independent foundation.
Financial data (yr. ended 12/31/05): Assets,
$47,542,448 (M); expenditures, $2,476,807;
qualifying distributions, $2,416,807; giving
activities include $2,410,000 for 99 grants (high:
$115,000; low: $2,500).
Purpose and activities: Emphasis on cultural
programs, hospitals and health associations,
education, social service agencies, community
funds, and environmental associations.
Fields of interest: Arts; Elementary/secondary
education; Higher education; Environment;
Hospitals (general); Health organizations,
association; Medical research, institute; Human
services; Federated giving programs.
Limitations: Applications not accepted. Giving
primarily in Chicago, IL. No grants to individuals.
Application information: Contributes only to
pre-selected organizations.
Board meeting date(s): Fall
Officers: Kenneth H. Buchanan, Pres.; G.M. Walsh,
V.P. and Secy.; Huntington Eldridge, Jr., Treas.
Directors: John A. Andersen; Kent Chandler, Jr.
EIN: 366160998
Selected grants: The following grants were reported
in 2004.
$115,000 to Opportunity, Highland Park, IL. For
general operating support.
$110,000 to Lake Forest College, Lake Forest, IL.
For general operating support.
$70,000 to Childrens Memorial Hospital, Chicago,
IL. For general operating support.
$70,000 to Northwestern Memorial Hospital,
Chicago, IL. For general operating support.
$70,000 to Rehabilitation Institute of Chicago,
Chicago, IL. For general operating support.
$70,000 to Rush-Presbyterian-Saint Lukes Medical
Center, Chicago, IL. For general operating
support.
$50,000 to Art Institute of Chicago, Chicago, IL. For
general operating support.
$50,000 to Lake Forest Open Lands Association,
Lake Forest, IL. For general operating support.
$43,000 to Field Museum of Natural History,
Chicago, IL. For general operating support.
$40,000 to Museum of Science and Industry,
Chicago, IL. For general operating support.

2638

Buehler Family Foundation ✧

(formerly A. C. Buehler Foundation)
c/o Bank of America, N. A.
231 S. LaSalle St.
Chicago, IL 60697 (312) 828-1785
Contact: M. Catherine Ryan, Asst. Secy-Treas.

Incorporated in 1972 in IL.

Donor: Albert C. Buehler.
Foundation type: Independent foundation.
Financial data (yr. ended 12/31/05): Assets,
$13,172,541 (M); expenditures, $1,465,937;
qualifying distributions, $1,383,935; giving
activities include $1,367,500 for 9 grants (high:
$597,500; low: $10,000).
Purpose and activities: Giving primarily for health
care, including a center on aging, as well as for
education, the arts, and environmental
conservation.
Fields of interest: Museums; Higher education;
Botanical gardens; Hospitals (general); Human
services; Family services; Residential/custodial
care, senior continuing care; Aging, centers/
services.
Type of support: Equipment; Research.
Limitations: Giving primarily in the metropolitan
Chicago, IL, area, and FL.
Application information: Application form not
required.
Initial approach: Letter
Deadline(s): None
Officers and Directors:* Patricia Buehler,* Pres.;
Dale Park, Jr.,* Secy.; M. James Termondt,* Treas.;
Pamela Varner.
EIN: 237166014

2639

Howard G. Buffett Foundation ✧

158 W. Prairie Ave., Ste. 107
Decatur, IL 62523

Established in 1999 in IL and NE.
Donors: E. Buffett; Warren E. Buffett; Susan T.
Buffett‡.
Foundation type: Independent foundation.
Financial data (yr. ended 12/31/05): Assets,
$129,950,979 (M); expenditures, $6,621,198;
qualifying distributions, $6,484,870; giving
activities include $5,994,766 for 38 grants (high:
$2,050,000; low: $1,000; average: $2,000–
$200,000).
Fields of interest: Education; Environment;
Animals/wildlife; Human services.
Limitations: Applications not accepted. Giving
primarily in IL. No grants to individuals.
Application information: Contributes only to
pre-selected organizations.
Officers and Directors:* Howard G. Buffett,* Pres.;
Ronald O. Olson,* Secy.; Devon G. Buffett,* Treas.;
Susan S. Bell; Michael D. Walter.
EIN: 470824756
Selected grants: The following grants were reported
in 2005.
$2,050,000 to Nature Conservation Trust, South
Africa. .
$1,075,624 to World Vision, Federal Way, WA.
$504,250 to Decatur Public Schools Foundation,
Decatur, IL.
$230,000 to Baby Talk, Decatur, IL.
$97,500 to Catholic Relief Services, Baltimore, MD.
For CRS/Mexico in Tucson, AZ.
$50,000 to University of Nebraska, Lincoln, NE.

2640

Rebecca Susan Buffett Foundation ✧

c/o L. Bettanin
548 Hyacinth Pl.
Highland Park, IL 60035

Established in 1998 in IL.
Foundation type: Independent foundation.
Financial data (yr. ended 12/31/05): Assets,
$8,381,004 (M); expenditures, $1,084,731;
qualifying distributions, $1,076,729; giving
activities include $1,076,729 for 23 grants (high:
$252,729; low: $500).
Fields of interest: Education; Hospitals (general);
Mental health, association; Roman Catholic
agencies & churches.
Limitations: Applications not accepted. No grants to
individuals.
Application information: Contributes only to
pre-selected organizations.
Officers and Directors:* Pamela Buffett,* Pres. and
Treas.; Allen Greenberg,* Secy.; Sarah Buffett.
EIN: 364201771

2641

Bunning Family Foundation ✧ ☆

225 E. Deerpath Rd., Ste. 210
Lake Forest, IL 60045

Established in 2005 in IL.
Donor: David G. Bunning.
Foundation type: Independent foundation.
Financial data (yr. ended 6/30/05): Assets,
$1,924,502 (M); gifts received, $4,000,000;
expenditures, $2,090,164; qualifying distributions,
$2,088,716; giving activities include $2,082,000
for 6 grants (high: $2,000,000; low: $500).
Purpose and activities: Giving primarily for
education; support also for an alopecia areata
foundation.
Fields of interest: Elementary/secondary
education; Higher education; Skin disorders.
Limitations: Applications not accepted. Giving
primarily in Cambridge, MA; some giving also in CA
and IL.
Application information: Contributes only to
pre-selected organizations.
Officers and Directors:* David G. Bunning,* Pres.
and Treas.; Denise A. Bunning,* V.P. and Secy.;
Michael Bunning; Steve Bunning.
EIN: 201919538

2642

Bunning Food Allergy Foundation ✧ ☆

225 E. Deerpath Rd., Ste. 210
Lake Forest, IL 60045

Established in 2002 in IL.
Donors: David G. Bunning; Denise A. Bunning.
Foundation type: Independent foundation.
Financial data (yr. ended 6/30/05): Assets,
$6,376,680 (M); gifts received, $7,337,399;
expenditures, $4,951,902; qualifying distributions,
$4,940,816; giving activities include $4,903,581
for 5 grants (high: $2,502,000; low: $10,000).
Fields of interest: Allergies; Allergies research.
Limitations: Applications not accepted. Giving
primarily in IL and Fairfax, VA. No grants to
individuals.
Application information: Contributes only to
pre-selected organizations.
Officers and Directors:* David G. Bunning,* Pres.
and Treas.; Denise A. Bunning,* V.P. and Secy.;
Barbara K. Bunning; James E. Bunning; Michael
Bunning.
EIN: 421564861

2643
Dean L. & Rosemarie Buntrock
    Foundation ◇
Oakbrook Terrace Twr.
1 Tower Ln., Ste. 2242
Oakbrook Terrace, IL 60181-4636

Established in 1979 in IL.
Donor: Dean L. Buntrock.
Foundation type: Independent foundation.
Financial data (yr. ended 12/31/05): Assets, $10,242,462 (M); expenditures, $1,651,408; qualifying distributions, $1,471,989; giving activities include $1,471,989 for 169 grants (high: $300,000; low: $25).
Purpose and activities: Giving primarily for arts, education, and health care, including a children's hospital, Christian ministries and schools, and children, youth, and social services, including a homeless shelter and programs for the blind.
Fields of interest: Arts education; Museums; Performing arts; Historic preservation/historical societies; Arts; Education, public education; Elementary/secondary education; Higher education; Libraries (public); Education; Environment; Animal welfare; Hospitals (general); Health organizations, association; Medical research, institute; Neuroscience research; Human services; Children/youth, services; Homeless, human services; Christian agencies & churches; Blind/visually impaired.
Limitations: Applications not accepted. Giving on a national basis, with some emphasis on IL, particularly Chicago. No grants to individuals.
Application information: Contributes only to pre-selected organizations.
Officer: Donovan A. Langford III, Treas.
Directors: Dean L. Buntrock; Rosemarie Buntrock; Peer Pedersen.
EIN: 363001925
Selected grants: The following grants were reported in 2003.
$400,000 to Millennium Park, Chicago, IL. For general operating support.
$63,000 to Joffrey Ballet, New York, NY. For general operating support.
$60,000 to Chicago Symphony Orchestra, Chicago, IL. For general operating support.
$50,000 to Converse College, Spartanburg, SC. For capital campaign.
$40,000 to Restoration Ministries, Harvey, IL. For general operating support.
$25,000 to Horatio Alger Association of Distinguished Americans, Alexandria, VA. For general operating support.
$25,000 to Trinity Lutheran Seminary, Columbus, OH. For general operating support.
$20,000 to United Way of Metropolitan Chicago, Chicago, IL. For general operating support.
$16,000 to Chicagoland Lutheran Educational Foundation, Chicago, IL. For general operating support.
$15,000 to Rush-Presbyterian-Saint Lukes Medical Center, Chicago, IL. For general operating support.

2644
Burlington Northern Santa Fe
    Foundation ▼ ◇
(formerly Santa Fe Pacific Foundation)
5601 W. 26th St.
Cicero, IL 60804 (708) 924-5615
Contact: Richard A. Russack, Pres.

Incorporated in 1953 in IL.
Donors: Santa Fe Pacific Corp.; Burlington Northern Santa Fe Corp.
Foundation type: Company-sponsored foundation.
Financial data (yr. ended 12/31/05): Assets, $563,202 (M); gifts received, $4,559,748; expenditures, $6,288,874; qualifying distributions, $6,288,063; giving activities include $5,521,183 for 550 grants (high: $1,000,000; low: $100), and $762,374 for 575 employee matching gifts.
Purpose and activities: The foundation supports organizations involved with arts and culture, higher education, financial aid, health, legal services, employment, hunger, youth development, human services, economic freedom, civic affairs, senior citizens, physically and mentally disabled people, minorities, economically disadvantaged people, and homeless people and awards college scholarships to high school seniors and Native Americans.
Fields of interest: Museums; Performing arts; Performing arts, dance; Performing arts, theater; Arts; Higher education; Scholarships/financial aid; Public health; Health care; Legal services; Employment, training; Employment; Food services; Youth development; Family services, domestic violence; Human services; Business/industry; Public policy, research; Public affairs, citizen participation; Public affairs; Aging; Physically disabled; Mentally disabled; Minorities; Native Americans/American Indians; Economically disadvantaged; Homeless.
Type of support: General/operating support; Continuing support; Annual campaigns; Building/renovation; Program development; Scholarship funds; Employee matching gifts; Employee-related scholarships; Scholarships—to individuals.
Limitations: Giving on a national basis in areas of company operations. No support for religious organizations not of direct benefit to the entire community, public educational institutions, preschools, or primary or secondary educational institutions, political, fraternal, or veterans' organizations, national health or cultural organizations, or community or other grantmaking foundations. No grants to individuals (except for scholarships), or for conferences, seminars, travel, testimonial dinners, endowments, capital campaigns, salaries, administrative expenses, computer-related projects, or television or film production.
Publications: Application guidelines.
Application information: Application form required.
    Initial approach: Letter of inquiry for application form
    Copies of proposal: 1
    Deadline(s): None
    Board meeting date(s): Monthly
    Final notification: Varies
Officers: Richard A. Russack,* Pres.; S.E. Forsberg, V.P.; P.D. Hiatte, V.P.; Sharon M. Heft, Secy.; Linda J. Hurt, Treas.
Directors: Thomas N. Hund; Jeffrey Moreland; Matt Rose.
Number of staff: 2 full-time professional.
EIN: 366051896

Selected grants: The following grants were reported in 2005.
$1,000,000 to American Red Cross, National Headquarters, DC. For relief effort for Hurricane Katrina.
$311,843 to United Way of Metropolitan Tarrant County, Fort Worth, TX. For general support.
$284,625 to Scholarship Program Administrators, Nashville, TN. For general support.
$197,480 to United Way of America, Alexandria, VA. For employee matching for Hurricane Katrina.
$100,000 to Boys and Girls Clubs of America, Atlanta, GA. For general support.
$100,000 to Omaha Performing Arts Society, Omaha, NE. For general support.
$51,000 to Future Farmers of America Foundation, National, Indianapolis, IN. For general support.
$45,000 to University of Denver, Denver, CO. For general support.
$30,000 to Artrain USA, Ann Arbor, MI. For general support.
$12,000 to United Way of the Mid-South, Memphis, TN. For general support.

2645
Leo Burnett Company Charitable
    Foundation ◇
35 W. Wacker Dr.
Chicago, IL 60601 (312) 220-5959
Contact: Chris Kimball

Established in 1985 in IL.
Donor: Leo Burnett Co., Inc.
Foundation type: Company-sponsored foundation.
Financial data (yr. ended 12/31/04): Assets, $1,327,369 (M); gifts received, $300,000; expenditures, $549,086; qualifying distributions, $547,586; giving activities include $269,107 for 26 grants (high: $150,000; low: $50), and $278,154 for 545 employee matching gifts.
Purpose and activities: The foundation supports organizations involved with arts and culture, education, health, human services, urban community development, economically disadvantaged people, and homeless people.
Fields of interest: Arts; Higher education; Education; Health care; Homeless, human services; Human services; Urban/community development; Economically disadvantaged; Homeless.
Limitations: Giving on a national basis. No grants to individuals.
Application information: Application form not required.
    Initial approach: Proposal
    Deadline(s): None
    Board meeting date(s): Biannually
Officers: Kristin Anderson, Sr. V.P.; Cheryl R. Berman, V.P.; Richard Meehan, V.P.; Sondra Thorson, V.P.; Robert Westphal, V.P.; Carla R. Michelotti, Secy.; Bob Maloney, Treas.
Number of staff: 1 full-time professional; 1 part-time professional; 1 full-time support.
EIN: 363379336
Selected grants: The following grants were reported in 2004.
$150,000 to United Way of Metropolitan Chicago, Chicago, IL.
$10,000 to Foundation Fighting Blindness, Owings Mills, MD.
$10,000 to Goodman Theater, Chicago, IL.
$5,950 to Atlanta Ronald McDonald House Charities, Atlanta, GA.
$5,000 to Latin School of Chicago, Chicago, IL.

$295 to Stage Left Theater, Chicago, IL.

$275 to Lewis University, Romeoville, IL.

$180 to Christian Foundation for Children and Aging, Kansas City, KS.

$100 to American Brain Tumor Association, Des Plaines, IL.

$100 to Evanston Community Foundation, Evanston, IL.

2646
Butler Family Foundation
1550 Northwest Hwy., Ste. 108-D
Park Ridge, IL 60068-1482 (847) 299-2244
Contact: Rhett W. Butler, Tr.

Established in 1953 in IL.
Donor: Butler Charitable Lead Trust.
Foundation type: Independent foundation.
Financial data (yr. ended 12/31/05): Assets, $11,611,690 (M); gifts received, $585,834; expenditures, $544,470; qualifying distributions, $494,477; giving activities include $480,750 for 96 grants (high: $50,000; low: $500; average: $500–$50,000).
Purpose and activities: Giving primarily for education and health and human services.
Fields of interest: Arts; Theological school/education; Education; Environment; Medical research, institute; Human services; Protestant agencies & churches.
Type of support: General/operating support; Continuing support; Annual campaigns; Capital campaigns; Building/renovation; Endowments; Program development; Fellowships; Internship funds; Scholarship funds; Research; Program-related investments/loans; Matching/challenge support.
Limitations: Giving primarily in Chicago, IL. No grants to individuals.
Publications: Application guidelines.
Application information: Unsolicited proposals are not encouraged. If there is interest, the foundation will request an on-site visit, after which a full proposal may be requested. Application form not required.
Initial approach: Letter (1-2 pages)
Deadline(s): None
Board meeting date(s): 3 times per year
Trustees: Lynne Butler Adams; Rhett W. Butler.
Number of staff: 1 part-time professional; 1 part-time support.
EIN: 366101775

2647
William Butterworth Memorial Trust ◇
c/o First Midwest Bank
P.O. Box 990
Moline, IL 61266-0990
Contact: Stephen Dembosky

Trust established in 1951 in IL.
Donor: Katherine Deere Butterworth†.
Foundation type: Independent foundation.
Financial data (yr. ended 12/31/04): Assets, $37,735,383 (M); gifts received, $15,378; expenditures, $1,530,079; qualifying distributions, $1,380,232; giving activities include $400,000 for 1 grant, $30,350 for grants to individuals, and $892,716 for 1 foundation-administered program.
Purpose and activities: Giving primarily to operate and maintain Butterworth Center and Deere/Wiman

House in support of diverse charitable, literary and educational interests in the city of Moline, IL; some scholarship awards to residents of Moline, IL.
Fields of interest: Human services.
Type of support: General/operating support; Scholarships—to individuals.
Limitations: Applications not accepted. Giving limited to Moline, IL.
Application information: Unsolicited requests for funds not accepted.
Officers: Pamela M. Anderson, Co-Chair.; Frank S. Cottrell, Co-Chair.; Mark R. McLaughlin, Secy.; Nathan J. Jones, Treas.
EIN: 362255481

2648
Horace C. Cabe Foundation ◇
c/o Northern Trust Bank of Texas, Agent
P.O. Box 803878
Chicago, IL 60680

Established in 1991 in TX.
Donor: Horace C. Cabe†.
Foundation type: Independent foundation.
Financial data (yr. ended 6/30/05): Assets, $40,726,681 (M); expenditures, $2,401,768; qualifying distributions, $2,068,744; giving activities include $1,989,141 for 157 grants (high: $100,000; low: $100).
Fields of interest: Arts; Higher education; Education; Hospitals (general); Health care; Boy scouts; Human services; Children/youth, services; Christian agencies & churches.
Limitations: Applications not accepted. Giving primarily in AR and TX. No grants to individuals.
Application information: Contributes only to pre-selected organizations.
Officers: Charles Lee "Sandy" Cabe, Pres.; Marianne C. Long, V.P.; Lucille T. Cook, Secy.
Directors: Charles L. Cabe, Jr.; Thomas H. Cabe; William Slicker.
EIN: 752402852
Selected grants: The following grants were reported in 2004.
$100,000 to Arkansas Childrens Hospital Foundation, Little Rock, AR.
$100,000 to Presbyterian Healthcare Foundation, Dallas, TX.
$100,000 to Watersprings Ranch, Texarkana, AR.
$50,000 to Children are a Gift Foundation, Tyler, TX.
$50,000 to Southwestern Medical Foundation, Dallas, TX.
$40,000 to Childrens Medical Center of Dallas, Dallas, TX.
$38,100 to Stephen F. Austin State University, Nacogdoches, TX.
$30,000 to Henderson State University, Arkadelphia, AR.
$10,000 to American Parkinson Disease Association, Dallas, TX.
$2,500 to Brook Hill School, Bullard, TX.

2649
Apollos Camp and Bennet Humiston Trust ◇
300 W. Washington St.
Pontiac, IL 61764-0710
Contact: Neil C. Bach, Chair.

Established in 1925 in IL.
Foundation type: Independent foundation.

Financial data (yr. ended 4/30/05): Assets, $8,299,031 (M); expenditures, $475,389; qualifying distributions, $414,615; giving activities include $379,695 for 16 grants (high: $68,975; low: $750).
Purpose and activities: Giving primarily for children, youth and social services, and community development.
Fields of interest: Education; Environment, natural resources; Health care; Recreation; Boys & girls clubs; Human services; Children/youth, services; Community development.
Type of support: General/operating support; Building/renovation; Equipment.
Limitations: Giving limited to Pontiac, IL. No grants to individuals.
Application information:
Initial approach: Proposal
Deadline(s): None
Officer: Neil C. Bach, Chair.
Trustees: Victoria P. Glennon; David R. Harding; William C. Harris; Louis Lyons.
EIN: 370701044
Selected grants: The following grants were reported in 2003.
$91,000 to Boys and Girls Club of Livingston County, Pontiac, IL. 2 grants: $60,000 (For operating support), $31,000 (For renovations).
$62,209 to Humiston Woods Nature Center, Pontiac, IL. 2 grants: $5,889, $56,320 (For operating support).
$35,300 to Livingston County Special Services Unit, Pontiac, IL. For wheelchair accessible bus.
$33,000 to Pontiac Township High School, Pontiac, IL. 2 grants: $20,000 (For outdoor track), $13,000 (For band and choir trip).
$20,000 to Livingston County Mutual Aid Association, Pontiac, IL. For equipment.
$12,000 to Pontiac School District 429, Pontiac, IL. For playground equipment.
$10,000 to Pontiac Daily Leader Needy Kids Fund, Pontiac, IL. For operating support.

2650
The Canning Foundation ◇
1650 W. Dublin Ct.
Inverness, IL 60067

Established in 1993 in IL.
Donors: John A. Canning, Jr.; Rita Canning.
Foundation type: Independent foundation.
Financial data (yr. ended 11/30/05): Assets, $1,087,301 (M); expenditures, $936,563; qualifying distributions, $933,929; giving activities include $931,091 for 56 grants (high: $226,000; low: $50).
Purpose and activities: Giving primarily for education; some giving also for human services and youth organizations.
Fields of interest: Education; Health organizations, association; Youth development, centers/clubs; Human services; Federated giving programs; Christian agencies & churches.
Limitations: Applications not accepted. Giving primarily in IL. No grants to individuals.
Application information: Contributes only to pre-selected organizations.
Officers: John A. Canning, Jr., Pres.; Rita Canning, V.P. and Secy.
Director: Sharon J. Kulak.
EIN: 363913323
Selected grants: The following grants were reported in 2005.

$60,000 to Saint Francis de Sales High School, Chicago, IL.

$50,000 to Teach for America, New York, NY.

$48,000 to Maria High School, Chicago, IL.

$43,000 to WINGS Program, Arlington Heights, IL.

$40,000 to Music and Dance Theater Chicago, Chicago, IL.

$37,500 to Hales Franciscan High School, Chicago, IL.

$25,000 to American Jewish Committee, New York, NY.

$25,000 to United Way.

$15,000 to Make-A-Wish Foundation of Wisconsin, Butler, WI.

$14,000 to Seton Academy, South Holland, IL.

2651
Gerald and Janet Carrus Foundation ✧

c/o Bank of America, N.A.
231 S. LaSalle St.
Chicago, IL 60697
Contact: Charles Slamer, Jr.

Established in 1997.
Donors: Janet Carrus; Gerald Carrus†.
Foundation type: Independent foundation.
Financial data (yr. ended 12/31/03): Assets, $12,960,191 (M); expenditures, $740,012; qualifying distributions, $688,322; giving activities include $661,953 for 10 grants (high: $250,000; low: $6,000).
Fields of interest: Higher education.
Limitations: Giving primarily in NY. No grants to individuals.
Application information: Application form not required.
Initial approach: Letter of inquiry
Deadline(s): None
Final notification: Positive responses only
Director: Janet Carrus.
EIN: 133929249

2652
Carylon Foundation ✧

2500 W. Arthington St.
Chicago, IL 60612
Contact: Marcie Mervis, Dir.

Established in 1956 in IL.
Donor: Julius Hemmelstein.
Foundation type: Independent foundation.
Financial data (yr. ended 6/30/05): Assets, $16,250,693 (M); gifts received, $981,000; expenditures, $626,126; qualifying distributions, $618,966; giving activities include $618,696 for 76 grants (high: $250,000; low: $10).
Purpose and activities: The foundation supports Jewish agencies and temples and organizations involved with arts and culture, education, health, and human services.
Fields of interest: Museums; Arts; Education; Hospitals (general); Health organizations, association; Human services; Jewish federated giving programs; Philanthropy/voluntarism; Jewish agencies & temples.
Limitations: Giving on a national basis. No grants to individuals.
Application information: Application form not required.
Initial approach: Proposal
Deadline(s): None

Directors: J. Hemmelstein; Marcie Mervis.
EIN: 366033583
Selected grants: The following grants were reported in 2004.
$50,000 to American Friends of Israel Arts and Science Academy, Chicago, IL.
$50,000 to Jewish United Fund of Metropolitan Chicago, Chicago, IL.
$10,000 to Stanford University, Stanford, CA.
$1,000 to Chicago Public Library Foundation, Chicago, IL.
$1,000 to Lakeside Foundation, Brockport, NY.
$500 to Palliative Care Center and Hospice of the North Shore, Evanston, IL.
$250 to Greater Chicago Food Depository, Chicago, IL.
$100 to AIDS Foundation of Chicago, Chicago, IL.
$100 to San Jose Obrero Mission, Chicago, IL.
$100 to W B E Z, Chicago, IL.

2653
Caterpillar Foundation ▼ ✧

100 N.E. Adams St.
Peoria, IL 61629-1480 (309) 675-4464
URL: http://www.cat.com/foundation

Established in 1952 in IL.
Donor: Caterpillar Inc.
Foundation type: Company-sponsored foundation.
Financial data (yr. ended 12/31/05): Assets, $44,707,911 (M); gifts received, $23,929,800; expenditures, $24,115,731; qualifying distributions, $23,978,101; giving activities include $22,591,062 for 506 grants (high: $2,540,000; low: $32), and $1,323,200 for employee matching gifts.
Purpose and activities: The foundation supports organizations involved with arts and culture, education, the environment, health, human services, and civic affairs.
Fields of interest: Arts; Higher education; Education; Environment; Health care; Human services; Federated giving programs; Government/public administration; Public affairs.
Type of support: Annual campaigns; Capital campaigns; Program development; Employee matching gifts.
Limitations: Giving primarily in areas of company operations. No support for fraternal organizations, religious organizations not of direct benefit to the entire community, or United Way-supported organizations. No grants to individuals, or for general operating support, tickets or advertising for fundraising benefits, or political activities.
Publications: Application guidelines; Corporate giving report; Program policy statement.
Application information: Proposals should be brief. Application form not required.
Initial approach: Proposal to nearest company facility
Copies of proposal: 1
Deadline(s): None
Board meeting date(s): Dec. 1
Final notification: 2 months
Officers and Directors:* J.W. Owens,* Pres.; S.C. Banwart, V.P.; T.L. Elder,* V.P.; H.W. Holling, V.P.; S.L. Levenick,* V.P.; T.L. May, V.P.; J.B. Buda, Secy.; R.D. Beran, Treas.
EIN: 376022314
Selected grants: The following grants were reported in 2004.
$1,051,500 to Illinois State University, Normal, IL.
$850,000 to Bradley University, Peoria, IL.

$400,000 to Valparaiso University, Valparaiso, IN.
$342,010 to YMCA.
$207,500 to Salvation Army.
$204,963 to Center for Prevention of Abuse, Peoria, IL.
$200,000 to Abraham Lincoln Presidential Library Foundation, Springfield, IL.
$200,000 to Vanderbilt University, Nashville, TN.
$189,000 to Illinois Central College Foundation, East Peoria, IL.
$150,000 to Monmouth College, Monmouth, IL.

2654
CH2M Hill Foundation ✧

P.O. Box 803878
Chicago, IL 60680

Established in 1992.
Donors: James W. Poirot; CH2M Hill.
Foundation type: Independent foundation.
Financial data (yr. ended 12/31/05): Assets, $2,055,119 (M); gifts received, $579,650; expenditures, $526,333; qualifying distributions, $504,255; giving activities include $500,869 for 86 grants (high: $75,000; low: $500).
Purpose and activities: Giving primarily for undergraduate and graduate engineering and science programs. Support also for technology initiatives that promote sustainable communities, clean water, a healthy environment, safe transportation systems, renewable energy, and efficient industry.
Fields of interest: Higher education; Engineering.
Type of support: General/operating support; Capital campaigns; Scholarship funds.
Limitations: Applications not accepted. Giving on a national basis. No grants to individuals.
Publications: Annual report; Informational brochure.
Application information: Contributes only to pre-selected organizations.
Board meeting date(s): Varies
Officers: Joseph A. Ahern, Chair.; L.L. Nelson, Treas.
Directors: Sam Iapalucci; Michael D. Kennedy; Ralph Peterson.
EIN: 841227384
Selected grants: The following grants were reported in 2004.
$40,000 to Manitou Institute, Crestone, CO. 4 grants: $10,000 each
$20,000 to University of Denver, Denver, CO.
$16,700 to Purdue Foundation, West Lafayette, IN.
$16,350 to University of Illinois Foundation, Urbana, IL.
$9,000 to American Society for Engineering Education, DC.
$8,350 to University of California, Davis, CA.
$1,000 to Virginia Polytechnic Institute and State University, Blacksburg, VA.

2655
Harry F. and Elaine Chaddick Foundation, Inc. ✧

19 S. LaSalle St., Ste. 1100
Chicago, IL 60603

Established in 1986 in IL.
Donors: Harry F. Chaddick†; Elaine M. Chaddick†.
Foundation type: Independent foundation.
Financial data (yr. ended 6/30/05): Assets, $14,536,204 (M); expenditures, $965,813; qualifying distributions, $865,493; giving activities

include $654,780 for 92 grants (high: $68,650; low: $100).

Purpose and activities: Giving primarily for higher education, health associations, particularly for cancer, children, youth, and social services, and to Christian organizations and churches.

Fields of interest: Media, radio; Higher education; Education; Zoos/zoological societies; Health care; Health organizations, association; Cancer research; Human services; Children/youth, services; Christian agencies & churches.

Type of support: Continuing support; Building/renovation; Equipment; Program development; Conferences/seminars; Curriculum development; Scholarship funds; Research.

Limitations: Applications not accepted. Giving primarily in the metropolitan Chicago, IL, area. No grants to individuals.

Application information: Contributes only to pre-selected organizations.

Board meeting date(s): June and as necessary

Officers and Directors:* Mari Hatzenbuehler Craven,* Pres.; Suzanne Hudson,* V.P.; Wayne Moretti,* Treas.

Number of staff: 1 part-time professional; 1 full-time support.

EIN: 363320988

Selected grants: The following grants were reported in 2005.

$68,650 to DePaul University, Chicago, IL.

$27,200 to Lincoln Park Zoo, Chicago, IL.

$25,000 to Chicago Symphony Orchestra, Chicago, IL.

$25,000 to Medical Research Institute Council, Chicago, IL.

$24,000 to Leap Learning Systems, Chicago, IL.

$15,000 to Starlight Starbright Childrens Foundation, Los Angeles, CA.

$10,000 to Alzheimers Association, Chicago, IL.

$7,500 to Merit School of Music, Chicago, IL.

$5,100 to Literacy Chicago, Chicago, IL.

$5,000 to Child Advocacy Services Center, Kansas City, MO.

2656
Norman and Joan Chapman
Foundation ◇ ☆

2 Woodley Rd.
Winnetka, IL 60093
Contact: Norman Chapman, Pres.

Established in 1986 in IL.

Donors: Joan Chapman; Norman Chapman.

Foundation type: Independent foundation.

Financial data (yr. ended 11/30/05): Assets, $5,595,512 (M); gifts received, $636,930; expenditures, $401,749; qualifying distributions, $399,224; giving activities include $391,915 for 28 grants (high: $250,000; low: $40).

Purpose and activities: Giving primarily for the arts, health and human services; funding also to Jewish organizations.

Fields of interest: Arts; Education; Health organizations, association; Human services; Jewish federated giving programs; Jewish agencies & temples.

Limitations: Giving primarily in Chicago, IL. No support for private or operating foundations. No grants to individuals.

Application information: Application form not required.

Initial approach: Letter
Deadline(s): None

Officers: Norman Chapman, Pres.; Joan Chapman, Secy.-Treas.

EIN: 363480507

Selected grants: The following grants were reported in 2005.

$35,000 to Altamaha Riverkeeper, Darien, GA.

$2,000 to American Red Cross.

$1,000 to Holocaust Education Foundation, Chicago, IL.

$250 to American Cancer Society, Atlanta, GA.

$200 to American Institute of Philanthropy, Chicago, IL.

$100 to American Association of Retired Persons (AARP), DC.

$100 to Smile Train, New York, NY.

2657
Charleston Area Charitable Foundation

6029 Park Dr.
P.O. Box 677
Charleston, IL 61920

Established in 1985 in IL.

Donors: Blanche Linder Trust; Mary Linder Trust; Lewis Linder Trust; Dorothy M. Woodyard Trust; Virginia L. Moore.

Foundation type: Independent foundation.

Financial data (yr. ended 6/30/06): Assets, $9,260,635 (M); gifts received, $300; expenditures, $410,947; qualifying distributions, $364,636; giving activities include $364,636 for grants.

Purpose and activities: Giving primarily for community development, education, the arts, and children and youth services.

Fields of interest: Performing arts, orchestra (symphony); Arts; Elementary/secondary education; Higher education; Education; Recreation, community facilities; Children/youth, services; Community development; Federated giving programs; Government/public administration.

Type of support: General/operating support; Annual campaigns; Building/renovation; Scholarship funds; Exchange programs.

Limitations: Giving limited to Charleston and the Coles County, IL, area. No grants to individuals.

Publications: Application guidelines.

Application information: Application form required.

Initial approach: Letter
Copies of proposal: 1
Deadline(s): Jan. 15, Apr. 15, July 15, and Oct. 15
Board meeting date(s): 1st Mon. in Aug., Nov., Feb., and May

Officers: Michael J. Metzger, Pres.; Henry E. Kramer, V.P.; Mark Bluhm, Secy.; Richard J. Williams, Treas.

Directors: Jan Grewell; Jeff Horn; Dolly McFarland.

Number of staff: None.

EIN: 371172293

2658
Elizabeth F. Cheney Foundation

120 S. LaSalle St., Ste. 1740
Chicago, IL 60603
Contact: Elisabeth Geraghty, Admin. Dir.
FAX: (312) 782-1242;
E-mail: egeraghty@cheneyfoundation.org;
URL: http://www.cheneyfoundation.org

Established in 1985 in IL.

Donor: Elizabeth F. Cheney Trust.

Foundation type: Independent foundation.

Financial data (yr. ended 5/31/05): Assets, $13,636,144 (M); expenditures, $874,913; qualifying distributions, $830,949; giving activities include $677,615 for 97 grants (high: $50,000; low: $500), and $50,000 for 25 employee matching gifts.

Purpose and activities: The Elizabeth F. Cheney Foundation is a private independent foundation. Its principal focus is to support the arts and cultural organizations. Organizations supported include, but are not limited to, musical performance organizations, theatre and dance companies, historical societies and museums. The overall grant making focus of the foundation is on artistic achievement in presentation or performance rather than education enrichment or outreach.

Fields of interest: Visual arts; Museums; Performing arts, dance; Performing arts, theater; Performing arts, music; Literature.

Type of support: Program development.

Limitations: Giving primarily in the metropolitan Chicago, IL, area. No grants to individuals.

Publications: Application guidelines; Annual report; Grants list.

Application information: Unsolicited requests for funds will be considered only for organizations in the Chicago, IL, metropolitan area. See Foundation Web site for application guidelines and to download application form. Application form required.

Initial approach: Letter or E-mail
Copies of proposal: 1
Deadline(s): Feb. 1 for museums and literary arts; Apr. 1 for music; Aug. 1 for dramatic arts; Oct. 1 for dance
Board meeting date(s): Mar., May, Sept., and Nov.
Final notification: Six weeks

Officers and Directors:* Lawrence L. Belles,* Pres.; Howard McCue III,* Secy.; Allan Drebin,* Treas.

Number of staff: 1 part-time professional.

EIN: 363375377

Selected grants: The following grants were reported in 2004.

$50,000 to Chicago Symphony Orchestra, Chicago, IL. For Civic Orchestra programs.

$50,000 to Lyric Opera of Chicago, Chicago, IL. For Lyric at Grant Park and Rising Stars Concert.

$50,000 to Ravinia Festival Association, Highland Park, IL. For Emerson String Quartet and Postludes.

$6,000 to Civic Orchestra of Chicago, Chicago, IL. For scholarships.

$5,000 to Music Institute of Chicago, Winnetka, IL. For Lincoln Trio.

$3,000 to Rochester Philharmonic Orchestra, Rochester, NY.

$1,000 to Art Institute of Chicago, Chicago, IL.

$1,000 to Evanston Art Center, Evanston, IL.

$1,000 to Light Opera Works, Evanston, IL.

$1,000 to Zephyr Dance Ensemble, Chicago, IL.

2659
Jack Chester Foundation ◇

c/o Northern Trust Bank of Florida, N.A.
P.O. Box 803878
Chicago, IL 60680

Established in 2001 in FL.

Donor: Jack Chester‡.

Foundation type: Independent foundation.

Financial data (yr. ended 12/31/05): Assets, $11,590,659 (M); expenditures, $735,850; qualifying distributions, $621,439; giving activities

include $556,500 for 46 grants (high: $150,000; low: $2,000).

Purpose and activities: Giving primarily to Jewish agencies, temples, and schools.

Fields of interest: Higher education; Education; Human services; Jewish federated giving programs; Jewish agencies & temples.

Limitations: Applications not accepted. Giving primarily in FL and NY.

Application information: Contributes only to pre-selected organizations.

Trustees: Isodoro Lerman; Jorge Lerman; Norman H. Lipoff; Bernardo Pedro Szwarc.

EIN: 316660664

Selected grants: The following grants were reported in 2004.

$150,000 to Jewish Federation of Greater Miami, Miami, FL. For general support.

$48,000 to Holocaust Memorial Committee, Miami, FL. For general support.

$43,000 to Friends of the Israel Defense Forces, New York, NY. For general support.

$40,000 to Cuban Hebrew Congregation, Miami Beach, FL. For general support.

$20,000 to Hadassah, The Womens Zionist Organization of America, New York, NY. For general support.

$20,000 to P.E.F. Israel Endowment Funds, New York, NY. For general support.

$15,000 to Dave and Mary Alper Jewish Community Center, Miami, FL. For general support.

$15,000 to Miami Jewish Home and Hospital for the Aged, Miami, FL. For general support.

$15,000 to Michael-Ann Russell Jewish Community Center, North Miami Beach, FL. For general support.

$10,000 to Talmudic College of Florida, Miami Beach, FL. For general support.

2660
Chicago Board of Trade Foundation ✧

141 W. Jackson Blvd.
Chicago, IL 60604 (312) 435-3500
Contact: Ellen Paparelli, Admin.

Established in 1984 in IL.

Donor: Chicago Board of Trade.

Foundation type: Company-sponsored foundation.

Financial data (yr. ended 6/30/06): Assets, $4,234,421 (M); gifts received, $401,615; expenditures, $696,004; qualifying distributions, $649,115; giving activities include $649,115 for grants.

Purpose and activities: The foundation supports zoos, Christian agencies and churches, and organizations involved with health, cancer, children and youth, and human services.

Fields of interest: Zoos/zoological societies; Health care; Cancer; Children/youth, services; Youth, services; Human services; Christian agencies & churches.

Type of support: Scholarship funds; General/operating support; Continuing support; Annual campaigns; Capital campaigns; Endowments.

Limitations: Giving primarily in Chicago, IL. No grants to individuals.

Application information: Application form not required.

Initial approach: Proposal
Copies of proposal: 1
Deadline(s): None
Board meeting date(s): 1st quarter annually
Final notification: Within 30 days

Officers and Directors:* Charles P. Carey,* Chair.; Robert Corvino,* Vice-Chair.; Jill A. Harley, Treas.; Ellen Paparelli, Admin.; Thomas P. Cunningham; Michael J. Daley; Nickolas Neubauer.

EIN: 363348469

Selected grants: The following grants were reported in 2005.

$20,000 to INFANT, Inc., Winnetka, IL.

$10,000 to Chicago Zoological Society, Brookfield, IL.

$10,000 to Sunshine Gospel Ministries, Chicago, IL.

$6,500 to Seguin Services, Cicero, IL.

$6,000 to Santas Anonymous of East Dupage, Chicago, IL.

$5,000 to Girl Scouts of the U.S.A., Chicago, IL.

$5,000 to Little City Foundation, Palatine, IL.

$2,500 to Big Shoulders Fund, Chicago, IL.

$2,500 to Blessed Sacrament Youth Center, Chicago, IL.

2661
The Chicago Community Trust ▼

111 E. Wacker Dr., Ste. 1400
Chicago, IL 60601 (312) 616-8000
Contact: For grants: Ms. Sandy Phelps, Grants Mgr.
FAX: (312) 616-7955; E-mail: info@cct.org; TDD: (312) 856-1703; Grant inquiries E-mail: grants@cct.org; URL: http://www.cct.org

Established in 1915 in IL by bank resolution and declaration of trust.

Donors: Albert W. Harris; and members of the Harris family.

Foundation type: Community foundation.

Financial data (yr. ended 9/30/05): Assets, $1,503,994,247 (M); gifts received, $81,325,064; expenditures, $87,451,959; giving activities include $75,988,536 for grants.

Purpose and activities: Established for such charitable purposes as will best make for the mental, moral, intellectual and physical improvement, assistance and relief of the inhabitants of the County of Cook, State of Illinois. Grants for both general operating support and specific programs and projects in the areas of health, basic human needs, education, arts and humanities, and community development; awards fellowships to individuals in leadership positions in local community service organizations.

Fields of interest: Visual arts; Performing arts; Humanities; Historic preservation/historical societies; Arts; Child development, education; Elementary school/education; Secondary school/education; Higher education; Libraries/library science; Education; Health care; AIDS; Employment, training; Housing/shelter, development; Youth development, services; Children/youth, services; Child development, services; Aging, centers/services; Women, centers/services; Minorities/immigrants, centers/services; Homeless, human services; Human services; Economic development; Community development; Public policy, research; Government/public administration; Leadership development; Aging; Disabilities, people with; Minorities; Women; Homeless.

Type of support: General/operating support; Continuing support; Income development; Management development/capacity building; Capital campaigns; Building/renovation; Equipment; Land acquisition; Emergency funds; Program development; Seed money; Curriculum development; Fellowships; Research; Technical

assistance; Consulting services; Program evaluation; Program-related investments/loans; Employee matching gifts; Matching/challenge support.

Limitations: Giving primarily in Cook County and the adjacent 5 counties of northeastern, IL. No support for religious purposes. No grants to individuals (except for limited fellowship programs), or for annual campaigns, deficit financing, endowment funds, publications, conferences, or scholarships; no support for the purchase of computer hardware; no general operating support for agencies or institutions whose program activities substantially duplicate those already undertaken by others.

Publications: Application guidelines; Annual report; Financial statement; Grants list.

Application information: Visit foundation Web site for Letter of Inquiry forms and application guidelines. Full proposals are not considered unless the foundation has sent an invitation to the organization based on their Letter of Inquiry. Faxed or e-mailed applications are not accepted. Application form required.

Initial approach: Complete online Letter of Inquiry form
Copies of proposal: 1
Deadline(s): Mar. 17, July 14, and Nov. 10 for Letters of Inquiry
Board meeting date(s): Jan., May, and Sept.
Final notification: Apr. 19, Aug. 16, and Dec. 13 for notification of LOI results; approx. 2 weeks after Exec. Comm. meetings for grant notification

Officers and Executive Committee:* Prudence R. Beidler,* Chair.; Marshall Field V, Vice-Chair.; Terry Mazany, C.E.O. and Pres.; Anne Blanton, Exec. V.P., Admin.; Carol Y. Crenshaw, V.P., Finance and C.F.O.; Merri Ex, V.P., Philanthropic Svcs.; Frank Soo Hoo, Cont.; Maria C. Bechily; Heather Bilandic Black; John A. Canning, Jr.; Adela Cepeda; Frank M. Clark; Paula Hannaway Crown; Judy Erwin; Jack M. Greenberg; King W. Harris; Mercedes A. Laing; Quintin E. Primo III.

Trustees: Bank of America, Illinois; Harris Bank, N.A.; JPMorgan Chase Bank, N.A.; LaSalle Bank, N.A.; The Northern Trust Co.; The Park National Bank; U.S. Bank, N.A.

Number of staff: 32 full-time professional; 11 full-time support.

EIN: 362167000

Selected grants: The following grants were reported in 2005.

$2,000,000 to Children First Fund: The Chicago Public Schools Foundation, Chicago, IL. For scaling up of Advanced Reading Development Demonstration Project. Grant made through Searle Funds.

$2,000,000 to University of Chicago, Chicago, IL. For renovation of Searle Chemistry Laboratory. Grant made through Searle Funds.

$1,550,442 to Chicago Community Foundation, Chicago, IL. 2 grants: $310,000 (For Arts Education Initiative for evaluation and professional development for academic year and implementation grants), $1,240,442.

$500,000 to Local Initiatives Support Corporation (LISC), Chicago, IL. For economic development projects. Grant made through Searle Funds, payable over 5 years.

$250,000 to Catholic Charities Housing Development Corporation (CCHDC), Chicago, IL. For development of Saint Leo Residence for Veterans. Grant made through Searle Funds.

$250,000 to Centers for New Horizons, Chicago, IL. For construction of Effie Ellis Center for Children and Community.

$200,000 to Childrens Memorial Medical Center, Chicago, IL. For continued support of Consortium to Lower Obesity in Chicago Children (CLOCC).

$30,000 to Northlight Theater, Skokie, IL. For creation of literacy focused in-school programs.

$25,000 to Arts and Business Council of Chicago, Chicago, IL. For upgrades to Web-based survey-data compilation-reporting tool.

2662
Chicago Mercantile Exchange Foundation ✧

(also known as CME Foundation)
20 S. Wacker Dr.
Chicago, IL 60606-7499 (800) 331-3332
Contact: Kristin K. Wood, Mgr., Public and Community Rels.
E-mail: info@cme.com; URL: http://www.cme.com/about/ins/cf/index.html

Established in 2001 in IL.
Donor: Chicago Mercantile Exchange Inc.
Foundation type: Company-sponsored foundation.
Financial data (yr. ended 12/31/03): Assets, $0 (M); gifts received, $370; expenditures, $420,504; qualifying distributions, $420,492; giving activities include $400,000 for 5 grants (high: $200,000; low: $50,000).
Purpose and activities: The foundation supports organizations involved with education, health, disaster relief, human services, and children and youth.
Fields of interest: Education; Health care; Disasters, 9/11/01; Safety/disasters; Human services; Children/youth.
Limitations: Giving primarily in Chicago, IL, New York, NY, and Washington, DC.
Application information: Proposals should be no longer than 5 pages.
  Initial approach: Proposal
  Final notification: Within 4 to 6 weeks
Officers and Directors:* Craig S. Donohue,* Pres.; Kathleen M. Cronin, Secy.; David G. Gomach,* Treas.; Kristin K. Wood, Mgr., Public and Community Rels.; Terrence A. Duffy; Phupinder S. Gill; E. Beth Keeve; David P. Prosperi.
EIN: 364468353
Selected grants: The following grants were reported in 2003.
$250,000 to Saint Vincents Hospital and Medical Center of New York, New York, NY. 2 grants: $200,000 (For Rudolph W. Guiliani Trauma Center), $50,000 (For general support).
$50,000 to Tuesdays Children, Manhasset, NY. For general support.
$50,000 to Washington Hospital Center Foundation, DC. For Burn Center.
$50,000 to YMCA of the USA, Armed Services, Alexandria, VA. For general support.

2663
Chicago Tribune Foundation ✧

c/o Community Rels.
435 N. Michigan Ave., 2nd Fl.
Chicago, IL 60611-4041 (312) 222-4300
Contact: Jan Ellen Woelffer, Prog. Off.
FAX: (312) 222-3751;
E-mail: ctcommunityrelations@tribune.com;

URL: http://about.chicagotribune.com/community/foundation.htm

Incorporated in 1958 in IL.
Donor: Chicago Tribune Co.
Foundation type: Company-sponsored foundation.
Financial data (yr. ended 12/31/04): Assets, $4,425,784 (M); expenditures, $830,986; qualifying distributions, $829,026; giving activities include $646,430 for 85 grants (high: $40,000; low: $250); $131,096 for employee matching gifts, and $51,500 for 2 foundation-administered programs.
Purpose and activities: The foundation supports organizations involved with journalism, arts and culture, and civic affairs.
Fields of interest: Media, journalism/publishing; Arts; Civil rights, equal rights; Civil liberties, first amendment; Public affairs.
Type of support: Program development; General/operating support; Employee matching gifts.
Limitations: Giving primarily in the metropolitan Chicago, IL, area; giving also to national organizations for Journalism. No support for high school or college newspapers or international organizations. No grants to individuals, or for capital campaigns.
Publications: Application guidelines; Corporate giving report; Grants list.
Application information: Proposals may be submitted using the Chicago Area Grant Application Form. Unsolicited requests for Civic grants are not accepted. Unsolicited requests for non-diversity Journalism grants from organizations located in the metropolitan Chicago, IL, area are not accepted. Support is limited to 3 years in length. Proposals should be no longer than 2 to 5 pages. Application form not required.
  Initial approach: Proposal
  Copies of proposal: 1
  Deadline(s): Feb. 1 for Culture; June 1 for Journalism
  Board meeting date(s): June for Culture; Sept. for Journalism
  Final notification: Following board meetings
Officers and Directors:* David Hiller, Chair.; Frank Gihan,* Pres.; Don Wycliff; Owen Youngman.
EIN: 366050792
Selected grants: The following grants were reported in 2004.
$40,000 to Chicago Symphony Orchestra, Chicago, IL.
$25,000 to Spanish Coalition for Jobs, Chicago, IL.
$25,000 to United Negro College Fund, Fairfax, VA.
$15,000 to Chicago United, Chicago, IL.
$15,000 to Community Renewal Society, Chicago, IL.
$15,000 to National Association of Hispanic Journalists, DC.
$7,500 to Near South Planning Board, Chicago, IL.
$7,500 to Reading in Motion, Chicago, IL.
$5,000 to ETA Creative Arts Foundation, Chicago, IL.
$5,000 to Rainbow House, Chicago, IL.

2664
The Children's Care Foundation ✧

333 N. Michigan Ave., Ste. 2131
Chicago, IL 60601-4110
Contact: Robert L. Campbell, Exec. Dir.

Established in 1990 in IL.

Donors: Mary L. Medlock Trust; William J. Watson Trust; C. Lydia Frederick Trust; Hobart W. Williams Trust; Ava W. Farwell Trust; Robert & Janet McMurdy Fund; George J. Williams Charitable Trust.
Foundation type: Independent foundation.
Financial data (yr. ended 6/30/05): Assets, $42,469,084 (M); gifts received, $156,728; expenditures, $2,075,194; qualifying distributions, $2,367,280; giving activities include $1,810,025 for 44 grants (high: $350,000; low: $3,000).
Purpose and activities: Support limited to organizations that benefit children in the state of Illinois.
Fields of interest: Hospitals (general); Human services; Children/youth, services.
Type of support: Program-related investments/loans; Matching/challenge support.
Limitations: Giving limited to IL. No grants to individuals.
Publications: Informational brochure (including application guidelines).
Application information: Application form not required.
  Initial approach: Proposal
  Copies of proposal: 1
  Deadline(s): None
  Board meeting date(s): Twice a year
  Final notification: By letter following board action
Officers and Directors:* R. Bruce P. Bagge,* Chair.; Joseph S. Johnson,* Pres.; Bruce E. Huey,* V.P.; Anthony Pertile,* V.P.; George S. Trees, Jr.,* V.P.; Roxanne M. Warble,* V.P.; Justin Stanley, Secy.-Treas.; Robert L. Campbell,* Exec. Dir.; Edward X. Clinton; Marvin Kamensky; Michael E. Reed; Samuel H. Young.
Number of staff: 1 full-time professional.
EIN: 366088708
Selected grants: The following grants were reported in 2003.
$425,000 to Saint Bernard Hospital and Health Care Center, Chicago, IL.
$344,603 to Loyola University Medical Center, Maywood, IL.
$100,000 to Chicago Youth Centers, Chicago, IL.
$61,573 to Rush-Presbyterian-Saint Lukes Medical Center, Chicago, IL.
$50,000 to Allendale Association, Lake Villa, IL.
$47,333 to Boy Scouts of America, Calumet Council, Munster, IN.
$40,000 to Children of Peace School, Chicago, IL.
$36,527 to Community Mennonite Day Care Center, Markham, IL.
$36,000 to Illinois Fatherhood Initiative, Chicago, IL.
$30,000 to Chinese American Service League, Chicago, IL.

2665
Jay and Doris Christopher Foundation ✧ ☆

323 Hillcrest Ave.
Hinsdale, IL 60521-4737

Established around 1995 in IL.
Foundation type: Independent foundation.
Financial data (yr. ended 12/31/05): Assets, $2,748,010 (M); gifts received, $2,004,200; expenditures, $417,466; qualifying distributions, $413,000; giving activities include $413,000 for 8 grants (high: $100,000; low: $15,000).
Purpose and activities: Giving for education and Lutheran organizations.

Fields of interest: Higher education; Education; Human services; Family services; Protestant agencies & churches.
Limitations: Applications not accepted. Giving primarily in IL. No grants to individuals.
Application information: Contributes only to pre-selected organizations.
Trustees: Doris K. Christopher; Jay W. Christopher; Julie A. Christopher.
EIN: 367092282

2666
Circle of Service Foundation
P.O. Box 6067
Vernon Hills, IL   60061
Contact: Susan Karlinsky, Admin.
E-mail: susan@circleofservicefoundation.org;
URL: http://www.circleofservicefoundation.org

Established in 1997 in IL.
Donor: Michael P. Krasny.
Foundation type: Independent foundation.
Financial data (yr. ended 12/31/05): Assets, $95,745,259 (M); gifts received, $1,000,000; expenditures, $7,621,103; qualifying distributions, $5,106,713; giving activities include $3,657,238 for 154 grants (high: $500,000; low: $300), $23,675 for 20 employee matching gifts, and $1,250,000 for 1 loan/program-related investment.
Purpose and activities: Giving primarily for human services, technology and Jewish concerns.
Fields of interest: Education; Health organizations, association; Human services; Children/youth, services.
Type of support: General/operating support; Continuing support; Annual campaigns; Capital campaigns; Building/renovation; Equipment; Matching/challenge support.
Limitations: Giving primarily in Cook and Lake counties, IL, with funding also in Chicago. No grants to individuals, or for travel or international purposes, or for the funding of policy research.
Publications: Application guidelines; Annual report; Grants list; Program policy statement.
Application information: See Web site for guidelines. Application form not required.
Initial approach: Electronically through a link on the Grant Guidelines page of Web site
Copies of proposal: 1
Deadline(s): Varies
Board meeting date(s): 4 times a year
Final notification: 60-90 days
Officers and Directors:* Michael P. Krasny,* Pres. and Secy.; Adam Levine,* Treas.; Gary Kash; Janet Krasny; Steven S. Lowenstein; Amy B. Stein; Michael S. Tepper.
Number of staff: 1 full-time professional.
EIN: 364185939
Selected grants: The following grants were reported in 2004.
$750,000 to Howard Area Community Center, Chicago, IL.
$510,000 to Crohns and Colitis Foundation of America, Des Plaines, IL.
$500,000 to Holocaust Memorial Foundation of Illinois, Skokie, IL.
$420,000 to Greater Chicago Food Depository, Chicago, IL. 2 grants: $400,000 and $20,000
$30,000 to KESHET, Northbrook, IL.
$25,000 to Cancer Wellness Center, Northbrook, IL.
$20,000 to Erikson Institute, Chicago, IL.
$10,000 to Chicago Sinfonietta, Chicago, IL.
$7,500 to North Shore Senior Center, Northfield, IL.

2667
Citadel Group Foundation ✧ ☆
131 S. Dearborn St.
Chicago, IL   60604

Established in 2001 in IL.
Donor: Kenneth C. Griffin.
Foundation type: Independent foundation.
Financial data (yr. ended 12/31/05): Assets, $317,210 (M); gifts received, $1,296,000; expenditures, $1,457,159; qualifying distributions, $1,457,155; giving activities include $1,448,872 for 36 grants (high: $250,000; low: $350).
Fields of interest: Human services; Foundations (public).
Limitations: Applications not accepted. Giving primarily in Chicago, IL and New York, NY. No grants to individuals.
Application information: Contributes only to pre-selected organizations.
Officers and Directors:* Kenneth C. Griffin,* Pres.; Alec Litowitz,* Secy.-Treas.
EIN: 364482467

2668
Cless Family Foundation ✧
(formerly Karl Cless Foundation)
2100 Mallard Dr.
Northbrook, IL   60062

Established in 1991 in IL.
Donor: Gerhard Cless.
Foundation type: Independent foundation.
Financial data (yr. ended 12/31/05): Assets, $10,892,765 (M); expenditures, $422,894; qualifying distributions, $408,000; giving activities include $408,000 for 14 grants (high: $120,000; low: $1,000).
Purpose and activities: Giving primarily for higher and other education including medical research; some funding for children, youth, and family services.
Fields of interest: Secondary school/education; Higher education; Education; Medical research; Human services; Children/youth, services; Family services.
Limitations: Applications not accepted. Giving primarily in IL; some funding nationally. No grants to individuals.
Application information: Contributes only to pre-selected organizations.
Officers: Gerhard Cless, Pres. and Treas.; Ruth I. Cless, V.P. and Secy.
Directors: Bryan C. Cless; Jennifer U. Cless; Martin Cless; Stephen G. Cless.
EIN: 363796675
Selected grants: The following grants were reported in 2003.
$105,000 to Duke University, Durham, NC. For medical research.
$102,000 to University of Illinois at Urbana-Champaign, Urbana, IL. For medical research.
$70,000 to Golden Apple Foundation, Chicago, IL.
$60,000 to Evangelical Lutheran Church in America, Chicago, IL.
$15,000 to Education Foundation of Collier County, Naples, FL.
$15,000 to Young Womens Leadership Charter School of Chicago, Chicago, IL.
$10,000 to Family Guidance Centers, Chicago, IL.
$10,000 to LEARN Charter School, Chicago, IL.

$8,000 to American Brain Tumor Association, Des Plaines, IL. For medical research.
$6,000 to Bottomless Closet, Chicago, IL.

2669
Clingen Foundation, Ltd. ✧ ☆
c/o Brian T. Clingen
5101 Darmstadt Rd.
Hillside, IL   60162

Established in 1997 in IL.
Donor: Brian T. Clingen.
Foundation type: Independent foundation.
Financial data (yr. ended 12/31/05): Assets, $833,516 (M); expenditures, $340,843; qualifying distributions, $340,350; giving activities include $340,350 for 29 grants (high: $73,400; low: $200).
Purpose and activities: Giving primarily for education and youth services.
Fields of interest: Higher education; Youth development, centers/clubs; Children/youth, services.
Limitations: Applications not accepted. Giving primarily in IL. No grants to individuals.
Application information: Contributes only to pre-selected organizations.
Officers and Directors:* Brian T. Clingen,* Pres. and Treas.; Kenneth W. Clingen,* Secy.; Deidre M. Clingen.
EIN: 364200766
Selected grants: The following grants were reported in 2004.
$50,000 to Mercy Home for Boys and Girls, Chicago, IL. 2 grants: $25,000 each
$10,000 to Sue Duncan Childrens Center, Chicago, IL.
$5,000 to Boys and Girls Club of West Cook County, Bellwood, IL.
$4,000 to Benet Academy, Lisle, IL. 2 grants: $1,500, $2,500
$1,000 to Kids in Need, Bloomingdale, IL.
$1,000 to Saint Marys University, San Antonio, TX.

2670
CNA Foundation ▼ ✧
(formerly CNA Insurance Companies Foundation)
333 S. Wabash Ave., 44th Fl.
Chicago, IL   60604
Contact: Gina Lockhart, Prog. Coord.
E-mail: gina.lockhart@cna.com; Additional contact: Marlene Rotstein, Dir., tel.: (312) 822-7065, E-mail: marlene.rotstein@cna.com; Additional E-mail: cna_foundation@cna.com; URL: http://www.cna.com/cnaeportal/eportal/site/cna/menuitem.7204aaf0316757e8715f09f6556631a0/?vgnextoid=b1e940fa11056010VgnVCM1000005566130aRCRD

Established in 1995.
Donor: CNA Financial Corp.
Foundation type: Company-sponsored foundation.
Financial data (yr. ended 12/31/05): Assets, $9,454,165 (M); expenditures, $3,556,587; qualifying distributions, $3,556,587; giving activities include $2,910,515 for 85+ grants (high: $534,840), $26,891 for 9 grants to individuals (high: $3,000; low: $2,891), and $519,197 for employee matching gifts.

Purpose and activities: The foundation supports organizations involved with education, employment, and economically disadvantaged people.

Fields of interest: Elementary/secondary education; Vocational education; Education; Employment, training; Employment; Children; Economically disadvantaged.

Type of support: Continuing support; Program development; Employee matching gifts; Grants to individuals.

Limitations: Giving primarily in Chicago, IL. No support for political organizations, professional associations, labor, alumni, or fraternal organizations or social clubs, religious organizations not of direct benefit to the entire community, discriminatory organizations, or grantmaking foundations. No grants to individuals (except for employee-related emergency disaster relief grants), or for political, legislative, lobbying, or advocacy efforts, endowed chairs or professorships, endowments, advertising or raffles, tickets for testimonial events or similar benefit events from which only a portion of the revenue reaches the sponsor, or dinners or golf tournaments.

Publications: Application guidelines; Annual report; Corporate giving report.

Application information: Additional information may be requested at a later date. Multi-year funding is not automatic. Application form required.

> *Initial approach:* Download application form and mail proposal and application form to foundation
> *Copies of proposal:* 1
> *Deadline(s):* None
> *Final notification:* 6 months

Officers and Directors:* Stephen W. Lilienthal,* Chair.; Tom Pontarelli,* Pres.; Sandra Wagman, V.P. and Secy.; Dennis Hemme, V.P.; Steve Westman, V.P.; Joyce Donaly, Treas.; Sarah Pang, Exec. Dir.; Lori Komstadius; Jim Lewis; Craig Mense; Peter Wilson.

Number of staff: 2 part-time professional.

EIN: 364029026

Selected grants: The following grants were reported in 2004.

$200,000 to Millennium Park, Chicago, IL.
$200,000 to World Business Chicago, Chicago, IL.
$175,000 to Boys and Girls Clubs of Chicago, Chicago, IL.
$173,466 to National Merit Scholarship Corporation, Evanston, IL.
$72,000 to Metropolitan Family Services, Chicago, IL.
$50,000 to Goodman Theater, Chicago, IL.
$50,000 to PLUS Foundation, Minneapolis, MN.
$15,000 to Skinner Classical School, Chicago, IL.
$10,000 to Hispanic Chamber of Commerce of the U.S., DC.
$10,000 to Korean American Association of Chicago, Chicago, IL.

2671
The Code Family Foundation ✧
c/o Blake Thoele
10 S. Wacker Dr., Ste. 3175
Chicago, IL 60606-7407

Established in 1997 in IL.

Donor: Andrew W. Code.

Foundation type: Independent foundation.

Financial data (yr. ended 12/31/05): Assets, $12,836,593 (M); gifts received, $3,056,000; expenditures, $1,538,479; qualifying distributions,

$936,557; giving activities include $918,083 for 48 grants (high: $300,000; low: $250).

Fields of interest: Education; Health organizations, association; Children/youth, services; Christian agencies & churches.

Limitations: Applications not accepted. No support for organizations that the foundation is not involved with or connected to in some way.

Application information: Unsolicited requests for funds not accepted.

> *Board meeting date(s):* Annually during the 4th quarter

Officers: Andrew W. Code, Pres.; Susan K. Code, V.P. and Secy.; Blake Thoele, Treas.

Number of staff: None.

EIN: 364159492

Selected grants: The following grants were reported in 2004.

$40,000 to Latin School of Chicago, Chicago, IL.
$20,000 to Greater Chicago Food Depository, Chicago, IL.
$20,000 to Kanakuk Ministries, Branson, MO.
$11,200 to University of Iowa Foundation, Iowa City, IA.
$8,500 to Young Life.
$5,000 to Circle Urban Ministries, Chicago, IL.
$2,500 to Giant Steps Illinois, Westmont, IL.
$1,000 to Canine Companions for Independence.
$1,000 to Communities in Schools, Alexandria, VA.
$1,000 to YWCA of Metropolitan Chicago, Chicago, IL.

2672
Jerome and Ilene Cole Foundation, Inc. ✧
975 North Ave.
Deerfield, IL 60015 (847) 945-3362
Contact: Jerome J. Cole, Pres.

Established in 1995 in IL.

Donors: Jerome J. Cole; Ilene S. Cole†.

Foundation type: Independent foundation.

Financial data (yr. ended 12/31/05): Assets, $18,135,416 (M); gifts received, $252,934; expenditures, $1,029,392; qualifying distributions, $884,020; giving activities include $884,000 for 28 grants (high: $150,000; low: $3,000).

Purpose and activities: Giving primarily to hospitals and health associations.

Fields of interest: Hospitals (general); Health organizations, association; Medical research, association; Human services; Jewish federated giving programs.

Limitations: Giving primarily in Chicago, IL; some funding also in FL and NY. No grants to individuals.

Application information: Application form not required.

> *Deadline(s):* None

Officers and Directors:* Jerome J. Cole,* Pres. and Treas.; Ilene S. Cole,* V.P. and Secy.; Jennifer R. Cole,* V.P.; Julie L. Cole,* V.P.

EIN: 364039363

2673
The Coleman Foundation, Inc. ▼
651 W. Washington Blvd., Ste. 306
Chicago, IL 60661 (312) 902-7120
Contact: Michael W. Hennessy, C.E.O.
FAX: (313) 902-7124;
E-mail: info@colemanfoundation.org; *URL:* http://www.colemanfoundation.org

Trust established in 1951 in IL.

Donors: J.D. Stetson Coleman†; Dorothy W. Coleman†.

Foundation type: Independent foundation.

Financial data (yr. ended 12/31/05): Assets, $157,066,582 (M); expenditures, $8,108,562; qualifying distributions, $7,040,207; giving activities include $6,253,640 for 143 grants (high: $529,500; low: $2,500; average: $10,000–$100,000).

Purpose and activities: Giving for postsecondary, community, secondary and elementary education programs which focus on developing awareness of self-employment, and other selected postsecondary, secondary, and elementary education projects. Support also for cancer research and care as well as for programs to aid the developmentally disabled in the metropolitan Chicago area.

Fields of interest: Elementary school/education; Secondary school/education; Higher education; Business school/education; Adult/continuing education; Education; Medical care, rehabilitation; Cancer; Cancer research; Human services; Community development, small businesses; Community development; Disabilities, people with; Economically disadvantaged.

Type of support: General/operating support; Income development; Capital campaigns; Building/renovation; Equipment; Program development; Conferences/seminars; Professorships; Curriculum development; Scholarship funds; Research; Program-related investments/loans; Matching/challenge support.

Limitations: Giving primarily in the Midwest, with emphasis on the metropolitan Chicago, IL, area; support outside the Midwest is only for selected programs. No support for religious or political organizations. No grants to individuals, or for deficit financing, ticket purchases, or student loans to individuals.

Publications: Application guidelines; Financial statement; Grants list; Occasional report.

Application information: Brochures, videotapes, CDs and other attachments should not be sent with the letter of inquiry. Full grant proposals should only be submitted upon invitation by the foundation. Refer to website for application requirements. Application form not required.

> *Initial approach:* Concise letter of inquiry
> *Copies of proposal:* 1
> *Deadline(s):* Rolling deadline schedule with quarterly consideration
> *Board meeting date(s):* Usually in Feb., May, Aug., and Nov.
> *Final notification:* 3 months

Officers and Directors:* Michael W. Hennessy,* C.E.O. and Pres.; James H. Jones,* Secy.; Trevor C. Davies,* C.F.O. and Treas.; John E. Hughes,* Chair. Emeritus; C. Hugh Albers; R. Michael Furlong.

Number of staff: 4 full-time professional; 1 full-time support.

EIN: 363025967

Selected grants: The following grants were reported in 2004.

$600,000 to Park Lawn Association, Oak Lawn, IL. For program support.
$250,000 to Northwestern University, Feinberg School of Medicine, Evanston, IL. For salaries in Chicago.
$250,000 to Providence Saint Mel School, Chicago, IL. For capital support.
$150,000 to Columbia College, Chicago, IL. For salaries.

$150,000 to Cristo Rey Jesuit High School, Chicago, IL. For capital support.

$146,140 to DePaul University, Chicago, IL. For program support.

$145,000 to U.S. Association for Small Business and Entrepreneurship, Madison, WI. For program support.

$100,000 to University of Illinois at Chicago, College of Business Administration, Chicago, IL. For program support for Institute of Entrepreneurial Studies.

$93,635 to Millikin University, Decatur, IL. For program support.

$81,000 to Institute for Entrepreneurship, Milwaukee, WI. For program support.

2674
Earle M. & Virginia M. Combs Foundation ◇
141 W. Jackson Blvd., Ste. 3302
Chicago, IL 60604

Established in 1967 in IL.
Donors: Earle M. Combs III; Virginia M. Combs; Earle M. Combs IV.
Foundation type: Independent foundation.
Financial data (yr. ended 12/31/05): Assets, $9,188,105 (M); gifts received, $250; expenditures, $444,097; qualifying distributions, $419,922; giving activities include $356,151 for 71 grants (high: $65,218; low: $250).
Purpose and activities: Giving primarily for Christian and Baptist organizations; funding also for education and human services, including a YMCA.
Fields of interest: Higher education; Theological school/education; Human services; YM/YWCAs & YM/YWHAs; Youth, services; Christian agencies & churches; Protestant agencies & churches.
Type of support: General/operating support.
Limitations: Applications not accepted. Giving primarily in the U.S., with emphasis on IL and WI; funding also in Australia, Fiji, the United Kingdom, and Zambia. No grants to individuals.
Application information: Contributes only to pre-selected organizations.
Officers and Directors:* Earle M. Combs III,* Pres.; Virginia M. Combs, Secy.-Treas.; Earle M. Combs IV; Eric C. Combs; Bonnie C. Etters.
EIN: 366168454
Selected grants: The following grants were reported in 2004.
$90,015 to John Stott Ministries, Carol Stream, IL.
$16,800 to International Teams, Elgin, IL.
$9,900 to Common Hope, Saint Paul, MN.
$8,900 to Chicago Symphony Orchestra, Chicago, IL.
$6,200 to Opportunity International, Oak Brook, IL.
$4,803 to Campus Crusade for Christ, Miami, FL.
$2,000 to Heritage Hill Foundation, Green Bay, WI.
$1,120 to Adler Planetarium, Chicago, IL.
$1,000 to Pacific Garden Mission, Chicago, IL.
$1,000 to UFM International, Bala Cynwyd, PA.

2675
The Comer Foundation
c/o Neal Gerber & Eisenberg
2 N. LaSalle St.
Chicago, IL 60602
Contact: Stephanie Comer, Pres.

Established in 1986 in IL.

Donors: Gary C. Comer‡; Frances Comer.
Foundation type: Independent foundation.
Financial data (yr. ended 12/31/05): Assets, $14,206,479 (M); gifts received, $1,396,742; expenditures, $1,811,026; qualifying distributions, $1,746,483; giving activities include $1,692,455 for 54 grants (high: $300,000; low: $1,000).
Purpose and activities: Giving primarily for environmental protection, medicine, arts and cultural organizations, human services, and education.
Fields of interest: Museums; Arts; Libraries/library science; Education; Environment, natural resources; Zoos/zoological societies; Hospitals (general); Public health; AIDS; Human services; Children/youth, services.
Type of support: General/operating support; Continuing support; Program development; Internship funds; Scholarship funds.
Limitations: Applications not accepted. Giving primarily in Chicago, IL. No grants to individuals.
Application information: Contributes only to pre-selected organizations.
Officers: Stephanie Comer, Pres.; Frances Comer, V.P. and Secy.; Gary C. Comer, Treas.
Number of staff: 1 full-time professional.
EIN: 363522486
Selected grants: The following grants were reported in 2004.
$268,078 to Millennium Park, Chicago, IL.
$87,500 to Harm Reduction Coalition, Oakland, CA.
$43,240 to Scholarship America, Saint Peter, MN.
$42,500 to Positive Health Project, New York, NY.
$30,000 to Clean Needles Now, Los Angeles, CA.
$30,000 to Friends of Acadia, Bar Harbor, ME.
$20,000 to AIDS Network, Madison, WI.
$17,000 to Dodgeville Scholarship Fund, Dodgeville, WI.
$15,000 to After Hours Project, Brooklyn, NY.
$15,000 to HIV Alliance, Eugene, OR.

2676
Comer Science & Education Foundation ▼ ◇
c/o Lawrence Richman
2 N. LaSalle St., No. 2200
Chicago, IL 60602

Established in 1998 in IL.
Donors: Gary Comer‡; The Comer Foundation.
Foundation type: Independent foundation.
Financial data (yr. ended 12/31/05): Assets, $55,866,574 (M); gifts received, $1,826,749; expenditures, $21,364,613; qualifying distributions, $20,758,842; giving activities include $17,404,646 for 71 grants (high: $3,000,000; low: $500; average: $110,000–$1,000,000).
Purpose and activities: Giving primarily for higher education.
Fields of interest: Museums; Museums (natural history); Higher education; Hospitals (general).
Limitations: Applications not accepted. Giving primarily in Chicago, IL. No grants to individuals.
Application information: Contributes only to pre-selected organizations.
Officers and Directors: Guy Comer,* V.P.; Stephanie Comer, V.P.; William T. Schleicher,* V.P.; Gregory Mooney, Exec. Dir.
EIN: 364244783
Selected grants: The following grants were reported in 2004.
$3,333,000 to University of Chicago Hospitals, Chicago, IL. For general support.

$1,398,359 to Paul Revere Elementary School, Chicago, IL. For general support.
$1,003,750 to San Miguel School, Chicago, IL. For general support.
$585,000 to University of California, Berkeley, CA. For general support.
$382,716 to Columbia University, New York, NY. For general support.
$170,000 to South Shore Drill Team and Performing Arts Ensemble, Chicago, IL. For general support.
$165,000 to Pennsylvania State University, University Park, PA. For general support.
$165,000 to Princeton University, Princeton, NJ. For general support.
$165,000 to University of Maine, Office of Research and Sponsored Programs, Orono, ME. For general support.
$150,000 to University of Chicago, Chicago, IL. For general support.

2677
Community Foundation of Central Illinois ◇
(formerly Peoria Area Community Foundation)
331 Fulton St., Ste. 310
Peoria, IL 61602 (309) 674-8730
Contact: Shanna Miller, Exec. Dir.
FAX: (309) 674-8754;
E-mail: jim@communityfoundationci.org;
URL: http://www.communityfoundationci.org

Incorporated in 1987 in IL.
Foundation type: Community foundation.
Financial data (yr. ended 6/30/04): Assets, $11,130,226 (M); gifts received, $893,104; expenditures, $709,803; giving activities include $365,628 for 203 grants (high: $30,000; low: $40), and $71,500 for 31 grants to individuals (high: $6,000; low: $500).
Purpose and activities: The foundation seeks to serve the Central Illinois area by providing an intelligent bridge between needs and resources through a growing endowment, entrepreneurial grantmaking service to the nonprofit sector, and promotion of philanthropy. Primary areas of interest include community development, the arts and humanities, education, health, and human services.
Fields of interest: Visual arts; Museums; Performing arts; Performing arts, dance; Humanities; Historic preservation/historical societies; Arts; Education, early childhood education; Child development, education; Elementary school/education; Secondary school/education; Higher education; Adult/continuing education; Adult education—literacy, basic skills & GED; Education, reading; Education; Environment, natural resources; Environment; Animal welfare; Animals/wildlife, preservation/protection; Reproductive health, family planning; Medical care, rehabilitation; Health care; Substance abuse, services; Mental health/crisis services; Health organizations, association; Cancer; Heart & circulatory diseases; AIDS; Alcoholism; Cancer research; Heart & circulatory research; AIDS research; Crime/violence prevention, youth; Food services; Nutrition; Recreation; Youth development, services; Children/youth, services; Child development, services; Family services; Aging, centers/services; Homeless, human services; Human services; Civil rights; Urban/community development; Community development; Voluntarism promotion; Federated giving programs; Social sciences; Government/public administration; Leadership development;

Aging; Disabilities, people with; Minorities; Economically disadvantaged; Homeless.

Type of support: General/operating support; Capital campaigns; Equipment; Program development; Conferences/seminars; Seed money; Scholarship funds; Employee matching gifts; In-kind gifts; Matching/challenge support.

Limitations: Giving limited to the central IL area. No support for sectarian religious purposes. No grants to individuals (except for scholarships), or for annual campaigns or endowments; no loans.

Publications: Application guidelines; Annual report (including application guidelines); Financial statement; Informational brochure; Newsletter.

Application information: Visit foundation Web site for application form and application guidelines. Application form required.

> *Initial approach:* Submit application and attachments
> *Copies of proposal:* 1
> *Deadline(s):* Jan. 15, Apr. 15, and Sept. 15
> *Board meeting date(s):* Monthly
> *Final notification:* Within 1 month

Officers and Directors:* Terry Machetti,* Pres.; Karl Kuppler,* V.P.; Shelley Epstein,* Secy.; Debra Bowers,* Treas.; James Sullivan, Exec. Dir.; Mary Ardapple; Eldon Arnold; Scott Cisel; James Fassino; Steve Gosselin; Neal Johnson; Deborah Anne Lane; Steve Montez; Andrea Parker; Michael Quine; James Rinkenberger; Robert Stevenson III; Valerie Umholtz; Jan Wright Vergon; Jennifer Wilfong; Thomas Wyman, M.D.

Number of staff: 2 full-time professional; 1 part-time professional.

EIN: 371185713

2678
The Community Foundation of Decatur/ Macon County ✧

125 N. Water St., Ste. 200
Decatur, IL 62523-1309 (217) 429-3000
Contact: Lucy Murphy, Exec. Dir.
FAX: (217) 429-3001;
E-mail: lmurphy@endowdecatur.org; URL: http://www.endowdecatur.org

Established in 1998 in IL.

Foundation type: Community foundation.

Financial data (yr. ended 12/31/04): Assets, $3,427,423 (M); expenditures, $474,707; giving activities include $317,570 for grants.

Purpose and activities: The foundation seeks to increase the permanent charitable capital available in Decatur and Macon County, IL.

Fields of interest: Arts; Education; Environment; Health care; Community development; Youth.

Limitations: Giving primarily in Decatur and Macon County, IL.

Publications: Application guidelines; Annual report; Financial statement; Grants list; Informational brochure; Newsletter; Occasional report; Program policy statement.

Application information: Application form not required.

> *Board meeting date(s):* Quarterly

Officers and Directors:* Larry Haab,* Chair.; Doug Schmalz,* Vice-Chair; Peg Luy,* Secy.; Pat Mohan,* Treas.; Lucy Murphy, Exec. Dir.; Dale Arnold; Rod Bussell; Kit Paulin; Troy Swinford; Guy Williams.

Number of staff: 1 full-time professional; 1 part-time professional.

EIN: 371372729

2679
Community Foundation of Northern Illinois ✧

(formerly Rockford Community Foundation)
946 N. 2nd St.
Rockford, IL 61107 (815) 962-2110
Contact: Gloria Lundin, Pres.; For grants: Barbara Nelson, V.P.
FAX: (815) 962-2116; E-mail: info@cfnil.org; Additional E-mail: glundin@cfnil.org; Grant application tel.: (815) 962-2110, ext. 15 and e-mail: bnelson@cfnil.org; URL: http://www.cfnil.org

Established in 1953 in IL.

Foundation type: Community foundation.

Financial data (yr. ended 6/30/05): Assets, $46,111,822 (M); gifts received, $3,535,252; expenditures, $4,195,556; giving activities include $3,549,791 for 902 grants (high: $448,600; low: $5).

Purpose and activities: The foundation seeks to serve the four-county area through philanthropy, to provide leadership in meeting charitable needs, and to be a responsible steward to donors of the endowment. Giving primarily for social services; support also for arts and culture, education, health services, and housing, neighborhoods, economic and community development, youth, children, and families. In Youth We Trust group of the foundation supports programs initiated by and operated for people under 21.

Fields of interest: Humanities; Arts; Education; Health care; Housing/shelter; Youth, services; Child development, services; Family services; Human services; Economic development; Community development; Youth.

Type of support: Building/renovation; Equipment; Emergency funds; Seed money; Scholarship funds; Technical assistance; Program evaluation; Program-related investments/loans; Scholarships —to individuals; Matching/challenge support.

Limitations: Giving primarily in the metropolitan Rockford, IL, area, including Boone, Ogle, Stephenson, and Winnebago. No grants to individuals (except for scholarships), or for ongoing project support or operating support, annual or capital campaigns, budget deficit, endowments, or regranting of funds.

Publications: Application guidelines; Annual report; Grants list; Informational brochure (including application guidelines); Newsletter; Program policy statement.

Application information: Visit foundation Web site for application forms and additional guidelines per grant type. Applicant may attend a Grant Seekers meeting held on the 1st Tues. of every June or Dec.; call for reservations. Application form required.

> *Initial approach:* Submit application for grants of up to $7,500; a preliminary application is required for grants over $7,500 for Arts and Humanities and Community Needs grants
> *Copies of proposal:* 1
> *Deadline(s):* Jan. 15 and July 15 for Arts and Humanities and Community Needs grants; Feb. 1 and Oct. 15 for In Youth We Trust grants
> *Board meeting date(s):* Feb., Apr., May, Aug., Sept., Oct., and Nov.
> *Final notification:* Varies

Officers and Trustees:* Sue Grans,* Chair.; James Pirages,* Vice-Chair.; Gloria Lundin,* Pres.; Barbara I. Nelson, V.P. and Sr. Prog. Off.; Michael E. Abate; Elise Cadigan; Monica R. Calcott; Patrick T. Derry; Gary Ecklund; Darlene J. Furst; Terrie E. Hall; Robert M. Hammes, Jr.; Suzanne R. Lukas; Kent A.

Mallquist; Nate Martin; Michael R. Perry; James A. Powers; Forest W. Price; Howard E. Sorenson; David A. Thompson; Jean E. Vitale.

Trustee Bank: JPMorgan Chase Bank, N.A.

Number of staff: 5 full-time professional; 2 part-time professional.

EIN: 364402089

2680
Community Foundation of the Fox River Valley

(formerly The Aurora Foundation)
111 W. Downer Pl., Ste. 312
Aurora, IL 60506-5136 (630) 896-7800
Contact: Sharon Stredde, C.E.O.
FAX: (630) 896-7811;
E-mail: info@CommunityFoundationFRV.org;
Additional E-mails: sstredde@communityfoundationfrv.org and grant@communityfoundationfrv.org; URL: http://www.communityfoundationfrv.org

Incorporated in 1948 in IL.

Foundation type: Community foundation.

Financial data (yr. ended 12/31/05): Assets, $35,692,953 (M); gifts received, $3,396,700; expenditures, $1,813,535; giving activities include $937,274 for 265 grants (high: $100,000; low: $25), and $447,850 for grants to individuals.

Purpose and activities: The foundation is a collection of individual funds and resources given by local citizens to enhance and support the quality of life in the Greater Aurora area. Foundation funds are used to provide grants to nonprofit organizations and scholarships to area students.

Fields of interest: Humanities; Arts; Higher education; Education; Hospitals (general); Health care; Health organizations, association; Children/ youth, services; Human services.

Type of support: Capital campaigns; Building/ renovation; Equipment; Seed money; Scholarship funds; Scholarships—to individuals; Matching/ challenge support; Student loans—to individuals.

Limitations: Giving limited to residents in the immediate Aurora, IL, area, including southern Kane and Kendall counties. No support for private foundations, sectarian or religious purposes, or for organizations operated primarily for the benefit of their own membership. No grants to individuals (except for scholarships), or for operating budgets, research, annual campaigns, continuing support, endowments, contingency funds, reserves, deficits, tickets, or national fundraising efforts.

Publications: Application guidelines; Annual report; Newsletter.

Application information: Contact foundation for eligibility requirements and application forms. Application form required.

> *Initial approach:* Telephone or e-mail
> *Copies of proposal:* 8
> *Deadline(s):* Jan. 1 and Aug. 1 for grants; varies for scholarships
> *Board meeting date(s):* Mar. and Sept.; executive committee meets as required
> *Final notification:* Varies

Officers and Directors:* Hilary K. Brennan,* Chair.; Ralph D. Voris,* Vice-Chair.; Sharon Stredde, C.E.O. and Pres.; Mark E. Truemper,* Treas.; Thomas S. Alexander; Roger O. Anderson; Daniel Barreiro; Gretta E. Bieber; Robert E. Brent; Warren F. Cannon; Marilyn A. Foote; F. James Garbe; Anne S. Goldsmith; Bruce L. Goldsmith; Peter H. Henning;

Robert P. Hubbard; Darrell L. Jordan; V. Gregory McKnight; Frank R. Miller; Calvin R. Myers; Neal Ormond III; Gerald Palmer; Mac Salazar; William B. Skoglund; Peter K. Whinfrey.

Number of staff: 1 full-time professional; 1 full-time support.

EIN: 366086742

2681

Community Memorial Foundation ▼ ✧

15 Spinning Wheel Rd., Ste. 326
Hinsdale, IL 60521 (630) 654-4729
Contact: James Durkan, C.E.O. and Pres.
FAX: (630) 654-3402; E-mail: info@cmfdn.org;
URL: http://cmfdn.org/

Established in 1995 in IL; converted from sale of La Grange Memorial Hospital to Columbia/HCA.

Donors: Helen Prempas Trust; LaGrange Memorial Health System; Marion O. Crion Trust; Harris Associates.

Foundation type: Independent foundation.

Financial data (yr. ended 12/31/04): Assets, $86,038,181 (M); expenditures, $5,181,440; qualifying distributions, $4,858,849; giving activities include $4,087,890 for 59 grants (high: $1,000,000; low: $955; average: $10,000–$50,000).

Purpose and activities: The foundation is dedicated to improving the health and well being of people who live and work in the western suburbs of Chicago, IL.

Fields of interest: Health care; Youth development; Family services; Community development; Aging.

Type of support: Consulting services; Seed money; General/operating support; Continuing support; Program development; Conferences/seminars; Technical assistance; Program evaluation; Program-related investments/loans; Matching/challenge support.

Limitations: Giving limited to the 27 communities in western Cook and southeastern DuPage counties in IL. No support for organizations which limit services to any one religious group or members of a specific sectarian perspective. No grants to individuals, or for endowments, in-patient care, capital projects, sponsoring dinners, or advertising space.

Publications: Annual report (including application guidelines); Grants list.

Application information: Call, write, or E-mail for grant guidelines. See foundation Web site for downloadable General Grant Application Packet. Application form required.

Initial approach: Telephone or proposal
Copies of proposal: 3
Deadline(s): Mar. 31 and Sept. 30 (If either date falls on a weekend, proposals must be received by 5 PM on following Monday)
Board meeting date(s): Varies
Final notification: June and Dec.

Officers and Directors:* Allyson Z. Zak,* Chair.; C. Roger Brown,* Vice-Chair.; James Durkan,* C.E.O and Pres.; Irene Frye, V.P.; Ruth Ann Althaus, Ph.D.; Sam Balark; Richard J. Carroll, M.D.; Linda M. Eastman; Jeffrey J. Frommelt; Donald J. Gralen; John J. Maden; Paul Naffah, M.D.; Maria del Socorro Pesquiera; Timothy R. Ricordati, Ed.D.

Number of staff: 5 full-time professional.

EIN: 364012380

Selected grants: The following grants were reported in 2004.

$355,519 to Pillars Community Services, LaGrange Park, IL. 2 grants: $284,644 (For Infant-Toddler Program serving children ages birth to three

years), $70,875 (To expand Families and Schools Together (FAST) Program into Wharton Elementary School in Summit).

$342,988 to Community Nurse Health Association, La Grange, IL. 2 grants: $180,537 (For Pediatric/Adolescent and Dental Clinics), $162,451 (For Healthy Beginnings Program that provides comprehensive health care to undeserved pregnant women and families).

$250,000 to Suburban Primary Health Care Council, Westchester, IL. For primary health care services to low-income, uninsured residents in western Cook County.

$140,200 to Lyons Township High School, Lyons, IL. For Families and Schools Together (FAST) Program in school districts 102, 105, and 106.

$114,700 to Access DuPage, Oakbrook Terrace, IL. To link low-income uninsured people to primary care services, access to diagnostic testing, specialty care and prescription drugs.

$90,325 to Access Community Health Network, Chicago, IL. For Enhanced Perinatal Program at Des Plaines Valley Health Center in Summit.

$73,000 to DuPage Community Clinic, Wheaton, IL. For Diabetic, Hypertension, and Dental Clinics.

$50,000 to Family Shelter Service, Wheaton, IL. For new Community Counseling Program satellite site in southeast county that offers support programs and parenting education to victims of domestic violence.

2682

Robert J. and Loretta W. Cooney Family Foundation ✧

c/o Robert J. Cooney, Jr.
120 N. LaSalle St., 30th Fl.
Chicago, IL 60602

Established in 2000 in IL.

Donors: Loretta W. Cooney; Robert J. Cooney.

Foundation type: Independent foundation.

Financial data (yr. ended 12/31/05): Assets, $4,288,864 (M); gifts received, $3,425,837; expenditures, $355,819; qualifying distributions, $346,779; giving activities include $346,779 for 37 grants (high: $142,857; low: $100).

Fields of interest: Arts; Education; Human services; Philanthropy/voluntarism.

Limitations: Applications not accepted. No grants to individuals.

Application information: Contributes only to pre-selected organizations.

Directors: Loretta W. Cooney; Robert J. Cooney, Jr.

EIN: 364408645

Selected grants: The following grants were reported in 2003.

$50,000 to Boston College, Chestnut Hill, MA.

$29,000 to Daniel Murphy Scholarship Foundation, Chicago, IL.

$10,000 to Saint Lukes School.

$5,300 to Cinn Foundation, Chicago, IL.

$500 to Brighter Futures, Chicago, IL.

2683

Cooper Family Foundation ✧

(formerly Richard W. Cooper Foundation)
611 Enterprise Dr.
Oak Brook, IL 60523

Established in 1969 in IL.

Donors: Richard H. Cooper; Cooperfund, Inc.

Foundation type: Independent foundation.

Financial data (yr. ended 12/31/05): Assets, $8,677,494 (M); expenditures, $491,074; qualifying distributions, $426,400; giving activities include $426,400 for 5 grants (high: $200,000; low: $200).

Purpose and activities: Giving primarily for health associations; funding also for the arts, including an orchestral association, and for social services and community development.

Fields of interest: Arts, association; Museums (art); Animal welfare; Health organizations, association; Lupus research; Human services; International affairs, foreign policy; Community development.

Type of support: General/operating support.

Limitations: Applications not accepted. Giving primarily in IL, with emphasis on Chicago. No grants to individuals.

Application information: Contributes only to pre-selected organizations.

Officer and Director:* Jean Frandsen,* Pres.

EIN: 237024516

Selected grants: The following grants were reported in 2003.

$150,000 to Museum of Contemporary Art, Chicago, IL.

$100,000 to Orchestral Association, Chicago, IL.

$57,000 to Museum of Contemporary Photography, Chicago, IL.

$15,000 to Music and Dance Theater Chicago, Chicago, IL.

$5,075 to Lupus Foundation of America, Chicago, IL.

$1,500 to Art Institute of Chicago, Chicago, IL.

$1,250 to Chicago Humanities Festival, Chicago, IL.

$700 to Lymphoma Research Foundation, New York, NY.

$500 to PAWS Chicago, Chicago, IL.

$70 to School of the Art Institute of Chicago, Chicago, IL.

2684

Philip H. Corboy Foundation ✧

30 N. LaSalle St., Ste. 4200
Chicago, IL 60602

Established in 1983 in IL.

Donors: Philip H. Corboy; James Epstein Investment Trust.

Foundation type: Independent foundation.

Financial data (yr. ended 12/31/05): Assets, $14,083,501 (M); gifts received, $150,000; expenditures, $798,791; qualifying distributions, $633,040; giving activities include $633,040 for 143 grants (high: $50,000; low: $40).

Purpose and activities: Support primarily for higher education and human services.

Fields of interest: Arts; Law school/education; Education; Health care; Health organizations, association; Recreation; Human services; Children/youth, services; Christian agencies & churches; Roman Catholic agencies & churches.

Limitations: Applications not accepted. Giving primarily in Chicago, IL. No grants to individuals.

Application information: Contributes only to pre-selected organizations.

Officers and Directors:* Thomas J. Durkin,* Pres.; Mary A. Dempsey,* Secy.-Treas.; Howard M. Denenberg.

EIN: 363211607

2685
Alverin M. Cornell Foundation ◇
1827 Walden Office Sq., Ste. 104
Schaumburg, IL 60173

Established in 2001 in IL.
Donor: Alverin Cornell Marital Trust.
Foundation type: Independent foundation.
Financial data (yr. ended 12/31/05): Assets, $24,402,913 (M); gifts received, $142,065; expenditures, $1,525,594; qualifying distributions, $1,318,334; giving activities include $1,186,436 for 145 grants (high: $25,000; low: $500).
Fields of interest: Education; Health organizations, association; Christian agencies & churches.
Limitations: Applications not accepted. No grants to individuals.
Application information: Contributes only to pre-selected organizations.
Officers and Directors:* William H. Brewer,* Pres.; Charles H. Brewer,* V.P. and Treas.; David Jackson,* Secy.
EIN: 367371436
Selected grants: The following grants were reported in 2005.
$100,000 to Storehouse, Albuquerque, NM. 2 grants: $50,000 each
$25,000 to Culver Educational Foundation, Culver, IN.
$25,000 to Willow Creek Community Church, South Barrington, IL.
$17,500 to World Vision, Federal Way, WA. 2 grants: $7,500, $10,000
$15,000 to Childrens Memorial Hospital, Chicago, IL.
$15,000 to Outward Bound, Garrison, NY.
$10,000 to Aurora University, Aurora, IL.
$5,000 to Fairygodmother Foundation, Chicago, IL.

2686
The Coydog Foundation ◇
191 N. Wacker Dr., Ste. 1500
Chicago, IL 60606-1899 (312) 621-0590

Established in 1986 in IL.
Donors: Irving B. Harris; William Harris Trust.
Foundation type: Independent foundation.
Financial data (yr. ended 12/31/04): Assets, $16,919,878 (M); expenditures, $1,061,272; qualifying distributions, $816,868; giving activities include $816,843 for 32 grants (high: $120,000; low: $650).
Fields of interest: Arts; Higher education; Human services.
Limitations: Applications not accepted. Giving primarily in Washington DC, MA and NY. No grants to individuals.
Application information: Contributes only to pre-selected organizations. Unsolicited requests for funds not accepted.
Officers and Directors:* William W. Harris,* Pres. and Treas.; Roberta Harris,* V.P.; Boardman Lloyd,* V.P.; Jack Polsky,* Secy.; Michael Resnick.
EIN: 363479461

2687
Crane Foundation, Inc. ◇
c/o M. Gelineau
1908 Kingsbrook Ct., Ste. B
Wheaton, IL 60187

Established in 1951 in MO.
Donor: Crane Co.
Foundation type: Company-sponsored foundation.
Financial data (yr. ended 12/31/05): Assets, $6,757,979 (M); expenditures, $415,179; qualifying distributions, $353,756; giving activities include $258,820 for 81 grants (high: $15,000; low: $250), and $65,463 for employee matching gifts.
Purpose and activities: The foundation supports organizations involved with performing arts, K-12 and higher education, health, recreation, human services, philanthropy and voluntarism, and minorities.
Fields of interest: Performing arts; Elementary/secondary education; Higher education; Health care; Recreation; Children/youth, services; Child development, services; Family services; Human services; Philanthropy/voluntarism; Minorities.
International interests: Canada.
Type of support: General/operating support; Continuing support; Annual campaigns; Scholarship funds; Employee matching gifts.
Limitations: Applications not accepted. Giving limited to areas of company operations, including in Canada. No grants to individuals, or for endowments, capital campaigns, or research; no loans.
Application information: Contributes only to pre-selected organizations.
Board meeting date(s): As required
Officers and Directors:* Robert S. Evans,* Chair.; Eric C. Fast,* Pres.; Augustus I. DuPont,* V.P., Secy., and General Counsel; E.M. Kopczick, V.P.; T.M. Noonan, V.P.; J.R. Vipond,* V.P.; Gil A. Dickoff, Treas.
EIN: 436051752

2688
Crane Fund for Widows and Children ◇
1908 Kingsbrook Ct.
Wheaton, IL 60187
Contact: M. Gellineau

Established in 1914 in IL.
Foundation type: Independent foundation.
Financial data (yr. ended 12/31/05): Assets, $30,397,433 (M); expenditures, $1,155,015; qualifying distributions, $1,024,937; giving activities include $960,575 for 213 grants.
Purpose and activities: Support for community funds, hospitals, and higher education for the needy; limited support also to organizations in Canada.
Fields of interest: Higher education; Hospitals (general); Federated giving programs; Economically disadvantaged.
Type of support: Continuing support; Annual campaigns; Scholarship funds.
Limitations: Applications not accepted. Giving primarily in the U.S.; some giving also in Canada. No grants to individuals.
Application information: Unsolicited requests for funds not accepted.
Trustees: G.A. Dickoff; A.I. duPont; E.M. Kopczick; G.S. Scimone.
EIN: 366116543

2689
The Bryan C. & Christina I. Cressey Foundation ◇ ☆
c/o Rosen & Cohen
555 Skokie Blvd., Ste. 260
Northbrook, IL 60062 (847) 897-8900
Contact: Bryan C. Cressey, Pres. and Treas.

Established in 1986 in IL.
Donors: Bryan C. Cressey; Christina I. Cressey.
Foundation type: Independent foundation.
Financial data (yr. ended 12/31/05): Assets, $822,371 (M); gifts received, $1,992; expenditures, $675,574; qualifying distributions, $670,500; giving activities include $670,500 for 48 grants (high: $150,000; low: $500).
Purpose and activities: Giving primarily for Christian and Protestant churches, particularly Episcopal churches; funding also for education and human services.
Fields of interest: Arts education; Humanities; Higher education; Business school/education; Animals/wildlife; Health organizations, association; Recreation; Human services; American Red Cross; Residential/custodial care, hospices; Women, centers/services; Christian agencies & churches.
Type of support: General/operating support.
Limitations: Giving primarily in the Chicago, IL, area. No grants to individuals.
Application information: Application form not required.
Deadline(s): None
Officers: Bryan C. Cressey, Pres. and Treas.; Christina I. Cressey, V.P. and Secy.
EIN: 363486617
Selected grants: The following grants were reported in 2004.
$86,000 to Saint Michaels Episcopal Church. For unrestricted support.
$25,000 to Harvard University, Business School, Cambridge, MA. For unrestricted support.
$25,000 to International SeaKeepers Society, Miami, FL. For unrestricted support.
$25,000 to Reed College, Portland, OR. For unrestricted support.
$17,500 to Adler Planetarium, Chicago, IL. For unrestricted support.
$15,300 to Junior Achievement of Chicago, Chicago, IL. For unrestricted support.
$15,000 to Lake Forest Academy, Lake Forest, IL. For unrestricted support.
$6,000 to Cathedral Shelter of Chicago, Chicago, IL. For unrestricted support.
$1,500 to Art Institute of Chicago, Chicago, IL. For unrestricted support.
$1,000 to Equestrian Land Conservation Resource, Elizabeth, IL. For unrestricted support.

2690
Mary Jane Crowe Foundation ◇
c/o Bank of America, N.A.
231 S. LaSalle St.
Chicago, IL 60697 (312) 828-1785
Contact: M.C. Ryan

Established in 1955.
Donor: Mary Jane Crowe Trust.
Foundation type: Independent foundation.
Financial data (yr. ended 12/31/05): Assets, $8,563,774 (M); expenditures, $856,877; qualifying distributions, $777,707; giving activities include $728,500 for 4 grants (high: $715,000; low: $3,500).

Purpose and activities: Giving primarily for higher education.

Fields of interest: Higher education; Education; American Red Cross; Children/youth, services; Family services, single parents; Roman Catholic agencies & churches.

Limitations: Giving primarily in FL, IL, and MT.

Application information:

Initial approach: Proposal

Deadline(s): None

Trustees: Linda Crowe Tate; Bank of America, N.A.

EIN: 356020626

2691
Arie and Ida Crown Memorial ▼
222 N. LaSalle St., Ste. 2000
Chicago, IL   60601-1109   (312) 236-6300
Contact: Susan Crown, Pres.
FAX: (312) 984-1499;
E-mail: aicm@crown-chicago.com; URL: http://www.crownmemorial.org/

Incorporated in 1947 in IL.

Donor: members of the Crown family.

Foundation type: Independent foundation.

Financial data (yr. ended 12/31/04): Assets, $262,850,484 (M); gifts received, $548,981; expenditures, $10,205,434; qualifying distributions, $9,190,018; giving activities include $9,190,018 for 680 grants (high: $646,586; low: $15; average: $1,000–$200,000).

Purpose and activities: Broad mandate with focus on opportunity building; emphasis on Jewish issues, education, human services, health care, youth agencies, and inner-city welfare.

Fields of interest: Arts; Education; Health care; Human services; Public affairs; Jewish agencies & temples.

International interests: Israel.

Type of support: General/operating support; Continuing support; Annual campaigns; Capital campaigns; Building/renovation; Equipment; Endowments; Program development; Professorships; Fellowships; Scholarship funds; Employee matching gifts; Matching/challenge support.

Limitations: Giving primarily in metropolitan Chicago, IL. No support for government-sponsored programs. No grants to individuals, or for consulting services, conferences, or film or documentary projects; no loans.

Publications: Application guidelines.

Application information: Application form not required.

Initial approach: Letter of inquiry

Copies of proposal: 1

Deadline(s): Jan. 31 and July 31

Board meeting date(s): Spring and fall

Officers and Directors:* Susan Crown,* Pres.; A. Steven Crown,* V.P.; James S. Crown,* V.P.; Rebecca Crown,* V.P.; William Crown,* V.P.; Charles Goodman,* V.P.; Barbara Goodman Manilow,* V.P.; Sara Crown Star,* V.P.; Arnold Weber,* V.P.; Lester Crown,* Treas.; Jennifer Jacoby Hurd,* Exec. Dir.

Number of staff: 5 full-time professional.

EIN: 366076088

Selected grants: The following grants were reported in 2004.

$646,586 to JPF Foundation, Chicago, IL.

$366,000 to Covenant Foundation, New York, NY.

$250,000 to Magen David Adom, New York, NY.

$110,000 to American Friends of the Israel Museum, New York, NY.

$100,000 to Jewish Federation of Metropolitan Chicago, Dina and Eli Field EZRA Multi-Service Center, Chicago, IL.

$100,000 to World of Hope, DC.

$5,000 to Jewish Funders Network, New York, NY.

$5,000 to John F. Kennedy Center for the Performing Arts, DC.

$3,600 to Duke University, Durham, NC.

$2,500 to Resurrection Home Health Foundation, Niles, IL.

2692
The Cuneo Foundation
9101 N. Greenwood Ave., Ste. 210
Niles, IL   60714
Contact: John F. Cuneo, Jr., Pres.

Incorporated in 1945 in IL.

Donors: John F. Cuneo; Milwaukee Golf Development Corp.

Foundation type: Independent foundation.

Financial data (yr. ended 12/31/04): Assets, $35,539,189 (M); expenditures, $2,290,009; qualifying distributions, $1,792,229; giving activities include $755,082 for 103 grants (high: $56,000; low: $1,000), and $1,054,931 for 1 foundation-administered program.

Purpose and activities: Giving primarily for Roman Catholic church support and church-related organizations; funding also for health care, education, and children, youth and social services.

Fields of interest: Elementary/secondary education; Higher education; Health care; Health organizations, association; Human services; Children/youth, services; Roman Catholic agencies & churches; Blind/visually impaired.

Type of support: General/operating support; Continuing support; Building/renovation; Equipment; Scholarship funds; Matching/challenge support.

Limitations: Giving primarily in the metropolitan Chicago, IL, area. No grants to individuals, or for fellowships, or research projects; no loans.

Publications: Annual report.

Application information: Application form not required.

Initial approach: Letter

Copies of proposal: 1

Deadline(s): None

Board meeting date(s): May and Oct.

Final notification: 2 months

Officers and Directors:* John F. Cuneo, Jr.,* Pres.; Herta Cuneo,* V.P.; John F. Tomisek, Secy.-Treas.; Leonard P. Diorio; Andrea Hasten; James J. Hasten; Bishop George Rassas; Joan E. Steel; Katherine White.

EIN: 362261606

Selected grants: The following grants were reported in 2004.

$56,000 to Holy Family Preservation Society, Chicago, IL.

$25,000 to Benedictine University, Lisle, IL.

$25,000 to Big Shoulders Fund, Chicago, IL.

$15,000 to Catholic Charities.

$15,000 to YMCA.

$10,000 to Lumen Christi Institute, Chicago, IL.

$10,000 to Saint Mary of the Angels Parish, Chicago, IL.

$5,000 to Chicago Jesuit Academy, Chicago, IL.

$5,000 to Salvation Army.

$3,000 to Chicago Bible Society, Chicago, IL.

2693
D and R Fund ◇
500 W. Monroe St., Ste. 2660
Chicago, IL   60661-3630   (312) 621-6216
Contact: James J. Glasser, Treas.

Incorporated in 1951 in IL.

Donors: Samuel R. Rosenthal†; Marie-Louise Rosenthal; Carolyn S. Dreyfus†; Alice L. Dreyfus†.

Foundation type: Independent foundation.

Financial data (yr. ended 12/31/04): Assets, $13,657,673 (M); gifts received, $344,798; expenditures, $1,105,583; qualifying distributions, $923,000; giving activities include $923,000 for 10 + grants (high: $150,000).

Purpose and activities: Giving for civic affairs, culture, education and organizations dealing with urban problems.

Fields of interest: Arts; Education; Medical care, rehabilitation; Health care; Mental health/crisis services; Housing/shelter; Youth development, services; Human services; Civil rights; Community development.

Limitations: Applications not accepted. Giving primarily in the Chicago, IL, metropolitan area. No grants to individuals, or for building or endowment funds or operating budgets.

Application information: Contributes only to pre-selected organizations.

Board meeting date(s): As necessary

Officers and Directors:* Marie-Louise Rosenthal,* Pres.; Louise R. Glasser,* V.P.; Babette H. Rosenthal,* V.P.; James J. Glasser,* Treas.; Emily Glasser; Samuel L. Rosenthal.

EIN: 366057159

2694
D.A.S. Charitable Fund for the Preservation of Feline Animal Life ◇
1580 S. Milwaukee Ave., Ste. 410
Libertyville, IL   60048
Contact: Dennis Ryan, Tr.

Established in 2002 in IL.

Donor: Steven C. Pearson†.

Foundation type: Independent foundation.

Financial data (yr. ended 12/31/05): Assets, $8,749,938 (M); expenditures, $694,951; qualifying distributions, $643,075; giving activities include $496,423 for 27 grants (high: $75,000; low: $2,500).

Purpose and activities: Giving limited to the promotion and preservation of animal life.

Fields of interest: Animal welfare.

Limitations: Giving limited to Lake County, IL. No grants to individuals.

Application information:

Initial approach: Letter

Final notification: None

Trustee: Dennis Ryan.

EIN: 300068578

2695
D.H.R. Foundation ◇
333 W. Wacker Dr., Ste. 830
Chicago, IL   60606

Donors: Donald H. Rumsfeld; Joyce P. Rumsfeld.

Foundation type: Independent foundation.

Financial data (yr. ended 12/31/04): Assets, $14,887,309 (M); expenditures, $489,964;

qualifying distributions, $459,970; giving activities include $444,950 for 66 grants (high: $50,000; low: $200).

Fields of interest: Museums (art); Historic preservation/historical societies; Arts; Education, single organization support; Higher education; Education; Substance abuse, treatment; Human services; Children/youth, services; International relief; Federated giving programs; American studies; Protestant agencies & churches.

Limitations: Applications not accepted. Giving primarily in CA, Washington, DC, IL, with emphasis on Chicago, Taos, NM, and New York, NY; some limited funding nationally. No grants to individuals.

Application information: Contributes only to pre-selected organizations.

Officers: Donald H. Rumsfeld, Pres.; Joyce P. Rumsfeld, V.P.; James M. Denny, Secy.-Treas.

EIN: 364283822

Selected grants: The following grants were reported in 2004.

$50,000 to Santa Fe Waldorf School, Santa Fe, NM. For unrestricted support.

$30,000 to Gerald R. Ford Foundation, Grand Rapids, MI. For unrestricted support.

$25,000 to American Enterprise Institute for Public Policy Research, DC. For unrestricted support.

$25,000 to Chicago Foundation for Education, Chicago, IL. For unrestricted support.

$25,000 to National D-Day Museum, New Orleans, LA. For unrestricted support.

$25,000 to Special Operations Fund, Arlington, VA. For unrestricted support.

$20,000 to Christ Church, DC. For unrestricted support.

$20,000 to National Park Foundation, DC. For unrestricted support.

$20,000 to W E T A-FM, DC.

$11,000 to Princeton University, Princeton, NJ. For unrestricted support.

2696
Davee Foundation ▼ ✧

c/o Chas Stern - Wildman, Harrold, Allen
225 W. Wacker Dr., Ste. 3000
Chicago, IL 60606-1229
Contact: Ruth D. Davee, Pres.

Established in 1964 in IL.

Donor: Ken M. Davee.

Foundation type: Independent foundation.

Financial data (yr. ended 12/31/05): Assets, $129,871,161 (M); expenditures, $3,677,110; qualifying distributions, $3,497,071; giving activities include $3,457,500 for 75 grants (high: $1,000,000; low: $1,000; average: $5,000–$50,000).

Purpose and activities: Support primarily for a university; emphasis also on the arts, hospitals, higher education, social services, and civil rights organizations.

Fields of interest: Arts; Higher education; Medical school/education; Hospitals (general); Human services; Civil rights.

Type of support: General/operating support; Professorships; Research.

Limitations: Applications not accepted. Giving primarily in IL. No grants to individuals.

Application information: Contributes only to pre-selected organizations.

Officer: Ruth D. Davee, Pres.

Directors: J.W. Dugdale, Jr.; Nancy Hensel; Charles A. Stern.

EIN: 366124598

Selected grants: The following grants were reported in 2004.

$1,000,000 to Northwestern University, Medical School, Evanston, IL. For educational and medical research.

$761,000 to Rehabilitation Institute of Chicago, Chicago, IL. For general support.

$500,000 to Childrens Memorial Foundation, Chicago, IL. For general support.

$425,000 to Northwestern Memorial Hospital, Chicago, IL. For general support.

$100,000 to Chicago Symphony Orchestra, Chicago, IL. For general support.

$50,000 to Illinois Philharmonic Orchestra, Park Forest, IL. For general support.

$50,000 to International Music Foundation, Chicago, IL. For general support.

$30,000 to People for the American Way, DC. For general support.

$25,000 to Art Institute of Chicago, Chicago, IL. For general support.

$25,000 to Goodman Theater, Chicago, IL. For general support.

2697
Yosef Davis Family Foundation ✧

3553 W. Peterson Ave., Ste. 300
Chicago, IL 60659-3273

Established in 1999 in IL.

Donor: Yosef Davis.

Foundation type: Independent foundation.

Financial data (yr. ended 12/31/04): Assets, $57,845 (L); gifts received, $364,200; expenditures, $449,735; qualifying distributions, $449,573; giving activities include $449,573 for 336 grants (high: $29,608; low: $3).

Purpose and activities: Giving primarily to Jewish temples and agencies and yeshivas.

Fields of interest: Elementary/secondary education; Jewish agencies & temples.

Limitations: Applications not accepted. Giving on a national basis. No grants to individuals.

Application information: Contributes only to pre-selected organizations.

Directors: Edie Davis; Moshe Davis; Yosef Davis.

EIN: 364262401

2698
Doris & Victor Day Foundation, Inc.

1705 2nd Ave., Ste. 424
Rock Island, IL 61201-8718 (309) 788-2300
Contact: Alan L. Egly, Exec. Dir.
FAX: (309) 788-3298;
E-mail: day.rauch@sbcglobal.net; URL: http://www.dayfoundation.org

Established in 1965 in IL.

Donors: Doris D. Day‡; Victor B. Day‡.

Foundation type: Independent foundation.

Financial data (yr. ended 6/30/05): Assets, $15,395,328 (M); expenditures, $875,371; qualifying distributions, $800,111; giving activities include $696,784 for 103 grants (high: $100,000; low: $165), and $2,000 for 1 employee matching gift.

Purpose and activities: Giving primarily for social services, including child welfare and the homeless.

Fields of interest: Education; Health organizations, association; Employment, services; Employment, training; Housing/shelter, development; Youth development, adult & child programs; Human services; Children/youth, services; Homeless, human services; Minorities; Homeless.

Type of support: General/operating support; Building/renovation; Equipment; Emergency funds; Seed money; Scholarship funds.

Limitations: Giving limited to Scott County, IA, and Rock Island County, IL. No support for religious purposes (except for non-sectarian, community serving programs of religious organizations). No grants to individuals, or for endowment funds.

Publications: Annual report (including application guidelines); Grants list.

Application information: Application form available on foundation Web site. Application form required.
Initial approach: Letter or telephone
Copies of proposal: 1
Deadline(s): May 1
Final notification: Sept. 1

Officers and Directors:* Samuel M. Gilman,* Pres.; Charles Wilson,* V.P.; William R. Stengel, Jr.,* Secy.-Treas.; Alan L. Egly, Exec. Dir.

Number of staff: 1 full-time professional.

EIN: 366131596

Selected grants: The following grants were reported in 2006.

$100,000 to Churches United of the Quad Cities Area, Rock Island, IL. For women and childrens emergency shelter.

$75,000 to Supplemental Emergency Assistance Program.

$43,500 to Rebuilding Together Quad Cities, Davenport, IA. For PROJECT IMPACT Rehab.

$35,000 to Iowa Medical Aid Fund, Cedar Rapids, IA.

$20,000 to Community Health Care, Davenport, IA. For Dental Workforce Development program.

$20,000 to Western Illinois University Foundation, Macomb, IL.

$11,010 to Oak Glen Home Auxiliary. For purchasing ten riser beds.

$6,250 to Planned Parenthood of East Central Iowa, Cedar Rapids, IA. For capital campaign and privacy landscaping.

$5,000 to Prairie State Legal Services, Rockford, IL. For operating support.

$2,000 to Black Hawk College Foundation, Moline, IL. For Adult Education GED fees.

2699
John Deere Foundation ▼

1 John Deere Pl.
Moline, IL 61265 (309) 748-7960
Contact: John W. Bustle, Mgr., Strategic Philanthropy
FAX: (309) 748-7953;
E-mail: bustlejohnw@johndeere.com; URL: http://www.deere.com/en_US/compinfo/csr/community/found.html

Incorporated in 1948 in IL.

Donor: Deere & Co.

Foundation type: Company-sponsored foundation.

Financial data (yr. ended 10/31/05): Assets, $44,372,919 (M); gifts received, $12,204,750; expenditures, $9,644,432; qualifying distributions, $9,617,069; giving activities include $9,274,433 for 224 grants (high: $1,000,000; low: $500), and $559,286 for 2 foundation-administered programs.

Purpose and activities: The foundation supports organizations involved with arts and culture,

education, health, human services, and community development.

Fields of interest: Arts; Education; Health care; Human services; Community development.

Type of support: General/operating support; Continuing support; Annual campaigns; Capital campaigns; Building/renovation; Emergency funds; Program development; Seed money; Fellowships; Scholarship funds; Research; Loaned talent.

Limitations: Giving primarily in areas of company operations in IL, IA, NC, and WI. No support for religious organizations, athletic organizations, political organizations, foundations, tax-supported organizations, or fraternal organizations or sororities. No grants to individuals, or for sports programs, political campaigns, advertising, or marketing; no loans.

Publications: Corporate giving report (including application guidelines).

Application information: Application form not required.

> *Initial approach:* Proposal
> *Copies of proposal:* 1
> *Deadline(s):* None
> *Board meeting date(s):* Quarterly
> *Final notification:* 30 days following board meetings

Officers and Directors: Robert W. Lane,* Chair.; James H. Collins,* Pres.; Mark A. Howze, Secy.; Dennis R. Schwartz, Treas.; Samuel R. Allen; Frances B. Emerson; James R. Jenkins; Michael J. Mack, Jr.; H.J. Markley; Marie Z. Ziegler.

EIN: 366051024

Selected grants: The following grants were reported in 2005.

$1,500,000 to American Red Cross, National Headquarters, DC. 2 grants: $1,000,000, $500,000 (For relief effort for Hurricane Katrina).

$1,000,000 to Kickstart-International, San Francisco, CA. For general support.

$824,350 to United Way of the Quad Cities Area, Davenport, IA.

$750,000 to Lincoln Park Zoo, Chicago, IL. For general support.

$350,000 to United Way, Cedar Valley, Waterloo, IA.

$200,000 to Abraham Lincoln Presidential Library Foundation, Springfield, IL.

$25,000 to American Red Cross of the Quad Cities Area, Moline, IL.

$25,000 to Dartmouth College, Tuck School of Business, Hanover, NH. For general support.

$20,000 to United Way of the Central Savannah River Area, Augusta, GA.

2700
Deering Foundation ✧
410 N. Michigan Ave., Rm. 590
Chicago, IL 60611

Incorporated in 1956 in IL.

Donors: Barbara D. Danielson; Richard E. Danielson, Jr.; Marion D. Campbell; Miami Corp.

Foundation type: Independent foundation.

Financial data (yr. ended 11/30/05): Assets, $15,068,237 (L); expenditures, $827,301; qualifying distributions, $735,277; giving activities include $705,000 for 3 grants (high: $235,000; low: $235,000).

Purpose and activities: Giving primarily for the arts and education.

Fields of interest: Arts education; Performing arts centers; Arts; Higher education; Environment,

natural resources; Hospitals (general); Federated giving programs.

Type of support: General/operating support.

Limitations: Applications not accepted. Giving primarily in IL. No grants to individuals, or for scholarships or fellowships; no loans.

Application information: Contributes only to pre-selected organizations.

Officers and Directors: John Rau,* Pres.; Candida D. Burnap,* V.P.; Barbara S. Danielson,* V.P.; Charles E. Schroeder,* Secy.-Treas.; Charles E. Seitz; Richard Strachan; Stephen M. Strachan; Jocelyn D. Tennille.

EIN: 366051876

2701
DeKalb County Community Foundation ✧
The Atrium Office Ctr.
2600 DeKalb Ave., Ste. J
Sycamore, IL 60178 (815) 748-5383
Contact: Jerome A. Smith, Secy.
FAX: (815) 748-5873;
E-mail: jerry@dekalbcountyfoundation.org;
URL: http://www.dekalbcountyfoundation.org

Established in 1991 in IL; re-incorporated in 1993 under current name.

Foundation type: Community foundation.

Financial data (yr. ended 12/31/05): Assets, $20,149,664 (M); gifts received, $2,301,427; expenditures, $1,118,403; giving activities include $760,016 for 122+ grants, and $72,457 for 44 grants to individuals.

Purpose and activities: The foundation seeks to enhance the quality of life for the citizens of DeKalb County, IL, by: 1) serving donors in achieving their philanthropic objectives; 2) creating and building a lasting source of revenue to benefit the residents of the local community; and 3) providing leadership and resources in addressing community needs.

Fields of interest: Arts; Education; Health care; Human services; Community development.

Type of support: Building/renovation; Equipment; Seed money; Matching/challenge support.

Limitations: Giving primarily in DeKalb County, IL. No support for religious purposes. No grants for capital campaigns, operational phases of established programs, debt reduction, or advertising.

Publications: Application guidelines; Annual report; Informational brochure; Newsletter; Occasional report.

Application information: Visit foundation Web site for application form and guidelines. Application form required.

> *Initial approach:* Contact foundation
> *Copies of proposal:* 7
> *Deadline(s):* Feb. 23 or Sept. 1
> *Board meeting date(s):* Jan., Apr., July, and Oct.
> *Final notification:* Approx. 60 days

Officers and Directors: William R. Mullins,* Pres.; Bradley V. Brown,* V.P.; Jerome A. Smith,* Secy. and Exec. Dir.; Thomas J. Matya,* Treas.; Larry D. Bolles; Micki Chulick; Evelina J. Cichy; Gary W. Cordes; Edward Davis; Peter Dell; Tim Dunlop; Joan Fenstermaker; Elroy E. Golden; Daniel Gudmunson; Lana Haines; Margy Hill; Suzanne Juday; Jane Ovitz; Mary E. Pritchard; Jesus Romero; Mariam Wassmann; Thomas R. Weber.

Number of staff: 1 full-time professional; 1 full-time support.

EIN: 363788167

2702
N. Demos Foundation, Inc. ✧
c/o The Northern Trust Co.
50 S. LaSalle St.
Chicago, IL 60675 (312) 630-6000
Contact: Diane Day, Secy.
FAX: (312) 444-4122; E-mail: ddm@ntrs.com;
Additional tel.: (312) 444-5933

Incorporated in 1964 in NY.

Donor: Nicholas Demos†.

Foundation type: Independent foundation.

Financial data (yr. ended 6/30/05): Assets, $4,258,430 (M); expenditures, $411,545; qualifying distributions, $378,261; giving activities include $362,999 for 29 grants (high: $48,600; low: $5,400).

Purpose and activities: Grants for educational projects, social work activities, and health care assistance in Greece.

Fields of interest: Education; Children/youth, services.

International interests: Greece.

Type of support: General/operating support; Scholarship funds.

Limitations: Giving limited to Greece. No grants to individuals.

Publications: Application guidelines.

Application information: Application form required.

> *Initial approach:* Letter
> *Copies of proposal:* 1
> *Deadline(s):* Sept. 1
> *Board meeting date(s):* Fall
> *Final notification:* Dec. 31

Officers: Robert F. Reusche, Chair.; Charles Gray, Pres.; Diane Day, Secy.; Hugh Magill, Treas.

Directors: Mrs. Desi Bakalis; Elizabeth Gebhard; Metropolitan Iakovos; Hon. Paul C. Lillios.

EIN: 366165689

Selected grants: The following grants were reported in 2004.

$40,000 to Cerebral Palsy Greece, Argyroupoli, Greece. .

$38,000 to Social Work Foundation, Attika, Greece. .

$25,000 to Anatolia College, Thessaloniki, Greece. .

$15,000 to American Farm School, Thessaloniki, Greece. .

$15,000 to Patriarchal Institute for Patristic Studies, Thessaloniki, Greece. .

$12,500 to American School of Classical Studies at Athens, Athens, Greece. .

$10,000 to American College of Greece, Athens, Greece. .

$8,000 to Spastics Society, Athens, Greece. .

$5,000 to Saint Tabitha Orphanage, Greece. .

$5,000 to Sofir Orphanage, Greece. .

2703
James and Catherine Denny Foundation ✧
1 N. Wacker Dr., Ste. 4055
Chicago, IL 60606

Established in 1993 in IL.

Donors: James M. Denny; Catherine M. Denny.

Foundation type: Independent foundation.

Financial data (yr. ended 12/31/04): Assets, $1,808,761 (M); gifts received, $735,858; expenditures, $674,457; qualifying distributions, $662,377; giving activities include $662,377 for 45 grants (high: $333,172; low: $100).

Purpose and activities: Giving primarily to Roman Catholic agencies.
Fields of interest: Elementary/secondary education; Roman Catholic agencies & churches.
Limitations: Applications not accepted. Giving primarily in Chicago, IL. No grants to individuals.
Application information: Contributes only to pre-selected organizations.
Trustees: Catherine M. Denny; James M. Denny.
EIN: 367067862

2704
Dillon Foundation ▼ ◇
P.O. Box 537
Sterling, IL   61081   (815) 626-9000
Contact: Peter W. Dillon, Pres.

Incorporated in 1953 in IL.
Donor: members of the Dillon family.
Foundation type: Independent foundation.
Financial data (yr. ended 10/31/05): Assets, $85,900,701 (M); expenditures, $5,073,560; qualifying distributions, $4,281,264; giving activities include $4,173,792 for 153 grants (high: $870,102; low: $250; average: $1,000–$25,000).
Purpose and activities: Support for local community economic development and civic and urban affairs; technology and other education; social services and youth; historic preservation and museums; recreation; and libraries in and around Sterling, IL.
Fields of interest: Museums; Historic preservation/historical societies; Vocational education, post-secondary; Libraries/library science; Education; Employment; Recreation; Human services; Children/youth, services; Community development; Government/public administration.
Type of support: General/operating support; Continuing support; Annual campaigns; Capital campaigns; Building/renovation; Equipment; Land acquisition; Endowments; Emergency funds; Program development; Seed money; Scholarship funds; In-kind gifts; Matching/challenge support.
Limitations: Giving primarily in the Sterling, IL, area. No grants to individuals; no loans.
Application information: Application form not required.
 Initial approach: Letter
 Copies of proposal: 1
 Deadline(s): None
 Board meeting date(s): Feb. and Aug.
 Final notification: As soon as possible
Officers and Directors:* Peter W. Dillon,* Pres.; James M. Boesen,* Secy.; Margo Dillon; Patrick Dillon; Gale D. Inglee; Mark Inglee; Molly Dillion-McGee; Christine Montgomery.
Number of staff: 1 part-time support.
EIN: 366059349
Selected grants: The following grants were reported in 2005.
$870,102 to Sterling Park District, Sterling, IL.
$525,494 to Sterling, City of, Sterling, IL.
$525,173 to Greater Sterling Development Corporation, Sterling, IL.
$505,058 to Community Unit School District 5, Sterling, IL.
$408,595 to YMCA, Sterling-Rock Falls Family, Sterling, IL. 2 grants: $70,833 (For Woodlawn Arts Academy), $337,762 (For Woodlawn Arts Academy).
$75,151 to Sauk Valley College Foundation, Dixon, IL.
$6,500 to Rock Falls Public Library, Rock Falls, IL.
$5,000 to River Cities Rollers, Sterling, IL.

$2,650 to Freedoms Foundation at Valley Forge, Valley Forge, PA.

2705
Domanada Foundation ◇
c/o David E. Sveen
1749 S. Naperville Rd., Ste. 206
Wheaton, IL   60187

Established in 1989 in IL.
Donors: Donald E. Sveen; Marjorie L. Sveen.
Foundation type: Independent foundation.
Financial data (yr. ended 12/31/05): Assets, $25,221,692 (M); gifts received, $250,000; expenditures, $1,581,410; qualifying distributions, $1,408,327; giving activities include $1,180,800 for 46 grants (high: $110,000; low: $1,000).
Purpose and activities: Giving primarily for human services and Christian agencies and churches.
Fields of interest: Higher education; Theological school/education; Hospitals (general); Human services; Religious federated giving programs; Christian agencies & churches.
Limitations: Applications not accepted. Giving primarily in IL. No grants to individuals.
Application information: Contributes only to pre-selected organizations.
Trustees: Nancy L. Jackson; David E. Sveen; Donald E. Sveen; Marjorie L. Sveen.
EIN: 366916790
Selected grants: The following grants were reported in 2003.
$100,000 to North Park Theological Seminary, Chicago, IL.
$40,000 to Church Resource Ministries, Anaheim, CA. 2 grants: $20,000 each
$35,000 to Josiah Venture, Wheaton, IL.
$25,000 to Breakthrough Urban Ministries, Chicago, IL.
$25,000 to Chicago Humanities Festival, Chicago, IL.
$25,000 to Covenant Bible College, Windsor, CO.
$25,000 to Outreach Community Ministries, Wheaton, IL.
$15,000 to Evangelical Covenant Church, Chicago, IL.
$14,000 to John Stott Ministries, Carol Stream, IL.

2706
Gaylord and Dorothy Donnelley Foundation ◇
35 E. Wacker Dr., Ste. 2600
Chicago, IL   60601-2102   (312) 977-2700
Contact: Judith M. Stockdale, Exec. Dir.
FAX: (312) 977-1686; E-mail: gddf@gddf.org;
URL: http://www.gddf.org

Incorporated in 1952 in IL.
Donors: Gaylord Donnelley†; Dorothy Ranney Donnelley†; Anthony Dean; Inanna Donnelley.
Foundation type: Independent foundation.
Financial data (yr. ended 12/31/04): Assets, $140,003,213 (M); gifts received, $13,403,341; expenditures, $4,877,674; qualifying distributions, $4,629,110; giving activities include $3,256,938 for grants.
Purpose and activities: Primary areas of interest include conservation and environment, education, arts and culture, and short term food and shelter programs.

Fields of interest: Arts; Education; Environment, natural resources; Environment; Housing/shelter, development; Youth development.
Type of support: Employee matching gifts; General/operating support; Program development.
Limitations: Giving primarily in the Chicago, IL, area and in the Lowcountry area of SC. No support for religious purposes. No grants to individuals, or for pledges, endowments, capital campaigns, benefits, conferences, meetings, eradication of deficits, research, or studies, publications, films, videos or fundraising events; no loans.
Publications: Application guidelines; Annual report; Grants list.
Application information: The foundation does not accept unsolicited proposals under its Adolescent Education and Community Welfare areas at this time. Complete guidelines for each program are available on foundation Web site. Telephone or fax requests not considered. Application form required.
 Initial approach: Letter requesting guidelines
 Copies of proposal: 1
 Deadline(s): None
 Board meeting date(s): Mar., June, and Nov.
 Final notification: 1 month after board review
Officers and Directors:* Laura Donnelley-Morton,* Chair.; Strachan Donnelley, Ph.D.*, Vice-Chair.; Shawn M. Donnelley,* Secy.-Treas.; Judith M. Stockdale, Exec. Dir.; Elliott R. Donnelley,* Life Dir.; Jane Rishel, Life Dir.; Gerald Adelmann; James B. Edwards; Ronne Hartfield; Coy Johnston; Nancy F. Talbot; Max E. Wheeler.
Number of staff: 4 full-time professional.
EIN: 366108460

2707
R. R. Donnelley Foundation
77 W. Wacker Dr., 9th Fl.
Chicago, IL   60601-1696   (312) 326-8102
Contact: Susan M. Levy
FAX: (312) 326-8262; E-mail: susan.levy@rrd.com;
URL: http://www.rrd.com/wwwRRD/AboutUs/Community/CommunityInvolvement.asp

Established in 2000 in IL.
Donor: R.R. Donnelley & Sons Co.
Foundation type: Company-sponsored foundation.
Financial data (yr. ended 12/31/04): Assets, $708,115 (M); gifts received, $500,200; expenditures, $966,082; qualifying distributions, $964,780; giving activities include $963,394 for grants.
Purpose and activities: The foundation supports organizations involved with literacy and reading.
Fields of interest: Education, reading.
Type of support: General/operating support; Employee volunteer services; Sponsorships; Employee-related scholarships.
Limitations: Giving on a national basis. No support for religious organizations. No grants to individuals (except for employee-related scholarships), or for television, radio, film, video, medical research, or equipment.
Application information: Application form not required.
 Initial approach: Proposal
 Deadline(s): Jan. 1 through Nov. 1
 Board meeting date(s): Quarterly
Officers: Calvin G. Butler, Pres.; Suzanne S. Bettman, Secy.; Thomas J. Quinlan, Treas.
EIN: 364398696

2708
The Donnelley Foundation
c/o Thomas E. Donnelley, II
360 N. Michigan Ave., Ste. 1009
Chicago, IL 60601-3803

Incorporated in 1954 in IL.
Donors: Elliott Donnelley†; Ann S. Hardy†; Thomas E. Donnelley II; James R. Donnelley; Barbara C. Donnelley; Nina H. Donnelley; Robert G. Donnelley; Miranda S. Donnelley; David E. Donnelley.
Foundation type: Independent foundation.
Financial data (yr. ended 12/31/05): Assets, $15,662,636 (M); gifts received, $26,528; expenditures, $1,140,719; qualifying distributions, $956,430; giving activities include $929,680 for 159 grants (high: $85,000; low: $50).
Purpose and activities: Giving primarily to wildlife conservation, youth welfare, libraries, historic preservation, and educational and medical institutions with which the foundation directors have long-term relationships and/or serve on the boards.
Fields of interest: Museums; Historic preservation/historical societies; Libraries/library science; Education; Animals/wildlife, preservation/protection; Hospitals (general); Children/youth, services.
Type of support: General/operating support; Continuing support; Annual campaigns; Capital campaigns; Building/renovation; Endowments; Seed money; Matching/challenge support.
Limitations: Applications not accepted. Giving primarily in CA, CT, IL, MA, MT, OR and VT. No support for political organizations. No grants to individuals, or for pledges or multi-year grants.
Application information: Contributes only to pre-selected organizations.
Board meeting date(s): As required
Officers and Directors:* Thomas E. Donnelley II,* Pres.; James R. Donnelley,* 1st V.P.; David E. Donnelley,* V.P. and Secy.; Robert G. Donnelley,* V.P. and Treas.
EIN: 366066894
Selected grants: The following grants were reported in 2005.
$21,000 to National Trust for Historic Preservation, DC. 2 grants: $20,000, $1,000
$15,000 to Lake Forest College, Lake Forest, IL.
$13,000 to Sonoma Valley Education Foundation, Sonoma, CA.
$10,000 to Chicago Youth Centers, Chicago, IL.
$10,000 to United Way International, Alexandria, VA.
$7,500 to Friends of Ryerson Woods, Deerfield, IL.
$4,000 to Sarah Lawrence College, Bronxville, NY.
$2,500 to Lake Forest Open Lands Association, Lake Forest, IL.
$1,500 to Chicago Foundation for Women, Chicago, IL.

2709
Sally and James Dowdle Family Foundation ◇
c/o Madden, Jiganti, Moore & Sinars
190 S. LaSalle St., Ste. 1700
Chicago, IL 60603

Established in 1997 in IL.
Donor: James C. Dowdle.
Foundation type: Independent foundation.
Financial data (yr. ended 3/31/06): Assets, $1,026,186 (M); gifts received, $4,938; expenditures, $464,613; qualifying distributions,

$447,750; giving activities include $447,750 for 30 grants (high: $200,000; low: $250).
Purpose and activities: Giving primarily for education, Roman Catholic agencies and churches, health and human services, and youth organizations.
Fields of interest: Secondary school/education; Theological school/education; Education; Hospitals (general); Health care; Health organizations, association; Youth development; Human services; Roman Catholic agencies & churches.
Limitations: Applications not accepted. Giving primarily in IL. No grants to individuals.
Application information: Contributes only to pre-selected organizations.
Officers and Directors:* Sally S. Dowdle,* Pres.; Colleen D. Burke,* V.P.; James C. Dowdle, Jr.,* V.P.; Jeanne D. Dwyer,* V.P.; Sarah D. Tyrrell,* V.P.; James C. Dowdle,* Secy.-Treas.
EIN: 364157838

2710
The Richard H. Driehaus Foundation ▼ ◇
203 N. Wabash Ave., Ste. 1800
Chicago, IL 60601-2417 (312) 641-5772
Contact: Sunny Fischer, Exec. Dir.
FAX: (312) 641-5736;
E-mail: driehausfoundation@ameritech.net;
URL: http://www.driehausfoundation.org

Established in 1983 in IL.
Donors: Richard H. Driehaus; John D. and Catherine T. MacArthur Foundation; Reva and David Logan Foundation; Leveraging Investment in Creativity.
Foundation type: Independent foundation.
Financial data (yr. ended 12/31/04): Assets, $58,561,854 (M); gifts received, $454,610; expenditures, $12,655,887; qualifying distributions, $12,134,849; giving activities include $11,457,513 for 328 grants (high: $1,000,000; low: $200; average: $1,000–$50,000), and $30,000 for 3 grants to individuals.
Purpose and activities: The foundation benefits individuals and communities primarily by preserving and enhancing built and natural environments through historic preservation, recognition of quality community and landscape design, and conserving open space. The foundation also supports the performing and visual arts and helps organizations that provide opportunities for economically disadvantaged individuals.
Fields of interest: Visual arts, design; Historic preservation/historical societies; Arts; Housing/shelter, development; Human services; Economic development.
International interests: Scotland.
Type of support: Grants to individuals; General/operating support; Capital campaigns; Emergency funds; Program development; Publication; Seed money; Matching/challenge support.
Limitations: Giving primarily in the Chicago, IL, area. Generally, no support for arts education or arts outreach, community theater or community dance, public, private or parochial education, or health care.
Publications: Biennial report.
Application information: For general funding areas, the foundation accepts no unsolicited proposals, but welcomes letters of inquiry and phone calls. Arts organizations with budgets under $500,000, as well as theater and dance groups with budgets under $150,000 wishing to apply should call for an

application or download application from the foundation's Web site.
Final notification: 4 - 5 months
Officers and Directors:* Richard H. Driehaus,* Pres.; Elizabeth Driehaus,* Secy.; Dorothy Mellin,* Treas.; Sunny Fischer, Exec. Dir.
Number of staff: 2 full-time professional; 1 full-time support.
EIN: 363261347
Selected grants: The following grants were reported in 2004.
$6,100,000 to Richard H. Driehaus Museum, Chicago, IL. 7 grants: $1,000,000, $1,000,000 (For renovation of Nickerson Mansion), $100,000 (For renovation of Nickerson Mansion), $1,000,000 (For renovation of Nickerson Mansion), $1,000,000 (For renovation of Nickerson Mansion), $1,000,000 (For renovation of Nickerson Mansion), $1,000,000 (For renovation of Nickerson Mansion).
$200,000 to Millennium Park, Chicago, IL.
$59,393 to Local Initiatives Support Corporation (LISC), Chicago, IL. For Chicago Neighborhood Development Awards.
$50,000 to W B E Z, Chicago, IL. For Annual Third Coast International Audio Festival.

2711
The Duchossois Family Foundation ◇
(formerly The Duchossois Foundation)
203 N. Wabash, Ste. 1800
Chicago, IL 60601 (312) 641-5765
Contact: Iris Krieg, Exec. Dir.

Established in 1984 in IL.
Donors: Duchossois Industries, Inc.; Thrall Car Manufacturing Co.; Duchossois TECnology Partners, LLC; Chamberlain Group, Inc.
Foundation type: Company-sponsored foundation.
Financial data (yr. ended 12/31/04): Assets, $6,229,102 (M); gifts received, $5,000,000; expenditures, $1,500,121; qualifying distributions, $1,487,149; giving activities include $1,351,699 for 52 grants (high: $1,000,000; low: $500).
Purpose and activities: The foundation supports organizations involved with arts and culture, mental health, cancer, HIV/AIDS, and human services.
Fields of interest: Arts; Mental health/crisis services; Cancer; AIDS; Cancer research; AIDS research; Human services.
Type of support: General/operating support; Annual campaigns; Capital campaigns; Research.
Limitations: Applications not accepted. Giving primarily in the metropolitan Chicago, IL, area.
Application information: Contributes only to pre-selected organizations.
Board meeting date(s): 4 times per year
Officers and Directors:* Kimberly Duchossois,* Pres.; Craig J. Duchossois,* V.P.; R. Bruce Duchossois,* V.P.; Dayle Duchossois Fortino; Richard L. Duchossois.
Number of staff: 3 part-time professional; 1 part-time support.
EIN: 363327987
Selected grants: The following grants were reported in 2004.
$1,041,000 to American Cancer Society, Chicago, IL. 3 grants: $25,000, $1,000,000, $16,000
$4,308 to Susan G. Komen Breast Cancer Foundation, Hartland, WI.

2712
Dunard Fund USA, Ltd. ✦
555 Skokie Blvd., Ste. 555
Northbrook, IL 60062-2845

Established around 1993 in IL.
Donors: Consolidated Electrical Distributors, Inc.; LCR-M Corp.
Foundation type: Company-sponsored foundation.
Financial data (yr. ended 12/31/04): Assets, $19,160,543 (M); gifts received, $1,576,739; expenditures, $2,693,684; qualifying distributions, $2,605,832; giving activities include $2,605,535 for 35 grants (high: $1,000,000; low: $500).
Purpose and activities: The foundation supports organizations involved with visual and performing arts, music, education, and human services.
Fields of interest: Visual arts; Performing arts, music; Performing arts, education; Education; Human services.
Type of support: General/operating support; Continuing support; Capital campaigns; Building/renovation; Endowments; Scholarship funds.
Limitations: Applications not accepted. Giving on a national basis, with emphasis on Los Angeles, CA, and New York, NY. No grants to individuals.
Application information: Contributes only to organizations referred by known and highly respected figures.
Board meeting date(s): Weekly
Officers and Directors:* Carol C. Hogel,* Pres.; Pamela B. Johnson,* Secy.; Catherine C. Hogel; Elisabeth W. Norman.
EIN: 980087034
Selected grants: The following grants were reported in 2003.
$400,315 to Los Angeles Philharmonic Association, Los Angeles, CA. For Edinburgh International Festival.
$25,000 to Beginning with Children Foundation, New York, NY. For general support.
$25,000 to Virginia Opera Association, Norfolk, VA. For operating support.
$7,000 to Schneider Fund for Young Musicians, Marlboro, NJ. For scholarships.
$6,446 to Metropolitan Museum of Art, New York, NY. For annual support.
$5,000 to Museum of Contemporary Art (MOCA), Los Angeles, CA. For annual support.
$5,000 to New York City Ballet, New York, NY. For operating support.
$4,345 to Los Angeles County Museum of Art, Los Angeles, CA. For operating support.
$2,000 to American Youth Symphony, Los Angeles, CA. For endowment.
$500 to K U S C-FM, Los Angeles, CA. For annual support.

2713
The DuPage Community Foundation
2100 Manchester Rd., Bldg. A, Ste. 303
Wheaton, IL 60187-4584 (630) 665-5556
Contact: David M. McGowan, Pres.; For grants: Bonnie L. Heydorn, Dir., Grants
FAX: (630) 665-9571; E-mail: dmm@dcfdn.org; Additional E-mail: cadams@dcfdn.org; Grant application E-mail: bheydorn@dcfdn.org;
URL: http://www.dcfdn.org

Established in 1986 in IL as fund of Chicago Community Trust; became a separate entity in 1994.
Foundation type: Community foundation.

Financial data (yr. ended 6/30/05): Assets, $17,644,331 (M); gifts received, $2,355,504; expenditures, $1,113,027; giving activities include $569,820 for grants.
Purpose and activities: The foundation was created to benefit the residents of DuPage County, IL. It receives contributions and bequests into a permanent endowment that continues to grow and help meet the needs of its community. Priorities in grantmaking are arts and culture, civic and environmental affairs, education, health, and human services.
Fields of interest: Historic preservation/historical societies; Arts; Education; Environment, pollution control; Environmental education; Environment; Animals/wildlife, preservation/protection; Health care; Mental health/crisis services; Children/youth, services; Human services; Civil rights.
Type of support: General/operating support; Building/renovation; Equipment; Program development; Seed money; Scholarship funds; Matching/challenge support.
Limitations: Giving primarily in DuPage County, IL. No support for religious purposes, disease-specific organizations, or private foundations or private operating foundations. No grants to individuals (except from designated scholarship funds) or for endowment.
Publications: Application guidelines; Annual report; Financial statement; Grants list; Informational brochure; Newsletter.
Application information: Visit foundation Web site for application form and guidelines. Application form required.
Initial approach: Telephone
Copies of proposal: 2
Deadline(s): Feb. and Aug.
Board meeting date(s): Bimonthly
Officers and Trustees:* Jack E. Mensching,* Chair.; David P. Aldridge,* Vice-Chair.; David M. McGowan, Pres.; Carson R. Yeager, Secy.; Norman J. Beles,* Treas.; Anna C. Ball; Dalip Bammi; Joseph Beavers; Betty Bradshaw; Cleve E. Carney; George N. Gilkerson, Jr.; Janet A. Hodge; Frank C. Hudetz; Emmett P. Malloy, Jr.; Laurie K. McMahon; Raymond C. Mines; Vincent A. Naccarato; Nancy E. Sindelar; Joyce Van Der Moben.
Number of staff: 3 full-time professional; 2 part-time professional.
EIN: 363978733

2714
Eddema Foundation ✦ ☆
700 N. Linden Ave.
Oak Park, IL 60302

Established in 1991 in IL.
Donor: Edward Petrick.
Foundation type: Independent foundation.
Financial data (yr. ended 12/31/05): Assets, $8,413,609 (M); expenditures, $414,107; qualifying distributions, $380,732; giving activities include $380,732 for 4 grants (high: $315,000; low: $5,732).
Purpose and activities: Focus is on land conservation, including individual grants to low income persons ages 11-18 years to learn how to stay in a different environment.
Fields of interest: Environment, land resources; Youth development.
Limitations: Applications not accepted. Giving primarily in Oak Park, IL; giving also in MI. No grants to individuals.

Application information: Contributes only to pre-selected organizations.
Officer: Edward Petrick, Mgr.
EIN: 363781866

2715
Edwardson Family Foundation ✦
(formerly 747 Foundation)
c/o CDW Corp.
200 N. Milwaukee Ave.
Vernon Hills, IL 60061-1517

Established in 1990 in IL.
Donors: John A. Edwardson; Catherine O. Edwardson.
Foundation type: Independent foundation.
Financial data (yr. ended 12/31/05): Assets, $4,769,589 (M); gifts received, $284,175; expenditures, $553,301; qualifying distributions, $538,431; giving activities include $538,329 for 59 grants (high: $200,000; low: $50; average: $1,000–$10,000).
Purpose and activities: Giving primarily for education, as well as for human services, particularly to a food depository, and for the arts, including a music school.
Fields of interest: Arts education; Arts; Higher education; Health organizations, association; Food services; Children/youth, services; Christian agencies & churches.
Limitations: Applications not accepted. Giving primarily in IL, with emphasis on Chicago; giving also in West Lafayette, IN. No grants to individuals.
Application information: Contributes only to pre-selected organizations.
Trustee: John A. Edwardson.
EIN: 363757845
Selected grants: The following grants were reported in 2004.
$500,000 to Purdue University, West Lafayette, IN. 2 grants: $250,000 each
$60,000 to Ravinia Festival Association, Highland Park, IL. 2 grants: $10,000, $50,000
$50,000 to University of Chicago, Chicago, IL.
$42,500 to Habitat for Humanity, Morristown, NJ.
$40,000 to Music Institute of Chicago, Winnetka, IL. 2 grants: $20,000 each
$10,000 to Purdue Foundation, West Lafayette, IN.
$5,000 to Art Institute of Chicago, Chicago, IL.

2716
George M. Eisenberg Foundation for Charities ✦
(formerly Eisenberg Foundation for Charities)
2340 S. Arlington Heights Rd., Ste. 615
Arlington Heights, IL 60005 (847) 981-0545
Contact: James Marousis, Treas.

Established in 1989 in IL.
Donor: George M. Eisenberg‡.
Foundation type: Independent foundation.
Financial data (yr. ended 12/31/05): Assets, $60,232,705 (M); expenditures, $3,465,508; qualifying distributions, $3,045,943; giving activities include $2,854,500 for 130 grants (high: $1,025,000; low: $500).
Purpose and activities: Giving primarily for medicine, health, education, and physical, emotional, and social assistance for the benefit of underprivileged youth and the elderly.

Fields of interest: Elementary/secondary education; Higher education; Hospitals (general); Medical care, rehabilitation; Public health; Medical research, institute; Youth development, services; Human services; Children/youth, services; Aging, centers/services; Religion.

Type of support: General/operating support; Capital campaigns.

Limitations: Giving limited to IL and MN, with emphasis on metropolitan Chicago and DuPage County, IL, and Rochester, MN. No support for political organizations, elementary or secondary schools, public colleges or universities (unless related to medical care), churches, or religious education. No grants to individuals, or for endowment funds, advertising, or purchasing of tickets for fundraising.

Application information: Application form not required.

Initial approach: 1- to 2-page letter

Deadline(s): July 31

Board meeting date(s): Eight or more times per year

Final notification: Nov. or Dec.

Officers and Directors:* Thomas Spelsberg,* Pres.; Thomas E. O'Brien,* Secy.; James Marousis,* Treas.; Helen Banas; James Murphy.

EIN: 363689650

Selected grants: The following grants were reported in 2005.

$1,025,000 to Mayo Foundation for Medical Education and Research, Rochester, MN.

$175,000 to Maryville Academy, Des Plaines, IL.

$87,500 to Boys and Girls Clubs of Chicago, Chicago, IL.

$50,000 to Childrens Memorial Foundation, Chicago, IL.

$50,000 to Marklund Childrens Home, Glendale Heights, IL.

$50,000 to Northwest Home for the Aged, Chicago, IL.

$30,000 to La Rabida Childrens Hospital, Chicago, IL.

$5,000 to Saint Jude Childrens Research Hospital, Memphis, TN.

$4,000 to Little Sisters of the Poor, Chicago, IL.

$3,000 to Blessed Sacrament Youth Center, Chicago, IL.

2717
Elgin Financial Foundation ✧

1695 Larkin Ave.
Elgin, IL 60123 (847) 741-3900
Contact: Ursula Wilson, Secy.

Established in 1998 in DE and IL.

Donors: Elgin Financial Savings Bank; EFC Bancorp, Inc.

Foundation type: Company-sponsored foundation.

Financial data (yr. ended 12/31/03): Assets, $10,610,852 (M); expenditures, $528,894; qualifying distributions, $521,836; giving activities include $504,648 for 87 grants (high: $60,000; low: $200).

Purpose and activities: The foundation supports organizations involved with arts and culture, education, health, housing, youth development, human services, community development, and religion.

Fields of interest: Arts; Education; Health care; Housing/shelter; Youth development; Human services; Community development; Religion.

Limitations: Giving limited to areas of company operations in IL.

Application information: Application form required.

Initial approach: Contact foundation for application form

Deadline(s): Feb. 28, June 30, and Oct. 31

Final notification: Within 2 months

Officers and Directors:* Leo M. Flanagan, Jr.,* Chair.; Thomas I. Anderson,* Vice-Chair.; Barrett J. O'Connor,* C.E.O. and Pres.; James J. Kovac,* Sr. V.P., Treas., and C.F.O.; Ursula Wilson, Secy.; James A. Alpeter; Randolph W. Brittain; Larry Narum; Vincent C. Norton; Peter A. Traeger.

EIN: 364219647

2718
Gail G. Ellis Foundation, Inc. ✧ ☆

c/o David Friedlander
2801 Lakeside Dr., 3rd Fl.
Bannockburn, IL 60015

Established in 1995 in IL.

Donor: Gail G. Ellis.

Foundation type: Independent foundation.

Financial data (yr. ended 12/31/05): Assets, $9,948,699 (M); gifts received, $10,002,877; expenditures, $409,675; qualifying distributions, $409,000; giving activities include $409,000 for 59 grants (high: $100,000; low: $1,000).

Fields of interest: Arts; Higher education; Education; Health care; Health organizations, association; Human services.

Limitations: Applications not accepted. No grants to individuals.

Application information: Contributes only to pre-selected organizations.

Directors: Gail G. Ellis; Brian C. Sullivan; Carrie E. Sullivan.

EIN: 364076867

2719
Emerson Directors and Officers Charitable Trust ✧

c/o The Northern Trust Co.
P.O. Box 803878
Chicago, IL 60680

Established in 1986 in MO.

Foundation type: Independent foundation.

Financial data (yr. ended 12/31/04): Assets, $2,240,239 (M); gifts received, $21,027; expenditures, $914,872; qualifying distributions, $894,872; giving activities include $894,872 for 116 grants (high: $200,000; low: $25).

Purpose and activities: Giving primarily for higher and other education; support also for children and youth services, including children's health; funding also for other health associations, and to Christian and Protestant churches and organizations.

Fields of interest: Arts; Secondary school/education; Higher education; Education; Health care; Health organizations, association; Boy scouts; Children/youth, services; Federated giving programs; Christian agencies & churches; Protestant agencies & churches.

Type of support: Continuing support; Annual campaigns; Endowments.

Limitations: Giving primarily in St. Louis, MO.

Application information:

Deadline(s): None

Trustees: Robert W. Staley; and 16 additional trustees.

EIN: 436316003

Selected grants: The following grants were reported in 2003.

$103,383 to University of Notre Dame, Notre Dame, IN.

$100,000 to Cornell University, Ithaca, NY.

$100,000 to Wake Forest University, Winston-Salem, NC.

$40,000 to Duke University, Durham, NC.

$15,000 to Drury University, Springfield, MO.

$5,000 to Saint Louis University, Saint Louis, MO.

$5,000 to University of Illinois at Urbana-Champaign, Urbana, IL.

$4,000 to United Way of Greater Saint Louis, Saint Louis, MO.

$1,525 to Boy Scouts of America, Saint Louis, MO.

$1,471 to University of Wisconsin, Madison, WI.

2720
Endless Education, Inc. ✧

3131 Greenhead Dr., Ste. D
Springfield, IL 62711 (217) 793-7866
Application address: c/o Christopher Richardson, C.E.O. and Pres., 7227 N. 16th St., Phoenix, AZ 85020, tel.: (866) 539-9036

Established in 2003 in IL.

Donors: Gail Richardson; 21st Century Learning, LLC; Community Quest, LLC; Edisco Education.

Foundation type: Operating foundation.

Financial data (yr. ended 12/31/05): Assets, $392 (M); gifts received, $343,400; expenditures, $346,737; qualifying distributions, $344,087; giving activities include $344,087 for 9 grants (high: $116,511; low: $3,000).

Purpose and activities: Giving primarily for scholarships for individuals to obtain a degree in education at an accredited university or college, as well as to promote continuing education of individuals involved in the education of children in the classroom and school; funding also for Roman Catholic education and churches.

Fields of interest: Scholarships/financial aid; Children, services; Roman Catholic agencies & churches.

Application information: Application form required.

Initial approach: Letter requesting application form

Final notification: Forty-five days before the applicable semester beginning date

Officers and Directors:* Christopher Richardson,* C.E.O. and Pres.; Brent Richardson,* Exec. V.P.; Dennis Little,* C.F.O.

EIN: 412076555

2721
Energizer Charitable Trust ✧

c/o The Northern Trust Co.
P.O. Box 803878
Chicago, IL 60680
Application address: c/o Barb LeClere, Energizer Charitable Trust, 533 Maryville University Dr., St. Louis, MO 63141

Established in 2000 in MO.

Donors: Ralston Purina Trust Fund; Energizer Holdings, Inc.

Foundation type: Company-sponsored foundation.

Financial data (yr. ended 9/30/05): Assets, $10,747,597 (M); gifts received, $2,000,000; expenditures, $1,224,486; qualifying distributions, $1,218,436; giving activities include $1,218,436 for 302 grants (high: $240,000).

Purpose and activities: The trust supports organizations involved with arts and culture, education, human services, international relief, science, and economically disadvantaged people.

Fields of interest: Museums (science/technology); Arts; Secondary school/education; Higher education; Education; YM/YWCAs & YM/YWHAs; Children/youth, services; Human services; International relief; Federated giving programs; Science; Economically disadvantaged.

Type of support: Scholarship funds; Employee matching gifts; Program development; General/operating support.

Limitations: Giving on a national basis, with emphasis on St. Louis, MO. No support for veterans' or fraternal organizations not of direct benefit to the entire community. No grants to individuals, or for religious or politically partisan purposes, investment funds, tickets for dinners, benefits, exhibits, conferences, sports events, or other short term activities, advertisements, or debt reduction or post-event needs; no loans.

Publications: Application guidelines; Program policy statement.

Application information: Application form not required.

Initial approach: Proposal
Deadline(s): None
Board meeting date(s): Quarterly

Trustees: Buron Buffkin; Jacqueline E. Burwitz; Dan Carpenter; William C. Fox; Mark A. Schafale; Joseph J. Tisone; Jeff Ziminski.

EIN: 367324191

Selected grants: The following grants were reported in 2004.

$365,000 to United Way of Greater Saint Louis, Saint Louis, MO. 2 grants: $200,000, $165,000

$100,000 to Saint Louis Science Center, Saint Louis, MO.

$90,000 to American Youth Foundation, Saint Louis, MO. 2 grants: $50,000, $40,000

$50,000 to Vashon Education Compact, Saint Louis, MO.

$50,000 to Webster University, Saint Louis, MO.

$6,000 to Junior Achievement of Mississippi Valley, Chesterfield, MO.

$250 to Hopkins School, New Haven, CT.

$105 to Cleveland Museum of Art, Cleveland, OH.

2722
The Excelsior! Foundation ◇
c/o John McGovern
225 W. Wacker Dr., Ste. 2800
Chicago, IL 60606

Donor: Barbara Olin Taylor.
Foundation type: Independent foundation.
Financial data (yr. ended 12/31/05): Assets, $2,171,858 (M); gifts received, $2,539,140; expenditures, $500,697; qualifying distributions, $470,030; giving activities include $446,810 for 12 grants (high: $225,000; low: $500).

Purpose and activities: Giving primarily for education and human services.

Fields of interest: Education, administration/regulation; Higher education; Education; Environment, natural resources; Health care; Human services; Federated giving programs;

Philanthropy/voluntarism; Christian agencies & churches.

Limitations: Applications not accepted. Giving on a national basis. No grants to individuals.

Application information: Contributes only to pre-selected organizations.

Officers and Directors:* Barbara Olin Taylor,* Pres. and Treas.; Frederick M. Taylor III, V.P.; James W. Taylor, V.P.; Spencer O. Taylor, V.P.; John E. McGovern, Jr.; F. Morgan Taylor, Jr.

EIN: 363812346

Selected grants: The following grants were reported in 2003.

$140,537 to National Center for Effective Schools Research and Development, Okemos, MI. 2 grants: $50,248, $90,289

$140,000 to Lake Forest College, Lake Forest, IL. 2 grants: $15,000 (For annual fund), $125,000 (For Library/Learning Resource Center Project).

$28,500 to Winnie Palmer Nature Reserve, Latrobe, PA.

$25,000 to Synergos Institute, New York, NY.

$19,000 to Church of the Holy Spirit, Lake Forest, IL. 2 grants: $10,000, $9,000

$5,000 to John Burroughs School, Saint Louis, MO.

$5,000 to Jupiter Island Medical Fund, Hobe Sound, FL.

2723
Fairwyn Fund ◇
(formerly The ServiceMaster Foundation)
1755 S. Naperville Rd.
Wheaton, IL 60187   (630) 663-2202
Contact: C. William Pollard, Pres.

Established as a company-sponsored foundation in 1987 in IL; status changed to independent foundation in 2002.

Donors: ServiceMaster L.P.; ServiceMaster Venture Fund L.L.C; The ServiceMaster Co.

Foundation type: Independent foundation.
Financial data (yr. ended 12/31/03): Assets, $6,531,596 (M); expenditures, $741,108; qualifying distributions, $741,000; giving activities include $741,000 for 27 grants (high: $125,000; low: $538).

Purpose and activities: The foundation supports Christian agencies and churches and organizations involved with education and international agricultural development.

Fields of interest: Higher education; Education; International economic development; Christian agencies & churches.

International interests: Asia.

Limitations: Giving on a national and international basis. No grants to individuals.

Application information: Application form not required.

Initial approach: Contact foundation for application information
Deadline(s): None

Officers and Directors:* C. William Pollard, Jr.,* Pres.; Vernon T. Squires, V.P. and Secy.; Charles W. Pollard III; Brian C. Pollard; Judy Pollard.

EIN: 363529559

Selected grants: The following grants were reported in 2003.

$125,000 to Moody Bible Institute of Chicago, Chicago, IL.

$50,000 to Wheaton College, Wheaton, IL.

$40,000 to DuPage Community Foundation, Wheaton, IL.

$25,000 to Indiana Wesleyan University, Marion, IN.

$25,000 to Leader to Leader Institute, New York, NY.

$25,000 to W G B H Educational Foundation, Boston, MA.

$21,000 to Daystar U.S., Edina, MN.

$10,000 to Claremont University Center and Graduate School, Claremont, CA.

$10,000 to Koinonia House, Jackson, MI.

$5,000 to Americans United for Life, Chicago, IL.

2724
Dr. Ralph and Marian Falk Medical Research Trust ▼ ◇
c/o Bank of America, N.A.
231 S. LaSalle St.
Chicago, IL 60697   (312) 828-1785
Contact: M.C. Ryan

Established in 1991 in IL.
Donor: Marian Citron Falk Trust.
Foundation type: Independent foundation.
Financial data (yr. ended 11/30/05): Assets, $152,900,071 (M); expenditures, $6,321,987; qualifying distributions, $5,515,018; giving activities include $5,364,806 for 11 grants (high: $1,007,120; low: $58,693; average: $106,700–$1,000,000).

Purpose and activities: Support for medical research in the area of diseases for which no definite cure is known.

Fields of interest: Medical research, institute.

Limitations: Giving in the U.S., with emphasis on IL. No grants to individuals.

Application information: Application form not required.

Deadline(s): None

Trustee: Bank of America, N.A.

EIN: 366975534

Selected grants: The following grants were reported in 2005.

$1,106,700 to Northwestern University, Evanston, IL. 2 grants: $106,700 (For medical research), $1,000,000 to Falk Center for Molecular Therapeutics (For research).

$1,007,120 to Loyola University Medical Center, Maywood, IL. For medical research.

$1,000,000 to Thomas Jefferson University, Philadelphia, PA. For medical research.

$866,668 to Childrens Memorial Hospital, Chicago, IL. For medical research.

$550,000 to Northwestern Memorial Foundation, Chicago, IL. For medical research.

$333,000 to Brown University, Providence, RI. For medical research.

$234,250 to University of Illinois at Chicago, Chicago, IL. For medical research.

$138,375 to Medical College of Wisconsin, Milwaukee, WI. For medical research.

$70,000 to Citizens United for Research in Epilepsy (CURE), Burr Ridge, IL. For research.

2725
The Farrell Foundation ◇ ☆
1051 Meadow Ln.
Lake Forest, IL 60045

Established in 1996 in IL.
Donors: Maxine P. Farrell; W. James Farrell.
Foundation type: Independent foundation.
Financial data (yr. ended 12/31/05): Assets, $1,825,793 (M); gifts received, $2,001,302;

expenditures, $878,791; qualifying distributions, $877,023; giving activities include $875,270 for 36 grants (high: $500,022; low: $500).

Fields of interest: Museums (science/technology); Performing arts, theater; Performing arts, orchestra (symphony); Performing arts, opera; Boys & girls clubs; Federated giving programs.

Limitations: Applications not accepted. Giving primarily in Chicago, IL. No grants to individuals.

Application information: Contributes only to pre-selected organizations.

Officers: Maxine P. Farrell, Pres.; W. James Farrell, Secy.

Directors: Kathleen Esposito; David J. Farrell; James M. Farrell; Andrew L. Powell; Julie Simak.

EIN: 364120660

Selected grants: The following grants were reported in 2005.

$525,022 to Lyric Opera of Chicago, Chicago, IL. 2 grants: $500,022, $25,000

$10,135 to Midland Montessori School, Midland, MI.

$10,006 to Northwestern University, Evanston, IL. 2 grants: $5,000, $5,006

$10,000 to Avon Old Farms School, Avon, CT.

$10,000 to Big Shoulders Fund, Chicago, IL.

$5,044 to Midland Center for the Arts, Midland, MI.

$5,044 to Saint Lawrence University, Canton, NY.

$5,000 to ETA Creative Arts Foundation, Chicago, IL.

2726
Peter & Paula Fasseas Foundation ◇

c/o Peter Fasseas
1110 W. 35th St.
Chicago, IL 60609

Established in 1995 in IL.

Donors: Alpha Bancorp; Metropolitan Bancorp; Plaza Bancorp; Metropolitan Bank Group; North Community Bank.

Foundation type: Company-sponsored foundation.

Financial data (yr. ended 12/31/05): Assets, $24,877,522 (M); gifts received, $5,166,313; expenditures, $689,534; qualifying distributions, $681,701; giving activities include $676,500 for 7 grants (high: $600,000; low: $1,200).

Purpose and activities: The foundation supports organizations involved with higher education, animal welfare, recreation, youth development, and children and youth.

Fields of interest: Higher education; Animal welfare; Recreation; Youth development, centers/clubs; Children/youth, services.

Type of support: General/operating support.

Limitations: Applications not accepted. Giving limited to Chicago, IL. No grants to individuals.

Application information: Contributes only to pre-selected organizations.

Officer and Directors: Peter A. Fasseas, Pres.; Alexis Fasseas; Drew Fasseas; Paula Fasseas.

EIN: 364010374

2727
Joseph and Bessie Feinberg Foundation ▼ ◇

505 N. Lake Shore Dr., Ste. 1005
Chicago, IL 60611

Established in 1969 in IL.

Donor: Reuben Feinberg‡.

Foundation type: Independent foundation.

Financial data (yr. ended 10/31/05): Assets, $121,670,214 (M); gifts received, $6,956,049; expenditures, $6,469,503; qualifying distributions, $6,072,083; giving activities include $5,862,800 for 51 grants (high: $4,000,000; low: $500; average: $1,000–$50,000).

Purpose and activities: Giving primarily for Jewish welfare and education; support also for a local television station.

Fields of interest: Media/communications; Education; Human services; Jewish federated giving programs.

Limitations: Applications not accepted. Giving primarily in IL. No grants to individuals.

Application information: Contributes only to pre-selected organizations.

Officer: Paul Goldberg, Secy.-Treas.

Trustees: Beatrice Crain; Janice Feinberg; Joseph Feinberg; Michael Maling.

EIN: 237028857

Selected grants: The following grants were reported in 2005.

$4,000,000 to Northwestern University, Medical School, Evanston, IL.

$1,000,000 to Spertus Institute of Jewish Studies, Chicago, IL.

$400,000 to Jewish United Fund of Metropolitan Chicago, Chicago, IL. 6 grants: $50,000, $50,000, $75,000, $75,000, $75,000, $75,000

$50,000 to Hebrew Theological College, Skokie, IL.

$50,000 to Jewish Theological Seminary of America, New York, NY.

2728
The Field Foundation of Illinois, Inc. ◇

200 S. Wacker Dr., Ste. 3860
Chicago, IL 60606 (312) 831-0910
Contact: Aurie A. Pennick, Exec. Dir.
FAX: (312) 831-0961; URL: http://www.fieldfoundation.org

Incorporated in 1960 in IL.

Donor: Marshall Field IV‡.

Foundation type: Independent foundation.

Financial data (yr. ended 4/30/05): Assets, $55,518,327 (M); expenditures, $3,500,345; qualifying distributions, $3,006,469; giving activities include $2,160,063 for grants.

Purpose and activities: Giving in the fields of health, community welfare, primary and secondary education, cultural activities, conservation, and urban and community affairs.

Fields of interest: Museums; Arts; Education, early childhood education; Elementary school/education; Secondary school/education; Adult education—literacy, basic skills & GED; Education; Environment; Health care; Substance abuse, services; Mental health/crisis services; AIDS; Employment; Food services; Human services; Children/youth, services; Aging, centers/services; Homeless, human services; Civil rights, race/intergroup relations; Community development; Public policy, research; Public affairs; Aging; Economically disadvantaged; Homeless.

Type of support: General/operating support; Capital campaigns; Building/renovation; Equipment; Land acquisition; Emergency funds; Program development; Seed money; Curriculum development; Technical assistance; Employee matching gifts.

Limitations: Giving primarily in the Chicago, IL, area. No support for member agencies of community funds, medical research, national health agencies, neighborhood health clinics, small cultural groups, or religious purposes. No grants to individuals, or for endowment funds, continuing operating support, conferences, operating support of day care centers, fundraising events, advertising, scholarships, printed materials or video equipment, or fellowships; no loans.

Publications: Biennial report (including application guidelines); Informational brochure (including application guidelines); Occasional report.

Application information: Application form not required.

Initial approach: Proposal
Copies of proposal: 1
Deadline(s): Jan. 15, May 15, and Sept. 15
Board meeting date(s): 3 times per year
Final notification: Within 4 months

Officers and Directors:* Christine M. Tchen,* Chair.; Gary H. Kline,* Secy.; Aurie A. Pennick, Treas. and Exec. Dir.; Judith S. Block; Burlean Miller Burris; Marshall Field; Philip Wayne Hummer; Lyle Logan; F. Oliver Nicklin; George A. Ranney, Jr.

Number of staff: 4 full-time professional; 1 part-time professional; 1 full-time support; 1 part-time support.

EIN: 366059408

Selected grants: The following grants were reported in 2003.

$25,000 to Muntu Dance Theater, Chicago, IL. For Muntu Center for the Performing Arts.

$25,000 to Music and Dance Theater Chicago, Chicago, IL. 2 grants: $12,500 each (For capital campaign).

$10,000 to Chicago Opera Theater, Chicago, IL. For Participatory Opera Program.

$10,000 to Erikson Institute, Chicago, IL. For Learning and Teaching Assessment System (LTAS) Program.

$10,000 to Housing Opportunities for Women, Chicago, IL. For Permanent Supportive Housing program.

$10,000 to Illinois Center for Violence Prevention, Chicago, IL. For Evaluation Resource Institute.

$10,000 to Inspiration Corporation, Inspiration Cafe, Chicago, IL. For Cafe Too Job Training Program.

$10,000 to Lawndale Christian Health Center, Chicago, IL. For Psychosocial Service Triage Program.

$10,000 to Merit School of Music, Chicago, IL. For Preparatory Program.

2729
Roger S. Firestone Foundation ◇

c/o Bank of America, N.A.
231 S. LaSalle St., Rm. 0340
Chicago, IL 60697
Contact: M. Catherine Ryan

Established in 1983 in OH.

Foundation type: Independent foundation.

Financial data (yr. ended 12/31/04): Assets, $12,937,646 (M); expenditures, $623,307; qualifying distributions, $559,138; giving activities include $505,000 for 27 grants (high: $55,000; low: $4,000).

Purpose and activities: Emphasis on urban issues, housing, and cultural programs; support also for social service agencies.

Fields of interest: Arts; Education; Housing/shelter, development; Human services; Urban/community development.
Type of support: General/operating support; Continuing support; Annual campaigns; Capital campaigns.
Limitations: Giving primarily in AZ, CA and Washington, DC. No grants to individuals, including scholarships.
Publications: Application guidelines; Multi-year report.
Application information: Application form not required.
  Initial approach: Proposal
  Copies of proposal: 1
  Deadline(s): None
  Board meeting date(s): Mar. and Oct.
Officers and Trustees:* John D. Firestone,* Chair.; Gay F. Wray,* Pres.; Lisa S. Firestone,* Treas.; Susan F. Semegen; Tim F. Wray.
EIN: 341388255

2730
Fites Family Charitable Trust ◇

602 E. High Point
Peoria, IL 61614

Established in 1999 in IL.
Donors: Donald V. Fites; Sylvia D. Fites.
Foundation type: Independent foundation.
Financial data (yr. ended 12/31/05): Assets, $10,563,479 (M); gifts received, $307,242; expenditures, $1,147,195; qualifying distributions, $1,035,959; giving activities include $1,035,959 for 34 grants (high: $624,550; low: $100).
Purpose and activities: Giving primarily for higher education as well as for the arts, a wildlife refuge, and health and human services.
Fields of interest: Arts education; Historical activities, war memorials; Higher education; Education; Animals/wildlife, preservation/protection; Hospitals (general); Human services; Protestant agencies & churches.
Limitations: Applications not accepted. No grants to individuals.
Application information: Contributes only to pre-selected organizations.
Trustees: Donald V. Fites; Linda F. Reed.
EIN: 371375732
Selected grants: The following grants were reported in 2005.
$624,550 to Valparaiso University, Valparaiso, IN.
$25,000 to Alzheimers Association, Chicago, IL.
$8,000 to Salvation Army.
$5,000 to YWCA.
$2,400 to Notre Dame University, Philippines. .
$2,000 to Opera Illinois, Peoria, IL.
$2,000 to United Way.
$250 to Boy Scouts of America.

2731
Flagg Creek Foundation ☆

c/o Emily H. King
745 McClintock Dr.
Burr Ridge, IL 60527

Established in 1995 in IL.
Donor: Robert E. King.
Foundation type: Independent foundation.
Financial data (yr. ended 9/30/05): Assets, $3,732,238 (M); expenditures, $460,338;

qualifying distributions, $434,980; giving activities include $434,980 for 59 grants (high: $55,000; low: $100).
Purpose and activities: Giving primarily for the arts, education, and health.
Fields of interest: Performing arts; Arts; Education; Health care; Human services.
Type of support: Building/renovation; Annual campaigns; General/operating support; Continuing support; Capital campaigns; Endowments; Emergency funds; Program development; Curriculum development; Scholarship funds; Technical assistance.
Limitations: Applications not accepted. Giving primarily in IL. No grants to individuals.
Application information: Contributes only to pre-selected organizations.
Officers: Emily H. King, Pres.; Robert E. King, Jr., V.P.
Directors: Elizabeth K. Alden; Robert E. King; Heather K. Pines.
Number of staff: None.
EIN: 363991717
Selected grants: The following grants were reported in 2005.
$55,000 to African Wildlife Foundation, DC.
$10,000 to American Red Cross, National Headquarters, DC.
$10,000 to Association House of Chicago, Chicago, IL.
$6,000 to DuPage Community Foundation, Wheaton, IL.
$6,000 to Golden Apple Foundation, Chicago, IL.
$2,400 to San Miguel School, Chicago, IL.
$2,080 to Futures for Children, Albuquerque, NM.
$1,500 to Lincoln Park Zoo, Chicago, IL.
$1,000 to Hull House Association, Chicago, IL.
$1,000 to Humane Society of Hinsdale, Hinsdale, IL.

2732
Foundation for the Education & Research in Neurological Emergencies ◇ ☆

c/o UIC Dept. EM(MC724)
808 S. Wood St., Ste. 471H
Chicago, IL 60612-7354   (312) 355-1651
Contact: Charrise O'Neill, Exec. Dir.
FAX: (312) 355-1269; E-mail: ferne@ferne.org;
URL: http://www.FERNE.org

Established in 1999 in DE.
Donors: Pfizer/Warner Lambert; Abbott Laboratories.
Foundation type: Independent foundation.
Financial data (yr. ended 12/31/05): Assets, $732,901 (M); gifts received, $1,205,980; expenditures, $684,635; qualifying distributions, $508,416; giving activities include $508,416 for grants.
Purpose and activities: Giving for education and research in neurologic emergencies.
Fields of interest: Medical school/education; Neuroscience research.
Type of support: Conferences/seminars; Seed money; Research.
Limitations: Giving on a national basis. No grants to individuals.
Application information: See Web site for application information.
  Deadline(s): None

Officers: Edward Sloan, Pres.; J. Stephen Huff, Secy.; Andy Jagoda, Treas.; Charrise O'Neill, Exec. Dir.
EIN: 134062989

2733
J. S. Frank Foundation ◇

666 Garland Pl.
Des Plaines, IL 60016-4725
Contact: James S. Frank, Pres.

Established in IL.
Donors: James S. Frank; Frank Consolidated Enterprises.
Foundation type: Independent foundation.
Financial data (yr. ended 12/31/05): Assets, $352,376 (M); gifts received, $725,000; expenditures, $706,865; qualifying distributions, $706,850; giving activities include $706,850 for 17 grants (high: $500,000; low: $100).
Purpose and activities: Giving primarily for higher education and the arts.
Fields of interest: Arts; Higher education; Hospitals (general); Human services; Federated giving programs.
Limitations: Giving primarily in IL. No grants to individuals.
Application information:
  Initial approach: Letter
  Deadline(s): None
Officers: James S. Frank, Pres.; Karen Frank, Secy.
EIN: 237376410
Selected grants: The following grants were reported in 2004.
$50,000 to W T T W Channel 11, Chicago, IL. For general support.
$40,000 to Hebrew Union College-Jewish Institute of Religion, Cincinnati, OH. For general support.
$30,000 to Ravinia Festival Association, Highland Park, IL. For general support.
$25,000 to Dartmouth College, Hanover, NH. For general support.
$20,000 to Jewish Community Centers of Chicago, Chicago, IL. For general support.
$20,000 to Northwestern University, Evanston, IL. For general support.
$16,000 to Thresholds, Chicago, IL. For general support.
$13,500 to Anderson Ranch Arts Center, Snowmass Village, CO. For general support.
$11,000 to Chicago Shakespeare Theater, Chicago, IL.
$9,300 to University of Chicago, Chicago, IL. For general support.

2734
Franke Family Charitable Foundation ◇

400 N. Michigan Ave., Ste. 300
Chicago, IL 60611   (312) 917-7778
Contact: Richard J. Franke, Tr.

Established in 1989 in IL.
Donors: Richard J. Franke; Barbara E. Franke.
Foundation type: Independent foundation.
Financial data (yr. ended 6/30/05): Assets, $48,029,330 (M); gifts received, $60,320; expenditures, $2,329,096; qualifying distributions, $2,295,576; giving activities include $2,280,625 for 88 grants (high: $533,216; low: $50).

Purpose and activities: Giving primarily for higher education, and the performing arts with an emphasis on theater and a humanities festival.
Fields of interest: Arts education; Museums (art); Performing arts; Humanities; Arts; Higher education; Education; Federated giving programs.
Type of support: Annual campaigns; Capital campaigns.
Limitations: Giving primarily in IL, with emphasis on Chicago and Evanston; some giving also in New Haven, CT and New York, NY, and nationally. No grants to individuals.
Application information:
  Initial approach: Letter
  Deadline(s): None
Trustees: Barbara E. Franke; Richard J. Franke; Jane Franke-Molner.
EIN: 363662848
Selected grants: The following grants were reported in 2003.
$639,688 to University of Chicago, Chicago, IL. 2 grants: $231,100 to Frank Institute for the Humanities (For unrestricted support), $408,588 (For grant made in form of stock).
$211,000 to Yale University, New Haven, CT. For unrestricted support.
$200,000 to Northwestern University, Evanston, IL. For unrestricted support.
$50,000 to Chicago Humanities Festival, Chicago, IL. 2 grants: $20,000 (For endowment), $30,000 (For unrestricted support).
$50,000 to Chicago Shakespeare Theater, Chicago, IL. For unrestricted support.
$44,800 to North Shore Country Day School, Winnetka, IL. For unrestricted support.
$37,500 to Chicago Symphony Orchestra, Chicago, IL. For unrestricted support.
$23,820 to Court Theater, Chicago, IL. For unrestricted support.

2735
Julius N. Frankel Foundation ◇
(formerly Frankel Foundation)
c/o Harris Trust and Savings Bank, Tax Div.
P.O. Box 755
Chicago, IL 60690 (312) 461-2655
Contact: Foundation Admin.

Established in 1959 in IL.
Donors: Gerald Frankel‡; Gustav Frankel‡; Julius N. Frankel‡.
Foundation type: Independent foundation.
Financial data (yr. ended 10/31/05): Assets, $52,582,531 (M); expenditures, $2,772,238; qualifying distributions, $2,424,129; giving activities include $2,115,000 for 46 grants (high: $230,000; low: $10,000).
Purpose and activities: Giving primarily for higher education, hospitals, arts and culture, and social services, including recordings for the blind and services for the deaf.
Fields of interest: Media, television; Performing arts; Arts; Higher education; Hospitals (general); Recreation, fairs/festivals; Human services; Children/youth, services; Family services.
Limitations: Giving primarily in Chicago, IL. No grants to individuals.
Application information: Application form not required.
  Initial approach: Letter
  Deadline(s): None
  Board meeting date(s): At least 5 times annually
  Final notification: Immediately following meetings

Trustees: Nelson D. Cornelius; John L. Georgas; Harris Bank, N.A.
EIN: 366765844
Selected grants: The following grants were reported in 2005.
$230,000 to Lyric Opera of Chicago, Chicago, IL.
$150,000 to Chicago Symphony Orchestra, Chicago, IL.
$125,000 to W T T W Channel 11, Chicago, IL.
$100,000 to Childrens Memorial Foundation, Chicago, IL.
$75,000 to Roosevelt University, Chicago, IL.
$50,000 to Goodman Theater, Chicago, IL.
$45,000 to Thresholds, Chicago, IL.
$40,000 to Infant Welfare Society of Chicago, Chicago, IL.
$30,000 to Mercy Home for Boys and Girls, Chicago, IL.
$25,000 to Teach for America, Chicago, IL.

2736
Freed Family Foundation ◇ ☆
220 N. Smith St., Ste. 300
Palatine, IL 60067 (847) 215-5500
Contact: Laurance Freed, Pres.

Established in 1994 in IL.
Donors: Daniel J. Freed; Laurance Freed; Debra F. Ruderman; Joseph Freed.
Foundation type: Independent foundation.
Financial data (yr. ended 12/31/05): Assets, $10,367 (M); gifts received, $363,601; expenditures, $369,277; qualifying distributions, $369,068; giving activities include $369,068 for grants.
Purpose and activities: Giving for medical and health services, the arts, and Jewish organizations and federated giving programs.
Fields of interest: Arts; Higher education; Health organizations; Jewish federated giving programs; Jewish agencies & temples.
Limitations: Giving primarily in IL. No grants to individuals.
Application information: Application form not required.
  Initial approach: Letter
  Deadline(s): None
Officers: Laurance Freed, Pres.; Paul Homer, Secy.; Gerald Frishman, Treas.
Directors: Daniel S. Freed; Debra F. Ruderman.
EIN: 363978482
Selected grants: The following grants were reported in 2005.
$56,533 to City Year Chicago, Chicago, IL.
$35,000 to Chicago Community Foundation, Chicago, IL.
$18,217 to American Red Cross.
$10,000 to Austin Jewish Academy, Austin, TX.
$5,036 to Jewish Community Association of Austin, Austin, TX.
$2,500 to Erie Neighborhood House, Chicago, IL.
$500 to Harvard University, Cambridge, MA.
$500 to United Way, WI.
$250 to Austin Public Library Foundation, Austin, TX.
$100 to Yale Alumni Fund, New Haven, CT.

2737
Norman & Edna Freehling Foundation ◇ ☆
c/o Paul Freehling
55 E. Monroe St., Ste. 4200
Chicago, IL 60603-5803

Established in 1953 in IL.
Foundation type: Independent foundation.
Financial data (yr. ended 9/30/05): Assets, $177,372 (M); expenditures, $775,375; qualifying distributions, $765,247; giving activities include $762,450 for 47 grants (high: $230,000; low: $100).
Purpose and activities: Giving primarily for arts and culture and higher education.
Fields of interest: Arts; Higher education; Education; Human services; Foundations (private grantmaking); Jewish federated giving programs; Jewish agencies & temples.
Type of support: Annual campaigns; Capital campaigns; Endowments; Professorships.
Limitations: Applications not accepted. Giving primarily in Chicago, IL. No grants to individuals.
Application information: Contributes only to pre-selected organizations.
Trustee: Paul Freehling.
EIN: 366058353
Selected grants: The following grants were reported in 2005.
$25,000 to Alzheimers Association, Chicago, IL.
$25,000 to Chicago Foundation for Women, Chicago, IL.
$25,000 to Chicago Opera Theater, Chicago, IL.
$25,000 to Frank Lloyd Wright Preservation Trust, Oak Park, IL.
$25,000 to Wellesley College, Wellesley, MA.
$10,000 to Chicago Botanic Garden, Glencoe, IL.
$10,000 to Landmarks Preservation Council of Illinois, Chicago, IL.
$10,000 to Nature Conservancy, Arlington, VA.
$10,000 to Roosevelt University, Chicago, IL.
$10,000 to United Way.

2738
Philip M. Friedmann Family Charitable Trust ◇
2430 N. Lakeview Ave.
Chicago, IL 60614

Established in 1998 in IL.
Donors: Philip M. Friedmann; Recycled Paper Greetings, Inc.
Foundation type: Independent foundation.
Financial data (yr. ended 12/31/05): Assets, $22,097,726 (M); gifts received, $5,600,000; expenditures, $804,415; qualifying distributions, $698,186; giving activities include $698,186 for 150 grants (high: $75,000; low: $100).
Fields of interest: Higher education, college; Neuroscience; Neuroscience research; Big Brothers/Big Sisters; Youth development, services; Public affairs; Jewish agencies & temples; Aging.
Limitations: Applications not accepted. Giving on a national basis, with some emphasis on the Chicago, IL area, and the greater metropolitan Washington, DC, area.
Application information: Contributes only to pre-selected organizations.
Manager: Albert B. Friedmann.
Trustee: Philip M. Friedmann.
EIN: 367252117
Selected grants: The following grants were reported in 2004.
$100,000 to Foundation for Neurological Diseases, New York, NY. For general support.
$50,000 to Cato Institute, DC. For general support.
$50,000 to Parents Television Council, Los Angeles, CA. For general support.

$25,000 to Heartland Institute, Chicago, IL. For general support.
$25,000 to Institute for Justice, DC. For general support.
$25,000 to Media Research Center, Alexandria, VA. For general support.
$15,000 to Francis W. Parker School, Chicago, IL. For general support.
$12,500 to New Moms, Chicago, IL. For general support.
$10,000 to Heritage Foundation, DC. For general support.
$10,000 to Simon Wiesenthal Center, Los Angeles, CA. For general support.

2739
Helen V. Froehlich Foundation ✧
c/o The Northern Trust Co.
P.O. Box 803878
Chicago, IL 60680

Established in 1993 in IL.
Foundation type: Independent foundation.
Financial data (yr. ended 5/31/05): Assets, $31,181,139 (M); expenditures, $1,981,587; qualifying distributions, $1,897,170; giving activities include $1,875,600 for 7 grants (high: $475,000; low: $80,000).
Purpose and activities: Giving primarily to botanical gardens in IL and NY, and for natural resource conservation.
Fields of interest: Environment, natural resources; Environment, water resources; Environment, land resources; Botanical gardens.
Limitations: Applications not accepted. Giving primarily in Chicago, IL, and NY, with emphasis on Brooklyn, and Lake George. No grants to individuals.
Application information: Contributes only to pre-selected organizations.
Trustee: The Northern Trust Co.
EIN: 367033137
Selected grants: The following grants were reported in 2004.
$500,000 to Brooklyn Botanic Garden, Brooklyn, NY. For general support.
$500,000 to Chicago Botanic Garden, Glencoe, IL. For general support.
$406,000 to Lake George Association, Lake George, NY. For general support.
$250,000 to Rensselaer Polytechnic Institute, Darrin Fresh Water Institute, Troy, NY. For general support.
$100,000 to Lake George Land Conservancy, Bolton Landing, NY. For general support.
$60,000 to Fund for Lake George, Lake George, NY. For general support.

2740
Lloyd A. Fry Foundation ▼ ✧
120 S. LaSalle St., Ste. 1950
Chicago, IL 60603-3419 (312) 580-0310
Contact: Unmi Song, Secy. and Exec. Dir.
FAX: (312) 580-0980;
E-mail: usong@fryfoundation.org; URL: http://www.fryfoundation.org

Established in 1959 in IL.
Donor: Lloyd A. Fry‡.
Foundation type: Independent foundation.
Financial data (yr. ended 6/30/05): Assets, $168,649,397 (M); gifts received, $865,563; expenditures, $10,151,717; qualifying distributions, $9,416,217; giving activities include $7,586,441 for 347 grants (high: $200,000; low: $200; average: $10,000–$100,000).
Purpose and activities: The foundation supports organizations with the strength and commitment to address persistent problems of urban Chicago resulting from poverty, violence, ignorance and despair. The foundation seeks to build the capacity of individuals and the systems that serve them. The vision is of a Chicago that offers education, prosperity and hope for all.
Fields of interest: Arts; Elementary school/education; Secondary school/education; Education; Health care; AIDS; Employment; Minorities/immigrants, centers/services; Minorities; Economically disadvantaged.
Type of support: General/operating support; Continuing support; Program development; Curriculum development; Technical assistance; Program evaluation.
Limitations: Giving generally limited to Chicago, IL. No support for medical research, religious purposes, governmental bodies, or tax-supported educational institutions for services that fall within their responsibilities. No grants to individuals, or for general operating support for new grantees, annual campaigns, emergency funds, deficit financing, building funds, fundraising benefits, land acquisition, renovation projects, or endowment funds; no loans.
Publications: Application guidelines; Annual report (including application guidelines); Grants list.
Application information: Organizations outside of Chicago, IL are rarely funded. Application form not required.
Initial approach: Letter of inquiry
Copies of proposal: 1
Deadline(s): Mar. 1, June 1, Sept. 1, and Dec. 1
Board meeting date(s): Feb., May, Aug., and Nov.
Final notification: 3 months
Officers and Directors:* Howard M. McCue III,* Chair.; Lloyd A. Fry III,* Vice-Chair.; M. James Termondt,* Pres. and Treas.; David A. Donovan,* V.P.; Stephanie Pace Marshall,* V.P.; Unmi Song, Secy. and Exec. Dir.; Diane Sotiros, Cont.
Number of staff: 5 full-time professional; 3 full-time support; 1 part-time support.
EIN: 366108775
Selected grants: The following grants were reported in 2005.
$150,000 to Big Shoulders Fund, Chicago, IL. For scholarships, technology, and professional development.
$100,000 to Doctors Without Borders USA, New York, NY. For Emergency Relief Fund.
$70,000 to W T T W Channel 11, Chicago, IL. For Artbeat Chicago.
$67,045 to Women Employed Institute, Chicago, IL. For creation of career development and educational counseling program to help low-income women plan and manage careers.
$36,000 to Carole Robertson Center for Learning, Chicago, IL. For Family Health Education Program.
$25,000 to Chinese American Service League, Chicago, IL. For Community Health Program.
$20,000 to Life Span, Chicago, IL. For Employment Services for Domestic Violence Victims.
$20,000 to Urban Gateways: The Center for Arts in Education, Chicago, IL. For Summer Institute for Chicago public school teachers.
$15,000 to Fourth Presbyterian Church, Chicago, IL. For Project Light, to provide support for programs to/with financially disadvantaged residents of Cabrini Green and surrounding areas.
$10,000 to Puerto Rican Arts Alliance, Chicago, IL. For Cuatro and Spanish Guitar lessons.

2741
Paul A. Funk Foundation ✧
115 W. Jefferson St., Ste. 200
Bloomington, IL 61702-3217

Established in 1967 in IL.
Foundation type: Independent foundation.
Financial data (yr. ended 6/30/05): Assets, $7,696,688 (M); expenditures, $620,992; qualifying distributions, $612,954; giving activities include $594,500 for 67 grants (high: $200,000; low: $500).
Purpose and activities: Funding primarily for community development, education, and human services.
Fields of interest: Higher education; Hospitals (general); Health organizations, association; Human services; Community development.
Limitations: Applications not accepted. Giving primarily in McLean County, IL. No grants to individuals.
Application information: Unsolicited requests for funds not accepted.
Trustees: Duncan Funk; John L. Funk; Rey Jannusch; Justin McLaughlin; Clint Rehtmeyer; Eugene A. Roth.
EIN: 376075515
Selected grants: The following grants were reported in 2004.
$100,000 to Sugar Grove Foundation, McLean, IL. For general support.
$30,000 to University of Illinois at Urbana-Champaign, Urbana, IL. For Paul A. Fund Awards.
$10,000 to Childrens Foundation, Bloomington, IL. For general support.
$10,000 to Four-H Foundation, Illinois, Champaign, IL. For general support.
$10,000 to McLean County Historical Society, Bloomington, IL. For general support.
$10,000 to Mid Central Community Action, Bloomington, IL. For general support.
$10,000 to United Way of McLean County, Bloomington, IL. For general support.
$3,000 to Salvation Army of Bloomington, Bloomington, IL. For general support.
$2,500 to Girl Scouts of the U.S.A., Bloomington, IL. For general support.
$1,500 to American Lung Association of Illinois-Iowa, Springfield, IL. For general support.

2742
Galashiels Fund, Ltd. ✧
555 Skokie Blvd., Ste. 555
Northbrook, IL 60062-2845

Established in 1988 in IL.
Donors: Consolidated Electrical Distributors, Inc.; RCK Properties; Rolled Alloys, Inc.
Foundation type: Independent foundation.
Financial data (yr. ended 12/31/04): Assets, $58,445,117 (L); gifts received, $2,787,802; expenditures, $3,477,871; qualifying distributions, $3,025,481; giving activities include $3,022,897 for 36 grants (high: $785,000; low: $5,000).

Purpose and activities: Giving primarily for education, particularly to a private academy; funding also for the arts, with emphasis on theater.

Fields of interest: Museums (art); Performing arts; Performing arts, theater; Arts; Secondary school/education; Higher education; Foundations (private grantmaking).

Type of support: General/operating support; Continuing support.

Limitations: Applications not accepted. Giving on a national basis.

Application information: Contributes only to pre-selected organizations.

Officers and Directors:* Keith W. Colburn,* Pres.; Betsy P. Colburn,* V.P.; David T. Bradford,* Secy.

EIN: 943059858

Selected grants: The following grants were reported in 2003.

$1,000,000 to Phillips Exeter Academy, Exeter, NH. For K. S. O'Donnell Scholarship Fund.

$100,000 to Beginning with Children Foundation, New York, NY. For annual support.

$100,000 to Merit School of Music, Chicago, IL. For capital campaign.

$50,000 to Winnetka Community House, Winnetka, IL. For capital campaign.

$30,000 to Wellesley College, Wellesley, MA. For Friends of Art endowment.

$25,000 to PUENTE Learning Center: People United to Enrich the Neighborhood Through Education, Los Angeles, CA. For endowment.

$15,000 to Museum of Contemporary Art, Chicago, IL. For annual fund.

$10,000 to Colburn School of the Performing Arts, Los Angeles, CA. For general support.

$10,000 to Cristo Rey Jesuit High School, Chicago, IL. For Michael D O'Halleran Scholarship Fund.

$10,000 to Harvard College Fund, Cambridge, MA. For annual support.

2743
The Robert E. Gallagher Charitable Trust ◇
c/o Arthur J. Gallagher & Co.
2 Pierce Pl.
Itasca, IL 60143-3141

Established in 1997 in IL.

Donor: Robert E. Gallagher.

Foundation type: Operating foundation.

Financial data (yr. ended 12/31/03): Assets, $13,063,306 (L); gifts received, $166,100; expenditures, $664,628; qualifying distributions, $658,960; giving activities include $649,500 for 49 grants (high: $400,000; low: $500).

Purpose and activities: Giving primarily to Roman Catholic organizations and churches.

Fields of interest: Roman Catholic agencies & churches.

Limitations: Applications not accepted. Giving primarily in Chicago, IL. No grants to individuals.

Application information: Contributes only to pre-selected organizations.

Trustee: Robert E. Gallagher.

EIN: 367180671

Selected grants: The following grants were reported in 2004.

$500,000 to Cornell University, Ithaca, NY.

$10,000 to Boston College, Chestnut Hill, MA. For general support.

$10,000 to Catholic Charities of the Archdiocese of Chicago, Chicago, IL. For general support.

$10,000 to Cornell Catholic Community, Ithaca, NY. For general support.

$10,000 to Cristo Rey Jesuit High School, Chicago, IL.

$10,000 to Jesuit International Missions, Chicago, IL. For general support.

$10,000 to Josephinum High School, Chicago, IL.

$10,000 to Sisters of Providence of Saint Mary of the Woods, Saint Mary of the Woods, IN. For general support.

$10,000 to Woodlands Academy of the Sacred Heart, Lake Forest, IL.

$5,000 to Saint James Catholic School, Chicago, IL.

2744
Arthur J. Gallagher Foundation
c/o Arthur J. Gallagher & Co.
2 Pierce Pl.
Itasca, IL 60143-3141

Donor: Arthur J. Gallagher & Co.

Foundation type: Independent foundation.

Financial data (yr. ended 12/31/05): Assets, $2,858,195 (M); gifts received, $1,669,209; expenditures, $1,851,930; qualifying distributions, $1,844,307; giving activities include $1,840,376 for grants.

Purpose and activities: The foundation disburses employee-matching gifts only.

Fields of interest: Arts; Education; Environment; Human services; Christian agencies & churches; Disabilities, people with.

Type of support: Employee matching gifts.

Limitations: Applications not accepted. Giving on a national basis. No support for domestic animal shelters. No grants to individuals.

Publications: Informational brochure.

Application information: Contributes only to pre-selected organizations.

Board meeting date(s): Quarterly

Trustees: J. Patrick Gallagher, Jr.; Robert E. Gallagher.

Number of staff: 1 part-time support.

EIN: 366082304

2745
The Galter Foundation ◇
55 E. Superior St., 3rd Fl.
Chicago, IL 60611

Incorporated in 1943 in IL.

Donors: Dollie Galter†; Jack Galter†; William Galter†; Spartus Corp.

Foundation type: Independent foundation.

Financial data (yr. ended 12/31/04): Assets, $13,531,458 (M); gifts received, $1,139,966; expenditures, $1,209,346; qualifying distributions, $1,029,273; giving activities include $1,028,707 for 42 grants (high: $200,000; low: $100).

Purpose and activities: Giving for Jewish welfare funds and temple support, hospitals, higher education, and the handicapped.

Fields of interest: Hospitals (general); Health organizations, association; Human services; Jewish federated giving programs; Jewish agencies & temples; Disabilities, people with.

Limitations: Applications not accepted. Giving primarily in IL. No grants to individuals; no loans or program-related investments.

Application information: Contributes only to pre-selected organizations.

Directors: Karen Goodman; Robert Joseph; Theodore Netzky.

EIN: 366082419

Selected grants: The following grants were reported in 2003.

$200,000 to Swedish Covenant Hospital, Chicago, IL.

$50,000 to Jewish Community Centers of Chicago, Chicago, IL.

$50,000 to Rehabilitation Institute of Chicago, Chicago, IL.

$25,000 to Anixter Center, Chicago, IL.

$25,000 to Temple Shomer Emunim, Sylvania, OH.

$15,000 to Lynn Sage Cancer Research Fund, Chicago, IL.

$10,000 to Israel Childrens Centers, Deerfield Beach, FL.

$10,000 to Mount Sinai Medical Center Foundation, Miami Beach, FL.

$10,000 to Tourette Syndrome Association, Bayside, NY.

$10,000 to UCLA Foundation, Los Angeles, CA.

2746
Helen M. Galvin Charitable Trust ◇
71 S. Wacker Dr., Ste. 3575
Chicago, IL 60606

Established in 1989 in AZ.

Donor: Helen M. Galvin†.

Foundation type: Independent foundation.

Financial data (yr. ended 12/31/05): Assets, $69,672,592 (M); expenditures, $2,798,921; qualifying distributions, $2,767,403; giving activities include $2,748,085 for 22 grants (high: $998,085; low: $25,000).

Purpose and activities: Giving primarily for health associations, and human services.

Fields of interest: Elementary/secondary education; Higher education; Hospitals (general); Health organizations, association; Medical research, institute; Children/youth, services.

Limitations: Applications not accepted. Giving primarily in AZ and IL. No grants to individuals.

Application information: Contributes only to pre-selected organizations.

Trustees: Christopher Galvin; Robert Galvin.

EIN: 866182808

Selected grants: The following grants were reported in 2004.

$75,000 to Kidspace, A Participatory Museum, Pasadena, CA.

$50,000 to Boys and Girls Clubs of Scottsdale, Scottsdale, AZ.

$50,000 to Center for Strategic and International Studies, DC.

$50,000 to Crisis Nursery, Phoenix, AZ.

$50,000 to University of Virginia, Charlottesville, VA.

$40,000 to American Enterprise Institute for Public Policy Research, DC.

$40,000 to Rehabilitation Institute of Chicago, Chicago, IL. For Women's Board.

$20,000 to Mobile CARE (Childrens Asthma Research and Education) Foundation, Evanston, IL.

$10,000 to John F. Kennedy Center for the Performing Arts, DC.

$10,000 to University of Southern California, Marshall School of Business, Los Angeles, CA.

2747
Robert W. Galvin Foundation ✧
1295 E. Algonquin Rd.
Schaumburg, IL 60196
Contact: Robert W. Galvin, Pres.

Incorporated in 1953 in IL.
Donor: Robert W. Galvin.
Foundation type: Independent foundation.
Financial data (yr. ended 12/31/05): Assets,
$23,396,812 (M); gifts received, $2,501,775;
expenditures, $3,937,295; qualifying distributions,
$3,937,285; giving activities include $3,934,643
for 156 grants (high: $250,163; low: $100).
Purpose and activities: Giving primarily for higher
and other education as well as for the arts, health
care, and children, youth, and social services.
Fields of interest: Museums; Performing arts;
Performing arts centers; Historic preservation/
historical societies; Arts; Elementary/secondary
education; Vocational education; Human services;
Children/youth, services; Federated giving
programs; Science.
Limitations: Giving primarily in IL, with emphasis on
Chicago; some funding nationally. No grants to
individuals.
Application information: Application form not
required.
  Initial approach: Letter
  Deadline(s): None
  Board meeting date(s): Annually
Officers: Robert W. Galvin, Pres.; Christopher B.
Galvin, V.P.; Mary G. Galvin, Secy.-Treas.
EIN: 366065560
Selected grants: The following grants were reported
in 2004.
$100,030 to Mobile CARE (Childrens Asthma
  Research and Education) Foundation, Evanston,
  IL.
$60,368 to John F. Kennedy Center for the
  Performing Arts, DC.
$50,250 to Joffrey Ballet of Chicago, Chicago, IL.
$50,181 to Lyric Opera of Chicago, Chicago, IL.
$50,181 to Northwestern University, School of
  Medicine, Evanston, IL.
$50,181 to University of Chicago, Chicago, IL.
$50,024 to University of Minnesota Foundation,
  Minneapolis, MN. For Joseph M. Juran Center for
  Leadership in Quality.
$40,388 to United Way of Metropolitan Chicago,
  Chicago, IL.
$30,184 to Art Institute of Chicago, Chicago, IL.
$25,090 to Santa Fe Institute, Santa Fe, NM.

2748
Gantz Family Foundation ✧ ☆
72 Indian Hill Rd.
Winnetka, IL 60093

Established in 1986 in IL.
Donors: Wilbur H. Gantz; Linda Gantz.
Foundation type: Operating foundation.
Financial data (yr. ended 12/31/05): Assets,
$882,875 (M); gifts received, $142,279;
expenditures, $731,294; qualifying distributions,
$731,294; giving activities include $729,654 for 54
grants (high: $389,000; low: $50).
Fields of interest: Arts education; Higher education;
Engineering school/education; Hospitals (general);
Recreation, social clubs; Boys & girls clubs;
Protestant agencies & churches.
Limitations: Applications not accepted. Giving
primarily in Chicago, IL. No grants to individuals.

Application information: Contributes only to
pre-selected organizations.
Officers and Directors:* Wilbur H. Gantz,* Pres.;
Linda T. Gantz,* V.P. and Secy.; Matthew J. Gantz.
EIN: 363484258

2749
James & Zita Gavin Foundation, Inc. ✧
161 Thorntree Ln.
Winnetka, IL 60093

Established in 1983 in IL.
Donors: James J. Gavin, Jr.; Zita C. Gavin.
Foundation type: Independent foundation.
Financial data (yr. ended 12/31/05): Assets,
$7,627,835 (M); expenditures, $496,418;
qualifying distributions, $490,075; giving activities
include $490,000 for 7 grants (high: $135,000;
low: $5,000; average: $50,000–$100,000).
Purpose and activities: Support primarily for Roman
Catholic education and charities.
Fields of interest: Elementary/secondary
education; Roman Catholic agencies & churches.
Limitations: Applications not accepted. Giving on a
national basis. No grants to individuals.
Application information: Contributes only to
pre-selected organizations.
Officers: James J. Gavin, Jr., Pres.; Zita C. Gavin,
V.P.; Steven J. Gavin, Secy.; Kevin P. Gavin, Treas.
EIN: 363256613

2750
Geneseo Foundation ✧
c/o Central Bank Illinois, Trust Dept.
P.O. Box 89
Geneseo, IL 61254
Contact: John DuBois, Trust Off., Central Bank
Illinois
Application address: c/o Central Bank Illinois, 101
N. State St., Geneseo, IL 61254

Established in 1961 in IL.
Donors: George B. Dedrick; Catherine Cambell†;
Walter & Carol Keppy Memorial Trust.
Foundation type: Independent foundation.
Financial data (yr. ended 3/31/06): Assets,
$6,778,149 (M); gifts received, $48,133;
expenditures, $435,311; qualifying distributions,
$407,026; giving activities include $376,477 for 34
grants (high: $80,000; low: $750), and $17,625 for
grants to individuals.
Purpose and activities: Giving for civic
organizations, social services, youth, recreation,
and education, including for scholarships for
graduates of Geneseo High School.
Fields of interest: Arts; Education; Recreation;
Human services; Children/youth, services;
Community development; Government/public
administration.
Type of support: General/operating support;
Scholarships—to individuals.
Limitations: Giving primarily in Geneseo, IL.
Application information: Scholarships limited to
graduates of Geneseo High School. Application form
required.
  Initial approach: Letter or telephone to request
    application form
  Copies of proposal: 1
  Deadline(s): 1st week of the month; June 1 for
    scholarships
  Board meeting date(s): Monthly

Managers: Alan C. Anderson; Bryce B. Chamberlain;
A. Dean Decker; Bruce R. Fehlman; Michael L.
Gernant; John T. Greenwood; Mark E. Lohman;
Robert E. Schaefer; Todd W. Sieben.
EIN: 366079604
Selected grants: The following grants were reported
in 2005.
$80,000 to Geneseo School Facility Enhancement
  Foundation, Geneseo, IL.
$50,000 to Geneseo Community Park District,
  Geneseo, IL.
$20,000 to Abilities Plus, Kewanee, IL.
$5,000 to Good Shepherd Foundation, Longview,
  TX.
$3,000 to Cambridge Historical Society, Cambridge,
  MA.
$2,000 to Quad City Arts, Rock Island, IL.
$1,000 to Big Brothers/Big Sisters.

2751
Elizabeth Morse Genius Charitable Trust
c/o Bank of America, N.A.
231 S. LaSalle St.
Chicago, IL 60697 (312) 828-1029
Contact: Kristin Carlson Vogen

Established in 1992 in IL.
Foundation type: Independent foundation.
Financial data (yr. ended 11/30/04): Assets,
$60,483,589 (M); expenditures, $2,868,141;
qualifying distributions, $2,605,426; giving
activities include $2,216,052 for 60 grants (high:
$300,000; low: $10,000).
Purpose and activities: Giving primarily for
individual self-reliance, the relief of human suffering,
and the fostering of individual self-worth, with an
emphasis on the classical fine arts, the
development of physical health and spiritual
well-being, and the promotion of world peace
through the improvement of travel.
Fields of interest: Media, radio; Performing arts,
orchestra (symphony); Higher education;
Residential/custodial care, half-way house.
Limitations: Giving limited to Chicago, IL,
metropolitan area.
Publications: Application guidelines.
Application information: Application form required.
  Initial approach: Telephone for guidelines
  Copies of proposal: 2
  Deadline(s): None
  Board meeting date(s): Ongoing
  Final notification: 9 months
Trustees: James L. Alexander; Bank of America,
N.A.
EIN: 367010559
Selected grants: The following grants were reported
in 2004.
$300,000 to Field Museum of Natural History,
  Chicago, IL.
$300,000 to Lyric Opera of Chicago, Chicago, IL.
$160,000 to Ravinia Festival Association, Highland
  Park, IL.
$83,825 to Music and Dance Theater Chicago,
  Chicago, IL.
$50,000 to Chicago Public Library, Chicago, IL.
$50,000 to Chicago Shakespeare Theater, Chicago,
  IL.
$50,000 to Whirlwind Performance Company,
  Chicago, IL.
$25,000 to Peoples Music School, Chicago, IL.
$25,000 to Roseland Training Center, Chicago, IL.
$15,000 to Music of the Baroque, Chicago, IL.

2752
Geraldi Norton Memorial Corporation ◇
c/o Hackbarth & Hudson, PC
20 N. Wacker Dr., Ste. 1520
Chicago, IL 60606
Contact: Christopher S. Eklund, Treas.

Incorporated in 1952 in IL.
Donor: Grace Geraldi Norton†.
Foundation type: Independent foundation.
Financial data (yr. ended 12/31/05): Assets,
$4,351,078 (M); expenditures, $396,616;
qualifying distributions, $375,937; giving
activities include $343,500 for 34 grants (high: $250,000;
low: $1,000).
Purpose and activities: Giving primarily for
education, health and human services.
Fields of interest: Arts; Higher education;
Education; Hospitals (general); Health
organizations, association; Medical research,
institute; Human services; Children/youth, services;
Community development, neighborhood
development.
Type of support: General/operating support; Annual
campaigns; Capital campaigns; Building/
renovation; Professorships; Research.
Limitations: Giving primarily in the Chicago, IL, area.
No grants to individuals.
Application information: Application form required.
Initial approach: Letter
Deadline(s): None
Board meeting date(s): Dec. 19
Final notification: Generally in Dec.
Officers and Directors:* Sally S. Eklund,* Pres.;
Katherine Wise,* Secy.; Christopher S. Eklund,*
Treas.; Peter H. Eklund.
EIN: 366069997

2753
The Getz Foundation ◇
(formerly Emma & Oscar Getz Foundation)
55 E. Monroe St., Ste. 4200
Chicago, IL 60603

Established in 1966 in IL.
Donors: Oscar Getz‡; Emma Getz.
Foundation type: Independent foundation.
Financial data (yr. ended 12/31/05): Assets,
$6,434,524 (M); expenditures, $1,002,745;
qualifying distributions, $855,195; giving activities
include $816,650 for 65 grants (high: $100,000;
low: $250).
Purpose and activities: Giving primarily for the arts,
particularly a jazz festival; funding also for
education, health, social services, community
foundations, and Jewish organizations.
Fields of interest: Museums; Performing arts,
theater; Performing arts, music; Arts; Elementary/
secondary education; Higher education; Education;
Environment, land resources; Health organizations;
Medical research, institute; Human services;
Foundations (community); Jewish agencies &
temples.
Limitations: Applications not accepted. Giving
primarily in Aspen, CO, and Chicago, IL. No grants to
individuals.
Application information: Contributes only to
pre-selected organizations.
Officers and Directors:* William M. Getz,* Pres.;
Ralph D. Silver,* V.P. and Secy.; H. Debra Levin,*
Treas.
EIN: 366150787

2754
**Christina and Ronald Gidwitz Charitable
Foundation** ◇
200 S. Wacker Dr.
Chicago, IL 60606

Established in 2001 in IL.
Donors: Christina K. Gidwitz; Ronald J. Gidwitz.
Foundation type: Independent foundation.
Financial data (yr. ended 12/31/05): Assets,
$7,424 (M); gifts received, $494,168;
expenditures, $497,778; qualifying distributions,
$493,334; giving activities include $493,334 for 9
grants (high: $250,000; low: $5,000).
Purpose and activities: Giving primarily to a
museum; funding also for theater, educational
organizations, including elementary education, a
Roman Catholic church, and to a YMCA.
Fields of interest: Museums; Performing arts,
theater; Education, management/technical aid;
Elementary school/education; YM/YWCAs & YM/
YWHAs; Roman Catholic agencies & churches.
Limitations: Giving primarily in Chicago, IL.
Application information:
Initial approach: Letter
Deadline(s): None
Officers: Christina K. Gidwitz, Chair.; Ronald J.
Gidwitz, Pres.; Herbert Halperin, Treas.
EIN: 364430172

2755
Gidwitz Family Foundation ◇
200 S. Wacker Dr., Ste. 4000
Chicago, IL 60606

Established in 1996 in IL.
Donors: James G. Gidwitz; Jane B. Gidwitz; Nancy
Gidwitz; Ronald J. Gidwitz.
Foundation type: Independent foundation.
Financial data (yr. ended 12/31/05): Assets,
$3,011,599 (M); gifts received, $161,504;
expenditures, $576,580; qualifying distributions,
$532,835; giving activities include $532,835 for 55
grants (high: $153,000; low: $75).
Purpose and activities: Giving primarily for arts and
culture, higher education, youth programs, and
Jewish organizations.
Fields of interest: Museums; Museums (science/
technology); Performing arts, theater; Performing
arts, opera; Higher education; Boys & girls clubs;
Jewish federated giving programs; Jewish agencies
& temples.
Limitations: Giving primarily in IL.
Application information: Application form not
required.
Initial approach: Letter
Deadline(s): None
Officers and Directors:* Betsy R. Gidwitz,* Pres.;
Ronald J. Gidwitz,* V.P.; Nancy Gidwitz,*
Secy.-Treas.; Alan K. Gidwitz; James G. Gidwitz;
Peter E. Gidwitz; Ralph W. Gidwitz; Teri Gidwitz;
Thomas R. Gidwitz; Linda Karamitis.
EIN: 364118455
Selected grants: The following grants were reported
in 2005.
$35,000 to Hotchkiss School, Lakeville, CT.
$25,000 to Lyric Opera of Chicago, Chicago, IL.
$16,000 to American Red Cross. 2 grants: $6,000,
$10,000
$5,000 to Chicago Foundation for Women, Chicago,
IL.
$5,000 to Jump Rhythm Jazz Project, Evanston, IL.

$3,000 to Chicago Jazz Ensemble, Chicago, IL.
$1,000 to Erikson Institute, Chicago, IL.
$1,000 to Jewish Federation.
$1,000 to Jewish Federation of Metropolitan
Chicago, Chicago, IL.

2756
**Joseph L. & Emily K. Gidwitz Memorial
Foundation** ◇
(formerly Division Fund)
200 S. Wacker Dr., Ste. 4000
Chicago, IL 60606-1274
Contact: Kevin O'Keefe

Established in 1983 as the Division Foundation.
Donor: Joseph L. Gidwitz.
Foundation type: Independent foundation.
Financial data (yr. ended 12/31/05): Assets,
$21,674,563 (M); expenditures, $907,696;
qualifying distributions, $630,000; giving activities
include $630,000 for 9 grants (high: $300,000;
low: $10,000).
Fields of interest: Museums; Human services;
Jewish federated giving programs.
International interests: Israel.
Limitations: Giving primarily in Chicago, IL.
Application information:
Initial approach: Letter
Deadline(s): None
Officers: Betsy R. Gidwitz, Pres.; Ronald J. Gidwitz,
Secy.
Director: Richard M. Horwood.
EIN: 363209007
Selected grants: The following grants were reported
in 2003.
$300,000 to Jewish United Fund of Metropolitan
Chicago, Chicago, IL. For general support.
$150,000 to Israel Emergency Fund. For general
support.
$100,000 to Field Museum of Natural History,
Chicago, IL. For general support.
$25,000 to American Jewish Committee, Chicago,
IL. For general support.
$17,500 to Anti-Defamation League of Bnai Brith,
Chicago, IL. For general support.

2757
Girl's Best Friend Foundation ◇
900 N. Franklin St., Ste. 210
Chicago, IL 60610 (312) 266-2842
Contact: Christine Plautz, Admin. and Grants Mgr.
TTY: (800) 526-0844; *FAX:* (312) 266-2972;
E-mail: contact@girlsbestfriend.org; *URL:* http://
www.girlsbestfriend.org

Established in 1994 in IL.
Donor: Cyndie McLachlan.
Foundation type: Independent foundation.
Financial data (yr. ended 6/30/05): Assets,
$2,214,550 (M); gifts received, $986,471;
expenditures, $1,691,194; qualifying distributions,
$1,682,499; giving activities include $1,039,606
for 102 grants (high: $23,000; low: $50).
Purpose and activities: The mission of the
foundation is to promote and protect the human
rights of girls in the Chicago, IL, area by advancing
and sustaining policies and programs that ensure
girls' self-determination, power, and well-being.
Fields of interest: Education; Youth development,
adult & child programs; Children/youth, services;
Women.

Type of support: General/operating support; Continuing support; Program development; Conferences/seminars; Research; Technical assistance; Program evaluation; Matching/challenge support.
Limitations: Giving primarily in the Chicago, IL, metropolitan area including Cook, DuPage, Kane, Lake, McHenry, and Will counties. No support for medical research organizations or to religious organizations. No grants to individuals, or for fund-raising events, endowments, capital fund drives, scholarships, fellowships, or debt reduction.
Publications: Application guidelines; Grants list; Informational brochure; Newsletter; Occasional report.
Application information: Application guidelines available on foundation Web site. Proposals sent by fax will not be accepted. In 2008, the foundation will award its final grants. Application form required.
Initial approach: Letter (not exceeding 3 pages)
Copies of proposal: 1
Deadline(s): 1st Mon. in Aug.
Board meeting date(s): Mar., June, Sept., and Dec.
Final notification: Jan.
Officers and Board Members:* Stephanie Kanter,* Co-Chair.; Mona Noriega,* Co-Chair.; Kate McLachlan,* Secy.; Tiffany Chiang,* Treas.; Alice Cottingham, Exec. Dir.; Nikita Buckhoy; Tracy Fischman; Cheryl Graves; Linda Hannah; Lesley Kennedy; Presita May; Cyndie McLachlan; Suleyma Perez.
Number of staff: 4 full-time professional; 1 part-time professional; 1 full-time support.
EIN: 363991813
Selected grants: The following grants were reported in 2005.
$51,000 to Illinois Caucus for Adolescent Health, Chicago, IL. 2 grants: $34,500, $16,500
$30,000 to Project Exploration, Chicago, IL.
$30,000 to Young Chicago Authors, Chicago, IL.
$21,375 to Girl Scouts of the U.S.A., Chicago, IL.
$20,000 to Blocks Together, Chicago, IL.
$20,000 to Family Matters, Chicago, IL.
$16,500 to Music Theater Workshop, Chicago, IL.
$16,500 to Young Womens Empowerment Project, Chicago, IL.
$3,300 to Community Extension Project, La Grange, IL.

2758
GKN Foundation ✧
(formerly Interlake Foundation)
550 Warrenville Rd.
Lisle, IL 60532-4387 (630) 719-7272
Contact: Hugo Perez, Treas.

Incorporated in 1951 in IL.
Donor: The Interlake Corp.
Foundation type: Company-sponsored foundation.
Financial data (yr. ended 12/31/05): Assets, $7,151,525 (M); expenditures, $514,536; qualifying distributions, $487,010; giving activities include $414,300 for 180 grants (high: $25,000; low: $150), $33,170 for grants to individuals, and $39,540 for employee matching gifts.
Purpose and activities: The foundation supports organizations involved with arts and culture, education, health, youth development, human services, and community development.
Fields of interest: Arts; Higher education; Libraries (public); Education; Hospitals (general); Health care; Health organizations, association; Cancer; Food

services; Youth development; Human services; Children/youth, services; Residential/custodial care, hospices; Community development; Federated giving programs.
Type of support: General/operating support; Continuing support; Capital campaigns; Scholarship funds; Research; Employee matching gifts; Matching/challenge support.
Limitations: Applications not accepted. Giving primarily in areas of company operations, with emphasis on IL. No support for political, religious, or athletics organizations.
Application information: Contributes only to pre-selected organizations.
Officers and Directors:* Stephen R. Smith,* V.P., Secy., and Gen. Counsel; Hugo Perez,* Treas.
EIN: 362590617

2759
Sidney and Lisa Glenner Foundation ✧
5454 W. Fargo Ave.
Skokie, IL 60077 (847) 674-5454
Contact: Sidney Glenner, Pres.

Established in 1986 in IL.
Donor: Sidney Glenner.
Foundation type: Independent foundation.
Financial data (yr. ended 11/30/05): Assets, $262,809 (M); gifts received, $1,450,000; expenditures, $2,690,902; qualifying distributions, $2,670,553; giving activities include $2,670,553 for 546 grants (high: $150,000; low: $10).
Purpose and activities: Giving primarily to Jewish temples and organizations including yeshivas.
Fields of interest: Education, management/technical aid; Jewish agencies & temples.
Type of support: General/operating support.
Limitations: Giving in the U.S. and Israel.
Application information:
Initial approach: Letter
Deadline(s): None
Officers and Directors:* Sidney Glenner,* Pres.; Lisa Glenner,* Secy.
EIN: 363557155

2760
Gloyd Family Foundation ✧
809 W. Detweiller Dr.
Peoria, IL 61615 (309) 691-0034
Contact: Cheryl Kuppler
Application address: c/o Sheryl J. Burdick, 6135 N. Black Oak Ct., Peoria, IL, 61615, tel.: (309) 693-1809

Established in 1997 in IL.
Donor: Lawrence E. Gloyd.
Foundation type: Independent foundation.
Financial data (yr. ended 12/31/05): Assets, $5,346,826 (M); expenditures, $423,752; qualifying distributions, $423,752; giving activities include $351,975 for 61 grants (high: $100,000; low: $100).
Purpose and activities: Giving primarily to a Presbyterian church. Support also for the arts, education, and children and youth services.
Fields of interest: Arts; Education; Big Brothers/Big Sisters; Human services; YM/YWCAs & YM/YWHAs; Children/youth, services; Protestant agencies & churches.

Limitations: Giving primarily in the greater Rockford, IL area. No support for political campaigns. No grants to individuals, or for loans.
Application information: Contact the foundation at least 2 weeks before applications are due to provide preliminary information. If it is determined that a request falls within the foundation's guidelines, an application will be supplied. Application form required.
Initial approach: Letter
Copies of proposal: 5
Deadline(s): May 1 and Nov. 1
Final notification: June 30 and Dec. 31
Officers and Directors:* Delma M. Gloyd,* Pres.; Lawrence E. Gloyd,* V.P.; Sheryl J. Burdick,* Secy.-Treas. and Mgr.; Julia G. Buchanan; Susan M. Crowell.
EIN: 364140796
Selected grants: The following grants were reported in 2005.
$80,000 to Rockford College, Rockford, IL.
$20,000 to Salvation Army. 3 grants: $10,000, $5,000, $5,000
$12,500 to United Way.
$10,000 to Girl Scouts of the U.S.A..
$3,000 to Hanover College, Hanover, IN.
$3,000 to Rockford Day Nursery, Rockford, IL.
$3,000 to YMCA.
$1,000 to Boys and Girls Club.

2761
The Milton D. and Madeline L. Goldberg Family Foundation ✧
(formerly ISGO Foundation)
c/o RSM McGladrey, Inc.
20 N. Martingale Rd., Ste. 500
Schaumburg, IL 60173

Incorporated in 1953 in IL.
Donors: Madeline L. Goldberg; ISGO Corp.
Foundation type: Independent foundation.
Financial data (yr. ended 5/31/05): Assets, $8,381,304 (M); expenditures, $367,586; qualifying distributions, $330,556; giving activities include $325,307 for 62 grants (high: $51,000; low: $50).
Purpose and activities: Giving primarily for Jewish organizations and federated giving programs, the arts, and human services.
Fields of interest: Museums (art); Museums (specialized); Performing arts; Higher education; Health care, formal/general education; Medical care, outpatient care; Health organizations, association; Human services; Residential/custodial care, hospices; Aging, centers/services; Civil rights; Jewish federated giving programs; Jewish agencies & temples.
Limitations: Applications not accepted. Giving primarily in San Diego, CA. No grants to individuals.
Application information: Contributes only to pre-selected organizations.
Officers: Madeline L. Goldberg, Pres. and Treas.; James W. Sansone, Secy.
Director: Hamilton Loeb.
EIN: 366064876
Selected grants: The following grants were reported in 2004.
$65,100 to Seacrest Village, CA.
$55,000 to San Diego Symphony Orchestra, San Diego, CA.
$45,300 to Jewish Family Services.
$35,000 to American Jewish Joint Distribution Committee, New York, NY.

$35,000 to Anti-Defamation League of Bnai Brith, San Diego, CA.

$35,000 to Jewish United Fund.

$10,050 to San Diego Hospice and Palliative Care, San Diego, CA.

$10,000 to La Jolla Playhouse, La Jolla, CA.

$10,000 to Museum of Photographic Arts, San Diego, CA.

$6,000 to San Diego Museum of Art, San Diego, CA.

2762
Golder Family Foundation ✧
254 Scott Ave.
Winnetka, IL   60093
Contact: Joan J. Golder, Pres.

Established in 1985 in IL.

Donors: Stanley C. Golder; Joan J. Golder.

Foundation type: Independent foundation.

Financial data (yr. ended 12/31/05): Assets, $6,030,827 (L); gifts received, $100,000; expenditures, $460,935; qualifying distributions, $411,152; giving activities include $398,658 for 17 grants (high: $65,000; low: $2,500).

Fields of interest: Education; Human services; Children/youth, services; Jewish federated giving programs; Jewish agencies & temples.

Limitations: Giving primarily in the Chicago, IL, area; some funding also in New York, NY. No grants to individuals.

Application information: Application form not required.

Deadline(s): None

Officers: Joan J. Golder, Pres. and Secy.; David B. Golder, V.P. and Treas.; Kenneth Golder, V.P.; Nancy Northrip, V.P.

EIN: 363485592

Selected grants: The following grants were reported in 2003.

$65,000 to Golden Apple Foundation, Chicago, IL. For unrestricted support.

$50,000 to Museum of Science and Industry, Chicago, IL. For unrestricted support.

$50,000 to Temple Jeremiah, Northfield, IL.

$45,000 to Hebrew Seminary of the Deaf, Skokie, IL.

$30,000 to YMCA, Greater Lake County Family, Waukegan, IL. For unrestricted support.

$25,000 to American Jewish Committee, Chicago, IL. For unrestricted support.

$25,000 to Jewish United Fund of Metropolitan Chicago, Chicago, IL. For unrestricted support.

$8,000 to Link Unlimited, Chicago, IL. For unrestricted support.

$5,000 to Drake University, Des Moines, IA. For unrestricted support.

$5,000 to Make-A-Wish Foundation of Northern Illinois, Chicago, IL. For unrestricted support.

2763
Goldman Philanthropic Partnerships ✧ ☆
(formerly Judith and George Goldman Foundation for Fighting Catastrophic Diseases)
70 W. Madison, No. 1500
Chicago, IL   60602   (312) 601-8855
Contact: Jerry Glashagel
URL: http://www.goldmanpartnerships.org

Established in 1998 in IL. Classified as a private operating foundation in 2000.

Donors: George N. Goldman; Mark Soriano; Merv Dukatt; Steve Dukatt.

Foundation type: Operating foundation.

Financial data (yr. ended 3/31/05): Assets, $2,239,978 (M); gifts received, $1,714,418; expenditures, $2,228,902; qualifying distributions, $2,222,031; giving activities include $1,609,000 for 30+ grants (high: $108,000), and $591,850 for foundation-administered programs.

Purpose and activities: Giving primarily for medical research.

Fields of interest: Education; Health care; Medical research, institute.

Type of support: Research.

Limitations: Giving primarily in CA and MN.

Application information:

Initial approach: Letter

Deadline(s): None

Officers: Roberta LaPorte, C.E.O; Judith Goldman, Pres.; George N. Goldman, V.P.; Michael Diamond, V.P.

Directors: Stephen Goldman; Nanci Goldman-Soriano; Perry Snyderman.

EIN: 364258390

Selected grants: The following grants were reported in 2005.

$108,000 to Columbia University, New York, NY.

$108,000 to Johns Hopkins University, Baltimore, MD.

$108,000 to Washington University, Saint Louis, MO.

$25,000 to Brown University, Providence, RI.

$25,000 to Childrens Hospital.

$25,000 to Purdue University, West Lafayette, IN.

$25,000 to University of California, Albany, CA.

$25,000 to University of Chicago, Chicago, IL.

$25,000 to University of Utah, Salt Lake City, UT.

2764
Walter & Karla Goldschmidt Foundation ✧
465 Lakeside Terr.
Glencoe, IL   60022-1760
Contact: Susan Goldschmidt, Treas.

Established in 1974 in IL.

Donors: Walter Goldschmidt; Karla Goldschmidt.

Foundation type: Independent foundation.

Financial data (yr. ended 11/30/05): Assets, $2,720,780 (M); expenditures, $328,042; qualifying distributions, $327,876; giving activities include $326,050 for 48 grants (high: $200,000; low: $25).

Purpose and activities: Giving to Jewish agencies, cultural institutes and for education.

Fields of interest: Arts, multipurpose centers/ programs; Performing arts, orchestra (symphony); Arts; Higher education, university; Health organizations, association; Medical research, institute; Human services; Jewish agencies & temples.

Limitations: Giving primarily in IL.

Application information: Application form not required.

Initial approach: Letter

Deadline(s): None

Officers: Walter Goldschmidt, Pres.; Karla Goldschmidt, V.P.; Susan Goldschmidt, Treas.

EIN: 237410867

Selected grants: The following grants were reported in 2003.

$80,000 to Project Lifeline, Glencoe, IL.

$10,000 to Jewish United Fund of Metropolitan Chicago, Chicago, IL.

$7,000 to Scottsdale Museum of Contemporary Art, Scottsdale, AZ.

$5,625 to Self-Help Action of Chicago, Chicago, IL.

$5,000 to SculptureCenter, Long Island City, NY.

$4,000 to Ravinia Festival Association, Highland Park, IL.

$2,347 to North Shore Congregation Israel, Glencoe, IL.

$1,000 to Chicago Symphony Orchestra, Chicago, IL.

$1,000 to New York University, Tisch School of the Arts, New York, NY.

$100 to United Way of Glencoe, Glencoe, IL.

2765
Gillian and Ellis Goodman Foundation ✧
69 Park Ave.
Glencoe, IL   60022

Established in 1987 in IL.

Donors: Gillian Goodman; Ellis M. Goodman; Paul Goodman.

Foundation type: Independent foundation.

Financial data (yr. ended 12/31/04): Assets, $9,062,404 (M); gifts received, $135,000; expenditures, $877,189; qualifying distributions, $848,676; giving activities include $848,676 for 72 grants (high: $250,000; low: $75).

Purpose and activities: Giving primarily for Jewish agencies and federated giving programs, the arts, education, and health and human services.

Fields of interest: Performing arts; Performing arts, theater; Arts; Higher education; Law school/ education; Health organizations, association; Human services; Neighborhood centers; Civil rights; Jewish federated giving programs.

Limitations: Applications not accepted. Giving primarily on a national basis, with some emphasis on Chicago and Glencoe, IL; funding also in London, England. No grants to individuals.

Application information: Contributes only to pre-selected organizations.

Officers: Ellis M. Goodman, Pres. and Treas.; Gillian Goodman, V.P. and Secy.

EIN: 363566590

Selected grants: The following grants were reported in 2003.

$300,000 to Jewish United Fund of Metropolitan Chicago, Chicago, IL.

$128,600 to Sustain, Chicago, IL.

$68,500 to Writers Theater, Glencoe, IL.

$25,000 to Joffrey Ballet of Chicago, Chicago, IL.

$15,000 to Anti-Defamation League of Bnai Brith, New York, NY.

$10,000 to Brandeis University, Waltham, MA.

$10,000 to University of Michigan, Ann Arbor, MI.

$2,000 to Cancer Prevention Coalition, Chicago, IL.

$1,500 to Rehabilitation Institute of Chicago, Chicago, IL.

$250 to Between Friends, Chicago, IL.

2766
Grace Foundation ▼ ✧
290 S. County Farm Rd., 3rd Fl.
Wheaton, IL   60187

Established in 1985 in IL.

Donor: Robert Van Kampen†.

Foundation type: Independent foundation.

Financial data (yr. ended 12/31/04): Assets, $29,503,697 (M); expenditures, $3,940,367;

qualifying distributions, $3,940,367; giving activities include $3,925,636 for 15 grants (high: $2,221,500; low: $1,200; average: $25,000–$200,000).

Purpose and activities: Giving primarily to Christian agencies, churches, and schools.

Fields of interest: Elementary/secondary education; Theological school/education; Christian agencies & churches.

Limitations: Applications not accepted. Giving primarily in IL. No grants to individuals.

Application information: Contributes only to pre-selected organizations.

Officers: Dean H. Tisch, V.P.; Jerald A. Trannel, Treas.; Scott Pierre, Exec. Dir.

Directors: Judith Van Kampen; Karla Van Kampen-Pierre; Kristen Wisen.

EIN: 363374325

Selected grants: The following grants were reported in 2004.

$2,221,500 to Sola Scriptura, Orlando, FL.
$629,174 to Zions Hope, Orlando, FL.
$455,162 to Masters Mission, Robbinsville, NC.
$230,000 to Hachotam Publishing House, Israel. .
$150,000 to Walk in the Word Ministries, Rolling Meadows, IL.
$110,000 to Josiah Venture, Wheaton, IL.
$39,000 to Van Kampen Foundation, Wheaton, IL.
$15,000 to World Harvest Ministries, Freeland, MI.

2767

Graham Foundation for Advanced Studies in the Fine Arts ◇

4 W. Burton Pl.
Chicago, IL 60610-1416 (312) 787-4071
Contact: Patricia Snyder, Admin.
E-mail: info@grahamfoundation.org; URL: http://www.grahamfoundation.org

Incorporated in 1956 in IL.
Donor: Ernest R. Graham†.
Foundation type: Independent foundation.
Financial data (yr. ended 12/31/05): Assets, $38,829,572 (M); expenditures, $2,078,108; qualifying distributions, $1,689,151; giving activities include $532,383 for 58 grants (high: $15,000), and $536,750 for 81 grants to individuals (high: $10,500).
Purpose and activities: Grants for advanced research in contemporary architecture, design, and the study of urban planning, principally to Americans working within the U.S. who have demonstrated mature, creative talent and have specific work objectives. Fellows are selected by the trustees on the recommendation of the director and special advisors. Some support for exhibitions, publications, lectures, and architectural and urban studies.
Fields of interest: Visual arts, architecture.
International interests: Canada.
Type of support: Program development; Conferences/seminars; Publication; Curriculum development; Fellowships; Research; Grants to individuals.
Limitations: Giving primarily in the U.S. and Canada. No grants for building or endowment funds, annual operating expenses, construction or architectural fees in support of construction or renovation projects, scholarships or projects done in pursuit of academic degrees (with the exception of the Carter Manny Award for doctoral candidates), or matching gifts; no loans.

Publications: Application guidelines; Annual report (including application guidelines); Grants list.
Application information: The foundation will not accept applications sent by fax or e-mail. Application guidelines available on foundation Web site. Application form not required.
Initial approach: Proposal with summary sheet
Copies of proposal: 1
Deadline(s): Mar. 15 for Carter Manny Award; July 15 and Jan. 15 for other grants
Board meeting date(s): Nov. and May
Final notification: 4 months for Carter Manny Award; 5 months for other grants
Director: Sarah Herda.
Trustees: Susan Bielstein; Roberta Feldman; Sunny Fischer; Henry H. Kuehn; James Nagle; John Syvertsen; Martha Thorne; Ben Weese; Daniel Wheeler; Robert Wislow.
Number of staff: 4 full-time professional; 2 full-time support.
EIN: 362356089

2768

The Grainger Foundation Inc. ▼

100 Grainger Pkwy.
Lake Forest, IL 60045-5201 (847) 535-1000
Contact: Lee J. Flory, V.P. and Exec. Dir.

Incorporated in 1967 in IL as successor to the Grainger Charitable Trust established in 1949.
Donors: William W. Grainger†; Hally W. Grainger†; David W. Grainger.
Foundation type: Independent foundation.
Financial data (yr. ended 12/31/05): Assets, $41,723,269 (M); expenditures, $7,770,463; qualifying distributions, $7,321,500; giving activities include $7,321,500 for 26 grants (high: $1,500,000; low: $2,500; average: $20,000–$300,000).
Purpose and activities: Emphasis on capital funds, and special program funds for higher education (colleges and universities), cultural and historical institutions (the arts, symphony orchestras, and museums), hospitals, and human service organizations.
Fields of interest: Museums; Historic preservation/historical societies; Arts; Higher education; Hospitals (general); Medical research; Human services; Engineering.
Type of support: General/operating support; Continuing support; Capital campaigns; Building/renovation; Equipment; Endowments; Program development; Professorships; Fellowships; Scholarship funds; Research.
Limitations: Applications not accepted. Giving primarily in the Chicago, IL, area. No grants to individuals, or for seed money, emergency funds, deficit financing, publications, conferences, or matching gifts; no loans.
Application information: The foundation contributes only to pre-selected charitable organizations as determined by its directors and officers. For this reason, and due to staffing constraints, grant requests received from organizations other than those first contacted by The Grainger Foundation cannot be reviewed or acknowledged.
Board meeting date(s): Periodically
Officers and Directors:* David W. Grainger,* Pres. and Treas.; Gloria J. Sinclair, V.P. and Secy.; Lee J. Flory,* V.P. and Exec. Dir.; William B. Hayden, V.P.; John S. Chapman; Richard L. Keyser.
Number of staff: 3 part-time professional.
EIN: 366192971

Selected grants: The following grants were reported in 2005.

$1,500,000 to Colonial Williamsburg Foundation, Williamsburg, VA. For Special Program Funds.
$1,429,500 to University of Missouri, Rolla, MO. For Special Program Fund.
$1,000,000 to Rensselaer Polytechnic Institute, Troy, NY. For Special Program Fund.
$1,000,000 to University of Washington, Seattle, WA. For Special Program Fund.
$383,900 to Museum of Science and Industry, Chicago, IL. For Special Program Fund.
$300,000 to Massachusetts Institute of Technology, Cambridge, MA. For Special Program Fund.
$250,000 to Salvation Army of Chicago, Chicago, IL. For Special Program Fund.
$200,000 to United Service Organization, DC. For Special Program Fund.
$105,000 to University of Wisconsin Foundation, Madison, WI. For Special Program Funds.
$75,000 to Science and Technology Interactive Center (SciTech), Aurora, IL. For Special Program Fund.

2769

Grand Victoria Foundation ▼

230 W. Monroe St., Ste. 2530
Chicago, IL 60606 (312) 609-0200
Contact: Nancy Fishman, Exec. Dir.
FAX: (312) 658-0738;
E-mail: nancyf@grandvictoriafdn.org; Application address for Elgin Grantworks: 60 S. Grove Ave., Elgin, IL 60120, tel.: (847) 289-8575, FAX: (847) 289-8576; Additional E-mail: info@grandvictoriafdn.org; URL: http://www.grandvictoriafdn.org

Established in 1996 in IL.
Donors: Grand Victoria Casino; Elgin Riverboat Resort.
Foundation type: Company-sponsored foundation.
Financial data (yr. ended 12/31/05): Assets, $118,765,585 (M); gifts received, $14,386,560; expenditures, $8,283,216; qualifying distributions, $8,018,839; giving activities include $6,765,044 for 161 grants (high: $385,084; low: $250), and $4,300 for 12 employee matching gifts.
Purpose and activities: The foundation supports organizations involved with education, the environment, employment, housing, youth development, children's day care, economic development, business and industry, and transportation.
Fields of interest: Education, equal rights; Education, early childhood education; Teacher school/education; Education; Environment, public education; Environment, pollution control; Environment, natural resources; Environment, water resources; Environment, land resources; Environment, energy; Environmental education; Environment; Employment; Housing/shelter; Youth development; Children, day care; Economic development; Business/industry; Transportation.
Type of support: General/operating support; Management development/capacity building; Land acquisition; Program development; Scholarship funds; Technical assistance; Program-related investments/loans; Employee matching gifts; Matching/challenge support.
Limitations: Giving limited to IL, with emphasis on the Chicago metropolitan area, Elgin, and southern Cook, DeKalb, DuPage, Kane, Kendall, Lake,

McHenry, Winnebago, and Will counties. No support for grantmaking organizations or federated funds. No grants to individuals, or for endowments, fundraising events, debt reduction, political campaigns, or religious programs; generally, no grants for research or planning projects.
Publications: Application guidelines; Financial statement; Grants list; Informational brochure; Newsletter.
Application information: An application form is required for Elgin Grantworks.
Initial approach: Letter of inquiry for Education, Economic Development, and Environment; download application form and mail proposal and application form to application address for Elgin Grantworks
Deadline(s): 1st Fri. in May and Oct. for Education, Economic Development, and Environment; 1st Fri. in Feb., June, and Oct. for Elgin Grantworks
Board meeting date(s): Quarterly
Final notification: 10 business days for Education, Economic Development, and Environment; 8 to 10 weeks for Elgin Grantworks
Officers and Directors:* Nicholas J. Pritzker,* Pres.; Richard L. Schulze, Exec. V.P.; Merlinda Gallegos,* Secy.; Antonio Gracias,* Treas.; Nancy Fishman, Exec. Dir.; Dan Azark; Zelema Harris; Taffy Hoffer; Gary Jacobs; John Redmond.
Number of staff: 2 full-time professional; 2 full-time support.
EIN: 364107162
Selected grants: The following grants were reported in 2005.
$385,084 to Illinois Facilities Fund, Chicago, IL. For program support.
$215,000 to Chicago Jobs Council, Chicago, IL. For program support.
$200,000 to Moline Foundation, Moline, IL. For challenge grant.
$95,000 to Illinois Mathematics and Science Academy, Aurora, IL. For program support.
$90,000 to Nature Conservancy, Chicago, IL. For program support.
$75,000 to Illinois Network of Child Care Resource and Referral Agencies, Bloomington, IL. For program support.
$60,000 to De Kalb County Community Foundation, Sycamore, IL. For general operating support.
$41,000 to Conservation Foundation of DuPage County, Naperville, IL. For program support.
$31,100 to Bright Beginnings Childcare, Aledo, IL. For program support.
$30,000 to ACCION Chicago, Chicago, IL. For program support.

2770
Grant Healthcare Foundation
500 N. Western Ave., Ste. 204
Lake Forest, IL   60045   (847) 735-1590
Contact: Joan Eldridge Ridell, Exec. Dir.
E-mail: granthealthcare@sbcglobal.net; FAX: (847) 735-8770; URL: http://www.granthealthcare.org

Established in 1996 in IL.
Foundation type: Independent foundation.
Financial data (yr. ended 12/31/05): Assets, $29,393,742 (M); expenditures, $2,047,244; qualifying distributions, $1,703,241; giving activities include $1,703,241 for 46 grants (high: $150,000; low: $150).
Purpose and activities: Giving primarily for hospitals and healthcare organizations in the greater Chicago, IL, area.

Fields of interest: Hospitals (general); Reproductive health; Health care; Medical research, institute.
Type of support: General/operating support; Building/renovation; Equipment; Program development; Seed money; Research.
Limitations: Giving primarily in Chicago, IL, and the surrounding metropolitan area. No support for religious and political organizations. No grants to individuals.
Publications: Application guidelines; Grants list.
Application information: Application form required.
Initial approach: Preliminary grant inquiry
Copies of proposal: 7
Deadline(s): Preliminary grants: July 20, Sept. 1 final deadline
Board meeting date(s): Monthly, except Jan. and Feb.
Final notification: Dec. 15
Officers and Directors:* Robert F. Carr III,* Chair.; George M. Covington,* Secy.-Treas.; Joan Eldridge Ridell, Exec. Dir.; Joseph S. Carr; Robert Friedlander; Lawrence D. Glass; Richard M. Norton.
Number of staff: 1 full-time professional.
EIN: 362167090
Selected grants: The following grants were reported in 2004.
$175,000 to University of Chicago Childrens Hospital, Chicago, IL. 2 grants: $50,000, $125,000
$100,000 to Chicago Botanic Garden, Glencoe, IL.
$100,000 to Childrens Memorial Hospital, Chicago, IL.
$100,000 to Lincoln Park Zoo, Chicago, IL.
$60,000 to Young Womens Leadership Charter School of Chicago, Chicago, IL.
$50,000 to Access Community Health Network, Chicago, IL.
$45,000 to Horizon Hospice and Palliative Care, Chicago, IL.
$40,000 to Hadley School for the Blind, Winnetka, IL.
$25,000 to Chicago Hearing Society, Chicago, IL.

2771
Richard and Mary Gray Foundation
875 N. Michigan Ave., Ste. 2503
Chicago, IL   60611-3103
Contact: Richard Gray, Pres.
E-mail: rgray@richardgraygallery.com

Established in 1987 in IL.
Donors: Richard Gray; Graycor, Inc.
Foundation type: Independent foundation.
Financial data (yr. ended 12/31/05): Assets, $11,902,827 (M); gifts received, $288,315; expenditures, $687,604; qualifying distributions, $498,595; giving activities include $498,595 for grants.
Purpose and activities: Giving for arts and culture and human services.
Fields of interest: Visual arts, architecture; Museums; Performing arts; Performing arts, music; Historic preservation/historical societies; Arts; Higher education.
Type of support: General/operating support; Annual campaigns; Capital campaigns; Endowments.
Limitations: Applications not accepted. Giving primarily in Chicago, IL. No grants to individuals.
Application information: Unsolicited requests for funds not accepted.
Officers: Richard Gray, Pres.; Mary L. Gray, V.P.
EIN: 363485580

2772
David Green and Mary Winton Green Foundation ◇
(formerly Quartet Foundation in Honor of David and Mary W. Green)
650 Dundee Rd., No. 456
Northbrook, IL   60062

Donors: David Green; Mary Winton Green; Quartet Manufacturing Co.
Foundation type: Independent foundation.
Financial data (yr. ended 12/31/05): Assets, $1,394,915 (M); expenditures, $5,705,861; qualifying distributions, $5,681,422; giving activities include $5,670,000 for 6 grants (high: $4,010,000; low: $10,000).
Purpose and activities: Giving primarily for higher education and the performing arts, particularly theater.
Fields of interest: Performing arts, theater; Higher education.
Limitations: Applications not accepted. Giving primarily in Chicago, IL. No grants to individuals.
Application information: Contributes only to pre-selected organizations.
Trustees: David Green; Mary Winton Green.
EIN: 363776779

2773
John C. Griswold Foundation
c/o James Donnelley, Stet and Query, LP
360 N. Michigan Ave., Ste. 1009
Chicago, IL   60601   (312) 827-1201
Contact: James R. Donnelley, V.P. and Treas.
FAX: (312) 827-1234;
E-mail: james.donnelley@stetandquery.com

Established in 1978 in NY.
Donor: John C. Griswold†.
Foundation type: Independent foundation.
Financial data (yr. ended 11/30/05): Assets, $13,639,397 (M); gifts received, $500,000; expenditures, $934,032; qualifying distributions, $813,408; giving activities include $772,000 for 68 grants (high: $160,000; low: $500).
Purpose and activities: Giving only to organizations in which family and outside trustees have an interest.
Type of support: General/operating support; Continuing support; Annual campaigns; Building/renovation.
Limitations: Applications not accepted. No grants to individuals.
Application information: Support limited to charities which are already known to the trustees.
Board meeting date(s): Varies
Officers and Trustees:* Jacqueline G. Moore,* Chair.; Jeffrey W. Earls,* Pres.; D. Ross Griswold, Jr., V.P.; Allyson Griswold Dayak, V.P.; James R. Donnelley,* Treas.
Advisory Committee: Christopher B. Earls; Christopher J. Earls; David Earls; John G. Earls; Keith Earls; Michael B. Earls; Stephanie Earls; Mark Griswold.
Number of staff: 1 part-time support.
EIN: 132978937

2774
David F. and Margaret T. Grohne Family Foundation ◇
907 Lawn Ct.
Western Springs, IL 60558
Contact: David Grohne, Pres.

Established in 1995 in IL.
Donors: David Grohne; Margaret Grohne.
Foundation type: Independent foundation.
Financial data (yr. ended 12/31/05): Assets, $40,278,457 (M); gifts received, $9,765,562; expenditures, $1,453,789; qualifying distributions, $1,305,700; giving activities include $1,305,700 for 10 grants (high: $1,000,000; low: $100).
Fields of interest: Animals/wildlife, preservation/protection; Animals/wildlife, bird preserves.
Limitations: Giving primarily in TN. No grants to individuals.
Application information: Application form not required.
Deadline(s): None
Officers: David Grohne, Pres.; Margaret Grohne, V.P.
Director: Jeffrey Grohne.
EIN: 364061509

2775
The Guth Foundation Charitable Trust ◇
(formerly The Guth Foundation)
c/o Bank of America, N.A.
231 S. LaSalle St., IL1-231-14-19
Chicago, IL 60697

Established in 1993 in MO.
Donor: James Black Guth.
Foundation type: Independent foundation.
Financial data (yr. ended 12/31/05): Assets, $6,787,931 (M); expenditures, $610,268; qualifying distributions, $529,395; giving activities include $505,000 for 28 grants (high: $100,000; low: $5,000).
Purpose and activities: Giving primarily for health associations, children and youth services, including children's hospitals, and human services, including services for people who are blind or deaf.
Fields of interest: Hospitals (general); Health organizations; Youth development, centers/clubs; Human services; YM/YWCAs & YM/YWHAs; Children/youth, services.
Limitations: Applications not accepted. Giving primarily in St. Louis, MO. No grants to individuals.
Application information: Contributes only to pre-selected organizations.
Trustee: Mark J. Bade; Sally C. Coleman; Edward J. Costigan, III, Jr.; Bank of America, N.A.
EIN: 436462823

2776
The Leo S. Guthman Fund ◇ ☆
c/o Iris Krieg Assocs.
203 N. Wabash Ave., No. 1800
Chicago, IL 60601

Established in 2004 in IL.
Foundation type: Independent foundation.
Financial data (yr. ended 12/31/04): Assets, $4,355,947 (M); expenditures, $1,084,976; qualifying distributions, $1,074,013; giving activities include $1,021,647 for 102 grants (high: $50,000; low: $475).

Purpose and activities: Giving primarily for Jewish organizations, including Jewish family services, and to women's organizations and services; funding also for children, youth and social services.
Fields of interest: Museums; Human services; Children/youth, services; Family services; Jewish agencies & temples; Women.
Limitations: Applications not accepted. Giving primarily in CA and IL; some funding nationally. No grants to individuals.
Application information: Contributes only to pre-selected organizations.
Officer and Director:* Harold D. Shapiro,* Secy.
Trustees: Lynne Rosenthal; Patti Silver.
EIN: 611459002

2777
The H.B.B. Foundation ◇
400 N. Michigan Ave., Ste. 1120
Chicago, IL 60611

Established in 1964 in IL.
Donor: Elizabeth Babson Tieken Charitable Lead Trust.
Foundation type: Independent foundation.
Financial data (yr. ended 12/31/05): Assets, $12,469,180 (M); gifts received, $909,967; expenditures, $621,736; qualifying distributions, $596,130; giving activities include $525,000 for 56 grants (high: $60,000; low: $500).
Purpose and activities: Giving primarily for health services and the arts.
Fields of interest: Museums; Arts; Education; Environment; Hospitals (general); Health organizations, association; Human services; Children/youth, services.
Limitations: Applications not accepted. Giving in the U.S., with emphasis on IL; some giving also in CO, MA, and VA. No grants to individuals.
Application information: Contributes only to pre-selected organizations.
Officers and Directors:* Theodore D. Tieken, Jr.,* Pres.; Mark Stephenitch,* Treas.; Elizabeth Kirkpatrick; Nancy B. Tieken.
EIN: 366104969

2778
William M. Hales Foundation ◇
120 W. Madison St., Ste. 700-E
Chicago, IL 60602

Established in 1991 in IL.
Donors: William M. Hales; Mary C. Hales; Lynn H. Jacob; John W. Hales.
Foundation type: Independent foundation.
Financial data (yr. ended 12/31/05): Assets, $6,138,764 (M); expenditures, $367,863; qualifying distributions, $329,289; giving activities include $325,400 for 37 grants (high: $93,000; low: $500).
Fields of interest: Arts; Higher education; Health care; Human services; Federated giving programs.
Limitations: Giving primarily in IL, with emphasis on Chicago. No grants to individuals.
Application information: Application form not required.
Deadline(s): None
Officers and Directors:* Mary C. Hales,* Pres.; John W. Hales,* Secy.-Treas.; Catherine L. Hales; Erick W. Hales.
EIN: 363735095

Selected grants: The following grants were reported in 2005.
$93,000 to Beloit College, Beloit, WI.
$75,000 to Urantia Foundation, Chicago, IL.
$5,000 to Oglala Lakota College, Kyle, SD.
$4,500 to Winnetka Congregational Church, Winnetka, IL.
$500 to Hadley School for the Blind, Winnetka, IL.
$500 to Newberry Library, Chicago, IL.

2779
John R. Halligan Charitable Fund
c/o Neal, Gerber & Eisenberg, LLP
2 N. LaSalle St., Ste. 2200
Chicago, IL 60602
Contact: Norman J. Gantz, Pres.
E-mail: ngantz@ngelaw.com

Established in 1963 in IL.
Donor: John R. Halligan†.
Foundation type: Independent foundation.
Financial data (yr. ended 12/31/05): Assets, $25,611,114 (M); expenditures, $1,332,351; qualifying distributions, $1,196,332; giving activities include $1,119,369 for 63 grants (high: $162,269; low: $2,500).
Purpose and activities: Giving for the arts, civic and cultural institutes.
Fields of interest: Museums; Historic preservation/historical societies; Arts; Animals/wildlife.
Type of support: General/operating support; Continuing support; Annual campaigns.
Limitations: Applications not accepted. Giving primarily in Honolulu, HI, and Chicago, IL. No grants to individuals.
Application information: Contributes only to pre-selected organizations.
Officers and Directors:* Norman J. Gantz,* Pres.; Norman Kellerman,* Treas.; Lawrence Richman.
EIN: 366078591
Selected grants: The following grants were reported in 2005.
$162,269 to Lyric Opera of Chicago, Chicago, IL.
$40,000 to Bishop Museum, Honolulu, HI.
$40,000 to Hawaii Opera Theater, Honolulu, HI.
$40,000 to Honolulu Symphony, Honolulu, HI.
$40,000 to Humane Society.
$35,000 to Chicago Historical Society, Chicago, IL.
$20,000 to Lincoln Park Zoo, Chicago, IL.
$17,500 to Chicago Zoological Society, Brookfield, IL.
$7,500 to Joffrey Ballet of Chicago, Chicago, IL.
$5,000 to PAWS Chicago, Chicago, IL.

2780
Hamill Family Foundation ◇
(formerly Happy Hollow Fund)
c/o Corwith Hamill
P.O. Box 206
Wayne, IL 60184-0206

Established in 1963.
Donors: Corwith Hamill; Joan B. Hamill†; Jonathan C. Hamill.
Foundation type: Independent foundation.
Financial data (yr. ended 12/31/05): Assets, $26,127,750 (M); gifts received, $7,172; expenditures, $1,830,903; qualifying distributions, $1,679,175; giving activities include $1,663,468 for 207 grants.

Purpose and activities: Giving primarily for the environment and animal welfare; giving also for education, the arts, and health and human services.
Fields of interest: Arts; Higher education; Environment; Human services; Christian agencies & churches.
Type of support: General/operating support; Continuing support; Capital campaigns; Endowments; Debt reduction; Matching/challenge support.
Limitations: Applications not accepted. Giving primarily in IL. No grants to individuals.
Application information: Contributes only to pre-selected organizations.
Officers and Directors:* Corwith Hamill,* Chair.; Elizabeth C. Bramsen,* V.P.; Nancy C.H. Winter,* V.P.; Jonathan C. Hamill,* Secy.-Treas.
EIN: 366096808

2781
Charles & Carol Hammersmith Family Foundation ✧
400 W. 1st St.
Elmhurst, IL 60126

Established in 1999 in IL.
Donors: Charles P. Hammersmith, Jr.; Carol D. Hammersmith.
Foundation type: Independent foundation.
Financial data (yr. ended 12/31/04): Assets, $1,973,761 (M); expenditures, $477,172; qualifying distributions, $466,350; giving activities include $466,350 for 17 grants (high: $300,000; low: $100).
Fields of interest: Education, special; Higher education; Youth development, adult & child programs.
Limitations: Applications not accepted. Giving primarily in IL. No grants to individuals.
Application information: Contributes only to pre-selected organizations.
Officers and Directors:* Charles P. Hammersmith, Jr.,* Pres.; Kenneth J. Lahner,* V.P.; Carol Hammersmith,* Secy.-Treas.; Charles P. Hammersmith, Sr.
EIN: 364334722

2782
Hansen-Furnas Foundation, Inc. ✧
(formerly Furnas Foundation, Inc.)
28 S. Water St., Ste. 310
Batavia, IL 60510

Incorporated in 1960 in IL.
Donors: W.C. Furnas†; Leto M. Furnas†.
Foundation type: Independent foundation.
Financial data (yr. ended 12/31/05): Assets, $904,072 (M); gifts received, $460,000; expenditures, $541,791; qualifying distributions, $540,666; giving activities include $243,597 for grants, and $247,244 for grants to individuals.
Purpose and activities: Emphasis on higher education, including a scholarship program for undergraduate study; support also for health and family agencies, hospices, and community funds.
Fields of interest: Higher education; Health care; Family services; Residential/custodial care, hospices.
Type of support: Annual campaigns; Capital campaigns; Building/renovation; Equipment;

Scholarships—to individuals; Matching/challenge support.
Limitations: Giving primarily in IA and IL; giving limited to Clarke County, IA, and within 15 miles of Batavia, IL, for scholarships. No grants to individuals (except for scholarships); no loans.
Publications: Application guidelines; Informational brochure; Program policy statement.
Application information: Application form required for scholarships; request form from scholarship committee.
 Initial approach: Proposal or letter
 Copies of proposal: 1
 Deadline(s): Mar. 1
 Board meeting date(s): Jan., Apr., July, and Oct.
 Final notification: May 15
Officers: Joanne B. Hansen, Pres.; Gilbert R. Nary, Treas.
Directors: Kirsten Hansen Barkley; Thomas F. Caughlin; James Hansen; Lisa Hansen; Richard W. Hansen; Robert F. Peterson; Britt Hansen Phillips.
EIN: 366049894
Selected grants: The following grants were reported in 2003.
$28,250 to Iowa State University, Ames, IA. For scholarships.
$17,640 to Purdue University, West Lafayette, IN. For scholarships.
$15,000 to Lazarus House, Saint Charles, IL. For general support.
$15,000 to Rose-Hulman Institute of Technology, Terre Haute, IN. For scholarships.
$15,000 to Suicide Prevention Services, Batavia, IL. For general support.
$15,000 to Tri-City Health Partnership, Saint Charles, IL. For general support.
$10,100 to Northern Illinois University, De Kalb, IL. For scholarships.
$10,000 to Delnor Health Care Foundation, Saint Charles, IL. For general support.
$10,000 to TriCity Family Services, Geneva, IL. For general support.
$7,032 to Aurora University, Aurora, IL. For scholarships.

2783
Alice G. Hanson Family Foundation, Inc. ✧
c/o The Northern Trust Co.
P.O. Box 803878
Chicago, IL 60680

Foundation type: Independent foundation.
Financial data (yr. ended 12/31/04): Assets, $10,806,147 (M); expenditures, $565,677; qualifying distributions, $466,770; giving activities include $437,500 for 8 grants (high: $250,000; low: $2,500).
Fields of interest: Higher education, university; Hospitals (general); Jewish agencies & temples.
Limitations: Applications not accepted. Giving primarily in FL and NY. No grants to individuals.
Application information: Contributes only to pre-selected organizations.
Officers and Directors:* Burton Rottman,* Pres.; Howard Rottman,* Secy.; Michael Rottman,* Treas.
EIN: 363215192

2784
George and Barbara Hanus Foundation ✧
333 W. Wacker Dr., Ste. 2700
Chicago, IL 60606

Established in 1986 in IL.
Donor: George D. Hanus.
Foundation type: Independent foundation.
Financial data (yr. ended 11/30/05): Assets, $807,571 (M); gifts received, $1,095,941; expenditures, $1,221,839; qualifying distributions, $1,221,839; giving activities include $1,177,605 for 20+ grants (high: $524,385).
Purpose and activities: Giving primarily to Jewish organizations, including a Jewish broadcasting network and a Jewish publication; funding also for scholarships and yeshivas.
Fields of interest: Elementary/secondary education; Higher education; Scholarships/financial aid; Jewish agencies & temples.
Limitations: Applications not accepted. Giving primarily in IL. No grants to individuals.
Application information: Contributes only to pre-selected organizations. Unsolicited requests for funds not considered.
Directors: Barbara A. Hanus; George D. Hanus; Magda Hanus.
EIN: 363485278

2785
Marguerite Delaney Hark Foundation ✧
325 W. Wellington Ave.
Chicago, IL 60657

Established in 1988 in IL.
Donor: Marguerite D. Hark.
Foundation type: Independent foundation.
Financial data (yr. ended 12/31/05): Assets, $4,408,134 (M); gifts received, $360,653; expenditures, $505,133; qualifying distributions, $480,149; giving activities include $470,000 for 5 grants (high: $200,000; low: $20,000).
Purpose and activities: Giving primarily for housing and community development.
Fields of interest: Higher education; Housing/shelter, development; Human services; Children/youth, services.
Limitations: Applications not accepted. Giving primarily in IL. No grants to individuals.
Application information: Contributes only to pre-selected organizations.
Trustees: William P. Eftax; Marguerite Delany Hark; Thomas Royce Leach; Richard C. Ruwe.
EIN: 363617116

2786
Philip S. Harper Foundation ✧
c/o Harper-Wyman Co.
930 N. York Rd., Ste. 204
Hinsdale, IL 60521-2913 (630) 887-8688
Contact: Charles C. Lamar, Secy.-Treas.

Incorporated in 1953 in IL.
Donors: Philip S. Harper; Harper-Wyman Co.
Foundation type: Independent foundation.
Financial data (yr. ended 9/30/05): Assets, $7,755,162 (M); expenditures, $424,577; qualifying distributions, $358,569; giving activities include $337,950 for 172 grants (high: $25,000; low: $250).
Purpose and activities: Giving primarily for the arts, education, Protestant churches and organizations, and for human services.
Fields of interest: Media/communications; Arts; Elementary/secondary education; Higher education; Environment, natural resources; Health care;

Medical research, institute; Legal services; Human services; Children/youth, services; Public affairs; Christian agencies & churches; Protestant agencies & churches.

Limitations: Applications not accepted. Giving on a national basis. No grants to individuals.

Application information: Unsolicited requests for funds not accepted.

Officers: Philip S. Harper, Jr., Pres.; Lamar Harper Williams, V.P.; Charles C. Lamar, Secy.-Treas.

EIN: 366049875

2787
Harris Bank Foundation ✧

P.O. Box 755
Chicago, IL 60690-0755 (312) 461-5834
Contact: Mary H. Houpt, Secy.-Treas.

Incorporated in 1953 in IL.

Donors: Harris Bankcorp, Inc.; Harris Trust and Savings Bank.

Foundation type: Company-sponsored foundation.

Financial data (yr. ended 12/31/05): Assets, $2,727,889 (M); gifts received, $1,500,000; expenditures, $2,529,366; qualifying distributions, $2,608,337; giving activities include $1,796,509 for 96 grants (high: $215,000; low: $500), and $397,141 for employee matching gifts.

Purpose and activities: The foundation supports organizations involved with education, employment, social services, community development, and civic affairs.

Fields of interest: Education; Employment; Human services; Community development; Public affairs.

Type of support: Employee volunteer services; General/operating support; Continuing support; Annual campaigns; Capital campaigns; Building/ renovation; Equipment; Program development; Seed money; Technical assistance; Program-related investments/loans; Employee matching gifts; Employee-related scholarships; In-kind gifts; Matching/challenge support.

Limitations: Giving limited to the greater metropolitan Chicago, IL, area, with emphasis on the neighborhood of North Lawndale. No support for sectarian or religious organizations, fraternal organizations, political organizations, hospitals, national health organizations, or private elementary or secondary schools. No grants to individuals (except for employee-related scholarships), or for research, publications, sponsorships, conferences, testimonials, or advertisements.

Publications: Application guidelines; Program policy statement.

Application information: The Chicago Area Common Grant Application Form is required. Organizations receiving support are asked to provide periodic progress reports. Application form required.

Initial approach: Mail application form to foundation
Copies of proposal: 1
Deadline(s): None
Board meeting date(s): As needed
Final notification: 2 weeks following board meetings

Officers and Directors:* Robin S. Coffey,* Pres.; Joseph Teller, V.P.; Mary H. Houpt,* Secy.-Treas.; Anne Coon,* Recording Secy.; Michael Chin; Daniela O'Leary Gill; Angela Smith.

Number of staff: 1 full-time professional; 1 part-time professional; 1 full-time support.

EIN: 366033888

2788
Harris Family Foundation ✧

200 S. Wacker Dr., Ste. 3900
Chicago, IL 60606 (312) 831-4130

Incorporated in 1957 in IL.

Donors: Nelson Harris‡; KPH Trust; KWWH Trust; THP Trust; King W. Harris.

Foundation type: Independent foundation.

Financial data (yr. ended 2/28/05): Assets, $53,896,244 (M); gifts received, $963,809; expenditures, $3,377,099; qualifying distributions, $3,150,151; giving activities include $3,150,151 for 126 grants (high: $500,000; low: $100; average: $500–$5,000).

Purpose and activities: Giving primarily for education, arts and culture, botanical gardens, zoos, hospitals and medical research, human services, children and family services, and Jewish organizations and temples.

Fields of interest: Arts; Higher education; Education; Botanical gardens; Zoos/zoological societies; Hospitals (general); Medical care, rehabilitation; Health organizations, association; Medical research, institute; Human services; Children/youth, services; Family services; Jewish federated giving programs; Jewish agencies & temples.

Type of support: General/operating support; Continuing support; Annual campaigns; Capital campaigns; Building/renovation; Conferences/ seminars; Professorships; Internship funds; Scholarship funds.

Limitations: Giving primarily in the Chicago, IL, area. No grants to individuals.

Application information: Application form not required.

Initial approach: Letter
Copies of proposal: 1
Deadline(s): None
Board meeting date(s): May and Nov.
Final notification: 30 days

Officer and Directors:* Edward Schwartz,* Secy.-Treas.; Bette D. Harris; Katherine Harris; King W. Harris; Toni H. Paul.

EIN: 366054378

Selected grants: The following grants were reported in 2003.

$500,000 to Phillips Academy, Andover, MA.
$425,000 to Jewish United Fund of Metropolitan Chicago, Chicago, IL.
$400,000 to Family Institute of Chicago, Chicago, IL.
$350,000 to Illinois Mathematics and Science Academy, Aurora, IL.
$200,000 to Yale University, New Haven, CT.
$150,000 to Ounce of Prevention Fund, Chicago, IL.
$135,000 to University of Chicago, Chicago, IL.
$94,000 to Museum of Contemporary Art, Chicago, IL.
$50,000 to Music and Dance Theater Chicago, Chicago, IL.
$40,000 to Art Institute of Chicago, Chicago, IL.

2789
The Irving Harris Foundation ▼

(formerly The Harris Foundation)
191 N. Wacker Dr., Ste. 1500
Chicago, IL 60606-1899 (312) 621-0566
Contact: For Arts Proposals: Joan W. Harris, Chair.; For all other proposals: June Matayoshi, Grants Admin.

Incorporated in 1945 in MN.

Donors: Joan W. Harris; Members of the Harris family; Alliance Capital Management Corp.

Foundation type: Independent foundation.

Financial data (yr. ended 12/31/04): Assets, $153,596,227 (M); gifts received, $1,838,790; expenditures, $12,640,293; qualifying distributions, $9,927,470; giving activities include $9,284,638 for 262 grants (high: $1,000,000; low: $100; average: $1,000–$500,000), and $17,980 for 71 employee matching gifts.

Purpose and activities: Interests include demonstration programs in prevention of family dysfunction; prevention of teenage pregnancy and infant mortality and morbidity; infant mental health and early childhood development; Jewish charities; and the arts and educational television.

Fields of interest: Arts; Education, early childhood education; Child development, education; Reproductive health, family planning; Human services; Children/youth, services; Child development, services; Family services; Jewish federated giving programs.

Type of support: General/operating support; Program development; Employee matching gifts.

Publications: Financial statement.

Application information: Generally contributes to pre-selected organizations. Application form not required for those who still wish to apply. The foundation is currently in transition, so board meeting dates are not consistent. Call for latest information. Application form not required.

Initial approach: Letter of inquiry
Copies of proposal: 1
Deadline(s): Apr. 1 and Sept. 1
Board meeting date(s): May/June and Sept./Oct.
Final notification: Following board meetings, approximately Apr./May and Oct./Nov.

Officer and Trustees:* Joan W. Harris,* Chair.; Benjamin Harris; David Harris; Alicia Lieberman; Daniel Meyer; Harriet Meyer; Nancy Meyer; Charles Polsky; Jack Polsky.

Number of staff: 3 full-time professional; 1 full-time support; 2 part-time support.

EIN: 366055115

Selected grants: The following grants were reported in 2004.

$1,000,000 to University of Chicago, Chicago, IL. For scholarships and fellowships.
$600,000 to Planned Parenthood/Chicago Area, Chicago, IL. For institutional support.
$500,000 to Jewish United Fund of Metropolitan Chicago, Chicago, IL. For project support.
$231,000 to Foundation for Children at Risk, Tel Aviv, Israel. For project support.
$225,000 to Chicago Childrens Museum, Chicago, IL. For institutional support.
$34,000 to Zero to Three: National Center for Infants, Toddlers and Families, DC. For project support.
$20,000 to M. B. Fund, DC. For institutional support.
$15,000 to Crossroads Fund, Chicago, IL. For institutional support.
$10,000 to Spertus Institute of Jewish Studies, Chicago, IL. For institutional support.
$2,500 to Theater for a New Audience, New York, NY. For institutional support.

2790
Fred G. Harrison Foundation ✦ ☆
101 S. Park Ave.
Herrin, IL 62948-3609
Application address: The Bank of Herrin, P.O. Box B, Herrin, IL 62948, tel.: (618) 942-6666

Established in 1969 in IL.
Donors: Julia Harrison Bruce†; Fred G. Harrison†.
Foundation type: Independent foundation.
Financial data (yr. ended 12/31/05): Assets, $16,088,084 (M); expenditures, $901,984; qualifying distributions, $567,356; giving activities include $537,411 for 11 grants (high: $124,764; low: $300), and $4,000 for 4 grants to individuals (high: $1,000; low: $1,000).
Purpose and activities: Support primarily for social services, education, civic improvements, and churches; scholarships awarded to high school seniors.
Fields of interest: Libraries/library science; Education; Human services; Community development, civic centers; Government/public administration.
Type of support: General/operating support; Scholarships—to individuals.
Limitations: Giving primarily in Herrin, IL.
Application information: Application form not required.
  Initial approach: Letter or telephone
  Deadline(s): None
Advisors: Carl Goodwin; Ed Goodwin; Barbara Jacobs; Dorothy Mercer.
Trustee: The Bank of Herrin.
EIN: 376085205

2791
Helen M. Harrison Foundation, Inc. ✦ ☆
70 W. Madison, Ste. 620
Chicago, IL 60602

Incorporated in 2005 in IL as successor to Helen M. Harrison Foundation established in 1986 in IL.
Donor: Helen M. Harrison Foundation.
Foundation type: Independent foundation.
Financial data (yr. ended 12/31/05): Assets, $13,025,597 (M); expenditures, $623,707; qualifying distributions, $553,796; giving activities include $470,000 for 54 grants (high: $60,000; low: $1,000).
Fields of interest: Arts; Secondary school/education; Higher education; Libraries/library science; Hospitals (general); Health organizations; Diabetes; Children/youth, services; Community development; Foundations (community); Christian agencies & churches.
Limitations: Applications not accepted. Giving primarily in Chicago and Oak Park, IL. No grants to individuals.
Application information: Contributes only to pre-selected organizations.
Trustees: Katherine Burno; Philip M. Burno; Timothy G. Carroll; Raymond Kratzer.
EIN: 421668546

2792
The Selma J. Hartke Community Foundation ✦
c/o U.S. Bank, N.A.
P.O. Box 19264
Springfield, IL 62794
Application address: c/o Edwin E. Hardt, 13105 E. 1st Rd., Litchfield, IL 62056

Established in 2001 in IL.
Donor: Selma Hartke†.
Foundation type: Independent foundation.
Financial data (yr. ended 3/31/06): Assets, $10,233,491 (M); expenditures, $667,634; qualifying distributions, $609,552; giving activities include $99,500 for 10 grants (high: $45,000; low: $2,250), and $433,250 for 289 grants to individuals (high: $6,000; low: $125).
Purpose and activities: Giving primarily for social services including food services for the homeless and needy, and heating services for low-income families. Also giving scholarships for higher education.
Fields of interest: Education; Agriculture/food; Human services; Salvation Army; Pregnancy centers; Developmentally disabled, centers & services; Christian agencies & churches.
Type of support: Scholarships—to individuals.
Limitations: Giving limited to the greater Litchfield, IL, area.
Application information:
  Initial approach: Letter
  Deadline(s): None
Directors: Dorothy A. Ernst; Edwin E. Hardt; Karl W. Hardt.
EIN: 371406237

2793
Hartman Family Foundation ✦
c/o Itex Co.
6633 N. Lincoln Ave.
Lincolnwood, IL 60712-3625

Established in 1991 in IL.
Donor: Robert Hartman.
Foundation type: Independent foundation.
Financial data (yr. ended 12/31/03): Assets, $1,491,564 (M); gifts received, $400,000; expenditures, $644,997; qualifying distributions, $534,424; giving activities include $534,424 for 54 grants (high: $100,000; low: $500).
Purpose and activities: Giving primarily to Jewish organizations, and for the promotion of democracy.
Fields of interest: Jewish agencies & temples.
Limitations: Applications not accepted. No grants to individuals.
Application information: Contributes only to pre-selected organizations.
Officers: Robert Hartman, Pres.; Debra F. Hartman, Secy.
EIN: 364120697

2794
Hartmarx Charitable Foundation ✦ ☆
101 N. Wacker Dr., 23rd Fl.
Chicago, IL 60606   (312) 372-6300
Contact: Kay C. Nalbach, Pres.

Incorporated in 1966 in IL.
Donor: Hartmarx Corp.
Foundation type: Company-sponsored foundation.

Financial data (yr. ended 11/30/05): Assets, $38,628 (M); gifts received, $320,881; expenditures, $331,286; qualifying distributions, $331,286; giving activities include $330,287 for 146 grants (high: $35,000).
Purpose and activities: The foundation supports organizations involved with arts and culture, education, and human services.
Fields of interest: Performing arts, orchestra (symphony); Performing arts, music (choral); Historical activities; Arts; Higher education; Business school/education; Education; American Red Cross; Neighborhood centers; Homeless, human services; Human services; Federated giving programs.
Type of support: General/operating support; Program development; Scholarship funds; Employee matching gifts.
Limitations: Giving primarily in IL, IN, and NY. No support for religious or lobbying organizations. No grants to individuals, or for political activities, or advertising for fundraising benefits.
Publications: Application guidelines.
Application information: Application form not required.
  Initial approach: Proposal
  Copies of proposal: 1
  Deadline(s): None
  Board meeting date(s): Dec., Mar., June, and Sept.
Officers and Directors:* Kay C. Nalbach,* Pres.; Glenn R. Morgan,* V.P.; Andrew A. Zahr, V.P.; Taras R. Proczko,* Secy.; June M. Johnson, Treas.
EIN: 366152745
Selected grants: The following grants were reported in 2005.
$35,000 to United Way of Metropolitan Chicago, Chicago, IL.
$27,180 to American Red Cross, Chicago, IL.
$15,000 to Music of the Baroque, Chicago, IL.
$10,700 to American Red Cross.
$7,500 to Robert T. Jones, Jr. Memorial Scholarship Fund, New York, NY.
$7,000 to United Way of Buffalo and Erie County, Buffalo, NY.
$3,000 to United Way of Southeast Missouri, Cape Girardeau, MO.
$2,000 to Thresholds, Chicago, IL.
$1,200 to Memorial Art Gallery of the University of Rochester, Rochester, NY.
$200 to Michigan City Public Library, Michigan City, IN.

2795
Helen's Hope Foundation ✦ ☆
41 W. 872 White Oak Ln.
St. Charles, IL 60175

Established in 2003.
Donors: William Bertsche; Daniel Bertsche; Lorraine Miller.
Foundation type: Independent foundation.
Financial data (yr. ended 12/31/05): Assets, $0 (M); gifts received, $541,503; expenditures, $335,388; qualifying distributions, $335,388; giving activities include $335,388 for 12 grants (high: $150,000; low: $1,000).
Trustees: Bernard B. Bertsche; Jeanne Bertsche; Michael Bertsche.
EIN: 542135918

2796
Carl Hendrickson Family Foundation
c/o Bank of America, N.A.
231 S. LaSalle St.
Chicago, IL 60697 (312) 828-1029
Contact: Kristin Carlson Vogen, Treas.

Established in 1981 in IL.
Donor: Virginia Hendrickson‡.
Foundation type: Independent foundation.
Financial data (yr. ended 12/31/04): Assets,
$11,687,925 (M); expenditures, $600,996;
qualifying distributions, $533,690; giving activities
include $492,000 for 32 grants (high: $97,000;
low: $5,000).
Purpose and activities: Funding for higher education
and Christian organizations; funding also for human
services and health associations.
Fields of interest: Higher education; Health
organizations, association; Human services;
Christian agencies & churches.
Limitations: Giving primarily in CO and IL; some
funding also in CA.
Publications: Application guidelines.
Application information: Application form required.
Initial approach: Telephone for guidelines
Copies of proposal: 2
Deadline(s): Aug. 31
Board meeting date(s): Oct.
Final notification: Jan.
Officers: Charles Slamar, Jr., Pres.; David J. Zeller,
Secy.; Kristin Carlson Vogen, Treas.
EIN: 366736213

2797
The Heritage Foundation of First Security Federal Savings Bank, Inc. ◆
2329 W. Chicago Ave.
Chicago, IL 60622-4723 (773) 486-6645
Contact: Julian E. Kulas, Pres.

Established in 1997 in IL.
Donor: First Security Federal Savings Bank.
Foundation type: Company-sponsored foundation.
Financial data (yr. ended 12/31/05): Assets,
$12,472,273 (M); expenditures, $649,142;
qualifying distributions, $564,804; giving activities
include $564,804 for 100 grants (high: $30,250;
low: $100).
Purpose and activities: The foundation supports
programs designed to preserve Ukrainian culture
and heritage; and promote democracy and a free
market economy.
Fields of interest: Arts, cultural/ethnic awareness;
Public affairs, alliance.
International interests: Ukraine.
Type of support: Conferences/seminars;
Publication.
Limitations: Applications not accepted. Giving
primarily in IL. No grants to individuals.
Application information: Contributes only to
pre-selected organizations.
Officers: Julian E. Kulas, Pres.; Paul Nadzikewycz,
V.P.; Terry Gawryk, Secy.
Number of staff: 1 part-time support.
EIN: 364135415

2798
The Grover Hermann Foundation ◆
1000 Hillgrove Ave., Ste. 200
Western Springs, IL 60558 (708) 246-8331
Contact: Katheryn V. Rhoads, Dir.

Incorporated in 1955 in IL.
Donor: Grover M. Hermann.
Foundation type: Independent foundation.
Financial data (yr. ended 12/31/05): Assets,
$12,055,092 (M); expenditures, $1,167,942;
qualifying distributions, $1,064,855; giving
activities include $938,000 for 64 grants (high:
$250,000; low: $500).
Purpose and activities: Grants largely for higher
education, social services, community
development, health, public policy organizations,
and religious organizations, solely for assistance in
furthering well-defined secular causes.
Fields of interest: Higher education; Health care;
Health organizations, association; Human services;
Community development; Public policy, research;
Religion.
Type of support: General/operating support; Annual
campaigns; Building/renovation; Equipment;
Endowments; Program development; Seed money;
Scholarship funds.
Limitations: Giving limited to Monterey County, CA,
and Chicago, IL for social services and community
development; other programs funded nationwide.
No support for fraternal, athletic, or foreign
organizations or private foundations. No grants to
individuals; generally no support for operating
budgets, except for national health organizations.
Publications: Application guidelines.
Application information: Application form not
required.
Initial approach: Letter (telephone inquiries not
considered)
Copies of proposal: 3
Deadline(s): None
Board meeting date(s): Quarterly; Mar., June,
Sept. and Dec.
Final notification: Within one to two weeks
following board meeting
Officers and Directors:* Paul K. Rhoads,* Pres.;
Katheryn V. Rhoads,* Exec. Dir.; Marianne K.
Calhoun.
EIN: 366064489
Selected grants: The following grants were reported
in 2003.
$250,000 to Community Foundation for Monterey
County, Monterey, CA. For Hermann Foundation
Fund.
$200,000 to Heritage Foundation, DC. For fellow in
Federal Budgetary Affairs.
$25,000 to Alice Lloyd College, Pippa Passes, KY.
For scholarships.
$20,000 to Daniel Murphy Scholarship Foundation,
Chicago, IL. For scholarships.
$20,000 to Intercollegiate Studies Institute,
Wilmington, DE. For honors fellowships.
$20,000 to Philanthropy Roundtable, DC.
$15,000 to Capital Research Center, DC. For
Foundation Watch newsletter.
$15,000 to Interplast, Mountain View, CA. For
Visiting Educator Program.
$15,000 to Reason Foundation, Los Angeles, CA.
For program support.
$15,000 to Salt Creek Ballet Company, Westmont,
IL. For performance programming.

2799
The David Herro Charitable Foundation ◆ ☆
65 E. Goethe, Ste. 3W
Chicago, IL 60610

Donor: David Herro.
Foundation type: Independent foundation.
Financial data (yr. ended 12/31/05): Assets,
$1,932,227 (M); gifts received, $690,150;
expenditures, $1,068,926; qualifying distributions,
$1,054,209; giving activities include $1,054,209
for grants.
Fields of interest: Education; Children, services.
Limitations: Applications not accepted. Giving
primarily in Chicago, IL.
Application information: Contributes only to
pre-selected organizations.
Trustee: David Herro.
EIN: 364121681

2800
Armin & Esther Hirsch Foundation ◆
4400 S. Kildare Ave.
Chicago, IL 60632-4356

Established in 1991 in IL.
Donors: Esther Hirsch; Richard Hirsch.
Foundation type: Independent foundation.
Financial data (yr. ended 12/31/05): Assets,
$6,490,981 (M); expenditures, $430,107;
qualifying distributions, $379,736; giving activities
include $374,824 for 87 grants (high: $40,000;
low: $176), $3,104 for 1 grant to an individual, and
$1,808 for 1 employee matching gift.
Purpose and activities: Funding primarily for human
services and education. The foundation also
contributes to an employee scholarship program,
which is administered by an outside organization.
Fields of interest: Scholarships/financial aid;
Education; Cancer; AIDS; Human services;
Children/youth, services.
Limitations: Applications not accepted. Giving
primarily in IL.
Application information: Contributes only to
pre-selected organizations.
Directors: David Hirsch; Paul Hirsch; Richard Hirsch;
Robert Hirsch.
EIN: 363774078

2801
Eleanor and Henry Hitchcock Charitable Foundation ◆
c/o Bank of America, N.A.
231 S. LaSalle St., IL1-231-14-19
Chicago, IL 60697

Established in 2002 in MO.
Donor: Eleanor H. Hitchcock Trust.
Foundation type: Independent foundation.
Financial data (yr. ended 12/31/03): Assets,
$12,837,866 (M); expenditures, $404,717;
qualifying distributions, $358,287; giving activities
include $362,500 for 10 grants (high: $250,000;
low: $500).
Fields of interest: Performing arts, theater; Arts;
Higher education; Environment.
Limitations: Applications not accepted. Giving
primarily in CO. No grants to individuals.
Application information: Contributes only to
pre-selected organizations.

Trustee: Harrison N. Augur.
EIN: 316672533
Selected grants: The following grants were reported in 2004.
$315,000 to Creede Repertory Theater, Creede, CO. For general support.
$35,000 to Growing Gardens of Boulder County, Boulder, CO. For general support.
$30,000 to University of Southern Maine, Portland, ME. For general support.
$20,000 to Creede, City of, Creede, CO.
$12,000 to Franklin Furnace Archive, New York, NY. For general support.
$5,000 to San Luis Valley Ecosystem Council, Alamosa, CO. For general support.

2802
The Hobbs Foundation ✧
102 N. Westgate Ave., Ste. A
Jacksonville, IL 62650-1718

Established in 1986 in AL.
Donor: Ioka Fund.
Foundation type: Independent foundation.
Financial data (yr. ended 12/31/05): Assets, $11,450,166 (M); expenditures, $545,225; qualifying distributions, $545,225; giving activities include $540,000 for 97 grants (high: $56,500; low: $200).
Fields of interest: Performing arts, orchestra (symphony); Historical activities; Higher education; Education; Zoos/zoological societies; Animals/wildlife; Boys & girls clubs; Human services; Federated giving programs; Protestant agencies & churches.
Type of support: Capital campaigns; Building/renovation.
Limitations: Applications not accepted. Giving primarily in Montgomery, AL. No grants to individuals.
Application information: Contributes only to pre-selected organizations.
Officer: Truman M. Hobbs, Pres.
Directors: Joyce C. Hobbs; Truman M. Hobbs, Jr.
EIN: 630952482

2803
Hochberg Family Foundation ✧
400 Skokie Blvd., Ste. 800
Northbrook, IL 60062
Contact: Larry J. Hochberg, Dir.
Additional address: 275 N. Deere Park E., Highland Park, IL 60035

Established in 1981 in IL.
Donors: Larry J. Hochberg; Joseph Hochberg; Sanford Cantor; Andrew S. Hochberg.
Foundation type: Independent foundation.
Financial data (yr. ended 11/30/05): Assets, $4,540,969 (M); gifts received, $270,000; expenditures, $426,279; qualifying distributions, $376,147; giving activities include $373,190 for 19 grants (high: $312,400; low: $50).
Purpose and activities: Giving primarily for education, community services, and Jewish institutions.
Fields of interest: Education; Medical research, institute; Human services; Jewish federated giving programs; Jewish agencies & temples.
Limitations: Applications not accepted. Giving primarily in Chicago, IL.

Application information: Unsolicited requests for funds not accepted.
Directors: Andrew S. Hochberg; Larry J. Hochberg.
EIN: 363152002

2804
Hospira Foundation ✧ ☆
275 N. Field Dr., Dept. 051N, H-1
Lake Forest, IL 60045-2579
URL: http://www.hospira.com/InTheCommunity/default.aspx

Established in 2004 in IL.
Donor: Hospira, Inc.
Foundation type: Company-sponsored foundation.
Financial data (yr. ended 11/30/05): Assets, $2,798,586 (M); gifts received, $3,675,000; expenditures, $939,585; qualifying distributions, $933,039; giving activities include $634,698 for 26 grants (high: $300,000; low: $1,000), and $296,841 for employee matching gifts.
Purpose and activities: The foundation supports organizations involved with health and other areas. Special emphasis is directed toward programs designed to advance wellness.
Fields of interest: Public health; Health care; General charitable giving.
Type of support: Continuing support; Program development; Employee matching gifts; Donated products.
Limitations: Giving primarily in Morgan Hill, CA, Lake County, IL, McPherson, KS, Buffalo, NY, Clayton and Rocky Mount, NC, Ashland, OH, Austin, TX, and Kenosha County, WI; giving also to national organizations. No support for veterans', labor, or political organizations, fraternal, athletic, or social organizations, or organizations posing a conflict of interest with Hospira's code of business conduct or corporate policies. No grants to individuals, or for capital campaigns, endowments, general operating support, equipment, charity event attendance, debt reduction, political campaigns, or religious or sectarian causes; no loans.
Application information: Proposals should be no longer than 2 pages. Multi-year funding is not automatic. Application form not required.
Initial approach: Contact nearest company facility; proposal to foundation for national organizations and organizations located in Lake County, IL, and Kenosha County, WI
Copies of proposal: 1
Deadline(s): None
Final notification: 6 weeks for national organizations and organizations located in Lake County, IL, and Kenosha County, WI
Directors: Christopher Begley; Lon Carlson; Stacey Eisen; Terrence Kearney; Henry Weishaar.
EIN: 202039190

2805
John R. Houlsby Foundation ✧
212 Bridle Path Cir.
Oak Brook, IL 60523 (630) 986-5645
Contact: Judy Louthan, Admin. Dir.

Established in 1996.
Donor: John R. Houlsby‡.
Foundation type: Independent foundation.
Financial data (yr. ended 12/31/05): Assets, $11,538,489 (M); expenditures, $1,495,244; qualifying distributions, $1,406,100; giving

activities include $1,323,100 for 58 grants (high: $200,000; low: $5,000).
Purpose and activities: Giving primarily for community welfare, including the arts and youth services.
Fields of interest: Arts; Mental health, treatment; Children, services; Community development.
Type of support: Continuing support; Emergency funds; Program development; Scholarship funds.
Limitations: Giving limited to Cook and Lake counties, IL. No grants to individuals.
Publications: Application guidelines.
Application information: Application form required.
Initial approach: Request application
Copies of proposal: 1
Deadline(s): None
Board meeting date(s): 6 times a year
Final notification: 10-12 weeks from receipt
Officers and Directors:* David E. Mason,* Pres.; Matthew Kass,* Secy.; Maree G. Bullock; Katherine L. Fox; Mary L. Fox.
Number of staff: 1 full-time professional.
EIN: 363915186

2806
Huizenga Foundation ✧
2215 York Rd., Ste. 500
Oak Brook, IL 60523

Established in 1988 in IL.
Donor: Peter H. Huizenga.
Foundation type: Independent foundation.
Financial data (yr. ended 12/31/04): Assets, $6,069,827 (M); gifts received, $45,000; expenditures, $1,549,530; qualifying distributions, $1,396,056; giving activities include $1,396,056 for 146 grants (high: $156,000; low: $25).
Purpose and activities: Giving primarily to Protestant organizations, including a prison ministry, and churches, and for Protestant education, as well as for higher education, environmental conservation, and for children, youth, families, and social services.
Fields of interest: Historic preservation/historical societies; Arts; Elementary/secondary education; Higher education; Theological school/education; Environment; Animals/wildlife, preservation/protection; Human services; Family services; Christian agencies & churches.
Limitations: Applications not accepted. Giving in the U.S., primarily in IL, Washington, DC, PA, and MI. No grants to individuals.
Application information: Contributes only to pre-selected organizations.
Officers and Directors:* Peter H. Huizenga,* Pres.; David A. Bradley, Secy.; Heidi A. Huizenga,* Treas.; Betsy Bradley; Greta Giesen; P.J. Huizenga; Tim Huizenga.
EIN: 363582536
Selected grants: The following grants were reported in 2003.
$186,100 to Christ Church of Oak Brook, Oak Brook, IL. For general support.
$140,100 to Hope College, Holland, MI. For general support.
$110,100 to Trinity Christian College, Palos Heights, IL. For general support.
$25,000 to Loyola University of Chicago, Chicago, IL. For general support.
$15,000 to DePauw University, Greencastle, IN. For general support.
$10,000 to University of Illinois Foundation, Champaign, IL. For general support.

$1,000 to North Central College, Naperville, IL. For general support.

$950 to Friends of Conservation, Oak Brook, IL. For general support.

$250 to Nature Conservancy, Chicago, IL. For general support.

$200 to Conservation Foundation of DuPage County, Naperville, IL. For general support.

2807
Hull Family Foundation ◇

(formerly M. Blair Hull, Jr. Foundation)
141 W. Jackson Blvd., Ste. 340
Chicago, IL 60604-3124

Established in 1998 in IL.
Donors: M. Blair Hull, Jr.; Matlock Capital, LLC.
Foundation type: Independent foundation.
Financial data (yr. ended 12/31/05): Assets, $15,211,426 (M); gifts received, $1,143,481; expenditures, $527,692; qualifying distributions, $491,292; giving activities include $425,300 for 90 grants (high: $50,000; low: $500).
Purpose and activities: Giving primarily for the arts, and children, youth, and social services; funding also for education and sports foundations and organizations.
Fields of interest: Museums; Arts; Education; Recreation; Human services; Children/youth, services; Foundations (private grantmaking); Women.
Limitations: Applications not accepted. Giving on a national basis, with some emphasis on the greater Chicago, IL, area. No grants to individuals.
Application information: Contributes only to pre-selected organizations.
Officers: Edward B. Chez, Treas.; M. Blair Hull, Jr., Mgr.
EIN: 364227476
Selected grants: The following grants were reported in 2003.
$100,920 to Womens Sports Foundation, East Meadow, NY.
$10,000 to Womens Business Development Center, Chicago, IL.
$7,000 to Resource Generation, Cambridge, MA.
$6,000 to Prevent Child Abuse Illinois, Springfield, IL.
$5,000 to Brown University, Providence, RI. For annual fund.
$3,000 to Chicago Coalition for the Homeless, Chicago, IL.
$1,000 to After-School All-Stars, Los Angeles, CA.
$1,000 to Andre Agassi Charitable Foundation, Las Vegas, NV.
$1,000 to Girls Inc., New York, NY.
$1,000 to Team-Up for Youth, Oakland, CA.

2808
Perkins Malo Hunter Foundation ◇

311 S. Wacker Dr., Ste. 6000
Chicago, IL 60606

Established in 1996 in IL.
Donors: Robert H. Perkins; Nancy A. Perkins; Kenneth V. Perkins; Patrick Perkins; Greg Wolf; Todd Perkins; Gregory Grosh; Curtis L. Stine; Jill Perkins; Nancy Perkins Trust; Robert H. Perkins Trust; Phillip Perkins Trust; Todd Perkins Trust.
Foundation type: Independent foundation.

Financial data (yr. ended 12/31/05): Assets, $26,991,894 (M); gifts received, $106,006; expenditures, $1,061,661; qualifying distributions, $1,006,493; giving activities include $1,006,493 for 39 grants (high: $199,011; low: $70).
Purpose and activities: Giving primarily for children, youth, adult, and social services including programs for early childhood education, homelessness, job training, and the elderly; some funding also for education.
Fields of interest: Elementary/secondary education; Higher education; Education; Animal welfare; Human services; Children/youth, services; Christian agencies & churches.
Limitations: Applications not accepted. Giving primarily in IL. No grants to individuals.
Application information: Contributes only to pre-selected organizations.
Directors: Jill Perkins; Laurie Perkins; Phillip M. Perkins; Robert H. Perkins; Todd Perkins; Curtis L. Stine.
EIN: 364098513
Selected grants: The following grants were reported in 2003.
$234,408 to Marcy-Newberry Association, Chicago, IL. 4 grants: $69,408, $75,000, $40,000, $50,000
$45,000 to Saint Agnes Parish, Greenwich, CT.
$40,000 to Himalayan Cataract Project, Burlington, VT.
$40,000 to Potters House, Grand Rapids, MI. 2 grants: $20,000 each
$5,000 to FUTURE Foundation Youth Services, Ford Heights, IL.
$5,000 to Salvation Army.

2809
The James Huntington Foundation ◇

c/o Samuel H. Ellis
10 S. Wacker Dr., Ste. 2675
Chicago, IL 60606-7453

Established in 1987 in IL.
Donor: Samuel H. Ellis.
Foundation type: Independent foundation.
Financial data (yr. ended 12/31/05): Assets, $14,078,465 (M); expenditures, $1,096,830; qualifying distributions, $602,100; giving activities include $602,100 for 68 grants (high: $127,500; low: $500).
Purpose and activities: Giving primarily for the arts, and for hospitals and health associations.
Fields of interest: Arts; Elementary/secondary education; Higher education; Environment, natural resources; Animals/wildlife, preservation/protection; Hospitals (general); Health organizations, association; Human services.
Limitations: Applications not accepted. Giving primarily in IL. No grants to individuals.
Application information: Contributes only to pre-selected organizations.
Trustee: Samuel H. Ellis.
EIN: 363553345

2810
Hyatt Foundation ◇

71 S. Wacker Dr., Ste. 4600
Chicago, IL 60606
Contact: Carol A. Bock, Asst. Secy.

Established in 1978 in IL.

Donors: Allen M. Turner; HT-Hotel Equities, Inc.; Asworth Corp.; Hyatt Corporation; Pritzker Foundation.
Foundation type: Independent foundation.
Financial data (yr. ended 7/31/05): Assets, $16,453,432 (M); expenditures, $684,287; qualifying distributions, $486,583; giving activities include $437,512 for grants to individuals, and $7,444 for foundation-administered programs.
Purpose and activities: Annual Pritzker Architectural Prize awarded to an individual for significant contribution to humanity through architecture.
Fields of interest: Visual arts, architecture.
Application information: Applications accepted for Award only. Unsolicited requests for funds not accepted. No posthumous awards are given.
Initial approach: Letter
Deadline(s): Jan. 31
Officers and Trustees:* Thomas J. Pritzker,* Chair. and Pres.; Allen Turner,* V.P. and Secy.; Glen Miller, V.P. and Treas.; Marian Pritzker,* V.P.; Nicholas J. Pritzker, V.P.
EIN: 362981565
Selected grants: The following grants were reported in 2004.
$35,000 to American Friends of the State Hermitage Museum, New York, NY.

2811
I and G Charitable Foundation ◇

c/o Roger Brown
225 W. Washington St., Ste. 1650
Chicago, IL 60606-3418

Incorporated in 1945 in IL.
Donors: Roger O. Brown; Barbara Brown; GB 30 Year Char. Trust; Roger O. Brown Char. Trust.
Foundation type: Independent foundation.
Financial data (yr. ended 12/31/04): Assets, $8,891,047 (M); gifts received, $64,440; expenditures, $653,190; qualifying distributions, $536,030; giving activities include $236,030 for 71 grants (high: $55,000; low: $100).
Fields of interest: Arts; Higher education; Human services; Community development.
Limitations: Applications not accepted. Giving primarily in CA, and Chicago, IL; some funding nationally, particularly in the Minneapolis-St. Paul, MN, area. No support for hospitals or schools. No grants to individuals.
Application information: Contributes only to pre-selected organizations.
Officers and Directors:* Owen Brown,* Pres. and Treas.; Gail Feiger Brown,* V.P. and Secy.; Joan Jensen, V.P.; Andrew Brown; Barbara Brown; Henry Brown; Jeffrey R. Brown; Roger O. Brown; Vanessa J.B. McGuire.
EIN: 366069174
Selected grants: The following grants were reported in 2003.
$75,000 to Target Hope, Chicago, IL.
$34,000 to Will Feed Community Organization, Chicago, IL.
$30,000 to Saint Leonards Ministries, Chicago, IL.
$16,000 to Breakthrough Urban Ministries, Chicago, IL.
$5,000 to Opportunity, Highland Park, IL.
$2,375 to University of Chicago, Chicago, IL.
$700 to Mercy Housing Lakefront, Chicago, IL.
$700 to Off the Street Club, Chicago, IL.
$500 to Becker House, Chicago, IL.
$500 to Community Supportive Living Systems, Chicago, IL.

2812
Illinois Children's Healthcare Foundation
15 Spinning Wheel Rd., Ste. 228
Hinsdale, IL   60521   (630) 655-2873
FAX: (630) 655-4725; E-mail: info@ilchf.org;
URL: http://www.ilchf.org

Established in 2002 in IL.
Donor: Health Care Services Corp.
Foundation type: Independent foundation.
Financial data (yr. ended 12/31/05): Assets, $129,684,632 (M); gifts received, $1,938; expenditures, $6,744,198; qualifying distributions, $6,439,410; giving activities include $5,972,465 for 48 grants (high: $400,000; low: $7,000; average: $20,000–$150,000).
Purpose and activities: The foundation (ILCHF) has a single mission: to ensure that every child in Illinois has access to affordable and quality health care. As such, its grantmaking is designed to close the gap between children who have access to care and those who are underserved. ILCHF focuses its giving in three specific areas: 1) improving the oral health of underserved children; 2) addressing the mental health needs of children; and 3) increasing the incidence of developmental screening in young children. In addition, the foundation monitors emerging and other compelling health issues that the board of directors may select as focus areas in the future.
Fields of interest: Dental care; Health care; Mental health/crisis services; Children.
Type of support: Building/renovation; Equipment; Emergency funds; Program development; Curriculum development; Research; Program evaluation.
Limitations: Giving limited to IL. No support for intermediary funding agencies, partisan, lobbying, political or denominational organizations, or for organizations not determined to be public charities. No grants to individuals, or for endowments or, general medical research.
Publications: Annual report; Financial statement; Grants list; IRS Form 990-PF.
Application information: Unsolicited requests for funds not accepted. Funding is through requests for proposals only.
   Initial approach: See foundation Web site for RFP information
   Board meeting date(s): Generally six times per year
Officers and Directors:* Peter E. Doris,* Chair.; Kathleen L. Halloran,* Vice-Chair.; J. Kevin Dorsey,* Secy.; Charles E. Box,* Treas.; Louise Coleman; Rey B. Gonzalez; Bennett L. Leventhal, M.D.; Mary McGrath; Margaret O'Flynn; Floyd Perkins; C. William Pollard; Jim Ryan; Jerome Stermer.
Number of staff: 4 full-time professional.
EIN: 030503425
Selected grants: The following grants were reported in 2004.
$545,382 to Childrens Memorial Hospital, Chicago, IL.
$500,000 to University of Chicago, Chicago, IL.
$200,000 to Horizon Hospice and Palliative Care, Chicago, IL.
$173,832 to Ounce of Prevention Fund, Chicago, IL.
$170,000 to Fight Crime: Invest in Kids Illinois, Chicago, IL.
$150,000 to La Rabida Childrens Hospital, Chicago, IL.
$145,749 to Chapin Hall Center for Children, Chicago, IL.
$125,000 to Erie Neighborhood House, Chicago, IL.

$100,000 to Hope School, Springfield, IL.
$84,755 to Rush University Medical Center, Chicago, IL.

2813
Illinois Tool Works Foundation ▼ ✧
3600 W. Lake Ave.
Glenview, IL   60025-5811   (847) 724-7500
Contact: Mary Ann Mallahan, Secy.
FAX: (847) 657-4505; E-mail: mmallahan@itw.com; URL: http://www.itw.com/itw_foundation.html

Incorporated in 1954 in IL.
Donor: Illinois Tool Works Inc.
Foundation type: Company-sponsored foundation.
Financial data (yr. ended 2/28/06): Assets, $26,547,048 (M); gifts received, $14,520,500; expenditures, $11,074,216; qualifying distributions, $11,050,746; giving activities include $6,540,633 for 477 grants (high: $844,942; low: $75), and $4,457,293 for 10,712 employee matching gifts.
Purpose and activities: The foundation supports organizations involved with arts and culture, education, human services, and youth.
Fields of interest: Arts; Education; Human services; Youth.
Type of support: Continuing support; Annual campaigns; Employee matching gifts; Employee-related scholarships.
Limitations: Giving primarily in areas of company operations, with emphasis on Chicago, IL. No grants to individuals (except for employee-related scholarships), or for endowments or research; no loans.
Publications: Newsletter.
Application information: Application form not required.
   Initial approach: Proposal
   Copies of proposal: 1
   Deadline(s): None
   Board meeting date(s): May and Dec.
   Final notification: May and Dec.
Officers and Directors: Harold Byron Smith, Jr., Pres.; Mary Ann Mallahan, Secy.; Felix L. Rodriquez, Treas.; Robert Callahan; W. James Farrell; Michael J. Lynch; David Speer; James Wooten.
Number of staff: 1 full-time support.
EIN: 366087160
Selected grants: The following grants were reported in 2005.
$987,200 to United Way of Metropolitan Chicago, Chicago, IL. 2 grants: $200,000 (For capital campaign), $787,200 (For general operating support).
$351,270 to Scholarship America, Saint Peter, MN. For general operating support.
$200,000 to Northwestern University, Evanston, IL. For capital campaign.
$57,504 to Ralph Wilson Youth Clubs, Temple, TX. For general operating support.
$50,000 to Chicago Historical Society, Chicago, IL. For capital campaign.
$50,000 to Lake Forest Graduate School of Management, Chicago, IL.
$20,000 to Junior Achievement Worldwide, Colorado Springs, CO. For general operating support.
$20,000 to Music and Dance Theater Chicago, Chicago, IL. For capital campaign.
$13,899 to United Way, Watertown Area, Watertown, SD. For general operating support.

2814
Irwin Family Foundation ✧
2825 Denton Ct.
Westchester, IL   60154   (708) 751-5597
Contact: Robert W. Lynch, Tr.

Established in 1977.
Donors: Richard D. Irwin Trust No. 1; Richard D. Irwin Charitable Remainder Annuity Trust.
Foundation type: Independent foundation.
Financial data (yr. ended 12/31/05): Assets, $18,328,315 (M); gifts received, $2,861,927; expenditures, $1,092,593; qualifying distributions, $1,063,620; giving activities include $1,035,000 for 7 grants (high: $500,000; low: $20,000).
Purpose and activities: Giving primarily for education and health associations, including a cancer support center.
Fields of interest: Higher education; Business school/education; Hospitals (general); Health organizations, association; Federated giving programs.
Type of support: Capital campaigns; Program development; Fellowships; Scholarship funds.
Application information: Application form not required.
   Initial approach: Letter
   Deadline(s): None
   Board meeting date(s): As required
Trustees: George Allen; Donald G. Kind; Robert W. Lynch; Jacqueline Pipher.
EIN: 362913193
Selected grants: The following grants were reported in 2003.
$150,000 to Ingalls Memorial Hospital, Harvey, IL. For program support.
$140,000 to University of Illinois at Urbana-Champaign, Urbana, IL. For scholarships.
$75,000 to Cancer Support Center, Homewood, IL. For program support.
$20,000 to Literacy Council of Bonita Springs, Bonita Springs, FL. For program support.
$15,000 to Cornerstone Academy, Oak Park, IL. For program support.

2815
Verne G. and Judith A. Istock Foundation ✧
Chase Tower
10 S. Dearborn, Ste. 0554
Chicago, IL   60603-2003

Established in 2001 in IL.
Donor: Verne G. Istock.
Foundation type: Independent foundation.
Financial data (yr. ended 12/31/05): Assets, $2,152,646 (M); gifts received, $275,239; expenditures, $425,164; qualifying distributions, $415,940; giving activities include $412,940 for 54 grants (high: $73,000; low: $500).
Fields of interest: Arts; Higher education; Environment; Boys & girls clubs; Federated giving programs.
Limitations: Applications not accepted. Giving primarily in Chicago, IL. No grants to individuals.
Application information: Contributes only to pre-selected organizations.
Trustees: Judith A. Istock; Verne G. Istock.
EIN: 367362355

2816
Reinhardt H. & Shirley R. Jahn Foundation ◇ ☆
2737 Eastwood Ave.
Evanston, IL 60201-1544
Contact: Shirley R. Jahn, Pres.

Established in 1992 in IL.
Donors: Shirley R. Jahn; Reinhardt H. Jahn†.
Foundation type: Independent foundation.
Financial data (yr. ended 12/31/05): Assets, $3,002,189 (M); expenditures, $393,413; qualifying distributions, $373,500; giving activities include $373,500 for grants.
Fields of interest: Arts; Botanical gardens; Environment; Boys & girls clubs.
Limitations: Applications not accepted. Giving primarily in IL. No grants to individuals.
Application information: Contributes only to pre-selected organizations.
Officer and Directors:* Shirley R. Jahn,* Pres.; Carolyn L. Jahn; Charles L. Jahn; Reinhardt E. Jahn.
EIN: 363857635
Selected grants: The following grants were reported in 2005.
$30,000 to International Crane Foundation, Baraboo, WI.
$10,000 to Art Institute of Chicago, Chicago, IL.
$10,000 to Chicago Symphony Orchestra, Chicago, IL.
$5,000 to Salvation Army, Port Huron, MI.

2817
JM Freedom Foundation ◇ ☆
485 Half Day Rd., Ste. 200
Buffalo Grove, IL 60089 (847) 883-9700
Contact: Eric F. Achepohl, V.P. and Treas.

Donors: Jack Miller Charitable Trust; Audrey & Jack Miller Family Charitable Foundation.
Foundation type: Independent foundation.
Financial data (yr. ended 12/31/05): Assets, $161,087 (M); gifts received, $579,459; expenditures, $495,026; qualifying distributions, $482,616; giving activities include $482,500 for 5 grants (high: $402,500; low: $25,000).
Fields of interest: Education; Public policy, research; Public affairs, public education.
Limitations: Giving on a national basis.
Application information: Application form not required.
Initial approach: Letter
Deadline(s): None
Officers and Directors:* Goldie Wolf Miller,* Pres.; Eric F. Achepohl,* V.P. and Treas.; Judith N. Joy; Sharon A. Miller.
EIN: 201930482

2818
JMR Charities, Inc. ◇
333 W. 35th St.
Chicago, IL 60616

Established in IL.
Donor: Jerry Reinsdorf.
Foundation type: Independent foundation.
Financial data (yr. ended 12/31/05): Assets, $89,994 (M); gifts received, $200,000; expenditures, $315,882; qualifying distributions, $315,739; giving activities include $315,739 for grants.

Purpose and activities: Giving for the arts, education, health, and Jewish organizations; funding also for art and craft kits for children in various hospitals in Phoenix, AZ.
Fields of interest: Arts; Education; Animal welfare; Health care; Health organizations, association; Youth development; Human services; Children/youth, services; Voluntarism promotion; Jewish federated giving programs; Jewish agencies & temples.
Limitations: Applications not accepted. Giving on a national basis. No grants to individuals.
Application information: Contributes only to pre-selected organizations.
Officers: Jerry Reinsdorf, Pres.; Allan Muchin, Secy.
Director: Gerald Penner.
EIN: 363218989
Selected grants: The following grants were reported in 2005.
$5,000 to Hugh OBrian Youth Leadership.
$2,000 to Shalva, Chicago, IL.
$2,000 to Young Peoples Leadership Foundation, New York, NY.
$1,000 to Gastro-Intestinal Research Foundation, Chicago, IL.
$1,000 to Illinois College, Jacksonville, IL.
$1,000 to Mayors Fund to Advance New York City, New York, NY.
$1,000 to Multiple Myeloma Research Foundation, Norwalk, CT.
$1,000 to Wendy Will Case Cancer Fund, Chicago, IL.
$975 to National Constitution Center, Philadelphia, PA.
$500 to Boys and Girls Club of Chicago, Chicago, IL.

2819
Violet M. Johnson Family Foundation ◇ ☆
c/o Northern Trust Bank N.A.
P.O. Box 803878
Chicago, IL 60680

Foundation type: Independent foundation.
Financial data (yr. ended 7/31/05): Assets, $11,863,723 (M); expenditures, $431,030; qualifying distributions, $385,134; giving activities include $345,000 for 18 grants (high: $35,000; low: $5,000).
Fields of interest: Cancer; Food banks; Housing/shelter, development; Human services; American Red Cross; Christian agencies & churches.
Limitations: Applications not accepted. Giving on a national basis.
Application information: Contributes only to pre-selected organizations.
Officers: Loren Thomas Halverstadt, Jr., Pres. and Treas.; Karen Halverstadt Miller, V.P. and Secy.
Director: Douglas Halverstadt.
EIN: 200128534

2820
The Joyce Foundation ▼
70 W. Madison St., Ste. 2750
Chicago, IL 60602 (312) 782-2464
Contact: Prog. Staff
FAX: (312) 782-4160; *E-mail:* info@joycefdn.org;
URL: http://www.joycefdn.org

Incorporated in 1948 in IL.
Donor: Beatrice Joyce Kean†.
Foundation type: Independent foundation.

Financial data (yr. ended 12/31/05): Assets, $892,492,212 (M); expenditures, $36,887,080; qualifying distributions, $30,571,102; giving activities include $30,571,102 for grants.
Purpose and activities: The foundation supports efforts to protect the natural environment of the Great Lakes, to reduce poverty and violence in the region, and to ensure that its people have access to good schools, decent jobs, and a diverse and thriving culture. It is especially interested in improving public policies, because public systems such as education and welfare directly affect the lives of so many people, and because public policies help shape private sector decisions about jobs, the environment, and the health of our communities. To ensure that public policies truly reflect public rather than private interests, the foundation supports efforts to reform the system of financing election campaigns.
Fields of interest: Arts; Education; Environment; Crime/violence prevention; Crime/violence prevention, gun control; Employment; Public affairs, finance; Public affairs, political organizations.
Type of support: General/operating support; Continuing support; Program development; Conferences/seminars; Research; Program evaluation; Employee matching gifts.
Limitations: Giving primarily in the Great Lakes region, including IL, IN, MI, MN, OH, and WI; limited number of environment grants made in Canada; culture grants are primarily restricted to the metropolitan Chicago, IL, area. No support for religious activities, or for political organizations. No grants for endowment campaigns, scholarships, direct service programs, or capital proposals.
Publications: Annual report (including application guidelines); Financial statement; Newsletter; Occasional report.
Application information: Program policy and grant proposal guidelines reviewed annually in Dec. Proposals in all program areas will be considered at each board meeting. Applicants are encouraged to submit their proposals for the Apr. or July meeting, since most grant funds will be distributed at those times. Proposal cover sheet available on foundation Web site. Online proposals will not be considered. Application form required.
Initial approach: Contact foundation for application guidelines prior to submitting 2- to 3-page letter of inquiry
Copies of proposal: 1
Deadline(s): Letter of inquiry required at least 6 to 8 weeks before proposal deadlines. For formal proposals: Dec. 11 (for Apr. meeting); Apr. 16 (for July meeting); Aug. 15 (for Dec. meeting)
Board meeting date(s): Apr., July, and Dec.
Final notification: 2 weeks after meeting
Officers and Directors:* John T. Anderson,* Chair.; Charles U. Daly, Vice.-Chair.; Ellen S. Alberding,* Pres.; Deborah Gillespie, V.P., Finance and Admin.; Lawrence N. Hansen, V.P. and Prog. Off., Money and Politics; Gil M. Sarmiento, Cont.; Robert G. Bottoms; Michael F. Brewer; Roger R. Fross; Howard L. Fuller; Carlton L. Guthrie; Marion T. Hall; Valerie B. Jarrett; Daniel P. Kearney; Paula Wolff.
Number of staff: 14 full-time professional; 4 part-time professional; 6 full-time support.
EIN: 366079185
Selected grants: The following grants were reported in 2005.
$800,000 to American Farmland Trust, DC. To conduct research and disseminate information about benefits of rewarding farmers for

environmental stewardship rather than production of commodities, payable over 2 years.

$798,975 to University of Chicago, Consortium on Chicago School Research, Chicago, IL. To study Chicago teacher turnover patterns, new teacher support programs, and teacher and school effectiveness, payable over 2 years.

$700,000 to Harvard University, Cambridge, MA. For Harvard Injury Control Research Center's technical assistance (coordinated through School of Public Health in Boston) to National Violent Death Reporting System, to conduct policy-relevant firearm research, and to increase communications capacity, payable over 2 years.

$540,000 to Illinois Campaign for Political Reform, Chicago, IL. For policy research, development, advocacy, and public education activities on range of campaign finance, governmental ethics, judicial independence, and media reform issues, payable over 2 years.

$500,000 to Women Employed Institute, Chicago, IL. For advocacy efforts to improve access to training and education opportunities for low-wage workers in Illinois, payable over 2 years.

$400,000 to Environmental Defense, New York, NY. To develop, in partnership with American Farmland Trust, diverse alliance to analyze and advocate for reforms in federal agriculture support programs that promise to improve environmental stewardship, payable over 2 years.

$400,000 to Local Initiatives Support Corporation (LISC), New York, NY. For Building Community Through the Arts project, new initiative to develop cultural plans for three Chicago neighborhoods: South Chicago, Humboldt Park, and Albany Park, payable over 2 years.

$181,117 to Johns Hopkins University, School of Hygiene and Public Health, Center for Gun Policy and Research, Baltimore, MD. To share research findings with Chicago and Milwaukee city officials, law enforcement, advocates, and media on beneficial effects of undercover police stings of gun stores in reducing flow of guns to illicit markets, payable over 2 years.

$168,475 to Center for Teaching Quality, Chapel Hill, NC. To create TeacherSoultions as means to have nations most accomplished teachers develop new compensation models that will help local, state, and federal policymakers understand what those in classroom believe is necessary.

$100,000 to Minnesota Environmental Partnership, Saint Paul, MN. To lead and coordinate efforts to advance state-level policies that protect and restore Minnesota's waters; and to organize public participation and policy-maker education around Great Lakes issues such as proposed water withdrawal rules and Great Lakes.

2821
JYN Foundation ◇
c/o Kinship Trust Co.
400 Skokie Blvd., Ste. 300
Northbrook, IL   60062

Established in 1999 in OR.
Donors: Carolynn D. Loacker; John R. Loacker.
Foundation type: Independent foundation.
Financial data (yr. ended 12/31/04): Assets, $1,619,369 (M); expenditures, $448,167; qualifying distributions, $436,500; giving activities

include $436,500 for 10 grants (high: $150,000; low: $1,500).
Fields of interest: Performing arts, orchestra (symphony); Education; Animals/wildlife, preservation/protection; Medical research, single organization support; Community development.
Limitations: Applications not accepted. Giving primarily in IL and OR. No grants to individuals.
Application information: Contributes only to pre-selected organizations.
Trustees: Carolynn D. Loacker; John R. Loacker.
EIN: 931267230

2822
Kainz Family Foundation ◇
(formerly Joseph A. & Susan J. Kainz Foundation)
c/o KRD
1101 Perimeter Dr., No. 760
Schaumburg, IL   60173

Established in 2000 in IL.
Donors: Joseph A. Kainz; Susan J. Kainz.
Foundation type: Independent foundation.
Financial data (yr. ended 6/30/05): Assets, $4,617,948 (M); expenditures, $523,433; qualifying distributions, $475,943; giving activities include $475,943 for 14 grants (high: $243,411; low: $5,000).
Purpose and activities: Giving primarily for children's services including health care.
Fields of interest: Environment, natural resources; Environment; Zoos/zoological societies; Hospitals (general); Health care; Children, services; Residential/custodial care, hospices.
Limitations: Applications not accepted. Giving primarily in IL, MT, and VA. No grants to individuals.
Application information: Contributes only to pre-selected organizations.
Directors: John Kainz; Joseph A. Kainz; Michael J. Kainz; Patrick J. Kainz; Susan J. Kainz.
EIN: 364394506
Selected grants: The following grants were reported in 2003.
$27,000 to Eagle Mount Bozeman, Bozeman, MT. For unrestricted support.
$25,000 to Lincoln Park Zoo, Chicago, IL. For unrestricted support.
$25,000 to Operation Smile International, Norfolk, VA. For unrestricted support.
$14,110 to Make-A-Wish Foundation of Northern Illinois, Chicago, IL. For unrestricted support.
$10,000 to Hospice of Northeastern Illinois, Barrington, IL. For unrestricted support.
$5,000 to Home of the Sparrow McHenry County Interfaith Shelter Program, McHenry, IL. For unrestricted support.
$5,000 to Wellness Place, Palatine, IL. For unrestricted support.

2823
Mayer and Morris Kaplan Family Foundation ◇
1780 Green Bay Rd., Ste. 205
Highland Park, IL   60035   (847) 926-8350
Contact: Jason Heeney, Exec. Dir.
E-mail: Jheeney@kapfam.com

Incorporated in 1957 in IL.
Donors: Burton B. Kaplan; Morris Kaplan.
Foundation type: Independent foundation.

Financial data (yr. ended 12/31/05): Assets, $34,800,823 (M); gifts received, $1,031,914; expenditures, $4,294,465; qualifying distributions, $3,500,664; giving activities include $3,304,990 for grants.
Purpose and activities: Primary areas of interest include community organizations, education, the arts, family programs, and Jewish organizations within Chicago, IL.
Fields of interest: Visual arts; Museums; Performing arts; Performing arts, dance; Performing arts, theater; Performing arts, music; Humanities; Arts; Elementary school/education; Secondary school/ education; Education; Reproductive health, family planning; Children/youth, services; Family services; Minorities/immigrants, centers/services; Civil liberties, reproductive rights; Civil rights; Jewish agencies & temples; Minorities; Economically disadvantaged.
Type of support: General/operating support; Continuing support; Program development; Seed money.
Limitations: Giving primarily in the Chicago, IL, area. No support for religious organizations. No grants to individuals, or for capital campaigns, building funds, equipment or materials, land acquisition, general endowments, research, publications, conferences and seminars, or films.
Publications: Application guidelines; Annual report.
Application information: Application form not required.
   Initial approach: Request guidelines
   Copies of proposal: 1
   Deadline(s): Jan. 15, May 15, and Sept. 15
   Board meeting date(s): 3 times per year
   Final notification: 3-4 months
Officers and Directors:* Robert Kaplan,* Chair.; Jessica Lundevall,* Secy.; Burton B. Kaplan,* Treas.; Jason Heeney, Exec. Dir.; Aura de la Fuente; Anne Kaplan; Charlie Kaplan; Curt Kaplan; David Kaplan; Hilary Kaplan; Jean Kaplan; Mike Kaplan; Morris A. Kaplan; Sarah Kaplan; Beth Karmin.
Number of staff: 3 full-time professional.
EIN: 366099675
Selected grants: The following grants were reported in 2003.
$120,000 to New Israel Fund, DC. For general support.
$75,000 to Chicago Symphony Orchestra, Chicago, IL.
$50,000 to North Lawndale College Preparatory Charter High School, Chicago, IL. For general operating support.
$40,000 to Jewish Council on Urban Affairs, Chicago, IL.
$30,000 to Tel Aviv Foundation, New York, NY. For Hemda project.
$25,000 to Chicago Humanities Festival, Chicago, IL. For general operating support.
$25,000 to Joffrey Ballet of Chicago, Chicago, IL. For general support.
$25,000 to Teach for America, Chicago, IL. For general support.
$20,000 to Albany Park Neighborhood Council, Chicago, IL. For general operating support.
$20,000 to Brighton Park Neighborhood Council, Chicago, IL. For general operating support.

2824
Kaplan Foundation
25 Lakewood Pl.
Highland Park, IL 60035-5007
Application address: c/o Chicago Community Trust, 111 E. Wacker Dr., Ste. 1400, Chicago, IL 60601; tel.: (312) 616-8000, fax: (312) 616-7955, e-mail: info@cct.org

Established in 1991 in IL.
Donor: Edward Kaplan.
Foundation type: Independent foundation.
Financial data (yr. ended 12/31/05): Assets, $15,325,747 (M); expenditures, $1,149,057; qualifying distributions, $1,042,217; giving activities include $1,033,425 for 19 grants (high: $1,000,000; low: $100).
Purpose and activities: Giving primarily to Jewish organizations, education, and health and human services.
Fields of interest: Museums; Performing arts, orchestra (symphony); Education; Hospitals (general); Health organizations, association; Youth development, centers/clubs; Human services; Jewish federated giving programs; Jewish agencies & temples.
Limitations: Applications not accepted. Giving primarily in IL. No grants to individuals.
Application information: Contributes only to pre-selected organizations. Unsolicited requests for funds not accepted.
Officers: Carol K. Kaplan, Pres.; Edward Kaplan, Secy.-Treas.
Directors: Alan Kaplan; Martin Kaplan.
EIN: 363796516
Selected grants: The following grants were reported in 2004.
$1,050,000 to Chicago Community Trust, Chicago, IL.
$6,000 to Jewish National Fund, New York, NY.
$6,000 to Ravinia Festival Association, Highland Park, IL.
$3,500 to Erikson Institute, Chicago, IL.
$1,000 to AIDS Walk Chicago, Chicago, IL.
$1,000 to American Jewish Committee, New York, NY.
$1,000 to Association of Small Foundations, DC.
$100 to Chicago Women in Philanthropy, Chicago, IL.

2825
John and Editha Kapoor Charitable Foundation
(formerly Kapoor Charitable Foundation)
c/o Mary Gauwitz
225 E. Deerpath Rd., Ste. 250
Lake Forest, IL 60045
E-mail: mgauwitz@ejfinancial.com

Established in 1990 in IL.
Donors: Editha Sue Kapoor†; John N. Kapoor.
Foundation type: Independent foundation.
Financial data (yr. ended 12/31/05): Assets, $5,859,152 (M); gifts received, $209,007; expenditures, $1,078,276; qualifying distributions, $1,070,931; giving activities include $1,057,500 for 19 grants (high: $1,000,000; low: $500).
Purpose and activities: Giving primarily for education and human services.
Fields of interest: Cancer; AIDS; Cancer research; AIDS research; Food banks; Nutrition; Human services; Youth, pregnancy prevention; Homeless.

Limitations: Giving primarily in AZ, IL and NY. No grants to individuals.
Trustee: John N. Kapoor.
EIN: 366923817
Selected grants: The following grants were reported in 2005.
$1,000,000 to University of Buffalo Foundation, Buffalo, NY.
$10,000 to Brophy College Preparatory, Phoenix, AZ.
$6,000 to Northwestern University, Evanston, IL.
$5,000 to Woodlands Academy of the Sacred Heart, Lake Forest, IL.
$1,000 to United Negro College Fund, New York, NY.

2826
Katten Muchin Zavis Rosenman Foundation, Inc. ◇
(formerly Katten Muchin & Zavis Foundation, Inc.)
525 W. Monroe St., Ste. 1900
Chicago, IL 60661-3693 (312) 902-5200
Contact: Mark P. Broutman

Established about 1982 in IL.
Donors: Katten Muchin Zavis; Katten Muchin Zavis Rosenman; Katten Muchin Rosenman LLP.
Foundation type: Company-sponsored foundation.
Financial data (yr. ended 12/30/04): Assets, $121,584 (M); gifts received, $1,577,100; expenditures, $1,646,791; qualifying distributions, $1,646,789; giving activities include $1,646,656 for 287 grants (high: $146,828; low: $30).
Purpose and activities: The foundation supports Jewish agencies and organizations involved with arts and culture, education, health, legal services, children and youth, human services, civil rights, and community development.
Fields of interest: Performing arts; Performing arts, opera; Arts; Education; Health care; Cancer; Diabetes research; Legal services; Children/youth, services; Human services; Civil rights; Community development; Federated giving programs; Roman Catholic federated giving programs; Jewish federated giving programs; Jewish agencies & temples.
Limitations: Giving primarily in the Chicago, IL, area. No grants to individuals.
Application information: Application form not required.
Initial approach: Letter of inquiry
Deadline(s): None
Officers and Directors: Vincent A.F. Sergi,* Pres.; Herbert S. Wander,* Secy.; Arthur W. Hahn; Howard S. Jacobs; David H. Kistenbroker; Howard S. Lanznar; Nina B. Matis; Steven V. Napolitano; William Natbony; Saul E. Rudo; Joshua S. Rubenstein; David Schwinger; Gail Migdal Title; Joel A. Yunis.
EIN: 363165216
Selected grants: The following grants were reported in 2004.
$146,828 to Lyric Opera of Chicago, Chicago, IL.
$135,000 to United Way of Metropolitan Chicago, Chicago, IL.
$49,160 to Legal Assistance Foundation of Chicago, Chicago, IL.
$43,707 to American Cancer Society, Atlanta, GA.
$25,000 to Catholic Charities.
$24,450 to Boys and Girls Club.
$24,000 to Fulfillment Fund, Los Angeles, CA.
$4,400 to Facets Multimedia, Chicago, IL.
$3,500 to Cabrini Green Legal Aid Clinic, Chicago, IL.

$1,000 to Dallas Jewish Community Foundation, Dallas, TX.

2827
Kazma Family Foundation ◇
4343 Commerce Ct., Ste. 610
Lisle, IL 60532
Contact: Leigh-Anne Kazma, Pres.

Established in 1997 in IL.
Donors: Gerald Kazma; Amzak Corp.
Foundation type: Independent foundation.
Financial data (yr. ended 4/30/06): Assets, $1,283,297 (M); gifts received, $442,000; expenditures, $454,794; qualifying distributions, $453,368; giving activities include $453,368 for 14 grants (high: $248,000; low: $380).
Purpose and activities: Giving primarily to Roman Catholic schools and organizations, and for social services.
Fields of interest: Elementary/secondary education; Higher education; Education; Human services; Children, services; Roman Catholic federated giving programs; Roman Catholic agencies & churches.
Limitations: Giving primarily in Chicago, IL.
Officers: Leigh-Anne Kazma, Pres.; Gerald Kazma, Treas.
Directors: Margaret Kazma; Michael Kazma.
EIN: 364206371
Selected grants: The following grants were reported in 2004.
$360,000 to Big Shoulders Fund, Chicago, IL.
$223,250 to Diocese of Joliet, Joliet, IL. 2 grants: $221,250, $2,000 (For annual campaign).
$66,042 to Josephinum High School, Chicago, IL.
$50,000 to Mercy Home for Boys and Girls, Chicago, IL.
$10,000 to Bradley University, Peoria, IL.
$10,000 to DuPage Childrens Museum, Naperville, IL.
$2,500 to Starlight Starbright Childrens Foundation, Chicago, IL.
$1,000 to Boy Scouts of America, Chicago Area Council, Chicago, IL.
$650 to Cristo Rey Jesuit High School, Chicago, IL.

2828
Michael L. Keiser and Rosalind C. Keiser Charitable Trust ◇
2450 N. Lakeview Ave.
Chicago, IL 60614-2794

Established in 1990 in IL.
Donors: Michael L. Keiser; Rosalind C. Keiser; Helen Douglas Hart†; Recycled Paper Greetings, Inc.
Foundation type: Independent foundation.
Financial data (yr. ended 12/31/05): Assets, $13,893,438 (M); gifts received, $6,000,000; expenditures, $799,871; qualifying distributions, $752,775; giving activities include $752,660 for 160 grants (high: $90,000; low: $50).
Purpose and activities: Primary area of interest is in public policy issues.
Fields of interest: Secondary school/education; Crime/law enforcement; Human services; International human rights; Civil rights; Public policy, research; Government/public administration.
Limitations: Applications not accepted. Giving primarily in Chicago, IL, giving also nationally with

emphasis on Washington, DC, and VA. No grants to individuals.
Application information: Contributes only to pre-selected organizations.
Trustees: Michael L. Keiser; Rosalind C. Keiser.
EIN: 366943606
Selected grants: The following grants were reported in 2004.
$25,000 to Catholic Charities of the Archdiocese of Chicago, Chicago, IL.
$25,000 to Saint Ignatius High School, Chicago, IL.
$25,000 to William and Mary Athletic Educational Foundation, Williamsburg, VA.
$15,000 to Committee for Justice, DC.
$15,000 to Prep for Prep, New York, NY.
$10,500 to Lincoln Park Zoo, Chicago, IL.
$10,000 to Art Institute of Chicago, Chicago, IL.
$10,000 to Foundation for Neurological Diseases, New York, NY.
$10,000 to Providence Saint Mel School, Chicago, IL.
$10,000 to Santa Clara University, Santa Clara, CA.

2829
Keller Family Foundation ✧
c/o Ginsberg Myers
1264 Derby Ln.
Mundelein, IL   60060-4619

Established in 1997 in IL.
Donor: Dennis J. Keller.
Foundation type: Independent foundation.
Financial data (yr. ended 12/31/04): Assets, $352,387 (M); gifts received, $383,600; expenditures, $891,229; qualifying distributions, $888,337; giving activities include $888,337 for grants (high: $582,600).
Purpose and activities: Giving primarily for education, conservation, and health and human services.
Fields of interest: Arts; Education; Environment; Animals/wildlife; Health care; Human services.
Limitations: Applications not accepted. Giving on a national basis, with emphasis on IL. No grants to individuals.
Application information: Contributes only to pre-selected organizations.
Trustees: Constance T. Keller; David M. Keller; Dennis J. Keller; Jeffrey B. Keller; John T. Keller.
EIN: 364209206

2830
Donald P. and Byrd M. Kelly Foundation ✧
701 Harger Rd.
Oak Brook, IL   60523   (630) 575-2344
Contact: Laura K. McGrath, Treas.

Established in 1985 in IL.
Donors: Donald P. Kelly; Byrd M. Kelly; Patrick J. Kelly; Thomas N. Kelly; Laura K. McGrath.
Foundation type: Independent foundation.
Financial data (yr. ended 6/30/05): Assets, $5,927,668 (M); gifts received, $336,795; expenditures, $677,235; qualifying distributions, $661,926; giving activities include $642,316 for 113 grants (high: $72,114; low: $500).
Purpose and activities: Support for organizations, institutions, and individuals who are involved in providing or seeking formal education.
Fields of interest: Education, association; Education, research; Education, fund raising/fund

distribution; Education, early childhood education; Elementary school/education; Secondary school/education; Higher education; Adult/continuing education; Education; Minorities.
Type of support: General/operating support; Continuing support; Endowments; Scholarship funds.
Limitations: Giving primarily in IL, with emphasis on Chicago. No grants to individuals.
Publications: Application guidelines.
Application information: Application form required.
   Initial approach: Request application
   Copies of proposal: 1
   Deadline(s): Sept. 1 and Feb. 1
   Board meeting date(s): Sept., Feb., and Apr.
   Final notification: Oct. 31 and Mar. 31
Officers and Directors:* Byrd M. Kelly, Pres.; Patrick J. Kelly,* V.P.; Thomas N. Kelly, Secy.; Laura K. McGrath,* Treas.
EIN: 363444536

2831
Kemper Educational and Charitable Fund ✧
1001 Green Bay Rd., PMB 186
Winnetka, IL   60093-1721   (847) 441-2043

Incorporated in 1961 in IL.
Donor: James Scott Kemper‡.
Foundation type: Independent foundation.
Financial data (yr. ended 12/31/04): Assets, $11,005,122 (M); expenditures, $636,412; qualifying distributions, $534,224; giving activities include $504,395 for 28 grants (high: $104,280; low: $100).
Purpose and activities: Giving primarily for health associations as well as for children, youth, and social services; some funding for education and the arts.
Fields of interest: Performing arts, music; Historic preservation/historical societies; Arts; Secondary school/education; Higher education; Medical school/education; Education; Botanical gardens; Zoos/zoological societies; Health care; Health organizations, association; Human services; Children/youth, services; Family services; Christian agencies & churches.
Type of support: General/operating support; Continuing support; Building/renovation; Equipment; Program development; Curriculum development; Scholarship funds; Research.
Limitations: Applications not accepted. Giving primarily in the metropolitan Chicago, IL, area and adjoining states. No grants to individuals; no loans.
Application information: Contributes only to pre-selected organizations.
   Board meeting date(s): Annually and as required
Officers and Trustees:* John Van Cleave,* Chair.; Dale Park, Jr.,* Secy.; Patricia Van Cleave, Exec. Dir.; Margaret M. Archambault; Brian Van Cleave.
Number of staff: 1 part-time professional; 1 part-time support.
EIN: 366054499
Selected grants: The following grants were reported in 2004.
$104,280 to Lawrence Hall Youth Services, Chicago, IL.
$100,000 to Lincoln Park Zoo, Chicago, IL.
$50,350 to Chicago Botanic Garden, Glencoe, IL.
$50,000 to Night Ministry, Chicago, IL.
$37,500 to Perspectives Charter School, Chicago, IL.

$37,500 to Winnetka Historical Society, Winnetka, IL.
$35,000 to Winnetka Community House, Winnetka, IL.
$4,500 to Chicago Zoological Society, Brookfield, IL.
$3,500 to Museum of Science and Industry, Chicago, IL.
$1,500 to Art Institute of Chicago, Chicago, IL.

2832
James S. Kemper Foundation
20 N. Wacker Dr., Ste. 1823
Chicago, IL   60606   (312) 332-3114
Contact: Ryan LaHurd, Pres. and Exec. Dir.
URL: http://www.jskemper.org

Incorporated in 1942 in IL.
Donors: James Scott Kemper‡; Lumbermens Mutual Casualty Co.; American Motorists Insurance Co.; American Manufacturers Mutual Insurance Co.
Foundation type: Independent foundation.
Financial data (yr. ended 7/31/05): Assets, $40,678,462 (M); expenditures, $2,132,251; qualifying distributions, $1,555,650; giving activities include $1,076,426 for grants.
Purpose and activities: The mission of the James S. Kemper Foundation is to promote liberal arts education as an ideal preparation for life and work, especially in administration and business. The foundation focuses primarily on small, private liberal arts colleges, though it maintains a secondary commitment to undergraduate opportunities at Chicago's cultural organizations. The foundation partners with fifteen private colleges in a special scholarship/internship program, the Kemper Scholars Program, and it also makes project grants to small private colleges and some of Chicago's cultural organizations.
Fields of interest: Arts; Higher education, college.
Type of support: Seed money; Program development; Internship funds; Conferences/seminars; Curriculum development.
Limitations: Giving on a national basis. No support for public institutions, large universities, cultural organizations outside of Chicago, or international organizations. No grants to individuals or for capital purposes.
Publications: Application guidelines; Grants list; Program policy statement.
Application information: The Kemper Scholar Grant program is administered by selection committees at participating colleges and universities. The committee on each campus publicizes the program to enrolled freshman students who are oriented toward a career in business, accepts applications, and screens the applicants. Liberal Arts colleges are given preference. Application information also available on foundation Web site. Full proposals will be accepted by invitation only. Application form not required.
   Initial approach: Letter of inquiry (not to exceed 3 pages)
   Copies of proposal: 1
   Deadline(s): Oct. 15 for letters of inquiry; Dec. 1 for invited proposals
   Board meeting date(s): Feb.
   Final notification: Early Mar.
Officers and Trustees:* David B. Mathis,* Chair.; Ryan LaHurd, Pres. and Exec. Dir.; John K. Conway,* Secy.; E.B. Smith, Jr., Treas.; Genl. John T. Chain, Jr.; J. Reed Coleman; Peter B. Hamilton; George R. Lewis; John E. Porter.

Number of staff: 2 full-time professional; 1 part-time professional.
EIN: 366007812
Selected grants: The following grants were reported in 2005.
$50,000 to Anderson University, Anderson, IN.
$38,436 to University of Evansville, Evansville, IN.
$37,500 to Shimer College, Waukegan, IL.
$35,000 to Lake Forest College, Lake Forest, IL.
$25,000 to Chicago Shakespeare Theater, Chicago, IL.
$25,000 to Chicago Symphony Orchestra, Chicago, IL.
$25,000 to Lyric Opera of Chicago, Chicago, IL.
$20,000 to Air Force Memorial Foundation, Arlington, VA.
$9,216 to Poetry Center of Chicago, Chicago, IL.
$8,000 to La Salle University, Philadelphia, PA.

2833
The George R. Kendall Foundation ◇
c/o JPMorgan Chase Bank, N.A.
P.O. Box 1308
Wilmette, IL 60091
Contact: Wendy J. Hayes, V.P. and Trust Off., JPMorgan Chase Bank, N.A.
Application address: c/o JP Morgan Chase Bank, N. A., 1200 Central St., Wilmette, IL 60091, tel: (847) 853-2730

Trust established in 1969 in IL.
Donor: George R. Kendall, Sr.‡.
Foundation type: Independent foundation.
Financial data (yr. ended 11/30/05): Assets, $16,467,687 (M); expenditures, $991,744; qualifying distributions, $854,010; giving activities include $773,000 for 17 grants (high: $217,000; low: $5,000).
Fields of interest: Child development, education; Higher education; Human services; Children/youth, services; Child development, services.
Type of support: General/operating support; Program development; Curriculum development.
Limitations: Giving primarily in the North Shore suburbs, north of Chicago, IL. No grants to individuals, or for endowment funds, scholarships, fellowships, or matching gifts; no loans.
Application information: Application form not required.
Initial approach: Proposal
Copies of proposal: 1
Deadline(s): Mar. 1
Board meeting date(s): Oct.
Final notification: Positive responses only
Trustees: George Kendall, Jr.; Helen Kendall; Thomas Kendall; JPMorgan Chase Bank, N.A.
EIN: 366403376

2834
George D. Kennedy & Valerie P. Kennedy Charitable Trust ◇
789 Humbolot Ave.
Winnetka, IL 60093-1948

Established in 1992 in IL.
Donors: George D. Kennedy; Valerie P. Kennedy.
Foundation type: Independent foundation.
Financial data (yr. ended 12/31/05): Assets, $18,995 (M); gifts received, $195,141; expenditures, $337,780; qualifying distributions,

$327,700; giving activities include $327,000 for 9 grants (high: $100,000; low: $1,000).
Purpose and activities: Giving for the arts, higher education, and hospitals.
Fields of interest: Performing arts; Historic preservation/historical societies; Arts; Higher education; Hospitals (general); Federated giving programs.
Limitations: Applications not accepted. Giving limited to IL and MA. No grants to individuals.
Application information: Contributes only to pre-selected organizations.
Trustees: George D. Kennedy; Valerie P. Kennedy.
EIN: 367014327
Selected grants: The following grants were reported in 2005.
$36,000 to Chicago Symphony Orchestra, Chicago, IL.
$25,000 to Saint Johns Episcopal Church, Williamstown, MA.
$25,000 to Williamstown Theater Festival, Williamstown, MA.
$5,700 to Childrens Memorial Hospital, Chicago, IL.

2835
Kenny's Kids ◇
(formerly Comdisco Foundation)
c/o Nicholas K. Pontikes
1212 W. Lill St.
Chicago, IL 60614

Established in 1994 in IL.
Donor: Comdisco, Inc.
Foundation type: Independent foundation.
Financial data (yr. ended 9/30/05): Assets, $12,557,052 (M); expenditures, $744,961; qualifying distributions, $543,962; giving activities include $542,162 for 9 grants (high: $175,000; low: $1,000).
Purpose and activities: The primary target of grants is giving support to organizations which seek to give youth greater opportunities outside of the classroom to learn and grow, to teach them skills that will enable them to thrive in a technology-oriented society, and to offer them the guidance and attention necessary to develop such skills. Also consideration for youth-oriented organizations and other organizations that promote the welfare of youth, such as those that offer hope and encouragement to the sick and terminally ill, protect those who have suffered from abuse, and offer after-school programs for the underprivileged.
Fields of interest: Education; Hospitals (general); Sickle cell disease; Youth development, services; Children/youth, services; Children, services.
Type of support: General/operating support; Annual campaigns; Program development.
Limitations: Giving primarily in the Chicago, IL, area. No support for private foundations, schools (public or private), or corporations, political campaigns. No grants to individuals, film, video, or audio productions.
Application information: Grant requests are processed monthly.
Initial approach: Proposal
Board meeting date(s): Quarterly
Officers and Directors: * Nicholas K. Pontikes,* Pres.; Melissa S. Scanlon,* Secy.; Victoria L. Gallegos,* Treas.
EIN: 363977234

2836
The Kensington Square Foundation ◇
1418 N. Lake Shore Dr., Ste. 9
Chicago, IL 60610
Contact: Richard C. Carr, Pres.

Established in 1999 in IL.
Donors: Richard C. Carr; Ann K. Carr.
Foundation type: Independent foundation.
Financial data (yr. ended 12/31/05): Assets, $10,304,835 (M); gifts received, $15; expenditures, $526,353; qualifying distributions, $516,400; giving activities include $516,400 for 52 grants (high: $100,000; low: $500; average: $2,500–$10,000).
Fields of interest: Arts; Higher education; Education; Human services.
Limitations: Giving primarily in IL. No grants to individuals.
Application information:
Initial approach: Letter
Officers and Directors: * Richard C. Carr,* Pres.; Ann K. Carr,* Secy.
EIN: 367291505

2837
Kern Foundation Trust ◇
c/o The Northern Trust Co.
P.O. Box 803878
Chicago, IL 60680
Application address: c/o The Northern Trust Co., 50 S. LaSalle St., Chicago, IL 06075, tel.: (312) 630-6000

Established in 1959 in IL.
Donors: Herbert A. Kern‡; Theosophical Society in America; Krotona Institute of Theosophy; Happy Valley School; The Theosophical Book Gift Institute; Theosophical Order of Service.
Foundation type: Independent foundation.
Financial data (yr. ended 12/31/05): Assets, $26,204,829 (M); gifts received, $21,000; expenditures, $1,463,603; qualifying distributions, $1,387,427; giving activities include $1,286,032 for 3 grants (high: $1,147,000; low: $1,000).
Purpose and activities: To aid the spiritual enlightenment of as many people as practical by exposing them to the theosophical philosophy, particularly through support of the Theosophical Society in America and the Krotona Institute of Theosophy.
Fields of interest: Religion.
Limitations: Giving primarily in CA and IL. No grants to individuals, or for building funds.
Publications: Program policy statement.
Application information: Application form not required.
Deadline(s): None
Trustees: John C. Kern; The Northern Trust Co.
EIN: 366107250

2838
Kersten Family Foundation ◇
701 W. Erie St.
Chicago, IL 60610-3973

Established in 1959 in IL.
Donors: Samuel Kersten, Jr.‡; Steven Kersten; Priscilla Kersten.
Foundation type: Independent foundation.

Financial data (yr. ended 12/31/05): Assets, $14,119,531 (M); gifts received, $3,000,000; expenditures, $368,948; qualifying distributions, $334,850; giving activities include $334,850 for 47 grants (high: $130,000; low: $100).
Purpose and activities: Funding primarily for Jewish federated giving programs, Jewish agencies, higher education and human services.
Fields of interest: Arts; Higher education; Education; Health organizations, association; Human services; Jewish federated giving programs; Jewish agencies & temples.
Limitations: Applications not accepted. Giving primarily in Chicago, IL. No grants to individuals.
Application information: Contributes only to pre-selected organizations.
Officers and Directors:* Priscilla Kersten,* Pres.; Steven A. Kersten,* Secy.-Treas.; Walter Roth.
EIN: 366068835

2839
Khesed Foundation ◇
c/o The Northern Trust Co.
P.O. Box 803878
Chicago, IL 60680

Established in 2001 in IL.
Donors: Janet Willis; Scott Willis.
Foundation type: Independent foundation.
Financial data (yr. ended 1/31/06): Assets, $7,547,768 (M); expenditures, $466,620; qualifying distributions, $447,401; giving activities include $446,570 for 4 grants (high: $275,000; low: $2,500).
Purpose and activities: Giving primarily to Christian ministries.
Fields of interest: Christian agencies & churches.
Limitations: Applications not accepted. Giving primarily in IL. No grants to individuals.
Application information: Contributes only to pre-selected organizations.
Directors: Amy Willis Moody; Daniel Willis; Janet Willis; Scott Willis; Toby Willis.
EIN: 260036863

2840
The Kipper Family Foundation ◇
(formerly Chas. and Ruth Levy Foundation)
1930 George St., Unit 1
Melrose Park, IL 60160

Incorporated in 1959 in IL.
Donors: Barbara Levy Kipper; David Kipper.
Foundation type: Independent foundation.
Financial data (yr. ended 6/30/05): Assets, $1,318,520 (M); expenditures, $451,474; qualifying distributions, $430,180; giving activities include $430,180 for 41 grants (high: $65,000; low: $200).
Purpose and activities: Giving primarily for the arts, education, social services, and to Jewish causes.
Fields of interest: Performing arts, ballet; Performing arts, theater; Historic preservation/historical societies; Arts; Education; Human services; Federated giving programs; Jewish federated giving programs; Jewish agencies & temples; Women.
Type of support: General/operating support.
Limitations: Applications not accepted. Giving primarily in Chicago, IL. No grants to individuals.

Application information: Contributes only to pre-selected organizations.
Directors: Linda C. Harris; Barbara Levy Kipper; David Kipper; Donald Lubin.
EIN: 366032324

2841
The Jules and Gwen Knapp Charitable Foundation ◇
333 Surfside Pl.
Glencoe, IL 60022 (847) 835-8898
Contact: Gwen Knapp, Pres.

Established in 1985 in IL.
Donors: Jules Knapp; Gwen Knapp.
Foundation type: Independent foundation.
Financial data (yr. ended 12/31/05): Assets, $2,563,670 (M); gifts received, $500,000; expenditures, $750,096; qualifying distributions, $747,616; giving activities include $747,616 for 45 grants (high: $616,646; low: $20).
Fields of interest: Museums (history); Arts; Higher education; Health organizations, association; Jewish federated giving programs; Jewish agencies & temples.
Limitations: Giving primarily in FL and IL; some giving also in CA and NY. No grants to individuals.
Application information:
   Initial approach: Letter
   Deadline(s): None
Officers: Gwen Knapp, Pres.; Jules Knapp, Secy.
Directors: Susan Knapp Schulman; Elyse Knapp Sollender.
EIN: 363381401
Selected grants: The following grants were reported in 2005.
$11,000 to Martin Memorial Foundation, Stuart, FL.
$8,925 to Chicago Botanic Garden, Glencoe, IL.
$3,000 to La Jolla Country Day School, La Jolla, CA.
$2,500 to Ravinia Festival Association, Highland Park, IL.
$2,300 to Florida Oceanographic Society, Stuart, FL.
$1,000 to Womens American ORT, New York, NY.
$500 to W P B T Channel 2, Miami, FL.

2842
Winifred H. Knox Private Foundation ◇
108 Elm St.
Franklin Grove, IL 61031
Contact: Stephen B. Saathoff, Dir.

Established in 1998 in IL.
Foundation type: Independent foundation.
Financial data (yr. ended 12/31/04): Assets, $10,493,013 (M); expenditures, $566,999; qualifying distributions, $400,000; giving activities include $400,000 for 2 grants (high: $200,000; low: $200,000).
Fields of interest: Libraries (public); Residential/custodial care, senior continuing care.
Limitations: Giving limited to U.S. citizens or entities, with emphasis on IL.
Application information: Generally contributes to pre-selected organizations.
Director: Steve Saathoff.
EIN: 367288681
Selected grants: The following grants were reported in 2004.
$200,000 to Franklin Grove Public Library, Franklin Grove, IL.

2843
Gerald A. & Karen A. Kolschowsky Foundation, Inc. ◇
1225 Corporate Blvd., Ste. 103
Aurora, IL 60504-6409

Incorporated in 1986 in IL.
Donor: Gerald A. Kolschowsky.
Foundation type: Independent foundation.
Financial data (yr. ended 12/31/05): Assets, $4,390,241 (M); gifts received, $1,000,000; expenditures, $431,480; qualifying distributions, $427,827; giving activities include $409,200 for 133 grants (high: $66,000; low: $100).
Purpose and activities: Giving primarily for Lutheran churches; support also for health associations and hospitals, and social services, including child welfare.
Fields of interest: Higher education; Hospitals (general); Health organizations, association; Human services; Children/youth, services; Protestant agencies & churches.
Type of support: General/operating support.
Limitations: Applications not accepted. Giving primarily in IL. No grants to individuals.
Application information: Contributes only to pre-selected organizations.
Officers and Directors:* Karen A. Kolschowsky,* Pres.; Michael J. Kolschowsky,* V.P.; Timothy J. Kolschowsky,* V.P.; Gerald A. Kolschowsky,* Secy.-Treas.
EIN: 363505302

2844
Kovler Family Foundation ◇
(formerly Harry and Maribel G. Blum Foundation)
875 N. Michigan Ave., Ste. 3400
Chicago, IL 60611 (312) 664-5050
Contact: H.H. Bregar, Secy.

Established in 1967 in IL.
Donors: Harry Blum†; Everett Kovler.
Foundation type: Independent foundation.
Financial data (yr. ended 12/31/05): Assets, $42,537,226 (M); expenditures, $2,283,527; qualifying distributions, $2,077,928; giving activities include $2,030,950 for 23 grants (high: $850,000; low: $100).
Purpose and activities: Giving primarily for university medical research, a Jewish welfare fund, a zoological society, and an art museum.
Fields of interest: Museums (art); Higher education; Zoos/zoological societies; Medical research, institute; Human services; Jewish federated giving programs.
Type of support: General/operating support; Research.
Limitations: Giving primarily in Chicago, IL. No grants to individuals.
Application information: Application form not required.
   Initial approach: Letter or proposal
   Copies of proposal: 1
   Deadline(s): None
   Board meeting date(s): As required
Officers and Directors:* H. Jonathan Kovler,* Pres.; H.H. Bregar,* Secy.
Number of staff: 2 full-time professional; 2 part-time professional.
EIN: 366152744
Selected grants: The following grants were reported in 2004.

$250,000 to Northwestern Memorial Hospital, Chicago, IL.
$209,566 to Museum of Contemporary Art, Chicago, IL.
$200,000 to Chicago Historical Society, Chicago, IL.
$100,000 to Francis W. Parker School, Chicago, IL.
$10,000 to Erikson Institute, Chicago, IL.
$5,000 to Aspen Art Museum, Aspen, CO.
$5,000 to Chicago Center for Family Health, Chicago, IL.
$1,000 to Columbia College, Chicago, IL.
$1,000 to National Student Partnerships, DC.

2845
Krehbiel Family Foundation ◇ ☆
c/o Robert J. Reichner & Assoc., Inc.
807 Chestnut Ave.
Wilmette, IL 60091

Established in 2003 in IL as s successor to the original Krehbiel Family Foundation.
Foundation type: Independent foundation.
Financial data (yr. ended 10/31/05): Assets, $7,783,918 (M); expenditures, $424,897; qualifying distributions, $359,195; giving activities include $355,000 for 9 grants (high: $70,000; low: $10,000).
Fields of interest: Performing arts, music; Higher education; Environment; Youth development, adult & child programs.
Limitations: Applications not accepted. Giving primarily in IL and NY.
Application information: Unsolicited requests for funds not accepted.
Officers and Directors:* Margaret V. Krehbiel-Ellsworth,* Pres.; William V. Krehbiel,* Treas.; Frederick A. Krehbiel; Frederick L. Krehbiel; Jay F. Krehbiel; John H. Krehbiel, Jr.; John H. Krehbiel III.
EIN: 841621866

2846
The Anstiss & Ronald Krueck Foundation ◇ ☆
18 E. Pearson St.
Chicago, IL 60611
Contact: Ronald Krueck, Pres.

Established in 1992 in IL.
Donors: Ronald Krueck; Anstiss Krueck.
Foundation type: Independent foundation.
Financial data (yr. ended 12/31/05): Assets, $1,240,046 (M); gifts received, $19,750; expenditures, $363,727; qualifying distributions, $329,064; giving activities include $329,064 for 25 grants (high: $266,030; low: $50).
Fields of interest: Visual arts, photography; Museums (art); Performing arts; Performing arts, theater; Arts; Higher education; Health care, clinics/centers; Recreation, parks/playgrounds; Human services.
Limitations: Giving primarily in Chicago, IL.
Application information: Application form not required.
Deadline(s): None
Officer and Trustees:* Ronald Krueck,* Pres.; Anstiss Krueck.
EIN: 363855553

2847
Landau Family Foundation ◇
P.O. Box 577880
Chicago, IL 60657-7880

Established in 1955 in IL.
Donor: Howard M. Landau‡.
Foundation type: Independent foundation.
Financial data (yr. ended 11/30/05): Assets, $9,488,651 (M); expenditures, $486,799; qualifying distributions, $400,500; giving activities include $400,500 for 30 grants (high: $50,000; low: $2,000).
Purpose and activities: Support primarily for social and economic justice.
Fields of interest: Legal services, public interest law; Housing/shelter, public housing; Human services; International peace/security; Jewish federated giving programs; Jewish agencies & temples.
International interests: Israel; Middle East.
Type of support: General/operating support; Continuing support; Emergency funds; Program development; Seed money; Program-related investments/loans.
Limitations: Giving primarily in Chicago, IL. No grants to individuals.
Application information: Application form not required.
Deadline(s): None
Officers and Board Members:* Kenneth Landau,* Secy.; Kay Berkson,* Treas.; Daniel Berkson; Sidney Hollander.
EIN: 366089098
Selected grants: The following grants were reported in 2003.
$50,000 to Americans for Peace Now, DC. For unrestricted support.
$50,000 to Jewish Council on Urban Affairs, Chicago, IL. For unrestricted support.
$35,000 to Jewish United Fund of Metropolitan Chicago, Chicago, IL. For unrestricted support.
$25,000 to New Israel Fund, DC. For unrestricted support.
$15,000 to Chicago Coalition for the Homeless, Chicago, IL. For unrestricted support.
$10,000 to Jewish Fund for Justice, New York, NY. For unrestricted support.
$10,000 to Partnership to End Homelessness, Chicago, IL. For unrestricted support.
$10,000 to People for the American Way Foundation, DC. For unrestricted support.
$10,000 to Roger Baldwin Foundation of the American Civil Liberties Union, Chicago, IL. For unrestricted support.
$10,000 to United for a Fair Economy, Boston, MA. For unrestricted support.

2848
Lange Burk Fund ◇
c/o Bank of America, N.A.
231 S. LaSalle St.
Chicago, IL 60697 (312) 828-8028
Contact: Charles Slamar, Jr.
Additional contact: Kristin Carlson Vogen, tel.: (312) 828-1029

Established in 1995 in IL.
Donor: Henrietta Lange Burk Trust.
Foundation type: Independent foundation.
Financial data (yr. ended 9/30/05): Assets, $8,915,548 (M); expenditures, $494,621; qualifying distributions, $454,842; giving activities

include $435,344 for 29 grants (high: $75,000; low: $4,800).
Purpose and activities: Giving primarily for the arts and human services.
Fields of interest: Arts; Education; Human services; Children/youth, services; Religion.
Limitations: Giving primarily in Chicago, IL.
Application information: Application form required.
Initial approach: Telephone
Copies of proposal: 1
Deadline(s): Jan. 31 and July 30
Final notification: Varies
Trustee: Bank of America, N.A.
EIN: 367092200
Selected grants: The following grants were reported in 2005.
$50,000 to Civic Orchestra of Chicago, Chicago, IL.
$25,000 to Donors Forum of Chicago, Chicago, IL.
$20,000 to Juvenile Protective Association, Chicago, IL.
$20,000 to Northwestern University, Evanston, IL.
$15,000 to Actors Gymnasium, Evanston, IL.
$15,000 to Casa Central, Chicago, IL.
$15,000 to Deborahs Place, Chicago, IL.
$10,000 to Association House of Chicago, Chicago, IL.
$10,000 to Infant Welfare Society of Chicago, Chicago, IL.
$10,000 to Resurrection Home Health Services, Skokie, IL.

2849
Lavin Family Foundation ◇
(formerly Leonard H. Lavin Foundation)
411 Lakeside Terr.
Glencoe, IL 60022-1710
Contact: Leonard H. Lavin, Pres.

Established around 1964.
Donor: Leonard H. Lavin.
Foundation type: Independent foundation.
Financial data (yr. ended 12/31/04): Assets, $50,559,043 (M); expenditures, $5,266,470; qualifying distributions, $5,259,343; giving activities include $5,257,200 for 24 grants (high: $5,000,000; low: $500).
Purpose and activities: Giving primarily for higher and other education, as well as for human services.
Fields of interest: Higher education; Education; Medical research, institute; Human services.
Limitations: Giving primarily in Chicago, IL. No grants to individuals.
Application information: Application form not required.
Initial approach: Letter
Deadline(s): None
Officers: Leonard H. Lavin, Pres.; Carol L. Bernick, V.P.; Bernice E. Lavin, Secy.-Treas.
EIN: 366106074

2850
The Lea Charitable Trust ◇ ☆
1500 Primrose Ln.
Glenview, IL 60026

Established in 1986 in IL.
Donors: L. Bates Lea; Marcia W. Lea.
Foundation type: Independent foundation.
Financial data (yr. ended 12/31/05): Assets, $8,292,505 (M); gifts received, $3,000,456; expenditures, $355,792; qualifying distributions,

$355,792; giving activities include $322,000 for 28 grants (high: $130,000; low: $1,000).

Fields of interest: Arts education; Visual arts; Performing arts, orchestra (symphony); Arts; Education; Cancer; Human services; Foundations (community); Federated giving programs.

Limitations: Applications not accepted. Giving primarily in IL and FL. No grants to individuals.

Application information: Contributes only to pre-selected organizations.

Trustees: Victoria Lea Chaney; Christopher G. Lea; L. Bates Lea; Marcia W. Lea; Jennifer Lea Robinson.

EIN: 363486285

Selected grants: The following grants were reported in 2004.

$105,000 to Community Foundation of Collier County, Naples, FL. For general support.

$50,000 to Northwestern University, Cancer Center, Evanston, IL. For general support.

$20,000 to Massachusetts Institute of Technology, Cambridge, MA. For general support.

$6,000 to Metropolitan Family Services, Chicago, IL. For general support.

$5,000 to Art Institute of Chicago, Chicago, IL. For general support.

$3,000 to Chicago Botanic Garden, Glencoe, IL. For general support.

$2,500 to University of Michigan, Ann Arbor, MI. For general support.

$1,000 to American Red Cross, Chicago, IL. For general support.

$1,000 to Chicago House and Social Service Agency, Chicago, IL. For general support.

$1,000 to Denison University, Granville, OH. For general support.

2851

The Francis L. Lederer Foundation ◇

120 S. Riverside Plz., Ste. 1200
Chicago, IL 60606-3913 (312) 876-7855
Contact: Robert I. Ury, V.P.

Established in 1966 in IL.

Foundation type: Independent foundation.

Financial data (yr. ended 12/31/05): Assets, $4,326,441 (M); expenditures, $456,518; qualifying distributions, $390,518; giving activities include $367,500 for 25 grants (high: $200,000; low: $1,000).

Purpose and activities: Giving primarily for esophageal cancer research, for the arts, and to a Jewish temple.

Fields of interest: Arts; Health organizations, association; Medical research, institute; Crime/violence prevention, child abuse; Jewish federated giving programs; Jewish agencies & temples.

Limitations: Giving primarily in Chicago, IL. No grants to individuals.

Application information:

Initial approach: Proposal
Deadline(s): None

Officers and Directors:* Adrienne Lederer,* Pres.; Robert I. Ury,* V.P. and Secy.; Lawrence D. Silverman,* Treas.; Mitchell Lederer; Sharon Lederer.

EIN: 362594937

2852

Anne P. Lederer Research Institute ◇

c/o Blooma Stark
1 IBM Plz., Rm. 3000
Chicago, IL 60611

Established in 1980 in IL.

Donor: Anne P. Lederer†.

Foundation type: Independent foundation.

Financial data (yr. ended 12/31/05): Assets, $1,388,734 (M); expenditures, $598,117; qualifying distributions, $567,730; giving activities include $567,730 for 39 grants (high: $99,750; low: $300).

Purpose and activities: Grants primarily for music, health, including mental health, and human services.

Fields of interest: Performing arts, music; Education; Mental health, treatment; Human services; Psychology/behavioral science; Jewish agencies & temples.

Type of support: Scholarship funds.

Limitations: Applications not accepted. Giving primarily in IL. No grants to individuals.

Application information: Contributes only to pre-selected organizations. Unsolicited requests for funds not considered.

Officers: Paul V. Anglin, Pres.; Laurence S. Kaplan, V.P. and Treas.; Blooma Stark, Secy.

Director: Audrey G. Ratner.

EIN: 363076805

Selected grants: The following grants were reported in 2004.

$99,750 to Council for Jewish Elderly, Chicago, IL. For program support.

$75,000 to Lyric Opera Center for American Artists, Chicago, IL.

$40,000 to International Music Foundation, Chicago, IL.

$30,000 to Musical Arts Association, Cleveland, OH.

$25,000 to Deborahs Place, Chicago, IL.

$25,000 to Hinsdale Community Service, Hinsdale, IL.

$25,000 to Weizmann Institute of Science, Rehovot, Israel. .

$20,000 to Shalva, Chicago, IL.

$20,000 to Thresholds, Chicago, IL.

$10,000 to Loras College, Dubuque, IA.

2853

Daniel and Karen Lee Family Foundation ◇ ☆

c/o Daniel R. Lee
555 Skokie Blvd., Ste. 345
Northbrook, IL 60062-2827

Established in 1998 in IL.

Donors: Daniel R. Lee; Karen K. Lee.

Foundation type: Independent foundation.

Financial data (yr. ended 12/31/05): Assets, $392,048 (M); expenditures, $437,949; qualifying distributions, $434,490; giving activities include $434,490 for 37 grants (high: $250,000; low: $50).

Fields of interest: Health organizations, association; Human services; Jewish agencies & temples.

Limitations: Applications not accepted. Giving primarily in IL. No grants to individuals.

Application information: Contributes only to pre-selected organizations.

Officers: Daniel R. Lee, Pres. and Treas.; Karen K. Lee, Secy.

Director: Joel H. Fenchel.

EIN: 364157608

Selected grants: The following grants were reported in 2005.

$5,000 to Rush University Medical Center, Chicago, IL.

$1,000 to Jewish Community Centers, Boston, MA.

$800 to American Cancer Society, Atlanta, GA. 4 grants: $550, $50, $100, $100

$320 to March of Dimes Birth Defects Foundation, White Plains, NY.

$300 to Multiple Sclerosis Society, National, New York, NY. 2 grants: $150 each

2854

Sheldon L. and Pearl R. Leibowitz Foundation ◇

2800 Lakeside Dr.
Bannockburn, IL 60015

Established in 1986 in IL.

Donors: Sheldon L. Leibowitz; Pearl R. Leibowitz.

Foundation type: Independent foundation.

Financial data (yr. ended 9/30/05): Assets, $3,308,924 (M); gifts received, $50,000; expenditures, $356,143; qualifying distributions, $356,123; giving activities include $356,000 for 76 grants (high: $30,000; low: $500).

Purpose and activities: Giving to human services, Jewish federated programs, and to health associations.

Fields of interest: Arts; Theological school/education; Education; Health organizations, association; Human services; Jewish federated giving programs; Jewish agencies & temples.

Limitations: Applications not accepted. Giving primarily in Chicago, IL. No grants to individuals.

Application information: Contributes only to pre-selected organizations.

Officer: Sheldon L. Leibowitz, Pres.

Directors: Dale Leibowitz; Lew Leibowitz; Todd Leibowitz.

EIN: 363480213

2855

Levi, Ray & Shoup Foundation ◇ ☆

2401 W. Monroe St.
Springfield, IL 62704

Established in 2001 in IL.

Donor: Levi, Ray & Shoup, Inc.

Foundation type: Company-sponsored foundation.

Financial data (yr. ended 7/31/05): Assets, $5,121,825 (M); gifts received, $1,000,000; expenditures, $575,193; qualifying distributions, $561,515; giving activities include $561,500 for 23 grants (high: $450,000; low: $500).

Purpose and activities: The foundation supports organizations involved with arts and culture, education, parks, and human services.

Fields of interest: Arts; Higher education; Education; Recreation, parks/playgrounds; Human services; Federated giving programs.

Type of support: General/operating support; Building/renovation.

Limitations: Applications not accepted. Giving limited to Springfield, IL. No grants to individuals.

Application information: Contributes only to pre-selected organizations.

Trustees: Agnes E. Levi; Richard H. Levi; Ryan M. Levi; Lindsay M. Matthews.
EIN: 326007063

2856
The Carole & Joseph Levy, Jr.
Foundation ✧
3340 W. Main St.
Skokie, IL 60076

Established in 1999 in IL.
Donors: Joseph Levy, Jr. Trust; Max Madsen; Levy Venture Mgmt., Inc.
Foundation type: Independent foundation.
Financial data (yr. ended 6/30/05): Assets, $1,301,238 (M); gifts received, $98,999; expenditures, $425,024; qualifying distributions, $418,169; giving activities include $418,919 for 18 grants (high: $134,969; low: $100).
Purpose and activities: Giving primarily for Jewish agencies and temples and for education.
Fields of interest: Education; Hospitals (general); Health organizations, association; Human services; Jewish federated giving programs; Jewish agencies & temples.
Limitations: Applications not accepted. Giving primarily in IL, with some emphasis on Chicago. No grants to individuals.
Application information: Contributes only to pre-selected organizations.
Directors: James R. Hardt; Carole Levy; Joseph Levy, Jr.
EIN: 364251966

2857
Lewis-Sebring Family Foundation ✧
2735 Sheridan Rd.
Evanston, IL 60201

Established in 1996 in IL.
Donors: Charles A. Lewis; Penny Bender Sebring.
Foundation type: Independent foundation.
Financial data (yr. ended 11/30/05): Assets, $4,818,785 (M); expenditures, $1,662,458; qualifying distributions, $1,658,147; giving activities include $1,658,043 for 42 grants (high: $1,000,000; low: $250).
Fields of interest: Performing arts, orchestra (symphony); Arts; Education, public education; Higher education; Diabetes research; Human services; YM/YWCAs & YM/YWHAs; Children/youth, services; Federated giving programs.
Limitations: Applications not accepted. Giving primarily in Evanston and Chicago, IL. No grants to individuals.
Application information: Contributes only to pre-selected organizations.
Officers and Directors:* Charles A. Lewis,* Chair.; Penny Bender Sebring,* Pres.; Lisa S. Carreras,* V.P.; Kathryn Lewis Varela, Secy.; Peter C. Lewis,* Treas.
EIN: 364120411
Selected grants: The following grants were reported in 2004.
$200,000 to University of Chicago, Chicago, IL. 2 grants: $100,000 each (For capital campaign).
$130,000 to Grinnell College, Grinnell, IA. 2 grants: $30,000 (For annual fund), $100,000 (For capital campaign).
$100,000 to Chicago Public Education Fund, Chicago, IL. For capital campaign.

$100,000 to YMCA of Evanston, McGaw Family Branch, Evanston, IL. For capital campaign.
$80,000 to Chicago Symphony Orchestra, Chicago, IL. 2 grants: $30,000 (For annual fund), $50,000 (For annual fund).
$50,000 to Amherst College, Amherst, MA. For capital campaign.
$42,000 to Juvenile Diabetes Research Foundation International, Chicago, IL. For annual fund.

2858
The Libra Foundation
1700 W. Irving Park Rd., Rm. 203
Chicago, IL 60613
URL: http://www.thelibrafoundation.org

Established in 2002 in IL.
Donor: Pritzker Foundation.
Foundation type: Independent foundation.
Financial data (yr. ended 12/31/05): Assets, $41,846,264 (M); expenditures, $1,958,725; qualifying distributions, $1,771,420; giving activities include $1,601,300 for 51 grants (high: $125,000; low: $2,500; average: $15,000–$50,000).
Purpose and activities: The foundation seeks to support programs that contribute to improving the quality of life and promoting human rights and social justice for the disenfranchised or marginalized populations, as well as those initiatives that protect and sustain the ecosystems that surround us. Emphasis is on organizations in the Chicago, IL and San Francisco, CA areas whose work is national in scope.
Fields of interest: Human services; Civil rights; Community development; Economically disadvantaged.
Limitations: Giving primarily in San Francisco, CA and Chicago, IL. No grants to individuals.
Publications: Application guidelines; Grants list.
Application information: In general, the foundation does not accept unsolicited proposals. Brief letters of inquiry are accepted however, on a rolling basis. Refer to foundation Web site for complete application information and guidelines. Application form required.
   Initial approach: Letter of Inquiry only
   Deadline(s): None
Officers and Directors:* Susan S. Pritzker,* Pres.; Regan Pritzker,* Secy.; Nicholas J. Pritzker,* Treas.; Jacob Pritzker; Joseph Pritzker.
Number of staff: 1 full-time professional; 1 part-time professional; 1 part-time support.
EIN: 300031117
Selected grants: The following grants were reported in 2004.
$125,000 to Pitzer College, Claremont, CA.
$75,000 to Global Greengrants Fund, Boulder, CO.
$75,000 to Population Council, New York, NY.
$75,000 to Stanford University, Stanford, CA.
$70,000 to Women of Color Resource Center, Oakland, CA.
$65,000 to Chicago Foundation for Women, Chicago, IL.
$60,000 to Global Fund for Women, San Francisco, CA.
$30,000 to Center for Women Policy Studies, DC.
$25,000 to Amnesty International USA, New York, NY.
$20,000 to Sustain, Chicago, IL.

2859
Little Angel Foundation ✧
(formerly Little Angel Perpetual Charitable Trust)
P.O. Box 96
Hinsdale, IL 60522-0096 (630) 679-4980
Contact: Carol K. Mason, Exec. Dir.
E-mail: info@littleangelfoundation.org; URL: http://www.littleangelfoundation.org

Established in 2001 in IL.
Foundation type: Independent foundation.
Financial data (yr. ended 12/31/05): Assets, $3,093,343 (M); gifts received, $1,615; expenditures, $1,234,518; qualifying distributions, $1,234,518; giving activities include $101,049 for 48 grants (high: $71,000; low: $1,338), and $90,209 for foundation-administered programs.
Purpose and activities: Giving for the benefit of battered women and abused and orphaned children; giving also for youth development and afterschool programming.
Fields of interest: Crime/violence prevention, child abuse; Family services, domestic violence.
International interests: Bahamas.
Type of support: General/operating support; Continuing support; Equipment; Program development; Conferences/seminars; Program evaluation; Grants to individuals; Scholarships—to individuals.
Limitations: Giving primarily in the greater Chicago, IL, area.
Publications: Application guidelines.
Application information: See foundation Web site for application guidelines.
   Initial approach: Letter
   Deadline(s): May 1 and Oct. 1
   Board meeting date(s): June and Nov.
Officers: Ernest H. Huntzinger, Chair.; Carol K. Mason, Exec. Dir.
Trustee: Nick Madori.
Number of staff: None.
EIN: 367362956

2860
Reva and David Logan Foundation ☆
c/o David S. Logan
980 N. Michigan Ave., Ste. 1122
Chicago, IL 60611
FAX: (312) 664-9103; E-mail: dalo@loganfdn.org; URL: http://www.loganfdn.org

Established in 1965.
Donors: David Logan; Daniel Logan; Richard Logan; Jonathan Logan.
Foundation type: Independent foundation.
Financial data (yr. ended 12/31/05): Assets, $937,817 (M); gifts received, $997,455; expenditures, $700,784; qualifying distributions, $688,061; giving activities include $666,805 for 39 grants (high: $250,000; low: $35).
Purpose and activities: Giving primarily for education, community and social welfare, Jewish life and concerns, public service and civil society, and the upkeep and support of a library of modern illustrated and photographic books.
Fields of interest: Media/communications; Literature; Arts; Education; Aging, centers/services; Philanthropy/voluntarism; Leadership development; Jewish agencies & temples; Children; LGBTQ.
Type of support: General/operating support; Annual campaigns; Building/renovation; Endowments; Publication; Curriculum development; Research; Matching/challenge support.

Limitations: Applications not accepted. Giving primarily in the metropolitan areas of San Francisco, CA, and Chicago, IL. No grants to individuals.
Application information: Unsolicited requests for funds not accepted. However, a short letter of introduction describing an organization's services and future projects will be accepted.
Officers and Trustees:* Jonathan Logan,* Pres.; Daniel Logan,* V.P.; Richard Logan,* V.P.; David Logan,* Secy.-Treas.; Jeff Abt; Ben Rothblatt; Sherwin Zuckerman.
Number of staff: None.
EIN: 366139439
Selected grants: The following grants were reported in 2006.
$250,000 to Center for Investigative Reporting, Berkeley, CA.
$110,000 to Center for Documentary Studies, Durham, NC.
$37,500 to Richard H. Driehaus Foundation, Chicago, IL.
$21,219 to East Bay Community Foundation, Oakland, CA.
$18,411 to Ark, The, Chicago, IL.
$18,012 to Columbia College, Chicago, IL.
$16,000 to Our Family Coalition, San Francisco, CA.
$10,000 to Institute for Public Accuracy, San Francisco, CA.
$7,500 to Children of Lesbians and Gays Everywhere (COLAGE), San Francisco, CA.
$6,000 to San Francisco Museum of Modern Art, San Francisco, CA.

2861
Michael W. Louis Charitable Trust ◇
200 W. Adams St., Ste. 2600
Chicago, IL   60606-5233

Established in 1998 in IL.
Donor: Michael W. Louis.
Foundation type: Independent foundation.
Financial data (yr. ended 12/31/04): Assets, $4,855,855 (M); gifts received, $2,212,630; expenditures, $691,951; qualifying distributions, $690,929; giving activities include $688,889 for 2 grants (high: $500,000; low: $188,889).
Fields of interest: Scholarships/financial aid; Hospitals (specialty).
Limitations: Applications not accepted. Giving primarily in IL; giving also in AZ. No grants to individuals.
Application information: Contributes only to pre-selected organizations.
Trustee: Herbert J. Louis.
EIN: 367216588

2862
Josephine P. & John J. Louis Foundation ◇
(formerly John J. Louis, Jr. Foundation)
c/o Frye-Louis Capital Mgmt.
225 W. Wacker Dr., Ste. 1000
Chicago, IL   60606
Contact: Jennifer M. Millhouse, Admin.

Established in 1992 in IL as partial successor to John J. Louis Foundation.
Donors: John J. Louis, Jr.†; Josephine P. Louis; John J. Louis Foundation.
Foundation type: Independent foundation.
Financial data (yr. ended 12/31/04): Assets, $5,282,074 (M); gifts received, $744,502;

expenditures, $898,228; qualifying distributions, $837,955; giving activities include $837,955 for 49 grants (high: $233,333; low: $50)).
Purpose and activities: Giving primarily for education, health care, and religion.
Fields of interest: Arts; Elementary/secondary education; Environment; Hospitals (general); Human services; Government/public administration; Religion.
International interests: United Kingdom.
Type of support: General/operating support; Continuing support; Annual campaigns; Capital campaigns; Building/renovation; Endowments.
Limitations: Applications not accepted. Giving primarily in the Chicago, IL, area; limited giving to United Kingdom organizations. No grants to individuals, or for scholarships or fellowships.
Application information: Contributes only to pre-selected organizations.
   Board meeting date(s): Mid to late Oct.
Officers and Directors:* Josephine P. Louis,* V.P.; J. Jeffry Louis III,* Secy.-Treas.; Tracy Louis Merrill; Kimberly Louis Stewart.
EIN: 363837993

2863
Edward K. Love Conservation
Foundation ◇
231 S. LaSalle St., IL1-231-14-19
Chicago, IL   60697
Contact: Andrew S. Love, Jr., Governor
Application address: c/o Love Realty, 515 Olive St., Ste. 1400, St. Louis, MO 63101, tel.: (314) 621-1200

Established in MO.
Foundation type: Independent foundation.
Financial data (yr. ended 9/30/05): Assets, $8,285,486 (M); expenditures, $440,880; qualifying distributions, $378,096; giving activities include $373,710 for 4 grants (high: $248,710; low: $25,000).
Purpose and activities: Support is limited to recipients who aid in the protection and conservation of wildlife in Missouri.
Fields of interest: Higher education; Environment, natural resources; Animals/wildlife, preservation/protection.
Limitations: Giving limited to MO.
Application information:
   Initial approach: Proposal
   Deadline(s): None
Board of Governors: Andrew Sproule Love, Jr.; Daniel Spoule Love; Lowell Mohler; Scott Schnuck.
Trustee: Bank of America, N.A.
EIN: 436022352
Selected grants: The following grants were reported in 2003.
$200,000 to Saint Louis Zoo, Saint Louis, MO. For general support.
$50,000 to Nature Conservancy, Saint Louis, MO. For general support.
$45,000 to Center for Plant Conservation, Saint Louis, MO. For general support.
$25,000 to Conservation Foundation of Missouri Charitable Trust, Jefferson City, MO. For general support.
$25,000 to Missouri Prairie Foundation, Columbia, MO. For general support.
$25,000 to University of Missouri, Columbia, MO. For general support.

$8,682 to Missouri Botanical Garden, Saint Louis, MO. For general support.

2864
The Lumpkin Family Foundation
121 S. 17th St.
Mattoon, IL   61938   (217) 235-3361
Contact: Bruce Karmazin, Exec. Dir.
FAX: (217) 258-8444;
E-mail: info@lumpkinfoundation.org; URL: http://www.lumpkinfoundation.org/

Incorporated in 1953 in IL.
Donors: Besse Adamson Lumpkin†; Mary G. Lumpkin†; Richard Adamson Lumpkin†; Illinois Consolidated Telephone Co.; Richard Anthony Lumpkin; Mary Lee Sparks; Margaret L. Keon; Elizabeth Lumpkin Celio.
Foundation type: Independent foundation.
Financial data (yr. ended 12/31/05): Assets, $45,910,818 (M); gifts received, $1,080,239; expenditures, $2,515,563; qualifying distributions, $2,194,271; giving activities include $1,714,318 for 156 grants (high: $260,000; low: $50)).
Purpose and activities: The foundation is dedicated to supporting education, preserving and protecting the environment, and fostering opportunities for leadership, with special consideration for its heritage in central IL.
Fields of interest: Libraries (public); Education; Environment, natural resources; Human services; Children, services.
Type of support: General/operating support; Management development/capacity building; Annual campaigns; Program development; Seed money; Internship funds; Technical assistance; Program evaluation; Employee matching gifts; Matching/challenge support.
Limitations: Giving primarily in central IL; giving also in the San Francisco Bay Area, CA, Albuquerque, NM, Chicago, IL, Philadelphia, PA, the Jamestown area in western NY, and Wilton, CT. No support for religious organizations, political causes, or organizations who influence legislation. No grants to individuals.
Publications: Application guidelines; Annual report.
Application information: Application form required.
   Initial approach: Letter
   Copies of proposal: 1
   Deadline(s): Apr. 15, May 16, and Oct. 15
   Board meeting date(s): Feb., Apr., June, Sept. and Nov.
   Final notification: May, June, and Nov.
Officers and Directors:* Elizabeth Lumpkin Celio, Pres.; Susan Keon DeWyngaert, V.P.; Barbara Federico, V.P.; S.L. Grissom, Secy.; Richard Anthony Lumpkin,* Treas.; Bruce Karmazin, Exec. Dir.; John W. Sparks; Richard De Wyngaert.
Number of staff: 2 full-time professional; 1 full-time support.
EIN: 237423640
Selected grants: The following grants were reported in 2005.
$10,000 to Arts Council for Chautauqua County, Jamestown, NY. For Radio Apprentice Program.

2865
Ann and Robert H. Lurie Foundation ▼ ◇
(formerly Ann and Robert H. Lurie Family Foundation)
2 N. Riverside Plz., Ste. 1500
Chicago, IL 60606 (312) 466-3997
Contact: Ann Lurie, Pres. and Treas.

Established in 1986 in IL.
Donors: Ann Lurie; Robert Lurie†; Robert H. & Ann Lurie Trust.
Foundation type: Independent foundation.
Financial data (yr. ended 12/31/05): Assets, $18,740,468 (M); gifts received, $3,675,503; expenditures, $4,789,352; qualifying distributions, $4,730,158; giving activities include $4,730,158 for 27 grants (high: $3,000,000; low: $1,500; average: $10,000–$400,000).
Purpose and activities: Giving primarily for education, human services, and health.
Fields of interest: Higher education; Environment, research; Environment, natural resources; Health care; Health organizations, association; Children/ youth, services.
Type of support: Endowments.
Limitations: Applications not accepted. Giving primarily in Chicago, IL, and MI. No grants to individuals.
Application information: Contributes only to pre-selected organizations.
Officers and Directors:* Ann Lurie,* Pres. and Treas.; Andrew Lurie,* V.P.; Benjamin Lurie,* V.P.; Mark Slezak,* V.P.; Sheli Z. Rosenberg,* Secy.
EIN: 363486274
Selected grants: The following grants were reported in 2004.
$2,500,000 to University of Michigan, College of Engineering, Ann Arbor, MI. For unrestricted support.
$1,771,190 to Africa Infectious Disease Village Clinics, Chicago, IL. For unrestricted support.
$244,563 to Riders for Health II, Rockville, MD. 2 grants: $219,563 (For unrestricted support), $25,000 (For unrestricted support).
$155,000 to Infant Welfare Society of Chicago, Chicago, IL. For unrestricted support.
$50,000 to Chicago Public Library Foundation, Chicago, IL. For unrestricted support.
$50,000 to Choate Rosemary Hall, Wallingford, CT. For unrestricted support.
$47,000 to Childrens Memorial Foundation, Chicago, IL. 2 grants: $35,000 (For unrestricted support), $12,000 (For unrestricted support).
$25,000 to Children Affected by AIDS Foundation, Los Angeles, CA. For unrestricted support.

2866
The Lyon Family Foundation ◇
225 W. Wacker Dr., No. 2400
Chicago, IL 60606

Established in 2000 in IL.
Donor: Robert H. Lyon.
Foundation type: Independent foundation.
Financial data (yr. ended 12/31/05): Assets, $1,464,793 (M); gifts received, $419,995; expenditures, $408,983; qualifying distributions, $408,700; giving activities include $408,700 for 17 grants (high: $150,000; low: $1,000).
Purpose and activities: Giving primarily for Christian ministries, and human services.
Fields of interest: Human services; YM/YWCAs & YM/YWHAs; Christian agencies & churches.

Limitations: Applications not accepted. Giving primarily in IL. No grants to individuals.
Application information: Contributes only to pre-selected organizations.
Officers: Robert H. Lyon, Pres.; Donna M. Lyon, Secy.
EIN: 364386801

2867
J. Roderick MacArthur Foundation ▼ ◇
9333 N. Milwaukee Ave.
Niles, IL 60714

Established in 1976 in IL.
Donors: J. Roderick MacArthur†; Solange D. MacArthur; Bradford Exchange, Ltd.
Foundation type: Independent foundation.
Financial data (yr. ended 12/31/05): Assets, $16,636,923 (M); expenditures, $4,826,343; qualifying distributions, $4,695,330; giving activities include $4,581,302 for 5 grants (high: $2,200,000; low: $25,000; average: $120,000–$200,000).
Purpose and activities: The primary aims of the foundation in fulfilling its charitable, scientific, literary and educational purposes are to protect and encourage freedom of expression, human rights, civil liberties and social justice.
Fields of interest: Civil rights.
Type of support: General/operating support; Program development; Publication; Seed money.
Limitations: Applications not accepted.
Publications: Grants list.
Application information: Unsolicited requests for funds not considered or acknowledged. A major commitment has been made to 3 specific projects.
Board meeting date(s): Approximately every 2 months
Officers and Directors:* Solange D. MacArthur,* Chair.; John R. MacArthur,* Vice-Chair. and Secy.; James D. Liggett,* Pres.; Marylou Bane, Treas. and Admin.
Number of staff: 1 full-time professional.
EIN: 510214450
Selected grants: The following grants were reported in 2005.
$3,150,000 to Harpers Magazine Foundation, New York, NY. For continuing operating support for Harper's Magazine.
$730,007 to University of Chicago, MacArthur Justice Center at School of Law, Chicago, IL. For general support.
$500,000 to American Dance Institute, Rockville, MD. 2 grants: $340,000 (For dance programs), $160,000 (For dance programs).
$201,295 to Death Penalty Information Center, DC. For general support.

2868
John D. and Catherine T. MacArthur Foundation ▼
140 S. Dearborn St., Ste. 1200
Chicago, IL 60603-5285 (312) 726-8000
Contact: Richard J. Kaplan, Assoc. V.P., Institutional Research and Dir., Grants Mgmt.
FAX: (312) 920-6258;
E-mail: 4answers@macfound.org; TDD: (312) 920-6285; URL: http://www.macfound.org

Incorporated in 1970 in IL.

Donors: John D. MacArthur†; Catherine T. MacArthur†.
Foundation type: Independent foundation.
Financial data (yr. ended 12/31/05): Assets, $5,490,449,000 (M); expenditures, $225,774,000; qualifying distributions, $194,500,000; giving activities include $194,500,000 for grants.
Purpose and activities: The foundation is a private, independent grantmaking institution dedicated to helping groups and individuals foster lasting improvement in the human condition. The foundation seeks the development of healthy individuals and effective communities; peace within and among nations; responsible choices about human reproduction; and a global ecosystem capable of supporting healthy human societies. The foundation pursues this mission by supporting research, policy development, dissemination, education and training, and practice.
Fields of interest: Media/communications; Media, film/video; Education, public education; Higher education; Environment, natural resources; Reproductive health; Mental health/crisis services, public policy; Crime/violence prevention, youth; International peace/security; International affairs, foreign policy; International human rights; International affairs; Community development, neighborhood development; Public policy, research.
International interests: Africa; India; Mexico; Nigeria; Russia.
Type of support: General/operating support; Program development; Fellowships; Research; Program-related investments/loans; Employee matching gifts; Matching/challenge support.
Limitations: Giving on a national and international basis, with emphasis on Chicago, IL. No support for religious programs, political activities or campaigns. No grants for capital or endowment funds, equipment purchases, plant construction, conferences, publications, debt retirement, development campaigns, fundraising appeals, tuition expenses, scholarships, or fellowships (other than those sponsored by the foundation).
Publications: Annual report; Newsletter.
Application information: Please do not send the letter of inquiry by fax. Send it by mail to the office of Grants Management or by E-mail. Direct applications for MacArthur Fellows programs not accepted. Grants increasingly initiated by the board. Application form not required.
Initial approach: Letter of inquiry (2 to 3 pages) and one-page summary
Copies of proposal: 1
Deadline(s): None
Board meeting date(s): Mar., June, Sept., and Dec.
Final notification: 8 to 10 weeks
Officers and Directors:* Sara Lawrence-Lightfoot,* Chair.; Robert E. Denham, Chair.- Elect; Jonathan F. Fanton,* Pres.; Arthur M. Sussman, V.P. and Secy.; Susan Manske, V.P. and C.I.O.; Joshua J. Mintz, V.P. and Genl. Counsel; John Hurley, V.P., Prog. on Global Security and Sustainability; William E. Lowry, V.P., Human Resources and Admin.; Elspeth A. Revere, V.P., Genl. Prog.; Julia M. Stasch, V.P., Prog. on Human and Community Devel.; Marc P. Yanchura, Treas.; Lloyd Axworthy; John Seely Brown; Drew Saunders Days III; Jamie S. Gorelick; Mary Graham; Donald R. Hopkins, M.D.; Will Miller; Mario J. Molina; Marjorie M. Scardino; Thomas C. Theobold.

Number of staff: 92 full-time professional; 85 full-time support.
EIN: 237093598
Selected grants: The following grants were reported in 2005.

$12,000,000 to Energy Foundation, San Francisco, CA. For general operating support, payable over 3 years.

$10,000,000 to U.S. Civilian Research and Development Foundation for the Independent States, Arlington, VA. For Program on Basic Research and Higher Education in Russia, payable over 5 years.

$2,250,000 to Princeton University, Woodrow Wilson School of Public and International Affairs, Princeton, NJ. For research, training, and collaboration with independent analysts worldwide on issues at intersection of science, technology, and security, payable over 5 years.

$1,600,000 to Population Council, New York, NY. For programs on reducing maternal mortality and advancing young people's reproductive health in Mexico, India, and globally, payable over 3 years.

$1,500,000 to National Council of Juvenile and Family Court Judges, Reno, NV. For technical assistance, documentation, and coordination for Models for Change initiative, efforts to improve juvenile justice system in Illinois for children and youth, payable over 2 years.

$1,000,000 to Community Builders, Boston, MA. For efforts at Oakwood Shores to help ensure successful mixed-income development and broader community revitalization, payable over 3 years.

$700,000 to World Wildlife Fund, DC. To assist Royal Government of Bhutan in strengthening corridor system connecting protected areas of Bhutan into single continuous landscape, payable over 3 years.

$250,000 to Fundacion Cayetano Heredia, Lima, Peru. To establish first graduate program in conservation science in Peru, payable over 3 years.

$215,000 to Committee of Vice-Chancellors of Nigerian Federal Universities, Abuja, Nigeria. To re-engineer and strengthen capacity and influence in sector, payable over 2 years.

$200,000 to Perm Civic Chamber, Perm, Russia. For activities to promote human rights community in Russian Federation, payable over 2 years.

2869
Madigan Family Foundation ✧
c/o Madden, Jiganti, Moore & Sinars
190 S. LaSalle St., Ste. 1700
Chicago, IL 60603

Established in 1997 in IL.
Donor: John W. Madigan.
Foundation type: Independent foundation.
Financial data (yr. ended 3/31/06): Assets, $2,579,952 (M); expenditures, $583,297; qualifying distributions, $558,855; giving activities include $558,855 for 104 grants (high: $100,000; low: $100).
Purpose and activities: Giving primarily for health including hospitals and medical research as well as for education, the arts, environmental conservation, and for children, youth, and social services.
Fields of interest: Arts education; Museums (art); Museums (children's); Museums (specialized); Performing arts; Performing arts centers; Arts; Higher education, university; Business school/

education; Education; Environment, natural resources; Environment; Animals/wildlife, preservation/protection; Hospitals (general); Health organizations, association; Medical research, institute; Human services; Children/youth, services; International affairs, foreign policy; Federated giving programs; Public affairs, research; Christian agencies & churches.
Limitations: Applications not accepted. Giving primarily in IL. No grants to individuals.
Application information: Contributes only to pre-selected organizations.
Officers and Directors:* Holly W. Madigan,* Pres.; John W. Madigan,* Secy.-Treas.; John J. Jiganti.
EIN: 364155300
Selected grants: The following grants were reported in 2004.

$100,000 to Family Institute, Evanston, IL. 2 grants: $50,000 each
$50,000 to Smithsonian Institution, DC.
$50,000 to United Way.
$49,748 to Ravinia Festival Association, Highland Park, IL. 2 grants: $24,748, $25,000
$25,000 to Chicago Council on Foreign Relations, Chicago, IL.
$25,000 to Hoover Institution on War, Revolution and Peace, Stanford, CA.
$20,000 to Rush-Presbyterian-Saint Lukes Medical Center, Chicago, IL. For Woman's Board.
$10,000 to Museum of Television and Radio, New York, NY.

2870
Magnus Charitable Trust ✧ ☆
600 W. Rand Rd.
Arlington Heights, IL 60004

Established in 1995 in IL.
Donors: Alexander B. Magnus, Jr.; The Magnus Asset Management Trust.
Foundation type: Independent foundation.
Financial data (yr. ended 12/31/05): Assets, $9,348,008 (M); gifts received, $137,459; expenditures, $1,423,536; qualifying distributions, $532,748; giving activities include $316,031 for 6 grants (high: $156,000; low: $380), and $170,700 for 49 grants to individuals.
Purpose and activities: Giving primarily for Christian and public policy organizations, including an organization which promotes responsible media; funding also for human services.
Fields of interest: Media/communications; Scholarships/financial aid; Education; Human services; Public affairs, finance; Christian agencies & churches.
Limitations: Applications not accepted. Giving on a national basis, with emphasis on Chicago, IL.
Application information: Unsolicited requests for funds not accepted.
Trustees: Maria Magnus; Krzysztof Swewczul.
EIN: 364049284

2871
Makray Family Foundation ✧
c/o David P. Buckley, Jr.
231 W. Main St.
Barrington, IL 60010

Established in IL.
Donor: Paul Makray.
Foundation type: Independent foundation.

Financial data (yr. ended 1/31/05): Assets, $15,852,770 (M); expenditures, $924,913; qualifying distributions, $850,000; giving activities include $850,000 for 35 grants (high: $95,000; low: $5,000).
Purpose and activities: Giving primarily for natural resource conservation, and animal welfare.
Fields of interest: Environment, natural resources; Animal welfare; Zoos/zoological societies; Human services; Christian agencies & churches.
Limitations: Applications not accepted. Giving primarily in IL. No grants to individuals.
Application information: Contributes only to pre-selected organizations.
Officers and Directors:* Nancy Harney,* Pres.; Christine Brownstein,* V.P.; Carol Donohoe,* V.P.; Robert Harney, Secy.; Paul Makray, Jr.,* Treas.; David P. Buckley, Jr.; Robert F. Lamping.
EIN: 364298517
Selected grants: The following grants were reported in 2005.

$95,000 to Lincoln Park Zoological Society, Chicago, IL.
$60,000 to Nature Conservancy, Arlington, VA.
$50,000 to Biblical Counseling Center, Jenison, MI.
$50,000 to International Crane Foundation, Baraboo, WI. 2 grants: $25,000 each
$25,000 to Geneva Lake Conservancy, Lake Geneva, WI.
$20,000 to Humane Society.
$18,000 to American Humane Association, Englewood, CO.
$16,000 to National Parks Conservation Association, DC.
$15,000 to For the Children, Cleveland, OH.

2872
Malott Family Foundation ✧
(formerly Camalott Charitable Foundation)
200 E. Randolph Dr.
Chicago, IL 60601
Contact: Elizabeth Malott Pohle, Dir.

Established in 1989 in IL.
Donor: Robert H. Malott.
Foundation type: Independent foundation.
Financial data (yr. ended 12/31/05): Assets, $31,838,915 (M); gifts received, $2,952,243; expenditures, $1,788,220; qualifying distributions, $1,568,133; giving activities include $1,477,328 for 58 grants (high: $300,000; low: $250).
Purpose and activities: Funding primarily for arts and culture, and education; some funding also for human services and health care.
Fields of interest: Performing arts; Performing arts, opera; Arts; Higher education; Graduate/professional education; Education; Botanical gardens; Environment; Zoos/zoological societies; Health care; Federated giving programs; Public policy, research.
Limitations: Applications not accepted. Giving primarily in IL. No support for religious organizations. No grants to individuals.
Application information: Unsolicited requests for funds not considered.
Officers: Robert H. Malott, Pres.; Barbara H. Malott Kizziah, Secy.
Directors: Robert Deane Malott; Elizabeth Malott Pohle.
Number of staff: 1 full-time professional; 1 part-time professional.
EIN: 363680666

2873
Walter S. Mander Foundation ◇
c/o Goschi & Goschi
120 S. LaSalle St., Ste. 1720
Chicago, IL 60603

Established in 1994 in IL.
Donor: Walter S. Mander†.
Foundation type: Independent foundation.
Financial data (yr. ended 3/31/06): Assets,
$13,228,671 (M); expenditures, $932,108;
qualifying distributions, $815,930; giving activities
include $815,930 for 35 grants (high: $200,000;
low: $500).
Purpose and activities: Giving primarily for health
and to Jewish organizations.
Fields of interest: Hospitals (general); Jewish
federated giving programs; Jewish agencies &
temples.
Type of support: General/operating support.
Limitations: Applications not accepted. Giving
primarily in Chicago, IL. No grants to individuals.
Application information: Contributes only to
pre-selected organizations.
Officers and Directors:* C.B. Wolf,* Pres.; James J.
Stevens,* V.P.; P.E. Goschi,* Secy.; Hilde Wolf.
EIN: 363961599

2874
Bert W. Martin Foundation ◇
c/o The Northern Trust Co.
P.O. Box 803878
Chicago, IL 60680 (312) 630-6000
Application address: c/o Tom James, 50 S. La Salle
St., Chicago, IL, 60675

Incorporated in 1946 in IL.
Donors: Bert W. Martin; Ada La May Martin; Bert
Martin Charitable Fund.
Foundation type: Independent foundation.
Financial data (yr. ended 12/31/05): Assets,
$40,484,701 (M); gifts received, $255,412;
expenditures, $2,920,264; qualifying distributions,
$2,810,576; giving activities include $2,793,710
for 14 grants (high: $1,000,000; low: $7,128).
Purpose and activities: Giving primarily for higher
education, health care, and human services.
Fields of interest: Museums; Higher education;
Health care; Big Brothers/Big Sisters; Human
services; Federated giving programs; Science.
Limitations: Giving primarily in CA and FL. No grants
to individuals.
Application information: Application form not
required.
   Deadline(s): None
Officers and Directors:* Winifred M. Warden,*
Pres.; Chandler D. Warden,* V.P.; F. Andrew
Warden,* V.P.; Thomas M. James, Secy.
EIN: 366060591
Selected grants: The following grants were reported
in 2003.
$405,250 to Rollins College, Winter Park, FL. For
   general support.
$400,000 to Orlando Regional Healthcare
   Foundation, Orlando, FL. For general support.
$150,000 to Arizona-Sonora Desert Museum,
   Tucson, AZ. For general support.
$100,000 to Central Florida Zoological Society,
   Lake Monroe, FL. For general support.
$50,000 to Black Stallion Literacy Project,
   Kissimmee, FL. For general support.
$50,000 to University of Florida, Gainesville, FL. For
   general support.

$30,000 to Big Brothers Big Sisters of Tucson,
   Tucson, AZ. For general support.
$25,000 to California State Polytechnic University,
   Pomona, CA. For general support.
$25,000 to Columbia University, New York, NY. For
   general support.
$13,500 to Morris K. Udall Foundation, Tucson, AZ.
   For general support.

2875
**Master Educational Assistance
   Foundation** ◇ ☆
747 S. Euclid Ave.
Oak Park, IL 60304-1243 (847) 431-5590
Contact: James F. Zangrilli, Exec. Dir.

Established in 1987 in IL.
Donor: Valerian Schultz.
Foundation type: Independent foundation.
Financial data (yr. ended 12/31/05): Assets,
$5,536,904 (M); gifts received, $224,000;
expenditures, $479,290; qualifying distributions,
$479,290; giving activities include $253,131 for 27
+ grants (high: $45,230; low: $500), and $144,247
for grants to individuals.
Purpose and activities: Giving primarily for
education and for scholarship awards and other
educational assistance to financially disadvantaged
and/or physically or mentally disabled inner city
residents; support also for health care.
Fields of interest: Education; Hospitals (general);
Cancer; Blind/visually impaired.
Type of support: Scholarships—to individuals.
Limitations: Giving primarily to residents of IL.
Application information: Application form not
required.
   Initial approach: Submit completed copy of
   FAFSA, brochures, letters, etc.
   Deadline(s): None
Officer: James F. Zangrilli, Exec. Dir.
EIN: 363542174
Selected grants: The following grants were reported
in 2004.
$14,647 to San Miguel Education Center,
   Providence, RI.
$6,000 to National Federation of the Blind,
   Baltimore, MD.
$5,556 to El Hogar del Nino, Chicago, IL.
$4,500 to Saint Agatha School, Portland, OR.
$3,500 to Resurrection Project, Chicago, IL.

2876
**Oscar G. and Elsa S. Mayer Family
   Foundation** ◇
c/o Barbara J. Pope
115 S. LaSalle St., Ste. 2285
Chicago, IL 60603

Established in 1996.
Foundation type: Independent foundation.
Financial data (yr. ended 12/31/04): Assets,
$17,279,407 (M); expenditures, $1,166,133;
qualifying distributions, $970,913; giving activities
include $923,553 for grants.
Fields of interest: Children/youth, services.
Type of support: Program development.
Limitations: Applications not accepted. Giving
primarily in IL. No grants to individuals.

Application information: Applications only accepted
from organizations a foundation director is involved
with. Unsolicited requests for funds not accepted.
   Board meeting date(s): Feb.
Officers and Directors:* Harold F. Mayer, Pres.;
Allan C. Mayer,* V.P.; Harold M. Mayer,* V.P.; Oscar
G. Mayer,* V.P.; Allison M. Shetter,* Secy.-Treas.;
Gregory K. Mayer; Oscar H. Mayer; Robert O. Mayer.
Number of staff: 1 part-time support.
EIN: 364035204
Selected grants: The following grants were reported
in 2003.
$70,000 to Providence Saint Mel School, Chicago,
   IL. For Science Lab.
$70,000 to University of Wisconsin Foundation,
   Madison, WI. For Child Emotion Research
   Project.
$50,000 to Prison Fellowship Ministries, DC. For
   Angel Tree Camp.
$50,000 to Uhlich Childrens Advantage Network,
   Chicago, IL. For STARS Program.
$41,100 to Western Resource Advocates, Boulder,
   CO. For Rudd Mayer Memorial Fund.
$40,000 to Denver Center for the Performing Arts,
   Denver, CO.
$35,000 to Ounce of Prevention Fund, Chicago, IL.
   For children's programs.
$35,000 to Pepperdine University, Malibu, CA. For
   Jumpstart program.
$25,000 to Beloit College, Beloit, WI. For Beloit
   Academy.
$25,000 to Lyric Opera of Chicago, Chicago, IL.

2877
Mazza Foundation ◇
30 S. Wacker Dr., Ste. 2600
Chicago, IL 60606 (312) 855-4055
Contact: Mary Jane Rubinelli, Pres.

Incorporated in 1957 in IL.
Donors: Leonard M. Lavezzorio†; Louise T. Mazza
Trust.
Foundation type: Independent foundation.
Financial data (yr. ended 11/30/05): Assets,
$36,548,388 (M); expenditures, $1,728,189;
qualifying distributions, $1,546,455; giving
activities include $1,521,000 for 57 grants (high:
$500,000; low: $1,000).
Purpose and activities: Giving primarily for
education, health associations, children and youth
services, including a children's hospital, as well as
for social services and, Roman Catholic
organizations and churches.
Fields of interest: Museums (specialized); Arts;
Elementary/secondary education; Higher education;
Education; Hospitals (specialty); Health care; Health
organizations, association; Human services;
Children/youth, services; Roman Catholic agencies
& churches.
Limitations: Giving primarily in Chicago, IL.
Application information: Application form not
required.
   Deadline(s): None
Officers and Directors:* Mary Jane Rubinelli,*
Pres.; Joseph O. Rubinelli, Jr.,* V.P. and Secy.;
Nicholas J. Lavezzorio,* V.P. and Treas.; Joan F.
Lavezzorio,* V.P.
EIN: 366054751

2878
Chauncey and Marion Deering McCormick Foundation ✧

410 N. Michigan Ave., Rm. 590
Chicago, IL 60611-4252 (312) 644-6720
Contact: John Rau, Pres.

Incorporated in 1957 in IL.
Donors: Brooks McCormick; Brooks McCormick Trust; Charles Deering McCormick Trust; Roger McCormick Trust.
Foundation type: Independent foundation.
Financial data (yr. ended 7/31/05): Assets, $61,323,507 (M); gifts received, $276,139; expenditures, $2,699,015; qualifying distributions, $2,656,258; giving activities include $2,630,000 for 53 grants (high: $1,000,000; low: $5,000; average: $20,000–$100,000).
Purpose and activities: Emphasis on higher and secondary education, hospitals, and cultural institutions, including an art institute and a museum; support also for conservation and child welfare.
Fields of interest: Museums; Arts; Higher education; Environment, natural resources; Zoos/zoological societies; Hospitals (general); Children/youth, services.
Type of support: General/operating support.
Limitations: Giving primarily in Chicago, IL. No grants to individuals.
Application information: Application form not required.
  Deadline(s): None
Officers and Trustees: * Brooks McCormick,* Chair.; John Rau,* Pres.; Charlotte Deering McCormick,* V.P.; Charles E. Schroeder,* Secy.-Treas.; Christopher Hunt; Fiona M. Hunt; Ian C. Hunt; Blair Collins Maus; Nancy V.T. McCormick; Hilary H. McCutcheon; Lisa Collins Meaney; Abby McCormick O'Neil.
EIN: 366054815
Selected grants: The following grants were reported in 2004.
$2,000,000 to Music and Dance Theater Chicago, Chicago, IL. For unrestricted support.
$1,500,000 to Rush-Presbyterian-Saint Lukes Medical Center, Neonatal Intensive Care Unit, Chicago, IL. For unrestricted support.
$500,000 to Field Museum of Natural History, Chicago, IL. For unrestricted support.
$345,000 to YMCA of Metropolitan Chicago, Lawson YMCA, Chicago, IL. For unrestricted support.
$250,000 to San Francisco Child Abuse Prevention Center, San Francisco, CA. For unrestricted support.
$200,000 to Northwestern University, Evanston, IL. 2 grants: $100,000 to Kellogg Graduate School of Business (For unrestricted support), $100,000 (For Deering Library Fund).
$100,000 to Morton Arboretum, Lisle, IL. For unrestricted support.
$75,000 to Lyric Opera of Chicago, Chicago, IL. For unrestricted support.
$50,000 to American Hospital of Paris Foundation, New York, NY. For unrestricted support.

2879
Flora S. McCourtney Trust ✧

c/o Bank of America, N.A.
231 S. LaSalle St., IL1-231-14-19
Chicago, IL 60697
Contact: Christine Secorsky
Application address: c/o Bank of America, N.A., 100 N. Broadway, P.O. Box 14737, St. Louis, MO 63178. tel.: (314) 466-4417

Established in 1953 in IL.
Donors: Plato McCourtney†; Flora McCourtney†.
Foundation type: Independent foundation.
Financial data (yr. ended 9/30/05): Assets, $7,917,179 (M); gifts received, $545; expenditures, $387,201; qualifying distributions, $353,349; giving activities include $351,000 for 48 grants (high: $117,500; low: $1,000).
Purpose and activities: The trust awards scholarships only to graduating seniors of high schools in Sangamon County, IL, who wish to continue their education. Scholarships are awarded on the basis of scholastic ability.
Fields of interest: Higher education.
Type of support: Scholarship funds.
Limitations: Giving limited to Sangamon County, IL.
Application information: Application form available at qualifying high schools. Application form required.
  Initial approach: Completed application
  Deadline(s): None
  Board meeting date(s): Early Apr.
  Final notification: May
Trustee: Bank of America, N.A.
EIN: 436023586
Selected grants: The following grants were reported in 2005.
$27,000 to Northwestern University, Evanston, IL.
$16,000 to Bradley University, Peoria, IL.
$11,000 to Butler University, Indianapolis, IN.
$11,000 to Cornell University, Ithaca, NY.
$10,000 to Rice University, Houston, TX.
$10,000 to Saint Louis University, Saint Louis, MO.
$7,000 to Illinois Wesleyan University, Bloomington, IL.
$6,000 to Wheaton College, Wheaton, IL.
$5,000 to Arizona State University, Tempe, AZ.
$4,500 to Purdue University, West Lafayette, IN.

2880
Ronald L. McDaniel Foundation ✧

8005 Woodside Ln.
Burr Ridge, IL 60527

Established in 1995 in IL.
Donor: Ronald L. McDaniel.
Foundation type: Independent foundation.
Financial data (yr. ended 12/31/05): Assets, $8,350,442 (M); gifts received, $525,000; expenditures, $390,663; qualifying distributions, $361,172; giving activities include $361,172 for 8 grants (high: $333,333; low: $500).
Purpose and activities: Giving primarily for higher education.
Fields of interest: Higher education, college; Salvation Army; Children/youth, services; Children, services; Christian agencies & churches.
Limitations: Applications not accepted. Giving primarily in IL and IN. No grants to individuals.
Application information: Contributes only to pre-selected organizations.
Officers: Ronald McDaniel, Pres.; Barbara Gulick, V.P.; Julia Vincer, Secy.; Brenda Jacobs, Treas.
EIN: 364012153

2881
McDougal Family Foundation

400 N. Michigan Ave., Ste. 300
Chicago, IL 60611-4212 (312) 836-1243
Contact: Peter Mich
FAX: (312) 836-1217;
E-mail: pmich.mff@ameritech.net

Established in 1994.
Donor: Alfred L. McDougal.
Foundation type: Independent foundation.
Financial data (yr. ended 12/31/04): Assets, $15,710,640 (M); expenditures, $880,766; qualifying distributions, $723,543; giving activities include $543,584 for 23 grants (high: $75,000; low: $500).
Purpose and activities: Giving primarily for teacher professional development programs in Chicago Public Schools, Chicago, IL.
Fields of interest: Elementary/secondary education; Teacher school/education.
Type of support: General/operating support; Continuing support; Program development; Conferences/seminars; Curriculum development.
Limitations: Giving primarily in Chicago, IL. No support for individual schools. No grants for scholarships for individuals, special events, or capital campaigns.
Publications: Application guidelines; Grants list.
Application information: Application form required.
  Initial approach: Telephone and letter of inquiry
  Copies of proposal: 1
  Board meeting date(s): Varies
  Final notification: 2 weeks
Officers: Alfred L. McDougal, Pres. and Treas.; Nancy A. Lauter, V.P.; Thomas McDougal, Secy.
Directors: Sarah Duncan; Jan McDougal; Stephen McDougal.
Number of staff: 1 full-time professional; 1 part-time support.
EIN: 363943431

2882
McGraw Foundation

653 Landwehr Rd.
Northbrook, IL 60062-2309 (847) 291-9810
Contact: James F. Quilter, V.P.
FAX: (847) 291-9811;
E-mail: maxmcgraw@worldnet.att.net

Incorporated in 1948 in IL.
Donors: Alfred Bersted†; Carol Jean Root†; Maxine Elrod†; Donald S. Elrod†; Max McGraw†; Richard F. McGraw†; McGraw-Edison Co.; and others.
Foundation type: Independent foundation.
Financial data (yr. ended 12/31/05): Assets, $13,423,020 (M); expenditures, $808,003; qualifying distributions, $738,270; giving activities include $512,980 for 60 grants (high: $50,000; low: $1,000), and $90,137 for 55 employee matching gifts.
Purpose and activities: Primary areas of interest include education, particularly in scientific and environmental fields, including higher education, human services, cultural programs, health and medical research and the arts.
Fields of interest: Humanities; Arts; Education, special; Higher education; Environment; Medical research; Human services; Science.
Type of support: General/operating support; Continuing support; Annual campaigns; Capital campaigns; Building/renovation; Professorships; Seed money; Scholarship funds; Research;

Employee matching gifts; Matching/challenge support.

Limitations: Giving primarily in the Chicago, IL, area. No support for religious purposes. No grants to individuals.

Publications: Application guidelines; Program policy statement.

Application information: Grant requests sent by e-mail or fax will not be accepted. Application form not required.

Initial approach: Letter or telephone
Copies of proposal: 1
Deadline(s): Mail between Dec. 1 and Feb. 1
Board meeting date(s): June; grant committee meets annually in Mar.
Final notification: 30 days to 1 year

Officers and Directors:* William W. Mauritz, Pres.; James F. Quilter,* V.P., Secy.-Treas., and Exec. Dir.; J. Bradley Davis; Scott M. Elrod; Dennis W. Fitzgerald; Jerry D. Jones; Gordon Labounty; Carol E. Moorman; Cathryn B. Nelson; Bernard B. Rinella.

Number of staff: 1 full-time professional; 1 full-time support.

EIN: 362490000

2883
McIntosh Foundation, Inc. ◇
525 Sheridan Rd.
Kenilworth, IL 60043-1222

Established in 1985 in IL.
Donor: William A. McIntosh.
Foundation type: Independent foundation.
Financial data (yr. ended 4/30/06): Assets, $13,621,973 (M); expenditures, $471,898; qualifying distributions, $454,470; giving activities include $452,000 for 15 grants (high: $100,000; low: $1,000).
Purpose and activities: Support primarily for programs of an archdiocese and other Roman Catholic parishes, schools, and charities; giving also for other education and social services.
Fields of interest: Performing arts, ballet; Elementary/secondary education; Higher education; Education; Human services; YM/YWCAs & YM/YWHAs; Roman Catholic federated giving programs; Roman Catholic agencies & churches.
Limitations: Applications not accepted. Giving primarily in IL, with emphasis on Chicago, and New York, NY; some funding nationally. No grants to individuals.
Application information: Contributes only to pre-selected organizations.
Officers: William A. McIntosh, Pres. and Treas.; Kathleen M. Clarke, V.P. and Secy.
Directors: Anne Atzeff; David McIntosh; Michael McIntosh; Julia A. Smith.
EIN: 363358483
Selected grants: The following grants were reported in 2003.
$200,000 to Big Shoulders Fund, Chicago, IL. For general support.
$100,000 to Missionaries of Charity, New York, NY. For general support.
$50,000 to Archdiocese of Chicago, Chicago, IL. For general support.
$50,000 to Fairfield University, Fairfield, CT. For general support.
$30,000 to Faith Community of Saint Sabina, Chicago, IL. For general support.
$25,000 to YWCA, Evanston/North Shore, Evanston, IL. For general support.

$10,000 to Archdiocese of Washington, DC. For general support.
$10,000 to Jewish United Fund of Metropolitan Chicago, Chicago, IL. For general support.
$10,000 to Papal Foundation, Philadelphia, PA. For general support.
$10,000 to United Way of Metropolitan Chicago, Chicago, IL. For general support.

2884
James and Milton McMullan Foundation ◇ ☆
800 S. Ridge Rd.
Lake Forest, IL 60045
Application address: c/o Newton High School, Attn.: Ms. Cille Norman, Newton, MS 39345

Established in IL.
Donors: James M. McMullan; Milton McMullan; Madeleine McMullan; Carlette McMullan.
Foundation type: Independent foundation.
Financial data (yr. ended 12/31/05): Assets, $2,308,973 (M); gifts received, $125,296; expenditures, $322,082; qualifying distributions, $320,000; giving activities include $315,000 for 6 grants (high: $50,000; low: $15,000), and $5,000 for 4 grants to individuals (high: $1,250; low: $1,250).
Purpose and activities: Giving primarily for education and religion.
Fields of interest: Higher education; Libraries/library science; Scholarships/financial aid; Children/youth, services; Religion.
Type of support: General/operating support; Scholarships—to individuals.
Limitations: Giving limited to residents of Newton, MS.
Application information: Application form required.
Deadline(s): Apr. 1
Trustees: Carlette McMullan; James M. McMullan; Madeleine McMullan; Margaret McMullan.
EIN: 363506203

2885
Andrew & Jeanine McNally Charitable Foundation ◇
333 N. Michigan Ave., Ste. 2200
Chicago, IL 60601-4104

Established in 1993 in IL.
Donor: A. McNally III Trust.
Foundation type: Independent foundation.
Financial data (yr. ended 6/30/05): Assets, $170,173 (M); gifts received, $423,359; expenditures, $412,735; qualifying distributions, $412,167; giving activities include $412,200 for 33 grants (high: $120,000; low: $250).
Purpose and activities: Giving primarily for education including libraries, as well as for the arts, and for animal preservation and protection; some funding for health care, and children, youth and social services.
Fields of interest: Museums (marine/maritime); Museums (natural history); Performing arts; Arts; Secondary school/education; Higher education; Libraries/library science; Zoos/zoological societies; Animals/wildlife; Hospitals (general); Medical care, rehabilitation; Human services; Community development, neighborhood development; Foundations (community); Disabilities, people with.

Limitations: Applications not accepted. Giving primarily in Chicago, IL and NY. No grants to individuals.
Application information: Contributes only to pre-selected organizations.
Trustees: Andrew McNally IV; Jeanine S. McNally.
EIN: 367056039

2886
The McNamara Purcell Foundation ◇
(formerly The Anne McNamara Purcell Foundation)
27 W. 332 Churchill Rd.
Winfield, IL 60190

Established in 1999 in IL.
Donors: Philip J. Purcell; Anne McNamara Purcell.
Foundation type: Independent foundation.
Financial data (yr. ended 12/31/05): Assets, $11,771,343 (M); expenditures, $486,710; qualifying distributions, $484,215; giving activities include $480,200 for 22 grants (high: $100,000; low: $5,000).
Purpose and activities: Giving primarily for education and health.
Fields of interest: Secondary school/education; Higher education, university; Hospitals (general); Medical research, institute.
Limitations: Applications not accepted. Giving primarily in Chicago, IL; some funding nationally. No grants to individuals.
Application information: Contributes only to pre-selected organizations.
Manager: Philip J. Purcell.
Trustees: David P. Purcell; Michael J. Purcell; Paul M. Purcell.
EIN: 367293187

2887
Col. Stanley R. McNeil Foundation ◇
c/o Bank of America, N.A.
231 S. LaSalle St.
Chicago, IL 60697-0246   (312) 828-8028
Contact: Charles Slamar, Jr., V.P., Bank of America, N.A.

Established in 1992 in IL.
Donor: Stanley McNeil.
Foundation type: Independent foundation.
Financial data (yr. ended 11/30/05): Assets, $19,203,303 (M); expenditures, $986,448; qualifying distributions, $911,147; giving activities include $899,014 for 46 grants (high: $50,000; low: $3,000).
Fields of interest: Education; Health care; Children/youth, services.
Type of support: General/operating support; Building/renovation; Equipment; Program development; Curriculum development; Scholarship funds; Research; Matching/challenge support.
Limitations: Giving primarily in the Chicago, IL, area. No grants to individuals.
Application information: Application form not required.
Copies of proposal: 1
Deadline(s): None
Final notification: Varies
Trustee: Bank of America, N.A.
Number of staff: 1 full-time professional; 3 full-time support.
EIN: 367016333

2888
D. Richard Mead Charitable Foundation ✧ ☆
c/o Northern Trust Bank of Florida, N.A.
P.O. Box 803878
Chicago, IL 60680

Established in 1992 in FL.
Donor: D.R. Mead, Sr.
Foundation type: Independent foundation.
Financial data (yr. ended 12/31/05): Assets, $2,451,346 (M); expenditures, $535,662; qualifying distributions, $526,306; giving activities include $525,076 for 26 grants (high: $444,688; low: $250).
Fields of interest: Higher education; Business school/education; Health care; Human services; American Red Cross; Children/youth, services.
Limitations: Applications not accepted. Giving primarily in FL, with emphasis on Miami. No grants to individuals.
Application information: Contributes only to pre-selected organizations.
Trustees: Mary Catherine Hamil; D. Richard Mead, Jr.; Stanley Budge Mead; The Northern Trust Co.
EIN: 656106335
Selected grants: The following grants were reported in 2004.
$50,000 to Duke University, Fuqua School of Business, Durham, NC. For general support.
$10,000 to Baptist Health South Florida, Coral Gables, FL. For general support.
$8,250 to Fairchild Tropical Garden, Coral Gables, FL. For general support.
$4,900 to American Red Cross, Miami, FL. For general support.
$2,500 to Boy Scouts of America, South Florida Council, Miami, FL. For general support.
$2,500 to Boys and Girls Clubs of Miami, Miami, FL. For general support.
$2,500 to Goodwill Industries of South Florida, Miami, FL. For general support.
$2,000 to Childrens Home Society of Florida, Jacksonville, FL. For general support.
$1,250 to American Heart Association, Dallas, TX. For general support.
$1,000 to Dade Community Foundation, Miami, FL. For general support.

2889
The Medline Foundation ✧ ☆
1 Medline Pl.
Mundelein, IL 60060

Established in 2002 in IL.
Donor: Medline Industries, Inc.
Foundation type: Company-sponsored foundation.
Financial data (yr. ended 12/31/05): Assets, $4,322,129 (M); gifts received, $1,026,960; expenditures, $526,164; qualifying distributions, $515,890; giving activities include $515,890 for grants.
Purpose and activities: The foundation supports organizations involved with health and human services.
Fields of interest: Health care; Human services; Federated giving programs.
Type of support: Employee-related scholarships; Scholarships—to individuals.
Limitations: Giving primarily in areas of company operations in IL.
Application information:

Initial approach: Proposal
Deadline(s): None
Officers and Directors:* Jon Mills,* Pres.; James Mills,* Secy.; James Abrams; Andrew Mills; Charlie Mills.
EIN: 421563666
Selected grants: The following grants were reported in 2005.
$50,000 to National Breast Cancer Foundation, Addison, TX.
$33,333 to Los Angeles Jewish Home for the Aging, Reseda, CA.
$20,000 to University of Detroit Mercy, Detroit, MI.
$18,000 to Golden Rule Foundation, Maitland, FL.
$15,000 to Rutherford Hospital Foundation, Rutherfordton, NC.
$10,000 to Long Beach Medical Center, Long Beach, NY.
$5,000 to American Lung Association of Kentucky, Louisville, KY.
$4,625 to Childrens Miracle Network, Salt Lake City, UT.
$4,300 to Resurrection Development Foundation, Chicago, IL.
$632 to Winchester Medical Center Foundation, Winchester, VA.

2890
Edward Arthur Mellinger Educational Foundation, Inc. ✧
1025 E. Broadway
P.O. Box 770
Monmouth, IL 61462 (309) 734-2419
FAX: (309) 734-4435; E-mail: info@mellinger.org;
URL: http://www.mellinger.org/

Incorporated in 1959 in DE.
Donor: Inez M. Hensleigh†.
Foundation type: Independent foundation.
Financial data (yr. ended 12/31/05): Assets, $22,521,676 (M); gifts received, $200; expenditures, $1,069,422; qualifying distributions, $906,797; giving activities include $754,831 for grants to individuals, and $43,750 for loans to individuals.
Purpose and activities: The Mellinger Foundation is committed to the support of education. Accordingly, the Foundation devotes a major portion of its resources to providing scholarship and loan assistance to young men and women from western Illinois and eastern Iowa who attend colleges and universities throughout the nation. In addition, the Foundation offers support to a variety of educational organizations and programs in its local area.
Type of support: Seed money; Scholarships—to individuals; Student loans—to individuals.
Limitations: Giving limited to students residing in western IL.
Publications: Application guidelines; Program policy statement.
Application information: Application form available on foundation Web site. Application form required.
Initial approach: Request application form
Copies of proposal: 1
Deadline(s): May 1 for new applicants
Board meeting date(s): Scholarship committee meets in June
Final notification: 1 month after meeting
Officers and Trustees:* David D. Fleming,* Pres.; Tom Johnson,* Secy.; Mary Frances Miller; Charles Slamar; Gary D. Willhardt.

Number of staff: 1 part-time professional; 4 part-time support.
EIN: 362428421

2891
Richard & Martha Melman Foundation ✧
c/o Lettuce Entertain You Entertainment
5419 N. Sheridan Rd.
Chicago, IL 60640
Contact: Tom Muno

Established in 1996 in IL.
Donor: Richard Melman.
Foundation type: Independent foundation.
Financial data (yr. ended 12/31/05): Assets, $410,013 (M); gifts received, $116,628; expenditures, $505,500; qualifying distributions, $494,285; giving activities include $494,285 for 78 grants (high: $25,000; low: $250).
Purpose and activities: Giving primarily for youth services and Jewish organizations.
Fields of interest: Human services; Children/youth, services; Jewish agencies & temples.
Limitations: Applications not accepted. No grants to individuals.
Application information: Contributes only to pre-selected organizations.
Directors: Martha Melman; Richard Melman; R.J. Melman.
EIN: 364140849
Selected grants: The following grants were reported in 2005.
$100,000 to University of Chicago Hospitals, Chicago, IL.
$25,000 to Northwestern Memorial Hospital, Chicago, IL.
$5,000 to Rush University Medical Center, Chicago, IL.

2892
The Melrene Fund ✧ ☆
P.O. Box 272
North Aurora, IL 60542 (630) 851-0989
Contact: Melvin Goldman, Pres.

Established in 1958 in IL.
Donor: Melvin Goldman.
Foundation type: Independent foundation.
Financial data (yr. ended 12/31/05): Assets, $3,812,530 (M); expenditures, $1,470,428; qualifying distributions, $1,420,688; giving activities include $1,420,688 for grants.
Purpose and activities: Funding for the arts, Jewish organizations, and human services.
Fields of interest: Arts education; Museums; Performing arts, orchestra (symphony); Arts; Human services; Jewish agencies & temples.
Limitations: Giving primarily in IL; some giving in Denver, CO. No grants to individuals.
Application information:
Initial approach: Typed letter
Officers and Directors:* Melvin Goldman,* Pres.; Irene Goldman,* Secy.; Susan Carson; Peggy Goldman; Stephen Goldman; Jeffrey B. Shamis.
EIN: 363056828

2893
Tyler Meriweather Perpetual Charitable Trust ◇ ☆
c/o First National Bank of Decatur
130 N. Water St.
Decatur, IL 62523

Established in 2003 in IL.
Foundation type: Independent foundation.
Financial data (yr. ended 12/31/05): Assets, $481,523 (M); expenditures, $345,634; qualifying distributions, $325,000; giving activities include $325,000 for 1 grant.
Purpose and activities: Giving primarily to an animal shelter.
Fields of interest: Animal welfare.
Limitations: Applications not accepted. Giving primarily in Decatur, IL. No grants to individuals.
Application information: Contributes only to pre-selected organizations.
Trustee: First National Bank of Decatur.
EIN: 836056889

2894
Mesirow Charitable Foundation ◇ ☆
610 Central Ave., No. 200
Highland Park, IL 60035 (847) 681-2300
Contact: Richard Mesirow, Mgr.

Established in 1958 in IL.
Donor: Members of the Mesirow family.
Foundation type: Independent foundation.
Financial data (yr. ended 12/31/05): Assets, $572,802 (M); gifts received, $351,603; expenditures, $406,196; qualifying distributions, $404,263; giving activities include $404,263 for 35 grants (high: $187,818; low: $250).
Fields of interest: Education; Health care; Children/youth, services; Family services; Jewish federated giving programs; Philanthropy/voluntarism; Jewish agencies & temples.
Limitations: Giving primarily in Chicago, IL. No grants to individuals, or for major public charities.
Application information: Application form not required.
   Deadline(s): None
Officer: Richard Mesirow, Mgr.
EIN: 366060923
Selected grants: The following grants were reported in 2004.
$100,000 to Jewish United Fund of Metropolitan Chicago, Chicago, IL.
$2,500 to Ravinia Festival Association, Highland Park, IL.
$2,000 to Highland Park Community Foundation, Highland Park, IL.
$1,500 to Anti-Defamation League of Bnai Brith, Chicago, IL.
$1,000 to American Jewish Committee, Chicago, IL.
$1,000 to Chicago Foundation for Women, Chicago, IL.
$1,000 to College Bound, Chicago, IL.
$1,000 to Northwestern Memorial Foundation, Chicago, IL.
$1,000 to Northwestern University, Evanston, IL.
$1,000 to Planned Parenthood/Chicago Area, Chicago, IL.

2895
The Meyer Charitable Foundation ◇
100 W. University Ave., Ste. 401
Champaign, IL 61820

Established in 1996 in IL.
Donor: A.C. Meyer, Jr.
Foundation type: Independent foundation.
Financial data (yr. ended 5/31/05): Assets, $9,128,777 (M); expenditures, $493,785; qualifying distributions, $459,720; giving activities include $459,720 for grants.
Purpose and activities: Giving primarily to federated giving programs and for higher and other education; funding also for the arts, health associations, and children, youth and social services.
Fields of interest: Arts; Higher education; Libraries (public); Education; Health organizations; Boy scouts; Human services; American Red Cross; Children/youth, services; Federated giving programs.
Limitations: Applications not accepted. Giving primarily in CA, and Champaign, IL. No grants to individuals.
Application information: Contributes only to pre-selected organizations.
Officers: Karen H. Meyer, Pres.; Gregory A. Kimmel, V.P.; August C.F. Meyer, V.P.; A.C. Meyer, Jr., Secy.-Treas.
EIN: 364152268

2896
C. Louis Meyer Family Foundation ◇
(formerly Oakleaf Foundation)
c/o Carol Barrett, Admin.
P.O. Box 854
Huntley, IL 60142
E-mail: CLMFF@foxvalley.net

Established in 1999 in IL.
Foundation type: Independent foundation.
Financial data (yr. ended 12/31/03): Assets, $8,660,515 (M); gifts received, $50,216; expenditures, $765,656; qualifying distributions, $679,843; giving activities include $530,987 for 63 grants (high: $75,000; low: $200).
Fields of interest: Arts; Education; Health care; Health organizations, association; Human services; Youth, services; Christian agencies & churches.
Type of support: Matching/challenge support; General/operating support; Continuing support; Capital campaigns; Building/renovation; Endowments; Emergency funds; Program development; Scholarship funds; Research.
Limitations: Applications not accepted. Giving primarily in Chicago, IL, Pinehust, NC, and NY. No grants to individuals.
Publications: Grants list.
Application information: Contributes only to pre-selected organizations.
   Board meeting date(s): Quarterly, dates vary within each quarter
Officers and Directors:* C. Foster Brown III,* Pres.; Louis M. Brown, Exec. V.P.; Louis M. Brown, Jr., Secy.; Angeline Brown Leonard, Treas.
Number of staff: 1 full-time professional; 1 part-time support.
EIN: 364304695

2897
Adah K. Millard Charitable Trust ◇
c/o The Northern Trust Co.
P.O. Box 803878
Chicago, IL 60680

Established in 1976 in IL.
Donor: Adah K. Millard†.
Foundation type: Independent foundation.
Financial data (yr. ended 12/31/05): Assets, $6,997,737 (M); expenditures, $455,743; qualifying distributions, $430,585; giving activities include $420,000 for 20 grants (high: $52,500; low: $3,000).
Purpose and activities: Giving primarily for human services including children and youth services, and the arts.
Fields of interest: Museums (art); Performing arts centers; Arts; Higher education; Education; Animal welfare; Hospitals (general); Food banks; Human services; YM/YWCAs & YM/YWHAs; Children/youth, services; Federated giving programs; Christian agencies & churches.
Type of support: General/operating support; Continuing support; Building/renovation; Equipment; Program development; Seed money.
Limitations: Applications not accepted. Giving limited to Douglas County, NE. No grants to individuals, or for endowment funds, scholarships, or fellowships; generally no grants for operating budgets; no loans.
Application information: Contributes only to pre-selected organizations.
   Board meeting date(s): Apr. and Nov.
Trustee: The Northern Trust Co.
EIN: 366629069
Selected grants: The following grants were reported in 2005.
$50,000 to Durham Western Heritage Museum, Omaha, NE.
$50,000 to Omaha Childrens Museum, Omaha, NE.
$36,000 to United Way of the Midlands, Omaha, NE.
$32,500 to Siena/Francis House, Omaha, NE.
$25,000 to Grace University, Omaha, NE.
$20,000 to Strategic Air and Space Museum, Ashland, NE.
$15,000 to Douglas County Historical Society, Omaha, NE.
$10,000 to Girl Scouts of the U.S.A., Omaha, NE.
$5,000 to Nebraska Jewish Historical Society, Omaha, NE.
$4,000 to North Omaha Foundation for Human Development, Omaha, NE.

2898
Audrey and Jack Miller Family Charitable Foundation ◇
485 E. Half Day Rd., Ste. 200
Buffalo Grove, IL 60089 (847) 883-9700
Contact: Jack Miller, Pres.

Established in 1987 in IL.
Donor: Jack Miller.
Foundation type: Independent foundation.
Financial data (yr. ended 12/31/05): Assets, $5,957,460 (M); gifts received, $214,078; expenditures, $1,531,569; qualifying distributions, $1,463,824; giving activities include $1,431,508 for 36 grants (high: $477,500; low: $95).
Purpose and activities: Giving primarily for education and health and human services.
Fields of interest: Arts; Higher education; Hospitals (specialty); Health organizations, association;

Medical research, institute; Human services; Jewish federated giving programs.
Limitations: Giving primarily in CA and IL.
Application information: Application form not required.
Initial approach: Letter
Deadline(s): None
Officers and Directors:* Jack Miller,* Pres.; Judith N. Joy,* V.P.; Sharon A. Miller,* V.P.; Eric F. Achepohl, Treas.
EIN: 363563806
Selected grants: The following grants were reported in 2005.
$477,500 to Childrens Memorial Foundation, Chicago, IL.
$25,000 to City of Hope, Los Angeles, CA.
$1,000 to Saint Jude Childrens Research Hospital, Memphis, TN.

2899
Jack and Goldie Wolfe Miller Foundation ◇ ☆
485 Half Day Rd., Ste. 200
Buffalo Grove, IL   60089   (847) 883-9700
Contact: Goldie Wolfe Miller, Pres.

Established in 2004 in IL.
Donors: Audrey and Jack Miller Family Charitable Fund; Jack Miller Charitable Trust.
Foundation type: Independent foundation.
Financial data (yr. ended 12/31/05): Assets, $232,046 (M); gifts received, $562,072; expenditures, $507,752; qualifying distributions, $501,830; giving activities include $501,600 for 18 grants (high: $225,000; low: $100).
Fields of interest: Arts; Education; Medical research, institute; Nerve, muscle & bone research; Human services; Jewish federated giving programs; Jewish agencies & temples.
Limitations: Giving primarily in IL, with emphasis on Chicago. No grants to individuals.
Application information: Application form not required.
Deadline(s): None
Officers and Directors:* Goldie Wolfe Miller,* Pres.; Eric F. Achepohl, V.P. and Treas.; Judith N. Joy; Sharon A. Miller; Alicia Oberman.
EIN: 201930514

2900
James Millikin Trust ◇
P.O. Box 1278
Decatur, IL   62525-1813   (217) 429-4253
Application address: c/o James Uhl, 295 N. Franklin St., Decatur, IL 26523-1390, tel.: (217) 429-2391

Established in 1910 in IL.
Donor: James Millikin†.
Foundation type: Independent foundation.
Financial data (yr. ended 12/31/05): Assets, $17,616,266 (M); expenditures, $884,103; qualifying distributions, $802,986; giving activities include $772,650 for 11 grants (high: $362,500; low: $5,000).
Purpose and activities: Support for a university and other educational organizations; giving also to a community fund and youth services.
Fields of interest: Elementary/secondary education; Higher education, university; Children/youth, services.
Type of support: General/operating support.

Limitations: Giving primarily in Decatur, IL.
Application information: Application form not required.
Initial approach: Proposal
Deadline(s): None
Board meeting date(s): 3rd Wed. of each month
Trustees: Larry Altenbaumer; John Cobb; James E. Masey; Phillip C. Wise; H. Gale Zacheis.
EIN: 370661226
Selected grants: The following grants were reported in 2003.
$375,000 to Millikin University, Decatur, IL.
$84,250 to Baby Talk, Decatur, IL.
$70,000 to Webster-Cantrell Hall, Decatur, IL.
$50,000 to Decatur Area Arts Council, Decatur, IL.
$50,000 to Richland Community College, Decatur, IL.
$35,000 to Decatur Day Care Center, Decatur, IL.
$25,000 to Lutheran School Association of Decatur, Decatur, IL.
$25,000 to Robertson Charter School, Decatur, IL.
$20,000 to United Way of Decatur and Mid-Illinois, Decatur, IL.
$19,000 to School District No. 61, Decatur, IL.

2901
Mills Family Charitable Foundation ◇
1600 Eastwood Ave.
Highland Park, IL   60035

Established in 2001 in IL.
Donors: James D. Abrams; Andrew J. Mills.
Foundation type: Independent foundation.
Financial data (yr. ended 12/31/05): Assets, $5,441,230 (M); expenditures, $669,188; qualifying distributions, $653,960; giving activities include $653,945 for 109 grants (high: $185,000; low: $25).
Fields of interest: Arts; Education; Health care; Human services; Jewish agencies & temples.
Limitations: Applications not accepted. Giving primarily in IL. No grants to individuals.
Application information: Contributes only to pre-selected organizations.
Trustee: Jonathan M. Mills.
EIN: 306000363
Selected grants: The following grants were reported in 2005.
$185,000 to Holocaust Education Foundation, Chicago, IL.
$25,000 to United Way.
$20,000 to John Howard Association, Chicago, IL.
$18,000 to Casa Central, Chicago, IL.
$15,000 to Lake County Center for Independent Living, Mundelein, IL.
$13,500 to Invest in Kids, Denver, CO. 2 grants: $3,500, $10,000
$6,000 to Hebrew Theological College, Skokie, IL.
$3,000 to Belle Center of Chicago, Chicago, IL.
$3,000 to Writers Theater, Glencoe, IL.

2902
The Moline Foundation ◇
817 11th Ave.
Moline, IL   61265
Contact: Joy Boruff, Exec. Dir.
FAX: (309) 736-3721;
E-mail: molinefoundation@qconline.com;
URL: http://www.molinefoundation.org

Established in 1953 in Illinois.

Foundation type: Community foundation.
Financial data (yr. ended 9/30/04): Assets, $10,422,964 (M); gifts received, $268,829; expenditures, $670,166; giving activities include $444,450 for grants, and $28,550 for grants to individuals.
Purpose and activities: The foundation is a community-based, nonprofit organization which provides grants to health, human services, education, community development, the arts, and other charitable organizations which benefit the citizens of Moline and the Quad Cities, IL, region.
Fields of interest: Arts; Education; Health care; Human services; Community development, neighborhood development.
Type of support: Scholarship funds.
Limitations: Giving limited to the Quad Cities area of eastern IA and western IL.
Application information: Visit foundation Web site for grant application guidelines. Application form not required.
Initial approach: Letter
Copies of proposal: 9
Deadline(s): Jan. 31, Apr. 15, and Aug. 31
Board meeting date(s): Scheduled as needed
Final notification: Within 4 weeks of interview
Officers and Trustees:* Dennis Fox,* Chair.; Gene Blanc,* Vice-Chair.; Dennis Schwartz,* Secy.; Joy Boruff, Exec. Dir.; Paula Arnell; Karen Getz; Sandra Kramer; Jon Tunberg.
EIN: 366036867

2903
Kenneth & Harle Montgomery Foundation ◇
c/o Cynthia Kobel
2150 N. Lincoln Park W., Ste. 406
Chicago, IL   60614

Established in 1993 in IL.
Donor: Harle G. Montgomery.
Foundation type: Independent foundation.
Financial data (yr. ended 12/31/05): Assets, $4,341,035 (M); gifts received, $415,690; expenditures, $666,050; qualifying distributions, $524,482; giving activities include $524,482 for 86 grants (high: $75,000; low: $125).
Fields of interest: Arts; Education; International affairs.
Limitations: Applications not accepted. Giving primarily in IL. No grants to individuals.
Application information: Contributes only to pre-selected organizations.
Officers and Directors:* Harle G. Montgomery,* Pres.; Bryant G. Garth,* V.P.; Walter W. Bell,* Secy.-Treas.; Cynthia Kobel.
EIN: 363871012
Selected grants: The following grants were reported in 2003.
$850,000 to La Jolla Branch Library, Friends of, La Jolla, CA. For general support.
$50,000 to La Jolla Playhouse, La Jolla, CA. For general support.
$25,000 to Stanford University, Stanford, CA. For general support.
$17,500 to Goodman Theater, Chicago, IL. For general support.
$16,134 to Safer Foundation, Chicago, IL. For general support.
$15,000 to Northwestern University, School of Law, Evanston, IL. For general support.

$15,000 to Steppenwolf Theater Company, Chicago, IL. For general support.

$12,500 to Facets Multimedia, Chicago, IL. For general support.

$10,000 to Carter Center, Atlanta, GA. For general support.

$10,000 to Health and Medicine Policy Research Group, Chicago, IL. For general support.

2904
The Monticello College Foundation

The Evergreens
5800 Godfrey Rd.
Godfrey, IL 62035 (618) 468-2370
Contact: Linda K. Nevlin, Exec. Dir.
E-mail: lnevlin@lc.edu

Incorporated in 1843 in IL as Monticello College; reorganized as a foundation in 1971.

Donors: H. Barnett Trust; Spencer T. and Ann W. Olin Foundation.

Foundation type: Independent foundation.

Financial data (yr. ended 6/30/05): Assets, $11,986,772 (M); gifts received, $100,130; expenditures, $428,238; qualifying distributions, $368,234; giving activities include $351,050 for 22 grants (high: $110,000; low: $1,000).

Purpose and activities: Support for programs that assist in advancing education for women.

Fields of interest: Higher education; Education; Women.

Type of support: Endowments; Fellowships; Internship funds; Scholarship funds.

Limitations: Giving primarily in the Midwest. No support for private foundations, social service agencies, foreign schools, or foreign-based American schools. No grants to individuals (including exchange students), or for capital funds, bricks and mortar, current operating expenses, or endowed chairs.

Publications: Annual report (including application guidelines).

Application information: Proposals may be stapled, but please do not place them in folders or other binders. Application form not required.

Initial approach: Proposal
Copies of proposal: 18
Deadline(s): Submit proposal preferably by end of Aug. or end of Feb.; deadline 8 weeks before board meeting
Board meeting date(s): Oct. and Apr.
Final notification: 2 weeks after board meeting

Officers and Trustees:* Janet Biermann,* Chair.; Norella Huggins,* Vice-Chair.; Kay Morrill,* Secy.; Karl K. Hoagland, Jr.,* Treas.; Linda K. Nevlin, Exec. Dir.; Alice Barnard; Sara Hoagland; Christopher Kreid; Cathy K. Maude; George S. Milnor II; Alice Norton; Barbara P. Pierce; Mary Dell Pritzlaff; Jenny Sadow; Dianne P. Saul; Janet Schweppe; Mary Vogt; Julie Williams.

Number of staff: 1 part-time professional.

EIN: 370681538

Selected grants: The following grants were reported in 2004.

$277,900 to Washington University, Saint Louis, MO. For Olin Fellowship.

$18,000 to California Institute of Technology, Pasadena, CA. For summer internships.

$15,000 to Blackburn College, Carlinville, IL. For scholarships.

$15,000 to Webster University, Saint Louis, MO. For music school scholarship.

$12,500 to Lewis and Clark Community College, Godfrey, IL. For athletic scholarships.

$11,380 to Central College, Pella, IA. For research scholarships.

$10,000 to Alice Lloyd College, Pippa Passes, KY. For women workshops.

$8,000 to Beloit College, Beloit, WI. For scholarships for science majors.

$6,000 to Vincent Gray Alternative High School, East Saint Louis, IL. For scholarships.

$4,000 to New Opportunity School for Women, Berea, KY. For scholarships.

2905
Mark Morton Memorial Fund ✧

123 N. Wacker Dr.
Chicago, IL 60606-1743

Established in 1951 in IL.

Foundation type: Independent foundation.

Financial data (yr. ended 12/31/05): Assets, $23,551,262 (M); expenditures, $1,611,319; qualifying distributions, $1,412,627; giving activities include $735,000 for 101 grants (high: $150,000; low: $80,000), and $510,847 for 36 grants to individuals (high: $25,657; low: $60).

Purpose and activities: Grants to individuals are limited to those who have been verifiable employees of the Morton Salt Co. before June 30, 1971, to assist with hospital, medical, and surgical expenses, as well as assistance to the aged, blind, or disabled. Organizational support focuses on the environment and human services, with emphasis on women and domestic violence.

Fields of interest: Environment, natural resources; Crime/violence prevention, domestic violence; Human services; Women.

Type of support: Grants to individuals.

Limitations: Giving primarily to organizations in IL and to residents of LA and TX.

Application information: Grant requests from people who are not employees of Morton Salt Company will not be accepted or acknowledged.

Officers and Directors:* Scott Ellwood,* Pres.; William J. Cooney,* V.P.; Arthur J. McGivern, V.P.; Davis H. Roenisch,* V.P.; Leonard E. Zak,* V.P.

Number of staff: 2

EIN: 237181380

2906
Motorola Foundation ▼ ✧

1303 E. Algonquin Rd.
Schaumburg, IL 60196 (847) 576-6200
FAX: (847) 576-9440; *E-mail:* giving@motorola.com;
URL: http://www.motorola.com/
MotorolaFoundation/

Incorporated in 1953 in IL.

Donor: Motorola, Inc.

Foundation type: Company-sponsored foundation.

Financial data (yr. ended 12/31/05): Assets, $71,908,153 (M); expenditures, $7,425,454; qualifying distributions, $7,344,928; giving activities include $7,298,873 for 1,160 grants (high: $1,000,000).

Purpose and activities: The foundation supports organizations involved with arts and culture, education, human services, and community development. Special emphasis is directed toward programs designed to promote math, science, and engineering education.

Fields of interest: Arts; Elementary/secondary education; Higher education; Education; Human services; Community development; Federated giving programs; Science, formal/general education; Mathematics; Engineering/technology.

Type of support: General/operating support; Continuing support; Employee volunteer services; Employee matching gifts; Employee-related scholarships.

Limitations: Giving on a national and international basis in areas of company operations, with emphasis on Huntsville, AL, Phoenix, AZ, Boynton Beach and Fort Lauderdale, FL, IL, and Austin and Sequin, TX. No support for political or lobbying organizations, political candidates, trade schools, or private foundations. No grants to individuals (except for employee-related scholarships), or for political campaigns, endowments, sports sponsorships, fundraising events, conferences, benefits, sponsorships, dinners, tickets, courtesy advertising, capital campaigns, or media projects; no product or equipment donations.

Publications: Application guidelines; Grants list; Program policy statement.

Application information: Unsolicited requests from organizations located outside the U.S. are not accepted. Application form required.

Initial approach: Complete online application form
Board meeting date(s): Monthly and as required

Officers and Directors:* Edward J. Zander,* Pres.; David Devonshire, V.P. and Treas.; Ruth Fattori, V.P.; A. Peter Lawson, Secy.; Eileen Sweeney, Dir., Corp. and Fdn. Philanthropic Rels.

Number of staff: 1 part-time professional; 2 part-time support.

EIN: 366109323

Selected grants: The following grants were reported in 2004.

$2,400,000 to Massachusetts Institute of Technology, Cambridge, MA. 3 grants: $900,000, $900,000, $600,000

$400,000 to Abraham Lincoln Presidential Library Foundation, Springfield, IL.

$300,000 to Georgia Tech Foundation, Atlanta, GA.

$198,575 to National Merit Scholarship Corporation, Evanston, IL.

$80,000 to North Carolina A & T State University, Greensboro, NC.

$70,000 to Hispanic Engineer National Achievement Awards Conference (HENAAC), Monterey Park, CA.

$50,000 to FIRST LEGO League, Manchester, NH.

$50,000 to Purdue University, Center for Wireless Systems and Applications, West Lafayette, IN.

2907
The Mullen Family Foundation ✧

1955 N. Burling St.
Chicago, IL 60614

Established in 1998 in IL.

Donor: Timothy Mullen.

Foundation type: Independent foundation.

Financial data (yr. ended 9/30/05): Assets, $4,446,322 (M); expenditures, $457,656; qualifying distributions, $418,995; giving activities include $418,750 for 9 grants (high: $200,000; low: $250).

Fields of interest: Elementary/secondary education; Zoos/zoological societies; Human services.

Type of support: General/operating support.

Limitations: Applications not accepted. No grants to individuals.
Application information: Contributes only to pre-selected organizations.
Officers: Timothy Mullen, Pres. and Treas.; Alicia Mullen, V.P. and Secy.; Richard G. Mullen, V.P.
EIN: 364270223

2908
Salus Mundi Foundation ▼ ✧
P.O. Box 803878
Chicago, IL 60680

Established in 2000 in AZ.
Donor: Diebold Foundation.
Foundation type: Independent foundation.
Financial data (yr. ended 9/30/05): Assets, $10,790,946 (M); expenditures, $9,033,060; qualifying distributions, $8,993,034; giving activities include $8,988,634 for 28 grants (high: $5,000,000; low: $10,000; average: $25,000–$250,000).
Purpose and activities: Support primarily for higher education.
Fields of interest: Higher education; Children, services.
Type of support: General/operating support; Program development; Fellowships.
Limitations: Applications not accepted. Giving on a national basis. No grants to individuals.
Application information: Contributes only to pre-selected organizations.
Trustee: Northern Trust Bank, N.A.
EIN: 866289295
Selected grants: The following grants were reported in 2005.
$5,000,000 to University of California, Berkeley, CA. For Dean George Breslauer Fellowship.
$2,047,000 to University of Arizona Foundation, Tucson, AZ. For faculty lecture series and Asian anthropology.
$467,030 to University of Texas, Austin, TX. 2 grants: $224,925 (For Indo-European Language), $242,105 (For Early Indo-European Languages).
$250,000 to New School, New York, NY. For project of transregional demographic studies.
$125,000 to School of American Research, Santa Fe, NM. For Salus Mundi Foundation seminars.
$50,000 to Center for Desert Archaeology, Tucson, AZ. For archeological research.

2909
The Negaunee Foundation, Ltd. ✧
P.O. Box 1287
Northbrook, IL 60065-1287
Contact: Richard W. Colburn, Pres.

Established in 1987.
Foundation type: Independent foundation.
Financial data (yr. ended 12/31/03): Assets, $41,068,419 (M); gifts received, $4,300,000; expenditures, $2,134,298; qualifying distributions, $1,879,884; giving activities include $1,856,536 for 61 grants (high: $200,000; low: $500).
Purpose and activities: Giving primarily for museums and the performing arts.
Fields of interest: Performing arts, music; Arts; Higher education; Human services.
Type of support: General/operating support; Continuing support; Endowments.

Limitations: Applications not accepted. Giving primarily in Chicago, IL. No grants to individuals; no loans.
Application information: Contributes only to pre-selected organizations. Unsolicited requests for funds not considered.
Board meeting date(s): Dec.
Officers and Directors:* Richard W. Colburn,* Pres.; Robin Tennant Colburn,* V.P.
EIN: 363555046
Selected grants: The following grants were reported in 2004.
$125,000 to Salvation Army, Sterling, IL.
$100,000 to Ravinia Festival Association, Highland Park, IL.
$60,000 to Pacific Legal Foundation, Sacramento, CA.
$50,000 to Beginning with Children Foundation, New York, NY.
$35,000 to Orphans of the Storm, Deerfield, IL.
$25,000 to Nature Conservancy, Arlington, VA.
$25,000 to Peoples Music School, Chicago, IL.
$10,000 to Chicago Zoological Society, Brookfield, IL.
$10,000 to George Mason University Foundation, Fairfax, VA.
$6,000 to Night Ministry, Chicago, IL.

2910
The Neisser Fund ✧ ☆
c/o Cohen, Grossman, & Rosenson, LLC
233 N. Michigan Ave., Ste. 1720
Chicago, IL 60601

Established in 1964 in IL.
Donors: Edward Neisser; Judith E. Neisser.
Foundation type: Independent foundation.
Financial data (yr. ended 12/31/05): Assets, $361,440 (M); gifts received, $992,182; expenditures, $893,999; qualifying distributions, $884,626; giving activities include $884,626 for grants.
Purpose and activities: Giving primarily for the arts and education.
Fields of interest: Museums; Performing arts; Arts; Higher education; Health organizations, association.
Limitations: Applications not accepted. Giving primarily in Chicago, IL. No grants to individuals.
Application information: Contributes only to pre-selected organizations.
Officers and Directors:* Judith E. Neisser,* Pres. and Treas.; Katherine M. Neisser,* V.P.; Nathan Grossman; Sherwin Zuckerman.
EIN: 366054300
Selected grants: The following grants were reported in 2005.
$72,778 to Art Institute of Chicago, Chicago, IL. 2 grants: $71,428, $1,350
$37,300 to Aspen Institute, DC. 2 grants: $2,300, $35,000
$27,015 to Whitney Museum of American Art, New York, NY.
$25,000 to Archeworks, Chicago, IL.
$14,000 to Francis Parker School, San Diego, CA. 2 grants: $4,000, $10,000
$12,965 to Erikson Institute, Chicago, IL.
$12,500 to Music Associates of Aspen, Aspen, CO.

2911
James & Aune Nelson Foundation ✧
P.O. Box 5146
Godfrey, IL 62035

Donor: Aune Nelson†.
Foundation type: Independent foundation.
Financial data (yr. ended 12/31/05): Assets, $20,504,906 (M); expenditures, $485,093; qualifying distributions, $457,450; giving activities include $449,633 for 5 grants (high: $333,333; low: $9,300).
Purpose and activities: Giving primarily for conservation and the environment.
Fields of interest: Environment, natural resources.
Type of support: General/operating support; Land acquisition; Program development.
Limitations: Applications not accepted. Giving primarily in IL and CA. No grants to individuals.
Application information: Contributes only to pre-selected organizations.
Officers: David Pfeifer, Pres.; Robert Freeman, V.P.; William Hoagland, Secy.; Robert Larson, Treas.
Directors: Anita Cooper; Annie Hoagland; Don Huber; Dorothy Metzger; L. James Struif.
EIN: 371371840

2912
New Prospect Foundation ✧
c/o KKP Group LLC
1603 Orrington Ave., Ste. 1880
Evanston, IL 60201 (847) 328-2288
Contact: Paul Lehman, Dir.

Established in 1969 in IL.
Donors: Elliot Lehman; Frances Lehman; Fel-Pro Inc.
Foundation type: Independent foundation.
Financial data (yr. ended 12/31/04): Assets, $16,637,901 (M); expenditures, $1,808,893; qualifying distributions, $1,599,033; giving activities include $1,599,033 for 66 grants (high: $200,000; low: $1).
Purpose and activities: Support for advocacy directed toward the improvement of housing, employment, welfare, and the economic viability of urban and inner-city neighborhoods. Funding priority given to organizations with modest budgets that may not qualify for traditional sources of financial assistance; also supports efforts undertaken in the public interest through legal services. Additional areas of interest are pro-choice activities, human and civil rights, and Chicago, IL, public school reform.
Fields of interest: Museums (children's); Arts; Education, reform; Reproductive health, family planning; Legal services; Civil liberties, reproductive rights; Civil rights; Community development; Women; Economically disadvantaged.
Type of support: General/operating support; Continuing support; Program development; Seed money.
Limitations: Giving primarily in the metropolitan Chicago, IL, area. Generally no funding for the arts, higher education, health care, or human/social services. No grants to individuals, or for capital or endowment funds, basic research, scholarships, or fellowships; no loans.
Publications: Informational brochure.
Application information: Application form not required.
Initial approach: Letter
Deadline(s): None

Officers and Directors:* Paul Lehman,* Pres.; Kay Schlozman,* V.P.; Betsy Levisay,* Secy.; Frances Lehman,* Treas.; Elliot Lehman; Peter Lehman; Daniel Schlozman; Ronna Stamm.
Number of staff: 1 part-time professional.
EIN: 237032384

2913
The Newell Rubbermaid Scholarship Fund ◇

(formerly James R. Caldwell Scholarship Fund)
c/o The Northern Trust Co.
50 S. LaSalle St., L-5
Chicago, IL 60675
Application address: The Newell Rubbermaid Scholarship Fund, c/o Newell Rubbermaid Inc., 29 E. Stephenson St., Freeport, IL 61032

Donors: Rubbermaid Inc.; Newell Rubbermaid Inc.
Foundation type: Company-sponsored foundation.
Financial data (yr. ended 12/31/03): Assets, $0 (M); gifts received, $313,327; expenditures, $403,133; qualifying distributions, $403,097; giving activities include $403,133 for 181 grants to individuals (high: $5,000; low: $177).
Purpose and activities: The foundation awards college scholarships to the children of employees of Newell Rubbermaid.
Type of support: Employee-related scholarships.
Limitations: Applications not accepted. Giving limited to areas of company operations.
Application information: Contributes only through employee-related scholarships.
Trustee: The Northern Trust Co.
EIN: 346525539

2914
Niamogue Foundation ◇

c/o John McCartney
300 E. Randolph St., Ste. 2810
Chicago, IL 60601

Established in 1995 in IL.
Donor: John F. McCartney.
Foundation type: Independent foundation.
Financial data (yr. ended 12/31/05): Assets, $10,133,163 (L); expenditures, $1,527,128; qualifying distributions, $1,522,960; giving activities include $1,522,940 for 80 grants (high: $275,000; low: $1,000).
Purpose and activities: Giving primarily for higher education including a business school as well as for the arts, hospitals including medical research, and for human services.
Fields of interest: Museums (art); Performing arts; Arts; Education, public education; Higher education; Business school/education; Hospitals (general); Health organizations, association; Health organizations, research; Cancer; Food banks; Human services; Youth, services; Christian agencies & churches; Women.
Limitations: Applications not accepted. Giving on a national basis, with emphasis on Chicago, IL; funding also in Paris, France. No grants to individuals.
Application information: Contributes only to pre-selected organizations.
Officers: Clare M. Munana, Pres.; Harry L. Vincent, V.P.; John F. McCartney, Secy.-Treas.
EIN: 364054294

Selected grants: The following grants were reported in 2003.
$250,000 to University of Pennsylvania, Wharton School of Business, Philadelphia, PA. For general support.
$212,000 to Davidson College, Davidson, NC. For general support.
$200,000 to Lawrence Hall Youth Services, Chicago, IL. For general support.
$25,000 to Aspen Institute, DC. For general support.
$25,000 to Urban Pathways, New York, NY. For general support.
$16,219 to Chicago Public Schools, Chicago, IL. For general support.
$10,000 to Alivio Medical Center, Chicago, IL. For Web site development.
$10,000 to Chicago Humanities Festival, Chicago, IL. For general support.
$10,000 to Memorial Sloan-Kettering Cancer Center, New York, NY. For general support.
$2,500 to Southampton Hospital Association, Southampton, NY. For general support.

2915
NIB Foundation

1140 W. Erie
Chicago, IL 60622

Established in 2001 in IL.
Donors: Sonia Florian; William C. Florian.
Foundation type: Independent foundation.
Financial data (yr. ended 8/31/05): Assets, $16,587,920 (M); expenditures, $1,736,856; qualifying distributions, $1,556,669; giving activities include $1,437,500 for 53 grants (high: $450,000; low: $1,500).
Fields of interest: Arts; Education; Human services.
Limitations: Applications not accepted. No grants to individuals.
Application information: Contributes only to pre-selected organizations.
Officers and Directors:* William C. Florian,* Pres.; Sonia Florian,* Secy.
EIN: 364464875
Selected grants: The following grants were reported in 2005.
$450,000 to Lyric Opera of Chicago, Chicago, IL.
$150,000 to Puerto Rico Animal Welfare Society, Aguadilla, PR.
$50,000 to American Ballet Theater, New York, NY.
$50,000 to Light Opera Works, Evanston, IL.
$30,000 to Gene Siskel Film Center, Chicago, IL.
$25,000 to Bang On A Can, New York, NY.
$25,000 to Chicago Symphony Orchestra, Chicago, IL.
$25,000 to Ravinia Festival Association, Highland Park, IL.
$20,000 to Music in the Loft, Chicago, IL.
$10,000 to Music of the Baroque, Chicago, IL.

2916
John D. & Alexandria C. Nichols Family Foundation ◇

900 Mt. Pleasant Rd.
Winnetka, IL 60093

Established in 1992 in IL.
Donors: John D. Nichols; Alexandra Trust; Nichols Family Investment, LP.
Foundation type: Independent foundation.

Financial data (yr. ended 12/31/04): Assets, $32,988,437 (M); gifts received, $1,000,000; expenditures, $1,152,864; qualifying distributions, $1,063,467; giving activities include $1,063,467 for 145+ grants (high: $250,000).
Purpose and activities: Giving primarily for the arts and for education.
Fields of interest: Arts education; Arts; Education; Human services.
Limitations: Applications not accepted. Giving primarily in Chicago, IL. No grants to individuals.
Application information: Contributes only to pre-selected organizations.
Trustees: Alexandra C. Nichols; John D. Nichols.
EIN: 363858388

2917
Dellora A. & Lester J. Norris Foundation ◇

303 E. Main St.
P.O. Box 4325
St. Charles, IL 60174 (630) 584-2500
Contact: Eugene W. Butler, Treas.

Established in 1979 in IL.
Donors: Dellora A. Norris†; Lester J. Norris†.
Foundation type: Independent foundation.
Financial data (yr. ended 12/31/05): Assets, $36,184,860 (M); expenditures, $2,181,503; qualifying distributions, $1,892,910; giving activities include $1,850,700 for 87 grants (high: $200,000; low: $1,000).
Purpose and activities: Giving primarily for hospitals, higher and secondary education, and church support.
Fields of interest: Secondary school/education; Higher education; Hospitals (general); YM/YWCAs & YM/YWHAs; Religion.
Limitations: Giving on a national basis. No grants to individuals.
Application information: Support mainly for organizations started by donors and officers. Application form not required.
Initial approach: Letter
Deadline(s): None
Board meeting date(s): Quarterly
Officers and Directors:* Robert C. Norris,* Chair.; George N. Gaynor,* Pres.; Pamela Norris,* V.P.; Howard S. Tuthill, Secy.; Eugene W. Butler, Treas.; John R. Collins.
EIN: 363054939
Selected grants: The following grants were reported in 2004.
$288,000 to YMCA of Collier County, Bonita Springs, FL. 2 grants: $25,000, $263,000
$200,000 to Delnor-Community Health Care Foundation, Geneva, IL.
$130,000 to Denver Academy, Denver, CO.
$50,000 to Sayre School, Lexington, KY.
$25,000 to Tri-City Health Partnership, Saint Charles, IL.
$25,000 to Up With People, Broomfield, CO.
$15,000 to University of Denver, Denver, CO.
$10,000 to Bridgewood Farms, Conroe, TX.
$10,000 to Saint Charles Historical Society, Saint Charles, IL.

2918
The Northern Trust Company Charitable Trust ▼

c/o The Northern Trust Co., Community Affairs Div.
50 S. LaSalle St., L7
Chicago, IL 60675 (312) 630-1762
Contact: Chastity Davis
E-mail: northern_trust_charitable_trust@ntrs.com;
URL: http://www.northerntrust.com/pws/jsp/
display2.jsp?XML=pages/nt/
0601/1137700254265_667.xml

Trust established in 1966 in IL.
Donor: The Northern Trust Co.
Foundation type: Company-sponsored foundation.
Financial data (yr. ended 12/31/05): Assets,
$556,621 (M); gifts received, $4,449,617;
expenditures, $4,319,503; qualifying distributions,
$4,318,337; giving activities include $3,583,107
for 209+ grants (high: $212,500; low: $25), and
$734,871 for 928 employee matching gifts.
Purpose and activities: The trust supports
organizations involved with arts and culture,
education, and social welfare. Special emphasis is
directed toward programs designed to advance the
well being of disadvantaged women and children
and people with disabilities.
Fields of interest: Arts; Education; Human services;
Children; Disabilities, people with; Women;
Economically disadvantaged.
Type of support: General/operating support;
Continuing support; Annual campaigns; Capital
campaigns; Building/renovation; Endowments;
Program development; Employee volunteer
services; Employee matching gifts; Matching/
challenge support.
Limitations: Giving primarily in the Chicago, IL,
neighborhoods of Chatham, Englewood, Humboldt
Park, Logan Square, Loop, Washington Park, and
West Town. No support for United Way-supported
organizations (over 5 percent of budget), national
health organizations or the local affiliates of national
health organizations or research or disease
advocacy organizations, political, labor, or fraternal
organizations or social clubs, religious organizations
not of direct benefit to the entire community,
individual pre-K-12 schools, or organizations
established less than 2 years ago. No grants to
individuals, or for scholarships or fellowships,
fundraising events, advertising or marketing, sports,
athletic events, or athletic programs, travel-related
events, book, film, video, or television development
or production, memorial campaigns, or multi-year
general operating support.
Publications: Corporate giving report (including
application guidelines); Grants list.
Application information: Support is limited to 3
years. Application form required.
   Initial approach: Complete online letter of inquiry
   form; complete online application form for
   current grantees
   Deadline(s): Dec. 1 and June 30 for Social
   Welfare; Mar. 30 for Arts and Culture and
   Education; Jan. 12 and Aug. 10 for Social
   Welfare for current grantees; May 11 for Arts
   and Culture and Education for current grantees
   Board meeting date(s): Late Mar., July, and Oct.
   Final notification: 2 months
Trustee: The Northern Trust Co.
Number of staff: 2 full-time professional; 1 part-time
professional; 1 full-time support; 1 part-time
support.
EIN: 366147253

Selected grants: The following grants were reported
in 2003.
$50,000 to Advocate Charitable Foundation, Park
   Ridge, IL. For capital support.
$50,000 to Northwestern University, Evanston, IL.
   To endow Freshman Urban Program.
$35,000 to Big Shoulders Fund, Chicago, IL. For
   support for inner-city schools.
$33,000 to Chicago Public Education Fund,
   Chicago, IL. For operating support.
$30,000 to Local Initiatives Support Corporation
   (LISC), Chicago, IL. For Campaign for
   Communities.
$30,000 to Museum of Science and Industry,
   Chicago, IL. For Science Club Network.
$25,000 to Childrens Memorial Foundation,
   Chicago, IL. For program support.
$25,000 to DePaul University, Chicago, IL. For
   financial assistance for needy undergraduate
   students.
$25,000 to Kohl Childrens Museum of Greater
   Chicago, Glenview, IL. For capital support.
$25,000 to Roosevelt University, Chicago, IL. For
   financial assistance for students in Renaissance
   II programs.

2919
Rudolf Nureyev Dance Foundation ✧

c/o Barry L. Weinstein
311 W. Superior St., Ste. 525
Chicago, IL 60610 (312) 649-0700
Contact: Linda Pilkinton, Prog. Mgr.
FAX: (312) 573-0023;
E-mail: linda@rudolfnureyevdancefoundation.org;
URL: http://www.rudolfnureyevdancefoundation.org

Established in 1991 in IL.
Donor: Rudolf Nureyev†.
Foundation type: Independent foundation.
Financial data (yr. ended 6/30/06): Assets,
$6,587,720 (M); expenditures, $727,533;
qualifying distributions, $645,000; giving activities
include $645,000 for grants.
Purpose and activities: The foundation provides
grants in the U.S. for ballet and modern dance
performances, funds dance schools and dance
scholarships, provides financial assistance for the
creation of new choreography, and supports the
establishment of dance collections and film
archives to preserve the history, tradition and
appreciation of dance.
Fields of interest: Performing arts, dance;
Performing arts, ballet; Performing arts,
choreography.
Type of support: Scholarship funds.
Limitations: Applications not accepted. Giving on a
national basis. No support for health or medical
research. No grants to individuals, or for
maintenance, construction, office expenses, or for
administrative costs.
Application information: Contributes only to
pre-selected organizations.
Officers and Directors:* Barry L. Weinstein,* Pres.;
Jeannette Etheredge,* V.P.; Joyce A. Moffatt, V.P.;
Hilary Weinstein,* V.P.; Paul Horwitz, Secy.-Treas.
EIN: 363822516

2920
Bill Nygren Foundation ✧

(formerly William & Sara Nygren Charitable
Foundation)
2 N. LaSalle St., Ste. 500
Chicago, IL 60602

Established in 1994 in IL.
Donors: William C. Nygren; Sara Nygren.
Foundation type: Independent foundation.
Financial data (yr. ended 12/31/05): Assets,
$7,944,931 (M); expenditures, $422,263;
qualifying distributions, $414,000; giving activities
include $414,000 for 32 grants (high: $100,000;
low: $500).
Purpose and activities: Giving for art and cultural
institutes, federated giving programs, youth
services, and Christian churches.
Fields of interest: Museums; Human services;
Children/youth, services.
Limitations: Applications not accepted. Giving
primarily in Chicago, IL. No grants to individuals.
Application information: Contributes only to
pre-selected organizations.
Officer and Directors:* William C. Nygren,* Pres.
and Treas.; Henry Berghoef; Robert Levy.
EIN: 363987600
Selected grants: The following grants were reported
in 2004.
$75,000 to United Way, IL.
$30,000 to University of Wisconsin Foundation,
   Madison, WI.
$25,000 to Childrens Memorial Foundation,
   Chicago, IL.
$25,000 to LEARN Charter School, Chicago, IL.
$20,000 to Chicago Tribune Holiday Fund, Chicago,
   IL.
$12,000 to Hubbard Street Dance Chicago,
   Chicago, IL.
$10,000 to Erikson Institute, Chicago, IL.
$10,000 to Perspectives Charter School, Chicago,
   IL.
$5,000 to Community Support Services, Brookfield,
   IL.
$1,000 to Spare Key Foundation, South Saint Paul,
   MN.

2921
The William F. O'Connor Foundation ✧

c/o Ryan and Juraska
141 W. Jackson Blvd., Ste. 3520
Chicago, IL 60604 (312) 922-0062
Contact: Carol Hennessy, Treas.

Established in IL.
Donor: William F. O'Connor†.
Foundation type: Independent foundation.
Financial data (yr. ended 6/30/05): Assets,
$31,627,788 (M); gifts received, $1,003,338;
expenditures, $2,920,017; qualifying distributions,
$960,225; giving activities include $905,635 for 9
+ grants (high: $260,250).
Purpose and activities: Giving primarily for
education and human services; funding also for a
children's hospital, as well as an academic medical
center, and to a public media broadcast station in
Chicago, IL.
Fields of interest: Media/communications; Higher
education; Education; Hospitals (specialty); Roman
Catholic agencies & churches.
Limitations: Giving primarily in IL. No grants to
individuals.
Application information:

Initial approach: Letter
Deadline(s): None
Officers and Directors:* Mary Jane O'Connor,* Pres.; Carol Hennessy,* Treas.; Mark Cermack; Mary Jo McGuire; Joanne Unkovskoy.
EIN: 363593445

2922
Oak Park/River Forest Community Foundation ◇
1049 Lake St., No. 204
Oak Park, IL 60301 (708) 848-1560
Contact: For grants: David Weindling, Donor Svcs. Dir.
FAX: (708) 848-1531;
E-mail: advisors@oprfcommfd.org; URL: http://www.oprfcommfd.org

Established in 1958 in IL.
Foundation type: Community foundation.
Financial data (yr. ended 12/31/04): Assets, $8,986,824 (M); gifts received, $1,439,904; expenditures, $935,917; giving activities include $644,493 for grants.
Purpose and activities: The foundation supports community programs and services. Also provides away from home residential scholarships to 11-18 year-old children from low-income families in metropolitan Chicago, IL, and awards undergraduate scholarships to Oak Park and River Forest, IL, graduating seniors.
Fields of interest: Arts; Education; Environment; Health care; Crime/violence prevention; Housing/shelter; Recreation; Family services; Human services; Community development, neighborhood development; Community development; Children/youth; Aging; Disabilities, people with; Minorities.
Type of support: Income development; Program development; Seed money; Consulting services; Scholarships—to individuals; Matching/challenge support.
Limitations: Giving limited to Oak Park and River Forest, IL, for discretionary grantmaking. No grants to individuals (except for specific funds designated for scholarships), or for operating expenses, endowments, capital campaigns or for debt retirement.
Publications: Application guidelines; Annual report (including application guidelines); Grants list; Informational brochure; Newsletter; Occasional report.
Application information: Visit foundation Web site for application form and guidelines. Applications are sent to an extensive mailing list of Oak Park and River Forest organizations; to be placed on the list, organizations can call the foundation or E-mail staff. E-mailed or faxed applications are not accepted. Application form required.
Initial approach: Telephone or E-mail
Copies of proposal: 3
Deadline(s): May 1
Board meeting date(s): 2nd Tues. in Jan., Mar., May, Sept., and Nov.
Final notification: Oct. 1
Officers and Directors:* Dave Valenti,* Pres.; Boyd McDowell,* V.P.; Miriam Burkland,* Secy.; Lou Marchi,* Treas.; Theresa Amato, Exec. Dir.; Case Hoogendoorn, Counsel; Debbie Abrahamson; Bobbi Asher; Sharyn Austin; Beta Balgeman; Deborah Braxton; Harmon Brown; Mena Boulanger; Tom Dwyer; Bill Cragg; Julia Faust; Sara Faust; Barbara Furlong; Albert George; Bill Greffin; Matt Grote; Andy

Hibel; Emlee Hilliard-Smith; Werner Huget; Clarmarie Keenan; Rick King; Shirley Klem; Naomi Law; Carlotta Lucchesi; Virginia Martinez; Kevin McCole; Victor Mirelman; Rob Moore; Martin Noll; Chatka Ruggiero; Robert Sassetti; Bill Shorney; Doug Stewart; Jim Winikates.
Number of staff: 2 full-time professional; 1 part-time professional.
EIN: 364150724

2923
Oberweiler Foundation ◇
18 E. Dundee Rd., Bldg. 3, Ste. 204
Barrington, IL 60010
Contact: James R. Bartell, V.P. and Exec. Dir.

Established in 2000 in IL.
Donor: Siegfried Weiler.
Foundation type: Independent foundation.
Financial data (yr. ended 12/31/05): Assets, $13,302,314 (M); expenditures, $755,590; qualifying distributions, $530,675; giving activities include $413,817 for 22 grants (high: $50,000; low: $1,000).
Purpose and activities: Giving primarily to 1) help individuals achieve higher levels of wellness through the application of alternative medicine procedures, 2) prevent the demise of America's wilderness/wetlands as a result of private exploitation and/or public encroachment, and 3) assist disadvantaged, sick, and/or abused children.
Fields of interest: Environment; Health care; Health organizations, association; Children/youth, services.
Type of support: Equipment; Land acquisition; Internship funds; Scholarship funds; Research; Scholarships—to individuals; Matching/challenge support.
Limitations: Giving primarily in northern IL. No grants for operational support.
Publications: Application guidelines.
Application information:
Initial approach: Letter of inquiry (maximum 2 pages); foundation will respond either with a request to submit a detailed grant application form or an explanation of why the request was denied
Board meeting date(s): Feb.
Officers and Directors:* Siegfried Weiler,* Pres.; James R. Bartell,* V.P. and Exec. Dir.; Anna Weiler,* Secy.; Ruth S. Flynn; Martha Heylin; Ronald Ohlsen.
Number of staff: 1 full-time professional.
EIN: 364376705
Selected grants: The following grants were reported in 2004.
$30,240 to Alternative Medicine Foundation, Potomac, MD. For HerbMed Database and Information Resource Guides, to open public access to objective information to add clarity and integrity via database and resource guides.
$30,000 to Alliance for the Great Lakes, Chicago, IL. For Sustaining Our Great Lakes Waters and Waukegan Harbor Clean Up Project, promotion of long-term, sustainable water management policy by researching other water conservation practices around the world and educating public to call for strong, sustainable water use programs for the Great Lakes, for non-renewable resource that is being abused.
$25,000 to Association House of Chicago, Chicago, IL. For Healthy Lifestyles Initiative, for behavioral changes to reduce health problems such as obesity, diabetes, cardiovascular diseases, and

infant mortality that are result of poor nutrition and depravation.
$25,000 to Land Conservancy of McHenry County, Woodstock, IL. For Camp Algonquin Acquisition to purchase acres of open space in densely populated area of McHenry County, adjacent to Fox Bluff Conservation Area, resulting in preservation and management of greater area of Fox River Watershed.
$20,000 to Environmental Law and Policy Center of the Midwest, Chicago, IL. For Clean Water Initiative Program to protect Northern Illinois' threaded rivers, lakes and wetlands; advocating smart growth planning techniques that protect groundwater resources; and promote creation of new Great Lakes Restoration Fund.
$15,000 to Make-A-Wish Foundation of Northern Illinois, Chicago, IL. For At Risk Children's Wish Program.
$10,000 to Good News Partners, Chicago, IL. For Youth at Risk Program, for housing and support services for children who would be homeless and abused by poverty, racism, and inequality through mentoring program for boys 11-16 years of age, family reading coaches involvement program for first graders at risk for educational neglect, and New Life Shelter program of providing permanent housing for pervasive homelessness for high risk children.
$10,000 to Living Lands and Waters Restoration Organization, East Moline, IL. For Plum Island Restoration Project.
$10,000 to Night Ministry, Chicago, IL. For Youth Health Ministry Program, for health care services to underserved children, including nursing visits to area youth shelters and HIV/STD prevention and testing efforts to those at highest risk youth on nighttime streets of Chicago and marginal shelters where they stay.
$10,000 to Wetlands Initiative, Chicago, IL. For Midewin Tallgrass Prairie Restoration.

2924
The Offield Family Foundation ▼ ◇
400 N. Michigan Ave., Rm. 407
Chicago, IL 60611

Incorporated in 1940 in IL.
Donor: Dorothy Wrigley Offield.
Foundation type: Independent foundation.
Financial data (yr. ended 6/30/04): Assets, $101,000,616 (M); gifts received, $1,805,716; expenditures, $8,033,158; qualifying distributions, $7,321,310; giving activities include $7,241,133 for 68 grants (high: $1,026,369; low: $500; average: $5,000–$100,000).
Purpose and activities: Emphasis on hospitals, a family planning agency, education, and cultural programs.
Fields of interest: Arts; Education; Hospitals (general).
Limitations: Applications not accepted. Giving primarily in AZ, CA, the Chicago, IL, area and MI. No grants to individuals.
Application information: Contributes only to pre-selected organizations.
Officers and Directors:* Paxson H. Offield,* Pres.; James S. Offield,* V.P. and Treas.; Gail Hodge,* Secy.; Chase Offield; Meighan Offield.
EIN: 366066240
Selected grants: The following grants were reported in 2005.

$1,450,115 to Little Traverse Conservancy, Harbor Springs, MI.

$1,000,000 to Shaw Caring House, Edwards, CO.

$500,000 to Northern Michigan Hospital Foundation, Petoskey, MI.

$400,000 to Peregrine Fund, Boise, ID.

$300,000 to Harbor Springs Educational Foundation, Harbor Springs, MI.

$200,000 to Planned Parenthood Northern Michigan, Traverse City, MI.

$150,000 to Michigan Land Use Institute, Beulah, MI.

$123,000 to Bat Conservation International, Austin, TX.

$50,000 to Hospice of Little Traverse Bay, Harbor Springs, MI.

$25,000 to North Central Michigan College Foundation, Petoskey, MI.

2925

Olin Corporation Charitable Trust

427 N. Shamrock St.
East Alton, IL 62024 (618) 258-2000
Contact: Ann Pipkin, Mgr., Public Affairs
FAX: (618) 258-2028; URL: http://www.olin.com/about/charitable.asp

Established in 1945 in MO.
Donor: Olin Corp.
Foundation type: Company-sponsored foundation.
Financial data (yr. ended 12/31/03): Assets, $122,315 (M); gifts received, $400,000; expenditures, $343,222; qualifying distributions, $339,860; giving activities include $330,761 for 118 grants (high: $55,000; low: $50).
Purpose and activities: The foundation supports organizations involved with education, the environment, animals and wildlife, minorities, health, substance abuse, safety and disasters, human services, and civil rights.
Fields of interest: Elementary/secondary education; Higher education; Business school/education; Engineering school/education; Education; Environment, natural resources; Environmental education; Environment; Animals/wildlife, preservation/protection; Health care; Substance abuse, services; Safety/disasters; Youth, services; Human services; Civil rights; Federated giving programs; Science; Minorities; African Americans/Blacks.
Type of support: Employee-related scholarships; General/operating support; Continuing support; Annual campaigns; Capital campaigns; Building/renovation; Equipment; Land acquisition; Emergency funds; Program development; Conferences/seminars; Seed money; Curriculum development; Fellowships; Internship funds; Scholarship funds; Research; Employee matching gifts; Matching/challenge support.
Limitations: Giving primarily in areas of company operations in AL, CT, GA, IL, IN, NY, and TN. No grants to individuals (except for fellowships and employee-related scholarships), or for endowments; no loans.
Application information: Application form not required.
Initial approach: Proposal
Copies of proposal: 1
Deadline(s): Between Jan. and Aug. is preferred
Board meeting date(s): Dec.
Final notification: 2 to 3 months
Trustees: Donald W. Griffin; Peter C. Kosche, Jr.; Wachovia Bank, N.A.

Number of staff: 1 full-time professional; 1 part-time support.
EIN: 436022750
Selected grants: The following grants were reported in 2003.
$55,000 to Buffalo Bill Memorial Association, Cody, WY.
$20,000 to SoundWaters, Stamford, CT.
$9,809 to United Way of Williams County, Bryan, OH.
$9,000 to Conference Board, New York, NY.
$9,000 to United Way of Niagara, Niagara Falls, NY.
$5,485 to YMCA of Chattanooga, Chattanooga, TN.
$5,450 to United Way of Bradley County, Cleveland, TN.
$5,000 to Foundation for Student Communication, Princeton, NJ.
$5,000 to University of Missouri, Rolla, MO.
$5,000 to Yale-New Haven Hospital, New Haven, CT.

2926

Omron Foundation, Inc. ◇

c/o Omron Electronics LLC
1 E. Commerce Dr.
Schaumburg, IL 60173 (847) 843-7900
Contact: Nobuyuki Nakatani, Secy.-Treas.

Established in 1989 in IL.
Donors: Omron Electronics Inc.; Omron Electronics LLC; Omron Healthcare, Inc.
Foundation type: Company-sponsored foundation.
Financial data (yr. ended 3/31/06): Assets, $1,150,236 (M); gifts received, $295,710; expenditures, $405,975; qualifying distributions, $400,723; giving activities include $400,723 for 161 grants (high: $86,760; low: $25).
Purpose and activities: The foundation supports organizations involved with arts and culture, education, the environment, health, youth development, human services, civil rights, community development, and civic affairs.
Fields of interest: Performing arts; Arts; Secondary school/education; Higher education; Education; Environment; Health care; Youth development, citizenship; Youth development; American Red Cross; Human services; Civil rights; Community development; Federated giving programs; Public affairs.
International interests: Asia; Japan.
Type of support: General/operating support; Continuing support; Building/renovation; Scholarship funds; Employee matching gifts; Employee-related scholarships; In-kind gifts.
Limitations: Giving primarily in Chicago, IL. No grants to individuals (except for employee-related scholarships).
Application information: Application form not required.
Initial approach: Proposal
Deadline(s): None
Board meeting date(s): Quarterly
Officers and Directors: Tatsunoske Goto, Pres.; Takashi Kasai, Secy.-Treas.; Nobuyuki Nakatani, Secy.-Treas.; Craig Bauer; Kazuo Saito; K. Blake Thatcher.
EIN: 363644055
Selected grants: The following grants were reported in 2004.
$50,000 to American Heart Association, Westmont, IL.
$25,000 to Gleaners Community Food Bank, Detroit, MI.

$25,000 to Northern Illinois University, De Kalb, IL. For general support.
$15,000 to Augustana College, Rock Island, IL.
$15,000 to William Rainey Harper College, Palatine, IL.
$13,750 to National Merit Scholarship Corporation, Evanston, IL.
$11,730 to United Way of Greater Saint Charles and Elburn, Saint Charles, IL.
$10,000 to Direct Relief International, Santa Barbara, CA.
$5,000 to American Lung Association of Metropolitan Chicago, Chicago, IL.
$5,000 to Salvation Army, Geneva, IL.

2927

Edmond and Alice Opler Foundation ◇

(formerly Edmond Opler Foundation)
180 N. LaSalle St., Ste. 2700
Chicago, IL 60601
Contact: Lloyd S. Kupferberg, V.P.

Established in 1981.
Donor: Edmond Opler.
Foundation type: Independent foundation.
Financial data (yr. ended 12/31/04): Assets, $20,876,878 (M); expenditures, $1,328,226; qualifying distributions, $1,014,500; giving activities include $1,014,500 for 92 grants (high: $50,000; low: $1,000).
Purpose and activities: Giving primarily for health associations, social services, and children and youth services, including children's health organizations; funding also for education, and Jewish and Roman Catholic organizations.
Fields of interest: Museums; Arts; Education; Hospitals (general); Health organizations; Human services; Children, services; Family services; Roman Catholic agencies & churches; Jewish agencies & temples.
Limitations: Giving primarily in IL.
Application information:
Initial approach: Letter
Deadline(s): None
Officers: Lyle Olson, Pres. and Treas.; Lloyd S. Kupferberg, V.P. and Secy.; Rosemary Morris, V.P.
EIN: 363137745

2928

The Oppenheimer Family Foundation ◇

1501 N. State Pkwy., Ste. 11B
Chicago, IL 60610
Application address: c/o E.H. Oppenheimer, P.O. Box 14471, Chicago, IL 60614; FAX: (312) 943-9472

Incorporated in 1953 in IL.
Donors: Seymour Oppenheimer†; Edward H. Oppenheimer; James K. Oppenheimer; Harry D. Oppenheimer.
Foundation type: Independent foundation.
Financial data (yr. ended 12/31/04): Assets, $6,257,302 (M); gifts received, $25,773; expenditures, $609,916; qualifying distributions, $557,105; giving activities include $557,105 for 97 grants (high: $112,650; low: $400).
Fields of interest: Media/communications; Performing arts; Arts; Education; Human services; Children/youth, services; Federated giving programs; Jewish federated giving programs.
Limitations: Giving primarily in Chicago, IL.

Application information: Application form not required.

Initial approach: Letter
Copies of proposal: 1
Deadline(s): None

Officers and Directors:* Edward H. Oppenheimer,* Pres.; Harry J. Oppenheimer,* V.P.; James Oppenheimer,* V.P.; William J. Garmisa,* Secy.

EIN: 366054015

2929
The Owens Foundation

(formerly Thomas M. & Mary M. Owens Foundation)
7804 College Dr., Ste. 3SW
Palos Heights, IL   60463   (708) 361-8845
Contact: Mary M. Owens, Pres.

Established in 1985 in IL.
Donor: Thomas M. Owens.
Foundation type: Independent foundation.
Financial data (yr. ended 12/31/05): Assets, $23,784,396 (M); expenditures, $1,369,664; qualifying distributions, $1,248,156; giving activities include $1,110,697 for 78 grants (high: $19,209; low: $200), and $21,017 for foundation-administered programs.
Purpose and activities: Giving primarily in three areas: 1) programs that work with the homeless, the poor, and other disadvantaged populations, particularly those programs that deal with self-sufficiency through self-help, and programs that provide basic support, food, shelter and clothing, along with job training and employment, are given high priority; 2) homeless prevention - emergency funds administered independently by each agency for rents, most payments, utilities, and food, etc.; 3) private education, primarily secondary education for use for scholarships for poor and deserving students.
Fields of interest: Secondary school/education; Housing/shelter, development; Human services; Economically disadvantaged; Homeless.
Type of support: Emergency funds; General/operating support; Scholarship funds.
Limitations: Giving primarily in Chicago, IL. No grants to individuals directly, or for capital campaigns, building funds, or raffles.
Publications: Application guidelines; Program policy statement.
Application information: Application form required.

Initial approach: Letter or telephone requesting application guidelines
Copies of proposal: 1
Deadline(s): None
Board meeting date(s): Quarterly

Officers and Directors:* Mary M. Owens,* Pres. and Secy.; Thomas M. Owens,* V.P. and Treas.; Sharon M. McManaman; Julie Owens Mineman; Katie M. Mulcahy; Michael Owens; Thomas M. Owens, Jr.
Number of staff: 1 part-time professional; 1 part-time support.
EIN: 363429160
Selected grants: The following grants were reported in 2004.
$352,500 to CARA Program, Chicago, IL.
$41,000 to Old Saint Patricks Church, Chicago, IL.
$15,000 to Marist High School, Chicago, IL.
$15,000 to Missionaries of Charity, Chicago, IL.
$7,500 to Josephinum High School, Chicago, IL.
$7,500 to Mercy Home for Boys and Girls, Chicago, IL.
$5,000 to Boys Hope Girls Hope of Illinois, Wilmette, IL.

$5,000 to Family Rescue, Chicago, IL.
$5,000 to Franciscan Outreach Association, Chicago, IL.
$5,000 to HighSight, Chicago, IL.

2930
The Ozinga Foundation, Inc. ◇

15959 S. 108th Ave.
Orland Park, IL   60467   (708) 364-8201

Established in 1995 in IL.
Donors: Martin Ozinga III; Richard K. Ozinga; James A. Ozinga; Ozinga Bros., Inc.; Martin Ozinga, Jr.; American Service and Product Inc.; Beverly Ozinga.
Foundation type: Independent foundation.
Financial data (yr. ended 12/31/05): Assets, $1,491,739 (M); gifts received, $20,000; expenditures, $842,607; qualifying distributions, $842,607; giving activities include $832,871 for 65 grants (high: $130,000; low: $250).
Purpose and activities: Giving primarily for Christian agencies and churches and for Christian education.
Fields of interest: Education; Human services; Christian agencies & churches.
Limitations: Applications not accepted. Giving primarily in IL; some giving nationally. No grants to individuals.
Application information: Contributes only to pre-selected organizations.
Officers: Martin Ozinga III, Pres.; Richard K. Ozinga, Secy.; James A. Ozinga, Treas.
EIN: 364039338
Selected grants: The following grants were reported in 2004.
$410,000 to Trinity Christian College, Palos Heights, IL.
$103,000 to Bible League, Chicago, IL.
$100,000 to Calvin College, Grand Rapids, MI.
$90,000 to Chicago West Side Christian School, Chicago, IL.
$50,000 to Luke Society, Sioux Falls, SD.
$36,500 to Restoration Ministries, Harvey, IL.
$27,000 to Elim Christian Services, Palos Heights, IL.
$4,700 to Crisis Center for South Suburbia, Tinley Park, IL.
$3,500 to Family of Faith Church, Monee, IL.
$1,200 to Campus Crusade for Christ, Mission Viejo, CA.

2931
Dorothy C. and Richard A. Parks Foundation ◇

2321 Plainfield Rd.
Crest Hill, IL   60435

Established in 2001 in IL.
Donor: Dorothy C. Parks.
Foundation type: Independent foundation.
Financial data (yr. ended 12/31/05): Assets, $1,812,304 (M); expenditures, $560,891; qualifying distributions, $548,500; giving activities include $548,500 for 3 grants (high: $500,000; low: $20,000).
Purpose and activities: Giving primarily to a United Methodist church.
Fields of interest: Elementary/secondary education; Protestant agencies & churches.
Limitations: Applications not accepted. Giving primarily in IL. No grants to individuals.

Application information: Contributes only to pre-selected organizations.
Officers and Directors:* Donald L. Cordano,* Pres. and Treas.; Scott E. Nemanich,* V.P.; Gregory D. Severson,* Secy.
EIN: 364476024

2932
The John C. & Carolyn Noonan Parmer Private Foundation ◇

9 Woodley Rd.
Winnetka, IL   60093

Established in 1997 in IL.
Foundation type: Independent foundation.
Financial data (yr. ended 12/31/05): Assets, $20,404,423 (M); gifts received, $5,386,892; expenditures, $798,122; qualifying distributions, $695,015; giving activities include $695,000 for 40 grants (high: $200,500; low: $500).
Purpose and activities: Giving primarily for education, including a Roman Catholic seminary, health and human services, and to Roman Catholic agencies and churches.
Fields of interest: Theological school/education; Education; Health care; Human services; Roman Catholic agencies & churches.
Limitations: Applications not accepted. Giving primarily in IL; some funding nationally. No grants to individuals.
Application information: Contributes only to pre-selected organizations.
Trustees: Carolyn L. Parmer Larochelle; Carolyn Noonan Parmer; James W. Parmer; John F. Parmer; Raymond C. Parmer; Phyllis M. Parmer Plummer.
EIN: 364153563
Selected grants: The following grants were reported in 2003.
$150,000 to De La Salle Institute, Chicago, IL. For unrestricted support.
$102,500 to Link Unlimited, Chicago, IL. For unrestricted support.
$76,500 to Dominican University, River Forest, IL. For unrestricted support.
$52,000 to Catholic Theological Union at Chicago, Chicago, IL. For unrestricted support.
$52,000 to Saint Marys University of Minnesota, Winona, MN. For unrestricted support.
$50,000 to Misericordia Home, Chicago, IL. For unrestricted support.
$25,000 to Sinsinawa Dominicans, Sinsinawa, WI. For unrestricted support.
$15,000 to Saint Francis Hospital, Evanston, IL. For unrestricted support.
$12,500 to Deborahs Place, Chicago, IL. For unrestricted support.
$8,000 to Lamar Consolidated Independent School District, Rosenberg, TX. For unrestricted support.

2933
Pasquinelli Family Foundation ◇

6880 N. Frontage Rd., Ste. 100
Burr Ridge, IL   60527   (630) 455-5400
Contact: Bruno A. Pasquinelli, Dir.

Established in 1997 in IL.
Donors: Anthony R. Pasquinelli; Bruno A. Pasquinelli; Portrait Homes-North Carolina, LLC.
Foundation type: Independent foundation.
Financial data (yr. ended 12/31/04): Assets, $6,109,744 (M); gifts received, $1,201,049;

expenditures, $396,899; qualifying distributions, $396,899; giving activities include $378,038 for 46 grants (high: $129,000; low: $100).

Purpose and activities: Giving for children's services, higher and primary education, housing services, the arts, and for the disabled.

Fields of interest: Performing arts; Performing arts, orchestra (symphony); Secondary school/education; Education; Housing/shelter; Children, services.

Limitations: Giving primarily in IL.

Application information:

Initial approach: Letter

Deadline(s): May 1 and Nov. 1

Directors: Anthony R. Pasquinelli; Bruno A. Pasquinelli.

EIN: 364157643

Selected grants: The following grants were reported in 2004.

$33,222 to International School of Indiana, Indianapolis, IN.

$29,431 to University of Illinois Foundation, Urbana, IL.

$10,000 to Chicago Symphony Orchestra, Chicago, IL.

$10,000 to Lyric Opera of Chicago, Chicago, IL.

$5,000 to Dallas Symphony Orchestra, Dallas, TX.

$5,000 to Dore Academy, Charlotte, NC.

$2,500 to Glenwood School for Boys, Glenwood, IL.

$250 to Holocaust Documentation and Education Center, North Miami, FL.

2934

Frank E. Payne and Seba B. Payne Foundation ▼ ✧

c/o Bank of America, N.A.
231 S. LaSalle St.
Chicago, IL 60697 (312) 828-1785
Contact: M. Catherine Ryan, Sr. V.P., Bank of America, N.A.

Trust established in 1962 in IL.

Donor: Seba B. Payne†.

Foundation type: Independent foundation.

Financial data (yr. ended 6/30/05): Assets, $125,317,239 (M); expenditures, $6,705,654; qualifying distributions, $6,130,895; giving activities include $6,071,459 for 67 grants (high: $1,100,000; low: $5,000; average: $10,000–$50,000).

Purpose and activities: Support for education, hospitals, and cultural and religious programs; support also for the prevention of cruelty to children or animals.

Fields of interest: Arts; Education; Animal welfare; Hospitals (general); AIDS; AIDS research; Children/youth, services.

Type of support: General/operating support; Building/renovation; Equipment.

Limitations: Giving primarily in Bethlehem, PA. No grants to individuals, or for fellowships; generally no support for endowments; no loans.

Publications: Application guidelines.

Application information: Application form required.

Initial approach: Proposal

Copies of proposal: 1

Deadline(s): Mar. 15 and Oct. 15

Board meeting date(s): May and Nov., and as required

Final notification: 4 months

Trustees: Susan Hurd Cummings; Priscilla Payne Hurd; Bank of America, N.A.

EIN: 237435471

Selected grants: The following grants were reported in 2005.

$1,100,000 to Moravian College, Bethlehem, PA.

$1,000,000 to National Museum of Industrial History, Bethlehem, PA.

$1,000,000 to Saint Lukes Hospital of Bethlehem, Bethlehem, PA.

$250,000 to Allentown Art Museum, Allentown, PA.

$150,000 to Lehigh Valley Child Care, Allentown, PA.

$148,365 to Bethlehem Area Public Library, Bethlehem, PA.

$145,000 to Riegelsville-Palisades Emergency Medical Services, Riegelsville, PA.

$40,000 to Casa Guadalupe Center, Allentown, PA.

$30,000 to Holy Infancy School, Bethlehem, PA.

$25,000 to W T T W Channel 11, Chicago, IL.

2935

PDB Foundation, Inc. ✧ ☆

306 N. Main St., Ste. 3
Bloomington, IL 61701 (309) 829-3311

Established in 1993 in IL.

Donors: Paul D. Brown; American Builders Financial Corp.

Foundation type: Independent foundation.

Financial data (yr. ended 12/31/05): Assets, $498,027 (M); gifts received, $270; expenditures, $572,814; qualifying distributions, $571,781; giving activities include $500,000 for 1 grant, and $71,832 for foundation-administered programs.

Fields of interest: Christian agencies & churches.

Limitations: Applications not accepted. Giving primarily in Orlando, FL. No grants to individuals.

Application information: Contributes only to pre-selected organizations.

Officers and Directors: * Estelle Brown,* Pres.; Paul D. Brown,* Secy.-Treas.

EIN: 371309421

2936

Pepper Family Foundation ✧

c/o Richard S. Pepper
643 N. Orleans St.
Chicago, IL 60610

Established in 1987 in IL.

Donors: Richard S. Pepper; Roxelyn M. Pepper; The Pepper Cos., Inc.; Richard S. Pepper Trust.

Foundation type: Independent foundation.

Financial data (yr. ended 12/31/03): Assets, $3,015,483 (M); gifts received, $770,000; expenditures, $869,371; qualifying distributions, $869,371; giving activities include $866,808 for 32 grants (high: $250,000; low: $1,000).

Purpose and activities: Giving primarily for higher education and health care.

Fields of interest: Arts; Elementary/secondary education; Higher education; Engineering school/education; Hospitals (general); Roman Catholic agencies & churches.

Type of support: General/operating support; Scholarship funds.

Limitations: Applications not accepted. Giving primarily in IL. No grants to individuals.

Application information: Contributes only to pre-selected organizations.

Officers and Directors: * Richard S. Pepper,* Pres. and Treas.; Roxelyn M. Pepper,* V.P.; Thomas M. O'Leary, Secy.; Lynda Bollman; J. David Pepper; J. Stanley Pepper.

EIN: 363540747

Selected grants: The following grants were reported in 2005.

$50,000 to Lawrence Hall Youth Services, Chicago, IL.

$50,000 to Swedish Covenant Hospital, Chicago, IL.

$35,000 to Art Institute of Chicago, Chicago, IL.

$30,000 to Hospice Foundation of Northeastern Illinois, Barrington, IL.

$25,000 to Chicago Botanic Garden, Glencoe, IL.

$25,000 to Max McGraw Wildlife Foundation, Dundee, IL.

$25,000 to United Cerebral Palsy Association of Greater Chicago, Chicago, IL.

$20,000 to Central DuPage Hospital Association, Winfield, IL.

$20,000 to Elgin Academy, Elgin, IL.

$18,000 to Associated Colleges of Illinois, Chicago, IL.

2937

PepsiAmericas Foundation ✧

(formerly Whitman Corporation Foundation)
3501 Algonquin Rd.
Rolling Meadows, IL 60008-3103
Contact: Charles H. Connolly, Pres.

Established in 1988 in IL.

Donors: Whitman Corp.; PepsiAmericas, Inc.

Foundation type: Company-sponsored foundation.

Financial data (yr. ended 12/31/03): Assets, $1,421,310 (M); expenditures, $427,521; qualifying distributions, $427,493; giving activities include $427,493 for 175 grants (high: $111,000; low: $50).

Purpose and activities: The foundation supports organizations involved with arts and culture, education, and human services.

Fields of interest: Arts; Education; Human services.

Type of support: General/operating support; Continuing support; Annual campaigns; Employee matching gifts; Matching/challenge support.

Limitations: Giving primarily in Chicago, IL.

Application information: Telephone calls during the application process are not encouraged. Application form not required.

Initial approach: Proposal

Copies of proposal: 1

Deadline(s): None

Officers and Directors: * Randy Downing, Pres.; Timothy W. Gorman, V.P.; Brian D. Wenger,* Secy.; G. Michael Durkin,* Treas.; John F. Bierbaum; Robert C. Pohlad.

EIN: 363610784

2938

Harold L. Perlman Family Foundation ✧ ☆

(formerly Harold L. Perlman Foundation)
10 S. LaSalle St., Ste. 3450
Chicago, IL 60603
Contact: Jane Perlman, Pres.

Established in 1964 in IL.

Donors: Harold L. Perlman; Jane Perlman; Continental Sales & Enterprises, Inc.; Virgo Ventures, Inc.

Foundation type: Independent foundation.
Financial data (yr. ended 3/31/05): Assets, $2,658,897 (M); gifts received, $350,000; expenditures, $468,859; qualifying distributions, $394,515; giving activities include $394,515 for 20 grants (high: $300,000; low: $500).
Purpose and activities: Giving primarily for Jewish federated giving programs, human services, and education.
Fields of interest: Higher education; Education; Human services; Jewish federated giving programs.
Type of support: General/operating support.
Limitations: Giving primarily in Chicago, IL. No grants to individuals.
Application information:
  Initial approach: Letter
  Deadline(s): None
Officers: Jane Perlman, Pres.; Sherwyn L. Ehrlich, Secy.; Daniel L. Rosenberg, Treas.
Directors: Karen Ami; Mark Feinberg; David Rosenberg; Michael Rosenberg; Marjorie P. Shafton.
EIN: 362555314
Selected grants: The following grants were reported in 2005.
$5,000 to Florida Memorial University, Miami, FL.
$4,000 to Childrens Heart Foundation, Chicago, IL.
$3,000 to Council for Jewish Elderly, Chicago, IL.
$2,000 to Holocaust Memorial Foundation of Illinois, Skokie, IL.
$1,500 to Chicago Botanic Garden, Glencoe, IL.
$1,000 to PAWS Chicago, Chicago, IL.
$500 to Chicago Artists Coalition, Chicago, IL.

2939
Richard A. Perritt Charitable Foundation ✧
P.O. Box 433
Barrington, IL 60011-0433

Established in 1993 in IL.
Donor: Richard A. Perritt Char. Trust.
Foundation type: Independent foundation.
Financial data (yr. ended 12/31/05): Assets, $3,089,215 (M); gifts received, $673,268; expenditures, $913,368; qualifying distributions, $888,913; giving activities include $850,945 for 24 grants (high: $175,000; low: $1,000).
Purpose and activities: Giving primarily for health associations, with an emphasis on cancer research, and services for people who are visually impaired; funding also for children, youth and social services.
Fields of interest: Higher education; Medical school/education; Animals/wildlife, management/technical aid; Hospitals (general); Health care; Cancer research; Human services; Children/youth, services; Roman Catholic agencies & churches.
Limitations: Applications not accepted. Giving primarily in IL. No grants to individuals.
Application information: Contributes only to pre-selected organizations.
Officers and Directors:* Ronald A. Tyrpin,* Pres.; Diane A. Tyrpin,* V.P. and Secy.-Treas.; John C. Tyrpin,* V.P.; Mark A. Tyrpin,* V.P.
EIN: 363896125

2940
The Herman & Katherine Peters Foundation Corp. ✧ ☆
67 E. Madison St., Ste. 1515
Chicago, IL 60603-3014 (312) 782-4415
Contact: Scot A. Leonard, Pres.

Established in 1998 in IL.
Donors: Katherine Peters†; Katherine Peters Trust.
Foundation type: Independent foundation.
Financial data (yr. ended 12/31/05): Assets, $10,524,590 (M); gifts received, $615,321; expenditures, $514,595; qualifying distributions, $420,200; giving activities include $420,200 for grants.
Purpose and activities: Scholarship awards to financially needy students pursuing studies relating to environmental concerns or Christian-based religious instruction. Some giving for educational field trips for underprivileged children to heighten their awareness about the importance of conservation.
Fields of interest: Higher education; Environmental education; Christian agencies & churches.
Type of support: Scholarships—to individuals.
Limitations: Giving primarily in AZ, CO, IL, MI, and WI.
Application information: Application form required.
  Deadline(s): None
Officers and Directors:* Scot A. Leonard,* Pres.; James P. Devine, Jr.,* V.P.; Jeanine Holtsford,* Secy.-Treas.; George Carroll; Inge Dominis.
EIN: 364180010

2941
Esper A. Petersen Foundation ✧
3535 Washington St.
Gurnee, IL 60031

Incorporated in 1944 in IL.
Donor: Esper A. Petersen†.
Foundation type: Independent foundation.
Financial data (yr. ended 12/31/04): Assets, $9,012,382 (M); expenditures, $705,790; qualifying distributions, $355,018; giving activities include $355,018 for 32 grants (high: $77,680; low: $500).
Fields of interest: Arts; Education; Hospitals (general); Health care; Human services; Children/youth, services; Family services; Community development; Economically disadvantaged.
Type of support: General/operating support; Building/renovation; Research.
Limitations: Giving primarily in CA and IL. No grants to individuals.
Publications: Application guidelines.
Application information: Application form not required.
  Initial approach: Letter
  Deadline(s): None
  Board meeting date(s): July and Dec.
  Final notification: Dec. 31
Officers and Directors:* Esper A. Petersen,* Pres.; Ann Petersen,* V.P.; Steven Malato,* Secy.
EIN: 366125570

2942
Alan & Mildred Peterson Charitable Foundation ✧
150 S. Wacker Dr., Ste. 500
Chicago, IL 60606 (312) 849-9900
Contact: Alan E. Peterson, Dir.

Established in 1984.
Donors: Alan Peterson; Mildred Peterson.
Foundation type: Independent foundation.
Financial data (yr. ended 12/31/04): Assets, $1,376,796 (M); gifts received, $1,512,620;

expenditures, $351,792; qualifying distributions, $347,465; giving activities include $275,910 for 51 grants (high: $150,000; low: $25), and $60,000 for 17 grants to individuals (high: $4,000; low: $3,000).
Purpose and activities: Provides scholarships to students and grants to not-for-profit educational and community organizations.
Fields of interest: Higher education; Education.
Type of support: General/operating support; Scholarship funds; Scholarships—to individuals.
Limitations: Giving on a national basis.
Application information: Application form required for scholarship program. Scholarship payments paid directly to the educational institution on behalf of the individual recipients. Application form required.
  Deadline(s): None
Directors: Julie K. Knudson; Alan E. Peterson; Mildred A. Peterson.
EIN: 363355444
Selected grants: The following grants were reported in 2003.
$95,000 to Georgia Tech Foundation, Atlanta, GA. For AMP Tech Transfer Initiative.
$20,000 to College of William and Mary, Williamsburg, VA.
$10,000 to Central DuPage Hospital Association, Winfield, IL.
$10,000 to Metropolitan Family Services, Chicago, IL.
$200 to Big Shoulders Fund, Chicago, IL.
$100 to Gateway Foundation, Chicago, IL.
$100 to Museum of Science and Industry, Chicago, IL.
$100 to Smithsonian Institution, DC.
$100 to Urban Gateways: The Center for Arts in Education, Chicago, IL.
$50 to Hadley School for the Blind, Winnetka, IL.

2943
The Albert Pick, Jr. Fund ✧
30 N. Michigan Ave., Ste. 1002
Chicago, IL 60602 (312) 236-1192
Contact: Cleopatra B. Alexander, Exec. Dir.
E-mail: cleopatra@albertpickjrfund.org; URL: http://www.albertpickjrfund.org

Incorporated in 1947 in IL.
Donors: Albert Pick, Jr.†; Harris Associates.
Foundation type: Independent foundation.
Financial data (yr. ended 12/31/04): Assets, $21,179,547 (M); gifts received, $220,775; expenditures, $1,825,086; qualifying distributions, $1,616,598; giving activities include $1,474,998 for 94 grants (high: $100,000; low: $3,000).
Purpose and activities: Support within four major program categories: 1) Civic and community, including programs which enhance the environment, address the needs of minorities and the physically disabled, and/or promote good government and human relations; 2) Cultural organizations, especially projects which seek to expand audience access or educate new audiences through outreach activities; 3) Educational improvement and reform at the precollegiate level, especially early childhood education, tutoring, at-risk intervention, and in-job training and re-training; and 4) Health and human services, including wellness programs, community-based health care delivery, youth, family planning, or geriatric services, mental health, physical rehabilitation and shelter care services.
Fields of interest: Arts; Education; Health care; Human services; Community development.

Type of support: General/operating support; Continuing support; Program development; Technical assistance.

Limitations: Giving limited to Chicago, IL. No support for political or religious purposes, hospitals or local chapters of single-disease agencies, umbrella organizations, fraternal, veterans', labor, or athletic organizations, or local chapters of state, regional, or national organizations, professional groups with volunteer service programs, or for individual elementary or secondary schools. No grants to individuals, or for building or endowment funds, capital campaigns, deficit financing, long-term projects, travel, sponsorship, advertising, scholarships, or fundraising.

Publications: Application guidelines.

Application information: The fund will not review incomplete or late applications. Application guidelines available on fund's Web site. Application form required.

> *Initial approach:* Letter requesting guidelines
> *Copies of proposal:* 1
> *Deadline(s):* Jan. 21, Apr. 1, July 1, and Oct. 1
> *Board meeting date(s):* Mar., June, Sept., and Dec. Cultural proposals considered only at Sept. meeting; other categories considered at all meetings
> *Final notification:* Within 3 weeks of board meetings

Officers and Directors:* Robert B. Lifton,* Pres.; Burton B. Kaplan,* V.P. and Treas.; Albert Pick III,* V.P.; Gregory M. Darnieder,* Secy.; Cleopatra B. Alexander, Exec. Dir.; Janet Diederichs; Carolyn W. Meza; Gwendolyn M. Rice; David H. Voss.

Number of staff: 1 full-time professional.

EIN: 366071402

Selected grants: The following grants were reported in 2005.

$75,000 to Merit School of Music, Chicago, IL.
$35,000 to Chicago Childrens Museum, Chicago, IL.
$25,000 to Neighborhood Housing Services of Chicago, Chicago, IL.
$25,000 to Rochelle Lee Fund, Chicago, IL.
$20,000 to Good News Partners, Chicago, IL.
$20,000 to Teen Living Programs, Chicago, IL.
$15,000 to Communities in Schools, Alexandria, VA.
$15,000 to New Moms, Chicago, IL.
$10,000 to Erie Neighborhood House, Chicago, IL.
$10,000 to Lawyers for the Creative Arts, Chicago, IL.

2944
A. Franklin Pilchard Foundation ✧
508 N. Plum Grove Rd.
Palatine, IL 60067
Contact: Robert C. Pacilio, Treas.

Established in 1990 in IL.

Donor: A. Franklin Pilchard.

Foundation type: Independent foundation.

Financial data (yr. ended 6/30/05): Assets, $20,925,215 (M); expenditures, $1,098,387; qualifying distributions, $985,745; giving activities include $922,225 for 138 grants to individuals (high: $15,407; low: $325).

Purpose and activities: Scholarships awarded only to students who attend participating educational institutions in IL.

Fields of interest: Education.

Type of support: Scholarship funds.

Limitations: Giving limited to residents of IL.

Application information: Applications accepted only from those graduating from one of the high schools participating in the scholarship program in IL. Application form required.

> *Initial approach:* Request application form
> *Deadline(s):* Oct. 31

Officers and Directors:* Kevin J. Ryan,* Pres.; Donald R. Pawelski,* Secy.; Robert C. Pacilio,* Treas.

EIN: 363723290

2945
Ploughshares Foundation
108 W. Grand Ave.
Chicago, IL 60610 (312) 321-9700
Contact: Donald M. Ephraim, Pres.

Established in 1990 in IL.

Foundation type: Independent foundation.

Financial data (yr. ended 12/31/05): Assets, $33,593,085 (M); expenditures, $2,109,324; qualifying distributions, $1,947,000; giving activities include $1,947,000 for 99 grants (high: $202,000; low: $1,000).

Fields of interest: Environment; AIDS; Human services; Civil rights, race/intergroup relations; Homeless.

Type of support: General/operating support.

Limitations: Giving on a national basis. No grants to individuals.

Application information: Application form not required.

> *Initial approach:* Letter
> *Deadline(s):* None

Officer and Directors:* Donald M. Ephraim,* Pres.; Joseph F. Coyne; Eliot S. Ephraim.

EIN: 363739577

2946
Polk Bros. Foundation, Inc. ▼ ✧
20 W. Kinzie St., Ste. 1110
Chicago, IL 60610-4600 (312) 527-4684
Contact: Nikki W. Stein, Exec. Dir.; Suzanne Doornbos Kerbow, Assoc. Dir.
FAX: (312) 527-4681; E-mail: info@polkbrosfdn.org; URL: http://www.polkbrosfdn.org/

Incorporated in 1957 in IL.

Donors: David D. Polk‡; Harry Polk‡; Morris G. Polk‡; Samuel H. Polk‡; Sol Polk‡; and members of the Polk family; Rand Realty and Development Co.; Polk Bros., Inc.

Foundation type: Independent foundation.

Financial data (yr. ended 8/31/05): Assets, $387,169,673 (M); expenditures, $19,845,789; qualifying distributions, $16,938,367; giving activities include $14,631,250 for 501 grants (high: $250,000; low: $200; average: $15,000–$75,000), and $849,035 for 329 employee matching gifts.

Purpose and activities: Grants primarily for new or ongoing programs to organizations whose work is in the area of social service, education, arts and culture, and health care. Main emphasis is support for organizations in Chicago that serve needy populations in underserved communities.

Fields of interest: Museums; Performing arts; Performing arts, theater; Arts; Education, early childhood education; Child development, education; Vocational education; Higher education; Adult/continuing education; Adult education—literacy,

basic skills & GED; Education, reading; Education; Health care; Mental health/crisis services; Health organizations, association; AIDS; Crime/violence prevention, domestic violence; Legal services; Employment; Youth development, services; Human services; Children/youth, services; Child development, services; Family services; Women, centers/services; Minorities/immigrants, centers/services; Homeless, human services; Civil rights, race/intergroup relations; Urban/community development; Community development; Jewish federated giving programs; Leadership development; Jewish agencies & temples; Disabilities, people with; Minorities; Women; Economically disadvantaged; Homeless.

Type of support: General/operating support; Continuing support; Equipment; Program development; Curriculum development; Scholarship funds; Technical assistance; Program evaluation; Employee matching gifts.

Limitations: Giving primarily in Chicago, IL. No support for political organizations or religious institutions seeking support for programs whose participants are restricted by religious affiliation, or for tax-generating entities (municipalities and school districts) for services within their normal responsibilities. No grants to individuals, or for medical, scientific or academic research, or purchase of dinner or raffle tickets.

Publications: Annual report (including application guidelines).

Application information: An organization that has not previously received a grant from the foundation should first call or complete the pre-application form available on the foundation's Web site. Proposals for health-related services are reviewed at the spring and fall board meetings only. Application form required.

> *Initial approach:* Letter
> *Copies of proposal:* 1
> *Deadline(s):* None
> *Board meeting date(s):* Feb., May, Aug., and Nov.
> *Final notification:* 3 - 4 months

Officers and Directors:* Sandra P. Guthman,* C.E.O. and Pres.; J. Ira Harris,* V.P.; Raymond F. Simon,* V.P.; Gordon S. Prussian,* Secy.; Theodore S. Weymouth, C.F.O.; Sidney Epstein,* Treas.; Nikki Will Stein, Exec. Dir.; Bruce R. Bachmann; Howard J. Polk.

Number of staff: 8 full-time professional; 1 part-time professional; 2 full-time support.

EIN: 366108293

Selected grants: The following grants were reported in 2005.

$250,000 to New Schools for Chicago, Chicago, IL.
$150,000 to W T T W Channel 11, Chicago, IL.
$100,000 to Council for Jewish Elderly, Chicago, IL.
$80,000 to Mercy Housing Lakefront, Chicago, IL.
$75,000 to Local Initiatives Support Corporation (LISC), Chicago, IL.
$75,000 to Rehabilitation Institute of Chicago, Chicago, IL.
$40,000 to Golden Apple Foundation, Chicago, IL.
$35,000 to Chicago Health Corps, Chicago, IL.
$30,000 to Howard Area Community Center, Chicago, IL.
$25,000 to Hyde Park Art Center, Chicago, IL.

2947
Abra Prentice Foundation, Inc. ✧
c/o Harris Bank, N.A.
111 W. Monroe St., No. 6W
Chicago, IL 60603 (312) 461-7551
Contact: Ted Plis

Established in 1980 in IL.
Donor: Abra Prentice Wilkin.
Foundation type: Independent foundation.
Financial data (yr. ended 12/31/05): Assets, $16,728,145 (M); gifts received, $1,799,300; expenditures, $727,152; qualifying distributions, $611,622; giving activities include $600,000 for 5 grants (high: $250,000; low: $10,000).
Purpose and activities: Giving primarily for educational institutions.
Fields of interest: Secondary school/education; Education; Hospitals (general).
Type of support: General/operating support; Building/renovation.
Limitations: Giving primarily in Simsbury, CT, and Chicago, IL. No grants to individuals.
Application information: Application form not required.
Deadline(s): None
Officers: Abra Prentice Wilkin, Pres.; Don H. Reuben, Secy.
Director: Robert F. Carr III.
EIN: 363092281

2948
Prince Charitable Trusts ▼ ✧
303 W. Madison St., Ste. 1900
Chicago, IL 60606 (312) 419-8700
Contact: Benna Wilde, Managing Dir.; For RI Proposals: Sharon Robison, Grants Mgr.
FAX: (312) 419-8558;
E-mail: srobison@prince-trusts.org; Additional address: Prince Charitable Trusts, 816 Connecticut Ave. N.W., Washington, DC 20006, Tel.: (202) 728-0646, FAX: (202) 466-4726, E-mail: info@princetrusts.org (DC office); URL: http://www.foundationcenter.org/grantmaker/prince/

Frederick Henry Prince Trust dated July 9, 1947 established in 1947 in IL. Frederick Henry Prince Testamentary Trust established in 1947 in RI. Abbie Norman Prince Trust established in 1949 in IL.
Donor: Frederick Henry Prince†.
Foundation type: Independent foundation.
Financial data (yr. ended 12/31/04): Assets, $182,251,458 (M); expenditures, $8,917,193; qualifying distributions, $8,977,406; giving activities include $7,726,113 for 408 grants (high: $250,000; low: $100; average: $2,000–$25,000), and $250,000 for 1 loan/program-related investment.
Purpose and activities: Support for cultural programs, public school programming, youth organizations, social services, hospitals, hospital morale, rehabilitation, and environment.
Fields of interest: Arts; Education, early childhood education; Elementary school/education; Secondary school/education; Education; Environment, natural resources; Environment; Hospitals (general); Reproductive health, family planning; Medical care, rehabilitation; Health care; Human services; Children/youth, services; Youth, pregnancy prevention; Family services; Minorities; Economically disadvantaged; Homeless.
Type of support: General/operating support; Continuing support; Capital campaigns; Program

development; Seed money; Technical assistance; Program-related investments/loans; Employee matching gifts.
Limitations: Giving limited to local groups in Washington, DC, Chicago, IL, and RI, with emphasis on Aquidneck Island. No support for national organizations. No grants to individuals.
Publications: Application guidelines.
Application information: The DC office has its own application guidelines. All applications must include a cover sheet which can be found at the trust's Web site or by contacting the Grants Mgr. Rhode Island applications will not be accepted via fax or e-mail. Application form not required.
Initial approach: Letter and proposal (3 to 5 pages for proposal). Check foundation Web site for application guidelines
Copies of proposal: 1
Deadline(s): Chicago: Jan. 13 for Education, and Social Svcs., May 1 for Health, June 1 for Arts/Culture, Environment and Capital; Rhode Island: June 1; Washington, DC: Feb. 1 for Arts/Culture and Smart Growth, Sept. 1 for Health, Social Svcs., Youth or Environment
Board meeting date(s): Chicago: spring and fall; Rhode Island: summer; Washington, DC: late spring and late fall
Final notification: Within 5 months of proposal deadline
Trustees: Frederick Henry Prince IV; William Norman Wood Prince.
Number of staff: 3 full-time professional; 2 part-time professional; 1 full-time support; 1 part-time support.

2949
Prince Foundation ✧
c/o Trustees of Prince Charitable Trusts
303 W. Madison St., Ste. 1900
Chicago, IL 60606 (312) 419-8700

Incorporated in 1955 in IL.
Donors: F.H. Prince & Co., Inc.; John D. and Catherine T. MacArthur Foundation.
Foundation type: Company-sponsored foundation.
Financial data (yr. ended 12/31/04): Assets, $1,626,478 (M); gifts received, $750,000; expenditures, $859,654; qualifying distributions, $859,554; giving activities include $784,534 for 74 grants (high: $35,000; low: $100).
Purpose and activities: The foundation matches contributions made by employees of F.H. Prince & Company.
Type of support: Employee matching gifts.
Limitations: Applications not accepted. No grants to individuals.
Application information: Contributes only through employee matching gifts.
Officers and Trustees:* William Norman Wood Prince,* Pres.; Randall M. Highley,* V.P.; Frederick Henry Prince,* V.P.; Sarah A. Richardson, Secy.-Treas.
EIN: 366116507

2950
The Anthony Pritzker Family Foundation ✧
1603 Orrington Ave., Ste. 1600
Evanston, IL 60201

Established in 2002 in CA and IL.
Foundation type: Independent foundation.

Financial data (yr. ended 12/31/04): Assets, $46,196,776 (M); gifts received, $6,251; expenditures, $1,986,516; qualifying distributions, $1,635,736; giving activities include $1,631,733 for 67 grants (high: $500,000; low: $100).
Fields of interest: Health organizations, association; Human services; Jewish federated giving programs; Jewish agencies & temples.
Limitations: Applications not accepted. Giving primarily in CA. No grants to individuals.
Application information: Contributes only to pre-selected organizations.
Officers and Directors:* Anthony N. Pritzker,* Pres.; Judy Schroffel, Secy.; Allan Von Halle, Treas.; Jay Robert Pritzker; Jeanne Pritzker.
EIN: 300039840
Selected grants: The following grants were reported in 2004.
$363,148 to Wilshire Boulevard Temple, Los Angeles, CA. 2 grants: $6,005, $357,143
$250,000 to Brandeis-Bardin Institute, Brandeis, CA. 2 grants: $200,000, $50,000
$100,000 to Heal The Bay, Santa Monica, CA.
$62,500 to Center for Early Education, West Hollywood, CA.
$60,000 to Korean American Family Service Center, Los Angeles, CA. 2 grants: $10,000, $50,000
$40,000 to California Institute of the Arts, Valencia, CA.
$5,000 to Fulfillment Fund, Los Angeles, CA.

2951
Margot & Thomas Pritzker Family Foundation ✧
71 S. Wacker Dr., Ste. 4600
Chicago, IL 60606
Contact: Thomas J. Pritzker, Pres.

Foundation type: Independent foundation.
Financial data (yr. ended 10/31/05): Assets, $41,283,565 (M); gifts received, $362,267; expenditures, $1,784,095; qualifying distributions, $1,380,452; giving activities include $1,370,800 for 33 grants (high: $500,000; low: $100).
Fields of interest: Arts; Higher education, university; International affairs; Philanthropy/voluntarism.
Type of support: General/operating support.
Limitations: Applications not accepted. Giving on a national basis, with an emphasis on MA. No grants to individuals.
Application information: Contributes only to pre-selected organizations.
Board meeting date(s): Nov., and as necessary
Officers and Directors:* Thomas J. Pritzker,* Pres.; Thomas Dykstra,* V.P. and Treas.; Margot Pritzker,* V.P.; Marshall Eisenberg,* Secy.
EIN: 363852559
Selected grants: The following grants were reported in 2004.
$666,666 to Brandeis University, Waltham, MA.
$75,000 to Stanford University, Stanford, CA.
$50,000 to Center for Strategic and International Studies, DC.
$40,000 to Aspen Institute, Queenstown, MD.
$38,000 to University of California, Berkeley, CA.
$30,000 to Bernard Zell Anshe Emet Day School, Chicago, IL.
$11,000 to University of Chicago, Chicago, IL.
$1,000 to University of California at San Francisco Foundation, San Francisco, CA.

2952
Pritzker Foundation ▼ ✧

71 S. Wacker Dr., Ste. 4600
Chicago, IL 60606 (312) 577-2666
Contact: Glen Miller, V.P.

Incorporated in 1944 in IL.
Donors: Members of the Pritzker family; H. Group
Holding, Inc. and Subsidiaries; Marmon Holdings,
Inc. and Subsidiaries.
Foundation type: Independent foundation.
Financial data (yr. ended 12/31/04): Assets,
$334,092,615 (M); expenditures, $16,989,928;
qualifying distributions, $13,257,799; giving
activities include $13,198,383 for 78 grants (high:
$3,095,000; low: $200; average: $1,000–
$100,000).
Purpose and activities: Grants largely for higher
education, including medical education, and
religious welfare funds; giving also for hospitals,
temple support, and cultural programs.
Fields of interest: Arts; Higher education; Medical
school/education; Hospitals (general); Human
services; Religious federated giving programs;
Jewish agencies & temples.
Limitations: Applications not accepted. Giving on a
national basis, with some emphasis on Chicago, IL.
No grants to individuals.
Application information: Contributes only to
pre-selected organizations.
Board meeting date(s): Dec. and as required
Officers and Directors:* Robert A. Pritzker,* Pres.;
Mark Hoplamazian, V.P. and Secy.; Glen Miller, V.P.
and Treas.; Nicholas J. Pritzker,* V.P.; Penny S.
Pritzker,* V.P.; Thomas J. Pritzker,* V.P.
EIN: 366058062
Selected grants: The following grants were reported
in 2004.
$3,095,000 to University of Chicago, Chicago, IL.
For general operating support.
$3,005,000 to Stanford University, Stanford, CA.
For general operating support.
$1,012,500 to Art Institute of Chicago, Chicago, IL.
For general operating support.
$1,010,000 to Museum of Contemporary Art,
Chicago, IL. For general operating support.
$400,000 to Field Museum of Natural History,
Chicago, IL. For general operating support.
$300,000 to Chicago Childrens Museum, Chicago,
IL. For general operating support.
$200,000 to Childrens Memorial Hospital, Chicago,
IL. For general operating support and for Pediatric
Intensive Care.
$200,000 to Museum of Science and Industry,
Chicago, IL. For general operating support.
$200,000 to Rush-Presbyterian-Saint Lukes
Medical Center, Chicago, IL. For general
operating support.
$150,000 to Chicago Historical Society, Chicago, IL.
For general operating support.

2953
The Jay Pritzker Foundation ✧

c/o Eric Brandfonbrener
131 S. Dearborn St., Ste. 1700
Chicago, IL 60603

Established in 2002 in IL.
Foundation type: Independent foundation.
Financial data (yr. ended 12/31/03): Assets,
$31,483,956 (M); expenditures, $7,231,015;
qualifying distributions, $7,057,065; giving
activities include $7,057,065 for 27 grants (high:

$4,465,000; low: $1,000; average: $10,000–
$200,000).
Purpose and activities: Giving primarily for
education.
Fields of interest: Elementary school/education;
Higher education; Higher education, university;
Education.
Limitations: Applications not accepted. No grants to
individuals.
Application information: Contributes only to
pre-selected organizations.
Officers and Directors:* Daniel F. Pritzker,* Pres.;
Karen M. Pritzker,* Secy.; Leonard J. Loventhal,
Treas.; Diana E. Conway.
EIN: 020550210
Selected grants: The following grants were reported
in 2003.
$5,000,000 to Tufts University, Medford, MA. 2
grants: $4,465,000 (For general support),
$535,000 (For general support).
$995,000 to Providence Saint Mel School, Chicago,
IL. 4 grants: $200,000 (For general support),
$500,000 (For general support), $50,000 (For
general support), $245,000 (For general
support).
$661,425 to Ring Mountain Day School, Mill Valley,
CA. 4 grants: $95,000 (For general support),
$216,425 (For general support), $100,000 (For
general support), $250,000 (For general
support).

2954
The Pritzker Pucker Family Foundation ✧

(formerly The Vince Club Family Foundation)
c/o GiGi Pritzker Pucker
71 S. Wacker Dr., Ste. 4600
Chicago, IL 60606

Established in 2002 in IL.
Foundation type: Independent foundation.
Financial data (yr. ended 12/31/04): Assets,
$38,653,467 (M); gifts received, $3,543;
expenditures, $2,039,963; qualifying distributions,
$1,641,496; giving activities include $1,638,250
for 48 grants (high: $250,000; low: $1,000).
Fields of interest: Arts; Education; Jewish agencies
& temples.
Limitations: Applications not accepted. No grants to
individuals.
Application information: Contributes only to
pre-selected organizations.
Board meeting date(s): Annually
Officers and Directors:* GiGi Pritzker Pucker,*
Pres.; Marian F. Pritzker,* Secy.; Michael Pucker,*
Treas.
EIN: 300036022
Selected grants: The following grants were reported
in 2004.
$215,000 to Bernard Zell Anshe Emet Day School,
Chicago, IL.
$215,000 to Chicago Childrens Museum, Chicago,
IL.
$145,000 to Stanford University, Stanford, CA.
$75,000 to University of Illinois Foundation,
Chicago, IL.
$60,000 to Children Affected by AIDS Foundation,
Los Angeles, CA.
$52,500 to Victory Gardens Theater, Chicago, IL.
$50,000 to Commonwealth School, Boston, MA.
$50,000 to Southwest Organizing Project, Chicago,
IL.
$25,000 to Bethel New Life, Chicago, IL.

$25,000 to University of Wisconsin Foundation,
Madison, WI.

2955
The Pritzker Traubert Family Foundation ✧

(formerly The Bryan Traubert and Penny Pritzker
Charitable Foundation)
71 S. Wacker Dr., Ste. 4600
Chicago, IL 60606
Contact: Penny Pritzker, V.P.

Established in 2000 in IL.
Donors: Bryan Traubert; Penny Pritzker.
Foundation type: Independent foundation.
Financial data (yr. ended 12/31/04): Assets,
$39,257,932 (M); gifts received, $3,543;
expenditures, $2,109,091; qualifying distributions,
$1,677,538; giving activities include $1,663,350
for 66 grants (high: $625,000; low: $250).
Fields of interest: Education; Human services.
Limitations: Applications not accepted. No grants to
individuals.
Application information: Contributes only to
pre-selected organizations.
Board meeting date(s): Annually
Officers and Directors:* Bryan Traubert,* Pres.;
Penny Pritzker,* V.P.; Kevin Poorman,* Secy.-Treas.
EIN: 364347781
Selected grants: The following grants were reported
in 2004.
$625,000 to Citadel Foundation, Charleston, SC.
$215,000 to Stanford University, Stanford, CA.
$36,500 to University of Chicago, Chicago, IL.
$20,000 to Namaste Charter School, Chicago, IL.
$10,000 to Castilleja School, Palo Alto, CA.
$10,000 to Saint Chrysostoms Day School,
Chicago, IL.
$10,000 to University of Illinois Foundation, Urbana,
IL.
$5,000 to Perspectives Charter School, Chicago, IL.
$1,000 to High Jump, Chicago, IL.
$1,000 to Room to Read, San Francisco, CA.

2956
Progressive Education Foundation, Inc. ✧ ☆

c/o Northern Trust Bank Of Florida
P.O. Box 803878
Chicago, IL 60680

Established in 2005 in IL.
Donors: Robert C. Pew; Mary I. Pew.
Foundation type: Independent foundation.
Financial data (yr. ended 10/31/05): Assets,
$2,277,554 (M); gifts received, $2,814,469;
expenditures, $602,913; qualifying distributions,
$600,436; giving activities include $600,000 for 1
grant.
Purpose and activities: Giving primarily to a public
education fund trust.
Fields of interest: Education, public education.
Limitations: Applications not accepted. Giving
primarily in West Palm Beach, FL. No grants to
individuals.
Application information: Contributes only to
pre-selected organizations.
Directors: John E. Pew; Mary I. Pew; Robert C. Pew;
Robert C. Pew III; Kate Pew Wolters.
EIN: 300259919

2957
George M. Pullman Educational Foundation ✧

39 S. LaSalle St., Ste. 718
Chicago, IL 60603-1621 (312) 422-0444
FAX: (312) 422-0448; URL: http://
www.pullmanfoundation.org

Incorporated in 1949 in IL.
Donors: George Mortimer Pullman†; Harriet Sanger Pullman†.
Foundation type: Independent foundation.
Financial data (yr. ended 7/31/05): Assets, $26,955,435 (M); gifts received, $56,494; expenditures, $1,399,306; qualifying distributions, $1,291,156; giving activities include $806,909 for 100 grants (high: $85,843; low: $150).
Purpose and activities: The foundation has focused its resources on college scholarships and compensatory educational guidance programs. Residents of Cook County, IL, who are nominated by their high schools and children or grandchildren of graduates of the Pullman Free School of Manual Training are eligible for consideration for the scholarship program.
Fields of interest: Education.
Type of support: Program development; Scholarship funds.
Limitations: Giving primarily to residents of Cook County, IL.
Publications: Informational brochure.
Application information: Scholarship applicants must be referred by Cook County, IL, high schools; unsolicited requests for funds not considered. Application information available on foundation Web site. Application form required.
Board meeting date(s): Semiannually
Officers and Directors:* Phillip Lowden Miller,* Pres.; Christopher W. Nugent,* V.P.; Rev. Sam A. Portaro, Jr.,* Secy.; Edward McCormick Blair, Jr.,* Treas.; Sandra Blau, Exec. Dir.; Robert W. Bennett; Edward McCormick Blair, Sr.; Nelvia M. Brady, Ph.D.; Manford Byrd, Jr.; Mary Lee Leahy; Barbara H. Miller; Warren Pullman Miller; Harry M. Oliver, Jr.
Number of staff: 3 full-time professional; 2 full-time support.
EIN: 362216171
Selected grants: The following grants were reported in 2004.
$64,107 to DePaul University, Chicago, IL.
$54,784 to University of Chicago, Chicago, IL.
$53,900 to Loyola University of Chicago, Chicago, IL.
$28,000 to Saint Xavier University, Chicago, IL.
$25,026 to Chicago State University, Chicago, IL.
$24,333 to Northwestern University, Evanston, IL.
$23,350 to Howard University, DC.
$13,100 to Alabama State University, Montgomery, AL.
$12,500 to Butler University, Indianapolis, IN.
$10,000 to Spelman College, Atlanta, GA.

2958
Rajchenbach Family Foundation ✧

6633 N. Lincoln Ave.
Lincolnwood, IL 60712

Established in 1995 in IL.
Donors: Jack Rajchenbach; Judith Rajchenbach; JLR Management Corp.; J & J Partnership.
Foundation type: Independent foundation.
Financial data (yr. ended 12/31/05): Assets, $0 (M); gifts received, $867,000; expenditures,

$894,591; qualifying distributions, $886,030; giving activities include $886,030 for 960 grants (high: $25,000; low: $18).
Purpose and activities: Giving primarily to Jewish agencies, temples, and schools.
Fields of interest: Elementary/secondary education; Theological school/education; Jewish agencies & temples.
Limitations: Applications not accepted. No grants to individuals.
Application information: Contributes only to pre-selected organizations.
Officers: Jack Rajchenbach, Pres.; Judith Rajchenbach, V.P.
EIN: 363990464
Selected grants: The following grants were reported in 2003.
$27,000 to Congregation Tiferes Tsvi, Brooklyn, NY.
$7,500 to Bais Yaakov High School.
$6,000 to Hanna Sacks Bais Yaakov High School, Chicago, IL.
$3,600 to Congregation Ahavas Tzdokah V Chesed, Brooklyn, NY.
$3,000 to KESHET, Northbrook, IL.
$2,500 to Chicago Chesed Fund, Chicago, IL.
$2,500 to Hebrew Theological College, Skokie, IL.
$360 to Etz Chaim Center for Jewish Studies, Baltimore, MD.
$100 to Daughters of Israel Geriatric Center, West Orange, NJ.
$20 to Chai Lifeline, Skokie, IL.

2959
Red Bird Hollow Foundation ✧

1340 N. Waukegan Rd.
Lake Forest, IL 60045

Established in 1991 in IL.
Donors: John Lillard; Paula Polk Lillard.
Foundation type: Independent foundation.
Financial data (yr. ended 6/30/05): Assets, $2,064,270 (M); gifts received, $543,300; expenditures, $619,875; qualifying distributions, $589,908; giving activities include $589,908 for 51 grants (high: $150,000; low: $250).
Purpose and activities: Giving primarily for education and youth programs.
Fields of interest: Arts; Elementary/secondary education; Higher education; Education; Children/youth, services; Christian agencies & churches.
Limitations: Applications not accepted. Giving primarily in IL. No grants to individuals.
Application information: Contributes only to pre-selected organizations.
Officers: Paula Polk Lillard, Pres.; Howard Jessen, V.P. and Treas.; John Lillard, V.P.; Helen Jessen, Secy.
EIN: 363747664
Selected grants: The following grants were reported in 2004.
$125,000 to University of Chicago, Chicago, IL.
$55,000 to Forest Bluff School, Lake Bluff, IL. 2 grants: $25,000, $30,000
$50,000 to Lake Forest Academy, Lake Forest, IL.
$32,500 to University of Virginia, Charlottesville, VA. 3 grants: $25,000, $2,500, $5,000
$10,000 to Lake Forest College, Lake Forest, IL.
$4,500 to Skidmore College, Saratoga Springs, NY.
$1,000 to Xavier University, Cincinnati, OH.

2960
Redhill Foundation - Rothberg Family Charitable Trust ✧

301 S.W. Adams St., Ste. 700
Peoria, IL 61602-1574

Established in 1987 in IL.
Donors: Samuel Rothberg; Lee Patrick Rothberg; Kathleen M. Barnett; Heidi B. Munday.
Foundation type: Independent foundation.
Financial data (yr. ended 12/31/04): Assets, $8,790,668 (M); expenditures, $515,298; qualifying distributions, $422,676; giving activities include $422,676 for 24+ grants (high: $250,000; low: $1,000).
Fields of interest: Education; Jewish federated giving programs; Jewish agencies & temples.
Type of support: General/operating support; Scholarship funds; Research.
Limitations: Applications not accepted. Giving primarily in IL. No grants to individuals.
Application information: Contributes only to pre-selected organizations.
Trustees: Kathleen M. Barnett; Heidi B. Rothberg; Jean C. Rothberg; Lee Patrick Rothberg; Michael Rothberg; Samuel Rothberg.
EIN: 371217165

2961
Michael Reese Health Trust ▼

(formerly Michael Reese Hospital Foundation)
20 N. Wacker Dr., Ste. 760
Chicago, IL 60606 (312) 726-1008
Contact: Dorothy H. Gardner, Pres.
FAX: (312) 726-2797;
E-mail: programs@healthtrust.net; URL: http://
www.healthtrust.net

Established in 1995 in IL; converted from sale of Michael Reese Hospital to Humana (now Columbia/HCA).
Donors: Foreman Trust; Lazarus Charitable Fund; Kirchheimer Trust; Blum Trust; Alice Schimburg.
Foundation type: Independent foundation.
Financial data (yr. ended 6/30/05): Assets, $109,628,378 (M); gifts received, $390,667; expenditures, $5,533,249; qualifying distributions, $4,741,685; giving activities include $3,896,575 for 126 grants (high: $273,929; low: $600; average: $10,000–$50,000), and $153,553 for foundation-administered programs.
Purpose and activities: The trust seeks to improve the health of people in Chicago's metropolitan communities through effective grantmaking in health care, health education, and health research. A portion of its funding will focus on Jewish institutions and issues to fulfill the 110-year legacy of Michael Reese Hospital, founded and supported primarily by the Jewish community. In fulfilling its Jewish responsibilities to participate in the arena of general community needs and problem solving, the trust will strive to serve the healthcare needs of vulnerable and underserved Chicagoans of all races and ethnic origins.
Fields of interest: Health care, research; Medicine/medical care, public education; Public health; Health care; Medical research, institute; Children/youth, services; Civil rights, disabled; Jewish agencies & temples; Aging; Disabilities, people with; Immigrants/refugees.
Type of support: General/operating support; Program development; Research; Technical assistance; Program evaluation.

Limitations: Giving limited to the metropolitan Chicago, IL, area with emphasis on the city of Chicago. No support for private foundations. No grants to individuals, or for capital campaigns, endowment funds, fundraising events, debt reduction, or scholarships.

Publications: Biennial report; Grants list.

Application information: If an organization's letter of inquiry is accepted, a full proposal will be invited. Application form not required.

> *Initial approach:* Letter of inquiry (4 copies) by mail
> *Copies of proposal:* 7
> *Deadline(s):* Dec. 15 and June 15 for receipt of letter of inquiry
> *Board meeting date(s):* Twice per year
> *Final notification:* Within 30 days of receipt of letter of inquiry

Officers and Trustees:* John F. Benjamin,* Chair.; Herbert S. Wander,* Vice-Chair.; Dorothy H. Gardner,* Pres.; Walter R. Nathan, Secy.; Ellard Pfaelzer, Jr., Treas.; and 21 additional trustees.

Number of staff: 4 full-time professional.

EIN: 362170910

Selected grants: The following grants were reported in 2005.

$556,358 to Jewish Federation of Metropolitan Chicago, Chicago, IL. 3 grants: $67,500 (For Chicago Center for Jewish Genetic Disorders in provision of information and education programming about Jewish genetic disorders, referrals, screenings and genetic counseling), $214,929 (For Midgal Oaz group home for adults with disabilities and Dina and Eli Field EZRA Multi-Service Center to meet needs of economically disadvantaged families and individuals residing in Chicago), $273,929 (For Fund for Innovation in Health, which funds innovative programs and services to address health needs of Jewish populations in Chicago).

$100,000 to Illinois Department of Public Aid, Chicago, IL. For using Medicaid data and involving community agencies and universities in designing and implementing pilot projects to decrease negative birth outcomes and to improve children's oral health.

$62,500 to Illinois Center for Violence Prevention, Chicago, IL. For Advancing Violence Prevention Through Evaluation Capacity to evaluate and describe interventions used to develop evaluation capacity of Chicago-area organizations with violence prevention programs.

$50,000 to Heartland Alliance for Human Needs and Human Rights, Chicago, IL. For Marjorie Kovler Center for Treatment of Survivors of Torture which provides comprehensive medical and mental health care, as well as case management services, to survivors of torture.

$49,200 to Access Community Health Network, Chicago, IL. For diabetes care management program at clinic sites. Supports salaries of personnel-project manager, medical assistant, dietician.

$30,000 to Community Health, Chicago, IL. For general operating support.

$25,000 to DePaul University, College of Law Family Law Center, Chicago, IL. For evaluating effectiveness and coordination of criminal justice, court, social service and health systems response to victims of domestic violence and sexual assault and to advocate for systemic change.

$25,000 to Erikson Institute, Chicago, IL. For Fussy Baby Network to provide support to parents and children who experience excessive crying, ultimately preventing child abuse; program is collaboration with at-risk families supported by Healthy Families Illinois.

2962
The Regenstein Foundation ✧
8600 W. Bryn Mawr Ave., Ste. 560N
Chicago, IL 60631-3541 (773) 693-6464
Contact: Susan Regenstein Frank, Chair.

Incorporated in 1950 in IL as the Joseph & Helen Regenstein Foundation; in 1981 merged into Regenstein Foundation which was incorporated in DE.

Donors: Joseph Regenstein†; Helen Regenstein†; Velsicol Corporation; Arvey Corporation.

Foundation type: Independent foundation.

Financial data (yr. ended 12/31/04): Assets, $75,171,237 (M); expenditures, $3,518,483; qualifying distributions, $2,744,208; giving activities include $2,700,000 for 22 grants (high: $1,500,000; low: $2,000; average: $5,000–$30,000).

Fields of interest: Human services.

Type of support: Capital campaigns; Building/renovation; Equipment; Program development; Research.

Limitations: Giving primarily in the metropolitan Chicago, IL, area. No grants to individuals, or for scholarships, fellowships, annual campaigns, seed money, emergency funds, deficit financing, publications, conferences, or matching gifts; no loans.

Publications: Application guidelines; Program policy statement.

Application information: Most grants made on the initiative of the directors. Application form not required.

> *Initial approach:* Letter
> *Copies of proposal:* 1
> *Deadline(s):* Mar. 31 and Sept. 30
> *Board meeting date(s):* May and as required
> *Final notification:* 30 days

Officers and Directors:* Susan Regenstein Frank,* Chair. and Acting Pres.; Thomas A. Staszak, V.P. and Treas.; Joan Gorsuch, Secy.; Robert F. Carr; Marshall Field V; Thomas G. Opferman; Joseph Regenstein III.

Number of staff: 3 full-time professional; 1 part-time support.

EIN: 363152531

Selected grants: The following grants were reported in 2004.

$1,530,000 to Lincoln Park Zoological Society, Chicago, IL. 2 grants: $30,000 (For annual fund), $1,500,000 (For demolition and rebuilding of Great Ape House).

$1,025,000 to Chicago Botanic Garden, Glencoe, IL. 2 grants: $25,000 (For general operating support), $1,000,000 (For construction of Joseph Regenstein, Jr. School).

$20,000 to Rehabilitation Institute of Chicago, Chicago, IL. For operating support.

$15,000 to Rush University Medical Center, Chicago, IL. For operating support.

$13,000 to Childrens Memorial Hospital, Chicago, IL. For operating support.

$10,000 to Art Institute of Chicago, Chicago, IL. For general operating support.

$10,000 to Shelter for Abused Women of Collier County, Naples, FL. For operating support.

$5,000 to Lake Forest Hospital, Lake Forest, IL. For addition to hospital.

2963
Relations Foundation
203 N. Wabash Ave., Ste. 1800
Chicago, IL 60601 (312) 641-5765
Contact: Iris Krieg, Admin.
FAX: (312) 641-5736; E-mail: iriskrieg1@aol.com

Established in 1969 in IL.

Donors: Barbara Kessler; Dennis L. Kessler; Lewis C. Weinberg.

Foundation type: Independent foundation.

Financial data (yr. ended 12/31/05): Assets, $5,120,793 (M); expenditures, $664,753; qualifying distributions, $664,753; giving activities include $603,194 for 54 grants (high: $110,000; low: $250).

Purpose and activities: Giving primarily to assist low income people, and to Jewish causes.

Fields of interest: Environment; Human services; Civil liberties, reproductive rights; Jewish agencies & temples; Women.

International interests: Israel.

Type of support: General/operating support; Continuing support; Program development; Seed money; Matching/challenge support.

Limitations: Giving primarily in the Chicago, IL, area; funding also in Israel. No support for fraternal or veterans' groups, or for private foundations. No grants to individuals, or for endowment funds, capital campaigns, or tickets for fundraising events; no loans.

Publications: Application guidelines.

Application information: Application form not required.

> *Initial approach:* Proposal
> *Copies of proposal:* 1
> *Deadline(s):* Apr. 1, July 1, and Oct. 1
> *Board meeting date(s):* May, Aug., and Dec.

Officers and Directors:* Barbara Kessler,* Pres.; Dennis L. Kessler,* V.P.; Jerry Newton,* Secy.; David A. Weinberg,* Treas.; Joseph Radov; Sylvia M. Radov; Lewis C. Weinberg.

EIN: 237032294

Selected grants: The following grants were reported in 2005.

$55,000 to New Israel Fund, DC.

$20,000 to Sargent Shriver National Center on Poverty Law, Chicago, IL.

$15,000 to Chicago Public Education Fund, Chicago, IL.

$12,500 to Business and Professional People for the Public Interest, Chicago, IL.

$12,500 to Spertus Institute of Jewish Studies, Chicago, IL.

$12,000 to Chicago Foundation for Women, Chicago, IL.

$10,000 to Friends of the Chicago River, Chicago, IL.

$9,000 to Ark, The, Chicago, IL.

$7,000 to Emergency Fund for Needy People, Chicago, IL.

$4,000 to Chicago Coalition for the Homeless, Chicago, IL.

2964
The Retirement Research Foundation ▼

8765 W. Higgins Rd., Ste. 430
Chicago, IL 60631-4170 (773) 714-8080
Contact: Marilyn Hennessy, Pres.
FAX: (773) 714-8089; E-mail: info@rrf.org;
Additional E-mail (for Marilyn Hennessy):
hennessy@rrf.org; URL: http://www.rrf.org

Incorporated in 1950 in MI.
Donor: John D. MacArthur†.
Foundation type: Independent foundation.
Financial data (yr. ended 12/31/05): Assets, $165,060,129 (M); expenditures, $10,329,989; qualifying distributions, $8,836,547; giving activities include $7,051,295 for 233 grants (high: $100,000; low: $1,000; average: $25,000–$50,000), and $159,745 for 96 employee matching gifts.
Purpose and activities: Support principally to improve the quality of life of older persons in the U.S. Priority interests are innovative model projects and research designed to: 1) improve the availability and quality of community-based long-term care by: increasing the availability and effectiveness of community programs designed to maintain older persons in their own homes, as well as those in residential settings; improving the quality of nursing home care; and integrating the provision of acute and long-term care for older persons with chronic conditions by supporting efforts that provide continuity of care, prevention, early intervention, and client education; 2) provide new and expanded opportunities for older adults to engage in meaningful roles in society such as employment and voluntarism, that will strengthen the community through activities including, but not limited to, advocacy, community leadership, community services, and intergenerational programs; 3) seek causes and solutions to significant problems of older adults through support of selected applied and policy research for which federal funding is not available; and 4) increase the number of professionals and paraprofessionals adequately prepared to serve the elderly population through support of selected education and training initiatives that enhance knowledge and skills of participants.
Fields of interest: Health care; Mental health/crisis services; Health organizations, association; Geriatrics; Medical research, institute; Employment; Nutrition; Human services; Aging, centers/services; Homeless, human services; Social sciences; Public policy, research; Aging; Homeless.
Type of support: Management development/capacity building; Equipment; Program development; Seed money; Curriculum development; Research; Technical assistance; Program evaluation; Program-related investments/loans; Matching/challenge support.
Limitations: Giving limited to the Midwest (IA, IL, IN, KY, MO, WI) and FL for direct service projects not having the potential of national impact. No support for governmental agencies (except area agencies on aging). No grants to individuals, or for computers, construction, general operating expenses of established organizations, endowment or developmental campaigns, emergency funds, deficit financing, land acquisition, publications, conferences, scholarships, media productions, dissertation research, annual campaigns, or biomedical research. Publications and conference support is generally limited to those which are components of larger foundation funded projects.

Publications: Application guidelines; Grants list; Informational brochure; Occasional report.
Application information: All proposals must relate to aged population. Application form not required.
  Initial approach: Letter or proposal
  Copies of proposal: 3
  Deadline(s): Submit proposal preferably in Jan., Apr., or July; deadlines Feb. 1, May 1, and Aug. 1
  Board meeting date(s): Feb., May, Aug., and Oct.
  Final notification: 6 months
Officers and Trustees:* Edward J. Kelly,* Chair.; Marilyn Hennessy, Pres.; Sharon F. Markham, Assoc. V.P.; Ruth Ann Watkins,* Secy.; William J. Gentle,* Treas.; Webster H. Hurley; Nathaniel P. McParland, M.D.; Marvin Meyerson; Bart T. Murphy; John F. Santos, Ph.D.; Sr. Stella Louise Slomka, C.S.F.N.
Number of staff: 4 full-time professional; 1 part-time professional; 4 full-time support.
EIN: 362429540
Selected grants: The following grants were reported in 2006.
$277,376 to Community Catalyst, Boston, MA. For Special Needs Plan Consumer Education Project, to involve consumers in development and implementation of Medicare Advantage Special Needs Plans (SNPs), payable over 2 years.
$262,150 to Wayne State University, Detroit, MI. For Building Occupational Therapy Skills and Competencies to Advance Mental Health Practices with Older Adults, payable over 2 years.
$249,568 to Wider Opportunities for Women (WOW), DC. For pilot phase of project to gain use of Elder Economic Security Standard, a measure of minimum economic security for seniors, payable over 1.50 years.
$215,462 to Ohio State University Research Foundation, Columbus, OH. For study of employer-sponsored eldercare programs and their effectiveness at helping employees and employers address increasing caregiving duties of employees with older relatives, payable over 2 years.
$189,000 to Generations of Hope, Rantoul, IL. For installing new carpeting and furnaces in housing for older adults at Hope Meadows, to improve energy efficiency and safety.
$182,446 to National Religious Retirement Office, DC. For pilot training and education project in Person-Centered Care Best Practices for U.S. Catholic Retired Women and Men Religious, payable over 1.25 years.
$75,000 to Coalition of Limited English Speaking Elderly (CLESE), Chicago, IL. For Depression in Ethnic Elderly: Understanding and Accepting Treatment.
$68,000 to Interdependent Living Solutions Center, Evergreen Park, IL. For continued support to recruit, train, and place certified nurse assistants in long-term care settings.
$65,009 to Portland State University, Portland, OR. For Health Care Utilization in Canada and United States: Study of Near Elderly and Elderly Populations.
$50,000 to Polish American Association, Chicago, IL. For Senior Services Program.

2965
Otto L. and Hazel T. Rhoades Fund ◇

8000 Sears Twr.
Chicago, IL 60606

Established in 1978 in IL.
Donors: Otto L. Rhoades†; Hazel T. Rhoades†.
Foundation type: Independent foundation.
Financial data (yr. ended 12/31/05): Assets, $14,188,743 (M); expenditures, $848,936; qualifying distributions, $682,700; giving activities include $682,700 for 85 grants (high: $30,000; low: $100).
Purpose and activities: Giving primarily for health care and the arts.
Fields of interest: Performing arts; Arts; Higher education; Education; Hospitals (general); Human services; Children/youth, services; Christian agencies & churches; Disabilities, people with.
Limitations: Applications not accepted. Giving primarily in IL. No grants to individuals.
Application information: Contributes only to pre-selected organizations.
  Board meeting date(s): 1st week of Mar. and Dec.
Officers and Directors:* Julius Lewis,* Pres.; H. Allan Stark,* V.P. and Secy.; James F. Oates,* Treas.
EIN: 362994856
Selected grants: The following grants were reported in 2004.
$80,000 to Alliance Francaise de Chicago, Chicago, IL. 3 grants: $25,000, $5,000, $50,000
$50,000 to Art Institute of Chicago, Chicago, IL.
$25,000 to Chicago Opera Theater, Chicago, IL.
$20,000 to Greater Chicago Food Depository, Chicago, IL.
$20,000 to Holy Family Ministries Foundation, Northfield, IL.
$10,000 to Salvation Army. 2 grants: $5,000 each
$2,500 to Vital Bridges, Chicago, IL.

2966
Rice Foundation ▼ ◇

8600 Gross Point Rd.
Skokie, IL 60077-2151 (847) 581-9999
Contact: Peter Nolan, Pres.

Incorporated in 1947 in IL.
Donors: Daniel F. Rice†; Ada Rice†.
Foundation type: Independent foundation.
Financial data (yr. ended 12/31/05): Assets, $84,346,365 (M); expenditures, $5,966,801; qualifying distributions, $5,220,623; giving activities include $4,676,201 for 153 grants (high: $500,000; low: $400; average: $5,000–$50,000).
Purpose and activities: Emphasis on higher education, including medical education, hospitals, and youth agencies.
Fields of interest: Higher education; Medical school/education; Hospitals (general); Children/youth, services; Government/public administration.
Type of support: General/operating support.
Limitations: Giving primarily in IL. No grants to individuals.
Application information:
  Initial approach: Proposal
  Deadline(s): None
Officers and Directors:* Peter G. Nolan,* Pres.; Cori Nolan,* V.P. and Secy.; Robin G. Nolan, V.P.; Richard T. Shroeder,* Treas.; Marilynn A. Alsdorf; John D. Gray; David J. Winchester.
EIN: 366043160
Selected grants: The following grants were reported in 2005.
$1,000,000 to John G. Shedd Aquarium, Chicago, IL. For general support.
$500,000 to Field Museum of Natural History, Chicago, IL. For general support.

$386,700 to Northwestern University, Evanston, IL. For general support.

$330,000 to Saint Scholastica Academy, Chicago, IL. For general support.

$275,000 to Night Ministry, Chicago, IL. 2 grants: $250,000 (For general support), $25,000 (For general support).

$250,000 to Kohl Childrens Museum of Greater Chicago, Glenview, IL. For general support.

$128,506 to PAWS Chicago, Chicago, IL. For general support.

$50,000 to Lincoln Park Zoo, Chicago, IL. For general support.

$30,000 to Big Shoulders Fund, Chicago, IL. For general support.

2967
The William R. Rich Foundation ◇

9450 Bryn Mawr Ave., Ste. 310
Rosemont, IL 60018-5272
Contact: Lynne Kaplan, Tr.

Established in 1993 in IL.
Foundation type: Independent foundation.
Financial data (yr. ended 12/31/05): Assets, $6,613,748 (M); expenditures, $372,530; qualifying distributions, $315,000; giving activities include $315,000 for 7 grants.
Fields of interest: Medical school/education; Education; Cancer research; Children/youth, services; Women, centers/services.
Limitations: Applications not accepted. Giving limited to Chicago, IL. No grants to individuals.
Application information: Contributes only to pre-selected organizations.
Trustees: Lynne Kaplan; Elizabeth Reardon; Mark Reardon.
EIN: 363885448
Selected grants: The following grants were reported in 2003.
$130,000 to Northwestern University, Feinberg School of Medicine, Evanston, IL.
$50,000 to Educational Foundation of Orinda, Orinda, CA. For program support.
$35,000 to National Childrens Cancer Society, Saint Louis, MO.
$35,000 to Okizu Foundation, Novato, CA.
$10,000 to Cancer League of California, Piedmont, CA.
$10,000 to Childrens Hospital and Research Center Foundation, Oakland, CA.

2968
Elyse Meredith Roberts and Raymond John Roberts Charitable Foundation ◇

88 Brinker Rd.
Barrington, IL 60010

Established in 2001 in IL.
Donors: Elyse Meredith Roberts; Raymond J. Roberts; Allison Roberts Greene.
Foundation type: Independent foundation.
Financial data (yr. ended 7/31/05): Assets, $10,430,466 (M); expenditures, $566,288; qualifying distributions, $527,019; giving activities include $527,019 for 27 grants (high: $150,000; low: $500).
Fields of interest: Performing arts, opera; Arts; Health care; Recreation, camps; Youth development, community service clubs; Children/youth, services; Protestant agencies & churches.

Limitations: Applications not accepted. Giving primarily in IL. No grants to individuals.
Application information: Contributes only to pre-selected organizations.
Directors: Allison Roberts Greene; Elyse Meredith Roberts.
EIN: 522333799
Selected grants: The following grants were reported in 2005.
$150,000 to San Francisco Art Institute, San Francisco, CA.
$52,000 to Crohns and Colitis Foundation of America, New York, NY.
$34,500 to Barrington Area Arts Council, Barrington, IL.
$20,000 to Raue Center for the Arts, Crystal Lake, IL.
$15,000 to Sweet Briar College, Sweet Briar, VA.
$10,000 to Barrington Youth Dance Ensemble, Barrington, IL.
$1,500 to Art Institute of Chicago, Chicago, IL.

2969
The Rochetta-Wessies Scholarship Foundation ◇ ☆

c/o Carleton M. Tower & Co., Ltd.
10 S. LaSalle St., No. 3450
Chicago, IL 60603
Application address: Rev. John McGivern, Pres., c/o St. Edmund Church, 188 S. Oak Park Ave., Oak Park, IL 60302

Established in 1994 in IL.
Donors: Bruce V. Rauner; Diana Rauner; Rosemarie Wessies.
Foundation type: Independent foundation.
Financial data (yr. ended 9/30/05): Assets, $522,972 (M); expenditures, $460,309; qualifying distributions, $458,278; giving activities include $456,250 for 7 grants (high: $400,000; low: $1,000).
Purpose and activities: Scholarship awards to graduates in St. Edmund's parochial school system, Oak Park, IL.
Fields of interest: Scholarships/financial aid.
Type of support: Scholarships—to individuals.
Limitations: Giving primarily to Oak Park, IL.
Application information: Application form not required.
  Deadline(s): None
Officers: Rev. John McGivern, Pres.; Patricia Fernholz, Secy.; Donald Giannetti, Treas.
Directors: Nora Schenk; Alan Schmitt; Sr. Collette Mary White, O.P.
EIN: 363853007

2970
Benjamin J. Rosenthal Foundation ◇

P.O. Box 166037
Chicago, IL 60616-6037

Incorporated in 1922 in IL.
Donor: Benjamin J. Rosenthal†.
Foundation type: Independent foundation.
Financial data (yr. ended 12/31/04): Assets, $5,451,860 (M); expenditures, $475,652; qualifying distributions, $411,920; giving activities include $339,900 for 128 grants (high: $103,000; low: $500).

Purpose and activities: Support primarily for youth, child welfare, human services, arts and culture, and protection of animals.
Fields of interest: Arts; Scholarships/financial aid; Education; Environment, natural resources; Animal welfare; Animals/wildlife, preservation/protection; Human services; Children/youth, services.
Limitations: Applications not accepted. Giving on a national basis, with emphasis on Chicago, IL, and Washington, DC. No grants to individuals.
Application information: Contributes only to pre-selected organizations.
Officers: Elaine Broadhead, Chair.; Melissa Foulke, Pres. and Treas.; Walter Roth, Secy.
Trustee: Joseph Glossberg.
EIN: 362523643
Selected grants: The following grants were reported in 2004.
$18,000 to Chicago Youth Centers, Chicago, IL. 2 grants: $3,000, $15,000
$15,000 to Principia Corporation, Saint Louis, MO.
$10,000 to Center for Food Safety, DC.
$10,000 to Family Rescue, Chicago, IL.
$10,000 to Ravinia Festival Association, Highland Park, IL.
$5,000 to Chicago Humanities Festival, Chicago, IL.
$5,000 to Greenpeace Fund, DC.
$2,500 to Alice Lloyd College, Pippa Passes, KY.
$2,000 to Covenant House, New York, NY.

2971
Hulda B. & Maurice L. Rothschild Foundation ◇

c/o The Northern Trust Co.
P.O. Box 803878
Chicago, IL 60680
Application address: c/o Northern Trust, 50 S. LaSalle St., Admin. on B-3, Chicago, IL 60675

Established in 1981 in IL.
Donor: Hulda B. Rothschild†.
Foundation type: Independent foundation.
Financial data (yr. ended 12/31/05): Assets, $14,841,607 (M); expenditures, $665,129; qualifying distributions, $517,939; giving activities include $444,500 for 32 grants (high: $105,559; low: $908).
Purpose and activities: To improve the quality of life for older adults in the Chicago, IL, metropolitan area; the foundation is interested in innovative projects which develop and/or demonstrate new approaches and creative solutions to the problems of older adults and which have the potential for significant impact, especially programs of cultural outreach.
Fields of interest: Museums (art); Performing arts; Arts; Higher education; Human services; Federated giving programs.
Type of support: Program development; Publication; Seed money; Research; Matching/challenge support.
Limitations: Giving primarily in the metropolitan Chicago, IL, area. No support for projects outside the U.S. No grants to individuals, or for general purposes, operating budgets, endowment or development campaigns, or scholarships; no loans.
Publications: Application guidelines; Program policy statement.
Application information: Priority given to organizations which have clear objectives, well-defined outcomes or impact, and cost effective approaches. Application form not required.
  Initial approach: Letter
  Copies of proposal: 1

Deadline(s): None
Final notification: 30 to 45 days
Trustees: Beatrice Mayer; Robert N. Mayer; The Northern Trust Co.
EIN: 366752787

2972
Rotonda Foundation ✧

(formerly Irving Harris Foundation A)
191 N. Wacker Dr., Ste. 1500
Chicago, IL 60606-1899

Established in 1993 in IL.
Donor: Roxanne H. Frank.
Foundation type: Independent foundation.
Financial data (yr. ended 12/31/04): Assets, $18,922,949 (M); gifts received, $12,906; expenditures, $1,633,059; qualifying distributions, $1,175,489; giving activities include $1,175,004 for 64 grants (high: $200,000; low: $500).
Fields of interest: Performing arts, music; Education; AIDS; Jewish federated giving programs.
Limitations: Applications not accepted. Giving primarily in St. Louis, MO. No grants to individuals.
Publications: Annual report.
Application information: Contributes only to pre-selected organizations.
Officers and Directors: * Roxanne H. Frank,* Pres. and Secy.; Daniel Meyer,* V.P.; Nancy Meyer,* V.P.; Thomas Meyer,* V.P.; Jack Polsky, V.P.; Michael Resnick, Treas.
EIN: 363866527
Selected grants: The following grants were reported in 2004.
$300,000 to Saint Louis Art Museum Foundation, Saint Louis, MO. 2 grants: $200,000, $100,000
$105,000 to StreetSquash, New York, NY.
$75,000 to Research Foundation of the State University of New York, Brooklyn, NY.
$50,000 to Madison Square Park Conservancy, New York, NY.
$25,000 to Contemporary Art Museum Saint Louis, Saint Louis, MO.
$25,000 to People for the American Way Foundation, DC.
$10,000 to Museum of Modern Art, New York, NY.
$10,000 to Project Vote/Voting for America, Little Rock, AR.
$7,500 to University of Missouri, Saint Louis, MO.

2973
The Dennis and Joyce Ruben Foundation ✧

6519 N. Central Park Ave.
Lincolnwood, IL 60712-4013

Established in 1986 in IL.
Donors: Dennis Ruben; Joyce Ruben.
Foundation type: Independent foundation.
Financial data (yr. ended 12/31/05): Assets, $1,668,136 (M); gifts received, $2,238,000; expenditures, $726,289; qualifying distributions, $719,241; giving activities include $719,241 for 214 grants (high: $150,000; low: $10).
Purpose and activities: Giving for Jewish organizations, including yeshivas.
Fields of interest: Elementary/secondary education; Human services; Jewish agencies & temples.
Limitations: Applications not accepted. Giving primarily in IL and NY. No grants to individuals.

Application information: Contributes only to pre-selected organizations.
Trustees: Dennis Ruben; Joyce Ruben.
EIN: 363486610

2974
Robert E. & Judith O. Rubin Foundation ✧

c/o The Northern Trust Co.
P.O. Box 803878
Chicago, IL 60680-3828

Established in 1980 in NY.
Donor: Robert E. Rubin.
Foundation type: Independent foundation.
Financial data (yr. ended 8/31/05): Assets, $451 (M); gifts received, $1,018,500; expenditures, $1,021,887; qualifying distributions, $1,021,875; giving activities include $1,021,850 for 39 grants (high: $250,000; low: $1,000).
Purpose and activities: Giving primarily for higher education and the arts.
Fields of interest: Media/communications; Media, radio; Performing arts, theater; Arts; Higher education; Education; Hospitals (general); Jewish agencies & temples.
Limitations: Applications not accepted. Giving primarily in New York, NY; some funding nationally. No grants to individuals.
Application information: Contributes only to pre-selected organizations.
Trustees: Judith O. Rubin; Robert E. Rubin; Roy E. Zuckerberg.
EIN: 133050749
Selected grants: The following grants were reported in 2004.
$500,000 to Mount Sinai Medical Center, New York, NY. For general support.
$148,500 to Playwrights Horizons, New York, NY. 2 grants: $10,000 (For general support), $138,500 (For general support).
$91,250 to Public Radio International, Minneapolis, MN. 2 grants: $56,250 (For general support), $35,000 (For general support).
$50,000 to Center for American Progress, DC. For general support.
$35,000 to Council on Foreign Relations, New York, NY. For general support.
$25,000 to Concord Coalition, Arlington, VA. For general support.
$21,500 to Theater Communications Group, New York, NY. For general support.
$20,000 to Phipps Houses, New York, NY. For general support.

2975
Paul A. and Joan S. Rubschlager Foundation ✧

800 N. Michigan Ave., Unit 3002
Chicago, IL 60611

Established in 1986 in IL.
Donors: Paul A. Rubschlager; Joan S. Rubschlager.
Foundation type: Independent foundation.
Financial data (yr. ended 10/31/05): Assets, $10,132,040 (M); gifts received, $1,000,000; expenditures, $536,702; qualifying distributions, $534,335; giving activities include $534,335 for 27 grants (high: $360,000; low: $500).
Fields of interest: Health organizations, association; Human services.

Limitations: Applications not accepted. Giving primarily in IL. No grants to individuals.
Application information: Contributes only to pre-selected organizations.
Trustees: Joan S. Rubschlager; Paul A. Rubschlager.
EIN: 363487448
Selected grants: The following grants were reported in 2005.
$20,750 to American Heart Association, Chicago, IL.
$17,120 to Alzheimers Association, Chicago, IL.
$10,000 to University of Chicago Cancer Research Foundation, Chicago, IL.
$7,250 to American Cancer Society, Chicago, IL.
$6,100 to Easter Seal Society, Peoria, IL.
$6,000 to National Kidney Foundation, Chicago, IL.
$5,000 to American Diabetes Association, Chicago, IL.
$5,000 to American Lung Association of Metropolitan Chicago, Chicago, IL.
$3,000 to Epilepsy Foundation of Greater Chicago, Chicago, IL.

2976
Tom Russell Charitable Foundation, Inc. ✧

2 Transam Plz. Dr., Ste. 200
Oakbrook Terrace, IL 60181-4296
(630) 916-0123
Contact: Thomas A. Hearn, Pres.

Incorporated in 1960 in IL.
Donors: Thomas C. Russell‡; Wrap-On Co., Inc.; Huron & Orleans Building Corp.; F.D. Russell Trust f/b/o Mary J. Dickie.
Foundation type: Independent foundation.
Financial data (yr. ended 8/31/05): Assets, $15,366,648 (M); expenditures, $995,248; qualifying distributions, $795,825; giving activities include $650,100 for 70 grants (high: $75,000; low: $100).
Purpose and activities: Giving primarily for education, children and youth services, including services for disadvantaged youth, and for health, and human services.
Fields of interest: Education; Health care; Health organizations, association; Cancer research; Boys & girls clubs; Big Brothers/Big Sisters; Human services; Children/youth, services; Family services; Community development; Federated giving programs; Religion.
Limitations: Giving primarily in the metropolitan Chicago, IL area; funding also in NC, and OK. No grants to individuals.
Publications: Application guidelines.
Application information: Application form not required.
Initial approach: Proposal
Copies of proposal: 1
Final notification: July or Aug.
Officers and Directors: * Thomas A. Hearn,* Pres.; J. Kirby Aiken,* V.P.; David S. Lindquist,* V.P.; John L. Bishop,* Treas.; Frank S. Scarlati, Jr.
EIN: 366082517
Selected grants: The following grants were reported in 2005.
$50,000 to Northwestern University, Evanston, IL.
$30,000 to Independent Living Services for Youth, Norman, OK.
$20,000 to Saint Jude House, Crown Point, IN.
$15,000 to Beacon Therapeutic School, Chicago, IL.
$15,000 to Central Oklahoma Community Action Agency, Shawnee, OK.

$10,000 to Rehabilitation Institute of Chicago, Chicago, IL.
$5,000 to DuPage Community Clinic, Wheaton, IL.
$5,000 to National Relief Charities, Elkwood, VA.
$5,000 to Queen of Angels Montessori School, Cincinnati, OH.
$5,000 to Saint Jude Childrens Research Hospital, Memphis, TN.

2977
Patrick G. & Shirley W. Ryan Foundation ◇ ☆
150 N. Michigan Ave., Ste. 2100
Chicago, IL   60601

Established in 1984 in IL.
Donors: Patrick G. Ryan; Shirley W. Ryan; Ryan Holding Corp. of Illinois; Ryan Enterprises Corp. of Illinois.
Foundation type: Independent foundation.
Financial data (yr. ended 11/30/05): Assets, $35,681,652 (M); gifts received, $47,241; expenditures, $359,544; qualifying distributions, $348,972; giving activities include $348,972 for grants.
Purpose and activities: Giving primarily to education, the arts, and Roman Catholic churches.
Fields of interest: Arts; Education; Human services; Federated giving programs; Roman Catholic agencies & churches.
Limitations: Applications not accepted. Giving primarily in IL. No grants to individuals.
Application information: Contributes only to pre-selected organizations.
Officers: Shirley W. Ryan, Pres. and Treas.; Patrick G. Ryan, V.P.; Mary Ignell, Secy.
Directors: Patrick G. Ryan, Jr.; Robert J.W. Ryan.
EIN: 363305162
Selected grants: The following grants were reported in 2005.
$114,222 to Lyric Opera of Chicago, Chicago, IL.
$25,000 to Sacred Heart Church, Winnetka, IL.
$15,000 to National Center for Learning Disabilities, New York, NY.
$10,000 to Chicago Foundation for Education, Chicago, IL.
$10,000 to Horizon Hospice and Palliative Care, Chicago, IL.
$10,000 to United Cerebral Palsy Association of Greater Chicago, Chicago, IL.
$5,000 to Homan Square Community Center Foundation, Chicago, IL.
$1,500 to Sacred Heart Schools, Chicago, IL.
$1,000 to Chicago Historical Society, Chicago, IL.
$1,000 to Childrens Place Association, Chicago, IL.

2978
William G. and Mary A. Ryan Foundation ◇ ☆
12 Salt Creek Ln., Ste. 200
Hinsdale, IL   60521

Established around 1993 in IL.
Donors: Mary A. Ryan; William G. Ryan.
Foundation type: Independent foundation.
Financial data (yr. ended 11/30/05): Assets, $7,240,426 (M); gifts received, $6,502,937; expenditures, $654,586; qualifying distributions, $638,143; giving activities include $638,143 for 46 grants (high: $500,000; low: $100).

Fields of interest: Museums; Performing arts; Education; Health care; Human services; Federated giving programs; Roman Catholic agencies & churches.
Limitations: Applications not accepted. Giving on a national basis. No grants to individuals.
Application information: Contributes only to pre-selected organizations.
Directors: Mary A. Ryan; William G. Ryan.
EIN: 363870010
Selected grants: The following grants were reported in 2005.
$12,500 to Nicklaus Childrens Health Care Foundation, West Palm Beach, FL.
$5,000 to Chicago Symphony Orchestra, Chicago, IL.
$5,000 to Wellness House, Hinsdale, IL.
$4,000 to Evans Scholars Foundation, Golf, IL.
$2,000 to Community House, Hinsdale, IL.
$1,250 to Salvation Army, Sterling, IL.
$1,000 to 626 Landmark Foundation, Chicago, IL.
$350 to Art Institute of Chicago, Chicago, IL.
$300 to Misericordia Home, Chicago, IL.
$250 to Hinsdale Center for the Arts, Hinsdale, IL.

2979
Sacks Family Foundation ◇
c/o Michael Sacks
1850 2nd St., Ste. 201
Highland Park, IL   60035

Established in 2001 in IL.
Donors: Michael Sacks; Judd Malkin; Stephen S. Malkin; Cari A. Sacks.
Foundation type: Independent foundation.
Financial data (yr. ended 12/31/04): Assets, $1,483,925 (M); gifts received, $1,000,000; expenditures, $901,349; qualifying distributions, $899,133; giving activities include $899,133 for 84 grants (high: $150,000; low: $250).
Fields of interest: Arts; Higher education; Hospitals (general); Cancer; Human services; Jewish federated giving programs; Jewish agencies & temples.
Limitations: Applications not accepted. Giving primarily in Chicago, IL.
Application information: Contributes only to pre-selected organizations.
Officers: Michael Sacks, Pres. and Treas.; Kenneth Sacks, Secy.
Director: A. Lee Sacks.
EIN: 364053778
Selected grants: The following grants were reported in 2005.
$235,121 to Food Allergy and Anaphylaxis Network, Fairfax, VA.
$110,000 to University of Chicago Childrens Hospital, Chicago, IL.
$97,790 to Survivors of the Shoah Visual History Foundation, Los Angeles, CA.
$54,700 to KESHET, Northbrook, IL.
$21,000 to Merit School of Music, Chicago, IL.
$10,000 to High Jump, Chicago, IL.
$5,500 to Cystic Fibrosis Foundation, Bethesda, MD.
$5,000 to Rush University Medical Center, Chicago, IL.
$5,000 to Womens American ORT, New York, NY.
$2,850 to Childrens Memorial Foundation, Chicago, IL.

2980
The Samaritan Foundation ◇
33 W. Higgins Rd., Rm. 610
South Barrington, IL   60010

Established in 1999 in IL.
Donors: Edward T. Owens; Samaritan Asset Management, Inc.
Foundation type: Operating foundation.
Financial data (yr. ended 12/31/04): Assets, $5,417 (M); gifts received, $479,325; expenditures, $524,571; qualifying distributions, $524,570; giving activities include $454,179 for 149 grants (high: $35,000; low: $100).
Purpose and activities: Giving primarily for international affairs and relief, and for religious agencies.
Fields of interest: International relief; Christian agencies & churches.
Type of support: Program-related investments/loans; Employee matching gifts; Matching/challenge support.
Limitations: Applications not accepted. Giving on a national basis. No grants to individuals.
Application information: Contributes only to pre-selected organizations.
Officer and Directors: Edward T. Owens, Pres.; Dimple Owens; Jeannine Owens.
Number of staff: 1 full-time support.
EIN: 364295983
Selected grants: The following grants were reported in 2005.
$30,000 to Harvest Bible Chapel, Rolling Meadows, IL.
$18,000 to Arab World Ministries, Upper Darby, PA. 2 grants: $9,000 each
$9,500 to Campus Crusade for Christ, Miami, FL.
$5,000 to Ravi Zacharias International Ministries, Norcross, GA.
$5,000 to Wheaton Academy, West Chicago, IL.
$2,250 to Jews for Jesus, San Francisco, CA.
$1,000 to Global Action, Colorado Springs, CO.

2981
Sangre De Christo Charitable Trust ◇ ☆
(formerly Bernard J. and Joyce M. Hank, Jr. Charitable Trust)
2000 52nd Ave., Ste. 2
Moline, IL   61265

Established in 1993 in IL.
Donors: Bernard J. Hank, Jr.; Joyce M. Hank.
Foundation type: Independent foundation.
Financial data (yr. ended 12/31/05): Assets, $1,515,103 (M); expenditures, $474,690; qualifying distributions, $462,500; giving activities include $462,500 for 13 grants (high: $210,000; low: $2,500).
Purpose and activities: Funding primarily for higher education. Funding also for Roman Catholic agencies, and human services.
Fields of interest: Museums (art); Higher education; Libraries (public); Children/youth, services; Federated giving programs; Roman Catholic agencies & churches.
Limitations: Applications not accepted. Giving primarily in IA, IL, and IN. No grants to individuals.
Application information: Contributes only to pre-selected organizations.
Trustees: Bernard J. Hank, Jr.; Joyce M. Hank.
EIN: 367042588
Selected grants: The following grants were reported in 2003.

$150,000 to Saint Marys College, Notre Dame, IN. For general support.

$26,250 to Priests of the Holy Cross, Notre Dame, IN. For general support.

$15,000 to Christian Friendliness Association, Moline, IL. For general support.

$10,000 to Junior Achievement of the Quad Cities, Davenport, IA. For general support.

$10,000 to United Way of the Quad Cities Area, Rock Island, IL. For general support.

$5,000 to University of Notre Dame, Notre Dame, IN. For general support.

$5,000 to YMCA of Moline, Moline, IL. For general support.

$4,375 to Quad City Arts, Rock Island, IL. For general support.

$2,500 to Childrens Therapy Center of the Quad Cities, Moline, IL. For general support.

2982
Sara Lee Foundation ▼ ✧
c/o Direct Grants Prog.
3 First National Plz.
Chicago, IL 60602-4260
URL: http://www.saraleefoundation.org

Incorporated in 1981 in IL.
Donor: Sara Lee Corp.
Foundation type: Company-sponsored foundation.
Financial data (yr. ended 7/2/05): Assets, $1,846,556 (M); gifts received, $630,443; expenditures, $8,629,546; qualifying distributions, $8,623,867; giving activities include $6,224,152 for 210 grants (high: $350,000; low: $350), and $1,218,071 for 1,252 employee matching gifts.
Purpose and activities: The foundation supports organizations involved with arts and culture, employment, hunger, nutrition, diversity, minorities, and women.
Fields of interest: Arts, equal rights; Visual arts; Museums; Performing arts; Performing arts, dance; Performing arts, theater; Performing arts, music; Arts; Employment, training; Employment; Food services; Nutrition; Civil rights, equal rights; Minorities; Women.
Type of support: General/operating support; Annual campaigns; Program development; Employee volunteer services; Sponsorships; Employee matching gifts; Donated products.
Limitations: Giving primarily in areas of company operations, with emphasis on the greater metropolitan Chicago, IL, area. No support for organizations with an accumulated deficit, organizations with a limited constituency, religious organizations not of direct benefit to the entire community, political or lobbying organizations, government units, disease-specific hospitals or health organizations, community development corporations, or discriminatory organizations. No grants for sports-related events or sponsorships.
Publications: Application guidelines; Annual report; Biennial report; Grants list; Program policy statement (including application guidelines).
Application information: General operating support generally does not exceed $15,000. Support is limited to 1 contribution per organization during any given year.
Initial approach: Complete online letter of inquiry form for organizations located in the Chicago, IL, area; proposal to nearest company facility for organizations located outside the Chicago, IL, area; complete online application form for table sponsorships

Copies of proposal: 1
Deadline(s): None
Final notification: 3 weeks
Officers and Directors:* Randy White, Pres.; Roderick A. Palmore, V.P. and Secy.; L.M. "Theo" de Kool,* V.P. and Treas.; C.J. Fraleigh,* V.P.; Jim Nolan,* V.P.; Brenda C. Barnes; Adriaan Nuhn.
Number of staff: 6 full-time professional.
EIN: 363150460
Selected grants: The following grants were reported in 2005.

$350,000 to United Way of Metropolitan Chicago, Chicago, IL. For general operating support.

$312,500 to Forsyth Medical Center Foundation, Winston-Salem, NC. For Sara Lee Center for Women's Health.

$250,000 to Chicago Symphony Orchestra, Chicago, IL. For Symphony Center Presents Sara Lee Series.

$200,000 to Music and Dance Theater Chicago, Chicago, IL. For general operating support.

$200,000 to New Schools for Chicago, Chicago, IL. For Commercial Club Foundation.

$50,000 to Southwest Women Working Together, Chicago, IL. For Spirit of a Woman event.

$25,000 to Arts and Business Council of Chicago, Chicago, IL. For Anniversary Outreach.

$25,000 to Charities Aid Foundation (CAF) America, Alexandria, VA. For general operating support.

$15,000 to Chicago Legal Clinic, Chicago, IL. For Domestic Violence Program, Pilsen office.

$10,000 to University of Chicago, Chicago, IL. For general operating support.

2983
The Satter Family Foundation ✧
500 N. Michigan Ave., Ste. 1700
Chicago, IL 60611

Established in 1997 in NY.
Donor: Muneer A. Satter.
Foundation type: Independent foundation.
Financial data (yr. ended 12/31/05): Assets, $26,297,739 (M); gifts received, $2,993,548; expenditures, $800,103; qualifying distributions, $682,515; giving activities include $677,240 for 39 grants (high: $225,500; low: $40).
Fields of interest: Arts; Higher education; Environment, natural resources; Botanical gardens; Human services.
Limitations: Applications not accepted. Giving on a national basis. No grants to individuals.
Application information: Contributes only to pre-selected organizations.
Trustees: Kristen Hertel; Muneer A. Satter; Michael J. Schierl.
EIN: 133936468
Selected grants: The following grants were reported in 2005.

$225,500 to Nature Conservancy, Arlington, VA.

$102,000 to Room to Read, San Francisco, CA.

$30,000 to Berea College, Berea, KY.

$29,200 to Link Unlimited, Chicago, IL.

$25,000 to United Way.

$20,000 to Northwestern University, Evanston, IL.

$10,000 to Trust for Public Land, San Francisco, CA.

$3,500 to Montessori School.

$1,000 to Chicago Botanic Garden, Glencoe, IL.

$1,000 to Rainforest Alliance, New York, NY.

2984
The Clarence W. and Marilyn G. Schawk Family Foundation ✧
1695 River Rd.
Des Plaines, IL 60018

Established in 1995 in IL.
Donors: Clarence W. Schawk; Marilyn G. Schawk.
Foundation type: Independent foundation.
Financial data (yr. ended 12/31/04): Assets, $7,008,411 (M); expenditures, $711,583; qualifying distributions, $699,950; giving activities include $697,122 for 50 grants (high: $418,620; low: $200).
Purpose and activities: Giving primarily to Christian agencies and for education.
Fields of interest: Education; Hospitals (general); Human services; Federated giving programs; Protestant agencies & churches; Religion.
Limitations: Applications not accepted. Giving primarily in IL. No grants to individuals.
Application information: Contributes only to pre-selected organizations.
Trustees: Clarence W. Schawk; Marilyn G. Schawk.
EIN: 363996543

2985
The Schield Family Foundation, Inc. ✧
P.O. Box 221
Wilmette, IL 60091-0221
Contact: Michael A. Schield, Pres.

Established around 1967 in WI.
Donors: William H. Schield, Jr.‡; Charlotte H. Schield‡.
Foundation type: Independent foundation.
Financial data (yr. ended 12/31/05): Assets, $7,699,103 (M); expenditures, $1,169,416; qualifying distributions, $1,169,259; giving activities include $1,164,133 for 70 grants (high: $300,217; low: $14).
Purpose and activities: Giving primarily for higher education, particularly to a medical college; funding also for the arts, health associations, and federated giving programs.
Fields of interest: Museums (art); Performing arts; Performing arts, theater; Arts; Higher education; Medical school/education; Education; Health organizations, association; Human services; Foundations (community).
Limitations: Applications not accepted. Giving primarily in Milwaukee, WI; some giving also in the New York, NY, area. No grants to individuals.
Application information: Unsolicited requests for funds not accepted.
Officers and Directors:* Michael A. Schield,* Pres. and Treas.; Michael Hamilton,* V.P.; Marianne Epstein, Secy.
EIN: 396105207

2986
William E. Schmidt Charitable Foundation ✧
605 Westpark Dr.
Columbia, IL 62236

Established in 1981 in IL.
Donors: William E. Schmidt; John F. Schmidt.
Foundation type: Independent foundation.
Financial data (yr. ended 4/30/05): Assets, $9,325,834 (M); gifts received, $191;

expenditures, $479,784; qualifying distributions, $464,000; giving activities include $464,000 for 69 grants (high: $50,000; low: $1,000).

Purpose and activities: Giving primarily for higher education, cancer research, human services, and to Christian and Protestant organizations and churches.

Fields of interest: Arts; Higher education; Education; Health care; Cancer research; Human services; YM/YWCAs & YM/YWHAs; Children, services; Christian agencies & churches; Protestant agencies & churches.

Limitations: Applications not accepted. Giving primarily in AZ and IL. No grants to individuals.

Application information: Contributes only to pre-selected organizations.

Officers: John Schmidt, Pres.; Margaret C. Schmidt, Secy.

Director: Thomas Schmidt.

EIN: 371098426

Selected grants: The following grants were reported in 2005.

$80,000 to YMCA of Southwest Illinois, Belleville, IL. 2 grants: $50,000 (For program support), $30,000 (For program support).

$30,000 to Blackburn College, Carlinville, IL.

$30,000 to McKendree College, Lebanon, IL.

$30,000 to Washington University, Saint Louis, MO.

$25,000 to Southern Illinois University at Edwardsville Foundation, Edwardsville, IL.

$25,000 to University of Arizona Foundation, Tucson, AZ.

$15,000 to Evangelical Lutheran Church, Gillespie, IL.

$5,000 to Kids First, Nashville, TN.

$5,000 to Ronald McDonald House, Tucson, AZ.

2987
Arthur J. Schmitt Foundation
P.O. Box 520
Wilmette, IL 60091
Contact: John A. Donahue, Exec. Dir.

Incorporated in 1941 in IL.

Donor: Arthur J. Schmitt†.

Foundation type: Independent foundation.

Financial data (yr. ended 6/30/05): Assets, $20,982,109 (M); expenditures, $1,681,500; qualifying distributions, $1,318,453; giving activities include $1,282,000 for 34 grants (high: $125,000; low: $5,000).

Purpose and activities: Giving primarily to Catholic educational institutions for scholarships and fellowships established at certain selected universities to aid students in pursuing graduate degrees; grants to a few Catholic secondary schools; grants to three mentoring and scholarship programs for high school students; grants also to charitable agencies to help alleviate poverty, homelessness, drug addictions, illiteracy, racism and other social ills and to aid in cultural programs, all in the Chicago, IL, area.

Fields of interest: Education; Human services.

Type of support: General/operating support; Continuing support; Fellowships; Scholarship funds.

Limitations: Giving limited to the metropolitan Chicago, IL, area, except for two universities. No grants to individuals, or for capital or building funds, research, or matching gifts; no loans.

Publications: Application guidelines; Informational brochure.

Application information: Application form required.

Initial approach: Letter

Copies of proposal: 1

Deadline(s): Submit proposal preferably in July, Oct., Jan., or Apr.

Board meeting date(s): Sept., Dec., Mar., and June

Final notification: 1 month after board meeting

Officers and Directors: * Richard C. Becker,* Pres.; Daniel E. Mayworm,* V.P.; Peter J. Wrenn,* V.P.; Patricia A. Shevlin,* Secy.; John J. Gearen,* Treas.; John A. Donahue, Exec. Dir.; Mary M. Dwyer.

Number of staff: 1 part-time professional.

EIN: 362217999

Selected grants: The following grants were reported in 2003.

$125,000 to Daniel Murphy Scholarship Foundation, Chicago, IL.

$125,000 to Link Unlimited, Chicago, IL.

$60,000 to Lewis University, Romeoville, IL.

$60,000 to Saint Xavier University, Chicago, IL.

$60,000 to University of Saint Francis, Joliet, IL.

$50,000 to Benedictine University, Lisle, IL.

$50,000 to Dominican University, River Forest, IL.

$25,000 to Catholic Theological Union at Chicago, Chicago, IL.

$25,000 to Hales Franciscan High School, Chicago, IL.

$20,000 to Marquette University, Milwaukee, WI.

2988
John D. and Minnie R. Schneider Charitable Trust ◇ ☆
(formerly John D. Schneider Charitable Trust)
c/o Richard T. Zwirner
130 E. Randolph St., Ste. 3800
Chicago, IL 60601

Established in 1985 in IL.

Foundation type: Independent foundation.

Financial data (yr. ended 12/31/05): Assets, $6,318,525 (M); gifts received, $108,311; expenditures, $397,882; qualifying distributions, $375,000; giving activities include $375,000 for 3 grants (high: $225,000; low: $50,000).

Fields of interest: Higher education; Disasters, Hurricane Katrina; International relief, 2004 tsunami.

Limitations: Applications not accepted. Giving primarily in IL. No grants to individuals.

Application information: Contributes only to pre-selected organizations.

Officer and Trustees: * Richard T. Zwirner,* Pres.; Loretta L. Stempinski.

EIN: 363388493

2989
Dr. Scholl Foundation
1033 Skokie Blvd., Ste. 230
Northbrook, IL 60062 (847) 559-7430
Contact: Pamela Scholl, Pres.
URL: http://www.drschollfoundation.com

Incorporated in 1947 in IL.

Donor: William M. Scholl, M.D.†.

Foundation type: Independent foundation.

Financial data (yr. ended 12/31/05): Assets, $170,428,674 (M); expenditures, $7,462,890; qualifying distributions, $5,135,440; giving activities include $4,068,000 for 237 grants (high: $250,000; average: $5,000–$50,000).

Purpose and activities: Support for private education at all levels, including elementary,

secondary, and postsecondary schools, colleges and universities, and medical and nursing institutions; general charitable programs, including grants to hospitals, and programs for children, the developmentally disabled, and senior citizens; and civic, cultural, social welfare, economic, and religious activities.

Fields of interest: General charitable giving.

Type of support: Research; Scholarship funds; Internship funds; Fellowships; Program development; Equipment; Continuing support; General/operating support.

Limitations: Giving primarily in the U.S., with some emphasis on the Chicago, IL area. No support for public education, political organizations, or political action committees. No grants to individuals, or for deficit financing, or unrestricted purposes, or to endowments, or capital campaigns, event sponsorship, liquidation of debt; no loans.

Publications: Application guidelines; Informational brochure.

Application information: Applications sent by fax or E-mail not accepted; only one request per organization, per year is permitted. Application form required.

Initial approach: Letter on organization letterhead

Copies of proposal: 1

Deadline(s): Mar. 1

Board meeting date(s): Feb., May, Aug., and Nov.

Final notification: Nov. 1 to Mar. 1

Officers and Directors: * Pamela Scholl,* Chair. and Pres.; Jeanne M. Scholl,* V.P.; Jack E. Scholl,* Secy.; John A. Nitschke, Treas.; Mary Ann Hynes; Richard B. Patterson; David L. Royalty; Daniel Scholl; Susan Scholl.

Number of staff: 3 full-time professional; 1 part-time professional; 2 full-time support.

EIN: 366068724

Selected grants: The following grants were reported in 2004.

$600,000 to Big Shoulders Fund, Chicago, IL. Toward scholarship program.

$171,000 to Cambridge Foundation, Cambridge, England. For Professorship at Cambridge Centre for Brain Repair.

$100,000 to Millennium Park, Chicago, IL. For endowment.

$50,000 to Lyric Opera of Chicago, Chicago, IL. For Student Matinees program.

$50,000 to Mayo Foundation, Rochester, MN. For research and Dr. Scholl Scholars program.

$50,000 to Metropolitan Family Services, Chicago, IL. For Family Counseling Room and Critical Response Team.

$47,000 to Rush University Medical Center, Chicago, IL. For medical research project.

$20,000 to YMCA, Green County Family, Monroe, WI. Toward construction of Fitness Center.

$15,000 to Music Institute of Chicago, Winnetka, IL. For financial assistance program.

$15,000 to Saint Xavier University, Chicago, IL. For scholarships for undergraduate minority nursing students.

2990
Schuler Family Foundation ◇ ☆
28161 N. Keith Dr.
Lake Forest, IL 60045
E-mail: info@schulerfoundation.org; *URL:* http://www.schulerfoundation.org/SFF/index.htm
Scholarship program application address: 6547 N. Chicora Ave., Chicago, IL, 60646

Established in 1997 in IL.
Donor: Jack W. Schuler.
Foundation type: Independent foundation.
Financial data (yr. ended 12/31/05): Assets, $12,996,562 (M); expenditures, $469,611; qualifying distributions, $466,826; giving activities include $185,750 for 44 grants (high: $85,000; low: $250), and $142,500 for grants to individuals.
Purpose and activities: The foundation sponsors a scholarship program to motivate and change behavior of high potential students to strive towards a goal of graduating from college, recognizing that even high potential students are vulnerable to outside influences during high school and college years. Schuler Scholars are students selected at the end of the freshman year in high school. They are offered a 4 year college scholarship of $5,000 per year provided they maintain the requirements of the Scholar program for their remaining 3 years of high school and 4 years of college. Each student will have a team of advisors, including her/his parents to help him or her navigate through high school and college. Currently only freshman from Waukegan, IL, can apply for this scholarship.
Fields of interest: Arts; Higher education; Health care; Human services; Children/youth, services.
Limitations: Giving primarily in Waukegan, IL.
Application information: Contributes only to pre-selected organizations for general grants; see foundation Web site for Schuler Scholar guidelines and application. Application form required.
Deadline(s): Varies; see foundation Web site for current deadline
Officers: Jack W. Schuler, Pres. and Secy.; Therese H. Schuler, V.P.; Tino H. Schuler, V.P.; Renate R. Schuler, Treas.
Director: Tanya E. Schuler.
EIN: 364154510
Selected grants: The following grants were reported in 2005.
$90,000 to Carleton College, Northfield, MN. 2 grants: $85,000, $5,000
$6,500 to Knox College, Galesburg, IL.
$2,000 to Admission Possible, Saint Paul, MN.
$2,000 to Art Institute of Chicago, Chicago, IL.
$2,000 to Lake Forest Symphony, Lake Forest, IL.
$2,000 to Lyric Opera of Chicago, Chicago, IL.
$2,000 to Moab Music Festival, Moab, UT.
$500 to Northwestern University, Evanston, IL.
$500 to W T T W Channel 11, Chicago, IL.

2991
Theodore G. Schwartz Family Foundation ✧
(formerly Theodore G. and M. Christine Schwartz Family Foundation)
c/o TCS Group, LLC
650 Dundee Rd., Ste. 450
Northbrook, IL 60062

Established in 1996 in IL.
Donors: Theodore G. Schwartz; M. Christine Schwartz.
Foundation type: Independent foundation.
Financial data (yr. ended 12/31/05): Assets, $1,392,591 (M); gifts received, $2,000,000; expenditures, $1,629,350; qualifying distributions, $1,629,350; giving activities include $1,627,218 for 24 grants (high: $216,000; low: $100).
Purpose and activities: Giving to 1) promote self-esteem, self-confidence and a sense of pride in Jewish youth, emphasizing Jewish identity and historical accomplishments, and to promote causes

to benefit the State of Israel; 2) to encourage measures for raising standards of research and prevention or suppression of mental illness and related disorders, including establishing or maintaining transitional living resources for afflicted individuals, to assist them in building confidence and the necessary tools for successful re-entry into the mainstream; 3) to promote resources to enable and empower deserving youth in broken homes and dysfunctional environments to develop self-esteem and self-confidence while assisting them to become productive adults; 4) to promote alternative transitional resources to enable and empower people in abusive relationships to develop self-esteem, and to allow them to productively improve their lives and eliminate abuse; 5) to promote conservation of natural resources, and the advancement of farming, by providing education to deserving students and funding research to benefit responsible farmers; 6) to encourage measures for preservation and conservation of wildlife, including the enhancement of animal life and promotion of animal welfare; 7) to match resources with the homeless whose private resources are inadequate, including financial assistance for the erection and operation of housing, and the opportunity for a better future; 8) to promote education by providing resources and financial assistance to enable motivated responsible individuals to secure an education; 9) to promote scientific and medical research for the alleviation of human suffering, including promoting a better quality of life and sense of dignity when encountering adversity; 10) to encourage measures for raising standards of medical care, research and prevention or suppression of disease; and 11) to promote public appreciation of literature, music, painting, dance and other fine arts.
Fields of interest: Higher education; Human services; Community development; Jewish agencies & temples.
Limitations: Applications not accepted. Giving primarily in Coral Gables, FL, and IL. No grants to individuals; or for political campaigns.
Application information: Contributes only to pre-selected organizations.
Officers and Directors:* M. Christine Schwartz,* Pres.; Tracy Schwartz,* Secy.; Theodore G. Schwartz,* Treas.; Steven A. Schlensky; Todd Schwartz.
EIN: 311490195
Selected grants: The following grants were reported in 2004.
$1,000,000 to University of Miami, Coral Gables, FL.
$250,000 to Jewish United Fund of Metropolitan Chicago, Chicago, IL.
$7,500 to American Committee for the Weizmann Institute of Science, Chicago, IL.
$3,000 to University of Illinois Foundation, Champaign, IL.
$2,500 to Tulane University, New Orleans, LA.
$2,000 to American Jewish Committee, Chicago, IL.
$500 to Cancer Wellness Center, Northbrook, IL.
$300 to Canine Companions for Independence, Santa Rosa, CA.
$300 to Youth Services of Glenview/Northbrook, Glenview, IL.
$250 to American Cancer Society, Evanston, IL.

2992
The Joseph C. and Judith A. Scully Foundation ✧ ☆
2120 N. Fremont Ave.
Chicago, IL 60614
Contact: Joseph C. Scully, Tr.

Established in 1999 in IL.
Foundation type: Independent foundation.
Financial data (yr. ended 12/31/05): Assets, $2,692,809 (M); expenditures, $358,363; qualifying distributions, $340,200; giving activities include $340,200 for grants.
Fields of interest: Education; Human services; Religion.
Limitations: Giving primarily in Chicago, IL. No grants to individuals.
Application information: Application form not required.
Deadline(s): None
Trustees: Joseph C. Scully; Judith A. Scully.
EIN: 367295474
Selected grants: The following grants were reported in 2004.
$101,800 to Link Unlimited, Chicago, IL.
$65,000 to CARA Program, Chicago, IL.
$10,000 to CARE, Chicago, IL.
$5,000 to Hephzibah Childrens Association, Oak Park, IL.
$2,000 to Circle Urban Ministries, Chicago, IL.
$1,500 to Art Institute of Chicago, Chicago, IL.
$1,500 to Goodman Theater, Chicago, IL.
$1,000 to Salvation Army, Sterling, IL.

2993
The Seabury Foundation ✧
1111 N. Wells St., Ste. 503
Chicago, IL 60610
Contact: Boyd McDowell III
FAX: (312) 587-7332;
E-mail: seabury@seaburyfoundation.org

Trust established in 1947 in IL.
Donors: Charles Ward Seabury†; Louise Lovett Seabury†.
Foundation type: Independent foundation.
Financial data (yr. ended 12/31/05): Assets, $25,868,022 (M); gifts received, $825,000; expenditures, $1,932,432; qualifying distributions, $1,900,212; giving activities include $1,640,500 for 78 grants (high: $825,000; low: $2,000).
Purpose and activities: Giving primarily for community and social services.
Fields of interest: Performing arts, theater; Arts; Secondary school/education; Higher education; Education; Environment; Health care; Employment, training; Human services; Children/youth, services; Family services; Community development.
Type of support: Seed money; Matching/challenge support; Equipment; General/operating support; Program development; Scholarship funds; Technical assistance.
Limitations: Giving primarily in Chicago, IL; giving also in MI. No grants to individuals, or for benefits; no loans.
Publications: Application guidelines; Program policy statement; Program policy statement (including application guidelines).
Application information: See application guidelines. Application form not required.
Initial approach: Letter of inquiry at least 30 days in advance of deadlines

Copies of proposal: 1
Deadline(s): Nov. 1, Mar. 1, and Aug. 1
Board meeting date(s): Feb., May, and Oct.
Final notification: Feb. 28, May 31, and Oct. 31
Officers and Trustees:* Louise F. Morris,* Exec.
Secy.; Seabury J. Hibben, Exec. Dir.; Robert S.
Boone; Charles B. Fisk; Richard D. Fisk; William C.
Fisk; Deborah S. Holloway; The Northern Trust Co.
Director: Boyd McDowell III.
Number of staff: 2 full-time professional.
EIN: 366027398

2994
Searle Freedom Trust ◇
(formerly D & D Foundation)
c/o D.C. Searle
400 Skokie Blvd., Ste. 300
Northbrook, IL 60062

Established in 1999 in IL.
Foundation type: Independent foundation.
Financial data (yr. ended 12/31/05): Assets,
$90,877,336 (M); gifts received, $65,338,154;
expenditures, $1,927,076; qualifying distributions,
$1,547,081; giving activities include $1,547,081
for 23 grants (high: $215,000; low: $5).
Fields of interest: Human services.
Type of support: Conferences/seminars;
Publication; Fellowships; Research.
Limitations: Applications not accepted. Giving on a
national basis. No grants to individuals, or for
endowments, operating support or annual
campaigns.
Application information: Contributes only to
pre-selected organizations.
Trustees: Kimberly O. Dennis, Exec. Dir.;
Christopher DeMuth; Steven F. Hayward; Stephen
Moore; D.C. Searle; D. Gideon Searle; Michael D.
Searle.
EIN: 367244615
Selected grants: The following grants were reported
in 2004.
$100,000 to Heritage Foundation, DC.
$100,000 to Institute for Humane Studies,
Arlington, VA.
$100,000 to Institute for Justice, DC.
$100,000 to Manhattan Institute for Policy
Research, New York, NY.
$100,000 to Reason Foundation, Los Angeles, CA.
$99,150 to National Council on Teacher Quality, DC.
$75,000 to University of Chicago, Chicago, IL.
$50,000 to American Legislative Exchange Council,
DC.
$50,000 to Donors Trust, Alexandria, VA.
$50,000 to Philanthropy Roundtable, DC.

2995
Segal Family Foundation II ◇
1250 Techny Rd.
Northbrook, IL 60062

Established in 2000 in IL.
Donors: Carole B. Segal; Gordon I. Segal Income
Trust.
Foundation type: Independent foundation.
Financial data (yr. ended 12/31/05): Assets,
$5,270,664 (M); gifts received, $2,114,736;
expenditures, $1,213,774; qualifying distributions,
$1,188,881; giving activities include $1,188,881
for 46 grants (high: $586,000; low: $81).

Purpose and activities: Giving primarily in the area
of arthritis.
Fields of interest: Arts; Education; Health
organizations, association; Arthritis; Christian
agencies & churches.
Limitations: Applications not accepted. No grants to
individuals.
Application information: Contributes only to
pre-selected organizations.
Officers and Directors:* Carole B. Segal,* Pres. and
Treas.; Harvey J. Silverstone, Secy.; Katherine
Frekko; Robert Segal.
EIN: 364330990

2996
Barbara and Barre Seid Foundation ◇
(formerly Barre Seid Foundation)
1111 W. 35th St., 12th Fl.
Chicago, IL 60609-1404 (773) 869-1111
Contact: Barre Seid, Pres.

Established in 1985 in IL.
Donor: Barre Seid.
Foundation type: Independent foundation.
Financial data (yr. ended 12/31/05): Assets,
$9,248,800 (M); expenditures, $3,153,513;
qualifying distributions, $3,102,332; giving
activities include $3,102,332 for 70 grants (high:
$400,000; low: $100).
Purpose and activities: Support primarily for
education, cultural organizations and the arts, and
philanthropic associations.
Fields of interest: Performing arts, music; Arts;
Higher education; Education; Human services;
Jewish federated giving programs; Jewish agencies
& temples.
Limitations: Applications not accepted. Giving
primarily in Chicago, IL. No grants to individuals.
Application information: Contributes only to
pre-selected organizations.
Officers: Barre Seid, Pres. and Treas.; Barbara
Landis-Seid, Secy.
Directors: Steve Baer; Joan Frontczak.
EIN: 363342443
Selected grants: The following grants were reported
in 2004.
$176,788 to Heartland Institute, Chicago, IL.
$87,500 to Lincoln Legal Foundation, Chicago, IL. 3
grants: $50,000, $12,500, $25,000
$26,220 to Chicago Opera Theater, Chicago, IL.
$25,700 to Competitive Enterprise Institute, DC.
$20,000 to Illinois Taxpayer Education Foundation,
Chicago, IL. 2 grants: $10,000 each
$10,000 to Santa Fe Opera, Santa Fe, NM.
$5,000 to Contemporary Art Workshop, Chicago, IL.

2997
Seigle Family Foundation ◇
1331 Davis Rd.
Elgin, IL 60123
Contact: Mark Seigle, Treas.

Established in 1981 in IL.
Donors: Harold T. Seigle†; Lora Seigle; Seigles Inc.
Foundation type: Independent foundation.
Financial data (yr. ended 12/31/05): Assets,
$1,240,685 (M); gifts received, $692,967;
expenditures, $346,949; qualifying distributions,
$343,969; giving activities include $343,969 for 74
grants (high: $16,666; low: $25).

Purpose and activities: Giving primarily for
education, health care, housing, community
development, and social services.
Fields of interest: Education; Health care; Human
services; Community development, neighborhood
development.
Limitations: Giving primarily in the metropolitan
Chicago, IL, area. No grants to individuals.
Publications: Application guidelines.
Application information: Application form not
required.
Initial approach: Letter
Deadline(s): None
Officers: Harry J. Seigle, Pres.; Mark S. Seigle,
Treas.
EIN: 363112783
Selected grants: The following grants were reported
in 2004.
$31,666 to Steppenwolf Theater Company,
Chicago, IL. 2 grants: $16,666, $15,000
$25,000 to Ecker Center for Mental Health, Elgin,
IL.
$15,000 to Elgin Symphony Orchestra, Elgin, IL.
$15,000 to United Way of Elgin, Elgin, IL.
$12,500 to Larkin Center, Elgin, IL.
$10,000 to American Jewish Committee, Chicago,
IL.
$5,500 to Elgin Academy, Elgin, IL.
$2,500 to Elgin Choral Union, Elgin, IL.
$1,000 to DayOneNetwork, Batavia, IL.

2998
SF Foundation ◇
(formerly Simon Family Foundation)
c/o Blackman Kallick Bartelstein, LLP
10 S. Riverside Plz., Rm. 900
Chicago, IL 60606

Established in 1997 in IL.
Donor: Daniel L. Simon.
Foundation type: Independent foundation.
Financial data (yr. ended 12/31/05): Assets,
$18,377,365 (M); expenditures, $1,112,454;
qualifying distributions, $1,087,794; giving
activities include $1,067,100 for 14 grants (high:
$1,002,000; low: $100).
Purpose and activities: Giving primarily for higher
education; funding also for human services.
Fields of interest: Higher education; Human
services; Children/youth, services; Family services;
Economically disadvantaged.
Limitations: Applications not accepted. Giving
primarily in IL and MN; some funding nationally. No
grants to individuals.
Application information: Contributes only to
pre-selected organizations.
Directors: Daniel L. Simon; Joseph Simon; Kelly
Simon; Paul G. Simon; Sandra Simon.
EIN: 364146804
Selected grants: The following grants were reported
in 2004.
$1,000,000 to Fairfield University, Fairfield, CT.
$20,000 to Big Shoulders Fund, Chicago, IL.
$1,000 to Chicago Zoological Society, Brookfield,
IL.

2999
Joseph R. and Helen Shaker Family Foundation ✧
(formerly The Shaker Family Foundation)
1100 W. Lake St.
Oak Park, IL 60301-1015 (708) 524-0800

Established in 1986 in IL.
Donors: Anthony R. Shaker; Joseph R. Shaker; Shaker Advertising Agency, Inc.; Elizabeth Shaker; Joseph G. Shaker; John E. Shaker; Catherine Breit.
Foundation type: Independent foundation.
Financial data (yr. ended 11/30/05): Assets, $1,948,685 (M); gifts received, $1,895,010; expenditures, $1,401,801; qualifying distributions, $1,401,801; giving activities include $1,331,907 for 203 grants (high: $454,433; low: $20).
Purpose and activities: Giving for education, religion, relief services, and for the prevention of cruelty to women and children.
Fields of interest: Arts; Education; Hospitals (general); Human services; Christian agencies & churches.
Type of support: General/operating support; Annual campaigns; Building/renovation; Scholarship funds.
Limitations: Giving primarily in IL, with some emphasis on the Chicago area. No grants to individuals.
Trustee: Anthony R. Shaker.
Number of staff: 1
EIN: 363572999
Selected grants: The following grants were reported in 2005.
$56,674 to AmeriCares, Stamford, CT.
$41,572 to Americas Second Harvest, Chicago, IL.
$20,000 to Catholic Relief Services, Baltimore, MD.
$20,000 to Direct Relief International, Santa Barbara, CA.
$11,000 to Catholic Charities, Harvey, IL.
$10,000 to CARE, Chicago, IL.
$10,000 to First Book, DC.
$10,000 to National Coalition for the Homeless, DC.
$1,000 to Association House of Chicago, Chicago, IL.
$1,000 to University of Michigan, Ann Arbor, MI.

3000
Lester & Edna Shapiro Family Foundation
799 Central Ave., Ste. 350
Highland Park, IL 60035

Established in 1968.
Donors: Lester Shapiro†; Nathan Shapiro; Norton Shapiro; Robert Shapiro; Daniel Shapiro; Sherwin Begoun; NS Associates, Inc.
Foundation type: Independent foundation.
Financial data (yr. ended 9/30/05): Assets, $1,154,839 (M); gifts received, $318,558; expenditures, $670,856; qualifying distributions, $669,269; giving activities include $669,269 for grants.
Fields of interest: Elementary/secondary education; Jewish agencies & temples.
Limitations: Applications not accepted. No grants to individuals.
Application information: Contributes only to pre-selected organizations.
Trustees: Nathan Shapiro; Norton Shapiro; Robert Shapiro.
EIN: 363985971

3001
Charles and M. R. Shapiro Foundation, Inc. ✧
(formerly Fern G. Shapiro, Morris R. Shapiro, and Charles Shapiro Foundation, Inc.)
191 N. Wacker Dr., Ste. 1800
Chicago, IL 60606-1615

Incorporated in 1958 in IL.
Donors: Charles Shapiro†; Mary Shapiro†; Molly Shapiro†; Morris R. Shapiro†.
Foundation type: Independent foundation.
Financial data (yr. ended 7/31/05): Assets, $38,851,686 (M); expenditures, $2,072,461; qualifying distributions, $1,885,943; giving activities include $1,714,500 for 73 grants (high: $135,000; low: $2,000).
Purpose and activities: Giving primarily to Jewish organizations and for human services.
Fields of interest: Arts; Higher education; Health organizations, association; Medical research, institute; Human services; Youth, services; Jewish federated giving programs; Jewish agencies & temples.
Limitations: Applications not accepted. Giving primarily in Chicago, IL; funding also in New York, NY. No grants to individuals.
Application information: Contributes only to pre-selected organizations.
Officers and Directors:* Norman A. Shubert,* Pres.; Joan Pines,* V.P. and Secy.; Michael D. Vick,* Treas.
EIN: 366109757

3002
The Sharpe Family Foundation ✧
c/o Amy E. Szostak, Northern Trust Co.
50 S. LaSalle St.
Chicago, IL 60675
Contact: Henry D. Sharpe, Jr., Tr.

Established in 1966 in RI.
Donors: Mary Elizabeth Sharpe†; Henry D. Sharpe, Jr.
Foundation type: Independent foundation.
Financial data (yr. ended 12/31/05): Assets, $31,341,104 (M); gifts received, $400,000; expenditures, $1,652,469; qualifying distributions, $1,396,900; giving activities include $1,396,900 for 102 grants (high: $315,000; low: $500).
Purpose and activities: Giving primarily for higher and other education, particularly to a school of design, as well as for art and culture, nature conservation, and health.
Fields of interest: Museums; Arts; Secondary school/education; Higher education; Education; Environment, natural resources; Health organizations, association; Christian agencies & churches.
Limitations: Giving primarily in RI. No grants to individuals.
Application information:
  Initial approach: Letter
  Deadline(s): None
Trustees: Henry D. Sharpe, Jr.; Peggy B. Sharpe.
EIN: 136208422
Selected grants: The following grants were reported in 2005.
$315,000 to Rhode Island School of Design, Providence, RI.
$210,000 to Rocky Hill School, East Greenwich, RI.
$50,000 to Robert Abbe Museum, Bar Harbor, ME.

$41,000 to Planned Parenthood Federation of America, New York, NY.
$38,000 to Rhode Island Natural History Survey, Kingston, RI.
$12,000 to Conservation Law Foundation, Providence, RI.
$5,000 to Looking Glass Theater, Providence, RI.
$5,000 to Miriam Hospital, Providence, RI.
$5,000 to Sarah Lawrence College, Bronxville, NY.
$4,200 to Groundwork Providence, Providence, RI.

3003
Seyfarth Shaw Charitable Foundation ✧ ☆
55 E. Monroe St., Ste. 4200
Chicago, IL 60603 (312) 621-8734
Contact: Marisa Williams

Established in 2004 in IL.
Donors: Joel Kaplan; Seyfarth Shaw LLP.
Foundation type: Independent foundation.
Financial data (yr. ended 7/31/05): Assets, $14,405 (M); gifts received, $640,533; expenditures, $630,231; qualifying distributions, $630,231; giving activities include $630,140 for 22 grants (high: $18,000; low: $100).
Fields of interest: Arts; Health organizations, association; Human services.
Limitations: Giving on a national basis.
Application information:
  Initial approach: Letter
  Deadline(s): None
Officers: Andrew R. Laidlaw, Pres.; Gilmore F. Diekmann, Jr., V.P.; Richard D. Ostrow, V.P.; Robert Somma, V.P.; Nathaniel Sack, Secy.
EIN: 201076114

3004
Walden W. & Jean Young Shaw Foundation ✧
55 E. Monroe St., Ste. 4200
Chicago, IL 60603

Established in 1967 in IL.
Donors: Walden W. Shaw; Jean Young Shaw.
Foundation type: Independent foundation.
Financial data (yr. ended 6/30/05): Assets, $12,019,301 (M); expenditures, $892,873; qualifying distributions, $831,508; giving activities include $741,200 for 7 grants (high: $225,000; low: $24,200).
Purpose and activities: Giving limited to hospitals and other medical facilities, including medical facilities for children, as well as for other children's services.
Fields of interest: Hospitals (general); Mental health, treatment; Cancer; Medical research, institute; Cancer research; Children/youth, services.
Limitations: Applications not accepted. Giving primarily in Chicago, IL, CA, and OR. No grants to individuals.
Application information: Contributes only to pre-selected organizations.
Officers: N. Carey Iler, Jr., Pres.; Robert Gordon Iler, V.P.; Walter Roth, Secy.-Treas.
Directors: Donald Carey Iler; Robert Gordon Iler, Jr.; Cheryl Kennedy; Sharon Jean Stone.
EIN: 366162196
Selected grants: The following grants were reported in 2003.

$225,000 to Mercy Foundation, Roseburg, OR. To purchase equipment.

$225,000 to University of Chicago, Child Psychiatry Clinic, Chicago, IL. For general support.

$125,000 to Childrens Memorial Hospital, Chicago, IL. For research.

$100,000 to Pediatric Cancer Research Foundation, Irvine, CA. For research.

$90,000 to Erikson Institute, Chicago, IL. For general support.

$60,000 to Hoag Hospital Foundation, Newport Beach, CA. To purchase equipment.

$40,000 to Childrens Hospital of Orange County (CHOC) Foundation, Orange, CA. For general support.

$25,300 to Burn Institute, San Diego, CA. For general support.

3005
The Sheba Foundation ✧ ☆
c/o Sheldon Lavin
1225 Corporate Blvd.
Aurora, IL 60504-6408

Established in 1994 in IL.
Donors: Sheldon Lavin; Sylvia Lavin.
Foundation type: Independent foundation.
Financial data (yr. ended 12/31/05): Assets, $16,695,088 (M); gifts received, $3,294,240; expenditures, $1,469,282; qualifying distributions, $1,414,800; giving activities include $1,414,200 for 16 grants (high: $1,000,000; low: $100).
Purpose and activities: Giving primarily for health, Jewish federated giving programs and human services.
Fields of interest: Philosophy/ethics; Education, early childhood education; Hospitals (general); Health care, infants; Health care, patient services; Multiple sclerosis; Cancer research; Jewish federated giving programs; Jewish agencies & temples.
Limitations: Applications not accepted. Giving primarily in IL. No grants to individuals.
Application information: Contributes only to pre-selected organizations.
Officers and Directors:* Sheldon Lavin,* Pres.; Sylvia Lavin,* Secy.-Treas.; Jerold Lavin; Steven Lavin; Deborah Rosenberg.
EIN: 363976909
Selected grants: The following grants were reported in 2003.
$50,000 to Jewish United Fund of Metropolitan Chicago, Chicago, IL.
$28,400 to Goodman Theater, Chicago, IL.
$25,000 to National Fish and Wildlife Foundation, DC.
$25,000 to University of Chicago, Department of Pediatrics, Chicago, IL. For research.
$4,630 to Multiple Sclerosis Society, National, Chicago, IL. For research.
$1,000 to Chicago Public Education Fund, Chicago, IL.
$1,000 to Macula Vision Research Foundation, Bala Cynwyd, PA.
$500 to Field Museum of Natural History, Chicago, IL.
$500 to KESHET, Northbrook, IL.
$250 to Memorial Sloan-Kettering Cancer Center, New York, NY.

3006
The Shifting Foundation ✧
c/o Ostron, Reisin, Berk & Abrams, Ltd.
455 N. City Front Plz. Dr., Ste. 2600
Chicago, IL 60611

Established in 1982 in IL.
Donors: Julie Breskin; David Breskin.
Foundation type: Independent foundation.
Financial data (yr. ended 12/31/05): Assets, $8,291,413 (M); gifts received, $200,369; expenditures, $483,979; qualifying distributions, $398,279; giving activities include $397,129 for 35 grants (high: $30,000; low: $2,910).
Purpose and activities: Support primarily for the economically disadvantaged, hunger relief, social services, health organizations, human and civil rights, environmental and anti-nuclear interests, and Third World development.
Fields of interest: Visual arts; Museums; Performing arts; Performing arts, music; Literature; Arts; Education; Environment; Animals/wildlife, preservation/protection; Reproductive health, family planning; Health care; Children/youth, services; Women, centers/services; Minorities/ immigrants, centers/services; Homeless, human services; International relief; International peace/ security; International affairs, arms control; International human rights; Civil rights, race/ intergroup relations; Civil rights; Community development; Minorities; Women; Economically disadvantaged; Homeless.
Type of support: General/operating support; Continuing support; Capital campaigns; Program development.
Limitations: Applications not accepted. Giving on a national basis. No grants to individuals.
Application information: Contributes only to pre-selected organizations.
Officers and Directors:* David Breskin,* Pres.; Julie Breskin,* V.P.; Brian Israel, Secy.; Richard Reisin, Treas.
EIN: 366108560
Selected grants: The following grants were reported in 2005.
$30,000 to Boys Club of San Francisco, Omega, San Francisco, CA.
$25,000 to Environmental Defense, New York, NY.
$25,000 to Natural Resources Defense Council, New York, NY.
$25,000 to Oxfam America, Boston, MA.
$15,000 to Doctors Without Borders USA, New York, NY.
$15,000 to International Rescue Committee, New York, NY.
$15,000 to Union of Concerned Scientists, Cambridge, MA.
$11,000 to Little School, San Francisco, CA.
$10,000 to Childrens Defense Fund, DC.
$10,000 to Poetry in Review Foundation, New York, NY.

3007
The Russell and Betty Shirk Foundation ✧
P.O. Box 1549
Bloomington, IL 61702-1549

Established in 1968.
Donors: Russell O. Shirk; James A. Shirk; Betty Shirk.
Foundation type: Independent foundation.
Financial data (yr. ended 12/31/05): Assets, $13,494,070 (M); gifts received, $205,000;

expenditures, $643,292; qualifying distributions, $629,158; giving activities include $628,000 for 13 grants (high: $550,000; low: $250).
Fields of interest: Higher education; Education; Health organizations, association; Athletics/sports; school programs; Human services; YM/YWCAs & YM/YWHAs; Children/youth, services.
Type of support: General/operating support; Scholarship funds.
Limitations: Applications not accepted. Giving primarily in IL, with emphasis on Bloomington. No grants to individuals.
Application information: Contributes only to pre-selected organizations.
Officers and Directors:* James A. Shirk,* Pres.; Betty J. Shirk, Secy.; Merrick C. Hayes.
EIN: 237022709
Selected grants: The following grants were reported in 2005.
$550,000 to Illinois Wesleyan University, Bloomington, IL.
$50,000 to YMCA of McLean County, Bloomington, IL.
$6,000 to University of Illinois, Springfield, IL.
$2,500 to United Way of McLean County, Bloomington, IL.
$2,000 to Boy Scouts of America, Peoria, IL.
$1,500 to Lake Land College, Mattoon, IL.
$1,000 to American Red Cross, Bloomington, IL.

3008
The Simmons Family Foundation ✧ ☆
12 Danforth Rd.
Alton, IL 62002
Contact: John D. Simmons, Tr.; Jayne Simmons

Donors: John D. Simmons; Jayne Simmons.
Foundation type: Independent foundation.
Financial data (yr. ended 12/31/05): Assets, $886,933 (M); gifts received, $1,000; expenditures, $2,721,773; qualifying distributions, $2,709,353; giving activities include $2,709,353 for 11+ grants (high: $1,760,264).
Purpose and activities: Giving primarily to a Baptist church and to Protestant ministries, schools, and churches; some funding for children, youth, and social services.
Fields of interest: Higher education; Education; Animal welfare; Health organizations, association; Athletics/sports, school programs; Children/youth, services; Protestant agencies & churches.
Limitations: Giving primarily in IL and MO; some funding nationally.
Application information:
Initial approach: Letter
Trustee: John D. Simmons.
EIN: 206093255

3009
The Siragusa Foundation
875 N. Michigan Ave., Ste. 3216
Chicago, IL 60611 (312) 280-0833
Contact: Irene S. Phelps, Pres.
FAX: (312) 943-4489;
E-mail: information@siragusa.org; URL: http://
www.siragusa.org

Trust established in 1950 in IL; incorporated in 1980.
Donor: Ross D. Siragusa†.
Foundation type: Independent foundation.

Financial data (yr. ended 12/31/05): Assets, $32,988,516 (M); expenditures, $2,108,740; qualifying distributions, $1,693,032; giving activities include $1,326,074 for 163 grants (high: $20,000; low: $500).

Purpose and activities: The foundation is committed to honoring founder Ross D. Siragusa by sustaining and developing Chicago, IL's nonprofit resources. Through its program areas, the foundation funds organizations and projects that provide specialized services to populations with defined needs. The foundation strives to improve the quality of life for people living in the metropolitan Chicago, IL, area.

Fields of interest: Humanities; Arts; Child development, education; Higher education; Education; Environment; Hospitals (general); Health care; Health organizations, association; Breast cancer; Heart & circulatory diseases; Arthritis; Medical research, institute; Cancer research; Heart & circulatory research; Brain research; Human services; Youth, services; Child development, services; Aging, centers/services; Homeless, human services; Disabilities, people with; Economically disadvantaged; Homeless.

Type of support: General/operating support; Annual campaigns; Equipment; Program development; Fellowships; Scholarship funds; Research; Matching/challenge support.

Limitations: Giving primarily in the Midwest, with emphasis on the metropolitan Chicago, IL, area. No support for political advocacy programs. No grants to individuals, or for endowment funds; no loans.

Publications: Financial statement; Grants list.

Application information: Refer to foundation Web site for future giving deadlines. After reviewing the letter of inquiry, the foundation may request a formal proposal. The foundation does not accept proposals submitted online or via e-mail. The foundation does not accept unsolicited proposals from outside the Chicago, IL, area. Application form required.

Initial approach: Letter of inquiry (2 pages)
Copies of proposal: 1
Board meeting date(s): Apr. and Nov.
Final notification: Sept. 1

Officers and Directors:* John R. Siragusa,* Chair.; Irene S. Phelps, Pres.; Richard D. Siragusa,* Secy.; George E. Driscoll, Dir. Emeritus; James Durkan; Jennifer I. Hicks; John E. Hicks, Jr.; Melvyn H. Schneider; Alexander C. Siragusa; Ross D. Siragusa, Jr.; Ross D. Siragusa III; Sinclair C. Siragusa; James B. Wilson.

Number of staff: 2 full-time professional; 1 full-time support.

EIN: 363100492

Selected grants: The following grants were reported in 2006.

$10,000 to Cove School, Northbrook, IL. For scholarships.

$7,500 to Art Resources in Teaching (ART), Chicago, IL. For expansion of visual arts residency programs.

$7,500 to BUILD, Chicago, IL. For Project BUILD.

$7,500 to Hadley School for the Blind, Winnetka, IL. For development of two educational programs.

$7,500 to Neumann Association, Chicago, IL. For Neumann Neighbors jobs training and placement program.

$5,000 to Emergency Fund for Needy People, Chicago, IL. For Financial Assistance Program.

$1,500 to Literature for All of Us, Evanston, IL.

3010
Sirius Fund

(formerly Peter and Virginia Foreman Family Foundation)
225 W. Washington St., Ste. 1650
Chicago, IL 60606
Contact: Peter B. Foreman, Pres.

Established in 1990 in IL.

Donors: Christopher Foreman; Peter B. Foreman.

Foundation type: Independent foundation.

Financial data (yr. ended 6/30/05): Assets, $13,845,319 (M); gifts received, $20,076; expenditures, $757,746; qualifying distributions, $744,551; giving activities include $699,066 for 97 grants (high: $219,980; low: $25).

Purpose and activities: Giving primarily for the arts, education, health, and human services; also support for Jewish organizations.

Fields of interest: Museums; Performing arts, theater; Arts; Higher education; Education; Environment, natural resources; Botanical gardens; Hospitals (general); Health care; Health organizations, association; Recreation, parks/ playgrounds; Human services; Children/youth, services; Women, centers/services; Community development, neighborhood development; Jewish federated giving programs.

Limitations: Applications not accepted. Giving primarily in Chicago, IL. No grants to individuals.

Application information: Unsolicited requests for funds not accepted.

Officers: Peter B. Foreman, Pres.; Virginia Foreman, V.P.; Rhonda Keysor, V.P.

Directors: Christopher Foreman; Jeffrey Foreman.

EIN: 363712587

Selected grants: The following grants were reported in 2004.

$236,829 to Merit School of Music, Chicago, IL.

$15,100 to John G. Shedd Aquarium, Chicago, IL.

$5,000 to Cystic Fibrosis Foundation, Chicago, IL.

$2,670 to Art Institute of Chicago, Chicago, IL.

$2,250 to North Lawndale College Preparatory Charter High School, Chicago, IL.

$600 to Museum of Contemporary Art, Chicago, IL.

$500 to Access Living of Metropolitan Chicago, Chicago, IL.

$500 to Childrens Memorial Hospital, Chicago, IL.

$250 to Chicago Cares, Chicago, IL.

$250 to Infant Welfare Society of Chicago, Chicago, IL.

3011
Harry L. & John L. Smysor Memorial Fund ◇ ☆

c/o First Mid-Illinois Bank & Trust
P.O. Box 499
Mattoon, IL 61938-3932
Application address: c/o Gary Kuhns, First Mid-Illinois Bank & Trust, 1515 Charleston Ave., Mattoon, IL 61938, tel.: (217) 234-7454

Established in 1982 in IL.

Donors: Catherine H. Smysor†; John L. Smysor†.

Foundation type: Independent foundation.

Financial data (yr. ended 5/31/06): Assets, $4,546,878 (M); expenditures, $712,690; qualifying distributions, $468,480; giving activities include $468,480 for grants to individuals.

Purpose and activities: Awards scholarships to high school students for higher education.

Type of support: Scholarships—to individuals.

Limitations: Giving primarily to residents of IL.

Application information: Application form available from Windsor, IL, high school or from trustee bank. Application form required.

Deadline(s): Apr. 15

Trustees: Lyle Huffmaster; Orris Seng; First Mid-Illinois Bank & Trust.

EIN: 371160678

3012
Fred B. Snite Foundation ◇

550 W. Frontage Rd., Ste. 3745
Northfield, IL 60093-1289
Contact: Margaret Sackley, Pres.

Incorporated in 1945 in IL.

Donors: Fred B. Snite†; Local Loan Co.

Foundation type: Independent foundation.

Financial data (yr. ended 6/30/05): Assets, $18,164,871 (M); expenditures, $899,293; qualifying distributions, $800,491; giving activities include $776,675 for 27 grants (high: $153,107; low: $5,000).

Purpose and activities: Giving primarily for Roman Catholic church support and church-related educational institutions; funding also for human services.

Fields of interest: Secondary school/education; Higher education; Education; Hospitals (general); Human services; Roman Catholic agencies & churches; Disabilities, people with.

Limitations: Giving primarily in CA and IL. No grants to individuals.

Application information:

Initial approach: Letter
Deadline(s): None

Officers and Directors:* Margaret Sackley,* Pres.; Katherine B. Meszklevitz,* Exec. V.P.; Teresa Bratton,* V.P.; Theresa Rassas,* V.P.; Patrick Sackley, V.P.; Joanne Ward, V.P.; Lance Williams, V.P.; Patricia Nahigian, Secy.; A.E. Eliot, Treas.

EIN: 366084839

Selected grants: The following grants were reported in 2004.

$50,000 to Eisenhower Medical Center, Rancho Mirage, CA.

$20,000 to University of Notre Dame, Notre Dame, IN.

$15,000 to Cristo Rey Jesuit High School, Chicago, IL.

$15,000 to Saint Joseph College Seminary, Chicago, IL.

$15,000 to Saint Vincent de Paul Center, Chicago, IL.

$10,000 to Greater Chicago Food Depository, Chicago, IL.

$10,000 to La Rabida Childrens Hospital, Chicago, IL.

$10,000 to Lewis University, Romeoville, IL.

$10,000 to Nurturing Network, White Salmon, WA.

$10,000 to Rehabilitation Institute of Chicago, Chicago, IL.

3013
Souder Family Foundation ◇

c/o The Northern Trust Bank of FL
P.O. Box 803878
Chicago, IL 60680
Application address: c/o The Northern Trust Bank of FL, 700 Brickell Ave., Miami, FL 33131

Established in 1986 in FL.

Donors: William F. Souder, Jr. Charitable Lead Trust; Susanna J. Souder.
Foundation type: Independent foundation.
Financial data (yr. ended 12/31/04): Assets, $12,728,098 (M); gifts received, $565,513; expenditures, $629,445; qualifying distributions, $558,101; giving activities include $556,271 for 37 grants (high: $115,000; low: $500).
Purpose and activities: Giving primarily for education and health care, and to Protestant organizations, particularly to a Presbyterian church.
Fields of interest: Museums (children's); Historic preservation/historical societies; Higher education; Medical school/education; Education; Zoos/zoological societies; Aquariums; Hospitals (general); Health care; Human services; Children/youth, services; Protestant agencies & churches.
Type of support: General/operating support; Annual campaigns; Building/renovation.
Limitations: Giving primarily in FL, IL, MI, and WI. No grants to individuals.
Application information: Application form not required.
  Deadline(s): None
Directors: Paul Schwab; Susanna J. Souder; William F. Souder, Jr.
EIN: 391560019

3014
Albert J. & Claire R. Speh Foundation
10700 W. Higgins Rd., Ste. 250
Rosemont, IL   60018   (847) 299-7011
Contact: Kevin Malinger, Exec. Dir.
FAX: (847) 299-7044; E-mail: info@speh.org;
URL: http://www.speh.org

Established in 1996 in IL.
Donors: Albert J. Speh, Jr.†; Claire R. Speh.
Foundation type: Independent foundation.
Financial data (yr. ended 12/31/05): Assets, $13,289,973 (M); expenditures, $1,052,589; qualifying distributions, $869,919; giving activities include $682,679 for 55 grants (high: $75,000; low: $500).
Purpose and activities: Giving primarily for youth services.
Fields of interest: Education; Youth development; Children/youth, services; Family services.
Type of support: General/operating support; Continuing support; Management development/capacity building; Annual campaigns; Capital campaigns; Building/renovation; Equipment; Emergency funds; Program development; Seed money; Curriculum development; Internship funds; Scholarship funds; Technical assistance; Consulting services; Program-related investments/loans; Employee-related scholarships; Matching/challenge support.
Limitations: Giving primarily in Chicago, and in Cook, Lake, McHenry, Will and DuPage counties, IL. No grants for research.
Publications: Grants list; Informational brochure (including application guidelines).
Application information: Chicago Area Grant Application Form accepted, and can be downloaded from foundation Web site. Application form required.
  Initial approach: Letter of inquiry (no longer than 2 typewritten pages. Attachments, brochures, reports, articles, etc., will not be accepted)
  Copies of proposal: 1
  Deadline(s): Mar. 15 and July 15 for applications
  Board meeting date(s): Feb., June, and Oct.
  Final notification: June 30 and Oct. 30

Officers and Trustees:* Claire R. Speh,* Pres.; Kathleen M. Malinger,* Treas.; Kevin Malinger, Exec. Dir.; Justin Bennett; Alanna Golden; Erik Jorgenson; Megan Jorgenson; Lorene Malinger; Lynette Malinger; Shannon Neal; Matthew Sharko; Michelle Sharko; Albert J. Speh III; Albert J. Speh IV; Lawrence J. Speh.
Number of staff: 2 full-time professional; 1 part-time support.
EIN: 364118596

3015
The Spencer Foundation ▼
625 N. Michigan Ave., Ste. 1600
Chicago, IL   60611   (312) 337-7000
Contact: Michael S. McPherson, Pres.
FAX: (312) 337-0282;
E-mail: information@spencer.org; URL: http://www.spencer.org

Incorporated in 1962 in IL.
Donor: Lyle M. Spencer†.
Foundation type: Independent foundation.
Financial data (yr. ended 3/31/05): Assets, $411,018,768 (M); expenditures, $20,592,979; qualifying distributions, $18,312,242; giving activities include $12,217,563 for 123 grants (high: $1,500,000; low: $2,500), $1,981,760 for 11 grants to individuals (high: $681,600; low: $37,500), $197,765 for employee matching gifts, and $669,743 for foundation-administered programs.
Purpose and activities: The foundation is committed to supporting high-quality investigation of education through its research programs and to strengthening and renewing the educational research community through its fellowship and training programs and related activities.
Fields of interest: Education, research.
Type of support: Fellowships; Research; Employee matching gifts.
Limitations: Giving on a national and international basis. No grants to individuals (except those working under the auspices of an institution), or for capital funds, general purposes, operating or continuing support, sabbatical supplements, work in instructional or curriculum development, any kind of training or service program, scholarships, travel fellowships, endowment funds, or pre-doctoral research; no loans.
Publications: Annual report.
Application information: Submit full proposal only upon request. Information on program and application form required for Spencer Post-doctoral Fellowships should be requested from the National Academy of Education, 500 5th St. N.W., No. 1049, Washington, DC 20001. Application form not required.
  Initial approach: Initial proposal
  Copies of proposal: 4
  Deadline(s): None for initial proposal
  Board meeting date(s): Jan., June, and Oct.
  Final notification: Varies depending on the amount requested
Officers and Directors:* Derek C. Bok,* Chair.; Kenji Hakuta,* Vice-Chair.; Michael S. McPherson,* Pres.; Paul D. Goren, V.P.; Mary J. Cahillane, C.F.O. and Treas.; Maria H. Carlos, Cont.; Howard E. Gardner; Cynthia Greenleaf; Christopher Jencks; Carol R. Johnson; Lyle Logan; Richard J. Shavelson.
Number of staff: 7 full-time professional; 11 full-time support; 1 part-time support.
EIN: 366078558

Selected grants: The following grants were reported in 2005.
$4,559,000 to National Academy of Education, New York, NY. For Postdoctoral Fellowship Program.
$1,387,425 to Harvard University, Cambridge, MA. 2 grants: $312,425 (For research project, The High School Work Transition in Japan: Its Transformation and Consequences), $1,075,000 (For Forum for Excellence in Higher Education).
$881,500 to University of California, Berkeley, CA. 2 grants: $480,250 (For research project, Patterns of Change and Control: Specifying What to Teach on the Basis of Scientific Research), $401,250 (For research project, Effective Preschooling for Latino Children Identifying Discontinuities between Home and Preschool).
$440,325 to Princeton University, Princeton, NJ. For research project, Higher Educational Opportunity in Texas: The Top 10 Percent Plan in the Shadows of Hopwood, Grutter and Gratz.
$428,925 to Duke University, Durham, NC. For research project, Teacher Quality and Public Policy.
$318,775 to University of Georgia, Athens, GA. For research project, A Freed People's Education: Learners, Classrooms, and Teachers.
$39,950 to University of North Carolina, Charlotte, NC. For research project, The Conflicting Goals of Public School Choice and Performance-Based Incentives.
$39,800 to Stanford University, Stanford, CA. For research project, Famous Americans: Changes in Historical Consciousness across the American Century.

3016
The Otho S. A. Sprague Memorial Institute
P.O. Box 806214
Chicago, IL   60680-4123
Contact: James N. Alexander, Exec. Dir.
URL: http://www.spragueinstitute.org

Incorporated in 1910 in IL.
Donor: Members of the Sprague family.
Foundation type: Independent foundation.
Financial data (yr. ended 12/31/05): Assets, $34,201,319 (M); expenditures, $1,799,757; qualifying distributions, $1,588,532; giving activities include $1,448,590 for 13 grants (high: $468,011; low: $2,750).
Purpose and activities: Giving for the investigation of the causes of disease and the prevention and relief of human suffering. In accordance with the wishes of the founder, support is restricted to nonprofits and programs within Chicago, IL.
Fields of interest: Health care, reform; Public health; Health care; Pediatrics research; American Red Cross.
Type of support: General/operating support; Program development; Publication; Seed money; Curriculum development; Research; Technical assistance.
Limitations: Applications not accepted. Giving limited to Chicago, IL. No grants to individuals, or for building or endowment funds, general purposes, scholarships, fellowships, or matching gifts; no loans.
Publications: Annual report.
Application information: Unsolicited requests for funds not accepted. Application by invitation only.
  Board meeting date(s): May and Dec.

Officers and Directors:* Whitney Wood Addington, M.D.*, Pres.; Edward K. Chandler,* V.P.; Michelle R. Obama,* Secy.; John A. Svoboda,* Treas.; James N. Alexander, Exec. Dir.; Vernon Armour, Life Dir.; Charles F. Clarke, Jr., Life Dir.; Stewart S. Dixon, Life Dir.; Charles C. Haffner III, Life Dir.; William E. Bennett; Tariq H. Butt, M.D.; Caswell Evans, DDS; Rodney L. Goldstein; Ada Mary Gugenheim; Arthur G. Jones, M.D.; Susan C. Scrimshaw; Rebecca M. Wurtz, M.D.
Number of staff: 1 part-time professional.
EIN: 366068723

3017
Spreading the Good News of Salvation Foundation ✦
4355 Weaver Pkwy.
Warrenville, IL 60555-4028
Contact: Kenneth Neumann, Dir.; Jean Neumann, Dir.

Established in 2002 in IL.
Donors: Jean Neumann; Kenneth Neumann.
Foundation type: Independent foundation.
Financial data (yr. ended 12/31/05): Assets, $277,518 (M); expenditures, $1,169,090; qualifying distributions, $1,169,079; giving activities include $1,167,000 for 5 grants (high: $515,000; low: $1,000).
Fields of interest: Protestant agencies & churches; Religion.
Limitations: Giving on a national basis. No grants to individuals.
Application information:
  Initial approach: Letter
  Deadline(s): None
Directors: Jean L. Neumann; Kenneth P. Neumann.
EIN: 046965300
Selected grants: The following grants were reported in 2003.
$250,000 to Pastoral Leadership Institute, Santa Ana, CA. For program support.
$200,000 to Wisconsin Evangelical Lutheran Synod Kingdom Workers, Wauwatosa, WI. 2 grants: $100,000 (For India Outreach Mission), $100,000 (For Hope School).
$2,000 to Clef Scholarship Campaign. For scholarships.

3018
Square D Foundation ✦
1415 S. Roselle Rd.
Palatine, IL 60067 (847) 397-2600
Contact: Harry Wilson, Secy.

Incorporated in 1956 in MI.
Donor: Square D Co.
Foundation type: Company-sponsored foundation.
Financial data (yr. ended 12/31/03): Assets, $112,579 (M); gifts received, $1,566,714; expenditures, $1,546,759; qualifying distributions, $1,542,609; giving activities include $1,542,609 for grants.
Purpose and activities: The foundation supports organizations involved with arts and culture, education, health, human services, community development, senior citizens, disabled people, and economically disadvantaged people.
Fields of interest: Arts; Education; Health care; Youth, services; Human services; Community

development; Aging; Disabilities, people with; Economically disadvantaged.
Type of support: General/operating support; Continuing support; Annual campaigns; Capital campaigns; Building/renovation; Emergency funds; Professorships; Scholarship funds; Employee matching gifts; In-kind gifts; Matching/challenge support.
Limitations: Giving primarily in areas of company operations, with emphasis on IA, IL, IN, KY, MO, NC, NE, OH, SC, TN, and TX. No support for United Way-supported organizations, religious organizations, labor unions, or political organizations. No grants to individuals.
Publications: Application guidelines; Program policy statement.
Application information: Telephone calls are not encouraged. Application form not required.
  Initial approach: Proposal to nearest company facility
  Copies of proposal: 1
  Deadline(s): June to Aug.
  Board meeting date(s): As necessary
  Final notification: Mar.
Officers and Directors:* W.W. Kurczewski,* Pres.; R.P. Fiorani,* V.P.; Peggy P. Gann, V.P.; Chris Richardson, V.P.; H. Wilson,* Secy.-Treas.
EIN: 366054195

3019
State Farm Companies Foundation ▼
1 State Farm Plz.
Bloomington, IL 61710 (309) 766-2161
Contact: Kristy Funk, Asst. Secy.
FAX: (309) 766-2314;
E-mail: kristy.funk.cm3n@statefarm.com; Additional E-mail: home.sf-foundation.
494b00@statefarm.com; URL: http://www.statefarm.com/foundati/foundati.htm
Address for Hispanic College Fund: 55 2nd St., Ste. 1500, San Francisco, CA 94105, tel.: (877) 473-4636

Incorporated in 1963 in IL.
Donor: State Farm Mutual Automobile Insurance Co.
Foundation type: Company-sponsored foundation.
Financial data (yr. ended 12/31/05): Assets, $11,607,830 (M); gifts received, $21,071,939; expenditures, $20,692,480; qualifying distributions, $20,423,725; giving activities include $17,430,339 for 811+ grants (high: $1,769,725), $60,000 for 6 grants to individuals, and $2,933,386 for employee matching gifts.
Purpose and activities: The foundation supports organizations involved with K-12 and higher education and awards fellowships to doctoral students and college scholarships to African Americans, Hispanics, Native Americans, and high school students.
Fields of interest: Elementary/secondary education; Higher education; Business school/education; Minorities; African Americans/Blacks; Hispanics/Latinos; Native Americans/American Indians.
International interests: Canada.
Type of support: General/operating support; Program development; Curriculum development; Fellowships; Internship funds; Scholarship funds; Employee volunteer services; Employee matching gifts; Employee-related scholarships; Scholarships—to individuals.

Limitations: Giving on a national basis and in Canada. No support for teams or clubs, political organizations, or religious organizations. No grants to individuals (except for Doctoral Dissertation Awards and scholarships), or for one-time events, capital campaigns, or banquets, tours, or competitions.
Publications: Corporate giving report (including application guidelines); Informational brochure.
Application information: An application form is required for the Doctoral Dissertation Award and the Hispanic Scholarship Fund Scholarship Program. Support is limited to 1 contribution per organization during any given year. Proposals should be submitted using organization letterhead.
  Initial approach: Proposal to nearest company facility; download application form for Doctoral Dissertation Award; contact Hispanic College Fund for application form for Hispanic Scholarship Fund Scholarship Program
  Deadline(s): Mar. 31 for Doctoral Dissertation Award; postmarked by Oct. 16 for Hispanic Scholarship Fund Scholarship Program
  Final notification: May for Doctoral Dissertation Award
Officers and Directors:* Edward B. Rust, Jr.,* Chair. and Pres.; Barbara Cowden,* V.P. and Secy.; Don Heltner, V.P., Fixed Income; Barbara Kirchgasler, V.P., Progs.; Willie Brown,* V.P.; Michael L. Tipsord, Treas.; Brian Boyden; W.H. Knight, Jr.; Susan M. Phillips.
EIN: 366110423
Selected grants: The following grants were reported in 2005.
$1,769,725 to National Merit Scholarship Corporation, Evanston, IL.
$1,380,836 to Youth Service America, DC.
$1,250,000 to National Youth Leadership Council, Saint Paul, MN.
$1,008,000 to Illinois Wesleyan University, Bloomington, IL.
$600,000 to Smithsonian Institution Fund, DC.
$396,656 to United Way of McLean County, Bloomington, IL.
$85,000 to Operation Respect, New York, NY.
$24,508 to United Way, Columbia Area, Columbia, MO.
$20,000 to Public Education Foundation, Salt Lake City, UT.
$14,000 to National Liberty Museum, Philadelphia, PA.

3020
Kent D. & Mary L. Steadley Memorial Trust ✦
c/o Bank of America, N.A.
231 S. LaSalle St.
Chicago, IL 60697-0001
Application address: Lareta Garnier, c/o Bank of America, N.A., P.O. Box 8300, Springfield, MO, 65801-8300, tel.: (417) 227-6237

Established in 1970.
Donor: K.D. & M.L. Steadley Irrevocable Trust.
Foundation type: Independent foundation.
Financial data (yr. ended 12/31/05): Assets, $23,040,526 (M); gifts received, $1,830,624; expenditures, $1,006,578; qualifying distributions, $901,671; giving activities include $876,728 for 13 grants (high: $200,000; low: $1,500).
Purpose and activities: Funds shall be distributed exclusively in and near the city of Carthage, MO, to promote community well-being.

Fields of interest: Elementary/secondary education; Youth development, scouting agencies (general); Human services; Community development.
Limitations: Giving limited to the Carthage, MO, area. No grants to individuals, or for national fundraising events.
Application information: Application form required.
  Initial approach: Letter requesting application materials
  Deadline(s): None
  Final notification: Usually within 6 months
Trustee: Bank of America, N.A.
EIN: 436120866
Selected grants: The following grants were reported in 2004.
$405,000 to Carthage, City of, Carthage, MO. 4 grants: $5,000, $150,000, $200,000, $50,000
$50,000 to Innovative Industries, Carthage, MO.
$50,000 to YMCA, Fair Acres Family, Carthage, MO.
$15,000 to Humane Society, Carthage, Carthage, MO.
$15,000 to Saint Anns School, Carthage, MO.
$650 to Boy Scouts of America, Joplin, MO.

3021
Steans Family Foundation
River Plz., P2 S.
405 N. Wabash Ave.
Chicago, IL   60611   (312) 467-5900, ext. 1500
Contact: Reginald Jones, Exec. Dir.
FAX: (312) 467-1229; E-mail: sffinfo@fic-sff.com;
E-mail: cgriffith@fic-sff.com (for Chindaly Griffith, Grants Mgr.); URL: http://
www.steansfamilyfoundation.org

Established in 1986 in IL.
Donors: Heather Steans; Robin Steans; Jennifer W. Steans; Harrison Steans; MacArthur Foundation; Princeton in Chicago; Chicago Community Foundation; Harold M. & Adeline Morrison Family; Lennar Foundation.
Foundation type: Independent foundation.
Financial data (yr. ended 12/31/05): Assets, $25,374,461 (M); gifts received, $276,202; expenditures, $4,118,802; qualifying distributions, $2,377,701; giving activities include $2,377,701 for 156 grants (high: $100,000; low: $250), and $17,000 for 1 loan/program-related investment.
Purpose and activities: The foundation's mission is to concentrate its grantmaking and programs in North Lawndale, IL, a revitalizing neighborhood on Chicago, IL's, west side, and working in partnership with local residents and institutions to build and enhance the North Lawndale community. Giving primarily for education and youth services; support also for community services.
Fields of interest: Higher education; Education; Health care; Employment, formal/general education; Employment, services; Housing/shelter; Human services; Children/youth, services; Family services; Urban/community development; Community development; Philanthropy/voluntarism; Public affairs.
Type of support: Technical assistance; Program-related investments/loans; Management development/capacity building; Fellowships; Curriculum development; Continuing support; General/operating support; Building/renovation; Program development; Seed money.
Limitations: Giving primarily in Chicago and North Lawndale, IL. No grants to individuals.
Publications: Annual report.

Application information: Accepts Chicago Area Grant Application. Contributes only to pre-selected organizations in North Lawndale, IL.
  Initial approach: Telephone to Prog. Off.
  Copies of proposal: 1
  Deadline(s): Refer to website
  Board meeting date(s): Bimonthly and as needed
  Final notification: 4-6 weeks
Officers and Trustees:* Harrison I. Steans,* C.E.O. and Pres.; Reginald Jones, Exec. Dir.; Gregory M. Darnieder; Leonard A. Gail; James P. Kastenholz; Leo A. Smith; Heather A. Steans; Jennifer Steans; Lois M. Steans; Robin M. Steans.
Number of staff: 6 full-time professional; 2 full-time support.
EIN: 363486843

3022
Avy and Marcie Stein Foundation ◇
1 N. Wacker Dr., Ste. 4800
Chicago, IL   60606

Established in 1995 in IL.
Donors: Avy Stein; Marcie Stein.
Foundation type: Independent foundation.
Financial data (yr. ended 12/31/05): Assets, $0 (L); gifts received, $462,956; expenditures, $590,176; qualifying distributions, $588,934; giving activities include $587,436 for 74 grants (high: $122,000; low: $36).
Purpose and activities: Giving primarily for the arts, education, and health organizations, including children's health; funding also for other children's services, and to Jewish organizations.
Fields of interest: Arts; Higher education; Education; Health organizations; Children/youth, services; Jewish federated giving programs; Jewish agencies & temples.
Limitations: Applications not accepted. Giving primarily in IL. No grants to individuals.
Application information: Contributes only to pre-selected organizations.
Directors: Avy Stein; Marcie Stein.
EIN: 363993406

3023
Irvin Stern Foundation ◇
116 W. Illinois St., No. 2E
Chicago, IL   60610   (312) 321-9402
E-mail: info@irvinstern.org; URL: http://
www.irvinstern.org

Established in 1957 in IL.
Donor: Irvin Stern†.
Foundation type: Independent foundation.
Financial data (yr. ended 9/30/05): Assets, $12,675,450 (M); expenditures, $1,096,615; qualifying distributions, $938,117; giving activities include $890,000 for 69 grants (high: $80,000; low: $2,500).
Purpose and activities: Grants for human services, particularly aid to the underserved, the poor and disadvantaged, via innovative social service programs, physical and mental health outreach, literacy and vocational training; civic affairs aimed at improving the quality of life in urban communities through grass roots and neighborhood organizations; and for the enhancement of the Jewish community through education and spirituality.

Fields of interest: Education; Mental health/crisis services; Food services; Human services; Homeless, human services; Community development; Jewish federated giving programs; Public affairs.
International interests: Israel.
Type of support: General/operating support; Building/renovation; Equipment; Emergency funds; Program development; Seed money.
Limitations: Giving primarily in Chicago, IL and New York, NY. No grants to individuals, or for endowment funds, deficit financing, building funds, capital campaigns, construction projects, medical research, or advertising or program books.
Publications: Application guidelines; Program policy statement.
Application information: Letter of inquiry form available on foundation Web site. (If organization's goals are within the foundation's guidelines, a letter of inquiry may be submitted online or by mail). Application form required.
  Initial approach: Brief letter of inquiry, online preferred
  Copies of proposal: 1
  Deadline(s): Submit proposal preferably in Mar. or Aug.; deadlines Apr. 1 and Sept. 1
  Board meeting date(s): Apr. and Oct.
Trustee: Jeffrey R. Epstein.
Number of staff: 1 part-time professional.
EIN: 366047947
Selected grants: The following grants were reported in 2003.
$160,000 to Jewish United Fund of Metropolitan Chicago, Chicago, IL. For general operating support.
$50,000 to New Israel Fund, DC. For general operating support.
$25,000 to San Diego Hospice and Palliative Care, San Diego, CA.
$25,000 to UNICEF of the Greater Chicago Area, Chicago, IL. For programs for children affected by HIV/AIDS around the world.
$25,000 to University of Michigan, Ann Arbor, MI. For undergraduate research opportunity program.
$20,000 to Brady Center to Prevent Gun Violence, DC. For Legal Action Project.
$15,000 to American Jewish Joint Distribution Committee, New York, NY. For Reach Out and Read program.
$15,000 to Association of Community Employment Programs for the Homeless (ACE), New York, NY. For project Comback, a work readiness program for the homeless.
$15,000 to Hand in Hand, American Friends of the Center for Jewish-Arab Education in Israel, Portland, OR. For general operating support.
$15,000 to Jewish Community Centers Association, Saint Louis, MO.

3024
Stewart Foundation ◇
515 Redwood Dr.
Aurora, IL   60507

Established in 1984 in IL.
Donors: John Alexander; Thomas S. Alexander; Alexander S. Rudolph; Geoffrey E. Rudolph; Emily H. Alexander; Martha J. Alexander; Brett W. Barnes; Kenneth W. Barnes; Eliza A. Cummings; Walter Alexander; Chris Barnes; American Livestock Insurance Co.; Alexander-Stewart Lumber Co.
Foundation type: Independent foundation.

Financial data (yr. ended 8/31/05): Assets, $2,824,183 (M); gifts received, $8,514; expenditures, $1,121,770; qualifying distributions, $1,121,700; giving activities include $1,121,700 for 45 grants (high: $615,000; low: $200).
Purpose and activities: Giving primarily for higher education, wildlife conservation and to zoos.
Fields of interest: Arts education; Higher education, university; Zoos/zoological societies; Aquariums; Animals/wildlife; Mental health/crisis services, suicide; Youth, services.
Limitations: Applications not accepted. Giving primarily in IL and NY; some funding nationally. No grants to individuals.
Application information: Contributes only to pre-selected organizations.
Officers and Directors: * John Alexander,* Pres.; Geoffrey E. Rudolph,* Secy.; Thomas S. Alexander,* Treas.
EIN: 363339135

3025
Jerome H. Stone Family Foundation ◇

150 N. Michigan Ave.
Chicago, IL 60601 (312) 580-4607
Contact: Jerome H. Stone, Pres.

Established in 1963 in IL.
Donors: Jerome H. Stone; Cynthia Raskin; Ellen Stone Belic; Cynthia Stone; James H. Stone.
Foundation type: Independent foundation.
Financial data (yr. ended 12/31/05): Assets, $2,918,330 (M); gifts received, $224,449; expenditures, $391,578; qualifying distributions, $370,322; giving activities include $367,691 for 115 grants (high: $35,000; low: $20).
Fields of interest: Museums; Arts; Higher education; Education; Health organizations, association; Human services.
Limitations: Giving primarily in IL, with emphasis on Chicago. No grants to individuals.
Application information:
Initial approach: Letter
Officers: Jerome H. Stone, Pres.; Ellen Stone Belic, V.P.; Cynthia Raskin, Secy.; James H. Stone, Treas.
EIN: 366061300
Selected grants: The following grants were reported in 2004.
$65,000 to Jewish United Fund of Metropolitan Chicago, Chicago, IL. 3 grants: $15,000, $35,000, $15,000
$36,600 to Columbia College, Chicago, IL. 2 grants: $20,000, $16,600
$20,000 to Museum of Contemporary Art, Chicago, IL.
$20,000 to Palm Springs Art Museum, Palm Springs, CA.
$10,000 to Eisenhower Medical Center, Rancho Mirage, CA.
$5,000 to Alzheimers Association, Chicago, IL.
$5,000 to Music and Dance Theater Chicago, Chicago, IL.

3026
Roger and Susan Stone Family Foundation ◇ ☆

c/o Roger Stone
1 Northfield Plz., Ste. 480
Northfield, IL 60093

Established in 1969 in IL.

Donor: Roger Stone.
Foundation type: Independent foundation.
Financial data (yr. ended 12/31/05): Assets, $5,226,516 (M); expenditures, $581,403; qualifying distributions, $528,520; giving activities include $525,200 for 100 grants (high: $70,000; low: $50).
Purpose and activities: Giving for health, Jewish organizations, and education.
Fields of interest: Arts; Education; Botanical gardens; Health care; Health organizations; Boys & girls clubs; Human services; Federated giving programs; Jewish agencies & temples.
Limitations: Applications not accepted. Giving primarily in Chicago, IL. No grants to individuals.
Application information: Contributes only to pre-selected organizations.
Directors: Roger Stone; Susan Stone.
EIN: 237026711
Selected grants: The following grants were reported in 2004.
$73,100 to Chicago Botanic Garden, Glencoe, IL.
$25,000 to United Way, IL.
$12,600 to Nature Conservancy, Chicago, IL.
$12,500 to Boys and Girls Clubs of Chicago, Chicago, IL.
$12,500 to North Shore Country Day School, Winnetka, IL.
$10,000 to Chicago Symphony Orchestra, Chicago, IL.
$6,000 to Cato Institute, DC.
$5,000 to Alliance Francaise de Chicago, Chicago, IL.
$5,000 to Media Research Center, Alexandria, VA.
$1,000 to Georgia Institute of Technology, Atlanta, GA.

3027
Straus Quintas Foundation ◇

c/o Bethia G. Straus
9429 Avers Ave.
Evanston, IL 60203-1314

Established in 1997 in IL.
Donor: Bethia G. Straus.
Foundation type: Independent foundation.
Financial data (yr. ended 12/31/05): Assets, $714,447 (M); gifts received, $30,000; expenditures, $317,817; qualifying distributions, $317,333; giving activities include $315,950 for 19 grants (high: $50,900; low: $2,000).
Purpose and activities: Giving for Jewish education and organizations.
Fields of interest: Education; Jewish agencies & temples.
Limitations: Applications not accepted. Giving primarily in IL and NY. No grants to individuals.
Application information: Contributes only to pre-selected organizations.
Trustees: Paul Z. Quintas; Bethia G. Straus.
EIN: 137124402
Selected grants: The following grants were reported in 2004.
$250,000 to Drisha Institute for Jewish Education, New York, NY.
$43,000 to American Friends of Nishmat, New York, NY.
$35,400 to Hillel Torah North Suburban Day School, Skokie, IL.
$31,250 to EDAH, New York, NY.
$31,250 to Yad Avraham Institute, New York, NY.
$25,000 to Camp Moshava, Skokie, IL.
$25,000 to Central Fund of Israel, New York, NY.

$25,000 to Jewish Orthodox Feminist Alliance, New York, NY.
$25,000 to Kollel Torah Mitzion, Chicago, IL.
$24,000 to Congregation Or Torah, Skokie, IL.

3028
Stuart Family Foundation ◇

(formerly The Barbara and Robert Stuart Foundation)
150 Field Dr., Ste. 100
Lake Forest, IL 60045-2597
Contact: Truman O. Anderson, Exec. Dir.

Established in 1985 in IL.
Donor: Robert D. Stuart, Jr.
Foundation type: Independent foundation.
Financial data (yr. ended 12/31/05): Assets, $19,510,436 (M); gifts received, $1,542,977; expenditures, $3,178,247; qualifying distributions, $3,003,064; giving activities include $2,726,341 for 157 grants (high: $169,789; low: $250; average: $1,000–$100,000).
Fields of interest: Media/communications; Arts; Education; International affairs, goodwill promotion; Civil rights, race/intergroup relations.
Type of support: General/operating support; Continuing support; Annual campaigns; Capital campaigns.
Limitations: Applications not accepted. Giving primarily in Chicago, IL. No grants to individuals.
Application information: Contributes only to pre-selected organizations.
Board meeting date(s): Nov.
Officers and Directors: * Robert D. Stuart, Jr.,* Pres.; Marian S. Pillsbury,* V.P.; Alexander D. Stuart,* Secy.; Teresa Acuna,* Treas.; Truman O. Anderson, Exec. Dir.; Donaldson C. Pillsbury.
Number of staff: 1 full-time professional; 3 part-time professional.
EIN: 363422731
Selected grants: The following grants were reported in 2004.
$150,000 to Center for Media and Public Affairs, DC.
$137,670 to Center for Strategic and International Studies, DC.
$100,000 to Campaign Legal Center, DC.
$75,000 to American Council of Trustees and Alumni, DC.
$75,000 to Intercollegiate Studies Institute, Wilmington, DE.
$75,000 to Jamestown Foundation, DC.
$50,000 to Institute of World Politics, DC.
$20,000 to Alliance for Better Campaigns, DC.
$2,500 to Ragdale Foundation, Lake Forest, IL.
$1,500 to Providence Saint Mel School, Chicago, IL.

3029
Sudix Foundation ◇

400 Skokie Blvd., Ste. 300
Northbrook, IL 60062
Contact: Wesley M. Dixon, Jr., Pres.

Established in 1985 in IL.
Donor: Wesley M. Dixon, Jr.
Foundation type: Independent foundation.
Financial data (yr. ended 12/31/04): Assets, $1,799,250 (M); expenditures, $502,892; qualifying distributions, $490,000; giving activities include $490,000 for 8 grants (high: $200,000; low: $20,000).

Purpose and activities: Giving primarily to higher education.

Fields of interest: Arts; Higher education; Botanical gardens; Protestant agencies & churches.

Limitations: Applications not accepted. Giving primarily in IL. No grants to individuals.

Application information: Contributes only to pre-selected organizations.

Officers: Wesley M. Dixon, Jr., Pres.; Suzanne S. Dixon, V.P. and Secy.-Treas.

Director: Pamela Bolton.

EIN: 363377946

3030

Susman and Asher Foundation ◇ ☆

225 W. Washington St., No. 1440
Chicago, IL 60606 (312) 782-1660
Contact: Donald Asher, Pres.

Incorporated in 1949 in IL.

Donors: Louis Susman; and members of the Asher family.

Foundation type: Independent foundation.

Financial data (yr. ended 12/31/05): Assets, $557,237 (M); gifts received, $176,133; expenditures, $327,761; qualifying distributions, $327,284; giving activities include $327,284 for grants.

Purpose and activities: Emphasis on higher education, religion, and Jewish welfare funds; support also for health and hospitals.

Fields of interest: Higher education; Theological school/education; Hospitals (general); Health care; Health organizations, association; Human services; Jewish federated giving programs; Jewish agencies & temples.

Type of support: General/operating support; Scholarship funds.

Limitations: Applications not accepted. Giving primarily in IL. No grants to individuals.

Application information: Contributes only to pre-selected organizations.

Officers: Donald Asher, Pres. and Treas.; David L. Asher, V.P.; Gilbert Asher, V.P.; Rebecca Johnston, Secy.

EIN: 366049760

3031

Gertrude and Walter E. Swanson, Jr. Foundation ◇

c/o Lawrence X. Pusateri
1212 N. Lake Shore Dr., Ste. 18BS
Chicago, IL 60610-6671

Established in 1995 in IL.

Foundation type: Independent foundation.

Financial data (yr. ended 12/31/04): Assets, $14,356,933 (M); expenditures, $644,489; qualifying distributions, $504,359; giving activities include $504,359 for 10 grants (high: $100,871; low: $25,218).

Purpose and activities: Giving primarily to health associations and hospitals.

Fields of interest: Higher education; Hospitals (general); Cancer; Heart & circulatory diseases; American Red Cross; Salvation Army; Christian agencies & churches.

Limitations: Applications not accepted. Giving primarily in Chicago, IL. No grants to individuals.

Application information: Contributes only to pre-selected organizations.

Trustee: Lawrence X. Pusateri.

EIN: 363994250

3032

Takiff Family Foundation ◇

(formerly Sanford & Bobette Takiff Charities, Ltd.)
313 Shoreline Ct.
Glencoe, IL 60022
Contact: Elizabeth Scheinfeld, Dir.

Established in 1984 in IL.

Donors: Bobette Takiff; Sanford Takiff.

Foundation type: Independent foundation.

Financial data (yr. ended 12/31/05): Assets, $8,979,202 (M); expenditures, $499,905; qualifying distributions, $471,703; giving activities include $469,798 for 62 grants (high: $160,025; low: $15).

Purpose and activities: Giving primarily for Jewish organizations including education and health.

Fields of interest: Museums; Arts; Education; Health organizations, association; Human services; Children/youth, services; International affairs; Civil rights, advocacy; Jewish federated giving programs; Jewish agencies & temples.

Type of support: Continuing support; Annual campaigns; Capital campaigns; Building/ renovation; Program development; Curriculum development; Scholarship funds.

Limitations: Applications not accepted. Giving primarily in Chicago, IL. No grants to individuals.

Application information: Unsolicited requests for funds not accepted.

Board meeting date(s): 3rd Tues. of each month

Directors: Jill Hirsh; Elizabeth Scheinfeld; Bobette Takiff; Sanford Takiff; Sherri Zirlin.

EIN: 363307589

Selected grants: The following grants were reported in 2004.

$210,000 to Spertus Institute of Jewish Studies, Chicago, IL.

$50,000 to Chicago Humanities Festival, Chicago, IL.

$36,039 to Jewish Community Centers Association, Saint Louis, MO.

$500 to Lawyers for the Creative Arts, Chicago, IL.

$98 to Brandeis University, Waltham, MA.

$90 to AMIT Women, New York, NY.

$40 to Art Institute of Chicago, Chicago, IL.

3033

The Tawani Foundation ◇

(also known as Colonel (IL) James N. Pritzker Charitable Distribution Fund)
610 N. Fairbanks Ct., 2nd Fl.
Chicago, IL 60604 (312) 587-7917
Contact: Edward C. Tracy, Exec. Dir.
FAX: (312) 587-7311;
E-mail: etracy@tawanifoundation.net

Established in 2002 in IL.

Donors: Pritzker Foundation; Pritzker Cousins Foundation.

Foundation type: Independent foundation.

Financial data (yr. ended 12/31/05): Assets, $40,752,330 (M); gifts received, $362,267; expenditures, $2,562,650; qualifying distributions, $2,074,450; giving activities include $1,700,763 for 163 grants (high: $300,000; low: $13; average: $10,000–$25,000).

Type of support: Research; Publication; Matching/ challenge support; Program development; Professorships; General/operating support; Capital campaigns; Building/renovation.

Publications: Application guidelines; Grants list; Program policy statement.

Application information: Proposals will be invited by the foundation after letter of inquiry is successfully evaluated. Application form required.

Initial approach: Letter of inquiry

Board meeting date(s): Fall and spring

Final notification: 90 days

Directors: Charles E. Dobrusin; Jane Feerers; James N. Pritzker.

Number of staff: 5 full-time professional.

EIN: 300040386

3034

Tellabs Foundation ◇

1415 W. Diehl Rd., M.S. 10
Naperville, IL 60563 (630) 798-2506
Contact: Meredith Hilt, Exec. Dir.
FAX: (630) 798-4778;
E-mail: meredith.hilt@tellabs.com; URL: http://www.tellabs.com/about/foundation.shtml

Established in 1997 in IL.

Donor: Tellabs, Inc.

Foundation type: Company-sponsored foundation.

Financial data (yr. ended 12/31/04): Assets, $27,612,576 (M); expenditures, $1,569,863; qualifying distributions, $1,327,418; giving activities include $1,324,793 for 33 grants (high: $150,000; low: $500).

Purpose and activities: The foundation supports organizations involved with education, the environment, health, and medical research.

Fields of interest: Engineering school/education; Education; Environment, air pollution; Environment, water pollution; Environment, waste management; Environment; Public health; Health care; Medical research; Mathematics; Science.

Type of support: Building/renovation; Land acquisition; Program development; Conferences/ seminars; Professorships; Seed money; Curriculum development; Fellowships; Research.

Limitations: Giving on a national basis, with emphasis on Sunrise, FL, Bolingbrook and Naperville, IL, and Ashburn, VA. No support for political or lobbying organizations, labor organizations, service organizations raising money for community purposes, local or national alumni groups, clubs or fraternities, individual churches or synagogues or other religious organizations, or organizations not of direct benefit to the entire community or discriminatory organizations. No grants to individuals, or for local athletic or sports programs, travel, tours, expeditions, or trips, institutional memberships or subscription fees for publications, or benefit events, raffle tickets, or fundraising efforts returning value to the donor.

Publications: Application guidelines; Informational brochure (including application guidelines).

Application information: Letters of inquiry should be no longer than 1 to 2 pages. Application form not required.

Initial approach: Mail letter of inquiry to foundation

Deadline(s): 4 weeks prior to board meetings

Board meeting date(s): Quarterly

Officers and Directors:* Michael Birck,* Pres. and Treas.; Denise Callarman,* V.P.; Carol Gavin,* V.P.;

Stephanie P. Marshall,* V.P.; Meredith Hilt,* Exec. Dir.
EIN: 364037547
Selected grants: The following grants were reported in 2005.
$100,000 to American Cancer Society, Chicago, IL.
$100,000 to Illinois Institute of Technology, Chicago, IL.
$100,000 to Nature Conservancy, Chicago, IL.
$50,000 to American Red Cross, National Headquarters, DC. For relief efforts for Hurricane Katrina.
$50,000 to Morton Arboretum, Lisle, IL.
$45,000 to Central DuPage Health Foundation, Winfield, IL.
$45,000 to United Cerebral Palsy Association of Greater Chicago, Chicago, IL.
$45,000 to United Negro College Fund, Chicago, IL.
$43,135 to Hales Franciscan High School, Chicago, IL.
$15,000 to American Lung Association of Illinois, Northeast Service Area, Wheaton, IL.

3035
The Carl & Marilynn Thoma Foundation ◇ ☆
724 12th St.
Wilmette, IL 60091-2641

Established in 1986 in IL.
Donors: Carl D. Thoma; Marilynn J. Thoma.
Foundation type: Independent foundation.
Financial data (yr. ended 12/31/05): Assets, $3,623,764 (M); gifts received, $3,053,950; expenditures, $367,738; qualifying distributions, $365,931; giving activities include $364,661 for 31 grants (high: $100,000; low: $100).
Purpose and activities: Giving primarily to higher education.
Fields of interest: Performing arts, theater; Performing arts, opera; Higher education, college; Education; Medical care, rehabilitation; Disabilities, people with.
Limitations: Applications not accepted. Giving primarily in IL. No grants to individuals.
Application information: Contributes only to pre-selected organizations.
Officers: Carl D. Thoma, Pres.; Marilynn J. Thoma, V.P. and Treas.
EIN: 363486549

3036
Robert H. Torstenson Family Foundation ◇ ☆
c/o Jan H. Ohlander
2902 McFarland Rd.
Rockford, IL 61107

Established in 2001 in IL.
Donors: Robert H. Torstenson†; Leslie M. Torstenson.
Foundation type: Independent foundation.
Financial data (yr. ended 9/30/05): Assets, $1,011,471 (M); gifts received, $640,668; expenditures, $720,405; qualifying distributions, $710,737; giving activities include $710,737 for 2 grants (high: $640,668; low: $70,069).
Fields of interest: Animals/wildlife, preservation/protection.

Limitations: Applications not accepted. Giving primarily in Dundee, IL, and Missoula, MT. No grants to individuals.
Application information: Contributes only to pre-selected organizations.
Officers and Directors:* Leslie M. Torstenson,* Pres.; Brooke J. Torstenson,* V.P.; Eric C. Torstenson,* V.P.; Jan H. Ohlander,* Secy.; Betsy Mathison,* Treas.
EIN: 611418226

3037
Tracy Family Foundation ◇
c/o Dot Foods, Inc.
P.O. Box 192, Rte. 99
Mount Sterling, IL 62353 (217) 773-4411
Contact: Sharon Mosey
URL: http://www.tracyfoundation.org

Established in 1997 in IL.
Donor: Dot Foods, Inc.
Foundation type: Company-sponsored foundation.
Financial data (yr. ended 12/31/05): Assets, $2,286,723 (M); gifts received, $1,386,250; expenditures, $742,681; qualifying distributions, $741,118; giving activities include $656,774 for grants.
Purpose and activities: The foundation supports organizations involved with education, youth development, and human services.
Fields of interest: Education; Youth development; Children/youth, services; Family services; Human services.
Type of support: General/operating support.
Limitations: Giving primarily in Brown County, IL. No grants to individuals.
Application information: Application form required.
Initial approach: Contact foundation for application form
Deadline(s): July 1 and Oct. 15
Board meeting date(s): Mar., July, and Nov.
Officers and Trustees:* Jean C. Buckley,* Pres.; Jay Sullivan,* Treas.; Maureen Schuering; Patrick J. Smith; Adina Tracy; Dick Tracy; Pam Tracy; Wanda Tracy.
EIN: 364163760

3038
The Traders Foundation ◇ ☆
1 N. Wacker Dr., 31st Fl.
Chicago, IL 60606

Established in 1984 in IL.
Donors: John Bollero, Jr.; James Hofheimer; Steve Lawrence; Robert B. Moore; John Moore; Robert Jeffs Kollar.
Foundation type: Independent foundation.
Financial data (yr. ended 12/31/03): Assets, $0 (M); gifts received, $2,000; expenditures, $550,953; qualifying distributions, $549,944; giving activities include $549,944 for grants.
Purpose and activities: Giving primarily for children and youth services and for medical research.
Fields of interest: Medical research, association; Children/youth, services; Christian agencies & churches.
Limitations: Giving primarily in Chicago, IL. No grants to individuals.
Officers: Michael J. Daley, Chair.; Peter Sandquist, Vice-Chair.

Trustees: Robert Corvino; Justin Nolan; William Noyes; Chess Obermeier; Paul Pantola; Mike Ryan; William Weldon; Keith Yavitt.
EIN: 366795846

3039
Trustmark Foundation ◇
(formerly BTL Foundation)
400 Field Dr.
Lake Forest, IL 60045-4809

Established in 1985.
Donor: Trustmark Insurance Co.
Foundation type: Company-sponsored foundation.
Financial data (yr. ended 12/31/03): Assets, $1,092,188 (M); gifts received, $831,373; expenditures, $621,516; qualifying distributions, $621,516; giving activities include $588,324 for grants (high: $100,000), and $32,623 for in-kind gifts.
Purpose and activities: The foundation supports organizations involved with arts and culture, education, health, human services, and children and youth services.
Fields of interest: Arts; Education; Health organizations, association; Human services; Children/youth, services; Federated giving programs.
Type of support: General/operating support.
Limitations: Applications not accepted. Giving primarily in IL. No grants to individuals.
Application information: Contributes only to pre-selected organizations.
Trustees: Denise Battles; Michael French; Frank G. Gramm; Michelle Jones; David McDonough; Donald M. Peterson; Cindy Preller; Warren Schreier; Deborah Smart, M.D.; J. Grover Thomas, Jr.
EIN: 363330631

3040
Tully Family Foundation ◇ ☆
33 N. Dearborn St., No. 2450
Chicago, IL 60602-3109

Established in 1997 in IL.
Donor: Thomas M. Tully.
Foundation type: Operating foundation.
Financial data (yr. ended 12/31/05): Assets, $1,302,228 (M); gifts received, $40,000; expenditures, $319,701; qualifying distributions, $315,857; giving activities include $315,857 for 51 grants (high: $200,000; low: $100).
Fields of interest: Higher education, university; Education; Health organizations, association; Children, services; Family services.
Limitations: Applications not accepted. Giving primarily in IL; giving also in OH. No grants to individuals.
Application information: Contributes only to pre-selected organizations.
Officers and Directors:* Thomas M. Tully,* Pres. and Treas.; Ellen Danaher Tully,* V.P. and Secy.; Kenneth G. Pigott.
EIN: 364156972
Selected grants: The following grants were reported in 2003.
$32,360 to John Carroll University, University Heights, OH. For general support.
$25,000 to Saint Ignatius High School, Chicago, IL. For general support.

$10,000 to Childrens Memorial Foundation, Chicago, IL. For general support.

$5,000 to Big Shoulders Fund, Chicago, IL. For general support.

$5,000 to Chicago City Day School, Chicago, IL. For general support.

$2,500 to Mercy Hospital and Medical Center, Chicago, IL. For general support.

$1,000 to Brain Research Foundation, Chicago, IL. For general support.

$1,000 to DePaul University, College of Law, Chicago, IL. For general support.

$500 to KESHET, Northbrook, IL. For recreational programs.

$500 to Special Childrens Charities, Chicago, IL. For general support.

3041
Walter & Mary Tuohy Foundation ✧
c/o John L. Tuohy
111 W. Monroe St., Ste. 1400
Chicago, IL   60603-4011   (312) 845-3752

Established in 1960 in OH.
Donors: Mary Frances Tuohy‡; Walter Joseph Tuohy‡.
Foundation type: Independent foundation.
Financial data (yr. ended 12/31/05): Assets, $1,530,583 (M); expenditures, $377,288; qualifying distributions, $368,000; giving activities include $368,000 for 54 grants (high: $110,000; low: $500).
Purpose and activities: Primary areas of interest include secondary and higher education, welfare, and housing.
Fields of interest: Visual arts; Performing arts; Arts; Higher education; Education; Substance abuse, services; Mental health/crisis services; Medical research; Housing/shelter, development; Human services; Family services; Homeless, human services; Religion; Economically disadvantaged; Homeless.
Type of support: Annual campaigns; Capital campaigns; Building/renovation; Curriculum development; Research.
Limitations: Applications not accepted. Giving on a national basis, with some emphasis on Chicago, IL, Denver, CO, and NM. No grants to individuals.
Application information: Unsolicited requests for funds not accepted.
Officers and Trustees:* John L. Tuohy,* Pres. and Treas.; Walter J. Tuohy, Jr.,* V.P. and Secy.; Patricia J. Tuohy,* V.P.; Mary Ann Kundtz,* V.P.
EIN: 346558081

3042
Tyndale House Foundation ✧
351 Executive Dr.
Carol Stream, IL   60188-2420   (630) 668-8300
Contact: Mary Kleine Yehling, Exec. Dir.

Established in 1964 in IL.
Donors: Howard A. Elkind; Kenneth N. Taylor; ENB Charitable Trust; Elizabeth Taylor Char. Trust.
Foundation type: Independent foundation.
Financial data (yr. ended 12/31/04): Assets, $74,439,127 (M); gifts received, $1,368,501; expenditures, $3,219,517; qualifying distributions, $3,049,467; giving activities include $3,008,900 for 117 grants (high: $310,000; low: $1,000).

Purpose and activities: To promote the gospel through Christian literature projects, Bible translations, and Christian services and activities in the U.S. and abroad.
Fields of interest: Language/linguistics; Literature; Human services; Religious federated giving programs; Christian agencies & churches; Protestant agencies & churches.
Type of support: General/operating support; Program development; Conferences/seminars; Publication; Matching/challenge support.
Limitations: Giving on a national and international basis. No support for libraries. No grants to individuals, or for building or endowment funds, scholarships, fellowships, or personnel support.
Publications: Financial statement; Informational brochure (including application guidelines).
Application information: Application form not required.
Initial approach: Letter or telephone
Copies of proposal: 10
Deadline(s): Dec. 31
Board meeting date(s): Early Nov. for grantmaking, and as required for administrative business
Officers: Doug C. McConnell, Pres.; Mark D. Taylor, V.P. and Treas.; Margaret W. Taylor, Secy.; Mary Kleine Yehling, Exec. Dir.
Directors: Edward Elliott; Edwin L. Frizen, Jr.; Dave M. Howard; Ted Noble; Robert B. Reekie; Kenneth N. Taylor; Peter W. Taylor.
Number of staff: 1 part-time professional.
EIN: 362555516

3043
John Ullrich Foundation Trust ✧ ☆
c/o Main Street Bank & Trust
130 N. Water St.
Decatur, IL   62523

Foundation type: Independent foundation.
Financial data (yr. ended 12/31/05): Assets, $16,433,320 (M); expenditures, $1,010,354; qualifying distributions, $716,686; giving activities include $716,686 for 14 grants (high: $400,000; low: $5,080).
Fields of interest: Museums (children's); Higher education, college (community/junior).
Type of support: General/operating support.
Limitations: Applications not accepted. Giving primarily in IL. No grants to individuals.
Application information: Contributes only to pre-selected organizations.
Trustee: Main Street Bank & Trust.
EIN: 376279232
Selected grants: The following grants were reported in 2005.
$50,145 to Webster-Cantrell Hall, Decatur, IL.
$47,000 to American Red Cross.
$37,602 to United Way. 3 grants: $12,277, $12,277, $13,048
$30,000 to Childrens Museum.
$25,000 to Millikin University, Decatur, IL.

3044
United Airlines Foundation ✧
(formerly UAL Foundation)
P.O. Box 66100
Chicago, IL   60666
FAX: (847) 700-7345; Application address: c/o United Airlines WHQPR, Corp. Social Investment, 1200 E. Algonquin Rd., Elk Grove Village, IL 60007

Incorporated in 1951 in IL.
Donor: United Air Lines, Inc.
Foundation type: Company-sponsored foundation.
Financial data (yr. ended 12/31/04): Assets, $2,714,593 (M); gifts received, $123,164; expenditures, $869,515; qualifying distributions, $869,515; giving activities include $867,989 for 66 grants (high: $100,000; low: $1,000).
Purpose and activities: The foundation supports organizations involved with arts and culture, education, health, children and youth services, human services, and religion.
Fields of interest: Arts; Education, research; Higher education; Education; Health care; Children/youth, services; Human services; Federated giving programs; Religion.
Type of support: General/operating support; Annual campaigns; Capital campaigns; Research.
Limitations: Applications not accepted. Giving primarily in areas of company operations in Los Angeles and San Francisco, CA, Denver, CO, Chicago, IL, and Washington, DC. No support for political or fraternal organizations, United Way-supported organizations, religious organizations, or individual public or private schools. No grants to individuals, or for capital campaigns or development campaigns.
Application information: Contributes only to pre-selected organizations.
Board meeting date(s): Mar., June, Sept., and Dec.
Officers and Directors:* Sonya Jackson,* Pres.; Peter D. McDonald,* V.P.; Frederic F. Brace,* Treas.; Graham D. Atkinson; Sara A. Fields; Rosemary Moore; John H. Walker.
Number of staff: 2
EIN: 366109873

3045
United Stationers Foundation ✧ ☆
2200 E. Golf Rd.
Des Plaines, IL   60016-1267   (847) 699-5000
Contact: Brian S. Cooper, Sr. V.P.

Established around 1988 in IL.
Donor: United Stationers Inc.
Foundation type: Company-sponsored foundation.
Financial data (yr. ended 8/31/05): Assets, $0 (M); expenditures, $361,778; qualifying distributions, $361,770; giving activities include $361,770 for 35 grants (high: $144,584; low: $150).
Purpose and activities: The foundation supports organizations involved with education, health, and human services.
Fields of interest: Education; Health care; Human services.
Type of support: General/operating support.
Limitations: Giving on a national basis. No grants to individuals.
Application information: Application form not required.
Initial approach: Proposal
Deadline(s): None
Board meeting date(s): Quarterly
Officers: Richard W. Gochnauer, C.E.O. and Pres.; Kathleen S. Dvorak, Sr. V.P. and C.F.O.; Brian S. Cooper, Sr. V.P. and Treas.; John T. Sloan, Sr. V.P.
EIN: 363458832
Selected grants: The following grants were reported in 2003.
$86,130 to City of Hope, Skokie, IL.
$18,400 to Computers for Children, Buffalo, NY.

$7,500 to Anti-Defamation League of Bnai Brith, Chicago, IL.

$6,500 to American Cancer Society of Des Plaines, Des Plaines, IL.

$4,750 to UJA-Federation of New York, New York, NY.

$2,500 to Hospice of West Alabama, Tuscaloosa, AL.

$2,000 to Conservation Fund, Arlington, VA.

$1,000 to Cabrini Connections, Chicago, IL.

$1,000 to Maryville Academy, Des Plaines, IL.

$1,000 to United Way, Northwest Suburban, Des Plaines, IL.

3046
USG Foundation, Inc. ✧
125 S. Franklin St.
Chicago, IL 60606-4678 (312) 606-4021
Contact: Peter K. Maitland, Pres.
FAX: (312) 606-5316; Additional tel.: (312) 606-4024

Incorporated in 1978 in IL.
Donors: USG Corp.; Chicago Tourism Fund.
Foundation type: Company-sponsored foundation.
Financial data (yr. ended 12/31/05): Assets, $1,936,689 (M); gifts received, $1,100,000; expenditures, $896,658; qualifying distributions, $896,658; giving activities include $822,576 for 62 grants (high: $82,500; low: $1,000), and $67,886 for employee matching gifts.
Purpose and activities: The foundation supports organizations involved with arts and culture, higher education, health, human services, community development, and civic affairs.
Fields of interest: Arts; Higher education; Hospitals (general); Health care; Children/youth, services; Human services; Community development; Federated giving programs; Public affairs.
Type of support: General/operating support; Continuing support; Annual campaigns; Capital campaigns; Building/renovation; Equipment; Program development; Scholarship funds; Research; Technical assistance; Employee matching gifts.
Limitations: Giving primarily in areas of company operations. No support for sectarian organizations not of direct benefit to the entire community, political organizations, fraternal or veterans' organizations, or primary or secondary schools; generally, no support for united fund-supported organizations. No grants to individuals, or for courtesy advertising; no loans.
Publications: Program policy statement (including application guidelines).
Application information: Multi-year funding is not automatic. Application form not required.
Initial approach: Proposal
Copies of proposal: 1
Deadline(s): None
Board meeting date(s): Quarterly
Officers: Peter K. Maitland, Pres.; B.J. Cook, V.P.; R.H. Fleming, V.P.; Marcia S. Kaminsky, V.P.; J.S. Metcalf, V.P.; J.P. Rodewald, V.P.; S.K. Torrey, Secy.
Number of staff: 1 full-time professional.
EIN: 362984045
Selected grants: The following grants were reported in 2004.
$80,000 to American Red Cross.
$46,379 to United Way. 2 grants: $36,954, $9,425
$30,000 to Robert Crown Center for Health Education, Hinsdale, IL.
$25,000 to Chicago United, Chicago, IL.

$20,000 to Victory Gardens Theater, Chicago, IL.
$15,000 to Armed Forces Relief Trust, DC.
$10,000 to DuPage Childrens Museum, Naperville, IL.
$10,000 to Naperville Heritage Society, Naperville, IL.
$5,000 to Equip for Equality, Chicago, IL.

3047
Vermilion Healthcare Foundation ✧
702 N. Logan Ave.
Danville, IL 61832-4323 (217) 431-7021
Contact: Valeria Saikley

Established in 1994.
Foundation type: Independent foundation.
Financial data (yr. ended 9/30/05): Assets, $10,459,053 (M); expenditures $683,549; qualifying distributions, $614,284; giving activities include $605,649 for 16 grants (high: $226,344; low: $4,250).
Purpose and activities: Support primarily for a medical center; giving also for research, education, and social and youth services.
Fields of interest: Libraries/library science; Education; Hospitals (general); Human services; Children/youth, services.
Limitations: Giving limited to Danville, IL. No grants to individuals.
Publications: Application guidelines; Program policy statement.
Application information:
Initial approach: Telephone
Copies of proposal: 8
Deadline(s): Mar. 15, June 15, Sept. 15, and Dec. 15
Board meeting date(s): Last Wed. in Jan., Apr., July, and Oct.
Officers and Directors:* Judd Peck,* Chair.; Rebecca Schlecht, Vice-Chair.; James D. Anderson, Secy.-Treas.; Mary Michael Bateman; Thomas Bott; Neil M. Ehrlich; H. Michael Finkle; Cheryl Harmon; Robert Kesler; Bruce Meachum; Melvin Myers; Michael J. O'Brien; W. John Shane; Tom Wodetzki.
EIN: 371225688

3048
Vibern Foundation ✧
c/o Northern Trust Co.
P.O. Box 803878
Chicago, IL 60680

Established around 1995 in IL.
Donor: Viola D. Hank.
Foundation type: Independent foundation.
Financial data (yr. ended 12/31/05): Assets, $6,679,844 (M); gifts received, $156,023; expenditures, $371,771; qualifying distributions, $350,015; giving activities include $350,000 for 7 grants (high: $60,000; low: $25,000).
Fields of interest: Education; Christian agencies & churches.
Limitations: Applications not accepted. Giving limited to IL. No grants to individuals.
Application information: Contributes only to pre-selected organizations.
Trustees: Jeanne M. Dale; William J. Hank; Marie T. McKellar.
EIN: 363996796
Selected grants: The following grants were reported in 2003.

$50,000 to Fenwick High School, Oak Park, IL.
$30,000 to Mount Saint Joseph, Lake Zurich, IL.
$30,000 to Sisters of Mercy, Hartsdale, NY. For high school.
$25,000 to Midtown Educational Foundation, Chicago, IL.
$20,000 to Andrean High School, Merrillville, IN.
$20,000 to Mary, Seat of Wisdom School, Park Ridge, IL.
$20,000 to Mercy Home for Boys and Girls, Chicago, IL.
$20,000 to Saint Mary of Celle Catholic Church and School, Berwyn, IL.
$15,000 to Dominican Sisters of Saint Mary of the Springs, Dominican Learning Center, Columbus, OH.
$14,000 to Our Lady of Charity School, Brookhaven, PA.

3049
VNA Foundation
(formerly Visiting Nurse Association of Chicago)
20 N. Wacker Dr., Ste. 3118
Chicago, IL 60606 (312) 214-1521
Contact: Robert N. DiLeonardi, Exec. Dir.
FAX: (312) 214-1529; E-mail: vnafund@aol.com;
URL: http://www.vnafoundation.net

Established in 1995 in IL; converted from the transfer of VNA-C operations to CareMed Chicago; status changed to a private foundation in July 1998.
Foundation type: Independent foundation.
Financial data (yr. ended 6/30/06): Assets, $49,302,595 (M); gifts received, $34,490; expenditures, $2,735,096; qualifying distributions, $2,410,005; giving activities include $1,955,931 for 53 grants (high: $72,285; low: $3,415; average: $20,000–$60,000).
Purpose and activities: The grantmaking goal of the foundation is to support home- and community-based health care and health services for the medically underserved in Cook and the collar counties, IL, with a focus on Chicago. Capital, program and general operating grants to support home, health, community and school-based services, prevention and health promotion, and early intervention are available to nonprofits. Priority is given to programs in which care is provided by nurses.
Fields of interest: Nursing care; Health care, home services; Health care.
Type of support: General/operating support; Capital campaigns; Equipment; Program development; Seed money; Program evaluation; Program-related investments/loans; Matching/challenge support.
Limitations: Giving primarily in Cook, DuPage, Kane, Lake, Will, and McHenry counties, IL.
Publications: Application guidelines; Annual report (including application guidelines); Grants list.
Application information: Accepts the Chicago Area Grant Application Form. Application form required.
Initial approach: Telephone (calls are encouraged), letter of intent or full proposals invited
Copies of proposal: 2
Deadline(s): Call for deadlines or see foundation Web site
Board meeting date(s): Quarterly
Final notification: 7 weeks
Officers and Directors:* Julia Cowell,* Chair.; Brigid Kenney,* Vice-Chair; Suzanne McWilliams, Secy.; Nancy Jones Emrich, Treas.; Robert N. DiLeonardi,

Exec. Dir.; Janet Cabot; Anne Davis; Dian Lansenhorst; Katherine H. Miller.

Number of staff: 2 full-time professional; 1 part-time professional.

EIN: 362167943

Selected grants: The following grants were reported in 2004.

$69,355 to Helping Hands Health Center, Chicago, IL. For salary support for nurse practitioner.

$33,000 to Health and Medicine Policy Research Group, Chicago, IL. For Albert Schweitzer nursing fellowships.

$30,000 to Horizon Hospice and Palliative Care, Chicago, IL. For care of low-income patients.

$30,000 to Suburban Primary Health Care Council, Westchester, IL. For care for uninsured patients.

$26,726 to Breakthrough Urban Ministries, Chicago, IL. For healthcare services.

$25,000 to Infant Welfare Society of Chicago, Chicago, IL. For computer equipment.

$25,000 to Lake Forest Hospital, Lake Forest, IL. For Care Coach.

$21,000 to Community Health, Chicago, IL. For computer equipment.

$3,846 to Donors Forum of Chicago, Chicago, IL. For general operating support.

$2,000 to Council on Foundations, DC. For general operating support.

3050

Wadsworth Golf Charities Foundation ✧

1901 N. Van Dyke Rd.
Plainfield, IL 60544-7727
FAX: (815) 436-8404; Application address: c/o Richard S. Slagle, 3201 Milton Rd., Middletown, OH 45042; tel.: (513) 424-3701

Established in 1995 in IL.

Donors: Brenton H. Wadsworth; Jean Wadsworth.

Foundation type: Independent foundation.

Financial data (yr. ended 12/31/05): Assets, $11,136,495 (M); gifts received, $602,745; expenditures, $511,888; qualifying distributions, $465,150; giving activities include $420,000 for 39 grants (high: $30,000; low: $500).

Purpose and activities: Giving primarily to programs related to golf and recreation that offers positive alternatives for the disadvantaged or handicapped.

Fields of interest: Health organizations; Athletics/sports, golf; Human services.

Type of support: Program development.

Limitations: Giving on a national basis.

Publications: Informational brochure.

Application information: Application form not required.

Initial approach: Letter
Copies of proposal: 1
Deadline(s): None
Board meeting date(s): As necessary

Officers: Brenton H. Wadsworth, Pres.; Leslie Wadsworth, Secy.; Leon McNair, Treas.; Richard Slagle, Exec. Dir.

Director: John Cotter.

EIN: 364028075

Selected grants: The following grants were reported in 2004.

$50,000 to Cantigny Foundation, Chicago, IL. 2 grants: $25,000 each

$30,000 to Clearview Legacy Foundation, East Canton, OH.

$10,000 to Aurora University, Aurora, IL.

$10,000 to Woodlands Foundation, Wexford, PA.

$7,500 to Fore Hope, Galloway, OH.

$5,000 to City Parks Foundation, New York, NY.

$5,000 to Mount Washington Pediatric Hospital, Baltimore, MD.

$400 to Middletown Community Foundation, Middletown, OH.

3051

Walgreen Benefit Fund ✧

200 Wilmot Rd., Ste. 2270
Deerfield, IL 60015
Contact: E.H. King, V.P.
Application address: Ruth D. Crane, Corp. 104, Wilmot Rd., M.S. 1444, Deerfield, IL 60015, tel.: (847) 315-4663,
E-mail: ruth.crane@walgreen.com

Incorporated in 1939 in IL.

Donors: Walgreen Co.; C.R. Walgreen, Jr.; L. Daniel Jorndt.

Foundation type: Company-sponsored foundation.

Financial data (yr. ended 4/30/06): Assets, $22,183,488 (M); gifts received, $657,753; expenditures, $1,663,892; qualifying distributions, $1,647,768; giving activities include $1,645,594 for 2,522 grants to individuals (high: $5,191; low: $1).

Purpose and activities: The fund awards grants to needy employees and former employees and the family members of employees and former employees of Walgreen.

Type of support: Grants to individuals.

Limitations: Giving on a national basis.

Publications: Application guidelines; Annual report.

Application information: Application form not required.

Initial approach: Contact fund for application information
Copies of proposal: 1
Deadline(s): None
Board meeting date(s): Monthly
Final notification: 4 to 6 weeks

Officers and Directors:* E.H. King,* V.P.; D.R. O'Dell, V.P.; N.J. Godfrey,* Secy.-Treas.; R.J. Hans; Kevin Walgreen; K.R. Weigand.

Number of staff: 1 part-time professional; 1 part-time support.

EIN: 366051130

3052

The Kathleen and Charles R. Walgreen Foundation ✧

(formerly Airdrie Foundation)
P.O. Box 465
Deerfield, IL 60015
Contact: Nancy J. Godfrey

Established in 1987 in IL.

Foundation type: Independent foundation.

Financial data (yr. ended 12/31/05): Assets, $7,037,694 (M); expenditures, $420,589; qualifying distributions, $395,925; giving activities include $374,550 for 47 grants (high: $110,000; low: $250; average: $1,000–$10,000).

Fields of interest: Arts; Higher education; Education; Hospitals (general); Health care; Children/youth, services; Roman Catholic federated giving programs; Roman Catholic agencies & churches.

Limitations: Giving primarily in IL. No grants to individuals.

Application information:

Initial approach: Letter
Deadline(s): Sept. 30

Officers: Charles R. Walgreen III, Pres.; Kathleen B. Walgreen, V.P.; Edward H. King, Secy.

EIN: 363486435

Selected grants: The following grants were reported in 2005.

$110,000 to Our Lady of Mercy High School, Rochester, NY.

$26,500 to Lake Forest Hospital, Lake Forest, IL.

$20,000 to Woodlands Academy of the Sacred Heart, Lake Forest, IL.

$15,000 to Library Foundation of Martin County, Stuart, FL.

$10,500 to Lake Forest Country Day School, Lake Forest, IL.

$10,000 to Saint Andrew Catholic Church, Stuart, FL.

$1,000 to American Foundation for Pharmaceutical Education, Rockville, MD.

$1,000 to Central American Ministries, Toledo, OH.

$1,000 to Evans Scholars Foundation, Golf, IL.

$500 to Northwestern Memorial Foundation, Chicago, IL.

3053

Maurice Walk Fine Arts Foundation ✧ ☆

c/o Bell Jones Quinlisk
200 W. Adams St., Ste. 2600
Chicago, IL 60606

Established in 1999 in IL.

Donor: Maurice Walk Charitable Lead Annuity Trust.

Foundation type: Operating foundation.

Financial data (yr. ended 12/31/05): Assets, $5,931,979 (M); gifts received, $523,627; expenditures, $562,801; qualifying distributions, $506,000; giving activities include $506,000 for 4 grants (high: $450,000; low: $1,000).

Fields of interest: Arts education; Museums (art); Performing arts; music; Performing arts, music ensembles/groups.

Limitations: Applications not accepted. Giving primarily in WY. No grants to individuals.

Application information: Contributes only to pre-selected organizations.

Officers: Marguerite Walk, Pres.; Cynthia Walk Wolfinger, Secy.; Margaretha Walk, Treas.

EIN: 364327696

3054

Walnut Foundation ✧

c/o Henry Dale Smith, Sr.
5 Washington Pl.
Springfield, IL 62702-4634

Established in 1984.

Donor: Henry Dale Smith, Sr.

Foundation type: Independent foundation.

Financial data (yr. ended 12/31/05): Assets, $10,015,224 (M); gifts received, $903,623; expenditures, $732,285; qualifying distributions, $720,218; giving activities include $720,218 for 137 grants (high: $60,000; low: $100).

Purpose and activities: Giving primarily for the matching of H.D. Smith Associates gifts.

Fields of interest: Education; Human services; Christian agencies & churches; Protestant agencies & churches.

Limitations: Applications not accepted. Giving primarily in IL. No grants to individuals.

Application information: Contributes only to pre-selected organizations.
Trustees: Henry Dale Smith, Sr.; Henry Dale Smith, Jr.; James Christopher Smith.
EIN: 371138383

3055
The Walsh Foundation ◇
c/o Madden, Jiganti, Moore & Sinars
190 S. LaSalle St., Ste. 1700
Chicago, IL 60603

Established around 1995 in IL.
Donors: The Walsh Construction Co. of Illinois; A-W Contractors.
Foundation type: Independent foundation.
Financial data (yr. ended 12/31/05): Assets, $31,101,163 (M); gifts received, $4,756,721; expenditures, $1,447,227; qualifying distributions, $1,321,000; giving activities include $1,321,000 for grants.
Purpose and activities: Giving primarily for higher education, as well as for Roman Catholic churches, organizations and education; funding also for the arts, and children's social services.
Fields of interest: Performing arts, theater; Arts; Secondary school/education; Higher education; Education; Medical research, institute; Human services; Children, services; Residential/custodial care; Roman Catholic agencies & churches.
Limitations: Applications not accepted. Giving primarily in IL, with emphasis on Chicago. No grants to individuals.
Application information: Contributes only to pre-selected organizations.
Officers and Directors:* Matthew M. Walsh,* C.E.O.; Daniel J. Walsh, Pres.; Patricia R. Walsh,* Secy.; Joyce S. Walsh,* Treas.; E. Bryan Dunigan.
EIN: 363994447

3056
The A. Montgomery Ward Foundation ◇
c/o Bank of America, N.A.
231 S. LaSalle St.
Chicago, IL 60697 (312) 828-1785
Contact: M. Catherine Ryan, Trust Off., Bank of America, N.A.

Trust established in 1959 in IL.
Donor: Marjorie Montgomery Ward Baker‡.
Foundation type: Independent foundation.
Financial data (yr. ended 6/30/05): Assets, $15,910,184 (M); expenditures, $978,058; qualifying distributions, $877,351; giving activities include $746,369 for 61 grants (high: $150,000; low: $3,000).
Purpose and activities: The foundation's grantmaking emphasizes those institutions in the Chicago, IL, area which provide its many citizens with high-quality, well established educational and cultural activities, with emphasis on museums; funding also for children, youth, families, women, and social services including recordings for the blind and dyslexic, and treatment for families where child abuse and neglect have occurred, focusing on children from birth to 5 years.
Fields of interest: Media, television; Media, radio; Museums (natural history); Museums (science/technology); Planetarium; Arts; Elementary/secondary education; Secondary school/education; Higher education; Education; Hospitals (specialty);

Health care; Health organizations, association; Crime/violence prevention, child abuse; Housing/shelter, development; Human services; Children/youth, services; Family services; Roman Catholic federated giving programs; Philanthropy/voluntarism.
Type of support: General/operating support; Capital campaigns; Scholarship funds.
Limitations: Giving primarily in Chicago, IL, and surrounding metropolitan areas. No grants to individuals.
Publications: Application guidelines.
Application information:
Initial approach: Proposal
Copies of proposal: 2
Deadline(s): None
Board meeting date(s): May and Nov.
Final notification: Apr. 30 and Oct. 31
Trustees: Jack Hutchings; Richard Oloffson; Bank of America, N.A.
EIN: 362417437
Selected grants: The following grants were reported in 2005.
$150,000 to Museum of Science and Industry, Chicago, IL.
$60,000 to Associated Colleges of Illinois, Chicago, IL.
$27,000 to Juvenile Protective Association, Chicago, IL.
$25,000 to W T T W Channel 11, Chicago, IL.
$20,000 to Association House of Chicago, Chicago, IL.
$20,000 to Hales Franciscan High School, Chicago, IL.
$11,369 to Little City Foundation, Palatine, IL.
$10,000 to Chicago Humanities Festival, Chicago, IL.
$10,000 to Field Museum of Natural History, Chicago, IL.
$10,000 to High Jump, Chicago, IL.

3057
David M. Wark and Mary Ann Barrows Wark Foundation ◇
191 N. Wacker Dr., Ste. 1500
Chicago, IL 60606

Established in 2000 in IL.
Donor: Mary Ann Barrows Wark.
Foundation type: Independent foundation.
Financial data (yr. ended 12/31/04): Assets, $1,363,373 (M); gifts received, $1,703; expenditures, $773,474; qualifying distributions, $755,020; giving activities include $755,000 for 15 grants (high: $200,000; low: $2,500).
Purpose and activities: Giving primarily to Jewish agencies and temples, including Jewish federated giving programs, and for Jewish education; funding also for other higher education.
Fields of interest: Higher education; Children/youth, services; Jewish federated giving programs; Jewish agencies & temples.
Limitations: Applications not accepted. Giving primarily in St. Paul, MN. No grants to individuals.
Application information: Contributes only to pre-selected organizations.
Officers and Directors:* Mary Ann Barrows Wark,* Pres.; David M. Wark,* V.P.; Jack R. Polsky,* Secy.-Treas.
EIN: 364383745
Selected grants: The following grants were reported in 2004.

$250,000 to Resources for Child Caring, Saint Paul, MN. 2 grants: $200,000, $50,000
$164,000 to United Jewish Fund and Council, Saint Paul, MN. 2 grants: $60,000, $104,000
$150,000 to Saint Paul Academy and Summit School, Saint Paul, MN. 2 grants: $100,000, $50,000
$125,000 to MacPhail Center for Music, Minneapolis, MN.
$5,000 to Saint Paul Chamber Orchestra Society, Saint Paul, MN.
$3,500 to Family Focus, Chicago, IL.

3058
Washington Square Health Foundation, Inc. ◇
875 N. Michigan Ave., Ste. 3516
Chicago, IL 60611 (312) 664-6488
Contact: Howard Nochumson, Exec. Dir.
FAX: (312) 664-7787; E-mail: washington@wshf.org;
URL: http://www.wshf.org

Established in 1985 in IL; converted from Henrotin Hospital.
Donors: Henrotin Hospital; George Zendt Charitable Trust.
Foundation type: Independent foundation.
Financial data (yr. ended 9/30/05): Assets, $24,429,037 (M); gifts received, $6,305; expenditures, $1,585,477; qualifying distributions, $1,455,068; giving activities include $1,017,258 for 97 grants (high: $48,068; low: $100).
Purpose and activities: To promote and maintain access to adequate primary health care, through grants for medical and nursing education scholarships, medical research, and direct healthcare services.
Fields of interest: Medical school/education; Nursing school/education; Nursing care; Nursing home/convalescent facility; Health care; AIDS; Medical research, institute; AIDS research; Crime/violence prevention, domestic violence; Aging; Disabilities, people with; Minorities; Women; AIDS, people with; LGBTQ; Immigrants/refugees; Homeless.
Type of support: Equipment; Program development; Seed money; Fellowships; Scholarship funds; Research; Program-related investments/loans; Matching/challenge support.
Limitations: Giving primarily in the Chicago, IL, area for direct healthcare services; giving nationally for medical research and education grants. No grants to individuals, or for general operating or administrative expenses, land acquisition, or construction.
Publications: Application guidelines; Annual report.
Application information: Annual report is available on foundation Web site, as well as application guidelines, procedures, and grant application form. Application form required.
Initial approach: Send in application
Copies of proposal: 4
Deadline(s): June 1 and Dec. 1
Board meeting date(s): Jan., May, Aug., Dec.
Final notification: Within 1-month of board meeting
Officers and Directors:* Angelo P. Creticos, M.D.*, Pres.; Mrs. Arthur M. Wirtz, Jr.,* V.P.; William B. Friedeman,* Secy.; John C. York,* Treas.; Howard Nochumson,* Exec. Dir.; Howard M. McCue III, Legal Counsel; Richard B. Patterson; James M. Snyder; William N. Werner, M.D.; Bill G. Wiley.

Number of staff: 2 full-time professional; 1 part-time support.
EIN: 361210140
Selected grants: The following grants were reported in 2003.

$50,000 to Roseland Christian Health Ministries, Chicago, IL. For Chicago Youth Programs, to establish new health care clinic for new South Side Chicago site.

$25,000 to Gildas Club Chicago, Chicago, IL. For Latino Coordinator position and for Illinois Hispanic Nurses Association meetings.

$12,500 to Coordinating Action for Childrens Health (COACH), Naperville, IL. To establish Transitional Care Center which has significantly lowered hospital length-of-stay of clients while incorporating life skills training to parents to prepare them to care for their children with special health care needs.

$12,246 to Chicago Hearing Society, Chicago, IL. To establish Latino Outreach program.

$3,000 to Access Community Health Network, Chicago, IL. To conduct variety of Diabetes Prevention and Control programs at a number of their sites, in order to see what method works best.

3059
Wavering Family Charitable Foundation ✧
c/o The Northern Trust Co.
P.O. Box 803878
Chicago, IL 60680

Established in 1990 in IL.
Donor: Emer H. Wavering.
Foundation type: Independent foundation.
Financial data (yr. ended 12/31/05): Assets, $13,674,745 (M); expenditures, $705,814; qualifying distributions, $674,386; giving activities include $671,000 for 5 grants (high: $361,000; low: $10,000).
Purpose and activities: Giving for higher education and for a day school.
Fields of interest: Elementary/secondary education; Higher education.
Limitations: Giving primarily in IA and IL.
Application information: Application form not required.
Deadline(s): None
Trustee: The Northern Trust Co.
EIN: 366940417

3060
Wein Family Foundation ✧
(formerly Hyman & Susan Wein Foundation)
1550 W. Carroll Ave.
Chicago, IL 60607-1012

Donors: Irving L. Wein; Zahava Wein.
Foundation type: Independent foundation.
Financial data (yr. ended 12/31/05): Assets, $5,553,158 (M); gifts received, $250,000; expenditures, $528,372; qualifying distributions, $465,064; giving activities include $462,113 for 53 grants (high: $127,348; low: $50).
Fields of interest: Arts; Higher education; Children/youth, services; Jewish agencies & temples.
International interests: Israel.
Limitations: Applications not accepted. Giving primarily in Chicago, IL. No grants to individuals.

Application information: Contributes only to pre-selected organizations.
Officers: Joseph Wein, Pres.; Susan Wein-Bernhardt, Secy.; Zahava Wein, Treas.
EIN: 366065421
Selected grants: The following grants were reported in 2004.

$11,000 to Jewish United Fund of Metropolitan Chicago, Chicago, IL.

$10,500 to American Committee for the Weizmann Institute of Science, New York, NY.

$10,000 to Washington Institute for Near East Policy, DC.

$3,000 to American Friends of Shalom Hartman Institute, New York, NY.

$3,000 to Jewish Federation of Metropolitan Chicago, Chicago, IL.

$3,000 to Nature Conservancy, Arlington, VA.

$2,000 to Francis W. Parker School, Chicago, IL.

$2,000 to Friends of Yemin Orde, DC.

$2,000 to Middle East Media Research Institute, DC.

$2,000 to Oprahs Angel Network, Chicago, IL.

3061
Judd A. & Marjorie G. Weinberg Family Foundation ✧
21 S. Clark St., Ste. 3140
Chicago, IL 60603-2003

Established in 1977.
Donors: Marjorie G. Weinberg; Judd A. Weinberg; and other members of the Weinberg family.
Foundation type: Independent foundation.
Financial data (yr. ended 12/31/05): Assets, $8,907,527 (M); expenditures, $697,863; qualifying distributions, $654,544; giving activities include $649,249 for 85 grants (high: $200,000; low: $100).
Purpose and activities: Giving primarily for higher education; funding also for medical research, the arts and Jewish welfare.
Fields of interest: Arts; Higher education; Cancer; Medical research, institute; Cancer research; Human services; Jewish federated giving programs; Jewish agencies & temples.
Limitations: Applications not accepted. Giving primarily in IL, with emphasis on Chicago. No grants to individuals.
Application information: Contributes only to pre-selected organizations.
Officers and Directors:* Judd A. Weinberg,* Chair.; Richard G. Weinberg, Pres.; David B. Weinberg,* V.P.; Jack A. Weinberg,* V.P.
EIN: 362934515

3062
William L. and Josephine B. Weiss Family Foundation ✧
21 S. Clark St.
Chicago, IL 60603-2006

Established in 1986 in IL.
Donors: William L. Weiss; Josephine B. Weiss.
Foundation type: Independent foundation.
Financial data (yr. ended 12/31/03): Assets, $7,746,663 (M); expenditures, $488,071; qualifying distributions, $438,084; giving activities include $436,600 for 14 grants (high: $368,000; low: $100).

Purpose and activities: Giving primarily for higher education, as well as for health and child care, and Christian and Presbyterian churches.
Fields of interest: Higher education; Health care, clinics/centers; Children, day care; Community development; Federated giving programs; Christian agencies & churches; Protestant agencies & churches.
Limitations: Applications not accepted. Giving on a national basis, with emphasis on FL, IL, NC, and PA. No grants to individuals.
Application information: Contributes only to pre-selected organizations.
Officers: William L. Weiss, Pres.; Josephine B. Weiss, V.P. and Secy.-Treas.; Steven P. Weiss, V.P.
Directors: Susan L. Miller; David W. Weiss.
EIN: 363478679

3063
Herbert C. Wenske Foundation ✧
1 S. Wacker Dr., Ste. 800
Chicago, IL 60606 (312) 207-2800
Contact: Howard L. Stone, Pres.

Established in 1957 in IL.
Donors: Florence Wenske; Herbert C. Wenske†; Wenske Enterprises, Inc.
Foundation type: Independent foundation.
Financial data (yr. ended 12/31/05): Assets, $10,268,403 (M); expenditures, $1,037,967; qualifying distributions, $929,794; giving activities include $826,870 for 42 grants (high: $80,000; low: $1,000).
Purpose and activities: Giving primarily for religious and educational purposes; support also for hospitals and health care.
Fields of interest: Medical school/education; Education; Hospitals (general); Health organizations, association; Children/youth, services; Family services, domestic violence; Religion.
Limitations: Giving primarily in Chicago, IL. No grants to individuals.
Application information: Application form not required.
Deadline(s): None
Officers: Howard L. Stone, Pres.; Loren R. Stone, Secy.; Harvey Gaffen, Treas.
EIN: 366055643
Selected grants: The following grants were reported in 2003.

$125,000 to Northwestern University, School of Medicine, Evanston, IL.

$75,000 to Jewish United Fund of Metropolitan Chicago, Chicago, IL. For unrestricted support.

$51,000 to Holocaust Educational Foundation, Wilmette, IL.

$50,000 to Rush-Presbyterian-Saint Lukes Medical Center, Chicago, IL.

$25,000 to Boys Town Jerusalem Foundation of America, New York, NY.

$20,000 to Evanston Northwestern Healthcare, Evanston, IL. For unrestricted support.

$18,750 to United Cerebral Palsy Association of Greater Chicago, Chicago, IL.

$17,500 to Holy Family Ministries Foundation, Northfield, IL. For unrestricted support.

$12,000 to Visitation Scholarship Program, Chicago, IL. For unrestricted support.

$10,000 to Institute for Clinical Social Work, Chicago, IL. For unrestricted support.

3064
Wessner Foundation ✧
200 W. Adams St., Ste. 2600
Chicago, IL 60606-5233

Established in 1994 in MN.
Donor: Norma C. Wessner.
Foundation type: Independent foundation.
Financial data (yr. ended 12/31/05): Assets, $14,018,207 (M); expenditures, $732,017; qualifying distributions, $667,450; giving activities include $667,450 for 14 grants (high: $150,000; low: $10,000).
Purpose and activities: Giving primarily for Christian organizations; support also for higher education.
Fields of interest: Higher education; Christian agencies & churches.
Limitations: Applications not accepted. Giving on a national basis, with some emphasis on IL. No grants to individuals.
Application information: Contributes only to pre-selected organizations.
Officers and Directors:* David K. Wessner,* Pres.; Barbara W. Anderson,* V.P. and Secy.; Norma C. Wessner,* Treas.; Ross E. Anderson; Patricia A. Wessner.
EIN: 363480120

3065
West Suburban Sentinel Corporation ✧ ☆
1001 Lake St.
Oak Park, IL 60301-1101

Established in 2004 in IL.
Foundation type: Independent foundation.
Financial data (yr. ended 12/31/05): Assets, $1,513,947 (M); expenditures, $567,712; qualifying distributions, $552,854; giving activities include $552,854 for 1 grant.
Purpose and activities: Giving primarily to a community wellness center.
Fields of interest: Health care.
Limitations: Applications not accepted. Giving primarily in Oak Park, IL.
Application information: Contributes only to pre-selected organizations.
Officers and Directors:* Martin J. Noll,* Pres.; Arthur M. Morris, M.D.*, V.P.; Chester L. Stewart,* Secy.-Treas.; Michael E. Kelly; Allan O. Muehrcke, M.D.; J. Kevin O'Donoghue, M.D.; Marianne Schiavone; James Winikates.
EIN: 200671544

3066
Westlake Health Foundation ✧ ☆
1 Lincoln Ctr.
18 W. 140 Butterfield Rd., Ste. 1660
Oakbrook Terrace, IL 60181 (630) 495-3800
Contact: Leonard J. Muller, Pres.
E-mail: info@westlakehf.com; URL: http://www.westlakehf.com

Established in 1998 in IL; converted from Westlake Hospital.
Foundation type: Independent foundation.
Financial data (yr. ended 12/31/05): Assets, $105,340,242 (M); expenditures, $5,585,785; qualifying distributions, $4,942,695; giving activities include $4,511,438 for 28 grants (high: $2,250,000; low: $5,000).
Purpose and activities: The foundation supports and encourages the development of healthcare services by making grants to nonprofit community organizations.
Fields of interest: Health care.
Limitations: Giving primarily in west suburban Cook County, IL. No support for direct religious activities; fraternal societies; or fundraising. No grants to individuals; or endowment campaigns.
Application information: See Web site for additional application guidelines.
Deadline(s): May 1 and Nov. 1
Board meeting date(s): June and Dec.
Officers and Trustees:* Arthur T. Dalton,* Chair.; Leonard J. Muller,* Pres.; John P. Goedert,* Secy.; John A. Fogle,* Treas.; Earl C. Bird; Frank J. McGarr; Richard M. Montalbano, Sr.; Raul Villasuso, M.D.
EIN: 363104071
Selected grants: The following grants were reported in 2004.
$230,000 to Way Back Inn, Maywood, IL. 2 grants: $200,000, $30,000
$203,864 to Triton College, River Grove, IL.
$125,000 to Aspire of Illinois, Westchester, IL.
$75,000 to Community Care Options, Berwyn, IL.
$55,000 to Community Support Services, Brookfield, IL.
$40,000 to Suburban Primary Health Care Council, Westchester, IL.
$10,000 to Sarahs Inn, Oak Park, IL. 2 grants: $5,000 each

3067
W. P. and H. B. White Foundation
540 Frontage Rd., Ste. 3240
Northfield, IL 60093 (847) 446-1441
Contact: M. Margaret Blandford, Exec. Dir.

Incorporated in 1953 in IL.
Donors: William P. White†; Hazel B. White†.
Foundation type: Independent foundation.
Financial data (yr. ended 12/31/05): Assets, $27,439,500 (M); expenditures, $1,837,477; qualifying distributions, $1,743,975; giving activities include $1,471,700 for grants (low: $3,200).
Purpose and activities: Funding to organizations in the metropolitan Chicago, IL area that contribute to the future good of the country, primarily in the areas of education, health, and human services, with an emphasis on helping those most in need.
Fields of interest: Secondary school/education; Higher education; Adult/continuing education; Education; Health care; Housing/shelter, development; Human services; Children/youth, services; Urban/community development; Minorities; Economically disadvantaged.
Type of support: General/operating support; Continuing support; Annual campaigns; Program development; Scholarship funds.
Limitations: Giving primarily in the metropolitan Chicago, IL, area. No grants to individuals, or for land acquisition, endowment funds, publications, conferences, deficit financing, or visual or performing arts; no loans.
Publications: Application guidelines.
Application information: Application form not required.
Initial approach: Proposal
Copies of proposal: 1
Deadline(s): Feb. 1, May 1, Aug. 1, Nov. 1
Board meeting date(s): Mar., June, Sept., and Dec.
Final notification: Several weeks
Officers and Directors:* Roger B. White,* Pres.; Philip O. White,* V.P. and Treas.; Steven R. White,* Secy.; M. Margaret Blandford, Exec. Dir.; John J. McCarthy; William P. White III.
Number of staff: 1 full-time professional; 1 full-time support.
EIN: 362601558
Selected grants: The following grants were reported in 2005.
$35,000 to Golden Apple Foundation, Chicago, IL.
$35,000 to Holy Trinity High School, Chicago, IL.
$25,000 to Infant Welfare Society of Chicago, Chicago, IL.
$22,000 to Carole Robertson Center for Learning, Chicago, IL.
$20,000 to Chicago Youth Programs, Chicago, IL.
$20,000 to Interfaith House, Chicago, IL.
$17,000 to Queen of Peace High School, Burbank, IL.
$15,000 to Deborahs Place, Chicago, IL.
$15,000 to Erie Family Health Center, Chicago, IL.
$12,000 to Chicago Abused Women Coalition, Chicago, IL.

3068
David & Barbara Whitwam Foundation, Inc. ✧ ☆
c/o Northern Trust Co.
P.O. Box 803878
Chicago, IL 60680
Application address: c/o David R. Whitwam, 1408 Manley Ct., St. Joseph, MI 49085, tel.: (269) 923-3150

Established in 1986 in MI.
Donors: David R. Whitwam; Barbara Whitwam.
Foundation type: Independent foundation.
Financial data (yr. ended 12/31/05): Assets, $4,668,456 (M); expenditures, $392,943; qualifying distributions, $339,050; giving activities include $339,050 for 23 grants (high: $200,000; low: $250).
Fields of interest: Education; Human services; Federated giving programs; Christian agencies & churches.
Limitations: Giving primarily in Benton Harbor, Stevensville, and St. Joseph, MI. No grants to individuals.
Application information: Application form not required.
Deadline(s): None
Officer and Directors:* David R. Whitwam,* Pres.; Barbara Whitwam.
EIN: 382712616
Selected grants: The following grants were reported in 2005.
$200,000 to Lake Michigan College Foundation, Benton Harbor, MI.
$13,000 to Boys and Girls Club of Benton Harbor, Benton Harbor, MI.
$6,000 to Readiness Center, Benton Harbor, MI.
$500 to Boy Scouts of America, Kalamazoo, MI.
$500 to Junior Achievement, East Lansing, MI.

3069
Wieboldt Foundation ✧
53 W. Jackson Blvd., Ste. 838
Chicago, IL 60604 (312) 786-9377
Contact: Carmen Prieto, Assoc. Dir.
FAX: (312) 786-9232; E-mail: info@wieboldt.org;
URL: http://www.wieboldtfoundation.org

Incorporated in 1921 in IL.
Donors: William A. Wieboldt†; Anna Krueger
Wieboldt†; The Ford Foundation.
Foundation type: Independent foundation.
Financial data (yr. ended 12/31/05): Assets,
$22,378,654 (M); expenditures, $1,301,915;
qualifying distributions, $1,043,846; giving
activities include $721,660 for 44 grants (high:
$40,000; low: $1,000).
Purpose and activities: The foundation's highest
priority is the support of multi-issue community
organizations that work in low-income
neighborhoods, that are accountable to
neighborhood residents, and through which people
are empowered to have a major voice in shaping
decisions that affect their lives. A second priority is
given to organizations that support community
organizations through training, technical
assistance, legal strategies, coalition building,
advocacy, and policy development.
Fields of interest: Human services; Community
development; Public affairs.
Type of support: General/operating support;
Continuing support; Program-related investments/
loans.
Limitations: Giving limited to the metropolitan
Chicago, IL, and IN areas. No grants to individuals,
or for endowment funds, studies and research,
capital campaigns, scholarships, fellowships,
conferences, direct service projects, or economic
development.
Publications: Annual report (including application
guidelines); Grants list.
Application information: Proposals submitted by fax
not accepted. See foundation Web site for
application guidelines and procedures. Application
form not required.
   Initial approach: Proposal (no more than 10
      pages)
   Copies of proposal: 1
   Deadline(s): End of each month for grants and
      PRIs
   Board meeting date(s): Monthly, except Apr., Aug.,
      and Dec.
   Final notification: 2 months after receipt of
      proposal
Officers and Directors:* Jennifer S. Corrigan,*
Pres.; William W. Davis,* V.P.; Regina McGraw,*
Secy. and Exec. Dir.; Nancy Wieboldt,* Treas.; Anne
W. Burghard; Anita S. Darrow; Jessica Darrow; Philip
Darrow; Rev. Calvin S. Morris; Rita Simo; John W.
Straub; Dorian T. Warren.
Number of staff: 2 full-time professional.
EIN: 362167955

3070
Wilemal Fund ✧
1275 N. Greenbay Rd.
Lake Forest, IL 60045-2427

Established in 1964.
Donor: Elizabeth Byron Brown.
Foundation type: Independent foundation.
Financial data (yr. ended 12/31/05): Assets,
$24,412,217 (M); expenditures, $1,023,375;

qualifying distributions, $939,681; giving activities
include $926,334 for 29 grants (high: $120,000;
low: $1,000).
Purpose and activities: Giving primarily for the arts,
education, social services, and Christian churches.
Fields of interest: Arts education; Media, television;
Visual arts, architecture; Performing arts, orchestra
(symphony); Arts; Higher education; Zoos/zoological
societies; Community development; Christian
agencies & churches.
Limitations: Applications not accepted. Giving
primarily in FL, IL, with emphasis on Chicago, and
Winston-Salem, NC. No grants to individuals.
Application information: Contributes only to
pre-selected organizations. Unsolicited requests for
funds not accepted.
Officers and Directors:* William Gardner Brown,*
Pres. and Secy.; Malcolm McDougal Brown,* V.P.
and Treas.; Solange Pezon Brown.
EIN: 366098849

3071
Wilkie Brothers Foundation ✧ ☆
254 N. Laurel Ave.
Des Plaines, IL 60016-4321 (847) 824-1122
Contact: Michael L. Wilkie, V.P.

Incorporated in 1951 in IL.
Donors: Leighton A. Wilkie†; Robert J. Wilkie; James
W. Wilkie†.
Foundation type: Independent foundation.
Financial data (yr. ended 12/31/05): Assets,
$529,090 (M); expenditures, $431,243; qualifying
distributions, $424,120; giving activities include
$424,120 for 6 grants (high: $300,000; low:
$1,000).
Purpose and activities: Giving primarily for the arts,
with emphasis on museums, as well as for wildlife
preservation and protection; some funding for
education.
Fields of interest: Museums (natural history);
Museums (specialized); Arts; Higher education;
Animals/wildlife.
Limitations: Giving on a national basis, with
emphasis on CA and MN. No grants to individuals.
Application information: Application form not
required.
   Initial approach: Letter or proposal
   Deadline(s): None
Officers and Directors:* Jonathan P. Wilkie,* Pres.;
Michael L. Wilkie,* V.P.; Tim Moran,* Secy.; Richard
Hermann, Treas.
EIN: 362226189

3072
Wilkins Foundation, Inc. ✧ ☆
P.O. Box 3073
Barrington, IL 60011 (800) 713-2275
Contact: Helen N. Wilkins, Pres.

Donors: Helen N. Wilkins; Floyd V. Wilkins Trust;
HNW Charitable Trust.
Foundation type: Independent foundation.
Financial data (yr. ended 12/31/05): Assets,
$610,875 (M); gifts received, $122,041;
expenditures, $596,351; qualifying distributions,
$596,351; giving activities include $503,834 for 4
grants (high: $288,174; low: $1,060).
Fields of interest: Christian agencies & churches.
Limitations: Giving primarily in FL and TX.
Application information:

Initial approach: Letter
Deadline(s): None
Officers and Directors:* Helen N. Wilkins,* Pres.;
Ronald N. Wilkins,* V.P; John Vanderveld.
EIN: 222676848
Selected grants: The following grants were reported
in 2004.
$98,000 to Living Light Ministries, Plano, TX.
$15,430 to Lamplighter School, Dallas, TX.
$5,100 to SR Horse Sanctuary, Venice, FL.
$4,000 to Straight Way Ministries, Gainesville, FL.
$2,050 to North American Ministries, Inverness, IL.

3073
Howard L. Willett Foundation, Inc. ✧
111 W. Washington St., Ste. 1900
Chicago, IL 60602-2713 (312) 407-7800
Contact: Arthur H. Anderson, Jr., Pres.

Incorporated in 1973 in IL.
Donors: Howard L. Willett†; Howard L. Willett, Jr.†.
Foundation type: Independent foundation.
Financial data (yr. ended 12/31/03): Assets,
$2,525,300 (M); expenditures, $418,081;
qualifying distributions, $410,627; giving activities
include $405,013 for 138 grants (high: $32,500;
low: $50).
Purpose and activities: Giving primarily for the arts,
education, health organizations and human
services.
Fields of interest: Arts; Higher education; Health
care; Health organizations, association; Human
services.
Limitations: Giving primarily in the metropolitan
Chicago, IL, area. No grants to individuals.
Application information: Application form not
required.
   Initial approach: Letter
   Deadline(s): None
Officers and Directors:* Arthur H. Anderson, Jr.,*
Pres.; Arthur J. Bruen, Jr.,* V.P. and Secy.; Irwin W.
Hart, Jr.,* V.P. and Treas.; John R. Covington,* V.P.;
Nancy Spore,* V.P.; Phyliss Willett,* V.P.
EIN: 237311429
Selected grants: The following grants were reported
in 2004.
$56,200 to Chinese American Service League,
   Chicago, IL.
$29,500 to Lake Forest College, Lake Forest, IL.
$12,500 to Lake Forest Symphony Association,
   Lake Forest, IL.
$9,000 to Glenwood School for Boys, Glenwood, IL.
$6,000 to Thresholds, Chicago, IL.
$5,000 to Kenilworth Union Church, Kenilworth, IL.
$4,000 to Siesta Key Chapel, Sarasota, FL.
$2,500 to Latin School of Chicago, Chicago, IL.
$2,000 to Adler Planetarium, Chicago, IL.
$1,500 to A Safe Place, Oakland, CA.

3074
Willow Springs Foundation ✧
(also known as Donald and Barbara Brodie
Charitable Foundation)
10897 S. Rte. 78
Mount Carroll, IL 61053

Established in 1995 in IL.
Donors: Donald Brodie; Barbara Brodie.
Foundation type: Independent foundation.
Financial data (yr. ended 12/31/04): Assets,
$14,274,202 (M); expenditures, $1,456,121;

qualifying distributions, $1,354,500; giving activities include $1,354,500 for 29 grants (high: $250,000; low: $2,000).

Purpose and activities: Giving primarily for higher education, the arts, and children and youth services.

Fields of interest: Arts; Higher education; Education; Big Brothers/Big Sisters; Human services; Children/youth, services; Family services.

Type of support: General/operating support.

Limitations: Applications not accepted. Giving on a national basis. No grants to individuals.

Application information: Contributes only to pre-selected organizations.

Officers and Directors:* Kent Brodie,* Pres.; Jenny B. Stoddard,* Secy.; Greg Andresen,* Treas.

Trustees: Sara Smock Foszcz; Suzy Brodie Volger.

EIN: 364054428

Selected grants: The following grants were reported in 2003.

$770,000 to University of Illinois Foundation, Urbana, IL.

$150,000 to Edgewood Center for Children and Families, San Francisco, CA.

$50,000 to Raue Center for the Arts, Crystal Lake, IL.

$30,000 to Elgin Symphony Orchestra, Elgin, IL.

$25,000 to Eastern Illinois University, Charleston, IL.

$20,600 to Big Brothers/Big Sisters of McHenry County, McHenry, IL.

$15,000 to Home of the Sparrow McHenry County Interfaith Shelter Program, McHenry, IL.

$15,000 to San Francisco Zoological Society, San Francisco, CA.

$10,000 to Bozeman Public Library, Bozeman, MT.

$4,991 to McHenry County College, Crystal Lake, IL.

3075
Anne Potter Wilson Foundation ◇

c/o Bank of America, N.A.
231 S. LaSalle St., IL1-231-14-19
Chicago, IL 60697-1411
Contact: Stephanie Edwards
Application address: c/o Bank of America, N.A., 414 Union St., Nashville, TN 37219, tel.: (615) 749-4344

Established in 1996 in TN.

Foundation type: Independent foundation.

Financial data (yr. ended 12/31/05): Assets, $22,725,801 (M); expenditures, $1,289,670; qualifying distributions, $1,152,755; giving activities include $1,140,000 for 9 grants (high: $250,000; low: $50,000).

Purpose and activities: Giving primarily for higher education.

Fields of interest: Performing arts, orchestra (symphony); Historic preservation/historical societies; Higher education; Libraries (public); Botanical gardens; Zoos/zoological societies; Human services.

Limitations: Giving primarily in Nashville, TN. No grants to individuals.

Application information: Application form not required.

Initial approach: Letter
Deadline(s): None

Trustee: Bank of America, N.A.

Committee Members: Blair J. Wilson; David K. Wilson; Justin P. Wilson; William M. Wilson.

EIN: 626306576

3076
Wine & Spirits Distributors of Illinois Charitable Foundation ◇

27 E. Monroe St., Ste. 1200
Chicago, IL 60603-5672 (312) 782-7820
Contact: Teresa Kelly, Dep. Dir.

Established in 1998 in IL.

Donors: Wine & Spirits Distributors of Illinois; Union Beverage Co.; Judge & Dolph, Ltd.

Foundation type: Independent foundation.

Financial data (yr. ended 12/31/05): Assets, $60,131 (M); gifts received, $277,500; expenditures, $430,030; qualifying distributions, $430,030; giving activities include $361,123 for grants.

Fields of interest: Education; Medical research, institute; Human services.

Limitations: Giving primarily in IL. No grants to individuals.

Application information:

Initial approach: Letter
Deadline(s): 6 weeks prior (contact foundation for deadline)
Board meeting date(s): Monthly

Directors: Lou DeFalco; Paul Jenkins; Donald G. Pydo.

EIN: 364330942

Selected grants: The following grants were reported in 2004.

$20,000 to Equality Illinois Education Project, Chicago, IL.

$10,000 to Chicago International Film Festival, Chicago, IL.

$7,500 to Horizons Community Services, Chicago, IL.

$4,750 to Cystic Fibrosis Foundation, Bethesda, MD. 2 grants: $2,750, $2,000

$2,250 to Loyola Academy, Wilmette, IL.

$1,500 to Childrens Hospital.

$1,500 to Childrens Place Association, Chicago, IL.

$1,500 to Fenwick High School, Oak Park, IL.

$1,000 to Grant Park Orchestral Association, Chicago, IL.

3077
The Oprah Winfrey Foundation ▼ ◇

(formerly For a Better Life Foundation)
110 N. Carpenter St.
Chicago, IL 60607
Contact: Oprah G. Winfrey, Chair.

Established in 1995 in IL.

Donors: Harpo, Inc.; Harpo Productions, Inc.

Foundation type: Independent foundation.

Financial data (yr. ended 12/31/04): Assets, $140,321,830 (M); gifts received, $45,000,000; expenditures, $8,531,097; qualifying distributions, $8,087,040; giving activities include $7,717,946 for 34 grants (high: $3,500,000; low: $2,620; average: $10,000–$100,000).

Purpose and activities: The purpose of the foundation is to focus on education, and empowering women, children, and families.

Fields of interest: Arts; Education; Hospitals (specialty); Health care; Health organizations; Boys & girls clubs; Human services; Children, services; Family services; Community development; Women.

Limitations: Applications not accepted. Giving on a national basis, with emphasis on Chicago, IL.

Application information: Contributes only to pre-selected organizations.

Officers and Directors:* Oprah G. Winfrey,* Pres.; Tim Bennett,* V.P.; Letty Tanchum,* Treas.; Caren Yanis, Exec. Dir.; Mary Kay Clinton; Gayle King; Harriet Seitler.

EIN: 363976230

Selected grants: The following grants were reported in 2004.

$3,500,000 to Morehouse College, Atlanta, GA. For scholarships.

$500,000 to Alvin Ailey Dance Foundation, New York, NY. For scholarship for dance program.

$500,000 to National Underground Railroad Freedom Center, Cincinnati, OH. For capital campaign and project support.

$458,060 to Boys and Girls Club of Kosciusko and Attala County, Kosciusko, MS. 2 grants: $358,060 (For youth center building project), $100,000 (For general operating support for youth center).

$425,000 to Help the Afghan Children, Vienna, VA. For school building projects in Afghanistan.

$348,676 to Jackson State University, Jackson, MS. For scholarships for teaching programs.

$250,000 to Museum of Broadcast Communications, Chicago, IL. For curriculum development.

$100,000 to Tyrese Gibson Watts Foundation, Beverly Hills, CA. For capital campaign for youth center in South Central Los Angeles.

$86,712 to Mississippi Institutions of Higher Learning, Jackson, MS. For scholarships for teaching programs.

3078
Wohlers Family Foundation ◇ ☆

c/o The Northern Trust Co.
P.O. Box 803878
Chicago, IL 60680

Established in 2002 in IL.

Donor: Albert H. Wohlers.

Foundation type: Independent foundation.

Financial data (yr. ended 12/31/05): Assets, $1,843,759 (M); gifts received, $1,000,000; expenditures, $663,062; qualifying distributions, $656,470; giving activities include $655,500 for 52 grants (high: $250,000; low: $1,000).

Fields of interest: Hospitals (general); Health care; Health organizations; Human services.

Limitations: Applications not accepted. Giving primarily in IL. No grants to individuals.

Application information: Contributes only to pre-selected organizations.

Officers: James R. Malik, Mgr.; Thomas Moran, Mgr.; Albert H. Wohlers, Mgr.

Trustee: The Northern Trust Co.

EIN: 367393288

3079
Marie E. Wolf Charitable Trust ◇ ☆

c/o Harris Trust and Savings Bank
P.O. Box 755
Chicago, IL 60690

Established in 1996 in IL.

Foundation type: Independent foundation.

Financial data (yr. ended 12/31/05): Assets, $6,308,432 (M); expenditures, $433,458; qualifying distributions, $382,706; giving activities include $360,309 for 5 grants (high: $144,123; low: $36,030).

Purpose and activities: To distribute funds to specified charitable organizations.

Fields of interest: Higher education, college; Hospitals (general); Salvation Army; Christian agencies & churches.

Limitations: Applications not accepted. Giving primarily in IL. No grants to individuals.

Application information: Unsolicited requests for funds not considered.

Trustee: Harris Trust and Savings Bank.

EIN: 367160372

Selected grants: The following grants were reported in 2005.

$72,063 to Saint Xavier University, Chicago, IL.

$54,046 to Saints Faith, Hope and Charity, Winnetka, IL.

$36,030 to Salvation Army, Sterling, IL.

3080
Wonderful Life Foundation ✧
(formerly M. Jude & Lori W. Reyes Foundation)
9500 W. Bryn Mawr Ave., Ste. 700
Rosemont, IL 60018

Established in 2000 in VA.

Donors: M. Jude Reyes; Lori W. Reyes.

Foundation type: Independent foundation.

Financial data (yr. ended 12/31/05): Assets, $1,561,615 (M); gifts received, $179,755; expenditures, $582,469; qualifying distributions, $576,150; giving activities include $576,150 for 62 grants (high: $100,000; low: $500).

Purpose and activities: Giving primarily to hospitals, including a children's hospital, and for education.

Fields of interest: Education; Hospitals (specialty); Health organizations; Human services; Children, services.

Limitations: Applications not accepted. Giving primarily in Washington, DC, MD, and VA. No grants to individuals.

Application information: Contributes only to pre-selected organizations.

Directors: Lori W. Reyes; M. Jude Reyes.

EIN: 541995591

Selected grants: The following grants were reported in 2004.

$100,000 to Childrens National Medical Center, DC.

$60,000 to Rehabilitation Institute of Chicago, Chicago, IL. 2 grants: $50,000, $10,000

$40,000 to Evanston Northwestern Healthcare, Evanston, IL.

$40,000 to North Shore Country Day School, Winnetka, IL.

$30,000 to National Rehabilitation Hospital, DC.

$20,000 to Bethel New Life, Chicago, IL.

$10,000 to Link Unlimited, Chicago, IL. 2 grants: $5,000 each

3081
L. S. Wood Charitable Trust ✧
c/o Bank of America, N.A.
231 S. LaSalle St.
Chicago, IL 60697 (312) 828-1785
Application address: c/o Donald H. Parkison, Admin., 1317 Grand Ave., Ste. 228, Glenwood Springs, CO 81601, tel.: (970) 945-4952, FAX: (970) 947-9215, E-mail: parkison@sopris.net

Foundation type: Independent foundation.

Financial data (yr. ended 12/31/05): Assets, $8,815,605 (M); expenditures, $673,978; qualifying distributions, $671,857; giving activities include $542,398 for grants to individuals.

Purpose and activities: Awards scholarships to individuals for undergraduate degree programs.

Type of support: Scholarships—to individuals.

Limitations: Giving on a national basis.

Application information: Applications are available at the Trust's office, or through high school counselors beginning Nov. 1. Application form required.

> *Deadline(s):* Feb. 1
> *Final notification:* July

Trustees: Frederick G. Acker; Thomas E. Gibbs; Joseph Edward Harker; John A. Reeves; Bank of America, N.A.

EIN: 366146230

3082
Woodbury Foundation
c/o Christine M. Rhode
222 N. LaSalle St., 24th Fl.
Chicago, IL 60601
Application address: c/o Dean of Admissions, Warren Wilson College, Swannanoa, NC 28778, tel.: (704) 298-3325

Established in 1990.

Donors: Christiana L. Ransom†; Christiana Ransom Irrevocable Trust.

Foundation type: Independent foundation.

Financial data (yr. ended 5/31/05): Assets, $18,642,560 (M); expenditures, $810,154; qualifying distributions, $728,617; giving activities include $592,600 for 19 grants (high: $106,900; low: $2,000), and $123,800 for grants to individuals.

Purpose and activities: Scholarships for study at Warren Wilson College, preference given to students from Charlevoix, Emmet, Cheboygan and Antrim counties, MI. Giving also for churches and drug rehabilitation centers.

Fields of interest: Historic preservation/historical societies; Higher education; Substance abuse, services; Substance abuse, treatment; Human services; Children, services.

Type of support: General/operating support; Building/renovation; Endowments; Scholarships—to individuals.

Limitations: Applications not accepted. Giving on a national basis.

Application information: Scholarship application available only from Warren Wilson College. Unsolicited requests for funds are not accepted.

> *Board meeting date(s):* April

Officers and Directors: * Myron P. Boon,* Pres.; F. Conrad Fischer,* V.P.; Sophia Iannaccone, Secy.; Christina Lopez,* Treas.; Priscilla M. Anderson; Jennifer Melton; Earl Ransom.

EIN: 363715828

3083
Abbey Woods Foundation ✧ ☆
P.O. Box 1119
Frankfort, IL 60423-1119

Established in 2000 in IL.

Donors: Linda Kay Mitchell; James J. Mitchell.

Foundation type: Independent foundation.

Financial data (yr. ended 12/31/05): Assets, $2,081,727 (M); gifts received, $572,152; expenditures, $546,806; qualifying distributions, $519,625; giving activities include $516,850 for 9 grants (high: $200,000; low: $2,000).

Fields of interest: Higher education; Animals/wildlife, special services; Alzheimer's disease; Crime/violence prevention, domestic violence; Human services; Developmentally disabled, centers & services; Women, centers/services; Protestant agencies & churches; Religion.

Limitations: Giving primarily in IL.

Trustees: James J. Mitchell III; Linda Kay Mitchell.

EIN: 367336271

Selected grants: The following grants were reported in 2004.

$50,000 to Park Lawn Association, Oak Lawn, IL.

$20,000 to Little Brothers - Friends of the Elderly, Chicago, IL.

$10,000 to Community Mennonite Day Care Center, Markham, IL.

$10,000 to Little Sisters of the Poor, Palatine, IL.

$10,000 to Night Ministry, Chicago, IL.

$5,000 to Free Street Programs, Chicago, IL.

$5,000 to Guardian Angel Home of Joliet, Joliet, IL.

$5,000 to Sarahs Circle, Chicago, IL.

$5,000 to South Suburban Family Shelter, Homewood, IL.

$5,000 to Will County Center for Community Concerns, Joliet, IL.

3084
Woods Fund of Chicago ▼ ✧
360 N. Michigan Ave., Ste. 1600
Chicago, IL 60601-3806 (312) 782-2698
Contact: Deborah D. Clark, Grants and Opers. Mgr.
FAX: (312) 782-4155;
E-mail: application@woodsfund.org; URL: http://www.woodsfund.org

Established in 1994 in IL.

Donors: Woods Charitable Fund, Inc.; The Ford Foundation; East Chicago Development Foundation, Inc.; Twin City Education Foundation, Inc.

Foundation type: Independent foundation.

Financial data (yr. ended 12/31/04): Assets, $67,268,475 (M); expenditures, $4,779,891; qualifying distributions, $4,541,691; giving activities include $3,509,750 for 132 grants (high: $170,000; low: $300; average: $1,000–$50,000).

Purpose and activities: The fund's goal is to increase opportunities for less advantaged people and communities in the metropolitan Chicago, IL, area, including the opportunity to contribute to decisions affecting them. Working primarily as a funding partner with nonprofit organizations, the fund supports them in their important roles of engaging people in civic life, addressing the causes of poverty and other challenges facing the region, promoting more effective public policies, reducing barriers to equal opportunity, and building a sense of community and common ground. The grants are concentrated into two main program areas: Community Organizing, and Public Policy. In addition, a limited number of grants are awarded for Arts and Culture.

Fields of interest: Arts; Community development, public policy; Community development, citizen coalitions; Public policy, research; Welfare policy/reform; Public affairs.

Type of support: Research; General/operating support; Continuing support; Program development.

Limitations: Giving limited to the metropolitan Chicago, IL, area. No support for social services, residential care, counseling programs, clinics, recreation programs, housing construction or rehabilitation, religious programs, business or economic development practitioners, healthcare institutions, or programs in or for individual schools. No grants to individuals, or for capital campaigns and projects, fundraising benefits, program advertising, endowments, scholarships, fellowships, or medical and scientific research.

Publications: Application guidelines; Annual report.

Application information: Application guidelines and inquiry form available on foundation Web site. Form must be submitted as either a 3.5 diskette or CD, or can be sent as an electronic attachment via E-mail. Application form required.

> *Initial approach:* Prospective grantees should first submit an inquiry form. Full applications accepted by invitation only
> *Deadline(s):* Arts and Culture: Jan. 31; Deadline for all other programs: Jan. 31 and July 31
> *Board meeting date(s):* June and Dec.
> *Final notification:* Jan. or July for inquiry forms; June and Dec. for final grant decisions

Officers and Directors: * William C. Ayers,* Chair.; Laura S. Washington,* Vice-Chair.; Deborah Harrington, Pres.; Kristin Patton, Secy.; Suzanne R. Boyle; Lee Bey; Doris Salomon Chagin; Jesus G. Garcia; Beth E. Richie; Charles N. Wheatley.

Number of staff: 5 full-time professional; 1 full-time support.

EIN: 363917968

Selected grants: The following grants were reported in 2004.

$170,000 to Sargent Shriver National Center on Poverty Law, Chicago, IL. For general support.

$110,000 to Chicago Rehab Network, Chicago, IL. For Housing Policy Analysis and Action Center.

$75,000 to Center for Tax and Budget Accountability, Chicago, IL. For general support.

$70,000 to Association of Community Organizations for Reform Now (ACORN), Chicago, IL. For general operating support for work on issues of education reform, living wage, anti-predatory lending, immigration reform, and responsiveness to neighborhood needs. Grant made through American Institute for Social Justice.

$70,000 to Women Employed Institute, Chicago, IL. For career pathways system aimed at enabling educationally and economically disadvantaged individuals to obtain skills training and education leading to higher wage jobs.

$60,000 to Strategic Learning Initiatives, Chicago, IL. Toward research-based model of whole school improvement that aims to accelerate systemic improvement in Chicago public schools.

$45,000 to Chicago Coalition for the Homeless, Chicago, IL. For general support.

$35,000 to Chicago Arts Partnerships in Education (CAPE), Chicago, IL. For general support.

$30,000 to Bickerdike Redevelopment Corporation, Chicago, IL. For general support.

$30,000 to Westside Health Authority, Chicago, IL. For efforts to connect local merchants, institutions, police and park district officials with community residents for problem solving in predominantly African-American community.

3085
Woodward Governor Company Charitable Trust ✧

5001 N. 2nd St.
Rockford, IL 61125-7001
Contact: Pam Johnson, Chair., Contribs. Comm.

Established in 1947 in IL.

Donor: Woodward Governor Co.

Foundation type: Company-sponsored foundation.

Financial data (yr. ended 12/31/05): Assets, $16,080,836 (M); gifts received, $200,000; expenditures, $939,159; qualifying distributions, $863,901; giving activities include $832,100 for 67 grants (high: $150,000; low: $500).

Purpose and activities: The trust supports organizations involved with arts and culture, education, health, youth crime prevention, hunger, housing, human services, community development, disabled people, minorities, homeless people, and economically disadvantaged people.

Fields of interest: Museums; Arts; Vocational education; Adult education—literacy, basic skills & GED; Education, reading; Education; Health care; Crime/violence prevention, youth; Food services; Housing/shelter; Children/youth, services; Residential/custodial care, hospices; Minorities/immigrants, centers/services; Homeless, human services; Human services; Community development; Federated giving programs; Disabilities, people with; Minorities; Economically disadvantaged; Homeless.

Type of support: General/operating support; Continuing support; Annual campaigns; Capital campaigns; Equipment; Emergency funds; Seed money.

Limitations: Giving primarily in areas of company operations, with emphasis on Fort Collins, CO, Rockford, IL, and Stevens Point, WI. No grants to individuals, or for endowments, research, scholarships, fellowships, special projects, publications, or conferences; no loans; no matching gifts.

Application information: Application form not required.

> *Initial approach:* Proposal
> *Copies of proposal:* 1
> *Deadline(s):* Mar. or July is preferred
> *Board meeting date(s):* As required
> *Final notification:* 8 weeks

Trustees: Vern H. Cassens; Dan Loescher; George Mittendorf; Robert E. Reuterfors; Phil Turner.

EIN: 846025403

3086
Geneva & Gordon Worley Charitable Trust ✧

c/o Gordon R. Worley
332 Regent Wood Rd.
Northfield, IL 60093-2762

Established in 1983 in IL.

Donors: Gordon R. Worley; Geneva B. Worley.

Foundation type: Independent foundation.

Financial data (yr. ended 12/31/04): Assets, $940,091 (M); gifts received, $234,364; expenditures, $550,363; qualifying distributions, $540,400; giving activities include $535,900 for 44 grants (high: $372,500; low: $400).

Fields of interest: Hospitals (general); Health organizations, association; Human services; Protestant agencies & churches.

Type of support: General/operating support; Continuing support; Endowments; Research.

Limitations: Applications not accepted. Giving primarily in Naples, FL and Chicago, IL. No grants to individuals.

Application information: Contributes only to pre-selected organizations.

Officer and Trustees: * Gordon R. Worley,* Pres.; Geneva B. Worley.

Number of staff: 1 part-time professional; 1 part-time support.

EIN: 366784812

3087
WPW Family Foundation ✧ ☆

4920 S. Greenwood Ave.
Chicago, IL 60615-2816

Established in 1997 in IL.

Donor: Wayne Whalen.

Foundation type: Independent foundation.

Financial data (yr. ended 12/31/05): Assets, $180,150 (M); gifts received, $1,084; expenditures, $791,415; qualifying distributions, $790,831; giving activities include $790,831 for 14 grants (high: $766,006; low: $75).

Fields of interest: Higher education; Education; Hospitals (general); Human services.

Limitations: Applications not accepted. Giving primarily in Chicago, IL. No grants to individuals.

Application information: Contributes only to pre-selected organizations.

Trustees: Wayne Whalen; Paula Wolff.

EIN: 364199287

3088
Wm. Wrigley Jr. Company Foundation ✧

410 N. Michigan Ave.
Chicago, IL 60611 (312) 645-4089
Contact: Anne Vela-Wagner, Prog. Dir.

Established in 1986 in IL.

Donor: Wm. Wrigley Jr. Co.

Foundation type: Company-sponsored foundation.

Financial data (yr. ended 12/31/05): Assets, $67,443,792 (M); gifts received, $15,227,643; expenditures, $2,877,039; qualifying distributions, $2,702,256; giving activities include $2,351,250 for 70 grants (high: $350,000; low: $60), and $305,393 for employee matching gifts.

Purpose and activities: The foundation supports organizations involved with education, youth, and youth development. Special emphasis is directed toward programs designed to improve the academic performance of young people.

Fields of interest: Elementary/secondary education; Education; Youth development; Youth, services; Federated giving programs.

Type of support: General/operating support; Employee matching gifts.

Limitations: Giving on a national basis, with emphasis on areas of company operations; giving also to national organizations. No grants to individuals.

Application information: Application form not required.

> *Initial approach:* Proposal
> *Deadline(s):* Oct. 1

Officers and Directors: * William Wrigley, Jr.,* Chair.; Ronald V. Waters,* Pres.; Christopher

Perille,* V.P.; Allyson Boulden, Secy.; Alan J. Schneider, Treas.; Anne Vela-Wagner, Prog. Dir.
EIN: 363486958
Selected grants: The following grants were reported in 2004.
$301,200 to United Way. 4 grants: $102,000, $127,500, $50,000, $21,700
$100,000 to American Red Cross.
$50,000 to Commercial Club Foundation, Chicago, IL.
$50,000 to United Negro College Fund, Fairfax, VA.
$35,000 to Keep America Beautiful, Stamford, CT.
$25,000 to Chicago Public Education Fund, Chicago, IL.
$15,000 to Student Conservation Association, Charlestown, NH.

3089
Morton and Helen Yulman Charitable Trust ◇

(formerly Yulman Foundation)
c/o Northern Trust Bank of Florida, N.A.
50 S. LaSalle St., Ste. L-5
Chicago, IL 60675

Established in 1955.
Donors: Morton Yulman; Helen Yulman.
Foundation type: Independent foundation.
Financial data (yr. ended 12/31/03): Assets, $8,451,524 (M); expenditures, $410,175; qualifying distributions, $366,230; giving activities include $365,920 for 19 grants (high: $136,000; low: $250).
Purpose and activities: Giving primarily for arts, education and Jewish organizations.
Fields of interest: Arts; Higher education; Human services; Jewish agencies & temples.
Limitations: Applications not accepted. Giving primarily in FL and upstate NY. No grants to individuals.
Application information: Contributes only to pre-selected organizations.
Trustee: Morton Yulman.
EIN: 146015572
Selected grants: The following grants were reported in 2004.
$110,000 to United Way of Miami-Dade, Miami, FL.
$47,500 to Jewish Federation of Greater Miami, Miami, FL.
$10,000 to Union College, Schenectady, NY.
$1,200 to Saratoga Springs Performing Arts Center, Saratoga Springs, NY.
$250 to Norton Museum of Art, West Palm Beach, FL.
$250 to Palm Beach Civic Association, Palm Beach, FL.

3090
Zell Family Foundation ▼ ◇

(formerly Samuel Zell Family)
2 N. Riverside Plz., Ste. 600
Chicago, IL 60606-2639   (312) 466-3852

Established in 1986 in IL.
Donor: Samuel Zell.
Foundation type: Independent foundation.
Financial data (yr. ended 12/31/05): Assets, $15,079,874 (M); gifts received, $9,486,780; expenditures, $9,918,352; qualifying distributions, $9,861,558; giving activities include $9,849,745 for 120 grants (high: $1,000,000; low: $500).

Purpose and activities: Giving primarily for the arts, education, medicine, cancer research, recreation, youth development, and human service organizations.
Fields of interest: Arts; Education; Health care; Cancer research; Recreation; Youth development; Human services.
Limitations: Applications not accepted. Giving primarily in Chicago, IL. No grants to individuals.
Application information: Contributes only to pre-selected organizations.
Officers and Directors:* Samuel Zell,* Pres.; Donald J. Liebentritt, V.P.; Helen H. Zell,* V.P.; Joann L. Zell,* V.P.; Kellie Zell,* V.P.; Matthew M. Zell,* V.P.; Carleen Schreder, Secy.; James Bunegar, Treas.
EIN: 363487811
Selected grants: The following grants were reported in 2005.
$2,000,000 to Museum of Contemporary Art, Chicago, IL. 2 grants: $1,000,000 each (For Bridge Gift).
$1,600,000 to Northwestern University, Evanston, IL. 2 grants: $1,000,000 (For Robert H. Lurie Comprehensive Cancer Center), $600,000 to Kellogg School of Management.
$1,500,000 to University of Michigan, Ann Arbor, MI. 2 grants: $1,000,000 to Institute for Entrepreneurial Studies, $500,000 (For graduate student support).
$500,000 to Jewish United Fund.
$33,000 to John F. Kennedy Center for the Performing Arts, DC.
$10,000 to National Kidney Foundation, Chicago, IL.
$10,000 to Robert Toigo Foundation, Oakland, CA.

3091
Zerrusen Family Foundation ◇

902 W. Main St.
Teutopolis, IL 62467

Established in 2003 in IL.
Donor: Three Z Printing Co.
Foundation type: Company-sponsored foundation.
Financial data (yr. ended 12/31/05): Assets, $7,937,125 (M); gifts received, $3,000,000; expenditures, $410,201; qualifying distributions, $405,640; giving activities include $405,640 for grants.
Purpose and activities: The foundation supports organizations involved with human services and Christianity.
Fields of interest: Human services; Christian agencies & churches.
Limitations: Applications not accepted. Giving primarily in IL. No grants to individuals.
Application information: Contributes only to pre-selected organizations.
Trustee: Lorraine E. Zerrusen.
EIN: 200484359

3092
William J. Zimmerman Foundation ◇

35 W. Wacker Dr., Ste. 4200
Chicago, IL 60601-9703

Established in 1983 in IL.
Donor: Zimmerman Family Trust, No. 1.
Foundation type: Independent foundation.

Financial data (yr. ended 12/31/04): Assets, $13,195,254 (M); gifts received, $785,167; expenditures, $597,381; qualifying distributions, $435,540; giving activities include $400,000 for 12 grants (high: $100,000; low: $2,500).
Fields of interest: Education; Human services.
Limitations: Applications not accepted. Giving on a national basis, with some emphasis on CA. No grants to individuals.
Application information: Contributes only to pre-selected organizations.
Officers and Directors:* Christopher J. Podoll,* Pres.; William M. Doyle, Jr.,* Secy.; David J. Johnson,* Treas.; Marc S. Zimmerman.
EIN: 421223262
Selected grants: The following grants were reported in 2004.
$100,000 to National Foundation for Teaching Entrepreneurship, New York, NY.
$40,000 to Consumer Policy Institute, Yonkers, NY.
$30,000 to Food Project, Lincoln, MA.
$25,000 to Roots of Change Fund, San Francisco, CA.
$15,000 to University of Iowa, Iowa City, IA.
$12,500 to Childrens Hospital Foundation, Seattle, WA.
$12,500 to Marin County Bicycle Coalition, Fairfax, CA.

3093
The Zurich U.S. Foundation ◇

(formerly The Zurich American Foundation)
1400 American Ln.
Schaumburg, IL 60196
Contact: Mark E. Johnson, Exec. Dir.
FAX: (847) 605-3436; *URL:* http://www.zurich.com/main/aboutus/corporateresponsibility/corporatecitizenship/communityinvolvement/theunitedstatesofamerica.htm

Established in 1988 in IL.
Donors: Zurich Insurance Co.; Zurich American Insurance Co.; Zurich Financial Svcs.
Foundation type: Company-sponsored foundation.
Financial data (yr. ended 12/31/04): Assets, $555,605 (M); gifts received, $1,030,000; expenditures, $811,438; qualifying distributions, $811,402; giving activities include $731,615 for 640 grants (high: $100,000; low: $10), and $64,236 for 274 employee matching gifts.
Purpose and activities: The foundation supports organizations involved with post-secondary insurance education and children.
Fields of interest: Higher education; Children, services; Human services, financial counseling.
Type of support: Employee volunteer services; Employee matching gifts; Employee-related scholarships; Scholarships—to individuals.
Limitations: Giving primarily in areas of company operations. No support for arts organizations, political organizations, or strictly sectarian organizations. No grants for benefit events or advertising.
Application information: Application form required.
Initial approach: Contact foundation for application form
Copies of proposal: 1
Deadline(s): None
Board meeting date(s): Quarterly
Final notification: Within 2 months
Officers and Board Members:* Sue Harold, Pres.; Chris Haarmann, V.P.; Gerald Ladner, V.P.; Stephen

Gohmann, Secy.; Eric Daniel, Treas.; Mark E. Johnson, Exec. Dir.; John Malek; Don Skypech.

EIN: 363602244

Selected grants: The following grants were reported in 2004.

$50,000 to Roosevelt University, Chicago, IL.

$33,884 to Saint Jude Childrens Research Hospital, Memphis, TN.

$30,000 to Boys Hope Girls Hope of Illinois, Wilmette, IL.

$25,272 to United Way, IL.

$10,635 to American Heart Association, Chicago, IL.

$500 to Boys and Girls Harbor, New York, NY.

$275 to American Cancer Society, Framingham, MA.

$250 to Princeton University, Princeton, NJ.

$250 to United Way of Central Maryland, Baltimore, MD.

$225 to Advocate Charitable Foundation, Park Ridge, IL.

INDIANA

3094

1st Source Foundation ✧

c/o 1st Source Bank
100 N. Michigan St.
South Bend, IN 46601
Contact: Lee Morton

Established in 1952 in IN.
Donors: 1st Source Bank; 1st Source Bank Charitable Trust.
Foundation type: Company-sponsored foundation.
Financial data (yr. ended 12/31/05): Assets, $19,857,864 (M); expenditures, $986,602; qualifying distributions, $876,148; giving activities include $876,148 for 82 grants (high: $250,000; low: $114).
Purpose and activities: The foundation supports community foundations and organizations involved with medical education, health, human services, and civic affairs.
Fields of interest: Medical school/education; Hospitals (general); YM/YWCAs & YM/YWHAs; Human services; Foundations (community); Federated giving programs; Public affairs.
Limitations: Giving primarily in IN.
Application information: Application form not required.
  Initial approach: Proposal
  Deadline(s): None
Directors: Terry Gerber; W.D. Jones III; Rex Martin; Christopher J. Murphy III.
Trustee: 1st Source Bank.
EIN: 356034211
Selected grants: The following grants were reported in 2004.
$105,000 to Saint Marys College.
$100,000 to Boy Scouts of America, South Bend, IN.
$100,000 to Diocese of Fort Wayne-South Bend, Fort Wayne, IN.
$100,000 to Indiana University, South Bend, IN.
$100,000 to Studebaker National Museum, South Bend, IN.
$46,000 to United Way of Saint Joseph County, South Bend, IN.
$35,000 to W N I T-TV, Channel 34, Elkhart, IN.
$25,000 to Morris Entertainment, South Bend, IN.
$13,000 to Independent Colleges of Indiana, Indianapolis, IN.
$543 to United Way of Kosciusko County, Warsaw, IN.

3095

Adams County Community Foundation ✧

102 N. 2nd St.
Decatur, IN 46733-1660 (260) 724-3939
Contact: Coni Mayer, Exec. Dir.
FAX: (260) 724-2299;
E-mail: accfoundation@earthlink.com

Established in 1991 in Indiana.
Foundation type: Community foundation.
Financial data (yr. ended 12/31/04): Assets, $7,663,766 (M); gifts received, $1,290,998; expenditures, $563,693; giving activities include $332,945 for 78 grants (high: $52,410; low: $48), and $10,819 for 37 grants to individuals.

Purpose and activities: Giving for education, civic and cultural affairs, social services and for health and medical services.
Fields of interest: Arts; Elementary/secondary education; Education, early childhood education; Secondary school/education; Education, special; Higher education; Scholarships/financial aid; Hospitals (general); Health care; Employment; Children/youth, services; Aging, centers/services; Human services; Community development.
Type of support: Equipment; Seed money; Scholarship funds; Scholarships—to individuals.
Limitations: Giving limited to Adams County, IN. No support for sectarian religious purposes. No grants for endowments, or for grants to attend seminars or take trips that do not benefit the community.
Publications: Annual report.
Application information: Application form available in the foundation office or each of the Adams County public libraries. Application form required.
  Initial approach: Submit application form
  Copies of proposal: 10
  Deadline(s): Apr. 1 and Oct. 7; Feb. 3 for scholarships
  Board meeting date(s): 4th Wed. of each month
Officers and Directors:* James Howenstine,* Pres.; David Collier,* V.P.; Alice Rhoades,* Secy.; Timothy Baker,* Treas.; Coni Mayer, Exec. Dir.; Frederick A. Lehman; Douglas Milligan; Wayne Porter; Sylvia Scheumann; Cathy Stucky; Dr. Roger Thompson; Roger Weadock.
Number of staff: 1 full-time professional; 1 part-time support.
EIN: 351834664

3096

John & Hester Adams Trust ✧

P.O. Box 1248
Marion, IN 46952
Contact: Dick Buchanan, Trust Off., STAR Financial Bank

Established in 1984 in IN.
Donor: Hester Adams†.
Foundation type: Independent foundation.
Financial data (yr. ended 5/31/05): Assets, $177,188 (M); expenditures, $489,237; qualifying distributions, $488,094; giving activities include $478,255 for 18 grants (high: $284,255; low: $500).
Purpose and activities: Support primarily for civic and community needs.
Fields of interest: Historic preservation/historical societies; Human services.
Type of support: Scholarship funds; Scholarships—to individuals.
Limitations: Giving limited to Columbia City and Whitley County, IN.
Application information: Application form required.
  Deadline(s): June 30th
Officer: Jo Ellen McConnell, Chair.
Committee Members: Paul Anders; Ralph Bailey; Mick Long; Glenn Miller; Joe Zickgraf.
Trustee: STAR Financial Bank.
EIN: 356376209

3097

ADL Charitable Trust ✧

8910 Purdue Rd., Ste. 230
Indianapolis, IN 46268
Contact: Alexander C. Lange, Tr.

Established in 1997 in IN.
Donor: Alexander C. Lange.
Foundation type: Independent foundation.
Financial data (yr. ended 12/31/04): Assets, $6,664,078 (M); expenditures, $492,340; qualifying distributions, $424,002; giving activities include $299,925 for 18 grants (high: $100,000; low: $250), and $102,750 for 2 employee matching gifts.
Fields of interest: Arts; Elementary/secondary education; Education; Boy scouts; Human services; Christian agencies & churches.
Limitations: Applications not accepted. Giving primarily in IN, with emphasis on Indianapolis.
Application information: Unsolicited requests for funds not accepted.
Trustees: Alexander C. Lange; Alexander T. Lange; Cynthia M. Lange; Dorothea L. Morton.
EIN: 352033079
Selected grants: The following grants were reported in 2003.
$200,000 to University High School of Indiana, Carmel, IN. 2 grants: $165,000 (For capital campaign), $35,000 (For annual support).
$125,000 to Hope Evangelical Covenant Church, Indianapolis, IN. For general support.
$35,000 to Sycamore School, Indianapolis, IN. For annual support.
$20,000 to Nathans Battle Foundation, Greenwood, IN.
$11,000 to Milton and Rose D. Friedman Foundation, Indianapolis, IN. For Educational Choice.
$5,000 to Boy Scouts of America, Crossroads of America Council, Indianapolis, IN. For capital campaign.
$1,500 to Campus Crusade for Christ International, Orlando, FL. For general support.
$1,000 to Eiteljorg Museum of American Indians and Western Art, Indianapolis, IN. For capital campaign.
$1,000 to Indiana Symphony Society, Indianapolis, IN. For annual support.

3098

American General Finance Foundation, Inc. ✧

(formerly American General Finance, Inc.—Richard E. Meier Foundation, Inc.)
601 N.W. 2nd St.
P.O. Box 59
Evansville, IN 47701-0059 (812) 468-5413
Contact: Michelle Dixon, Mgr., Mktg. Prog.

Incorporated in 1958 in IN.
Donors: American General Finance, Inc.; and subsidiaries.
Foundation type: Company-sponsored foundation.
Financial data (yr. ended 12/31/04): Assets, $97,776 (M); gifts received, $450,000; expenditures, $426,802; qualifying distributions, $426,802; giving activities include $404,595 for 20 + grants, and $22,000 for 11 grants to individuals (high: $2,000; low: $2,000).
Purpose and activities: The foundation supports organizations involved with arts and culture, education, youth development, safety, human services, and civic affairs.
Fields of interest: Museums (science/technology); Arts; Higher education; Education; Safety/ disasters; Youth development; Human services; Federated giving programs; Government/public administration.

Type of support: General/operating support; Continuing support; Annual campaigns; Building/renovation; Employee matching gifts; Employee-related scholarships.

Limitations: Giving primarily in Evansville, IN. No support for religious organizations not of direct benefit to the entire community or health care organizations. No grants to individuals (except for employee-related scholarships), or for start-up needs, emergency needs or endowments, debt reduction, equipment, land acquisition, special projects, research, publications, tickets or advertising for benefit purposes, or conferences; no loans; no matching or challenge grants.

Publications: Application guidelines.

Application information: Application form not required.

Initial approach: Proposal

Copies of proposal: 1

Deadline(s): None

Board meeting date(s): Quarterly

Final notification: 4 to 6 weeks

Officers and Directors:* Frederick W. Geissinger,* Chair., C.E.O., and Pres.; Timothy M. Hayes, Sr. V.P., Secy., and Gen. Counsel; Donald R. Breivogel, Jr.,* Sr. V.P. and C.F.O.; Robert A. Cole, Sr. V.P.; Jerry L. Gilpin, Sr. V.P.; Bryan A. Binyon, V.P. and Treas.; George W. Schmidt, V.P. and Cont.

EIN: 356042566

3099
John W. Anderson Foundation ▼

402 Wall St.

Valparaiso, IN 46383 (219) 462-4611

Contact: William N. Vinovich, Vice-Chair.

Trust established in 1967 in IN.

Donor: John W. Anderson†.

Foundation type: Independent foundation.

Financial data (yr. ended 12/31/05): Assets, $204,218,483 (M); expenditures, $9,775,435; qualifying distributions, $8,935,658; giving activities include $8,365,629 for 262 grants (high: $2,091,940; low: $320; average: $5,000–$50,000).

Purpose and activities: Giving primarily to organizations serving youth; higher educational institutions; community funds; scientific or medical research for the purpose of alleviating suffering; care of needy, crippled or orphaned children; care of needy persons who are sick, aged or helpless; improving the health, and quality of life of all persons; human services; and the arts and humanities.

Fields of interest: Arts; Higher education; Health care; Medical research, institute; Human services; Children/youth, services; Developmentally disabled, centers & services; Community development, neighborhood development; Federated giving programs; Disabilities, people with.

Type of support: General/operating support; Continuing support; Annual campaigns; Program development; Scholarship funds; Research.

Limitations: Giving primarily in Lake and Porter counties in northwest IN. No support for elementary and secondary schools, or for business or any for-profit organization. No grants to individuals, or for endowment funds, fundraising events, advertising, seed money, deficit financing; no loans.

Publications: Application guidelines; Informational brochure (including application guidelines).

Application information: Applications sent by fax not considered. Application form not required.

Initial approach: Letter

Copies of proposal: 6

Deadline(s): Jan. 20, Mar. 20, May 20, July 20, Sept. 20, and Nov. 20

Board meeting date(s): Feb., Apr., June, Aug., Oct., and Dec.

Final notification: In writing, 2 to 3 weeks after board meeting

Officers and Trustees:* Bruce W. Wargo,* Chair. and Treas.; William N. Vinovich,* Vice-Chair.; William L. Staehle,* Secy.; Clyde D. Compton; Charles W. Conover.

Number of staff: 2 full-time professional; 3 part-time professional; 1 part-time support.

EIN: 356070695

Selected grants: The following grants were reported in 2005.

$2,091,940 to Boys and Girls Clubs of Northwest Indiana, Gary, IN. For capital and operating support.

$1,071,400 to Boys and Girls Clubs of Porter County, Valparaiso, IN. For capital and operating support.

$450,000 to United Way, Lake Area, Griffith, IN. For operating support.

$225,000 to Purdue University, West Lafayette, IN. For capital and operating support.

$200,000 to Independent Colleges of Indiana Foundation, Indianapolis, IN. For operating support.

$100,000 to Crisis Center, Gary, IN. For operating support.

$40,000 to Calumet College of Saint Joseph, Whiting, IN. For capital support.

$30,000 to YMCA of Portage Township, Portage, IN. For operating support.

$25,000 to Girl Scouts of the U.S.A., Drifting Dunes Council, Merrillville, IN. For operating support.

$10,000 to Crown Point Community Foundation, Crown Point, IN. For operating support for Memorial Charities.

3100
The R. B. Annis Educational Foundation ◇

3265 E. Tulip Dr.

Indianapolis, IN 46227

Established in 1996 in IN.

Donors: Robert B. Annis†; Ralph Stahl.

Foundation type: Independent foundation.

Financial data (yr. ended 12/31/05): Assets, $13,221,610 (M); expenditures, $638,570; qualifying distributions, $572,225; giving activities include $512,250 for 35 grants (high: $140,000; low: $250).

Fields of interest: Museums; Arts; Higher education; Libraries (public); Girl scouts; Human services.

Limitations: Applications not accepted. Giving primarily in IN. No grants to individuals.

Application information: Contributes only to pre-selected organizations.

Trustees: Charles D. Angus; Elmira F. Annis; Wayne E. Weber; C. Daniel Yates.

EIN: 356627460

Selected grants: The following grants were reported in 2005.

$53,500 to Indianapolis Zoological Society, Indianapolis, IN.

$51,500 to Interlochen Center for the Arts, Interlochen, MI.

$50,000 to Jameson Camp, Indianapolis, IN.

$25,000 to Grand Valley State University, Grand Rapids, MI.

$15,000 to Sterling College, Craftsbury Common, VT.

$13,000 to University of Indianapolis, Indianapolis, IN.

$10,000 to President Benjamin Harrison Foundation, Indianapolis, IN.

$2,000 to Michigan State University, East Lansing, MI.

$250 to Metropolitan Indianapolis Public Broadcasting, Indianapolis, IN.

3101
Anthem Foundation, Inc. ◇

120 Monument Cir.

Indianapolis, IN 46204

Contact: Vicki Perkins, Exec. Dir.

Established in 2000 in IN.

Donors: Anthem Insurance Cos., Inc.; Anthem Health Plans of New Hampshire, Inc.; Anthem, Inc.; WellPoint, Inc.

Foundation type: Company-sponsored foundation.

Financial data (yr. ended 12/31/05): Assets, $57,088,728 (M); expenditures, $3,806,710; qualifying distributions, $3,686,040; giving activities include $3,478,315 for 64 grants (high: $350,000; low: $1,511).

Purpose and activities: The foundation supports organizations involved with education, health, and human services.

Fields of interest: Higher education; Education; Health care; Human services; Federated giving programs.

Limitations: Giving on a national basis.

Application information: Application form required.

Initial approach: Contact foundation for application form

Deadline(s): None

Officers and Directors:* Larry C. Glasscock,* Pres.; Nancy L. Purcell, Secy.; R. David Kretschmer, Treas.; Vicki L. Perkins, Exec. Dir.; Angela F. Braly; David C. Colby; Keith R. Faller.

EIN: 352122763

Selected grants: The following grants were reported in 2004.

$610,339 to United Way. 4 grants: $119,368, $116,081, $309,248, $65,642

$310,000 to Penobscot Community Health Center, Bangor, ME.

$120,000 to Saint Francis Healthcare Foundation, Beech Grove, IN.

$107,550 to Bon Secours Richmond Health Care Foundation, Richmond, VA.

$100,000 to Learning Well, Indianapolis, IN.

$75,000 to Foundation for Healthy Communities, Concord, NH.

$50,000 to Ammonoosuc Community Health Services, Littleton, NH.

3102
Anthem Foundation, Inc. ◇

(formerly Southeastern Group Foundation, Inc.)

120 Monument Cir.

Indianapolis, IN 46204 (800) 563-5465

Contact: Vicki L. Perkins, Exec. Dir.

Established in 1990 in KY.

Donors: Southeastern Mutual Insurance Co.; SpectraCare, Inc.

Foundation type: Company-sponsored foundation.
Financial data (yr. ended 12/31/05): Assets, $5,764,464 (L); gifts received, $6,000; expenditures, $479,408; qualifying distributions, $486,738; giving activities include $486,738 for 14 grants (high: $250,000; low: $25).
Purpose and activities: The foundation supports organizations involved with education, health, human services, and economic development.
Fields of interest: Higher education; Education; Health care; Human services; Economic development; Federated giving programs.
Type of support: General/operating support; Employee matching gifts.
Limitations: Giving limited to KY, with emphasis on Louisville.
Application information: Application form required.
  Initial approach: Contact foundation for application form
  Deadline(s): None
Officers and Directors: * Larry C. Glasscock,* Pres.; Nancy L. Purcell, Secy.; R. David Kretschmer, Treas.; Vicki L. Perkins, Exec. Dir.; Angela F. Braly; David C. Colby; Keith R. Faller.
EIN: 611191499
Selected grants: The following grants were reported in 2004.
$296,925 to United Way of Central Indiana, Indianapolis, IN.
$126,647 to United Way, Warren County.
$100,000 to Muhammad Ali Museum and Education Center, Louisville, KY.
$94,179 to United Way, Metro, Louisville, KY.
$52,680 to Public Radio Partnership, Louisville, KY.
$50,000 to American Cancer Society, Logan Unit, Louisville, KY.
$50,000 to National Center on Addiction and Substance Abuse at Columbia University, New York, NY.
$34,125 to United Way of Franklin County, Frankfort, KY.
$25,000 to National Association of Free Clinics, DC.
$14,800 to American Diabetes Association, Louisville, KY.

3103
Ball Brothers Foundation ▼

P.O. Box 1408
Muncie, IN 47308 (765) 741-5500
Contact: Jud Fisher, Assoc. Exec. Dir.
FAX: (765) 741-5518; E-mail: info@ballfdn.org; Additional address: 222 S. Mulberry St., Muncie, IN 47305; E-mail: jud.fisher@ballfdn.org; Additional E-mail: donna.munchel@ballfdn.org; URL: http://www.ballfdn.org

Incorporated in 1926 in IN.
Donors: Edmund B. Ball†; Frank C. Ball†; George A. Ball†; Lucius L. Ball, M.D.†; William A. Ball†.
Foundation type: Independent foundation.
Financial data (yr. ended 12/31/04): Assets, $130,752,875 (M); expenditures, $6,219,721; qualifying distributions, $5,351,900; giving activities include $3,984,299 for 34 grants (high: $2,440,985; low: $1,500; average: $1,000–$10,000), and $995,303 for in-kind gifts.
Purpose and activities: Support for the humanities and cultural programs, higher and other education, health and medical education, youth, and family and social services.
Fields of interest: Museums; Humanities; Arts; Elementary school/education; Secondary school/education; Higher education; Medical school/

education; Adult education—literacy, basic skills & GED; Education, reading; Education; Environment; Hospitals (general); Health care; Health organizations, association; Human services; Children/youth, services; Family services; Community development; Public affairs.
Type of support: General/operating support; Annual campaigns; Capital campaigns; Building/renovation; Endowments; Program development; Conferences/seminars; Professorships; Publication; Curriculum development; Research; Technical assistance; In-kind gifts; Matching/challenge support.
Limitations: Giving limited to IN. No support for non-secular religious programs or booster organizations. No grants to individuals.
Publications: Application guidelines; Annual report; Informational brochure.
Application information: See foundation's Web site for application forms and more information. Application form required.
  Initial approach: Proposal with cover sheet
  Copies of proposal: 1
  Deadline(s): Submit proposal preferably before June; no set deadline
  Board meeting date(s): Quarterly and as necessary
  Final notification: Varies
Officers and Directors: * John W. Fisher,* Chair. and Pres.; Frank E. Ball,* Vice-Chair. and V.P.; Douglas A. Bakken,* C.O.O. and Exec. V.P.; William L. Skinner,* Secy.; Douglas J. Foy,* Treas.; William M. Bracken; Nancy B. Keilty; Judith F. Oetinger; John J. Pruis; Terry L. Walker.
Number of staff: 6
EIN: 350882856
Selected grants: The following grants were reported in 2004.
$2,440,985 to Minnetrista Cultural Foundation, Muncie, IN.
$330,000 to Ball State University Foundation, Muncie, IN.
$145,000 to Purdue University, West Lafayette, IN.
$55,000 to Independent Colleges of Indiana Foundation, Indianapolis, IN.
$50,000 to DePauw University, Greencastle, IN.
$50,000 to Ivy Tech Foundation, Indianapolis, IN.
$41,000 to Muncie Symphony Orchestra, Muncie, IN.
$35,000 to Paramount Theater Center and Ballroom, Anderson, IN.
$21,000 to Muncie Community Schools, Muncie, IN.
$2,314 to Delaware County Historical Society, Muncie, IN.

3104
George and Frances Ball Foundation ▼

P.O. Box 1408
Muncie, IN 47308 (765) 741-5500
Contact: Joyce Beck, Exec. Asst.
Additional address: 222 S. Mulberry St., Muncie, IN 47305; FAX: (765) 741-5518;
E-mail: jjpruis@iquest.net

Incorporated in 1937 in IN.
Donor: George A. Ball†.
Foundation type: Independent foundation.
Financial data (yr. ended 12/31/05): Assets, $95,569,421 (M); expenditures, $5,117,077; qualifying distributions, $4,758,724; giving activities include $4,684,654 for 58 grants (high:

$1,042,490; low: $1,500; average: $2,500–$250,000).
Purpose and activities: Emphasis on higher education and community programs.
Fields of interest: Arts; Education; Environment, natural resources; Environment; Health care; Human services; Community development, neighborhood development.
Type of support: Scholarship funds; Capital campaigns; Building/renovation; Equipment; Program development; Professorships; Matching/challenge support.
Limitations: Giving primarily in Muncie and Delaware County, IN. No support for religious or political organizations. No grants to individuals.
Application information: Application form not required.
  Initial approach: Letter and proposal
  Copies of proposal: 1
  Deadline(s): None
  Board meeting date(s): Varies
  Final notification: Following board review
Officers and Directors: * Frank A. Bracken,* Pres.; John J. Pruis,* Exec. V.P.; Joan H. McKee,* Secy.; Douglas J. Foy, Treas.; Stefan S. Anderson; Ronald K. Fauquher; Jon H. Moll; Robert M. Smitson.
Number of staff: 1 part-time professional; 1 part-time support.
EIN: 356033917
Selected grants: The following grants were reported in 2005.
$1,250,000 to Ball State University Foundation, Muncie, IN. 3 grants: $250,000 (For academic excellence programs), $250,000 (For Endowed Chair), $750,000 (To renovate stadium).
$1,200,000 to Keuka College, Keuka Park, NY. 2 grants: $200,000 (For Experiential Learning Center), $1,000,000 (To renovate Ball Hall, College's original building, which carries name of Rev. Dr. George Harvey Ball, founder and first president).
$1,042,490 to Minnetrista Cultural Foundation, Muncie, IN. For Oakhurst Gardens.
$110,000 to Ivy Tech Community College East Central, Muncie, IN. For Academic Support Center.
$60,000 to Leelanau Conservancy, Leland, MI. For capital campaign.
$60,000 to Nature Conservancy, Indianapolis, IN. For Natures Treasures: Saving Indiana's Last Great Places campaign.
$28,000 to Boy Scouts of America, Crossroads Council, Muncie, IN. For Camp Redwing.

3105
Edmund F. and Virginia B. Ball Foundation, Inc.

P.O. Box 1408
Muncie, IN 47308-1408
Contact: Kris Gross

Established in 1994 in IN.
Donors: Edmund F. Ball†; Virginia B. Ball†.
Foundation type: Independent foundation.
Financial data (yr. ended 9/30/05): Assets, $27,300,514 (M); expenditures, $1,020,053; qualifying distributions, $869,330; giving activities include $869,087 for 7 grants (high: $350,000; low: $250).
Fields of interest: Arts; Education; Recreation; Children/youth, services.
Limitations: Giving primarily in MI and IN. No grants to individuals.

Application information:
Initial approach: Proposal
Deadline(s): None
Officers and Directors:* Frank E. Ball,* Pres.;
Robert B. Ball,* V.P.; Douglas J. Foy,* Secy.-Treas.;
Douglas A. Bakken.
EIN: 351911169
Selected grants: The following grants were reported
in 2003.
$240,000 to Ball State University, Muncie, IN. For
Muncie Center for the Arts.
$235,000 to Minnetrista Cultural Foundation,
Muncie, IN. 2 grants: $200,000 (For catalyst
sculpture), $35,000 (For publications fund).
$100,000 to Interlochen Center for the Arts,
Interlochen, MI.
$35,000 to Asheville School, Asheville, NC. For
endowed chair for archives.
$25,000 to Muncie Center for the Arts, Muncie, IN.
For Interlochen scholarship.
$15,000 to Indiana Humanities Council,
Indianapolis, IN.
$10,000 to Johns Hopkins University, Wilmer
Ophthalmological Institute, Baltimore, MD. For
Directors Discovery Fund.
$10,000 to Unitarian Universalist Church, Muncie,
IN.
$1,000 to Ball Memorial Hospital Foundation,
Muncie, IN.

3106
The Biomet Foundation, Inc.

P.O. Box 587
Warsaw, IN 46581-0587
Contact: Darlene K. Whaley, Secy.

Established in 1990 in IN.
Donors: Biomet, Inc.; Dane A. Miller; Mrs. Dane A.
Miller; Jerry L. Ferguson; Mrs. Jerry L. Ferguson.
Foundation type: Company-sponsored foundation.
Financial data (yr. ended 12/31/05): Assets,
$7,059,548 (M); expenditures, $371,261;
qualifying distributions, $369,859.
Purpose and activities: The foundation supports
hospitals and organizations involved with arts and
culture, education, recreation, and human services.
Fields of interest: Arts; Education; Hospitals
(general); Recreation; Children/youth, services;
Human services; Federated giving programs.
Type of support: Annual campaigns;
Employee-related scholarships.
Limitations: Giving primarily in Warsaw, IN. No
support for political or religious organizations.
Publications: Informational brochure.
Application information: Application form not
required.
Initial approach: Proposal
Copies of proposal: 1
Board meeting date(s): Quarterly
Final notification: Up to 3 months
Officers and Directors:* Mrs. Dane A. Miller,* Pres.;
Mrs. Jerry L. Ferguson,* V.P.; Darlene K. Whaley,
Secy.; Patrick S. Scheets, Treas.; Joel P. Pratt.
EIN: 351806314
Selected grants: The following grants were reported
in 2005.
$100,000 to Grace College and Seminary, Winona
Lake, IN.
$25,000 to Indiana State Museum, Indianapolis, IN.
$10,000 to Science Central, Fort Wayne, IN.
$5,000 to Carriage House, Breckenridge, CO.
$4,000 to American Red Cross.

$3,000 to Lakeland Community Services, Syracuse,
IN.
$2,500 to Cardinal Center, Warsaw, IN.
$2,000 to LeTourneau University, Longview, TX.

3107
The Blue River Community Foundation, Inc.

(formerly The Blue River Foundation, Inc.)
54 W. Broadway, Ste. 1
P.O. Box 808
Shelbyville, IN 46176 (317) 392-7955
Contact: For grant applications: Lynne Ensminger,
Prog. Admin.
FAX: (317) 392-4545;
E-mail: brf@blueriverfoundation.com; Grant
application E-mail:
lensminger@blueriverfoundation.com; URL: http://
www.blueriverfoundation.com

Established in 1988 in IN.
Foundation type: Community foundation.
Financial data (yr. ended 12/31/05): Assets,
$14,833,818 (M); gifts received, $2,828,166;
expenditures, $814,963; giving activities include
$259,818 for 107 grants (high: $21,000; low: $16),
and $144,640 for 136 grants to individuals (high:
$2,300; low: $15).
Purpose and activities: The foundation seeks to
serve and assist charitable endeavors in Shelby
County, IN, and to promote leadership to address
community issues.
Fields of interest: Arts; Education; Health care;
Recreation; Human services; Community
development.
Type of support: Capital campaigns; Building/
renovation; Equipment; Endowments; Program
development; Seed money; Curriculum
development; Scholarship funds; Technical
assistance; Consulting services; Grants to
individuals; Scholarships—to individuals; In-kind
gifts; Matching/challenge support.
Limitations: Giving limited to Shelby County, IN. No
support for religious organizations for religious
purposes. No grants to individuals (except for
scholarships), or for travel or endowments
(generally).
Publications: Application guidelines; Annual report;
Financial statement; Informational brochure.
Application information: Visit foundation Web site
for application form and guidelines. Application form
required.
Initial approach: Submit Grant Interest form
Copies of proposal: 1
Deadline(s): Feb. 1, June 1, and Oct. 1
Board meeting date(s): 4th Wed. of each month
Final notification: One month after deadline
Officers and Directors:* Todd Plymate,* Pres.; Nick
Runnebohm,* V.P.; Chris King,* Secy.; Steve
Plunkett,* Treas.; Elaine Haehl, Exec. Dir.; Bob
Britton; Robert Claxton; John DePrez, Jr.; Joe
Hauersperger; Nisa Hensley; Rita D. Mohr; Linda
Muegge; Lori Tennell.
Number of staff: 2 full-time professional; 1 part-time
professional; 1 part-time support.
EIN: 351756331

3108
The Boren Foundation, Inc.

P.O. Box 218
Upland, IN 46989-0218
Contact: Lori L. Meyers, Pres.

Established in 1982 in IN.
Donors: Leland E. Boren; LaRita R. Boren.
Foundation type: Independent foundation.
Financial data (yr. ended 9/30/05): Assets,
$13,058,097 (M); expenditures, $689,967;
qualifying distributions, $677,371; giving activities
include $639,735 for 16 grants (high: $161,250;
low: $2,500).
Purpose and activities: Giving primarily for the arts,
health care, and education.
Fields of interest: Media, film/video; Elementary
school/education; Education; Hospitals (general);
Christian agencies & churches.
Type of support: General/operating support; Capital
campaigns; Matching/challenge support.
Limitations: Giving primarily in IN. No grants to
individuals.
Publications: Financial statement; Program policy
statement (including application guidelines).
Application information: Telephone calls are not
accepted. Application form not required.
Initial approach: Typewritten letter
Copies of proposal: 1
Deadline(s): None
Board meeting date(s): Apr. and Sept.
Final notification: 60-90 days
Officers and Directors:* Lori L. Meyers, Pres.;
LaRita R. Boren,* V.P.; Angela Taylor, Secy.; Danyel
Miller, Treas.; Lael Boren; Leland E. Boren; Thomas
Logan.
Number of staff: None.
EIN: 351557058
Selected grants: The following grants were reported
in 2003.
$100,000 to Heartland Film Festival, Indianapolis,
IN.
$100,000 to Nathans Battle Foundation,
Greenwood, IN. For medical research.
$62,295 to Upland Elementary School, Upland, IN.
For sponsor writing workshop.
$50,000 to Child Advocacy Center of Allen County,
Fort Wayne, IN. For general support.
$25,000 to Matthews, Town of, Matthews, IN.
$22,752 to Van Buren Elementary School, Van
Buren, IN. For sponsor writing workshop.
$18,500 to Marion Philharmonic Association,
Marion, OH. For general support.
$15,000 to Fort Wayne Childrens Zoo, Fort Wayne,
IN. For general support.
$10,000 to Taylor University, Upland, IN. For general
support.
$5,000 to Wheeler Mission Ministries, Indianapolis,
IN.

3109
The Elba L. and Gene Portteus Branigin Foundation, Inc. ◇

c/o Gene Henderson, First Indiana Plz.
135 N. Pennsylvania St., Ste. 2700
Indianapolis, IN 46204

Established in 1987 in IN.
Foundation type: Independent foundation.
Financial data (yr. ended 12/31/04): Assets,
$5,928,918 (M); expenditures, $682,514;
qualifying distributions, $631,397; giving activities

include $611,000 for 15 grants (high: $411,500; low: $200).

Purpose and activities: Giving primarily for higher education.

Fields of interest: Higher education; Human services; Foundations (community); Christian agencies & churches.

Type of support: General/operating support; Endowments; Scholarship funds.

Limitations: Applications not accepted. Giving primarily in Franklin, IN. No grants to individuals.

Application information: Contributes only to pre-selected organizations.

Officers and Directors:* Eugene L. Henderson,* Pres. and Secy.; John M. Chiarotti,* Treas.

EIN: 351697364

3110
Brown County Community Foundation, Inc. ☆

96 S. Jefferson St.
P.O. Box 191
Nashville, IN   47448   (812) 988-4882
Contact: For grants: Michelle Flinn, Exec. Asst.; For scholarships: Judy Bowling, Office and Financial Mgr.
FAX: (812) 988-0299;
E-mail: judy@browncountycommunityfoundation.org;
Grant application E-mail:
mflinn@browncountycommunityfoundation.org;
URL: http://www.browncountycommunityfoundation.org

Established in 1993 in IN.

Foundation type: Community foundation.

Financial data (yr. ended 12/31/05): Assets, $7,652,245 (M); gifts received, $728,196; expenditures, $619,237; giving activities include $324,336 for 84+ grants.

Purpose and activities: The foundation seeks to receive, hold, and distribute funds for charity. Primary areas of focus include arts and humanities, education, the environment, health care, human services, and community development.

Fields of interest: Humanities; Arts; Higher education; Education; Environment; Health care; Human services; Community development.

Type of support: Continuing support; Capital campaigns; Building/renovation; Equipment; Land acquisition; Emergency funds; Program development; Seed money; Scholarship funds; Technical assistance; Scholarships—to individuals; Matching/challenge support.

Limitations: Giving primarily in Brown County, IN. No support for religious organizations. No grants for operating expenses (generally).

Publications: Application guidelines; Annual report; Informational brochure (including application guidelines); Newsletter.

Application information: Visit foundation Web site for application form and guidelines. Application form required.
Initial approach: Submit application form and attachments
Copies of proposal: 8
Deadline(s): Late May for grants; Jan. for scholarships
Board meeting date(s): 4th Monday of every month
Final notification: Late June

Officers and Directors:* Robert Wright,* Chair.; F. Andrew Rogers,* Vice-Chair.; Lisa Terry, C.E.O. and

Exec. Dir.; Jeff McCabe,* Secy.; Ken Birkemeier; Diane Cantrell; Richard Greeno; Ken Harker; Steve Marshall; James Moore; Donna Ormiston; Rachel Perry; Suzannah Zody.

Number of staff: 3 full-time professional.

EIN: 351960379

3111
Bussing-Koch Foundation, Inc.

2905 Bayard Park Dr.
Evansville, IN   47714
Contact: Wilfred C. Bussing III, Pres.

Established in 1995 in IN.

Donor: Loretta M. Koch†.

Foundation type: Independent foundation.

Financial data (yr. ended 12/31/05): Assets, $6,625,423 (M); gifts received, $127; expenditures, $868,896; qualifying distributions, $806,133; giving activities include $806,133 for grants.

Fields of interest: Museums (art); Arts; Higher education; Medical care, rehabilitation; Girl scouts; American Red Cross; YM/YWCAs & YM/YWHAs; Youth, services; Roman Catholic agencies & churches.

Type of support: General/operating support; Continuing support; Annual campaigns; Capital campaigns; Building/renovation; Equipment; Land acquisition; Endowments; Debt reduction; Emergency funds; Program development; Conferences/seminars; Professorships; Publication; Seed money; Curriculum development; Fellowships; Scholarship funds; Research; Technical assistance; Program evaluation.

Limitations: Applications not accepted. Giving primarily in southwestern IN.

Application information: Unsolicited requests for funds not accepted.
Board meeting date(s): As needed

Officers: Wilfred C. Bussing III, Pres.; Wilfred C. Bussing, Jr., V.P.; Constance K. Bussing, Secy.; Marie A. Bussing-Burks, Treas.

EIN: 351780862

Selected grants: The following grants were reported in 2003.

$55,000 to Saint Marys Medical Center Memorial Foundation, Evansville, IN. For capital campaign.

$30,000 to YMCA of Southwestern Indiana, Evansville, IN. For capital campaign.

$25,000 to University of Evansville, Evansville, IN. For capital campaign.

$20,250 to Evansville Museum of Arts, History and Science, Evansville, IN. For general operating support.

$10,000 to American Red Cross, Evansville, IN. For capital campaign.

$8,500 to Evansville Philharmonic Orchestra, Evansville, IN. For general operating support.

$1,000 to Boys and Girls Club of Evansville, Evansville, IN. For general operating support.

$500 to Saint Mary of the Woods College, Saint Mary of the Woods, IN. For general operating support.

$300 to Arts Council of Southwestern Indiana, Evansville, IN. For general operating support.

$250 to Marian College, Indianapolis, IN. For general operating support.

3112
BVM Foundation, Inc. ✧ ☆

c/o Daniel R. Tekulve
2056 Shrine Rd.
Batesville, IN   47006

Established in 2004 in IN.

Donors: Daniel R. Tekulve; Albert H. Langenkamp.

Foundation type: Independent foundation.

Financial data (yr. ended 12/31/05): Assets, $1,526,199 (M); gifts received, $19,770; expenditures, $961,743; qualifying distributions, $822,821; giving activities include $812,821 for 26 grants (high: $497,887; low: $3,000).

Fields of interest: Human services; Roman Catholic agencies & churches.

Limitations: Applications not accepted. Giving on a national basis. No grants to individuals.

Application information: Contributes only to pre-selected organizations.

Officers and Directors:* Daniel R. Tekulve,* Pres.; Cheryl A. Tekulve,* Secy.-Treas.; Kevin B. McCarthy.

EIN: 201155875

3113
Carmichael Foundation, Inc. ✧

c/o 1st Source Bank, Trust Dept.
100 N. Michigan St.
P.O. Box 1602
South Bend, IN   46601   (574) 235-2790
Contact: Lee Morton

Incorporated in 1967 in IN.

Donors: Christopher J. Murphy III; Carmen C. Murphy.

Foundation type: Independent foundation.

Financial data (yr. ended 12/31/05): Assets, $10,413,888 (M); gifts received, $7,905; expenditures, $453,632; qualifying distributions, $425,141; giving activities include $425,141 for 17 grants (high: $122,940; low: $500).

Purpose and activities: Support primarily for the arts, and higher education.

Fields of interest: Performing arts, orchestra (symphony); Higher education; Human services; Foundations (community); Federated giving programs.

Limitations: Giving primarily in South Bend, IN. No grants to individuals.

Application information: Application form not required.
Initial approach: Letter
Deadline(s): None

Trustee: 1st Source Bank.

EIN: 356069904

Selected grants: The following grants were reported in 2005.

$47,500 to South Bend Symphony Orchestra, South Bend, IN.

$45,000 to Saint Marys College, Notre Dame, IN.

$36,291 to Northern Indiana Center for History, South Bend, IN.

$25,000 to Goshen College, Goshen, IN.

$11,000 to United Way of Saint Joseph County, South Bend, IN.

$8,700 to Boys and Girls Club of Saint Joseph County, South Bend, IN.

$3,710 to First Presbyterian Church, Fort Wayne, IN.

$1,000 to Memorial Health Foundation, South Bend, IN.

3114
Florence V. Carroll Charitable Trust
c/o Wells Fargo Bank Indiana, N.A.
112 W. Jefferson Blvd.
South Bend, IN 46601 (574) 237-3475
Contact: Charles F. Nelson, V.P.

Established in 1989 in IN.
Donor: Florence V. Carroll Trust.
Foundation type: Independent foundation.
Financial data (yr. ended 6/30/05): Assets,
$9,704,955 (M); expenditures, $532,776;
qualifying distributions, $472,655; giving activities
include $455,131 for 25 grants (high: $100,000;
low: $2,500).
Fields of interest: Arts; Higher education; Human
services.
Limitations: Giving limited to St. Joseph County, IN.
Application information: Application form not
required.
Initial approach: Letter
Copies of proposal: 7
Deadline(s): Apr. 1 and Oct. 1
Board meeting date(s): May and Nov.
Final notification: May and Nov.
Trustee: Wells Fargo Bank, N.A.
EIN: 356495556

3115
Cass County Community Foundation, Inc.
1 National City Plz., 3rd Fl.
P.O. Box 441
Logansport, IN 46947 (574) 722-2200
FAX: (574) 732-0301;
E-mail: cccf@cassfoundation.com; Additional E-mail:
dcrispen@cassfoundation.com; URL: http://
www.cassfoundation.com

Foundation type: Community foundation.
Financial data (yr. ended 12/31/05): Assets,
$9,428,744 (M); gifts received, $681,121;
expenditures, $637,691; giving activities include
$327,113 for 28+ grants.
Purpose and activities: The foundation honors the
spirit of giving and assists donors in building
enduring sources of charitable assets to promote
education, enhance humanity and advance
community development throughout Cass County,
IN.
Fields of interest: Education; Human services;
Community development.
Type of support: Equipment; Scholarships—to
individuals.
Limitations: Giving primarily in Cass County, IN. No
support for public schools.
Publications: Application guidelines; Annual report;
Informational brochure.
Application information: Scholarship Orientation
Session mandatory for scholarships. Visit
foundation Web site for application form and
application information. Application form required.
Initial approach: Contact foundation
Copies of proposal: 6
Deadline(s): June 30
Officers and Board Members:* Elizabeth Billman,*
Pres.; Randy Head,* V.P.; Kevin Crook,* Secy.; Bill
Cuppy,* Treas.; Deanna Crispen, Exec. Dir.; Alan
Biggs; Joyce Eshelman; Carol Sue Hayworth; Tom
Heckard; Dan Layman; Barrie McClain; Jon Myers;
Jesse Robinson; Dick Rusk; Brian Shockney.

Number of staff: 1 full-time professional; 1 part-time
professional; 1 full-time support.
EIN: 352125727

3116
Central Indiana Community Foundation, Inc. ✧
615 N. Alabama St., Ste. 119
Indianapolis, IN 46204-1498 (317) 634-2423
Contact: Brian Payne, Pres.
FAX: (317) 684-0943; E-mail: program@cicf.org;
Additional tel.: (317) 634-7497; URL: http://
www.cicf.org

Established in 1997 in IN through a partnership
between the Indianapolis Foundation and the Legacy
Fund of Hamilton County.
Foundation type: Community foundation.
Financial data (yr. ended 12/31/05): Assets,
$535,352,484 (M); gifts received, $30,422,416;
expenditures, $31,693,842; giving activities
include $21,688,138 for grants.
Purpose and activities: The foundation is
committed to improving and strengthening the
metropolitan region community, with grantmaking
focused on helping where the needs are greatest
and the benefits to the region are most extensive.
Fields of interest: Arts, cultural/ethnic awareness;
Arts; Education; Health care; Mental health/crisis
services; Health organizations, association;
Housing/shelter; Children/youth, services; Family
services; Human services, emergency aid; Aging,
centers/services; Human services; Community
development, neighborhood development;
Economic development; Economic development,
visitors/convention bureau/tourism promotion;
Community development, business promotion;
Community development; Philanthropy/voluntarism;
Government/public administration; Disabilities,
people with.
Type of support: General/operating support; Annual
campaigns; Capital campaigns; Building/
renovation; Equipment; Land acquisition;
Emergency funds; Program development;
Conferences/seminars; Publication; Seed money;
Curriculum development; Scholarship funds;
Technical assistance; Consulting services; Program
evaluation; Scholarships—to individuals; Matching/
challenge support.
Limitations: Giving limited to the central IN region.
No support for religious or sectarian purposes, or for
post-event or after-the-fact situations. No grants for
long-term operating support, endowment funds,
medical, scientific or academic research,
publications, travel, fundraising events, annual
appeals, or membership contributions.
Publications: Application guidelines; Annual report;
Financial statement; Grants list; Informational
brochure; Newsletter.
Application information: Visit foundation Web site
for application form and guidelines. Applicants must
first submit an application to the foundation before
potentially being asked to submit a full grant
proposal. Application form required.
Initial approach: Submit an application form
Copies of proposal: 1
Deadline(s): None for initial application form
Board meeting date(s): Feb., May., Sept., and
Nov.
Final notification: Within 60 days for initial
response

Officers and Directors:* Michael L. Smith,* Chair.;
J. Murray Clark,* Vice-Chair.; Brian Payne,* Pres.;
Rosemary Dorsa, Exec. V.P.; Gregory E. Lynn,* V.P.,
Real Estate and Facilities; Rob MacPherson, V.P.,
Devel.; Greg McMillen, V.P. and C.I.O.; Robert H.
Reynolds,* Secy.; Janet Haley, C.F.O.; John J.
Quinn,* Treas.; Brenda Delaney, Cont.; David
Becker; Lori Efroymson-Aguilera; Robert J. Laikin;
Alan A. Levin; D. William Moreau, Jr.; Peggy O.
Monson; Ann D. Murtlow; Sarah Wilson Otte; Myrta
J. Pulliam; Pat Garrett Rooney; Cynthia Simon
Skjodt; George P. Sweet; Milton O. Thompson.

3117
Chancellor Foundation, Inc. ✧ ☆
P.O. Box 5669
Evansville, IN 47716-5669

Established in 2004 in IN.
Donor: Steven E. Chancellor.
Foundation type: Independent foundation.
Financial data (yr. ended 12/31/05): Assets,
$12,010 (M); gifts received, $691,000;
expenditures, $679,938; qualifying distributions,
$679,938; giving activities include $679,908 for 41
grants (high: $112,500; low: $100).
Fields of interest: Elementary/secondary
education; Animal welfare; Health organizations;
Children/youth, services.
Limitations: Applications not accepted. Giving
primarily in Evansville, IN. No grants to individuals.
Application information: Contributes only to
pre-selected organizations.
Officers: Steven E. Chancellor, Pres. and Treas.;
Shane A. Chancellor, V.P.; Stephen E. Weitzel, Secy.
EIN: 201327280

3118
The Citizens Savings Foundation ✧
c/o Charles Cole
707 Ridge Rd.
Munster, IN 46321 (219) 836-5500
Contact: Monica F. Sullivan, Secy.
URL: http://www.cfsbancorp.com/about/
community.asp

Established in 1998 in IN.
Donors: CFS Bancorp, Inc.; Citizens Helping
Citizens Fund.
Foundation type: Company-sponsored foundation.
Financial data (yr. ended 6/30/03): Assets,
$3,652,892 (M); expenditures, $326,176;
qualifying distributions, $320,414; giving activities
include $319,493 for 117 grants (high: $11,300;
low: $100).
Purpose and activities: The foundation supports
organizations involved with arts and culture,
education, youth development, human services, and
community involvement.
Fields of interest: Arts; Education; Health care; Boys
& girls clubs; Youth development; Human services;
Children/youth, services; Community development;
Federated giving programs; Roman Catholic
agencies & churches.
Type of support: Employee matching gifts.
Limitations: Giving primarily in southern Cook
County, IL, and Lake and Porter counties, IN. No
grants to individuals.
Application information: Application form required.

Initial approach: Contact foundation for application form

Deadline(s): None

Officers: Thomas F. Prisby, C.E.O. and Pres.; Monica F. Sullivan, Secy.; John T. Stephens, Treas.

Directors: Peter J. Doherty; Bruce E. Huey; Timothy D. Johnson; Rocharda Moore-Morris; Jerome J. Reppa.

EIN: 352056076

Selected grants: The following grants were reported in 2004.

$12,500 to Bishop Noll Institute Foundation, Hammond, IN.

$12,500 to Saint Thomas More Elementary School, Munster, IN.

$12,500 to TradeWinds Rehabilitation Center, Gary, IN.

$10,025 to Purdue University-Calumet, Hammond, IN.

$10,000 to Habitat for Humanity, Northwest, Hammond, IN.

$9,500 to Blue Cap, Blue Island, IL.

$9,000 to Twin City Community Services, East Chicago, IN.

$7,650 to Restoration Ministries, Harvey, IL.

$7,500 to Hospice of Calumet Area, Munster, IN.

$7,500 to Saint Josephs Home for Boys, Saint Louis, MO.

3119

Allen Whitehill Clowes Charitable Foundation, Inc. ▼ ✧

320 N. Meridian St., Ste. 811
Indianapolis, IN   46204   (317) 955-0138
Contact: William H. Marshall, Pres.

Established in 1990 in IN.

Donor: Allen W. Clowes†.

Foundation type: Independent foundation.

Financial data (yr. ended 12/31/05): Assets, $113,804,443 (M); expenditures, $5,483,710; qualifying distributions, $5,412,547; giving activities include $5,186,800 for 53 grants (high: $4,000,000; low: $4,000; average: $10,000–$50,000).

Purpose and activities: The foundation supports charitable organizations that promote or preserve the arts and humanities. Priority will be given, primarily, to those located in central Indiana.

Fields of interest: Humanities; Arts.

Type of support: General/operating support; Building/renovation; Equipment; Program development; Publication; Research; Program evaluation; Matching/challenge support.

Limitations: Giving primarily in central IN. No grants for endowments.

Publications: Application guidelines.

Application information: Application form required.

Initial approach: Letter

Copies of proposal: 2

Deadline(s): Feb. 28 and June 30

Board meeting date(s): Apr. and Aug.

Final notification: 3 months

Officers and Directors:* William H. Marshall,* Pres. and Treas.; Bret Waller,* V.P.; Betty Roberts,* Secy.; Ben W. Blanton; Danny R. Dean; James B. Lemler; Thomas J. Loften; Beth Slaninka; Anna Seim White.

Number of staff: 1 part-time professional; 1 part-time support.

EIN: 351812631

Selected grants: The following grants were reported in 2005.

$4,000,000 to Indianapolis-Marion County Public Library Foundation, Indianapolis, IN. For library expansion.

$50,000 to Athenaeum Foundation, Indianapolis, IN. For operating support.

$50,000 to Indianapolis Opera, Indianapolis, IN. For operating support.

$45,000 to Heartland Film Festival, Indianapolis, IN. For operating support.

$40,000 to Indiana University Foundation, Bloomington, IN. For operating support.

$40,000 to Young Audiences of Indiana, Indianapolis, IN. For operating support.

$20,000 to Cathedral Arts, Indianapolis, IN. For operating support.

$10,000 to Charles A. Tindley Accelerated School, Charter of Accelerated Learning, Indianapolis, IN. For operating support.

$10,000 to Metropolitan School District of Perry Township, Indianapolis, IN. For operating support.

$10,000 to University of the Cumberlands, Williamsburg, KY. For operating support.

3120

The Clowes Fund, Inc.

320 N. Meridian St., Ste. 316
Indianapolis, IN   46204-1722
Contact: Elizabeth A. Casselman, Exec. Dir.
FAX: (317) 833-0145; E-mail: staff@clowesfund.org; Additional tel.: (800) 943-7209; Additional fax: (800) 943-7286; URL: http://www.clowesfund.org

Incorporated in 1952 in IN.

Donors: Edith W. Clowes†; George H.A. Clowes†; Allen W. Clowes†; George H.A. Clowes, Jr.†.

Foundation type: Independent foundation.

Financial data (yr. ended 12/31/05): Assets, $73,837,477 (M); expenditures, $3,307,847; qualifying distributions, $2,980,727; giving activities include $2,672,576 for 145 grants (high: $100,000; low: $25).

Purpose and activities: The Clowes Fund, a family foundation, seeks to enhance the common good by encouraging organizations and projects that help to build a just and equitable society, create opportunities for initiative, foster creativity and the growth of knowledge, and promote appreciation of the natural environment. The fund pursues these goals by awarding grants in three areas: the arts, education and social services. It also recognizes the special value of efforts that create links among these areas. The fund has a special interest in supporting projects that strengthen the communities in which Clowes family members and the fund's directors live and work. The fund is interested in supporting efforts to address the economic, legal, cultural, and psychological hurdles that immigrants and refugees face during their integration into American society. Its interest in workplace development is to ensure that all individuals have available the support and services necessary to enable them to participate fully in the economic life of their community.

Fields of interest: Performing arts; Performing arts, music; Arts; Elementary/secondary education; Human services.

Type of support: General/operating support; Income development; Management development/capacity building; Capital campaigns; Building/renovation; Equipment; Endowments; Emergency funds;

Program development; Professorships; Seed money; Fellowships; Internship funds; Program evaluation; Employee matching gifts; Matching/challenge support.

Limitations: Giving primarily in Indianapolis, IN, MA, Seattle, WA, and parts of northern New England. No support for foreign organizations, unsolicited colleges or universities, or programs promoting specific religious doctrine. No grants to individuals, or for videos, publications, conferences, or seminars; no operating support for unsolicited organizations; no loans.

Publications: Application guidelines; Grants list; Program policy statement.

Application information: Organizations without prior history with the fund should consult with fund staff before submitting a proposal. Application forms available on foundation Web site. The fund will periodically update deadlines and priority areas of funding. Please check the fund's Web site at that time for information. Requests for funding are limited to one request per organization per calendar year. Application form required.

Initial approach: Preliminary proposal via e-mail or through eGrant Web site

Copies of proposal: 1

Deadline(s): Preliminary proposal, Nov. 1; Jan. 31 for final proposal

Board meeting date(s): Annually, between Apr. 1 and June 1

Final notification: By June 1

Officers and Directors:* Alexander W. Clowes,* Pres.; Jonathan J. Clowes,* V.P.; Margaret C. Bowles,* Secy.; William H. Marshall,* Treas.; Elizabeth A. Casselman, Exec. Dir.; Margaret J. Clowes, Dir. Emeritus; Ben W. Blanton; Edith W. Clowes; Lynn L. Clowes; Thomas J. Clowes; Donna L. Wiley.

Number of staff: 2 full-time professional; 1 full-time support; 1 part-time support.

EIN: 351079679

Selected grants: The following grants were reported in 2005.

$200,000 to Marine Biological Laboratory, Woods Hole, MA. For endowment challenge.

$150,000 to Planned Parenthood of Indiana, Indianapolis, IN. For endowment and operating support.

$100,000 to United Way of Central Indiana, Indianapolis, IN. For agency capacity building fund.

$50,000 to School on Wheels, Indianapolis, IN. For operating support.

$50,000 to Seattle Art Museum, Seattle, WA. For restoring and installing Italian room.

$45,000 to Indiana Youth Institute, Indianapolis, IN. For Youth Service Toolkit.

$30,000 to College Mentors for Kids, Indianapolis, IN. For operating support.

$20,000 to International Center of Indianapolis, Indianapolis, IN. For Somali Bantu Refugees Program.

$15,000 to New Hampshire Community Loan Fund, Concord, NH. For immigration and New Hampshire Entrepreneurship.

$5,000 to Women United in Action, Dorchester, MA. For ESOL II/Bridge to College or Work class.

3121

Olive B. Cole Foundation, Inc. ✧

6207 Constitution Dr.
Fort Wayne, IN   46804
Contact: Maclyn T. Parker, Pres.

Incorporated in 1954 in IN.

Donors: Richard R. Cole†; Olive B. Cole†.

Foundation type: Independent foundation.

Financial data (yr. ended 3/31/06): Assets, $33,905,220 (M); expenditures, $1,641,274; qualifying distributions, $1,446,611; giving activities include $1,032,454 for 61 grants (high: $300,000; low: $50), $217,900 for 234 grants to individuals (high: $1,000; low: $800), and $75,009 for 2 foundation-administered programs.

Purpose and activities: Grants largely for education, including student aid for graduates of Noble County, IN, high schools, hospitals, civic affairs, youth agencies, and cultural programs.

Fields of interest: Arts; Higher education; Hospitals (general); Youth, services; Government/public administration.

Type of support: General/operating support; Continuing support; Building/renovation; Equipment; Land acquisition; Seed money; Scholarships—to individuals; Matching/challenge support.

Limitations: Giving limited to Noble County, IN, and immediate adjacent areas in northern IN. No grants for endowment funds or research.

Publications: Application guidelines; Program policy statement.

Application information: Scholarship applications available through foundation and at all Noble County, IN, secondary schools. Application form required.

Initial approach: Letter
Copies of proposal: 7
Deadline(s): None
Board meeting date(s): Feb., May, Aug., and Nov.
Final notification: 4 months

Officers and Directors:* John N. Pichon, Jr.,* Chair.; Maclyn T. Parker,* Pres.; John E. Hogan, Exec. V.P. and Treas.; Emily E. Pichon, Secy.; Jack Hunter; Samuel Patton.

Scholarship Administrator: Gwen I. Tipton.

Number of staff: 1 full-time professional; 1 full-time support.

EIN: 356040491

3122
Community Foundation Alliance, Inc. ✧

123 N.W. 4th Ave., Ste. 322
Evansville, IN 47708-1712 (812) 429-1191
Contact: Marilyn J. Klenck, C.E.O.; Carol M. Pace, Mgr., Comms. and Donor Svcs.
FAX: (812) 429-0840; E-mail: info@alliance9.org; Additional Tel.: (877) 429-1191; Additional E-mail: mklenck@alliance9.org; URL: http://www.alliance9.org

Established in 1991 in IN.

Foundation type: Community foundation.

Financial data (yr. ended 6/30/05): Assets, $55,005,990 (M); gifts received, $2,290,279; expenditures, $2,944,667; giving activities include $1,037,084 for 186+ grants, and $816,066 for 73 grants to individuals.

Purpose and activities: The alliance seeks to provide leadership and support for member community foundations as they promote philanthropy and build endowments to serve their communities.

Fields of interest: Humanities; Historic preservation/historical societies; Arts; Education; Botanical/horticulture/landscape services; Environment, beautification programs; Animal welfare; Animals/wildlife, preservation/protection;

Zoos/zoological societies; Animals/wildlife, special services; Health care; Mental health/crisis services; Food services; Housing/shelter; Recreation; Youth development; Human services; Civil rights; Community development; Public affairs.

Type of support: Management development/ capacity building.

Limitations: Giving limited to Daviess, Gibson, Knox, Perry, Pike, Posey, Spencer, Vanderburgh, and Warrick counties, IN.

Publications: Application guidelines; Annual report; Financial statement; Grants list; Informational brochure; Newsletter.

Application information: Visit foundation Web site or contact foundation for application forms, deadlines, and guidelines. Application form required.

Initial approach: Telephone
Deadline(s): Varies according to county
Board meeting date(s): 2nd Tues. of each month

Officers and Trustees:* Donald M. Aronoff,* Chair.; Cynthia Gaskins,* Vice-Chair.; Marilyn J. Klenck,* C.E.O. and Pres.; Donald Hauke, C.F.O.; Matt Volkman,* Treas.; Sharen Buyher; Mark Ewing; James H. Gislason; Joe Kress; Eric Lane; Ralph Mallory; Joe Malone; Norman Miller; Carole D. Rust; Steve Smith; Deron Steiner; Jim Swinney; Kristen Tucker; Kent E. Utt; Robert G. Waddle; Barbara Wood; Jeffrey L. Zook.

Number of staff: 2 full-time professional; 8 full-time support; 2 part-time support.

EIN: 351830262

3123
Community Foundation of Boone County, Inc. ✧

60 E. Cedar St.
P.O. Box 92
Zionsville, IN 46077 (317) 873-0210
Contact: Lisa Latz John, Exec. Dir.
FAX: (317) 873-0219; E-mail: cfbc@in-motion.net; Additional tel.: (765) 482-0024; URL: http://www.bccn.boone.in.us/cf

Established in 1991 in IN.

Foundation type: Community foundation.

Financial data (yr. ended 12/31/04): Assets, $13,945,414 (M); gifts received, $582,269; expenditures, $799,043; giving activities include $471,526 for 175 grants (high: $49,000; low: $8), and $9,740 for 13 grants to individuals (high: $1,200; low: $100).

Purpose and activities: The foundation was established in order to serve as the central philanthropic vehicle to address the needs of the Boone County, Indiana community.

Fields of interest: Arts; Education; Environment; Health care; Recreation; Children/youth, services; Human services; Public affairs; Youth; Aging; Disabilities, people with; Economically disadvantaged.

Type of support: Emergency funds; Program development; Seed money; Scholarship funds; Technical assistance; Program-related investments/loans; Grants to individuals; Scholarships—to individuals; Matching/challenge support; Student loans—to individuals.

Limitations: Giving limited to the residents of Boone County, IN, area. No support for religious purposes. No grants to individuals (except for designated scholarship funds), or for general operating expenses, salaries of existing staff, or international travel.

Publications: Application guidelines; Annual report; Informational brochure; Newsletter.

Application information: Visit foundation Web site for application format and guidelines. Application form not required.

Initial approach: Proposal (not to exceed 10 pages)
Copies of proposal: 5
Deadline(s): None
Board meeting date(s): Monthly

Officers and Directors:* Eric Ragsdale,* Pres.; Brett Bayston,* V.P.; Tom Easterday,* Secy.; Mike Caldwell,* Treas.; Lisa Latz John, Exec. Dir.; Phil Bainbridge; Nancy Beesley; Bill Haggstrom; Gary Heck; Charles M. Keenan; Wendell McBurney; Colleen Moran; Barbara Portell; Alan Quick; Mark Ransom; Bill Stanczykiewicz.

Number of staff: 2 full-time professional; 1 part-time professional.

EIN: 351829585

3124
Community Foundation of Grant County

505 W. 3rd St.
Marion, IN 46952 (765) 662-0065
Contact: Elizabeth Wright, Exec. Dir.
FAX: (765) 662-1438;
E-mail: foundationoffice@comfdn.org; URL: http://www.comfdn.org

Incorporated in 1984 in IN.

Foundation type: Community foundation.

Financial data (yr. ended 3/31/06): Assets, $17,713,689 (M); gifts received, $1,493,572; expenditures, $1,551,848; giving activities include $1,041,384 for 195 grants (high: $25,000; low: $25).

Purpose and activities: The foundation offers creative and imaginative grantmaking, coupled with strict volunteer review that assures responsible funding.

Fields of interest: Arts; Education; Environment, beautification programs; Health care; Mental health/crisis services; Recreation, parks/playgrounds; Youth development, services; Youth development; Children/youth, services; Family services; Aging, centers/services; Human services; Community development, neighborhood associations; Economic development; Community development; Philanthropy/voluntarism.

Type of support: Equipment; Building/renovation; Annual campaigns; Emergency funds; Program development; Conferences/seminars; Seed money; Scholarship funds; Technical assistance; Scholarships—to individuals; Matching/challenge support.

Limitations: Giving limited to Grant County, IN. No support for sectarian or religious purposes. No grants for endowments or salaries.

Publications: Application guidelines; Annual report; Financial statement; Newsletter.

Application information: Visit foundation Web site for proposal summary form and guidelines. Application form required.

Initial approach: Telephone or letter
Copies of proposal: 12
Deadline(s): Last Friday of Jan., Apr., July, and Oct.
Board meeting date(s): Feb., May, Aug., and Nov.
Final notification: Feb., May, Aug., and Nov.

Officers and Directors:* Beth Kachel,* Pres.; Tom Gearhart,* V.P.; Steve Wampner,* Secy.; Joe Certain,* Treas.; Elizabeth Wright, Exec. Dir.; Janet

Barnett; Yvette Breckenridge; Nancy Cole; David Crouse; Martin Harker; Jeff Harris; Ross Hoffman; Alex Huskey; Gene Johnson; Chris Oliver; Mike Powell; Sam Small; Dennis Smith; Federa Smith; Ralph Spencer; Wilbur Webb; Wanda Williams.
Number of staff: 4 full-time professional; 3 full-time support; 2 part-time support.
EIN: 311117791

3125
Community Foundation of Greater Fort Wayne, Inc. ▼
(formerly Fort Wayne Community Foundation)
701 S. Clinton St., Ste. 210
Fort Wayne, IN   46802   (260) 426-4083
Contact: David J. Bennett, Exec. Dir.; For grant application: Christine Meek, Prog. Off.
FAX: (260) 424-0114; E-mail: info@cfgfw.org; Additional E-mail: dbennett@cfgfw.org; Grant application tel.: (260) 426-4083, ext. 318 and E-mail: cmeek@cfgfw.org; URL: http://www.cfgfw.org

Incorporated in 1956 in IN.
Foundation type: Community foundation.
Financial data (yr. ended 12/31/05): Assets, $88,006,008 (M); gifts received, $6,423,555; expenditures, $7,461,434; giving activities include $6,294,982 for grants, and $597,409 for 248 grants to individuals (high: $6,000; low: $250).
Purpose and activities: Discretionary grantmaking preference given to projects expected to generate substantial benefits for the greater Fort Wayne, IN, area, including capital projects, demonstration projects, and projects promoting effective management, efficient use of community resources, or volunteer participation. Areas of interest include social services, education, community development, health services, and the arts.
Fields of interest: Arts; Education, early childhood education; Business school/education; Adult education—literacy, basic skills & GED; Education; Health care; Substance abuse, services; Health organizations, association; Food services; Youth development, services; Youth, services; Family services; Homeless, human services; Human services; Community development; Voluntarism promotion; Science; Leadership development; Disabilities, people with; Minorities; Economically disadvantaged; Homeless.
Type of support: Scholarships—to individuals; General/operating support; Management development/capacity building; Capital campaigns; Building/renovation; Equipment; Land acquisition; Emergency funds; Program development; Seed money; Scholarship funds; Technical assistance; Consulting services; Program evaluation; Matching/challenge support.
Limitations: Giving primarily in the Fort Wayne and Allen County, IN, areas. No support for religious purposes, hospitals, or private, public, or parochial schools. No grants to individuals (except for scholarships), or for operating budgets, continuing support, annual campaigns, deficit financing, endowment funds (except for Endowment-Building matching grants for funds), fellowships, medical or academic research, sponsorships, special events, advertising, films or videos, television programs, conferences, or group uniforms or group trips; no loans.
Publications: Application guidelines; Annual report; Financial statement; Grants list; Informational brochure; Informational brochure (including

application guidelines); Newsletter; Occasional report.
Application information: Visit foundation Web site for concept letter fact sheet, guidelines, and specific deadlines; application by invitation only after consideration of concept letter. Faxed or e-mailed concept letters are not accepted. Application form required.
Initial approach: Mail concept letter
Copies of proposal: 5
Deadline(s): First 3 quarters of year
Board meeting date(s): Feb., May, Aug., and Nov.
Final notification: 3 months for grant determination
Officers and Board Members:* Larry S. Adelman,* Pres.; Kathy Friend,* V.P.; Howard L. Chapman,* Secy.; Glynn A. Hines,* Treas.; David J. Bennett, Exec. Dir.; Keith Busse; Kathy Callen; Derrick K. Hayes; Greg A. Johnson; Thomas M. Kimbrough; Tracie Martin; Tracy L. Shellabarger; Marcia Tapp-Sanders; Rise Taylor; James M. Vann; W. Paul Wolf.
Number of staff: 3 full-time professional; 3 part-time professional; 2 full-time support; 4 part-time support.
EIN: 351119450
Selected grants: The following grants were reported in 2005.
$50,000 to Easter Seals ARC of Northeast Indiana, Fort Wayne, IN. For One Campus, One Heart Capital Campaign.
$50,000 to Fort Wayne Park Foundation, Fort Wayne, IN. For Lifetime Sports Academy.
$50,000 to Harold W. McMillen Center for Health Education, Fort Wayne, IN. For Facility Roof Project.
$50,000 to Turnstone Center for Disabled Children and Adults, Fort Wayne, IN. For Kimbrough Early Learning Center.
$50,000 to Visiting Nurse and Hospice Home, Fort Wayne, IN. For laptop computers for Clinical Staff.
$43,000 to Wellspring Interfaith Social Services, Fort Wayne, IN. For Older Adult Services.
$36,500 to Vincent House, Fort Wayne, IN. For salary support for Program Director.
$32,908 to Hoagland Area Advancement Association, Hoagland, IN. To build restroom and concession building.
$26,823 to Catholic Charities of the Diocese of Fort Wayne-South Bend, Fort Wayne, IN. For Immigration Program.
$20,000 to American Red Cross, Fort Wayne, IN. For Emergency Services Program.

3126
The Community Foundation of Howard County, Inc. ✧
202 N. Main St.
Kokomo, IN   46901-4624   (765) 454-7298
Contact: Hilda Burns, V.P.
FAX: (765) 868-4123; E-mail: hilda@cfhoward.org; Additional tel.: (800) 964-0508; URL: http://www.cfhoward.org

Established in 1991 in IN.
Foundation type: Community foundation.
Financial data (yr. ended 12/31/04): Assets, $26,555,173 (M); gifts received, $354,175; expenditures, $823,620; giving activities include $394,691 for grants, and $98,524 for 81 grants to individuals.

Purpose and activities: The foundation seeks to improve the quality of life in the community through the accumulation and stewardship of enduring charitable gifts. Primary areas of interest include health, social services, education, cultural affairs, and civic affairs.
Fields of interest: Historic preservation/historical societies; Arts; Elementary/secondary education; Education, early childhood education; Education, special; Higher education; Education; Hospitals (general); Health care; Employment; Youth, services; Human services; Community development; Leadership development.
Type of support: Capital campaigns; Building/renovation; Equipment; Program development; Seed money; Scholarship funds; Scholarships—to individuals; Matching/challenge support.
Limitations: Giving limited to Carroll, Clinton, and Howard counties, IN. No support for sectarian religious purposes. No grants to individuals (except for scholarships), or for seminars, equipment, normal operating expenses or salaries, or endowments.
Publications: Application guidelines; Annual report (including application guidelines); Informational brochure; Newsletter.
Application information: Visit foundation Web site for application form and guidelines. All applicants must receive pre-qualification prior to submitting an application; visit Web site for details. Application form required.
Initial approach: Letter of Inquiry
Copies of proposal: 21
Deadline(s): Feb. 3, Apr. 12, Aug. 11, and Oct. 13 for letter of inquiry; Mar. 1, May 3, Sept. 6, and Nov. 1 for full application
Board meeting date(s): Monthly
Final notification: Within 90 days
Officers and Directors:* Jim McIntyre,* Chair.; Rex Gingerich,* Vice-Chair.; Ron Harper, Pres.; Hilda Burns, V.P.; Mike Spear,* Secy.-Treas.; Janet Ayers; Bill Bersbach; Cynthia Cavanaugh; Tonya Goodier; Lindan Hill; Bob Hingst; Betsy Hoshaw; Ron McClughen; Herbert Miller; Sally Myers; Jim Santori; Marilyn Skinner; Rick Smith; Bill Stifle; Walter Wolff; Jeff Zollman.
Number of staff: 1 full-time professional.
EIN: 351844891

3127
Community Foundation of Madison and Jefferson County, Inc.
214 E. Main St.
P.O. Box 306
Madison, IN   47250-0306   (812) 265-3327
Contact: Louise Markel, C.E.O.
FAX: (812) 273-0181; E-mail: jeffcom@cfmjc.org; URL: http://www.cfmjc.org

Established in 1992 in IN.
Foundation type: Community foundation.
Financial data (yr. ended 12/31/05): Assets, $14,746,800 (M); gifts received, $1,586,408; expenditures, $991,881; giving activities include $386,000 for grants (high: $45,000; low: $100), and $30,900 for grants to individuals.
Purpose and activities: The mission of the foundation is to build a strong, vibrant community by helping donors provide perpetual funding for the people, projects and passions of Jefferson County, IN.

Fields of interest: Arts; Education; Environment; Health organizations, association; Human services; Community development.
Type of support: Building/renovation; Management development/capacity building; Capital campaigns; Equipment; Endowments; Emergency funds; Program development; Conferences/seminars; Seed money; Scholarship funds; Technical assistance; Consulting services; Scholarships—to individuals; Matching/challenge support.
Limitations: Giving limited to Jefferson County, IN. No support for religious purposes or programs requiring religious participation, public or private educational institutions, or government agencies. No grants for debt reduction, annual appeals or membership contribution, ongoing operating expenses or regular programming of well-established agencies, or travel expenses.
Publications: Application guidelines; Annual report; Financial statement; Grants list; Informational brochure; Newsletter; Program policy statement.
Application information: Visit foundation Web site for application guidelines. Initial proposals are accepted via mail, fax, or hand delivery. Application form required.
  Initial approach: Submit initial proposal (1 page)
  Copies of proposal: 7
  Deadline(s): Mar. 15 and Aug. 15 for initial proposal; Apr. 15 and Sept. 15 for full applications
  Board meeting date(s): 1st Wed. of each month
  Final notification: Up to 2 months
Officers and Directors:* Bill Hensler,* Chair.; Jim Braun,* Vice-Chair.; Louise Markel, C.E.O. and Pres.; Gerry Michl,* Secy.; Donald L. McCauley,* Treas.; Timothy Breeding; Kathleen Huffman; Alice Carlson Jackson; Jane Jakoubek; Fred Koehler; Betty L. Sebree; Tom Solomon; Mark Wynn.
Number of staff: 1 full-time professional; 1 full-time support.
EIN: 351847297

3128
The Community Foundation of Muncie and Delaware County, Inc. ✧

P.O. Box 807
Muncie, IN 47308-0807 (765) 747-7181
Contact: Roni Johnson, Pres.
FAX: (765) 289-7770;
E-mail: commfound@cfmdin.org; URL: http://www.cfmdin.org

Incorporated in 1985 in IN.
Foundation type: Community foundation.
Financial data (yr. ended 12/31/05): Assets, $36,383,474 (M); gifts received, $2,029,221; expenditures, $3,700,920; giving activities include $3,026,962 for 274 grants (high: $200,000; low: $25), and $191,359 for 71 grants to individuals (high: $15,830; low: $150).
Purpose and activities: The foundation seeks to encourage philanthropy, assist donors in building and enduring source of charitable assets, and exercise leadership in directing resources to enhance the quality of life of the residents of Muncie and Delaware County, Indiana.
Fields of interest: Performing arts, theater; Arts; Education, association; Libraries/library science; Education; Environment; Health care; Health organizations, association; Crime/law enforcement; Youth, services; Minorities/immigrants, centers/

services; Human services; Economic development; Community development; Economics; Minorities.
Type of support: General/operating support; Capital campaigns; Building/renovation; Equipment; Emergency funds; Program development; Conferences/seminars; Seed money; Scholarship funds; Technical assistance; Consulting services; Scholarships—to individuals; In-kind gifts; Matching/challenge support.
Limitations: Giving limited to Muncie and Delaware County, IN. No support for religious purposes or public agency projects. No grants to individuals (except for scholarships), or for endowment support, travel, fundraising events, or budget deficits.
Publications: Application guidelines; Annual report; Financial statement; Grants list; Informational brochure; Newsletter; Occasional report.
Application information: Visit foundation Web site for application form and specific guidelines per grant type. Application form required.
  Initial approach: Telephone
  Copies of proposal: 18
  Deadline(s): 2nd Fri. of Jan., Apr., July, and Oct.
  Board meeting date(s): 3rd Mon. of each month
  Final notification: 3rd Mon. of Feb., May, Aug., and Nov.
Officers and Trustees:* John D. Littler,* Chair.; Terry L. Walker,* Vice-Chair.; Roni Johnson, Pres.; Ermalene M. Faulkner,* Secy.; Gordon D. Cox,* Treas.; Ramon Avila; Jack E. Buckles; Marilyn Cleary; Ron Fauquher; Suzanne Gresham; Kelly Stanley.
Number of staff: 2 full-time professional; 1 part-time professional; 2 full-time support.
EIN: 351640051

3129
Community Foundation of Northwest Indiana, Inc. ✧

(formerly Community Foundation, Inc.)
901 MacArthur Blvd., Ste. 606
Munster, IN 46321-1721
Contact: John W. Mybeck, Sr. V.P.

Established in IN.
Foundation type: Community foundation.
Financial data (yr. ended 6/30/04): Assets, $200,769,671 (M); gifts received, $58,443,892; expenditures, $4,318,627; giving activities include $602,300 for 2 grants (high: $402,300; low: $200,000).
Purpose and activities: The foundation makes grants to improve the health and welfare of the community.
Fields of interest: Arts; Education; Cancer; Human services; Community development.
Limitations: Giving limited to the Lake County, IN, area. No grants to individuals.
Application information:
  Board meeting date(s): 3rd Wed. or each month
Officers and Directors:* Donald S. Powers,* Chair. and Pres.; David McCoy, Sr. V.P., Fin. and C.F.O.; John W. Mybeck, Sr. V.P. and C.A.O.; John Gorski, Sr. V.P., Hospital Operations; Frankie Fesko,* V.P.; James Richards,* Secy.; David Wickland,* Treas.; Steven Beering, M.D.; Albert J. Costello; Donald Fesko, M.D.; Alan Harre, Ph.D.; Richard McClaughry; Joseph Morrow; Sr. Kathleen Quinn; Donald Sands; William Schenck; Msgr. Joseph Semancik; Nabil Shabeeb, M.D.; Palmer Singleton, Jr.; Robert Welsh; Edward Williams, Ph.D.; Joe Williamson.
EIN: 311128781

3130
Community Foundation of Southern Indiana ✧

4104 Charlestown Rd.
New Albany, IN 47150 (812) 948-4662
Contact: Laura Hansen Dean, C.E.O.; For grants: Christine Harbeson, Prog. Off.
FAX: (812) 948-4678;
E-mail: info@cfsouthernindiana.com; Additional tel.: (888) 388-2374; Grant inquiry E-mail: CHarbeson@CFSouthernIndiana.com; URL: http://www.cfsouthernindiana.com

Established in 1991 in IN.
Foundation type: Community foundation.
Financial data (yr. ended 6/30/05): Assets, $21,936,207 (M); gifts received, $2,590,111; expenditures, $1,937,122; giving activities include $577,296 for grants.
Purpose and activities: The foundation uses its funds to assist and benefit people in Clark, Crawford, Floyd, and Harrison, IN, through funding of health, education, cultural, civic and recreational programs. The mission of the foundation is to foster philanthropy and build assets for the common good, now and forever.
Fields of interest: Arts; Education; Environment; Health care; Recreation; Public affairs.
Type of support: Management development/capacity building; Capital campaigns; Building/renovation; Emergency funds; Program development; Conferences/seminars; Seed money; Scholarship funds; Scholarships—to individuals; Matching/challenge support.
Limitations: Giving limited to Clark, Crawford, Floyd, and Harrison counties, IN. No support for religious or sectarian purposes. No grants to individuals (except for designated scholarship funds), or for existing obligations, travel expenses, or repeat funding; no loans.
Publications: Annual report (including application guidelines); Financial statement; Informational brochure.
Application information: Visit foundation Web site for application forms and guidelines. Application form required.
  Initial approach: Submit application forms and attachments
  Copies of proposal: 2
  Deadline(s): Sept. 1
  Board meeting date(s): Bimonthly
Officers and Directors:* Don Day,* Chair.; Michael Waiz,* Vice-Chair.; Laura Hansen Dean, C.E.O. and Pres.; Rita Shourds,* Secy.; Douglas York,* Treas.; Sherry Huffman, Cont.; Leslie Vidra, Legal Counsel; Les Albro; Stephen Bodney; Joyce Brown; J. Terrence Cody; Uric Dufrene; Laurie Eckart; Robert E. Kleehamer; Tom Lindley; Kyle Ridout; Leslie Robertson; Barbara Williams.
Number of staff: 3 full-time professional; 5 full-time support.
EIN: 351827813

3131
Community Foundation of St. Joseph County

205 W. Jefferson Blvd.
P.O. Box 837
South Bend, IN 46624-0837 (574) 232-0041
Contact: Angela Butiste, Sr. Prog. Off.

FAX: (574) 233-1906; E-mail: info@cfsjc.org; Additional E-mail: angela@cfsjc.org; URL: http://www.cfsjc.org

Established in 1991 in IN.
Foundation type: Community foundation.
Financial data (yr. ended 6/30/06): Assets, $101,594,651 (M); gifts received, $24,741,280; expenditures, $4,743,411; giving activities include $3,873,543 for 146 grants (high: $340,000; low: $250).
Purpose and activities: The foundation seeks to improve the quality of life for the citizens of St. Joseph County and their succeeding generations. Currently, the foundation awards challenge grants, offering $1 for every $1 raised.
Fields of interest: Arts; Higher education; Education; Health care; Recreation, parks/playgrounds; Recreation; Human services; Community development, neighborhood development; Youth.
Type of support: Scholarships—to individuals; Matching/challenge support.
Limitations: Giving limited to St. Joseph County, IN. No support for religious organizations for religious purposes, or development or public relations activities. No grants to individuals (except for scholarships), or for operational phases of established programs, endowment campaigns, retirement of debts, camperships, annual appeals or membership contributions, travel, post-event or after the fact situations, or computers (unless presented as a necessary component of larger program or objective).
Publications: Application guidelines; Financial statement; Grants list; Newsletter.
Application information: Visit foundation Web site for application Cover Sheet and guidelines. Application form required.
  Initial approach: Submit Grant Cover Sheet and attachments
  Copies of proposal: 1
  Deadline(s): Mar. 1 and Oct. 1
  Board meeting date(s): Mar., June, Sept., and Dec.
  Final notification: Following May Exec. Comm. meeting and Dec. board meetings
Officers and Directors:* Edwina Kintner,* Chair.; Myrtle Wilson,* Vice-Chair.; Rose Meissner,* Pres.; Anita Echevarria, V.P., Admin.; Christopher Nanni,* V.P., Progs.; Margaret King,* Secy.; Albert Brown-Gort; Phil Byrd; Thomas Cassady, Jr.; Angie Chamblee; Mike Donovan; Linda Dosh; Carol Evans; Marion Fulce; Alfred Guillaume, Jr.; Anne Hillman; Joseph Iams; Nancy Ickler; Jim Keenan; Robert Kill; Nancy King; Donald Kyle; Jon Laidig; Barbara Lobdell; David Ray; Chuck Roemer; Rick Rice; Tim Sexton; Bonnie Shaffer; Dr. Dean Strycker; Thomas Varga; Karen White.
Number of staff: 9 full-time professional.
EIN: 237365930

3132
Community Foundation of Wabash County
(formerly North Manchester Community Foundation)
218 E. Main St.
P.O. Box 98
North Manchester, IN 46962-0098
(260) 982-4824
Contact: Steve Mason, Exec. Dir.
FAX: (260) 982-8644; E-mail: steve@cfwabash.org;
URL: http://www.cfwabash.org

Established in 1954 in IN as North Manchester Community Foundation; current name adopted in 1992.
Foundation type: Community foundation.
Financial data (yr. ended 12/31/05): Assets, $19,123,812 (M); gifts received, $2,603,443; expenditures, $1,999,165; giving activities include $1,667,327 for 425 grants (high: $631,588; low: $10), and $97,307 for 56 grants to individuals (high: $13,029; low: $100).
Purpose and activities: The foundation serves the citizens of Wabash County by implementing their charitable aspirations, making grants, investing and safeguarding charitable assets, providing information regarding charitable endeavors, and convening citizens and linking resources to address issues confronting residents' shared lives.
Fields of interest: Arts; Higher education; Education; Environment; Health care; Recreation; Human services; Community development; Social sciences.
Type of support: Scholarships—to individuals; General/operating support; Continuing support; Building/renovation; Equipment; Endowments; Program development; Seed money; Curriculum development; Scholarship funds; Technical assistance; Program evaluation; Matching/challenge support.
Limitations: Giving limited to Wabash County, IN. No support for religious activities, or for national organizations (except for local chapters serving Wabash County). No grants to individuals (except for scholarships), or for annual fund campaigns, or programs or products produced for resale.
Publications: Application guidelines; Annual report (including application guidelines); Informational brochure; Newsletter.
Application information: Visit foundation Web site for application form and additional guidelines per grant type. The foundation's Financial Aid & Scholarship Handbook is available at any Wabash County high school guidance office, or by calling the foundation; other locations where the Handbook may be obtained are listed on Web site. Application form required.
  Initial approach: Mail application form and attachments
  Copies of proposal: 1
  Deadline(s): Mar. 15, July 15, and Nov. 15
  Board meeting date(s): Quarterly
  Final notification: One month after deadline
Officers and Directors:* Dave McFadden,* Pres.; Pam Higgins,* V.P.; Mary Anne Bain,* Secy.; Ralph Naragon, Treas.; Steve Mason, Exec. Dir.; Joe Burgos; Chris Daughtry; Brent Dawes; Nick Ferry; Steve Ford; Chris Garber; Cathy Gatchel; Patty Grant; Steve Hentgen; Bonnie Ingraham; Dave Mann; Kerri Mattern; Ken Perkins; Albert Schlitt; Robin Shepherd; Steve Van Voorhis; Rose Wenrich.
Number of staff: 3 full-time professional.
EIN: 356019016

3133
Community Foundation Partnership, Inc. ☆
(doing business as Lawrence County Community Foundation)
(also known as Martin County Community Foundation)
1016 15th St.
P.O. Box 1235
Bedford, IN 47421
Contact: Hope Flores, Exec. Dir.
FAX: (812) 279-1984; E-mail: lccf@kiva.net;
URL: http://www.Kiva.net/~lccf

Established in 1992 in IN.
Foundation type: Community foundation.
Financial data (yr. ended 12/31/05): Assets, $6,317,176 (M); gifts received, $1,295,958; expenditures, $787,863; giving activities include $508,089 for 194 grants (high: $100,000; low: $50).
Purpose and activities: The foundation's mission is to enhance the quality of life for the citizens of Lawrence and Martin Counties, IN, in the areas of education, health and human services, civic and historical affairs, the arts and culture, and recreational activities.
Fields of interest: Historical activities; Arts; Education; Health care; Recreation; Human services; Community development.
Type of support: Scholarship funds; Matching/challenge support.
Limitations: Giving primarily in Lawrence and Martin counties, IN. No support for religious instruction or doctrine. No grants to individuals (except for scholarships), or for debt retirement, capital campaigns, or endowments.
Publications: Annual report; Informational brochure; Newsletter.
Application information: Visit foundation Web site for application forms and guidelines. The foundation offers Grantseeker Workshops approximately 1 month prior to grant application deadline; attendance is strongly encouraged. Application form required.
  Initial approach: Contact foundation Prog. Off.
  Copies of proposal: 9
  Deadline(s): Varies
  Final notification: Varies
Officers and Directors:* George McNichols,* Pres.; Ann Ackerman,* V.P.; William Shobe,* Secy.; Terri Owens,* Treas.; Hope Flores, Exec. Dir.; Kenny Fye; Anthony Nonte; James Oswalt.
Number of staff: 2 full-time professional; 2 full-time support.
EIN: 351889139

3134
Cornelius Family Foundation, Inc. ✧
111 Monument Cir., Ste. 4700
P.O. Box 44906
Indianapolis, IN 46244-0906
Contact: James M. Cornelius, Pres.

Established in 1997 in IN.
Donor: James M. Cornelius.
Foundation type: Independent foundation.
Financial data (yr. ended 12/31/05): Assets, $5,633,540 (M); gifts received, $2,774,707; expenditures, $2,711,194; qualifying distributions, $2,639,911; giving activities include $2,600,591 for 41 grants (high: $2,000,000; low: $41).

Purpose and activities: Giving primarily for higher education, federated giving programs, and to Roman Catholic churches.

Fields of interest: Museums; Arts; Higher education; Education; Human services; Federated giving programs; Roman Catholic agencies & churches.

Limitations: Giving primarily in MI and IN.

Application information: Application form not required.

Deadline(s): None

Officers: James M. Cornelius, Pres.; Kathleen M. Cornelius, V.P. and Secy.

Directors: Andrew James Cornelius; Lindsay Anne Cornelius.

EIN: 352030709

Selected grants: The following grants were reported in 2004.

$30,000 to Little Sisters of the Poor, Indianapolis, IN.

$25,000 to Saint Paul Hermitage, Beech Grove, IN.

$15,000 to National Medical Fellowships, New York, NY.

$12,500 to DePauw University, Greencastle, IN.

$10,000 to Indianapolis Art Center, Indianapolis, IN.

$5,000 to Marian College, Indianapolis, IN.

$2,500 to International Center of Indianapolis, Indianapolis, IN.

$2,500 to Saint Elizabeths Home, Indianapolis, IN.

$1,000 to Conner Prairie, an Earlham Museum, Fishers, IN.

$1,000 to Indiana Symphony Society, Indianapolis, IN.

3135
Crown Point Community Foundation

Courthouse Sq., Ste. 302
P.O. Box 522
Crown Point, IN 46308-0522 (219) 662-7252
Contact: Patricia Huber, Pres.
FAX: (219) 662-9493; E-mail: cpcf@sbcglobal.net;
URL: http://www.crownpointcommunityfoundation.org

Established in 1990 in IN.

Foundation type: Community foundation.

Financial data (yr. ended 12/31/05): Assets, $7,852,343 (M); gifts received, $620,086; expenditures, $569,494; giving activities include $351,813 for grants, and $96,672 for grants to individuals.

Purpose and activities: The foundation serves as a facilitator for community good, builds endowments, allocates grants, and awards scholarships to better serve Crown Point and South Lake County area in Indiana. Funding is provided for arts and culture, community development, education, health, and human services.

Fields of interest: Historic preservation/historical societies; Arts; Higher education; Education; Environment; Health care; Crime/violence prevention; Housing/shelter; Recreation; Youth development; Human services; Community development; Philanthropy/voluntarism; Religion.

Type of support: General/operating support; Continuing support; Annual campaigns; Capital campaigns; Equipment; Emergency funds; Scholarship funds; Scholarships—to individuals.

Limitations: Giving limited to northwestern IN, including the Crown Point area. No support for religious organizations for religious purposes. No grants for endowments.

Publications: Application guidelines; Annual report; Informational brochure; Newsletter.

Application information: Visit foundation Web site for application form and application information. Application form required.

Initial approach: Letter
Copies of proposal: 7
Deadline(s): June 1, Sept. 1, and Dec. 1
Board meeting date(s): 4 times per-year, plus annual dinner meeting
Final notification: 1 month

Officers and Directors:* Joseph Allegretti,* Chair.; Ron Borto,* 1st Vice-Chair.; John Diederich,* 2nd Vice-Chair.; Patricia Huber,* Pres. and Exec. Dir.; Timothy R. Sendak,* Secy.; Joseph Beckman,* Treas.; Mary Ann Abraham; John Barney; Mark Bates; Dave Batusic; Jack Esala; Gregory Forsythe; Marge Kerr; Darryl Miller; Sally Nalbor; Karen Raab; Daniel R. Root; William Rosenbower; Gil Stiener; Bonnie Vinovich.

Number of staff: 1 full-time professional; 2 part-time support.

EIN: 310247014

3136
The Cummins Foundation ✦

(formerly Cummins Engine Foundation)
500 Jackson St., M.C. 60633
Columbus, IN 47201 (812) 377-3114
Contact: Gayle Dudley Nay
FAX: (812) 377-7897; Mailing address: Box 3005, M.C. 60633, Columbus, IN 47202-3005;
URL: http://www.cummins.com/na/pages/en/whoweare/foundation.cfm

Incorporated in 1954 in IN.

Donors: Cummins Engine Co., Inc.; Fleetguard, Inc.; Cummins Inc.

Foundation type: Company-sponsored foundation.

Financial data (yr. ended 12/31/04): Assets, $5,269,661 (M); gifts received, $5,157,549; expenditures, $1,717,728; qualifying distributions, $1,717,728; giving activities include $1,438,192 for 95 grants (high: $200,000; low: $1,000), $1,000 for 1 grant to an individual, and $16,830 for employee matching gifts.

Purpose and activities: The foundation focuses primarily on local communities and providing the tools and means to help individuals left out of society overcome the barriers they face.

Fields of interest: Visual arts, architecture; Arts; Elementary school/education; Secondary school/education; Education; Youth, services; Minorities/immigrants, centers/services; Civil rights; Community development; Federated giving programs; Public policy, research; Minorities.

International interests: Brazil; China; India; Mexico.

Type of support: Employee matching gifts; General/operating support; Continuing support; Annual campaigns; Capital campaigns; Building/renovation; Endowments; Emergency funds; Program development; Publication; Technical assistance.

Limitations: Giving primarily in areas of company operations, with emphasis on Lakemills, IA, the Columbus and Seymour, IN, areas, Fridley, MN, Rocky Mount, NC, Jamestown, NY, Charleston, SC, Cookeville, Memphis, and Nashville, TN, El Paso, TX, and in Brazil, China, India, and Mexico; giving also to national organizations. No support for sectarian religious organizations or political candidates. No grants to individuals, or for business start-up needs or political causes; no loans.

Publications: Corporate giving report (including application guidelines).

Application information: Application form not required.

Initial approach: Proposal
Copies of proposal: 1
Deadline(s): None
Board meeting date(s): Varies from 3 to 4 meetings per year
Final notification: Varies by board meeting cycle

Officers and Directors:* Theodore M. Solso,* Chair.; Tracy H. Souza, Pres.; Steve Chapman, V.P., International; John Wall, V.P., Chief Tech. Off.; Jean Blackwell,* Secy.-Treas.; Thomas Linebarger; F. Joseph Loughrey; William I. Miller; Rick J. Mills.

Number of staff: 2 full-time professional; 1 full-time support.

EIN: 356042373

Selected grants: The following grants were reported in 2004.

$500,000 to United Way of Bartholomew County, Columbus, IN. 3 grants: $100,000, $200,000, $200,000

$180,000 to Bartholomew Consolidated School Corporation, Columbus, IN. 2 grants: $10,000, $170,000

$50,000 to National Civil Rights Museum, Memphis, TN.

$25,000 to EARTH University Foundation, Atlanta, GA.

$25,000 to Robert H. Jackson Center, Jamestown, NY.

$13,495 to United Way of Johnson County, Franklin, IN.

$4,670 to Memphis Cultural Arts Enrichment Center, Memphis, TN.

3137
Dearborn Community Foundation ✦

(formerly Dearborn County Community Foundation)
204 Short St.
Lawrenceburg, IN 47025 (812) 539-4115
Contact: Fred McCarter, Exec. Dir.; For grants: Alyson K. Glaze, Dir., Progs.
FAX: (812) 539-4119; E-mail: info@dearborncf.org;
Grant information E-mail: dcf@suscom.net;
URL: http://www.dearborncf.org

Established in 1997 in IN.

Donors: The Greater Cincinnati Foundation; Lilly Endowment; Rising Sun Regional Foundation.

Foundation type: Community foundation.

Financial data (yr. ended 12/31/04): Assets, $10,307,228 (M); gifts received, $3,003,500; expenditures, $3,503,505; giving activities include $2,503,224 for 95+ grants, and $681,437 for grants to individuals.

Purpose and activities: The foundation is a dynamic, creative force with the goal of advancing social, educational, and cultural opportunities while preserving the community's heritage.

Fields of interest: Arts; Elementary/secondary education; Education; Environment, natural resources; Environment; Hospitals (general); Health care; Crime/law enforcement, government agencies; Human services; Community development; Children/youth.

Type of support: Building/renovation; Equipment; Program development; Seed money; Scholarships—to individuals; Matching/challenge support.

Limitations: Giving limited to Dearborn County, IN. No support for sectarian or religious purposes. No grants to individuals (except for scholarships), or exclusively for endowment creation or debt reduction, or for travel expenses or after-the-fact funding.

Publications: Annual report; Newsletter.

Application information: Visit foundation Web site for application cover form and guidelines per grant type. Application form required.

    Initial approach: Submit grant application cover form and attachments

    Copies of proposal: 1

    Deadline(s): Varies for grants; Jan. 11 for scholarships

    Board meeting date(s): 4th Thurs. of every month except Apr., July, and Dec.

    Final notification: Varies

Officers and Directors:* Michael Hollenbeck,* Chair.; Mike Heffelmire,* Pres.; Jim Deaton,* V.P.; Joseph Stephens,* Secy.; Brad Rupel,* Treas.; Fred McCarter, Exec. Dir.; Lisa DeHart Lehner, Counsel; Jada Ankenbauer; Charles Blankenship; Frank Frable; Luree Ketcham; Elaine Kroger; Karleen McGraw; Gerald Nixon; Jane Ohlmansiek; Ron Powell; Margaret Stewart.

Number of staff: 3 full-time professional; 1 full-time support.

EIN: 352036110

3138
Decatur County Community Foundation, Inc. ✧

101 E. Main St., Ste. 1
P.O. Box 72
Greensburg, IN 47240 (812) 662-6364
Contact: Sharon Hollowell, Exec. Dir.
FAX: (812) 662-8704;
E-mail: contact@dccfound.org; URL: http://www.dccfound.org

Established in 1992 in IN.

Foundation type: Community foundation.

Financial data (yr. ended 12/31/05): Assets, $14,380,244 (M); gifts received, $375,863; expenditures, $760,918; giving activities include $585,504 for grants.

Purpose and activities: The foundation seeks to provide a general depository for charitable contributions that will service Decatur County. The foundation supports the following areas of interest: civic and community, education, health and human services, arts and literacy, historic preservation, safety, and youth and recreation.

Fields of interest: Historic preservation/historical societies; Arts; Education, reading; Education; Public health; Health care; Safety, education; Recreation; Youth development, services; Human services; Community development.

Type of support: Building/renovation; Equipment; Emergency funds; Program development; Seed money; Scholarship funds; Technical assistance; Program-related investments/loans; Scholarships —to individuals; Matching/challenge support.

Limitations: Giving primarily in Decatur County, IN. No support for religious purposes. No grants for debt reduction, post-event or after the fact funding, make-up operating deficits, or ongoing operating expenses.

Publications: Application guidelines; Annual report (including application guidelines); Financial statement; Informational brochure; Informational brochure (including application guidelines); Newsletter; Occasional report.

Application information: Visit foundation Web site for Letter of Intent form and additional guidelines per grant type. Upon approval of Letter of Intent, grant applications will be sent to eligible applicants. Organization may not receive foundation grants more than once in a 12-month period; maximum grant amount $25,000. Application form required.

    Initial approach: Submit Letter of Intent form

    Copies of proposal: 10

    Deadline(s): Feb. 15, May 15, and Sept. 15 for large community grants

    Board meeting date(s): 3rd Fri. monthly

    Final notification: Normally within 2 months

Officers and Directors:* Dale Crites,* Pres.; Don Wickens,* V.P.; Norm Denny,* Secy.-Treas.; Sharon Hollowell, Exec. Dir.; Jay Hatton; Margaret Lowe; Ernestine McIntyre; Jennifer Sturges; Glenn Tebbe; Sandi Westhafer.

Number of staff: 1 full-time professional; 1 part-time support.

EIN: 351870979

3139
Arthur J. Decio Foundation ✧ ☆

c/o Skyline Corp.
2520 Bypass Rd.
Elkhart, IN 46515 (574) 294-6521
Contact: Ronald F. Kloska, Tr.

Established in 1970 in IN.

Donor: Arthur J. Decio.

Foundation type: Independent foundation.

Financial data (yr. ended 9/30/05): Assets, $3,397,744 (M); gifts received, $315,000; expenditures, $460,787; qualifying distributions, $458,764; giving activities include $458,400 for 56 grants (high: $130,000; low: $250).

Purpose and activities: Giving primarily for higher education and public television.

Fields of interest: Media, television; Arts; Higher education; Christian agencies & churches.

Limitations: Giving primarily in IN.

Application information:

    Initial approach: Letter

    Deadline(s): None

Trustees: Arthur J. Decio; Patricia C. Decio; Terrence M. Decio; Ronald F. Kloska; Richard M. Treckelo.

EIN: 237083597

Selected grants: The following grants were reported in 2005.

$130,000 to Diocese of Fort Wayne-South Bend, Fort Wayne, IN.

$25,000 to United Way of Elkhart County, Elkhart, IN.

$20,000 to Ara Parseghian Medical Research Foundation, Tucson, AZ.

$20,000 to Saint Thomas the Apostle Church, Los Angeles, CA.

$16,000 to Salvation Army.

$10,000 to Northern Indiana Center for History, South Bend, IN.

$5,000 to College Football Hall of Fame, South Bend, IN.

$5,000 to RV/MH Heritage Foundation, Elkhart, IN.

$4,000 to Premier Arts, Elkhart, IN.

$3,500 to Studebaker National Museum, South Bend, IN.

3140
Christel DeHaan Family Foundation ✧
(formerly RCI Foundation)

10 W. Market St., Ste. 1990
Indianapolis, IN 46204 (317) 464-2038
Contact: Karen K. Witt, Dir.
FAX: (317) 464-2039; E-mail: kwitt@cde-ltd.com

Established in 1992 in IN.

Donor: Christel DeHaan.

Foundation type: Independent foundation.

Financial data (yr. ended 12/31/04): Assets, $41,709,816 (M); gifts received, $2,400; expenditures, $3,917,093; qualifying distributions, $3,502,302; giving activities include $2,826,013 for 69 grants (high: $1,000,000; low: $218), and $88,350 for 25 grants to individuals (high: $8,000; low: $50).

Purpose and activities: Giving to support arts and culture in central IN.

Fields of interest: Arts.

Type of support: Endowments; Program development; Capital campaigns; General/operating support; Continuing support; Annual campaigns; Matching/challenge support.

Limitations: Giving primarily in central IN. No support for religious organizations, political candidates, parties or lobbyists, federal/state/local governmental bodies, or for other private foundations. No grants for individual artistic endeavors, media advertising, or public awareness campaigns.

Publications: Application guidelines.

Application information: Telephone, fax or E-mail for Letter of Inquiry format detailed in Foundation Guidelines. Application form required.

    Initial approach: Letter of inquiry

    Copies of proposal: 1

    Deadline(s): Apr. 1

    Board meeting date(s): June and Dec.

    Final notification: 90 days

Officers and Directors:* Christel DeHaan,* Pres.; Cheryl J. Wendling,* V.P. and Secy.; Keith A. DeHaan,* V.P.; Kirsten A. DeHaan,* V.P.; Timothy E. DeHaan,* V.P.; Lisa Kipper, V.P.; Steve Miller,* C.F.O. and Treas.; Karen K. Witt.

Number of staff: 1 full-time professional; 1 full-time support.

EIN: 351939960

Selected grants: The following grants were reported in 2003.

$119,227 to American Pianists Association, Indianapolis, IN. For operating support.

$50,000 to Indiana University, School of Music, Bloomington, IN. For operating support.

$29,828 to Indianapolis Opera Company Foundation, Indianapolis, IN. For operating support.

$23,784 to American Cabaret Theater, Indianapolis, IN. For operating support.

$5,000 to Indianapolis Downtown, Indianapolis, IN. For operating support.

$5,000 to Midwest Academy, Carmel, IN. J. Reed award.

$2,000 to Covenant Christian High School, Indianapolis, IN. For teacher award.

$2,000 to Perry Meridian High School, Indianapolis, IN. For teacher award.

$1,096 to Educational Choice Charitable Trust, Indianapolis, IN. For operating support.

$375 to Indiana Symphony Society, Indianapolis, IN. For operating support.

3141
DeKalb County Community Foundation, Inc.
650 W. North St.
P.O. Box 285
Auburn, IN 46706 (260) 925-0311
Contact: Wendy Oberlin, Exec. Dir.; For grants: Doreen Brown, Prog. Mgr.; Diane Wilson, Admin. Asst.
FAX: (260) 925-0383;
E-mail: woberlin@dekalbfoundation.org; Additional tel.: (888) 727-3834; Additional E-mail: dwilson@dekalbfoundation.org; Grant application E-mail: dbrown@dekalbfoundation.org; URL: http://www.dekalbfoundation.org

Established in 1996 in IN.
Foundation type: Community foundation.
Financial data (yr. ended 12/31/05): Assets, $10,250,542 (M); gifts received, $1,678,460; expenditures, $827,724; giving activities include $330,166 for 185 grants (high: $20,000; low: $3), $94,693 for 110 grants to individuals (high: $4,000; low: $250), and $183,311 for foundation-administered programs.
Purpose and activities: The foundation is an asset builder and grantmaker whose purpose is to improve the quality of life in the DeKalb County, IN, community.
Fields of interest: Arts; Higher education; Education; Environment; Health care; Youth development; Human services; Community development.
Type of support: General/operating support; Capital campaigns; Building/renovation; Equipment; Program development; Scholarships—to individuals.
Limitations: Giving limited to projects/programs that benefit residents of DeKalb County, IN.
Publications: Application guidelines; Annual report; Informational brochure; Newsletter.
Application information: Visit foundation Web site for application form and guidelines. Handwritten proposals are not accepted. The foundation offers free 60-minute workshops to help grantseekers understand the application process and how to submit a request; contact Prog. Mgr. to register. Application form required.
  Initial approach: Contact foundation to schedule meeting
  Copies of proposal: 1
  Deadline(s): June 1 and Oct. 1
  Board meeting date(s): Varies
Officers and Directors:* J. Bryan Nugen,* Pres.; Donna Martin Boseker,* V.P.; Christine Rowe,* Secy.; Michael J. Tullis,* Treas.; Wendy Oberlin, Exec. Dir.; Fred L. Brown; Jeffrey Burns; Sherry Crisp-Ridge; Randall J. Deetz; Michael Douglas; David M. Hawkins; Robert B. Keifer; Robert Menzie; Connie Miles; Brian D. Ruegsegger; Peg Yoder.
Number of staff: 3 full-time professional; 2 full-time support; 1 part-time support.
EIN: 351992897

3142
Dekko Foundation, Inc. ▼
P.O. Box 548
Kendallville, IN 46755-0548 (260) 347-1278
Contact: Thomas Leedy, Pres.
FAX: (260) 347-7103;
E-mail: dekko@dekkofoundation.org; URL: http://www.dekkofoundation.org

Established in 1981 in IN.
Donor: Chester E. Dekko†.
Foundation type: Independent foundation.
Financial data (yr. ended 8/31/05): Assets, $238,402,917 (M); gifts received, $3,790,721; expenditures, $12,300,327; qualifying distributions, $11,151,340; giving activities include $10,037,526 for 250 grants (high: $1,100,000; low: $60; average: $1,000–$200,000), and $192,105 for 5 foundation-administered programs.
Purpose and activities: Support primarily for philanthropy, community as it applies to youth ages 0-18, child-centered choices in schools for youth ages 6-18, and developmentally appropriate child care for ages 0-5.
Fields of interest: Education, early childhood education; Elementary school/education; Secondary school/education; Libraries (public); Libraries (school); Education; Youth development.
Type of support: Land acquisition; Building/renovation; Management development/capacity building; Continuing support; General/operating support; Capital campaigns; Equipment; Endowments; Program development; Conferences/seminars; Seed money; Curriculum development; Technical assistance; Consulting services; Matching/challenge support.
Limitations: Giving primarily in Limestone County, AL; Clarke, Decatur, Lucas, Ringgold, and Union counties, IA; and DeKalb, Kosciousko, LaGrange, Noble, Steuben, and Whitley counties, IN. No grants to individuals.
Publications: Application guidelines; Annual report.
Application information: See foundation's Web site to apply online. Application form not required.
  Initial approach: Letter or E-mail
  Copies of proposal: 1
  Deadline(s): None
  Board meeting date(s): Six times per year
  Final notification: 3-4 months
Officers and Directors:* Lorene Dekko Salsbery,* C.E.O.; Thomas Leedy, Pres.; Robin McCormick, Cont.; Chester E. Dekko, Jr.; Erica D. Dekko.
Number of staff: 7 full-time professional; 1 full-time support; 2 part-time support.
EIN: 351528135
Selected grants: The following grants were reported in 2005.
$1,100,000 to Oak Farm School, Kendallville, IN. For Middle School Project.
$846,111 to Kendallville Public Library, Kendallville, IN. For building project.
$620,000 to Garrett Community Center, Garrett, IN. For Community Center.
$312,450 to East Noble School Corporation, Kendallville, IN. For All-Write program.
$309,920 to Early Childhood Alliance, Fort Wayne, IN. For Triumph Program.
$300,000 to Girl Scouts of the U.S.A., Limberlost Council, Fort Wayne, IN. For capital campaign.
$17,500 to South Central Iowa Community Foundation, Osceola, IA. For Youth Pod.
$15,000 to Mentone Daycare Center, Mentone, IN. For operating support.
$4,000 to Limestone County Board of Education, Athens, AL. For Teach to Reach program.
$2,763 to Lakewood Park Christian School, Auburn, IN. For Music Program.

3143
Duneland Health Council, Inc. ✧
P.O. Box 9327
Michigan City, IN 46361 (219) 874-4193
Contact: Grants Comm.

Established in 1997 in IN.
Donor: Alverno Health Care Corp.
Foundation type: Independent foundation.
Financial data (yr. ended 12/31/05): Assets, $7,891,348 (M); gifts received, $300; expenditures, $524,999; qualifying distributions, $361,451; giving activities include $361,451 for 11 grants (high: $188,999; low: $2,000).
Purpose and activities: To improve the health and general welfare of the greater Michigan City, IN, community.
Fields of interest: Education; Health care, clinics/centers; Health care; Human services; Salvation Army; Family services; Community development.
Limitations: Giving primarily in the metropolitan Michigan City, IN, area. No support for religious organizations. No grants to individuals, or for fund-raising, endowments, or advertising.
Application information: Duneland Health Council Grant Application Form required. Application form required.
  Initial approach: Completed application form
  Deadline(s): None
Officers: Burton B. Ruby, Chair.; George R. Averitt, Vice-Chair.; George E. Todd, Secy.; Roger J. McKee, Treas.; Norman D. Steider, Exec. Dir.
Directors: Linda Anast-May; Linda Bechinski; Michael Harding; Judy Jacobi; H. Fred Miller; Gil R. Pontius; Gene Simmons.
EIN: 352021548
Selected grants: The following grants were reported in 2003.
$73,912 to Open Door Health Center, Michigan City, IN. For pharmacy program and extended care.
$45,000 to La Porte County Child Abuse Prevention Council, Michigan City, IN. For salary support.
$10,000 to Sinai Sunday Evening Forum, Michigan City, IN. For speaker fees.
$9,000 to Samaritan Counseling Centers, Michigan City, IN. For general support.
$4,730 to Michigan City High School, Michigan City, IN. For AED units.
$4,000 to Marquette High School, Michigan City, IN. For two AED units.

3144
East Chicago Community Development Foundation, Inc. ✧
905 W. Chicago Ave.
East Chicago, IN 46312 (219) 392-4225
FAX: (219) 392-4245;
E-mail: grantinfo@foundationsec.org; URL: http://www.foundationsec.org/

Established in 1997 in IN.
Donor: Showboat Marina Partnership.
Foundation type: Company-sponsored foundation.
Financial data (yr. ended 12/31/04): Assets, $11,643,613 (M); gifts received, $3,144,134; expenditures, $2,491,044; qualifying distributions, $963,305; giving activities include $1,456,833 for grants.
Purpose and activities: The foundation supports organizations involved with safety, employment, human services, and community development.

Fields of interest: Crime/law enforcement; Employment, services; Employment; Family services; Human services; Economic development; Business/industry; Community development.
Limitations: Giving limited to East Chicago, IN.
Publications: Application guidelines.
Application information: Additional information may be requested at a later date. Application form not required.

Initial approach: Letter of inquiry
Deadline(s): Jan. 6, Apr. 7, July 7, and Oct. 7
Final notification: 4 months

Officer and Directors:* Rev. Vincent McCutcheon,* Pres.; Nadyne Kokot,* V.P.; George Weems,* Secy.; Sally Anguiano; Antonio Barreda; Charles Comer; Fred de Cristobal; Gilbert Diaz; Robert Hoggs; Rev. James Hunter; Michael Monagan; Anthony Mrvan; Joseph Rivich; Mark A. Sanders; James R. Scott; Joseph Semancik.
EIN: 352025208

3145
Elkhart County Community Foundation, Inc. ✧

KeyBank Bldg.
101 S. Main St., P.O. Box 2932
Elkhart, IN 46515-2932 (574) 295-8761
Contact: W. Earl Taylor, Pres.
FAX: (574) 389-7497; E-mail: elk.ccf@verizon.net; Additional E-mail: weteccf@aol.com; URL: http://www.elkhartccf.org

Established in 1987 in IN; incorporated in 1989.
Foundation type: Community foundation.
Financial data (yr. ended 6/30/04): Assets, $34,205,947 (M); gifts received, $2,320,285; expenditures, $2,007,517; giving activities include $1,225,907 for 258+ grants, and $300,320 for 75 grants to individuals.
Purpose and activities: The foundation seeks to maintain funding in the areas of arts and culture, community development, education, health, and human services.
Fields of interest: Arts; Education; Health care; Youth development; Human services; Community development.
Type of support: General/operating support; Continuing support; Equipment; Endowments; Program development; Seed money; Scholarship funds; Technical assistance; Scholarships—to individuals; In-kind gifts; Matching/challenge support.
Limitations: Giving limited to Elkhart County, IN. No support for religious or sectarian purposes. No grants to individuals (except for scholarships), or for operating budgets or budget deficits, annual funds, conferences, scholarly research, endowments, personal travel, or films.
Publications: Application guidelines; Annual report (including application guidelines); Grants list; Informational brochure; Newsletter; Occasional report.
Application information: Visit foundation Web site for application forms and guidelines. The foundation strongly recommends first filing a letter of interest before preparing a complete grant application. Application form required.

Initial approach: Letter of Interest (no longer than 2 pages)
Copies of proposal: 16

Deadline(s): Last Fridays of Mar., June, Aug., and Dec. for Letters of Interest; Mar. 1, June 1, Sept. 1, and Nov. 1 for application form
Board meeting date(s): Quarterly
Final notification: Within 3 weeks for Letter of Interest; Apr., July, Oct., and Dec. for grant determination

Officers and Directors:* John Leavitt,* Chair.; John Fidler,* Vice-Chair.; W. Earl Taylor,* Pres.; Nancy Banks,* Secy.; John Wolf,* Treas.; Rebecca Ball-Miller; Wilbur Bontrager; Sarah Chocola; Andy Frech; Craig Fulmer; Tom Irions; Randall Jacobs; Toni Johnson; Michael Kubacki; Allan Ludwig; Rex Martin; Elizabeth Naquin-Borger; William Phillips; Mike Pianowski; Don Pletcher; Richard Snyder; Jerry Trolz.
Number of staff: 1 full-time professional; 1 part-time professional; 1 full-time support; 1 part-time support.
EIN: 311255886
Selected grants: The following grants were reported in 2005.
$32,500 to ADEC, Bristol, IN. For Corporate Guardianship Program.
$15,000 to La Casa of Goshen, Goshen, IN. For community outreach position.
$15,000 to Life Treatment Centers, South Bend, IN. For intake/treatment coordinator.
$15,000 to North Central Indiana Food Bank, South Bend, IN. For capital improvement plan.
$13,000 to Faith Mission of Elkhart, Elkhart, IN. To purchase passenger van.
$6,425 to Youth for Christ of Elkhart County, Elkhart, IN. For expansion of at-risk youth program.
$5,000 to Elkhart Symphony Society, Elkhart, IN. For general support.
$3,000 to Midwest Museum of American Art, Elkhart, IN. For Smithsonian Institution traveling exhibition entitled, The Art of the Stamp.
$2,228 to Lifeline Youth and Family Services, Fort Wayne, IN. For CARE Program's home based services.
$2,000 to American Red Cross, Elkhart, IN. To purchase BAT program supplies to expand Elkhart Schools.

3146
English-Bonter-Mitchell Foundation ▼ ✧

c/o National City Bank
110 W. Berry St.
Fort Wayne, IN 46802-2316

Established in 1972 in IN.
Donors: Mary Tower English; Louise Bonter; and others.
Foundation type: Independent foundation.
Financial data (yr. ended 12/31/04): Assets, $124,297,302 (M); expenditures, $6,230,983; qualifying distributions, $5,713,867; giving activities include $5,394,000 for 141 grants (high: $270,749; low: $500; average: $5,000–$50,000).
Purpose and activities: Giving primarily for cultural programs and programs for youth; support also for higher education, hospitals, churches and religious organizations, social services, health, and community development.
Fields of interest: Arts; Higher education; Hospitals (general); Health care; Health organizations, association; Human services; Children/youth, services; Community development; Christian agencies & churches.

Limitations: Applications not accepted. Giving primarily in Fort Wayne, IN. No grants to individuals.
Application information: Contributes only to pre-selected organizations.
Trustee: National City Bank.
EIN: 356247168
Selected grants: The following grants were reported in 2004.
$270,749 to Auburn Automotive Heritage, Auburn, IN. For matching grant for operating support.
$215,000 to Fort Wayne Park Foundation, Fort Wayne, IN. For matching grant for skateboard park and Lifetime Sports Academy.
$195,000 to Indiana University-Purdue University at Fort Wayne Foundation, Fort Wayne, IN. For dorm pledge and various programs.
$140,000 to United Way of Allen County, Fort Wayne, IN. For operating support.
$75,000 to Girl Scouts of the U.S.A., Limberlost Council, Fort Wayne, IN. For operating support.
$75,000 to YMCA of Metropolitan Fort Wayne, Fort Wayne, IN. For operating support.
$30,000 to Allen County Local Education Fund, Fort Wayne, IN. For operating support.
$30,000 to Youth for Christ, Fort Wayne, IN. For operating support.
$25,000 to Indiana Humanities Council, Indianapolis, IN. For operating support.
$25,000 to YMCA, Cole Center Family, Kendallville, IN. For operating support.

3147
Richard M. Fairbanks Foundation, Inc. ▼
(formerly Fairbanks Foundation, Inc.)

9292 N. Meridan St., Ste. 304
Indianapolis, IN 46260 (317) 846-7111
Contact: Betsy Bikoff, V.P. and Chief Grantmaking Off.
FAX: (317) 844-0167; e-mail (for Betsy Bikoff): Bikoff@rmfairbanksfoundation.org; URL: http://www.rmfairbanksfoundation.org

Established in 1986 in IN.
Donor: Richard M. Fairbanks†.
Foundation type: Independent foundation.
Financial data (yr. ended 12/31/04): Assets, $302,315,761 (M); expenditures, $12,341,908; qualifying distributions, $10,652,388; giving activities include $10,457,799 for 85 grants (high: $2,600,000; low: $150; average: $10,000–$500,000).
Purpose and activities: Support primarily for health care, human services and local public benefit.
Fields of interest: Health care; Human services; Community development.
Type of support: General/operating support; Continuing support; Annual campaigns; Capital campaigns; Building/renovation; Equipment; Endowments; Program development; Seed money; Research; Technical assistance; Program evaluation; Matching/challenge support.
Limitations: Giving primarily in greater Indianapolis, IN. No support for political organizations. No grants to individuals.
Publications: Application guidelines; Financial statement; Grants list; Newsletter.
Application information: Proposals should be submitted to the foundation only upon request. Unsolicited full proposals will not be accepted. Application form not required.

Initial approach: Telephone or letter of inquiry (2-3 pages)
Copies of proposal: 1

Deadline(s): March 1, July 10, Oct. 15
Board meeting date(s): Spring, summer, and fall
Final notification: Day after board meetings
Officers and Directors:* Leonard J. Betley,* Chair., C.E.O. and Pres.; Mary E. "Betsy" Bikoff, V.P. and Chief Grantmaking Off.; Thomas H. Ristine,* Secy.; Roger S. Snowdon,* Treas.; Daniel C. Appel; Christopher M. Callahan, M.D.; Jonathan B. Fairbanks; Elizabeth N. Mann.
Number of staff: 3 full-time professional; 1 full-time support.
EIN: 311189885
Selected grants: The following grants were reported in 2005.
$10,000,000 to Central Indiana Corporate Partnership Foundation, Indianapolis, IN. For Fairbanks Institute, new entity in Indianapolis which will work to predict, prevent and treat common diseases affecting many Americans.
$3,000,000 to University High School of Indiana, Carmel, IN. For Phase II construction of Fairbanks Hall Classroom Building.
$2,000,000 to Indiana Health Information Exchange, Indianapolis, IN. For development of clinical quality support services.
$1,680,000 to Layalina Productions, DC. For program support.
$250,000 to Saint Christopher Center, Indianapolis, IN. For capital project.
$150,000 to Greater Educational Opportunities (GEO) Foundation, Indianapolis, IN. For Indiana Charter Schools Services Center.
$25,000 to Indiana State Museum Foundation, Indianapolis, IN. For renovation of Broadcasters Hall of Fame area and Global Indiana Gallery.
$15,000 to College Mentors for Kids, Indianapolis, IN. For college students mentoring at-risk elementary students.
$15,000 to Good News Mission, Indianapolis, IN. For Good Samaritan Health Clinic.
$10,000 to United Christmas Service, Indianapolis, IN. For general operating support.

3148
Finish Line Youth Foundation, Inc. ✧
3308 N. Mitthoeffer Rd.
Indianapolis, IN   46235-2332   (317) 899-1022
Contact: David Klapper, Dir.
URL: http://www.finishline.com/store/corporate_info/youthfoundation.jsp

Established in 1998 in IN.
Donors: The Finish Line, Inc.; The Sablosky Family Foundation, Inc.; Reebok International Ltd.; The Cohen Family Foundation, Inc.
Foundation type: Company-sponsored foundation.
Financial data (yr. ended 12/31/04): Assets, $2,397,460 (M); gifts received, $1,295,966; expenditures, $556,190; qualifying distributions, $544,748; giving activities include $333,717 for 59 grants (high: $110,151; low: $700).
Purpose and activities: The foundation supports organizations involved with athletics and children and youth. Special emphasis is directed toward programs designed to promote education, sports, and exercise; place importance on living a healthy lifestyle; bolster confidence and leadership skills; and teach the importance of teamwork.
Fields of interest: Recreation; Children/youth, services.
Type of support: Program development.
Limitations: Applications not accepted. Giving primarily in areas of company operations. No

support for religious or political organizations, fraternal, labor, or veterans' organizations, or foundations affiliated with a for-profit company. No grants to individuals, or for endowments, debt reduction, beauty or talent contests, or travel.
Application information:
Board meeting date(s): Feb., May, Aug., and Nov.
Officers and Directors:* Kevin Flynn,* Pres.; Gary D. Cohen,* V.P.; Nancy Zinger, Secy.; Kevin Wampler,* Treas.; Alan Cohen; Bob Edwards; Marianna Hagen; David Klapper; Mark Lallathin; Mike Marchetti; Larry Sablosky.
EIN: 352059749
Selected grants: The following grants were reported in 2004.
$11,000 to United Negro College Fund, Indianapolis, IN.
$5,760 to Special Olympics of Indiana, Indianapolis, IN.
$5,000 to Big Brothers/Big Sisters of Central Indiana, Indianapolis, IN.
$5,000 to Childrens Cancer Association, Portland, OR.
$5,000 to Fine Arts Society of Indianapolis, Indianapolis, IN.
$5,000 to Partners in Neighborhood Growth, Birmingham, AL.
$5,000 to University of Indianapolis, Indianapolis, IN.
$4,487 to DePelchin Childrens Center, Houston, TX.
$2,660 to Cincinnati Childrens Hospital Medical Center, Cincinnati, OH.
$2,500 to Camp Twin Lakes, Atlanta, GA.

3149
Foellinger Foundation, Inc. ▼
520 E. Berry St.
Fort Wayne, IN   46802   (260) 422-2900
Contact: Cheryl K. Taylor, C.E.O.
FAX: (260) 422-9436; *E-mail:* info@foellinger.org; *E-mail* (for Cheryl K. Taylor): cheryl@foellinger.org;
URL: http://www.foellinger.org

Incorporated in 1958 in IN.
Donors: Esther A. Foellinger†; Helene R. Foellinger†.
Foundation type: Independent foundation.
Financial data (yr. ended 8/31/05): Assets, $167,306,981 (M); expenditures, $8,751,485; qualifying distributions, $8,103,214; giving activities include $7,213,439 for 150 grants (high: $380,000; low: $3,000; average: $2,000–$100,000), and $175,398 for 3 foundation-administered programs.
Purpose and activities: Giving primarily in Allen County, IN, for early childhood development, youth development and family development, especially for the economically disadvantaged, and organizational effectiveness.
Fields of interest: Children/youth, services; Family services; Economically disadvantaged.
Type of support: Continuing support; General/operating support; Capital campaigns; Building/renovation; Equipment; Land acquisition; Program development; Research; Technical assistance; Consulting services; Program evaluation; Matching/challenge support.
Limitations: Giving primarily in the Allen County, IN, area. Generally, no grants for religious groups for religious purposes, elementary or secondary schools independent of their school systems, or purposes taxpayers are expected to support. No grants to individuals, or for endowments, deficit

financing, sponsorships, special events, conferences, commercial advertising, or group trips.
Publications: Application guidelines; Annual report; Grants list; Informational brochure (including application guidelines); Newsletter; Occasional report.
Application information: See foundation's Web site for downloadable grant guideline packet. Application form not required.
Initial approach: Grant application
Copies of proposal: 1
Deadline(s): First working day in Feb., Aug. or Nov., exceptions to deadlines for invited applications
Board meeting date(s): Quarterly in Feb., May, Aug., and Nov.
Final notification: One week after board meeting
Officers and Directors:* Barbara A. Burt,* Chair.; Carolyn R. Hughes,* Vice-Chair. and Secy.; Cheryl K. Taylor,* C.E.O. and Pres.; David A. Bobilya, Treas.; Mary F. Barksdale; Thomas J. Felts; Joanne B. Lantz, Ph.D.; Richard B. Pierce.
Number of staff: 3 full-time professional; 3 full-time support.
EIN: 356027059
Selected grants: The following grants were reported in 2005.
$500,000 to Lutheran Homes, Fort Wayne, IN. For capital support for intergenerational program, payable over 4 years.
$300,000 to Wellspring Interfaith Social Services, Fort Wayne, IN. payable over 2 years.
$225,000 to Literacy Alliance, Fort Wayne, IN. For operating support, payable over 3 years.
$200,000 to Visiting Nurse and Hospice Home, Fort Wayne, IN. For capital support for building expansion, payable over 3 years.
$150,000 to Arts United of Greater Fort Wayne, Fort Wayne, IN. For operating support.
$150,000 to Community Foundation of Greater Fort Wayne, Fort Wayne, IN. For program support of Strategic Resource Development plan, payable over 2 years.
$100,000 to Catholic Charities of the Diocese of Fort Wayne-South Bend, Fort Wayne, IN. For teen parenting program support, payable over 2 years.
$50,000 to Youth for Christ, Fort Wayne, IN. For Charla De Chicas program support, payable over 2 years.
$43,950 to Fort Wayne Museum of Art, Fort Wayne, IN. For project support for building relationships for success, payable over 3.50 years.
$28,000 to East Allen County Schools, Fort Wayne, IN. For New Haven Elementary School.

3150
Ford Meter Box Foundation, Inc.
775 Manchester Ave.
P.O. Box 443
Wabash, IN   46992-0443
Contact: Thomas G. Vanosdol, Chair.

Established in 1988 in IN.
Donor: The Ford Meter Box Co., Inc.
Foundation type: Company-sponsored foundation.
Financial data (yr. ended 12/31/05): Assets, $3,232,899 (M); expenditures, $665,170; qualifying distributions, $644,319; giving activities include $644,085 for 47 grants (high: $500,000; low: $150).
Purpose and activities: The foundation supports organizations involved with arts and culture,

education, health, youth development, community development, and Christianity.

Fields of interest: Arts; Education; Health care; Youth development; Community development; Christian agencies & churches.

Type of support: Capital campaigns; Building/renovation; General/operating support.

Limitations: Giving primarily in Wabash County, IN.

Publications: Application guidelines.

Application information: Application form not required.

Initial approach: Proposal
Copies of proposal: 1
Deadline(s): None

Officers and Board Members:* Thomas G. Vanosdol,* Chair.; Daniel H. Ford, Vice-Chair.; Marta D. Gidley,* Secy.; Steven R. Ford,* Treas.

EIN: 351253080

Selected grants: The following grants were reported in 2005.

$500,000 to Honeywell Foundation, Wabash, IN.

$30,000 to Independent Colleges of Indiana, Indianapolis, IN.

$2,500 to Community Foundation of Wabash County, North Manchester, IN.

$500 to Indiana Wesleyan University, Marion, IN.

3151

Four D Foundation, Inc. ◇

2000 N. Wells St., Bldg. 2
Fort Wayne, IN 46808

Established in 2002 in IN.

Donors: Donald R. Willis; Doris D. Willis; Devin R. Willis; Brenda Willis.

Foundation type: Independent foundation.

Financial data (yr. ended 12/31/05): Assets, $336,598 (M); gifts received, $1,775,000; expenditures, $1,850,645; qualifying distributions, $1,840,000; giving activities include $1,840,000 for 3 grants (high: $1,705,000; low: $10,000).

Fields of interest: Education; Community development.

Limitations: Applications not accepted. Giving primarily in IN. No grants to individuals.

Application information: Contributes only to pre-selected organizations.

Directors: Dacia D. Michael; Devin R. Willis; Donald R. Willis; Doris D. Willis.

EIN: 113665492

3152

Freedom 22 Foundation ◇

c/o The Trust Co. of Oxford
P.O. Box 40856
Indianapolis, IN 46240-0856

Established in 1997 in IN.

Donors: Charles Asher; Barbara Asher.

Foundation type: Independent foundation.

Financial data (yr. ended 12/31/05): Assets, $3,948,619 (M); expenditures, $472,686; qualifying distributions, $457,581; giving activities include $453,167 for 51 grants (high: $32,325; low: $400).

Purpose and activities: Giving primarily for Christian schools.

Fields of interest: Education; Christian agencies & churches.

Limitations: Applications not accepted. Giving primarily in IN. No grants to individuals.

Application information: Contributes only to pre-selected organizations.

Managers: Barbara Asher; Charles Asher.

EIN: 356653987

Selected grants: The following grants were reported in 2005.

$40,650 to Christian Center, Anderson, IN. 2 grants: $19,425, $21,225

$16,000 to Earlham School of Religion, Richmond, IN.

$7,250 to Montessori School.

$5,500 to Montessori Academy, Arlington, TX. 2 grants: $2,500, $3,000

$5,000 to Earlham College, Richmond, IN.

$2,000 to Logan Community Resources, South Bend, IN.

$500 to Christian Center School, Hayden, ID.

3153

The Froderman Foundation, Inc. ◇

4325 U.S. Highway 41 S.
P.O. Box 10039
Terre Haute, IN 47801 (812) 232-2364
Contact: Mark Fuson, Pres.
FAX: (812) 232-8414;
E-mail: markfuson@drivefuson.com; *URL:* http://www.frodermanfoundation.com

Established in 1962 in IN.

Donors: Harvey Froderman‡; Mrs. Harvey Froderman.

Foundation type: Independent foundation.

Financial data (yr. ended 6/30/05): Assets, $11,401,904 (M); expenditures, $425,509; qualifying distributions, $370,595; giving activities include $370,595 for 29 grants (high: $50,000; low: $900).

Purpose and activities: Funding primarily for religion, higher education, hospitals and human services.

Fields of interest: Higher education; Hospitals (general); Human services; Christian agencies & churches.

Type of support: Building/renovation; Equipment; Publication; Scholarship funds.

Limitations: Giving primarily in IN. No grants to individuals, or for operating budgets.

Application information: Application form available upon request. Application form required.

Initial approach: Letter
Copies of proposal: 1
Deadline(s): None
Board meeting date(s): Apr., June, Sept., and Dec.

Officers: Mark J. Fuson, Pres.; Carl M. Froderman, V.P.; Esten Fuson, Secy.-Treas.

EIN: 356025283

Selected grants: The following grants were reported in 2003.

$55,667 to Union Hospital Foundation, Terre Haute, IN.

$50,000 to Saint Vincent Hospital Foundation, Saint Vincent Children's Hospital, Indianapolis, IN.

$50,000 to World Gospel Church, Terre Haute, IN. For Missionary Fund.

$25,000 to Special Olympics of Indiana, Indianapolis, IN.

$10,000 to Indiana State University Foundation, Terre Haute, IN. For Medical School Baccalaureate Program.

$8,624 to Fellowship of Christian Athletes, Marshall, IN.

$7,500 to Light House Mission, Terre Haute, IN.

$7,000 to Wheeler Mission Ministries, Indianapolis, IN.

$5,000 to Fairbanks Hospital, Indianapolis, IN.

$1,355 to Saint Lukes United Methodist Church, Indianapolis, IN. For preschool.

3154

Garcia Family Charitable Foundation Trust ◇ ☆

c/o KeyBank N.A., Trust Div.
202 S. Michigan St.
South Bend, IN 46601

Established in 1998 in IN.

Donor: Juan C. Garcia, M.D.

Foundation type: Independent foundation.

Financial data (yr. ended 12/31/05): Assets, $1,945,638 (M); gifts received, $367,200; expenditures, $561,309; qualifying distributions, $553,034; giving activities include $544,215 for 31 grants (high: $226,365; low: $1,000).

Purpose and activities: Giving for education, health and family services, and for human services.

Fields of interest: Education; Health care; Cancer; Residential/custodial care, hospices; Federated giving programs; Roman Catholic agencies & churches.

Limitations: Applications not accepted. Giving primarily in IN. No grants to individuals.

Application information: Contributes only to pre-selected organizations.

Advisors: Juan C. Garcia, M.D.; Maria N. Garcia.

Trustee: KeyBank N.A.

EIN: 356664933

Selected grants: The following grants were reported in 2004.

$70,000 to Team Tobati, New Britain, CT.

$23,000 to American Cancer Society, Mishawaka, IN.

$10,000 to United Health Services of Saint Joseph County, South Bend, IN.

$5,000 to Goshen Hospital Association, Goshen, IN.

$5,000 to Health Visions Midwest, East Chicago, IN.

$5,000 to Logan Community Resources, South Bend, IN.

$5,000 to Maple City Health Care Center, Goshen, IN.

$5,000 to March of Dimes Birth Defects Foundation, South Bend, IN.

$5,000 to Servants of the Streets Ministries, Elkhart, IN.

$3,000 to Boy Scouts of America, La Salle Council, South Bend, IN.

3155

Eugene and Marilyn Glick Foundation Corporation ▼ ◇

P.O. Box 40177
Indianapolis, IN 46240
Contact: Sharon Kibbe, Dir.

Established in 1982.

Donors: Eugene B. Glick; Marilyn K. Glick.

Foundation type: Independent foundation.

Financial data (yr. ended 11/30/05): Assets, $108,209,029 (M); gifts received, $12,952,732; expenditures, $5,212,569; qualifying distributions, $4,896,260; giving activities include $4,872,865 for 155 grants (high: $3,850,000; low: $40; average: $100–$1,000).

Purpose and activities: Giving primarily for higher education, and for youth development, community development, and the arts.

Fields of interest: Arts; Higher education; Education; Health organizations, association; Recreation; Human services; Children/youth, services; Foundations (community); Federated giving programs; Christian agencies & churches; Jewish agencies & temples.

Type of support: General/operating support; Capital campaigns; Program development; Matching/challenge support.

Limitations: Giving primarily in Indianapolis, IN. No grants to individuals.

Application information:

  Initial approach: Letter

  Deadline(s): None

Officers: Eugene B. Glick, Pres.; Marilyn K. Glick, Secy.-Treas.

Directors: James T. Bisesi; Sharon Kibbe.

Number of staff: 1 full-time professional.

EIN: 351549707

Selected grants: The following grants were reported in 2005.

$3,850,000 to Central Indiana Community Foundation, Indianapolis, IN. For Eugene and Marilyn Glick Foundation Fund.

$250,000 to Crooked Creek Service Center, Indianapolis, IN. For Fay Biccard Glick Center and Family Pavilion.

$250,000 to Second Helpings, Indianapolis, IN. For capital campaign.

$204,000 to Childrens Bureau of Indianapolis, Indianapolis, IN. 3 grants: $91,000 (For Fay Biccard Glick Family Place and Rachel Glick Courage Center), $100,000 (For PRO-100 program), $13,000 (For arborist program).

$100,000 to Indianapolis Art Center, Indianapolis, IN. For Marilyn K. Glick Center.

$50,000 to Indiana Historical Society, Indianapolis, IN. For Fay Biccard Glick Jewish History of Indiana Fund.

$33,334 to Indianapolis-Marion County Public Library Foundation, Indianapolis, IN. For computer training lab.

$20,000 to United Way of Central Indiana, Indianapolis, IN. For annual support.

3156
Robert Goldstine Foundation, Inc. ◇

c/o Lloyd Ehmcke
2020 E. Washington Blvd., Ste. 400
Fort Wayne, IN   46803

Established in 2002 in IN.

Donor: Robert I. Goldstine†.

Foundation type: Independent foundation.

Financial data (yr. ended 12/31/05): Assets, $10,108,968 (M); expenditures, $515,222; qualifying distributions, $468,750; giving activities include $468,750 for 21 grants (high: $60,000; low: $1,500).

Fields of interest: Performing arts, orchestra (symphony); Higher education; Human services, travelers' aid; Federated giving programs.

Limitations: Applications not accepted. Giving primarily in Fort Wayne, IN. No grants to individuals.

Application information: Contributes only to pre-selected organizations.

Officers: Stephen J. Wesner, Pres.; Lloyd E. Ehmcke, Secy.

Directors: Philip L. Carson; Stephanie Kaskel McCormick; Donald F. Schenkel.

EIN: 352151920

3157
Pierre F. and Enid Goodrich Foundation

(formerly Thirty Five Twenty, Inc.)
8335 Allison Pointe Trail, Ste. 300
Indianapolis, IN   46250-1687   (317) 842-0880
Contact: Emilio J. Pacheco, Pres.

Incorporated in 1965 in IN.

Donors: Enid Goodrich†; Pierre F. Goodrich†.

Foundation type: Independent foundation.

Financial data (yr. ended 4/30/06): Assets, $20,593,380 (M); expenditures, $1,022,642; qualifying distributions, $955,461; giving activities include $836,000 for 37 grants (high: $55,000; low: $10,000).

Purpose and activities: The foundation makes grants for general support and special projects that support further educational activities that are concerned with human liberty and individual freedom within a free society.

Fields of interest: Humanities; Education; Economics; Political science.

Type of support: General/operating support; Program development; Conferences/seminars; Research.

Limitations: Giving on a national basis. No support for government agencies, or schools and universities, hospitals or medical research facilities. No grants to individuals, or for annual campaigns, emergency funds, deficit financing, capital or endowment funds, scholarships, fellowships, matching gifts, or demonstration projects; no loans.

Application information: Application form required.

  Initial approach: Letter

  Copies of proposal: 1

  Deadline(s): None

  Board meeting date(s): Apr. and Oct.

  Final notification: Within 1 month, if denied

Officers and Directors:* T. Alan Russell,* Chair.; Emilio J. Pacheco, Pres.; Sandra J. Schaller, Secy. and Cont.; Chris L. Talley,* Treas.; Manuel F. Ayau; Ruth E. Connolly; Richard W. Duesenberg; Helen W. Garlotte.

Number of staff: 5 part-time professional; 2 part-time support.

EIN: 356056960

Selected grants: The following grants were reported in 2004.

$60,000 to Mont Pelerin Society, Alexandria, VA.

$40,000 to Federalist Society for Law and Public Policy Studies, DC.

$25,000 to International Foundation for Research in Experimental Economics (IFREE), Tucson, AZ.

$20,000 to Foundation for Individual Rights in Education, Philadelphia, PA.

$20,000 to Property and Environment Research Center, Bozeman, MT.

$20,000 to Santa Clara University, Civil Society Institute, Santa Clara, CA.

$15,000 to Acton Institute for the Study of Religion and Liberty, Grand Rapids, MI.

$15,000 to Institute of Economic Affairs, London, England. .

$10,000 to Fraser Institute, Vancouver, Canada. .

$10,000 to Instituto Liberal do Rio de Janeiro, Rio de Janeiro, Brazil. .

3158
The W. C. Griffith Foundation ◇

320 High St.
Muncie, IN   47305   (812) 461-9789
Application address: c/o Old National Trust, 101 W. Ohio St., No. 1450, Indianapolis, IN 46204, tel.: (317) 693-2504

Established in 1959 in IN.

Donors: William C. Griffith†; Ruth Perry Griffith†.

Foundation type: Independent foundation.

Financial data (yr. ended 11/30/05): Assets, $12,839,183 (M); gifts received, $767,192; expenditures, $602,374; qualifying distributions, $533,120; giving activities include $528,500 for 98 grants (high: $45,000; low: $500).

Purpose and activities: Support primarily for hospitals, health associations, medical and cancer research, the arts, including music and museums, community funds and development, higher, secondary, and other education, family planning services, child welfare, the homeless, the environment, libraries, and Christian religious organizations.

Fields of interest: Museums; Performing arts, music; Arts; Secondary school/education; Higher education; Libraries/library science; Education; Environment; Hospitals (general); Reproductive health, family planning; Health organizations, association; Cancer; Medical research, institute; Cancer research; Children/youth, services; Homeless, human services; Community development; Federated giving programs; Christian agencies & churches; Minorities; Homeless.

Type of support: Continuing support; Capital campaigns; Building/renovation.

Limitations: Giving primarily in Indianapolis, IN. No grants to individuals, or for scholarships or fellowships.

Application information: Application form not required.

  Initial approach: Letter

  Copies of proposal: 1

  Deadline(s): None

  Board meeting date(s): June and Nov.

Advisors: Ruthelen Griffith Burns; Charles P. Griffith, Jr.; Walter S. Griffith; William C. Griffith III; Wendy Griffith Kortepeter.

Trustee: Old National Trust Co.

Number of staff: 1 part-time support.

EIN: 356007742

Selected grants: The following grants were reported in 2003.

$50,000 to James Whitcomb Riley Memorial Association, Indianapolis, IN. For operating support.

$45,000 to YMCA Camp Tecumseh, Brookston, IN. For operating support.

$35,000 to Brebeuf Preparatory School, Indianapolis, IN. For operating support.

$25,000 to Eiteljorg Museum of American Indians and Western Art, Indianapolis, IN. For operating support.

$20,000 to Indianapolis Senior Citizens Center, Indianapolis, IN. For operating support.

$16,500 to Indiana Repertory Theater, Indianapolis, IN. For operating support.

$10,000 to Indianapolis Downtown, Indianapolis, IN. For operating support.

$10,000 to Oaks Academy, Indianapolis, IN. For operating support.

$5,000 to Museum of Art, Fort Lauderdale, FL. For operating support.

$5,000 to Orchard School, Indianapolis, IN. For operating support.

3159
Guidant Foundation ▼ ✧
111 Monument Cir., Ste. 2900
Indianapolis, IN 46204 (317) 971-2272
Contact: Pat Kuhl
FAX: (317) 971-2118; E-mail: pkuhl@guidant.com;
URL: http://www.guidant.com/foundation/

Established in 1996 in IN.
Donors: Guidant Corp.; Advanced Cardiovascular Systems, Inc.; Intermedics, Inc.
Foundation type: Company-sponsored foundation.
Financial data (yr. ended 12/31/05): Assets, $1,815,514 (M); gifts received, $13,000,000; expenditures, $14,135,369; qualifying distributions, $14,135,368; giving activities include $13,122,065 for 409 grants (high: $1,039,000; low: $33), and $728,437 for 20 employee matching gifts.
Purpose and activities: The foundation supports organizations involved with arts and culture, education, health, cardiovascular patient education and advocacy, and human services.
Fields of interest: Arts; Higher education; Education; Health care; Heart & circulatory diseases; Human services.
Type of support: General/operating support; Program development; Conferences/seminars; Curriculum development; Fellowships; Employee volunteer services; Employee matching gifts; Matching/challenge support.
Limitations: Giving on a national basis, with emphasis on areas of company operations. No support for political organizations. No grants to individuals, or for surgery, medical equipment, hospitalization costs, travel expenses, honorariums, construction, debt reduction, fundraising activities related to individual sponsorships, or memorials.
Publications: Application guidelines; Grants list.
Application information: Unsolicited requests from arts organizations located outside areas of company operations are not accepted. Application form required.
Initial approach: Complete online application form
Deadline(s): May 30 and Nov. 30; none for organizations located in areas of company operations
Board meeting date(s): Jan. and July
Final notification: 2 weeks following board meetings; within 90 days for organizations located in areas of company operations
Officers and Trustees:* James R. Baumgardt, Pres.; Keith E. Brauer,* V.P.; Ronald W. Dollens,* V.P.; Fred McCoy,* V.P.; Guido Neels, V.P.; Rob Allen, Secy.
Number of staff: 1 full-time professional; 1 full-time support.
EIN: 351969142
Selected grants: The following grants were reported in 2004.
$1,700,000 to Indiana University-Purdue University, Indianapolis, IN. For endowment.
$1,000,000 to Duke University, Durham, NC. For endowment.
$638,000 to Heart Rhythm Foundation, DC. For North American Society of Pacing and Electrophysiology (NASPE) Fellowship.
$350,000 to Cardiovascular and Interventional Radiology Research and Education Foundation,

Legs for Life, Fairfax, VA. For Patient Advocacy Initiative, Legs for Life, national leg pain screening campaign for peripheral vascular disease.
$250,000 to American Diabetes Association, National Service Center, Alexandria, VA. For Patient Advocacy Initiatives.
$200,000 to Stanford University, Stanford, CA. For Heart Health Network Program.
$130,000 to Purdue University, West Lafayette, IN.
$120,000 to Association of Black Cardiologists, Atlanta, GA. For Physician Fellowships.
$75,000 to Heart Failure Society of America, Saint Paul, MN. For Physician Fellowships.
$25,000 to Florida A & M University, Tallahassee, FL.

3160
Hancock County Community Foundation, Inc. ✧
312 E. Main St.
Greenfield, IN 46140 (317) 462-8870
Contact: Mary Gibble, Pres.
FAX: (317) 467-3330; E-mail: mgibble@hccf.cc;
URL: http://www.hccf.cc

Established in 1992 in IN.
Foundation type: Community foundation.
Financial data (yr. ended 12/31/05): Assets, $12,428,953 (M); gifts received, $854,380; expenditures, $1,221,529; giving activities include $880,240 for grants.
Purpose and activities: The foundation provides philanthropic leadership to effectively manage and direct the resources of community donors in ways which enrich and enhance the quality of life in Hancock County, IN.
Fields of interest: Arts; Education; Health care; Children/youth, services; Human services; Community development; Youth.
Type of support: Equipment; Conferences/seminars; Seed money; Curriculum development; Scholarship funds; Technical assistance; Consulting services; Matching/challenge support.
Limitations: Giving limited to Hancock County, IN. No support for sectarian religious purposes. No grants to individuals.
Publications: Application guidelines; Annual report; Informational brochure; Newsletter.
Application information: Visit foundation Web site for application guidelines. The foundation requests full proposals based on letters of intent. Application form required.
Initial approach: Letter of intent
Copies of proposal: 3
Deadline(s): Feb. 2 for letter of intent; Mar. 2 for full proposal
Board meeting date(s): 2nd Thur. of each month
Final notification: Apr.
Officers and Directors:* Rick Edwards,* Chair.; Gregg Morelock,* Vice-Chair.; Mary Gibble, Pres.; Ann Vail,* Secy.; Jim Miller,* Treas.; Phyllis Polizotto, Cont.; Wayne Beck; Cherie L. Burrow; Dennis Chapman; Jaclyn L. Davis; Howard Green; Jaris Hammond; Pam Hayes; Chris McQueeney; David R. O'Donnell; Patty Paxton; Darlene Seifert; Tom Seng; Darrell Thomas; David Woods.
Number of staff: 3 full-time professional; 1 part-time professional; 1 full-time support.
EIN: 351837729

3161
Harrison County Community Foundation, Inc.
405 N. Capitol, Ste. 104
P.O. Box 279
Corydon, IN 47112 (812) 738-6668
Contact: Steve A. Gilliland, Exec. Dir.
FAX: (812) 738-6864;
E-mail: steveg@hccfindiana.org; Additional E-mail: staff@hccfindiana.org; URL: http://www.hccfindiana.org

Established in 1996 in IN.
Foundation type: Community foundation.
Financial data (yr. ended 12/31/05): Assets, $55,935,763 (M); gifts received, $12,293,088; expenditures, $6,281,733; giving activities include $2,695,326 for grants, and $210,365 for 140 grants to individuals (high: $6,000; low: $1,000).
Purpose and activities: The foundation was established for the receipt of donations and distribution of income from permanent endowments for the philanthropic purposes of Harrison County, IN. Giving primarily for higher and secondary education; support also for youth activities, health care, the arts, and human services.
Fields of interest: Historic preservation/historical societies; Arts; Secondary school/education; Higher education; Adult education—literacy, basic skills & GED; Scholarships/financial aid; Education; Environment; Health care; Recreation; Youth development; Human services; Community development; Aging; Homeless.
Type of support: General/operating support; Continuing support; Management development/capacity building; Capital campaigns; Building/renovation; Equipment; Land acquisition; Emergency funds; Program development; Conferences/seminars; Publication; Seed money; Curriculum development; Research; Consulting services; Program evaluation; Employee-related scholarships; Scholarships—to individuals; Matching/challenge support.
Limitations: Giving limited to Harrison County, IN. No support for religious organizations for the purpose of furthering their religion. No grants to individuals (except for scholarships), or for transportation costs.
Publications: Application guidelines; Annual report; Financial statement; Grants list; Informational brochure; Multi-year report; Newsletter.
Application information: Visit foundation Web site for application forms and guidelines. No mini-grant request may exceed $1,500. The foundation's staff provides grant training sessions in May and Nov. each year; visit Web site, watch the local newspaper, or contact the staff for specific dates, times and location of these workshops. Application form required.
Initial approach: Submit application and attachments; 1 page letter for mini-grants
Copies of proposal: 6
Deadline(s): Jan. 15 and July 15; prior to monthly board meetings for mini-grants
Board meeting date(s): Monthly, first Mon.
Final notification: Mar. 15 and Sept. 15
Officers and Directors:* Jane Kraft, Pres.; Qudsia Davis,* V.P.; Norbert Rawert,* Secy.; Joel E. Voyles,* Treas.; Steve A. Gilliland, Exec. Dir.; Maryland L. Austin; Paul Beckort; Joyce Bliss; Steven Bodney; Chris Byrd; Brian Churchill; Deborah L. Coleman; Judy G. Hess; Donna Lloyd; Charles E. Lynch; J. Gordon Pendleton; Peter J. Schickel; Sandy

Sherman; Mark Shireman; Bill Thomas; Dale E. Watson; H. Lloyd Whitis.
Number of staff: 1 full-time professional; 2 full-time support.
EIN: 351986569

3162

Hart N. and Simona Hasten Family Foundation, Inc. ◇
3901 W. 86th St., Ste. 470
Indianapolis, IN 46268 (317) 872-0044
Contact: Hart N. Hasten, Dir.

Established in 1996 in IN.
Donor: Hart N. Hasten.
Foundation type: Independent foundation.
Financial data (yr. ended 12/31/04): Assets, $1,694,384 (M); gifts received, $346,640; expenditures, $385,463; qualifying distributions, $380,196; giving activities include $380,516 for 47 grants (high: $97,117; low: $50).
Purpose and activities: Giving primarily to Jewish agencies.
Fields of interest: Higher education; Education; Jewish agencies & temples; Religion.
Limitations: Giving primarily in IN and NY.
Application information:
  Deadline(s): None
Officers and Directors:* Renee Hasten Halevy,* Pres.; Joshua Hasten,* V.P.; Bernard Hasten,* Secy.-Treas.; Hart N. Hasten; Simona Hasten.
EIN: 351998919
Selected grants: The following grants were reported in 2004.
$23,500 to Congregation Bnai Torah, Indianapolis, IN.
$20,000 to Jerusalem Foundation, New York, NY.
$10,000 to Central Fund of Israel, New York, NY.
$5,000 to Indiana University Foundation, Bloomington, IN.
$2,500 to Etz Jacob Hebrew Academy, Los Angeles, CA.
$2,000 to Girls and Boys Town, Boys Town, NE.
$500 to American Friends of Ohel Sarah.
$100 to Jewish National Fund, New York, NY.
$50 to First Christian Church, Bedford, IN.

3163

Mark and Anna Ruth Hasten Family Foundation, Inc. ◇
3901 W. 86th St., Ste. 470
Indianapolis, IN 46268 (317) 872-3345
Contact: Mark Hasten, Dir.

Established in 1996 in IN.
Donors: Mark Hasten; Anna Ruth Hasten.
Foundation type: Independent foundation.
Financial data (yr. ended 12/31/05): Assets, $581,159 (M); gifts received, $60,000; expenditures, $490,304; qualifying distributions, $439,630; giving activities include $439,630 for 118 grants (high: $95,880; low: $10; average: $1,000–$10,000).
Fields of interest: Education; Jewish federated giving programs; Jewish agencies & temples.
International interests: Canada; Israel.
Limitations: Giving primarily in the U.S., with some emphasis on IN and NY; giving also in Israel and Canada.
Application information:

Initial approach: Letter
Deadline(s): None
Officers and Directors:* Edward Hasten,* Pres.; Judith Hasten,* V.P.; Michael Hasten,* V.P.; Monica Hasten Rosenfeld,* Secy.; Anna Ruth Hasten; Mark Hasten.
EIN: 351998923
Selected grants: The following grants were reported in 2004.
$239,600 to Touro College, New York, NY.
$146,398 to Hebrew Academy Foundation of Indianapolis, Indianapolis, IN.
$54,000 to Jewish Federation of Greater Indianapolis, Indianapolis, IN.
$50,000 to Congregation Mosdosh Tash, Boisbriand, Canada. .
$18,190 to Congregation Bnai Torah, Indianapolis, IN.
$11,000 to Mayo Foundation for Medical Education and Research, Rochester, MN.
$5,262 to Jewish Community Center of Indianapolis, Indianapolis, IN.
$2,000 to Bikur Cholim Hospital, Jerusalem, Israel. .
$1,500 to Hadassah University Hospital, Jerusalem, Israel. .
$1,080 to Yeshiva Minchas Eluzar, Brooklyn, NY.

3164

The Health Foundation of Greater Indianapolis, Inc.
429 E. Vermont St., Ste. 300
Indianapolis, IN 46202 (317) 630-1805
Contact: Betty H. Wilson, C.E.O. and Pres.
FAX: (317) 630-1806; *E-mail:* steve@thfgi.org;
URL: http://www.thfgi.org

Established as a private foundation in 1985 in IN; converted from an HMO, Metro Health.
Donors: Deborah Simon; James Spain; AIDSERVE Indiana; Anthem, Inc.; Broadway Cares; Cooke Investment Group; Community Hospitals of Indiana; Indiana Thrift for AIDS; Endagered Species Chocolate; The National Bank of Indianapolis; National City Bank; Efromyson Fund; Central Indiana Community Foundation; Christel DeHaan Family Foundation; Joseph F. Miller Foundation; Indiana State Dept. of Health; Marion County Health Department; Indy Pride; St. Francis Hospital; The Indianapolis Foundation.
Foundation type: Independent foundation.
Financial data (yr. ended 12/31/05): Assets, $33,611,015 (L); gifts received, $578,825; expenditures, $3,489,729; qualifying distributions, $2,473,981; giving activities include $2,473,981 for 55 grants (high: $1,000,000; low: $1,000).
Purpose and activities: Primary areas of focus are adolescent health, including childhood obesity and school-based health clinics, and HIV/AIDS education and services. Grants will be made to neighborhood-based service centers such as neighborhood health centers, multi-service centers, churches, and other not-for-profit agencies and organizations.
Fields of interest: Health care; AIDS; Nutrition; Human services; Children/youth, services; Minorities; African Americans/Blacks; Hispanics/Latinos; Women; AIDS, people with; Economically disadvantaged.
Type of support: General/operating support; Continuing support; Equipment; Program development; Conferences/seminars; Seed money; Technical assistance.

Limitations: Giving limited to Marion County, IN and the seven contiguous counties. No support for sectarian or religious purposes. No grants to individuals, or for advertising, event tickets, research, payment of financial deficit, production and design of educational materials that are currently available for purchase, endowments, or short- or long- term loans.
Publications: Application guidelines; Grants list; Informational brochure; Informational brochure (including application guidelines); Occasional report.
Application information: Application guidelines available on foundation Web site. Application form required.
  Initial approach: Telephone or letter
  Copies of proposal: 18
  Deadline(s): Varies, see foundation Web site for current dates
  Board meeting date(s): 2nd Thur. of Jan., Mar., May and July
Officers and Directors:* Betty H. Wilson, C.E.O. and Pres.; Virginia A. Caine, M.D.*, V.P.; G. Elaine Johnson,* Secy.; David Kelleher,* Treas.; Betty A. Conner; Thomas J. Feeney; Cynthia B. Gardner; Terence P. Kahn; C. Phillip Love; Robert L. North; Robert D. Robinson, M.D.; Lawrence M. Ryan.
Number of staff: 3 full-time professional; 3 full-time support.
EIN: 356203550

3165

Henry County Community Foundation, Inc.
P.O. Box 6006
New Castle, IN 47362 (765) 529-2235
Contact: Jerry Schaeffer, Exec. Dir.
FAX: (765) 529-2284;
E-mail: jerry@henrycountycf.org; *URL:* http://www.henrycountycf.org

Established in 1985 in IN.
Foundation type: Community foundation.
Financial data (yr. ended 12/31/05): Assets, $24,422,841 (M); gifts received, $2,638,781; expenditures, $1,115,233; giving activities include $508,103 for 74 grants (high: $10,000; low: $220).
Purpose and activities: The mission of the foundation is to help where the needs are greatest, and the benefits to the community and its citizens are most substantial. To provide public-spirited donors a vehicle for using their gifts in the best possible way now and in the future, and to provide stewardship for those gifts.
Fields of interest: Arts; Education; Health care; Human services; Government/public administration.
Type of support: Seed money; Research; Publication; Continuing support; Consulting services; Capital campaigns; Building/renovation; Equipment; Emergency funds; Program development; Conferences/seminars; Scholarship funds; Scholarships—to individuals; Exchange programs; Matching/challenge support.
Limitations: Giving limited to Henry County, IN. No grants for operating costs including salaries.
Publications: Application guidelines; Annual report; Grants list; Informational brochure (including application guidelines); Newsletter.
Application information: Attendance at the foundation's grantmaking workshop is required. Application form required.
  Initial approach: Letter, telephone, or in person
  Copies of proposal: 14

Deadline(s): Mar. 31 and Aug. 31
Board meeting date(s): Monthly
Final notification: Within 30 days
Officers and Directors:* Herb Bunch,* Pres.;
Richard Armstrong,* V.P.; Bill Aitchison,* Treas.;
Jerry Schaeffer, Exec. Dir.; Elizabeth Adams; Donald
C. Danielson; Susan Falek-Neal; Jeff Galyen; John
Kellam; David McCord; Ann McGlothlin; Dick Myers;
Dr. Ray Pavy; Steve Pfenninger; James Ray; Jeff
Smiley.
Number of staff: 2 full-time professional; 1 full-time
support; 1 part-time support.
EIN: 311170412
Selected grants: The following grants were reported
in 2005.
$10,000 to Cadiz-Harrison Township Volunteer Fire
   Department, New Castle, IN. For equipment
   update.
$10,000 to Christian Love Help Center, New Castle,
   IN.
$10,000 to Healthy Communities of Henry County,
   New Castle, IN. For Connectivity Plan.
$10,000 to Mooreland Volunteer Fire Department,
   Mooreland, IN. For Self-Contained Breathing
   Apparatus (SCBA) Packs/Air Packs.
$5,000 to Dare to Dream Camp, New Castle, IN.
$4,000 to Second Harvest Food Bank, Anderson, IN.
   For deliveries.
$3,100 to New Castle Police Department, New
   Castle, IN. For SWAT bulletproof vests.
$2,500 to Make a Difference Knightstown,
   Knightstown, IN. For beautification of town
   square.
$1,170 to Spiceland-Dunreith Volunteer Fire
   Department, IN. For external defibrillator.
$220 to Cadiz, Town of, Cadiz, IN. For tornado siren
   installation.

3166

Heritage Fund - The Community Foundation of Bartholomew County ◇

(formerly Heritage Fund of Bartholomew County,
Inc.)
538 Franklin St.
P.O. Box 1547
Columbus, IN 47202-1547 (812) 376-7772
Contact: Sharon Risk Stark, C.E.O. and Pres.; For
grants: Lyn Morgan, Prog. Off.
FAX: (812) 376-0051;
E-mail: hfgrants@sbcglobal.net; Additional E-mail:
hfceo@sbcglobal.net; URL: http://
www.heritagefundbc.com

Incorporated in 1976 in IN.
Foundation type: Community foundation.
Financial data (yr. ended 12/31/04): Assets,
$41,418,537 (M); gifts received, $1,163,574;
expenditures, $3,715,478; giving activities include
$2,403,062 for 96 grants (high: $523,035; low:
$100), and $105,806 for 79 grants to individuals
(high: $8,500; low: $250).
Purpose and activities: The foundation addressed
the broad needs of residents of Bartholomew County
which fall generally into five categories: 1)
Education, including support for programs in
preschool, elementary and secondary education,
higher education, scholarships, and for special
education-related projects; 2) Social services; 3)
Civic affairs, including support of programs related
to economic and community development, criminal
justice, citizen involvement, leadership training, and
other related community activities; 4) Cultural
Affairs, including programs designed to establish a

diversified county cultural program that offers
widespread opportunities for participation and
appreciation; and 5) Health, including support of
hospitals and other medical-related programs.
Emphasis is given to change-oriented and
problem-solving grants which serve as seed money
or pilot project support.
Fields of interest: Arts; Education; Health care;
Health organizations, association; Offenders/
ex-offenders, rehabilitation; Employment; Children/
youth, services; Human services; Community
development; Public affairs; Aging.
Type of support: Management development/
capacity building; Capital campaigns; Building/
renovation; Equipment; Land acquisition;
Emergency funds; Program development;
Conferences/seminars; Publication; Seed money;
Scholarship funds; Research; Technical assistance;
Consulting services; Matching/challenge support.
Limitations: Giving limited to Bartholomew County,
IN. No support for sectarian religious purposes. No
grants to individuals (except for scholarships and
special educational programs), or for annual
campaigns, endowment funds, seminars or trips
(unless there are special circumstances which will
benefit the community), or operating support
(generally); no loans.
Publications: Application guidelines; Annual report;
Informational brochure; Newsletter; Program policy
statement.
Application information: Visit foundation Web site
for application form and guidelines. An organization
will be invited to submit a formal request based on
initial contact with the foundation. Scholarship
payments are made to the educational institutions
for the benefit of the individual recipients.
Application form required.
   Initial approach: Letter or telephone to Prog. Off.
   Copies of proposal: 13
   Deadline(s): Mar. 1, June 1, Sept. 1, and Dec. 1
   Board meeting date(s): Quarterly
   Final notification: Within 3 months
Officers and Directors:* Douglas Leonard,* Chair.;
Rick Johnson,* Vice-Chair.; Sharon Risk Stark,*
C.E.O. and Pres.; Richard B. Pease,* Secy.; Loretta
M. Burd,* Treas.; Fred L. Armstrong; Dan Arnholt;
Linda F. Behrman; Jeffrey N. Brown; Dan Daniel;
Dominic W. Glover; Richard E. Harris, Sr.; V. William
Hunt; Sarla Kalsi; Mickey Kim; Larry Kleinhenz;
William I. Miller; Yoshimitsu "Yoshi" Ogihara; Adolfo
"Rudy" Olivio; Douglas G. Otto; John Quick; Tim
Solso; Tracy H. Souza; Richard A. Stenner, Jr.;
Barbara Stevens; Madhu Vedak.
Number of staff: 4 full-time professional; 2 part-time
professional.
EIN: 351343903

3167

The Hilbert Foundation ◇

P.O. Box 90198
Indianapolis, IN 46290-0198 (317) 848-3146
Contact: Phillip S. Scheffsky

Established in 1996 in IN.
Donors: Stephen C. Hilbert; Tomisue S. Hilbert.
Foundation type: Independent foundation.
Financial data (yr. ended 12/31/03): Assets,
$100,212 (M); gifts received, $5,000;
expenditures, $401,558; qualifying distributions,
$400,059; giving activities include $394,199 for 5
grants (high: $211,539; low: $160).

Fields of interest: Performing arts, theater; Arts;
Zoos/zoological societies; Hospitals (general);
Protestant agencies & churches.
Limitations: Giving primarily in Indianapolis, IN.
Application information: Application form not
required.
   Initial approach: Proposal
   Deadline(s): None
Trustees: Stephen C. Hilbert; Tomisue S. Hilbert.
EIN: 352002703

3168

Holiday Management Foundation, Inc. ◇

(formerly Holiday Home Foundation of Evansville,
Inc.)
c/o Larry Dunigan
1202 W. Buena Vista Rd.
Evansville, IN 47710

Established in 1974 in IN.
Donors: Sharon Dunigan; Larry Dunigan; Holiday
Home Health Care Corp. of Evansville; Holiday
Leasing Corp.; Holiday Retirement Village; NSPB
Corp.; 3-D Corp.
Foundation type: Independent foundation.
Financial data (yr. ended 9/30/05): Assets,
$16,063,952 (M); gifts received, $240,700;
expenditures, $864,648; qualifying distributions,
$853,805; giving activities include $847,750 for 41
grants (high: $225,000; low: $200).
Purpose and activities: Giving primarily to
education, youth organizations, and to health and
human services.
Fields of interest: Higher education; Health
organizations, association; Youth development;
Human services; YM/YWCAs & YM/YWHAs;
Christian agencies & churches.
Limitations: Applications not accepted. Giving
primarily in Evansville, IN. Generally no grants to
individuals.
Application information: Contributes only to
pre-selected organizations. Unsolicited requests for
funds not considered.
Officers: Larry Dunigan, Pres.; Helen Dunigan, V.P.;
Sharon Dunigan, Secy.-Treas.
EIN: 237414999

3169

Hoover Family Foundation

860 E. 86th St., Ste. 5
Indianapolis, IN 46240 (317) 815-9553
Contact: David C. Hoover, Exec. Dir., Indianapolis,
IN; Glen H. Friedman, Exec. Dir., Portland, OR
FAX: (317) 815-9663; Additional tel.: (503)
699-1363; additional fax: (503) 699-1751

Established in 1992 in IN.
Donors: James E. Hoover; Katherine C. Hoover†;
Mildred M. Hoover†.
Foundation type: Independent foundation.
Financial data (yr. ended 6/30/05): Assets,
$16,346,362 (M); expenditures, $872,465;
qualifying distributions, $865,918; giving activities
include $672,994 for 110 grants (high: $30,000;
low: $1,000).
Purpose and activities: Giving primarily for human
services and promoting self-sufficiency.
Fields of interest: Education; Human services.
Limitations: Giving primarily in Indianapolis, IN, and
Portland, OR. No support for religious or sectarian
organizations. No grants to individuals, or for

operating budgets, continuous support, capital campaigns, event (or post event) funding, multi-year funding, college scholarships, medical research, private foundations or endowment funds, or for long term funding.

Publications: Application guidelines.

Application information: Application form not required.

Initial approach: Letter of inquiry
Copies of proposal: 3
Deadline(s): Mar. 1, July 1, and Nov. 1
Board meeting date(s): Jan., May, and Sept.
Final notification: 3-4 months

Officers and Directors:* James E. Hoover,* Pres.; Cynthia K. Hoover,* V.P.; David C. Hoover,* Secy.-Treas. and Exec. Dir. for Indiana; Glen H. Friedman, Exec. Dir. for Oregon.

Number of staff: 2 full-time professional; 1 part-time professional; 1 part-time support.

EIN: 351873953

Selected grants: The following grants were reported in 2005.

$30,000 to Indianapolis Foundation, Indianapolis, IN.

$10,000 to Executive Service Corps, Indianapolis, IN.

$10,000 to Fairbanks Hospital, Indianapolis, IN.

$10,000 to Jubilee Partnerships, Indianapolis, IN.

$10,000 to Saint Francis Healthcare Foundation, Beech Grove, IN.

$8,000 to College Mentors for Kids, Indianapolis, IN.

$7,500 to Ballet Internationale, Indianapolis, IN.

$6,000 to Growing Gardens, Portland, OR.

$5,000 to Tears of Joy Theater, Portland, OR.

$5,000 to YMCA of Columbia-Willamette, Portland, OR.

3170

The Hux Family Charitable Trust ◇

P.O. Box 1027
Riley, IN 47871-1027
Application address: c/o Cynthia S. Martin, 5451 Riley Rd., Terre Haute, IN 47802-8875, tel.: (812) 849-2096

Established in 1992 in IN.

Donor: Vernon E. Hux†.

Foundation type: Independent foundation.

Financial data (yr. ended 9/30/05): Assets, $7,622,408 (M); expenditures, $404,266; qualifying distributions, $364,777; giving activities include $368,337 for 60 grants (high: $35,437; low: $100).

Purpose and activities: Giving primarily for education, health associations, human services, and Christian and Roman Catholic organizations and churches; funding also for a United Methodist church.

Fields of interest: Elementary/secondary education; Higher education; Education; Hospitals (general); Health organizations, association; Human services; Children/youth, services; Roman Catholic federated giving programs; Christian agencies & churches; Protestant agencies & churches; Roman Catholic agencies & churches.

Limitations: Giving primarily in IN. No grants to individuals.

Application information:

Initial approach: Proposal
Deadline(s): None

Trustees: David H. Goeller; Cynthia S. Martin; Kathy A. Perry.

EIN: 356562911

Selected grants: The following grants were reported in 2005.

$50,000 to Ivy Tech Foundation, Terre Haute, IN.

$37,500 to Ocean View United Methodist Church, Oak Island, NC. 2 grants: $10,000, $27,500

$25,000 to Union Hospital Foundation, Terre Haute, IN.

$20,800 to Vigo County School Corporation, Terre Haute, IN. 3 grants: $6,400, $6,400, $8,000

$20,000 to Saint Mary of the Woods College, Saint Mary of the Woods, IN.

$10,000 to Catholic Relief Services, Baltimore, MD.

$5,000 to Lords Place, West Palm Beach, FL.

3171

IFSA Foundation, Inc. ◇ ☆

3815 River Crossing Pkwy., Ste. 100
Indianapolis, IN 46240-7766 (317) 566-2193
FAX: (317) 566-2056; E-mail for electronic applications: apply@theifsafoundation.org;
URL: http://www.theifsafoundation.org

Established in 2004 in IN.

Foundation type: Independent foundation.

Financial data (yr. ended 5/31/05): Assets, $5,392,842 (M); gifts received, $1,200,000; expenditures, $1,008,885; qualifying distributions, $676,662; giving activities include $437,688 for grants.

Purpose and activities: The purpose of the foundation is to assist and continue the advancement of international education through direct and indirect support of study abroad by undergraduate students. Grants are limited to accredited colleges, universities, or organizations with the mission to further international education.

Fields of interest: Higher education; International exchange, students.

Limitations: Giving primarily in the U.S.

Application information: Application form required.

Initial approach: Check foundation Web site for application guidelines
Deadline(s): Mar. 15 and Oct. 1
Final notification: May 1 and Dec. 1

Officers: Tom Roberts, Pres.; David Gray, Secy.; M. Jean White, Treas.

EIN: 201238211

3172

IMMI Word & Deed Foundation, Inc. ◇

18881 U.S. Hwy. 31 N.
P.O. Box 408
Westfield, IN 46074
Contact: Suzanne Anthony Wilhelm, Dir.

Established in 1991 in IN.

Donors: Indiana Mills & Manufacturing, Inc.; Beverly S. Anthony; James R. Anthony.

Foundation type: Independent foundation.

Financial data (yr. ended 11/30/05): Assets, $3,381,225 (M); gifts received, $1,955,249; expenditures, $1,171,112; qualifying distributions, $1,158,490; giving activities include $1,158,480 for 110 grants (high: $558,075; low: $100).

Purpose and activities: The foundation supports organizations involved with Christianity.

Fields of interest: Christian agencies & churches.

Limitations: Giving on a national basis. No grants to individuals.

Application information: Application form required.

Initial approach: Contact foundation for application form
Deadline(s): None

Officers: James R. Anthony, Pres.; Beverly S. Anthony, Secy.

Director: Suzanne Anthony Wilhelm.

EIN: 351859427

Selected grants: The following grants were reported in 2004.

$437,100 to Campus Crusade for Christ International, Orlando, FL.

$17,000 to River Oaks Community Church, Carmel, IN.

$12,000 to Insight for Living, Plano, TX.

$12,000 to Samaritans Purse, Boone, NC.

$10,000 to Oak Brook Community Church, Oak Brook, IL.

$6,000 to Billy Graham Evangelistic Association, Charlotte, NC.

3173

Indiana Chemical Trust ◇

c/o Old National Trust Co.
P.O. Box 1447
Terre Haute, IN 47808-1447 (812) 462-7255
Contact: Brenda Voll

Established in 1953 in IN.

Donors: Terre Haute Gas Corp.; Indiana Gas and Chemical Corp.; Tribune-Star Publishing Co.

Foundation type: Company-sponsored foundation.

Financial data (yr. ended 12/31/05): Assets, $8,856,353 (M); expenditures, $486,933; qualifying distributions, $453,327; giving activities include $452,000 for 34 grants (high: $70,000; low: $1,000).

Purpose and activities: The foundation supports children's museums and organizations involved with education, animals and wildlife, recreation, human services, and Catholicism.

Fields of interest: Museums (children's); Education; Animals/wildlife, preservation/protection; Zoos/zoological societies; Recreation; Children/youth, services; Human services; Roman Catholic agencies & churches.

Type of support: General/operating support.

Limitations: Giving primarily in Vigo County, IN. No grants to individuals.

Application information: Application form not required.

Initial approach: Proposal
Deadline(s): None
Board meeting date(s): Dec.

Committee Members: W. Curtis Brighton; Anton Hulman George; Mari Hulman George.

Trustee: Old National Trust Co.

EIN: 356024816

3174

Irwin Financial Foundation ◇ ☆

500 Washington St.
Columbus, IN 47201 (812) 376-1909
Application address: c/o Em Rodway, Prog. Off., Irwin Management Co., 301 Washington St., Columbus, IN 47201, tel.: (812) 376-3331

Established in 1992 in IN.

Donors: Irwin Financial Corp.; Irwin Mortgage Corp.; Irwin Union Bank & Trust Co.

Foundation type: Company-sponsored foundation.

Financial data (yr. ended 12/31/05): Assets, $2,797,221 (M); gifts received, $648,014; expenditures, $540,262; qualifying distributions, $474,000; giving activities include $474,000 for grants.

Purpose and activities: The foundation supports organizations involved with arts and culture, K-12 education, housing, youth, civil liberties, and neighborhood development.

Fields of interest: Arts; Elementary/secondary education; Housing/shelter; Youth, services; Civil liberties, advocacy; Community development, neighborhood development.

Type of support: General/operating support; Seed money.

Limitations: Giving primarily in areas of company operations, with emphasis on Columbus, IN.

Publications: Application guidelines; Biennial report.

Application information: Application form not required.

  Initial approach: Proposal
  Copies of proposal: 1
  Deadline(s): None
  Board meeting date(s): Quarterly

Officers and Directors:* William I. Miller,* Chair.; John A. Nash,* Pres.; Matthew F. Souza, Secy.; Marie S. Ameis, Treas.; Claude E. Davis; Elena Delgado; Rick McGuire; Michael F. Ryan; Thomas D. Washburn.

EIN: 351843700

3175
Irwin-Sweeney-Miller Foundation ◈

P.O. Box 808
Columbus, IN 47202-0808 (812) 372-0251
Contact: Sarla Kalsi, V.P.

Incorporated in 1952 in IN.

Donors: Xenia S. Miller; Members of the Irwin, Sweeney, and Miller families.

Foundation type: Independent foundation.

Financial data (yr. ended 12/31/04): Assets, $28,192,454 (M); expenditures, $1,755,092; qualifying distributions, $1,581,255; giving activities include $1,026,749 for 58 grants (high: $346,999; low: $200).

Purpose and activities: Support for creative programs in social justice, education, religion, the arts, and improving family stability; funding also for people who are disadvantaged and are working toward self-sufficiency, child welfare, social services, and community development.

Fields of interest: Arts; Education; Youth development; Human services; Children/youth, services; Community development; Christian agencies & churches; Protestant agencies & churches; Economically disadvantaged.

Type of support: General/operating support; Continuing support; Annual campaigns; Building/renovation; Emergency funds; Program development; Conferences/seminars; Seed money; Technical assistance; Consulting services; Matching/challenge support.

Limitations: Giving primarily in the Columbus, IN, area for new funding. No grants to individuals, or for deficit financing, research, scholarships, or fellowships; no loans.

Publications: Biennial report.

Application information: Application form not required.

  Initial approach: Letter with proposal
  Copies of proposal: 1
  Deadline(s): Mar. 1 and Sept. 1
  Board meeting date(s): May and Oct.
  Final notification: 1 month

Officers and Directors:* Lynne M. Maguire,* Chair.; Xenia S. Miller,* Pres.; Sarla Kalsi,* V.P., Treas., and Exec. Dir.; Em Rodway, Secy. and Prog. Off.; Robert Alan Melting; Catherine G. Miller; Elizabeth G. Miller; Hugh Thomas Miller; Margaret I. Miller; William I. Miller; Thomas N. Patch; Carolyn S. Tangeman; John T. Tangeman.

EIN: 356014513

Selected grants: The following grants were reported in 2003.

$286,337 to Columbus, City of, Columbus, IN. For The Commons.

$50,000 to Community Education Coalition, Columbus, IN. For fund drive.

$20,000 to ABC Learning Center, Columbus, IN. For general support.

$20,000 to Columbus Area Arts Council, Columbus, IN. For general support.

$20,000 to Columbus Indiana Philharmonic, Columbus, IN. For general support.

$2,000 to Indianapolis Museum of Art, Indianapolis, IN. For general support.

$2,000 to United Negro College Fund, Fairfax, VA. For general support.

$1,000 to Girl Scouts of the U.S.A., Bloomington, IN. For general support.

$1,000 to Independent Colleges of Indiana, Indianapolis, IN. For general support.

$500 to Urban League, National, New York, NY. For general support.

3176
Ispat Inland Foundation, Inc. ◈

3210 Watling St.
East Chicago, IN 46312
Contact: J. Medellin, V.P.

Established in 2000 in IN.

Foundation type: Independent foundation.

Financial data (yr. ended 12/31/05): Assets, $0 (M); gifts received, $654,562; expenditures, $654,562; qualifying distributions, $654,562; giving activities include $618,288 for 86 grants (high: $215,748; low: $30), and $228,249 for foundation-administered programs.

Purpose and activities: Giving for scholarships to dependents of active and retired employees of Ispat Inland Inc.

Fields of interest: Higher education; Human services.

Limitations: Giving primarily in IN.

Application information:

  Initial approach: Letter
  Deadline(s): None

Officers and Directors:* William Mundell,* Pres. and Treas.; Joseph Medellin,* V.P.; John Nielsen,* V.P.; Marc Jeske,* Secy.

EIN: 352121803

3177
Jasper Foundation, Inc. ◈

P.O. Box 295
Rensselaer, IN 47978 (219) 866-5899
Contact: Linda Reiners, Exec. Dir.

FAX: (219) 866-0555; E-mail: jasper@liljasper.com; URL: http://www.jasperfdn.org

Established in 1992 in IN.

Foundation type: Community foundation.

Financial data (yr. ended 12/31/04): Assets, $6,866,547 (M); gifts received, $335,377; expenditures, $568,499; giving activities include $178,739 for grants, and $199,563 for grants to individuals.

Purpose and activities: The foundation seeks to assist donors in creating a source of assets to meet the ongoing and changing charitable needs and interests of the people living in all of the Jasper County communities. The foundation seeks to make philanthropic grants in response to community needs for education, arts and culture, health, social concerns, and historic preservation.

Fields of interest: Historic preservation/historical societies; Arts; Higher education; Scholarships/financial aid; Education; Hospitals (general); Health care; Community development.

Type of support: Matching/challenge support; Seed money; Scholarship funds.

Limitations: Giving limited to Jasper County, IN. No support for religious purposes. No grants for budget deficits, endowments, or for projects normally the responsibility of a government agency; generally no grants for travel.

Application information: Visit foundation Web site for application form and guidelines. Application form required.

  Initial approach: Contact foundation
  Deadline(s): Apr. 1 and Oct. 1

Officers and Directors:* James H. Flickner,* Pres.; Kathy Parkison,* V.P.; Judy Hauser,* Secy.; David F. Schrum,* Treas.; Linda Reiners, Exec. Dir.; Gene Bell; Norman Chappell; John B. Egan; Pastor Keith Kincaid; Stephen J. Kinsell; Robert G. Lewis; Barb Morgin; Bev Randle; Sally Snow; Rodney Urbano.

EIN: 351842404

3178
Johnson County Community Foundation, Inc.

(formerly Greater Johnson County Community Foundation)
398 S. Main St.
P.O. Box 217
Franklin, IN 46131-2311 (317) 738-2213
Contact: Sandy Daniels, C.E.O.
FAX: (317) 738-9113; E-mail: sandyd@jccf.org; URL: http://www.jccf.org

Established in 1991 in IN.

Foundation type: Community foundation.

Financial data (yr. ended 12/31/05): Assets, $12,521,820 (M); gifts received, $1,056,291; expenditures, $837,799; giving activities include $222,175 for 112 grants (high: $13,685; low: $11), and $215,960 for 90 grants to individuals (high: $15,771; low: $250).

Purpose and activities: The foundation exists to encourage local philanthropy and to improve the quality of life in the Johnson County community through leadership and grant support to local nonprofit organizations. Scholarships are awarded to high school seniors from specific high schools primarily in Johnson County, IN, and/or students enrolled at specific IN colleges or universities.

Fields of interest: Arts; Higher education; Education; Environment; Health care; Disasters,

Hurricane Katrina; Human services; Community development.

Type of support: General/operating support; Management development/capacity building; Building/renovation; Equipment; Emergency funds; Program development; Seed money; Scholarship funds; Technical assistance; Consulting services; Program evaluation; Scholarships—to individuals; Matching/challenge support.

Limitations: Giving limited to Johnson County, IN, and vicinity. No support for sectarian or religious programs. No grants to individuals (except for scholarships), or for endowments, conferences, travel, publications or media projects, annual campaigns, capital campaigns, ongoing operating budgets, fundraising events, deficit funding, equipment, construction and renovation, land acquisition, public school services required by state law, repeat funding supported through prior grants, or athletic leagues or teams.

Publications: Application guidelines; Annual report (including application guidelines); Informational brochure (including application guidelines); Newsletter.

Application information: Visit foundation Web site for application information. If the grant request meets funding guidelines, the foundation will invite the organization to submit an application. Application form required.

Initial approach: Letter or telephone
Copies of proposal: 1
Deadline(s): Mar. 1, May 1, and Sept. 1
Board meeting date(s): 4 times per year
Final notification: Within 30 days

Officers and Directors: * Pat Van Valer,* Chair.; Sandy Daniels, C.E.O. and Pres.; Janette Koon,* Secy.; Susan Haines,* Treas.; Dean Abplanalp; Marian Callon; Dolores McGovern Dunn; Jeff Eggers; Jerry Engle; Mike Jarvis; Larry Koenes; Mitzi Martin; Gail Richards; Craig Wells; Anne Young.

Number of staff: 4 full-time professional; 2 part-time professional.

EIN: 351797437

3179
The Scott A. Jones Foundation, Inc. ✧
1150 W. 116th St.
Carmel, IN 46032

Established in 1994 in MA.
Donor: Scott A. Jones.
Foundation type: Independent foundation.
Financial data (yr. ended 12/31/04): Assets, $3,627,693 (M); expenditures, $1,412,194; qualifying distributions, $1,408,889; giving activities include $1,406,055 for 18 grants (high: $1,250,000; low: $100).
Purpose and activities: Giving primarily for human services, the arts, and education.
Fields of interest: Museums (children's); Secondary school/education; Education; Zoos/zoological societies; Human services; Children/youth, services.
Limitations: Applications not accepted. Giving primarily in IN. No grants to individuals.
Application information: Contributes only to pre-selected organizations.
Officers: Scott A. Jones, Pres.; Thomas P. Jalkut, Clerk; Lisa Hull, Treas.
EIN: 223295174
Selected grants: The following grants were reported in 2004.

$1,250,000 to Childrens Museum of Indianapolis, Indianapolis, IN. For general support.
$102,500 to Sycamore School, Indianapolis, IN. For general support.
$30,000 to Indianapolis Zoological Society, Indianapolis, IN. For general support.
$6,000 to Make-A-Wish Foundation of Indiana, Indianapolis, IN. For general support.
$2,500 to Simon Youth Foundation, Indianapolis, IN. For general support.
$1,320 to Domestic Violence Network of Greater Indianapolis, Indianapolis, IN. For general support.
$1,185 to Young Entrepreneurs Organization, Arlington, VA. For general support.
$1,000 to Owls Head Transportation Museum, Owls Head, ME. For general support.
$1,000 to Saint Vincent Hospital Foundation, Indianapolis, IN. For general support.
$500 to Planned Parenthood of Indiana, Indianapolis, IN. For general support.

3180
Arthur Jordan Foundation ✧
1230 N. Delaware St.
Indianapolis, IN 46202 (317) 635-1378
Contact: Margaret F. Sallee, Admin. Asst.
FAX: (317) 632-5488;
E-mail: msallee@arthurjordanfoundation.org;
URL: http://www.arthurjordanfoundation.org

Trust established in 1928 in IN.
Donor: Arthur Jordan†.
Foundation type: Independent foundation.
Financial data (yr. ended 12/31/04): Assets, $18,263,686 (M); expenditures, $781,401; qualifying distributions, $658,238; giving activities include $537,000 for 45 grants (high: $200,000; low: $1,000).
Fields of interest: Performing arts; Higher education.
Type of support: General/operating support; Annual campaigns; Capital campaigns; Building/renovation; Matching/challenge support.
Limitations: Giving limited to Marion County, IN. No support for medical research. No grants to individuals, or for endowment funds, multi-year grants, research, scholarships, or fellowships; no loans.
Publications: Application guidelines; Grants list.
Application information: Application guidelines and cover sheet available on foundation Web site. Application form required.
Initial approach: 1-2 page letter
Copies of proposal: 1
Deadline(s): Mar. 1
Board meeting date(s): May
Final notification: 90 days
Officers and Trustees: * Joseph D. Barnette, Jr.,* Chair.; Thomas P. Ewbank,* Vice. Chair.; Don R. DeMars,* Secy.; Sara B. Cobb, Treas.; Garcia J. Floyd; Thomas A. King; Samuel L. Odle.
Number of staff: 1 part-time professional.
EIN: 350428850

3181
Journal-Gazette Foundation, Inc. ✧
701 S. Clinton St.
Fort Wayne, IN 46802-1883 (260) 424-5257
Contact: Jerry D. Fox, Secy.-Treas.

Established in 1985 in IN.
Donors: Journal-Gazette Co.; Richard G. Inskeep; Harriett J. Inskeep.
Foundation type: Company-sponsored foundation.
Financial data (yr. ended 12/31/03): Assets, $12,700,468 (M); gifts received, $648,504; expenditures, $564,119; qualifying distributions, $554,556; giving activities include $553,174 for 90 grants (high: $112,000; low: $25).
Purpose and activities: The foundation supports organizations involved with arts and culture, education, health, youth development, and human services.
Fields of interest: Arts; Higher education; Education; Health care; Food banks; Recreation, parks/playgrounds; Youth development, business; Youth development; Human services; YM/YWCAs & YM/YWHAs; Foundations (community); Federated giving programs; Christian agencies & churches.
Type of support: General/operating support; Capital campaigns.
Limitations: Giving limited to northeastern IN. No grants to individuals.
Application information:
Initial approach: Proposal
Deadline(s): None
Board meeting date(s): Quarterly
Officers and Directors: * Richard G. Inskeep,* Pres.; Jerry D. Fox, Secy.-Treas.; Harriett Jane Inskeep; Thomas R. Inskeep; Julie Inskeep Simpson.
EIN: 311134237

3182
The Kimball International—Habig Foundation, Inc.
(formerly The Habig Foundation)
1600 Royal St.
Jasper, IN 47549 (812) 482-8263
E-mail: mgogel@kimball.com

Established in 1951 in IN.
Donor: Kimball International, Inc.
Foundation type: Company-sponsored foundation.
Financial data (yr. ended 6/30/05): Assets, $1,636,101 (M); gifts received, $250,000; expenditures, $437,621; qualifying distributions, $437,143; giving activities include $307,395 for 212 grants (high: $60,000; low: $50), and $128,700 for 87 grants to individuals (high: $1,500; low: $600).
Purpose and activities: The foundation supports religious institutions and organizations involved with arts and culture, education, health, human services, and civic and community.
Fields of interest: Arts; Education; Hospitals (general); Health care; Children/youth, services; Human services; Community development, service clubs; Community development; Public affairs; Religion.
Type of support: General/operating support; Employee-related scholarships.
Limitations: Applications not accepted. Giving limited to areas of company operations.
Application information: Contributes only to pre-selected organizations.
Officers and Directors: * Douglas A. Habig,* Chair.; James C. Thyen,* Pres.; John H. Kahle, Secy.-Treas.
Number of staff: 2
EIN: 356022535
Selected grants: The following grants were reported in 2005.
$60,000 to Indiana State Museum, Indianapolis, IN.

$30,000 to Sisters of Saint Benedict, Ferdinand, IN.

$20,000 to Indiana University Foundation, Bloomington, IN. 2 grants: $15,000, $5,000

$20,000 to Saint Meinrad Archabbey, Saint Meinrad, IN.

$10,000 to Boy Scouts of America, Buffalo Trace Council, Evansville, IN.

$7,500 to Girl Scouts of the U.S.A., Raintree Council, Evansville, IN.

$6,000 to Friends of the Arts, Jasper, IN.

$3,500 to Memorial Hospital Foundation, Jasper, IN.

$3,000 to Gonzaga University, Spokane, WA.

3183
The Klapper Family Foundation, Inc. ✧ ☆
3308 Mitthoeffer Rd.
Indianapolis, IN   46236   (317) 899-1022
Contact: David I. Klapper, Pres.

Established in 1996 in IN.
Donor: David I. Klapper.
Foundation type: Independent foundation.
Financial data (yr. ended 12/31/05): Assets, $8,255,189 (M); expenditures, $480,756; qualifying distributions, $351,475; giving activities include $345,215 for 37 grants (high: $150,000; low: $75).
Fields of interest: Performing arts, theater; Arts; Higher education; Education; Health organizations; Human services; Jewish agencies & temples.
Limitations: Giving primarily in Indianapolis, IN.
Application information: Application form not required.
Deadline(s): None
Officers: David I. Klapper, Pres. and Treas.; Mary Elizabeth Klapper, V.P. and Secy.
Director: Alan H. Cohen.
EIN: 351999306
Selected grants: The following grants were reported in 2003.

$123,000 to Indiana University Foundation, Bloomington, IN. For operating support.

$8,333 to Big Brothers/Big Sisters of Central Indiana, Indianapolis, IN. For operating support.

$8,100 to Indiana Repertory Theater, Indianapolis, IN. For operating support.

$5,000 to Dress for Success Indianapolis, Indianapolis, IN. For operating support.

$5,000 to W F Y I-Metropolitan Indianapolis Public Broadcasting, Indianapolis, IN. For operating support.

$2,850 to Indiana University, Bloomington, IN. For scholarships.

$2,000 to Childrens Bureau of Indianapolis, Indianapolis, IN. For operating support.

$1,667 to Matt White Cure ALS Foundation, Chicago, IL. For operating support.

$1,108 to Meals on Wheels of Indianapolis, Indianapolis, IN. For operating support.

$1,000 to Central Indiana Community Foundation, Indianapolis, IN. For Kevin G. Flynn Leadership Fund.

3184
Koch Foundation, Inc.
(formerly George Koch Sons Foundation, Inc.)
10 S. 11th Ave.
Evansville, IN   47744
Contact: Jennifer K. Slade, Secy.

URL: http://www.kochenterprises.com/corporate/foundation.htm

Incorporated in 1945 in IN.
Donors: George Koch Sons, Inc.; George Koch Sons, LLC; Gibbs Die Casting Corp.; Koch Enterprises, Inc.
Foundation type: Company-sponsored foundation.
Financial data (yr. ended 12/31/05): Assets, $21,547,940 (M); gifts received, $1,025,000; expenditures, $820,818; qualifying distributions, $723,423; giving activities include $722,862 for 126 grants (high: $115,253; low: $50).
Purpose and activities: The foundation supports organizations involved with arts and culture, education, health, human services, civic affairs, and religion. Special emphasis is directed toward organizations with which employees of Koch Enterprises are involved.
Fields of interest: Arts; Education; Health care; Human services; Public affairs; Religion.
Type of support: Employee volunteer services; Annual campaigns; Capital campaigns; Building/renovation; Program development; Research; Sponsorships; Employee matching gifts; Employee-related scholarships; Matching/challenge support.
Limitations: Giving limited to IN, KY, MO, Elko, NV, Harligen and Schertz, TX, Beckley, WV, and Casper, WY, with emphasis on the Evansville and Vanderburgh County, IN, area. No grants to individuals (except for employee-related scholarships).
Application information: Application form not required.
Initial approach: Proposal
Copies of proposal: 1
Deadline(s): None
Board meeting date(s): Sept. 5 and Dec. 12
Final notification: 3 months
Officers and Directors:* Robert L. Koch II,* Pres.; James H. Muehlbauer,* V.P.; Jennifer K. Slade, Secy.; Susan E. Parsons, Treas.; Steve A. Church; David M. Koch; Kevin R. Koch; Brad Muehlbauer.
Number of staff: 2 part-time support.
EIN: 356023372
Selected grants: The following grants were reported in 2006.

$200,000 to Evansville Catholic High Schools, Evansville, IN. For capital campaign.

$100,000 to Signature School, Evansville, IN. For renovation.

$20,000 to YMCA of Southwestern Indiana, Evansville, IN. For capital campaign.

3185
Kosciusko 21st Century Foundation, Inc.
117 W. Center St., Ste. C
P.O. Box 1810
Warsaw, IN   46581-1810   (574) 269-5188
FAX: (574) 269-5193;
E-mail: holly@k21foundation.org; URL: http://www.k21foundation.org

Established in 1999 in IN from the proceeds of the sale of Kosciusko Community Hospital to Quorum Health Group, Inc.
Foundation type: Independent foundation.
Financial data (yr. ended 12/31/04): Assets, $65,934,748 (M); gifts received, $187,652; expenditures, $2,612,505; qualifying distributions, $2,189,220; giving activities include $1,968,367 for 176 grants (high: $200,000; low: $100).

Purpose and activities: The foundation is dedicated to maintaining an endowment to ensure healthcare facilities remain in Kosciusko County, IN, and it is committed to improving community health and wellness through investments and grants.
Fields of interest: Medical care, community health systems; Hospitals (general); Health care; Mental health/crisis services; Disasters, preparedness/services; Residential/custodial care, hospices.
Limitations: Giving primarily in Kosciusko County, IN.
Publications: Grants list.
Application information: Application form available on foundation Web site. Application form required.
Copies of proposal: 1
Deadline(s): Feb. 1, May 1, Aug. 1, and Nov. 1
Officers: George Gilbert, Chair.; Willis Alt, Pres.
Directors: Joe Banks; Becky Doll; George Haymond, M.D.; Lee Heyde; Carol Lyn Jansen; Jo Lemon; Kathleen Mason; Ray Monteith; David Morales; Chuck Niemier; Erin Jungbauer, M.D.; Dennis Reeve; Steve Sands; Peggy Shively; Jon Sroufe; Marie Trump.
Number of staff: 1 full-time professional; 1 full-time support.
EIN: 351187105

3186
Kosciusko County Community Foundation, Inc.
102 E. Market St.
Warsaw, IN   46580   (574) 267-1901
Contact: Suzanne M. Light, Exec. Dir.
FAX: (574) 268-9780; E-mail: kcf@kcfoundation.org;
URL: http://www.kcfoundation.org

Established in 1968 by the Warsaw Chamber of Commerce as the Greater Warsaw Foundation. In 1972, after reorganization to include the entire county, the name was changed. In 2002, the current name was adopted.
Foundation type: Community foundation.
Financial data (yr. ended 6/30/06): Assets, $30,008,645 (M); gifts received, $3,412,069; expenditures, $1,897,890; giving activities include $1,259,114 for 662 grants, and $131,153 for 791 grants to individuals.
Purpose and activities: By bringing caring people and charitable endeavors together, the foundation makes donors dreams shine for the good of the community by: serving as the vehicle for donors' charitable dreams; awarding grants to charitable projects and organizations; and addressing community needs as a catalyst and convener.
Fields of interest: Arts; Education; Environment; Health care; Recreation; Human services; Public affairs.
Type of support: Management development/capacity building; Capital campaigns; Building/renovation; Program development; Seed money; Scholarships—to individuals; Matching/challenge support.
Limitations: Giving limited to Kosciusko County, IN. No support for sectarian or religious groups, or national organizations (unless the monies are to be used solely to benefit citizens of Kosciusko County). No grants to individuals (except for scholarships), or for operating budgets, endowment funds, fundraising projects, or long-term funding.
Publications: Application guidelines; Annual report (including application guidelines); Newsletter.

Application information: Visit foundation Web site for application form and guidelines. Application form required.

 Initial approach: Telephone
 Copies of proposal: 7
 Deadline(s): Jan. 15, May 15, and Sept. 15
 Board meeting date(s): Every 2 months
 Final notification: 9 weeks after deadline

Officers and Directors:* Robert C. Condon,* Pres.; Craig Tidball,* V.P.; Mindy Truex,* Secy.; Alan Wuthrich,* Treas.; Suzanne M. Light,* Exec. Dir.; Alan Alderfer; Carolyn Anderson; Brad Bishop; Jerry Clevenger; Marsha Cook; Antony "Tony" Garza; Richard Green; Jeanne Grossnickle; Zoe Howard; Barbara Kissane; Beth Krull; Dr. Ron Manahan; Jean Northenor; Greg Sasso; Rita Schobert; Rita Price Simpson; Sharon Sommers; Cara Tucker; Rev. Gerald Yoder.

Number of staff: 3 full-time professional; 4 full-time support.

EIN: 356086777

3187

Charles W. Kuhne Foundation Trust ✧ ☆

c/o Wells Fargo Bank N.A., MAC 8622-031
P.O. Box 960
Fort Wayne, IN 46801-6632
Contact: Alice Kopfer, V.P., Wells Fargo Bank, N.A.

Foundation type: Independent foundation.

Financial data (yr. ended 7/31/05): Assets, $7,361,642 (M); expenditures, $381,912; qualifying distributions, $350,210; giving activities include $323,541 for 22 grants (high: $50,000; low: $1,000).

Purpose and activities: Giving primarily for education, the arts, particularly theater and public television, community development, and social services.

Fields of interest: Museums (history); Arts; Higher education; Education; Food banks; Human services; YM/YWCAs & YM/YWHAs; Children/youth, services; Community development.

Type of support: General/operating support; Annual campaigns; Capital campaigns; Building/renovation; Equipment; Program development; Matching/challenge support.

Limitations: Giving limited to Allen County, IN. No support for elementary or high schools. No grants to individuals, or for scholarships or seminars.

Application information: Application form not required.

 Initial approach: Letter
 Deadline(s): None
 Board meeting date(s): Quarterly

Trustee: Wells Fargo Bank, N.A.

EIN: 356011137

Selected grants: The following grants were reported in 2004.

$30,000 to Urban League of Fort Wayne, Fort Wayne, IN. For capital campaign.

$25,000 to Arts United of Greater Fort Wayne, Fort Wayne, IN. For annual campaign for Arts Plaza Project.

$25,000 to Childrens Hope, Fort Wayne, IN.

$20,000 to Indiana Institute of Technology, Fort Wayne, IN. For capital campaign.

$19,000 to United Hispanic Americans, Fort Wayne, IN. For van.

$15,500 to Cancer Services of Allen County, Fort Wayne, IN. For general support.

$12,000 to Independent Colleges of Indiana, Indianapolis, IN. For general support.

$10,000 to Crossroad/Fort Wayne Childrens Home, Fort Wayne, IN. To purchase car.

$10,000 to Fort Wayne Clubhouse, Fort Wayne, IN. For Carries House-Copies and Notes.

$10,000 to Saint Vincent de Paul Society, Fort Wayne, IN. To purchase truck.

3188

Greater Lafayette Community Foundation

1114 State St.
Lafayette, IN 47905-1219 (765) 742-9078
Contact: Cheryl A. Ubelhor, Prog. Dir.; James E. Klusman, C.E.O.
FAX: (765) 742-2428; E-mail: info@glcfonline.org; Additional E-mails: cheryl@glcfonline.org, jklusman@glcfonline.org, and angela@glcfonline.org; URL: http://www.glcfonline.org

Established in 1970 in IN.

Foundation type: Community foundation.

Financial data (yr. ended 12/31/05): Assets, $24,169,670 (M); gifts received, $1,726,568; expenditures, $1,058,718; giving activities include $553,621 for grants, and $24,800 for 23 grants to individuals (high: $5,000; low: $500).

Purpose and activities: The mission of the foundation is to enhance the quality of life in the region through philanthropic leadership.

Fields of interest: Humanities; Arts; Higher education; Education; Environment, beautification programs; Environment; Health care; Substance abuse, services; Mental health/crisis services; Food services; Housing/shelter, homeless; Housing/shelter; Children, day care; Human services; Community development, neighborhood development; Youth.

Type of support: Scholarships—to individuals; Capital campaigns; Equipment; Emergency funds; Seed money; Scholarship funds.

Limitations: Giving primarily in Tippecanoe County and the greater Lafayette, IN, area, including the surrounding counties. No support for government agencies or public institutions, or sectarian or religious purposes. No grants to individuals (except for scholarships), or for ongoing expenses, endowments, special events, multi-year grants, debt or deficit reduction, or operating support.

Publications: Application guidelines; Annual report; Informational brochure; Newsletter.

Application information: Visit foundation Web site for application form and guidelines. Application form required.

 Initial approach: Mail grant proposal form and attachments
 Copies of proposal: 8
 Deadline(s): Mar. 1, June 1, and Sept. 1 (or first business day following)
 Board meeting date(s): Last Thurs. of each month except June and Dec.
 Final notification: Apr. 30, July 31, and Oct. 31

Officers and Directors:* Linda Bowman,* Chair.; Tom Parent,* Vice-Chair.; James E. Klusman,* C.E.O. and Pres.; Alysa C. Rollock,* Secy.; Liz Solberg,* Treas.; Mary Ilu Altman; William P. Gettings; Patty Jischke; David McGaughey; Betty Nelson; Sandy Pearlman; Charlene Sullivan; James Taylor.

Number of staff: 4 full-time professional; 1 full-time support; 1 part-time support.

EIN: 237147996

3189

Legacy Foundation, Inc.

1000 E. 80th Pl., S. Tower, Ste. 302
Merrillville, IN 46410-5644 (219) 736-1880
Contact: Nancy K. Johnson, Pres.
FAX: (219) 736-1940;
E-mail: info@legacyfoundationlakeco.org;
URL: http://www.legacyfoundationlakeco.org

Established in 1992 in IN.

Foundation type: Community foundation.

Financial data (yr. ended 6/30/05): Assets, $20,617,233 (M); gifts received, $2,421,667; expenditures, $1,003,947; giving activities include $416,535 for 73 grants, and $246,324 for 182 grants to individuals.

Purpose and activities: The foundation exists to encourage community philanthropy. It will seek and accept endowments from public and private sources and distribute the income for community enhancing projects and other charitable purposes.

Fields of interest: Arts; Education; Environment; Public health; Health care; Youth, services; Human services; Community development, neighborhood development; Community development; Philanthropy/voluntarism; Public affairs.

Type of support: Building/renovation; Equipment; Program development; Seed money; Scholarship funds; Technical assistance; Scholarships—to individuals; Matching/challenge support.

Limitations: Giving primarily in Lake County, IN. No support for sectarian religious programs or basic municipal or educational functions and services. No grants to individuals (except through designated scholarship funds), or for operating budgets, endowment funds, debt reduction, continuing support, general operating expenses (except for start up), annual campaigns, fundraising events, or travel; no multi-year grants or scholarly research grants.

Publications: Application guidelines; Annual report; Informational brochure; Newsletter.

Application information: Visit foundation Web site for application forms and guidelines. All proposals should be paper clipped. Application form required.

 Initial approach: Contact foundation
 Copies of proposal: 1
 Deadline(s): Mar. 15, June 15, Sept. 15, and Dec. 15
 Board meeting date(s): 1st Tues. of Feb., Apr., June, Aug., Oct., and Dec.
 Final notification: 60-90 days

Officers and Directors:* Tory Prasco,* Chair.; David Bochnowski,* Vice-Chair.; Nancy K. Johnson, Pres. and Exec. Dir.; James Greiner,* Secy.; Kenneth Krupinski,* Treas.; Robert Anadell,* Chair., Investment Comm.; Joe Medellin,* Chair., Grants Comm.; Nancy Clifford; Fredricka Davidson; Frankie Fesko; Stephanie Gerdes; Christopher Morrow; Robert Nickovich; Michael O'Donnell; Richard Oesterle; Stephen Place; Cynthia Powers; Jack Primich; David Ross, M.D.; John Rudy; Robert Scott; Verne Seehausen; Steve Simpson, M.D.; Jennifer Vinovich; W.F. Wellman.

Number of staff: 3 full-time professional; 1 full-time support.

EIN: 351872803

3190
Judd Leighton Foundation, Inc. ✧
211 W. Washington Ave., Ste. 2400
South Bend, IN 46601 (574) 287-5977
Contact: James F. Keenan, Pres.

Established in 2000 in IN.
Donor: Judd Leighton.
Foundation type: Independent foundation.
Financial data (yr. ended 12/31/05): Assets, $28,834,507 (M); expenditures, $1,499,874; qualifying distributions, $1,400,000; giving activities include $1,400,000 for 3 grants (high: $500,000; low: $400,000).
Fields of interest: Higher education; Human services; Homeless, human services; Foundations (community).
Limitations: Giving primarily in IN. No grants to individuals.
Application information: Application form required.
  Initial approach: Letter
  Deadline(s): None
Officers and Directors:* James F. Keenan,* Pres. and Treas.; Marilyn Bussewitz,* V.P.; Mary Stanfield,* Secy.
EIN: 352120550
Selected grants: The following grants were reported in 2003.
$1,355,745 to University of Notre Dame, Notre Dame, IN. For directorship endowment.
$500 to Eisenhower Medical Center, Rancho Mirage, CA. For general support.

3191
Leighton-Oare Foundation, Inc. ✧
211 W. Washington Ave., Ste. 2400
South Bend, IN 46601
Contact: James F. Keenan, Pres.

Incorporated in 1955 in IN.
Donors: Mary Morris Leighton; Judd C. Leighton.
Foundation type: Independent foundation.
Financial data (yr. ended 12/31/05): Assets, $22,844,380 (M); expenditures, $1,348,246; qualifying distributions, $1,027,400; giving activities include $1,027,400 for 16 grants (high: $500,000; low: $500).
Purpose and activities: Giving primarily to a symphony orchestra and for the arts; major support also for a law school, higher education and health.
Fields of interest: Arts, multipurpose centers/ programs; Performing arts, orchestra (symphony); Historic preservation/historical societies; Higher education, college; Law school/education; Health care, fund raising/fund distribution; Health care, clinics/centers.
Type of support: General/operating support; Continuing support; Building/renovation; Endowments.
Limitations: Giving primarily in IN. No grants to individuals.
Application information: Application form not required.
  Initial approach: Letter
  Deadline(s): None
  Board meeting date(s): Feb., May, Aug., and Nov.
  Final notification: 90 to 120 days
Officers: James F. Keenan, Pres.; Marilyn Bussewitz, V.P.; Mary Stanfield, Secy.
EIN: 356034243

3192
Eli Lilly and Company Foundation ▼
Lilly Corporate Ctr., D.C. 1627
Indianapolis, IN 46285
Contact: Robert L. Smith, Pres.
URL: http://www.lilly.com/products/access/ foundation.html

Incorporated in 1968 in IN.
Donor: Eli Lilly and Co.
Foundation type: Company-sponsored foundation.
Financial data (yr. ended 12/31/05): Assets, $96,129,760 (M); gifts received, $50,000,000; expenditures, $27,059,448; qualifying distributions, $26,853,326; giving activities include $21,243,458 for grants, and $5,556,419 for employee matching gifts.
Purpose and activities: The foundation supports organizations involved with arts and culture, K-12 education reform, mental health, disease, youth development, community development, diversity, and public policy research.
Fields of interest: Arts, cultural/ethnic awareness; Arts; Education, reform; Elementary/secondary education; Mental health, depression; Mental health, schizophrenia; Mental health/crisis services; Cancer; Heart & circulatory diseases; Nerve, muscle & bone diseases; Diabetes; Health organizations; Youth development; Civil rights, race/intergroup relations; Community development; Public policy, research; Women.
Type of support: Employee volunteer services; General/operating support; Continuing support; Annual campaigns; Capital campaigns; Equipment; Fellowships; Employee matching gifts; Donated products; Matching/challenge support.
Limitations: Giving on a national and international basis, with emphasis on areas of company operations, including Indianapolis, IN. No support for religious or sectarian organizations not of direct benefit to the entire community, fraternal, labor, athletic, or veterans' organizations or bands, or non-accredited educational organizations. No grants to individuals, or for scholarships or travel, endowments, debt reduction, beauty or talent contests, fundraising activities related to individual sponsorship, conferences or media production, or memorials; no loans; no political contributions.
Publications: Application guidelines; Corporate giving report; Informational brochure (including application guidelines).
Application information: Application form not required.
  Initial approach: Proposal
  Deadline(s): June 30 and Dec. 31
  Board meeting date(s): 1st quarter and 3rd quarter
  Final notification: Following board meetings
Officer and Directors:* Robert L. Smith,* Pres.; Robert A. Armitage; Scott A. Canute; Deirdre Connelly; Charles E. Golden; John C. Lechleiter, Ph.D.; Steven M. Paul, M.D.; Derica Rice; Gino Santini; Lorenzo Tallarigo, M.D.; Sidney Taurel.
Number of staff: 1 full-time professional; 3 full-time support.
EIN: 356202479
Selected grants: The following grants were reported in 2004.
$2,049,758 to United Way of Central Indiana, Indianapolis, IN. For program support and match of gifts made by Indianapolis and Greenfield employees and retirees during annual campaign.
$1,000,000 to Brigham and Womens Hospital, Boston, MA. To establish comprehensive,

practice-based hub for research and training on drug-resistant tuberculosis in South Africa, Russia, and China.
$500,000 to Indiana University, School of Medicine, Indianapolis, IN. For construction of new facility to house research programs.
$500,000 to Mental Health Association, National, Alexandria, VA. For Adult Mental Health Services.
$250,000 to American Diabetes Association, National Service Center, Alexandria, VA. To expand educational programming of Latino Health Care Provider (HCP) CME Project.
$225,000 to Indiana Symphony Society, Indianapolis Symphony Orchestra, Indianapolis, IN. For endowment campaign.
$100,000 to National Institutes of Health, Foundation for the, Bethesda, MD. For The Best Pharmaceuticals for Children Fund.
$50,000 to United Way International, Alexandria, VA. For general operating support.
$50,000 to World Health Organization, Geneva, Switzerland. For continued support for development of mental health services and strengthening health policies.
$25,000 to Harvard University, School of Public Health, Cambridge, MA. For minority fellowship in biostatistics at School of Public Health in Boston.

3193
Lilly Cares Foundation, Inc. ✧
c/o Eli Lilly and Co.
893 S. Delaware St., Lilly Corporate Ctr.
Indianapolis, IN 46285 (800) 545-6962
Application address: P.O. Box 230999, Centerville, VA 20120; URL: http://www.lillycares.com

Established as a company-sponsored operating foundation in 1996 in IN.
Donor: Eli Lilly and Co.
Foundation type: Operating foundation.
Financial data (yr. ended 12/31/04): Assets, $1,377 (M); gifts received, $98,246,623; expenditures, $146,701,709; qualifying distributions, $146,701,709; giving activities include $146,701,709 for grants to individuals.
Purpose and activities: The foundation distributes pharmaceuticals to the ill, the needy, the indigent, and infants.
International interests: Developing countries.
Type of support: Donated products; Grants to individuals.
Limitations: Giving on a national and international basis.
Application information: Application form required.
  Initial approach: Telephone foundation for application form
  Deadline(s): None
Officer: Thomas A. King, Pres.
Directors: Robert A. Armitage; Charles E. Golden; Pedro P. Granadillo; John C. Lechleiter, Ph.D.; Steven M. Paul, M.D.; Gino Santini; Lorenzo Tallarigo, M.D.; Sidney Taurel.
EIN: 352027985

3194
Lilly Endowment Inc. ▼
2801 N. Meridian St.
P.O. Box 88068
Indianapolis, IN 46208-0068 (317) 924-5471
Contact: Sue Ellen Walker, Comms. Assoc.

FAX: (317) 926-4431; URL: http://www.lillyendowment.org

Incorporated in June 1937 in IN.
Donors: J.K. Lilly, Sr.†; Eli Lilly†; J.K. Lilly, Jr.†; Ruth Lilly.
Foundation type: Independent foundation.
Financial data (yr. ended 12/31/05): Assets, $8,360,760,584 (M); gifts received, $17,317,562; expenditures, $445,763,815; qualifying distributions, $441,383,906; giving activities include $421,342,727 for 825 grants (high: $22,000,000; low: $1,000; average: $25,000–$1,000,000), $960,000 for 120 grants to individuals, $5,162,472 for 1,258 employee matching gifts, and $107,583 for 2 foundation-administered programs.
Purpose and activities: Support for religion, education, and community development, with special concentration on programs that benefit youth and develop leadership. Giving emphasizes charitable organizations that depend on private support, with a limited number of grants to government institutions and tax-supported programs. Also supports limited grant programs in public policy research.
Fields of interest: Museums; Historic preservation/historical societies; Arts; Education, research; Elementary/secondary education; Higher education; Theological school/education; Housing/shelter; Recreation; Youth development, services; Human services; Community development; Philanthropy/voluntarism, research; Voluntarism promotion; Public policy, research; Economically disadvantaged.
Type of support: Consulting services; Internship funds; Professorships; Management development/capacity building; General/operating support; Continuing support; Annual campaigns; Capital campaigns; Building/renovation; Equipment; Land acquisition; Endowments; Emergency funds; Program development; Conferences/seminars; Publication; Seed money; Curriculum development; Fellowships; Scholarship funds; Research; Technical assistance; Program evaluation; Employee matching gifts; Matching/challenge support.
Limitations: Giving limited to IN, with emphasis on Indianapolis, for community development projects (including the arts, preservation, capital building funds, operating funds, and social services). Education funding focused principally on Indiana under invitational grant programs. National giving in religion, philanthropic studies, leadership education, and selected higher education initiatives, principally to increase educational opportunities for minorities. Generally, no support for healthcare programs, or mass media projects; libraries, elementary/secondary schools or for human service projects. No grants to individuals (except for fellowships awarded under special programs) or endowments (except for community foundations in Indiana or in the context of special initiatives) or for building campaigns or operating funds.
Publications: Application guidelines; Annual report (including application guidelines); Occasional report; Program policy statement.
Application information: Requests submitted via fax or E-mail will not be considered. Application form not required.
Initial approach: Letter (no more than 2 pages)
Copies of proposal: 1

Board meeting date(s): Feb., Mar., May, June, July, Sept., Nov., and Dec.
Final notification: Generally 3 to 6 months after formal proposal is submitted
Officers and Directors:* Thomas M. Lofton,* Chair.; N. Clay Robbins,* Pres.; Craig R. Dykstra, Sr. V.P., Religion; Sara B. Cobb, V.P., Education; William M. Goodwin, V.P., Community Devel.; David D. Biber, Secy.-Treas.; Eugene F. Ratliff, Dir. Emeritus; Otis R. Bowen; Daniel P. Carmichael; William G. Enright, Ph.D.; Eli Lilly II; Mary K. Lisher.
Number of staff: 21 full-time professional; 23 full-time support.
EIN: 350868122
Selected grants: The following grants were reported in 2005.
$22,000,000 to Butler University, Indianapolis, IN. For creation of Butler Business Accelerator.
$19,979,940 to Ball State University Foundation, Muncie, IN. For supplemental support for iCommunication: The Media Design Initiative, effort to enhance opportunities for students and faculty to develop expertise in providing leadership and innovative content for digital communications.
$18,600,000 to Independent Colleges of Indiana, Indianapolis, IN. For Lilly Endowment Community Scholarship Program.
$10,000,000 to American Red Cross, National Headquarters, DC. For relief effort for Hurricane Katrina.
$8,171,433 to Indianapolis Center for Congregations, Indianapolis, IN. For operating support.
$6,250,000 to Educational Broadcasting Corporation, New York, NY. For continued support for broadcast of Religion and Ethics NewsWeekly.
$3,700,000 to Heartland Film Festival, Indianapolis, IN. For expanded operating support plan and special promotional initiatives.
$1,000,000 to Vincennes University Foundation, Vincennes, IN. For technical assistance for Phase II of Initiative to Strengthen Philanthropy for Indiana Higher Education Institutions.
$499,979 to Calvin College, Grand Rapids, MI. For Continuation of Kingdom Apprentices project.
$44,875 to Saint Celestine Roman Catholic Church, Elmwood Park, IL. For Clergy renewal program.

3195
Lincoln Financial Group Foundation ▼ ✧
(formerly The Lincoln National Foundation, Inc.)
1300 S. Clinton St.
P.O. Box 7863
Fort Wayne, IN 46801-7863   (260) 455-3879
Contact: Sandra Kemmish, Prog. Off.
FAX: (260) 455-4004; E-mail: skemmish@lnc.com; URL: http://www.lfg.com/lfg/ipc/abt/cgv/index.html

Established in 1962 in IN as a company-sponsored operating foundation.
Donors: Lincoln National Corp.; The Lincoln National Life Insurance Co.
Foundation type: Operating foundation.
Financial data (yr. ended 12/31/05): Assets, $16,220,954 (M); gifts received, $8,453,991; expenditures, $11,698,650; qualifying distributions, $11,430,962; giving activities include $9,745,924 for 587 grants (high: $500,000; low: $300), $277,359 for 240 employee matching gifts,

and $1,599,648 for foundation-administered programs.
Purpose and activities: The foundation supports organizations involved with arts and culture, education, and human services.
Fields of interest: Arts; Education; Human services.
International interests: United Kingdom.
Type of support: Annual campaigns; Capital campaigns; Building/renovation; Equipment; Land acquisition; Emergency funds; Program development; Conferences/seminars; Seed money; Scholarship funds; Technical assistance; Consulting services; Program evaluation; Employee matching gifts; Matching/challenge support.
Limitations: Giving limited to areas of company operations, with emphasis on Hartford, CT, Schaumburg and the Chicago, IL, area, Fort Wayne, IN, Portland, ME, Omaha, NE, Concord, NH, Greensboro, NC, Philadelphia, PA, and London, United Kingdom. No support for religious or political organizations, public or private elementary or secondary schools or school foundations, hospitals, hospital foundations, or nursing homes, veterans' or fraternal organizations, or pass-through organizations. No grants to individuals, or for endowments, continuing support, general operating support, debt reduction, marketing programs, sporting events or tournaments, or fundraising for national organizations; generally, no grants for tickets, corporate tables, or testimonial events.
Publications: Application guidelines; Grants list.
Application information: Visit Web site for nearest application address. Application form required.
Initial approach: Complete online application form or download application form and mail to nearest application address
Copies of proposal: 1
Deadline(s): Jan. 6 for Arts and Culture; Apr. 6 for Education; and July 6 for Human Services
Board meeting date(s): Quarterly
Final notification: Within 1 week following board meetings
Officers and Directors:* Jon A. Boscia,* Pres.; Priscilla S. Brown,* V.P.; Richard C. Vaughan,* V.P.; C. Suzanne Womack,* Secy.; Janet C. Chrzan,* Treas.; George E. Davis; Barbara S. Kowalczyk.
EIN: 356042099
Selected grants: The following grants were reported in 2005.
$500,000 to Junior Achievement of Northern Indiana, Fort Wayne, IN. For Lincoln Finance Park (Centennial Gift).
$431,000 to W H Y Y, Philadelphia, PA. For Lincoln Financial Digital Education Studio (Centennial Gift).
$280,000 to United Way of Allen County, Fort Wayne, IN. For corporate pledge and initiative support.
$250,000 to Fort Wayne Central Improvement Foundation, Fort Wayne, IN. For Grand Wayne Center expansion.
$100,000 to Teach for America, Philadelphia, PA. For Vision 2008.
$75,000 to YMCA of Philadelphia and Vicinity, Philadelphia, PA. For Saturday Fun Club.
$25,000 to Educational Opportunity and Talent Search Center, Fort Wayne, IN. For Technology Improvement and Instructional Support.
$20,000 to Allen County Fort Wayne Historical Society, Fort Wayne, IN. For creation of Interactive History Cases.
$20,000 to Congreso de Latinos Unidos, Philadelphia, PA. For Calle Americana CareerLink.

$20,000 to Junior Achievement of Southwest New England, Hartford, CT. For Partnership for Economic Education.

3196
Lumina Foundation for Education, Inc. ▼
P.O. Box 1806
Indianapolis, IN 46206-1806 (317) 951-5300
Contact: Prog. Office
FAX: (317) 951-5063; URL: http://www.luminafoundation.org

Established in 2000.
Donors: USA Group, Inc.; SLM Holding Corp.
Foundation type: Independent foundation.
Financial data (yr. ended 12/31/05): Assets, $1,235,598,231 (M); expenditures, $90,805,634; qualifying distributions, $48,457,322; giving activities include $48,457,322 for grants.
Purpose and activities: Giving primarily to support and expand access to postsecondary education in the United States, particularly for students of low income or other underrepresented groups. The three main themes focused on are: access, success, and adult learners.
Fields of interest: Higher education; Economically disadvantaged.
Type of support: Program development; Publication; Seed money; Research; Program evaluation; Employee matching gifts; Matching/challenge support.
Limitations: Giving on a national basis. No support for K-12 education reform, discipline-specific schools of study and training or religious activities (except for activities that promote educational access and success and that serve diverse recipients without regard to their religious background). No grants to individuals (except for employee matching gifts), or for scholarships, fundraisers, corporate sponsorships, meetings and conferences (except for those related to a strategic initiative of the foundation), capital campaigns, or endowment funds.
Publications: Application guidelines; Annual report; Financial statement; Informational brochure (including application guidelines); Newsletter.
Application information: Application form required.
  Initial approach: Letter of inquiry
  Copies of proposal: 1
  Deadline(s): None
  Final notification: 3 to 6 months
Officers and Directors:* John M. Mutz,* Chair.; Martha D. Lamkin,* C.E.O. and Pres.; Susan O. Conner, Exec. V.P., Impact Strategy; Holiday Hart McKiernan, Sr. V.P., Secy., and Genl. Counsel; J. David Maas, Sr. V.P., C.F.O., and Treas.; Leah Meyer Austin, Sr. V.P., Research and Progs.; Robert C. Dickeson, Sr. V.P., Policy and Organizational Learning; Nathan E. Fischer, V.P., Investments; David A. Brown, Cont.; Rev. E. William Beauchamp; Gerald L. Bepko; Norris Darrell, Jr.; James C. Lintzenich; Edward A. McCabe; Marie V. McDemmond; William R. Neale; J. Bonnie Newman; Richard J. Ramsden; Edward R. Schmidt; Randolph H. Waterfield, Jr.
Number of staff: 30 full-time professional; 2 part-time professional; 8 full-time support.
EIN: 351813228
Selected grants: The following grants were reported in 2004.
$2,683,700 to American Association of Community Colleges, DC. To serve as partner in Achieving the

Dream: Community Colleges Count initiative, payable over 1.50 years.
$2,400,000 to MDRC, New York, NY. To increase low-income and nontraditional student success and persistence by testing innovative interventions at selected community colleges, payable over 3 years.
$1,798,300 to Jobs for the Future, Boston, MA. To serve as partner in Achieving the Dream: Community Colleges Count initiative.
$1,755,000 to University of Texas, Austin, TX. To serve as partner in Achieving the Dream: Community Colleges Count Initiative, payable over 1.50 years.
$1,585,900 to Hispanic Scholarship Fund, San Francisco, CA. To increase enrollment of Latino students at four-year colleges by adding an access component to Scholar Chapters targeting community college students and high school students, payable over 3 years.
$1,180,000 to Central Indiana Corporate Partnership Foundation, Indianapolis, IN. To expand access to postsecondary education for Indiana students who aspire to work in life sciences and medical manufacturing sectors, payable over 2 years.
$1,027,600 to Teachers College Columbia University, New York, NY. To serve as partner in Achieving the Dream: Community Colleges Count initiative by helping colleges use data to conduct self-assessments, payable over 1.50 years.
$1,020,000 to College Summit, DC. To enroll more promising, low-income youth in college and develop strategies to increase college enrollment over time, payable over 3 years.
$960,500 to Indiana University-Purdue University, Indianapolis, IN. For Breaking the Cycle grants supporting programs that aim to improve the postsecondary access and attainment of foster youth in and out of care, ages 14-24, payable over 2 years.
$899,700 to Council for Adult and Experiential Learning, Chicago, IL. To increase and expand adult students' attainment in community colleges by improving institutional effectiveness and state policies that affect adults' postsecondary access and success, payable over 3 years.

3197
Madison County Community Foundation ◇
33 W. 10th St.
P.O. Box 1056
Anderson, IN 46015-1056 (765) 644-0002
Contact: Sally A. DeVoe, Exec. Dir.
FAX: (765) 644-3392; E-mail: info@madisonccf.org;
Additional E-mail: sdevoe@madisonccf.org;
URL: http://www.madisonccf.org

Established in 1992 in Indiana.
Foundation type: Community foundation.
Financial data (yr. ended 12/31/05): Assets, $12,008,765 (M); gifts received, $605,529; expenditures, $838,191; giving activities include $493,016 for grants.
Purpose and activities: The foundation seeks to enhance the quality of life of the citizens of Madison County, Indiana, by attracting charitable gifts, making philanthropic grants, providing responsible financial stewardship and community leadership.
Fields of interest: Arts; Education; Health care; Human services; Economic development; Public affairs.

Type of support: Emergency funds; General/operating support; Capital campaigns; Building/renovation; Equipment; Program development; Curriculum development; Scholarship funds; Scholarships—to individuals; Matching/challenge support.
Limitations: Giving limited to Madison County, IN. No support for religious or sectarian activities. No grants to individuals (except for scholarships), for budget deficits, annual fund campaigns, capital debt reduction, endowments, medical, scientific, or health research, or travel; no student loans.
Publications: Annual report (including application guidelines); Informational brochure; Newsletter.
Application information: Visit foundation Web site for application form, guidelines, and specific deadlines. Application form required.
  Initial approach: Letter
  Copies of proposal: 12
  Deadline(s): Spring and fall
  Board meeting date(s): 6 times a year
  Final notification: Within 6 weeks
Officers and Directors:* Robert J. Pensec,* Pres.; Joseph R. Kilmer,* V.P.; Renee Allen,* Secy.; Jay B. Ricker,* Treas.; Sally A. DeVoe,* Exec. Dir.; James F. Ault; Sherry Contos; Charles Dickmann; Dr. James L. Edwards; Roderick English; Jeff Jenness; Herbert G. Likens; Carlton C. Montague; Lynn Rowley; Kelly Schmink; William L. Surbaugh.
Number of staff: 1 full-time professional; 1 part-time professional; 1 full-time support.
EIN: 351859959

3198
The Elizabeth A. Mahnken Foundation, Inc. ◇ ☆
12210 N. Mariposa Dr.
Syracuse, IN 46567-8773 (574) 457-5365
Contact: Sally M. Mahnken, Exec. Dir.

Established in 1993 in IN.
Donors: Richard Mahnken, Jr.; sally Mahnken.
Foundation type: Independent foundation.
Financial data (yr. ended 12/31/05): Assets, $929,006 (M); gifts received, $97,586; expenditures, $329,834; qualifying distributions, $328,554; giving activities include $327,723 for 58 grants to individuals (high: $13,478; low: $400).
Purpose and activities: Scholarships only to Kosciusko County, IN, residents, who are attending a state-supported university or college, and who are seeking a four-year degree.
Type of support: Scholarships—to individuals.
Limitations: Giving limited to residents of Kosciusko County, IN.
Application information: Application form required.
  Initial approach: Request application
  Deadline(s): Mar. 1
Officer and Directors:* Sally M. Mahnken,* Exec. Dir.; David C. Cates; Deborah Gillum; Mary J. Lines; Stephen R. Snyder.
EIN: 351873161

3199
Marshall County Community Foundation, Inc.
2701 N. Michigan St.
P.O. Box 716
Plymouth, IN 46563 (574) 935-5159
Contact: Jayne Gibson

FAX: (574) 936-8040;
E-mail: info@marshallcountycf.org; Additional
E-mail: jayne@marshallcountycf.org; URL: http://
www.marshallcountycf.org

Established in 1991 in IN.
Foundation type: Community foundation.
Financial data (yr. ended 6/30/05): Assets,
$20,310,357 (M); gifts received, $166,923;
expenditures, $984,667; giving activities include
$568,460 for 85 grants (high: $206,400; low: $50).
Purpose and activities: The mission of the
foundation is to assist individuals within the
Marshall County, IN community in the building and
administration of endowment and planned giving
resulting in an enriched quality of life for all current
and future citizens.
Fields of interest: Arts; Secondary school/
education; Higher education; Libraries (public);
Scholarships/financial aid; Animals/wildlife,
preservation/protection; Hospitals (general);
Recreation, parks/playgrounds; Recreation;
Community development; Government/public
administration.
Type of support: Publication; Seed money;
Consulting services; Scholarships—to individuals.
Limitations: Giving limited to Marshall County, IN.
No support for sectarian or religious purposes. No
grants to individuals (except for scholarships), or for
operating expenses, long-term funding or for
endowments.
Publications: Application guidelines; Annual report
(including application guidelines); Financial
statement; Grants list; Informational brochure
(including application guidelines); Newsletter;
Program policy statement.
Application information: Visit foundation Web site
for application form and guidelines. Application form
required.
  Initial approach: Submit application form and
    attachments
  Copies of proposal: 3
  Deadline(s): Feb. 1 and Aug. 1
  Board meeting date(s): Jan., Mar., May, July,
    Sept., and Dec.
  Final notification: Within 90 days
Officers and Directors:* Bruce Jennings,* Pres.;
Tammy Houin,* V.P.; Sarah Smith,* Secy.; Richard
Parker,* Treas.; Jennifer S. Maddox, Exec. Dir.; Roy
Michael Roush, Legal Counsel; Matt Benedict;
James D. Bonine; Michael D. Burroughs; Judy Delp;
Frank DeSantis; James Erwin; Kathy Fick; Verna Kay
Finlay; Jayne Gibson; Jack Jordan; Patti Kitch;
Latham Lawson; Louise Mason; Amy Middaugh;
Greg Miller; Shannon Samuelson; Ben Schaller;
Brad Schuldt; Roger Umbaugh; Jon VanDerWeele;
Beverly Van Gilder; Leon Verhaeghe; Susan Wagner;
Fran Wilkins; John Zeglis.
Number of staff: 2 full-time professional; 1 part-time
professional.
EIN: 351826870

3200
Rex and Alice A. Martin Foundation ✧
1516 Middlebury St.
Elkhart, IN 46516-4740
URL: http://www.nibco.com/cms.do?id=550

Established in 2000 in IN.
Donors: Rex Martin; Alice A. Martin; NIBCO, Inc.
Foundation type: Operating foundation.
Financial data (yr. ended 6/30/05): Assets,
$11,602,749 (M); gifts received, $5,000;

expenditures, $540,204; qualifying distributions,
$429,924; giving activities include $382,073 for 16
grants (high: $150,000; low: $2,500).
Purpose and activities: Giving primarily for
secondary education.
Fields of interest: Media, television; Arts; Higher
education; Children/youth, services.
Limitations: Applications not accepted. No grants to
individuals.
Application information: Contributes only to
pre-selected organizations.
Officer and Directors:* Alice A. Martin,* Pres.; Rex
Martin.
EIN: 352117025
Selected grants: The following grants were reported
in 2004.
$150,000 to Middlesex School, Concord, MA. For
  Martin Mathematics classroom.
$50,000 to Carlock Christian Church, Carlock, IL.
  For stained glass windows.
$50,000 to Elkhart, City of, Elkhart, IN. For Martin
  Skate Park.
$25,000 to London Symphony Orchestra, London,
  England. For operating support.
$10,000 to American Red Cross, Augusta, GA. For
  disaster relief.
$10,000 to Boys and Girls Clubs of Deep East
  Texas, Nacogdoches, TX. For operating support.
$10,000 to Indiana Youth Institute, Indianapolis, IN.
  For kids' conference.
$10,000 to Midwest Museum of American Art,
  Elkhart, IN. For operating support.
$5,000 to Virginia Living Museum, Newport News,
  VA. For NIBCO Observatory staircase.
$2,500 to Marian High School, Mishawaka, IN. For
  Jubilee Auction.

3201
Master Works Foundation, Inc. ✧
2879 E. Dupont Rd.
Fort Wayne, IN 46825 (260) 485-1139
Contact: Laurie L. Doden, Exec. Dir.

Established in 1988 in IN.
Donor: Daryle L. Doden.
Foundation type: Independent foundation.
Financial data (yr. ended 12/31/05): Assets,
$2,015,535 (M); gifts received, $1,007,282;
expenditures, $841,494; qualifying distributions,
$709,063; giving activities include $499,656 for 43
grants (high: $59,904; low: $530), $6,495 for 2
employee matching gifts, and $4,000 for 1 in-kind
gift.
Purpose and activities: Giving primarily for Christian
education, agencies and churches; funding also for
Baptist churches.
Fields of interest: Higher education; Theological
school/education; Education; Christian agencies &
churches; Protestant agencies & churches.
Limitations: Giving on a national basis.
Application information: Application form not
required.
  Deadline(s): None
Officers: Daryle L. Doden, Pres.; Brenda J. Doden,
Secy.; Laurie Doden, Exec. Dir.
Director: Eric R. Doden.
EIN: 351752152

3202
Alfred J. McAllister and Dorothy N. McAllister Foundation ✧
1401 S. 9th St.
Lafayette, IN 47905-1858

Established in 2000 in IN.
Donor: Dorothy N. McAllister.
Foundation type: Independent foundation.
Financial data (yr. ended 12/31/05): Assets,
$12,649,533 (M); expenditures, $724,805;
qualifying distributions, $596,589; giving activities
include $510,900 for 13 grants (high: $130,000;
low: $4,700).
Fields of interest: Secondary school/education;
Food banks; Human services; Children/youth,
services; Community development.
Limitations: Applications not accepted. Giving
primarily in Lafayette, IN. No grants to individuals.
Application information: Contributes only to
pre-selected organizations.
Trustees: Charles Max Layden; William J. McCaw; J.
David Webb; Wayne E. Weber.
EIN: 352050825
Selected grants: The following grants were reported
in 2003.
$200,000 to Jefferson High School, Lafayette, IN.
$89,500 to Lafayette School Corporation,
  Lafayette, IN.
$41,500 to YWCA of Greater Lafayette, Lafayette,
  IN.
$35,000 to Wabash Center, Lafayette, IN.
$34,000 to Ivy Tech Foundation, Lafayette, IN.
$25,750 to Tippecanoe County Historical
  Association, Lafayette, IN.
$18,700 to Tippecanoe, County of, Department of
  Parks, Lafayette, IN.
$10,750 to Food Finders Food Bank, Lafayette, IN.
$8,000 to Boy Scouts of America, Sagamore
  Council, Kokomo, IN.
$3,000 to Pleasantview Christian School, West
  Lafayette, IN.

3203
McMillen Foundation, Inc. ✧
1302 S. Creighton Dr.
Fort Wayne, IN 46803 (260) 484-8631
Application address: c/o John F. McMillen, Pres.,
6610 Mutual Dr., Fort Wayne, IN 46825-4236

Incorporated in 1947 in IN.
Donors: Dale W. McMillen†; and members of the
McMillen family.
Foundation type: Independent foundation.
Financial data (yr. ended 12/31/04): Assets,
$27,822,773 (M); expenditures, $1,363,886;
qualifying distributions, $1,094,910; giving
activities include $1,094,910 for 22 grants (high:
$200,000; low: $2,000).
Purpose and activities: Emphasis on recreation
associations and youth agencies; some support
also for education, and health associations.
Fields of interest: Education; Health care; Health
organizations, association; Recreation; Children/
youth, services; Community development.
Type of support: Building/renovation; Program
development.
Limitations: Giving limited to Fort Wayne and Allen
County, IN. No support for churches or religious
groups. No grants to individuals.
Publications: Application guidelines.
Application information: Application form not
required.

Initial approach: Letter
Copies of proposal: 1
Deadline(s): None
Board meeting date(s): Annual meeting in midsummer; and executive committee meets near year end
Officers and Directors:* John F. McMillen,* Pres.; Thomas M. Shoaff,* V.P.; Dorothy J. Robinson, Secy.-Treas.; Thomas A. Irmscher; Dale W. McMillen III; N. Reed Silliman.
EIN: 356021003
Selected grants: The following grants were reported in 2003.
$100,000 to Fort Wayne Park Foundation, Fort Wayne, IN. For capital campaign.
$100,000 to YMCA of Metropolitan Fort Wayne, Fort Wayne, IN. For Jorgensen Family capital campaign.
$25,000 to Big Brothers/Big Sisters of Northeast Indiana, Fort Wayne, IN. For growth initiative campaign.
$25,000 to Childrens Hope, Fort Wayne, IN. For capital campaign.
$25,000 to Urban League of Fort Wayne, Fort Wayne, IN. For diversity and activity center capital campaign.
$10,000 to Educational Opportunity and Talent Search Center, Fort Wayne, IN. For building project.
$5,000 to Cornerstone Youth Center, Monroeville, IN. Toward purchase of facility.
$5,000 to Habitat for Humanity, Fort Wayne, Fort Wayne, IN. For new phone system.
$4,500 to Fort Wayne Community Schools, Fort Wayne, IN. For vision assistance program.
$2,000 to Community Foundation of Greater Fort Wayne, Fort Wayne, IN. For annual support.

3204
Met Foundation, Inc. ◇
7406 N. Washington Blvd.
Indianapolis, IN 46240 (317) 259-0717
Contact: Susan M. Tolbert, Pres. and Treas.

Established in 1997 in IN.
Donor: Sue Anne McVie.
Foundation type: Independent foundation.
Financial data (yr. ended 12/31/05): Assets, $13,573,852 (M); expenditures, $741,470; qualifying distributions, $690,585; giving activities include $677,243 for 50 grants (high: $131,000; low: $500).
Purpose and activities: Giving for the arts, youth services, and animal welfare.
Fields of interest: Museums; Higher education; Environment, natural resources; Environment, land resources; Animals/wildlife, preservation/ protection; Alzheimer's disease; Boy scouts; Youth, services; Protestant agencies & churches.
Limitations: Giving primarily in Indianapolis, IN.
Application information: Application form not required.
Deadline(s): None
Officers and Directors:* Susan M. Tolbert,* Pres. and Treas.; Douglas S. McVie,* V.P.; Alexander M. McVie III,* Secy.
EIN: 351995120
Selected grants: The following grants were reported in 2004.
$75,720 to Second Presbyterian Church, Indianapolis, IN.
$38,000 to Arizona Open Land Trust, Tucson, AZ.

$35,500 to National Sports Center for the Disabled, Winter Park, CO.
$25,000 to Alzheimers Disease and Related Disorders Association, Columbus, IN.
$25,000 to Defenders of Wildlife, DC.
$25,000 to Regis Jesuit High School, Aurora, CO.
$25,000 to Wabash College, Crawfordsville, IN.
$10,000 to Fox Tucson Theater Foundation, Tucson, AZ.
$5,000 to Educational Choice Charitable Trust, Indianapolis, IN.
$5,000 to Sky Island Alliance, Tucson, AZ.

3205
Michigan City Community Enrichment Corporation ◇
100 E. Michigan Blvd.
Michigan City, IN 46360 (219) 873-1408, ext. 382

Established in 1998 in IN.
Donor: Blue Chip Casino, Inc.
Foundation type: Company-sponsored foundation.
Financial data (yr. ended 12/31/04): Assets, $124,002 (M); gifts received, $750,000; expenditures, $758,758; qualifying distributions, $758,758; giving activities include $746,648 for 48 grants (high: $100,000; low: $3,000).
Purpose and activities: The foundation supports zoos, parks, and organizations involved with education, health, and community development.
Fields of interest: Education; Zoos/zoological societies; Health care; Recreation, parks/ playgrounds; Boys & girls clubs; Salvation Army; Community development.
Limitations: Giving primarily in Michigan City, IN. No grants to individuals.
Application information: Application form required.
Initial approach: Contact foundation for application form
Deadline(s): Varies
Officers and Directors:* Steven Gonzalez,* Chair.; Eddie Newson,* Vice-Chair.; Andrea Smith, Secy.; Sue Yadavia, Treas.; Jim Knitzele; Stephanie Oberlie; Arthur Payne; Freddi Valdez; Nate Williams; Bob Worek.
EIN: 352036426

3206
Montgomery County Community Foundation ◇
118 E. Main St.
P.O. Box 334
Crawfordsville, IN 47933 (765) 362-1267
Contact: L. Ann Malott, Exec. Dir.
FAX: (765) 361-0562; E-mail: ann@mc-cf.org; URL: http://www.mc-cf.org

Established in 1991 in Crawfordsville, IN.
Foundation type: Community foundation.
Financial data (yr. ended 12/31/05): Assets, $28,490,978 (M); gifts received, $312,314; expenditures, $1,119,889; giving activities include $605,677 for grants.
Purpose and activities: The foundation provides grants and scholarships to the Montgomery County community.
Fields of interest: Historic preservation/historical societies; Arts; Higher education; Education; Environment; Disabilities, people with.

Type of support: Annual campaigns; Capital campaigns; Building/renovation; Equipment; Program development; Conferences/seminars; Seed money; Scholarship funds; Scholarships—to individuals; Matching/challenge support.
Limitations: Giving limited to Montgomery County, IN. No support for religious organizations. No grants to individuals (except for scholarships), or for endowments, operating budgets, special events, or existing obligations.
Publications: Application guidelines; Annual report; Grants list; Informational brochure (including application guidelines); Newsletter.
Application information: Visit foundation Web site for application forms and guidelines. Grant requests over $5,000 require a long-form grant application; visit Web site for additional guidelines. Faxed applications are not accepted. Application form required.
Initial approach: Submit application form and attachments
Copies of proposal: 12
Deadline(s): May 12 and Oct. 13
Board meeting date(s): June and Nov.
Final notification: June and Nov.
Officers and Directors:* Kathleen Steele,* Pres.; Mike Grant,* V.P.; Susan Jeffery,* Secy.; Steve Loy,* Treas.; L. Ann Malott, Exec. Dir.; Charles Arvin; Roselie Bambrey; Anne Dantzig; Nancy Doemel; Lucinda Huffaker; Roy Kaser; Don Livingston; Suanne Milligan; Mike Mitchell; Gail Pebworth; Mike Plant; George Spencer.
EIN: 351836315

3207
Moore Foundation ◇
9100 Keystone Crossing, Ste. 390
Indianapolis, IN 46240 (317) 848-2013
Contact: Martin J. Moore, Pres.

Incorporated in 1960 in IN.
Donor: Frank M. Moore†.
Foundation type: Independent foundation.
Financial data (yr. ended 3/31/06): Assets, $2,953,635 (M); gifts received, $125; expenditures, $1,077,037; qualifying distributions, $739,251; giving activities include $739,251 for grants.
Purpose and activities: Support of the free enterprise system, the development of curriculum at the elementary and secondary school levels, and the support of religious organizations oriented toward youth.
Fields of interest: Elementary school/education; Secondary school/education; Higher education; Business school/education; Youth development, services; Human services; Children/youth, services; Community development; Economics; Leadership development; Christian agencies & churches; Religion; Economically disadvantaged.
Type of support: Continuing support; Program development.
Limitations: Giving primarily in Indianapolis, IN. No grants to individuals, or for capital or endowment funds, seed money, building funds, renovations, emergency funds, deficit financing, scholarships, or fellowships; no loans.
Publications: Informational brochure (including application guidelines).
Application information: Application form not required.
Initial approach: Telephone
Copies of proposal: 2

Deadline(s): Mar. 1, May 1, Sept. 1, and Dec. 1
Board meeting date(s): Jan., Apr., June, Oct.
Final notification: Within 1 month
Officers and Directors:* Martin J. Moore,* Pres.;
Stephen L. Keith,* V.P. and Treas.; Larry J. Hannah;
Edward C. McKeown; Susan J. Moore.
Number of staff: 2 full-time professional; 2 part-time
support.
EIN: 356013824
Selected grants: The following grants were reported
in 2004.
$303,500 to Benevolent Friends of African
Charities, Indianapolis, IN. For general operating
support.
$15,000 to Indianapolis Foundation, Indianapolis,
IN. For general support.
$12,500 to Indiana University Foundation,
Indianapolis, IN. For Moi Agri project.
$10,000 to Central Indiana Community Foundation,
Indianapolis, IN. For general support.
$10,000 to Lawndale Community Church, Chicago,
IL. For Hope House Program.
$8,000 to Impact America Foundation, Indianapolis,
IN. For YPII Consulting.
$6,000 to Gordon College, Wenham, MA. For African
Student scholarships.
$6,000 to Indiana Grantmakers Alliance,
Indianapolis, IN. For general support.
$5,000 to Angel Flight Central, Kansas City, MO. For
general support.
$5,000 to Community Partnerships with Youth, Fort
Wayne, IN. For general support.

3208
The Morgan Foundation ✧
(formerly The Charles P. and Roxanna L. Morgan
Foundation)
4670 Haven Point Blvd.
Indianapolis, IN   46280

Donors: Charles P. Morgan; Roxanna L. Morgan.
Foundation type: Independent foundation.
Financial data (yr. ended 12/31/05): Assets,
$238,810 (M); gifts received, $417,441;
expenditures, $1,192,605; qualifying distributions,
$1,192,500; giving activities include $1,191,500
for 23 grants (high: $770,000; low: $500).
Purpose and activities: Giving primarily to Christian
and Protestant churches, including Baptist and
Presbyterian churches; funding also for human
services.
Fields of interest: Human services; Protestant
agencies & churches.
Limitations: Applications not accepted. Giving
primarily in Colorado Springs, CO. No grants to
individuals.
Application information: Contributes only to
pre-selected organizations.
Trustees: Charles P. Morgan; Roxanna L. Morgan.
EIN: 352124850
Selected grants: The following grants were reported
in 2004.
$150,000 to Focus on the Family, Colorado Springs,
CO.
$125,000 to Insight for Living.
$105,000 to Young Life, Indianapolis, IN.
$50,000 to Family Research Council, DC.
$35,000 to Central Indiana Crisis Pregnancy Center,
Indianapolis, IN.
$26,800 to Dallas Theological Seminary, Dallas, TX.
$25,000 to Alliance for Marriage, Merrifield, VA.
$15,500 to River Oaks Community Church, Carmel,
IN.

$15,000 to Crisis Pregnancy Center of Bloomington,
Bloomington, IN.
$10,000 to Council for National Policy, Arlington,
VA.

3209
**Arthur K. Muselman Family Foundation,
Inc.** ✧ ☆
1275 Emmental Dr.
Berne, IN   46711

Established in 1978.
Donors: Arthur K. Muselman; Gloria E. Muselman.
Foundation type: Independent foundation.
Financial data (yr. ended 12/31/05): Assets,
$2,653,669 (M); gifts received, $188,319;
expenditures, $670,445; qualifying distributions,
$666,097; giving activities include $666,097 for 18
grants (high: $500,050; low: $100).
Fields of interest: Secondary school/education;
Higher education; Theological school/education;
Human services; Youth, services; Christian
agencies & churches; Religion.
Limitations: Applications not accepted. Giving
primarily in IN. No grants to individuals.
Application information: Contributes only to
pre-selected organizations.
Officers: Arthur K. Muselman, Pres.; Gloria E.
Muselman, V.P.; Tyler Kitt, C.F.O.
EIN: 310941468

3210
**Mutual Federal Savings Bank Charitable
Foundation, Inc.** ✧ ☆
110 E. Charles St.
P.O. Box 551
Muncie, IN   47308-0551

Established in 1998 in IN.
Donor: Mutual Federal Savings Bank.
Foundation type: Company-sponsored foundation.
Financial data (yr. ended 6/30/05): Assets,
$6,830,443 (M); expenditures, $374,154;
qualifying distributions, $370,836; giving activities
include $365,221 for 41 grants (high: $55,000;
low: $200).
Purpose and activities: The foundation supports
organizations involved with visual and performing
arts, education, health, and economic development.
Fields of interest: Visual arts; Performing arts;
Education; Health care; Economic development.
Type of support: General/operating support.
Limitations: Giving primarily in Delaware, Grant,
Kosciusko, and Randolph counties, IN. No grants to
individuals.
Publications: Annual report.
Application information: Application form required.
Initial approach: Contact foundation for
application form
Copies of proposal: 2
Deadline(s): Varies
Board meeting date(s): Quarterly
Final notification: Following board meetings
Officers: R. Donn Roberts, Pres.; Patrick Botts, V.P.;
David Heeter, Secy.; Lori Ritchey, Treas.
Directors: G. Richard Benson; Linn A. Crull; Earl R.
Williams.
EIN: 352064221
Selected grants: The following grants were reported
in 2005.

$45,900 to Ball State University, Muncie, IN. 2
grants: $40,000, $5,900
$24,500 to United Way of Delaware County, Muncie,
IN.
$20,000 to Ivy Tech Foundation, Muncie, IN.
$15,000 to Delaware Greenways, Muncie, IN.
$10,259 to Isanogel Center, Muncie, IN.
$10,000 to Minnetrista Cultural Foundation,
Muncie, IN.
$8,700 to Hillcroft Services, Muncie, IN.
$7,800 to Boys and Girls Club of Muncie, Muncie,
IN.
$7,600 to Muncie Childrens Museum, Muncie, IN.

3211
Clinton E. Newman Foundation ✧
c/o Salin Bank and Trust Co.
110 W. Main St.
Fort Wayne, IN   46802
Contact: Michele Herald, V.P., Trust Off.

Established in 2001 in IN.
Foundation type: Independent foundation.
Financial data (yr. ended 12/31/05): Assets,
$2,644,983 (M); expenditures, $383,423;
qualifying distributions, $352,775; giving activities
include $352,500 for 17 grants (high: $65,000;
low: $2,500).
Fields of interest: Historical activities; Arts.
Limitations: Giving limited to Allen County and Fort
Wayne, IN.
Application information: Unsolicited requests for
funds not accepted.
Trustee: Salin Bank and Trust Co.
EIN: 341955380

3212
Daniel M. Niblick Family Foundation ✧
c/o Galen D. Maust
3705 Rupp Dr., Ste. 201
Fort Wayne, IN   46815-4525

Established in 1997 in IN.
Donor: Harold W. Niblick.
Foundation type: Independent foundation.
Financial data (yr. ended 6/30/05): Assets,
$4,035,532 (M); expenditures, $747,875;
qualifying distributions, $741,875; giving activities
include $732,715 for 20 grants (high: $207,115;
low: $250).
Purpose and activities: Giving primarily for youth
organizations, Christian causes, and educational
scholarships.
Fields of interest: Arts; Higher education; Higher
education, university; Hospitals (general); Youth
development; Human services; Federated giving
programs; Christian agencies & churches.
Limitations: Applications not accepted. Giving
primarily in IN. No grants to individuals.
Application information: Contributes only to
pre-selected organizations.
Trustee: Galen D. Maust.
EIN: 352005094

3213

NiSource Charitable Foundation ◇

(formerly Columbia Gas Foundation)
c/o NiSource Corp. Citizenship
801 E. 86th Ave.
Merrillville, IN 46410 (219) 647-6204
E-mail: questions@nisource.com; URL: http://
www.nisource.com/about/corpcit/index.asp

Established in 1990 in DE.
Donors: The Columbia Gas System, Inc.; Columbia
Energy Group; Columbia Gas of Ohio, Inc.; NiSource
Corporate Services Co.
Foundation type: Company-sponsored foundation.
Financial data (yr. ended 12/31/04): Assets,
$4,514,615 (M); expenditures, $1,221,892;
qualifying distributions, $1,221,892; giving
activities include $1,221,892 for 221 grants (high:
$172,496; low: $20).
Purpose and activities: The foundation supports
organizations involved with education, the
environment, economic development, human
services, and public safety.
Fields of interest: Education; Environment; Crime/
law enforcement; Youth, services; Human services;
Community development; Federated giving
programs; Government/public administration.
Type of support: Continuing support; Annual
campaigns; Building/renovation.
Limitations: Giving limited to areas of company
operations. No support for religious organizations,
political organizations, or discriminatory
organizations. No grants to individuals, or for sports
sponsorships or goodwill advertising.
Publications: Application guidelines.
Application information: Application form required.
Initial approach: Download application form and
mail to foundation
Copies of proposal: 1
Deadline(s): None
Board meeting date(s): May and Oct.
Officers and Trustees:* Gary W. Pottorff, Secy.;
Susanne Taylor, Treas.; Kirsten L. Falzone-Scott,*
Exec. Dir.; Stephen Adik; Barbara S. McKay; Gary L.
Neale; Michael W. O'Donnell; Robert C. Skaggs, Jr.
EIN: 510324200
Selected grants: The following grants were reported
in 2004.
$72,740 to United Negro College Fund, DC.
$65,000 to United Way of Central Ohio, Columbus,
OH.
$34,533 to Marietta College, Marietta, OH.
$26,347 to United Way, Lake Area, Griffith, IN.
$25,000 to Northern Indiana Arts Association,
Munster, IN.
$25,000 to Ohio Energy Project, Columbus, OH.
$20,000 to Brockton City Arts, Brockton, MA.
$20,000 to Greater Kanawha Valley Foundation,
Charleston, WV.
$500 to Columbus Childrens Theater, Columbus,
OH.
$225 to Wheeling Jesuit University, Wheeling, WV.

3214

Noble County Community Foundation

1599 Lincolnway S.
Ligonier, IN 46767 (260) 894-3335
Contact: Dave Knopp, Exec. Dir.; For grant
applications: Jennifer Myers, Prog. Off.
FAX: (260) 894-9020; E-mail: nccf@ligtel.com;
E-mail for grants applications: grants@ligtel.com;
URL: http://www.noblecounty.org/cf_about_it.html

Established in 1991 in IN.
Foundation type: Community foundation.
Financial data (yr. ended 12/31/05): Assets,
$20,244,181 (M); gifts received, $1,398,721;
expenditures, $2,114,805; giving activities include
$928,243 for 358 grants (high: $54,961; low: $1);
$179,577 for 149 grants to individuals (high:
$15,771; low: $8), and $246,476 for 6
foundation-administered programs.
Purpose and activities: The foundation seeks to
improve the quality of life in Noble County by serving
as a catalyst for positive change, enabling donors to
carry out charitable intent, and making grants.
Primary areas of interest include health, human
services, education, arts and culture, and civic
affairs.
Fields of interest: Arts, cultural/ethnic awareness;
Arts; Education; Health care; Safety/disasters;
Youth development, services; Family services,
parent education; Human services; Community
development; Public affairs; Girls.
Type of support: Consulting services; Conferences/
seminars; Capital campaigns; General/operating
support; Building/renovation; Equipment; Land
acquisition; Emergency funds; Program
development; Seed money; Scholarship funds;
Technical assistance; Scholarships—to individuals;
Matching/challenge support.
Limitations: Giving limited to Noble County, IN. No
support for sectarian religious purposes, or for
conduit organizations. No grants for annual fund
campaigns, routine operating support for ongoing
programs, multi-year funding, travel, augmenting
endowments, deficit spending, underwriting for
fundraising events, or research; no loans.
Publications: Annual report; Informational brochure
(including application guidelines); Newsletter.
Application information: Visit foundation Web site
for application guidelines. Faxed proposals are not
accepted. The foundation offers a free grant writing
workshop from time to time; e-mail or call Prog. Off.
to register. Application form not required.
Initial approach: Telephone or letter of intent
Copies of proposal: 1
Deadline(s): Mar. 2, May 2, July 2, and Nov. 2
Board meeting date(s): 4th Wed. in Feb., Apr.,
June, Aug., Oct., and 3rd Wed. in Dec.
Final notification: 60 days after deadline
Officers and Directors:* Cathy Seymoure,* Pres.;
Chuck Shull,* V.P.; Mary Wysong,* Secy.; Martha
Ayres,* Treas.; Dave Knopp, Exec. Dir.; Joe Atz;
Brian Baker; Larry Baker; Jeanna Hagen; Daniel
Parker; Brenda Patton; Robert Probst; Jim Shrock;
Deb Spidel.
Number of staff: 3 full-time professional; 2 full-time
support.
EIN: 351827247
Selected grants: The following grants were reported
in 2004.
$10,000 to Parkview Noble Hospital Foundation,
Kendallville, IN. For Cardio-Pulmonary Testing
room in new hospital.
$5,000 to Four-H Exhibit Corporation of Noble
County. Toward building Beef and Dairy Steer
Barn.
$5,000 to Sweet Church Community Organization.
To repair two corners of building that have settled
enough to become serious structural problems.
$3,000 to Black Pine Animal Park, Albion, IN. To
acquire needed equipment to implement
environmentally friendly practice of composing
waste materials.
$2,000 to Fort Wayne Philharmonic Orchestra, Fort
Wayne, IN. To provide concerts at East Noble,

West Noble and Central Noble schools and two
community shows.
$1,217 to Otis R. Bowen Center for Human
Services, Warsaw, IN. To purchase an Automated
External Defibrillator (AED) for Albion outpatient.
$1,000 to Garrett Community Center, Garrett, IN.
Toward building new Garrett Community Center.
$750 to Early Childhood Alliance, Fort Wayne, IN. To
provide family child care retreat for family child
care providers.
$517 to Community Harvest Food Bank of Northeast
Indiana, Fort Wayne, IN. For Farm Wagon
program.
$490 to Central Noble School Corporation, Albion,
IN. To purchase entire fiction novel collection
from the Indiana Reading List.

3215

Northern Indiana Community Foundation, Inc.

800 Main St.
P.O. Box 807
Rochester, IN 46975 (574) 223-2227
Contact: Terri L. Johnson, Exec. Dir.
FAX: (574) 224-3709; E-mail: terri@nicf.org;
Additional tel.: (877) 432-6423; URL: http://
www.nicf.org

Established in 1993 in IN.
Foundation type: Community foundation.
Financial data (yr. ended 12/31/05): Assets,
$14,786,140 (M); gifts received, $1,409,738;
expenditures, $920,113; giving activities include
$545,982 for 591 grants (high: $29,332; low: $62),
and $132,569 for foundation-administered
programs.
Purpose and activities: The foundation seeks to
improve the quality of life in the community by
assisting donors in fulfilling their philanthropic
wishes.
Fields of interest: Arts; Education; Environment;
Health organizations, association; Recreation;
Youth development; Human services; Community
development; Youth.
Type of support: General/operating support;
Building/renovation; Equipment; Endowments;
Emergency funds; Program development; Seed
money; Scholarship funds; Consulting services;
Matching/challenge support.
Limitations: Giving limited to Fulton, Miami, and
Starke counties, IN. No support for sectarian or
religious organizations operated primarily for the
benefit of their own members. No grants to
individuals (except for scholarships), or for annual
fundraisers or campaigns, ongoing operating
expenses, deficits, direct or grass-roots lobbying,
sponsorships, special events, commercial
advertising, films or videos, television, conferences,
or group uniforms or trips.
Publications: Application guidelines; Annual report;
Informational brochure; Newsletter.
Application information: Visit foundation Web site
for specific county application forms, guidelines,
and deadlines. Application form required.
Initial approach: Telephone or fax
Copies of proposal: 1
Deadline(s): Varies
Board meeting date(s): 3rd Wed. of each month
Final notification: Approx. 6 weeks
Officers and Directors:* Mat Swanson,* Pres.; Bob
Hoffman,* V.P.; Susie Perkins,* Secy.; Alan
Terrell,* Treas.; Terri L. Johnson, Exec. Dir.; Debbie
Balsbaugh; Joanne Bendall; Ron Douglas; Dennis

Eller; Marilyn Fritts; James Hardesty; Max Hattery; Brad Lawrence; Barbara McLaughlin; Lance Nelson; Sandy Sawyer; Fred Vorm; Tyra Walker.
Number of staff: 1 full-time professional; 2 full-time support; 4 part-time support.
EIN: 351912317
Selected grants: The following grants were reported in 2005.
$14,000 to Ole Olsen Memorial Theater, Peru, IN. For renovation of toll house.
$13,200 to Lions International, Akron Lions Club, Akron, IN. For Akron Community Center Fund, raising kick-off program.
$7,500 to Coalition Against Domestic Abuse, Knox, IN. For construction of garage at Phoenix House.
$6,410 to Hickory Creek Healthcare Foundation, Rochester, IN. For new bird aviary.
$4,400 to YMCA, Miami County, Peru, IN. For new doors for teen room.
$4,100 to Hoosier Valley Railroad Museum, North Judson, IN. For rehab of track and development of public trail path.
$3,800 to Kewannas HEART, Kewanna, IN. For trees for town of Kewanna.
$3,115 to Liberty Township Park, Fulton, IN. For new sidewalks and handicap accessibility.
$2,000 to North Judson Main Street Committee, North Judson, IN. For street clock for downtown North Judson.

3216
Nicholas H. Noyes, Jr. Memorial Foundation, Inc. ✧
1950 E. Greyhound Pass, No. 18, PMB 356
Carmel, IN   46033-7730   (317) 844-8009
Contact: Kelly Mills, Exec. Admin.
FAX: (317) 844-8099;
E-mail: admin@noyesfoundation.org; URL: http://www.noyesfoundation.org

Incorporated in 1951 in IN.
Donors: Nicholas H. Noyes†; Marguerite Lilly Noyes†.
Foundation type: Independent foundation.
Financial data (yr. ended 12/31/05): Assets, $49,116,508 (M); gifts received, $1,693; expenditures, $2,670,430; qualifying distributions, $2,632,411; giving activities include $2,542,300 for 136 grants (high: $150,000; low: $2,000).
Purpose and activities: Primary areas of interest include education, the arts, family services, and other general charitable activities; organizations in Indianapolis, IN are primary focus.
Fields of interest: Museums; Performing arts; Arts; Education, early childhood education; Elementary school/education; Secondary school/education; Higher education; Education; Hospitals (general); Health care; Health organizations, association; Human services; Children/youth, services; Family services; Community development; Disabilities, people with; Minorities; Economically disadvantaged.
Type of support: General/operating support; Continuing support; Annual campaigns; Capital campaigns; Program development; Scholarship funds.
Limitations: Giving primarily in Indianapolis, IN. No support for political organizations or lobbying organizations. No grants to individuals, no loans.
Publications: Application guidelines.
Application information: Application form available on foundation Web site. Requests must be mailed. Application form required.

Initial approach: Full proposal per guidelines
Copies of proposal: 12
Deadline(s): Varies, refer to foundation Web site for latest deadlines
Board meeting date(s): Semiannually
Final notification: Grantseeker follows up 3 months after deadline
Officers and Directors:* Nancy Ayres,* Pres.; Robert H. Reynolds,* V.P. and Secy.; L. Gene Tanner, Treas.; Kelly L. Mills,* Exec. Admin.; Avery Augustine; Lisa A. Carrington; Elizabeth H. Noyes; Evan L. Noyes, Jr.; Henry S. Noyes; Nicholas S. Noyes.
Number of staff: 1 full-time professional; 1 part-time professional.
EIN: 351003699
Selected grants: The following grants were reported in 2005.
$180,000 to United Way of Central Indiana, Indianapolis, IN. 2 grants: $100,000, $80,000
$150,000 to Ballet Internationale, Indianapolis, IN.
$100,000 to Independent Colleges of Indiana Foundation, Indianapolis, IN.
$100,000 to Indianapolis Museum of Art, Indianapolis, IN.
$75,000 to United Negro College Fund, Indianapolis, IN.
$70,000 to Riley Childrens Foundation, Indianapolis, IN.
$20,000 to Saint Richards School, Indianapolis, IN.
$10,000 to Horizon House, Indianapolis, IN.
$10,000 to Indianapolis Chamber Orchestra, Indianapolis, IN.

3217
Hollie & Anna Oakley Foundation, Inc. ✧
18 S. 16th St.
Terre Haute, IN   47807   (812) 232-4437

Established in 1954 in IN.
Donor: Hollie N. Oakley†.
Foundation type: Independent foundation.
Financial data (yr. ended 12/31/04): Assets, $8,482,338 (M); expenditures, $559,492; qualifying distributions, $417,700; giving activities include $417,700 for 24 grants (high: $150,000; low: $500).
Purpose and activities: Giving primarily for education and human service.
Fields of interest: Arts; Higher education; Health organizations, association; Boy scouts; Youth development, business; Youth development; Human services; Community development.
Type of support: General/operating support; Scholarship funds.
Limitations: Giving primarily in IN. No grants to individuals.
Application information:
Initial approach: Letter
Deadline(s): None
Officers: Alice Ann Perry, Pres.; Eston L. Perry, V.P. and Treas.; Julie Perry Heck, Secy.
Director: Doris Kiburis.
EIN: 237008034
Selected grants: The following grants were reported in 2003.
$120,000 to Rose-Hulman Institute of Technology, Terre Haute, IN. For unrestricted support.
$100,000 to Terre Haute, City of, Terre Haute, IN. For unrestricted support.
$40,000 to Saint Mary of the Woods College, Saint Mary of the Woods, IN. For unrestricted support.

$25,000 to Salk Institute for Biological Studies, San Diego, CA. For unrestricted support.
$23,000 to Indiana University Foundation, Bloomington, IN. For unrestricted support.
$15,000 to Orlando Philharmonic Orchestra, Orlando, FL. For unrestricted support.
$12,500 to Vigo County Public Schools Education Foundation, Terre Haute, IN. For unrestricted support.
$10,000 to Indiana State University Foundation, Terre Haute, IN. For unrestricted support.
$10,000 to Terre Haute Symphony Orchestra, Terre Haute, IN. For unrestricted support.
$10,000 to University of Central Florida, Orlando, FL. For unrestricted support.

3218
Paul Ogle Foundation, Inc. ▼ ✧
323 E. Court Ave.
P.O. Box 946
Jeffersonville, IN   47130
Contact: Robert W. Lanum, Chair.
FAX: (812) 284-5519; E-mail: rlanum@stites.com; URL: http://www.ogle-fdn.org

Established in 1980 in IN.
Donor: Paul W. Ogle†.
Foundation type: Independent foundation.
Financial data (yr. ended 12/31/05): Assets, $69,187,047 (M); expenditures, $3,460,016; qualifying distributions, $3,205,068; giving activities include $3,136,500 for 38 grants (high: $578,000; low: $1,000; average: $10,000–$250,000).
Purpose and activities: The primary categories of funding by the foundation are education (primarily higher education), civic, economic development, humanities and health and general welfare. Historically, the foundation has supported projects with an emphasis on bricks and mortar, equipment purchases, and pre-selected scholarship funds.
Fields of interest: Arts; Higher education; Education; Human services; Community development.
Type of support: Building/renovation; Endowments; Scholarship funds; Matching/challenge support.
Limitations: Giving primarily in southern IN. No support for research programs, churches and related activities, private foundations, or public or private elementary or secondary school programs. No grants to individuals, or for ongoing, general operating expenses or existing deficits; no loans.
Publications: Application guidelines.
Application information: Based on review of the letter of inquiry, the foundation may request a full proposal. Applicants may apply for grant funds only once in 36 months. Application form required.
Initial approach: Letter of inquiry (no more than 4 pages)
Deadline(s): None
Board meeting date(s): Bimonthly
Final notification: 6 months
Officers and Directors:* Robert W. Lanum,* Chair. and C.E.O.; Willis Charles,* V.P.; Roy W. Nett,* Treas.; Norman Pfau; John Ragland; W.T. Sullivan.
Number of staff: 1 part-time professional; 1 part-time support.
EIN: 310988988
Selected grants: The following grants were reported in 2003.
$750,000 to YMCA of Southern Indiana, Jeffersonville, IN. For general support.

$250,000 to YMCA of Harrison County, Clarksburg, WV. For general support.

$175,000 to American Red Cross, National Headquarters, DC. For general support.

$125,000 to Spalding University, Louisville, KY. For general support.

$100,000 to J. B. Speed Art Museum, Louisville, KY. For general support.

$100,000 to Leadership Louisville Foundation, Louisville, KY. For general support.

$100,000 to Locust Grove Historic Home Museum, Louisville, KY. For general support.

$80,000 to Jeffersonville, City of, Department of Redevelopment, Jeffersonville, IN. For general support.

$75,000 to Clark County Historical Society and Howard Steamboat Museum, Jeffersonville, IN. For general support.

$50,000 to Mary Anderson Center for the Arts, Mount Saint Francis, IN. For general support.

3219

Oliver Memorial Trust Foundation

c/o Wells Fargo Bank Indiana, N.A.
112 W. Jefferson Blvd.
South Bend, IN   46601   (574) 237-3475
Contact: Charles F. Nelson, Trust Off., Wells Fargo Bank, N.A.

Trust established in 1959 in IN.
Donors: C. Frederick Cunningham†; Gertrude Oliver Cunningham†; Walter C. Steenburg†; Jane Cunningham Warriner; J. Oliver Cunningham.
Foundation type: Independent foundation.
Financial data (yr. ended 12/31/05): Assets, $9,812,983 (M); gifts received, $20,022; expenditures, $446,564; qualifying distributions, $411,694; giving activities include $401,281 for 19 grants (high: $177,481; low: $300).
Purpose and activities: Emphasis on hospitals, higher education, particularly college endowments, community funds, and youth agencies.
Fields of interest: Higher education; Hospitals (general); Youth, services; Federated giving programs.
Type of support: Continuing support; Annual campaigns; Capital campaigns; Building/renovation; Equipment; Endowments; Program development; Seed money; Research; Matching/challenge support.
Limitations: Applications not accepted. Giving primarily in the South Bend, IN, area. No grants to individuals, or for land acquisition, conferences, scholarships, or fellowships; no loans.
Application information: Unsolicited requests for funds not accepted.
   Board meeting date(s): Quarterly or as required
Trustee: Wells Fargo Bank Indiana, N.A.
EIN: 356013076
Selected grants: The following grants were reported in 2005.

$50,000 to University of Notre Dame, Notre Dame, IN.

$25,000 to Bethel College, Mishawaka, IN.

$25,000 to Community Foundation of Saint Joseph County, South Bend, IN.

$25,000 to Logan Community Resources, South Bend, IN.

$20,000 to Ray Bird Ministries, Fort Wayne, IN.

$10,000 to Saint Marys College, Notre Dame, IN.

$5,000 to United Negro College Fund, Fairfax, VA.

$3,500 to Independent Colleges of Indiana, Indianapolis, IN.

$300 to Union Theological Seminary, New York, NY.

3220

OneAmerica Foundation, Inc. ✧

(formerly AUL Foundation, Inc.)
c/o Sandy Charnstrom
P.O. Box 368
Indianapolis, IN   46206-4257   (317) 285-4652

Established in 1985 in IN.
Donor: American United Life Insurance Co.
Foundation type: Company-sponsored foundation.
Financial data (yr. ended 12/31/04): Assets, $5,711,567 (M); gifts received, $295,609; expenditures, $547,349; qualifying distributions, $538,750; giving activities include $538,750 for 29 grants (high: $112,500; low: $500).
Purpose and activities: The foundation supports organizations involved with education and health.
Fields of interest: Education; Health care.
Type of support: Capital campaigns; Endowments; Scholarship funds.
Limitations: Applications not accepted. Giving limited to the Indianapolis, IN, area. No grants to individuals.
Application information: Contributes only to pre-selected organizations.
Officers and Directors:* Jerry D. Semler,* Pres. and V.P.; Kaye Palmer, Secy.; Ronald A. Fritz, Treas.; James E. Dora; David W. Goodrich; James T. Morris; R. Stephen Radcliffe; William R. Riggs; John C. Scully.
EIN: 311146437

3221

Mary K. Peabody Foundation

c/o Tower Trust Co.
P.O. Box 11080
Fort Wayne, IN   46855-1080
Contact: David Fee

Established in 1991 in IN.
Foundation type: Independent foundation.
Financial data (yr. ended 7/31/06): Assets, $3,101,819 (M); expenditures, $520,754; qualifying distributions, $459,000; giving activities include $459,000 for grants.
Fields of interest: Foundations (community).
Type of support: Building/renovation; Equipment.
Limitations: Applications not accepted. Giving primarily in Manchester and Fort Wayne, IN. No grants to individuals.
Application information: Contributes only to pre-selected organizations.
Distribution Committee: Frances H. Fisher; Robert Wagner.
Trustee: Tower Bank.
EIN: 356546371
Selected grants: The following grants were reported in 2004.

$318,000 to Community Foundation of Wabash County, North Manchester, IN. 2 grants: $250,000 (For Roann Library addition), $68,000 (For Roann Library addition).

$250,000 to Manchester College, North Manchester, IN. For Peabody Scholarship Fund.

$5,500 to Boyne District Library, Boyne City, MI. For library addition.

$2,849 to Roann Library, Fort Wayne, IN. For library addition.

3222

Perelman Charitable Foundation, Inc. ✧ ☆

8751 Jaffa Ct. E. Dr., No. 16
Indianapolis, IN   46260
Contact: Dr. Melvin Perelman, Pres.

Established in 1991 in IN.
Donor: Melvin Perelman.
Foundation type: Independent foundation.
Financial data (yr. ended 12/31/05): Assets, $3,256,620 (M); gifts received, $250,000; expenditures, $421,258; qualifying distributions, $420,918; giving activities include $417,750 for 12 grants (high: $350,500; low: $50).
Purpose and activities: Giving for museums, public broadcasting, higher education, animal welfare organizations and federated giving programs.
Fields of interest: Museums; Higher education; Medical school/education; Zoos/zoological societies; Federated giving programs.
Limitations: Giving primarily in IN. No grants to individuals.
Application information: Application form not required.
   Initial approach: Letter
   Copies of proposal: 1
   Deadline(s): None
Officers: Melvin Perelman, Pres. and Treas.; Joan B. Perelman, Secy.
Director: Jeffrey H. Thomasson.
Number of staff: None.
EIN: 351838295

3223

The Portland Foundation

112 E. Main St.
Portland, IN   47371   (260) 726-4260
Contact: Douglas L. Inman, Exec. Dir.
FAX: (260) 726-4273;
E-mail: tpf@portlandfoundation.org; URL: http://www.portlandfoundation.org

Established in 1951 in IN.
Foundation type: Community foundation.
Financial data (yr. ended 12/31/05): Assets, $17,307,928 (M); gifts received, $1,074,440; expenditures, $1,592,481; giving activities include $1,131,665 for grants, and $190,832 for 79 grants to individuals.
Purpose and activities: The foundation provides support for all aspects of the quality of life in the Jay County, IN, community.
Fields of interest: Arts; Child development, education; Higher education; Education; Health care; Children/youth, services; Human services; Community development; Youth.
Type of support: Capital campaigns; Building/renovation; Equipment; Program development; Seed money; Scholarship funds; Scholarships—to individuals; Matching/challenge support.
Limitations: Giving limited to Jay County, IN. No support for religious or sectarian purposes. No grants to individuals (except through designated scholarship funds); generally no grants for regular operating budgets, operating costs, operating deficits, after-the-fact funds, endowments, or long-term funding; no loans.
Publications: Application guidelines; Annual report; Newsletter.
Application information: Visit foundation Web site for application form and guidelines. Applications must be typed; handwritten copies will not be accepted. Application form required.

Initial approach: Submit application form and attachments
Copies of proposal: 10
Deadline(s): Jan. and July
Board meeting date(s): Bimonthly
Final notification: Feb. and Aug.
Officers and Directors:* Marianne Horn,* Pres.; Mark Haggenjos, V.P.; Rosalie Clamme,* Secy.-Treas.; Douglas L. Inman, Exec. Dir.; Julie Barber; Julie Forcum; Phil Frantz; Ron Freeman; Giles Laux; Eric Reynolds.
Number of staff: 1 full-time professional; 1 part-time professional; 1 part-time support.
EIN: 356028362

3224
Myrta J. Pulliam Charitable Trust ✧
c/o Holly Pantzer
201 N. Illinois St., Ste. 700
Indianapolis, IN 46204

Established in 2001 in IN.
Donors: Myrta J. Pulliam; Jane B. Pulliam†.
Foundation type: Independent foundation.
Financial data (yr. ended 12/31/05): Assets, $10,189,982 (M); gifts received, $867,667; expenditures, $712,453; qualifying distributions, $665,591; giving activities include $661,750 for 22 grants (high: $500,000; low: $250).
Fields of interest: Higher education; Health care; Foundations (community); Women.
Type of support: Program development; Scholarship funds.
Limitations: Applications not accepted. Giving primarily in IN. No grants to individuals.
Application information: Contributes only to pre-selected organizations.
Trustee: Myrta J. Pulliam.
EIN: 356712560

3225
Nina Mason Pulliam Charitable Trust ▼
135 N. Pennsylvania St., Ste. 1200
Indianapolis, IN 46204 (317) 231-6075
Contact: Mary K. Price, Dir., Grants Admin.
FAX: (317) 231-9208; E-mail: mprice@nmpct.org;
Application address for Arizona organizations: 2201 E. Camelback Rd., Ste. 600B, Phoenix, AZ 85016, tel.: (602) 955-3000, FAX: (602) 955-8029;
URL: http://www.ninapulliamtrust.org

Established in 1997.
Foundation type: Independent foundation.
Financial data (yr. ended 12/31/05): Assets, $361,932,460 (M); expenditures, $18,840,977; qualifying distributions, $16,660,243; giving activities include $13,704,419 for 240 grants (high: $351,984; low: $2,000; average: $10,000–$100,000).
Purpose and activities: The trust seeks to help people in need, especially women, children and families; to protect animals and nature; and to enrich community life in the metropolitan areas of Indianapolis, IN, and Phoenix, AZ.
Fields of interest: Museums; Arts; Education; Environment, natural resources; Animal welfare; Health care; Eye diseases; Food banks; Human services; Children/youth, services; Family services; Community development; Disabilities, people with.

Type of support: Annual campaigns; Capital campaigns; Building/renovation; Equipment; Land acquisition; Endowments; Curriculum development.
Limitations: Giving primarily in Phoenix, AZ, and Indianapolis, IN. No grants to individuals, or for academic research, non-operating private foundations, or international activities.
Publications: Application guidelines; Annual report (including application guidelines); Financial statement; Grants list; Newsletter.
Application information: See the foundation's Web site for an application. Requests for funding are limited to one request per organization per year. Preliminary proposals may be submitted online via the foundation's Web site. Application form required.
Initial approach: Preliminary proposal letter and application form
Copies of proposal: 5
Deadline(s): Jan. 4; May 4 and Sept. 4
Board meeting date(s): Feb., June, Oct., and Dec.
Final notification: June 29, Oct. 31, and Feb. 28
Officers: Harriet M. Ivey, C.E.O. and Pres.; Robert L. Lowry, C.O.O. and C.F.O.
Trustees: Frank E. Russell; Nancy M. Russell; Carol P. Schilling.
Number of staff: 9 full-time professional; 7 full-time support.
EIN: 356644088
Selected grants: The following grants were reported in 2005.
$481,900 to Maricopa Colleges Foundation, Tempe, AZ. For Nina Mason Pulliam Legacy Scholars program.
$300,000 to Hacienda de Los Angeles, Phoenix, AZ. For construction of skilled nursing facility in south Phoenix to expand capacity of beds for infants, children and young adults with acute or chronic medical physical and intellectual impairments and/or developmental disabilities.
$250,000 to Childsplay, Tempe, AZ. To create Campus for Imagination and Wonder at former Mitchell Elementary School in Tempe.
$200,000 to John H. Boner Community Center, Indianapolis, IN. To expand facility to create one-stop neighborhood resource center to better serve Indianapolis clients on near east side.
$150,000 to Boyce Thompson Southwestern Arboretum, Superior, AZ. For construction of Children's Horticultural Garden.
$150,000 to Fairbanks Hospital, Indianapolis, IN. To renovate and expand residential facility to provide services for more adolescents in need of alcohol and drug addiction treatment services in local community.
$75,000 to Health and Hospital Corporation of Marion County, Indianapolis, IN. For Marion County Health Department to collect health data of IPS school students to address problem of childhood obesity.
$75,000 to Indianapolis Public Schools Education Foundation, Indianapolis, IN. To complete Classroom Take-Home Libraries for IPS first-grade students in effort to increase reading skills.
$60,000 to Hoosier Heartland Resource Conservation and Development Council, Indianapolis, IN. To launch Plant a Million Trees program, environmental education/public awareness campaign for general public of metropolitan Indianapolis.
$50,000 to Foster Angels of Arizona Serving Together, Gilbert, AZ. For Kids Learn FAST program, providing both academic and personal

guidance to children in Child Protective Services care by matching them with trained tutors/mentors.

3226
M. E. Raker Foundation, Inc.
6207 Constitution Dr.
Fort Wayne, IN 46804
Contact: Jennifer Pickard, Grants Coord.

Established in 1984 in IN.
Donor: M.E. Raker†.
Foundation type: Independent foundation.
Financial data (yr. ended 6/30/05): Assets, $9,838,961 (M); expenditures, $626,136; qualifying distributions, $509,848; giving activities include $408,296 for 59 grants (high: $20,000; low: $1,500).
Fields of interest: Historic preservation/historical societies; Education; Environment, natural resources; Health care; Human services; Children/youth, services; Disabilities, people with.
Type of support: Program development; Matching/challenge support; General/operating support; Building/renovation.
Limitations: Giving primarily in Allen County, IN. No support for the arts. No grants to individuals.
Application information: Application form required.
Initial approach: Letter requesting application
Deadline(s): None
Directors: Emily Pichon; John N. Pichon; Stephen J. Williams.
EIN: 311040474
Selected grants: The following grants were reported in 2005.
$20,000 to Fort Wayne Public Television, Fort Wayne, IN.
$15,000 to Cancer Services of Allen County, Fort Wayne, IN.
$14,400 to Bishop Luers High School, Fort Wayne, IN.
$10,000 to Allen County Council on Aging, Fort Wayne, IN.
$10,000 to Bishop Dwenger High School, Fort Wayne, IN.
$10,000 to Childrens Hope, Fort Wayne, IN.
$7,500 to Shepherds House, Fort Wayne, IN.
$7,500 to Super Shot, Fort Wayne, IN.
$5,000 to University of Saint Francis, Fort Wayne, IN.
$4,500 to Audiences Unlimited, Fort Wayne, IN.

3227
Carl Marshall Reeves and Mildred Almen Reeves Foundation, Inc. ✧ ☆
3435 Duffer Dr.
Columbus, IN 47203 (812) 372-1073
Contact: Mary Ann Nunn, Secy.-Treas.

Established in 1997 in IN.
Foundation type: Independent foundation.
Financial data (yr. ended 12/31/05): Assets, $12,759,413 (M); expenditures, $392,165; qualifying distributions, $364,205; giving activities include $355,867 for 17 grants (high: $60,000; low: $1,173).
Fields of interest: Education; Health care; Eye research; Crime/law enforcement.
Application information: Application form required.
Initial approach: Proposal
Copies of proposal: 6

Deadline(s): Prior to board meeting
Board meeting date(s): Annually
Officers: Larry E. Nunn, Pres.; Mary Ann Nunn, Secy.-Treas.
Directors: Tom Bigley; W. George Brueggemann; Emily A. Mabe; Mary Lu Orr.
EIN: 352026200
Selected grants: The following grants were reported in 2005.
$56,569 to Washington University, Saint Louis, MO. 2 grants: $27,959, $28,610
$56,000 to Community Education Coalition, Columbus, IN. 2 grants: $50,000, $6,000
$30,000 to Foundation for Youth, Columbus, IN.
$25,000 to Vanderbilt University, Nashville, TN.
$1,173 to Hospice of South Central Indiana, Columbus, IN.

3228
Regenstrief Foundation, Inc.
9292 N. Meridian, Ste. 202
Indianapolis, IN   46260
Contact: Joanne Fox, Secy.
FAX: (317) 848-9586;
E-mail: jfox@regenstrieffdn.org

Established in IN in 1969.
Foundation type: Independent foundation.
Financial data (yr. ended 6/30/05): Assets, $142,634,164 (M); expenditures, $4,625,001; qualifying distributions, $3,760,568; giving activities include $3,583,063 for 2 grants (high: $3,298,734; low: $284,329).
Purpose and activities: Giving for innovative research directed toward improving the efficiency, quality, and accessibility of health care.
Fields of interest: Higher education; Medical research, institute; Medical research, information services; Medical research, formal/general education.
Type of support: Research.
Limitations: Applications not accepted. Giving primarily in Indianapolis, IN.
Application information: Unsolicited requests for funds not considered.
Board meeting date(s): Jan. and June
Officers: Leonard J. Betley, Pres.; Jack R. Shaw, V.P. and Treas.; Harvey Feigenbaum, M.D., V.P.; Joanne K. Fox, Secy.
Directors: Allan L. Cohn; Walter J. Daly, M.D.; Stephen L. Ferguson; and 8 additional directors.
Number of staff: 2 part-time professional; 3 part-time support.
EIN: 356066023

3229
Gilmore and Golda Reynolds Foundation ✧
c/o Steve Gloyd
136 S. Buckeye St.
Osgood, IN   47037

Established in 1990 in IN.
Donor: Golda Reynolds.
Foundation type: Independent foundation.
Financial data (yr. ended 12/31/05): Assets, $19,037,507 (M); gifts received, $302,690; expenditures, $1,169,584; qualifying distributions, $1,010,249; giving activities include $796,886 for 14 grants (high: $643,179; low: $400), and $81,015 for loans/program-related investments.

Purpose and activities: Giving for community volunteer services.
Fields of interest: Secondary school/education; Safety/disasters, volunteer services; Disasters, fire prevention/control; Human services.
Limitations: Applications not accepted. Giving primarily in Osgood, IN. No grants to individuals.
Application information: Contributes only to pre-selected organizations.
Officers: Michael Black, Pres.; Dwight Hooter, V.P.; Neil Comer, Secy.; Douglas Thayer, Treas.; Steve Gloyd, M.D., Exec. Dir.
EIN: 356525698

3230
Ripley County Community Foundation, Inc. ✧
132 S. Main St.
P.O. Box 279
Batesville, IN   47006   (812) 933-1098
Contact: Sally Morris, Exec. Dir.
FAX: (812) 933-0096; *E-mail:* rccfound@nalu.net; Additional tel.: (887) 234-5220; Additional E-mail: smorris@rccfonline.org; URL: http://www.rccfonline.org

Established in 1997 in IN.
Foundation type: Community foundation.
Financial data (yr. ended 12/31/04): Assets, $6,451,059 (M); gifts received, $136,390; expenditures, $579,622; giving activities include $254,398 for 54+ grants, and $103,017 for grants to individuals.
Purpose and activities: The foundation seeks to assist donors to build an enduring source of charitable assets to benefit Ripley County; to provide responsible stewardship of the gifts donated; to promote leadership in addressing Ripley County's issues; and to make grants in the fields of community service, social service, education, health, environment, and the arts.
Fields of interest: Arts; Education; Environment; Health care; Human services; Community development.
Type of support: Matching/challenge support; General/operating support; Seed money.
Limitations: Giving limited to Ripley County, IN. No support for sectarian religious purposes. No grants to individuals (except for scholarships), or for seminars, trips, or endowments.
Application information: Visit foundation Web site for application guidelines. The foundation offers Grantwriting Workshops to help nonprofits with the application process; attendance to one workshop is mandatory. Intent to Apply forms will be available at the Grantwriting Workshops. Application form required.
Initial approach: Telephone or letter of inquiry
Copies of proposal: 11
Deadline(s): Aug. for Intent to Apply form; Sept. for grant application
Final notification: Within 2 weeks for Intent to Apply determination
Officers and Board Members:* Kris Schneider,* Pres.; Dan Schantz,* V.P.; Linda Chandler,* Secy.; Ron Knueven, Treas.; Sally Morris, Exec. Dir.: George Brinkmoeller; Jennifer Darnold; Deb Hellman; George Junker II; Clarence "Bud" McGowan; Gene Pitts; Laura Lee Spaulding; Mike Stephens; Steve Todd; Bill Van Hook.
EIN: 352048001

3231
Ian & Mimi Rolland Foundation, Inc.
4228 Reservation Trail
Fort Wayne, IN   46814
Contact: Ian Rolland, Pres.

Established in 1995 in IN.
Donors: Ian Rolland; Miriam Rolland.
Foundation type: Independent foundation.
Financial data (yr. ended 6/30/05): Assets, $8,061,935 (M); gifts received, $50; expenditures, $422,143; qualifying distributions, $379,241; giving activities include $366,833 for 80 grants (high: $38,000; low: $500).
Purpose and activities: Giving for the arts, education, and social services.
Fields of interest: Arts; Education; Human services.
Type of support: General/operating support; Annual campaigns; Capital campaigns; Building/ renovation; Endowments; Emergency funds; Program development; Professorships; Scholarship funds; Research.
Limitations: Giving primarily in IN, with emphasis on Fort Wayne. No grants to individuals.
Application information: Application form not required.
Initial approach: Letter
Copies of proposal: 1
Deadline(s): None
Board meeting date(s): Quarterly
Officers: Ian Rolland, Pres.; Miriam Rolland, V.P.; Ann White, Secy.
Number of staff: None.
EIN: 351944302
Selected grants: The following grants were reported in 2005.
$21,000 to United Way of Allen County, Fort Wayne, IN.
$10,000 to Science Central, Fort Wayne, IN.
$10,000 to YWCA.
$9,500 to Salvation Army, New Albany, IN.
$7,500 to Headwaters Park Alliance, Fort Wayne, IN.
$5,000 to Fort Wayne Park Foundation, Fort Wayne, IN.
$5,000 to Kendallville Public Library, Kendallville, IN.
$3,000 to American Red Cross.
$2,000 to Learning and Development Center, Fort Wayne, IN.
$1,500 to Audiences Unlimited, Fort Wayne, IN.

3232
Franklin I. and Irene List Saemann Foundation ✧
(formerly Franklin I. Saemann Foundation)
119 E. Center St.
Warsaw, IN   46580
Application address: P.O. Box 105, Morrison, IL 61270

Established in 1983 in IN.
Donors: Franklin I. Saemann†; Irene L. Saemann†.
Foundation type: Independent foundation.
Financial data (yr. ended 6/30/05): Assets, $8,180,371 (M); expenditures, $857,467; qualifying distributions, $426,500; giving activities include $409,500 for 20 grants (high: $272,000; low: $100).
Purpose and activities: Giving primarily for education and human services, with an emphasis on funding for libraries and literacy programs.

Fields of interest: Arts; Higher education; Libraries (public); Health organizations, association; Human services; Youth, services; Federated giving programs.
Limitations: Giving primarily in Waverly, IA, Warsaw, IN, and Kenosha, WI. No grants to individuals.
Publications: Informational brochure (including application guidelines).
Application information: Application form not required.
Initial approach: Letter
Deadline(s): Apr. 1
Board meeting date(s): Quarterly; June for considering grant applications
Trustees: Amy C. Kilgus Chamley; Katherine A. Kauffman; Joann A. Kilgus; Thomas E. List; June I. Waller.
Number of staff: 1 full-time professional; 3 full-time support.
EIN: 626171002
Selected grants: The following grants were reported in 2004.
$255,000 to Wartburg College, Waverly, IA.
$105,000 to Carthage College, Kenosha, WI.
$10,000 to Charleston Carnegie Public Library, Charleston, IL.
$10,000 to List Academy of Music and Arts, Newport, RI.
$5,000 to Champaign Public Library, Champaign, IL.
$5,000 to Heartline Pregnancy Center, Warsaw, IN.
$5,000 to United Way of Kosciusko County, Warsaw, IN.
$2,500 to North Webster Community Center, North Webster, IN.
$2,000 to American Poetry and Literacy Project, DC.
$1,000 to Kosciusko County Community Foundation, Warsaw, IN.

3233
Saltsburg Fund Charitable Trust ✧
P.O. Box 40669
Indianapolis, IN 46240-0669
Contact: Donald W. Buttrey, Tr.

Established in 2000 in IN.
Donors: Donald W. Buttrey; Karen Lake Buttrey.
Foundation type: Independent foundation.
Financial data (yr. ended 12/31/04): Assets, $6,259,518 (M); expenditures, $662,608; qualifying distributions, $648,361; giving activities include $644,828 for 61 grants (high: $381,000; low: $100).
Fields of interest: Arts; Human services.
Limitations: Giving primarily in Indianapolis, IN.
Application information: Application form required.
Initial approach: Letter
Deadline(s): None
Trustees: Donald W. Buttrey; Karen Lake Buttrey.
EIN: 912044415
Selected grants: The following grants were reported in 2004.
$381,000 to Indiana University Foundation, Bloomington, IN.
$45,000 to Chatham College, Pittsburgh, PA.
$25,000 to Neighborhood Christian Legal Clinic, Indianapolis, IN.
$21,000 to Salvation Army, New Albany, IN.
$5,000 to American Red Cross, Indianapolis, IN.
$5,000 to Indiana State University Foundation, Terre Haute, IN.
$1,000 to Park Tudor School, Indianapolis, IN.
$500 to American Bar Foundation, Chicago, IL.
$500 to Indiana Bar Foundation, Indianapolis, IN.

$500 to Wheeler Mission Ministries, Indianapolis, IN.

3234
Samerian Foundation, Inc. ☆
9910 Towne Rd.
Carmel, IN 46032
Contact: Fonda Crandall, Secy.-Treas.

Established in 2002 in IN.
Donor: Cynthia Simon Skjodt.
Foundation type: Independent foundation.
Financial data (yr. ended 12/31/05): Assets, $434,737 (M); gifts received, $740,000; expenditures, $484,962; qualifying distributions, $481,783; giving activities include $481,783 for 43 grants (high: $100,000; low: $100).
Fields of interest: Elementary school/education; Scholarships/financial aid; Environment; Children, services; Jewish agencies & temples.
Type of support: Scholarships—to individuals; Grants to individuals; General/operating support; Continuing support; Annual campaigns; Capital campaigns.
Limitations: Giving primarily in IN. No support for political organizations.
Application information: Application form required.
Initial approach: Letter
Deadline(s): None
Final notification: 60 days
Officers: Paul Skjodt, Chair.; Cynthia Simon Skjodt, Pres.; Fonda Crandall, Secy.-Treas.
Number of staff: None.
EIN: 371439047
Selected grants: The following grants were reported in 2004.
$50,000 to Indianapolis-Marion County Public Library, Indianapolis, IN.
$25,000 to Boys and Girls Clubs of Indianapolis, Indianapolis, IN. 2 grants: $5,000, $20,000
$25,000 to Butler University, Indianapolis, IN.
$25,000 to United Way of Central Indiana, Indianapolis, IN.
$16,950 to Congregation Beth-El Zedeck, Indianapolis, IN.
$15,000 to Childrens Bureau of Indianapolis, Indianapolis, IN.
$12,500 to Park Tudor School, Indianapolis, IN.
$5,000 to Oprahs Angel Network, Chicago, IL.
$2,000 to Indiana Childrens Wish Fund, Indianapolis, IN.

3235
The Scheumann Foundation, Inc. ✧ ☆
P.O. Box 811
Lafayette, IN 47902

Established in 2002 in IN.
Donor: John B. Scheumann.
Foundation type: Independent foundation.
Financial data (yr. ended 12/31/05): Assets, $5,598,518 (M); expenditures, $1,749,747; qualifying distributions, $1,750,250; giving activities include $1,750,250 for grants.
Fields of interest: Secondary school/education; YM/YWCAs & YM/YWHAs.
Limitations: Giving primarily in IN.
Officers: John B. Scheumann, Pres. and Treas.; John B. Scheumann II, Secy.
EIN: 300129316

3236
The Melvin and Bren Simon Charitable Foundation Number One ✧
P.O. Box 7033
Indianapolis, IN 46207-7033 (317) 636-1600
Contact: Deborah Simon

Established in 1998 in IN.
Donors: Melvin Simon; Melvin Simon and Associates, Inc.
Foundation type: Independent foundation.
Financial data (yr. ended 6/30/05): Assets, $19,364,701 (M); gifts received, $19,064,418; expenditures, $3,643,226; qualifying distributions, $3,560,961; giving activities include $3,560,961 for 122 grants (high: $200,000; low: $500).
Purpose and activities: Giving primarily for Jewish organizations, as well as for health associations, particularly for prostate cancer research; funding also for education, museums, and federated giving programs.
Fields of interest: Museums (specialized); Performing arts, orchestra (symphony); Higher education; Health organizations; Cancer research; Disasters, fire prevention/control; Girl scouts; Federated giving programs; Jewish federated giving programs; Jewish agencies & temples.
Limitations: Giving on a national basis, with emphasis on Indianapolis, IN, West Palm Beach, FL, and CA. No grants to individuals.
Application information:
Initial approach: Proposal
Deadline(s): None
Trustees: Bren Simon; Melvin Simon.
EIN: 352049367
Selected grants: The following grants were reported in 2004.
$201,875 to Jewish Federation of Greater Indianapolis, Indianapolis, IN. 2 grants: $171,875, $30,000
$148,635 to New Hope Charities, West Palm Beach, FL. 2 grants: $84,164, $64,471
$145,000 to International AIDS Trust, DC. 2 grants: $100,000, $45,000
$132,700 to Foundation of Indy Festivals, Indianapolis, IN.
$100,000 to University of Judaism, Los Angeles, CA.
$50,000 to Congregation Beth-El Zedeck, Indianapolis, IN.
$1,000 to University of Indianapolis, Indianapolis, IN.

3237
David E. Simon & Jacqueline S. Simon Charitable Foundation ✧ ☆
10555 Hussey Ln.
Carmel, IN 46032

Established in 2003 in IN.
Donor: David E. Simon.
Foundation type: Independent foundation.
Financial data (yr. ended 12/31/04): Assets, $1,786,884 (M); gifts received, $1,007,085; expenditures, $649,676; qualifying distributions, $611,062; giving activities include $611,062 for 28 grants (high: $375,000; low: $150).
Fields of interest: Higher education; Libraries (public); Health care; Youth development; Jewish federated giving programs; Jewish agencies & temples.

Limitations: Applications not accepted. Giving on a national basis, with emphasis on Indianapolis, IN. No grants to individuals.

Application information: Contributes only to pre-selected organizations.

Trustees: David E. Simon; Jacqueline S. Simon.

EIN: 141859319

3238
Deborah Joy Simon Charitable Foundation ◇

950 Laurelwood
Carmel, IN 46032-8738
Contact: Deborah Joy Simon, Tr.

Established in 2002 in IN.

Foundation type: Independent foundation.

Financial data (yr. ended 12/31/04): Assets, $3,126,679 (M); gifts received, $1,394,044; expenditures, $890,047; qualifying distributions, $834,540; giving activities include $834,540 for 39 grants (high: $200,000; low: $100).

Fields of interest: Libraries/library science; Education; Health care; Children/youth, services; Jewish agencies & temples.

Limitations: Giving primarily in IN.

Application information:
  Initial approach: Letter
  Deadline(s): None

Trustee: Deborah Joy Simon.

EIN: 300125798

3239
The Max Simon Charitable Foundation ◇

115 W. Washington St.
Indianapolis, IN 46204
Application address: c/o Melvin Simon, Tr., P.O. Box 7033, Indianapolis, IN 46207, tel.: (317) 636-1600

Established in 1999 in IN.

Donors: Cynthia Simon Skjodt; Deborah Simon; Melvin Simon.

Foundation type: Independent foundation.

Financial data (yr. ended 12/31/04): Assets, $8,546,032 (M); gifts received, $5,090; expenditures, $789,307; qualifying distributions, $621,911; giving activities include $621,911 for 11 grants (high: $250,000; low: $1,000).

Purpose and activities: Giving primarily for education, human services, and the arts, particularly to a museum for African-American history, and a film festival.

Fields of interest: Media, film/video; Museums (ethnic/folk arts); Arts; Higher education; Human services.

Type of support: General/operating support.

Limitations: Giving primarily in Indianapolis, IN.

Application information:
  Initial approach: Letter
  Deadline(s): None

Trustees: Tamme K. "Descouteau" McCauley; Bren Simon; David E. Simon; Deborah J. Simon; Melvin Simon; Cynthia A. Simon Skjodt.

EIN: 356692310

Selected grants: The following grants were reported in 2004.

$250,000 to Indiana Museum of African American History, Indianapolis, IN.
$178,911 to New Hope Charities, West Palm Beach, FL.

$100,000 to Heartland Film Festival, Indianapolis, IN.
$60,000 to Bard College, Annandale on Hudson, NY. 2 grants: $10,000, $50,000
$10,000 to Aspen Country Day School, Aspen, CO.
$10,000 to Brookside United Methodist Church, Indianapolis, IN.
$10,000 to Dance Kaleidoscope, Indianapolis, IN.
$1,000 to Damar Services, Camby, IN.

3240
The Herbert Simon Family Foundation ◇

P.O. Box 7033
Indianapolis, IN 46207-7033   (317) 636-1600
Contact: Stephen H. Simon, Tr.

Established in 1998 in IN.

Donor: Herbert Simon.

Foundation type: Independent foundation.

Financial data (yr. ended 6/30/05): Assets, $8,574,732 (M); expenditures, $1,606,047; qualifying distributions, $1,317,500; giving activities include $1,317,500 for 45 grants (high: $450,000; low: $1,000).

Fields of interest: Higher education; Education; Environment, land resources; Health care; Human services; Youth, services; Federated giving programs; Jewish federated giving programs; Jewish agencies & temples.

Limitations: Giving primarily in CA and IN.

Application information:
  Initial approach: Letter
  Deadline(s): None

Trustees: Herbert Simon; Jennifer K. Simon; Stephen H. Simon.

EIN: 943302950

3241
Steuben County Community Foundation

207 S. Wayne, Ste. A
Angola, IN 46703   (260) 665-6656
Contact: Sharon E. Stroh, C.E.O.
FAX: (260) 665-8420; E-mail: sccf@locl.net;
URL: http://www.steubenfoundation.org

Established in 1992 in IN.

Foundation type: Community foundation.

Financial data (yr. ended 6/30/05): Assets, $13,139,264 (M); gifts received, $2,185,452; expenditures, $813,722; giving activities include $430,644 for 315 grants (high: $30,000; low: $100).

Purpose and activities: The foundation works to preserve and enhance the lifestyle and assets of Steuben County, IN, for all current and future generations by providing ongoing assessment and financial support of identified needs through philanthropic giving and endowment building.

Fields of interest: Arts; Higher education; Education; Environment; Health care; Recreation; Human services; Community development.

Type of support: Scholarships—to individuals; Capital campaigns; Building/renovation; Equipment; Land acquisition; Endowments; Program development; Conferences/seminars; Seed money; Curriculum development; Scholarship funds; Technical assistance; Matching/challenge support.

Limitations: Giving limited to Steuben County, IN. No support for private schools, or religious or sectarian causes. No grants to individuals (except for scholarships), or for general operating funds,

second- or multi-year funding, budget deficits, travel, advertising, or annual campaigns; no loans.

Publications: Application guidelines; Annual report; Financial statement; Informational brochure (including application guidelines); Newsletter; Occasional report.

Application information: Visit foundation Web site for Grant Application Cover Sheet and application guidelines. Application form required.
  Initial approach: Letter or telephone
  Copies of proposal: 1
  Deadline(s): Last day of Feb., Apr., June, Aug., Oct., and Dec.
  Board meeting date(s): 3rd Thurs. of each month
  Final notification: Generally 3 weeks

Officers and Directors:* Todd Stock,* Chair.; Ellen Bisson,* Vice-Chair.; Sharon E. Stroh, C.E.O. and Pres.; Kim Tubergen,* Secy.; Bill Geiger,* Treas.; Melanie Harmon; Judy Manahan; Chuck Nedele; Tom Simons; Tony Smith; Carl Swift; Christopher Wheeler.

Number of staff: 3 full-time professional; 1 full-time support.

EIN: 351857065

3242
The Storehouse Charitable Trust ◇

c/o Russell B. Pulliam, Tr.
1025 W 52nd St.
Indianapolis, IN 46228

Established in 2001 in IN.

Donors: Russell B. Pulliam; Jane B. Pulliam.

Foundation type: Independent foundation.

Financial data (yr. ended 12/31/04): Assets, $0 (M); gifts received, $1,869,279; expenditures, $1,869,279; qualifying distributions, $1,869,279; giving activities include $1,866,667 for 1 grant.

Fields of interest: Community development; Foundations (community).

Limitations: Applications not accepted. Giving primarily in Indianapolis, IN. No grants to individuals.

Application information: Contributes only to pre-selected organizations.

Trustee: Russell B. Pulliam.

EIN: 916533016

3243
Tipton County Foundation, Inc.

1020 W. Jefferson St.
P.O. Box 412
Tipton, IN 46072-0412   (765) 675-8480
Contact: Frank M. Giammarino, Exec. Dir.
FAX: (765) 675-8488; E-mail: tcf@tiptontel.com;
URL: http://www.tiptoncf.org

Established in 1986 in IN.

Foundation type: Community foundation.

Financial data (yr. ended 12/31/05): Assets, $18,271,912 (M); gifts received, $655,524; expenditures, $843,165; giving activities include $454,766 for 30+ grants (high: $218,288; low: $310), and $83,279 for 12 grants to individuals (high: $38,411).

Purpose and activities: The foundation is a nonprofit public charity established in 1986 to serve donors, award grants, and provide leadership to improve the quality of life in Tipton County.

Fields of interest: Arts; Education; Recreation; Youth development; Human services; Community development; Public affairs.

Type of support: Consulting services; Equipment; Capital campaigns; Building/renovation; Income development; Management development/capacity building; Program development; Annual campaigns; Emergency funds; Conferences/seminars; Seed money; Curriculum development; Scholarship funds; Scholarships—to individuals; Matching/challenge support.

Limitations: Giving limited to Tipton County, IN. No support for religious purposes. No grants for ongoing operating expenses, debt reduction, annual appeals or membership contributions, travel, or endowment building.

Publications: Annual report; Financial statement; Grants list; Informational brochure; Newsletter; Occasional report.

Application information: Visit foundation Web site for application form and guidelines. Application form required.

Initial approach: Submit application form and attachments
Copies of proposal: 1
Deadline(s): Jan. 20, Apr. 14, July 7, and Oct. 13
Board meeting date(s): 2nd Tues. of Feb., May, July, and Nov.
Final notification: 1 month after deadline

Officers and Directors:* Tom McKinney,* Pres.; Virginia Chambers,* V.P.; Ron Warren,* V.P., Finance; Judy Burton,* Secy.; Frank M. Giammarino, Exec. Dir.; Mark Baird; Joe Cottingham; Rex Craig; Tom Dolezal; Brad Nichols; Nancy A. Nicholson; Mark Raver.

Number of staff: 1 full-time professional; 1 part-time support.

EIN: 311175045

3244
Randall L. & Marianne W. Tobias Fund ◇
500 E. 96th St., Ste. 110
Indianapolis, IN   46220

Established in 1999 in IN.
Donor: Randall L. Tobias.
Foundation type: Independent foundation.
Financial data (yr. ended 12/31/05): Assets, $2,182,250 (M); expenditures, $605,099; qualifying distributions, $601,945; giving activities include $599,475 for 23 grants (high: $335,000; low: $100).

Purpose and activities: Giving primarily for the arts, particularly the symphony, as well as for a school of music; funding also for higher and other education, human services, and a Presbyterian church.

Fields of interest: Arts, association; Arts, formal/general education; Performing arts, orchestra (symphony); Higher education; Libraries (public); Education; Human services; Protestant agencies & churches.

Limitations: Applications not accepted. Giving primarily in Indianapolis, IN. No grants to individuals.

Application information: Contributes only to pre-selected organizations.

Officer: Marianne W. Tobias, Pres. and Treas.
EIN: 352086313

3245
Twin City Education Foundation, Inc. ◇
905 W. Chicago Ave.
East Chicago, IN   46312   (219) 392-4225
FAX: (219) 392-4245;
E-mail: grantinfo@foundationsec.org; URL: http://www.foundationsec.org

Established in 1997 in IN.
Donor: Showboat Marina Partnership.
Foundation type: Company-sponsored foundation.
Financial data (yr. ended 12/31/04): Assets, $8,703,574 (M); gifts received, $3,144,134; expenditures, $2,338,245; qualifying distributions, $2,277,514; giving activities include $1,436,140 for grants.

Purpose and activities: The foundation supports organizations involved with education, employment, and human services.

Fields of interest: Education; Employment, services; Employment; Family services; Human services.

Limitations: Giving limited to East Chicago, IN.
Publications: Application guidelines.
Application information: Additional information may be requested at a later date. Application form not required.

Initial approach: Letter of inquiry
Deadline(s): Jan. 6, Apr. 7, July 7, and Oct. 7
Final notification: 4 months

Officers and Directors:* Norman Comer,* Pres.; Fernando Trevino,* V.P.; James Rajchel,* Secy.; Rev. David Blakely; John Flores; R. Louie Gonzalez; Cora Jones; Will Long; Pauline Morgan; Sylvia Morrisroe; Anna Delia Nunez-Deguits; Kathy Oppolo; Mario Palacios; Richard Peterson; Amparo Porras; Dan Rios; Peter Smith; Joseph Verduzco; Edward Williams.

EIN: 352025210

3246
Tyson Fund ◇
c/o Tyson United Methodist Church
324 W. Tyson St.
P.O. Box 446
Versailles, IN   47042

Trust established in 1930 in IN.
Donor: James H. Tyson.
Foundation type: Independent foundation.
Financial data (yr. ended 8/31/05): Assets, $19,008,404 (M); expenditures, $973,950; qualifying distributions, $919,654; giving activities include $919,654 for 4 grants (high: $474,000; low: $57,827).

Fields of interest: Libraries (public); Community development; Christian agencies & churches.

Type of support: General/operating support; Building/renovation; Equipment.

Limitations: Applications not accepted. Giving limited to Versailles, IN. No grants to individuals.

Application information: Contributes only to pre-selected organizations.

Officers: David E. Westmeyer, Pres.; Judith A. Sanders, Secy.
Trustee: Bank One, N.A.
EIN: 356009973
Selected grants: The following grants were reported in 2004.

$411,342 to Tyson United Methodist Church, Versailles, IN. For renovation, repairs and general fund.

$80,242 to Tyson Library, Versailles, IN. For new library building.

3247
Unity Foundation of La Porte County, Inc.
619 Franklin St.
P.O. Box 527
Michigan City, IN   46360-0527   (219) 879-0327
Contact: Margaret A. Spartz, Pres.
FAX: (219) 873-2416; E-mail: unity@uflc.net;
Additional tel.: (888) 89-UNITY; URL: http://www.uflc.net

Established in 1992 in IN.
Foundation type: Community foundation.
Financial data (yr. ended 12/31/04): Assets, $16,429,012 (M); gifts received, $716,063; expenditures, $1,127,438; giving activities include $244,094 for 142 grants (high: $23,729; low: $22), and $267,182 for 106 grants to individuals (high: $21,000; low: $100).

Purpose and activities: The foundation seeks to accept and pool charitable contributions from a variety of resources, and use the proceeds to support other charitable activities and organizations to benefit the residents of La Porte County, IN. The foundation makes discretionary and field of interest grants to charitable organizations in the area of the arts, education, health and human services, the environment, and the community.

Fields of interest: Arts; Education; Environment; Health care; Housing/shelter, homeless; Housing/shelter; Youth development; Children/youth, services; Human services; Community development.

Type of support: Land acquisition; Endowments; Building/renovation; Equipment; Program development; Conferences/seminars; Seed money; Scholarship funds; Technical assistance; Employee matching gifts.

Limitations: Giving limited to residents of La Porte County, IN. No support for sectarian religious programs. No grants to individuals (except for scholarship funds), or for operating budgets, basic municipal or educational functions and services, debt reduction, long-term funding, or after-the-fact funding.

Publications: Application guidelines; Annual report; Annual report (including application guidelines); Financial statement; Grants list; Newsletter.

Application information: Visit foundation Web site for application forms and guidelines. The foundation offers grantseeking/writing workshops; call foundation for information. Application form required.

Initial approach: Submit letter and attachments
Copies of proposal: 1
Deadline(s): July 15
Board meeting date(s): 1st Mon. of month
Final notification: Within 90 days

Officers and Directors:* Michael Brennan,* Co-Chair.; Edward Volk,* Co-Chair.; Margaret A. Spartz, Pres.; Arlene Dunn,* Secy.; Romona Hay; Margaret F. Hiler; Jim Jessup; Robert Johnson; Jerry Kabelin; Vidya Kora, M.D.; Robert Lake; Daniel E. Lewis, Jr.; Mary Lou Linnen; Burton B. Ruby; Michael Salmon; Robert Schaefer; Marti Swanson.

Number of staff: 2 full-time professional; 1 part-time professional; 2 part-time support.

EIN: 351658674

3248
Valiant Foundation, Inc. ✧
c/o Wells Fargo Bank Indiana, N.A.
P.O. Box 960
Fort Wayne, IN   46801-6632

Established in 1986 in IN.
Donor: Joe R. Gerson.
Foundation type: Independent foundation.
Financial data (yr. ended 9/30/05): Assets, $2,200,457 (M); gifts received, $1,788,119; expenditures, $571,790; qualifying distributions, $561,983; giving activities include $555,100 for 125 grants (high: $40,000; low: $500).
Purpose and activities: Giving to higher education, art institutes, and Jewish agencies and temples and Christian churches. Giving also for medical and health services.
Fields of interest: Higher education; Health organizations, association; Human services; Children/youth, services; Jewish federated giving programs; Protestant agencies & churches; Roman Catholic agencies & churches; Jewish agencies & temples.
Limitations: Applications not accepted. Giving primarily in Fort Wayne, IN. No grants to individuals.
Application information: Contributes only to pre-selected organizations.
Trustee: Wells Fargo Bank Indiana, N.A.
EIN: 351727123
Selected grants: The following grants were reported in 2005.
$5,000 to Indiana Institute of Technology, Fort Wayne, IN.
$5,000 to Lincoln Museum, Fort Wayne, IN.
$5,000 to Parkview Foundation, Fort Wayne, IN.
$5,000 to Turnstone Center for Disabled Children and Adults, Fort Wayne, IN.
$4,000 to Indianapolis Hebrew Congregation, Indianapolis, IN.
$3,500 to Cancer Services of Allen County, Fort Wayne, IN.
$3,500 to Embassy Theater Foundation, Fort Wayne, IN.
$3,000 to Fort Wayne Zoological Society, Fort Wayne, IN.
$3,000 to Indiana Repertory Theater, Indianapolis, IN.
$2,500 to Daybreak, Fort Wayne, IN.

3249
Vectren Foundation, Inc. ✧
(formerly Indiana Energy Foundation, Inc.)
1 Vectren Sq.
Evansville, IN   47708   (812) 491-4176
Contact: Mark Miller
E-mail: mmiller@vectren.com; Application address: P.O. Box 209, Evansville, IN 47702-0209; URL: http://www.vectren.com/web/holding/discover/foundation/foundation_i.jsp

Established in 1995 in IN.
Donors: Indiana Energy, Inc.; Vectren Corp.
Foundation type: Company-sponsored foundation.
Financial data (yr. ended 12/31/04): Assets, $33,375 (M); gifts received, $1,176,600; expenditures, $1,316,967; qualifying distributions, $1,316,299; giving activities include $1,316,299 for 558 grants (high: $79,860; low: $18).
Purpose and activities: The foundation supports organizations involved with arts and culture, education, natural resources, environmental education, health, mental health, employment, human services, and community development.
Fields of interest: Visual arts; Performing arts; Historical activities; Arts; Elementary/secondary education; Higher education; Education; Environment, natural resources; Environmental education; Hospitals (general); Health care; Mental health/crisis services; Employment; Human services; Community development, business promotion; Nonprofit management; Community development; Federated giving programs.
Type of support: General/operating support; Capital campaigns; Equipment; Program development; Employee volunteer services; Employee matching gifts.
Limitations: Giving limited to areas of company operations in IN. No support for political, religious, fraternal, labor, or veterans' organizations or issue-oriented organizations. No grants to individuals.
Publications: Application guidelines; Annual report.
Application information: Application form required.
Initial approach: Download application form and mail to foundation
Deadline(s): None
Final notification: 90 days
Officers and Directors:* Niel C. Ellerbrook,* Pres.; Ronald E. Christian, V.P. and Secy.; Jeffrey W. Whiteside,* V.P. and Treas.; Gregg M. McManus, V.P.; Jerome A. Benkert, Jr.; John M. Bohls.
EIN: 351950691
Selected grants: The following grants were reported in 2004.
$81,816 to United Way. 2 grants: $79,860, $1,956
$59,668 to United Way of Southwestern Indiana, Evansville, IN.
$50,000 to Indiana State Museum Foundation, Indianapolis, IN.
$30,000 to Signature Learning Center, Evansville, IN.
$25,000 to Evansville Philharmonic Orchestra, Evansville, IN.
$25,000 to YMCA.
$1,400 to Evansville Museum of Arts, History and Science, Evansville, IN.
$1,000 to Salvation Army.
$500 to Purdue University Foundation, West Lafayette, IN.

3250
Wabash Valley Community Foundation, Inc.
2901 Ohio Blvd., Ste. 153
Terre Haute, IN   47803-2239   (812) 232-2234
Contact: Beth A.A. Tevlin, Exec. Dir.
FAX: (812) 234-4853; E-mail: info@wvcf.com; Additional E-mails: beth@wvcf.com and rose@wvcf.com; URL: http://www.wvcf.com

Established in 1991 in IN.
Foundation type: Community foundation.
Financial data (yr. ended 9/30/05): Assets, $22,223,214 (M); gifts received, $1,171,501; expenditures, $1,123,607; giving activities include $593,318 for 217 grants (high: $10,000; low: $140), and $78,454 for 62 grants to individuals.
Purpose and activities: The foundation's mission is to promote community investment for a better tomorrow. Giving primarily for arts and culture, education, human services, community development, and religion in west central IN, specifically in Clay, Sullivan and Vigo counties.
Fields of interest: Arts; Education; Youth, services; Human services; Community development; Religion.
Type of support: Scholarships—to individuals; General/operating support; Capital campaigns; Equipment; Emergency funds; Seed money; Scholarship funds.
Limitations: Giving primarily in Clay, Sullivan, and Vigo counties, IN; requests from other counties occasionally considered.
Publications: Application guidelines; Annual report; Grants list; Informational brochure; Newsletter.
Application information: Visit foundation Web site for application guidelines, varying per grant type. 17 to 22 copies depending on grant cycle. Application form required.
Initial approach: Letter of Intent (1 page)
Copies of proposal: 16
Deadline(s): Jan. 15 and July 15 for full proposal; Dec. 15 for scholarships; varies for youth grants
Board meeting date(s): Jan., Mar., May, July, Sept., and Nov.
Final notification: Approx. 2 to 4 months
Officers and Directors:* Cynthia Cox,* Pres.; Ron Rich,* V.P.; Dean Cooke,* Secy.; Patrick Cahill,* Treas.; Beth A.A. Tevlin, Exec. Dir.; Hon. David R. Bolk; Mary Ann Carroll; Tom S. Clary; John Driscoll; Jerry Einstandig; Thomas L. Francis; John R. Heaton; Marlene Johnson-Hill; Ronald Jones; Mary McLaughlin; Malinda Medsker; Gary L. Morris; C. Don Nattkemper; Joseph F. Osborn; Gary W. Schomer; Oscar B. Session; William W. Sisson; Stanley Smith; Paul M. Thrift.
Number of staff: 2 full-time professional; 1 part-time professional; 1 full-time support; 1 part-time support.
EIN: 351848649

3251
Watanabe Family Foundation, Inc. ✧ ☆
10666 Winterwood
Carmel, IN   46032   (317) 517-0318
Contact: August M. Watanabe, Pres.

Established in 2001 in IN.
Donor: August M. Watanabe.
Foundation type: Independent foundation.
Financial data (yr. ended 12/31/05): Assets, $646,105 (M); gifts received, $502,832; expenditures, $534,240; qualifying distributions, $534,012; giving activities include $534,012 for 5 grants (high: $233,351; low: $5,040).
Fields of interest: Arts; Education; Health organizations, association; Human services; Children/youth, services.
Limitations: Giving primarily in IN.
Application information: Applications for scholarships should include some or all of the following: an essay including a description of applicant's interests and aspirations, description of past involvement in extracurricular activities, and a list of academic honors and recognitions, a transcript of prior academic achievements, report of performance on tests designed to measure ability and aptitude for academic work, description of financial need, written recommendations by individuals not related to the applicant, and the names of the institutions of higher education to which the applicant intends to apply. Application form not required.
Deadline(s): None

Officers and Directors:* August M. Watanabe,* Pres.; Margaret R. Watanabe,* Secy.-Treas.; Mary Ellen Raff.
EIN: 352143597

3252
Waterfield Foundation, Inc.

P.O. Box 40200
Fort Wayne, IN   46804-0200
Contact: Howard L. Chapman, Pres.

Established in 1992 in IN.
Donors: Anne K. Waterfield†; Elizabeth W. Chapman; Frances L. Swanson; Richard D. Waterfield.
Foundation type: Independent foundation.
Financial data (yr. ended 12/31/05): Assets, $3,948,187 (M); expenditures, $419,684; qualifying distributions, $392,390; giving activities include $390,835 for 59 grants (high: $106,550; low: $50).
Purpose and activities: Giving primarily for housing, recreation, youth development, the environment, and services for people who are handicapped.
Fields of interest: Arts, cultural/ethnic awareness; Performing arts; Education; Housing/shelter, development; Recreation, parks/playgrounds; Athletics/sports, training; Youth development, centers/clubs.
Type of support: General/operating support; Continuing support; Annual campaigns; Capital campaigns; Building/renovation; Equipment; Land acquisition; Endowments; Emergency funds; Program development; Seed money; Scholarship funds; Exchange programs.
Limitations: Giving primarily in northeastern IN. No support for non-501(c)(3) organizations.
Application information: Application form not required.
  Initial approach: Written requests only
  Copies of proposal: 1
  Deadline(s): None
  Board meeting date(s): Quarterly
  Final notification: After quarterly board meeting, only to approved grant applicants
Officers and Directors:* Richard D. Waterfield,* Chair. and Treas.; Howard L. Chapman, Pres.; Frances L. Swanson,* V.P.; Elizabeth W. Chapman,* Secy.
Number of staff: 2 part-time support.
EIN: 351872984
Selected grants: The following grants were reported in 2005.
$40,000 to Fort Wayne Park Foundation, Fort Wayne, IN.
$13,500 to United Way.
$5,000 to Boys and Girls Club.
$5,000 to Fort Wayne Ballet, Fort Wayne, IN.
$5,000 to SCAN.
$3,000 to American Red Cross.
$3,000 to YWCA.
$2,500 to Little River Wetlands Project, Fort Wayne, IN.
$2,500 to Nature Conservancy, Arlington, VA.
$1,000 to Heartland Chamber Chorale, Fort Wayne, IN.

3253
Wayne County, Indiana Foundation, Inc.

33 S. 7th St., Ste. 1
Richmond, IN   47374-5423   (765) 962-1638
Contact: Steven C. Borchers, Exec. Dir.
FAX: (765) 966-0882;
E-mail: info@waynecountyfoundation.org; Additional E-mail: steve@waynecountyfoundation.org;
URL: http://www.waynecountyfoundation.org

Established in 1979 in IN.
Foundation type: Community foundation.
Financial data (yr. ended 12/31/05): Assets, $28,994,267 (M); gifts received, $1,087,099; expenditures, $1,486,515; giving activities include $621,299 for 54+ grants, and $362,422 for 215 grants to individuals (high: $28,554; low: $100).
Purpose and activities: The foundation exists to foster and encourage private philanthropic giving, to enhance the spirit of community, and to improve the quality of life in the Wayne County, IN, area now and for future generations. Scholarships through restricted funds are awarded to deserving graduates of Wayne County, IN, high schools.
Fields of interest: Visual arts; Museums; Performing arts; Historic preservation/historical societies; Arts; Higher education; Adult education—literacy, basic skills & GED; Education, reading; Education; Environment; Animal welfare; Mental health/crisis services; Health organizations, association; Cancer research; Crime/violence prevention, youth; Crime/violence prevention, child abuse; Children/youth, services; Human services; Community development; Aging; Disabilities, people with.
Type of support: Equipment; Program development; Conferences/seminars; Publication; Seed money; Scholarship funds; Scholarships—to individuals; Matching/challenge support.
Limitations: Giving limited to Wayne County, IN. No support for religious organizations for sectarian purposes, organizations normally funded by the government, or for operating costs of non-public schools. No grants to individuals (except through restricted funds and scholarships), or for annual campaigns or operating funds, endowment funds, travel, or operating deficits or capital debt reduction.
Publications: Annual report; Informational brochure (including application guidelines); Newsletter.
Application information: Visit foundation Web site for grant application Cover Sheet and guidelines. Scholarship applications are available at local school guidance offices. Application form required.
  Initial approach: Submit application Cover Sheet and proposal
  Copies of proposal: 5
  Deadline(s): Apr. 3 for Arts, Youth, and Macy Museum Funds, Aug. 1 for Community Activities and Education, and Oct. 3 for Health, Human Service, Seniors, and Environment Preservation
  Board meeting date(s): 2nd Fri. of each month
  Final notification: May, Sept., and Nov.
Officers and Directors:* Rob Quigg,* Chair.; Alan Spears,* Vice-Chair.; Carol McKey,* Secy.; Carol Hinshaw,* Treas.; Stephen C. Borchers, Exec. Dir.; Thomas P. Alberts; Jon A. Ford; Dave Gethers; Shelley Miller; Sara Jane Moyer; Michael Nottingham; Robert Ramsey; Richard Smith; Charles K. Todd; Tammy Williamson; Benjamin Young.
Number of staff: 3 full-time professional; 2 part-time professional; 1 part-time support.
EIN: 351406033

3254
Welborn Baptist Foundation, Inc. ☆
(formerly Welborn Foundation, Inc.)

21 S.E. 3rd St., Ste. 610
Evansville, IN   47708-1418   (812) 437-8260
Contact: Garz W. Bauer, C.F.O.
FAX: (812) 437-8269; E-mail: info@welbornfdn.org;
URL: http://www.welbornfdn.org

Established in 1999 in IN; converted from Welborn Hospital.
Donor: WBH Evansville, Inc.
Foundation type: Independent foundation.
Financial data (yr. ended 12/31/05): Assets, $107,342,342 (M); gifts received, $2,915; expenditures, $4,954,158; qualifying distributions, $4,107,179; giving activities include $3,193,219 for 78 grants (high: $420,000; low: $1,000; average: $10,000–$420,000).
Purpose and activities: Giving primarily to apply Christian principles in support of improved community health, well being and quality of life for all members of the Tri-State Community.
Fields of interest: Health care; Substance abuse, services; Crime/violence prevention; Nutrition; Youth development; Community development; Religion.
Type of support: Matching/challenge support; Curriculum development; Conferences/seminars; Program development; Equipment; Building/renovation; Capital campaigns.
Limitations: Giving limited to Gallatin, Saline, Wabash, Wayne and White counties, IL; Dubois, Gibson, Perry, Pike, Posey, Spencer, Vanderburgh, and Warrick counties, IN; and Henderson County, KY. No support for basic scientific research. No grants to individuals, or for endowments, annual fund drives, debt service, deficit spending, scholarships, fellowships, general operating costs, venture capital or fund-raising; no loans.
Publications: Annual report; Financial statement; Multi-year report; Program policy statement.
Application information: Application guidelines available on Web site.
  Board meeting date(s): Varies
Officers and Directors:* John M. Dunn,* Vice-Chair.; E. Lynn Johnson, 1st Vice-Chair.; James R. Price, Secy.; Ronald Romain,* 2nd Vice Chair.; Marjorie Soyugenc, C.E.O. and Exec. Dir.; Gary W. Bauer, C.F.O.; W. Harold Calloway, Secy.; Jack E. "Ted" Sheppe, Treas.; Rita Eykamp; Mark Hubbard; Robert Hopper; Marilyn Klenck; James Murray, Ph.D.; Connie K. Nass; Ronald G. Reherman; Thomas M. Smythe; Ann Voliva; John O. Wells; Jaleigh White.
Number of staff: 4 full-time professional; 1 part-time professional; 1 full-time support.
EIN: 352056720

3255
The Wells County Foundation, Inc. ✧

109 N. Scott St.
Bluffton, IN   46714-0060
Contact: Bette Erxleben, C.E.O.
E-mail: wellscountyfound@wellscountyfound.org;
Additional E-mail: berxleben@parlorcity.com;
URL: http://www.wellscountyfound.org

Established in 1957 in IN.
Foundation type: Community foundation.
Financial data (yr. ended 12/31/04): Assets, $13,501,400 (M); gifts received, $275,375; expenditures, $1,081,070; giving activities include

$615,810 for grants, and $249,947 for grants to individuals.

Purpose and activities: The foundation seeks to enhance the quality of life of the Wells County, IN, community through the generation and prudent administration of entrusted donor funds to meet present and future changing community needs. Grantmaking fields of interest include arts and culture, education, economic and community development, health and human services, and other charitable purposes.

Fields of interest: Arts; Scholarships/financial aid; Education; Health care; Recreation; Human services; Economic development; Community development; Public affairs.

Type of support: Building/renovation; Equipment; Emergency funds; Program development; Seed money; Technical assistance; Scholarships—to individuals; Matching/challenge support.

Limitations: Giving primarily in Wells County, IN. No support for religious organizations for religious purposes. No grants to individuals (except for scholarships); no multi-year funding.

Publications: Application guidelines; Annual report; Informational brochure.

Application information: Visit foundation Web site for grant application format and guidelines. Scholarships only to residents of Wells County, IN; application guidelines available upon request. Application form not required.

> *Initial approach:* Letter or telephone
> *Copies of proposal:* 1
> *Deadline(s):* Feb. 15 and Aug. 15

Officers and Directors: * Bette Erxleben, C.E.O.; Peter Confer,* Pres.; Timothy Babcock,* V.P.; James Van Winkle,* Secy.; Brad Johnson, Treas.; Vicki Hanselman,* Chair., Strategic Planning Comm.; Thomas Stogdill,* Chair., Grants Comm.; John Whicker,* Chair., Finance Comm.; Mike Chaney; Stephanie Davis; Glennis Dick; Ted Ellis; Sandy Garcia; Kim Gentis; Gloria Shinn; Rick Singer; Phil Swain.

Number of staff: 1 full-time professional.
EIN: 356042815

3256
West Foundation, Inc.

c/o JPMorgan Chase Bank, N.A.
111 Monument Cir., Ste. 220
Indianapolis, IN   46204-5168   (317) 972-0204
Contact: Emily A. West, Dir.
Application address: 4120 N. Illinois St., Indianapolis, IN 46208

Established in 1954.
Donors: Stephen R. West; Phyllis M. West.
Foundation type: Independent foundation.
Financial data (yr. ended 12/31/05): Assets, $8,408,618 (M); expenditures, $1,069,138; qualifying distributions, $1,080,976; giving activities include $1,012,400 for 40 grants (high: $60,000; low: $1,500).

Purpose and activities: Emphasis is on international community development and problem-youth agencies and alcohol and drug abuse programs.

Fields of interest: Substance abuse, services; Alcoholism; Youth, services; International economic development.

International interests: Africa; Europe; South America.

Type of support: General/operating support; Annual campaigns; Capital campaigns; Matching/challenge support.

Limitations: Giving primarily in central IN; some giving also in Europe, South America, and Africa. No grants to individuals.

Publications: Application guidelines.

Application information: Application form not required.

> *Copies of proposal:* 1
> *Deadline(s):* None
> *Board meeting date(s):* Feb., May, Aug., and Nov.

Officers: Stephen R. West, Pres. and Treas.; Phyllis M. West, V.P.
Director: Emily A. West.
EIN: 237416727

Selected grants: The following grants were reported in 2005.

$60,000 to ProLiteracy Worldwide, Syracuse, NY.
$50,000 to Aspen Institute, DC.
$50,000 to MAP International, Brunswick, GA.
$50,000 to Resource Foundation, Larchmont, NY.
$50,000 to TechnoServe, Norwalk, CT.
$40,000 to Aid to Artisans, Hartford, CT.
$40,000 to HealthStore Foundation, Minneapolis, MN.
$35,000 to International Child Resource Institute, Berkeley, CA.
$30,000 to Village Enterprise Fund, San Carlos, CA.
$25,000 to Hesperian Foundation, Berkeley, CA.

3257
Dean & Barbara White Family Foundation, Inc. ◇ ☆

1000 E. 80th Pl., Ste. 700 N
Merrillville, IN   46410

Established in 1997.
Donors: Dean V. White; Barbara E. White.
Foundation type: Independent foundation.
Financial data (yr. ended 12/31/05): Assets, $14,527,306 (M); gifts received, $80,000; expenditures, $1,437,285; qualifying distributions, $1,196,781; giving activities include $1,196,781 for grants.

Purpose and activities: Giving primarily for human, social, and community services.

Fields of interest: Museums; Health organizations, association; Housing/shelter; Human services; Children/youth, services; Community development.

Limitations: Applications not accepted. Giving primarily in northwestern IN. No grants to individuals.

Application information: Contributes only to pre-selected organizations.

> *Board meeting date(s):* Dec.

Officers: Dean V. White, Pres.; Craig White, V.P. and Secy.; Barbara E. White, V.P. and Treas.
EIN: 352015808

Selected grants: The following grants were reported in 2005.

$250,000 to Northwest Indiana Symphony Society, Munster, IN.
$244,000 to Northwest Indiana Forum Foundation, Portage, IN. 2 grants: $122,000 each
$100,000 to American Maritime History Project, Kings Point, NY.
$50,000 to Indiana State Museum Foundation, Indianapolis, IN.

$10,000 to Northwest Indiana Quality of Life Council, Gary, IN.
$8,000 to Northern Indiana Arts Association, Munster, IN. 2 grants: $5,000, $3,000
$7,500 to Ridgewood Arts Foundation, Munster, IN. 2 grants: $5,000, $2,500

3258
Whitley County Community Foundation

400 N. Whitley St.
P.O. Box 527
Columbia City, IN   46725-0527   (260) 244-5224
Contact: September McConnell, Exec. Dir.; For grant applications: John Slavich, Prog. Off.
FAX: (260) 244-5724; E-mail: wccf@kconline.com;
URL: http://whitleycountycommunityfoundation.org

Established in 1992 in IN.
Foundation type: Community foundation.
Financial data (yr. ended 12/31/05): Assets, $13,950,135 (M); gifts received, $523,287; expenditures, $1,263,440; giving activities include $624,505 for 813 grants (high: $50,000; low: $1); $220,000 for grants to individuals, and $367,521 for 90 loans to individuals (high: $6,000; low: $500).

Purpose and activities: The mission of the foundation is to champion the spirit of philanthropy and grow permanent endowments. Utilizing collaborative leadership, it will assess and address local needs and direct funding to best meet community aspirations. Funding categories include: arts and culture, health, civic affairs, recreation, community development, welfare, and education.

Fields of interest: Arts; Education; Health care; Recreation; Human services; Community development, neighborhood development; Community development; Voluntarism promotion; Public affairs.

Type of support: Capital campaigns; Endowments; Emergency funds; Seed money; Scholarships—to individuals; Matching/challenge support; Student loans—to individuals.

Limitations: Giving limited to Whitley County, IN. No support for private schools, or religious or sectarian causes. No grants for operating budgets, budget deficits, annual campaigns, advertising, or debt retirement.

Publications: Application guidelines; Biennial report; Informational brochure (including application guidelines); Newsletter.

Application information: Visit foundation Web site for application form and guidelines. Application form required.

> *Initial approach:* Submit application form and attachments
> *Copies of proposal:* 1
> *Deadline(s):* May 1 and Dec. 1
> *Board meeting date(s):* 2nd Thurs. of each month

Officers and Directors: * Todd Jones,* Pres.; Aileen Meien,* V.P.; Rosemary Steiner,* Secy.; Clark Waterfall,* Treas.; September McConnell, Exec. Dir.; Ralph Bailey; Dale Duncan; John Leferer; Harold Norman; C. Taron Smith; Dave Smith; John Whiteleather.

Number of staff: 4 full-time professional; 1 full-time support.

EIN: 351860518

IOWA

3259
AEGON Transamerica Foundation ▼ ✧
(formerly AEGON USA Charitable Foundation, Inc.)
c/o Tax Dept.
4333 Edgewood Rd., N.E.
Cedar Rapids, IA 52499-3210

Established around 1994.
Donor: AEGON USA, Inc.
Foundation type: Company-sponsored foundation.
Financial data (yr. ended 12/31/05): Assets,
$108,861,302 (M); gifts received, $2,196,070;
expenditures, $6,809,943; qualifying distributions,
$6,265,342; giving activities include $5,860,031
for 336 grants (high: $1,000,000; low: $150), and
$405,311 for 847 employee matching gifts.
Purpose and activities: The foundation supports
organizations involved with arts and culture,
education, health, human services, business, and
government and public administration.
Fields of interest: Arts; Higher education;
Education; Health care; YM/YWCAs & YM/YWHAs;
Human services; Business/industry; Federated
giving programs; Government/public administration.
Type of support: General/operating support;
Employee matching gifts.
Limitations: Applications not accepted. Giving on a
national basis, with emphasis on areas of company
operations. No grants to individuals.
Application information: Contributes only to
pre-selected organizations.
Officers: Donald J. Shepard, Chair.; David
Blankenship, Pres.; Henry Hagan, V.P.; Kate
Modzelewski, V.P.; Marie Swope, V.P.; Craig Vermie,
Secy.; Diane Meiners, Treas.
EIN: 421415998
Selected grants: The following grants were reported
in 2005.
$1,000,000 to National Chamber Foundation, DC.
$334,000 to Sidney Kimmel Cancer Center, San
   Diego, CA.
$320,278 to United Way of East Central Iowa, Cedar
   Rapids, IA. 2 grants: $160,139 each
$317,541 to American Red Cross, Grantwood Area
   Chapter, Cedar Rapids, IA.
$317,541 to Habitat for Humanity, DC, DC.
$60,000 to Arts and Science Council of
   Charlotte-Mecklenburg, Charlotte, NC.
$52,181 to United Way, Heart of America, Kansas
   City, MO.
$43,750 to University of North Carolina at Charlotte
   Foundation, Charlotte, NC.
$20,000 to Aging Services, Cedar Rapids, IA.

3260
The Claude W. & Dolly Ahrens Foundation
1510 Penrose St.
P.O. Box 284
Grinnell, IA 50112 (641) 236-5518
Contact: Julie Gosselink, C.E.O. and Pres.
FAX: (641) 236-5590;
E-mail: grantinformation@ahrensfamilyfoundation.o
rg; URL: http://www.ahrensfamilyfoundation.org/

Established in 1993 in IA.
Donor: Claude W. Ahrens†.
Foundation type: Independent foundation.

Financial data (yr. ended 10/31/05): Assets,
$16,774,440 (M); expenditures, $1,713,342;
qualifying distributions, $1,463,739; giving
activities include $1,264,050 for 39 grants (high:
$500,000; low: $131).
Purpose and activities: Giving primarily for
education and recreation.
Fields of interest: Arts; Education; Health care;
Recreation, parks/playgrounds; Human services;
Youth, services.
Type of support: Capital campaigns; Building/
renovation; Equipment; Program development;
Conferences/seminars; Seed money; Technical
assistance; Matching/challenge support.
Limitations: Giving limited to central IA. No support
for religious and political organizations. No grants to
individuals, or for scholarships, general operating
support, or international.
Publications: Application guidelines; Annual report;
Grants list; Informational brochure; Informational
brochure (including application guidelines).
Application information: Formal grant application by
invitation only; see foundation Web site for
guidelines and procedures. Application form not
required.
   Initial approach: Letter of inquiry
   Copies of proposal: 1
   Deadline(s): Feb. 1, Apr. 1, Jun. 1, Aug. 1, Oct. 1,
      Dec. 1
   Board meeting date(s): Jan., Mar., May, July,
      Sept., and Nov.
   Final notification: 1 month
Officers and Trustees:* Julie Gosselink,* C.E.O.
and Pres.; Chad W. Ahrens,* V.P.; Susan E. Ahrens
Witt,* V.P.; Shannon Fitzgerald-Schultz,
Secy.-Treas.; David Clay.
Number of staff: 3 full-time professional.
EIN: 391906775
Selected grants: The following grants were reported
in 2004.
$500,000 to Greater Poweshiek Community
   Foundation, Grinnell, IA.
$335,000 to Grinnell Athletic and Recreation
   Center, Grinnell, IA.
$100,000 to Grinnell Regional Medical Center,
   Grinnell, IA.
$50,000 to University of Northern Iowa Foundation,
   Cedar Falls, IA.
$33,333 to Iowa Valley Community College,
   Marshalltown, IA.
$10,000 to Iowa Childrens Museum, Coralville, IA.
$10,000 to University of Iowa Foundation, Iowa City,
   IA.

3261
AmerUs Group Charitable Foundation
(formerly American Mutual Life/AmerUs Charitable
Foundation)
699 Walnut St., 20th Fl.
Des Moines, IA 50309 (515) 557-3910
Contact: Jonna M. LaToure, Asst. Secy.
URL: http://www.amerus.com/foundation/
index.cfm

Established in 1994 in IA.
Donors: American Mutual Life Insurance Co.;
AmerUs Group Co.
Foundation type: Company-sponsored foundation.
Financial data (yr. ended 12/31/05): Assets,
$5,680,158 (M); expenditures, $707,187;
qualifying distributions, $667,505; giving activities
include $658,267 for 86 grants (high: $334,367;
low: $50).

Purpose and activities: The foundation supports
organizations involved with arts and culture,
education, community development, and civic
affairs.
Fields of interest: Arts; Education; Community
development; Public affairs.
Type of support: General/operating support.
Limitations: Giving primarily in Indianapolis, IN, Des
Moines, IA, Topeka, KS, and Long Island, NY. No
grants to individuals.
Publications: Application guidelines; Program policy
statement.
Application information: Application form required.
   Initial approach: Download application form and
      mail to foundation
   Copies of proposal: 1
   Deadline(s): Varies
Officers and Directors:* Thomas C. Godlasky,*
Pres.; Roger D. Fors, V.P., Investments; James A.
Smallenberger, Secy.; Melinda S. Urion,* Treas.;
Mark V. Heitz; Christopher J. Littlefield; Gary R.
McPhail.
Number of staff: 2 part-time professional.
EIN: 421431745

3262
Andringa Family Foundation, Inc. ✧ ☆
10682 N.E. 46th Ave.
Mitchellville, IA 50169

Established in IA.
Donors: Dale J. Andringa; Mary A. Andringa.
Foundation type: Independent foundation.
Financial data (yr. ended 12/31/05): Assets,
$135,924 (M); gifts received, $299,675;
expenditures, $332,432; qualifying distributions,
$330,000; giving activities include $330,000 for 5
grants (high: $100,000; low: $30,000).
Fields of interest: Higher education; Theological
school/education; Religion.
Type of support: General/operating support.
Limitations: Applications not accepted. Giving on a
national basis. No grants to individuals.
Application information: Contributes only to
pre-selected organizations.
Officers and Directors:* Dale J. Andringa,* Pres.;
Mary A. Andringa,* Secy.-Treas.; Franklin Vanden
Bosch; Mindi Vanden Bosch.
EIN: 421240932

3263
Marie H. Bechtel Charitable Remainder
Uni-Trust ✧
(formerly Marie H. Bechtel Charitable Trust)
201 W. 2nd St., Ste. 1000
Davenport, IA 52801
Contact: R. Richard Bittner, Tr.

Established in 1987 in IA.
Foundation type: Independent foundation.
Financial data (yr. ended 12/31/04): Assets,
$37,473,594 (M); expenditures, $1,683,115;
qualifying distributions, $1,560,987; giving
activities include $1,506,968 for 27 grants (high:
$268,000; low: $1,768).
Purpose and activities: Giving primarily for youth
services and education; support also for the
advancement of health care, maintenance of
community cultural activities, and enhancement of
the community by restoring its vitality and creating
meaningful employment.

Fields of interest: Museums; Higher education; Education; Youth, services; Community development.
Limitations: Giving limited to Scott County, IA. No grants for endowment funds, past operating deficit or debt retirement, general or continuing operating support, or basic scholarly research.
Application information: Application form required.
  Initial approach: Contact foundation for application forms
  Deadline(s): None
Trustee: R. Richard Bittner.
EIN: 426288500
Selected grants: The following grants were reported in 2004.
$268,000 to Saint Ambrose University, Davenport, IA.
$150,000 to Davenport, City of, Davenport, IA.
$150,000 to River Music Experience, Davenport, IA. 2 grants: $50,000, $100,000
$50,000 to Center for Aging Services, Davenport, IA.
$35,000 to Junior Achievement, Quad Cities Area, Moline, IL.
$25,000 to Hand in Hand, Davenport, IA.
$25,000 to Skip-A-Long Child Development Services, Elgin, IL.
$1,768 to Hillcrest Family Services, Dubuque, IA.

3264
Harold R. Bechtel Charitable Remainder Uni-Trust ◇

201 W. 2nd St., Ste. 1000
Davenport, IA   52801
Contact: R. Richard Bittner, Tr.

Established in 1987 in IA.
Foundation type: Independent foundation.
Financial data (yr. ended 4/30/05): Assets, $27,261,449 (M); expenditures, $1,259,990; qualifying distributions, $1,134,458; giving activities include $1,084,522 for 20 grants (high: $187,000; low: $2,000), and $125,000 for 1 loan/program-related investment.
Purpose and activities: Giving primarily for health associations, education, and for children, youth, and social services.
Fields of interest: Education; Health organizations, association; Heart & circulatory research; Human services; YM/YWCAs & YM/YWHAs; Children/youth, services; Family services; Community development.
Type of support: Building/renovation.
Limitations: Giving limited to Scott County, IA. Generally no grants to individuals, or for endowment funds, debt retirement, past operating deficit, general or continuing support, or for scholarly research in an established discipline.
Application information: Application form required.
  Initial approach: Letter requesting application form
  Deadline(s): None
Trustee: R. Richard Bittner.
EIN: 426288501
Selected grants: The following grants were reported in 2005.
$187,000 to Saint Ambrose University, Davenport, IA.
$150,000 to Davenport, City of, Davenport, IA.
$50,000 to Family Resources, Davenport, IA.
$50,000 to River Music Experience, Davenport, IA.
$35,000 to Quad City Arts, Rock Island, IL.
$10,000 to American Heart Association, Des Moines, IA.

$10,000 to Youth Sports Foundation, Muscatine, IA.
$3,500 to Student Hunger Drive, Davenport, IA.

3265
Harold R. Bechtel Testamentary Charitable Trust ◇

201 W. 2nd St., Ste. 1000
Davenport, IA   52801   (563) 328-3333
Contact: R. Richard Bittner, Tr.

Established in 1989 in IA.
Donor: Harold Bechtel†.
Foundation type: Independent foundation.
Financial data (yr. ended 10/31/05): Assets, $8,562,279 (M); expenditures, $589,726; qualifying distributions, $538,841; giving activities include $503,400 for 18 grants (high: $125,000; low: $3,200).
Fields of interest: Arts; Higher education; Human services; Children/youth, services; Family services; Community development; Christian agencies & churches.
Limitations: Giving primarily in IA and IL. No grants to individuals, or for endowment funds, debt retirement, past operating deficit, general or continuing support, or for scholarly research in an established discipline.
Application information: Application form required.
  Initial approach: Letter or telephone requesting application form
  Deadline(s): None
Trustee: R. Richard Bittner.
EIN: 426428369
Selected grants: The following grants were reported in 2005.
$100,000 to University of Iowa Foundation, Iowa City, IA. 3 grants: $30,000, $50,000, $20,000
$40,000 to Quad City Botanical Center, Rock Island, IL.
$31,700 to Quad City Arts, Rock Island, IL. 2 grants: $3,200, $28,500
$30,000 to Augustana College, Rock Island, IL.
$20,000 to Niabi Zoological Society, Coal Valley, IL.
$15,000 to Saint Ambrose University, Davenport, IA.
$4,000 to University of Dubuque, Dubuque, IA.

3266
F. William Beckwith & Leola I. Beckwith Charitable Foundation

P.O. Box 70
Boone, IA   50036-0070
Contact: F. William Beckwith, Pres.

Established in 1995.
Donors: F. William Beckwith; Leola I. Beckwith†.
Foundation type: Operating foundation.
Financial data (yr. ended 12/31/03): Assets, $3,064,425 (M); gifts received, $450,000; expenditures, $344,896; qualifying distributions, $343,733; giving activities include $342,200 for 9 grants (high: $130,000; low: $4,000).
Purpose and activities: Giving primarily for education and family services.
Fields of interest: Libraries (public); Education; Botanical gardens; Recreation, camps; Youth development, agriculture; Family services; Christian agencies & churches.
Limitations: Giving primarily in IA. No grants to individuals.
Application information:

Initial approach: Letter
  Deadline(s): None
Officer: F. William Beckwith, Pres. and Treas.
EIN: 421448419

3267
Bedell World Citizenship Fund ◇ ☆

12019 240th Ave.
P.O. Box 557
Spirit Lake, IA   51360

Established in 2003 in IA.
Donor: Thomas W. Bedell.
Foundation type: Independent foundation.
Financial data (yr. ended 12/31/05): Assets, $2,347,312 (M); expenditures, $440,763; qualifying distributions, $411,500; giving activities include $411,500 for grants.
Fields of interest: Foundations (public).
Limitations: Applications not accepted. Giving primarily in IA. No grants to individuals.
Application information: Contributes only to pre-selected organizations.
Officers: Thomas W. Bedell, Pres. and Secy.; Karen L. Ridenour, V.P.; Thomas L. Heneke, Treas.
EIN: 200418324

3268
Myron & Jacqueline Blank Fund ◇

(formerly The Myron and Jacqueline Blank Charity Fund)
414 Insurance Exchange Bldg.
505 5th Ave.
Des Moines, IA   50309
Contact: Sandy Fein, Assoc.

Incorporated in 1948 in IA.
Donors: A.H. Blank†; Myron N. Blank.
Foundation type: Independent foundation.
Financial data (yr. ended 12/31/04): Assets, $9,187,461 (M); gifts received, $345; expenditures, $4,333,397; qualifying distributions, $4,288,918; giving activities include $4,286,921 for 16 grants (high: $1,675,000; low: $100).
Purpose and activities: Giving primarily to a zoo foundation, as well as for the arts, human services, health, federated giving programs, and Jewish organizations.
Fields of interest: Arts; Zoos/zoological societies; Reproductive health, family planning; Health care; Human services; Federated giving programs; Jewish federated giving programs; Jewish agencies & temples.
Type of support: Annual campaigns; Building/renovation; Endowments; Professorships.
Limitations: Applications not accepted. Giving primarily in Des Moines, IA. No grants to individuals.
Application information: Contributes only to pre-selected organizations.
Director: Myron N. Blank*.
Number of staff: 2 part-time professional.
EIN: 237423791

3269
The Bright Foundation ◇

c/o Brooks Lodden, PC
1441 29th St., Ste. 305
West Des Moines, IA   50266-1357

Established in 1974.

Donors: H. Dale Bright; Lois L. Bright.
Foundation type: Independent foundation.
Financial data (yr. ended 8/31/05): Assets, $10,562,295 (M); expenditures, $547,781; qualifying distributions, $384,698; giving activities include $335,733 for 21 grants (high: $93,434; low: $25).
Purpose and activities: Giving primarily for education, as well as for the arts, children's services, including a children's home and a hospital for crippled children; funding also for social services and Christian churches.
Fields of interest: Performing arts; Arts; Higher education; Libraries (public); Human services; Children, services; Residential/custodial care; Christian agencies & churches.
Type of support: General/operating support.
Limitations: Applications not accepted. Giving primarily in Des Moines, IA. No grants to individuals.
Application information: Contributes only to pre-selected organizations.
Officers and Directors:* Lois L. Bright,* Pres.; Carren Sturm,* V.P.; Gerry L. Rydell,* Secy.; Daniel M. Kelly,* Treas.; Wendy Carlson; Ellis E. Monk.
EIN: 426073848
Selected grants: The following grants were reported in 2005.
$45,000 to Buena Vista University, Storm Lake, IA.
$25,000 to Iowa College Foundation, Des Moines, IA.
$20,000 to Des Moines Metro Opera, Indianola, IA.
$20,000 to Drake University, Des Moines, IA.
$10,000 to Big Brothers/Big Sisters, Waterloo, IA.
$10,000 to Des Moines Art Center, Des Moines, IA.
$5,000 to Des Moines Area Religious Council, Des Moines, IA.
$5,000 to Iowa Stories 2000, Des Moines, IA.
$5,000 to Youth Homes of Mid-America, Johnston, IA.

3270
Brownell Family Foundation ✧ ☆
c/o Frank R. Brownell III
200 S. Front St.
Montezuma, IA 50171-1000

Established in 1986.
Donor: Frank R. Brownell III.
Foundation type: Independent foundation.
Financial data (yr. ended 12/31/05): Assets, $0 (M); gifts received, $877,796; expenditures, $842,199; qualifying distributions, $842,087; giving activities include $840,879 for 119 grants.
Purpose and activities: Giving to Christian agencies, higher education, the arts, and medical centers.
Fields of interest: Arts; Higher education; Hospitals (general); Christian agencies & churches.
Limitations: Applications not accepted. Giving primarily in IA. No grants to individuals.
Application information: Contributes only to pre-selected organizations.
Trustee: Frank R. Brownell III.
EIN: 421276134
Selected grants: The following grants were reported in 2005.
$15,000 to Des Moines Metro Opera, Indianola, IA.
$10,000 to Iowa Valley Community College, Marshalltown, IA.
$3,000 to Iowa College Foundation, Des Moines, IA.
$2,000 to University of Dubuque, Dubuque, IA.
$600 to Santa Fe Opera, Santa Fe, NM.
$300 to Biblical Archaeology Society, DC.

$250 to Lowell Observatory, Flagstaff, AZ.
$100 to Cystic Fibrosis Foundation, Bethesda, MD.
$100 to National Kidney Foundation, New York, NY.
$50 to Phi Beta Kappa Society, DC.

3271
Martin Bucksbaum Family Foundation ▼ ✧
(formerly Bucksbaum Foundation)
P.O. Box 498
Ankeny, IA 50021-0498

Established around 1968.
Donors: Maurice Bucksbaum; Martin Bucksbaum; Melva Bucksbaum; Mary Bucksbaum; Martin Investment Trust G.
Foundation type: Independent foundation.
Financial data (yr. ended 12/31/05): Assets, $821,564 (M); gifts received, $1,000,000; expenditures, $2,419,504; qualifying distributions, $2,411,492; giving activities include $2,411,492 for 15+ grants (high: $312,500; average: $34,500–$200,000).
Purpose and activities: Giving primarily for museums, arts and cultural programs, higher education, medical research, federated giving programs, Jewish federated giving programs, and religion.
Fields of interest: Museums (art); Museums (specialized); Arts; Higher education; Environment; Medical research, institute; Foundations (community); Federated giving programs; Jewish federated giving programs; Jewish agencies & temples.
Limitations: Applications not accepted. Giving primarily in IA and NY. No grants to individuals.
Application information: Contributes only to pre-selected organizations.
Officers and Directors:* Melva Bucksbaum,* Pres.; Mary Bucksbaum,* V.P.; Matthew Bucksbaum,* V.P.; Michael Greaves, Secy.
EIN: 426122182
Selected grants: The following grants were reported in 2004.
$749,428 to Whitney Museum of American Art, New York, NY.
$526,000 to Des Moines Art Center, Des Moines, IA.
$514,745 to Jewish Museum, New York, NY.
$200,000 to Baum Foundation, San Francisco, CA.
$120,000 to Smithsonian Institution, Hirshhorn Museum and Sculpture Garden, DC.
$100,000 to University of Pennsylvania, Wharton School of Business, Philadelphia, PA.
$73,350 to American Friends of the Israel Museum, New York, NY.
$63,485 to Music Associates of Aspen, Aspen, CO.
$53,750 to Drawing Center, New York, NY.
$50,500 to Temple Bnai Jeshurun, Des Moines, IA.

3272
Matthew and Carolyn Bucksbaum Family Foundation ✧
(formerly Matthew Bucksbaum Family Foundation)
P.O. Box 498
Ankeny, IA 50023

Established in 1994 in IA.
Donors: Matthew Bucksbaum; Carolyn Bucksbaum; John Bucksbaum; Ann B. Friedman; Orly D. Friedman; General Trust Co.; Jacolyn Bucksbaum.

Foundation type: Independent foundation.
Financial data (yr. ended 12/31/04): Assets, $53,647,303 (M); gifts received, $5,868,400; expenditures, $3,759,482; qualifying distributions, $3,759,482; giving activities include $3,651,604 for 21+ grants (high: $1,600,000; average: $25,000–$100,000).
Purpose and activities: Support primarily for health care, recreational activities, education, arts and culture, and Jewish giving.
Fields of interest: Arts; Federated giving programs; Jewish agencies & temples.
Limitations: Applications not accepted. Giving primarily in Des Moines, IA. No grants to individuals.
Application information: Contributes only to pre-selected organizations.
Officers and Directors:* Matthew Bucksbaum,* Pres.; Carolyn Bucksbaum,* V.P.; John Bucksbaum,* V.P.; Ann B. Friedman,* V.P.; Michael Greaves, Secy.; Thomas L. Friedman.
EIN: 421425846

3273
The Butler Family Foundation ✧
P.O. Box 28
Dubuque, IA 52004

Established in 1994 in IA.
Donors: John E. Butler; Alice L. Butler; Andrew J. Butler; Debra Butler; Cottlingham & Butler Insurance.
Foundation type: Independent foundation.
Financial data (yr. ended 12/31/05): Assets, $9,944,302 (M); gifts received, $732,700; expenditures, $1,265,529; qualifying distributions, $1,225,221; giving activities include $1,225,221 for 60 grants (high: $1,000,000; low: $100).
Purpose and activities: Giving primarily for education and youth services.
Fields of interest: Arts; Elementary/secondary education; Higher education; Youth development; Human services; Religion.
Limitations: Applications not accepted. Giving primarily in Dubuque, IA. No grants to individuals.
Application information: Contributes only to pre-selected organizations.
Officers: John E. Butler, Chair.; Alice L. Butler, Vice-Chair.; Marci Trost, Secy.; Brenda Hoefler, Treas.
EIN: 421429940
Selected grants: The following grants were reported in 2005.
$1,000,000 to University of Dubuque, Dubuque, IA.
$25,000 to Babson College, Babson Park, MA.
$12,500 to Clarke College, Dubuque, IA.
$5,000 to Wellesley College, Wellesley, MA.
$3,500 to Iowa College Foundation, Des Moines, IA.
$1,000 to Laurel School, Shaker Heights, OH.
$500 to Bryn Mawr College, Bryn Mawr, PA.

3274
Roy J. Carver Charitable Trust ▼ ✧
202 Iowa Ave.
Muscatine, IA 52761-3733 (563) 263-4010
Contact: Troy K. Ross Ph.D., Exec. Admin.
FAX: (563) 263-1547; E-mail: info@carvertrust.org;
URL: http://www.carvertrust.org

Established in 1982 in IA.
Donor: Roy J. Carver, Sr.‡.
Foundation type: Independent foundation.

Financial data (yr. ended 4/30/05): Assets, $285,237,001 (M); expenditures, $16,898,565; qualifying distributions, $14,785,049; giving activities include $14,215,706 for 133 grants (high: $4,350,000; low: $1,000; average: $10,000–$150,000).

Purpose and activities: Support primarily for biomedical and scientific research and programs addressing the educational needs of youth.

Fields of interest: Elementary/secondary education; Higher education; Libraries/library science; Biomedicine; Medical research, institute; Youth development; Science, research.

Type of support: Capital campaigns; Building/renovation; Equipment; Program development; Conferences/seminars; Professorships; Seed money; Curriculum development; Scholarship funds; Research.

Limitations: Giving primarily in IA. No support for religious activities or political organizations. No grants to individuals, or for endowments, fundraising benefits, program advertising, annual operating support.

Publications: Informational brochure (including application guidelines).

Application information: Proposals must be accompanied by a standardized cover sheet available on trust Web site. Application form not required.

   Initial approach: Letter (no more than 2 pages)
   Copies of proposal: 1
   Deadline(s): Feb. 15, May 15, Aug. 15, and Nov. 15
   Board meeting date(s): 3rd Fri. of Jan., Apr., July, and Oct.

Officers and Trustees:* Roy J. Carver, Jr.,* Chair.; J. Larry Griffith,* Vice-Chair.; William F. Cory,* Secy.; Troy K. Ross, Ph.D., Exec. Admin.; Willard L. Boyd; John A. Carver; D. Scott Ingstad; David M. Utley.

Number of staff: 4 full-time professional; 1 full-time support; 1 part-time support.

EIN: 421186589

Selected grants: The following grants were reported in 2005.

$4,350,000 to University of Iowa Foundation, College of Medicine, Iowa City, IA. For endowment and capital projects.

$1,000,000 to Figge Art Museum, Davenport, IA. To construct new building and develop web-based technology consortium.

$800,000 to Iowa State University Foundation, Ames, IA. For laboratory equipment for biomolecular research.

$650,000 to University of Illinois at Urbana-Champaign, Urbana, IL. 2 grants: $150,000 (To enhance bioinformatics and mass spectrometry resources within Biotechnology Center), $500,000 (To enhance bioinformatics and mass spectrometry resources within Biotechnology Center).

$500,000 to Muscatine Community School District, Muscatine, IA. For development of multi-use, synthetic turf field complex at Muscatine High School.

$200,000 to Camp Courageous of Iowa, Monticello, IA. To construct multipurpose facility on camp grounds.

$102,914 to University of Iowa, Department of Biology, Iowa City, IA. To investigate molecular evolution of sex chromosomes, using various species of fruit fly as comparative model systems.

$30,000 to Family Museum of Arts and Sciences Foundation, Bettendorf, IA. To renovate The Homestead exhibition gallery.

$7,699 to Wartburg College, Waverly, IA. To replace Carver Scholars grant.

3275
The Greater Cedar Rapids Community Foundation

(formerly The Greater Cedar Rapids Foundation)
200 1st St. S.W.
Cedar Rapids, IA   52404   (319) 366-2862
Contact: Daniel Baldwin, C.E.O.; For grants: Leslie Wright, Dir., Progs.
FAX: (319) 366-2912; E-mail: info@gcrcf.org; Additional E-mail: leslie.wright@gcrcf.org; URL: http://www.gcrcf.org

Established in 1949 in IA.

Foundation type: Community foundation.

Financial data (yr. ended 12/31/05): Assets, $47,933,480 (M); gifts received, $5,625,436; expenditures, $4,211,405; giving activities include $3,500,082 for 324 grants (high: $250,000; low: $250).

Purpose and activities: The foundation seeks to enhance the quality of life in the community by supporting creative and innovative programs, current or emerging charitable opportunities, services not presently offered, and occasional capital projects. The foundation serves as one of the most important resources in Linn County, funding activities in four essential program areas: Arts and Culture, Community Development and the Environment, Education, and Health and Human Services.

Fields of interest: Historic preservation/historical societies; Arts; Education; Environment; Health care; AIDS; Human services; Community development, neighborhood development; Community development.

Type of support: Capital campaigns; Building/renovation; Equipment; Emergency funds; Program development; Conferences/seminars; Publication; Seed money; Curriculum development; Scholarship funds; Technical assistance; Consulting services; Matching/challenge support.

Limitations: Giving limited to the greater Cedar Rapids and surrounding Linn County, IA, area. No support for religious activities of religious organizations (including parochial schools), or for crisis intervention. No grants to individuals (except for scholarships), or for annual operating budgets or travel; generally no grants for capital campaigns, endowment campaigns, one-time events, fundraising, equipment, scientific research, debt retirement, or deficit financing.

Publications: Application guidelines; Annual report; Informational brochure; Newsletter.

Application information: Visit foundation Web site for application Cover Sheet and guidelines. Application form required.

   Initial approach: Telephone
   Copies of proposal: 12
   Deadline(s): Feb. 15, June 15, and Oct. 16
   Board meeting date(s): Bimonthly
   Final notification: Apr., Aug., and Dec.

Officers and Directors:* Ann G. Hoffman,* Chair.; Gary Skogman,* Vice-Chair.; Daniel Baldwin, C.E.O and Pres.; Kathy L. Hall, V.P., Resource Devel.; Terry Trimpe,* Secy.; Larry Christy,* Treas.; Karen Nemecek, Cont.; Richard Altorfer; Bill Aossey; Lorna M. Barnes; J. Scott Bogguss; Swati A. Dandekar;

Katrina Garner; Kay L. Hegarty; Korlin Kazimour; Gerald T. Matchett; Doug Neumann; Greg Neumeyer; Ron Olson; Rich Patterson; Jay Petersen; Mary K. Quaas; John L. Wasta; Dr. Ruth E. White.

Number of staff: 6 full-time professional; 2 part-time professional; 1 full-time support.

EIN: 426053860

3276
The Clarinda Foundation ✧

213 E. Washington St.
P.O. Box 273
Clarinda, IA   51632   (712) 542-4412
Contact: Robert L. Caswell, Exec. Dir.
FAX: (712) 542-4412;
E-mail: clarindafound@iowatelecom.net;
URL: http://www.clarindafoundation.com

Established in 1986 in IA.

Foundation type: Community foundation.

Financial data (yr. ended 12/31/04): Assets, $1,256,738 (M); gifts received, $958,762; expenditures, $1,124,306; giving activities include $1,078,544 for 6+ grants (high: $890,980), and $13,540 for grants to individuals.

Purpose and activities: The foundation seeks to provide prospective donors an effective way to invest in the future of Clarinda, IA, and to maximize tax savings to the donors and their estates.

Fields of interest: Human services.

Limitations: Giving limited to within 15 miles of Clarinda, IA.

Publications: Newsletter.

Application information: Visit foundation Web site for grant application form. Application form required.

   Initial approach: Mail application form
   Deadline(s): Apr. 1 and Oct. 1

Officers and Directors:* Frederick V. Lisle,* Pres.; Dale McAllister, 1st V.P.; Mary Richardson, 2nd V.P.; Michael Anderson,* 3rd V.P.; Elaine Armstrong,* Secy.-Treas.; Robert L. Caswell, Exec. Dir.; Gary Beggs; Beth Gregory; Paul Honnold; Mark Lund; Marty Mattes; Ed Miller; Jim Millhone; Connie Richardson; Randall Schultz; John Woolson.

Number of staff: 1 part-time professional.

EIN: 421285187

3277
Community Foundation of the Great River Bend

(formerly Davenport Area Foundation)
111 E. 3rd St., Ste. 710
Davenport, IA   52801   (563) 326-2840
Contact: Susan S. Skora, C.E.O.
FAX: (563) 326-2870; E-mail: info@cfgrb.org;
Additional E-mail: susanskora@cfgrb.org;
URL: http://www.cfgrb.org

Established in 1964 in IA.

Foundation type: Community foundation.

Financial data (yr. ended 12/31/05): Assets, $37,752,608 (M); gifts received, $7,316,641; expenditures, $2,019,329; giving activities include $1,421,918 for 422 grants (high: $125,000; low: $200), $194,465 for 99 grants to individuals (high: $15,000; low: $250), $38,400 for 14 loans to individuals, and $37,000 for foundation-administered programs.

Purpose and activities: The foundation seeks to enhance the quality of life in the communities served by encouraging permanent charitable giving to meet the needs of present and future generations. Giving primarily for cultural activities, educational programs, health and human services, and economic development.

Fields of interest: Arts; Scholarships/financial aid; Education; Environment; Health care; Youth development, services; Human services; Economic development; Community development; Philanthropy/voluntarism; Youth.

Type of support: Continuing support; Management development/capacity building; Capital campaigns; Building/renovation; Equipment; Emergency funds; Conferences/seminars; Publication; Seed money; Technical assistance; Consulting services; Matching/challenge support.

Limitations: Giving limited to eastern IA and western IL. No support for sectarian purposes. No grants to individuals (except for scholarships), or for annual fundraising, endowment funds, or deficit financing; generally no multi-year grants.

Publications: Application guidelines; Annual report; Grants list; Informational brochure; Newsletter.

Application information: Visit foundation Web site for application form and guidelines. Grants $2,500 or under only require one copy of application, which can be e-mailed to the foundation. Application form required.

  Initial approach: Submit application form
  Copies of proposal: 7
  Deadline(s): None
  Board meeting date(s): 1st Tues. of each month
  Final notification: Varies

Officers and Trustees:* James D. Horstmann,* Chair.; Richard G. Kleine,* 1st Vice-Chair.; Diane B. Harris,* 2nd Vice-Chair.; Susan S. Skora, C.E.O. and Pres.; Tana S. Odean, V.P., Regional Progs.; Pete M. Wessels,* Secy.; Chris Wahlig,* Treas.; Edward J. Cervantes; David A. Dettmann; Michael K. Drymiller; Gregory B. Gackle; Dennis A. Norling; Frank L. Nowinski; Deann R. Thoms; Rita A. Vargas; Marie Ziegler.

Number of staff: 3 full-time professional; 2 part-time professional; 1 full-time support; 2 part-time support.

EIN: 426122716

3278
Community Foundation of Waterloo/
   Cedar Falls & Northeast Iowa

425 Cedar St., Ste. 310
P.O. Box 1176
Waterloo, IA 50704 (319) 287-9106
Contact: Mary Ann Burk, C.E.O.
FAX: (319) 287-9105;
E-mail: office@communityfoundationneiowa.com;
URL: http://www.communityfoundationneiowa.com

Incorporated in 1956 in IA.
Foundation type: Community foundation.
Financial data (yr. ended 4/30/05): Assets, $25,131,966 (M); gifts received, $3,170,730; expenditures, $1,802,220; giving activities include $1,437,739 for 836 grants (high: $59,280; low: $4), and $68,075 for 87 grants to individuals (high: $2,000; low: $250).

Purpose and activities: The foundation seeks to promote, encourage, and aid recreational, benevolent, charitable, medical, scientific, literary, educational, and research organizations' projects in the portions of northern and eastern Iowa.

Fields of interest: Historic preservation/historical societies; Arts; Child development, education;

Libraries/library science; Education; Environment, natural resources; Environment; Health care; Disasters, Hurricane Katrina; Recreation; Children/youth, services; Child development, services; Family services; Minorities/immigrants, centers/services; Human services; Community development.

Type of support: Management development/capacity building; General/operating support; Continuing support; Capital campaigns; Building/renovation; Equipment; Endowments; Emergency funds; Program development; Conferences/seminars; Publication; Seed money; Scholarship funds; Research; Program evaluation; Exchange programs; Matching/challenge support.

Limitations: Giving primarily in northeastern IA. No support for religious organizations. No grants to individuals (except for scholarships), or for annual campaigns.

Publications: Application guidelines; Annual report; Financial statement; Grants list; Informational brochure (including application guidelines); Newsletter.

Application information: Visit foundation Web site for Grant Request Summary form and guidelines. Application form required.

  Initial approach: Telephone
  Copies of proposal: 12
  Deadline(s): Apr. 1 and Oct. 1
  Board meeting date(s): 1st Wed. in June and Dec.
  Final notification: June and Dec.

Officers and Trustees:* Thomas Porth,* Chair.; Mark Baldwin,* Vice-Chair.; Terri Walker,* 2nd Vice-Chair.; Mary Ann Burk,* C.E.O. and Pres.; Dee Vandeventer,* Secy.; Chuck Shirey,* Treas.; Berdena J. Beach; Gary Bertch; Robert P. Bradford; John Bunge; Dennis Clark; Dawn Duven; Maureen Elbert; John Goossen; John C. Larsen; Amy Lockard; Timothy L. Manatt; Susan Nelson; Barb Opheim; Lois Rupkey-Cohrt; Robert L. Smith, Jr.; David G. Sparks; Josef M. Vich; James Walsh; Katy Williams.

Number of staff: 5 full-time professional; 1 full-time support; 3 part-time support.

EIN: 426060414

3279
Gardner and Florence Call Cowles
   Foundation, Inc. ◆

c/o David Kruidenier
1915 Grand Ave.
Des Moines, IA 50309

Incorporated in 1934 in IA.
Donors: Gardner Cowles, Sr.†; Florence C. Cowles†.
Foundation type: Independent foundation.
Financial data (yr. ended 12/31/05): Assets, $8,194,712 (M); expenditures, $1,422,109; qualifying distributions, $1,179,497; giving activities include $1,179,497 for 3 grants (high: $600,000; low: $100,000).

Purpose and activities: Grants primarily for four-year private colleges; some support also for various cultural institutions and selected social service agencies.

Fields of interest: Arts; Education, fund raising/fund distribution; Higher education.

Type of support: General/operating support; Continuing support; Building/renovation; Endowments; Seed money; Matching/challenge support.

Limitations: Applications not accepted. Giving limited to IA, with emphasis on Des Moines. No

grants to individuals, or for scholarships or fellowships; no loans.

Publications: Annual report.

Application information: Contributes only to pre-selected organizations.

  Board meeting date(s): Annually, and as required

Officers and Trustees:* Charles C. Edwards, Jr.,* Pres.; Elizabeth Ballantine,* V.P.; Lisa Kruidenier, Secy.; Thomas R. Hutchison,* Treas.; Morley Cowles Ballantine; Jacqueline Easley; Luther L. Hill, Jr.*; David Kruidenier; Elizabeth S. Kruidenier.

EIN: 426054609

Selected grants: The following grants were reported in 2004.

$600,000 to Des Moines Art Center, Des Moines, IA.

$30,000 to Des Moines Metro Opera, Indianola, IA.

3280
The Catherine Vincent Deardorf Charitable
   Foundation

c/o First American Bank
P.O. Box 798
Fort Dodge, IA 50501-0798 (515) 955-0670
Contact: Maureen Merrill, Tr.

Established in 1994 in IA.
Foundation type: Independent foundation.
Financial data (yr. ended 12/31/05): Assets, $8,318,809 (M); expenditures, $460,585; qualifying distributions, $386,109; giving activities include $365,951 for 32 grants (high: $64,000; low: $327).

Purpose and activities: Giving primarily for the community, including arts and culture, education, and health and human services.

Fields of interest: Arts, multipurpose centers/programs; Performing arts; Elementary/secondary education; Libraries/library science; Reproductive health; Human services; Children/youth, services.

Limitations: Giving limited to Webster County, IA. No support for religious activities and groups. No grants to individuals.

Application information: Application form required.

  Initial approach: Letter or telephone
  Copies of proposal: 1
  Deadline(s): None

Officers: Hans Nielsen, Pres.; Jane Gibb, V.P.; Judy Perkins, Secy.

Trustees: Dolores Garst; Maureen Merrill.

EIN: 426496438

Selected grants: The following grants were reported in 2003.

$60,000 to Harlan and Hazel Rogers Sports Complex, Fort Dodge, IA. For park improvements.

$54,000 to Fort Dodge Community Foundation, Fort Dodge, IA. For Oleson Park Bandshell renovation and Park.

$45,297 to Domestic-Sexual Assault Outreach Center, Fort Dodge, IA.

$29,850 to Fort Dodge, City of, Fort Dodge, IA. For summer reading assistance and parks initiative.

$25,000 to Humane Society of Webster County, Fort Dodge, IA. For building fund.

$21,465 to YMCA of Fort Dodge, Fort Dodge, IA. For building repair and uniforms.

$20,000 to Friends of Oleson Park Zoo, Fort Dodge, IA. For winter quarters for zoo animals.

$20,000 to United Way, Fort Dodge, Fort Dodge, IA. For Local campaign drive.

$15,000 to W. H. Johnston Foundation, Fort Dodge, IA. For Director incentive compensation.

$8,803 to Community Day Care and Preschool Center, Fort Dodge, IA. For curriculum enhancement.

3281
The Greater Des Moines Community Foundation ▼
(formerly Des Moines Community Foundation)
1915 Grand Ave.
Des Moines, IA 50309 (515) 883-2626
Contact: Johnny Danos, Pres.; For grants: Kristi Knous, V.P., Donor Rels. and Progs.
FAX: (515) 883-2630;
E-mail: info@desmoinesfoundation.org; Additional E-mail: knous@desmoinesfoundation.org; Grant request tel.: (515) 883-2703; URL: http://www.desmoinesfoundation.org

Incorporated in 1969 in IA.
Foundation type: Community foundation.
Financial data (yr. ended 12/31/05): Assets, $83,988,979 (M); gifts received, $29,394,651; expenditures, $17,303,504; giving activities include $16,510,117 for grants.
Purpose and activities: The foundation seeks to improve the quality of life in the Greater Des Moines, IA, area, by initiating programs, coordinating resources, and supporting organizations that enhance education, community betterment, arts and culture, health, and human services.
Fields of interest: Arts; Education; Health care; Children/youth, services; Human services; Community development.
Type of support: Scholarships—to individuals; Program development; Seed money; Scholarship funds; Technical assistance; Matching/challenge support.
Limitations: Giving primarily in the Greater Des Moines, IA, area. No support for sectarian religious purposes. No grants to individuals (except for scholarships), or for continuing support, or annual, building, capital, or endowment campaigns, capital infrastructure projects (bricks and mortar), or fundraising feasibility studies.
Publications: Application guidelines; Annual report; Informational brochure (including application guidelines).
Application information: Visit foundation Web site for application guidelines per grant type and Community Impact Grant cover letter page. Letters of intent are reviewed by the foundation to determine if projects merit further consideration; if the projects are determined to meet eligibility requirements, the organizations will receive an invitation to submit a full grant application. Application form required.
Initial approach: Letter of Intent
Copies of proposal: 3
Deadline(s): Mar. 31 and Sept. 1 for Community Impact Grants; none for others
Board meeting date(s): Quarterly
Final notification: Varies
Officers and Directors:* Madelyn M. Levitt,* Chair.; Allison Fleming,* Vice-Chair.; Kyle Krause,* Vice-Chair.; Johnny Danos,* Pres.; Kristi Knous, V.P., Donor Rels. and Progs.; J. Edward Power,* Secy.-Treas.; Margo Blumenthal; Roger K. Brooks; Robert Burnett; Teree Caldwell-Johnson; James S. Cownie; Patricia J. Crawford; Charles C. Edwards, Jr.; William Friedman, Jr.; Michele Griswell; Linda Koehn; Mary Middleton; Mell Meredith; Mary O'Keefe; Mark Oman; Thomas E. Press; Kurt

Rasmussen; Doug Reichardt; Stan J. Reynolds; Janis Ruan; Dawn Taylor; Ted Townsend.
Number of staff: 4 full-time professional; 2 full-time support.
EIN: 426139033
Selected grants: The following grants were reported in 2005.
$135,000 to Human Services Planning Alliance, Des Moines, IA. 2 grants: $100,000 (For Circles of Support), $35,000 (For operational support).
$50,000 to Des Moines Art Center, Des Moines, IA. For All Gates Project.
$50,000 to Downtown Events Group, Des Moines, IA. For World Food Festival.
$50,000 to Polk County Housing Trust Fund, Des Moines, IA. For housing supportive services and capacity building.
$40,000 to Science Center of Iowa, Des Moines, IA. For Who Are We.
$34,083 to Greater New Orleans Foundation, New Orleans, LA. For Rebuild New Orleans Fund.
$25,000 to Institute for Character Development, Des Moines, IA.
$17,042 to Gulf Coast Community Foundation, Gulfport, MS. For Build Back Our Gulf Coast Fund.
$10,298 to Children and Families of Iowa, Des Moines, IA. For start-up support for Compass Project.

3282
Employers Mutual Charitable Foundation ◇
P.O. Box 712
Des Moines, IA 50303-0712 (515) 362-7601
Contact: Robert Morian

Established in 1989 in IA.
Donor: Employers Mutual Casualty Co.
Foundation type: Company-sponsored foundation.
Financial data (yr. ended 12/31/05): Assets, $1,648,899 (M); gifts received, $212,269; expenditures, $1,027,078; qualifying distributions, $1,007,873; giving activities include $1,007,873 for 96 grants (high: $216,910; low: $100).
Purpose and activities: The foundation supports organizations involved with arts and culture, education, health, and human services.
Fields of interest: Arts; Elementary/secondary education; Higher education; Education; Health care; American Red Cross; Children/youth, services; Human services; Federated giving programs.
Limitations: Giving limited to IA. No grants to individuals.
Application information: Application form not required.
Initial approach: Proposal
Deadline(s): None
Officers and Directors:* Bruce G. Kelley,* C.E.O. and Pres.; George W. Kochheiser, V.P.; Richard Hoffmann, Secy.; Ronald D. Herman, Treas.; Joseph A. Smith,* Mgr. and Exec. Dir.
EIN: 421343474

3283
Joan Kuyper Farver Foundation ◇ ☆
604 Liberty St., Ste. 311
Pella, IA 50219

Established in 1993 in CO.
Donor: Mary Joan Farver.
Foundation type: Independent foundation.

Financial data (yr. ended 12/31/05): Assets, $497,122 (M); gifts received, $360,766; expenditures, $399,427; qualifying distributions, $398,661; giving activities include $398,661 for grants.
Fields of interest: Arts; Higher education; Hospitals (general); Health care; Human services; Christian agencies & churches.
Type of support: Continuing support; Annual campaigns; Capital campaigns; Building/renovation; Endowments; Emergency funds; Curriculum development.
Limitations: Giving primarily in IA and CO. No grants to individuals.
Publications: Program policy statement.
Application information:
Initial approach: Letter
Deadline(s): None
Board meeting date(s): Apr. and as needed
Officers: Mary Joan Farver, Pres.; Charles E. Farver, V.P.; Mary Farver-Griffith, Secy.
EIN: 841205184
Selected grants: The following grants were reported in 2005.
$100,000 to Central College, Pella, IA.
$50,000 to Pella Christian High School, Pella, IA.
$7,250 to American Red Cross, Des Moines, IA.
$5,000 to Des Moines Metro Opera, Indianola, IA.
$5,000 to Grinnell College, Grinnell, IA.
$5,000 to Music Associates of Aspen, Aspen, CO.
$1,500 to Iowa College Foundation, Des Moines, IA.
$1,500 to Iowa Public Television, Johnston, IA.
$1,000 to Children and Families of Iowa, Des Moines, IA.
$1,000 to New Hope Village, Carroll, IA.

3284
V. O. Figge and Elizebeth Kahl Figge Charitable Foundation ▼ ◇
326 W. 3rd St, Ste. 714
Davenport, IA 52801 (563) 336-8902

Established in 1992 in IA.
Donor: Vivian Otto Figge†.
Foundation type: Independent foundation.
Financial data (yr. ended 12/31/05): Assets, $4,847,967 (M); expenditures, $4,228,876; qualifying distributions, $4,223,181; giving activities include $3,858,532 for 12 grants (high: $2,888,563; low: $90; average: $10,000–$75,000).
Purpose and activities: Giving primarily for education and Catholic agencies and services.
Fields of interest: Arts; Education; Health care; Human services; Roman Catholic agencies & churches.
Limitations: Giving primarily in IA.
Application information: Application form not required.
Initial approach: Letter
Deadline(s): None
Trustees: Thomas K. Figge; Elizabeth Haines; Richard Horst.
EIN: 421398444
Selected grants: The following grants were reported in 2004.
$4,031,922 to Figge Art Museum, Davenport, IA. 2 grants: $3,971,922, $60,000 (For museum director).
$300,000 to Putnam Museum, Moline, IL.
$162,500 to Fountain Valley School of Colorado, Colorado Springs, CO.

$75,000 to Rivermont Collegiate, Bettendorf, IA.

$62,500 to YMCA, Scott County Family, Davenport, IA.

$50,000 to National Trust for Historic Preservation, DC.

$47,467 to John Lewis Coffee Shop, Davenport, IA.

$40,000 to American Folk Art Museum, New York, NY.

$40,000 to Ward Museum of Wildfowl Art, Salisbury, MD. For Illinois River Decoy Exhibit.

3285
Gramma Fisher Foundation ✧

112 W. Church St.
Marshalltown, IA 50158
Application address: c/o Christine F. Hunter, Chair., 6967 Cooke's Hope Dr., Easton, MD 21601, tel.: (410) 822-8450

Incorporated in 1957 in IA.
Donors: J. William Fisher†; William T. Hunter.
Foundation type: Independent foundation.
Financial data (yr. ended 12/31/05): Assets, $22,043,454 (M); expenditures, $2,273,678; qualifying distributions, $2,089,226; giving activities include $2,089,226 for 7 grants (high: $1,824,031; low: $9).
Purpose and activities: Grants mainly for the support and sponsorship of opera.
Fields of interest: Performing arts; Performing arts centers; Performing arts, music; Performing arts, opera.
Limitations: Giving in the U.S., primarily in New York, NY. No grants to individuals.
Application information: Application form not required.
Deadline(s): None
Board meeting date(s): As necessary
Officers: Christine F. Hunter, Chair.; William T. Hunter, Treas.
EIN: 426068755
Selected grants: The following grants were reported in 2003.
$500,000 to Washington Opera, DC. For operating support.
$275,000 to Metropolitan Opera, New York, NY. For operating support.
$150,000 to Lyric Opera of Chicago, Chicago, IL. For operating support.

3286
The Gerdin Charitable Foundation ✧

2777 Heartland Dr.
Coralville, IA 52241

Established in 1996 in IA.
Donors: Russell A. Gerdin; Ann S. Gerdin.
Foundation type: Independent foundation.
Financial data (yr. ended 12/31/05): Assets, $30,171,172 (M); gifts received, $3,675,984; expenditures, $1,247,317; qualifying distributions, $1,240,000; giving activities include $1,240,000 for 6 grants (high: $1,000,000; low: $10,000).
Purpose and activities: Giving primarily for education.
Fields of interest: Higher education; Education.
Limitations: Applications not accepted. Giving primarily in IA. No grants to individuals.
Application information: Contributes only to pre-selected organizations.

Officers: Russell A. Gerdin, Pres.; Ann S. Gerdin, V.P.
EIN: 421462088

3287
Gilchrist Foundation ✧

c/o Security National Bank
P.O. Box 147
Sioux City, IA 51102-0147

Established in 1998 in IA.
Foundation type: Independent foundation.
Financial data (yr. ended 12/31/05): Assets, $22,731,150 (M); expenditures, $1,045,484; qualifying distributions, $880,000; giving activities include $870,000 for 14 grants (high: $150,000; low: $10,000).
Fields of interest: Arts, association; Media, television; Media, radio; Performing arts, orchestra (symphony); Arts; Environment, natural resources; Animal welfare; Health care, association; American Red Cross.
Type of support: General/operating support.
Limitations: Applications not accepted. Giving primarily in IA, with emphasis on Sioux City. No grants to individuals.
Application information: Contributes only to pre-selected organizations.
Trustee: Security National Bank.
EIN: 426578668

3288
Leonard A. Good Trust

2200 Hamilton Dr., No. 604
Ames, IA 50014-8275
Contact: Helen Miller, Tr.

Established in 1990 in IA.
Foundation type: Independent foundation.
Financial data (yr. ended 12/31/05): Assets, $9,656,722 (M); expenditures, $619,054; qualifying distributions, $597,112; giving activities include $592,387 for 36 grants (high: $91,183; low: $1,000).
Purpose and activities: Giving primarily for public affairs and human services.
Fields of interest: Elementary/secondary education; Human services; Public affairs, government agencies.
Limitations: Giving primarily in Boone County, IA. No grants to individuals.
Application information: Application form required.
Copies of proposal: 4
Deadline(s): None
Board meeting date(s): Varies
Trustees: J. Dale Burman; Helen Miller; Douglas E. Nebbe; Randall C. Reutter.
EIN: 426453227

3289
The John R. and Zelda Z. Grubb Charitable Foundation ✧

475 S. 50th St.
West Des Moines, IA 50265

Established in 1995 in IA.
Donors: John R. Grubb†; John R. Grubb, Inc.
Foundation type: Operating foundation.
Financial data (yr. ended 12/31/05): Assets, $9,977,847 (M); gifts received, $170;

expenditures, $4,198,826; qualifying distributions, $715,213; giving activities include $700,665 for 37 grants (high: $242,385; low: $100), and $3,186,561 for 2 foundation-administered programs.
Purpose and activities: Giving primarily for health, children's services, and the arts.
Fields of interest: Theological school/education; Health organizations; Salvation Army; Children/youth, services; Foundations (community); Federated giving programs; Protestant agencies & churches.
Limitations: Applications not accepted. Giving primarily in IA. No grants to individuals.
Application information: Contributes only to pre-selected organizations. Unsolicited requests for funds not accepted.
Trustees: John W. Grubb.
EIN: 426521745

3290
The Hall-Perrine Foundation, Inc. ▼ ✧

(formerly The Hall Foundation, Inc.)
115 3rd St., S.E., Ste. 803
Cedar Rapids, IA 52401-1222
Contact: Jack B. Evans, Pres.

Incorporated in 1953 in IA.
Donor: Members of the Hall family.
Foundation type: Independent foundation.
Financial data (yr. ended 12/31/05): Assets, $107,924,272 (M); expenditures, $6,305,696; qualifying distributions, $5,674,889; giving activities include $5,608,146 for 23 grants (high: $3,000,000; low: $1,000; average: $20,000–$450,000).
Purpose and activities: The foundation is dedicated to improving the quality of life for people in Linn County, IA by responding to changing social, economic, and cultural needs. Primary areas of interest include the arts, higher education, social services, community funds, and health care. Support also for cultural programs, including fine and performing art groups, youth agencies, and health services.
Fields of interest: Arts; Higher education; Health care; Youth, services; Human services.
Type of support: Capital campaigns; Building/renovation; Matching/challenge support.
Limitations: Giving limited to Linn County, IA. No support for churches or their programs, or elementary or secondary schools. No grants to individuals, or for deficit financing, endowment funds, continuing operating support, benefits, special events, conferences, or fellowships; no loans.
Application information: Application form required.
Initial approach: Letter
Copies of proposal: 1
Deadline(s): Varies according to meeting dates
Board meeting date(s): Varies
Final notification: After board meetings
Officers and Directors:* William P. Whipple,* Chair.; Jack B. Evans,* Pres.; Darrel A. Morf,* V.P.; Iris E. Muchmore,* Secy.; John G. Lidvall,* Treas.; Dennis L. Boatman; E.J. Buresh; Kathy E. Eno; Carleen Grandon; Alex A. Meyer; Charles M. Peters.
Number of staff: 2 full-time professional.
EIN: 426057097
Selected grants: The following grants were reported in 2005.
$3,000,000 to Cornell College, Mount Vernon, IA. For Student Center renovations.

$3,000,000 to Mercy Medical Center, Hall Radiation Center, Cedar Rapids, IA. For equipment.

$526,370 to United Way of East Central Iowa, Cedar Rapids, IA. For annual campaign.

$20,000 to Iowa College Foundation, Des Moines, IA. For annual support.

$12,070 to Council on Foundations, DC. For annual support.

3291
The John K. & Luise V. Hanson Foundation
(formerly The Hanson Foundation)
P.O. Box 450
Forest City, IA 50436
Contact: Linda Kay, Secy.-Treas.

Established in 1971 in IA.
Foundation type: Independent foundation.
Financial data (yr. ended 6/30/05): Assets, $59,897,120 (M); expenditures, $3,804,451; qualifying distributions, $3,529,079; giving activities include $3,518,526 for 196 grants (high: $575,000; low: $200; average: $5,000–$100,000).
Purpose and activities: Giving primarily to provide the means of enhancing the quality of life in the north central IA, area, through activities involving youth, parks, recreation, and governmental agencies.
Fields of interest: Historical activities; Arts; Health care; Recreation; Human services; Children/youth, services; Public affairs, government agencies.
Type of support: Matching/challenge support.
Limitations: Applications not accepted. Giving primarily in north central IA. No support for religious organizations, or political organizations. No grants to individuals.
Application information: Contributes only to pre-selected organizations.
Board meeting date(s): Mar., June, Sept., Dec.
Officers and Trustees: John V. Hanson, * Pres.; Mary Jo Boman, * V.P.; Linda Kay, Secy.-Treas.
Number of staff: 1 part-time support.
EIN: 421343843
Selected grants: The following grants were reported in 2005.
$975,000 to Waldorf College, Forest City, IA. 2 grants: $575,000 (For library), $400,000 (For library project).
$250,000 to RV/MH Heritage Foundation, Elkhart, IN. 2 grants: $50,000, $200,000
$220,000 to Mayo Foundation, Rochester, MN. 2 grants: $200,000, $20,000
$100,000 to Forest City Education Association, Forest City, IA. For scholarships.
$100,000 to Iowa Natural Heritage Foundation, Des Moines, IA. For shoreline conservation on west end of Clear Lake.
$100,000 to Winnebago Historical Society, Forest City, IA. For Heritage Park upgrades.
$40,000 to Clear Lake Development Foundation, Clear Lake, IA. For swimming pool.

3292
Bruce & Sandy Heerema Charitable Foundation ✧
c/o Bruce Heerema
1111 Sunset St.
Pella, IA 50219

Established in 1997.
Donors: Bruce Heerema; Sandy Heerema.
Foundation type: Independent foundation.
Financial data (yr. ended 12/31/05): Assets, $498,249 (M); gifts received, $123,217; expenditures, $336,851; qualifying distributions, $336,391; giving activities include $335,933 for 10 grants (high: $160,987; low: $500).
Purpose and activities: Giving primarily for Christian organizations and schools.
Fields of interest: Elementary/secondary education; Theological school/education; Christian agencies & churches.
Limitations: Applications not accepted. Giving primarily in IA.
Officers: Bruce Heerema, Pres.; Sandy Heerema, V.P.
Directors: M. Timothy Heerema; Steven Heerema; Julie Mueller.
EIN: 391910689

3293
HNI Charitable Foundation ✧
(formerly HON INDUSTRIES Charitable Foundation)
P.O. Box 1109
Muscatine, IA 52761-0071
Contact: Susan J. Cradick, Secy.-Treas.
Application address: 414 E. 3rd St., Muscatine, IA 52761-0071

Established in 1985 in IA.
Donors: HON INDUSTRIES Inc.; HNI Corp.
Foundation type: Company-sponsored foundation.
Financial data (yr. ended 12/31/05): Assets, $3,833,960 (M); gifts received, $2,719,050; expenditures, $2,897,349; qualifying distributions, $2,896,405; giving activities include $2,896,405 for 396 grants (high: $350,000; low: $30).
Purpose and activities: The foundation supports organizations involved with cultural and ethnic awareness, education, health, human services, and community development.
Fields of interest: Arts, cultural/ethnic awareness; Education; Health care; Human services; Community development; Federated giving programs.
Type of support: General/operating support; Capital campaigns; Building/renovation; Employee matching gifts.
Limitations: Giving limited to areas of company operations. No support for national, statewide, or religious organizations. No grants to individuals.
Application information: Application form not required.
Initial approach: Proposal or telephone
Copies of proposal: 1
Deadline(s): None
Officers: Jack D. Michaels, Pres.; Roger Behrens, V.P.; Jeffrey D. Fick, V.P.; Stanley M. Howe, V.P.; Susan J. Cradick, Secy.-Treas.
Number of staff: 1 full-time professional.
EIN: 421246787
Selected grants: The following grants were reported in 2004.
$390,000 to Historic Muscatine, Muscatine, IA.
$383,615 to University of Iowa Foundation, Iowa City, IA.
$111,875 to United Way of Muscatine, Muscatine, IA.
$40,000 to Iowa College Foundation, Des Moines, IA.
$33,000 to Saint Ambrose University, Davenport, IA.

$27,830 to Musser Public Library, Muscatine, IA.
$20,855 to United Way of King County, Seattle, WA.
$8,169 to United Way of the Southern Tier, Corning, NY.
$2,000 to Muscatine Community College, Muscatine, IA.
$1,500 to Quad City Arts, Rock Island, IL.

3294
Roland & Ruby Holden Foundation
c/o Charles W. Orr
821 Forest Hill Dr.
Coralville, IA 52241

Established in 1993 in IA.
Donors: Curtis L. Blythe; Mary Ann Blythe; Arlene Holden; Karol A. Holden; Ronald W. Holden; Ruby E. Holden; David McCurry; Susan McCurry.
Foundation type: Independent foundation.
Financial data (yr. ended 6/30/05): Assets, $58,996 (M); gifts received, $375,000; expenditures, $443,315; qualifying distributions, $443,041; giving activities include $443,000 for 2 grants (high: $393,000; low: $50,000).
Purpose and activities: Giving primarily for higher education, research, and community development.
Fields of interest: Education, research; Higher education; Education; Human services; Community development.
Limitations: Applications not accepted. Giving primarily in IA. No grants to individuals.
Application information: Contributes only to pre-selected organizations.
Officers and Directors: Ruby E. Holden,* Pres.; Susan H. McCurry,* V.P.; Curtis L. Blythe,* Secy.-Treas.; Charles W. Orr, Exec. Dir.; Mary Ann Blythe; Arlene Holden; Karol A. Holden; Ronald W. Holden; David G. McCurry.
EIN: 421410022

3295
Holthues Trust ✧
225 Iowa Ave.
Muscatine, IA 52761
Contact: Betty J. Anders, Admin.
E-mail: andersbetty@stanleygroup.com

Established in 1997 in IA.
Donor: The Stanley Foundation.
Foundation type: Independent foundation.
Financial data (yr. ended 12/31/04): Assets, $30,174,065 (M); expenditures, $1,272,239; qualifying distributions, $1,259,832; giving activities include $1,255,000 for 39 grants (high: $125,000; low: $2,000).
Purpose and activities: Supports projects that will advance the goals of peace, security, freedom and justice globally, as well as community services locally in Iowa.
Fields of interest: Education; Human services; International peace/security; International human rights; International affairs; Civil rights; Community development.
Limitations: Applications not accepted. Giving in the U.S., with emphasis on Washington, DC, IA, IL, MN, and NY. No support for private foundations. No grants to individuals.
Application information: Contributes only to pre-selected organizations.
Officers and Directors: Richard H. Stanley,* Pres.; Joseph H. Stanley,* V.P.; Betty Anders, Secy.; Dana

W. Pittman, Treas.; Elizabeth Shriver; Lynne E. Stanley.
EIN: 421466786
Selected grants: The following grants were reported in 2003.
$150,000 to Physicians for Human Rights, Cambridge, MA. For studies on gender discrimination in HIV/AIDS.
$140,000 to Center for Victims of Torture, Minneapolis, MN. For new tactics in human rights.
$100,000 to Doctors Without Borders USA, New York, NY. For humanitarian aid in Liberia.
$50,000 to Mississippi Center for Nonprofits, Jackson, MS.
$20,000 to American Refugee Committee, Minneapolis, MN.
$10,000 to American Farmland Trust, DC.
$10,000 to Center for Justice and Accountability, San Francisco, CA.
$10,000 to Reef Ball Foundation, Woodstock, GA.
$10,000 to SeaWeb, DC.
$10,000 to Seeds of Peace, New York, NY.

3296
The Howe Foundation ✧
c/o Stanley M. Howe
1124 Oakland Dr.
Muscatine, IA 52761-5564

Established in 1992 in IA.
Donor: Stanley M. Howe.
Foundation type: Independent foundation.
Financial data (yr. ended 6/30/05): Assets, $25,564,907 (M); gifts received, $1,891,785; expenditures, $1,588,039; qualifying distributions, $1,582,709; giving activities include $1,579,070 for 16 grants (high: $499,500; low: $500).
Purpose and activities: Giving primarily for higher education; funding also for human services.
Fields of interest: Historical activities; Higher education; Education; Human services; Community development.
Limitations: Applications not accepted. Giving primarily in IA. No grants to individuals.
Application information: Contributes only to pre-selected organizations.
Officers: Stanley M. Howe, Pres.; Helen H. Howe, Secy.
EIN: 421395312
Selected grants: The following grants were reported in 2004.
$400,000 to Iowa Wesleyan College, Mount Pleasant, IA.
$250,000 to University of Iowa Foundation, Business School, Iowa City, IA.
$50,000 to Historic Muscatine, Muscatine, IA.
$40,650 to Boy Scouts of America, Davenport, IA.
$25,000 to Rock in Prevention, Des Moines, IA.
$25,000 to Senior Resources, Muscatine, IA.
$10,000 to Iowa College Foundation, Des Moines, IA.
$10,000 to Junior Achievement, Quad Cities Area, Quad Cities Area Chapter, Moline, IL.
$500 to Salvation Army of Muscatine, Muscatine, IA.
$500 to YMCA of Muscatine, Muscatine, IA.

3297
James W. Hubbell, Jr. & Helen H. Hubbell Foundation ✧
P.O. Box 897
Des Moines, IA 50304-0897 (515) 245-2800
Contact: Mindy Nussbaum-Bell, V.P., Bankers Trust Co.

Established in 1976 in IA.
Donor: James W. Hubbell, Jr.
Foundation type: Independent foundation.
Financial data (yr. ended 6/30/05): Assets, $6,340,520 (M); gifts received, $285,700; expenditures, $461,190; qualifying distributions, $403,063; giving activities include $402,000 for 14 grants (high: $60,000; low: $500).
Purpose and activities: Giving primarily for higher education, children and youth services, social services, and to an art foundation.
Fields of interest: Higher education; Libraries (public); Human services; Children/youth, services; Foundations (private grantmaking); Federated giving programs.
Type of support: General/operating support; Continuing support; Annual campaigns; Capital campaigns; Endowments; Program development; Seed money; Internship funds; Matching/challenge support.
Limitations: Giving primarily in Des Moines, IA.
Application information:
Initial approach: Letter
Deadline(s): None
Trustees: James W. Hubbell, Jr.; Bankers Trust Co.
EIN: 426259130

3298
Iowa West Foundation ▼
25 Main Pl., Ste. 550
Council Bluffs, IA 51503 (712) 309-3003
FAX: (712) 322-2267;
E-mail: grantinfo@iowawestfoundation.org;
URL: http://www.iowawestfoundation.org

Established in 1992 in IA, began grant operations in 1994.
Donor: Iowa West Racing Assn.
Foundation type: Independent foundation.
Financial data (yr. ended 12/31/04): Assets, $307,889,409 (M); gifts received, $78,357,392; expenditures, $19,109,764; qualifying distributions, $17,474,932; giving activities include $15,924,419 for 133 grants (high: $3,000,000; low: $1,000; average: $100,000–$500,000), $500,000 for 25 grants to individuals, and $85,000 for foundation-administered programs.
Purpose and activities: The mission of the foundation is to improve lives and strengthen communities for present and future generations. The foundation strives to provide leadership, create partnerships, leverage resources and serve as a catalyst in identifying and supporting community needs. The foundation has a special interest in the areas of community development and beautification, economic development, education, and human and social needs.
Fields of interest: Education; Human services; Community development.
Type of support: Capital campaigns; Building/renovation; Equipment; Program development; Seed money; Scholarships—to individuals; Matching/challenge support.

Limitations: Giving primarily in southwest IA and the Council Bluffs, Omaha, NE, area. No support for medical research or church-affiliated organizations for religious purposes. No grants to individuals, or for scholarships (except for foundation scholarship programs) fundraising, benefit, and social events, capital requests (for improvements to school property or for hospitals, medical facilities, assisted living projects, nursing homes, independent care, and extended care facilities), publications, films, books, seminars, symposia or for conferences.
Publications: Application guidelines; Annual report; Quarterly report.
Application information: Letter of inquiry may be submitted by mail, fax, or through the foundation's Web site online submission form. Requests for application forms accepted up to a week before the deadline dates. Application form required.
Initial approach: Letter of inquiry (no more than 3 pages)
Copies of proposal: 1
Deadline(s): For letter of inquiry: Jan. 1, Apr. 1, July 1, and Oct. 1; For full proposal: Jan. 15, Apr. 15, July 15, and Oct. 15
Final notification: 3 months from full proposal deadline
Officers and Directors:* Lynn G. Grobe,* Pres.; David H. Kuper,* V.P.; Ronald N. Tekippe,* Secy.-Treas.; J. Todd Graham, Exec. Dir.; John M. Burns; Patricia A. Hannan; Joseph D. Lehan; Suellen Overton; Charles L. Smith; Gary D. Woods.
Number of staff: 6 full-time professional.
EIN: 421391990
Selected grants: The following grants were reported in 2004.
$9,065,962 to Council Bluffs, City of, Council Bluffs, IA. 7 grants: $500,000 (For adaptive re-use of historic commercial properties), $483,900 (For redevelopment of West Broadway commercial site), $800,000 (For Avenue G viaduct and corridor aesthetics), $2,817,062 (To donate land for Mid-America Center), $715,000 (To develop and enhance Riverfront), $750,000 (For South 24th Street corridor improvements), $3,000,000 (For economic development).
$1,000,000 to Pottawattamie County Board of Supervisors, Council Bluffs, IA. For CITIES (Community Improvement To Increase Economic Stability) Program.
$450,000 to Pottawattamie County Development Corporation, Council Bluffs, IA. For South Main redevelopment.
$384,941 to Loess Hills Area Education Agency, Council Bluffs, IA. For safety equipment and technology for students.

3299
Richard O. Jacobson Foundation, Inc. ✧
P.O. Box 224
Des Moines, IA 50301 (515) 265-6171
Contact: Richard O. Jacobson, Pres.

Established in 1976.
Donor: Richard O. Jacobson.
Foundation type: Independent foundation.
Financial data (yr. ended 10/31/05): Assets, $9,727,035 (M); gifts received, $390,000; expenditures, $473,580; qualifying distributions, $450,372; giving activities include $450,372 for 57 grants (high: $83,333; low: $80).
Purpose and activities: Giving primarily for higher education, and youth services.

Fields of interest: Higher education; Youth development, business; Youth development; Human services.
Limitations: Giving primarily in IA. No grants to individuals.
Application information: Application form not required.
Deadline(s): None
Officer: Richard O. Jacobson, Pres.
EIN: 510192624
Selected grants: The following grants were reported in 2005.
$75,000 to Iowa State Fair Blue Ribbon Foundation, Des Moines, IA.
$40,000 to Rock in Prevention, Des Moines, IA.
$15,333 to Iowa Health Foundation, Des Moines, IA. 2 grants: $8,333, $7,000
$10,000 to Planned Parenthood of Greater Iowa, Des Moines, IA.
$9,500 to Grand View College, Des Moines, IA.
$2,500 to Iowa State University Foundation, Ames, IA.
$500 to Iowa Games, Ames, IA.

3300
Kinney-Lindstrom Foundation, Inc. ◇ ☆
c/o Kent A. Hall
P.O. Box 520
Mason City, IA 50401

Incorporated in 1957 in IA.
Foundation type: Independent foundation.
Financial data (yr. ended 12/31/05): Assets, $5,002,000 (M); expenditures, $856,763; qualifying distributions, $333,316; giving activities include $333,316 for grants.
Purpose and activities: Support primarily for education, historical museums and other cultural programs, social services, youth and health agencies, and civic programs.
Fields of interest: Museums (history); Arts; Elementary/secondary education; Higher education; Health organizations, association; Human services; American Red Cross; Children/youth, services; Federated giving programs; Government/public administration.
Type of support: Building/renovation; Equipment.
Limitations: Applications not accepted. Giving primarily within a 25-mile radius of Mason City, IA. No grants to individuals, or for endowment funds, operating budgets, or research; no loans.
Application information: Contributes only to pre-selected organizations.
Board meeting date(s): Four meetings annually
Officer: Kent A Hall, Treas.
Trustees: John H. Greue; Patty J. Hall; Everett J. Hermanson.
Number of staff: 1 full-time professional.
EIN: 426037351
Selected grants: The following grants were reported in 2004.
$25,000 to Iowa College Foundation, Des Moines, IA. For Library Challenge.
$25,000 to Mercy Medical Center. For equipment for Cancer Center.
$25,000 to North Iowa Vocational Center (NIVC Services), Mason City, IA. For relocation.
$20,000 to North Iowa Area Community College, Mason City, IA. For acoustical sound shell.
$20,000 to Northern Lights Alliance for the Homeless, Mason City, IA. For building challenge.
$15,000 to United Way, IA. For annual fund.

$12,000 to North Central Human Services, Forest City, IA. For pool repairs.
$10,000 to North Iowa Fair Association, Mason City, IA. For Owen Schoolhouse restoration.
$10,000 to Waldorf College, Forest City, IA. For library technology.
$4,500 to Girl Scouts of the U.S.A., Mason City, IA. For camperships.

3301
William C. Knapp Charitable Foundation ◇
(formerly Iowa Realty Charitable Foundation)
4949 Westown Pkwy., Ste. 200
West Des Moines, IA 50266-6704

Established in 1987 in IA.
Donors: Allied Development; Knapp Realty Co.
Foundation type: Independent foundation.
Financial data (yr. ended 12/31/05): Assets, $2,122,619 (M); gifts received, $1,500,000; expenditures, $1,175,031; qualifying distributions, $1,168,315; giving activities include $1,166,415 for 104 grants (high: $333,333; low: $50).
Purpose and activities: Giving primarily for community development; some giving also for education, health associations, and federated giving programs.
Fields of interest: Arts; Education; Reproductive health, family planning; Health organizations, association; Human services; Community development; Federated giving programs; Religion.
Limitations: Applications not accepted. Giving primarily in Des Moines, IA. No grants to individuals.
Application information: Contributes only to pre-selected organizations.
Officers: William C. Knapp, Pres.; Gerard D. Neugent, Secy.
Directors: Virginia Haviland; Roger Knapp; WIlliam C. Knapp II.
EIN: 421234012
Selected grants: The following grants were reported in 2005.
$100,000 to United Way of Central Iowa, Des Moines, IA.
$33,333 to Science Center of Iowa, Des Moines, IA.
$30,000 to Muscular Dystrophy Association, Tucson, AZ. 3 grants: $10,000 each
$20,000 to Oakridge Neighborhood Services, Des Moines, IA.
$15,755 to American Red Cross. 2 grants: $10,000, $5,755
$5,000 to Harbor, Smithfield, NC.
$1,000 to Catholic Charities.

3302
Krause Gentle Foundation ◇ ☆
6400 Westown Pkwy.
West Des Moines, IA 50266

Established in 1994 in IA.
Donors: William A. Krause; KG Investments; Krause Gentle Corporation; Kum & Go LC; Cheiftain.
Foundation type: Independent foundation.
Financial data (yr. ended 12/31/05): Assets, $7,431,904 (M); gifts received, $3,568,568; expenditures, $658,834; qualifying distributions, $643,294; giving activities include $637,953 for 107 grants (high: $141,500; low: $25).
Purpose and activities: Giving for Catholic schools, churches and organizations; giving also for youth services and programs and for higher education.

Fields of interest: Visual arts; Performing arts, music (choral); Elementary/secondary education; Higher education; Animal welfare; Cystic fibrosis; Muscular dystrophy; Multiple sclerosis; Alzheimer's disease; Food services; Housing/shelter, development; Recreation, association; Recreation, camps; Boy scouts; Girl scouts; YM/YWCAs & YM/YWHAs; Youth, services; Residential/custodial care; Community development; Federated giving programs; Protestant agencies & churches; Roman Catholic agencies & churches.
Limitations: Giving on a national basis, with emphasis on IA. No grants to individuals.
Directors: Dennis Folden; William A. Krause.
EIN: 421414004
Selected grants: The following grants were reported in 2004.
$50,000 to University of Northern Iowa, Cedar Falls, IA.
$30,467 to United Way.
$26,900 to University of Iowa, Iowa City, IA.
$6,900 to Drake University, Des Moines, IA.
$6,500 to Greater Des Moines Community Foundation, Des Moines, IA.
$4,500 to Clarke College, Dubuque, IA.
$2,500 to YMCA.
$1,000 to Catholic Charities.
$1,000 to Children and Families of Iowa, Des Moines, IA.
$1,000 to New Hope Village, Carroll, IA.

3303
Kruidenier Charitable Foundation, Inc. ◇
715 Locust St.
Des Moines, IA 50309-3703   (515) 284-8117

Established in 1984 in IA.
Donors: David Kruidenier; Elizabeth Kruidenier; Lisa Kruidenier.
Foundation type: Independent foundation.
Financial data (yr. ended 12/31/05): Assets, $10,912,157 (M); expenditures, $1,699,288; qualifying distributions, $1,687,922; giving activities include $1,687,922 for 46 grants (high: $500,000; low: $500).
Purpose and activities: Giving primarily for community foundations, and arts and culture; funding also for human services, and religion.
Fields of interest: Arts; Higher education; Human services; Foundations (community); Religion.
Type of support: General/operating support.
Limitations: Applications not accepted. Giving primarily in Des Moines, IA. No grants to individuals.
Application information: Contributes only to pre-selected organizations.
Officers and Directors:* David Kruidenier,* Pres. and Treas.; Lisa Kruidenier,* V.P.; Elizabeth Kruidenier,* Secy.; Joe Scofield.
EIN: 421255071

3304
Peter H. and E. Lucille Gaass Kuyper Foundation ◇
c/o Pella Corp.
102 Main St.
Pella, IA 50219   (641) 621-6224
Contact: Mary Van Zante, Secy.-Treas.

Established in 1970 in IA.
Donors: Peter H. Kuyper†; E. Lucille Gaass Kuyper†; Joan Kuyper Farver.

Foundation type: Independent foundation.
Financial data (yr. ended 12/31/05): Assets, $11,606,063 (M); expenditures, $690,759; qualifying distributions, $581,524; giving activities include $451,874 for 31 grants (high: $160,000; low: $500), and $129,640 for 37 employee matching gifts.
Purpose and activities: Primarily general charitable giving, including the arts, education, Christian agencies, and health.
Fields of interest: Arts; Higher education; Hospitals (general); Christian agencies & churches.
Type of support: Annual campaigns; Capital campaigns; Building/renovation; Equipment; Endowments; Scholarship funds.
Limitations: Giving primarily in the Pella, IA, area. No grants to individuals.
Application information: Application form not required.
  Initial approach: Letter
  Copies of proposal: 1
  Deadline(s): None
  Board meeting date(s): Apr.
Officers and Directors:* Joan Kuyper Farver,* Chair. and Pres.; Charles Farver,* V.P.; Chip Griffith, V.P.; Mary Griffith,* V.P.; Ann F. Lennartz,* V.P.; Mary Van Zante,* Secy.-Treas.
EIN: 237068402
Selected grants: The following grants were reported in 2003.
$175,000 to Central College, Pella, IA. For scholarships.
$25,000 to Pella Opera House Commission, Pella, IA. For program support.
$20,000 to Iowa College Foundation, Des Moines, IA. For annual support.
$10,000 to Iowa State University Achievement Fund, Ames, IA. For scholarships.
$5,000 to Des Moines Art Center, Des Moines, IA. For annual support.
$5,000 to University of Northern Iowa, Cedar Falls, IA. For program support.
$3,000 to Iowa Natural Heritage Foundation, Des Moines, IA. For annual support.
$3,000 to Pella Public Library, Pella, IA. For annual support.
$1,000 to Prevent Blindness Iowa, Des Moines, IA. For annual support.
$500 to Ames International Orchestra Festival, Ames, IA. For annual support.

3305
Lee Endowment Foundation ✧
c/o First Citizens Trust Co., N.A.
2601 4th St., S.W.
P.O. Box 1708
Mason City, IA 50402-1708
Application address: c/o Howard Query, Chair., Charitable Fund Screening Comm., Globe-Gazette, Mason City, IA 50401, tel.: (641) 421-0507 (for Elizabeth Muse Norris Char. Fund and Lorraine & Ray Rorick Fund)

Established in 1978 in IA.
Donor: Elizabeth Norris†.
Foundation type: Independent foundation.
Financial data (yr. ended 12/31/05): Assets, $24,560,839 (M); expenditures, $1,710,799; qualifying distributions, $1,672,805; giving activities include $1,400,830 for 77 grants (high: $150,000; low: $306), and $268,164 for 216 grants to individuals (high: $1,300; low: $650).

Purpose and activities: Support for community development, higher education, health and social services, and for scholarships to individuals for postsecondary education.
Fields of interest: Arts; Education; Health care; Recreation; Human services; Community development.
Type of support: General/operating support; Scholarships—to individuals.
Limitations: Giving primarily to residents of Mason City and Cerro Gordo County, IA, for scholarships; in north central IA for other grants.
Application information: Application form required for scholarships.
  Deadline(s): Feb. 1 for scholarships; no deadline for charitable fund applications, but generally will be acted upon once annually, in Feb.
Officers and Directors:* Donald Harrer,* Pres.; Sanders Hook,* V.P.; Howard Kennedy,* V.P.; Lloyd Loers,* V.P.; Douglas Sherwin,* V.P.; Ronald L. Rickman,* Secy.-Treas.
EIN: 421074052

3306
Lee Foundation ✧
201 N. Harrison St., Ste. 600
Davenport, IA 52801
Contact: Carl Schmidt, Secy.-Treas.

Incorporated in 1962 in IA.
Donor: Lee Enterprises, Inc.
Foundation type: Company-sponsored foundation.
Financial data (yr. ended 9/30/05): Assets, $6,611,320 (M); expenditures, $588,688; qualifying distributions, $560,811; giving activities include $560,436 for 72 grants (high: $200,000; low: $250).
Purpose and activities: The foundation supports organizations involved with arts and culture, education, animal welfare, and child abuse prevention.
Fields of interest: Arts; Education; Animal welfare; Crime/violence prevention, child abuse.
Type of support: Capital campaigns; Building/renovation; Endowments.
Limitations: Giving primarily in areas of company operations in CA, ID, IA, IL, IN, KY, MN, MT, ND, NE, NY, NV, OR, PA, SC, SD, WA, WI, and WY. No grants to individuals.
Application information: Application form not required.
  Initial approach: Letter of inquiry to nearest company newspaper
  Copies of proposal: 5
  Deadline(s): None
  Final notification: Within 4 months
Officers and Directors:* Mary Junck,* Pres.; Carl Schmidt,* Secy.-Treas.; Greg Schermer; Greg Veon.
Number of staff: 1 part-time support.
EIN: 426057173

3307
Madelyn M. Levitt Foundation ✧
(formerly Madelyn L. Glazer Foundation)
6200 Aurora Ave., Ste. 310W
Urbandale, IA 50322-2838

Established in 1957 in Iowa.
Donor: Madelyn M. Levitt.
Foundation type: Independent foundation.

Financial data (yr. ended 12/31/05): Assets, $13,712,450 (M); gifts received, $468,132; expenditures, $714,770; qualifying distributions, $706,450; giving activities include $706,450 for 14 grants (high: $472,000; low: $500).
Purpose and activities: Giving primarily for the arts, education, and federated giving programs.
Fields of interest: Arts; Higher education; Higher education, university; Boys & girls clubs; Foundations (community); Federated giving programs; Jewish agencies & temples.
Limitations: Applications not accepted. Giving primarily in Des Moines, IA. No grants to individuals.
Application information: Contributes only to pre-selected organizations.
Officers: Madelyn M. Levitt, Pres. and Treas.; Jeffrey W. Glazer, V.P.; Richard S. Levitt, Secy.
EIN: 426052426

3308
Mansfield Charitable Foundation ✧
(formerly Wesley & Irene Mansfield Charitable Foundation)
823 13th St.
P.O. Box 283
Belle Plaine, IA 52208 (319) 444-3285
Contact: Larry Schlue, Tr.

Established in 1984 in IA.
Foundation type: Independent foundation.
Financial data (yr. ended 7/31/05): Assets, $14,622,054 (M); expenditures, $734,922; qualifying distributions, $634,611; giving activities include $614,611 for 18 grants (high: $112,261; low: $2,500).
Purpose and activities: Giving primarily for community development, including an historical society; funding also for higher education.
Fields of interest: Historic preservation/historical societies; Higher education; Community development; Foundations (private grantmaking); Government/public administration.
Type of support: General/operating support; Building/renovation; Scholarship funds.
Limitations: Giving primarily in IA; some funding also in NE. No grants to individuals.
Application information: Application form not required.
  Copies of proposal: 1
  Deadline(s): June 1
Trustees: M.D. Dreibelbis; Jeanne Mansfield; Larry Schlue.
EIN: 421226535

3309
Maytag Corporation Foundation
P.O. Box 39
403 W. 4th St. N.
Newton, IA 50208-0039 (641) 787-8357
Contact: Michele Walstrom, V.P.
FAX: (641) 787-8170; *Additional tel.:* (641) 787-6357; *URL:* http://www.maytag.com/mths/our_company/social_commitment.jsp

Incorporated in 1952 in IA.
Donor: Maytag Corp.
Foundation type: Company-sponsored foundation.
Financial data (yr. ended 12/31/05): Assets, $5,451,149 (M); expenditures, $1,601,337; qualifying distributions, $1,569,945; giving activities include $1,426,795 for 105 grants (high:

$240,657; low: $350), and $143,150 for employee matching gifts.

Purpose and activities: The foundation supports organizations involved with arts and culture, education, employment, human services, and community development.

Fields of interest: Visual arts; Performing arts; Arts; Education, early childhood education; Higher education; Business school/education; Engineering school/education; Education; Employment, training; Employment; Children, services; Family services; Human services; Economic development; Community development; Federated giving programs.

Type of support: General/operating support; Continuing support; Annual campaigns; Capital campaigns; Building/renovation; Seed money; Scholarship funds; Employee matching gifts; Employee-related scholarships; In-kind gifts; Matching/challenge support.

Limitations: Applications not accepted. Giving limited to areas of company operations, with emphasis on Searcy, AR, Herrin, IL, Amana and Newton, IA, North Canton, OH, Williston, SC, Cleveland and Jackson, TN, and El Paso, TX. No support for health agencies, churches, or fraternal organizations. No grants to individuals (except for employee-related scholarships), or for benefit dinners, complimentary advertising, or sponsorships, conferences, seminars, endowments, religious causes, or international relations; no loans.

Publications: Corporate giving report.

Application information:
 Board meeting date(s): Jan., July, and Nov.
Officers and Trustees:* Ralph F. Hake, Pres.; Michele Walstrom, V.P.; Patricia J. Martin,* Secy.; Gregory P. Irwin; Mark Krivorvchka; Karen Lynn; Michael A. Reusswig.
Number of staff: 1 full-time professional; 1 full-time support.
EIN: 426055722
Selected grants: The following grants were reported in 2004.
$226,717 to National Merit Scholarship Corporation, Evanston, IL.
$100,000 to Partners in Economic Progress, Des Moines, IA. For capital campaign.
$100,000 to Science Center of Iowa, Des Moines, IA.
$60,000 to Jasper Community Foundation, Jasper, TX. For Re-New Newton.
$50,000 to Friends of the Library of Barnwell County, Barnwell, SC.
$50,000 to Ohio Foundation of Independent Colleges, Columbus, OH. For annual support.
$50,000 to YMCA, Canton Area - North Canton Center Branch, North Canton, OH.
$35,000 to Des Moines Metro Opera, Indianola, IA.
$35,000 to Iowa Association of Business and Industry Foundation, Des Moines, IA. For Excellence in Teaching Institute and Leadership Institute for Administrators.
$30,000 to Hospice of Jasper County, Newton, IA. For hospice addition.

3310
The F. Maytag Family Foundation ✧
(formerly The Fred Maytag Family Foundation)
P.O. Box 366
Newton, IA 50208 (641) 792-1133
Contact: Ellen Bergeron, Secy.

Application address: c/o Maytag Dairy Farms, Inc., 2282 E. 8th St. N., Newton, IA 50208

Trust established in 1945 in IA.
Donors: Fred Maytag II†; and members of the Maytag family.
Foundation type: Independent foundation.
Financial data (yr. ended 12/31/05): Assets, $64,237,398 (M); expenditures, $4,837,107; qualifying distributions, $4,663,416; giving activities include $4,592,899 for 90 grants (high: $2,500,000; low: $175; average: $5,000–$50,000).
Purpose and activities: Giving for higher and other education, arts and culture, public affairs, social services, health, including cancer research, and aid for the handicapped.
Fields of interest: Arts; Higher education; Education; Environment, natural resources; Health care; Health organizations, association; Cancer; Cancer research; Human services; Community development; Science, research; Public affairs; Disabilities, people with.
Type of support: General/operating support; Continuing support; Annual campaigns; Capital campaigns; Building/renovation; Equipment; Land acquisition; Endowments; Emergency funds; Program development; Conferences/seminars; Professorships; Publication; Seed money; Curriculum development; Fellowships; Internship funds; Scholarship funds; Research; Technical assistance; Matching/challenge support.
Limitations: Giving primarily in Des Moines and Newton, IA. No grants to individuals, or for emergency funds, deficit financing, scholarships, fellowships, demonstration projects, or conferences; no loans.
Publications: Application guidelines.
Application information: Application form not required.
 Initial approach: Application
 Copies of proposal: 3
 Deadline(s): None
Officer: Ellen Bergeron, Secy.
Trustees: Frederick L. Maytag III; Kenneth P. Maytag; William C. Weinsheimer.
Number of staff: 2 full-time support.
EIN: 421444870
Selected grants: The following grants were reported in 2003.
$1,000,000 to Save-the-Redwoods League, San Francisco, CA. Toward land acquisitions.
$500,000 to Science Center of Iowa, Des Moines, IA. Toward capital improvements.
$100,000 to Iowa College Foundation, Des Moines, IA. Toward general operating support.
$75,000 to Nature Conservancy, Des Moines, IA. Toward land acquisitions.
$55,600 to Berea College, Berea, KY. Toward general operating support.
$50,000 to American Red Cross, National Headquarters, DC. Toward general support.
$50,000 to Friends of CRAFT (Center for Research into Anthropological Foundations of Technology), Bloomington, IN. Toward construction debt.
$50,000 to Iowa Barn Foundation, Nevada, IA. Toward restoration grants.
$50,000 to Property and Environment Research Center, Bozeman, MT. Toward general operating support.
$50,000 to Trust for Public Land, San Francisco, CA. Toward general operating support for Arizona Office.

3311
McCarthy Bush Foundation ✧ ☆
5401 Victoria Ave.
Davenport, IA 52807

Established in 1989 in IA.
Donors: McCarthy Bush Corp.; John L. Bush; McCarthy Improvement Co.; Linwood Mining & Minerals Corp.
Foundation type: Company-sponsored foundation.
Financial data (yr. ended 12/31/05): Assets, $23,030 (M); gifts received, $436,026; expenditures, $414,147; qualifying distributions, $395,771; giving activities include $395,771 for grants.
Purpose and activities: The foundation supports organizations involved with arts and culture, education, health, human services, and children and youth services.
Fields of interest: Arts; Higher education; Education; Health organizations, association; Human services; Children/youth, services; Federated giving programs.
Limitations: Applications not accepted. Giving primarily in Davenport, IA. No grants to individuals.
Application information: Contributes only to pre-selected organizations.
Officer: Patricia M. Bush, Pres.
Directors: John L. Bush; Lawrence P. Bush; Barbara J. Johnson; Mary Walsh.
EIN: 421322400
Selected grants: The following grants were reported in 2005.
$100,330 to Saint Ambrose University, Davenport, IA.
$30,000 to Figge Art Museum, Davenport, IA.
$14,138 to YMCA.
$10,250 to Clarke College, Dubuque, IA.
$5,000 to Palmer College of Chiropractic, Davenport, IA.
$4,925 to Handicapped Development Center, Davenport, IA.
$2,950 to Iowa Scholarship Fund, Iowa City, IA.
$2,000 to University of Iowa Foundation, Iowa City, IA.
$1,450 to Marquette Academy, Davenport, IA.
$1,304 to Variety Club.

3312
A. Y. McDonald Manufacturing Company Charitable Foundation ✧ ☆
c/o A.J. Wilherding
P.O. Box 508
Dubuque, IA 52004-0508 (563) 583-7311

Established in 1967 in IA.
Donor: A.Y. McDonald Industries, Inc.
Foundation type: Company-sponsored foundation.
Financial data (yr. ended 12/31/05): Assets, $2,851,419 (M); gifts received, $350,000; expenditures, $407,742; qualifying distributions, $406,980; giving activities include $406,980 for grants.
Purpose and activities: The foundation supports organizations involved with education, medical research, human services, children and youth services, and community development.
Fields of interest: Higher education; Education; Health care; Medical research; Youth development, business; Human services; Children/youth, services; Community development; Federated giving programs.

Limitations: Applications not accepted. Giving primarily in eastern IA, with emphasis on Dubuque. No grants to individuals.

Application information: Contributes only to pre-selected organizations.

Officers: R.D. McDonald, Pres.; W.A. Knapp, V.P.; J.M. McDonald III, V.P.; L.J. Sherman, V.P.; M.B. McDonald, Secy.

EIN: 426119514

Selected grants: The following grants were reported in 2004.

$31,832 to United Way Services, Dubuque, IA.

$25,000 to Clarke College, Dubuque, IA.

$25,000 to University of Dubuque, Dubuque, IA.

$10,000 to Loras College, Dubuque, IA.

$6,860 to Dubuque Symphony Orchestra, Dubuque, IA.

$5,500 to Girl Scouts of the U.S.A., Little Cloud Council, Dubuque, IA.

$5,000 to Hillcrest Family Services, Dubuque, IA.

$4,425 to Junior Achievement.

$4,000 to River Valley Initiative Foundation, Dubuque, IA.

$3,850 to Boy Scouts of America.

3313
R. J. McElroy Trust ✧
425 Cedar St., Ste. 312
Waterloo, IA 50701 (319) 287-9102
Contact: Linda L. Klinger, Exec. Dir.
FAX: (319) 287-9105;
E-mail: klinger@mcelroytrust.org; Additional E-mail: office@mcelroytrust.org; URL: http://www.mcelroytrust.org

Established in 1965 in IA; private foundation status attained in 1984.

Donor: R.J. McElroy†.

Foundation type: Independent foundation.

Financial data (yr. ended 12/31/05): Assets, $47,523,941 (M); expenditures, $2,835,367; qualifying distributions, $2,643,757; giving activities include $2,350,803 for 104 grants (high: $400,000; low: $300), and $87,000 for 35 grants to individuals (high: $10,000; low: $500).

Purpose and activities: Primary emphasis on education, especially scholarship and loan programs; public secondary education, particularly for the disadvantaged; early childhood and elementary education and programs for minorities; and youth, including internships. Giving also for the arts, recreation, and the environment; some support through matching funds and fellowships for graduate study.

Fields of interest: Visual arts; Performing arts; Arts; Education, early childhood education; Child development, education; Elementary school/education; Secondary school/education; Higher education; Education; Environment; Recreation; Youth development, services; Human services; Children/youth, services; Child development, services; Leadership development; Minorities; Economically disadvantaged.

Type of support: General/operating support; Capital campaigns; Building/renovation; Equipment; Emergency funds; Program development; Professorships; Seed money; Fellowships; Internship funds; Scholarship funds; Research; Matching/challenge support.

Limitations: Giving primarily in 19 counties in northeast IA (Allamakee, Benton, Black Hawk, Bremer, Buchanan, Butler, Chickasaw, Clayton, Delaware, Dubuque, Fayette, Floyd, Franklin,

Grundy, Howard, Hardin, Tama, Winneshiek, and rural Linn). No support for religious organizations. No grants to individuals (except for fellowship program).

Publications: Application guidelines; Grants list; Informational brochure; Informational brochure (including application guidelines); Program policy statement; Program policy statement (including application guidelines).

Application information: Application guidelines and form available on foundation Web site.

Initial approach: Letter or telephone

Copies of proposal: 1

Deadline(s): Mar. 1, June 1, Sept. 1, and Dec. 1

Board meeting date(s): Monthly

Final notification: May 1, Aug. 1, Nov. 1, and Feb. 1

Officers and Trustees:* Ross D. Christensen,* Chair.; Linda L. Klinger, Exec. Dir.; Raleigh D. Buckmaster; James B. Waterbury; Rick Young.

Number of staff: 1 full-time professional; 1 full-time support.

EIN: 426173496

3314
Meredith Corporation Foundation ✧
1716 Locust St.
Des Moines, IA 50309-3023
Contact: Cheri Cipperley

Established around 1994 in IA.

Donor: Meredith Corp.

Foundation type: Company-sponsored foundation.

Financial data (yr. ended 6/30/05): Assets, $13,162,745 (M); gifts received, $3,153,130; expenditures, $2,034,855; qualifying distributions, $2,032,539; giving activities include $2,032,332 for 768 grants (high: $578,712; low: $25).

Purpose and activities: The foundation supports organizations involved with arts and culture, education, and human services.

Fields of interest: Arts; Journalism school/education; Education; Human services; Federated giving programs.

Type of support: General/operating support; Program development; Employee volunteer services; Employee matching gifts.

Limitations: Giving primarily in the metropolitan Des Moines, IA, area. No grants to individuals, or for fundraising events or sports or health-related programs.

Application information: Application form not required.

Initial approach: Proposal

Deadline(s): Jan. 15 through Mar. 15 and July 15 through Sept. 15

Board meeting date(s): Apr. and Oct.

Officers and Directors:* Mell Meredith Frazier,* Chair.; William T. Kerr,* Pres.; Stephen Lacy,* V.P.; Arthur J. Slusark, Secy.; Sandra Cooney, Treas.; Suku V. Radia; John S. Zieser.

EIN: 421426258

Selected grants: The following grants were reported in 2003.

$116,670 to Des Moines Art Center, Des Moines, IA.

$115,000 to United Way of Central Iowa, Des Moines, IA.

$107,850 to Drake University, Des Moines, IA.

$103,785 to Public Library of Des Moines, Des Moines, IA.

$85,750 to Greater Des Moines Community Foundation, Des Moines, IA.

$50,000 to Rebuilding Together, DC.

$40,675 to Des Moines Symphony, Des Moines, IA.

$37,880 to American Red Cross, Des Moines, IA.

$24,070 to Science Center of Iowa, Des Moines, IA.

$21,475 to Civic Center of Greater Des Moines, Des Moines, IA.

3315
Edwin T. Meredith Foundation
1716 Locust St.
Des Moines, IA 50309-3023
Contact: Cheri Cipperley

Incorporated in 1946 in IA.

Donor: Meredith Publishing Co.

Foundation type: Independent foundation.

Financial data (yr. ended 12/31/05): Assets, $20,321,088 (M); expenditures, $826,263; qualifying distributions, $716,090; giving activities include $716,090 for 29 grants (high: $125,000; low: $500).

Purpose and activities: Grants largely for youth agencies, higher education, cultural programs, and a historic preservation area; some support for hospitals and health agencies, as well as for conservation.

Fields of interest: Arts; Higher education; Environment, natural resources; Health care; Children/youth, services.

Type of support: Annual campaigns; Capital campaigns; Building/renovation; Endowments.

Limitations: Applications not accepted. Giving primarily in IA. No grants to individuals.

Application information: Contributes only to pre-selected organizations.

Board meeting date(s): June

Officers: Katherine C. Meredith, Pres.; D. Mell Frazier, V.P.; E.T. Meredith IV, V.P.; John Zieser, Secy.; Marilyn J. Dillivan, Treas.

EIN: 426059818

Selected grants: The following grants were reported in 2003.

$415,000 to Science Center of Iowa, Des Moines, IA.

$100,000 to Drake University, Des Moines, IA.

$100,000 to Public Library of Des Moines, Des Moines, IA.

$50,000 to Boys and Girls Club of Des Moines, Des Moines, IA.

$47,500 to Nature Conservancy of Wyoming, Lander, WY.

$35,000 to Greater Des Moines Community Foundation, Des Moines, IA.

$30,000 to Iowa Natural Heritage Foundation, Des Moines, IA.

$30,000 to YMCA of Sheridan County, Sheridan, WY.

$15,000 to Saint Ambrose Cathedral, Des Moines, IA.

$12,500 to American Red Cross, Des Moines, IA.

3316
Mid-America Foundation ✧
4700 Westown Pkwy., Ste. 303
West Des Moines, IA 50266

Established in 1966.

Donor: Marvin A. Pomerantz.

Foundation type: Independent foundation.

Financial data (yr. ended 12/31/05): Assets, $401,086 (M); gifts received, $747,106;

expenditures, $626,164; qualifying distributions, $625,044; giving activities include $625,044 for 80 grants (high: $150,000; low: $25).

Purpose and activities: Giving primarily for education, health and human services, and to Jewish agencies and temples.

Fields of interest: Arts; Education; Health organizations, association; Medical research, institute; Human services; Federated giving programs; Jewish federated giving programs; Jewish agencies & temples.

Limitations: Applications not accepted. Giving primarily in IA. No grants to individuals; no loans.

Application information: Contributes only to pre-selected organizations.

Trustees: Steve Zumbach-Belin Lamson; Joseph E. Pierce; Marvin A. Pomerantz.

EIN: 426101963

3317

Mid-Iowa Health Foundation ✧

550 39th St., Ste. 305

Des Moines, IA 50312-3529 (515) 277-6411

Contact: Denise Swartz, Prog. Off.; Kathryn Bradley, Pres. and Exec. Dir.

E-mail: kbradley@midiowahealth.org; Additional E-mail: dswartz@midiowahealth.org; URL: http://www.midiowahealth.org

Established in 1983 in IA; converted from Northwest Community Hospital.

Foundation type: Independent foundation.

Financial data (yr. ended 12/31/05): Assets, $15,549,485 (M); expenditures, $947,370; qualifying distributions, $895,313; giving activities include $691,410 for 35 grants (high: $55,000; low: $1,270).

Purpose and activities: The foundation will be a catalyst for and sustainer of preventive health services for vulnerable populations in Des Moines, IA, and the surrounding communities.

Fields of interest: Medical care, community health systems; Health care, clinics/centers; Health care.

Type of support: General/operating support; Program development; Technical assistance.

Limitations: Giving limited to Polk, Warren, and Dallas counties, IA. No support for scientific or medical research, health camps, or religious organizations. No grants to individuals, or for research, fundraisers, conferences, endowments, debt reduction, capital campaigns, film, or for computer equipment.

Publications: Application guidelines; Annual report; Grants list; Informational brochure (including application guidelines).

Application information: Applications only accepted for Community Response Program. Application form available on foundation Web site. Application form required.

Initial approach: Letter, e-mail or telephone

Copies of proposal: 11

Deadline(s): Apr. 1 and Oct. 1

Board meeting date(s): Mar., June, Sept., and Dec.

Final notification: 6 to 8 weeks

Officers and Directors: * Ivan Johnson,* Chair.; Don C. Green,* Vice-Chair.; Kathryn Bradley,* Pres. and Exec. Dir.; T. Ward Phillips, Secy.-Treas.; Teree Caldwell-Johnson; Simon Casady; Nolden Gentry; Rob Hayes; Thomas Jeschke; Judith Vogel.

Number of staff: 2 full-time professional.

EIN: 421235348

3318

Muscatine Foods Corporation Charitable Foundation ✧

(formerly Kent-Stein Foundation)

c/o Grain Processing Corp.

1600 Oregon St.

Muscatine, IA 52761

Established in 1945 in IA.

Donor: Grain Processing Corp.

Foundation type: Independent foundation.

Financial data (yr. ended 12/31/05): Assets, $1,303,644 (M); expenditures, $497,608; qualifying distributions, $493,981; giving activities include $493,981 for 22 grants (high: $125,000; low: $1,000).

Fields of interest: Higher education; Human services; Community development; Federated giving programs.

Limitations: Applications not accepted. Giving primarily in IA, with some emphasis on Muscatine. No grants to individuals.

Application information: Contributes only to pre-selected college funds.

Trustees: John T. Kautz; J.H. Kent; Marion Kay Van Acker.

EIN: 426058939

Selected grants: The following grants were reported in 2003.

$133,333 to Muscatine, City of, Muscatine, IA. For operating support.

$94,500 to United Way of Muscatine, Muscatine, IA. For operating support.

$25,000 to Iowa College Foundation, Des Moines, IA. For operating support.

$10,000 to YM-YWCA of Muscatine, Muscatine, IA. For operating support.

$4,500 to Iowa Scholarship Fund, Iowa City, IA. For operating support.

$2,400 to United Way of Daviess County, Washington, IN. For operating support.

$2,000 to Muscatine Community College, Muscatine, IA. For operating support.

$1,300 to William Woods University, Fulton, MO. For operating support.

$1,300 to YMCA of Muscatine, Muscatine, IA. For operating support.

$1,000 to Muscatine Charities, Muscatine, IA. For operating support.

3319

New Hope Foundation ✧

2610 Park Ave.

Muscatine, IA 52761-5639

Established in 1992 in IA.

Donors: David M. Stanley; Jean Leu Stanley; E & M Charities.

Foundation type: Independent foundation.

Financial data (yr. ended 12/31/04): Assets, $22,561,125 (M); gifts received, $33,173; expenditures, $1,242,836; qualifying distributions, $1,227,865; giving activities include $781,000 for 116 grants (high: $77,000; low: $300), and $175,417 for 1 foundation-administered program.

Purpose and activities: Giving primarily to United Methodist organizations. Some support for other Protestant organizations and for education.

Fields of interest: Education; Health organizations, association; Human services; Federated giving programs; Christian agencies & churches; Protestant agencies & churches.

Limitations: Applications not accepted. Giving on a national basis, with some emphasis on IA, particularly Muscatine. No grants to individuals.

Application information: Contributes only to pre-selected organizations.

Officers and Directors: * David M. Stanley,* Pres. and Treas.; Jean Leu Stanley,* V.P. and Secy.; Robert H. Solt,* V.P. and Treas.; Kevin J. Burns,* V.P., Invest. Mgmt.; Jeffrey R. Boeyink,* V.P.; Andrea S. Failor, V.P.; Edward D. Failor, Sr.,* V.P.; I. Maurene Failor, V.P.; Christopher A. Hoffman, V.P.; Dana D. Solt, V.P.; Richard G. Andersen; Edward D. Failor, Jr.; Harry L. Knutsen.

EIN: 421395902

3320

Northeast Iowa Charitable Foundation ✧

14 E. Charles St.

Oelwein, IA 50662

Contact: Char DeHaven, Dir.

Established in 1989 in IA.

Donor: Churchill Williams.

Foundation type: Independent foundation.

Financial data (yr. ended 12/31/05): Assets, $7,229,454 (M); expenditures, $414,108; qualifying distributions, $376,830; giving activities include $324,330 for 16 grants (high: $100,000; low: $500), and $52,500 for grants to individuals.

Fields of interest: Education; Hospitals (general).

Type of support: Equipment; Scholarship funds; Scholarships—to individuals.

Limitations: Giving primarily in northeastern IA.

Application information:

Initial approach: Letter

Deadline(s): None

Directors: Andrew Cubit; Marilyn Dahl; Char DeHaven; Alan Jamison; Maureen Nolan; James R. Ridihalgh; Churchill Williams; Marval Williams.

EIN: 421341188

Selected grants: The following grants were reported in 2004.

$180,000 to Greater Oelwein Area Charitable Foundation, Oelwein, IA. 2 grants: $150,000, $30,000

$32,000 to UNI Foundation, Cedar Falls, IA.

$32,000 to Upper Iowa University, Fayette, IA.

$12,955 to Oelwein Community Schools, Oelwein, IA. 2 grants: $10,000, $2,955

$12,000 to Oelwein Area Historical Society, Oelwein, IA.

$8,000 to American Legion of Iowa, Des Moines, IA.

$8,000 to Herbert Hoover Presidential Library Association, West Branch, IA.

$2,250 to Sacred Heart School, Oelwein, IA.

3321

Ochylski Family Foundation ✧

300 Walnut St., Ste. 295A

Des Moines, IA 50309 (515) 244-6040

Contact: Kathy Hovey

Established in 1996 in IL.

Donors: Edward Ochylski; Mrs. Edward Ochylski.

Foundation type: Independent foundation.

Financial data (yr. ended 12/31/05): Assets, $11,521,957 (M); gifts received, $1,000,000; expenditures, $3,289,775; qualifying distributions, $3,252,500; giving activities include $3,252,500 for 15 grants (high: $1,000,000; low: $10,000).

Purpose and activities: Giving primarily for The Holy See, Vatican City.
Fields of interest: Education; Children/youth, services; Roman Catholic agencies & churches.
International interests: Vatican City.
Limitations: Giving on a national basis; funding also in Vatican City.
Application information: Application form not required.
  Initial approach: Letter
  Deadline(s): Oct. 1
Officers and Directors:* Edward Ochylski,* Pres.; Kelly Ochylski Butler, V.P.; Gabrielle Klein, V.P.; Daniel Ochylski, V.P.; Edward Ochylski III, V.P.; Juliana Ochylski, V.P.; Mary C. Ochylski-Wertsch, V.P.; Jessica Stark, V.P.; Eleanor Ochylski,* Secy.-Treas.; Victor Bezman.
EIN: 364110483
Selected grants: The following grants were reported in 2003.
$420,000 to Pontifical Council for Justice and Peace, Vatican City. .
$250,000 to San Miguel School, Chicago, IL.
$100,000 to Des Moines Symphony Association, Des Moines, IA.

3322
John & Mary Pappajohn Scholarship Foundation ◇
2116 Financial Ctr.
Des Moines, IA 50309

Established in 1996 in IA.
Foundation type: Independent foundation.
Financial data (yr. ended 9/30/04): Assets, $430,479 (M); expenditures, $352,822; qualifying distributions, $350,504; giving activities include $350,000 for 19 grants (high: $161,500; low: $250).
Purpose and activities: Giving primarily for higher education.
Fields of interest: Higher education; Scholarships/ financial aid; Religion.
Limitations: Applications not accepted. Giving primarily in IA. No grants to individuals.
Application information: Contributes only to pre-selected organizations.
Directors: John Pappajohn; Mary Pappajohn; Ann Vassiliou.
EIN: 421645551
Selected grants: The following grants were reported in 2005.
$20,000 to Hellenic Times Scholarship Fund, New York, NY.
$20,000 to University of Iowa Foundation, Iowa City, IA.
$10,000 to Anatolia College, Boston, MA.
$10,000 to Des Moines Art Center, Des Moines, IA.
$10,000 to Iowa State University, Ames, IA.
$10,000 to Pine Manor College, Chestnut Hill, MA.
$10,000 to University of Minnesota Foundation, Minneapolis, MN.
$5,000 to Phi Gamma Delta Educational Foundation, Lexington, KY.
$250 to Piney Woods School, Piney Woods, MS.

3323
Pella Rolscreen Foundation
102 Main St.
Pella, IA 50219
Contact: Mary A. Van Zante, Dir.

FAX: (641) 621-6950; *E-mail:* mavzante@pella.com;
URL: http://www.pellarolscreen.org

Trust established in 1952 in IA.
Donor: Pella Corp.
Foundation type: Company-sponsored foundation.
Financial data (yr. ended 12/31/04): Assets, $16,419,636 (M); gifts received, $2,054,668; expenditures, $1,997,364; qualifying distributions, $1,830,448; giving activities include $947,614 for 280 grants (high: $181,800; low: $100), $183,000 for 97 grants to individuals (high: $6,000; low: $1,500), and $699,834 for 471 employee matching gifts.
Purpose and activities: The foundation supports organizations involved with arts and culture, higher education, and human services.
Fields of interest: Arts; Higher education; Human services.
Type of support: Employee volunteer services; Capital campaigns; Building/renovation; Endowments; Program development; Scholarship funds; Employee matching gifts; Employee-related scholarships.
Limitations: Giving primarily in areas of company manufacturing operations. No support for religious or political organizations or organizations with a narrow scope. No grants to individuals (except for employee-related scholarships); no loans.
Publications: Application guidelines; Annual report.
Application information: Application form required.
  Initial approach: Download application form and mail to foundation
  Copies of proposal: 1
  Deadline(s): None
  Board meeting date(s): Quarterly
  Final notification: 1 to 3 months
Officers and Directors:* Melvin Haught,* Chair. and Pres.; Charles Farver,* Treas.; Joan Farver; Mary A. Van Zante.
Number of staff: 2 part-time support.
EIN: 237043881

3324
Pioneer Hi-Bred International, Inc. Foundation ☆
c/o Pioneer Hi-Bred International, Inc.
P.O. Box 1014
Johnston, IA 50131-1014
Contact: Steve Schaaf, V.P.
Additional address: c/o Community Investment, 9550 White Oak Ln., Ste. 100, P.O. Box 1014, Johnston, IA 50131-1014; *URL:* http:// www.pioneer.com/pioneer_info/corporate/ci.htm

Established in 1992.
Donor: Pioneer Hi-Bred International, Inc.
Foundation type: Company-sponsored foundation.
Financial data (yr. ended 12/31/04): Assets, $23,250 (M); gifts received, $706,852; expenditures, $683,602; qualifying distributions, $683,602; giving activities include $683,568 for 33 grants (high: $250,000; low: $750).
Purpose and activities: The foundation supports organizations involved with education, agriculture, food, nutrition, farm safety, and science and technology.
Fields of interest: Education; Agriculture; Food services; Nutrition; Safety, education; Science.
International interests: Africa; Europe; Mexico; South America.

Type of support: Research; Program development; Matching/challenge support; Employee matching gifts.
Limitations: Giving on a national and international basis, including in Africa, Europe, Mexico, and South America. No support for religious or political organizations. No grants to individuals, or for marketing or advertising.
Application information: Application form required.
  Initial approach: Download application form and mail to nearest company facility
  Copies of proposal: 1
  Deadline(s): None
Officers and Directors:* Dean C. Oestreich,* V.P.; Thomas Phillips,* V.P.; Steve Schaaf,* V.P.; Tom West, V.P.; Dean C. Mohr, Secy.; Daniel E. Jacobi.
EIN: 421388269

3325
Greater Poweshiek Community Foundation ☆
1510 Penrose St.
P.O. Box 344
Grinnell, IA 50112 (641) 236-5518
Contact: Todd Nelson, Pres.
FAX: (641) 236-5590;
E-mail: greaterpoweshiek@yahoo.com; *URL:* http:// www.greaterpcf.org

Established in 1989 in IA.
Foundation type: Community foundation.
Financial data (yr. ended 12/31/05): Assets, $942,731 (M); gifts received, $1,388,747; expenditures, $2,096,418; giving activities include $2,060,402 for 6 grants (high: $2,000,000; low: $250), and $26,050 for 72 grants to individuals (high: $4,000; low: $200).
Purpose and activities: The foundation seeks to strengthen the community by building charitable endowments, assisting donors, making effective grants and providing for county needs. The foundation primarily provides support for education, the environment, health care, human services, and community and economic development.
Fields of interest: Education; Environment; Health care; Human services; Community development, neighborhood development; Economic development.
Type of support: Endowments; Program development; Seed money; Scholarship funds; Scholarships—to individuals.
Limitations: Giving primarily in Poweshiek County, IA. No grants for debt reduction, conferences, or annual meetings; no loans.
Application information: Application form required.
  Initial approach: Contact foundation
  Board meeting date(s): Quarterly
Officers and Directors:* Todd Nelson,* Pres.; Dion Schrack,* V.P.; Clem Bodensteiner,* Secy.; Hutch Kracht,* Treas.; John F. "Rick" Bierman; George Drake; Jenny Erickson; Jeffery Garland; Rich Gogg; Neill Goltz; F. Austin Jones; Gerald LaLonde; Tim Marsho; Orlan Mitchell; Martha Pinder; Laura Van Cleve.
EIN: 421298055

3326
Principal Financial Group Foundation, Inc. ▼ ✧

711 High St.
Des Moines, IA 50392-0150 (515) 247-7227
Contact: Laura Sauser
FAX: (515) 246-5475;
E-mail: murphy.jodi@principal.com; URL: http://www.principal.com/about/giving

Established in 1987 in IA.
Donor: Principal Life Insurance Co.
Foundation type: Company-sponsored foundation.
Financial data (yr. ended 12/31/05): Assets, $56,093,108 (M); expenditures, $10,489,576; qualifying distributions, $10,350,576; giving activities include $10,350,576 for 903 grants (high: $1,000,000).
Purpose and activities: The foundation supports organizations involved with arts and culture, education, health, substance abuse, disease, employment training, nutrition, housing, recreation and tourism, youth development, human services, community development, babies, and senior citizens.
Fields of interest: Arts, equal rights; Arts, cultural/ethnic awareness; Arts; Education, equal rights; Child development, education; Higher education; Business school/education; Education; Health care, equal rights; Public health; Health care; Substance abuse, services; Health organizations, public education; Geriatrics; Employment, training; Nutrition; Housing/shelter; Recreation; Youth development, adult & child programs; Youth development; Family services; Human services, financial counseling; Human services; Community development; Computer science; Infants/toddlers; Aging.
Type of support: General/operating support; Continuing support; Annual campaigns; Capital campaigns; Building/renovation; Program development; Professorships; Seed money; Curriculum development; Scholarship funds; Program evaluation; Employee matching gifts.
Limitations: Giving limited to Des Moines, IA, and areas of company operations in Phoenix, AZ, Middletown, CT, Wilmington, DE, Cedar Falls, Mason City, Ottumwa, and Pella, IA, Indianapolis, IN, Grand Island, NE, Spokane, WA, and Appleton, WI. No support for athletic organizations, fraternal organizations, individual K-12 schools, libraries, pass-through organizations, partisan political organizations, private foundations, sectarian, religious, or denominational organizations, social organizations, tax-supported city, county, or state organizations, trade, industry, or professional associations, or veterans' organizations. No grants to individuals, or for conference or seminar attendance, courtesy or goodwill advertising in benefit publications, endowments or memorials, fellowships, festival participation, hospital or health care facility capital campaigns, or United Way-funded programs.
Publications: Application guidelines; Biennial report; Corporate giving report; Grants list; Program policy statement.
Application information: Video submissions are not encouraged. Multi-year funding is not automatic. Application form required.
Initial approach: Download application form and mail proposal and application form to foundation
Copies of proposal: 11

Deadline(s): Mar. 1 for Health and Human Services; June 1 for Education; Sept. 1 for Arts and Culture; and Dec. 1 for Recreation and Tourism
Board meeting date(s): Quarterly
Final notification: 6 weeks
Officers and Directors:* J. Barry Griswell,* Chair. and C.E.O.; Mary O'Keefe,* Sr. V.P.; Libby Jacobs,* Secy.; Jed Fisk,* Treas.; John Aichenbrenner; Mike Gersie; Joyce Hoffman; Mark Movic.
EIN: 421312301
Selected grants: The following grants were reported in 2004.
$555,915 to Greater Des Moines Community Foundation, Des Moines, IA. 2 grants: $55,915, $500,000
$361,773 to United Way of Central Iowa, Des Moines, IA.
$300,000 to Des Moines Public Library Foundation, Des Moines, IA.
$300,000 to Science Center of Iowa, Des Moines, IA.
$135,000 to Drake University, Des Moines, IA.
$50,000 to Hope Ministries, Des Moines, IA.
$21,055 to University of Iowa Foundation, Iowa City, IA.
$20,000 to Des Moines Playhouse, Des Moines, IA.
$10,000 to Young Womens Resource Center, Des Moines, IA.

3327
R & R Realty Group Foundation ✧ ☆

1225 Jordan Creek Pkwy., Ste. 200
West Des Moines, IA 50266

Established in 1999 in IA.
Donors: R&R Investors Inc.; Daniel P. Rupprecht.
Foundation type: Company-sponsored foundation.
Financial data (yr. ended 6/30/06): Assets, $5,023 (M); gifts received, $497,185; expenditures, $491,868; qualifying distributions, $490,140; giving activities include $490,140 for grants.
Purpose and activities: The foundation supports Roman Catholic agencies and churches and organizations involved with arts and culture, education, health, youth development, and human services.
Fields of interest: Arts; Higher education; Education; Nursing home/convalescent facility; Health care; Diabetes; Youth development; Human services; Federated giving programs; Roman Catholic agencies & churches.
Type of support: General/operating support.
Limitations: Applications not accepted. Giving primarily in Des Moines and West Des Moines, IA. No grants to individuals.
Application information: Contributes only to pre-selected organizations.
Trustees: Daniel P. Rupprecht; Phyllis M. Rupprecht.
EIN: 421494641

3328
Rockwell Collins Charitable Corporation ✧

400 Collins Rd., N.E., M.S. 124-302
Cedar Rapids, IA 52498-0001
Contact: Cindy Dietz, Mgr., Community Rels.
FAX: (319) 295-9374;
E-mail: cmdietz@rockwellcollins.com; Additional E-mail: communityrelations@rockwellcollins.com; URL: http://www.rockwellcollins.com/about/

community/charitable_giving/charitable_corporation/index.html

Established in 2001 in IA.
Donor: Rockwell Collins, Inc.
Foundation type: Company-sponsored foundation.
Financial data (yr. ended 9/30/05): Assets, $5,326,041 (M); gifts received, $4,000,000; expenditures, $2,644,494; qualifying distributions, $2,619,852; giving activities include $2,222,800 for 115 grants (high: $285,000; low: $500), and $397,052 for employee matching gifts.
Purpose and activities: The foundation supports organizations involved with arts and culture, education, the environment, health, human services, and civic affairs. Special emphasis is directed toward programs designed to promote math, science, engineering, and technology education and arts and culture education for young people.
Fields of interest: Arts education; Arts; Engineering school/education; Education; Environment; Health care; Human services; Science, formal/general education; Mathematics; Public affairs; Youth.
Type of support: Continuing support; Capital campaigns; Program development; Scholarship funds; Employee matching gifts.
Limitations: Giving on a national and international basis in areas of company operations, with emphasis on Pomona, San Jose, and Tustin, CA, Melbourne, FL, IA, Portland, OR, and Richardson, TX. No support for private foundations, religious organizations not of direct benefit to the entire community, or fraternal or social organizations. No grants to individuals, or for endowments, debt reduction, or federated campaigns.
Publications: Application guidelines.
Application information: Organizations receiving Green Communities grants are asked to provide a final report. Application form required.
Initial approach: Telephone or E-mail foundation; download application form and mail to foundation for organizations located in IA; download application form and mail to nearest company facility for organizations located outside IA
Copies of proposal: 1
Deadline(s): Sept. 1; Jan. 2 to Mar. 3 for Green Communities Program
Board meeting date(s): Oct.
Final notification: 3 months; May 22 for Green Communities Program
Officers: Ronald W. Kirchenbauer, Pres.; Clayton Jones, V.P.; Gary R. Chadick, Secy.; Patrick E. Allen, Treas.
EIN: 421526774
Selected grants: The following grants were reported in 2005.
$397,052 to JK Group, Plainsboro, NJ.
$285,000 to United Way of East Central Iowa, Cedar Rapids, IA. For annual campaign.
$115,000 to Greater Cedar Rapids Community Foundation, Cedar Rapids, IA. For K-12 and REACT (Rockwell Educational Access to Computer Technology) programs.
$100,000 to Air Force Memorial Foundation, Arlington, VA. For capital campaign.
$100,000 to American Red Cross, National Headquarters, DC. For Tsunami Relief.
$100,000 to Iowa State University Foundation, Ames, IA. For Coover Hall and female/minority scholarships.
$50,000 to Four Oaks Foundation, Cedar Rapids, IA. For Changing Lives Together Campaign.

$20,000 to South Dakota School of Mines and Technology, Rapid City, SD. For antennas and applied electromagnetics.

$15,000 to African-American Heritage Foundation, Cedar Rapids, IA. For educational programming on ICN.

$15,000 to Purdue Foundation, West Lafayette, IN. For Armstrong Engineering Center.

3329
John Ruan Foundation Trust ◇
3200 Ruan Ctr.
666 Grand Ave.
Des Moines, IA 50309 (515) 245-2555
Contact: John Ruan, Tr.

Established in 1955 in IA.
Donors: RUAN Transport Management Systems; John Ruan.
Foundation type: Company-sponsored foundation.
Financial data (yr. ended 6/30/05): Assets, $13,248,862 (M); gifts received, $200,000; expenditures, $734,446; qualifying distributions, $725,802; giving activities include $725,420 for 59 grants (high: $107,500; low: $100).
Purpose and activities: The foundation supports organizations involved with arts and culture, education, health, youth development, human services, and Christianity.
Fields of interest: Historic preservation/historical societies; Arts; Education; Health care; Youth development; Children/youth, services; Human services; Christian agencies & churches.
Limitations: Applications not accepted. Giving primarily in Des Moines, IA. No grants to individuals.
Application information: Contributes only to pre-selected organizations.
Trustees: Elizabeth Ruan; John Ruan.
EIN: 426059463
Selected grants: The following grants were reported in 2005.
$107,500 to Culver Educational Foundation, Culver, IN.
$100,000 to Northwestern University, Evanston, IL.
$100,000 to Public Library of Des Moines, Des Moines, IA.
$100,000 to World Food Prize, Des Moines, IA.
$50,500 to Science Center of Iowa, Des Moines, IA.
$50,000 to Chinese Cultural Center of America, Ames, IA.
$25,000 to Hoyt Sherman Place Foundation, Des Moines, IA.
$17,000 to Salisbury House Foundation, Des Moines, IA.
$10,000 to University of Iowa Foundation, Iowa City, IA.
$5,000 to Des Moines Arts Festival, Des Moines, IA.

3330
Sehgal Family Foundation ◇
700 Walnut St., Ste. 1600
Des Moines, IA 50309-3899

Established in 1998 in IA.
Donors: Edda G. Sehgal; Surinder M. Sehgal.
Foundation type: Independent foundation.
Financial data (yr. ended 12/31/05): Assets, $54,246,572 (M); gifts received, $25,219; expenditures, $2,445,226; qualifying distributions, $2,737,571; giving activities include $1,052,533

for 24 grants (high: $500,000; low: $500), and $467,265 for foundation-administered programs.
Purpose and activities: Giving primarily for the environment and natural resource conservation. The foundation also works to address issues in India, such as gender inequality, low literacy, and awareness of reproductive health and family planning. Additionally, the foundation works to facilitate Gurgaon, India villagers in assessing their perceived, met, unmet, hidden health care, and other domestic needs, and it also works to ensure that safe drinking water is available throughout rural Gurgaon, and to promote water literacy. The foundation also works to create village level institutions in India which generate both employment and income, and assist in start up farm production activities.
Fields of interest: Environment, natural resources; Environment; International development; Foundations (community).
International interests: India.
Limitations: Applications not accepted. Giving in the U.S. and India. No grants to individuals.
Application information: Contributes only to pre-selected organizations.
Officers and Trustees: * Surinder M. Sehgal,* Chair., Pres., and Treas.; Edda G. Sehgal,* V.P. and Secy.; Rajat M. Sehgal, Exec. Dir.; Arvind Bahl; Nishat Farooq; Y.C. Nanda; AVM S. Sahni; Jay Sehgal; Jagadish Shukla; Om Thanvi.
EIN: 421477858
Selected grants: The following grants were reported in 2003.
$1,000,000 to International Crops Research Institute for the Semi-Arid Tropics, Hyderabad, India. For research.
$750,000 to Greater Des Moines Community Foundation, Des Moines, IA.
$250,000 to Trees for Life, Wichita, KS.
$30,000 to Institute of Global Environment and Society, Calverton, MD.
$13,037 to Westminster College, Fulton, MO.
$10,000 to Ashoka Trust for Research in Ecology and the Environment, Belmont, MA. For research.
$10,000 to Association for Indias Development (AID), College Park, MD.
$10,000 to Iowa State University, Ames, IA.
$10,000 to Swaraj Foundation, Willowbrook, IL.
$10,000 to United Nations Foundation, DC.

3331
The Seidler Foundation ◇
P.O. Box 1297
Des Moines, IA 50305
Contact: Stanley B. Seidler, Pres.

Established in 1982 in IA.
Donors: Iowa Periodicals, Inc.; Stanley B. Seidler; Excell Mktg.
Foundation type: Company-sponsored foundation.
Financial data (yr. ended 12/31/03): Assets, $5,393,982 (M); gifts received, $700,100; expenditures, $357,289; qualifying distributions, $347,372; giving activities include $346,465 for 53 grants (high: $68,280; low: $100).
Purpose and activities: The foundation supports organizations involved with arts and culture, higher education, and Judaism.
Fields of interest: Performing arts; Arts; Higher education; Scholarships/financial aid; Jewish federated giving programs; Jewish agencies & temples.

Type of support: General/operating support; Scholarship funds.
Limitations: Giving on a national basis, with emphasis on IA.
Application information: Application form not required.
Initial approach: Proposal
Deadline(s): None
Officer and Directors: * Stanley B. Seidler,* Pres.; Carol Mavrakis; Susan Seidler.
EIN: 421209825
Selected grants: The following grants were reported in 2005.
$28,272 to Temple Bnai Jeshurun, Des Moines, IA.
$27,866 to University of Iowa Foundation, Iowa City, IA.
$22,030 to Des Moines Art Center, Des Moines, IA.
$15,000 to Cornell College, Mount Vernon, IA.
$9,750 to Grand Teton Music Festival, Teton Village, WY.
$8,000 to Des Moines Metro Opera, Indianola, IA.
$7,500 to Lyric Opera of Chicago, Chicago, IL.
$5,250 to Des Moines Public Library Foundation, Des Moines, IA.
$5,000 to United Way of Central Iowa, Des Moines, IA.
$4,000 to Community Foundation of Jackson Hole, Jackson, WY.

3332
Siouxland Community Foundation ☆
(formerly Siouxland Foundation)
505 5th St., Ste. 412
Sioux City, IA 51101-1507
Contact: Debbie Hubbard, Exec. Dir.
FAX: (712) 293-3303;
E-mail: office@siouxlandcommunityfoundation.org;
URL: http:// www.siouxlandcommunityfoundation.org

Established in 1988 in IA.
Foundation type: Community foundation.
Financial data (yr. ended 12/31/05): Assets, $7,999,728 (M); gifts received, $2,313,926; expenditures, $564,585; giving activities include $392,491 for 107 grants (high: $18,194; low: $115), and $51,378 for 25 grants to individuals (high: $12,000; low: $250).
Purpose and activities: The foundation awards grants to social-service agencies that offer assistance with addiction, domestic violence and other issues. Giving also for arts and culture, education, civic affairs, and health.
Fields of interest: Performing arts, music; Arts; Education, early childhood education; Child development, education; Medical school/ education; Adult education—literacy, basic skills & GED; Education, reading; Education; Nursing care; Health care; Substance abuse, services; Mental health/crisis services; Health organizations, association; Alcoholism; Crime/violence prevention, domestic violence; Safety/disasters; Recreation; Children/youth, services; Child development, services; Family services; Aging, centers/services; Minorities/immigrants, centers/ services; Human services; Government/public administration; Aging; Disabilities, people with; Minorities; Asians/Pacific Islanders; African Americans/Blacks; Hispanics/Latinos; Native Americans/American Indians; Economically disadvantaged; Homeless.
Type of support: Scholarships—to individuals; Building/renovation; Equipment; Program

development; Conferences/seminars; Seed money; Scholarship funds; Research; Employee-related scholarships.

Limitations: Giving limited to the greater Sioux City, IA, tri-state area (within a 50-mile radius of Sioux City, including NE and SD). No support for religious or political purposes. No grants to individuals (except for scholarships), or for endowment funds, deficit financing, fundraising campaigns, capital campaigns, general operating support, or school playground equipment or uniforms.

Publications: Application guidelines; Annual report (including application guidelines); Informational brochure (including application guidelines); Newsletter.

Application information: Application form required.
Initial approach: Letter or telephone
Copies of proposal: 4
Deadline(s): Jan. 15 and May 15
Board meeting date(s): Mar., June, Sept., and Dec.
Final notification: Mar. 31 and June 30

Officers and Directors:* John W. Gleeson,* Pres.; Lynn Persinger, V.P.; Daniel D. Dykstra,* Secy.; Joseph P. Delperdang,* Treas.; Debbie Hubbard, Exec. Dir.; Barry E. Backhaus; Craig S. Berenstein; Colin C. Jensen; Don "Skip" Meisner; Nancy R. Metz; Maurice B. Nieland; Delaine C. Peterson; R. Scott Rager; John C. Reynders; James M. Yanney.

Number of staff: 1 full-time professional; 1 part-time professional.

EIN: 421323904

3333
South Central Iowa Community Foundation ✧

P.O. Box 258
Leon, IA 50144
Contact: Diane Rouse

Established in 1993 in IA.

Foundation type: Community foundation.

Financial data (yr. ended 6/30/05): Assets, $5,208,647 (M); gifts received, $463,104; expenditures, $414,068; giving activities include $322,101 for grants.

Purpose and activities: The foundation provides grants to various charitable and community organizations for support of community projects and improvements for community betterment.

Limitations: Giving primarily in Clarke, Decatur, Lucas, Ringgold, and Union counties in southern IA.

Application information: Application form required.
Initial approach: Contact foundation
Copies of proposal: 6

Officers and Directors:* Don Sheridan,* Pres.; Betty Hansen,* V.P.; Michell Ricker,* Secy.; Jeff DeForest,* Treas.; Sue Beck; Karen Bender; James Brown; Emily Forquer; Mike Frost; Kay Herring; Judy Hopkins; Connie Kent; Mary Ellen Kimball; Tom Morain; Joe Novak; Gloria Salsman; Arlene Sobotka; Sharon South; Clint Spurnor; Dave Stafford; Roger Struve; Ray Thurlby; Kay Vaughan; Jim Wright.

Number of staff: 1 full-time professional; 1 full-time support.

EIN: 421411234

3334
C. Richard Stark, Jr. & Joan E. Stark Foundation ✧ ☆

2 Ruan Ctr.
601 Locust, Ste. 1100
Des Moines, IA 50309

Established in 1989 in IA.

Donor: C. Richard Stark, Jr.

Foundation type: Independent foundation.

Financial data (yr. ended 12/31/05): Assets, $4,017,748 (M); expenditures, $424,279; qualifying distributions, $371,500; giving activities include $371,500 for 18 grants (high: $100,000; low: $1,000).

Purpose and activities: Giving for Christian organizations, education, health, and youth services.

Fields of interest: Elementary/secondary education; Health care; Children/youth, services; Roman Catholic agencies & churches; Religion.

Limitations: Applications not accepted. Giving primarily in IA. No grants to individuals.

Application information: Contributes only to pre-selected organizations.

Directors: C. Richard Stark, Jr.; Joan E. Stark.

EIN: 421345092

3335
Stine Family Foundation ✧

2225 Laredo Trail
Adel, IA 50003

Established in 1999 in IA.

Donor: Harry H. Stine.

Foundation type: Independent foundation.

Financial data (yr. ended 6/30/05): Assets, $10,859,377 (M); expenditures, $546,653; qualifying distributions, $535,825; giving activities include $525,000 for 9 grants (high: $430,000; low: $2,000).

Purpose and activities: Giving primarily for an institute that mobilizes community-based character development; some giving also for education.

Fields of interest: Higher education; Education.

Type of support: General/operating support.

Limitations: Applications not accepted. Giving primarily in McPherson, KS and in IA. No grants to individuals.

Application information: Contributes only to pre-selected organizations.

Officers and Directors:* Harry H. Stine,* Pres.; Jerald L. Reichling, C.F.O. and Treas.; Michael L. Peterson; John Reiher; Molly S. Stine.

EIN: 421497513

Selected grants: The following grants were reported in 2003.
$240,000 to Cedars, Inc., McPherson, KS. For capital support.
$14,000 to Minburn Area Firefighters, Minburn, IA. To purchase truck.
$8,000 to Spurgeon Manor, Dallas Center, IA. For building renovations.
$3,000 to Church of the Brethren, Dallas Center, IA. To fund missions.

3336
The Sukup Family Foundation ✧ ☆

1379 Beets Lake Dr.
Hampton, IA 50441

Established in 1999 in IA.

Donors: Eugene Sukup; Mary Sukup; Charles Sukup.

Foundation type: Independent foundation.

Financial data (yr. ended 12/31/05): Assets, $118,694 (M); gifts received, $495,000; expenditures, $606,739; qualifying distributions, $606,193; giving activities include $606,193 for grants.

Fields of interest: Higher education; Protestant agencies & churches.

Limitations: Applications not accepted. Giving primarily in IA. No grants to individuals.

Application information: Contributes only to pre-selected organizations.

Officers: Eugene Sukup, Pres.; Charles Sukup, V.P.; Mary Sukup, Secy.; Steven Sukup, Treas.

EIN: 421488675

Selected grants: The following grants were reported in 2004.
$84,000 to Hampton Community Christian Daycare, Hampton, IA.
$20,000 to Tentmakers, Minneapolis, MN.
$10,000 to Youth for Christ.
$5,000 to Riverside Lutheran Bible Camp, Story City, IA.
$5,000 to Wartburg College, Waverly, IA.

3337
Martha-Ellen Tye Foundation ✧

16 E. Main St., Ste. 260
Marshalltown, IA 50158-4936   (641) 752-8340
Contact: Susan Martin, Exec. Dir.
FAX: (641) 752-8341;
E-mail: metf@thewebunwired.com

Established in 1976 in IA.

Donor: Martha-Ellen Tye†.

Foundation type: Independent foundation.

Financial data (yr. ended 12/31/05): Assets, $27,063,554 (M); expenditures, $1,427,101; qualifying distributions, $1,232,419; giving activities include $1,044,559 for 56 grants (high: $185,000; low: $1,000).

Purpose and activities: Giving primarily for arts and culture, and education; funding also for new residents, human service needs, and community betterment.

Fields of interest: Performing arts; Historic preservation/historical societies; Education; Youth development.

Type of support: Program development; Curriculum development; Capital campaigns; Building/renovation; Equipment; Matching/challenge support.

Limitations: Giving primarily in Marshalltown, IA, and the surrounding county; limited giving in San Antonio, TX. No support for religious organizations. No grants to individuals.

Publications: Application guidelines; Program policy statement.

Application information: Application form required.
Initial approach: Letter, telephone or E-mail
Copies of proposal: 1
Deadline(s): Mar. 1, June 1, Sept.1, and Dec. 1
Board meeting date(s): Late Apr. and late Oct.
Final notification: Within 6 weeks of application deadline

Officers and Directors:* Dennis A. O'Toole,* Pres.; William M. Tank,* V.P.; Rex J. Ryden,* Secy.-Treas.; Terry Buzbee; R.W. Fisher; Maureen Lyons; Betsy Macke; Loras Neuroth; Thomas O'Toole; Joe B. Tye, Jr.

Number of staff: 1 full-time professional; 1 part-time support.
EIN: 421055988

3338

United Fire Group Foundation ◇

118 2nd Ave. S.E.
Cedar Rapids, IA 52401

Established in 2001 in IA.
Donor: United Fire & Casualty Co.
Foundation type: Company-sponsored foundation.
Financial data (yr. ended 12/31/03): Assets,
$7,879 (M); gifts received, $14,802; expenditures,
$318,126; qualifying distributions, $312,465;
giving activities include $315,085 for 45 grants
(high: $100,000; low: $25).
Purpose and activities: The foundation supports
organizations involved with arts and culture,
education, and human services.
Fields of interest: Arts; Education; Human services;
Federated giving programs.
Limitations: Applications not accepted. Giving
primarily in IA. No grants to individuals.
Application information: Contributes only to
pre-selected organizations.
Officers and Directors:* John Scott McIntrye, Jr.,*
Pres.; John Arthur Rife,* Secy.; Kent Gilbert Baker,*
Treas.
EIN: 421492320
Selected grants: The following grants were reported
in 2005.
$132,000 to United Way of East Central Iowa, Cedar
    Rapids, IA.
$25,000 to Iowa College Foundation, Des Moines,
    IA.
$12,500 to American Red Cross.
$12,500 to Community Health Free Clinic, Cedar
    Rapids, IA.
$12,500 to Tanager Place, Cedar Rapids, IA.
$10,000 to United Way of Galveston, Galveston, TX.
$8,000 to Kirkwood Community College, Cedar
    Rapids, IA.
$7,500 to Alternative Services, Cedar Rapids, IA.
$7,500 to Planned Parenthood of East Central Iowa,
    Cedar Rapids, IA.
$5,000 to Nebraska Independent College
    Foundation, Omaha, NE.

3339

Valley Community Foundation for Lifelong Learning ◇ ☆

22651 Canoe Rd.
Elgin, IA 52141

Established in 2003 in IA.
Foundation type: Independent foundation.
Financial data (yr. ended 12/31/05): Assets,
$394,357 (M); gifts received, $380,605;
expenditures, $380,150; qualifying distributions,
$380,150; giving activities include $380,150 for 3
grants (high: $380,000; low: $25).
Officer: Debra Kahler, Treas.
EIN: 421469525

3340

Arlan J. Van Wyk Family Foundation ◇ ☆

P.O. Box 389
Sheldon, IA 51201-0389
Contact: Arlan J. Van Wyk, Mgr.

Established in 1999 in IA.
Donor: Arlan J. Van Wyk.
Foundation type: Independent foundation.
Financial data (yr. ended 12/31/05): Assets,
$686,952 (M); gifts received, $810,000;
expenditures, $346,877; qualifying distributions,
$346,515; giving activities include $346,515 for 22
grants (high: $250,000; low: $100).
Fields of interest: Recreation; Children/youth,
services; Religion; Children/youth; Disabilities,
people with.
Limitations: Applications not accepted. Giving on a
national basis, with some emphasis on IA. No grants
to individuals.
Application information: Contributes only to
pre-selected organizations.
Officer: Arlan J. Van Wyk, Mgr.
EIN: 421484434
Selected grants: The following grants were reported
in 2005.
$5,000 to Hope Haven, Rock Valley, IA.
$2,200 to Bible League, Chicago, IL.
$2,000 to Northwestern College, Orange City, IA.
$1,000 to Alliance Defense Fund, Scottsdale, AZ.
$1,000 to Banquet, The, Sioux Falls, SD.
$1,000 to Homes for Our Troops, Taunton, MA.

3341

Vermeer Charitable Foundation, Inc.

c/o Vermeer Manufacturing Co.
1210 Vermeer Rd. E.
Pella, IA 50219
Contact: Lois J. Vermeer, Exec. Secy.
E-mail: charitablefoundation@vermeermfg.com;
URL: http://dealers.vermeermfg.com/
charitablefoundation/index.cfm

Established in 1977 in IA.
Donors: Vermeer Manufacturing Co.; Vermeer
Farms, Inc.
Foundation type: Company-sponsored foundation.
Financial data (yr. ended 12/31/05): Assets,
$7,115,419 (M); gifts received, $1,521,079;
expenditures, $2,441,854; qualifying distributions,
$2,429,482; giving activities include $2,429,482
for 130 grants (high: $1,305,800; low: $100).
Purpose and activities: The foundation supports
organizations involved with higher education,
Christianity, and senior citizens.
Fields of interest: Higher education; Christian
agencies & churches; Aging.
Type of support: Building/renovation; Seed money.
Limitations: Giving primarily in the Pella, IA, area. No
grants to individuals, or for endowments; no loans.
Application information: Application form required.
    Initial approach: Contact foundation for
        application form
    Copies of proposal: 2
    Deadline(s): Apr. and Nov.
    Board meeting date(s): Apr., Nov., and as required
Officers and Directors:* Gary J. Vermeer,* Pres.;
Matilda Vermeer,* V.P.; Lois J. Vermeer,* Exec.
Secy.; Robert L. Vermeer,* Treas.; Dale J. Andringa;
Jason Andringa; Mary A. Andringa; Christina
Vermeer; Daniel Vermeer.
Number of staff: 1 part-time professional; 2
part-time support.
EIN: 421087640
Selected grants: The following grants were reported
in 2005.
$1,305,800 to Pella Christian High School, Pella,
    IA.
$150,000 to Central College, Pella, IA.

$107,643 to Dordt College, Sioux Center, IA.
$100,000 to Calvin College, Grand Rapids, MI.
$100,000 to Fuller Theological Seminary,
    Pasadena, CA.
$50,000 to Rehoboth Christian School, Rehoboth,
    NM.
$36,250 to Pella Christian Grade School, Pella, IA.
$25,000 to Calvin Theological Seminary, Grand
    Rapids, MI.
$25,000 to Trinity Christian College, Palos Heights,
    IL.
$7,000 to Indian Hills Community College,
    Ottumwa, IA.

3342

The Wallace Research Foundation ▼ ◇

c/o RSM McGladrey, Inc.
221 3rd Ave. S.E., Ste. 300
Cedar Rapids, IA 52401
Contact: Joe Gevock

Established in 1996 in IA.
Donors: H.B. Wallace; Jocelyn M. Wallace; Henry D.
Wallace; Linda Wallace-Gray.
Foundation type: Independent foundation.
Financial data (yr. ended 12/31/04): Assets,
$88,389,203 (M); expenditures, $4,327,357;
qualifying distributions, $3,863,497; giving
activities include $3,815,958 for 47 grants (high:
$294,885; low: $5,000; average: $20,000–
$200,000).
Purpose and activities: Giving primarily for
education, the environment, and medical research.
Fields of interest: Higher education; Environment,
natural resources; Medical research.
Type of support: Research.
Limitations: Applications not accepted. No support
for religious or political purposes. No grants to
individuals.
Application information: Contributes only to
pre-selected organizations.
Officers: H.B. Wallace, Pres. and Secy.-Treas.;
Henry D. Wallace, V.P.; Jocelyn M. Wallace, V.P.;
Linda Wallace-Gray, V.P.
EIN: 426540579
Selected grants: The following grants were reported
in 2004.
$294,885 to Center for Desert Archaeology,
    Tucson, AZ.
$280,102 to University of Arizona, Tucson, AZ.
$259,000 to Nature Conservancy, Arlington, VA.
$221,318 to Dermatology Foundation of Miami,
    Miami, FL.
$200,000 to Dental Choice Support Fund, DC.
$200,000 to Harlan E. Moore Heart Research
    Foundation, Champaign, IL.
$120,000 to Center for Mind-Body Medicine, DC.
$70,000 to Humane Society of Tucson, Tucson, AZ.
$60,000 to Nature Conservancy, Nashville, TN.
$54,000 to University of Kentucky, Lexington, KY.

3343

The Wellmark Foundation ◇

(formerly The IASD Health Care Foundation)
636 Grand Ave., Ste. 150
P.O. Box 9232
Des Moines, IA 50309-9232 (515) 245-4819
Contact: Dr. Sheila Riggs, Exec. Dir.
FAX: (515) 235-4445;
E-mail: wmfoundation@wellmark.com; URL: http://
www.wellmark.com/foundation/index.asp

Established in 1991 in IA.

Donors: Blue Cross and Blue Shield of Iowa; Blue Cross and Blue Shield of South Dakota; Wellmark, Inc.

Foundation type: Company-sponsored foundation.

Financial data (yr. ended 12/31/04): Assets, $34,046,013 (M); gifts received, $4,498,799; expenditures, $1,926,269; qualifying distributions, $1,427,847; giving activities include $1,427,847 for 56 grants (high: $250,000; low: $800).

Purpose and activities: The foundation supports organizations involved with health.

Fields of interest: Health care.

Type of support: Program development; Seed money.

Limitations: Giving limited to IA and SD. No grants to individuals.

Publications: Grants list; Newsletter.

Application information: Application form not required.

Initial approach: Proposal

Copies of proposal: 9

Deadline(s): Feb. 28 and June 6

Board meeting date(s): Mar. 30, May 24, Aug. 11, and Nov. 1

Final notification: 8 weeks

Officers and Directors: John Forsyth, Chair.; F. Joseph DuBray, Secy.; Richard C. Anderson, Treas.; Thomas L. Aller; Thomas J. Huber, M.D.; Eldon Huston; Edward R. Lynn; Robert O'Connell; Robert Richard; Elaine E. Szymoniak; Roberta Wattlesworth.

Number of staff: 2 full-time professional; 1 part-time professional.

EIN: 421368650

3344

Winterhaven, Inc. ✦ ☆

119 19th St., Ste. 206

West Des Moines, IA 50265

Established in 1997 in IA.

Donors: Rocinda J. Green; Anthony S. Wilson; Nancy J. Wilson.

Foundation type: Independent foundation.

Financial data (yr. ended 12/31/05): Assets, $118,722 (M); gifts received, $1,016,443; expenditures, $940,748; qualifying distributions, $940,748; giving activities include $905,153 for 110 grants to individuals (high: $32,921; low: $1,700).

Purpose and activities: Giving primarily for assistance to help households purchase dwellings for use as their primary residence.

Fields of interest: Housing/shelter.

Limitations: Giving primarily in IA.

Officer: C. David Albright, Pres.

EIN: 421278027

KANSAS

3345
Earl Bane Foundation ◇
P.O. Box 201
Salina, KS 67402-0201
Application address: c/o Sandra Buster, Pres., 315
N. 9th St., Salina, KS 67401, tel.: (785) 827-1492

Established in 1994 in KS.
Donor: Earl Bane†.
Foundation type: Independent foundation.
Financial data (yr. ended 4/30/05): Assets,
$11,055,264 (M); expenditures, $689,756;
qualifying distributions, $647,010; giving activities
include $413,225 for 22 grants (high: $80,000;
low: $1,000), and $175,000 for 37 grants to
individuals (high: $5,000; low: $2,500).
Purpose and activities: Giving to educational,
economic, scientific, and religious organizations
generally for the benefit of persons in or from Salina
and Saline County, KS.
Fields of interest: Higher education; Education;
Human services; Science; Religion.
Type of support: Annual campaigns; Building/
renovation; Equipment; Endowments; Program
development; Scholarship funds; Program-related
investments/loans; Scholarships—to individuals.
Limitations: Giving primarily in Salina and Saline
County, KS.
Application information: Application form not
required.
  Initial approach: Letter or telephone
  Copies of proposal: 3
  Deadline(s): None
  Board meeting date(s): Mar., June, Sept. and Dec.
Officer and Trustees:* Sandra Buster,* Pres.;
Melanie Bailey; Robert Buster; Gerald L. Hunter;
Elna Sloop.
Number of staff: 1 part-time professional.
EIN: 481152429
Selected grants: The following grants were reported
in 2005.
$80,000 to Salina Education Foundation, Salina,
  KS. For Lift Program.
$65,000 to Boy Scouts of America, Salina, KS. 2
  grants: $15,000 to Coronado Area Council (For
  general support), $50,000 to Coronado Area
  Council (For office building and Camp Brown
  renovations).
$50,000 to Salina Regional Health Foundation,
  Salina, KS. For Cancer Center Building Project.
$25,000 to Episcopal Diocese of Western Kansas,
  Salina, KS. For Spirituality and Leadership
  Center.
$25,000 to Presbyterian Manors of Mid-America,
  Wichita, KS. For building renovation campaign.
$21,237 to Cloud County Community College,
  Concordia, KS. For equipment and materials for
  nursing and science.
$17,288 to Salina Community Theater, Salina, KS.
  For box office software upgrade.
$16,200 to Teen Town, Salina, KS. For Alive Youth
  Leadership Program.
$10,000 to Saint Francis Academy, Salina, KS. For
  operating support.

3346
Baughman Foundation ◇
P.O. Box 1356
Liberal, KS 67905-1356 (620) 624-1371
Contact: Carol Feather-Francis, Pres.

Incorporated in 1958 in KS.
Donors: Robert W. Baughman†; The John W.
Baughman Farms Co.
Foundation type: Independent foundation.
Financial data (yr. ended 12/31/05): Assets,
$25,788,567 (M); expenditures, $1,440,327;
qualifying distributions, $1,234,772; giving
activities include $1,134,279 for 56 grants (high:
$68,735; low: $1,160).
Fields of interest: Arts; Higher education; Hospitals
(general); Crime/law enforcement, police agencies;
Youth, services; Community development;
Government/public administration.
Type of support: General/operating support;
Building/renovation; Endowments; Program
development; Scholarship funds.
Limitations: Giving primarily in southeast CO,
southwest KS, and the OK Panhandle area. No
support for private foundations. No grants to
individuals.
Application information:
  Initial approach: Proposal
  Copies of proposal: 3
  Deadline(s): 1st Wed. of each month, before
    10AM central time
  Board meeting date(s): Monthly
  Final notification: 30 days
Officers: Carol Feather-Francis, Pres.; Richard
Yoxall, V.P.; James R. Yoxall, Secy.-Treas.
Number of staff: 1 part-time support.
EIN: 486108797
Selected grants: The following grants were reported
in 2004.
$20,000 to Childrens Center, Bethany, OK.
$20,000 to Liberal Memorial Library, Liberal, KS.
$20,000 to Prairie View, Newton, KS.
$20,000 to Saint Francis Academy, Salina, KS.
$15,000 to Heartspring, Wichita, KS.
$10,000 to Kansas Childrens Service League,
  Wichita, KS.
$10,000 to Kansas Independent College Fund,
  Topeka, KS.
$6,000 to Make-A-Wish Foundation, Wichita, KS.
$5,000 to Friends University, Wichita, KS.
$5,000 to Salvation Army, Kansas City, MO.

3347
Israel Henry Beren Charitable Trust ◇
P.O. Box 20380
Wichita, KS 67208
Contact: Robert M. Beren, Tr.

Established in 1995.
Donor: Israel Henry Beren†.
Foundation type: Independent foundation.
Financial data (yr. ended 12/31/04): Assets,
$47,487,130 (M); expenditures, $2,447,757;
qualifying distributions, $2,329,844; giving
activities include $2,328,500 for 14 grants (high:
$1,400,000; low: $2,500).
Fields of interest: Jewish agencies & temples.
Limitations: Applications not accepted. Giving
primarily in NY; some giving also in Israel. No grants
to individuals.
Application information: Contributes only to
pre-selected organizations.

Trustee: Robert M. Beren.
EIN: 486337836
Selected grants: The following grants were reported
in 2004.
$1,400,000 to Yeshiva University, New York, NY.
  For endowment fund.
$200,000 to Ohr Torah Stone Colleges and
  Graduate Programs, New York, NY. For Israel
  Henry Beren Residence Hall.
$175,000 to American Friends of Beit Morasha,
  Englewood, NJ. 2 grants: $100,000 (For general
  support), $75,000 (For general support).
$160,000 to Ner Israel Rabbinical College,
  Baltimore, MD. For Israel Henry Beren
  Scholarship Fund.
$150,000 to Jerusalem College of Technology,
  Jerusalem, Israel. For Israel Henry Beren
  Dormitory.
$100,000 to United Lubavitcher Yeshiva, Brooklyn,
  NY. 2 grants: $50,000 each (For Torah Center).
$50,000 to Machon Chana Womens Institute,
  Brooklyn, NY. For library and new building.
$18,000 to Chabad Lubavitch of North Broward and
  Palm Beach Counties, Coral Spring, FL. For library
  and improvements.

3348
Robert M. Beren Foundation, Inc. ◇
P.O. Box 20380
Wichita, KS 67208
Contact: Robert M. Beren, Pres.

Established in 1984 in KS.
Donors: Adolph Beren†; Robert M. Beren.
Foundation type: Independent foundation.
Financial data (yr. ended 10/31/05): Assets,
$52,175,729 (M); expenditures, $3,147,843;
qualifying distributions, $2,692,921; giving
activities include $2,685,870 for 39 grants (high:
$1,500,000; low: $100).
Purpose and activities: Giving primarily for religious,
educational, and welfare organizations, including
synagogues.
Fields of interest: Higher education; Human
services; Jewish federated giving programs; Jewish
agencies & temples.
Type of support: Fellowships; Building/renovation;
Emergency funds; General/operating support;
Annual campaigns.
Limitations: Applications not accepted. Giving on a
national basis. No grants to individuals.
Application information: Contributes only to
pre-selected organizations.
Officers: Robert M. Beren, Pres. and Treas.; Charles
B. Spradlin, Jr., Secy.
EIN: 480990309
Selected grants: The following grants were reported
in 2004.
$1,700,000 to Harvard University, Cambridge, MA.
$400,000 to Jewish Federation of Palm Beach
  County, West Palm Beach, FL. 2 grants:
  $150,000 (For general support), $250,000 (For
  emergency fund).
$175,000 to American Friends of Beit Morasha,
  Englewood, NJ. 2 grants: $100,000 (For general
  support), $75,000 (For general support).
$100,000 to AISH New York, New York, NY. 2
  grants: $50,000 each (For fellowships in
  Jerusalem).
$50,000 to Harvard Hillel, Cambridge, MA. For
  general support.
$50,000 to Robert M. Beren Academy, Houston, TX.
  For general support.

$25,000 to Palm Beach Orthodox Synagogue, Palm Beach, FL. For building.

3349
The Breidenthal-Snyder Foundation ◇
(formerly Ruth B. and Willard B. Snyder Foundation, Inc.)
8014 State Line Rd., Ste. 203
Shawnee Mission, KS   66208-3712
Contact: Willard B. Snyder, Pres.

Established around 1984.
Donors: Ruth B. Snyder†; Willard B. Snyder; Julie Breidenthal Gold†.
Foundation type: Independent foundation.
Financial data (yr. ended 12/31/05): Assets, $9,413,255 (M); expenditures, $414,847; qualifying distributions, $405,928; giving activities include $404,368 for 63 grants (high: $21,500; low: $500).
Limitations: Giving primarily in the Kansas City, KS, area. No grants to individuals.
Application information: Generally contributes only to pre-selected organizations. Only 1 grant to any recipient within a calendar year. Application form required.
   Initial approach: Letter requesting application
   Copies of proposal: 1
   Deadline(s): None
   Board meeting date(s): June and Dec.
   Final notification: Positive responses only
Officers and Directors:* Willard B. Snyder,* Pres.; Rolf D. Snyder,* Secy.-Treas.; Pat Lockerby; T.J. Snyder; Keith Wilson, Jr.
EIN: 480979412
Selected grants: The following grants were reported in 2004.
$20,000 to Liberty Memorial Association, Kansas City, MO.
$16,200 to Unicorn Theater, Kansas City, MO.
$15,000 to Friends of the Zoo, Kansas City, MO.
$15,000 to Naval War College Foundation, Newport, RI.
$14,000 to Salvation Army of Kansas City, Kansas City, KS.
$12,000 to Kansas City Community Kitchen, Kansas City, MO.
$10,000 to Donnelly College, Kansas City, KS.
$10,000 to Kansas City Friends of Alvin Ailey, Kansas City, MO.
$10,000 to Lyric Opera of Kansas City, Kansas City, MO.
$5,000 to Tufts University, Medford, MA.

3350
Capitol Federal Foundation
700 S. Kansas Ave., Ste. 517
Topeka, KS   66603   (785) 270-6040
Contact: Jack H. Hamilton, Pres.

Established in 1999 in KS.
Donor: Capitol Federal Financial.
Foundation type: Independent foundation.
Financial data (yr. ended 12/31/04): Assets, $68,095,748 (M); expenditures, $3,018,710; qualifying distributions, $2,792,593; giving activities include $2,752,236 for 322 grants (high: $500,000; low: $150).
Purpose and activities: Giving primarily for education and to affordable housing services;

funding also for health associations, youth services, community development, and the United Way.
Fields of interest: Performing arts centers; Education; Health organizations, association; Housing/shelter; Boys & girls clubs; Big Brothers/Big Sisters; Human services; Youth, services; Community development; Federated giving programs.
Type of support: General/operating support; Continuing support; Income development; Annual campaigns; Capital campaigns; Building/renovation; Equipment; Land acquisition; Emergency funds; Program development; Conferences/seminars; Professorships; Seed money; Fellowships; Internship funds; Scholarship funds; Employee matching gifts; Matching/challenge support.
Limitations: Giving limited to major metropolitan areas of central and northeastern KS.
Application information: Application form not required.
   Initial approach: Letter or telephone
   Copies of proposal: 1
   Deadline(s): None
   Board meeting date(s): Quarterly
   Final notification: 90-120 days
Officers: John C. Dicus, Chair.; Jack H. Hamilton, Pres.; John B. Dicus, Secy.-Treas.
Directors: Rick C. Jackson; Nancy Perry; Ron Roskens.
Number of staff: 1 full-time professional.
EIN: 481214952
Selected grants: The following grants were reported in 2004.
$500,000 to Kansas University Endowment Association, Lawrence, KS.
$100,000 to Kansas Newspaper Foundation, Topeka, KS.
$100,000 to Lets Help, Topeka, KS.
$100,000 to Stormont-Vail Foundation, Topeka, KS.
$89,000 to Family Service and Guidance Center of Topeka, Topeka, KS.
$75,000 to Boy Scouts of America, Jayhawk Area Council, Topeka, KS.
$56,000 to United Way of Greater Topeka, Topeka, KS.
$5,000 to Washburn Endowment Association, Topeka, KS.
$2,500 to TLC for Children and Families, Olathe, KS.
$2,500 to United Way, Salina Area, Salina, KS.

3351
Cessna Foundation, Inc. ◇
P.O. Box 7706
Wichita, KS   67277   (316) 517-7810
Contact: Marilyn Richwine, Secy.-Treas.

Incorporated in 1952 in KS.
Donor: The Cessna Aircraft Co.
Foundation type: Company-sponsored foundation.
Financial data (yr. ended 12/31/05): Assets, $18,686,907 (M); gifts received, $1,472,035; expenditures, $2,018,691; qualifying distributions, $1,898,795; giving activities include $1,682,470 for 67 grants (high: $400,000; low: $250), and $213,743 for employee matching gifts.
Purpose and activities: The foundation supports organizations involved with arts and culture, education, natural resources, human services, and community development.
Fields of interest: Arts; Education; Environment, natural resources; Human services; Community development.

Type of support: Annual campaigns; Capital campaigns; Building/renovation; Emergency funds; Program development; Scholarship funds; Employee matching gifts; Scholarships—to individuals.
Limitations: Giving limited to areas of company operations, with emphasis on Wichita, KS; giving also to regional and national organizations. No support for regional or national organizations not addressing specific local needs, fraternal or veterans' organizations, religious organizations, medical or other research organizations, or athletic teams, bands, or volunteer firefighting squads. No grants to individuals (except for scholarships), or for general operating support, political action, or legislative advocacy.
Publications: Application guidelines.
Application information: Application form not required.
   Initial approach: Proposal
   Copies of proposal: 1
   Deadline(s): None
   Board meeting date(s): Quarterly
   Final notification: 6 to 8 weeks
Officers and Trustees:* Russell W. Meyer, Jr.,* Pres.; John E. Moore,* V.P.; Marilyn Richwine,* Secy.-Treas.; Jordan L. Haines; Gary W. Hay; Charles B. Johnson; Ken Wagnon.
EIN: 486108801
Selected grants: The following grants were reported in 2004.
$655,500 to United Way of the Plains, Wichita, KS.
$50,000 to Big BrothersBig Sisters, Kansas, Wichita, KS. For Big Ambition.
$50,000 to Exploration Place, Wichita, KS.
$50,000 to Kansas University Endowment Association, College of Engineering, Lawrence, KS.
$33,333 to Catholic Charities of Wichita, Wichita, KS. For Harbor House.
$25,000 to K P T S Channel 8, Wichita, KS. For capital campaign.
$10,000 to Youth Entrepreneurs of Kansas, Wichita, KS.
$8,000 to LeTourneau University, Longview, TX. For scholarships.
$6,240 to Union Rescue Mission, Little Rock, AR.
$5,000 to United Way of the Chattahoochee Valley, Columbus, GA.

3352
Coleman Family Foundation, Inc. ◇ ☆
610 E. Jefferson St.
Pittsburg, KS   66762
Contact: H. Richard Coleman, Pres.

Established in 2002 in KS and MO.
Donors: Faith P. Coleman; H. Richard Coleman.
Foundation type: Independent foundation.
Financial data (yr. ended 12/31/05): Assets, $1,406,773 (M); gifts received, $1,351,644; expenditures, $1,212,385; qualifying distributions, $1,211,920; giving activities include $1,210,600 for grants (high: $300,000; low: $200).
Fields of interest: Elementary/secondary education; Higher education; Children/youth, services; Family services.
Limitations: Giving limited to Pittsburg, KS.
Application information:
   Initial approach: Letter
   Deadline(s): None
Officers: H. Richard Coleman, Pres. and Treas.; Faith P. Coleman, V.P.; Marcia A. Sorrick, Secy.
EIN: 431947299

Selected grants: The following grants were reported in 2005.

$25,000 to Greenbush Educational Foundation, Girard, KS.

$23,000 to Pittsburg State University, Pittsburg, KS.

$10,000 to YMCA of Pittsburg, Pittsburg, KS.

$5,000 to Childrens Mercy Hospital, Kansas City, MO.

$5,000 to First United Methodist Church, Lawrence, KS.

$5,000 to Pittsburg State University Foundation, Pittsburg, KS.

$3,700 to United Way of Crawford County, Pittsburg, KS.

$2,000 to Rose Brooks Center, Kansas City, MO.

$200 to Boy Scouts of America, Springfield, MO.

3353
The Cooper-Clark Foundation ◇
P.O. Box 2707
Liberal, KS 67905-2707 (620) 624-7699
Contact: Jay Hay, Secy.-Treas.

Established in 1983.
Donors: James Clark†; Lucille Clark†.
Foundation type: Independent foundation.
Financial data (yr. ended 12/31/05): Assets, $11,924,381 (M); expenditures, $699,372; qualifying distributions, $585,811; giving activities include $559,831 for 127 grants (high: $37,500; low: $135; average: $2,000–$10,000).
Purpose and activities: Giving primarily for social services.
Fields of interest: Arts; Elementary/secondary education; Human services; Aging, centers/services; Community development; Aging.
Type of support: General/operating support; Continuing support; Building/renovation; Equipment; Land acquisition; Emergency funds; Conferences/seminars; Seed money; Research; Technical assistance.
Limitations: Giving limited to Baca, Cheyenne, Kiowa, Kit Carson, and Lincoln counties, CO, and Grant, Haskell, Morton, Seward, and Stanton counties, KS. No grants to individuals.
Application information: Application form required.
Deadline(s): None
Board meeting date(s): Quarterly
Officers and Directors:* Lee Anderson,* Pres.; Bob Todd,* V.P.; Jay Hay,* Secy.-Treas.; Kay Hay; Sharon Todd.
Number of staff: 1 part-time professional.
EIN: 742252034

3354
Delta Dental Plan of Kansas Foundation, Inc. ◇ ☆
9300 W. 110th St., Bldg. 55, Ste. 450
Overland Park, KS 66210 (913) 327-3727
Contact: Karen Finstad, Exec. Dir.
FAX: (913) 381-8312;
E-mail: kfinstad@deltadentalks.com; URL: http://www.deltadentalksfoundation.org

Established in 2004 in KS.
Donor: Delta Dental Plan of Kansas, Inc.
Foundation type: Company-sponsored foundation.
Financial data (yr. ended 12/31/05): Assets, $1,956,090 (M); gifts received, $1,035,000; expenditures, $499,165; qualifying distributions,

$407,092; giving activities include $407,092 for grants.
Purpose and activities: The foundation supports organizations involved with dental education and dental care. Special emphasis is directed toward programs designed to raise public awareness of oral health issues; emphasize prevention; and improve access to dental services.
Fields of interest: Dental school/education; Dental care.
Type of support: General/operating support; Equipment; Program development; Donated products.
Limitations: Giving limited to KS. No support for political or lobbying organizations. No grants to individuals, or for ongoing programs, general operating support, or debt reduction or fundraising events.
Publications: Application guidelines.
Application information: Requests should be no longer than five pages. Application form required.
Initial approach: Download application form and mail to foundation
Copies of proposal: 11
Deadline(s): Apr. 3 and Oct. 2
Final notification: May and Nov.
Officers and Directors:* Ted Jowett,* Pres.; Brad Clothier,* V.P.; Mike Herbert,* Secy.-Treas.; Karen Finstad,* Exec. Dir.; Michael Clark; Sheila Floodman-McAllister; Elizabeth Kinch; Rodger Maechtlen; Marge Petty; Robert Starr; Stan Wint.
EIN: 680554527

3355
Deramus Foundation, Inc. ◇
(formerly Southern Foundation, Inc.)
c/o D. Zimmerman, Shughart Thomson & Kilroy, P.C.
9225 Indian Creek Pkwy., Bldg. 32, Ste. 1100
Overland Park, KS 66210
Contact: David N. Zimmerman

Established in 1966 in MO.
Foundation type: Independent foundation.
Financial data (yr. ended 12/31/05): Assets, $15,542,435 (M); expenditures, $804,490; qualifying distributions, $731,000; giving activities include $731,000 for 14 grants (high: $250,000; low: $1,000).
Fields of interest: Higher education; Education; Health organizations, association; Human services.
Limitations: Giving primarily in MO, with emphasis on Kansas City. No grants to individuals.
Application information:
Initial approach: Letter
Deadline(s): None
Officers and Directors:* William N. Deramus IV,* Pres. and Secy.; Patricia D. Bunch,* V.P. and Treas.; Jill D. Dean,* V.P.; Jean D. Dean,* V.P.
EIN: 436066776
Selected grants: The following grants were reported in 2003.

$250,000 to Friends of the Zoo, Kansas City, MO. For operating support.

$100,000 to Heritage Foundation, DC. For operating support.

$60,000 to University of Missouri, Kansas City, MO. For Law Foundation.

$50,000 to Bishop Spencer Place, Kansas City, MO.

$50,000 to Boys and Girls Clubs of Greater Kansas City, Kansas City, MO. For operating support.

$20,000 to American Heart Association, Dallas, TX. For operating support.

$20,000 to Meals on Wheels, Overland Park, KS. For operating support.

$10,000 to Salvation Army, Kansas City, MO. For operating support.

$6,650 to Dolphin Communcation Project, Oxnard, CA. For operating support.

$1,500 to American Red Cross, National Headquarters, DC. For operating support.

3356
The Devlin Family Foundation ◇
1313 N. Webb Rd., Rm. 100
Wichita, KS 67206-4070

Established in 2004 in KS.
Donor: Thomas R. Devlin.
Foundation type: Independent foundation.
Financial data (yr. ended 12/31/05): Assets, $190,202 (M); gifts received, $306,810; expenditures, $451,812; qualifying distributions, $437,925; giving activities include $437,925 for 36 grants (high: $200,000; low: $50; average: $100–$1,000).
Fields of interest: Higher education; Christian agencies & churches.
Limitations: Applications not accepted. Giving primarily in Wichita, KS. No grants to individuals.
Application information: Contributes only to pre-selected organizations.
Officers and Directors:* Thomas R. Devlin,* Pres.; David C. Nesbitt,* V.P. and Secy.; Thomas M. Mack,* V.P. and Treas.; Thomas R. Devlin, Jr.; Timothy J. Devlin.
EIN: 200959519

3357
DeVore Foundation, Inc. ◇
9020 E. 35th St. N., Ste. A
Wichita, KS 67226-2017
Contact: Richard A. DeVore, Pres.

Incorporated in 1953 in KS.
Donors: Floyd DeVore†; Richard A. DeVore; William D. DeVore; and their businesses.
Foundation type: Independent foundation.
Financial data (yr. ended 11/30/05): Assets, $7,521,202 (M); expenditures, $467,079; qualifying distributions, $362,663; giving activities include $361,537 for 77 grants (high: $184,000; low: $84).
Fields of interest: Arts; Higher education; Health care; Health organizations, association; Human services; Children/youth, services; Federated giving programs; Protestant agencies & churches.
Type of support: General/operating support; Continuing support; Annual campaigns; Capital campaigns; Building/renovation; Equipment; Endowments; Program development; Seed money.
Limitations: Giving restricted to the Wichita, KS, area.
Publications: Application guidelines; Annual report.
Application information: Application form not required.
Initial approach: Letter
Copies of proposal: 1
Deadline(s): None
Officers: Richard A. DeVore, Pres. and Secy.; William D. DeVore, V.P. and Treas.
EIN: 486109754

3358
Barry L. & Paula M. Downing Foundation ◇

8907 E. Shadowridge
Wichita, KS 67226-2136
Contact: Lisa Jackson, Tr.
Tel.: (316) 636-5050, ext. 709

Established in 1993 in KS.
Donor: Barry L. Downing.
Foundation type: Independent foundation.
Financial data (yr. ended 12/31/05): Assets, $4,315,202 (M); gifts received, $4,000,000; expenditures, $740,021; qualifying distributions, $626,800; giving activities include $626,800 for 29 grants (high: $272,000; low: $200).
Purpose and activities: Giving for education, the arts, and youth services.
Fields of interest: Arts, multipurpose centers/programs; Museums (art); Higher education; Education; Animal welfare; Zoos/zoological societies; Human services; Children/youth, services.
Limitations: Giving primarily in Wichita, KS.
Application information:
Initial approach: Letter
Deadline(s): None
Trustees: Barry L. Downing; Paula M. Downing; Lisa Jackson.
EIN: 481134459

3359
The Dreiseszun Family Foundation ◇

5600 W. 95th St., Ste. 110
Overland Park, KS 66207 (913) 649-9080
Contact: Sherman Dreiseszun, Tr.

Established in 1985 in MO.
Donors: Richard Dreiseszun; Sherman Dreiseszun.
Foundation type: Independent foundation.
Financial data (yr. ended 11/30/05): Assets, $8,592,359 (M); gifts received, $500,000; expenditures, $851,696; qualifying distributions, $670,640; giving activities include $670,640 for 84 grants (high: $337,000; low: $25).
Fields of interest: Arts; Education; Human services; Jewish federated giving programs; Jewish agencies & temples.
Limitations: Giving primarily in KS and MO. No grants to individuals.
Application information:
Initial approach: Letter
Deadline(s): Nov. 30
Trustees: Helene Abrahams; Irene Dreiseszun; Sherman Dreiseszun; Erica Fisher; Brooke Levy.
EIN: 481021776
Selected grants: The following grants were reported in 2005.
$25,000 to Ronald McDonald House Charities, Columbia, MO.
$11,000 to Salvation Army, Kansas City, MO.
$10,000 to American Red Cross, Kansas City, MO.
$10,000 to Jewish Family Service of Colorado, Denver, CO.
$10,000 to University Academy, Kansas City, MO.
$10,000 to Wexner Center for the Arts, Columbus, OH.
$2,500 to University of Iowa Foundation, Iowa City, IA.
$1,800 to Hyman Brand Hebrew Academy, Overland Park, KS.

$1,000 to American Friends of the Hebrew University, New York, NY.
$1,000 to Kansas City Friends of Alvin Ailey, Kansas City, MO.

3360
The DSSR Charitable Foundation, Inc. ◇

475 N. West Rd.
Wellington, KS 67152-5047
Contact: Bill Meridith, Pres.

Established in 1999 in KS.
Donor: Bill Bert Meridith.
Foundation type: Independent foundation.
Financial data (yr. ended 12/31/05): Assets, $4,493,993 (M); expenditures, $1,302,337; qualifying distributions, $1,280,410; giving activities include $1,280,410 for 5 grants (high: $1,273,410; low: $500).
Purpose and activities: Giving primarily to help children and their families through charity based on Christian principles.
Fields of interest: Higher education; Christian agencies & churches.
Limitations: Giving primarily in KS.
Application information: Application form required.
Initial approach: Proposal (less than 5 pages)
Deadline(s): Nov. 15
Officer: Bill Bert Meridith, Pres. and V.P.
Directors: Shelly L. Delice; Susan Hensey; Billy Ross Meridith; Deeta Strader.
EIN: 311677378

3361
The Ellis Foundation ◇ ☆

(formerly Danny and Willa Ellis Foundation)
P.O. Box 54
Fort Scott, KS 66701 (620) 223-2232
Contact: Danny Ellis, Pres.; Willa Ellis, Secy.-Treas.
FAX: (620) 223-2236;
E-mail: dan@theellisfoundation.org; Additional e-mails:chris@theellisfoundation.org; julie@theellisfoundation.org; URL: http://www.theellisfoundation.org

Established in 1991 in KS.
Donors: Danny Ellis; Willa Ellis; Charles W. Cooper; Medplans 2000, Inc.
Foundation type: Independent foundation.
Financial data (yr. ended 6/30/06): Assets, $3,497,960 (M); gifts received, $313,154; expenditures, $500,957; qualifying distributions, $427,313; giving activities include $25,000 for 2 grants (high: $24,000; low: $1,000), and $293,409 for grants to individuals.
Purpose and activities: Giving primarily for scholarships.
Fields of interest: Scholarships/financial aid; Human services.
Type of support: General/operating support.
Limitations: Giving primarily in Bourbon County, KS.
Application information: See foundation Web site.
Initial approach: Letter
Deadline(s): None
Officers: Danny Ellis, Pres.; Willa Ellis, Secy.-Treas.
Directors: James Banwart; Chris Ellis; Bob Patton.
EIN: 481093604

3362
Virginia H. Farah Foundation

P.O. Box 457
Wichita, KS 67201-0457
Contact: Eric S. Namee, Pres.
E-mail: contact@farahfoundation.org; URL: http://www.farahfoundation.org

Established in 1983.
Foundation type: Independent foundation.
Financial data (yr. ended 12/31/05): Assets, $2,827,698 (M); gifts received, $5,200; expenditures, $524,094; qualifying distributions, $401,050; giving activities include $401,050 for 27 grants (high: $70,000; low: $500).
Purpose and activities: Giving primarily for the maintenance and growth of the Orthodox Christian Church in the U.S. and the world. Giving also to Orthodox Christian agencies and churches, for the purpose of improving the lives of disadvantaged children and senior citizens; some giving also for higher education.
Type of support: Management development/capacity building; Capital campaigns; Building/renovation; Program development; Publication; Seed money.
Application information: Application available on foundation Web site. Application form required.
Initial approach: Letter
Copies of proposal: 4
Deadline(s): Sept. 1
Board meeting date(s): Fall and spring
Officers and Trustees:* Eric S. Namee,* Pres.; Valerie DeBolt,* V.P.; Tommie Peterson,* Secy.-Treas.
EIN: 760067300
Selected grants: The following grants were reported in 2003.
$101,000 to Wichita State University, Wichita, KS. For baseball program.
$50,000 to Yale University Press, New Haven, CT. For distribution of creeds and confessions.
$31,000 to Heartland Orthodox Christian Council, Topeka, KS.
$25,000 to Project Mexico of the Orthodox Church, Chula Vista, CA. For program support.
$12,500 to Saint Mary Orthodox Church, Wichita, KS. For program support.
$7,500 to Raphael House, San Francisco, CA. For Children's Program.
$5,000 to Saint George Orthodox Christian Church, Wichita, KS.
$1,000 to Saint Vladimirs Orthodox Theological Seminary, Crestwood, NY. For program support.
$1,000 to University of Kansas, Lawrence, KS. For program support.
$1,000 to Wichita State University Foundation, Wichita, KS. For program support.

3363
Jean and Willard Garvey Fund ◇

c/o Heritage Group
7309 E. 21st St. N., Ste. 120
Wichita, KS 67206-1080

Established in 1989 in KS.
Donors: Jean K. Garvey; Willard W. Garvey; Willard W. Garvey Charitable Trust No. 1; Willard W. Garvey Charitable Trust No. 2; Garvey, Inc.; Jean K. Garvey Revocable Trust.
Foundation type: Independent foundation.
Financial data (yr. ended 12/31/04): Assets, $831,950 (M); expenditures, $840,634; qualifying

distributions, $834,810; giving activities include $826,014 for 111 grants (high: $200,000; low: $50).

Fields of interest: Performing arts; Arts; Higher education; Education; Human services; Salvation Army; Community development, neighborhood development; Protestant agencies & churches.

Type of support: General/operating support; Building/renovation; Endowments; Scholarship funds.

Limitations: Applications not accepted. Giving primarily in Wichita, KS. No grants to individuals.

Application information: Contributes only to pre-selected organizations.

Trustee: Jean K. Garvey.

EIN: 481068307

3364
Olive White Garvey Trust ◇
c/o Heritage Group
7309 E. 21st St. N., Ste. 120
Wichita, KS 67206-1178 (316) 261-5379

Established in 1985 in KS.

Donor: Garvey Charitable Trust No. 11.

Foundation type: Independent foundation.

Financial data (yr. ended 12/31/04): Assets, $5,029,481 (M); expenditures, $1,105,454; qualifying distributions, $1,086,664; giving activities include $1,082,993 for 2 grants (high: $1,032,993; low: $50,000).

Purpose and activities: Giving primarily for a center of nutritional medicine and holistic healing; higher education, and public policy groups.

Fields of interest: Higher education; Health care; Social sciences.

Type of support: General/operating support; Scholarship funds.

Limitations: Applications not accepted. Giving primarily in Wichita, KS. No grants to individuals.

Application information: Contributes only to pre-selected organizations.

Trustee: Ruth G. Fink.

EIN: 486268131

Selected grants: The following grants were reported in 2004.

$1,032,993 to Center for the Improvement of Human Functioning International, Wichita, KS.
$50,000 to Independent Institute, Oakland, CA.

3365
Haglage Charitable Trust Agency ◇ ☆
5442 W. 100th Terr.
Overland Park, KS 66207

Donors: Dorothy Claire Haglage†; Daniel Hutchins.

Foundation type: Independent foundation.

Financial data (yr. ended 12/31/05): Assets, $4,570,941 (M); expenditures, $411,719; qualifying distributions, $381,581; giving activities include $370,576 for grants.

Fields of interest: Salvation Army; Christian agencies & churches; Protestant agencies & churches.

Limitations: Applications not accepted. Giving primarily in KS and MO. No grants to individuals.

Application information: Contributes only to pre-selected organizations.

Trustee: Daniel Hutchins.

EIN: 486375911

Selected grants: The following grants were reported in 2004.

$127,200 to Child Evangelism Fellowship, Warrenton, MO.
$48,300 to Operation Mobilization, Tyrone, GA.
$45,000 to City Union Mission, Kansas City, MO.
$15,000 to Salvation Army, Kansas City, MO.
$3,600 to Young Life Foundation, Colorado Springs, CO.

3366
Dane G. Hansen Foundation ◇
P.O. Box 187
Logan, KS 67646 (785) 699-4832
Contact: Don Stahr, Tr.
URL: http://www.hansenfoundationscholarships.com

Incorporated in 1965 in KS.

Donor: Dane G. Hansen†.

Foundation type: Independent foundation.

Financial data (yr. ended 9/30/05): Assets, $76,327,321 (M); gifts received, $8,778,562; expenditures, $3,080,115; qualifying distributions, $2,694,120; giving activities include $2,414,318 for 61 grants (high: $675,308; low: $150).

Purpose and activities: Grants largely for higher education, including undergraduate, graduate, theological, and vocational scholarships to individuals, civic affairs and public interest groups, youth agencies, services for the handicapped, and hospitals.

Fields of interest: Vocational education; Higher education; Hospitals (general); Youth, services; Public policy, research; Government/public administration; Disabilities, people with.

Type of support: General/operating support; Continuing support; Building/renovation; Equipment; Publication; Scholarship funds; Scholarships—to individuals.

Limitations: Giving primarily in Logan, Phillips County, and northwestern KS; scholarships limited to residents of 26 northwestern KS counties.

Application information: Scholarship seekers should call or write the foundation about eligibility requirements, application forms, and interviews. Application form required.

  Deadline(s): Sept. and Oct. for scholarships
  Board meeting date(s): Monthly
  Final notification: Within 2 weeks for grants to organizations; 30 days after graduation for scholarships

Officers and Trustees:* Carol Bales,* Pres.; Don Stahr,* V.P.; F. Doyle Fair,* Secy.-Treas.; Robert Hartman; Charles I. Moyer; Doyle D. Rahjas.

Number of staff: 7 full-time support.

EIN: 486121156

Selected grants: The following grants were reported in 2005.

$325,611 to Kansas State University, Manhattan, KS. 2 grants: $193,611 (For Dane G. Hansen Foundation Education Scholarship Program), $132,000 (For Presidents discretion).
$185,000 to Boy Scouts of America, Coronado Area Council, Salina, KS. For operation of Hansen Reservation.
$150,000 to Logan, City of, Logan, KS. For Hansen Memorial Plaza and Museum.
$108,000 to Fort Hays State University, Hays, KS. For program support.
$75,000 to Smoky Hill Public Television Corporation - K O O D 9, Bunker Hill, KS. For operating support.

$50,000 to Salvation Army Baltimore Area, Baltimore, MD. For hurricane victims.
$30,000 to Hospice Services, Phillipsburg, KS. For operating support.
$12,500 to Kansas Wesleyan University, Salina, KS. To establish Interactive TV System.
$12,500 to Nicodemus Historical Society, Nicodemus, KS. To re-open museum.

3367
Horejsi Charitable Foundation, Inc. ◇
200 S. Santa Fe Ave., Ste. 4
Salina, KS 67401-3963

Established in 1998 in KS.

Donors: Stewart Horejsi; Horejsi, Inc.

Foundation type: Independent foundation.

Financial data (yr. ended 12/31/05): Assets, $16,720,839 (M); gifts received, $31,932; expenditures, $1,038,609; qualifying distributions, $865,500; giving activities include $865,500 for 9 grants (high: $643,000; low: $1,000).

Purpose and activities: Giving primarily for education.

Fields of interest: Higher education; Education.

Limitations: Applications not accepted. Giving primarily in AZ and KS. No grants to individuals.

Application information: Contributes only to pre-selected organizations.

Officers and Directors:* Stewart Horejsi,* Pres.; Laura Rhodenbaugh, V.P. and Secy.-Treas.; Steve Miller, V.P.; Susan Ciciora; Larry Dunlap; John Horejsi.

EIN: 460447536

3368
Hutchinson Community Foundation
1 N. Main St., Ste. 501
P.O. Box 298
Hutchinson, KS 67504-0298 (620) 663-5293
Contact: Aubrey Abbott Patterson, Pres.; For grants: Christine Pechstein, Community Investment Off.
FAX: (620) 663-9277; *E-mail:* info@hutchcf.org;
Grant application E-mail: christine@hutchcf.org;
URL: http://www.hutchcf.org

Established in 1989 in KS.

Foundation type: Community foundation.

Financial data (yr. ended 12/31/05): Assets, $22,928,044 (M); gifts received, $4,051,089; expenditures, $8,058,100; giving activities include $7,789,162 for 937 grants (high: $3,709,470; low: $5), and $76,782 for grants to individuals.

Purpose and activities: The foundation connects donors to community needs and opportunities, increases philanthropy and provides community leadership. Giving primarily for arts, education, health care, mental health/crisis services, health associations, housing/shelter development, human services, children and youth services, hospices, aging centers and services, civil rights, community development, voluntarism promotion, federated giving programs, disabled, aging, economically disadvantaged, and general charitable giving.

Fields of interest: Visual arts; Performing arts; Performing arts, theater; Arts; Education, early childhood education; Higher education; Education; Health care; Substance abuse, services; Mental health/crisis services; Health organizations, association; Housing/shelter, development; Youth development; Children/youth, services; Child development, services; Residential/custodial care, hospices; Aging, centers/services; Human services; Civil rights; Economic development; Community development; Voluntarism promotion; Federated giving programs; Aging; Disabilities, people with; Men; Economically disadvantaged.

Type of support: Scholarships—to individuals; General/operating support; Continuing support; Annual campaigns; Capital campaigns; Equipment; Endowments; Debt reduction; Program development; Conferences/seminars; Seed money; Curriculum development; Scholarship funds; Technical assistance; Matching/challenge support.

Limitations: Giving primarily in Reno County, KS. No grants to individuals (except for scholarships).

Publications: Application guidelines; Annual report; Financial statement; Grants list; Informational brochure; Newsletter; Occasional report; Program policy statement.

Application information: Grant Proposal Application may be requested by e-mailing the foundation, but completed proposals must be submitted in hard copy. Application form required.
Initial approach: E-mail foundation for grant application form
Copies of proposal: 15
Deadline(s): Aug. 15
Board meeting date(s): Every other month

Officers and Directors:* Richard A. Manka,* Chair.; Aubrey Abbott Patterson, Pres. and Exec. Dir.; Terri L. Eisiminger,* V.P., Admin. and Secy.; Paul W. Dillon,* Treas.; Dave Claxton; Mark Coberly; Concha Duarte; Terry B. Edwards; Gerald L. Green; Skip Johnson; Bryana Kelley; Dave Kerr; Patricia Lemmon; William "Buck" Lyle; Marla J. McKee; Darla M. Neal; Barbara Nunns; John B. Swearer; John L. Withrow; Donna S. Zwick.

Number of staff: 3 full-time professional; 1 part-time support.

EIN: 481076910

3369
INTRUST Bank Charitable Trust

(formerly First National Bank in Wichita Charitable Trust)
c/o INTRUST Bank, N.A.
P.O. Box 1
Wichita, KS 67201 (316) 383-1489
Contact: Diane Iseman, V.P.

Established in 1952 in KS.
Donor: INTRUST Bank, N.A.
Foundation type: Company-sponsored foundation.
Financial data (yr. ended 12/31/03): Assets, $2,971 (M); gifts received, $360,000; expenditures, $405,696; qualifying distributions, $405,096; giving activities include $405,096 for 25 grants (high: $147,207; low: $250).
Purpose and activities: The foundation supports organizations involved with arts and culture, higher education, and human services.
Fields of interest: Arts; Higher education; Children/youth, services; Human services; Federated giving programs.
Type of support: General/operating support; Building/renovation.
Limitations: Giving limited to KS, with emphasis on Wichita.
Application information: Application form not required.
Initial approach: Proposal
Deadline(s): None

Trustees: Charles Q. Chandler; Charles Q. Chandler IV; J.V. Lentell; Rodney D. Pitts; Gary E. Proffitt; Susan Sullivan; Lyndon Wells.
EIN: 486102412
Selected grants: The following grants were reported in 2004.
$162,728 to United Way of the Plains, Wichita, KS.
$50,000 to Exploration Place, Wichita, KS.
$30,000 to Wichita State University Foundation, Wichita, KS.
$20,000 to Big BrothersBig Sisters, Kansas, Wichita, KS.
$10,000 to Girl Scouts of the U.S.A..
$10,000 to Heartspring, Wichita, KS.
$10,000 to YMCA of El Dorado, El Dorado, KS.
$6,000 to Lawrence Arts Center, Lawrence, KS.
$5,000 to Old Cowtown Museum, Wichita, KS.
$3,272 to United Way of El Dorado, El Dorado, KS.

3370
Walter S. and Evan C. Jones Foundation

(also known as Jones Foundation, Inc.)
527 Commercial St., Rm. 501
Emporia, KS 66801-4081
Contact: Sharon L. Tidwell, Exec. Dir.
FAX: (620) 342-4701; E-mail: dir@jonesfdn.org;
URL: http://www.jonesfdn.org

Established in 1974 in KS.
Donor: Walter S. and Evan C. Jones Trust.
Foundation type: Independent foundation.
Financial data (yr. ended 6/30/06): Assets, $83,429 (M); gifts received, $916,000; expenditures, $1,003,931; qualifying distributions, $886,869; giving activities include $879,969 for 788 grants to individuals.
Purpose and activities: Grants awarded are limited to educational and medical expenses of children of 3 specified counties who have resided there continuously for a minimum of 1 year.
Fields of interest: Education; Health care; Children/youth, services; Economically disadvantaged.
Type of support: Grants to individuals; Scholarships—to individuals.
Limitations: Giving limited to children who have resided continuously for a minimum of one year in Osage, Coffey, or Lyon counties, KS.
Publications: Informational brochure; Program policy statement.
Application information: Applicants must contact office prior to submitting an application. Must be under 21 for medical grants. Medical services must be pre-approved generally, except in emergency cases. Copy of current federal income tax return (both personal and business, if applicable), a minimum of 1 month's pay stubs, proof of all other income, and a copy of insurance card (if applicable) are required with application. Application form required.
Initial approach: Telephone
Deadline(s): None
Board meeting date(s): Monthly
Final notification: 1-2 months

Officers: J. Stephen Jones, Pres.; Tom Thomas, V.P.; Max Stewart, Jr., Secy.; Arnold Graham, Treas.; Sharon L. Tidwell, Exec. Dir.
Trustees: Megan A. Evans; Jeff Larsen; Jeff Longbine.
Number of staff: 1 full-time professional; 1 full-time support; 1 part-time support.
EIN: 237384087

3371
Verla Nesbitt Joscelyn Foundation ✧

P.O. Box 975
Salina, KS 67402-0975 (785) 825-4674

Established in 1968 in KS.
Donor: Verla Nesbitt Joscelyn.
Foundation type: Independent foundation.
Financial data (yr. ended 12/31/05): Assets, $9,069,167 (M); expenditures, $560,566; qualifying distributions, $388,450; giving activities include $388,450 for 32 grants (high: $50,000; low: $1,000).
Fields of interest: Arts; Higher education; Human services; YM/YWCAs & YM/YWHAs; Children/youth, services; Foundations (community); Federated giving programs; Protestant agencies & churches.
Limitations: Applications not accepted. Giving primarily in Salina, KS. No grants to individuals.
Application information: Contributes only to pre-selected organizations.
Officers: L.L. McAninch, Pres.; Janice L. Doherty, V.P. and Secy.-Treas.; Thomas W. Poos.
EIN: 237067278
Selected grants: The following grants were reported in 2005.
$50,000 to Salina Community Theater, Salina, KS.
$25,000 to First Presbyterian Church, Hutchinson, KS.
$25,000 to Salina Education Foundation, Salina, KS.
$25,000 to United Way, Salina Area, Salina, KS.
$15,000 to Salina Art Center, Salina, KS.
$10,000 to Kansas State University Foundation, Manhattan, KS.
$10,000 to Salvation Army, Olathe, KS.
$7,000 to Bethany College, Lindsborg, KS.
$5,000 to Domestic Violence Association of Central Kansas, Salina, KS.
$5,000 to Kansas Childrens Service League, Wichita, KS.

3372
Kansas Health Foundation ▼ ✧

(formerly Kansas Health Foundation/Kansas Health Trust)
309 E. Douglas
Wichita, KS 67202-3405 (316) 262-7676
Contact: Nancy Claassen, Grants Mgr.
FAX: (316) 262-2044; E-mail: info@khf.org;
Additional tel.: (800) 373-7681; E-mail (for Nancy Claassen): nclaassen@khf.org; URL: http://www.kansashealth.org

Established in 1978 in KS as the Wesley Medical Endowment Foundation; converted from funds resulting from the sale of Wesley Medical Center to HCA in 1985; current name adopted in 1991.
Foundation type: Independent foundation.
Financial data (yr. ended 12/31/05): Assets, $484,119,001 (M); gifts received, $12,000; expenditures, $23,623,058; qualifying distributions, $19,893,000; giving activities include $18,000,070 for grants, and $845,584 for 4 foundation-administered programs.
Purpose and activities: To improve the health of all Kansans through strategic grantmaking. Funding areas include public health, children's health, leadership, and policy.
Fields of interest: Health care, public policy; Public health; Children/youth, services; Public policy, research; Leadership development.

Type of support: General/operating support; Program development; Technical assistance.
Limitations: Giving limited to KS. No grants to individuals.
Publications: Annual report; Annual report (including application guidelines); Newsletter; Occasional report.
Application information: Application forms required for Recognition Grants. Forms are available on foundation Web site. For all other grants, applicants should visit the Web site. Application form required.
  Initial approach: Application through Recognition Grant program
  Copies of proposal: 7
  Deadline(s): Mar. 15 and Sept. 15 for Recognition Grants
  Board meeting date(s): Quarterly
  Final notification: 60 days for Recognition Grants
Officers and Directors:* Kermit Wedel, M.D.*, Chair.; Andy Tompkins,* Vice-Chair.; Marni Vliet,* C.E.O. and Pres.; Evan Meyers, V.P. and C.F.O.; Mary K. Campuzano, V.P., Progs.; Steve Coen, V.P., Admin.; Kathy Lawless, Cont.; Rev. Cheryl Jefferson Bell; Shelly Buhler; William R. Docking; Ronald G. Holt; Timothy E. McKee; Hon. Deanell Reece Tacha.
Number of staff: 9 full-time professional; 16 full-time support; 1 part-time support.
EIN: 480873431
Selected grants: The following grants were reported in 2004.
$8,100,000 to Wichita Community Foundation, Wichita, KS. 2 grants: $5,100,000 (For endowment for Kansas Community Leadership Initiative sites to build and sustain leadership and children's health initiatives at community level), $3,000,000 (To regrant to other community Foundations).
$3,700,000 to Kansas Health Institute, Topeka, KS. 2 grants: $3,300,000 (To provide information to policymakers and other leaders in state to improve health of Kansans), $400,000 (To increase collaboration and training in field of public health informatics to enhance availability of public health data).
$629,483 to Wichita State University Foundation, Wichita, KS. To oversee the revision and launch of Let's Take It Outside media campaign to reinforce public's understanding of dangers of second-hand smoke.
$175,000 to Tobacco Free Kansas Coalition, Shawnee, KS. For statewide initiative that focuses on reducing youth use of tobacco.
$35,000 to Council on Foundations, DC. For membership.
$25,000 to Kansas Public Telecommunications Service, Wichita, KS. To produce nine-part monthly series on key health issues in Kansas.
$25,000 to United Way, Salina Area, Salina, KS. To build stronger, healthier, and more caring community.
$1,000 to Unified School District No. 480, Liberal, KS. For drug and alcohol-free school celebration.

3373

Helen and Sam Kaplan Charitable Foundation ✦ ☆

c/o R. Caspermeyer
9400 Mission Rd.
Overland Park, KS 66206

Established in 2000 in MO.
Foundation type: Operating foundation.

Financial data (yr. ended 12/31/05): Assets, $1,127,612 (M); expenditures, $390,944; qualifying distributions, $368,480; giving activities include $367,500 for 25 grants (high: $60,000; low: $1,000).
Purpose and activities: Giving primarily for education and Jewish organizations, and to a children's hospital.
Fields of interest: Arts; Higher education; Hospitals (general); Jewish federated giving programs; Jewish agencies & temples.
Limitations: Applications not accepted. No grants to individuals.
Application information: Contributes only to pre-selected organizations.
Trustee: Country Club Bank.
Manager: Paragon Capital Mgmt.
EIN: 431862067

3374

The Fred C. and Mary R. Koch Foundation, Inc. ✦

(formerly The Fred C. Koch Foundation)
P.O. Box 2256
Wichita, KS 67201-2256 (316) 828-2646
Contact: Roger Ramseyer, V.P.
E-mail: ramseyer@kochind.com

Incorporated in 1953 in KS.
Donors: Fred C. Koch†; Mary R. Koch†; Koch Industries, Inc.
Foundation type: Independent foundation.
Financial data (yr. ended 12/31/03): Assets, $24,908,437 (M); gifts received, $570,000; expenditures, $1,230,075; qualifying distributions, $1,199,559; giving activities include $990,803 for 30 grants (high: $300,000; low: $1,000; average: $2,500–$10,000), and $109,000 for 109 grants to individuals (high: $1,000; low: $1,000).
Purpose and activities: Grants for the arts and art education, environmental stewardship, human services, and education in KS.
Fields of interest: Arts; Education.
Type of support: General/operating support; Continuing support; Program development; Scholarship funds; Research; Employee-related scholarships.
Limitations: Giving primarily in KS. No grants to individuals (except for dependents of Koch Industries employees).
Application information: Application required for scholarships. Application form not required.
  Initial approach: Letter for grants; scholarship applicants should send for guidelines
  Copies of proposal: 1
  Deadline(s): Submit proposal preferably in Feb. (Mar. 1 deadline for scholarship)
  Board meeting date(s): Mar.
Officers and Directors:* Elizabeth B. Koch,* Pres.; Roger Ramseyer,* V.P.; Tye Darland,* Secy.; Vonda Holliman, Treas.; Richard Fink; Charles G. Koch; David H. Koch; Michael Morgan.
EIN: 486113560
Selected grants: The following grants were reported in 2004.
$440,000 to Claude R. Lambe Charitable Foundation, DC. For educational grant programs.
$300,000 to Youth Entrepreneurs of Kansas, Wichita, KS. For program support.
$100,000 to University of Kansas, Center for Applied Economics, Lawrence, KS. For Kansas Model State Initiative.

$100,000 to Wichita Symphony Society, Wichita, KS. For Wichita Youth Symphony.
$75,000 to Wichita Childrens Home, Wichita, KS. For independent living program.
$20,000 to Kansas Council on Economic Education, Wichita, KS. For K-12 economic education programming.
$13,000 to Wichita Center for the Arts, Wichita, KS. For Ken Burns lecture on Frank Lloyd Wright.

3375

Harry J. Lloyd Charitable Trust

(formerly Share Foundation)
7200 W. 132nd St., Ste. 190
Overland Park, KS 66213 (913) 851-2174
Contact: Russell Brown, Pres.
E-mail: Ltrust@Ltrust.org

Established in 1965 in MO.
Donors: House of Lloyd, Inc.; Harry J. Lloyd†.
Foundation type: Independent foundation.
Financial data (yr. ended 12/31/04): Assets, $135,111,716 (M); expenditures, $11,092,167; qualifying distributions, $10,389,613; giving activities include $9,499,824 for grants.
Purpose and activities: The foundation concentrates its support on projects that have a spiritual dimension, with special attention given to evangelical work, especially in the foreign mission field. Interest also in human services and educational organizations that are Christian-based.
Fields of interest: Christian agencies & churches.
International interests: Africa; China; India; Latin America; Middle East.
Type of support: Program development; Seed money.
Application information: Application form not required.
  Initial approach: Proposal
  Copies of proposal: 1
  Deadline(s): Contact foundation for deadlines
  Board meeting date(s): Quarterly
Officer and Trustees:* Russell Brown,* Pres.; Janet Ashcroft; G. Richard Hastings; Jami Kay; Demi Lloyd; Jeanette Lloyd; Timothy J. Oxley.
Number of staff: 6 full-time support.
EIN: 436689416

3376

Don C. and Florence M. McCune Foundation ✦ ☆

P.O. Box 198
Salina, KS 67402-0198
Application address: c/o Sidney A. Reitz, 119 W. Iron Ave., United Bldg., 10th Fl., Salina, KS 67401-2600, tel.: (785) 827-7251

Established in 1995 in KS.
Donor: Florence M. McCune.
Foundation type: Independent foundation.
Financial data (yr. ended 6/30/06): Assets, $12,270,207 (M); expenditures, $490,109; qualifying distributions, $430,600; giving activities include $414,850 for 9 grants (high: $250,000; low: $1,000).
Purpose and activities: Giving primarily for higher education, and to Presbyterian churches and orgnanizations; some funding for the arts.
Fields of interest: Arts; Higher education; Protestant agencies & churches.

Limitations: Giving primarily in Salina, KS. No grants to individuals.
Application information: Application form not required.
Deadline(s): None
Trustees: Gerald L. Hunter; Sidney A. Reitz; Susan N. Reitz.
EIN: 481164218

3377
The Morgan Family Foundation ◇
P.O. Box 129
Shawnee Mission, KS   66201   (913) 831-2996
Contact: Mark A. Morgan, Pres.

Incorporated in 1985 in MO.
Donors: Frank Morgan; Frank Morgan Trust; Frank Morgan Charitable Lead Annuity Trust; Frank Morgan Charitable Lead Unitrust.
Foundation type: Independent foundation.
Financial data (yr. ended 11/30/04): Assets, $33,174,204 (M); gifts received, $2,525,714; expenditures, $1,546,947; qualifying distributions, $1,325,340; giving activities include $1,325,340 for 105 grants (high: $360,000; low: $340).
Purpose and activities: Giving primarily to Jewish and health organizations as well as for health and human services.
Fields of interest: Health care; Health organizations, association; Human services; Foundations (community); Jewish federated giving programs; Jewish agencies & temples.
Limitations: Giving primarily in Overland Park, KS and Kansas City, MO. No grants to individuals.
Application information:
Initial approach: Letter
Deadline(s): Nov. 30 for next fiscal year
Officers and Directors:* Mark A. Morgan,* Pres.; Marilyn J. Morgan,* V.P.; Thomas S. Morgan,* V.P.; Todd D. Morgan,* Secy.; Michael B. Morgan,* Treas.
EIN: 481024615
Selected grants: The following grants were reported in 2004.
$360,000 to United Methodist Church of the Resurrection, Leawood, KS.
$60,000 to Jewish Federation of Greater Kansas City, Overland Park, KS.
$50,000 to Jewish Community Center of Greater Kansas City, Overland Park, KS.
$50,000 to Ronald McDonald House Charities, Oak Brook, IL.
$41,500 to Childrens Place, Kansas City, MO.
$30,000 to Barstow School, Kansas City, MO.
$30,000 to Turning Point: The Center for Hope and Healing, Kansas City, MO.
$27,000 to National Council on Alcoholism and Drug Dependence, Kansas City, MO.
$25,000 to Synergy Services, Parkville, MO.
$25,000 to Vanderbilt University, Nashville, TN.

3378
Mark and Bette Morris Family Foundation
140 Fairlawn Rd.
Topeka, KS   66606
Contact: Mark L. Morris, Jr., Pres.
Additional address: 5500 S.W. 7th St., Topeka, KS 66606

Established in 1989 in KS.
Donors: Mark L. Morris, Jr.; Bette M. Morris.

Foundation type: Independent foundation.
Financial data (yr. ended 12/31/05): Assets, $24,801,057 (M); gifts received, $2,284,199; expenditures, $1,577,489; qualifying distributions, $1,111,445; giving activities include $1,111,445 for 14 grants (high: $353,845; low: $3,000).
Purpose and activities: Support only to pre-selected organizations that encourage the healthy development and well-being of persons and animals, and that are personally known by the donors.
Fields of interest: Performing arts, theater; Higher education; Theological school/education; Animal welfare; Children/youth, services; Federated giving programs; Protestant agencies & churches.
Limitations: Applications not accepted. Giving primarily in KS; some funding nationally, particularly in CO and MO. No grants to individuals.
Application information: Contributes only to pre-selected organizations that are personally known by the donors. Unsolicited requests for funds not considered.
Officers: Mark L. Morris, Jr., Pres. and Treas.; Bette M. Morris, V.P. and Secy.
EIN: 481077121
Selected grants: The following grants were reported in 2005.
$353,845 to Morris Animal Foundation, Englewood, CO.
$201,000 to Kansas Masonic Foundation, Topeka, KS.
$110,000 to Saint Paul School of Theology, Kansas City, MO.
$75,000 to University of Michigan, Ann Arbor, MI.
$53,600 to Topeka Civic Theater, Topeka, KS.
$27,000 to Kansas University Endowment Association, Lawrence, KS.
$5,000 to Auburn University Foundation, Auburn, AL.
$5,000 to Starlight Theater, Kansas City, MO.
$3,000 to Family Service and Guidance Center of Topeka, Topeka, KS.

3379
Muchnic Foundation ◇
704 N. 4th St.
P.O. Box 329
Atchison, KS   66002
Additional address: c/o David C. Mize, Secy., 104 S. Cascade Ave., Ste. 202, Colorado Springs, CO 80903

Trust established in 1946 in KS.
Donors: Valley Co., Inc.; Helen Q. Muchnic†; H.E. Muchnic†.
Foundation type: Independent foundation.
Financial data (yr. ended 11/30/05): Assets, $9,034,560 (M); expenditures, $470,712; qualifying distributions, $457,447; giving activities include $391,000 for 54 grants (high: $50,000; low: $1,000).
Purpose and activities: Giving primarily for higher education and cultural programs, including museums, and civic affairs; support also for health associations and medical research.
Fields of interest: Museums; Arts; Higher education; Health organizations, association; Medical research, institute.
Limitations: Giving on a national basis. No grants to individuals.
Application information: Large brochures are not helpful. Application form not required.
Initial approach: Letter

Deadline(s): Oct. 31
Board meeting date(s): As required
Officer: David C. Mize, Secy.
Directors: Ann Mize; Daphne Nan Muchnic.
Trustee: Elizabeth M. Elicker.
Number of staff: 1
EIN: 486102818
Selected grants: The following grants were reported in 2004.
$50,000 to Atchison Art Association, Atchison, KS. 2 grants: $35,000, $15,000
$35,000 to Kansas University Endowment Association, Lawrence, KS.
$20,000 to Saint Francis Academy, Salina, KS.
$15,000 to Benedictine College, Atchison, KS.
$10,000 to Cystic Fibrosis Foundation, Colorado Springs, CO.
$10,000 to Susan G. Komen Breast Cancer Foundation, Dallas, TX.
$5,000 to Academy of the Arts, Easton, MD.
$5,000 to Drexel University, Philadelphia, PA.
$5,000 to John F. Kennedy Center for the Performing Arts, DC.

3380
Payless ShoeSource Foundation ◇
3231 S.E. 6th Ave.
Topeka, KS   66607
Contact: Michael Morant
URL: http://63.240.117.243/en-US/Corporate/Foundation/Foundation.htm

Established in 1998 in KS and MO.
Donor: Payless ShoeSource, Inc.
Foundation type: Company-sponsored foundation.
Financial data (yr. ended 1/29/05): Assets, $1,027,310 (M); gifts received, $527,000; expenditures, $499,465; qualifying distributions, $495,898; giving activities include $488,765 for 184 grants (high: $30,500; low: $100).
Purpose and activities: The foundation supports organizations involved with arts and culture, education, health, and human services.
Fields of interest: Arts; Education; Health care; Human services; Federated giving programs.
Type of support: Annual campaigns; Scholarship funds; Sponsorships; General/operating support; Continuing support; Capital campaigns; Building/renovation; Program development; Conferences/seminars.
Limitations: Giving primarily in areas of company operations. No support for religious or political organizations; generally, no support for United Way member agencies. No grants to individuals.
Application information: Application form not required.
Initial approach: Proposal
Deadline(s): 60 days prior to need
Board meeting date(s): Quarterly
Final notification: 1 month following review
Officers and Directors:* Jay A. Lentz,* Pres.; Michael J. Massey,* V.P. and Secy.; Ullrich E. Porzig,* V.P. and Treas.; Steven J. Douglass, V.P.
EIN: 481196508
Selected grants: The following grants were reported in 2005.
$91,500 to United Way of Greater Topeka, Topeka, KS. 3 grants: $30,500 each
$30,000 to Kansas State University Foundation, Manhattan, KS.
$26,500 to Kansas University Endowment Association, Lawrence, KS.
$10,000 to Salvation Army, Olathe, KS.

$10,000 to Topeka Performing Arts Center, Topeka, KS.

$5,000 to Topeka Civic Theater, Topeka, KS.

$2,500 to Pittsburg State University Foundation, Pittsburg, KS.

$1,000 to UFA Widows and Childrens Fund, New York, NY.

3381
The Powell Family Foundation ✧
4350 Shawnee Mission Pkwy., Ste. 280
Fairway, KS 66205
Contact: Carrie Hoelscher, Secy. to the Board of Trustees

Established in 1969 in MO.
Donor: George E. Powell, Sr.†.
Foundation type: Independent foundation.
Financial data (yr. ended 12/31/05): Assets, $21,881,275 (M); expenditures, $1,774,614; qualifying distributions, $1,537,337; giving activities include $1,467,000 for 4 grants (high: $1,450,000; low: $1,500).
Purpose and activities: Grants for education, civic affairs, and youth agencies.
Fields of interest: Education; Youth, services; Community development, neighborhood development.
Type of support: General/operating support; Continuing support; Annual campaigns; Capital campaigns.
Limitations: Giving primarily in Kansas City, MO. No support for the arts, organizations in the medical field, social welfare, or organizations outside the continental U.S. No grants to individuals, or for endowment or building funds.
Publications: Application guidelines.
Application information: Application form not required.
Initial approach: Letter (no more than 2 pages)
Copies of proposal: 2
Deadline(s): 30 days preceding board meeting
Board meeting date(s): Usually in Fall
Final notification: 60 days
Officers and Trustees:* George E. Powell, Jr.,* Pres.; Nicholas K. Powell,* V.P.; Barbara Powell Allen,* Secy.; George E. Powell III,* Treas.
Number of staff: 2 part-time support.
EIN: 237023968

3382
Pritchett Foundation ✧
c/o United Bank & Trust
P.O. Box 709
Pittsburg, KS 66762-0709
Application address: c/o Julie Plank or Ken Webb, Gold Trust Co., 417 N. Broadway, Pittsburg, KS 66762, tel.: (620) 231-2000; FAX: (620) 231-3974

Established in 1994 in KS.
Donor: First State Bank & Trust.
Foundation type: Independent foundation.
Financial data (yr. ended 5/31/05): Assets, $8,175,271 (M); expenditures, $511,152; qualifying distributions, $430,965; giving activities include $423,971 for 31 grants (high: $95,300; low: $500).
Purpose and activities: The foundation's mission is to improve the quality of life in Pittsburg and Crawford County, KS, by strengthening children,

youth, and families, and by supporting projects that serve these populations.
Fields of interest: Arts; Education; Children/youth, services; Youth, services; Family services; Foundations (community).
Limitations: Giving limited to Crawford County and Pittsburg, KS. No grants to individuals.
Application information:
Initial approach: 1-page letter
Deadline(s): Dec. 31
Final notification: End of Feb.
Trustee: United Bank & Trust.
EIN: 481210113
Selected grants: The following grants were reported in 2003.
$97,000 to Pittsburg State University Foundation, Pittsburg, KS. 3 grants: $40,000 (For Veterans Memorial Amphitheater), $50,000 (For scholarships), $7,000 (For Young Authors Conference).
$50,800 to Unified School District No. 250, Pittsburg, KS. 3 grants: $6,000 to Pittsburg High School (For transportation for marching band), $25,000 (For ball park renovations), $19,800 (For Summer Learning program).
$25,000 to Pittsburg, City of, Pittsburg, KS. For playground equipment.
$20,000 to Pittsburg Community Foundation, Pittsburg, KS. For Immigrant Park Pavilion.
$7,500 to Boy Scouts of America, Ozark Trails Council, Joplin, MO.
$3,000 to Girard Public Library, Girard, KS. To purchase audio books.

3383
Elmer C. Rhoden Charitable Foundation ✧
3965 W. 83rd St., Ste. 350
Prairie Village, KS 66208-5308

Established in 1986 in MO and KS.
Foundation type: Independent foundation.
Financial data (yr. ended 7/31/05): Assets, $11,240,570 (M); expenditures, $494,126; qualifying distributions, $458,914; giving activities include $455,000 for 11 grants (high: $100,000; low: $10,000).
Purpose and activities: Giving primarily for higher education, children, youth and social services, and to a Presbyterian church.
Fields of interest: Higher education; Social work school/education; Education; Health organizations, association; Housing/shelter, development; Human services; Children/youth, services; Protestant agencies & churches.
Type of support: General/operating support; Building/renovation; Equipment; Program development; Conferences/seminars.
Limitations: Applications not accepted. Giving primarily in the bi-state metropolitan Kansas City area. No grants to individuals.
Application information: Contributes only to pre-selected organizations. Unsolicited requests for funds not considered.
Directors: Lois D. Lacy; Janet E. Rhoden Longenecker; Marilyn A. Rhoden.
EIN: 431337876

3384
Ethel and Raymond F. Rice Foundation
1617 St. Andrews Dr., No. 200A
Lawrence, KS 66047 (785) 841-9961
Contact: James W. Paddock, Pres.

Established about 1972.
Foundation type: Independent foundation.
Financial data (yr. ended 12/31/05): Assets, $14,272,755 (M); expenditures, $720,703; qualifying distributions, $790,778; giving activities include $605,000 for 32 grants (high: $176,000; low: $1,000).
Purpose and activities: Giving primarily for education and human services.
Fields of interest: Arts; Higher education; Human services; Children/youth, services.
Type of support: General/operating support; Capital campaigns; Building/renovation; Equipment; Scholarship funds; Research.
Limitations: Giving primarily in the Douglas County, KS, area. No grants to individuals, or for pledges for future support.
Publications: Annual report; Informational brochure (including application guidelines).
Application information: Grants are made in Dec. Application form required.
Initial approach: Letter
Copies of proposal: 1
Deadline(s): Sept. 1
Board meeting date(s): Quarterly
Officers and Trustees:* James W. Paddock,* Pres.; Joseph Kelly,* V.P.; Robert C. Johnson,* Secy.; Peter Curran,* Treas.
Number of staff: 1 part-time professional; 1 part-time support.
EIN: 237156608

3385
Rudd Foundation ✧
(formerly LGR Charitable Trust)
c/o LRCIO
P.O. Box 968
Wichita, KS 67201

Established in 1994 in NV.
Donor: Leslie G. Rudd.
Foundation type: Independent foundation.
Financial data (yr. ended 12/31/05): Assets, $11,914,242 (M); expenditures, $1,958,350; qualifying distributions, $1,620,362; giving activities include $1,619,675 for 36 grants (high: $1,500,000; low: $35).
Purpose and activities: Giving primarily for higher education; some funding also for the arts, and to children, youth, and families, and for social services.
Fields of interest: Performing arts; Elementary/secondary education; Higher education; Animal welfare; Hospitals (general); Human services; Children/youth, services; Jewish agencies & temples; Economically disadvantaged.
Type of support: Scholarship funds; Research.
Limitations: Applications not accepted. Giving primarily in CA, with emphasis on Napa, and Wichita, KS; some funding nationally. No grants to individuals.
Application information: Contributes only to pre-selected organizations.
Board meeting date(s): May 15
Trustee: Leslie G. Rudd.
EIN: 886059216
Selected grants: The following grants were reported in 2004.

$50,000 to Jerusalem Fund, DC.

$25,500 to Culinary Institute of America, Hyde Park, NY.

$10,000 to Jewish Federation of Greater Dallas, Dallas, TX.

$5,000 to American Red Cross.

$3,500 to Savannah College of Art and Design, Savannah, GA.

$1,000 to Furth Family Foundation, Healdsburg, CA.

$500 to Jewish Federation of Greater Long Beach and West Orange County, Long Beach, CA.

$100 to Hospice of Napa Valley, Napa, CA.

3386
Sabatini Family Foundation ✧
120 S.W. 6th St.
Topeka, KS 66603-3806 (785) 274-5761

Established in 1985 in KS.
Donors: Frank C. Sabatini; Alice C. Sabatini; Capital City Bankshares, Inc.; Frank C. Sabatini Cos., Inc.
Foundation type: Independent foundation.
Financial data (yr. ended 3/31/04): Assets, $1,991,922 (M); gifts received, $45,287; expenditures, $375,382; qualifying distributions, $372,285; giving activities include $373,956 for grants.
Purpose and activities: Giving for education, art and culture, and youth services.
Fields of interest: Elementary/secondary education; Higher education; Human services; Children/youth, services; Christian agencies & churches.
Type of support: Building/renovation; Endowments; Program development; Research; Scholarships—to individuals.
Limitations: Giving primarily in Topeka, KS.
Application information: Scholarship applications should be addressed to school. Others should go to the foundation. Application form not required.
Initial approach: Letter
Deadline(s): None
Trustee: Frank C. Sabatini.
EIN: 480966619

3387
Greater Salina Community Foundation
157 S. 7th St. (7th & Walnut)
P.O. Box 2876
Salina, KS 67402-2876 (785) 823-1800
E-mail: communityfoundation@gscf.org;
URL: http://www.gscf.org

Established in 1999 in KS.
Foundation type: Community foundation.
Financial data (yr. ended 6/30/06): Assets, $34,146,528 (M); gifts received, $18,390,304; expenditures, $1,234,456; giving activities include $1,024,740 for 340 grants.
Purpose and activities: The foundation seeks to enhance quality of life, both today and in the future, by enabling donors to fulfill their charitable desires, building a permanent endowment, facilitating prudent management and care of funds, and meeting needs through grants, awards, and scholarships.
Fields of interest: Visual arts; Performing arts; Arts; Scholarships/financial aid; Education; Environment; Health care; Employment, training; Human services.
Type of support: General/operating support; Management development/capacity building;

Capital campaigns; Equipment; Endowments; Emergency funds; Program development; Conferences/seminars; Publication; Seed money; Scholarship funds; Grants to individuals; Scholarships—to individuals.
Limitations: Giving primarily in Saline County, KS, and the surrounding area. No grants for operating deficits or retirement of debt.
Publications: Annual report; Financial statement; Newsletter.
Application information: Visit foundation Web site for application forms and additional guidelines per grant type. Contact the foundation for specific deadlines for the Fund for Salina County grants. Application form required.
Initial approach: Submit application form
Copies of proposal: 14
Deadline(s): Dec./Jan. and June/July for the Fund for Salina County grants; none for others
Board meeting date(s): Bi-monthly
Final notification: Spring and fall for Fund for Salina Co. grants
Officers and Directors:* Sid Reitz,* Chair.; Steve Ryan,* Vice-Chair.; Betsy Wearing,* Pres. and Exec. Dir.; Jim Trower,* Secy.-Treas.; Jim Allen; Jane Alsop; Kim Brown; Connie Burket; Tom Dill; John Divine; Roberto Garcia; Amanda Gutierrez; Gary Hunter; Stephanie Klingzel-Carlin; Corlene Lang; Margaret Logan; Brenda McDaniel; Ken Miller; John Mize; Betsy Scholten; Kristin Maxwell Seaton; Brenda R. Smith; Sydney Soderberg; Connie Stevens.
Number of staff: 1 full-time professional; 2 part-time professional; 2 part-time support.
EIN: 481215503

3388
The Schowalter Foundation, Inc. ✧
900 N. Poplar, Ste. 200
Newton, KS 67114
Contact: Willis Harder, Pres.

Incorporated in 1953 in KS.
Donor: J.A. Schowalter†.
Foundation type: Independent foundation.
Financial data (yr. ended 12/31/05): Assets, $12,582,367 (M); expenditures, $793,783; qualifying distributions, $558,312; giving activities include $516,525 for 69 grants (high: $30,000; low: $250).
Purpose and activities: To assist retired ministers and missionaries, and theological seminaries and church-related schools (including scholarships); grants also for peace and international cooperation, and for technical assistance abroad, and other activities of the 3 Mennonite denominations related to the foundation.
Fields of interest: Education; Christian agencies & churches.
Limitations: Applications not accepted. Giving limited to the Midwest. No grants to individuals, or for endowment funds, fellowships, operating budgets, travel, or matching gifts; no loans.
Application information: Unsolicited requests for funds not accepted.
Officer: Willis Harder, Pres.
EIN: 480623544
Selected grants: The following grants were reported in 2004.
$30,000 to Bethel College, North Newton, KS.
$30,000 to Bluffton College, Bluffton, OH.
$30,000 to Goshen College, Goshen, IN.

$30,000 to Hesston College, Hesston, KS. 3 grants: $8,000, $10,000, $12,000
$13,500 to Mennonite Central Committee, Akron, PA. 3 grants: $3,500, $5,000, $5,000
$10,000 to Health Ministries of Harvey County, Newton, KS.

3389
The Arthur E. & Cornelia C. Scroggins Foundation, Inc. ✧
P.O. Box 1112
Dodge City, KS 67801 (620) 662-5319

Established in 1983 in KS.
Foundation type: Independent foundation.
Financial data (yr. ended 12/31/04): Assets, $2,049,174 (M); gifts received, $1,000; expenditures, $706,829; qualifying distributions, $688,523; giving activities include $682,250 for 22 grants (high: $652,500; low: $500).
Purpose and activities: Giving for children's hospitals and services, human services, and education.
Fields of interest: Nursing school/education; Education; Health care; Health organizations, association; Human services; Children/youth, services.
Type of support: Scholarship funds.
Limitations: Giving primarily within Ford and Gray counties, KS. No support for veterans', labor, fraternal, or athletic organizations (except for specific projects that benefit the broad community). No grants to individuals, or for capital campaigns or fundraising events.
Application information: Application forms available from Fidelity State Bank & Trust Co. (Trust Dept.). Application form required.
Deadline(s): Dec. 31
Officers: Frank B. Mapel, Pres.; George Voss, V.P.; Sherry Maxwell, Secy.; Stanley D. Simpson, Treas. and Mgr.
Directors: Roderic Simpson; Marilynne VenJohn; Fidelity State Bank and Trust Co.
Number of staff: 1 part-time professional.
EIN: 480945437

3390
Security Benefit Life Insurance Company Charitable Trust ✧
c/o Security Benefit Corp.
1 Security Benefit Pl.
Topeka, KS 66636
Contact: Kris Robbins, Tr.

Established in 1976 in KS.
Donor: Security Benefit Life Insurance Co.
Foundation type: Company-sponsored foundation.
Financial data (yr. ended 12/31/04): Assets, $1,716,467 (M); gifts received, $1,010,612; expenditures, $526,541; qualifying distributions, $526,541; giving activities include $526,541 for 303 grants (high: $25,000; low: $25).
Purpose and activities: The foundation supports organizations involved with arts and culture, higher education, cancer, HIV/AIDS research, hunger, human services, women, economically disadvantaged people, and homeless people.
Fields of interest: Performing arts; Arts; Higher education; Cancer; AIDS research; Food services; Children/youth, services; Human services;

Voluntarism promotion; Women; Economically disadvantaged; Homeless.
Type of support: Continuing support; Annual campaigns; Capital campaigns; Equipment; Program-related investments/loans; Employee matching gifts.
Limitations: Giving limited to the Topeka, KS, area.
Application information: Application form not required.
  Initial approach: Proposal
  Copies of proposal: 1
  Deadline(s): None
Trustee: Kris A. Robbins.
EIN: 486211612

3391
Servant Foundation ▼ ✧
c/o Patricia A. Lloyd
P.O. Box 7127
Shawnee Mission, KS 66207
Contact: Patricia A. Lloyd, Pres.
E-mail: servantfound@aol.com; Application address: Shook, Hardy & Bacon, c/o Stan Weiner, 2555 Grand Blvd., Kansas City, MO 64108

Established in 1996 in KS.
Donor: Patricia A. Lloyd.
Foundation type: Independent foundation.
Financial data (yr. ended 12/31/05): Assets, $16,746 (M); expenditures, $5,861,500; qualifying distributions, $5,825,785; giving activities include $5,825,785 for 42 grants (high: $1,494,085; low: $100; average: $5,000–$250,000).
Purpose and activities: Giving primarily for Evangelical Christian agencies and churches.
Fields of interest: Christian agencies & churches.
International interests: China.
Type of support: Annual campaigns; Program development; Seed money; Matching/challenge support.
Limitations: Giving primarily in the Kansas City, MO, metropolitan area. No grants to individuals.
Application information:
  Initial approach: Letter
  Copies of proposal: 2
  Deadline(s): None
  Final notification: Usually within 2 months
Officers: Patricia A. Lloyd, Pres.; Jami Kay, V.P.; Stanley P. Weiner, Secy.; Demi Lloyd, Treas.
Number of staff: 1 part-time support.
EIN: 481189123
Selected grants: The following grants were reported in 2005.
$1,944,085 to Servant Christian Community Foundation, Olathe, KS. 2 grants: $450,000 (For operating support), $1,494,085 (For operating support).
$1,110,600 to Doulos Ministries, Littleton, CO. For Shelterwood, residential care facility for teenagers in crisis.
$700,000 to Westminster Academy, Overland Park, KS. 2 grants: $350,000 (For operating support), $350,000 (For education program).
$300,000 to Wings of Hope, Chesterfield, MO. For operating support.
$185,000 to Luis Palau Evangelistic Association, Portland, OR. 3 grants: $10,000 (For tsunami victims), $25,000 (For Next Generation Alliance), $150,000 (For operating support).
$31,000 to Hope House for Battered Women, Independence, MO. For Joe and Bethany Randa Foundation for operating support.

3392
The Ken and Jan Shannon Family Foundation ✧ ☆
820 N. Linden St.
Wichita, KS 67206-4002

Foundation type: Independent foundation.
Financial data (yr. ended 6/30/05): Assets, $28,746 (M); gifts received, $377,500; expenditures, $357,252; qualifying distributions, $357,250; giving activities include $357,250 for 20 grants (high: $300,000; low: $50).
Fields of interest: Human services; Community development; Christian agencies & churches.
Limitations: Applications not accepted. Giving primarily in Wichita, KS. No grants to individuals.
Application information: Contributes only to pre-selected organizations.
Officers and Directors:* Janet A. Shannon,* Pres.; Ken Shannon,* Secy.-Treas.; Kirsten Palmrose; David J. Shannon; Julie E. Shannon.
EIN: 200438918

3393
Kenneth L. & Eva S. Smith Foundation ✧
11000 King St., Ste. 200, Bldg. C
Overland Park, KS 66210
Contact: Thomas K. Jones, Tr.

Established in 1968 in KS.
Donors: Kenneth L. Smith†; Eva S. Smith†.
Foundation type: Independent foundation.
Financial data (yr. ended 12/31/05): Assets, $7,467,539 (M); gifts received, $16,502; expenditures, $551,353; qualifying distributions, $481,935; giving activities include $447,000 for 11 grants (high: $125,000; low: $1,000; average: $10,000–$25,000).
Purpose and activities: Giving primarily for health and human services.
Fields of interest: Hospitals (general); Residential/custodial care.
Type of support: Continuing support.
Limitations: Applications not accepted. Giving primarily in the greater Kansas City, MO, area. No grants to individuals.
Application information: Contributes only to pre-selected organizations.
Trustee: Thomas K. Jones.
EIN: 486142517
Selected grants: The following grants were reported in 2004.
$120,000 to Lakemary Center, Paola, KS.
$100,000 to Operation Breakthrough, Kansas City, MO.
$50,000 to Childrens Mercy Hospital, Kansas City, MO.
$10,000 to Saint Lukes Hospital Foundation, Kansas City, MO.

3394
Smoot Charitable Foundation ✧
P.O. Box 2567
Salina, KS 67402-2567 (785) 825-4674
Contact: Robert W. Weber M.D., Pres.

Established in 1976.
Foundation type: Independent foundation.
Financial data (yr. ended 6/30/05): Assets, $13,453,246 (M); expenditures, $856,924; qualifying distributions, $661,986; giving activities

include $657,094 for 36 grants (high: $328,844; low: $1,000).
Purpose and activities: Giving primarily for a YMCA; giving also for the arts, education, human services, and children and youth services.
Fields of interest: Arts; Higher education; Human services; YM/YWCAs & YM/YWHAs; Children/youth, services.
Limitations: Giving limited to Salina County, KS. No grants to individuals.
Application information: Application form not required.
  Initial approach: Letter
  Deadline(s): None
Officers: Robert W. Weber, M.D., Pres.; George W. Yarnevich, V.P.; Janice L. Doherty, Secy.; Tom A. Williamson, Treas.
Trustee: Thomas J. Kennedy.
EIN: 480851141
Selected grants: The following grants were reported in 2004.
$289,447 to YMCA, Salina Family, Salina, KS. For general support.
$90,000 to Kansas Wesleyan University, Salina, KS. For general support.
$54,000 to United Way, Salina Area, Salina, KS. For general support.
$30,000 to YWCA of Salina, Salina, KS. For general support.
$20,000 to Greater Salina Community Foundation, Salina, KS. For general support.
$15,000 to Salina Art Center, Salina, KS. For general support.
$5,000 to Occupational Center of Central Kansas, Salina, KS. For general support.
$3,000 to Salina Rescue Mission, Salina, KS. For general support.
$2,000 to Child Abuse Prevention Services, Salina, KS. For general support.
$2,000 to Salina Community Theater, Salina, KS. For general support.

3395
Sprint Foundation ▼ ✧
(formerly United Telecommunications Foundation)
6220 Sprint Pkwy.
Overland Park, KS 66251 (913) 762-3767
Contact: Ralph Reid, Secy. and Exec. Dir.
FAX: (913) 624-3490; Mailing address: P.O. Box 11315, Kansas City, MO 64112; E-mail for Sprint Achievement Prog.: education@sprint.com; URL: http://www.sprint.com/community/sprint_foundation

Established in 1989 in KS.
Donors: Sprint Corp.; Sprint Nextel Corp.; The United Telephone Co. of Pennsylvania.
Foundation type: Company-sponsored foundation.
Financial data (yr. ended 12/31/04): Assets, $10,121,843 (M); gifts received, $1,826,142; expenditures, $5,575,280; qualifying distributions, $5,444,815; giving activities include $5,444,815 for 1,551 grants (high: $700,217; low: $25).
Purpose and activities: The foundation supports organizations involved with arts and culture, K-12, business, and technology education, youth development, and civic affairs and awards grants to K-12 public school educators.
Fields of interest: Arts, equal rights; Visual arts; Museums; Performing arts; Performing arts, theater; Performing arts, orchestra (symphony); Arts; Elementary/secondary education; Business school/education; Youth development, adult & child

programs; Youth development, services; Youth development; Science, formal/general education; Public affairs; Youth; Minorities.

Type of support: General/operating support; Continuing support; Annual campaigns; Program development; Scholarship funds; Employee matching gifts; Grants to individuals.

Limitations: Giving primarily in Los Angeles and San Francisco, CA, Denver, CO, Washington, DC, Atlanta, GA, Chicago, IL, Kansas City, MO, New York, NY, and Dallas, TX; giving also to regional organizations active in areas of company operations and national organizations; giving limited to Cass, Clay, Jackson, and Platte counties, KS, and Johnson and Wyandotte counties, MO, for the Sprint Achievement Program. No support for discriminatory organizations, political organizations, private charities or foundations, religious organizations not of direct benefit to the entire community, international organizations, or school-affiliated teams, bands, or choirs. No grants to individuals (except for the Sprint Achievement Program), or for travel, film, music, television, video, or media production projects, school-affiliated events, marketing, sports, or event sponsorships, or scholarships; generally, no grants for endowments, capital campaigns, memorials, construction, or renovation projects.

Publications: Application guidelines; Annual report.

Application information: Application form required.
  Initial approach: Complete online application form
  Deadline(s): Jan. 2 to Nov. 30; Apr. 1 to Apr. 30 for Sprint Achievement Program
  Board meeting date(s): Quarterly
  Final notification: 90 days; June 1 to June 30 for Sprint Achievement Program

Officers and Directors:* Tom Murphy,* Chair. and Pres.; Ralph Reid,* Secy. and Exec. Dir.; John Garcia; Tom Gerke; Jim Kissinger; Denton Roberts; Steve Signoff; Kathy A. Walker.

EIN: 481062018

Selected grants: The following grants were reported in 2004.

$700,217 to United Way, Heart of America, Kansas City, MO.

$325,000 to Missouri Development Finance Board, Jefferson City, MO.

$200,000 to Nelson-Atkins Museum of Art, Kansas City, MO.

$162,620 to Park University, Parkville, MO.

$125,562 to American Red Cross, National Headquarters, DC.

$91,815 to Boy Scouts of America, Heart of America Council, Kansas City, MO.

$25,000 to Greater Kansas City Community Foundation, Kansas City, MO.

$25,000 to Urban League of Kansas City, Kansas City, MO.

$15,000 to Filmmakers Alliance, Los Angeles, CA.

$12,450 to Sacred Heart School, Shawnee, KS.

3396
Charles A. Sullivan Charitable Foundation ✧

(formerly Sullivan Charitable Foundation)
c/o Bank of Blue Valley
P.O. Box 26128
Overland Park, KS 66225-6128

Established in 1998 in MO.

Donors: Charles Sullivan; Jacqueline Sullivan.

Foundation type: Independent foundation.

Financial data (yr. ended 12/31/05): Assets, $8,762,528 (M); expenditures, $444,677; qualifying distributions, $410,293; giving activities include $377,585 for 26 grants (high: $84,000; low: $4,000).

Purpose and activities: Giving primarily to Roman Catholic churches, organizations, and schools.

Fields of interest: Education; Civil liberties, right to life; Roman Catholic agencies & churches.

Type of support: General/operating support; Capital campaigns; Endowments; Scholarship funds.

Limitations: Applications not accepted. Giving primarily in MO and OH. No grants to individuals.

Application information: Contributes only to pre-selected organizations.

Trustees: Charles Sullivan; Jacqueline Sullivan; Timothy Sullivan; Bank of Blue Valley; Country Club Trust Co.

EIN: 481196696

Selected grants: The following grants were reported in 2003.

$100,000 to Central Catholic High School, Toledo, OH. For general support.

$50,000 to Rider University, Lawrenceville, NJ. For scholarships and capital campaign.

$37,500 to Central City School Fund, Kansas City, MO. For scholarship.

$20,000 to Harvesters-The Community Food Network, Kansas City, MO. For general support.

$20,000 to Saint Martin de Porres Parish, Toledo, OH. For scholarships.

$10,000 to Bishop Sullivan Center, Kansas City, MO. For general support.

$10,000 to Catholic Charities of the Archdiocese of Kansas City Kansas, Kansas City, KS. For general support.

$10,000 to Moms House, Toledo, OH. For general support.

$10,000 to Mothers Choice - Refuge for the Pregnant and Unborn, Independence, MO. For general support.

$10,000 to Room at the Inn, Charlotte, NC. For general support.

3397
Sunderland Foundation ▼ ✧

(formerly Lester T. Sunderland Foundation)
11011 Cody St.
Overland Park, KS 66210 (913) 451-8900
Contact: Kent Sunderland, Pres.; James P. Sunderland, Secy.
E-mail: sunderlandfoundation@ashgrove.com;
URL: http://www.sunderlandfoundation.org

Incorporated in 1945 in MO.

Donors: Lester T. Sunderland†; Paul Sunderland†.

Foundation type: Independent foundation.

Financial data (yr. ended 12/31/05): Assets, $90,267,151 (M); expenditures, $4,536,323; qualifying distributions, $4,233,366; giving activities include $4,218,000 for 86 grants (high: $255,000; low: $2,000; average: $10,000–$200,000).

Purpose and activities: Emphasis on building funds for higher education; support also for youth agencies, hospitals, community funds and low income housing.

Fields of interest: Education, fund raising/fund distribution; Hospitals (general); Children/youth, services.

Type of support: General/operating support; Continuing support; Annual campaigns; Capital campaigns; Building/renovation; Equipment; Land acquisition; Endowments; Emergency funds.

Limitations: Giving primarily in AR, KS, MO, and NE. No grants to individuals or for scholarships; no loans.

Publications: Application guidelines; Program policy statement.

Application information: Application form not required.
  Initial approach: Letter
  Copies of proposal: 1
  Deadline(s): None
  Board meeting date(s): As required

Officers and Trustees:* Kent Sunderland,* Pres.; Charles Sunderland,* V.P.; James P. Sunderland,* Secy.; L.D. Sunderland; W.J. Sunderland.

Number of staff: 1 part-time support.

EIN: 446011082

Selected grants: The following grants were reported in 2005.

$255,000 to Johnson County Community College Foundation, Overland Park, KS. For general support.

$200,000 to Habitat for Humanity of Kaw Valley, Kansas City, KS. For general support.

$200,000 to Nelson Gallery Foundation, Kansas City, MO. For general support.

$200,000 to Saint Lukes Hospital Foundation, Kansas City, MO. For general support.

$125,000 to Liberty Memorial Association, Kansas City, MO. To construct Glass Bridge.

$60,000 to Bishop Spencer Place, Kansas City, MO. For capital campaign.

$40,000 to Bethel College, North Newton, KS. For general support.

$25,000 to Ronald McDonald House Charities of the Heart of America, Kansas City, MO. For general support.

$25,000 to Stormont-Vail Foundation, Topeka, KS. For general support.

$20,000 to Habitat for Humanity of Omaha, Omaha, NE. For general support.

3398
SYZYGY Foundation, Inc. ✧

5420 W. 61st Pl.
P.O. Box 918
Shawnee Mission, KS 66201

Established in 2001 in KS.

Donors: John C. Kornitzer; Jamie Lee Curtis Guest; Christopher Guest.

Foundation type: Independent foundation.

Financial data (yr. ended 12/31/04): Assets, $1,073,751 (M); gifts received, $1,004,464; expenditures, $1,062,913; qualifying distributions, $1,060,125; giving activities include $1,060,125 for 16 grants (high: $1,005,000; low: $1,000).

Fields of interest: Museums (history); Elementary/secondary education; Health organizations, association; Human services.

Limitations: Applications not accepted. Giving primarily in CA. No grants to individuals.

Application information: Contributes only to pre-selected organizations.

Officers: Jamie Lee Curtis Guest, Pres.; Christopher Guest, Secy.

EIN: 481250583

3399

Daniel J. Taylor Family Charitable Foundation ✧

1938 N. Woodlawn, Ste. 400
Wichita, KS 67208-1875

Established in 1998 in KS.
Donor: Daniel J. Taylor.
Foundation type: Independent foundation.
Financial data (yr. ended 12/31/05): Assets, $663,914 (M); expenditures, $333,020; qualifying distributions, $330,750; giving activities include $330,750 for 37 grants (high: $152,500; low: $200).
Purpose and activities: Giving primarily for education and human services.
Fields of interest: Education; Health care; Human services.
Limitations: Applications not accepted. Giving primarily in KS. No grants to individuals.
Application information: Contributes only to pre-selected organizations.
Officers and Directors:* Daniel J. Taylor,* Pres.; Kathleen Baer Taylor,* Secy.-Treas.; Daniel J. Taylor, Jr.
EIN: 481203060
Selected grants: The following grants were reported in 2005.
$50,000 to Wichita Collegiate School, Wichita, KS.
$12,500 to Lords Diner, Wichita, KS.
$5,000 to First Christian Church, Olathe, KS.
$3,000 to Fundamental Learning Center, Wichita, KS.
$1,000 to American Red Cross, Wichita, KS.
$1,000 to Horizon United Methodist Center, Arkansas City, KS.
$1,000 to Kansas Childrens Service League, Wichita, KS.
$1,000 to Salvation Army, Olathe, KS.
$1,000 to Victory in the Valley, Wichita, KS.
$1,000 to Wichita Childrens Home, Wichita, KS.

3400

Topeka Community Foundation ✧

5431 S.W. 29th St., Ste. 300
Topeka, KS 66614 (785) 272-4804
Contact: Chandler Moenius, Pres.
FAX: (785) 273-2467;
E-mail: info@topekacommunityfoundation.org;
Additional E-mail:
moenius@topekacommunityfoundation.org;
URL: http://www.topekacommunityfoundation.org

Incorporated in 1983 in KS.
Foundation type: Community foundation.
Financial data (yr. ended 12/31/04): Assets, $21,608,934 (M); gifts received, $1,978,053; expenditures, $1,783,146; giving activities include $1,323,924 for grants.
Purpose and activities: Primary area of interest is the arts, including fine and performing arts; social services, including family services; and civic affairs.
Fields of interest: Performing arts; Arts; Education, early childhood education; Education; Environment, natural resources; Environment; Public health; Substance abuse, services; Children/youth, services; Family services; Homeless, human services; Human services; Community development; Government/public administration; Homeless.
Type of support: General/operating support; Continuing support; Annual campaigns; Capital

campaigns; Building/renovation; Emergency funds; Program development; Seed money; Scholarship funds; Employee matching gifts; Scholarships—to individuals; In-kind gifts; Matching/challenge support.
Limitations: Giving limited to Topeka and Shawnee County, KS. No support for religious organizations for religious purposes. No grants to individuals (directly), or for ongoing general operating expenses or existing deficits, endowments, or fundraising events.
Publications: Application guidelines; Annual report; Financial statement; Informational brochure; Informational brochure (including application guidelines); Newsletter.
Application information: Visit foundation Web site for application forms and attachments. Faxed or e-mailed applications are not accepted. Application form required.
  Initial approach: Submit application and attachments
  Copies of proposal: 17
  Deadline(s): Aug. 18 for Safety and Prevention grants
  Board meeting date(s): Bimonthly, last Thurs. of month
  Final notification: May for Safety and Prevention grants
Officers and Directors:* James Schmank,* Chair.; James Haines,* Vice-Chair.; Chandler Moenius,* Pres. and Exec. Dir.; Gregory S. Schwerdt,* Secy.; Duane Bond,* Treas.; Gay Bauersfeld; John Hutton; Linda Jeffery; Jim Maag; Blanche C. Parks; Brady Robb; Alicia Salisbury; Mark Synovec, M.D.; Stephen Tempero, M.D.; Jeff Ungerer.
Number of staff: 1 full-time professional.
EIN: 480972106

3401

Robert & Gwen Tyler Charitable Foundation ✧ ☆

2701 Cabrillo Dr.
Winfield, KS 67156-8789

Established in 2003 in KS.
Donors: Robert D. Tyler; Gwendolyn Tyler.
Foundation type: Independent foundation.
Financial data (yr. ended 12/31/05): Assets, $1,222,324 (M); gifts received, $630,095; expenditures, $686,222; qualifying distributions, $681,666; giving activities include $681,666 for 3 grants (high: $666,666; low: $5,000).
Fields of interest: Higher education; Human services.
Limitations: Applications not accepted. Giving primarily in KS. No grants to individuals.
Application information: Contributes only to pre-selected organizations.
Officers: Robert D. Tyler, Pres. and Co-Treas.; Gwendolyn A. Tyler, Secy. and Co-Treas.
EIN: 200489246

3402

V & H Charitable Foundation ✧

P.O. Box 26128
Overland Park, KS 66225

Established in 1990 in KS.
Donors: Helen Regnier; Ranch Mart, Inc.
Foundation type: Operating foundation.

Financial data (yr. ended 3/31/06): Assets, $11,996,667 (M); expenditures, $544,217; qualifying distributions, $490,426; giving activities include $490,426 for 15 grants (high: $255,000; low: $1,500).
Purpose and activities: Giving primarily for higher and other education, as well as for children, youth and social services, and for health associations.
Fields of interest: Elementary/secondary education; Higher education; Education; Health organizations, association; Human services; Salvation Army; Children/youth, services.
Limitations: Applications not accepted. Giving primarily in Kansas City, MO, and Overland Park, KS. No grants to individuals.
Application information: Contributes only to pre-selected organizations.
Trustees: Catherine M. Regnier; Robert B. Regnier; Victor A. Regnier.
EIN: 436378149

3403

Westar Energy Foundation ✧

(formerly Western Resources Foundation, Inc.)
818 Kansas Ave.
Topeka, KS 66612 (785) 575-1544
Contact: Cynthia McCarvel, Pres.

Established in 1991 in KS.
Donors: Western Resources, Inc.; Westar Energy, Inc.
Foundation type: Company-sponsored foundation.
Financial data (yr. ended 12/31/05): Assets, $124,225 (L); gifts received, $450,000; expenditures, $544,634; qualifying distributions, $541,441; giving activities include $541,401 for 312 grants (high: $80,000; low: $100).
Purpose and activities: The foundation supports organizations involved with early childhood development.
Fields of interest: Child development, education.
Type of support: Emergency funds; Seed money; Scholarship funds; Research; Employee matching gifts; In-kind gifts.
Limitations: Giving primarily in areas of company operations in KS. No grants to individuals.
Publications: Application guidelines; Financial statement; Informational brochure.
Application information: Application form required.
  Initial approach: Contact foundation for application form
  Copies of proposal: 1
  Deadline(s): 6 months prior to need
  Board meeting date(s): Quarterly
Officers: Cynthia McCarvel, Pres.; Greg Greenwood, V.P. and Treas.; Carlene Barkley, Secy.
Directors: Larry Irick; Jim Ludwig; Bill Moore; Caroline Williams.
Number of staff: 2 full-time professional; 1 full-time support.
EIN: 481099341

3404

Wichita Community Foundation ✧

(formerly Greater Wichita Community Foundation)
200 W. Douglas, Ste. 250
Wichita, KS 67202-3002 (316) 264-4880
Contact: James D. Moore, Exec. Dir.
FAX: (316) 264-7592; E-mail: wcf@wichitacf.org;
URL: http://www.wichitacf.org

Incorporated in 1986 in KS.
Foundation type: Community foundation.
Financial data (yr. ended 6/30/05): Assets, $39,153,577 (M); gifts received, $9,498,335; expenditures, $4,761,529; giving activities include $4,316,729 for grants.
Purpose and activities: The foundation was established to build charitable endowments and help donors create funds that reflect their charitable goals. It consists of numerous permanent funds in its endowment built by many thoughtful individuals, families, and companies who care about the Wichita region. Grants are made from endowment earnings to a wide variety of nonprofit organizations to enhance life in the community.
Fields of interest: Humanities; Arts; Education; Environment, natural resources; Environment; Health care; Human services.
Type of support: Scholarships—to individuals; Matching/challenge support.
Limitations: Giving limited to the greater Wichita, KS, area. No support for religious organizations for religious purposes. No grants to individuals (except for scholarships), or for building projects, endowments, fellowships, debt reduction, administrative overhead, or fundraising campaigns.
Publications: Application guidelines; Annual report; Financial statement; Informational brochure; Newsletter.
Application information: Visit foundation Web site for grant application Cover Sheet and guidelines. Application form required.
Initial approach: Telephone
Copies of proposal: 8
Deadline(s): Aug. 15 for Unrestricted grants
Board meeting date(s): Apr. 16 and Oct. 24
Officers and Directors:* Donald L. Cordes,* Chair.; Phillip R. Neff,* Vice-Chair.; Dr. Dennis L. Ross,

M.D.*, Secy.; Bill Lucas,* Treas.; James D. Moore, Exec. Dir.; Shirley Beggs; Daniel M. Carney; Linda Constable; Chris Goebel; Lou Heldman; Vernell Jackson; Tony Madrigal; Gayle Malone; Nancy E. Martin; Sharol Rasberry.
Number of staff: 1 full-time professional; 1 part-time professional; 1 full-time support.
EIN: 481022361

3405
K. T. Wiedemann Foundation, Inc. ✧
10 Saint James Pl.
Wichita, KS   67206
Address for letters of inquiry: 8710 Shadowridge Cir., Wichita, KS 67226

Incorporated in 1959 in KS.
Donor: K.T. Wiedemann Trust.
Foundation type: Independent foundation.
Financial data (yr. ended 2/28/05): Assets, $15,984,516 (M); expenditures, $1,213,428; qualifying distributions, $1,052,420; giving activities include $1,028,420 for 70 grants (high: $50,000; low: $300).
Purpose and activities: Giving primarily for the arts, health, at-risk children and youth, the elderly, low-income people, the mentally ill and physically challenged people. Churches or religious organizations applying for grants must receive multi-denominational support which must include support from Lutheran, Episcopalian, or Presbyterian churches.
Fields of interest: Museums; Performing arts; Education; Health care; Health organizations, association; Youth development, centers/clubs; Children/youth, services; Aging, centers/services.

Type of support: General/operating support; Capital campaigns; Emergency funds; Program development.
Limitations: Giving primarily in Butler and Sedgwick counties, KS, with emphasis on Wichita. No grants to individuals, or for endowment funds.
Publications: Application guidelines.
Application information: Application form required.
Initial approach: 2-page letter of inquiry
Copies of proposal: 3
Deadline(s): Prior to board meeting dates
Board meeting date(s): Apr. 15, Aug. 15, and Dec. 15
Final notification: Response to letter of inquiry within 1 month of board meeting
Officers and Trustees:* Douglas S. Pringle,* Pres.; Lynne A. Hankins,* V.P.; Bruce A. Pringle,* Secy.-Treas.
EIN: 486117541
Selected grants: The following grants were reported in 2004.
$80,300 to Girl Scouts of the U.S.A., Golden Plains Council, Wichita, KS.
$80,000 to YMCA of Wichita, Wichita, KS.
$40,000 to Boy Scouts of America, Quivira Council, Wichita, KS.
$35,000 to Inter-Faith Ministries Wichita, Wichita, KS.
$32,000 to American Red Cross, Midway-Kansas Chapter, Wichita, KS.
$30,000 to Nature Conservancy of Kansas, Topeka, KS.
$25,150 to Big BrothersBig Sisters, Kansas, Wichita, KS.
$25,000 to Butler County Community College, El Dorado, KS.
$25,000 to Child Guidance Center of Wichita, Wichita, KS.
$20,000 to Salvation Army of Wichita, Wichita, KS.

KENTUCKY

3406

Bavarian Foundation Trust ✧

12764 McCoy Fork Rd.
Walton, KY 41094
Contact: Bernard Kunkel, Tr.

Established in 1999 in KY.
Donors: Bavarian Irrevocable Complex Trust; Bavarian Trucking Co., Inc.
Foundation type: Independent foundation.
Financial data (yr. ended 12/31/04): Assets, $253,321 (M); gifts received, $175,000; expenditures, $357,832; qualifying distributions, $357,011; giving activities include $305,646 for 44 grants (high: $60,000; low: $100), and $30,000 for 13 grants to individuals (high: $5,500; low: $500).
Fields of interest: Human services; Children/youth, services; Roman Catholic agencies & churches.
Type of support: Building/renovation; Program development; Grants to individuals.
Limitations: Giving primarily in KY and OH; some funding nationally.
Application information: Application form not required.
   Deadline(s): None
Trustees: Bernard Brueggemann; James Brueggemann; John Brueggemann; Bernard Kunkel.
EIN: 266007704

3407

Blue Grass Community Foundation, Inc.

(formerly Blue Grass Foundation, Inc.)
250 W. Main St., Ste. 1220
Lexington, KY 40507-1714 (859) 225-3343
Contact: For grant applications: Barbara A. Fischer, Grants Off.
FAX: (859) 243-0770; E-mail: info@bgcf.org; Grant information E-mail: bfischer@bgcf.org; URL: http://www.bgcf.org

Incorporated in 1967 in KY.
Foundation type: Community foundation.
Financial data (yr. ended 12/31/05): Assets, $26,221,968 (M); gifts received, $1,910,034; expenditures, $2,141,972; giving activities include $1,283,697 for 249 grants (high: $101,981; low: $100), $248,046 for 161 grants to individuals (high: $4,000; low: $140), and $322,604 for 2 foundation-administered programs.
Purpose and activities: The foundation receives gifts and gives grants to people and causes in central and eastern Kentucky.
Fields of interest: Humanities; Arts; Education; Environment; Health care; Health organizations, association; Housing/shelter, homeless; Housing/shelter; Disasters, Hurricane Katrina; Human services; Economic development; Community development; Public affairs; Religion.
Type of support: Management development/capacity building; Building/renovation; Equipment; Seed money; Employee-related scholarships; Scholarships—to individuals; Matching/challenge support.
Limitations: Giving limited to central and eastern KY.

Publications: Application guidelines; Annual report; Financial statement; Grants list; Informational brochure (including application guidelines).
Application information: Visit foundation Web site for application information. The foundation's grant committee will review all letters of inquiry and decide which agencies will be asked to complete a full application. Application form required.
   Initial approach: Letter of inquiry (1 to 2 pages)
   Copies of proposal: 1
   Deadline(s): Aug. 8 for letters of inquiry; Sept. 19 for full applications
   Board meeting date(s): Quarterly
   Final notification: Mid-Nov.
Officers and Directors:* John R. Hall,* Pres.; Jack R. Cunningham,* V.P.; Joan Gaines,* Secy.; Garland H. Barr III,* Treas.; Tom Ackerman; C.B. Akins, Sr.; Richard Alloo; Mira Ball; Samuel G. Barnes; Marilyn Clark; Robert N. Clay; John L. Flanagan; Melanie Glasscock-Simpson; Philip Lee Greer; Whitney Greer-Stokes; John M. Keith, Jr.; Timothy M. Kelly; Celeste Neuman; Doug Roederer; Arthur Salomon; Carla Van Meter; Eugene A. Woods.
Number of staff: 4 full-time professional.
EIN: 616053466

3408

Owsley Brown Charitable Foundation ✧

c/o Owsley Brown II
850 Dixie Hwy.
Louisville, KY 40210

Established in 1990 in KY.
Donors: Owsley Brown II; Mrs. W.L. Lyons Brown.
Foundation type: Independent foundation.
Financial data (yr. ended 12/31/05): Assets, $18,462,467 (M); gifts received, $2,000,000; expenditures, $1,189,155; qualifying distributions, $1,131,240; giving activities include $1,131,057 for 128 grants (high: $215,180; low: $50; average: $1,000–$10,000).
Purpose and activities: Giving primarily for the arts, and education.
Fields of interest: Performing arts; Performing arts, theater; Arts; Higher education; Education; Human services; Federated giving programs; Christian agencies & churches; Religion, interfaith issues.
Limitations: Applications not accepted. Giving primarily in KY. No grants to individuals.
Application information: Contributes only to pre-selected organizations.
Officers and Directors:* Owsley Brown II,* Pres.; Christina Lee Brown,* Secy.-Treas.; Brooke Lee Brown; Owsley Brown III.
EIN: 611189915
Selected grants: The following grants were reported in 2004.
$1,800,000 to Filson Club, Louisville, KY.
$104,000 to Actors Theater of Louisville, Louisville, KY.
$82,450 to Louisville Collegiate School, Louisville, KY.
$56,000 to Cathedral Heritage Foundation, Louisville, KY.
$34,000 to Westover School, Middlebury, CT.
$26,000 to Robert E. Lee Memorial Association, Stratford, VA.
$25,000 to Kentucky Opera Association, Louisville, KY.
$10,000 to Film Arts Foundation, San Francisco, CA.
$6,250 to Yale in Kentucky, Louisville, KY.
$5,000 to Childrens Storefront, New York, NY.

3409

James Graham Brown Foundation, Inc. ▼

4350 Brownsboro Rd., Ste. 200
Louisville, KY 40207 (502) 896-2440
Contact: Mason B. Rummel, Exec. Dir.
FAX: (502) 896-1774; E-mail: mason@jgbf.org; Additional tel.: (866) 896-5423; URL: http://www.jgbf.org

Trust established in 1943 in KY; incorporated in 1954.
Donors: J. Graham Brown‡; Agnes B. Duggan‡.
Foundation type: Independent foundation.
Financial data (yr. ended 12/31/05): Assets, $407,526,012 (M); expenditures, $20,814,209; qualifying distributions, $19,125,239; giving activities include $18,738,169 for 44 grants (high: $5,000,000; low: $500; average: $500,000–$1,000,000).
Purpose and activities: Giving primarily for higher education; support also for civic organizations, community and economic development, human service organizations, culture and humanities, and health.
Fields of interest: Museums; Historic preservation/historical societies; Higher education; Education; Health care; Human services; Youth, services; Homeless, human services; Urban/community development; Disabilities, people with; Homeless.
Type of support: Capital campaigns; Building/renovation; Equipment; Land acquisition; Endowments; Professorships; Scholarship funds; Research; Matching/challenge support.
Limitations: Giving primarily in KY, with emphasis on the Jefferson County and Louisville metropolitan areas. No support for private foundations or the performing arts, primary or secondary schooling, religious institutions for religious purposes, including theological seminaries, or political or national organizations. No grants to individuals, or for operating needs.
Publications: Application guidelines; Grants list; Informational brochure (including application guidelines).
Application information: Application form required if board approves request for permission to apply. Applications received after Oct. 1 will be considered for the following year. Application form required.
   Initial approach: Letter
   Copies of proposal: 1
   Deadline(s): None
   Board meeting date(s): Monthly
   Final notification: Applicants notified monthly; grants paid Dec. 31
Officers and Trustees:* Joe M. Rodes,* Pres.; R. Alex Rankin,* V.P.; Mason B. Rummel, Secy. and Exec. Dir.; Joan R. Dudley, Treas.; Ina B. Bond; Sylvia W. Jaegers; Graham B. Loper; W. Barrett Nichols; J.A. Paradis, III; Robert W. Rounsavall III; R. Ted Steinbock.
Number of staff: 2 full-time professional; 3 part-time professional.
EIN: 610724060
Selected grants: The following grants were reported in 2005.
$3,000,000 to Louisville Olmsted Parks Conservancy, Louisville, KY.
$1,000,000 to United Way, Metro, Louisville, KY.
$960,000 to Bellarmine University, Louisville, KY.
$953,706 to Centre College of Kentucky, Danville, KY.
$952,793 to Kentucky Wesleyan College, Owensboro, KY.

$850,000 to American Red Cross, Louisville Area Chapter, Louisville, KY.

$676,700 to Thomas More College, Crestview Hills, KY.

$635,000 to Community Foundation of Louisville, Louisville, KY.

$500,000 to Prichard Committee for Academic Excellence, Lexington, KY.

$30,000 to Association of Community Ministries, Louisville, KY.

3410
W. L. Lyons Brown Foundation ✧

Waterfront Plz., Ste. 1110
325 W. Main St.
Louisville, KY 40202
Contact: Susan V. Nicholson, Admin.
E-mail: susann@cflouisville.org

Incorporated in 1962 in KY.
Donors: W.L. Lyons Brown†; Sara S. Brown.
Foundation type: Independent foundation.
Financial data (yr. ended 12/31/05): Assets, $41,491,173 (M); expenditures, $1,485,522; qualifying distributions, $1,457,683; giving activities include $1,440,333 for 27 grants (high: $83,333; low: $1,000).
Purpose and activities: Giving primarily to organizations in KY seeking to improve quality of life, including museums, parks, educational institutions, and organizations supporting the arts.
Fields of interest: Museums; Arts; Higher education; Environment, natural resources.
Type of support: General/operating support; Annual campaigns; Capital campaigns; Building/renovation; Land acquisition.
Limitations: Applications not accepted. Giving primarily in the metropolitan Louisville, KY, area. No support for sectarian projects. No grants to individuals, or for scholarships or annual appeals; no loans.
Application information: Unsolicited requests for funds not accepted.
  Board meeting date(s): Oct.
Officers and Trustees:* Ina B. Bond,* Pres.; Martin S. Brown,* V.P.; Mrs. W.L. Lyons Brown,* Secy.; Owsley Brown II,* Treas.
EIN: 610598511

3411
W. L. Lyons Brown, Jr. Charitable Foundation ✧

c/o W.L. Lyons Brown, Jr.
320 Whittington Pkwy., Ste. 206
Louisville, KY 40222

Established in 1993 in KY.
Donors: Mrs. W.L. Lyons Brown; Sara Shallenberger Brown.
Foundation type: Independent foundation.
Financial data (yr. ended 12/31/05): Assets, $20,661,512 (M); gifts received, $2,000,000; expenditures, $952,970; qualifying distributions, $952,970; giving activities include $854,018 for 61 grants (high: $189,000; low: $250).
Purpose and activities: Giving primarily for the arts and education.
Fields of interest: Museums; Historic preservation/historical societies; Higher education; Education; Foundations (community); Federated giving programs.

Limitations: Applications not accepted. Giving on a national basis. No grants to individuals.
Application information: Contributes only to pre-selected organizations.
Officers and Directors:* Alice Cary Brown,* Pres.; W.L. Lyons Brown, Jr.,* Secy.-Treas.; Stuart R. Brown; A. Cary Brown Epstein.
EIN: 611233038

3412
The C.E. and S. Foundation, Inc.

1650 National City Twr.
Louisville, KY 40202 (502) 583-0546
Contact: Bruce A. Maza, Exec. Dir.
FAX: (502) 583-7648; URL: http://www.cesfoundation.com

Established in 1984 in FL.
Donors: David A. Jones; and family.
Foundation type: Independent foundation.
Financial data (yr. ended 12/31/04): Assets, $46,927,569 (M); gifts received, $25,000; expenditures, $2,690,145; qualifying distributions, $2,425,587; giving activities include $2,037,776 for 111 grants (high: $224,000; low: $250), and $159,790 for 6 employee matching gifts.
Purpose and activities: Giving primarily for higher education, (with a focus on undergraduate liberal arts programs in Louisville, KY), as well as for colleges and universities, and for disaster relief and prevention, international cooperation, Louisville's urban environment, and special projects initiated by the grants committee.
Fields of interest: Education; International affairs, goodwill promotion; Urban/community development.
Type of support: General/operating support; Income development; Management development/capacity building; Capital campaigns; Land acquisition; Emergency funds; Program development; Technical assistance; Program-related investments/loans.
Limitations: Giving primarily in Louisville, KY. No support for medical research organizations, or for political organizations. No grants to individuals.
Publications: Application guidelines; Annual report; Grants list; Program policy statement.
Application information:
  Initial approach: Letter, telephone, or Web site for guidelines
  Copies of proposal: 1
  Deadline(s): None
  Board meeting date(s): Jan., May, Sept. and Nov.
  Final notification: Up to two months
Officers and Trustee:* David A. Jones,* Pres.; Bruce A. Maza, Exec. Dir.
Number of staff: 1 full-time professional; 1 full-time support.
EIN: 592466943
Selected grants: The following grants were reported in 2004.
$183,000 to Middlebury College, Middlebury, VT. 2 grants: $150,000 (For new library), $33,000 (For Bread Loaf School of English summer fellowship program for Kentucky teachers).
$50,000 to David School, David, KY. For new resident development officer.
$50,000 to Yale University, Law School, New Haven, CT. For China Law Center, Phase II.
$45,000 to Jefferson County Public Schools, Louisville, KY. For Every1 Reads, phase II.
$38,360 to Americana Community Center, Louisville, KY. For Nonprofit Management Fellowship.

$30,000 to Jefferson County Public Education Foundation, Louisville, KY. For Sheltered Instruction Observation Protocol (SIOP) program, for ESL training.
$25,000 to Louisville Free Public Library Foundation, Louisville, KY. For phase II of Iroquois Library's programming with international populations.
$25,000 to Wayside Christian Mission, Louisville, KY. For 2003 capital campaign.
$20,000 to Harvard University, Cambridge, MA. For Sheffer Professorship in Allergic Diseases at Medical School.

3413
Chase Family Foundation ✧

3060 Ashley Dr.
Edgewood, KY 41017

Established in OH.
Donors: W. Rowell Chase; Alison Mason Chase; W. Rowell Chase Charitable Lead Annuity Trust.
Foundation type: Independent foundation.
Financial data (yr. ended 12/31/05): Assets, $14,145,918 (M); gifts received, $1,620,450; expenditures, $597,569; qualifying distributions, $526,161; giving activities include $489,114 for 103 grants (high: $50,000; low: $100).
Fields of interest: Arts; Higher education; Environment, natural resources; Environment, land resources; Human services; Federated giving programs; Christian agencies & churches; Protestant agencies & churches.
Limitations: Applications not accepted. Giving on a national basis. Generally no grants to individuals.
Application information: Contributes only to pre-selected organizations.
Officers and Trustees:* R. Kingsbury Chase,* Chair.; Alison Mason Chase,* Vice-Chair.; Charlene R. Connett,* Secy.; Barbara K. Chase; J. Michael Cooney; Joseph C. Hill.
EIN: 316038352

3414
The Community Foundation of Louisville, Inc. ▼

(formerly Louisville Community Foundation, Inc.)
Waterfront Plz. Bldg.
325 W. Main St., Ste. 1110
Louisville, KY 40202-4251 (502) 585-4649
Contact: C. Dennis Riggs, C.E.O.; For grants: Alexandra M. Spoelker, Dir., Grants
FAX: (502) 587-7484; E-mail: info@cflouisville.org; Grant application E-mail: alexs@cflouisville.org; URL: http://www.cflouisville.org

Established in 1916 in KY; reorganized in 1984.
Foundation type: Community foundation.
Financial data (yr. ended 6/30/05): Assets, $182,778,225 (M); gifts received, $9,074,766; expenditures, $15,127,545; giving activities include $8,952,116 for 1,462 grants (high: $250,000; low: $100; average: $100–$150,000), and $747,676 for 2 foundation-administered programs.
Purpose and activities: The mission of the foundation is to advance philanthropy by serving the charitable interests of donors, enabling increased charitable giving, and improving communities by being a permanent philanthropic resource for current and future needs. Giving for health and

human services, arts and humanities, education, and the environment; support also for scholarships. The current focus of grantmaking from unrestricted funds is to help children and families in poverty achieve self-sufficiency.

Fields of interest: Humanities; Historic preservation/historical societies; Arts; Education; Environment; Public health; Health care; Family services; Human services; Community development.

Type of support: General/operating support; Continuing support; Annual campaigns; Building/renovation; Equipment; Emergency funds; Program development; Publication; Seed money; Scholarship funds; Research; Technical assistance; Employee matching gifts; Scholarships—to individuals; Matching/challenge support.

Limitations: Giving primarily in Louisville and Jefferson County, KY. No support for sectarian purposes. No grants to individuals (except for scholarships), or generally for endowments or capital campaigns.

Publications: Annual report; Informational brochure; Newsletter; Program policy statement.

Application information: Visit foundation Web site for application forms and additional guidelines per grant type. Faxed or e-mailed applications are not accepted. Application form required.

Initial approach: Submit application form and attachments
Deadline(s): Nov. 1 for Community Grants
Board meeting date(s): Mar., June, Sept., and Dec.
Final notification: Mar. for Community Grants

Officers and Directors:* Olivia F. Kirtley,* Chair.; Daniel W. McMahan,* Vice-Chair.; C. Dennis Riggs, C.E.O. and Pres.; Susan V. Nicholson, V.P. and C.F.O.; Kathy B. Steward, V.P., Philanthropic Svcs.; Chris "Kit" Georgehead,* Secy.; Michael B. Mountjoy, Chair. Emeritus; Bonita K. Black; Carl Brazley; A. Francis Brennan, M.D., Ph.D.; Diane Cornwell; Laura M. Douglas; Adel S. Elmaghraby, Ph.D.; Robert R. Goodin, M.D.; F. Gerald Greenwell; Audwin A. Helton; Jay L. Klempner; Yung T. Nguyen; Elizabeth S. Peabody; Irvin W. Quesenberry; Sharon A. Receveur; Terry L. Singer, Ph.D.; Jude Thompson; Matthew A. Thornton; Mimi Zinniel.

Number of staff: 10 full-time professional; 5 full-time support.

EIN: 310997017

Selected grants: The following grants were reported in 2005.

$55,000 to Public Radio Partnership, Louisville, KY. For Instrumental Partners, donation and collection program for used musical instruments that are reconditioned, repaired and donated to Jefferson County Public Schools with high percentage of at-risk students.

$25,000 to Family Place, Louisville, KY. Toward specialized day care and preschool program for children, ages five and younger, with emotional and physical developmental delays resulting from abuse or neglect.

$25,000 to Legal Aid Society, Louisville, KY. For Children At-Risk Program, to avert disruption in development and education of school children by giving legal assistance to prevent loss of family rental housing.

$25,000 to YMCA, Safe Places Services. For Street Outreach Program, to educate homeless and runaway teens about available social services and provide emergency assistance such as food, clothing, and first aid.

$22,500 to Neighborhood House, Louisville, KY. Toward JCPS Every 1 Reads initiative for Portland-area youth in grades K-12.

$21,000 to Youth Alive, Louisville, KY. For after-school program offering group and one-on-one counseling, tutoring and mentoring opportunities for children, ages 10-17, from Park DuValle, Park Hill and Parkland neighborhoods.

$20,000 to Family and Childrens Counseling Center, Louisville, KY. Toward pilot homelessness-prevention program for children, ages 4-11, at Hazelwood Elementary School to address high transience rate of students.

$20,000 to Girl Scouts of the U.S.A., Kentuckiana Council, Louisville, KY. For 2B Girl Power, educational after-school program for girls, ages 11-17, that focuses on positive decision-making skills, health issues, peer pressure and social skills.

$18,500 to Saint George Community Center, Louisville, KY. For Innocent Echoes, comprehensive after-school program for youth, ages 11-14, including anger management training, conflict resolution and drama workshops to foster positively expressed feelings.

$1,000 to Mattingly Center, Louisville, KY. For music theater program serving disabled adults. Grant made through George and Mary Alice Hadley Fund.

3415
Community Foundation of West Kentucky ◇

(formerly Paducah Area Community Foundation)
P.O. Box 7901
Paducah, KY 42002-7901 (270) 442-8622
Contact: Tony Watkins, Exec. Dir.
FAX: (270) 442-8623; URL: http://jpf.org/community_foundation.htm

Established in 1995 in KY.
Foundation type: Community foundation.
Financial data (yr. ended 12/31/03): Assets, $5,142,636 (M); gifts received, $1,295,942; expenditures, $852,650; giving activities include $750,877 for 33+ grants (high: $152,094), and $4,600 for grants to individuals.
Purpose and activities: The foundation supports areas of art and culture, community development, education, environment, health and social needs.
Fields of interest: Arts, cultural/ethnic awareness; Arts; Education; Environment; Public health; Health care; Human services; Community development.
Type of support: Equipment; General/operating support; Annual campaigns; Capital campaigns; Endowments; Debt reduction; Emergency funds; Program development; Scholarship funds.
Limitations: Applications not accepted. Giving primarily in western KY and Massac County, IL. No grants to individuals.
Publications: Annual report; Informational brochure; Newsletter.
Application information:
Board meeting date(s): Quarterly in Feb., May, Aug., and Nov.
Officers and Directors:* George B. Shaw, Pres.; Geraldine Montgomery, V.P.; Jerry Severns,* Secy.-Treas.; Tony Watkins, Exec. Dir.; Ronald Jackson,* Chair., Finance and Investment; Carney Allen; Chris Black; Avery Crounse; Dan R. Ellison; Joseph H. Frampton; Brent Gregory; C. Ronald James; Eugene Katterjohn, Jr.; Vicki Ladt; Daniel P.

Murphy, Jr.; Fred Paxton; Scott Powell; Bonnie Schrock; Richard Smith; Ken Wheeler.
Number of staff: 1 full-time professional; 1 full-time support; 1 part-time support.
EIN: 611304905

3416
The Cralle Foundation, Inc.
614 W. Main St., Ste. 2500
Louisville, KY 40202
Contact: James T. Crain, Jr., Exec. Dir.

Incorporated in 1990 in KY as successor foundation to the Cralle Foundation.
Foundation type: Independent foundation.
Financial data (yr. ended 12/31/05): Assets, $10,974,416 (M); expenditures, $868,882; qualifying distributions, $792,680; giving activities include $655,230 for 60 grants (high: $30,000; low: $1,000; average: $5,000–$20,000).
Purpose and activities: Giving primarily for education and human services.
Fields of interest: Museums; Higher education; Education; Human services; Children/youth, services; Community development; Economically disadvantaged; Homeless.
Type of support: Continuing support; General/operating support; Capital campaigns; Building/renovation; Equipment; Endowments; Program development; Seed money; Scholarship funds.
Limitations: Giving primarily in KY, with emphasis on Louisville. No grants to individuals.
Application information: Application form required.
Initial approach: Letter requesting application form
Copies of proposal: 5
Board meeting date(s): Apr. and Oct.
Officer and Trustees:* James T. Crain, Jr.,* Exec. Dir.; Carolyn Day; Joan Cralle Day; Susan Day.
Number of staff: 1 full-time professional; 1 part-time support.
EIN: 611179672

3417
E.ON U.S. Foundation ◇
(formerly LG&E Energy Foundation, Inc.)
220 W. Main St.
Louisville, KY 40202
Contact: Elaine Ashcraft, Grants Admin.
FAX: (502) 627-3629; Application address: P.O. Box 32030, Louisville, KY 40232; URL: http://www.lgeenergy.com/foundation/default.asp

Established in 1994 in KY.
Donors: LG&E Energy Corp.; LG&E Energy LLC; E.ON U.S. LLC.
Foundation type: Company-sponsored foundation.
Financial data (yr. ended 12/31/04): Assets, $13,243,453 (M); expenditures, $2,416,833; qualifying distributions, $2,158,289; giving activities include $1,999,317 for 55 grants (high: $848,782; low: $500), and $158,972 for employee matching gifts.
Purpose and activities: The foundation supports organizations involved with education, diversity, the environment, and health and human services.
Fields of interest: Arts, cultural/ethnic awareness; Arts; Education; Environment; Health care; Health organizations, association; Human services; Community development.

Type of support: General/operating support; Building/renovation; Program development; Scholarship funds; Employee matching gifts; Matching/challenge support.

Limitations: Giving primarily in areas of company operations in KY. No support for political, fraternal, labor, or religious organizations or United Way or Fund for the Arts agencies. No grants to individuals, or for pageants or travel expenses, capital campaigns, medical research or disease campaigns/walks, or athletic sponsorships.

Publications: Application guidelines; Program policy statement.

Application information: Application form required.
Initial approach: Complete online application form
Copies of proposal: 1
Deadline(s): Nov. 1 to Nov. 30
Board meeting date(s): Annually

Officers and Directors:* Victor A. Stafferi,* Pres.; John R. McCall,* V.P. and Secy.; S. Bradford Rives,* V.P. and Treas.; Rudolph W. Keeling, V.P.

Number of staff: 1 full-time professional.

EIN: 611257368

Selected grants: The following grants were reported in 2004.

$162,261 to Greater Louisville Fund for the Arts, Louisville, KY.

$100,000 to Courier-Journal, Louisville, KY.

$84,000 to Energy Conservation Associates, Louisville, KY. For program support.

$75,000 to Cabbage Patch Settlement House, Louisville, KY. For program support.

$40,000 to Lexington Partnership for Workforce Development, Lexington, KY. For One Team One Vision.

$30,000 to Louisville Science Center, Louisville, KY. For The World Around Us.

$25,000 to J. B. Speed Art Museum, Louisville, KY. For children and family art education.

$25,000 to Kentucky Center for African American Heritage, Louisville, KY. For exhibits.

$20,000 to Daniel Pitino Foundation, Lexington, KY. For program support.

$20,000 to W H A S Crusade for Children, Louisville, KY. For program support.

3418
Fischer Family Foundation ◇

P.O. Box 17160
Fort Mitchell, KY 41017-0160

Established in 1996 in KY.

Donors: Henry K. Fischer; Elaine M. Fischer.

Foundation type: Independent foundation.

Financial data (yr. ended 11/30/05): Assets, $45,940,898 (M); gifts received, $4,350,969; expenditures, $2,437,504; qualifying distributions, $2,006,005; giving activities include $2,006,005 for 47 grants (high: $1,520,100; low: $30).

Purpose and activities: Giving primarily for residential care, health care, human services, and education.

Fields of interest: Arts; Secondary school/education; Higher education; Higher education, university; Health care; Human services; Children/youth, services; Residential/custodial care, hospices; Developmentally disabled, centers & services; Roman Catholic agencies & churches.

Limitations: Applications not accepted. Giving primarily in KY and OH. No grants to individuals.

Application information: Contributes only to pre-selected organizations.

Trustees: Elaine M. Fischer; Henry K. Fischer.

EIN: 586332121

Selected grants: The following grants were reported in 2005.

$1,530,100 to Boys and Girls Clubs of Greater Cincinnati, Cincinnati, OH. 2 grants: $1,520,100 (For general support), $10,000 (For general support).

$101,000 to Saint Joseph Orphanage, Cincinnati, OH. For general support.

$100,000 to Saint Elizabeth Medical Center, Covington, KY. For general support for hospice unit.

$50,000 to American Red Cross, National Headquarters, DC. For general support.

$50,000 to Welcome House of Northern Kentucky, Covington, KY. For general support.

$20,000 to Catholic Social Services of Northern Kentucky, Covington, KY. For general support.

$10,000 to Cincinnati Childrens Hospital Medical Center, Cincinnati, OH. For general support for Starshine Hospice.

3419
Gordon Ford Foundation, Inc. ☆

5915 Brittany Valley Rd.
Louisville, KY 40222
Contact: Mrs. Gordon Ford, Chair.
FAX: (502) 426-0078; *E-mail:* glendaford@aol.com

Established in 1958.

Donors: Gordon Ford; Southeastern Investment Trust, Inc.

Foundation type: Independent foundation.

Financial data (yr. ended 8/31/06): Assets, $1,323,794 (M); expenditures, $2,154,093; qualifying distributions, $2,141,534; giving activities include $2,131,625 for 16 grants (high: $2,000; low: $100).

Fields of interest: Education; Youth development; Federated giving programs; Christian agencies & churches.

Type of support: Annual campaigns; Capital campaigns; Scholarship funds.

Limitations: Applications not accepted. Giving primarily in KY. No grants to individuals.

Application information: Contributes only to pre-selected organizations.
Board meeting date(s): Dec.

Officers: Mrs. Gordon Ford, Chair., Pres., and Secy.; Helen Vittitow, V.P. and Treas.

EIN: 616034183

3420
Foundation for the Tri-State Community, Inc.

(formerly Greater Ashland Area Cultural and Economic Development Foundation, Inc.)
1999 Winchester Ave., 2nd Fl.
P.O. Box 2096
Ashland, KY 41105-2096 (606) 324-3888
Contact: Mary Witten Wiseman, Pres.
FAX: (606) 324-5961;
E-mail: ftsc_mwwiseman@yahoo.com; Additional
E-mail: ftsc_smartin@yahoo.com; *URL:* http://www.tristatefoundation.org

Incorporated in 1972 in KY.

Foundation type: Community foundation.

Financial data (yr. ended 12/31/04): Assets, $12,624,362 (M); gifts received, $619,681;

expenditures, $1,085,875; giving activities include $770,770 for 165+ grants.

Purpose and activities: The foundation makes grants for charitable, cultural, educational, and scientific purposes and seeks to respond to a wide variety of needs in the community.

Fields of interest: Arts; Education; Science.

Type of support: Building/renovation; Equipment; Emergency funds; Program development; Seed money; Scholarship funds; Technical assistance; Consulting services; Matching/challenge support.

Limitations: Giving limited to Boyd and Greenup counties, KY; Lawrence County, OH; and Cabell and Wayne counties, WV. No support for sectarian activities of religious organizations. No grants to individuals, or for deficit financing, operating support, or endowment funds.

Publications: Application guidelines; Annual report; Informational brochure.

Application information: Applications reviewed quarterly. Visit foundation Web site for application information. Application form required.
Initial approach: Letter, telephone, or proposal
Copies of proposal: 1
Deadline(s): None
Board meeting date(s): Quarterly

Officers and Trustees:* Ben R. Cooksey,* Chair. and V.P., KY; Curtis B. Anderson, Vice-Chair., OH; Michael J. Emerson, Vice-Chair., WV; Mary Whitten Wiseman, Pres.; Larry W. Jones, Secy.-Treas.; Jane H. Boylin; Dianne W. Clement; Donald L. Edwards; Michael W. Hobbs; Daniel B. Huffman; Henry M. Kayes; Kimberly L. Lewis; Fr. Thomas R. Nau; John F. Speer; Jack W. Strother, Jr.; Carolyn P. Warnock.

Number of staff: 2 full-time professional; 1 full-time support.

EIN: 610729266

3421
The Gheens Foundation, Inc. ▼

1 Riverfront Plz., Ste. 705
Louisville, KY 40202 (502) 584-4650
Contact: Carl M. Thomas, Exec. Dir.
FAX: (502) 584-4652;
E-mail: carl@gheensfoundation.org; *URL:* http://www.gheensfoundation.org

Incorporated in 1957 in KY.

Donors: C. Edwin Gheens†; Mary Jo Gheens Hill†.

Foundation type: Independent foundation.

Financial data (yr. ended 10/31/05): Assets, $80,509,156 (M); expenditures, $4,804,586; qualifying distributions, $3,711,016; giving activities include $3,377,198 for 77 grants (high: $500,000; low: $500; average: $10,000–$100,000).

Purpose and activities: Emphasis on higher and secondary education, ongoing teacher education, social service agencies, health associations, programs for the physically and mentally handicapped, and cultural programs.

Fields of interest: Arts; Secondary school/education; Higher education; Education; Mental health/crisis services; Health organizations, association; Human services; Disabilities, people with.

Type of support: General/operating support; Capital campaigns; Building/renovation; Equipment; Program development; Scholarship funds; Research.

Limitations: Giving primarily in Louisville, KY, and LaFourche and Terrebone parishes, LA. No support for private high schools. No grants to individuals.

Publications: Application guidelines; Grants list.
Application information: Application is available on the foundation's Web site. Application form required.
> *Initial approach:* Ask for application by letter, phone, fax, or E-mail
> *Copies of proposal:* 7
> *Deadline(s):* None
> *Board meeting date(s):* Quarterly
> *Final notification:* Within 90 days

Officers and Trustees:* Morton Boyd, Pres.; Michael B. Mountjoy,* V.P. and Treas.; William G. Duncan, Jr., Secy.; Carl M. Thomas, Exec. Dir.; Laman A. Gray; Phoebe A. Wood.
Number of staff: 2 full-time professional; 1 part-time professional; 3 full-time support.
EIN: 616031406
Selected grants: The following grants were reported in 2005.
$750,000 to University of Louisville Foundation, Louisville, KY. 2 grants: $500,000 (For medical research), $250,000 (For Outcomes Research Institute).
$250,000 to Jefferson County Public Education Foundation, Louisville, KY. For Every 1 Reads program.
$156,819 to Jefferson County Public Schools, Louisville, KY. 2 grants: $49,591 (For STARS program (Student Tracking Attendance Reporting System)), $107,228 (For STARS program (Student Tracking Attendance Reporting System)).
$125,000 to Muhammad Ali Museum and Education Center, Louisville, KY.
$100,000 to Greater Louisville Fund for the Arts, Louisville, KY.
$100,000 to National D-Day Museum Foundation, New Orleans, LA.
$100,000 to University of the Cumberlands, Williamsburg, KY.
$50,000 to Actors Theater of Louisville, Louisville, KY.

3422
Good Samaritan Foundation, Inc. ✧

270 S. Limestone St.
Lexington, KY 40508-2566
FAX: (859) 254-7337; E-mail: info@gsfky.org;
URL: http://www.gsfky.org/

Established in 1888 in KY, Incorporated as Good Samaritan Hospital of KY in 1929; Good Samaritan Foundation is a hospital conversion foundation.
Foundation type: Independent foundation.
Financial data (yr. ended 6/30/05): Assets, $23,327,619 (M); gifts received, $42,700; expenditures, $1,372,955; qualifying distributions, $1,042,890; giving activities include $832,240 for 27 grants (high: $303,033; low: $1,450).
Purpose and activities: The foundation, initiates, participates in, and supports activities which focus on improving the health status of Kentuckians.
Fields of interest: Health care.
Type of support: General/operating support; Equipment; Seed money; Curriculum development; Fellowships; Scholarship funds; Research.
Limitations: Giving limited to KY. No support for indirect costs. No grants to individuals or capital improvements or for endowment funds.
Publications: Application guidelines; Informational brochure (including application guidelines); Newsletter; Occasional report.
Application information:

Initial approach: Letter and application
Copies of proposal: 2
Deadline(s): Jan. 10
Final notification: No later than July
Officers and Trustees:* James W. Holsinger, Jr., M.D., Ph.D.*, Chair.; Sally L. Manning,* Vice-Chair.; Rev. Linda Rumpke,* Secy.; Charles B. Verrette,* Treas.; Samuel Barnes; R. Scott Davis; Ira L. Hemmings, Jr., M.D.; and 6 additional trustees.
Number of staff: 1 full-time support.
EIN: 311087598
Selected grants: The following grants were reported in 2005.
$437,364 to University of Kentucky, Lexington, KY. 7 grants: $303,033, $37,145, $48,332, $17,000, $8,000, $3,854, $20,000
$38,000 to University of Louisville, Louisville, KY.
$31,680 to Midway College, Midway, KY.
$22,400 to Lexington Community College, Lexington, KY.

3423
The Virginia Clark Hagan Charitable Foundation, Inc. ✧

250 W. Main St., Ste. 1600
Lexington, KY 40507-1726
Contact: Herbert D. Sledd, Pres.

Established in 2002.
Donors: Virginia Clark Hagan†; Hagan Unitrust.
Foundation type: Independent foundation.
Financial data (yr. ended 12/31/05): Assets, $14,641,383 (M); expenditures, $618,822; qualifying distributions, $513,935; giving activities include $497,000 for 5 grants (high: $150,000; low: $52,000).
Purpose and activities: Giving primarily for education and human services.
Fields of interest: Higher education; Adult education—literacy, basic skills & GED; Human services; Christian agencies & churches.
Limitations: Giving primarily in Lexington, KY.
Application information:
> *Initial approach:* Letter
> *Deadline(s):* None
Officers: Herbert D. Sledd, Pres.; Sarah Clark, V.P.; Charles L. Shearer, Secy.; Julius Clark, Treas.
EIN: 611184780

3424
The Claude and Betty Harris Foundation, Inc. ✧

1406 Browns Ln., 2nd Fl.
Louisville, KY 40207

Established in 2002 in KY.
Donor: Harris Charitable Lead Trust.
Foundation type: Independent foundation.
Financial data (yr. ended 12/31/05): Assets, $23,718,933 (M); gifts received, $5,399,373; expenditures, $1,079,343; qualifying distributions, $877,482; giving activities include $830,600 for 58 grants (high: $44,300; low: $1,000; average: $10,000–$20,000).
Fields of interest: Health care, clinics/centers; Food banks; Housing/shelter, development; Human services; Children/youth, services; Women, centers/services.
Limitations: Applications not accepted. No grants to individuals.

Application information: Contributes only to pre-selected organizations.
Officers: Theresa Jean Harris Moore, Chair.; Don Harris, Vice-Chair.; Paula Harris Stansell, Secy.
Directors: David Harris; Gary Harris; Gayla Harris; Timothy Harris.
Trustee: Cullinan Associates Inc. 1406.
EIN: 611400416

3425
Hayswood Foundation, Inc. ✧

1 W. McDonald Pkwy., Ste. 3A
Maysville, KY 41056   (606) 563-9333
Contact: Lloyd Schlitz, Exec. Dir.
FAX: (606) 563-9444;
E-mail: hayswoodfoundation@maysvilleky.net

Established in 1985.
Foundation type: Independent foundation.
Financial data (yr. ended 12/31/05): Assets, $9,378,877 (M); gifts received, $1,050; expenditures, $631,353; qualifying distributions, $521,743; giving activities include $521,743 for 15 grants (high: $138,813; low: $1,000).
Fields of interest: Education; Health care; Mental health/crisis services.
Type of support: General/operating support; Capital campaigns; Building/renovation; Equipment; Program development; Scholarship funds; Scholarships—to individuals; Matching/challenge support.
Limitations: Giving limited to Bracken, Fleming, Lewis, Mason, and Robertson counties, KY, and to Adams and Brown counties, OH. No support for religious or political organizations. No grants to individuals (except for scholarships) or for endowments.
Publications: Application guidelines.
Application information: Application forms are available starting June 1 of each year. Application form required.
> *Initial approach:* Contact foundation for application form and instructions
> *Copies of proposal:* 1
> *Deadline(s):* Aug. 1
> *Board meeting date(s):* Jan., May, Aug. and Oct.
> *Final notification:* Oct.
Officers and Directors:* Jay Andrews,* Pres.; Douglas Hendrickson,* V.P.; Dave Clark,* Secy.; Anne Pawsat,* Treas.; Robert Biddle; Robert Canada; Thomas Clark; Danita Lewis; William McNeill; Suzan Ross; Elizabeth Sewell; Debra Wallingford; Sally Walton; Deborah Weber; Robert D. Vance.
Number of staff: 1 part-time professional.
EIN: 237345996

3426
The Hep Foundation Business Trust ✧ ☆

c/o L Edwin Paulson, Jr.
209 E. High St.
Lexington, KY 40507

Established in 2004 in KY.
Donors: L. Edwin Paulson, Jr.; Jean Ellen Paulson.
Foundation type: Independent foundation.
Financial data (yr. ended 12/31/05): Assets, $522,335 (M); gifts received, $1,167,868; expenditures, $669,476; qualifying distributions, $668,731; giving activities include $668,731 for 21 grants (high: $529,946; low: $50).

Fields of interest: Elementary/secondary education; Higher education; Protestant agencies & churches.
Limitations: Applications not accepted. Giving primarily in Lexington, KY. No grants to individuals.
Application information: Contributes only to pre-selected organizations.
Trustees: Jean Ellen Paulson; L. Edwin Paulson, Jr.
EIN: 300200192

3427
Mildred V. Horn Foundation ✧
South Highway 53, Ste. 3, PMB 2028
La Grange, KY 40031-9119 (502) 895-2622
Contact: H. Scott Davis, Jr., Tr.

Established in 1988 in KY.
Donor: Mildred V. Horn†.
Foundation type: Independent foundation.
Financial data (yr. ended 12/31/05): Assets, $32,413,575 (M); expenditures, $1,772,638; qualifying distributions, $1,719,761; giving activities include $1,492,480 for 152 grants (high: $236,517; low: $500).
Purpose and activities: Giving primarily for preservation of historic homes (1760-1860) which are open to the public; giving also for homeless shelters and schools.
Fields of interest: Museums; Historic preservation/historical societies; Elementary/secondary education; Higher education; Human services; Family services; Homeless.
Type of support: General/operating support; Building/renovation.
Limitations: Giving primarily in KY (for homeless shelters and education) and historic homes open to the public in KY, IL, IN, MO, OH, TN, VA, and WV. No grants to individuals.
Publications: Application guidelines.
Application information: Application form not required.
  Initial approach: 1-to 2-page letter for requests under $5,000; 4-page form may be required for grants over $5,000
  Copies of proposal: 1
  Deadline(s): Dec. 31
  Board meeting date(s): Varies
Trustees: Walter T. Crutcher; H. Scott Davis, Jr.; Louisa M. Gaines.
Number of staff: 1 full-time professional; 3 part-time professional.
EIN: 616166544
Selected grants: The following grants were reported in 2005.
$236,517 to My Old Kentucky Home State Park Foundation, Bardstown, KY. For restoration and furnishings.
$104,345 to Riverside, The Farnsley-Moremen Landing, Louisville, KY. For furnishings and equipment.
$100,000 to 21st Century Parks, Louisville, KY. For house acquisition.
$66,035 to Louisville Free Public Library Foundation, Louisville, KY. For development software and director retention.
$62,000 to Saint Johns Center, Louisville, KY. For shelter and phone program.
$33,250 to Community Foundation of Louisville, Louisville, KY. For program support.
$31,000 to United Way, Metro, Louisville, KY. For operating support.
$24,780 to Friends of the Culbertson Mansion, New Albany, IN. For chandelier and draperies.

$20,000 to Wayside Christian Mission, Louisville, KY. For operating support.
$15,000 to Community Foundation of Southern Indiana, New Albany, IN. For Jefferson Carnegie Library Foundation.

3428
The Humana Foundation, Inc. ▼ ✧
500 W. Main St.
Louisville, KY 40202 (502) 580-3613
Contact: Barbara Wright; Virginia K. Judd, Exec. Dir.
FAX: (502) 580-1256;
E-mail: bwright@humana.com; URL: http://www.humanafoundation.org

Incorporated in 1981 in KY.
Donor: Humana Inc.
Foundation type: Company-sponsored foundation.
Financial data (yr. ended 12/31/05): Assets, $58,772,340 (M); expenditures, $6,793,557; qualifying distributions, $6,760,041; giving activities include $6,760,041 for 98 grants (high: $793,149; low: $250).
Purpose and activities: The foundation supports programs designed to promote healthy lives and healthy communities, with a focus on the needs of children, families, and seniors. Special emphasis is directed toward programs designed to promote health and fitness to better decisions and lifestyles; promote literacy to improve health experiences; and develop the technology, tools, and resources that lead to healthy communities.
Fields of interest: Education; Health care; Children, services; Family services; Human services; Aging.
International interests: Romania.
Type of support: General/operating support; Continuing support; Annual campaigns; Capital campaigns; Building/renovation; Conferences/seminars; Professorships; Curriculum development; Internship funds; Scholarship funds; Employee-related scholarships.
Limitations: Giving on a national and international basis in areas of company operations, with emphasis on Louisville, KY. No support for social, labor, political, veterans', or fraternal organizations. No grants for start up needs, lobbying efforts, or general operating support for religious organizations, construction or renovation of sanctuaries, or mission-focused activities.
Publications: Application guidelines; Newsletter.
Application information: Application form required.
  Initial approach: Complete online application form or download application form and mail to foundation; download application form and mail to nearest market office for organizations located outside Louisville, KY
  Copies of proposal: 1
  Deadline(s): Nov. 1 through Jan. 15 for organizations located in Louisville, KY; Nov. 1 through June 15 for organizations located outside of Louisville, KY
  Board meeting date(s): Every 2 months
  Final notification: Generally, 6 weeks to 2 months
Officers and Directors:* David A. Jones,* Chair., C.E.O., and Pres.; James H. Bloem, Sr. V.P., C.F.O., and Treas.; Arthur P. Hipwell, Sr. V.P.; George G. Bauernfeind, V.P.; Joan O. Lenahan, Secy.; Virginia K. Judd, Exec. Dir.; Michael E. Gellert; David A. Jones, Jr.; Michael B. McCallister.
EIN: 611004763
Selected grants: The following grants were reported in 2005.

$793,149 to American Red Cross, Louisville Area Chapter, Louisville, KY. For Hurricane Katrina relief.
$650,000 to Actors Theater of Louisville, Louisville, KY. For Humana Festival of New American Plays.
$504,225 to Scholarship America, Saint Peter, MN. For scholarships for children of Humana employees.
$301,500 to Greater Louisville Fund for the Arts, Louisville, KY. For Louisville Orchestra.
$300,000 to Community Foundation of Louisville, Louisville, KY. For Metro Future Fund.
$250,000 to University of Louisville Foundation, Louisville, KY. For Humana Endowment for International Pediatrics.
$243,000 to United Way, Metro, Louisville, KY. For annual support.
$25,000 to Murray State University Foundation, Murray, KY. For modern language fund.
$25,000 to Prichard Committee for Academic Excellence, Lexington, KY. For capital campaign.
$5,000 to Leukemia & Lymphoma Society, White Plains, NY.

3429
The J & L Foundation ✧
(formerly The Joan and Lee Thomas Foundation, Inc.)
2602 Grassland Dr.
Louisville, KY 40299-2524
Contact: Lee B. Thomas, Dir.

Established in 1989 in KY.
Donor: Lee B. Thomas.
Foundation type: Independent foundation.
Financial data (yr. ended 6/30/05): Assets, $21,481,571 (M); gifts received, $200,000; expenditures, $1,206,770; qualifying distributions, $1,118,436; giving activities include $1,113,040 for 30 grants (high: $175,000; low: $1,500).
Purpose and activities: Giving primarily for women's and family services and for education.
Fields of interest: Higher education; Adult education—literacy, basic skills & GED; Education, reading; Education; Family services; Women, centers/services; International peace/security; Economics; Women.
Limitations: Applications not accepted. Giving primarily in Louisville, KY. No grants to individuals.
Application information: Unsolicited requests for funds not accepted.
Directors: Glenn E. Thomas; Joan E. Thomas; Lee B. Thomas.
EIN: 611166955
Selected grants: The following grants were reported in 2006.
$150,000 to Home of the Innocents, Louisville, KY.
$115,000 to University of Louisville, Louisville, KY. 2 grants: $75,000, $40,000
$110,000 to Lincoln Foundation, Louisville, KY.
$100,000 to Center for Women and Families, Louisville, KY.
$100,000 to Friends Committee on National Legislation (FCNL) Education Fund, DC.
$75,000 to Bellarmine University, Louisville, KY.
$50,000 to Wilmington College, Wilmington, OH.
$30,000 to Friends School, Louisville, KY.
$30,000 to Neighborhood House, Louisville, KY.

3430
The Jones Family Charitable Foundation, Inc. ◇ ☆

6009 Brownsboro Park Blvd., Ste. H
Louisville, KY   40207   (502) 899-5995

Established in 2004 in KY.
Donors: Soterion Corp.; Robert N. Jones.
Foundation type: Independent foundation.
Financial data (yr. ended 12/31/05): Assets, $475,215 (M); expenditures, $730,154; qualifying distributions, $683,200; giving activities include $683,200 for 18 grants (high: $525,000; low: $100).
Fields of interest: Education; Human services; Christian agencies & churches.
Limitations: Giving on a national basis, with some emphasis on KY.
Application information:
   Initial approach: Letter or telephone
   Deadline(s): None
Officers: Robert N. Jones, Pres.; Margaret W. Jones, Secy.; Robert S. Jones, Treas.
EIN: 202059627

3431
The Frank and Mattie Justice Charitable Foundation ◇

P.O. Box 2230
Pikeville, KY   41502
Contact: Karla Corbin, Tr.

Established in 1999 in KY.
Donor: Frank Justice.
Foundation type: Independent foundation.
Financial data (yr. ended 12/31/05): Assets, $13,887,049 (M); expenditures, $516,756; qualifying distributions, $510,791; giving activities include $489,552 for 13 grants (high: $231,547; low: $1,600).
Fields of interest: Secondary school/education; Scholarships/financial aid.
Type of support: General/operating support; Building/renovation; Equipment.
Limitations: Giving primarily in the Appalachian area of KY. No support for religious organizations (except Churches of Christ).
Publications: Application guidelines; Grants list.
Application information: Application form required.
   Initial approach: Telephone for application
   Copies of proposal: 2
   Deadline(s): Sept. 1
   Board meeting date(s): Nov. 1
Trustees: Karla Corbin; Bridget Justice; Frank Justice; Frank Justice II; Jason Justice; Mattie Justice.
Number of staff: 1 part-time professional.
EIN: 597162579
Selected grants: The following grants were reported in 2004.
$50,400 to Pikeville College, Pikeville, KY.
$10,193 to YMCA.

3432
Keeneland Foundation, Inc.

4201 Versailles Rd.
P.O. Box 1690
Lexington, KY   40588-1690   (859) 288-4246
Contact: Fran Taylor, Exec. Dir.; Sandy Chin
FAX: (859) 255-2484;
E-mail: ftaylor@keeneland.com; Additional tel.:

(859) 288-4142; URL: http://www.keeneland.com/about/foundation.asp

Established in 1999 in KY.
Donors: Keeneland Association Inc.; Maker's Mark.
Foundation type: Company-sponsored foundation.
Financial data (yr. ended 6/30/05): Assets, $682,878 (M); gifts received, $672,049; expenditures, $845,121; qualifying distributions, $832,175; giving activities include $822,175 for 51 grants (high: $200,000; low: $1,000), and $10,000 for 1 employee matching gift.
Purpose and activities: The foundation supports organizations involved with higher education, health, and human services. Special emphasis is directed toward programs designed to serve the equine industry, specifically in the areas of thoroughbred breeding and racing.
Fields of interest: Higher education; Veterinary medicine; Health care; Human services.
Type of support: Research; General/operating support; Capital campaigns; Building/renovation; Equipment; Endowments; Program development; Scholarship funds; Employee matching gifts.
Limitations: Giving primarily in central KY. No support for political organizations, primary or secondary schools, fraternal or veterans' organizations not of direct benefit to the entire community, religious organizations not of direct benefit to the entire community, or youth sports leagues. No grants to individuals, or for courtesy advertising, annual campaigns, general operating support for hospitals or patient care institutions, or tickets or sponsorships; no ticket or dining space contributions.
Publications: Application guidelines; Annual report.
Application information: Proposals should be no longer than 3 pages. Board of directors lists should be no longer than 2 pages. Application form required.
   Initial approach: Download application form and mail proposal and application form to foundation
   Copies of proposal: 5
   Deadline(s): None
   Board meeting date(s): Quarterly
Officers: J.E. Bassett III, Pres.; L.L. Haggin III, V.P.; Harvie B. Wilkinson, Secy.; Jessica A. Green, Treas.; Fran Taylor, Exec. Dir.
Trustee: William Bishop.
EIN: 611358165
Selected grants: The following grants were reported in 2004.
$170,000 to Thoroughbred Retirement Foundation, Secretariat Center, Shrewsbury, NJ.
$50,000 to Kentucky Historical Society, Frankfort, KY. To sponsor Changing Exhibits Gallery at Kentucky History Center.
$50,000 to YMCA of Central Kentucky, Lexington, KY. For capital campaign.
$10,000 to American Cancer Society, Lexington, KY. For construction of Hope Lodge office complex.
$10,000 to Center for Women, Children and Families, Lexington, KY.
$5,000 to Bluegrass Conservancy, Lexington, KY. For public education.
$5,000 to Hope Center, Lexington, KY. For general support.
$3,000 to Young Life, Lexington, KY. For camp scholarships.
$1,000 to Buckhorn Childrens Foundation, Buckhorn, KY. For animal therapy program.

$1,000 to Kentucky Harvest, Louisville, KY. For general support.

3433
Kentucky Fund for Healthy Living, Inc. ◇ ☆

c/o Mark A. Modlin
130 Dudley Rd.
Edgewood, KY   41017-2396
Contact: Mark A. Modlin, Pres.

Established in 2003 in KY.
Donor: Boone Circuit Court.
Foundation type: Independent foundation.
Financial data (yr. ended 3/31/05): Assets, $20,498,339 (M); expenditures, $2,014,391; qualifying distributions, $1,593,895; giving activities include $1,452,595 for 30 grants (high: $150,000; low: $3,600).
Purpose and activities: Giving to promote healthy living.
Application information: Applicants should submit a letter of request, indicating how the grant will benefit or promote healthy living.
   Initial approach: Letter of request
   Deadline(s): None
Officers: Mark A. Modlin, Pres. and Mgr.; Melbourne Mills, Jr., V.P. and Secy.; Shirley A. Cunningham, Jr., V.P. and Treas.; William J. Gallion, V.P.
EIN: 300162664

3434
Kindred Foundation Inc. ☆

(formerly Vencor Foundation, Inc.)
c/o Kindred Healthcare, Inc.
680 S. 4th St.
Louisville, KY   40202-2412
Contact: Susan E. Moss, V.P.

Established in 1991 in KY.
Donors: Vencor, Inc.; Kindred Healthcare, Inc.; Ventas, Inc.; Kindred Healthcare Operating, Inc.; Kindred Hospice Charities, Inc.
Foundation type: Company-sponsored foundation.
Financial data (yr. ended 12/31/05): Assets, $14,787 (M); gifts received, $600,035; expenditures, $1,029,748; qualifying distributions, $1,029,715; giving activities include $1,029,715 for grants.
Purpose and activities: The foundation supports organizations involved with arts and culture, education, health, children and youth services, and human services.
Fields of interest: Performing arts, opera; Arts; Elementary/secondary education; Education, special; Education; Health care; Children/youth, services; Family services; Human services.
Limitations: Applications not accepted. Giving primarily in areas of company operations, with emphasis on Louisville, KY.
Application information: Contributes only to pre-selected organizations.
Officers and Directors:* Richard E. Chapman,* Pres.; Susan E. Moss,* V.P.; Joseph L. Landewich,* Secy.; John J. Lucchese, Treas.; Paul J. Diaz; Teri A. Hartlage; Donald H. Robinson.
EIN: 611204724
Selected grants: The following grants were reported in 2003.
$40,600 to Greater Louisville Inc., Louisville, KY. For general support.

$23,894 to United Way of New York City, New York, NY. For general support.

$15,000 to Johns Hopkins University, Baltimore, MD. For general support.

$14,480 to Health Enterprises Network, Louisville, KY. For general support.

$14,215 to Alzheimers Disease and Related Disorders Association, Louisville, KY. For general support.

$12,500 to American Lung Association of Kentucky, Louisville, KY. For general support.

$10,000 to Saint Elizabeths Regional Maternity Center, New Albany, IN. For general support.

$9,310 to American Cancer Society, Logan Unit, Louisville, KY. For general support.

$8,000 to Family and Children First, Louisville, KY. For general support.

$7,500 to Kentucky Derby Museum Corporation, Louisville, KY. For general support.

3435
The Klein Family Foundation, Inc. ✧

(formerly Julia & Isadore Klein Family Foundation, Inc.)
6714 Elmcroft Cir.
Louisville, KY 40241
Contact: Bertram W. Klein, Pres.

Established in 1965.
Donors: Bertram W. Klein; David Klein; Richard Klein; Stephen Klein.
Foundation type: Independent foundation.
Financial data (yr. ended 12/31/05): Assets, $8,457,361 (M); expenditures, $495,728; qualifying distributions, $433,194; giving activities include $433,194 for 203 grants (high: $100,000; low: $15).
Purpose and activities: Giving for arts, education, religion, and health and human services.
Fields of interest: Arts; Education; Health care; Human services; Jewish agencies & temples.
Type of support: General/operating support; Annual campaigns; Capital campaigns; Building/renovation.
Limitations: Giving primarily in Louisville, KY.
Application information: Application form not required.
Deadline(s): None
Officers and Directors:* Bertram W. Klein, Pres.; Beth Paxton Klein, Secy.; Richard Klein,* Treas.; David Klein; Elaine B. Klein; Stephen Klein.
EIN: 610648689
Selected grants: The following grants were reported in 2003.
$201,409 to Temple, The, Louisville, KY.
$18,500 to Kentucky Center for the Arts, Louisville, KY.
$8,000 to University of Louisville Foundation, Louisville, KY.
$4,165 to Kentucky Country Day School, Louisville, KY.
$3,600 to Actors Theater of Louisville, Louisville, KY.
$1,100 to Alzheimers Disease and Related Disorders Association, Louisville, KY.
$1,000 to American Diabetes Foundation, Louisville, KY.
$500 to Family and Childrens Counseling Center, Louisville, KY.
$200 to Cabbage Patch Settlement House, Louisville, KY.
$200 to Dare to Care Food Bank, Louisville, KY.

3436
Frank S. and Julia M. Ladner Family Foundation ✧

c/o John S. Lueken
3300 National City
Louisville, KY 40202-3197

Established in 1993 in KY.
Donors: Frank S. Ladner; Julia M. Ladner.
Foundation type: Independent foundation.
Financial data (yr. ended 12/31/05): Assets, $17,620,413 (M); gifts received, $11,452; expenditures, $1,296,893; qualifying distributions, $1,188,500; giving activities include $1,188,500 for 40 grants (high: $1,000,000; low: $500).
Purpose and activities: Giving primarily to Roman Catholic organizations and education.
Fields of interest: Education; Human services; Roman Catholic agencies & churches.
Limitations: Applications not accepted. No grants to individuals.
Application information: Contributes only to pre-selected organizations.
Officers and Directors:* Frank S. Ladner, Pres.; Julia M. Ladner,* Secy.-Treas.; Mary F.L. Bauer; Ann Marie Ladner; Julia M. Ladner; Margaret M. Ladner; Thomas M. Ladner; William P. Ladner.
EIN: 611248781

3437
The W. Paul & Lucille Caudill Little Foundation, Inc. ✧

c/o Bank of the Bluegrass
101 E. High St.
Lexington, KY 40507

Established in KY.
Donor: Lucille Caudill Little.
Foundation type: Independent foundation.
Financial data (yr. ended 12/31/05): Assets, $16,683,093 (M); expenditures, $1,556,365; qualifying distributions, $1,356,893; giving activities include $1,340,728 for 11 grants (high: $1,000,000; low: $5,000).
Purpose and activities: Giving primarily to a children's theater; funding also for higher education.
Fields of interest: Arts; Higher education; Education.
Type of support: Building/renovation.
Limitations: Applications not accepted. Giving primarily in Lexington, KY. No grants to individuals.
Application information: Contributes only to pre-selected organizations.
Officers: Charles A. Caudill, Pres.; Boone Procter Caudill, Secy.; Katharine M. Milby, Treas.
Directors: Dee Fizdale; Mark Herren; Clay Maupin; B.D. McDonald; Mark Neff; Charlotte Parrish; Delores N. Roberson; Gary L. Rohrer; Susan Skinner; Jo Smith.
EIN: 611250327
Selected grants: The following grants were reported in 2005.
$1,000,000 to Rowan, County of, Morehead, KY. For renovation and restoration of old courthouse.
$98,060 to Prichard Committee for Academic Excellence, Lexington, KY. For parents and teachers as arts partners.
$78,629 to Lexington Childrens Theater, Lexington, KY. For dramatic education outreach program.
$49,165 to Music Institute of Lexington, Lexington, KY.

$31,000 to Hospice of the Bluegrass, Lexington, KY. For using arts to help heal children.
$23,000 to Lexington Childrens Museum, Lexington, KY.
$19,826 to University of Louisville, Louisville, KY.
$18,189 to University of Kentucky, Lexington, KY.

3438
The Marshall Charitable Foundation, Inc. ✧ ☆

P.O. Box 7066
Louisville, KY 40257

Established in 1998 in KY.
Donors: Homestead Co.; Louisville Timber Co.; Maggie T. Marshall.
Foundation type: Independent foundation.
Financial data (yr. ended 12/31/05): Assets, $16,100,099 (M); gifts received, $9,222,402; expenditures, $564,330; qualifying distributions, $525,000; giving activities include $525,000 for grants.
Purpose and activities: Giving primarily for education.
Fields of interest: Secondary school/education; Education; Medical care, rehabilitation; Health care; Protestant agencies & churches.
Limitations: Applications not accepted. Giving primarily in KY. No grants to individuals.
Application information: Contributes only to pre-selected organizations.
Officers: Robert Wood Marshall, Sr., Pres.; Frank H. Thiemann III, V.P.; Sue Ellen Marshall, Secy.; Phillip H. Marshall, Sr., Treas.
Directors: Andrew M. Davidson; Martin P. Duffy; Clay M. Keeley; Phillip H. Marshall, Jr.; Robert Woodrow Marshall; Scott E. Sanders.
EIN: 611308522
Selected grants: The following grants were reported in 2004.
$60,000 to Trinity High School, Louisville, KY.
$5,000 to Youth Alive, Louisville, KY.

3439
Jessie Barker McKellar Charitable Foundation ✧

c/o The Glenview Trust Co.
4969 U.S. Hwy. 42, Ste. 2000
Louisville, KY 40222
Application address: c/o Douglas H. McKellar, Jr., 364 Saint Cloud Rd., Los Angeles, CA 90077-3423, tel.: (408) 626-2770

Established in 1997 in KY.
Foundation type: Independent foundation.
Financial data (yr. ended 12/31/05): Assets, $8,213,544 (M); expenditures, $409,262; qualifying distributions, $354,490; giving activities include $351,290 for 8 grants (high: $214,790; low: $5,000).
Fields of interest: Museums; Hospitals (general).
Limitations: Giving primarily in CA.
Application information:
Initial approach: Letter
Deadline(s): None
Trustee: The Glenview Trust Co.
EIN: 626323409
Selected grants: The following grants were reported in 2004.
$140,000 to Saint Johns Health Center Foundation, Santa Monica, CA.

$25,000 to House Ear Institute, Los Angeles, CA.
$15,000 to Home of the Innocents, Louisville, KY.
$10,000 to All Saints Episcopal Church, Pasadena, CA.

3440

The Mustard Seed Foundation ✧ ☆

200 Big Run Rd.
Lexington, KY   40503

Established in 2001 in KY.
Donors: Rick Ifland; John S. Sawyer.
Foundation type: Independent foundation.
Financial data (yr. ended 12/31/05): Assets, $13,252 (M); gifts received, $393,508; expenditures, $381,120; qualifying distributions, $381,120; giving activities include $20,258 for 2 grants (high: $18,358; low: $1,900), and $299,920 for 3 grants to individuals (high: $147,550; low: $46,870).
Fields of interest: Religion.
Type of support: Grants to individuals.
Limitations: Applications not accepted.
Application information: Unsolicited requests for funds not accepted.
Directors: T.H. Callahan; Rick Ifland; Robert V. Sartin; John S. Sawyer.
EIN: 611390910

3441

The Norton Foundation, Inc.

(formerly The George W. Norton Foundation, Inc.)
4350 Brownsboro Rd., Ste. 133
Louisville, KY   40207   (502) 893-9549
Contact: Lucy Crawford, Secy.-Treas.
FAX: (502) 896-9378;
E-mail: lcrawford@nortonfoundation.com;
URL: http://www.nortonfoundation.com

Incorporated in 1958 in KY.
Donor: Mrs. George W. Norton†.
Foundation type: Independent foundation.
Financial data (yr. ended 12/31/05): Assets, $16,519,589 (M); expenditures, $1,073,287; qualifying distributions, $901,221; giving activities include $731,032 for 37 grants (high: $60,000; low: $3,500).
Purpose and activities: The foundation's mission is to contribute to the improvement of the quality of life, and foster a favorable business climate in the company's communities in North America, consistent with and supportive of business objectives.
Fields of interest: Arts education; Education, early childhood education; Elementary school/education; Secondary school/education; Education, reading; Education; Human services; Children/youth, services; Family services; Minorities/immigrants, centers/services; Economically disadvantaged.
Type of support: General/operating support; Continuing support; Endowments; Program development; Seed money; Scholarship funds.
Limitations: Giving limited to the Louisville, KY, area. No grants to individuals.
Publications: Application guidelines; Financial statement; Grants list.
Application information: Application form required.
  Initial approach: Proposal
  Copies of proposal: 3
  Deadline(s): Quarterly

Board meeting date(s): Quarterly
Final notification: 1 month
Officers and Directors:* Jane Norton Newton,* Pres.; Robert W. Dulaney,* V.P.; Lucy Crawford,* Secy.-Treas. and Exec. Dir.; Richard H.C. Clay.
Number of staff: 1 full-time professional.
EIN: 616024040
Selected grants: The following grants were reported in 2004.
$75,000 to Kentucky Museum of Arts and Design, Louisville, KY.
$61,000 to Waldorf School of Louisville, Louisville, KY.
$52,900 to Jefferson County Public Schools, Louisville, KY.
$52,500 to Association of Waldorf Schools of North America, Minneapolis, MN.
$50,000 to Family Place, Louisville, KY.
$35,000 to J. B. Speed Art Museum, Louisville, KY.
$35,000 to Kentucky Center for the Arts, Louisville, KY.
$35,000 to Louisville Central Community Center, Louisville, KY.
$25,000 to Kentucky Collaborative for Teaching and Learning, Louisville, KY.
$20,000 to Americana Community Center, Louisville, KY.

3442

The David C. and Wendy L. Novak Foundation, Inc. ✧

13006 Osage Rd. N.
Anchorage, KY   40223

Established in 1999 in KY.
Donors: David C. Novak; Wendy L. Novak.
Foundation type: Independent foundation.
Financial data (yr. ended 12/31/05): Assets, $2,607,163 (M); gifts received, $990,499; expenditures, $363,711; qualifying distributions, $350,055; giving activities include $350,055 for 25 grants (high: $120,000; low: $30).
Purpose and activities: Giving primarily for Christian organizations, and for health associations.
Fields of interest: Arts; Health organizations, association; Youth, services; Federated giving programs; Christian agencies & churches.
Limitations: Applications not accepted. No grants to individuals.
Application information: Contributes only to pre-selected organizations.
Officers and Directors:* David C. Novak,* Pres.; Wendy L. Novak,* V.P. and Secy.-Treas.; Susan B. Novak.
EIN: 611359337

3443

Omnicare Charitable Foundation ✧

c/o Omnicare, Inc.
100 E. Rivercenter Blvd.
Covington, KY   41011
Application address: Vern Gideon, 2313 S. Mount Prospect Rd., Des Plaines, IL 60018, tel.: (847) 635-3000

Established in 1997 in OH.
Donors: Omnicare, Inc.; Omnicare Foundation.
Foundation type: Company-sponsored foundation.
Financial data (yr. ended 12/31/04): Assets, $13,500 (M); gifts received, $580,103; expenditures, $590,748; qualifying distributions,

$590,476; giving activities include $590,476 for 92 grants (high: $69,500; low: $18).
Purpose and activities: The foundation supports Jewish agencies and temples and organizations involved with senior citizens.
Fields of interest: Geriatrics; Aging, centers/services; Jewish agencies & temples; Aging.
Type of support: General/operating support.
Limitations: Giving primarily in Chicago, IL.
Application information: Application form not required.
  Initial approach: Proposal
  Deadline(s): None
Officers and Directors:* Joel F. Gemunder,* Pres.; Cheryl D. Hodges,* Secy.; Thomas R. Marsh, Treas.; Vern Gideon; Patrick E. Keefe.
EIN: 611314910

3444

Omnicare Foundation ✧

c/o Omnicare, Inc.
1600 River Center II
100 E. Rivercenter Blvd.
Covington, KY   41011   (859) 392-3331
Contact: Cheryl D. Hodges, Secy.

Established in 1993 in KY.
Donors: Omnicare, Inc.; Thomas R. Isgrig.
Foundation type: Company-sponsored foundation.
Financial data (yr. ended 12/31/04): Assets, $1,843,511 (M); gifts received, $2,775,489; expenditures, $1,134,882; qualifying distributions, $1,133,723; giving activities include $1,127,463 for 36 grants (high: $580,103; low: $1,000).
Purpose and activities: The foundation supports organizations involved with education, health, religion, and senior citizens.
Fields of interest: Elementary school/education; Higher education; Pharmacy/prescriptions; Health care; Geriatrics; Jewish federated giving programs; Religion; Aging.
Type of support: Program development; Sponsorships; Building/renovation; Scholarship funds; Capital campaigns.
Limitations: Giving on a national basis. No grants to individuals.
Application information: Application form not required.
  Initial approach: Letter of inquiry
  Deadline(s): None
Officers and Directors :* Joel F. Gemunder,* Pres.; Cheryl D. Hodges,* Secy.; Thomas R. Marsh, Treas.; Patrick E. Keefe.
EIN: 311389112

3445

Orleton Trust Fund ✧

c/o Anne Greene
324 Overton St.
Newport, KY   41071-1746

Trust established in 1944 in OH.
Donor: Mary E. Johnston†.
Foundation type: Independent foundation.
Financial data (yr. ended 12/31/04): Assets, $9,196,241 (M); expenditures, $505,688; qualifying distributions, $426,095; giving activities include $426,095 for 12 grants (high: $85,219; low: $17,044).
Fields of interest: Foundations (community); Federated giving programs.

Type of support: General/operating support; Building/renovation; Scholarship funds.
Limitations: Applications not accepted. Giving primarily in the San Francisco, CA, area, and Cincinnati, OH; some funding also in Tampa, FL. No grants to individuals.
Application information: Contributes only to pre-selected organizations.
Board meeting date(s): As required
Trustees: Edward Sawyer; John Sawyer.
EIN: 316024543
Selected grants: The following grants were reported in 2003.
$154,000 to Greater Cincinnati Foundation, Cincinnati, OH. 2 grants: $77,000 (For Ed Sawyer Fund), $77,000 (For John and Ruth Sawyer Fund).
$37,500 to Inventing Flight, Dayton, OH.
$25,000 to Girl Scouts of the U.S.A., Buckeye Trails Council, Dayton, OH.
$20,000 to Arts Center Foundation, Dayton, OH.
$20,000 to Community Blood Center, Dayton, OH.
$20,000 to United Way of the Greater Dayton Area, Dayton, OH.
$19,250 to Community Foundation of Tampa Bay, Tampa, FL. For Mary Elizabeth Smith Family Fund.
$15,000 to United Theological Seminary, Dayton, OH.
$5,000 to YWCA of Dayton, Dayton, OH.

3446
Raymond B. Preston Family Foundation ✧
P.O. Box 652
Henderson, KY 42420

Established in 1989 in MD.
Donors: Hattie L. Preston; Raymond B. Preston.
Foundation type: Independent foundation.
Financial data (yr. ended 12/31/05): Assets, $5,629,960 (M); gifts received, $232,234; expenditures, $564,225; qualifying distributions, $516,733; giving activities include $516,733 for 27 grants (high: $166,667; low: $1,000).
Purpose and activities: Giving primarily for education and religious purposes, particularly Christian and Episcopal organizations.
Fields of interest: Arts; Higher education; Libraries (public); Human services; YM/YWCAs & YM/YWHAs; Federated giving programs; Christian agencies & churches; Protestant agencies & churches; Religion.
Type of support: General/operating support; Building/renovation.
Limitations: Applications not accepted. Giving primarily in KY, with emphasis on Henderson and Louisville. No grants to individuals.
Application information: Contributes only to pre-selected organizations.
Directors: Charlotte Critser; Scott P. Davis; Viki Gurowitz; Sarah Morgan; Hattie L. Preston; Jennifer Preston; Leigh Anne Preston; Raymond B. Preston; Jerry Wischer.
EIN: 521676236

3447
Reed Foundation ✧
c/o David W. Reed
P.O. Box 67
Gilbertsville, KY 42044-0067

Established in 1990 in KY.

Donor: David W. Reed.
Foundation type: Independent foundation.
Financial data (yr. ended 12/31/05): Assets, $8,003,464 (M); expenditures, $668,251; qualifying distributions, $646,406; giving activities include $646,406 for 29 grants (high: $125,000; low: $1,000).
Purpose and activities: Giving primarily for education, and children, youth and social services.
Fields of interest: Performing arts centers; Secondary school/education; Higher education; Education; Human services; Children/youth, services; Federated giving programs.
Type of support: General/operating support; Building/renovation; Endowments.
Limitations: Applications not accepted. Giving limited to KY. No grants to individuals.
Application information: Contributes only to pre-selected organizations.
Trustee: David W. Reed.
EIN: 611189284

3448
The River Foundation, Inc. ✧
c/o First Southern Bancorp
P.O. Box 328
Stanford, KY 40484

Established in 1990 in KY.
Donors: Jess Correll; First Southern National Bank of Lincoln County; National Bank of Lancaster.
Foundation type: Independent foundation.
Financial data (yr. ended 12/31/04): Assets, $42,665 (M); gifts received, $547,984; expenditures, $1,001,960; qualifying distributions, $1,001,937; giving activities include $904,387 for 16 grants (high: $60,000; low: $1,000).
Fields of interest: YM/YWCAs & YM/YWHAs; Christian agencies & churches; Protestant agencies & churches; Economically disadvantaged.
Type of support: General/operating support.
Limitations: Applications not accepted. Giving primarily in KY. No grants to individuals.
Application information: Contributes only to pre-selected organizations.
Officers and Directors:* Jess Correll,* Pres.; Randall Attkisson,* V.P.; Betty England, Secy.-Treas.; Greg Correll, Exec. Dir.; Rusty Clark; Ward Correll; Dale Ditto; Doug Dockter; Dennis Kinlaw; Rockie Mason; Lystan Peebles; Gayle Toole.
EIN: 611190262
Selected grants: The following grants were reported in 2003.
$55,000 to Global Focus, Woodstock, GA.
$50,000 to Fidelity Investments Charitable Gift Fund, Boston, MA.
$50,000 to Servers International, Cary, NC.
$47,100 to Family Foundation of Kentucky, Lexington, KY.
$40,199 to Lyston Peebles Ministry, Raleigh, NC.
$35,200 to Southside Christian Church, Harrodsburg, KY.
$32,125 to Young Life, Lexington, KY.
$31,500 to Ministry Ventures, Roswell, GA.
$28,350 to Oak Ranch, Sanford, NC.
$26,507 to Prison Family Ministries, Wilmore, KY.

3449
E. O. Robinson Mountain Fund ✧
P.O. Box 54930
Lexington, KY 40555-4930
Contact: Juanita Stollings, Secy.-Treas.

Incorporated in 1922 in KY.
Donors: Edward O. Robinson†; University of Kentucky.
Foundation type: Independent foundation.
Financial data (yr. ended 6/30/05): Assets, $16,982,799 (M); expenditures, $701,347; qualifying distributions, $560,798; giving activities include $457,000 for 30 grants (high: $50,000; low: $3,000).
Purpose and activities: To promote the general welfare of the people of eastern KY in the areas of education, health care, and community programs.
Fields of interest: Higher education; Adult/continuing education; Libraries (public); Education; Speech/hearing centers; Health care; Crime/violence prevention, domestic violence; Food services; Community development; Christian agencies & churches.
Type of support: General/operating support; Continuing support; Building/renovation; Equipment; Scholarship funds; Matching/challenge support.
Limitations: Giving limited to 30 counties in eastern KY. No grants to individuals.
Publications: Informational brochure.
Application information: Application form not required.
Initial approach: Letter
Copies of proposal: 11
Deadline(s): None
Board meeting date(s): Every 4 months
Officers and Directors:* Hon. N. Mitchell Meade,* Chair.; Vinson A. Watts,* Vice-Chair.; Juanita Stollings,* Secy.-Treas.; J. Hagan Codell; Hon. Sara Walter Combs; Susan Duff; William Engle III; Judy Rose; J. Phil Smith.
Number of staff: 1 full-time professional; 2 full-time support.
EIN: 610449642
Selected grants: The following grants were reported in 2005.
$50,000 to Cardinal Hill Foundation, Lexington, KY.
$25,000 to Alice Lloyd College, Pippa Passes, KY.
$25,000 to Kentucky Mountain Bible College, Vancleve, KY.
$13,000 to Berea College, Berea, KY.
$12,500 to David School, David, KY.
$11,000 to Lindsey Wilson College, Columbia, KY.
$10,000 to Georgetown College, Georgetown, KY.
$10,000 to Morehead State University, Morehead, KY.
$10,000 to Pikeville College, Pikeville, KY.
$8,000 to Transylvania University, Lexington, KY.

3450
The Rosenthal Foundation, Inc. ✧
P.O. Box 54826
Lexington, KY 40555-4826

Established in 1989 in KY.
Donors: Warren W. Rosenthal; Betty M. Rosenthal.
Foundation type: Independent foundation.
Financial data (yr. ended 12/31/05): Assets, $4,321,159 (M); gifts received, $630,000; expenditures, $950,258; qualifying distributions, $945,576; giving activities include $945,576 for grants.

Purpose and activities: Giving primarily for arts, education, health associations, and youth services.

Fields of interest: Visual arts; Museums; Museums (children's); Historic preservation/historical societies; Arts; Elementary/secondary education; Higher education; Health care; Health organizations, association; Children/youth, services; Jewish agencies & temples.

Type of support: General/operating support; Land acquisition; Endowments.

Limitations: Applications not accepted. Giving primarily in Lexington, KY. No grants to individuals.

Application information: Contributes only to pre-selected organizations.

Officers: Warren W. Rosenthal, Pres. and Mgr.; Betty M. Rosenthal, Secy.-Treas.

EIN: 611161776

Selected grants: The following grants were reported in 2005.

$450,000 to Transylvania University, Lexington, KY.

$40,000 to Lourdes Hospital, Paducah, KY.

$7,000 to Sayre School, Lexington, KY.

$250 to National Jewish Medical and Research Center, Denver, CO.

$250 to Smile Train, New York, NY.

$200 to Lexington Public Library Foundation, Lexington, KY.

$100 to Navy Supply Corps Foundation, Athens, GA.

$100 to United Negro College Fund, Fairfax, VA.

3451
The Sutherland Foundation, Inc. ◇
7001 U.S. Hwy. 42
Louisville, KY 40241

Established in 1989 in KY.

Donor: Laura Lee Lyons Brown.

Foundation type: Independent foundation.

Financial data (yr. ended 3/31/05): Assets, $15,805,783 (M); gifts received, $206,000; expenditures, $1,074,769; qualifying distributions, $935,153; giving activities include $926,891 for 60 grants (high: $225,000; low: $25).

Purpose and activities: Giving primarily for arts and culture. Giving also for education, human services, Christian churches, and to environmental organizations.

Fields of interest: Arts; Education; Environment; Recreation; Human services; Community development; Christian agencies & churches.

Type of support: General/operating support; Continuing support; Annual campaigns; Capital campaigns; Building/renovation; Land acquisition; Endowments; Program development.

Limitations: Applications not accepted. Giving primarily in the greater Louisville, KY, area. No grants to individuals.

Application information: Contributes only to pre-selected organizations.

Officer: Laura Lee Lyons Brown, Pres. and Secy.-Treas.

EIN: 616175862

3452
Trager Family Foundation, Inc. ◇
601 W. Market St.
Louisville, KY 40202

Established in 1998 in KY.

Donor: Bernard M. Trager.

Foundation type: Independent foundation.

Financial data (yr. ended 12/31/05): Assets, $3,398,743 (M); gifts received, $687,531; expenditures, $335,400; qualifying distributions, $333,959; giving activities include $333,959 for 5 grants (high: $193,025; low: $10,000).

Fields of interest: Higher education; Hospitals (general); Jewish agencies & temples.

Type of support: General/operating support.

Limitations: Applications not accepted. Giving primarily in Louisville, KY. No grants to individuals.

Application information: Contributes only to pre-selected organizations.

Officers: Bernard M. Trager, Pres.; Steven E. Trager, V.P.; Shelley Trager Kusman, Secy.; Jean S. Trager, Treas.

EIN: 611337078

3453
Fred B. & Opal S. Woosley Foundation, Inc. ◇
900 Kentucky Home Life Bldg.
Louisville, KY 40202 (502) 588-1194
Application address: Arthur C. Peter c/o Hilliard Lyons Asset Mgmt., 501 S. 4th St., P.O. Box 32760, Louisville, KY 40232

Established in 1986 in KY.

Foundation type: Independent foundation.

Financial data (yr. ended 12/31/05): Assets, $6,941,012 (M); expenditures, $437,487; qualifying distributions, $437,487; giving activities include $396,000 for 50 grants (high: $34,000; low: $1,000).

Purpose and activities: Giving primarily for physically and mentally handicapped children in the Jefferson County, KY, area.

Fields of interest: Children, services; Disabilities, people with.

Limitations: Giving primarily in the Jefferson County, KY, area. No grants to individuals.

Application information: Application form not required.

Initial approach: Letter
Copies of proposal: 1
Deadline(s): None
Board meeting date(s): Dec.
Final notification: After board meeting; positive replies only

Officer and Directors:* Arthur C. Peter,* Pres.; John McFerran Barr; David A. Bell; Beverly S. Clark; Donald E. Meyer.

EIN: 611104319

3454
Marilyn & William Young Charitable Foundation, Inc. ◇
(formerly Marilyn & William Young Foundation)
P.O. Box 825
Owensboro, KY 42302-0549
Application address: c/o Sara Hemingway, P.O. Box 1860, Owensboro, KY 42302-1860

Established in 1993 in KY.

Donor: Marilyn F. Young.

Foundation type: Independent foundation.

Financial data (yr. ended 12/31/05): Assets, $12,122,622 (M); expenditures, $733,118; qualifying distributions, $652,104; giving activities include $643,686 for 68 grants (high: $80,000; low: $550).

Purpose and activities: Giving primarily for the arts, particularly to museums; funding also for health and social services.

Fields of interest: Museums; Museums (art); Museums (specialized); Performing arts centers; Performing arts, orchestra (symphony); Arts; Education; Boys & girls clubs; Human services; Developmentally disabled, centers & services; Community development.

Type of support: Scholarship funds.

Limitations: Giving primarily in Owensboro, KY.

Application information: Application form not required.

Deadline(s): None

Directors: Gayle S. Dorsey; E. Phillips Malone; William R. Young III.

EIN: 616175836

3455
W. T. Young Family Foundation, Inc. ◇
P.O. Box 1110
Lexington, KY 40589-1110

Established in 1981 in KY.

Donors: William T. Young; William T. Young, Jr.; The William T. Young Revocable Trust.

Foundation type: Independent foundation.

Financial data (yr. ended 12/31/05): Assets, $3,578,419 (M); gifts received, $2,801,445; expenditures, $2,138,930; qualifying distributions, $2,130,936; giving activities include $2,129,430 for 10 grants (high: $1,238,680; low: $1,250).

Purpose and activities: Giving primarily for higher education and the arts.

Fields of interest: Museums; Arts; Higher education; Cancer; Urban/community development.

Limitations: Applications not accepted. Giving primarily in KY, with emphasis on Lexington. No grants to individuals.

Application information: Contributes only to pre-selected organizations.

Officers: William T. Young, Pres.; Douglas Dean, V.P.; Robert Warren, Secy.-Treas.

Directors: Lucy Young Hamilton; Christopher H. Young; Meade C. Young.

EIN: 311020207

Selected grants: The following grants were reported in 2003.

$400,000 to Muhammad Ali Museum and Education Center, Louisville, KY.

$300,000 to Kentucky Educational Television, Lexington, KY.

$200,000 to Sayre School, Lexington, KY.

$200,000 to University of South Florida Foundation, Tampa, FL.

$55,000 to Shakertown at Pleasant Hill, Harrodsburg, KY.

$20,000 to Little Traverse Conservancy, Harbor Springs, MI.

$10,000 to Grayson-Jockey Club Research Foundation, New York, NY.

$10,000 to Kentucky Horse Park Foundation, Lexington, KY.

3456
John B. & Brownie Young Memorial Fund ◇
c/o BB&T
230 Frederica St.
Owensboro, KY 42301 (270) 688-7878

Established in 1961 in KY.
Foundation type: Independent foundation.
Financial data (yr. ended 12/31/05): Assets, $17,688,624 (M); expenditures, $1,193,530; qualifying distributions, $1,104,792; giving activities include $1,000,264 for grants to individuals.
Purpose and activities: Scholarships for students in school districts of Daviess, McClean, and Owensboro counties, KY.
Fields of interest: Education.
Type of support: Scholarships—to individuals.
Limitations: Giving limited to Daviess, McLean, and Owensboro school districts in KY.
Application information: Applications available at area high schools. Application form required.
   Deadline(s): Beginning of college year
Trustee: BB&T.
EIN: 616025137

3457
Yum! Brands Foundation ▼ ✧
(formerly Tricon Foundation, Inc.)
P.O. Box 35910
Louisville, KY 40232 (502) 874-8294
Contact: Mary Dossett

Application address: 1441 Gardiner Ln., Louisville, KY 40213-5910; URL: http://www.yum.com/responsibility/foundation.asp

Established in 1998 in KY and TX.
Donors: Tricon Global Restaurants, Inc.; Yum! Brands, Inc.
Foundation type: Company-sponsored foundation.
Financial data (yr. ended 12/31/05): Assets, $4,507,883 (M); gifts received, $8,918,836; expenditures, $4,604,885; qualifying distributions, $4,604,765; giving activities include $4,318,205 for 654 grants (high: $1,000,000; low: $25), and $281,261 for grants to individuals.
Purpose and activities: The foundation supports organizations involved with arts and culture, education, hunger, and youth development.
Fields of interest: Arts; Education; Food services; Food banks; Youth development.
Type of support: General/operating support; Loaned talent; Sponsorships; Employee matching gifts.
Limitations: Giving on a national basis, with some emphasis on Louisville, KY.
Application information: Application form required.

Initial approach: Contact foundation for application form
   Deadline(s): None
Officers and Directors:* David C. Novak,* Chair. and C.E.O.; Jonathan D. Blum,* Vice-Chair. and Pres.; Christian L. Campbell, V.P. and Secy.; Richard T. Carrucci, V.P. and Treas.; Greg Creed, V.P.; Donald Phillips, V.P.; W. Lawrence Gathof, C.F.O.; Brian J. Riendeau, Exec. Dir. and Admin.
EIN: 611327140
Selected grants: The following grants were reported in 2004.
$583,340 to United Way, Metro, Louisville, KY.
$528,698 to Fund for the Arts, Lexington, KY.
$250,000 to Scholarship America, Saint Peter, MN.
$244,113 to Dare to Care Food Bank, Louisville, KY.
$125,000 to Muhammad Ali Museum and Education Center, Louisville, KY.
$115,750 to Kentucky Opera, Louisville, KY.
$100,250 to J. B. Speed Art Museum, Louisville, KY.
$74,818 to United Way of the Bluegrass, Lexington, KY.
$34,295 to Saint Patrick School, Maysville, KY.
$25,000 to Gallopalooza, Louisville, KY.

LOUISIANA

3458
Yvonne & Red Adams Foundation ✧
228 St. Charles Ave., Ste. 707
New Orleans, LA 70130
Contact: Brad A. Adams

Established in 1994 in LA.
Donors: Byron A. "Red" Adams, Sr.; Yvonne B. Adams.
Foundation type: Independent foundation.
Financial data (yr. ended 12/31/05): Assets, $2,374,353 (M); gifts received, $250,000; expenditures, $619,165; qualifying distributions, $618,840; giving activities include $616,335 for 20 grants (high: $466,585; low: $2,500; average: $3,000–$25,000).
Purpose and activities: Giving primarily for religion, particularly Roman Catholic churches, organizations, and schools; funding also for human services.
Fields of interest: Secondary school/education; Higher education; Human services; Roman Catholic agencies & churches.
Limitations: Applications not accepted. Giving primarily in LA. No grants to individuals.
Application information: Contributes only to pre-selected organizations.
Officers: Yvonne B. Adams, Pres. and Treas.; Byron A. "Red" Adams, Sr., V.P. and Secy.
EIN: 721283535

3459
The Almar Foundation ☆
400 Poydras St., Ste. 1560
New Orleans, LA 70130
Contact: Susan Couvillon, Mgr.

Established in 1997 in LA.
Foundation type: Independent foundation.
Financial data (yr. ended 12/31/05): Assets, $21,098,340 (M); gifts received, $307,380; expenditures, $417,617; qualifying distributions, $386,211; giving activities include $373,275 for 43 grants (high: $100,000; low: $100).
Fields of interest: Education; Disasters, Hurricane Katrina; Religion.
Type of support: General/operating support; Endowments; Seed money; Scholarship funds.
Limitations: Giving primarily in New Orleans, LA. No support for political organizations. No grants to individuals.
Publications: Application guidelines; Program policy statement (including application guidelines).
Application information: Application form required.
Initial approach: Letter
Copies of proposal: 1
Deadline(s): Various
Board meeting date(s): May, Nov. and Feb.
Final notification: Various
Trustees: Alden Laborde; James Laborde; John Laborde; Margaret Laborde.
Number of staff: 1 part-time professional.
EIN: 721371702
Selected grants: The following grants were reported in 2003.
$40,000 to Jesuit High School, New Orleans, LA. For capital campaign.

$25,000 to Archbishops Community Appeal, New Orleans, LA. For witness program.
$10,000 to Catholic University of America, DC. For study of parochial schools.
$10,000 to Little Sisters of the Poor, New Orleans, LA. For operating support.
$5,000 to Big Brothers/Big Sisters of Southeast Louisiana, New Orleans, LA.
$5,000 to Covenant House New Orleans, New Orleans, LA. For Youth Shelter Crisis Center.
$5,000 to Junior Achievement of New Orleans, New Orleans, LA. For exchange city grant.
$5,000 to Parkway Partners Program, New Orleans, LA. For hot sauce production.
$5,000 to Saint Joseph Abbey, Saint Benedict, LA. For scholarships.
$5,000 to United Cerebral Palsy of Greater New Orleans, New Orleans, LA. For spasticity center.

3460
The Azby Fund ✧
650 Poydras St., Ste. 2521
New Orleans, LA 70130

Established in 1969 in LA.
Donors: Marion W. Harvey†; Herbert J. Harvey, Jr.†; Erminia Wadsworth†.
Foundation type: Independent foundation.
Financial data (yr. ended 12/31/05): Assets, $18,421,453 (M); expenditures, $2,271,479; qualifying distributions, $1,796,828; giving activities include $1,701,749 for 72 grants (high: $692,808; low: $1,000).
Fields of interest: Historic preservation/historical societies; Arts; Elementary/secondary education; Higher education; Education; Botanical gardens; Health care; Children/youth, services; Roman Catholic agencies & churches.
Limitations: Applications not accepted. Giving primarily in New Orleans, LA. No grants to individuals.
Application information: Contributes only to pre-selected organizations.
Officers and Directors: Ann Fitzmorris, Pres.; Stewart Farnet,* V.P.; Thomas B. Lemann,* Secy.-Treas.; Michael Liebaert,* Exec. Dir.; Samuel S. Farnet, Jr.; Patrick Wadsworth Fitzmorris.
EIN: 726049781

3461
Baptist Community Ministries ▼
400 Poydras St., Ste. 2950
New Orleans, LA 70130
Contact: Byron R. Harrell, Pres.
E-mail: info@bcm.org; URL: http://www.bcm.org/

Established in 1995 in LA; converted from the sale of the assets of Mercy-Baptist Medical Center.
Foundation type: Independent foundation.
Financial data (yr. ended 9/30/05): Assets, $232,261,973 (M); expenditures, $11,155,272; qualifying distributions, $9,478,056; giving activities include $6,787,415 for 44+ grants (high: $1,050,000; average: $5,000–$350,000), and $150,834 for employee matching gifts.
Purpose and activities: Baptist Community Ministries is committed to the development of a healthy community offering a wholesome quality of life to its residents and to improving the physical, mental, and spiritual health of the individuals it serves.

Fields of interest: Education; Health care; Safety/disasters.
Type of support: General/operating support; Continuing support; Program development; Seed money; Curriculum development; Research; Technical assistance; Program evaluation; Matching/challenge support.
Limitations: Giving primarily in Jefferson, Orleans, Plaquemines, St. Bernard, and St. Tammany parishes, LA. No grants to individuals.
Publications: Application guidelines; Annual report (including application guidelines); Informational brochure.
Application information: Provide material on standard 8-1/2 by 11 inch paper with 2 filing holes punched at top and secured with binder clips. Do not use staples, binders or folders. Application form required.
Initial approach: Check web site for updated application information before applying. Completed application from form available on foundation Web site
Copies of proposal: 3
Deadline(s): Mar. 1 through Mar. 15, and Sept. 1 through Sept. 15
Board meeting date(s): May and Nov.
Final notification: June and Dec.
Officers and Trustees: Janice M. Foster,* Chair.; Thomas L. Callicutt, Jr.,* Vice-Chair.; Charles E. Beasley, C.O.O. and V.P.; Byron R. Harrell, C.E.O. and Pres.; Laurie G. DeCuir, Cont.; Herschel L. Abbott, Jr.; Bobby C. Brannon; Nancy H. Calhoun; Jean C. Felts; John J. Graham; Robert E. Howson; Hans A.B. Jonassen; Kenneth E. Pickering; J. Gordon Reische; W. James Wilkinson; John M. Yarborough, Jr.
Number of staff: 11 full-time professional; 3 full-time support; 2 part-time support.
EIN: 721155847
Selected grants: The following grants were reported in 2004.
$1,210,888 to School Leadership Center of Greater New Orleans, New Orleans, LA. For core support.
$902,293 to Christian Health Ministries, New Orleans, LA. For core support.
$850,000 to Healthy Lifestyle Choices, New Orleans, LA. For core support.
$340,500 to Literacy Alliance of Greater New Orleans, New Orleans, LA.
$329,425 to Greater New Orleans Education Foundation, New Orleans, LA. For core support.
$241,901 to University of New Orleans Foundation, New Orleans, LA. For training teachers to recognize abuse.
$195,959 to American Heart Association, Dallas, TX. For Operation Heartbeat.
$176,718 to Jefferson Parish Public Schools, Harvey, LA. For alternative strategies for suspended youth.
$169,523 to United Negro College Fund, New Orleans, LA.
$158,000 to Dillard University, New Orleans, LA. For Out-of-School Time Project.

3462
Baton Rouge Area Foundation ▼ ✧
402 N. 4th St.
Baton Rouge, LA 70802 (225) 387-6126
Contact: John G. Davies, C.E.O.
FAX: (225) 387-6153; E-mail: jdavies@braf.org; Additional tel.: (877) 387-6126; Grant information E-mail: grantmaking@braf.org; URL: http://www.braf.org

Incorporated in 1964 in LA.

Foundation type: Community foundation.

Financial data (yr. ended 12/31/04): Assets, $363,767,711 (M); gifts received, $12,630,798; expenditures, $20,083,252; giving activities include $13,206,270 for grants, and $95,250 for grants to individuals.

Purpose and activities: The foundation funds programs in the areas of the arts and humanities, community development, education, the environment, human services, health and medical issues, and religion. Primary areas of interest include elementary and secondary education and health. Preference given to those projects which promise to affect a broad segment of the population or which tend to help a segment of the citizenry who are not being adequately served by the community's resources.

Fields of interest: Humanities; Arts; Child development, education; Elementary school/education; Secondary school/education; Medical school/education; Nursing school/education; Education; Environment; Health care; Health organizations, association; Disasters, Hurricane Katrina; Children/youth, services; Child development, services; Aging, centers/services; Women, centers/services; Human services; Community development; Religion; Aging; Disabilities, people with; Women; Economically disadvantaged.

Type of support: Capital campaigns; Building/renovation; Equipment; Endowments; Emergency funds; Program development; Seed money; Research; Program-related investments/loans; Scholarships—to individuals; Matching/challenge support.

Limitations: Giving limited to the Baton Rouge, LA, area, including East Baton Rouge, West Baton Rouge, Livingston, Ascension, Iberville, Pointe Coupee, East Feliciana, and West Feliciana parishes. No grants to individuals (except for scholarships), or for continuing support, annual campaigns, deficit financing, fellowships, or operating budgets.

Publications: Application guidelines; Annual report (including application guidelines); Informational brochure; Newsletter.

Application information: Visit foundation Web site for grant application information and specific application forms per grant type. Application form required.

Initial approach: Telephone
Copies of proposal: 1
Deadline(s): Feb. 1, May 1, Aug. 1, and Nov. 1 for Health Care grants; Jan. 1, Apr. 1, July 1, and Oct. 1 for Neighborhood Initiative grants; varies for others
Board meeting date(s): May, July, Sept., and Nov.
Final notification: Feb. 1, May 26, Aug. 1 and Nov. 17 for Health Care grants; Feb. 28, May 28, Aug. 28, and Nov. 28 for Neighborhood Initiative grants; varies for others

Officers and Directors:* Thomas H. Turner,* Chair.; Christel C. Slaughter, Ph.D.*, Vice-Chair.; John G. Davies,* C.E.O. and Pres.; John Spain, Exec. V.P.; Brace B. Godfrey, Jr.,* Secy.; Thomas A. Cotten,* Treas.; Courtney Saizan, Compt.; John W. Barton, Sr.,* Chair. Emeritus; Warren O. Birkett, Jr.; Thomas L. Frazer; Alice D. Greer; Richard F. Manship; Charles W. "Chuck" McCoy; Jennifer Eplett Reilly; H. Norman Saurage III; Charles L. Valluzzo; Jacqueline D. Vines; Paul S. West; Candance E. Wright.

Trustee Bank: JPMorgan Chase Bank, N.A.

Number of staff: 16 full-time professional.

EIN: 726030391

Selected grants: The following grants were reported in 2005.

$351,900 to City Year Louisiana, Baton Rouge, LA.

$248,984 to Academic Distinction Fund, Baton Rouge, LA.

$235,020 to Family Road of Greater Baton Rouge, Baton Rouge, LA. For Hurricane Katrina for client assistance funds to expecting parents and young families to pay for rent and essential supplies that they may not have access to otherwise.

$235,006 to Capital Area Human Services District, Baton Rouge, LA. For relief efforts for Hurricane Katrina.

$200,000 to Louisiana Cultural Economy Foundation, Baton Rouge, LA.

$146,634 to Diocese of Baton Rouge, Baton Rouge, LA.

$137,220 to Baton Rouge General Medical Center Foundation, Baton Rouge, LA.

$34,500 to Youth Oasis, Baton Rouge, LA.

$26,500 to Trinity Episcopal Church, Baton Rouge, LA.

$20,000 to West Feliciana Parish School Board, Saint Francisville, LA.

3463

The Biedenharn Foundation ◇
P.O. Box 577
Benton, LA   71006

Established in 1985 in LA.

Donors: R.Z. Biedenharn†; Catherine Susan Biedenharn†.

Foundation type: Independent foundation.

Financial data (yr. ended 11/30/05): Assets, $10,376,920 (M); expenditures, $703,363; qualifying distributions, $644,380; giving activities include $625,000 for 64 grants (high: $105,000; low: $2,000).

Purpose and activities: Giving primarily for human services and environmental conservation.

Fields of interest: Media, radio; Performing arts, theater; Higher education; Environment; Health care, research; Human services; Residential/custodial care, hospices.

Type of support: General/operating support; Annual campaigns; Endowments; Emergency funds; Research.

Limitations: Applications not accepted. Giving on a national basis. No grants to individuals.

Application information: Contributes only to pre-selected organizations.

Board meeting date(s): Varies

Officers and Board Members:* Sydney Biedenharn,* Chair.; David E. Tyrone,* Secy.-Treas.; Sue Brown Dykes; Gia Morgan; Mary Cobb Thompson; Randy Walker; Reina Walker.

Number of staff: 1 part-time support.

EIN: 721052971

Selected grants: The following grants were reported in 2005.

$105,000 to American Red Cross, Richmond, VA.

$25,000 to Humane Society of Northwest Louisiana, Shreveport, LA.

$20,000 to Providence House, Shreveport, LA.

$20,000 to World Wildlife Fund, DC.

$10,000 to Habitat for Humanity of Northwest Louisiana, Shreveport, LA.

$10,000 to Ocean Conservancy, DC.

$10,000 to Rainforest Action Network, San Francisco, CA.

$10,000 to Sierra Club Foundation, San Francisco, CA.

$5,000 to Canine Companions for Independence, Colorado Springs, CO.

$5,000 to National Wildlife Federation, DC.

3464

The Booth-Bricker Fund ◇
826 Union St., Ste. 300
New Orleans, LA   70112   (504) 581-2430
Contact: Gray S. Parker, Chair.

Established in 1966 in LA.

Donors: John F. Bricker†; Nina B. Bricker†.

Foundation type: Independent foundation.

Financial data (yr. ended 12/31/04): Assets, $37,004,015 (M); expenditures, $1,827,901; qualifying distributions, $1,457,354; giving activities include $1,225,561 for 75 grants (high: $50,500; low: $900), and $115,851 for 39 employee matching gifts.

Purpose and activities: Giving primarily for the purpose of promoting, developing, and fostering religious, charitable, scientific, literary, and educational programs.

Fields of interest: Visual arts; Museums; Performing arts; Performing arts, theater; Historic preservation/historical societies; Arts; Education, fund raising/fund distribution; Elementary/secondary education; Education, early childhood education; Child development, education; Secondary school/education; Higher education; Theological school/education; Adult education—literacy, basic skills & GED; Libraries/library science; Education, reading; Education; Environment; Hospitals (general); Speech/hearing centers; Health care; Mental health/crisis services; Health organizations, association; Cancer; Biomedicine; Medical research, institute; Cancer research; Crime/law enforcement; Food services; Human services; Youth, services; Child development, services; Family services; Aging, centers/services; Homeless, human services; Roman Catholic agencies & churches; Religion; Aging; Economically disadvantaged; Homeless.

Type of support: Capital campaigns; Building/renovation; Equipment; Endowments; Debt reduction; Professorships; Publication; Scholarship funds; Research; Employee matching gifts; Matching/challenge support.

Limitations: Giving primarily in LA, with emphasis on New Orleans. No grants to individuals, or for operating or maintenance costs.

Application information: Videotapes not accepted. Application form not required.

Initial approach: Letter or proposal
Copies of proposal: 1
Deadline(s): None
Board meeting date(s): Quarterly

Officers and Trustees:* Gray S. Parker,* Chair.; Ingrid C. Laffont, Secy.-Treas.; Robert L. Goodwin; Henry N. Kuechler III; Charles B. Mayer; Mary Kay Parker; Nathaniel P. Phillips, Jr.; H. Hunter White, Jr.

EIN: 720818077

3465
Joe W. & Dorothy Dorsett Brown Foundation ✧
c/o The Brown Foundation Center
320 Hammond Hwy., Ste. 500
Metairie, LA 70005 (504) 834-3433
Contact: Beth Buscher
Service Learning Program address: 320 Hammond Hwy., Ste. 502, Metairie, LA 70005; e-mail for Beth Buscher: BethBuscher@thebrownfoundation.org; URL: http://www.thebrownfoundation.org

Established in 1959 in LA.
Donors: Joe W. Brown†; Dorothy Dorsett Brown†.
Foundation type: Independent foundation.
Financial data (yr. ended 12/31/04): Assets, $125,466,546 (M); expenditures, $3,769,022; qualifying distributions, $4,646,392; giving activities include $2,483,419 for 118 grants (high: $390,000; low: $500), and $1,484,008 for 8 loans/program-related investments.
Purpose and activities: Giving primarily to fund medical research, housing for the homeless, organizations that care for the sick, hungry or helpless, religious and educational institutions, and organizations and groups that are concerned with improving the foundation's local community.
Fields of interest: Education; Environment, natural resources; Hospitals (general); Health care; Food services; Human services; Homeless, human services; Community development; Religion; Homeless.
Type of support: General/operating support; Continuing support; Scholarship funds; Research; Program-related investments/loans; Matching/challenge support.
Limitations: Giving limited to southern LA and the New Orleans area, and the Gulf Coast of MS. No support for organizations that are less than 3 years old. No grants to individuals, or for equipment, endowments, building funds, community-wide capital drives, multi-year grants, indirect grants to intermediary institutions, or for grants to offset budget mandated cutbacks.
Publications: Application guidelines; Grants list.
Application information: The foundation has discontinued awarding scholarships to individuals. Application form and guidelines are available on foundation Web site. All applications must be received at least 3 months before funds are required. Application form required.
  Initial approach: Proposal
  Copies of proposal: 1
  Deadline(s): Between Jan. 1 and Sept. 30
  Board meeting date(s): On Fridays mid-monthly
  Final notification: 1-2 months
Officers: D.P. Spencer, Pres.; V.C. Rodriguez, V.P.; B.G. Spencer, V.P.; D.B. Spencer, V.P.; E.K. Hunter, Secy.; B.M. Estopinal, Treas.
Number of staff: 4 full-time professional; 2 part-time professional.
EIN: 726027232
Selected grants: The following grants were reported in 2004.
$390,000 to Service Learning Action Program, Metairie, LA. For general program support.
$194,635 to University of New Orleans, New Orleans, LA. For Cellular Imaging Center.
$125,000 to Tulane University, Cancer Center, New Orleans, LA. For research fellowship.
$100,000 to Audubon Nature Institute, New Orleans, LA. For Butterflies in Flight.
$47,500 to Nature Conservancy, Baton Rouge, LA. To enhance science based conservation in Greater New Orleans Area.
$42,500 to Preservation Resource Center of New Orleans, New Orleans, LA. For general support.
$40,000 to Volunteers of America, Greater New Orleans Chapter, New Orleans, LA. For expansion of Lighthouse Program.
$20,000 to Saint Mary of the Angels Center, New Orleans, LA. For general program support.
$20,000 to Saint Mary of the Angels School, New Orleans, LA. For general program support.
$10,000 to Ochsner Clinic Foundation, New Orleans, LA. For ECMO Pediatric Unit Run.

3466
Richard A. Brunswick Charitable Foundation ✧
1100 Poydras St., Ste. 3200
New Orleans, LA 70163-3200

Established in 1995 in LA.
Donor: Richard A. Brunswick†.
Foundation type: Independent foundation.
Financial data (yr. ended 12/31/04): Assets, $667 (M); gifts received, $328,000; expenditures, $375,025; qualifying distributions, $375,000; giving activities include $375,000 for 14 grants (high: $200,000; low: $1,000).
Purpose and activities: Giving for children and youth services, with an emphasis on medical aid; some giving also for community organizations.
Fields of interest: Performing arts, orchestra (symphony); Education; Medical care, in-patient care; Hospitals (general); Cancer; Hematology.
Limitations: Applications not accepted. Giving primarily in ME and PA. No grants to individuals.
Application information: Contributes only to pre-selected organizations.
Trustees: Edward B. Brunswick; John Y. Pearce; Lois Farfel Stark.
EIN: 721294164
Selected grants: The following grants were reported in 2004.
$200,000 to Texas Childrens Hospital, Houston, TX.
$25,000 to Lafayette College, Easton, PA.
$25,000 to University of Texas M. D. Anderson Cancer Center, Houston, TX.
$20,000 to Franklin Memorial Hospital, Farmington, ME.
$20,000 to Philadelphia Orchestra Association, Philadelphia, PA.
$5,000 to Alzheimers Association, Chicago, IL.
$2,000 to Guadalupe Center, Immokalee, FL.

3467
The William T. and Ethel Lewis Burton Foundation ✧ ☆
641 W. Prien Lake Rd.
Lake Charles, LA 70601
Contact: William B. Lawton, Chair.

Incorporated in 1963 in LA.
Donors: William T. Burton; Wm. T. Burton Industries, Inc.
Foundation type: Independent foundation.
Financial data (yr. ended 5/31/06): Assets, $4,964,615 (M); expenditures, $347,260; qualifying distributions, $327,781; giving activities include $327,781 for grants.
Purpose and activities: Giving for scholarships restricted to southwest Louisiana high school seniors and McNeese State University football team.
Fields of interest: Human services; Protestant agencies & churches.
Type of support: General/operating support.
Limitations: Giving limited to southwest LA, with emphasis on Lake Charles. No grants for endowment funds or matching gifts; no loans.
Application information: Application form not required.
  Deadline(s): None
Officers and Directors:* William B. Lawton,* Chair.; Jack E. Lawton, Sr.,* Pres.; William T. Drost,* Secy.; Jack E. Lawton, Jr.; Billy Moses.
EIN: 726027957
Selected grants: The following grants were reported in 2004.
$50,000 to McNeese State University, Lake Charles, LA. 2 grants: $30,000 (For scholarships), $20,000.
$20,000 to Lake Charles Memorial Hospital, Lake Charles, LA.
$20,000 to Saint Patrick Hospital, Lake Charles, LA.
$20,000 to West Calcasieu Cameron Hospital, Sulphur, LA.
$6,000 to United Way of Southwest Louisiana, Lake Charles, LA.
$5,240 to Henning Memorial United Methodist Church, Sulphur, LA.
$5,000 to Our Lady of Prompt Succor Catholic Church, Alexandria, LA.
$400 to First Baptist Church, Sulphur, LA.
$121 to Sulphur High School, Sulphur, LA.

3468
Community Foundation of Acadiana ✧ ☆
600 Jefferson St., Ste. 402
P.O. Box 3892
Lafayette, LA 70502-3892 (337) 266-2145
Contact: For grants: Marilyn Lee, Donor Rels. Admin.
FAX: (337) 266-2162; E-mail: info@cfacadiana.org; URL: http://www.cfacadiana.org

Established in 2000 in LA.
Foundation type: Community foundation.
Financial data (yr. ended 12/31/04): Assets, $9,246,495 (M); gifts received, $6,412,052; expenditures, $783,763; giving activities include $580,513 for 12+ grants (high: $175,500).
Purpose and activities: The foundation provides leadership in facilitating the charitable and creative giving its donors in an effort to improve the quality of life for the citizens of Acadiana, LA.
Application information: The foundation does not currently have an unrestricted grants procedure as unrestricted funds are limited. Visit foundation Web site for Donor-Advised and Corporate Charitable funds grant information and application form. Application form required.
  Initial approach: Submit application form
  Deadline(s): None
Officers and Directors:* Barry F. Berthelot,* Chair.; Elaine D. Abell,* Vice-Chair.; Leonard K. Lemoine,* Secy.-Treas.; Raymond J. Hebert, Exec. Dir.; Kathy Ashworth; Odon Bacque; David T. Calhoun; Michael DeHart; Ernest Freyou; Michael J. Michot; Kevin Moody; Frank X. Neuner, Jr.; Raymond H. Pellerin; Hank Perret; Rae Robinson; Gail Romero; Robert Trahan; E. Warner Veillon; Janet Morein Wood.
EIN: 721493023

3469
The Community Foundation of
Shreveport-Bossier
401 Edwards St., Ste. 105
Shreveport, LA 71101 (318) 221-0582
Contact: Paula H. Hickman, Exec. Dir.; For grants:
Susan P. Adams, Dir., Progs.
FAX: (318) 221-7463;
E-mail: cfsb@comfoundsb.org; Additional E-mail:
hickman@comfoundsb.org; Grant application
E-mail: adams@comfoundsb.org; URL: http://
www.comfoundsb.org

Incorporated in 1961 in LA.
Foundation type: Community foundation.
Financial data (yr. ended 12/31/05): Assets,
$52,875,573 (M); gifts received, $11,362,176;
expenditures, $2,977,115; giving activities include
$2,345,069 for 138 grants (high: $74,622; low:
$500).
Purpose and activities: The foundation seeks to
promote philanthropy and improve the quality of life
in the Shreveport-Bossier communities by serving as
a permanent and growing resource of expertise and
funds.
Fields of interest: Arts; Higher education; Adult
education—literacy, basic skills & GED; Education,
reading; Education; Environment, natural resources;
Environment; Health care; Health organizations,
association; Youth, services; Aging, centers/
services; Homeless, human services; Human
services; Community development; Science; Aging;
Disabilities, people with; Women; Economically
disadvantaged; Homeless.
Type of support: Continuing support; Management
development/capacity building; Capital campaigns;
Building/renovation; Equipment; Land acquisition;
Emergency funds; Program development;
Conferences/seminars; Seed money; Curriculum
development; Scholarship funds; Technical
assistance; Matching/challenge support.
Limitations: Giving strictly limited to "Bossier and
Caddo" Parishes, LA (unless specifically named by
donor). No support for religious purposes. No grants
to individuals, or for debt retirement, endowment
funds, general operating expenses, annual
sustaining fund drives, or capital (brick and mortar)
campaigns.
Publications: Application guidelines; Annual report;
Annual report (including application guidelines);
Informational brochure; Informational brochure
(including application guidelines); Newsletter.
Application information: Visit foundation Web site
for application form and guidelines. All organizations
interested in submitting a proposal must send a
representative to attend one of the scheduled Grant
Overview Sessions prior to submission; reservations
are required by calling or e-mailing the foundation.
Application form required.
Initial approach: Telephone or e-mail
Copies of proposal: 8
Deadline(s): Feb. 28 and July 31
Board meeting date(s): May and Oct.
Final notification: Two weeks following board
meetings
Officers and Directors:* Maxine Sarpy,* Chair.; Joe
N. Averett, Jr.,* Vice-Chair.; Bobby Jelks,* Secy.;
Don E. Jones,* Treas.; Paula H. Hickman, Exec. Dir.;
Mike Alost; Edward Crawford III; Marion W. Weiss.
Trustee Banks: AmSouth Bank; JPMorgan Chase
Bank, N.A.
Number of staff: 3 full-time professional; 2 full-time
support.
EIN: 726022365

3470
Coughlin-Saunders Foundation, Inc. ✧
2010 Gus Kaplan Dr.
Alexandria, LA 71301 (318) 561-4070
Contact: Ed Crump, Dir.
FAX: (318) 487-7339;
E-mail: csfoundation@kricket.net

Incorporated in 1950 in LA.
Donors: Anne S. Coughlin†; R.R. Saunders†; F.H.
Coughlin†; J.A. Adams†; Carolyn Saunders†.
Foundation type: Independent foundation.
Financial data (yr. ended 11/30/05): Assets,
$13,809,848 (M); expenditures, $697,774;
qualifying distributions, $438,745; giving activities
include $430,405 for 137 grants (high: $50,000;
low: $100).
Purpose and activities: Giving primarily for
education, particularly to Episcopal, Christian and
Roman Catholic schools, as well as to churches;
funding also for Baptist churches, and for children,
youth and social services.
Fields of interest: Arts; Elementary/secondary
education; Education; Human services; Children/
youth, services; Christian agencies & churches;
Protestant agencies & churches; Roman Catholic
agencies & churches.
Type of support: General/operating support;
Continuing support; Capital campaigns; Building/
renovation; Equipment; Emergency funds; Program
development; Professorships; Scholarship funds.
Limitations: Giving limited to central LA. No grants
to individuals, or for matching gifts.
Publications: Application guidelines; Program policy
statement.
Application information: Application form not
required.
Initial approach: Letter
Copies of proposal: 1
Deadline(s): None
Board meeting date(s): Apr. and Sept.
Final notification: Between Mar. 31 and Oct. 31
Officers: Sally Cockerham, Co-Chair.; Ann Maynard,
Co-Chair.
Directors: Nell Adams; Homer Adler; Scott Brame;
Ed Crump.
EIN: 726027641
Selected grants: The following grants were reported
in 2005.
$26,000 to American Red Cross. 3 grants: $1,000,
$5,000, $20,000
$25,000 to Grace Christian Educational
Association, Watervliet, MI.
$25,000 to Saint Georges Episcopal School, New
Orleans, LA.
$8,000 to United Way.
$5,000 to Rhodes College, Memphis, TN.
$4,000 to Red River Radio, Shreveport, LA.
$1,000 to New Orleans Ballet Association, New
Orleans, LA.
$1,000 to United Jewish Communities, New York,
NY.

3471
Coypu Foundation ✧
c/o Whitney National Bank, Trust Dept.
P.O. Box 6120
New Orleans, LA 70161-1260
Contact: Peggy K. Scott
E-mail: pkscott@whitneybank.com

Established in 1988 in LA.
Donor: John S. McIlhenny.

Foundation type: Independent foundation.
Financial data (yr. ended 12/31/03): Assets,
$16,931,994 (M); gifts received, $14,465;
expenditures, $888,445; qualifying distributions,
$801,023; giving activities include $801,023 for 14
grants (high: $200,000; low: $7,922).
Fields of interest: Higher education; Environment,
natural resources; Animals/wildlife; Biomedicine
research.
Type of support: Program development;
Conferences/seminars; Professorships; Research.
Limitations: Giving primarily in LA. No grants to
individuals.
Application information: Application form required.
Initial approach: Letter or E-mail
Copies of proposal: 6
Deadline(s): July 31
Board meeting date(s): Quarterly
Final notification: 90 days after deadline
Trustees: William Callihan; Chris Hale; John
Hernandez; Eugenie Schwartz; Whitney National
Bank.
EIN: 581795856
Selected grants: The following grants were reported
in 2003.
$200,000 to Pennington Biomedical Research
Center, Baton Rouge, LA. For John S. McIlhenny
endowed chair in Health Wisdom.
$92,790 to Audubon Nature Institute, New Orleans,
LA. 2 grants: $42,540 (For conservation and
reproduction program for endangered cranes),
$50,250 (For construction of whooping crane
exhibit).
$80,000 to Louisiana State University and A & M
College Foundation, LSU Libraries, Baton Rouge,
LA. For acquisition of Gandy collection of
photographs.
$75,000 to Tulane University, Center for
Bioenvironmental Research, New Orleans, LA.
For Eugenie Schwartz Professorship in River and
Coastal Studies.
$71,000 to Southeastern Louisiana University,
Hammond, LA. For conservation of endangered
pine savanna plants in Louisiana.
$70,000 to Louisiana Society for the Prevention of
Cruelty to Animals, New Orleans, LA. For
crematorium.
$25,000 to Sul Ross State University, Department
of Natural Resource Management, Alpine, TX. For
study of ecology of Montezuma Quail.
$22,400 to University of New Orleans, Department
of Biological Sciences, New Orleans, LA. For
study of nutria in southern Louisiana.
$7,922 to Northwestern State University,
Natchitoches, LA. For population surveys using
pitfall traps.

3472
John W. & Bertie M. Deming
Foundation ✧ ☆
3600 Parliament Dr.
Alexandria, LA 71303 (318) 445-5472
Contact: Mamie Sterkx, Dir.

Foundation type: Independent foundation.
Financial data (yr. ended 10/31/05): Assets,
$8,812,832 (M); expenditures, $366,300;
qualifying distributions, $344,610; giving activities
include $342,540 for 76 grants (high: $80,000;
low: $25).
Fields of interest: Arts; Education; Human services;
Protestant agencies & churches.

Limitations: Giving primarily in LA. No grants to individuals.
Application information: Application form not required.
  Deadline(s): None
Directors: Brenner Sadler; Bertie Deming Smith; Mamie Sterkx.
EIN: 726041682
Selected grants: The following grants were reported in 2005.
$50,000 to Boys and Girls Club.
$35,000 to Rapides Symphony Orchestra, Alexandria, LA. 3 grants: $10,000, $10,000, $15,000
$10,000 to American Red Cross.
$10,000 to United Way.
$5,000 to Teach for America, New York, NY.
$1,000 to New Orleans Museum of Art, New Orleans, LA.
$500 to Pierpont Morgan Library, New York, NY.
$250 to Salvation Army.

3473
Collins C. Diboll Private Foundation ◇
201 Saint Charles Ave., 50th Fl.
New Orleans, LA 70170-5100 (504) 582-8103
Contact: Donald W. Diboll, Chair.

Established in 1989 in LA.
Donor: Collins C. Diboll†.
Foundation type: Independent foundation.
Financial data (yr. ended 12/31/04): Assets, $15,298,846 (M); expenditures, $810,598; qualifying distributions, $722,824; giving activities include $687,300 for 21 grants (high: $201,500; low: $300).
Fields of interest: Museums; Museums (art); Historic preservation/historical societies; Higher education; Education; Health care; Health organizations, association; Kidney research; Human services; Protestant agencies & churches; Roman Catholic agencies & churches.
Type of support: General/operating support; Capital campaigns; Building/renovation; Endowments.
Limitations: Giving primarily in LA. No grants to individuals.
Application information:
  Initial approach: Letter
  Deadline(s): None
Officer: Donald W. Diboll, Chair.
Trustees: David F. Edwards; Paul T. Westerfelt.
EIN: 726126376
Selected grants: The following grants were reported in 2004.
$201,500 to Tulane University, New Orleans, LA.
$120,000 to Junior Achievement.
$100,000 to New Orleans Museum of Art, New Orleans, LA.
$50,000 to Alton Ochsner Medical Foundation, New Orleans, LA.
$37,500 to Christ Episcopal School, Covington, LA.
$6,000 to Christ Church Mobile, Mobile, AL.
$5,000 to Archdiocese of New Orleans, New Orleans, LA.
$5,000 to Catholic Charities.

3474
Entergy Charitable Foundation ◇
639 Loyola Ave.
New Orleans, LA 70113 (877) 285-2006
E-mail: grants@entergy.com; *URL:* http://www.entergy.com/our_community/giving.aspx

Established in 2000 in AR and LA.
Donor: Entergy Corp.
Foundation type: Company-sponsored foundation.
Financial data (yr. ended 12/31/04): Assets, $1,124,405 (M); gifts received, $2,085,000; expenditures, $2,413,507; qualifying distributions, $2,413,507; giving activities include $2,409,007 for 160 grants (high: $500,000; low: $500).
Purpose and activities: The foundation supports programs designed to assist low-income families; and promote education and literacy.
Fields of interest: Adult education—literacy, basic skills & GED; Education; Economically disadvantaged.
Type of support: Program development.
Limitations: Giving primarily in areas of company operations in AR, LA, MA, MS, NH, NY, TX, and VT. No support for political organizations, religious organizations not of direct benefit to the entire community, or organizations owned or operated by an employee of Entergy. No grants to individuals, or for utility bills, administrative expenses or recurring expenses that exceed 15% of the requested amount, capital campaigns, gala events, testimonials, or fundraising meals, advertisements, or uniforms, equipment, or trips for school-related organizations or amateur sports teams; no loans.
Publications: Application guidelines.
Application information: Application form required.
  Initial approach: Complete online application form
  Deadline(s): Feb. 1, May 1, and Aug. 1
  Board meeting date(s): Three times per year
Officers and Directors:* Kay Kelley Arnold,* Chair., C.E.O., and Pres.; Leo P. Denault, Secy.-Treas.; Renae E. Conley; Curt L. Hebert, Jr.; J. Wayne Leonard; William E. Madison; Hugh T. McDonald; Richard J. Smith; Gary Taylor.
EIN: 710845366
Selected grants: The following grants were reported in 2004.
$500,000 to Xavier University of Louisiana, New Orleans, LA. For Entergy Presidential Scholarship Fund.
$200,000 to Ursuline Academy, New Orleans, LA. For capital campaign.
$166,666 to University of Arkansas for Medical Sciences Foundation, Little Rock, AR. For BioVentures Arkansas BioTechnology Business Incubator.
$65,419 to Texas A & M University, Nuclear Engineering Department, College Station, TX. For nuclear engineering recruiting and outreach program.
$55,000 to Habitat for Humanity International, New Orleans Area Chapter, New Orleans, LA. For New Habitat for Humanity House.
$50,000 to Foundation for American Communications, Pasadena, CA. For Journalism Education PACS Seminars for Working Journalists.
$25,000 to Ball State University Foundation, Miller College of Business, Muncie, IN. For general support.
$21,500 to Habitat For Humanity, Walker County, Huntsville, TX. For Putting on the Blitz.

$14,500 to New Orleans Youth Entrepreneurship Program, New Orleans, LA. For Uptown Youth Entrepreneurs Computer Training Program.
$12,500 to Historic New Orleans Collection, New Orleans, LA. For teaching American history in New Orleans.

3475
Eye, Ear, Nose and Throat Foundation ◇
111 Veterans Memorial Blvd., Ste. 702
Metairie, LA 70005-3035
Contact: William F. Finegan, Exec. Dir.

Donors: Eye, Ear, Nose and Throat Hospital; Isaac Stauffer Clinic.
Foundation type: Independent foundation.
Financial data (yr. ended 12/31/05): Assets, $59,316,894 (M); expenditures, $2,243,520; qualifying distributions, $1,833,865; giving activities include $1,747,963 for 15 grants (high: $616,449; low: $2,500).
Purpose and activities: Giving for eye and ear care for indigent residents of southeast Louisiana.
Fields of interest: Eye diseases; Ear & throat diseases; Economically disadvantaged.
Limitations: Giving limited to southeastern LA.
Application information: Application form not required.
  Initial approach: Letter
  Deadline(s): None
Officer and Trustees:* William F. Finegan,* Exec. Dir.; Ashley S. Bright; Crichton W. Brown; John D. Charbonnet; Michael D. Charbonnet; R. Foster Duncan; Charles N. Monsted III; Morgan S. Nalty; Michele Reed; St. Denis J. Villere.
EIN: 720928511
Selected grants: The following grants were reported in 2005.
$968,711 to Saint Thomas Health Services, New Orleans, LA. 2 grants: $352,262 (For eye and ear care to indigent residents of the Saint Thomas Housing Project and surrounding environs), $616,449 to Daughters of Charity Services of New Orleans (For prescription eyeglasses for indigent community residents).
$320,452 to Daughters of Charity Services of New Orleans, New Orleans, LA. For eye and ear care to indigent residents of the area.
$121,946 to Saint Vincent de Paul TriParish Community Pharmacy, Houma, LA. For eye and ear prescription medications for indigent residents of New Orleans.
$100,000 to Ochsner Clinic Foundation, New Orleans, LA. For eye and ear medical care to the indigent population displaced by Hurricane Katrina.
$35,000 to Program of All-Inclusive Care for the Elderly (PACE), New Orleans, LA. For equipment for an eye examination room at the Center at Saint Cecilia Church in New Orleans.
$32,707 to New Orleans Speech and Hearing Center, New Orleans, LA. For sight and hearing testing in pre-school and day care centers for low-income children.
$29,731 to Plaquemines Parish Medical Center, Port Sulphur, LA. For eye care to residents in the area.
$25,832 to Jean Lafitte, Town of, Jean Lafitte, LA. For eye clinic for indigent population in the area.

3476
Ben E. Factor Foundation ◇
106 Wilree St.
New Iberia, LA   70560
Contact: Annette F. White, Secy.

Established in 1987 in LA.
Donors: Robert N. White; Annette F. White; Keith White; Mrs. Keith White.
Foundation type: Independent foundation.
Financial data (yr. ended 12/31/05): Assets, $11,909,441 (M); gifts received, $381,200; expenditures, $669,817; qualifying distributions, $632,900; giving activities include $632,900 for 37 grants (high: $240,000; low: $500; average: $1,000–$4,000).
Fields of interest: Higher education; Human services; Christian agencies & churches; Protestant agencies & churches.
Limitations: Giving primarily in LA. No grants to individuals.
Application information:
  Initial approach: Proposal
Officers: Robert N. White, Pres.; Keith White, V.P.; R. Marc White, V.P.; Annette F. White, Secy.
EIN: 721086995
Selected grants: The following grants were reported in 2004.
$25,000 to North American Mission Board, SBC, Alpharetta, GA.
$20,000 to American Red Cross.
$12,000 to Grace to You, Valencia, CA.
$12,000 to Masters College, Santa Clarita, CA.
$12,000 to World Hunger Relief, Elm Mott, TX.
$8,000 to Gospel for Asia, Carrollton, TX.
$8,000 to Louisiana Baptist Childrens Home, Monroe, LA.
$5,000 to American Family Association, Tupelo, MS.
$4,050 to Love Worth Finding Ministries, Memphis, TN.
$4,000 to Bridges for Peace, Tulsa, OK.

3477
Ruth U. Fertel Foundation ◇ ☆
1010 Common St., Ste. 1810
New Orleans, LA   70112

Established in 2002 in LA.
Donor: Ruth U. Fertel Charitable Lead Unitrust.
Foundation type: Independent foundation.
Financial data (yr. ended 12/31/05): Assets, $15,896 (M); gifts received, $632,420; expenditures, $621,070; qualifying distributions, $621,070; giving activities include $620,000 for 19 grants (high: $110,000; low: $5,000).
Fields of interest: Elementary/secondary education; Higher education; Human services.
Limitations: Applications not accepted. Giving primarily in New Orleans, LA. No grants to individuals.
Application information: Contributes only to pre-selected organizations.
Officers and Directors:* Randy Fertel,* Pres.; James E. Ryder, Jr.,* Secy.-Treas.; Robert W. Merrick.
EIN: 710879051

3478
The Alta and John Franks Foundation ◇
(formerly The Franks Foundation)
P.O. Box 7665
Shreveport, LA   71137-7665

Established in LA.
Donors: John Franks†; Alta V. Franks.
Foundation type: Independent foundation.
Financial data (yr. ended 12/31/05): Assets, $633,987 (M); gifts received, $1,800,000; expenditures, $1,309,634; qualifying distributions, $1,308,929; giving activities include $1,308,929 for 67 grants.
Purpose and activities: Giving primarily for a Christian preparatory school program.
Fields of interest: Education; Christian agencies & churches.
Limitations: Applications not accepted. Giving primarily in LA. No grants to individuals.
Application information: Contributes only to pre-selected organizations.
Officers: Bobby E. Jelks, Pres.; Alta V. Franks, V.P.; Faith N. Gilbert, Secy.
EIN: 237422163

3479
Frazier Foundation, Inc. ◇
419 Homer Rd.
Minden, LA   71055-2933
Application address: P.O. Box 1175, Minden, LA 71058-1175, tel.: (318) 377-0182

Established in 1974 in LA.
Donor: J. Walter Frazier.
Foundation type: Independent foundation.
Financial data (yr. ended 11/30/05): Assets, $7,378,537 (M); expenditures, $1,086,872; qualifying distributions, $929,409; giving activities include $910,175 for 59 grants (high: $55,000; low: $3,600).
Purpose and activities: Support primarily for the Church of Christ, Christian religious organizations, child care, and educational institutions.
Fields of interest: Media, radio; Higher education; Education; Human services; Children/youth, services; Family services; Pregnancy centers; Christian agencies & churches.
Limitations: Giving primarily in TX; some funding nationally. No grants to individuals, or for endowment funds; no loans.
Publications: Application guidelines.
Application information: Do not fax applications. Application form required.
  Initial approach: Letter or proposal, on organization's letterhead
  Copies of proposal: 4
  Deadline(s): Submit proposal preferably in Apr. or Oct.; deadlines May 1 and Nov. 1
  Board meeting date(s): June and Dec.
  Final notification: Within 6 months
Officers: James Walter Frazier, Jr., Pres.; Rudith A. Drennan, V.P.; Sylvia L. Frazier, Secy.; A. Don Drennan, Treas.
EIN: 720760891
Selected grants: The following grants were reported in 2003.
$127,500 to Ohio Valley University, Vienna, WV.
$40,000 to Westover Hills Church of Christ, Austin, TX.
$30,000 to Abilene Christian University, Abilene, TX.

$25,000 to Healing Hands International, Abilene, TX.
$25,000 to Marriage Savers, Potomac, MD.
$25,000 to Missions Resource Network, Abilene, TX.
$25,000 to Sunset International Bible Institute, Lubbock, TX.
$20,000 to Church of Christ, Fort Worth, TX.
$15,000 to Harpeth Hills Church of Christ, Brentwood, TN.
$10,000 to Zambia Christian School, Zambia. .

3480
The Ella West Freeman Foundation
P.O. Box 13218
New Orleans, LA   70185-3218   (504) 895-1984
Contact: Louis M. Freeman, Chair.
FAX: (504) 895-1988; E-mail: info@ellawest.org;
URL: http://www.ellawest.org

Established about 1940 in LA.
Donors: Richard W. Freeman†; Alfred B. Freeman†.
Foundation type: Independent foundation.
Financial data (yr. ended 12/31/04): Assets, $28,854,930 (M); gifts received, $42,000; expenditures, $1,400,810; qualifying distributions, $1,241,849; giving activities include $1,209,004 for 21+ grants (high: $325,000).
Purpose and activities: Emphasis on higher education and civic affairs; support also for a museum, historic preservation, and the environment.
Fields of interest: Arts; Higher education; Human services; Government/public administration.
Type of support: Annual campaigns; Capital campaigns; Building/renovation; Endowments; Program development; Seed money.
Limitations: Giving primarily in the greater New Orleans, LA, area. No grants to individuals.
Publications: Application guidelines; Grants list.
Application information: Application form and guidelines available on foundation Web site. Application form required.
  Initial approach: Proposal (no more than 3 pages)
  Copies of proposal: 2
  Deadline(s): Mar. 1 and Oct. 15
  Board meeting date(s): Biannually beginning in spring
Officer and Trustees:* Louis M. Freeman,* Chair.; Richard W. Freeman, Jr.; R. West Freeman III; Virginia Rowan; Philip Woollam; Tina F. Woollam.
EIN: 726018322
Selected grants: The following grants were reported in 2005.
$100,000 to United Way for the Greater New Orleans Area, New Orleans, LA. For Emergency fund support.
$50,000 to Tulane University, New Orleans, LA. For unsolicited Hurricane Katrina emergency funds.
$30,000 to New Orleans Museum of Art, New Orleans, LA. For Katrina Emergency Operating Funds.
$25,000 to New Orleans Neighborhood Development Collaborative (NONDC), New Orleans, LA. For operating support.
$20,000 to Archbishop Rummel High School, Metairie, LA. For support for temporary Katrina Students.
$20,000 to Coalition to Restore Coastal Louisiana, Baton Rouge, LA. For unsolicited Hurricane Katrina emergency funds.

$20,000 to Louise McGehee School Fund, New Orleans, LA. For Hurricane Katrina emergency funds.

$15,000 to Bureau of Governmental Research, New Orleans, LA. For Hurricane Katrina emergency funds.

$10,000 to Nature Conservancy, Baton Rouge, LA. For Climate Change Education and Organizing.

$5,000 to Ogden Museum of Southern Art, New Orleans, LA.

3481
Freeport-McMoran Foundation ◇
1615 Poydras St.
New Orleans, LA 70112 (504) 582-1803
Contact: Cynthia M. Molyneux, Pres.

Established in 1996 in LA.
Foundation type: Independent foundation.
Financial data (yr. ended 12/31/05): Assets, $1,232,969 (M); gifts received, $2,461,568; expenditures, $2,423,651; qualifying distributions, $2,312,608; giving activities include $2,303,175 for grants.
Purpose and activities: The foundation is specifically organized for the charitable purpose of serving the community's needs by providing grants to qualified tax-exempt, health and social service, educational, cultural and arts, civic and environmental organizations primarily in the New Orleans, LA, area.
Fields of interest: Education; Environment; Health care; Human services.
Limitations: Giving primarily in the southern LA area. No support for political and fraternal organizations, or for churches and religious institutions (except where such organizations are providing services to the community at large). No grants to individuals.
Application information: Southern Louisiana Standard Submission Application Form can be requested from the foundation. Application form required.
   Initial approach: Telephone
   Copies of proposal: 1
   Deadline(s): June 30
   Board meeting date(s): As needed
   Final notification: Jan. or Feb. following the deadline
Officers and Trustees:* Cynthia M. Molyneux,* Pres.; Kathleen L. Quirk,* V.P. and Treas.; Dean T. Falgoust,* V.P.; Douglas N. Currault II, Secy.; Nancy L. Adkerson, Exec. Dir.; Richard C. Adkerson.
EIN: 721316308
Selected grants: The following grants were reported in 2004.
$219,000 to Horatio Alger Association of Distinguished Americans, Alexandria, VA. For unrestricted support.
$135,568 to United Way for the Greater New Orleans Area, New Orleans, LA. For unrestricted support.
$91,901 to W Y E S Greater New Orleans Educational Television, New Orleans, LA. For unrestricted support.
$80,000 to Richard C. Adkerson Family Foundation, New Orleans, LA. For unrestricted support.
$72,116 to Louisiana Philharmonic Orchestra, New Orleans, LA. For unrestricted support.
$65,000 to MetroVision Partnership Foundation, New Orleans, LA. For unrestricted support.
$61,000 to Teach for America, Greater New Orleans, New Orleans, LA. For unrestricted support.

$55,000 to United States Indonesia Society, DC. For annual fund and unrestricted support.
$53,800 to American Cancer Society, Kenner, LA. For unrestricted support.
$52,000 to Johns Hopkins University, Baltimore, MD. For unrestricted support.

3482
Wendell & Anne Gauthier Family Foundation ◇
3500 N. Hullen St.
Metairie, LA 70002

Established in 2002 in LA.
Donor: Anne S. Barrios Gauthier.
Foundation type: Independent foundation.
Financial data (yr. ended 12/31/03): Assets, $54 (M); gifts received, $1,500; expenditures, $501,446; qualifying distributions, $501,446; giving activities include $500,000 for 1 grant.
Fields of interest: Law school/education.
Limitations: Applications not accepted. Giving primarily in New Orleans, LA. No grants to individuals.
Application information: Contributes only to pre-selected organizations.
Directors: John C. Calhoun; Anne S. Barrios Gauthier; Celeste A. Gauthier; Cherie A. Gauthier; Michelle A. Gauthier; Deborah M. Sulzer.
EIN: 721518612

3483
German Protestant Orphan Asylum Association Foundation ◇
(also known as GPOA Foundation)
P.O. Box 158
Mandeville, LA 70470-0158 (985) 674-5328
Contact: Lisa M. Kaichen, Fdn. Mgr.
FAX: (985) 674-0490;
E-mail: gpoafoundation@aol.com; Additional tel.: New Orleans, LA, tel.: (504) 895-2361; URL: http://www.gpoafoundation.org/

Parent organization founded in 1855; foundation established in 1979 in LA.
Foundation type: Independent foundation.
Financial data (yr. ended 11/30/05): Assets, $12,109,901 (M); gifts received, $355; expenditures, $664,887; qualifying distributions, $592,395; giving activities include $481,235 for grants (average: $1,500–$50,000).
Purpose and activities: Grants only for the benefit and welfare of children and youth in Louisiana.
Fields of interest: Children/youth, services.
Type of support: General/operating support; Program development; Seed money; Matching/challenge support.
Limitations: Giving limited to LA. No support for programs not focused on children, or for out-of-state organizations (unless request is to serve LA children). No grants to individuals, or for capital campaigns, building or renovation expenses, computers, special events, or traditional scholarships.
Publications: Application guidelines; Annual report; Grants list.
Application information: Applications accepted by mail only. The foundation will also accept the Southern Grantmakers Common Application Form. Application form not required.
   Initial approach: 1-page concept letter

Copies of proposal: 12
Deadline(s): Feb. 1, May 1, Aug. 1, and Nov. 1
Board meeting date(s): Jan., Apr., July, and Oct.
Final notification: May 15 (for Feb. 1 deadline), Aug. 15 (for May 1 deadline), Nov. 15 (for Aug. 1 deadline), and Feb. 15 (for Nov. 1 deadline)
Officers and Directors:* J. Gary Haller,* Pres.; Charles B. Mayer,* V.P.; Walter C. Flower III,* Secy.; Robert L. Hattier,* Treas.; Ralph Cox; Price Crane; Paul Haygood; Charles Monsted III; Camille Strachan.
Number of staff: 2 part-time professional; 1 part-time support.
EIN: 720423621

3484
Goldring Family Foundation ▼ ◇
809 Jefferson Hwy.
Jefferson, LA 70121
Contact: Trudi Briede, Dir.
FAX: (504) 849-6515;
E-mail: trudibriede@rbc-usa.com; Application address: P.O. Box 53333, New Orleans, LA 70153

Incorporated in 1955 in LA.
Donors: Magnolia Liquor Co., Inc.; Sazerac Co., Inc.; Great Southern Liquor Co., Inc.; N. Goldring Corp.; and members of the Goldring family.
Foundation type: Independent foundation.
Financial data (yr. ended 11/30/05): Assets, $85,905,324 (M); expenditures, $4,647,248; qualifying distributions, $3,791,783; giving activities include $3,791,783 for grants.
Purpose and activities: Giving primarily to Jewish agencies and temples, education, and the arts.
Fields of interest: Arts; Higher education; Education; Health care; Human services; Jewish federated giving programs.
Type of support: General/operating support; Continuing support; Annual campaigns; Capital campaigns; Building/renovation; Equipment; Emergency funds; Program development; Research; Matching/challenge support.
Limitations: Giving primarily in the greater New Orleans, LA region. No support for political purposes.
Publications: Informational brochure (including application guidelines).
Application information: Application form not required.
   Initial approach: Letter of inquiry
   Deadline(s): Varies
   Board meeting date(s): Varies
   Final notification: Varies, usually 2 - 3 weeks after board meeting dates
Officers: William Goldring, Pres.; Jeffrey Goldring, V.P. and Secy.-Treas.
Number of staff: 1 part-time professional.
EIN: 726022666
Selected grants: The following grants were reported in 2004.
$200,000 to New Orleans Jazz Orchestra, New Orleans, LA.
$150,000 to Dillard University, New Orleans, LA.
$150,000 to Touro Infirmary Foundation, New Orleans, LA.
$125,000 to Jewish Federation of Greater New Orleans, Metairie, LA.
$100,000 to Catholic Charities Association, New Orleans, LA.
$100,000 to Hadassah, The Womens Zionist Organization of America, New York, NY.
$50,000 to Hazelden Foundation, Center City, MN.

$50,000 to National D-Day Museum, New Orleans, LA.

$40,000 to Covenant House New Orleans, New Orleans, LA.

$25,000 to Saint Michael Special School, New Orleans, LA.

3485
Juliet E. Hardtner Fund ◇ ☆

P.O. Box 1447
Lake Charles, LA 70602

Established in 1997 in LA.
Donor: Juliet E. Hardtner†.
Foundation type: Independent foundation.
Financial data (yr. ended 12/31/05): Assets, $8,267,107 (M); expenditures, $438,297; qualifying distributions, $389,000; giving activities include $389,000 for grants.
Purpose and activities: Funding for a state university foundation, for education including support for a school for terminally ill children and an Episcopal church.
Fields of interest: Elementary/secondary education; Higher education; Federated giving programs; Protestant agencies & churches.
Limitations: Applications not accepted. Giving primarily in Lake Charles, LA. No grants to individuals.
Application information: Contributes only to pre-selected organizations.
Trustee: William D. Blake.
EIN: 726187624
Selected grants: The following grants were reported in 2003.
$71,000 to Bishop Noland Episcopal Day School Fund, Lake Charles, LA.
$50,000 to Episcopal Theological Seminary of the Southwest, Austin, TX. For scholarships.
$32,130 to McNeese State University Foundation, Lake Charles, LA. For academic, endowments, departments and scholarships.
$25,000 to Prevent Child Abuse Louisiana, Baton Rouge, LA. For program support.
$20,000 to United Way of Southwest Louisiana, Lake Charles, LA.
$10,000 to Coastal Plains Conservancy, Lake Charles, LA. For program support.
$5,000 to Austin Waldorf School, Austin, TX. For program support.
$5,000 to Lake Charles Symphony, Lake Charles, LA.
$2,000 to Imperial Calcasieu Museum, Lake Charles, LA. For program support.
$693 to Urania, Town of, Urania, LA. For program support.

3486
The Helis Foundation ◇

228 St. Charles Ave., Ste. 912
New Orleans, LA 70130 (504) 523-1831
Contact: David A. Kerstein, V.P.

Incorporated in 1955 in LA.
Donor: Members of the William G. Helis family.
Foundation type: Independent foundation.
Financial data (yr. ended 12/31/03): Assets, $14,331,807 (M); expenditures, $863,435; qualifying distributions, $850,318; giving activities include $837,500 for 36 grants (high: $150,000; low: $250).

Purpose and activities: Giving primarily for higher education, health associations, and human services.
Fields of interest: Higher education; Hospitals (general); Hospitals (specialty); Health care; Health organizations, association; Cancer; Medical research, institute; Food banks; Human services; Children, services; Federated giving programs; Religion.
Limitations: Giving primarily in New Orleans, LA; funding also in New York, NY. No grants to individuals.
Application information:
  Initial approach: Typed letter
  Deadline(s): None
Officer: David A. Kerstein, V.P.
Trustees: Bettie Conley Helis; Esther Helis Henry; Adrienne Helis Malvin.
EIN: 726020536
Selected grants: The following grants were reported in 2003.
$150,000 to Columbia University, New York, NY.
$100,000 to Childrens Hospital, New Orleans, LA.
$50,000 to American Cancer Society, New Orleans, LA.
$30,000 to Second Harvest Food Bank of Greater New Orleans and Acadiana, New Orleans, LA.
$15,000 to Lighthouse for the Blind, New Orleans, LA.
$15,000 to Neighborhood Housing Services of New Orleans, New Orleans, LA.
$10,000 to Touro Infirmary Foundation, New Orleans, LA.
$7,500 to Covenant House New Orleans, New Orleans, LA.
$7,500 to Little Sisters of the Poor, New Orleans, LA.
$2,500 to Summerbridge New Orleans, a Breakthrough Program, New Orleans, LA.

3487
Heymann-Wolf Foundation ◇

1201 Canal St.
New Orleans, LA 70112

Incorporated in 1947 in LA.
Donors: Leon Heymann†; Mrs. Leon Heymann†; Leon M. Wolf†; May H. Wolf; Jimmy Heymann; Mrs. Jimmy Heymann; Jonas John Heymann; Krauss Co., Ltd.
Foundation type: Independent foundation.
Financial data (yr. ended 12/31/03): Assets, $12,558,481 (M); expenditures, $461,404; qualifying distributions, $388,250; giving activities include $387,350 for 21 grants (high: $250,000; low: $100).
Purpose and activities: Giving primarily for education, the arts, Jewish and other federated giving programs, and social services.
Fields of interest: Museums (art); Performing arts, theater; Performing arts, theater (playwriting); Arts; Elementary school/education; Higher education; Human services; Federated giving programs; Jewish federated giving programs.
Limitations: Applications not accepted. Giving primarily in New Orleans, LA, and New York, NY. No grants to individuals.
Application information: Contributes only to pre-selected organizations.
Officers: Jerry Heymann, Pres.; Jonas John Heymann, V.P.; Marjorie Heymann, V.P.
EIN: 726019363

Selected grants: The following grants were reported in 2003.
$250,000 to Tulane University, New Orleans, LA.
$25,000 to Columbia University, College of Physicians and Surgeons, New York, NY.
$10,000 to Village Community School, New York, NY.
$7,000 to New York Theater Workshop, New York, NY.
$5,000 to Loyola University, New Orleans, LA.
$2,500 to W N Y C Foundation, New York, NY.
$1,000 to Action Against Hunger - USA, New York, NY.
$1,000 to Haifa Foundation North America, New York, NY.
$1,000 to Isidore Newman School, New Orleans, LA.
$1,000 to Jewish Endowment Foundation, New Orleans, LA.

3488
Huie-Dellmon Trust ◇

P.O. Box 330
Alexandria, LA 71301
Contact: Richard L. Crowell, Jr., Tr.

Established around 1976.
Foundation type: Independent foundation.
Financial data (yr. ended 12/31/05): Assets, $10,322,960 (M); expenditures, $543,121; qualifying distributions, $460,785; giving activities include $435,347 for 35 grants (high: $100,000; low: $250).
Purpose and activities: Giving primarily to Christian and Protestant organizations, as well as to children, youth, and social services, historic preservation, and to a hospital foundation.
Fields of interest: Historic preservation/historical societies; Libraries/library science; Hospitals (general); Human services; Children/youth, services; Christian agencies & churches; Protestant agencies & churches.
Type of support: General/operating support; Continuing support; Annual campaigns; Capital campaigns; Building/renovation; Equipment; Endowments; Program development; Professorships; Scholarship funds; Research; Matching/challenge support.
Limitations: Giving primarily in central LA. No grants to individuals.
Application information: Application form not required.
  Initial approach: Letter
  Deadline(s): None
Trustees: Richard L. Crowell, Jr.; Nancy C. Owens.
EIN: 720809684
Selected grants: The following grants were reported in 2005.
$50,000 to Rapides Parish School Board, Alexandria, LA.
$30,000 to Southern Forest Heritage Museum and Research Center, Longleaf, LA.
$25,000 to Rapides Symphony Orchestra, Alexandria, LA.
$15,000 to Volunteers of America.
$10,000 to United Way.
$3,500 to Louisiana Baptist Childrens Home, Monroe, LA. 2 grants: $1,500, $2,000
$3,000 to Hope House for Battered Women, Independence, MO.
$2,000 to Fellowship of Christian Athletes, Kansas City, MO.

$500 to Hermann-Grima Historic House, New Orleans, LA.

3489
Institute of Mental Hygiene of the City of New Orleans ◇

1055 St. Charles Ave., Ste. 350
New Orleans, LA 70130-3995
Contact: Nancy Freeman, Exec. Dir.
FAX: (504) 566-1853; E-mail: imheimhno.org;
URL: http://www.imhno.org

Established in 1937 in LA.
Donor: Samuel Zemurray†.
Foundation type: Independent foundation.
Financial data (yr. ended 12/31/05): Assets, $20,095,694 (M); expenditures, $1,042,705; qualifying distributions, $952,316; giving activities include $758,487 for 26 grants (high: $75,000; low: $680).
Purpose and activities: Giving to improve mental health for children (emphasis on children aged 0-6 years).
Fields of interest: Mental health/crisis services; Youth development; Human services; Children, services.
Type of support: General/operating support; Continuing support; Program development; Conferences/seminars; Seed money; Research; Technical assistance; Program evaluation; Matching/challenge support.
Limitations: Giving limited to New Orleans, LA. No grants to individuals; or for capital campaigns.
Publications: Application guidelines; Biennial report; Grants list.
Application information: Application guidelines available on foundation Web site.
Copies of proposal: 2
Deadline(s): See foundation Web site for deadlines of various programs
Board meeting date(s): Late Feb., late June, and late Oct.
Final notification: Mar. 1, July 1, and Nov. 1
Officers and Directors:* Anthony Recasner, Ph.D.*, Pres.; Martin Drell, M.D.*, V.P.; Judith Watts, Secy.; Beverly Nichols, Treas.; Nancy Freeman, Exec. Dir.; Anthony Barczykowski, Sr.; Stephen Daste; Deena Gerber; Bonnie Goldblum; Elaine Joseph; Ruth Kullman; Catherine Pierson; Ted Quant; Charles Zeanah.
Number of staff: 1 full-time professional; 1 part-time support.
EIN: 720446138
Selected grants: The following grants were reported in 2005.
$50,000 to Agenda for Children, New Orleans, LA.
$50,000 to VIA LINK, New Orleans, LA.
$44,682 to Catholic Charities.
$6,135 to Hume Child Development Center, New Orleans, LA.
$3,566 to Bright School, Chattanooga, TN.
$3,180 to Council on Foundations, DC.

3490
Jaeger Foundation ◇ ☆

(formerly Jaeger Unruh Foundation)
P.O. Box 6917
Metairie, LA 70010

Established in 1997 in LA.

Donors: MCC Group; McDonnell Group Employee Relief Fund.
Foundation type: Independent foundation.
Financial data (yr. ended 12/31/05): Assets, $11,327 (M); gifts received, $498,335; expenditures, $489,998; qualifying distributions, $489,000; giving activities include $489,000 for grants.
Director: Jr. Joseph A. Jaeger.
EIN: 721341576

3491
Eugenie and Joseph Jones Family Foundation ◇

835 Union St., Ste. 333
New Orleans, LA 70112 (504) 581-1545
Contact: Eugenie Jones Huger, Pres.; Elaine F. Jones, V.P.; Susan Gundlach, V.P.

Incorporated in 1955 in LA.
Donors: Joseph M. Jones†; Eugenie P. Jones†.
Foundation type: Independent foundation.
Financial data (yr. ended 12/31/05): Assets, $20,245,871 (M); expenditures, $1,096,567; qualifying distributions, $957,006; giving activities include $884,933 for 87 grants (high: $83,333; low: $200).
Purpose and activities: Primary areas of interest include education, community development, health and human services, and arts and cultural programs.
Fields of interest: Museums; Arts; Education; Health care; Human services; Community development, neighborhood development; Community development; Protestant agencies & churches.
Type of support: General/operating support; Continuing support; Annual campaigns; Capital campaigns; Building/renovation; Equipment; Endowments; Program development; Professorships; Seed money; Fellowships; Scholarship funds; Matching/challenge support.
Limitations: Giving primarily in LA, especially in the greater New Orleans area. No grants to individuals, or for land acquisition, special projects, research, publications, conferences, start-up or emergency funds, or deficit financing; no loans.
Publications: Application guidelines.
Application information: Application form required.
Initial approach: Request guidelines from foundation
Copies of proposal: 1
Deadline(s): None
Board meeting date(s): Mar., June, Sept., and Dec.
Officers and Trustees:* Eugenie Jones Huger,* Pres.; Susan Jones Gundlach,* V.P.; Elaine F. Jones,* V.P.
Number of staff: 4 part-time support.
EIN: 720507534
Selected grants: The following grants were reported in 2003.
$60,000 to Contemporary Arts Center, New Orleans, LA. For general operating support.
$50,000 to Habitat for Humanity International, New Orleans, LA.
$50,000 to Junior League of New Orleans, New Orleans, LA. For endowment.
$30,000 to Isidore Newman School, New Orleans, LA.
$20,000 to Gallier House, New Orleans, LA. For endowment.

$19,000 to Planned Parenthood of Louisiana and the Mississippi Delta, New Orleans, LA.
$15,000 to Episcopal Diocese of Louisiana, Baton Rouge, LA. For capital campaign.
$12,500 to University of Virginia, Charlottesville, VA. For Jefferson Scholars Program.
$10,000 to Academy of the Sacred Heart, New Orleans, LA. For capital campaign.
$2,500 to New Orleans Art Review, New Orleans, LA.

3492
Lester E. Kabacoff Family Foundation ◇

2 Poydras St., 3rd Fl.
New Orleans, LA 70130-1656

Established in 1996.
Donors: Gloria S. Kabacoff; Lester E. Kabacoff.
Foundation type: Independent foundation.
Financial data (yr. ended 12/31/05): Assets, $2,719,549 (M); expenditures, $381,158; qualifying distributions, $360,230; giving activities include $282,538 for 59 grants (high: $80,130; low: $100), and $77,692 for 1 in-kind gift.
Fields of interest: Historic preservation/historical societies; Arts; Higher education; Reproductive health, family planning; Crime/law enforcement, police agencies; Human services.
Limitations: Giving primarily in New Orleans, LA. No grants to individuals.
Officers: Gloria S. Kabacoff, Pres.; Margot K. Thomas, V.P.; Maurice P. Kabacoff, Secy.-Treas.
EIN: 721307912

3493
Keller Family Foundation ◇

P.O. Box 13625
New Orleans, LA 70185-3625 (504) 861-3391
Contact: Mary Keller Zervigon, Pres.
URL: http://kellerfamilyfoundation.org/index.html

Established in 1949 in LA.
Donors: Charles Keller, Jr.†; Rosa F. Keller†.
Foundation type: Independent foundation.
Financial data (yr. ended 12/31/05): Assets, $13,334,144 (M); expenditures, $644,412; qualifying distributions, $630,795; giving activities include $630,795 for 1 grant.
Purpose and activities: The foundation has interests in education, youth development, human services, and public affairs.
Fields of interest: Arts; Higher education; Education; Human services; Community development; Federated giving programs.
Type of support: General/operating support; Capital campaigns.
Limitations: Giving primarily in New Orleans, LA. No grants to individuals, or for tickets or fundraisers.
Application information: Applicants must complete the Southeast Louisiana Association of Grantmakers Common Application Form or acceptable substitute from foundation Web site. Application form required.
Initial approach: 2-page proposal. See foundation Web site for guidelines
Copies of proposal: 2
Deadline(s): Feb. 1 for spring meeting, and Sept. 15 for fall meeting
Board meeting date(s): Apr. and Nov.
Officers and Directors:* Mary K. Zervigon,* Pres.; Luis C. Zervigon,* Secy.; Caroline K. Loughlin,*

Treas.; Julie F. Breitmeyer; Thomas K. Loughlin; Andres M. Zervigon.
EIN: 726027426

3494
Libby-Dufour Fund ✧
c/o Whitney National Bank
228 Saint Charles Ave.
New Orleans, LA 70130
Contact: M. Cleland Powell III, Treas.

Incorporated in 1952 in LA.
Donor: Edith Libby Dufour‡.
Foundation type: Independent foundation.
Financial data (yr. ended 12/31/05): Assets, $8,454,159 (M); expenditures, $638,359; qualifying distributions, $567,514; giving activities include $565,000 for 20 grants (high: $50,000; low: $5,000).
Purpose and activities: Giving primarily for Christian organizations, churches, and schools.
Fields of interest: Education; Hospitals (general); Human services; Christian agencies & churches.
Limitations: Giving limited to the New Orleans, LA, area. No grants to individuals, or for endowment funds or operating budgets.
Application information:
Initial approach: Proposal
Copies of proposal: 1
Deadline(s): None
Board meeting date(s): Quarterly
Officers: E. James Kock, Jr., Pres.; Denis H. McDonald, V.P.; Harry B. Kelleher, Jr., Secy.; M. Cleland Powell III, Treas.
Trustees: Clarence C. Clifton; Edward M. Simmons.
EIN: 726027406
Selected grants: The following grants were reported in 2003.
$100,000 to Loyola University, New Orleans, LA.
$50,000 to Maison Hospitaliere, New Orleans, LA.
$25,000 to De La Salle High School, New Orleans, LA.
$25,000 to Stuart Hall School, New Orleans, LA.
$20,000 to Louisiana Society for the Prevention of Cruelty to Animals, New Orleans, LA.
$20,000 to Ozanam Inn, New Orleans, LA.
$15,000 to National Society of the Colonial Dames of America, New Orleans, LA.
$15,000 to Second Harvest Food Bank of Greater New Orleans and Acadiana, New Orleans, LA.
$10,000 to Saint Anthony of Padua Catholic School, Greenville, SC.
$5,000 to Magnolia School, Jefferson, LA.

3495
Live Oak Foundation ✧
(formerly Frank & Mary Godchaux Foundation)
P.O. Box 269
Abbeville, LA 70511-0269

Donors: Frank A. Godchaux III; Charles R. Godchaux; Frank M. Godchaux.
Foundation type: Independent foundation.
Financial data (yr. ended 12/31/04): Assets, $3,369,197 (M); gifts received, $282,450; expenditures, $583,131; qualifying distributions, $567,100; giving activities include $567,100 for 47 grants.
Purpose and activities: Giving primarily for nursing school education, the environment, and federated giving programs.

Fields of interest: Nursing school/education; Education; Environment; Federated giving programs; Protestant agencies & churches; Cemeteries/burial services.
Limitations: Applications not accepted. Giving on a national basis. No grants to individuals.
Application information: Contributes only to pre-selected organizations.
Officers: Frank K. Godchaux, Pres.; Theresa G. Payne, V.P.; Leslie K. Godchaux, Secy.
EIN: 726042163
Selected grants: The following grants were reported in 2003.
$65,660 to Graceland Cemetery Association, Weston, MO.
$60,000 to Vanderbilt University, School of Nursing, Nashville, TN. For building fund.
$13,000 to Project Lazarus, New Orleans, LA.
$5,000 to Atlantic Salmon Federation, Calais, ME.
$5,000 to Nature Conservancy, Baton Rouge, LA.
$2,000 to Conservation International, DC.
$1,500 to Montgomery Bell Academy, Nashville, TN.
$1,000 to Taft School, Watertown, CT.
$1,000 to University of Louisiana at Lafayette, Lafayette, LA.
$1,000 to Woodberry Forest School, Woodberry Forest, VA.

3496
Lorio Foundation ✧
P.O. Box 895
Thibodaux, LA 70302 (985) 449-0380

Established in LA.
Foundation type: Independent foundation.
Financial data (yr. ended 12/31/05): Assets, $25,039,351; expenditures, $1,213,592; qualifying distributions, $1,173,597; giving activities include $1,132,318 for grants.
Fields of interest: Higher education, university; Animal welfare; Crime/law enforcement, correctional facilities; Crime/law enforcement, police agencies; Housing/shelter; Recreation, parks/playgrounds; Athletics/sports, football; Community development, volunteer services; Community development; Protestant agencies & churches; Roman Catholic agencies & churches.
Limitations: Giving limited to Thibodaux, LA.
Application information:
Initial approach: Letter
Deadline(s): None
Managers: Rita Dickie; Camille A. Morvant III; Christopher Terracina.
EIN: 721318244
Selected grants: The following grants were reported in 2004.
$150,000 to Thibodaux, City of, Thibodaux, LA. 2 grants: $20,000 (For Main Street Program), $130,000 (For Thibodaux/Lafourche Animal Shelter).
$129,300 to Lafourche Parish School Board, Thibodaux, LA. 2 grants: $100,000 (For playground equipment for three Thibodaux elementary schools), $29,300 (For Community Walking Program).
$100,000 to Nicholls State University, Thibodaux, LA. For band instruments.
$80,000 to Thibodaux Volunteer Fire Department, Thibodaux, LA. For construction of new station for VCH fire company.
$50,000 to E. D. White Catholic High School, Thibodaux, LA. For school Library.

$45,000 to Thibodaux High School, Thibodaux, LA. For construction of concession/Press Box/ Restroom facilities at baseball field.
$44,000 to Habitat for Humanity, Thibodaux Area, Thibodaux, LA. To purchase property.
$25,000 to Saint Vincent de Paul TriParish Community Pharmacy, Houma, LA. For medicine for elderly and poor in Thibodaux.

3497
Louisiana Outside Counsel Health & Ethics Foundation ✧
1419 Ryan St.
Lake Charles, LA 70601

Established in 2004 in LA.
Foundation type: Independent foundation.
Financial data (yr. ended 12/31/04): Assets, $0 (M); gifts received, $500,000; expenditures, $500,000; qualifying distributions, $500,000; giving activities include $500,000 for 6 grants (high: $300,000; low: $20,000).
Fields of interest: Higher education; Legal services; Crime/law enforcement; Human services.
Limitations: Applications not accepted. Giving in LA, primarily in Baton Rouge and New Orleans. No grants to individuals.
Application information: Contributes only to pre-selected organizations.
Directors: Ken Carter; Russ Herman; Don Kelly; Bob Wright; Drew Ranier; Richard Scruggs.
EIN: 010550123

3498
The Lupin Foundation ✧
(formerly Physicians New Orleans Foundation)
234 Metairie Rd.
Metairie, LA 70005 (504) 849-0518

Incorporated in 1981 in LA.
Foundation type: Independent foundation.
Financial data (yr. ended 12/31/04): Assets, $26,694,750 (M); expenditures, $1,432,587; qualifying distributions, $1,131,188; giving activities include $799,667 for 74 grants (high: $60,000; low: $1,000).
Purpose and activities: Giving primarily to Jewish agencies and temples; also support for health associations, education, and the arts.
Fields of interest: Museums; Arts; Higher education; Education; Hospitals (general); Health organizations, association; Medical research, institute; Cancer, leukemia research; Human services; Jewish federated giving programs; Jewish agencies & temples; Disabilities, people with.
Limitations: Giving primarily in LA. No grants to individuals; no loans.
Publications: Application guidelines.
Application information: Application form required.
Initial approach: Proposal
Copies of proposal: 1
Deadline(s): None
Board meeting date(s): 9 times yearly
Final notification: 2 weeks
Officer: Arnold M. Lupin, M.D., Pres.
Directors: Louis Levy II, M.D.; Jay S. Lupin, M.D.; Lisa Lupin; Louis Lupin; Ralph Lupin, M.D.; Samuel Lupin, M.D.; Timothy Lupin; Lois Salzman; Suzanne Stokar.
Number of staff: 1 full-time support.
EIN: 720940770

3499
Florence Mauboules Charitable Trust ◇
P.O. Drawer 449
Crowley, LA 70527-0449 (337) 783-7142
Contact: Kenneth O. Privat, Tr.
Application address: 525 W. Court Cir., Crowley, LA 70526

Established in 2004 in LA.
Donor: Florence Mauboules.
Foundation type: Independent foundation.
Financial data (yr. ended 12/31/05): Assets, $1,066,950 (M); gifts received, $957,000; expenditures, $423,534; qualifying distributions, $414,816; giving activities include $414,816 for 87 grants (high: $37,250; low: $70).
Fields of interest: Elementary/secondary education; Higher education; Human services; Christian agencies & churches.
Limitations: Giving primarily in LA.
Application information:
Initial approach: Letter
Deadline(s): None
Trustee: Kenneth O. Privat.
EIN: 201774892

3500
The Jess Merkle Foundation ◇ ☆
7717 Creswell Rd., Ste. 18
Shreveport, LA 71106

Established in 1997 in LA.
Donor: Lyda T. Merkle†.
Foundation type: Independent foundation.
Financial data (yr. ended 6/30/05): Assets, $6,025,830 (M); expenditures, $658,996; qualifying distributions, $566,566; giving activities include $565,196 for 9 grants (high: $325,000; low: $750).
Fields of interest: Secondary school/education; Substance abuse, services; Human services; Salvation Army.
Type of support: General/operating support; Endowments.
Limitations: Applications not accepted. Giving on a national basis, with some emphasis on LA. No grants to individuals.
Application information: Contributes only to pre-selected organizations.
Trustee: Paul Merkle.
EIN: 721336331
Selected grants: The following grants were reported in 2004.
$150,000 to Salvation Army National Headquarters, Alexandria, VA.
$22,549 to Saint Lukes United Methodist Church, DC.
$20,000 to Loyola College Preparatory School, Shreveport, LA.
$20,000 to Oakwood Home for Women, Shreveport, LA.
$20,000 to Shreveport-Bossier Community Renewal, Shreveport, LA.
$9,441 to 81st Street Early Education Center, Shreveport, LA.

3501
J. Edgar Monroe Foundation (1976) ◇
228 St. Charles Ave., Ste. 1402
New Orleans, LA 70130
Contact: Robert J. Monroe, Pres.

Established in 1976 in LA.
Donors: J. Edgar Monroe†; Robert J. Monroe.
Foundation type: Independent foundation.
Financial data (yr. ended 12/31/04): Assets, $8,581,032 (M); gifts received, $700,000; expenditures, $1,691,899; qualifying distributions, $1,273,235; giving activities include $1,257,335 for 80 grants (high: $725,000; low: $43).
Purpose and activities: Giving primarily for health, education, and the arts.
Fields of interest: Arts; Education, fund raising/fund distribution; Higher education; Hospitals (general); Human services; Roman Catholic agencies & churches.
Type of support: Annual campaigns; Capital campaigns; Building/renovation; Equipment; Emergency funds; Scholarship funds; Research; Matching/challenge support.
Limitations: Applications not accepted. Giving primarily in LA. No grants to individuals.
Application information: Contributes only to pre-selected organizations.
Board meeting date(s): Quarterly
Officer: Robert J. Monroe, Pres.
Directors: Marjorie Colomb; William F. Finegan; Joseph P. Monroe.
Number of staff: 2 full-time support.
EIN: 720784059
Selected grants: The following grants were reported in 2003.
$725,000 to Loyola University, New Orleans, LA.
$30,000 to New Orleans Museum of Art, New Orleans, LA.
$22,838 to Louisiana State University Health Sciences Center, New Orleans, LA.
$16,500 to Stuart Hall School, New Orleans, LA.
$6,000 to Saint Thomas Health Services, New Orleans, LA.
$5,880 to New Orleans Opera Association, New Orleans, LA.
$3,000 to Pendleton Memorial Methodist Hospital, New Orleans, LA.
$2,960 to Easter Seal Society of Louisiana, New Orleans, LA.
$398 to New Orleans Ballet Association, New Orleans, LA.
$70 to Tulane University Health Sciences Center, New Orleans, LA.

3502
Monteleone Family Foundation ◇
214 Royal St.
New Orleans, LA 70130-2201

Established in 2002 in LA.
Donor: New Hotel Monteleone, LLC.
Foundation type: Company-sponsored foundation.
Financial data (yr. ended 12/31/04): Assets, $412,259 (M); gifts received, $438,898; expenditures, $321,011; qualifying distributions, $320,994; giving activities include $320,994 for 4 grants (high: $300,076; low: $500).
Purpose and activities: The foundation supports Jewish agencies and temples and organizations involved with education.
Fields of interest: Elementary/secondary education; Higher education; Federated giving programs; Jewish agencies & temples.
Limitations: Applications not accepted. Giving primarily in New Orleans, LA, and Houston, TX. No grants to individuals.
Application information: Contributes only to pre-selected organizations.
Officers: William A. Monteleone, Jr., Pres.; Ronald Pincus, V.P.; Charles Lacinak, Jr., Secy.-Treas.
Directors: Anne Monteleone Burr; David G. Monteleone.
EIN: 820569392

3503
The Greater New Orleans Foundation ◇
1055 St. Charles Ave., Ste. 100
New Orleans, LA 70130 (504) 598-4663
Contact: Gregory Ben Johnson, C.E.O.; For grants: Samantha Bickham, Prog. Off.
FAX: (504) 598-4676; E-mail: benj@gnof.org; E-mail for Donor-Advised fund grant recommendations to the Rebuild New Orleans Fund: GNOFgrants@gnof.org; URL: http://www.gnof.org

Established in 1924 in LA as the Community Chest; became a community foundation in 1983.
Foundation type: Community foundation.
Financial data (yr. ended 12/31/05): Assets, $134,603,157 (M); gifts received, $16,927,205; expenditures, $10,664,495; giving activities include $8,659,432 for grants.
Purpose and activities: The foundation will respond to the New Orleans region with data-driven grantmaking in the areas of: 1) excellence in education; 2) economic expansion and job training; 3) affordable housing/neighborhood development; 4) race and equity; and 5) sustaining and developing nonprofit capacity.
Fields of interest: Arts; Education; Environment; Health care; Health organizations, association; Crime/violence prevention; Employment; Food services; Housing/shelter; Disasters, Hurricane Katrina; Recreation; Youth development; Human services; Economic development; Community development; Philanthropy/voluntarism; Public affairs.
Type of support: Management development/capacity building; Emergency funds; Program development; Seed money; Technical assistance; Program evaluation; Matching/challenge support.
Limitations: Giving limited to southeastern LA, including the greater New Orleans area. No support for religious activities. No grants to individuals, or for annual fund campaigns, capital expenditures, sponsorship of special events, trips, continuing support, endowment funds, equipment, building funds, or deficit financing.
Publications: Annual report; Informational brochure; Program policy statement.
Application information: Each competitive grantmaking fund is governed by different grantmaking priorities, criteria and guidelines. Visit foundation Web site for application information per grant type.
Deadline(s): Varies
Board meeting date(s): Quarterly
Final notification: Varies
Officers and Trustees:* M. Cleland Powell III,* Chair.; Myron E. Moorehead, M.D.*, Vice-Chair.; Gregory Ben Johnson, C.E.O. and Pres.; Kathleen Herbert, V.P., Finance and Admin.; Martha McDermott Landrum, V.P., Devel. and Comms.; Orlando C. Watkins, V.P., Progs.; Kim M. Boyle,* Secy.; Gary N. Solomon,* Treas.; Cherie F. Thompson, Cont.; Madlyn B. Bagneris; John D. Becker; Edgar L. Chase III; Philip F. Cossich, Jr.; Joseph Failla II; Ludovico Feoli; David Francis; Richard W. Freeman, Jr.; Philip J. Gunn; Paul M. Haygood; Scott P. Howard; Robert E. Howson; Henry M. Lambert; J. Thomas Lewis; Andree K. Moss;

Rajender K. Pannu; Leann O. Moss; Michael O. Read; Anthony Recasner, M.D.; Robert D. Reily; William H. Shane, Jr.; Gloria Richard-Davis, M.D.; Stephen L. Sontheimer; Phyllis M. Taylor; Cheryl R. Teamer; Frances G. Villere; David R. Voelker; Joseph E. Williams.
Number of staff: 5 full-time professional; 3 full-time support.
EIN: 720408921

3504
The Peltier Foundation ◇ ☆
101 St. Louis St.
Thibodaux, LA   70301   (985) 447-4033

Established in 1998 in LA.
Donor: Richard Peltier.
Foundation type: Independent foundation.
Financial data (yr. ended 12/31/05): Assets, $7,676,862 (M); expenditures, $339,090; qualifying distributions, $330,500; giving activities include $330,500 for 17 grants (high: $100,000; low: $1,000).
Fields of interest: Higher education; Health care; Housing/shelter; Human services; Government/public administration; Roman Catholic agencies & churches.
Limitations: Giving primarily in Thibodaux, LA. No grants to individuals.
Application information:
  Initial approach: Letter
  Deadline(s): None
Officers: Donald L. Peltier, Pres.; Bernice P. Harang, V.P.; James Peltier, Secy.
EIN: 721416778

3505
Irene W. & C. B. Pennington
Foundation ▼ ◇
2237 S. Acadian Thruway, Ste. 601
Baton Rouge, LA   70808   (225) 383-3412
Contact: William E. Hodgkins, Exec. Dir.; To Discuss Current or Proposed Projects: Lori Bertman, Prog. Off.
FAX: (225) 381-0128; Additional tel. for Lori Bertman: (225) 338-9386, E-mail: lori@penningtonfamilyfoundation.org; URL: http://www.penningtonfamilyfoundation.org

Established in 1982 in LA.
Donors: C.B. Pennington†; Irene W. Pennington†.
Foundation type: Independent foundation.
Financial data (yr. ended 12/31/05): Assets, $132,048,752 (M); gifts received, $11,894,485; expenditures, $12,223,840; qualifying distributions, $6,910,182; giving activities include $6,910,182 for 130 grants (high: $1,000,000; low: $500; average: $1,000–$100,000).
Purpose and activities: Giving primarily to provide philanthropic support to promote the overall well-being of families and communities.
Fields of interest: Secondary school/education; Medical specialty research; Youth development, centers/clubs; Human services; Youth, services.
Type of support: General/operating support; Capital campaigns; Building/renovation; Program development.
Limitations: Giving limited to communities within or near Baton Rouge, LA. No grants to individuals.
Publications: Application guidelines.

Application information: If the proposed project in the concept paper is of interest to the foundation, the organization will be invited to submit a full proposal due by Aug. 15. Faxed or e-mailed concept papers will not be accepted. Grants are awarded once a year - in late Oct. or early Nov. Application form required.
  Initial approach: Brief concept paper (1-2 pages)
  Copies of proposal: 3
  Deadline(s): May 15 for concept paper. All organizations, regardless of whether or not they have been funded in the past, must submit concept paper
  Final notification: June 30
Officer: William E. Hodgkins, Exec. Dir.
Trustees: Richard Blackstone; Paula P. Delabretonne; Claude B. Pennington III; Daryl B. Pennington, Sr.; Daryl B. Pennington, Jr.; Sharon Palmer Pennington.
Number of staff: 2
EIN: 720938097
Selected grants: The following grants were reported in 2004.
$750,000 to Louisiana State Laboratory School Foundation, Baton Rouge, LA. For general support.
$500,000 to Louisiana Art and Science Museum, Baton Rouge, LA. For general support.
$375,000 to Family Service of Greater Baton Rouge, Baton Rouge, LA. For general support.
$333,333 to East Feliciana Parish, Clinton, LA. For general support.
$250,000 to Pennington Biomedical Research Center Foundation, Baton Rouge, LA. For general support.
$210,000 to East Feliciana Parish Sheriffs Office, Clinton, LA. For general support.
$25,000 to Arts Council of Greater Baton Rouge, Baton Rouge, LA. For general support.
$25,000 to Slaughter Police Department, Slaughter, LA. For general support.
$20,000 to Saint Vincent de Paul Society, Baton Rouge, LA. For general support.
$15,000 to Slaughter Elementary School, Slaughter, LA. For general support.

3506
The Reily Foundation
640 Magazine St.
New Orleans, LA   70130-3406
Contact: Robert D. Reily, Dir.

Established in 1962.
Donor: Reily Foods Co.
Foundation type: Company-sponsored foundation.
Financial data (yr. ended 12/31/04): Assets, $18,631,003 (M); expenditures, $948,321; qualifying distributions, $819,400; giving activities include $816,300 for 66 grants (high: $80,000; low: $500).
Purpose and activities: The foundation supports organizations involved with arts and culture, education, health, human services, and civic affairs.
Fields of interest: Arts; Education; Health care; Children/youth, services; Human services; Federated giving programs; Public affairs.
Type of support: Income development; Equipment; General/operating support; Continuing support; Capital campaigns; Building/renovation.
Limitations: Giving primarily in the greater New Orleans, LA, area. No support for religious or political organizations. No grants to individuals.
Application information: Application form required.

Initial approach: Contact foundation for application form
Deadline(s): None
Board meeting date(s): Varies
Directors: Joan M. Coulter; Robert D. Reily; William B. Reily III.
EIN: 726029179

3507
The RosaMary Foundation
P.O. Box 13218
New Orleans, LA   70185-3218   (504) 895-1984
Contact: Richard W. Freeman, Jr., Chair.
FAX: (504) 895-1988; URL: http://www.rosamary.org

Trust established in 1939 in LA.
Donor: Members of the A.B. Freeman family.
Foundation type: Independent foundation.
Financial data (yr. ended 12/31/04): Assets, $50,523,103 (M); expenditures, $2,190,512; qualifying distributions, $1,986,124; giving activities include $1,937,708 for 47+ grants (high: $400,000).
Purpose and activities: Emphasis on a community fund, higher and secondary education, including church-related schools, social service agencies, civic affairs, and cultural programs.
Fields of interest: Arts; Secondary school/education; Higher education; Human services; Community development; Government/public administration.
Type of support: General/operating support; Continuing support; Annual campaigns; Capital campaigns; Building/renovation; Endowments; Program development; Seed money.
Limitations: Giving primarily in the greater New Orleans, LA, area. No grants to individuals.
Publications: Application guidelines.
Application information: Application form and summary sheet available on foundation Web site. Application form required.
  Initial approach: Proposal in letter form (no more than 3 pages)
  Copies of proposal: 1
  Deadline(s): Feb. 1 and Sept. 1
  Board meeting date(s): Approximately 2 times a year beginning in spring
Officer and Trustees:* Richard W. Freeman, Jr.,* Chair.; Adelaide Benjamin; Louis M. Freeman, Jr.; Tina Freeman; Caroline Loughlin; Andrew Wisdom; Betty Wisdom; Carlos Zervigon; Mary Zervigon.
EIN: 726024696
Selected grants: The following grants were reported in 2005.
$885,000 to Greater New Orleans Foundation, New Orleans, LA. 2 grants: $10,000 (For general support), $875,000 (For Donor Advised Fund).
$250,000 to United Way for the Greater New Orleans Area, New Orleans, LA. For renewal of annual support.
$90,000 to Parent-Teacher-Student Association, Robert Mills Lusher Alternative Elementary School, New Orleans, LA. For capital campaign, payable over 2 years.
$40,000 to United Negro College Fund, New Orleans, LA. For renewal of annual support.
$35,000 to Louisiana Philharmonic Orchestra, New Orleans, LA. For renewal of annual support.
$15,000 to Tipitinas Foundation, New Orleans, LA. For general operating support.

$10,000 to New Orleans Video Access Center (NOVAC), New Orleans, LA. For general operating support.

$8,000 to New Orleans Opera Association, New Orleans, LA. For operational support for season.

$7,000 to My House, New Orleans, LA. For Safe and Smart After-School and Summer Camp.

3508
Edward G. Schlieder Educational Foundation ✧
201 St. Charles Ave., Ste. 2508
New Orleans, LA 70170
Contact: Pierre F. Lapeyre, Consultant

Incorporated in 1945 in LA.
Donor: Edward G. Schlieder†.
Foundation type: Independent foundation.
Financial data (yr. ended 12/31/05): Assets, $55,998,416 (M); expenditures, $3,616,852; qualifying distributions, $2,750,873; giving activities include $2,676,820 for 27 grants (high: $310,000; low: $50,000).
Purpose and activities: Giving primarily to schools, colleges, and universities, with some emphasis on Episcopal schools and universities.
Fields of interest: Higher education; Education; Medical research, institute; Protestant agencies & churches.
Type of support: Capital campaigns; Equipment; Research.
Limitations: Giving limited to educational institutions in LA. No grants to individuals, or for general purposes, endowment funds, scholarships, fellowships, or operating budgets; no loans.
Publications: Annual report.
Application information: Application form not required.
   Initial approach: Letter
   Copies of proposal: 3
   Deadline(s): None
   Board meeting date(s): As required
   Final notification: 30 to 45 days
Officers: Elizabeth S. Nalty, Pres.; Thomas D. Westfeldt, V.P.; John M. Waid, Secy.; Jill K. Nalty, Treas.
Number of staff: 1 part-time professional; 1 part-time support.
EIN: 720408974
Selected grants: The following grants were reported in 2003.

$574,000 to Tulane University, New Orleans, LA. 3 grants: $334,000 (For Westfeldt Practice Competition Complex), $120,000 (For biomedical engineering chair), $120,000 (For surgical oncology chair).

$200,000 to Louise S. McGehee School, New Orleans, LA. For student center renovations.

$125,000 to Our Lady of Holy Cross College, New Orleans, LA. For Presidents Chair.

$120,000 to University of New Orleans, Ogden Museum of Southern Art, New Orleans, LA. To complete, furnish and equip orientation and lecture hall and research library.

$120,000 to Xavier University of Louisiana, New Orleans, LA. For pharmaceutical science chair.

$100,000 to Northwestern State University of Louisiana, Shreveport, LA. For education chair.

$66,667 to Christ Episcopal School, Covington, LA. For classroom building.

$62,500 to New Orleans Baptist Theological Seminary, New Orleans, LA. For renovation and expansion.

3509
Scott Foundation, Inc. ✧
P.O. Box 4948
Monroe, LA 71201 (318) 387-4160
Contact: T.H. Scott

Established in 1992 in LA.
Donors: Scott Truck & Tractor Co.; Gold Mine Gin, Inc.
Foundation type: Independent foundation.
Financial data (yr. ended 7/31/05): Assets, $28,762,060 (M); gifts received, $10,000; expenditures, $1,419,941; qualifying distributions, $1,095,700; giving activities include $1,085,892 for 472 grants (high: $100,000; low: $50).
Purpose and activities: Giving primarily to Christian churches, education, youth organizations, health care, human services, and civic organizations.
Fields of interest: Secondary school/education; Higher education; Health care; Medical research; Recreation; Human services; Youth, services; Community development; Protestant agencies & churches.
Type of support: Scholarship funds.
Limitations: Giving primarily in northern LA.
Application information: Application form not required.
   Deadline(s): None
Officers: Betty S. Cummins, Chair.; G.J. Bershen, Secy.-Treas.; Paula Brodnax, Secy.
Trustees: Sam Adams; Hugh McDonald; John Mullins; T.H. Scott, Jr.
EIN: 726027563

3510
Stuller Family Foundation ✧
1213 Terrace Hwy.
Broussard, LA 70518-7643 (337) 394-5432
Contact: Michael Dehart

Established in 1995.
Donor: Matthew G. Stuller.
Foundation type: Independent foundation.
Financial data (yr. ended 12/31/03): Assets, $32,095,803 (M); gifts received, $5,030,092; expenditures, $932,703; qualifying distributions, $632,062; giving activities include $632,062 for 71 grants (high: $200,000; low: $100).
Purpose and activities: Giving primarily for Roman Catholic causes.
Fields of interest: Education; Human services; Children/youth, services; Roman Catholic agencies & churches.
Limitations: Giving primarily in Lafayette, LA.
Application information:
   Initial approach: Proposal
   Copies of proposal: 4
   Board meeting date(s): Quarterly
Trustees: William P. Mills; Catharine O. Stuller; Matthew G. Stuller.
Number of staff: 1 part-time professional; 1 part-time support.
EIN: 721282688
Selected grants: The following grants were reported in 2003.

$200,000 to Gemological Institute of America, Carlsbad, CA.

$25,000 to Community Foundation of Acadiana, Lafayette, LA.

$16,500 to Boy Scouts of America, Lafayette, LA.

$10,000 to United Way of Acadiana, Lafayette, LA.

$5,000 to Love INC of Lafayette, Lafayette, LA.

$3,500 to University of Louisiana at Lafayette, Lafayette, LA.

$2,500 to Boys and Girls Clubs of Acadiana, Lafayette, LA.

$1,500 to YMCA of Lafayette, Lafayette, LA.

$1,000 to American Red Cross, Lafayette, LA.

$1,000 to Louisiana Public Broadcasting, Friends of, Baton Rouge, LA.

3511
The Patrick F. Taylor Foundation ✧
1615 Poydras St., Ste. 1100
New Orleans, LA 70112 (504) 581-5491
Contact: Phyllis M. Taylor, Pres.

Established in 1987 in LA.
Donors: Maj. Gen. L.F. Taylor; Taylor Energy Co.
Foundation type: Independent foundation.
Financial data (yr. ended 12/31/05): Assets, $918,807 (M); gifts received, $1,500,320; expenditures, $1,190,200; qualifying distributions, $1,154,481; giving activities include $1,148,455 for 120 grants (high: $350,000; low: $100).
Purpose and activities: Giving primarily for educational institutions; scholarship awards paid directly to the college or university for specific individuals to attend higher learning institutions.
Fields of interest: Museums; Arts; Secondary school/education; Higher education; Scholarships/financial aid; Roman Catholic agencies & churches.
Type of support: General/operating support; Scholarship funds.
Limitations: Giving primarily in New Orleans, LA. No grants to individuals directly.
Application information: Scholarship candidates are identified through written recommendation by an instructor, professor, or counselor, as to the candidates' academic ability, proposed contribution to original thinking, and financial need. Application form not required.
   Deadline(s): None
Officers: Phyllis M. Taylor, Pres.; Amb. Thomas C. Ferguson, V.P.; VADM. Diego E. Hernandez, Secy.; Marvin L. Jacobs, Treas.; James A. Callier, Exec. Dir.
Trustees: Morrison C. Bethea; Gen. Walter E. Boomer; Carol Wilson Suggs.
EIN: 581686754

3512
David Toms Charitable Foundation, Inc. ✧ ☆
1545 E. 70th St., Ste. 201
Shreveport, LA 71105 (318) 798-5437
Contact: Adam Young, Exec. Dir.
FAX: (318) 798-1616;
E-mail: Info@DavidTomsFoundation.com;
URL: http://www.davidtomsfoundation.com

Established in 2003 in LA.
Donors: Merrill Lynch, PFS; PGA; Achushnet; Ducks Unlimited; Pat Locke; Tommy Talbot; Blue Cross and Blue Shield; Brad Leinart; Sedgwick Claims Mgt. Services, Inc.; Pierremont Anesthesia Consultants.
Foundation type: Independent foundation.
Financial data (yr. ended 12/31/05): Assets, $1,330,905 (M); gifts received, $2,249,379; expenditures, $1,361,035; qualifying distributions, $1,215,831; giving activities include $1,215,831 for grants.
Purpose and activities: The foundation helps underprivileged, abused and abandoned children

through funding programs that are designed to enhance a child's character, self-esteem and career possibilities.

Fields of interest: Youth development; Children.

Application information:

Deadline(s): None

Officers: David Toms, Pres.; Robert A. Dunkelman, Secy.; Jack A. Smithwick, Treas.; Adam Young, Exec. Dir.

Directors: Chris Campbell; Donna Miciotto; Knox Ridley, Jr.; Sonya Toms.

EIN: 582670763

3513
TWL Foundation ✧

1100 Poydras St., Ste. 2200
New Orleans, LA 70163-2200

Established in 1995 in LA.

Donors: Harry B. Freeman; Mrs. Harry B. Freeman; W. Harrell Freeman.

Foundation type: Independent foundation.

Financial data (yr. ended 12/31/03): Assets, $6,430,190 (M); expenditures, $405,208; qualifying distributions, $404,605; giving activities include $404,000 for 5 grants (high: $336,000; low: $3,000).

Purpose and activities: Giving primarily to Christian agencies and churches, and for higher education.

Fields of interest: Higher education; Christian agencies & churches.

Limitations: Applications not accepted. Giving on a national basis, with some emphasis on Searcy, AR. No grants to individuals.

Application information: Contributes only to pre-selected organizations.

Officers: W. Harrell Freeman, Pres.; Carlton L. Freeman, Secy.

EIN: 721306709

Selected grants: The following grants were reported in 2003.

$336,000 to Harding University, Searcy, AR. For general support.

$40,000 to Faulkner University, Montgomery, AL. For general support.

$15,000 to Metropolitan Crime Commission of New Orleans, New Orleans, LA. For general support.

$10,000 to Right to Life Committee Educational Trust Fund, National, DC. For general support.

$3,000 to Hickory Knoll Church of Christ, New Orleans, LA. For general support.

3514
The Wheless Foundation ✧

c/o AmSouth Bank
333 Texas St., SH 2069
Shreveport, LA 71101
Contact: Barbara R. York, V.P. and Trust Off., AmSouth Bank

Established in 1945 in LA.

Donor: N. Hobson Wheless†.

Foundation type: Independent foundation.

Financial data (yr. ended 10/31/05): Assets, $6,592,085 (M); expenditures, $370,463; qualifying distributions, $322,551; giving activities include $315,450 for 56 grants (high: $51,000; low: $100).

Purpose and activities: Giving primarily for health and human services and to Christian churches.

Fields of interest: Higher education; Health organizations, association; Children/youth, services; Community development; Federated giving programs; Christian agencies & churches.

Type of support: General/operating support; Continuing support; Annual campaigns; Capital campaigns; Building/renovation; Program development; Research.

Limitations: Giving primarily in northwest LA. No grants to individuals.

Application information: Application form not required.

Initial approach: Letter
Copies of proposal: 1
Deadline(s): None
Board meeting date(s): Annually in Oct.

Board of Control: Jim Devane; Elise W. Hogan; Nicholas Hobson Wheless, Jr.

Trustee: AmSouth Bank.

EIN: 726017724

Selected grants: The following grants were reported in 2005.

$25,000 to Shreveport-Bossier Community Renewal, Shreveport, LA.

$15,100 to Providence House, Shreveport, LA.

$11,000 to Public Affairs Research Council of Louisiana, Baton Rouge, LA.

$11,000 to Shreveport Regional Arts Council, Shreveport, LA.

$10,000 to American Red Cross, Dallas, TX.

$10,000 to Humane Society of Louisiana, New Orleans, LA.

$2,500 to American Quarter Horse Foundation, Amarillo, TX.

$1,000 to Salvation Army, Santa Fe, NM.

$1,000 to Volunteers of America, New Orleans, LA.

3515
The Huey and Angelina Wilson Foundation ✧

3636 S. Sherwood Forest Blvd., Ste. 650
Baton Rouge, LA 70816-2298 (225) 292-1344
Contact: Gregory J. Cotter, Tr.
FAX: (225) 292-1589;
E-mail: wilsonfoundation@hwilson.org

Established in 1986 in LA.

Donors: Huey J. Wilson; Angelina M. Wilson.

Foundation type: Independent foundation.

Financial data (yr. ended 12/31/04): Assets, $29,223,026 (M); gifts received, $499,749; expenditures, $559,977; qualifying distributions, $465,000; giving activities include $465,000 for 33 grants (high: $49,000; low: $5,000; average: $5,000–$40,000).

Purpose and activities: Of particular interest to the foundation are the handicapped, both physical and mental, those afflicted with disease, disadvantaged youth, the hungry and the homeless. While care for the less fortunate is important to the foundation, the trustees will look particularly favorable on grantees addressing the root cause of the misfortunate. Where practical or possible, the foundation will assist their targeted group to become self-sufficient productive contributors to the community.

Fields of interest: Education; Health care; Hemophilia; Human services; Salvation Army; Children/youth, services; Protestant agencies & churches; Disabilities, people with; Homeless.

Type of support: General/operating support; Continuing support; Capital campaigns; Building/

renovation; Equipment; Emergency funds; Program development; Matching/challenge support.

Limitations: Giving limited to the Baton Rouge, LA, area. No grants to individuals.

Publications: Application guidelines.

Application information: Application form not required.

Initial approach: Telephone requesting guidelines
Copies of proposal: 1
Deadline(s): 4th Fri. in Feb. and Aug.
Board meeting date(s): 3rd Fri. in Apr. and Oct.
Final notification: May 1 and Nov. 1

Trustees: Daniel J. Bevan; Gregory J. Cotter; Ben R. Miller, Jr.; Donna Saurage; Angelina M. Wilson; Denver Wilson; Dianne Wilson; Huey J. Wilson; John Wilson.

EIN: 581714586

3516
The Woldenberg Foundation

(formerly Dorothy & Malcolm Woldenberg Foundation)
809 Jefferson Hwy.
Jefferson, LA 70121 (504) 849-6078
Contact: Trudi Briede, Dir.
FAX: (504) 849-6515; Application address: P.O. Box 53333, New Orleans, LA 70153

Incorporated in 1959 in LA as Woldenberg Charitable and Educational Foundation.

Donors: Malcolm Woldenberg†; Magnolia Liquor Co., Inc.; Sazerac Co., Inc.; Great Southern Liquor Co., Inc.; Duval Spirits, Inc.

Foundation type: Independent foundation.

Financial data (yr. ended 12/31/05): Assets, $45,603,262 (M); expenditures, $3,276,528; qualifying distributions, $2,670,883; giving activities include $2,670,883 for grants.

Purpose and activities: Giving primarily for education, and to Jewish organizations.

Fields of interest: Museums; Arts; Higher education; Human services; Jewish federated giving programs.

International interests: Israel.

Type of support: General/operating support; Continuing support; Capital campaigns; Building/renovation; Equipment; Emergency funds; Program development; Research.

Limitations: Giving primarily in the greater New Orleans, LA, area, with special interest in Miami, FL, the southeastern U.S., and Israel. No support for political organizations. No grants to individuals.

Publications: Application guidelines.

Application information: Application form required.

Initial approach: Letter of inquiry
Deadline(s): Varies
Board meeting date(s): Varies
Final notification: Varies - usually 2 to 3 weeks prior to board meeting dates

Officer and Trustees:* William Goldring,* Pres.; Minette Brown,* V.P.; Mark Halpern,* V.P.; Robert Steeg,* Secy.; Jeffrey Goldring.

Number of staff: 1 part-time professional.

EIN: 726022665

3517
William C. Woolf Foundation ✧

333 Texas St., SH 2069
Shreveport, LA 71101
Contact: Barbara York

Incorporated in 1959 in LA.
Donors: William C. Woolf†; Geraldine H. Woolf†.
Foundation type: Independent foundation.
Financial data (yr. ended 2/28/05): Assets, $8,397,651 (M); expenditures, $435,304; qualifying distributions, $370,608; giving activities include $362,589 for 40 grants (high: $100,000; low: $300).
Purpose and activities: Giving primarily for education, health and human services, and to Christian churches.
Fields of interest: Higher education; Medical research, institute; Human services; Children/ youth, services; Christian agencies & churches.
Type of support: General/operating support; Continuing support; Capital campaigns; Building/ renovation; Program development; Research.
Limitations: Giving primarily in Shreveport, LA. No grants to individuals.
Application information: Application form not required.
   Initial approach: Letter
   Copies of proposal: 1
   Board meeting date(s): Feb.
Trustees: Willis L. Meadows; C. Lane Sartor; Nicholas Hobson Wheless, Jr.
EIN: 726020630
Selected grants: The following grants were reported in 2003.
$45,500 to Centenary College of Louisiana, Shreveport, LA.
$40,000 to Biomedical Research Foundation of Northwest Louisiana, Shreveport, LA. For research.
$40,000 to Glen Oaks Retirement System, Shreveport, LA.
$40,000 to Sci-Port Discovery Center, Shreveport, LA.
$25,000 to Louisiana United Methodist Children and Family Services, Ruston, LA.
$17,000 to United Way of Northwest Louisiana, Shreveport, LA.
$10,000 to Louisiana Alliance for Education Reform, New Orleans, LA.
$5,000 to Boy Scouts of America, Norwela Council, Shreveport, LA.
$2,600 to Junior Achievement of North Louisiana, Shreveport, LA.
$1,250 to Shreveport Symphony, Shreveport, LA.

3518
The H. & B. Young Foundation ◇
(formerly The Morgan City Fund)
P.O. Box 889
Morgan City, LA 70381
Contact: Brenda B. Ayo, Secy.

Incorporated in 1955 in LA.
Donor: Byrnes M. Young†.
Foundation type: Independent foundation.
Financial data (yr. ended 12/31/03): Assets, $15,419,741 (M); expenditures, $791,586; qualifying distributions, $693,260; giving activities include $632,700 for 29 grants (high: $209,000; low: $300), and $6,000 for 1 grant to an individual.
Purpose and activities: Funding primarily for arts and cultural programs, education, with emphasis on a technical college, human services, community development, and Protestant churches.
Fields of interest: Arts; Secondary school/ education; Education; Human services; Community development; Government/public administration; Protestant agencies & churches.

Type of support: Grants to individuals; General/ operating support; Equipment.
Limitations: Giving limited to Morgan City, LA.
Application information:
   Initial approach: Letter
Officers: Eugene B. Garber, Sr., Pres.; George Eells, V.P.; Brenda B. Ayo, Secy.
EIN: 726029365
Selected grants: The following grants were reported in 2003.
$210,000 to Louisiana Technical University, Ruston, LA. 2 grants: $209,000 to Young Memorial Campus (For scholarships and for expansion of marine department), $1,000 (For scholarships).
$30,500 to Morgan City, City of, Morgan City, LA. 2 grants: $10,500 (For purchase of signs for Main Street), $20,000 to Recreation Department (For purchase of tennis court lights).
$30,000 to Saint Mary Outreach, Morgan City, LA. For general support.
$10,000 to Trinity Episcopal Church, Morgan City, LA. Toward repair of stained glass windows.
$6,000 to Central Catholic High School, Morgan City, LA. For scholarships.
$5,000 to Holy Cross Elementary School, Morgan City, LA. For computer upgrades.
$4,000 to Morgan City High School, Morgan City, LA. 2 grants: $1,000 (For library), $3,000 (For scholarships).

3519
Zemurray Foundation ◇
228 St. Charles Ave., Ste. 1024
New Orleans, LA 70130
Contact: Kimberley M. Quintana, Treas.

Incorporated in 1951 in LA.
Donor: Sarah W. Zemurray.
Foundation type: Independent foundation.
Financial data (yr. ended 12/31/03): Assets, $95,760,810 (M); expenditures, $7,426,695; qualifying distributions, $6,632,637; giving activities include $6,497,745 for 53 grants (high: $2,375,000; low: $1,000; average: $15,000–$150,000).
Purpose and activities: Grants primarily for education, particularly higher education, cultural programs, civic affairs, hospitals, and medical research.
Fields of interest: Arts; Higher education; Education; Hospitals (general); Medical research, institute; Government/public administration.
Limitations: Applications not accepted. Giving primarily in New Orleans, LA, and Cambridge, MA. No grants to individuals.
Application information: Contributes only to pre-selected organizations.
   Board meeting date(s): Usually in Nov.
Officers and Trustees: * Samuel Z. Stone,* Pres.; Stephanie Stone Feoli, V.P.; Alison Stone Golcher, V.P.; Haydee T. Stone, V.P.; Thomas B. Lemann, Secy.; Kimberley M. Quintana, Treas.; Ludovico Feoli; Alberto Golcher.
Number of staff: 1 full-time professional; 2 part-time support.
EIN: 720539603
Selected grants: The following grants were reported in 2003.
$500,000 to Tulane University, New Orleans, LA.
$300,000 to Ochsner Clinic Foundation, Alton Ochsner Medical Foundation, New Orleans, LA.

$250,000 to Louisiana Philharmonic Orchestra, New Orleans, LA.
$250,000 to Union College, Barbourville, KY.
$240,000 to University of New Orleans Foundation, New Orleans, LA.
$225,000 to Contemporary Arts Center, New Orleans, LA.
$212,500 to Isidore Newman School, New Orleans, LA.
$200,000 to Dillard University, New Orleans, LA.
$200,000 to School of American Research, Santa Fe, NM.
$167,000 to New Orleans Museum of Art, New Orleans, LA. For operating support.

3520
Fred B. and Ruth B. Zigler Foundation ◇
P.O. Box 986
Jennings, LA 70546-0986 (337) 824-2413
Contact: Julie G. Berry, Pres.

Incorporated in 1956 in LA.
Donors: Fred B. Zigler†; Ruth B. Zigler†.
Foundation type: Independent foundation.
Financial data (yr. ended 12/31/04): Assets, $8,031,266 (M); expenditures, $558,077; qualifying distributions, $404,495; giving activities include $374,437 for 42 grants (high: $58,750; low: $88).
Purpose and activities: Emphasis on higher and secondary education, including scholarships for local students, and youth agencies.
Fields of interest: Secondary school/education; Higher education; Children/youth, services.
Type of support: General/operating support; Building/renovation; Equipment; Program development; Research; Scholarships—to individuals; Matching/challenge support.
Limitations: Giving primarily in Jefferson Davis Parish, LA. No grants to individuals (except scholarships for graduates of Jefferson Davis Parish high schools).
Publications: Annual report.
Application information: Scholarship application forms available through Jefferson Davis Parish high schools. Application form required.
   Initial approach: Proposal or letter
   Copies of proposal: 1
   Deadline(s): 3 weeks prior to board meetings; scholarship deadline Mar. 10
   Board meeting date(s): Bimonthly beginning in Jan.
Officers and Trustees: * Julie G. Berry,* Pres.; Marie C. Romero, Secy.-Treas.; Paul E. Brummett II; Dale Elmore; John M. Elmore; Mark Fehl; Richard C. Oustalet; John Pipkin.
Number of staff: 1 full-time professional; 1 part-time professional.
EIN: 726019403
Selected grants: The following grants were reported in 2004.
$58,750 to McNeese State University, Lake Charles, LA.
$41,250 to Louisiana State University and A & M College, Baton Rouge, LA. 2 grants: $11,250, $30,000
$17,500 to University of Louisiana at Lafayette, Lafayette, LA.
$8,750 to Northwestern State University, Natchitoches, LA.
$7,500 to University of Louisiana at Monroe, Monroe, LA.
$1,250 to Ozark Christian College, Joplin, MO.

MAINE

3521

Harold Alfond Foundation ✧

c/o Dexter Enterprises
2 Monument Sq.
Portland, ME 04101
Contact: Gregory Powell, Tr.

Established in 1993 in ME as successor to Harold Alfond Trust.
Donor: Harold Alfond.
Foundation type: Independent foundation.
Financial data (yr. ended 12/31/05): Assets, $50,075,793 (M); gifts received, $25,772,778; expenditures, $3,748,383; qualifying distributions, $3,621,098; giving activities include $3,570,687 for 50 grants (high: $1,000,000; low: $25).
Purpose and activities: Support primarily for higher education, the arts, and health care.
Fields of interest: Arts; Elementary/secondary education; Higher education; Hospitals (general); Health organizations, association; Human services; Children/youth, services; Community development, business promotion; Jewish agencies & temples.
Type of support: Matching/challenge support; Scholarship funds; Research; Endowments; Building/renovation; Capital campaigns; Annual campaigns.
Limitations: Giving primarily in FL and ME. No grants to individuals.
Application information: Application form not required.
Initial approach: Letter (no more than 3 pages)
Copies of proposal: 1
Deadline(s): None
Final notification: 3-6 months
Trustees: Dorothy Alfond; Harold Alfond; Peter Alfond; Theodore Alfond; William Alfond; Gregory Powell.
EIN: 223281672
Selected grants: The following grants were reported in 2003.
$430,227 to Maine Childrens Home for Little Wanderers, Waterville, ME. For campus renovations.
$250,000 to University of Maine Foundation, Orono, ME. For coach achievement fund.
$249,515 to Husson College, Bangor, ME. For baseball stadium.
$199,799 to Governor Dummer Academy, Byfield, MA. For capital campaign.
$197,663 to University of Massachusetts, Isenberg School of Management, Amherst, MA. For building fund.
$150,000 to University of Maine, Orono, ME. For arena expansion.
$100,000 to Eaglebrook School, Deerfield, MA. For student ice arena.
$50,000 to Colby College, Waterville, ME. 2 grants: $25,000 each (For basketball expansion project).
$20,000 to Catherine McAuley High School, Portland, ME. For building fund.

3522

The Peter Alfond Foundation ✧

c/o Dexter Enterprises, Inc.
2 Monument Sq.
Portland, ME 04101
Contact: Gregory Powell, Mgr.

Established in 1993 in ME.
Donors: Peter G. Alfond; Berkshire Hathaway Inc.
Foundation type: Independent foundation.
Financial data (yr. ended 12/31/05): Assets, $9,695,146 (M); expenditures, $544,146; qualifying distributions, $519,596; giving activities include $495,190 for 13 grants (high: $386,090; low: $100).
Purpose and activities: Giving primarily for education, social services, conservation, and federated giving programs.
Fields of interest: Secondary school/education; Higher education; Libraries (public); Education; Environment, natural resources; Human services; Federated giving programs; Jewish agencies & temples.
Limitations: Applications not accepted. Giving primarily in FL, MA, ME, and PR. No grants to individuals.
Application information: Contributes only to pre-selected organizations.
Officer: Gregory Powell, Mgr.
Trustees: Peter G. Alfond; William Alfond.
EIN: 223267949
Selected grants: The following grants were reported in 2004.
$347,800 to Maine Community Foundation, Ellsworth, ME.
$7,500 to Rollins College, Winter Park, FL.

3523

The William and Joan Alfond Foundation ✧ ☆

(formerly William L. Alfond Foundation)
c/o Dexter Enterprises, Inc.
2 Monument Sq.
Portland, ME 04101
Contact: Gregory Powell, Secy.

Established in 1986 in NE.
Donors: William Alfond; Berkshire Hathaway Inc.
Foundation type: Independent foundation.
Financial data (yr. ended 12/31/05): Assets, $18,265,441 (M); expenditures, $688,447; qualifying distributions, $649,748; giving activities include $617,202 for 46 grants (high: $124,268; low: $50).
Purpose and activities: Giving primarily for education.
Fields of interest: Education; Hospitals (general); Community development; Federated giving programs.
Type of support: Scholarship funds; Endowments; Capital campaigns; Annual campaigns.
Limitations: Giving primarily in New England. No grants to individuals.
Application information: Application form not required.
Initial approach: Letter (no more than 3 pages)
Copies of proposal: 1
Deadline(s): None
Final notification: 3-6 months

Officers and Directors:* Joan Alfond,* Pres. and Treas.; Gregory Powell, Secy.; Justin Alfond; Kenden Alfond; Theodore Alfond; Reis Alfond.
EIN: 010421806
Selected grants: The following grants were reported in 2003.
$57,980 to Governor Dummer Academy, Byfield, MA. For fitness center.
$50,000 to Dartmouth College, Hanover, NH. For men's hockey.
$45,000 to Boys and Girls Club of Waterville, Waterville, ME. For Passamoquoddy Indians, Eastport Boys and Girls Club.
$25,000 to Alfond Youth Center, Waterville, ME. For annual support.
$10,000 to Good Will-Hinckley School, Hinckley, ME. For scholarships.
$10,000 to University of Maine Foundation, Ellen Loring Museum, Bangor, ME. For Ellen Loring Collection.
$5,000 to Massachusetts General Hospital, Boston, MA. For Gelfand research.
$1,000 to Chewonki Foundation, Wiscasset, ME. For unrestricted support.
$1,000 to Eaglebrook School, Deerfield, MA. For annual support.
$1,000 to Maine Childrens Home for Little Wanderers, Waterville, ME. For campus renovations and capital campaign.

3524

The Baker Conservation Trust ☆

c/o First Advisors
9 Bristol Rd.
Damariscotta, ME 04543
Application address: c/o First Advisors, Trust Dept., Main St., Damariscotta, ME 04543

Established in 1991 in ME.
Donor: Robert W. Baker.
Foundation type: Independent foundation.
Financial data (yr. ended 12/31/05): Assets, $2,989,987 (M); gifts received, $500,000; expenditures, $910,406; qualifying distributions, $900,000; giving activities include $900,000 for grants.
Purpose and activities: Giving primarily for natural resource conservation.
Fields of interest: Environment, natural resources; Environment.
Limitations: Giving primarily in ME.
Application information: Application form not required.
Deadline(s): None
Trustee: First Advisors.
EIN: 226560684
Selected grants: The following grants were reported in 2004.
$117,754 to Maine Community Foundation, Ellsworth, ME. For conservation and preservation of wild natural history.

3525

Bangor Savings Bank Foundation ✧

99 Franklin St.
Bangor, ME 04402 (207) 942-5211
Contact: John Moore; Darlene Hawkes

Established in 1996 in ME.
Donor: Bangor Savings Bank.
Foundation type: Company-sponsored foundation.

Financial data (yr. ended 3/31/05): Assets, $3,869,420 (M); gifts received, $200,500; expenditures, $400,479; qualifying distributions, $374,728; giving activities include $372,774 for 56 grants (high: $39,124; low: $1,000).
Purpose and activities: The foundation supports organizations involved with arts and culture, education, and health.
Fields of interest: Arts; Education; Health care.
Limitations: Giving limited to areas of company operations in ME. No grants to individuals.
Application information:
    Initial approach: Proposal
    Deadline(s): None
Directors: David M. Carlisle; P. James Dowe, Jr.; G. Clifton Eames; James H. Goff; Kenneth H. Hews; Martha G. Newman; Gary W. Smith; Robert A. Strong; Calvin E. True.
EIN: 043353896
Selected grants: The following grants were reported in 2005.
$39,124 to United Way of Eastern Maine, Bangor, ME.
$30,000 to Husson College, Bangor, ME.
$10,000 to Maine Development Foundation, Augusta, ME.
$10,000 to Maine Maritime Academy, Castine, ME.
$10,000 to Public Theater, Auburn, ME.
$5,000 to Central Maine Medical Center, Lewiston, ME.
$5,000 to Eastern Maine Medical Center, Bangor, ME.
$5,000 to Pittsfield Public Library, Pittsfield, ME.
$3,000 to Coastal Enterprises, Wiscasset, ME.
$3,000 to Penobscot Marine Museum, Searsport, ME.

3526
Arthur and Doris Berry Foundation ✦ ☆
c/o Ralph Hodgkins
3 Rocky Rd.
Westport Island, ME 04578   (207) 882-7573

Established in ME.
Donor: Doris Berry†.
Foundation type: Independent foundation.
Financial data (yr. ended 12/31/05): Assets, $146,543 (M); expenditures, $1,310,067; qualifying distributions, $1,304,760; giving activities include $1,302,910 for 7 grants (high: $512,910; low: $30,000).
Fields of interest: Higher education; Animal welfare; Housing/shelter, development; Protestant agencies & churches.
Type of support: Scholarship funds; General/operating support.
Limitations: Applications not accepted. Giving primarily in ME. No grants to individuals.
Application information: Contributes only to pre-selected organizations.
Directors: Methyl A. Hodgkins; Ralph L. Hodgkins, Jr.; Susan Matzell.
EIN: 010500960

3527
Margaret E. Burnham Charitable Trust ✦
c/o H.M. Payson & Co.
P.O. Box 31
Portland, ME   04112-0031   (207) 772-3761
Contact: Thomas M. Pierce, Tr.
URL: http://www.megrants.org/Burnham.html

Established in 1995 in ME.
Donor: Margaret E. Burnham†.
Foundation type: Independent foundation.
Financial data (yr. ended 12/31/05): Assets, $6,899,669 (M); expenditures, $395,987; qualifying distributions, $369,564; giving activities include $347,400 for 87 grants (high: $18,000; low: $1,000; average: $5,000–$10,000).
Purpose and activities: Giving primarily for the arts, education, the environment, and human services.
Fields of interest: Arts; Higher education; Environment; Hospitals (general); Human services; Federated giving programs.
Type of support: Continuing support; Annual campaigns; Capital campaigns; Building/renovation; Equipment; Land acquisition; Program development; Publication; Research.
Limitations: Giving limited to ME. No support for religious organizations. No grants to individuals.
Publications: Application guidelines.
Application information: Application guidelines and form available on foundation Web site. Application form required.
    Initial approach: Letter
    Copies of proposal: 1
    Deadline(s): Oct. 1
    Board meeting date(s): Dec.
    Final notification: Dec. 31
Trustees: Thomas M. Pierce; Clifford H. Sinnett.
EIN: 010496879
Selected grants: The following grants were reported in 2004.
$20,000 to United Way of Greater Portland, Portland, ME.
$15,000 to Spring Harbor Hospital, Westbrook, ME.
$10,000 to North Yarmouth Academy, Yarmouth, ME.
$10,000 to Northern Maine Development Commission, Caribou, ME.
$10,000 to Portland Museum of Art, Portland, ME.
$5,000 to Greater Portland Landmarks, Portland, ME.
$5,000 to Trust for Public Land, San Francisco, CA.
$5,000 to YMCA.
$2,500 to American Red Cross.
$2,500 to Maine Reads, Portland, ME.

3528
Grace Butnam Foundation ✦
P.O. Box 40
South Windham, ME   04082

Established in 1985 in NH.
Donors: Marilyn L. Goodreau; Lawrence J. Keddy Trust; Freda Ellis†.
Foundation type: Independent foundation.
Financial data (yr. ended 12/31/04): Assets, $5,599,497 (M); expenditures, $689,224; qualifying distributions, $522,011; giving activities include $453,200 for 10 grants (high: $444,000; low: $200).
Fields of interest: Animal welfare.
Type of support: General/operating support.
Limitations: Applications not accepted. Giving primarily in ME. No grants to individuals.
Application information: Contributes only to pre-selected organizations.
Officers: Marilyn L. Goodreau, Pres.; Nancy Proctor, Treas. and Exec. Dir.
Directors: David Hawkes; Erlon Jones; Dawn Winchester.
EIN: 222672858

Selected grants: The following grants were reported in 2003.
$496,891 to Maine State Society for the Protection of Animals, Windham, ME.

3529
The Catalyst Fund ✦ ☆
40 Twin Ponds Dr.
Falmouth, ME   04105-2099

Donor: Elisabeth Hoffman.
Foundation type: Independent foundation.
Financial data (yr. ended 12/31/04): Assets, $27,204,245 (M); expenditures, $520,308; qualifying distributions, $441,745; giving activities include $441,745 for 8 grants (high: $250,191; low: $5,000).
Fields of interest: Education; Environment.
Limitations: Applications not accepted.
Application information: Contributes only to pre-selected organizations.
Officers: Elisabeth Hoffman, Pres.; Seth Johnson, Secy.-Treas.
Directors: Alfred Hoffman, Jr.; Bruce Jeffrey; Cynthia Sampson.
EIN: 352202654

3530
The Crockett Foundation ✦ ☆
c/o Richard A. Liberty
23 N. Raymond Rd.
Gray, ME   04039-9744
Contact: Linda Liberty, Pres.

Established in 2002 in ME.
Donor: R.C. and Annie T. Crockett Unitrust.
Foundation type: Independent foundation.
Financial data (yr. ended 12/31/04): Assets, $40,007 (M); gifts received, $506,120; expenditures, $1,214,816; qualifying distributions, $1,200,358; giving activities include $1,200,358 for 9 grants (high: $654,509; low: $500).
Fields of interest: Elementary/secondary education.
Application information:
    Initial approach: Letter
    Deadline(s): Sept. 30
Officers: Linda Liberty, Pres.; Richard Liberty, Secy.-Treas.
Director: Jim Dalamater.
EIN: 010471523

3531
George P. Davenport Trust Fund
65 Front St.
Bath, ME   04530   (207) 443-3431
Contact: Barry M. Sturgeon, Tr.

Trust established in 1927 in ME.
Donor: George P. Davenport†.
Foundation type: Independent foundation.
Financial data (yr. ended 12/31/05): Assets, $6,293,440 (M); gifts received, $28,384; expenditures, $403,652; qualifying distributions, $357,023; giving activities include $339,340 for 122 grants (high: $40,000; low: $350).
Purpose and activities: Support for the benefit of young and needy children, and for religious, temperance, moral, educational, benevolent and charitable institutions and organizations.

Fields of interest: Higher education; Education; Health care; Human services; Community development; Religion.
Type of support: Scholarship funds; General/operating support; Building/renovation; Emergency funds; Seed money; Matching/challenge support.
Limitations: Giving limited to Bath, ME. No grants to individuals (other than student loans and scholarships to Bath, ME, area, high school graduates), or for continuing support, annual campaigns, deficit financing, research, demonstration projects, publications, or celebration events.
Application information: Now using Maine Philanthropy Center common grant application. Application form required.
  Initial approach: Telephone
  Copies of proposal: 1
  Deadline(s): None
  Board meeting date(s): Semimonthly
  Final notification: 1 month
Trustees: Roberta F. Banks; Richard E. Jackson; Barry M. Sturgeon.
Number of staff: 1 part-time support.
EIN: 016009246
Selected grants: The following grants were reported in 2005.
$10,000 to Maine Medical Center, Portland, ME.
$2,500 to Junior Achievement of Maine, Scarborough, ME.
$1,750 to Chop Point, Woolwich, ME.
$370 to Learning for Life, Portland, ME.
$350 to YMCA, Bath Area Family, Bath, ME.

3532
The Falcon Charitable Foundation ◇ ☆
c/o Robert B. Gregory
P.O. Box 760
Damariscotta, ME   04543

Established in 1994 in ME.
Donor: Mary F. Fiore.
Foundation type: Independent foundation.
Financial data (yr. ended 12/31/05): Assets, $3,171,130 (M); expenditures, $401,625; qualifying distributions, $374,000; giving activities include $374,000 for 50 grants (high: $35,000; low: $100).
Purpose and activities: Giving primarily for the arts and environmental conservation; funding also for human rights and civil liberties.
Fields of interest: Arts; Environment, natural resources; Hospitals (general); Human services; International human rights; Civil liberties, advocacy.
Limitations: Applications not accepted. Giving primarily in ME and NY. No grants to individuals.
Application information: Contributes only to pre-selected organizations.
Trustees: Joseph A. Fiore; Mary F. Fiore.
EIN: 223340779
Selected grants: The following grants were reported in 2004.
$22,000 to Medomak Valley Land Trust, Waldoboro, ME.
$20,000 to Damariscotta River Association, Damariscotta, ME.
$20,000 to Nature Conservancy, Maine Chapter, Brunswick, ME.
$17,550 to Round Top Center for the Arts, Damariscotta, ME.
$15,000 to Amnesty International USA, New York, NY.
$10,000 to Environmental Defense, New York, NY.

$2,000 to Bloomingdale School of Music, New York, NY.
$500 to Adirondack Council, Elizabethtown, NY.
$500 to Audubon Society of Maine, Falmouth, ME.
$500 to Lincoln County Community Theater and Orchestra, Damariscotta, ME.

3533
The Edward E. Ford Foundation ◇
66 Pearl St., Ste. 322
Portland, ME   04101   (207) 774-2346
Contact: Robert Hallett, Exec. Dir.
FAX: (207) 774-2348; E-mail: info@eeford.org;
URL: http://www.eeford.org

Trust established in 1957 in NY.
Donor: Edward E. Ford†.
Foundation type: Independent foundation.
Financial data (yr. ended 9/30/05): Assets, $67,306,507 (M); expenditures, $3,968,321; qualifying distributions, $3,492,464; giving activities include $3,041,314 for 62 grants (high: $104,000; low: $10,000).
Purpose and activities: Grants for independent secondary education only. Independent secondary schools must hold full and active membership in National Association of Independent Schools to be eligible for consideration.
Fields of interest: Secondary school/education.
Type of support: Annual campaigns; Capital campaigns; Building/renovation; Equipment; Endowments; Program development; Conferences/seminars; Seed money; Curriculum development; Scholarship funds; Research; Matching/challenge support.
Limitations: Giving limited to the U.S. and its protectorates. No support for public elementary or college-level schools, schools that have been applicants within the last three years, or schools that do not have individual membership in NAIS (National Association of Independent Schools). No grants to individuals, or for emergency funds or deficit financing.
Application information: Applicants must request space on agenda prior to submitting a proposal. Application form required.
  Initial approach: For application guidelines go to Web site
  Copies of proposal: 18
  Deadline(s): Submit proposal during months prior to stated deadlines: Feb. 1, Apr. 1, and Sept. 15; Sept. 15 for associations grant program
  Board meeting date(s): Apr., June, and Nov.
  Final notification: 6 weeks for formal reply; informal reply sooner
Officers and Advisory Board:* Phillips Smith,* Chair.; Walter Burgin,* Vice-Chair.; Robert Hallett,* Exec. Dir.; Gillian Attfield; Gillian R. Brooks; Nancy R. Cavanaugh; George J. Gillespie III; Philip V. Havens; Edward F. Menard; Julia F. Menard; Lyman W. Menard; William L. Menard; John K. Prentiss; H. Ward Reighley.
Trustee: JPMorgan Chase Bank, N.A.
Number of staff: 1 full-time professional; 1 full-time support.
EIN: 136047243

3534
Fore River Foundation ◇
P.O. Box 7525
Portland, ME   04112-7525

Established in 1986.
Donors: Kate Davis P. Quesada; Peter W. Quesada; T. Ricardo Quesada.
Foundation type: Independent foundation.
Financial data (yr. ended 11/30/05): Assets, $4,591,307 (M); gifts received, $166,683; expenditures, $490,927; qualifying distributions, $476,416; giving activities include $475,500 for grants.
Purpose and activities: Giving primarily for the arts, education, health and human services.
Fields of interest: Historic preservation/historical societies; Arts; Education; Environment, natural resources; Animals/wildlife, preservation/protection; Youth development, centers/clubs; Human services.
Type of support: General/operating support.
Limitations: Applications not accepted. Giving primarily in ME. No grants to individuals; no loans or program-related investments.
Application information: Contributes only to pre-selected organizations.
Officers and Directors:* T. Ricardo Quesada,* Pres.; Strand O. Quesada,* V.P.; Dennis C. Keeler, Jr.,* Secy.; Peter W. Quesada,* Treas.
EIN: 010421912
Selected grants: The following grants were reported in 2004.
$40,000 to Maine Coast Heritage Trust, Topsham, ME. For unrestricted support.
$30,000 to Foxcroft School, Middleburg, VA. For unrestricted support.
$30,000 to World Wildlife Fund, DC. For unrestricted support.
$25,000 to Childrens Hearing and Speech Center, DC. For unrestricted support.
$25,000 to North Yarmouth Academy, Yarmouth, ME. For unrestricted support.
$25,000 to Saint Marks School, San Rafael, CA. For unrestricted support.
$25,000 to Saint Timothys School, Stevenson, MD. For unrestricted support.
$20,000 to American Red Cross, Portland, ME. For unrestricted support.
$20,000 to Topsham Public Library, Topsham, ME. For unrestricted support.
$15,000 to Friends of Acadia, Bar Harbor, ME. For unrestricted support.

3535
The Lewis P. Gallagher Family Foundation ◇
26 Collinsbrook Rd.
Brunswick, ME   04011

Established in 1992 in ME.
Foundation type: Independent foundation.
Financial data (yr. ended 12/31/05): Assets, $9,821,558 (M); expenditures, $509,064; qualifying distributions, $456,707; giving activities include $442,500 for 7 grants (high: $150,000; low: $5,000).
Purpose and activities: Giving primarily for federated giving programs, and to Baptist and Christian organizations.
Fields of interest: Elementary/secondary education; Theological school/education; Youth development, religion; Federated giving programs; Christian agencies & churches; Protestant agencies & churches.
Type of support: Capital campaigns; Equipment; Scholarship funds.

Limitations: Applications not accepted. Giving in the U.S., primarily in MA, OH, and PA. No grants to individuals.
Application information: Contributes only to pre-selected organizations.
Officers: H.H. Fraser, Pres.; H.H. Fraser, Jr., V.P.; G.V. Kelling, Jr., Secy.; M.D. Custer III, Treas.
EIN: 010511466
Selected grants: The following grants were reported in 2004.
$180,000 to Fidelity Investments Charitable Gift Fund, Boston, MA.
$60,000 to Baptist Bible College and School of Theology, Clarks Summit, PA. For advanced classroom technology equipment.
$50,000 to Our Health, Winchester, VA. For capital improvements.
$50,000 to Shepherds Baptist Ministries, Union Grove, WI.
$25,000 to Child Evangelism Fellowship, Portland, ME. For acquisition of real property in Herman, Maine.
$10,000 to CareNet of Midcoast Maine, Brunswick, ME. For operating support.
$10,000 to New Testament Baptist Church, Royersford, PA. For Meghan Osborne Missionary Fund.
$5,000 to Kiwanis Foundation, Hudson, Hudson, OH. For recreational programs.

3536
Gardiner Savings Institution Charitable Foundation ◇
190 Water St.
Gardiner, ME 04345 (207) 582-5550
Contact: Arthur C. Markos, Pres.

Established in 1988 in ME.
Donor: Gardiner Savings Institution, F.S.B.
Foundation type: Company-sponsored foundation.
Financial data (yr. ended 12/31/05): Assets, $2,906,472 (M); gifts received, $374,000; expenditures, $586,275; qualifying distributions, $585,359; giving activities include $585,359 for 229 grants (high: $100,000; low: $41).
Purpose and activities: The foundation supports organizations involved with arts and culture, education, health, youth development, human services, community development, and religion.
Fields of interest: Arts; Education; Health care; Boys & girls clubs; Youth development; Family services; Human services; Community development; Federated giving programs; Religion.
Limitations: Giving primarily in Gardiner, ME.
Application information: Application form not required.
Initial approach: Proposal
Deadline(s): None
Officers and Directors:* George W. Heselton,* Chair.; Richard L. Goodwin, Vice-Chair.; Arthur C. Markos,* Pres.; Anita M. Nored, Treas.; Everett L. Ayer; Al C. Graceffa; Robert P. Lacasse; Paul F. McClay; John G. Rizzo.
Trustee: Gardiner Savings Institution, F.S.B.
EIN: 010446023
Selected grants: The following grants were reported in 2004.
$102,500 to YMCA. 2 grants: $100,000, $2,500
$25,000 to Johnson Hall, Gardiner, ME.
$13,785 to United Way of Kennebec Valley, Augusta, ME. 2 grants: $10,785, $3,000
$5,000 to Medical Care Development, Augusta, ME.

$5,000 to Saint Andrews Hospital, Boothbay Harbor, ME.
$2,000 to American Red Cross.
$1,000 to Maine State Museum, Augusta, ME.
$166 to Salvation Army.

3537
The Gateway Foundation ◇ ☆
1 Windward Way
Cape Elizabeth, ME 04107

Established in 1997 in ME.
Donors: Richard Kurtz; Glenn R. Kurtz; Virginia H. Kurtz.
Foundation type: Independent foundation.
Financial data (yr. ended 12/31/05): Assets, $1,288,057 (M); gifts received, $199,374; expenditures, $419,980; qualifying distributions, $398,885; giving activities include $398,885 for grants.
Fields of interest: Elementary/secondary education; Christian agencies & churches.
Type of support: General/operating support.
Limitations: Applications not accepted. No grants to individuals.
Application information: Contributes only to pre-selected organizations.
Trustees: Richard Kurtz; Virginia Hoyt Kurtz.
EIN: 043389228
Selected grants: The following grants were reported in 2004.
$11,470 to Agawam Council, Hanover, MA. For general support.
$10,000 to Greenwich Academy, Greenwich, CT. For general support.
$5,000 to Alliance Defense Fund, Scottsdale, AZ. For general support.
$5,000 to Focus on the Family, Colorado Springs, CO. For general support.
$2,500 to Mercy Ships, Garden Valley, TX. For general support.
$2,000 to Christian Education League, Augusta, ME. For general support.
$2,000 to Young Life, Portland, OR. For general support.
$1,000 to Campus Crusade for Christ International, Orlando, FL. For general support.
$1,000 to Christian Research Institute, Rancho Santa Margarita, CA. For general support.
$1,000 to Ligonier Ministries, Lake Mary, FL. For general support.

3538
The Golden Rule Foundation, Inc. ◇ ☆
P.O. Box 286
Belfast, ME 04915
Contact: Lissa Widoff, Mgr.
E-mail: goldenrule@prexar.com; URL: http://www.goldrule.org

Established in 1981 in DC.
Donor: Jack Evans†.
Foundation type: Independent foundation.
Financial data (yr. ended 10/31/05): Assets, $5,869,147 (M); expenditures, $457,075; qualifying distributions, $325,000; giving activities include $325,000 for grants.
Purpose and activities: Giving primarily for the arts, environmental programs, and social services.
Fields of interest: Arts; Education; Environment, alliance; Environment, toxics; Environment, natural

resources; Human services; Community development.
International interests: Mexico.
Type of support: General/operating support; Program development; Seed money.
Limitations: Applications not accepted. Giving primarily on the East Coast. No grants to individuals.
Publications: Informational brochure.
Application information: Unsolicited requests for funds not considered.
Board meeting date(s): Late Aug.
Officers and Directors:* Jean Evans,* Pres.; Gareth Evans,* Secy.; Sian Evans; Trevor Evans; Sal Messina; Tegan Stephen.
Number of staff: 1 part-time support.
EIN: 599207701
Selected grants: The following grants were reported in 2005.
$26,000 to Rhode Island School of Design, Providence, RI.
$15,000 to Tenants and Workers Support Committee, Alexandria, VA. 2 grants: $8,000, $7,000
$10,000 to Childrens Hospital, Richmond, VA.
$10,000 to Haystack Mountain School of Crafts, Deer Isle, ME.
$8,000 to Bargemusic, Brooklyn, NY.
$8,000 to Center for Book Arts, New York, NY.
$6,000 to Coastal Mountains Land Trust, Camden, ME.
$5,000 to A Gathering of the Tribes, New York, NY.
$3,000 to Waldo County Committee for Social Action, Belfast, ME.

3539
Great Bay Foundation for Social Entrepreneurship ◇
48 Free St.
Portland, ME 04101 (207) 774-2067
Contact: Peter W. Greenleaf, Pres.
FAX: (207) 774-6566;
E-mail: info@greatbayfoundation.org; URL: http://www.greatbayfoundation.org

Established in 1998.
Donors: James R. Singer; White Mountains Foundation.
Foundation type: Independent foundation.
Financial data (yr. ended 9/30/05): Assets, $13,645,213 (M); expenditures, $943,762; qualifying distributions, $914,026; giving activities include $583,500 for 11 grants (high: $123,000; low: $5,000).
Purpose and activities: Giving to increase individuals' self-reliance by encouraging principle-based social entrepreneurs. Great Bay makes grants to nonprofit organizations lead by individuals who have an entrepreneurial attitude, drive and vision, and who work toward social change in the areas of economic development, education and health care.
Fields of interest: Animals/wildlife, special services; Human services; Children/youth, services; Roman Catholic agencies & churches; Disabilities, people with.
Type of support: General/operating support.
Limitations: Giving primarily in ME and NH. No support for religious organizations, or for research projects, unless they lead toward self-sufficiency, public schools, colleges or universities, state agencies, or direct social service programs. No grants to individuals, or for travel or study, capital campaigns, or bricks and mortar.

Publications: Application guidelines.
Application information: Application guidelines available on foundation Web site. Application form required.
Initial approach: 1- to 3-page letter
Deadline(s): None
Officer: Peter W. Greenleaf, Pres.
Trustee: Marilyn Bronzi.
Director: Charles E. Vadakin.
EIN: 010519446
Selected grants: The following grants were reported in 2005.
$123,000 to Information Technology Exchange, Searsport, ME. For PC's for Maine program.
$89,612 to Platform Shoes Forum, Rockland, ME. To expand programs.
$87,100 to Rippleffect, Portland, ME. For Ripple Adventures program for at-risk youths.
$80,000 to My Wonderful Dog, Portland, ME. To expand animal training program.
$80,000 to York-Cumberland Association of Handicapped Persons, Portland, ME. To expand Maine WoodWorks furniture project and to purchase equipment.
$60,000 to Fannie Clac, Lebanon, NH. To expand low-income borrower automobile financing and financial literacy project.
$17,500 to Cathedral School, Portland, ME. To provide tuition subsidies, increase enrollment and upgrade computer center.
$10,000 to Independent Transportation Network, Westbrook, ME. For planning grant.

3540
Hannaford Charitable Foundation ◇
P.O. Box 1000
Portland, ME 04104
URL: http://www.hannaford.com/Contents/Our_Company/Community/charitable.shtml

Established in 1993 in ME.
Donor: Hannaford Bros. Co.
Foundation type: Company-sponsored foundation.
Financial data (yr. ended 12/31/05): Assets, $2,178,266 (M); gifts received, $1,142,250; expenditures, $1,089,199; qualifying distributions, $1,089,199; giving activities include $1,058,496 for 72 grants (high: $100,000; low: $275).
Purpose and activities: The foundation supports organizations involved with arts and culture, education, health, human services, and civic affairs.
Fields of interest: Museums; Arts; Higher education; Libraries (public); Education; Hospitals (general); Health care; Boys & girls clubs; YM/YWCAs & YM/YWHAs; Children/youth, services; Human services; Federated giving programs; Public affairs.
Type of support: Building/renovation; Employee-related scholarships; Capital campaigns.
Limitations: Giving primarily in areas of company operations in ME, MA, NH, NY, and VT. No support for tax-supported organizations or veterans', fraternal, or religious organizations not of direct benefit to the entire community. No grants to individuals (except for employee-related scholarships), or for advertising or general operating support.
Publications: Application guidelines.
Application information: Proposals should be submitted using organization letterhead. Additional information may be requested at a later date. Application form not required.
Initial approach: Proposal

Copies of proposal: 10
Deadline(s): 6 to 8 weeks prior to need
Final notification: 6 to 8 weeks for requests of under $50,000; 3 to 4 months for requests of over $50,000
Officers and Directors: Bradford A. Wise, Pres.; Donna J. Boyce, Secy.; Garrett D. Bowne, Treas.; Beth Newlands Campbell; Mark Doiron; Andy Mayo; Tod Pepin; Bob Schools.
EIN: 010483892

3541
Horizon Foundation, Inc.
1 Monument Way, 2nd Fl.
Portland, ME 04101-4078 (207) 773-5101
Contact: Alexander K. Buck, Jr., Pres.
FAX: (207) 773-5201;
E-mail: info@horizonfoundation.org; Additional *E-mail:* horizon@nii.net; *URL:* http://www.horizonfoundation.org

Established in 1997 in MA and PA.
Donors: Alexander K. Buck, Sr.; Alexander K. Buck, Jr.; N. Harrison Buck.
Foundation type: Independent foundation.
Financial data (yr. ended 6/30/06): Assets, $12,087,266 (M); gifts received, $2,118,977; expenditures, $426,686; qualifying distributions, $419,229; giving activities include $315,720 for 29 grants (high: $22,500; low: $1,520).
Purpose and activities: The foundation supports organizations that effect positive change among children, the adults who work with them, and the communities in which they live. The foundation will support programs and organizations that aspire to create and maintain sustainable and livable communities by protecting and conserving land and water resources, educating children and adults about being good stewards of the environment, promoting vibrant, child-oriented arts, teaching respect for and preservation of historic assets, enabling children and adults to lead their communities in thoughtful, creative, and healthy ways, and encouraging service to others. Giving primarily for education in the arts, history, the environment, and leadership training for children; funding also for community services and mentoring.
Fields of interest: Arts education; History/archaeology; Education; Environmental education; Leadership development.
Type of support: Equipment; Program development; Conferences/seminars; Seed money; Curriculum development; Internship funds; Program evaluation; Matching/challenge support.
Limitations: Giving limited to Barnstable County, MA, Cumberland, Franklin, Lincoln, and York counties, ME, and Mercer County, NJ. No support for religion, colleges and universities, or public and private schools. No grants to individuals, or for international or foreign affairs, state agencies, emergency requests, building, capital or endowment funds, or health/mental health.
Publications: Application guidelines; Annual report; Grants list; Informational brochure (including application guidelines).
Application information: Unsolicited proposals are not considered. Full proposals are accepted by invitation only. See foundation Web site for information. Application form not required.
Initial approach: 1-page letter of inquiry; no faxed or E-mailed letters of inquiry or proposals
Copies of proposal: 1

Deadline(s): See foundation Web site for latest deadlines; proposals arriving after deadlines will be considered in next awards cycle.
Board meeting date(s): May, July, and Nov.
Final notification: June 1 and Dec. 1
Officers: Alexander K. Buck, Sr., Chair.; Alexander K. Buck, Jr., Pres.; Nancy B. Buck, V.P.; Sara L. Buck, V.P.; Anne E. Buck, Secy.; N. Harrison Buck, Treas.
Number of staff: 1 part-time professional.
EIN: 232867116
Selected grants: The following grants were reported in 2005.
$25,000 to Delaware and Raritan Greenway, Princeton, NJ.
$25,000 to Forest Society of Maine, Bangor, ME.
$17,750 to Ipswich River Watershed Association, Ipswich, MA.
$15,000 to Damariscotta River Association, Damariscotta, ME.
$15,000 to Jobs for Maines Graduates, Farmingdale, ME.
$10,636 to Newburyport Maritime Society, Newburyport, MA.
$10,000 to Maine Coast Heritage Trust, Topsham, ME.
$10,000 to Plimoth Plantation, Plymouth, MA.
$6,500 to Cape Ann Historical Association, Gloucester, MA.
$6,500 to Young Audiences of New Jersey, Princeton, NJ.

3542
JTG Foundation ◇
184 Main St.
Lewiston, ME 04243-3070
Contact: Martha E. Greene
Application address: c/o Brann & Isaacson, P.O. Box 3070, Lewiston, ME 04243-3070, tel.: (207) 786-3566, e-mail: mgreene@brannlaw.com

Established in 1996 in ME.
Donor: John T. Gorman, Jr.
Foundation type: Independent foundation.
Financial data (yr. ended 12/31/05): Assets, $18,415,146 (M); gifts received, $4,048,451; expenditures, $630,842; qualifying distributions, $504,016; giving activities include $504,016 for grants.
Purpose and activities: Giving primarily to enhance mental health services, improve the care of those suffering from cancer, enhance the lives of the elderly, to provide for the unmet needs of low-income or otherwise disadvantaged children, and to enhance community services.
Fields of interest: Mental health/crisis services; Cancer; Children, services; Community development; Aging; Economically disadvantaged.
Type of support: General/operating support; Income development; Equipment; Program development; Seed money.
Limitations: Giving primarily in ME. No grants to individuals.
Application information: Application form required.
Initial approach: Letter, telephone or e-mail
Copies of proposal: 1
Deadline(s): None
Board meeting date(s): Usually in winter, spring and fall
Final notification: Following the next board meeting

Officers: John T. Gorman, Jr., Pres.; Irving Isaacson, Secy.; Weston Bonney, Treas.
EIN: 010498551
Selected grants: The following grants were reported in 2005.
$53,726 to Maine State Library, Augusta, ME.
$25,000 to AmeriCares, Stamford, CT.
$25,000 to Fairfield University, Fairfield, CT.
$25,000 to Sisters of Charity Health System, Lewiston, ME.
$25,000 to Youth Alternatives, Portland, ME.
$20,000 to Preble Street Resource Center, Portland, ME.
$12,000 to Autism Society of Maine, Winthrop, ME.
$10,000 to Humane Society of Bangor, Bangor, ME.

3543
Kennebec Savings Bank Foundation ◇ ☆
(formerly Kennebec Foundation)
c/o James R. Chase
P.O. Box 50
Augusta, ME   04332

Established in 1985 in ME.
Donor: Kennebec Savings Bank.
Foundation type: Independent foundation.
Financial data (yr. ended 12/31/05): Assets, $2,657,998 (M); gifts received, $506,910; expenditures, $729,530; qualifying distributions, $714,500; giving activities include $714,500 for grants.
Purpose and activities: Giving for human services.
Fields of interest: Arts; Human services; Youth, services; Community development.
Limitations: Applications not accepted. Giving limited to the Kennebec County, ME, area. No grants to individuals.
Application information: Contributes only to pre-selected organizations.
Trustee: Kennebec Savings Bank.
EIN: 222624600
Selected grants: The following grants were reported in 2003.
$50,000 to Team Cony, Augusta, ME.
$22,728 to United Way of Kennebec Valley, Augusta, ME.
$5,000 to Childrens Center Early Intervention and Family Support, Augusta, ME.
$5,000 to Cumston Hall, Friends of, Monmouth, ME.
$2,500 to MaineGeneral Health, Augusta, ME.
$1,500 to Big Brothers/Big Sisters of Kennebec Valley, Waterville, ME. For Bowl for Kids Sake.
$1,000 to Good Shepherd Food-Bank, Auburn, ME.
$1,000 to Lincoln Elementary School, Fremont, NE. For playground project.
$1,000 to Wayne Fire Department, Wayne, ME.
$500 to ElderCare Network of Lincoln County, Damariscotta, ME.

3544
Kennebunk Savings Bank Foundation ◇ ☆
104 Main St.
P.O. Box 28
Kennebunk, ME   04043-0028

Donor: Kennebunk Savings Bank.
Foundation type: Company-sponsored foundation.
Financial data (yr. ended 12/31/05): Assets, $573,598 (M); gifts received, $361,988; expenditures, $334,110; qualifying distributions,

$330,329; giving activities include $330,329 for grants.
Purpose and activities: The foundation supports organizations involved with arts and culture, education, the environment, and human services.
Fields of interest: Arts; Education; Environment; Children/youth, services; Human services.
Limitations: Giving primarily in ME.
Application information:
Initial approach: Proposal
Officers and Directors:* Andrew T. Furlong, Jr.,* Chair.; Joel W. Stevens,* Pres.; Wayne F. Manchester,* V.P.; Susan F. Hoctor, Secy.; Pamela J. Drew,* Treas.; Richard V. Bibber; James J. Keating III; Raymond E. Mailhot; Stephen A. Morris; Geofrey Titherington.
EIN: 010547392
Selected grants: The following grants were reported in 2004.
$58,617 to United Way of York County, Kennebunk, ME. 3 grants: $28,180, $2,257, $28,180
$20,000 to YMCA of Biddeford, Biddeford, ME.
$13,867 to Animal Welfare Society, West Kennebunk, ME.
$10,000 to Boy Scouts of America, Pine Tree Council, Portland, ME.
$10,000 to Maine Public Broadcasting Corporation, Lewiston, ME.
$3,141 to Center for Wildlife, Cape Neddick, ME.
$2,901 to Caring Unlimited, Sanford, ME.
$2,901 to Kennebunk Land Trust, Kennebunk, ME.

3545
Stephen and Tabitha King Foundation, Inc. ▼ ◇
49 Florida Ave.
Bangor, ME   04401   (207) 990-2910
Contact: Stephanie Leonard, Admin.
FAX: (207) 990-2975;
E-mail: info@stkfoundation.org; URL: http://www.stkfoundation.org

Established in 1986 in ME.
Donor: Stephen E. King.
Foundation type: Independent foundation.
Financial data (yr. ended 12/31/04): Assets, $2,266,034 (M); gifts received, $1,156,395; expenditures, $4,139,285; qualifying distributions, $4,128,941; giving activities include $4,124,786 for 184 grants (high: $250,000; low: $25; average: $5,000–$50,000).
Purpose and activities: Giving primarily for the arts, education (including libraries), and human services.
Fields of interest: Performing arts, orchestra (symphony); Arts; Higher education; Libraries (public); Education; Health organizations, association; Human services; Federated giving programs.
Type of support: Seed money; Research; Program development; Matching/challenge support; Land acquisition; General/operating support; Equipment; Endowments; Capital campaigns; Building/renovation.
Limitations: Applications not accepted. Giving limited to ME. No support for hospice programs or facilities, animal shelters/hospitals or rehabilitation centers. No grants to individuals, or for fellowships, scholarships, or for travel or sponsorships, student or athletic groups, graduation parties or events, renovations to churches or other religious properties or institutions, or renovations to historical society property unless connected to a library, or for film or video productions, transportation, book or

publishing projects, conferences, meetings, exhibits, or workshops, construction of playgrounds; no loans.
Application information: See foundation's Web site for information.
Board meeting date(s): Spring and fall
Officers: Stephen E. King, Pres.; Tabitha King, V.P.; Arthur B. Greene, Secy.; Stephanie Leonard, Admin.
Number of staff: 1 full-time professional.
EIN: 133364647
Selected grants: The following grants were reported in 2004.
$250,000 to Forest Society of Maine, Bangor, ME.
$100,000 to American Red Cross, Pine Tree Chapter, Bangor, ME.
$100,000 to Bridgton Hospital, Bridgton, ME.
$100,000 to Penobscot Theater Company, Bangor, ME.
$52,000 to Charlotte Hobbs Memorial Library, Lovell, ME.
$50,000 to YMCA of Bangor, Bangor, ME.
$47,000 to Alton Fire Department, Alton.
$40,000 to Warren Center for Communication and Learning, Bangor, ME.
$25,000 to Northeast Harbor Library, Northeast Harbor, ME.
$25,000 to Porter Memorial Library, Machias, ME.

3546
Libra Foundation ▼ ◇
3 Canal Plz.
P.O. Box 17516
Portland, ME   04112-8516   (207) 879-6280
Contact: Owen W. Wells, Pres. and Secy.
FAX: (207) 879-6281; URL: http://www.librafoundation.org

Established in 1989 in ME.
Donor: Elizabeth B. Noyce†.
Foundation type: Independent foundation.
Financial data (yr. ended 12/31/05): Assets, $153,395,950 (M); expenditures, $14,583,514; qualifying distributions, $16,003,936; giving activities include $12,241,340 for 48 grants (high: $4,632,863; low: $2,375; average: $5,000–$100,000), $26,300 for 1 foundation-administered program and $2,675,134 for 3 loans/program-related investments.
Purpose and activities: Giving primarily for arts and culture, science, recreation and sports, human services, education, environment, and public/society benefit.
Fields of interest: Arts; Education; Recreation; Human services; Science.
Type of support: General/operating support; Continuing support; Capital campaigns; Building/renovation; Equipment; Land acquisition; Endowments; Emergency funds; Program development; Seed money; Curriculum development; Research; Technical assistance; Program-related investments/loans.
Limitations: Giving limited to ME. No grants to individuals.
Publications: Application guidelines; Annual report; Financial statement; Grants list; Informational brochure (including application guidelines).
Application information: Application form required.
Initial approach: Letter or telephone
Copies of proposal: 1
Deadline(s): Feb. 15, May 15, Aug. 15, and Nov. 15

Board meeting date(s): Mar., June, Sept., and Dec.

Final notification: Within 1 week of board meeting

Officers and Trustees:* Pendred E. Noyce,* Chair.; Owen W. Wells,* C.E.O. and Pres.; Jere G. Michelson, V.P. and C.F.O.; Craig N. Denekas, V.P.; Henry G. Brooks,* Treas.; William J. Ryan.

Number of staff: 4 full-time professional; 3 full-time support.

EIN: 046626994

Selected grants: The following grants were reported in 2005.

$4,632,863 to Pineland Farms, New Gloucester, ME. To develop, operate, and staff Pineland Farms.

$1,827,037 to Maine Winter Sports Center, Limestone, ME. For development of world-class biathlon cross-country ski facilities and alpine ski areas and programs.

$1,420,443 to United Way of Greater Portland, Portland, ME. For Summer Champs Camp Program.

$1,041,140 to United Way of Androscoggin County, Lewiston, ME. For TOPS Camp Program.

$746,226 to United Way of Eastern Maine, Bangor, ME. For Camp Bangor Program.

$693,856 to MaineHealth, Portland, ME. For Raising Readers Program.

$187,500 to Big Rock, Mars Hill, ME. For capital development project.

$141,000 to Riding to the Top, Windham, ME. For Therapeutic Riding Programs.

$100,000 to Calais Regional Hospital, Calais, ME. To create replacement community hospital for Northeastern Washington County.

$50,000 to Boy Scouts of America, Bangor, ME. For expansion and enhancement of facilities at Camp Roosevelt.

3547
Lunder Foundation ✧

c/o Kenilworth, Inc.
2 Monument Sq., Ste. 704
Portland, ME 04101

Established in 1988 in ME.

Donors: Peter Lunder; Berkshire Hathaway Inc.

Foundation type: Independent foundation.

Financial data (yr. ended 12/31/05): Assets, $15,000,135 (M); gifts received, $797,805; expenditures, $754,322; qualifying distributions, $725,188; giving activities include $697,077 for 208 grants (high: $179,100; low: $25).

Purpose and activities: Giving primarily to higher education, the arts, hospitals and health associations, human services, children and youth services, and Jewish agencies and temples.

Fields of interest: Museums; Performing arts; Arts; Higher education; Education; Hospitals (general); Health organizations, association; Human services; Children/youth, services; Jewish agencies & temples.

Type of support: Scholarship funds; Capital campaigns; Annual campaigns; Matching/challenge support.

Limitations: Giving primarily in MA and central ME. No grants to individuals.

Application information:

Initial approach: Letter (no more than 3 pages)

Deadline(s): None

Officers: Peter Lunder, Pres.; Paula Lunder, V.P.

Directors: Marjorie L. Goldy; Alan Lunder; Marc Lunder; Steven Lunder.

EIN: 010437556

3548
The Maine Community Foundation, Inc. ▼

245 Main St.
Ellsworth, ME 04605 (207) 667-9735

Contact: For grants: Peter Taylor, Dir., Grantmaking; For scholarships: Jean Warren, Scholarship Funds Mgr.

FAX: (207) 667-0447; E-mail: info@mainecf.org; Additional tel: (877) 700-6800; Portland mailing address: 1 Monument Way, Ste. 200, P.O. Box 7380, Portland, ME 04101, tel.: (207) 761-2440, fax: (207) 773-8832; Grant information E-mail: ptaylor@mainecf.org; URL: http://www.mainecf.org

Incorporated in 1983 in ME.

Foundation type: Community foundation.

Financial data (yr. ended 12/31/05): Assets, $166,091,471 (M); gifts received, $12,331,539; expenditures, $18,559,265; giving activities include $14,354,958 for grants.

Purpose and activities: The foundation promotes active philanthropy by stewarding charitable funds and making effective grants. Primary areas of interest include the arts, child welfare and youth, the disadvantaged, education, health, community development, and sustainable development.

Fields of interest: Humanities; Arts; Education; Environment, natural resources; Environment; Health care; Health organizations, association; Youth development, services; Children/youth, services; Aging, centers/services; Human services; Urban/community development; Nonprofit management; Community development; Leadership development; Economically disadvantaged.

Type of support: Endowments; Management development/capacity building; Land acquisition; Program development; Seed money; Technical assistance; Grants to individuals; Scholarships—to individuals; Matching/challenge support.

Limitations: Giving limited to ME. No support for religious organizations for religious purposes. No grants to individuals (except for scholarship funds), or for equipment, annual campaigns for regular operations, or for capital campaigns.

Publications: Application guidelines; Annual report; Financial statement; Grants list; Informational brochure; Newsletter.

Application information: Visit foundation Web site for application form and guidelines. Faxed or e-mailed applications are not accepted. Application form required.

Initial approach: Submit application form and attachments

Copies of proposal: 1

Deadline(s): Jan. 15 and May 15 for Community Building Prog. (including County Fund Prog.); varies for others

Board meeting date(s): 3 times annually

Final notification: Within 10 weeks

Officers and Directors:* Robert Woodbury,* Chair.; Kenneth Spirer,* Vice-Chair.; Henry L.P. Schmelzer,* C.E.O. and Pres.; James E. Geary, V.P., Finance and Admin.; Meredith Jones, V.P., Prog. Devel. and Grantmaking Svcs.; Ellen Pope, V.P., Philanthropic Svcs.; Laura Young, V.P., Advancement; Elizabeth Hewlett, Cont.; Forrest Berkley; Stephanie A. Bunker; Tae Y. Chong; David M. Coit; Jean M. Deighan; David C. Dixon; Caroline G. Donnelly; Eileen M.L. Epstein; Sandra

Featherman; Elisabeth C. Heyward; Horace Hildreth; Anne O. Jackson; William H. Kieffer III; David W. King; Donna M. Loring; Carleton "Davis" Pike; Betty D. Robinson; Peter Rothschild; Mary "Polly" Saltonstall; Bruce Schatz; Curtis Scribner; Arthur Thompson; Calvin E. True; Anne L. Vartabedian.

Number of staff: 16 full-time professional; 3 full-time support; 1 part-time support.

EIN: 010391479

Selected grants: The following grants were reported in 2004.

$25,000 to Brown Memorial Library, East Baldwin, ME. To expand existing library.

$20,055 to Maine Sea Coast Missionary Society, Bar Harbor, ME. 2 grants: $10,055 (To develop series of in-depth community courses taught by local experts, community leaders, business people and organizational representatives, as part of effort to replicate EdGE program model and increase student enrollment and retention), $10,000 (To develop and implement series of in-depth community courses taught by local experts, community leaders, business people, as part of effort to increase and sustain older student enrollment and to replicate EdGE program).

$15,000 to GrowSmart Maine, Yarmouth, ME. For research project, which will focus on development and implementation of strategies to manage and direct growth in selected towns that will then serve as models for other communities.

$15,000 to Portland Trails, Portland, ME. To implement formal structure to carry Greening School Grounds program into future.

$12,500 to Maine School Administrative District No. 55, Hiram, ME. To expand educational experiences for Baldwin Consolidated School students by improving access to technology through purchase of laptop computers and additional software, and by increasing cultural opportunities such as field trips and presentations.

$12,000 to River Coalition, Old Town, ME. For summer program that will provide hands-on, experiential math and science activities and excursions for low-income middle-school youth, as extension of after-school Learning Without Borders program.

$10,000 to Childrens Museum of Maine, Portland, ME. For recruiting, training and hiring teenagers as environmental science educators for Youth Ranger program, to promote environmental education and advocacy, provide leadership opportunities with focus on minority youth and to broaden diversity.

$10,000 to Great Cranberry Island Historical Society, Cranberry Isles, ME. To ready lot for moving of historic Mountain View Inn building that will become permanent Historical Museum and Cultural Center and home.

$10,000 to Penobscot Marine Museum, Searsport, ME. For Lobstah exhibit, comprehensive museum-wide show.

3549
Maine Health Access Foundation ▼

150 Capitol St., Ste. 4
Augusta, ME 04330 (207) 620-8266

Contact: Wendy J. Wolf M.D., M.P.H., C.E.O. and Pres.

FAX: (207) 620-8269;
E-mail: mricker@mehaf.org;Cluce@meuaf.org;

Toll-free tel.: (866) 848-9210; URL: http://www.mehaf.org

Established in 2000 in ME.

Donor: Associated Hospital Service of Maine.

Foundation type: Independent foundation.

Financial data (yr. ended 12/31/05): Assets, $110,537,960 (M); expenditures, $4,721,658; qualifying distributions, $4,035,745; giving activities include $3,122,481 for 61 grants (high: $389,007; low: $1,000; average: $5,000–$100,000).

Purpose and activities: The mission of the foundation is to promote affordable and timely access to comprehensive, quality health care, and improve the health of every Maine resident. Moving forward, the foundation wants to direct their resources to transforming the current fragmented health care system into an integrated, patient-centered system that aligns incentives and support with the strategic and appropriate distribution of resources. These new priorities will include: Advancing care for Maine's uninsured, strengthening Maine's health care system, and advancing state-wide solutions.

Fields of interest: Health care, public policy; Health care.

Type of support: Equipment; Program development; Conferences/seminars; Curriculum development; Research; Technical assistance; Program evaluation.

Limitations: Giving primarily in ME. No support for private foundations, political candidates, or lobbying. No grants to individuals, or for endowments, debt retirement, annual appeals or membership campaigns, fundraising or social events, or public relations campaigns.

Publications: Application guidelines; Annual report; Grants list; Newsletter; Occasional report.

Application information: See foundation Web site for application guidelines and procedures, as well as new funding priorities. Application form required.

   Initial approach: Phone discussion with program staff
   Copies of proposal: 5
   Deadline(s): Variable depending on RFP
   Board meeting date(s): 3rd Thurs. monthly
   Final notification: Variable depending on type of grant

Officers and Trustees:* Maroulla Gleaton, M.D.*, Chair.; Kevin Gildart,* Vice-Chair.; Wendy J. Wolf, M.D., C.E.O. and Pres.; Wesley Davidson,* Secy.; Warren Kessler,* Treas.; Anne Johnson Cole Brown, M.D.; Jack Comart; Laurie Eddy; Lani F.B. Graham, M.D., M.P.H.; Richard Marston; Lisa Miller; Neil Rolde; Cheryl Rust; Diana C. Scully; Lee Webb.

Number of staff: 5 full-time professional; 1 full-time support.

EIN: 010535144

Selected grants: The following grants were reported in 2005.

$200,000 to Maine Office of the Governor, Augusta, ME. For Office of Health, Policy, and Finance and for technical assistance to implement Dingo Health, comprehensive state health plan, and to conduct study of costs at Maine hospitals and outreach activities.

$144,523 to Maine Department of Health and Human Services, Department of Health and Human Services, Augusta, ME. For telephone and in-person assistance in helping Elderly and Disabled (DEL) members decide if Part D is appropriate for them, applying for subsidies and the Medicare Savings Program if applicable, and

choosing the best Preferred Drug Plan (PDP) for each member.

$135,000 to Maine Medical Center, Portland, ME. For PIER pilot program, for early identification of psychotic disorders and access to state-of-the-art assessment and treatment services to those in early stages of psychosis.

$124,074 to Maine Equal Justice Partners, Augusta, ME. For advocacy initiative to preserve and maximize health care coverage for Maine's low-income populations through coverage of childless adults under MaineCare, implementation of Medicare Part D Prescription Drug Benefits, and alternatives to cost-cutting proposals in Medicaid budget.

$100,000 to Crisis and Counseling Centers, Augusta, ME. For Crisis OutReach Project, to create more flexible and responsive system for underserved individuals by linking crisis clients with clinical services and community supports, and by establishing crisis protocols with providers of chronically mentally ill.

$100,000 to University of Maine, Center on Aging, Orono, ME. For screening program to identify patients 60 years and older who may be at risk of elder abuse, neglect, or exploitation.

$99,966 to American Cancer Society, Brunswick, ME. To increase cancer patients' access to clinical and community services in rural areas, and to demonstrate how volunteers help to activate patients.

$97,776 to Eastern Maine Healthcare Systems, Bangor, ME. To use findings and recommendations of study documenting transportation as barrier to health care access to improve access to health care throughout Eastern Maine.

$88,916 to MaineHealth, Portland, ME. For AHI Asthma Health Community Collaborative (AHCC), bringing diverse community resources to bear to address asthma, including medical care, public health, and community-based organizations.

$88,211 to Amistad, Portland, ME. To establish overnight warm-line telephone service for individuals with mental illness to call when they need to speak with a peer.

3550
Melmac Education Foundation ✧ ☆
P.O. Box 58
Augusta, ME   04330

Established in 2001 in ME.

Foundation type: Independent foundation.

Financial data (yr. ended 12/31/05): Assets, $35,988,880 (M); expenditures, $1,606,880; qualifying distributions, $1,585,200; giving activities include $1,219,299 for 3 grants (high: $676,093; low: $50,000), and $133,000 for 133 grants to individuals (high: $1,000; low: $1,000).

Fields of interest: Higher education.

Type of support: Scholarships—to individuals.

Limitations: Applications not accepted. Giving primarily in ME.

Application information: Unsolicited requests for funds not accepted.

Officers and Directors:* Joseph H. Gambino, Jr.,* Chair.; John R. Huard,* Vice-Chair.; Sue Ann Huseman,* Secy.; Wendy L. Ault, Exec. Dir.; Roy Barry; James Grandmaison; Scott MacDonald; Patricia B. McNamara; Richard Tyler.

EIN: 010390854

3551
The Clarence E. Mulford Trust ✧
P.O. Box 290
Fryeburg, ME   04037-0290   (207) 935-2061
Contact: David R. Hastings II, Tr.

Established in 1950 in ME.

Donor: Clarence E. Mulford†.

Foundation type: Independent foundation.

Financial data (yr. ended 12/31/05): Assets, $10,545,953 (M); expenditures, $540,326; qualifying distributions, $496,677; giving activities include $464,507 for 27 grants (high: $341,557; low: $300).

Purpose and activities: Giving primarily to churches, hospitals, and animal welfare organizations; support also for education and community service.

Fields of interest: Secondary school/education; Libraries/library science; Education; Animal welfare; Human services; Community development; Christian agencies & churches.

Limitations: Giving primarily in Fryeburg, ME, and neighboring towns. No grants to individuals, or for building or endowment funds, scholarships, fellowships, or matching gifts; no loans.

Application information: Application form not required.

   Initial approach: Letter
   Copies of proposal: 3
   Deadline(s): Preferably in June or Dec., no later than July 10 or Jan. 10
   Board meeting date(s): Jan. and July
   Final notification: Positive replies only

Trustees: David R. Hastings II; Peter G. Hastings.

EIN: 010247648

3552
The Oak Foundation U.S.A. ▼
511 Congress St., Ste. 800
Portland, ME   04101
Contact: Karen Phair, Asst. to the Pres.
E-mail: info@oakfnd.org; URL: http://www.oakfnd.org

Established in 1986 in DE.

Donors: The Oak Trust; The Forest Trust.

Foundation type: Independent foundation.

Financial data (yr. ended 12/31/04): Assets, $320,455,621 (M); gifts received, $6,567,000; expenditures, $20,663,318; qualifying distributions, $17,205,751; giving activities include $16,388,530 for 87 grants (high: $5,570,990; low: $2,500; average: $10,000–$150,000).

Purpose and activities: The foundation's giving priorities include child abuse prevention, the environment, housing and homelessness, international human rights, issues affecting women, and learning disabilities.

Fields of interest: Environment, global warming; Environment, natural resources; Environment, water resources; Environment; Learning disorders; Crime/violence prevention, child abuse; Housing/shelter, homeless; International human rights; Women.

International interests: Africa; Asia; Central America; Europe; Latin America; South America; Zimbabwe.

Type of support: General/operating support; Continuing support; Building/renovation; Equipment; Program development; Research; Program evaluation; Matching/challenge support.

Limitations: Giving on a national and international basis. No support for Religious organizations for religious purposes; or for political candidates. No grants to individuals, fundraising drives, events or amounts under $25,000.

Publications: Application guidelines; Annual report (including application guidelines); Grants list; Program policy statement.

Application information: See foundation's Web site for more information. The foundation will respond within two months to inquiries, informing the applicant whether there is sufficient interest to pursue a proposal. Generally grants will not be given for under $25,000. Application form not required.

Initial approach: Inquiry via e-mail or letter
Copies of proposal: 1
Deadline(s): None
Final notification: Two months

Officers and Directors:* Jette Parker,* Chair.; Alan M. Parker,* Pres.; Gary Goodman, Secy.

Number of staff: 3 full-time professional.

EIN: 133321196

Selected grants: The following grants were reported in 2004.

$5,570,990 to Mercy Ships, Garden Valley, TX. For general support.

$1,333,333 to Global Fund for Women, San Francisco, CA. For general support.

$1,299,500 to Oceana, DC. For general support.

$1,000,000 to Robin Hood Foundation, New York, NY. For general support.

$873,777 to Harvard University, Cambridge, MA. For general support.

$330,350 to Alaska Conservation Foundation, Anchorage, AK. For general support.

$225,405 to Clean Energy Group, Montpelier, VT. For general support.

$172,818 to Physicians for Human Rights, Cambridge, MA. For general support.

$75,000 to Environmental Law and Policy Center of the Midwest, Chicago, IL. For general support.

$36,000 to EARTH University Foundation, Atlanta, GA. For general support.

3553
Dr. Clinton N. & Alice F. Peters Medical Education Trust Fund

c/o Merton G. Henry, Jensen Baird Gardner & Henry
10 Free St.
P.O. Box 450
Portland, ME   04112-4510
Contact: Merton G. Henry, Tr.
Scholarship application address: c/o Dir. of Financial Aid, Bowdoin College, Brunswick, ME 04011

Donors: Clinton N. Peters; Alice F. Peters.

Foundation type: Independent foundation.

Financial data (yr. ended 12/31/05): Assets, $6,112,996 (M); expenditures, $387,484; qualifying distributions, $325,000; giving activities include $325,000 for 1 grant.

Purpose and activities: Support only for a scholarship fund at Bowdoin College, ME, to benefit medical and pre-med students who were born in ME.

Fields of interest: Medical school/education.

Type of support: Scholarship funds.

Limitations: Applications not accepted. Giving limited to ME.

Application information: Unsolicited requests for funds not accepted; contact Bowdoin College for information.

Board meeting date(s): Dec. 1

Trustees: Merton G. Henry; Theodore H. Warner.

EIN: 222514405

Selected grants: The following grants were reported in 2004.

$300,000 to Bowdoin College, Brunswick, ME.

3554
River Rock Foundation

P.O. Box 14
South Freeport, ME   04078-0014
Contact: Marilyn T. Bronzi, Pres.

Established in 2000 in ME.

Donor: James R. Singer.

Foundation type: Independent foundation.

Financial data (yr. ended 12/31/05): Assets, $6,467,941 (M); expenditures, $817,147; qualifying distributions, $810,436; giving activities include $772,500 for 19 grants (high: $100,000; low: $8,000).

Purpose and activities: Giving primarily to end violence and racism, and to improve the lives of children and parents; funding also for education, social, economic and racial justice, and peace/non-violence restorative justice.

Type of support: General/operating support; Endowments; Program development; Conferences/seminars; Seed money; Research; Consulting services; Program evaluation; Matching/challenge support.

Limitations: Applications not accepted. Giving on a national basis. No grants to individuals.

Application information: Unsolicited requests for funds not accepted; proposals are invited.

Board meeting date(s): Monthly

Officer: Marilyn T. Bronzi, Pres.

Directors: Barbara Coughlin; Mary Lou Michael; Karen Moran; Carol Wishcamper.

Number of staff: None.

EIN: 010530269

Selected grants: The following grants were reported in 2004.

$33,000 to Amherst Writers and Artists, Amherst, MA.

$30,000 to Rippleffect, Portland, ME.

$30,000 to United Way of Greater Portland, Portland, ME.

$25,000 to East Harlem School at Exodus House, New York, NY.

$20,000 to Outright, Portland, ME.

$15,000 to Center for Young Womens Development, San Francisco, CA.

$15,000 to Immigrant Legal Advocacy Project, Portland, ME.

$14,000 to Maine Peace Fund, Portland, ME.

$14,000 to Spruce Run, Bangor, ME.

$5,000 to Chewonki Foundation, Wiscasset, ME.

3555
The Sandy River Charitable Foundation ◇

349 Voter Hill Rd.
Farmington, ME   04938
FAX: (207) 779-1901;
E-mail: info@srcfoundation.org; URL: http://www.srcfoundation.org

Established in 1997 in ME.

Donor: Berry Charitable Trust.

Foundation type: Independent foundation.

Financial data (yr. ended 5/31/05): Assets, $38,513,727 (M); expenditures, $3,029,299; qualifying distributions, $2,778,540; giving activities include $2,557,250 for 37 grants (high:

$200,000; low: $1,000), and $150,000 for 1 employee matching gift.

Purpose and activities: Giving primarily to disaster rehabilitation and hunger relief services; funding also for a community foundation in Ellsworth, ME, and a mountain alliance in Farmington, ME. Funding is also made for international and rural development, microfinancing, and adoption services.

Fields of interest: Environment; Food services; Disasters, preparedness/services; Children, adoption; Family services; International agricultural development; Rural development; Foundations (community).

Type of support: General/operating support; Continuing support; Income development; Management development/capacity building; Building/renovation; Equipment; Program evaluation; Program-related investments/loans; Matching/challenge support.

Limitations: Applications not accepted. Giving on an international and national basis, (particularly Board/staff areas), with a special emphasis on ME. No grants to individuals.

Application information: Contributes only to pre-selected organizations. Application provided with invitation. See foundation Web site for further information.

Board meeting date(s): June and Dec.

Officers: Archie W. Berry, Jr., Pres.; Nathanael W. Berry, V.P. and Secy.; Jon W. Berry, Treas.

Directors: Marla S. Berry; Nan Berry; Suphaporn V. Berry; Lillian Dox.

Number of staff: 1 full-time professional.

EIN: 522029911

Selected grants: The following grants were reported in 2005.

$360,000 to Holt International Childrens Services, Eugene, OR. 2 grants: $200,000 (For Eastern Europe Fund), $160,000 (For Guatemala and Ecuador programs).

$200,000 to Oxfam America, Boston, MA. For Center America Regional Program.

$200,000 to World Vision, Federal Way, WA. For Senegal Water Development.

$177,000 to Maine Community Foundation, Ellsworth, ME. For County Fund program.

$125,000 to Sustainable Long Island, Garden City, NY. For Coastal Enterprise.

$100,000 to Heifer Project International, Little Rock, AR. For Agro-Ecology Fund.

$100,000 to Wagner Free Institute of Science, Philadelphia, PA. For building restoration.

$50,000 to Western Mountains Alliance, Farmington, ME. For general operating support.

$25,000 to Maine Initiatives, Augusta, ME. For Bridge Grant.

3556
The Margaret Chase Smith Foundation

10 Free St.
P.O. Box 4510
Portland, ME   04112
Contact: Merton G. Henry, Pres.

Established in 1983 in ME.

Donors: Margaret Chase Smith†; Alden B. Dow Charitable Trust; Dexter Shoe Co.; Evelyn Shaw Trust; Muriel & Robert List Trusts.

Foundation type: Independent foundation.

Financial data (yr. ended 12/31/05): Assets, $11,272,583 (M); gifts received, $5,475; expenditures, $701,304; qualifying distributions,

$625,128; giving activities include $608,975 for 7 grants (high: $531,000; low: $2,975).

Purpose and activities: Giving primarily to support the Margaret Chase Smith Library in Skowhegan, ME, and the Margaret Chase Smith Center for Public Policy at the University of Maine in Orono, ME.

Fields of interest: Libraries (public); Education; Social sciences, public policy.

Type of support: General/operating support; Conferences/seminars; Publication; Fellowships.

Limitations: Applications not accepted. Giving primarily in ME. No grants to individuals.

Application information: Contributes only to pre-selected organizations.

Board meeting date(s): June and Dec.

Officers: Merton G. Henry, Pres.; Michael J. Quinlan, Secy.-Treas.

Directors: Davida D. Barter; John Bernier; Charles L. Cragin; David E. Fry; Georgia McKearly; Janet M. Mills.

EIN: 010388680

Selected grants: The following grants were reported in 2005.

$531,000 to Northwood University, Midland, MI.

$35,000 to University of Maine, Orono, ME.

$10,000 to United States Air Force Academy, Colorado Springs, CO.

$10,000 to United States Coast Guard Academy, New London, CT.

$10,000 to United States Military Academy, West Point, NY.

$10,000 to United States Naval Academy, Annapolis, MD.

3557
Robert and Patricia Switzer Foundation

(formerly Switzer Foundation)
P.O. Box 293
Belfast, ME 04915 (207) 338-5654
Contact: Lissa Widoff, Exec. Dir.
E-mail: lissa@switzernetwork.org; URL: http://www.switzernetwork.org/

Established in 1985 in OH.

Donors: Robert Switzer†; Patricia Switzer.

Foundation type: Independent foundation.

Financial data (yr. ended 6/30/05): Assets, $17,865,185 (M); expenditures, $882,461; qualifying distributions, $797,389; giving activities include $608,601 for 26 grants (high: $160,000; low: $750).

Purpose and activities: Graduate fellowships awarded for one year to individuals most apt to be leaders in environmental science and policy action. Only awarded to students in CA, and in New England through the Robert and Patricia Switzer Foundation. Grants also to environmental non-profits to hire Switzer Fellow(s) in leadership positions.

Fields of interest: Environment.

Type of support: Fellowships; Scholarship funds.

Limitations: Giving limited to CA, CT, MA, ME, NH, RI, and VT for fellowship program, leadership grants available on a national basis.

Publications: Informational brochure; Newsletter.

Application information: See foundation Web site for details before initiating contact. Leadership Grant Program requires participation of Switzer fellow.

Board meeting date(s): Varies

Officers and Trustees:* Cynthia R. Robinson,* Chair; Lissa Widoff, Exec. Dir.; Ashley Boren; Kevin Carley; Paulette Licht; Dara O'Rourke; Mark Switzer; Patricia D. Switzer; Peter Switzer.

Number of staff: 1 full-time professional; 2 part-time professional.

EIN: 341504501

Selected grants: The following grants were reported in 2005.

$40,000 to Green Empowerment, Portland, OR. For Catalyzing Renewable Energy Implementation in Mekong Region.

$40,000 to Two Countries One Forest, Halifax, Canada. For Northern Appalachian EcoTrends Project.

$30,000 to Audubon Society, Massachusetts, Lincoln, MA. For associate regional scientist for Southeastern Massachusetts.

$30,000 to University of California, Los Angeles, CA. For Scientific Environmental Assessment for Los Angeles Basin and Bay (SEA-LABB).

$20,000 to Sonoma Ecology Center, Sonoma, CA. For Phase III: Community-based restoration of Sonoma Creek.

3558
TD Banknorth Charitable Foundation ◇

(formerly Banknorth Charitable Foundation)
P.O. Box 9540
1 Portland Sq.
Portland, ME 04112-9540 (207) 828-7558
Contact: Julie McQuillan, Mgr., Community Rels.
E-mail: julie.mcquillan@tdbanknorth.com; Additional tel.: (207) 756-6947; URL: http://www.tdbanknorth.com/community/charitable_foundation.html

Established in 2002 in ME.

Donors: Banknorth Group, Inc.; TD Banknorth Inc.; American Savings Bank; Cape Cod Bank and Trust Co.

Foundation type: Company-sponsored foundation.

Financial data (yr. ended 12/31/04): Assets, $28,038,270 (M); gifts received, $697,000; expenditures, $2,496,739; qualifying distributions, $2,342,776; giving activities include $2,331,736 for 674 grants.

Purpose and activities: The foundation supports organizations involved with arts and culture, education, health, employment, housing, youth development, human services, and community development. Special emphasis is directed toward programs designed to support low- to moderate-income individuals by providing services, training, or education that improves the quality of life and provides opportunities for advancement.

Fields of interest: Arts; Education; Health care; Employment, services; Housing/shelter; Youth development; Youth, services; Human services, financial counseling; Human services; Community development; Federated giving programs; Economically disadvantaged.

Type of support: Capital campaigns; Program development; Employee volunteer services; Sponsorships; Employee matching gifts.

Limitations: Giving limited to CT, MA, ME, NH, NY, and VT. No support for political, fraternal, religious, or labor organizations or teams. No grants to individuals, or for research projects, events not open to members of the general public, endowments, tournaments, fundraising events, or debt reduction.

Publications: Application guidelines.

Application information: Visit Web site for application addresses. Application form required.

Initial approach: Download application form and mail to state community relations manager

Deadline(s): None

Board meeting date(s): 3rd week of every month

Officers: David J. Ott, Pres.; Elizabeth K. Warn, V.P.; John R. Opperman, Secy.; Stephen J. Boyle, Treas.

Directors: Scott Bacon; Mickey Greene.

EIN: 141864317

Selected grants: The following grants were reported in 2004.

$274,570 to United Way of Greater Portland, Portland, ME.

$250,000 to Thomas College, Waterville, ME.

$200,000 to New Britain General Hospital, New Britain, CT.

$100,000 to Androscoggin Home Health Services, Lewiston, ME.

$100,000 to Maine Medical Center, Portland, ME.

$100,000 to University of New England, Biddeford, ME.

$90,000 to March of Dimes Birth Defects Foundation, Falmouth, ME.

$75,000 to Klingberg Family Centers, New Britain, CT.

$50,000 to Burlington Community Land Trust, Burlington, VT.

$50,000 to Keene State College, Keene, NH.

MARYLAND

3559

The Abell Foundation, Inc. ▼
111 S. Calvert St., Ste. 2300
Baltimore, MD 21202-6174 (410) 547-1300
Contact: Robert C. Embry, Jr., Pres.
FAX: (410) 539-6579; E-mail: abell@abell.org;
URL: http://www.abell.org

Incorporated in 1953 in MD.
Donors: A.S. Abell Co.; Harry C. Black†; Gary Black, Sr.†; Douglas Koshland.
Foundation type: Independent foundation.
Financial data (yr. ended 12/31/05): Assets, $207,400,766 (M); gifts received, $10,135; expenditures, $14,990,026; qualifying distributions, $14,050,372; giving activities include $8,974,442 for grants, $219,958 for 205 employee matching gifts, $307,212 for 4 foundation-administered programs and $283,528 for 5 loans/program-related investments (high: $100,000; low: $5,000).
Purpose and activities: The foundation has seven broad program areas of interest: community development; workforce development criminal justice and addiction; education; health and human services; conservation and environment; and arts and culture. Within these areas, the foundation invites requests for demonstration projects, feasibility studies, strategic planning, capital improvements, new construction, and equipment, program development and enhancements, research, and program-related investments.
Fields of interest: Arts; Education, research; Education, early childhood education; Child development, education; Elementary school/ education; Environment, natural resources; Environment; Reproductive health, family planning; Health care; Substance abuse, services; Crime/ violence prevention; Offenders/ex-offenders, services; Employment, services; Employment; Food services; Youth development, services; Children/ youth, services; Family services; Community development; Leadership development; Minorities; Economically disadvantaged; Homeless.
Type of support: General/operating support; Capital campaigns; Building/renovation; Equipment; Land acquisition; Endowments; Program development; Conferences/seminars; Seed money; Curriculum development; Scholarship funds; Program-related investments/loans; Employee matching gifts; Matching/challenge support.
Limitations: Giving limited to MD, with emphasis on Baltimore. No support for educational programs at higher education institutions or medical facilities. No grants to individuals, or for scholarships, fellowships, endowments, travel, annual operating expenses, sponsorships, memberships, or deficit financing.
Publications: Application guidelines; Annual report (including application guidelines); Newsletter; Occasional report; Program policy statement.
Application information: Should the foundation be interested in the preliminary proposal, the applicant will be asked to submit a formal and detailed application. Downloadable application form is available on the foundation's Web site. Application form required.
  Initial approach: Letter (1-2 pages)
  Copies of proposal: 1

Deadline(s): Jan. 1, Mar. 1, May 1, Aug. 1, Sept. 1, and Nov. 1
Board meeting date(s): Bimonthly
Final notification: Within 1 week of board meetings
Officers and Trustees: * Gary Black, Jr.,* Chair.; Robert C. Embry, Jr.,* Pres.; Anne LaFarge Culman, V.P.; Frances Murray Keenan, V.P., Finance; Esthel M. Summerfield, Secy.; Eileen M. O'Rourke, Treas.; Ellen H. Mullan, Cont.; Walter Sondheim, Jr., Tr. Emeritus; W. Shepherdson Abell; George L. Bunting, Jr.; Robert Garrett; Jacqueline C. Hrabowski; Sally J. Michel.
Number of staff: 7 full-time professional; 5 part-time professional; 3 full-time support.
EIN: 526036106
Selected grants: The following grants were reported in 2005.
$500,000 to Catholic Charities of the Archdiocese of Baltimore, Baltimore, MD. Toward final construction costs of new Our Daily Bread Employment Center, providing meals, shelter, employment services, and travelers' aid for homeless individuals.
$477,259 to Mayors Office of Employment Development, Baltimore, MD. For Ex-Offender Re-Entry Center in Northwest Career Center.
$395,500 to Baltimore City Public Schools, Baltimore, MD. For planning and implementation of Early Identification and Intervention Project at Barclay Elementary/Middle School and Edgewood Elementary School.
$300,000 to Rose Street Community Center, Baltimore, MD. For continued support of rehabilitation services for ex-offenders, both adult residents recovering from substance abuse and youth residents at risk, including transitional housing, employment opportunities, stipends for living expenses, and opportunities for after-school and community activities.
$200,000 to American Civil Liberties Union Foundation of Maryland, Baltimore, MD. For continued support of Regional Equity in Housing Project.
$127,000 to Baltimore City Healthy Start, Baltimore, MD. For transitional housing and community outreach services for Recovery In Community (RIC) outpatient substance abuse treatment program.
$125,092 to Center for Fathers, Families and Work Force Development, Baltimore, MD. For Child Support Intervention Project, job training program to help low-income noncustodial fathers meet child support obligations.
$100,000 to Loading Dock, Baltimore, MD. For purchase, renovation, and relocation costs of new facility to provide affordable recycled building materials for housing and community improvement.
$56,490 to Prisoners Aid Association of Maryland, Baltimore, MD. For interim operating costs of Female Transitional House and Shelter Plus Care programs.
$30,000 to Partnership for Learning, Baltimore, MD. For education-based juvenile program for first-time offenders experiencing learning difficulties, to reduce recidivism and increase academic outcomes.

3560

William S. Abell Foundation, Inc. ✧
(formerly Charles S. Abell Foundation, Inc.)
8401 Connecticut Ave., Ste. 1204
Chevy Chase, MD 20815 (301) 652-2224
Contact: Carol Doolan, Exec. Dir.
FAX: (301) 652-9173;
E-mail: cdoolan@williamsabellfoundation.org;
URL: http://www.williamsabellfoundation.org

Established in 1985 in MD.
Donors: William S. Abell†; Patricia O'Callaghan Abell†.
Foundation type: Independent foundation.
Financial data (yr. ended 12/31/04): Assets, $69,025,095 (M); gifts received, $45,772,427; expenditures, $2,485,010; qualifying distributions, $1,752,903; giving activities include $1,752,903 for 59 grants (high: $65,000; low: $5,000).
Purpose and activities: The focus of the foundation is aiding the hungry, the mentally retarded, the homeless, abused women and children, and helping needy pregnant women in delivering and caring for their infants. The Foundation ordinarily will make grants to shelters and transitional housing, but not for permanent housing.
Fields of interest: Performing arts, ballet; Performing arts, theater; Crime/violence prevention, abuse prevention; Crime/violence prevention, child abuse; Food services; Human services; Women, centers/services; Homeless, human services; Mentally disabled; Women; Homeless.
Type of support: General/operating support; Program development; Matching/challenge support.
Limitations: Giving primarily in Washington, DC, and five nearby counties in MD. No support for organizations sponsoring or referring for abortion; or for national touring companies, even for performances in the Washington, DC, metropolitan area. No grants to individuals, or for capital or endowment campaigns, multi-year grants, grants in consecutive calendar years, or for the construction or improvement of buildings.
Publications: Application guidelines; Annual report; Grants list.
Application information: Proposal guidelines and Abortion Counseling Disclosure form available on foundation Web site. Application form not required.
  Initial approach: 2-page proposal
  Copies of proposal: 1
  Deadline(s): Jan. 15, Apr. 15, July 15, and Oct. 15
  Board meeting date(s): Mar., June, Sept., and Dec.
  Final notification: 2 weeks after board meeting
Officers and Trustees: * Christopher S. Abell,* Chair.; W. Shepherdson Abell,* Pres.; Marguerite Elaine Abell Nurmi, V.P.; Anthony F. Abell,* Secy.-Treas.; Carol Doolan, Exec. Dir.; Alicia M. Abell; Charles S. Abell; Gregory T. Abell; Kevin O'Callaghan Abell; Nancy Elbin Abell; Thomas D. Nurmi.
Number of staff: 1 part-time professional; 1 part-time support.
EIN: 521435573

3561

Abramson Family Foundation, Inc. ✧
(formerly Abramson Foundation, Inc.)
11501 Huff Ct.
Kensington, MD 20895-1043

Established in 1959 in MD.

Donors: Albert Abramson; Gary M. Abramson; Ronald D. Abramson; Dawson Development Co., LLC; Tower Capital, LLC.
Foundation type: Independent foundation.
Financial data (yr. ended 12/31/05): Assets, $35,565,579 (M); gifts received, $101,233; expenditures, $2,248,534; qualifying distributions, $2,079,624; giving activities include $2,079,230 for 102 grants (high: $300,500; low: $50).
Fields of interest: Visual arts; Museums (art); Performing arts; Graduate/professional education; Education; Medical research, institute; Jewish federated giving programs; Public policy, research; Jewish agencies & temples.
Type of support: General/operating support.
Limitations: Applications not accepted. Giving primarily in the greater Washington, DC, area, including MD; some funding nationally, particularly in FL and NY. No grants to individuals.
Application information: Contributes only to pre-selected organizations.
Officers: Albert Abramson, Pres.; Jeffrey Abramson, V.P.; Gary M. Abramson, Secy.; Ronald D. Abramson, Treas.
EIN: 526039192
Selected grants: The following grants were reported in 2004.
$184,000 to Corcoran Gallery of Art, DC.
$100,000 to American University, DC.
$96,250 to American Committee for the Weizmann Institute of Science, DC.
$94,700 to Yeshiva of Greater Washington, Silver Spring, MD.
$70,000 to Hebrew Home of Greater Washington, Rockville, MD.
$29,000 to Studio Theater, DC.
$27,500 to Washington Performing Arts Society, DC.
$25,000 to Folger Shakespeare Library, DC.
$5,000 to Childrens Hospital, DC.
$5,000 to Raymond F. Kravis Center for the Performing Arts, West Palm Beach, FL.

3562

The Adams Charitable Foundation, Inc. ✧
11049 Seven Hill Ln.
Potomac, MD 20854

Established in 1996 in MD.
Donor: Richard Adams.
Foundation type: Independent foundation.
Financial data (yr. ended 12/31/04): Assets, $38,330,713 (M); expenditures, $2,456,577; qualifying distributions, $2,107,000; giving activities include $2,107,000 for 9 grants (high: $475,000; low: $100,000).
Fields of interest: Museums (art); Museums (children's); Performing arts, music; Arts; Education; Computer science.
Limitations: Applications not accepted. Giving on a national basis. No grants to individuals.
Application information: Contributes only to pre-selected organizations.
Officers and Directors:* Donnalyn Frey Adams,* Pres.; Allan H. Frey,* V.P.; Richard L. Adams, Jr.,* Secy.-Treas.
EIN: 522002510
Selected grants: The following grants were reported in 2003.
$380,500 to Internet Software Consortium, Redwood City, CA.
$300,000 to Friends of the National Zoo, DC.

$250,000 to Electronic Frontier Foundation, San Francisco, CA.
$230,000 to Walters Art Gallery Endowment Foundation, Baltimore, MD.
$210,000 to Discovery Creek Childrens Museum of Washington, DC.
$200,000 to Music Maker Relief Foundation, Hillsborough, NC.
$175,000 to FreeBSD Foundation, Boulder, CO.
$132,000 to Field Museum of Natural History, Chicago, IL.
$50,000 to Glen Echo Park Foundation, Glen Echo, MD.
$10,000 to Edlin School, Reston, VA.

3563

Agilent Technologies Foundation ☆
20440 Century Blvd., Ste. 110
Germantown, MD 20874
Contact: Linda Ale, Admin., Grants
FAX: (202) 416-6253;
E-mail: linda_ale@agilent.com; URL: http://www.agilent.com/contributions/foundation.html

Established in 1999 in CA.
Donor: Agilent Technologies, Inc.
Foundation type: Company-sponsored foundation.
Financial data (yr. ended 10/31/05): Assets, $12,580,931 (M); gifts received, $13,326,000; expenditures, $2,445,099; qualifying distributions, $2,430,745; giving activities include $875,766 for 66 grants (high: $100,000; low: $500; average: $1,000–$100,000), and $1,424,301 for employee matching gifts.
Purpose and activities: The foundation supports organizations involved with K-12 science education and disaster relief.
Fields of interest: Elementary/secondary education; Disasters, preparedness/services; Science, formal/general education; Minorities; Women.
International interests: Asia; Europe.
Type of support: Annual campaigns; Employee matching gifts.
Limitations: Applications not accepted. Giving on a national and international basis in areas of company operations, including in Asia and Europe. No support for home schools, sectarian or denominational organizations, or discriminatory organizations. No grants to individuals, or for religious activities, political activities, or non-academic extracurricular activities.
Application information: Contributes only to pre-selected organizations.
Officers: William P. Sullivan, Chair. and 1st V.P.; D. Craig Nordlund, V.P. and Secy.; Adrian Dillon, V.P. and Treas.; Cynthia D. Johnson, V.P.; Karen R. Lewis, Exec. Dir.
Number of staff: 2 full-time professional; 1 full-time support.
EIN: 770532250
Selected grants: The following grants were reported in 2005.
$120,000 to Bay Area Air Quality Management District Employees Association, San Francisco, CA. For Clean Air Challenge (CAC) curriculum, instructional materials and lab supplies, and hold workshops that train teachers to deliver Clean Air Challenge curriculum classrooms in California, Colorado, Delaware, and in pilot program in China.

$100,000 to Biological Sciences Curriculum Study, Colorado Springs, CO. For National Academy for Curriculum Leadership (NACL).
$75,000 to Teachers Without Borders, Mercer Island, WA. For pilot project for professional development in science and science pedagogy in Chengdu-Sichuan Province in China.
$51,900 to EUN Partnership AISBL, Belgium. For development of web-based experiment that will allow secondary school students throughout Europe to participate in shared experiement experience.
$15,000 to Fudan University, Shanghai, China. For scholarships for female and minority students to complete their 4-year studies.
$15,000 to Tsinghua University, Beijing, China. For scholarships for female and minority students to complete their 4-year studies.

3564

Alcoholic Beverage Medical Research Foundation ✧
1122 Kenilworth Dr., Ste. 407
Baltimore, MD 21204 (410) 821-7066
Contact: Robin A. Kroft Ph.D., V.P.
FAX: (410) 821-7065; E-mail: info@abmrf.org;
URL: http://www.abmrf.org/

Established in 1982 in MD.
Donors: Beer Institute; Brewers Association of Canada.
Foundation type: Independent foundation.
Financial data (yr. ended 12/31/05): Assets, $3,725,395 (M); gifts received, $1,901,841; expenditures, $2,168,490; qualifying distributions, $2,117,056; giving activities include $1,499,087 for 41 grants (high: $56,548; low: $800), and $2,117,056 for foundation-administered programs.
Purpose and activities: The mission of the foundation is to achieve a better understanding of the effects of alcohol on the health and behavior of individuals; to provide the scientific basis for prevention and treatment of alcohol misuse and alcoholism; to fund innovative, high-quality research; to support promising new investigations; to communicate effectively with the research community and with other interested parties.
Fields of interest: Alcoholism.
International interests: Canada.
Type of support: Research.
Limitations: Giving primarily in the U.S. and Canada. No grants to individuals, or for education projects, public awareness efforts, treatment or referral services, training of pre- and post-doctoral fellows, undergraduates, graduate students, medical students, interns or residents, or for thesis or dissertation research.
Publications: Annual report; Financial statement; Grants list.
Application information: See foundation Web site for application form and guidelines. Application form required.
Initial approach: Download guidelines and application from Web site
Copies of proposal: 10
Deadline(s): Feb. 1 and Sept. 1
Board meeting date(s): Apr. and Nov.
Final notification: Within 2 weeks of board meeting
Officers and Trustees:* Ivan Diamond, M.D., Ph.D., Chair.; Sharon C. Wilsnack, Ph.D., Vice-Chair.; Mack C. Mitchell, Jr., M.D.*, Pres.; Bruce Ambler; Jeffrey

Becker; Anthony J. Cutaia, Ph.D.; R. Stuart Dickson; Buster C. Glosson; Richard Jessor, Ph.D.; Steven W. Leslie, Ph.D.; Louise Nadeau, Ph.D.; Jeff Newton; David K. Rehr, Ph.D.; John Sleeman; Alan R. Timothy.

Number of staff: 2 full-time professional; 2 part-time professional.

EIN: 521234277

Selected grants: The following grants were reported in 2004.

$58,715 to McGill University, Montreal, Canada. .

$50,000 to Thomas Jefferson University, Philadelphia, PA.

$50,000 to University of Illinois at Chicago, Chicago, IL.

$50,000 to University of Texas, Austin, TX.

$50,000 to Washington State University, Pullman, WA.

$49,700 to Kansas State University, Manhattan, KS.

$49,500 to University of Calgary, Calgary, Canada. .

$49,500 to Wake Forest University Health Sciences, Winston-Salem, NC.

$29,570 to University of British Columbia, Vancouver, Canada. .

$25,000 to Wake Forest University, Winston-Salem, NC.

3565

Allegis Group Foundation, Inc. ✧

(formerly Team Aerotek Foundation, Inc.)
7301 Parkway Dr.
Hanover, MD 21076 (410) 579-3509
Contact: Hilary Murray

Established in 1998 in MD.

Donors: Aerotek, Inc.; Allegis Group, Inc.

Foundation type: Company-sponsored foundation.

Financial data (yr. ended 12/31/04): Assets, $4,815,013 (M); gifts received, $918,630; expenditures, $711,227; qualifying distributions, $703,799; giving activities include $703,799 for 138 grants (high: $72,000; low: $30).

Purpose and activities: The foundation supports organizations involved with education, health, and youth development. Special emphasis is directed toward programs designed to assist underprivileged children.

Fields of interest: Education; Health care; Youth development; Children, services; Economically disadvantaged.

Type of support: General/operating support; Scholarship funds.

Limitations: Giving on a national basis, with emphasis on Baltimore, MD.

Application information: Application form not required.

Initial approach: Proposal

Deadline(s): None

Officers and Directors:* James C. Davis,* Pres.; Neil Mann, V.P. and Treas.; Randall D. Sones, Secy.; Stephen J. Bisciotti.

EIN: 311608900

Selected grants: The following grants were reported in 2004.

$135,000 to Mother Seton Academy, Baltimore, MD. 2 grants: $63,000, $72,000

$50,000 to Living Classrooms Foundation, Baltimore, MD.

$22,000 to Boy Scouts of America, Baltimore, MD.

$10,000 to American Cancer Society, Baltimore, MD.

$10,000 to Carol Jean Cancer Foundation, Silver Spring, MD.

$7,500 to ARC of Baltimore, Baltimore, MD.

$5,000 to Dyslexia Tutoring Program, Baltimore, MD.

$1,300 to Catholic Charities, Princess Anne, MD.

$560 to Cystic Fibrosis Foundation, Seattle, WA.

3566

Clayton Baker Trust

2 E. Read St., Ste. 100
Baltimore, MD 21202 (410) 837-3555
Contact: John B. Powell, Jr., Exec. Dir.
FAX: (410) 837-7711

Established in 1960 in MD.

Donor: Julia C. Baker†.

Foundation type: Independent foundation.

Financial data (yr. ended 12/31/05): Assets, $34,395,813 (M); expenditures, $1,800,028; qualifying distributions, $1,596,906; giving activities include $1,593,400 for 84 grants (high: $75,000; low: $2,000).

Purpose and activities: Supports organizations in Baltimore, Maryland that will improve the lives of persons who are financially poor with a strong emphasis on providing opportunities to children. Also supports organizations in Baltimore City that foster community development, and work to protect and improve the physical environment of the Baltimore, MD, region.

Fields of interest: Children, services; Community development.

Type of support: General/operating support; Building/renovation; Program development.

Limitations: Giving primarily in Baltimore, MD. No support for academic or scientific research, arts and culture, workshops or for specific diseases and disabilities, or local land trusts. No grants to individuals, or for deficit funding, endowments, fundraising events, publication or seminars.

Publications: Application guidelines.

Application information: Association of Baltimore Area Grantmakers Common Grant Application Form required. Application information available at http://www.abagmc.org. Application form required.

Initial approach: Letter requesting application form

Copies of proposal: 1

Deadline(s): Apr. 5, Aug. 5, and Dec. 5

Final notification: Within 60 days of deadline

Officer: John B. Powell, Jr., Exec. Dir.

EIN: 526054237

Selected grants: The following grants were reported in 2005.

$250,000 to Baltimore Community Foundation, Baltimore, MD. 2 grants: $200,000, $50,000

$80,000 to Baltimore School for the Arts Foundation, Baltimore, MD. 2 grants: $50,000, $30,000

$75,000 to Fund for Educational Excellence, Baltimore, MD.

$40,000 to Chesapeake Bay Foundation, Annapolis, MD.

$30,000 to Midtown Community Fund, Baltimore, MD.

$20,000 to South Baltimore Learning Center, Baltimore, MD.

$15,000 to Maryland Association of Nonprofit Organizations, Baltimore, MD.

$10,000 to Sustainable Development Institute, DC.

3567

The William G. Baker, Jr. Memorial Fund

2 E. Read St., 9th Fl.
Baltimore, MD 21202 (410) 332-4171
Contact: Melissa Warlow, Prog. Off.
URL: http://www.bcf.org/ourgrants/ourgrantsdetail.aspx?grid=1

Established in 1964 in MD.

Foundation type: Independent foundation.

Financial data (yr. ended 12/31/05): Assets, $29,008,752 (M); expenditures, $1,107,659; qualifying distributions, $953,386; giving activities include $841,810 for 124 grants (high: $40,000; low: $500).

Purpose and activities: Giving primarily for the arts, education and community development; support also for children and families, social services and health. Priority will be given to requests that support core grantee capacities and organizational efficiency and stability, priority fields of interest, key partners/grantees, special opportunities that arise, and strategic opportunities.

Fields of interest: Arts, alliance; Museums (art); Performing arts; Performing arts centers; Historic preservation/historical societies; Arts; Education; Health care; Mental health/crisis services; Human services; Children/youth, services; Community development.

Type of support: Program evaluation; Income development; Management development/capacity building; Equipment; Program development; Seed money; Technical assistance; Consulting services.

Limitations: Giving limited to 501(c)(3) organizations in the metropolitan Baltimore, MD, area. No grants to individuals, or for annual campaigns, event sponsorships, or deficit financing; no loans.

Publications: Application guidelines.

Application information: See Web site for 2007 deadlines. Application form not required.

Initial approach: Proposal (no more than 3-4 pages)

Copies of proposal: 5

Deadline(s): Mar. 3, Aug. 4, and Oct. 6

Board meeting date(s): Feb., May, Sept., and Dec.

Final notification: 2 months

Officer and Governors:* Connie E. Imboden,* Chair.; J. Marshall Reid; Walter Sondheim, Jr.; Semmes G. Walsh; Thomas Wilcox.

Corporate Trustee: Mercantile-Safe Deposit & Trust Co.

Number of staff: None.

EIN: 526057178

Selected grants: The following grants were reported in 2005.

$20,000 to Maryland Institute College of Art, Baltimore, MD.

$20,000 to United Way of Central Maryland, Baltimore, MD.

$15,000 to Holy Nativity and Saint Johns Development Corporation, Baltimore, MD.

$10,000 to Baltimore City Heritage Area Association, Baltimore, MD.

$10,000 to Maryland Association of Nonprofit Organizations, Baltimore, MD.

$7,500 to Advocates for Children and Youth, Baltimore, MD.

$7,500 to Baltimore Neighborhood Collaborative, Baltimore, MD.

$7,500 to Baltimore Theater Project, Baltimore, MD.

$5,000 to Hampden Family Center, Baltimore, MD.

$5,000 to Village Learning Place, Baltimore, MD.

3568

The Baltimore Community Foundation ▼

2 E. Read St., 9th Fl.
Baltimore, MD 21202 (410) 332-4171
Contact: Thomas E. Wilcox, C.E.O.; For grants: Aisha Samples, Prog. Asst.
FAX: (410) 837-4701; E-mail: questions@bcf.org; Additional E-mail: asamples@bcf.org; Grant application E-mail: grants@bcf.org; URL: http://www.bcf.org

Incorporated in 1972 in MD.
Foundation type: Community foundation.
Financial data (yr. ended 12/31/05): Assets, $166,036,468 (M); gifts received, $19,475,619; expenditures, $52,809,877; giving activities include $45,882,563 for 3,143 grants, and $390,000 for 310 grants to individuals.
Purpose and activities: The foundation's mission is to inspire donors to achieve their charitable goals from generation to generation and to improve the quality of life in the Baltimore region through grantmaking, enlightened civic leadership, and strategic investments. BCF's strategic grantmaking focuses on the areas of human services, youth, education, transportation, neighborhoods, diversity, environment, arts and culture, and promoting Baltimore, MD.
Fields of interest: Arts; Education; Environment; Human services; Community development, neighborhood development; Transportation; Youth; Aging.
Type of support: Income development; Management development/capacity building; Endowments; Program development; Seed money; Scholarship funds; Technical assistance; Consulting services; Scholarships—to individuals; Matching/challenge support.
Limitations: Giving primarily in Baltimore City and Baltimore County, MD. No support for religious or sectarian purposes. No grants to individuals (except for scholarships), or for capital campaigns, annual fund campaigns, or event sponsorships.
Publications: Application guidelines; Annual report; Financial statement; Grants list; Informational brochure; Newsletter.
Application information: Visit foundation Web site for application guidelines pertaining to specific areas. Applications begin with a brief letter of inquiry; Prog. Officer may request a full proposal upon review of the letter. Application form not required.
  Initial approach: Mail or e-mail letter of inquiry (2 pages)
  Copies of proposal: 1
  Deadline(s): None for letters of inquiry
  Board meeting date(s): Mar., June, Sept., and Dec.
  Final notification: Within 3 months of proposal deadlines
Officers and Trustees:* E. Robert Kent, Jr.,* Chair.; George L. Bunting, Jr.,* Vice-Chair.; Suzanne F. Cohen,* Vice-Chair.; Calman J. Zamoiski, Jr.,* Vice-Chair.; Thomas E. Wilcox,* C.E.O. and Pres.; Michael E. Cryor,* Secy.; Mark Hansen, C.F.O.; James C. Alban IV,* Treas.; William C. Baker; William R. Brody; Constance R. Caplan; Benjamin S. Carson, Sr., M.D.; Juliet A. Eurich; Mychelle Y. Farmer, M.D.; Redmond C.S. Finney; Sandra Levi Gerstung; Wilson T. Gildee; Sheldon Goldseker; Michael D. Hankin; Freeman A. Hrabowski III; Stephon A. Jackson; Harry S. Johnson; Susan B. Katzenberg; Douglas W. Nelson; Walter D. Pinkard, Jr.; Arnold I. Richman; Theo C. Rodgers; Pam

Shriver; Lenel Srochi-Meyerhoff; Marc B. Terrill; Donn Weinberg.
Number of staff: 25 full-time professional; 2 part-time professional; 3 full-time support.
EIN: 237180620
Selected grants: The following grants were reported in 2004.
$2,020,000 to Family League of Baltimore City, Baltimore, MD. For Reason to Believe initiative.
$977,773 to Associated Black Charities, Baltimore, MD. For turning the Corner Achievement Program. Grant made through Eddie C. and C. Sylvia Brown Family Foundation.
$297,965 to United Way of Central Maryland, Baltimore, MD. For Reason to Believe initiative.
$45,000 to Association of Baltimore Area Grantmakers, Baltimore, MD. Toward neighborhood revitaliztion grantmaking, which seeks to strengthen housing markets, increase affordable housing, improve economic conditions and increase investment in target neighborhoods.
$42,630 to Sankofa Center for Cultural Enrichment, Baltimore, MD. For African Drum, Dance and Stage Management programs.
$40,000 to Citizens Planning and Housing Association, Baltimore, MD. Toward Resource Center for Neighborhoods, which provides individualized assistance, resource library and volunteer bank.
$37,500 to Greater Homewood Community Corporation, Baltimore, MD.
$34,000 to Goodwill Industries of the Chesapeake, Baltimore, MD. For Reason to Believe initiative.
$32,000 to Kids on the Hill, Baltimore, MD.
$31,500 to Chemical People Task Force of Cherry Hill, Baltimore, MD. For African Drum and Dance Program.

3569

Helen S. & Merrill L. Bank Foundation, Inc. ◇

1829 Reisterstown Rd., Ste. 430
Baltimore, MD 21208
Contact: Herbert Bank, V.P.

Established about 1969 in MD.
Donors: Helen S. Bank; Merrill L. Bank.
Foundation type: Independent foundation.
Financial data (yr. ended 6/30/05): Assets, $10,531,346 (M); expenditures, $551,797; qualifying distributions, $502,150; giving activities include $502,150 for 65 grants (high: $98,000; low: $100).
Purpose and activities: Giving primarily to Jewish organizations and federated giving programs; giving also for education, and health and human services.
Fields of interest: Arts; Education; Hospitals (general); Health care; Health organizations, association; Human services; Jewish federated giving programs; Jewish agencies & temples.
Limitations: Giving primarily in Palm Beach, FL; some funding in Baltimore, MD.
Application information:
  Initial approach: Letter
  Deadline(s): None
Officers: Helen S. Bank, Pres.; Herbert Bank, V.P. and Secy.; Penny Bank, V.P. and Treas.
EIN: 237031791

3570

Herbert Bearman Foundation ◇

c/o A. Katz
9690 Deereco Rd., Ste. 500
Timonium, MD 21093 (561) 852-0587
Application address: c/o Sheldon Bearman, Pres. and Treas., 10525 Terra Lago Dr., West Palm Beach, FL 33412-3026, tel.: (561) 852-0587

Established in 2003 in MD.
Foundation type: Independent foundation.
Financial data (yr. ended 12/31/05): Assets, $41,298,879 (M); expenditures, $2,151,907; qualifying distributions, $1,804,552; giving activities include $1,681,791 for 64 grants (high: $185,000; low: $200).
Fields of interest: Higher education; Education; Health care; Human services; Jewish federated giving programs; Jewish agencies & temples.
Limitations: Giving on a national basis.
Application information: Application form not required.
  Deadline(s): None
Officers: Sheldon Bearman, Pres. and Treas.; Arlene Bearman, V.P. and Secy.
EIN: 311602562

3571

August and Marjorie C. Berlitz Charitable Trust ◇ ☆

c/o Noel Wilkinson
79 West St.
Annapolis, MD 21401

Established in 2002 in MD.
Donor: Marjorie C. Berlitz‡.
Foundation type: Independent foundation.
Financial data (yr. ended 12/31/05): Assets, $48,306 (M); expenditures, $1,378,475; qualifying distributions, $1,350,000; giving activities include $1,350,000 for 4 grants (high: $675,000; low: $75,000).
Fields of interest: Human services.
Limitations: Applications not accepted. Giving primarily in MD; some funding also in NM. No grants to individuals.
Application information: Contributes only to pre-selected organizations.
Trustee: Noel Wilkinson.
EIN: 036095072

3572

The Dennis Berman Family Foundation, Inc. ◇

(formerly The Robin and Dennis Berman Foundation, Inc.)
5410 Edson Ln., Ste. 220
Rockville, MD 20852-3195

Established in 1999 in MD.
Donors: Dennis Berman; Robin Ely Berman; Sylvia Ely Jacobs‡; Michael Epstein.
Foundation type: Independent foundation.
Financial data (yr. ended 12/31/05): Assets, $4,806,528 (M); gifts received, $1,245,223; expenditures, $1,079,747; qualifying distributions, $1,022,116; giving activities include $1,022,116 for 297+ grants (high: $115,000).
Purpose and activities: Giving primarily to Jewish organizations, temples and yeshivas; some giving for social services.

Fields of interest: Theological school/education; Education; Human services; Foundations (public); Jewish federated giving programs; Jewish agencies & temples.
International interests: Israel.
Limitations: Applications not accepted. Giving on a national and international basis, particularly in MD and NY; funding also in Israel, with emphasis on Jerusalem. No grants to individuals.
Application information: Contributes only to pre-selected organizations.
Director: Dennis Berman.
EIN: 311684732
Selected grants: The following grants were reported in 2005.
$115,000 to Melvin J. Berman Hebrew Academy, Rockville, MD.
$37,500 to Jewish Federation of Greater Washington, Rockville, MD.
$13,400 to Yeshiva of Greater Washington, Silver Spring, MD.
$12,000 to Central Fund of Israel, New York, NY.
$12,000 to Yeshiva Mir Yerushalayim, Brooklyn, NY.
$10,000 to Torah Schools for Israel, New York, NY.
$9,000 to Torah Institute of Baltimore, Baltimore, MD.
$7,500 to Yeshiva Chaim Berlin, Brooklyn, NY.
$5,000 to Aleph Society, New York, NY.
$2,500 to Gush Etzion Foundation, Manchester, NH.

3573
The Dollye and I. Wolford Berman Foundation, Inc. ✧
5410 Edison Ln., Ste. 220
Rockville, MD 20852

Established in 1998 in MD.
Donors: Dollye Berman†; Gary Berman; The Berman Charitable Trust; Berman Enterprises; Shenandoah Valley Products, Inc.
Foundation type: Independent foundation.
Financial data (yr. ended 12/31/05): Assets, $2,769,826 (M); expenditures, $917,128; qualifying distributions, $896,959; giving activities include $896,959 for 89 grants (high: $222,000; low: $22).
Purpose and activities: Giving primarily to Jewish organizations, including temples, yeshivas, and funds; some giving also to the performing arts and human services.
Fields of interest: Performing arts; Human services; Jewish agencies & temples.
Limitations: Applications not accepted. Giving primarily in Washington, DC, and MD. No grants to individuals.
Application information: Contributes only to pre-selected organizations.
Directors: Gary Berman; Elyse Vinitsky.
EIN: 522073364

3574
A. T. & Mary H. Blades Foundation
3400 Poplar Neck Rd.
Preston, MD 21655

Established in 1961.
Donors: A.T. Blades†; Mary H. Blades†.
Foundation type: Independent foundation.
Financial data (yr. ended 6/30/05): Assets, $26,220,748 (M); gifts received, $2,426,855;

expenditures, $1,152,770; qualifying distributions, $1,004,243; giving activities include $1,000,000 for 55 grants (high: $50,000; low: $2,000).
Purpose and activities: Giving primarily for health, human services and education.
Fields of interest: Education; Hospitals (general); Health organizations, association; Alcoholism research; Human services; Residential/custodial care, hospices; Christian agencies & churches.
Type of support: Scholarship funds; Research; Program development; Matching/challenge support; Land acquisition; General/operating support; Equipment; Emergency funds; Debt reduction; Continuing support; Capital campaigns; Building/renovation; Annual campaigns.
Limitations: Giving almost exclusively on the eastern shore of MD, with a focus on Caroline, Dorchester, and Talbot counties. No support for political organizations. No grants to individuals.
Application information: Application form not required.
Initial approach: Letter
Copies of proposal: 1
Deadline(s): Mar. 1
Board meeting date(s): May
Final notification: Positive responses only
Officers: Thomas Harper, Pres.; Jon Harper, Secy.; Mary Ellen Harper, Treas.
Trustee: David Harper, Jr.
Agent: David Harper, Jr.
EIN: 520794020
Selected grants: The following grants were reported in 2004.
$200,000 to Caroline Hospice Foundation, Denton, MD.
$45,000 to Copper Ridge, Sykesville, MD.
$30,000 to A. T. and Mary H. Blades Center for Clinical Practice and Research in Alcoholism, Baltimore, MD.
$25,000 to Dixon House, Easton, MD.
$15,000 to Dorchester General Hospital, Cambridge, MD.
$10,000 to Bay Hundred Community Volunteers, McDaniel, MD.
$10,000 to Easter Seals Delaware and Marylands Eastern Shore, Salisbury, MD.
$10,000 to Johns Hopkins Bayview Medical Center, Baltimore, MD.
$10,000 to Talbot Partnership for Alcohol and Other Drug Abuse Prevention, Easton, MD.
$5,000 to United Way of Caroline County, Denton, MD.

3575
The Jacob and Hilda Blaustein Foundation, Inc. ▼
10 E. Baltimore St., Ste. 1111
Baltimore, MD 21202-1630 (410) 347-7201
Contact: Betsy F. Ringel, Exec. Dir.
E-mail: info@blaufund.org; URL: http://www.blaufund.org/foundations/jacobandhilda_f.html

Incorporated in 1957 in MD.
Donors: Jacob Blaustein†; American Trading and Production Corp.; Barbara B. Hirschhorn; Elizabeth B. Roswell.
Foundation type: Independent foundation.
Financial data (yr. ended 12/31/05): Assets, $123,423,328 (M); gifts received, $925,000; expenditures, $8,457,427; qualifying distributions, $7,345,105; giving activities include $6,852,333

for 163 grants (high: $925,000; low: $1,000; average: $5,000–$50,000), $6,390 for 30 employee matching gifts, and $313,750 for 2 loans/program-related investments.
Purpose and activities: The foundation promotes social justice and human rights through its five program areas: Jewish life, strengthening Israeli democracy, health and mental health, educational opportunity, and human rights. The foundation supports organizations that promote systematic change; involve constituents in planning and decisionmaking; encourage volunteer and professional development; and engage in ongoing program evaluation.
Fields of interest: Arts education; Arts; Education, reform; Education, public education; Health care; Mental health, treatment; International human rights; Jewish federated giving programs; Jewish agencies & temples.
International interests: Israel.
Type of support: Employee matching gifts; General/operating support; Capital campaigns; Building/renovation; Endowments; Program development; Technical assistance; Program evaluation; Program-related investments/loans; Matching/challenge support.
Limitations: Giving primarily in MD (no local projects outside Baltimore, MD); giving also in Israel. No support for unaffiliated schools or synagogues. No grants to individuals, or for fundraising events, or direct mail solicitations; no loans (except for program-related investments).
Publications: Application guidelines; Grants list.
Application information: The foundation accepts applications that conform to the Association of Baltimore Area Grantmakers Common Grant Application. Application form not required.
Initial approach: Letter
Copies of proposal: 1
Deadline(s): None
Board meeting date(s): Quarterly
Final notification: 4 to 6 months
Officers and Trustees:* Michael J. Hirschhorn,* Pres.; Barbara B. Hirschhorn,* V.P.; Arthur E. Roswell,* V.P.; Elizabeth B. Roswell,* V.P.; Lynn Wintriss, Secy.; Maureen L. Stewart, Treas.; Betsy F. Ringel, Exec. Dir.; Gina B. Hirschhorn; Barbara S. Roswell; Sarah H. Shapiro; Judith R. Weinstein.
Number of staff: 1 part-time professional.
EIN: 526038382
Selected grants: The following grants were reported in 2004.
$880,000 to The Associated: Jewish Community Federation of Baltimore, Baltimore, MD. For unrestricted support.
$333,333 to Hebrew Union College-Jewish Institute of Religion, Cincinnati, OH. For unrestricted support.
$200,000 to American Jewish Committee, New York, NY. For unrestricted support.
$133,333 to LifeBridge Health, Baltimore, MD. For unrestricted support.
$87,500 to New Israel Fund, DC. For unrestricted support.
$75,000 to World Union for Progressive Judaism, New York, NY. For unrestricted support.
$30,000 to Center for Health and Gender Equity (CHANGE), Takoma Park, MD. For unrestricted support.
$25,000 to American Jewish World Service, New York, NY. For unrestricted support.
$10,000 to Jewish Womens Archive, Brookline, MA. For unrestricted support.

$5,500 to Association of Baltimore Area Grantmakers, Baltimore, MD. For unrestricted support.

3576
The Morton K. and Jane Blaustein Foundation, Inc.
10 E. Baltimore St., Ste. 1111
Baltimore, MD 21202 (410) 347-7206
Contact: Mary Jane Blaustein, Pres.
FAX: (410) 347-7210;
E-mail: therbick@blaufund.org; URL: http://www.blaufund.org/foundations/mortonandjane_f.html

Established in 1988 in MD.
Donors: Morton K. Blaustein†; Lord Baltimore Capital Corp.
Foundation type: Independent foundation.
Financial data (yr. ended 12/31/04): Assets, $59,273,154 (M); gifts received, $250,000; expenditures, $3,568,870; qualifying distributions, $3,344,583; giving activities include $3,149,881 for 79 grants.
Purpose and activities: The foundation is guided by the principle that people will develop and flourish best through equal opportunities in education, access to quality health care and the freedom to participate in a democratic society. Accordingly, grants are made in the areas of education, health and human rights and social justice.
Fields of interest: Education; Health care; Mental health/crisis services; International human rights.
Type of support: General/operating support; Continuing support; Emergency funds; Program development.
Limitations: Giving primarily in Washington, DC, Baltimore, MD, and New York, NY. No support for fundraising events, or direct mail solicitations. No grants to individuals, or for fundraising, capital campaigns or annual campaigns; no loans.
Application information: See foundation Web site for program guidelines. Application form not required.
  Initial approach: Letter
  Copies of proposal: 1
  Deadline(s): None
  Final notification: 4 to 6 months
Officers and Trustees:* Mary Jane Blaustein,* Pres.; Alan Berlow,* V.P.; Susan B. Berlow,* V.P.; Jeanne P. Blaustein,* V.P.; Peter Bokor,* V.P.; Lynn Wintriss, Secy.-Treas.; Betsy Ringel, Exec. Dir.
Number of staff: 1 full-time professional.
EIN: 521607300
Selected grants: The following grants were reported in 2004.
$300,000 to Johns Hopkins University, Baltimore, MD.
$250,000 to The Associated: Jewish Community Federation of Baltimore, Baltimore, MD.
$75,000 to Physicians for Human Rights, Cambridge, MA.
$66,667 to LifeBridge Health, Baltimore, MD.
$50,000 to Baltimore Community Foundation, Baltimore, MD.
$50,000 to Center for Public Integrity, DC.
$50,000 to Global Rights, DC.
$34,000 to Institute for Policy Studies, DC.
$30,000 to Center for Victims of Torture, Minneapolis, MN.
$25,000 to City Prep, Scarsdale, NY.

3577
The Lois and Irving Blum Foundation ◇
233 E. Redwood St., Ste. 100
Baltimore, MD 21202
Application address: c/o Lois Feinblatt, 3908 N. Charles St., Apt. 503, Baltimore, MD 21218, tel.: (410) 296-6300

Established about 1965 in MD.
Donors: Lois Blum Feinblatt; Irving Blum†.
Foundation type: Independent foundation.
Financial data (yr. ended 3/31/05): Assets, $15,403,681 (M); gifts received, $112,365; expenditures, $971,399; qualifying distributions, $856,304; giving activities include $856,304 for 91 grants (high: $160,000; low: $100).
Purpose and activities: Giving primarily for Jewish causes, the arts, and human services.
Fields of interest: Arts; Education; Health organizations, association; Human services; Federated giving programs; Jewish federated giving programs; Jewish agencies & temples.
Type of support: General/operating support.
Limitations: Giving primarily in Baltimore, MD. No support for private foundations. No grants to individuals.
Application information:
  Initial approach: Proposal
  Deadline(s): None
Officers: Lois Blum Feinblatt, Pres.; Lawrence A. Blum, V.P.; Carolyn P. Blum, Secy.; Jeffrey D. Blum, Treas.
EIN: 526057035

3578
Alex. Brown & Sons Charitable Foundation, Inc. ◇
P.O. Box 2257
Baltimore, MD 21203
Contact: Margaret Preston, Secy.

Established in 1954 in MD.
Donor: Alex. Brown & Sons Inc.
Foundation type: Company-sponsored foundation.
Financial data (yr. ended 12/31/04): Assets, $3,854,527 (M); expenditures, $1,084,135; qualifying distributions, $1,035,625; giving activities include $1,035,625 for 89 grants (high: $100,000; low: $500).
Purpose and activities: The foundation supports hospitals and organizations involved with arts and culture, education, the environment, health, youth development, and human services.
Fields of interest: Museums; Humanities; Arts; Higher education; Education; Environment; Hospitals (general); Health care; Youth development; Minorities/immigrants, centers/services; Human services.
Type of support: General/operating support; Continuing support; Annual campaigns; Capital campaigns; Building/renovation; Endowments; Scholarship funds.
Limitations: Applications not accepted. Giving primarily in MD. No support for private schools or churches. No grants to individuals.
Application information: Contributes only to pre-selected organizations.
Officers and Trustees: Mayo A. Shattuck III,* Pres.; Margaret Preston, Secy.; Thomas Schweizer.
EIN: 526054236

3579
Alvin I. & Peggy S. Brown Charitable Foundation ☆
c/o Charles Harab
7900 Wisconsin Ave., Ste. 403
Bethesda, MD 20814-3601 (301) 656-5998

Established about 1963.
Donors: Alvin I. Brown; Peggy S. Brown.
Foundation type: Independent foundation.
Financial data (yr. ended 3/31/06): Assets, $4,879,509 (M); gifts received, $577,000; expenditures, $612,261; qualifying distributions, $581,289; giving activities include $581,289 for grants.
Purpose and activities: Giving primarily to Jewish agencies and temples; some giving also to education.
Fields of interest: Museums; Education; Zoos/zoological societies; Health organizations, association; Medical research, institute; Human services; Jewish federated giving programs; Social sciences; Jewish agencies & temples.
Limitations: Applications not accepted. Giving on a national basis. No grants to individuals.
Application information: Unsolicited requests for funds not accepted.
  Board meeting date(s): Varies
Officers: Alvin I. Brown, Pres.; Peggy S. Brown, V.P.; Charles Harab, Secy.-Treas.; Larry N. Gandal, Secy.
EIN: 526041735
Selected grants: The following grants were reported in 2005.
$135,000 to Zoological Society of the Palm Beaches, West Palm Beach, FL. 4 grants: $27,500, $30,000, $67,500, $10,000
$60,000 to Jewish Federation of Palm Beach County, West Palm Beach, FL.
$56,100 to South Florida Science Museum, West Palm Beach, FL. 3 grants: $20,000, $5,000, $31,100
$20,000 to Southwestern College, Santa Fe, NM.
$1,000 to Cornell University, Ithaca, NY.

3580
Bunting Family Foundation, Inc. ◇
c/o Bunting Mgmt. Group
9690 Deerco Rd., Ste. 700
Timonium, MD 21093

Established in 1991 in MD.
Donors: George L. Bunting, Jr.; Dorothy W. Bunting; Mary C. Bunting; George L. Bunting, Sr.†.
Foundation type: Independent foundation.
Financial data (yr. ended 12/31/05): Assets, $11,856,578 (M); gifts received, $3,038,987; expenditures, $628,586; qualifying distributions, $611,137; giving activities include $593,208 for 60 grants (high: $115,000; low: $350).
Purpose and activities: Giving primarily for education, the arts, and human services.
Fields of interest: Arts; Education; Environment; Human services; Federated giving programs; Roman Catholic agencies & churches.
Limitations: Applications not accepted. Giving primarily in Baltimore, MD. No grants to individuals.
Application information: Contributes only to pre-selected organizations.
Officers and Directors:* George L. Bunting,* Chair.; Judith Needham, Pres.; Chris Bunting; Jeff Bunting; Marc Bunting; Mary C. Bunting; Mary Ellen Krazlin.
EIN: 521724988

3581
John Calvin Bible Foundation, Inc. ✧ ☆
P.O. Box 268
Jarrettsville, MD 21084

Established in 1998 in MD.
Donors: Robert Henderson; Todd Henderson; Troy Henderson.
Foundation type: Independent foundation.
Financial data (yr. ended 6/30/06): Assets, $1,345,854 (M); gifts received, $600,000; expenditures, $397,830; qualifying distributions, $397,830; giving activities include $395,000 for 29 + grants (high: $75,000).
Purpose and activities: Giving for Christian religious education and churches.
Fields of interest: Theological school/education; Christian agencies & churches.
Limitations: Applications not accepted. Giving on a national basis. No grants to individuals.
Application information: Contributes only to pre-selected organizations.
Trustees: Robert Henderson; Todd Henderson; Troy Henderson.
EIN: 522135959

3582
The Keith Campbell Foundation for the Environment, Inc. ✧
410 Severn Ave., Ste. 210
Annapolis, MD 21403 (410) 990-0900
Contact: Keith Campbell, Pres.
FAX: (410) 990-0988; For Chesapeake and Atlantic Coastal Bay proposals: Verna Harrison, E-mail: vharrisonkcf@verizon.net; for West Coast proposals: Samantha Campbell, E-mail: scampbellkcf@sbcglobal.net; URL: http://www.campbellfoundation.com

Established in 1998 in MD.
Donor: Keith Campbell.
Foundation type: Independent foundation.
Financial data (yr. ended 12/31/04): Assets, $89,327,934 (M); gifts received, $30,000,500; expenditures, $4,194,184; qualifying distributions, $4,442,751; giving activities include $3,671,856 for 58 grants (high: $1,121,430; low: $400), and $789,562 for loans/program-related investments.
Purpose and activities: The foundation promotes action to improve water quality, restore ecological balance, and foster an engaged citizenry within the watersheds of the Chesapeake Bay, Atlantic Coastal Bays and the West Coast. The foundation is also involved with The Living Shorelines Stewardship Initiative (LSSI), which is a collaborative project that is supported by several public and private entities. The overall goal of LSSI is to improve water quality and enhance habitat for living resources in the Chesapeake Bay through shoreline management efforts of individual waterfront property owners.
Fields of interest: Education; Environment; Medical research; Human services; Philanthropy/voluntarism.
Type of support: General/operating support.
Limitations: Giving primarily in MD. No grants to individuals.
Publications: Grants list.
Application information: The majority of funding will be allocated to grantees solicited by the foundation. Applications should be sent via e-mail. See

foundation Web site for application guidelines and form. Application form required.
Deadline(s): See foundation Web site for application deadlines
Officers and Director:* Keith Campbell,* Pres. and Secy.; Verna Harrison, Exec. Dir.; Samantha Campbell; Catherine Gray.
EIN: 522136842
Selected grants: The following grants were reported in 2003.
$1,031,450 to Chesapeake Bay Foundation, Annapolis, MD. For general operating support.
$25,000 to Conservation Fund, Arlington, VA. For general operating support.
$20,000 to Alliance for the Chesapeake Bay, Baltimore, MD. For general operating support.
$15,000 to Potomac Riverkeeper, Rockville, MD. For general operating support.
$10,000 to Living Classrooms Foundation, Baltimore, MD. For general operating support.
$10,000 to Potomac Conservancy, Silver Spring, MD. For general operating support.
$5,000 to 1000 Friends of Maryland, Baltimore, MD. For general operating support.
$1,000 to Atlantic General Hospital, Berlin, MD. For general operating support.
$500 to Multiple Sclerosis Society, National, DC. For general operating support.
$100 to Maryland Food Bank, Baltimore, MD. For general operating support.

3583
Anne Cannon Trust ✧ ☆
766 Old Hammonds Ferry Rd.
Linthicum, MD 21090
Application address: c/o Joseph Ferlise, Trust Off., Mercantile Safe Deposit & Trust Co., 2 Hopkins Plz., Baltimore, MD 21201, tel.: (410) 237-5673

Established in 2004 in MD.
Donor: Anne C. Forsyth Revocable Trust No. 1.
Foundation type: Independent foundation.
Financial data (yr. ended 12/31/05): Assets, $745,866 (M); expenditures, $1,402,207; qualifying distributions, $1,400,000; giving activities include $1,400,000 for 2 grants (high: $700,000; low: $700,000).
Fields of interest: Arts education; Higher education.
Limitations: Giving primarily in NC.
Application information: Application form not required.
Initial approach: Letter
Deadline(s): None
Trustees: John M. Ehle, Jr.; Vernon E. Jordan; Zachary Reynolds Tate; Mercantile-Safe Deposit & Trust Co.
EIN: 546603260

3584
Capital Gazette Foundation, Inc. ✧
c/o James Brown
2000 Capital Dr.
Annapolis, MD 21401-3155
Contact: Wilbert H. Sirota, Secy.

Established in 1986 in MD.
Donors: Capital Gazette Communications, Inc.; Washington Magazine, Inc.; The Washingtonian.
Foundation type: Independent foundation.
Financial data (yr. ended 12/31/04): Assets, $327,106 (M); gifts received, $396,000;

expenditures, $401,300; qualifying distributions, $401,000; giving activities include $401,000 for 33 grants (high: $200,000; low: $250).
Fields of interest: Arts; Higher education; Environment, natural resources; Health care; Human services; Federated giving programs.
Type of support: General/operating support; Matching/challenge support.
Limitations: Applications not accepted. Giving primarily in Washington, DC and MD. No grants to individuals.
Application information: Contributes only to pre-selected organizations.
Officers: Eleanor Merrill, Pres. and Treas.; Wilbert H. Sirota, Secy.
EIN: 521490576
Selected grants: The following grants were reported in 2003.
$200,000 to Chesapeake Bay Foundation, Annapolis, MD. For Phil Merrill Environment Center.
$84,000 to Johns Hopkins University, Baltimore, MD. For Paul H. Nitze School of Advanced International Studies in Washington, DC.
$50,000 to American Enterprise Institute for Public Policy Research, DC.
$15,000 to John F. Kennedy Center for the Performing Arts, DC.
$10,000 to Anne Arundel Medical Center Foundation, Annapolis, MD.
$10,000 to SEED Foundation, DC.
$10,000 to Severn School, Severna Park, MD.
$10,000 to Shakespeare Theater, DC.
$5,000 to Fords Theater, DC.
$4,000 to Barker Foundation, Cabin John, MD.

3585
The Annie E. Casey Foundation ▼
701 St. Paul St.
Baltimore, MD 21202 (410) 547-6600
Contact: Dana Vickers Shelly, Dir., Strategic Comms.; Tiffany Thomas Smith
FAX: (410) 547-6624; E-mail: webmail@aecf.org; URL: http://www.aecf.org

Incorporated in 1948 in CA.
Donors: Annie E. Casey†; James E. Casey†; and members of the Casey family.
Foundation type: Independent foundation.
Financial data (yr. ended 12/31/05): Assets, $3,152,516,760 (M); gifts received, $13,020,462; expenditures, $223,349,751; qualifying distributions, $227,823,782; giving activities include $173,118,671 for 1,337 grants (high: $42,443,436; low: $53; average: $1,000–$400,000), $21,208,926 for 85 foundation-administered programs and $37,300,000 for 13 loans/program-related investments (high: $18,900,000; low: $500,000; average: $500,000–$2,000,000).
Purpose and activities: The primary mission of the foundation is to foster public policies, human service reforms, and community supports that more effectively meet the needs of today's vulnerable children and families. In pursuit of this goal, the foundation makes grants that help states, cities, and communities fashion more innovative, cost-effective responses to these needs.
Fields of interest: Education; Youth development, services; Human services; Children/youth, services; Urban/community development; Public affairs; Economically disadvantaged.

Type of support: Management development/ capacity building; General/operating support; Program development; Conferences/seminars; Publication; Fellowships; Research; Technical assistance; Consulting services; Program evaluation; Program-related investments/loans; Grants to individuals.

Limitations: Giving primarily in Much of the investments are concentrated in the ten sites that make up the Making Connections initiative, as well as the foundation civic sites in Baltimore, New Haven and Atlanta. No support for political committees-529s (PACs). No grants to individuals (except for Casey Children and Family Fellowship Program), or for capital projects or medical research.

Publications: Financial statement; Informational brochure; Newsletter; Occasional report.

Application information: Most grantees are by invitation. All publications can be found on foundation Web site at http://www.aecf.org/ publications. Please see foundation Web site for giving areas and limitations. Application form not required.

Initial approach: Letter (no more than 3 pages)
Deadline(s): None
Board meeting date(s): 5 times annually
Final notification: Approximately 30 days after receiving letter

Officers and Trustees:* James P. Kelly,* Chair.; Michael L. Eskew,* Vice-Chair.; Douglas W. Nelson,* Pres., and Asst. Secy.-Treas.; Joseph R. Moderow,* Secy.; Robert J. Clanin,* Treas.; Raymond Torres, Exec. Dir., Casey Family Svcs.; John Engler; Constance Horner; Teri McClure; Gabriella Morris; Kent C. Nelson; Lea Soupata; Calvin E. Tyler, Jr.; D. Scott Davis.

Senior Staff: Ralph Smith, Sr. V.P.; Tony Cipollone, V.P., Asessment and Advocacy; Patrick McCarthy, V.P., System and Service Reform; Burton Sonenstein, V.P., Fin. and Admin.; Kathleen Feely, Managing Dir., Casey Strategic Consulting Group; Sherri Killins, Dir., Personnel and Opers.

Number of staff: 474 full-time professional; 40 full-time support.

EIN: 521951681

Selected grants: The following grants were reported in 2005.

$5,271,163 to Jim Casey Youth Opportunities Initiative, Saint Louis, MO. To develop Jim Casey Youth Opportunities Initiative, for youth transitioning from nation's foster care system, to help ensure that these young people have opportunities they need to become fulfilled and productive adults.

$1,750,000 to Living Cities: The National Community Development Initiative, New York, NY. To continue support for cutting-edge community development approaches, innovative financial investment strategies and products, and urban policy advocacy.

$1,340,000 to Urban Institute, DC. 2 grants: $340,000 (To fully implement Reentry Mapping Network in six sites and produce assessment report and guide book, and disseminate findings from twelve-site project), $1,000,000 (For continuation of Assessing the New Federalism Project, including analysis of third wave of National Survey of America's Families (NSAF)).

$350,000 to Foundations, Inc., Moorestown, NJ. To provide technical assistance in design, development, and operation of high quality schools of choice in Philadelphia, PA.

$250,000 to Corporate Voices for Working Families, DC.

$100,000 to Zero to Three: National Center for Infants, Toddlers and Families, DC.

$85,000 to North American Council on Adoptable Children, Saint Paul, MN. For identifying and recommending practice changes in the child welfare system in order to elimnate racial disparity for children and families and distribute findings to key audiences.

$80,000 to Rural School and Community Trust, Arlington, VA.

$79,500 to Youth Employment Partnership, Oakland, CA. For enhancing and expanding School-to-Career Partnership for youth in foster care.

$75,000 to Advocates for Children and Youth, Baltimore, MD. For policy analysis and advocacy by coalition of organizations, Maryland Juvenile Justice Coalition (MJJC), seeking to improve juvenile justice in Maryland.

$75,000 to Children First for Oregon, Portland, OR. For continued KIDS COUNT activities.

$75,000 to Families and Work Institute, New York, NY. For a partnership promoting school readiness through family, friends, and neighbor care.

$75,000 to W. Haywood Burns Institute, San Francisco, CA.

$50,000 to Arkansas Advocates for Children and Families, Little Rock, AR. Toward continuation of State Fiscal Analysis Initiative (SFAI), as part of state's KIDS COUNT project.

$50,000 to Center for Fathers, Families and Work Force Development, Baltimore, MD.

$50,000 to Congressional Coalition on Adoption Institute, McLean, VA. For the Congressional Foster Youth Internship program, connecting foster youth with opportunities to work with congressional leaders and increasing awareness among key officials about "aging out" of foster care.

$50,000 to Greatschools.net, San Francisco, CA. For GreatSchools Network pilot program that strengthens the ability of families to be involved in education improvement efforts.

$50,000 to National Womens Law Center, DC. To develop State Early Childhood Network.

$50,000 to United Way of the Bay Area, Oakland, CA. For Earn It, Keep It Campaign in Alameda County.

$30,000 to Public Children Services Association of Ohio, Columbus, OH. For effort to make lessons, experience, and tools of Family to Family (F2F) available on-site to new states and cities and to implement a parent advocacy program.

3586
Eugene B. Casey Foundation ▼ ✧

800 S. Frederick Ave., Ste. 100
Gaithersburg, MD 20877-4102 (301) 948-4595
Contact: Betty Brown Casey, Tr.

Established in 1981 in MD.
Foundation type: Independent foundation.
Financial data (yr. ended 8/31/05): Assets, $192,104,409 (M); expenditures, $7,806,305; qualifying distributions, $5,578,468; giving activities include $5,578,468 for 20 grants (high: $2,250,000; low: $1,000).
Purpose and activities: Support primarily for higher education and medical research; support also for the fine arts and community development.

Fields of interest: Visual arts; Performing arts; Higher education; Medical research, institute; Community development.
Type of support: General/operating support.
Limitations: Applications not accepted. Giving primarily in the greater Washington, DC, area, and MD.
Application information: Generally contributes only to the same pre-selected organizations each year.
Trustees: Betty Brown Casey; W. James Price IV; John S. Saia.
EIN: 526220316
Selected grants: The following grants were reported in 2005.

$3,500,000 to Suburban Hospital, Bethesda, MD. 4 grants: $250,000 (For Eugene B. Casey Joint Replacement Center), $500,000 (For endowment fund for diabetes center), $500,000 (For surgical renovation), $2,250,000 (To provide care for stroke patients).

$850,000 to Washington Opera, DC. 2 grants: $350,000 (For NPR Broadcasts), $500,000 (For Opening Night Gala).

$550,000 to W E T A-Greater Washington Educational Telecommunications Association, Arlington, VA. 2 grants: $450,000 (For Cezanne in Provence Video), $100,000 (For general support).

$30,000 to Cystic Fibrosis Foundation, Bethesda, MD. For general support.

$20,000 to Metropolitan Washington Ear, Silver Spring, MD. For audio services for blind, visually impaired and disabled.

3587
Eugene Chaney Foundation, Ltd. ✧ ☆

P.O. Box 548
Waldorf, MD 20604
Contact: Francis H. Chaney II, Pres.
URL: http://www.chaney-ent.com/ chaney_foundation/index.htm

Established in 1987 in MD.
Donors: Chaney Enterprises, L.P.; B.P.O.E.; Southstar, LP.
Foundation type: Company-sponsored foundation.
Financial data (yr. ended 12/31/05): Assets, $2,031,365 (M); gifts received, $524,994; expenditures, $598,797; qualifying distributions, $568,974; giving activities include $568,974 for grants.
Purpose and activities: The foundation supports organizations involved with arts and culture, education, the environment, health, children and youth services, community development, and religion.
Fields of interest: Arts; Education; Environment; Health organizations, association; Children/youth, services; Community development; Religion.
Type of support: General/operating support; Research; Employee matching gifts.
Limitations: Applications not accepted. Giving limited to southern MD. No grants to individuals.
Publications: Annual report.
Application information: Contributes only to pre-selected organizations.
Board meeting date(s): 3rd Mon. of Feb. and Sept.
Officers and Directors:* Francis H. Chaney II,* Pres.; William F. Childs IV,* V.P.; Carol Jackson,* Secy.; Bob Agee; Mary M. Chaney; Mike Mickelton.
EIN: 521525001
Selected grants: The following grants were reported in 2003.

$41,267 to American Cancer Society, Annapolis, MD.

$29,933 to Boys and Girls Club of Annapolis, Bywater, Annapolis, MD.

$25,000 to Key School, Annapolis, MD.

$20,000 to Calverton School, Huntingtown, MD.

$15,000 to Maryland Hall for the Creative Arts, Annapolis, MD.

$5,000 to Anne Arundel County Trust for Preservation, Annapolis, MD.

$5,000 to Mineral Information Institute, Englewood, CO.

$3,000 to Camp Blaze, Arnold, MD.

$1,000 to Calvert Memorial Hospital Foundation, Prince Frederick, MD.

$1,000 to Saint Marys Hospital Foundation, Leonardtown, MD.

3588

Charlotte's Web ✧ ☆

c/o Robert Philipson & Co.
8601 Georgia Ave., Ste. 1001
Silver Spring, MD 20910

Established in 1997 in MD.

Donor: Ann L. Weir.

Foundation type: Independent foundation.

Financial data (yr. ended 6/30/05): Assets, $3,294,781 (M); expenditures, $418,352; qualifying distributions, $378,600; giving activities include $378,600 for 1 grant.

Purpose and activities: Giving for a private secondary school scholarship program.

Fields of interest: Education; Animals/wildlife, single organization support.

Limitations: Applications not accepted. Giving primarily in Washington, DC and Andover, NH. No grants to individuals.

Application information: Contributes only to pre-selected organizations.

Trustees: Ann L. Weir; Matthew T. Weir.

EIN: 522007855

Selected grants: The following grants were reported in 2004.

$160,866 to African Wildlife Foundation, DC. For general support.

3589

Choice Hotels International Foundation

10750 Columbia Pike
Silver Spring, MD 20901 (301) 592-5000
Contact: Pat Murphy, Exec. Dir.
FAX: (301) 592-6677; URL: http://www.choicehotels.com/ires/en-US/html/ChoiceFoundation?sid=szWVM.AvZbigeLW.5

Established in 1999 in MD.

Donor: Choice Hotels International, Inc.

Foundation type: Company-sponsored foundation.

Financial data (yr. ended 12/31/04): Assets, $7,381 (M); gifts received, $440,000; expenditures, $429,722; qualifying distributions, $428,315; giving activities include $423,680 for 222 grants (high: $75,000; low: $10).

Purpose and activities: The foundation supports organizations involved with arts and culture, education, hunger, housing, human services, and community development.

Fields of interest: Arts; Education; Food services; Housing/shelter; Human services; Economic

development, visitors/convention bureau/tourism promotion; Community development.

Type of support: Employee-related scholarships; General/operating support; Capital campaigns; Program development; Scholarship funds; Research; Employee volunteer services; Employee matching gifts.

Limitations: Giving primarily in Phoenix, AZ, Grand Junction, CO, the Washington, DC and MD, area, and Minot, ND. No support for religious organizations, political organizations, or medical- or health-related organizations. No grants to individuals (except for employee-related scholarships).

Publications: Application guidelines; Annual report.

Application information: Application form required.

Initial approach: Download application form and mail proposal and application form to foundation

Copies of proposal: 1

Deadline(s): None

Board meeting date(s): Rolling

Final notification: 2 months

Officers and Trustees:* Charles A. Ledsinger, Jr.,* Pres.; Thomas Mirgon, Sr. V.P.; Michael J. DeSantis, Secy.; Joseph M. Squeri, Treas.; Pat Murphy, Exec. Dir.; Gary Thomson.

EIN: 522184905

Selected grants: The following grants were reported in 2004.

$50,000 to Strathmore Hall Arts Center, North Bethesda, MD. payable over 5 years.

$25,000 to Food and Friends, DC.

$5,000 to Arizona Hotel Foundation, Phoenix, AZ.

$5,000 to Kinetics Dance Theater, Ellicott City, MD.

$5,000 to STRIVE (Support and Training Result in Valuable Employees) DC, DC.

$5,000 to Thurgood Marshall Scholarship Fund, New York, NY.

$4,000 to Maryland Humanities Council, Baltimore, MD.

$2,500 to Hospice Caring, Gaithersburg, MD.

$1,000 to Cresthaven Elementary School PTA, Silver Spring, MD.

$1,000 to District of Columbia Public Schools, DC. For DC Boys Choir.

3590

Clark Charitable Foundation, Inc. ✧

Bethesda Metro Ctr.
7500 Old Georgetown Rd., 15th Fl.
Bethesda, MD 20814 (301) 657-7166
Contact: Courtney Clark Pastrick, Secy.

Incorporated in 1987 in MD.

Donors: A. James Clark; Lawrence C. Nussdorf; Aon Risk Services Co.; J & H Marsh & McLennan; The Clark Endowment.

Foundation type: Independent foundation.

Financial data (yr. ended 12/31/04): Assets, $40,990,516 (M); gifts received, $2,000,000; expenditures, $1,699,599; qualifying distributions, $1,568,553; giving activities include $1,568,553 for 82 grants (high: $200,000; low: $1,000).

Purpose and activities: Giving primarily for higher education and programs and services for children and youth; support also for health and hospitals, human services, education, and the arts.

Fields of interest: Arts; Higher education; Education; Hospitals (general); Health care; Human services; Children/youth, services.

Type of support: General/operating support.

Limitations: Applications not accepted. Giving limited to the U.S., primarily in Washington, DC, and MD. No support for organizations lacking nonprofit tax-exempt status. No grants to individuals.

Application information: Contributes only to pre-selected organizations.

Officers: A. James Clark, Pres.; Lawrence C. Nussdorf, V.P.; Courtney Clark Pastrick, Secy.

EIN: 521512330

Selected grants: The following grants were reported in 2004.

$100,000 to Childrens National Medical Center, DC.

$100,000 to Georgetown University, DC.

$100,000 to Samaritan Inns, DC.

$100,000 to Suburban Hospital Foundation, Bethesda, MD.

$50,000 to Historical Society of Washington, DC, DC.

$50,000 to Strathmore Hall Arts Center, North Bethesda, MD.

$25,000 to Marthas Table, DC.

$25,000 to Washington Episcopal Day School, Bethesda, MD.

$20,000 to District of Columbia College Access Program, DC.

$7,500 to Iona Senior Services, DC.

3591

Clark-Winchcole Foundation ▼ ✧

3 Bethesda Metro Ctr., Ste. 550
Bethesda, MD 20814-5358 (301) 654-3607
Contact: Vincent C. Burke, III, Pres.

Established in 1964 in DC.

Donors: Dorothy C. Winchcole†; Elizabeth G. Clark†.

Foundation type: Independent foundation.

Financial data (yr. ended 12/31/04): Assets, $110,505,903 (M); expenditures, $5,633,973; qualifying distributions, $4,637,327; giving activities include $4,326,275 for 218 grants (high: $170,000; low: $1,000; average: $5,000–$50,000).

Purpose and activities: Emphasis on higher education, hospitals, health agencies, cultural programs, social service and youth agencies, aid to the handicapped, and Protestant church support.

Fields of interest: Arts; Higher education; Hospitals (general); Health care; Human services; Youth, services; Protestant agencies & churches; Disabilities, people with.

Type of support: General/operating support; Building/renovation.

Limitations: Giving primarily in the Washington, DC, area. No support for private foundations. No grants to individuals.

Application information: Application form required.

Initial approach: Application

Deadline(s): None

Officers: Vincent C. Burke III, Chair. and Pres.; Grover B. Russell, V.P.; Thomas C. Thompson, Jr., V.P.; Gregory Oyler, Secy.; W. Craig Thompson, Treas.; Steve Ferrigno, Exec. Dir.

Trustee: Vincent C. Burke, Jr.

EIN: 526058340

Selected grants: The following grants were reported in 2004.

$170,000 to Wolf Trap Foundation for the Performing Arts, Vienna, VA. For annual fund and Center for Education.

$125,000 to Gallaudet University, DC. For new language and communication center.

$100,000 to First Baptist Church of the City of Washington DC, DC. For general operating support.

$100,000 to Georgetown Preparatory School, Rockville, MD. For Vision Capital Campaign's Endowment Scholarship Program.

$100,000 to Georgetown Visitation Preparatory School, DC. For scholarship fund.

$50,000 to Catholic Community Services of the Archdiocese of Washington, DC. For family service centers.

$25,000 to Higher Achievement Program, DC. For permanent office acquisition.

$25,000 to Saint Columbas Episcopal Church, DC. For Truesdell Education Partnership.

$15,000 to Ignatian Lay Volunteer Corps, Baltimore, MD. For Retired Senior Volunteer Corps.

$15,000 to National Theater Corporation, DC. For community programs.

3592
Ben & Zelda Cohen Charitable Foundation, Inc. ✧ ☆
1233 W. Mount Royal Ave.
Baltimore, MD 21217-4133 (410) 727-4586
Contact: Richard Davidson, Secy.-Treas.

Donors: Ben Cohen; Zelda G. Cohen†; Ben Cohen Trust.
Foundation type: Independent foundation.
Financial data (yr. ended 2/28/05): Assets, $9,688,690 (M); gifts received, $220,903; expenditures, $871,895; qualifying distributions, $793,600; giving activities include $793,600 for 10 grants.
Fields of interest: Education; Jewish agencies & temples.
Limitations: Giving primarily in Baltimore, MD. No grants to individuals.
Application information:
Initial approach: Letter
Deadline(s): None
Officers: Rosalee C. Davison, Pres.; Charlotte Cohen Weinberg, V.P.; Richard Davison, Secy.-Treas.
EIN: 526039179
Selected grants: The following grants were reported in 2003.
$200,000 to Shoresh, Baltimore, MD.
$25,000 to Temple Oheb Shalom, Baltimore, MD.

3593
The Ryna and Melvin Cohen Family Foundation, Inc. ✧
c/o Wayne Boggs
10501 Rhode Island Ave.
Beltsville, MD 20705 (301) 937-5300

Established in 1992 in MD.
Donors: Ryna G. Cohen; Melvin S. Cohen.
Foundation type: Independent foundation.
Financial data (yr. ended 12/31/05): Assets, $24,197,045 (M); gifts received, $2,300,000; expenditures, $3,284,787; qualifying distributions, $3,057,328; giving activities include $3,055,634 for 124 grants (high: $600,000; low: $50; average: $1,000–$10,000).
Purpose and activities: Giving primarily for the arts, higher education, human services and Jewish agencies and temples.

Fields of interest: Arts; Higher education; Human services; Jewish federated giving programs; Jewish agencies & temples.
Limitations: Applications not accepted. Giving primarily in the Washington, DC, area and MD; some giving nationally. No grants to individuals.
Application information: Contributes only to pre-selected organizations.
Officers: Melvin S. Cohen, Pres.; Ryna G. Cohen, V.P. and Treas.; Mark L. Cohen, V.P.; Neil D. Cohen, V.P.; Diane C. Zack, V.P.
EIN: 521800019
Selected grants: The following grants were reported in 2003.
$450,000 to Jewish Federation of Greater Washington, Rockville, MD.
$200,000 to Childrens National Medical Center, DC.
$200,000 to John F. Kennedy Center for the Performing Arts, DC.
$100,000 to SEED Foundation, DC.
$80,000 to Jewish Community Center of Greater Washington, Rockville, MD.
$53,500 to Washington Opera, DC.
$50,000 to National Gallery of Art, DC.
$37,500 to Hebrew Home of Greater Washington, Rockville, MD.
$22,500 to Boys and Girls Clubs of Greater Washington, Silver Spring, MD.
$21,000 to Fight for Children, DC.

3594
Naomi and Nehemiah Cohen Foundation ▼
P.O. Box 30100
Bethesda, MD 20824 (301) 652-2230
Contact: Alison McWilliams, Dir.
FAX: (301) 652-2260; *E-mail:* nncf@starpower.net

Incorporated in 1959 in DC.
Donors: Emanuel Cohen†; N.M. Cohen†; Naomi Cohen†; Israel Cohen†; Daniel Solomon; Lillian Cohen Solomon†; David Solomon; Stuart Brown; Diane Solomon Brown.
Foundation type: Independent foundation.
Financial data (yr. ended 12/31/05): Assets, $79,119,474 (M); gifts received, $20,000; expenditures, $3,581,549; qualifying distributions, $3,581,549; giving activities include $3,402,960 for 133 grants (high: $150,000; low: $1,800).
Purpose and activities: The focus of the foundation is on human services, health care and civic affairs in Washington, DC, and Jewish-Arab co-existence and civil rights in Israel.
Fields of interest: Environment; Youth development; Human services; International human rights; Civil rights; Community development.
International interests: Israel.
Type of support: General/operating support; Annual campaigns; Capital campaigns; Building/renovation; Program evaluation; Program-related investments/loans.
Limitations: Giving primarily in Washington, DC, and Israel. No grants to individuals.
Publications: Application guidelines; Grants list.
Application information: Washington Grantmakers Common Grant Application is accepted but not required. Application form not required.
Initial approach: Letter of intent
Copies of proposal: 1
Deadline(s): Quarterly
Board meeting date(s): Quarterly

Officers and Directors:* Daniel Solomon,* Pres.; Jane Solomon, V.P.; Stuart Brown, Treas.; Dr. Diane Solomon Brown.
Number of staff: 1 full-time professional; 1 part-time support.
EIN: 201135004
Selected grants: The following grants were reported in 2004.
$405,000 to P.E.F. Israel Endowment Funds, New York, NY.
$150,000 to Hand in Hand, American Friends of the Center for Jewish-Arab Education in Israel, Portland, OR.
$100,000 to Americans for Peace Now, DC.
$100,000 to Givat Haviva Educational Foundation, New York, NY.
$100,000 to Hadassah, The Womens Zionist Organization of America, New York, NY.
$100,000 to New Israel Fund, DC.
$60,000 to Jewish Social Service Agency of Metropolitan Washington, Rockville, MD.
$60,000 to Shefa Fund, Philadelphia, PA.
$50,000 to American Friends of Neve Shalom/Wahat al-Salam: The Oasis of Peace, Mount Laurel, NJ.
$50,000 to American Supporters of YEDID, New York, NY.

3595
The Columbia Foundation
10227 Wincopin Cir., G-15
Columbia, MD 21044-2624 (410) 730-7840
Contact: Barbara K. Lawson, C.E.O.
FAX: (410) 997-6021;
E-mail: info@columbiafoundation.org; Additional *E-mail:* bklawson@columbiafoundation.org;
URL: http://www.columbiafoundation.org

Incorporated in 1969 in MD.
Foundation type: Community foundation.
Financial data (yr. ended 12/31/05): Assets, $10,996,930 (M); gifts received, $1,071,756; expenditures, $933,982; giving activities include $609,477 for grants.
Purpose and activities: The foundation serves as a catalyst for building a more caring, creative, and effective community in Howard County, MD, by promoting and creating opportunities for personal and corporate philanthropy, managing endowments, anticipating and responding to community needs, and strategically granting funds.
Fields of interest: Performing arts; Performing arts, music; Historic preservation/historical societies; Arts; Education; Environment; Animals/wildlife; Health care; Housing/shelter, development; Disasters, Hurricane Katrina; Children/youth, services; Family services; Aging, centers/services; Human services; Community development; Aging; Disabilities, people with.
Type of support: Scholarship funds; General/operating support; Continuing support; Building/renovation; Equipment; Emergency funds; Program development; Conferences/seminars; Seed money; Curriculum development; Technical assistance; Consulting services; Program-related investments/loans; Matching/challenge support.
Limitations: Giving limited to Howard County, MD. No support for projects of a sectarian religious nature or medical research. No grants to individuals, or for annual campaigns, deficit financing, land acquisition, or general or special endowments.

Publications: Application guidelines; Annual report; Grants list; Informational brochure; Newsletter; Program policy statement.
Application information: Visit foundation Web site for application and additional guidelines per grant type. Application form required.

Initial approach: Submit grant application and attachments
Copies of proposal: 15
Deadline(s): 1st Fri. of Feb. for project grants; 1st Fri. of Sept. for operational grants
Board meeting date(s): 3rd Wed. of each month
Final notification: Late Apr. for project grants; late Nov. for operational grants

Officers and Trustees:* Michael W. Davis,* Chair.; Meg Moon,* Vice-Chair.; Barbara K. Lawson, C.E.O. and Pres.; Dorothy V. Harris,* Secy.; Brian S. Walter,* Treas.; Earl Armiger; Buffy Beaudoin-Schwartz; Steven K. Breeden; Rev. Harry E. Brunette; Hugh F. Cole, Jr.; Michael F. Croxson; Dorothy Doub; Karen Dwyer; Lawrence M. Fiorino; David E. Forester; Karen M. Geary; Mary E. Glagola; Dorothy V. Harris; Lenneal Henderson; Faith Horowitz; Beverly Koren; Dennis J. Lane; Tim Lordan; Malynda H. Madzel; Margaret Mauro; Sang W. Oh; Joseph E. Pipitone; Gary Rosenbaum; Bruce I. Rothschild; John A. Scaldara, Jr.; Mary Ann Scully; Richard W. Story; Brian Walter; Richard D. Zwaig.
Number of staff: 2 full-time professional; 1 full-time support.
EIN: 520937644

3596
Commonweal Foundation, Inc. ✧
10770 Columbia Pike, Ste. 150
Silver Spring, MD 20901 (240) 450-0000
Contact: Carole Prest, Exec. Dir.
FAX: (240) 450-4115; E-mail: gdairsow@cweal.org; Additional E-mail: jcarwell@cweal.org; URL: http://www.commonweal-foundation.org

Established in 1968 in Washington, DC.
Donor: Stewart Bainum, Sr.
Foundation type: Operating foundation.
Financial data (yr. ended 6/30/05): Assets, $95,922,247 (M); gifts received, $183,196; expenditures, $8,529,173; qualifying distributions, $9,320,429; giving activities include $2,573,634 for 122 grants (high: $350,000; low: $338), and $355,272 for 26 employee matching gifts.
Purpose and activities: The foundation supports educational programs and projects assisting disadvantaged youth. It focuses on secondary, and to a lesser extent, elementary education. The foundation also considers grants for educational research, and to a limited extent, health care.
Fields of interest: Child development, education; Elementary school/education; Secondary school/education; Human services; Children/youth, services; Child development, services; Minorities.
Type of support: General/operating support; Continuing support; Program development; Seed money; Scholarship funds; Matching/challenge support.
Limitations: Giving limited to Washington, DC, MD, and northern VA. No grants to individuals, or for endowments or building funds.
Publications: Application guidelines; Grants list; Program policy statement.
Application information: WG Common Grant Application Form accepted and can be downloaded via foundation Web site; Organizations with operating budget above 1 million will not be considered for funding. Application form not required.

Initial approach: Telephone for initial screening
Copies of proposal: 1
Deadline(s): Aug. 1 and Mar. 1
Board meeting date(s): June and Dec.
Final notification: 4 to 6 weeks after deadline

Officers and Directors:* Stewart Bainum, Sr.,* Chair.; Barbara Bainum,* Pres.; Carole Prest, Exec. Dir.; Bruce Bainum; Roberta Bainum; Scott Renschler; Christine A. Shreve.
Number of staff: 11 full-time professional; 4 full-time support.
EIN: 237000192
Selected grants: The following grants were reported in 2005.
$60,000 to American Indian College Fund, Denver, CO.
$50,075 to Capital Partners for Education, DC.
$50,000 to Pauls Place, Baltimore, MD.
$40,000 to Hope Village, Baltimore, MD.
$25,000 to Lawyers for Children America, DC.
$25,000 to Little Lights Urban Ministries, DC.
$15,000 to Teaching for Change, DC.
$10,000 to City at Peace, DC.
$10,000 to City Gate, DC.
$10,000 to Good Samaritan Foundation, DC.

3597
Community Foundation of Carroll County, Inc. ✧
255 Clifton Blvd.
Westminster, MD 21158 (410) 876-5505
FAX: (410) 871-9031;
E-mail: info@carrollcommunityfoundation.org;
URL: http://www.carrollcommunityfoundation.org

Established in 1994 in MD.
Foundation type: Community foundation.
Financial data (yr. ended 12/31/04): Assets, $3,250,302 (M); gifts received, $910,210; expenditures, $1,158,923; giving activities include $424,246 for 146 grants (high: $98,296; low: $48), and $41,952 for 51 grants to individuals (high: $7,685; low: $42).
Purpose and activities: The foundation seeks to maintain and enhance the quality of life in the community of Carroll County through philanthropic means. The foundation will receive, invest and distribute funds for charitable, cultural and educational purposes for the benefit of the citizens of Carroll County.
Fields of interest: Historic preservation/historical societies; Arts; Education; Health care; Recreation; Human services.
Limitations: Giving limited to Carroll County, MD. No support for sectarian religious programs. No grants for to individuals (except for scholarships), or for operational deficits, fundraisers, or debt retirement.
Application information: Visit foundation Web site for application form and guidelines. Application form required.

Initial approach: Contact foundation

Officers and Trustees:* Brian Lockard,* Chair.; Fred K. Teeter, Jr.,* Vice-Chair.; Harry Haight,* Secy.; Caroline Babylon,* Treas.; Audrey S. Cimino, Exec. Dir.; Carol Blackburn; Neil J. Borrelli, M.D.; Randi Buergenthal; Anne Burgan; Barbara Denton; Gregory Dorsey; Jill Gebhart; JoAnn Hunter; Paula Langmead; Nancy B. McCormick; James McPhillips,

M.D.; David Roush; Harry Sirinakis; Robin L. Weisse; Thomas Welliver; Missie Wilcox.
EIN: 521865244

3598
The Community Foundation of Frederick County, MD, Inc.
312 E. Church St.
Frederick, MD 21701 (301) 695-7660
Contact: Elizabeth Y. Day, Pres.
FAX: (301) 695-7775; E-mail: info@cffredco.org; Additional E-mail: donor.services@cffredco.org; URL: http://www.cffredco.org

Established in 1986 in MD.
Foundation type: Community foundation.
Financial data (yr. ended 6/30/05): Assets, $29,929,858 (M); gifts received, $4,025,992; expenditures, $2,605,918; giving activities include $1,690,976 for 379 grants (high: $124,000; low: $39), and $287,893 for 248 grants to individuals (high: $5,540; low: $57).
Purpose and activities: The mission of the foundation is to enhance the quality of life for all the people of Frederick County, MD, by serving as a community leader and a resource for philanthropy, by supporting a broad range of programs and projects, by helping people fulfill their charitable dreams, and by building permanent funds.
Fields of interest: Historic preservation/historical societies; Arts; Higher education; Education; Environment, pollution control; Health care; Human services; Community development; Religion.
Type of support: Capital campaigns; Building/renovation; Emergency funds; Program development; Publication; Seed money; Scholarship funds; Scholarships—to individuals.
Limitations: Giving limited to Frederick County, MD. No grants for operating costs, annual campaigns, endowments, or multi-year funding.
Publications: Application guidelines; Annual report; Grants list; Newsletter.
Application information: Visit foundation Web site for application guidelines. Application form not required.

Initial approach: Contact foundation
Copies of proposal: 1
Deadline(s): Oct. 1
Board meeting date(s): 4th Fri. of each month
Final notification: Mid-Dec.

Officers and Trustees:* D. Hunt Hendrickson,* Chair.; Edmond B. "Ted" Gregory,* 1st Vice Chair; Robert E. Kallstrom,* 2nd Vice-Chair.; Elizabeth Y. Day, Pres.; C. Richard Miller, Jr.,* Secy.; Gail M. Fitzgerald, C.F.O.; Kathleen M. Davis,* Treas.; Albert H. Cohen, Emeritus; Dennis E. Black, Ph.D.; Denise Hall Brown; Andrew Carpel; Gordon M. Cooley; Kathleen A. Costlow; Clyde C. Crum; Diane S. Ford, M.D.; Karlys Kline; Martin S. Lapera; George E. Lewis, Jr., Ph.D.; Ann Burnside Love; Rocky Mackintosh; Robert C. Mount; Kenneth W. Parker; John R. Ratnavale; Doug W. Selby; John E. "Jack" Tritt; Joseph S. Welty; Barbara Windsor.
Number of staff: 4 full-time professional; 3 full-time support.
EIN: 521488711

3599

Community Foundation of the Eastern Shore, Inc.

1324 Belmont Ave., Ste. 401
Salisbury, MD   21804-0000   (410) 742-9911
Contact: J. Spicer Bell, Pres.
FAX: (410) 742-6638; E-mail: cfes@cfes.org;
URL: http://www.cfes.org

Established in 1984 in MD.
Foundation type: Community foundation.
Financial data (yr. ended 6/30/05): Assets,
$51,402,669 (M); gifts received, $4,469,597;
expenditures, $2,771,353; giving activities include
$2,218,705 for 745 grants (high: $5,000; low:
$500), $90,000 for 60 grants to individuals (high:
$2,000; low: $500), and $420,894 for 3
foundation-administered programs.
Purpose and activities: The mission of the
foundation is to strengthen the community by
building charitable endowments, maximizing
benefits to donors, making effective grants and
providing leadership to address community needs.
Fields of interest: Historic preservation/historical
societies; Arts; Higher education; Education;
Environment; Health care; Human services;
Community development; Religion; Youth.
Type of support: Scholarships—to individuals;
Management development/capacity building;
Program development; Conferences/seminars;
Seed money; Scholarship funds; Technical
assistance; Consulting services; Matching/
challenge support.
Limitations: Giving limited to the Lower Eastern
Shore of MD, Somerset, Wicomico, and Worcester
counties. No grants to individuals (except for
scholarships), or for annual campaigns, building
campaigns, fundraising campaigns, major capital
campaigns, building or endowment funds,
continuing support, land acquisition, general
operating support, playground equipment, or debt
retirement or budget deficits; no program-related
investments.
Publications: Application guidelines; Annual report;
Financial statement; Informational brochure;
Newsletter.
Application information: Visit foundation Web site
for application form and guidelines. Application form
required.
  Initial approach: Letter or telephone
  Copies of proposal: 1
  Deadline(s): Apr. 1, Aug. 1, and Dec. 1
  Board meeting date(s): Apr., June, Aug., Oct., and
    Dec.
  Final notification: Feb., June, and Oct.
Officers and Directors:* Gregory L. Stein,* Chair.;
Arthur M. Cooley,* Vice-Chair.; J. Spicer Bell, Pres.;
Louis H. Taylor,* Secy.; Joseph R. Ollinger,* Treas.;
James W. Almand; Alden H. Balfany; James R.
Bergey, Jr.; Terrence F. Blades; Jacqueline R.
Cassidy; Jane R. Corcoran; Annemarie Dickerson;
Charles G. Goslee; Dr. Shirley Hymon-Parker; Karen
E. Lischick; Thomas E. Mahn; Bruce A. Moore;
James F. Morris; Susan D. North; Susan K. Purnell;
Pamela D. Stansell; John M. Stern, Jr.; Raymond M.
Thompson; Thelma B. Thompson; Jeffrey F. Turner.
Number of staff: 6 full-time professional.
EIN: 521326014

3600

Community Foundation of Washington County Maryland, Inc.

120 W. Washington St., Ste. 300
Hagerstown, MD   21740   (301) 745-5210
Contact: Brad Sell, Exec. Dir.
FAX: (301) 791-5752;
E-mail: brads@hagcomfound.org; URL: http://
www.hagcomfound.org

Established in 1996 in MD.
Foundation type: Community foundation.
Financial data (yr. ended 6/30/05): Assets,
$8,279,370 (M); gifts received, $2,526,604;
expenditures, $837,033; giving activities include
$617,730 for 35 grants (high: $176,216).
Purpose and activities: The foundation's mission
includes: 1) serving as a leader, resource, and
catalyst to enrich the quality of life in the community;
2) providing a variety of flexible and cost-effective
ways for donors to create permanent endowments;
3) providing donor services that allow the foundation
to respond to changing community needs and
opportunities; 4) making financial gifts to qualified
organizations and other community needs; and 5)
encouraging philanthropy at all levels.
Fields of interest: Arts; Education; Health care; Boys
& girls clubs; YM/YWCAs & YM/YWHAs; Children,
services; Human services; Federated giving
programs; Economically disadvantaged.
Type of support: Seed money; Scholarship funds;
Program development.
Limitations: Giving primarily in Washington County,
MD. No support for projects that would ordinarily
receive public tax support, sectarian religious
programs, or K-12 educational institutions. No
grants for annual operating expenses, or for
endowment campaigns, deficit retirement, special
fundraising events, or celebration functions.
Publications: Application guidelines; Annual report;
Newsletter.
Application information: Visit foundation Web site
for application information. Full proposals are
accepted only after invitation, based on
organization's Letter of Interest. Application form
required.
  Initial approach: Submit completed Letter of
    Interest form (supplied by the foundation)
  Copies of proposal: 6
  Deadline(s): Nov. 15 for Letter of Interest; Jan. 15
    for invited full proposal
  Board meeting date(s): 3rd Thurs. of each month
  Final notification: Early Dec. for full proposal
    invitation
Officers and Trustees:* Ross H. Rhoads,* Chair.;
David Beachley,* Vice-Chair.; Michael G. Day,*
Vice-Chair., and Chair., Edu., Mktg. and PR Comm.;
Merle S. Elliott,* Grants Allocation Chair.; Alan J.
Noia,* Investment Comm. Chair.; Richard W.
Phoebus, Sr.,* Secy.; Arthur R. Crumbacker, Treas.;
Bradley N. Sell,* Exec. Dir.; Wayne E. Alter, Jr.; John
F. Barr; Howard "Blackie" Bowen; Hugh J. Breslin III;
Adna Fulton; Donald R. Harsh, Jr.; John Hershey, Jr.;
Howard S. Kaylor; Mitesh Kothari, M.D.; Paul
Mellott, Jr.; Cynthia Perini; Spence Perry; James
Pierne; Jeanne Singer; J. Randall Thompson; John
M. Waltersdorf; William P. Young, Jr.
Number of staff: 1 full-time professional; 1 part-time
professional.
EIN: 522001455

3601

The Concordia Foundation

c/o Mercantile-Safe Deposit and Trust Co.
2 Hopkins Plz.
P.O. Box 2257
Baltimore, MD   21203   (410) 237-5673
Contact: Joseph Ferlise
FAX: (410) 237-5237;
E-mail: concordia.foundation@mercantile.com

Established in 1997 in MD.
Donor: John J. Roberts.
Foundation type: Independent foundation.
Financial data (yr. ended 12/31/05): Assets,
$34,459,761 (M); gifts received, $2,000,000;
expenditures, $1,734,361; qualifying distributions,
$1,673,517; giving activities include $1,461,572
for 48 grants (high: $75,000; low: $10,000).
Purpose and activities: Giving primarily for
scholarships, preserving the ecosystems of the
Eastern Shore of MD and Central NJ, social service
and arts organizations.
Fields of interest: Arts; Education; Environment,
natural resources.
Type of support: General/operating support; Capital
campaigns; Land acquisition; Program
development; Scholarship funds.
Limitations: Giving primarily in the eastern shore of
MD and central NJ. No support for religious
organizations or for medical research. No grants to
individuals, or for matching gifts; no loans.
Publications: Application guidelines.
Application information: Request an application
cover sheet and detailed application guidelines via
e-mail. Application form required.
  Initial approach: Letter with e-mail address
  Deadline(s): Aug. 1
  Final notification: 2-3 months
Trustees: Christopher L. Roberts; John J. Roberts;
Nancy L. Roberts; Rebecca B. Roberts.
Number of staff: 2 full-time professional; 1 part-time
support.
EIN: 311486126
Selected grants: The following grants were reported
in 2004.
$100,000 to New York University, New York, NY.
$100,000 to Princeton Healthcare System
  Foundation, Princeton, NJ.
$60,000 to Creative Capital Foundation, New York,
  NY.
$60,000 to Maryland Institute College of Art,
  Baltimore, MD.
$60,000 to Princeton Day School, Princeton, NJ.
$50,000 to Eastern Shore Land Conservancy,
  Queenstown, MD.
$50,000 to Institute for Advanced Study, Princeton,
  NJ.
$45,000 to Recording for the Blind and Dyslexic,
  Princeton, NJ.
$21,000 to Mercer Street Friends, Trenton, NJ.
$17,760 to Arts Council of Princeton, Princeton, NJ.

3602

Constellation Energy Group Foundation, Inc. ✧

(formerly Baltimore Gas and Electric Foundation,
Inc.)
111 Market Pl., 2nd Fl.
Baltimore, MD   21202   (888) 460-2002
Contact: Malinda B. Small, V.P.
FAX: (410) 230-5800;
E-mail: suzanne.c.mackenzie@constellation.com;

URL: http://www.constellation.com/portal/site/
constellation/menuitem.
94939662e40191875fb60610025166a0

Established in 1986 in MD.
Donors: Baltimore Gas and Electric Co.;
Constellation Energy Group, Inc.
Foundation type: Company-sponsored foundation.
Financial data (yr. ended 12/31/04): Assets,
$4,335,637 (M); gifts received, $2,000,000;
expenditures, $2,230,540; qualifying distributions,
$2,121,027; giving activities include $2,121,027
for 74+ grants (high: $286,339).
Purpose and activities: The foundation supports
organizations involved with education, energy
assistance, the environment, and economic
development.
Fields of interest: Education; Environment, energy;
Environment; Economic development; Economically
disadvantaged.
Type of support: General/operating support;
Continuing support; Capital campaigns; Building/
renovation; Equipment; Program development;
Scholarship funds; Employee matching gifts;
Matching/challenge support.
Limitations: Giving primarily in areas of company
operations, with emphasis on central MD. No
support for churches not of direct benefit to the
entire community or organizations actively opposing
Constellation's position on issues. No grants to
individuals, or for general operating or program
development support for United Way agencies,
start-up needs, or hospital operating campaigns.
Publications: Application guidelines; Informational
brochure (including application guidelines).
Application information: Support is limited to 1
contribution per organization during any given year.
Organizations receiving support are asked to provide
a final report. Proposals should be submitted using
organization letterhead. Proposals should be no
longer than 6 pages. Application form required.
  Initial approach: Download application form and
    mail proposal and application form to
    foundation
  Copies of proposal: 2
  Deadline(s): May 1 and Sept. 1 for requests of
    over $10,000
  Board meeting date(s): June and Oct.
  Final notification: 6 to 8 weeks for requests of
    under $10,000
Officers: Mayo A. Shattuck III, Chair.; Paul J. Allen,
Pres.; Malinda B. Small, V.P.; Charles A.
Berardesco, Secy.; Jeanne M. Blondia, Treas.
EIN: 521452037

3603
The Charles Crane Family Foundation, Inc. ✧
c/o DLA Piper Rudnick, LLP
6225 Smith Ave.
Baltimore, MD 21209-3600

Established in 1991 in MD.
Donors: Charles Crane; Howard S. Brown.
Foundation type: Independent foundation.
Financial data (yr. ended 12/31/05): Assets,
$42,729,317 (M); expenditures, $2,993,719;
qualifying distributions, $2,832,309; giving
activities include $2,823,669 for 25 grants (high:
$1,315,000; low: $37; average: $25,000–
$150,000).
Purpose and activities: Giving primarily for
education and Jewish organizations.

Fields of interest: Secondary school/education;
Higher education; Education; Hospitals (general);
Human services; Jewish federated giving programs;
Jewish agencies & temples.
Limitations: Applications not accepted. Giving
primarily in Baltimore, MD. No grants to individuals.
Application information: Contributes only to
pre-selected organizations.
Officers: Shale D. Stiller, Pres.; Darrell D. Friedman,
V.P. and Secy.; Dean Laurence M. Katz, V.P.; Amy
Macht, V.P.; P. McEvoy Cromwell, Treas.
EIN: 521755504
Selected grants: The following grants were reported
in 2003.
$592,250 to Center for Jewish Education of
  Baltimore, Baltimore, MD.
$490,000 to The Associated: Jewish Community
  Federation of Baltimore, Baltimore, MD.
$183,333 to Johns Hopkins University, Baltimore,
  MD.
$100,000 to Mercy Medical Center, Baltimore, MD.
$66,666 to Bais Hamedrash and Mesivta of
  Baltimore, Baltimore, MD.
$38,200 to House of Ruth Maryland, Baltimore, MD.
$33,333 to Bais Yaakov School for Girls, Owings
  Mills, MD.
$33,333 to Shoshana S. Cardin Jewish Community
  High School, Baltimore, MD.
$33,333 to Torah Institute of Baltimore, Baltimore,
  MD.
$1,800 to Talmudical Academy of Baltimore,
  Pikesville, MD.

3604
The Haron Dahan Foundation, Inc. ✧
2231 Conowingo Rd.
Bel Air, MD 21014 (410) 879-9194
Contact: Haron Dahan, Pres.

Established in 1986 in MD.
Donors: Haron Dahan; Caddie Homes, Inc.; Dahan
Homes, Inc.
Foundation type: Independent foundation.
Financial data (yr. ended 12/31/05): Assets,
$28,743,972 (M); expenditures, $1,415,121;
qualifying distributions, $1,411,950; giving
activities include $1,371,250 for 23 grants.
Purpose and activities: Giving primarily for Jewish
agencies and temples, including education,
hospitals, and social services.
Fields of interest: Higher education; Hospitals
(general); Human services; Jewish federated giving
programs; Jewish agencies & temples.
International interests: Israel.
Limitations: Giving in the U.S., primarily in Brooklyn
and New York, NY, Washington, DC, Baltimore, MD,
and in Jerusalem, Israel.
Application information:
  Initial approach: Letter
  Deadline(s): None
Officers: Haron Dahan, Pres.; Nissim Dahan, V.P.;
Alan Berkowitz, Secy.-Treas.
Number of staff: 1 part-time support.
EIN: 521473704

3605
Darby Foundation ☆
c/o Katherine D. Brady
P.O. Box 156
Trappe, MD 21673

Established in 1966 in NJ.
Donor: Nicholas F. Brady.
Foundation type: Independent foundation.
Financial data (yr. ended 12/31/05): Assets,
$5,893,482 (M); gifts received, $3,352,547;
expenditures, $404,143; qualifying distributions,
$394,000; giving activities include $394,000 for 21
grants (high: $200,000; low: $1,000).
Fields of interest: Museums; Historic preservation/
historical societies; Libraries/library science;
Human services; Children/youth, services; Roman
Catholic agencies & churches.
Type of support: Annual campaigns; Capital
campaigns.
Limitations: Applications not accepted. Giving
primarily in Washington, DC, NJ, and NY.
Application information: Unsolicited requests for
funds not accepted.
Trustees: Katherine D. Brady; Nicholas F. Brady.
Number of staff: None.
EIN: 136212178
Selected grants: The following grants were reported
in 2004.
$50,000 to Yale University, New Haven, CT. For
  Stone Trust.
$25,000 to Avalon Theater, Easton, MD. For
  operating support.
$20,000 to Lyford Cay Foundation, Nassau,
  Bahamas. .
$10,000 to Barbara Bush Foundation for Family
  Literacy, DC. For operating support.
$10,000 to Friends of Island Academy, New York,
  NY.
$10,000 to Juvenile Diabetes Research Foundation
  International, New York, NY.
$10,000 to National Gallery of Art, DC.
$10,000 to National Museum of Racing, Saratoga
  Springs, NY.
$10,000 to National Museum of Women in the Arts,
  DC.
$10,000 to Trappe Volunteer Fire Company, Trappe,
  MD. For operating support.

3606
The Davis Family Foundation, Inc. ✧
c/o Mr. & Mrs. James C. Davis
2008 W. Joppa Rd.
Lutherville, MD 21093

Established in 2002 in MD.
Donors: James C. Davis; Kimberly J. Davis.
Foundation type: Independent foundation.
Financial data (yr. ended 12/31/03): Assets,
$28,110,094 (M); gifts received, $12,002,959;
expenditures, $596,725; qualifying distributions,
$542,500; giving activities include $542,500 for 16
grants (high: $310,000; low: $1,000).
Fields of interest: Education; Boys & girls clubs;
Human services; Children/youth, services; Roman
Catholic agencies & churches.
Limitations: Applications not accepted. Giving
primarily in Baltimore, MD and in PA. No grants to
individuals.
Application information: Contributes only to
pre-selected organizations.
Officers and Directors:* James C. Davis,* Pres.;
Kimberly J. Davis,* V.P. and Secy.-Treas.
EIN: 010751429

3607
Cora & John H. Davis Foundation, Inc. ✧
1401 Rockville Pike, Ste. 560
Rockville, MD 20852
Application address: c/o Stuart L. Bindeman, 7101 Wisconsin Ave., Ste. 1203, Bethesda, MD 20814, tel.: (301) 907-7200

Established in 1983 in DC.
Donors: Cora Davis†; John H. Davis†.
Foundation type: Independent foundation.
Financial data (yr. ended 12/31/05): Assets, $9,834,786 (M); expenditures, $481,041; qualifying distributions, $442,167; giving activities include $368,700 for 33 grants (high: $40,000; low: $1,200).
Purpose and activities: Giving primarily for universities; support also for social services and youth, hospitals and health associations, and Jewish social service agencies.
Fields of interest: Performing arts; Higher education; Hospitals (general); Health organizations, association; Boys & girls clubs; Human services; Family services; Jewish agencies & temples.
Type of support: General/operating support; Continuing support; Annual campaigns; Capital campaigns; Building/renovation; Equipment; Emergency funds; Scholarship funds; Research.
Limitations: Giving primarily in the Washington, DC, area, including MD and VA.
Application information:
  Initial approach: Letter
  Copies of proposal: 1
  Deadline(s): None
Officers: Stuart L. Bindeman, Pres.; Harold Zirkin, V.P.; Michael F. Glazer, Secy.-Treas.
Number of staff: 3 part-time professional.
EIN: 521282054
Selected grants: The following grants were reported in 2004.
$25,000 to George Washington University, DC.
$10,000 to Arena Stage, DC.
$10,000 to Boys and Girls Clubs, Hammond, IN.
$10,000 to Red Auerbach Youth Foundation, Boston, MA.
$10,000 to Shady Grove Adventist Hospital, Rockville, MD.
$10,000 to Washington Hospital Center, DC.
$10,000 to Washington Performing Arts Society, DC.
$8,000 to Lab School of Washington, DC.
$8,000 to Recording for the Blind and Dyslexic, Princeton, NJ.
$7,500 to Muscular Dystrophy Association, Tucson, AZ.

3608
The Shelby Cullom Davis Foundation ▼ ✧
3 Bethesda Metro Ctr., Ste. 118
Bethesda, MD 20814 (301) 961-4000
FAX: (301) 961-4001;
E-mail: scdf@scdfoundation.org; URL: http://www.scdfoundation.org

Incorporated in 1962 in NY.
Donors: Shelby Cullom Davis†; Kathryn W. Davis.
Foundation type: Independent foundation.
Financial data (yr. ended 11/30/05): Assets, $111,311,064 (M); gifts received, $756,346; expenditures, $5,198,603; qualifying distributions, $5,070,741; giving activities include $4,321,614

for 151 grants (high: $100,000; low: $200; average: $1,000–$100,000).
Purpose and activities: The mission of the foundation is to promote entrepreneurship, self-reliance, global understanding, free enterprise, and to enhance the quality of life by supporting the arts, education, health advancements, and preservation of the environment.
Fields of interest: Arts; Higher education; Economics; Public policy, research.
Limitations: Applications not accepted. Giving on a national basis. No grants to individuals.
Application information: Contributes only to pre-selected organizations.
Officers: Diana Davis Spencer, Chair., Grants; Abby Spencer Moffat, Vice-Chair., Grants.
Trustees: Andrew Adams Davis; Christopher Cullom Davis; Kathryn W. Davis; Lansing A. Davis; Shelby Moore Cullom Davis; Victoria Davis; Kimberly F. LaManna.
Corporate Trustee: Bessemer Trust Co., N.A.
EIN: 136165382
Selected grants: The following grants were reported in 2005.
$387,000 to Wellesley College, Wellesley, MA. Toward Davis UWC Scholarship program.
$218,000 to Institute of World Politics, DC. For accreditation, library acquisitions, student recruitment and general support.
$100,000 to Huntington Library, Friends of the, San Marino, CA. For general support.
$100,000 to Maine Coast Heritage Trust, Topsham, ME. Toward Schoolhouse Ledge campaign.
$100,000 to Manhattan Institute for Policy Research, New York, NY. For general support of Center for Legal Policy.
$75,000 to Center for Security Policy, DC. For Islamist project and the Family Security Matters network.
$40,000 to Natural Resources Defense Council, New York, NY. For general operating support.
$30,000 to National Museum of Wildlife Art, Jackson, WY. For general operating support.
$26,500 to Read to Grow, Branford, CT. For Center for Literacy program and special event.
$25,000 to American Foreign Policy Council, DC. Toward Public Diplomacy Project.

3609
Richard & Rosalee C. Davison Foundation, Inc. ✧
1233 W. Mount Royal Ave.
Baltimore, MD 21217-4133 (410) 727-4586
Contact: Richard Davison, Pres.

Established in 1984 in MD.
Donors: Richard Davison; Rosalee C. Davison.
Foundation type: Independent foundation.
Financial data (yr. ended 7/31/05): Assets, $1,389,751 (M); gifts received, $8,574; expenditures, $864,763; qualifying distributions, $862,549; giving activities include $862,549 for 20 + grants (high: $278,600).
Purpose and activities: Giving primarily for education, the arts, and Jewish causes.
Fields of interest: Museums; Arts; Higher education; Education; Hospitals (general); Health care; Human services; Jewish federated giving programs; Jewish agencies & temples.
Limitations: Giving primarily in Baltimore, MD; some giving nationally.
Application information:

Initial approach: Proposal
Deadline(s): None
Officers: Richard Davison, Pres. and Treas.; Rosalee C. Davison, V.P. and Secy.
EIN: 521348965

3610
Joel Dean Foundation, Inc. ✧
c/o Jurrien Dean
7422 Hampden Ln.
Bethesda, MD 20814

Established in 1957 in NY.
Donors: Joel Dean; Joel Dean Assoc. Corp.
Foundation type: Independent foundation.
Financial data (yr. ended 12/31/05): Assets, $7,337,434 (M); expenditures, $407,670; qualifying distributions, $316,000; giving activities include $316,000 for 34 grants (high: $100,000; low: $500; average: $1,000–$10,000).
Purpose and activities: Giving primarily for education; some funding also for the arts.
Fields of interest: Arts; Secondary school/education; Higher education.
Type of support: General/operating support; Scholarship funds.
Limitations: Applications not accepted. Giving on a national basis, with some emphasis on CA, Washington, DC, MD, and New York, NY. No grants to individuals.
Application information: Contributes only to pre-selected organizations.
Officers and Directors:* Jurrien Dean, Pres. and Treas.; Gillian Dean,* V.P.; Joel Dean, Jr.,* V.P.
EIN: 136097306
Selected grants: The following grants were reported in 2003.
$53,000 to Green Acres School, Rockville, MD. For general support.
$51,000 to Columbia University, New York, NY. For scholarships.
$50,000 to ISB Foundation, Flemington, NJ. For computer labs.
$15,000 to Gordon Research Conferences, West Kingston, RI. For general support.
$15,000 to Whitman College, Walla Walla, WA. For general support.
$6,000 to Swarthmore College, Swarthmore, PA. For scholarships.
$5,000 to University of Chicago, Chicago, IL. For general support.
$1,000 to Bellarmine College Preparatory, San Jose, CA. For scholarships.
$1,000 to Montalvo Association, Saratoga, CA. For general support.
$1,000 to Saint Andrews School, Saratoga, CA. For general support.

3611
The Decesaris Foundation ✧
2001 Rosetta Way
Davidsonville, MD 21035

Established in 2001 in DE.
Donor: Geaton A. Decesaris, Jr.
Foundation type: Independent foundation.
Financial data (yr. ended 12/31/05): Assets, $5,376,381 (M); expenditures, $694,219; qualifying distributions, $677,219; giving activities include $664,400 for 14 grants (high: $300,000; low: $2,000).

Purpose and activities: Giving primarily for hospitals, particularly a women's hospital, as well as for social services.

Fields of interest: Education; Hospitals (general); Health organizations, association; Human services; Community development.

Limitations: Applications not accepted. Giving primarily in MD. No grants to individuals.

Application information: Contributes only to pre-selected organizations.

Officers: Geaton A. Decesaris, Jr., Chair.; Josephine A. Decesaris, Pres.; Kristine Decesaris, V.P.; Angela Duffy, V.P.; Elizabeth Decesaris, Secy.; Jo Ann Decesaris, Treas.

EIN: 522303477

3612
Lydia Collins deForest Charitable Trust ◇

c/o Bank of America, N.A.
10 Light St., MD4-302-17-06
Baltimore, MD 21202

Established in 2002 in NJ.

Donors: Lydia Collins deForest†; deForest Estate.

Foundation type: Independent foundation.

Financial data (yr. ended 2/28/06): Assets, $9,771,004 (M); expenditures, $484,764; qualifying distributions, $456,148; giving activities include $405,000 for 21 grants (high: $40,000; low: $5,000).

Purpose and activities: The trustees will give special consideration to institutions mentioned in Article V (c) of Mrs. deForest's will: The Lighthouse, Inc., in New York, NY, and other organizations that provide services to those who are visually limited; The Rector, Wardens, and Vestry of Calvary Episcopal Church in Summit, NJ, and other churches affiliated with the Protestant Episcopal Church in the United States of America and other religious organizations in union with or recognized by the Episcopal Church; and The Salvation Army, in Union, NJ, and other organizations that provide social services to those who are homeless, unemployed or substance-dependant.

Fields of interest: Education; Employment, services; Human services; Salvation Army; Family services; Protestant agencies & churches; Blind/visually impaired.

Limitations: Giving primarily in NJ and in the greater New York, NY metropolitan area. No grants to individuals.

Application information: Applicants should complete a Grant Application Coversheet.
Deadline(s): Oct.
Final notification: Feb.

Trustees: Robert B. Bourne; Jean F. Marano; Bank of America, N.A.

EIN: 030433603

3613
Elsie & Marvin Dekelboum Foundation, Inc. ◇

(formerly Elmar Foundation, Inc.)
4600 N. Park Ave., Plz. S.
Chevy Chase, MD 20815
Contact: Elsie Dekelboum, Pres.
Application address: 2770 S. Ocean Blvd., Apt. 502-S, Palm Beach, FL 33480-5595

Established in 1989 in FL.

Donors: Marvin Dekelboum; Elsie Dekelboum; Marvin Dekelboum Revocable Trust.

Foundation type: Independent foundation.

Financial data (yr. ended 12/31/04): Assets, $56,592,056 (M); gifts received, $7,145,845; expenditures, $755,747; qualifying distributions, $638,046; giving activities include $596,000 for 4 grants (high: $500,000; low: $10,000).

Fields of interest: Performing arts centers; Education; Hospitals (specialty); Human services; Jewish federated giving programs.

Limitations: Giving primarily in the Washington, DC, metropolitan area, and in south FL.

Application information: Application form required.
Initial approach: Letter
Deadline(s): Rolling deadline

Officers: Elsie Dekelboum, Pres.; Gail Hartstein, V.P.; Mark Hughes, V.P.; Neil S. Kaplan, V.P.; Steven H. Oram, Secy.; Bruno A. Kaelin III, Treas.

EIN: 650121068

3614
Delaplaine Foundation, Inc. ◇

c/o Great Southern Enterprises, Inc.
244 W. Patrick St.
P.O. Box 3829
Frederick, MD 21705 (301) 662-2753
Contact: Marlene B. Young, Tr.
FAX: (301) 620-1689;
E-mail: info@delaplainefoundation.org; URL: http://www.delaplainefoundation.org/

Established in 2001 in MD.

Donors: Edward S. Delaplaine; Elizabeth B. Delaplaine; George B. Delaplaine, Jr.; George B. Delaplaine III; James W. Delaplaine; John F. Delaplaine.

Foundation type: Independent foundation.

Financial data (yr. ended 12/31/05): Assets, $14,786,739 (M); expenditures, $884,971; qualifying distributions, $750,000; giving activities include $750,000 for 60 grants (high: $160,000; low: $500; average: $5,000–$20,000).

Purpose and activities: Giving primarily for historical exhibition and preservation, higher education, community services, health, and spiritual enrichment.

Fields of interest: Historic preservation/historical societies; Higher education; Health care; Community development; Religion.

Type of support: General/operating support; Continuing support; Annual campaigns; Capital campaigns; Endowments; Program development.

Limitations: Giving primarily in Frederick County, MD, and its surrounding area. No grants to individuals.

Publications: Application guidelines; Informational brochure (including application guidelines).

Application information: See foundation Web site for complete guidelines. Application form available on Web site. Application form required.
Copies of proposal: 1
Deadline(s): Nov. 1
Board meeting date(s): 1st Wed. in Nov.
Final notification: 4-6 weeks

Officers: George B. Delaplaine, Jr., Pres.; Elizabeth B. Delaplaine, V.P.; George B. Delaplaine III, Secy.-Treas.

Trustees: Edward S. Delaplaine; James W. Delaplaine; John F. Delaplaine; Philip W. Hammond; Marlene B. Young.

Number of staff: 2 part-time professional.

EIN: 522278038

Selected grants: The following grants were reported in 2004.

$160,000 to Delaplaine Visual Arts Education Center, Frederick, MD.

$20,000 to American Red Cross.

$15,000 to Mission of Mercy, Fairfield, PA.

$5,000 to Heartly House, Frederick, MD.

$5,000 to Maryland Food Bank, Baltimore, MD.

$5,000 to Smile Train, New York, NY.

3615
The Helen Pumphrey Denit Trust for Charitable and Educational Purposes ◇

c/o Bank of America, N.A.
10 Light St., MD4-302-17-06
Baltimore, MD 21202
Application address: c/o John Gilpin, Bank of America, N.A., 100 S. Charles St., MD4-325-09-04, Baltimore, MD 21201, tel.: (410) 547-4776

Established in 1989 in DC and MD.

Donor: Helen P. Denit†.

Foundation type: Independent foundation.

Financial data (yr. ended 6/30/05): Assets, $7,951,732 (M); expenditures, $467,327; qualifying distributions, $397,511; giving activities include $395,000 for 12 grants (high: $100,000; low: $5,000).

Purpose and activities: Giving primarily for scholarship funds, educational activities and programs, building funds, honors programs, programs to end hunger, religious programs, and research programs.

Fields of interest: Arts; Higher education; Theological school/education; Hospitals (general); Heart & circulatory diseases; Human services.

Limitations: Giving primarily in Baltimore, MD. No grants to individuals.

Application information:
Initial approach: Letter
Deadline(s): None

Trustee: Bank of America, N.A.

EIN: 526401248

Selected grants: The following grants were reported in 2005.

$100,000 to LifeBridge Health, Baltimore, MD. For unrestricted support.

$100,000 to University of Baltimore Educational Foundation, Baltimore, MD. For unrestricted support.

$50,000 to George Washington University, DC. For unrestricted support.

$50,000 to Montgomery General Hospital (MGH) Health Foundation, Olney, MD. For unrestricted support.

$50,000 to Wesley Theological Seminary, DC. For unrestricted support.

$10,000 to Center for Poverty Solutions, Baltimore, MD. For unrestricted support.

$10,000 to Center Stage, Baltimore, MD. For unrestricted support.

$5,000 to B and O Railroad Museum, Baltimore, MD. For unrestricted support.

$5,000 to Baltimore Museum of Art, Baltimore, MD. For unrestricted support.

$5,000 to Walters Art Museum, Baltimore, MD. For unrestricted support.

3616
Robert W. Deutsch Foundation
c/o Jane Brown
P.O. Box 907
Brooklandville, MD 21022
E-mail: jcbrown@rwd.com

Established in 1991 in MD.
Donor: Robert W. Deutsch.
Foundation type: Independent foundation.
Financial data (yr. ended 12/31/05): Assets, $9,177,971 (M); gifts received, $1,000,000; expenditures, $484,376; qualifying distributions, $443,535; giving activities include $346,519 for 3 grants (high: $165,000; low: $46,164).
Purpose and activities: To support higher education technology programs committed to community change.
Fields of interest: Media/communications; Higher education.
Type of support: General/operating support; Continuing support; Program development; Seed money; Curriculum development; Fellowships; Internship funds; Research; Consulting services.
Limitations: Applications not accepted. Giving primarily in MD. No support for religious or political organizations.
Application information: Unsolicited requests for funds not accepted.
Officers and Directors:* Robert W. Deutsch,* Pres.; Jane Brown,* Exec. Dir.; David Deutsch; Neil Didriksen; Laurens M. MacClure, Jr.
Number of staff: 1 part-time professional.
EIN: 521758252
Selected grants: The following grants were reported in 2003.
$115,000 to University of Baltimore Educational Foundation, Baltimore, MD.
$105,000 to Goucher College, Baltimore, MD.
$80,000 to University of Maryland Foundation, Catonsville, MD.
$5,000 to University of Maryland-Baltimore Foundation, Baltimore, MD.
$4,500 to Association of Baltimore Area Grantmakers, Baltimore, MD.
$3,500 to University of Maryland-College Park Foundation, College Park, MD.

3617
The Dresher Foundation, Inc.
4940 Campbell Blvd., Ste. 110
Baltimore, MD 21236 (410) 933-0384
Contact: Robin Platts, Exec. Dir.
FAX: (410) 931-9052;
E-mail: info@dresherfoundation.org; *URL:* http://www.dresherfoundation.org

Established in 1989 in MD.
Donor: James T. Dresher, Sr.†.
Foundation type: Independent foundation.
Financial data (yr. ended 12/31/04): Assets, $56,521,448 (M); expenditures, $2,445,817; qualifying distributions, $1,658,294; giving activities include $1,509,264 for 128 grants (high: $200,000; low: $500).
Purpose and activities: Giving primarily to education and human services.
Fields of interest: Elementary/secondary education; Human services; Youth, services; Economically disadvantaged; Homeless.
Type of support: General/operating support; Continuing support; Capital campaigns; Building/renovation; Equipment; Scholarship funds.

Limitations: Giving primarily in Baltimore and Harford counties, MD. No support for adult literacy, charter or public schools and political organizations, or for national/local chapters for specific diseases. No grants to individuals, or for annual campaigns, legal services, events or conferences.
Publications: Grants list.
Application information: Unsolicited proposals will not be accepted.
Board meeting date(s): Mar., May, Sept., and Nov.
Officers: Patti Dresher, Pres.; James T. Dresher, Jr., V.P.; Virginia M. Dresher, Secy.; Jeffrey M. Dresher, Treas.; Robin Platts, Exec. Dir.
Trustees: James R. Butcher; Jeanne D. Butcher; Patricia K. Dresher; Joshua Dresher; Michael Medi; Anthony J. Meoli; Marcie Michael; Susan Roarty; Melanie Robinson.
Number of staff: 1 full-time professional.
EIN: 521610465
Selected grants: The following grants were reported in 2003.
$221,000 to Upper Chesapeake Health Foundation, Bel Air, MD.
$50,000 to Essex Community College, Baltimore, MD.
$26,000 to John Carroll School, Bel Air, MD.
$25,000 to Family Tree, Baltimore, MD.
$10,000 to Abilities Network, Towson, MD.
$10,000 to Learning Independence Through Computers, Baltimore, MD.
$6,000 to Jemicy School, Owings Mills, MD.
$3,000 to Mother Seton Academy, Baltimore, MD.
$2,000 to Ronald McDonald House Charities of Baltimore, Baltimore, MD.
$1,000 to Sparrow House, Jarrettsville, MD.

3618
Dupkin Educational and Charitable Foundation, Inc. ✧
c/o The Exchange
1122 Kenilworth Dr., Ste. 317
Towson, MD 21204

Established in 2000 in MD.
Donors: Manuel Dupkin II; Carol N. Dupkin.
Foundation type: Independent foundation.
Financial data (yr. ended 12/31/05): Assets, $25,188,079 (M); expenditures, $1,240,594; qualifying distributions, $1,030,788; giving activities include $1,030,788 for 16 grants (high: $1,000,000; low: $11).
Purpose and activities: Giving primarily to a Jewish federated giving program, and to other Jewish organizations; funding also for education and human services.
Fields of interest: Elementary/secondary education; Higher education; Education; Mental health, residential care; Human services; Jewish federated giving programs; Jewish agencies & temples.
Limitations: Applications not accepted. Giving primarily in Baltimore, MD. No grants to individuals.
Application information: Contributes only to pre-selected organizations.
Officers and Trustees:* Manuel Dupkin II,* Pres.; Carol N. Dupkin,* V.P.; Sally P. Thanhouser,* Secy.-Treas.; Stanford Z. Rothschild, Jr.
EIN: 522277075

3619
The Richard Eaton Foundation, Inc. ✧
(formerly Eaton Foundation, Inc.)
8401 Connecticut Ave., Ste. 103
Chevy Chase, MD 20815

Established in 1952 in MD.
Foundation type: Independent foundation.
Financial data (yr. ended 12/31/04): Assets, $16,799,669 (M); expenditures, $916,163; qualifying distributions, $754,896; giving activities include $692,000 for 49 grants (high: $125,000; low: $5,000).
Fields of interest: Media/communications; Arts; Higher education; Education; Youth development, services; Human services; Children/youth, services.
Type of support: General/operating support; Building/renovation; Scholarship funds.
Limitations: Applications not accepted. Giving primarily in Washington, DC, MD, and VA; some giving also in CA and NH. No grants to individuals.
Application information: Contributes only to pre-selected organizations.
Trustees: Gerald J. Hroblak; Neil E. Johnson; John V. Pollock; Grover B. Russell.
EIN: 526040787
Selected grants: The following grants were reported in 2003.
$125,000 to George Washington University, DC. For scholarships.
$125,000 to University of Maryland-College Park Foundation, College Park, MD. For operating support.
$35,000 to Saint James School, Saint James, MD. For operating support.
$35,000 to Wolf Trap Foundation for the Performing Arts, Vienna, VA. For education program.
$25,000 to Christmas Pageant of Peace, DC. For operating support.
$20,000 to Mount Vernon Ladies Association, Mount Vernon, VA. For operating support.
$10,000 to Hispanic Scholarship Fund, San Francisco, CA. For scholarships.
$10,000 to Kidsnet, DC. For operating support.
$10,000 to Marymount University, Arlington, VA. For internships and operating support.
$8,000 to Kingsbury Center, DC. For operating support.

3620
The Eliasberg Family Foundation, Inc. ✧ ☆
7 St. Paul St., Ste. 710
Baltimore, MD 21202 (410) 752-7100
Contact: Richard A. Eliasberg, Pres.

Established in 1980 in MD.
Donor: Richard A. Eliasberg.
Foundation type: Independent foundation.
Financial data (yr. ended 12/31/05): Assets, $6,904,277 (M); expenditures, $424,329; qualifying distributions, $328,769; giving activities include $328,769 for grants.
Purpose and activities: Giving for the arts, education, health, and religious organizations.
Fields of interest: Museums; Performing arts, orchestra (symphony); Arts; Higher education; Health organizations, association; Jewish federated giving programs; Protestant agencies & churches; Religion.
Type of support: General/operating support; Annual campaigns; Endowments.
Limitations: Giving primarily in Baltimore, MD. No grants to individuals.

Application information: Contributions limited to $25,000 to any one organization in any one year.
Initial approach: Letter
Deadline(s): None
Board meeting date(s): Quarterly
Final notification: 30 days after board meeting
Officers and Trustees:* Richard A. Eliasberg,* Pres.; Hildegard V. Eliasberg,* V.P.; Gail E. Redtman,* Secy.; Ilona B. Winter,* Treas.
EIN: 521199165
Selected grants: The following grants were reported in 2004.
$35,700 to The Associated: Jewish Community Federation of Baltimore, Baltimore, MD. For general support.
$28,402 to Mount Washington Pediatric Foundation, Baltimore, MD. For general support.
$26,800 to University of Pennsylvania, Philadelphia, PA. For general support.
$6,700 to Temple Oheb Shalom, Baltimore, MD. For general support.
$1,600 to United Way of Central Maryland, Baltimore, MD. For general support.
$1,200 to Maryland Science Center, Baltimore, MD. For general support.
$1,070 to Walters Art Museum, Baltimore, MD. For general support.
$1,000 to American Heart Association, Baltimore, MD. For general support.
$1,000 to Baltimore Council on Foreign Affairs, Baltimore, MD. For general support.
$1,000 to Maryland Historical Society, Baltimore, MD. For general support.

3621
The Ellison Medical Foundation ▼
4710 Bethesda Ave., Ste. 204
Bethesda, MD 20814-5226 (301) 657-1830
Contact: Richard L. Sprott Ph.D., Exec. Dir.
FAX: (301) 657-1828;
E-mail: rsprott@ellisonfoundation.org; URL: http://www.ellisonfoundation.org

Established in 1997 in CA.
Donor: Lawrence J. Ellison.
Foundation type: Independent foundation.
Financial data (yr. ended 12/31/05): Assets, $17,400,804 (M); gifts received, $18,000,509; expenditures, $28,040,626; qualifying distributions, $27,515,557; giving activities include $5,971,105 for 37 grants (high: $1,165,009; low: $1,500), $20,294,068 for 134 grants to individuals (high: $697,268; low: $50,000), and $237,753 for 3 foundation-administered programs.
Purpose and activities: Giving primarily for basic biomedical research on aging relevant to understanding lifespan development processes and age-related diseases and disabilities.
Fields of interest: Medical research, institute; Biomedicine research; Geriatrics research; Aging.
Type of support: Conferences/seminars; Research; Grants to individuals.
Limitations: Giving limited to U.S. institutions only. No support for commercial or for-profit organizations.
Publications: Informational brochure; Newsletter.
Application information: See foundation Web site for additional information, including guidelines for Senior Scholar Letter. Application form required.
Initial approach: Submit Senior Scholar letter of intent via e-mail
Copies of proposal: 1

Deadline(s): Early spring
Final notification: Summer
Officers and Directors:* Lawrence J. Ellison,* Chair.; Andrew L. Dudnick, Corp. Secy.; Philip B. Simon, C.F.O.; Richard L. Sprott, Ph.D., Exec. Dir.; Melanie Craft Ellison.
Scientific Advisory Board: Barry R. Bloom; Eric R. Kandel; Joshua Lederberg; Arnold J. Levine; George M. Martin; Gerald Weissmann.
Number of staff: 2 full-time professional; 3 full-time support; 1 part-time support.
EIN: 943269827
Selected grants: The following grants were reported in 2005.
$1,406,009 to Marine Biological Laboratory, Woods Hole, MA. 2 grants: $241,000 (For Biology of Aging Summer Course), $1,165,009 (For Molecular Pathogenesis and Global Infectious Diseases).
$1,100,000 to Harvard University, Cambridge, MA. For career development, research, and training in global infectious diseases at Medical School in Boston.
$1,100,000 to Jackson Laboratory, Bar Harbor, ME. For Integrative Center for Genetic Regulation of Aging.
$636,945 to National Academy of Sciences, DC. 2 grants: $561,945 (For Resident Research Associateships Program in Molecular Pathogenesis and Global Infectious Disease Program), $75,000 (For Frontiers of Science Symposium Series).
$440,000 to University of Washington, Seattle, WA. For Consortium for the Determination of Public Pathways Regulating Longevity.
$324,000 to University of Virginia, Charlottesville, VA. For Center for Global Health.
$51,000 to Life Sciences Research Foundation, Baltimore, MD. For post-doctoral fellowship at Duke University.
$10,000 to Toxoplasmosis Research Institute, Chicago, IL. For Relevance of T. gondii to Fight Apicomplexan Diseases at International Congress on Toxoplasmosis.

3622
The Lois & Richard England Family Foundation, Inc.
(formerly The Lois & Richard England Foundation, Inc.)
P.O. Box 341077
Bethesda, MD 20827 (301) 767-9888
Contact: Monica Smith, Prog. Asst.
FAX: (301) 767-0361;
E-mail: england.familyfdn@verizon.net; URL: http://foundationcenter.org/grantmaker/england/

Established in 1990 in MD.
Donors: Richard England; Lois H. England.
Foundation type: Independent foundation.
Financial data (yr. ended 12/31/04): Assets, $10,835,296 (M); gifts received, $1,698,223; expenditures, $1,322,028; qualifying distributions, $1,234,959; giving activities include $1,161,493 for 111 grants (high: $300,000; low: $500).
Purpose and activities: The foundation is committed to the improvement of the lives of children living in underserved communities in Washington, DC. Its current focus is out of school time programs that provide academic support and enrichment, athletic activities, and/or arts education to children in grades 3 and above. The foundation also has a strong commitment to

strengthening Jewish life in the United States and internationally.
Fields of interest: Arts; Education; Human services; Community development, neighborhood development; Jewish agencies & temples.
International interests: Israel.
Type of support: General/operating support; Continuing support; Annual campaigns; Capital campaigns; Building/renovation; Program development; Publication; Seed money; Program evaluation; Program-related investments/loans; Matching/challenge support.
Limitations: Applications not accepted. Giving primarily in the Washington, DC, area. No grants to individuals.
Publications: Grants list.
Application information: Unsolicited requests for funds not accepted. The foundation may request letters of inquiry from organizations working in targeted areas of interest.
Board meeting date(s): May and Nov.
Officers and Board Members:* Catherine S. England,* Chair.; Richard England,* Pres.; Lois H. England,* V.P.; Richard England, Jr.,* Treas.; Larry Akman; Nonie Akman; Diana England.
Number of staff: 1 part-time support.
EIN: 521521418
Selected grants: The following grants were reported in 2003.
$20,000 to Beacon House Community Ministry, DC.
$20,000 to DC SCORES, DC.
$20,000 to For Love of Children (FLOC), DC.
$20,000 to Higher Achievement Program, DC.
$15,000 to Barker Foundation, Cabin John, MD.
$15,000 to Heads Up: A University Neighborhood Initiative, DC.
$12,500 to DeCordova Museum and Sculpture Park, Lincoln, MA.
$12,500 to Washington AIDS Partnership, DC.
$10,000 to Boys and Girls Clubs of Greater Washington, Silver Spring, MD.
$5,000 to La Clinica del Pueblo, DC.

3623
Diana and Michael David Epstein Family Foundation, Inc. ✧ ☆
5410 Edson Ln., No. 300
Rockville, MD 20852

Established in 2000 in MD.
Donors: Michael David Epstein; Diana Ely Epstein.
Foundation type: Independent foundation.
Financial data (yr. ended 12/31/05): Assets, $3,531,635 (M); expenditures, $466,547; qualifying distributions, $455,637; giving activities include $455,637 for 81 grants (high: $127,500; low: $5).
Fields of interest: Jewish federated giving programs; Jewish agencies & temples.
Limitations: Applications not accepted. Giving primarily in MD, Washington, DC and NY. No grants to individuals.
Application information: Contributes only to pre-selected organizations.
Officers and Directors:* Michael David Epstein,* Pres.; Diana Ely Epstein,* Secy.; Samantha Epstein.
EIN: 311684510
Selected grants: The following grants were reported in 2003.
$50,000 to Melvin J. Berman Hebrew Academy, Rockville, MD.
$19,396 to Beth Shalom Congregation, Potomac, MD.

$9,700 to American Committee for the Weizmann Institute of Science, New York, NY.

$8,100 to Jewish Community Center of Greater Washington, Rockville, MD.

$5,000 to Middle East Media Research Institute, DC.

$1,500 to Jewish Social Service Agency of Metropolitan Washington, Rockville, MD.

$1,200 to Young Israel of Scarsdale, Scarsdale, NY.

$1,000 to Operation Embrace, Potomac, MD.

$750 to Gesher School, Fairfax, VA.

$500 to Yeshiva of Rockland County - Rockland Hebrew Day School, Spring Valley, NY.

3624

The Erickson Foundation, Inc. ✧

701 Maiden Choice Ln.
Catonsville, MD 21228 (410) 737-8911
Contact: John M. Parrish Ph.D., Exec. Dir.
FAX: (410) 737-8856

Established in 1998 in MD.

Donors: John C. Erickson; Nancy A. Erickson.

Foundation type: Operating foundation.

Financial data (yr. ended 12/31/05): Assets, $74,707,224 (M); gifts received, $26,252,837; expenditures, $6,941,054; qualifying distributions, $35,836,110; giving activities include $2,000,000 for 1 grant, and $33,778,540 for 2 foundation-administered programs.

Purpose and activities: Giving primarily to a university for a school of aging studies.

Fields of interest: Higher education, university; Gerontology.

Limitations: Giving primarily in Baltimore, MD.

Publications: Informational brochure; Newsletter.

Application information:
 Initial approach: Letter
 Deadline(s): None

Officers and Trustees: * John C. Erickson,* Pres.; Nancy A. Erickson,* V.P. and Secy.; Jeffrey A. Jacobson, Treas.; John M. Parrish, Ph.D., Exec. Dir.; Craig A. Erickson; Mark P. Erickson; and 2 additional trustees.

Number of staff: 3 full-time professional; 1 full-time support.

EIN: 522112929

3625

Evergreen Foundation, Inc. ✧ ☆

c/o Allan M. Fox
8 W. Lenox St.
Chevy Chase, MD 20815-4209

Established in 1997 in MD.

Donor: Allan M. Fox.

Foundation type: Independent foundation.

Financial data (yr. ended 12/31/05): Assets, $1,613,390 (M); gifts received, $5,430; expenditures, $398,420; qualifying distributions, $375,000; giving activities include $375,000 for grants.

Purpose and activities: Giving primarily for Jewish federated giving programs.

Fields of interest: Education; Jewish federated giving programs.

Limitations: Applications not accepted. Giving primarily in Washington, DC. No grants to individuals.

Application information: Contributes only to pre-selected organizations.

Officer: Allan M. Fox, Pres.

EIN: 522010135

Selected grants: The following grants were reported in 2003.

$220,000 to Jewish Federation of Greater Washington, Rockville, MD. For general support.

$12,000 to Field School, DC. For general support.

3626

Frank M. Ewing Foundation, Inc. ✧

5610 Wisconsin Ave., Ste. PH20C
Chevy Chase, MD 20815 (301) 656-7337
Contact: Judith H. Ewing, Exec. V.P.

Established around 1994.

Donor: Frank M. Ewing.

Foundation type: Independent foundation.

Financial data (yr. ended 9/30/05): Assets, $8,935,792 (M); expenditures, $435,941; qualifying distributions, $430,000; giving activities include $430,000 for 20 grants (high: $100,000; low: $1,000).

Purpose and activities: Giving primarily for health and human services; support also for education.

Fields of interest: Elementary/secondary education; Medical care, rehabilitation; Cancer; YM/YWCAs & YM/YWHAs; Christian agencies & churches.

Type of support: Continuing support; Annual campaigns; Capital campaigns; Research.

Limitations: Giving on a national basis. No grants to individuals.

Application information: Application form not required.
 Initial approach: Letter
 Copies of proposal: 1
 Deadline(s): Aug.
 Board meeting date(s): Oct.
 Final notification: Oct.

Officers: Frank M. Ewing, Pres.; Judith H. Ewing, Exec. V.P.; Frances E. Tennery, V.P. and Secy.; Peggy E. Atherton, Treas.

Number of staff: 2 full-time professional.

EIN: 521902030

Selected grants: The following grants were reported in 2005.

$100,000 to American Red Cross, Washington, NC.

$100,000 to Norwood School, Bethesda, MD.

$10,000 to Nature Conservancy, Arlington, TX.

$10,000 to Paralyzed Veterans of America, DC.

$10,000 to Remedy, New Haven, CT.

3627

The Sherman Fairchild Foundation, Inc. ▼

5454 Wisconsin Ave., Ste. 1205
Chevy Chase, MD 20815 (301) 913-5990
Contact: Bonnie Himmelman, Pres.

Incorporated in 1955 in NY.

Donors: May Fairchild†; Sherman Fairchild†.

Foundation type: Independent foundation.

Financial data (yr. ended 12/31/04): Assets, $470,734,978 (M); expenditures, $25,995,733; qualifying distributions, $20,371,154; giving activities include $20,013,561 for 54 grants (high: $5,000,000; low: $15,000; average: $25,000–$100,000).

Purpose and activities: Emphasis on higher education and fine arts and cultural institutions; some support for medical research and social welfare.

Fields of interest: Visual arts; Performing arts; Arts; Higher education; Medical research, institute; Human services.

Limitations: Applications not accepted. Giving on a national basis.

Application information: Unsolicited requests for funds not accepted.

Officers and Directors: * Walter F. Burke III,* Chair. and V.P.; Bonnie Himmelman,* Pres.; Sandra Weiksner, Secy.; Walter Burke,* Treas.; Charles L. Biggs; Bruce M. Dresner; Michele Myers; Charles E. Pierce; Agnar Pytte; James Wright.

Number of staff: 3 full-time professional.

EIN: 131951698

Selected grants: The following grants were reported in 2004.

$10,000,000 to California Institute of Technology, Pasadena, CA. For Cahill Center for Astronomy and Astrophysics.

$10,000,000 to Dartmouth College, Hanover, NH. For Professorships in emerging fields.

$5,000,000 to Denison University, Granville, OH. For faculty enhancement program.

$3,653,104 to University of California, San Francisco, CA. For development of synthetic prion technology.

$857,956 to Huntington Library, Art Collections and Botanical Gardens, San Marino, CA. For construction of conservation laboratory.

$500,000 to Barnard College, New York, NY. For SEP Phase IX, science education program to benefit undergraduate research with laboratory equipment and full-time technician.

$500,000 to Metropolitan Museum of Art, Sherman Fairchild Center for Objects Conservation, New York, NY. For Sherman Fairchild Head Conservatorship.

$500,000 to Salvation Army of Greater New York, New York, NY. For general operating support.

$500,000 to Williams College, Williamstown, MA. For SEP Phase IX, science education program for development of interdisciplinary curriculum.

$500,000 to Xavier University of Louisiana, New Orleans, LA. For SEP Phase IX, science education program.

3628

FBW Foundation ✧

(formerly Ferris, Baker Watts Foundation)
8403 Colesville Rd., Ste. 900
Silver Spring, MD 20910

Established in 1992 in MD.

Donors: Ferris, Baker Watts, Inc.; Marshfield Assocs.

Foundation type: Company-sponsored foundation.

Financial data (yr. ended 2/28/05): Assets, $4,084,750 (M); expenditures, $555,097; qualifying distributions, $514,055; giving activities include $514,055 for 278 grants (high: $18,700; low: $25).

Purpose and activities: The foundation supports hospitals, museums, and organizations involved with arts and culture, education, health, human services, and children and youth.

Fields of interest: Museums; Arts; Higher education; Education; Hospitals (specialty); Health care; Children/youth, services; Human services; Federated giving programs.

Limitations: Applications not accepted. Giving primarily in the Washington, DC, area, including MD, with some emphasis on Baltimore. No grants to individuals.

Application information: Contributes only to pre-selected organizations.
Trustees: George M. Ferris, Jr.; Robin O. Oegerle; Theodore W. Urban.
EIN: 521805407

3629
Felburn Foundation ✧
c/o Robert Philipson & Co.
8601 Georgia Ave., No. 1001
Silver Spring, MD 20910

Established in 1978 in VA.
Donors: Phil Felburn†; The Aetna Freight Lines, Inc.
Foundation type: Independent foundation.
Financial data (yr. ended 12/31/04): Assets, $46,085,869 (M); gifts received, $220; expenditures, $2,312,301; qualifying distributions, $1,797,736; giving activities include $1,644,438 for 19 grants (high: $500,000; low: $25).
Purpose and activities: Giving primarily for natural resources conservation, the environment, and wildlife preservation and protection.
Fields of interest: Museums; Libraries/library science; Environment, natural resources; Animals/wildlife, preservation/protection; Animals/wildlife; Recreation, parks/playgrounds; Community development.
Limitations: Applications not accepted. Giving primarily in WI, MS, and FL. No grants to individuals.
Application information: Contributes only to pre-selected organizations.
Officers and Directors:* Charles Freeman, Chair. and Pres.; Elmyra F. Schiller, Vice-Chair. and Secy.-Treas.; Larry J. While, V.P.
EIN: 510234331
Selected grants: The following grants were reported in 2004.
$500,000 to Aldo Leopold Foundation, Baraboo, WI.
$237,400 to International Crane Foundation, Baraboo, WI.
$60,000 to Coastal Carolina University, Conway, SC.
$50,000 to Avian Research and Conservation Institute, Gainesville, FL.
$50,000 to International Snow Leopard Trust, Seattle, WA.

3630
Robert M. Fisher Memorial Foundation, Inc. ✧
c/o John J. Schofield
11140 Rockville Pike, Ste. 340
North Bethesda, MD 20852

Established in 1963 in DC.
Donors: Jess Fisher; Mildred D. Fisher.
Foundation type: Independent foundation.
Financial data (yr. ended 11/30/05): Assets, $23,515,014 (M); gifts received, $12,500,000; expenditures, $4,419,093; qualifying distributions, $4,341,702; giving activities include $4,326,500 for 5 grants (high: $4,210,000; low: $1,500).
Purpose and activities: Giving primarily to a university.
Fields of interest: Arts; Higher education, university; Human services.
Limitations: Applications not accepted. Giving primarily in Towson, MD; giving also in Washington, DC and VA. No grants to individuals.

Application information: Contributes only to pre-selected organizations.
Officers: John J. Schofield, Pres. and Treas.; Robert L. Jones, V.P.; Douglas Siegler, Secy.
EIN: 526054331

3631
Sid & Mary Foulger Foundation, Inc. ✧
9600 Blackwell Rd, Ste. 200
Rockville, MD 20850-3659

Established in 1997 in MD.
Donors: Mary Foulger; Sidney W. Foulger.
Foundation type: Independent foundation.
Financial data (yr. ended 12/31/04): Assets, $97,725 (M); gifts received, $409,139; expenditures, $521,112; qualifying distributions, $521,112; giving activities include $104,120 for 1 grant, and $414,072 for 47 grants to individuals (high: $40,000; low: $1,544).
Purpose and activities: Giving for higher education assistance.
Type of support: Scholarships—to individuals.
Limitations: Applications not accepted. Giving primarily to residents of UT.
Application information: Contributes only to pre-selected organizations.
Directors: Bryant F. Foulger; Clayton F. Foulger; Mary Foulger; Sidney W. Foulger; Brent K. Pratt.
EIN: 522062781

3632
France-Merrick Foundation ▼
The Exchange
1122 Kenilworth Dr., Ste. 118
Baltimore, MD 21204 (410) 832-5700
Contact: Robert W. Schaefer, Exec. Dir.

Established in 1962; merged with Jacob and Annita France Foundation, Inc. and assumed current name in 1998.
Donors: Robert G. Merrick, Sr.†; Robert G. Merrick, Jr.†; Anne M. Merrick†; Jacob France†; Annita France†.
Foundation type: Independent foundation.
Financial data (yr. ended 5/31/06): Assets, $233,715,080 (M); expenditures, $13,466,498; qualifying distributions, $11,489,760; giving activities include $10,380,920 for 127 grants (high: $1,000,000; low: $2,500; average: $10,000–$100,000), and $570,456 for 117 employee matching gifts.
Purpose and activities: Emphasis on civic and cultural activities, historic preservation, all levels of private, parochial and public education, community development, and conservation and the environment.
Fields of interest: Arts, cultural/ethnic awareness; Historic preservation/historical societies; Education; Environment, natural resources; Environment; Health care; Human services; Public affairs.
Type of support: Capital campaigns; Building/renovation; Equipment; Endowments; Program development; Seed money; Technical assistance; Employee matching gifts; Matching/challenge support.
Limitations: Giving primarily in the metropolitan Baltimore, MD, area. No grants for operating expenses, sponsorship of fundraising events,

symposiums, conferences, or annual giving campaigns.
Publications: Application guidelines.
Application information: ABAG application with inclusion of the foundation's specific requirements as outlined in the guidelines accepted. Application form not required.
 Initial approach: Letter
 Copies of proposal: 1
 Deadline(s): None
 Board meeting date(s): Mar., May, July, Oct., and Dec.
 Final notification: Letter from Exec. Dir. upon receipt of proposal
Officers and Directors:* Walter D. Pinkard, Jr.,* Pres.; Robert G. Merrick III,* V.P.; Robert M. Pinkard,* Secy.; Gregory C. Pinkard,* Treas.; Robert W. Schaefer, Exec. Dir.; Redmond C.S. Finney; Freeman A. Hrabowski III.
Number of staff: 1 full-time professional; 2 part-time professional; 1 full-time support; 2 part-time support.
EIN: 526072964
Selected grants: The following grants were reported in 2005.
$1,304,065 to Baltimore Community Foundation, Baltimore, MD.
$1,000,000 to Hippodrome Performing Arts Center, Baltimore, MD.
$540,000 to Nature Conservancy, Bethesda, MD.
$506,000 to University of Baltimore Educational Foundation, Baltimore, MD.
$500,000 to Towson University, Towson, MD. For endowment for scholastic-based scholarship program.
$300,000 to Historic East Baltimore Community Action Coalition (HEBCAC), Baltimore, MD. For facility renovation and neighborhood revitalization.
$300,000 to Learning, Inc., Baltimore, MD. For facility renovations.
$250,000 to Center Stage, Baltimore, MD. For technology and building renovation portion of capital campaign.
$250,000 to Garrett-Jacobs Mansion Endowment Fund, Baltimore, MD. To restore public rooms in historic mansion.
$160,000 to YMCA of Central Maryland, Baltimore, MD.
$100,333 to United Way of Central Maryland, Baltimore, MD.
$50,000 to Baltimore Choral Arts Society, Baltimore, MD.
$50,000 to Caroline Center, Baltimore, MD. For renovation of space to move and expand job creation facility.
$50,000 to Concert Artists of Baltimore, Baltimore, MD. To strengthen infrastructure.
$50,000 to Echo Hill Outdoor School, Worton, MD.
$50,000 to Friendship School, Eldersburg, MD. To construct new facility.
$50,000 to Junior League of Baltimore, Baltimore, MD. For facility renovation and expansion.
$10,500 to Hiding Place, Baltimore, MD.
$10,035 to Saint Timothys School, Stevenson, MD.
$10,000 to School 33 Art Center, Baltimore, MD. To purchase technology for capacity building.

3633
The Carl M. Freeman Foundation, Inc.
18330 Village Mart Dr., 2nd Fl.
Olney, MD 20832
Contact: Cheryl C. Kagan, Exec. Dir.

FAX: (240) 779-8180;
E-mail: cheryl@freemanfoundation.org; URL: http://www.freemanfoundation.org

Established in 1960.
Donor: Carl M. Freeman Charitable Lead Trust†.
Foundation type: Independent foundation.
Financial data (yr. ended 12/31/04): Assets, $13,496,112 (M); gifts received, $1,374,785; expenditures, $1,905,651; qualifying distributions, $1,126,987; giving activities include $1,103,156 for grants.
Purpose and activities: The Carl M. Freeman Foundation is committed to making a meaningful difference in the communities it serves. The foundation is particularly dedicated to supporting local arts, social service, religious, and educational organizations. Preference will be given to challenge grants and new initiatives that enhance existing programs.
Fields of interest: Performing arts; Performing arts centers; Arts; Education; Human services; Child development, services; Jewish federated giving programs; Jewish agencies & temples.
Type of support: Employee matching gifts; Equipment; General/operating support; Continuing support; Annual campaigns; Program development; Technical assistance; Matching/challenge support.
Limitations: Giving in the Washington, DC, area, including MD and VA, and Sussex County, DE. No support for religious organizations for religious work. No grants to individuals.
Publications: Application guidelines; Annual report; Grants list.
Application information: Application information and guidelines available on foundation Web site. Application form required.
  Deadline(s): See foundation Web site for current deadlines
  Board meeting date(s): Generally on a quarterly basis
Officers and Trustees:* Joshua M. Freeman,* Chair. and Pres.; Stephen B. Huttler,* Secy.; Christine A. Shreve,* Treas.; Cheryl C. Kagan, Exec. Dir.; Michelle D. Freeman.
Number of staff: 1 full-time professional; 1 part-time professional; 1 full-time support.
EIN: 526047536
Selected grants: The following grants were reported in 2003.
$250,000 to Boys and Girls Club, Olney, Olney, MD.
$200,000 to Washington Opera, DC.
$15,000 to Ivymount School, Rockville, MD.
$10,000 to National Gallery of Art, DC.
$8,000 to Our House, Brookeville, MD.
$1,700 to Montgomery County Coalition for the Homeless, Rockville, MD.
$1,500 to Adventure Theater, Glen Echo, MD.
$1,500 to American University, DC.
$1,000 to Community Bridges, Silver Spring, MD.
$1,000 to Dwelling Place, Gaithersburg, MD.

3634
GEICO Philanthropic Foundation ✧
c/o GEICO Corp.
5260 Western Ave.
Chevy Chase, MD 20815 (301) 986-3802
Contact: David L. Schindler, Chair.

Established in 1980 in DC.
Donor: Government Employees Insurance Co.
Foundation type: Company-sponsored foundation.

Financial data (yr. ended 12/31/05): Assets, $36,772,384 (M); gifts received, $7,566,073; expenditures, $3,695,100; qualifying distributions, $3,668,997; giving activities include $3,641,497 for 1,246 grants (high: $246,042; low: $15), and $27,500 for 11 grants to individuals (high: $2,500; low: $2,500).
Purpose and activities: The foundation supports organizations involved with substance abuse, safety, and the insurance industry and awards grants to active and retired federal employees.
Fields of interest: Substance abuse, services; Safety, education; Business/industry.
Type of support: General/operating support; Employee matching gifts; Grants to individuals.
Limitations: Giving primarily in San Diego, CA, Washington, DC, Lakeland, FL, Macon, GA, Long Island, NY, Dallas, TX, and Fredericksburg, VA. No support for political organizations or religious organizations not of direct benefit to the entire community. No grants to individuals (except for Public Service Awards).
Application information: Application form not required.
  Initial approach: Proposal
  Deadline(s): Oct. 1 for Public Service Awards
  Board meeting date(s): Quarterly
Officers and Directors:* David L. Schindler, Chair.; Charles R. Davies,* Pres. and Genl. Counsel; Jan C. Stewart, Secy.; Michael H. Campbell,* Treas.; Nancy L. Pierce; Rynthia M. Rost; Thomas A. Wells.
Number of staff: 1 full-time professional.
EIN: 521202740

3635
Lowell & Harriet Glazer Family Foundation ✧
(formerly Lowell R. Glazer Family Foundation)
9690 Deereco Rd., Ste. 500
Timonium, MD 21093

Established in 1989 in MD.
Donor: Lowell R. Glazer.
Foundation type: Independent foundation.
Financial data (yr. ended 12/31/05): Assets, $1,500,056 (M); gifts received, $430,210; expenditures, $630,398; qualifying distributions, $601,206; giving activities include $595,266 for 73 grants (high: $249,000; low: $50).
Purpose and activities: Giving for emergency relief services, Jewish organizations, a hospital, and higher education.
Fields of interest: Higher education; Education; Health care; Human services; Jewish agencies & temples.
Limitations: Applications not accepted. Giving primarily in MD. No grants to individuals.
Application information: Contributes only to pre-selected organizations.
Trustees: John P. Abosch; Lowell R. Glazer; Gerald M. Katz.
EIN: 521633239

3636
Morris Goldseker Foundation of Maryland, Inc. ▼ ✧
1040 Park Ave., Ste. 310
Baltimore, MD 21201 (410) 837-5100
Contact: Carol Gilbert, Prog. Off.

FAX: (410) 837-7927;
E-mail: cgilbert@goldsekerfoundation.org;
URL: http://www.goldsekerfoundation.org

Incorporated in 1973 in MD.
Donor: Morris Goldseker†.
Foundation type: Independent foundation.
Financial data (yr. ended 12/31/05): Assets, $97,697,131 (M); expenditures, $4,806,047; qualifying distributions, $4,163,683; giving activities include $3,241,375 for 98 grants (high: $200,000; low: $35; average: $5,000–$50,000).
Purpose and activities: In 2000, the Goldseker Foundation's Board of Trustees and its Selection Committee adopted a two-track approach to grantmaking. This approach designates priority areas that build on existing experience and investments, but it also retains the ability to respond to new ideas and opportunities within the established program areas. The foundation's grantmaking funds will focus on the first-track priority areas. In these areas - community development, regionalism, and the nonprofit sector - the foundation will be a more directly engaged and active partner. The existing grantmaking policies apply to the priority areas. Grants will include a mix of foundation initiatives and projects submitted independently by potential grantees. The second track focuses on the foundation's established program areas: neighborhood development, community affairs, human services, and education.
Fields of interest: Education; Human services; Community development, neighborhood development; Public affairs, association.
Type of support: Program development; Seed money; Technical assistance; Consulting services; Matching/challenge support.
Limitations: Giving limited to the Baltimore, MD, area. No support for advocacy or political action groups, religious purposes, arts or cultural affairs, specific diseases or disabilities, or for projects normally financed with public funds. No grants to individuals, or for building or endowment funds, deficit financing, annual campaigns, or publications.
Publications: Annual report; Informational brochure (including application guidelines).
Application information: Submit preliminary letter as early as possible before deadlines. Application form not required.
  Initial approach: Letter or telephone inquiry
  Copies of proposal: 1
  Deadline(s): Jan. 1, Apr. 1, and Aug. 1
  Board meeting date(s): Distribution committee meets 3 times a year (Mar., June, and Oct.)
  Final notification: Following committee meetings
Officers and Directors:* Sheldon Goldseker,* Chair.; Simon Goldseker,* Vice-Chair.; Timothy D. Armbruster, Ph.D., C.E.O. and Pres.; Sheila L. Purkey, V.P. and Secy-Treas.; Ana Goldseker; Deborah Goldseker; Sharna Goldseker; Susan B. Katzenberg; Howard M. Weiss.
Advisory Selection Committee: William R. Brody; Earl S. Richardson; Marc B. Terrill.
Number of staff: 2 full-time professional; 2 part-time professional; 1 full-time support.
EIN: 520983502
Selected grants: The following grants were reported in 2004.
$208,500 to Johns Hopkins University, Baltimore, MD. For Goldseker Scholars Program, providing financial aid to undergraduates from Baltimore metropolitan area.

$208,500 to Morgan State University, Baltimore, MD. For Goldseker Fellows Program and student participation in Morgan State University Academy of Finance at Lake Clifton-Eastern High School.

$208,500 to The Associated: Jewish Community Federation of Baltimore, Baltimore, MD. For continued support for Goldseker Foundation Aid and Education Fund, helping new immigrants settling in Baltimore region become independent and self-supporting.

$150,000 to Greater Homewood Community Corporation, Baltimore, MD. For continued support for general operating expenses and for community and economic development staff.

$150,000 to Healthy Neighborhoods, Baltimore, MD. For general support.

$125,000 to Baltimore Neighborhood Collaborative, Baltimore, MD. For new Regional Equity Initiative and continued support for Neighborhood Revitalization Fund.

$125,000 to East Baltimore Development, Baltimore, MD. For project planning and management for development of new community school.

$120,000 to Citizens Planning and Housing Association, Baltimore, MD. For support for staff working on transit and housing issues.

$90,000 to Southeast Community Development Corporation, Baltimore, MD. For revitalization staff, general operations, and organizational development.

$75,000 to Patterson Park Community Development Corporation, Baltimore, MD. For core staff support and general operations.

3637
The Goldsmith Family Foundation, Inc. ✧
1829 Reisterstown Rd., Ste. 430
Baltimore, MD   21208   (410) 484-7700
Contact: Alan Berkowitz, Secy.-Treas.

Established in 1990 in MD.
Foundation type: Independent foundation.
Financial data (yr. ended 9/30/05): Assets, $19,463,355 (M); gifts received, $250; expenditures, $1,301,364; qualifying distributions, $981,261; giving activities include $852,452 for 131 grants (high: $100,000; low: $100).
Purpose and activities: Giving primarily for elementary schools, the arts, health associations, human services, and Jewish organizations and temples.
Fields of interest: Arts; Elementary school/education; Higher education; Education; Health organizations, association; Human services; Children/youth, services; Federated giving programs; Jewish federated giving programs; Jewish agencies & temples.
Type of support: General/operating support; Scholarship funds.
Limitations: Giving primarily in Baltimore, MD.
Application information:
Initial approach: Letter
Deadline(s): None
Officers: Beth Goldsmith, Pres. and Mgr.; Raymond Altman, V.P.; Alan Berkowitz, Secy.-Treas.
EIN: 521714353

3638
W. R. Grace Foundation, Inc. ✧
7500 Grace Dr.
Columbia, MD   21044   (410) 531-4000
Contact: W. Brian McGowan, Chair.

Incorporated in 1996 in FL.
Donor: W.R. Grace & Co.
Foundation type: Company-sponsored foundation.
Financial data (yr. ended 12/31/04): Assets, $3,936,025 (M); expenditures, $1,184,224; qualifying distributions, $1,144,908; giving activities include $1,056,686 for 128 grants (high: $112,000; low: $61), and $87,193 for employee matching gifts.
Purpose and activities: The foundation supports organizations involved with arts and culture, education, conservation, health, human services, children and youth, community development, and civic affairs.
Fields of interest: Arts; Elementary/secondary education; Higher education; Education; Environment, natural resources; Health care; Children/youth, services; Human services; Community development; Federated giving programs; Government/public administration.
Type of support: Program development; Employee matching gifts; General/operating support.
Limitations: Giving primarily in areas of company operations.
Application information: Application form not required.
Initial approach: Proposal
Deadline(s): None
Officers: W. Brian McGowan, Chair.; William M. Corcoran, V.P.; Mark A. Shelnitz, Secy.; Robert M. Tarola, Treas.
EIN: 650630671
Selected grants: The following grants were reported in 2004.
$100,000 to Grace Institute, New York, NY.
$24,000 to Keystone Center, Keystone, CO.
$15,000 to Columbia Festival of the Arts, Columbia, MD.
$10,000 to Massachusetts State Science Fair, Lincoln, MA.
$10,000 to McNeese State University, Lake Charles, LA.
$10,000 to Middle Tennessee State University, Murfreesboro, TN.
$5,000 to Boston Lyric Opera Company, Boston, MA.
$5,000 to Boston Symphony Orchestra, Boston, MA.
$5,000 to Huntington Theater Company, Boston, MA.
$3,500 to Aiken Technical College, Aiken, SC.

3639
Monica and Hermen Greenberg Foundation ✧
7501 Wisconsin Ave., Ste. 1103
Bethesda, MD   20814   (301) 215-7997

Established in 1980 in DC.
Donors: Hermen Greenberg; Monica Greenberg.
Foundation type: Independent foundation.
Financial data (yr. ended 11/30/05): Assets, $503,650 (M); gifts received, $495,984; expenditures, $535,443; qualifying distributions, $533,905; giving activities include $532,576 for 76 grants (high: $111,844; low: $100).

Purpose and activities: Giving primarily for the arts and to Jewish organizations; funding also for health associations, and to horse shows.
Fields of interest: Museums (art); Performing arts; Performing arts centers; Performing arts, opera; Arts; Education; Health organizations, association; Recreation, parks/playgrounds; Athletics/sports, equestrianism; Jewish federated giving programs; Jewish agencies & temples.
Limitations: Giving primarily in the Washington, DC, metro area, including Bethesda, MD. No grants to individuals.
Application information:
Initial approach: Proposal
Deadline(s): None
Final notification: Within 2 months
Officers: Hermen Greenberg, Pres.; Monica Greenberg, V.P.
EIN: 521187884
Selected grants: The following grants were reported in 2004.
$95,000 to John F. Kennedy Center for the Performing Arts, DC. 3 grants: $45,000, $45,000, $5,000
$40,000 to National Gallery of Art, DC. 2 grants: $15,000, $25,000
$15,000 to Washington International Horse Show, Gaithersburg, MD.
$12,000 to Sibley Memorial Hospital, DC. 2 grants: $10,000, $2,000
$2,500 to Red Auerbach Youth Foundation, Boston, MA.
$2,000 to Suburban Hospital, Bethesda, MD.

3640
Louis H. Gross Foundation, Inc.
c/o B. Waldholtz
P.O. Box 217
Riderwood, MD   21139

Established in 1959 in NY.
Donor: Frank Sutland†.
Foundation type: Independent foundation.
Financial data (yr. ended 12/31/05): Assets, $8,922,630 (M); gifts received, $38,002; expenditures, $481,689; qualifying distributions, $455,475; giving activities include $455,475 for 38 grants (high: $82,500; low: $500).
Purpose and activities: Giving primarily for child welfare, including pediatric centers and programs for physically or learning disabled youth.
Fields of interest: Hospitals (general); Children/youth, services; Disabilities, people with.
Limitations: Applications not accepted. Giving primarily in Baltimore, MD, and New York, NY. No grants to individuals.
Application information: Contributes only to pre-selected organizations.
Board meeting date(s): Annually
Officers and Directors:* Sheila S. Pakula,* Pres.; Baila P. Waldholtz, Secy.; Annette Pakula; Lawrence Pakula; Dale E. Perreault.
EIN: 146018307

3641
The Homer and Martha Gudelsky Family Foundation, Inc. ✧
c/o Medda Gudelsky
11900 Tech Rd.
Silver Spring, MD   20904

Incorporated in 1968 in MD.
Donors: Members of the Gudelsky family; Percontee, Inc.
Foundation type: Independent foundation.
Financial data (yr. ended 12/31/05): Assets, $25,759,953 (M); expenditures, $1,486,916; qualifying distributions, $1,450,031; giving activities include $1,450,031 for 16 grants (high: $500,000; low: $31).
Fields of interest: Performing arts, theater; Higher education; Engineering school/education; Environment, research; Health care, information services; Health care.
Type of support: Annual campaigns; Capital campaigns; Building/renovation; Equipment; Scholarship funds; Research.
Limitations: Applications not accepted. Giving primarily in MD. No grants to individuals, or for books, movies or CD's.
Application information: Unsolicited requests for funds not accepted. Contributes only to pre-selected organizations.
Officers and Directors:* John Gudelsky,* Pres.; Martha Gudelsky,* V.P.; Medda Gudelsky,* V.P.; Rita Regino,* V.P.; Holly Stone,* V.P.; Jonathan Genn,* Secy.; Samuel Yedlin, Treas.
EIN: 520885969
Selected grants: The following grants were reported in 2003.
$500,000 to Hippodrome Performing Arts Center, Baltimore, MD.
$250,000 to University of Maryland-Baltimore County, Baltimore, MD.
$100,000 to Atlantic General Hospital, Berlin, MD.
$100,000 to Capitol College, Laurel, MD.
$30,000 to School 33 Art Center, Baltimore, MD.
$25,000 to University of Maryland Medical System Foundation, Baltimore, MD.
$20,000 to Enterprise Community Partners, Columbia, MD.
$10,000 to National Museum of Women in the Arts, DC.
$5,000 to Florence Fuller Child Development Center, Boca Raton, FL.
$1,000 to Boca Raton Community Hospital, Boca Raton, FL.

3642

The Hackerman Foundation, Inc. ✧
300 E. Joppa Rd., 8th Fl.
Baltimore, MD   21286-3048

Foundation type: Independent foundation.
Financial data (yr. ended 12/31/05): Assets, $7,019,493 (M); gifts received, $3,049,901; expenditures, $3,111,592; qualifying distributions, $3,111,592; giving activities include $3,100,000 for 9 grants (high: $500,000; low: $100,000).
Purpose and activities: Giving primarily for higher education and the National Archives.
Fields of interest: Higher education; Jewish federated giving programs.
Limitations: Applications not accepted. Giving primarily in Bethesda, MD. No grants to individuals.
Application information: Contributes only to pre-selected organizations.
Officers: Willard Hackerman, Pres.; Nancy Hackerman, V.P.; Steven Hackerman, V.P.; Lillian Hackerman, Secy.-Treas.
EIN: 521459149
Selected grants: The following grants were reported in 2005.

$500,000 to Case Western Reserve University, Cleveland, OH.
$500,000 to Johns Hopkins University, Baltimore, MD.
$500,000 to MedStar Health, Columbia, MD.
$150,000 to Baltimore School for the Arts, Baltimore, MD.

3643

LaVerna Hahn Charitable Trust ✧
7 Saint Paul St., Ste. 1400
Baltimore, MD   21202-1626   (410) 347-8786
Contact: Robert Sloan, Tr.

Established in 1987 in MD.
Foundation type: Independent foundation.
Financial data (yr. ended 11/30/05): Assets, $28,840,892 (M); expenditures, $1,417,098; qualifying distributions, $1,353,755; giving activities include $1,292,167 for 48 grants (high: $200,000; low: $1,500).
Purpose and activities: Giving primarily for health associations, higher education, and health care with emphasis on hospices; funding also for arts and culture, social services, and for religious purposes.
Fields of interest: Museums; Arts; Higher education; Hospitals (general); Health care; Health organizations, association; Cancer; Human services; Residential/custodial care, hospices; Women, centers/services; Federated giving programs; Religion.
Type of support: Capital campaigns; Building/renovation.
Limitations: Giving primarily in Baltimore, MD. No grants to individuals.
Application information: Application form not required.
   Initial approach: Letter
   Deadline(s): None
Trustee: Robert Sloan.
EIN: 521585047
Selected grants: The following grants were reported in 2005.
$391,667 to Hospice of Baltimore, Baltimore, MD. 3 grants: $125,000, $166,667, $100,000
$80,000 to Hopewell Cancer Support, Brooklandville, MD. 2 grants: $30,000, $50,000
$25,000 to Family and Childrens Services of Central Maryland, Baltimore, MD.
$25,000 to Saint Marys College of Maryland, Saint Marys City, MD.
$15,000 to Baltimore Opera Company, Baltimore, MD.
$10,000 to Enoch Pratt Free Library, Baltimore, MD.
$10,000 to Everyman Theater, Baltimore, MD.

3644

The Howard and Martha Head Foundation, Inc.
(formerly The Howard and Martha Head Fund, Inc.)
901 S. Bond St., Ste. 400
Baltimore, MD   21231

Established around 1989 in MD.
Donor: Howard Head†.
Foundation type: Independent foundation.
Financial data (yr. ended 12/31/05): Assets, $3,274,216 (M); expenditures, $432,584; qualifying distributions, $414,985; giving activities include $399,962 for 60 grants (high: $157,500; low: $30).

Purpose and activities: Giving primarily for federated giving programs, as well as for the arts, education, and human services.
Fields of interest: Arts; Higher education; Education; Zoos/zoological societies; Human services; Federated giving programs.
Type of support: Continuing support; Annual campaigns; Program development.
Limitations: Applications not accepted. Giving on a national basis, with some emphasis on Vail, CO. No grants to individuals.
Application information: Contributes only to pre-selected organizations.
Officers and Trustees:* Michael D. Hankin,* Pres.; Martha Head,* V.P.
EIN: 521268755

3645

The Hecht-Levi Foundation, Inc. ✧
c/o Mercantile-Safe Deposit & Trust Co.
766 Old Hammonds Ferry Rd.
Linthicum, MD   21090-1323
Contact: Blanche Roche
Application address: c/o Mercantile Safe Deposit & Trust Co., 2 Hopkins Plz., Baltimore, MD 21201

Incorporated in 1958 in MD.
Donors: Alexander Hecht†; Selma H. Hecht†; Robert H. Levi†; Ryda H. Levi.
Foundation type: Independent foundation.
Financial data (yr. ended 12/31/05): Assets, $17,622,424 (M); expenditures, $785,825; qualifying distributions, $721,033; giving activities include $720,333 for 77 grants (high: $125,000; low: $1,500; average: $2,000–$10,000).
Purpose and activities: Giving primarily for education and the arts.
Fields of interest: Visual arts; Performing arts; Performing arts, theater; Performing arts, music; Arts; Higher education; Human services; Jewish federated giving programs.
Limitations: Giving primarily in the metropolitan Baltimore, MD, area. No grants to individuals.
Application information: Application form not required.
   Initial approach: Proposal
   Copies of proposal: 1
   Deadline(s): Apr. 15 and Oct. 15
   Board meeting date(s): June and Dec.
   Final notification: 2-3 months after receipt of proposal
Officers and Directors:* Sandra L. Gerstung,* Pres.; Richard H. Levi,* V.P. and Treas.; Alexander H. Levi,* V.P.; Ryda H. Levi, V.P.; Wilbert H. Sirota,* Secy.
EIN: 526035023
Selected grants: The following grants were reported in 2005.
$125,000 to Baltimore Community Foundation, Baltimore, MD.
$50,000 to Baltimore Museum of Art, Baltimore, MD. 2 grants: $40,000, $10,000
$10,500 to Maryland Institute College of Art, Baltimore, MD. 2 grants: $3,000, $7,500
$7,500 to Conservation International, DC.
$6,250 to Environmental Defense, New York, NY.
$5,000 to United Way of Central Maryland, Baltimore, MD.
$5,000 to Wesleyan University, Middletown, CT.
$2,000 to Everyman Theater, Baltimore, MD.

3646
The Helena Foundation ✧
P.O. Box 625
Crownsville, MD   21032-0625

Established in 1987 in MD.
Donor: Margaret H. Earl†.
Foundation type: Independent foundation.
Financial data (yr. ended 12/31/05): Assets,
$28,152,462 (M); expenditures, $1,458,573;
qualifying distributions, $1,456,236; giving
activities include $1,456,236 for 25 grants (high:
$352,400; low: $1,000).
Purpose and activities: Giving primarily to colleges
and universities; some support also for elementary
and secondary education, the arts, and hospitals.
Fields of interest: Arts; Elementary/secondary
education; Higher education; Environment, land
resources; Hospitals (general).
Type of support: General/operating support; Capital
campaigns; Endowments.
Limitations: Applications not accepted. Giving
primarily in Boston, MA and MD. No grants to
individuals.
Application information: Contributes only to
pre-selected organizations.
Officers and Directors:* James A. Earl,* Pres. and
Treas.; Sylvia Earl,* V.P. and Secy.
EIN: 521522573
Selected grants: The following grants were reported
in 2005.
$352,400 to Anne Arundel Medical Center,
Annapolis, MD.
$179,100 to Wheelock College, Boston, MA.
$177,700 to Trust for Public Land, DC.
$176,310 to Massachusetts Institute of
Technology, Cambridge, MA.
$100,780 to Enoch Pratt Free Library, Baltimore,
MD.
$47,720 to University of Minnesota, Minneapolis,
MN.
$47,720 to University of Nebraska Foundation,
Omaha, NE.
$29,630 to Saint Johns College, Annapolis, MD.
$6,000 to Eastern Shore Land Conservancy,
Queenstown, MD.
$5,000 to Chesapeake Bay Foundation, Annapolis,
MD.

3647
John and Maureen Hendricks Charitable
Foundation ✧ ☆
1 Discovery Pl.
Silver Spring, MD   20910-3354

Established in 2001 in MD.
Donors: John S. Hendricks; Maureen D. Hendricks.
Foundation type: Operating foundation.
Financial data (yr. ended 3/31/05): Assets,
$16,364 (M); gifts received, $600,000;
expenditures, $595,000; qualifying distributions,
$595,000; giving activities include $595,000 for 24
grants (high: $100,000; low: $5,000).
Fields of interest: Visual arts; Education;
Environment, natural resources; Health care;
Human services; International relief; Rural
development; Physically disabled.
Type of support: General/operating support.
Limitations: Applications not accepted. Giving on a
national basis. No grants to individuals.
Application information: Contributes only to
pre-selected organizations.

Trustees: John S. Hendricks; Maureen D. Hendricks;
Eric W. Shaw.
EIN: 137180307

3648
The Richard A. Henson Foundation, Inc. ✧
P.O. Box 151
Salisbury, MD   21803-0151
Contact: Donna S. Ashby, Exec. Dir.
FAX: (410) 742-4036;
E-mail: dashby_md@yahoo.com; URL: http://
www.richardhensonfoundation.org

Established in 1989 in MD; funded in 1990.
Donor: Richard A. Henson†.
Foundation type: Independent foundation.
Financial data (yr. ended 12/31/05): Assets,
$31,586,130 (M); gifts received, $5,310;
expenditures, $1,740,345; qualifying distributions,
$1,300,548; giving activities include $1,254,608
for 19+ grants (high: $520,000).
Purpose and activities: To enrich the quality of life
primarily, but not exclusively, in the greater
Salisbury, MD, area.
Fields of interest: Arts; Higher education; Hospitals
(general); Children/youth, services; Federated giving
programs.
Type of support: Continuing support; Annual
campaigns; Capital campaigns; Building/
renovation; Equipment; Endowments; Scholarship
funds; In-kind gifts; Matching/challenge support.
Limitations: Giving primarily on the Eastern Shore
and the Salisbury, MD, area. No grants to
individuals.
Publications: Application guidelines; Financial
statement; Informational brochure.
Application information: Application information
and guidelines available on foundation Web site.
Submission of full application forms are by invitation
only.
Initial approach: Letter of inquiry (not to exceed 3
pages)
Copies of proposal: 8
Deadline(s): 30th of month
Board meeting date(s): Monthly
Final notification: Within 30 days
Officers and Trustees:* Jon P. Sherwell,*
Vice-Chair.; Thomas F. McCarthy,* Secy.; Thomas L.
Trice IV, Treas.; Donna S. Ashby, Exec. Dir.; Thomas
H. Evans; Stephen R. Farrow; Gordon D. Gladden;
Davis R. Ruark.
Number of staff: 1 full-time professional.
EIN: 521642558

3649
Corina Higginson Trust
3400 Bryan Point Rd.
Accokeek, MD   20607   (301) 283-2113
Contact: Wilton C. Corkern, Tr.
FAX: (301) 283-2049;
E-mail: wcockern@accokeek.org; URL: http://
www.corinahigginsontrust.org

Trust established in 1962 in DC.
Donor: Corina Higginson†.
Foundation type: Independent foundation.
Financial data (yr. ended 12/31/05): Assets,
$5,654,640 (M); expenditures, $467,121;
qualifying distributions, $410,474; giving activities
include $404,200 for 75 grants (high: $50,000;
low: $1,000; average: $5,000–$10,000).

Purpose and activities: The trust makes gifts
primarily for the benefit of the Washington, DC,
metropolitan area for charitable and educational
purposes.
Fields of interest: Arts; Education; Environment;
Human services.
Type of support: General/operating support;
Continuing support; Program development;
Conferences/seminars; Publication; Seed money;
Curriculum development; Internship funds;
Research; Exchange programs; Matching/challenge
support.
Limitations: Giving primarily in the Washington, DC,
area, including portions of MD and VA. No support
for medical or health-related programs or
organizations. No grants to individuals, or for
endowment funds or scholarship funds.
Publications: Application guidelines.
Application information: WG Common Grant
Application Form strongly encouraged. Application
form required.
Initial approach: Proposal, letter, or telephone
Copies of proposal: 7
Deadline(s): Mar. 1 and Sept. 1
Board meeting date(s): May and Nov.
Final notification: May and Nov
Trustees: Charles C. Abeles; Wilton C. Corkern, Jr.;
Alexander Mackay-Smith, Jr.; Virginia L.
Mackay-Smith; Floretta Dukes McKenzie.
EIN: 526055743

3650
The David and Barbara B. Hirschhorn
Foundation, Inc.
c/o AFS
10 E. Baltimore St., Ste. 1101
Baltimore, MD   21202-1620   (410) 347-7201
Contact: Betsy F. Ringel, Exec. Dir.
E-mail: info@blafund.org

Established in 1986 in MD.
Donors: Barbara B. Hirschhorn; David Hirschhorn†.
Foundation type: Independent foundation.
Financial data (yr. ended 12/31/05): Assets,
$39,011,653 (M); expenditures, $2,030,682;
qualifying distributions, $1,914,446; giving
activities include $1,834,492 for 96 grants (high:
$500,000; low: $683).
Fields of interest: Human services; International
relief; Civil rights, race/intergroup relations; Jewish
federated giving programs; Jewish agencies &
temples; Religion, interfaith issues.
Type of support: General/operating support; Annual
campaigns; Capital campaigns; Endowments.
Limitations: Giving primarily in the metropolitan
Baltimore, MD, area. No grants to individuals or for
fundraisers; no loans.
Application information: Application form not
required.
Initial approach: Letter
Copies of proposal: 1
Deadline(s): None
Final notification: 4 to 6 months
Officers and Trustees:* Barbara B. Hirschhorn,*
Chair.; Daniel B. Hirschhorn,* V.P.; Michael J.
Hirschhorn,* V.P.; Sarah H. Shapiro,* V.P.; Deborah
H. Vogelstein,* V.P.; Lynn Wintriss, Secy.; Maureen
Stewart, Treas.; Betsy F. Ringel, Exec. Dir.
EIN: 521489400
Selected grants: The following grants were reported
in 2004.
$66,666 to LifeBridge Health, Baltimore, MD.

$50,000 to Chizuk Amuno Congregation, Baltimore, MD.

$40,000 to Maimonides Academy of Baltimore, Baltimore, MD.

$35,000 to American Jewish Committee, New York, NY.

$31,500 to United Way of Central Maryland, Baltimore, MD.

$25,000 to Legal Aid Bureau, Baltimore, MD.

$20,000 to Kennedy Krieger Institute, Baltimore, MD.

$15,000 to Art With a Heart, Baltimore, MD.

$12,500 to AMIT Women, New York, NY.

$12,500 to Dystonia Medical Research Foundation, Chicago, IL.

3651
Hittman Family Foundation, Inc. ✧
3211 Keyser Rd.
Baltimore, MD   21208

Established in 1998 in MD.
Donors: Fred Hittman; Sandra Hittman.
Foundation type: Independent foundation.
Financial data (yr. ended 12/31/04): Assets, $4,570,749 (M); expenditures, $363,373; qualifying distributions, $330,219; giving activities include $320,000 for 26 grants (high: $100,000; low: $1,000).
Fields of interest: Performing arts, music; Animal welfare; Jewish agencies & temples.
Limitations: Applications not accepted. Giving primarily in MD. No grants to individuals.
Application information: Contributes only to pre-selected organizations.
Officers and Directors:* Stephen J. Hittman,* Pres.; Sandra Hittman, Secy.-Treas.; Karen E. Gober; Judith E. Hittman; Stanley E. Kosin; Shale D. Stiller.
EIN: 911937345
Selected grants: The following grants were reported in 2004.
$100,000 to American Society for Technion-Israel Institute of Technology, New York, NY.

$10,000 to Baltimore Opera Company, Baltimore, MD.

$9,000 to Food Allergy and Anaphylaxis Network, Fairfax, VA.

$5,000 to Glenelg Country School, Glenelg, MD.

$2,000 to Baltimore Museum of Art, Baltimore, MD.

$1,000 to Baltimore Symphony Orchestra, Baltimore, MD.

$1,000 to Everyman Theater, Baltimore, MD.

$1,000 to Shriver Hall Concert Series, Baltimore, MD.

$1,000 to Walters Art Museum, Baltimore, MD.

3652
Hoffberger Foundation, Inc.
101 W. Mount Royal Ave.
Baltimore, MD   21201-5781   (410) 369-9336
FAX: (410) 369-9337;
E-mail: info@hoffbergerfoundation.org; URL: http://www.hoffbergerfoundation.org/main.html

Incorporated in 1941 in MD.
Donor: The Hoffberger family.
Foundation type: Independent foundation.
Financial data (yr. ended 12/31/04): Assets, $21,826,318 (M); gifts received, $500; expenditures, $768,792; qualifying distributions,

$779,561; giving activities include $694,416 for 43 grants (high: $104,000; low: $300).
Purpose and activities: The foundation's mission is to respond with available resources to unmet needs in the greater Baltimore, MD, community, with a significant commitment to the Jewish community.
Fields of interest: Theological school/education; Education; Human services; Children/youth, services; Community development, neighborhood development; Economic development; Jewish federated giving programs; Jewish agencies & temples.
International interests: Israel.
Type of support: General/operating support; Continuing support; Building/renovation; Endowments; Program development; Seed money; Scholarship funds; Matching/challenge support.
Limitations: Giving primarily in Baltimore, MD. No grants to individuals; no loans.
Publications: Application guidelines; Grants list; Program policy statement; Program policy statement (including application guidelines).
Application information: Application form required.
    Initial approach: Letter of inquiry
    Copies of proposal: 1
    Deadline(s): Rolling
    Final notification: Varies
Officers and Directors:* LeRoy E. Hoffberger,* Chair.; Bruce Hoffberger,* Pres.; Sue Gross,* V.P.; David Hoffberger,* Secy.; Patricia A. Facetta, Cont.; Heller H. Zainman, Exec. Dir.; Louise Goodman; C. Peter Hoffberger.
Number of staff: 1 part-time professional; 1 part-time support.
EIN: 520794249

3653
HRLD Foundation, Inc. ✧
P.O. Box 2249
Columbia, MD   21045-1249   (443) 259-4011
Contact: David R. Huber, Dir.

Established in 1997 in MD.
Donors: David R. Huber; Debra Huber.
Foundation type: Independent foundation.
Financial data (yr. ended 12/31/03): Assets, $3,819,686 (M); expenditures, $864,848; qualifying distributions, $825,313; giving activities include $825,313 for 4 grants (high: $60,000; low: $10,000).
Purpose and activities: Giving primarily for higher education, particularly for electrical engineering; funding also for mental health services and the United Way.
Fields of interest: Higher education; Mental health/crisis services; Federated giving programs; Mormon agencies & churches.
Limitations: Giving on a national basis, with emphasis on MD, UT, and VA.
Application information:
    Initial approach: Letter
    Deadline(s): None
Directors: David R. Huber; Debra Huber.
EIN: 311531885

3654
Howard Hughes Medical Institute ✧
c/o Office of Grants and Special Progs.
4000 Jones Bridge Rd.
Chevy Chase, MD   20815-6789   (301) 215-8500
Contact: For general inquiries: Dr. Peter J. Bruns, V.P., Grants and Special Progs.; Dr. William R. Galey, Prog. Dir., Grad. Prog.; Stephen A. Barkanic, Prog. Dir., Undergrad Prog.; Dr. Jill G. Conley, Prog. Dir., International Prog., Precollege Prog., Research Resources Prog.; Dr. Dennis Liu, Prog. Dir., Educational Products
FAX: (301) 215-8888; E-mail: grantswww@hhmi.org; URL: http://www.hhmi.org
Additional tel.: (800) 448-4882

Incorporated in 1953 in DE.
Donor: Howard R. Hughes†.
Financial data (yr. ended 8/31/04): Assets, $15,396,735,408 (M); expenditures, $640,853,700; giving activities include $57,627,987 for 563 grants (high: $1,600,000; low: $114), and $446,782,710 for foundation-administered programs.
Purpose and activities: The purpose of the Institute is promotion of human knowledge within the field of basic sciences (chiefly medical research and education) and the effective application thereof to benefit mankind. The Institute is a medical research organization, not a private foundation, under federal tax codes. Through its Medical Research Program, the Institute's scientists conduct fundamental biomedical research throughout the U.S. in the fields of cell biology, computational biology, genetics, immunology, neuroscience, and structural biology. Through its Office of Grants and Special Programs, the Institute awards grants for education in biology and related sciences, funds research at medical schools, and supports fundamental research abroad. The emphasis of the grants program is graduate, undergraduate, and precollege and public science education. Graduate support is primarily awarded under two programs: 1) Research Training Fellowships for Med. Students. Deadline: early Jan.; 2) HHMI-NIH Research Scholars Program. Deadline: Jan. 10. The Undergraduate Science Education Program, awards grants to colleges and universities for 1) student research and expanding access in the sciences; 2) science equipment and lab renovations; 3) faculty and curriculum development; and 4) outreach programs in the sciences and mathematics with elementary and secondary schools, and with junior/community colleges. The HHMI Professors awards, an Undergraduate Program initiative, supports and empowers accomplished research scientists in transmitting the excitement and values of scientific research to undergraduate education. The Institute continues to monitor trends in science education and science, including public and private support. The Precollege Science Education Program addresses concerns about science literacy in the general population by engaging K-12 students, teachers, and families in science education.
Fields of interest: Secondary school/education; Higher education; Medical school/education; Education; Biomedicine; Medical research, institute; Biological sciences; Minorities; Asians/Pacific Islanders; African Americans/Blacks; Hispanics/Latinos; Native Americans/American Indians.
International interests: Argentina; Australia; Bangladesh; Brazil; Bulgaria; Canada; Chile; Czech Republic; Estonia; France; Germany; Greece;

Guinea; Hungary; India; Israel; Lithuania; Mexico; Poland; Russia; Slovakia; South Africa; Switzerland; Taiwan; Uganda; Ukraine; United Kingdom; Uruguay; Venezuela.

Type of support: Building/renovation; Equipment; Program development; Professorships; Curriculum development; Fellowships; Research; Program evaluation; Grants to individuals.

Limitations: Giving on a national and international basis. Graduate, undergraduate, and precollege grants are nationwide; grants to foreign scientists made in selected countries. Some graduate fellowships given outside the U.S. Research grants have gone to scientists in Canada and Mexico (1991), Australia, New Zealand, and the United Kingdom (1992), The Baltics, Cent. Europe, and the former Soviet Union (1995), Argentina, Brazil, Canada, Chile, Mexico, and Venezuela (1997), and Australia, Bangladesh, Bulgaria, Czech Republic, Estonia, France, Germany, Greece, Guinea, Hungary, India, Israel, Lithuania, Mexico, Poland, Russia, Slovak Republic, South Africa, Switzerland, Taiwan, Uganda, Ukraine, United Kingdom, Uruguay, Venezuela (2000). No support for biomedical research in the U.S., except to scientists employed by the Institute; no grants or fellowships except to individuals or institutions competing under established science education programs. No grants for conferences or publications.

Publications: Application guidelines; Annual report; Informational brochure (including application guidelines); Newsletter; Occasional report; Program policy statement.

Application information: Applicants should consult guidelines in program announcements prior to application. Fellowships and grants are awarded on the basis of national or international competitions. Proposals for Undergraduate Science Education Program and the Precollege Science Education Program are by invitation only. For the HHMI Professors awards, each invited institution may nominate up to two faculty members. In addition to the science education programs, grants are awarded to biomedical scientists in specified countries under the international program. Awards in all programs are based on peer review. Application form required.

Initial approach: Letter, proposal, or application, depending on program
Deadline(s): Request program announcements for program-specific deadlines
Board meeting date(s): Feb., May, Aug., and Nov.
Final notification: Each grants program has an individual notification date; program brochures and announcements should be consulted

Officers: Thomas R. Cech, Ph.D., Pres.; Peter J. Bruns, Ph.D., V.P., Grants and Special Progs.; David A. Clayton, Ph.D., V.P. and Chief Scientific Off.; Stephen M. Cohen, V.P. and C.F.O.; Joan S. Leonard, V.P. and Genl. Counsel; Avice A. Meehan, V.P. for Comm. and Pub. Affairs; Gerald M. Rubin, Ph.D., V.P. and Dir., Research Campus Janelia Farm; Nestor V. Santiago, V.P. and C.I.O.

Trustees: Hanna H. Gray, Ph.D., Chair.; James A. Baker III; Alexander G. Bearn, M.D.; Frank William Gay; Joseph L. Goldstein, M.D.; Garnett L. Keith; Jeremy R. Knowles, Ph.D.; William R. Lummis; Sir Paul Nurse; Anne M. Tatlock.

Number of staff: 2479 full-time professional; 64 part-time professional; 484 full-time support; 105 part-time support.

EIN: 590735717

3655
The Hussman Foundation, Inc. ✧ ☆
5136 Dorsey Hall Dr.
Ellicott City, MD 21042

Established in 2005 in MD.
Donor: John P. Hussman.
Foundation type: Independent foundation.
Financial data (yr. ended 6/30/05): Assets, $1,559,669 (M); gifts received, $1,944,121; expenditures, $386,066; qualifying distributions, $386,066; giving activities include $386,066 for 2 grants (high: $266,203; low: $119,863).
Fields of interest: Medical research.
Limitations: Applications not accepted. No grants to individuals.
Application information: Contributes only to pre-selected organizations.
Officers and Directors:* John P. Hussman,* Pres. and Treas.; John Kenney,* V.P. and Dir.; Brooke Steinau, Secy.; Paula Kluth.
EIN: 202062883

3656
ISE Cultural Foundation, Inc. ✧
P.O. Box 267
Galena, MD 21635-0267
Contact: Tomi Ise
Application address: 555 Broadway, New York, NY 10012, tel.: (212) 925-1649; FAX: (212) 226-9362; E-mail: info@isefoundation.org; URL: http://www.isefoundation.org

Established in 1983.
Donor: N.H. Ise.
Foundation type: Independent foundation.
Financial data (yr. ended 12/31/04): Assets, $169,642 (M); gifts received, $28,721; expenditures, $488,857; qualifying distributions, $485,994; giving activities include $485,994 for 13 grants (high: $324,544; low: $20).
Purpose and activities: The foundation supports exchanges of art and culture (mainly visual art) between the nations for its objective that enhances the devotion to development of Japanese esthetics and culture as well as deepens mutual understandings of culture in terms of demographically and ethnographically diverse society. Provides grants for cultural exchange activities between Japan and the U.S.
Fields of interest: Arts.
International interests: Japan.
Type of support: General/operating support; Fellowships.
Limitations: Giving primarily in NY.
Publications: Application guidelines; Informational brochure.
Application information: Application form not required.
Initial approach: Proposal
Deadline(s): The last business day of Feb. and Aug.
Final notification: 2-3 months
Officers and Trustees:* Isaac Shapiro,* Chair. and Secy.; Hikonobu Ise,* Pres.; Gerald Curtis, V.P.; Donald Keene,* V.P.; Ryuzo Sejima, V.P.; Seiji Tsutsumi,* V.P.
Number of staff: 2 full-time professional; 1 part-time professional.
EIN: 222530466

3657
The James M. Johnston Trust for Charitable and Educational Purposes ▼ ✧
2 Wisconsin Cir., Ste. 600
Chevy Chase, MD 20815 (301) 907-0135
Contact: Julie Sanders, Admin. Asst.

Trust established in 1968 in DC.
Donor: James M. Johnston†.
Foundation type: Independent foundation.
Financial data (yr. ended 12/31/04): Assets, $84,346,835 (M); expenditures, $4,848,063; qualifying distributions, $4,107,907; giving activities include $3,900,000 for 54 grants (high: $1,707,052; low: $10,000; average: $10,000–$50,000).
Purpose and activities: Grants largely to higher and secondary educational institutions located in Washington, DC, and NC. This includes support for scholarships, training of nurses, and faculty salaries.
Fields of interest: Secondary school/education; Higher education; Nursing school/education.
Type of support: Scholarship funds.
Limitations: Giving primarily in Washington, DC, and NC. No support for private foundations. No grants to individuals.
Application information: Application form required.
Initial approach: Letter
Copies of proposal: 1
Deadline(s): None
Board meeting date(s): Monthly
Final notification: 30 days
Trustees: Barnum L. Colton, Jr.; W. Dunbar Gram; Betty F. Hayes.
Number of staff: 1 full-time professional.
EIN: 237019796
Selected grants: The following grants were reported in 2004.
$2,085,000 to University of North Carolina, Chapel Hill, NC. 2 grants: $1,707,052 (For scholarships), $377,948 (For budget).
$185,000 to Wesleyan University, Middletown, CT. For scholarships.
$90,000 to Culver Educational Foundation, Culver, IN. For faculty salaries.
$70,000 to National Rehabilitation Hospital, DC. For nursing continuing education.
$60,000 to Trinity College, Hartford, CT. For scholarships.
$50,000 to Childrens National Medical Center, DC. For nursing continuing education.
$50,000 to Hospital for Sick Children, DC. For general support.
$45,000 to Sibley Memorial Hospital, DC. For nursing training.
$25,000 to Norwood School, Bethesda, MD. For faculty salaries.

3658
Jonan Foundation, Inc. ✧
701 Maiden Choice Ln.
Baltimore, MD 21228

Established in 1992 in MD.
Donor: John C. Erickson.
Foundation type: Independent foundation.
Financial data (yr. ended 12/31/04): Assets, $32,333 (M); gifts received, $349,000; expenditures, $343,700; qualifying distributions,

$343,547; giving activities include $343,550 for 23 grants (high: $100,000; low: $100).

Purpose and activities: Giving primarily for education, health associations, and human services.

Fields of interest: Elementary/secondary education; Education; Health organizations, association; Human services; Children/youth, services; Federated giving programs; Christian agencies & churches.

Limitations: Applications not accepted. Giving primarily in Baltimore, MD. No grants to individuals.

Application information: Contributes only to pre-selected organizations.

Officers and Directors: * John C. Erickson, Pres.; Nancy A. Erickson,* V.P.; Paul L. Erickson, Secy.; Andrea C. Erickson; Craig A. Erickson; Mark R. Erickson; Scott R. Erickson.

EIN: 521803663

Selected grants: The following grants were reported in 2003.

$20,000 to Saint Josephs Pro-Cathedral, Camden, NJ.

$20,000 to United Way of Central Maryland, Baltimore, MD.

$15,000 to Parks and People Foundation for Baltimore Recreation and Parks, Baltimore, MD.

$5,000 to Juvenile Diabetes Research Foundation International, New York, NY.

$2,500 to Catonsville Community College, Catonsville, MD.

$1,000 to Baltimore Freedom Academy, Baltimore, MD.

$1,000 to Baltimore School for the Arts, Baltimore, MD.

$630 to Saint Vincent de Paul Society, Baltimore, MD.

$140 to My Sisters Circle, Timonium, MD.

$100 to Little Sisters of the Poor, Baltimore, MD.

3659
Charles I. & Mary Kaplan Foundation ✧

6001 Montrose Rd., Ste. 403
Rockville, MD   20852-4872   (202) 293-6930
Contact: Edward H. Kaplan, Secy.-Treas.

Established in 1956 in DE.

Donors: Joan L. Gindes; Edward H. Kaplan; Jerome A. Kaplan.

Foundation type: Independent foundation.

Financial data (yr. ended 12/31/05): Assets, $25,409,120 (M); gifts received, $463,950; expenditures, $960,502; qualifying distributions, $605,000; giving activities include $605,000 for 3 grants (high: $455,000; low: $50,000).

Purpose and activities: Giving primarily to a Jewish federated giving program, as well as to other Jewish organizations, and a children's hospital.

Fields of interest: Hospitals (specialty); Human services; Jewish federated giving programs; Jewish agencies & temples.

Limitations: Giving primarily in New York, NY and Rockville, MD. No grants to individuals.

Application information:
   Initial approach: Letter
   Deadline(s): None

Officers: Jerome A. Kaplan, Pres.; Joan L. Gindes, V.P.; Irene Kaplan, V.P.; Edward H. Kaplan, Secy.-Treas.

EIN: 526043928

Selected grants: The following grants were reported in 2004.

$375,000 to Jewish Federation of Greater Washington, Rockville, MD.

3660
The Kay Family Foundation, Inc. ✧

(formerly L & S Foundation)
8720 Georgia Ave., Ste. 410
Silver Spring, MD   20910
Contact: Jack Kay, Pres.

Established in 1976 in MD.

Donors: Jack Kay; Ina Kay†; Lauren Hawkins; Shelley Joan Melrod.

Foundation type: Independent foundation.

Financial data (yr. ended 12/31/05): Assets, $14,170,966 (M); gifts received, $700,000; expenditures, $529,418; qualifying distributions, $483,260; giving activities include $483,260 for 31 grants (high: $142,000; low: $2,500; average: $5,000–$10,000).

Purpose and activities: Giving for education, health and human services, and for Jewish organizations.

Fields of interest: Performing arts, dance; Higher education; Hospitals (specialty); Cancer research; Human services; Jewish federated giving programs.

Limitations: Giving primarily in MD; some funding in New York, NY, and Washington, DC. No grants to individuals.

Application information:
   Initial approach: Letter
   Deadline(s): None

Officers: Jack Kay, Pres. and Treas.; Lauren K. Pollin, V.P.; Shelley Joan Melrod, Secy.

EIN: 521045650

3661
Grayce B. Kerr Fund, Inc. ✧

117 Bay St.
Easton, MD   21601   (410) 822-6652
Contact: Sheryl V. Kerr, Pres.
FAX: (410) 822-4546; E-mail: gbkf@bluecrab.org

Chartered in 1986 in OK; reincorporated in 1993 in MD.

Donors: Grayce B. Kerr Flynn†; Breene M. Kerr.

Foundation type: Independent foundation.

Financial data (yr. ended 12/31/04): Assets, $32,240,036 (M); expenditures, $2,458,399; qualifying distributions, $2,113,460; giving activities include $1,713,791 for 40+ grants (high: $250,000).

Purpose and activities: Major area of interest is education, including higher, secondary, elementary, and early childhood education; support also for environmental conservation, museums, public policy research, and nonprofit organizations focused on improving the quality of life.

Fields of interest: Museums; Museums (marine/maritime); Elementary/secondary education; Education, early childhood education; Higher education; Environment, natural resources; Cancer research; Medical research; Community development; Public policy, research.

Type of support: Capital campaigns; Building/renovation; Equipment; Endowments; Program development; Professorships; Publication; Curriculum development; Scholarship funds; Research; Employee matching gifts; Matching/challenge support.

Limitations: Giving primarily in MD. No grants to individuals, or for continuing support.

Publications: Application guidelines; Grants list; Multi-year report.

Application information: Application form required.
   Initial approach: Telephone
   Copies of proposal: 1
   Deadline(s): None
   Final notification: 3 months after final proposal is submitted

Officers: Breene M. Kerr, Chair.; Sheryl V. Kerr, Pres. and Secy.; James S. Maffitt, V.P.; John R. Valliant, Treas.

Trustees: Collin W. Scarborough; Marcy Kerr Yuknat.

Number of staff: 1 full-time professional; 1 full-time support.

EIN: 731256124

Selected grants: The following grants were reported in 2004.

$250,000 to Island Institute, Rockland, ME.

$200,000 to Massachusetts Institute of Technology, Cambridge, MA.

$150,000 to Chesapeake College, Wye Mills, MD.

$125,000 to Coastal Maine Botanical Gardens, Boothbay, ME.

$80,000 to Academy Art Museum, Easton, MD.

$64,633 to Marine Environmental Research Institute, Blue Hill, ME.

$40,000 to Country School, Easton, MD.

$8,118 to Washington College, Chestertown, MD.

$5,000 to Alliance for the Chesapeake Bay, Baltimore, MD.

$3,000 to Chesapeake Bay Maritime Museum, Saint Michaels, MD.

3662
The Ralph and Shirley Klein Foundation, Inc.

2101 Rockspring Rd.
Forest Hill, MD   21050
Contact: Shirley S. Klein, Secy.

Established in 1991 in MD.

Donors: Klein's Super Markets, Inc.; Colgate Investments; Shirley S. Klein.

Foundation type: Company-sponsored foundation.

Financial data (yr. ended 12/31/03): Assets, $1,746,041 (M); gifts received, $5,000; expenditures, $320,320; qualifying distributions, $319,508; giving activities include $319,940 for 32 grants (high: $200,000; low: $100).

Purpose and activities: The foundation supports organizations involved with arts and culture, education, health, human services, and Judaism.

Fields of interest: Arts; Higher education, college (community/junior); Education; Medical care, in-patient care; Health care; Children/youth, services; Human services; Federated giving programs; Jewish federated giving programs; Jewish agencies & temples.

Type of support: Continuing support; Annual campaigns; Capital campaigns; Curriculum development; Scholarship funds.

Limitations: Giving primarily in MD, with emphasis on Hartford County. No grants to individuals.

Publications: Occasional report.

Application information: Application form not required.
   Initial approach: Proposal
   Board meeting date(s): 1st of every month
   Final notification: 1 month

Officers and Director: Ralph L. Klein, Pres.; Howard S. Klein, V.P.; Michael J. Klein, V.P.; Shirley S. Klein, Secy.; Marshall Klein.

EIN: 521763518

Selected grants: The following grants were reported in 2003.

$200,000 to Upper Chesapeake Health Foundation, Bel Air, MD. For general support.

$35,000 to Jewish National Fund, New York, NY. For general support.

$25,000 to Harford Jewish Center, Havre de Grace, MD. For general support.

$10,000 to ARC, Northern Chesapeake Region, Aberdeen, MD. For general support.

$8,000 to YMCA, Harford County Family, Bel Air, MD. For general support.

$6,000 to John Carroll School, Bel Air, MD. For general support.

$5,000 to Franklin and Marshall College, Lancaster, PA. For general support.

$4,000 to University of Maryland-College Park Foundation, College Park, MD. For general support.

$2,004 to McDonogh School, Owings Mills, MD. For general support.

$2,000 to American Committee for Shaare Zedek Hospital in Jerusalem, Baltimore, MD. For general support.

3663

The John W. Kluge Foundation ▼ ✧

15004 Sunflower Ct.
Rockville, MD 20853-1748 (301) 929-9340
Contact: Edward A. Hopkins, Treas.

Established in 1990 in DE and MD.

Donor: John W. Kluge.

Foundation type: Independent foundation.

Financial data (yr. ended 9/30/05): Assets, $64,479,699 (M); gifts received, $280,000; expenditures, $5,851,523; qualifying distributions, $5,807,402; giving activities include $5,799,190 for 31 grants (high: $600,000; low: $1,000; average: $10,000–$500,000).

Purpose and activities: Giving primarily for higher education, medical research, and science.

Fields of interest: Higher education; Medical research; Science.

Type of support: Research; General/operating support; Scholarship funds; Grants to individuals.

Limitations: Applications not accepted.

Application information: Unsolicited requests for funds not accepted.

Officers and Trustees:* John W. Kluge,* Chair. and Pres.; David Finkelstein,* V.P.; Stuart Subotnick,* V.P.; Kevin J. O'Brien, Secy.; Edward A. Hopkins,* Treas.; Edward M. Campbell; Maria T. Kluge.

EIN: 521720688

Selected grants: The following grants were reported in 2005.

$1,396,635 to Library of Congress, DC. 3 grants: $500,000 (For National Digital Library), $500,000 (For Leadership Development Trust Fund), $396,635 (For Creative Space: Fifty Years of Robert Blackburn's Printmaking Workshop).

$700,000 to Archdiocese of Washington, DC. For general support.

$600,000 to Rockefeller University, New York, NY. For general support.

$500,000 to Exploring the Arts, New York, NY. For general support.

$390,000 to University of Massachusetts Medical School at Worcester, Worcester, MA. For general support for Medical School Fund.

$350,000 to Stone Barns Restoration Corporation, New York, NY. For general support.

$250,000 to Southern Methodist University, Dallas, TX. For general support.

$150,000 to American Academy in Berlin, New York, NY. For general support.

3664

Knapp Educational Fund, Inc.

P.O. Box O
St. Michaels, MD 21663

Established in 1979 in MD.

Donor: The Knapp Foundation, Inc.

Foundation type: Independent foundation.

Financial data (yr. ended 12/31/05): Assets, $5,081,612 (M); expenditures, $1,755,633; qualifying distributions, $1,737,000; giving activities include $1,689,319 for 12 grants (high: $1,350,000; low: $2,500).

Purpose and activities: Support for education, including scholarship awards for children of employees of Macmillan, Inc.

Fields of interest: Education.

Type of support: Employee-related scholarships.

Limitations: Applications not accepted. Giving primarily on the East Coast. No grants to individuals (except employee-related scholarships).

Application information: Unsolicited requests for funds not accepted.

Officers and Trustees:* Antoinette P. Vojvoda,* Pres.; Ruth M. Capranica,* V.P. and Secy.; Steven F. Capranica,* Treas.; Sylvia V. Penny.

EIN: 132970128

3665

The Knapp Foundation, Inc.

P.O. Box O
St. Michaels, MD 21663 (410) 745-5660
Contact: Ruth M. Capranica, V.P.

Incorporated in 1929 in NC.

Donor: Joseph Palmer Knapp‡.

Foundation type: Independent foundation.

Financial data (yr. ended 12/31/05): Assets, $20,815,627 (M); expenditures, $1,324,715; qualifying distributions, $1,170,234; giving activities include $1,027,657 for 32 grants (high: $285,000; low: $3,800).

Purpose and activities: Grants primarily for conservation and preservation of wildlife and wildfowl, and for assistance to college and university libraries in the purchasing of reading materials and equipment to improve education.

Fields of interest: Higher education; Libraries/library science; Animals/wildlife, preservation/protection.

Type of support: Equipment; Matching/challenge support.

Limitations: Giving limited to the U.S., primarily in the eastern region, including CT, DE, FL, GA, MA, MD, ME, NC, NH, NJ, NY, PA, RI, SC, VA, and VT. No support for foreign projects. No grants to individuals, or for endowment or building funds, operating budgets, or research.

Publications: Application guidelines.

Application information: Application form not required.

Initial approach: Letter
Copies of proposal: 1
Deadline(s): Quarterly
Board meeting date(s): Dec.; executive board meets quarterly
Final notification: 90 days

Officers and Trustees:* Antoinette P. Vojvoda,* Pres.; Ruth M. Capranica,* V.P. and Secy.; Steven F. Capranica,* Treas.; Krista L. Hodgkin; Margaret P. Newcombe; Sylvia V. Penny.

Number of staff: 1 part-time professional.

EIN: 136001167

Selected grants: The following grants were reported in 2004.

$500,000 to Nature Conservancy, Arlington, VA.

$43,275 to Philadelphia Zoo, Philadelphia, PA.

$36,500 to North Carolina Coastal Federation, Newport, NC.

$30,000 to Coalition for Buzzards Bay, New Bedford, MA.

$25,000 to Tufts University, Medford, MA.

$19,600 to Elmwood Park Zoo, Norristown, PA.

$14,500 to Mercer University, Macon, GA.

$12,830 to North Carolina Zoological Society, Asheboro, NC.

$12,600 to Keystone College, La Plume, PA.

$11,600 to Wetlands Institute, Stone Harbor, NJ.

3666

The Marion I. and Henry J. Knott Foundation, Inc.

3904 Hickory Ave.
Baltimore, MD 21211-1834 (410) 235-7068
Contact: Gregory Cantori, Exec. Dir.
FAX: (410) 889-2577;
E-mail: knott@knottfoundation.org; URL: http://www.knottfoundation.org

Established in 1977 in MD as successor to the first Marion I. and Henry J. Knott Foundation, Inc.

Donors: Marion I. Knott†; Henry J. Knott, Sr.†.

Foundation type: Independent foundation.

Financial data (yr. ended 12/31/05): Assets, $61,809,900 (M); gifts received, $402,307; expenditures, $2,997,549; qualifying distributions, $2,420,403; giving activities include $1,896,456 for 139 grants (high: $70,000; low: $10,000), and $50,000 for loans/program-related investments (high: $25,000; low: $12,500).

Purpose and activities: Giving for Roman Catholic activities and other charitable, cultural, educational, and health and human service organizations. Areas of interest include the fine and performing arts; Roman Catholic and non-sectarian private schools; higher, adult, and vocational education; hospitals and health services, including hospices and programs for the mentally ill; social and family services, including youth, the elderly, the handicapped, and the homeless; and community development and civic affairs.

Fields of interest: Humanities; Arts; Elementary school/education; Secondary school/education; Health care; Human services; Roman Catholic agencies & churches.

Type of support: General/operating support; Management development/capacity building; Capital campaigns; Building/renovation; Equipment; Land acquisition; Endowments; Emergency funds; Program development; Technical assistance; Program evaluation; Program-related investments/loans; Employee matching gifts; Matching/challenge support.

Limitations: Giving limited to Baltimore City and Allegheny, Anne Arundel, Baltimore, Carroll, Frederick, Garrett, Harford, Howard, and Washington counties, MD. No support for public education, public sector agencies, the environment, day care centers, single-disease organizations, pass-through agencies, pro-choice activities or reproductive health programs, or organizations in operation for less than one year. No grants to individuals, or for annual giving, medical research, legal services, endowment funds for the arts or humanities, one-time events, seminars, or workshops, or scholarships.
Publications: Financial statement; Grants list.
Application information: Application guidelines available on foundation Web site and upon request; do not fax or e-mail proposals. Application form not required.
  Copies of proposal: 2
  Deadline(s): Feb. 1 and Aug. 1
  Board meeting date(s): June and Dec.
  Final notification: 1 month
Officers: Martin F. Porter, Pres.; Owen M. Knott, V.P; Margie Riehl, Secy.; Marion I. Knott, Treas.; Gregory Cantori, Exec. Dir.
Trustees: Lindsay R. Gallagher; Kelly L. Harris; Eric C. Knott; Marion I. Knott; Martin G. Knott, Sr.; Martin G. Knott, Jr.; Owen M. Knott; Ann Lindsay Marsh; Peter R. McGill; David L. Porter; Joanna O. Porter; Martin F. Porter; Margie M. Riehl; Brooke Rodgers; Patrick Rodgers; Geralynn D. Smyth; John C. Smyth; Patrick J. Smyth; Peggy Smyth; Jan Steendam; Alice K. Voelkel.
Number of staff: 1 full-time professional; 2 full-time support; 1 part-time support.
EIN: 521517876

3667
Koppel Family Charitable Foundation ◇
c/o Grace Anne Dorney Koppel
10701 Ardnave Pl.
Potomac, MD 20854-1261

Established in 1999 in MD.
Donors: Edward J. Koppel; Grace Anne Dorney Koppel; Boston University.
Foundation type: Independent foundation.
Financial data (yr. ended 12/31/04): Assets, $1,903,310 (M); gifts received, $637,798; expenditures, $530,811; qualifying distributions, $525,000; giving activities include $525,000 for 13 grants (high: $75,000; low: $20,000).
Fields of interest: Human services.
Limitations: Applications not accepted. Giving primarily in Washington, DC, MA, MD, and New York, NY. No grants to individuals.
Application information: Contributes only to pre-selected organizations.
Officers and Directors:* Grace Anne Dorney Koppel,* Pres.; Edward J. Koppel,* V.P.
EIN: 522214925
Selected grants: The following grants were reported in 2003.
$75,000 to Luther Place Memorial Church, DC. For general support.
$75,000 to So Others Might Eat (SOME), DC. For general support.
$30,000 to House of Hope, Oakland, MD. For general support.

3668
The Abraham and Ruth Krieger Family Foundation, Inc. ◇
(formerly The Krieger Fund, Inc.)
3908 N. Charles St., Ste. 303
Baltimore, MD 21218
Contact: Howard K. Cohen, V.P.

Incorporated in 1944 in MD.
Donors: Abraham Krieger†; Jane K. Shapiro; Howard K. Cohen.
Foundation type: Independent foundation.
Financial data (yr. ended 12/31/05): Assets, $7,106,742 (M); expenditures, $400,371; qualifying distributions, $329,123; giving activities include $323,660 for 29 grants (high: $143,660; low: $500).
Purpose and activities: Emphasis on Jewish welfare funds; support also for secondary education, higher education and human services.
Fields of interest: Secondary school/education; Higher education; Human services; Jewish federated giving programs; Jewish agencies & temples.
Limitations: Applications not accepted. Giving primarily in Baltimore, MD. No grants to individuals.
Application information: Unsolicited requests for funds not accepted.
  Board meeting date(s): As required
Officers: Jane K. Shapiro, Pres.; Joann C. Fruchtman, V.P. and Secy.; Howard K. Cohen, V.P. and Treas.
Trustees: Nancy Cohen; Jack Fruchtman, Jr.; Liana Fruchtman; Alyssa C. Zelman.
EIN: 526035537

3669
Krongard Foundation, Inc. ◇
(formerly The Albert & Gloria Lion Foundation)
901 S. Bond St.
Baltimore, MD 21231
Application address: c/o A.B. Krongard, 1400 W. Seminary Ave., Lutherville, MD 21093

Established in 1956.
Donors: A.B. Krongard; Patricia L. Krongard.
Foundation type: Independent foundation.
Financial data (yr. ended 12/31/05): Assets, $234,544 (M); expenditures, $370,757; qualifying distributions, $370,000; giving activities include $370,000 for 5 grants (high: $200,000; low: $10,000).
Fields of interest: Elementary school/education; Medical school/education.
Limitations: Giving primarily in Baltimore, MD. No grants to individuals.
Application information:
  Initial approach: Letter
  Deadline(s): None
Officers: Timothy L. Krongard, Pres.; Alexander L. Krongard, V.P.; A.B. Krongard, Secy.; Randall H. Krongard, Treas.
EIN: 526054495

3670
George H. Langenfelder Charitable Trust ◇ ☆
c/o Bank Of America, N.A.
10 Light St., MD4-302-17-06
Baltimore, MD 21202

Established in 2005 in MD.
Foundation type: Independent foundation.
Financial data (yr. ended 6/30/05): Assets, $12,970,674 (M); gifts received, $7,039,666; expenditures, $579,739; qualifying distributions, $474,636; giving activities include $474,136 for 6 grants (high: $79,024; low: $79,020).
Fields of interest: Health care; Health organizations.
Limitations: Applications not accepted. Giving primarily in MD. No grants to individuals.
Application information: Contributes only to pre-selected organizations.
Trustees: Barbara Ann Spicer; Bank of America, N.A.
EIN: 546548865

3671
Lawless Family Foundation ◇ ☆
c/o M.S. Hellauer
6225 Smith Ave.
Baltimore, MD 21209-3600

Established in 2002 in MD.
Donor: Robert J. Lawless.
Foundation type: Independent foundation.
Financial data (yr. ended 12/31/05): Assets, $2,260,801 (M); gifts received, $69,836; expenditures, $584,273; qualifying distributions, $574,000; giving activities include $559,000 for 5 grants (high: $250,000; low: $15,000).
Purpose and activities: Giving primarily for higher education.
Fields of interest: Higher education; Roman Catholic federated giving programs.
Limitations: Giving primarily in Baltimore and Hunt Valley, MD, and Lookout Mountain, GA. No grants to individuals.
Application information:
  Initial approach: Letter
  Deadline(s): None
Officer: Kristin Susan Lawless Miniotos, Exec. Dir.
Trustee: Robert J. Lawless.
EIN: 030486725

3672
Legg Mason Charitable Foundation, Inc. ◇
100 Light St.
Baltimore, MD 21202 (410) 539-0000
Contact: Carol Gay, Secy.

Donor: Legg Mason, Inc.
Foundation type: Company-sponsored foundation.
Financial data (yr. ended 3/31/04): Assets, $5,419,932 (M); gifts received, $3,713,167; expenditures, $1,339,015; qualifying distributions, $1,339,015; giving activities include $1,339,015 for 60 grants (high: $228,500; low: $75).
Purpose and activities: The foundation supports Christian agencies and churches and organizations involved with arts and culture, education, health, youth development, and human services.
Fields of interest: Museums (art); Performing arts, orchestra (symphony); Arts; Higher education; Education; Health organizations, association; Crime/law enforcement, police agencies; Youth development; Residential/custodial care, hospices; Human services; Federated giving programs; Christian agencies & churches.
Limitations: Giving primarily in Baltimore, MD.
Application information: Application form not required.

Initial approach: Telephone
Deadline(s): None
Officers: Raymond Mason, Pres.; Peter L. Bain, V.P.; Carol Gay, Secy.; Charles J. Daley, Treas.
EIN: 311738146

3673
John J. Leidy Foundation, Inc. ◆
305 W. Chesapeake Ave., Ste. 308
Towson, MD 21204 (410) 821-3006
Contact: W. Michel Pierson, Pres.
E-mail: Leidyfd@attglobal.net

Incorporated in 1957 in MD.
Donor: John J. Leidy†.
Foundation type: Independent foundation.
Financial data (yr. ended 12/31/04): Assets, $12,432,633 (M); expenditures, $541,509; qualifying distributions, $501,116; giving activities include $447,350 for 76 grants (high: $50,000; low: $350).
Fields of interest: Higher education; Food services; Human services; Children/youth, services; Federated giving programs; Disabilities, people with.
Type of support: General/operating support; Building/renovation; Equipment; Program development; Scholarship funds.
Limitations: Giving primarily in the metropolitan Baltimore, MD, area. No grants to individuals.
Application information: Application form not required.
Initial approach: Proposal
Copies of proposal: 5
Deadline(s): None
Board meeting date(s): Monthly
Officers: W. Michel Pierson, Pres.; Ruth C. Pear, V.P.; Robert Pierson, Secy.; Henry E. Pear, Treas.
EIN: 526034785
Selected grants: The following grants were reported in 2003.
$54,000 to Maryland Institute College of Art, Baltimore, MD. 2 grants: $4,000, $50,000
$50,000 to Baltimore Hebrew Congregation, Baltimore, MD.
$29,000 to Associated Jewish Charities of Baltimore, Baltimore, MD.
$13,500 to Govans Ecumenical Development Corporation, Baltimore, MD.
$10,000 to Community Law Center, Baltimore, MD.
$10,000 to Northwest Hospital Center, Randallstown, MD.
$7,500 to Baltimore Station, Baltimore, MD.
$7,500 to Shepherds Clinic, Baltimore, MD.
$7,000 to Mission of Mercy, Emmitsburg, MD.

3674
Lerner Family Foundation ◆
c/o Jeffrey K. Gonya
1829 Reisterstown Rd., Ste. 420
Baltimore, MD 21208

Established in 1997 in MD.
Donor: Mark Lerner.
Foundation type: Independent foundation.
Financial data (yr. ended 11/30/05): Assets, $6,417,509 (M); gifts received, $3,000,000; expenditures, $1,045,131; qualifying distributions, $1,020,762; giving activities include $1,018,019 for 40 grants (high: $318,000; low: $100).
Fields of interest: Education; Hospitals (general); Hospitals (specialty); Human services; Jewish

federated giving programs; Jewish agencies & temples.
Type of support: General/operating support; Capital campaigns.
Limitations: Applications not accepted. Giving primarily in Baltimore, MD. No grants to individuals.
Application information: Contributes only to pre-selected organizations.
Trustees: Mark Lerner; Traci Lerner.
EIN: 522073256
Selected grants: The following grants were reported in 2005.
$100,000 to Capital Camps, Rockville, MD.
$68,529 to Chizuk Amuno Foundation, Baltimore, MD.
$20,000 to Teach for America, New York, NY.
$8,500 to Hillel of Greater Baltimore, Baltimore, MD.
$5,250 to American Society for Technion-Israel Institute of Technology, New York, NY.
$250 to Students in Free Enterprise, Springfield, MO.

3675
Annette M. and Theodore N. Lerner Family Foundation, Inc. ◆
11501 Huff Ct.
Kensington, MD 20895-1094 (301) 984-1500

Established in 1986 in MD.
Donors: Edward L. Cohen; Mark D. Lerner; Theodore N. Lerner; Robert K. Tanenbaum; Annette M. Lerner; Debra L. Cohen; Marla L. Tanenbaum.
Foundation type: Independent foundation.
Financial data (yr. ended 12/31/04): Assets, $4,011,715 (M); expenditures, $2,075,029; qualifying distributions, $2,071,016; giving activities include $2,070,600 for 52 grants (high: $500,000; low: $250).
Purpose and activities: Giving for education and Jewish organizations.
Fields of interest: Arts; Elementary/secondary education; Higher education, university; Theological school/education; Human services; Jewish federated giving programs; Jewish agencies & temples.
Type of support: General/operating support.
Limitations: Applications not accepted. Giving primarily in Washington, DC, and MD. No grants to individuals.
Application information: Contributes only to pre-selected organizations.
Officers and Directors: * Marla L. Tanenbaum, Pres.; Mark D. Lerner,* V.P.; Debra L. Cohen,* Secy.; Annette M. Lerner,* Treas.; Theodore N. Lerner.
EIN: 521528436

3676
The Levitt Foundation ◆
(formerly Richard S. Levitt Foundation)
c/o Richard S. Levitt
6001 Montrose Rd., Ste. 600
Rockville, MD 20852

Established in 1957 in IA.
Donor: Members of the Levitt Family.
Foundation type: Independent foundation.
Financial data (yr. ended 12/31/04): Assets, $12,934,894 (M); gifts received, $96,796; expenditures, $1,568,657; qualifying distributions,

$1,491,001; giving activities include $1,491,001 for 102 grants (high: $422,500; low: $15).
Purpose and activities: Giving primarily for Jewish agencies and federated giving programs; some support also for the performing arts and other cultural programs, higher education, and social services.
Fields of interest: Performing arts; Arts; Higher education; Human services; Jewish federated giving programs; Jewish agencies & temples.
Type of support: Annual campaigns.
Limitations: Applications not accepted. Giving primarily in Washington, DC, Des Moines, IA, Chicago, IL, and Minneapolis, MN. No grants to individuals.
Application information: Contributes only to pre-selected organizations.
Officers: Richard S. Levitt, Pres. and Treas.; Mark Levitt, V.P.; Randall Levitt, V.P.; Jeanne Levitt, Secy.
EIN: 426052427
Selected grants: The following grants were reported in 2003.
$413,000 to Walker Art Center, Minneapolis, MN.
$409,830 to Des Moines Art Center, Des Moines, IA.
$105,025 to University of Iowa Foundation, Iowa City, IA.
$35,000 to Minneapolis Institute of Arts, Minneapolis, MN.
$29,000 to Jewish United Fund of Metropolitan Chicago, Chicago, IL.
$10,000 to United Way of Central Iowa, Des Moines, IA.
$5,000 to Brandeis University, Waltham, MA.
$1,800 to Jewish Community Center of Greater Washington, Rockville, MD.
$1,000 to Hillel of Greater Washington, Rockville, MD.
$430 to Yeshiva of Greater Washington, Silver Spring, MD.

3677
Life Sciences Research Foundation ◆
3520 San Martin Dr.
Baltimore, MD 21218 (410) 467-2597
Contact: Christine Pratt, Treas.
E-mail: lsrf@ciwemb.edu; URL: http://www.lsrf.org
Application address: Susan DiRenzo, Life Sciences Research Foundation, c/o Lewis Thomas Laboratory, Princeton University, Washington Rd., Princeton, NJ 08544, tel.: (609) 258-3551, E-mail: sdirenzo@molbio.princeton.edu

Changed status to a private foundation in 1984 in MD.
Donors: Linda W. Brown; Dept. of Energy, Energy Biosciences Research Division; The Bristol-Myers Squibb Pharmaceutical Research Institute; The Burroughs Wellcome Fund; Merck Research Laboratories; GlaxoSmithKline; Wyeth; Abbott Laboratories; Amgen Inc.; Ellison Medical Foundation; Lilly Research Foundation; Rett Syndrome Research Foundation; Pfizer Inc.; The O'Donnell Foundation; Gilead Sciences, Inc.; Johnson and Johnson; Lilly Research Laboratories; Novartis Corp.
Foundation type: Independent foundation.
Financial data (yr. ended 5/31/05): Assets, $1,526,592 (M); gifts received, $1,693,623; expenditures, $1,465,942; qualifying distributions, $1,465,942; giving activities include $1,410,000 for 34 grants to individuals (high: $62,500; low: $10,000).

Purpose and activities: Awards postdoctoral research fellowships to graduates of medical schools and graduate schools in the biological sciences.

Fields of interest: Graduate/professional education; Medical research, institute; Biological sciences.

Type of support: Fellowships; Research.

Limitations: Giving on a national basis.

Publications: Application guidelines; Annual report; Financial statement; Grants list; Informational brochure.

Application information: In the spring of each year an e-mail application notice is sent to every graduate school in biology and every medical school in the U.S. A list of these schools may be obtained from the "Graduate Programs and Admissions Manual, Volume A" put out by the Graduate Record Examination Board or by directly requesting an application form from the foundation. Applications must be submitted online through the foundation's Web site. Paper applications will no longer be accepted. Complete guidelines are available from foundation Web site. Please do not call the Administrative office with questions pertaining to the submission of applications and application materials. The application process is handled by the Scientific office (Susan DiRenzo, Asst. Dir.). Application form required.

Initial approach: Online
Copies of proposal: 3
Deadline(s): Oct. 1, including supporting letters
Final notification: Mar. to May

Officers and Directors:* Douglas E. Koshland,* Chair.; Donald D. Brown,* Pres.; Christine Pratt, Treas.; James Broach; Thomas Silhavy; Solomon H. Snyder.

Advisory Board of Trustees: David Baltimore; Paul Berg; Michael S. Brown; Purnell Choppin; Pedro Cuatrecasas; James E. Darnell, Jr.; Mark Fishman; Alfred G. Gilman; David V. Goeddel; Joseph L. Goldstein; Jeffrey Leiden; Steven L. McKnight; Cecil Pickett; William Rutter; Edward M. Scolnick; Donald W. Seldin; Phillip A. Sharp; Maxine F. Singer; Shirley M. Tilghman; Robert Tjian; James Watson; James Watson.

EIN: 521231801

3678
Linehan Family Foundation, Inc. ✧

515 Fairmont Ave., Ste. 400
Towson, MD 21286

Established in 1993 in MD.
Donor: Earl L. Linehan.
Foundation type: Independent foundation.
Financial data (yr. ended 12/31/05): Assets, $5,475,126 (M); gifts received, $1,203,362; expenditures, $822,029; qualifying distributions, $768,584; giving activities include $767,200 for 74 grants (high: $100,000; low: $100).
Fields of interest: Arts; Higher education; Education; Human services; Federated giving programs; Roman Catholic federated giving programs; Roman Catholic agencies & churches.
Type of support: Annual campaigns; Capital campaigns; Building/renovation; Scholarship funds.
Limitations: Applications not accepted. Giving primarily in Baltimore, MD. No grants to individuals.
Application information: Contributes only to pre-selected organizations.
Board meeting date(s): Dec.

Officers: Darielle D. Linehan, Pres.; Earl L. Linehan, Secy.-Treas.
Trustees: Brendan E. Linehan; Charles M. Linehan; John D. Linehan.
EIN: 521853307
Selected grants: The following grants were reported in 2003.
$75,000 to Mercy Medical Center, Baltimore, MD. For general support.
$28,500 to Calvert School, Baltimore, MD. For general support.
$24,000 to Saint Marys Seminary and University, Baltimore, MD. For general support.
$19,000 to Gilman School, Baltimore, MD. For general support.
$15,000 to University of Maryland-Baltimore Foundation, Baltimore, MD. For general support.
$5,500 to Saint Ignatius Loyola Academy, Baltimore, MD. For general support.
$5,000 to Parks and People Foundation for Baltimore Recreation and Parks, Baltimore, MD. For general support.
$3,500 to Center Stage, Baltimore, MD. For general support.
$2,500 to American Visionary Art Museum, Baltimore, MD. For general support.
$2,500 to Baltimore Symphony Orchestra, Baltimore, MD. For general support.

3679
The Little Family Foundation, Inc. ✧ ☆

13010 Jerome Jay Dr.
Hunt Valley, MD 21030

Established in 2004 in MD.
Foundation type: Independent foundation.
Financial data (yr. ended 12/31/05): Assets, $3,229,815 (M); gifts received, $3,500,000; expenditures, $1,476,098; qualifying distributions, $1,440,000; giving activities include $1,440,000 for 24 grants (high: $327,000; low: $1,000).
Purpose and activities: Giving primarily for Christian education, agencies, and churches.
Fields of interest: Education; Christian agencies & churches.
Limitations: Applications not accepted. Giving on a national basis. No grants to individuals.
Application information: Contributes only to pre-selected organizations.
Director: Arthur F. Bell, Jr.
EIN: 201965919

3680
The Locke Family Foundation, Inc. ✧ ☆

c/o James D. Locke
6219 Kennedy St.
Chevy Chase, MD 20815

Established in 2003 in MD.
Donor: James Locke.
Foundation type: Operating foundation.
Financial data (yr. ended 6/30/05): Assets, $0 (M); gifts received, $308,500; expenditures, $361,845; qualifying distributions, $359,545; giving activities include $355,000 for grants.
Limitations: Applications not accepted. No grants to individuals.
Application information: Contributes only to pre-selected organizations.
Trustee: James Locke.
EIN: 260069404

3681
Lockhart Vaughan Foundation, Inc.

2 E. Read St., Ste. 100
Baltimore, MD 21202 (410) 837-9400
Contact: John B. Powell, Jr., Exec. Dir.

Established in 1990 in MD; funded in 1991.
Donors: The McAshan Foundation, Inc.; Julia C. Baker‡.
Foundation type: Independent foundation.
Financial data (yr. ended 12/31/05): Assets, $32,382,105 (M); expenditures, $1,552,460; qualifying distributions, $1,486,662; giving activities include $1,457,431 for 60 grants (high: $100,000; low: $2,500).
Purpose and activities: The foundation directs its giving toward its 4 goals for the city of Baltimore, MD: 1) quality public education; 2) more educational choices; 3) better environment; and 4) vibrant neighborhoods.
Fields of interest: Children/youth, services; Community development.
Type of support: General/operating support; Capital campaigns; Program development.
Limitations: Giving limited to Baltimore, MD.
Publications: Application guidelines.
Application information: Applications must be on Association of Baltimore Area Grantmakers (ABAG) Common Grant Form. Application information available at http://www.abagmc.org. Application form required.
Initial approach: Letter requesting application form
Copies of proposal: 2
Deadline(s): Feb. 20, June 20, and Oct. 20
Final notification: Within 60 days of deadline
Officer: John B. Powell, Jr., Exec. Dir.
Number of staff: None.
EIN: 521693184
Selected grants: The following grants were reported in 2003.
$75,000 to Fund for Educational Excellence, Baltimore, MD. For Baltimore high school reform.
$50,000 to American Civil Liberties Union Foundation of Maryland, Baltimore, MD. For campaign to achieve full public funding of public schools.
$50,000 to Maryland Zoological Society, Baltimore, MD. For capital campaign for Baltimore Zoo.
$42,000 to New Song Urban Ministries, Baltimore, MD. For debt reduction for New Song Urban Community Learning Center.
$42,000 to Saint Ignatius Loyola Academy, Baltimore, MD. For endowment fund.
$35,000 to Johns Hopkins University, Baltimore, MD. For Language and Literacy project at Baltimore Head Start Center for improve reading readiness.
$30,000 to Enoch Pratt Free Library, Baltimore, MD. For summer reading program.
$25,000 to American Red Cross of Central Baltimore, Baltimore, MD.
$25,000 to Teach for America, Baltimore, MD. For recruiting and training teachers for public schools.
$15,000 to Advocates for Children and Youth, Baltimore, MD.

3682
Lockheed Martin Corporation Foundation ▼ ✧

(formerly Martin Marietta Corporation Foundation)
6801 Rockledge Dr.
Bethesda, MD 20817
Contact: David Phillips, Secy.

Trust established in 1955 in MD; current name adopted in 1996 following the merger of Lockheed Corp with Martin Marietta Corp.
Donors: Martin Marietta Corp.; Lockheed Martin Corp.
Foundation type: Company-sponsored foundation.
Financial data (yr. ended 12/31/04): Assets, $1,960,348 (M); gifts received, $7,000,000; expenditures, $7,183,885; qualifying distributions, $7,168,885; giving activities include $7,052,605 for 250 grants (high: $644,450; low: $250).
Purpose and activities: The foundation supports organizations involved with arts and culture, education, health, youth development, human services, and community development.
Fields of interest: Arts; Education; Health organizations, association; Youth development; Human services; Community development; Voluntarism promotion.
Type of support: General/operating support; Program development; Employee matching gifts; Employee-related scholarships.
Limitations: Giving primarily in areas of company operations. No support for religious organizations not of direct benefit to the entire community, professional associations, labor or fraternal organizations, social clubs, or athletic organizations. No grants to individuals (except for employee-related scholarships), or for booklet, yearbook, or journal advertising, or home-based child care or educational services.
Publications: Application guidelines.
Application information: Proposals should be no longer than 2 pages. Support is limited to 1 contribution per organization during any given year. Application form not required.
   Initial approach: Proposal to nearest company facility
   Copies of proposal: 1
   Deadline(s): None
   Final notification: 1 month
Officer: David Phillips, Secy.
Trustees: Dennis Boxx; Ed Taft; Robert Trice; Peter F. Warren, Jr.
Number of staff: 1 full-time professional; 1 full-time support.
EIN: 136161566
Selected grants: The following grants were reported in 2004.
$1,900,000 to Scholarship Foundation, Cherry Hill, NJ.
$644,450 to National Merit Scholarship Corporation, Evanston, IL.
$300,000 to District of Columbia College Access Program, DC.
$250,000 to United Negro College Fund, Fairfax, VA.
$200,000 to Smithsonian Institution, National Air and Space Museum, DC.
$150,000 to Maryland Science Center, Baltimore, MD.
$125,000 to Tufts University, Medford, MA.
$110,000 to Strathmore Hall Arts Center, North Bethesda, MD.
$32,000 to Pennsylvania State University, University Park, PA.

$20,000 to Baltimore Museum of Art, Baltimore, MD.

3683
Morton and Sophia Macht Foundation, Inc. ✧

15 E. Fayette St.
Baltimore, MD 21202-1606 (410) 539-2370
Contact: Amy Macht, Pres.
FAX: (410) 752-7813;
E-mail: mbishoff@regionalmgmt.com

Established in 1956 in MD.
Donors: Sophia Macht†; Westland Gardens Co.; Mallview; Queensgate; Windsor; Automatic Service; Baltoland Inc.; Conwill Co.; Dahley Co.; Builders; Compression; Developers; Halldane; Maxwell; Patience; Realsearch; Tracery; Transmaryland; Huron; Outpost; Raintree; Scholar; Stranden; Lodestone; Masterplan; Northrail; Tensiltech Corp.; Walden Co.; Talltimber; Thunderwood; Wolfwind; College Gardens; Elmcroft; Welsh Construction; Gradient; Folcroft; Cosmo Co.; Lawford Co.; Cedlair Corp.; Park Grove Realty Co.
Foundation type: Independent foundation.
Financial data (yr. ended 4/30/06): Assets, $1,516,005 (M); gifts received, $370,200; expenditures, $404,625; qualifying distributions, $373,540; giving activities include $372,729 for 125 grants (high: $107,000; low: $25).
Purpose and activities: Giving primarily for arts and culture, higher education, and human services.
Fields of interest: Arts; Higher education; Education; Environment; Human services.
Type of support: General/operating support; Continuing support; Annual campaigns; Capital campaigns; Equipment; Program development; Conferences/seminars; Publication; Seed money; Scholarship funds; Research.
Limitations: Giving primarily in the metropolitan Baltimore, MD, area. No grants to individuals.
Application information: Application form not required.
   Initial approach: Proposal
   Copies of proposal: 1
   Deadline(s): None
   Final notification: Letter
Officers and Trustees:* Amy Macht,* Pres.; Katherine Kelly Howard,* V.P. and Secy.; Jill Gansler,* V.P. and Treas.; Bette D. Cohen,* V.P.; William A. Goodhardt,* V.P.; Philip Macht,* V.P.; Robert W. Mastropieri,* V.P.
EIN: 526035753
Selected grants: The following grants were reported in 2005.
$79,712 to Civic Works, Baltimore, MD. 3 grants: $27,616, $32,096, $20,000
$77,637 to YMCA of Central Maryland, Baltimore, MD.
$20,000 to University of Maryland Foundation, Adelphi, MD.
$12,600 to Rosedale Recreation and Parks Council, Baltimore, MD. 2 grants: $6,300 each
$2,500 to Washington University, Saint Louis, MO.
$600 to Community Assistance Network, Baltimore, MD.
$500 to Maryland Committee for Children, Baltimore, MD.

3684
MARPAT Foundation, Inc.

P.O. Box 1769
Silver Spring, MD 20915-1769
Contact: Joan F. Koven, Secy.-Treas.
E-mail: jkoven@marpatfoundation.org; URL: http://foundationcenter.org/grantmaker/marpat/

Incorporated in 1985 in MD.
Donor: Marvin Breckinridge Patterson†.
Foundation type: Independent foundation.
Financial data (yr. ended 12/31/05): Assets, $33,147,444 (M); gifts received, $10,106; expenditures, $3,218,605; qualifying distributions, $2,626,898; giving activities include $2,491,000 for 141 grants (high: $75,000; low: $5,000), and $10,000 for 1 in-kind gift.
Purpose and activities: Grants will be made primarily to established charitable organizations whose activities are personally known to the directors and based in or benefiting the greater Washington, DC, metropolitan area. Grants will be made to the following: organizations that advance international understanding, museums, and libraries for the advancement and diffusion of knowledge; organizations and schools that sponsor programs that advocate and encourage family planning, or promote or provide health care; organizations promoting or conducting scientific programs and research projects; organizations providing services and/or education designed to preserve natural and historical resources, and advance the knowledge of mankind's history and cultural past; and organizations that promote volunteer participation in, and citizen involvement with such organizations.
Fields of interest: Visual arts; Museums; Performing arts; Historic preservation/historical societies; Arts; Libraries/library science; Education; Environment, natural resources; Reproductive health, family planning; Health care; Human services; Voluntarism promotion.
Type of support: General/operating support; Continuing support; Building/renovation; Equipment; Land acquisition; Program development; Publication; Matching/challenge support.
Limitations: Giving primarily in the metropolitan Washington, DC, area. No support for projects or organizations for any weapons development, or for medical research. No grants to individuals, or for endowment funds.
Publications: Application guidelines; Grants list.
Application information: Application form and summary sheet available on Web site. Full proposals by invitation only. Application form required.
   Initial approach: Stage one application form
   Copies of proposal: 1
   Deadline(s): May for Stage One Summary; Aug. 15 for applicants invited to submit Stage Two Application
   Board meeting date(s): Dec.
   Final notification: End of June for Stage One response
Officers and Directors:* Samuel N. Stokes,* Pres.; Ellen Bozman, V.P.; Joan F. Koven,* Secy.-Treas.; Isabella G. Breckinridge; Sherrill M. Houghton; Christine Minter-Dowd; Charles E. Yonkers.
Number of staff: 1 part-time professional; 1 part-time support.
EIN: 521358159

3685
Nancy Peery Marriott Foundation, Inc.

10400 Fernwood Rd., Dept. 901-01
Bethesda, MD 20817
Contact: Nancie Suzuki, Fdn. Admin.
FAX: (301) 380-6993;
E-mail: nancie.suzuki@hosthotels.com

Established in 2002 in MD.
Foundation type: Independent foundation.
Financial data (yr. ended 9/30/05): Assets,
$14,417,743 (M); expenditures, $724,166;
qualifying distributions, $650,900; giving
activities include $650,900 for 49 grants (high:
$100,000; low: $200).
Fields of interest: Museums; Arts; Higher
education; Hospitals (specialty); Cancer research.
Limitations: Applications not accepted. Giving in the
U.S., with emphasis on MD and Washington, DC. No
grants to individuals.
Application information: Contributes only to
pre-selected organizations.
   Board meeting date(s): July
Officers and Directors:* Nancy Perry Marriott,*
Pres. and Treas.; Richard E. Marriott,* Exec. V.P.;
James A. Poulos, Secy.; Sandra Peery Marriott
Bertha; Mary Alice Marriott Hatch; Julie Ann Marriott
Keenan; Karen Christine Marriott.
EIN: 522003744

3686
Richard E. & Nancy P. Marriott Foundation, Inc.

10400 Fernwood Rd., Dept. 901
Bethesda, MD 20817
Contact: Nancie Suzuki, Fdn. Admin.
FAX: (301) 380-6993;
E-mail: nancie.suzuki@hosthotels.com

Established in 1999 in MD.
Donors: Richard E. Marriott; Alice S. Marriott
Lifetime Trust; J. Willard Marriott, Jr. Foundation.
Foundation type: Independent foundation.
Financial data (yr. ended 12/31/05): Assets,
$30,075,291 (M); gifts received, $31;
expenditures, $1,066,615; qualifying distributions,
$1,051,600; giving activities include $1,047,050
for 76 grants (high: $150,000; low: $200).
Fields of interest: Education; Youth development,
adult & child programs.
Limitations: Giving on a national basis. No grants to
individuals.
Application information: Telephone calls not
accepted. Application form not required.
   Initial approach: Proposal
   Copies of proposal: 1
   Deadline(s): None
   Board meeting date(s): June and Nov.
Officers and Directors:* Richard E. Marriott,* Pres.;
Ralph W. Handy, Jr.,* Secy.; Nancy P. Marriott,*
Treas.
Number of staff: 1 part-time professional.
EIN: 521953832
Selected grants: The following grants were reported
in 2004.
$150,000 to PAIRS Foundation, Weston, FL.
$50,000 to Brigham Young University, Provo, UT. 2
   grants: $25,000 (For International Internship),
   $25,000 (For Center for International
   Entrepreneurship).
$50,000 to Enterprise Mentors International,
   Chesterfield, MO.

$30,000 to University of Maryland-College Park,
   Robert Smith School of Business, College Park,
   MD.
$25,000 to Called to Serve Foundation, Provo, UT.
$25,000 to National Ability Center of Park City, Park
   City, UT.
$25,000 to Unitas Therapeutic Community, Bronx,
   NY.
$15,000 to Park City Foundation for the Arts and
   Humanities, Park City, UT. For Ski Utah School
   Program.
$10,000 to Gallaudet University, DC.

3687
George Preston Marshall Foundation ✧
(also known as Redskin Foundation, Inc.)
4300 Montgomery Ave., Ste. 104
Bethesda, MD 20814 (301) 654-7774
Contact: Elizabeth B. Frazier, Exec. Dir.

Incorporated in 1972 in DC.
Donors: George Preston Marshall†; George Preston
Marshall Trust.
Foundation type: Independent foundation.
Financial data (yr. ended 12/31/05): Assets,
$77,761 (M); gifts received, $576,000;
expenditures, $606,266; qualifying distributions,
$606,266; giving activities include $460,822 for 57
grants (high: $21,000; low: $1,000).
Purpose and activities: Giving only for programs
benefiting children in areas of welfare, health,
mental health, education, arts, and recreation in
Washington, DC, MD, and VA.
Fields of interest: Children/youth, services.
Type of support: General/operating support; Capital
campaigns; Building/renovation; Equipment; Land
acquisition; Publication; Seed money; Scholarship
funds; Matching/challenge support.
Limitations: Giving limited to Washington, DC, MD,
and VA. No support for programs which do not
directly benefit children. No grants to individuals.
Publications: Application guidelines; Annual report.
Application information: Application form not
required.
   Initial approach: Proposal (no more than 5 pages)
   Copies of proposal: 1
   Deadline(s): None
   Board meeting date(s): 5 times per year
Officers and Directors:* James C. McKay,* Pres.;
William D. Foote, Jr.,* V.P.; Ellin J. Nolan,* Secy.; G.
Dewey Arnold III, Treas.; Elizabeth B. Frazier, Exec.
Dir.
Number of staff: 1 part-time professional.
EIN: 237173302
Selected grants: The following grants were reported
in 2004.
$30,000 to Rosemount Center, DC.
$30,000 to Treatment and Learning Centers (TLC),
   Rockville, MD.
$25,000 to Kingsbury Center, DC.
$25,000 to SEED Foundation, DC.
$24,000 to Girl Scouts of the U.S.A., Council of the
   Nations Capital, DC.
$20,000 to Levine School of Music, DC.
$15,500 to Crossway Community, Kensington, MD.
$15,000 to Community of Hope, DC.
$14,000 to Barker Foundation, Cabin John, MD.
$12,140 to Madeira School, McLean, VA.

3688
The Sumner T. McKnight Foundation
901 S. Bond St., Ste. 400
Baltimore, MD 21231

Incorporated in 1956 in MN.
Donors: Sumner T. McKnight; H. Turney McKnight.
Foundation type: Independent foundation.
Financial data (yr. ended 12/31/05): Assets,
$4,159,930 (M); expenditures, $432,458;
qualifying distributions, $400,592; giving activities
include $400,000 for 30 grants (high: $125,000;
low: $500).
Fields of interest: Environment, natural resources;
Environment.
Limitations: Applications not accepted. Giving
primarily in MD. No support for religion. No grants to
individuals, or for endowment or capital funds or
trips or tours.
Application information: Contributes only to
pre-selected organizations.
   Board meeting date(s): Apr.
Directors: Christina McKnight Kippen; H. Turney
McKnight; Sumner T. McKnight; John T. Westrum.
Number of staff: 1
EIN: 416022360

3689
The Merrill Foundation, Inc. ✧
c/o Wilbert H. Sirota
6225 Smith Ave.
Baltimore, MD 21209-3600

Established in 1986 in MD.
Donors: Philip Merrill; Eleanor Merrill; Capital
Gazette Communications, Inc.; Washington
Magazine, Inc.; Merrill Charitable Lead Trust.
Foundation type: Independent foundation.
Financial data (yr. ended 12/31/04): Assets,
$19,382,520 (M); gifts received, $2,946,774;
expenditures, $1,383,478; qualifying distributions,
$1,239,350; giving activities include $1,239,350
for 21 grants (high: $535,600; low: $250).
Purpose and activities: Giving primarily for higher
education and medical research.
Fields of interest: Higher education; Business
school/education; Environment; Medical research,
institute.
Limitations: Applications not accepted. Giving
primarily in Washington, DC. No grants to
individuals.
Application information: Contributes only to
pre-selected organizations.
Officers: Eleanor Merrill, Pres. and Treas.; Wilbert H.
Sirota, Secy.
EIN: 521490571
Selected grants: The following grants were reported
in 2004.
$375,000 to Johns Hopkins University, Baltimore,
   MD.
$125,000 to Aspen Institute, DC.
$38,000 to Cornell University, Ithaca, NY.
$38,000 to Dickinson College, Carlisle, PA.
$10,000 to Foundation for the National Archives,
   DC.

3690
Robert & Jane Meyerhoff Foundation, Inc. ✧
1025 Cranbrook Rd.
Cockeysville, MD 21030

Established in 1980 in MD.
Donor: Robert E. Meyerhoff.
Foundation type: Independent foundation.
Financial data (yr. ended 12/31/03): Assets, $1,324,780 (M); expenditures, $477,983; qualifying distributions, $470,286; giving activities include $470,000 for 3 grants (high: $450,000; low: $10,000).
Purpose and activities: Giving to higher education, and the arts.
Fields of interest: Museums (art); Performing arts, music; Education.
Limitations: Applications not accepted. Giving primarily in MD. No grants to individuals.
Application information: Contributes only to pre-selected organizations.
Officers and Directors:* Robert E. Meyerhoff,* Pres. and Treas.; Jane B. Meyerhoff, V.P. and Secy.; Neil A. Meyerhoff, V.P.; Herbert Goldman; Rose Ellen Greene.
EIN: 521176421
Selected grants: The following grants were reported in 2003.
$450,000 to University of Maryland Foundation, Adelphi, MD. For annual support.
$10,000 to Marylanders Against Handgun Abuse, Baltimore, MD. For annual support.
$10,000 to University of Miami, Coral Gables, FL. For annual support.

3691
The Harvey M. Meyerhoff Fund, Inc.
25 S. Charles St.
Baltimore, MD   21201

Established in 1994 in MD.
Foundation type: Independent foundation.
Financial data (yr. ended 12/31/04): Assets, $9,657,194 (M); expenditures, $485,501; qualifying distributions, $458,070; giving activities include $451,808 for 36 grants (high: $100,000; low: $500).
Purpose and activities: Giving primarily for the arts, education, and health services; support also for Jewish organizations and agencies.
Fields of interest: Performing arts, orchestra (symphony); Libraries/library science; Scholarships/financial aid; Health organizations, association; Jewish agencies & temples.
International interests: Israel.
Type of support: General/operating support; Continuing support; Annual campaigns; Capital campaigns; Building/renovation; Equipment; Endowments; Emergency funds; Program development; Conferences/seminars; Professorships; Curriculum development; Scholarship funds; Research; Program evaluation; Matching/challenge support.
Limitations: Applications not accepted. Giving primarily in MD. No grants to individuals.
Application information: Contributes only to pre-selected organizations.
Officers: Harvey M. Meyerhoff, Pres.; Lee M. Hendler, V.P. and Secy.; Terry M. Rubenstein, V.P. and Treas.
Trustees: Jill M. Hieronimus; Joseph Meyerhoff II.
EIN: 521904818
Selected grants: The following grants were reported in 2004.
$125,000 to Johns Hopkins University, Baltimore, MD. 3 grants: $100,000, $5,000, $20,000
$100,000 to Baltimore Symphony Orchestra, Baltimore, MD.

$48,208 to The Associated: Jewish Community Federation of Baltimore, Baltimore, MD. 2 grants: $23,208, $25,000
$25,000 to Concord Coalition, Arlington, VA.
$25,000 to Johns Hopkins Hospital, Baltimore, MD.
$15,000 to Walters Art Museum, Baltimore, MD.
$6,500 to Center Stage, Baltimore, MD.

3692
The Joseph Meyerhoff Fund, Inc.
25 S. Charles St.
Baltimore, MD   21201

Incorporated in 1953 in MD.
Donors: Joseph Meyerhoff†; Mrs. Joseph Meyerhoff; Meyerhoff Charitable Income Trust; Katz Charitable Income Trust; Meyerhoff Charitable Income Trust II; Katz Charitable Income Trust II.
Foundation type: Independent foundation.
Financial data (yr. ended 12/31/04): Assets, $71,550,118 (M); expenditures, $3,390,048; qualifying distributions, $2,996,207; giving activities include $2,770,724 for 144 grants (high: $355,344; low: $1,000).
Purpose and activities: Giving primarily to support and encourage cultural and higher educational programs and institutions and to facilitate immigration and absorption of new immigrants into Israel.
Fields of interest: Arts; Higher education; Human services; Jewish federated giving programs; Jewish agencies & temples; Immigrants/refugees.
International interests: Israel.
Type of support: General/operating support; Continuing support; Annual campaigns; Capital campaigns; Building/renovation; Equipment; Land acquisition; Endowments; Debt reduction; Emergency funds; Program development; Professorships; Publication; Seed money; Fellowships; Scholarship funds; Research; Matching/challenge support.
Limitations: Applications not accepted. Giving primarily in Baltimore, MD, New York, NY; some funding also to organizations in Israel. No grants to individuals.
Application information: Contributes only to pre-selected organizations.
Board meeting date(s): May and Oct.
Officers: Harvey M. Meyerhoff, Pres.; Terry Rubenstein, V.P. and Secy.; Lee M. Hendler, V.P. and Treas.; Eleanor M. Katz, V.P.
Number of staff: 1 part-time professional; 1 part-time support.
EIN: 526035997

3693
Mid-Shore Community Foundation, Inc.
c/o Bullitt House
102 E. Dover St.
Easton, MD   21601   (410) 820-8175
Contact: Robbin F. Hill, Dir., Fdn. Progs.
FAX: (410) 820-8729; E-mail: info@mscf.org;
Additional E-mail: robbin@mscf.org; URL: http://www.mscf.org

Established in 1992 in MD.
Foundation type: Community foundation.
Financial data (yr. ended 6/30/05): Assets, $28,313,919 (M); gifts received, $1,234,112; expenditures, $1,087,412; giving activities include $679,492 for 56 grants (high: $100,000; low: $50).

Purpose and activities: The foundation connects private resources with public needs to enhance the quality of life for the citizens of Caroline, Dorchester, Kent, Queen Anne's and Talbot counties, MD.
Fields of interest: Community development.
Type of support: Program development; Management development/capacity building; Employee matching gifts; Curriculum development; General/operating support; Capital campaigns; Building/renovation; Equipment; Land acquisition; Emergency funds; Seed money; Scholarship funds; In-kind gifts; Matching/challenge support.
Limitations: Giving limited to the mid-shore and eastern-shore areas of MD (Caroline, Dorchester, Kent, Queen Anne, and Talbot counties). No support for veterans groups or fraternal organizations. No grants to individuals (except for scholarships), or for fundraisers, conferences, public relations, publications, or for multi-year commitments.
Publications: Application guidelines; Annual report; Financial statement; Informational brochure; Newsletter.
Application information: Visit foundation Web site for application form and guidelines. Application form required.
Initial approach: Submit application form and attachments
Copies of proposal: 1
Deadline(s): Apr. 1 and Oct. 1
Board meeting date(s): Mar., June, Sept., and Dec.
Final notification: June 30 and Dec. 30
Officers and Directors:* Charles T. Capute,* Chair.; F. Graham Lee, Pres.; W. Moorhead Vermilye,* Secy.; Lloyd L. Beatty, Sr.,* Treas.; Joseph B. Stevens, Jr., Dir. Emeritus; Charles E. Wheeler, Dir. Emeritus; James A. Adkins; Wheeler R. Baker; Alice R. Bower; John W. Dillon; Stuart "Mickey" Elsberg; Mrs. Russell J. Ferree; Richard C. Granville; William T. Hunter, Jr.; Charles W. Kelly; Charles L. Lea, Jr.; David B. Nagel; Hamish S. Osborne; Dr. Harry C. Rhodes; J. Thomas Rhodes, Jr.; Dr. Baird Tipson; Willie G. Woods, Ph.D.
Number of staff: 2 full-time professional; 1 full-time support.
EIN: 521782373

3694
Middendorf Foundation, Inc.
2 E. Read St., 5th Fl.
Baltimore, MD   21202
Contact: Laura A. Holter, Grants Admin.

Incorporated in 1953 in MD.
Donors: J. William Middendorf, Jr.†; Alice C. Middendorf†.
Foundation type: Independent foundation.
Financial data (yr. ended 3/31/05): Assets, $31,731,504 (M); expenditures, $1,830,860; qualifying distributions, $1,648,723; giving activities include $1,593,390 for 35 grants (high: $250,000; low: $500), and $5,000 for 1 employee matching gift.
Purpose and activities: Giving primarily for higher education, particularly to scholarship funds, and for community and social services.
Fields of interest: Museums (art); Historic preservation/historical societies; Higher education; Libraries (public); Hospitals (general); Employment, job counseling; Human services; Residential/custodial care, hospices.

Type of support: General/operating support; Capital campaigns; Building/renovation; Endowments; Professorships; Matching/challenge support.

Limitations: Giving primarily in MD, with emphasis on Baltimore. No support for political organizations, or for programs. No grants to individuals, or for annual funds.

Application information: Application form not required.

  Initial approach: Letter
  Copies of proposal: 1
  Deadline(s): None
  Board meeting date(s): Quarterly (Apr., July, Sept. and Dec.)
  Final notification: 2 weeks for acknowledgement, 1 week after trustee meetings for determination

Officers and Trustees:* Craig Lewis,* Pres.; Forrest F. Bramble, Jr.,* V.P.; Theresa N. Knell,* Secy.; Benjamin F. Lucas II,* Treas.; Phillips Hathaway; Sealy H. Hopkinson.

Number of staff: 2 part-time professional.

EIN: 526048944

Selected grants: The following grants were reported in 2005.

$250,000 to Walters Art Museum, Baltimore, MD.

$200,000 to Living Classrooms Foundation, Baltimore, MD.

$150,000 to Maryland Science Center, Baltimore, MD.

$140,000 to Institute of Notre Dame, Baltimore, MD.

$100,000 to AmeriCares, Stamford, CT.

$100,000 to Baltimore Museum of Art, Baltimore, MD.

$100,000 to Ladew Topiary Gardens, Monkton, MD.

$100,000 to Salvation Army, Lutz, FL.

$50,000 to Marine Corps Scholarship Foundation, Alexandria, VA.

$25,000 to Family and Childrens Services of Central Maryland, Baltimore, MD.

3695
The Morningstar Foundation

4550 Montgomery Ave., Ste. 650 N.
Bethesda, MD 20814
Contact: Michael C. Gelman, V.P.

Established in 1982 in DC and MD.

Donors: Michael C. Gelman; Susan R. Gelman; Richard Goldman 1997 Charitable Lead Annuity Trust; Susan R. Gelman Charitable Lead Trust.

Foundation type: Independent foundation.

Financial data (yr. ended 12/31/04): Assets, $19,933,779 (M); gifts received, $4,126,703; expenditures, $3,024,828; qualifying distributions, $2,899,536; giving activities include $2,877,860 for 137 grants (high: $700,000; low: $300).

Fields of interest: Arts; Education; Environment; Human services; International peace/security; Jewish agencies & temples.

International interests: Israel.

Type of support: General/operating support; Annual campaigns; Capital campaigns.

Limitations: Applications not accepted. Giving primarily in the greater Washington, DC, area and in Israel. No grants to individuals.

Application information: Contributes only to pre-selected organizations. Unsolicited requests for funds not accepted.

  Board meeting date(s): Quarterly

Officers: Susan R. Gelman, Pres.; Michael C. Gelman, V.P.; George P. Levendis, Secy.

Number of staff: 1 part-time support.

EIN: 521270464

Selected grants: The following grants were reported in 2003.

$1,000,000 to Jewish Federation of Greater Washington, Rockville, MD.

$30,000 to National Gallery of Art, DC.

$12,500 to Chesapeake Bay Foundation, Annapolis, MD.

$10,000 to Bard College, Annandale on Hudson, NY.

$10,000 to DC Wheel Productions, Dance Place, DC.

$5,000 to Human Rights Campaign Foundation, DC.

$5,000 to P.E.F. Israel Endowment Funds, New York, NY.

$5,000 to University of Maryland-College Park Foundation, College Park, MD.

$3,750 to Shakespeare Theater, DC.

$2,500 to Capitol Hill Arts Workshop, DC.

3696
Vincent Mulford Foundation ◇

c/o Mercantile-Safe Deposit & Trust Co.
766 Old Hammonds Ferry Rd.
Linthicum, MD 21090
Contact: Christian R. Sonne, Tr.
E-mail: info@mulfordfdn.org; Application address: P.O. Box 635, Tuxedo Park, NY 10987; URL: http://www.mulfordfdn.org

Trust established in 1951 in NJ.

Donors: Walter Moor†; Vincent S. Mulford†; Edith Mulford†; Donald Mulford†; Vincent S. Mulford, Jr.†.

Foundation type: Independent foundation.

Financial data (yr. ended 12/31/04): Assets, $15,436,952 (M); expenditures, $764,712; qualifying distributions, $737,148; giving activities include $717,000 for 110 grants (high: $60,000; low: $500).

Purpose and activities: To improve the lives of others, particularly the least fortunate. Giving primarily for providing permanent and transitional housing for homeless; programs helping homeless find and move into permanent and transitional housing and to support efforts of those at risk of losing their housing to retain it.

Fields of interest: Housing/shelter, public education; Housing/shelter, homeless; Housing/shelter; Homeless, human services.

Type of support: Seed money; General/operating support; Continuing support; Annual campaigns; Capital campaigns; Building/renovation; Emergency funds; Matching/challenge support.

Limitations: Giving generally limited to Boston, MA, and its western suburbs, and New York, NY. No support for governmental organizations or advocacy groups. No grants to individuals.

Publications: Application guidelines; Informational brochure (including application guidelines).

Application information: A substantial portion of available funding is already committed in program areas long supported by family members, including emergency services, support of micro-enterprise and provision of educational and social tools to disadvantaged individuals. The foundation is not currently accepting proposals in these program areas from organizations that are new to the foundation. Please send proposals in duplicate. Proposals sent by fax or e-mail will not be accepted. Application form required.

  Initial approach: Letter or proposal
  Copies of proposal: 2

  Deadline(s): Mar. 1 and Sept. 1
  Final notification: Early June and early Dec.

Trustees: Madeleine B. Grant; Christian R. Sonne.

Number of staff: 1 part-time support.

EIN: 226043594

3697
Jerome S. & Grace H. Murray Foundation ◇

P.O. Box 227
Owings, MD 20736
Contact: Kim Harrison, Admin.
FAX: (410) 257-5526; E-mail: kimjgmf@msn.com; URL: http://www.jgmurrayfoundation.org

Established in 1980 in FL.

Donors: Grace H. Murray; Jerome S. Murray; Grace Healy Murray Irrevocable Trust.

Foundation type: Independent foundation.

Financial data (yr. ended 12/31/04): Assets, $14,185,713 (M); gifts received, $5,488; expenditures, $801,223; qualifying distributions, $625,056; giving activities include $625,056 for 33 grants (high: $111,017; low: $5,843).

Purpose and activities: Funding primarily for the care, training and education of physically, mentally, and emotionally disturbed children and adults, and the training and education of those who will help them.

Fields of interest: Education, special.

Limitations: Giving on a national basis.

Publications: Application guidelines; Annual report; Grants list.

Application information: All grant applications must be sponsored by a Jerome S. & Grace H. Murray lineal descendant, age 18 and over. A copy of current IRS 501(c)(3) determination letter, and most recent annual financial statement (audited if possible) must be mailed or faxed. Application form required.

  Initial approach: E-mail proposal. Applicants may E-mail Kim Harrison, Fdn. Admin., prior to submission
  Deadline(s): Sept. 15
  Board meeting date(s): Sept.

Trustees: Steve Althoff; Eileen M. Dillon; Reilly Murray.

Number of staff: 1 full-time professional.

EIN: 521805567

3698
The Israel & Mollie Myers Foundation, Inc. ◇

P.O. Box 32338
Baltimore, MD 21282-2338
Contact: Judith Langenthal, Co-Pres.; Jonathan P. Myers, Co-Pres.

Established in 1961.

Donors: Israel Myers†; Jonathan P. Myers; Herschel L. Langenthal; Judith Lagenthal; Beverly Meyers.

Foundation type: Independent foundation.

Financial data (yr. ended 12/31/03): Assets, $7,656,857 (M); gifts received, $381,537; expenditures, $627,171; qualifying distributions, $537,048; giving activities include $496,639 for 124 grants (high: $190,000; low: $25).

Purpose and activities: Giving primarily for Jewish organizations, including welfare services; support also for secondary and higher education, and the performing arts.

Fields of interest: Secondary school/education; Higher education; Hospitals (general); Jewish agencies & temples.
Limitations: Giving primarily in Baltimore, MD.
Application information: Application form not required.
Initial approach: Letter
Copies of proposal: 1
Deadline(s): None
Officers: Judith Langenthal, Co-Pres.; Jonathan P. Myers, Co-Pres.; Herschel L. Langenthal, V.P.; Beverly Myers, V.P.; Carol Rogers, Secy.; David Goldner, Treas.
EIN: 521314430
Selected grants: The following grants were reported in 2003.
$210,000 to The Associated: Jewish Community Federation of Baltimore, Baltimore, MD. 3 grants: $190,000 (For unrestricted support), $10,000 (For unrestricted support), $10,000 (For unrestricted support).
$50,000 to Harbour School, Annapolis, MD. For unrestricted support.
$20,000 to Beth El Congregation, Baltimore, MD. For unrestricted support.
$20,000 to McDaniel College, Westminster, MD. For unrestricted support.
$15,000 to Jewish Museum of Maryland, Baltimore, MD. For unrestricted support.
$10,000 to Baltimore Hebrew University, Baltimore, MD. For unrestricted support.
$10,000 to Jewish Community Center of Baltimore, Baltimore, MD. For unrestricted support.
$2,000 to Scotts Valley Unified School District, Scotts Valley, CA. For unrestricted support.

3699
The Nabit Foundation, Inc. ✧
17 Commerce St.
Baltimore, MD 21202 (410) 727-2404
FAX: (410) 625-1531

Donors: Merwin J. Nabit; Charles J. Nabit; Great Chesapeake Bay Swim, Inc.
Foundation type: Independent foundation.
Financial data (yr. ended 6/30/05): Assets, $1,422,218 (M); gifts received, $170,000; expenditures, $432,977; qualifying distributions, $417,500; giving activities include $417,500 for 17 grants (high: $245,000; low: $250).
Purpose and activities: Giving primarily for higher education; funding also for the arts.
Fields of interest: Arts; Higher education; Cystic fibrosis; Jewish agencies & temples.
Limitations: Applications not accepted. Giving primarily in Sewanee, TN; some funding also in Baltimore, MD. No grants to individuals.
Application information: Contributes only to pre-selected organizations.
Board meeting date(s): Periodically
Officers and Directors:* Merwin J. Nabit,* Pres.; Charles J. Nabit,* Secy.; Michael C. Hodes.
EIN: 521756376
Selected grants: The following grants were reported in 2005.
$245,000 to University of the South, Sewanee, TN.
$25,000 to Notre Dame Preparatory School, Towson, MD.
$20,000 to Chesapeake Bay Trust, Annapolis, MD.
$20,000 to Hippodrome Foundation, Baltimore, MD.
$20,000 to University of Maryland Medical System, Baltimore, MD.

$15,000 to Maryland Art Place, Baltimore, MD.
$5,000 to Baltimore School for the Arts, Baltimore, MD.
$1,000 to Marine Corps Scholarship Foundation, Princeton, NJ.

3700
The Nasdaq Stock Market Educational Foundation, Inc. ✧
9513 Key West Ave.
Rockville, MD 20850-3389 (800) 842-0356
E-mail: foundation@nasdaq.com; Application address: 1801 K St., N.W., 8th Fl., Washington, DC 20006; URL: http://www.nasdaq.com/services/education_initiatives.stm

Established in 1993 in MD and DE.
Donor: The Nasdaq Stock Market, Inc.
Foundation type: Company-sponsored foundation.
Financial data (yr. ended 12/31/03): Assets, $34,766,786 (M); expenditures, $1,386,820; qualifying distributions, $1,139,450; giving activities include $1,139,450 for 24 grants (high: $230,000; low: $10,000).
Purpose and activities: The foundation supports organizations involved with financial markets literacy and awards fellowships to individuals for the purpose of conducting independent academic study or research on financial markets.
Fields of interest: Human services, financial counseling.
Type of support: Program development; Curriculum development; Fellowships; Research.
Limitations: Giving on a national basis for fellowships.
Application information: Unsolicited requests from organizations are not accepted.
Initial approach: Visit Web site for application information for fellowships
Officers and Directors:* Robert Greifeld, Chair.; Michael Casey; Joan C. Conley; Lois de Menil; Joseph R. Hardiman.
EIN: 521864429

3701
The W. O'Neil Foundation ✧
5454 Wisconsin Ave., Ste. 730
Chevy Chase, MD 20815
Contact: Helene O'Neil Cobb, Pres.

Incorporated in 1948 in OH.
Donors: William O'Neil†; Grace O'Neil†; John J. O'Neil†; Grace O'Neil Regan; and others.
Foundation type: Independent foundation.
Financial data (yr. ended 12/31/03): Assets, $49,414,291 (M); expenditures, $2,489,611; qualifying distributions, $2,370,669; giving activities include $2,362,460 for 74 grants (high: $300,000; low: $2,500).
Purpose and activities: Grants primarily given to Roman Catholic Church-related organizations for international emergency relief and for programs that bring food, clothing, shelter, basic medical care, and basic education to the poor of the world, preferably through projects that help the poor help themselves toward these goals. International assistance grants are only made to U.S.-based charities.
Fields of interest: Human services; Human services, emergency aid; Homeless, human services; International development; Roman Catholic agencies & churches; Homeless.

Type of support: General/operating support; Equipment; Program development.
Limitations: Giving primarily in Washington, DC, and New York, NY. No grants to individuals, or for endowment funds, church and school renovations, capital campaigns, administrative overhead, research, conferences, seminars, or matching gifts; no loans.
Publications: Application guidelines.
Application information: If project coincides with the foundation's interests, a proposal will be requested. Application form not required.
Initial approach: Letter of inquiry
Copies of proposal: 1
Deadline(s): None
Board meeting date(s): Feb., Apr., June, and Sept.
Officers and Trustees:* Helene O'Neil Cobb,* Chair. and Pres.; Helene Connellan O'Neil,* Vice-Chair. and V.P.; Jane Wieder,* V.P. and Treas.; Grace O'Neil Regan,* V.P.; Ann O'Neil Gradowski,* Secy.; John J. O'Neil, Jr.; Ann Regan; Mary Regan.
EIN: 346516969
Selected grants: The following grants were reported in 2004.
$1,200,000 to Catholic Relief Services, Baltimore, MD. 4 grants: $350,000 (For emergency relief fund), $350,000 (For emergency relief in Sudan and South Asia), $200,000 (For Caribbean hurricane relief), $300,000 (For emergency relief for victims).
$50,000 to Diocese of Pensacola-Tallahassee, Pensacola, FL. For emergency relief for victims of hurricanes.
$50,000 to Haitian Health Foundation, Norwich, CT. For housing project for clinic patients in Jeremie, Haiti.
$50,000 to Washington Middle School for Girls, DC. For general support for tuition-free school for impoverished girls.
$40,000 to Georgetown University Medical Center, DC. For KIDS Mobile Medical Clinic.
$40,000 to Operation Smile International, Norfolk, VA. For medical missions in Vietnam and India.
$30,000 to Capital Interfaith Hospitality Network, DC.

3702
The Orokawa Foundation, Inc. ✧ ☆
c/o Martin J. Eby
305 Washington Ave., No. 204
Towson, MD 21204

Established in 2005 in MD.
Foundation type: Independent foundation.
Financial data (yr. ended 6/30/05): Assets, $28,432,954 (M); gifts received, $27,975,000; expenditures, $754,751; qualifying distributions, $700,000; giving activities include $700,000 for 2 grants (high: $450,000; low: $250,000).
Purpose and activities: Giving primarily for leukemia and lymphoma research; funding also for a camp for children with life-threatening illnesses.
Fields of interest: Cancer, leukemia research; Recreation, camps.
Limitations: Applications not accepted. Giving primarily in Casco, ME, and White Plains, NY. No grants to individuals.
Application information: Contributes only to pre-selected organizations.
Officers: Bruce Cleland, Pres. and Treas.; Isobel Cleland, V.P. and Secy.
EIN: 201850543

3703
The Osprey Foundation ◇

305 Washington Ave., Ste. 204
Baltimore, MD   21204-4740

Established in 2002 in MD.
Donors: William C. Clark III; Mrs. William C. Clarke III.
Foundation type: Independent foundation.
Financial data (yr. ended 6/30/05): Assets, $19,753,916 (M); gifts received, $11,590,939; expenditures, $833,583; qualifying distributions, $739,500; giving activities include $739,500 for 34 grants (high: $50,000; low: $3,000).
Purpose and activities: Giving primarily for higher education and educational programs, as well as for health care, including medical research, Presbyterian ministries and children, youth, women, and family services, as well as for human services, including a community kitchen.
Fields of interest: Arts; Higher education; Education; Health care; Health organizations, association; Cancer research; Housing/shelter, development; Boy scouts; Human services; Children/youth, services; Women, centers/ services; International human rights; Christian agencies & churches.
Type of support: General/operating support; Scholarship funds.
Limitations: Applications not accepted. Giving primarily in Baltimore, MD. No grants to individuals.
Application information: Contributes only to pre-selected organizations.
Officers and Directors:* William C. Clarke III, Chair. and Pres.; Bonnie A. Clarke,* Secy.-Treas.; Lindsey B. Clarke; Meredith A. Clarke; Steven W. Clarke.
EIN: 141862154
Selected grants: The following grants were reported in 2005.
$40,000 to Boy Scouts of America, Baltimore, MD.
$40,000 to Family Tree, Baltimore, MD.
$30,000 to Coalition to End Childhood Lead Poisoning, Baltimore, MD.
$30,000 to Living Classrooms Foundation, Baltimore, MD.
$22,000 to University of Richmond, Richmond, VA.
$20,000 to House of Ruth Maryland, Baltimore, MD.
$15,000 to Carter Center, Atlanta, GA.
$15,000 to Leukemia & Lymphoma Society, Baltimore, MD.
$15,000 to Penn-Mar Organization, Maryland Line, MD.
$10,000 to Interchurch Medical Assistance, New Windsor, MD.

3704
The Anne Lindsey Otenasek Charitable Foundation, Inc. ◇ ☆

405 E. Joppa Rd., Ste. 100
Baltimore, MD   21286

Established in 2004 in MD.
Donors: Margaret B. Otenasek; Francis H. Otenasek; Catherine Otenasek Levitas; Richard J. Otenasek III.
Foundation type: Independent foundation.
Financial data (yr. ended 12/31/05): Assets, $6,068,860 (M); expenditures, $443,117; qualifying distributions, $439,783; giving activities include $400,000 for 5 grants (high: $130,500; low: $14,000).
Fields of interest: Education; Mental health, residential care; Safety/disasters.

Type of support: Building/renovation.
Limitations: Applications not accepted. Giving primarily to national organizations in MD and VA. No grants to individuals.
Application information: Contributes only to pre-selected organizations.
Officers and Directors:* Margaret B. Otenasek,* Pres.; John P. Hull,* Secy.; Harry J. Leonard,* Treas.; Page O. Kozak; Catherine O. Levitas; Francis H. Otenasek; John H. Otenasek; Richard J. Otenasek III.
EIN: 200702156

3705
Arthur W. Perdue Foundation, Inc. ◇

P.O. Box 1537
Salisbury, MD   21802   (410) 543-3217
Contact: Howard L. Millard

Donor: Franklin P. Perdue.
Foundation type: Independent foundation.
Financial data (yr. ended 12/31/05): Assets, $2,271,469 (M); expenditures, $348,192; qualifying distributions, $314,986; giving activities include $314,986 for grants.
Fields of interest: Libraries/library science; Education; Health care; Human services; Community development.
Limitations: Giving primarily in AL, CT, DE, IN, KY, MD, NC, SC, VA, TN, and WV. No grants to individuals.
Application information:
   Initial approach: Letter
   Deadline(s): None
Officers and Directors:* Franklin P. Perdue,* Pres.; James A. Perdue,* V.P.; Eileen F. Burza, Secy.-Treas.; Thomas E. Mahn; Mary H. Perdue.
EIN: 526054332
Selected grants: The following grants were reported in 2003.
$1,000,000 to Community Foundation of the Eastern Shore, Salisbury, MD.
$25,000 to Wor-Wic Community College, Salisbury, MD. For program support.
$20,000 to Shore Memorial Hospital, Nassawadox, VA. For radiation therapy.
$12,500 to Van Horn Community Christian Shelter, Van Horn, TX. For refrigeration and freezer.
$11,000 to Peninsula Regional Medical Center, Salisbury, MD. 2 grants: $1,000 (For monitoring system for trauma center), $10,000 (For image checker equipment).
$10,000 to Junior Achievement of the Eastern Shore, Salisbury, MD. For program support.
$10,000 to YMCA of Greater Charlotte, Charlotte, NC. For Ridge Campaign.
$4,500 to Association of Baltimore Area Grantmakers, Baltimore, MD. For program support.

3706
Clarence Manger & Audrey Cordero Plitt Trust ◇

c/o M&T Bank
25 S. Charles St., M.S. 101-621
Baltimore, MD   21203
Application address: c/o Mary M. Kirgan, 508 Woodside Rd., Baltimore, MD 21229, tel.: (410) 566-0914

Established in 1979 in MD.

Donor: Clarence M. Plitt†.
Foundation type: Independent foundation.
Financial data (yr. ended 8/31/05): Assets, $12,124,920 (M); expenditures, $710,482; qualifying distributions, $642,500; giving activities include $550,000 for 3 grants (high: $500,000; low: $25,000).
Purpose and activities: Grants to educational institutions for student loans.
Fields of interest: Secondary school/education; Higher education.
Type of support: Program-related investments/ loans; Matching/challenge support; Student loans —to individuals.
Limitations: Giving primarily in MA and NY.
Publications: Annual report.
Application information: Application form required.
   Initial approach: Letter
   Copies of proposal: 2
   Deadline(s): May 31
Officers: Mary Anne Kirgan, Mgr.; Robert S. Kirgan, Mgr.
Trustee: M&T Bank.
Number of staff: 1 full-time professional.
EIN: 526195778
Selected grants: The following grants were reported in 2005.
$500,000 to Wellesley College, Wellesley, MA.
$25,000 to School of the Holy Child, Rye, NY.
$25,000 to Trinity-Pawling School, Pawling, NY.

3707
The John J. Pohanka Family Foundation ◇ ☆

4608 St. Barnabas Rd.
Marlow Heights, MD   20748

Established in 1996 in MD.
Donor: John J. Pohanka.
Foundation type: Independent foundation.
Financial data (yr. ended 11/30/04): Assets, $7,512,585 (M); gifts received, $1,648,486; expenditures, $719,447; qualifying distributions, $687,900; giving activities include $687,900 for 34 grants (high: $500,000; low: $100).
Purpose and activities: Giving primarily for the arts, as well as for historical preservation; funding also for education and social services.
Fields of interest: Performing arts, opera; Historic preservation/historical societies; Arts; Elementary/ secondary education; Education; Human services.
Trustees: Steven Parker; Geoffrey Pohanka; John J. Pohanka.
EIN: 566784266

3708
Howard and Geraldine Polinger Family Foundation

(formerly Howard and Geraldine Polinger Foundation)
5530 Wisconsin Ave., Ste. 1000
Chevy Chase, MD   20815
Contact: Lorre Polinger, Pres.
E-mail: Polingerfoundation@polingerco.com; Tel./ fax: (617) 964-6199; URL: http:// foundationcenter.org/grantmaker/polinger/

Incorporated in 1968 in MD.
Donors: Howard Polinger; Geraldine Polinger.
Foundation type: Independent foundation.

Financial data (yr. ended 6/30/05): Assets, $19,722,133 (M); gifts received, $1,657,848; expenditures, $832,587; qualifying distributions, $692,273; giving activities include $621,900 for 67 grants (high: $118,000; low: $500).
Purpose and activities: Support for organizations that strengthen Jewish life, locally and in Israel. Foundation grants focus primarily on the Washington, DC, metropolitan area, and concentrate on providing opportunity and access to quality education, cultural arts, and services to enhance family well being.
Fields of interest: Arts; Education; Jewish agencies & temples.
International interests: Israel.
Type of support: General/operating support; Continuing support; Capital campaigns; Endowments; Program development; Curriculum development; Program evaluation; Matching/challenge support.
Limitations: Giving primarily in the Washington, DC, and Montgomery County, MD, area. No grants to individuals.
Publications: Application guidelines; Grants list.
Application information: Eligible organizations will be invited to submit a full proposal. See foundation Web site for application guidelines. Material sent by e-mail or fax will not be accepted. Application form required.
Initial approach: Letter of inquiry (no more than 2 pages)
Copies of proposal: 1
Deadline(s): None
Board meeting date(s): Spring and fall
Final notification: 1 month after board meeting
Officers and Directors:* Lorre Polinger,* Pres.; Arnold Polinger,* V.P.; Jan Polinger,* V.P.; Margaret Siegel, Secy.; David Polinger,* Treas.
Number of staff: 2 part-time professional; 1 part-time support.
EIN: 526078041
Selected grants: The following grants were reported in 2005.
$45,000 to Round House Theater, Bethesda, MD. 2 grants: $5,000, $40,000
$30,000 to Abraham Fund Initiatives, New York, NY.
$30,000 to Israel Project, DC.
$17,400 to Temple Sinai, DC. 3 grants: $2,000, $10,000, $5,400
$10,000 to Goucher College, Baltimore, MD.
$5,000 to McLean School of Maryland, Potomac, MD.
$5,000 to National Foundation for Jewish Culture, New York, NY.

3709
T. Rowe Price Associates Foundation, Inc. ✧
100 E. Pratt St.
Baltimore, MD 21202 (410) 345-3603
Contact: Christine D. Stein, Prog. Dir.

Established in 1981 in MD.
Donors: T. Rowe Price Associates, Inc.; T. Rowe Price Group, Inc.
Foundation type: Company-sponsored foundation.
Financial data (yr. ended 12/31/05): Assets, $39,002,588 (M); gifts received, $10,006,946; expenditures, $4,019,538; qualifying distributions, $3,961,961; giving activities include $3,924,524 for 827 grants (high: $344,004).

Purpose and activities: The foundation supports organizations involved with arts and culture, education, human services, and community development.
Fields of interest: Arts; Secondary school/education; Higher education; Education; Human services; Community development; Federated giving programs.
Type of support: General/operating support; Continuing support; Capital campaigns; Program development; Scholarship funds; Employee volunteer services; Employee matching gifts.
Limitations: Giving primarily in the metropolitan Baltimore, MD, area. No support for religious or political organizations, hospitals, health care providers, recreational sports leagues, or private foundations. No grants to individuals, or for sports-related fundraisers.
Publications: Application guidelines; Financial statement.
Application information: Application form not required.
Initial approach: Proposal
Copies of proposal: 1
Deadline(s): None
Board meeting date(s): Quarterly
Final notification: Several weeks following board meetings
Officers and Directors:* A.C. Hubbard, Jr.,* Pres.; Ann Allston Boyce,* V.P.; Jacqueline C. Hrabowski,* V.P.; Mary J. Miller,* V.P.; Brian C. Rogers,* V.P.; William F. Wendler II,* V.P.; Stephen W. Boesel,* Secy.-Treas.
Number of staff: 1 full-time professional; 1 full-time support.
EIN: 521231953

3710
Jerold & Marjorie Principato Foundation ✧ ☆
10401 Old Georgetown Rd., Ste. 408
Bethesda, MD 20814

Established in 1996 in MD.
Donor: International Medical and Educational Data LINK, Inc.
Foundation type: Company-sponsored foundation.
Financial data (yr. ended 12/31/05): Assets, $3,566,338 (M); expenditures, $534,312; qualifying distributions, $523,585; giving activities include $485,500 for 42 grants (high: $200,000; low: $100).
Purpose and activities: The foundation supports cemeteries and organizations involved with arts and culture, education, the environment, health, human services, and Christianity.
Fields of interest: Arts; Elementary/secondary education; Higher education; Education; Environment; Health care; Human services; Christian agencies & churches; Cemeteries/burial services.
Type of support: Annual campaigns; Capital campaigns.
Limitations: Applications not accepted. Giving primarily in Washington, DC, MD, and VA. No grants to individuals.
Application information: Contributes only to pre-selected organizations.
Directors: Deborah Lindsey; Jerold Principato; Marjorie Principato.
EIN: 521960863

Selected grants: The following grants were reported in 2004.
$39,500 to Saint Albans School, DC.
$34,500 to Beauvoir National Cathedral Elementary School, DC.
$11,500 to National Cathedral School, DC.
$7,500 to National Museum of Natural History, DC.
$3,500 to Washington Opera, DC.
$2,500 to Fauquier Hospital Foundation, Warrenton, VA.
$2,500 to National Gallery of Art, DC.
$1,000 to American University, DC.
$500 to Phillips Collection, DC.
$250 to National Trust for Historic Preservation, DC.

3711
The Procter & Gamble Cosmetics Foundation, Inc. ✧
(formerly The Procter & Gamble Cosmetics and Fragrance Foundation, Inc.)
11050 York Rd.
Hunt Valley, MD 21030-2098 (410) 785-5598
Contact: Carroll A. Bodie, Pres. and Secy.

Incorporated in 1951 in MD.
Donor: Noxell Corp.
Foundation type: Company-sponsored foundation.
Financial data (yr. ended 6/30/05): Assets, $992,283 (M); gifts received, $200,000; expenditures, $380,435; qualifying distributions, $366,952; giving activities include $359,366 for grants.
Purpose and activities: The foundation supports organizations involved with arts and culture, education, health, children and youth, human services, and civic affairs.
Fields of interest: Museums; Arts; Education; Health care; Children/youth, services; Human services; Federated giving programs; Public affairs.
Type of support: Annual campaigns; Capital campaigns; Building/renovation; Equipment; Land acquisition; Endowments; Emergency funds; Seed money; Internship funds; Scholarship funds; Research; Employee matching gifts; Matching/challenge support.
Limitations: Giving limited to the greater Baltimore, MD, area and New York, NY. No support for political organizations. No grants to individuals, or for general operating support or debt reduction; no loans.
Application information: Application form not required.
Initial approach: Proposal
Copies of proposal: 1
Deadline(s): None
Board meeting date(s): Quarterly
Final notification: 3 months
Officers: Carroll A. Bodie, Pres. and Secy.; Mason A. Brown, V.P. and Treas.; Cheryl G. Hudgins,* V.P.
EIN: 526041435
Selected grants: The following grants were reported in 2003.
$50,000 to Baltimore Symphony Orchestra, Baltimore, MD. 2 grants: $15,000, $35,000
$35,000 to Ruxton Country School, Baltimore, MD.
$27,500 to Independent College Fund of Maryland, Baltimore, MD.
$25,829 to Center Stage, Baltimore, MD.
$14,102 to United Way of Central Maryland, Baltimore, MD.
$13,200 to Junior Achievement of Central Maryland, Owings Mills, MD.

$12,500 to Kennedy Krieger Institute, Baltimore, MD.
$10,000 to House of Ruth, Louisville, KY.
$10,000 to Susan G. Komen Breast Cancer Foundation, Baltimore, MD.

3712
Provident Bank/Skip Johnson Charitable Foundation, Inc. ✧

114 E. Lexington St., M.C. 456
Baltimore, MD 21202-1703 (410) 277-2063
Contact: Vicki Cox, V.P.

Established in 1995 in MD.
Donors: Provident Bank of Maryland; The Provident Bank.
Foundation type: Company-sponsored foundation.
Financial data (yr. ended 12/31/03): Assets, $3,196 (M); gifts received, $382,500; expenditures, $373,134; qualifying distributions, $373,132; giving activities include $372,715 for 83 grants (high: $55,000; low: $100).
Purpose and activities: The foundation supports organizations involved with arts and culture, education, health, human services, and economic development.
Fields of interest: Arts; Education; Health organizations, association; Human services; Economic development.
Type of support: General/operating support; Continuing support; Annual campaigns; Capital campaigns; Building/renovation; Equipment; Emergency funds; Program development; Curriculum development; Scholarship funds; Research; In-kind gifts.
Limitations: Applications not accepted. Giving primarily in the greater Washington, DC, area and the greater Baltimore, MD, area. No support for churches not of direct benefit to the entire community. No grants to individuals, or for start-up needs.
Application information: Contributes only to pre-selected organizations.
Officers: Richard J. Oppitz, Pres.; Lillian S. Kilroy, V.P.; Robert L. Davis, Secy.; Karen Malecki, Treas.
EIN: 521954579
Selected grants: The following grants were reported in 2004.
$10,000 to Catholic Charities.
$10,000 to Economic Alliance of Greater Baltimore, Baltimore, MD.
$10,000 to Teach for America, New York, NY.
$8,150 to Mount Saint Joseph High School, Baltimore, MD.
$6,000 to Habitat for Humanity International.
$5,000 to Girl Scouts of the U.S.A..
$5,000 to Independent College Fund of Maryland, Baltimore, MD.
$5,000 to Kennedy Krieger Institute, Baltimore, MD.
$5,000 to Maryland Science Center, Baltimore, MD.
$5,000 to Urban League.

3713
John A. Quinn Foundation, Inc. ✧ ☆

(formerly John A. Quinn Foundation)
5020 Nicholson Ct., Ste. 207A
Kensington, MD 20895-1007
Contact: William Redfern

Established in 1968.
Foundation type: Independent foundation.

Financial data (yr. ended 12/31/05): Assets, $4,267,868 (M); expenditures, $1,648,870; qualifying distributions, $1,348,500; giving activities include $1,348,500 for grants.
Purpose and activities: Giving primarily for Roman Catholic education, churches, and social services.
Fields of interest: Performing arts, opera; Secondary school/education; Higher education; Aging, centers/services; Roman Catholic agencies & churches.
Limitations: Giving primarily in Washington, DC, and MD. No grants to individuals.
Application information:
  Initial approach: Letter
  Deadline(s): None
Officers: Eileen S. Quinn, Pres.; Robert F. Comstock, Secy.
Directors: Lauren L. Bailey; George J. Quinn, Jr.; Kathleen M. Quinn; Kimberly B. Shaughnessy.
EIN: 526081612
Selected grants: The following grants were reported in 2004.
$215,000 to Archdiocese of Washington, Baltimore, MD.
$65,200 to Catholic University of America, DC.
$2,500 to Actors Fund of America, New York, NY.

3714
The Bill Raskob Foundation, Inc. ✧

P.O. Box 507
Crownsville, MD 21032-0507 (410) 879-0500
Contact: Edward H. Robinson, Corp. Secy.
E-mail: info@billraskob.org; Additional E-mail: ed@billraskob.org; URL: http://www.billraskob.org

Incorporated in 1928 in DE.
Donors: John J. Raskob†; Helena S. Raskob Corcoran†.
Foundation type: Independent foundation.
Financial data (yr. ended 12/31/05): Assets, $5,223,809 (M); expenditures, $554,137; qualifying distributions, $437,970; giving activities include $368,459 for grants.
Purpose and activities: Giving limited to no-interest loans to finance education for American citizens currently enrolled at accredited institutions within the U.S.
Type of support: Student loans—to individuals.
Limitations: Giving on a national basis. No grants for scholarships, first year studies for undergraduates or medical students, or for foreign students.
Publications: Application guidelines; Program policy statement.
Application information: The foundation strongly suggests all applicants first apply for government loans or grants. Application form and guidelines available on foundation Web site. Application form required.
  Initial approach: Letter and SASE
  Copies of proposal: 1
  Deadline(s): Request application between Jan. 1 and Apr. 1; deadline May 1
  Board meeting date(s): Annually
  Final notification: Before Sept.
Officers and Directors:* Theodore H. Bremekamp III,* Pres.; Anthony L. Robinson,* 1st V.P.; Edward H. Robinson,* Corp. Secy.; Kathleen D. Smith,* Treas.; Noelle Fracyon; Sr. Pat Geuting; Thomas Geuting; Patrick McGrory; Timothy T. Raskob; Eddie Robinson; Lucia Robinson; Maria Rosa Robinson; Peter Robinson.

Number of staff: 1 full-time professional.
EIN: 510110185

3715
The Rathmann Family Foundation ✧

c/o WindCrest Mgmt., LLC
1290 Bay Dale Dr., PMB No. 352
Arnold, MD 21012 (410) 349-2376
Contact: Rick Rathmann

Established in 1991 in WA.
Donors: George Rathmann; Joy Rathmann.
Foundation type: Independent foundation.
Financial data (yr. ended 12/31/04): Assets, $47,295,980 (M); expenditures, $2,687,485; qualifying distributions, $2,571,854; giving activities include $2,383,778 for 102 grants (high: $211,000; low: $100).
Purpose and activities: The mission (or purpose) of the foundation is to promote and support innovation, development and excellence in science, technology, education and the environment. The foundation funds organizations and programs which apply research, science, technology and education to improving lives and strengthening communities and the nation. The foundation's educational interests extend from elementary through post-secondary years and focus primarily on science, math, technology, the environment, medicine and the arts. Related areas of foundation interest include biotechnology and conservation of the environment and open spaces for low impact use, such as hiking, walking and off-leash recreation.
Fields of interest: Arts; Education; Environment; Health care; Health organizations, association; Children/youth, services; Science, research; Science, public education; Mathematics; Economically disadvantaged.
Type of support: General/operating support; Continuing support; Capital campaigns; Equipment; Endowments; Program development; Conferences/seminars; Seed money; Curriculum development; Fellowships; Internship funds; Scholarship funds; Research; Program evaluation; Program-related investments/loans; Matching/challenge support.
Limitations: Applications not accepted. Giving primarily in the San Francisco Bay Area, CA, Annapolis, MD, the metropolitan Minneapolis-St. Paul, MN, area, Philadelphia, PA, and Seattle, WA. No support for private foundations, religious organizations for religious activities, civil rights, social action, or advocacy organizations, fraternal, labor, or veterans' groups, political purposes, or mental health counseling. No grants to individuals, or for fundraising, media events, public relations, propaganda, or annual appeals.
Application information: The foundation will fund only board-initiated or solicited programs and, in selected cases, organizations and programs in which it has previously invested. Unsolicited requests for funds not accepted.
Officers and Directors:* George B. Rathmann,* Chair.; Margaret Crosby Rathmann,* Pres.; James Louis Rathmann,* V.P.; Laura Jean Rathmann,* V.P.; Frances Joy Rathmann,* Secy.; Sally Rathmann Kadifa, M.D.*, Treas.; Richard G. Rathmann,* Exec. Dir.
EIN: 521757445
Selected grants: The following grants were reported in 2004.
$202,000 to Princeton University, Princeton, NJ.
$125,000 to National Science and Technology Medals Foundation, DC.

$120,000 to Nicasio School Foundation, Nicasio, CA.

$115,979 to Stanford University, Stanford, CA.

$93,000 to Key School, Annapolis, MD.

$85,500 to Marin Organic, Point Reyes Station, CA.

$40,000 to Science Museum of Minnesota, Saint Paul, MN.

$30,000 to Peoples Light and Theater Company, Malvern, PA.

$25,000 to Alumnae Association of Smith College, Northampton, MA.

$5,000 to Guthrie Theater, Minneapolis, MN.

3716
RFI Foundation ◇ ☆
7200 Wisconsin Ave., Ste. 1006
Bethesda, MD 20814-4885

Established in 2002 in MD.
Donors: Joshua B. Rales; Debra Rales.
Foundation type: Independent foundation.
Financial data (yr. ended 12/31/05): Assets, $1,014,890 (M); gifts received, $200,000; expenditures, $353,787; qualifying distributions, $351,014; giving activities include $351,014 for grants.
Fields of interest: Medical school/education; Education; Medical research; Jewish agencies & temples.
Limitations: Applications not accepted. Giving primarily in MD; giving also in Washington, DC, NY, and VA. No grants to individuals.
Application information: Contributes only to pre-selected organizations.
Officers: Joshua B. Rales, Pres. and Treas.; Debra L. Rales, Secy.
Director: Norman Freidkin.
EIN: 542076962
Selected grants: The following grants were reported in 2004.
$90,000 to Montgomery County Public Schools Educational Foundation, Rockville, MD.

$10,128 to Hadassah, Silver Spring, MD.

$10,000 to Johns Hopkins University, School of Medicine, Department of Pediatrics, Baltimore, MD.

$10,000 to University of Virginia, Center for Politics, Charlottesville, VA.

$7,000 to Norwood School, Bethesda, MD.

$5,250 to Washington Hospital Center Foundation, DC.

$5,000 to Hebrew Home of Greater Washington, Rockville, MD.

$5,000 to Melvin J. Berman Hebrew Academy, Rockville, MD.

$250 to Jewish Women International, DC.

$100 to Suburban Hospital Foundation, Bethesda, MD.

3717
The Rock Springs Foundation ◇
6903 Rockledge Dr., Ste. 214
Bethesda, MD 20817

Established in 1998 in MD.
Donor: Chester Davenport.
Foundation type: Independent foundation.
Financial data (yr. ended 12/31/04): Assets, $4,414,227 (M); gifts received, $30,000; expenditures, $693,366; qualifying distributions,

$627,990; giving activities include $598,333 for 11 grants (high: $275,000; low: $5,000).
Purpose and activities: Support primarily for education and civil rights.
Fields of interest: Higher education; Education; Civil rights, minorities; African Americans/Blacks; Economically disadvantaged.
Limitations: Applications not accepted. Giving primarily in the metropolitan Washington, DC, area, including portions of MD and VA; giving also in Atlanta, GA, and Chicago, IL. No grants to individuals.
Application information: Contributes only to pre-selected organizations.
Officer: Chester Davenport, Pres.
EIN: 223624934

3718
Rollins-Luetkemeyer Foundation, Inc. ◇
(formerly The Rollins-Luetkemeyer Charitable Foundation, Inc.)
1427 Clarkview Rd., Ste. 500
Baltimore, MD 21209-2100 (443) 921-4358
Contact: John A. Luetkemeyer, Jr., Pres.

Established in 1961 in MD.
Foundation type: Independent foundation.
Financial data (yr. ended 12/31/05): Assets, $63,517,315 (M); expenditures, $2,855,162; qualifying distributions, $2,263,480; giving activities include $2,233,480 for 20 grants (high: $1,360,480; low: $5,000).
Purpose and activities: At least 70 percent of future giving will be for building funds for early childhood, elementary and secondary schools; support also for certain hospitals and institutions, social service agencies, health organizations, and historical preservation.
Fields of interest: Historic preservation/historical societies; Education, early childhood education; Elementary school/education; Higher education; Education; Hospitals (general); Health care; Health organizations, association; Human services; Protestant agencies & churches.
Type of support: General/operating support; Annual campaigns; Building/renovation.
Limitations: Giving primarily in the Baltimore, MD, area. No grants to individuals.
Application information: Funds largely to organizations in which donors have a direct interest. Application form not required.
Initial approach: Letter
Deadline(s): None
Officers and Directors:* John A. Luetkemeyer, Jr.,* Pres.; Anne L. Stone,* V.P.; Richard E. Levine,* Secy.; Esther Templeton, Treas.
Number of staff: 2 part-time professional.
EIN: 526041536
Selected grants: The following grants were reported in 2005.
$1,360,480 to McDonogh School, Owings Mills, MD.

$300,000 to Lawrenceville School, Lawrenceville, NJ.

$205,000 to Williams College, Williamstown, MA.

$28,000 to Dickinson College, Carlisle, PA.

$25,000 to Wesley Theological Seminary, DC.

$10,000 to Washington and Lee University, Lexington, VA.

$5,000 to Maryvale Preparatory School, Brooklandville, MD.

3719
The Henry and Ruth Blaustein Rosenberg Foundation, Inc. ◇
10 E. Baltimore St., Ste. 1111
Baltimore, MD 21202 (410) 347-7201
Contact: Henry A. Rosenberg, Jr., Pres.
FAX: (410) 347-7210; E-mail: info@blaufund.org;
URL: http://www.blaufund.org/foundations/henryandruth_f.html

Incorporated in 1959 in MD.
Donors: Ruth Blaustein Rosenberg†; Henry A. Rosenberg, Jr.; Ruth R. Marder; American Trading and Production Corp.; Rosemore, Inc.
Foundation type: Independent foundation.
Financial data (yr. ended 12/31/05): Assets, $29,580,839 (M); gifts received, $594,881; expenditures, $2,050,978; qualifying distributions, $1,822,085; giving activities include $1,723,417 for 81 grants (high: $475,000; low: $1,500).
Purpose and activities: The mission of the foundation is to improve the human condition through promoting life-long educational opportunities, research advances and a spectrum of cultural programming.
Fields of interest: Arts; Adult education—literacy, basic skills & GED; Health care; Employment, services; Youth development, adult & child programs.
Type of support: General/operating support; Annual campaigns; Capital campaigns; Building/renovation; Matching/challenge support.
Limitations: Giving primarily in the greater Baltimore, MD, area. No support for unaffiliated schools. No grants to individuals, or for fundraising events, direct mail solicitations; no loans.
Publications: Application guidelines; Grants list.
Application information: The foundation does not accept unsolicited proposals for health research. Complete application guidelines available on foundation Web site. Application form not required.
Initial approach: Letter
Copies of proposal: 1
Deadline(s): None
Board meeting date(s): Semiannually
Final notification: 4 to 6 months
Officers and Trustees:* Henry A. Rosenberg, Jr.,* Pres.; Judith R. Hoffberger,* V.P.; Ruth R. Marder,* V.P.; Betsy F. Ringel, Secy.; Barry L. Miller, Treas.
EIN: 526038384
Selected grants: The following grants were reported in 2003.
$712,500 to The Associated: Jewish Community Federation of Baltimore, Baltimore, MD. 2 grants: $237,500 (For unrestricted support), $475,000 (For unrestricted support).

$300,000 to Kennedy Krieger Institute, Baltimore, MD. For unrestricted support.

$100,000 to Walters Art Gallery Endowment Foundation, Baltimore, MD. 2 grants: $50,000 each (For unrestricted support).

$78,500 to Baltimore Symphony Orchestra, Baltimore, MD. For unrestricted support.

$70,000 to Maryland Zoological Society, Baltimore, MD. For unrestricted support.

$50,000 to B and O Railroad Museum, Baltimore, MD. For unrestricted support.

$50,000 to Johns Hopkins Hospital, Baltimore, MD. For unrestricted support.

$30,000 to Family Tree, Baltimore, MD. For unrestricted support.

3720
The Dorothy L. & Henry A. Rosenberg, Jr. Foundation, Inc.

1 N. Charles St., 22nd Fl.
Baltimore, MD 21201
Contact: Henry A. Rosenberg, Jr., Pres.

Established in 1999 in MD.
Donor: Henry A. Rosenberg, Jr.
Foundation type: Independent foundation.
Financial data (yr. ended 12/31/05): Assets, $822,335 (M); gifts received, $550,687; expenditures, $925,664; qualifying distributions, $920,164; giving activities include $915,450 for 44 grants (high: $500,000; low: $1,000).
Fields of interest: Arts; Higher education; Zoos/zoological societies; Boy scouts; Children, services; Foundations (community).
Limitations: Applications not accepted. Giving primarily in MD. No grants to individuals.
Application information: Unsolicited requests for funds not accepted.
Officers and Trustees:* Henry A. Rosenberg, Jr.,* Pres.; Dorothy L. Rosenberg,* V.P.; Frank B. Rosenberg, Secy.
EIN: 522185213
Selected grants: The following grants were reported in 2005.
$500,000 to McDonogh School, Owings Mills, MD.
$50,000 to Barbara Bush Foundation for Family Literacy, DC.
$20,000 to Johns Hopkins University, Baltimore, MD. 3 grants: $10,000, $5,000, $5,000
$16,000 to Saint Marys College of Maryland Foundation, Saint Marys City, MD.
$12,500 to Goucher College, Baltimore, MD.
$10,000 to Carson Scholars Fund, Towson, MD.
$10,000 to Notre Dame Preparatory School, Towson, MD.
$5,000 to Institute of Notre Dame, Baltimore, MD.

3721
Ben & Esther Rosenbloom Foundation, Inc.

Reservoir Cir., Ste. 202
Baltimore, MD 21208
Contact: Howard Rosenbloom, Exec. Dir.

Established in 1982 in MD.
Donor: Ben Rosenbloom†.
Foundation type: Independent foundation.
Financial data (yr. ended 12/31/04): Assets, $35,314,028 (M); expenditures, $2,018,143; qualifying distributions, $1,646,589; giving activities include $1,478,705 for 80 grants (high: $450,000; low: $215).
Purpose and activities: Giving primarily to higher education, human services, Jewish federated giving programs and Jewish agencies.
Fields of interest: Higher education; Human services; Jewish federated giving programs; Jewish agencies & temples.
Limitations: Giving primarily in Baltimore, MD. No support for disease specific research, advocacy, the environment, or for social work or psychology. No grants to individuals, or for endowments.
Application information: Application form not required.
Initial approach: Proposal
Copies of proposal: 1
Deadline(s): None
Final notification: Positive responses only

Officers and Directors:* Esther Rosenbloom,* Pres.; Robert Rosenbloom,* Secy.; Keith Rosenbloom,* Treas.; Howard Rosenbloom, Exec. Dir.; Michelle G. Rosenbloom, Medical Dir.
Number of staff: 1 full-time professional.
EIN: 521258672
Selected grants: The following grants were reported in 2003.
$550,000 to Shoshana S. Cardin Jewish Community High School, Baltimore, MD.
$25,000 to American Israel Education Foundation (AIEF), DC.
$25,000 to Hillel of Greater Baltimore, Baltimore, MD.
$25,000 to United Way of Central Maryland, Baltimore, MD.
$16,668 to Johns Hopkins University, Baltimore, MD.
$15,000 to Hadassah, The Womens Zionist Organization of America, New York, NY.
$12,000 to Torah Institute of Baltimore, Baltimore, MD.
$10,000 to Aleph Society, New York, NY.
$10,000 to Chizuk Amuno Congregation, Baltimore, MD.
$5,000 to Gush Etzion Foundation, Manchester, NH.

3722
Elizabeth B. and Arthur E. Roswell Foundation, Inc.

c/o Betsy Ringel
10 E. Baltimore St., Ste. 1111
Baltimore, MD 21202-1620
Contact: Arthur E. Roswell, Pres.
E-mail: info@blafund.org

Incorporated in 1986 in MD.
Donor: Elizabeth B. Roswell.
Foundation type: Independent foundation.
Financial data (yr. ended 12/31/05): Assets, $10,294,396 (M); expenditures, $626,652; qualifying distributions, $577,215; giving activities include $533,666 for 62 grants (high: $66,666; low: $500; average: $1,000–$30,000).
Purpose and activities: Giving primarily for basic human needs and the environment.
Fields of interest: Environment, natural resources; Health care; Human services; Family services.
Type of support: General/operating support; Annual campaigns.
Limitations: Applications not accepted. Giving primarily in Baltimore, MD, NJ, and southeastern PA. No grants to individuals, or for fundraising or direct mailings; no loans.
Application information: Unsolicited requests for funds not accepted.
Officers and Trustees:* Elizabeth B. Roswell,* Chair.; Arthur E. Roswell,* Pres.; Barbara Roswell,* V.P.; Marjorie B. Roswell,* V.P.; Robert A. Roswell,* V.P.; Judith E. Weinstein,* V.P.; Kenneth C. Weinstein,* V.P.; Lynn Wintriss, Secy.; Maureen L. Stewart, Treas.
EIN: 521490498
Selected grants: The following grants were reported in 2005.
$66,666 to LifeBridge Health, Baltimore, MD.
$50,000 to Mount Sinai School of Medicine of New York University, New York, NY.
$30,000 to American Society for the Protection of Nature in Israel, Great Neck, NY.
$20,000 to Fusion Partnerships, Baltimore, MD.

$18,000 to Hillel of Greater Baltimore, Baltimore, MD.
$15,000 to Environmental Defense, New York, NY.
$12,500 to Philadelphia Citizens for Children and Youth, Philadelphia, PA.
$10,000 to People for the American Way Foundation, DC.
$10,000 to Physicians Committee for Responsible Medicine, DC.
$8,000 to Herring Run Watershed Association, Baltimore, MD.

3723
The Rothschild Charitable Foundation, Inc. ✧

1122 Kenilworth Ave., Ste. 317
Baltimore, MD 21202

Established in 1986 in MD.
Donor: Stanford Z. Rothschild, Jr.
Foundation type: Independent foundation.
Financial data (yr. ended 12/31/04): Assets, $5,940,997 (M); gifts received, $417,354; expenditures, $486,373; qualifying distributions, $439,877; giving activities include $439,877 for grants.
Fields of interest: Museums; Performing arts, music; Education; Health organizations, association; Human services; Federated giving programs; Jewish federated giving programs; Jewish agencies & temples.
Limitations: Applications not accepted. Giving primarily in Baltimore, MD. No grants to individuals; no loans or program-related investments.
Application information: Contributes only to pre-selected organizations.
Officers and Directors:* Stanford Z. Rothschild, Jr.,* Pres. and Treas.; Cory Rothschild,* V.P. and Secy.; Manuel Dupkin II; David Rothschild; Frederick Steinmann.
EIN: 521492357

3724
Rouse Company Foundation, Inc. ✧

10275 Little Patuxent Pkwy.
Columbia, MD 21044
Contact: Margaret P. Mauro, V.P. and Secy.
E-mail: mmauro@therousecompany.com

Established in 1967 in MD.
Donors: The Rouse Co.; The Hughes Corp.; The Rouse Company Incentive Compensation Statutory Trust; General Growth Properties, Inc.
Foundation type: Company-sponsored foundation.
Financial data (yr. ended 12/31/04): Assets, $27,961,412 (M); gifts received, $21,139,029; expenditures, $1,910,759; qualifying distributions, $1,847,234; giving activities include $1,847,234 for 308 grants (high: $200,000; low: $25).
Purpose and activities: The foundation supports organizations involved with arts and culture, education, health, housing, human services, and community development.
Fields of interest: Visual arts; Museums (art); Museums (children's); Performing arts; Arts; Elementary/secondary education; Higher education; Education; Hospitals (general); Health care; Housing/shelter; Children/youth, services; Human services; Economic development; Community development; Federated giving programs.

Type of support: Annual campaigns; Capital campaigns; Building/renovation; Program development.
Limitations: Giving primarily in the central MD area. No support for religious or political organizations. No grants to individuals, or for endowments, disability- or disease-specific research, publications, promotional campaigns, or predominately government-supported projects.
Publications: Informational brochure (including application guidelines).
Application information: Application form not required.
> *Initial approach:* Mail or E-mail proposal to foundation
> *Copies of proposal:* 1
> *Deadline(s):* None

Officers and Trustees:* Anthony W. Deering,* Chair., Pres., and Treas.; Margaret P. Mauro, V.P. and Secy.; Heather Crosby,* Exec. Dir.; Gordon H. Glenn; Alton J. Scavo.
Number of staff: 1 full-time professional; 1 part-time professional.
EIN: 526056273
Selected grants: The following grants were reported in 2004.
$325,000 to New Song Community Learning Center, Baltimore, MD. 2 grants: $200,000, $125,000
$160,000 to United Way. 2 grants: $60,000, $100,000
$75,000 to Baltimore Museum of Art, Baltimore, MD.
$75,000 to Hippodrome Foundation, Baltimore, MD.
$42,857 to Howard Hospital Foundation, Columbia, MD.
$20,000 to Kennedy Krieger Institute, Baltimore, MD.
$10,000 to American Visionary Art Museum, Baltimore, MD.
$400 to Marquette University, Milwaukee, WI.

3725
The Herman and Walter Samuelson Foundation ✧
c/o Friedman & Friedman, LLP
409 Washington Ave., Ste. 900
Towson, MD 21204-4905

Established in 1995 in MD.
Donor: Herman Samuelson.
Foundation type: Independent foundation.
Financial data (yr. ended 12/31/05): Assets, $15,330,104 (M); expenditures, $800,937; qualifying distributions, $743,868; giving activities include $720,500 for 19 grants (high: $300,000; low: $1,000).
Purpose and activities: Giving primarily to hospitals and health associations, including an oncology center; funding also for higher education and Jewish organizations and temples.
Fields of interest: Higher education; Law school/education; Hospitals (general); Health organizations, association; Cancer; Jewish agencies & temples.
Limitations: Applications not accepted. Giving primarily in Baltimore, MD. No grants to individuals.
Application information: Contributes only to pre-selected organizations.
Trustees: Robert Damie; Louis F. Friedman.
EIN: 521921761

3726
Schifter Family Foundation ✧ ☆
c/o R. Philipson Co.
8601 Georgia Ave., Ste. 1001
Silver Spring, MD 20910

Established in 2000 in DC.
Donors: Richard P. Schifter; Jennifer Schifter.
Foundation type: Independent foundation.
Financial data (yr. ended 12/31/05): Assets, $1,960,267 (M); expenditures, $555,809; qualifying distributions, $414,650; giving activities include $414,650 for grants.
Purpose and activities: Giving primarily for education, environmental conservation groups, and Jewish organizations.
Fields of interest: Elementary/secondary education; Higher education; Environment, natural resources; Human services; Youth, services; Jewish agencies & temples.
Limitations: Applications not accepted. Giving on a national basis, with emphasis on New York, NY, and Washington, DC. No grants to individuals.
Application information: Contributes only to pre-selected organizations.
Trustees: Jennifer Schifter; Richard P. Schifter.
EIN: 134148941
Selected grants: The following grants were reported in 2004.
$25,000 to National Cathedral School, DC.
$25,000 to Youth, INC, DC.
$20,000 to Amherst College, Amherst, MA.
$11,000 to William Wendt Center for Loss and Healing, DC.
$10,000 to Robert Packard Foundation for ALS Research, San Francisco, CA.
$5,000 to Colgate University, Hamilton, NY.
$5,000 to Fight Crime: Invest in Kids, DC.
$5,000 to Nature Conservancy, New York, NY.
$1,500 to Marthas Vineyard Preservation Trust, Edgartown, MA.
$1,000 to Island Affordable Housing Fund, Vineyard Haven, MA.

3727
The Shared Earth Foundation
113 Hoffman Ln.
Chestertown, MD 21620 (410) 778-6868
Contact: Caroline D. Gabel, C.E.O. and Pres.
FAX: (410) 778-9050;
E-mail: sharedearth@aol.com; URL: http://www.sharedearth.org/

Established in 1999 in MD.
Donor: Caroline D. Gabel.
Foundation type: Independent foundation.
Financial data (yr. ended 3/31/05): Assets, $7,132,472 (M); gifts received, $1,296,072; expenditures, $488,266; qualifying distributions, $454,200; giving activities include $447,685 for 32 grants (high: $40,000; low: $1,000).
Purpose and activities: Support for the environment, biodiversity, the protection and enhancement of the natural habitat, and the protection of wildlife and endangered species.
Fields of interest: Environment, natural resources; Environment, land resources; Environment; Animals/wildlife, preservation/protection; Animals/wildlife, endangered species.
International interests: Bolivia; Canada; Ecuador; Guatemala; India; Indonesia; Malaysia; Mexico; Pakistan; Peru.

Type of support: General/operating support; Continuing support; Program development; Research; Technical assistance; Matching/challenge support.
Limitations: Applications not accepted. Giving on a national and international basis. No grants to individuals, or for scholarships, fellowships, or financial aid.
Publications: Annual report.
Application information: Unsolicited requests for funds not accepted. Applications are by invitation only. See foundation Web site for information.
> *Board meeting date(s):* Quarterly

Officer: Caroline D. Gabel, C.E.O. and Pres.
EIN: 522151843
Selected grants: The following grants were reported in 2004.
$35,000 to Nature Conservancy, Arlington, VA. For program support in Bolivia.
$25,000 to American Rivers, DC. For Corps Reform Campaign.
$25,000 to Defenders of Wildlife, DC. For general support.
$25,000 to National Parks Conservation Association, DC. For motorized abuse program to prevent further damage to national Parks from unregulated motorized.
$25,000 to Orangutan Foundation International, Los Angeles, CA. To establish patrols to protect the Orangutans within the Tanjung Putting National Park.
$25,000 to Rachels Network, DC. For general support.
$20,000 to African Wildlife Foundation, DC. For Heartlands Science Unit.
$20,000 to American Forests, DC. For Community Forestry Education program.
$20,000 to Center for Policy Alternatives, DC.
$16,000 to Worldwatch Institute, DC. For World Summit for sustainable development.

3728
The Shattuck Family Foundation, Inc. ✧
20 Blythewood Rd.
Baltimore, MD 21210

Established in 1999 in MD.
Donor: Mayo A. Shattuck III.
Foundation type: Independent foundation.
Financial data (yr. ended 12/31/05): Assets, $731,574 (M); gifts received, $39,542; expenditures, $347,053; qualifying distributions, $339,075; giving activities include $335,575 for 28 grants (high: $100,000; low: $200; average: $5,000–$10,000).
Purpose and activities: Giving for higher education and medical research; funding also for the arts and social services.
Fields of interest: Museums (art); Higher education; Education; Health organizations; Medical research, institute; Human services; Federated giving programs.
Limitations: Applications not accepted. Giving primarily in Baltimore, MD; some funding nationally. No grants to individuals.
Application information: Contributes only to pre-selected organizations.
Officers and Trustees:* Mayo A. Shattuck III,* Pres.; Molly Ann George Shattuck,* Secy.-Treas.; Mayo A. Shattuck IV.
EIN: 522165454
Selected grants: The following grants were reported in 2005.

$100,000 to Williams College, Williamstown, MA.

$50,000 to Baltimore School for the Arts, Baltimore, MD.

$35,000 to United Way of Central Maryland, Baltimore, MD.

$25,000 to Calvert School, Baltimore, MD.

$10,000 to Baltimore School for the Arts Foundation, Baltimore, MD.

$5,600 to Maryland Institute College of Art, Baltimore, MD.

3729
The Thomas B. and Elizabeth M. Sheridan Foundation, Inc.
Executive Plz. II
11350 McCormick Rd., Ste. 704
Hunt Valley, MD 21031 (410) 771-0475
Contact: James L. Sinclair, Pres.

Incorporated in 1962 in MD.
Donors: Thomas B. Sheridan†; Elizabeth M. Sheridan†.
Foundation type: Independent foundation.
Financial data (yr. ended 12/31/05): Assets, $20,598,524 (M); expenditures, $1,061,138; qualifying distributions, $895,362; giving activities include $773,656 for 17 grants (high: $150,000; low: $3,900; average: $15,000–$50,000).
Purpose and activities: Emphasis on private secondary schools and cultural organizations in the greater Baltimore, MD, area.
Fields of interest: Arts; Secondary school/education.
Type of support: Continuing support; Annual campaigns; Capital campaigns; Building/renovation; Equipment; Endowments; Program development; Matching/challenge support.
Limitations: Giving primarily in the greater Baltimore, MD, area. No grants to individuals, or for employee matching gifts; no loans.
Publications: Application guidelines; Program policy statement.
Application information: Application form required.
  Initial approach: Letter
  Copies of proposal: 2
  Deadline(s): None
  Board meeting date(s): Mar., June, Sept., and Dec.
Officers and Trustees:* James L. Sinclair,* Pres.; L. Patrick Deering,* V.P.; John B. Sinclair,* Secy.; Philip D. English,* Treas.; Mark R. Fetting.
Number of staff: 1 full-time professional; 1 part-time support.
EIN: 526075270
Selected grants: The following grants were reported in 2004.
$155,000 to Mother Seton Academy, Baltimore, MD.
$125,000 to Loyola Blakefield High School, Towson, MD.
$100,000 to Archbishop Curley High School, Baltimore, MD.
$100,000 to Institute of Notre Dame, Baltimore, MD.
$100,000 to John Carroll School, Bel Air, MD.
$100,000 to Maryvale Preparatory School, Brooklandville, MD.
$100,000 to Park School of Baltimore, Brooklandville, MD.
$50,000 to Bryn Mawr School, Baltimore, MD.
$30,000 to School Sisters of Notre Dame, Baltimore, MD.

$20,000 to Johns Hopkins University, Baltimore, MD.

3730
The George L. Shields Foundation, Inc. ◇
11140 Rockville Pike, Ste. 620
Rockville, MD 20852-3177
Contact: Robert M. Reiner, Secy.-Treas.

Established in 1993 in DC.
Donor: George L. Shields†.
Foundation type: Independent foundation.
Financial data (yr. ended 12/31/04): Assets, $35,238,219 (M); gifts received, $4,138,553; expenditures, $1,221,152; qualifying distributions, $893,000; giving activities include $893,000 for 74 grants (high: $300,000; low: $1,000).
Fields of interest: Museums; Performing arts; Arts; Higher education; Youth development; Human services; Children/youth, services; Homeless, human services.
Limitations: Applications not accepted. Giving on a national basis, with some emphasis on the greater metropolitan Washington, DC, area.
Application information: Contributes only to pre-selected organizations.
Officers and Directors:* Ann Schein Carlyss,* Pres.; Robert M. Reiner, Secy.-Treas.; Robert Brenengen; Bruce MacDonald; Carolyn Moore; Laszlo Steven Medgyesy, M.D.
EIN: 521851638

3731
Shrensky Foundation, Inc. ◇ ☆
10708 Balantre Ln.
Potomac, MD 20854

Established in 2000 in MD.
Donors: Lewis Shrensky; Barbara Shrensky.
Foundation type: Independent foundation.
Financial data (yr. ended 12/31/05): Assets, $291,391 (M); gifts received, $140,000; expenditures, $401,568; qualifying distributions, $400,000; giving activities include $400,000 for 1 grant.
Fields of interest: Jewish agencies & temples.
Limitations: Applications not accepted. Giving primarily in Potomac, MD. No grants to individuals.
Application information: Contributes only to pre-selected organizations.
Officers: Lewis F. Shrensky, Pres. and Treas.; Barbara Shrensky, V.P. and Secy.
EIN: 522284925

3732
The Bernard E. Shultz Foundation, Inc. ◇
15022 Snowden Dr.
Silver Spring, MD 20905 (301) 989-1511
Contact: Jerold J. Samet, Pres.

Established in 2001 in MD.
Donors: Bernard Shultz Trust; Youth Leaders International.
Foundation type: Independent foundation.
Financial data (yr. ended 12/31/04): Assets, $4,994,514 (M); gifts received, $33,110; expenditures, $923,329; qualifying distributions, $904,054; giving activities include $890,000 for 1 grant, and $11,550 for 8 grants to individuals (high: $10,000; low: $100).
Purpose and activities: Giving for children's charities, youth activities, and promoting international and cultural exchanges for youths and young adults.
Fields of interest: Youth development, adult & child programs; Children/youth, services; Children/youth.
Application information: Application form not required.
  Deadline(s): None
Officers and Directors:* Jerold J. Samet,* Pres.; Michael L. Dixon,* V.P.; Paul M. Bessel, Secy.; Thomas A. Russo,* Treas.
EIN: 521994346

3733
The Carlynn and Lawrence Silverman Family Foundation, Inc. ◇ ☆
5630 Wisconsin Ave., Ste. 104
Chevy Chase, MD 20815

Established in 1996 in MD.
Donors: Carlynn Silverman; Lawrence Silverman.
Foundation type: Independent foundation.
Financial data (yr. ended 12/31/05): Assets, $3,101,469 (M); gifts received, $233; expenditures, $387,265; qualifying distributions, $357,373; giving activities include $357,373 for grants.
Purpose and activities: Giving primarily to Jewish agencies.
Fields of interest: Higher education; Hospitals (general); Jewish agencies & temples.
Limitations: Applications not accepted. Giving primarily in Washington, DC, and MD. No grants to individuals.
Application information: Contributes only to pre-selected organizations.
Officers: Carlynn Silverman, Pres.; Lawrence Silverman, V.P. and Secy.; Amy Louise Dickstein, V.P.; Lisa Ivy Harwood, V.P.
EIN: 522002734
Selected grants: The following grants were reported in 2003.
$54,783 to Washington Hebrew Congregation, DC.
$25,000 to Jewish Federation of Greater Washington, Rockville, MD.
$25,000 to Johns Hopkins University, Baltimore, MD.
$10,000 to Sibley Memorial Hospital, DC.
$5,000 to Bullis School, Potomac, MD. For Finishing the Foundation Campaign.
$5,000 to Hadassah, Silver Spring, MD.
$5,000 to Jewish Foundation for Group Homes, Rockville, MD.

3734
Albert & Lillian Small Foundation, Inc. ◇
7501 Wisconsin Ave., No. 1103
Bethesda, MD 20814-6515 (301) 215-7997
Contact: Albert H. Small, Pres.

Established in 1981 in DC.
Foundation type: Independent foundation.
Financial data (yr. ended 12/31/05): Assets, $10,319,658 (M); expenditures, $553,391; qualifying distributions, $516,577; giving activities include $509,123 for 74 grants (high: $45,873; low: $500).
Purpose and activities: Giving primarily for Jewish organizations, as well as for education and health

associations; funding also for the arts and human services.

Fields of interest: Historic preservation/historical societies; Arts; Higher education; Education; Health organizations, association; Human services; Jewish federated giving programs; Jewish agencies & temples.

Type of support: General/operating support.

Limitations: Giving primarily in Washington, DC, and FL; some funding nationally. No grants to individuals.

Application information:

Initial approach: Letter

Deadline(s): None

Officers: Albert H. Small, Pres.; Shirley Small, V.P.; Albert H. Small, Jr., Treas.

EIN: 521266289

3735

Small-Alper Family Foundation ◇

7501 Wisconsin Ave., Ste. 1103
Bethesda, MD   20814   (301) 215-7997
Contact: Alpert H. Small, Mgr.

Established in 1994 in DC.

Donor: Lillian Small.

Foundation type: Independent foundation.

Financial data (yr. ended 12/31/05): Assets, $10,383,024 (M); expenditures, $518,544; qualifying distributions, $479,577; giving activities include $472,123 for 38 grants (high: $51,373; low: $1,000).

Fields of interest: Museums (art); Performing arts, theater; Historic preservation/historical societies; Arts; Higher education; Jewish agencies & temples.

Type of support: Annual campaigns; Capital campaigns; Endowments.

Limitations: Giving primarily in Washington, DC, and MD. No grants to individuals.

Application information:

Initial approach: Letter

Deadline(s): None

Managers: Carolyn Alper; Albert H. Small; Lillian Small.

EIN: 521898610

Selected grants: The following grants were reported in 2004.

$50,000 to Washington Hebrew Congregation, DC.

$49,277 to Jewish Historical Society of Greater Washington, DC.

$35,000 to National Gallery of Art, DC.

$30,650 to Woolly Mammoth Theater Company, DC.

$24,000 to Corcoran Gallery of Art, DC.

$23,000 to National Foundation for Teaching Entrepreneurship, DC.

$10,000 to American University, DC.

$10,000 to Arena Stage, DC.

$10,000 to Studio Theater, DC.

$7,500 to Levine School of Music, DC.

3736

Gordon V. & Helen C. Smith Foundation ◇

8716 Crider Brook Way
Potomac, MD   20854   (301) 469-8597
Contact: Gordon V. Smith, Pres.

Established in 1986 in MD.

Donors: Gordon V. Smith; Helen C. Smith; Douglas I. Smith; Anne U. Smith; Miller and Smith, Inc.

Foundation type: Independent foundation.

Financial data (yr. ended 12/31/05): Assets, $44,873,302 (M); gifts received, $932,202; expenditures, $3,302,226; qualifying distributions, $3,573,666; giving activities include $2,959,959 for 53 grants (high: $847,500; low: $250; average: $1,000–$50,000).

Purpose and activities: Support primarily for education; also for Christian and health organizations in which family members are currently involved.

Fields of interest: Higher education; Theological school/education; Health care; Christian agencies & churches; Religion.

Type of support: General/operating support; Building/renovation; Scholarship funds.

Limitations: Giving on a national basis. No grants to individuals.

Application information: Application form not required.

Deadline(s): None

Officers: Gordon V. Smith, Pres.; Helen C. Smith, V.P.

Directors: Cynthia J. Skarbek; Bruce G. Smith; Douglas I. Smith.

EIN: 521440846

Selected grants: The following grants were reported in 2004.

$456,792 to Ohio Wesleyan University, Delaware, OH. 4 grants: $250,000, $83,000, $73,792, $50,000

$155,290 to Wesley Theological Seminary, DC. 2 grants: $51,250, $104,040

$50,000 to Acton Institute for the Study of Religion and Liberty, Grand Rapids, MI.

$50,000 to Cato Institute, DC.

$17,500 to DePauw University, Greencastle, IN.

$6,000 to Woodrow Wilson International Center for Scholars, DC.

3737

The Robert H. Smith School of Business Foundation, Inc. ◇ ☆

c/o University of Maryland
Van Munching Hall, Rm. 2570
College Park, MD   20742

Foundation type: Independent foundation.

Financial data (yr. ended 6/30/05): Assets, $3,859,032 (M); gifts received, $202,507; expenditures, $1,665,606; qualifying distributions, $354,116; giving activities include $320,699 for 1 grant.

Fields of interest: Higher education.

Limitations: Applications not accepted. Giving limited to MD. No grants to individuals.

Application information: Contributes only to pre-selected organizations.

Officers: B. Gary Dando, Pres.; John Boyle, V.P.

EIN: 237332043

3738

The Aaron Straus & Lillie Straus Foundation, Inc. ▼

2 E. Read St., Ste. 100
Baltimore, MD   21202   (410) 539-8308
Contact: Jan Rivitz, Exec. Dir.
FAX: (410) 837-7711;
E-mail: info@strausfoundation.org; URL: http://www.strausfoundation.org

Established in 1926 in MD.

Foundation type: Independent foundation.

Financial data (yr. ended 12/31/04): Assets, $64,924,783 (M); expenditures, $4,303,486; qualifying distributions, $3,547,168; giving activities include $3,295,109 for 101 grants (high: $750,000; low: $100; average: $1,000–$150,000).

Purpose and activities: Giving primarily for education, human services, and public policy.

Fields of interest: Education, public policy; Human services; Children, services; Family services; Federated giving programs; Public policy, research.

Type of support: General/operating support; Income development; Annual campaigns; Capital campaigns; Building/renovation; Program development; Seed money; Scholarship funds; Technical assistance; Consulting services; Program evaluation.

Limitations: Giving primarily in Baltimore, MD. No grants to individuals, or for endowments.

Publications: Application guidelines; Informational brochure; Program policy statement (including application guidelines).

Application information: The foundation requires the Common Grant Application Form of the Association of Baltimore Area Grantmakers. This form is available on the foundation's Web site. Unsolicited applications not accepted for Arts and Culture. Application form required.

Initial approach: Proposal

Copies of proposal: 1

Deadline(s): Feb. 1, July 1, and Oct. 1

Final notification: 8-10 weeks

Officer: Jan Rivitz, Pres. and Exec. Dir.

Number of staff: 1 full-time professional.

EIN: 522040073

Selected grants: The following grants were reported in 2003.

$1,783,300 to The Associated: Jewish Community Federation of Baltimore, Baltimore, MD. 2 grants: $750,000 (For general support), $1,033,300 (For general support).

$250,000 to University of Maryland-Baltimore County, Baltimore, MD. For general support of Sondheim Public Affairs Program.

$150,000 to Central Scholarship Bureau, Baltimore, MD. For general support.

$150,000 to Crossroads School, New York, NY. For general support.

$150,000 to Teach for America, New York, NY. For general support.

$100,000 to Fund for Educational Excellence, Baltimore, MD. For general support.

$100,000 to Planned Parenthood Federation of America, New York, NY. For capital campaign.

$50,000 to Childrens Aid Society, New York, NY. For general support of Carrera Model Replication for sexual education.

$50,000 to Institute for Responsible Citizenship, DC. For general support.

3739

Leonard and Helen R. Stulman Charitable Foundation, Inc.

6225 Smith Ave.
Baltimore, MD   21209
Contact: Shale D. Stiller, Pres.
E-mail: lcrosley@bcf.org; Application address: c/o Laurie Baker Crosley, Dir. of Donor Svcs., Baltimore Community Foundation, 2 E. Read St., Baltimore, MD 21202; E-mail: lcrosley@bcf.org; URL: http://www.bcf.org

Established in 1986 in MD.
Donor: Leonard Stulman†.
Foundation type: Independent foundation.
Financial data (yr. ended 12/31/05): Assets, $3,706,057 (M); gifts received, $1,892,176; expenditures, $1,535,897; qualifying distributions, $1,385,336; giving activities include $1,385,336 for 19 grants (high: $500,000; low: $9,500).
Purpose and activities: Supports programs in research and treatment for mental illness, aging, health care, and broad-based charitable endeavors in MD.
Fields of interest: Mental health, treatment; Mental health, schizophrenia; Mental health, association; Allergies research; Civil rights, aging; Gerontology; Jewish agencies & temples.
Type of support: General/operating support.
Limitations: Giving primarily in Baltimore, MD. No support for organizations that further religious doctrine. No grants to individuals, or for debt retirement, membership campaigns, public primary and secondary education, or conferences/seminars.
Application information: See Web site of Baltimore Community Foundation for application guidelines, procedures, and application deadlines. Application form not required.
  Initial approach: Letter of inquiry
  Copies of proposal: 1
  Deadline(s): Rolling
  Board meeting date(s): Varies
  Final notification: 3 to 6 months
Officers: Shale D. Stiller, Pres.; Frank T. Gray, V.P. and Secy.; Walter D. Pinkard, Jr., Treas.
Number of staff: None.
EIN: 521491609
Selected grants: The following grants were reported in 2004.
$2,416,500 to Baltimore Community Foundation, Baltimore, MD.

3740
Sunrise Charitable Foundation Trust ◇
c/o Antoine Van Agtmael
7906 Springer Rd.
Bethesda, MD 20817-5547

Established in 1992 in MD.
Donor: Antoine Van Agtmael.
Foundation type: Independent foundation.
Financial data (yr. ended 12/31/04): Assets, $8,919,211 (M); gifts received, $2,300,830; expenditures, $388,137; qualifying distributions, $379,700; giving activities include $379,700 for 14 grants (high: $160,000; low: $4,000).
Fields of interest: Elementary/secondary education; Higher education; Scholarships/financial aid.
Type of support: Research; General/operating support; Scholarship funds.
Limitations: Applications not accepted. Giving primarily in New Haven, CT, Washington, DC, MD, and VA. No grants to individuals.
Application information: Contributes only to pre-selected organizations.
Trustees: Antoine Van Agtmael; Emily Van Agtmael.
EIN: 526560157

3741
Sylvan/Laureate Foundation, Inc.
(formerly The Sylvan Learning Foundation, Inc.)
1001 Fleet St.
Baltimore, MD 21202-4382
Contact: Carol Maivelett, Admin.

Established in 1997 in MD.
Donors: Sylvan Learning Systems, Inc.; Laureate Education, Inc.
Foundation type: Company-sponsored foundation.
Financial data (yr. ended 12/31/03): Assets, $8,825,213 (M); gifts received, $71,113; expenditures, $1,123,186; qualifying distributions, $1,116,095; giving activities include $1,042,530 for grants.
Purpose and activities: The foundation supports organizations involved with arts and culture, health, parks and playgrounds, children and youth, and Judaism.
Fields of interest: Arts; Elementary/secondary education; Higher education; Education; Health care; Recreation, parks/playgrounds; Children/youth, services; Voluntarism promotion; Federated giving programs; Jewish agencies & temples.
Limitations: Giving primarily in Baltimore, MD. No support for religious organizations or political or lobbying organizations. No grants to individuals.
Publications: Application guidelines.
Application information:
  Initial approach: Contact foundation for application information
  Board meeting date(s): Apr., July, Oct., and Jan.
Officers and Trustees:* Douglas L. Becker,* Pres.; R. Christopher Hoehn-Saric,* 1st V.P.; Robert W. Zentz, 2nd V.P. and Secy.; Peter Cohen, 2nd V.P.
EIN: 522044008
Selected grants: The following grants were reported in 2003.
$500,000 to Book Adventure Foundation, Baltimore, MD. For general support.
$85,000 to Johns Hopkins University, Baltimore, MD. For general support.
$52,140 to Baltimore Community Foundation, Baltimore, MD. For general support.
$10,000 to Baltimore School for the Arts, Baltimore, MD. For general support.
$10,000 to Everyman Theater, Baltimore, MD. For general support.
$10,000 to Teach for America, Baltimore, MD. For general support.
$10,000 to William S. Baer School No. 301, Baltimore, MD. For general support.
$5,000 to University of Maryland-Baltimore, Baltimore, MD. For general support.
$3,000 to American Cancer Society, Baltimore, MD. For general support.
$2,500 to Harford-Belair Community Mental Health Center, Baltimore, MD. For general support.

3742
The Laszlo N. Tauber Family Foundation ☆
5110 Ridgefield Rd., Ste. 413
Bethesda, MD 20816

Established in 2004 in MD.
Donor: Laszlo N. Tauber†.
Foundation type: Independent foundation.
Financial data (yr. ended 12/31/05): Assets, $94,242,402 (M); gifts received, $68,500,000; expenditures, $2,558,514; qualifying distributions, $2,121,800; giving activities include $2,121,800 for grants.

Fields of interest: Elementary/secondary education; Medical research; Jewish agencies & temples.
Limitations: Applications not accepted. Giving primarily in Baltimore, MD. No grants to individuals.
Application information: Contributes only to pre-selected organizations.
Officers and Directors:* Alfred I. Tauber,* Pres.; Ingrid D. Tauber,* Secy.-Treas.
Number of staff: 2 full-time professional.
EIN: 300208793

3743
Ten Talents Foundation, Inc. ◇ ☆
P.O. Box 43547
Baltimore, MD 21236
Contact: Robert P. Dushel, Treas.

Established in 2004 in MD.
Donors: Thomas Barbera; Mary Poppert Barbera.
Foundation type: Independent foundation.
Financial data (yr. ended 12/31/05): Assets, $4,829,705 (M); expenditures, $597,233; qualifying distributions, $520,000; giving activities include $520,000 for grants.
Fields of interest: Education; Human services; Children, services; Christian agencies & churches.
Application information:
  Initial approach: Letter
  Deadline(s): None
Officers and Directors:* Thomas Barbera,* Pres.; Mary Poppert Barbera,* V.P. and Secy.; Robert P. Dushel,* Treas.; Concetta Barbera; Rachel Curtis; William Curtis; Andrew Truszkowski; Madeline Truszkowski.
EIN: 300266863

3744
The Alvin and Fanny Blaustein Thalheimer Foundation, Inc.
10 E. Baltimore St., Ste. 1111
Baltimore, MD 21202 (410) 347-7201
Contact: Betsy F. Ringel, Exec. Dir.
FAX: (410) 347-7210; E-mail: info@blaufund.org; URL: http://www.blaufund.org/foundations/alvinandfanny_f.html

Incorporated in 1958 in MD.
Donors: American Trading and Production Corp.; Lord Baltimore Capital Corp.
Foundation type: Independent foundation.
Financial data (yr. ended 12/31/04): Assets, $26,286,839 (M); gifts received, $250,000; expenditures, $1,519,408; qualifying distributions, $1,297,570; giving activities include $1,296,500 for 34 grants (high: $250,000; low: $4,000; average: $10,000–$45,000).
Purpose and activities: Support primarily for higher educational institutions and Jewish organizations.
Fields of interest: Arts; Employment; Human services; Economic development; Jewish agencies & temples.
Type of support: Capital campaigns; Building/renovation; Program development; Conferences/seminars; Curriculum development.
Limitations: Giving primarily in the Baltimore, MD, metropolitan area. No grants to individuals or for fundraising events or direct mail solicitations; no loans.
Publications: Application guidelines; Grants list.

Application information: The foundation accepts the Association of Baltimore Area Grantmakers Common grant application. Application will be acknowledged by postcard within 2 weeks. Application form not required.

Initial approach: Letter of inquiry (2 - 3 pages)
Copies of proposal: 1
Deadline(s): None
Board meeting date(s): Semiannually
Final notification: 4 to 6 months

Officers and Trustees:* Louis B. Thalheimer,* Pres.; Elizabeth T. Wachs, V.P.; Betsy F. Ringel, Exec. Dir.; Marjorie Thalheimer Coleman.
EIN: 526038383
Selected grants: The following grants were reported in 2003.
$200,000 to Jewish Family Services of Central Maryland, Baltimore, MD.
$50,000 to Temple Oheb Shalom, Baltimore, MD. For general support.
$25,000 to Center for Fathers, Families and Work Force Development, Baltimore, MD. For general support.
$20,000 to Job Opportunities Task Force, Baltimore, MD. For general support.

3745
Columbus W. Thorn, Jr. Foundation
109 E. Main St.
Elkton, MD 21921 (410) 398-0611
Contact: Trustees

Established in 1971 in MD.
Donor: Columbus W. Thorn†.
Foundation type: Independent foundation.
Financial data (yr. ended 12/31/05): Assets, $16,784,668 (M); gifts received, $446,474; expenditures, $882,564; qualifying distributions, $882,564; giving activities include $741,418 for 126 loans to individuals (high: $7,000; low: $500).
Purpose and activities: Awards educational loans to high school graduates of Cecil County, MD.
Fields of interest: Adult/continuing education.
Type of support: Student loans—to individuals.
Limitations: Giving limited to residents of Cecil County, MD.
Publications: Application guidelines.
Application information: Application form required.
Initial approach: Letter, telephone, or in person
Deadline(s): None
Trustees: Charles L. Scott; Doris P. Scott.
Number of staff: 1 part-time support.
EIN: 237153983

3746
Thunder Bay Charities Foundation ◇
901 S. Bond St.
Baltimore, MD 21231

Established in 1997 in MD.
Foundation type: Independent foundation.
Financial data (yr. ended 12/31/05): Assets, $789,089 (M); expenditures, $455,676; qualifying distributions, $445,000; giving activities include $445,000 for 3 grants (high: $250,000; low: $25,000).
Fields of interest: Elementary/secondary education; Boys & girls clubs.
Limitations: Applications not accepted. Giving primarily in Atlanta, GA. No grants to individuals.

Application information: Contributes only to pre-selected organizations.
Officers: Peter J. Kight, Chair.; John H. Lahey, Secy.; Teresa J. Kight, Treas.
EIN: 586435475
Selected grants: The following grants were reported in 2004.
$250,000 to Woodward Academy, College Park, GA.
$120,000 to Boys and Girls Club, Warren Memorial, Atlanta, GA.

3747
TKF Foundation
(formerly Open Spaces, Sacred Places)
410 Severn Ave., Ste. 216
Annapolis, MD 21403
Contact: Mary F. Wyatt, Exec. Dir.
FAX: (410) 268-1379; E-mail: mwyatt@tkffdn.org; URL: http://www.tkffdn.org

Established in 1985 in IA.
Donors: Thomas H. Stoner; Katharine E. Stoner.
Foundation type: Independent foundation.
Financial data (yr. ended 12/31/05): Assets, $12,229,827 (M); gifts received, $261,428; expenditures, $910,976; qualifying distributions, $733,935; giving activities include $578,511 for grants.
Purpose and activities: To provide the opportunity for a deeper human experience by supporting the creation of public greenspaces that offers a temporary place of sanctuary, encourages reflection, provides solace, and engenders peace.
Fields of interest: Arts; Environment, natural resources; Community development.
Type of support: Continuing support; Program development; Seed money; Technical assistance; Matching/challenge support.
Limitations: Giving limited to Washington, DC, and Annapolis and Baltimore, MD. No grants to individuals or for endowments, debt reduction, ongoing operating costs, special projects or capital campaigns.
Publications: Application guidelines; Annual report; Informational brochure (including application guidelines).
Application information: Association of Baltimore Area Grantmakers Common Grant Application Form required. Additional application information and application guidelines available on foundation Web site. Application form required.
Initial approach: 1-page Screening letter
Copies of proposal: 3
Deadline(s): Oct. 1 for Open Spaces, Sacred Places, Community Greening deadline Aug. 1, Nov. 1 for pre-approved organizations
Board meeting date(s): Bi-annual
Final notification: Jan. 30 for Open Spaces, Sacred Places; Nov. 1 for Community Greening
Officers and Directors:* Thomas H. Stoner,* Pres. and Treas.; Katharine E. Stoner,* V.P.; Mary F. Wyatt, Secy. and Exec. Dir.; Jack Bloodgood; Chuck Foster; Alden Stoner; Chelle Stoner.
Number of staff: 2 full-time professional; 1 part-time professional; 1 part-time support.
EIN: 421263576
Selected grants: The following grants were reported in 2004.
$160,000 to Citizens for Georgetown Fund, DC.
$100,091 to University of Pennsylvania, Philadelphia, PA.
$50,000 to Annapolis, City of, Annapolis, MD.
$15,000 to Garden Resources of Washington, DC.

$15,000 to Washington Parks and People, DC.
$10,000 to Kids on the Hill, Baltimore, MD.
$6,000 to Providence Health Foundation, DC.
$320 to Friends of Patterson Park, Baltimore, MD.

3748
Robert E. Torray and Anne P. Torray Family Foundation ◇ ☆
7501 Wisconsin Ave., Ste. 1100
Bethesda, MD 20814-6523

Established in 1998 in MD.
Donors: Robert E. Torray; Anne P. Torray.
Foundation type: Independent foundation.
Financial data (yr. ended 5/31/05): Assets, $308,353 (M); gifts received, $579,538; expenditures, $533,081; qualifying distributions, $533,050; giving activities include $533,050 for 6 grants (high: $225,000; low: $1,000).
Fields of interest: Higher education; Education; Crime/violence prevention, domestic violence; Food services, commodity distribution; Human services.
Limitations: Applications not accepted. Giving primarily in Washington, DC, and NY. No grants to individuals.
Application information: Contributes only to pre-selected organizations.
Trustees: Anne P. Torray; Robert E. Torray.
EIN: 526930570

3749
Town Creek Foundation, Inc. ◇
121 N. West St.
Easton, MD 21601 (410) 763-8171
Contact: Stuart A. Clarke, Exec. Dir.
FAX: (410) 763-8172;
E-mail: info@towncreekfdn.org; URL: http://www.towncreekfdn.org

Established in 1981 in MD.
Donor: Edmund A. Stanley, Jr.
Foundation type: Independent foundation.
Financial data (yr. ended 12/31/05): Assets, $58,207,794 (M); expenditures, $3,073,770; qualifying distributions, $2,813,484; giving activities include $2,465,500 for 84 grants (high: $75,000; low: $2,000).
Purpose and activities: The foundation is dedicated to a sustainable environment, a strong democracy, and a peaceful world. It makes grants to nonprofit organizations that work to protect our natural resources, to deepen public discussion of public policy issues, and to encourage public debate about how to reduce the risks and costs of war. The foundation also supports a number of social service initiatives in Talbot County, MD.
Fields of interest: Media/communications; Environment, natural resources; Environment; International peace/security.
Type of support: General/operating support; Continuing support; Program development; Seed money; Matching/challenge support.
Limitations: Giving primarily in the Mid Atlantic region, the southern Appalachian National Forests, and in Talbot County, MD. No support for primary or secondary schools, hospitals, healthcare institutions, or religious organizations. No support for colleges or universities except when some aspect of their work is an integral part of a program supported by the foundation, or for government organizations. No grants to individuals, or for

endowment, capital, or building fund campaigns, purchase of land or buildings, research, scholarship programs, conferences, the publication of books or periodicals, or visual or performing arts projects.
Publications: Application guidelines; Grants list.
Application information: Application guidelines available upon request; include SASE (regular business-sized envelope). Applications sent by fax or e-mail not considered. Application form not required.

Initial approach: Letter of inquiry, up to 2 pages, may be submitted before a full proposal. Letter may be sent by fax or e-mail
Copies of proposal: 1
Deadline(s): Letters of inquiry are due Nov. 17, for spring 2007 and Mar. 16, for summer 2007; invited proposals are due Aug. 18, for fall 2006, Dec. 15, for spring 2007, and Apr. 13, for summer 2007
Board meeting date(s): Mar., July, and Nov.
Final notification: Late Nov., for fall 2006, mid-Mar., for spring 2007, and mid-July, for summer 2007

Officers and Trustees:* Jennifer Stanley,* Pres.; Lisa A. Stanley, V.P.; Philip E.L. Dietz, Jr.,* Secy.-Treas.; Stuart A. Clark, Exec. Dir.; Edmund A. Stanley, Jr.; Betsy Taylor.
Number of staff: 1 full-time professional; 1 part-time professional; 1 part-time support.
EIN: 521222703

3750
Marcia Brady Tucker Foundation, Inc. ◇
P.O. Box 1149
Easton, MD 21601
Contact: Luther Tucker, Jr., Pres.

Incorporated in 1941 in NY.
Donor: Marcia Brady Tucker†.
Foundation type: Independent foundation.
Financial data (yr. ended 12/31/04): Assets, $12,365,615 (M); expenditures, $578,890; qualifying distributions, $478,392; giving activities include $402,207 for 131 grants (high: $25,000; low: $100).
Purpose and activities: Giving primarily for the arts, education, the environment, social services, and religious institutions.
Fields of interest: Museums; Arts; Higher education; Theological school/education; Environment; Hospitals (general); Human services; Christian agencies & churches; Jewish agencies & temples; Religion.
Type of support: General/operating support; Annual campaigns; Capital campaigns; Building/renovation; Endowments; Program development; Seed money; Matching/challenge support.
Limitations: Applications not accepted. Giving primarily in CA, CO, MD, NY, and OH. No grants to individuals.
Application information: Contributes only to pre-selected organizations. Unsolicited requests for funds not accepted.

Board meeting date(s): Spring and fall
Officers and Directors:* Luther Tucker, Jr.,* Pres.; Toinette Tucker, V.P.; Marcia B. Loughran, Secy.; David Randell, Treas.; Marcia Boogaard; Tom Boogaard; Sarah House; Barbara Randell; Elizabeth Sanders; Carll Tucker III; Gary Tucker-Duncan.
Number of staff: 1 part-time support.
EIN: 136161561
Selected grants: The following grants were reported in 2004.

$25,000 to Church of the Redeemer, Cincinnati, OH.
$12,500 to National Sports Center for the Disabled, Denver, CO.
$10,400 to Chesapeake Wildlife Heritage, Easton, MD.
$10,000 to Charities Aid Foundation (CAF) America, Alexandria, VA.
$8,000 to Part of the Solution, Bronx, NY.
$5,000 to Saint Matthews Church, Bedford, NY.
$4,400 to Queen City Foundation, Cincinnati, OH.
$2,600 to Natural Resources Defense Council, DC.
$2,600 to UNICEF, New York, NY.
$600 to United Fund of Talbot County, Easton, MD.

3751
The Tzedakah Fund ◇ ☆
c/o O. Hirschman
6006 Berkeley Ave.
Baltimore, MD 21209

Established in 2003 in MD.
Donors: Orin Z. Hirschman; Hershel Berkowitz; Ettil Berkowitz.
Foundation type: Independent foundation.
Financial data (yr. ended 12/31/05): Assets, $1,390,461 (M); gifts received, $1,463,000; expenditures, $2,986,227; qualifying distributions, $2,980,905; giving activities include $2,980,905 for grants.
Fields of interest: Jewish agencies & temples.
Limitations: Applications not accepted. Giving primarily in NY; some giving in MD and NJ. No grants to individuals.
Application information: Contributes only to pre-selected organizations.
Trustees: Esther Hirschman; Orin Z. Hirschman.
EIN: 200386456

3752
Richard D. Van Lunen Charitable Foundation ◇
c/o Peacock, Condron, Anderson & Co.
6851 Oak Hall Ln., Ste. 300
Columbia, MD 21045 (410) 720-5220
Contact: David Condron

Established in 1985 in DE and MD.
Donor: Richard D. Van Lunen†.
Foundation type: Independent foundation.
Financial data (yr. ended 12/31/05): Assets, $69,009,425 (M); gifts received, $500,000; expenditures, $5,830,511; qualifying distributions, $4,721,536; giving activities include $4,549,035 for grants.
Purpose and activities: Giving primarily for Christian churches and education.
Fields of interest: Higher education; Christian agencies & churches.
Limitations: Giving on a national basis, with emphasis on MD. No grants to individuals.
Application information:
Initial approach: Letter
Deadline(s): None
Officer: James Achterhof, Exec. Dir.
Trustees: James Ellis; Gordon Van Der Brug.
EIN: 521419025
Selected grants: The following grants were reported in 2004.
$805,000 to Lexington Christian Academy, Lexington, MA.

$202,000 to Baltimore Christian School, Baltimore, MD.
$125,000 to Calvin College, Grand Rapids, MI.
$100,000 to Chicago West Side Christian School, Chicago, IL.
$55,000 to Roseland Christian School, Chicago, IL.
$30,000 to Christian Schools International, Grand Rapids, MI.

3753
Viragh Family Foundation ◇
c/o Young, Brophy & Duncan, PC
10211 Wincopin Cir., No. 450
Columbia, MD 21044

Established in 2000 in MD.
Donors: Albert P. Viragh†; Robert J. Viragh; Mark S. Viragh; Katherine Viragh; Jean M. Dahl.
Foundation type: Independent foundation.
Financial data (yr. ended 6/30/05): Assets, $37,718,033 (M); gifts received, $315,500; expenditures, $1,633,813; qualifying distributions, $1,298,590; giving activities include $1,298,590 for 26 grants (high: $100,000; low: $10,000).
Purpose and activities: Giving primarily for education, and human services, including services for people who are homeless, especially housing services; funding also for children and youth services, including homeless children, children with serious illnesses, and abused and neglected children. Support also for health care and medical research, including pancreatic cancer research, and multiple sclerosis research.
Fields of interest: Higher education; Education; Health care; Cancer research; Medical research; Housing/shelter, services; Human services; Children/youth, services.
Limitations: Applications not accepted. Giving primarily in MD, MO, and TX. No grants to individuals.
Application information: Contributes only to pre-selected organizations.
Officers: Mark S. Viragh, Pres.; Roger E. Young, V.P.; Susan B. Rankin, Secy.; Katherine A. Viragh, Treas.
Directors: Jean M. Dahl; Robert J. Viragh; Paula Virgah Williams.
EIN: 522284009
Selected grants: The following grants were reported in 2003.
$233,500 to Johns Hopkins University, Baltimore, MD. For Pancreatic Cancer Research.
$44,500 to Saint Louis Crisis Nursery, Saint Louis, MO.

3754
The Robert A. Waidner Foundation ◇ ☆
c/o Robert Sloan
7 St. Paul St., Ste. 1400
Baltimore, MD 21202-1626

Established in 2001 in MD.
Foundation type: Independent foundation.
Financial data (yr. ended 12/31/05): Assets, $23,150,042 (M); expenditures, $5,608,417; qualifying distributions, $5,466,814; giving activities include $5,446,214 for 3 grants (high: $3,491,163; low: $209,470).
Fields of interest: Performing arts, orchestra (symphony); Higher education; Health care.
Limitations: Applications not accepted. Giving primarily in MD and PA. No grants to individuals.

Application information: Contributes only to pre-selected organizations.

Trustees: Frederick Singley Koontz; Robert Sloan.

EIN: 527195462

3755
Dorothy Wagner Wallis Charitable Trust ✧

7 Saint Paul St., Ste. 1400
Baltimore, MD 21202-1626   (410) 347-8770
Contact: Frederick Singley Koontz, Tr.

Established in 1993.

Foundation type: Independent foundation.

Financial data (yr. ended 12/31/05): Assets, $5,837,716 (M); expenditures, $372,309; qualifying distributions, $321,296; giving activities include $316,822 for 13 grants (high: $100,000; low: $5,000).

Purpose and activities: Giving primarily for historic preservation, art, higher education, and human services.

Fields of interest: Historic preservation/historical societies; Arts; Higher education; Animal welfare; Human services.

Limitations: Giving primarily in Baltimore, MD. No grants to individuals.

Application information:
Initial approach: Proposal
Deadline(s): None

Trustee: Frederick Singley Koontz.

EIN: 526605828

3756
E. C. Wareheim Foundation ✧

c/o M & T Bank, Trust Dept.
25 S. Charles St.
Baltimore, MD 21201
Application address: c/o William L. Mathers, Exec. Dir., P.O. Box 3444, Virginia Beach, VA 23454, tel.: (804) 481-3166

Established in 1956 in MD.

Foundation type: Independent foundation.

Financial data (yr. ended 12/31/05): Assets, $11,399,403 (M); gifts received, $16,853; expenditures, $639,736; qualifying distributions, $572,982; giving activities include $472,100 for 76 grants (high: $50,000; low: $500).

Purpose and activities: Giving primarily for children and youth development and services, including youth at risk; support also for education.

Fields of interest: Elementary/secondary education; Courts/judicial administration; Legal services; Human services; Children/youth, services; Family services.

Limitations: Giving primarily in VA; some giving also in MD. No grants to individuals.

Application information: Application form required.
Initial approach: Letter
Deadline(s): None

Officer: William L. Mathers, Exec. Dir.

Trustee: M & T Bank.

EIN: 526033212

Selected grants: The following grants were reported in 2003.

$75,000 to Virginia Military Institute Foundation, Lexington, VA. For general operating support.

$30,000 to American Red Cross of Southeastern Virginia, Tidewater Chapter, Norfolk, VA. For general operating support.

$28,000 to Chesapeake Bay Foundation, Annapolis, MD. For general operating support.

$23,000 to Sugar Plum Bakery, Virginia Beach, VA. For general operating support.

$22,300 to United Cerebral Palsy of Southern and Central Virginia, Virginia Beach, VA. For general operating support.

$22,000 to Chapel Hill Training Outreach Project, Chapel Hill, NC. For general operating support.

$22,000 to Maryland Mentoring Partnership, Baltimore, MD. For general operating support.

$22,000 to YMCA of South Hampton Roads, Norfolk, VA. For general operating support.

$20,000 to Mother Seton House, Virginia Beach, VA. For general operating support.

$18,000 to College Bound, DC. For general operating support.

3757
George Wasserman Family Foundation, Inc. ✧

(formerly George Wasserman Foundation, Inc.)
c/o Grossberg Co.
6707 Democracy Blvd., Ste. 300
Bethesda, MD 20817
Contact: Janice W. Goldsten, Pres.
Application address: 8 Harborage Isle Rd., Fort Lauderdale, FL 33316

Established in 1948.

Donor: George Wasserman†.

Foundation type: Independent foundation.

Financial data (yr. ended 12/31/05): Assets, $8,653,948 (M); expenditures, $437,031; qualifying distributions, $393,208; giving activities include $390,750 for 40 grants (high: $113,000; low: $1,000).

Purpose and activities: Grants primarily for Jewish welfare funds, theological studies, and temple support; giving also for the performing arts, human services, and health.

Fields of interest: Performing arts; Nursing home/convalescent facility; Health care; Human services; Jewish federated giving programs; Jewish agencies & temples.

Type of support: General/operating support; Continuing support; Annual campaigns; Building/renovation; Endowments; Program development; Seed money; Scholarship funds; Research; Technical assistance; Exchange programs.

Limitations: Giving primarily in Washington, DC, and MD. No grants to individuals.

Application information:
Initial approach: Letter
Deadline(s): None

Officers: Janice W. Goldsten, Pres. and Treas.; Carolyn Stopak, V.P. and Secy.; Lisa W. Gill, V.P.

EIN: 526035888

Selected grants: The following grants were reported in 2005.

$25,000 to United States Holocaust Memorial Museum, DC.

$20,000 to Multicultural Career Intern Program, DC.

$10,000 to Iona Senior Services, DC.

$10,000 to N Street Village, DC.

$10,000 to Nova Southeastern University, Fort Lauderdale, FL.

$5,000 to Duke Ellington School of the Arts, DC.

$5,000 to Jewish Historical Society of Greater Washington, DC.

$5,000 to Jewish Women International, DC.

$5,000 to Lab School of Washington, DC.

$5,000 to Phillips Collection, DC.

3758
The Ellen W. P. Wasserman Foundation ✧

3416 Garrison Farms Rd.
Pikesville, MD 21208
Application address: c/o George W. Cox, 4 N. Park Dr., Ste. 121, Hunt Valley, MD 21030, tel.: (410) 771-8033

Established in 1997 in MD.

Donors: Ellen W.P. Wasserman; Cox, Ferber & Associates, LLC.

Foundation type: Independent foundation.

Financial data (yr. ended 3/31/06): Assets, $15,671,908 (M); gifts received, $1,583,050; expenditures, $773,527; qualifying distributions, $651,957; giving activities include $651,957 for 15 grants (high: $329,492; low: $511).

Purpose and activities: Giving primarily to Jewish federated giving programs, as well as to Jewish organizations including a hospital; funding also for the performing arts.

Fields of interest: Museums (art); Performing arts, orchestra (symphony); Performing arts, opera; Hospitals (general); Physical therapy; Human services; Jewish federated giving programs; Computer science; Jewish agencies & temples.

Limitations: Giving primarily in Baltimore, MD. No grants to individuals.

Application information:
Initial approach: Written proposal
Deadline(s): None

Trustee: Ellen W.P. Wasserman.

EIN: 522038129

Selected grants: The following grants were reported in 2006.

$329,492 to Sinai Hospital of Baltimore, Baltimore, MD.

$25,102 to Baltimore Opera Company, Baltimore, MD.

$25,060 to Baltimore Symphony Orchestra, Baltimore, MD.

$13,067 to Temple Oheb Shalom, Baltimore, MD.

$10,105 to Dyslexia Tutoring Program, Baltimore, MD.

$10,105 to Learning Independence Through Computers, Baltimore, MD.

3759
The Harry and Jeanette Weinberg Foundation, Inc. ▼

7 Park Center Ct.
Owings Mills, MD 21117-4200   (410) 654-8500
Contact: Ki Held, Grants Mgr. and Database Admin.
FAX: (410) 654-4900;
E-mail: info@theweinbergfoundation.org;
URL: http://www.hjweinbergfoundation.org

Incorporated in 1959 in MD.

Donors: Harry Weinberg†; and various companies.

Foundation type: Independent foundation.

Financial data (yr. ended 2/28/06): Assets, $2,154,005,108 (M); expenditures, $114,176,438; qualifying distributions, $93,630,682; giving activities include $93,630,682 for grants.

Purpose and activities: To contribute to charitable organizations which will use the distribution to benefit those whose financial resources are less than the financial resources of fifty percent of the members of the relevant community to which such beneficiaries belong.

Fields of interest: Food services; Human services; Aging, centers/services; Aging; Disabilities, people with; Economically disadvantaged.

Type of support: Capital campaigns; Building/renovation; Equipment; Endowments; Matching/challenge support.

Limitations: Giving on a national basis. No support for political organizations, colleges, universities, think tanks, or for arts organizations. No grants to individuals, or for deficit financing, annual giving, publications or for scholarships.

Application information: Unsolicited full proposals will not be accepted. The foundation will invite appropriate proposals following submission of LOI. Guidelines for LOI and invited proposals available on foundation Web site. Application form not required.

   Initial approach: Letter of Inquiry (LOI) no more than 3 pages
   Deadline(s): None
   Board meeting date(s): Periodically
   Final notification: Within 90 days

Officers and Directors:* Shale D. Stiller, Pres.; Rachel Garbow Monroe, C.O.O.; Alvin Awaya,* V.P.; Timothy P. Kelly,* V.P.; Donn Weinberg,* V.P.; Barry I. Schloss,* Treas.

Number of staff: 4 full-time professional.

EIN: 526037034

Selected grants: The following grants were reported in 2005.

$2,000,000 to Maryland Food Bank, Baltimore, MD.
$1,000,000 to YMCA of Central Maryland, Baltimore, MD.
$900,000 to Ezer Mizion, Bnei Brak, Israel. .
$654,000 to Catholic Charities of the Archdiocese of Baltimore, Baltimore, MD.
$525,000 to Mental Health Kokua, Honolulu, HI.
$500,000 to Beth Sholom Home of Eastern Virginia, Virginia Beach, VA.
$500,000 to Childhaven, Seattle, WA.
$500,000 to Jewish Community Centers Association of North America, New York, NY.
$500,000 to Jewish Community Centers of South Broward, David Posnack Jewish Community Center, Davie, FL.
$425,000 to Center for Fathers, Families and Work Force Development, Baltimore, MD.

3760
The Weiss Foundation

c/o Gelman Rosenberg & Freedman
4550 Montgomery Ave., Ste. 650 N.
Bethesda, MD 20814-3250

Established in 1993 in DC.
Donor: Stanley Weiss.
Foundation type: Operating foundation.
Financial data (yr. ended 9/30/05): Assets, $415,147 (M); gifts received, $348,178; expenditures, $823,165; qualifying distributions, $810,698; giving activities include $662,020 for 22 grants (high: $430,000; low: $500), and $430,000 for foundation-administered programs.
Purpose and activities: Focus on educating the public on issues concerning national and international security, including matters of defense policy and the promotion of democratic institutions and societies.

Fields of interest: Children/youth, services; International affairs, arms control; International affairs; Public policy, research.
Type of support: Continuing support; Endowments; Program development; Research.
Limitations: Applications not accepted. Giving primarily in the greater metropolitan Washington, DC, area, and New York, NY. No grants to individuals.
Publications: Financial statement.
Application information: Contributes only to pre-selected organizations.
Officers: Stanley Weiss, Pres.; Lisa Weiss, V.P.; Anthony Weiss, Secy.
Director: Lori Christina Lurie.
Number of staff: 1 full-time professional; 1 part-time professional.
EIN: 521848413

3761
Thomas Wilson Sanitarium for Children of Baltimore City ◇

P.O. Box 2766
Baltimore, MD 21225 (410) 360-9510
Contact: Kenneth Schuberth, Pres.

Trust established in 1879 in MD.
Donor: Thomas Wilson†.
Foundation type: Independent foundation.
Financial data (yr. ended 1/31/06): Assets, $12,180,452 (M); expenditures, $695,812; qualifying distributions, $686,435; giving activities include $597,822 for 41 grants (high: $30,000; low: $3,000).
Purpose and activities: Giving primarily for hospitals, medical and educational research, and social services, entirely relating to children of Baltimore, MD. Giving also for children's social and medical programs.
Fields of interest: Medical research, institute; Children/youth, services.
Type of support: Equipment; Program development; Seed money; Research.
Limitations: Giving limited to Baltimore, MD.
Application information: Application form not required.
   Initial approach: Letter
   Deadline(s): None
   Board meeting date(s): May
Officers and Trustees:* Kenneth Schuberth, M.D.*, Pres.; Kinloch N. Yellott III,* V.P.; Perry J. Bolton, Treas.; Robert D. Hopkins; Michael J. McCarthy; Melchijah Spragins, M.D.; Charles L. Stout; Francis H. Trimble, M.D.; J. Ronald Walcher, M.D.; Christopher R. West; Ralph N. Willis.
Number of staff: 1 part-time support.
EIN: 526044885

3762
Wright Family Foundation ◇

21619 Gunpowder Rd.
Lineboro CPO, MD 21102-2415
Contact: Vernon H.C. Wright, Tr.
E-mail: Wrightmbna@aol.com

Established in 2000 in MD.
Donor: Vernon H.C. Wright.
Foundation type: Independent foundation.
Financial data (yr. ended 12/31/04): Assets, $5,842,159 (M); gifts received, $4,588,824; expenditures, $562,885; qualifying distributions, $560,245; giving activities include $560,245 for 9 grants (high: $422,025; low: $1,000).
Fields of interest: Arts; Elementary/secondary education; Higher education; Human services.
Type of support: Building/renovation; Curriculum development; Research.
Limitations: Applications not accepted. Giving primarily in MD. No grants to individuals.
Application information: Unsolicited requests for funds not accepted.
Trustees: Lucy Babb Wright; Vernon H.C. Wright.
EIN: 522278319

3763
Zickler Family Foundation, Inc. ◇ ☆

c/o Leo E. Zickler
7200 Wisconsin Ave., Ste. 1100
Bethesda, MD 20814

Established in 2000.
Donors: Leo E. Zickler; Judy Zickler.
Foundation type: Independent foundation.
Financial data (yr. ended 12/31/04): Assets, $5,213,502 (M); gifts received, $253,354; expenditures, $456,768; qualifying distributions, $454,915; giving activities include $454,750 for grants (high: $100,000).
Fields of interest: Arts; Elementary/secondary education; Education; Health care; Medical research; Human services.
Type of support: General/operating support; Continuing support; Management development/capacity building; Annual campaigns; Capital campaigns; Building/renovation; Endowments; Seed money; Curriculum development; Research; Matching/challenge support.
Limitations: Applications not accepted. Giving on a national basis, primarily along the East Coast and in CA. No grants to individuals.
Application information: Contributes only to pre-selected organizations.
Officers and Director:* Leo E. Zickler,* Chair. and Secy.-Treas.; Judy Zickler, Pres.
Number of staff: 1 part-time support.
EIN: 522283882
Selected grants: The following grants were reported in 2004.
$100,000 to Phillips Collection, DC.
$50,000 to SEED Foundation, DC.
$27,500 to Woolly Mammoth Theater Company, DC.
$20,000 to George Mason University Foundation, Fairfax, VA.
$5,000 to Bardavon 1869 Opera House, Poughkeepsie, NY.
$5,000 to Windrush School, El Cerrito, CA.
$5,000 to Young Playwrights Theater, DC.
$3,334 to Free Arts for Abused Children, Los Angeles, CA.
$2,500 to Capitol Hill Day School, DC.
$2,500 to Signature Theater, Arlington, VA.

MASSACHUSETTS

3764
The A & A Fund ✧
(formerly Alexander and Adelaide Hixon Fund for
Religion and Education)
c/o R. Brinckerhoff Lowery
21 Milk St., 3rd Fl.
Boston, MA   02109-5408

Established in 1991 in MA.
Donor: Alexander P. Hixon.
Foundation type: Independent foundation.
Financial data (yr. ended 12/31/03): Assets,
$7,681,784 (M); expenditures, $416,437;
qualifying distributions, $355,417; giving activities
include $353,376 for 22 grants (high: $123,875;
low: $500).
Fields of interest: Human services; Christian
agencies & churches; Buddhism; Religion.
Limitations: Applications not accepted. Giving on a
national basis. No grants to individuals.
Application information: Contributes only to
pre-selected organizations.
Trustee: R. Brinckerhoff Lowery.
Advisory Board: Alexandra H. Ballard; Dylan H.
Hixon; Shanti S. Hixon; Sheila K. Hixon; India T.
Radfar.
EIN: 043127721
Selected grants: The following grants were reported
in 2004.
$158,400 to Peacemaker Community, Santa
    Barbara, CA. 3 grants: $30,000, $78,400,
    $50,000
$10,000 to Jewel Heart Corporation, Ann Arbor, MI.
$5,000 to Garrison Institute, Garrison, NY.
$5,000 to La Crosse County Historical Society, La
    Crosse, WI.

3765
A Child Waits Foundation
1136 Barker Rd., No. 12
Pittsfield, MA   01201   (866) 999-2445
Contact: Cynthia Nelson, Pres.; Randolph Nelson,
V.P.
FAX: (518) 794-6243;
E-mail: cnelson@achildwaits.org; Additional E-mail:
rgriffin@achildwaits.org (Raymona Griffin, Prog.
Dir.); URL: http://www.achildwaits.org

Established in 1998 in NY.
Donors: Cynthia Nelson; Randolph Nelson; Ira and
Beth Leventhal Foundation; Dove Givings
Foundation.
Foundation type: Independent foundation.
Financial data (yr. ended 12/31/05): Assets,
$2,012,789 (M); gifts received, $1,220;
expenditures, $620,878; qualifying distributions,
$333,000; giving activities include $333,000 for 88
grants, and $205,400 for 24 loans to individuals
(high: $10,000; low: $1,800).
Purpose and activities: Giving primarily to provide
financial assistance to individuals adopting
foreign-born children. Support for adoption, adoption
funding, international adoption and child welfare.
Fields of interest: Children/youth, services;
Children, adoption.
Type of support: Grants to individuals.
Limitations: Giving on a national basis.

Publications: Application guidelines; Informational
brochure.
Application information: See foundation Web site
for application guidelines and forms. A child must
meet special needs criteria, and adoptive family
must meet financial criteria. Application form
required.
    Initial approach: E-mail, letter or telephone
    Copies of proposal: 1
    Deadline(s): None
    Board meeting date(s): Weekly
    Final notification: 2-4 weeks
Officers: Cynthia Nelson, Pres.; Randolph Nelson,
V.P.; Richard Cayne, Secy.
Number of staff: 2 full-time professional.
EIN: 133978652
Selected grants: The following grants were reported
in 2004.
$30,000 to Focus on the Children, Durango, CO.
$18,500 to Bethany Christian Services.
$13,000 to Dillon International, Tulsa, OK.
$7,000 to Childrens Home Society.
$5,000 to Catholic Charities.
$3,500 to Helping Hand, Countryside, IL.
$2,500 to All Gods Children United Methodist
    Church, Aulander, NC.
$2,500 to His Kids, Highland, IL.

3766
The A.M. Fund ✧ ☆
c/o The Stride Rite Fdn.
400 Atlantic Ave.
Boston, MA   02110

Established in 2001 in MA.
Donors: Arnold S. Hiatt; Fallen Angel Corp.; Autumn
Ventures.
Foundation type: Independent foundation.
Financial data (yr. ended 12/31/05): Assets,
$3,761,422 (M); gifts received, $510,614;
expenditures, $415,680; qualifying distributions,
$384,037; giving activities include $383,862 for 15
grants (high: $125,000; low: $1,000).
Fields of interest: Education; Human services;
Jewish agencies & temples.
Limitations: Applications not accepted. Giving
primarily in MA. No grants to individuals.
Application information: Contributes only to
pre-selected organizations.
Trustees: Amy R. Hiatt; Arnold S. Hiatt; Matthew T.
Hiatt.
EIN: 046956130

3767
The Aaron Foundation ✧
(formerly The Stop & Shop Charitable Foundation)
225 Franklin St., Ste. 2700
Boston, MA   02110-2804   (617) 695-1300
Contact: Avram J. Goldberg, Tr.

Trust established in 1951 in MA.
Donors: The Stop & Shop Cos., Inc.; The Stop &
Shop Supermarket Co.; Avram J. Goldberg.
Foundation type: Independent foundation.
Financial data (yr. ended 12/31/05): Assets,
$12,233,340 (M); expenditures, $726,695;
qualifying distributions, $624,154; giving activities
include $564,333 for 16 grants (high: $140,000;
low: $1,000).
Fields of interest: Arts; Higher education;
Education; Human services; Youth, services;

Federated giving programs; Jewish federated giving
programs; Jewish agencies & temples.
Limitations: Giving primarily in CT, MA, and RI. No
grants to individuals.
Application information: Application form not
required.
    Initial approach: Letter
    Copies of proposal: 1
    Deadline(s): None
Trustees: Hope R. Edison; Avram J. Goldberg; Carol
R. Goldberg; James M. Rabb; Jane M. Rabb; Betty
R. Schafer.
Number of staff: 1 full-time professional; 2 full-time
support.
EIN: 046039593

3768
Amy & David Abrams Foundation ✧ ☆
20 Lowell Ln.
Brookline, MA   02445
Contact: Amy Abrams, Tr.; David C. Abrams, Tr.

Established in 1997 in MA.
Donor: David C. Abrams.
Foundation type: Independent foundation.
Financial data (yr. ended 12/31/05): Assets,
$12,892,333 (M); gifts received, $6,550,000;
expenditures, $712,080; qualifying distributions,
$700,250; giving activities include $700,000 for 17
grants (high: $100,000; low: $10,000).
Fields of interest: Higher education, university;
Human services; Jewish agencies & temples.
Type of support: General/operating support.
Limitations: Giving primarily in NY. No grants to
individuals.
Application information:
    Initial approach: Letter
    Deadline(s): None
Trustees: Amy Abrams; David C. Abrams.
EIN: 046856820
Selected grants: The following grants were reported
in 2005.
$110,000 to Combined Jewish Philanthropies of
    Greater Boston, Boston, MA.
$100,000 to David Project, Newtonville, MA.
$55,000 to Milton Academy, Milton, MA.
$50,000 to Brown University, Providence, RI.
$50,000 to Israel Project, DC.
$50,000 to Vietnam Veterans of America
    Foundation, DC.
$40,000 to University of Pennsylvania, Philadelphia,
    PA.
$25,000 to New Profit, Cambridge, MA.
$10,000 to Link Community School, Newark, NJ.
$10,000 to Museum of Science, Boston, MA.

3769
Acorn Foundation ✧
1 Chestnut St.
Weston, MA   02493

Established in 1993 in MA.
Donors: Theodore Alfond; Berkshire Hathaway Inc.
Foundation type: Independent foundation.
Financial data (yr. ended 12/31/05): Assets,
$8,324,708 (M); gifts received, $854,631;
expenditures, $887,835; qualifying distributions,
$868,992; giving activities include $847,949 for 58
grants (high: $250,000; low: $50).
Purpose and activities: Giving primarily for
education and the arts.

Fields of interest: Arts; Elementary/secondary education; Higher education; Health care.
Limitations: Applications not accepted. Giving primarily in New England, with emphasis on MA, ME, and RI, some giving also in Winter Park, FL. No grants to individuals.
Application information: Contributes only to pre-selected organizations.
Trustees: Barbara Alfond; Michael M. Davis.
EIN: 043201916

3770
The Acushnet Foundation ✧
c/o Seamark Fin. Svcs.
P.O. Box 1498
Mattapoisett, MA 02739 (508) 758-6159
Contact: R. William Blasdale, Tr.

Trust established in 1953 in MA.
Foundation type: Independent foundation.
Financial data (yr. ended 6/30/05): Assets, $102,690 (M); expenditures, $5,917,609; qualifying distributions, $5,878,052; giving activities include $5,864,313 for 42 grants (high: $5,444,313; low: $1,000).
Fields of interest: Historic preservation/historical societies; Secondary school/education; Education; Animal welfare; Hospitals (general); Boys & girls clubs; Human services; YM/YWCAs & YM/YWHAs; Children/youth, services; Family services; Foundations (community); Federated giving programs.
Type of support: Continuing support; Annual campaigns; Capital campaigns; Building/renovation; Emergency funds; Seed money; Scholarship funds.
Limitations: Giving generally limited to the greater New Bedford, MA, area. No grants to individuals, or for endowment funds, operating budgets, deficit financing, or matching gifts.
Application information: Application form not required.
   Initial approach: Letter
   Copies of proposal: 1
   Deadline(s): None
   Board meeting date(s): As required
   Final notification: 4 to 6 weeks
Trustees: R. William Blasdale; Mrs. R. William Blasdale; Graeme L. Flanders; Carl Ribeiro; Mrs. Carl Ribeiro; Richard B. Young; William E. Young.
Number of staff: 1 part-time support.
EIN: 046032197

3771
The C. F. Adams Charitable Trust ✧
c/o Lowell, Blake & Assocs., Inc.
141 Tremont St., Ste. 200
Boston, MA 02111-1209 (617) 951-7586
Contact: Janet C. Taylor, Tr.

Established in 1986 in MA.
Donor: Charles F. Adams†.
Foundation type: Independent foundation.
Financial data (yr. ended 12/31/05): Assets, $15,921,215 (M); expenditures, $983,916; qualifying distributions, $929,612; giving activities include $899,300 for 50 grants (high: $150,000; low: $400; average: $500–$50,000).
Fields of interest: Historic preservation/historical societies; Environment; Human services; Children,

services; Community development; Philanthropy/voluntarism.
Type of support: Program development; Management development/capacity building; Income development; General/operating support.
Limitations: Applications not accepted. Giving primarily in eastern MA and down east ME. No grants to individuals.
Application information: Contributes only to pre-selected organizations.
Trustees: Beatrice D. Adams; Edward P. Lawrence; James H. Lowell II; Janet C. Taylor.
EIN: 046556188

3772
Charles E. & Caroline J. Adams Trust ✧
(formerly Frank W. and Carl S. Adams Memorial Fund)
c/o Bank of America, N.A., Philanthropic Mgmt.
100 Federal St., MA5-100-05-01
Boston, MA 02110 (617) 434-4846
Contact: Kerry H. Sullivan, Sr. V.P., Bank of America, Philanthropic Mgmt.

Established in 1955 in MA.
Donors: Charles E. Adams†; Caroline J. Adams†.
Foundation type: Independent foundation.
Financial data (yr. ended 5/31/05): Assets, $14,180,285 (M); expenditures, $711,051; qualifying distributions, $657,756; giving activities include $605,562 for 8 grants (high: $152,781; low: $15,000).
Purpose and activities: One half of the net income is distributed for general purposes, in the fields of health, welfare, the humanities, and education; the balance of the income is designated to assist needy and deserving students selected by Massachusetts Institute of Technology and the Harvard Medical School.
Fields of interest: Medical school/education; Engineering school/education; Adult education—literacy, basic skills & GED; Education; Employment, labor unions/organizations; Foundations (community).
Type of support: General/operating support; Capital campaigns; Building/renovation; Seed money.
Limitations: Giving primarily in Boston and Cambridge, MA. No support for national organizations. No grants to individuals, or for conferences, film production, travel, research projects, or publications; no loans.
Application information: AGM Common Proposal Format accepted. Grant Application Coversheet required.
   Initial approach: Proposal
   Copies of proposal: 1
   Deadline(s): Feb. 3
   Board meeting date(s): Mar., June, Sept., and Dec.
   Final notification: Apr.
Trustee: Bank of America, N.A.
EIN: 046011995
Selected grants: The following grants were reported in 2004.
$131,181 to Harvard University, School of Medicine, Cambridge, MA. For general support.
$131,181 to Massachusetts Institute of Technology, Cambridge, MA. For general support.
$100,000 to Boston Adult Literacy Fund, Boston, MA. For general support.
$50,000 to Massachusetts Institute for a New Commonwealth (MassINC), Boston, MA. For general support.

$35,000 to STRIVE (Support and Training Result in Valuable Employees)/Boston Employment Service, Boston, MA. For general support.
$30,000 to Boston Workforce Development Coalition, Boston, MA. For general support.
$25,000 to Cambridge Community Foundation, Cambridge, MA. For general support.
$25,000 to Camp Fire USA, Eastern Massachusetts Council, Boston, MA. For general support.
$5,000 to Home for Little Wanderers, Boston, MA. For general support.
$5,000 to Tutoring Plus of Cambridge, Cambridge, MA. For general support.

3773
Noubar & Anna Afeyan Foundation ✧ ☆
1 Sunset Ridge
Lexington, MA 02421

Established in 1999 in MA.
Donor: Noubar Afeyan.
Foundation type: Independent foundation.
Financial data (yr. ended 12/31/05): Assets, $334,007 (M); gifts received, $138,461; expenditures, $341,025; qualifying distributions, $334,615; giving activities include $334,615 for 22 grants (high: $75,000; low: $175).
Purpose and activities: Giving primarily for Armenian related projects and issues.
Fields of interest: Education; Human services; Religion.
International interests: Armenia.
Limitations: Applications not accepted. Giving primarily in Armenia, with some giving in MA. No grants to individuals.
Application information: Contributes only to pre-selected organizations.
Trustees: Noubar Afeyan; Anna Karin M. Gunnarson.
EIN: 043489109

3774
Mary H. Agostine Trust ✧ ☆
c/o Bank of America, N.A., P.C. Group
P.O. Box 55886
Boston, MA 02205-5886

Established in 1983 in MA.
Foundation type: Independent foundation.
Financial data (yr. ended 12/31/05): Assets, $1,002,538 (M); expenditures, $343,554; qualifying distributions, $341,548; giving activities include $318,066 for 1 grant.
Fields of interest: Libraries/library science.
Type of support: General/operating support.
Limitations: Applications not accepted. Giving on an international basis, primarily in Italy. No grants to individuals.
Application information: Contributes only to pre-selected organizations.
Trustee: Bank of America, N.A.
EIN: 046489996

3775
The Alchemy Foundation ☆
c/o Kyra Montagu
76 Walnut Pl.
Brookline, MA 02445

Established in 2000 in MA.
Donors: Jean Montagu; Kyra Montagu.

Foundation type: Independent foundation.
Financial data (yr. ended 12/31/05): Assets, $4,591,652 (M); expenditures, $377,928; qualifying distributions, $344,085; giving activities include $344,085 for grants.
Purpose and activities: Giving primarily to international refugee projects in Africa, and health initiatives in Vietnam and internationally.
Fields of interest: Arts; Education; Human services.
International interests: Africa; Vietnam.
Type of support: Program development.
Limitations: Applications not accepted. Giving on a national basis (with emphasis on MA) and on an international basis (with emphasis on Africa and Vietnam). No grants to individuals, or for capital.
Application information: Contributes only to pre-selected organizations.
    Board meeting date(s): Oct.
Trustees: Mohammed Ali; Doan Ngoc Diep; Jean Montagu; Kyra Montagu; Sasha Montagu.
EIN: 043541830

3776
The George I. Alden Trust ▼ ✧
370 Main St.
Worcester, MA 01608-1779 (508) 798-8621, ext. 3374
Contact: Susan B. Woodbury, Chair.
FAX: (508) 791-6454;
E-mail: trustees@aldentrust.org; Additional tel.: (508) 798-8621, ext. 3303; URL: http://www.aldentrust.org

Trust established in 1912 in MA.
Donor: George I. Alden†.
Foundation type: Independent foundation.
Financial data (yr. ended 12/31/04): Assets, $171,013,321 (M); expenditures, $9,282,599; qualifying distributions, $8,595,867; giving activities include $8,449,157 for 103 grants (high: $400,000; low: $6,000; average: $15,000–$150,000).
Purpose and activities: To support private, independent education, primarily in colleges in New York, New Jersey, Pennsylvania, and the six New England states, with consideration also given to Massachusetts YMCA's. Occasional grants to Worcester area educational and cultural institutions. Giving primarily for capital projects and permanent restricted endowments for the educational benefit of students and faculty.
Fields of interest: Vocational education; Higher education; Education; YM/YWCAs & YM/YWHAs.
Type of support: Capital campaigns; Building/renovation; Equipment; Endowments; Professorships; Scholarship funds.
Limitations: Giving limited to NY, NJ, PA and the six New England states. No grants to individuals; no loans.
Publications: Annual report (including application guidelines); Financial statement; Grants list; Informational brochure (including application guidelines).
Application information: Application form not required.
    Initial approach: Proposal with cover letter
    Copies of proposal: 1
    Deadline(s): Feb. 1, May 1, Aug. 1, Oct. 1, and Dec. 1
    Board meeting date(s): Feb., May, Aug., Oct., and Dec.
    Final notification: Within a week of grants meeting

Officers and Trustees: * Susan B. Woodbury,* Chair.; Richard P. Traina,* Vice-Chair.; Warner S. Fletcher,* Clerk; James E. Collins,* Treas.
Number of staff: 4 part-time professional; 2 part-time support.
EIN: 046023784
Selected grants: The following grants were reported in 2005.
$800,000 to Boys and Girls Club of Worcester, Worcester, MA. 2 grants: $300,000, $500,000
$800,000 to YMCA of Greater Worcester, Worcester, MA.
$250,000 to Higgins Armory Museum, Worcester, MA.
$200,000 to Bates College, Lewiston, ME.
$200,000 to Franklin and Marshall College, Lancaster, PA.
$200,000 to YMCA of Central Massachusetts, Worcester, MA.
$125,000 to College of Saint Rose, Albany, NY.
$18,000 to Mechanics Hall, Worcester, MA.
$18,000 to Southeast Asian Coalition of Central Massachusetts, Worcester, MA.

3777
John W. Alden Trust ✧
c/o U.S. Trust
225 Franklin St.
Boston, MA 02110 (617) 951-1108
Contact: Susan T. Monahan, Grants Coord.
E-mail: stm@rackmann.com; URL: http://www.cybergrants.com/alden

Established in 1986 in MA.
Donor: Priscilla Alden†.
Foundation type: Independent foundation.
Financial data (yr. ended 9/30/05): Assets, $10,312,376 (M); expenditures, $546,737; qualifying distributions, $489,124; giving activities include $426,807 for 37 grants (high: $25,000; low: $1,088).
Purpose and activities: Grant support directed toward organizations providing care and administering to the needs of children who are blind, retarded, disabled, or who are either mentally or physically ill, or to organizations engaged in medical and scientific research, directed toward the prevention or cure of diseases and disabilities particularly affecting children.
Fields of interest: Arts education; Child development, education; Hospitals (general); Medical research, institute; Children/youth, services; Child development, services; Disabilities, people with.
Type of support: Program development; Seed money; Research.
Limitations: Giving primarily in eastern MA. No grants to individuals.
Publications: Application guidelines.
Application information: Applications must be submitted online through the foundation's Web site. Application form not required.
    Initial approach: Letter
    Deadline(s): Jan. 15, Apr. 15, July 15, and Oct. 15
    Board meeting date(s): Feb., May, Aug., and Nov.
    Final notification: Within 1 month
Trustees: William B. Tyler; U.S. Trust.
Number of staff: 1 part-time professional; 1 part-time support.
EIN: 222719727
Selected grants: The following grants were reported in 2004.

$25,000 to Lesley University, Cambridge, MA. For Threshold Program Scholarship Endowment.
$25,000 to Northeastern University, Boston, MA. For research on psychological and neurological status of children admitted to intensive care unit.
$20,000 to Family Service Association of Greater Boston, Jamaica Plain, MA. For Trauma Services Program.
$20,000 to Franciscan Childrens Hospital and Rehabilitation Center, Boston, MA. For community fitness programs for disabled youth.
$19,650 to South Shore Mental Health Center, Quincy, MA. For expansion of Super Employable People program to include court involved adolescents with mental illnesses.
$17,200 to Cotting School, Lexington, MA. For specialized adaptive equipment.
$15,000 to Adolescent Consultation Services, Cambridge, MA. For Education and Advocacy Program.
$15,000 to Boston Urban Youth Foundation, Boston, MA. For expansion of School Success Truancy Program.
$10,000 to James F. Farr Academy, Cambridge, MA. For Expansion of the Arts Education Program.
$10,000 to Jeannie Lindheims Hospital Clown Troupe, Brookline Village, MA. For hospital clown visits to ill and disabled children.

3778
Alvord Family Foundation ✧ ☆
c/o Joel B. Alvord
75 Federal St., 18th Fl.
Boston, MA 02110

Established in 1996 in MA.
Donor: Joel B. Alvord.
Foundation type: Independent foundation.
Financial data (yr. ended 11/30/05): Assets, $1,253,243 (M); gifts received, $300,000; expenditures, $542,171; qualifying distributions, $511,838; giving activities include $511,838 for grants.
Purpose and activities: Giving primarily for the arts, as well as for education, children and youth services, including a children's medical center, social services and federated giving programs.
Fields of interest: Museums; Performing arts, theater; Arts; Higher education; Education; Hospitals (general); Human services; Children/youth, services; Federated giving programs.
Limitations: Applications not accepted. Giving primarily in MA. No grants to individuals.
Application information: Contributes only to pre-selected organizations.
Trustees: Joel B. Alvord; Sarah H. Alvord; Seth W. Alvord.
EIN: 046820195
Selected grants: The following grants were reported in 2004.
$10,000 to Wesleyan University, Middletown, CT.
$5,000 to Boston Symphony Orchestra, Boston, MA.
$5,000 to Teen Center of Wilton, Wilton, CT.
$3,250 to Seton Hall University, South Orange, NJ.
$2,000 to Greater Boston Youth Symphony Orchestra, Boston, MA.
$1,000 to Museum of the City of New York, New York, NY.
$800 to Boys Club of New York, New York, NY.

3779
Ronald M. Ansin Foundation ✧
(formerly Ronald M. Ansin Private Foundation)
1 Main St.
Leominster, MA   01453
Contact: Ronald M. Ansin, Tr.

Established in 1984 in MA.
Donor: Ronald M. Ansin.
Foundation type: Independent foundation.
Financial data (yr. ended 11/30/05): Assets,
$9,620,295 (M); expenditures, $954,765;
qualifying distributions, $938,346; giving activities
include $938,346 for 88 grants (high: $100,000;
low: $100).
Fields of interest: Museums; Performing arts,
theater; Performing arts, orchestra (symphony);
Arts; Education; Hospitals (general); Health care;
AIDS; Youth development, services; Human
services; Civil rights; Community development;
Jewish agencies & temples.
Limitations: Giving primarily in MA. No grants to
individuals.
Application information:
Initial approach: Letter
Deadline(s): None
Trustee: Ronald M. Ansin.
EIN: 042786469
Selected grants: The following grants were reported
in 2004.
$170,000 to Applewild School, Fitchburg, MA. 2
grants: $20,000, $150,000
$75,000 to Lawrence Academy, Groton, MA.
$60,000 to Fenway Community Health Center,
Boston, MA.
$50,000 to Victory Programs, Boston, MA.
$46,000 to Our Fathers House, Fitchburg, MA.
$36,950 to Merrimack Repertory Theater, Lowell,
MA.
$25,000 to United Way.
$15,000 to PrideFest Philadelphia, Philadelphia,
PA.
$5,000 to Florida Stage, Manalapan, FL.

3780
Arbella Charitable Foundation, Inc. ✧ ☆
101 Arch St., Ste. 1860
Boston, MA   02110
Contact: Beverly Kenneally, Clerk

Established in 2004 in MA.
Donor: Arbella, Inc.
Foundation type: Independent foundation.
Financial data (yr. ended 12/31/05): Assets,
$7,816,097 (M); gifts received, $4,000,000;
expenditures, $446,111; qualifying distributions,
$429,093; giving activities include $429,093 for
grants.
Officers: John F. Donohue, Pres.; Robert P. Medwid,
Treas.; Beverly T. Kenneally, Clerk.
Directors: Patricia B. Bailey; Francis X. Bellotti; Anne
DeFrancesco; Edmund J. Doherty; J. Robert Dowling;
William H. DuMouchel; Andrea Gargiulo; David W.
Hattman; Thomas R. Kiley; Jeannette M. Orsino.
EIN: 050613355

3781
The ASD Foundation ✧
c/o Steven B. Dodge and Anne N. Dodge
239 Summer St.
Manchester, MA   01944

Established in 1998 in MA.
Donors: Anne N. Dodge; Steven B. Dodge.
Foundation type: Independent foundation.
Financial data (yr. ended 6/30/04): Assets,
$7,781,799 (M); expenditures, $646,526;
qualifying distributions, $585,606; giving activities
include $585,525 for 50 grants (high: $100,000;
low: $100).
Fields of interest: Higher education; Education;
Hospitals (general); Health organizations,
association; Human services; Federated giving
programs.
Limitations: Giving primarily in Boston, MA.
Application information:
Initial approach: Letter
Deadline(s): None
Trustees: Anne N. Dodge; Steven B. Dodge.
EIN: 043446318

3782
Elisha V. Ashton Trust ✧
c/o Choate, Hall & Stewart
2 International Pl.
Boston, MA   02110

Established in 1884 in MA.
Foundation type: Independent foundation.
Financial data (yr. ended 10/31/05): Assets,
$17,405,300 (M); expenditures, $976,832;
qualifying distributions, $873,898; giving activities
include $851,000 for 23 grants (high: $37,000;
low: $37,000).
Purpose and activities: Giving primarily for social
services, especially organizations which aid and
house the needy, indigent, aged, and women and
children; support also for hospitals and animal
welfare.
Fields of interest: Animal welfare; Hospitals
(general); Human services; Children/youth,
services; Family services; Residential/custodial
care; Aging, centers/services; Women, centers/
services; Aging; Women.
Limitations: Applications not accepted. Giving
primarily in the Boston, MA, area. No grants to
individuals.
Application information: Contributes only to
pre-selected organizations.
Trustees: John M. Cornish; James R. Nichols.
EIN: 046016303

3783
**Association for the Relief of Aged Women
of New Bedford** ✧
1140 State Rd.
P.O. Box 819
Westport, MA   02790

Established in 1866.
Foundation type: Operating foundation.
Financial data (yr. ended 3/31/06): Assets,
$17,912,593 (M); gifts received, $3,600;
expenditures, $1,069,507; qualifying distributions,
$1,019,009; giving activities include $644,484 for
9 grants, and $285,752 for 111 grants to
individuals.
Purpose and activities: A private operating
foundation; furnishes assistance to and promotes
the welfare and relief of elderly women in New
Bedford, Dartmouth, Fairhaven, and Acushnet, MA.
Applicants for aid must be 60 years of age or older,
have liquid assets under $5,000, and live alone.

Only women who have been residents of the above
named towns for at least five years are eligible.
Fields of interest: Children, services; Family
services; Aging; Women; Economically
disadvantaged.
Type of support: Grants to individuals.
Limitations: Applications not accepted. Giving
limited to residents of New Bedford, Dartmouth,
Fairhaven, and Acushnet, MA.
Application information: Unsolicited requests for
funds not accepted.
Board meeting date(s): 1st Mon. of each month
Officers and Directors:* Mary Little,* Pres.; Ellen
Williams,* Secy.; Nancy Kurtz,* Treas.; Hope
Atkinson; Mary Barrows; Mary Elinore Davies;
Sandra Fogg; and 11 additional directors.
EIN: 046056367

3784
**The Robert and Michelle Cooke Atchinson
Foundation** ✧ ☆
3 Burroughs Rd.
Lexington, MA   02420

Established in 1998 in MA.
Donors: Robert G. Atchinson; Michelle Cooke
Atchinson.
Foundation type: Independent foundation.
Financial data (yr. ended 12/31/05): Assets,
$6,786,169 (M); gifts received, $1,693,890;
expenditures, $484,321; qualifying distributions,
$429,515; giving activities include $429,515 for
grants.
Fields of interest: Education; Human services.
Type of support: General/operating support.
Limitations: Applications not accepted. Giving
primarily in MA. No grants to individuals.
Application information: Contributes only to
pre-selected organizations.
Trustees: Michelle Cooke Atchinson; Robert G.
Atchinson.
EIN: 046875099

3785
Alice S. Ayling Scholarship Foundation ✧
c/o Tyler & Reynolds
77 Summer St.
Boston, MA   02110   (617) 695-9799
Contact: Richard P. Hamel, Tr.

Established in 1987 in MA.
Donor: Alice S. Ayling.
Foundation type: Independent foundation.
Financial data (yr. ended 12/31/05): Assets,
$13,130,990 (M); expenditures, $774,841;
qualifying distributions, $700,898; giving activities
include $645,250 for 15 grants (high: $62,000;
low: $11,000).
Purpose and activities: Giving to colleges and
universities which recommend scholarship
candidates who are engaged in full-time studies, for
assistance at their sole discretion. Strong attention
given to scholarships relating to the field of
humanities.
Fields of interest: Humanities; Scholarships/
financial aid.
Type of support: Scholarship funds.
Limitations: Giving primarily in MA, ME, NH, and VT.
No grants to individuals.

Application information: Direct applications from individuals not considered. Application form required.

   Deadline(s): May 15

Officer: Geoffrey C. Andrews, Exec. Dir.

Trustees: Richard P. Hamel; Gerald B. O'Grady.

EIN: 222808952

Selected grants: The following grants were reported in 2004.

$59,000 to Keene State College, Keene, NH.

$59,000 to Northeastern University, Boston, MA.

$57,500 to Bates College, Lewiston, ME.

$53,500 to Clark University, Worcester, MA.

$51,000 to University of Maine, Orono, ME.

$51,000 to University of Vermont, Burlington, VT.

$50,500 to Simmons College, Boston, MA.

$43,500 to Colby College, Waterville, ME.

$42,500 to Middlebury College, Middlebury, VT.

$40,500 to Bowdoin College, Brunswick, ME.

3786
Azadoutioun Foundation

c/o Gravestar, Inc.
160 2nd St.
Cambridge, MA 02142-1515
Contact: Laurie Le Blanc
Application address: 10 Madison Ave., Groveland, MA 01834-1143

Established in 1985 in MA.

Donor: Carolyn G. Mugar.

Foundation type: Independent foundation.

Financial data (yr. ended 12/31/04): Assets, $2,652,157 (M); gifts received, $30,000; expenditures, $1,170,942; qualifying distributions, $996,224; giving activities include $496,817 for 9 grants (high: $407,817; low: $1,000).

Purpose and activities: Giving primarily for education and human services.

Fields of interest: Adult education—literacy, basic skills & GED; Education, reading; Environment; Human services; International economic development.

Type of support: General/operating support; Program development.

Limitations: Giving on a national basis. No grants to individuals; no loans.

Application information: Application form not required.

   Initial approach: Letter outlining request

   Copies of proposal: 1

   Deadline(s): None

   Board meeting date(s): Annually

Trustees: Janet Corpus; Carolyn G. Mugar; Sidney Peck; Sharryn Ross.

Number of staff: 1 part-time professional; 1 part-time support.

EIN: 042876245

3787
The Paul and Edith Babson Foundation ◇

c/o Nichols & Pratt
50 Congress St., Ste. 832
Boston, MA 02109-4017
Contact: Elizabeth D. Nichols, Prog. Off.
FAX: (617) 523-8949;
E-mail: pebabsonfdn@babsonfoundations.org;
Elizabeth D. Nichols, Prog. Off. tel.: (617) 523-8368 (Wed. and Thurs.); Rashetta Ulness, Fdn. Asst. tel.: (617) 523-6800 (any day);
URL: http://www.babsonfoundations.org

Trust established in 1957 in MA.

Donor: Paul T. Babson‡.

Foundation type: Independent foundation.

Financial data (yr. ended 12/31/05): Assets, $12,191,929 (M); expenditures, $595,564; qualifying distributions, $581,258; giving activities include $548,503 for 81 grants (high: $26,000; low: $1,000).

Purpose and activities: The competitive grant program focuses on providing opportunities for the people of Greater Boston, MA, through grants in four program areas: entrepreneurship and economic development, culture, education and leadership development, environment and community building, and health and social services.

Fields of interest: Performing arts, theater; Performing arts, music; Arts; Education; Environment, beautification programs; AIDS; Crime/violence prevention, domestic violence; Youth, services; Economic development; Urban/community development; Community development, small businesses.

Type of support: General/operating support; Program development; Scholarship funds.

Limitations: Giving limited to the greater Boston, MA, area as generally defined by Route 128. No grants to individuals, or for individual scholarships, conferences, films, fundraising, or donor cultivations.

Publications: Application guidelines; Grants list; Program policy statement.

Application information: After review of concept letter, proposal submissions will be invited from a limited number of applicants. New applicants are encouraged to telephone Elizabeth D. Nichols, Prog. Off. or Rashetta Ulness, Fdn. Asst. Summary Sheets available on foundation Web site. Application form required.

   Initial approach: 2- to 3-page concept letter with Summary Sheet

   Copies of proposal: 2

   Deadline(s): Feb. 6 and Sept. 9

   Board meeting date(s): Late May and early Dec.

   Final notification: Within 6 weeks

Trustees: James A. Babson; James R. Nichols; Katherine L. Nichols.

EIN: 046037891

3788
William W. Bain, Jr. Charitable Trust ◇

c/o Ropes & Gray, LLP
1 International Pl., 21st Fl.
Boston, MA 02110-2624
Contact: William W. Bain, Jr., Tr.

Established in 1986 in MA.

Donor: William W. Bain, Jr.

Foundation type: Independent foundation.

Financial data (yr. ended 11/30/05): Assets, $1,033,123 (M); expenditures, $677,446; qualifying distributions, $659,564; giving activities include $648,500 for 9 grants (high: $300,000; low: $5,000).

Purpose and activities: Giving primarily for children and youth services, particularly to a children's hospital; funding also for education.

Fields of interest: Education; Hospitals (specialty); Boys & girls clubs; Children/youth, services; Foundations (private grantmaking).

Limitations: Applications not accepted. Giving primarily in MA, with emphasis on Boston. No grants to individuals.

Application information: Contributes only to pre-selected organizations.

Trustees: William W. Bain, Jr.; William A. Truslow.

EIN: 046572942

Selected grants: The following grants were reported in 2005.

$300,000 to Vanderbilt University, Nashville, TN.

$25,000 to Boys and Girls Club of Boston, Chinatown, Boston, MA.

$25,000 to Milton Academy, Milton, MA.

$10,000 to Boston Celtics Shamrock Foundation, Boston, MA.

$5,000 to NCH Healthcare System Foundation, Naples, FL.

3789
The A. W. Baldwin Charitable Foundation, Inc. ◇

(formerly Baldwin Charitable Foundation, Inc.)
c/o Fiduciary Trust Co.
P.O. Box 55806
Boston, MA 02205-5806

Established in 1969 in MA.

Donor: Alfred W. Baldwin.

Foundation type: Independent foundation.

Financial data (yr. ended 12/31/05): Assets, $25,444,293 (M); expenditures, $1,403,302; qualifying distributions, $1,271,195; giving activities include $1,270,000 for 19 grants (high: $200,000; low: $15,000).

Fields of interest: Education; Hospitals (general); Health organizations, association.

Limitations: Applications not accepted. Giving primarily in Boston, MA. No grants to individuals.

Application information: Contributes only to pre-selected organizations.

Officers: Janet D. Wilson, Pres.; Andrew C. Bailey, Clerk; Sofie Zivulovic, Treas.

EIN: 237004131

3790
L. G. Balfour Foundation ▼

c/o Bank of America, N.A., Philanthropic Management
100 Federal St., MA5-100-05-01
Boston, MA 02110 (617) 434-4846
Contact: Kerry Herlihy Sullivan, Sr. V.P., Bank of America, N.A., Philanthropic Management
Additional tel.: (617) 434-4941

Established in 1973 in MA.

Donor: L.G. Balfour‡.

Foundation type: Independent foundation.

Financial data (yr. ended 3/31/05): Assets, $98,765,263 (M); expenditures, $4,706,739; qualifying distributions, $4,438,410; giving activities include $4,160,000 for 64 grants (high: $450,000; low: $5,000; average: $25,000–$75,000).

Purpose and activities: Giving primarily for programs that provide access to education, and for charitable contributions in the city of Attleboro.

Fields of interest: Education.

Type of support: General/operating support; Program development.

Limitations: Giving primarily in New England, with emphasis on Attleboro, MA. No grants to individuals.

Publications: Application guidelines.

Application information: Do not send videotapes. Please number each section as indicated on the Grant Application. Application form required.

Initial approach: Full proposal using AGM Common Proposal Format. Applicants must also complete a Grant Application Coversheet which may be downloaded from the foundation Web site

Copies of proposal: 1

Deadline(s): Feb. 3; Ongoing for general education only

Final notification: Apr.; Ongoing for general education only

Trustee: Bank of America, N.A.

Number of staff: 5

EIN: 222751372

Selected grants: The following grants were reported in 2005.

$450,000 to Sigma Chi Foundation, Evanston, IL. For Balfour Leadership Training Workshop and fellowship programs.

$200,000 to Boston Plan for Excellence in the Public Schools, Boston, MA. For middle grades teacher network and literacy coaching initiative.

$140,000 to Sturdy Memorial Foundation, Attleboro, MA. For emergency care unit.

$100,000 to Crotched Mountain Foundation, Greenfield, NH. For Community Transitions Project.

$75,000 to Boston Symphony Orchestra, Boston, MA. For Education Resource Center.

$75,000 to Elms College, Chicopee, MA. For Standing on a Foundation Success Project.

$50,000 to Boston Childrens Chorus, Boston, MA. For general operating support.

$50,000 to Boston Institute for Arts Therapy, Boston, MA. For Artsreach program with Attleboro Museum.

$50,000 to YMCA of Attleboro, Attleboro, MA. For YLight program.

$25,000 to University of New Hampshire, Institute on Disabilities, Concord, NH. For New Hampshire Family Leadership Series.

3791

Barr Foundation ▼

(formerly The Hostetter Foundation)
The Pilot House
Lewis Wharf
Boston, MA 02110 (617) 854-3500
Contact: Kerri Hurley, Grants Mgr.
FAX: (617) 854-3501;
E-mail: info@barrfoundation.org; URL: http://www.barrfoundation.org

Established in 1987 in MA.

Donors: Amos B. Hostetter, Jr.; Barbara W. Hostetter.

Foundation type: Independent foundation.

Financial data (yr. ended 12/31/05): Assets, $857,054,761 (M); expenditures, $47,756,530; qualifying distributions, $40,022,156; giving activities include $37,643,279 for 377 grants (high: $2,000,000; low: $500; average: $1,000–$200,000).

Purpose and activities: The foundation is committed to enhancing the quality of life for all of the citizens of Boston, MA. Its primary areas of emphasis are education and the environment, and it also provides support to arts and cultural activities.

Fields of interest: Arts; Elementary school/education; Education; Environment, natural resources; Environment; Community development.

Type of support: General/operating support; Annual campaigns; Capital campaigns; Building/renovation; Land acquisition; Endowments; Emergency funds; Program development; Conferences/seminars; Fellowships; Research; Technical assistance; Consulting services; Program evaluation; Matching/challenge support.

Limitations: Applications not accepted. Giving primarily in the greater Boston, MA, area. No grants to individuals.

Application information: Unsolicited requests for funds not accepted.

Board meeting date(s): Quarterly

Officers: Marion Kane, Exec. Dir.

Trustees: Amos B. Hostetter, Jr.; Barbara W. Hostetter.

Number of staff: 7 full-time professional; 2 full-time support.

EIN: 046579815

Selected grants: The following grants were reported in 2004.

$2,000,000 to Newton-Wellesley Hospital Charitable Foundation, Newton, MA.

$1,000,000 to Institute of Contemporary Art, Boston, MA.

$945,947 to Amherst College, Amherst, MA.

$750,000 to Boston Community Capital, Boston, MA.

$691,500 to Child Care Capital Investment Fund, Boston, MA.

$600,000 to Boston Foundation, Boston, MA.

$296,129 to Charles River Watershed Association, Waltham, MA.

$100,000 to Boston Education Development Foundation, Boston, MA.

$60,000 to Boston Medical Center, Boston, MA.

$59,700 to Multicultural Youth Tour of What's Now (MYTOWN), Boston, MA.

3792

The Barron Family Charitable Foundation ◇ ☆

c/o Deloitte & Touche, LLP
200 Berkeley St.
Boston, MA 02116
Contact: Norman W. Barron, Tr.

Established in 1987 in MA.

Donor: Norman W. Barron.

Foundation type: Independent foundation.

Financial data (yr. ended 12/31/05): Assets, $1,866,561 (M); gifts received, $190,000; expenditures, $386,468; qualifying distributions, $374,520; giving activities include $374,520 for grants.

Purpose and activities: Giving primarily for hospitals and Jewish organizations.

Fields of interest: Hospitals (general); Medical research, institute; Jewish federated giving programs; Jewish agencies & temples.

Limitations: Giving primarily in Boca Raton, FL.

Application information: Application form not required.

Initial approach: Letter

Deadline(s): None

Trustees: Adele L. Barron; Douglas S. Barron; Norman W. Barron; Scott V. Barron; Frederick W. Shaw.

EIN: 042981078

Selected grants: The following grants were reported in 2003.

$30,000 to Jewish Federation of the North Shore, Marblehead, MA. For general support.

$20,000 to Jewish Federation of South Palm Beach County, Boca Raton, FL. For general support.

$15,000 to Massachusetts General Hospital, Boston, MA.

$10,000 to Boston University, Boston, MA.

$10,000 to Lown Cardiovascular Research Foundation, Brookline, MA.

$5,000 to North Shore Medical Center, Salem, MA.

$1,000 to Anti-Defamation League of Bnai Brith, New York, NY.

$1,000 to Boca Raton Community Hospital Foundation, Boca Raton, FL. For general support.

$1,000 to Hospice by the Sea, Boca Raton, FL.

$1,000 to Susan G. Komen Breast Cancer Foundation, Dallas, TX.

3793

Richard Allan Barry Charitable Foundation ◇

c/o Lourie & Cutler
60 State St.
Boston, MA 02109

Established in 2000 in MA.

Donor: Richard Allen Barry.

Foundation type: Independent foundation.

Financial data (yr. ended 12/31/05): Assets, $7,854,139 (M); expenditures, $390,357; qualifying distributions, $390,427; giving activities include $326,500 for 16 grants (high: $100,000; low: $1,000).

Purpose and activities: Giving primarily for medical research, human rights, and youth development.

Fields of interest: Parkinson's disease; AIDS; Alzheimer's disease; Autism; Youth development, centers/clubs; Human services; Civil liberties, advocacy.

Limitations: Applications not accepted. Giving primarily in MA; some funding nationally. No grants to individuals.

Application information: Contributes only to pre-selected organizations.

Trustee: Richard Allen Barry.

EIN: 046920279

Selected grants: The following grants were reported in 2005.

$100,000 to Massachusetts Institute of Technology, Cambridge, MA.

$50,000 to American Civil Liberties Union (ACLU), New York, NY.

$25,000 to George Washington University, DC.

$25,000 to Habitat for Humanity International.

$10,000 to Boston Foundation, Boston, MA.

$2,500 to Boys and Girls Club of Venice, Venice, CA.

$1,000 to Alzheimers Association, Chicago, IL.

$1,000 to National Alliance for Autism Research, Princeton, NJ.

3794

The Bay State Federal Savings Charitable Foundation ◇

55 Cambridge Pkwy.
Cambridge, MA 02142 (617) 225-6945
Contact: Jill W. Power, Corp. Secy.
FAX: (617) 225-2822;
E-mail: info@baystatecharitable.com; URL: http://www.baystatecharitable.com

Established in 1997 in MA as a company-sponsored operating foundation.

Donors: Bay State Bancorp, Inc.; Bay State Federal Savings Bank.

Foundation type: Operating foundation.

Financial data (yr. ended 3/31/06): Assets, $13,561,543 (M); expenditures, $727,802; qualifying distributions, $691,531; giving activities include $400,790 for 235 grants (high: $50,000; low: $80).

Purpose and activities: Giving for youth services and development, education, health associations, health care, including hospitals and medical research, community organizations that contribute to the quality of life, and social services, including a senior center, and a shelter for the homeless.

Fields of interest: Arts; Elementary/secondary education; Higher education; Education; Environment; Hospitals (general); Health organizations, association; Health organizations; Medical research, institute; Cancer research; Housing/shelter; Youth development; Human services; Children/youth, services; Christian agencies & churches; Aging.

Limitations: Giving primarily in MA. No grants to individuals.

Application information:

Initial approach: Letter or proposal

Deadline(s): None

Officers and Directors:* John F. Murphy, Chair., C.E.O., and Treas.; Denise M. Renaghan,* Pres. and Exec. Dir.; Jill W. Power, Corp. Secy.; Anthony F. Caruso; Phyllis M. Penta.

Special Advisor: Michael O. Gilles.

EIN: 043415547

Selected grants: The following grants were reported in 2006.

$50,000 to Brookline Senior Center, Brookline, MA.

$8,000 to Brookline Community Fund, Brookline, MA. 2 grants: $3,000, $5,000

$5,000 to North Cambridge Catholic High School, Cambridge, MA.

$3,000 to Arsenal Center for the Arts, Watertown, MA.

$3,000 to Childrens Law Center of Massachusetts, Lynn, MA.

$2,500 to American Cancer Society, Boston, MA.

$1,500 to Saint Francis House, Boston, MA.

$1,500 to Triangle, Inc., Malden, MA.

$1,000 to Presentation of Mary Academy, Methuen, MA.

3795
Adelaide Breed Bayrd Foundation

28 Pilgrim Rd.

Melrose, MA 02176 (781) 662-7971

Contact: Russell E. Watts M.D., Pres.

FAX: (781) 662-7342; Additional tel.: (781) 662-7971

Incorporated in 1927 in MA.

Donors: Frank A. Bayrd‡; Blanche S. Bayrd‡.

Foundation type: Independent foundation.

Financial data (yr. ended 12/31/05): Assets, $3,977,405 (M); gifts received, $615,000; expenditures, $602,322; qualifying distributions, $547,007; giving activities include $523,630 for grants.

Purpose and activities: Giving to support primarily those activities in which the donors' mother took an active interest. This includes local hospitals, social welfare concerns, libraries, youth-oriented programs, and cultural activities. The foundation

does not grant individual scholarships but does fund ten scholarships annually through the Malden High School in MA. All grants must in some manner benefit the citizens of Malden, MA.

Fields of interest: Arts; Adult/continuing education; Libraries/library science; Education; Hospitals (general); Health care; Health organizations, association; Human services; Children/youth, services; Family services; Residential/custodial care, hospices; Aging, centers/services; Community development; Aging.

Type of support: Annual campaigns; Capital campaigns; Building/renovation; Equipment; Emergency funds; Program development; Scholarship funds.

Limitations: Giving limited to the metropolitan Boston, MA, area, with emphasis on Malden. No support for national or out-of-state organizations or the performing arts (except certain educational programs). No grants to individuals (except for scholarships supplementary to the will of Blanche Bayrd), or for matching or challenge grants, demonstration projects, conferences, publications, research or endowment funds; no loans.

Publications: Annual report (including application guidelines).

Application information: Application form not required.

Initial approach: Proposal

Copies of proposal: 1

Deadline(s): Submit proposal before annual meeting on the 2nd Tues. in Feb.

Board meeting date(s): 2nd Tues. in Feb.; special meetings usually held in Apr. or May to consider grant requests

Final notification: Generally in Apr. or May

Officers and Trustees:* Russell E. Watts, M.D.*, Pres.; Susan C. Mansur,* Treas.; Francis K. Brown II; Richard R. Burns, Jr.; C. Henry Kezer; Fred I. Lamson; William H. Marshall; Jean H. Stearns; H. Allen Stevens.

Number of staff: 1 part-time professional; 1 part-time support.

EIN: 046051258

3796
The Behrakis Foundation ✧

c/o Stephanie Behrakis-Liakos

80 Hayden Ave., Ste. 100

Lexington, MA 02421-7303 (781) 861-9114

E-mail: sbliakos@behrprivfdn.com

Established in 1996 in MA.

Donor: George D. Behrakis.

Foundation type: Independent foundation.

Financial data (yr. ended 9/30/05): Assets, $5,531,692 (M); expenditures, $510,085; qualifying distributions, $387,802; giving activities include $387,802 for 44 grants (high: $50,000; low: $200).

Purpose and activities: Giving primarily for education, Eastern Orthodox Christian churches, museums, and for health care.

Fields of interest: Arts; Education; Health care; Christian agencies & churches.

Type of support: Continuing support; Capital campaigns; Building/renovation; Program development; Conferences/seminars; Scholarship funds; Research; Program-related investments/loans; Matching/challenge support.

Limitations: Giving primarily in Merrimack Valley, MA. No grants to individuals.

Publications: Informational brochure (including application guidelines).

Application information: Application form required.

Initial approach: Letter

Copies of proposal: 1

Deadline(s): June 30

Board meeting date(s): Quarterly

Final notification: Within 3 months

Trustees: Drake Behrakis; George D. Behrakis; Margo Behrakis; Stephanie Behrakis-Liakos.

Number of staff: 1 full-time professional.

EIN: 043348263

Selected grants: The following grants were reported in 2003.

$50,000 to Brigham and Womens Hospital, Boston, MA.

$50,000 to Museum of Fine Arts, Boston, MA.

$35,000 to Boys and Girls Club of Greater Lowell, Lowell, MA. 2 grants: $25,000, $10,000

$33,333 to Mother Caroline Academy and Education Center, Dorchester, MA.

$15,000 to Johns Hopkins Bayview Medical Center, Baltimore, MD. For Asthma and Allergy Center.

$8,000 to Massachusetts Society for the Prevention of Cruelty to Children, Boston, MA.

$6,000 to Asthma and Allergy Foundation of America, Chestnut Hill, MA.

$3,333 to Challenge Unlimited, Andover, MA.

$3,000 to Immigrant Learning Center, Malden, MA.

3797
Benfamil Charitable Trust ✧

c/o Calibre Advisory Svcs., Inc., attn.: David L. Beatty

800 South St., Ste. 195

Waltham, MA 02453

Established in 1962 in MA.

Donors: George F. Bennett, Sr.; George F. Bennett, Jr.; Peter C. Bennett; Robert B. Bennett.

Foundation type: Independent foundation.

Financial data (yr. ended 12/31/04): Assets, $5,053,033 (M); gifts received, $214,548; expenditures, $1,064,064; qualifying distributions, $1,025,133; giving activities include $1,013,806 for 79 grants (high: $201,198; low: $1,000).

Purpose and activities: Support primarily for Protestant organizations of various denominations, including schools, churches, and missions.

Fields of interest: Elementary/secondary education; Higher education; Education; Human services; Children/youth, services; Family services; Protestant agencies & churches.

Limitations: Applications not accepted. Giving primarily in MA. No grants to individuals.

Application information: Contributes only to pre-selected organizations.

Trustees: David L. Beatty; George F. Bennett, Sr.; George F. Bennett, Jr.; Peter C. Bennett; Robert B. Bennett.

EIN: 046079101

3798
The Doris L. Benz Trust ✧ ☆

c/o Wendell P. Weyland

309 Ipswich Rd.

Boxford, MA 01921-1505

Application address: c/o New Hampshire Charitable Foundation, Attn: Student Aid Office, 37 Pleasant St., Concord, NH 03301-4005

Established in 1984 in NH.

Donor: Doris L. Benz†.

Foundation type: Independent foundation.

Financial data (yr. ended 6/30/05): Assets, $9,139,709 (M); expenditures, $784,514; qualifying distributions, $716,546; giving activities include $691,597 for 28 grants (high: $349,397; low: $500).

Purpose and activities: One half of income of trust to be used for student scholarships disbursed through New Hampshire Charitable Fund, and the remaining half to be distributed to charitable organizations.

Fields of interest: Higher education; Education; Hospitals (general); Human services; Foundations (community).

Type of support: General/operating support; Scholarship funds.

Limitations: Giving primarily in MA and NH; scholarship funds limited to residents of NH. No support for religious purposes.

Application information: Scholarships administered by New Hampshire Charitable Foundation. Application form required for scholarships. Application form required.

　Initial approach: Letter
　Deadline(s): Apr. 26 for scholarships; none for other grants

Directors: Janet Brown; Claire Lyons; Janice C. Sinclair; Ronald P. Weyland; Wendell P. Weyland.

EIN: 046504871

Selected grants: The following grants were reported in 2004.

$162,404 to New Hampshire Charitable Foundation, Concord, NH. For college scholarships.

$10,000 to ARC, North Shore, Danvers, MA. For capital support.

$10,000 to Hospice of the North Shore, Danvers, MA. For capital support.

$10,000 to North Shore Medical Center, Salem, MA. For capital support.

$6,000 to Holy Family Hospital and Medical Center, Methuen, MA. For capital support.

$5,000 to Help for Abused Women and Their Children, Salem, MA. For capital support.

$5,000 to New Hampshire Public Television, Durham, NH. For capital support.

$4,000 to Gibson Center for Senior Services, Conway, NH. For adult tuition program.

$2,000 to Pine Manor College, Chestnut Hill, MA. For Cancer Walk.

$200 to Special Olympics of Massachusetts, Danvers, MA. For capital support.

3799
Theodore W. & Evelyn G. Berenson Charitable Foundation ◇

c/o Goulston & Storrs
400 Atlantic Ave., Rm. 401
Boston, MA   02110

Established in 1953 in MA.

Donors: Evelyn G. Berenson; Theodore W. Berenson†; Helaine B. Allen.

Foundation type: Independent foundation.

Financial data (yr. ended 11/30/05): Assets, $4,905,037; expenditures, $529,580; qualifying distributions, $447,075; giving activities include $447,075 for 30 grants (high: $100,000; low: $500).

Purpose and activities: Giving primarily for higher education, as well as for Jewish organizations,

hospitals, including a children's hospital, health associations and social services.

Fields of interest: Performing arts; Higher education; Hospitals (general); Health organizations, association; Cancer research; Eye research; Human services; Aging, centers/services; Jewish federated giving programs; Jewish agencies & temples.

Limitations: Applications not accepted. Giving primarily in MA. No grants to individuals.

Application information: Contributes only to pre-selected organizations.

Trustees: Helaine B. Allen; Alan W. Rottenberg; Marvin Sparrow.

EIN: 046068512

Selected grants: The following grants were reported in 2004.

$125,000 to Brandeis University, Waltham, MA. 2 grants: $100,000, $25,000

$80,000 to Beth Israel Deaconess Medical Center, Boston, MA. 2 grants: $70,000, $10,000

$61,000 to Hebrew College, Newton Centre, MA.

$56,000 to Boston Symphony Orchestra, Boston, MA. 2 grants: $6,000, $50,000

$27,500 to Beth Israel Hospital Association, Passaic, NJ.

$1,000 to Childrens Hospital Medical Center.

$1,000 to Proctor Academy, Andover, NH.

3800
Berkshire Bank Foundation ◇

(formerly Berkshire Hills Foundation)
c/o Admin.
P.O. Box 1308
Pittsfield, MA   01202-1308   (413) 447-1724
Contact: Mary Ellen Puntin
URL: http://www.berkshirebank.com/about/foundations.asp

Established in 2000 in MA.

Donor: Berkshire Hills Bancorp, Inc.

Foundation type: Company-sponsored foundation.

Financial data (yr. ended 12/31/05): Assets, $19,152,044 (M); expenditures, $1,844,041; qualifying distributions, $1,548,063; giving activities include $1,464,409 for 412+ grants (high: $125,000).

Purpose and activities: The foundation supports organizations involved with arts and culture, education, housing, human services, and community development.

Fields of interest: Arts; Education; Housing/shelter; Human services; Community development.

Limitations: Giving limited to Berkshire County, MA. No support for religious organizations not of direct benefit to the entire community or labor, fraternal, or political organizations. No grants to individuals, or for trips or tours or endowments.

Publications: Application guidelines.

Application information: Application form required.

　Initial approach: Download application form and mail to foundation

Officers and Directors:* Michael P. Daly,* Chair and Pres.; Thomas W. Barney, V.P.; Gayle P. Fawcett, V.P.; Linda A. Johnston, V.P.; Gerald A. Denmark, Secy.; Catherine B. Miller, Clerk; Wayne F. Patenaude, Treas.; Catherine B. Miller; Corydon L. Thurston; Ann H. Trabulsi; Robert A. Wells.

EIN: 043521179

3801
Berkshire Taconic Community Foundation ▼

(formerly Berkshire-Taconic Foundation)
271 Main St., Ste. 3
Great Barrington, MA   01230-1972
(413) 528-8039
Contact: Jennifer Dowley, Pres.; Jill S. Gellert, V.P., Finance and Admin.; For grants: Maeve M. O'Dea, Prog. Dir.
FAX: (413) 528-8158;
E-mail: info@berkshiretaconic.org; Additional tel.: (413) 528-8039; Grant inquiry E-mail: maeve@berkshiretaconic.org; URL: http://www.berkshiretaconic.org

Established in 1987 in CT.

Foundation type: Community foundation.

Financial data (yr. ended 12/31/05): Assets, $66,101,365 (M); gifts received, $9,862,377; expenditures, $7,918,031; giving activities include $6,866,249 for 3,292 grants (high: $150,291; low: $1), $250,997 for 155 grants to individuals (high: $10,000; low: $75), and $1,425 for 2 loans to individuals (high: $1,125; low: $300).

Purpose and activities: The foundation primarily provides support for education, the arts, the environment, and health and human services.

Fields of interest: Arts; Education; Environment; Health care; Human services.

Type of support: General/operating support; Equipment; Endowments; Emergency funds; Program development; Conferences/seminars; Publication; Seed money; Curriculum development; Fellowships; Scholarship funds; Technical assistance; Consulting services; Program evaluation; Employee-related scholarships; Scholarships—to individuals; Matching/challenge support; Student loans—to individuals.

Limitations: Giving limited to northwest Litchfield County, CT, Berkshire County, MA, and Columbia County and northeast Dutchess County, NY.

Publications: Application guidelines; Annual report; Financial statement; Informational brochure (including application guidelines); Occasional report.

Application information: Visit foundation Web site for application forms, deadlines, and specific guidelines per grant type. Application form required.

　Initial approach: Telephone
　Copies of proposal: 1
　Deadline(s): Oct. 1 for Community Fund grants; varies for others
　Board meeting date(s): Quarterly
　Final notification: Within 3 months for Community Fund grants; varies for others

Officers and Directors:* David L. Klausmeyer,* Chair.; Carmi Rapport, Vice-Chair.; Jennifer Dowley, Pres.; Jill S. Gellert, V.P., Finance and Admin.; Jane Allen Waters,* Secy.; Gail L.K. Cashen,* Treas.; Sia Arnason; Sally W. Berg; Lo-Yi Chan; J. Williar "Bill" Dunlaevy; Joan B. Dunlop; Thomas P. Falus; Rachel G. Fletcher; Richard C. Lamb; Neil M. McCarthy; Patrick J. Mele, Jr.; Arthur S. Rosenblatt; Virginia Stanton Smith; Sarah S. Stack; Nancy Ireland Stahl; John P. Tuke; Andrew C. Vickery.

Number of staff: 6 full-time professional; 3 full-time support; 1 part-time support.

EIN: 061254469

Selected grants: The following grants were reported in 2005.

$100,000 to Barrington Stage Company, Sheffield, MA. For general operating support.

$99,800 to Hudson City School District, Hudson, NY. For general operating support.

$82,000 to Columbia Land Conservancy, Chatham, NY. 2 grants: $67,000 (For general operating support), $15,000 (For general operating support).

$60,000 to Scoville Memorial Library Association, Salisbury, CT. For building renovations.

$50,000 to Saint Johns Episcopal Church, Williamstown, MA. For capital campaign.

$45,000 to Boston Symphony Orchestra, Boston, MA. For general operating support.

$20,000 to Saint James Episcopal Church, Great Barrington, MA. For annual campaign.

$15,000 to Williams College, Williamstown, MA. For general operating support.

$10,100 to American Friends of the Israel Philharmonic Orchestra, New York, NY.

3802
Carol and Alan J. Bernon Family Foundation ✧
(formerly Alan J. Bernon Family Foundation)
124 Grove St., Ste. 100
Franklin, MA 02038

Established in 1991 in MA.
Donor: Alan J. Bernon.
Foundation type: Independent foundation.
Financial data (yr. ended 12/31/04): Assets, $7,807,129 (M); expenditures, $711,362; qualifying distributions, $601,712; giving activities include $601,712 for 32 grants (high: $125,000; low: $1,000).
Fields of interest: Education; Cancer research; Human services; Jewish agencies & temples.
Limitations: Applications not accepted. Giving primarily in MA. No grants to individuals.
Application information: Contributes only to pre-selected organizations.
Trustee: Alan J. Bernon.
EIN: 046661364
Selected grants: The following grants were reported in 2003.
$500,000 to New York University, New York, NY.
$100,000 to Worcester Academy, Worcester, MA.
$100,000 to YMCA of the Hockomock Area, North Attleboro, MA.
$65,000 to Combined Jewish Philanthropies of Greater Boston, Boston, MA.
$50,000 to Noble and Greenough School, Dedham, MA.
$50,000 to Wellesley Free Library, Wellesley, MA. For building fund.
$25,000 to Fessenden School, West Newton, MA.
$20,000 to Dean College, Franklin, MA.
$10,000 to Hofstra University, Hempstead, NY.
$10,000 to Metrowest Jewish Day School, Framingham, MA.

3803
Berthiaume Family Foundation, Inc. ✧ ☆
18 Buttonwood Dr.
Andover, MA 01810
Contact: Douglas A. Berthiaume, Pres.

Established in 2005 in MA.
Donor: Douglas A. Berthiaume.
Foundation type: Independent foundation.
Financial data (yr. ended 6/30/06): Assets, $17,991,627 (M); expenditures, $970,000;

qualifying distributions, $950,000; giving activities include $950,000 for 2 grants (high: $900,000; low: $50,000).
Purpose and activities: Giving primarily for a children's hospital; funding also for higher education.
Fields of interest: Higher education; Hospitals (specialty).
Limitations: Giving primarily in MA.
Application information:
Initial approach: Letter
Officers and Directors:* Douglas A. Berthiaume,* Pres.; Diana M. Berthiaume,* Treas. and Clerk.
EIN: 331095606

3804
Bertolon Family Foundation
80 City Sq.
Boston, MA 02129
Contact: Henry J. Bertolon, Jr., Tr.

Established in 2000 in MA.
Donors: Donna Bertolon; Henry J. Bertolon, Jr.
Foundation type: Independent foundation.
Financial data (yr. ended 12/31/05): Assets, $11,625 (M); gifts received, $300,000; expenditures, $317,227; qualifying distributions, $316,960; giving activities include $316,960 for 24 grants (high: $250,000; low: $40).
Fields of interest: Elementary/secondary education; Boys & girls clubs; Human services.
Type of support: General/operating support; Continuing support; Annual campaigns; Capital campaigns.
Limitations: Applications not accepted. Giving primarily in MA.
Publications: Annual report.
Application information: Unsolicited requests for funds not accepted.
Trustees: Donna Bertolon; Henry J. Bertolon, Jr.
EIN: 046917944

3805
Bilezikian Family Foundation, Inc. ✧ ☆
c/o State Street Bank & Trust Co.
1 Lincoln St., SSFC24
Boston, MA 02111-2900

Established in MA.
Donors: Charles G. Bilezikian; Doreen Bilezikian.
Foundation type: Independent foundation.
Financial data (yr. ended 12/31/05): Assets, $14,975,993 (M); gifts received, $2,030,130; expenditures, $825,100; qualifying distributions, $726,692; giving activities include $693,605 for 24 grants (high: $135,360; low: $1,000).
Fields of interest: Education; Environment, water resources; Human services; Children/youth, services.
Limitations: Applications not accepted. Giving primarily in Boston and Cape Cod, MA.
Application information: Contributes only to pre-selected organizations.
Officers and Directors:* Doreen Bilezikian,* Pres.; Gregory C. Bilezikian,* V.P.; Jeffrey D. Bilezikian,* V.P.; Henry L. Murphy, Jr.,* Clerk; Charles G. Bilezikian,* Treas.
EIN: 043504021
Selected grants: The following grants were reported in 2004.

$10,500 to Penikese Island School, Woods Hole, MA.

$10,000 to Cape Cod Free Clinic in Falmouth, Falmouth, MA.

$10,000 to Emerald Necklace Conservancy, Brookline, MA.

$8,490 to Boston Cares, Boston, MA.

$8,000 to Loomis Chaffee School, Windsor, CT.

3806
Biogen Idec Foundation Inc.
(formerly Biogen Foundation, Inc.)
14 Cambridge Ctr.
Cambridge, MA 02142 (617) 679-2851
Contact: Kathryn R. Bloom

Established in 2002 in MA.
Donor: Biogen, Inc.
Foundation type: Company-sponsored foundation.
Financial data (yr. ended 12/31/05): Assets, $26,620,562 (M); expenditures, $1,960,959; qualifying distributions, $1,845,765; giving activities include $1,620,250 for 134 grants (high: $500,000; low: $125).
Purpose and activities: The foundation supports organizations involved with science education.
Fields of interest: Education; Science.
Type of support: General/operating support; Annual campaigns; Employee matching gifts.
Limitations: Giving primarily in San Diego, CA, Cambridge and greater Boston, MA, and Durham and Raleigh, NC. No support for religious or political organizations. No grants to individuals, or for special events.
Application information: Application form not required.
Initial approach: Proposal
Copies of proposal: 1
Deadline(s): None
Board meeting date(s): Twice per year
Officers: Peter N. Kellogg, Chair.; Michael F. Phelps, Treas.
Directors: Connie Matsui; James C. Mullen; Hon. Lynn Schenk.
Trustee Bank: Bank of America, N.A.
Number of staff: 1 full-time professional.
EIN: 161636254

3807
Birmingham Foundation ✧
1 International Pl., 11th Fl.
Boston, MA 02110-2602

Established about 1954.
Donor: John P. Birmingham†.
Foundation type: Independent foundation.
Financial data (yr. ended 12/31/05): Assets, $4,736,592 (M); expenditures, $452,157; qualifying distributions, $407,860; giving activities include $402,000 for 25 grants (high: $100,000; low: $1,000).
Purpose and activities: Giving primarily for Roman Catholic education and organizations; funding also for health care, including hospitals and medical research, education, and youth services.
Fields of interest: Elementary/secondary education; Higher education; Education; Hospitals (general); Health care; Health organizations, association; Cancer research; Boys & girls clubs; Human services; Children/youth, services; Roman Catholic agencies & churches.

Type of support: Program development; Seed money; Scholarship funds.
Limitations: Applications not accepted. Giving primarily in Boston, MA. No grants to individuals.
Application information: Contributes only to pre-selected organizations.
Trustees: Paul J. Birmingham; Lois I. Wrightson.
EIN: 046050748
Selected grants: The following grants were reported in 2005.

$56,000 to Mercy Hospital of Pittsburgh, Children's Hospital, Pittsburgh, PA. To provide a safe and structured program for 100 youth aged nine through eighteen residing within the South side communities of Pittsburgh.

$50,000 to Goodwill Industries of Pittsburgh, Pittsburgh, PA. To restructure and further develop the youth council to effectively equip youth to engage the community and workforce.

$50,000 to YouthWorks, Pittsburgh, PA. To provide services for youth in leadership and career development activities that will decrease their vulnerability to involvement in violence.

$35,000 to Greater Pittsburgh Community Food Bank, Duquesne, PA. To increase capacity of local food pantries and food programs to meet needs of families through lines of credit at food bank.

$32,000 to Pittsburgh Action Against Rape, Pittsburgh, PA. To deliver trauma based empowerment counseling to south Pittsburgh communities.

$30,000 to Nazareth Housing, New York, NY. To assist low-income seniors to age in place by addressing critical home repairs and provide home ownership education and opportunities for low income families in South Pittsburgh.

$30,000 to YWCA of Greater Pittsburgh, Pittsburgh, PA. To improve financial knowledge of South Pittsburgh residents, through improved access to education, to become financially stable and self-sufficient.

$29,000 to Center for Victims of Violence and Crime, Pittsburgh, PA. To establish a comprehensive school and community based violence prevention program that provides structured opportunities for youths to participate in peace building and violence prevention activities with their peers and in partnership with adults and community members.

$24,000 to Lutheran Service Society of Western Pennsylvania, Pittsburgh, PA. To maintain continued nutrition assessment and intervention to at-risk seniors referred from community and food programs and enhance wellness of seniors through nutrition prevention programs at local senior centers.

$20,000 to Travelers Aid Society of Pittsburgh, Pittsburgh, PA. To increase access to behavioral health treatment and support services for local consumers through transportation assistance program in order to improve attendance and outcomes.

3808
The Black Mountain Foundation ✧ ☆
c/o Ropes & Gray
1 Intl. Pl.
Boston, MA 02110

Established in 1997 in MA.
Donor: W. Nicholas Thorndike.
Foundation type: Independent foundation.

Financial data (yr. ended 12/31/05): Assets, $574,304 (M); expenditures, $773,422; qualifying distributions, $765,000; giving activities include $765,000 for grants.
Fields of interest: Media, television; Scholarships/financial aid; Human services.
Type of support: Scholarship funds.
Limitations: Applications not accepted. Giving primarily in MA. No grants to individuals.
Application information: Contributes only to pre-selected organizations.
Trustees: Edward P. Lawrence; Alexander L. Thorndike; Joan I. Thorndike; W. Nicholas Thorndike; William N. Thorndike, Jr.
EIN: 046825487

3809
Leonard X. Bosack and Bette M. Kruger Charitable Foundation, Inc.
21 Eliot St.
Natick, MA 01760
Contact: Emily Goldfarb, Prog. Assoc.
FAX: (508) 907-6261; E-mail: info@bkfoundation.org

Re-established in 2002 in MA.
Donors: Leonard Bosack; Sandy Lerner; The Leonard X. Bosack & Bette M. Kruger Foundation, CA.
Foundation type: Independent foundation.
Financial data (yr. ended 12/31/04): Assets, $21,122,999 (M); expenditures, $2,905,483; qualifying distributions, $2,575,492; giving activities include $2,218,023 for 50 grants (high: $287,595; low: $500).
Purpose and activities: Funding specifically in support of scientific education and the promotion of animal welfare, with a special emphasis on the welfare of captive wildlife, humane alternatives in veterinary education, collaborative spay and neuter programs, and protection of wild carnivores; funding also for the preservation and study of works by 17th, 18th, and early 19th century women writers.
Fields of interest: Higher education; Libraries/library science; Animal welfare; Engineering/technology; Science.
Type of support: Building/renovation; Equipment; Emergency funds; Program development; Conferences/seminars; Research.
Limitations: Applications not accepted. Giving primarily on a national basis. No grants to individuals, or for operating budgets.
Application information: Contributes only to pre-selected organizations.
Board meeting date(s): Varies
Officers and Directors:* Sandy Lerner,* Chair. and Pres.; Leonard Bosack,* V.P. and Secy.; Kathleen Savesky, Exec. Dir.; Robert Liebscher.
Number of staff: 2 full-time professional.
EIN: 753089497
Selected grants: The following grants were reported in 2003.

$5,260,580 to Chawton House Library, Alton, England. 3 grants: $2,435,608 (For program support), $2,690,199 (For book donations), $134,773 (For donation of furnishings).

$310,000 to Tufts University, Medford, MA. For construction and equipment for Luke and Lily Lerner Spay and Neuter Clinic at School of Veterinary Medicine in Grafton.

$186,228 to Western University of Health Sciences, College of Veterinary Medicine, Pomona, CA. For mobile clinic to serve community.

$164,446 to Stanford University, Stanford, CA. For graduate student support in Wavelet Research at STARLab (Space, Telecommunications and Radio Science Laboratory).

$66,000 to Harvard University, Department of Physics, Cambridge, MA. To support graduate student study in optical Search for Extraterrestrial Intelligence (SETI) research.

$56,672 to Achievement Rewards for College Scientists (ARCS) Foundation, Seattle Chapter, Seattle, WA. For graduate student support for ice and water studies at University of Washington.

$51,765 to University of California, School of Veterinary Medicine, Davis, CA. For study at Center for Equine Health of chronic progressive lymphedema in draft horses.

$49,338 to Earth Action Network, Norwalk, CT. For articles and major cover story and secondary media distribution for E Magazine.

3810
BOSE Foundation, Inc. ✧ ☆
c/o BOSE Corp.
The Mountain, Ste. MS6B1
Framingham, MA 01701-9168 (508) 879-7330

Established in 1987 in MA.
Donor: BOSE Corp.
Foundation type: Company-sponsored foundation.
Financial data (yr. ended 3/25/06): Assets, $1,317,681 (M); gifts received, $480,000; expenditures, $410,064; qualifying distributions, $410,064; giving activities include $409,883 for 113 grants (high: $96,789; low: $100).
Purpose and activities: The foundation supports organizations involved with performing arts and higher education and awards research grants to academic institutions in the areas of electric engineering, business, and computer science.
Fields of interest: Performing arts; Performing arts, orchestra (symphony); Higher education; American Red Cross; Federated giving programs.
Type of support: General/operating support; Research.
Limitations: Applications not accepted. Giving limited to MD and MA.
Application information: Contributes only to pre-selected organizations.
Officers: Robert Maresca, Pres.; Mark E. Sullivan, Clerk; Herbert Batchelder, Treas.
EIN: 042967717
Selected grants: The following grants were reported in 2005.

$58,960 to Massachusetts Institute of Technology, Cambridge, MA. 2 grants: $5,000, $53,960

$56,564 to American Red Cross.

$45,700 to United Way. 2 grants: $35,000, $10,700

$1,000 to Madonna University, Livonia, MI.

$500 to Cambridge School Volunteers, Cambridge, MA.

$500 to Childrens Room, Waterbury, VT.

$500 to Recording for the Blind and Dyslexic, Princeton, NJ.

$150 to Alternatives Unlimited, Whitinsville, MA.

3811
Boston Fatherless & Widows Society
Exchange Pl., Ste. 2200
Boston, MA 02109-2881 (617) 570-1130
Contact: George W. Butterworth III, Treas.

FAX: (617) 227-8591;
E-mail: gbutterworth@goodwinprocter.com

Established in 1817 in MA; incorporated in 1837.
Foundation type: Independent foundation.
Financial data (yr. ended 11/30/05): Assets, $6,901,645 (M); gifts received, $37,000; expenditures, $443,241; qualifying distributions, $387,006; giving activities include $113,000 for 25 grants (high: $12,000; low: $1,000), and $272,844 for grants to individuals.
Purpose and activities: Aid to elderly indigent widows in the greater Boston, MA, area.
Fields of interest: Aging; Women; Economically disadvantaged.
Type of support: General/operating support; Grants to individuals.
Limitations: Giving limited to the greater Boston, MA, area.
Application information: Application form not required.
   Initial approach: Letter
   Deadline(s): None
Officers and Trustees:* Mrs. H. Stephen Kott,* Pres.; Mrs. Robert B. Bachman,* V.P.; Mrs. John R. Johnston,* Secy.; George W. Butterworth III, Treas.; Mrs. Allen N. Clapp; Mrs. E. Raymond Corey; Mrs. Richard Gordon; Mrs. Willard S. Levings; Mrs. Jacob H. Martin; Mrs. Richard W. Russell; Mrs. Charles Staples; Mrs. Robert H. Welsh.
EIN: 046006506
Selected grants: The following grants were reported in 2005.
$10,000 to Walker Home and School, Needham, MA.
$9,000 to Women of Means, Wellesley, MA.
$7,000 to Womens Lunch Place, Boston, MA.
$5,000 to Boston Rescue Mission, Boston, MA.
$4,000 to Carroll Center for the Blind, Newton, MA.
$4,000 to Solutions at Work, Cambridge, MA.
$2,000 to Community Family Center, Highland Park, IL.

3812
Boston Foundation, Inc. ▼

75 Arlington St.,10th Fl.
Boston, MA 02116   (617) 338-1700
Contact: David Trueblood, Dir., Public Rels.; For grants: Corey L. Davis, Grants Mgr.
FAX: (617) 338-1604; E-mail: info@tbf.org;
Additional E-mails: david.trueblood@tbf.org and cld@tbf.org; URL: http://www.tbf.org

Established in 1915 in MA by agreement and declaration of trust; incorporated in 1917.
Foundation type: Community foundation.
Financial data (yr. ended 6/30/06): Assets, $769,807,869 (M); gifts received, $73,560,736; expenditures, $74,388,860; giving activities include $63,914,314 for grants.
Purpose and activities: The foundation seeks to nurture a sense of community among the people of Greater Boston and reinforce shared values, encourage mutual respect, develop practices of common concern, and enable all people to realize their full potential.
Fields of interest: Arts; Education, early childhood education; Child development, education; Elementary school/education; Secondary school/education; Adult/continuing education; Adult education—literacy, basic skills & GED; Education, reading; Education; Health care; Health organizations, association; AIDS; Crime/violence

prevention, youth; Employment; Nutrition; Housing/shelter, development; Youth development, services; Children/youth, services; Child development, services; Family services; Aging, centers/services; Women, centers/services; Minorities/immigrants, centers/services; Homeless, human services; Human services; Civil rights, race/intergroup relations; Civil rights; Urban/community development; Community development; Voluntarism promotion; Public policy, research; Leadership development; Aging; Disabilities, people with; Minorities; Women; Immigrants/refugees; Economically disadvantaged; Homeless.
Type of support: Program development; Seed money; Technical assistance; Consulting services; Employee matching gifts; Matching/challenge support.
Limitations: Giving from discretionary funds limited to the greater Boston, MA, area. No support for religious purposes, city or state government agencies or departments, private schools, municipalities, or national or international programs. No grants to individuals, or for scientific or academic research, books or articles, films, radio, or television programs, equipment, travel, endowments, scholarships, fellowships, conferences, or symposia or capital campaigns; no loans.
Publications: Application guidelines; Annual report (including application guidelines); Financial statement; Grants list; Informational brochure (including application guidelines); Newsletter; Occasional report.
Application information: The foundation will invite submission of full proposals based on its review of the Pre-Application Form, but will not consider uninvited proposals. Visit the foundation Web site for Pre-Application Form and guidelines. Pre-Application Form may be completed online or mailed to the foundation in hard-copy form; faxed or e-mailed applications not accepted. Application form required.
   Initial approach: Submit Pre-Application Form
   Copies of proposal: 1
   Deadline(s): Jan. 5 and July 1 for Pre-Application Form; Mar. 15 and Sept. 15 for full proposal
   Board meeting date(s): Mar., June, Sept., and Dec.
   Final notification: Invitation for full proposal within 6 weeks of Pre-Application Form
Officers and Board Members:* Rev. Ray Hammond,* Chair.; Carol F. Anderson,* Vice-Chair.; Paul S. Grogan,* Pres.; Kate Guedj, V.P., Philanthropic and Donor Svcs.; Terry Saunders Lane, V.P., Prog.; Mary Jo Meisner, V.P., Comms., Community Rels. and Public Affairs; Ruben Orduna, V.P., Devel.; Gail Snowden, V.P., Finance and Opers., and Treas.; Timothy B. Gassert, Corp. Secy.; Hope C. Groves, Cont.; Richard M. Burnes; Louis Casagrande; Gerald Chertavian; Catherine D'Amato; Richard B. DeWolfe; Atsuko Toko Fish; Jackie Jenkins-Scott; Michael Keating; Myra Kraft; Paul La Camera; Jack R. Meyer; Herbert E. Morse; Kevin C. Phelan; Binkley Shorts; Micho F. Spring; Benaree P. Wiley.
Number of staff: 24 full-time professional; 1 part-time professional; 13 full-time support; 4 part-time support.
EIN: 042104021
Selected grants: The following grants were reported in 2005.
$2,400,000 to Harvard University, Cambridge, MA. For general operating support.

$2,198,411 to JK Group, Plainsboro, NJ. 4 grants: $691,476 (For general operating support), $620,099 (For general operating support), $487,065 (For general operating support), $399,771 (For general operating support).
$833,500 to Phillips Academy, Andover, MA. For general operating support.
$750,000 to Boston Plan for Excellence in the Public Schools, Boston, MA. For general operating support.
$500,000 to Childrens Museum, Boston, MA. For general operating support.
$500,000 to Institute of Contemporary Art, Boston, MA. For general operating support.
$500,000 to Williams College, Williamstown, MA. For general operating support.

3813
Boston Scientific Foundation, Inc. ✧

1 Boston Scientific Pl., M.S. C14
Natick, MA 01760-1537   (508) 650-8554
Contact: Faye Harrington

Established in 2001 in MA.
Donors: Boston Scientific Corp.; John Abele; G. David Jang.
Foundation type: Company-sponsored foundation.
Financial data (yr. ended 12/31/05): Assets, $21,013,134 (M); expenditures, $1,504,688; qualifying distributions, $1,504,688; giving activities include $1,176,749 for 111 grants (high: $75,000; low: $250).
Purpose and activities: The foundation supports organizations involved with education, health, youth development, and human services.
Fields of interest: Education; Health care; Boys & girls clubs; Youth development; Children/youth, services; Human services.
Limitations: Giving primarily in MA and MN. No grants to individuals.
Application information: Application form required.
   Initial approach: Contact foundation for application form
   Copies of proposal: 2
   Deadline(s): None
   Final notification: 3 to 6 months
Officers: Paul Donovan, Pres.; Milan Kofol, Treas.; Paul Sandman, Clerk.
EIN: 043556844
Selected grants: The following grants were reported in 2004.
$1,000,000 to Doctors Without Borders USA, New York, NY. For anniversary commemorative gift.
$75,000 to Boston Health Care for the Homeless Program, Boston, MA. For Diabetes collaborative.
$75,000 to Fremont Community Health Services, Minneapolis, MN. For Stroke Prevention Collaborative.
$75,000 to Great Brook Valley Health Center, Worcester, MA. For Hypertension Collaborative.
$75,000 to Helen B. Bentley Family Health Center, Miami, FL. For Cardiovascular Disease Collaborative.
$75,000 to Plainfield Health Center, Plainfield, NJ. For Pediatric Obesity Collaborative.
$23,000 to Smart School, Lauderhill, FL. For Extended Day Program.
$20,000 to BestPrep, Brooklyn Park, MN. For Tech Corps.
$20,000 to Clara-Mateo Alliance, Menlo Park, CA. For children and family services program.
$10,000 to Tri-City Homeless Coalition, Fremont, CA. For HOPE project.

3814
Harry L. Bradley, Jr. Charitable Fund ✧
c/o Robert J. Morrissey
2 International Pl., Ste. 3500
Boston, MA 02110-4102

Established in 1981 in MA.
Donor: Mark S. Bradley Trust.
Foundation type: Independent foundation.
Financial data (yr. ended 6/30/05): Assets,
$1,311 (M); gifts received, $1,304,500;
expenditures, $1,321,778; qualifying distributions,
$1,314,700; giving activities include $1,314,700
for 23 grants (high: $1,028,000; low: $200).
Purpose and activities: Giving primarily for higher
education, health associations, and to Roman
Catholic churches and organizations.
Fields of interest: Arts; Higher education;
Theological school/education; Health care; Health
organizations, association; Roman Catholic
agencies & churches.
Type of support: General/operating support.
Limitations: Applications not accepted. Giving
primarily in MA, with emphasis on Chestnut Hill and
Boston. No grants to individuals.
Application information: Contributes only to
pre-selected organizations. Unsolicited requests for
funds not accepted.
Trustee: Robert J. Morrissey.
EIN: 042747025
Selected grants: The following grants were reported
in 2004.
$818,000 to Boston College, Chestnut Hill, MA. For
general support.
$139,000 to Inner-City Scholarship Fund, Boston,
MA. For general support.
$45,000 to Maryknoll Fathers and Brothers,
Maryknoll, NY. For general support.
$30,000 to American Ireland Fund, Boston, MA. For
general support.
$25,000 to Museum of Fine Arts, Boston, MA. For
general support.
$25,000 to Weston Jesuit School of Theology,
Cambridge, MA. For general support.
$15,000 to Dana Hall School, Wellesley, MA. For
general support.
$10,000 to Opportunity, West Palm Beach, FL. For
general support.
$4,000 to Society of Jesus of New England, Boston,
MA. For general support.
$3,000 to Partners in Health, Boston, MA. For
general support.

3815
The Bressler Family Foundation ✧ ☆
(formerly The Alan S. Bressler and Lorraine D.
Bressler Foundation)
76 Scotch Pine Rd.
Weston, MA 02493

Established in 1997 in MA.
Donors: Alan S. Bressler; Lorraine D. Bressler.
Foundation type: Independent foundation.
Financial data (yr. ended 12/31/05): Assets,
$2,581,193 (M); expenditures, $588,602;
qualifying distributions, $548,500; giving activities
include $548,500 for grants.
Fields of interest: Museums (art); Performing arts,
music; Arts; Education; Health care, research;
Health care; Health organizations, association;
Human services; Jewish agencies & temples.
Limitations: Applications not accepted. No grants to
individuals.

Application information: Contributes only to
pre-selected organizations.
Trustees: Alan S. Bressler; Daryl Bressler; Karen S.
Bressler; Lorraine D. Bressler; Nancy
Bressler-Starn.
EIN: 046837456
Selected grants: The following grants were reported
in 2003.
$56,496 to Boston Latin School Association,
Boston, MA. 2 grants: $46,496 (For general
support), $10,000 (For general support).
$25,000 to Boston Symphony Orchestra, Boston,
MA. For general support.
$10,000 to Boston Chamber Music Society,
Cambridge, MA. For general support.
$10,000 to Museum of Fine Arts, Boston, MA. For
general support.
$5,000 to Temple Emeth, Chestnut Hill, MA. For
general support.
$4,000 to Meadowbrook School, Weston, MA. For
general support.
$2,000 to Jewish National Fund, New York, NY. For
general support.
$1,500 to School of the Museum of Fine Arts,
Boston, MA. For general support.
$1,000 to Creative Time, New York, NY. For general
support.

3816
Bristol County Savings Charitable
Foundation, Inc. ✧
35 Broadway
Taunton, MA 02780
Contact: Michele L. Fortier, Clerk
Application address: 29 Broadway, 2nd Fl., Taunton,
MA 02780, tel.: (508) 462-3106

Established in 1996 in MA.
Donor: Bristol County Savings Bank.
Foundation type: Company-sponsored foundation.
Financial data (yr. ended 10/31/04): Assets,
$7,663,958 (M); gifts received, $43,315;
expenditures, $553,900; qualifying distributions,
$499,951; giving activities include $499,951 for 90
grants (high: $58,600; low: $125).
Purpose and activities: The foundation supports
organizations involved with arts and culture,
education, health, youth development, human
services, and religion.
Fields of interest: Museums; Historic preservation/
historical societies; Arts; Secondary school/
education; Education; Health care, clinics/centers;
Health care; Recreation; Boys & girls clubs; Youth
development; YM/YWCAs & YM/YWHAs; Human
services; Federated giving programs; Christian
agencies & churches; Religion.
Type of support: General/operating support.
Limitations: Giving limited to the greater
Attleboro-Taunton, MA, area.
Application information: Application form required.
Initial approach: Contact foundation for
application form
Officers and Trustees: E. Dennis Kelley, Jr., Pres.;
Michele L. Fortier, Clerk; Patrick J. Murray, Jr.,
Treas.; Dennis M. Cody; J. Jerome Coogan; William
J. Gloekler; Marjorie L. Largey; Edward P. Pariseau;
Joseph I. Quinn; Louis M. Ricciardi; Charles P. Terry;
Suzanne Withers.
EIN: 043332966
Selected grants: The following grants were reported
in 2003.
$96,250 to Morton Hospital and Medical Center,
Taunton, MA. For operating support.

$83,100 to United Way of Greater Attleboro/
Taunton, Attleboro, MA. For operating support.
$44,200 to Boys and Girls Club of Taunton,
Taunton, MA. For operating support.
$30,340 to Sturdy Memorial Foundation, Attleboro,
MA. For operating support.
$14,600 to YMCA of North Attleboro, Attleboro, MA.
For operating support.
$12,500 to Fire Department of Taunton, Taunton,
MA. For operating support.
$8,700 to Girl Scouts of the U.S.A., Taunton, MA.
For operating support.
$8,000 to Charles E. Shea High School, Pawtucket,
RI. For operating support.
$8,000 to Community Counseling of Bristol County,
Taunton, MA. For operating support.
$7,700 to Saint Francis Samaritan House of Greater
Taunton, Taunton, MA. For operating support.

3817
The Bromley Charitable Trust ✧
299 Clapboardtree St.
Westwood, MA 02090

Established in 1994 in MA.
Donors: Duncan M. McFarland; Elizabeth M.
McFarland; Ellen B. McFarland.
Foundation type: Independent foundation.
Financial data (yr. ended 12/31/05): Assets,
$4,443,493 (M); gifts received, $3,058,084;
expenditures, $2,258,199; qualifying distributions,
$2,241,995; giving activities include $2,241,995
for 60 grants (high: $625,000; low: $100; average:
$1,000–$25,000).
Fields of interest: Elementary/secondary
education; Environment, natural resources;
Hospitals (general); Health organizations,
association; Human services; Community
development.
Limitations: Applications not accepted. Giving on a
national basis. No grants to individuals.
Application information: Contributes only to
pre-selected organizations.
Trustees: Duncan M. McFarland; Ellen B.
McFarland; Nancy E. Dempze; William A. Oates, Jr.
EIN: 043237138
Selected grants: The following grants were reported
in 2004.
$323,353 to Westwood Land Trust, Westwood, MA.
$50,000 to Hualalai Academy, Kailua Kona, HI.
$35,000 to Kona Hospital Foundation, Kealakekua,
HI.
$25,000 to New England Aquarium, Boston, MA.
$20,000 to Room to Grow, New York, NY.
$12,500 to EARTH University Foundation, Atlanta,
GA.
$10,000 to Conservation International, DC.
$5,000 to Christmas in the City, Hingham, MA.
$5,000 to Saint Barnabas Episcopal School,
Philadelphia, PA.
$1,000 to Audubon Society, National, New York, NY.

3818
Brookfield Arts Foundation, Inc. ✧ ☆
82 Devonshire St., Ste. F9A3
Boston, MA 02109-3605

Established in 1995 in MA.
Donors: Edward C. Johnson III; Edward C. Johnson
Fund; Fidelity Ventures Ltd.
Foundation type: Operating foundation.

Financial data (yr. ended 12/31/05): Assets, $54,032,625 (M); gifts received, $10,475,187; expenditures, $16,034,883; qualifying distributions, $26,578,164; giving activities include $15,458,526 for 2 grants (high: $15,452,036; low: $6,490), and $11,155,007 for foundation-administered programs.
Fields of interest: Museums; Museums (art).
Limitations: Applications not accepted. Giving primarily in Boston and Salem, MA. No grants to individuals.
Application information: Contributes only to pre-selected organizations.
Officers and Directors:* Edward C. Johnson III,* Pres.; Tara Cederholm, V.P.; Patricia R. Hurley, Secy.; Richard G. Weidmann, Treas.; Christopher C. Curtis.
EIN: 311681603

3819
Bruner Foundation, Inc.
130 Prospect St.
Cambridge, MA 02139 (617) 492-8404
Contact: Emily Axelrod, Exec. Dir.
FAX: (617) 876-4002;
E-mail: info@brunerfoundation.org; URL: http://www.brunerfoundation.org

Incorporated in 1967 in NY.
Donors: Rudy Bruner†; Martha Bruner†.
Foundation type: Independent foundation.
Financial data (yr. ended 12/31/05): Assets, $8,324,727 (M); expenditures, $639,759; qualifying distributions, $544,497; giving activities include $368,184 for grants.
Purpose and activities: Support primarily for the Rudy Bruner Award for Excellence and evaluation of nonprofit service delivery.
Fields of interest: Visual arts, architecture; Arts; Urban/community development; Nonprofit management; Community development.
Type of support: Conferences/seminars; Program development; Research.
Limitations: Giving on a national basis within the lower 48 states only. No grants to individuals, or for general support, building or endowment funds, scholarships, or fellowships.
Publications: Application guidelines; Informational brochure (including application guidelines); Program policy statement.
Application information: The foundation is not currently making any new grants. See foundation Web site for application guidelines, procedures, and publications for the Rudy Bruner Award.
　Initial approach: Request application for Rudy Bruner Award by telephone, fax, e-mail or foundation Web site in fall of even-numbered years
　Copies of proposal: 1
　Deadline(s): Dec. of even-numbered years for Rudy Bruner Award; no applications accepted for other grants
　Board meeting date(s): As required
　Final notification: Apr./May of odd-numbered years
Officers: Joshua E. Bruner, Pres.; Richard J.L. Herson, Secy.; R. Simeon Bruner, Treas.; Emily Axelrod, Exec. Dir.
Number of staff: 1 part-time professional; 1 part-time support.
EIN: 136180803

3820
William and Bernice E. Bumpus Foundation ◈
c/o WCPH and Dorr, LLP
P.O. Box 9350
Boston, MA 02114

Established in 2000 in MA.
Donor: Bernice E. Bumpus Revocable Trust.
Foundation type: Independent foundation.
Financial data (yr. ended 1/31/06): Assets, $11,079,713 (M); expenditures, $653,849; qualifying distributions, $553,972; giving activities include $546,864 for 2 grants (high: $276,864; low: $270,000).
Fields of interest: Parkinson's disease research.
Limitations: Applications not accepted. Giving primarily in CT and MA. No grants to individuals.
Application information: Contributes only to pre-selected organizations.
Trustee: William H. Schmidt.
EIN: 043410822

3821
The Byrnes Family Foundation ◈
c/o Christopher C. Curtis, Sullivan & Worcester, LLP
1 P.O. Sq.
Boston, MA 02109

Established in 1984.
Donors: William L. Byrnes; Mary Elizabeth Byrnes; Randall W. Byrnes.
Foundation type: Independent foundation.
Financial data (yr. ended 12/31/04): Assets, $8,436,963 (M); gifts received, $357,872; expenditures, $415,322; qualifying distributions, $376,420; giving activities include $371,800 for 14 grants (high: $75,900; low: $500).
Purpose and activities: Giving primarily for education.
Fields of interest: Elementary/secondary education; Higher education; Education; Hospitals (general); Boys & girls clubs; Protestant agencies & churches.
Limitations: Applications not accepted. Giving primarily in MA. No grants to individuals.
Application information: Contributes only to pre-selected organizations.
Trustees: Mary Elizabeth Byrnes; Randall W. Byrnes; William L. Byrnes.
EIN: 222544803
Selected grants: The following grants were reported in 2004.
$77,500 to Kearns-Saint Ann School, Salt Lake City, UT.
$31,000 to Trinity-by-the-Cove Episcopal Church, Naples, FL.
$10,000 to Belmont Hill School, Belmont, MA.
$7,300 to Potomac School, McLean, VA.
$6,000 to Alzheimers Support Network, Naples, FL.
$5,500 to Guiding Eyes for the Blind.
$3,000 to Foundation for Neurologic Diseases, Newburyport, MA.
$2,500 to Southeastern Guide Dogs, Palmetto, FL.
$2,500 to Woods Academy, Bethesda, MD.
$2,000 to Council for the Spanish Speaking, Milwaukee, WI.

3822
The Edmund & Betsy Cabot Charitable Foundation ◈ ☆
c/o Cabot Wellington, LLC
70 Federal St.
Boston, MA 02110

Established in 1985 in MA.
Donors: Edmund B. Cabot; Elizabeth W. Cabot.
Foundation type: Independent foundation.
Financial data (yr. ended 9/30/05): Assets, $3,063,814 (M); gifts received, $1,400,679; expenditures, $381,006; qualifying distributions, $358,927; giving activities include $351,752 for 50 grants (high: $265,002; low: $250).
Purpose and activities: Giving to arts, culture and education.
Fields of interest: Arts; Education; Environment.
Limitations: Applications not accepted. Giving primarily in CO, MA, and ME. No grants to individuals.
Application information: Contributes only to pre-selected organizations.
Trustees: Edmund B. Cabot; Elizabeth W. Cabot.
EIN: 042900424
Selected grants: The following grants were reported in 2005.
$15,000 to Huntington Theater Company, Boston, MA.
$5,000 to Dana Hall School, Wellesley, MA.
$5,000 to Maine Coast Heritage Trust, Topsham, ME.
$5,000 to Rocky Mountain Elk Foundation, Missoula, MT.
$3,000 to Handel and Haydn Society, Boston, MA.
$2,500 to Phillips Academy, Andover, MA.
$1,000 to Boston Athenaeum, Boston, MA.
$1,000 to Cantata Singers, Cambridge, MA.
$1,000 to Nature Conservancy, Arlington, VA.
$500 to New England Aquarium, Boston, MA.

3823
Cabot Corporation Foundation, Inc. ◈
2 Seaport Ln., Ste. 1300
Boston, MA 02210 (617) 342-6002
Contact: Dorothy L. Forbes, Exec. Dir.
Additional tel.: (617) 342-6004;
E-mail: dorothy_forbes@cabot-corp.com;
URL: http://w1.cabot-corp.com/controller.jsp?N=21+3030

Incorporated in 1953 in MA.
Donor: Cabot Corp.
Foundation type: Company-sponsored foundation.
Financial data (yr. ended 9/30/05): Assets, $187,122 (L); expenditures, $954,668; qualifying distributions, $949,582; giving activities include $949,582 for 65 grants (high: $400,000; low: $1,000).
Purpose and activities: The foundation supports organizations involved with arts and culture, education, the environment, health, families, community development, science and technology, and disabled people.
Fields of interest: Arts; Education, research; Education, fund raising/fund distribution; Elementary/secondary education; Education, early childhood/education; Higher education; Business school/education; Adult/continuing education; Education; Environment, natural resources; Environment; Health care; Family services; Community development; Federated giving programs; Chemistry; Mathematics; Engineering/

technology; Computer science; Biological sciences; Science; Disabilities, people with.

Type of support: General/operating support; Annual campaigns; Capital campaigns; Building/renovation; Equipment; Program development; Seed money; Scholarship funds; Research; Technical assistance; Employee volunteer services; Employee matching gifts; In-kind gifts; Matching/challenge support.

Limitations: Giving limited to areas of company operations in Douglas County, IL, Evangeline and St. Mary parishes, LA, Billerica, Boston, and Everett, MA, Boyertown, PA, Pampa, TX, and Waverly, WV. No support for religious organizations not of direct benefit to the entire community or political or fraternal organizations. No grants to individuals, or for capital campaigns or endowments, advertising, or dinners.

Publications: Annual report (including application guidelines); Occasional report.

Application information: Proposals should be no longer than 2 pages in length. Application form not required.

　Initial approach: Proposal or telephone
　Copies of proposal: 1
　Deadline(s): 1 month prior to board meetings
　Board meeting date(s): Mar., June, Sept., and
　　Dec.
　Final notification: 3 months

Officers and Directors:* Kennett F. Burnes,* Pres.; Karen Morrissey,* V.P.; John J. Lawler,* Treas.; Dorothy L. Forbes, Exec. Dir.; Christina Bramante; Charles D. Gerlinger*; Charles A. Gray; Peter S. Gregory*; Ho-il Kim; Robbie D. Sisco; Scott E. Squillace.

EIN: 046035227

3824
Cabot Family Charitable Trust ◇

c/o Cabot-Wellington, LLC
70 Federal St., 7th Fl.
Boston, MA　02110　(617) 451-1744
Contact: Nike F. Speltz, Exec. Dir.
FAX: (617) 451-1733; E-mail: nspeltz@cabwel.com;
Tel. for Nike F. Speltz: (617) 451-1855, ext. 205,
fax: (617) 451-1724; URL: http://
www.cabwel.com/cabot_home_page.htm

Trust established in 1942 in MA.
Donor: Godfrey L. Cabot†.
Foundation type: Independent foundation.
Financial data (yr. ended 12/31/05): Assets, $44,355,669 (M); expenditures, $2,071,445; qualifying distributions, $1,894,064; giving activities include $1,594,946 for 76 grants (high: $100,000; low: $3,500).

Purpose and activities: Program includes a wide range of organizations and activities important to the Boston, MA, area and the New England region, as well as nonprofit programs that represent particular family interests.

Type of support: General/operating support; Continuing support; Management development/capacity building; Annual campaigns; Capital campaigns; Building/renovation; Endowments; Program development; Seed money; Matching/challenge support.

Limitations: Giving primarily in the Boston, MA, area, and New England. No support for religious institutions for sectarian purposes, and fraternal organizations. No grants to individuals, or for research, event sponsorship, or matching gifts.

Publications: Application guidelines; Annual report.

Application information: Associated Grantmakers of Massachusetts Common Proposal Form also accepted, and can be downloaded from http://www.agmconnect.org. Application information also available on foundation Web site. Application form required.

　Initial approach: Proposal (6-8 pages)
　Copies of proposal: 2
　Deadline(s): Feb. 1 and Sept. 1
　Board meeting date(s): May. and Nov.
　Final notification: 2 weeks after board meeting

Officers and Trustees:* John G.L. Cabot,* Chair.; Nike F. Speltz, Exec. Dir.; Jane C. Bradley; Louis W. Cabot; Mary Schneider Enriquez; Greenfield Sluder.

Number of staff: 1 part-time professional; 1 part-time support.

EIN: 046036446

3825
The Virginia Wellington Cabot Foundation

c/o Cabot-Wellington, LLC
70 Federal St., 7th Fl.
Boston, MA　02110　(617) 451-1744
Contact: Joan M. Whelton, Exec. Dir.
FAX: (617) 451-1724; E-mail: Jowhelton@aol.com;
URL: http://www.cabwel.com/
v_w_cabot_foundation.htm

Established in 1992 in MA.
Donors: Thomas D. Cabot, Jr.; Thomas D. Cabot 1986 Conduit Trust; Thomas D. Cabot 1994 Charitable Lead Unitrust; Virginia W. Cabot Revocable Trust; Virginia W. Cabot 1996 Charitable Lead Unitrust.
Foundation type: Independent foundation.
Financial data (yr. ended 12/31/04): Assets, $37,486,308 (M); gifts received, $400; expenditures, $2,032,154; qualifying distributions, $1,737,071; giving activities include $1,431,031 for 125 grants (high: $100,000; low: $500; average: $5–$25,000).

Purpose and activities: The foundation grants program includes a wide range of organizations and activities that represent particular interests of family members.

Fields of interest: Arts; Secondary school/education; Higher education; Education; Environment; Youth development; Human services; Public affairs.

Type of support: General/operating support; Annual campaigns; Capital campaigns; Building/renovation; Endowments; Program development; Fellowships; Scholarship funds; Matching/challenge support.

Limitations: No support for religious or political organizations. No grants for one-time events.

Publications: Application guidelines.

Application information: Unsolicited applications are generally not accepted. All grant applications are sponsored by family members who initiate the process. Application form required.

　Copies of proposal: 1
　Deadline(s): Mar. 1, and Sept. 13
　Board meeting date(s): Semiannually
　Final notification: 1 week after meeting

Officers: Amanda Cabot, Chair.; Joan M. Whelton, Exec. Dir.

Trustees: Alison Arshad; Jeremy Black; Sophie Black; Betsy Cabot; Mabel Cabot; Mithran Cabot; Penny Cabot; Thomas D. Cabot III; Virginia Cabot; Chris Carrigan.

EIN: 046728351

Selected grants: The following grants were reported in 2003.

$125,000 to Island Institute, Rockland, ME. 2 grants: $25,000, $100,000

$100,000 to American Academy of Arts and Sciences, Cambridge, MA.

$60,000 to Conservation International, DC.

$51,071 to Tides Foundation, San Francisco, CA.

$50,000 to Community Therapeutic Day School, Lexington, MA.

$50,000 to Rocky Mountain Elk Foundation, Missoula, MT.

$30,000 to Woods Hole Oceanographic Institution, Woods Hole, MA.

$27,500 to Outdoor Explorations, Medford, MA.

$20,000 to Stroud Water Research Center, Avondale, PA.

3826
Calderwood Charitable Foundation ◇

c/o Choate Hall & Stewart
2 International Plz.
Boston, MA　02110

Established in 1968 in MA.
Donor: Stanford M. Calderwood.
Foundation type: Independent foundation.
Financial data (yr. ended 12/31/05): Assets, $8,364,436 (M); gifts received, $1,100,000; expenditures, $2,364,179; qualifying distributions, $2,328,753; giving activities include $2,324,122 for 7 grants (high: $1,250,000; low: $1,500).

Purpose and activities: Giving for art and cultural programs, and for public television.

Fields of interest: Media/communications; Museums; Performing arts, theater; Libraries (special).

Limitations: Applications not accepted. Giving primarily in Boston, MA. No grants to individuals.

Application information: Contributes only to pre-selected organizations.

Trustees: John M. Cornish; William A. Lowell.

EIN: 046186166

3827
Caldwell Foundation ◇

c/o Robert G. Stewart, PC
3 Heritage Way, Ste. 1
Gloucester, MA　01930

Established in 1999 in MA.
Donors: Alexander L.M. Dingee; Susan J. Gray.
Foundation type: Independent foundation.
Financial data (yr. ended 12/31/05): Assets, $7,249,441 (M); expenditures, $384,666; qualifying distributions, $384,666; giving activities include $372,500 for 11 grants (high: $134,000; low: $5,000).

Purpose and activities: Giving primarily for environmental conservation, and the arts, including a museum for film and television.

Fields of interest: Museums; Performing arts; Libraries (public); Environment; Human services; YM/YWCAs & YM/YWHAs; Children/youth, services.

Limitations: Applications not accepted. Giving primarily in MA, with emphasis on Gloucester. No grants to individuals.

Application information: Contributes only to pre-selected organizations.

Trustees: Alexander L.M. Dingee; Susan J. Gray; Robert G. Stewart.
EIN: 046902006

3828
Cambridge Community Foundation ✧
(formerly The Cambridge Foundation)
99 Bishop Allen Dr.
Cambridge, MA 02139 (617) 576-9966
Contact: Robert S. Hurlbut, Jr., Exec. Dir.
FAX: (617) 876-8187; *E-mail:* cambridgecf@igc.org

Established in 1916 in MA by declaration of trust.
Foundation type: Community foundation.
Financial data (yr. ended 6/30/05): Assets, $17,315,465 (M); gifts received, $793,210; expenditures, $1,017,989; giving activities include $618,333 for 181 grants (high: $25,546; low: $25), and $6,346 for 8 grants to individuals (high: $1,500; low: $100).
Purpose and activities: The foundation seeks to promote the mental, moral, and physical welfare of the inhabitants of Cambridge, MA (or elsewhere, if specified by the donor), through grants to community agencies, generally for: 1) social services - child welfare and development, emergency aid, employment and job training, legal assistance, and family services; 2) education - elementary and secondary education and ESL/GED programs; 3) health - hospice and home care, mental health and counseling, and substance abuse programs; and 4) housing and shelter - home improvement and repair, housing development, and shelter and transitional housing. Other areas of focus include gender issues, volunteer services, and community and capacity building.
Fields of interest: Education; Health care; Mental health/crisis services; Health organizations, association; Housing/shelter, development; Children/youth, services; Human services.
Type of support: General/operating support; Emergency funds; Program development; Seed money; Curriculum development; Scholarship funds; Technical assistance.
Limitations: Giving primarily in Cambridge, MA, except as specified by donors. No support for municipal, state, or federal agencies. No grants for research studies, conferences, films, or capital fund drives; no loans.
Publications: Application guidelines; Annual report; Program policy statement.
Application information: Application form required.
  Initial approach: Telephone or letter requesting guidelines
  Copies of proposal: 6
  Deadline(s): Submit proposal preferably Feb. through Apr. and Sept. through Oct.; deadline Apr. 15 for June consideration and Oct. 15 for Dec. consideration
  Board meeting date(s): Distribution Committee meets in June and Dec.
  Final notification: June and Dec.
Officers and Overseers:* Betty Bardige,* Pres.; Geneva T. Malenfant,* V.P.; Paul J. Gallagher,* Treas.; Robert S. Hurlbut, Jr., Exec. Dir.; Elizabeth Dowling Bartle; Casimir de Rham, Jr.; Francis H. Duehay; Wambui B. Githiora-Updike; Nan Haar; Richard A. Harriman; Jill M. Herold; Melville T. Hodder; Rev. Kevin J. O'Leary; Daniel A. Phillips; Frank B. Porter, Jr.; Dr. Peter B. Randolph; Sylvia Saavedra-Keber; Nan Stone; Janie Victoria Ward; Ann Marie Wilkins; Gwill E. York; Geraldine Zetzel.

Trustees: Cambridge Trust Co.; Bank of America, N.A.
Number of staff: 2 full-time professional.
EIN: 046012492

3829
Cammarata Family Foundation ✧
P.O. Box 248
Concord, MA 01742

Established in 1997 in MA.
Donor: Bernard Cammarata.
Foundation type: Independent foundation.
Financial data (yr. ended 12/31/04): Assets, $4,526,678 (M); gifts received, $170,000; expenditures, $927,191; qualifying distributions, $756,068; giving activities include $756,068 for 15 grants (high: $324,608; low: $500).
Fields of interest: Higher education; Environment, land resources; Health care; Human services.
Limitations: Applications not accepted. Giving primarily in MA. No grants to individuals.
Application information: Contributes only to pre-selected organizations.
Trustee: Bernard Cammarata.
EIN: 043374858

3830
Bushrod H. Campbell and Adah F. Hall Charity Fund ✧
c/o Palmer & Dodge
Prudential Ctr.
111 Huntington Ave.
Boston, MA 02199-7613 (617) 239-0556
Contact: Brenda K. Taylor

Established in 1956 in MA.
Donors: Bushrod H. Campbell†; Adah F. Hall†.
Foundation type: Independent foundation.
Financial data (yr. ended 5/31/05): Assets, $19,834,910 (M); expenditures, $1,026,609; qualifying distributions, $930,125; giving activities include $806,344 for 108 grants (high: $55,000; low: $3,000).
Purpose and activities: Grants limited to organizations and/or their projects devoted to aid the elderly, population studies, and health care.
Fields of interest: Reproductive health, family planning; Health organizations, association; Medical research, institute; Aging, centers/services; Aging.
Type of support: General/operating support; Continuing support; Building/renovation; Program development; Seed money; Research.
Limitations: Giving limited to the greater Boston, MA, area (within Route 128 and Boston); giving on a national basis to organizations dealing with population control. No grants to individuals, or for annual campaigns, emergency funds, deficit financing, land acquisition, publications, or general endowments; no loans.
Publications: Application guidelines; Grants list; Informational brochure.
Application information: Application form required.
  Initial approach: Proposal
  Copies of proposal: 1
  Deadline(s): Jan. 15, Apr. 15, Aug. 15, and Oct. 15
  Board meeting date(s): Feb., May, Sept., and Nov.
  Final notification: By mail only

Trustees: Casimir de Rham, Jr.; Arthur B. Page; Curtis Prout, M.D.
Number of staff: 1 part-time professional.
EIN: 046013598

3831
Canaday Family Charitable Trust ✧ ☆
c/o U.S. Trust Co. of Boston
P.O. Box 55122
Boston, MA 02205-8670

Established in 2004 in MA.
Foundation type: Independent foundation.
Financial data (yr. ended 12/31/05): Assets, $15,599,006 (M); gifts received, $401,558; expenditures, $965,087; qualifying distributions, $833,974; giving activities include $749,117 for 13 grants (high: $212,400; low: $10,000).
Fields of interest: Environment; Animals/wildlife; Health care.
Type of support: General/operating support.
Limitations: Applications not accepted. No grants to individuals.
Application information: Contributes only to pre-selected organizations.
Trustees: Family Capital Trust Company, N.A.; U.S. Trust Co. of Boston.
EIN: 912158408

3832
Cape Cod Five Cents Savings Bank Charitable Trust ✧
P.O. Box 10
Orleans, MA 02653-0010 (508) 247-2223
Contact: David B. Williard, Secy.

Established in 1998 in MA.
Donor: Cape Cod Five Cents Savings Bank.
Foundation type: Company-sponsored foundation.
Financial data (yr. ended 12/31/04): Assets, $12,378,298 (M); gifts received, $2,500,440; expenditures, $502,780; qualifying distributions, $471,460; giving activities include $452,762 for 168 grants (high: $29,321; low: $200).
Purpose and activities: The foundation supports organizations involved with arts and culture, education, the environment, health, and human services.
Fields of interest: Arts; Education; Environment; Health care; Human services; Children/youth, services.
Type of support: Continuing support; Capital campaigns; Building/renovation; Land acquisition; Program development; Conferences/seminars; Scholarship funds.
Limitations: Giving limited to MA. No support for general operating support, fundraisers, third party events, or field trips.
Application information: Application form required.
  Initial approach: Contact foundation for application form
  Copies of proposal: 1
  Board meeting date(s): Every 7 weeks
Officers: Elliott Carr, Chair.; David Williard, Secy.; Ronald Reed, Treas.
EIN: 043423249
Selected grants: The following grants were reported in 2003.
$14,590 to Cape Cod Community College, Barnstable, MA. 2 grants: $10,000, $4,590 (For program support).

$10,000 to Cape Cod Healthcare Foundation, Hyannis, MA. For renovations.

$5,000 to Barnstable Land Trust, Cotuit, MA. For capital support.

$5,000 to Wellfleet Conservation Trust, Wellfleet, MA.

$3,500 to Cape Museum of Fine Arts, Dennis, MA.

$3,334 to Center for Coastal Studies, Provincetown, MA.

$2,500 to Cape Cod Symphony Orchestra Association, Yarmouth Port, MA.

$1,700 to Boch Center for the Performing Arts, Mashpee, MA.

$1,000 to Academy of Performing Arts, Orleans, MA.

3833
The Cape Cod Foundation

(formerly The Community Foundation of Cape Cod)
259 Willow St.
P.O. Box 406
Yarmouthport, MA   02675   (508) 790-3040
Contact: Elizabeth Gawron, Pres.
FAX: (508) 790-4069;
E-mail: info@capecodfoundation.org; Additional tel.: (800) 947-2322; Additional E-mail: egawron@capecodfoundation.org; URL: http://www.capecodfoundation.org

Established in 1989 in MA.
Foundation type: Community foundation.
Financial data (yr. ended 12/31/05): Assets, $30,591,782 (M); gifts received, $4,013,008; expenditures, $10,159,143; giving activities include $9,568,510 for 172+ grants.
Purpose and activities: The foundation seeks to build a permanent resource supporting educational and charitable programs for all of Cape Cod.
Fields of interest: Humanities; Arts; Education; Environment; Health care; Youth development, community service clubs; Youth, services; Human services; Economic development; Nonprofit management; Community development; Economically disadvantaged.
Type of support: Land acquisition; General/operating support; Emergency funds; Consulting services; Conferences/seminars; Capital campaigns; Building/renovation; Annual campaigns; Continuing support; Management development/capacity building; Equipment; Seed money; Scholarship funds; Technical assistance; Grants to individuals; Scholarships—to individuals; In-kind gifts; Matching/challenge support; Student loans—to individuals.
Limitations: Giving limited to Barnstable, Duke, and Nantucket counties, MA.
Publications: Application guidelines; Annual report; Informational brochure; Newsletter.
Application information: Visit foundation Web site for application Cover Sheet and guidelines. Faxed or e-mailed applications are not accepted. Application form required.
Initial approach: Mail Cover Sheet and proposal to foundation
Copies of proposal: 11
Deadline(s): Apr. 1 and Oct. 1
Board meeting date(s): Bimonthly; Grant Review meetings are held semiannually
Final notification: 2 to 3 months
Officers and Directors:* Joseph A. Signore,* Chair.; Brooks S. Thayer,* Vice-Chair.; Elizabeth Gawron, Pres.; Gene Kennedy,* Clerk; Earle Batchelder,* Treas.; Mary Cotoia; George Dillon; Roger W. Ludwig; Brian O'Connell; Thomas J. O'Neill, Jr.; Richard M.

Page; Bertram Perkel; Jennifer S.D. Roberts; Lois Taylor; James Vaccaro; Linda Zammer.
Number of staff: 4 full-time professional; 1 full-time support; 1 part-time support.
EIN: 510140462

3834
Cardinal Brook Trust ◇ ☆

(formerly Karen & David Davis Charitable Fund)
95 Maple Ln.
Petersham, MA   01366

Established in 1988 in MA.
Donors: David Davis; Karen Davis.
Foundation type: Independent foundation.
Financial data (yr. ended 12/31/04): Assets, $5,410,973 (M); gifts received, $1,208,250; expenditures, $438,063; qualifying distributions, $384,692; giving activities include $382,200 for 46 grants (high: $59,500; low: $200).
Fields of interest: Elementary/secondary education; Higher education, college; Environment, natural resources; Environment, forests; Human services.
Limitations: Applications not accepted. Giving primarily in MA. No grants to individuals.
Application information: Contributes only to pre-selected organizations.
Trustees: David Davis; Karen Davis.
EIN: 043050557

3835
Carlee Charitable Trust ◇ ☆

c/o Loring, Wolcott, & Coolidge
230 Congress St.
Boston, MA   02110   (617) 523-6531
Contact: Frederick D. Ballou, Tr.

Established in 1995 in MA.
Donor: Jane H. Carlee.
Foundation type: Independent foundation.
Financial data (yr. ended 12/31/05): Assets, $3,574,449 (M); expenditures, $344,879; qualifying distributions, $319,514; giving activities include $315,000 for 3 grants (high: $200,000; low: $25,000).
Purpose and activities: Giving for the protection and care of domestic animals, the protection of natural wildlife species, the conservation of areas of natural habitat and beauty, and the preservation of historic architecture in the New England area.
Fields of interest: Environment, natural resources; Animals/wildlife.
Type of support: Capital campaigns; Land acquisition; Seed money.
Limitations: Giving primarily in MA. No grants to individuals.
Application information:
Initial approach: Letter or telephone call
Trustees: Frederick D. Ballou; William H. Hays III; Patricia H. Loring.
EIN: 046796657
Selected grants: The following grants were reported in 2003.
$100,000 to New England Wildlife Center, Hingham, MA. For general support.
$56,250 to Massachusetts Society for the Prevention of Cruelty to Children, Boston, MA. For general support.
$50,000 to Nantucket Land Council, Nantucket, MA. For general support.

3836
The Carleton Family Foundation, Inc. ◇

288 Fox Hill Rd.
Needham, MA   02492

Established in 2004 in MA.
Donors: James T. Carleton; Sharon E. Carleton.
Foundation type: Independent foundation.
Financial data (yr. ended 12/31/04): Assets, $302,161 (M); gifts received, $1,400,000; expenditures, $1,100,000; qualifying distributions, $1,100,000; giving activities include $1,100,000 for 2 grants (high: $600,000; low: $500,000).
Fields of interest: Elementary/secondary education; Higher education.
Limitations: Applications not accepted. Giving primarily in MA. No grants to individuals.
Application information: Contributes only to pre-selected organizations.
Officers and Directors:* James T. Carleton,* Pres.; Sharon E. Carleton,* Treas.
EIN: 201281898

3837
Patrick Carney Foundation ◇

c/o Claremont Management Co.
1 Lakeshore Ctr.
Bridgewater, MA   02324   (508) 279-4300
Contact: Patrick Carney, Dir.

Established in 1988 in MA.
Donor: Patrick Carney.
Foundation type: Independent foundation.
Financial data (yr. ended 12/31/05): Assets, $3,000,989 (M); gifts received, $3,058,200; expenditures, $336,974; qualifying distributions, $336,780; giving activities include $336,780 for 25 grants (high: $200,000; low: $100).
Purpose and activities: Giving for education, including a scholarship fund, as well as for Roman Catholic churches, schools, and organization; some funding for health care, and human services.
Fields of interest: Museums; Elementary/secondary education; Higher education; Education; Hospitals (specialty); Health organizations, association; Human services; Family services; Roman Catholic agencies & churches.
Type of support: General/operating support; Annual campaigns; Capital campaigns.
Limitations: Giving primarily in MA, with emphasis on Boston and New Bedford; some funding nationally. No grants to individuals.
Application information:
Initial approach: Letter on organization letterhead
Deadline(s): None
Director: Patrick Carney.
EIN: 046614314

3838
Gregory C. Carr Foundation, Inc. ◇

975 Memorial Dr., Ste. 1008
Cambridge, MA   02138
Contact: Megan Grey, Admin. Asst.
E-mail: MLgray@prodigy.net

Established in 1999 in MA.
Donor: Gregory C. Carr.
Foundation type: Independent foundation.
Financial data (yr. ended 6/30/05): Assets, $51,528,984 (M); gifts received, $6,315,640; expenditures, $5,523,031; qualifying distributions,

$5,174,094; giving activities include $1,407,995 for 38 grants (high: $100,000; low: $100), and $8,000 for 5 grants to individuals (high: $2,000; low: $1,000).

Purpose and activities: Giving primarily to further public education in the area of human rights.

Fields of interest: Higher education; Human services; International human rights.

Limitations: Giving primarily in MA.

Application information: Application form not required.

Initial approach: Letter
Copies of proposal: 8
Deadline(s): None

Officer: Gregory C. Carr, Pres. and Treas.

EIN: 043452643

3839
Casty-Dunn Families Charitable Foundation ◇ ☆
850 Boylston St., Ste. 428
Chestnut Hill, MA 02467

Established in 1962 in MA.

Donor: Norman S. Dunn.

Foundation type: Independent foundation.

Financial data (yr. ended 11/30/05): Assets, $1,080,218 (M); gifts received, $100,000; expenditures, $1,251,802; qualifying distributions, $1,251,802; giving activities include $1,239,180 for 19 grants (high: $300,000; low: $180).

Purpose and activities: Giving primarily to Jewish organizations and temples, as well as for higher education, health associations and human services.

Fields of interest: Performing arts, ballet; Higher education; Health organizations, association; Disasters, 9/11/01; Human services; Federated giving programs; Jewish federated giving programs; Jewish agencies & temples.

Limitations: Applications not accepted. Giving primarily in Boston, MA. No grants to individuals.

Application information: Contributes only to pre-selected organizations.

Trustees: Arthur Altman; Ronald G. Casty; Norman S. Dunn.

EIN: 046074905

Selected grants: The following grants were reported in 2003.

$50,000 to Combined Jewish Philanthropies of Greater Boston, Boston, MA.

$10,000 to Boys and Girls Clubs of Boston, Boston, MA.

$10,000 to Hebrew College, Newton Centre, MA.

$10,000 to Providence College, Providence, RI.

$4,500 to Beth Israel Deaconess Medical Center, Boston, MA.

$3,000 to Boston Arts Academy, Boston, MA.

$1,500 to Childrens Hospital League, Boston, MA.

$1,500 to Dana-Farber Cancer Institute, Friends of, Boston, MA.

$1,000 to Alzheimers Association, Massachusetts Chapter, Cambridge, MA.

$1,000 to Greater Boston Aid to the Blind, West Roxbury, MA.

3840
Cedar Tree Foundation ▼ ◇
(formerly David H. Smith Foundation)
10 Milk St., Ste. 401
Boston, MA 02108 (617) 695-6767
E-mail: info@cedartreefound.org; URL: http://www.cedartreefound.org

Established in 1994 in DE.

Donors: Dr. David H. Smith‡; Andrea L. Smith; Rachel A. Smith; Jennifer L. Smith.

Foundation type: Independent foundation.

Financial data (yr. ended 12/31/04): Assets, $83,517,451 (M); gifts received, $3,759,436; expenditures, $5,792,784; qualifying distributions, $5,006,980; giving activities include $4,158,000 for 48 grants (high: $636,000; low: $5,000; average: $10,000–$100,000).

Purpose and activities: The foundation focuses on the following areas of concern: sustainable agriculture, environmental education, and environmental health. The foundation will give particular consideration to proposals demonstrating strong elements of environmental justice, and conservation.

Fields of interest: Environment, legal rights; Environment, formal/general education; Environment; Agriculture.

Limitations: Giving primarily in NY. No grants to individuals.

Publications: Grants list.

Application information: The foundation will review letters of inquiry and request additional information or a proposal if interested. Letters of inquiry are not accepted via fax or e-mail.

Initial approach: Letter of inquiry (no more than 3 pages)
Deadline(s): None

Officers: Joan M. Smith, Pres.; Andrea L. Smith, V.P.; Jennifer L. Smith, Secy.; Rachel A. Smith, Treas.; Martin Teitel, Ph.D., Exec. Dir.

EIN: 133601934

Selected grants: The following grants were reported in 2004.

$636,000 to Pesticide Action Network (PAN), North America Regional Center, San Francisco, CA. For project support for Persistent Pesticides Campaign.

$270,000 to Slow Food USA, Brooklyn, NY. For project support for Renewing America's Food Traditions.

$250,000 to Natural Resources Council of Maine, Augusta, ME. For project support for North Woods Project and Penobscot River Restoration Project.

$250,000 to Tides Center, San Francisco, CA. For general support for National Voice Campaign, coalition of nonprofit and community groups working to maximize public participation in nation's democratic process.

$220,000 to USAction Education Fund, DC. For project support for non-partisan regional voter education efforts.

$200,000 to Earth Day Network, DC. For Campaign for Communities.

$100,000 to Farm School, Athol, MA. For project support for Apprentice Program.

$80,000 to Center for Food Safety, DC. For general support.

$75,000 to Wisconsin Citizen Action Fund, Milwaukee, WI. For general support.

$65,000 to Arizona League of Conservation Voters, Tucson, AZ. For general support.

3841
Center for Biomedical Science & Engineering Trust ◇
30 Warren St.
Brookline, MA 02445

Established in 1996 in MA. Classified as a private operating foundation in 1997.

Donors: Boston Scientific; Cardiac Dimensions; Cardiomind; Conor Medsystems; Cordis; Guidant; Labcoat Limited; Medinol; Medtronic Danvers; Mitralign; Percardia, Inc.; Possis Medical, Inc.; Xtent; Angioscore, Inc.; Biotegra, Inc.; Cappella, Inc.; WL Gore & Assoc.; Isis Pharmaceuticals; Medtronic Vascular, Inc.; Tepha; Viacor.

Foundation type: Operating foundation.

Financial data (yr. ended 12/31/05): Assets, $6,679,531 (M); gifts received, $3,741,529; expenditures, $3,238,901; qualifying distributions, $1,923,299; giving activities include $1,923,299 for 2 grants (high: $1,591,638; low: $331,661).

Purpose and activities: The foundation pays the expenses for sponsored researchers to conduct research involving the root causes of accelerated disease of blood vessels, the response of blood vessels to injury, and the mechanisms of vascular repair.

Fields of interest: Medical research, association.

Limitations: Applications not accepted. Giving primarily in MA. No grants to individuals.

Application information: Contributes only to pre-selected organizations.

Trustees and Director:* Cheryl A. Edelman; Elazer R. Edelman*.

EIN: 043299490

Selected grants: The following grants were reported in 2003.

$1,421,268 to Brigham and Womens Hospital, Boston, MA. For research.

$828,671 to Massachusetts Institute of Technology, Harvard Health Sciences, Cambridge, MA. For research.

3842
Irwin Chafetz Family Charitable Trust ◇
300 1st Ave.
Needham, MA 02494

Established in 1995 in MA.

Donors: Irwin Chafetz; Howard Chafetz.

Foundation type: Independent foundation.

Financial data (yr. ended 12/31/04): Assets, $1,996,210 (M); gifts received, $912,114; expenditures, $1,166,744; qualifying distributions, $962,208; giving activities include $962,208 for 79 grants (high: $241,250; low: $100).

Purpose and activities: Giving primarily to Jewish causes and to health organizations; funding also for social services.

Fields of interest: Arts; Education; Medical care, community health systems; Health organizations, association; Human services; Children, services; Jewish federated giving programs; Jewish agencies & temples.

Limitations: Applications not accepted. Giving primarily in MA, with emphasis on Boston; some funding nationally. No grants to individuals.

Application information: Contributes only to pre-selected organizations.

Trustees: Howard Chafetz; Irwin Chafetz; Laurence Chafetz; Roberta Chafetz.

EIN: 043282073

Selected grants: The following grants were reported in 2003.

$435,000 to Combined Jewish Philanthropies of Greater Boston, Boston, MA.

$100,000 to Hebrew College, Newton Centre, MA.

$20,000 to Massachusetts General Hospital, Boston, MA.

$20,000 to Stonehill College, Easton, MA.

$15,000 to Jewish Community Housing for the Elderly, Brighton, MA.

$3,000 to Crohns and Colitis Foundation of America, Needham, MA.

$2,500 to Jewish Community Day School, Newton, MA.

$2,100 to Project Bread - The Walk for Hunger, Boston, MA.

$1,000 to Beth Israel Deaconess Medical Center, Boston, MA.

$750 to Pine Street Inn, Boston, MA.

3843
The Chahara Foundation, Inc. ✧

612 Columbia Rd.
Dorchester, MA   02125   (617) 287-0200
Contact: Deahdra Butler-Henderson, Exec. Dir.
FAX: (617) 287-0206; E-mail: carol@chahara.org;
Additional FAX: (617) 247-7177; Additional e-mail:
deahdra@chahara.org; URL: http://
www.chahara.org

Established in 1999 in NY.
Donor: Karen Pittelman.
Foundation type: Independent foundation.
Financial data (yr. ended 12/31/04): Assets,
$1,016,672 (M); gifts received, $144,000;
expenditures, $769,060; qualifying distributions,
$713,531; giving activities include $375,635 for 29
grants (high: $42,135; low: $1,000).
Purpose and activities: Giving primarily to support
radical grassroots non-profits run by and for
low-income women in the greater Boston, MA, area.
Special focus is placed on the amplification of
women's voices as they fight to shape public opinion
and policy around the issue of economic
oppression.
Fields of interest: Women.
Type of support: General/operating support;
Continuing support; Emergency funds;
Conferences/seminars; Research; Technical
assistance.
Limitations: Giving primarily in the greater Boston,
MA, area. No grants to individuals.
Publications: Grants list.
Application information: Grant requests are not to
exceed $20,000. Application guidelines available
on foundation Web site. The foundation will accept
applications in foreign languages. Application form
required.
  Initial approach: Proposal (1-3 pages in length)
  Deadline(s): Sept.
  Board meeting date(s): Dec.
Officer: Karen Pittelman, Pres.
Directors: Yoav Bergner; Carol Pittelman.
Number of staff: 2 full-time professional.
EIN: 043479691
Selected grants: The following grants were reported
in 2004.

$20,000 to Association of Haitian Women in Boston, Dorchester, MA.

$10,000 to Freedom House, Dorchester, MA.

$5,000 to Chinese Progressive Association, Boston, MA.

$5,000 to Tieng Xanh: Voice, Dorchester, MA.

3844
Charles River Laboratories Foundation, Inc. ✧ ☆

(formerly Charles River Foundation)
251 Ballardvale St.
Wilmington, MA   01887   (978) 658-6000
Contact: Marilyn Brown, Pres.

Donor: Charles River Laboratories, Inc.
Foundation type: Company-sponsored foundation.
Financial data (yr. ended 10/31/05): Assets,
$10,202 (M); gifts received, $517,293;
expenditures, $507,638; qualifying distributions,
$507,638; giving activities include $489,444 for 44
grants (high: $89,282; low: $275), and $9,913 for
10 grants to individuals (high: $2,500; low: $500).
Purpose and activities: The foundation supports
organizations involved with animal welfare,
biomedical and medical research, and children.
Fields of interest: Animal welfare; Biomedicine
research; Medical research; American Red Cross;
Children, services.
Type of support: Grants to individuals; Scholarships
—to individuals; General/operating support;
Research.
Limitations: Giving primarily in MA.
Application information: Application form not
required.
  Initial approach: Proposal
  Deadline(s): None
Officers and Directors:* Marilyn Brown, Pres.;
James C. Foster,* Treas.; Henry L. Foster, D.V.M.
EIN: 510188208
Selected grants: The following grants were reported
in 2004.

$100,000 to Northeastern University, Boston, MA.

$25,000 to States United for Biomedical Research, Raleigh, NC.

$20,000 to American College of Laboratory Animal Medicine, Chester, NH. 3 grants: $5,000, $10,000, $5,000

$10,000 to Minneapolis Heart Institute Foundation, Minneapolis, MN.

$10,000 to Research America, Alexandria, VA. 2 grants: $5,000 each

$7,500 to Massachusetts Society for Medical Research, Waltham, MA.

$6,000 to Foundation for Biomedical Research, DC.

3845
Charlesbank Homes ✧

c/o Watch Hill Co.
63 Shore Rd., Ste. 35
Winchester, MA   01890
Contact: Richard H. Sayre, Pres.
E-mail: rhsayre@juno.com

Established in 1911.
Donor: Edwin Ginn†.
Foundation type: Independent foundation.
Financial data (yr. ended 4/30/05): Assets,
$16,141,858 (M); expenditures, $818,872;
qualifying distributions, $698,653; giving activities
include $693,300 for grants.
Purpose and activities: Emphasis on bricks and
mortar projects for low- and moderate-income
housing.
Fields of interest: Housing/shelter.
Type of support: Building/renovation.
Limitations: Giving primarily in MA. No support for
medically oriented housing/shelter. No grants to
individuals, or for operating budgets.

Application information: Application guidelines
available via E-mail. Application form not required.
  Initial approach: Letter or telephone
  Copies of proposal: 1
  Deadline(s): None
  Board meeting date(s): Quarterly
  Final notification: 1 week following board vote
Officers and Trustees:* Richard D. Driscoll,* Chair.;
Richard H. Sayre,* Pres.; Frederick L. Worcester,*
Treas.; Thomas W. Cornu; Susan K. Keller; Sarah
Leggat; M. Chrysa Long; George Macomber; J. Louis
Newell; Philip J. Notopoulos*; R. Bruce Taylor.
Number of staff: None.
EIN: 042103755
Selected grants: The following grants were reported
in 2004.

$70,000 to United South End Settlements, Boston, MA. 2 grants: $35,000 each

$50,000 to Boston Rescue Mission, Boston, MA.

$50,000 to Brookview House, Boston, MA.

$50,000 to Jamaica Plain Neighborhood House Association, Jamaica Plain, MA.

$35,000 to Just a Start, Cambridge, MA.

$35,000 to Saint Francis House, Boston, MA.

$30,000 to Saint Marys Women and Childrens Center of Dorchester, Dorchester, MA.

$25,000 to Second Step, Newton, MA.

$25,000 to Tri-City Community Action Program, Malden, MA.

3846
Earle P. Charlton, Jr. Discretionary Charitable Trust ✧

(formerly Earle P. Charlton, Jr. Charitable Trust)
P.O. Box 55886
Boston, MA   02205-5886
Application address: c/o Lauren Cerullo, Bank of
America, N.A., Fdn. and Philanthropic Svcs., 100
Federal St., Boston, MA 02110, tel.: (617)
434-0225

Established in 1973 in MA.
Donor: Earle P. Charlton, Jr.†.
Foundation type: Independent foundation.
Financial data (yr. ended 12/31/05): Assets,
$7,713,861 (M); expenditures, $405,808;
qualifying distributions, $383,279; giving activities
include $357,840 for 7 grants (high: $200,000;
low: $10,000).
Purpose and activities: Giving primarily for
rehabilitation and education.
Fields of interest: Higher education; Medical care,
rehabilitation; Human services; Federated giving
programs; Protestant agencies & churches.
Limitations: Giving primarily in Boston and Fall
River, MA. No grants to individuals.
Application information: Associated Grantmakers
Common Proposal Format accepted.
  Initial approach: Letter
  Deadline(s): None
Trustees: Earle P. Charlton, Jr.; Bank of America,
N.A.
EIN: 046334412
Selected grants: The following grants were reported
in 2004.

$200,000 to Southcoast Health System, New Bedford, MA. For general support.

$150,000 to University of Massachusetts, North Dartmouth, MA. For general support.

3847

The Alfred E. Chase Charity Foundation ✧
c/o Bank of America, N.A., Fdn. and Philanthropic
Svcs.
100 Federal St., MA5-100-20-06
Boston, MA 02110 (617) 434-4846
Contact: Kerry Herlihy Sullivan, Dir., Bank of
America, N.A., Fdn. & Philanthropic Svcs.
E-mail: kerry.h.sullivan@bankofamerica.com

Established in 1956 in MA.
Donor: Alfred E. Chase†.
Foundation type: Independent foundation.
Financial data (yr. ended 10/31/05): Assets,
$8,239,691 (M); expenditures, $427,651;
qualifying distributions, $400,822; giving activities
include $366,000 for grants.
Purpose and activities: Giving primarily for children
and youth services (including year-round
recreationally-linked educational programs) as well
as for community services, and education.
Fields of interest: Education; Health care;
Recreation, camps; Recreation, community
facilities; Recreation; Human services; Children/
youth, services; Family services; Human services,
mind/body enrichment; Community development;
Federated giving programs.
Type of support: General/operating support; Annual
campaigns; Equipment; Program development;
Technical assistance.
Limitations: Giving limited to MA, with emphasis on
Lynne and North Shore areas. No grants to
individuals, or for research, scholarships, or
fellowships; no loans.
Publications: Application guidelines.
Application information: AGM Common Grant
Application accepted. Applicants should complete a
Grant Application coversheet. Only 1 proposal per
organization may be submitted per 12-month period.
No hand deliveries of proposals or video tapes will
be accepted. Application form required.
  Initial approach: Proposal with cover sheet
  Copies of proposal: 1
  Deadline(s): Apr. 7
  Board meeting date(s): May
  Final notification: June
Trustee: Bank of America, N.A.
EIN: 046026314
Selected grants: The following grants were reported
in 2003.
$50,000 to Catholic Schools Foundation, Boston,
  MA. For general support.
$40,000 to Cambridge Health Alliance, Cambridge,
  MA. For general support.
$37,500 to South End Community Health Center,
  Boston, MA. For general support.
$20,000 to Boys and Girls Club of Lynn, Lynn, MA.
  For general support.
$17,500 to Home for Little Wanderers, Boston, MA.
  For general support.
$15,000 to Boston Ten Point Coalition, Boston, MA.
  For general support.
$15,000 to Fitchburg Art Museum, Fitchburg, MA.
  For general support.
$10,000 to Agassiz Village, Lexington, MA. For
  general support.
$10,000 to Dorchester Super Summer, Dorchester,
  MA. For general support.
$5,000 to Camp Allen, Bedford, NH. For general
  support.

3848

**Roberta M. Childs Charitable
  Foundation** ✧ ☆
P.O. Box 639
North Andover, MA 01845-0639
(978) 685-4113
Contact: John R.D. McClintock, Tr.

Established in 1978 in MA.
Donor: Roberta M. Childs†.
Foundation type: Independent foundation.
Financial data (yr. ended 3/31/06): Assets,
$7,116,229 (M); expenditures, $430,798;
qualifying distributions, $386,500; giving activities
include $386,500 for grants.
Fields of interest: Education; Environment, natural
resources; Animal welfare; Hospitals (general);
Human services; Children/youth, services; Family
services; Marine science.
Type of support: General/operating support;
Continuing support.
Limitations: Giving primarily in MA. No grants to
individuals.
Application information: Application form not
required.
  Initial approach: Letter
  Copies of proposal: 1
  Deadline(s): None
  Board meeting date(s): Varies
Trustee: John R.D. McClintock.
EIN: 042660275
Selected grants: The following grants were reported
in 2005.
$25,000 to Baylor College of Medicine, Houston,
  TX.
$25,000 to Brigham and Womens Hospital, Boston,
  MA.
$10,000 to Nantucket Land Council, Nantucket,
  MA.
$5,000 to Adolescent Consultation Services,
  Cambridge, MA.
$5,000 to Hibiscus Childrens Center, Jensen
  Beach, FL.
$5,000 to Nantucket Conservation Foundation,
  Nantucket, MA.
$4,000 to American Indian College Fund, Denver,
  CO.
$4,000 to Nantucket Cottage Hospital, Nantucket,
  MA.
$4,000 to New England Wildlife Center, Hingham,
  MA.
$3,000 to Hearts United for Animals, Auburn, NE.

3849

John Clarke Trust ✧ ☆
c/o Bank of America, N.A.
P.O. Box 55886
Boston, MA 02205-5886
Application address: c/o Bank of America, N.A., 100
Federal St., Boston, MA 02110

Established in 1676 in Rhode Island.
Donor: John Clark†.
Foundation type: Independent foundation.
Financial data (yr. ended 12/31/05): Assets,
$7,608,053 (M); gifts received, $730;
expenditures, $399,243; qualifying distributions,
$381,443; giving activities include $359,863 for 65
grants (high: $35,000; low: $319).
Fields of interest: Higher education; Education;
Health care, clinics/centers; Human services;
Youth, services; Community development.

Type of support: General/operating support;
Equipment; Program development; Curriculum
development; Scholarship funds; Matching/
challenge support.
Limitations: Giving primarily in RI.
Application information: Application form not
required.
  Copies of proposal: 1
  Deadline(s): None
  Board meeting date(s): May, Aug., and Dec.
Trustees: William W. Corcoran; Barbara N.
Watterson; Bank of America, N.A.
EIN: 056006062
Selected grants: The following grants were reported
in 2004.
$10,000 to Community Preparatory School,
  Providence, RI.
$10,000 to Lucys Hearth, Middletown, RI.
$10,000 to Newport Hospital Foundation, Newport,
  RI.
$10,000 to Rogers High School, Newport, RI.
$6,000 to Salve Regina University, Newport, RI.
$6,000 to San Miguel Education Center,
  Providence, RI.
$5,000 to Boys and Girls Clubs of Providence,
  Providence, RI.
$5,000 to Portsmouth High School, Portsmouth, RI.
$3,000 to Davisville Free Library Association, North
  Kingstown, RI.
$1,000 to Big Sisters of Rhode Island, Cranston, RI.

3850

Clipper Ship Foundation, Inc. ✧
c/o Grants Mgmt. Assocs.
77 Summer St., 8th Fl.
Boston, MA 02110 (617) 426-7080, ext. 317
Contact: Ms. Tegin Teich, Clerk
FAX: (617) 426-7087;
E-mail: tteich@grantsmanagement.com;
URL: http://www.agmconnect.org/clipper1.html

Established in 1979 in MA.
Donor: David Parmely Weatherhead†.
Foundation type: Independent foundation.
Financial data (yr. ended 10/31/05): Assets,
$27,510,253 (M); expenditures, $1,492,071;
qualifying distributions, $1,383,597; giving
activities include $1,304,750 for 207 grants (high:
$30,150; low: $500).
Purpose and activities: Priority given to
organizations devoted to helping the homeless, the
destitute, the handicapped, children and the aged,
or supplying the special needs of minority,
low-income individuals and families. Special
consideration also given to emergency disaster
situations worldwide.
Fields of interest: Food services; Food banks;
Housing/shelter, development; Disasters,
preparedness/services; Human services; Children/
youth, services; Aging, centers/services;
Minorities/immigrants, centers/services;
Homeless, human services; Community
development; Public affairs; Aging; Disabilities,
people with; Minorities; Homeless.
Type of support: General/operating support;
Continuing support; Capital campaigns; Building/
renovation; Equipment; Emergency funds; Program
development; Technical assistance; Consulting
services; Matching/challenge support.
Limitations: Giving primarily in Brockton, Lawrence,
and the greater Boston, MA, area (in cities and
towns lying on or within Rte. 128). No support for
religion, hospitals, higher education, legal services,

or advocacy programs. No grants to individuals, campaigns for endowment funds; for the production of motion pictures, television, video tapes or film strips; for conferences or conventions; for consulting, research, scholarships, fellowships, student loans or travel; for the writing or publishing of books or articles.

Publications: Application guidelines; Annual report (including application guidelines); Financial statement; Grants list; Informational brochure (including application guidelines).
Application information: Associated Grantmakers of MA Common Proposal Format required. Associated Grantmakers of MA Cover Summary required. See AGM URL: http://www.agmconnect.org. Only 1 proposal per applicant will be considered each calendar year. Application form required.

   Initial approach: Proposal, telephone or E-mail
   Copies of proposal: 1
   Deadline(s): Mar. 1, May 10, Aug. 10, and Nov. 15
   Board meeting date(s): Jan, Apr., July, and Oct.
   Final notification: Within 2 months

Officers and Directors: * Benjamin H. Lacy,* Chair.; Nicholas S.F. Carter,* Pres. and Treas.; John B. Newhall,* V.P.; Tegin Teich,* Clerk; Brian S. Kelley; Sarah R. Newbury; George F. Pennington; Mayra Rodriguez-Howard.
Number of staff: 1 part-time professional.
EIN: 042687384
Selected grants: The following grants were reported in 2004.
$27,000 to Associated Grant Makers, Boston, MA. For camps.
$15,000 to Centro Hispano de Chelsea, Chelsea, MA. For program operating support.
$15,000 to Chelsea Human Services Collaborative, Chelsea, MA. For operating support.
$15,000 to Lawrence Community Works, Lawrence, MA. For general operating support.
$15,000 to YMCA, Old Colony, Brockton, MA. For project support for Family Life Center in Brockton.
$12,000 to Edward Brooke Charter School, Brighton, MA. For Permanent Facility Project.
$10,000 to Boston Collegiate Charter School, Dorchester, MA. For new school in Dorchester.
$10,000 to Boston Symphony Orchestra, Boston, MA. For Youth Concerts Program.
$10,000 to Boys and Girls Club of Brockton, Brockton, MA. For operating support.
$10,000 to Greater Lawrence Educational Collaborative, Lawrence, MA. For Multicultural Enrichment Partnership.

3851
Cogan Family Foundation ✦
c/o WCPH and D, LLP
P.O. Box 9350
Boston, MA 02114

Established in 2000 in MA.
Donor: John F. Cogan, Jr.
Foundation type: Independent foundation.
Financial data (yr. ended 8/31/05): Assets, $20,997,495 (M); expenditures, $1,166,893; qualifying distributions, $924,125; giving activities include $924,000 for 69 grants (high: $100,000; low: $1,500).
Purpose and activities: Giving primarily for the arts, particularly to an art museum, as well as for education, including a school for the blind, legal services, medical care, children, youth, and family

services, and social services including a shelter for the homeless.
Fields of interest: Media, radio; Museums (art); Performing arts; Arts; Elementary/secondary education; Higher education; Law school/education; Libraries/library science; Education; Hospitals (general); Medical research, institute; Legal services; Food banks; Housing/shelter, development; Human services; Children/youth, services; Family services; Homeless, human services; Federated giving programs.
Limitations: Applications not accepted. Giving primarily in CA, MA, and NY. No grants to individuals.
Application information: Contributes only to pre-selected organizations.
Trustees: Gregory Cogan; John F. Cogan, Jr.; Mary Cornille; Pamela Cogan Riddle.
EIN: 046923387

3852
Colombe Foundation ✦
101 University Dr., Ste. A2
Amherst, MA 01002 (413) 256-0349
Contact: Amy Clough, Grants Mgr.
FAX: (413) 256-3536;
E-mail: aclough@proteusfund.org; URL: http://www.proteusfund.org/grantmaking/colombe/

Established in 1996 in DE.
Donor: Edith W. Allen.
Foundation type: Independent foundation.
Financial data (yr. ended 6/30/05): Assets, $9,648,795 (M); expenditures, $998,170; qualifying distributions, $890,000; giving activities include $890,000 for 29 grants (high: $100,000; low: $10,000).
Purpose and activities: The foundation seeks to create a peaceful world through changes in American policy. It works for the elimination of weapons of mass destruction, a shift from war and aggression to conflict prevention and conflict resolution, and a shift from wasteful military spending to investments in programs addressing poverty, environmental degradation and other root causes of violence. The foundation currently makes grants to organizations in the U.S. that share its mission and use these strategies: 1) grassroots organizations working to educate the public and influence decision makers; 2) peace advocacy organizations promoting alternative policies; and 3) organizations initiating media coverage.
Fields of interest: Education, public education; Environment, research; International affairs, information services; International peace/security; Social sciences, public policy; Social sciences, government agencies; Social sciences, formal/general education; Political science.
Publications: Application guidelines; Grants list.
Application information: 2 copies required if mailed, only 1 required if sent via e-mail. Standard cover sheet, to be sent with proposal, can be downloaded on foundation Web site.
   Initial approach: Proposal with standard cover sheet
   Copies of proposal: 2
   Deadline(s): Mar. 9 for the spring, and Aug. 1 for the fall
   Final notification: Spring and Fall
Officers: Edith W. Allen, Pres.; Frederick Allen, Secy.
EIN: 137103356
Selected grants: The following grants were reported in 2004.

$135,000 to Womens Action for New Directions (WAND) Education Fund, Arlington, MA. For general support.
$50,000 to Center for Arms Control and Non-Proliferation, DC. For general support.
$50,000 to National Priorities Project, Northampton, MA. For general support.
$45,000 to GlobalSecurity.org, Alexandria, VA. For general support.
$40,000 to New School, New York, NY. For general support.
$40,000 to Physicians for Social Responsibility, DC. For general support.
$40,000 to Project on Government Oversight, DC. For general support.
$35,000 to Educators for Social Responsibility Metropolitan Area, New York, NY. For general support.
$30,000 to Alliance for Nuclear Accountability, Seattle, WA. For general support.
$30,000 to Institute for Energy and Environmental Research, Takoma Park, MD. For general support.

3853
Common Stream, Inc. ✦ ☆
c/o Nutter, McClennen & Fish, LLP
P.O. Box 51400
Boston, MA 02205

Established in MA.
Foundation type: Independent foundation.
Financial data (yr. ended 12/31/05): Assets, $22,462,310 (M); expenditures, $1,977,773; qualifying distributions, $1,834,422; giving activities include $1,640,000 for 82 grants (high: $35,000; low: $2,000).
Purpose and activities: Giving primarily for environmental causes; funding also for youth services and human services.
Fields of interest: Environment; Human services; Youth, services.
Limitations: Applications not accepted. Giving primarily in AK, ME, and MA. No grants to individuals.
Application information: Contributes only to pre-selected organizations.
Officers: Julia Satti Cosentino, Pres.; Derek Davis, Clerk; Mary Ryan, Treas.
EIN: 721556093

3854
Community Foundation of Southeastern Massachusetts ✦
227 Union St., Ste. 609
New Bedford, MA 02740 (508) 996-8253
Contact: Craig J. Dutra, Pres.
FAX: (508) 996-8254; E-mail: info@cfsema.org; URL: http://www.cfsema.org

Established in 1995 in MA.
Foundation type: Community foundation.
Financial data (yr. ended 12/31/03): Assets, $4,086,313 (M); gifts received, $681,994; expenditures, $848,069; giving activities include $444,920 for grants.
Purpose and activities: The foundation seeks to support programs that improve the quality of life for residents of the 41 towns and cities in Southeastern MA.

Fields of interest: Historic preservation/historical societies; Arts; Child development, education; Education; Environment; Health care; Mental health, treatment; Medical research, institute; Housing/shelter; Disasters, preparedness/services; Children/youth, services; Children, services; Child development, services; Family services; Human services; Economic development; Community development; Leadership development.

Type of support: Technical assistance; General/operating support; Management development/capacity building; Building/renovation; Emergency funds; Program development; Seed money; Scholarship funds.

Limitations: Giving primarily in southeastern MA.

Publications: Financial statement; Informational brochure; Multi-year report.

Application information: The foundation does not currently have any discretionary funds available; visit foundation Web site for discretionary fund updates, NewBAD (New Bedford Against Drugs) request for proposal information, and scholarship information.

Board meeting date(s): Monthly

Officers and Directors:* Elizabeth Isherwood,* Chair.; Samuel McFadden,* Vice-Chair.; Craig J. Dutra,* Pres.; John J. Feitelberg,* Clerk; Mary Louise Nunes,* Treas.; C. Eric Lindell, Dir. Emeritus; Lori L. Anderson-Martin; Linda Bodenmann; Peter Bullard; Kim Clark; John J. Feitelberg; Seth Garfield; Sr. Kathleen Harrington; Peter T. Kavanaugh; William T. Kennedy; Rev. Robert P. Lawrence; Albert E. Lees III; Thomas F. Lyons; Calvin Siegal; June A. Smith; Elsie Souza; Robert Ward; David F. Westgate.

Number of staff: 3 full-time professional; 1 full-time support; 1 part-time support.

EIN: 043280353

3855
Community Foundation of Western Massachusetts ▼

1500 Main St., Ste. 2300
P.O. Box 15769
Springfield, MA   01115   (413) 732-2858
Contact: Kent W. Faerber, C.E.O.
FAX: (413) 733-8565;
E-mail: wmass@communityfoundation.org;
Additional E-mail:
kfaerber@communityfoundation.org; Grant
information for
grants@communityfoundation.org; URL: http://
www.communityfoundation.org

Established in 1991 in MA.

Foundation type: Community foundation.

Financial data (yr. ended 3/31/05): Assets, $78,276,453 (M); gifts received, $6,178,306; expenditures, $5,964,370; giving activities include $4,774,264 for 604+ grants (high: $166,050).

Purpose and activities: The foundation seeks to enrich the quality of life of the people of Hampden, Hampshire, and Franklin counties in Western Massachusetts by: encouraging philanthropy; developing a permanent, flexible endowment; assessing and responding to emerging and changing needs; serving as a resource, catalyst, and coordinator for charitable activities; and promoting efficiency in the management of charitable funds.

Fields of interest: Performing arts; Historic preservation/historical societies; Arts; Education, fund raising/fund distribution; Adult/continuing education; Adult education—literacy, basic skills & GED; Libraries/library science; Education, reading; Education; Environment, natural resources;

Environment; Animals/wildlife, preservation/protection; Hospitals (general); Reproductive health, family planning; Medical care, rehabilitation; Health care; Substance abuse, services; Health organizations, association; Cancer; Heart & circulatory diseases; AIDS; Crime/violence prevention, youth; Crime/law enforcement; Housing/shelter, development; Safety/disasters; Recreation; Children/youth, services; Aging, centers/services; Women, centers/services; Minorities/immigrants, centers/services; Human services; Civil rights; Community development; Voluntarism promotion; Public policy, research; Public affairs; Aging; Disabilities, people with; Minorities; Native Americans/American Indians; Women; LGBTQ; Economically disadvantaged.

Type of support: Student loans—to individuals; Land acquisition; Capital campaigns; Building/renovation; Equipment; Program development; Conferences/seminars; Publication; Seed money; Scholarship funds; Technical assistance; Scholarships—to individuals; Matching/challenge support.

Limitations: Giving limited to western MA, including Franklin County, Hampden County, and Hampshire County. No support for religious purposes, or private education. No grants to individuals directly, or for operating budgets, endowments, fundraising events, tickets for benefits, courtesy advertising, academic or medical research or multi-year funding.

Publications: Application guidelines; Annual report; Grants list; Informational brochure; Newsletter.

Application information: Visit foundation Web site for application cover page and guidelines. Faxed or e-mailed applications are not accepted. The foundation offers a Small Group Grant Orientation for those new to grantseeking or new to the Community Foundation of Western MA; space is limited, reservations required. Application form required.

Initial approach: Telephone
Copies of proposal: 3
Deadline(s): Jan. 20 and Aug. 21
Board meeting date(s): Bimonthly
Final notification: Within 4 months

Officers and Trustees:* Carol Leary, Ph.D., Chair.; Stephen Davis, Vice-Chair.; Kent W. Faerber, C.E.O. and Pres.; Nancy Reiche, V.P., Progs.; Michael Riley, C.F.O. and C.A.O.; Dana R. Barrows; Bruce Brown; Marcia Burick; Robert S. Carroll; Ruth Constantine; Michael Fritz; Orlando Isaza; Sonia Nieto; Sandon S. Pearson; Timothy S. Rice; M. Trish Robinson; Elizabeth D. Scheibel; Mary Ellen Scott; Charlena Seymour; Richard B. Steele, Jr.; Linda Silva Thompson; R. Lyman Wood; Margaret Woods; Richard Zilewicz.

Number of staff: 4 full-time professional; 3 part-time professional; 5 full-time support.

EIN: 223089640

Selected grants: The following grants were reported in 2005.

$55,000 to Springfield School Volunteers, Springfield, MA. 2 grants: $25,000 (For Adult English Language Learners Pilot Program), $30,000 (For Springfield Oral Health Initiative Renovation).

$50,000 to Food Bank of Western Massachusetts, Hatfield, MA. For capital campaign.

$50,000 to Jose N. Gandara Mental Health Center, Springfield, MA. For building purchase and renovations.

$35,000 to YMCA of Metropolitan Springfield, Springfield, MA. For capital campaign.

$25,000 to Business Friends of the Arts, Springfield, MA. For Springfield Symphony Hall Renovation.

$15,000 to American Red Cross, Pioneer Valley Chapter, Springfield, MA. For health, emergency, and community support.

$14,000 to Northfield Mount Hermon School, Northfield, MA. For transitional support for 9th graders.

$10,000 to Organization of American Kodaly Educators, Moorhead, MN. For community concert.

$10,000 to Springfield Southwest Community Health Center, Springfield, MA. For Prescription Drug Access Pilot Project.

3856
The William F. Connell Charitable Trust ▼ ✧

c/o Lynch, Brewer, Hoffman & Sands, LLP
101 Federal St., 22nd Fl.
Boston, MA   02110

Established in 1986 in MA.

Donor: William F. Connell.

Foundation type: Independent foundation.

Financial data (yr. ended 12/31/05): Assets, $135,726 (M); gifts received, $1,098,539; expenditures, $3,716,827; qualifying distributions, $3,692,714; giving activities include $3,692,714 for 7 grants (high: $2,000,000; low: $10,000; average: $200,000–$1,000,000).

Purpose and activities: Giving primarily for higher education, a hospital, and federated giving programs.

Fields of interest: Secondary school/education; Higher education; Business school/education; Medical school/education; Libraries/library science; Hospitals (general); Cancer; Boy scouts; Federated giving programs.

Limitations: Applications not accepted. Giving primarily in MA. No grants to individuals.

Application information: Contributes only to pre-selected organizations.

Trustees: Courtenay E. Connell; Terence A. Connell; Timothy P. Connell; William C. Connell; Monica C. Healey; Lisa T. McNamara.

EIN: 222778156

Selected grants: The following grants were reported in 2005.

$2,000,000 to Boston College, Chestnut Hill, MA.

$1,000,000 to Caritas Saint Elizabeths Medical Center of Boston, Boston, MA.

$572,714 to Harvard University, Business School, Cambridge, MA. For research and using funds to benefit those in need.

$50,000 to John F. Kennedy Library Foundation, Boston, MA.

$50,000 to University of Massachusetts, Boston, MA.

$10,000 to Agganis Foundation, Lynn, MA.

$10,000 to William F. Connell Golf Fund, Norton, MA.

3857
The Connolly Family Foundation ✧

775 Monument St.
Concord, MA   01742

Established in 1997 in MA.

Donor: Richard F. Connolly, Jr.

Foundation type: Independent foundation.
Financial data (yr. ended 12/31/05): Assets, $974,699 (M); expenditures, $909,956; qualifying distributions, $883,605; giving activities include $883,605 for 74 grants (high: $165,300; low: $25).
Fields of interest: Museums; Libraries/library science; Hospitals (general); Health organizations, association; Human services; Federated giving programs.
Limitations: Applications not accepted. No grants to individuals.
Application information: Contributes only to pre-selected organizations.
Trustee: Richard F. Connolly, Jr.
EIN: 043367902
Selected grants: The following grants were reported in 2005.
$75,000 to Fenn School, Concord, MA. 2 grants: $25,000, $50,000
$55,000 to Colby College, Waterville, ME.
$50,000 to Laboure College, Boston, MA.
$25,125 to College of the Holy Cross, Worcester, MA.
$25,000 to Babson College, Babson Park, MA.
$25,000 to Middlesex School, Concord, MA.
$20,500 to Davidson College, Davidson, NC. 2 grants: $20,000, $500
$10,000 to Concord Free Public Library, Concord, MA.

3858
Conservation, Food and Health Foundation, Inc. ✧

c/o Grants Mgmt. Assocs.
77 Summer St., 8th Fl.
Boston, MA 02110 (617) 426-7080, ext. 307
Contact: Prentice Zinn, Admin.
FAX: (617) 426-7087;
E-mail: pzinn@grantsmanagement.com;
URL: http://www.grantsmanagement.com/cfhguide.html

Established in 1985 in MA.
Foundation type: Independent foundation.
Financial data (yr. ended 12/31/05): Assets, $15,533,241 (M); gifts received, $80,000; expenditures, $1,731,991; qualifying distributions, $827,481; giving activities include $799,878 for 44 grants (high: $30,000; low: $8,500).
Purpose and activities: The purpose of the foundation is to assist in the conservation of natural resources, the production and distribution of food, and the improvement and promotion of health in the developing world. The foundation is especially interested in supporting projects which lead to the transfer of responsibility to the citizens of developing countries for managing and solving their own problems and for developing the capacity of local organizations. Preference will be given to projects, including research projects, in areas that tend to be under-funded.
Fields of interest: Environment, natural resources; Environment; Animals/wildlife, preservation/protection; Health care; Agriculture; Agriculture/food.
International interests: Developing countries.
Type of support: Program development; Seed money; Research; Technical assistance.
Limitations: Giving limited to benefit Third World countries. No support for famine, emergency relief, or for overhead expenses of large institutions. No grants to individuals (except for research efforts sponsored by organizations and institutions), or for

building or land purchase, endowments, fundraising activities, scholarships, tuition, and travel grants or general operating support.
Publications: Application guidelines; Grants list.
Application information: Faxed or e-mailed proposals will not be accepted. In order to try to reduce the number of applicants who are turned down for lack of available funds, and to save time loss and expense to the applicants, the foundation has adopted a 2-phase application system, comprised of a short concept application, followed by a limited number of full proposals, at the invitation of the foundation. This system is designed to screen out, at the concept application level, projects which appear unlikely to receive final funding. Application guidelines available on foundation Web site. Application form required.
  Initial approach: Letter of inquiry or concept paper
  Copies of proposal: 5
  Deadline(s): Feb. 1 and Aug. 1 for concept applications; Mar. 1 and Sept. 1 for requests for proposal; Apr. 1 and Oct. 1 for proposals
  Board meeting date(s): Apr. and Oct.
  Final notification: June 1 and Dec. 1
Officer: Philip M. Fearnside, Pres.
EIN: 222625024

3859
Copeland Family Foundation, Inc. ✧

1183 Randolph Ave.
Milton, MA 02186 (617) 698-5980
Contact: Martha Verdone, Pres.

Established around 1983 in MA.
Foundation type: Independent foundation.
Financial data (yr. ended 12/31/05): Assets, $18,821,483 (M); expenditures, $2,784,191; qualifying distributions, $1,479,024; giving activities include $1,479,024 for 233 grants (high: $450,000; low: $350; average: $5,000–$20,000).
Purpose and activities: Giving primarily for education, animal welfare, hospitals, health associations, human services, community development, and Christian agencies and churches.
Fields of interest: Education; Animal welfare; Hospitals (general); Health organizations, association; Food services; Human services; Children/youth, services; Community development; Christian agencies & churches.
Limitations: Giving primarily in MA, with emphasis on Milton.
Application information:
  Initial approach: Letter
  Deadline(s): None
Officers and Directors:* Martha Verdone,* Pres.; Joyce Tobin,* Secy.; John Tobin,* Treas.; A. Gladys Copeland; Elizabeth Verdone.
EIN: 222474056

3860
The John and Mary Corcoran Family Foundation ✧

(formerly The 1991 Corcoran Foundation)
100 Grandview Rd., Ste. 207
Braintree, MA 02184-2600

Established in 1991 in MA.
Donor: John M. Corcoran.
Foundation type: Independent foundation.
Financial data (yr. ended 12/31/05): Assets, $5,142,025 (M); gifts received, $500,000;

expenditures, $1,174,765; qualifying distributions, $1,158,199; giving activities include $1,123,526 for 45 grants (high: $365,000; low: $1,000; average: $10,000–$50,000).
Purpose and activities: Giving primarily for human services and Roman Catholic education.
Fields of interest: Elementary/secondary education; Human services; Philanthropy/voluntarism; Roman Catholic agencies & churches.
Limitations: Applications not accepted. Giving primarily in MA, with emphasis on Boston. No grants to individuals.
Application information: Contributes only to pre-selected organizations.
Trustees: John M. Corcoran, Jr.; Thomas M. Corcoran.
EIN: 046689934
Selected grants: The following grants were reported in 2004.
$200,000 to Inner-City Scholarship Fund, Boston, MA.
$150,000 to Caritas Communities, Braintree, MA.
$150,000 to Partners in Health, Boston, MA.
$49,000 to Odwin Learning Center, Dorchester, MA.
$40,000 to Mass Mentoring Partnership, Boston, MA.
$20,000 to Cathedral High School, Boston, MA.
$20,000 to Pine Street Inn, Boston, MA.
$20,000 to Saint Francis House, Boston, MA.
$10,000 to Bridge Over Troubled Waters, Boston, MA.
$5,000 to Montrose School, Natick, MA.

3861
Robert Lloyd Corkin Charitable Foundation ✧ ☆

c/o The Entwistle Co.
Bigelow St.
Hudson, MA 01749

Established in 1985 in RI.
Donors: John J. Bradley; Howab Trust; Global Securities, Inc.
Foundation type: Independent foundation.
Financial data (yr. ended 12/31/05): Assets, $12,252,634 (M); gifts received, $1,915,200; expenditures, $651,110; qualifying distributions, $634,735; giving activities include $634,735 for grants.
Fields of interest: Secondary school/education; Higher education; Dental school/education; Hospitals (general); Health care; Health organizations, association; Youth, services; Federated giving programs; Jewish agencies & temples.
Limitations: Applications not accepted. Giving primarily in MA. No grants to individuals.
Application information: Contributes only to pre-selected organizations.
Trustee: Herbert Corkin.
EIN: 056022654
Selected grants: The following grants were reported in 2003.
$75,000 to Childrens Hospital Corporation, Boston, MA. For general support.
$50,000 to Brimmer and May School, Chestnut Hill, MA. For general support.
$10,000 to Boston University, School of Dental Medicine, Boston, MA. For general support.
$5,000 to Snow College, Ephraim, UT. For general support.
$1,500 to Dana-Farber Cancer Institute, Friends of, Boston, MA. For general support.

$1,500 to Jewish Family and Childrens Service, Waltham, MA. For general support.

$1,000 to Brain Tumor Society, Watertown, MA. For general support.

$500 to Hebrew Rehabilitation Center for Aged, Boston, MA. For general support.

$100 to Greater Boston Aid to the Blind, West Roxbury, MA. For general support.

$100 to New England Baptist Hospital, Boston, MA. For general support.

3862
The Fannie Cox Foundation ✧
P.O. Box 690
Southborough, MA 01772

Established in 1991 in NH.
Donors: Gardner C. Hendrie; Karen Johansen.
Foundation type: Independent foundation.
Financial data (yr. ended 12/31/05): Assets, $8,183,795 (M); expenditures, $336,636; qualifying distributions, $334,192; giving activities include $334,192 for 31 grants (high: $100,000; low: $1,000).
Purpose and activities: Giving primarily for education and the arts.
Fields of interest: Museums; Arts; Higher education, university; Education.
Type of support: General/operating support.
Limitations: Applications not accepted. Giving primarily in MA. No grants to individuals.
Application information: Contributes only to pre-selected organizations.
Trustees: Gardner C. Hendrie; Karen Johansen.
EIN: 026086221

3863
Cox Foundation, Inc. ✧
c/o Hemenway & Barnes
P.O. Box 961209
Boston, MA 02196-1209
Contact: Michael J. Puzo, Dir.

Established in 1970.
Donor: William C. Cox, Jr.
Foundation type: Independent foundation.
Financial data (yr. ended 12/31/05): Assets, $26,672,751 (M); expenditures, $1,382,368; qualifying distributions, $1,265,364; giving activities include $1,234,570 for 57 grants (high: $225,000; low: $1,000; average: $5,000–$50,000).
Purpose and activities: Giving primarily for education, conservation, and human services.
Fields of interest: Museums; Arts; Secondary school/education; Environment, natural resources; Environment; Hospitals (general); Medical research, institute.
Type of support: General/operating support; Continuing support; Annual campaigns; Capital campaigns; Land acquisition; Program development; Research.
Limitations: Applications not accepted. Giving primarily in FL and MA. No grants to individuals.
Application information: Contributes only to pre-selected organizations.
Board meeting date(s): Dec.
Officers: William C. Cox, Jr., Pres.; Martha W. Cox, Treas.
Directors: Roy A. Hammer; Michael J. Puzo.
EIN: 237068786

3864
Crane & Co. Fund
c/o Elizabeth M. Pomeroy
30 South St.
Dalton, MA 01226
Contact: John R. Schulte, Tr.

Established in 1953 in MA.
Donors: Crane & Co., Inc.; Byron-Weston Co.
Foundation type: Company-sponsored foundation.
Financial data (yr. ended 12/31/03): Assets, $0 (M); gifts received, $323,900; expenditures, $323,900; qualifying distributions, $323,900; giving activities include $323,900 for 25 grants (high: $93,000; low: $100).
Purpose and activities: The foundation supports organizations involved with arts and culture, education, environmental conservation, health, human services, and government and public administration.
Fields of interest: Museums; Arts; Education; Environment, natural resources; Health care; Human services; Federated giving programs; Government/public administration.
Type of support: General/operating support; Annual campaigns; Capital campaigns.
Limitations: Giving limited to Berkshire County, MA. No grants to individuals, or for scholarships.
Application information: Application form not required.
Initial approach: Letter of inquiry
Copies of proposal: 1
Trustees: Douglas A. Crane; Timothy T. Crane; Richard C. Kendall; John R. Schulte.
EIN: 046057388
Selected grants: The following grants were reported in 2005.
$100,200 to United Way. 2 grants: $93,000, $7,200
$25,000 to Berkshire Medical Center, Pittsfield, MA.
$4,000 to Berkshire Natural Resources Council, Pittsfield, MA.
$3,000 to Berkshire Museum, Pittsfield, MA.
$3,000 to Upper Housatonic Valley National Heritage Area, Lakeville, CT.
$1,000 to American Cancer Society, Atlanta, GA.
$1,000 to Berkshire Music School, Pittsfield, MA.
$1,000 to Christian Center, Anderson, IN.
$500 to Recording for the Blind and Dyslexic, Princeton, NJ.

3865
Josephine B. Crane Foundation ✧
c/o William K. Mackey
P.O. Box 901
Falmouth, MA 02541

Incorporated in 1955 in NY.
Donors: Josephine B. Crane†; Davis Crane Greene.
Foundation type: Independent foundation.
Financial data (yr. ended 12/31/05): Assets, $6,135,492 (M); expenditures, $345,042; qualifying distributions, $322,043; giving activities include $315,000 for 9 grants (high: $65,000; low: $5,000).
Fields of interest: Human services.
Type of support: General/operating support; Continuing support; Capital campaigns.
Limitations: Applications not accepted. Giving primarily in Dalton and in Berkshire and Barnstable counties, MA. No grants to individuals.

Application information: Contributes only to pre-selected organizations. Unsolicited requests for funds not considered.
Officers and Directors:* Davis Crane Greene,* Pres.; Winnie Crane Mackey,* V.P.; William K. Mackey,* Secy.-Treas.; Josephine B. Greene.
EIN: 136156264
Selected grants: The following grants were reported in 2005.
$50,000 to Boys and Girls Club of Pittsfield, Pittsfield, MA.
$50,000 to Outward Bound, Garrison, NY.
$25,000 to Berkshire Medical Center, Pittsfield, MA.
$25,000 to Berkshire Museum, Pittsfield, MA.
$20,000 to Sierra Club Foundation, San Francisco, CA.
$5,000 to Boston Living Center, Boston, MA.

3866
Louise Crane Foundation ✧
P.O. Box 901
Falmouth, MA 02541

Established in 1963 in NY.
Donor: Louise Crane†.
Foundation type: Independent foundation.
Financial data (yr. ended 12/31/04): Assets, $62,446,862 (M); gifts received, $24,481,136; expenditures, $2,622,869; qualifying distributions, $2,400,750; giving activities include $2,400,000 for 30 grants (high: $350,000; low: $5,000).
Purpose and activities: Giving primarily for health care, education, and community development.
Fields of interest: Arts; Education; Hospitals (general); Mental health/crisis services; Health organizations, association; Boys & girls clubs; Community development; Federated giving programs.
Type of support: General/operating support; Continuing support; Capital campaigns.
Limitations: Applications not accepted. Giving primarily in MA, with emphasis on the Falmouth and Pittsfield areas. No grants to individuals.
Application information: Contributes only to pre-selected organizations. Unsolicited requests for funds not considered.
Officers and Directors:* Davis C. Greene,* Pres.; Winnie C. Mackey,* V.P.; William K. Mackey,* Secy.-Treas.
EIN: 136119886
Selected grants: The following grants were reported in 2003.
$200,000 to Boston University, Center for Psychiatric Rehabilitation, Boston, MA.
$200,000 to McLean Hospital, Belmont, MA.
$200,000 to Milton Academy, Milton, MA.
$75,000 to Childrens Hospital Corporation, Boston, MA.
$75,000 to Sierra Club Foundation, San Francisco, CA.
$75,000 to Visiting Nurse Association of Cape Cod Foundation, South Dennis, MA.
$50,000 to Falmouth Hospital Foundation, Falmouth, MA.
$30,000 to Berkshire Medical Center, Pittsfield, MA.
$25,000 to Berkshire Museum, Pittsfield, MA.
$10,000 to Falmouth Service Center, Falmouth, MA.

3867

The Crawford Idema Family Foundation
(formerly The Crawford Idema Foundation)
100 Main St., Ste. 325
Concord, MA 01742 (978) 318-0505
Contact: Philip VanDerWilden, Exec. Dir.

Established in 1997 in CA.
Foundation type: Independent foundation.
Financial data (yr. ended 12/31/04): Assets, $10,286,561 (M); expenditures, $721,450; qualifying distributions, $533,691; giving activities include $454,660 for 47 grants (high: $35,000; low: $1,000).
Fields of interest: Environment, natural resources; Substance abuse, prevention; Human services; Child development, services; LGBTQ; Economically disadvantaged; Homeless.
Type of support: General/operating support; Continuing support; Curriculum development.
Limitations: Applications not accepted. Giving limited to the Santa Barbara, CA and Concord, MA areas. No support for religious activities or programs that serve religious groups or denominations, or political candidates. No grants to individuals, general fund raising drives, endowment funds, or for debt reduction.
Publications: Informational brochure; Occasional report.
Application information:
Board meeting date(s): Nov.
Officers and Directors:* Thomas Crawford, Jr.,* Pres.; Nancy S. Crawford,* Secy. and C.F.O.; Philip VanDerWilden, Exec. Dir.; Rob Adams; Susan C. Adams; Nancy R. Crawford; Peter T. Crawford; Thomas Crawford IV; Mary-Wren VanDerWilden; Peter Van Meeuwen.
Number of staff: 1 full-time professional.
EIN: 043473310

3868

The Croll Foundation ◇
c/o Goodwin, Proctor, LLP
Exchange Pl.
Boston, MA 02109-2881

Established in 1987 in MA.
Donors: David D. Croll; Victoria B. Croll.
Foundation type: Independent foundation.
Financial data (yr. ended 10/31/05): Assets, $15,219,280 (M); expenditures, $1,611,155; qualifying distributions, $1,604,821; giving activities include $1,604,821 for 55 grants (high: $426,800; low: $100).
Fields of interest: Museums; Museums (art); Higher education; Education; Human services.
Type of support: Scholarship funds.
Limitations: Applications not accepted. Giving primarily in MA, with some emphasis on Boston. No grants to individuals.
Application information: Contributes only to pre-selected organizations.
Trustees: David D. Croll; Victoria B. Croll.
EIN: 222946282
Selected grants: The following grants were reported in 2005.
$426,800 to Museum of Fine Arts, Boston, MA.
$330,000 to Cornell University, Ithaca, NY.
$100,750 to Middlesex School, Concord, MA.
$100,000 to Milton Academy, Milton, MA.
$60,000 to Park School, Brookline, MA.
$25,000 to Mount Holyoke College, South Hadley, MA.

$25,000 to Ohio Wesleyan University, Delaware, OH.
$8,000 to Peabody Essex Museum, Salem, MA.
$5,000 to New Bedford Whaling Museum, New Bedford, MA.
$600 to School of the Museum of Fine Arts, Boston, MA.

3869

Crossroads Community Foundation, Inc.
21 Eliot St.
Natick, MA 01760 (508) 647-2260
FAX: (508) 647-2288; E-mail: INFO@ccfdn.org;
URL: http://www.ccfdn.org

Established in 1995 in MA.
Foundation type: Community foundation.
Financial data (yr. ended 12/31/04): Assets, $5,073,938 (M); gifts received, $583,140; expenditures, $836,070; giving activities include $467,010 for grants.
Purpose and activities: The foundation's mission is to improve the quality of life in the Metrowest area by increasing the level and spirit of philanthropy in the region.
Fields of interest: Youth, services; General charitable giving.
Type of support: General/operating support; Management development/capacity building; Capital campaigns; Building/renovation; Equipment; Endowments; Program development; Conferences/seminars; Publication; Seed money; Curriculum development; Technical assistance; Consulting services.
Limitations: Giving primarily in Acton, Ashland, Boxborough, Concord, Dover, Framingham, Holliston, Hopkinton, Hudson, Lincoln, Marlborough, Maynard, Medfield, Medway, Milford, Millis, Natick, Needham, Sherborn, Southborough, Stow, Sudbury, Waltham, Wayland, Wellesley, Westborough, and Weston, MA. No support for religious organizations or sectarian programs. No grants to individuals.
Publications: Annual report; Informational brochure.
Application information: Visit foundation Web site for application cover sheets, deadlines, and specific guidelines per grant type. Faxed applications are not accepted. Application form required.
Initial approach: Letter or e-mail
Copies of proposal: 3
Deadline(s): Sept. for Capacity Building grants; varies for others
Board meeting date(s): Quarterly
Final notification: Within 4 or 5 months of each deadline
Officers and Trustees:* John H. Schwarz,* Chair. and Treas.; Judith Salerno, Co-Exec. Dir.; Kathan Tracy, Co-Exec. Dir.; Kay Hodge, Clerk; Peter Bentinck-Smith; Robert B. Brack; Woolsey S. Conover; Rudman J. Ham; Katherine McHugh; Arthur H. Nelson; Robert D. Rands.
Number of staff: 4 part-time professional; 1 part-time support.
EIN: 043266789

3870

The Crotty Family Foundation, Inc. ◇ ☆
c/o Battery Ventures
20 William St., Ste. 200
Wellesley, MA 02481

Donors: Thomas J. Crotty; Sharolyn K. Crotty.
Foundation type: Independent foundation.
Financial data (yr. ended 12/31/05): Assets, $1,624,146 (M); expenditures, $404,552; qualifying distributions, $397,188; giving activities include $397,188 for grants.
Fields of interest: Higher education, university; Education; Health organizations; Human services; Children/youth, services.
Limitations: Applications not accepted. Giving primarily in NH. No grants to individuals.
Application information: Contributes only to pre-selected organizations.
Officers: Thomas J. Crotty, Pres.; Sharolyn K. Crotty, Clerk.
EIN: 830368529

3871

Cummings Foundation ◇
(formerly New Horizons at Choate, Inc.)
200 W. Cummings Park
Woburn, MA 01801 (781) 935-8000
FAX: (781) 935-1990; URL: http://www.cummingsfoundation.org

Established in 1986 in MA.
Donors: Joyce M. Cummings; William S. Cummings; Cummings Properties Foundation; W.S. Cummings Realty Trust; J. & M. Forsyth.
Foundation type: Operating foundation.
Financial data (yr. ended 12/31/05): Assets, $539,853,361 (M); gifts received, $13,956,259; expenditures, $58,884,584; qualifying distributions, $54,811,370; giving activities include $584,552 for 229 grants (high: $50,000; low: $28), and $54,226,817 for 3 foundation-administered programs.
Fields of interest: Higher education; Education; Hospitals (general); Health organizations; Boys & girls clubs; Human services; Children/youth, services.
Type of support: Scholarship funds.
Limitations: Applications not accepted. Giving primarily in MA. No grants to individuals.
Publications: Annual report.
Application information: Contributes only to pre-selected organizations.
Officers and Trustees:* William S. Cummings,* Pres.; Patricia A. Cummings,* V.P.; Joyce M. Cummings, Treas.; Robert F.P. Nigro,* Exec. Dir.; Robert D. O'Connor,* Exec. Dir.; Joseph A. Abate, M.D.; Lawrence S. Bacow, Ph.D.; Hon. Margot Botsford; Paul C. Casey; Carol A. Donovan; Philip C. Kosch, Ph.D.; Jason Z. Morris, Ph.D.; Marilyn C. Morris, M.D.; Richard C. Ockerbloom; Janet M. Pavliska.
EIN: 043073023
Selected grants: The following grants were reported in 2003.
$50,000 to Hospice Care, Stoneham, MA.
$33,000 to North Shore Community College Foundation, Beverly, MA.
$30,000 to Winchester Hospital, Winchester, MA.
$20,000 to Solutions for Living, Medford, MA. 2 grants: $10,000 each
$10,000 to Catholic Charities Archdiocese of Boston, Boston, MA.
$10,000 to Massachusetts Eye and Ear Infirmary, Boston, MA.
$10,000 to Middlesex Community College, Bedford, MA. For scholarships.
$10,000 to United Way of Massachusetts Bay, Boston, MA.

$5,000 to University of Massachusetts, Boston, MA.

3872

Theodore H. Cutler Family Charitable Trust ◇

300 1st Ave.
Needham, MA 02494-2703

Established in 1994 in MA.
Donors: Theodore H. Cutler; Robert Cutler; Joan H. Cutler.
Foundation type: Independent foundation.
Financial data (yr. ended 12/31/04): Assets, $2,198,152 (M); gifts received, $487,153; expenditures, $844,849; qualifying distributions, $843,103; giving activities include $843,103 for 34 grants (high: $272,500; low: $250).
Purpose and activities: Giving primarily for the arts and education, and to Jewish organizations.
Fields of interest: Performing arts; Arts; Elementary/secondary education; Health organizations; Medical research, institute; Jewish federated giving programs; Jewish agencies & temples.
Limitations: Giving primarily in MA, with emphasis on Boston.
Trustees: Joan H. Cutler; Theodore H. Cutler.
EIN: 046773335
Selected grants: The following grants were reported in 2003.
$260,000 to Emerson College, Boston, MA.
$220,000 to Combined Jewish Philanthropies of Greater Boston, Boston, MA.
$100,000 to Hebrew College, Newton Centre, MA.
$35,100 to Boston Ballet, Boston, MA.
$25,250 to Brandeis University, Waltham, MA.
$10,000 to Museum of Fine Arts, Boston, MA.
$7,000 to Boston Lyric Opera Company, Boston, MA.
$5,000 to Rashi School, Newton, MA.
$2,500 to Boston Center for the Arts, Boston, MA.
$2,500 to Boston Jewish Film Festival, West Newton, MA.

3873

Herman Dana Charitable Trust ◇

1340 Centre St., Ste. 101
Newton, MA 02459-2453 (617) 928-1700
Contact: Marshall A. Dana, Tr.

Established in 1969 in MA.
Donor: Herman Dana†.
Foundation type: Independent foundation.
Financial data (yr. ended 12/31/04): Assets, $14,181,182 (M); expenditures, $1,910,298; qualifying distributions, $1,059,208; giving activities include $1,031,684 for 13 grants (high: $275,000; low: $6,644).
Purpose and activities: Grants to participating organizations of the Combined Jewish Philanthropies of greater Boston, MA, for capital purposes or urgent current needs, domestic organizations doing overseas work, and Jewish charitable or educational institutions; support also for organizations and institutions, with the grant to be used for the cost of psychiatric care and counseling of undergraduate students at Harvard University.

Fields of interest: Hospitals (general); Human services; International relief; Jewish federated giving programs; Jewish agencies & temples.
Limitations: Giving primarily in MA and NY. No grants to individuals.
Application information:
  Initial approach: Detailed proposal
  Deadline(s): None
Trustees: Marshall A. Dana; David L. Stone.
EIN: 046209497
Selected grants: The following grants were reported in 2003.
$150,000 to Beth Israel Deaconess Medical Center, Boston, MA.
$150,000 to Hadassah Medical Relief Association, New York, NY.
$138,897 to Combined Jewish Philanthropies of Greater Boston, Boston, MA.
$75,000 to Jewish Family and Childrens Service, Waltham, MA.
$50,000 to Anti-Defamation League of Bnai Brith, Boston, MA.
$50,000 to World Union for Progressive Judaism, New York, NY.
$50,000 to Yeshiva University, Albert Einstein College of Medicine, New York, NY.
$25,000 to Tufts University, Medford, MA. For Hillel Foundation.
$20,000 to Facing History and Ourselves National Foundation, Brookline, MA.
$10,000 to Frances Jacobson Early Childhood Center, Boston, MA.

3874

The Davis Family Foundation ◇ ☆

7 Wyndemere Dr.
Southborough, MA 01772

Established in 1999 in MA.
Donor: Robert J. Davis.
Foundation type: Independent foundation.
Financial data (yr. ended 12/31/05): Assets, $396,719 (M); gifts received, $2,604; expenditures, $323,264; qualifying distributions, $320,436; giving activities include $320,366 for 22 grants (high: $100,000; low: $66).
Fields of interest: Education; Hospitals (general); Food banks; Athletics/sports, baseball; Children, services; Christian agencies & churches.
Limitations: Applications not accepted. Giving primarily in MA. No grants to individuals.
Application information: Contributes only to pre-selected organizations.
Trustees: Rita M. Davis; Robert J. Davis.
EIN: 046907384
Selected grants: The following grants were reported in 2004.
$21,400 to Saint Marks Church, Dorchester, MA. 2 grants: $20,000, $1,400
$1,000 to Boys and Girls Club of Boston, Chinatown, Boston, MA.
$250 to American Cancer Society, Boston, MA.

3875

Irene E. and George A. Davis Foundation ▼

1 Monarch Pl., Ste. 1450
Springfield, MA 01144-1450 (413) 734-8336
Contact: Mary E. Walachy, Exec. Dir.
FAX: (413) 734-7845; E-mail: info@davisfdn.org;
Additional E-mail (for Mary E. Walachy):

mwalachy@davisfdn.org; URL: http://www.davisfdn.org

Established in 1970 in MA.
Foundation type: Independent foundation.
Financial data (yr. ended 12/31/04): Assets, $67,918,382 (M); gifts received, $60,295; expenditures, $5,463,368; qualifying distributions, $5,126,106; giving activities include $4,604,669 for 209 grants (high: $250,000; low: $25; average: $5,000–$50,000).
Purpose and activities: The mission of the foundation is to strengthen the capacity of individuals, families, and organizations in Hampden County predominantly through strengthening the quality of education for children and youth; ensuring the well-being of at-risk children, youth and families; and enhancing the management, leadership and governance capabilities of nonprofit organizations in order to assist them in achieving their diverse missions.
Fields of interest: Elementary/secondary education; Education, early childhood education; Human services; Children/youth, services; Community development; Economically disadvantaged.
Type of support: General/operating support; Continuing support; Annual campaigns; Capital campaigns; Building/renovation; Equipment; Land acquisition; Emergency funds; Program development; Seed money; Technical assistance; Consulting services; Program evaluation; Matching/challenge support.
Limitations: Giving primarily in Hampden County, MA. No support for private foundations. No grants to individuals, or for scholarships, internships, continuing support of current programs, debt reduction, or endowments; no program-related investments or loans.
Publications: Application guidelines.
Application information: Letter of intent form available on foundation's Web site. Application form required.
  Initial approach: Letter of intent
  Copies of proposal: 1
  Deadline(s): Feb. 1, May 1, Aug. 1, and Nov. 1 for grants
  Board meeting date(s): Mar., June, Sept., and Dec.
  Final notification: 2 weeks after board meeting
Officer: Mary E. Walachy, Exec. Dir.
Trustees: John H. Davis; Stephen A. Davis; Jane Davis-Kusek.
Number of staff: 2 full-time professional.
EIN: 237102734
Selected grants: The following grants were reported in 2004.
$250,000 to YWCA of Western Massachusetts, Springfield, MA. For capital campaign.
$225,000 to American International College, Springfield, MA. For capital fund drive, the New Millennium Campaign.
$200,000 to Nantucket Historical Association, Nantucket, MA. For general operating support.
$200,000 to Western New England College, Springfield, MA. For campaign for Law and Business Center for Advancing Entrepreneurship.
$100,000 to College of Our Lady of the Elms, Chicopee, MA. For construction of Science/Technology Center and Improvement of Athletic Fields.
$100,000 to YMCA of Metropolitan Springfield, Springfield, MA. For grant made through John and Robyn Davis Foundation, payable over 5 years.

$25,000 to Regional Technology Corporation (RTC), Springfield, MA. For general operating support.

$15,000 to New England Adolescent Research Institute, Holyoke, MA. For building assets and learning support.

$10,000 to Community Music School of Springfield, Springfield, MA. For annual operating support.

$10,000 to Downey Side, Springfield, MA. For general operating support.

3876
V. Eugene and Rosalie DeFreitas Charitable Foundation ◇

c/o Eastern Bank & Trust Co.
605 Broadway, LF41-RMW
Saugus, MA 01906   (781) 581-4274
Contact: Robert M. Wallask, V.P., Eastern Bank & Trust Co.

Established in 1994 in MA.
Donors: V. Eugene DeFreitas; Rosalie DeFreitas.
Foundation type: Independent foundation.
Financial data (yr. ended 11/30/05): Assets, $9,830,829 (M); expenditures, $544,373; qualifying distributions, $485,189; giving activities include $455,000 for 13 grants (high: $50,000; low: $25,000).
Purpose and activities: Support to colleges and seminaries without regard to religious denomination within the Christian beliefs, for the purpose of teaching and training Christian missionaries. Preference is given to the teaching and training of ministers for foreign missions.
Fields of interest: Elementary/secondary education; Theological school/education; Christian agencies & churches.
Type of support: Endowments.
Limitations: Giving primarily in MA. No grants to individuals.
Application information: Application form required.
  Initial approach: Letter requesting application form and guidelines
  Deadline(s): None
  Final notification: July 31
Trustee: Eastern Bank & Trust Co.
EIN: 046714542
Selected grants: The following grants were reported in 2004.

$50,000 to Eastern Nazarene College, Quincy, MA. For unrestricted support.

$40,000 to Gordon-Conwell Theological Seminary, South Hamilton, MA. For unrestricted support.

$40,000 to Weston Jesuit School of Theology, Cambridge, MA. For unrestricted support.

$35,000 to Pacific Rim Bible College, Honolulu, HI. For unrestricted support.

$30,000 to Assumption College, Worcester, MA. For unrestricted support.

$30,000 to Boston University, School of Theology, Boston, MA. For unrestricted support.

$25,000 to Blessed John XXIII National Seminary, Weston, MA. For unrestricted support.

$25,000 to Episcopal Divinity School, Cambridge, MA. For unrestricted support.

$25,000 to Gordon College, Wenham, MA. For unrestricted support.

$25,000 to Northwest Baptist Seminary, Tacoma, WA. For unrestricted support.

3877
The DeLuca Family Charitable Trust ◇ ☆

P.O. Box 3069
Andover, MA 01810

Established in 1997 in MA.
Donors: Richard Hindlian; Lease and Rental Mgmt. Corp., Inc.
Foundation type: Independent foundation.
Financial data (yr. ended 12/31/05): Assets, $982,771 (M); gifts received, $325,000; expenditures, $325,213; qualifying distributions, $323,733; giving activities include $323,733 for 11 grants (high: $258,833; low: $400).
Fields of interest: Elementary/secondary education; Boys & girls clubs; Christian agencies & churches; Aging.
Type of support: General/operating support.
Limitations: Applications not accepted. Giving primarily in MA. No grants to individuals.
Application information: Contributes only to pre-selected organizations.
Trustees: Kathleen M. DeLuca; William P. DeLuca.
EIN: 046846332
Selected grants: The following grants were reported in 2005.

$258,833 to Boys and Girls Club of Lawrence, Lawrence, MA.

$15,000 to Central Catholic High School, Lawrence, MA.

$15,000 to Shelter, Inc., Cambridge, MA.

$5,000 to Childrens Hospital Trust, Boston, MA.

$5,000 to Lawrence General Hospital, Lawrence, MA.

$400 to Massachusetts General Hospital, Boston, MA.

3878
Demoulas Foundation ◇

286 Chelmsford St.
Chelmsford, MA 01824   (978) 244-1024
Contact: Telemachus A. Demoulas, Tr.

Established in 1964 in MA.
Donors: Demoulas Super Markets, Inc.; and members of the Demoulas family.
Foundation type: Company-sponsored foundation.
Financial data (yr. ended 12/31/03): Assets, $35,513,383 (L); expenditures, $2,019,731; qualifying distributions, $1,935,819; giving activities include $1,897,205 for 181 grants (high: $1,000,000; low: $250).
Purpose and activities: The foundation supports organizations involved with arts and culture, K-12 and higher education, health, youth development, civic affairs, and religion.
Fields of interest: Arts; Elementary/secondary education; Higher education; Medical care, in-patient care; Health care; Youth development; Public affairs; Christian agencies & churches; Jewish agencies & temples; Religion.
Limitations: Giving primarily in MA.
Application information: Application form not required.
  Initial approach: Proposal
  Deadline(s): None
Trustees: Arthur T. Demoulas; D. Harold Sullivan.
EIN: 042723441
Selected grants: The following grants were reported in 2003.

$1,000,000 to Boston College, Chestnut Hill, MA.

$30,000 to Central Catholic High School, Lawrence, MA.

$25,000 to Catholic Schools Foundation, Boston, MA.

$25,000 to Massachusetts General Hospital, Boston, MA. For Roman W. Sanctis, MD. Clinical Scholar Fund.

$15,000 to Hellenic College/Holy Cross, School of Theology, Brookline, MA.

$14,500 to Celebrity Series of Boston, Boston, MA.

$10,000 to Lawrence General Hospital, Lawrence, MA.

$10,000 to Merrimack College, North Andover, MA.

$10,000 to Pingree School, South Hamilton, MA.

$10,000 to United Negro College Fund, Boston, MA.

3879
Telemachus A. and Irene Demoulas Foundation ◇

286 Chelmsford St.
Chelmsford, MA 01824   (978) 244-1024
Contact: Arthur T. Demoulas, Tr.

Established in 2001 in MA.
Donors: Telemachus A. Demoulas; Irene Demoulas; Arthur T. Demoulas; Frances Demoulas Kettenbach; Glorianne Demoulas Farnham; Caren Demoulas Pasquale.
Foundation type: Independent foundation.
Financial data (yr. ended 12/31/05): Assets, $42,324,561 (M); gifts received, $202,000; expenditures, $2,031,250; qualifying distributions, $2,002,750; giving activities include $1,960,000 for 10 grants (high: $1,250,000; low: $10,000).
Purpose and activities: Giving primarily to Greek Orthodox churches; funding also for a hospital and schools.
Fields of interest: Education; Hospitals (general); Community development; Christian agencies & churches.
Limitations: Giving primarily in St. Concord, MA. No grants to individuals.
Application information:
  Initial approach: Letter
  Deadline(s): None
Trustees: Arthur T. Demoulas; Irene Demoulas; D. Harold Sullivan.
EIN: 043582759
Selected grants: The following grants were reported in 2003.

$1,000,000 to Bentley College, Waltham, MA.

$100,000 to Massachusetts General Hospital, Boston, MA.

$10,000 to Leadership 100, New York, NY. For endowment fund.

3880
Paul W. DiMaura Charitable Trust ◇ ☆

c/o Lourie & Cutler, P.C.
60 State St.
Boston, MA 02109

Established in 1992 in MA.
Donor: Paul W. DiMaura.
Foundation type: Independent foundation.
Financial data (yr. ended 12/31/05): Assets, $256,078 (M); expenditures, $1,043,573; qualifying distributions, $1,030,435; giving activities include $1,030,435 for 27 grants (high: $1,000,000; low: $25).
Purpose and activities: Giving for higher education, hospitals, health and medical treatment, and research.

Fields of interest: Higher education, university; Environment, forests; Hospitals (general); Health organizations; Human services.
Limitations: Applications not accepted. No grants to individuals.
Application information: Contributes only to pre-selected organizations.
Trustees: Karen S. DiMaura; Paul W. DiMaura.
EIN: 046720853
Selected grants: The following grants were reported in 2003.
$50,000 to Genesis Fund, Canton, MA.
$50,000 to University of Pennsylvania, Philadelphia, PA.
$10,500 to Guanacaste Dry Forest Conservation Fund, Philadelphia, PA.
$10,000 to Massachusetts General Hospital, Boston, MA.
$800 to Christmas in the City, Hingham, MA.
$750 to Jimmy Fund, Boston, MA.
$500 to Jewish Vocational School.
$250 to AIDS Action Committee of Massachusetts, Boston, MA.
$250 to Florida Keys Childrens Shelter, Tavernier, FL.
$250 to Littlewand.

3881
Richard K. & Nancy L. Donahue Charitable Foundation
c/o Nancy L. and Richard K. Donahue
52 Belmont Ave.
Lowell, MA 01852
Contact: Nancy L. Donahue, Tr.
E-mail: nldonahue@comcast.net

Established in 1991 in MA.
Donors: Richard K. Donahue; Nancy L. Donahue.
Foundation type: Independent foundation.
Financial data (yr. ended 12/31/05): Assets, $4,369,586 (M); gifts received, $3,943; expenditures, $585,058; qualifying distributions, $569,519; giving activities include $569,519 for 25 grants (high: $401,453; low: $500).
Purpose and activities: Giving for the arts, education, and human services.
Fields of interest: Museums; Performing arts, theater; Arts; Higher education; Education; Health organizations, association; Human services; Foundations (community).
Type of support: General/operating support; Continuing support; Annual campaigns; Capital campaigns; Endowments; Debt reduction; Curriculum development.
Limitations: Giving primarily in the greater Lowell, MA, area. No grants to individuals.
Application information: Application form not required.
Initial approach: Letter
Copies of proposal: 3
Deadline(s): None
Board meeting date(s): Varies
Final notification: 2 weeks
Trustees: David W. Donahue; Nancy L. Donahue; Richard K. Donahue, Jr.
EIN: 043133049
Selected grants: The following grants were reported in 2004.
$1,000,000 to Greater Lowell Community Foundation, Lowell, MA.
$15,000 to Challenge Unlimited, Andover, MA.

$15,000 to Merrimack Repertory Theater, Lowell, MA.
$10,000 to Community Family, Everett, MA.
$10,000 to Lawrence Academy, Groton, MA.
$10,000 to Retarded Adult Rehabilitative Association, Lowell, MA.
$3,000 to Merrimack Valley Housing Partnership, Lowell, MA.
$1,000 to Community Teamwork, Lowell, MA.
$1,000 to Girls Inc., Taunton, MA.

3882
The Downs Foundation ✧ ☆
c/o Bingham Dana
150 Federal St.
Boston, MA 02110

Established in 2000 in MA.
Donor: Frederick S. Downs, Jr.
Foundation type: Independent foundation.
Financial data (yr. ended 12/31/05): Assets, $706,281 (M); expenditures, $365,667; qualifying distributions, $329,800; giving activities include $329,800 for grants.
Fields of interest: Higher education.
Limitations: Applications not accepted. Giving primarily in VA. No grants to individuals.
Application information: Contributes only to pre-selected organizations.
Director: Frederick S. Downs, Jr.
EIN: 043541593
Selected grants: The following grants were reported in 2004.
$50,000 to Brewster Baptist Church, Brewster, MA. For unrestricted support.
$25,000 to KW International, Mukilteo, WA. For unrestricted support.
$15,000 to Delhi Council for Child Welfare, Delhi, India. For unrestricted support.
$15,000 to Roxbury Latin School, West Roxbury, MA. For unrestricted support.
$10,000 to HelpAge India, New Delhi, India. For unrestricted support.
$10,000 to Oberlin College, Oberlin, OH. For unrestricted support.
$10,000 to Tenacre Country Day School, Wellesley, MA. For unrestricted support.
$5,000 to University of Virginia, Law School, Charlottesville, VA.

3883
Druker Charitable Foundation ✧ ☆
c/o Goulston & Storrs
400 Atlantic Ave., Rm. 401
Boston, MA 02110

Established in 1982 in MA.
Donor: Bertram A. Drucker‡.
Foundation type: Independent foundation.
Financial data (yr. ended 9/30/05): Assets, $10,836,508 (M); expenditures, $509,159; qualifying distributions, $421,125; giving activities include $421,125 for grants.
Purpose and activities: Giving for medical centers and higher education.
Fields of interest: Higher education, college; Hospitals (general).
Limitations: Applications not accepted. Giving primarily in the greater Boston, MA, area. No grants to individuals.

Application information: Contributes only to pre-selected organizations.
Trustees: Ronald M. Druker; Phillip J. Nexon.
EIN: 042751060
Selected grants: The following grants were reported in 2004.
$90,000 to Huntington Theater Company, Boston, MA.
$2,500 to Newton-Wellesley Hospital, Newton, MA.

3884
Dunn Family Charitable Foundation ✧
c/o AHI
119 Russell St., Rm. 22
Littleton, MA 01460

Established in 1993 in MA.
Donor: Raymond J. Dunn III.
Foundation type: Independent foundation.
Financial data (yr. ended 10/31/05): Assets, $12,189,929 (M); expenditures, $657,302; qualifying distributions, $646,158; giving activities include $600,635 for 80 grants (high: $100,000; low: $35).
Fields of interest: Higher education; Education; Health organizations; Human services; Children/youth, services; Community development; Federated giving programs.
Limitations: Applications not accepted. Giving primarily in MA. No grants to individuals.
Application information: Contributes only to pre-selected organizations.
Officers and Trustees:* William J. Chase,* Cont.; Raymond J. Dunn III,* Mgr.; Louise Dunn III; Margaret Dunn; Martin Dunn; Peter Dunn; Raymond J. Dunn IV.
EIN: 043251269

3885
The Dusky Foundation ✧ ☆
c/o Robert S. Gulick
50 Congress St., Ste. 925
Boston, MA 02109-4075

Established in 1991 in MA.
Foundation type: Independent foundation.
Financial data (yr. ended 12/31/05): Assets, $2,873,232 (M); gifts received, $88,853; expenditures, $513,108; qualifying distributions, $491,500; giving activities include $491,500 for 37 grants (high: $105,000; low: $2,000).
Purpose and activities: Giving primarily for education, social, cultural, and inner-city.
Fields of interest: Performing arts, music; Arts; Higher education; Education; Environment, natural resources; Children/youth, services.
Type of support: General/operating support; Continuing support; Capital campaigns; Building/renovation; Equipment.
Limitations: Applications not accepted. Giving primarily in New England, with emphasis on Boston, MA. No grants to individuals.
Application information: Contributes only to pre-selected organizations.
Board meeting date(s): Quarterly
Trustees: J. Linzee Coolidge; Robert S. Gulick.
EIN: 043122206
Selected grants: The following grants were reported in 2004.
$33,000 to Brantwood Camp, Boston, MA.

$15,000 to Walker Home and School, Needham, MA.

$10,000 to Essex County Community Foundation, Danvers, MA. 2 grants: $5,000 each

$10,000 to Our Lady of Lourdes School, Boston, MA.

$10,000 to Womens Educational and Industrial Union, Boston, MA.

$8,000 to Camp Howe, Goshen, MA.

$6,000 to Childrens Literacy Foundation, Hanover, NH.

$5,000 to Associated Early Care and Education, Boston, MA.

$3,000 to Saint Marks School, Southborough, MA.

3886
Eastern Bank Charitable Foundation ✦

195 Market St., EP5-02
Lynn, MA 01901 (781) 598-7888
Contact: Laura Kurzrok, Exec. Dir.
FAX: (781) 596-4445;
E-mail: l.kurzrok@easternbk.com; TDD/TTY tel.: (781) 596-4408; URL: http://www.easternbank.com/a_charitable_foundation.html

Established in 1985 in MA.
Donor: Eastern Bank.
Foundation type: Company-sponsored foundation.
Financial data (yr. ended 12/31/05): Assets, $39,411,411 (M); gifts received, $6,500,000; expenditures, $4,199,948; qualifying distributions, $3,939,341; giving activities include $3,760,657 for 1,201 grants (high: $100,000), and $171,649 for employee matching gifts.
Purpose and activities: The foundation supports organizations involved with education, health, affordable housing, human services, community development, and science.
Fields of interest: Education; Health care; Housing/shelter; Children, services; Family services; Human services; Community development; Federated giving programs; Science.
Type of support: General/operating support; Annual campaigns; Capital campaigns; Building/renovation; Program development; Scholarship funds; Sponsorships; Employee matching gifts.
Limitations: Giving primarily in eastern MA.
Publications: Annual report (including application guidelines); Corporate report.
Application information: Community Donations are grants less than $10,000; Eastern Bank Grants are grants greater than $10,000; Eastern Bank Grants generally do not exceed $25,000. The Associated Grantmakers of Massachusetts Common Proposal Form is required for Eastern Bank Grants. Proposals should be submitted using organization letterhead. Eastern Bank Grants are limited to 1 contribution per organization during any given 3-year period. Application form required.
Initial approach: Download application form and mail or E-mail proposal and application form to foundation for Community Donations; download application form and Associated Grantmakers of Massachusetts Common Proposal Form for Eastern Bank Grants
Copies of proposal: 1
Deadline(s): None for Community Donations; Apr. 1 and Oct. 1 for Eastern Bank Grants

Board meeting date(s): Monthly for Community Donations; June and Dec. for Eastern Bank Grants
Final notification: 60 days for Community Donations; within 30 days following board meetings for Eastern Bank Grants
Trustees: Richard C. Bane; William F. Collins, Jr.; Daryl A. Hellman; Deborah C. Jackson; Andre C. Jasse, Jr.; Wendell J. Knox; Stanley J. Lukowski; George E. Massaro; Nils P. Peterson; Roger D. Scoville; Michael B. Sherman.
Number of staff: 1 full-time professional; 1 part-time support.
EIN: 223317340
Selected grants: The following grants were reported in 2003.
$100,000 to Salem State College Foundation, Salem, MA. For capital campaign.
$75,000 to Peabody Essex Museum, Salem, MA. For capital campaign.
$25,000 to Saint Marys High School, Westfield, MA. For capital campaign.
$10,000 to Boys and Girls Club of Waltham, Waltham, MA. For capital campaign.
$4,900 to YMCA, South Shore, Quincy, MA. For annual support.
$2,500 to Casa Myrna Vasquez, Boston, MA. For program support.
$2,500 to My Brothers Table, Lynn, MA. For annual campaign.
$2,500 to United Way, North Shore, Beverly, MA. For annual support.
$500 to Quincy Community Action Programs, Quincy, MA. For general support.
$100 to Beverly Bootstraps Food Pantry, Beverly, MA. For annual support.

3887
Easthampton Savings Foundation ✦ ☆

36 Main St.
Easthampton, MA 01027 (413) 527-4111
Contact: Richard W. Kozak, Treas.

Established in 1997 in MA.
Donor: Easthampton Savings Bank.
Foundation type: Company-sponsored foundation.
Financial data (yr. ended 12/31/05): Assets, $743,795 (M); gifts received, $220,000; expenditures, $346,721; qualifying distributions, $346,721; giving activities include $346,636 for 249 grants (high: $100,000; low: $25).
Purpose and activities: The foundation supports organizations involved with arts and culture, education, athletics, human services, and disabled people.
Fields of interest: Arts; Higher education; Education, services; Education; Hospitals (general); Health care; Athletics/sports, amateur leagues; Athletics/sports, golf; Human services; Disabilities, people with.
Type of support: General/operating support; Annual campaigns; Capital campaigns; Building/renovation; Program development; Sponsorships.
Limitations: Giving primarily in MA.
Application information: Application form required.
Initial approach: Contact foundation for application form
Officers and Directors: William S. Horgan, Jr., Pres.; Kenneth S. Cernak,* Clerk; Richard W. Kozak,* Treas.; Richard A. Boulanger; David J. Fagnand; James G. Hayden, D.V.M.
EIN: 043371592

3888
Georgiana Goddard Eaton Memorial Fund ✦

c/o Welch & Forbes LLC
45 School St.
Boston, MA 02108
Contact: Philip Hall, Admin.
Application address: c/o Grants Mgmt. Assocs., 77 Summer St., 8th Fl., Boston, MA 02110-1006; tel.: (617) 426-7080, FAX: (617) 426-7087; E-mail: phall@grantsmanagement.com; URL: http://www.grantsmanagement.com/eatonnoapps.html

Trust established in 1917 in MA.
Foundation type: Independent foundation.
Financial data (yr. ended 6/30/06): Assets, $11,589,539 (M); expenditures, $661,871; qualifying distributions, $488,937; giving activities include $432,002 for 1 grant, and $44,418 for 3 grants to individuals (high: $20,328; low: $7,247).
Purpose and activities: Giving to agencies dedicated to improving the lives of low-income individuals of Boston, MA, including support for a named charity, and a rehabilitation agency.
Fields of interest: Education; Legal services; Employment; Housing/shelter; Human services; Family services; Homeless, human services; Urban/community development.
Type of support: General/operating support; Program development; Seed money.
Limitations: Giving limited to Boston, MA. No grants to individuals (except former employees of Community Workshops, Inc.), or for endowment funds, or matching gifts; no loans.
Publications: Application guidelines.
Application information: Application guidelines are available on the fund's Web site. Application form not required.
Initial approach: Telephone
Copies of proposal: 1
Deadline(s): Mar. 1 and Sept. 1
Board meeting date(s): May/June and Nov./Dec.
Final notification: June and Dec.
Trustees: Thomas N. Dabney; Oliver A. Spalding.
Number of staff: 2 part-time professional; 1 part-time support.
EIN: 046112820
Selected grants: The following grants were reported in 2005.
$320,418 to Community Work Services, Boston, MA.

3889
The Edgerly Foundation ✦

(formerly Foundation for Partnerships Trust)
c/o Ropes & Gray, attn.: Truman S. Casner, et al.
1 International Pl.
Boston, MA 02110-2624

Established in 1992 in MA.
Donors: William S. Edgerly; Lois Stiles Edgerly.
Foundation type: Independent foundation.
Financial data (yr. ended 12/31/04): Assets, $5,870,399 (M); expenditures, $443,558; qualifying distributions, $404,650; giving activities include $405,500 for grants.
Purpose and activities: Giving primarily for education and community development.
Fields of interest: Elementary/secondary education; Education; Legal services; Employment, labor unions/organizations; International affairs,

foreign policy; Community development; Federated giving programs.

Limitations: Applications not accepted. Giving primarily in MA. No grants to individuals.

Application information: Contributes only to pre-selected organizations.

Trustees: Truman S. Casner; Lois Stiles Edgerly; William S. Edgerly.

EIN: 043165980

3890
Egan Family Foundation ✧
116 Flanders Rd., Ste. 3000
Westborough, MA   01581

Established in 1993 in MA.

Donor: Maureen E. Egan.

Foundation type: Independent foundation.

Financial data (yr. ended 9/30/05): Assets, $12,166,029 (M); gifts received, $500; expenditures, $1,275,619; qualifying distributions, $1,064,769; giving activities include $963,717 for 50 grants (high: $275,000; low: $100).

Purpose and activities: Support primarily for health care, education, and for children, youth and social services.

Fields of interest: Education; Environment, natural resources; Health organizations, association; Human services; Children/youth, services.

Limitations: Applications not accepted. Giving primarily in MA; some funding nationally. No grants to individuals.

Application information: Contributes only to pre-selected organizations. Unsolicited requests for funds not accepted.

Officer: Catherine E. Walkey, Exec. Dir.

Trustees: Christopher F. Egan; John R. Egan; Michael J. Egan; Maureen E. Petracca.

EIN: 043211653

Selected grants: The following grants were reported in 2004.

$300,000 to Alliance to Protect Nantucket Sound, Hyannis, MA.

$100,000 to Diocese of Helena, Helena, MT.

$100,000 to Marine Corps Heritage Foundation, Quantico, VA.

$60,000 to Fay School, Southborough, MA.

$50,000 to Inner-City Scholarship Fund, Boston, MA.

$19,500 to Boston Symphony Orchestra, Boston, MA.

$15,000 to Massachusetts Charter School Association, Haydenville, MA.

$10,000 to Bridge Over Troubled Waters, Boston, MA.

$10,000 to Museum of the City of New York, New York, NY.

$5,000 to Lazarus House, Lawrence, MA.

3891
The Ellison Foundation ▼ ✧
c/o David L. Babson Co.
1 Memorial Dr.
Cambridge, MA   02142-1300
Contact: Elton F. Drew, Tr.

Established in 1952 in MA.

Donors: Eben H. Ellison†; William P. Ellison†; Harriot Ellison Rogers†.

Foundation type: Independent foundation.

Financial data (yr. ended 12/31/04): Assets, $82,959,611 (M); expenditures, $5,192,147; qualifying distributions, $4,261,484; giving activities include $4,153,000 for 33 grants (high: $1,000,000; low: $5,000; average: $20,000–$100,000).

Purpose and activities: Emphasis on a hospital; support also for higher education.

Fields of interest: Higher education; Hospitals (general).

Limitations: Applications not accepted. Giving primarily in MA. No grants to individuals.

Application information: Contributes only to pre-selected organizations. Generally awards are made to the same organizations year to year, with occasional one-time grants made to organizations solicited by the foundation.

Trustees: Francis L. Coolidge; Elton F. Drew; Andrew Silverman.

EIN: 046050704

Selected grants: The following grants were reported in 2004.

$1,000,000 to American Cancer Society, Framingham, MA.

$1,000,000 to Massachusetts General Hospital, Boston, MA.

$750,000 to Newton-Wellesley Hospital, Newton, MA.

$200,000 to Harvard University, Cambridge, MA. For Harvard Center for Cancer Prevention at School of Public Health in Boston.

$108,000 to University of Massachusetts Memorial Medical Center, Worcester, MA.

$100,000 to Dana-Farber Cancer Institute, Boston, MA.

$85,000 to 200 Foundation, Framingham, MA.

$65,000 to Salvation Army of Boston, Boston, MA.

$40,000 to Two/Ten International Footwear Foundation (TTF), Waltham, MA.

$30,000 to Make-A-Wish Foundation of Greater Boston, Boston, MA.

3892
Ruth H. and Warren A. Ellsworth Foundation ✧
370 Main St., 12th Fl., Ste. 1250
Worcester, MA   01608   (508) 798-8621
Contact: Sumner B. Tilton, Jr., Tr.

Trust established in 1964 in MA.

Donor: Ruth H. Ellsworth†.

Foundation type: Independent foundation.

Financial data (yr. ended 12/31/05): Assets, $20,861,643 (M); expenditures, $1,034,492; qualifying distributions, $968,650; giving activities include $799,150 for 93 grants (high: $125,000; low: $250).

Purpose and activities: Emphasis on higher education, scientific research, youth agencies, and hospitals.

Fields of interest: Visual arts; Performing arts; Arts; Education, fund raising/fund distribution; Child development, education; Higher education; Education; Hospitals (general); Health care; Substance abuse, services; Health organizations, association; Human services; Children/youth, services; Child development, services; Family services; Community development; Engineering/technology; Science; Economically disadvantaged.

Type of support: General/operating support; Continuing support; Annual campaigns; Building/renovation; Equipment; Land acquisition; Debt reduction; Emergency funds; Seed money.

Limitations: Giving primarily in the Worcester, MA, area. No grants to individuals, or for endowment funds, scholarships, fellowships, research, publications, conferences, or matching gifts; no loans.

Application information: Application form not required.

Initial approach: Letter
Copies of proposal: 1
Deadline(s): June 1
Board meeting date(s): June and Dec.
Final notification: By Dec. 28

Trustees: David H. Ellsworth; Joyce Wetzel Hall; Sumner B. Tilton, Jr.; Mark R. Wetzel; Todd H. Wetzel.

Number of staff: 1 part-time professional.

EIN: 046113491

3893
The Elqui Valley Foundation ✧ ☆
c/o Choate, Hall & Stewart
2 International Pl.
Boston, MA   02110

Established in 1999 in MA.

Donor: Maria J. Grasso.

Foundation type: Independent foundation.

Financial data (yr. ended 6/30/05): Assets, $3,468,975 (M); expenditures, $493,548; qualifying distributions, $485,112; giving activities include $481,750 for 4 grants (high: $220,000; low: $11,750).

Purpose and activities: Giving primarily to Adventist relief organizations and schools.

Limitations: Applications not accepted. Giving primarily in MA and MD. No grants to individuals.

Application information: Contributes only to pre-selected organizations.

Trustees: Angelo J. Grasso; Maria J. Grasso; Ana Maria Patterson.

EIN: 043484088

3894
Encourage, Inc. ✧
1400 Computer Dr., Ste. 300
Westborough, MA   01581

Established in 1986 in FL.

Donors: Edward W. Poitras; Kay G. Poitras.

Foundation type: Independent foundation.

Financial data (yr. ended 11/30/04): Assets, $63,702 (M); gifts received, $650,000; expenditures, $659,495; qualifying distributions, $658,836; giving activities include $653,874 for 29 grants (high: $45,000; low: $3,000).

Fields of interest: Christian agencies & churches; Protestant agencies & churches.

Limitations: Applications not accepted. No grants to individuals.

Application information: Contributes only to pre-selected organizations.

Officer: Paula Miner, Treas. and Convener.

Trustees: Edward W. Poitras; Kay G. Poitras; David Bryan; G. Comforted Keen; Jay Lauer; Francis MacNutt; Thomas G. Riley.

EIN: 592752833

3895
Endowment for Biblical Research, Boston ◇ ☆
2 Boulder Top
Rockport, MA 01966 (978) 546-5284
Contact: Virginia Stopfel, Secy.

Established in 1920 in MA.
Donor: Mary Beecher Longyear†.
Foundation type: Independent foundation.
Financial data (yr. ended 12/31/04): Assets, $3,289,928 (M); expenditures, $358,411; qualifying distributions, $334,461; giving activities include $327,000 for 1 grant.
Purpose and activities: To facilitate and advance research on the Bible and to increase public understanding of the Bible, its application to human needs, and biblically related religious history.
Fields of interest: Theology.
Type of support: Research.
Limitations: Giving primarily in Cambridge, MA. No support for denominational and non-biblical education.
Publications: Informational brochure (including application guidelines).
Application information: Funds largely committed, but proposals invited. Application form not required.
Initial approach: Proposal (no more than 2 pages) on organization letterhead
Copies of proposal: 1
Deadline(s): Mar. 1 and Sept. 1
Board meeting date(s): Apr. and Oct.
Final notification: May and Nov.
Officers and Trustees:* Virginia B. Stopfel,* Secy.; Charles A. Stocking,* Treas.; Bruce Butterfield; Lance Carden; Stephen R. Howard; Heather Williams.
Number of staff: 1 part-time professional.
EIN: 042104439

3896
EOS Foundation ◇
13 Cameron Rd.
Harvard, MA 01451
Contact: Kenneth S. Nickerson, Tr.

Established in 1999 in MA.
Donors: Kenneth S. Nickerson; Katherine A. Deyst.
Foundation type: Independent foundation.
Financial data (yr. ended 6/30/05): Assets, $13,534,490 (M); gifts received, $380,000; expenditures, $1,347,220; qualifying distributions, $1,345,000; giving activities include $1,345,000 for 10 grants (high: $250,000; low: $25,000).
Fields of interest: Hospitals (general); Food services; Housing/shelter, development.
Limitations: Applications not accepted.
Application information: Unsolicited requests for funds not accepted.
Trustees: Katherine A. Deyst; Kenneth S. Nickerson.
EIN: 043494831
Selected grants: The following grants were reported in 2005.
$250,000 to Food Project, Lincoln, MA.
$250,000 to Phillips Exeter Academy, Exeter, NH.
$200,000 to Boston Medical Center, Boston, MA.
$200,000 to Center for Women and Enterprise, Boston, MA.
$200,000 to Docs for Tots, DC.
$40,000 to Living Independently Forever, Hyannis, MA.

3897
Essex County Community Foundation, Inc.
15 Cherry St.
Danvers, MA 01923 (978) 777-8876
FAX: (978) 777-9454; *E-mail:* info@eccf.org; Grants update E-mail: response@eccf.org; *URL:* http://www.eccf.org

Established in 1998 in MA.
Foundation type: Community foundation.
Financial data (yr. ended 6/30/05): Assets, $6,597,089 (M); gifts received, $2,763,733; expenditures, $1,511,596; giving activities include $886,005 for 186 grants (high: $60,000; low: $250).
Purpose and activities: The mission of the foundation is to foster connections across Essex County, MA between those who offer of themselves and those in need through philanthropy, endowment, advocacy, collaboration, and education.
Fields of interest: Arts; Education; Environment; Youth development; Human services.
Type of support: Equipment; Emergency funds; Program development; Seed money; Scholarship funds; Technical assistance; Program evaluation.
Limitations: Giving limited to Essex County, MA. No support for sectarian or religious purposes. No grants to individuals, or for debt or deficit reduction.
Publications: Application guidelines; Annual report; Informational brochure.
Application information: The focus of the foundation's discretionary fund is being redesigned; visit foundation Web site for application information and updates. Application form required.
Board meeting date(s): Usually held in Mar., June, Sept., and Dec.
Officers and Directors:* Joseph Trustey,* Chair.; Paula Shorts,* Vice-Chair.; Ashley Allison,* C.E.O. and Pres.; Chuck von Bruns,* Treas.; Steve Bergholtz; Ken Block; Tom Burger; Susan Coffin; Christopher Corbett; Christopher Cowans; Kathleen Hines; Juliet Nagle; Michael Prior; Richard Purinton; William Rogers; Deborah Pechet Quinan; Debra Silberstein; Tesa Van Munching.
Number of staff: 1 full-time professional; 1 full-time support.
EIN: 043407816

3898
The Evans Family Foundation ◇
82 Lenox St.
Newton, MA 02465-3014

Established in 2000 in MA.
Donors: Bruce R. Evans; Bridgitt B. Evans.
Foundation type: Independent foundation.
Financial data (yr. ended 12/31/05): Assets, $3,702,747 (M); gifts received, $1,446,400; expenditures, $488,059; qualifying distributions, $472,258; giving activities include $472,258 for 30 grants (high: $125,000; low: $100).
Fields of interest: Museums (art); Elementary/secondary education; Business school/education; Education; Health organizations, association; Human services; Christian agencies & churches.
Type of support: General/operating support; Annual campaigns.
Limitations: Applications not accepted. Giving on a national basis, primarily in MA and New York, NY. No grants to individuals.
Application information: Contributes only to pre-selected organizations.

Trustees: Bridgitt B. Evans; Bruce R. Evans.
EIN: 043523698
Selected grants: The following grants were reported in 2004.
$125,000 to Winsor School, Boston, MA.
$40,000 to Fessenden School, West Newton, MA.
$15,000 to City Year.
$5,000 to Telluride Academy, Telluride, CO.
$2,000 to Boys and Girls Club.
$1,500 to Harvard Business School Fund, Boston, MA.
$500 to Sigma Chi Foundation, Evanston, IL.

3899
Charles H. Farnsworth Trust
c/o U.S. Trust Co. of Boston
225 Franklin St.
Boston, MA 02110
Contact: Marilyn E. Wales

Trust established in 1930; became a charitable trust in 1978.
Donor: Charles H. Farnsworth†.
Foundation type: Independent foundation.
Financial data (yr. ended 9/30/05): Assets, $28,340,685 (M); expenditures, $1,684,500; qualifying distributions, $1,615,942; giving activities include $1,537,812 for 34 grants.
Purpose and activities: To assist elderly persons to live with dignity and independence. Special focus on services which help prevent premature institutionalization. Grants fostering the development of housing for the elderly are of special interest.
Fields of interest: Housing/shelter, development; Aging, centers/services; Aging.
Type of support: General/operating support; Capital campaigns; Building/renovation; Equipment; Program development; Seed money; Technical assistance.
Limitations: Giving limited to MA. No grants to individuals.
Publications: Application guidelines; Grants list.
Application information: Application form not required.
Initial approach: Proposal
Copies of proposal: 1
Deadline(s): Feb. 1, May 1, Aug. 1, and Nov. 1
Board meeting date(s): Mar., June, Sept., and Dec.
Final notification: Within 1 month of meeting
Trustee: U.S. Trust Co. of Boston.
Number of staff: 2 part-time support.
EIN: 046096075

3900
The Fassino Foundation, Inc. ◇ ☆
42 Eliot Hill Rd.
Natick, MA 01760
Contact: Edward G. Fassino, Pres.
E-mail: efassino@mediaone.net

Established in 1992 in MA.
Donor: Edward G. Fassino.
Foundation type: Independent foundation.
Financial data (yr. ended 9/30/05): Assets, $3,431,388 (M); expenditures, $327,700; qualifying distributions, $322,450; giving activities include $276,450 for 15+ grants (high: $50,000), and $46,000 for 10 grants to individuals (high: $5,000; low: $4,000).

Purpose and activities: Support for community-based organizations that aid homeless, abused, and disabled children and their families. The foundation also grants college scholarships to specific high schools.

Fields of interest: Education; Crime/violence prevention, domestic violence; Children/youth, services; Family services; Disabilities, people with; Homeless.

Limitations: Giving primarily in the greater Boston, MA, area.

Application information: Application form required.

Initial approach: Letter
Deadline(s): None

Officers: Edward G. Fassino, Pres.; Alan L. Stanzler, Clerk; Lillian M. Fassino, Treas.

EIN: 043177633

3901
The Feldberg Family Foundation ◇
P.O. Box 9175
Framingham, MA   01701

Established in 1951 in MA.

Donors: Max Feldberg; Morris Feldberg†.

Foundation type: Independent foundation.

Financial data (yr. ended 12/31/04): Assets, $1,253,617 (M); expenditures, $1,019,153; qualifying distributions, $990,000; giving activities include $990,000 for 4 grants (high: $575,000; low: $15,000).

Purpose and activities: Giving primarily to Jewish federated giving programs, as well as to a university.

Fields of interest: Higher education; Human services; Jewish federated giving programs.

Limitations: Applications not accepted. Giving primarily in MA. No grants to individuals.

Application information: Contributes only to pre-selected organizations.

Board meeting date(s): As required

Trustees: Stanley H. Feldberg; Sumner Feldberg; Barbara Stern.

EIN: 046065393

3902
F. Felix Foundation ◇
100 Larkspur Dr.
Amherst, MA   01002

Established in 2000 in DE and MA.

Foundation type: Independent foundation.

Financial data (yr. ended 9/30/05): Assets, $9,062,159 (M); expenditures, $637,371; qualifying distributions, $587,607; giving activities include $488,810 for 23 grants (high: $281,000; low: $100).

Fields of interest: Human services.

Limitations: Applications not accepted. Giving primarily in MA; some funding nationally. No grants to individuals.

Application information: Contributes only to pre-selected organizations.

Officers and Directors:* Robert Mazer,* Pres.; Magdalena Mazer,* V.P.; Thomas R. Asher, Secy.

EIN: 043464255

Selected grants: The following grants were reported in 2004.

$300,312 to Stop It Now, Northampton, MA.
$100,000 to Proteus Fund, Amherst, MA.
$25,000 to Spirit in Action, Belchertown, MA.
$5,000 to Peace Development Fund, Amherst, MA.

$2,000 to Coalition for Equality in New Mexico, Santa Fe, NM.
$1,000 to Generation Five, San Francisco, CA.
$500 to National Priorities Project, Northampton, MA.

3903
The Elizabeth T. Fessenden Charitable Foundation ◇
c/o Northeast Investment Mgmt., Inc.
150 Federal St., Ste. 1000
Boston, MA   02110-1870

Established in 1995 in MA.

Foundation type: Independent foundation.

Financial data (yr. ended 7/31/05): Assets, $6,367,404 (M); expenditures, $464,539; qualifying distributions, $426,743; giving activities include $415,000 for 20 grants (high: $30,000; low: $5,000).

Purpose and activities: Giving primarily for education and theater.

Fields of interest: Media, television; Museums (art); Performing arts, orchestra (symphony); Historic preservation/historical societies; Higher education; Libraries (public); Education; Environment, natural resources; Botanical gardens; Horticulture/garden clubs; Hospitals (general); Reproductive health, family planning.

Limitations: Applications not accepted. Giving limited to MA. No grants to individuals.

Application information: Contributes only to pre-selected organizations.

Trustees: Katherine C. Ferguson; Neil W. Rice; Louise C. Riemer.

EIN: 223432161

3904
Fidelity Foundation ▼
82 Devonshire St., S2
Boston, MA   02109-3614   (617) 563-6806
Contact: Margaret H. Morton, Sr. V.P., Prog.
URL: http://www.fidelityfoundation.org

Trust established in 1965 in MA.

Donors: FMR Corp.; Fidelity Ventures Ltd.

Foundation type: Company-sponsored foundation.

Financial data (yr. ended 12/31/05): Assets, $372,237,853 (M); gifts received, $4,101,465; expenditures, $16,393,507; qualifying distributions, $15,386,320; giving activities include $13,914,788 for grants.

Purpose and activities: The foundation supports organizations involved with arts and culture, education, health, medical research, human services, and community development.

Fields of interest: Arts; Education; Health care; Medical research, institute; Human services; Community development.

International interests: Canada.

Type of support: Building/renovation; Equipment; Land acquisition; Endowments; Program development; Conferences/seminars; Publication; Curriculum development; Research; Technical assistance; Consulting services; Employee matching gifts; Matching/challenge support.

Limitations: Giving on a national basis and in Canada, with emphasis on areas of company operations, including Northern KY, Boston and Marlborough, MA, Merrimack, NH, Jersey City, NJ, lower Manhattan, NY, NC, Cincinnati, OH,

Smithfield, RI, Dallas, Fort Worth, and northern TX, Salt Lake City, UT, and Toronto, Canada. No support for start-up, sectarian, or civic organizations, public school systems, or disease-specific organizations. No grants to individuals, or for general operating support, sponsorships, scholarships, benefits, corporate memberships, or video or film projects.

Publications: Application guidelines; Informational brochure (including application guidelines).

Application information: Additional information may be requested at a later date. Application form required.

Initial approach: Download application form and mail to nearest regional office
Copies of proposal: 1
Deadline(s): None
Final notification: 3 to 6 months

Officers and Trustees:* Anne-Marie Soulliere,* Pres.; Margaret H. Morton, Sr. V.P., Prog.; Eve K. Nichols, V.P., Science; Thomas P. Ruddy, V.P., Plan. and Admin.; Abigail P. Johnson; Edward C. Johnson III; Ross E. Sherbrooke.

Number of staff: 4 full-time professional; 3 full-time support.

EIN: 046131201

Selected grants: The following grants were reported in 2004.

$2,500,000 to Boston Symphony Orchestra, Boston, MA. For performances.
$1,000,000 to Boys and Girls Clubs of Boston, Boston, MA. For endowment.
$1,000,000 to Museum of Fine Arts, Boston, MA. For acquisitions.
$500,000 to Northern Kentucky University Foundation, Highland Heights, KY. For construction and renovation.
$250,000 to Cathedral High School, Boston, MA. For new construction.
$100,000 to Rogerson Communities, Boston, MA. For equipment.
$75,000 to Thomas More College, Crestview Hills, KY. For construction and renovation.
$50,000 to Big Brothers Big Sisters of North Texas, Arlington, TX. For information technology equipment.
$35,000 to Cincinnati Institute of Fine Arts, Cincinnati, OH. For program support.
$25,000 to YMCA, Merrimack Valley, Lawrence, MA. For construction and renovation.

3905
Fields Pond Foundation, Inc.
5 Turner St.
P.O. Box 540667
Waltham, MA   02454-0667   (781) 899-9990
Contact: Brian H. Rehrig, V.P.
FAX: (781) 899-2819; *E-mail:* info@fieldspond.org;
URL: http://www.fieldspond.org

Established in 1993 in MA.

Foundation type: Independent foundation.

Financial data (yr. ended 12/31/05): Assets, $9,534,281 (M); expenditures, $491,154; qualifying distributions, $468,881; giving activities include $416,250 for 63 grants (high: $15,000; low: $300; average: $1,000–$10,000).

Purpose and activities: Provides assistance to nature and land conservation organizations which are community based, and which serve to increase environmental awareness by involving local residents in conservation issues. The foundation makes grants under the following priorities: 1) project grants for trailmaking and other enhancement of public access to conservation lands, rivers, coastlines, and other natural resources; 2) land acquisition for conservation; 3) assistance in the establishment of endowments as a means of funding stewardship of conservation areas; and 4) related education programs and publications. The foundation encourages proposals from municipal government agencies. It may also consider short-term loans to conservation groups for the purpose of acquiring conservation lands. Outside of the primary mission, it will also consider grant requests from other not-for-profit organizations that have a demonstrated local impact on precollegiate education.

Fields of interest: Elementary/secondary education; Environment, natural resources; Environment.

Type of support: Capital campaigns; Land acquisition; Endowments; Emergency funds; Seed money; Matching/challenge support.

Limitations: Giving primarily in New England. No support for sectarian religious activities. No grants to individuals; or for deficit financing, routine operating budgets, or for funding usually supported by public subscription or through national appeals.

Publications: Application guidelines; Grants list.

Application information: AGM Common Proposal Format is accepted. Application form not required.
  Initial approach: Telephone or submit a 1-page outline prior to submitting full proposal
  Copies of proposal: 2
  Deadline(s): None
  Board meeting date(s): Bimonthly
  Final notification: 3-4 weeks

Officers and Directors:* Leon H. Cohen,* Pres. and Treas.; Brian H. Rehrig,* V.P.; Rhoda R. Cohen,* Clerk; Elizabeth S. Bercow; Nina R. Cohen; Russell A. Cohen.

Number of staff: 1 part-time professional; 1 part-time support.

EIN: 043196041

Selected grants: The following grants were reported in 2005.
$16,000 to Nature Conservancy, Maine Chapter, Brunswick, ME. Toward protection of forest land along Spring and Narraguagus Rivers in Hancock County.
$9,000 to Appalachian Mountain Club, Boston, MA. Toward trail improvements in and around Katahdin Ironworks area of Maine.
$8,000 to Dartmouth Natural Resources Trust, Dartmouth, MA. Toward acquisition of 40-acre addition to protected lands in Little River watershed.
$8,000 to Kestrel Trust, Amherst, MA. Toward aquisition of two additional parcels of Great Meadow, an agricultural area.
$6,000 to 300 Committee, Falmouth, MA. Toward acquisition of 8-acre parcel on Quashnet River.
$2,750 to Maine Coast Heritage Trust, Topsham, ME. Toward trail work at Western Head Preserve in Cutller.

3906

Fieldstone Foundation, Inc. ✧

(formerly Meetinghouse Foundation, Inc.)
636 Great Rd., Ste. 202
Stow, MA   01775

Established in 1990 in MA.
Donor: Thomas R. Shepherd.
Foundation type: Independent foundation.

Financial data (yr. ended 12/31/04): Assets, $4,320,298 (M); expenditures, $471,626; qualifying distributions, $424,326; giving activities include $424,326 for 46 grants (high: $110,000; low: $5).

Fields of interest: Elementary/secondary education; Education, early childhood education; Higher education; Environment.

Limitations: Applications not accepted. Giving primarily in MA and VT. No grants to individuals.

Application information: Contributes only to pre-selected organizations.

Officers and Directors:* Nancy Shepherd,* Pres.; Katharine S. Furney,* Clerk; Thomas R. Shepherd,* Treas.; Elizabeth R. Beneche; Ruth H. Shepherd; T. Nathanial Shepherd.

EIN: 223111728

Selected grants: The following grants were reported in 2004.
$110,000 to Washington and Lee University, Lexington, VA.
$25,000 to Doctor Franklin Perkins School, Lancaster, MA.
$25,000 to Sudbury Valley Trustees, Wayland, MA.
$25,000 to United Way of Massachusetts Bay, Boston, MA.
$8,000 to Notre Dame Education Center, South Boston, MA.
$6,000 to Committee on Temporary Shelter, Burlington, VT.
$6,000 to Wilderness Society, Boston, MA.
$5,000 to Boston Partners in Education, Boston, MA.
$5,000 to ReCycle North, Burlington, VT.
$5,000 to Rosies Place, Boston, MA.

3907

Lincoln and Therese Filene Foundation, Inc.

c/o Nutter, McClennen & Fish, LLP
PO Box 51400
Boston, MA   02205   (617) 439-2000
Contact: Alane H. Wallis
URL: http://www.prephosting.org/filene/grantapp.pdf

Incorporated in 1937 in MA.
Donor: Lincoln Filene†.
Foundation type: Independent foundation.

Financial data (yr. ended 12/31/05): Assets, $21,279,823 (M); expenditures, $1,317,668; qualifying distributions, $1,186,944; giving activities include $1,122,768 for 42 grants (high: $236,668; low: $100).

Purpose and activities: General purposes; grants primarily for civic education, human development and self-sufficiency, music and performing arts education, citizenship, and public education. Funds largely committed to long-term support of existing projects.

Fields of interest: Performing arts; Performing arts, music; Higher education; Education; Youth development, citizenship; Jewish federated giving programs; Public affairs, citizen participation.

Type of support: Program development.

Limitations: Giving limited to the New England area. No support for political groups. No grants to individuals, or for endowment funds, capital campaigns, operating costs, scholarships, fellowships, or religious groups; no loans.

Publications: Application guidelines.

Application information: Funds largely committed. Application guidelines available on foundation Web site. Application form required.
  Initial approach: Letter
  Copies of proposal: 1
  Deadline(s): March 1 and Sept. 1
  Board meeting date(s): May and Nov.
  Final notification: After next semiannual meeting

Officers and Directors:* David A. Robertson, Jr.,* Pres.; Rev. David J. Ladd,* V.P.; Peter A. Brown, Secy.-Treas.; Kimberly Dietel; J. Scott Ladd; John D. Ladd; Lincoln F. Ladd; Robert M. Ladd; Michael E. Mooney; Joan D. Tolley, Jr.

EIN: 237423946

3908

Neal F. Finnegan Charitable Trust ✧

c/o Neal F. Finnegan
87 Atlantic Ave.
Cohasset, MA   02025-1810

Established in 1999 in MA.
Donor: Neal F. Finnegan.
Foundation type: Independent foundation.

Financial data (yr. ended 7/31/05): Assets, $497,398 (M); gifts received, $2,152; expenditures, $363,228; qualifying distributions, $362,600; giving activities include $362,600 for 31 grants (high: $200,000; low: $50).

Fields of interest: Higher education; Health organizations, association; Human services; Federated giving programs; Roman Catholic agencies & churches.

Limitations: Applications not accepted. No grants to individuals.

Application information: Contributes only to pre-selected organizations.

Trustee: Neal F. Finnegan.

EIN: 046898030

Selected grants: The following grants were reported in 2005.
$200,000 to Northeastern University, Boston, MA.
$20,000 to Babson College, Babson Park, MA.
$10,500 to Catholic Charities.
$5,000 to Northwestern University, Evanston, IL.
$5,000 to Rodman Ride for Kids, Foxboro, MA.
$500 to Laboure Center, Boston, MA.

3909

The Paul and Phyllis Fireman Charitable Foundation ✧

c/o A. Mullen
186 South St., 4th Fl.
Boston, MA   02111

Established in 1985 in MA.
Foundation type: Independent foundation.

Financial data (yr. ended 12/31/04): Assets, $112,040,000 (M); gifts received, $4,875; expenditures, $2,783,935; qualifying distributions, $2,882,924; giving activities include $2,445,450 for 92 grants (high: $1,000,000; low: $100), and $220,000 for 1 loan/program-related investment.

Purpose and activities: Giving primarily for performing arts centers, hospitals, human services, and Jewish agencies and temples.

Fields of interest: Performing arts centers; Hospitals (general); Human services; Jewish agencies & temples.

Type of support: Continuing support; Program-related investments/loans.

Limitations: Applications not accepted. Giving primarily in MA. No grants to individuals.
Application information: Contributes only to pre-selected organizations. Unsolicited requests for funds not considered or acknowledged.
Officer: Melinda Marble, Exec. Dir.
Trustees: Paul Fireman; Phyllis Fireman.
EIN: 222677986
Selected grants: The following grants were reported in 2003.
$1,303,025 to One Family Campaign, Boston, MA.
$500,000 to Combined Jewish Philanthropies of Greater Boston, Boston, MA.
$100,000 to Treehouse Foundation, Sharon, MA.
$100,000 to YWCA of Boston, Boston, MA.
$75,000 to Center for Victims of Torture, Minneapolis, MN.
$75,000 to Travelers Aid Family Services, Boston, MA.
$60,000 to Little Sisters of the Assumption, Boston, MA.
$50,100 to Dana-Farber Cancer Institute, Boston, MA.
$50,000 to Willowbend Pro-Am Childrens Charity Golf Tournament, Mashpee, MA.
$35,000 to Massachusetts Coalition for the Homeless, Boston, MA.

3910
The Simon C. Fireman Charitable Foundation ◇
525 Bodwell St.
Avon, MA 02322 (617) 328-4080
Contact: Simon C. Fireman, Tr.
URL: http://www.firemanfoundation.org

Established in 1995 in MA.
Donor: Simon C. Fireman.
Foundation type: Independent foundation.
Financial data (yr. ended 12/31/03): Assets, $684,375 (M); gifts received, $1,673,291; expenditures, $1,520,205; qualifying distributions, $1,515,286; giving activities include $1,403,699 for 30 grants (high: $200,000; low: $350).
Purpose and activities: Giving primarily to health care and to services for the elderly and children; funding also for the performing arts.
Fields of interest: Performing arts, ballet; Performing arts, orchestra (symphony); Hospitals (general); Health care; Health organizations, association; Cancer; Diabetes research; Jewish agencies & temples.
Limitations: Giving primarily in FL and MA. No grants to individuals.
Application information:
Initial approach: Letter
Deadline(s): None
Trustee: Simon C. Fireman.
EIN: 046774656
Selected grants: The following grants were reported in 2003.
$200,000 to Hebrew Rehabilitation Center for Aged, Boston, MA. For general support.
$200,000 to Quincy Medical Center Foundation, Quincy, MA. For general support.
$157,004 to Florida Ballet, Jacksonville, FL. For general support.
$118,100 to American Cancer Society, Atlanta, GA. For general support.
$100,000 to Cystic Fibrosis Foundation, Bethesda, MD. For general support.
$25,000 to Salvation Army National Headquarters, Alexandria, VA. For general support.

$12,500 to Palm Beach Pops Orchestra, West Palm Beach, FL. For general support.
$10,300 to Leukemia & Lymphoma Society, White Plains, NY. For general support.
$10,000 to American Heart Association, Dallas, TX. For general support.
$3,000 to American Lung Association, New York, NY. For general support.

3911
The Flatley Foundation ▼ ◇
50 Braintree Hill Office Park
Braintree, MA 02184-8754 (781) 848-2000

Established in 1982 in MA.
Donor: Thomas J. Flatley.
Foundation type: Independent foundation.
Financial data (yr. ended 12/31/05): Assets, $178,732,183 (M); gifts received, $15,000,000; expenditures, $7,657,681; qualifying distributions, $7,043,200; giving activities include $7,043,200 for 101 grants (high: $2,650,000; low: $200; average: $10,000–$100,000).
Purpose and activities: Giving primarily for education and health care; some giving to Christian organizations.
Fields of interest: Elementary/secondary education; Higher education; Human services; International affairs; Christian agencies & churches.
Limitations: Applications not accepted. Giving primarily in MA. No grants to individuals.
Application information: Contributes only to pre-selected organizations.
Trustee: Thomas J. Flatley.
EIN: 042763837
Selected grants: The following grants were reported in 2005.
$2,650,000 to Fidelity Investments Charitable Gift Fund, Boston, MA. For unrestricted support.
$1,010,000 to Missionaries of Charity, Bronx, NY. For unrestricted support.
$1,000,000 to AmeriCares, Stamford, CT. For unrestricted support.
$400,000 to Catholic Schools Foundation, Boston, MA. For unrestricted support of Inner City Scholarship Fund.
$220,000 to American Ireland Fund, Boston, MA. For unrestricted support.
$200,000 to Roxbury Presbyterian Church, Roxbury, MA. For rebuilding fund.
$125,000 to Salvation Army of Boston, Boston, MA. For unrestricted support.
$40,000 to Elizabeth Seton Academy, Dorchester, MA. For unrestricted support.
$25,000 to Saint Patricks Church, Roxbury, MA. For unrestricted support.
$15,000 to Life Focus Center of Charlestown, Charlestown, MA. For unrestricted support.

3912
Fletcher Foundation ◇
370 Main St., 12th Fl.
Worcester, MA 01608 (508) 459-8000
Contact: Warner S. Fletcher, Secy.-Treas.

Established in 1981 in MA.
Donor: Paris Fletcher†.
Foundation type: Independent foundation.
Financial data (yr. ended 12/31/05): Assets, $27,947,492 (M); expenditures, $1,457,262; qualifying distributions, $1,361,738; giving

activities include $1,313,000 for 72 grants (high: $225,000; low: $1,000).
Purpose and activities: Giving primarily for education, the arts, community development, and human services.
Fields of interest: Arts; Education; Health care; Human services; Children/youth, services; Community development.
Type of support: Seed money; Land acquisition; Equipment; Capital campaigns; Building/renovation; General/operating support.
Limitations: Giving limited to Worcester County, MA, with an emphasis on the city of Worcester. No support for religious organizations. No grants to individuals.
Application information: Application form not required.
Initial approach: Letter and telephone
Copies of proposal: 5
Deadline(s): June 1 and Dec. 1
Board meeting date(s): June and Dec.
Final notification: Within 1 month of distribution meeting
Officers and Trustees:* Allen W. Fletcher,* Chair.; Warner S. Fletcher,* Secy.-Treas.; Mary F. Fletcher; Patricia A. Fletcher.
EIN: 046470890
Selected grants: The following grants were reported in 2004.
$300,000 to Worcester Historical Museum, Worcester, MA.
$100,000 to Boys and Girls Club of Worcester, Worcester, MA.
$75,000 to Worcester Youth Center, Worcester, MA.
$50,000 to American Red Cross, Concord, NH.
$50,000 to Dynamy, Worcester, MA.
$50,000 to Massachusetts College of Pharmacy and Health Sciences, Boston, MA.
$40,000 to Music Worcester, Worcester, MA.
$30,000 to Clark University, Worcester, MA.
$7,500 to Youthnet, Medford, MA.
$5,000 to Higgins Armory Museum, Worcester, MA.

3913
Joseph F. and Clara Ford Foundation ◇ ☆
c/o Leslie K. Lerner
77 Pond Ave., Ste. 801
Brookline, MA 02445-7114

Established in 1946 in MA.
Donors: Clara Ford†; Joseph F. Ford†; Charles A. Fortus†.
Foundation type: Independent foundation.
Financial data (yr. ended 7/31/05): Assets, $1,658,300 (M); expenditures, $647,329; qualifying distributions, $639,011; giving activities include $600,000 for 12 grants (high: $271,056; low: $8,380).
Purpose and activities: Giving primarily for colleges and universities, including medical schools and a Jewish theological seminary; support also for hospitals and Jewish organizations.
Fields of interest: Higher education; Medical school/education; Theological school/education; Hospitals (general); Jewish federated giving programs; Aging.
Limitations: Applications not accepted. Giving primarily in MA. No grants to individuals.
Application information: Contributes only to pre-selected organizations.
Officer: Leslie Lerner, Admin.
EIN: 046111820

3914

Henry & Lois Foster Charitable Foundation ◇

251 Ballardvale St.
Wilmington, MA 01887

Established in 1984 in MA.
Donors: Henry L. Foster; Mrs. Henry L. Foster; Charles River Laboratories, Inc.
Foundation type: Independent foundation.
Financial data (yr. ended 12/31/05): Assets, $2,170,388 (M); expenditures, $374,370; qualifying distributions, $367,720; giving activities include $367,720 for 16 grants (high: $86,000; low: $100).
Purpose and activities: Giving primarily for higher education; funding also for health associations and human services.
Fields of interest: Higher education; Health organizations, association; Human services.
Type of support: General/operating support.
Limitations: Applications not accepted. Giving primarily in MA. No grants to individuals.
Application information: Contributes only to pre-selected organizations.
Trustees: Henry L. Foster; Lois Foster.
EIN: 222572061
Selected grants: The following grants were reported in 2003.
$750,000 to Emerson College, Boston, MA.
$55,000 to Brandeis University, Waltham, MA.
$25,000 to Massachusetts Society for Medical Research, Waltham, MA.
$25,000 to Museum of Fine Arts, Boston, MA.
$10,000 to Americans for Medical Progress Educational Foundation, Alexandria, VA.
$10,000 to Foundation for Biomedical Research, DC.
$10,000 to Massachusetts General Hospital, Boston, MA.
$6,000 to Anti-Defamation League of Bnai Brith, Boston, MA.
$2,500 to Childrens Hospital League, Boston, MA.
$1,200 to Institute of Contemporary Art, Boston, MA.

3915

Foundation for Research in Cell Biology and Cancer ◇

c/o Kurt J. Isselbacher
P.O. Box 290088
Charlestown, MA 02129-3502

Established as a public charity in 1996 in MA; reclassified in 2001.
Donors: Milton Sender; Laune Schwartz; Carmen Family Charitable Foundation; Mrs. John Sullivan; Robert Samuels.
Foundation type: Independent foundation.
Financial data (yr. ended 12/31/05): Assets, $3,463,361 (M); gifts received, $996,158; expenditures, $797,830; qualifying distributions, $789,655; giving activities include $725,000 for 2 grants (high: $700,000; low: $25,000).
Purpose and activities: Gives for marine biological research and to a local hospital.
Fields of interest: Medical school/education; Cancer; Biomedicine; Children, services.
Limitations: Applications not accepted. Giving primarily in Charlestown, MA.
Application information: Contributes only to pre-selected organizations.

Trustees: Roy A. Goldberg, M.B.A., Ph.D.; Eric Isselbacher; Kurt J. Isselbacher, M.D.; Walter Salmon; Laurel Schwartz.
EIN: 042660137
Selected grants: The following grants were reported in 2003.
$340,000 to Massachusetts General Hospital, Children Center, Boston, MA.
$10,000 to Marine Biological Laboratory, Woods Hole, MA.

3916

Foundation M ◇ ☆

P.O. Box 3219
Andover, MA 01810-0804

Established in 2000 in MA.
Donors: Casper Martin; Martin Foundation, Inc.
Foundation type: Independent foundation.
Financial data (yr. ended 6/30/05): Assets, $11,704,944 (M); expenditures, $603,339; qualifying distributions, $518,500; giving activities include $518,500 for 34 grants (high: $50,000; low: $3,500).
Fields of interest: Environment; Animals/wildlife, association; Boys & girls clubs; Human services; YM/YWCAs & YM/YWHAs; Women.
Limitations: Applications not accepted. Giving primarily in MA. No grants to individuals.
Application information: Contributes only to pre-selected organizations.
Trustees: Casper Martin; Linda Woolford.
EIN: 043559359

3917

Fraser Family Foundation, Inc. ◇

c/o Rinet Co., LLC
101 Federal St., 14th Fl.
Boston, MA 02110

Established in 1988 in MA.
Donors: Richard M. Fraser; Richard M. & Helen T. Fraser Foundation.
Foundation type: Independent foundation.
Financial data (yr. ended 12/31/05): Assets, $6,539,885 (M); expenditures, $855,072; qualifying distributions, $812,500; giving activities include $812,500 for 29 grants (high: $500,000; low: $500).
Purpose and activities: Giving primarily for the arts, museums, hospitals, and health associations.
Fields of interest: Media/communications; Museums; Museums (marine/maritime); Performing arts, orchestra (symphony); Education; Hospitals (general); Health organizations, association; Federated giving programs.
Limitations: Applications not accepted. Giving primarily in MA; funding also in FL. Some funding nationally. No grants to individuals.
Application information: Contributes only to pre-selected organizations.
Officers: Richard M. Fraser, Pres.; Helen T. Fraser, Treas.
EIN: 043005593
Selected grants: The following grants were reported in 2004.
$550,000 to W G B H Educational Foundation, Boston, MA. 2 grants: $500,000 (For unrestricted support), $50,000 (For unrestricted support).

$100,000 to Bermuda Maritime Museum, Friends of, Bermuda. For unrestricted support.
$100,000 to Bermuda National Trust, Hamilton, Bermuda. For unrestricted support.
$100,000 to Boca Grande Health Clinic, Boca Grande, FL. For unrestricted support.
$50,000 to Isabella Stewart Gardner Museum, Boston, MA. For unrestricted support.
$25,000 to Bermuda Artworks Foundation, New York, NY. For unrestricted support.
$25,000 to Emory University, Atlanta, GA. For unrestricted support.
$25,000 to Massachusetts General Hospital, Boston, MA. For unrestricted support.
$25,000 to Saint Andrews Church, Boca Grande, FL. For unrestricted support.

3918

The George F. and Sybil H. Fuller Foundation ▼ ◇

370 Main St., Ste. 660
Worcester, MA 01608 (508) 755-1684
Contact: Mark W. Fuller, Chair.
FAX: (508) 755-2634;
E-mail: info@gsfullerfoundation.org; URL: http://www.gsfullerfoundation.org

Trust established in 1955 in MA.
Donors: George Freeman Fuller‡; Sybil H. Fuller.
Foundation type: Independent foundation.
Financial data (yr. ended 12/31/05): Assets, $65,262,488 (M); expenditures, $3,872,058; qualifying distributions, $3,620,000; giving activities include $3,509,000 for 121 grants (high: $250,000; low: $1,000; average: $10,000–$55,000).
Purpose and activities: The foundation's program interests include: 1) Culture - area museums and arts institutions; 2) Education - area colleges; 3) Health care - hospital and support agencies; 4) Social Services - recreation and youth development; and 5) Religious Institutions. The types of projects supported include capital campaigns; new construction; building renovations; historic preservation; equipment, including computer hardware and software; and building furnishings. The foundation occasionally supports scholarship funds, church renovation projects, continuing support, disaster relief, emergency funds, and research.
Fields of interest: Museums; Arts; Higher education; Higher education, university; Health care; Human services.
Type of support: Continuing support; Annual campaigns; Capital campaigns; Building/renovation; Equipment; Land acquisition; Emergency funds; Seed money; Scholarship funds; Research; Matching/challenge support.
Limitations: Giving primarily in MA, with emphasis on Worcester. No grants to individuals, or for endowments, conferences, seminars, cash reserve management programs, or technical assistance or consulting; no loans.
Publications: Application guidelines; Grants list.
Application information: Application form not required.
Initial approach: Telephone or letter of inquiry
Copies of proposal: 1
Deadline(s): 2 weeks before board meeting
Board meeting date(s): Feb., Apr., June, Aug., Oct., and Dec.
Final notification: 1 to 2 months

Officers and Trustees:* Mark W. Fuller,* Chair. and Treas.; Joyce I. Fuller,* Vice-Chair.; Diane H. Robbins,* Secy.; Janice L. Fuller; Lincoln E. Fuller; David P. Hallock.
Number of staff: 1 part-time support.
EIN: 046125606
Selected grants: The following grants were reported in 2003.
$259,000 to EcoTarium, Worcester, MA.
$210,000 to Assumption College, Worcester, MA.
$210,000 to Worcester Polytechnic Institute, Worcester, MA.
$200,000 to Boylston Historical Society and Museum, Boylston, MA.
$200,000 to Worcester Art Museum, Worcester, MA.
$110,000 to Anna Maria College for Men and Women, Paxton, MA.
$110,000 to Becker College, Worcester, MA.
$110,000 to Clark University, Worcester, MA.
$105,000 to Joy of Music Program, Worcester, MA.
$100,000 to American Red Cross, Worcester, MA.

3919
The Gabrieli Family Foundation ✧
c/o Frederick A. Tilton, III
65 Pye Brook Ln.
Boxford, MA   01921

Established in 1991 in CA.
Donors: Christopher F.O. Gabrieli; Hilary B. Gabrieli.
Foundation type: Independent foundation.
Financial data (yr. ended 12/31/04): Assets, $969,517 (M); gifts received, $1,063,715; expenditures, $1,029,515; qualifying distributions, $1,022,250; giving activities include $1,022,250 for 55 grants (high: $870,000; low: $100).
Purpose and activities: Giving primarily for education, particularly for the improvement of educational and economic opportunities for children and families; funding also for the arts and human services.
Fields of interest: Arts; Education; Boys & girls clubs; Human services; Children/youth, services; Family services.
Type of support: Scholarship funds.
Limitations: Applications not accepted. Giving primarily in Boston, MA. No grants to individuals.
Application information: Contributes only to pre-selected organizations.
Officers and Directors: * Christopher F.O. Gabrieli,* Pres.; Frederick A. Tilton III, Treas.; Hilary B. Gabrieli; John D.E. Gabrieli; Lila Gabrieli.
EIN: 770309791
Selected grants: The following grants were reported in 2003.
$850,000 to Massachusetts 2020 Foundation, Boston, MA.
$7,000 to Winsor School, Boston, MA.
$2,500 to Fessenden School, West Newton, MA.
$1,000 to City on a Hill Charter School, Boston, MA.
$1,000 to Jane Doe, The Massachusetts Coalition Against Sexual Assault and Domestic Violence, Boston, MA.
$1,000 to Southfield School, Brookline, MA.
$750 to Pine Street Inn, Boston, MA.
$750 to Rosies Place, Boston, MA.
$500 to Art Institute of Boston, Boston, MA.
$250 to Museum of Fine Arts, Boston, MA.

3920
Gardinor-Prunaret Foundation ✧ ☆
P.O. Box 639
North Andover, MA   01845-0639

Donors: Mildred Gardinor Prunaret†; Henri Prunaret Trust.
Foundation type: Independent foundation.
Financial data (yr. ended 3/31/06): Assets, $5,411,083 (M); expenditures, $390,510; qualifying distributions, $358,000; giving activities include $358,000 for grants.
Fields of interest: Hospitals (general); Health organizations, research; Human services; Children/youth, services.
Type of support: General/operating support.
Limitations: Applications not accepted. Giving primarily in MA. No grants to individuals.
Application information: Contributes only to pre-selected organizations.
Trustee: John R.D. McClintock.
EIN: 042598211
Selected grants: The following grants were reported in 2003.
$120,000 to Morse Institute Library, Natick, MA.
$100,000 to Francis Ouimet Caddie Scholarship Fund, Norton, MA.
$10,000 to Nantucket Land Council, Nantucket, MA.
$5,000 to Boys and Girls Club of Nantucket, Nantucket, MA.
$5,000 to Jackson Laboratory, Bar Harbor, ME.
$5,000 to Visiting Nurse Association, Natick, MA.

3921
The Garfield Foundation ✧
208 Warcham Rd., Ste. 2A
Marion, MA   02738-1146
Contact: Jennie Curtis, Exec. Dir.
FAX: (508) 748-3607;
E-mail: inquiry@garfieldfoundation.org

Established in 1980.
Foundation type: Independent foundation.
Financial data (yr. ended 11/30/04): Assets, $58,276,457 (M); expenditures, $3,793,514; qualifying distributions, $3,469,495; giving activities include $2,929,180 for 77 grants.
Purpose and activities: To stimulate systemic-level solutions to progress towards a more equitable, economically prosperous and environmentally sustainable global society. Grantmaking priorities include sustainable production and consumption, biodiversity conservation, animal welfare and toxic metal pollutant source reduction, and community revitalization. Biodiversity conservation projects are limited to South America, specifically Amazonia and Bolivian Gran Chaco regions.
Fields of interest: Environment, toxics; Environment, natural resources; Animal welfare; Youth development; Economic development; Community development.
International interests: South America.
Limitations: Applications not accepted. No grants to individuals.
Application information: Contributes only to pre-selected organizations.
Trustees: Michael Baldwin; Ronald Berman; Brian Garfield.
Number of staff: 2 full-time professional.
EIN: 222285358
Selected grants: The following grants were reported in 2003.

$250,000 to Natural Step, San Francisco, CA. For general support.
$150,000 to Local Initiatives Support Corporation (LISC), New York, NY. For general support.
$100,000 to Wildlife Waystation, Sylmar, CA. For general support.
$89,500 to Childrens Village, Dobbs Ferry, NY. For general support.
$75,000 to National Wildlife Federation, DC. For general support.
$62,500 to Fight Crime: Invest in Kids, DC. For general support.
$50,000 to Sustainable Cotton Project, Oroville, CA. For general support.
$20,000 to Environmental Grantmakers Association, New York, NY. For general support.
$10,000 to Government Accountability Project (GAP), DC. For general support.
$5,000 to Anti-Defamation League of Bnai Brith, Los Angeles, CA. For general support.

3922
Genzyme Charitable Foundation, Inc. ✧
15 Pleasant St. Connector
Framingham, MA   01701
Application address: 500 Kendall St., Cambridge, MA 02142, tel.: (617) 768-9009

Established as a company-sponsored operating foundation in 1997 in MA.
Donor: Genzyme Corp.
Foundation type: Operating foundation.
Financial data (yr. ended 12/31/05): Assets, $0 (M); gifts received, $43,689,450; expenditures, $43,689,450; qualifying distributions, $43,689,150; giving activities include $43,689,150 for grants.
Purpose and activities: The foundation donates prescription medications Cerezyme for the treatment of Gaucher disease; Fabrazyme, for Fabry disease; and Aldurazyme, for MPS 1 disease, to patients in need.
Type of support: Grants to individuals; Donated products.
Application information: Application form required.
Initial approach: Telephone foundation for application form
Deadline(s): None
Board meeting date(s): Monthly
Officers and Directors: * Henri A. Termeer,* Pres.; Peter Wirth,* Clerk; Michael S. Wyzga,* Treas.
EIN: 043236375

3923
Gerard Health Foundation ✧
21 Eliot St.
Natick, MA   01760

Donor: Raymond & Marilyn Ruddy Charitable Trust.
Foundation type: Independent foundation.
Financial data (yr. ended 12/31/04): Assets, $0 (M); gifts received, $2,450,000; expenditures, $2,580,947; qualifying distributions, $2,501,772; giving activities include $1,996,796 for 28 grants (high: $392,304; low: $225).
Fields of interest: Reproductive health; Human services; Children/youth, services; Family services; Civil rights; Women.
Limitations: Applications not accepted. Giving primarily in MA. No grants to individuals.

Application information: Contributes only to pre-selected organizations.
Officers: Raymond B. Ruddy, Pres.; John M. Malloy, Secy.; Ginger A. Ruddy, Treas.
EIN: 043580039

3924

Germeshausen Foundation, Inc. ✦
60 State St.
Boston, MA 02109 (617) 526-6610
Contact: Martin S. Kaplan, Tr.

Established in 1999 in MA.
Foundation type: Independent foundation.
Financial data (yr. ended 12/31/04): Assets, $14,410,783 (M); expenditures, $944,058; qualifying distributions, $821,914; giving activities include $594,000 for 21 grants (high: $150,000; low: $500).
Purpose and activities: Giving primarily to arts and cultural programs, education, and human services.
Fields of interest: Arts; Education; Human services.
Type of support: General/operating support.
Limitations: Giving primarily in Boston, MA. No grants to individuals.
Publications: Application guidelines.
Application information: Application form not required.
Initial approach: Letter of inquiry
Copies of proposal: 1
Deadline(s): None
Board meeting date(s): As needed
Officers: Nancy G. Klavans, Pres.; Martin S. Kaplan, Secy.-Treas.
EIN: 043485516

3925

Gerondelis Foundation, Inc. ✦
c/o Gregory C. Demakis
56 Central Ave., Ste. 201
Lynn, MA 01901 (781) 595-3311

Established in 1966 in MA.
Foundation type: Independent foundation.
Financial data (yr. ended 12/31/05): Assets, $4,975,341 (M); expenditures, $478,606; qualifying distributions, $478,465; giving activities include $314,000 for 33 grants (high: $100,000; low: $1,000), and $78,000 for 26 grants to individuals (high: $3,000; low: $3,000).
Purpose and activities: Giving primarily for education; funding also for Greek Orthodox churches.
Fields of interest: Higher education; Medical school/education; Education; Hospitals (general); Orthodox Catholic agencies & churches.
International interests: Greece.
Type of support: Scholarship funds.
Limitations: Applications not accepted. Giving primarily in MA. No grants to individuals.
Application information: Contributes only to pre-selected organizations.
Board meeting date(s): 2nd Tues. in Jan., Apr., July, and Oct.
Directors: Phillip Comenos; Gregory C. Demakis; John N. Demakis; Paul C. Demakis; Thomas C. Demakis; Thomas L. Demakis; George J. Macropoulous; Christopher Scangas; Russell Smith; Nicholas T. Zervas, M.D.
Number of staff: 1 part-time support.
EIN: 046130871

Selected grants: The following grants were reported in 2004.
$10,500 to Georgia Institute of Technology, Atlanta, GA.
$7,000 to Massachusetts Institute of Technology, Cambridge, MA.
$7,000 to Northwestern University, Evanston, IL.
$7,000 to University of Southern California, Los Angeles, CA.
$3,500 to Boys and Girls Club of Lynn, Lynn, MA.
$3,500 to Georgia State University, Atlanta, GA.
$3,500 to Hofstra University, Hempstead, NY.
$3,500 to Longy School of Music, Cambridge, MA.
$3,500 to New York University, New York, NY.
$3,500 to University of Central Florida, Orlando, FL.

3926

Israel and Matilda Goldberg Family Foundation ✦
c/o Jomar Co.
209 W. Central St., Ste. 202
Natick, MA 01760

Established in 1952 in MA.
Donors: Israel Goldberg; Albert S. Goldberg; Herbert A. Goldberg.
Foundation type: Independent foundation.
Financial data (yr. ended 12/31/05): Assets, $2,159,881 (M); expenditures, $585,926; qualifying distributions, $578,790; giving activities include $573,505 for 3 grants (high: $250,000; low: $73,505).
Purpose and activities: Emphasis on Jewish welfare funds and temple support.
Fields of interest: Education; Human services; Jewish federated giving programs; Jewish agencies & temples.
Limitations: Applications not accepted. Giving primarily in Holyoke, MA, and FL. No grants to individuals.
Application information: Contributes only to pre-selected organizations.
Trustees: Albert S. Goldberg; Barbara S. Goldberg; Harvey E. Goldberg; Herbert A. Goldberg.
EIN: 046047066

3927

The Goldberg Family Foundation ✦
(formerly Avram & Carol Goldberg Charitable Foundation)
225 Franklin St., Ste. 2700
Boston, MA 02110-2804 (617) 695-1300
Contact: Avram J. Goldberg, Tr.

Established in 1961 in MA.
Foundation type: Independent foundation.
Financial data (yr. ended 12/31/05): Assets, $18,163,933 (M); gifts received, $670,034; expenditures, $823,053; qualifying distributions, $729,290; giving activities include $673,479 for 231 grants (high: $73,000; low: $5).
Purpose and activities: Giving to various charitable endeavors, with emphasis on Jewish agencies and temples.
Fields of interest: Museums; Performing arts; Performing arts, orchestra (symphony); Higher education; Education; Hospitals (general); Health care; Health organizations, association; Human services; Children/youth, services; Family services; Women, centers/services; Federated giving programs; Jewish federated giving programs;

Government/public administration; Jewish agencies & temples; Women; Economically disadvantaged.
International interests: Israel.
Type of support: General/operating support; Continuing support; Annual campaigns; Capital campaigns; Building/renovation; Endowments.
Limitations: Giving primarily in the greater Boston, MA, area. No support for advocacy groups. No grants to individuals; no loans.
Application information: Application form not required.
Initial approach: Letter
Deadline(s): None
Board meeting date(s): Varies
Trustees: Avram J. Goldberg; Carol R. Goldberg; Deborah B. Goldberg; Joshua R. Goldberg.
EIN: 046039556

3928

Gordon Family Foundation ✦
c/o Michael S. Gordon
260 Franklin St., Ste. 1900
Boston, MA 02110

Established in 1997 in MA.
Donor: Michael S. Gordon.
Foundation type: Independent foundation.
Financial data (yr. ended 12/31/05): Assets, $16,351,751 (M); gifts received, $4,000,000; expenditures, $871,494; qualifying distributions, $867,000; giving activities include $867,000 for 26 grants (high: $200,000; low: $1,000).
Purpose and activities: Giving for education and Jewish organizations.
Fields of interest: Education; Foundations (public); Jewish agencies & temples.
Type of support: General/operating support; Scholarship funds.
Limitations: Applications not accepted. Giving primarily in MA. No grants to individuals.
Application information: Contributes only to pre-selected organizations.
Trustees: Christina M. Gordon; Michael S. Gordon.
EIN: 137130595
Selected grants: The following grants were reported in 2004.
$226,000 to Chestnut Hill School, Chestnut Hill, MA.
$130,000 to Red Sox Foundation, Boston, MA.
$20,000 to Project Bread - The Walk for Hunger, Boston, MA.
$10,000 to ROSE Fund, Boston, MA.
$5,000 to Boys and Girls Club.
$5,000 to Casa Myrna Vasquez, Boston, MA.
$1,000 to Baltimore Hebrew Congregation, Baltimore, MD.
$100 to Brookline Music School, Brookline, MA.

3929

Grand Circle Foundation, Inc. ✦
347 Congress St.
Boston, MA 02210 (617) 346-6602
Contact: Jean Kenney, Mgr.
FAX: (617) 346-6030; E-mail: jkenney@gct.com; URL: http://www.gct.com/gcc/general/default.aspx?oid=72100

Established in 1993 in MA.
Donors: Grand Circle Corp.; Overseas Adventure Travel; Alan Lewis; Harriet Lewis.
Foundation type: Company-sponsored foundation.

Financial data (yr. ended 12/31/04): Assets, $2,013,309 (M); gifts received, $3,777,555; expenditures, $3,111,569; qualifying distributions, $2,933,796; giving activities include $2,933,796 for 134 grants (high: $868,508; low: $250).
Purpose and activities: The foundation supports organizations involved with arts and culture, education, health, youth development, human services, and the elderly.
Fields of interest: Arts; Education; Youth development; Human services; Aging.
International interests: Africa; Asia; Australia; Central America; Europe; Fiji; Mexico; New Zealand; South America.
Type of support: Program development.
Limitations: Giving limited to Boston, MA; giving also on an international basis. No support for discriminatory, political, or religious organizations. No grants to individuals, or for general operating support, advertising, or dinner table sponsorship.
Publications: Application guidelines; Grants list.
Application information: Proposals should be no longer than 2 pages. Application form not required.
   Initial approach: Proposal
   Deadline(s): Mar. 31, Jul. 31, and Nov. 30
   Board meeting date(s): May, Aug., and Dec.
Officer and Directors: Harriet R. Lewis,* Chair.; Mark Frevert; Alan E. Lewis.
Number of staff: 2 full-time professional.
EIN: 043175434
Selected grants: The following grants were reported in 2004.
$868,508 to Boys and Girls Club of Allston-Brighton, West End House, Allston, MA. For general support.
$225,000 to Artists for Humanity, Boston, MA. For general support.
$200,000 to Childrens Museum, Boston, MA. For general support.
$180,000 to Thompson Island Outward Bound Education Center, Boston, MA. For general support.
$110,000 to Anti-Defamation League of Bnai Brith, Boston, MA. For general support.
$104,000 to Combined Jewish Philanthropies of Greater Boston, Boston, MA. For general support.
$88,000 to Beth Israel Deaconess Medical Center, Boston, MA. For general support.
$45,000 to Rivers School, Weston, MA. For general support.
$30,000 to Little Brothers - Friends of the Elderly, Jamaica Plain, MA. For general support.
$20,000 to SquashBusters, Roxbury Crossing, MA. For general support.

3930
Grantham Foundation for the Protection of the Environment ◇

(formerly Jeremy and Hannelore Grantham Charitable Trust)
40 Rowes Wharf
Boston, MA   02110   (617) 346-7693
Contact: Jeremy Grantham, Tr.

Established in 1997 in MA.
Donor: R. Jeremy Grantham.
Foundation type: Independent foundation.
Financial data (yr. ended 12/31/04): Assets, $59,698,398 (M); gifts received, $15,571,000; expenditures, $1,699,136; qualifying distributions, $1,601,500; giving activities include $1,601,500 for grants.

Fields of interest: Environment, natural resources; Environment.
Limitations: Applications not accepted. No grants to individuals.
Application information: Contributes only to pre-selected organizations.
Trustee: Jeremy Grantham.
EIN: 046856456

3931
The Grass Foundation

400 Franklin St., Ste. 302
Braintree, MA   02184   (541) 346-3540
Contact: Janis C. Weeks, Pres.
FAX: (541) 346-4548;
E-mail: info@grassfoundation.org; URL: http://www.grassfoundation.org

Incorporated in 1957 in MA.
Donors: Albert M. Grass†; Ellen R. Grass†; Grass Instrument Co.; Cannon Manufacturing Co.; The Ellen R. Grass Trust.
Foundation type: Independent foundation.
Financial data (yr. ended 12/31/05): Assets, $21,741,575 (M); expenditures, $1,089,902; qualifying distributions, $994,389; giving activities include $851,374 for grants.
Purpose and activities: To encourage research in neurophysiology and the neurosciences; grants primarily for fellowships for summer study at a marine biological laboratory, lectureships, and for higher education.
Fields of interest: Biomedicine; Neuroscience; Medical research; Biological sciences.
International interests: Africa; Latin America.
Type of support: Fellowships; Research.
Limitations: Giving internationally, but primarily focused in the United States.
Publications: Application guidelines; Informational brochure (including application guidelines); Program policy statement.
Application information: Application formats and deadlines depend upon type of grant; specific information will be sent upon request. Application guidelines are available on foundation Web site. Application form not required.
   Initial approach: Letter
   Board meeting date(s): Jan. and July
Officers and Trustees: Janis C. Weeks, Ph.D., Pres.; Bernice Grafstein, Ph.D.*, V.P.; Louis Ptacek, M.D., Clerk; Richard Larkin, C.P.A., Treas.; John Burris, Ph.D.; David Cohen, Ph.D.; Donald Faber, Ph.D.; Henry J. Grass, M.D.; John G. Hildebrand, Ph.D.; Ronald Hoy, Ph.D.; Donald L. Price, M.D.; Stephen C. Reingold, Ph.D.; Felix Schweizer, Ph.D.; Amy Segal; Steven J. Zottoli, Ph.D.
Number of staff: 2 part-time support.
EIN: 046049529

3932
Grayson Family Foundation, Inc. ◇ ☆

c/o ABS Ventures
890 Winter St., Ste. 225
Waltham, MA   02451
Contact: Bruns H. Grayson, Pres.

Established in 1996 in MD.
Donor: Bruns H. Grayson.
Foundation type: Independent foundation.
Financial data (yr. ended 12/31/05): Assets, $7,176,932 (M); gifts received, $644,056;

expenditures, $464,815; qualifying distributions, $464,000; giving activities include $464,000 for grants.
Purpose and activities: Giving primarily for education.
Fields of interest: Arts; Elementary/secondary education; Higher education; Federated giving programs; Christian agencies & churches.
Type of support: General/operating support; Annual campaigns.
Limitations: Giving primarily in MD. No grants to individuals.
Application information:
   Initial approach: Letter
   Deadline(s): None
Officers: Bruns H. Grayson, Pres.; Perrin M. Grayson, Secy.-Treas.
EIN: 522007478

3933
Helen Wade Greene Charitable Trust ◇

c/o Bank of America, N.A.
P.O. Box 55886
Boston, MA   02205-5886

Established in 1957 in OH.
Foundation type: Independent foundation.
Financial data (yr. ended 12/31/05): Assets, $12,020,046 (M); expenditures, $880,339; qualifying distributions, $817,220; giving activities include $700,000 for 15 grants (high: $200,000; low: $5,000).
Fields of interest: Arts, association; Museums (art); Arts; Higher education; Nursing school/education; Education; Hospitals (general); Human services; Federated giving programs.
Type of support: General/operating support.
Limitations: Applications not accepted. Giving primarily in Boston, MA. No grants to individuals.
Application information: Contributes only to pre-selected organizations.
Trustee: Bank of America, N.A.
EIN: 346527172

3934
Grimshaw-Gudewicz Charitable Foundation ◇

c/o A. Shabshelowitz
P.O. Box 789
Fall River, MA   02722
Contact: Anne Fazendeiro, Tr.
Application address: 173 Auburn St., New Bedford, MA 02740

Established in 1995 in NH.
Foundation type: Independent foundation.
Financial data (yr. ended 12/31/05): Assets, $27,374,144 (M); expenditures, $1,476,410; qualifying distributions, $1,419,637; giving activities include $1,200,000 for 88 grants (high: $120,000; low: $500).
Purpose and activities: Giving primarily for the arts, and education, particularly education aimed at the enhancement of business and entrepreneurial skills; funding also for health care, and the preservation of local culture. The foundation's trustees also favor organizations that will provide a lasting named memorial whenever possible.
Fields of interest: Arts; Secondary school/education; Higher education; Education; Health organizations, association.

Limitations: Giving primarily in Bristol County, MA, RI, and Peterborough, NH. No grants to individuals.
Application information:
Initial approach: Letter
Deadline(s): None
Trustees: Anne Fazendeiro; Arthur Parker; Barry Robbins; Andrew Shabshelowitz; Bernard A.G. Taradash.
EIN: 046778721
Selected grants: The following grants were reported in 2004.
$115,000 to Brown University, Providence, RI.
$115,000 to Franklin Pierce College, Rindge, NH.
$115,000 to Masonic Education and Charity Trust, Boston, MA.
$115,000 to New Hampshire Association for the Blind, Concord, NH.
$115,000 to Schepens Eye Research Institute, Boston, MA.
$27,500 to New Bedford Whaling Museum, New Bedford, MA.
$20,000 to Eastern Nazarene College, Quincy, MA.
$20,000 to Lown Cardiovascular Research Foundation, Brookline, MA.
$5,000 to Saint Andrews School, Barrington, RI.
$2,000 to Newport Art Museum and Art Association, Newport, RI.

3935
The Harold Grinspoon Charitable Foundation ✧
380 Union St.
West Springfield, MA 01089 (413) 736-2552
Contact: Joanna S. Ballantine, Exec. Dir.
FAX: (413) 732-2632; URL: http://www.hgcf.org

Established in 1986 in MA.
Donors: Harold Grinspoon; Massmutual Financial Group.
Foundation type: Independent foundation.
Financial data (yr. ended 8/31/05): Assets, $2,504,786 (M); gifts received, $812,217; expenditures, $920,788; qualifying distributions, $812,239; giving activities include $706,421 for 515 grants (high: $50,000; low: $8).
Purpose and activities: The foundation focuses on the following areas: 1) rewarding excellence in teaching ; 2) encouraging young people to reach their academic and leadership potential; 3) encouraging entrepreneurship among young people; and 4) promoting literacy and early childhood education.
Fields of interest: Arts; Education; Cancer research; Youth development; Human services; Jewish agencies & temples; Women.
International interests: Israel.
Type of support: General/operating support; Annual campaigns; Endowments; Program development; Scholarship funds; Program-related investments/ loans.
Limitations: Applications not accepted. Giving primarily in western MA, with emphasis on Springfield. No grants to individuals (except for research projects), or for scholarships or student aid.
Publications: Financial statement.
Application information: Unsolicited requests for funds not accepted.
Officer: Joanna S. Ballantine, Exec. Dir.
Trustees: Jeffrey Grinspoon; Harold Grinspoon; Steven Grinspoon; Alissa Korn; Jeremy Pava; Diane Troderman.

Number of staff: 2 full-time professional; 2 part-time support.
EIN: 222738277

3936
The Phillip and Elizabeth Gross Family Foundation ✧
c/o Howland Capital Mgmt., Inc.
75 Federal St., Ste. 1100
Boston, MA 02110-1911

Established in 1998 in MA.
Donors: Phillip T. Gross; Elizabeth Cochary Gross.
Foundation type: Independent foundation.
Financial data (yr. ended 12/31/05): Assets, $9,575,178 (M); expenditures, $768,466; qualifying distributions, $809,346; giving activities include $758,873 for 6 grants (high: $624,937; low: $1,000).
Fields of interest: Elementary/secondary education; Higher education; Education; Philanthropy/voluntarism.
Limitations: Applications not accepted. Giving primarily in MA, with emphasis on Boston and Concord. No grants to individuals.
Application information: Contributes only to pre-selected organizations.
Trustees: Elizabeth Cochary Gross; Phillip T. Gross; Thomas V. Quirk.
EIN: 046878795

3937
The Julia & Seymour Gross Foundation, Inc. ✧
P.O. Box 506
Weston, MA 02493-0003

Established in NY and MA.
Donor: Inez Gross.
Foundation type: Independent foundation.
Financial data (yr. ended 6/30/05): Assets, $6,272,245 (M); expenditures, $450,948; qualifying distributions, $446,281; giving activities include $398,750 for 47 grants (high: $227,000; low: $25).
Purpose and activities: Giving for education.
Fields of interest: Higher education; Medical school/education; Hospitals (general).
Type of support: General/operating support.
Limitations: Applications not accepted. Giving primarily in NY. No grants to individuals.
Application information: Contributes only to pre-selected organizations.
Officers: Menard M. Gertler, M.D., Pres. and Treas.; Jonathan P. Gertler, M.D., V.P.; Mark D. Berlin, Secy.
Board Members: Jane Rogers Clark; Anna P. Gertler; Clark Chessin Gertler; David Paul Schiffer.
EIN: 136122092
Selected grants: The following grants were reported in 2004.
$211,000 to Weill Medical College of Cornell University, New York, NY. For general support.
$25,000 to McGill University, Montreal, Canada. For general support.
$25,000 to University of Saskatchewan, Saskatoon, Canada. For general support.
$15,000 to Belmont Hill School, Belmont, MA. For general support.
$5,000 to Reconstructionist Rabbinical College, Wyncote, PA. For general support.

$1,500 to Metropolitan Opera, New York, NY. For general support.
$100 to Avenue Association, New York, NY. For general support.
$100 to Fund for Park Avenue, New York, NY. For general support.
$100 to Greenwich Hospital, Greenwich, CT. For general support.
$50 to Lighthouse International, New York, NY. For general support.

3938
The Hagerty Family Foundation ✧
256 Beacon St., Rm. 4
Boston, MA 02116

Foundation type: Independent foundation.
Financial data (yr. ended 12/31/05): Assets, $462,946 (M); expenditures, $570,000; qualifying distributions, $570,000; giving activities include $570,000 for 7 grants (high: $315,000; low: $5,000).
Fields of interest: Performing arts, theater; Higher education; Hospitals (specialty); Diabetes research; Foundations (community); Roman Catholic agencies & churches.
Limitations: Applications not accepted. Giving primarily in Boston, MA; some funding nationally. No grants to individuals.
Application information: Contributes only to pre-selected organizations.
Trustees: Robert G. Bannish; Jeanne M. Hagerty; Thomas M. Hagerty.
EIN: 200509132

3939
Haley Family Foundation ✧
c/o Steven and Kathleen P. Haley
P.O. Box 395
Dover, MA 02030-0395

Established in 1998 in MA.
Donors: Steven Haley; Kathleen Powers Haley.
Foundation type: Independent foundation.
Financial data (yr. ended 12/31/04): Assets, $9,699,112 (M); expenditures, $629,390; qualifying distributions, $582,250; giving activities include $582,250 for 8 grants (high: $300,000; low: $250).
Purpose and activities: Giving primarily for education and youth services.
Fields of interest: Performing arts; Elementary/ secondary education; Higher education; Environment, water resources; Health organizations; Boys & girls clubs; Human services.
Limitations: Applications not accepted. Giving primarily in MA. No grants to individuals.
Application information: Contributes only to pre-selected organizations.
Trustees: Kathleen Powers Haley; Steven Haley.
EIN: 043356222

3940
Kendall C. and Anna Ham Charitable Foundation, Inc. ✧
c/o Paul L. Brigham
10 Park St.
Northborough, MA 01532
Application address: c/o Robert J. Murphy, P.O. Box 2853, North Conway, NH 03860

Established in 1994.
Foundation type: Independent foundation.
Financial data (yr. ended 12/31/04): Assets, $10,388,819 (M); expenditures, $524,714; qualifying distributions, $468,966; giving activities include $414,258 for 44 grants (high: $225,000; low: $100).
Purpose and activities: Giving to better community life in Bridgton, ME, and Mount Washington Valley, NH.
Fields of interest: Historic preservation/historical societies; Libraries/library science; Health care; Housing/shelter; Human services.
Type of support: Annual campaigns; Capital campaigns; Building/renovation; Equipment; Land acquisition; Endowments; Debt reduction; Program development; Seed money; Scholarships—to individuals; In-kind gifts; Matching/challenge support.
Limitations: Giving limited to Bridgton, ME, and the Mount Washington Valley area of NH.
Publications: Application guidelines; Annual report; Program policy statement.
Application information: Application form required.
  Initial approach: In person or telephone
  Copies of proposal: 1
  Deadline(s): 90 days prior to board meeting
  Board meeting date(s): Apr. and Oct.
  Final notification: Following meeting
Officers and Directors:* Paul L. Brigham,* Pres.; Frank J. Connolly, Jr., Secy.; Bruce A. Chalmers; Robert J. Murphy; Alan Ordway; Dorothea M. Seybold.
Number of staff: 1 full-time professional; 1 part-time support.
EIN: 223080012

3941
The Hanover Insurance Group Foundation, Inc. ✧

(formerly Allmerica Financial Charitable Foundation, Inc.)
440 Lincoln St.
Worcester, MA 01653 (508) 855-1000
URL: http://www.hanover.com/thg/about/community/grant.htm

Established in 1990 in MA.
Donors: First Allmerica Financial Life Insurance Co.; The Hanover Insurance Co.
Foundation type: Company-sponsored foundation.
Financial data (yr. ended 12/31/05): Assets, $8,044,656 (M); gifts received, $4,000,000; expenditures, $1,182,204; qualifying distributions, $1,181,679; giving activities include $1,181,679 for 275 grants (high: $200,000; low: $15).
Purpose and activities: The foundation supports organizations involved with arts and culture, education, health, recreation, and human services.
Fields of interest: Arts; Elementary/secondary education; Higher education; Education; Health care; Health organizations, association; Recreation; Human services; Children/youth, services; Federated giving programs.
Type of support: Scholarship funds.
Limitations: Giving primarily in Worcester, MA, and MI. No grants to individuals.
Application information: Application form required.
  Initial approach: Download application form
  Deadline(s): None

Officers and Directors:* Cheryl M. Lapriore,* Pres.; K. David Nunley, V.P.; Laura Gobron, Treas.; Richard Lavey; Joseph W. MacDougall, Jr.*.
EIN: 043105650
Selected grants: The following grants were reported in 2004.
$102,500 to United Way of Central Massachusetts, Worcester, MA. 2 grants: $52,500, $50,000
$30,000 to Student Leadership Services, Waterford, MI.
$15,000 to Junior Achievement of Worcester, Worcester, MA.
$15,000 to Salvation Army of Worcester, Worcester, MA.
$7,500 to Childrens Friend, Worcester, MA.
$5,000 to Boys and Girls Club of Worcester, Worcester, MA.
$5,000 to Worcester Public Schools, Worcester, MA.
$3,000 to Friendly House, Worcester, MA.
$200 to Brown University, Providence, RI.

3942
Esmond Harmsworth 1997 Charitable Foundation ✧
535 Boylston St., Ste. 1103
Boston, MA 02116

Established in 1998 in MA.
Donor: Esmond Harmsworth.
Foundation type: Independent foundation.
Financial data (yr. ended 4/30/06): Assets, $47,642 (M); gifts received, $300,000; expenditures, $548,500; qualifying distributions, $545,000; giving activities include $545,000 for 18 grants (high: $150,000; low: $10,000).
Purpose and activities: Giving primarily for education, AIDS research, gay and lesbian organizations, and social services.
Fields of interest: Education, special; Education; AIDS research; Human services; Civil rights, gays/lesbians; LGBTQ.
Limitations: Applications not accepted. Giving primarily in Boston, MA; some funding also in Washington, DC, and New York, NY. No grants to individuals.
Application information: Contributes only to pre-selected organizations.
Trustees: Esmond Harmsworth; James Richardson.
EIN: 046838152
Selected grants: The following grants were reported in 2005.
$125,000 to Eagle Hill School, Hardwick, MA.
$25,000 to Fenway Community Health Center, Boston, MA.
$25,000 to Museum of Fine Arts, Boston, MA.
$25,000 to W G B H Educational Foundation, Boston, MA.
$20,000 to Woods Hole Research Center, Woods Hole, MA.
$10,000 to Pine Street Inn, Boston, MA.
$10,000 to Thompson Island Outward Bound Education Center, Boston, MA.
$5,000 to Servicemembers Legal Defense Network, DC.

3943
Francis A. & Jacquelyn H. Harrington Foundation ✧
370 Main St., 12th Fl.
Worcester, MA 01608 (508) 798-8621
Contact: Sumner B. Tilton, Jr., Tr.

Established in 1965 in MA.
Donors: Francis A. Harrington†; Jacquelyn H. Harrington†.
Foundation type: Independent foundation.
Financial data (yr. ended 12/31/04): Assets, $13,390,367 (M); expenditures, $661,107; qualifying distributions, $618,418; giving activities include $536,000 for 11 grants (high: $25,000; low: $5,000).
Fields of interest: Secondary school/education; Higher education; Medical research, institute; Community development; Science.
Type of support: General/operating support; Capital campaigns; Equipment; Program development.
Limitations: Giving primarily in Worcester, MA. No grants to individuals, or for scholarships; no loans.
Application information: Application form not required.
  Initial approach: Letter
  Copies of proposal: 1
  Deadline(s): June 1
  Board meeting date(s): June and Dec. 15
  Final notification: Dec. 31
Trustees: Francis A. Harrington, Jr.; James H. Harrington; Phyllis Harrington; Sumner B. Tilton, Jr.
Number of staff: 1 part-time professional.
EIN: 046125088

3944
William H. Harris Foundation ✧
19 Windemere Cir.
Braintree, MA 02184

Donors: William H. Harris, M.D.; Johanna H. Harris.
Foundation type: Independent foundation.
Financial data (yr. ended 12/31/04): Assets, $6,079,513 (M); gifts received, $3,750; expenditures, $1,690,346; qualifying distributions, $1,367,127; giving activities include $1,149,118 for 7 grants (high: $388,118; low: $2,000).
Purpose and activities: Support for higher education, environmental sciences, and medical research.
Fields of interest: Higher education; Environment, natural resources; Animals/wildlife; Medical research.
Type of support: Research.
Limitations: Applications not accepted. Giving on a national basis, with some emphasis on MA and PA. No grants to individuals.
Application information: Contributes only to pre-selected organizations.
Trustees: Johanna H. Harris; William H. Harris, M.D.
EIN: 046197960

3945
The Ulf B. Heide and Elizabeth C. Heide Foundation Charitable Trust ✧ ☆
c/o Frank P. Conrad
8 Cedar Rd.
Weston, MA 02493

Established in 1991 in MA.
Donor: Ulf B. Heide.

Foundation type: Independent foundation.
Financial data (yr. ended 12/31/05): Assets, $1,434,952 (M); gifts received, $200,000; expenditures, $320,150; qualifying distributions, $317,654; giving activities include $317,654 for 18 grants (high: $221,900; low: $40).
Purpose and activities: Giving primarily for the arts, particularly to an art museum; funding also for education and human services.
Fields of interest: Museums (art); Performing arts, orchestra (symphony); Higher education; Education; Human services.
Limitations: Applications not accepted. Giving primarily in MA. No grants to individuals.
Application information: Contributes only to pre-selected organizations.
Trustees: Frank P. Conrad; Elizabeth C. Heide; Ulf B. Heide.
EIN: 046665830
Selected grants: The following grants were reported in 2004.
$216,000 to Museum of Fine Arts, Boston, MA. For general support.
$12,600 to Peabody Essex Museum, Salem, MA. For general support.
$6,000 to Boston Symphony Orchestra, Boston, MA. For general support.
$5,500 to Harvard University, Radcliffe Institute for Advanced Study, Cambridge, MA. For general support.
$5,000 to Holderness School, Plymouth, NH. For general support.
$5,000 to YMCA, Marblehead/Swampscott, Marblehead, MA. For general support.
$2,000 to Ellis Memorial and Eldredge House, Boston, MA. For general support.
$1,600 to Old North Church, Boston, MA. For general support.
$550 to My Brothers Table, Lynn, MA. For general support.
$200 to Salvation Army of Boston, Boston, MA. For general support.

3946
Henderson Foundation ◇ ☆
P.O. Box 420
Sudbury, MA   01776-0420
Contact: Ernest Henderson III

Trust established in 1947 in MA.
Donors: Ernest Henderson†; George B. Henderson†; J. Brooks Fenno†; Ernest Henderson III.
Foundation type: Independent foundation.
Financial data (yr. ended 12/31/05): Assets, $10,064,511 (M); expenditures, $807,990; qualifying distributions, $674,000; giving activities include $674,000 for grants.
Purpose and activities: Support for public policy organizations in the fields of foreign policy, defense, peace, and media issues, and higher and precollege education; minor support for medical research.
Fields of interest: Arts; Higher education; Medical research, institute; Human services; Public policy, research.
Type of support: General/operating support; Continuing support; Research.
Limitations: Giving primarily in Washington DC, MA, MD, NH and NY. No grants to individuals, or for scholarships or fellowships.
Application information:
  Initial approach: Letter
  Deadline(s): None

Trustees: Barclay Henderson; Ernest Henderson III; Joseph Petrone.
Number of staff: 1 part-time professional.
EIN: 046051095
Selected grants: The following grants were reported in 2004.
$51,000 to National Center on Family Homelessness, Newton Centre, MA.
$10,000 to Japan Society of Boston, Boston, MA.
$2,000 to Wellesley Community Center, Wellesley, MA.
$1,000 to Cape Cod Hospital Foundation, Hyannis, MA.

3947
The Stephen J. Hendrickson Foundation, Inc. ◇ ☆
P.O. Box 6000
Peabody, MA   01961-6000

Established in 1991 in MA.
Donor: Stephen J. Hendrickson.
Foundation type: Independent foundation.
Financial data (yr. ended 6/30/05): Assets, $10,187,689 (M); gifts received, $5,800,000; expenditures, $2,374,150; qualifying distributions, $2,280,000; giving activities include $2,280,000 for grants.
Fields of interest: Theological school/education; Religion.
Limitations: Applications not accepted. Giving primarily in Chicago, IL. No grants to individuals.
Application information: Contributes only to pre-selected organizations.
Directors: Stephen J. Hendrickson; G. Timothy Johnson, M.D.; T. Kirkland Ware III.
EIN: 043140238

3948
Hermann Foundation, Inc. ◇
c/o Charles F. Dodson
370 Main St., Ste. 925
Worcester, MA   01608   (508) 756-4657
Contact: Henry Lusardi, Treas.

Established in 2003 in MA.
Donors: Francoise Hermann Charitable Remainder Trust 2000; Francoise Hermann†.
Foundation type: Independent foundation.
Financial data (yr. ended 12/31/04): Assets, $27,105,269 (M); gifts received, $12,743,766; expenditures, $569,019; qualifying distributions, $460,100; giving activities include $460,100 for 18 grants (high: $75,000; low: $100).
Fields of interest: Arts; Education; Health care; Human services.
Limitations: Giving primarily in MA. No grants to individuals.
Application information:
  Initial approach: Letter
  Deadline(s): None
Officers: Charles F. Dodson, Pres.; Henry Lusardi, Treas.
Directors: Melissa Dodson; Maria Starzyk.
EIN: 562385301

3949
The Hershey Family Foundation ◇
(formerly Barry J. Hershey Foundation)
c/o Ropes & Gray
1 International Pl.
Boston, MA   02110-2624

Established around 1988 in MA.
Donor: Barry J. Hershey.
Foundation type: Independent foundation.
Financial data (yr. ended 12/31/04): Assets, $60,057,753 (M); expenditures, $2,848,043; qualifying distributions, $2,762,115; giving activities include $2,746,665 for 27 grants (high: $665,000; low: $10,000).
Purpose and activities: Giving primarily for the arts, education, health associations, human services, Buddhist-related organizations, as well as to a Montreal, Canada-based organization devoted to Tibetan culture.
Fields of interest: Performing arts, theater; Arts; Elementary/secondary education; Libraries (public); Animals/wildlife; Hospitals (general); Health organizations, association; Food services; Human services; International affairs; Public affairs, public education; Buddhism.
International interests: Canada.
Limitations: Applications not accepted. Giving on a national and international basis, primarily in CA and MA, as well as in Montreal, Canada. Generally, no grants to individuals.
Application information: Contributes only to pre-selected organizations. Unsolicited requests for funds not accepted.
Trustees: Barry J. Hershey; Connie Hershey.
EIN: 341574366
Selected grants: The following grants were reported in 2003.
$665,000 to Partners in Health, Boston, MA.
$200,000 to Beth Israel Deaconess Medical Center, Boston, MA.
$125,000 to Hunger Project, New York, NY.
$100,000 to Oxfam America, Boston, MA.
$80,000 to University of Washington, School of Nursing, Seattle, WA.
$70,000 to American Repertory Theater, Cambridge, MA.
$50,000 to Electronic Frontier Foundation, San Francisco, CA.
$50,000 to WildAid, San Francisco, CA.
$20,000 to Greater Boston Food Bank, Boston, MA.
$15,000 to Emerson Umbrella, Concord, MA.

3950
High Meadow Foundation, Inc. ◇
c/o Country Curtains, Inc.
30 Main St.
Stockbridge, MA   01262   (413) 298-5565
Contact: John H. Fitzpatrick, Pres.; Jane P. Fitzpatrick, Treas.

Established in 1984 in MA.
Donors: John H. Fitzpatrick; Jane P. Fitzpatrick; Country Curtains, Inc.; Housatonic Curtain Co.; Red Lion Inn; Country Curtains Retail; Fitzpatrick Companies, Inc.
Foundation type: Independent foundation.
Financial data (yr. ended 9/30/05): Assets, $1,859,940 (M); gifts received, $1,065,013; expenditures, $1,254,222; qualifying distributions, $1,254,222; giving activities include $1,226,227 for 134 grants (high: $122,000; low: $100), and

$10,500 for 16 grants to individuals (high: $1,000; low: $500).

Purpose and activities: Support primarily for the performing arts, especially theater and music, and other cultural organizations; giving also for health, social services, and education.

Fields of interest: Visual arts; Museums; Performing arts; Performing arts, theater; Performing arts, music; Humanities; Arts; Education, fund raising/fund distribution; Elementary school/education; Higher education; Libraries/library science; Reproductive health, family planning; Health care; Mental health/crisis services; Health organizations, association; Cancer; Medical research, institute; Cancer research; Human services; Children/youth, services; Family services; Women, centers/services; Homeless, human services; International relief; Community development; Religion; Native Americans/American Indians; Women; Homeless.

Type of support: Continuing support; Annual campaigns; Capital campaigns; Building/renovation; Equipment; Debt reduction; Emergency funds; Program development; Program-related investments/loans; Employee-related scholarships; Matching/challenge support.

Limitations: Giving primarily in Berkshire County, MA.

Application information: Application form not required.

Initial approach: Letter
Deadline(s): None

Officers and Directors:* John H. Fitzpatrick,* Pres.; Jane P. Fitzpatrick,* Treas.; Laura Topping,* Clerk; JoAnn Fitzpatrick Brown; Nancy J. Fitzpatrick; Tamara T. Stevens; Robert B. Trask.

Number of staff: 1

EIN: 222527419

Selected grants: The following grants were reported in 2003.

$147,735 to Boston Symphony Orchestra, Boston, MA. For general support.

$50,000 to Norman Rockwell Museum at Stockbridge, Stockbridge, MA. For general support.

$50,000 to Visiting Nurse Association, Lee Regional, Lee, MA. For general support.

$40,000 to United Way, Berkshire, Pittsfield, MA. For general support.

$25,000 to Buckley School, New York, NY. For general support.

$25,000 to Central Park Conservancy, New York, NY. For general support.

$25,000 to First Congregational Church of Stockbridge, Stockbridge, MA. For general support.

$25,000 to Massachusetts College of Liberal Arts, North Adams, MA. For library.

$25,000 to Massachusetts Museum of Contemporary Art, North Adams, MA. For general support.

$20,000 to Junior Achievement of Western Massachusetts, Springfield, MA. For general support.

3951

The Highland Street Connection ▼

(also known as The Highland Street Foundation)
463 Worcester Rd., Ste. 403
Framingham, MA 01701 (508) 820-1151
Contact: Mari Brennan Barrera, Exec. Dir.
FAX: (508) 820-1152;
E-mail: info@highlandstreet.org; URL: http://www.highlandstreet.org

Established in 1989 in MA.

Donor: David J. McGrath, Jr.‡.

Foundation type: Independent foundation.

Financial data (yr. ended 12/31/04): Assets, $189,148,838 (M); gifts received, $1,494,504; expenditures, $12,009,877; qualifying distributions, $10,167,719; giving activities include $8,996,020 for 302 grants (high: $950,000; low: $100; average: $1,000–$100,000), and $572,958 for 2 loans/program-related investments.

Purpose and activities: The Highland Street Foundation is a family foundation currently awarding grants to nonprofit organizations located predominantly in Massachusetts. The trustees have focused on providing assistance to disadvantaged and underserved children through the funding of programs that support education and mentoring. Grants have also been awarded in the areas of the environment, health care, housing, the arts, and social services.

Fields of interest: Arts; Education; Health care; Youth development; Community development; Religion.

Type of support: General/operating support; Continuing support; Annual campaigns; Capital campaigns; Building/renovation; Endowments; Program development; Scholarship funds; Program-related investments/loans; In-kind gifts; Matching/challenge support.

Limitations: Applications not accepted. Giving primarily in MA. No grants to individuals.

Publications: Grants list.

Application information: Contributes only to pre-selected organizations. Unsolicited proposals are not accepted.

Board meeting date(s): The board meets six times a year

Trustees: Christopher R. McGrath; David J. McGrath III; Holly L. McGrath; JoAnn McGrath; Scott J. McGrath; Sean P. McGrath.

EIN: 043048298

Selected grants: The following grants were reported in 2004.

$1,000,000 to Caritas Saint Elizabeths Medical Center of Boston, Boston, MA. For capital support.

$950,000 to Catholic Schools Foundation, Boston, MA. For program support.

$874,460 to Womens Institute for Housing and Economic Development, Boston, MA. 2 grants: $865,000 (For real estate), $9,460 (For general operating support).

$500,000 to Appalachian Mountain Club, Boston, MA. For challenge and capital support.

$200,000 to McCallum Theater, Palm Desert, CA. For general operating support.

$15,000 to Meadowbrook School, Weston, MA. For general operating support.

$8,000 to Childrens Hospital Trust, Boston, MA. For general operating support.

$5,000 to Hyde Park Main Streets, Hyde Park, MA. For general operating support.

$1,200 to Fund for Parks and Recreation in Boston, Boston, MA. For program support.

3952

The Hinduja Foundation, U.S. ✧ ☆

c/o Ropes & Gray
1 International Pl.
Boston, MA 02110-2624

Established in 1984 in MA.

Donors: Hinduja Trust; Amas Limited; Hinduja Family Foundation.

Foundation type: Independent foundation.

Financial data (yr. ended 12/31/05): Assets, $5,044 (M); gifts received, $342,500; expenditures, $337,675; qualifying distributions, $337,500; giving activities include $337,500 for grants.

Purpose and activities: Giving primarily for health care, research, education and conflict management as they relate to India. Funding also for trained physicians of Indian origin to serve indigent patients in the Hinduja National Hospital in Mumbia, India.

Fields of interest: Higher education; Higher education, university; Human services.

International interests: India.

Type of support: General/operating support; Research.

Limitations: Applications not accepted. Giving primarily in Baltimore, MD, and New York, NY. No grants to individuals.

Publications: Newsletter.

Application information: Contributes only to pre-selected organizations.

Officer: Kenneth D. Peterson, Pres.

Trustees: G.P. Hinduja; P.P. Hinduja; S.P. Hinduja.

Number of staff: 1 full-time professional; 1 part-time support.

EIN: 222570780

Selected grants: The following grants were reported in 2003.

$200,000 to Columbia University, New York, NY. For general support.

$1,100 to Iskon. For general support.

$288 to Children, Inc., Richmond, VA. For general support.

3953

The Hirschtick Family Foundation ✧

c/o Jon and Melissa Hirschtick
10 Porter Ln.
Lexington, MA 02420

Established in 1998 in MA.

Donors: Jon K. Hirschtick; Melissa H. Hirschtick.

Foundation type: Independent foundation.

Financial data (yr. ended 12/31/05): Assets, $24,175 (M); gifts received, $348,323; expenditures, $354,917; qualifying distributions, $343,754; giving activities include $343,754 for 16 grants (high: $181,565; low: $100).

Purpose and activities: Primarily gives to Jewish agencies and temples.

Fields of interest: Media, television; Animal welfare; Youth development, scouting agencies (general); Human services; Engineering/technology; Jewish agencies & temples.

Limitations: Applications not accepted. Giving primarily in MA. No grants to individuals.

Application information: Contributes only to pre-selected organizations.

Trustees: Jon K. Hirschtick; Melissa H. Hirschtick.

EIN: 046868401

Selected grants: The following grants were reported in 2004.

$10,000 to Massachusetts Institute of Technology, Cambridge, MA.

$5,250 to American Society for Technion-Israel Institute of Technology, New York, NY.

$2,500 to Animal Rescue League of Boston, Boston, MA.

$1,600 to YMCA.

$1,500 to W G B H Educational Foundation, Boston, MA.

$500 to Northeast Animal Shelter, Salem, MA.

3954
The Hoche-Scofield Foundation ✧

c/o Bank of America, N.A.
P.O. Box 55886
Boston, MA 02205-5886 (508) 770-7152
Contact: Dorothy Dudley, Trust Off., Bank of America, N.A.

Established in 1983 in MA.
Donor: William B. Scofield†.
Foundation type: Independent foundation.
Financial data (yr. ended 12/31/05): Assets, $17,403,476 (M); expenditures, $902,528; qualifying distributions, $839,908; giving activities include $770,489 for 111 grants (high: $20,000; low: $2,000).
Purpose and activities: Giving primarily for education and community and social services in Worcester, MA.
Fields of interest: Arts; Higher education; Health care; Health organizations, association; Human services; Children/youth, services; Women, centers/services; Community development; Federated giving programs; Women; Economically disadvantaged.
Type of support: Continuing support; Capital campaigns; Equipment; Program development; Seed money.
Limitations: Giving limited to the City and County of Worcester, MA.
Publications: Application guidelines.
Application information: Application form required.
 Initial approach: Letter
 Copies of proposal: 5
 Deadline(s): Feb. 15, May 15, Aug. 15, and Nov. 15
 Board meeting date(s): Mar. 15, June 15, Sept. 15, and Dec. 15
 Final notification: Apr. 15, July 15, Oct. 15, and Jan. 15
Trustees: Henry B. Dewey; Warner S. Fletcher; Lois B. Green; Bank of America, N.A.
EIN: 222519554
Selected grants: The following grants were reported in 2004.
$39,018 to Clark University, Worcester, MA.
$20,000 to Joy of Music Program, Worcester, MA. For Share the Joy capital campaign.
$15,000 to Becker College, Worcester, MA. For Blackboard Learning System and Community Portal.
$10,000 to Community Healthlink, Worcester Youth Guidance Center, Worcester, MA. For Youth Leadership Program.
$10,000 to Worcester Regional Research Bureau, Worcester, MA. For research and education program.
$7,000 to Childrens Friend, Worcester, MA. For Ellsworth Child and Family Counseling Center.
$5,000 to YMCA, Tri-Community, Southbridge, MA. For Children and Families First Renovation Program.
$4,000 to Easter Seal Society of Massachusetts, Worcester, MA. For summer camp program for disabled youngsters.
$4,000 to Oak Hill Community Development Corporation, Worcester, MA. For Neighborhood Revitalization Initiative.

$2,000 to Friendly House, Worcester, MA. For Pleasant Street Neighborhood Network Center.

3955
Hoffman Family Foundation ✧

(formerly The John Ernest Hoffman Foundation)
c/o Loring, Wolcott & Coolidge Office
230 Congress St.
Boston, MA 02110

Established in 1985 in MA.
Donor: Effe K.D. Hoffman†.
Foundation type: Independent foundation.
Financial data (yr. ended 12/31/05): Assets, $5,356,798 (M); expenditures, $446,305; qualifying distributions, $418,152; giving activities include $412,500 for 23 grants (high: $100,000; low: $1,000).
Purpose and activities: Giving primarily for the arts, particularly a center for chamber music; funding also for natural resource conservation, health associations, human services, federated giving programs, and Christian churches.
Fields of interest: Performing arts centers; Performing arts, music; Performing arts, orchestra (symphony); Arts; Higher education; Education; Environment, natural resources; Environment, forests; Health organizations; Human services; Foundations (community); Federated giving programs; Christian agencies & churches.
Type of support: General/operating support; Continuing support; Annual campaigns; Capital campaigns; Building/renovation.
Limitations: Applications not accepted. Giving primarily in MA and NH; some funding also in CT. No grants to individuals.
Application information: Contributes only to pre-selected organizations. Unsolicited requests for funds not considered.
 Board meeting date(s): As needed
Trustees: John E. Hoffman, Jr.; Stephen A. Moore; Roger M. Thomas.
EIN: 222677966
Selected grants: The following grants were reported in 2004.
$145,000 to Apple Hill Center for Chamber Music, Sullivan, NH.
$40,000 to New Hampshire Charitable Foundation, Concord, NH.
$30,000 to United Way, Monadnock, Keene, NH.
$25,000 to Monadnock Family Services, Keene, NH.
$20,000 to Keene State College, Keene, NH.
$13,500 to Harris Center for Conservation Education, Hancock, NH.
$6,000 to Monadnock Music, Peterborough, NH.
$5,000 to Choate Rosemary Hall, Wallingford, CT.
$5,000 to Monadnock Conservancy, Keene, NH.
$5,000 to Moving Company Dance Center, Keene, NH.

3956
Charles H. Hood Foundation

95 Berkeley St., Ste. 208
Boston, MA 02116
Contact: Ray Considine, Exec. Dir.
E-mail: glickwood@tmfnet.org; URL: http://www.tmfnet.org/grantmake.html

Fund established in 1931; incorporated in 1942 in NH.

Donor: Charles H. Hood†.
Foundation type: Independent foundation.
Financial data (yr. ended 12/31/05): Assets, $56,088,083 (M); expenditures, $3,145,577; qualifying distributions, $2,888,427; giving activities include $2,682,969 for 28 grants (high: $1,705,152; low: $43,500).
Purpose and activities: The foundation supports newly appointed independent faculty in New England whose research focuses on child health. Clinical, basic science, public health, and epidemiologic research projects must be hypothesis-driven with direct relevance to pediatric diseases. Grants are competitively reviewed by the Foundation's Scientific Advisory Committee.
Fields of interest: Pediatrics research.
Type of support: Research.
Limitations: Giving limited to New England. No support for mental health, education, or social or general welfare. No grants to individuals, or for building or endowment funds, operating budgets, general support, publications, scholarships, fundraising campaigns, or matching gifts; no loans.
Publications: Application guidelines; Annual report.
Application information: Generally, the foundation does not accept unsolicited applications. See application guidelines at http://www.tmfhealth.org/grantmake.html. Application form required.
 Copies of proposal: 12
 Deadline(s): Contact foundation for deadlines
 Board meeting date(s): Usually in June and Dec.
 Final notification: 6 weeks
Officers and Trustees:* Charles H. Hood II,* Pres. and Treas.; John O. Parker, Clerk; Ray Considine, Exec. Dir.; Jeffrey H. Boutwell, Ph.D.; Henry M. Sanders; J. Neil Smiley.
Number of staff: 3 part-time professional; 1 part-time support.
EIN: 043507847
Selected grants: The following grants were reported in 2005.
$300,000 to Childrens Hospital Corporation, Boston, MA. 4 grants: $75,000 (For promotion of mammalian cardia regeneration through cardiomyocyte proliferation), $75,000 (For novel comutational modeling of dynamic afterload and ventriculo-arterial coupling in coarctation of aorta), $75,000 (For genetics of bilateral frontoparietal polymicrogyria and epilepsy, payable over 2 years), $75,000 (For VIA-Overweight and At Risk (OAR)).
$150,000 to Massachusetts General Hospital, Boston, MA. 2 grants: $75,000 (For role of cdx genes and their downstream targets in hematoppoietic stem cell formation), $75,000 (For dissection of molecular pathways mediating epigenetic gene modification, payable over 2 years).
$75,000 to CBR Institute for Biomedical Research, Boston, MA. For identification of genetic defect causing immunodeficiency, myopathy and ectodermal dysplasia.
$75,000 to Dana-Farber Cancer Institute, Boston, MA. For chemical genomic approaches for pediatric leukemia, payable over 2 years.
$75,000 to Harvard Pilgrim Health Care, Boston, MA. For Children in High-Deductible Health Plans: Health Care Use and Impact of Chronic Conditions.
$75,000 to Northeastern University, Boston, MA. For development of novel skin substitute to promote dermal regeneration, payable over 2 years.

$75,000 to Rhode Island Hospital, Providence, RI. For mechanism of MAP Kinase Phosphatase 3 (MKP3) induced gluconeogenesis in obesity and diabetes.

$67,582 to Harvard University, Medical School, Cambridge, MA. For impact of isoniazid prophylaxis to prevent tuberculosis in children, payable over 2 years.

3957
Charles H. Hood Fund ✧ ☆
90 Everett Ave., Ste. 200
Chelsea, MA   02150-2310   (617) 887-8475
Contact: Linda Thompson, Clerk

Established in 1981 in MA.
Foundation type: Independent foundation.
Financial data (yr. ended 12/31/05): Assets, $2,188,332 (M); expenditures, $1,111,734; qualifying distributions, $1,076,881; giving activities include $1,000,000 for 1 grant, and $71,885 for 28 grants to individuals (high: $4,000; low: $1,885).
Purpose and activities: Giving for college scholarships which are limited to children of employees (of at least one year preceding Dec. 1st of year in which the applicant is a high school senior) of H.P. Hood, Inc.; awards up to $4,000 per year, per student for four years, provided curriculum is leading to a Bachelor's Degree, or a program for a certificate or degree as a registered nurse.
Fields of interest: Scholarships/financial aid.
Type of support: Employee-related scholarships.
Limitations: Giving primarily in MA and NY.
Publications: Application guidelines.
Application information: Application form required.
  Deadline(s): Feb. 15
  Final notification: May
Officers and Directors:* Charles H. Hood,* Chair. and Pres.; Linda Thompson,* Clerk; Theresa Bresten, Treas.; Camille M. DiCocco; Barbara N. Tobey.
EIN: 046036788

3958
The Hopedale Foundation ✧
43 Hope St.
P.O. Box 123
Hopedale, MA   01747-0123
Contact: Vincent J. Arone, Treas.

Trust established in 1946 in MA.
Donors: Draper Corp.; Thomas H. West†; John D. Gannett†.
Foundation type: Independent foundation.
Financial data (yr. ended 10/31/05): Assets, $8,631,889 (M); expenditures, $424,809; qualifying distributions, $421,488; giving activities include $231,852 for 24 grants (high: $100,000; low: $500), $10,000 for 4 grants to individuals (high: $2,500; low: $2,500), and $135,485 for loans to individuals.
Purpose and activities: Emphasis on area community funds and hospitals; support also for museums and other cultural programs, health agencies, youth services, and higher education; student loans limited to Hopedale High School graduates. New grants only to organizations having direct impact on the local community.
Fields of interest: Museums; Arts; Education, association; Higher education; Hospitals (general);

Health care; Children/youth, services; Federated giving programs; Social sciences.
Type of support: General/operating support; Annual campaigns; Capital campaigns; Student loans—to individuals.
Limitations: Giving primarily in MA, with emphasis on Hopedale and Milford. No grants for endowment funds.
Application information: Application form not required.
  Initial approach: Letter
  Copies of proposal: 1
  Deadline(s): June 1 for student loans; no set deadline for grants
  Board meeting date(s): Feb., June, and Oct.
Officers and Trustees:* William B. Gannett,* Chair.; Peter S. Ellis,* Vice-Chair.; W. Gregory Burrill,* Secy.; Vincent J. Arone,* Treas.; Alfred H. Sparling, Jr.; Thomas H. West, Jr.
Number of staff: 1 part-time professional.
EIN: 046044779

3959
The Mark D. Hostetter and Alexander N. Habib Foundation ✧
c/o Mark D. Hostetter, Vinik Asset Mgmt.
260 Franklin St., Ste. 1900
Boston, MA   02110

Established in 1997 in MA.
Donor: Mark D. Hostetter.
Foundation type: Independent foundation.
Financial data (yr. ended 12/31/05): Assets, $19,772,484 (M); gifts received, $1,000,000; expenditures, $589,957; qualifying distributions, $587,113; giving activities include $585,200 for 27 grants (high: $328,000; low: $500).
Purpose and activities: Giving to Presbyterian agencies and churches, and for gay and lesbian concerns.
Fields of interest: Hospitals (specialty); End of life care; Health care; Recreation; Protestant agencies & churches; LGBTQ.
Limitations: Applications not accepted. Giving on a national basis, with some emphasis on New York, NY. No grants to individuals.
Application information: Contributes only to pre-selected organizations.
Trustees: Alexander N. Habib; Mark D. Hostetter.
EIN: 043386858
Selected grants: The following grants were reported in 2004.
$43,100 to Family Pride Coalition, DC.
$40,000 to Presbyterian Conference Association, Holmes, NY.
$5,000 to New York Theological Seminary, New York, NY.
$5,000 to Wissahickon Hospice, Bala Cynwyd, PA.
$5,000 to Zion Lutheran Church, Bristol, PA.
$4,500 to Living Pulpit, Bronx, NY.
$1,000 to Church of the Covenant, Boston, MA.
$1,000 to First Presbyterian Church, Oyster Bay, NY.
$1,000 to Presbyterian Senior Services, New York, NY.
$500 to Sacred Hearts Academy, Honolulu, HI.

3960
Franklin and Alice Hoyt Charitable Foundation ✧
c/o Bingham Legg Advisors, LLC
45 Milk St.
Boston, MA   02109-5105

Established in 2001 in MA.
Donors: Franklin K. Hoyt; Alice P. Hoyt.
Foundation type: Independent foundation.
Financial data (yr. ended 12/31/04): Assets, $1,228,035 (M); expenditures, $538,227; qualifying distributions, $519,186; giving activities include $519,186 for 19 grants (high: $254,108; low: $500).
Fields of interest: Elementary/secondary education; Environment, natural resources; Environment; Human services.
Limitations: Applications not accepted. Giving primarily in MA and ME. No grants to individuals.
Application information: Contributes only to pre-selected organizations.
Trustees: Alice H. Hall; F. Sherman Hoyt; Marian Morgan.
EIN: 043554961

3961
The Hyams Foundation, Inc. ▼ ✧
(formerly Sarah A. Hyams Fund)
50 Federal St., 9th Fl.
Boston, MA   02110   (617) 426-5600
Contact: Elizabeth B. Smith, Exec. Dir.
FAX: (617) 426-5696;
E-mail: info@hyamsfoundation.org; Additional e-mail for questions regarding application process: sperry@hyamsfoundation.org; URL: http://www.hyamsfoundation.org

Established in 1929 in MA as the Sarah A. Hyams Fund; in 1991 merged with the Godfrey Hyams Trust and adopted current name.
Donors: Godfrey M. Hyams†; Sarah A. Hyams†.
Foundation type: Independent foundation.
Financial data (yr. ended 12/31/04): Assets, $123,841,735 (M); gifts received, $50,000; expenditures, $7,051,398; qualifying distributions, $6,843,186; giving activities include $5,102,840 for 147 grants (high: $100,000; low: $500; average: $25,000–$50,000), $172,821 for 4 foundation-administered programs and $660,000 for 1 loan/program-related investment.
Purpose and activities: The mission of the foundation is to increase economic, social justice and power within low-income communities. The foundation believes that investing in strategies that enable low-income people to increase their communities will have the greatest social return in these times. The foundation will carry out its mission by: supporting civic participation by low-income communities; promoting economic development that benefits low-income neighborhoods and their residents; and developing the talents and skills of low-income youth.
Fields of interest: Adult/continuing education; Reproductive health, family planning; AIDS; Housing/shelter, development; Human services; Youth, services; Family services; Homeless, human services; Civil rights, race/intergroup relations; Urban/community development; Community development; Aging; Disabilities, people with; Asians/Pacific Islanders; African Americans/Blacks; Hispanics/Latinos; Native Americans/

American Indians; AIDS, people with; LGBTQ; Immigrants/refugees; Economically disadvantaged.

Type of support: General/operating support; Continuing support; Program development; Technical assistance; Program-related investments/loans; Matching/challenge support.

Limitations: Giving primarily in Boston and Chelsea, MA. No support for municipal, state, or federal agencies; institutions of higher learning for standard educational programs; religious organizations for sectarian religious purposes; or national or regional health organizations; support for medical research is being phased out. No grants to individuals, or for endowment funds, hospitals and health centers, capital campaigns, fellowships, publications, conferences, films or videos or curriculum development.

Publications: Annual report; Grants list; Informational brochure (including application guidelines).

Application information: The foundation accepts the Associated Grantmakers of Massachusetts' Common Proposal Form. See foundation's Web site for application form and guidelines. Application form required.

Initial approach: 2-page letter of interest or proposal, no more than 10 pages
Copies of proposal: 1
Deadline(s): Mar. 1, July 7 and Nov. 15
Board meeting date(s): Feb., June., and Oct.
Final notification: 3 to 4 months

Officers and Trustees:* John H. Clymer,* Chair.; Meizhu Lui,* Vice-Chair.; Barbara E. Casey,* Clerk; Roslyn M. Watson,* Treas.; Elizabeth B. Smith, Exec. Dir.; Iris Gomez; Karen L. Mapp; Long Nguyen; John H. Sarvey; Adam D. Seitchik; Edward M. Swan, Jr.; Martella Wilson-Taylor.

Number of staff: 6 full-time professional; 2 full-time support; 1 part-time support.

EIN: 046013680

Selected grants: The following grants were reported in 2004.

$115,000 to Boston Foundation, Boston, MA. 2 grants: $75,000, $40,000

$100,000 to Institute for Responsive Education, Boston, MA.

$75,000 to Chelsea Human Services Collaborative, Chelsea, MA.

$60,000 to Allston-Brighton Community Development Corporation, Allston, MA.

$50,000 to Boston Urban Youth Foundation, Boston, MA.

$35,000 to Third Sector New England, Boston, MA.

$30,000 to Catholic Charitable Bureau of the Archdiocese of Boston, Boston, MA.

$30,000 to Project Hip-Hop, Boston, MA.

$25,000 to Massachusetts Advocates for Children, Task Force on Children Out of School, Boston, MA.

3962
The Lawrence H. Hyde, Jr. Charitable Trust
P.O. Box 854
Harwich Port, MA 02646

Established in 1993 in MA.
Donor: Lawrence H. Hyde, Jr.
Foundation type: Independent foundation.
Financial data (yr. ended 12/31/05): Assets, $3,656,314 (M); expenditures, $474,983; qualifying distributions, $452,000; giving activities include $452,000 for 15 grants (high: $132,000; low: $1,000).

Purpose and activities: Support of Catholic seminaries in impoverished areas.

Fields of interest: Roman Catholic agencies & churches.

International interests: Africa; Asia; South America.

Type of support: Continuing support.

Limitations: Applications not accepted. No grants to individuals.

Application information: Contributes only to pre-selected organizations.

Officer: Lawrence H. Hyde, Jr., Pres.

EIN: 137024608

3963
The Iacocca Foundation
17 Arlington St.
Boston, MA 02116 (617) 267-7747
Contact: Dana Ball
URL: http://www.iacoccafoundation.org

Established in 1984 in MA and MI.
Donor: Lido A. Iacocca.
Foundation type: Independent foundation.
Financial data (yr. ended 12/31/04): Assets, $44,770,907 (M); gifts received, $665,619; expenditures, $2,895,910; qualifying distributions, $2,583,763; giving activities include $1,664,774 for 49 grants (high: $724,053; low: $350).

Purpose and activities: The primary purpose of the foundation is to fund innovative and promising diabetes research programs and projects that will lead to a cure for the disease and alleviate complications caused by it.

Fields of interest: Hospitals (general); Diabetes; Diabetes research.

Type of support: Equipment; Conferences/ seminars; Professorships; Fellowships; Research; Matching/challenge support.

Limitations: Giving on a national basis. No grants for start-up funds, buildings or capital improvements, stem cell research employing embryonic cloning, hospital and university general fund drives, or for general operating costs of hospitals, research institutes, buildings, clinical care clinics, etc.

Publications: Application guidelines.

Application information: See foundation Web site for full application guidelines and requirements, including downloadable application form. Application form submitted by fax not accepted. Application form required.

Initial approach: Completed application form
Copies of proposal: 6
Deadline(s): Mar. 1
Board meeting date(s): Spring
Final notification: June 1

Officers and Trustees:* Kathryn Iacocca Hentz, Pres.; Lido A. Iacocca,* V.P.; Louis E. Lataif; Glenn White; William R. Winn.

Number of staff: 3 full-time professional.

EIN: 386071154

Selected grants: The following grants were reported in 2004.

$1,330,372 to Iacocca Foundation, Boston, MA. 5 grants: $20,000, $500,000, $724,053, $44,700, $41,619

3964
Inavale Foundation, Inc. ▼ ◇
c/o Hemenway & Barnes
P.O. Box 961209
Boston, MA 02196-1209

Established in 1998 in MA.
Donor: Katherine Buffett.
Foundation type: Independent foundation.
Financial data (yr. ended 12/31/04): Assets, $16,443,619 (M); gifts received, $10,000,000; expenditures, $5,108,566; qualifying distributions, $5,100,917; giving activities include $5,100,800 for 38 grants (high: $4,130,800; low: $1,000; average: $1,000–$10,000).

Purpose and activities: Giving primarily for community foundations, education, the arts, Baptist and Lutheran churches, and Jewish organizations and temples.

Fields of interest: Museums (children's); Higher education; Education; Human services; Foundations (community); Protestant agencies & churches; Jewish agencies & temples.

Limitations: Applications not accepted. Giving primarily in MA, ME, and MC; some funding nationally. No grants to individuals.

Application information: Contributes only to pre-selected organizations.

Officers and Directors:* William N. Buffett,* Pres.; Susan Kennedy,* Treas.; Thomas M. Buffett; Wendy O. Buffett; Noah E. Buffett-Kennedy.

EIN: 043409789

Selected grants: The following grants were reported in 2004.

$4,130,800 to Carleton College, Northfield, MN. For general support.

$516,000 to Posse Foundation, New York, NY. 2 grants: $16,000 (For general support), $500,000 (For general support).

$60,000 to Old Cambridge Baptist Church, Cambridge, MA. For general support.

$30,000 to Beyt Tikkun, San Francisco, CA. For general support.

$30,000 to Musica Sacra, Cambridge, MA. For general support.

$25,000 to Buckingham Browne and Nichols School, Cambridge, MA. For general support.

$25,000 to Omaha Schools Foundation, Omaha, NE. For general support.

$25,000 to Trinity Lutheran Church, Omaha, NE. For general support.

$18,000 to Boston Education Development Foundation, Boston, MA. For general support.

3965
Island Foundation, Inc. ◇
589 Mill St.
Marion, MA 02738-1553 (508) 748-2809
Contact: Michael Moore, Pres.
FAX: (508) 748-0991;
E-mail: islandfdn@earthlink.net

Incorporated in 1980 in MA as Ram Island, Inc.; current entity formed in 1986 by merger with Green Island, Inc.
Donor: W. Van Alan Clark, Jr.‡
Foundation type: Independent foundation.
Financial data (yr. ended 12/31/04): Assets, $40,477,232 (M); expenditures, $2,007,509; qualifying distributions, $1,877,610; giving activities include $1,756,270 for 78 grants (high: $160,000; low: $1,200).

Purpose and activities: Giving primarily for: 1) coastal water protection in New England environmental projects: right whale research, impact of toxins on wildlife-research, land use conservation in southeast MA, and 2) building the capacity of individuals and neighborhoods in the city of New Bedford, MA; and 3) alternative education programs.

Fields of interest: Education; Environment, natural resources; Environment; Animals/wildlife, preservation/protection; Economic development; Community development; Marine science; Biological sciences; Public policy, research.

Type of support: General/operating support; Capital campaigns; Equipment; Land acquisition; Program development; Curriculum development; Internship funds; Research; Technical assistance; Program-related investments/loans; Exchange programs; Matching/challenge support.

Limitations: Giving primarily in New Bedford, MA, for economic and community development, MA, ME, and RI for environmental programs. No support for religious organizations for sectarian purposes or political organizations. No grants to individuals.

Publications: Annual report (including application guidelines).

Application information: Full proposals by invitation only. Associated Grantmakers of MA Common Proposal Format accepted. Application form not required.

Initial approach: Telephone or letter
Copies of proposal: 1
Deadline(s): Rolling
Board meeting date(s): Annually and as needed

Officers: Michael Moore, Pres.; Douglas Watson, V.P.; Peter Nesbeda, Treas.; Julie A. Early, Exec. Dir.

Directors: K. Clark; Stephen Clark; Hannah Moore; Christopher Tupper; Cricket Tupper; Jo-Ann Watson.

Number of staff: 1 full-time professional.

EIN: 042670567

Selected grants: The following grants were reported in 2004.

$160,000 to YMCA, Southcoast, New Bedford, MA.
$125,000 to Community Boating Center, New Bedford, MA.
$50,000 to Center for Coastal Studies, Provincetown, MA.
$50,000 to Save the Bay, Providence, RI.
$40,000 to Cape Cod Stranding Network, Buzzards Bay, MA.
$40,000 to Penikese Island School, Woods Hole, MA.
$35,000 to United Way of Greater New Bedford, New Bedford, MA.
$35,000 to Waterfront Historic Area League, New Bedford, MA.
$25,000 to Land Trust Alliance, DC.
$15,000 to Coalition Against Poverty, New Bedford, MA.

3966
Ruth H. Jackson Charitable Trust ✧ ☆
34 Proctor St.
Manchester, MA 01944-1446
Contact: Polly J. Townsend, Tr.

Established in 1951 in PA.
Foundation type: Independent foundation.
Financial data (yr. ended 12/31/05): Assets, $12,458 (M); expenditures, $3,190,484; qualifying distributions, $3,176,997; giving activities include $3,176,997 for grants.

Purpose and activities: Giving to higher education, religion, and public service agencies.
Fields of interest: Arts; Education; Human services; Philanthropy/voluntarism; Christian agencies & churches.
Limitations: Giving primarily in PA.
Application information:
Initial approach: Letter
Deadline(s): None
Trustees: W. Richard Jackson; Polly J. Townsend.
Number of staff: 1
EIN: 256065763

3967
The Jacobson Family Trust Foundation ✧
14 Highfields Rd.
Wayland, MA 01778

Established in 1997 in MA.
Donor: Jonathon Jacobson.
Foundation type: Independent foundation.
Financial data (yr. ended 12/31/03): Assets, $36,583,824 (M); gifts received, $3,009,038; expenditures, $2,344,621; qualifying distributions, $2,342,085; giving activities include $2,340,084 for 44 grants (high: $750,000; low: $500).
Fields of interest: Secondary school/education; Education; Health organizations; Big Brothers/Big Sisters; Human services; Children, services; Federated giving programs; Jewish federated giving programs.
Limitations: Applications not accepted. Giving primarily in MA. No grants to individuals.
Application information: Contributes only to pre-selected organizations.
Trustees: Joanna Jacobson; Jonathon Jacobson.
EIN: 046836735
Selected grants: The following grants were reported in 2004.
$168,500 to Steppingstone Foundation, Boston, MA.
$150,000 to Brigham and Womens Hospital, Boston, MA.
$75,000 to David Project, Newtonville, MA.
$50,600 to Gilman School, Baltimore, MD.
$50,000 to One Family Campaign, Boston, MA.
$50,000 to Robin Hood Foundation, New York, NY.
$36,000 to Hadassah, Worcester, MA.
$30,500 to Fessenden School, West Newton, MA.
$10,000 to Harvard University, Cambridge, MA.
$3,500 to Tenacre Country Day School, Wellesley, MA.

3968
The Janey Fund Charitable Trust ✧
c/o Samet & Co., PC
1330 Boylston St.
Chestnut Hill, MA 02467

Established in 1986 in MA.
Donor: Daniel E. Rothenberg.
Foundation type: Independent foundation.
Financial data (yr. ended 6/30/05): Assets, $4,621,852 (M); gifts received, $712,500; expenditures, $727,557; qualifying distributions, $724,000; giving activities include $722,500 for 43 grants (high: $100,000; low: $5,000).
Purpose and activities: Giving primarily for arts and culture, education, and social services.

Fields of interest: Arts; Higher education; Medical care, rehabilitation; Human services; Community development.
Type of support: General/operating support.
Limitations: Applications not accepted. Giving primarily in MA and NY. No grants to individuals.
Application information: Contributes only to pre-selected organizations.
Trustees: William Buckley; Julian Cohen; Allen W. Rothenberg; Ann Rothenberg; Daniel E. Rothenberg; Edward Rothenberg; Susan Rothenberg; Theodore S. Samet.
EIN: 112836564

3969
The Jebediah Foundation ✧
c/o Bingham Legg Advisors, LLC
45 Milk St.
Boston, MA 02109-5105
Application address: c/o Colin S. Marshall, Bingham, McCutchen, LLP, 150 Federal St., Boston, MA 02110-1726, tel.: (617) 951-8576

Established in 1989 in MA.
Donor: Eunice Taylor Vanderhoef†.
Foundation type: Independent foundation.
Financial data (yr. ended 12/31/05): Assets, $11,129,885 (M); expenditures, $671,685; qualifying distributions, $605,666; giving activities include $578,000 for 117 grants (high: $50,000; low: $300).
Purpose and activities: Giving primarily for the arts, education, health and human services.
Fields of interest: Media, radio; Performing arts, theater; Arts; Higher education; Education; Health care; Human services; Protestant agencies & churches.
Type of support: General/operating support; Building/renovation.
Limitations: Giving primarily on the East Coast. No grants to individuals.
Application information: Application form not required.
Deadline(s): None
Trustees: Daniel Amory; Mary Amory; Robert Amory; Colin S. Marshall.
EIN: 222999430

3970
Edward C. Johnson Fund ▼ ✧
82 Devonshire St., Ste. S3
Boston, MA 02109-3614 (617) 563-6806
Contact: Anne-Marie Soulliere, Pres.

Trust established in 1964 in MA.
Donors: Edward C. Johnson II†; Edward C. Johnson III; Abigail P. Johnson; Edward C. Johnson IV; Elizabeth L. Johnson; Abel Partners; FMR Corp.
Foundation type: Independent foundation.
Financial data (yr. ended 12/31/04): Assets, $314,102,086 (M); gifts received, $5,230,273; expenditures, $23,857,005; qualifying distributions, $23,078,867; giving activities include $22,323,219 for 74 grants (high: $15,450,000; low: $525; average: $15,000–$200,000).
Purpose and activities: Emphasis on museums, historical societies, medical institutions, and some youth programs. Support also for the visual arts, historic preservation, higher education, elementary and secondary schools, and environmental organizations.

Fields of interest: Visual arts; Museums; Performing arts; Historic preservation/historical societies; Arts; Environment; Health care; Medical research, institute; Youth, services.

Type of support: Capital campaigns; Building/renovation; Endowments; Program development; Research.

Limitations: Giving limited to the greater Boston, MA, area. No grants to individuals, or for scholarships.

Publications: Application guidelines.

Application information: Applicants to the Edward C. Johnson Fund may not submit proposals simultaneously to the Fidelity Foundation nor to the Fidelity Nonprofit Management Foundation. Application form required.

Initial approach: Letter of inquiry
Copies of proposal: 1
Deadline(s): Mar. 30 and Oct. 30
Board meeting date(s): June and Dec.

Officers and Directors:* Edward C. Johnson III,* Chair.; Anne-Marie Soulliere, Pres.; Patricia R. Hurley, Secy.; Jeffrey P. Resnik, Treas.; Abigail P. Johnson; Edward C. Johnson IV; Elizabeth L. Johnson.

EIN: 046108344

Selected grants: The following grants were reported in 2004.

$15,450,000 to Brookfield Arts Foundation, Boston, MA. For art acquisition.

$1,181,190 to Peabody Essex Museum, Salem, MA. 4 grants: $250,000 (For art acquisition), $352,522 (For operating support), $450,000 (For art acquisition), $128,668 (For art acquisition).

$750,000 to Boys and Girls Club of Allston-Brighton, West End House, Allston, MA. For construction and renovation.

$500,000 to Trinity Boston Foundation, Boston, MA. For preservation of buildings.

$300,000 to Winterthur Museum, Garden and Library, Winterthur, DE. For art acquisition.

$200,000 to Harbor House, Southwest Harbor, ME. For construction and renovation.

$184,754 to National Trust, London, England. For public spaces and art.

3971

The Gerald R. Jordan Foundation ◇

75 State St., Rm. 2410
Boston, MA 02109

Established in 1996 in MA.

Foundation type: Independent foundation.

Financial data (yr. ended 12/31/05): Assets, $25,539,857 (M); expenditures, $1,115,727; qualifying distributions, $851,104; giving activities include $851,104 for 52 grants (high: $200,000; low: $200).

Purpose and activities: Giving primarily for the arts, education, health, and youth services.

Fields of interest: Museums; Historic preservation/historical societies; Higher education; Education; Aquariums; Hospitals (general); Health care; Cancer research; Boys & girls clubs; Federated giving programs.

Type of support: Scholarship funds.

Limitations: Applications not accepted. Giving primarily in New England. No grants to individuals.

Application information: Contributes only to pre-selected organizations.

Trustee: Gerald R. Jordan, Jr.

EIN: 043293081

3972

JSJN Children's Charitable Trust ◇ ☆

(formerly Webster Charitable Trust)
c/o Bain Capital, LLC
111 Huntington Ave., 35th Fl.
Boston, MA 02199

Established in 1998 in MA.

Donor: Stephen Pagliuca.

Foundation type: Independent foundation.

Financial data (yr. ended 9/30/05): Assets, $2,193,347 (M); gifts received, $302,046; expenditures, $388,500; qualifying distributions, $388,500; giving activities include $388,500 for 3 grants (high: $300,000; low: $20,000).

Fields of interest: Higher education; Children/youth, services.

Limitations: Applications not accepted. Giving primarily in MA and NC. No grants to individuals.

Application information: Contributes only to pre-selected organizations.

Trustee: Stephen G. Pagliuca.

EIN: 046893292

3973

Kahn Charitable Foundation ◇

(formerly JED Charitable Foundation)
c/o Atlantic Trust Co., N.A.
100 Federal St., 37th Fl.
Boston, MA 02110

Established in 1992 in MA.

Donor: The Jed Trust.

Foundation type: Independent foundation.

Financial data (yr. ended 6/30/05): Assets, $14,415,514 (M); expenditures, $548,978; qualifying distributions, $542,352; giving activities include $522,000 for 28 grants (high: $90,000; low: $2,500).

Fields of interest: Elementary/secondary education; Higher education, university; Environment, natural resources; Environment, water resources; Animal welfare.

Limitations: Applications not accepted. Giving limited to Cambridge, MA. No grants to individuals.

Application information: Contributes only to pre-selected organizations.

Trustees: Joseph Kahn; Edward I. Rudman.

EIN: 046718867

Selected grants: The following grants were reported in 2005.

$25,000 to National Public Radio, DC.

$21,000 to Multiple Sclerosis Society, National, New York, NY.

$10,000 to Childrens Hospital.

$10,000 to Hole in the Wall Gang Fund, New Haven, CT.

$10,000 to Peabody Essex Museum, Salem, MA.

$2,500 to Middlesex School, Concord, MA.

3974

Karp Family Foundation ◇

c/o New England Development
1 Wells Ave.
Newton, MA 02459
Contact: Jill E. Karp, Tr.; Stephen R. Karp, Tr.

Established in 1994 in MA.

Donor: Stephen R. Karp.

Foundation type: Independent foundation.

Financial data (yr. ended 2/28/04): Assets, $7,511,405 (M); gifts received, $1,184,464; expenditures, $821,530; qualifying distributions, $819,747; giving activities include $819,747 for 24 grants (high: $290,000; low: $500).

Fields of interest: Secondary school/education; Higher education, college; Aquariums; Hospitals (general); Cancer; Multiple sclerosis; Human services; Jewish agencies & temples.

Limitations: Applications not accepted. Giving primarily in MA. No grants to individuals.

Application information: Contributes only to pre-selected organizations.

Trustees: Jill E. Karp; Stephen R. Karp.

EIN: 043226725

3975

Keane Family Foundation ◇

c/o Weston Financial Group
40 William St., Ste. 100
Wellesley, MA 02481

Established in 1993 in MA.

Donors: John Keane; Marilyn Keane.

Foundation type: Independent foundation.

Financial data (yr. ended 12/31/05): Assets, $8,686,032 (M); expenditures, $471,444; qualifying distributions, $426,150; giving activities include $426,150 for 40 grants (high: $150,000; low: $100).

Purpose and activities: Giving primarily for the arts particularly art museums as well as for higher education including a business school; some giving also for children, youth, hospitals, and social services including a school for the blind.

Fields of interest: Media, television; Museums (art); Performing arts; Arts; Higher education; Business school/education; Education; Aquariums; Health care; Human services; Children/youth, services; Federated giving programs.

Limitations: Applications not accepted. Giving primarily in Boston, MA. No grants to individuals.

Application information: Contributes only to pre-selected organizations. Unsolicited requests for funds not accepted.

Trustees: John Keane; Marilyn Keane.

EIN: 046743248

3976

The Keel Foundation ◇

c/o Peter A. Wilson, Palmer & Dodge, LLP
111 Huntington Ave.
Boston, MA 02199 (617) 239-0771
Contact: Diane Gilchrist, Exec. Dir.

Established in 1992 in MA.

Foundation type: Independent foundation.

Financial data (yr. ended 12/31/05): Assets, $3,433,957 (M); expenditures, $355,818; qualifying distributions, $336,923; giving activities include $330,000 for 4 grants (high: $100,000; low: $30,000).

Fields of interest: Higher education.

Limitations: Giving primarily in CT and MA. No support for religious organizations. No grants to individuals.

Application information: Application form required.

Initial approach: Letter or telephone requesting application form
Deadline(s): None

Trustees: Mark M. Christopher; Kenneth H. Olsen; Peter A. Wilson.
EIN: 043166698
Selected grants: The following grants were reported in 2004.
$200,000 to Assumption College, Worcester, MA.
$50,000 to Connecticut College, New London, CT.

3977
The Henry P. Kendall Foundation
176 Federal St.
Boston, MA 02110 (617) 951-2525
Contact: Theodore M. Smith, Exec. Dir.
FAX: (617) 951-2556;
E-mail: request_info@kendall.org; URL: http://www.kendall.org

Trust established in 1957 in MA.
Donors: Henry Kendall†; Henry Way Kendall Trust; and members of the Henry P. Kendall family.
Foundation type: Independent foundation.
Financial data (yr. ended 12/31/05): Assets, $75,258,403 (M); gifts received, $54,000; expenditures, $9,627,437; qualifying distributions, $8,939,569; giving activities include $8,211,888 for grants, and $23,821 for foundation-administered programs.
Purpose and activities: Emphasis on strategic environmental policies/ecosystem management.
Fields of interest: Environment, natural resources.
International interests: Canada.
Type of support: Management development/capacity building; Research; General/operating support; Program development; Seed money; Internship funds.
Limitations: Applications not accepted. Giving primarily in western Canada and in New England, the Northeast and the Northwestern United States. No support for waste clean-ups, toxic or air/water pollution prevention or pollution monitoring initiatives, land trusts, or species-specific preservation efforts. No grants to individuals, or for capital or endowment funds, building construction/operation, basic research, scholarships, fellowships, equipment, debt reduction, or conference participation/travel.
Publications: Biennial report.
Application information: Unsolicited proposals and inquiries will not be reviewed.
Board meeting date(s): Mar., June, and Nov.
Officer: Theodore M. Smith, Exec. Dir.
Trustees: Andrew W. Kendall; John P. Kendall; Phoebe Winder.
Number of staff: 6 full-time professional.
EIN: 046029103

3978
Kessler Family Foundation ◇
c/o Tanager Financial Svcs.
800 South St., Ste. 195
Waltham, MA 02453
Contact: Antoinette Russell

Established in 1993 in MA.
Donors: Howard J. Kessler; Patricia M. Kessler.
Foundation type: Independent foundation.
Financial data (yr. ended 12/31/03): Assets, $24,758,897 (M); gifts received, $8,688,097; expenditures, $1,458,896; qualifying distributions, $1,390,425; giving activities include $1,322,277 for 94 grants (high: $225,000; low: $100).

Purpose and activities: Giving primarily for education, medical research, and human services; funding also for Jewish and other federated giving programs.
Fields of interest: Higher education; Education; Hospitals (general); Health organizations; Medical research, institute; Cancer research; Boys & girls clubs; Human services; American Red Cross; Federated giving programs; Jewish federated giving programs.
Limitations: Applications not accepted. Giving primarily in MA and FL. No grants to individuals.
Application information: Contributes only to pre-selected organizations.
Trustees: Howard J. Kessler; Patricia M. Kessler.
EIN: 043213614

3979
Michael R. Kidder 1996 Charitable Trust ◇
c/o Edwards Angell, Palmer & Dodge, LLP
P.O. Box 990129, Private Client Dept.
Boston, MA 02199-0129

Established in 1996 in MA.
Donor: Michael R. Kidder.
Foundation type: Independent foundation.
Financial data (yr. ended 8/31/05): Assets, $9,982,203 (M); expenditures, $789,480; qualifying distributions, $721,447; giving activities include $713,972 for 5 grants (high: $284,972; low: $87,906).
Fields of interest: Education; Environment.
Limitations: Applications not accepted. Giving primarily in Martha's Vineyard, MA. No grants to individuals.
Application information: Contributes only to pre-selected organizations.
Trustee: Michael R. Kidder.
EIN: 046824225
Selected grants: The following grants were reported in 2004.
$154,000 to FARM Institute, Edgartown, MA.
$42,500 to Featherstone Center for the Arts, Oak Bluffs, MA.
$20,000 to HGM Development, Keene, NH.
$20,000 to Marthas Vineyard Preservation Trust, Edgartown, MA.
$13,000 to Sheriffs Meadow Foundation, Vineyard Haven, MA.
$10,000 to Vineyard Voyagers, Edgartown, MA.
$10,000 to Yard, The, Chilmark, MA.
$5,000 to Marthas Vineyard Community Services, Vineyard Haven, MA.
$2,000 to Marthas Vineyard Hospital, Oak Bluffs, MA.
$500 to Massachusetts General Hospital, Boston, MA.

3980
Constance Killam Trust ◇
c/o Nutter, McClennen & Fish, LLP
155 Seaport Blvd., World Trade Ctr., W.
Boston, MA 02210-2604 (617) 439-2000
Contact: Thomas P. Jalkut, Tr.

Established in 1977 in MA.
Donor: Constance Killam†.
Foundation type: Independent foundation.
Financial data (yr. ended 4/30/06): Assets, $6,008,248 (M); expenditures, $448,138;

qualifying distributions, $390,000; giving activities include $390,000 for grants.
Purpose and activities: Giving primarily to protect the environment.
Fields of interest: Arts; Higher education; Environment, natural resources; Animals/wildlife, preservation/protection.
Limitations: Giving primarily in MA. No grants to individuals.
Application information:
Initial approach: Letter
Deadline(s): None
Trustees: Thomas P. Jalkut; John B. Newhall.
EIN: 046420685
Selected grants: The following grants were reported in 2006.
$25,000 to Saint Francis Xavier University, Antigonish, Canada. .
$25,000 to University of Vermont, Burlington, VT.
$10,000 to Arcadia University, Glenside, PA.
$10,000 to Dalhousie University, Halifax, Canada. .
$10,000 to McGill University, Montreal, Canada. .
$5,000 to Boston Symphony Orchestra, Boston, MA.

3981
Charles A. King Trust ◇
c/o Bank of America, N.A.
100 Federal St., MADE10020B
Boston, MA 02110 (617) 434-4847
Contact: Kerry H. Sullivan, V.P.
Application address: Deborah Pearce, c/o Bank of America, N.A., 75 State St., Boston, MA 02109; tels.: (617) 451-0049 or (617) 434-4846

Established in 1938 in MA.
Donor: Charles A. King†.
Foundation type: Independent foundation.
Financial data (yr. ended 12/31/05): Assets, $20,435,066 (M); expenditures, $1,020,509; qualifying distributions, $981,951; giving activities include $906,894 for 1 grant.
Purpose and activities: To encourage and support medical and surgical research projects carried on by charitable or educational corporations. Grants are awarded solely for postdoctoral research fellowships.
Fields of interest: Medical research, institute.
Type of support: Fellowships; Research.
Limitations: Giving limited to MA.
Publications: Application guidelines.
Application information: Fellowships are paid directly to sponsoring institutions. Visit The Medical Foundation's URL: http://www.tmfnet.org/grantmake.html. Application form required.
Initial approach: Telephone
Deadline(s): Dec.
Board meeting date(s): Dec.
Final notification: July
Trustees: Edward M. Dane; Richard H. Lovell; Bank of America, N.A.
EIN: 046012742

3982
Kingsbury Road Charitable Foundation ◇
P.O. Box 140
Mansfield, MA 02048-0140
Additional addresses: Roger B. Hunt, c/o Sullivan and Worcester, 1 Post Office Sq., Boston, MA 02109, Edward W. Weld, c/o Boston Family Office, 88 Broad St., Boston, MA 02110

Established in 1996 in MA.
Donors: Hamilton Osgood†; G. Grandchamps
Charitable Remainder Trust; R.L. Christmas
Charitable Remainder Trust.
Foundation type: Independent foundation.
Financial data (yr. ended 12/31/05): Assets,
$7,232,480 (M); gifts received, $36,539;
expenditures, $399,676; qualifying distributions,
$352,756; giving activities include $334,000 for 17
grants (high: $30,000; low: $7,000).
Purpose and activities: Giving primarily for the arts,
as well as for education, and human services.
Fields of interest: Media, television; Performing
arts, music; Performing arts, orchestra (symphony);
Elementary/secondary education; Education;
Animal welfare; Human services.
Type of support: General/operating support.
Limitations: Applications not accepted. Giving
primarily in MA. No grants to individuals.
Application information: Contributes only to
pre-selected organizations. Unsolicited requests for
funds not accepted.
Trustees: Roger B. Hunt; Edward W. Weld.
EIN: 046820320

3983

The Kittredge Foundation ✧
c/o Tanager Financial Services, Inc.
P.O. Box 540151
Waltham, MA   02454

Established in 2000 in MA.
Donors: Michael Kittredge; Lisa Kittredge.
Foundation type: Independent foundation.
Financial data (yr. ended 4/30/05): Assets,
$7,077,871 (M); expenditures, $1,060,524;
qualifying distributions, $1,007,796; giving
activities include $990,150 for 33 grants (high:
$500,000; low: $200).
Fields of interest: Education; Hospitals (general);
Cancer; Children/youth, services; Religion.
Limitations: Applications not accepted. Giving
primarily in MA. No grants to individuals.
Application information: Unsolicited requests for
funds not accepted.
Trustees: David Beatty; Lisa Kittredge; Michael
Kittredge; Steve Oliver.
EIN: 046911444
Selected grants: The following grants were reported
in 2005.
$50,000 to Bement School, Deerfield, MA.
$10,000 to American Heart Association, Dallas, TX.
$10,000 to Mercy Corps, Portland, OR.
$6,000 to YMCA. 2 grants: $5,000, $1,000
$5,000 to Northampton Community Music Center,
   Northampton, MA.
$5,000 to University of Hartford, West Hartford, CT.
$1,000 to American Cancer Society, Atlanta, GA.
$1,000 to Doc Hurley Scholarship Foundation,
   Hartford, CT.
$1,000 to Franklin Community Action Corporation,
   Greenfield, MA.

3984

The Kiva Foundation ✧ ☆
c/o Northstar
1000 Winter St., Box 203
Waltham, MA   02451-1448

Established in 1998.
Donor: Norman C. Payson.

Foundation type: Independent foundation.
Financial data (yr. ended 12/31/05): Assets,
$19,867,152 (M); expenditures, $1,151,619;
qualifying distributions, $893,594; giving activities
include $893,594 for grants.
Fields of interest: Hospitals (general).
Limitations: Applications not accepted. No grants to
individuals.
Application information: Contributes only to
pre-selected organizations.
Trustees: Robert L. Carson; Melinda B. Payson;
Norman C. Payson.
EIN: 043428609

3985

Klarman Family Foundation
(formerly The Seth A. & Beth S. Klarman Foundation)
1244 Boylston St., Ste. 309
Chestnut Hill, MA   02467-2116

Established in 1990 in MA.
Donors: Seth A. Klarman; Beth S. Klarman.
Foundation type: Independent foundation.
Financial data (yr. ended 12/31/04): Assets,
$55,651,590 (M); gifts received, $6,000,000;
expenditures, $4,580,181; qualifying distributions,
$3,983,324; giving activities include $3,887,952
for 165 grants (high: $571,500; low: $28).
Purpose and activities: Giving primarily for the arts,
Jewish organizations, education, and healing,
including children's hospitals, and human services.
Fields of interest: Education; Hospitals (general);
Boys & girls clubs; Human services; Children/youth,
services; Jewish federated giving programs.
Limitations: Applications not accepted. Giving
primarily in MA. No support for political
organizations. No grants to individuals, or for
endowments.
Application information: Contributes only to
pre-selected organizations.
Trustees: Beth S. Klarman; Seth A. Klarman.
Number of staff: 1 full-time professional; 1 full-time
support.
EIN: 043105768

3986

Knez Family Charitable Foundation ✧
c/o Castanea Partners
3 Newton Executive Park, Ste. 304
Newton, MA   02462

Established in 2001 in MA.
Donors: Brian J. Knez; Debra Smith Knez.
Foundation type: Independent foundation.
Financial data (yr. ended 11/30/05): Assets,
$6,603,788 (M); gifts received, $5,371,484;
expenditures, $373,970; qualifying distributions,
$373,970; giving activities include $369,876 for 35
grants (high: $207,376; low: $500).
Purpose and activities: Giving primarily for
education, social services and medical research.
Fields of interest: Education; Medical research,
institute; Boys & girls clubs; Human services;
Federated giving programs.
Limitations: Applications not accepted. No grants to
individuals.
Application information: Contributes only to
pre-selected organizations.
Trustees: Brian J. Knez; Debra Smith Knez.
EIN: 223850785

Selected grants: The following grants were reported
in 2005.
$207,376 to Boys and Girls Clubs of Boston,
   Boston, MA.
$12,500 to United Way.
$10,000 to Boston Medical Center, Boston, MA.
$5,000 to Childrens Museum.
$5,000 to Vermont Land Trust, Montpelier, VT.
$1,000 to Humane Society.
$1,000 to Meadowbrook School, Weston, MA.
$1,000 to Woodstock Historical Society,
   Woodstock, VT.

3987

Norman Knight Charitable Foundation ✧
63 Bay State Rd.
Boston, MA   02215   (617) 262-1950
Contact: Norman Knight, Tr.

Established in 1959 in MA.
Donor: Norman Knight.
Foundation type: Independent foundation.
Financial data (yr. ended 12/31/05): Assets,
$6,682,977 (M); gifts received, $48,358;
expenditures, $560,348; qualifying distributions,
$527,550; giving activities include $527,550 for 44
grants (high: $210,000; low: $300).
Fields of interest: Museums; Performing arts;
Higher education; Hospitals (general); Health
organizations, association; Recreation; Boys & girls
clubs; Human services; Youth, services; Community
development; Federated giving programs; Roman
Catholic agencies & churches.
Limitations: Applications not accepted. Giving
primarily in Boston, MA. No grants to individuals.
Application information: Unsolicited requests for
funds not accepted.
Trustee: Norman Knight.
EIN: 046056824
Selected grants: The following grants were reported
in 2005.
$210,000 to Massachusetts Eye and Ear Infirmary,
   Boston, MA.
$29,500 to Broadcasters Foundation, Greenwich,
   CT. 3 grants: $5,000, $12,000, $12,500
$25,000 to Emerson College, Boston, MA.
$20,000 to Massachusetts General Hospital,
   Boston, MA.
$10,000 to Worcester Academy, Worcester, MA.
$8,000 to Genesis Fund, Canton, MA.
$5,000 to Belmont Hill School, Belmont, MA.
$5,000 to Perkins School for the Blind, Watertown,
   MA.

3988

The Kobren Family Charitable Trust
c/o Lynch, Brewer, Hoffman & Fink, LLP
101 Federal St., 22nd Fl.
Boston, MA   02110-1800
Contact: Peter W. Fink, Tr.

Established in 1999 in MA.
Donor: Eric M. Kobren.
Foundation type: Independent foundation.
Financial data (yr. ended 9/30/05): Assets,
$2,938,728 (M); gifts received, $307,885;
expenditures, $457,158; qualifying distributions,
$447,025; giving activities include $447,025 for 2
+ grants (high: $316,825).
Fields of interest: Education; Hospitals (general);
Jewish agencies & temples.

Limitations: Applications not accepted. Giving primarily in MA and NY.
Application information: Unsolicited requests for funds not accepted.
Trustees: Peter W. Fink; Catherine S. Kobren.
EIN: 046885196

3989
Robert and Myra Kraft Family Foundation, Inc. ✧

(formerly Robert and Myra Kraft and J. Hiatt Foundation, Inc.)
c/o Kraft Group
1 Patriot Pl.
Foxboro, MA 02035-1388 (508) 698-4618
Contact: Robert K. Kraft, Pres.

Incorporated in 1951 in MA.
Donors: Jacob Hiatt; Frances L. Hiatt; Robert Kraft; Myra Kraft; Estey Charitable Income Trust; Rand-Whitney Packaging Corp.
Foundation type: Independent foundation.
Financial data (yr. ended 12/31/05): Assets, $37,387,324 (M); gifts received, $5,805,958; expenditures, $1,039,290; qualifying distributions, $988,893; giving activities include $988,893 for 53 grants (high: $145,000; low: $2).
Purpose and activities: Giving primarily for higher education.
Fields of interest: Higher education; Education; Health care; Children, services; Federated giving programs.
Limitations: Giving primarily in MA.
Application information: Application form not required.
Initial approach: Letter
Deadline(s): None
Officers: Robert K. Kraft, Pres.; Myra H. Kraft, Clerk.
Directors: Daniel A. Kraft; David H. Kraft; Jonathan A. Kraft; Joshua W. Kraft.
EIN: 046050716

3990
The Vernon K. Krieble Foundation, Inc. ✧ ☆

306 Main St.
P.O. Box 15034
Worcester, MA 01615-0034 (303) 758-3956
Contact: Helen E. Krieble, Pres.

Established in 1985 in CT.
Donor: Gladys V.K. Delmas†.
Foundation type: Independent foundation.
Financial data (yr. ended 12/31/05): Assets, $19,611,527 (M); expenditures, $779,511; qualifying distributions, $576,907; giving activities include $424,350 for 51 grants (high: $77,500; low: $600).
Purpose and activities: Giving primarily for recognized 501(c)(3) public policy organizations, including government, national security, and civil rights issues; support also for universities in the U.S. and Canada, art schools and organizations, and hospitals.
Fields of interest: Performing arts; Historic preservation/historical societies; Arts; Higher education; Education; Hospitals (general); Youth development, services; Civil rights; Public policy, research; Government/public administration; Leadership development; Public affairs.

International interests: Canada; Turks & Caicos Islands.
Limitations: Giving on a national and international basis; primarily in the U.S. No grants to individuals.
Publications: Annual report (including application guidelines).
Application information: Application form not required.
Initial approach: Letter
Copies of proposal: 1
Deadline(s): None
Board meeting date(s): June and Dec.
Officers: Helen E. Krieble,* Pres.; Frederick Krieble, V.P.; Amanda C. Fusscas,* Secy.; Christopher P. Fusscas,* Treas.
Director: Frederick B. Fusscas.
Number of staff: 1 part-time support.
EIN: 222538914
Selected grants: The following grants were reported in 2003.
$55,000 to Center for the Study of Popular Culture, Los Angeles, CA. For general support.
$10,000 to American Foreign Policy Council, DC. For general support.
$5,000 to Connecticut Childrens Medical Center, Hartford, CT. For general support.
$5,000 to Federalist Society for Law and Public Policy Studies, DC. For general support.
$5,000 to National Center for Policy Analysis, Dallas, TX. For general support.
$2,000 to University of Hartford, Hartford Art School, West Hartford, CT. For general support.
$1,750 to Council for National Policy, Arlington, VA. For general support.
$1,000 to American Enterprise Institute for Public Policy Research, DC. For general support.
$1,000 to Center for Security Policy, DC. For general support.
$1,000 to Harvard University, Cambridge, MA. For general support.

3991
The Judith & Douglas Krupp Family Charitable Foundation ✧

1 Beacon St., Ste. 1500
Boston, MA 02108

Established in 1996 in MA.
Donors: Douglas Krupp; Judith Krupp.
Foundation type: Independent foundation.
Financial data (yr. ended 12/31/05): Assets, $3,072,997 (M); gifts received, $3,299,650; expenditures, $405,025; qualifying distributions, $406,025; giving activities include $405,900 for grants.
Purpose and activities: Giving primarily to medical associations, and for education and to Jewish organizations.
Fields of interest: Performing arts; History/archaeology; Education; Hospitals (general); Jewish federated giving programs; Jewish agencies & temples.
Limitations: Applications not accepted. Giving primarily in MA, and RI. No grants to individuals.
Application information: Contributes only to pre-selected organizations.
Trustees: Douglas Krupp; Judith Krupp; Lawrence I. Silverstein.
EIN: 043294086
Selected grants: The following grants were reported in 2003.
$400,000 to Bryant University, Smithfield, RI. For general support.

$225,000 to Combined Jewish Philanthropies of Greater Boston, Boston, MA. For general support.
$160,000 to Huntington Theater Company, Boston, MA. For general support.
$34,000 to Berkshire Hills Music Academy, Newton, MA. For general support.
$25,000 to Commonwealth Shakespeare Company, Boston, MA. For general support.
$20,000 to Anti-Defamation League of Bnai Brith, New York, NY. For general support.
$6,500 to Franciscan Hospital for Children, Brighton, MA. For general support.
$2,500 to Dana-Farber Cancer Institute, Friends of, Boston, MA. For general support.
$1,000 to Boy Scouts of America, Narragansett Council, Providence, RI. For general support.
$1,000 to Museum of Science, Boston, MA. For general support.

3992
Helen & George Ladd Charitable Corporation ✧

c/o Nutter, McClennen, & Fish, LLP
World Trade Ctr. West
155 Seaport Blvd.
Boston, MA 02210-2604
Contact: Charles A. Rosebrock, Clerk

Established in 1984 in MA.
Donor: George E. Ladd, Jr. Charitable Trust.
Foundation type: Independent foundation.
Financial data (yr. ended 12/31/05): Assets, $10,077,012 (M); expenditures, $573,314; qualifying distributions, $518,057; giving activities include $501,000 for 67 grants (high: $70,500; low: $50).
Purpose and activities: Giving primarily for education and human services.
Fields of interest: Performing arts, theater; Arts; Higher education; Education; Health organizations, association; Human services; Community development; Public affairs, government agencies.
Limitations: Giving primarily in ME.
Application information:
Initial approach: Letter
Deadline(s): None
Officers and Directors: Robert M. Ladd,* Pres.; Charles A. Rosebrock,* Clerk; George E. Ladd III; Lincoln F. Ladd.
Trustee: Nutter, McClennen & Fish, LLP.
EIN: 042767890

3993
The Lalor Foundation

c/o Grants Mgmt. Assocs.
77 Summer St., 8th Fl.
Boston, MA 02110-1006 (617) 426-7080, ext. 314
Contact: Pamela Labonte Maksy, Admin.
FAX: (617) 426-7087;
E-mail: pmaksy@grantsmanagement.com;
URL: http://www.lalorfound.org

Incorporated in 1935 in DE.
Donors: Willard A. Lalor†; and members of the Lalor family.
Foundation type: Independent foundation.
Financial data (yr. ended 9/30/05): Assets, $12,451,528 (M); expenditures, $920,668; qualifying distributions, $853,933; giving activities

include $771,037 for 27 grants (high: $35,000; low: $5,000).

Purpose and activities: Support for programs that seek to educate young women about human reproduction, focus is particularly young women who have inadequate access.

Fields of interest: Reproductive health, family planning.

Type of support: Program development.

Limitations: Giving on a national and international basis. No support for private organizations. No grants to individuals directly, or for operating budgets, capital or endowment funds, continuing support, annual campaigns, seed money, emergency funds, deficit financing, or matching gifts; no loans.

Publications: Application guidelines; Grants list; Informational brochure (including application guidelines).

Application information: Requests received by fax or e-mail not considered. Application guidelines and form available on foundation Web site. Application form required.

Initial approach: Letter, visit Web site or E-mail
Copies of proposal: 1
Deadline(s): See Web site for application deadlines
Board meeting date(s): June and Dec.
Final notification: June 30 or Dec. 31

Officers and Trustees:* Cynthia B. Patterson,* Pres.; Sally H. Zeckhauser,* V.P.; Lalor Burdick,* Secy.-Treas.; Andrew G. Braun; Christopher Burdick; Carol Chandler.

EIN: 516000153

3994

The Peter and Deborah Lamm Foundation ✧

(formerly Peter Lamm Foundation)
c/o Ropes & Gray LLP
1 International Pl.
Boston, MA   02110-2624
Contact: R. Bradford Malt, Tr.

Established in 1997 in MA.
Donor: Peter Lamm.
Foundation type: Independent foundation.
Financial data (yr. ended 12/31/05): Assets, $30,497 (M); gifts received, $342,500; expenditures, $358,409; qualifying distributions, $357,500; giving activities include $357,500 for 68 grants (high: $50,000; low: $500).
Purpose and activities: Giving primarily for health organizations, human services, and the arts.
Fields of interest: Arts; Education; Hospitals (general); Health organizations, association; Housing/shelter, search services; Human services.
Limitations: Applications not accepted. Giving primarily in Boston, MA, and New York, NY. No grants to individuals.
Application information: Contributes only to pre-selected organizations.
Trustees: Peter Lamm; R. Bradford Malt.
EIN: 043406251

3995

C. Kevin Landry Charitable Foundation ✧ ☆

c/o Ernest J. Grassey
50 Cole Pkwy., No. 27
Scituate, MA   02066
Contact: C. Kevin Landry, Dir.

Established in 1986 in MA.
Donor: C. Kevin Landry.
Foundation type: Operating foundation.
Financial data (yr. ended 12/31/04): Assets, $8,247,846 (M); expenditures, $566,756; qualifying distributions, $550,000; giving activities include $550,000 for 23 grants (high: $400,000; low: $500).
Purpose and activities: Giving primarily for education and the arts.
Fields of interest: Museums (art); Arts; Elementary/ secondary education; Higher education; Scholarships/financial aid; Hospitals (general); Philanthropy/voluntarism.
Limitations: Giving primarily in MA. No grants to individuals.
Application information:
Initial approach: Letter
Deadline(s): None
Directors: Ernest J. Grassey; C. Kevin Landry.
EIN: 042943405
Selected grants: The following grants were reported in 2004.
$450,000 to Harvard University, Cambridge, MA. 3 grants: $25,000, $400,000, $25,000
$5,000 to Roxbury Preparatory Charter School, Roxbury, MA.
$2,500 to Sears House Association, Boston, MA.
$2,500 to Womens Commission for Refugee Women and Children, New York, NY.
$1,000 to Cato Institute, DC.
$1,000 to Middlesex School, Concord, MA.

3996

The Landsman Charitable Trust ✧ ☆

P.O. Box 227
Swampscott, MA   01907-0327

Established in 1994 in MA.
Donor: Emanuel E. Landsman.
Foundation type: Independent foundation.
Financial data (yr. ended 12/31/05): Assets, $8,501,000 (M); expenditures, $435,340; qualifying distributions, $345,240; giving activities include $345,240 for 12 grants (high: $150,000; low: $1,000).
Purpose and activities: Giving primarily for education, and Jewish agencies and temples.
Fields of interest: Higher education; Education; Health organizations, association; Jewish agencies & temples.
Limitations: Applications not accepted. Giving primarily in MA. No grants to individuals.
Application information: Contributes only to pre-selected organizations.
Trustees: Samuel Denbo; Emanuel E. Landsman; Sheila E. Landsman.
EIN: 043236716

3997

Robert I. Lappin Charitable Foundation ✧

29 Congress St.
P.O. Box 986
Salem, MA   01970

Established in 1988 in MA.
Donor: Robert I. Lappin.
Foundation type: Independent foundation.
Financial data (yr. ended 12/31/03): Assets, $6,335,228 (M); gifts received, $24,413; expenditures, $969,327; qualifying distributions, $966,173; giving activities include $694,036 for 16 grants (high: $584,252; low: $500).
Fields of interest: Neighborhood centers; Jewish federated giving programs; Jewish agencies & temples.
Limitations: Applications not accepted. Giving primarily in MA. No grants to individuals.
Application information: Contributes only to pre-selected organizations.
Trustee: Robert I. Lappin.
EIN: 046579206

3998

Larson Family Foundation ✧

4 Sudbury Rd.
Wellesley, MA   02481
Contact: Jeffrey B. Larson, Tr.

Established in 2000 in MA.
Donors: Jeffrey B. Larson; Janet B. Larson.
Foundation type: Independent foundation.
Financial data (yr. ended 12/31/05): Assets, $13,408,156 (M); gifts received, $1,002,500; expenditures, $4,027,775; qualifying distributions, $4,016,825; giving activities include $4,016,825 for 13 grants (high: $3,150,000; low: $5,000).
Fields of interest: Arts; Children/youth, services.
Limitations: Applications not accepted. Giving primarily in MA. No grants to individuals.
Application information: The foundation does not accept unsolicited applications.
Trustees: Janet B. Larson; Jeffrey B. Larson.
EIN: 043533712

3999

Leaves of Grass Fund ✧

P.O. Box 233
Lincoln, MA   01773

Established in 1987 in MA.
Donor: Community TV Corp.
Foundation type: Independent foundation.
Financial data (yr. ended 12/31/04): Assets, $18,864,946 (M); expenditures, $933,286; qualifying distributions, $869,670; giving activities include $854,367 for 12 grants (high: $456,034; low: $25).
Fields of interest: Performing arts, music; Higher education; Hospitals (general); Family services.
Limitations: Applications not accepted. Giving primarily in NH. No grants to individuals.
Application information: Contributes only to pre-selected organizations.
Trustees: Eleanor W. Herzog; James Herzog; Barbara White; Harmon S.B. White; Henry S. White.
EIN: 222824793

4000
Leclerc Charity Fund ✧
19 Water St.
Leominster, MA 01453-3216

Established in 1968 in MA.
Donors: Raymond Leclerc; Ray Plastic, Inc.
Foundation type: Independent foundation.
Financial data (yr. ended 12/31/05): Assets, $8,531,694 (M); gifts received, $400,000; expenditures, $411,783; qualifying distributions, $401,010; giving activities include $401,010 for 42 grants (high: $100,000; low: $200).
Purpose and activities: Giving primarily to Roman Catholic agencies, churches, and schools.
Fields of interest: Education; Health organizations, association; Human services; Christian agencies & churches; Roman Catholic agencies & churches; Disabilities, people with.
Type of support: General/operating support.
Limitations: Applications not accepted. Giving primarily in MA. No grants to individuals.
Application information: Contributes only to pre-selected organizations.
Manager: Raymond Leclerc.
Trustee: Francis S. Wyman.
EIN: 046183548

4001
Barbara Lee Family Foundation, Inc. ✧
131 Mt. Auburn St., 2nd Fl.
Cambridge, MA 02138 (617) 234-0355
FAX: (617) 234-0357;
E-mail: requests@leefamilyoffice.com; URL: http://www.barbaraleefoundation.org

Established in 1999 in MA.
Donor: Barbara Lee.
Foundation type: Independent foundation.
Financial data (yr. ended 12/31/05): Assets, $934,535 (M); gifts received, $1,487,545; expenditures, $1,081,019; qualifying distributions, $1,050,925; giving activities include $931,935 for 40 grants (high: $500,000; low: $100).
Purpose and activities: Giving primarily to support progressive initiatives in the areas of women in politics and the contemporary arts.
Fields of interest: Museums (art); Higher education, university; Women.
Type of support: General/operating support; Continuing support; Capital campaigns; Program development; Conferences/seminars; Curriculum development; Research; Matching/challenge support.
Limitations: Giving primarily in MA and NY. No grants to individuals or for scholarship programs; or for international or foreign-based programs, political campaigns, or projects delivering direct social services.
Publications: Application guidelines.
Application information: Please send one hard copy and one electronic copy of application. Application form required.
Initial approach: See Web site for application guidelines
Copies of proposal: 2
Deadline(s): See Web site for current deadline
Officer: Barbara Fish Lee, Pres.
Board Members: David Damroth; Joel A. Kozol; Robert S. Lee; S. Zachary Lee; Fran Seegull.
Number of staff: 9 part-time professional.
EIN: 043473585

4002
The Richard and Clare Lesser Family Foundation ✧
358 Cartwright Rd.
Wellesley, MA 02482

Established in 2001 in MA.
Donors: Richard G. Lesser; Clare E. Lesser.
Foundation type: Independent foundation.
Financial data (yr. ended 12/31/05): Assets, $877,682 (M); gifts received, $725,212; expenditures, $467,168; qualifying distributions, $464,329; giving activities include $464,329 for 43 grants (high: $175,000; low: $50).
Fields of interest: Education; Health care; Human services; Jewish agencies & temples.
Limitations: Applications not accepted. Giving primarily in MA. No grants to individuals.
Application information: Contributes only to pre-selected organizations.
Trustees: Clare E. Lesser; Richard G. Lesser.
EIN: 046961280
Selected grants: The following grants were reported in 2003.
$100,000 to Combined Jewish Philanthropies of Greater Boston, Boston, MA. For unrestricted support.
$75,000 to Northeastern University, Boston, MA. For unrestricted support.
$25,100 to Brigham and Womens Hospital, Boston, MA. For unrestricted support.
$25,000 to Massachusetts General Hospital, Boston, MA. For cardiac research.
$11,144 to Anti-Defamation League of Bnai Brith, New York, NY. For unrestricted support.
$11,000 to Dana-Farber Cancer Institute, Boston, MA. For unrestricted support.
$5,000 to American Jewish Historical Society, New York, NY. For unrestricted support.
$5,000 to Brady Center to Prevent Gun Violence, DC. For unrestricted support.
$1,000 to Hebrew College, Newton Centre, MA. For unrestricted support.
$1,000 to Roxbury Community College Foundation, Boston, MA. For unrestricted support.

4003
The Kenneth and Lorraine Levine Charitable Foundation ✧ ☆
(formerly The Kenneth and Rachel Levine Charitable Foundation)
c/o O'Connor & Drew
1515 Hancock St.
Quincy, MA 02169

Established in 1990 in NH.
Donor: Kenneth R. Levine.
Foundation type: Independent foundation.
Financial data (yr. ended 12/31/05): Assets, $40,741 (M); gifts received, $686,125; expenditures, $1,179,521; qualifying distributions, $1,172,637; giving activities include $1,172,500 for 7 grants (high: $917,500; low: $10,000).
Fields of interest: Museums; Elementary/secondary education; Jewish agencies & temples.
Limitations: Applications not accepted. Giving primarily in MA. No grants to individuals.
Application information: Contributes only to pre-selected organizations.
Trustee: Kenneth R. Levine.
EIN: 043105767

4004
The Levine Family Charitable Trust ✧
c/o O'Connor & Drew, PC
1515 Hancock St.
Quincy, MA 02169

Established in 1989 in MA.
Donor: S. Robert Levine.
Foundation type: Independent foundation.
Financial data (yr. ended 12/31/05): Assets, $2,825,927 (M); expenditures, $556,005; qualifying distributions, $549,834; giving activities include $549,705 for 24 grants (high: $150,000; low: $250; average: $10,000–$50,000).
Purpose and activities: Giving primarily for education and health care.
Fields of interest: Higher education, university; Education; Hospitals (general); Cancer; Human services; Philanthropy/voluntarism.
Limitations: Applications not accepted. Giving primarily in MA; some funding nationally. No grants to individuals.
Application information: Contributes only to pre-selected organizations.
Trustee: Robert Levine.
EIN: 043071725

4005
June Rockwell Levy Foundation, Inc. ✧
c/o Fiduciary Trust Co.
175 Federal St.
Boston, MA 02110-2289 (617) 574-3426
Contact: Jonathan B. Loring, Pres.

Incorporated in 1947 in CT.
Donor: Austin T. Levy†.
Foundation type: Independent foundation.
Financial data (yr. ended 12/31/05): Assets, $27,344,019 (M); expenditures, $1,506,178; qualifying distributions, $1,382,036; giving activities include $1,317,750 for 86 grants (high: $125,000; low: $2,000).
Purpose and activities: Grants largely for hospitals, medical research, and higher and secondary education; support also for youth agencies, cultural programs, and the handicapped.
Fields of interest: Arts; Secondary school/education; Higher education; Hospitals (general); Medical research, institute; Boy scouts; Children/youth, services; Disabilities, people with.
Type of support: General/operating support; Continuing support; Capital campaigns; Building/renovation; Equipment; Seed money; Scholarship funds; Research.
Limitations: Giving primarily in MA and RI. No support for religious purposes. No grants to individuals.
Application information: Application form required.
Initial approach: Letter
Copies of proposal: 1
Deadline(s): None
Board meeting date(s): Starting in Feb., 1st Tues. of every other month
Officers and Trustees:* Jonathan B. Loring,* Pres.; Paul F. Greene,* Secy.; Nancy B. Smith, Treas.; James K. Edwards; Francis J. Lanctot; Raymond G. Leveille, Jr.; Raymond N. Menard; Edward H. Osgood; Thomas H. Quill, Jr.
EIN: 046074284
Selected grants: The following grants were reported in 2005.
$125,000 to Landmark Medical Center, Woonsocket, RI.

$50,000 to Providence Public Library, Providence, RI.

$50,000 to Rhode Island Hospital Foundation, Providence, RI.

$25,000 to Pawtucket Armory Association, Pawtucket, RI.

$20,000 to San Miguel Education Center, Providence, RI.

$20,000 to Senior Services, Woonsocket, RI.

$18,000 to Community Preparatory School, Providence, RI.

$12,000 to Adoption Rhode Island, Pawtucket, RI.

$10,000 to Boston Symphony Orchestra, Boston, MA.

$10,000 to Sargent Rehabilitation Center, Warwick, RI.

4006
The Liberty Mutual Foundation, Inc. ◇
175 Berkeley St.
Boston, MA 02117
URL: http://www.libertymutual.com/omapps/ContentServer?cid=1003349317246&pagename=CorporateInternet%2FPage%2FStandardDarkBlue&c=Page

Established in 2003 in MA.
Donor: Liberty Mutual Insurance Co.
Foundation type: Company-sponsored foundation.
Financial data (yr. ended 12/31/05): Assets, $909,766 (M); gifts received, $6,366,555; expenditures, $6,199,063; qualifying distributions, $6,015,673; giving activities include $5,999,909 for 366 grants (high: $925,000; low: $33).
Purpose and activities: The foundation supports organizations involved with arts and culture, education, health, human services, community development, and religion.
Fields of interest: Arts; Education; Health care; Human services; Community development; Federated giving programs; Religion.
Type of support: General/operating support; Program development; Scholarship funds; Employee matching gifts; Continuing support; Capital campaigns.
Limitations: Giving primarily in the greater Boston, MA, area. No support for grantmaking foundations, religious organizations not of direct benefit to the entire community, or fraternal, social, or political organizations. No grants to individuals, or for sponsorships, dinners or memberships, trips, tours, or transportation, debt reduction, or conferences, forums, or special events.
Publications: Grants list.
Application information: Application form required.
  Initial approach: Complete online application form
  Deadline(s): None
  Board meeting date(s): Monthly
Officers and Directors:* Edmund F. Kelly,* Pres.; Mellissa MacDonnell,* V.P.; Dexter R. Legg, Secy.; Dennis Langwell,* Treas.; A. Alexander Fontanes; Christopher C. Mansfield.
EIN: 141893520

4007
Linde Family Foundation ▼ ◇
(formerly Linde Family Charitable Trust)
c/o Philanthropic Advisors
400 Atlantic Ave.
Boston, MA 02110
Contact: Lauren Goldberg, Dir., Progs.

E-mail: lgoldberg@philanthropicadvisors.com

Established in 2000 in MA.
Donor: Edward H. Linde.
Foundation type: Independent foundation.
Financial data (yr. ended 12/31/05): Assets, $33,707,633 (M); gifts received, $15,802,371; expenditures, $4,986,692; qualifying distributions, $4,875,190; giving activities include $4,492,545 for 32 grants (high: $1,190,000; low: $5,000; average: $10,000–$75,000).
Purpose and activities: Giving primarily for children's services, education, and the arts.
Fields of interest: Arts; Education; Children/youth, services.
Type of support: General/operating support; Annual campaigns; Capital campaigns; Building/renovation; Endowments; Program development; Curriculum development.
Limitations: Giving primarily in MA. No grants to individuals.
Application information: Application form not required.
  Deadline(s): None
Trustees: Carol Croft Linde; Douglas T. Linde; Edward H. Linde; Joyce Linde; Jeffrey N. Packman; Karen Linde Packman.
EIN: 046904949
Selected grants: The following grants were reported in 2004.
$850,000 to Museum of Fine Arts, Boston, MA. For general support.
$800,000 to Massachusetts Institute of Technology, Cambridge, MA. For general support.
$500,000 to Dana-Farber Cancer Institute, Boston, MA. 2 grants: $250,000 (For general support), $250,000 (For Acute Lymphoblastic Leukemia Fund).
$300,000 to DeCordova Museum and Sculpture Park, Lincoln, MA. For general support.
$80,000 to Horizons for Homeless Children, Dorchester, MA. 2 grants: $75,000 (For general support), $5,000 (For general support).
$25,000 to Alzheimers Association, Massachusetts Chapter, Cambridge, MA. For general support.
$25,000 to Posse Foundation, New York, NY. For general support.
$2,500 to Project Step, Boston, MA. For general support.

4008
The Linden Foundation, Inc. ◇
c/o Grants Mgmt. Assocs.
77 Summer St., 8th Fl.
Boston, MA 02110-1006 (617) 426-7080
Contact: Brinda Maira, Prog. Asst.
FAX: (617) 426-7087;
E-mail: bmaira@grantsmanagement.com;
URL: http://www.lindenfoundation.org

Established in 1996.
Foundation type: Independent foundation.
Financial data (yr. ended 12/31/05): Assets, $10,520,364 (M); expenditures, $782,345; qualifying distributions, $740,600; giving activities include $719,350 for 46 grants (high: $33,000; low: $5,000).
Purpose and activities: The mission of the foundation is to help disadvantaged families achieve a better quality of life through programs that help to nurture, build, and strengthen family relationships, as well as through workforce

development, and support for organizations that provide housing services.
Fields of interest: Family services; Homeless, human services.
Type of support: General/operating support; Program development; Matching/challenge support.
Limitations: Giving primarily in northern Boston and the North Shore, MA, northern NJ, the New York City area with emphasis on the Bronx and Westchester County, and the counties of the Lakes Region and northern NH. No support for public schools, charter schools or universities, or for community organizing or political lobbying efforts. No grants to individuals, or for tickets to artistic performances, computer centers, or operating support for community centers.
Publications: Application guidelines; Grants list.
Application information: Full applications by invite only. Application form required.
  Initial approach: Letter of inquiry (no more than 2 pages)
  Deadline(s): Dec. 1 for spring, and June 1 for fall
  Board meeting date(s): 2 times during the year
Officers and Directors:* Thomas V.A. Kelsey,* Pres. and Treas.; Elizabeth S. Kelsey, Secy.; G. Lea Dobbs Kelsey; Margen Kelsey; Suzanne V.A. Kelsey; William Kelsey; Mark J. Pine; Kenneth Siegert.
Number of staff: 2 part-time professional.
EIN: 226678640
Selected grants: The following grants were reported in 2004.
$95,000 to New Hampshire Charitable Foundation, Concord, NH.
$25,200 to Interfaith Council for the Homeless of Union County, Plainfield, NJ.
$25,000 to Greyston Foundation, Yonkers, NY.
$25,000 to Osborne Association, Long Island City, NY.
$23,100 to Wellspring House, Gloucester, MA.
$20,000 to Urban League of Hudson County, Jersey City, NJ.
$15,000 to Boys Hope Girls Hope of New York, Staten Island, NY.
$15,000 to Tri-City Family Housing, Malden, MA.
$13,000 to Action, Inc., Gloucester, MA.
$5,400 to Associated Grant Makers, Boston, MA.

4009
The Margaret Stewart Lindsay Foundation-1989 ◇ ☆
P.O. Box 55806
Boston, MA 02205-5806

Established in MA.
Donors: Margaret S. Lindsay; Edwin B. Lindsay; Elizabeth S. Lindsay.
Foundation type: Independent foundation.
Financial data (yr. ended 12/31/05): Assets, $6,863,275 (M); gifts received, $285,961; expenditures, $441,541; qualifying distributions, $381,195; giving activities include $380,000 for 9 grants (high: $100,000; low: $15,000).
Fields of interest: Performing arts, music ensembles/groups; Historic preservation/historical societies; Higher education; Animals/wildlife, management/technical aid; Mental health/crisis services, suicide; Children, services; Blind/visually impaired.
Limitations: Applications not accepted. Giving primarily in MA. No grants to individuals.
Application information: Contributes only to pre-selected organizations.

Trustees: Kathleen M. McCarthy; J. Brian Potts; Fiduciary Trust Co.

EIN: 043382858

Selected grants: The following grants were reported in 2005.

$100,000 to Samaritans, Providence, RI.

$50,000 to Community Music Center of Boston, Boston, MA.

$25,000 to Boston Childrens Chorus, Boston, MA.

$25,000 to Perkins School for the Blind, Watertown, MA.

4010

Joseph M. and Thelma Linsey Foundation ✧

(formerly Joseph M. Linsey Foundation)
60 Wells Ave.
Newton, MA 02459

Established in 1947 in MA.

Donors: Joseph M. Linsey; Thelma R. Linsey.

Foundation type: Independent foundation.

Financial data (yr. ended 12/31/05): Assets, $896,094 (M); expenditures, $452,693; qualifying distributions, $434,899; giving activities include $434,899 for 16 grants (high: $346,285; low: $100).

Purpose and activities: Support for Jewish religious, cultural, educational, and welfare organizations; support also for a university.

Fields of interest: Education; Hospitals (general); Human services; Jewish federated giving programs; Jewish agencies & temples; Economically disadvantaged.

Limitations: Applications not accepted. Giving primarily in MA. No grants to individuals.

Application information: Contributes only to pre-selected organizations.

Trustees: Thelma R. Linsey; Alfred S. Ross.

EIN: 046038331

4011

The Loebs Family Foundation ✧ ☆

c/o Welch & Forbes
45 School St., 5th Fl.
Boston, MA 02108

Established in 2000 in RI.

Donor: Edith S.S. Loebs.

Foundation type: Independent foundation.

Financial data (yr. ended 12/31/05): Assets, $4,396,711 (M); expenditures, $432,945; qualifying distributions, $407,710; giving activities include $405,000 for 6 grants (high: $200,000; low: $25,000).

Fields of interest: Arts; Education; Environment, natural resources; Health care; Christian agencies & churches.

Limitations: Applications not accepted. Giving primarily in Newport, RI. No grants to individuals.

Application information: Contributes only to pre-selected organizations.

Trustees: Stephen A. Haire; Richard C. Loebs, Jr.

EIN: 316653452

Selected grants: The following grants were reported in 2004.

$100,000 to Aquidneck Island Land Trust, Middletown, RI. For unrestricted support.

$75,000 to Rhode Island Hospital Foundation, Providence, RI. For unrestricted support.

$50,000 to Saint Georges School, Newport, RI. For unrestricted support.

$10,000 to Preserve Rhode Island, Providence, RI. For unrestricted support.

4012

The Lost and Foundation, Inc. ✧ ☆

(formerly The O. & C. Curme Family Foundation)
455 Glen Rd.
Weston, MA 02493

Established in 2000 in MA.

Donors: Oliver D. Curme; Cynthia K. Curme.

Foundation type: Independent foundation.

Financial data (yr. ended 12/31/05): Assets, $772,262 (M); gifts received, $432,875; expenditures, $320,284; qualifying distributions, $319,613; giving activities include $319,613 for grants.

Fields of interest: Performing arts, music; Performing arts, orchestra (symphony); Education; Human services; Roman Catholic agencies & churches.

Limitations: Applications not accepted. Giving primarily in MA. No grants to individuals.

Application information: Contributes only to pre-selected organizations.

Officers: Cynthia K. Curme, Pres. and Clerk; Oliver D. Curme, Treas.

EIN: 043527006

4013

Lovett/Woodsum Family Charitable Foundation, Inc. ✧

c/o Summit Partners
222 Berkeley St., 18th Fl.
Boston, MA 02116

Established in 1986 in MA.

Donors: Anne B. Lovett; Stephen G. Woodsum.

Foundation type: Independent foundation.

Financial data (yr. ended 11/30/03): Assets, $24,675,087 (M); gifts received, $2,500; expenditures, $1,177,429; qualifying distributions, $1,157,007; giving activities include $1,157,007 for 111 grants (high: $500,000; low: $75).

Fields of interest: Arts; Higher education; Education; Human services; Children/youth, services; Federated giving programs.

Limitations: Applications not accepted. Giving primarily in MA and NH. No grants to individuals.

Application information: Contributes only to pre-selected organizations.

Officers: Stephen G. Woodsum, Pres. and Treas.; Anne R. Lovett, Secy.

EIN: 042944183

Selected grants: The following grants were reported in 2003.

$500,000 to Yale University, New Haven, CT.

$30,000 to Childrens Museum, Boston, MA.

$10,000 to Isabella Stewart Gardner Museum, Boston, MA.

$10,000 to W G B H Educational Foundation, Boston, MA.

$9,500 to Museum of Fine Arts, Boston, MA.

$5,000 to New Hampshire Public Television, Durham, NH.

$2,500 to Massachusetts General Hospital, Boston, MA.

$1,000 to AIDS Action Committee of Massachusetts, Boston, MA.

$1,000 to Andover Newton Theological School, Newton Centre, MA.

$250 to New Hampshire Music Festival, Gilford, NH.

4014

Greater Lowell Community Foundation ✧

169 Merrimack St., 5th Fl.
Lowell, MA 01852-1723 (978) 970-1600
Contact: David Kronberg, Exec. Dir.
FAX: (978) 970-2444; E-mail: dave.glcf@verizon.net;
URL: http://www.glcfoundation.org

Established in 1996 in MA.

Donors: Joe Donahue; Richard K. Donahue, Sr.; Human Svcs. Corp.; Lowell Museum Corp.; The Theodore Edson Parker Foundation.

Foundation type: Community foundation.

Financial data (yr. ended 3/31/05): Assets, $10,614,940 (M); gifts received, $2,579,037; expenditures, $706,292; giving activities include $370,820 for grants.

Purpose and activities: The foundation seeks to improve the quality of life in the greater Lowell, MA, area by attracting funds, distributing grants, making loans and striving as a catalyst and leader among funders, agencies and individuals to address identified and emerging community needs.

Fields of interest: Arts; Education; Environment, water pollution; Environment, water resources; Environment; Health care; Human services; Economic development; Community development; Voluntarism promotion.

Type of support: Income development; Management development/capacity building.

Limitations: Giving limited to the greater Lowell, Nashoba, and Western Merrimack Valley, MA, regions. No support for religious organizations or government agencies. No grants to individuals, or for continuing support, operating expenses, building funds or endowment funds; no multi-year commitments.

Application information: Visit foundation Web site for application forms and guidelines. All applications must be submitted by conventional postage or ground delivery. Application form required.

Initial approach: Submit Proposal Summary and application form

Deadline(s): Mar. 15

Final notification: May 25

Officers and Directors:* George L. Duncan,* Pres.; James F. Conway III,* V.P.; James Shannon,* Treas.; David Kronberg,* Exec. Dir.; Chester G. Atkins; Robert A. Caruso; Richard K. Donahue, Sr.; Kay Doyle; Winslow H. Duke; Mary Jo Leahy; Arnold S. Lerner; Jaqueline F. Moloney; Luis Pedroso; AnnMarie Roark; James H. Reichheld; Lura Smith; Brian Stafford; Chanrithy Uong.

EIN: 043401997

4015

The Lowell Institute ✧

c/o Choate, Hall and Stewart LLP
2 International Pl.
Boston, MA 02110-4104

Established in 1836 in MA.

Donor: John Lowell‡.

Foundation type: Independent foundation.

Financial data (yr. ended 7/31/05): Assets, $41,756,944 (M); expenditures, $2,040,986; qualifying distributions, $1,936,372; giving

activities include $1,846,500 for 29 grants (high: $325,000; low: $2,000).
Fields of interest: Arts; Elementary school/education; Higher education; Adult/continuing education; Education; Engineering/technology; Science; Religion.
Type of support: Continuing support; Conferences/seminars; Curriculum development; Scholarship funds; Matching/challenge support.
Limitations: Applications not accepted. Giving primarily in the greater Boston, MA, area. No grants to individuals, or for operating budgets, building or endowment funds; no loans.
Publications: Informational brochure.
Application information: Contributes only to pre-selected organizations.
Trustee: John Lowell.
EIN: 042105771
Selected grants: The following grants were reported in 2004.
$325,000 to Museum of Science, Boston, MA. For programs and exhibit.
$325,000 to W G B H Educational Foundation, Boston, MA. For operating support.
$200,000 to Northeastern University, School of Engineering, Boston, MA. For program support.
$170,000 to Museum of Fine Arts, Boston, MA. For programs and exhibits.
$160,000 to New England Aquarium, Boston, MA. For programs and exhibits.
$93,000 to Harvard University, Cambridge, MA. For programs and lecture.
$50,000 to Boston Public Library, Boston, MA. For Lecture Series.
$45,000 to Wang Center for the Performing Arts, Boston, MA. For Suskind Young at Arts Program.
$35,000 to Boston Symphony Orchestra, Boston, MA. For Metropolitan Youth Series Concerts.
$30,000 to Cambridge Forum, Cambridge, MA. For Lecture Series.

4016
The Richard K. Lubin Family Foundation ◇
(formerly The Richard K. Lubin Charitable Trust)
17 Ascenta Terr.
West Newton, MA 02465

Established in 1986 in MA.
Donor: Richard K. Lubin.
Foundation type: Independent foundation.
Financial data (yr. ended 12/31/05): Assets, $3,964,300 (M); gifts received, $2,035,880; expenditures, $638,889; qualifying distributions, $614,116; giving activities include $614,116 for 51 grants (high: $200,000; low: $500).
Purpose and activities: Giving for education, Jewish organizations and federated giving programs.
Fields of interest: Elementary/secondary education; Higher education; Graduate/professional education; Hospitals (general); Boys & girls clubs; Human services; Federated giving programs; Jewish agencies & temples.
Limitations: Applications not accepted. Giving primarily in MA. No grants to individuals.
Application information: Contributes only to pre-selected organizations.
Trustees: Kate E. Lubin; Nancy K. Lubin; Richard K. Lubin; Emily L. Woods.
EIN: 222773808
Selected grants: The following grants were reported in 2003.
$101,000 to Bowdoin College, Brunswick, ME.
$60,000 to Winsor School, Boston, MA.

$50,000 to Combined Jewish Philanthropies of Greater Boston, Boston, MA.
$47,000 to Museum of Fine Arts, Boston, MA.
$10,000 to Dana-Farber Cancer Institute, Boston, MA.
$10,000 to United Way.
$10,000 to Wheaton College, Norton, MA.
$8,334 to SquashBusters, Roxbury Crossing, MA.
$5,000 to Harvard Eating Disorders Center, Cambridge, MA.
$5,000 to University of Pennsylvania, Philadelphia, PA.

4017
The Ludcke Foundation ◇ ☆
c/o Fiduciary Trust Co.
175 Federal St.
Boston, MA 02110
Application address: Jonathan Strong, c/o Ropes & Gray, 1 International Pl., Boston, MA 02110

Established in 1991 in MA.
Donors: Gipp L. Ludcke; Eleanor R. Ludcke.
Foundation type: Independent foundation.
Financial data (yr. ended 12/31/05): Assets, $46,791,042 (M); gifts received, $8,601,389; expenditures, $1,019,946; qualifying distributions, $836,225; giving activities include $792,500 for 21 grants (high: $100,000; low: $25,000).
Fields of interest: Performing arts, theater; Education; Animals/wildlife; Hospitals (general); Salvation Army; YM/YWCAs & YM/YWHAs.
Limitations: Giving limited to MA. No grants to individuals.
Application information: Application form not required.
  Initial approach: Letter
  Deadline(s): None
Trustees: Constance Huebner; Jonathan Strong; John L. Thorndike; Fiduciary Trust Co.
EIN: 046663582
Selected grants: The following grants were reported in 2005.
$100,000 to Medical Foundation, Boston, MA.
$50,000 to Associated Grant Makers, Boston, MA.
$50,000 to Boston Medical Center, Boston, MA.
$35,000 to Project Hope, Brooklyn, NY.
$25,000 to Huntington Theater Company, Boston, MA.
$25,000 to Junior Achievement.
$25,000 to Travelers Aid Family Services, Boston, MA.
$25,000 to United South End Settlements, Boston, MA.
$25,000 to United Way.
$25,000 to YMCA of Greater Boston, Boston, MA.

4018
Manitou Foundation, Inc. ◇
c/o Loring, Wolcott & Coolidge
230 Congress St.
Boston, MA 02110

Established in MA.
Donor: Horace H. Irvine II.
Foundation type: Independent foundation.
Financial data (yr. ended 11/30/05): Assets, $16,185 (M); expenditures, $362,815; qualifying distributions, $353,015; giving activities include $352,000 for 15 grants (high: $200,000; low: $1,000).

Purpose and activities: Giving primarily for the arts; some funding also for a hospital.
Fields of interest: Museums (art); Performing arts; Performing arts, theater; Performing arts, music; Performing arts, opera; Arts; Hospitals (general).
Limitations: Applications not accepted. Giving limited to MA and MN. No grants to individuals.
Application information: Contributes only to pre-selected organizations.
Officers: Horace H. Irvine II, Pres. and Treas.; James C. Hamilton, Clerk.
EIN: 510188184
Selected grants: The following grants were reported in 2005.
$200,000 to Boston Lyric Opera Company, Boston, MA.
$84,000 to Vincent Memorial Hospital, Boston, MA.
$35,000 to Huntington Theater Company, Boston, MA.
$10,000 to American Repertory Theater, Cambridge, MA.
$5,000 to Boston Landmarks Orchestra, Cambridge, MA.
$5,000 to From the Top, Boston, MA.
$5,000 to Ocean Reef Cultural Center, Key Largo, FL.
$1,000 to Ordway Center for the Performing Arts, Saint Paul, MN.

4019
Mannion Family Foundation ◇
c/o Rice, Heard & Bigelow
50 Congress St., Ste. 1025
Boston, MA 02109

Established in 2000 in MA.
Donors: Martin J. Mannion; Mrs. Martin J. Mannion.
Foundation type: Independent foundation.
Financial data (yr. ended 12/31/05): Assets, $3,934,177 (M); gifts received, $915,000; expenditures, $1,743,449; qualifying distributions, $1,732,146; giving activities include $1,732,146 for 21 grants (high: $283,334; low: $5,000).
Purpose and activities: Giving primarily for education, and to a children's hospital.
Fields of interest: Secondary school/education; Hospitals (specialty); Human services.
Limitations: Applications not accepted. No grants to individuals.
Application information: Contributes only to pre-selected organizations.
Trustees: Robert G. Bannish; Martin J. Mannion; Tristin Mannion.
EIN: 043522053

4020
Many Voices Foundation ◇ ☆
c/o Maximilian Dana Stone
4 Buttercup Ln.
Dover, MA 02030

Established in 2000 in DE.
Donor: Maximilian Dana Stone.
Foundation type: Independent foundation.
Financial data (yr. ended 12/31/05): Assets, $16,232,735 (M); gifts received, $8,024,060; expenditures, $418,240; qualifying distributions, $350,000; giving activities include $350,000 for grants.
Fields of interest: Environment, natural resources; Human services.

Limitations: Applications not accepted. Giving primarily in MA. No grants to individuals.
Application information: Contributes only to pre-selected organizations.
Officers and Directors:* Maximilian Dana Stone,* Pres. and Treas.; Cecilia V. Stone,* Secy.
EIN: 134144617
Selected grants: The following grants were reported in 2003.
$200,000 to Robin Hood Foundation, New York, NY. For general support.

4021
The Manzi Family Charitable Fund ◇
c/o Forman, Itzkowitz, Berenson & LaGreca, PC
404 Wyman St., Ste. 275
Waltham, MA   02451

Established in 1995 in MA.
Donor: Jim P. Manzi.
Foundation type: Independent foundation.
Financial data (yr. ended 5/31/05): Assets, $54,933 (M); expenditures, $442,830; qualifying distributions, $442,800; giving activities include $442,800 for grants.
Fields of interest: Higher education; Theological school/education; Education; Hospitals (general); Health organizations; Human services; Family services; Community development, neighborhood development; Foundations (private grantmaking); Jewish agencies & temples.
Limitations: Applications not accepted. Giving primarily in MA. No grants to individuals.
Application information: Contributes only to pre-selected organizations. Unsolicited requests for funds not accepted.
Trustees: Glenda B. Manzi; Jim P. Manzi; Robert J. Morrissey.
EIN: 046785692
Selected grants: The following grants were reported in 2005.
$200,000 to Julies Family Learning Program, South Boston, MA.
$30,000 to Park School, Brookline, MA.
$15,000 to Colgate University, Hamilton, NY.
$10,000 to Boston Medical Center, Boston, MA.
$2,500 to Brookline Music School, Brookline, MA.
$1,000 to International Institute of Boston, Boston, MA.
$1,000 to Red Sox Foundation, Boston, MA.

4022
William and Cynthia Marcus Family Charitable Trust ◇
(formerly Marcus Family Charitable Trust)
99-50 Florence St., Apt. 5B
Chestnut Hill, MA   02467-1941
Contact: William M. Marcus, Tr.

Established in 1985 MA.
Donor: William M. Marcus.
Foundation type: Independent foundation.
Financial data (yr. ended 3/31/05): Assets, $1,812,365 (M); gifts received, $244,555; expenditures, $514,887; qualifying distributions, $494,091; giving activities include $493,012 for 77 grants (high: $91,450; low: $25).
Fields of interest: History/archaeology; Education; Hospitals (general); Jewish federated giving programs; Jewish agencies & temples.

Type of support: General/operating support; Annual campaigns; Capital campaigns; Research.
Limitations: Applications not accepted. Giving primarily in MA. No grants to individuals.
Application information: Contributes only to pre-selected organizations. Funds fully committed.
Trustees: Cynthia S. Marcus; Daniel H. Marcus; Melanie L. Marcus; Richard S. Marcus; William M. Marcus.
EIN: 046042910

4023
The Roger M. & Michelle S. Marino Charitable Foundation ◇ ☆
254 Westfield St.
Dedham, MA   02026

Established in 1994 in MA.
Donors: Roger M. Marino; Michelle S. Marino.
Foundation type: Independent foundation.
Financial data (yr. ended 12/31/04): Assets, $5,525,583 (M); gifts received, $732,125; expenditures, $421,938; qualifying distributions, $375,335; giving activities include $375,335 for 28 grants (high: $100,000; low: $50; average: $500–$5,000).
Purpose and activities: Giving primarily for education.
Fields of interest: Education; Health care; Medical research, institute; Children/youth, services; Aging.
Limitations: Applications not accepted. Giving primarily in MA.
Application information: Unsolicited requests for funds not accepted.
Trustees: Michelle S. Marino; Roger M. Marino.
EIN: 046773605

4024
The Nancy Lurie Marks Family Foundation ◇
(formerly Nancy Lurie Marks Charitable Foundation)
c/o Goulston & Storrs
1244 Boylston St., Ste. 307
Chestnut Hill, MA   02467

Established in 1976 in MA.
Donors: Nancy Lurie Marks; Marian Smith†.
Foundation type: Independent foundation.
Financial data (yr. ended 10/31/04): Assets, $56,325,706 (M); expenditures, $3,439,140; qualifying distributions, $2,842,554; giving activities include $1,998,057 for 72 grants (high: $316,054; low: $100).
Purpose and activities: Giving primarily for education, museums, and Jewish federated giving programs.
Fields of interest: Museums; Arts; Higher education; Hospitals (general); Medical research, institute; Human services; Jewish federated giving programs; Social sciences.
Limitations: Applications not accepted. Giving primarily in Boston, MA. No grants to individuals; no loans or program-related investments.
Application information: Contributes only to pre-selected organizations.
Trustees: Mark D. Balk; Harvey E. Cushing; Cathy J. Lurie; Christina Lurie; Jeffrey R. Lurie; Nancy L. Marks.
EIN: 042607232
Selected grants: The following grants were reported in 2004.

$316,053 to Childrens Hospital.
$261,240 to Oxford University, Oxford, England. 2 grants: $130,620 each.
$60,000 to Childrens Hospital of Philadelphia, Philadelphia, PA.
$60,000 to Massachusetts Advocates for Children, Boston, MA.
$51,068 to Lesley University, Cambridge, MA.
$46,005 to Boston University, Boston, MA.
$38,034 to Brandeis University, Waltham, MA.
$23,750 to Massachusetts Institute of Technology, Cambridge, MA.
$10,000 to Curtis Institute of Music, Philadelphia, PA.

4025
Massachusetts 2020 Foundation, Inc. ◇
1 Beacon St., 34th Fl.
Boston, MA   02108   (617) 723-6747
FAX: (617) 723-6747; E-mail: info@mass2020.org; For extended-time schools initiative and after-school literacy coaching initiative: David Farbman, tel.: (617) 723-6747, ext. 3922, e-mail: david@mass2020.org; For school sites initiative: Jennifer Davis, tel.: (617) 723-6747, ext. 3923, e-mail: jennifer@mass2020.org; For middle school initiative: Susan Kirwan, tel.: (617) 723-6747, ext. 3921, e-mail: susan@mass2020.org; URL: http://www.mass2020.org

Established in 2000 in MA.
Donors: Christopher F. Gabrieli; Gabrieli Family Foundation; Nellie Mae Foundation; L.G. Balfour Foundation; United Way of MA Bay.
Foundation type: Operating foundation.
Financial data (yr. ended 12/31/04): Assets, $2,138,312 (M); gifts received, $1,453,958; expenditures, $1,789,808; qualifying distributions, $1,790,818; giving activities include $1,056,942 for grants.
Purpose and activities: The foundation serves as an initiative which is focused on improving and expanding educational and economic opportunities for children and families across MA. The foundation's initiatives include: 1) Extended-time schools initiative; 2) Boston's after-school for all partnership; 3) School sites initiative; 4) After-school literacy coaching initiative; and 5) The middle school initiative.
Fields of interest: Education; Human services; Children/youth, services; Federated giving programs.
Limitations: Applications not accepted. Giving primarily in MA, with emphasis on Boston and Dorchester. No grants to individuals.
Publications: Newsletter.
Application information: Contributes only to pre-selected organizations. Information about the foundation's initiatives can be found on the foundation Web site.
Officers and Directors:* Christopher F. Gabrieli,* Chair.; Jennifer Davis,* Pres.; Cheryl M. Cronin, Secy.; Frederick A. Tilton III, Treas.; Kelly Fitzsimmons; Andrea Kramer; John Palfney.
EIN: 043534001

4026
Massachusetts Automobile Dealers Charitable Foundation ☆
59 Temple Pl., Ste. 505
Boston, MA 02111 (617) 451-1051
Contact: Martha Bartle
FAX: (617) 451-9309; E-mail: mbartle@msada.org;
URL: http://www.skidschool.org

Established in 1998 in MA.
Donor: Massachusetts State Automobile Dealers Association, Inc.
Foundation type: Independent foundation.
Financial data (yr. ended 12/31/05): Assets, $219,568 (L); gifts received, $223,352; expenditures, $570,573; qualifying distributions, $549,830; giving activities include $389,863 for 7 grants (high: $268,663; low: $1,000).
Purpose and activities: Giving primarily for education. Scholarships for aspiring auto technicians to attend 2-year, degree-granting manufacturer-backed institutions.
Fields of interest: Higher education, college.
Type of support: Scholarship funds; General/operating support.
Limitations: Applications not accepted. Giving primarily in MA.
Application information: Unsolicited requests for funds not accepted.
Trustees: Carole Berotte-Joseph; Jim Boyle; Jerry Chase; Raymond J. Ciccolo; Marshall Jespersen; Thomas R. Keery II; Lionel Lamoureux; Richard Mastria; Steve Mitus.
Number of staff: 1 full-time professional; 1 full-time support.
EIN: 043402210
Selected grants: The following grants were reported in 2003.
$181,826 to Student Safe Driving Program. For general support.
$30,671 to Scholarship America, Saint Peter, MN. For general support.
$14,000 to Massachusetts Bay Community College, Wellesley Hills, MA. For general support.
$3,000 to Springfield Technical Community College, Springfield, MA. For general support.
$2,000 to Hudson Valley Community College, Troy, NY. For general support.
$1,000 to Quinsigamond Community College, Worcester, MA. For general support.
$775 to Upper Cape Cod Regional Technical School, Bourne, MA. For general support.
$725 to Greater New York Tech, NY. For scholarships.

4027
Massiah Foundation, Inc. ◇
c/o Deloitte & Touche
200 Berkeley St.
Boston, MA 02116

Established in 2000 in MA.
Donor: Fariborz Maseeh.
Foundation type: Independent foundation.
Financial data (yr. ended 12/31/04): Assets, $27,314,790 (M); gifts received, $500; expenditures, $3,039,018; qualifying distributions, $3,006,813; giving activities include $2,915,302 for 16 grants (high: $1,000,000; low: $1,000).
Purpose and activities: Giving primarily for higher and other education; support also for health and human services.

Fields of interest: Secondary school/education; Higher education; Education; Hospitals (general); Human services.
Limitations: Applications not accepted. Giving on a national basis, with some emphasis on the greater Boston, MA, area. No grants to individuals.
Application information: Contributes only to pre-selected organizations.
Officer: Fariborz Maseeh, Pres.
EIN: 043536335
Selected grants: The following grants were reported in 2004.
$2,000,000 to Portland State University, Portland, OR. 3 grants: $500,000, $1,000,000, $500,000
$800,000 to Massachusetts Institute of Technology, Cambridge, MA.
$10,000 to Childrens Hospital of Orange County (CHOC) Foundation, Orange, CA.
$10,000 to Collage New Music, Boston, MA.
$1,000 to AIDS Walk Boston, Boston, MA.

4028
Mazar Family Charitable Foundation ◇
c/o The Colony Group
2 Atlantic Ave.
Boston, MA 02110

Established in 1997 in MA.
Donors: Anne Mazar; Brian Mazar.
Foundation type: Independent foundation.
Financial data (yr. ended 12/31/05): Assets, $2,260,448 (M); gifts received, $11,850; expenditures, $542,654; qualifying distributions, $541,519; giving activities include $541,519 for 67 grants (high: $344,679; low: $25; average: $1,000–$5,000).
Fields of interest: Environment, natural resources; Health care; Human services; Children/youth, services; International development; Federated giving programs.
Limitations: Applications not accepted. Giving primarily in MA. No grants to individuals.
Application information: Contributes only to pre-selected organizations.
Trustees: Anne Mazar; Brian Mazar.
EIN: 043344681
Selected grants: The following grants were reported in 2004.
$1,020,000 to Nature Conservancy, Arlington, VA.
$3,500 to Rainforest Alliance, New York, NY.
$2,500 to Great Pond Foundation, Edgartown, MA.
$2,500 to Student Conservation Association, Charlestown, NH.
$2,000 to Earthjustice, Oakland, CA.
$1,500 to Trust for Public Land, San Francisco, CA.
$1,000 to Ocean Conservancy, DC.
$425 to Vineyard Energy Project, West Tisbury, MA. 2 grants: $325, $100
$50 to Natural Resources Defense Council, New York, NY.

4029
The McCallum Family Foundation ◇
(formerly The McCallum Foundation)
100 Vesper Executive Park
Tyngsboro, MA 01879 (978) 649-5626
Contact: Donna McCallum, Tr.

Established around 1986.

Donors: Elkin McCallum; Donna McCallum; Joan Fabrics Corp.
Foundation type: Independent foundation.
Financial data (yr. ended 12/31/04): Assets, $40,708,920 (M); expenditures, $1,631,532; qualifying distributions, $1,226,708; giving activities include $1,226,708 for 20 grants (high: $879,068; low: $250).
Purpose and activities: Giving primarily for higher education, as well as for health, and human services, and to a United Methodist church.
Fields of interest: Performing arts, theater; Higher education; Education; Hospitals (general); Human services; Foundations (community); Protestant agencies & churches.
Type of support: Scholarship funds.
Limitations: Giving primarily in MA.
Application information:
Initial approach: Letter or telephone
Deadline(s): None
Trustees: Donna McCallum; Elkin McCallum.
EIN: 222721718
Selected grants: The following grants were reported in 2003.
$924,561 to Bentley College, Waltham, MA. For scholarships.
$105,000 to Centralville United Methodist Church, Lowell, MA. For general support.
$25,000 to Lenoir-Rhyne College, Hickory, NC. For scholarships.
$25,000 to Lowell General Hospital, Lowell, MA. For general support.
$15,000 to Augusta State University Foundation, Augusta, GA. For scholarships.
$15,000 to Middlesex Community College Foundation, Bedford, MA. For scholarships.
$7,500 to Lowell Catholic High School, Lowell, MA. For general support.
$2,500 to Beth Israel Deaconess Medical Center, Boston, MA. For general support.
$1,250 to Girls Inc. of Greater Lowell, Lowell, MA. For general support.
$1,000 to Dana-Farber Cancer Institute, Boston, MA. For general support.

4030
The McCance Foundation ◇
c/o Greylock
880 Winter St.
Waltham, MA 02451
Application address: Keith S. Jennings, c/o Beach Investment Counsel, Inc., 3 Radnor Corp. Ctr., Radnor, PA 19087

Established in 1994 in MA.
Foundation type: Independent foundation.
Financial data (yr. ended 12/31/05): Assets, $7,371,171 (M); expenditures, $388,796; qualifying distributions, $365,500; giving activities include $365,500 for 39 grants (high: $100,000; low: $1,000).
Purpose and activities: Giving primarily for higher education, health associations, particularly for Alzheimer's disease, and human services.
Fields of interest: Higher education; Libraries/library science; Health care; Alzheimer's disease; Human services.
Limitations: Giving primarily in MA.
Application information: Application form not required.
Initial approach: Letter
Deadline(s): None

Trustees: Keith S. Jennings; Allison J. McCance; Henry F. McCance.
EIN: 046772532

4031
James S. McDonnell Family Foundation, Inc. ✧
c/o State Street Bank & Trust Co.
P.O. Box 5300
Boston, MA 02206-5300

Established in 2002 in MA.
Donors: James S. McDonnell Charitable Trust A; James S. McDonnell Charitable Trust B.
Foundation type: Independent foundation.
Financial data (yr. ended 12/31/05): Assets, $25,326,977 (M); gifts received, $5,802,692; expenditures, $1,037,834; qualifying distributions, $996,850; giving activities include $990,277 for 12 grants (high: $460,000; low: $10,000).
Purpose and activities: Giving primarily for community development and education.
Fields of interest: Arts; Elementary/secondary education; Higher education; Urban/community development.
Limitations: Applications not accepted. Giving in the U.S., primarily in MO. No grants to individuals.
Application information: Contributes only to pre-selected organizations.
Officers and Directors:* Holly M. James,* Pres. and Clerk; Catherine M. Rogers, Treas.; Alicia S. McDonnell; James S. McDonnell III; John F. McDonnell.
EIN: 364507175

4032
Mildred H. McEvoy Foundation ✧
370 Main St., 12th Fl., Ste. 1250
Worcester, MA 01608-1779
Contact: Sumner B. Tilton, Jr., Tr.

Trust established in 1963 in MA.
Donor: Mildred H. McEvoy‡.
Foundation type: Independent foundation.
Financial data (yr. ended 12/31/05): Assets, $26,338,735 (M); expenditures, $1,213,078; qualifying distributions, $1,157,535; giving activities include $956,535 for 62 grants (high: $60,000; low: $9), and $37,500 for 11 employee matching gifts.
Purpose and activities: Giving to health, educational, cultural, and human service organizations based in Worcester, MA, and Boothbay, ME.
Fields of interest: Museums; Historic preservation/historical societies; Education, association; Higher education; Health sciences school/education; Animals/wildlife, preservation/protection; Hospitals (general); Health organizations, association; Medical research, institute; Human services; Children/youth, services; Community development; Engineering/technology.
Limitations: Giving primarily in Worcester, MA, and the Boothbay Harbor, ME, area. No grants to individuals, or for endowment funds.
Application information: Application form not required.
Initial approach: Letter
Copies of proposal: 1
Deadline(s): June 1

Board meeting date(s): During the summer and in Dec.
Final notification: Dec. 31
Trustees: George H. McEvoy; Paul R. Rossley; Sumner B. Tilton, Jr.
Number of staff: 1 part-time professional.
EIN: 046069958
Selected grants: The following grants were reported in 2004.
$62,000 to Worcester Academy, Worcester, MA. 2 grants: $50,000, $12,000
$60,000 to Boys and Girls Club of Worcester, Worcester, MA.
$60,000 to Maine Maritime Museum, Bath, ME. 2 grants: $30,000 each
$35,000 to Worcester Art Museum, Worcester, MA.
$20,000 to Massachusetts College of Pharmacy and Health Sciences, Boston, MA.
$15,000 to Saint Andrews Hospital, Boothbay Harbor, ME.
$7,500 to Rangeley Region Health Center, Rangeley, ME.
$5,000 to Quoddy Tides Foundation, Eastport, ME.

4033
The McLane/Harper Charitable Foundation, Inc. ✧ ☆
c/o P. Andrews McLane
125 High St., Ste. 2500
Boston, MA 02110

Established in 1986 in MA.
Donors: P. Andrews McLane; Linda Harper McLane.
Foundation type: Independent foundation.
Financial data (yr. ended 11/30/05): Assets, $11,545,147 (M); expenditures, $2,001,746; qualifying distributions, $2,000,000; giving activities include $2,000,000 for 1 grant.
Fields of interest: Higher education, college.
Limitations: Applications not accepted. Giving primarily in Hanover, NH. No grants to individuals.
Application information: Contributes only to pre-selected organizations.
Officers: P. Andrews McLane, Pres.; Mary Ann Rooney, Clerk; Linda Harper McLane, Treas.
EIN: 042944189

4034
The Melville Charitable Trust ▼
160 Federal St., 8th Fl.
Boston, MA 02110 (617) 338-2590
Contact: Robert Hohler, Exec. Dir.
FAX: (617) 338-2591; E-mail: mct@tpi.org;
URL: http://www.melvilletrust.org

Established in 1987 in NY.
Donor: Dorothy Melville‡.
Foundation type: Independent foundation.
Financial data (yr. ended 12/31/05): Assets, $151,683,725 (M); gifts received, $4,000,000; expenditures, $8,838,791; qualifying distributions, $14,046,316; giving activities include $6,885,275 for 44 grants (high: $1,057,971; low: $7,500; average: $25,000–$400,000), and $5,672,209 for 2 loans/program-related investments.
Purpose and activities: The trust concentrates its efforts on finding and fighting the causes of homelessness. The trust supports service and housing programs in Connecticut that can serve as models throughout the country. The trust also funds

educational, research and advocacy initiatives in the state and on the national level.
Fields of interest: Employment, training; Employment; Housing/shelter, development; Housing/shelter, services; Homeless, human services; Community development, neighborhood development; Economic development.
Type of support: General/operating support; Management development/capacity building; Building/renovation; Equipment; Land acquisition; Program development; Conferences/seminars; Publication; Seed money; Research; Technical assistance; Consulting services; Program evaluation; Program-related investments/loans; Matching/challenge support.
Limitations: Giving primarily in CT. No support for religious organizations for religious purposes. No grants to individuals, for scholarships, budget deficits, or general fundraising drives or events.
Publications: Application guidelines; Annual report; Biennial report (including application guidelines); Grants list.
Application information: See foundation Web site. Application form not required.
Initial approach: Concept paper
Copies of proposal: 1
Deadline(s): Rolling
Board meeting date(s): Varies
Final notification: Varies
Officers and Board Members:* Stephen Melville,* Chair.; Robert Hohler, Exec. Dir.; John R. Gibb; Ben Maiden; Allen Melville; Frank Melville; Ruth Melville.
Trustee: Peter Weston, V.P.; Bank of America, N.A.
Number of staff: 3 full-time professional; 1 part-time support.
EIN: 133415258
Selected grants: The following grants were reported in 2005.
$1,057,971 to Corporation for Supportive Housing, Oakland, CA. To continue support of leadership and staffing, launch new supportive housing demonstration program, continue building national supportive housing Resource Center, support public policy reform efforts, and improve communications and fund development activities.
$738,800 to Technical Assistance Collaborative, Boston, MA. 2 grants: $560,000 (To sustain public policy, publication, and technical assistance activities to address and end homelessness among people with disabilities), $178,800 (To identify and take advantage of opportunities to expand affordable and permanent supportive housing for people below 30 percent of median income as integral part of long-term recovery and rebuilding strategies in Greater New Orleans area).
$653,034 to Partnership for Strong Communities, Hartford, CT. For program support for ongoing activities and operations of Partnership and Lyceum Resource and Conference Center.
$500,000 to Fellowship Place, New Haven, CT. For lead gift for Development Campaign, to provide resources for renovations, new construction, and equipment, developing new programs, and starting endowment.
$400,000 to Chapel Haven, Westville, CT. To purchase apartment house for Asperger's Syndrome Adult Residential Program.
$297,950 to Connecticut Legal Rights Project, Middletown, CT. To continue outreach, intervention, and advocacy activities for Helping Others Maintain Equity in Housing (HOME) project for adults with mental illness having

housing problems related to maintenance, discrimination, and inadequate support services.

$240,000 to National Low Income Housing Coalition and Low Income Housing Information Service, DC. To establish National Housing Trust Fund.

$175,000 to AIDS Housing Corporation, Boston, MA. To build capacity and support advocacy initiatives of United Disability Housing Partnership.

$130,000 to Alderhouse Residential Communities, Middletown, CT. For capacity building.

4035

Merck Family Fund

303 Adams St.
Milton, MA 02186 (617) 696-3580
Contact: Jenny Russell, Exec. Dir.
FAX: (617) 696-7262; E-mail: merck@merckff.org;
URL: http://www.merckff.org

Incorporated in 1954 in NJ.

Donor: Members of the Merck family.

Foundation type: Independent foundation.

Financial data (yr. ended 12/31/04): Assets, $61,213,830 (M); gifts received, $19,850; expenditures, $3,988,867; qualifying distributions, $3,458,765; giving activities include $3,006,332 for 96 grants (high: $250,000; low: $1,000).

Purpose and activities: To restore and protect the natural environment, and to strengthen the social fabric and physical landscape of the urban community. Primary areas of interest are: 1) Protecting and restoring vital eastern U.S. ecosystems and promoting sustainable economic practices; and 2) Strengthening the urban community, concentrating on green and open space programs and youth organizing in Boston, MA, Providence, RI, and New York City.

Fields of interest: Environment; Youth development; Children/youth, services; Community development; neighborhood development; Economics; Economically disadvantaged.

Type of support: General/operating support; Continuing support; Land acquisition; Program development; Conferences/seminars; Seed money; Matching/challenge support.

Limitations: Giving primarily in Boston, MA, New York, NY, and Providence, RI, for Urban Program; the Northern Forest of ME, NH, and VT, southern Appalachia, and SC coastal areas, for Eastern Ecosystems; and nationally for Economics Program. No support for sectarian or religious purposes, for-profit organizations, or for projects intended to support candidates for political office. No grants to individuals, or for endowments, debt reduction, annual fundraising campaigns, capital construction, equipment, land acquisition, or film or video projects; generally no grants for academic research or books.

Publications: Application guidelines; Annual report (including application guidelines); Grants list.

Application information: Full proposals by invitation only. Application form not required.

Initial approach: Letter of inquiry (not to exceed 2 pages); invited proposals should not exceed 8 pages on 100 percent recycled paper

Copies of proposal: 1

Deadline(s): Varies annually, approximately Mar. 1 and Aug. 1.

Board meeting date(s): Feb., May and Nov.

Final notification: Within 1 week of board decision

Officers and Trustees:* Wilhelm M. Merck,* Pres.; Serena Whitridge,* V.P.; Antony M. Merck, Secy.; Sharman Altshuler,* Treas.; Jenny Russell, Exec. Dir.; Nat Chamberlin; Patience M. Chamberlin; Oona Coy; Josephine A. Merck.

Number of staff: 3 full-time professional.

EIN: 226063382

Selected grants: The following grants were reported in 2004.

$250,000 to Food Project, Lincoln, MA.

$75,000 to Appalachian Mountain Club, Boston, MA.

$75,000 to Northern Forest Center, Concord, NH.

$50,534 to Northern Forest Alliance, Montpelier, VT.

$50,395 to Forest Society of Maine, Bangor, ME.

$50,000 to National Parks Conservation Association, DC.

$35,179 to Allston-Brighton Community Development Corporation, Allston, MA.

$25,274 to Sustainable South Bronx, Bronx, NY.

$25,000 to City Parks Foundation, New York, NY.

$25,000 to Point Community Development Corporation, Bronx, NY.

4036

The John Merck Fund ▼ ✧

47 Winter St., 7th Fl.
Boston, MA 02108
Contact: Ruth G. Hennig, Exec. Dir.
FAX: (617) 556-4130; E-mail: info@jmfund.org;
URL: http://www.jmfund.org

Established in 1970 in NY as a trust.

Donor: Serena S. Merck†.

Foundation type: Independent foundation.

Financial data (yr. ended 12/31/04): Assets, $198,646,948 (M); expenditures, $15,678,753; qualifying distributions, $13,461,994; giving activities include $12,379,000 for 193 grants (high: $475,000; low: $1,000; average: $15,000–$100,000).

Purpose and activities: Grants are made in the following areas: for medical research on developmentally disabled children; to preserve environmental quality in rural New England and globally; to support reproductive health and rights initiatives; to advance human rights in Latin America; and to support job creation and training in the New England area of the U.S.

Fields of interest: Environment, public policy; Environment, toxics; Environment, global warming; Environment; Reproductive health; Employment, services; International human rights; Civil liberties, reproductive rights.

International interests: Latin America.

Type of support: Program development.

Limitations: Giving on a national basis in the areas of reproductive health, the environment, and job opportunities; giving in Latin America in the area of human rights. Generally, no support for large organizations with well-established funding sources. No grants to individuals, or for endowment or capital fund projects, generally no general support grants.

Publications: Grants list; Program policy statement.

Application information: The fund does not encourage the submission of unsolicited applications for grants. The fund prefers to request a grant proposal after receiving preliminary written or verbal information about a project.

Initial approach: Letter of inquiry

Deadline(s): 2nd Wed. of Jan., Mar., May, Aug., and Nov.

Board meeting date(s): Feb., Apr., June, Sept., and Dec.

Officers and Trustees:* Francis W. Hatch,* Chair.; Ruth G. Hennig, Secy. and Exec. Dir.; Huyler C. Held,* Treas.; Katherine Arthaud, Advisory Tr.; Olivia H. Farr, Advisory Tr.; David Altshuler; Judith M. Buechner; Arnold Hiatt; Serena M. Hatch; Robert M. Pennoyer; Frederica Perera; Anne Stetson.

Number of staff: 3 full-time professional.

EIN: 237082558

Selected grants: The following grants were reported in 2004.

$350,000 to Clean Air Task Force, Boston, MA. To work with state partner groups in six to twelve states over next year to advance diesel engine cleanup in US through number of strategies at local, state, and national levels.

$250,000 to Clean Water Fund, Boston, MA. To achieve fundamental reform in state-level decision-making about chemicals use that stresses prevention of harm to public health and environment, and coordinate New England-wide effort to achieve virtual elimination of mercury emissions in the region by 2010 and prevent human exposure to mercury.

$210,000 to Center for Food Safety, DC. To launch Agricultural Biotechnology Media and Information Center, which will design and implement media and rapid response strategy for genetically engineered food and agriculture advocacy community, organize second genetically engineered foods strategy meeting in DC, and to protect human health and the environment by ensuring appropriate testing and regulation of all genetically engineered crops and organisms.

$175,000 to Commonweal, Bolinas, CA. To develop state and national alliances of constituencies with health problems linked to chemical exposures and health professionals who support them and alliances within learning and developmental disability communities nationally, and to create centralized source of information about biomonitoring projects, data, collection protocols, and communications strategies for organizations interested in chemical body burden and environmental testing.

$167,500 to Human Rights Watch, New York, NY. For general program support and to support threatened human rights advocates.

$152,000 to Human Rights First, New York, NY. For legal representation to asylum seekers, supporting International Criminal Court, human rights defenders, and promoting US security policy that upholds rule of law, and provide emergency travel and living support to family members of murdered Iraqi human rights activist.

$80,000 to Mexican Commission for the Defense and Promotion of Human Rights, Mexico City, Mexico. To promote human rights and rule of law in Mexico, through litigating cases of violations before national and international judicial bodies.

$50,000 to Ecology Center, Ann Arbor, MI. To move major automobile manufacturers toward elimination of persistent bioaccumulative toxic chemicals and use of safer alternatives.

$50,000 to National Network of Abortion Funds, Amherst, MA. For small grants to member funds to increase knowledge of and access to emergency contraception, with emphasis on reaching women of color, rural women and Spanish-speaking women.

$45,000 to Vermont Land Trust, Montpelier, VT. For Working Landscapes, project that provides business planning and development skills to increase financial viability of small farmers in Vermont.

4037
Middlecott Foundation ✧
c/o William L. Saltonstall
50 Congress St., Ste. 800
Boston, MA 02109

Established in 1967 in MA.
Donors: Sarah H.C. Ambler; Ames Byrd; Emily J. Byrd; Harry F. Byrd; Leverett S. Bryd; Richard E. Byrd III; Eleanor L. Campbell; Eleanor S. Campbell; Levin H. Campbell, Jr.; Emily S. Lewis; Lisa S. Lewis; Lynn Lewis; Deborah S. Pease; Roland F. Pease, Sr.; Roland F. Pease, Jr.; Alice W. Saltonstall; G. West Saltonstall; Patrick G. Saltonstall; Timothy Saltonstall; William L. Saltonstall, Jr.; and members of the Saltonstall family.
Foundation type: Independent foundation.
Financial data (yr. ended 12/31/04): Assets, $1,681,251 (M); gifts received, $610,233; expenditures, $719,951; qualifying distributions, $698,912; giving activities include $693,867 for 555 grants (high: $90,000; low: $50).
Purpose and activities: Giving primarily for education, arts and culture, health (including hospitals), and human services.
Fields of interest: Museums (art); Historic preservation/historical societies; Arts; Education; Hospitals (general); Health organizations, association; Human services; Children/youth, services.
Limitations: Applications not accepted. No grants to individuals.
Application information: Contributes only to pre-selected organizations. All grants are donor-directed.
Trustees: George Lewis; William L. Saltonstall; Neil L. Thompson.
Number of staff: 1 part-time support.
EIN: 046155699
Selected grants: The following grants were reported in 2003.
$250,000 to Peabody Essex Museum, Salem, MA.
$5,000 to Harvard University, Cambridge, MA.
$2,000 to Bowdoin College, Brunswick, ME.
$2,000 to Massachusetts General Hospital, Boston, MA.
$1,000 to Save the Children Federation, Westport, CT.
$750 to Newton-Wellesley Hospital, Newton, MA.
$500 to Museum of Fine Arts, Boston, MA.
$250 to Tufts University, Medford, MA.
$250 to Wellesley College, Center for Women, Wellesley, MA.
$100 to Rosies Place, Boston, MA.

4038
George H. & Jane A. Mifflin Memorial Fund
c/o Loring, Wolcott & Coolidge
230 Congress St.
Boston, MA 02110 (617) 622-2355
Contact: Barbara L. Carr, Admin.
FAX: (617) 523-6535; E-mail: bcarr@lwcotrust.com

Established in 1974 in Massachusetts.
Foundation type: Independent foundation.

Financial data (yr. ended 9/30/05): Assets, $33,018,407 (M); expenditures, $1,863,550; qualifying distributions, $1,721,808; giving activities include $1,676,355 for 99 grants (high: $120,000; low: $5,000).
Purpose and activities: Giving primarily for education. Some giving also for human services and environmental conservation.
Fields of interest: Education; Environment, natural resources; Legal services; Human services; Economically disadvantaged.
Type of support: General/operating support; Capital campaigns; Building/renovation; Land acquisition; Scholarship funds; Matching/challenge support.
Limitations: Giving primarily in MA. No grants to individuals.
Application information: Application form not required.
Initial approach: Proposal
Copies of proposal: 5
Deadline(s): Apr. 15
Board meeting date(s): Sept.
Final notification: Sept. 30
Trustees: John G. Brooks; Lawrence Coolidge; Peter B. Loring.
EIN: 046384983
Selected grants: The following grants were reported in 2005.
$200,000 to Boston Collegiate Charter School, Dorchester, MA. 2 grants: $120,000, $80,000
$80,000 to Peabody Essex Museum, Salem, MA.
$70,000 to Greater Boston Legal Services, Boston, MA.
$50,000 to Boston Museum Project, Boston, MA.
$25,000 to Bostonian Society, Boston, MA.
$25,000 to Essex County Greenbelt Association, Essex, MA.
$25,000 to Volunteer Lawyers Project of the Boston Bar Association, Boston, MA.
$20,000 to Morehouse College, Atlanta, GA.
$10,000 to Alaska Marine Conservation Council, Anchorage, AK.

4039
Herman and Frieda L. Miller Foundation
c/o Grants Mgt. Assoc.
77 Summer St., Ste. 800
Boston, MA 02110-1006 (617) 426-7080, ext. 304
Contact: Amy Segal Shorey, Admin.
FAX: (617) 426-7087;
E-mail: ashorey@grantsmanagement.com;
Application address: Yasmin Shah, Fdn. Asst., tel.: (617) 426-7080, ext. 317; e-mail: yshah@grantsmanagement.com; URL: http://www.grantsmanagement.com/millerguide.html

Established in 1997 in MA.
Donor: Herman Miller‡.
Foundation type: Independent foundation.
Financial data (yr. ended 11/30/05): Assets, $45,386,522 (M); expenditures, $2,604,855; qualifying distributions, $2,572,266; giving activities include $2,518,952 for 60 grants (high: $179,997; low: $5,000).
Purpose and activities: Giving primarily for arts and cultural programs, the environment, and human services.
Fields of interest: Arts; Environment, natural resources; Environment; Human services; Women, centers/services; Community development.

Type of support: General/operating support; Annual campaigns; Capital campaigns; Building/renovation; Matching/challenge support.
Limitations: Applications not accepted. Giving primarily in Boston, MA. No grants to individuals.
Application information: Unsolicited requests for funds not accepted.
Board meeting date(s): Varies
Trustee: Myron Miller.
Number of staff: None.
EIN: 137131926
Selected grants: The following grants were reported in 2005.
$200,000 to Boston Community Capital, Boston, MA.
$90,000 to Boston Foundation, Boston, MA.
$70,000 to Lawrence Community Works, Lawrence, MA.
$50,000 to City Life/Vida Urbana, Jamaica Plain, MA.
$50,000 to Greater Boston Interfaith Organization, Dorchester, MA.
$50,000 to United South End Settlements, Boston, MA.
$40,875 to On the Rise, Cambridge, MA.
$40,000 to Organizing and Leadership Training Center, Boston, MA.
$35,000 to Madison Park Development Corporation, Roxbury, MA.
$30,000 to Boston Cares, Boston, MA.

4040
The Millipore Foundation ✧
290 Concord Rd.
Billerica, MA 01821 (978) 715-1268
Contact: Debra Hilbert
FAX: (978) 715-1382;
E-mail: debra_hilbert@millipore.com; URL: http://www.millipore.com/foundation

Established in 1985 in MA.
Donor: Millipore Corp.
Foundation type: Company-sponsored foundation.
Financial data (yr. ended 9/30/05): Assets, $19,184 (M); gifts received, $1,088,692; expenditures, $1,240,588; qualifying distributions, $1,240,588; giving activities include $905,434 for 105 grants (high: $150,000; low: $250), and $315,403 for 491 employee matching gifts.
Purpose and activities: The foundation supports organizations involved with arts and culture, K-12 education, health, youth development, science research, science education, public policy, and minorities.
Fields of interest: Arts; Elementary/secondary education; Hospitals (general); Health care; Youth development; Science, research; Science, formal/general education; Biological sciences; Public policy, research; Youth; Aging; Minorities; Economically disadvantaged.
Type of support: General/operating support; Program development; Curriculum development; Scholarship funds; Employee volunteer services; Employee matching gifts; Employee-related scholarships; In-kind gifts; Matching/challenge support.
Limitations: Giving primarily in areas of company operations, with emphasis on MA; giving also to national organizations. No support for religious or political organizations. No grants to individuals (except for employee-related scholarships), or for endowments or conferences or seminars; no student loans; generally, no continuing support.

Publications: Financial statement; Grants list.
Application information: Proposals may be submitted using the AGM Common Grant Proposal Form. Application form not required.

Initial approach: Proposal
Copies of proposal: 1
Deadline(s): None
Board meeting date(s): Quarterly
Final notification: Within 1 month

Officer and Trustees:* Geoffrey Nunes,* Chair.; Jeffrey Rudin.
EIN: 222583952
Selected grants: The following grants were reported in 2005.
$150,000 to American Red Cross, Boston, MA.
$70,473 to City Year, Boston, MA.
$35,000 to Scholarship America, Saint Peter, MN.
$26,370 to Boston Partners in Education, Boston, MA.
$25,000 to Museum of Science, Boston, MA.
$10,000 to Adolescent Consultation Services, Cambridge, MA.
$10,000 to Boys and Girls Club of Greater Billerica, Billerica, MA.
$7,000 to Talking Information Center, Marshfield, MA.
$6,500 to Everybody Wins Metro Boston, Cambridge, MA.
$5,000 to Museum of Afro-American History, Boston, MA.

4041
John Mirak Foundation ✦ ☆
438 Massachusetts Ave., No. 127
Arlington, MA   02474

Established in 1972 in MA.
Donors: John Mirak; Arlington Center Service and Garage, Inc.; Mirak Building Trust; Artemis Mirak‡.
Foundation type: Independent foundation.
Financial data (yr. ended 12/31/05): Assets, $6,743,388 (M); gifts received, $1,943; expenditures, $726,014; qualifying distributions, $324,945; giving activities include $324,945 for grants.
Purpose and activities: Giving primarily for an Armenian cultural foundation and other Armenian organizations.
Fields of interest: Arts; Education; Orthodox Catholic agencies & churches.
Limitations: Applications not accepted. No grants to individuals.
Application information: Contributes only to pre-selected organizations.
Officer: Robert Mirak, Mgr.
EIN: 237161662

4042
Monsweag Foundation ✦
194 Simon Willard Rd.
Concord, MA   01742

Established in 2002 in MA.
Donors: John A. Webster, Jr.; Ann S. Webster.
Foundation type: Independent foundation.
Financial data (yr. ended 12/31/05): Assets, $4,739,824 (M); gifts received, $6,683; expenditures, $526,253; qualifying distributions, $480,070; giving activities include $480,000 for 2 grants (high: $250,000; low: $230,000).

Purpose and activities: Giving primarily to an institute of laryngology and voice restoration, as well as to a children's hospital.
Fields of interest: Hospitals (specialty); Ear & throat diseases; Foundations (private grantmaking).
Limitations: Applications not accepted. No grants to individuals.
Application information: Contributes only to pre-selected organizations.
Trustees: Ann S. Webster; John A. Webster, Jr.
EIN: 223887737
Selected grants: The following grants were reported in 2003.
$250,000 to Childrens Hospital Corporation, Boston, MA. For general support.
$250,000 to Veterinary Scholarship Trust of New England, MA. For general support.
$25,000 to Louisa May Alcott Memorial Association, Concord, MA. For general support.

4043
The Morningside Foundation ✦
(formerly Morningside-Springfield Foundation, Inc.)
1188 Centre St.
Newton Center, MA   02459

Established in 1996 in DE and MA.
Donors: Bill Fung; Springfield Financial Asset Mgmt., Inc.; Onyx Holdings, Inc.; Barley, Inc.; Geranium, Inc.; Watercress, Inc.; Stonecorner Corp.; Kadesh Investments Ltd.
Foundation type: Independent foundation.
Financial data (yr. ended 12/31/04): Assets, $16,990,239 (M); gifts received, $1,100,000; expenditures, $1,964,325; qualifying distributions, $1,212,334; giving activities include $1,212,334 for 13 grants (high: $348,334; low: $1,000).
Purpose and activities: Giving primarily for education, as well as for Christian ministries and organizations; support also for an Asia society.
Fields of interest: Arts, cultural/ethnic awareness; Elementary/secondary education; Higher education; Education; Hospitals (specialty); International affairs; Christian agencies & churches; Religion.
Limitations: Applications not accepted. No grants to individuals.
Application information: Contributes only to pre-selected organizations.
Officers: Paula E. Turnbull, V.P.; David Widener, V.P.
Directors: Gerald Chan; Ronnie Chan.
EIN: 043339572
Selected grants: The following grants were reported in 2004.
$348,334 to University of Southern California, Los Angeles, CA.
$100,000 to Asia Society, New York, NY.
$35,000 to Committee of 100, New York, NY.
$25,000 to Cold Spring Harbor Laboratory, Cold Spring Harbor, NY.
$20,000 to Harvard University, Cambridge, MA.

4044
Richard P. & Claire W. Morse Foundation ✦
240 Lee St.
Brookline, MA   02445

Established in 1966 in MA.
Donors: Ruth Morse‡; Richard P. Morse; Claire W. Morse.
Foundation type: Independent foundation.

Financial data (yr. ended 12/31/05): Assets, $5,100,243 (M); gifts received, $251,317; expenditures, $486,768; qualifying distributions, $474,468; giving activities include $472,843 for 35 grants (high: $123,458; low: $65).
Purpose and activities: Giving primarily to museums, and the symphony; funding also for higher education, and Jewish federated giving programs.
Fields of interest: Museums; Performing arts, orchestra (symphony); Education; Hospitals (general); Jewish federated giving programs.
Type of support: General/operating support; Continuing support; Annual campaigns; Capital campaigns; Building/renovation; Equipment; Endowments; Emergency funds; Program development; Seed money; Curriculum development; Fellowships; Internship funds; Program evaluation.
Limitations: Applications not accepted. Giving primarily in Boston, MA. No grants to individuals.
Application information: Contributes only to pre-selected organizations. Funds are fully committed for the next several years.
Trustees: Claire W. Morse; Richard P. Morse.
EIN: 046142794
Selected grants: The following grants were reported in 2004.
$120,000 to Museum of Fine Arts, Boston, MA. For unrestricted support.
$75,000 to Combined Jewish Philanthropies of Greater Boston, Boston, MA. For unrestricted support.
$62,000 to New England Conservatory of Music, Boston, MA. For unrestricted support.
$38,000 to Boston Symphony Orchestra, Boston, MA. For unrestricted support.
$10,200 to Dana-Farber Cancer Institute, Boston, MA. For unrestricted support.
$5,000 to Brigham and Womens Hospital, Boston, MA. For unrestricted support.
$5,000 to Grand Teton Music Festival, Teton Village, WY. For unrestricted support.
$3,000 to Facing History and Ourselves National Foundation, Brookline, MA. For unrestricted support.
$2,500 to Dana-Farber Cancer Institute, Friends of, Boston, MA. For unrestricted support.
$2,000 to School of the Museum of Fine Arts, Boston, MA. For unrestricted support.

4045
The Murray Family Charitable Foundation ✦
c/o Bank of America, N.A, Fdn. and Philanthropic Svcs.
100 Federal St., MA 100-20-06
Boston, MA   02110
Contact: Jane Grayhurst
E-mail: kerry.h.sullivan@bankofamerica.com;
URL: http://www.bankofamerica.com

Established in 1993 in RI.
Donors: Terrence Murray; Murray Family Annuity.
Foundation type: Independent foundation.
Financial data (yr. ended 12/31/04): Assets, $13,317,010 (M); gifts received, $2,232,500; expenditures, $806,243; qualifying distributions, $780,675; giving activities include $751,050 for 91 grants (high: $50,000; low: $100).
Purpose and activities: Giving primarily to hospitals, and for education and human services.

Fields of interest: Museums (art); Elementary/secondary education; Higher education; Education; Hospitals (general); Human services; Federated giving programs.

Limitations: Giving primarily in RI.

Application information: Application form not required.

Initial approach: Proposal with coversheet
Deadline(s): None

Officers and Trustees: * Colleen M. Coggins,* Pres. and Treas.; Paula McNamara,* Exec. V.P.; Terrence Murray,* Exec. V.P.; Megan Murray.

Agent: Bank of America, N.A.

EIN: 050475089

Selected grants: The following grants were reported in 2003.

$125,000 to Rhode Island College Foundation, Providence, RI.

$100,000 to Museum of Fine Arts, Boston, MA.

$67,100 to Providence Country Day School, East Providence, RI. 2 grants: $50,000, $17,100 (For Middle Scholarship Fund).

$25,000 to United Way of Rhode Island, Providence, RI.

$20,000 to United Ways of New England, Boston, MA.

$12,000 to Lincoln School, Providence, RI.

$10,000 to Brigham and Womens Hospital, Boston, MA. For annual fund.

$10,000 to Community Chest-United Way of Palm Beach, Palm Beach, FL.

$10,000 to Pomfret School, Pomfret, CT.

4046
MWC Foundation, Inc.

c/o Nutter, McClennen & Fish, LLP
World Trade Ctr. West
155 Seaport Blvd.
Boston, MA 02210-2604
Contact: Thomas P. Jalkut, Clerk

Established in 1988 in MA.

Foundation type: Independent foundation.

Financial data (yr. ended 12/31/05): Assets, $33,350,321 (M); expenditures, $1,417,031; qualifying distributions, $1,257,000; giving activities include $1,257,000 for grants.

Purpose and activities: Giving primarily for social services.

Fields of interest: Environment; Human services; Community development.

Limitations: Giving primarily in New England. No grants to individuals.

Application information: Contributes primarily to pre-selected organizations. Due to existing commitments, very few unsolicited requests receive favorable consideration.

Initial approach: Letter

Officer: Thomas P. Jalkut, Clerk and Treas.

Director: Richard N. Finlayson.

EIN: 222914691

4047
The Creighton Narada Foundation ✧

c/o Day, Berry & Howard, LLP
260 Franklin St.
Boston, MA 02110

Established in 1994 in MA.

Donors: Albert M. Creighton, Jr.; Charitable Lead Unitrust.

Foundation type: Independent foundation.

Financial data (yr. ended 12/31/05): Assets, $11,828,569 (M); gifts received, $84,091; expenditures, $569,431; qualifying distributions, $526,280; giving activities include $512,000 for 18 grants (high: $230,000; low: $1,500).

Purpose and activities: Giving primarily for land conservation and social services.

Fields of interest: Museums; Higher education; Environment, natural resources; Environment, land resources; Boys & girls clubs; Human services.

Limitations: Applications not accepted. Giving primarily in MA; substantial giving also in ME. No grants to individuals.

Application information: Contributes only to pre-selected organizations.

Trustees: Albert M. Creighton, Jr.; Albert M. Creighton III; Hilary H. Creighton; Peter H. Creighton.

EIN: 043243114

4048
NBT Charitable Trust ✧ ☆

c/o Nichols and Pratt
50 Congress St., Rm. 832
Boston, MA 02109 (617) 523-6800
Contact: James R. Nichols, Tr.

Established in 1991 in MA.

Foundation type: Independent foundation.

Financial data (yr. ended 12/31/05): Assets, $4,420,909 (M); expenditures, $907,543; qualifying distributions, $882,421; giving activities include $867,500 for 8 grants (high: $500,000; low: $2,500).

Purpose and activities: Scholarship awards to educational organizations to cover tuition and related expenses for students studying art or music; giving also to museums.

Fields of interest: Arts education; Museums; Scholarships/financial aid.

Publications: Financial statement; Informational brochure.

Application information:

Initial approach: Letter
Deadline(s): None

Trustees: James R. Nichols; Nancy B. Tieken.

EIN: 046677641

Selected grants: The following grants were reported in 2005.

$600,000 to Institute of Contemporary Art, Boston, MA. 2 grants: $100,000, $500,000

$110,000 to Museum of Contemporary Art San Diego, La Jolla, CA.

$70,000 to Atlantic Center for the Arts, New Smyrna Beach, FL.

$5,000 to Nashoba Brooks School, Concord, MA.

4049
Neighborhood Partners Fund, Inc. ✧

35 Blake St.
Cambridge, MA 02140

Established in 1999 in MA.

Donors: Debra Fox; William Traynor; RAF Foundation.

Foundation type: Operating foundation.

Financial data (yr. ended 12/31/04): Assets, $604,509 (M); gifts received, $504,980; expenditures, $610,374; qualifying distributions, $571,417; giving activities include $483,000 for 3 grants (high: $470,000; low: $5,000), and $88,417 for foundation-administered programs.

Fields of interest: Community development.

Limitations: Applications not accepted. Giving primarily in MA. No grants to individuals.

Application information: Contributes only to pre-selected organizations.

Officers: William Traynor, Pres.; Debra Fox, Secy.-Treas.

EIN: 043476677

4050
New Balance Foundation ▼ ✧

Brighton Landing
20 Guest St.
Boston, MA 02135 (617) 783-4000
Contact: Anne M. Davis, Tr.

Established in 1981 in MA.

Donor: New Balance Athletic Shoe, Inc.

Foundation type: Company-sponsored foundation.

Financial data (yr. ended 11/30/05): Assets, $86,282,973 (M); gifts received, $14,300,000; expenditures, $4,912,868; qualifying distributions, $4,603,014; giving activities include $4,602,764 for 84 grants (high: $1,000,000; low: $800).

Purpose and activities: The foundation supports organizations involved with arts and culture, education, health, youth development, and human services.

Fields of interest: Museums; Arts; Child development, education; Education; Health care; Youth development; Child development, services; Human services; Federated giving programs.

Type of support: General/operating support; Continuing support; Scholarship funds; Matching/challenge support.

Limitations: Giving primarily in MA and ME. No grants to individuals, or for conferences, sporting events, or conventions.

Publications: Financial statement.

Application information: Application form not required.

Initial approach: Proposal
Copies of proposal: 1

Trustees: Anne M. Davis; James S. Davis; Paul R. Gauron.

EIN: 046470644

Selected grants: The following grants were reported in 2005.

$1,000,000 to Habitat for Humanity International. For general support.

$500,000 to Tufts University, Gerald and Dorothy Friedman School of Nutrition, Medford, MA. For general support for program in Boston, MA.

$333,333 to Alfond Youth Center, Waterville, ME. For general support of Boys and Girls Club and YMCA.

$333,333 to Boston Medical Center, Boston, MA. For general support.

$105,890 to American Red Cross of Massachusetts Bay, Boston, MA. For general support.

$60,000 to Boys and Girls Club of Lawrence, Lawrence, MA. For general support.

$25,000 to Lawrence Community Works, Lawrence, MA. For general support.

$25,000 to Stephens Memorial Hospital, Norway, ME. For general support.

$10,000 to Jane Doe, The Massachusetts Coalition Against Sexual Assault and Domestic Violence, Boston, MA. For general support.

$10,000 to Perkins School for the Blind, Watertown, MA. For general support.

4051

New Breeze Foundation ✧
c/o Robert T. Hale, Jr.
8 Olmstead Dr.
Hingham, MA   02043

Established in 2000 in MA.
Donors: Robert T. Hale, Jr.; Robert Hale, Sr.; Judith Hale.
Foundation type: Independent foundation.
Financial data (yr. ended 12/31/05): Assets, $458,857 (M); gifts received, $600,000; expenditures, $657,099; qualifying distributions, $651,677; giving activities include $649,490 for 15 grants (high: $467,610; low: $50).
Fields of interest: Elementary/secondary education; Education; Human services.
Limitations: Applications not accepted. Giving primarily in Quincy, MA. No grants to individuals.
Application information: Contributes only to pre-selected organizations.
Trustees: Karen R. Hale; Robert T. Hale, Jr.
EIN: 043510635

4052

New England Biolabs Foundation
8 Enon St., No. 2B
Beverly, MA   01915-1116   (978) 927-2404
Contact: Martine Kellett, Exec. Dir.; Susan Foster, Asst. Dir.
FAX: (978) 998-6837; E-mail: fosters@nebf.org; Additional E-mail: kellett@nebf.org; URL: http://www.nebf.org

Established in 1982 in MA.
Donors: New England Biolabs, Inc.; Donald G. Combs; Martine Kellett.
Foundation type: Company-sponsored foundation.
Financial data (yr. ended 12/31/04): Assets, $8,179,330 (M); gifts received, $125,818; expenditures, $544,971; qualifying distributions, $516,342; giving activities include $351,017 for 93 grants.
Purpose and activities: The foundation supports organizations involved with elementary school environmental education, marine conservation and estuary protection, sustainable organic agriculture, and sustainable economic development and awards grants to individuals for environmental research. Special emphasis is directed toward programs designed to communicate their message through art and culture; and address environmental protection and education in Papua New Guinea.
Fields of interest: Elementary school/education; Environment, research; Environment, water resources; Environmental education; Agriculture, soil/water issues; Economic development.
International interests: Cameroon; Caribbean; Central America; Ghana; Guatemala; Madagascar; Papua New Guinea; South America; Tanzania.
Type of support: Program development; Seed money; Curriculum development; Research; Grants to individuals; Matching/challenge support.
Limitations: Giving primarily in New England, with emphasis on the Boston, MA, area, particularly the North Shore area of MA, and on an international basis in Cameroon, the Caribbean, Central America, Ghana, Guatemala, Madagascar, Papua New Guinea, South America, and Tanzania. No support for organizations located in Argentina, Belize, Brazil, Chile, Columbia, Costa Rica, French Guiana, Mexico, Panama, the Philippines, Suriname, Uruguay, Venezuela, or Vietnam or private schools. No grants

to individuals (except for environmental research), or for non-marine issues in the Caribbean or Madagascar, non-environmental education projects in Guatemala, non-environmental projects in Ghana, educational or community projects of U.S. organizations not located in the Boston, MA, area, art projects located outside the immediate community, capital campaigns, conferences, workshops, or travel, videos, movies, or books, religious activities, general operating support, scholarships, fellowships, or internships, scientific research eligible for funding by major agencies, services for senior citizens, economically disadvantaged people, or disabled people, or species-specific projects.
Publications: Application guidelines; Grants list; Informational brochure (including application guidelines).
Application information: Letters of inquiry should be no longer than 1 page. Letters of inquiry may be submitted using the NNG Common Grant Proposal Form. Grants generally do not exceed $10,000. Organizations receiving support are asked to provide a final report. Application form not required.
Initial approach: Telephone or mail or E-mail letter of inquiry to foundation; visit Web site for application information for grants to individuals
Copies of proposal: 1
Deadline(s): Postmarked by Mar. 1 and Sept. 1
Board meeting date(s): Apr. and Oct.
Final notification: 2 months following board meetings
Officer: Martine Kellett, Exec. Dir.
Trustees: David Comb; Ellen Lutz; Henry P. Paulus, Ph.D.; William Sargent.
Number of staff: 2 part-time professional.
EIN: 042776213

4053

The New England Foundation ✧
c/o Joseph McNay
125 High St., 29th Fl.
Boston, MA   02110

Established in 1986 in MA.
Donor: Joseph C. McNay.
Foundation type: Independent foundation.
Financial data (yr. ended 12/31/04): Assets, $18,882,894 (M); gifts received, $2,098; expenditures, $1,782,987; qualifying distributions, $1,690,028; giving activities include $1,665,550 for 40 grants (high: $806,800; low: $500).
Purpose and activities: Giving primarily for the arts and education.
Fields of interest: Media, radio; Arts; Secondary school/education; Higher education; Hospitals (general); Health care; Human services.
Limitations: Applications not accepted. Giving limited to New England. No grants to individuals.
Application information: Contributes only to pre-selected organizations.
Trustees: Colin McNay; Joseph C. McNay.
EIN: 222757391
Selected grants: The following grants were reported in 2004.
$806,800 to Wellesley College, Wellesley, MA.
$350,000 to Yale University, New Haven, CT.
$100,000 to Isabella Stewart Gardner Museum, Boston, MA.
$35,000 to National Public Radio, DC.
$25,000 to Roxbury Latin School, West Roxbury, MA.

$22,500 to Boston Symphony Orchestra, Boston, MA.
$20,000 to New-York Historical Society, New York, NY.
$2,500 to Boston Ballet, Boston, MA.
$2,500 to W G B H Educational Foundation, Boston, MA.
$2,000 to John F. Kennedy Library Foundation, Boston, MA.

4054

The New England Patriots Charitable Foundation, Inc. ✧ ☆
c/o Donation Requests
1 Patriot Pl.
Foxboro, MA   02035-1388
URL: http://www.patriots.com/charitable/

Established in 1994 in MA.
Donor: New England Patriots LP.
Foundation type: Company-sponsored foundation.
Financial data (yr. ended 12/31/05): Assets, $2,128,438 (M); gifts received, $2,391,102; expenditures, $1,866,116; qualifying distributions, $1,755,291; giving activities include $1,755,291 for grants.
Purpose and activities: The foundation supports organizations involved with education, health, human services, and women.
Fields of interest: Education; Health care; Children/youth, services; Human services; Federated giving programs; Women.
Type of support: Continuing support; Equipment; Program development; Curriculum development; Scholarship funds; Technical assistance; In-kind gifts.
Limitations: Giving limited to New England. No support for religious organizations. No grants to individuals, or for online auctions.
Application information: Proposals should be submitted using organization letterhead. Application form not required.
Initial approach: Mail proposal to foundation
Deadline(s): None
Officers: Robert K. Kraft, Chair.; Myra H. Kraft, Pres.; Joshua M. Kraft, Treas.
Directors: Daniel A. Kraft; David H. Kraft; Jonathan A. Kraft.
EIN: 043244069
Selected grants: The following grants were reported in 2004.
$160,500 to Boys and Girls Clubs of Boston, Boston, MA.
$125,000 to United Way of Massachusetts Bay, Boston, MA.
$50,000 to Inner-City Scholarship Fund, Boston, MA.
$25,000 to Boys and Girls Club of Cape Cod, Mashpee, MA.
$25,000 to Bridge Over Troubled Waters, Boston, MA.
$25,000 to Brookline High School, Brookline, MA.
$20,000 to Big Brothers of Massachusetts Bay, Boston, MA.
$10,000 to Wellspring House, Gloucester, MA.
$3,000 to Boston Public Schools, Boston, MA.
$500 to Desert Community Foundation, Palm Desert, CA.

4055
N. Woodburn Nichols Foundation, Inc.
18 King St.
Groveland, MA   01834

Established in 2002 in MA.
Donor: N. Woodburn Nichols†.
Foundation type: Independent foundation.
Financial data (yr. ended 12/31/05): Assets, $25,774,839 (M); expenditures, $1,660,754; qualifying distributions, $1,448,633; giving activities include $1,390,000 for 1 grant.
Purpose and activities: To support Nichols Village, Inc., a senior retirement community.
Fields of interest: Residential/custodial care, senior continuing care; Aging.
Limitations: Applications not accepted. Giving primarily in Groveland, MA. No support for research. No grants to individuals.
Application information:
Board meeting date(s): Dec. 24
Officers and Directors:* Richard N. Cammett,* Pres. and Treas.; Eileen I. Cammett,* Clerk; David B. Cammett; Richard N. Cammett, Jr.; Susan V. Cammett; Joanne Hayden; Lisa Hayden; Stephen Hayden; Janice Lane.
EIN: 651162899
Selected grants: The following grants were reported in 2005.
$2,564,872 to Nichols Village, Groveland, MA.

4056
Noorii-Iman Charitable Foundation, Inc. ◇
c/o MFA
793 Turnpike St.
North Andover, MA   01845

Established in 2000 in MA.
Donor: Ashraf Dahod.
Foundation type: Independent foundation.
Financial data (yr. ended 12/31/04): Assets, $142,038 (M); gifts received, $265; expenditures, $1,759,511; qualifying distributions, $1,752,000; giving activities include $1,752,000 for 8 grants (high: $1,356,000; low: $5,000).
Fields of interest: Education; Human services.
Limitations: Applications not accepted. Giving primarily in MA. No grants to individuals.
Application information: Contributes only to pre-selected organizations.
Trustee: Ashraf Dahod.
EIN: 043524114

4057
North Central Massachusetts Community Foundation, Inc.
285 John Fitch Hwy., Ste. 1
Fitchburg, MA   01420-5998   (978) 345-8383
Contact: Philip M. Grzewinski, Pres.
FAX: (978) 345-1459; E-mail: info@cfncm.org;
URL: http://www.cfncm.org

Established in 2000 in MA.
Foundation type: Community foundation.
Financial data (yr. ended 6/30/05): Assets, $5,079,844 (M); gifts received, $1,185,695; expenditures, $1,176,925; giving activities include $976,410 for 23 grants (high: $214,000; low: $245).

Purpose and activities: Giving to organizations that meet the needs and improve the quality of life for residents of north central Massachusetts.
Fields of interest: Arts; Education; Environment; Health care; Human services; Economic development; Community development.
Type of support: General/operating support; Endowments; Scholarship funds.
Limitations: Giving primarily in north central MA.
Publications: Annual report; Informational brochure; Newsletter.
Application information: Visit foundation Web site for grant information.
Officers and Trustees:* Thomas F. Bagley III,* Chair.; Charles Gelinas,* Vice-Chair.; Philip M. Grzewinski,* Pres. and Recording Secy.; Steve L. Stone,* Treas.; Robert C. Alario; Ronald M. Ansin; William E. Aubuchon III; Norman Boudreau; Paul Brown; Richard A. Cella; Jan Cochran; Martin F. Connors; George Gantz; James Garrison; David McKeehan; Kevin Miller; Richard W. Nobile; Sergio Paez; C. Deborah Phillips; Timothy W. Richards; Albert Stone.
EIN: 043537449

4058
James W. O'Brien Foundation, Inc. ◇ ☆
c/o McInnis Law Offices
807 Turnpike St.
North Andover, MA   01845-6131

Foundation type: Independent foundation.
Financial data (yr. ended 9/30/05): Assets, $17,680,600 (M); expenditures, $1,125,823; qualifying distributions, $780,752; giving activities include $683,912 for 66 grants (high: $300,000; low: $100).
Fields of interest: Secondary school/education; Higher education; Human services; Community development.
Limitations: Giving primarily in MA.
Trustees: Carl Diamati; Andrew Fila; James J. McInnis; Marybeth McInnis; Richard Santigati.
EIN: 043528495

4059
Joseph & Katherine O'Donnell Charitable Trust ◇
c/o Lourie & Cutler, PC
60 State St.
Boston, MA   02109

Established in 1997 in MA.
Donors: Joseph O'Donnell; Katherine O'Donnell.
Foundation type: Independent foundation.
Financial data (yr. ended 12/31/05): Assets, $1,688,514 (M); gifts received, $1,583,300; expenditures, $783,571; qualifying distributions, $777,850; giving activities include $777,850 for 14 grants (high: $200,000; low: $100).
Fields of interest: Higher education; Health care; Religion, formal/general education; Roman Catholic agencies & churches.
Limitations: Applications not accepted. No grants to individuals.
Application information: Contributes only to pre-selected organizations.
Trustee: William Eisen.
EIN: 046828957

4060
OneBeacon Charitable Trust ◇
(formerly CGU Charitable Trust)
1 Beacon St.
Boston, MA   02108   (617) 725-6165

Established in 1987 in PA.
Donor: General Accident Insurance Co. of America.
Foundation type: Company-sponsored foundation.
Financial data (yr. ended 12/31/05): Assets, $3,369,452 (M); expenditures, $710,664; qualifying distributions, $710,386; giving activities include $693,480 for grants.
Purpose and activities: The foundation supports organizations involved with arts and culture, higher education, health, human services, children and youth services, community development, and government and public administration.
Fields of interest: Arts; Higher education; Health organizations, association; Human services; Children/youth, services; Community development; Federated giving programs; Government/public administration.
Type of support: Employee matching gifts.
Limitations: Applications not accepted. Giving on a national basis. No grants to individuals.
Application information: Contributes only to pre-selected organizations.
Trustees: Roger M. Singer.
EIN: 232441567
Selected grants: The following grants were reported in 2003.
$20,274 to Public Broadcasting Association, New York, NY.
$20,000 to Boys Club of New York, New York, NY.
$10,000 to Northern Stage Company, White River Junction, VT.
$500 to Dynamy, Worcester, MA.
$500 to Muscular Dystrophy Association, Tucson, AZ.
$300 to Greyhound Friends, Hopkinton, MA.
$200 to American Lung Association, New York, NY.
$150 to Wellness Community-Philadelphia, Philadelphia, PA.
$100 to Boy Scouts of America, Lancaster, MA.
$100 to Shriners Hospitals for Children, Springfield, MA.

4061
Oral Health Services Foundation, Inc. ◇
465 Medford St.
Boston, MA   02129-1454   (617) 886-1700
FAX: (617) 886-1799;
E-mail: ohf@deltadentalma.com; Contacts: Implementation and Clinical Equipment Capacity Grants: Kathy Myers, Exec. Dir., Progs., tel.: (617) 886-1113, E-mail: kmyers@deltadentalma.com; Planning Grants: Judith Foley, Prog. Off., tel.: (617) 886-1466, E-mail: jfoley@deltadentalma.com; URL: http://www.oralhealthfoundation.org

Donor: Delta Dental Plan of Massachusetts.
Foundation type: Company-sponsored foundation.
Financial data (yr. ended 12/31/05): Assets, $16,524,254 (M); gifts received, $4,530,000; expenditures, $2,198,608; qualifying distributions, $2,114,561; giving activities include $1,609,125 for 19 grants (high: $218,200; low: $19,729).
Purpose and activities: The foundation supports programs designed to enhance access to appropriate oral health prevention and disease management services for underserved residents in Massachusetts; develop community-based,

sustainable preventive oral health service delivery plans that address the unmet oral health needs of areas and populations in Massachusetts; promote effective and innovative models of preventive oral health care; raise awareness of the importance of oral health; and strengthen oral health training and education to increase the number of culturally-competent health professionals.

Fields of interest: Dental school/education; Health care, equal rights; Medicine/medical care, public education; Dental care; Aging; Homeless.

Type of support: General/operating support; Management development/capacity building; Building/renovation; Equipment; Program development; Consulting services.

Limitations: Giving limited to MA. No grants for new building or endowments, direct individual scholarships, lobbying or political activities, debt reduction, fundraising events, or replacement of public, private, or indirect funding.

Publications: Application guidelines; Annual report; Grants list.

Application information: Unsolicited requests for Planning Grants are not accepted. Application form required.

  Initial approach: Download application form and mail to foundation
  Deadline(s): Mar. 1 for Implementation Grants; Mar. 30 for Clinical Equipment Capacity Grants
  Final notification: Sept. for Implementation Grants; July for Clinical Equipment Capacity Grants

Officers and Directors:* Chester W. Douglas, DMD,* Chair.; Ralph Fuccillo,* Pres.; Neil B. Epstein, DMD; Shepard Goldstein, DMD; Douglas B. Harding; Judith A. Jones, DDS; Roderick E. King, MD; Clare D. McGorrian; Mike Nacey; Marylou Sudders.

EIN: 043265080

4062
The Orchard Foundation ◇

c/o M. Gordon Ehrlich
Bingham McCutchen LLP
150 Federal St.
Boston, MA 02110
Contact: Brigitte L. Kingsbury, Exec. Dir.
E-mail: orchard@maine.rr.com; Application address: P.O. Box 2587, South Portland, ME 04116, tel.: (207) 799-0686; URL: http://www.orchardfoundation.org

Established in 1990 in MA.

Donors: Moose Mountain Trust; Leigh Fibers, Inc.; Leigh Fibers Holdings, Inc.

Foundation type: Company-sponsored foundation.

Financial data (yr. ended 12/31/04): Assets, $16,453,794 (M); gifts received, $925,500; expenditures, $1,175,413; qualifying distributions, $1,077,745; giving activities include $1,030,952 for 99 grants (high: $100,000; low: $400).

Purpose and activities: The foundation supports organizations involved with literacy, the environment, child and family advocacy, and campaign finance reform.

Fields of interest: Education, reading; Environment; Human services, alliance; Campaign finance reform.

Type of support: Continuing support; Program development; Seed money.

Limitations: Giving limited to CT, ME, MA, NH, NY, RI, and VT. No support for museums or religious organizations. No grants to individuals, or for endowments, annual campaigns, conferences or travel unrelated to a current grant, scholarships,

fellowships, building, equipment, or film or video projects; no loans.

Publications: Application guidelines; Grants list; Program policy statement.

Application information: Letters of inquiry should be no longer than 1 page. Support is limited to 1 contribution per organization during any given year. Organizations receiving support are asked to provide a final report. Express mail is not encouraged. Video or audio submissions are not encouraged. Application form not required.

  Initial approach: Mail or E-mail letter of inquiry
  Copies of proposal: 1
  Deadline(s): Postmarked by Jan. 15

Officer and Trustees:* Brigitte L. Kingsbury,* Exec. Dir.; M. Gordon Ehrlich; Carl P. Lehner; Heidi Lehner.

Number of staff: 1 part-time professional.

EIN: 046660214

Selected grants: The following grants were reported in 2004.

$100,000 to McLean Hospital, Center for Neuroregeneration Laboratory, Belmont, MA. For Parkinson's disease challenge grant.

$90,000 to Childrens Medical Center Corporation, Boston, MA. For Pediatric Rheumatology Clinical Fellowship.

$75,000 to Harvard University, Cambridge, MA. 2 grants: $25,000 to David Rockefeller Center for Latin American Studies (For general operating support), $50,000 (For capital campaign).

$30,000 to Massachusetts Institute of Technology, Mechanical Engineering Department, Cambridge, MA.

$25,000 to Amherst College, Amherst, MA. For Geology Building.

$20,000 to Black Warrior Riverkeeper, Birmingham, AL. For general operating support.

$20,000 to Lahey Clinic Foundation, Burlington, MA. For Institute of Urology and Institute of Orthopedics.

$20,000 to Union of Concerned Scientists, Cambridge, MA. For Northeast Carbon Offsets Project.

$20,000 to Well School, Peterborough, NH. For general operating support.

$15,000 to Clean Water Fund, Providence, RI. For New England Zero Mercury Campaign.

$15,000 to Forest Watch, Montpelier, VT. For protecting New England's forests from acid deposition and harmful logging practices.

$15,000 to Friends of Casco Bay, South Portland, ME. For stopping cruise ship pollution in Casco Bay.

$15,000 to Reach Out and Read of Greater New York, New York, NY. For coordinator internship program.

$10,000 to Childrens Hospital Corporation, Boston, MA. For childrens advocacy network.

$10,000 to Generations, Boston, MA. For classroom literacy coach.

$10,000 to Northern Forest Alliance, Montpelier, VT. For Northern Forest Public Funding Initiative.

$10,000 to Planned Parenthood League of Massachusetts, Boston, MA. For advancing comprehensive sex education in Massachusetts.

4063
Oristaglio Family Foundation ◇ ☆

(formerly Cristaglio Social Responsibility Family Foundation)
287 Commonwealth Ave., Ste. 4
Boston, MA 02115
Contact: Jeryl Oristaglio, Tr.

Established in 2000 in MA.

Donor: Stephen Oristaglio.

Foundation type: Independent foundation.

Financial data (yr. ended 12/31/05): Assets, $236,561 (M); gifts received, $710,000; expenditures, $521,309; qualifying distributions, $518,893; giving activities include $518,893 for 46 grants (high: $102,840; low: $250).

Fields of interest: Education; Hospitals (general); Health organizations, association; Federated giving programs.

Application information:
  Initial approach: Letter
  Deadline(s): None

Trustee: Jeryl Oristaglio.

EIN: 043541069

Selected grants: The following grants were reported in 2004.

$86,000 to Esplanade Association, Boston, MA.

$25,000 to City Year.

$15,350 to Boston Medical Center, Boston, MA.

$10,100 to Friends of the Public Gardens, Halifax, Canada. .

$10,000 to Horizons for Homeless Children, Dorchester, MA.

$7,500 to Boston Ballet, Boston, MA.

$5,400 to Rashi School, Newton, MA.

$5,000 to International Institute of Boston, Boston, MA.

$5,000 to Project Hope, Brooklyn, NY.

$2,500 to Rosemont College, Rosemont, PA.

4064
Edith H. Overly Foundation ◇

c/o Choate, Hall & Stewart
2 International Pl.
Boston, MA 02110

Established in 1990 in MA.

Donor: Edith H. Overly.

Foundation type: Independent foundation.

Financial data (yr. ended 12/31/05): Assets, $8,513,636 (M); gifts received, $142,815; expenditures, $614,973; qualifying distributions, $563,999; giving activities include $558,500 for 28 grants (high: $50,000; low: $1,000).

Fields of interest: Media/communications; Museums; Performing arts, music; Arts; Medical school/education; Education; Animals/wildlife, formal/general education; Medical research, institute; Cancer research.

Limitations: Applications not accepted. Giving primarily in Boston, MA. No grants to individuals.

Application information: Contributes only to pre-selected organizations.

Trustees: F. Davis Dassori; Edith H. Overly.

EIN: 223043340

Selected grants: The following grants were reported in 2004.

$50,000 to American Alpine Club, Golden, CO.

$35,000 to American Cancer Society, Framingham, MA.

$30,000 to Boston Athenaeum, Boston, MA.

$30,000 to W G B H Educational Foundation, Boston, MA.

$25,000 to Museum of Science, Boston, MA.

$20,000 to Appalachian Mountain Club, Boston, MA.

$20,000 to Museum of Fine Arts, Boston, MA.

$20,000 to Nature Conservancy, Boston, MA.

$15,000 to Shady Hill School, Cambridge, MA.

$15,000 to Winsor School, Boston, MA.

4065
Dorothy Pace Foundation, Inc. ✧

c/o Prince, Lobel, Glovsky & Tye
585 Commercial St.
Boston, MA 02109

Established in 2004 in MA.
Donor: Dorothy Pace.
Foundation type: Operating foundation.
Financial data (yr. ended 12/31/04): Assets,
$20,705 (M); gifts received, $490,514;
expenditures, $472,347; qualifying distributions,
$472,347; giving activities include $460,375 for
grants.
Purpose and activities: Support for The Cotting
School in Lexington, MA.
Fields of interest: Education, special.
Limitations: Applications not accepted. Giving
primarily in Lexington, MA. No grants to individuals.
Application information: Contributes only to
pre-selected organizations.
Director: Donald Adler.
EIN: 043462028

4066
Thomas Anthony Pappas Charitable Foundation, Inc. ✧

c/o S. Wolfberg Brown Rudnick Freed
P.O. Box 463
Belmont, MA 02478-0004 (781) 862-2802
Contact: John C. Pappas, V.P.

Incorporated in 1975 in MA.
Donor: Thomas Anthony Pappas†.
Foundation type: Independent foundation.
Financial data (yr. ended 12/31/04): Assets,
$21,408,382 (M); expenditures, $1,219,827;
qualifying distributions, $983,085; giving activities
include $774,000 for 42 grants (high: $250,000;
low: $1,000).
Purpose and activities: Emphasis on higher
education, hospitals and health associations,
cultural programs, Greek Orthodox church support,
religious associations, and youth and social service
agencies.
Fields of interest: Arts; Higher education;
Education; Hospitals (general); Health care; Health
organizations, association; Medical research,
institute; Human services; Children/youth, services;
Orthodox Catholic agencies & churches.
Type of support: Continuing support; Annual
campaigns; Building/renovation; Endowments;
Professorships; Fellowships; Scholarship funds;
Research.
Limitations: Giving primarily in MA. No grants to
individuals.
Publications: Application guidelines; Program policy
statement.
Application information: Application form not
required.
   Initial approach: Letter or proposal
   Deadline(s): Sept. 30
   Board meeting date(s): Mar., June, Sept., Dec.,
     and as required
   Final notification: Dec. 31
Officers and Directors:* Helen K. Pappas,* Pres.;
John Pappas,* V.P.; Betsy Demirjian; Thomas C.
Pappas; Sophia Sacher; Donald Young.
Number of staff: 3 full-time professional.
EIN: 510153284

4067
Arthur M. & Martha R. Pappas Foundation ✧

c/o R.N. Lusardi, CPA
271 Main St., Rm. 203
Stoneham, MA 02180-3580

Established in 1988 in MA.
Donors: Arthur M. Pappas; Martha R. Pappas.
Foundation type: Independent foundation.
Financial data (yr. ended 12/31/05): Assets,
$9,970,369 (M); gifts received, $200,000;
expenditures, $498,199; qualifying distributions,
$489,450; giving activities include $486,100 for 59
grants (high: $200,000; low: $25).
Purpose and activities: Giving for the arts,
education, the environment, health, and human
services.
Fields of interest: Arts; Education; Environment;
Health care; Health organizations, association;
Medical research; Human services; Christian
agencies & churches.
Limitations: Applications not accepted. Giving
primarily in MA. No grants to individuals.
Application information: Contributes only to
pre-selected organizations.
Trustees: Arthur M. Pappas; Martha R. Pappas.
EIN: 222967957
Selected grants: The following grants were reported
in 2005.
$25,000 to Massachusetts Hospital School,
   Canton, MA.
$25,000 to Wellesley College, Wellesley, MA.
$10,800 to Music Worcester, Worcester, MA.
$2,000 to Worcester Art Museum, Worcester, MA.
$1,000 to Mechanics Hall, Worcester, MA.
$500 to Boston Childrens Chorus, Boston, MA.
$500 to Haystack Mountain School of Crafts, Deer
   Isle, ME.
$500 to W G B H Educational Foundation, Boston,
   MA.
$100 to Boston Medical Center, Boston, MA.
$100 to Worcester District Medical Society,
   Worcester, MA.

4068
Samuel P. Pardoe Foundation ✧

c/o Grants Mgmt. Assoc., Inc.
77 Summer St., 8th Fl.
Boston, MA 02110-1006 (617) 426-7080
Contact: Mary Phillips
FAX: (617) 426-7087;
E-mail: mphillips@grantsmanagement.com;
URL: http://www.grantsmanagement.com/Pardoe/
pardoeguide.html

Established in 1989 in DC.
Donors: Samuel P. Pardoe†; Helen P. Pardoe Trust.
Foundation type: Independent foundation.
Financial data (yr. ended 6/30/05): Assets,
$10,532,157 (M); expenditures, $1,073,789;
qualifying distributions, $1,255,467; giving
activities include $963,720 for 28 grants (high:
$695,000; low: $500), and $249,000 for 1 loan/
program-related investment.
Purpose and activities: Support primarily for
programs that provide educational and economic
opportunities for underprivileged persons. Other
areas of interest include health and social services,
cultural programs, community development
activities, education, and land and resource
management.

Fields of interest: Education; Environment, land
resources; Human services.
Type of support: Capital campaigns; Building/
renovation; Equipment; Program development.
Limitations: Giving limited to the Lakes Region of
NH. No support for religious or sectarian purposes.
No grants to individuals, or for operating expenses,
endowments, scholarships, deficit financing,
advertising, special events, or fundraising activities;
no loans.
Publications: Application guidelines.
Application information: Application guidelines and
form available on foundation Web site. Application
form required.
   Initial approach: Letter with proposal cover sheet
     or telephone
   Copies of proposal: 2
   Deadline(s): Jan. 15
   Board meeting date(s): Spring and fall
   Final notification: Apr. 30
Officers and Directors:* Charles H. Pardoe II,*
Pres.; P. Bruce Pardoe,* V.P.; E. Spencer Pardoe
Ballou,* Secy.; Charles E. Pardoe,* Treas.
Number of staff: 2 part-time professional; 1
part-time support.
EIN: 521660757
Selected grants: The following grants were reported
in 2005.
$695,000 to Prescott Conservancy, Boston, MA.
$115,000 to Audubon Society of New Hampshire,
   Concord, NH.
$15,000 to Vermont Institute of Natural Science,
   Woodstock, VT.
$5,000 to Vinalhaven Land Trust, Vinalhaven, ME.
$1,000 to Maine Coast Heritage Trust, Topsham,
   ME.

4069
The Theodore Edson Parker Foundation

c/o Grants Mgmt. Assocs., Inc.
77 Summer St., 8th Fl.
Boston, MA 02110-1006 (617) 426-7080, ext.
309
Contact: Brinda Maira, Fdn. Asst.
FAX: (617) 426-7087;
E-mail: phall@grantsmanagement.com; URL: http://
www.grantsmanagement.com/
parkerfoundation.html

Incorporated in 1944 in MA.
Donor: Theodore Edson Parker†.
Foundation type: Independent foundation.
Financial data (yr. ended 12/31/05): Assets,
$21,500,670 (M); expenditures, $1,202,672;
qualifying distributions, $1,149,265; giving
activities include $1,007,830 for 43 grants (high:
$50,000; low: $300).
Purpose and activities: The foundation's primary
goal is to make effective grants that benefit the city
of Lowell, MA, and its residents. Giving for a variety
of purposes including social services, cultural
programs, community development activities,
education, community health needs and urban
environmental projects.
Fields of interest: Arts; Education; Environment;
Health care; Substance abuse, services;
Employment; Housing/shelter, development;
Human services; Children/youth, services;
Minorities/immigrants, centers/services;
Community development; Public affairs; Minorities;
Economically disadvantaged.
Type of support: Capital campaigns; Building/
renovation; Equipment; Land acquisition; Program

development; Seed money; Research; Consulting services; Program-related investments/loans; Matching/challenge support.

Limitations: Giving primarily in Lowell, MA. No grants to individuals, or for operating budgets, matching gifts, continuing support, annual campaigns, emergency funds, deficit financing, scholarships, or fellowships.

Publications: Application guidelines; Grants list.

Application information: Applicants are limited to 1 application per year. See foundation Web site for application guidelines and procedures. Please use the common proposal format developed by Associated Grant Makers (formerly Associated Grantmakers of MA) available at the Parker Foundation office and online at http://www.agmconnect.org. The foundation accepts unsolicited applications if focused on Lowell, MA. Application form not required.

 Initial approach: Telephone, proposal, or letter
 Copies of proposal: 1
 Deadline(s): Jan. 15, May 15, and Sept. 15
 Board meeting date(s): Apr. or May; Sept., and Dec.
 Final notification: 4 months

Officers and Trustees:* Newell Flather,* Pres.; Andrew C. Bailey,* Secy.-Treas.; Philip Hall,* Admin.; Karen H. Carpenter; Thomas E. Leggat.

EIN: 046036092

Selected grants: The following grants were reported in 2004.

$530,000 to Greater Lowell Community Foundation, Lowell, MA.

$321,000 to Lowell Parks and Conservation Trust, Lowell, MA. 2 grants: $20,000, $301,000

$50,000 to Community Teamwork, Lowell, MA.

$35,000 to YMCA, Greater Lowell Family, Lowell, MA.

$30,000 to International Institute of Boston, Boston, MA.

$25,000 to United Way of Merrimack Valley, Ward Hill, MA.

$20,000 to Justice Resource Institute, Boston, MA.

$15,000 to Boston Foundation, Boston, MA.

$15,000 to Massachusetts Alliance of Portuguese Speakers, Cambridge, MA.

4070

Albert N. Parlin Trust ✧

c/o Hemenway & Barnes
P.O. Box 961209
Boston, MA 02196-1209

Foundation type: Independent foundation.

Financial data (yr. ended 12/31/04): Assets, $5,207,217 (M); expenditures, $545,874; qualifying distributions, $522,496; giving activities include $522,491 for 2 grants (high: $420,100; low: $102,391).

Fields of interest: Human services; Foundations (private operating).

Limitations: Applications not accepted. Giving limited to Boston and Somerville, MA. No grants to individuals.

Application information: Contributes only to pre-selected organizations.

Trustees: Timothy F. Fidgeon; Kurt F. Somerville.

EIN: 510150855

4071

Partnership for Excellence in Jewish Education ✧

c/o Stephane Acel, Grant Admin.
88 Broad St., 6th Fl.
Boston, MA 02110 (617) 367-0001
FAX: (617) 367-0029; E-mail: info@peje.org;
URL: http://www.peje.org

Established in 1996 in MA.

Donors: E. Jesselson; M. Jesselson; Jim Joseph†; Morton Mandel; Michael Steinhardt; Abramson Family Foundation; Leslie H. Wexner; United Jewish Appeal-Federation of New York; S. Bronfman Foundation, Inc.; Harold Grinspoon Foundation.

Foundation type: Independent foundation.

Financial data (yr. ended 8/31/03): Assets, $7,330,329 (M); gifts received, $4,872,661; expenditures, $6,669,970; qualifying distributions, $6,976,697; giving activities include $1,854,367 for 82 grants (high: $100,000; low: $2,000).

Purpose and activities: The Partnership for Excellence in Jewish Education (PEJE) is a collaborative initiative of philanthropic partners committed to strengthening Jewish day school education in North America. Through grant making, expertise delivery, and advocacy, PEJE works to assist individual schools, promote excellence in the field at large, and increase awareness and support of day schools in the broader Jewish community.

Fields of interest: Elementary/secondary education; Education; Jewish agencies & temples.

Type of support: Conferences/seminars; Publication; Curriculum development; Technical assistance.

Limitations: Applications not accepted. Giving on a national basis. No grants to individuals.

Publications: Newsletter.

Application information: Contributes only to pre-selected organizations.

Officers: Michael Steinhardt, Pres.; Michael Bohnen, Clerk; Charles Schusterman, Treas.; Rabbi Joshua Elkin, Exec. Dir.

Directors: Charles R. Bronfman; Edgar M. Bronfman; Billie Gold; Harold Grinspoon; Erica Jesselson; Michael Jesselson; Morton Mandel; Henry Taub; Leslie H. Wexner.

EIN: 043365815

Selected grants: The following grants were reported in 2003.

$60,000 to Contra Costa Jewish Day School, Lafayette, CA.

$60,000 to Torah Academy of Suffolk County, Commack, NY.

$50,000 to Ben Porat Yosef, Leonia, NJ.

$50,000 to Chicago Jewish Day School, Chicago, IL.

$40,000 to Jewish Community Day School, Newton, MA.

$40,000 to San Diego Jewish Academy, San Diego, CA.

$40,000 to Solomon Schechter Day School, NJ.

$20,000 to Brandeis School, Lawrence, NY.

$20,000 to Torah Academy of Minneapolis, Saint Louis Park, MN.

$15,000 to Hebrew Academy of Long Beach, Long Beach, NY.

4072

Amelia Peabody Charitable Fund ▼

10 Post Office Sq. N., Ste. 995
Boston, MA 02109-4603 (617) 451-6178
Contact: Cheryl A. Gideon, Admin.

Established in 1974.

Donors: Amelia Peabody†; Eaton Foundation.

Foundation type: Independent foundation.

Financial data (yr. ended 12/31/04): Assets, $165,585,886 (M); gifts received, $76,000; expenditures, $8,935,531; qualifying distributions, $8,181,584; giving activities include $7,890,095 for 165 grants (high: $500,000; low: $2,500; average: $10,000–$150,000).

Purpose and activities: Grants primarily for hospitals, medical research, health and family services, and the environment.

Fields of interest: Museums; Arts; Environment; Hospitals (general); Health care, support services; Youth, services; Family services.

Type of support: Capital campaigns; Building/renovation; Equipment; Land acquisition; Research; Matching/challenge support.

Limitations: Giving primarily in New England with emphasis on MA. No support for tax-supported municipal or government organizations or religious groups. No grants to individuals, or for salaries, start-up funds or operating expenses.

Publications: Application guidelines; Grants list.

Application information: Accepts AGM Format for Proposals. Application form not required.

 Initial approach: Letter with proposal
 Copies of proposal: 3
 Deadline(s): Feb. 1, June 1, and Oct. 1 by 2:00 pm; if deadline falls on Sat. or Sun., the proposal is due the following Mon.
 Board meeting date(s): More than 15 times annually
 Final notification: Generally, 8 to 12 weeks from deadline

Trustees: Jo Anne Borek; Caleb Loring III; William A. Lowell; J. Elisabeth Rice.

Number of staff: 1 full-time support.

EIN: 237364949

Selected grants: The following grants were reported in 2004.

$500,000 to Massachusetts Eye and Ear Infirmary, Boston, MA. For research.

$250,000 to Institute of Contemporary Art, Boston, MA. For construction.

$250,000 to Nature Conservancy, Maine Chapter, Brunswick, ME. For land purchase.

$150,000 to Tufts University, Medford, MA. For construction.

$100,000 to Germaine Lawrence Incorporated, Arlington, MA. For construction.

$100,000 to Home for Little Wanderers, Boston, MA. For construction.

$50,000 to Androscoggin Home Health Services, Lewiston, ME. For construction.

$40,000 to Central Massachusetts Symphony Orchestra, Worcester, MA. For purchase of piano.

$30,000 to Woods Hole Research Center, Woods Hole, MA. For instruments.

$25,000 to Family Service Association of Greater Boston, Jamaica Plain, MA. For equipment.

4073

Amelia Peabody Foundation ▼

1 Hollis St.
Wellesley, MA 02482
Contact: Margaret N. St. Clair, Co-Managing Tr.; Bayard D. Waring, Co-Managing Tr.
URL: http://www.ameliapeabody.org

Trust established in 1942 in MA; absorbed a share of the assets of The Eaton Foundation, MA, in 1985.

Donor: Amelia Peabody†.

Foundation type: Independent foundation.
Financial data (yr. ended 12/31/04): Assets, $172,898,185 (M); expenditures, $9,477,657; qualifying distributions, $8,082,584; giving activities include $7,187,000 for 118 grants (high: $250,000; low: $15,000; average: $25,000–$100,000).
Purpose and activities: The primary mission of the foundation is to increase the number, range and depth of positive learning expeirences available to materially disadvantaged young people living in the cities and towns of Massachusetts.
Fields of interest: Child development, education; Education; Children/youth, services; Youth, services; Child development, services.
Type of support: General/operating support; Capital campaigns; Building/renovation; Equipment; Program development; Seed money; Matching/challenge support.
Limitations: Giving limited to MA. No support for lobbying organizations. No grants to individuals, or for endowment funds, performances, conferences, research, filmmaking or videos, publications, or fellowships; no loans or program-related investments.
Publications: Application guidelines.
Application information: Application form is not required but is preferred. One original proposal with attachments and 6 additional copies of narrative and program budget only. Some portions of application can be emailed. Check website for details. Application form not required.
  Initial approach: See Web site for full application form
  Copies of proposal: 7
  Deadline(s): Varies, see foundation website for details
  Board meeting date(s): Quarterly
  Final notification: 8 weeks after deadline
Officers and Trustees:* Margaret N. St. Clair,* Co-Managing Tr.; Bayard D. Waring,* Co-Managing Tr.; Philip B. Waring,* V.P., Grantmaking; Thomas B. St. Clair,* Prog. Dir., Grantmaking; Deborah Carlson.
Number of staff: 6 full-time professional; 1 full-time support.
EIN: 046036558
Selected grants: The following grants were reported in 2004.
$400,000 to MATCH School Foundation, Boston, MA. For Media and Technology Charter High (MATCH) Corps program.
$250,000 to Boys and Girls Club of Worcester, Worcester, MA. For Heart of the Neighborhood Soul of the City capital campaign.
$213,000 to Adelante Youth Center, Lawrence, MA. For School Success operating support, and high school scholarships.
$200,000 to MetroLacrosse, Boston, MA. For operating support.
$110,000 to Boys and Girls Club of Greater Holyoke, Holyoke, MA. For satellite units in Holyoke Housing Authority Communities.
$100,000 to Boston Chinatown Neighborhood Center, Boston, MA. For capital campaign.
$90,000 to Horizons for Youth, Sharon, MA. For operating support.
$50,000 to Action, Inc., Gloucester, MA. For Compass Center renovations.
$50,000 to Dorchester Youth Collaborative, Dorchester, MA. For general operating support.
$40,000 to Community Day Care of Lawrence, Lawrence, MA. For Data Analysis Model for Community Day Charter School.

4074
The Peabody Foundation, Inc. ✧
c/o Choate, Hall & Stewart
2 International Pl., 34th Fl.
Boston, MA 02110
Contact: William V. Tripp III, Pres.

Established in 1894 in MA.
Donors: Kay Manson†; Emma Flecter Trust; L.S. Fiske Trust.
Foundation type: Independent foundation.
Financial data (yr. ended 9/30/05): Assets, $21,293,591 (M); gifts received, $10,369; expenditures, $998,476; qualifying distributions, $1,030,882; giving activities include $897,855 for 21 grants (high: $225,000; low: $250).
Purpose and activities: Grants limited to providing care, treatment, rehabilitation, education, and assistance to children with physical disabilities, and to encourage and support medical research in the causes of crippling disease, particularly in children.
Fields of interest: Medical research, institute; Children/youth, services; Disabilities, people with.
Type of support: Research.
Limitations: Giving limited to MA, with emphasis on the Boston area. No grants to individuals.
Application information: Application form not required.
  Copies of proposal: 1
  Deadline(s): None
Officers and Trustees:* William V. Tripp III,* Pres.; Norman C. Nicholson,* V.P.; John E.A. Safford,* Treas.; Harry C. Barr; Sally Cave; Mrs. John L. Damon; Joseph C. Donnelly, Jr.; Kenneth L. Harvey; Sally D. Hurlbut; Andrew G. Jessiman; Mrs. Stephen D. Paine; Christopher D. Perry; David Simmons, M.D.; Sylvia L. Stephens; Mrs. W. Nicholas Thorndike; Mary Liz Van Dyck.
EIN: 042104767
Selected grants: The following grants were reported in 2003.
$235,000 to Childrens Hospital Corporation, Boston, MA.
$100,000 to Joslin Diabetes Center, Boston, MA.
$75,000 to Boston Medical Center, Boston, MA.
$40,339 to Massachusetts General Hospital, Boston, MA.
$30,000 to Outdoor Explorations, Medford, MA.
$28,500 to New England Medical Center, Boston, MA.
$25,000 to Brigham and Womens Hospital, Boston, MA.
$23,700 to Cotting School, Lexington, MA.
$23,000 to Agassiz Village, Lexington, MA.
$15,000 to Huntington Theater Company, Boston, MA.

4075
Mary Elizabeth Pearce Foundation Trust ✧
c/o McClintock
P.O. Box 639
North Andover, MA 01845-0639

Established in 1976.
Foundation type: Independent foundation.
Financial data (yr. ended 3/31/06): Assets, $14,042,728 (M); expenditures, $584,938; qualifying distributions, $521,600; giving activities include $512,000 for 20 grants (high: $150,000; low: $5,000).
Purpose and activities: Giving primarily for health care, medical schools, and medical research.

Fields of interest: Medical school/education; Hospitals (general); Medical research, institute; Biomedicine research; Human services.
Limitations: Applications not accepted. Giving primarily in New England. No grants to individuals.
Application information: Contributes only to pre-selected organizations.
Trustee: John R.D. McClintock.
EIN: 046382377

4076
Peppercorn Foundation ✧
c/o Wilmer Cutler Pickering Hale and Dorr, LLP
P.O. Box 9350
Boston, MA 02209
Contact: Michael L. Fay

Established in 1999 in MA.
Donor: Alan Rabinowitz.
Foundation type: Independent foundation.
Financial data (yr. ended 12/31/05): Assets, $4,879,371 (M); expenditures, $479,974; qualifying distributions, $439,270; giving activities include $340,000 for 7 grants (high: $67,000; low: $40,000).
Purpose and activities: To support childhood educational initiatives.
Fields of interest: Education, early childhood education; Education; Environmental education; Children/youth, services.
Limitations: Applications not accepted. Giving on a national basis. No grants to individuals.
Application information: Contributes only to pre-selected organizations.
Trustees: Jennifer Ladd; Alan Rabinowitz; Andrea Rabinowitz.
EIN: 043487843
Selected grants: The following grants were reported in 2003.
$75,000 to Praxis Institute for Early Childhood Education, Seattle, WA.
$50,000 to Economic Opportunity Institute, Seattle, WA. For general support.
$50,000 to Federation of Child Care Centers of Alabama (FOCAL), Montgomery, AL. For general support.
$50,000 to Rethinking Schools, Milwaukee, WI. For general support.
$40,000 to National Coalition of Education Activists, Philadelphia, PA. For general support.
$30,000 to Pacific Oaks College, Pasadena, CA.
$30,000 to Stand for Children Leadership Center, DC. For general support.
$30,000 to Teaching for Change, DC.
$10,000 to Alliance for Early Childhood Equity, DC. For general support.

4077
PerkinElmer Foundation ✧
(formerly EG&G Foundation)
c/o PerkinElmer, Inc.
45 William St.
Wellesley, MA 02481-4078 (781) 237-5100
Contact: Patricia Cucinotta, Admin.

Established in 1979 in MA.
Donors: EG&G, Inc.; PerkinElmer, Inc.
Foundation type: Company-sponsored foundation.
Financial data (yr. ended 6/30/05): Assets, $8,425,455 (M); expenditures, $497,925; qualifying distributions, $440,150; giving activities

include $440,150 for 46 grants (high: $83,333; low: $125).

Purpose and activities: The foundation supports organizations involved with arts and culture, education, health, human services, community development, and civic affairs.

Fields of interest: Arts; Education; Health care; Human services; Community development; Public affairs.

Type of support: General/operating support.

Limitations: Giving on a national basis. No grants to individuals.

Application information: Application form not required.

> *Initial approach:* Letter of inquiry
> *Deadline(s):* None

Officer and Trustees: Patricia Cucinotta, Admin.; Robert F. Friel; Gregory L. Summe; Richard F. Walsh.

EIN: 042683042

Selected grants: The following grants were reported in 2005.

$135,113 to March of Dimes Birth Defects Foundation, White Plains, NY. 4 grants: $25,000, $83,333, $3,780, $23,000

$100,000 to American Red Cross. 2 grants: $25,000, $75,000

$50,000 to Noble and Greenough School, Dedham, MA.

$11,500 to Walnut Hill School, Natick, MA. 2 grants: $4,000, $7,500

$10,000 to American Heart Association, Dallas, TX.

4078
Perpetual Trust for Charitable Giving ◇

c/o Bank of America, N.A., Fdn. and Philanthropic Svcs.
100 Federal St., MA5-100-20-06
Boston, MA 02110 (617) 434-4846
Contact: Kerry Herlihy Sullivan, Dir., Bank of America, N.A., Fdn. and Philanthropic Svcs.
E-mail: kerry.h.sullivan@bankofamerica.com

Established in 1957 in MA.

Foundation type: Independent foundation.

Financial data (yr. ended 12/31/03): Assets, $20,812,671 (M); expenditures, $1,043,004; qualifying distributions, $974,928; giving activities include $835,733 for 75 grants (high: $50,000; low: $333).

Purpose and activities: Giving primarily to organizations that support education, health care, and family services.

Fields of interest: Arts; Education; Health care; Multiple sclerosis research; Human services; Children/youth, services; Family services; Christian agencies & churches; Women; Girls; Homeless.

Type of support: General/operating support; Program development.

Limitations: Giving limited to MA. No grants to individuals.

Publications: Application guidelines.

Application information: AGM Common Proposal accepted. Applicants should complete a Grant Application Coversheet. Only 1 proposal per organization may be submitted per 12-month period. No hand deliveries of proposals, or video tapes will be accepted. Application form required.

> *Initial approach:* Proposal with cover sheet
> *Copies of proposal:* 1
> *Deadline(s):* Sept. 8
> *Board meeting date(s):* Nov.
> *Final notification:* Nov.

Trustee: Bank of America, N.A.

EIN: 046026301

Selected grants: The following grants were reported in 2004.

$88,538 to Boston Medical Center, Boston, MA. 4 grants: $18,856, $18,353, $16,329, $35,000

$45,000 to Massachusetts General Hospital, Boston, MA.

$35,000 to Education Resources Institute, Boston, MA. For CKP program.

$30,000 to Morton Hospital and Medical Center, Taunton, MA. For operating support.

$30,000 to Pine Street Inn, Boston, MA. For program support.

$29,000 to Cape Cod Healthcare Foundation, Hyannis, MA. For general operating support.

$20,000 to Jumpstart for Young Children, Boston, MA. For general operating support.

4079
The Edward Lee and Slocumb Hollis Perry Foundation ◇

120 Water St., 5th Fl.
Boston, MA 02109
Contact: Walter S. Burrage, Jr., Secy.

Established in 1998 in MA.

Donors: Edward Lee Perry; Helen Wade Green Charitable Trust.

Foundation type: Independent foundation.

Financial data (yr. ended 12/31/05): Assets, $48,929 (M); gifts received, $535,000; expenditures, $497,632; qualifying distributions, $496,000; giving activities include $496,000 for 15 grants (high: $190,000; low: $2,500).

Purpose and activities: Giving for the arts, medical and educational purposes.

Fields of interest: Museums; Museums (art); Performing arts, theater; Performing arts, orchestra (symphony); Performing arts, opera; Arts; Education; Health care.

Limitations: Giving primarily in the greater Boston, MA, area. No grants to individuals.

Application information:

> *Initial approach:* Letter
> *Deadline(s):* None

Officers and Trustees:* Edward Lee Perry,* Pres.; Walter S. Burrage, Jr.,* Secy.; Slocumb Hollis Perry,* Treas.

EIN: 311621824

4080
Joseph Persky Foundation ◇

c/o Singer & Lusardi
370 Main St., Ste. 925
Worcester, MA 01608

Incorporated in 1944 in MA.

Donors: David A. Persky; Hardwick Knitted Fabrics, Inc.

Foundation type: Independent foundation.

Financial data (yr. ended 12/31/05): Assets, $7,851,904 (L); expenditures, $433,117; qualifying distributions, $375,085; giving activities include $375,000 for 41 grants (high: $60,000; low: $500).

Purpose and activities: Grants largely for Jewish welfare funds; support also for higher education, hospitals and health agencies.

Fields of interest: Education; Hospitals (general); Human services; Federated giving programs; Jewish

---

federated giving programs; Jewish agencies & temples.

Limitations: Applications not accepted. Giving primarily in MA; some giving in Sarasota, FL. No grants to individuals.

Application information: Contributes only to pre-selected organizations.

Officers: David A. Persky, Pres. and Treas.; Marlene Persky, Secy.

Directors: Marguerite Persky; Warren E. Persky; Suzanne G. Persky Tompkins.

EIN: 046057747

Selected grants: The following grants were reported in 2004.

$90,000 to Jewish Federation of Central Massachusetts, Worcester, MA.

$50,000 to Jewish Community Center, Worcester, MA.

$17,000 to United Way of Central Massachusetts, Worcester, MA.

$16,000 to Institute of Contemporary Art, Boston, MA.

$13,000 to University of Massachusetts Memorial Medical Center Foundation, Worcester, MA.

$10,000 to Clark University, Worcester, MA.

$10,000 to Jewish Federation, Sarasota-Manatee, Sarasota, FL.

$8,000 to Worcester Art Museum, Worcester, MA.

$5,000 to Bancroft School, Worcester, MA.

$5,000 to Worcester Foundation for Biomedical Research, Worcester, MA.

4081
Frank R. Peters Trust ◇

P.O. Box 55886
Boston, MA 02205-5886
Contact: Kerry Herlihy Sullivan, Dir., Foundation & Philanthropic Svcs.
E-mail: kerrry.h.sullivan@bankofamerica.com;
Application address: c/o Bank of America, N.A., Foundation & Philanthropic Svcs., 100 Federal St., MA5-100-20-06, Boston, MA 02110, tel.: (617) 434-4846

Established in 1935 in MA.

Foundation type: Independent foundation.

Financial data (yr. ended 12/31/05): Assets, $9,014,503 (M); expenditures, $475,808; qualifying distributions, $448,278; giving activities include $420,000 for 27 grants (high: $100,000; low: $3,500).

Purpose and activities: Giving primarily for human services, focusing on the needs of children and families, adolescents, and the elderly; community development, health and education.

Fields of interest: Education; Health care; Human services; YM/YWCAs & YM/YWHAs; Children/youth, services; Family services; Community development; Federated giving programs.

Limitations: Giving limited to the greater Boston, MA, area. No grants to individuals, for independent research projects, or for publications or national organizations.

Application information: Associated Grantmakers Common Proposal Format accepted, and can be downloaded at http://www.agmconnect.org. Application form not required.

> *Initial approach:* Brief proposal
> *Deadline(s):* Jan. 15, May 15, and Sept. 15
> *Board meeting date(s):* Mar., July, and Nov.
> *Final notification:* 1st week of the month following meetings

---

Trustee: Bank of America, N.A.
EIN: 046012009
Selected grants: The following grants were reported in 2004.
$30,000 to Big Sister Association of Greater Boston, Boston, MA. For general support.
$30,000 to Boys and Girls Club of Allston-Brighton, West End House, Allston, MA. For Project Learn.
$30,000 to Bridge Over Troubled Waters, Boston, MA. For program support.
$25,000 to Treehouse Foundation, Sharon, MA. For general operating support.
$20,000 to Multicultural Youth Tour of What's Now (MYTOWN), Boston, MA. For general operating support.
$15,000 to Center for Teen Empowerment, Boston, MA.
$15,000 to Youthnet of Worcester, Worcester, MA.
$10,000 to Crossroads Community Foundation, Natick, MA.
$9,000 to Cotting School, Lexington, MA. For general operating support.
$5,000 to Elizabeth Peabody House Association, Somerville, MA. For Day Camp.

4082
Edwin Phillips Foundation ◇

P.O. 610075
Newton Highlands, MA 02461

Donor: Edwin Phillips†.
Foundation type: Independent foundation.
Financial data (yr. ended 12/31/04): Assets, $11,986,214 (M); expenditures, $609,244; qualifying distributions, $573,458; giving activities include $162,421 for grants, and $302,607 for grants to individuals.
Purpose and activities: Giving strictly limited to help children with disabilities in Plymouth County, MA, only.
Fields of interest: Children/youth, services; Disabilities, people with.
Limitations: Giving limited to Plymouth County, MA.
Application information: Unsolicited requests for funds not accepted from anyone outside of Plymouth County, MA. Application form not required.
　Initial approach: Proposal
　Copies of proposal: 1
　Deadline(s): Oct. 1 and Apr. 1
　Board meeting date(s): As needed
Trustees: Robert E. Galvin; Wilma Rae Goodhue; Grace Hill; Philip Johnson; Bank of America, N.A.
EIN: 046025549

4083
Stephen Phillips Memorial Charitable Trust ◇

P.O. Box 870
Salem, MA 01970
Contact: Karen Emery, Scholarship Coord.
FAX: (978) 744-0456;
E-mail: info@phillips-scholarship.org; URL: http://www.phillips-scholarship.org/
Additional E-mail: kemery@spscholars.org

Established in 1973.
Donor: Bessie Wright Phillips†.
Foundation type: Independent foundation.
Financial data (yr. ended 12/31/05): Assets, $70,868,304 (M); gifts received, $4,595; expenditures, $3,663,306; qualifying distributions,

$3,258,182; giving activities include $2,777,204 for grants to individuals.
Purpose and activities: Awards scholarships to individuals for undergraduate education.
Type of support: Scholarships—to individuals.
Limitations: Giving to New England and Mid-Atlantic states. Open to all U.S. citizens and resident aliens.
Publications: Application guidelines; Informational brochure (including application guidelines).
Application information: The application and application guidelines are available on foundation Web site. Letters are mailed to award recipients in mid-June, and the list of award winners is posted on the foundation Web site by June 24. Application form required.
　Initial approach: Letter
　Deadline(s): Apr. 30 for new applicants and Apr. 1 for renewals
　Final notification: Mid-June
Trustees: Lawrence Coolidge; Arthur H. Emery; John H. Finley IV; Richard Gross; Robert M. Randolph.
Number of staff: 2 full-time professional; 1 part-time professional.
EIN: 237235347

4084
The Harold Whitworth Pierce Charitable Trust ◇

c/o Nichols and Pratt
50 Congress St., Ste. 832
Boston, MA 02109-4017 (617) 523-8368
Contact: Elizabeth D. Nichols, Prog. Dir.
FAX: (617) 523-8949;
E-mail: piercetrust@nichols-pratt.com

Trust established in 1960 in MA.
Donor: Harold Whitworth Pierce†.
Foundation type: Independent foundation.
Financial data (yr. ended 12/31/04): Assets, $24,807,331 (M); expenditures, $1,249,030; qualifying distributions, $1,141,758; giving activities include $1,116,255 for 42 grants (high: $100,000; low: $1,000).
Purpose and activities: The Harold Whitworth Pierce Charitable Trust offers grants primarily for projects that will produce long-range benefits through leverage of the trust's resources. Grants are made for specific programs, for seed money, and for capital projects, especially those which can reduce operating costs. Occasional grants are made for operating support. Grants are focused on institutions and programs in the Boston, MA, area.
Fields of interest: Teacher school/education; Education; Environment; Community development.
Type of support: General/operating support; Capital campaigns; Building/renovation; Endowments; Seed money; Scholarship funds; Research.
Limitations: Giving primarily in the Boston, MA, area. No grants to individuals, or for scholarships for individuals, fund-raising events, fund-raising training, films, videos, travel, or advocacy.
Publications: Grants list; Informational brochure (including application guidelines).
Application information: Concept letter and cover sheet. No more than 2 pages accepted. Proposals invited from among concept letters. Grants are occasionally made for medical research and arts education; unsolicited proposals are not accepted for these areas. Application form not required.
　Initial approach: Letter or telephone
　Copies of proposal: 1

　Deadline(s): Mar. 1 and Sept. 15 for concept letters; Mid-Apr. and mid-Oct. for invited proposals
　Board meeting date(s): Mar., June, Sept., and Nov.
　Final notification: June 1 and Dec. 1
Trustees: James R. Nichols; Harold I. Pratt.
EIN: 046019896
Selected grants: The following grants were reported in 2005.
$66,000 to Boston Foundation, Boston, MA.
$50,000 to Boston Museum Project, Boston, MA.
$50,000 to New England Aquarium, Boston, MA.
$45,000 to Medical Foundation, Boston, MA.
$25,000 to Appalachian Mountain Club, Boston, MA.
$25,000 to Literacy Project, Greenfield, MA.
$25,000 to Wheelock College, Boston, MA.
$20,000 to Neighborhood House Charter School, Dorchester, MA.
$15,000 to Boston Schoolyard Initiative, Boston, MA.
$15,000 to Hubbard Brook Research Foundation, Hanover, NH.

4085
The Plymouth Rock Foundation ◇ ☆

695 Atlantic Ave.
Boston, MA 02111

Established in 1993 in MA.
Donors: Plymouth Rock Assurance Corporation; High Point Safety and Management Corp.
Foundation type: Independent foundation.
Financial data (yr. ended 12/31/05): Assets, $53,713 (M); gifts received, $292,000; expenditures, $327,147; qualifying distributions, $326,127; giving activities include $326,127 for grants.
Fields of interest: Higher education; Libraries/library science; Health organizations, association; Human services; Children/youth, services; Federated giving programs.
Limitations: Applications not accepted. Giving primarily in the greater Boston, MA, area. No grants to individuals.
Application information: Contributes only to pre-selected organizations.
Trustees: Lee Englert; Maureen Fidler; Paula Gold.
EIN: 046739902
Selected grants: The following grants were reported in 2005.
$10,050 to New England Shelter for Homeless Veterans, Boston, MA.
$10,000 to Artists for Humanity, Boston, MA.
$10,000 to Bottom Line, Jamaica Plain, MA.
$10,000 to United Way of Massachusetts Bay, Boston, MA.
$5,000 to Sportsmens Tennis Club, Dorchester, MA.
$3,800 to Boston Medical Center, Boston, MA.
$2,400 to American Liver Foundation, New York, NY.
$700 to Museum of Fine Arts, Boston, MA.
$600 to Rosies Place, Boston, MA.
$400 to Belmont Hill School, Belmont, MA.

4086
William J. & Lia G. Poorvu Foundation ◇

c/o William J. Poorvu, Tr.
P.O. Box 380828
Cambridge, MA 02238

Established in 1978.
Donor: William J. Poorvu.
Foundation type: Independent foundation.
Financial data (yr. ended 12/31/03): Assets, $18,113,290 (M); gifts received, $2,375,277; expenditures, $910,161; qualifying distributions, $683,250; giving activities include $680,750 for 40 grants (high: $125,000; low: $500).
Purpose and activities: Giving primarily for higher education; support also for cultural programs.
Fields of interest: Arts; Higher education.
Limitations: Applications not accepted. Giving primarily in MA. No grants to individuals.
Application information: Contributes only to pre-selected organizations. Unsolicited requests for funds not considered.
Trustees: Lia G. Poorvu; William J. Poorvu.
EIN: 042651199

4087
The Poss Family Foundation ✧
(formerly The Poss Kapor Familly Foundation)
c/o Eileen M. Poss
450 Warren St.
Brookline, MA   02445   (617) 531-6907

Established in 1998 in MA.
Donor: Ellen M. Poss.
Foundation type: Independent foundation.
Financial data (yr. ended 12/31/05): Assets, $15,419,376 (M); gifts received, $788,694; expenditures, $1,476,737; qualifying distributions, $1,328,000; giving activities include $1,328,000 for 13 grants (high: $550,000; low: $10,000).
Fields of interest: Performing arts, dance; Education; Human services; Civil rights, race/intergroup relations.
Type of support: General/operating support; Continuing support; Annual campaigns; Capital campaigns; Professorships; Curriculum development; Matching/challenge support.
Limitations: Applications not accepted. Giving primarily in MA. No grants to individuals.
Application information: Contributes only to pre-selected organizations. Unsolicited requests for funds will not be acknowledged or returned.
Trustee: Ellen M. Poss.
EIN: 043412829

4088
The Putnam Investments Foundation ✧
1 Post Office Sq., Ste. A-16-B
Boston, MA   02109
Contact: C. Nancy Fisher, Tr.

Established in 1992 in MA.
Donor: Putnam Investments, Inc.
Foundation type: Company-sponsored foundation.
Financial data (yr. ended 12/31/04): Assets, $1,920,515 (M); gifts received, $500,500; expenditures, $1,126,681; qualifying distributions, $1,126,681; giving activities include $1,126,431 for 191 grants (high: $195,000; low: $50).
Purpose and activities: The foundation supports organizations involved with arts and culture, animal welfare, health, human services, and community development.
Fields of interest: Museums; Arts; Animal welfare; Health care; Children/youth, services; Human services; Community development; Federated giving programs.

Type of support: General/operating support.
Limitations: Applications not accepted. Giving primarily in the greater metropolitan Boston, MA, area. No grants to individuals.
Application information: Contributes only to pre-selected organizations.
Trustees: C. Nancy Fisher; Richard S. Robie III.
EIN: 043175266
Selected grants: The following grants were reported in 2005.
$150,000 to Boston Medical Center, Boston, MA.
$125,000 to United Way of Massachusetts Bay, Boston, MA.
$80,000 to Wayside Youth and Family Support Network, Framingham, MA.
$75,000 to Year Up, Boston, MA.
$65,000 to American Red Cross. 2 grants: $50,000, $15,000
$60,000 to Habitat for Humanity International.
$50,000 to National Foundation for Teaching Entrepreneurship, New York, NY.
$25,000 to Boston Public Library Foundation, Boston, MA.
$7,800 to Associated Grant Makers, Boston, MA.

4089
William Lowell Putnam Prize Fund for the Promotion of Scholarship ✧
c/o Ropes & Gray
1 International Pl.
Boston, MA   02110-2624

Foundation type: Independent foundation.
Financial data (yr. ended 12/31/04): Assets, $9,888,800 (M); expenditures, $749,888; qualifying distributions, $675,747; giving activities include $545,000 for 6 grants (high: $470,000; low: $5,000), $36,000 for 33 grants to individuals (high: $3,500; low: $200), and $99,409 for 1 foundation-administered program.
Purpose and activities: Giving primarily for higher education. The Putnam Prize Fund provides funds for mathematics competition and awards prizes to individuals and their schools.
Fields of interest: Higher education.
Type of support: Grants to individuals.
Limitations: Applications not accepted. Giving primarily in MA.
Application information: Unsolicited requests for funds not accepted.
Trustees: George Putnam; George Putnam III.
EIN: 043414102

4090
Sidney & Esther Rabb Charitable Foundation ✧
225 Franklin St., Ste. 2700
Boston, MA   02110-2804   (617) 695-1946
Contact: Carol R. Goldberg, Tr.

Established in 1952 in MA.
Donor: Sidney R. Rabb†.
Foundation type: Independent foundation.
Financial data (yr. ended 12/31/05): Assets, $8,579,580 (M); expenditures, $432,982; qualifying distributions, $379,813; giving activities include $346,460 for 34 grants (high: $116,500; low: $1,000).
Purpose and activities: Giving primarily for Jewish agencies, temples, federated giving programs, and for human services.

Fields of interest: Arts; Education; Hospitals (general); Human services; Jewish federated giving programs; Jewish agencies & temples.
Limitations: Giving primarily in Boston, MA.
Application information: Application form not required.
Initial approach: Letter
Deadline(s): None
Trustees: Avram J. Goldberg; Carol R. Goldberg; Deborah B. Goldberg; Joshua R. Goldberg.
EIN: 046039595
Selected grants: The following grants were reported in 2005.
$18,975 to Hebrew Seniorlife, Boston, MA.
$15,825 to W G B H Educational Foundation, Boston, MA.
$14,765 to Beth Israel Deaconess Medical Center, Boston, MA.
$12,660 to Hebrew College, Newton Centre, MA.
$12,000 to Park School, Brookline, MA.
$10,550 to Boston Jewish Community Womens Fund, Boston, MA.
$10,000 to Putney School, Putney, VT.
$7,900 to Museum of Fine Arts, Boston, MA.
$7,570 to Kenneth B. Schwartz Center, Boston, MA.
$7,150 to Hospice of Naples, Naples, FL.

4091
Sidney R. Rabb Charitable Trust ✧
(formerly Esther V. & Sidney R. Rabb Family Trust)
225 Franklin St., Ste. 2700
Boston, MA   02110-2804   (617) 695-1946
Contact: Carol R. Goldberg, Tr.

Established in 1952.
Donor: Esther V. Rabb.
Foundation type: Independent foundation.
Financial data (yr. ended 12/31/05): Assets, $18,544,958 (M); expenditures, $955,639; qualifying distributions, $846,456; giving activities include $765,973 for 30 grants (high: $290,000; low: $2,000).
Purpose and activities: Giving primarily for education, hospitals, and Jewish causes.
Fields of interest: Performing arts, orchestra (symphony); Education; Hospitals (general); Jewish federated giving programs; Jewish agencies & temples.
Type of support: Building/renovation.
Limitations: Giving primarily in MA. No grants to individuals.
Application information: Application form not required.
Initial approach: Proposal
Deadline(s): None
Board meeting date(s): Aug.
Trustees: Nancy L. Cahners; M. Gordon Ehrlich; Carol R. Goldberg; Arthur B. Page.
EIN: 222754563

4092
The Radley Family Foundation ✧
225 Country Club Rd.
Dedham, MA   02026   (781) 237-4455
Contact: James A. Radley, Tr.

Established in 1997 in MA.
Donors: Gail C. Radley; James A. Radley; Eastern Casualty Insurance Co.
Foundation type: Independent foundation.

Financial data (yr. ended 12/31/04): Assets, $2,133,261 (M); gifts received, $3,500,000; expenditures, $1,493,208; qualifying distributions, $1,491,350; giving activities include $1,491,350 for 9 grants (high: $500,000).

Purpose and activities: Giving primarily to a children's hospital; funding also for education and human services.

Fields of interest: Education; Environment, land resources; Hospitals (specialty); Health organizations, association; Human services.

Limitations: Applications not accepted. Giving primarily in MA. No grants to individuals.

Application information: Contributes only to pre-selected organizations.

Trustees: Gail C. Radley; James A. Radley.

EIN: 043371968

4093
Jerome Lyle Rappaport Charitable Foundation ✧

60 State St., Ste. 1650
Boston, MA 02109-1803   (617) 878-7773
Contact: Jerome Lyle Rappaport, Tr.
FAX: (617) 227-4727; E-mail: jlrcf@aol.com;
URL: http://www.rappaportcharitablefoundation.com

Established in 1996 in FL.
Donor: Jerome Lyle Rappaport.
Foundation type: Independent foundation.
Financial data (yr. ended 9/30/05): Assets, $9,335,137 (M); expenditures, $587,608; qualifying distributions, $521,172; giving activities include $392,600 for 13 grants (high: $250,000; low: $1,000).

Purpose and activities: Giving primarily for higher education including fellowships and scholarships, particularly in neuroscience, mental health and Alzheimer's disease, and for museums.

Fields of interest: Arts; Higher education; Education; Environment, natural resources; Hospitals (general); Reproductive health, family planning; Jewish federated giving programs; Jewish agencies & temples.

Type of support: Fellowships; Grants to individuals.

Limitations: Giving primarily in the greater Boston, MA, area.

Publications: Informational brochure.

Application information: Application form not required.

Deadline(s): None

Officer: Lesa Lessard Pearson, Exec. Dir.

Trustees: Jill Glist; James W. Rappaport; Jerome Lyle Rappaport; Phyllis E. Rappaport.

Number of staff: 1 full-time professional.

EIN: 311485041

Selected grants: The following grants were reported in 2004.

$51,000 to DeCordova Museum and Sculpture Park, Lincoln, MA.
$50,000 to Harvard University, Cambridge, MA.
$40,000 to Suffolk University, Boston, MA.
$21,312 to Temple Beit Hayam, Stuart, FL.
$13,600 to Dana-Farber Cancer Institute, Boston, MA.
$5,000 to Northeastern University, Boston, MA.
$2,500 to Nantucket Cottage Hospital, Nantucket, MA.
$2,500 to Smith College, Northampton, MA.
$2,000 to Larchmont Temple, Larchmont, NY.

$1,000 to Brigham and Womens Hospital, Boston, MA.

4094
V. Kann Rasmussen Foundation ▼

c/o Wilmer Cutler Pickering Hale and Dorr LLP
60 State St.
Boston, MA 02109   (617) 526-6610
Contact: Martin S. Kaplan, Tr.
FAX: (617) 526-5000;
E-mail: mkaplantrustee@vkrf.org; Additional address: c/o Wilmer Cutler Pickering Hale and Dorr, LLP, 399 Park Ave., New York, NY, 10022, tel.: (212) 937-7272, FAX: (212) 230-8888;
URL: http://www.vkrf.org/

Established in 1991 in MA.
Donor: The Velux Trust.
Foundation type: Independent foundation.
Financial data (yr. ended 6/30/05): Assets, $93,026,461 (M); expenditures, $9,365,951; qualifying distributions, $8,731,326; giving activities include $7,707,736 for 52 grants (high: $937,500; low: $4,700; average: $20,000–$500,000).

Purpose and activities: Giving primarily for the environment.

Fields of interest: Higher education; Environment, natural resources; Environment; Medical research, institute.

Type of support: Program development; General/operating support.

Publications: Informational brochure; Occasional report.

Application information: During 2006 and 2007 the foundation will allocate time and resources to evaluating both its grantmaking strategy and the programs of its many grantees. During this period, the foundation will only make grantmaking decisions in Apr. 2006 relating to those applicants who were invited to submit proposals from the Nov. 2005 letter of inquiry process. The foundation will not have an open letter of inquiry process or a grantmaking round in fall 2006, except for submissions specifically invited by the foundation. Please check the foundation Web site periodically during 2006 for information updates including dates of the next open letter of inquiry period.

Initial approach: Letter of inquiry
Copies of proposal: 1
Deadline(s): See foundation Web site for current deadlines
Board meeting date(s): Mar./Apr. and Oct./Nov.
Final notification: 30 days or see foundation Web site

Officer and Trustees: Hans Kann Rasmussen,* Chair.; Martin S. Kaplan; Anne-Margrete Ogstrup-Pedersen; Aino Kann Rasmussen; Astrid Kann Rasmussen; Lois E. H. Smith, Ph.D., M.D.; Julie Kann Wilson.

EIN: 223101266

Selected grants: The following grants were reported in 2005.

$937,500 to Wildlife Trust, New York, NY. For environmental program.
$900,000 to Columbia University, New York, NY. For Center for Environmental Research.
$750,000 to Grist Magazine, Seattle, WA. For environmental program.
$345,000 to Harvard University, Cambridge, MA. For Committee on Environment.

$300,000 to Massachusetts Institute of Technology, Cambridge, MA. For Environmental Alliance for Global Sustainment.
$300,000 to Self Regional Healthcare, Greenwood, SC. For general support.
$300,000 to Thomas Berry Foundation, Boston, MA. For Center for Ethics and Environment.
$262,116 to Childrens Hospital Corporation, Boston, MA. For eye research.
$100,000 to Public Education Center, DC. For educational program.
$100,000 to University of Miami, Miami, FL. For environmental research.

4095
A.C. Ratshesky Foundation ✧ ☆

c/o Grants Mgmt. Assocs.
77 Summer St., 8th Fl.
Boston, MA 02110-1006   (617) 426-7080, ext. 323
Contact: Susan Haff, Fdn. Asst.
FAX: (617) 426-7087;
E-mail: ratsheskyfoundation@grantsmanagement.com; URL: http://www.grantsmanagement.com/ratshesky.html

Incorporated in 1916 in MA.
Donors: A.C. Ratshesky†; and family.
Foundation type: Independent foundation.
Financial data (yr. ended 12/31/05): Assets, $7,005,879 (M); expenditures, $462,220; qualifying distributions, $351,500; giving activities include $351,500 for grants.

Purpose and activities: Giving for education, including adult and vocational education, and academic enrichment programs for youth. Funding also for the performing arts and other cultural programs, child care, family services, employment, minorities, women, and immigrants and refugees. Some support also for Jewish organizations.

Fields of interest: Arts education; Arts; Vocational education; Adult education—literacy, basic skills & GED; Education, services; Education; Employment, services; Children/youth, services; Family services; Economically disadvantaged.

Type of support: General/operating support; Continuing support; Program development; Seed money.

Limitations: Giving limited to the metro Boston, MA, area, within Rte. 128. No support for public schools, or for health programs, national organizations, municipal, state or federal agencies, or religious programs. No grants to individuals, or for annual campaigns, general endowments, deficit financing, land acquisition, Web sites, scientific or other research, publications, or conferences; no loans.

Publications: Application guidelines; Grants list.

Application information: Associated Grant Makers (AGM) Common Proposal Summary Sheet required. AGM Common Proposal Form accepted; and can be downloaded at www.agmconnect.org; do not submit proposals in folders, binders or report covers; E-mailed or faxed proposals not accepted. Application form required.

Initial approach: Proposal or telephone
Copies of proposal: 1
Deadline(s): Mar. 1, Sept. 1, and Dec. 1
Board meeting date(s): Mar., June, and Nov.
Final notification: Following board meetings

Officers and Trustees:* Eric Robert Morse,* Pres.; Laurie Morse Sprague, V.P.; Linda Ortwein,* Secy.; John Morse, Jr.,* Treas.; Roberta Morse Levy; Alan

R. Morse, Jr.; Timothy Morse; Rebecca Morse Steinfield.
Number of staff: 2 part-time professional.
EIN: 046017426

4096
Red Acre Farm, Inc.
P.O. Box 278
Stow, MA 01775
Contact: Carolyn Bird, Exec. Dir.
URL: http://www.redacrefoundation.org

Established in 1903 in MA.
Donors: Helen Hardenbrook†; Josephine Kibbey†.
Foundation type: Independent foundation.
Financial data (yr. ended 9/30/05): Assets, $8,245,370 (M); gifts received, $19,196; expenditures, $499,640; qualifying distributions, $402,334; giving activities include $375,000 for 39 grants (high: $21,500; low: $3,500).
Purpose and activities: Giving primarily to a conservation trust for animal welfare, wildlife protection, and human and animal bond efforts.
Fields of interest: Environment, natural resources; Animal welfare; Animals/wildlife, preservation/protection.
Limitations: Giving limited to southern New England, southern AZ, and some areas in southwestern CO. No grants to individuals.
Application information: See foundation Web site for application guidelines and procedures. Application form required.
  Initial approach: Request for proposal form
  Copies of proposal: 1
  Deadline(s): Varies
  Board meeting date(s): Summer and winter
Officers and Directors:* David Ayer,* Pres.; Nathanael Shepherd,* V.P.; Walter M. Bird III,* Secy.; Walter M. Bird, Jr.,* Treas.; Carolyn G. Bird, Exec. Dir.; Helen B. Guidotti; Leonard W. Johnson; David M. Pinkham.
EIN: 042119492

4097
The Michael Redstone Charitable Trust ◇ ☆
200 Elm St.
P.O. Box 9126
Dedham, MA 02027-9126   (781) 461-1600
Contact: Sumner M. Redstone, Tr.

Established around 1970.
Foundation type: Independent foundation.
Financial data (yr. ended 12/31/05): Assets, $295,280 (M); expenditures, $505,253; qualifying distributions, $500,000; giving activities include $500,000 for 6 grants (high: $200,000; low: $10,000).
Purpose and activities: Giving primarily for health care, including medical research, and Jewish federated giving programs.
Fields of interest: Education; Hospitals (general); Medical research, institute; Cancer research; Jewish federated giving programs.
Limitations: Giving primarily in MA.
Application information: Application form not required.
  Deadline(s): None
Trustees: Edward Redstone; Sumner M. Redstone.
EIN: 046040806

4098
The Reebok Human Rights Foundation
(formerly The Reebok Foundation)
c/o Reebok International Ltd.
1895 J.W. Foster Blvd.
Canton, MA 02021   (781) 401-7707
Contact: Geri Noonan, Assoc. Exec. Dir.
FAX: (781) 401-7550;
E-mail: rhrfoundation@reebok.com; Address for Human Rights Award: Dir., Reebok Human Rights Award Prog., Reebok International Ltd., 1895 J.W. Foster Blvd., Canton, MA 02021, tel.: (781) 401-4377; Additional tel.: (781) 401-5000; URL: http://www.reebok.com/Static/global/initiatives/rights/foundation/index.html

Established in 1986 in MA.
Donor: Reebok International Ltd.
Foundation type: Company-sponsored foundation.
Financial data (yr. ended 12/31/05): Assets, $31,951 (M); gifts received, $2,079,156; expenditures, $2,157,546; qualifying distributions, $2,153,473; giving activities include $1,796,438 for 150 grants (average: $5,000–$25,000), and $293,497 for 2,067 employee matching gifts.
Purpose and activities: The foundation supports organizations involved with inner-city youth, human rights, and minorities.
Fields of interest: Youth, services; International human rights; Civil rights, public education; Civil rights; Youth; Minorities.
Type of support: General/operating support; Program development; Seed money; Technical assistance; Employee matching gifts.
Limitations: Giving on a national and international basis, with emphasis on countries of company operations; giving primarily in areas of company operations, with emphasis on greater Boston, MA, for Communities First Grants; giving also to national and international organizations. No grants to individuals, or for seminars or conferences, documentaries or media projects, publications, medical research or other research, or political projects; no product donations; no loans.
Publications: Application guidelines; Annual report.
Application information: Unsolicited requests from national organizations are not accepted. Application form not required.
  Initial approach: Letter of inquiry for grants
  Copies of proposal: 1
  Deadline(s): None
  Board meeting date(s): Biannually
Officer and Trustees: Paul Foster, Exec. Dir.; Paul Harrington; Sharon Bryan.
Number of staff: 2 full-time professional; 1 full-time support; 1 part-time support.
EIN: 043073548
Selected grants: The following grants were reported in 2005.
$50,000 to Building Educated Leaders for Life (BELL) Foundation, Dorchester, MA. For program support.
$50,000 to Carter Center, Atlanta, GA. For program support.
$40,000 to Georgetown University, Center for Social Justice Research, Teaching and Service, DC. For program support.
$40,000 to Global Rights, DC. For Initiative Against Trafficking in Persons project.
$22,000 to Womens Commission for Refugee Women and Children, New York, NY. For program support.
$20,000 to Amnesty International USA, Somerville, MA. For general support.

$20,000 to Global Fund for Women, San Francisco, CA. For program support.
$15,000 to Shelburne Community Council, Roxbury, MA. For Reebok Educational Athletic Partnership.
$10,000 to Robert F. Kennedy Memorial, DC. For Speak Truth to Power.
$10,000 to Summerbridge Cambridge, a Breakthrough Program, Cambridge, MA. For program support.

4099
The Reeder Foundation ◇
c/o Bingham McCutchen, LLP
150 Federal St.
Boston, MA 02110

Established in 2000 in MA.
Donor: Paul A. Reeder.
Foundation type: Independent foundation.
Financial data (yr. ended 12/31/05): Assets, $6,370,794 (M); gifts received, $1,003,643; expenditures, $590,785; qualifying distributions, $440,250; giving activities include $440,000 for 7 grants (high: $300,000; low: $5,000).
Purpose and activities: Giving primarily for higher education, particularly to an institute of technology.
Fields of interest: Higher education.
Limitations: Applications not accepted. Giving primarily in MA; some giving also in OH. No grants to individuals.
Application information: Contributes only to pre-selected organizations.
Director: Paul A. Reeder III.
EIN: 043542100

4100
Remillard Family Foundation, Inc. ◇
211 Main St.
Webster, MA 01570   (508) 949-4122
Contact: Arthur Remillard, Jr., Pres.

Established in 1997 in MA.
Donor: Arthur J. Remillard, Jr.
Foundation type: Independent foundation.
Financial data (yr. ended 12/31/04): Assets, $11,005,904 (M); gifts received, $1,196,600; expenditures, $577,365; qualifying distributions, $557,225; giving activities include $556,667 for 5 grants (high: $250,000; low: $16,667).
Fields of interest: Boys & girls clubs; Human services; American Red Cross; Salvation Army.
Limitations: Giving on a national basis. No grants to individuals.
Application information:
  Initial approach: Letter
  Deadline(s): None
Officer and Directors:* Arthur J. Remillard, Jr.,* Pres., Clerk and Treas.; Renee A. Granger; Danielle A. Haxton; Arthur J. Remillard III; Regan P. Remillard; Robert P. Remillard.
EIN: 043367614
Selected grants: The following grants were reported in 2004.
$250,000 to Boys and Girls Club.
$170,000 to American Red Cross.
$20,000 to Salvation Army.

4101
Marjorie Harris Reynolds Foundation ◇ ☆
c/o Atlantic Trust Co., N.A.
100 Federal St., 37th Fl.
Boston, MA   02110

Established in 1996 in MA.
Donor: Eric Oddleifson.
Foundation type: Independent foundation.
Financial data (yr. ended 12/31/05): Assets, $2,020,103 (M); expenditures, $359,417; qualifying distributions, $339,500; giving activities include $339,500 for grants.
Purpose and activities: Giving primarily for education.
Fields of interest: Libraries/library science; Education; Human services.
Limitations: Applications not accepted. Giving primarily in MA. No grants to individuals.
Application information: Contributes only to pre-selected organizations.
Trustees: Eric Oddleifson; Janna Oddleifson.
EIN: 046820699

4102
The Charles K. and Patricia F. Ribakoff Charitable Trust ◇
(formerly The Charles K. Ribakoff II Charitable Trust)
274 Beacon St., Ste. 9R
Boston, MA   02116

Established in 1986 in MA.
Donors: Charles K. Ribakoff II; The American Jewish Joint Distribution Committee, Inc.; Allard Ventures Group, LLC.
Foundation type: Independent foundation.
Financial data (yr. ended 9/30/05): Assets, $13,040 (M); gifts received, $523,000; expenditures, $414,167; qualifying distributions, $412,167; giving activities include $412,167 for 29 grants (high: $213,150; low: $500).
Purpose and activities: Giving primarily to Jewish organizations, as well as for education, health care and social services.
Fields of interest: Education, early childhood education; Higher education; Education; Hospitals (general); Health organizations, association; Human services; Jewish federated giving programs; Jewish agencies & temples.
Type of support: General/operating support.
Limitations: Applications not accepted. Giving primarily in MA. No grants to individuals.
Application information: Contributes only to pre-selected organizations.
Trustees: Charles K. Ribakoff II; Eugene J. Ribakoff; Patricia F. Ribakoff.
EIN: 046553859
Selected grants: The following grants were reported in 2005.
$25,000 to Smith College, Northampton, MA.
$20,000 to Boston Medical Center, Boston, MA.
$10,875 to United Way of Central Massachusetts, Worcester, MA.
$10,000 to Crohns and Colitis Foundation of America, Needham, MA.
$7,202 to Temple Israel, Boston, MA.
$5,000 to Chestnut Hill School, Chestnut Hill, MA.
$5,000 to Hill House, Boston, MA.
$5,000 to Museum of Fine Arts, Boston, MA.
$2,500 to Mount Ida College, Newton Centre, MA.
$1,000 to Temple Shir Tikva, Wayland, MA.

4103
Ribakoff Family Foundation ◇ ☆
(formerly Eugene J. and Corinne A. Ribakoff Charitable Foundation)
c/o GRKB
306 Main St., Ste. 400
Worcester, MA   01615-0034

Trust established in 1960 in MA.
Donors: Eugene J. Ribakoff; Auto Rental Corp.; Trucklease Corp.
Foundation type: Independent foundation.
Financial data (yr. ended 5/31/05): Assets, $2,456,347 (M); gifts received, $15,625; expenditures, $1,192,034; qualifying distributions, $1,174,780; giving activities include $1,174,780 for 46 grants (high: $465,000; low: $100).
Purpose and activities: Giving primarily to Jewish temples and federated giving programs.
Fields of interest: Jewish agencies & temples.
Limitations: Applications not accepted. Giving primarily in FL and MA. No grants to individuals.
Application information: Contributes only to pre-selected organizations.
Trustees: Charles K. Ribakoff; Eugene J. Ribakoff; Betsey R. Sheerr.
EIN: 046055498
Selected grants: The following grants were reported in 2005.
$465,000 to Jewish Federation of Palm Beach County, West Palm Beach, FL.
$225,000 to Brandeis University, Waltham, MA.
$5,000 to Bruce and Marsha Moskowitz Foundation, Palm Beach, FL.
$1,000 to Palm Beach Community College Foundation, Lake Worth, FL.

4104
The Mabel Louise Riley Foundation
(also known as The Riley Foundation)
77 Summer St., 8th Fl.
Boston, MA   02110-1006   (617) 399-1850
Contact: Nancy A. Saunders, Admin. Mgr.
FAX: (617) 399-1851;
E-mail: info@rileyfoundation.com; URL: http://www.rileyfoundation.com

Established in 1971 in MA as the Mabel Louise Riley Charitable Trust.
Donor: Mabel Louise Riley†.
Foundation type: Independent foundation.
Financial data (yr. ended 12/31/04): Assets, $57,933,339 (M); expenditures, $2,741,788; qualifying distributions, $2,525,588; giving activities include $2,268,925 for 73 grants (high: $100,000; low: $48).
Purpose and activities: Interest in new approaches to important problems, with an emphasis on improved social services and race relations; special interest in programs for children, youth, and families; support for educational programs, community and neighborhood development, employment, housing programs and cultural activities.
Fields of interest: Arts; Education; Employment; Housing/shelter, development; Human services; Children/youth, services; Family services; Minorities/immigrants, centers/services; Community development; Minorities.
Type of support: Capital campaigns; Building/renovation; Equipment; Program development; Seed money; Curriculum development; Technical assistance; Matching/challenge support.

Limitations: Giving limited to the greater Boston, MA, area, with strong emphasis on Boston. No support for political or sectarian religious purposes, or for national organizations. No grants to individuals, or for operating budgets, continuing support, annual campaigns, emergency funds, deficit financing, research, publications, conferences, professorships, scholarships, travel, internships, exchange programs, fellowships, no loans.
Publications: Application guidelines; Annual report; Grants list.
Application information: Proposals will come at the invitation of the foundation only, following review of concept paper. Unsolicited proposals will not be accepted. Application form not required.
Initial approach: Concept paper not more than 2 pages
Copies of proposal: 1
Deadline(s): None for initial concept paper
Board meeting date(s): Mar., June, Sept., and Dec.
Final notification: 1-2 weeks maximum
Officer: Nancy A. Saunders, Admin. Mgr.
Trustees: Andrew C. Bailey; Douglas Danner; Margaret B. Harrison; Robert W. Holmes, Jr.
Number of staff: 1 full-time support.
EIN: 046278857

4105
The Robb Charitable Trust ◇
c/o Richard Robb
56 Pilgrim Rd.
Marblehead, MA   01945

Established in 1990 in MA.
Donor: Walter Robb.
Foundation type: Independent foundation.
Financial data (yr. ended 12/31/04): Assets, $13,999,260 (M); expenditures, $1,026,954; qualifying distributions, $829,625; giving activities include $829,625 for 72 grants (high: $131,000; low: $50).
Fields of interest: Higher education; Youth development.
Limitations: Applications not accepted. Giving primarily in PA. No grants to individuals.
Application information: Contributes only to pre-selected organizations.
Trustees: Anne Robb; Kim Robb; Lindsey Robb; Marge Robb; Richard Robb; Steve Robb; Walter Robb.
EIN: 223087631
Selected grants: The following grants were reported in 2004.
$201,000 to First Reformed Church, Lynden, WA. 3 grants: $131,000, $20,000, $50,000
$75,000 to National Academy of Engineering, DC.
$53,000 to Johns Hopkins University, Baltimore, MD.
$50,000 to Ellis Hospital, Schenectady, NY.
$50,000 to Proctors Theater, Schenectady, NY.
$50,000 to Sage Colleges, Troy, NY.
$15,000 to Joy of Music Program, Worcester, MA.
$12,000 to United Way.

4106
The Robbins-De Beaumont Foundation ✧
c/o Sullivan & Worcester LLP
1 Post Office Sq.
Boston, MA   02109   (617) 338-2816
Contact: Joseph C. Robbins, Tr.

Established in 1992 in MA.
Donors: Joseph C. Robbins; Mary Deland de Beaumont; Mary Deland de Beaumont Trust.
Foundation type: Independent foundation.
Financial data (yr. ended 12/31/05): Assets, $9,441,211 (M); expenditures, $509,408; qualifying distributions, $473,146; giving activities include $446,500 for 33 grants (high: $44,000; low: $2,000).
Purpose and activities: The foundation seeks nonprofit organizations whose goals are helping people reach their full potential as contributing members of their family, neighborhoods, and society at large. Limited funds are available for unsolicited grants for new, innovative projects which address identified needs of the community served and have relatively modest operating budgets. The foundation also has an interest in the education of children and adults in the areas of parenting, volunteerism, employment/life skills, preservation of the environment, the performing and visual arts, and substance abuse.
Fields of interest: Visual arts; Performing arts; Arts; Education; Environment, natural resources; Employment; Human services; Youth, services; Community development.
Type of support: Seed money.
Limitations: Giving primarily in MA; some giving also in ME and New York, NY. No support for organizations whose primary focus is mental health, medical training, physical and mental disabilities, or for organizations whose annual operating budget exceeds $1,000,000, or which have been in existence for over 10 years. No grants to individuals, or for capital campaigns, debt reduction or cash reserves, endowments, or multi-year pledges.
Application information: Use Associated Grantmakers of Massachusetts Common Proposal Format for formal proposals. Application procedures available on foundation Web site.
   Initial approach: Telephone, letter of inquiry or concept paper, (not to exceed 2 pages) before submission of a formal proposal
   Deadline(s): Mar. 1 for concept paper; June 30 for proposal
   Board meeting date(s): Semiannually, grant determinations usually in Nov.
Trustees: Joan Hudson Kopperl; Joseph C. Robbins.
EIN: 046719809

4107
Byron Robinson Education Foundation, Inc. ✧
315 Blue Hill Ave.
Milton, MA   02186   (617) 698-1100
Contact: Byron Robinson, Chair.

Established in 1991 in MA.
Donors: Byron Robinson, D.D.S.; Dorothea Robinson; Mark A. Robinson; Stacey C. Robinson.
Foundation type: Operating foundation.
Financial data (yr. ended 12/31/03): Assets, $3,816,349 (M); expenditures, $949,877; qualifying distributions, $586,387; giving activities include $582,159 for 11 grants (high: $356,216; low: $2,000).

Fields of interest: Higher education; Education; Human services.
International interests: Caribbean.
Type of support: Scholarship funds.
Limitations: Giving in the U.S. and in the Caribbean. No grants to individuals.
Application information:
   Initial approach: Letter
   Deadline(s): None
Officers: Byron C. Robinson, Chair.; Mark A. Robinson, Pres.; Dorothea Robinson, Clerk; Cle Robinson-Holly, Treas.
EIN: 043119780

4108
Fred M. Roddy Foundation, Inc. ✧
c/o Bank of America, N.A., Fdn. and Philanthropic Svcs.
100 Federal St., MA5-100-20-06
Boston, MA   02110   (617) 434-8237
Contact: Kerry H. Sullivan, Dir., Bank of America, N.A.
E-mail: kerry.h.sullivan@bankofamerica.com

Trust established in 1969.
Donor: Fred M. Roddy‡.
Foundation type: Independent foundation.
Financial data (yr. ended 12/31/05): Assets, $15,787,753 (M); expenditures, $794,632; qualifying distributions, $725,100; giving activities include $685,471 for 30 grants (high: $125,000; low: $5,000).
Purpose and activities: Giving primarily to a children's home, as well as for other children and family services, health associations, education, and social services.
Fields of interest: Secondary school/education; Higher education; Medical school/education; Hospitals (general); Health organizations, association; Human services; Children, services; Family services; Residential/custodial care.
Limitations: Giving primarily in MA and RI. No grants to individuals.
Application information: Associated Grantmakers Common Proposal Format accepted. Application form required.
   Initial approach: Proposal
   Copies of proposal: 1
   Deadline(s): None
Officers and Directors:* David I. McIntyre,* Pres.; Mrs. Lee Kintzel,* V.P.; Shawn P. Buckless, Clerk; Richard B. LaFleur, Treas.
Trustee: Bank of America, N.A.
EIN: 056037528

4109
Elizabeth Killam Rodgers Trust
c/o Nutter, McClennen & Fish, LLP
P.O. Box 51400
Boston, MA   02205-8982   (617) 439-2000
Contact: Thomas P. Jalkut, Tr.

Established in 1975 in MA.
Donor: Elizabeth Killam Rodgers‡.
Foundation type: Independent foundation.
Financial data (yr. ended 4/30/05): Assets, $7,989,118 (M); expenditures, $670,704; qualifying distributions, $622,848; giving activities include $600,500 for 4 grants (high: $400,000; low: $500).

Fields of interest: Higher education; International exchange, students.
Limitations: Giving in the U.S., with emphasis on MA and CT; funding also in Nova Scotia, Canada. No grants to individuals.
Application information:
   Initial approach: Letter
   Deadline(s): None
Trustees: Thomas P. Jalkut; John B. Newhall.
EIN: 046385523

4110
Thomas A. Rodgers, Jr. Family Foundation ✧
P.O. Box 2509
Fall River, MA   02722
Application address: 111 Durfree St., Fall River, MA 02722, tel.: (508) 679-6451

Established in 1998 in RI.
Donors: Thomas A. Rodgers, Jr.; Thomas A. Rodgers III; Christine Fennelly; Geraldine Roos; Maureen Bateman.
Foundation type: Independent foundation.
Financial data (yr. ended 12/31/05): Assets, $18,944,356 (M); expenditures, $956,175; qualifying distributions, $929,813; giving activities include $747,100 for 72 grants (high: $100,000; low: $250).
Purpose and activities: Giving primarily for education and human services.
Fields of interest: Arts; Elementary/secondary education; Higher education; Hospitals (general); Heart & circulatory research; Human services; Federated giving programs; Roman Catholic federated giving programs; Roman Catholic agencies & churches.
Type of support: General/operating support; Annual campaigns; Building/renovation; Curriculum development.
Limitations: Giving on a national basis, with emphasis on MA and RI.
Application information:
   Initial approach: Letter
   Deadline(s): None
Officers: Thomas A. Rodgers, Jr., Pres.; Thomas A. Rodgers III, V.P. and Secy.; Myron Wilner, Treas.
EIN: 043442439
Selected grants: The following grants were reported in 2004.
$75,000 to Saint Philomena School, Portsmouth, RI.
$75,000 to Salve Regina University, Newport, RI.
$75,000 to United Way of Greater Fall River, Fall River, MA.
$50,000 to Catholic Relief Services, Baltimore, MD.
$50,000 to Patronato Beneficio Oriental of the United States, Miami, FL.
$50,000 to Saint Annes Hospital, Fall River, MA.
$25,000 to Bristol Community College, Fall River, MA.
$25,000 to Brown University, Providence, RI.
$25,000 to Diocese of Fall River, Fall River, MA.
$20,000 to Residential Care Consortium, Fall River, MA.

4111
Rodman Ford Sales, Inc. Charitable Trust ✧

Rte. 1
Foxboro, MA   02035
Contact: Donald E. Rodman, Tr.

Established in 1986 in MA.
Donors: Donald E. Rodman; Rodman Ford Sales, Inc.; R. & R. Realty Co.; Rodman Five Realty Trust.
Foundation type: Company-sponsored foundation.
Financial data (yr. ended 12/31/04): Assets, $872,759 (M); gifts received, $322,116; expenditures, $447,192; qualifying distributions, $446,940; giving activities include $446,940 for 81 + grants (high: $67,500).
Purpose and activities: The foundation supports organizations involved with arts and culture, education, health, and human services.
Fields of interest: Arts; Education; Health care; Children/youth, services; Human services.
Limitations: Giving primarily in MA. No grants to individuals.
Application information: Application form not required.
  Initial approach: Proposal
  Deadline(s): None
Trustees: Curtis Rodman; Donald E. Rodman.
EIN: 222780804
Selected grants: The following grants were reported in 2004.
$67,500 to Rodman Ride for Kids, Foxboro, MA.
$22,000 to Catholic Charities.
$15,668 to Project RISE, Braintree, MA.
$12,250 to Boys and Girls Club. 2 grants: $11,250, $1,000
$9,000 to Red Sox Foundation, Boston, MA.
$2,000 to United Way.
$1,000 to YMCA.

4112
The Rogers Family Foundation ✧

29 Water St., Ste. 214B
Newburyport, MA   01950   (978) 465-6100
Contact: Stephen H. Rogers, Pres.
E-mail: srogers@rogersfamilyfoundation.com;
URL: http://www.rogersfamilyfoundation.com

Established in 1957 in MA.
Donors: Irving E. Rogers†; Martha B. Rogers†; Eagle-Tribune Publishing Co.; Andover Publishing Co.; Rogers Investment Corp.; Consolidated Press, Inc.; Derry Publishing Co.
Foundation type: Independent foundation.
Financial data (yr. ended 12/31/05): Assets, $20,882,730 (M); expenditures, $1,086,228; qualifying distributions, $1,033,923; giving activities include $908,264 for 45 grants (high: $200,000; low: $500; average: $5,000–$25,000).
Purpose and activities: Giving primarily for education, religion, medicine, and the arts.
Fields of interest: Museums; Secondary school/ education; Education; Hospitals (general); Human services; Community development; Christian agencies & churches.
Type of support: General/operating support; Capital campaigns.
Limitations: Giving limited to Essex County, MA and to southeastern NH. No grants to individuals, or for research, scholarships, fellowships, or matching gifts; no loans.

Publications: Application guidelines; Annual report; Grants list; Program policy statement.
Application information: See foundation Web site for application requirements. Application form required.
  Initial approach: Letter
  Copies of proposal: 2
  Deadline(s): 1 month prior to applicable meeting
  Board meeting date(s): Feb. 15, July 15, and Nov. 15
  Final notification: 1 month
Officer and Trustees:* Stephen H. Rogers,* Pres.; Amy R. Dittrich; Deborah R. Doherty.
Number of staff: 1 full-time professional.
EIN: 046063152

4113
The Rosse Family Charitable Foundation ✧

(formerly Thomas A. Rosse Family Charitable Foundation)
c/o Rosse Enterprises
10 Speen St., Ste. 4
Framingham, MA   01701-4661
Contact: Thomas A. Rosse, Pres.

Established in 1978 in MA.
Donor: Thomas A. Rosse.
Foundation type: Independent foundation.
Financial data (yr. ended 11/30/05): Assets, $10,009,994 (M); expenditures, $579,135; qualifying distributions, $515,494; giving activities include $515,365 for 49 grants (high: $220,000; low: $15).
Purpose and activities: Giving primarily for education, the arts, and health care.
Fields of interest: Arts; Higher education; Education; Hospitals (general); Medical research, institute.
Type of support: Annual campaigns; Scholarship funds; Research.
Limitations: Applications not accepted. Giving primarily in Boston, MA. No grants to individuals.
Application information: Contributes only to pre-selected organizations.
Officers and Directors:* Thomas A. Rosse,* Pres.; Anthony N. Fiore, Jr., Secy.; Bennett S. Yee, Treas.; Florence M. Rosse.
EIN: 042659411
Selected grants: The following grants were reported in 2005.
$220,000 to Middlesex School, Concord, MA.
$41,500 to Boston Medical Center, Boston, MA.
$25,000 to Boston College, Chestnut Hill, MA.
$25,000 to Fenn School, Concord, MA.
$25,000 to Nashoba Brooks School, Concord, MA.
$10,000 to Belmont Hill School, Belmont, MA.
$10,000 to Concord Free Public Library, Concord, MA.
$10,000 to Northeastern University, Boston, MA.
$500 to Emerson Hospital, Concord, MA.
$500 to Partners in Health, Boston, MA.

4114
Adelard A. and Valeda Lea Roy Foundation ✧

c/o Spencer & Stone
1500 Worcester Rd.
Framingham, MA   01702
Contact: Nancy S. Smith, Managing Tr.

Established in 1990 in MA.
Donor: Adelard A. Roy†.
Foundation type: Independent foundation.
Financial data (yr. ended 12/31/05): Assets, $9,410,288 (M); expenditures, $621,702; qualifying distributions, $550,500; giving activities include $550,500 for 58 grants (high: $30,000; low: $1,000).
Fields of interest: Museums; Elementary/ secondary education; Hospitals (general); Christian agencies & churches.
Type of support: General/operating support; Capital campaigns; Building/renovation.
Limitations: Giving primarily in MA.
Application information: Application form not required.
  Deadline(s): Oct. 31
Trustees: Nancy S. Smith, Managing Tr.; Francis Sabourin; Elizabeth M. Valliere.
Agent: Spencer & Stone.
EIN: 046652923

4115
Lawrence J. and Anne Rubenstein Charitable Foundation ✧

c/o Ridgeway Advisors
10 Post Office Sq.
Boston, MA   02109   (617) 279-8052
Contact: Susan W. Hunnewell
FAX: (617) 279-8059;
E-mail: shunnewelle@ridgewayadvisors.com

Established in 1963 in MA.
Donors: Lawrence J. Rubenstein†; Anne C. Rubenstein†.
Foundation type: Independent foundation.
Financial data (yr. ended 12/31/05): Assets, $18,597,650 (M); expenditures, $1,070,057; qualifying distributions, $965,797; giving activities include $908,900 for 36 grants (high: $180,000; low: $5,000; average: $10,000–$50,000).
Purpose and activities: Giving primarily for early childhood services and higher education, support also for programs for school preparedness.
Fields of interest: Elementary/secondary education; Children/youth, services; Child development, services; Homeless, human services.
Type of support: General/operating support; Equipment; Emergency funds; Program development; Curriculum development; Scholarship funds.
Limitations: Giving primarily in Boston, MA and Philadelphia, PA. No grants to individuals.
Application information: Write, call or e-mail for application procedures and forms. Application form required.
  Initial approach: Letter of inquiry
  Copies of proposal: 1
  Deadline(s): Apr. 15 and Oct. 15
  Board meeting date(s): Quarterly
  Final notification: Up to 1 year
Trustees: Joycellen Auritt; Andrew M. Cable; Steven Perlmutter.
Number of staff: 1 part-time professional.
EIN: 046087371
Selected grants: The following grants were reported in 2004.
$129,250 to Jewish Family Service Associates, Long Beach, CA.
$70,000 to Brandeis University, Waltham, MA.
$65,000 to Childrens Hospital. 2 grants: $50,000, $15,000

$50,000 to University of Massachusetts Medical School, Shrewsbury, MA.

$5,000 to Berklee College of Music, Boston, MA.

$5,000 to Childrens Hospital League, Boston, MA.

4116

Harold Rubenstein Family Charitable Foundation ✧ ☆

c/o Raphael & Raphael
52 Church St.
Boston, MA   02116

Established in 1952 in MA.

Donors: Harold Rubenstein†; Brockton Wholesale Beverage Co., Inc.

Foundation type: Independent foundation.

Financial data (yr. ended 2/28/06): Assets, $6,141,483 (M); expenditures, $420,507; qualifying distributions, $364,413; giving activities include $364,413 for grants.

Purpose and activities: Giving primarily for education, community and health service organizations, youth, and women's services.

Fields of interest: Historic preservation/historical societies; Arts; Higher education; Business school/education; Law school/education; Education; Health care; Boys & girls clubs; Human services; Children/youth, services; Women, centers/services; Jewish agencies & temples.

Type of support: General/operating support.

Limitations: Applications not accepted. Giving primarily in MA; some giving also in Washington, DC. No grants to individuals.

Application information: Contributes only to pre-selected organizations.

Trustee: Bonnie Cohen.

EIN: 046041597

Selected grants: The following grants were reported in 2005.

$6,000 to Folger Shakespeare Library, DC.

$6,000 to Washington Opera, DC.

$5,000 to New Israel Fund, DC.

$5,000 to World Monuments Fund, New York, NY.

$3,000 to National Gallery of Art, DC.

$3,000 to Saint Albans School, DC.

$2,500 to American Rivers, DC.

$2,500 to National Council for the Traditional Arts, Silver Spring, MD.

$2,250 to Mount Vernon Ladies Association, Mount Vernon, VA.

$1,000 to Hoop Dreams Scholarship Fund, DC.

4117

Cele H. and William B. Rubin Family Fund, Inc. ✧

32 Monadnock Rd.
Wellesley Hills, MA   02481
Contact: Ellen R. Gordon, Pres.

Incorporated in 1943 in NY.

Donors: The Sweets Co. of America, Inc.; Joseph Rubin and Sons, Inc.; Tootsie Roll Industries, Inc.; Melvin J. Gordon; Ellen R. Gordon.

Foundation type: Independent foundation.

Financial data (yr. ended 12/31/05): Assets, $60,096,266 (M); gifts received, $1,550,000; expenditures, $3,166,011; qualifying distributions, $2,865,449; giving activities include $2,843,658 for 91 grants (high: $2,041,500; low: $25).

Purpose and activities: Giving primarily to a community foundation and colleges and universities.

Fields of interest: Higher education; Education; Health organizations, association; Human services; Federated giving programs.

Limitations: Giving primarily in IL, MA, and NY. No grants to individuals.

Application information: Application form not required.

Deadline(s): None

Officers and Directors:* Ellen R. Gordon,* Pres.; Melvin J. Gordon,* V.P.

EIN: 116026235

Selected grants: The following grants were reported in 2005.

$2,041,500 to Fleet Charitable Gift Fund, Boston, MA.

$78,000 to Combined Jewish Philanthropies of Greater Boston, Boston, MA.

$2,000 to United Way of Massachusetts Bay, Boston, MA.

4118

Raymond & Marilyn Ruddy Charitable Trust ✧

c/o Ginger A. Ruddy
99 Pine Hill Rd.
Southborough, MA   01772

Established in 2001 in MA.

Donors: Raymond B. Ruddy; Marilyn A. Ruddy.

Foundation type: Independent foundation.

Financial data (yr. ended 12/31/04): Assets, $8,566,572 (M); expenditures, $2,493,451; qualifying distributions, $2,451,500; giving activities include $2,451,500 for 2 grants (high: $2,450,000; low: $1,500).

Purpose and activities: Giving primarily to right-to-life causes, and for health care and human services.

Fields of interest: Health care; Human services; Civil liberties, right to life; Roman Catholic federated giving programs.

Limitations: Applications not accepted. Giving primarily in MA. No grants to individuals.

Application information: Contributes only to pre-selected organizations.

Trustees: Marilyn A. Ruddy; Raymond B. Ruddy.

EIN: 046946674

4119

The Ruettgers Family Charitable Foundation ✧

c/o Atlantic Trust Co., N.A.
100 Federal St., 37th Fl.
Boston, MA   02110

Established in 1997 in MA.

Foundation type: Independent foundation.

Financial data (yr. ended 9/30/04): Assets, $10,705,123 (M); expenditures, $553,015; qualifying distributions, $467,307; giving activities include $451,000 for 3 grants (high: $350,000; low: $1,000).

Purpose and activities: Giving primarily to a public media broadcast station in Boston, MA, and to a U.S.-based organization for the construction of a public library in Rwanda.

Fields of interest: Media/communications; Libraries (public).

International interests: Rwanda.

Limitations: Applications not accepted. Giving on a national basis. No grants to individuals.

Application information: Contributes only pre-selected organizations.

Trustees: Abagail Ruettgers; Christopher Ruettgers; Maureen Ruettgers; Michael Ruettgers; Polly Ruettgers.

EIN: 043340951

4120

Rx Foundation ✧

63 Pinckney St.
Boston, MA   02114

Established in 2002 in MA and DE.

Foundation type: Independent foundation.

Financial data (yr. ended 12/31/05): Assets, $35,264,888 (M); expenditures, $1,697,666; qualifying distributions, $1,311,915; giving activities include $1,311,915 for grants.

Purpose and activities: Giving primarily to an institute for healthcare improvement.

Limitations: Applications not accepted. Giving primarily in Boston, MA. No grants to individuals.

Application information: Contributes only to pre-selected organizations.

Officers and Directors:* Serena M. Hatch,* Pres.; Francis W. Hatch,* V.P. and Secy.-Treas.; Anne Stetson, Secy.-Treas.; George Hatch; Howard Hiatt.

EIN: 810556499

4121

The William Sadowsky Family Foundation ✧ ☆

c/o Virginia Levsky
215 Pendleton Ln.
Longmeadow, MA   01106

Established in 1959 in MA.

Donor: Williams Distributing Corp.

Foundation type: Independent foundation.

Financial data (yr. ended 8/31/05): Assets, $898,665 (M); expenditures, $1,244,144; qualifying distributions, $1,237,728; giving activities include $1,237,728 for 2 grants (high: $1,037,728; low: $200,000).

Purpose and activities: Giving primarily for the arts, health, and Jewish organizations.

Fields of interest: Higher education; Jewish agencies & temples.

Type of support: Endowments.

Limitations: Applications not accepted. Giving primarily in MA. No grants to individuals.

Application information: Contributes only to pre-selected organizations.

Board meeting date(s): Quarterly

Trustees: Jill Docking; Virginia Levsky; James Sadowsky; Ronald Sadowsky.

EIN: 046112178

4122

The Sager Family Traveling Foundation and Road Show, Inc. ✧

80 City Sq.
Boston, MA   02129-3742

Established in 2000 in MA.

Donors: Robert C. Sager; Elaine H. Sager; Tess Sager; Shane E. Sager.

Foundation type: Independent foundation.
Financial data (yr. ended 7/31/04): Assets, $1,566,767 (M); gifts received, $450,000; expenditures, $502,359; qualifying distributions, $512,082; giving activities include $440,330 for 23 grants (high: $139,999; low: $250), and $453,911 for 3 foundation-administered programs.
Fields of interest: Higher education; Education; Environment; Human services; International affairs.
International interests: England; Nepal; South Africa; Sub-Saharan Africa.
Limitations: Applications not accepted. Giving on a national and international basis, particularly MA, PA, Dover, England, Nepal, Rwanda, and South Africa. No grants to individuals.
Application information: Contributes only to pre-selected organizations.
Officers and Directors:* Robert C. Sager,* Pres.; Elaine H. Sager,* V.P.; Brian D. Ferullo, Secy.-Treas.; Michael J. Byrne, Exec. Dir.
EIN: 043528688

4123
Sailors' Snug Harbor of Boston, Inc. ✧

c/o Grants Mgmt. Assocs.
77 Summer St., 8th Fl.
Boston, MA   02110-1006   (617) 426-7172
Contact: Patricia McAlpine, Fdn. Asst.
FAX: (617) 426-5441;
E-mail: philanthropy@grantsmanagement.com;
URL: http://www.sailorssnugharbor.org

Established in 1852 in MA.
Foundation type: Independent foundation.
Financial data (yr. ended 4/30/05): Assets, $7,673,809 (M); expenditures, $517,652; qualifying distributions, $452,438; giving activities include $404,766 for 34 grants (high: $30,000; low: $500).
Purpose and activities: Grants to institutions for the relief and support of aged sailors and other elderly persons.
Fields of interest: Health care; Health organizations, association; Human services; Family services; Aging, centers/services; Aging; Economically disadvantaged.
Limitations: Giving primarily in the Boston, MA, area. No grants to individuals.
Publications: Annual report (including application guidelines); Grants list.
Application information: The foundation accepts the Associated Grant Makers Common Proposal Format, which can be downloaded from the foundation Web site. All grantmaking guidelines are available on foundation Web site. Application form not required.
 Initial approach: Proposal
 Deadline(s): In time for approval at board meetings
 Board meeting date(s): Nov. 15, Feb. 15, and Apr. 15
Officers and Trustees:* George B. Motley,* Pres.; Arthur Page,* Secy.; Pamela S. Cutrell,* Treas.; William N. Bancroft; Courtney Coles; William C. Eaton; Charles R. Eddy; Stephen Little; Robert W. Loring; Everett Morss; William B. Perkins; Thomas Rogerson; G. West Saltonstall; William Saltonstall; Amy E. Saltonstall-Isace; Jo-Ann Watson; Benjamin J. Williams.
EIN: 042104430

4124
James and Beatrice Salah Family Foundation for the Town of Canton, Inc. ✧ ☆

c/o Salah M. James
100 Hudson Rd.
Canton, MA   02021-1435

Established in 1995 in MA.
Donors: Beatrice Salah; James M. Salah.
Foundation type: Independent foundation.
Financial data (yr. ended 12/31/04): Assets, $2,070,359 (M); gifts received, $248,997; expenditures, $357,282; qualifying distributions, $356,783; giving activities include $250,000 for 1 grant, and $95,000 for 19 grants to individuals (high: $5,000; low: $5,000).
Purpose and activities: Giving for educational scholarships and civic organizations.
Fields of interest: Arts; Education; Youth development; American Red Cross; Community development.
Type of support: Scholarship funds; Scholarships—to individuals.
Limitations: Applications not accepted. Giving limited to residents of Canton, MA.
Application information: Unsolicited requests for funds not accepted.
Trustees: Paul Carrol; James M. Salah; Edward Sullivan.
EIN: 043292638

4125
Salem Five Charitable Foundation, Inc. ✧ ☆

210 Essex St.
Salem, MA   01970   (978) 720-5766
Contact: Janice Lento, Admin. Asst.
FAX: (978) 720-5715; URL: http://www.directbanking.com/aboutUs/charitableFoundation.html

Established in 1996 in MA.
Donor: Salem Five Cents Savings Bank.
Foundation type: Company-sponsored foundation.
Financial data (yr. ended 12/31/05): Assets, $955,641 (M); gifts received, $20,500; expenditures, $378,426; qualifying distributions, $376,874; giving activities include $376,874 for grants.
Purpose and activities: The foundation supports organizations involved with arts and culture, education, health, affordable housing, human services, and community development. Special emphasis is directed toward programs designed to support the well being of families, youth, and elders in the North Shore, Massachusetts, area.
Fields of interest: Arts; Education; Housing/shelter; Family services; Human services; Community development; Youth; Aging.
Type of support: Sponsorships; Program development.
Limitations: Giving primarily in the North Shore, MA, area, with emphasis on Salem. No support for discriminatory organizations. No grants for capital campaigns, equipment, or general operating support.
Application information: Proposals should be submitted using organization letterhead. Application form required.

Initial approach: Complete online application form and mail or FAX proposal to foundation
 Board meeting date(s): Monthly
Officers and Directors: Joseph M. Gibbons, Pres.; Nicholas A. Caporale, Clerk; Ping Yin Chai, Treas.; David H. Caldwell; Richard Gourdeau; Timothy J. Hunt; William J. Lundregan III; William H. Mitchelson.
EIN: 043342405
Selected grants: The following grants were reported in 2005.
$11,995 to American Red Cross.
$11,000 to Salem Partnership, Salem, MA. 2 grants: $6,000, $5,000
$10,500 to Boys and Girls Club of Greater Salem, Salem, MA. 2 grants: $500, $10,000
$10,000 to Beverly School for the Deaf, Beverly, MA.
$10,000 to Lynn Community Health Center, Lynn, MA.
$3,000 to North Shore Music Theater, Beverly, MA.
$1,000 to Bishop Fenwick High School, Middletown, OH.
$1,000 to YMCA.

4126
Richard Saltonstall Charitable Foundation

c/o Saltonstall & Co., Inc.
50 Congress St., Rm. 800
Boston, MA   02109   (617) 227-8660

Established in 1964 in MA.
Donor: Richard Saltonstall‡.
Foundation type: Independent foundation.
Financial data (yr. ended 12/31/05): Assets, $25,380,638 (M); expenditures, $1,306,168; qualifying distributions, $1,185,508; giving activities include $1,080,187 for 33 grants (high: $175,000; low: $5,000).
Fields of interest: Media/communications; Museums; Performing arts, orchestra (symphony); Higher education; Education; Environment, natural resources; Hospitals (general); Alzheimer's disease research; Human services; Federated giving programs.
Limitations: Giving primarily in MA, with some emphasis on Boston.
Application information: Application form not required.
 Initial approach: Letter
 Deadline(s): None
 Board meeting date(s): Nov. and Dec.
 Final notification: Dec.
Trustees: Robert A. Lawrence; Emily S. Lewis; Dudley H. Willis; Sally S. Willis.
Number of staff: 1 full-time professional; 1 full-time support.
EIN: 046078934
Selected grants: The following grants were reported in 2004.
$215,000 to United Way. 2 grants: $40,000, $175,000
$60,000 to Boston Symphony Orchestra, Boston, MA.
$50,000 to W G B H Educational Foundation, Boston, MA.
$35,000 to Penobscot Marine Museum, Searsport, ME.
$25,000 to Conservation Law Foundation, Boston, MA.
$25,000 to Peabody Essex Museum, Salem, MA.
$20,000 to Massachusetts Historical Society, Boston, MA.

$20,000 to Thompson Island Outward Bound Education Center, Boston, MA.

$10,000 to Nature Conservancy, Arlington, VA.

4127
Saquish Foundation ◇

c/o Hunter Assocs.
75 Federal St., Rm. 2005
Boston, MA 02110

Donor: Charles M. Werly†.
Foundation type: Independent foundation.
Financial data (yr. ended 12/31/05): Assets, $16,972,300 (M); expenditures, $921,939; qualifying distributions, $827,350; giving activities include $747,600 for 51 grants (high: $110,000; low: $12,000).
Purpose and activities: Giving for the arts, education, the environment, hospitals, and youth programs.
Fields of interest: Arts; Education; Environment; Hospitals (general); Health organizations; Human services; Children/youth, services; Federated giving programs.
Limitations: Applications not accepted. Giving on a national basis. No grants to individuals.
Application information: Contributes only to pre-selected organizations.
Trustees: Horace S. Nichols; John Werly.
EIN: 046136550

4128
Sawyer Charitable Foundation ◇

200 Newbury St., 4th Fl.
Boston, MA 02116-2504 (617) 267-2414
Contact: Carol S. Parks, Tr.

Established in 1957 in MA.
Donors: Frank Sawyer; Mildred E. Sawyer; William Sawyer; The Brattle Co. Corp.; St. Botolph Holding Co.; First Franklin Parking Corp.; First Federal Packing Corp.; and others.
Foundation type: Independent foundation.
Financial data (yr. ended 12/31/04): Assets, $4,677,720 (M); expenditures, $468,901; qualifying distributions, $391,446; giving activities include $357,025 for 91 grants (high: $50,000; low: $150).
Purpose and activities: Giving primarily for human services, including services for people who are blind; funding also for health associations, the arts, and children and youth services.
Fields of interest: Arts; Higher education; Environment; Health care; Health organizations, association; Human services; Children/youth, services; Blind/visually impaired.
Limitations: Giving primarily in the New England states, with some emphasis on MA, particularly the Boston area. No grants to individuals, or for operating budgets, building funds, payroll or administration.
Application information:
Initial approach: Proposal
Deadline(s): Oct. 15
Officers and Trustees:* James P. Milone, V.P. and C.F.O.; Carol S. Parks,* Mgr.; Joseph A. Parks, Jr.,* Mgr.; Mary S. Quinn, Mgr.
EIN: 046088774

4129
The Michael & Helen Schaffer Foundation ◇

6 Whittier Pl., Ste. 14N
Boston, MA 02114

Established in 2002 in MA.
Foundation type: Operating foundation.
Financial data (yr. ended 7/31/05): Assets, $11,733,635 (M); expenditures, $822,131; qualifying distributions, $779,064; giving activities include $678,400 for 30 grants.
Fields of interest: Media, television; Performing arts, music; Arts; Medical school/education; Human services; Military/veterans' organizations.
Limitations: Applications not accepted. Giving primarily in MA and NY. No grants to individuals.
Application information: Contributes only to pre-selected organizations.
Trustee: Wendy Appel.
EIN: 020534424
Selected grants: The following grants were reported in 2005.
$350,000 to Manjushri Center.
$30,000 to Fidelity Investments Charitable Gift Fund, Boston, MA.
$30,000 to Greater Lowell Community Foundation, Lowell, MA.
$25,000 to National Alliance for the Mentally Ill (NAMI), Boston, MA.
$25,000 to Sakya Institute for Buddhist Studies, Cambridge, MA.
$25,000 to Vietnam Veterans of America Foundation, New York, NY.
$20,000 to Tufts University, School of Medicine, Medford, MA.
$13,200 to George London Foundation for Singers, New York, NY.
$10,000 to John F. Kennedy Medical Center, Edison, NJ.
$10,000 to Nativity-Boston, Jamaica Plain, MA.

4130
Schoen Family Foundation ◇

c/o RH & B, Inc.
50 Congress St., Ste. 1025
Boston, MA 02109

Established in 2000 in MA.
Donors: Scott A. Schoen; Laurie G. Schoen.
Foundation type: Independent foundation.
Financial data (yr. ended 12/31/04): Assets, $641,001 (M); expenditures, $682,838; qualifying distributions, $668,037; giving activities include $666,250 for 30 grants (high: $300,000; low: $500).
Fields of interest: Higher education; Health care; Human services; Jewish federated giving programs; Jewish agencies & temples.
Limitations: Applications not accepted. Giving primarily in West Palm Beach, FL. No grants to individuals.
Application information: Contributes only to pre-selected organizations.
Trustees: Robert G. Bannish; Laurie G. Schoen; Scott A. Schoen.
EIN: 046771174
Selected grants: The following grants were reported in 2003.
$200,000 to United Way of Massachusetts Bay, Boston, MA.
$100,000 to Yale University, New Haven, CT.

$10,000 to Combined Jewish Philanthropies of Greater Boston, Boston, MA.
$2,500 to DeCordova Museum and Sculpture Park, Lincoln, MA.
$2,500 to Lesley University, Cambridge, MA.
$1,000 to Big Brothers of Massachusetts Bay, Boston, MA.
$1,000 to Childrens Hospital League, Boston, MA.
$1,000 to Horizons for Homeless Children, Dorchester, MA.
$1,000 to Jimmy Fund, Boston, MA.
$500 to American Brain Tumor Association, Des Plaines, IL.

4131
The Schooner Foundation ◇

(formerly Ryan Family Charitable Foundation)
c/o Schooner Capital LLC
745 Atlantic Ave., 10th Fl.
Boston, MA 02111
Contact: Cynthia Ryan, Tr.
E-mail: cryan@schoonercapital.com

Established in 1996 in MA.
Donor: Vincent J. Ryan.
Foundation type: Independent foundation.
Financial data (yr. ended 12/31/04): Assets, $8,833,465 (M); gifts received, $10,000; expenditures, $476,401; qualifying distributions, $440,976; giving activities include $410,150 for 5 grants (high: $250,000; low: $150).
Fields of interest: International relief; International peace/security; Civil rights; Disabilities, people with; Women.
International interests: Africa.
Type of support: General/operating support; Income development; Capital campaigns; Endowments; Program development; Professorships; Seed money; Fellowships; Scholarship funds; Consulting services; Matching/challenge support.
Limitations: Applications not accepted. Giving on a national basis. No grants to individuals.
Application information: Contributes only to pre-selected organizations.
Officer: Stephen D. Maiocco, Treas.
Trustee: Kimberly R. Dano; Stephanie R. Ditenhafer; Jennifer R. Flynn; Carla E. Meyer; Cynthia A. Ryan; Vincent J. Ryan.
Number of staff: 1 full-time professional.
EIN: 043347626
Selected grants: The following grants were reported in 2003.
$638,500 to Isabella Stewart Gardner Museum, Boston, MA. For general support and centennial program fund.
$250,000 to Physicians for Human Rights, Cambridge, MA.
$203,660 to Trinity College, DC. For general support.
$150,000 to Harvard University, Cambridge, MA. 2 grants: $25,000 to Belfer Center for Science and International Affairs (For annual support), $125,000.
$102,500 to Beaver Country Day School, Chestnut Hill, MA. For capital campaign and annual fund.
$100,000 to Thayer Academy, Braintree, MA. For Swain Fund.
$25,000 to Women for Women International, DC. For general support.
$21,000 to Boston University, School of Social Work, Boston, MA. For scholarships.
$20,000 to Block Island Conservancy, Block Island, RI.

4132
Caroline & Sigmund Schott Fund ✧
(formerly Caroline & Sigmund Schott Foundation, Inc.)
678 Massachusetts Ave., Ste. 301
Cambridge, MA 02139 (617) 876-7700
Contact: Grants Mgr.

Established in 1986 in DE.
Donors: Liselotte J. Leeds; Gerald G. Leeds.
Foundation type: Independent foundation.
Financial data (yr. ended 6/30/05): Assets, $49,754,148 (M); expenditures, $3,800,937; qualifying distributions, $3,460,716; giving activities include $3,288,253 for 8 grants (high: $3,185,253; low: $1,000).
Purpose and activities: Giving primarily for early childhood care, and for education.
Fields of interest: Education, public policy; Education, reform; Education, public education; Elementary/secondary education; Education, early childhood education; Child development, education; Higher education; Education; Girls clubs; Children, services.
Type of support: General/operating support; Continuing support; Program development; Conferences/seminars; Publication; Research; Technical assistance; Program evaluation; Program-related investments/loans.
Limitations: Applications not accepted. Giving primarily in MA and NY. No support for service organizations. No grants to individuals, or for services or service delivery.
Publications: Occasional report.
Application information: Contributes only to pre-selected organizations.
Officers and Board Members:* Greg Jobin-Leeds,* Chair.; Liselotte J. Leeds,* Vice-Chair. and Treas.; Rosa A. Smith, Pres.; Maria Jobin-Leeds,* V.P. and Secy.; Gerard G. Leeds,* V.P.
Number of staff: 3 full-time professional; 1 part-time professional; 1 full-time support.
EIN: 112856561

4133
William E. Schrafft and Bertha E. Schrafft Charitable Trust
P.O. Box 961449
Boston, MA 02196
Contact: Karen Faulkner, Exec. Dir.
E-mail: funding@schrafftcharitable.org; URL: http://www.schrafftcharitable.org

Trust established in 1946 in MA.
Donors: William E. Schrafft†; Bertha E. Schrafft†.
Foundation type: Independent foundation.
Financial data (yr. ended 12/31/05): Assets, $32,619,924 (M); expenditures, $1,721,851; qualifying distributions, $1,646,202; giving activities include $1,599,000 for 107 grants (high: $200,000; low: $3,000).
Purpose and activities: Grants primarily for educational programs in the Boston, MA, inner-city area, for minorities and higher and secondary education; support also for community funds, cultural programs, and youth agencies.
Fields of interest: Arts; Elementary school/education; Secondary school/education; Higher education; Children/youth, services; Youth, services; Minorities; Economically disadvantaged.
Type of support: Continuing support; Scholarship funds.

Limitations: Giving limited to the metropolitan Boston, MA, area. No grants to individuals, or for matching gifts, seed money, emergency funds, capital campaigns, or deficit financing; no loans.
Publications: Application guidelines; Annual report (including application guidelines); Grants list.
Application information: Applicants should use the Associated Grantmakers of Massachusetts Common Proposal Format, which is available through the trust's Web site. Application form not required.
  Initial approach: Proposal
  Copies of proposal: 1
  Deadline(s): None
  Board meeting date(s): About 6 times per year
  Final notification: 2 months
Officer: Karen Faulkner, Exec. Dir.
Trustees: Lavinia B. Chase; Kristen J. McCormack; Arthur H. Parker.
EIN: 046065605
Selected grants: The following grants were reported in 2004.
$200,000 to United Way. 2 grants: $25,000, $175,000
$45,000 to Gordon College, Wenham, MA.
$35,000 to Neighborhood House Charter School, Dorchester, MA.
$30,000 to Big Sister Association of Greater Boston, Boston, MA.
$30,000 to Boston Symphony Orchestra, Boston, MA.
$30,000 to Plimoth Plantation, Plymouth, MA.
$15,000 to Mother Caroline Academy and Education Center, Dorchester, MA.
$13,000 to Longy School of Music, Cambridge, MA.
$10,000 to Boys and Girls Club.

4134
The SDSC Global Foundation ✧
2 Possum Hollow Rd.
Andover, MA 01810

Established in 2000 in MA.
Donors: Chikong Shue; Susan Shue.
Foundation type: Independent foundation.
Financial data (yr. ended 12/31/04): Assets, $14,446,848 (M); expenditures, $773,782; qualifying distributions, $685,500; giving activities include $685,500 for 20 grants (high: $200,000; low: $1,500).
Purpose and activities: Giving primarily to a Chinese Bible church, and other Chinese religious organizations. Funding also for other religious purposes.
Fields of interest: Theological school/education; Christian agencies & churches.
Limitations: Applications not accepted. Giving primarily in CA and MA. No grants to individuals.
Application information: Contributes only to pre-selected organizations.
Trustees: Chikong Shue; Susan Shue.
EIN: 046911403

4135
Abraham Shapiro Charity Fund Trust ✧
c/o Morris & Morris
32 Kearney Rd.
Needham, MA 02494-2521

Established in 1945 in MA.
Donor: Abraham Shapiro.

Foundation type: Independent foundation.
Financial data (yr. ended 12/31/05): Assets, $4,707,891 (M); expenditures, $633,112; qualifying distributions, $620,450; giving activities include $620,450 for 10+ grants (high: $300,000).
Purpose and activities: Giving primarily for education; funding also for human services, and Jewish agencies.
Fields of interest: Higher education; Hospitals (general); Health organizations, association; Eye research; Human services; Jewish federated giving programs; Jewish agencies & temples.
Limitations: Applications not accepted. Giving primarily in MA, with emphasis on Boston, Brookline, and Waltham. No grants to individuals, or for scholarships, fellowships, or matching gifts; no loans.
Application information: Contributes only to pre-selected organizations.
  Board meeting date(s): Quarterly
Trustees: Joseph Michelson; Robert Shapiro; Philip Shir.
EIN: 046043588

4136
Carl and Ruth Shapiro Family Foundation
(formerly Carl and Ruth Shapiro Foundation)
399 Boylston St.
Boston, MA 02116 (617) 778-7999
Contact: Jean S. Whitney, Exec. Dir.

Established in 1961 in DE as Carl Shapiro Foundation.
Donors: Carl Shapiro; Ruth Shapiro.
Foundation type: Independent foundation.
Financial data (yr. ended 12/31/05): Assets, $194,385,748 (M); gifts received, $14,077,399; expenditures, $6,767,234; qualifying distributions, $6,706,051; giving activities include $6,514,100 for 163 grants (high: $1,600,000; low: $15; average: $5,000–$50,000).
Purpose and activities: Grants primarily for arts and culture, health and hospitals, education, human services and Jewish-sponsored interests.
Fields of interest: Museums; Performing arts, dance; Performing arts, theater; Performing arts, music; Arts; Higher education; Education; Hospitals (general); Cancer research; Medical research; Youth development; Human services; Jewish federated giving programs; Economics; Disabilities, people with.
Type of support: Technical assistance; Matching/challenge support; General/operating support; Annual campaigns; Capital campaigns; Building/renovation; Equipment; Program development; Conferences/seminars; Fellowships; Scholarship funds; Research.
Limitations: Applications not accepted. Giving primarily in greater Boston, MA, and Palm Beach County, FL. No support for sectarian purposes (except Jewish). No grants to individuals.
Application information: Contributes only to pre-selected organizations.
  Board meeting date(s): 3 times per year
Officers and Trustees:* Carl Shapiro,* Chair.; Rhonda Zinner,* Pres.; Jean S. Whitney, Exec. Dir.; Ruth Shapiro, Tr. Emeritus; Ellen Jaffe; Linda Waintrup.
Number of staff: 1 full-time professional; 2 part-time professional.
EIN: 046135027
Selected grants: The following grants were reported in 2005.

$2,132,000 to Brigham and Womens Hospital, Boston, MA. 2 grants: $1,600,000 (For capital support), $532,000 (For project support).

$680,000 to Museum of Fine Arts, Boston, MA. For capital support.

$350,000 to Brandeis University, Waltham, MA. For capital support.

$300,000 to Raymond F. Kravis Center for the Performing Arts, West Palm Beach, FL. For capital support.

$214,000 to Combined Jewish Philanthropies of Greater Boston, Boston, MA. For operating support.

$40,000 to Park School, Brookline, MA. For operating support.

$25,000 to Boston Medical Center, Boston, MA. For project support.

$25,000 to Huntington Theater Company, Boston, MA. For capital support.

$20,000 to Associated Grant Makers, Boston, MA. For project support.

4137
Jean S. & Frederic A. Sharf Fund ◇
155 Heath St.
Chestnut Hill, MA 02467-2805
Contact: Frederic A. Sharf, Tr.

Established in 1965 in MA.
Donors: Frederic A. Sharf; Jean S. Sharf; Evelyn P. Strouse†.
Foundation type: Independent foundation.
Financial data (yr. ended 12/31/05): Assets, $17,907 (M); gifts received, $429,651; expenditures, $435,845; qualifying distributions, $435,700; giving activities include $434,950 for grants (high: $225,500; low: $100).
Purpose and activities: Giving primarily to art museums, and for health care, and education.
Fields of interest: Museums (art); Arts; Higher education; Education; Hospitals (general); Cancer; Jewish federated giving programs; Philanthropy/voluntarism.
Type of support: Annual campaigns; Capital campaigns; Program development; Publication; Program-related investments/loans.
Limitations: Applications not accepted. Giving primarily in MA. No grants to individuals.
Application information: Contributes only to pre-selected organizations in which trustees have some interest and involvement.
Trustees: Frederic A. Sharf; Jean S. Sharf.
EIN: 236406343

4138
The Clinton H. & Wilma T. Shattuck
Charitable Trust ◇ ☆
c/o Kirkpatrick & Lockhart
75 State St.
Boston, MA 02109

Established in 1985 in MA.
Foundation type: Independent foundation.
Financial data (yr. ended 8/31/06): Assets, $7,505,814 (M); expenditures, $374,312; qualifying distributions, $318,500; giving activities include $318,500 for grants.
Purpose and activities: Giving primarily for education and youth programs.
Fields of interest: Education; Children/youth, services; Residential/custodial care, hospices.

Limitations: Applications not accepted. Giving on a national basis. No grants to individuals.
Application information: Contributes only to pre-selected organizations.
Trustees: Walter G. Van Dorn; William Williams II.
EIN: 222659654
Selected grants: The following grants were reported in 2005.

$12,000 to Pioneer Institute for Public Policy Research, Boston, MA.

$10,000 to Discovering Justice: James D. Saint Clair Court Public Education Project, Boston, MA.

$10,000 to Doctors Without Borders USA, New York, NY.

$10,000 to Germaine Lawrence Incorporated, Arlington, MA.

$10,000 to National Judicial College, Reno, NV.

$10,000 to Project Bread - The Walk for Hunger, Boston, MA.

$10,000 to Thompson Island Outward Bound Education Center, Boston, MA.

$10,000 to University of Pennsylvania, Philadelphia, PA.

$10,000 to Wellfleet Conservation Trust, Wellfleet, MA.

$10,000 to YWCA of Boston, Boston, MA.

4139
Gardiner Howland Shaw Foundation
10 Lincoln Rd., 2nd Fl.
Foxboro, MA 02035 (781) 455-8303
Contact: Thomas Coury, Exec. Dir.
FAX: (781) 433-0980; E-mail: ghsfound@aol.com;
URL: http://www.shawfoundation.org

Trust established in 1959 in MA.
Donor: Gardiner Howland Shaw†.
Foundation type: Independent foundation.
Financial data (yr. ended 4/30/05): Assets, $17,770,078 (M); expenditures, $865,344; qualifying distributions, $769,224; giving activities include $529,660 for 43 grants (high: $53,000; low: $250).
Purpose and activities: The study of prevention, correction, and alleviation of crime and delinquency and the rehabilitation of adult and juvenile offenders. The foundation is particularly interested in supporting projects which demonstrate a current awareness of the major issues confronting our criminal justice system, with the following funding priorities: 1) programs which can effectively divert court-involved youth and juvenile offenders from escalating involvement in the criminal justice system; 2) programs which promote the use and acceptance of alternatives to incarceration and intermediate criminal sanctions; 3) innovative and effective approaches to rehabilitation for detained and incarcerated juvenile and adult offenders; 4) methods which improve the administration of justice and the quality of services for individuals appearing before the criminal court; and 5) initiatives which can impact current public policy in the field of criminal justice through education, training and effective advocacy.
Fields of interest: Crime/law enforcement, reform; Crime/violence prevention, youth; Offenders/ex-offenders, rehabilitation.
Type of support: General/operating support; Continuing support; Program development; Seed money; Technical assistance.
Limitations: Giving limited to MA. No support for drug or mental health programs or the arts. No grants to individuals, or for capital or building funds,

equipment, land acquisition, renovations, endowment funds, scholarships, or fellowships.
Publications: Application guidelines; Annual report (including application guidelines); Grants list; Occasional report; Program policy statement (including application guidelines).
Application information: The foundation accepts the Associated Grantmakers Common Proposal format. Application form required.
   Initial approach: Letter or telephone
   Copies of proposal: 1
   Deadline(s): Feb. 1
   Board meeting date(s): Feb., May, and Oct. Funding decisions are made in May
   Final notification: May 31
Officer: Thomas Coury, Exec. Dir.
Trustees: M. Lynn Brennan; James D. Colt; Theodore E. Ober; Benjamin Williams; Welch & Forbes.
Number of staff: 1 full-time professional; 1 part-time support.
EIN: 046111826
Selected grants: The following grants were reported in 2005.

$111,000 to Community Resources for Justice, Boston, MA.

$28,000 to Childrens Law Center of Massachusetts, Lynn, MA.

$26,000 to Citizens for Juvenile Justice, Boston, MA.

$20,000 to Massachusetts Correctional Legal Services, Boston, MA.

$20,000 to University of Massachusetts Medical School, Shrewsbury, MA.

$18,000 to Catholic Charities Center of the Old Colony Area, Brockton, MA.

$18,000 to Massachusetts Advocates for Children, Boston, MA.

$17,410 to Friends of Bostons Homeless, Boston, MA.

$10,000 to Salvation Army, MA.

$5,000 to Suffolk University, Boston, MA.

4140
Sheehan Family Foundation ◇
P.O. Box K
Kingston, MA 02364
Contact: Laura Gang, Prog. Advisor
E-mail: lgang2@comcast.net

Established in 1993.
Donor: L. Knife & Son, Inc.
Foundation type: Operating foundation.
Financial data (yr. ended 12/31/05): Assets, $4,242,603 (M); gifts received, $13,348; expenditures, $1,054,564; qualifying distributions, $1,021,211; giving activities include $1,021,211 for 50 grants (high: $208,761; low: $300).
Purpose and activities: Giving primarily for education, including after school programs and natural resource protection.
Fields of interest: Education, early childhood education; Education; Environment, natural resources.
Type of support: General/operating support; Continuing support; Land acquisition; Conferences/seminars; Curriculum development; Scholarship funds; Technical assistance; Program evaluation; Matching/challenge support.
Limitations: Applications not accepted. Giving limited to Essex, Middlesex, Plymouth, Barnstable, Dukes, and Nantucket counties, MA. No grants to individuals.

Publications: Annual report.
Application information: Contributes only to pre-selected organizations.
Board meeting date(s): Jan., May and Sept.
Officer: Elizabeth Sheehan, Exec. Dir.
Trustees: Anne Sheehan Landers; Margaret Sheehan.
EIN: 043197325

4141
George and Beatrice Sherman Family Charitable Trust ◇
c/o G & S
400 Atlantic Ave., Ste. 401
Boston, MA 02110-3333

Established in 1969 in MA.
Donors: Beatrice B. Sherman†; George Sherman†.
Foundation type: Independent foundation.
Financial data (yr. ended 6/30/05): Assets, $2,419,906 (M); expenditures, $427,292; qualifying distributions, $404,432; giving activities include $392,791 for 78 grants (high: $71,500; low: $100).
Purpose and activities: Emphasis on higher education; support also for Jewish welfare funds, temple support, hospitals, and family and children's services.
Fields of interest: Education; Health care; Health organizations, association; Human services; Family services; Jewish federated giving programs; Jewish agencies & temples.
Limitations: Applications not accepted. Giving primarily in MA. No grants to individuals.
Application information: Contributes only to pre-selected organizations.
Trustees: Robert P. Goldman; Alan W. Rottenberg; Claire B. Sherman; Norton L. Sherman; Marvin Sparrow.
EIN: 046223350
Selected grants: The following grants were reported in 2004.
$60,000 to American Society for Technion-Israel Institute of Technology, Newton, MA.
$15,000 to Hebrew College, Newton Centre, MA.
$5,000 to Beth Israel Deaconess Medical Center, Boston, MA.
$2,500 to Emerson College, Boston, MA.
$2,200 to Temple Israel, Boston, MA.
$2,000 to Rosies Place, Boston, MA.
$750 to Bridge Over Troubled Waters, Boston, MA.
$500 to Joslin Diabetes Center, Boston, MA.
$500 to McLean Hospital, Belmont, MA.
$200 to Wesleyan University, Middletown, CT.

4142
The Shillman Foundation ◇
841 Worcester Rd., Ste. 357
Natick, MA 01760-2016

Established in 2000 in MA.
Donor: Robert J. Shillman.
Foundation type: Independent foundation.
Financial data (yr. ended 12/31/05): Assets, $5,012,274 (M); gifts received, $1,872; expenditures, $661,868; qualifying distributions, $637,718; giving activities include $617,718 for 8 grants (high: $250,000; low: $7,300).
Fields of interest: Education; Health care; Human services; Jewish federated giving programs; Jewish agencies & temples.

Limitations: Applications not accepted. Giving primarily in MA. No grants to individuals.
Application information: Contributes only to pre-selected organizations.
Trustees: Dianne Parrotte; Robert J. Shillman.
EIN: 043511089

4143
The Shipley Family Foundation, Inc. ◇
c/o Nutter, McClennen & Fish, LLP
P.O. Box 51400
Boston, MA 02205

Established in 1969 in MA.
Donors: Charles R. Shipley, Jr.; Lucia H. Shipley.
Foundation type: Independent foundation.
Financial data (yr. ended 12/31/05): Assets, $13,666,024 (M); gifts received, $488,900; expenditures, $905,115; qualifying distributions, $803,589; giving activities include $745,675 for 9 grants (high: $530,000; low: $1,000).
Fields of interest: Secondary school/education; Higher education; Hospitals (general); Health care; Health organizations, association; Human services.
Limitations: Applications not accepted. Giving primarily in MA.
Application information: Contributes only to pre-selected organizations.
Officers and Directors:* Charles R. Shipley, Jr., Pres.; William H. MacCrellish, Jr.,* Clerk; Thomas P. Jalkut,* Treas.; Lucia H. Shipley.
EIN: 237015570

4144
Joseph & Agatha Sicari Charitable Trust
c/o David Taylor
141 Kendall Hill Rd.
Sterling, MA 01564

Established in 2000 in MA.
Donor: Helen Sicari†.
Foundation type: Independent foundation.
Financial data (yr. ended 12/31/05): Assets, $9,543,878 (M); expenditures, $660,864; qualifying distributions, $507,500; giving activities include $507,500 for 11 grants (high: $175,000; low: $1,000).
Fields of interest: Elementary/secondary education; Christian agencies & churches.
Limitations: Applications not accepted. Giving primarily in MA.
Application information: Unsolicited requests for funds not accepted.
Trustee: David Taylor.
Number of staff: 1 part-time professional; 1 part-time support.
EIN: 046922636

4145
Siff Charitable Foundation ◇
255 Park Ave., Rm. 1101
Worcester, MA 01609

Established in 1953 in MA.
Donors: Robert M. Siff; B-W Footwear Co., Inc.
Foundation type: Independent foundation.
Financial data (yr. ended 12/31/05): Assets, $2,537,848 (M); expenditures, $348,427; qualifying distributions, $344,653; giving activities

include $344,653 for 154 grants (high: $150,000; low: $18).
Purpose and activities: Support primarily for Jewish welfare; some support for education, health, and medical research.
Fields of interest: Arts; Education; Hospitals (general); Health care; Health organizations, association; Medical research, institute; Human services; Jewish federated giving programs; Jewish agencies & temples.
Type of support: General/operating support.
Limitations: Applications not accepted. Giving primarily in MA. No grants to individuals.
Application information: Contributes only to pre-selected organizations.
Trustees: Lawrence Siff; Robert M. Siff; Shirley S. Siff; Karen Siff-Exkorn.
EIN: 046112346
Selected grants: The following grants were reported in 2004.
$15,500 to Temple Beth Avodah, Newton Centre, MA. 2 grants: $500, $15,000
$12,000 to United Way of Central Massachusetts, Worcester, MA. 3 grants: $5,500, $1,000, $5,500
$10,000 to EcoTarium, Worcester, MA.
$10,000 to Yale Child Study Center, New Haven, CT.
$2,500 to Worcester Academy, Worcester, MA.
$1,000 to Lown Cardiovascular Research Foundation, Brookline, MA.
$100 to United States Holocaust Memorial Museum, DC.

4146
Lois and Norman Silverman Foundation, Inc. ◇
1 Commonwealth Ave.
Boston, MA 02116

Established in 1994 in MA.
Donors: Lois Silverman; Norman Silverman.
Foundation type: Independent foundation.
Financial data (yr. ended 12/31/05): Assets, $1,813,934 (M); gifts received, $672,134; expenditures, $561,164; qualifying distributions, $538,747; giving activities include $529,497 for 125+ grants (high: $100,000).
Purpose and activities: Giving primarily for higher education, and the arts, particularly opera; funding also for health associations, as well as for Jewish organizations.
Fields of interest: Performing arts, opera; Arts; Higher education; Medical school/education; Health organizations, association; Federated giving programs; Jewish federated giving programs; Jewish agencies & temples.
Limitations: Giving primarily in MA. No grants to individuals.
Application information: Application form not required.
Initial approach: Letter
Deadline(s): None
Officers: Lois Silverman, Pres.; Norman Silverman, Clerk and Treas.
EIN: 043234201

4147
Joanne B. Simches Charitable Foundation ◇ ☆

(formerly Safety Insurance Foundation)
c/o Wolf & Co., P.C.
1 International Pl.
Boston, MA   02110

Established in 1990 in MA.
Donor: Thomas Black Insurance Agency, Inc.
Foundation type: Independent foundation.
Financial data (yr. ended 12/31/05): Assets, $7,791 (M); expenditures, $3,735,650; qualifying distributions, $3,725,000; giving activities include $3,725,000 for grants.
Fields of interest: Hospitals (general); Human services.
Type of support: Seed money.
Limitations: Applications not accepted. Giving primarily in MA. No grants to individuals.
Application information: Contributes only to pre-selected organizations.
Trustees: Deborah S. Kay; Sherri A. Mahne; Lorri S. Owades; Richard B. Simches; S. Nancy Simches.
EIN: 043110677

4148
Richard & Susan Smith 1990 Charitable Trust ☆

(formerly R. & S. Smith Charitable Trust)
c/o Richard A. Smith and Susan F. Smith
1280 Boylston St.
Chestnut Hill, MA   02467-2112

Established in 1990 in MA.
Donors: Richard A. Smith; Susan F. Smith.
Foundation type: Independent foundation.
Financial data (yr. ended 12/31/05): Assets, $99,616,655 (M); gifts received, $52,033,250; expenditures, $987,087; qualifying distributions, $915,045; giving activities include $909,825 for 37 grants.
Purpose and activities: Giving to a university and a cancer institute.
Fields of interest: Higher education; Cancer; Medical research, institute.
Type of support: Capital campaigns; Building/renovation.
Limitations: Applications not accepted. Giving limited to MA.
Application information: Unsolicited requests for funds not accepted.
Trustees: Richard A. Smith; Susan F. Smith.
Number of staff: 1
EIN: 223048829
Selected grants: The following grants were reported in 2004.
$50,000 to Dana-Farber Cancer Institute, Boston, MA.
$25,000 to Boston Symphony Orchestra, Boston, MA.
$15,000 to Dana-Farber Cancer Institute, Friends of, Boston, MA.
$10,000 to Boston Public Library, Boston, MA.
$10,000 to Falmouth Hospital, Falmouth, MA.
$10,000 to Huntington Theater Company, Boston, MA.
$10,000 to Joslin Diabetes Center, Boston, MA.
$10,000 to Massachusetts Eye and Ear Infirmary Foundation, Boston, MA. For general support.
$10,000 to Tufts University, Medford, MA.

$10,000 to Year Up, Boston, MA. For general support.

4149
Robert and Dana Smith Charitable Foundation ◇ ☆

c/o Castanea Partners
3 Newton Executive Park, Ste. 304
Newton, MA   02462

Established in 2001 in MA.
Donors: Dana Smith; Robert Smith.
Foundation type: Independent foundation.
Financial data (yr. ended 11/30/05): Assets, $9,994,951 (M); gifts received, $8,993,366; expenditures, $447,934; qualifying distributions, $447,934; giving activities include $447,859 for 47 grants (high: $150,000; low: $200).
Fields of interest: Higher education; Education; Hospitals (general); Health care; Boys & girls clubs; Human services.
Limitations: Applications not accepted. Giving primarily in the Boston, MA area. No grants to individuals.
Application information: Contributes only to pre-selected organizations.
Trustees: Dana Weiss Smith; Robert A. Smith.
EIN: 223850789
Selected grants: The following grants were reported in 2005.
$158,000 to Boys and Girls Club. 2 grants: $8,000, $150,000
$8,009 to Childrens Hospital.
$5,000 to Julies Family Learning Program, South Boston, MA.
$3,000 to Associates of the Boston Public Library, Boston, MA.
$2,500 to Beth Israel Deaconess Medical Center, Boston, MA.
$2,500 to Bridger Clinic, Bozeman, MT.
$2,500 to Harvard-Westlake School, North Hollywood, CA. 2 grants: $1,000, $1,500

4150
Richard and Susan Smith Family Foundation ▼

1280 Boylston St., Ste. 100
Chestnut Hill, MA   02467   (617) 278-5200
Contact: David Ford, Exec. Dir.
FAX: (617) 278-5250;
E-mail: dford@smithfamilyfoundation.net;
URL: http://www.smithfamilyfoundation.net

Trust established in 1970 in MA.
Donors: Marian Smith†; Richard A. Smith; Susan F. Smith.
Foundation type: Independent foundation.
Financial data (yr. ended 4/30/06): Assets, $185,863,888 (M); gifts received, $18,830,243; expenditures, $11,171,336; qualifying distributions, $9,165,888; giving activities include $8,258,120 for 92 grants.
Purpose and activities: Grants for health, education, and for children and youth; the arts are a secondary field of interest. Of particular interest are organizations providing opportunities for economically disadvantaged populations, especially children and youth.
Fields of interest: Museums; Arts; Education, early childhood education; Elementary school/education; Higher education; Education; Hospitals (general);

Medical research; Human services; Children/youth, services; Homeless, human services; Minorities; Economically disadvantaged; Homeless.
Type of support: Program evaluation; Research; Equipment; General/operating support; Annual campaigns; Capital campaigns; Building/renovation; Program development; Seed money; Curriculum development.
Limitations: Giving limited to greater Boston, MA. No support for sectarian religious activities, political causes, or for film or video efforts supported by either the general public or by the Combined Jewish Philanthropies. No support for efforts in which the foundation may become the sole source of funding. No grants to individuals, or for deficit financing, or endowment funds.
Publications: Application guidelines; Grants list.
Application information: Visit foundation Web site to see if foundation's priorities are pertinent to request for funding. Application form not required.
   Initial approach: Letter
   Copies of proposal: 1
   Deadline(s): Depends on program, see website
   Board meeting date(s): As needed, 4 or more times per year
   Final notification: After board meeting
Officer: David Ford, Exec. Dir.
Trustees: Amy S. Berylson; James Berylson; Jennifer Berylson; John G. Berylson; Brian J. Knez; Debra S. Knez; Dana W. Smith; Richard A. Smith; Robert A. Smith; Susan F. Smith.
Number of staff: 2 full-time professional; 1 part-time support.
EIN: 237090011
Selected grants: The following grants were reported in 2005.
$500,000 to Combined Jewish Philanthropies of Greater Boston, Boston, MA.
$437,000 to American Diabetes Association, National Service Center, Alexandria, VA.
$350,000 to Temple Israel, Boston, MA.
$313,000 to Harvard University, Cambridge, MA.
$307,500 to Dana-Farber Cancer Institute, Boston, MA. For medical research.
$195,437 to Facing History and Ourselves National Foundation, Brookline, MA.
$181,000 to Chicago Academy of Sciences, Chicago, IL.
$118,427 to Park School, Brookline, MA.
$100,000 to Massachusetts General Hospital, Boston, MA. For medical research.
$63,500 to United Way of Massachusetts Bay, Boston, MA.

4151
The Donald R. Sohn Foundation ◇

Kendall Sq. Sta.
P.O. Box 425-104
Cambridge, MA   02142-0003
Contact: Donald R. Sohn, Tr.

Established in 1993 in MA.
Donors: Clara Bergoff; Donald R. Sohn.
Foundation type: Independent foundation.
Financial data (yr. ended 12/31/04): Assets, $1,047,982 (M); expenditures, $597,878; qualifying distributions, $579,832; giving activities include $568,097 for 34 grants (high: $56,000; low: $40).
Purpose and activities: Giving primarily for higher education, and human services.
Fields of interest: Higher education; Human services; Federated giving programs; Religion.

Limitations: Applications not accepted. Giving primarily in MA.
Application information: Unsolicited requests for funds not accepted.
Trustees: William A. King; Donald R. Sohn.
EIN: 046718410

4152
Alan D. and Susan Lewis Solomont Family Foundation ◇
c/o Rinet Co. LLC
101 Federal St., 14th Fl.
Boston, MA 02110

Established in 1998 in MA.
Donor: Alan D. Solomont.
Foundation type: Independent foundation.
Financial data (yr. ended 12/31/04): Assets, $373,838 (M); gifts received, $82,523; expenditures, $327,187; qualifying distributions, $319,892; giving activities include $321,041 for 185 grants (high: $40,000; low: $25,000).
Purpose and activities: Giving primarily for education, hospitals and health care, human services, and Jewish agencies and temples.
Fields of interest: Higher education; Libraries (special); Education; Aquariums; Hospitals (general); Health care; Health organizations, association; Human services; Jewish federated giving programs; Jewish agencies & temples.
Limitations: Applications not accepted. Giving primarily in Boston, MA and New York, NY. No grants to individuals.
Application information: Contributes only to pre-selected organizations.
Trustee: Alan D. Solomont.
EIN: 043388562
Selected grants: The following grants were reported in 2004.
$32,150 to Boston Medical Center, Boston, MA.
$22,500 to New Israel Fund, DC.
$12,500 to John F. Kennedy Library Foundation, Boston, MA.
$10,000 to Jewish Fund for Justice, New York, NY.
$5,500 to Hebrew College, Newton Centre, MA. 2 grants: $500, $5,000
$5,000 to Silent Spring Institute, Newton, MA.
$1,000 to Roxbury Comprehensive Community Health Center, Roxbury, MA.
$500 to Family to Family, Carroll, IA.
$500 to Jewish Funders Network, New York, NY.

4153
South Mountain Company Foundation ◇ ☆
Red Arrow Rd.
P.O. Box 1260
West Tisbury, MA 02575-1260

Established in 2002 in MA.
Donor: John Abrams.
Foundation type: Company-sponsored foundation.
Financial data (yr. ended 4/30/06): Assets, $4,958 (M); gifts received, $318,570; expenditures, $321,697; qualifying distributions, $319,876; giving activities include $319,876 for grants.
Limitations: Applications not accepted. No grants to individuals.
Application information: Contributes only to pre-selected organizations.

Trustees: John Abrams; Deirdre L. Bohan; Peter D'Angelo; Michael H. Drezner.
EIN: 161628987

4154
Cheryl Spencer Memorial Foundation ◇ ☆
100 Charles Park Rd.
West Roxbury, MA 02132-4985
Additional address: c/o Aaron Spencer, 69 Farlow Rd., Newton, MA 02158, tel.: (617) 323-9200

Established in 1986 in MA.
Donor: Aaron Spencer.
Foundation type: Independent foundation.
Financial data (yr. ended 12/31/05): Assets, $6,363,105 (M); gifts received, $5,000,000; expenditures, $703,756; qualifying distributions, $655,874; giving activities include $655,804 for 28 grants (high: $260,000; low: $50).
Fields of interest: Higher education; Hospitals (general); Jewish federated giving programs; Jewish agencies & temples; Aging.
Limitations: Giving primarily in MA. No grants to individuals.
Application information: Application form not required.
Deadline(s): None
Trustees: Jack Calechman; Aaron Spencer.
EIN: 046360057

4155
Stamps Family Charitable Foundation, Inc. ◇
c/o Summit Partners
222 Berkeley St., 18th Fl.
Boston, MA 02116

Donors: Penelope W. Stamps; E. Roe Stamps IV.
Foundation type: Independent foundation.
Financial data (yr. ended 11/30/04): Assets, $51,463,338 (M); gifts received, $7,360,656; expenditures, $2,628,616; qualifying distributions, $2,563,350; giving activities include $2,563,350 for 64 grants (high: $750,000; low: $40).
Purpose and activities: Giving primarily for the arts and education.
Fields of interest: Museums (specialized); Performing arts; Arts; Higher education; Education; Botanical gardens; Health care; Human services; American Red Cross; Children, services; Federated giving programs.
Limitations: Applications not accepted. Giving primarily in MA. No grants to individuals.
Application information: Contributes only to pre-selected organizations.
Officers: Penelope Stamps, Pres.; E. Roe Stamps IV, Treas.
EIN: 042943910

4156
Staples Foundation for Learning, Inc.
500 Staples Dr., 4 W.
Framingham, MA 01702
FAX: (508) 253-9600
E-mail: foundationinfo@staples.com; *URL:* http://www.staplesfoundation.org

Established in 2002 in MA.
Donor: Staples, Inc.
Foundation type: Company-sponsored foundation.

Financial data (yr. ended 1/31/05): Assets, $210,830 (M); gifts received, $1,820,411; expenditures, $1,809,355; qualifying distributions, $1,809,157; giving activities include $1,809,157 for 92 grants (high: $500,000; low: $500).
Purpose and activities: The foundation supports organizations involved with education and job skills. Special emphasis is directed toward programs designed to support disadvantaged youth.
Fields of interest: Education; Employment, training; Youth; Economically disadvantaged.
Limitations: Giving on a national basis. No support for discriminatory organizations, international organizations, political organizations, religious organizations not of direct benefit to the entire community, or fraternal organizations, veterans' organizations, professional associations, or similar membership groups. No grants to individuals, or for travel or conferences or conventions, medical research projects, public or commercial broadcasting programs, or books, research papers, or articles in professional journals; no student loans.
Publications: Application guidelines; Corporate giving report; Informational brochure (including application guidelines).
Application information: Support is limited to 1 contribution per organization during any given 12-month period. Application form required.
Initial approach: Complete online application form
Deadline(s): Mar. 2, June 1, and Aug. 31
Board meeting date(s): May
Final notification: 1 to 2 weeks following board meeting
Officers and Directors: Ronald L. Sargent, Pres.; Shira G. Goodman, V.P.; Mark Buckley; John Burke; Joy Errico; Sally Everett; Patrick Lacchia; Bob Muldoon; Leslie Prinz; Royce Reed; Nan Stout; Weber Torres; Doug Woodard.
Number of staff: 2
EIN: 470867951

4157
The Stare Fund ◇ ☆
c/o Ropes & Gray
1 International Pl.
Boston, MA 02110-2624

Established in 1959 in MA.
Donor: Fredrick J. Stare†.
Foundation type: Independent foundation.
Financial data (yr. ended 11/30/05): Assets, $8,257,886 (M); expenditures, $382,679; qualifying distributions, $348,371; giving activities include $348,371 for grants.
Purpose and activities: Giving for public health including nutrition, hospitals, associations and research; also some giving for the arts and higher education.
Fields of interest: Arts; Education; Hospitals (general); Health organizations, association; Nutrition; Human services; Children/youth, services; Family services.
International interests: South America.
Limitations: Applications not accepted. Giving primarily in MA. No grants to individuals.
Application information: Contributes only to pre-selected organizations.
Trustees: David S. Stare; Fredrick A. Stare; Irene M. Stare; Mary S. Wilkinson.
EIN: 046026648
Selected grants: The following grants were reported in 2003.

$61,000 to Harvard University, Cambridge, MA. 2 grants: $15,000 to School of Public Health, Department of Nutrition (For Nutrition Center), $46,000 to School of Public Health, Department of Nutrition (For I. M. and F. J. Stare Scholarship Fund).

$20,000 to Lown Cardiovascular Research Foundation, Brookline, MA.

$13,000 to Clark University, Worcester, MA.

$2,000 to Boston Symphony Orchestra, Boston, MA.

$2,000 to Lahey Clinic Foundation, Burlington, MA. For Dr. Charles Fager Endowment Fund.

$2,000 to Museum of Fine Arts, Boston, MA.

$2,000 to Visiting Nurse Association, Natick, MA.

$1,000 to Newton-Wellesley Hospital, Newton, MA.

$1,000 to Wellesley Symphony Orchestra, Wellesley, MA.

4158

State Street Foundation ▼ ✧

c/o Community Affairs Div.
225 Franklin St., 12th Fl.
Boston, MA 02110-2884 (617) 664-1937
Contact: George A. Bowman, Jr., V.P. and Mgr.
E-mail: epsilvoy@statestreet.com; *URL:* http://www.statestreet.com/company/community_affairs/global_philanthropy/overview.html

Trust established in 1963 in MA.
Donors: State Street Boston Corp.; State Street Corp.; State Street Bank and Trust Co.
Foundation type: Company-sponsored foundation.
Financial data (yr. ended 12/31/05): Assets, $5,017,945 (M); gifts received, $11,019,396; expenditures, $12,741,963; qualifying distributions, $12,734,631; giving activities include $10,598,571 for 533 grants (high: $529,567; low: $200), and $806,659 for 1,997 employee matching gifts.
Purpose and activities: The foundation supports organizations involved with arts and culture, education, health, employment, housing, youth development, human services, and community development.
Fields of interest: Arts; Secondary school/education; Vocational education; Education, drop-out prevention; Education, reading; Education; Health care; Employment, training; Employment; Housing/shelter; Youth development; Youth, pregnancy prevention; Family services, adolescent parents; Human services; Community development; Federated giving programs.
Type of support: Continuing support; Annual campaigns; Building/renovation; Land acquisition; Emergency funds; Program development; Technical assistance; Program-related investments/loans; Employee matching gifts; Matching/challenge support.
Limitations: Giving on a national and international basis, with emphasis on the greater Boston, MA, area. No support for political organizations or religious organizations not of direct benefit to the entire community. No grants to individuals, or for general operating support, endowments or capital campaigns, equipment, hospital programs, medical research, or disease-specific initiatives, travel, or television or film projects.
Publications: Application guidelines.
Application information: Proposals should be submitted using organization letterhead. Proposals

should be no longer than 7 pages. Multi-year funding is not automatic. Application form required.
Initial approach: Download application form and E-mail to foundation; mail proposal to foundation
Copies of proposal: 1
Deadline(s): Jan. 15, Apr. 15, July 15, and Oct. 15
Board meeting date(s): Quarterly
Final notification: 90 days
Officers: George A. Bowman, Jr., V.P.; Judith Mullen, V.P.; Amanda Northrop, Off.; Erin Silvoy, Off.; Heejin Yoon, Off.
Trustee: State Street Bank and Trust Co.
Number of staff: 2 full-time professional; 2 full-time support.
EIN: 046401847
Selected grants: The following grants were reported in 2005.
$529,567 to United Way of Massachusetts Bay, Boston, MA. For Campaign Corporate Contribution.
$300,000 to American Red Cross, National Headquarters, Disaster Relief Emergency Assistance Fund, DC. For response to Southeast Asia 2004 earthquake and tsunami.
$200,000 to Roman Catholic Archdiocese of Boston, Planning Office for Urban Affairs, Boston, MA. For affordable housing in Greater Boston area.
$175,000 to Project Bread - The Walk for Hunger, Boston, MA. For Food Stamps Online Program serving low-income individuals and families.
$100,000 to Fund for Boston Neighborhoods, Boston, MA. For Boston's 375th Anniversary Celebration.
$100,000 to Massachusetts Institute of Technology, Cambridge, MA. For FutureBoston, What Next for Boston in First Decades of 21st Century Project.
$100,000 to Northeastern University, Boston, MA. For Project Teamwork and MathPower programs serving low to moderate income (LMI) youth.
$100,000 to Salvation Army of Massachusetts, Boston, MA. For Capital Campaign.
$30,000 to Associated Grant Makers, Boston, MA. For Resource Center for Philanthropy.
$18,223 to Crisis, London, England. For Open Christmas which will provide food, shelter, medical services, and counseling to over 1500 homeless people in London.

4159

Anna B. Stearns Charitable Foundation, Inc.

c/o Grants Mgmt. Assocs., Inc.
77 Summer St., 8th Fl.
Boston, MA 02110-1006 (617) 426-7080, ext. 304
Contact: Amy Segal Shorey, Admin.
FAX: (617) 426-7087;
E-mail: ashorey@grantsmanagement.com;
Application address for NH: New Hampshire Charitable Fdn., Martha Abbott Hill, Prog. Off., 37 Pleasant St., P.O. Box 1335, Concord, NH 03302-1335, tel.: (603) 225-6641. MA contact: Yasmin Shah, Fdn. Asst., tel.: (617) 426-7080, ext. 317, e-mail: yshah@grantsmanagement.com; *URL:* http://www.grantsmanagement.com/absguide.html

Established in 1966 in MA.
Donor: Anna B. Stearns†.
Foundation type: Independent foundation.

Financial data (yr. ended 12/31/05): Assets, $14,162,702 (M); expenditures, $803,777; qualifying distributions, $732,566; giving activities include $638,000 for 49 grants (high: $35,000; low: $5,000).
Purpose and activities: The foundation supports projects and organizations that address one or more of the foundation's major interests: 1) to strengthen the education, independence and capabilities of young people, especially girls, and of women and their children; 2) to support the healthy development of girls as the foundation for their adult lives; and 3) to protect and preserve the natural environment.
Fields of interest: Environment; Children/youth, services; Family services; Women, centers/services; Girls.
Type of support: General/operating support; Continuing support; Program development; Technical assistance; Matching/challenge support.
Limitations: Giving in the City of Boston, and Cambridge, Somerville, and Chelsea, MA; funding also in northern NH. No support for statewide initiatives, or for individual day care programs, crises intervention, family preservation programs, homeless shelters, housing development, medical services, substance abuse, ex-offender programs, or for core educational programs of public, private, parochial or charter schools. No grants for capital campaigns or endowments.
Publications: Application guidelines; Grants list.
Application information: Massachusetts Common Proposal Form/cover summary sheet required; AGM Common Proposal Form may be used for application. Proposals for summer programs will only be considered in the winter round (Nov. 1 deadline). Application guidelines are also available on foundation Web site. Application form required.
Initial approach: Proposal or telephone call
Copies of proposal: 1
Deadline(s): May 1 and Nov. 1
Board meeting date(s): During 1st and 3rd quarters
Final notification: Within 1 month of board meeting
Officers and Directors:* Sylvia Simmons,* Pres.; Katherine L. Babson, Jr.,* Clerk and Treas.; Leonard W. Johnson; Miren Uriarte; Kathryn A. Wheeler.
Number of staff: 2 part-time professional.
EIN: 046144732

4160

Stearns Charitable Trust

66 Commonwealth Ave.
Concord, MA 01742
Contact: Russell S. Beede, Tr.

Trust established in 1947 in MA.
Donor: Russell B. Stearns†.
Foundation type: Independent foundation.
Financial data (yr. ended 12/31/05): Assets, $7,461,367 (M); expenditures, $460,037; qualifying distributions, $396,753; giving activities include $377,000 for 70 grants (high: $59,500; low: $500).
Purpose and activities: Emphasis on cultural programs, including a science museum; support also for libraries, community funds, the environment, an aquarium, and social services.
Fields of interest: Museums; Arts; Libraries/library science; Environment; Alcoholism; Human services; Federated giving programs.
Type of support: General/operating support; Continuing support; Annual campaigns; Capital

campaigns; Building/renovation; Land acquisition; Program development.
Limitations: Applications not accepted. Giving primarily in IL, MA, and RI. No grants to individuals.
Application information: Contributes primarily to pre-selected organizations.
  Board meeting date(s): As required
Trustees: Russell S. Beede; James Gassel; Anne B. Jencks.
EIN: 046036697

4161
The Stemberg Family Charitable Trust ◇
c/o Atlantic Trust Co., N.A.
100 Federal St., 37th Fl.
Boston, MA   02110   (617) 357-9600

Established in 1994 in MA.
Foundation type: Independent foundation.
Financial data (yr. ended 11/30/05): Assets, $12,764,244 (M); expenditures, $642,035; qualifying distributions, $571,328; giving activities include $552,100 for 27 grants (high: $102,500; low: $500).
Fields of interest: Museums (specialized); Performing arts, orchestra (symphony); Historic preservation/historical societies; Education; Hospitals (general); Youth development, scouting agencies (general); Federated giving programs; Roman Catholic agencies & churches.
Limitations: Applications not accepted. Giving primarily in MA. No grants to individuals.
Application information: Contributes only to pre-selected organizations. Unsolicited requests for funds not accepted.
Trustees: Dola H. Stemberg; Thomas G. Stemberg.
EIN: 046772174
Selected grants: The following grants were reported in 2005.
$102,500 to Boston Symphony Orchestra, Boston, MA.
$40,000 to Museum of Fine Arts, Boston, MA.
$30,000 to New England Aquarium, Boston, MA.
$22,500 to Dexter School, Brookline, MA.
$20,000 to Boys and Girls Club of Boston, Chinatown, Boston, MA.
$10,000 to Massachusetts Golf Association, Norton, MA.
$500 to Marion Institute, Marion, MA.

4162
Stern Family Foundation ◇ ☆
c/o Feldberg Family Office
P.O. Box 9175
Framingham, MA   01701

Established in 1989 in MA.
Donors: Burton S. Stern; Barbara F. Stern; Elizabeth Feldberg.
Foundation type: Independent foundation.
Financial data (yr. ended 12/31/05): Assets, $1,810,189 (M); gifts received, $234,000; expenditures, $483,307; qualifying distributions, $446,140; giving activities include $444,500 for 10 grants (high: $200,000; low: $500).
Purpose and activities: Giving for health and medical services.
Fields of interest: Education; Hospitals (general); Health organizations, association; Medical research, institute; Jewish federated giving programs.

Limitations: Applications not accepted. Giving primarily on the East Coast. No grants to individuals.
Application information: Contributes only to pre-selected organizations.
Trustees: Barbara F. Stern; Burton S. Stern.
EIN: 223073966

4163
The Abbot and Dorothy H. Stevens Foundation ◇
P.O. Box 111
North Andover, MA   01845   (978) 688-7211
Contact: Josh Miner, Exec. Dir.

Trust established in 1953 in MA.
Donor: Abbot Stevens†.
Foundation type: Independent foundation.
Financial data (yr. ended 12/31/04): Assets, $23,945,249 (M); expenditures, $1,763,117; qualifying distributions, $1,665,310; giving activities include $1,599,200 for 95 grants (high: $250,000; low: $100).
Purpose and activities: Giving primarily for the arts, education, conservation, and health and human services.
Fields of interest: Museums; Humanities; Historic preservation/historical societies; Arts; Medical school/education; Education; Environment, natural resources; Health care; Health organizations, association; Crime/violence prevention, domestic violence; Human services; Children/youth, services; Aging; Disabilities, people with; African Americans/Blacks; Hispanics/Latinos; Immigrants/refugees; Economically disadvantaged.
Type of support: General/operating support; Continuing support; Capital campaigns; Building/renovation; Equipment; Endowments; Program development; Seed money; Technical assistance; Program-related investments/loans; Matching/challenge support.
Limitations: Giving limited to MA, with emphasis on the greater Lawrence area. No support for national organizations, or for state or federal agencies. No grants to individuals, or for annual campaigns, deficit financing, exchange programs, internships, professorships, scholarships, or fellowships.
Publications: Application guidelines; Program policy statement.
Application information: Accepts Associated Grantmakers Common Proposal Form. Application form not required.
  Initial approach: Proposal
  Copies of proposal: 1
  Deadline(s): None
  Board meeting date(s): Monthly except in July and Aug.
  Final notification: 1 week following board meetings
Officer: Josh Miner, Exec. Dir.
Trustees: Phebe S. Miner; Christopher W. Rogers; Samuel S. Rogers.
Number of staff: 1 full-time professional; 1 part-time support.
EIN: 046107991
Selected grants: The following grants were reported in 2004.
$250,000 to Lawrence General Hospital, Lawrence, MA.
$75,000 to YMCA.
$60,000 to Merrimack College, North Andover, MA.
$50,000 to Tabor Academy, Marion, MA.

$30,000 to Essex County Community Foundation, Danvers, MA.
$20,000 to YMCA of Haverhill, Haverhill, MA.
$15,000 to KidsCommons Columbus Community Childrens Museum, Columbus, IN.
$15,000 to United Way of Merrimack Valley, Ward Hill, MA.
$4,000 to Handel and Haydn Society, Boston, MA.
$1,000 to Pine Manor College, Chestnut Hill, MA.

4164
The Nathaniel and Elizabeth P. Stevens Foundation ◇
P.O. Box 111
North Andover, MA   01845   (978) 688-7211
Contact: Josh Miner, Exec. Dir.

Trust established in 1943 in MA.
Donor: Nathaniel Stevens†.
Foundation type: Independent foundation.
Financial data (yr. ended 12/31/04): Assets, $17,098,344 (M); expenditures, $1,343,560; qualifying distributions, $1,164,422; giving activities include $1,112,777 for 111 grants (high: $250,000; low: $250).
Fields of interest: Museums; Historic preservation/historical societies; Arts; Medical school/education; Education; Environment, natural resources; Hospitals (general); Health care; Health organizations, association; Crime/violence prevention, domestic violence; Housing/shelter, development; Human services; Minorities/immigrants, centers/services; Aging; Disabilities, people with; Minorities; African Americans/Blacks; Hispanics/Latinos; Immigrants/refugees; Economically disadvantaged.
Type of support: General/operating support; Continuing support; Capital campaigns; Building/renovation; Equipment; Land acquisition; Endowments; Emergency funds; Program development; Conferences/seminars; Seed money; Technical assistance; Consulting services; Matching/challenge support.
Limitations: Giving limited to MA, with emphasis on the greater Lawrence and Merrimack Valley areas. No support for national organizations, or for state or federal agencies. No grants to individuals, or for deficit financing, exchange programs, internships, lectureships, research, professorships, scholarships, fellowships, or annual campaigns.
Publications: Application guidelines; Program policy statement.
Application information: Accepts Associated Grantmakers Common Proposal Form. Application form required.
  Initial approach: Proposal
  Copies of proposal: 1
  Deadline(s): None
  Board meeting date(s): Monthly except July and Aug.
  Final notification: 1 week after monthly meeting
Trustees: Joshua L. Miner IV; Phebe S. Miner; Samuel S. Rogers.
EIN: 042236996
Selected grants: The following grants were reported in 2004.
$350,000 to American Textile History Museum, Lowell, MA. 2 grants: $100,000, $250,000
$150,000 to Lawrence Community Works, Lawrence, MA.
$50,000 to Pike School, Andover, MA.
$26,000 to Essex Art Center, Lawrence, MA.
$20,000 to YMCA. 2 grants: $5,000, $15,000

$5,000 to Bartlett Museum, Amesbury, MA.

$5,000 to Bryn Mawr College, Bryn Mawr, PA.

$3,000 to Merrimack Valley Housing Partnership, Lowell, MA.

4165

The Stoddard Charitable Trust ▼ ◇

370 Main St.
Worcester, MA 01608-1779 (508) 459-8000
Contact: Warner S. Fletcher, Chair.

Trust established in 1939 in MA.
Donor: Harry G. Stoddard†.
Foundation type: Independent foundation.
Financial data (yr. ended 12/31/05): Assets, $76,400,324 (M); expenditures, $3,542,380; qualifying distributions, $3,344,111; giving activities include $3,227,111 for 72 grants (high: $500,000; average: $10,000–$100,000).
Purpose and activities: Emphasis on education, cultural programs, historical associations, youth agencies, and a community fund; support also for social service agencies, environmental concerns, and health associations. The trust's primary focus is on support for private nonprofits and on support other than operating support.
Fields of interest: Arts; Education; Environment; Health organizations, association; Human services; Youth, services; Community development.
Type of support: General/operating support; Continuing support; Annual campaigns; Capital campaigns; Building/renovation; Equipment; Land acquisition; Emergency funds; Seed money; Matching/challenge support.
Limitations: Giving almost exclusively in the Worcester, MA area, with primary focus in the city of Wooster. No support for religious or political organizations. No grants to individuals.
Application information: Initial approach by telephone is recommended for potential new grant recipients. Application form not required.
   Initial approach: Letter or telephone
   Copies of proposal: 4
   Deadline(s): Mar. 1, June 1, Sept. 1, and Dec. 1
   Board meeting date(s): Mar., June, Sept., and Dec.
   Final notification: Within one month of distribution meeting at which grant request is considered
Officers and Trustees: Warner S. Fletcher,* Chair.; Valerie S. Loring,* Secy.; Judith S. King,* Treas.; Allen W. Fletcher.
EIN: 046023791
Selected grants: The following grants were reported in 2003.
$350,000 to Bancroft School, Worcester, MA. Toward initiative to establish unrestricted endowment.
$150,000 to American Red Cross, Central Massachusetts Division, Worcester, MA. Toward construction of new headquarters building.
$150,000 to University of Massachusetts Memorial Medical Center, Worcester, MA. Toward construction of Ambulatory Surgery Center at Hahnemann campus.
$150,000 to Youth Opportunities Upheld, Worcester, MA. For improvements to Cottage Hill Academy in Baldwinville.
$100,000 to American Antiquarian Society, Worcester, MA. Toward building addition and renovations.
$100,000 to Anna Maria College for Men and Women, Paxton, MA. Toward additions and renovations at Miriam Hall.

$100,000 to Audubon Society, Massachusetts, Broad Meadow Brook Conservation Center and Wildlife Sanctuary, Worcester, MA. Toward acquisition of property to be added to Sanctuary.
$100,000 to Bridge of Central Massachusetts, Worcester, MA. For general program support.
$100,000 to Clark University, Hiatt Center for Urban Education, Worcester, MA. For literacy and school development.
$100,000 to Massachusetts College of Pharmacy and Health Sciences, Boston, MA. Toward renovation of Living and Learning Center.

4166

Robert F. Stoico/FIRSTFED Charitable Foundation

(formerly The FIRSTFED Charitable Foundation)
P.O. Box 438
Swansea, MA 02777 (508) 235-1368
Contact: Stacie Charbonneau, Mgr.
FAX: (508) 672-0190;
E-mail: stacie@stoicofirstfed.org; URL: http://www.stoicofirstfed.org

Established in 1997 in MA.
Donor: FIRSTFED America Bancorp, INC.
Foundation type: Independent foundation.
Financial data (yr. ended 3/31/05): Assets, $29,840,453 (M); expenditures, $1,581,600; qualifying distributions, $1,324,777; giving activities include $1,107,175 for 173 grants (high: $200,000; low: $50).
Purpose and activities: The foundation supports organizations involved with arts and culture, education, health, employment, and housing.
Fields of interest: Arts; Education; Health care; Employment, training; Housing/shelter, development.
Type of support: General/operating support; Continuing support; Annual campaigns; Capital campaigns; Building/renovation; Scholarship funds.
Limitations: Giving primarily in southeastern MA and RI. No support for individual schools or athletic or political organizations. No grants to individuals.
Publications: Application guidelines; Annual report; Grants list.
Application information: For grant requests under $5,000 a brief description of request and a copy of 501(c)(3) are necessary, along with current financial information. Application information available on foundation Web site. Application form required.
   Initial approach: Letter, e-mail, or telephone
   Copies of proposal: 1
   Deadline(s): None
   Board meeting date(s): Feb., Apr., July., and Oct.
   Final notification: 6 to 8 weeks
Officers and Directors: Robert F. Stoico,* Chair., C.E.O. and Pres.; Stacie Charbonneau, Secy. and Mgr.; Peter Panaggio, Treas.
Number of staff: 2 full-time professional; 1 part-time professional.
EIN: 043343529
Selected grants: The following grants were reported in 2005.
$200,000 to Saint Annes Hospital, Fall River, MA.
$52,500 to Boys and Girls Club. 2 grants: $50,000, $2,500
$50,000 to Roger Williams University, Bristol, RI.
$25,000 to Crossroads Rhode Island, Providence, RI.
$25,000 to Providence Performing Arts Center, Providence, RI.

$2,500 to New Bedford Whaling Museum, New Bedford, MA.
$2,340 to Visiting Nurse Association of Southeastern Massachusetts, Fall River, MA.
$1,000 to Attleboro Scholarship Foundation, Attleboro, MA.
$1,000 to YMCA.

4167

James M. Stoneman Charitable Fund ◇

(formerly James and Selma Stoneman Charitable Fund)
c/o R.J. Morrissey
2 International Pl., Ste. 3500
Boston, MA 02110-4102

Established in 1981 in MA.
Donors: James M. Stoneman; Marjorie R. Zuckerwar.
Foundation type: Independent foundation.
Financial data (yr. ended 6/30/05): Assets, $27,643,302 (M); gifts received, $21,268,686; expenditures, $395,523; qualifying distributions, $384,496; giving activities include $380,496 for 55 grants (high: $200,000; low: $20).
Purpose and activities: Giving for hospitals, health, and education.
Fields of interest: Performing arts; Higher education; Hospitals (general); Health organizations; Athletics/sports, racquet sports; Human services; Children/youth, services; Jewish federated giving programs; Jewish agencies & temples.
Limitations: Applications not accepted. Giving primarily in MA. No grants to individuals.
Application information: Contributes only to pre-selected organizations.
Trustees: Robert J. Morrissey; James M. Stoneman.
EIN: 042741931

4168

Stoneman Family Foundation ◇

(formerly Anne and David Stoneman Charitable Foundation, Inc.)
c/o Philanthropic Advisors, LLC
400 Atlantic Ave.
Boston, MA 02110-3333
Contact: Julia M. Toulmin
E-mail: jtoulmin@philanthropicadvisors.com

Incorporated in 1957 in MA.
Donors: Sidney Stoneman†; Miriam Stoneman.
Foundation type: Independent foundation.
Financial data (yr. ended 9/30/05): Assets, $29,083,877 (M); expenditures, $1,546,978; qualifying distributions, $1,317,312; giving activities include $1,105,000 for 11 grants (high: $250,000; low: $5,000).
Purpose and activities: To help low-income people achieve independence and economic self-sufficiency, and to improve the well-being of society by promoting economic justice.
Fields of interest: Hospitals (general); Human services; Community development, neighborhood associations.
Type of support: General/operating support; Program development.
Limitations: Applications not accepted. No grants to individuals.
Application information: Contributes only to pre-selected organizations.

Officers and Directors: * Elizabeth Deknatel,* Chair.; Eric Stein, V.P.; Joshua Stein, Treas.; Gabriel Deknatel; Maria Deknatel; Alan Rottenberg; Robert Smith; Gerda Stein; Jane Stein; Miriam H. Stoneman.
Number of staff: None.
EIN: 046047379
Selected grants: The following grants were reported in 2005.
$250,000 to Center on Budget and Policy Priorities, DC.
$175,000 to Connecticut Voices for Children, New Haven, CT.
$150,000 to Community Action Project, Brooklyn, NY.
$100,000 to Center for Employment Opportunities, New York, NY.
$100,000 to My Turn, Brockton, MA.
$100,000 to Vocational Foundation, Brooklyn, NY.
$50,000 to Iowa Policy Project, Mount Vernon, IA.
$50,000 to Kentucky Youth Advocates, Jeffersontown, KY.
$50,000 to Rhode Island College, Providence, RI.
$5,000 to Brandeis University, Waltham, MA.

4169
Strategic Grant Partners, Inc. ✧ ☆
128 First Ave.
Needham, MA   02494

Established in 2002 in MA.
Foundation type: Independent foundation.
Financial data (yr. ended 6/30/05): Assets, $98,277 (M); gifts received, $3,113,712; expenditures, $3,048,201; qualifying distributions, $3,019,077; giving activities include $3,019,077 for 5 grants (high: $1,076,200; low: $35,000).
Fields of interest: Human services; Children/youth, services.
Limitations: Applications not accepted. Giving primarily in MA. No grants to individuals.
Application information: Contributes only to pre-selected organizations.
Officers: Joanna Jacobson, Pres.; Stephanie Dodson, Clerk; Phil Gross, Treas.
EIN: 460512638

4170
The Stratford Foundation ▼ ✧
c/o Edwards Angell Palmer & Dodge LLP
111 Huntington Ave.
Boston, MA   02199   (617) 239-0778
Contact: Peter A. Wilson, Exec. Dir.

Established in 1983 in MA.
Donor: Kenneth H. Olsen.
Foundation type: Independent foundation.
Financial data (yr. ended 12/31/04): Assets, $31,091,194 (M); expenditures, $8,933,791; qualifying distributions, $8,646,038; giving activities include $8,614,197 for 85 grants (high: $770,000; low: $2,000; average: $5,000–$250,000).
Purpose and activities: Grants primarily to institutions closely associated with the donor and the donor's family. However, non-donor associated grants may be considered.
Publications: Application guidelines.
Application information: Application form required.
Initial approach: Telephone
Copies of proposal: 1

Deadline(s): None
Board meeting date(s): Periodically
Officer and Trustees: * Peter A. Wilson,* Exec. Dir.; Ava-Lisa Memmen; Eeva-Liisa Aulikki Olsen; Kenneth H. Olsen.
EIN: 222524023
Selected grants: The following grants were reported in 2004.
$1,383,000 to Central Indiana Community Foundation, Indianapolis, IN. 2 grants: $553,000 (For WFYI Project), $830,000 (For Successful Parenting).
$770,475 to Gordon College, Wenham, MA.
$500,000 to Project Mercy, Fort Wayne, IN.
$450,000 to Heartland Film Festival, Indianapolis, IN.
$350,000 to First Presbyterian Church of Hollywood, Hollywood, CA.
$100,000 to InterVarsity Press, Downers Grove, IL.
$50,000 to Covenant Christian High School, Indianapolis, IN.
$50,000 to YMCA, Chelsea Community, Chelsea, MA.
$30,000 to New Harmony Project, Indianapolis, IN.

4171
The Stride Rite Charitable Foundation, Inc. ✧
400 Atlantic Ave.
Boston, MA   02110
Contact: Ellen Sahl, Treas.

Incorporated in 1953 in MA as J.A. and Bessie Slosberg Charitable Foundation, Inc.
Donors: The Stride Rite Corp.; The Stride Rite Philanthropic Foundation.
Foundation type: Company-sponsored foundation.
Financial data (yr. ended 9/30/04): Assets, $5,580,987 (M); gifts received, $144,404; expenditures, $1,254,262; qualifying distributions, $799,190; giving activities include $787,339 for 69 grants (high: $193,952; low: $750), and $11,851 for 35 employee matching gifts.
Purpose and activities: The foundation supports organizations involved with arts and culture, human services, and community development.
Fields of interest: Arts; Children/youth, services; Human services; Community development.
Type of support: Employee matching gifts; General/operating support; Continuing support; Annual campaigns.
Limitations: Giving limited to the Boston-Cambridge, MA, area. No grants to individuals.
Publications: Application guidelines.
Application information: Application form not required.
Initial approach: Contact foundation for application information
Copies of proposal: 1
Deadline(s): None
Board meeting date(s): Approximately every 6 to 8 weeks
Officers and Directors: * Arnold Hiatt,* Pres.; Ellen Sahl,* Treas.; Andrew Bernstein.
EIN: 046059887

4172
The Stride Rite Philanthropic Foundation ✧
191 Spring St.
P.O. Box 9191
Lexington, MA   02420-9191

Established in 1993 in MA.
Donors: The Stride Rite Corp.; The Stride Rite Charitable Foundation, Inc.
Foundation type: Company-sponsored foundation.
Financial data (yr. ended 9/30/04): Assets, $574,540 (M); expenditures, $344,325; qualifying distributions, $342,907; giving activities include $343,591 for 10+ grants (high: $213,157).
Purpose and activities: The foundation supports organizations involved with arts and culture, education, health, and children and youth.
Fields of interest: Museums; Arts; Education; Health care; Children/youth, services; Foundations (private grantmaking); Federated giving programs.
Limitations: Giving primarily in the greater Boston, MA, area. No grants to individuals.
Application information: Application form not required.
Initial approach: Proposal
Deadline(s): None
Officers and Directors: * David M. Chamberlain,* Pres.; Frank A. Caruso,* Treas.; Janet Depiero*.
EIN: 043183600
Selected grants: The following grants were reported in 2005.
$25,000 to United Way of Massachusetts Bay, Boston, MA.
$5,000 to Boston Ballet, Boston, MA.
$2,500 to Penikese Island School, Woods Hole, MA.
$1,500 to Girl Scouts of the U.S.A..
$1,000 to Count Me In, El Paso, TX.
$1,000 to March of Dimes Birth Defects Foundation, White Plains, NY.
$1,000 to YMCA.
$500 to American Red Cross.

4173
Sudbury Foundation ✧
278 Old Sudbury Rd.
Sudbury, MA   01776   (978) 443-0849
Contact: Marilyn Martino, Exec. Dir.
FAX: (978) 579-9536;
E-mail: contact@sudburyfoundation.org;
URL: http://www.sudburyfoundation.org

Trust established in 1952 in MA.
Donors: Esther M. Atkinson†; Herbert J. Atkinson†.
Foundation type: Independent foundation.
Financial data (yr. ended 12/31/05): Assets, $29,646,683 (M); expenditures, $1,277,007; qualifying distributions, $1,252,078; giving activities include $676,993 for 33 grants (high: $100,000; low: $250), and $283,100 for 60 grants to individuals (high: $7,300; low: $800).
Purpose and activities: Scholarships to residents of Sudbury or Metrowest, MA, who are graduates of Lincoln-Sudbury Regional High School or are dependents of employees of the Town of Sudbury; support also for community building and civic issues, the environment, local social services, public elementary and secondary education, and arts and culture.
Fields of interest: Arts; Elementary school/education; Secondary school/education;

Environment; Human services; Community development; Government/public administration.
Type of support: Seed money; Scholarships—to individuals; Matching/challenge support.
Limitations: Giving primarily to Sudbury, MA. No support for sectarian religious activities. No grants to individuals (except for the scholarship program), or for ongoing operating support, deficit financing, general appeals, or graduate study.
Publications: Application guidelines; Biennial report; Informational brochure; Program policy statement.
Application information: Program and application information and forms are available on foundation Web site. Application form required.
 Initial approach: Send Proposal. Telephone inquiries and concept papers are welcome prior to proposal submission
 Deadline(s): Feb. 1 for Atkinson Scholarships; Jan. 1, Apr. 1, July 1, and Oct. 1 for The Sudbury Program, The Regional Program, and The Environmental Program
 Board meeting date(s): Dates available on request
 Final notification: Mid-Dec.
Officer: Marilyn Martino, Exec. Dir.
Trustees: Richard H. Davison; Susan Iuliano; Jill M. Stansky; John E. Taft; Bank of America, N.A.
EIN: 046037026

4174
Swanee Hunt Family Foundation
(formerly The Hunt Alternatives Fund)
625 Mount Auburn St.
Cambridge, MA 02138
FAX: (617) 995-1982;
E-mail: info@huntalternatives.org

Established in 1981 in TX; merged in July 2000 as Swanee Hunt Family Foundation.
Donor: Swanee Hunt.
Foundation type: Independent foundation.
Financial data (yr. ended 11/30/03): Assets, $37,556,267 (M); gifts received, $2,193,806; expenditures, $2,562,012; qualifying distributions, $2,301,238; giving activities include $2,228,300 for 97 grants (high: $1,600,000; low: $120; average: $10,000–$250,000).
Fields of interest: Women.
Limitations: Applications not accepted. No grants to individuals.
Publications: Grants list; Informational brochure.
Application information: Contributes only to pre-selected organizations.
Officers and Directors:* Swanee Hunt,* Pres.; Henry Ansbacher,* V.P.; Charles Ansbacher,* Treas.; Katherine Archuleta; Tish Emerson; Marva Hammons; Lillian Hunt-Meeks; Jane Holl Lute; John Miller; Fern Portnoy.
Number of staff: 25
EIN: 841101901

4175
Swartz Foundation ▼ ✧
c/o Ropes & Gray LLP
1 International Pl.
Boston, MA 02110-2624
Contact: Janet C. Taylor, Philanthropic Advisor

Established in 1994 in MA.
Donors: Sidney W. Swartz; Judith W. Swartz.
Foundation type: Independent foundation.

Financial data (yr. ended 12/31/04): Assets, $131,057,278 (M); gifts received, $12,110,000; expenditures, $9,679,091; qualifying distributions, $8,323,088; giving activities include $8,256,800 for 40 grants (high: $2,100,000; low: $1,000; average: $5,000–$500,000).
Purpose and activities: Giving primarily to Jewish organizations for medical research, as well as to Jewish temples and federated giving programs; funding also for social services, and education.
Fields of interest: Medical research, institute; Human services; Jewish federated giving programs; Jewish agencies & temples; Women.
Type of support: General/operating support; Capital campaigns; Program development.
Limitations: Applications not accepted. Giving primarily in eastern MA, and Palm Beach, FL. No grants to individuals.
Application information: Contributes only to pre-selected organizations.
Trustees: John E. Beard; Robert N. Shapiro.
EIN: 043255974
Selected grants: The following grants were reported in 2004.
 $2,100,000 to Combined Jewish Philanthropies of Greater Boston, Boston, MA. For general support.
 $1,100,000 to Brandeis University, Waltham, MA. For general support.
 $1,000,000 to Gann Academy New Jewish High School, Waltham, MA. For general support.
 $851,000 to Hadassah, The Womens Zionist Organization of America, New York, NY. For general support.
 $600,000 to Hebrew College, Newton Centre, MA. For general support.
 $500,000 to City Year, Boston, MA. For general support.
 $500,000 to Harlem Childrens Zone, New York, NY. For general support.
 $500,000 to Share Our Strength (SOS), DC. For general support.
 $425,000 to Congregation Shaarei Tefillah, Newton, MA. For general support.
 $5,000 to Boston University, Boston, MA.

4176
Sweet Water Trust ☆
Faneuil Hall Marketplace
4 S. Market Pl., Bldg. 4th Fl.
Boston, MA 02109-1610 (617) 263-7776
Contact: Nancy Smith, Exec Dir.
FAX: (617) 263-7774; E-mail: watersweet@aol.com;
URL: http://www.sweetwatertrust.org

Established in 1991 in MA.
Donors: Walker G. Buckner, Jr.; Foundation for the Needs of Others, Inc.
Foundation type: Independent foundation.
Financial data (yr. ended 12/31/05): Assets, $25,003,324 (M); expenditures, $1,279,437; qualifying distributions, $1,240,250; giving activities include $1,240,250 for 14 grants (high: $500,000; low: $1,000).
Purpose and activities: Support for environmental preservation through its Land Protection Program: Wild Land; Wild Water - to help purchase land and conservation easements. The trust seeks partners (land trusts, government agencies, businesses and individuals) to work toward the ecological and biotic health of New England by establishing, enlarging, and connecting reserve areas. Grants range from $1,000-$1,000,000 for land acquisition.

Fields of interest: Environment, natural resources; Environment, water resources; Environment, land resources; Animals/wildlife, preservation/ protection; Biological sciences.
Type of support: Land acquisition; Technical assistance; Matching/challenge support.
Limitations: Giving generally limited to New England and upstate NY; giving also to Canada. No support for projects for the protection of farmland, timberlands, parks, and trails unless they are a small part of a reserve design of a natural area which exceeds 10,000 acres. No grants to individuals, or for operating support.
Publications: Grants list.
Application information: After preliminary telephone interview and review of concept paper, grant application is by invitation only. Grant guidelines are available on foundation Web site. Application form not required.
 Initial approach: Telephone
 Copies of proposal: 1
 Deadline(s): None
 Board meeting date(s): Monthly
 Final notification: Varies
Officer: Nancy Smith, Exec. Dir.
Trustee: Walker G. Buckner, Jr.
Number of staff: 1 full-time professional; 4 part-time professional; 2 part-time support.
EIN: 043118545

4177
Sidney A. Swensrud Foundation ✧
(formerly Sidney A. Swensrud Charitable Trust)
88 Broad St.
Boston, MA 02110-3407

Established in 1955 in MA.
Donors: Jeffrey F. Swegler; Leslie R. Swensrud; S. Blake Swensrud II; Anthony S. Swensrud.
Foundation type: Independent foundation.
Financial data (yr. ended 12/31/05): Assets, $17,888,986 (M); expenditures, $1,007,168; qualifying distributions, $857,000; giving activities include $857,000 for 14 grants (high: $250,000; low: $500).
Purpose and activities: Giving primarily for higher education, historical preservation, hospitals, including children's hospitals, and public policy, including immigration reform.
Fields of interest: Historic preservation/historical societies; Higher education; Hospitals (specialty); Health care; Human services; Public policy, research; Public affairs; Immigrants/refugees.
Limitations: Applications not accepted. Giving on a national basis, with some emphasis on Washington, DC, and MA. No grants to individuals.
Application information: Contributes only to pre-selected organizations.
Trustees: Nancy S. Anthony; Stephen B. Swensrud.
EIN: 256050238

4178
Talbots Charitable Foundation, Inc. ✧
1 Talbots Dr.
Hingham, MA 02043

Established in 2001.
Donor: The Talbots, Inc.
Foundation type: Company-sponsored foundation.
Financial data (yr. ended 1/29/05): Assets, $17,194 (M); gifts received, $400,000;

expenditures, $411,836; qualifying distributions, $411,836; giving activities include $387,343 for 162 grants (high: $63,600; low: $30).
Purpose and activities: The foundation supports organizations involved with arts and culture, education, health, and human services.
Fields of interest: Arts; Education; Health care; Human services; Federated giving programs.
Type of support: General/operating support; Program development; Research; Scholarships—to individuals.
Publications: Application guidelines.
Application information: An application form is required for scholarships.
> *Initial approach:* Proposal; download application form for scholarships
> *Deadline(s):* None
> *Final notification:* 6 to 8 weeks

Officers and Directors:* Arnold B. Zetcher,* Chair. and Pres.; Richard T. O'Connell, Jr.,* Sr. V.P. and Secy.; Edward L. Larsen,* Sr. V.P. and Treas.; Margery Myers,* V.P.; Carol Gordon Stone,* V.P.; Warren J. Casey.
EIN: 043547221
Selected grants: The following grants were reported in 2006.
$141,773 to Scholarship America, Saint Peter, MN. 2 grants: $77,223, $64,550
$54,900 to W G B H Educational Foundation, Boston, MA. 4 grants: $13,650, $13,750, $13,750, $13,750
$6,000 to United Way of Massachusetts Bay, Boston, MA.
$4,500 to United Way.
$2,500 to Kids Corporation, Newark, NJ.
$1,525 to United Way of Greater Knoxville, Knoxville, TN.

4179
The Tara Foundation ✧
c/o Michael Baldwin
3 Barnabas Rd.
Marion, MA   02738

Established in 1989 in NY.
Donor: Bokara Legendre.
Foundation type: Independent foundation.
Financial data (yr. ended 12/31/05): Assets, $65,440 (M); gifts received, $1,054,392; expenditures, $1,034,777; qualifying distributions, $1,027,882; giving activities include $1,027,655 for 46 grants (high: $358,135; low: $100).
Purpose and activities: Giving primarily for spiritual studies, interconnectedness, and meditation; funding also for Buddhist organizations, as well as for the arts and human services.
Fields of interest: Arts; Environment; Animals/ wildlife; Human services; Roman Catholic agencies & churches; Buddhism.
Limitations: Applications not accepted. Giving primarily in CA and New York, NY; some giving nationally. No grants or loans to individuals.
Application information: Contributes only to pre-selected organizations.
Trustees: Michael Baldwin; Bokara Legendre.
EIN: 133524901

4180
Technical Training Foundation ✧
1551 Osgood St.
North Andover, MA   01845
Contact: Ibrahim Hefni, Tr.

Established in 1985 in MA.
Donors: Ibrahim Hefni; Wensley Hefni.
Foundation type: Independent foundation.
Financial data (yr. ended 8/31/03): Assets, $48,534,925 (M); gifts received, $225,000; expenditures, $1,753,023; qualifying distributions, $1,632,132; giving activities include $349,000 for 8 grants (high: $150,000; low: $1,000), and $643,325 for 67 grants to individuals (high: $128,334; low: $287).
Purpose and activities: Support primarily for minorities and immigrants through scholarship programs in science and engineering at institutions of higher education and technical training.
Fields of interest: Higher education; Minorities/ immigrants, centers/services; Engineering/ technology; Science; Minorities; Economically disadvantaged.
International interests: Middle East.
Type of support: Scholarship funds; Scholarships—to individuals.
Limitations: Giving on a national basis.
Application information: Application form required.
> *Initial approach:* Letter
> *Copies of proposal:* 1
> *Deadline(s):* None
> *Board meeting date(s):* As necessary

Trustees: Denis Hamboyan; Ibrahim Hefni; Wensley Hefni.
Number of staff: 2 part-time professional.
EIN: 042864138

4181
Thomas Thompson Trust ✧
1 Financial Ctr., 29th Fl.
Boston, MA   02111   (617) 951-1108
Contact: Susan T. Monahan, Grants. Coord.
FAX: (617) 542-7437; E-mail: stm@rackemann.com; URL: http://www.cybergrants.com/thompson/ grant.html

Trust established in 1869 in MA.
Donor: Thomas Thompson†.
Foundation type: Independent foundation.
Financial data (yr. ended 5/31/05): Assets, $15,046,442 (M); expenditures, $860,625; qualifying distributions, $776,513; giving activities include $659,280 for 35 grants (high: $100,000; low: $2,250), and $41,565 for 3 employee matching gifts.
Purpose and activities: The foundation makes grants to charitable organizations whose work and purposes promote health, education or the general social or civic betterment in the stated geographical areas. However, the foundation will continue to place particular emphasis on healthcare and other social services.
Fields of interest: Arts; Libraries/library science; Education; Health care; Human services; Community development.
Type of support: Capital campaigns; Building/ renovation; Equipment; Emergency funds; Program development; Matching/challenge support.
Limitations: Giving limited to Dutchess County, NY, primarily in Rhinebeck, and in Windham County, VT, primarily in Brattleboro. No grants to individuals (except for designated women), or for operating

budgets, continuing support, seed money, deficit financing, endowment funds, scholarships, or fellowships; no loans.
Publications: Application guidelines.
Application information: Grants awarded only to organizations that have been in operation for 3 consecutive years. Application form available on foundation Web site. Application form required.
> *Initial approach:* Telephone or e-mail
> *Copies of proposal:* 1
> *Deadline(s):* 1st of month in which there is a meeting
> *Board meeting date(s):* Quarterly in Jan., Apr., July and Oct.

Trustees: Daniel W. Fawcett; Albert M. Fortier, Jr.; William B. Tyler.
Number of staff: 1 part-time professional.
EIN: 030179429
Selected grants: The following grants were reported in 2005.
$75,000 to Marlboro College, Marlboro, VT. 2 grants: $25,000, $50,000
$25,000 to Health Care and Rehabilitation Services of Southeastern Vermont, Bellows Falls, VT.
$25,000 to Rescue, Inc., Brattleboro, VT.
$25,000 to Wilderstein Preservation, Rhinebeck, NY.
$20,000 to Compass School, Westminster Station, VT.
$16,000 to Brattleboro Area Community Land Trust, Brattleboro, VT.
$15,000 to Vermont Center for the Deaf and Hard of Hearing, Brattleboro, VT.
$12,870 to Brattleboro Museum and Art Center, Brattleboro, VT.
$9,500 to Bard College, Annandale on Hudson, NY.

4182
Willard C. Tilson Foundation ✧ ☆
30 Western Ave.
Gloucester, MA   01930   (978) 283-0643
Contact: Bayard D. Waring, Tr.

Established in 1956 in MA.
Foundation type: Independent foundation.
Financial data (yr. ended 12/31/05): Assets, $5,568,227 (M); expenditures, $406,260; qualifying distributions, $345,378; giving activities include $332,000 for 3 grants (high: $162,500; low: $35,000).
Purpose and activities: Giving limited to programs helping brain-injured young people.
Fields of interest: Elementary/secondary education; Autism.
Limitations: Giving limited to MA.
Application information: Application form not required.
> *Initial approach:* Letter
> *Copies of proposal:* 1
> *Deadline(s):* None
> *Board meeting date(s):* Mar., June, Sept., and Dec.

Trustees: Bayard D. Waring; Philip B. Waring.
Number of staff: 1 full-time professional; 4 part-time professional.
EIN: 046036556

4183
The TJX Foundation, Inc. ▼
(formerly Zayre Foundation, Inc.)
c/o The TJX Cos., Inc.
770 Cochituate Rd., Rte. 1E
Framingham, MA 01701 (508) 390-3199
Contact: Christine A. Strickland, Mgr.
URL: http://www.tjx.com/corprespons/
commsupp.html

Incorporated in 1966 in MA.
Donors: The TJX Cos., Inc.; Marshalls of MA, Inc.
Foundation type: Company-sponsored foundation.
Financial data (yr. ended 1/28/06): Assets,
$15,986,118 (M); gifts received, $8,607,783;
expenditures, $5,905,903; qualifying distributions,
$5,737,561; giving activities include $5,737,561
for 862 grants (high: $400,000; low: $100).
Purpose and activities: The foundation supports
organizations involved with domestic violence,
disadvantaged families and children, disabled
people, women, and homeless people.
Fields of interest: Crime/violence prevention,
domestic violence; Children, services; Family
services; Disabilities, people with; Women;
Economically disadvantaged; Homeless.
Type of support: Continuing support.
Limitations: Giving on a national basis. No support
for political organizations or fraternal organizations.
No grants to individuals, or for capital campaigns.
Publications: Application guidelines; Annual report.
Application information: Application form required.
Initial approach: Telephone foundation for
application form
Copies of proposal: 1
Deadline(s): 4 weeks prior to board meetings
Board meeting date(s): Bimonthly
Officers and Directors:* Paul Kangas, V.P.; Mary B.
Reynolds, V.P.; Jeffrey Naylor,* Treas.; Bernard
Cammarata.
Number of staff: 3 full-time professional.
EIN: 042399760
Selected grants: The following grants were reported
in 2005.
$234,432 to Save the Children Federation,
Brookline, MA.
$125,000 to Family Violence Prevention Fund, San
Francisco, CA.
$100,000 to American Red Cross, National
Headquarters, DC.
$100,000 to Special Olympics, DC.
$50,000 to American Red Cross of Massachusetts
Bay, Boston, MA.
$40,000 to American Cancer Society, Atlanta, GA.
$25,000 to Beth Israel Deaconess Medical Center,
Boston, MA.
$25,000 to Metropolitan Council for Educational
Opportunity (METCO), Roxbury, MA.
$25,000 to Wang Center for the Performing Arts,
Boston, MA.
$15,000 to DSS Kids Fund, Boston, MA.

4184
Charles Irwin Travelli Fund ◇
c/o Tyler & Reynolds
77 Summer St.
Boston, MA 02110
Contact: Sumner R. Andrews, Pres.

Incorporated in 1914 in MA.
Donors: Charles I. Travelli†; Emma R. Travelli†.
Foundation type: Independent foundation.

Financial data (yr. ended 11/30/04): Assets,
$2,480,274 (M); gifts received, $1,195,883;
expenditures, $1,634,538; qualifying distributions,
$1,623,820; giving activities include $178,000 for
grants, and $1,409,700 for grants to individuals.
Purpose and activities: Grants for aid and comfort
to the deserving poor; contributes to the support of
other MA charitable corporations or associations,
and generally for the doing and carrying on of
educational, charitable, benevolent and religious
work. Grants largely for higher and other education;
minor support also for hospitals and social services.
Fields of interest: Higher education; Education;
Hospitals (general); Human services.
Type of support: Scholarship funds.
Limitations: Giving primarily in the New England
area for higher education; grants to other
organizations mainly in MA, with emphasis on
Boston.
Application information: Scholarship application
forms available at participating educational
institutions. Application form not required.
Initial approach: Letter
Deadline(s): None
Board meeting date(s): As required
Officers and Directors:* Sumner R. Andrews,*
Pres.; Sumner R. Andrews, Jr.,* Treas.; Geoffrey C.
Andrews, Exec. Dir.
Number of staff: 1 part-time professional.
EIN: 042260155

4185
Trefler Foundation ◇
233 Needham St., Rm. 420
Newton, MA 02464 (617) 454-1135
Contact: Pamela Trefler, Tr.

Established in 1997 in MA.
Donors: Alan N. Trefler; Pamela L. Trefler.
Foundation type: Independent foundation.
Financial data (yr. ended 12/31/04): Assets,
$520,732 (M); expenditures, $1,244,953;
qualifying distributions, $958,924; giving activities
include $647,838 for 25 grants (high: $110,000;
low: $435).
Purpose and activities: Giving primarily for
education.
Fields of interest: Education.
Type of support: Scholarships—to individuals.
Limitations: Giving primarily to residents of Boston,
MA.
Application information: Application guidelines
available from the foundation.
Trustees: Alan N. Trefler; Pamela L. Trefler.
EIN: 043369962
Selected grants: The following grants were reported
in 2004.
$110,000 to Center for Teen Empowerment,
Boston, MA.
$50,000 to Boston Foundation, Boston, MA.
$50,000 to Boston Partners in Education, Boston,
MA.
$46,633 to Dorchester High School, Boston, MA.
$33,170 to Fenway High School, Boston, MA.
$32,900 to Cambridge College, Cambridge, MA. 2
grants: $25,000, $7,900
$5,000 to Boston Education Development
Foundation, Boston, MA.
$1,657 to Boston Creative Action, Boston, MA.
$1,000 to Associated Grant Makers, Boston, MA.

4186
The Tupancy-Harris Foundation of 1986
P.O. Box 55806
Boston, MA 02205-5806
Contact: Robert N. Karelitz, V.P., Fiduciary Trust Co.
FAX: (617) 482-2078;
E-mail: karelitz@fiduciary-trust.com; Application
address: 175 Federal St., Boston, MA 02110, tel.:
(617) 482-5270

Established in 1986 in MA.
Donor: Oswald A. Tupancy†.
Foundation type: Independent foundation.
Financial data (yr. ended 12/31/05): Assets,
$25,803,847 (M); expenditures, $1,659,181;
qualifying distributions, $1,427,553; giving
activities include $1,426,289 for 32 grants (high:
$700,000; low: $1,000).
Purpose and activities: Support for the activities of
the Nantucket Conservation Foundation and the
Nantucket Historical Association.
Fields of interest: Media/communications; Historic
preservation/historical societies; Higher education;
Environment, natural resources; Hospitals (general);
Medical research, institute; Human services;
Children/youth, services.
Type of support: Annual campaigns; Capital
campaigns; Building/renovation.
Limitations: Giving limited to Nantucket, MA.
Application information: Application form not
required.
Initial approach: Letter
Copies of proposal: 1
Deadline(s): None
Trustee: Fiduciary Trust Co.
EIN: 046547989
Selected grants: The following grants were reported
in 2004.
$731,887 to Nantucket Conservation Foundation,
Nantucket, MA.
$90,763 to Nantucket Historical Association,
Nantucket, MA.
$50,000 to Nantucket Atheneum, Nantucket, MA.
$20,000 to Nantucket Community Music Center,
Nantucket, MA.
$20,000 to Nantucket Lighthouse School,
Nantucket, MA.
$1,000 to University of Michigan, Ann Arbor, MI.
$1,000 to W G B H Educational Foundation, Boston,
MA.

4187
Ray Tye Medical Aid Foundation ◇
175 Campanelli Dr.
Braintree, MA 02185 (781) 348-8000

Established in 2002 in MA.
Donors: Harvey R. Chaplin; Maurice Halter
Foundation; National Distributing Co., Inc.
Foundation type: Independent foundation.
Financial data (yr. ended 12/31/05): Assets,
$2,035,663 (M); gifts received, $1,071,868;
expenditures, $1,032,654; qualifying distributions,
$936,761; giving activities include $874,008 for 22
grants (high: $302,647; low: $695), and $62,753
for 9 grants to individuals (high: $38,200; low:
$205).
Purpose and activities: Giving primarily to hospitals,
and for the medical care of individuals who are not
otherwise eligible.
Fields of interest: Hospitals (general); Health care.

Limitations: Giving primarily in the Boston, MA, area, including Cambridge; funding also in Cape Cod.

Application information:

Initial approach: Letter

Officers: A. Raymond Tye, Pres.; Eileen Tye, V.P.

EIN: 046958143

4188
Uperetes Foundation ✧ ☆
320 Parker Rd.
Osterville, MA   02655

Established in 1998 in MA.

Donor: John Jendricks.

Foundation type: Independent foundation.

Financial data (yr. ended 6/30/06): Assets, $5,573,163 (M); gifts received, $450,000; expenditures, $7,091,023; qualifying distributions, $7,711,619; giving activities include $7,711,619 for 6 grants (high: $67,719,086,000).

Purpose and activities: Giving primarily to Baptist churches and to Baptist Bible colleges.

Fields of interest: Theological school/education; Education; Protestant agencies & churches.

Limitations: Applications not accepted. Giving on a national basis, with some emphasis on MA. No grants to individuals.

Application information: Contributes only to pre-selected organizations.

Officers and Trustees:* John Jendricks,* Pres.; Elizabeth C. Jendricks,* Treas.

EIN: 770470323

Selected grants: The following grants were reported in 2004.

$66,000 to First Baptist Community Church, Monte Sereno, CA. 2 grants: $31,000 (For missionary trip), $35,000 (For missionary van).

$34,000 to Faith Baptist Church, Osterville, MA. 2 grants: $10,000 (For parsonage building), $24,000 (For general support).

$25,000 to Campbell Christian School, Campbell, CA. For salary support.

4189
The Michael and Helen Valerio Charitable
Remainder Foundation ✧ ☆
4390 Main St.
P.O. Box 193
Cummaquid, MA   02637

Established in 1999 in MA.

Donors: Michael Valerio; Helen Valerio.

Foundation type: Independent foundation.

Financial data (yr. ended 9/30/05): Assets, $2,095,119 (M); gifts received, $460,000; expenditures, $393,338; qualifying distributions, $324,515; giving activities include $324,515 for 1 + grant (high: $264,000).

Fields of interest: Education; Roman Catholic agencies & churches.

Limitations: Applications not accepted. Giving primarily in MA.

Application information: Unsolicited requests for funds not accepted.

Trustees: Helen Valerio; Michael Valerio.

EIN: 046903625

4190
Van Sloun Foundation ✧
Scotch Pine Ln.
P.O. Box 116
Westport, MA   02790
Contact: Neil J. Van Sloun, Tr.

Established in 1991 in MA.

Donors: Neil J. Van Sloun; Sylvia Van Sloun.

Foundation type: Independent foundation.

Financial data (yr. ended 12/31/05): Assets, $6,827,822 (M); gifts received, $329,914; expenditures, $440,724; qualifying distributions, $404,125; giving activities include $379,000 for 49 grants (high: $60,000; low: $250).

Fields of interest: Secondary school/education; Higher education; Environment, natural resources; Animal welfare; Cancer; Cancer research; YM/YWCAs & YM/YWHAs.

Limitations: Giving primarily in MA. No grants to individuals.

Application information:

Initial approach: Letter

Deadline(s): None

Trustees: David B. Titus; Dennis L. Van Sloun; Joseph Van Sloun; Neil J. Van Sloun; Sylvia Van Sloun.

EIN: 046691809

Selected grants: The following grants were reported in 2005.

$25,000 to Minnesota Landscape Arboretum, Chaska, MN.

$20,000 to Berea College, Berea, KY. 2 grants: $10,000 each

$20,000 to University of Pennsylvania, Philadelphia, PA.

$10,000 to Alice Lloyd College, Pippa Passes, KY.

$10,000 to Audubon Society, National, New York, NY.

$10,000 to Connecticut College, New London, CT.

$10,000 to Ducks Unlimited, Memphis, TN.

$10,000 to National Education for Assistance Dog Services (NEADS), West Boylston, MA.

$6,000 to Student Conservation Association, Charlestown, NH.

4191
Robert C. Vance Charitable Foundation
P.O. Box 55886
Boston, MA   02205-5886
Contact: Herbert E. Carlson, Jr., Chair.

Established in 1960 in CT.

Donor: Robert C. Vance†.

Foundation type: Independent foundation.

Financial data (yr. ended 1/31/06): Assets, $8,622,910 (M); expenditures, $436,584; qualifying distributions, $427,363; giving activities include $412,625 for 14 grants (high: $255,525; low: $1,000; average: $2,500–$10,000).

Purpose and activities: Giving primarily for the arts, hospitals, and higher education.

Fields of interest: Museums; Performing arts; Higher education; Education; Hospitals (general); Federated giving programs.

Type of support: Annual campaigns; Capital campaigns; Building/renovation.

Limitations: Giving limited to the New Britain-Berlin, CT, area. No grants to individuals.

Publications: Application guidelines.

Application information: Application form not required.

Deadline(s): None

Officers and Directors:* Herbert E. Carlson, Jr.,* Chair. and Pres.; Cheryl C. Carlson,* Secy.; Rita H. Beaulieu,* Treas.; Robert E. Dragon, M.D.

Trustee: Bank of America, N.A.

EIN: 066050188

Selected grants: The following grants were reported in 2005.

$240,000 to Central Connecticut State University Foundation, New Britain, CT. 2 grants: $225,000, $15,000

$68,000 to United Way.

$25,000 to New Britain Museum of American Art, New Britain, CT.

$5,000 to Mooreland Hill School, Kensington, CT.

4192
The Vingo III Trust ✧
c/o Loring, Wolcott & Coolidge
230 Congress St.
Boston, MA   02110   (617) 434-4644

Established in 1991 in MA.

Foundation type: Independent foundation.

Financial data (yr. ended 12/31/04): Assets, $7,799,027 (M); expenditures, $535,105; qualifying distributions, $434,235; giving activities include $422,049 for 34 grants (high: $200,000; low: $100).

Purpose and activities: Giving primarily for education.

Fields of interest: Museums; Historic preservation/historical societies; Higher education; Education; Environment.

Limitations: Applications not accepted. Giving primarily in MA. No grants to individuals.

Application information: Contributes only to pre-selected organizations.

Trustees: David W. Fitts; Catherine C. Lastavica; John Lastavica.

EIN: 223106692

Selected grants: The following grants were reported in 2003.

$1,022,000 to Trustees of Reservations, Beverly, MA. For general support.

$140,800 to Peabody Essex Museum, Salem, MA. For general support.

$30,000 to Museum of Fine Arts, Boston, MA. For general support.

$10,000 to Essex County Greenbelt Association, Essex, MA. For general support.

$10,000 to Landing School of Boatbuilding and Design, Kennebunkport, ME. For general support.

$5,000 to Tufts University, School of Veterinary Medicine, Medford, MA. For general support.

$2,500 to Isabella Stewart Gardner Museum, Boston, MA. For general support.

$2,000 to Winsor School, Boston, MA. For general support.

$1,000 to North Bennet Street School, Boston, MA. For general support.

$1,000 to Wenham Historical Association and Museum, Wenham, MA. For general support.

4193
Vinik Family Foundation ▼ ✧
67 Byron Rd.
Weston, MA   02493
Contact: Jeffrey N. Vinik, Tr.

Established in 1998 in MA.

Donor: Jeffrey N. Vinik.
Foundation type: Independent foundation.
Financial data (yr. ended 12/31/05): Assets, $61,845,339 (M); gifts received, $34,000,000; expenditures, $3,398,421; qualifying distributions, $3,332,824; giving activities include $3,329,537 for 49 grants (high: $1,137,599; low: $250; average: $2,500–$250,000).
Purpose and activities: Giving primarily for Protestant organizations and human services.
Fields of interest: Human services; Protestant agencies & churches.
Limitations: Applications not accepted. No grants to individuals.
Application information: Contributes only to pre-selected organizations.
Trustees: Jeffrey N. Vinik; Mary Penny Vinik.
EIN: 911917506
Selected grants: The following grants were reported in 2004.
$440,000 to Catholic Foundation of the Archdiocese of Boston, Boston, MA. For general support of Promise for Tomorrow capital fund.
$225,500 to Combined Jewish Philanthropies of Greater Boston, Boston, MA. For general support.
$105,000 to Alliance for Children, Wellesley, MA. For general support.
$50,000 to American Red Cross, National Headquarters, DC. For general support.
$50,000 to Red Sox Foundation, Boston, MA. For general support.
$30,000 to Childrens Fund. For general support and Children's Hospital.
$25,000 to Saint Julia Church, Weston, MA. For general support.
$10,000 to Boston Globe Santa, Boston, MA. For general support of Globe Santa Fund.
$10,000 to Massachusetts Society for the Prevention of Cruelty to Children, Boston, MA. For general support.

4194
George C. Wadleigh Foundation, Inc.
(formerly George C. Wadleigh Home for Aged Men, Inc.)
P.O. Box 226
Groveland, MA 01834
Contact: Edmund J. Cote, Jr., Pres.

Established in 1981 in MA.
Donor: George C. Wadleigh†.
Foundation type: Independent foundation.
Financial data (yr. ended 12/31/05): Assets, $11,947,989 (M); expenditures, $683,767; qualifying distributions, $564,476; giving activities include $549,778 for 17 grants (high: $60,191; low: $8,892).
Purpose and activities: Grants primarily to organizations benefiting aged and indigent individuals in the greater Haverhill, MA, area.
Fields of interest: Human services; Aging, centers/services; Aging.
Type of support: Seed money; Equipment; Building/renovation.
Limitations: Giving primarily in the greater Haverhill, MA, area. No grants to individuals, or for general operating expenses, or research.
Publications: Application guidelines; Informational brochure.
Application information: Application form required.
Initial approach: Letter
Copies of proposal: 1
Deadline(s): Aug. 30

Board meeting date(s): 2nd Tues. of Feb., May, Aug., and Nov.
Final notification: Dec.
Officers and Directors:* Edmund J. Cote, Jr.,* Pres.; A. Bruce McGregor,* Secy.; Richard Cammett,* Treas.; David Hindle; William Kluber; Donald Ruhl; Charles Traver; Zoe Veasey.
Number of staff: None.
EIN: 042720087
Selected grants: The following grants were reported in 2005.
$60,191 to Home Care Associates, Boston, MA.
$60,000 to Elder Services of the Merrimack Valley, Lawrence, MA.
$51,300 to Penacook Place, Haverhill, MA.
$50,000 to Bethany Community Services, Haverhill, MA.
$50,000 to YMCA, Northeast Family, Haverhill, MA.
$40,000 to Community Action, Drop-In Center, Haverhill, MA.
$25,000 to Emmaus, Haverhill, MA.
$25,000 to Housing Support, Newburyport, MA.
$10,440 to VNA Care Network, Danvers, MA.
$10,000 to Rebuilding Together with Christmas in April - Haverhill, Haverhill, MA.

4195
The George R. Wallace Foundation
c/o Goodwin Procter LLP
1 Exchange Pl.
Boston, MA 02109-2881 (617) 570-1735
Contact: William Parizeau, Clerk
E-mail: wparizeau@goodwinprocter.com

Trust established in 1963 in MA.
Donor: George R. Wallace†.
Foundation type: Independent foundation.
Financial data (yr. ended 12/31/05): Assets, $7,591,282 (M); expenditures, $467,382; qualifying distributions, $417,472; giving activities include $370,000 for 8 grants (high: $60,000; low: $10,000).
Purpose and activities: Support for education, particularly for programs that benefit low-income students. Giving also for museums and libraries, particularly those serving the Fitchburg/Leominster, MA, area.
Fields of interest: Arts; Higher education; Education; Environment, natural resources; Human services.
Type of support: General/operating support; Annual campaigns; Capital campaigns; Building/renovation; Equipment; Endowments; Seed money; Matching/challenge support.
Limitations: Giving primarily in the Fitchburg, MA, area. No support for religious organizations, except for grants to support the education of disadvantaged and/or disabled children. No grants to individuals, or for scholarships or fellowships; no loans.
Application information: Application form not required.
Initial approach: Letter, telephone or e-mail
Copies of proposal: 4
Deadline(s): None
Board meeting date(s): Semiannually
Final notification: 6 months
Officer and Trustees:* William M. Parizeau,* Clerk; Andre A. Gelinas; John Grado, Jr.; Regina M. Pisa.
EIN: 046130518

4196
The Walske Charitable Foundation ◇
(formerly Walske-Longtine Foundation)
164 Chestnut Hill Rd.
Chestnut Hill, MA 02467 (617) 738-6948
Contact: Steven C. Walske, Tr.
Application address: 263 Hammond St., Chestnut Hill, MA 02467-3950

Established in 1997 in MA.
Donor: Steven Walske.
Foundation type: Independent foundation.
Financial data (yr. ended 12/31/05): Assets, $5,878,658 (M); expenditures, $336,333; qualifying distributions, $336,333; giving activities include $336,333 for 16 grants (high: $50,000; low: $2,500).
Fields of interest: Museums; Historic preservation/historical societies; Higher education, college; Education; Reproductive health, family planning; Women, centers/services; Urban/community development.
Limitations: Giving primarily in Boston, MA.
Application information: Application form not required.
Trustees: Jennifer C. Walske; Steven C. Walske.
EIN: 046818329
Selected grants: The following grants were reported in 2005.
$50,000 to Isabella Stewart Gardner Museum, Boston, MA.
$50,000 to Park School, Brookline, MA.
$50,000 to Princeton University, Princeton, NJ.
$38,000 to Boston Ballet, Boston, MA.
$33,333 to W G B H Educational Foundation, Boston, MA.
$30,000 to Commonwealth School, Boston, MA.
$25,000 to Max Warburg Courage Curriculum, Boston, MA.
$10,000 to Babson College, Babson Park, MA.
$10,000 to Harvard University, Cambridge, MA.
$7,500 to Beaver Country Day School, Chestnut Hill, MA.

4197
The Wang Foundation ◇
c/o Goodwin, Proctor & Hoar LLP
Exchange Pl.
Boston, MA 02109-2881
Contact: Mary Kathleen O'Connell, Tr.

Established in 1987 in MA.
Donor: An Wang†.
Foundation type: Independent foundation.
Financial data (yr. ended 12/31/05): Assets, $7,924,328 (M); expenditures, $556,076; qualifying distributions, $494,619; giving activities include $482,050 for 35 grants (high: $110,000; low: $100).
Fields of interest: Education; Hospitals (general); Health care; YM/YWCAs & YM/YWHAs.
Limitations: Applications not accepted. Giving on a national basis, with some emphasis on the greater metropolitan Boston, MA, area. No grants to individuals.
Application information: Contributes only to pre-selected organizations.
Trustees: Juliette W. Coombs; Mary Kathleen O'Connell; Courtney S. Wang; Frederick A. Wang; Lorraine C. Wang.
EIN: 222858458
Selected grants: The following grants were reported in 2004.

$111,000 to Hockaday School, Dallas, TX.
$100,000 to YMCA.
$25,000 to Boston Chinatown Neighborhood Center, Boston, MA.
$25,000 to Crystal Charity Ball, Dallas, TX.
$25,000 to Governor Dummer Academy, Byfield, MA.
$25,000 to YMCA of Greater Boston, Boston, MA.
$20,000 to Primary Source, Watertown, MA.
$5,000 to John F. Kennedy Library Foundation, Boston, MA.
$2,500 to Wellesley College, Wellesley, MA.

4198
Bernard E. & Edith B. Waterman Charitable Foundation ◇

(formerly Waterman Broadcasting Corporation Charitable Foundation)
370 Main St., Ste. 1250
Worcester, MA 01608
Contact: Arthur H. Miller, Tr.
FAX: (508) 791-1201; E-mail: amiller@ftwlaw.com

Established in 1984 in MA.
Donors: Bernard E. Waterman; Waterman Broadcasting Corp.
Foundation type: Independent foundation.
Financial data (yr. ended 6/30/05): Assets, $1,594,616 (M); gifts received, $350,000; expenditures, $1,003,431; qualifying distributions, $1,002,810; giving activities include $1,002,500 for 5 grants (high: $1,000,000; low: $500).
Fields of interest: Education; Environment; Medical research, institute; Genetics/birth defects research; Cancer research; Christian agencies & churches.
Type of support: General/operating support; Scholarship funds.
Limitations: Applications not accepted. Giving on a national basis. No grants to individuals.
Application information: Contributes only to pre-selected organizations.
Board meeting date(s): As required
Trustees: Arthur H. Miller; Bernard E. Waterman; Edith B. Waterman.
EIN: 223088264

4199
Stanley W. Watson Foundation ◇

c/o William K. Mackey
P.O. Box 901
Falmouth, MA 02541

Established in 1997 in MA.
Donor: Stanley W. Watson.
Foundation type: Independent foundation.
Financial data (yr. ended 12/31/04): Assets, $34,846,470 (M); expenditures, $1,608,831; qualifying distributions, $1,343,750; giving activities include $1,343,500 for 13 grants (high: $800,000; low: $1,000).
Purpose and activities: Giving primarily to local charities.
Fields of interest: Education; Health care; Marine science.
Limitations: Applications not accepted. Giving primarily in MA. No grants to individuals.
Application information: Contributes only to pre-selected organizations.
Trustees: William K. Mackey; Frederica W. Valois.
EIN: 223100750

Selected grants: The following grants were reported in 2003.
$810,500 to Woods Hole Oceanographic Institution, Woods Hole, MA.
$375,000 to Cape Cod Community College Educational Foundation, West Barnstable, MA.
$101,000 to Visiting Nurses Association, South Dennis, MA.
$100,000 to Falmouth Hospital Foundation, Falmouth, MA.
$75,000 to Penikese Island School, Woods Hole, MA.
$50,000 to Cape Cod Free Clinic in Falmouth, Falmouth, MA.
$25,000 to Falmouth Service Center, Falmouth, MA.
$25,000 to Historic Highfield, Falmouth, MA.
$25,000 to Woods Hole Research Center, Woods Hole, MA.
$1,500 to Woods Hole Community Association, Woods Hole, MA.

4200
The Frederick E. Weber Charities Corporation ◇

175 Federal St.
Boston, MA 02110 (617) 292-6264
Contact: Mary Ann Daily, Pres.

Incorporated in 1902 in MA.
Donor: Frederick E. Weber†.
Foundation type: Independent foundation.
Financial data (yr. ended 3/31/05): Assets, $7,259,599 (L); expenditures, $470,866; qualifying distributions, $408,841; giving activities include $369,500 for 59 grants (high: $50,000; low: $1,000).
Purpose and activities: Giving primarily to social service agencies for emergency financial assistance to indigent families or individuals.
Fields of interest: Hospitals (general); Health care; Food services; Nutrition; Children/youth, services; Family services; Homeless, human services; Federated giving programs; Economically disadvantaged; Homeless.
Type of support: Emergency funds; Grants to individuals.
Limitations: Giving limited to MA, with emphasis on Boston. No grants for research, capital projects, or equipment.
Publications: Annual report; Program policy statement.
Application information: Application form not required.
Initial approach: Letter
Copies of proposal: 1
Deadline(s): None
Board meeting date(s): Weekly except in Aug.
Final notification: 30 days
Officers: Mary Ann Daily, Pres.; Daniel A. Phillips, V.P. and Treas.; Janet W. Eustis, Clerk.
Directors: Lawrence Coolidge; Mary Huse; William C. Swan; Daniel P. Wise.
Number of staff: 1 part-time support.
EIN: 042133244

4201
Edwin S. Webster Foundation ◇

c/o Grants Mgmt. Assocs., Inc.
77 Summer St., 8th Fl.
Boston, MA 02110 (617) 426-7080
Contact: Michelle Jenney

FAX: (617) 426-7087;
E-mail: mjenney@grants.management.com

Established in 1948 in MA.
Donor: Edwin S. Webster†.
Foundation type: Independent foundation.
Financial data (yr. ended 12/31/04): Assets, $35,712,580 (M); expenditures, $2,221,677; qualifying distributions, $2,162,785; giving activities include $2,135,000 for 60 grants (high: $150,000; low: $5,000).
Purpose and activities: Giving primarily for education, arts, medicine, and human services.
Fields of interest: Arts; Education; Hospitals (general); Medical research, institute; Human services; Children/youth, services; Minorities/immigrants, centers/services; Minorities.
Type of support: General/operating support; Capital campaigns; Building/renovation; Endowments; Program development; Research.
Limitations: Giving primarily in New England, with an emphasis on the Boston, MA, area. No grants to individuals, or for emergency funds, deficit financing, publications, or conferences; no loans.
Publications: Application guidelines.
Application information: The foundation supports organizations that are well-known to the trustees. Application form not required.
Initial approach: Proposal
Copies of proposal: 1
Deadline(s): Submit proposal preferably by Apr. 15 or Sept. 30
Board meeting date(s): June and Dec.
Final notification: 15 days after meetings on grant proposals
Officer and Trustees:* Richard Harte, Jr.,* Secy.; Henry U. Harris, Jr.; Henry U. Harris III; Alexander W. Hiam.
Number of staff: 1 part-time professional.
EIN: 046000647
Selected grants: The following grants were reported in 2004.
$150,000 to Massachusetts General Hospital, Boston, MA.
$150,000 to New England Aquarium, Boston, MA.
$100,000 to United Way of Massachusetts Bay, Boston, MA.
$100,000 to Woods Hole Oceanographic Institution, Woods Hole, MA.
$80,000 to Museum of Science, Boston, MA.
$70,000 to United Negro College Fund, Boston, MA.
$50,000 to New York Botanical Garden, Bronx, NY.
$30,000 to Brigham and Womens Hospital, Boston, MA.
$25,000 to Medical College of Hampton Roads, Norfolk, VA.
$20,000 to Portland Concert Association, Portland, ME.

4202
The John F. Welch, Jr. Foundation ◇

40 Beacon St., Ste. 300
Boston, MA 02108-3614

Established in 1986 in CT.
Donors: John F. Welch, Jr.; Executive Focus International; General Electric, Inc.
Foundation type: Independent foundation.
Financial data (yr. ended 12/31/05): Assets, $16,569,635 (M); gifts received, $76,170; expenditures, $1,443,222; qualifying distributions, $1,413,550; giving activities include $1,413,550 for 122 grants (high: $120,000; low: $150).

Purpose and activities: Giving primarily for human services, higher education, and hospitals.

Fields of interest: Higher education; Hospitals (general); Human services; Children/youth, services; Federated giving programs; Roman Catholic agencies & churches.

Limitations: Applications not accepted. Giving primarily in CT, including Bridgeport, and Fairfield; some giving also in MA, NY, and elsewhere in the U.S. No grants to individuals.

Application information: Contributes only to pre-selected organizations.

Trustee: John F. Welch, Jr.

EIN: 222801492

Selected grants: The following grants were reported in 2004.

$100,000 to Nantucket Cottage Hospital, Nantucket, MA.

$100,000 to National Center for the American Revolution, Wayne, PA.

$100,000 to New York City Leadership Academy, New York, NY.

$50,000 to American Red Cross, National Headquarters, DC.

$50,000 to Cardinal Shehan Center, Bridgeport, CT.

$25,000 to Elfun Community Foundation, Fairfield, CT.

$25,000 to Inner-City Foundation for Charity and Education, Bridgeport, CT.

$10,000 to Student Sponsor Partners, New York, NY.

$5,000 to Cincinnati Childrens Hospital Medical Center, Cincinnati, OH.

$4,000 to Winchester Community Music School, Winchester, MA.

4203
Weld Foundation ◇

c/o Loring, Wolcott & Coolidge
230 Congress St.
Boston, MA 02110-2437

Trust established in 1952 in MA.

Donor: Mary Weld Pingree†.

Foundation type: Independent foundation.

Financial data (yr. ended 12/31/05): Assets, $9,823,200 (M); expenditures, $519,865; qualifying distributions, $483,017; giving activities include $477,000 for 17 grants (high: $125,000; low: $1,000).

Purpose and activities: Giving primarily for education and museums; support also for health and social services.

Fields of interest: Museums; Elementary/secondary education; Secondary school/education; Environment, natural resources; Health care; Religion.

Limitations: Applications not accepted. Giving primarily in MA. No grants to individuals.

Application information: Contributes only to pre-selected organizations.

Trustees: Frederick D. Ballou; Peter B. Loring; Charles W. Pingree.

EIN: 046039173

Selected grants: The following grants were reported in 2004.

$150,000 to Pingree School, South Hamilton, MA.

$125,000 to Essex Institute, Salem, MA.

$50,000 to North Shore Medical Center, Salem, MA.

$30,000 to Maine Coast Heritage Trust, Topsham, ME.

$30,000 to Schepens Eye Research Institute, Boston, MA.

$20,000 to Spaulding Rehabilitation Hospital, Boston, MA.

$15,000 to Massachusetts General Hospital, Boston, MA.

$15,000 to United Way of Massachusetts Bay, Boston, MA.

$10,000 to Windrush Farm Therapeutic Equitation, Boxford, MA.

$1,000 to North Haven Historical Society, North Haven, ME.

4204
David P. Wheatland Charitable Trust ◇

c/o Acadia Mgmt. Co., Inc.
111 Devonshire St., Ste. 620
Boston, MA 02109 (617) 426-5755
Contact: Richard Wheatland, Tr.

Established in 1993 in MA.

Donor: David P. Wheatland Trust.

Foundation type: Independent foundation.

Financial data (yr. ended 12/31/05): Assets, $8,043,236 (M); expenditures, $364,709; qualifying distributions, $364,709; giving activities include $332,500 for 6 grants (high: $100,000; low: $2,500).

Purpose and activities: Giving primarily to a museum of art, architecture and culture, as well as for a university historical science center; funding also for a marine mammal center.

Fields of interest: Museums (art); Historical activities; Animal welfare; Foundations (community).

Type of support: General/operating support.

Limitations: Giving primarily in MA. No grants to individuals.

Application information: Preference given to organizations historically supported by the donor and members of his family.

Deadline(s): None

Trustees: Eileen M. Balthazard; Timothy B. Biglow; Martha W. Lunt; Peter O. Stauffer; Barbara Wheatland; Rebecca Wheatland; Richard Wheatland.

EIN: 046744379

Selected grants: The following grants were reported in 2003.

$150,000 to Peabody Essex Museum, Salem, MA. 2 grants: $100,000 (For building fund), $50,000 (For Gardner Pingree House Endowment).

$125,000 to Harvard University, Cambridge, MA. For relocation of historical scientific instruments.

$25,000 to Essex County Community Foundation, Danvers, MA. For general support.

$22,000 to Marine Mammal Center, Sausalito, CA. For capital improvements.

4205
The Wilson Family Foundation ◇

c/o Fortis Management Group, LLC
20 Walnut St., Ste. 313
Wellesley Hills, MA 02481

Established in 1994 in MA.

Donors: James M. Wilson; M. Jane Wilson.

Foundation type: Independent foundation.

Financial data (yr. ended 4/30/05): Assets, $2,432,642 (M); expenditures, $976,075; qualifying distributions, $963,805; giving activities

include $963,805 for 12 grants (high: $250,000; low: $1,000).

Purpose and activities: Giving for the performing arts and cultural institutes, and children, youth, and social services.

Fields of interest: Performing arts, ballet; Education; Boys & girls clubs; Salvation Army; Children/youth, services.

Limitations: Applications not accepted. Giving primarily in Boston, MA. No grants to individuals.

Application information: Contributes only to pre-selected organizations.

Trustees: James M. Wilson; M. Jane Wilson.

EIN: 046773530

Selected grants: The following grants were reported in 2004.

$324,100 to Boston Ballet, Boston, MA.

$267,000 to Salvation Army of Boston, Boston, MA.

$167,000 to Trinity Church, Boston, MA.

$167,000 to United Way of Massachusetts Bay, Boston, MA.

$85,000 to Park School, Brookline, MA.

$25,000 to Handel and Haydn Society, Boston, MA.

$20,000 to International Institute of Boston, Boston, MA.

$10,000 to Cambridge in America, New York, NY.

$18 to Boston Ventures, Boston, MA.

4206
Louis E. Wolfson Foundation

c/o Gilmore, Rees & Carlson, PC
20 Walnut St., Ste. 200
Wellesley, MA 02481-2104
Contact: Paul Bishop

Trust established in 1951 in MA.

Donor: Louis E. Wolfson, M.D.†.

Foundation type: Independent foundation.

Financial data (yr. ended 6/30/05): Assets, $24,755,494 (M); expenditures, $1,344,266; qualifying distributions, $1,207,109; giving activities include $1,050,000 for 3 grants (high: $350,000; low: $350,000).

Purpose and activities: Two-thirds of income is restricted to the support of student aid endowments at the medical schools of Boston University, Harvard University, and Tufts University; remaining grants generally restricted to supporting the education of M.D. degree candidates at medical schools.

Fields of interest: Medical school/education.

Limitations: Giving primarily in Boston, MA. No grants to individuals.

Publications: Application guidelines.

Application information: Generally contributes to pre-selected organizations. Application form required.

Initial approach: Letter
Copies of proposal: 1
Deadline(s): None
Board meeting date(s): Varies; grants paid in late fall and in early spring
Final notification: Within 3 months

Trustees: Henry H. Banks, M.D.; Aram Chobanian, M.D.; Herbert Cohne; Albert F. Cullen; Jules Dienstag, M.D.; Jack London; John Penn, M.D.

Number of staff: 1 part-time support.

EIN: 046053295

Selected grants: The following grants were reported in 2003.

$350,027 to Boston University, School of Medicine, Boston, MA.

$350,027 to Harvard University, School of Medicine, Cambridge, MA.

$350,027 to Tufts University, School of Medicine, Medford, MA.

4207
The Wood Foundation of Chambersburg, PA ✧
1 Brattle Sq., 4th Fl.
Cambridge, MA   02138
Contact: C.O. Wood III, Dir.

Established in 1989 as successor foundation to the Wood Foundation of Chambersburg, PA.
Foundation type: Independent foundation.
Financial data (yr. ended 12/31/05): Assets, $8,793,412 (M); expenditures, $854,406; qualifying distributions, $796,190; giving activities include $743,445 for 37 grants (high: $113,334; low: $500).
Purpose and activities: Giving primarily for the arts and human services.
Fields of interest: Museums; Arts; Secondary school/education; Higher education; Hospitals (general); Human services.
Limitations: Giving primarily in Chambersburg and Franklin counties, PA.
Application information: Application form not required.
Initial approach: Proposal
Deadline(s): None
Directors: Emilie W. Robinson; C.O. Wood III; David S. Wood; Miriam M. Wood.
EIN: 251607838
Selected grants: The following grants were reported in 2003.
$360,433 to Franklin County Foundation to Improve Resources for Students, Russellville, AL. 5 grants: $25,000 (For building construction), $50,000 (For Youth Arts Initiative), $89,600 (For Center Stage Theater), $133,333 (For endowment), $62,500.
$25,000 to Aurora Theater Company, Berkeley, CA.
$25,000 to Celebrity Series of Boston, Boston, MA. For endowment campaign.
$20,000 to Community Foundation of the Eastern Shore, Salisbury, MD. For unrestricted support.
$15,000 to Isabella Stewart Gardner Museum, Boston, MA. For annual support.
$12,500 to Winterthur Museum, Garden and Library, Winterthur, DE.

4208
Charles O. Wood III & Miriam M. Wood Foundation ✧ ☆
c/o Wood Holdings
1 Brattle Sq.
Cambridge, MA   02138

Established in 1987 in PA.
Donors: Charles O. Wood III; Miriam M. Wood.
Foundation type: Independent foundation.
Financial data (yr. ended 12/31/05): Assets, $768,097 (M); expenditures, $340,897; qualifying distributions, $339,112; giving activities include $339,112 for 59 grants (high: $125,000; low: $55).
Purpose and activities: Giving to art and cultural institutes, and to higher education.
Fields of interest: Museums; Arts; Higher education; Education; Human services; Federated giving programs.
Type of support: Annual campaigns; Equipment.

Limitations: Applications not accepted. Giving on a national basis, with emphasis on MA and FL. No grants to individuals.
Application information: Contributes only to pre-selected organizations.
Trustees: Charles O. Wood III; Miriam M. Wood.
EIN: 251568770
Selected grants: The following grants were reported in 2004.
$125,000 to Harvard University, Art Museums, Cambridge, MA.
$5,000 to Hockaday School, Dallas, TX.
$5,000 to Wellesley College, Wellesley, MA. For annual campaign.
$2,112 to Museum of Fine Arts, Boston, MA.
$1,000 to Handel and Haydn Society, Boston, MA.
$430 to Whitney Museum of American Art, New York, NY.
$200 to W B U R, Boston, MA.
$125 to W G B H Educational Foundation, Boston, MA.
$75 to Museum of Modern Art, New York, NY.
$25 to Metropolitan Museum of Art, New York, NY.

4209
Greater Worcester Community Foundation, Inc. ✧
370 Main St., Ste. 650
Worcester, MA   01608-1738   (508) 755-0980
Contact: Ann T. Lisi, Exec. Dir.; For grants: Kerry L. Conaghan, Grants Mgr.
FAX: (508) 755-3406;
E-mail: gwcf@greaterworcester.org; Additional
E-mail: atlisi@greaterworcester.org; Grant application E-mail: conaghan@greaterworcester.org;
URL: http://www.greaterworcester.org

Incorporated in 1975 in MA.
Foundation type: Community foundation.
Financial data (yr. ended 12/31/05): Assets, $108,413,915 (M); gifts received, $3,491,861; expenditures, $5,097,779; giving activities include $3,719,620 for 321 grants, and $435,128 for 322 grants to individuals.
Purpose and activities: The foundation's mission is to increase philanthropy and build healthy and vibrant communities throughout Central Massachusetts. The foundation achieves its mission in four primary ways: 1) works with donor on tailored giving programs; 2) invests in local nonprofit organizations through grants and technical support; 3) convenes people and organizations with shared goals to solve problems; and 4) safeguards the assets in its trust.
Fields of interest: Humanities; Arts; Medical school/education; Nursing school/education; Education; Environment; Health care; Health organizations, association; Crime/violence prevention, abuse prevention; Housing/shelter, development; Youth development; Children/youth, services; Family services; Aging, centers/services; Homeless, human services; Human services; Community development; Government/public administration; Public affairs; Aging; Disabilities, people with; African Americans/Blacks; AIDS, people with; Economically disadvantaged; Homeless.
Type of support: Program development; Seed money; Scholarship funds; Technical assistance; Program evaluation; Scholarships—to individuals.
Limitations: Giving limited to Worcester County, MA. No grants to individuals (except for designated

scholarship funds), or for general operating expenses, capital campaigns, or endowments.
Publications: Application guidelines; Annual report; Newsletter.
Application information: Visit foundation Web site for application forms and guidelines. Faxed or e-mailed applications are not accepted. Scholarships are for residents of Worcester County, MA, only. Application form required.
Initial approach: Telephone
Copies of proposal: 2
Deadline(s): Mar. 15 and Sept. 15 for discretionary grants; varies for others
Board meeting date(s): Monthly
Final notification: 3 months
Officers and Directors:* Robert K. "Ross" Dik,* Pres.; James E. Collins,* V.P.; Ellen S. Dunlap,* Clerk; Dix F. Davis,* Treas.; Ann T. Lisi, Exec. Dir.; Sara Trillo Adams; Pamela K. Boisvert; Daniel de la Torre, Jr.; Warner S. Fletcher; Gerald "Lee" Gaudette III; Dennis Gorman; Mary E. Kett; Peter H. Levine, M.D.; Janet Wilson Moore; Frederic H. Mulligan; Martha R. Pappas; Paul R. Rossley; R. Joseph Salois; Roberta R. Schaefer; Robert L. Thomas; Carlton A. Watson.
Distribution Committee: Brian M. Chandley; Bettina M. Cullina; Richard P. Cusson; John C. Fray, Ph.D.; Kevin R. Kearney.
Number of staff: 7 full-time professional; 2 full-time support; 1 part-time support.
EIN: 042572276

4210
Woronoco Savings Charitable Foundation ✧
c/o Berkshire Bank
24 North St.
Pittsfield, MA   01201   (413) 236-3195
Contact: Wayne Patenaude

Established in 1999 in MA.
Donor: Woronoco Savings Bank.
Foundation type: Company-sponsored foundation.
Financial data (yr. ended 12/31/03): Assets, $13,813,386 (M); expenditures, $713,989; qualifying distributions, $704,908; giving activities include $670,144 for 87 grants (high: $225,000; low: $100).
Purpose and activities: The foundation supports organizations involved with education, human services, and community development.
Fields of interest: Education; Boys & girls clubs; Human services; Community development.
Limitations: Applications not accepted. Giving limited to western MA. No support for religious organizations or fraternal organizations. No grants to individuals.
Application information: Contributes only to pre-selected organizations.
Board meeting date(s): 3rd Wed. every other month
Officers and Directors:* Agastino J. Calheno,* Pres.; Debra L. Murphy,* Treas.; Barbara Braem, Exec. Dir.; William Aiken; Cornelius D. Mahoney; Ann V. Schultz; D. Jeffrey Templeton; Richard Pomeroy.
EIN: 043458037

4211
Yawkey Foundation II ▼ ✧
(also known as The Jean R. Yawkey Foundation)
990 Washington St.
Dedham, MA 02026-6716 (781) 329-7470
Contact: Nancy Keilty-Brodnicki
URL: http://www.yawkeyfoundation.org

Established in 1983 in MA.
Donor: Jean R. Yawkey†.
Foundation type: Independent foundation.
Financial data (yr. ended 12/31/05): Assets, $458,492,742 (M); gifts received, $2,000,000; expenditures, $47,382,051; qualifying distributions, $43,274,811; giving activities include $41,114,600 for 310 grants.
Purpose and activities: The mission of the foundation is to make grants that provide an immediate, significant and positive impact on the quality of life of youth, families and the underserved.
Fields of interest: Arts; Higher education; Adult education—literacy, basic skills & GED; Scholarships/financial aid; Education, services; Education; Environment; Animals/wildlife; Hospitals (general); Health care; Housing/shelter; Recreation; Human services; Children/youth, services; Children/youth; Economically disadvantaged.
Type of support: Scholarship funds.
Limitations: Giving primarily in MA, with emphasis on the greater metropolitan Boston area. Generally, no support for private foundations, political, fraternal, trade, civic or labor organizations, religious organizations for sectarian purposes, public schools or districts, charter schools, community or economic development corporations or programs, advocacy groups, pass-through or intermediary organizations, or workforce development programs. No grants to individuals.

Generally, no grants for operating deficits, retirement of debt, endowments, capital campaigns, events, conferences, seminars, group travel, awards, prizes, monuments, music, video, or film production, feasibility or research studies.
Application information: The foundation encourages applicants to review grant guidelines on the foundation Web site prior to applying for grants. Application form not required.
  Initial approach: Letter of inquiry (no more than 2 pages)
  Deadline(s): None
  Final notification: 60 days
Officer and Trustees:* John L. Harrington,* Pres.; Eleanor S. Armstrong; Charles I. Clough, Jr.; William B. Gutfarb; Rev. Ray Hammond; James P. Healey; Edward F. Kenney; James G. Maguire; Judy Walden Scarafile.
EIN: 042768239
Selected grants: The following grants were reported in 2005.
$4,000,000 to Boston College, Chestnut Hill, MA. 2 grants: $1,000,000 (For education and student programming), $3,000,000 (For construction of Athletic Center).
$3,000,000 to Massachusetts General Hospital, Boston, MA. For construction of outpatient care center.
$1,000,000 to Catholic Charities Archdiocese of Boston, Boston, MA. For construction of multi-service community center.
$525,000 to Emmanuel College, Boston, MA. For construction of student center.
$500,000 to After-School for All Partnership, Boston, MA. For school site and faith-based after-school education programs.

$500,000 to Georgetown County Memorial Hospital, Georgetown, SC. For construction of new medical center for cancer patients.
$500,000 to Melmark New England, Woburn, MA. For construction and renovation project.
$475,000 to National Baseball Hall of Fame and Museum, Cooperstown, NY. For preservation and archiving projects at museum.
$400,000 to Cape Cod Baseball League, Yarmouth Port, MA. For field improvement project and support for young men's summer baseball league.

4212
Zwanziger/Goldstein Foundation ✧
148 Dartmouth St.
West Newton, MA 02465

Established in 1994 in MA.
Donors: Orit Goldstein; Ron Zwanziger; Jeffrey Goldstein; Janet Zwanziger.
Foundation type: Independent foundation.
Financial data (yr. ended 12/31/05): Assets, $764,611 (M); gifts received, $75,218; expenditures, $482,562; qualifying distributions, $474,390; giving activities include $471,868 for 34 grants (high: $250,000; low: $36).
Purpose and activities: Giving primarily to hospitals, Jewish agencies, and for education.
Fields of interest: Education; Hospitals (general); Human services; Jewish agencies & temples.
Limitations: Applications not accepted. Giving primarily in MA. No grants to individuals.
Application information: Contributes only to pre-selected organizations.
Trustees: Michael L. Brown; Jeffrey Goldstein; Orit Goldstein; Janet Zwanziger; Ron Zwanziger.
EIN: 043246337

MICHIGAN

4213

Talbert & Leota Abrams Foundation
P.O. Box 27337
Lansing, MI 48909-7337
Contact: Joe C. Foster, Jr., Secy.

Established in 1960 in MI.
Donors: Leota Abrams†; Talbert Abrams†.
Foundation type: Independent foundation.
Financial data (yr. ended 12/31/05): Assets,
$9,924,766 (M); expenditures, $569,091;
qualifying distributions, $442,417; giving activities
include $326,500 for 10 grants (high: $144,000;
low: $2,000).
Purpose and activities: Support primarily for a
library and an educational science program; giving
also for universities and colleges and community
funds.
Fields of interest: Higher education; Adult education
—literacy, basic skills & GED; Libraries/library
science; Education, reading; Federated giving
programs.
Type of support: Program development; Scholarship
funds; Research.
Limitations: Giving primarily in central MI. No
support for churches for sectarian use, or for athletic
activities. No grants to individuals, or for operating
or traveling expenses; no loans.
Publications: Annual report.
Application information: Application form not
required.
Initial approach: 2-page letter
Copies of proposal: 1
Deadline(s): May 31 for next calendar year
Board meeting date(s): June
Officers and Directors:* Barbara J. Brown,* Pres.;
Kyle C. Abbott,* Exec. V.P.; Joe C. Foster, Jr.,*
Secy.; Craig C. Brown,* Treas.; Shane A. Patzer;
Tiffany L. Patzer.
Number of staff: 5 part-time professional.
EIN: 386082194
Selected grants: The following grants were reported
in 2005.
$144,000 to Library of Michigan Foundation,
Lansing, MI.
$10,500 to Michigan Historical Center Foundation,
Lansing, MI.
$6,000 to Lansing Community College Foundation,
Lansing, MI.
$5,000 to Junior Achievement, East Lansing, MI.
$5,000 to Rotary Club of Lansing Foundation,
Lansing, MI.
$2,000 to Michigan State University, East Lansing,
MI.

4214

James C. Acheson Foundation ☆
c/o Donna Niester
600 Fort St., Ste. 101
Port Huron, MI 48060

Established in 1999 in MI.
Donor: James C. Acheson.
Foundation type: Independent foundation.
Financial data (yr. ended 12/31/04): Assets,
$16,482,673 (M); gifts received, $10,000;
expenditures, $998,774; qualifying distributions,

$899,635; giving activities include $864,844 for 13
grants (high: $660,000; low: $450).
Purpose and activities: Support for the arts, health,
the environment, human services, and community
development.
Fields of interest: Museums; Environment; Health
care; Mental health/crisis services; Human
services; American Red Cross; Community
development; Federated giving programs.
Limitations: Applications not accepted. Giving
primarily in MI. No grants to individuals.
Application information: Contributes only to
pre-selected organizations.
Officers: James C. Acheson, Pres.; Douglas R.
Austin, Secy.-Treas.; Donna M. Niester, Mgr.
EIN: 383463509

4215

**The Ann and Bob Aikens Family
Foundation** ◇ ☆
(formerly The Aikens Family Foundation)
350 N. Old Woodward, Ste. 300
Birmingham, MI 48009

Established in 1999 in MI.
Foundation type: Independent foundation.
Financial data (yr. ended 11/30/05): Assets,
$678,108 (M); expenditures, $334,485; qualifying
distributions, $324,167; giving activities include
$322,855 for 15 grants (high: $100,000; low:
$200).
Fields of interest: Higher education; Education;
Environment; Hospitals (general); Health care;
Christian agencies & churches.
Limitations: Applications not accepted. Giving on a
national basis. No grants to individuals.
Application information: Contributes only to
pre-selected organizations.
Officers and Directors:* Robert B. Aikens,* Pres.;
Kimberly Aikens Levanovich, Secy.; Ann S. Aikens,*
Treas.
EIN: 383475628
Selected grants: The following grants were reported
in 2005.
$59,105 to Christ Church Cranbrook, Bloomfield
Hills, MI.
$5,000 to Our Lady of the Mississippi Abbey,
Dubuque, IA.
$1,250 to Little Traverse Conservancy, Harbor
Springs, MI.
$1,000 to Jackson Hole Land Trust, Jackson, WY.
$1,000 to National Museum of Wildlife Art, Jackson,
WY.

4216

The Alix Foundation
(formerly Jay & Maryanne Alix Foundation)
c/o Jean A. Wiley
2000 Town Ctr., Ste. 2400
Southfield, MI 48075
E-mail: jwiley@alixpartners.com

Established in 1994 in MI.
Donors: Jay Alix; Maryanne Alix†.
Foundation type: Independent foundation.
Financial data (yr. ended 12/31/04): Assets,
$1,059,559 (M); gifts received, $1,140,603;
expenditures, $1,348,591; qualifying distributions,
$1,347,080; giving activities include $1,344,782
for 23 grants (high: $110,000; low: $250).

Purpose and activities: Giving primarily for health
care, with an emphasis on cancer; funding also for
education and human services.
Fields of interest: Elementary/secondary
education; Higher education; Health care; Cancer;
Human services; Jewish agencies & temples.
Limitations: Applications not accepted. Giving
primarily in MI. No grants to individuals.
Application information: Contributes only to
pre-selected organizations.
Officers: Jay Alix, Pres.; Jean Wiley, Secy.
EIN: 383171122
Selected grants: The following grants were reported
in 2003.
$76,500 to Lighthouse P.A.T.H., Pontiac, MI. For
general support.
$50,000 to Common Ground, Royal Oak, MI. For
general support.
$50,000 to Henry Ford Health System, Detroit, MI.
$33,334 to Heinz C. Prechter Bipolar Research
Fund, Southgate, MI.
$25,000 to Teikyo Post University, Waterbury, CT.
$25,000 to William J. Clinton Presidential
Foundation, Little Rock, AR.
$20,000 to Edison Institute, Dearborn, MI.
$20,000 to Interfaith Hospitality Network of Greater
Grand Rapids, Grand Rapids, MI.
$15,167 to Detroit Country Day School, Beverly
Hills, MI.
$10,000 to Michigan State University, East Lansing,
MI.

4217

Allen Foundation, Inc.
P.O. Box 1606
Midland, MI 48641-1606
Contact: Dale Baum, Secy.
FAX: (989) 832-8842; *URL:* http://
www.allenfoundation.org/

Established in 1975 in MI.
Foundation type: Independent foundation.
Financial data (yr. ended 12/31/05): Assets,
$12,283,170 (M); expenditures, $412,450;
qualifying distributions, $349,763; giving activities
include $337,641 for 7 grants (high: $79,828; low:
$15,190).

Purpose and activities: The foundation focuses on
projects that benefit nutritional programs in the
areas of education, training and research. A lower
priority is given to proposals that help solve
immediate or emergency hunger and malnutrition
problems.
Fields of interest: Higher education; Hospitals
(general); Nutrition.
Limitations: Giving on a national basis. No grants to
individuals.
Publications: Application guidelines; Annual report;
Grants list.
Application information: Application forms and
latest information available on foundation Web site.
All applications are to be submitted online.
Application form not required.
Initial approach: See Web site
Deadline(s): Dec. 31
Board meeting date(s): Annually
Final notification: June
Officers and Trustees:* Gail E. Lanphear,* Chair.;
Mark Ostahowski, M.D.*, Pres.; William
Lauderbach,* V.P., Finance; Dale Baum,* Secy.;
William James Allen; Laurie Bouwman; Leslie
Hildebrandt, Ph.D.; Ann F. Jay; Pat Oriel, Ph.D.

Number of staff: 1 part-time support.
EIN: 510152562

4218

Americana Foundation

28115 Meadowbrook Rd.
Novi, MI 48377-3128 (248) 347-3863
Contact: Marlene J. Fluharty, Exec. Dir.
FAX: (248) 347-3349; E-mail: fluhart5@msu.edu

Established in 1978 in MI.
Donors: Adolph H. Meyer†; Ida M. Meyer†.
Foundation type: Independent foundation.
Financial data (yr. ended 12/31/05): Assets,
$20,764,640 (M); expenditures, $1,220,393;
qualifying distributions, $1,081,694; giving
activities include $762,510 for 36 grants (high:
$67,500; low: $250).
Purpose and activities: Support for education and
advocacy programs that address issues of
conserving agriculture and natural resources, and
the preservation of the American heritage.
Fields of interest: Museums (history); Historic
preservation/historical societies; Environment;
Agriculture.
Type of support: General/operating support;
Building/renovation; Program development;
Conferences/seminars; Publication; Internship
funds; Technical assistance; Matching/challenge
support.
Limitations: Giving primarily in MI. No support for
private foundations or for political purposes. No
grants to individuals, or for fundraising events,
tables, or scholarships.
Publications: Annual report (including application
guidelines); Grants list; Informational brochure
(including application guidelines).
Application information: Application form not
required.
　Initial approach: Letter or telephone
　Copies of proposal: 1
　Deadline(s): Middle of Jan., Apr., July, and Oct.
　Board meeting date(s): Quarterly
　Final notification: 3 months
Officers and Trustees:* Robert Janson,* Pres.;
Jonathan Thomas,* V.P.; Thomas F. Ranger,*
Treas.; Marlene J. Fluharty, Exec. Dir.; Norman
Brown; Kathryn Eckert; Kate Harper; Gary Rentrop.
Number of staff: 1 full-time professional; 1 part-time
support.
EIN: 382269431
Selected grants: The following grants were reported
in 2004.
$66,570 to Michigan State University, East Lansing,
　MI. For restoration needed at Tollgate Farm.
$50,000 to Metropolitan Museum of Art, New York,
　NY. For exhibition of colonial cabinetmaker, John
　Townsend.
$35,000 to Michigan Environmental Council,
　Lansing, MI. To unify grassroots action for land
　preservation.
$33,900 to Michigan Society of Planning Officials,
　Rochester, MI. To educate planners and elected
　officials in farmland preservation.
$30,000 to Mackinac Associates, Mackinaw City,
　MI. For restoration of historic lighthouse barn.
$30,000 to Michigan Land Use Institute, Beulah,
　MI. To inform citizens and encourage governor to
　view sprawl as high priority.
$30,000 to Museum of Fine Arts, Houston,
　Houston, TX. For internship for Bayou Bend.
$25,000 to Michigan Lighthouse Fund, Dewitt, MI.
　To offer stewards training and assistance.

$23,400 to Michigan Technological University,
　Houghton, MI. For development of county
　land-use plan.
$20,000 to Keeweenaw Land Trust, Houghton, MI.
　For project specialist for land protection projects.
$15,000 to Pewabic Pottery, Detroit, MI. To
　catalogue and conserve archived materials.
$1,200 to Michigan Barn Preservation Network,
　Mount Pleasant, MI. To upgrade current Barn
　Preservation Display.

4219

Frank N. Andersen Foundation ◇

P.O. Box 225
Bridgeport, MI 48722-0225 (989) 777-2361
Contact: Gerald Barber, V.P.

Established in 1955 in MI.
Donor: Frank N. Andersen†.
Foundation type: Independent foundation.
Financial data (yr. ended 12/31/05): Assets,
$10,788,972 (M); expenditures, $893,028;
qualifying distributions, $809,169; giving activities
include $809,169 for 32 grants (high: $200,000;
low: $1,000).
Purpose and activities: Emphasis on human
services and higher education; support also for arts
and humanities.
Fields of interest: Performing arts; Historic
preservation/historical societies; Higher education;
Education; Food services; Human services.
Type of support: Capital campaigns; Building/
renovation; Equipment; Scholarship funds.
Limitations: Giving limited to Saginaw and Bay
counties, MI. No grants to individuals.
Application information: Application form required.
　Initial approach: Letter requesting application
　　form
　Deadline(s): None
　Board meeting date(s): Quarterly
Officers and Trustees:* William McNally,* Pres.;
Gerald Barber,* V.P.; R. Ronald Zeros,*
Secy.-Treas.; John Gilmour; Arnold L. Johnson;
Barbara Lincoln; Paul Wendler.
Number of staff: 2 part-time professional.
EIN: 386062616
Selected grants: The following grants were reported
in 2004.
$400,000 to Delta College, University Center, MI.
$305,000 to Saginaw Valley State University,
　University Center, MI. 3 grants: $99,500,
　$50,000, $155,500
$250,000 to Delta College Foundation, University
　Center, MI. 2 grants: $200,000, $50,000
$125,000 to Saginaw Art Museum, Saginaw, MI.
$2,000 to Saginaw Choral Society, Saginaw, MI.
$1,200 to Read Association of Saginaw County,
　Saginaw, MI.

4220

The Andrah Foundation ◇

c/o Edward H. Koster
117 N. 1st St., Ste. 111
Ann Arbor, MI 48104

Established in 1996 in MI.
Donors: Thomas Knoll; Ruth Knoll.
Foundation type: Independent foundation.
Financial data (yr. ended 12/31/04): Assets, $0
(M); expenditures, $378,770; qualifying
distributions, $348,487; giving activities include

$348,487 for 13 grants (high: $289,637; low:
$500).
Purpose and activities: Support primarily for a
school.
Fields of interest: Elementary/secondary
education.
Limitations: Applications not accepted. Giving
primarily in Ann Arbor, MI. No grants to individuals.
Application information: Contributes only to
pre-selected organizations.
Officers: Thomas Knoll, Pres. and Treas.; Ruth
Knoll, Secy.
EIN: 383267840

4221

Ann Arbor Area Community Foundation

(formerly Ann Arbor Area Foundation)
301 N. Main St., Ste. 300
Ann Arbor, MI 48104-1133 (734) 663-0401
Contact: Cheryl W. Elliott, C.E.O.; For grants: Phil
D'Anieri, Prog. Dir.
FAX: (734) 663-3514; E-mail: info@aaacf.org;
Additional E-mail: pdanieri@aaacf.org; URL: http://
www.aaacf.org

Incorporated in 1963 in MI.
Foundation type: Community foundation.
Financial data (yr. ended 12/31/05): Assets,
$40,146,458 (M); gifts received, $3,915,272;
expenditures, $2,127,135; giving activities include
$1,241,053 for grants.
Purpose and activities: The mission of the
foundation is to enrich the quality of life in the
greater Ann Arbor, MI, area through building a
permanent endowment, providing a flexible vehicle
for donors, and acting as a leader for the
philanthropic community.
Fields of interest: Visual arts; Performing arts;
Performing arts, theater; Arts; Higher education;
Education; Environment, natural resources;
Environment; Health care; Health organizations,
association; Crime/violence prevention, domestic
violence; Disasters, Hurricane Katrina; Children/
youth, services; Family services; Aging, centers/
services; Homeless, human services; Human
services; Economic development; Community
development; Aging; Homeless.
Type of support: Income development; Management
development/capacity building; Emergency funds;
Program development; Conferences/seminars;
Publication; Seed money; Scholarship funds;
Research; Matching/challenge support.
Limitations: Giving limited to Washtenaw County,
MI. No support for religious or sectarian purposes.
No grants to individuals (except from designated
funds), or for normal operating expenses (except for
start-up purposes), construction projects, computer
hardware equipment, annual campaigns, or capital
campaigns; no loans.
Publications: Application guidelines; Annual report
(including application guidelines); Newsletter;
Program policy statement.
Application information: Visit foundation Web site
for application guidelines and specific deadlines.
Applicants must log on to http://
www.communitygrants.org to create an online
agency profile and complete the Short Community
Grants Application. Application form required.
　Initial approach: Create an online agency profile
　Deadline(s): 2nd Wed. of Feb. and 1st Wed. of
　　Oct. for grants; Sept. for youth projects

Board meeting date(s): Jan., Mar., May, July, Sept., and Nov.

Final notification: May and Dec. for grants

Officers and Trustees: * Bill Kinley,* Chair.; Deborah Beuche,* Vice-Chair.; Cheryl W. Elliot, C.E.O. and Pres.; Martha L. Bloom, V.P., Prog.; Kevin McDonald,* Secy.; Doug Weber, C.F.O.; Hugh Morgan,* Treas.; Sue Sharra, Cont.; Dr. D.J. Boehm; Jyoti Gupta; Gary Hahn; John Martin; Betsy McCallister; John W. Reed; Timothy Wadhams; Marc Weiser; Sandra L. White; Roy Wilbanks.

Number of staff: 1 full-time professional; 2 part-time professional; 1 full-time support; 1 part-time support.

EIN: 386087967

4222

The Eugene Applebaum Family Foundation ◇

39400 Woodward Ave., Ste. 100
Bloomfield Hills, MI 48304
Contact: Pamela Applebaum Wyett, Treas.

Donors: Pamela Applebaum Wyett; Eugene Applebaum Charitable Lead Trust; Lisa S. Applebaum.

Foundation type: Independent foundation.

Financial data (yr. ended 11/30/05): Assets, $10,308,373 (M); gifts received, $9,417,791; expenditures, $4,026,120; qualifying distributions, $3,960,670; giving activities include $3,925,218 for 134 grants (high: $1,533,333; low: $20; average: $5,000–$250,000).

Purpose and activities: Giving primarily to Jewish organizations, including federated giving programs; support also for education, the arts, and health care.

Fields of interest: Arts; Elementary/secondary education; Higher education; Education; Health care; Jewish federated giving programs; Jewish agencies & temples.

Limitations: Giving primarily in MI, and New York, NY; some funding nationally.

Application information:

Deadline(s): None

Officers: Eugene Applebaum, Pres.; Marcia Applebaum, V.P.; Lisa Applebaum Haddad, Secy.; Pamela Applebaum Wyett, Treas.

EIN: 382782955

Selected grants: The following grants were reported in 2005.

$1,750,000 to Mayo Foundation, Rochester, MN. 2 grants: $550,000, $1,200,000

$500,000 to Beaumont Foundation, Southfield, MI. 2 grants: $200,000, $300,000

$200,000 to Detroit Institute of Arts, Detroit, MI.

$100,000 to Michigan Opera Theater, Detroit, MI.

$95,000 to Hillel Day School of Metropolitan Detroit, Farmington Hills, MI. 2 grants: $70,000, $25,000

$75,000 to Wayne State University, Detroit, MI.

$70,000 to Detroit Symphony Orchestra, Detroit, MI.

4223

Arcus Foundation ▼

(formerly Jon L. Stryker Foundation)
402 E. Michigan Ave.
Kalamazoo, MI 49007 (269) 373-4373
Contact: Daniel Schwartz, Board Member

E-mail: contact@arcusfoundation.org; New York address: 119 W. 24th St., 9th Fl., New York, NY 10011, tel.: (212) 488-3000; URL: http://www.arcusfoundation.org

Established in 1997 in MI.

Donor: Jon L. Stryker.

Foundation type: Independent foundation.

Financial data (yr. ended 12/31/05): Assets, $72,827,720 (M); gifts received, $61,880,962; expenditures, $18,328,731; qualifying distributions, $17,852,484; giving activities include $16,657,143 for 89 grants (high: $5,151,456; low: $25; average: $10,000–$500,000).

Purpose and activities: Support for programs that fight prejudice and discrimination and protect and defend human and civil rights for the gay, lesbian, bisexual and transgender community. Giving also for Great Apes Sanctuary and Conservation.

Fields of interest: Animals/wildlife, endangered species; Animals/wildlife, sanctuaries; Animals/wildlife, special services; Civil rights, gays/lesbians; Civil rights; LGBTQ.

Type of support: General/operating support; Continuing support; Annual campaigns; Capital campaigns; Building/renovation; Endowments; Program development; Conferences/seminars; Publication; Curriculum development; Technical assistance; Consulting services; Program evaluation; Program-related investments/loans; Employee matching gifts; Matching/challenge support.

Limitations: Giving on a national basis, with emphasis on Kalamazoo, MI for some programs. No grants to individuals, of for religious or political activities, medical research or film/video production.

Publications: Annual report (including application guidelines); Newsletter.

Application information: For funding applications only use the foundation's Michigan address. Formal proposal accepted by invitation only following letter of inquiry process. See foundation Web site for complete formal proposal requirements. Application form not required.

Initial approach: Letter, no more than 2 pages

Copies of proposal: 4

Deadline(s): Feb. 15 and July 1 for letter of inquiry; Apr. 1 and Aug. 15 for invited proposals

Board meeting date(s): June and Dec.

Final notification: Mid-July and mid-Nov.

Officers: Jon L. Stryker, Pres.; Jeff Arnstein, C.F.O.; Urvashi Vaid, Exec. Dir.

Board Members: Cathy J. Cohen; Daniel Schwartz.

Number of staff: 12 full-time professional; 10 part-time professional.

EIN: 383332791

Selected grants: The following grants were reported in 2005.

$4,645,385 to Center for Captive Chimpanzee Care, Fort Pierce, FL. For construction and general operating support of world's largest chimpanzee sanctuary.

$2,000,000 to National Gay and Lesbian Task Force (NGLTF) Foundation, New York, NY.

$1,476,505 to Center for Orangutan and Chimpanzee Conservation, Center for Great Apes, Wauchula, FL. For sanctuary support including transferring, housing and caring for chimpanzees and orangutans rescued from entertainment industry.

$333,333 to Auburn University, Auburn, AL. For John Wilford Brown Endowed Chair in Chemical Engineering.

$300,000 to Park Square Advocates, Boston, MA. For general operating support for work in New England states working toward marriage rights, payable over 2 years.

$250,000 to American Civil Liberties Union Foundation, New York, NY. For general operating support for Lesbian and Gay Rights Project, which fights discrimination against GLBT people and families and works to move public opinion through the legal system, the media, and educational outreach.

$250,000 to Fauna Sanctuary, Champlain, NY. For general operating support related to caring for former biomedical chimpanzees at Fauna Foundation in Quebec, payable over 5 years.

$150,000 to Kalamazoo College, Kalamazoo, MI. For Upjohn Library Commons Renovation and Expansion Project.

$75,000 to WildAid, San Francisco, CA. For Wilderness Protection Mobile Unit to protect Southwest Cambodia's remaining wild gibbon population by confiscating illegally captured gibbons, providing them with intermediary medical care, food and shelter at Phnom Tamao Wildlife Rescue Center and reintroducing them into the wild.

$50,000 to Soulforce, Lynchburg, VA. For Equality Ride, bus tour bringing GLBT and ally youth activists to colleges throughout the U.S. which ban enrollment and employment of openly GLBT people.

4224

ArvinMeritor Trust Foundation ◇

(formerly Meritor Automotive, Inc. Trust)
c/o Community Rels.
2135 W. Maple Rd.
Troy, MI 48084-7186 (248) 435-7907
Contact: Jerry Rush, Sr. Dir., Govt. Rels.
FAX: (248) 435-1031;
E-mail: jerry.rush@arvinmeritor.com; URL: http://www.arvinmeritor.com/community/community.asp

Established in 1997 in MI.

Donors: Meritor Automotive, Inc.; ArvinMeritor, Inc.

Foundation type: Company-sponsored foundation.

Financial data (yr. ended 10/2/05): Assets, $102,297 (M); gifts received, $1,565,272; expenditures, $1,508,610; qualifying distributions, $1,508,610; giving activities include $1,405,277 for 236 grants (high: $200,000; low: $500), and $103,333 for 141 employee matching gifts.

Purpose and activities: The foundation supports organizations involved with arts and culture, education, health, medical research, safety, youth development, human services, community development, and civic affairs.

Fields of interest: Arts; Engineering school/education; Education; Public health; Health care, cost containment; Health care; Medical research; Safety, education; Youth development; Human services; Community development; Science, formal/general education; Public affairs; Youth.

Type of support: Program development; Employee-related scholarships.

Limitations: Giving primarily in areas of company operations. No support for discriminatory organizations, religious or sectarian organizations not of direct benefit to the entire community, labor, political, or veterans' organizations, or fraternal, athletic, or social clubs. No grants to individuals (except for employee-related scholarships), or for general operating support for local United Way agencies, sponsorship of fundraising activities for individuals, debt reduction, or seminars, conferences, trips, or tours; no loans.

Publications: Informational brochure (including application guidelines).

Application information: Application form not required.

Initial approach: Proposal

Deadline(s): Aug.

Officers and Trustees: Larry Yost, Chair. and C.E.O.; Terry O'Rourke, C.O.O. and Pres.; Vernon Baker, Sr. V.P., Secy., and General Counsel; Carl Soderstrom,* Sr. V.P. and C.F.O.; Lin Cummins,* Sr. V.P., Communications; Juan De La Riva,* Sr. V.P., Corp. Develop and Strategy; Ernie Whitus, Sr. V.P., Human Resources; Diane Bullock, V.P. and Cont.

EIN: 522089611

4225

The Ave Maria Foundation ▼ ✧

(formerly The Mater Christi Foundation)

1 Ave Maria Dr.

P.O. Box 373

Ann Arbor, MI 48106-0373 (734) 930-3150

URL: http://www.avemariafoundation.org

Established in 1983 in MI.

Donors: Domino's Pizza, Inc.; Thomas S. Monaghan; Elaine McInerney; Martin McInerney; Albert Schaller; Marilyn Schaller; Kimberly Gates; James Gates; Dennis Ardi; William McIntyre.

Foundation type: Independent foundation.

Financial data (yr. ended 12/31/05): Assets, $121,385,829 (M); gifts received, $11,983; expenditures, $37,203,918; qualifying distributions, $33,140,817; giving activities include $33,140,817 for 16 grants (high: $20,069,013; low: $1,516; average: $26,600–$7,200,326), and $500 for 1 foundation-administered program.

Purpose and activities: Support primarily for a variety of organizations which bring Catholic life and culture to the world.

Fields of interest: Education; Human services; Roman Catholic agencies & churches; Religion.

Type of support: Program development.

Limitations: Applications not accepted. Giving primarily in MI. No grants to individuals.

Application information: Unsolicited applications not considered.

Board meeting date(s): Annually

Officers and Director: Thomas S. Monaghan,* Pres.; Jeff Randolph, Secy.; Paul Roney, Treas.

Number of staff: 1 part-time professional.

EIN: 382514364

Selected grants: The following grants were reported in 2004.

$73,084,645 to Ave Maria University, Naples, FL. For construction and start-up support.

$8,247,895 to Ave Maria School of Law, Ann Arbor, MI. For general support.

$4,550,120 to Ave Maria College, Ypsilanti, MI. For general support.

$1,373,784 to Spiritus Sanctus Academy, Ann Arbor, MI. 2 grants: $1,345,610 (For general support), $28,174 (For general support).

$250,103 to Saint Marys College, Orchard Lake, MI. For general support.

$55,450 to National Association of Private Catholic Independent Schools (NAPCIS), Sacramento, CA. For general support.

$37,004 to Father Gabriel Richard High School, Ann Arbor, MI. For general support.

$30,000 to Catholic Schools Textbook Project, Ventura, CA. For general support.

$24,700 to Shepherd Montessori Center, Ann Arbor, MI. For general support.

4226

The Howard Baker Foundation ✧

4057 Pioneer Dr., Ste. 500

Walled Lake, MI 48390

Application address: c/o Michele Baker, Exec. Dir., P.O. Box 441453, Detroit, MI 48244, tel.: (313) 587-6207,

e-mail: mbaker@howardbakerfoundation.org;

URL: http://www.howardbakerfoundation.org

Established in 1992 in MI.

Donor: Howard Baker Trust.

Foundation type: Independent foundation.

Financial data (yr. ended 9/30/05): Assets, $3,643,668 (M); expenditures, $669,100; qualifying distributions, $564,662; giving activities include $564,662 for 9 grants (high: $234,662; low: $5,000).

Purpose and activities: Giving primarily for human services, as well as to a fund that has been established to provide assistance to residents of Detroit, MI, in financing their education at Wayne State University, and to encourage continued progress towards a degree.

Fields of interest: Higher education, university; Human services.

Type of support: General/operating support; Scholarship funds.

Limitations: Giving primarily in Detroit, and southeastern MI. No grants to individuals.

Application information: See foundation Web site for scholarship guidelines.

Initial approach: Proposal

Officers: Charlie J. Williams, Pres.; Ronald F. Michaels, V.P.; Dennis Gabrian, Secy.; O'Neal O. Wright, Treas.; Michelle L. Baker, Exec. Dir.

Directors: Paul J. Gampka; John J. Howe.

EIN: 383083465

4227

Barry Community Foundation

629 W. State St., Ste. 201

Hastings, MI 49058-0644 (269) 945-0526

Contact: Bonnie Hildreth, Pres.

FAX: (269) 945-0826; E-mail: bonnie@barrycf.org; Additional E-mail: grants@barrycf.org; URL: http://www.barrycf.org

Established in 1996 in MI.

Foundation type: Community foundation.

Financial data (yr. ended 6/30/05): Assets, $8,257,821 (M); gifts received, $1,148,648; expenditures, $598,870; giving activities include $427,253 for grants.

Purpose and activities: The mission of the foundation is to develop and manage endowed funds for helping and involving the people of Barry County, MI, to make a positive difference in their lives.

Fields of interest: Arts; Education; Environment, natural resources; Hospitals (general); Children/youth, services; Human services; Community development, neighborhood development; Community development.

Type of support: General/operating support; Annual campaigns; Capital campaigns; Building/

renovation; Equipment; Endowments; Program development; Conferences/seminars; Seed money; Curriculum development; Scholarship funds; Research; Technical assistance; Consulting services; Program evaluation; Matching/challenge support.

Limitations: Giving limited to Barry County, MI. No support for private organizations, including churches. No grants to individuals (except for scholarships), or for operating expenses or regularly upgrading equipment.

Publications: Application guidelines; Annual report; Informational brochure; Newsletter.

Application information: Visit foundation Web site for application form and guidelines. Number of copies vary per grant type. Application form required.

Initial approach: Telephone

Copies of proposal: 15

Deadline(s): Oct. 15; Jan. 15, Apr. 15, and July 15 for interim grants up to $3,000

Board meeting date(s): 3rd Thurs. monthly

Final notification: Within 8 weeks

Officers and Directors: Fred Jacobs, Chair.; Bonnie Hildreth,* Pres.; Jennifer Richards,* V.P.; Kathy Johnson,* Secy.; Jim Toburen,* Treas.; Bob Byington; Maggie Coleman; Don Drummond; Jan Hartough; Karen Heath; Pat Markle; Deb McKeown; Kim Norris; Jon Simpson.

Number of staff: 1 full-time professional; 1 full-time support; 1 part-time support.

EIN: 383246131

4228

Battle Creek Community Foundation ✧

(formerly Greater Battle Creek Foundation)

1 Riverwalk Ctr.

34 W. Jackson St.

Battle Creek, MI 49017-3505 (269) 962-2181

Contact: Brenda L. Hunt, C.E.O.; For grants: Kelly Boles Chapman, V.P., Progs.

FAX: (269) 962-2182;

E-mail: bccf@bccfoundation.org; Grant inquiry E-mail: kelly@bccfoundation.org; URL: http://www.bccfoundation.org

Established in 1974 in MI.

Foundation type: Community foundation.

Financial data (yr. ended 3/31/05): Assets, $82,360,581 (M); gifts received, $19,960,388; expenditures, $5,203,743; giving activities include $2,498,459 for grants, and $202,052 for grants to individuals.

Purpose and activities: The foundation seeks to promote giving, build endowment, and provide leadership to improve quality of life. Grantmaking for programming in the Battle Creek, MI, area serves the citizens of the community through education, health, human services, arts, public affairs, and community development; scholarships are also available to students residing in the greater Battle Creek area.

Fields of interest: Arts; Child development, education; Adult education—literacy, basic skills & GED; Education, reading; Education; Animal welfare; Hospitals (general); Health care; Health organizations, association; Children/youth, services; Child development, services; Minorities/immigrants, centers/services; Human services; Community development; Public affairs; Youth; Minorities.

Type of support: Building/renovation; Equipment; Land acquisition; Emergency funds; Program development; Conferences/seminars; Publication;

Seed money; Curriculum development; Scholarship funds; Technical assistance; Program evaluation; Program-related investments/loans; Scholarships —to individuals; Matching/challenge support.

Limitations: Giving limited to the greater Battle Creek, MI, area. No grants for operating budgets, deficit financing, endowments, or research; no loans (except for program-related investments).

Publications: Application guidelines; Annual report; Biennial report (including application guidelines); Financial statement; Grants list; Informational brochure; Newsletter; Program policy statement.

Application information: Visit foundation Web site for grant application packets, guidelines per grant type, and specific deadlines. Contact high school counselors for scholarship applications and guidelines. Application form required.

Initial approach: Letter or telephone
Copies of proposal: 20
Deadline(s): Mar., June, Sept., and Dec.
Board meeting date(s): Monthly
Final notification: Within 2 months

Officers and Trustees:* David L. Schweitzer,* Chair.; Betsy L. Briere,* Vice-Chair.; Brenda Jackson,* 2nd Vice-Chair.; Brenda L. Hunt, C.E.O. and Pres.; Kelly Boles Chapman, V.P., Progs.; Kimberly L. Holley, V.P., Mktg. and Comms.; Shelly Miller, V.P., Finance; Mahesh Karamchandani, M.D.*, Secy.; Robert G. Byelich, Treas.; Carolyn Ballard; John R. Bromley; Charles A. Cooper, Jr.; B. Scott Durham; David H. Eddy; Tim Kool; Denise Little; David P. Lucas; Victor R. Sanchez; James K. Sholl; Colleen Starring; Morgan Steely; Terris Eugene Todd.

Number of staff: 12 full-time professional; 2 part-time professional; 3 full-time support; 1 part-time support.

EIN: 382045459

Selected grants: The following grants were reported in 2005.

$517,500 to Battle Creek Health System, Battle Creek, MI.

$344,650 to Burnham Brook Center, Battle Creek, MI.

$147,964 to Music Center of South Central Michigan, Battle Creek, MI.

$133,315 to United Arts Council of Calhoun County, Battle Creek, MI.

$83,300 to Battle Creek Area Catholic Schools Foundation, Battle Creek, MI.

$83,150 to Humane Society-Calhoun Area, Battle Creek, MI.

$64,200 to Lifespan, Battle Creek, MI.

$46,400 to Kingman Museum, Battle Creek, MI.

$28,974 to Athens Area Schools, Athens, MI.

$25,000 to Marian E. Burch Adult Day Care and Rehabilitation Center, Battle Creek, MI.

4229
Bay Area Community Foundation ◇

703 Washington Ave.
Bay City, MI 48708-5732 (989) 893-4438
Contact: Roger Merrifield, C.E.O.; For grants: Ashley Morse, Prog. Off.
FAX: (989) 893-4448;
E-mail: bacfnd@bayfoundation.org; Additional tel.: (800) 926-3217; Addition E-mail: ashleym@bayfoundation.org; URL: http://www.bayfoundation.org

Established in 1982 in MI.
Foundation type: Community foundation.

Financial data (yr. ended 12/31/05): Assets, $27,868,887 (M); gifts received, $2,182,084; expenditures, $1,753,645; giving activities include $1,253,218 for grants.

Purpose and activities: The foundation seeks to fulfill a wide array of donors' charitable wishes by building permanent endowment funds and serving as a leader for community improvement through effective grantmaking and collaboration. Priority will be given to projects that focus on the following areas: charitable; cultural; educational; and environmental for Michigan's Bay and Arenac counties.

Fields of interest: Visual arts; Performing arts; Arts; Education; Environment, energy; Environment; Health care; Housing/shelter; Recreation; Human services; Community development; Science; Youth.

Type of support: Building/renovation; Program development; Seed money; Curriculum development; Internship funds; Scholarship funds; Research; Technical assistance; Matching/challenge support.

Limitations: Giving limited to Bay and Arenac counties, MI. No grants to individuals (excluding scholarships), or for capital campaigns, existing obligations, endowments, or fundraising events.

Publications: Annual report; Financial statement; Grants list; Informational brochure.

Application information: Visit foundation Web site for application form and guidelines. Applications sent by fax will not be accepted. Application form required.

Initial approach: Telephone
Deadline(s): Varies
Board meeting date(s): Monthly, except in June, Aug., and Dec.

Officers and Trustees:* Gary Labadie,* Chair.; Diane Demers,* Vice-Chair.; Roger Merrifield, C.E.O. and Pres.; Michael Stoner,* Secy.; Mike Hanisko,* Treas.; Gary Bosco; Charles B. Curtiss; Mike Dewey; Kevin Dykema; Jane Hagen; Robert Hetzler; Lucy Horak; Ruth Jaffe; Michael Kasperski; Mike Kelly; Steve Kessler; John Lore; Gary Manthey; Pamela Monastiere; Robert Monroe; Abel Torres; Carolyn Wierda; Jerome Yantz.

Number of staff: 3 full-time professional; 2 part-time support.

EIN: 382418086

4230
Mandell L. and Madeleine H. Berman Foundation

(formerly Madeleine and Mandell L. Berman Foundation)
c/o Sarai Brachman Shoup
29100 Northwestern Hwy., Ste. 370
Southfield, MI 48034

Established in 1994 in MI.
Foundation type: Independent foundation.

Financial data (yr. ended 12/31/04): Assets, $12,387,014 (M); gifts received, $1,467,250; expenditures, $971,808; qualifying distributions, $638,453; giving activities include $596,829 for grants.

Fields of interest: Arts; Animal welfare; Jewish agencies & temples; Disabilities, people with.

International interests: Israel.

Limitations: Applications not accepted. Giving on a national and international basis, and in the Detroit, MI, area. No grants to individuals.

Application information: Contributes only to pre-selected organizations.

Trustee: Mandell L. Berman.
Number of staff: 2 part-time professional.
EIN: 386644875

4231
Berrien Community Foundation, Inc.

2900 S. State St., Ste. 2E
St. Joseph, MI 49085 (269) 983-3486, ext. 1
Contact: Dr. Nanette Keiser, Pres.
FAX: (269) 983-4939;
E-mail: bcf@BerrienCommunity.org; Grant application tel.: (269) 983-3304, ext. 2; Additional E-mail: AnneMcCausland@BerrienCommunity.org; Grant application E-mail: NanetteKeiser@BerrienCommunity.org; URL: http://www.berriencommunity.org

Incorporated in 1952 in MI.
Foundation type: Community foundation.

Financial data (yr. ended 12/31/05): Assets, $17,419,418 (M); gifts received, $1,300,795; expenditures, $876,810; giving activities include $599,889 for 289 grants (high: $20,000; low: $100).

Purpose and activities: The mission of the foundation is to promote philanthropy, to build a spirit of community, and to enhance the quality of life in Berrien County through its stewardship of permanently endowed and other funds. The foundation shall accomplish this mission by: building permanent endowments and other funds, and providing a broad range of flexible and cost-effective donor services; investing and managing funds prudently and professionally; making grants to support a broad range of projects and programs that address community needs, with a focus on building a spirit of community/arts and culture, nurturing children, and youth leadership and development; and serving as a facilitative leader, catalyst, and resource for local communities.

Fields of interest: Historic preservation/historical societies; Arts; Education; Health care; Substance abuse, prevention; Housing/shelter; Youth development; Children, day care; Youth, pregnancy prevention; Family services; Human services; Community development; Youth; Aging.

Type of support: Program development; Seed money; Curriculum development; Scholarship funds; Matching/challenge support.

Limitations: Giving primarily in Berrien County, MI for Undesignated and Field-of-Interest funds; giving in the U.S. for Advised funds. No support for sectarian religious purposes. No grants to individuals (except for scholarships), or for consulting services for grant writing, ongoing operating funds, deficit financing, national fundraising efforts, annual fund drives, or program-related investments.

Publications: Financial statement; Informational brochure (including application guidelines); Occasional report.

Application information: Visit foundation Web site for application information; guidelines and forms are available on request. 20 copies of application required for youth-oriented projects only. Application form required.

Initial approach: Telephone (ext. 2) or e-mail
Copies of proposal: 15
Deadline(s): Sept. 1
Board meeting date(s): Oct.
Final notification: 10 to 14 weeks

Officers and Trustees:* Joanne Sims,* Chair.; Gregory C. Vaughn,* Vice-Chair.; Dr. Nanette Keiser, Pres.; Robert D. Gottlieb,* Secy.; Sharon Vargo,*

Treas.; Hillary Bubb; Rev. James Childs; Patricia Forbes; Nadra Kissman; Brenda Layne; Jane Marohn; Tim Passaro; Gladys Peeples-Burks, Ph.D.; Allan J. Westmaas.
Number of staff: 2.5 full-time professional.
EIN: 386057160

4232
Besser Foundation ✧
123 N. 2nd Ave., Ste. 3
Alpena, MI 49707-2801 (989) 354-4722
Contact: J. Richard Wilson, Pres.
FAX: (989) 354-8099; E-mail: bessfdtn@freeway.net

Incorporated in 1944 in MI.
Donors: J.H. Besser†; Besser Co.
Foundation type: Independent foundation.
Financial data (yr. ended 12/31/04): Assets, $17,289,894 (M); expenditures, $1,028,176; qualifying distributions, $952,110; giving activities include $874,908 for 46 grants (high: $220,000; low: $600; average: $300–$448,353).
Purpose and activities: Grants primarily to local schools and colleges and health and social service agencies; giving also to Africare for projects in underdeveloped nations in Africa. In addition, the foundation partially supports the Jesse Besser Museum, a local historical and art museum.
Fields of interest: Museums; Arts; Education; Human services; Children/youth, services.
Type of support: General/operating support; Continuing support; Capital campaigns; Building/renovation; Matching/challenge support.
Limitations: Giving limited to the Alpena, MI, area. No support for video projects. No grants to individuals, or for endowment funds, meeting or conference expenses, travel, or research.
Publications: Annual report (including application guidelines).
Application information: Applications sent via fax accepted. Application form not required.
  Initial approach: Letter of introduction
  Copies of proposal: 1
  Deadline(s): End of 1st month in each calendar quarter
  Board meeting date(s): Quarterly beginning in Mar.
Officers and Trustees:* J. Richard Wilson,* Pres. and Treas.; James C. Park,* V.P.; Patricia Gardner,* Secy.; Gary Dawley; Carl E. Reitz; Harold A. Ruemenapp.
Number of staff: 2 part-time support.
EIN: 386071938

4233
Guido A. & Elizabeth H. Binda Foundation
1415 Heritage Twr.
Battle Creek, MI 49017
Contact: Elizabeth H. Binda, Pres.

Established in 1977 in MI.
Donor: Guido A. Binda†.
Foundation type: Independent foundation.
Financial data (yr. ended 6/30/05): Assets, $15,362,290 (M); expenditures, $956,772; qualifying distributions, $792,221; giving activities include $766,545 for 75 grants (high: $100,000; low: $100).
Purpose and activities: Giving primarily for education; support also for health care, community development, and human services.

Fields of interest: Visual arts, architecture; Arts; Elementary school/education; Secondary school/education; Higher education; Adult education—literacy, basic skills & GED; Scholarships/financial aid; Education, reading; Education; Environment; Health care; Substance abuse, services; Human services; Community development; Minorities; Economically disadvantaged.
Type of support: Program development; Seed money; Curriculum development; Scholarship funds.
Limitations: Giving limited to Battle Creek and southwestern MI. No grants to individuals, or for endowments or capital campaigns.
Publications: Application guidelines; Informational brochure (including application guidelines).
Application information: Application form required.
  Initial approach: Letter or telephone
  Copies of proposal: 11
  Deadline(s): Dec. 1 to May 1
  Board meeting date(s): Jan. and June
  Final notification: 10 days
Officers and Trustees:* Elizabeth H. Binda,* Pres. and Secy.; Richard Tsoumas,* V.P.; E. James Swan,* Treas.; Robert Binda; LaVerne H. Boss; Norman Brown; Chris T. Christ; John Hosking; Joel Orosz; Cindy S. Ruble.
Number of staff: 1 part-time support.
EIN: 382184423

4234
Harold & Penny B. Blumenstein Foundation Corporation ✧
32400 Telegraph Rd., Ste. 202
Bingham Farms, MI 48025

Established in 1986 in MI.
Donors: Harold Blumenstein; Penny B. Blumenstein.
Foundation type: Independent foundation.
Financial data (yr. ended 12/31/05): Assets, $5,328,393 (M); gifts received, $1,100,000; expenditures, $1,446,248; qualifying distributions, $1,429,247; giving activities include $1,429,247 for 110 grants (high: $225,000; low: $18).
Purpose and activities: Giving primarily for Jewish agencies and federated giving programs.
Fields of interest: Arts; Education; Health organizations, association; Jewish federated giving programs; Jewish agencies & temples.
Limitations: Applications not accepted. Giving primarily in MI. No grants to individuals.
Application information: Contributes only to pre-selected organizations.
Officers: Harold Blumenstein, Pres.; Penny B. Blumenstein, V.P. and Secy.; Richard C. Blumenstein, V.P.; Lauren A. Cohen, V.P.; Randall S. Blumenstein, Treas.
EIN: 382710389

4235
John A. & Marlene L. Boll Foundation ✧
100 Maple Park Blvd., Ste. 118
St. Clair Shores, MI 48081
Contact: Kristine Boll Mestdagh, Dir.

Established in 1986 in MI.
Donors: John A. Boll; Marlene L. Boll.
Foundation type: Independent foundation.
Financial data (yr. ended 12/31/04): Assets, $18,498,845 (M); expenditures, $1,727,777; qualifying distributions, $1,466,165; giving

activities include $1,466,165 for 132 grants (high: $200,000; low: $30).
Purpose and activities: Giving educational scholarships to institutions with curriculum based, in part, on Judeo-Christian traditions.
Fields of interest: Arts; Higher education; Scholarships/financial aid; Health care; Human services; Christian agencies & churches.
Type of support: General/operating support.
Limitations: Giving primarily in MI. No grants to individuals.
Application information: Letters of recommendation for scholarship candidates are required for further review. Application form not required.
  Deadline(s): None
Directors: John A. Boll; Marlene L. Boll; Kristine B. Mestdagh.
EIN: 382708121
Selected grants: The following grants were reported in 2004.
$50,000 to Family Research Council, DC.
$50,000 to Make-A-Wish Foundation of Michigan, Lansing, MI.
$45,000 to Vail Valley Foundation, Vail, CO. 2 grants: $25,000, $20,000
$25,000 to Make-A-Wish Foundation of America, Phoenix, AZ.
$10,000 to Ecumenical Theological Seminary, Detroit, MI.
$7,000 to Ocean Reef Cultural Center, Key Largo, FL.
$5,000 to Family Learning Center, Boulder, CO.
$5,000 to Matrix Human Services, Detroit, MI.
$2,500 to Michigan Opera Theater, Detroit, MI.

4236
Boutell Memorial Fund ✧
(formerly Arnold and Gertrude Boutell Memorial Fund)
c/o Citizens Bank Wealth Mgmt., N.A.
328 S. Saginaw St., M/C 002072
Flint, MI 48502
Application address: c/o Helen James, Citizens Bank Wealth Mgmt., N.A., 101 N. Washington Ave., Saginaw, MI 48607, tel.: (989) 776-7368

Established in 1961 in MI.
Donors: Arnold Boutell†; Gertrude Boutell†.
Foundation type: Independent foundation.
Financial data (yr. ended 3/31/06): Assets, $12,414,223 (M); expenditures, $690,605; qualifying distributions, $575,701; giving activities include $560,164 for 26 grants (high: $100,000; low: $1,000).
Purpose and activities: Giving primarily for children, youth and social services, and for community development.
Fields of interest: Performing arts; Health care; Human services; Children/youth, services; Community development; Foundations (community).
Type of support: Equipment; Program development.
Limitations: Giving limited to Saginaw County, MI. No grants to individuals, or for endowment funds.
Application information: Application form required.
  Initial approach: Letter
  Copies of proposal: 1
  Deadline(s): None
  Board meeting date(s): 3rd Wed. of Mar., June, Sept., and Dec.
Trustee: Citizens Bank.
EIN: 386040492

Selected grants: The following grants were reported in 2005.

$262,500 to Hidden Harvest, Saginaw, MI. 2 grants: $175,000, $87,500

$35,000 to Saginaw Future, Saginaw, MI.

$33,333 to Delta College, University Center, MI.

$14,100 to Saginaw Community Foundation, Saginaw, MI. 3 grants: $10,000, $2,500, $1,600

$11,500 to United Way of Saginaw County, Saginaw, MI.

4237
Branch County Community Foundation

2 W. Chicago St., Ste. E-1
Coldwater, MI 49036-1602 (517) 278-4517
Contact: Colleen Knight, Exec. Dir.
FAX: (517) 279-2319;
E-mail: info@brcofoundation.org; Additional E-mail: colleen@brcofoundation.org; URL: http://www.brcofoundation.org

Established in 1991 in MI.
Foundation type: Community foundation.
Financial data (yr. ended 9/30/05): Assets, $4,057,246 (M); gifts received, $2,714,104; expenditures, $2,912,569; giving activities include $2,728,581 for grants.
Purpose and activities: The foundation seeks to build a permanent endowment by attracting funds from and providing services to a wide range of donors, and to grant the income from those funds to serve the community.
Fields of interest: Humanities; Arts; Education; Environment; Health care; Housing/shelter, homeless; Human services; Community development.
Type of support: General/operating support; Equipment; Endowments; Conferences/seminars; Scholarship funds; Technical assistance; In-kind gifts; Matching/challenge support.
Limitations: Giving limited to Branch County and Bronson, Coldwater, Colon, Quincy, and Union City, MI. No support for sectarian religious programs. No grants to individuals (except for scholarships); no loans or program-related investments.
Publications: Application guidelines; Annual report; Financial statement; Informational brochure; Newsletter; Occasional report.
Application information: Visit foundation Web site for grant application information. Application form required.
  Initial approach: Telephone, fax, or e-mail foundation for application packets
  Deadline(s): Varies
  Board meeting date(s): Monthly
  Final notification: 2 months
Officers and Directors:* M. Joe Ganger,* Pres.; Bruce Bloom,* V.P.; Hillary Eley,* Secy.; Edward Callahan,* Treas.; Colleen Knight, Exec. Dir.; Susan Sparrow, Cont.; Patricia Klein-Shoemaker, Dir. Emeritus; Bob Mayer, Dir. Emeritus; Ray Bregger; Paul Creal; Sandra Davis; Klaudia Fisher; Nancy Hutchins; Sandra Jackson; Mary Jo Kranz; Remus Rigg; Dave Wright; Bruce Young.
Number of staff: 1 full-time professional; 1 full-time support.
EIN: 383021071

4238
The Hilda E. Bretzlaff Foundation, Inc.

1550 N. Milford Rd.
Milford, MI 48381
Contact: Janelle M. Radtke, V.P.
E-mail: jradtke@hebf.org; Additional E-mail: klindbeck@hebf.org; URL: http://www.hebf.org

Established in 1994 in MI.
Donor: Hilda E. Bretzlaff†.
Foundation type: Independent foundation.
Financial data (yr. ended 12/31/05): Assets, $26,212,343 (M); gifts received, $100; expenditures, $1,311,838; qualifying distributions, $1,049,203; giving activities include $685,540 for 39 grants (high: $50,000; low: $2,500), and $82,138 for grants to individuals (high: $3,750; low: $200).
Purpose and activities: The foundation provides educational grants to assist students in attending educational institutions in the United States or England that promote high educational, moral, and conservative ideals.
Fields of interest: Scholarships/financial aid.
Type of support: Scholarship funds.
Limitations: Applications not accepted. Giving primarily for the benefit of U.S. citizens or individuals in the process of becoming U.S. citizens. Some giving also in England. No support for schools that are not conservative. No grants to individuals directly.
Application information: Funds administered through educational institutions. Applicants must have and maintain a minimum of 2.0 GPA. The foundation's mission statement indicates that all applicants must be financially needy, moral, conservative, and a credit to America.
  Board meeting date(s): Bimonthly
Officers: Gerald W. Radtke, Pres.; Susan J. Vogt, V.P. and Secy.; Janelle M. Radtke, V.P.; Kathleen M. Lindbeck, Mgr.
Number of staff: 4 part-time professional.
EIN: 382619845

4239
Peter D. and Dorothy S. Brown Charitable Trust ◇

3631 Wabeek Lake Dr. W.
Bloomfield Hills, MI 48302-1273

Established in 1987 in FL.
Donors: Peter D. Brown; Dorothy S. Brown; A. Bart Lewis; Susan Lewis.
Foundation type: Independent foundation.
Financial data (yr. ended 12/31/05): Assets, $10,394,020 (M); expenditures, $723,333; qualifying distributions, $601,100; giving activities include $592,350 for 6 grants (high: $250,000; low: $550).
Fields of interest: Jewish federated giving programs; Jewish agencies & temples.
Limitations: Applications not accepted. Giving primarily in MI; some funding also in FL. No grants to individuals.
Application information: Contributes only to pre-selected organizations.
Trustees: Dorothy S. Brown; A. Bart Lewis.
EIN: 386517224
Selected grants: The following grants were reported in 2004.
$257,500 to United Jewish Foundation, Bloomfield Hills, MI.

4240
The John and Rosemary Brown Family Foundation ◇

490 W. South St.
Kalamazoo, MI 49007

Established in 1997 in MI.
Donors: John W. Brown; Rosemary K. Brown.
Foundation type: Independent foundation.
Financial data (yr. ended 12/31/05): Assets, $13,635,285 (M); gifts received, $1,598,450; expenditures, $842,900; qualifying distributions, $841,475; giving activities include $840,500 for 40 grants (high: $400,000; low: $500).
Purpose and activities: Giving primarily for higher education, economic development, and Christian churches; funding also for health associations, the arts, and children, youth, and social services.
Fields of interest: Arts; Higher education; Education; Health organizations, association; Medical research, institute; Human services; Children/youth, services; Economic development; Community development; Federated giving programs; Christian agencies & churches.
Limitations: Applications not accepted. Giving primarily in MI, with emphasis on Kalamazoo. No grants to individuals.
Application information: Contributes only to pre-selected organizations.
Trustees: John W. Brown; Rosemary K. Brown.
EIN: 586343478

4241
The Burdick-Thorne Foundation

136 E. Michigan Ave., Ste. 1201
Kalamazoo, MI 49007-3936
Contact: David S. Kruis, Treas.

Established in 1990 in MI.
Donors: James M. Thorne†; Mary B. Thorne†.
Foundation type: Independent foundation.
Financial data (yr. ended 12/31/05): Assets, $10,585,747 (M); gifts received, $7,281; expenditures, $553,407; qualifying distributions, $518,578; giving activities include $439,000 for 49 grants (high: $80,000; low: $1,000).
Purpose and activities: Giving for higher education, the arts, social services, and natural resource preservation and enhancement.
Fields of interest: Arts councils; Performing arts; Performing arts, music; Higher education; Environment, natural resources; Human services.
Type of support: General/operating support; Continuing support; Annual campaigns; Capital campaigns; Building/renovation.
Limitations: Applications not accepted. Giving limited to Kalamazoo, MI. No grants to individuals.
Application information: Contributes only to pre-selected organizations.
  Board meeting date(s): Varies
Officers and Trustees:* James S. Hilboldt,* Pres.; James C. Melvin,* V.P.; Loyal A. Eldridge III,* Secy.; David S. Kruis, Treas.; Andrea M. Thorne; Betsy V. Thorne.
EIN: 382904527
Selected grants: The following grants were reported in 2003.
$70,000 to Kalamazoo College, Kalamazoo, MI. For recital hall.
$22,000 to Arts Council of Greater Kalamazoo, Kalamazoo, MI. For general operating support.
$11,500 to Fontana Chamber Arts, Kalamazoo, MI. For general operating support.

$5,000 to Birmingham-Bloomfield Symphony Orchestra, Birmingham, MI. For general operating support.

$5,000 to Michigan Youth Arts Festival, Kalamazoo, MI. For general operating support.

$3,000 to Salvation Army of Kalamazoo, Kalamazoo, MI. For general operating support.

$3,000 to YMCA of Kalamazoo, Kalamazoo, MI. For general operating support.

$2,000 to Crescendo Academy of Music, Kalamazoo, MI. For scholarships.

$2,000 to Kalamazoo Junior Symphony, Kalamazoo, MI. For scholarships.

$1,000 to New Vic Theatricals, Kalamazoo, MI. For general operating support.

4242
Burt Foundation ◇
c/o Erik H. Serr, Miller Canfield
101 N. Main St., 7th Fl.
Ann Arbor, MI 48104

Established in 1996 in MI.
Donor: Andrea L. Holmes.
Foundation type: Independent foundation.
Financial data (yr. ended 12/31/05): Assets, $4,784,260 (M); gifts received, $182,517; expenditures, $605,651; qualifying distributions, $580,000; giving activities include $580,000 for 20 grants (high: $250,000; low: $5,000).
Purpose and activities: Giving primarily for animal welfare; funding also for health care, human services and the environment.
Fields of interest: Environment; Animal welfare; Animals/wildlife, preservation/protection; Animals/wildlife, sanctuaries; Health care; Human services; Aging, centers/services.
Limitations: Applications not accepted. Giving primarily in MI. No grants to individuals.
Application information: Contributes only to pre-selected organizations.
Officer: Andrea L. Holmes, Pres. and Treas.
EIN: 383309907

4243
Capital Region Community Foundation
6035 Executive Dr., Ste. 104
Lansing, MI 48911 (517) 272-2870
Contact: Dennis W. Fliehman, Pres.
FAX: (517) 272-2871;
E-mail: dfliehman@crcfoundation.org; URL: http://www.crcfoundation.org

Established in 1987 in MI.
Foundation type: Community foundation.
Financial data (yr. ended 12/31/05): Assets, $52,383,547 (M); gifts received, $3,255,752; expenditures, $2,711,751; giving activities include $2,042,200 for 509 grants (high: $779,369; low: $38).
Purpose and activities: The purpose of the foundation is to build the number and size of permanent endowment funds, income from which is used for grants that meet the charitable needs of Clinton, Eaton, and Ingham counties, MI. The foundation provides support for humanities, education, environment, health care, human services, and public benefit.
Fields of interest: Humanities; Education; Environment; Health care; Children/youth, services;

Human services; Community development; Public affairs.
Type of support: Management development/capacity building; General/operating support; Capital campaigns; Building/renovation; Equipment; Program development; Seed money; Technical assistance; Matching/challenge support.
Limitations: Giving limited to Clinton, Eaton, and Ingham counties, MI. No support for international organizations, religious programs, or sectarian purposes. No grants to individuals (except for scholarships), or for endowment funds, administrative costs of fundraising campaigns, annual meetings, routine operating expenses, or for existing obligations, debts, or liabilities.
Publications: Application guidelines; Annual report; Financial statement; Newsletter.
Application information: Visit foundation Web site for application form and guidelines. Faxed or e-mailed applications are not accepted. Application form required.
   Initial approach: Telephone
   Copies of proposal: 2
   Deadline(s): Apr. 1 for grants; Jan. 30 for Youth Fund
   Board meeting date(s): Bimonthly
   Final notification: Oct. 1 for grants
Officers and Trustees:* David Donovan,* Chair.; Chris Laverty,* Chair.-Elect; Dennis W. Fliehman,* Pres.; Julia Oliver, V.P., Finance; Charles Blockett, Jr.,* Secy.; Gregg Cornell,* Treas.; Diana Rodriguez Algra; Mark Alley; John Arehart; Joan Bauer; Rolland Bethards, M.D.; Michael Clark, M.D.; Sam L. Davis; Hon. R. George Economy; Nancy A. Elwood; Eugenio Fernandez; Vincent J. Ferris; Mark Hooper; Nancy L. Little; Dorothy E. Maxwell; Douglas A. Mielock; Suzanne B. Mills; Rachelle Neal; Debra Pozega Osburn, Ph.D.; Mary J. Schafer; Mary Ellen Sheets; Sherry Solomon.
Number of staff: 4 full-time professional; 1 full-time support.
EIN: 382776652

4244
The Carls Foundation ▼ ◇
333 W. Fort St., Ste. 1940
Detroit, MI 48226 (313) 965-0990
Contact: Elizabeth A. Stieg, Exec. Dir.
FAX: (313) 965-0547; URL: http://www.carlsfdn.org

Established in 1961 in MI.
Donor: William Carls‡.
Foundation type: Independent foundation.
Financial data (yr. ended 12/31/05): Assets, $117,703,559 (M); expenditures, $6,099,742; qualifying distributions, $5,590,203; giving activities include $4,937,070 for 66 grants (high: $1,000,000; low: $1,164; average: $10,000–$100,000).
Purpose and activities: The principal purpose and mission of the foundation is: 1) Children's Welfare including: health care facilities and programs, with special emphasis on the prevention and treatment of hearing impairment, and recreational, educational, and welfare programs especially for children who are disadvantaged for economic and/or health reasons; and 2) Preservation of natural areas, open space and historic buildings and areas having special natural beauty or significance in maintaining America's heritage and historic ideals, through assistance to land trusts and land conservancies and directly related environmental educational programs.

Fields of interest: Historic preservation/historical societies; Education; Environment, natural resources; Hospitals (general); Speech/hearing centers; Health care; Recreation; Children/youth, services.
Type of support: Capital campaigns; Seed money.
Limitations: Giving primarily in MI. No grants to individuals, or for publications, film, research, endowments, fellowships, travel, conferences, special event sponsorships, playground or athletic facilities, or seminars; no educational loans.
Publications: Annual report.
Application information: Letter of inquiry is not required and phone calls are welcome. Use of the CMF Common Grant Application Form is optional and acceptable. Application form not required.
   Initial approach: Proposal
   Copies of proposal: 1
   Deadline(s): Mar. 1, July 1, and Nov. 1
   Board meeting date(s): Jan., May, and Sept.
   Final notification: Notification letter sent to all applicants
Officers and Trustees:* Arthur B. Derisley,* Pres. and Treas.; Harold E. Stieg,* V.P. and Secy.; Elizabeth A. Stieg, Exec. Dir.; Henry Fleischer; Teresa R. Krieger.
Advisory Board: Brian A. Derisley; Homer E. Nye; Rev. Delayne H. Pauling; Robert A. Sajdak; Edward C. Stieg.
Number of staff: 1 full-time professional; 1 part-time professional; 1 full-time support.
EIN: 386099935
Selected grants: The following grants were reported in 2005.

$1,000,000 to Beaumont Foundation, Southfield, MI. For capital campaign to create children's medical/pediatric center at Royal Oak facility.

$600,000 to YMCA of Metropolitan Detroit, Detroit, MI. For capital campaign earmarked to construct a full-service facility for Huron Valley YMCA.

$500,000 to Grand Traverse Regional Land Conservancy, Traverse City, MI. For land acquisition, purchase of developmental rights, and establishment of revolving fund for future purchases.

$400,000 to Nature Conservancy, Lansing, MI. For leadership grant to preserve 390 acres in Upper Peninsula.

$150,000 to Judson Center, Royal Oak, MI. For creation of Autism Center to service children and adults with autism in Metropolitan Detroit.

$100,000 to Detroit Rescue Mission Ministries, Detroit, MI. For construction of new bath house to serve youth at Wildwood Ranch.

$100,000 to Henry Ford Health System, Detroit, MI. For establishment of Pediatric Dermatology Emergency Needs to provide care for children with chronic dermatological conditions who lack insurance or resources.

$54,515 to Guidance Center, Southgate, MI. For purchase of hearing and vision equipment as well as supplies to provide screenings for children aged 0-5.

$25,000 to Hospice of Michigan, Detroit, MI. For funding needed for staff, supplies and medication to provide hospice services to pediatric patients.

$10,000 to Peace Neighborhood Center, Ann Arbor, MI. For summer day camp program serving economically disadvantaged children from Ann Arbor area.

4245
Cascade Hemophilia Consortium ✧
210 E. Huron St., Ste. D
Ann Arbor, MI 48104
Contact: William T. Sparrow, Exec. Dir.

Established in 1996 in MI.
Foundation type: Operating foundation.
Financial data (yr. ended 12/31/04): Assets, $0 (M); gifts received, $550; expenditures, $1,449,529; qualifying distributions, $999,225; giving activities include $999,225 for 33 grants (high: $276,016; low: $48).
Purpose and activities: Support limited to the medical care and research of hemophilia.
Fields of interest: Hemophilia; Hemophilia research.
Limitations: Applications not accepted. Giving primarily in MI and OH. No grants to individuals.
Application information: Foundation sends out Requests for Proposals and does not accept unsolicited requests for funds.
Officers: William Berk, M.D., Pres.; Stephen Pokoj, J.D., V.P.; Stephen Munk, Ph.D., Secy.; Carrie Voegtle, Treas.; William T. Sparrow, Exec. Dir.
Directors: Judith Andersen, M.D.; Tom Bills; Jane Dinnen, R.N.; Anne Eccles; Shelley Gerson; Ivan Harner; Phil Kucab; Caterine McClure, J.D.; Andy Muir; James Munn, R.N.; Linda Wacha, R.N.
EIN: 383199649
Selected grants: The following grants were reported in 2004.
$70,956 to Hemophilia Foundation of Michigan, Ann Arbor, MI. For camp rental, travel, administrative fees, Labtracker support and other regional services.
$48,500 to Indiana Hemophilia and Thrombosis Center, Indianapolis, IN. For nursing, physical therapy and social work.
$42,500 to Harper Hospital, Detroit, MI. For nursing, physical therapy, social work, genetic counseling, and dietician.
$35,500 to Ohio State University Medical Center, Columbus, OH. For Adult Hemophilia Treatment Center.
$34,000 to Munson Medical Center, Traverse City, MI. For social work, dietician, dental services and phlebotomist.
$33,000 to University Hospitals of Cleveland, Cleveland, OH. For nursing and social work.
$32,750 to University of Michigan Hospitals, Ann Arbor, MI. For Hemophilia Treatment Center.
$32,000 to Childrens Hospital Medical Center of Akron, Akron, OH. For nursing and social work.
$28,500 to Hurley Medical Center, Flint, MI.
$23,187 to Childrens Hospital of Michigan, Detroit, MI. For nursing and project assistant.

4246
Charlevoix County Community Foundation
507 Water St.
P.O. Box 718
East Jordan, MI 49727 (231) 536-2440
Contact: Robert G. Tambellini, C.E.O.
FAX: (231) 536-2640; E-mail: info@c3f.org;
URL: http://www.c3f.org

Established in 1992 in MI.
Foundation type: Community foundation.
Financial data (yr. ended 12/31/05): Assets, $18,113,170 (M); gifts received, $2,044,365; expenditures, $1,384,316; giving activities include $1,045,910 for 156 grants (high: $204,402; low:

$50), and $5,646 for 3 grants to individuals (high: $4,000; low: $95).
Purpose and activities: The foundation seeks to enhance the quality of life in Charlevoix County, MI, now and for generations to come, by building a permanent charitable endowment from a wide range of donors, addressing needs through grantmaking, and providing leadership on matters of community concern. The foundation provides support for worthwhile programs and projects focusing on the arts, education, environmental preservation, human services, wellness, civic improvement, and economic development.
Fields of interest: Arts; Higher education; Education; Environment; Health care; Recreation; Children/youth, services; Human services; Economic development; Community development; Government/public administration.
Type of support: Scholarships—to individuals; Endowments; Emergency funds; Program development; Seed money; Scholarship funds; Technical assistance; Consulting services.
Limitations: Giving limited to Charlevoix County, MI. No support for sectarian purposes. No grants to individuals (except for scholarships), or for ongoing operations, deficit spending, office equipment, or fundraising projects; no loans.
Publications: Application guidelines.
Application information: Visit foundation Web site for grant application cover sheet and guidelines. Application form required.
Initial approach: Telephone
Copies of proposal: 21
Deadline(s): Apr. 1 and Oct. 1
Board meeting date(s): 4th Mon. of the month, 5 times per year
Final notification: June and Dec.
Officers and Trustees:* Jim Howell,* Chair.; Don Spencer,* Vice-Chair.; Robert G. Tambellini, C.E.O. and Pres.; Bill Lorne,* Corp. Secy.; Kirk Jabara,* Treas.; Rhea Dow; Sally Fogg; Tom Hanna; Kay Heise; Bruce Herbert; Tom Irwin; Pat Poineau; Barbara Pritchard; Jeff Rogers; Nancy Wright.
Number of staff: 2 full-time professional; 1 full-time support.
EIN: 383033739

4247
Christian Evangelical Foundation ✧
618 Kenmoor Ave. S.E., Rm. 120
Grand Rapids, MI 49546

Established in 1987 in IL.
Donors: John C. Huizenga; Elizabeth I. Huizenga Foundation.
Foundation type: Independent foundation.
Financial data (yr. ended 12/31/04): Assets, $2,972,480 (M); gifts received, $13,230; expenditures, $1,236,543; qualifying distributions, $1,206,850; giving activities include $1,206,850 for 49 grants (high: $250,000; low: $100).
Purpose and activities: Giving primarily to Christian organizations and for Christian education.
Fields of interest: Higher education; Education; Human services; Children, services; Family services; Christian agencies & churches.
Type of support: General/operating support.
Limitations: Applications not accepted. Giving on a national basis with emphasis on MI. No grants to individuals.
Application information: Contributes only to pre-selected organizations. Unsolicited requests for funds not accepted.

Officers: John C. Huizenga, Pres. and Mgr.; John Grant, Secy.; Laura B. Huizenga, Treas.
EIN: 363501198
Selected grants: The following grants were reported in 2003.
$250,000 to Haggai Institute for Advanced Leadership Training, Atlanta, GA. For general support.
$102,000 to Geneva Camp and Retreat Center, Holland, MI. For general support.
$63,740 to Campus Crusade for Christ, Dallas, TX. For general support.
$40,000 to Young Life in Grand Rapids, Grand Rapids, MI. For general support.
$25,000 to Calvin College, Grand Rapids, MI. For general support.
$25,000 to Inner City Impact, Chicago, IL. For general support.
$25,000 to Kids Hope USA, Holland, MI. For general support.
$21,000 to Potters House, Grand Rapids, MI. For general support.
$15,000 to Open Doors International, Santa Ana, CA. For general support.
$15,000 to Pine Rest Foundation, Grand Rapids, MI. For general support.

4248
Citizens Banking Corporation Charitable Foundation ✧
c/o Citizens Bank Wealth Management, N.A.
328 S. Saginaw St., M.C. 002072
Flint, MI 48502

Established in 1999 in MI.
Donor: Citizens Banking Corp.
Foundation type: Company-sponsored foundation.
Financial data (yr. ended 12/31/05): Assets, $508,152 (M); gifts received, $69,326; expenditures, $1,055,994; qualifying distributions, $1,040,533; giving activities include $1,038,951 for 363 grants (high: $75,000; low: $250).
Purpose and activities: The foundation supports organizations involved with arts and culture, education, health, human services, and community development.
Fields of interest: Arts; Education; Hospitals (general); Health care; Youth, services; Human services; Community development; Federated giving programs.
Limitations: Applications not accepted. Giving primarily in IA, MI, and WI. No grants to individuals.
Application information: Contributes only to pre-selected organizations.
Trustee: Citizens Bank Wealth Management, N.A.
EIN: 386742630

4249
Citizens First Foundation, Inc. ✧
(formerly Citizens First Savings Charitable Foundation, Inc.)
525 Water St.
Port Huron, MI 48060

Established in 1998 in MI.
Donor: Citizens First Savings Bank.
Foundation type: Company-sponsored foundation.
Financial data (yr. ended 12/31/04): Assets, $23,163,631 (M); expenditures, $1,048,810; qualifying distributions, $1,035,284; giving

activities include $1,023,740 for 118 grants (high: $473,860; low: $50).

Purpose and activities: The foundation supports hospitals, community foundations, and organizations involved with arts and culture, education, heart and circulatory diseases, and human services.

Fields of interest: Arts; Education; Hospitals (general); Heart & circulatory diseases; Human services; Foundations (community); Federated giving programs.

Type of support: General/operating support.

Limitations: Applications not accepted. Giving primarily in MI. No grants to individuals.

Application information: Contributes only to pre-selected organizations.

Officers and Directors: Marshall J. Campbell, Pres.; Timothy D. Regan, Secy.-Treas.; Ronald W. Cooley; David C. Devendorf; Christopher A. Kellerman.

EIN: 383401243

Selected grants: The following grants were reported in 2004.

$708,125 to United Way of Saint Clair County, Port Huron, MI. 4 grants: $687,500, $6,875, $6,875, $6,875

$473,860 to Sanilac County Community Foundation, Sandusky, MI.

$105,000 to Saint Clair County Community College, Port Huron, MI. 2 grants: $5,000, $100,000

$13,000 to United Way of Sanilac County, Lexington, MI. 2 grants: $3,000, $10,000

$2,000 to United Way.

4250

The Cold Heading Foundation ✧

(formerly DeSeranno Educational Foundation, Inc.)

c/o Edward Miller

21777 Hoover Rd.

Warren, MI 48089

Established in 1968 in MI.

Donors: Cold Heading Co.; Ajax Metal Processing, Inc.; Beachlawn Mortgage Co.

Foundation type: Independent foundation.

Financial data (yr. ended 12/31/05): Assets, $29,265,309 (M); expenditures, $1,658,673; qualifying distributions, $1,385,705; giving activities include $1,227,450 for 41+ grants (high: $550,000).

Purpose and activities: Giving primarily for education, as well as for health associations, and to Roman Catholic churches and organizations.

Fields of interest: Higher education; Health care; Health organizations, association; Foundations (private grantmaking); Roman Catholic agencies & churches.

Type of support: General/operating support.

Limitations: Applications not accepted. Giving primarily in MI.

Application information: Unsolicited requests for funds not accepted.

Officers: Derek Stevens, Pres.; Elizabeth Stevens, V.P. and Secy.; Gregory Stevens, Treas.

Trustee: Aline DeSerrano.

Number of staff: 3 part-time support.

EIN: 237005737

Selected grants: The following grants were reported in 2004.

$120,000 to Steuben County Community Foundation, Angola, IN.

$100,000 to Madonna University, Livonia, MI.

$50,000 to Grosse Pointe Park Foundation, Grosse Pointe, MI.

$25,000 to Detroit Athletic Club Foundation, Detroit, MI.

$20,500 to New Common School Foundation, Detroit, MI.

$14,000 to United Way.

$2,500 to Lawrence Technological University, Southfield, MI.

$2,000 to Gonzaga University, Spokane, WA.

4251

Comerica Charitable Foundation ▼ ✧

c/o Comerica Inc.

P.O. Box 75000, M.C. 3390

Detroit, MI 48275-3390 (313) 222-7356

Contact: Caroline E. Chambers, Secy.

FAX: (313) 222-5555; Application addresses: Michigan: Michigan Comerica Corp. Contribs. Mgr., M.C. 3390, P.O. Box 75000, Detroit, MI 48275-3390, West Division: Comerica Corp. Contribs. Mgr., M.C. 4805, 333 W. Santa Clara St., San Jose, CA 95113, Dallas, TX, area: Comerica Corp. Contribs. Mgr., M.C. 6500, P.O. Box 650282, Dallas, TX 75265-0282, Houston, TX, area: Comerica Corp. Contribs. Mgr., M.C. 6623, P.O. Box 4167, Houston, TX 77210-4167, Florida: Randy Nobles, Comerica Corp. Contribs. Mgr., M.C. 5172, 1800 Corporate Blvd. N.W., Boca Raton, FL 33431-7394; URL: http://www.comerica.com/vgn-ext-templating/v/index.jsp?vgnextoid=374970d75d994010VgnVCM1000004502a8c0RCRD

Established in 1997 in MI.

Donors: Comerica Bank; Comerica Inc.

Foundation type: Company-sponsored foundation.

Financial data (yr. ended 12/31/05): Assets, $3,469,528 (M); gifts received, $7,107,837; expenditures, $9,293,467; qualifying distributions, $9,293,467; giving activities include $9,293,467 for 666 grants (high: $870,000; low: $43).

Purpose and activities: The foundation supports organizations involved with arts and culture, business education, literacy, health, mental health, employment, housing, financial literacy, community development, and economically disadvantaged people.

Fields of interest: Arts, equal rights; Performing arts; Arts; Business school/education; Adult education—literacy, basic skills & GED; Education, reading; Health care; Mental health/crisis services; Employment, training; Employment; Housing/shelter; Human services, financial counseling; Community development, small businesses; Community development; Economically disadvantaged.

Type of support: General/operating support; Capital campaigns; Scholarship funds.

Limitations: Giving in areas of company operations, with emphasis on MI.

Publications: Application guidelines; Annual report.

Application information: The Council of Michigan Foundations Common Grant Application form is available online at www.cmif.org. Application form required.

Initial approach: Download the Council of Michigan Foundations Common Grant Application form and mail proposal and application form to application address

Deadline(s): None; Jan. 1 to Oct. 1 for organizations located in Michigan

Final notification: 60 days

Officers: Richard A. Collister, Pres.; Caroline E. Chambers, Secy.; Megan Burkhart, Treas.

Directors: Elizabeth S. Acton; Frank DeAramas; Linda Forte; Mike Fulton; James Garavaglia; John Haggerty; Ron Marcinelli; Sharon McMurray; Albert Taylor; Mark Yonkman.

EIN: 383373052

Selected grants: The following grants were reported in 2004.

$971,000 to United Way for Southeastern Michigan, Detroit, MI. 2 grants: $805,000 (For Torch Drive Corporate Campaign), $166,000 (For New Detroit Fund).

$500,000 to Detroit Renaissance, Detroit, MI. For Downtown Development Initiative.

$250,000 to ACCION San Diego, San Diego, CA.

$250,000 to Community Financial Resource Center, Los Angeles, CA.

$200,000 to Greenlining Institute, Berkeley, CA. For capital campaign.

$187,500 to Local Initiatives Support Corporation (LISC), Detroit, MI.

$167,000 to Charles H. Wright Museum of African-American History, Detroit, MI.

$167,000 to Michigan Opera Theater, Detroit, MI. For New Century Fund Campaign.

$150,000 to Detroit Regional Chamber, Detroit, MI. For partnership.

4252

Community Foundation for Muskegon County ✧

(formerly Muskegon County Community Foundation, Inc.)

425 W. Western Ave., Ste. 200

Muskegon, MI 49440 (231) 722-4538

Contact: Chris Ann McGuigan, C.E.O.; For grants: Arnold "Arn" Boezaart, V.P., Grant Progs.

FAX: (231) 722-4616; E-mail: info@cffmc.org; Grant application E-mail: aboezaart@cffmc.org; URL: http://www.cffmc.org

Incorporated in 1961 in MI.

Donors: Alta Daetz†; Harold Frauenthal†; Charles Goodnow†; George Hilt; Jack Hilt; John Hilt; Paul C. Johnson†; Henry Klooster†; Ernest Settle†.

Foundation type: Community foundation.

Financial data (yr. ended 12/31/04): Assets, $88,320,829 (M); gifts received, $3,449,419; expenditures, $4,879,031; giving activities include $2,726,558 for 1,148 grants (high: $85,000; low: $4).

Purpose and activities: The foundation seeks to assist worthwhile projects, with emphasis on health and human services, arts and culture, education, community development, and youth. Of particular interest are pilot programs and collaborative projects.

Fields of interest: Arts education; Performing arts, theater; Arts; Scholarships/financial aid; Education; Environment, air pollution; Environment, water pollution; Environment, land resources; Environment; Health care; Health organizations, association; Youth development; Youth, pregnancy prevention; Human services; Economic development; Urban/community development; Community development; Infants/toddlers; Children.

Type of support: Continuing support; Building/renovation; Equipment; Emergency funds; Program development; Conferences/seminars; Professorships; Publication; Seed money; Internship funds; Scholarship funds; Research; Consulting services; Program-related investments/

---

loans; Scholarships—to individuals; Exchange programs; Matching/challenge support.
Limitations: Giving limited to Muskegon County, MI. No support for sectarian religious programs, or individual schools or districts. No grants to individuals (except for scholarships), or for deficit financing, routine operating expenses, capital equipment, endowment campaigns, special fundraising events, conferences, camps, publications, videos, films, television or radio programs, or for advertising.
Publications: Application guidelines; Annual report (including application guidelines); Financial statement; Grants list; Informational brochure (including application guidelines); Newsletter; Program policy statement.
Application Information: Visit foundation Web site for grant information; call the foundation for proposal guidelines and specific deadlines.
   Initial approach: Telephone
   Deadline(s): Varies
   Board meeting date(s): Feb., Apr., June, Aug., Oct., and Dec.
   Final notification: 3 months
Officers and Trustees:* Michael Bozym, Ph.D.*, Chair.; Patricia B. Johnson,* Vice-Chair. and Pres. Emeritus; Peter M. Turner,* Vice-Chair.; Chris Ann McGuigan,* C.E.O., Pres., and Secy.; Arnold "Arn" Boezaart, V.P., Grant Progs.; Robert Chapla, V.P., Devel.; Ann Van Tassel, V.P., Finance; Scott Musselman,* Treas.; Tim Achterhoft; B. Dennis Albrechtsen; Nancy L. Crandall; Lowell B. Dana; Barbara L. DeBruyn; Holly J. Hughes; Dr. John L. Mixer; Stephen G. Olsen; Michael A. Pepper; Hon. Greg C. Pittman; Rev. Charles Poole; Bruce C. Rice; Arthur V. Scott; John W. Swanson II; Sue Wierengo; Judith L. Wilcox; John Workman.
Trustee Banks: Comerica Bank; Fifth Third Bank; The Huntington National Bank; National City Bank.
Number of staff: 7 full-time professional; 5 full-time support.
EIN: 386114135
Selected grants: The following grants were reported in 2004.
$110,000 to Frauenthal Center for the Performing Arts, Muskegon, MI. For operating subsidy for theater which is operated as service to community.
$100,000 to Muskegon Area First, Muskegon, MI. For re-development of downtown.
$50,000 to MGH Family Health Center, Muskegon Family Care, Muskegon, MI. For construction of new health care facility.
$40,000 to Downtown Muskegon Development Corporation, Muskegon, MI. For consulting work for former Muskegon Mall property.
$30,000 to Hospice of Muskegon-Oceana, Muskegon, MI. For Poppen Hospice Residence.
$30,000 to Senior Resources of West Michigan, Muskegon Heights, MI. For development of Mukegon County 2-1-1.
$25,000 to Hackley Hospital, Muskegon, MI. For Hackley Emergency Center.
$20,000 to Hackley Public Library, Friends of, Muskegon, MI. For Stained Glass Window Repair.
$17,500 to Muskegon, City of, Muskegon, MI. For matching funds for Michigan Economic Development Corporation.
$11,000 to Salvation Army, Muskegon, MI. For shelter and utility assistance to City of Muskegon residents.

4253
Community Foundation for Northeast Michigan

(doing business as North Central Michigan Community Foundation)
(formerly Northeast Michigan Community Foundation)
111 Water St.
P.O. Box 495
Alpena, MI 49707 (989) 354-6881
Contact: Barbara A. Willyard, Exec. Dir.
FAX: (989) 356-3319; E-mail: bwillyard@cfnem.org;
Additional tel.: (877) 354-6881; URL: http://www.cfnem.org

Incorporated in 1974 in MI.
Foundation type: Community foundation.
Financial data (yr. ended 9/30/05): Assets, $22,968,969 (M); gifts received, $4,927,192; expenditures, $999,172; giving activities include $716,392 for 540 grants (high: $200,000; low: $100).
Purpose and activities: The foundation seeks to serve the community and to preserve the charitable goals of a wide range of donors now and for generations to come.
Fields of interest: Humanities; Arts; Libraries/library science; Education; Environment; Health care; Health organizations, association; Children/youth, services; Human services; Government/public administration.
Type of support: Building/renovation; Equipment; Program development; Conferences/seminars; Seed money; Scholarship funds; Technical assistance.
Limitations: Giving limited to Alcona, Alpena, Montmorency, and Presque Isle counties, and through affiliates: Crawford, Cheboygan, Iosco, Ogemaw, and Oscoda counties, MI. No support for religious or sectarian purposes. No grants to individuals (except for scholarships), or for annual giving campaigns or capital campaigns, normal operating expenses, or multi-year or sustained funding; no loans.
Publications: Application guidelines; Annual report; Financial statement; Grants list; Informational brochure; Newsletter; Program policy statement.
Application information: Visit foundation Web site for application forms and guidelines. For grants of $300 or less, organizations should use the 2-page mini-grant application and follow its specific guidelines. Application form required.
   Initial approach: Submit application forms and attachments
   Copies of proposal: 1
   Deadline(s): Feb. 1, Aug. 1, and Nov. 1
   Board meeting date(s): Quarterly
   Final notification: Within 6 weeks
Officers and Trustees:* Steve Lappan,* Pres.; Nancy Coombs,* V.P.; Bill Morford,* Secy.; Georgene Hildebrand,* Treas.; Barbara A. Willyard, Exec. Dir.; Marcia Aten; Benjamin Bolser; Carolyn Brummund; Larry Bruski; Ann Burton; Hugo Burzlaff; George "Ted" Cavin; Beach Hall; Carl Huebner; Sue Keller; Jennie Kerr; Chuck Manning; Damone Sorenson; Bill Speer.
Number of staff: 4 full-time professional.
EIN: 237384822

4254
Community Foundation for Southeast Michigan ▼

(formerly Community Foundation for Southeastern Michigan)
333 W. Fort St., Ste. 2010
Detroit, MI 48226 (313) 961-6675
Contact: Mariam C. Noland, Pres.
FAX: (313) 961-2886; E-mail: cfsem@cfsem.org;
URL: http://www.cfsem.org

Established in 1984 in MI.
Foundation type: Community foundation.
Financial data (yr. ended 12/31/05): Assets, $454,103,157 (M); gifts received, $47,470,217; expenditures, $33,870,694; giving activities include $27,473,684 for grants.
Purpose and activities: The foundation strengthens the region's quality of life by: 1) building "community capital"; 2) enhancing the region's quality of life; 3) engaging people and organizations in philanthropy; 4) convening, planning and working for positive change; and 5) supporting and launching new initiatives. Supports projects in the areas of civic affairs, social services, arts and culture, health, education, environment and land use, neighborhood and regional economic development and workforce development.
Fields of interest: Arts; Education; Environment; Health care; Health organizations, association; Youth development, services; Youth, services; Human services; Civil rights, race/intergroup relations; Economic development; Community development; Government/public administration; Leadership development; Public affairs; Economically disadvantaged.
Type of support: Program development; Seed money; Scholarship funds; Technical assistance; Scholarships—to individuals.
Limitations: Giving limited to Livingston, Macomb, Monroe, Oakland, St. Clair, Washtenaw, and Wayne counties, MI. No support for sectarian religious programs. No grants to individuals (from unrestricted funds), or for capital projects, endowments, annual campaigns, general operating support, conferences, computers and computer systems, fundraising, annual meetings, buildings, or equipment.
Publications: Application guidelines; Annual report (including application guidelines); Grants list; Informational brochure (including application guidelines); Newsletter.
Application information: There may be separate grantmaking guidelines for targeted grantmaking projects. These guidelines and special application forms are available by contacting the foundation or consulting the foundation's Guidelines for Grantmaking. Visit foundation Web site for general grant application guidelines. Application form not required.
   Initial approach: Telephone
   Copies of proposal: 2
   Deadline(s): Feb. 15, May 15, Aug. 15, and Nov. 15
   Board meeting date(s): Mar., June, Sept., and Dec.
   Final notification: 3 months after submission of proposal
Officers and Trustees:* Allan D. Gilmour,* Chair.; Alfred R. Glancy III,* Vice-Chair.; Alan E. Schwartz,* Vice-Chair.; Mariam C. Noland, Pres.; Robin D. Ferriby, V.P., Philanthropic Svcs.; Cassandra Joubert, Sc.D., V.P., Community Investment; Karen L. Leppanen, V.P., Finance and Admin.; Anne S.

Weekley, V.P., Comms.; Hon. Anna Diggs Taylor,* Secy.; Michael T. Monahan,* Treas.; Penny B. Blumenstein,* Chair., Prog. and Distrib.; Frederick M. Adams, Jr.; Margaret Acheson Allesee; Hon. Dennis W. Archer; Norma C. Barfield; Albert M. Berriz; Andrew L. Camden; Julie Fisher Cummings; Tarik S. Daoud; Paul R. Dimond; Deborah I. Dingell; Anthony F. Earley, Jr.; Irma B. Elder; David T. Fischer; Phillip W. Fischer; W. Frank Fountain; Steven K. Hamp; David M. Hempstead; William M. Hermann; William K. Howenstein; Joseph L. Hudson, Jr.; John D. Lewis; Dana M. Locniskar; Ben C. Maibach III; Florine Mark; Jack Martin; Kathleen McCree-Lewis; Edward J. Miller; Eugene A. Miller; James B. Nicholson; Bruce E. Nyberg; David K. Page; Cynthia J. Pasky; William F. Pickard; Sandra E. Pierce; John Rakolta, Jr.; Jack A. Robinson; Pamela Rodgers; Howard F. Sims; Vivian Day Stroh; Gary Torgow; Reginald M. Turner; Barbara C. Van Dusen; Ken Whipple; Tom Wilson.

Number of staff: 17 full-time professional; 1 part-time professional; 9 full-time support; 1 part-time support.

EIN: 382530980

Selected grants: The following grants were reported in 2005.

$1,000,000 to Detroit Riverfront Conservancy, Detroit, MI. For construction of Detroit RiverWalk.

$1,000,000 to Princeton University, Princeton, NJ. For program support.

$500,000 to Detroit Symphony Orchestra, Detroit, MI. For capital campaign.

$348,761 to Archdiocese of Detroit, Detroit, MI. For program support.

$100,000 to American Red Cross, Washtenaw County Chapter, Ann Arbor, MI. For program support.

$96,000 to Preserve Our Parks, Hamtramck, MI. For planning and design of trail connecting Veterans Memorial Park in Hamtramck to Dequindre Cut.

$25,000 to American Indian College Fund, Denver, CO. For program support.

4255

Community Foundation of Greater Flint

502 Church St.
Flint, MI 48502-1206 (810) 767-8270
Contact: Kathi Horton, Pres.
FAX: (810) 767-0496; E-mail: cfgf@cfgf.org;
Additional E-mail: khorton@cfgf.org; URL: http://www.cfgf.org

Established in 1988 in MI.
Foundation type: Community foundation.
Financial data (yr. ended 12/31/05): Assets, $117,794,673 (M); gifts received, $3,762,963; expenditures, $7,753,362; giving activities include $5,369,711 for 648 grants (high: $403,331), and $347,382 for 24 foundation-administered programs.
Purpose and activities: The foundation serves the common good in Genesee County, building a strong community by engaging people in philanthropy and developing the community's permanent endowment, now and for generations to come. The foundation seeks to respond to current or emerging needs in the local area in conservation and the environment, arts and humanities, education, health and human services, and leadership development.
Fields of interest: Humanities; Arts; Education; Environment, natural resources; Environment; Health care; Youth development, services;

Children/youth, services; Human services; Leadership development; Children/youth; Economically disadvantaged.
Type of support: General/operating support; Management development/capacity building; Program development; Seed money; Scholarship funds; Technical assistance; Program evaluation; Matching/challenge support.
Limitations: Giving primarily in Genesee County, MI. No support for sectarian religious purposes (generally). No grants to individuals (except for scholarships), or for deficit reduction, routine operating expenses of existing organizations, or endowments.
Publications: Application guidelines; Annual report; Financial statement; Grants list; Informational brochure; Occasional report; Program policy statement.
Application information: Visit foundation Web site for application guidelines. There are separate grantmaking guidelines for several special grantmaking projects. These guidelines and special application forms are available by contacting the foundation. Application form required.
Initial approach: Telephone or personal contact
Copies of proposal: 4
Deadline(s): Varies
Board meeting date(s): Feb., Apr., June, Aug., Oct., and Dec.
Officers and Trustees:* Lawrence E. Moon,* Chair.; Sherri E. Stephens,* Vice-Chair.; Kathi Horton, Pres.; Mary Ittigson, V.P., Finance and Admin.; Tanya Jefferson, V.P., Community Impact; AnnMarie VanDuyne, V.P., Philanthropic Svcs.; Jo Anne G. Mondowney,* Secy.; Daniel Coffield,* Treas.; Rudy V. Collins; Samuel Cox; F. James Cummins; Shannon M. Easter; Cheryl A. Gifford; Nancy Hanflik; Nina M. Jones; Timothy H. Knecht; Stanley Liberty; Juan Mestas; William Morgan; Bobby Mukkamala; Clarence Sevillian II; Susan Tippett.
Number of staff: 9 full-time professional; 3 full-time support.
EIN: 382190667

4256

Community Foundation of Greater Rochester ◇

(formerly Greater Rochester Area Community Foundation)
P.O. Box 80431
Rochester, MI 48308-0431 (248) 608-2804
Contact: Peggy Hamilton, Exec. Dir.
FAX: (248) 608-2826; E-mail: cfound@cfound.org;
URL: http://www.cfound.org
Scholarship application address for hand delivery: Community Fdn. Office, 127 W. University Dr., Rochester, MI 48307

Incorporated in 1983 in MI.
Foundation type: Community foundation.
Financial data (yr. ended 12/31/04): Assets, $0 (M); gifts received, $930,288; expenditures, $845,111; giving activities include $518,882 for 82 grants (high: $57,637; low: $50), and $141,587 for 98 grants to individuals (high: $4,000; low: $63).
Purpose and activities: The foundation seeks to enhance the quality of life for community residents within the following funding categories: arts and culture, education, youth, civic beautification, health, recreation, human services, and community development.
Fields of interest: Museums; Performing arts; Performing arts, music; Arts; Elementary school/

education; Education; Environment, natural resources; Environment; Health care; Recreation; Youth, services; Family services; Human services; Economic development; Community development; Youth; Disabilities, people with.
Type of support: General/operating support; Annual campaigns; Building/renovation; Equipment; Endowments; Emergency funds; Seed money; Scholarship funds; Scholarships—to individuals; Matching/challenge support.
Limitations: Giving limited to the greater Rochester, MI, area. No grants to individuals (except for designated scholarship funds), or for operating budgets.
Publications: Annual report (including application guidelines); Financial statement; Informational brochure; Newsletter.
Application information: Visit the foundation Web site for application forms and specific guidelines per grant type. Application form required.
Initial approach: Letter of Intent or telephone
Copies of proposal: 7
Deadline(s): Mar. 31 and Sept. 30 for grant application forms; Mar. 18 for scholarships
Board meeting date(s): Quarterly
Officers and Trustees:* Edward A. Golick,* Chair.; David de Steiger, Vice-Chair., Devel.; Linda Preede,* Vice-Chair., Investment; George Seifert,* Vice-Chair., Pro Tem; Patricia Botkin,* Secy.; Mary Ann Reidinger,* Treas.; Peggy Hamilton, Exec. Dir.; Kenneth D. Bilodeau; Joseph Champagne; Jack DiFranco; Gail Duncan; Michael Glass; Brian Hunter; Vern Pixley; Dave Shellenbarger.
Members: Johanna Allen; Corey Bordine; Frank Cardimen; Gerald Carvey; Jerry Collins; Penny Crissman; Kathy Dziurman; Tom Finnerty; Lois Haack; Robert Justin; Bruce Kresge; Richard Maibauer; Patrick McKay; Ed McKibbon; Sid Mittra; Pamela Mitzelfeld; John Modetz; Don Pixley; Katy Plummer; John Schultz; Russ Shelton; Marty Sibert; Mary Beth Snyder; Lawrence Ternan; Brad Upton.
Number of staff: 1 full-time professional; 1 part-time support.
EIN: 382476777

4257

Community Foundation of St. Clair County

516 McMorran Blvd.
Port Huron, MI 48060 (810) 984-4761
Contact: Randy D. Maiers, C.E.O.
FAX: (810) 984-3394;
E-mail: info@stclairfoundation.org; Grant application
E-mail: grants@stclairfoundation.org; Additional
E-mail: randy@stclairfoundation.org; URL: http://www.stclairfoundation.org

Established in 1944 in MI.
Foundation type: Community foundation.
Financial data (yr. ended 12/31/05): Assets, $29,339,308 (M); gifts received, $2,505,756; expenditures, $2,448,351; giving activities include $1,823,765 for grants, and $65,145 for 60 grants to individuals (high: $5,000; low: $300).
Purpose and activities: The foundation seeks to serve the charitable needs and enhance the quality of life of the community by: providing a flexible and convenient vehicle for donors having a variety of charitable goals and needs; receiving and investing contributions to build permanent endowments; responding to changing and emerging community needs; serving as a steward for individuals, families, foundations, and organizations entrusting assets to its care; and providing grants to philanthropic

organizations, social services, civic concerns, education, arts and culture, recreation and youth.

Fields of interest: Arts; Education; Recreation; Family services; Human services; Economic development; Community development; Youth; Aging.

Type of support: Technical assistance; Program-related investments/loans; Management development/capacity building; Building/renovation; Equipment; Program development; Publication; Seed money; Scholarship funds; Scholarships—to individuals; Matching/challenge support.

Limitations: Giving limited to St. Clair County, MI. No support for religious activities. No grants to individuals directly, or for endowments, equipment, annual meetings, conferences, travel expenses, venture capital funds, or film, video, or TV projects, deficit reduction, annual fundraising, capital campaigns, marketing or public relations, general operating expenses, or land use.

Publications: Application guidelines; Annual report; Financial statement; Grants list; Informational brochure; Newsletter.

Application information: Visit foundation Web site for application form and guidelines. Application form required.

Initial approach: Contact foundation
Copies of proposal: 1
Deadline(s): Jan. 1, Apr. 1, July 1, and Oct. 1
Board meeting date(s): Quarterly
Final notification: Mar., June, Sept., and Dec.

Officers and Board Members:* Frederick S. Moore,* Chair.; Charles G. Kelly,* Vice-Chair.; Randy D. Maiers, C.E.O. and Pres.; Marshall J. Campbell,* Secy.; Don C. Fletcher,* Treas.; Karen Lee, Cont.; Douglas R. Austin; Beth Belanger; Rose B. Bellanca; Heather Bokram; Ronald W. Cooley; Gary Fletcher; Lee C. Hanson; Steve Hill; Thomas A. Hunter; Roy W. Klecha; Gerald J. Kramer; John R. Monaghan; Franklin H. Moore; Donna M. Niester; David P. O'Connor; Will Oldford; Bill Robinson; Lynne M. Secory; John W. Shier; Douglas S. Touma; Joseph A. Vito; Martin E. Weiss; Cathy Wilkinson.

Number of staff: 4 full-time professional; 1 full-time support; 2 part-time support.

EIN: 381872132

4258

The Community Foundation of the Holland/Zeeland Area

(formerly Holland Community Foundation, Inc.)
70 W. 8th St., Ste. 100
Holland, MI 49423 (616) 396-6590
Contact: Janet DeYoung, Exec. Dir.
FAX: (616) 396-3573; E-mail: info@cfhz.org;
Additional E-mail: janet@cfhz.org; URL: http://www.cfhz.org

Incorporated in 1951 in MI.

Foundation type: Community foundation.

Financial data (yr. ended 12/31/05): Assets, $26,332,805 (M); gifts received, $5,203,323; expenditures, $3,546,505; giving activities include $3,100,985 for 331+ grants (high: $450,000; low: $80), and $139,353 for 119 grants to individuals.

Purpose and activities: The foundation seeks to make the greater Holland/Zeeland area a better place in which to live and work by enhancing the quality of life for all its citizens through the use of permanent endowments built from a wide variety of donors.

Fields of interest: Visual arts, art conservation; Historic preservation/historical societies; Arts; Education; Environment; Health care; Housing/shelter; Recreation; Children/youth, services; Human services; Economic development; Community development; Youth; Aging.

Type of support: Capital campaigns; Building/renovation; Equipment; Program development; Seed money; Curriculum development; Scholarship funds; Technical assistance; Program evaluation; Employee-related scholarships; In-kind gifts.

Limitations: Giving limited to the Holland/Zeeland, MI, area and surrounding townships. No support for sectarian religious programs. No grants for endowment funds, operating budgets, expenses for established programs, fundraising drives, capital equipment, conference attendance, salaries, stipends, sabbatical leaves, debt reduction, research, fellowships, matching gifts, travel, or computers, video equipment, or vehicles; no loans.

Publications: Application guidelines; Annual report; Informational brochure (including application guidelines); Newsletter.

Application information: Visit foundation Web site for application guidelines. Letter of intent is mandatory for invitation of full proposal from foundation (10 copies required). 35 copies of the application are required if the project is of primary benefit of youth programming for people under 21 years of age. Application form required.

Initial approach: Telephone
Copies of proposal: 15
Deadline(s): Oct. 26 for letter of intent; Jan. 18 for grant application
Board meeting date(s): Feb., Apr., Aug., and Oct.
Final notification: Within 1 month for letter of intent determination; Apr. for grant determination

Officers and Trustees:* Thun Champassak,* Chair., Investment Comm.; Melissa Kamara,* Chair., Devel.; Peter Neydon,* Pres.; John R. Marquis,* 1st V.P.; Donna VanIwaarden,* 2nd V.P.; Carla Masselink,* Secy.; Janet De Young, Exec. Dir.; Char Amante; Kenneth Bing; Susan Den Herder; Frank Garcia; Jeff Helder; Jim Jurries; Matthew Lepard; Hannes Meyers, Jr.; Grace Van Haitsma.

Number of staff: 3 full-time professional; 2 part-time professional.

EIN: 386095283

4259

Community Foundation of the Upper Peninsula

(formerly Upper Peninsula Community Foundation Alliance)
2500 7th Ave. S., Ste. 103
Escanaba, MI 49829-1176 (906) 789-5972
Contact: Gary LaPlant, Exec. Dir.
FAX: (906) 786-9124; E-mail: cfup@chartermi.net;
URL: http://cfup.org/about_CFUP.htm

Established in 1994 in MI.

Foundation type: Community foundation.

Financial data (yr. ended 12/31/05): Assets, $16,898,190 (M); gifts received, $7,949,108; expenditures, $1,032,146; giving activities include $608,214 for 382 grants (high: $100,000; low: $7), and $53,050 for 91 grants to individuals (high: $2,500; low: $100).

Purpose and activities: The foundation seeks to enhance the quality of life in the Upper Peninsula of MI. The foundation will provide its own U.P.-wide philanthropy and that of its geographic affiliate

members through growth of permanent endowment funds from a wide range of donors. The CFUP also provides financial, administrative, communication, and other support services to its affiliate members and to other U.P. community foundations.

Fields of interest: Historic preservation/historical societies; Environment; Health care; Human services; Economic development; Youth.

Type of support: Capital campaigns; Scholarship funds; Technical assistance; Scholarships—to individuals.

Limitations: Giving limited to the Upper Peninsula, MI, area, including Chippewa County, Schoolcraft County, Gogebic County, Alger, Cedarville, Delta, Ontonagon, Paradise, St. Ignace, Watersmeet County areas. No support for religious or sectarian purposes. No grants to individuals (except for scholarships), or for memberships, memorials, endowments, fundraising, social events, exhibits, or deficits in operating budgets or normal operating expenses, construction of buildings, or maintenance.

Publications: Application guidelines; Annual report; Financial statement; Informational brochure; Informational brochure (including application guidelines).

Application information: Visit foundation Web site for application Cover Sheet and guidelines. Application form required.

Initial approach: Submit Cover Sheet and attachments
Copies of proposal: 8
Deadline(s): Spring
Board meeting date(s): Feb., Apr., July, and Oct.
Final notification: By mail

Officers and Trustees:* Dr. Kenneth Drenth,* Co-Pres.; William W. Lake,* Co-Pres.; Kerry O'Connor,* V.P.; Bonnie Wenick-Kutz,* V.P.; Mary Bowerman,* Secy.; Tom Luckey,* Treas.; Gary LaPlant, Exec. Dir.; Elio Argentati; Margaret LaPonsie; William LeMire III, M.D.; John MacFarlane III; Dr. K. Gerald Marsden; Keith Neve; Walter North; Francis E. Paoli; Matt Smith, Jr.

Number of staff: 2 full-time professional; 2 part-time professional; 1 part-time support.

EIN: 383227080

4260

Consumers Energy Foundation ◇

(formerly Consumers Power Foundation)
1 Energy Plz., Rm. EP8-210
Jackson, MI 49201 (517) 788-0432
Contact: Carolyn A. Bloodworth, Secy.-Treas.
FAX: (517) 788-2281;
E-mail: foundation@consumersenergy.com;
Additional tel.: (877) 501-4952; URL: http://www.consumersenergy.com/foundation

Established in 1990 in MI.

Donors: Consumers Power Co.; Consumers Energy Co.

Foundation type: Company-sponsored foundation.

Financial data (yr. ended 12/31/04): Assets, $2,520,448 (M); gifts received, $1,000,000; expenditures, $587,945; qualifying distributions, $587,945; giving activities include $587,925 for 327 grants (high: $25,000; low: $50).

Purpose and activities: The foundation supports organizations involved with arts and culture, education, the environment, human services, and community development.

Fields of interest: Arts; Higher education; Education; Environment; Human services; Community development.

Type of support: General/operating support; Capital campaigns; Building/renovation; Employee matching gifts.

Limitations: Giving primarily in MI; some giving also on a national and international basis. No support for religious organizations not of direct benefit to the entire community, labor, political, or veterans' organizations, fraternal or social clubs, or United Way-supported organizations. No grants to individuals, or for endowments, debt reduction, sports tournaments, talent or beauty contests, or tickets for fundraising events; no loans for small businesses.

Publications: Application guidelines; Informational brochure.

Application information: The CMF Common Grant Application Form is required. Application form required.

> *Initial approach:* Mail proposal and application form to foundation
> *Copies of proposal:* 1
> *Deadline(s):* None
> *Board meeting date(s):* Quarterly
> *Final notification:* 6 to 8 weeks

Officers and Directors:* Kenneth Whipple,* Chair.; David Mengebier,* Pres.; Carolyn A. Bloodworth, Secy.-Treas.; David W. Joos; John G. Russell; S. Kinnie Smith, Jr.; Thomas T. Webb.

Number of staff: 2 full-time professional; 2 full-time support.

EIN: 382935534

Selected grants: The following grants were reported in 2003.

$99,500 to United Way of Jackson County, Jackson, MI.

$50,000 to Detroit Institute of Arts, Detroit, MI.

$18,000 to United Way, Greater Kalamazoo, Kalamazoo, MI.

$6,000 to Nature Conservancy, Lansing, MI.

$5,000 to Community Foundation for Muskegon County, Muskegon, MI.

$5,000 to Davenport University, Grand Rapids, MI.

$5,000 to Disability Connections, Jackson, MI.

$5,000 to Leila Arboretum Society, Battle Creek, MI.

$5,000 to Michigan Opera Theater, Detroit, MI.

$5,000 to Western Michigan University Foundation, Kalamazoo, MI.

4261
Cook Charitable Foundation ✧

618 Kenmoor Ave. S.E., Ste. 100
Grand Rapids, MI 49546
Contact: Peter C. Cook, Pres.

Established in 1987.

Donors: Peter C. Cook; Emajean Cook; Peter C. Cook Trust.

Foundation type: Independent foundation.

Financial data (yr. ended 12/31/05): Assets, $4,637,929 (M); gifts received, $27,500; expenditures, $1,098,775; qualifying distributions, $1,010,956; giving activities include $1,010,956 for 64 grants (high: $125,000; low: $100).

Purpose and activities: Giving primarily for education and religious organizations. Some support also for human service organizations, health associations, and arts and cultural organizations.

Fields of interest: Arts; Health organizations, association; Human services; Human services, mind/body enrichment; Christian agencies & churches.

Type of support: General/operating support.

Limitations: Applications not accepted. Giving limited to the Grand Rapids, MI, area. No grants to individuals.

Application information: Contributes only to pre-selected organizations.

Officers and Directors:* Peter C. Cook,* Pres.; Robert D. Brower,* Secy.; Carrie L. Boer; Thomas H. Claus; Thomas M. Cook.

EIN: 382752251

Selected grants: The following grants were reported in 2004.

$410,000 to Hope College, Holland, MI.

$250,000 to Calvin College, Grand Rapids, MI.

$101,000 to Van Andel Institute, Grand Rapids, MI.

$100,000 to Western Theological Seminary, Holland, MI.

$77,000 to Holland Home, Grand Rapids, MI.

$75,025 to Potters House, Grand Rapids, MI.

$50,000 to Camp Geneva, Holland, MI.

$50,000 to Grand Rapids Art Museum, Grand Rapids, MI.

$5,000 to Grand Rapids Childrens Museum, Grand Rapids, MI.

$5,000 to South End Community Outreach Ministries, Grand Rapids, MI.

4262
Cook Family Foundation ✧

P.O. Box 278
Owosso, MI 48867-0578 (989) 725-1621
Contact: Bruce L. Cook, Pres.
FAX: (989) 725-3138;
E-mail: tom_cook@chartermi.net

Established in 1979 in MI.

Donors: Donald O. Cook†; Florence-Etta Cook†; Donald O. Cook Charitable Trust; Wolverine Sign Works.

Foundation type: Independent foundation.

Financial data (yr. ended 12/31/05): Assets, $10,548,733 (M); expenditures, $532,484; qualifying distributions, $514,235; giving activities include $459,850 for 24+ grants (high: $74,244).

Purpose and activities: Giving primarily for education and youth programs.

Fields of interest: Historic preservation/historical societies; Higher education; Environmental education; Children/youth, services.

Type of support: General/operating support; Annual campaigns; Capital campaigns; Building/renovation; Program development; Internship funds; Scholarship funds.

Limitations: Applications not accepted. Giving limited to MI. No grants to individuals.

Publications: Annual report; Informational brochure.

Application information: Contributes only to pre-selected organizations.

> *Board meeting date(s):* Quarterly

Officers: Bruce L. Cook, Pres.; Laurie Caszatt Cook, V.P.; Thomas B. Cook, Secy.-Treas.

Trustees: Jacqueline P. Cook; Paul C. Cook; Anna E. Owens.

Number of staff: 1 part-time professional.

EIN: 382283809

4263
Peter J. & Constance M. Cracchiolo Foundation ✧

24055 Jefferson Ave., Ste. 200
St. Clair Shores, MI 48080-1514

Established in 1984 in MI.

Donors: Peter J. Cracchiolo; Constance M. Cracchiolo.

Foundation type: Independent foundation.

Financial data (yr. ended 6/30/05): Assets, $11,300,795 (M); gifts received, $214,980; expenditures, $512,180; qualifying distributions, $454,343; giving activities include $435,102 for 43 grants (high: $86,150; low: $100).

Purpose and activities: Giving primarily to Roman Catholic agencies and churches.

Fields of interest: Education; Hospitals (general); Health organizations, association; Human services; Roman Catholic agencies & churches.

Type of support: General/operating support.

Limitations: Applications not accepted. Giving primarily in MI. No grants to individuals.

Application information: Contributes only to pre-selected organizations.

Officers: Peter J. Cracchiolo, Pres.; Constance M. Cracchiolo, Secy.; Peter T. Cracchiolo, Treas.

EIN: 382561770

Selected grants: The following grants were reported in 2005.

$86,150 to De La Salle Collegiate High School, Warren, MI.

$51,000 to Covenant House Michigan, Detroit, MI.

$40,000 to Saint John Hospital and Medical Center, Detroit, MI.

$17,000 to Most Holy Trinity School, Detroit, MI.

$4,000 to Cornerstone Schools Association, Detroit, MI.

$3,000 to Holy Cross Childrens Services, Clinton, MI.

$1,000 to Sacred Heart Major Seminary, Detroit, MI.

$500 to Capuchin Seminary Guild, Detroit, MI.

$300 to Lutheran Special Education Ministries, Detroit, MI.

4264
Thomas and Carol Cracchiolo Foundation ✧

24055 Jefferson Ave., Ste. 200
St. Clair Shores, MI 48080-1514

Established in 1984 in MI.

Donors: Carol A. Cracchiolo; Thomas A. Cracchiolo.

Foundation type: Independent foundation.

Financial data (yr. ended 6/30/05): Assets, $10,315,749 (M); gifts received, $342,000; expenditures, $478,345; qualifying distributions, $445,924; giving activities include $420,260 for 45 grants (high: $82,000; low: $25).

Purpose and activities: Giving primarily for health and human services, and to Roman Catholic agencies and churches.

Fields of interest: Education; Hospitals (general); Health organizations, association; Children/youth, services; Roman Catholic agencies & churches.

Type of support: General/operating support.

Limitations: Applications not accepted. Giving primarily in MI. No grants to individuals.

Application information: Contributes only to pre-selected organizations.

Officers and Directors:* Thomas A. Cracchiolo,* Pres.; Carol A. Cracchiolo,* V.P.; Ann M. Caraway,*

Secy.; Lisa A. Peracchio,* Treas.; Bernadette Cracchiolo Hanauske; Carol N. Laub.
EIN: 382543263
Selected grants: The following grants were reported in 2005.
$82,000 to Holy Cross Childrens Services, Clinton, MI. For operating support.
$75,200 to Saint John Health Foundation, Madison Heights, MI. For operating support.
$50,800 to Solanus Casey Center, Detroit, MI. For capital campaign.
$35,333 to Pope John Paul II Cultural Foundation, Detroit, MI. For operating support.
$26,500 to Our Lady Star of the Sea Parish, Grosse Pointe, MI. 2 grants: $11,500 (For operating support), $15,000 (For operating support).
$20,000 to Saint Cecilia School, Detroit, MI. For operating support.
$12,000 to Camp Sancta Maria Trust, Gaylord, MI. For operating support.
$12,000 to Most Holy Trinity School, Detroit, MI. For operating support.
$4,000 to Cornerstone Schools Association, Detroit, MI. For operating support.

4265
DaimlerChrysler Corporation Fund ▼ ✧
(formerly Chrysler Corporation Fund)
CIMS: 485-10-94
1000 Chrysler Dr.
Auburn Hills, MI 48326-2766 (248) 512-2502
Contact: Brian G. Glowiak, V.P. and Secy.
FAX: (248) 512-2503; E-mail: mek@dcx.com;
URL: http://www2.daimlerchrysler.com/dccfund/

Incorporated in 1953 in MI.
Donors: Chrysler Corp.; DaimlerChrysler Corp.
Foundation type: Company-sponsored foundation.
Financial data (yr. ended 12/31/05): Assets, $37,859,586 (M); gifts received, $35,000,000; expenditures, $27,102,579; qualifying distributions, $27,081,543; giving activities include $25,954,013 for 1,190 grants (high: $1,850,769).
Purpose and activities: The fund supports organizations involved with arts and culture, vocational, higher education, business, and engineering education, the environment, employment, highway safety, human services, community development, science, and transportation.
Fields of interest: Arts, cultural/ethnic awareness; Arts; Vocational education; Higher education; Business school/education; Engineering school/ education; Education; Environment, energy; Environment; Employment, training; Safety, automotive safety; Human services; Economic development; Business/industry; Science; Public policy, research; Transportation.
Type of support: General/operating support; Continuing support; Annual campaigns; Emergency funds; Program development; Curriculum development; Employee matching gifts; Employee-related scholarships.
Limitations: Giving primarily in areas of company operations in Wittman, AZ, Irvine, CA, Englewood, CO, Newark, DE, Washington, DC, Orlando, FL, Belvidere and Lisle, IL, Indianapolis and Kokomo, IN, Elkridge, MD, Detroit, MI, Fenton, MO, Syracuse and Tappan, NY, Perrysburg, Toledo, and Twinsburg, OH, and Addison, TX, Kenosha, WI; giving also to regional and national organizations. No support for discriminatory organizations or private or corporate foundations. No grants to individuals (except for

employee-related scholarships), or for endowments, general operating support for local United Way agencies, direct health care delivery programs, additions or renovations to real estate, fundraising activities related to individual sponsorship, debt reduction, religious or sectarian programs, athletic programs involving individual teams; no loans; no vehicle donations.
Publications: Application guidelines; Annual report (including application guidelines).
Application information: Multi-year funding is not automatic. Application form required.
Initial approach: Complete online application form
Deadline(s): Nov. 1
Board meeting date(s): As required, usually quarterly
Final notification: 4 months
Officers and Trustees: * W. Frank Fountain,* Pres.; Brian G. Glowiak, V.P. and Secy.; Timothy P. Dykstra, V.P. and Treas.; E.S. "Steve" Harris, Cont.; Joachim W. Eberhardt; Frank J. Ewasyshyn; Frank O. Klegon; Robert G. Liberatore; Nancy A. Rae; Thomas W. Sidlik; Jason H. Vines; Jurgen Walker.
Number of staff: 2 full-time professional; 5 full-time support; 1 part-time support.
EIN: 386087371
Selected grants: The following grants were reported in 2004.
$2,444,700 to United Way for Southeastern Michigan, Detroit, MI. For Torch Drive pledge and Automotive Business Match.
$1,596,300 to Detroit Renaissance Foundation, Detroit, MI. For Directors Contributions.
$1,073,303 to Detroit Institute of Arts, Detroit, MI. For Century Campaign.
$685,300 to Scholarship America, Saint Peter, MN. For DCCF Scholarship Program Awards.
$500,000 to Focus: Hope, Detroit, MI. For Center for Advanced Technologies (CAT), educating students in manufacturing while they work toward bachelor and associate engineering degrees.
$67,000 to United Way of Summit County, Akron, OH. For corporate contribution.
$50,000 to Executive Service Corps of Detroit, Southfield, MI. For Management Assistance Program.
$31,960 to Pennsylvania State University, University Park, PA. For Aid to Higher Education Program: for Society of Black Engineers.
$25,000 to Hispanic Association of Colleges and Universities, San Antonio, TX. For Aid to Higher Education Program: Diversity grant.
$25,000 to Toledo Cultural Arts Center, Toledo, OH. For season sponsorship of productions.

4266
Dorothy U. Dalton Foundation, Inc. ✧
c/o Greenleaf Trust
100 W. Michigan Ave., Ste. 100
Kalamazoo, MI 49007 (269) 388-9800
Contact: Ronald N. Kilgore, Secy.-Treas.

Incorporated in 1978 in MI as successor to Dorothy U. Dalton Foundation Trust.
Donor: Dorothy U. Dalton†.
Foundation type: Independent foundation.
Financial data (yr. ended 12/31/04): Assets, $38,574,100 (M); expenditures, $2,234,074; qualifying distributions, $2,141,197; giving activities include $2,077,442 for 80 grants (high: $250,000; low: $1,000; average: $1,000– $15,000).

Purpose and activities: Emphasis on higher education, mental health, social service and youth agencies, and cultural programs.
Fields of interest: Performing arts; Performing arts, theater; Performing arts, music; Arts; Environment; Hospitals (general); Mental health/crisis services; Housing/shelter, development; Recreation, parks/ playgrounds; Human services; Youth, services; Community development.
Type of support: General/operating support; Continuing support; Capital campaigns; Building/ renovation; Equipment; Land acquisition; Debt reduction; Emergency funds; Program development; Seed money; Research; Matching/challenge support.
Limitations: Giving primarily in Kalamazoo County, MI. No support for religious organizations. No grants to individuals, or for annual campaigns, scholarships, fellowships, publications, or conferences; no loans.
Application information: Application form required.
Initial approach: Proposal
Copies of proposal: 5
Deadline(s): Submit proposal preferably in Apr. and Oct.
Board meeting date(s): May and Nov.
Final notification: 30 days after board meetings
Officers and Directors: * Suzanne D. Parish,* Pres.; Howard Kalleward,* V.P.; Ronald N. Kilgore,* Secy.-Treas.; Thompson Bennett.
EIN: 382240062
Selected grants: The following grants were reported in 2004.
$200,000 to Kalamazoo Aviation History Museum, Kalamazoo, MI.
$100,000 to Kalamazoo Nature Center, Kalamazoo, MI.
$88,000 to Borgess Medical Center, Kalamazoo, MI.
$75,000 to Lakeside, Kalamazoo, MI.
$70,000 to United Way.
$50,000 to Kalamazoo Valley Community College, Kalamazoo, MI.
$35,000 to YWCA.
$25,000 to Kairos Dwelling, Kalamazoo, MI.
$25,000 to Northside Economic Potential Group, Kalamazoo, MI.
$10,000 to Arts Council of Greater Kalamazoo, Kalamazoo, MI.

4267
The Dart Foundation
(formerly Solid Waste Management Foundation)
500 Hogsback Rd.
Mason, MI 48854-9547 (517) 244-2190
Contact: Claudia Deschaine, Grants Mgr.
FAX: (517) 244-2631;
E-mail: claudia_deschaine@dart.biz

Established in 1989 in MI.
Donor: W.A. Dart Foundation.
Foundation type: Independent foundation.
Financial data (yr. ended 10/31/05): Assets, $3,838,086 (M); gifts received, $5,323,000; expenditures, $4,125,041; qualifying distributions, $4,124,641; giving activities include $3,859,666 for 111 grants (high: $800,000; low: $250; average: $1,000–$100,000), and $250,355 for 4 foundation-administered programs.
Purpose and activities: The Dart Foundation is a privately funded organization committed to supporting public purposes.

Fields of interest: Performing arts, theater; Higher education; Education; Hospitals (general); Health organizations, association; Alzheimer's disease research; Boys & girls clubs; Human services; YM/YWCAs & YM/YWHAs; Children/youth, services; Federated giving programs; Engineering/technology; Public affairs.

Type of support: General/operating support; Continuing support; Building/renovation; Program development; Conferences/seminars; Publication; Curriculum development; Research; Matching/challenge support.

Limitations: Giving primarily in Sarasota, FL and central MI. No grants to individuals.

Application information: Application form not required.

Initial approach: Letter
Copies of proposal: 1
Deadline(s): None

Officers and Directors:* William A. Dart,* Pres. and Secy.; Claire T. Dart,* V.P. and Treas.; Kenneth B. Dart,* V.P.; Robert C. Dart,* V.P.; James D. Lammers, V.P.

EIN: 382849841

Selected grants: The following grants were reported in 2006.

$1,100,000 to University of Washington, Dart Center For Journalism and Trauma, Seattle, WA.

$500,000 to Cayman Islands National Recovery Fund, George Town, Cayman Islands. .

$250,000 to Lahey Clinic Foundation, Department of Urology, Burlington, MA.

$100,000 to Alzheimers Association, Chicago, IL.

$30,000 to Nature Conservancy, Arlington, VA.

$25,000 to Kentucky Repertory Theater, Horse Cave, KY.

4268
Richard E. & Sandra J. Dauch Family Foundation ✧
223 Bridge St.
P.O. Box 227
Charlevoix, MI 49720 (231) 547-4602
Contact: Thomas G. Bickersteth, Secy.

Established in 2002 in MI.
Donors: Richard E. Dauch; Sandra J. Dauch; Helen R. Dauch Trust.
Foundation type: Operating foundation.
Financial data (yr. ended 4/30/05): Assets, $11,863,229 (M); gifts received, $284,000; expenditures, $1,633,246; qualifying distributions, $1,551,567; giving activities include $1,520,620 for 13 grants (high: $963,968; low: $2,000).
Fields of interest: Higher education; Medical care, rehabilitation; Diabetes research; Recreation, fairs/festivals; Boys & girls clubs; Civil rights; Protestant agencies & churches.
Limitations: Giving primarily in MI and OH.
Application information:
Initial approach: Letter
Deadline(s): None
Officers: Richard E. Dauch, Pres.; Sandra J. Dauch, V.P. and Treas.; Thomas G. Bickersteth, Secy.
EIN: 300074517
Selected grants: The following grants were reported in 2004.
$1,973,621 to Ashland University, Ashland, OH. 2 grants: $1,000,000 to College of Economics, $973,621 to College of Economics
$50,000 to Boys and Girls Clubs of Southeastern Michigan, Farmington Hills, MI. For program support.

$50,000 to Focus: Hope, Detroit, MI. For Machinist Training Project.

$25,000 to Trinity Lutheran Church, Ashland, OH. For program support.

$3,000 to Charlevoix Venetian Festival, Charlevoix, MI. For operating support.

$2,000 to Bloomfield Hills School District, Bloomfield Hills, MI. For Booster Club.

$1,000 to Ashland County Community Foundation, Ashland, OH. For program support.

4269
M. E. Davenport Foundation
415 E. Fulton St., Warren Hall, Main Fl.
Grand Rapids, MI 49503 (616) 732-1098
Contact: Margaret E. Moceri, Chair. and C.E.O
FAX: (616) 732-1147;
E-mail: pmoceri@davenport.edu; URL: http://www.medavenport.org

Established in 1986 in MI.
Donors: Robert W. and Margaret D. Sneden Foundation; Margaret Moceri; Gregory Moceri; Kathleen Sneden; Mary Sneden Sullivan; Watson Pierce; Elsie Pierce; Barbara DeMoor.
Foundation type: Independent foundation.
Financial data (yr. ended 9/30/05): Assets, $14,135,534 (M); gifts received, $1,358; expenditures, $913,649; qualifying distributions, $765,621; giving activities include $664,979 for 12 grants (high: $533,979; low: $1,000).
Purpose and activities: Support primarily for private institutions of higher education, and specific social and community needs, usually related to business education, training, employment, and community stability, such as housing.
Fields of interest: Higher education; Employment, training; Youth development, business.
Type of support: Building/renovation; Capital campaigns; Program development; Seed money; Curriculum development.
Limitations: Giving primarily in western lower MI. No support for religious or political agendas. No grants to individuals, debt retirement, and taxable organizations or activities.
Publications: Application guidelines; Annual report; Financial statement; Grants list; Occasional report.
Application information: Application form required.
Initial approach: Letter
Copies of proposal: 1
Deadline(s): None
Board meeting date(s): Triannually
Final notification: 30-45 days
Officers and Trustees:* Margaret E. Moceri,* Chair. and C.E.O.; Gregory C. Moceri, V.P.; Mary P. Sullivan, Secy.; Kathleen M. Sneden; Marcia A. Sneden.
Number of staff: 2 full-time professional.
EIN: 382646809
Selected grants: The following grants were reported in 2005.
$533,979 to Davenport University, Grand Rapids, MI.
$30,000 to Potters House, Grand Rapids, MI.
$10,000 to American Red Cross.
$2,500 to Council of Michigan Foundations, Grand Haven, MI.
$1,000 to Northwoods Wilderness Recovery, Marquette, MI.

4270
Degroot Family Foundation ✧
5530 N. Coloma Rd.
P.O. Box 934
Coloma, MI 49038

Established in 2002 in MI.
Donor: Louise Degroot.
Foundation type: Independent foundation.
Financial data (yr. ended 12/31/05): Assets, $1,133,344 (M); expenditures, $333,234; qualifying distributions, $323,643; giving activities include $320,000 for 6 grants (high: $100,000; low: $10,000).
Purpose and activities: Giving for cancer research and aid to disenfranchised women and children.
Fields of interest: Pediatrics; Cancer research; Housing/shelter, homeless; Children/youth, services.
Limitations: Applications not accepted. Giving on a national basis. No grants to individuals.
Application information: Contributes only to pre-selected organizations.
Officers: Louise Degroot, Chair.; Shirley Leith, Pres.; Eric Brown, Secy.
EIN: 061654753

4271
Delphi Foundation, Inc.
5725 Delphi Dr., M.C. 483-400-501
Troy, MI 48098
URL: http://delphi.com/about/social/delphifoundation

Established in 1998 in MI.
Donors: General Motors Foundation, Inc.; Delphi Automotive Systems Corp.; Delphi Corp.
Foundation type: Company-sponsored foundation.
Financial data (yr. ended 12/31/04): Assets, $17,728,304 (M); expenditures, $1,034,308; qualifying distributions, $783,218; giving activities include $777,608 for 192 grants (high: $65,000; low: $100).
Purpose and activities: The foundation supports organizations involved with science and technology education and other areas related to Delphi's business objectives.
Fields of interest: Education; General charitable giving.
Limitations: Applications not accepted. Giving on a national basis. No support for political, lobbying, or fraternal organizations, private foundations, hospitals, health care institutions, schools, or religious organizations. No grants to individuals, or for endowments, capital campaigns, general operating support, debt reduction, or conferences, workshops, or seminars not directly related to Delphi's business interests.
Publications: IRS Form 990-PF.
Application information: The foundation utilizes an invitation only Request For Proposal (RFP) process. Unsolicited requests are not accepted.
Officers and Trustees:* Karen L. Healy,* Chair.; Nancy Moss, Secy.; John Arle, Treas.; Ronald L. Beeber; Mary Beth Inaciak; James P. Whitson.
EIN: 383442971

4272
DENSO North America Foundation
24777 DENSO Dr.
Southfield, MI 48033 (248) 372-8233
Contact: John Voorhorst, Pres.
FAX: (248) 213-2550;
E-mail: densofoundation@denso-diam.com;
URL: http://www.densofoundation.org

Established in 2001 in MI.
Donor: DENSO International America, Inc.
Foundation type: Company-sponsored foundation.
Financial data (yr. ended 12/31/05): Assets, $7,570,508 (M); expenditures, $374,612; qualifying distributions, $372,074; giving activities include $373,500 for grants.
Purpose and activities: The foundation supports organizations involved with engineering education and related business areas. Special emphasis is directed toward programs designed to advance automotive engineering and supply-side business practices.
Fields of interest: Business school/education; Engineering school/education.
International interests: Canada; Mexico.
Type of support: Building/renovation; Equipment; Program development.
Limitations: Applications not accepted. Giving on a national basis, with emphasis on CA, MI, and TN, and in Canada and Mexico. No grants to individuals.
Application information: The foundation utilizes an invitation only Request For Proposal (RFP) process; unsolicited requests are not accepted.
Board meeting date(s): May and Oct.
Officers and Directors: John Voorhorst, Pres.; Barbara Wertheimer, Secy.; Kim Madaj, Treas.; David Cole; Stanley Tooley; James Woroniecki.
Number of staff: 1 full-time professional.
EIN: 383547055
Selected grants: The following grants were reported in 2005.
$50,000 to Pellissippi State Technical Community College, Knoxville, TN. For equipment.
$50,000 to Robert B. Miller College, Battle Creek, MI. For equipment.
$50,000 to University of Michigan, Dearborn, MI. For building improvement.
$45,000 to Lawrence Technological University, Southfield, MI. For building improvement.
$41,000 to California State University, Long Beach, CA. For equipment.
$37,500 to Tennessee Technological University, Cookeville, TN. For building improvement.
$30,000 to Michigan Technological University, Houghton, MI. For program support.
$25,000 to American Red Cross, National Headquarters, DC. For disaster relief for Hurricane Katrina.
$25,000 to University of Tennessee, Knoxville, TN. For equipment.
$20,000 to Kettering University, Flint, MI. For building improvement.

4273
DeRoy Testamentary Foundation ✧
26999 Central Park Blvd., Ste. 160N
Southfield, MI 48076 (248) 827-0920
Contact: Julie A. Rodecker Holly, V.P. and Prog. Off.
FAX: (248) 827-0922; *E-mail:* deroyfdtn@aol.com

Established in 1979 in MI.
Donor: Helen L. DeRoy†.
Foundation type: Independent foundation.

Financial data (yr. ended 12/31/05): Assets, $50,962,525 (M); expenditures, $2,966,903; qualifying distributions, $2,560,810; giving activities include $2,274,637 for 127 grants (high: $700,000; low: $1,000).
Purpose and activities: Giving primarily for the arts, education, human services, and health care.
Fields of interest: Arts education; Arts; Higher education; Education; Hospitals (general); Human services; Children/youth, services; Jewish federated giving programs; Jewish agencies & temples.
Type of support: Program development.
Limitations: Giving primarily in MI. No grants to individuals.
Application information:
Deadline(s): None
Board meeting date(s): Monthly
Officers and Trustees:* Arthur Rodecker,* Pres.; Julie A.Rodecker Holly,* V.P. and Prog. Off.; Gregg D. Watkins,* Secy.; Sarah W. Keidan, Treas.
EIN: 382208833
Selected grants: The following grants were reported in 2003.
$100,000 to Detroit Science Center, Detroit, MI.
$100,000 to Detroit Zoological Society, Royal Oak, MI.
$100,000 to National Jewish Medical and Research Center, Denver, CO.
$97,000 to Oakland Family Services, Pontiac, MI.
$75,000 to Huron Valley-Sinai Hospital, Commerce Township, MI.
$70,000 to Hospice of Michigan, Detroit, MI.
$50,000 to Alzheimers Association, Southfield, MI.
$50,000 to YMCA of Metropolitan Detroit, Detroit, MI.
$35,000 to Childrens Museum Friends, Detroit, MI.
$30,000 to Detroit Symphony Orchestra, Detroit, MI.

4274
The Richard C. Devereaux Foundation ✧
39533 Woodward Ave., Ste. 200
Bloomfield Hills, MI 48304

Donors: Mrs. Richard C. Devereaux; S.W. Smith; Adelyn Devereaux Trust.
Foundation type: Independent foundation.
Financial data (yr. ended 8/31/05): Assets, $6,930,655 (M); gifts received, $84,721; expenditures, $919,146; qualifying distributions, $885,332; giving activities include $852,500 for 19 grants (high: $100,000; low: $10,000).
Purpose and activities: Giving primarily for education, health organizations, particularly for cancer research, and wildlife preservation; funding also for human services and for a public television station.
Fields of interest: Media, television; Higher education; Animals/wildlife, preservation/ protection; Health organizations; Cancer research; Human services.
Type of support: General/operating support.
Limitations: Applications not accepted. Giving primarily in Washington, DC, IL, MI, and VA. No grants to individuals.
Application information: Contributes only to pre-selected organizations.
Officers: Leslie C. Devereaux, Pres. and Treas.; Sidney W. Smith, Jr., V.P.; Curtis J. Mann, Secy.
EIN: 382638858
Selected grants: The following grants were reported in 2003.

$100,000 to Barbara Ann Karmanos Cancer Institute, Detroit, MI. For operating support.
$90,000 to Paralyzed Veterans of America, DC. For operating support.
$60,000 to Cancer Research and Prevention Foundation, Alexandria, VA. For operating support.
$50,000 to Alzheimers Association, Chicago, IL. For operating support.
$40,000 to World Wildlife Fund, DC. For general support.
$37,500 to Nature Conservancy, Baltimore, MD. For operating support.
$35,000 to African Wildlife Foundation, DC. For operating support.
$15,000 to National Geographic Society, DC. For operating support.
$10,000 to Detroit Educational Television Foundation-W T V S Channel 56, Detroit, MI. For operating support.
$10,000 to Hospice of Michigan, Detroit, MI. For operating support.

4275
The DeVlieg Foundation ✧
(formerly The Charles DeVlieg Foundation)
500 Woodward Ave., Ste. 2500
Detroit, MI 48226
Contact: Curtis J. DeRoo, Secy.-Treas.

Incorporated in 1961 in MI.
Donors: Charles B. DeVlieg†; Charles R. DeVlieg†; Kathryn S. DeVlieg†; DeVlieg Machine Co.
Foundation type: Independent foundation.
Financial data (yr. ended 12/31/05): Assets, $9,016,429 (M); expenditures, $673,420; qualifying distributions, $534,385; giving activities include $419,850 for 33 grants (high: $83,300; low: $550; average: $10,000–$20,000).
Purpose and activities: Support largely for higher and other education, including grants to a university for fellowships and a scholarship program for engineering, wildlife education, youth agencies, the arts, environmental organizations, and science and technology.
Fields of interest: Arts; Higher education; Engineering school/education; Environment, natural resources; Environment; Youth, services; Engineering/technology; Engineering; Science.
Type of support: General/operating support; Professorships; Scholarship funds.
Limitations: Giving primarily in ID, southeastern MI, and WA. No grants to individuals, or for endowment funds; no loans.
Publications: Annual report (including application guidelines).
Application information: Application form required.
Initial approach: Letter
Copies of proposal: 2
Deadline(s): None
Board meeting date(s): Semiannually
Officers and Directors:* Janet DeVlieg Pope,* Pres.; Curtis J. DeRoo,* Secy.; Julia DeVlieg; Richard A. Jerue; Gary Stetler; Gerald Stetler.
Number of staff: 1 part-time professional.
EIN: 386075696
Selected grants: The following grants were reported in 2003.
$130,000 to University of Idaho, Moscow, ID. 2 grants: $35,000 to College of Engineering, $95,000 to College of Natural Resources
$30,000 to Michigan Colleges Foundation, Southfield, MI. For general support.

$20,000 to Michigan State University, College of Engineering, East Lansing, MI.

$20,000 to Michigan Technological University, Houghton, MI.

$20,000 to Oakland University, Department of Engineering, Rochester, MI.

$20,000 to Wayne State University, College of Engineering, Detroit, MI.

$17,000 to Kettle Falls School District, Kettle Falls, WA. For general support.

$10,000 to Chief Joseph Foundation, Lapwai, ID. For general support.

$10,000 to Michigan Wildlife Habitat Foundation, Lansing, MI.

4276
Daniel and Pamella DeVos Foundation
P.O. Box 230257
Grand Rapids, MI 49523-0257 (616) 643-4700
Contact: Ginny Vander Hart, Exec. Dir.
FAX: (616) 774-0116; E-mail: virginiav@rdvcorp.com

Established in 1992 in MI.
Donor: The Richard and Helen DeVos Foundation.
Foundation type: Independent foundation.
Financial data (yr. ended 12/31/04): Assets, $730,939 (M); expenditures, $773,193; qualifying distributions, $752,631; giving activities include $703,589 for 67 grants (high: $209,980; low: $200).
Purpose and activities: Giving for museums, performing arts centers, arts and culture, education, human services and Christian agencies.
Fields of interest: Museums; Performing arts centers; Arts; Libraries/library science; Education; Human services; Children/youth, services; Christian agencies & churches.
Type of support: General/operating support; Continuing support; Annual campaigns; Capital campaigns; Building/renovation; Program development; Seed money; Matching/challenge support.
Limitations: Giving primarily in Grand Rapids, MI. No grants to individuals.
Publications: Informational brochure (including application guidelines).
Application information: Application form not required.
  Initial approach: Letter
  Copies of proposal: 1
  Deadline(s): None
  Final notification: 3 to 5 months
Officers: Daniel G. DeVos, Pres.; Pamella DeVos, V.P.; Jerry L. Tubergen, Secy.-Treas.
EIN: 383035976

4277
Dick & Betsy DeVos Foundation ▼
P.O. Box 230257
Grand Rapids, MI 49523-0257 (616) 643-4700
Contact: Ginny Vander Hart, Exec. Dir.; Sue Volkers, Fdn. Admin.
FAX (for Ginny Vander Hart): (616) 774-0116; E-mail (for Ginny Vander Hart): virginiav@rdvcorp.com

Established in 1989 in MI.
Donors: Dick DeVos; Betsy DeVos; Prince Foundation.
Foundation type: Independent foundation.
Financial data (yr. ended 12/31/04): Assets, $27,126,765 (M); gifts received, $14,005,615;

expenditures, $3,549,065; qualifying distributions, $3,366,407; giving activities include $3,239,999 for 133 grants (high: $453,349; low: $250; average: $1,000–$25,000).
Purpose and activities: The foundation seeks to create a legacy of caring and stewardship through its support of projects that build a strong community. To demonstrate this commitment, the foundation concentrates its funding in support of various initiatives that promote a healthier community, with a focus on the arts, health and children's causes.
Fields of interest: Arts; Education; Children/youth, services; Family services; Public policy, research; Christian agencies & churches.
Type of support: General/operating support; Continuing support; Annual campaigns; Capital campaigns.
Limitations: Giving primarily in west MI. No grants to individuals.
Publications: Application guidelines.
Application information: Application form not required.
  Initial approach: Letter
  Copies of proposal: 1
  Deadline(s): 2 weeks prior to review
  Board meeting date(s): Quarterly
  Final notification: 4 to 5 months
Officers and Directors:* Jerry L. Tubergen,* C.O.O., V.P. and Secy.; Richard M. DeVos, Jr.,* Pres.; Elisabeth DeVos,* V.P.; Robert H. Schierbeek, Treas.; Ginny Vander Hart, Exec. Dir. and Fdn. Dir.
EIN: 382902412
Selected grants: The following grants were reported in 2004.
$453,349 to Flannel, Grand Rapids, MI. For general support.
$303,000 to Education Freedom Fund, Grand Rapids, MI. For general support.
$150,000 to Institute for Marriage and Public Policy (iMAPP), DC. For general support.
$100,000 to Blodgett Butterworth Health Care Foundation, Grand Rapids, MI. For general support.
$30,000 to Act One, Los Angeles, CA. For general support.
$25,000 to CURE International, Harrisburg, PA. For general support.
$10,000 to English Language Institute in China, San Dimas, CA. For general support.
$10,000 to Snow Bible Church, Kent City, MI. For general support.
$5,000 to Grand Rapids Christian High School, Grand Rapids, MI.
$5,000 to Van Andel Institute, Grand Rapids, MI.

4278
Douglas & Maria DeVos Foundation
P.O. Box 230257
Grand Rapids, MI 49523-0257 (616) 643-4700
Contact: Ginny Vander Hart, Exec. Dir.
FAX: (616) 774-0116; E-mail: virginiav@rdvcorp.com

Established in 1992 in MI.
Donors: Douglas DeVos; Maria DeVos.
Foundation type: Independent foundation.
Financial data (yr. ended 12/31/04): Assets, $16,703,303 (M); gifts received, $14,500,000; expenditures, $1,650,558; qualifying distributions, $1,621,249; giving activities include $1,574,291 for grants.
Purpose and activities: The foundation hopes to build a legacy of caring and stewardship that

combines the heart and skill of philanthropy in order to improve the quality of people's lives and build a stronger community. Its focus is on organizations, projects, or programs that demonstrate Christian charity to meet both the spiritual and physical needs of people. Its primary commitment is to the support of the Grand Rapids, MI, community with goals of strengthening the bond of families, rebuilding strong neighborhoods, and providing opportunity for disadvantaged youth.
Fields of interest: Health care; Human services; Family services; Christian agencies & churches.
Type of support: General/operating support; Continuing support; Annual campaigns; Capital campaigns; Building/renovation; Program development; Matching/challenge support.
Limitations: Giving primarily in west MI.
Publications: Application guidelines.
Application information: Application form not required.
  Initial approach: Letter
  Copies of proposal: 1
  Deadline(s): 2 weeks prior to review
  Board meeting date(s): Quarterly
  Final notification: Within 3 to 5 months
Officers: Douglas DeVos, Pres.; Maria DeVos, V.P.; Jerry L. Tubergen, Secy.-Treas.
EIN: 383035972

4279
The Richard and Helen DeVos Foundation ▼
P.O. Box 230257
Grand Rapids, MI 49523-0257 (616) 643-4700
Contact: Ginny Vander Hart, Exec. Dir.

Incorporated in 1969 in MI.
Donors: Richard M. DeVos; Helen J. DeVos; Alticor Inc.
Foundation type: Independent foundation.
Financial data (yr. ended 12/31/04): Assets, $80,290,190 (M); gifts received, $4,066,394; expenditures, $36,983,711; qualifying distributions, $36,175,698; giving activities include $34,548,985 for 176 grants (high: $3,600,000; low: $500; average: $5,000–$50,000), and $806,662 for 1 foundation-administered program.
Purpose and activities: The foundation primarily supports the work of religious agencies, churches, and schools in ministry, outreach, and education. Its secondary focus includes social outreach, the arts, public policy, and health care. The foundation focuses its funding in the areas of western Michigan and central Florida.
Fields of interest: Arts; Health care; Social sciences; Public policy, research; Religion.
Type of support: General/operating support; Continuing support; Annual campaigns; Capital campaigns; Building/renovation; Program development; Seed money; Matching/challenge support.
Limitations: Giving primarily in central FL and western MI. No grants to individuals.
Publications: Application guidelines.
Application information: Application form not required.
  Initial approach: Letter
  Copies of proposal: 1
  Deadline(s): 2 weeks prior to review
  Board meeting date(s): Every 3 months
  Final notification: 4 to 5 months

Officers: Helen J. DeVos, Pres.; Jerry L. Tubergen, V.P. and Secy.; Robert H. Schierbeek, Treas.; Ginny Vander Hart, Exec. Dir.

EIN: 237066873

Selected grants: The following grants were reported in 2004.

$3,000,000 to National Constitution Center, Philadelphia, PA. For general support.

$2,500,000 to Gospel Communications International, Muskegon, MI. For general support.

$2,005,000 to DeVos Childrens Hospital Foundation, Grand Rapids, MI. For general support.

$1,510,000 to Coral Ridge Presbyterian Church, Fort Lauderdale, FL. For general support.

$1,250,000 to Grand Rapids Symphony, Grand Rapids, MI. For general support.

$1,000,000 to Prison Fellowship Ministries, Lansdowne, VA. For general support.

$600,000 to Heritage Foundation, DC. For general support.

$500,000 to Focus on the Family, Colorado Springs, CO. For general support.

$500,000 to George Washingtons Mount Vernon Estate and Gardens, Mount Vernon, VA. For general support.

$500,000 to Haggai Institute for Advanced Leadership Training, Atlanta, GA. For general support.

4280
DeWitt Families Conduit Foundation ◇
280 N. River Ave., Ste. B
Holland, MI 49424

Established in 1987 in MI.

Donors: Brian DeWitt; Lisa DeWitt; Dawn Brinks; Kurt Brinks; Deb Koop; J.P. Koop; Donald DeWitt; Minnie DeWitt; Gary D. DeWitt; Joyce DeWitt; Julia M. Morrison; Kathy Muyskens; Chris Muyskens; Keith DeWitt; Mary E. DeWitt; Kelly DeWitt; Kristin DeWitt; Kerri Sue Smits; James Smits; Lisa Vanderkolk; Jon Vanderkolk; Marilyn Norman; Thomas Norman; Marvin G. DeWitt; Jerene L. DeWitt; Merle DeWitt; Sheri DeWitt; Shirley Dedoes; William DeWitt, Jr.; Mary DeWitt; and members of the DeWitt family.

Foundation type: Independent foundation.

Financial data (yr. ended 12/31/05): Assets, $15,513 (M); gifts received, $1,057,416; expenditures, $1,053,733; qualifying distributions, $1,041,040; giving activities include $1,036,898 for 131 grants (high: $114,919; low: $100).

Purpose and activities: Giving for Christian churches, religious missionary organizations, and educational institutions.

Fields of interest: Elementary/secondary education; Higher education; Theological school/education; Education; Youth, services; Family services; Christian agencies & churches.

Limitations: Applications not accepted. Giving on a national basis, with some emphasis on MI. No grants to individuals.

Application information: Contributes only to pre-selected organizations.

Officers and Trustees: Marvin G. DeWitt,* Pres.; Gary D. DeWitt,* V.P.; William G. DeWitt,* V.P.; William J. DeWitt,* Secy.-Treas.

EIN: 382761226

Selected grants: The following grants were reported in 2003.

$287,340 to Western Theological Seminary, Holland, MI. For annual support.

$260,730 to Hope College, Holland, MI. For annual support.

$228,900 to Geneva Camp and Retreat Center, Holland, MI. For annual support.

$192,650 to Community Reformed Church, Holland, MI. For annual support.

$132,800 to Focus on the Family, Colorado Springs, CO. For annual support.

$104,397 to Ottawa Reformed Church, West Olive, MI. For annual support.

$64,000 to Lakeshore Pregnancy Center, Holland, MI. For annual support.

$45,000 to Northwestern College, Orange City, IA. For annual support.

$20,000 to Eastmanville United Reformed Church, Coopersville, MI. For annual support.

$15,000 to Campus Crusade for Christ, Lebanon, OH. For annual support.

4281
The Angelo & Margaret DiPonio Foundation ◇ ☆
14800 Farmington Rd., Ste. 102
Livonia, MI 48154
Contact: Ralph H. Houghton, Jr., Dir.

Established in 1987 in MI.

Donor: Margaret E. DiPonio.

Foundation type: Independent foundation.

Financial data (yr. ended 10/31/05): Assets, $3,722,610 (M); expenditures, $622,383; qualifying distributions, $593,125; giving activities include $593,125 for 9 grants (high: $500,000; low: $125).

Purpose and activities: Giving primarily for higher education, medical research, organizations providing medical assistance or treatment, and organizations providing assistance for persons temporarily out of work or homeless.

Fields of interest: Cancer; Human services; Family services; Family services, domestic violence; Christian agencies & churches.

Type of support: Building/renovation.

Limitations: Giving limited to MI. No grants to individuals.

Application information: Telephone inquiries will not be accepted.

  Initial approach: Proposal
  Deadline(s): None

Directors: Charles E. Bietler; Margaret E. DiPonio; Ralph H. Houghton, Jr.

EIN: 382828486

4282
The Dogwood Foundation
c/o Susan Meyers, Warner, Norcross & Judd
111 Lyon St. N.W., Ste. 900
Grand Rapids, MI 49503

Established in 1994 in FL.

Donors: Dorothy Scott Merrill†; Dorothy Scott Merrill Charitable Lead Unitrust.

Foundation type: Independent foundation.

Financial data (yr. ended 12/31/04): Assets, $14,694,113 (M); gifts received, $398,728; expenditures, $889,161; qualifying distributions, $857,012; giving activities include $784,568 for 15 grants (high: $479,159; low: $2,500).

Purpose and activities: Giving primarily for community foundations, education, particularly a military academy, the arts, and human services.

Fields of interest: Museums (specialized); Performing arts, theater; Historic preservation/historical societies; Arts; Libraries/library science; Education; Crime/violence prevention, domestic violence; Human services; Foundations (community).

Limitations: Applications not accepted. Giving on a national basis, with emphasis on FL, MI, TX, and the Midwest. No grants to individuals.

Application information: Contributes only to pre-selected organizations.

Trustees: Kyle Merrill Converse; John H. Martin; Danielle Merrill; Frank G. Merrill; Holly S. Merrill.

EIN: 650499552

Selected grants: The following grants were reported in 2004.

$479,159 to Fremont Area Community Foundation, Fremont, MI.

$70,409 to American Quarter Horse Foundation, Amarillo, TX.

$25,000 to Fremont Area District Library, Fremont, MI.

$25,000 to Key West Art and Historical Society, Key West, FL.

$15,000 to Reef Relief, Key West, FL.

$10,000 to Community Foundation of the Florida Keys, Key West, FL.

$2,500 to Boy Scouts of America, Grand Rapids, MI.

4283
The Doornink Foundation ◇
c/o Jeffrey B. Power, Warner, Norcross & Judd LLP
111 Lyon St. N.W., Ste. 900
Grand Rapids, MI 49503-2487

Established in 1997 in MI.

Donor: Mary Welch Corl.

Foundation type: Independent foundation.

Financial data (yr. ended 12/31/05): Assets, $13,912,524 (M); gifts received, $100,000; expenditures, $630,993; qualifying distributions, $598,110; giving activities include $594,000 for 12 grants (high: $250,000; low: $1,500).

Fields of interest: Museums (art); Arts; Education; Mental health, counseling/support groups; Human services; Children/youth, services; Federated giving programs.

Type of support: General/operating support; Capital campaigns; Program development.

Limitations: Applications not accepted. Giving primarily in Grand Rapids, MI.

Application information: Unsolicited requests for funds not accepted.

Officers and Trustees: Mary W. Corl,* Pres.; Robert W. Corl, Jr.,* V.P.; Jeffrey B. Power,* Secy.-Treas.; James M. Corl; Jeanne L. Corl; Kelli R. Corl; Robert W. Corl III.

EIN: 383386701

Selected grants: The following grants were reported in 2003.

$300,000 to East Grand Rapids, City of, East Grand Rapids, MI. For public works project.

$100,000 to United Way, Heart of West Michigan, Grand Rapids, MI. For general support.

$16,000 to Indian Trails Camp, Grand Rapids, MI. For market analysis.

$10,000 to Grand Rapids Ballet Company, Grand Rapids, MI. For expansion of ballet corps.

$10,000 to North Hills Classical Academy, Grand Rapids, MI. For general support.

$1,500 to Emma Willard School, Troy, NY. For general support.
$1,000 to ArtWorks, Grand Rapids, MI. For general support.

4284
The Dow Chemical Company Foundation ▼

2030 Dow Ctr.
Midland, MI 48674
Contact: R.N. "Bo" Miller, Pres. and Exec. Dir.
URL: http://www.dow.com/about/corp/social/social.htm

Established in 1979 in MI.
Donor: The Dow Chemical Co.
Foundation type: Company-sponsored foundation.
Financial data (yr. ended 12/31/05): Assets, $115,244,709 (M); gifts received, $125,000,000; expenditures, $15,955,345; qualifying distributions, $15,953,729; giving activities include $15,953,729 for 711 grants (high: $3,920,000; low: $25).
Purpose and activities: The foundation supports organizations involved with K-12 education, the environment, community development, and chemistry.
Fields of interest: Elementary/secondary education; Environment; Community development; Chemistry.
Type of support: In-kind gifts; General/operating support; Program development; Employee matching gifts.
Limitations: Giving primarily in areas of company operations. No support for political or religious organizations. No grants to individuals, or for travel or administrative costs.
Publications: Informational brochure.
Application information: Application form not required.
  Initial approach: Letter of inquiry
  Copies of proposal: 1
  Deadline(s): None
  Board meeting date(s): Usually 4 times per year
  Final notification: 2 to 3 months
Officers and Trustees:* Andrew N. Liveris,* Chair.; R.N. "Bo" Miller,* Pres. and Exec. Dir.; V.A. Gilfeather, Secy.; G.J. McGuire, Treas.; Bill Banholzer; Gregory Freiwald; Julie Fasone Holder; J. McIlvenny; Geoffrey E. Merszei.
Number of staff: 1 part-time professional; 1 part-time support.
EIN: 382314603
Selected grants: The following grants were reported in 2005.
$2,920,000 to American Red Cross, National Headquarters, DC. 2 grants: $1,000,000 (For relief efforts for Hurricane Katrina), $1,920,000.
$799,806 to United States Association for International Migration, DC.
$706,000 to United Way of Midland County, Midland, MI.
$500,000 to University of Michigan, Business School, Ann Arbor, MI.
$250,000 to Committee to Encourage Corporate Philanthropy, New York, NY. For South Asia Earthquake Relief Fund.
$71,000 to Solar Oven Society, Minneapolis, MN.
$23,000 to Greater Kanawha Valley Foundation, Charleston, WV.
$20,000 to Assistance League of Indianapolis, Indianapolis, IN.

$20,000 to Detroit Area Pre-College Engineering Program, Detroit, MI.

4285
Dow Corning Foundation ◇

2200 W. Salzburg Rd., Mail No. C01252
Midland, MI 48686-0994 (989) 496-6290
Contact: Anne M. DeBoer, Exec. Dir.
E-mail: community@dowcorning.com; URL: http://www.dowcorning.com/content/about/aboutcomm/aboutcomm_globalgivingstrategy1.asp

Established in 1982 in MI.
Donor: Dow Corning Corp.
Foundation type: Company-sponsored foundation.
Financial data (yr. ended 12/31/04): Assets, $17,446,131 (M); gifts received, $2,500,000; expenditures, $1,721,245; qualifying distributions, $1,714,994; giving activities include $1,324,967 for 74 grants (high: $235,000; low: $100), and $287,039 for 318 employee matching gifts.
Purpose and activities: The foundation supports organizations involved with K-12 education. Special emphasis is directed toward programs designed to increase access to math, science, and technology education.
Fields of interest: Elementary/secondary education.
International interests: Belgium; Brazil; China; Germany; India; Japan; South Korea; Wales.
Type of support: Capital campaigns; Building/renovation; Equipment; Program development; Seed money; Curriculum development; Employee matching gifts.
Limitations: Giving on a national and international basis in areas of company operations, with emphasis on Noble and Switzerland counties, IN, Carroll and Hardin counties, KY, Bay, Midland, and Saginaw counties, MI, Guilford County, NC, Seneffe, Belgium, Campinas, Brazil, Songjiang, China, Wiesbaden, Germany, Pune, India, Chiba, Fukui, and Yamakita, Japan, Jincheon, South Korea, and Barry, Wales. No support for veterans', religious, or political organizations. No grants to individuals, or for general operating support, conferences, dinners, fundraising events, or public advertisements.
Publications: Application guidelines.
Application information: An application form will be sent following a telephone or personal interview. Application form required.
  Initial approach: E-mail or telephone foundation
  Deadline(s): None
  Board meeting date(s): Quarterly
Officers and Trustees:* Marie N. Eckstein,* Pres.; Thomas H. Lane, V.P.; Paul A. Marcela, Secy.; Brad E. Sauve, Treas.; Mohamed A. Ahmed; Scott E. Fuson; Kim R. Houston-Philpot; Feifei Lin; James W. White.
Number of staff: 1 part-time professional; 1 part-time support.
EIN: 382376485
Selected grants: The following grants were reported in 2004.
$235,000 to United Way of Midland County, Midland, MI.
$100,000 to Delta College Foundation, University Center, MI.
$50,000 to Mid-Michigan Childrens Museum, Saginaw, MI.
$50,000 to North Midland Family Center, Midland, MI.
$43,000 to Midland Community Center, Midland, MI.

$31,000 to United Way of Bay County, Bay City, MI.
$27,500 to Saginaw Art Museum, Saginaw, MI.
$23,000 to Michigan Technological University, Houghton, MI.
$20,000 to Midland Area Community Foundation, Midland, MI.
$7,000 to Hemlock Public Schools, Hemlock, MI.

4286
Herbert H. and Barbara C. Dow Foundation ◇

P.O. Box 393
Frankfort, MI 49635-0393

Incorporated in 1957 in MI.
Donors: Herbert H. Dow†; Barbara C. Dow†; Dow 2005 Charitable Annuity Trust.
Foundation type: Independent foundation.
Financial data (yr. ended 12/31/05): Assets, $23,262,552 (M); gifts received, $164,376; expenditures, $1,234,299; qualifying distributions, $1,171,417; giving activities include $1,164,691 for 35 grants (high: $101,441; low: $1,000).
Purpose and activities: Support primarily for the arts, higher education, the environment, neuroscience and other medical research, and Christian ministries and organizations.
Fields of interest: Museums (art); Arts; Higher education; Environment, natural resources; Hospitals (specialty); Nursing care; Health care; Cancer research; Alzheimer's disease research; Neuroscience research; Medical research; Human services; Children/youth, services; Family services; Christian agencies & churches.
Type of support: General/operating support; Continuing support; Capital campaigns; Building/renovation; Endowments; Program development; Scholarship funds; Research.
Limitations: Applications not accepted. Giving primarily in AZ, MI, OH and TX; some giving nationally. No grants to individuals.
Application information: Contributes only to pre-selected organizations.
  Board meeting date(s): Annually
Officers and Trustees:* Willard H. Dow II,* Pres.; Dana D. Schuler,* Secy.; Pamela G. Dow,* Treas.
EIN: 386058513
Selected grants: The following grants were reported in 2003.
$75,000 to Focus on the Family, Colorado Springs, CO. For general operating support.
$65,000 to Habitat for Humanity, Dallas Area, Dallas, TX. For general operating support.
$50,000 to Grand Traverse Regional Land Conservancy, Traverse City, MI. For coastal campaign.
$50,000 to Hillsdale College, Hillsdale, MI. For campus speakers program.
$50,000 to National Coalition for the Protection of Children and Families, Cincinnati, OH. For general operating support.
$50,000 to Phoenix Art Museum, Phoenix, AZ. For general operating support.
$50,000 to Scottsdale Healthcare Foundation, Scottsdale, AZ. For Virginia G. Piper Cancer Center.
$40,000 to Barrow Neurological Foundation, Phoenix, AZ. For Alzheimer's research.
$35,000 to Paul Oliver Memorial Hospital Foundation, Frankfort, MI. For campaign for advanced life support.
$25,000 to Baylor Health Care System Foundation, Dallas, TX. For Psoriasis research.

4287
The Herbert H. and Grace A. Dow
Foundation ▼ ✧
1018 W. Main St.
Midland, MI 48640-4292 (989) 631-3699
Contact: Margaret Ann Riecker, Pres.
FAX: (989) 631-0675;
E-mail: info@hhdowfoundation.org; URL: http://
www.hhdowfoundation.org

Trust established in 1936 in MI.
Donor: Grace A. Dow‡.
Foundation type: Independent foundation.
Financial data (yr. ended 12/31/04): Assets,
$548,526,968 (M); expenditures, $23,230,223;
qualifying distributions, $23,570,047; giving
activities include $19,050,685 for 229 grants (high:
$1,500,000; low: $1,000; average: $212–
$500,000), and $1,270,657 for
foundation-administered programs.
Purpose and activities: Support for religious,
charitable, scientific, literacy, or educational
purposes for the public benefaction of the
inhabitants of the city of Midland and of the people
of the state of Michigan. Grants largely for
education, particularly higher education, community
and social services, civic improvement,
conservation, scientific research, church support
(only in Midland County, MI), and cultural programs;
maintains Dow Gardens, a public horticultural
garden.
Fields of interest: Arts; Higher education; Libraries/
library science; Education; Environment, natural
resources; Human services; Community
development; Engineering/technology; Science.
Type of support: General/operating support;
Building/renovation; Equipment; Endowments;
Program development; Seed money; Research;
Matching/challenge support.
Limitations: Giving limited to MI, with emphasis on
Midland County. No support for political
organizations or sectarian religious organizations or
programs, other than churches in Midland County.
No grants to individuals, or for travel or conferences;
no loans.
Publications: Annual report (including application
guidelines); Financial statement; Grants list.
Application information: Application form not
required.
Initial approach: Proposal
Copies of proposal: 1
Deadline(s): None
Board meeting date(s): Bimonthly
Final notification: 2 months
Officers and Trustees:* Margaret Ann Riecker,*
Pres.; Michael Lloyd Dow,* V.P.; Margaret E.
Thompson,* Secy.; Macauley Whiting, Jr.,* Treas.;
Jenee Velasquez, Exec. Dir.; Julie Carol Arbury;
Diane Dow Hullet; Andrew N. Liveris; Bonnie B.
Matheson; Terence F. Moore; Ruth B. Wheeler;
Helen Dow Whiting.
EIN: 381437485
Selected grants: The following grants were reported
in 2004.
$1,500,000 to Nature Conservancy, Lansing, MI.
For land purchase.
$1,002,502 to Hope College, Holland, MI. For
science facility.
$998,312 to Midland County Historical Society,
Midland, MI. 2 grants: $502,681 (For historical
museum), $495,631 (For historical museum).
$996,409 to Central Michigan University, Mount
Pleasant, MI. For operating support.

$625,000 to FACE - Truth and Clarity on Alcohol,
Clare, MI. For operating support.
$578,178 to Little Forks Conservancy, Midland, MI.
For operating support.
$498,973 to Saginaw Valley State University,
University Center, MI. For Regional Education
Center.
$495,631 to Midland Center for the Arts, Midland,
MI. For operating support.
$487,496 to Education and Training Connection,
Midland, MI. For facility renovation.

4288
Alden & Vada Dow Fund ✧
315 Post St.
Midland, MI 48640-2658
Contact: Craig McDonald, Grants Coord.

Established in 1960 in MI.
Donors: Alden Dow‡; Vada Dow‡; Vada B. Dow
Charitable Unitrust.
Foundation type: Independent foundation.
Financial data (yr. ended 12/31/05): Assets,
$9,709,190 (M); gifts received, $500,000;
expenditures, $730,525; qualifying distributions,
$558,975; giving activities include $482,415 for 28
grants (high: $50,000; low: $2,500).
Purpose and activities: Giving primarily for social
services, particularly children, youth, family and
community; some giving also for the arts, and
education.
Fields of interest: Performing arts, theater;
Performing arts, music; Arts; Elementary/secondary
education; Education; Environment; Zoos/
zoological societies; Health care; Food services,
congregate meals; Recreation, fairs/festivals;
Athletics/sports, baseball; Recreation; Human
services; American Red Cross; Children/youth,
services; Youth, services; Family services; Women,
centers/services.
Type of support: General/operating support;
Continuing support; Annual campaigns; Capital
campaigns; Equipment; Endowments;
Conferences/seminars.
Limitations: Applications not accepted. Giving
primarily in MI. No grants to individuals.
Application information: Contributes only to
pre-selected organizations.
Board meeting date(s): Feb. 15 and Sept. 15
Officers and Trustees:* Michael Lloyd Dow,* Pres.;
Steven Carras,* Secy.; Lloyd Mills,* Treas.; Barbara
D. Carras; Diane Hullet; Chris Mills.
Number of staff: 1 part-time professional.
EIN: 386058512

4289
DTE Energy Foundation ▼
(formerly Detroit Edison Foundation)
2000 2nd Ave., Rm. 1046 WCB
Detroit, MI 48226-1279
Contact: Karla Hall, V.P. and Secy.
URL: http://www.dteenergy.com/about/
community/foundation/foundationSupport.html

Established in 1986 in MI.
Donor: The Detroit Edison Co.
Foundation type: Company-sponsored foundation.
Financial data (yr. ended 12/31/04): Assets,
$22,311,575 (M); expenditures, $6,641,424;
qualifying distributions, $6,543,066; giving
activities include $6,096,623 for 443 grants (high:

$502,632; low: $70), and $313,349 for 204
employee matching gifts.
Purpose and activities: The foundation supports
organizations involved with education, the
environment, diversity, community development,
engineering, and leadership development.
Fields of interest: Elementary/secondary
education; Higher education; Engineering school/
education; Education; Environment, air pollution;
Environment, water pollution; Environment, energy;
Environmental education; Environment; Civil rights,
equal rights; Urban/community development;
Community development; Engineering; Leadership
development.
Type of support: Employee volunteer services;
General/operating support; Capital campaigns;
Employee matching gifts.
Limitations: Giving limited to MI. No support for
political organizations, religious organizations not of
direct benefit to the entire community, or
disease-specific health organizations. No grants to
individuals, or for student group trips or capital
campaigns or equipment for hospitals.
Publications: Informational brochure (including
application guidelines); Program policy statement.
Application information: Application form required.
Initial approach: Download application form and
mail proposal and application form to
foundation
Copies of proposal: 1
Deadline(s): Apr. 15, Aug. 15, and Dec. 15; Jan.
31 for Achieving Excellence
Board meeting date(s): 3 times per year
Final notification: 60 to 90 days
Officers and Directors:* Frederick E. Shell, Pres.;
Karla Hall,* V.P. and Secy.; Naif A. Khouri,* Treas.;
Chris Brown; Robert J. Buckler; Lynne Ellyn; Stephen
E. Ewing; Joyce Hayes-Giles; Paul Hillegonds; Bruce
Peterson; Michael C. Porter; Larry E. Steward.
Number of staff: 1 full-time professional; 2 full-time
support.
EIN: 382708636
Selected grants: The following grants were reported
in 2004.
$690,132 to United Way for Southeastern Michigan,
Detroit, MI. 2 grants: $502,632, $187,500
$500,000 to Detroit Renaissance Foundation,
Detroit, MI.
$255,000 to Detroit Symphony Orchestra, Detroit,
MI.
$200,000 to New Detroit, Detroit, MI.
$150,000 to Wayne State University, Detroit, MI.
$45,000 to University Cultural Center Association,
Detroit, MI.
$40,000 to Detroit Science Center, Detroit, MI.
$27,468 to Eastern Michigan University, Ypsilanti,
MI.
$25,000 to Upper Peninsula Community
Foundation, Gladstone, MI.

4290
The Duffy Foundation ✧
c/o Miller Canfield, Attn.: Erik H. Serr
101 N. Main St., 7th Fl.
Ann Arbor, MI 48104

Established in 1989 in MI.
Donors: Howard S. Holmes; Andrea L. Holmes; Mary
B. Holmes.
Foundation type: Independent foundation.
Financial data (yr. ended 12/31/05): Assets,
$45,090,284 (M); expenditures, $3,690,981;
qualifying distributions, $3,552,500; giving

activities include $3,552,500 for 52 grants (high: $1,500,000; low: $2,500).

Purpose and activities: Giving primarily to a hospital; giving also to animal protection organizations, environmental conservation, human services, and services for the elderly.

Fields of interest: Arts; Environment, natural resources; Animal welfare; Animals/wildlife, special services; Hospitals (general); Crime/violence prevention, domestic violence; Food services; YM/YWCAs & YM/YWHAs; Children/youth, services; Aging.

Limitations: Applications not accepted. Giving primarily in MI, with emphasis on Ann Arbor and Washtenaw County. No grants to individuals.

Application information: Contributes only to pre-selected organizations.

Officers and Directors:* Andrea L. Holmes,* Pres. and Treas.; Christine M. Holmes,* V.P.; Kathryn W. Holmes,* V.P.

EIN: 382908719

Selected grants: The following grants were reported in 2005.

$1,500,000 to Saint Joseph Mercy Hospital, Ann Arbor, MI.

$105,000 to Humane Society. 2 grants: $30,000, $75,000

$100,000 to Arbor Hospice, Ann Arbor, MI.

$85,000 to Washtenaw Land Trust, Ann Arbor, MI.

$75,000 to YMCA.

$40,000 to Recycle Ann Arbor, Ann Arbor, MI.

$35,000 to Ozone House, Ann Arbor, MI.

$30,000 to American Red Cross.

$25,000 to Horses Haven, South Lyon, MI.

4291
Earhart Foundation ▼

2200 Green Rd., Ste. H
Ann Arbor, MI 48105
Contact: Ingrid A. Gregg, Pres.

Incorporated in 1929 in MI.

Donor: Harry Boyd Earhart†.

Foundation type: Independent foundation.

Financial data (yr. ended 12/31/05): Assets, $61,971,515 (M); expenditures, $12,735,116; qualifying distributions, $12,423,221; giving activities include $7,671,934 for 306 grants (high: $1,722,048; low: $400; average: $5,000–$50,000), and $3,769,590 for 304 grants to individuals (high: $41,800; low: $375; average: $6,700–$25,000).

Purpose and activities: H.B. Earhart Fellowships for graduate study awarded through a special nominating process for which direct applications will not be accepted; research fellowships for individual projects in economics, history, philosophy, international affairs, and political science awarded upon direct application to faculty members; grants also to educational and research organizations legally qualified for private foundation support.

Fields of interest: History/archaeology; Philosophy/ethics; Graduate/professional education; Economics; Political science; International studies.

Type of support: Conferences/seminars; Publication; Curriculum development; Fellowships; Research; Grants to individuals; Scholarships—to individuals.

Publications: Annual report (including application guidelines).

Application information: Direct applications from candidates or uninvited sponsors for H.B. Earhart

Fellowships (for graduate study) are not accepted. Application form not required.

> *Initial approach:* Letter
> *Copies of proposal:* 1
> *Deadline(s):* Proposal should be submitted at least 120 days before beginning of project work period
> *Board meeting date(s):* Monthly except in Aug.

Officers and Trustees:* Dennis L. Bark,* Chair.; John H. Moore,* Vice-Chair.; Ingrid A. Gregg,* Pres.; Montgomery B. Brown, Secy. and Dir., Progs.; Kathleen B. Mason, Treas.; Peter B. Clark, Tr. Emeritus; Paul W. McCracken, Tr. Emeritus; Richard A. Ware, Tr. Emeritus; Thomas J. Bray; Kimberly O. Dennis; Earl I. Heenan III; Ann K. Irish; David B. Kennedy; Robert L. Queller.

Number of staff: 2 full-time professional; 3 full-time support.

EIN: 386008273

Selected grants: The following grants were reported in 2004.

$75,000 to Intercollegiate Studies Institute, Wilmington, DE. For fellowships.

$60,000 to Social Philosophy and Policy Foundation, Bowling Green, OH. For visiting scholars in fields of history and philosophy.

$55,100 to Jamestown Foundation, DC. For publication of Terrorism Focus.

$50,000 to Citizens Research Council of Michigan, Livonia, MI. For project, Facilitating Michigan Local Government Response to Financial Pressures.

$33,841 to University of Chicago, Law School, Chicago, IL. For visiting fellowship in Law, Economics and Government.

$27,273 to Mississippi State University, Center for International Security and Strategic Studies, Mississippi State, MS. For International Cooperation in War Against Terror in Asia-Pacific Region.

$25,000 to Philadelphia Society, Chicago, IL. For travel by graduate students and/or junior faculty to attend National Meeting in Chicago, Illinois and Regional Meeting in Philadelphia, Pennsylvania.

$15,000 to Sarah Lawrence College, Bronxville, NY. For Benardete Archive for graduate student's assistance in organizing and archival of Seth Benardete Papers housed in Raymond Fogelman Library of New School University.

$13,925 to Tufts University, Fletcher School of Law and Diplomacy, Medford, MA. For graduate fellowship in International Security Studies.

$13,000 to Westminster Theological Seminary, Department of Church History, Glenside, PA. For graduate fellowship in Religion.

4292
C. K. Eddy Family Memorial Fund ◇

c/o Citizens Bank Wealth Mgmt., N.A.
328 S. Saginaw St., M/C 002072
Flint, MI 48502
Application address: Helen James, Trust Off., c/o Citizens Bank Wealth Mgmt., N.A., 101 N. Washington Ave., Saginaw, MI 48007, tel.: (989) 776-7368

Trust established in 1925 in MI.

Donor: Arthur D. Eddy†.

Foundation type: Independent foundation.

Financial data (yr. ended 6/30/06): Assets, $16,030,358 (M); expenditures, $1,007,346; qualifying distributions, $1,151,286; giving

activities include $782,000 for 8 grants (high: $450,000; low: $28,500), and $181,500 for 51 loans to individuals (high: $4,000; low: $2,700).

Purpose and activities: Giving primarily for student loans and community programs.

Fields of interest: Arts; Education; Boys & girls clubs; Human services; YM/YWCAs & YM/YWHAs; Children/youth, services; Community development; Federated giving programs.

Type of support: Equipment; Program development; Student loans—to individuals.

Limitations: Giving limited to Saginaw County, MI, with some emphasis on the city of Saginaw.

Publications: Application guidelines.

Application information: Application form required.

> *Deadline(s):* None for grants; May 1 for student loans
> *Board meeting date(s):* 3rd Wed. of Mar., June, Sept., and Dec.

Trustee: Citizens Bank, N.A.

EIN: 386040506

Selected grants: The following grants were reported in 2005.

$101,000 to Saginaw Eddy Concert Band, Pinckney, MI.

$100,000 to Saginaw Community Foundation, Saginaw, MI. 2 grants: $50,000 each

$87,500 to Hidden Harvest, Saginaw, MI.

$60,000 to United Way of Saginaw County, Saginaw, MI.

$50,000 to Habitat for Humanity International, Saginaw, MI.

$30,500 to Hartley Outdoor Education Center, Saint Charles, MI.

$19,666 to Underground Railroad, Saginaw, MI.

$7,500 to East Side Soup Kitchen, Saginaw, MI.

$7,500 to Salvation Army, Port Huron, MI.

4293
Fabri-Kal Foundation ◇

c/o Fabri-Kal Corp.
Plastics Pl.
Kalamazoo, MI 49001   (269) 385-5050
Contact: Robert P. Kittredge, Pres.

Established in 1969 in MI.

Donor: Fabri-Kal Corp.

Foundation type: Company-sponsored foundation.

Financial data (yr. ended 12/31/05): Assets, $103 (M); gifts received, $466,470; expenditures, $466,564; qualifying distributions, $466,564; giving activities include $152,277 for 20 grants (high: $35,789; low: $1,000), and $314,195 for 77 grants to individuals (high: $16,112; low: $40).

Purpose and activities: The foundation supports organizations involved with arts and culture, education, human services, and Christianity.

Fields of interest: Arts; Education; Human services; Federated giving programs; Christian agencies & churches.

Type of support: Capital campaigns; Building/renovation; Equipment; Employee-related scholarships.

Limitations: Giving limited to Kalamazoo, MI, Hazleton, PA, and Greenville, SC.

Application information: Application form not required.

> *Initial approach:* Proposal
> *Deadline(s):* None
> *Board meeting date(s):* May

Officers: Robert P. Kittredge, Pres.; R.L. Weyhing III, Secy.; Gary Galia, Treas.

EIN: 237003366

4294
The Farbman Family Foundation ✧
(formerly The Farbman Foundation)
28400 Northwestern Hwy., 4th Fl.
Southfield, MI 48034-1839

Established in 1997 in MI.
Donors: Burton D. Farbman; Susan B. Farbman; The Farbman Group.
Foundation type: Independent foundation.
Financial data (yr. ended 12/31/05): Assets, $120,720 (M); gifts received, $496,500; expenditures, $432,239; qualifying distributions, $432,104; giving activities include $432,084 for 15 grants (high: $143,334; low: $1,000; average: $2,000–$40,000).
Fields of interest: Education; Zoos/zoological societies; YM/YWCAs & YM/YWHAs; Jewish federated giving programs; Jewish agencies & temples.
Limitations: Applications not accepted. Giving primarily in MI, with emphasis on Detroit. No grants to individuals.
Application information: Contributes only to pre-selected organizations.
Directors: Andrew V. Farbman; Burton D. Farbman; David S. Farbman; Susan B. Farbman.
EIN: 383345578
Selected grants: The following grants were reported in 2003.
$60,000 to Jewish Federation of Metropolitan Detroit, Bloomfield Hills, MI. For general support.
$35,000 to YMCA of Metropolitan Detroit, Detroit, MI. For general support.
$5,500 to College for Creative Studies, Detroit, MI. For general support.
$5,000 to Detroit Zoological Society, Royal Oak, MI. For general support.
$1,500 to University of Michigan, Ann Arbor, MI. For general support.
$1,000 to Crooked Tree Arts Council, Crooked Tree Arts Center, Petoskey, MI.
$1,000 to Detroit Historical Society, Detroit, MI. For general support.
$1,000 to Karmanos Cancer Foundation, Lathrup Village, MI. For general support.
$1,000 to Mosaic Youth Theater of Detroit, Detroit, MI. For general support.
$500 to Food Bank of Oakland County, Pontiac, MI. For general support.

4295
The Farver Foundation ✧
626 Depot St.
Blissfield, MI 49228-1399
Contact: Lori Mount, Admin. Asst.

Established in 1988 in MI.
Donors: Orville W. Farver†; Constance Farver; Herbert Farver.
Foundation type: Independent foundation.
Financial data (yr. ended 12/31/04): Assets, $5,143,536 (M); expenditures, $419,793; qualifying distributions, $382,003; giving activities include $384,550 for 57 grants (high: $25,000; low: $50).
Fields of interest: Education; Athletics/sports, baseball; Human services; Community development.
Type of support: General/operating support; Continuing support; Annual campaigns; Capital campaigns; Building/renovation; Equipment; Emergency funds.

Limitations: Giving primarily in Lenawee County, MI, with emphasis on the Adrian and Blissfield areas. No grants to individuals.
Application information: Application form not required.
Initial approach: Letter
Deadline(s): None
Trustees: Constance Farver; O. Herbert Farver.
EIN: 386540398
Selected grants: The following grants were reported in 2004.
$25,000 to Bixby Community Health Foundation, Adrian, MI.
$20,000 to Siena Heights University, Adrian, MI.
$15,000 to Little League Baseball.
$15,000 to Overlanders Association, Adrian, MI.
$15,000 to United Way.
$10,000 to Boys and Girls Club of Lenawee, Adrian, MI.
$10,000 to Habitat for Humanity of Lenawee County, Adrian, MI.
$10,000 to Lenawee County Education Foundation, Adrian, MI.
$10,000 to YMCA of Lenawee County, Adrian, MI.
$5,500 to Adrian Public Schools, Adrian, MI.

4296
The Miriam & Fred Ferber Foundation ✧
3000 Pontiac Trail
Commerce Township, MI 48390
(248) 863-3001, ext. 1274
Contact: Roman Ferber, Pres.

Established in 2002 in MI.
Donors: Annette Adalman; Brian Adalman.
Foundation type: Independent foundation.
Financial data (yr. ended 12/31/04): Assets, $94,298 (M); gifts received, $300,000; expenditures, $694,726; qualifying distributions, $694,300; giving activities include $694,300 for 11 grants (high: $365,000; low: $1,000).
Purpose and activities: Giving primarily to Jewish organizations.
Fields of interest: Health care; Jewish federated giving programs; Jewish agencies & temples.
Limitations: Giving on a national basis, with some emphasis on MI. No grants to individuals.
Application information:
Initial approach: Letter
Deadline(s): None
Officers and Directors:* Roman Ferber,* Pres. and Secy.; Alon Kaufman,* V.P. and Treas.
EIN: 371432758
Selected grants: The following grants were reported in 2003.
$400,000 to Jewish Federation of Metropolitan Detroit, Bloomfield Hills, MI. For program support.
$100,000 to Friendship Circle, West Bloomfield, MI. For program support.
$50,000 to Chabad. For program support.
$40,000 to Friends of the Israel Defense Forces, New York, NY. For program support.
$20,000 to Henry Ford Health System, Detroit, MI. For program support.
$20,000 to Hillel Day School of Metropolitan Detroit, Farmington Hills, MI. For program support.
$19,000 to Jewish Hospice and Chaplaincy Network, Bloomfield, MI. For program support.
$6,000 to Friends of AKIM USA, New York, NY. For program support.

4297
John E. Fetzer Institute, Inc. ✧
(formerly John E. Fetzer Foundation, Inc.)
9292 West KL Ave.
Kalamazoo, MI 49009-9398
Contact: Thomas F. Beech, C.E.O. and Pres.
FAX: (269) 372-2163; E-mail: info@fetzer.org;
URL: http://www.fetzer.org

Established in 1956.
Donors: John E. Fetzer†; John E. Fetzer Memorial Trust; Institute for Research on Unlimited Love; Shinnyo-En Foundation.
Foundation type: Operating foundation.
Financial data (yr. ended 7/31/05): Assets, $374,178,286 (M); gifts received, $3,208,720; expenditures, $14,140,624; qualifying distributions, $12,596,966; giving activities include $751,945 for 24 grants (high: $210,000), and $2,987,174 for 4 foundation-administered programs.
Purpose and activities: The institute is a nonprofit, private operating foundation with an interest in exploring the relationship between the inner life of mind and spirit and action and service in the world. The institute's mission is to foster awareness of the power of love and forgiveness in the emerging global community through research, education, and service programs.
Fields of interest: Education; Health care; Children/ youth, services; Philanthropy/voluntarism; Social sciences, research; Law/international law; Social sciences.
Type of support: General/operating support; Program development; Conferences/seminars; Research; Program evaluation; Grants to individuals; Matching/challenge support.
Limitations: Applications not accepted. Giving on a national basis.
Publications: Informational brochure; Newsletter; Occasional report; Program policy statement.
Application information: Contributes only to pre-selected organizations.
Board meeting date(s): Mar., June, Oct., and Dec.
Officers and Trustees:* Robert F. Lehman,* Chair.; Janis A. Claflin,* Vice-Chair.; Thomas F. Beech, Ed.D.,* C.E.O. and Pres.; Christina M. Adams, V.P., Finance and Admin.; Timothy J. Jones, V.P., Opers.; Shirley H. Showalter, Ph.D., V.P., Progs.; Kathleen M. Cavanaugh, Secy.; Bruce F. Fetzer,* Treas.; Angeles Arrien, Ph.D.; Carolyn Thompson Brown, Ph.D.; Bruce M. Carlson, M.D., Ph.D.; Lawrence E. Sullivan, Ph.D.; Lynn W. Twist; Frances E. Vaughan.
Number of staff: 24 full-time professional; 4 part-time professional; 17 full-time support; 6 part-time support.
EIN: 386052788

4298
John E. Fetzer Memorial Trust Fund ✧ ☆
c/o Michael C. Gergely
P.O. Box 117
Vicksburg, MI 49097-0117

Established in 1991 in MI.
Donor: J.E. Fetzer Revocable Trust.
Foundation type: Independent foundation.
Financial data (yr. ended 6/30/05): Assets, $75,803,696 (M); gifts received, $1,000,000; expenditures, $3,675,421; qualifying distributions, $3,460,243; giving activities include $3,000,000 for 1 grant.

Fields of interest: Higher education; Human services, mind/body enrichment; Voluntarism promotion; Psychology/behavioral science.
Type of support: General/operating support; Research.
Limitations: Applications not accepted. Giving primarily to Kalamazoo, MI, also and some giving in San Francisco, CA. No grants to individuals.
Application information: Contributes only to 2 pre-selected organizations.
Officers: Robert Lehman, Pres.; Bruce Fetzer, Exec. V.P.; Thomas Beaver, V.P.; Michael Gergely, Secy.; Louis Leeburg, Treas.
Number of staff: 1 full-time professional.
EIN: 383010714

4299
Max M. and Marjorie S. Fisher Foundation, Inc. ✧
2 Towne Sq., Ste. 920
Southfield, MI 48075-3761

Established in 1955 in MI.
Donors: Max M. Fisher‡; Marjorie M. Fisher; Martinique Hotel, Inc.
Foundation type: Independent foundation.
Financial data (yr. ended 11/30/05): Assets, $13,414,218 (M); gifts received, $7,569,630; expenditures, $4,762,402; qualifying distributions, $4,616,657; giving activities include $4,611,027 for 105 grants (high: $2,608,410; low: $100; average: $1,000–$300,000).
Purpose and activities: Giving primarily for education, with emphasis on a university; funding also for Jewish organizations, the arts, including a symphony orchestra, and human services.
Fields of interest: Museums; Performing arts; Arts; Elementary/secondary education; Higher education; Education; Health organizations; Human services; Federated giving programs; Jewish federated giving programs; Jewish agencies & temples.
Limitations: Applications not accepted. Giving on a national basis, with emphasis on MI, OH, and NY. No grants to individuals.
Application information: Contributes only to pre-selected organizations.
Officers and Directors:* Marjorie S. Fisher,* Pres.; Phillip William Fisher,* V.P.; Douglas Stewart, Exec. Dir.; Julie F. Cummings; Marjorie M. Fisher; Mary D. Fisher; Jane Ellen Sherman.
EIN: 381784340
Selected grants: The following grants were reported in 2005.
$2,608,410 to Detroit Symphony Orchestra, Detroit, MI.
$300,000 to University of Alabama, Birmingham, AL.
$255,000 to Beaumont Foundation, Southfield, MI.
$243,082 to United Jewish Foundation, Bloomfield Hills, MI.
$81,000 to United Way for Southeastern Michigan, Detroit, MI.

4300
William & Lisa Ford Foundation
1901 Saint Antoine St., 6th Fl.
Detroit, MI 48226 (313) 259-7777
Contact: David M. Hempstead, Secy.

Established in 1998 in MI.
Donors: William Clay Ford, Jr.; Lisa V. Ford.

Foundation type: Independent foundation.
Financial data (yr. ended 12/31/05): Assets, $10,828,359; expenditures, $465,188; qualifying distributions, $412,162; giving activities include $410,000 for 17 grants (high: $250,000; low: $1,000).
Purpose and activities: Giving primarily for children's services and higher education; funding also for human services.
Fields of interest: Museums; Higher education; Education; Environment, land resources; Health care; Human services; Children, services; Federated giving programs; Buddhism.
Limitations: Giving primarily in MI. No grants to individuals.
Application information: Awards are generally limited to charitable organizations already known and of interest to the foundation.
Initial approach: Letter
Deadline(s): None
Board meeting date(s): As necessary
Officers and Trustee:* William Clay Ford, Jr.,* Pres. and Dir.; Lisa V. Ford, V.P.; David M. Hempstead, Secy.; George A. Straitor, Treas.
EIN: 383441138
Selected grants: The following grants were reported in 2004.
$153,500 to Greenhills School, Ann Arbor, MI.
$50,000 to Telluride Foundation, Telluride, CO.
$40,000 to Spirit Rock Meditation Center, Woodacre, CA.
$10,000 to Michigan Environmental Council, Lansing, MI.
$5,500 to Huron River Watershed Council, Ann Arbor, MI.
$5,000 to Hotchkiss School, Lakeville, CT.
$4,000 to Universidad Metropolitana, Rio Piedras, PR.
$2,500 to Telluride Academy, Telluride, CO.
$1,000 to Albion College, Albion, MI.
$1,000 to National Outdoor Leadership School, Lander, WY.

4301
Benson and Edith Ford Fund
1901 Saint Antoine St., 6th Fl.
Detroit, MI 48226 (313) 259-7777
Contact: David M. Hempstead, Secy.

Incorporated in 1943 in MI as the Hotchkiss Fund.
Donor: Benson Ford‡.
Foundation type: Independent foundation.
Financial data (yr. ended 12/31/05): Assets, $34,280,463 (M); expenditures, $1,976,757; qualifying distributions, $1,819,510; giving activities include $1,815,000 for 44 grants (high: $485,000; low: $2,000).
Purpose and activities: Support for health, human services, education, and arts and culture.
Fields of interest: Arts; Education; Hospitals (general); Youth development, services; Children/youth, services; Federated giving programs; Jewish agencies & temples.
Limitations: Giving primarily in MI. No grants to individuals.
Application information: Awards generally limited to charities already favorably known to substantial contributors of the foundation.
Initial approach: Letter
Deadline(s): None

Officers and Trustees:* Lynn F. Alandt,* Pres.; Benson Ford, Jr.,* V.P.; David M. Hempstead,* Secy.; George A. Straitor, Treas.
EIN: 386066333
Selected grants: The following grants were reported in 2005.
$485,000 to Henry Ford Health System, Detroit, MI.
$250,000 to Detroit 300 Conservancy, Detroit, MI.
$100,000 to Detroit Institute of Arts, Detroit, MI.
$100,000 to Detroit Zoological Society, Royal Oak, MI.
$80,000 to College for Creative Studies, Detroit, MI.
$25,000 to Saint John Health System, Detroit, MI.
$15,000 to Detroit Institute for Children, Detroit, MI.
$10,000 to LocalMotion, Ann Arbor, MI.
$5,000 to Detroit Artists Market, Detroit, MI.
$5,000 to Masters School, Dobbs Ferry, NY.

4302
Eleanor and Edsel Ford Fund
c/o David M. Hempstead
1901 Saint Antoine St., 6th Fl.
Detroit, MI 48226

Incorporated in 1944 in MI.
Donor: Eleanor Clay Ford‡.
Foundation type: Independent foundation.
Financial data (yr. ended 12/31/05): Assets, $21,508,135 (M); expenditures, $1,427,674; qualifying distributions, $1,391,117; giving activities include $1,390,000 for 7 grants (high: $325,000; low: $20,000).
Purpose and activities: Grants are limited to organizations selected by the trustees from among the charities with which Eleanor Clay Ford was prominently associated during her lifetime.
Fields of interest: Museums; Performing arts; Arts; Elementary/secondary education; Higher education; Medical care, in-patient care; Protestant agencies & churches.
Type of support: General/operating support; Building/renovation; Scholarship funds.
Limitations: Applications not accepted. Giving primarily in MI, with emphasis on Detroit, MI. No grants to individuals.
Application information: Contributes only to pre-selected organizations. Unsolicited requests for funds not considered.
Officers and Trustees:* William Clay Ford,* Pres.; David M. Hempstead,* Secy.; George A. Straitor, Treas.
EIN: 386066331

4303
Walter and Josephine Ford Fund
Ford Field
1901 Saint Antoine St., 6th Fl.
Detroit, MI 48226
Contact: David M. Hempstead, Secy.

Incorporated in 1951 in MI.
Donors: Josephine F. Ford‡; Walter B. Ford II.
Foundation type: Independent foundation.
Financial data (yr. ended 12/31/05): Assets, $4,436,805 (M); gifts received, $206,170; expenditures, $1,317,331; qualifying distributions, $1,302,218; giving activities include $1,298,500 for 45 grants (high: $400,000; low: $500).
Purpose and activities: Giving primarily for arts and culture, particularly to a center for creative studies, as well as for education, health associations,

children and youth services, social services, federated giving programs, religious purposes, and for the prevention of cruelty to children and animals.

Fields of interest: Arts; Higher education; Education; Hospitals (general); Health organizations, association; Medical research, institute; Human services; Children/youth, services; Federated giving programs; Religion.

Limitations: Giving primarily in ME, with some emphasis on Northeast Harbor, and MI, with emphasis on Detroit. No grants to individuals.

Application information: Awards generally limited to charities already favorably known to substantial contributors of the foundation.

Initial approach: Letter

Deadline(s): None

Board meeting date(s): Varies

Officers and Trustees: * Walter B. Ford III, V.P.; David M. Hempstead,* Secy.; George A. Straitor, Treas.

EIN: 386066334

Selected grants: The following grants were reported in 2004.

$250,000 to College for Creative Studies, Detroit, MI.

$85,000 to Detroit Zoological Society, Royal Oak, MI.

$50,000 to Friends of Acadia, Bar Harbor, ME.

$15,000 to Henry Ford Health System, Detroit, MI.

$15,000 to Neighborhood House, Northeast Harbor, ME.

$5,000 to Ark, The, Cherryfield, ME.

$5,000 to Detroit Institute for Children, Detroit, MI.

$5,000 to Henry Ford Village, Dearborn, MI.

$5,000 to U.S. Sportsmens Alliance Foundation, Columbus, OH.

$5,000 to United Negro College Fund, Fairfax, VA.

4304
William and Martha Ford Fund

1901 Saint Antoine St., 6th Fl.
Detroit, MI   48226   (313) 259-7777
Contact: David M. Hempstead, Secy.

Incorporated in 1953 in MI.

Donors: William Clay Ford; Martha Firestone Ford.

Foundation type: Independent foundation.

Financial data (yr. ended 12/31/05): Assets, $6,728,675 (M); expenditures, $1,317,283; qualifying distributions, $1,286,653; giving activities include $1,285,000 for 63 grants (high: $401,750; low: $250).

Purpose and activities: The fund provides financial support to corporations, trusts, community chests, funds or foundations, organized and operated solely for religious, charitable, scientific, literary or educational purposes, or for the prevention of cruelty to children or animals.

Fields of interest: Museums; Arts; Higher education; Zoos/zoological societies; Hospitals (general); Health care; Substance abuse, services; Boys & girls clubs; Human services; Foundations (community); Federated giving programs.

Limitations: Giving primarily in MI; some giving nationally. No grants to individuals.

Application information: Awards generally limited to charities already favorably known to substantial contributors of the foundation.

Initial approach: Letter

Deadline(s): None

Officers and Trustees: * William Clay Ford,* Pres.; David M. Hempstead,* Secy.; George A. Straitor, Treas.; Martha F. Ford.

EIN: 386066335

Selected grants: The following grants were reported in 2004.

$417,000 to Henry Ford Health System, Detroit, MI.

$65,000 to Freedom Institute, New York, NY.

$51,500 to Detroit Zoological Society, Royal Oak, MI.

$30,000 to Saint Lukes Episcopal Hospital, Houston, TX.

$28,000 to College for Creative Studies, Detroit, MI.

$25,000 to East Hampton Healthcare Foundation, East Hampton, NY.

$25,000 to National Council on Alcoholism and Drug Dependence, New York, NY.

$20,000 to Childrens Home of Detroit, Grosse Pointe Woods, MI.

$5,000 to Bon Secours Cottage Health Services Foundation, Grosse Pointe, MI.

$5,000 to University Liggett School, Grosse Pointe, MI.

4305
Edsel B. Ford II Fund

6th Fl. at Ford Field
1901 Saint Antoine St.
Detroit, MI   48226   (313) 259-7777
Contact: David M. Hempstead, Secy.

Established in 1993 in MI.

Donor: Edsel B. Ford II.

Foundation type: Independent foundation.

Financial data (yr. ended 12/31/05): Assets, $7,328,302 (M); expenditures, $335,155; qualifying distributions, $321,960; giving activities include $321,550 for 43 grants (high: $31,000; low: $500).

Purpose and activities: Giving primarily for higher education, health, social services, children and youth services, particularly juvenile diabetes, federated giving programs, and a Presbyterian church.

Fields of interest: Arts; Higher education; Education; Zoos/zoological societies; Hospitals (general); Health care; Diabetes; Human services; Children/youth, services; Federated giving programs; Protestant agencies & churches.

Limitations: Giving primarily in MI. No grants to individuals.

Application information: Generally contributes to organizations already known to the donor.

Initial approach: Letter

Deadline(s): None

Board meeting date(s): As needed

Officers and Director: * Edsel B. Ford II,* Pres.; David M. Hempstead, Secy.; George A. Straitor, Treas.

EIN: 383153050

4306
The Henry Ford II Fund

Ford Field
1901 Saint Antoine St., 6th Fl.
Detroit, MI   48226   (313) 259-7777
Contact: David M. Hempstead, Secy.

Incorporated in 1953 in MI.

Donor: Henry Ford II†.

Foundation type: Independent foundation.

Financial data (yr. ended 12/31/05): Assets, $30,804,263 (M); expenditures, $2,226,055; qualifying distributions, $2,101,629; giving activities include $2,100,000 for 24 grants (high: $650,000; low: $2,500).

Purpose and activities: Giving primarily for education, social services, federated giving programs, and for the prevention of cruelty to children and animals.

Fields of interest: Higher education; Education; Health care; Human services; Federated giving programs.

Limitations: Applications not accepted. Giving primarily in MI, with emphasis on Dearborn, Detroit, and Grosse Pointe Woods. No grants to individuals.

Application information: Unsolicited requests for funds not accepted.

Board meeting date(s): As necessary

Officers and Trustees: * Edsel B. Ford II,* Pres.; David M. Hempstead,* Secy.; George A. Straitor,* Treas.

EIN: 386066332

Selected grants: The following grants were reported in 2005.

$500,000 to Salvation Army, Port Huron, MI.

$250,000 to Detroit 300 Conservancy, Detroit, MI.

$200,000 to Childrens Hospital of Michigan Foundation, Detroit, MI.

$100,000 to Detroit Zoological Society, Royal Oak, MI.

$100,000 to Focus: Hope, Detroit, MI.

$50,000 to Detroit Institute for Children, Detroit, MI.

$30,000 to CATCH, Detroit, MI.

$10,000 to Detroit Riverfront Conservancy, Detroit, MI.

$10,000 to Greening of Detroit, Detroit, MI.

4307
Ford Motor Company Fund ▼

1 American Rd.
P.O. Box 1899
Dearborn, MI   48126-2798   (313) 248-4745
FAX: (313) 594-7001; *E-mail:* fordfund@ford.com;
Additional tel.: (888) 313-0102; *URL:* http://www.ford.com/go/fordfund

Incorporated in 1949 in MI.

Donor: Ford Motor Co.

Foundation type: Company-sponsored foundation.

Financial data (yr. ended 12/31/04): Assets, $107,283,149 (M); gifts received, $81,500,000; expenditures, $40,236,667; qualifying distributions, $77,946,735; giving activities include $77,916,903 for 1,546+ grants (high: $4,100,000).

Purpose and activities: The fund supports organizations involved with arts and culture, education, auto industry environmental issues, health, auto safety, youth development, human services, diversity education, community development, public affairs, and minorities.

Fields of interest: Arts; Higher education; Business school/education; Engineering school/education; Education; Environment, air pollution; Environment; Hospitals (general); Health care; Safety, automotive safety; Youth development; Human services; Civil rights, public education; Community development; Science, formal/general education; Mathematics; Engineering/technology; Public affairs, alliance; Minorities.

Type of support: Employee-related scholarships; Continuing support; Annual campaigns; Capital campaigns; Equipment; Emergency funds; Program development; Conferences/seminars; Curriculum development; Scholarship funds; Research; Employee matching gifts; In-kind gifts; Matching/challenge support.

Limitations: Giving primarily in areas of company operations, with emphasis on southeastern MI. No support for religious organizations not of direct benefit to the entire community, political or fraternal organizations, animal rights organizations, labor groups, private schools, or species-specific organizations. No grants to individuals (except for employee-related scholarships), or for fellowships, endowments, debt reduction, general operating support, or beauty or talent contests; no loans or program-related investments; no vehicle donations.

Publications: Application guidelines; Annual report; Corporate giving report; Informational brochure.

Application information: Application form required.

Initial approach: Download application form and mail, fax, or E-mail to foundation

Copies of proposal: 1

Deadline(s): None

Board meeting date(s): Apr. and Oct.

Final notification: Within 6 weeks

Officers and Trustees:* James G. Vella,* Chair. and Pres.; Susan M. Cischke, V.P.; Peter Sherry, Jr., Secy.; Ann Marie Petach, Treas.; Alfred B. Ford; Sheila Ford Hamp; Timothy O'Brian; Ziad Ojakli.

Number of staff: 11 full-time professional; 10 full-time support.

EIN: 381459376

Selected grants: The following grants were reported in 2004.

$4,100,000 to Conservation International, DC.

$2,000,000 to Georgia Institute of Technology, Atlanta, GA.

$2,000,000 to Northwestern University, Evanston, IL.

$2,000,000 to Smith College, Northampton, MA.

$1,400,000 to Mount Vernon Ladies Association, Mount Vernon, VA.

$1,200,000 to Chicagos Environmental Fund, Chicago, IL.

$1,026,000 to Berry College, Mount Berry, GA.

$1,000,000 to Dearborn Community Fund, Dearborn, MI.

$1,000,000 to Detroit Renaissance Foundation, Detroit, MI.

$1,000,000 to Muhammad Ali Museum and Education Center, Louisville, KY.

4308
William C. Ford, Jr. Scholarship Program ✧ ☆

Ford Field
1901 Saint Antoine St., 6th Fl.
Detroit, MI 48226
Application address: c/o Scholarship America (William C. Ford, Jr. Pres.) P.O. Box 297, Saint Peter, MN 56082, tel.: (800) 537-4180

Established in 2005 in MI.

Donor: William C. Ford, Jr.

Foundation type: Independent foundation.

Financial data (yr. ended 12/31/05): Assets, $773,135 (M); gifts received, $1,412,328; expenditures, $522,983; qualifying distributions, $507,142; giving activities include $460,500 for 307 grants to individuals (high: $1,500; low: $1,500).

Fields of interest: Higher education.

Type of support: Scholarship funds.

Limitations: Giving primarily to children of company employees.

Application information: Application form required.

Initial approach: Application forms are available from Scholarship America. Applications must include a college transcript from the student's freshman year.

Deadline(s): July 1

Officers: William C. Ford, Jr., Pres.; David M. Hempstead, Secy.; James G. Vella, Treas.

EIN: 202462203

4309
Foundation for Theological Education in Southeast Asia ✧

c/o Norman Donkersloot
119 Oak Valley Dr.
Holland, MI 49424
FAX: (616) 355-4370; E-mail: jmhoff@egl.net

Established in 1934 in NY.

Foundation type: Independent foundation.

Financial data (yr. ended 12/31/05): Assets, $13,345,124 (M); gifts received, $3,504; expenditures, $738,614; qualifying distributions, $685,854; giving activities include $457,277 for 66 grants (high: $70,000; low: $1,500; average: $5,000–$10,000).

Purpose and activities: Giving primarily for theological education institutions in Southeast Asia, especially China.

Fields of interest: Theological school/education.

International interests: China.

Type of support: Professorships; Curriculum development.

Limitations: Applications not accepted. Giving on a national and international basis, with emphasis on Southeast Asia and China. No grants to individuals.

Application information: Contributes only to pre-selected organizations.

Board meeting date(s): Dec.

Officers: Norman Donkersloot, Treas.; Rev. Marvin D. Hoff, Exec. Dir.

Trustees: Gerald Anderson; Bill Browne, Rev.; Rev. Charles Clark; Glory Dharmana; Franklin Idshida, Rev.; Stanley Murray, Rev.; Letty Russell; Choon-Leong Seow; Martha Smalley; Ron Wallace, Rev.; Sze-Kar Wan; Greer Anne Wenh-in Ng; Xiaoling Zhu.

Number of staff: 1 full-time professional; 1 part-time support.

EIN: 237362344

4310
Four County Community Foundation

(formerly Four County Foundation)
231 E. Saint Clair St.
P.O. Box 539
Almont, MI 48003-0539 (810) 798-0909
Contact: Janet Bauer, Exec. Dir.
FAX: (810) 798-0908; E-mail: info@4ccf.org;
Additional E-mail: janet@4ccf.org; URL: http://www.4ccf.org

Established in 1987 in MI; originally converted from Community Hospital Foundation and sold to Saint Joseph Mercy of Macomb North.

Foundation type: Community foundation.

Financial data (yr. ended 12/31/05): Assets, $9,563,324 (M); gifts received, $179,310;

expenditures, $492,273; giving activities include $329,983 for 99 grants (high: $19,000; low: $100).

Purpose and activities: The foundation is dedicated to bringing together human and financial resources to support progressive ideas in education, health, community, youth and adult programs.

Fields of interest: Education; Environment; Health care; Health organizations, association; Recreation; Children/youth, services; Community development.

Type of support: Continuing support; Equipment; Program development; Conferences/seminars; Scholarship funds; Matching/challenge support.

Limitations: Giving limited to northwest Oakland, northwest Macomb, southeast Lapeer, and southwest St. Clair counties, MI. No support for sectarian religious programs. No grants to individuals, or for operating expenses or basic educational or municipal functions (generally).

Publications: Application guidelines; Annual report; Newsletter; Program policy statement.

Application information: Visit foundation Web site for application forms and additional guidelines per grant type. Faxed applications are not accepted. Application form required.

Initial approach: Submit application form

Copies of proposal: 9

Deadline(s): Jan. 1, Apr. 1, July 1, and Oct. 1

Board meeting date(s): 6 meetings per year

Final notification: Within 1 month

Officers and Trustees:* Charles Schiedegger,* Pres.; Joseph Salas,* V.P.; Kim Jorgensen,* Secy.; Barbara Quain,* Treas.; Janet Bauer, Exec. Dir.; Judy Czerepowicz; William R. Duggan, Jr.; Timothy Edwards; Katherine Eschenburg; Schaeffer Greene; Henry Malburg; Hank Nichols; Sean O'Bryan; Brenda K. Pinskey; Laura Schapman; Barbara Stremler; Al Verlinde.

Number of staff: 1 full-time professional; 2 part-time support.

EIN: 382736601

4311
Stanley and Judith Frankel Family Foundation ✧

2301 W. Big Beaver Rd., Ste. 900
Troy, MI 48084

Established in 2000 in MI.

Donors: Stanley Frankel; Judith Frankel.

Foundation type: Independent foundation.

Financial data (yr. ended 2/28/06): Assets, $5,447,482 (M); gifts received, $100,000; expenditures, $980,350; qualifying distributions, $946,850; giving activities include $946,850 for 13 grants (high: $350,000; low: $100).

Purpose and activities: Giving primarily for higher education and to Jewish organizations.

Fields of interest: Performing arts; Higher education; Education; Jewish federated giving programs.

Limitations: Applications not accepted. Giving limited to MI. No grants to individuals.

Application information: Contributes only to pre-selected organizations.

Officers: Stanley Frankel, Pres.; Judith Frankel, V.P.; Arthur Weiss, Secy.

EIN: 383531285

4312
Maxine and Stuart Frankel Foundation ✧
2301 W. Big Beaver Rd., Ste. 510
Troy, MI   48084

Established in 1998 in MI.
Donors: Maxine Frankel; Stuart Frankel; Jean Frankel; Samuel Frankel.
Foundation type: Independent foundation.
Financial data (yr. ended 12/31/05): Assets, $9,080,488 (M); gifts received, $5,000,000; expenditures, $481,189; qualifying distributions, $479,076; giving activities include $479,076 for 73 + grants (high: $84,825).
Purpose and activities: Giving primarily for the arts, education, health, particularly a children's hospital, as well as for youth, family and social services, and Jewish organizations.
Fields of interest: Museums (art); Arts; Higher education; Education; Hospitals (specialty); Health organizations, association; Human services; Children/youth, services; Family services; Jewish federated giving programs; Jewish agencies & temples.
Limitations: Applications not accepted. Giving primarily in MI. No grants to individuals.
Application information: Contributes only to pre-selected organizations.
Officers: Maxine Frankel, Pres.; Stuart Frankel, Secy.-Treas.
EIN: 383445379
Selected grants: The following grants were reported in 2003.
$204,400 to Childrens Hospital of Michigan, Detroit, MI. For general support.
$100,000 to New Common School Foundation, Detroit, MI. For general support.
$35,000 to Common Ground Sanctuary, Bloomfield Hills, MI. For general support.
$32,500 to Jewish Federation of Metropolitan Detroit, Bloomfield Hills, MI. For general support.
$20,150 to Independent Curators International, New York, NY. For general support.
$12,500 to Storm King Art Center, Mountainville, NY. For general support.
$6,000 to Planned Parenthood Federation of America, New York, NY. For general support.
$4,000 to University of Michigan, Ann Arbor, MI. For general support.
$3,500 to American Friends of the Israel Museum, New York, NY. For general support.
$1,000 to Gildas Club Worldwide, New York, NY. For general support.

4313
Samuel & Jean Frankel Foundation ✧
3875 Lakeland Ln.
Bloomfield Hills, MI   48302

Established around 1970.
Donors: Samuel Frankel; Jean Frankel.
Foundation type: Independent foundation.
Financial data (yr. ended 12/31/05): Assets, $29,691,848 (M); gifts received, $2,252,816; expenditures, $8,064,973; qualifying distributions, $7,998,494; giving activities include $7,998,494 for 138 grants (high: $5,000,000; low: $25).
Purpose and activities: Giving primarily for Jewish services, the fine and performing arts, higher education, health organizations, and human services.
Fields of interest: Museums; Performing arts; Education; Health organizations; Youth

development, services; Human services; Federated giving programs; Jewish federated giving programs; Jewish agencies & temples.
Limitations: Applications not accepted. Giving primarily in MI; some funding nationally. No grants to individuals.
Application information: Contributes only to pre-selected organizations.
Officers: Samuel Frankel, Pres.; Jean Frankel, V.P. and Secy.; Stanley Frankel, Treas.
Trustees: Bruce Frankel; Stuart Frankel; Joelyn Nyman; Arthur Weiss.
EIN: 386088399

4314
The Samuel and Jean Frankel Jewish Heritage Foundation ✧ ☆
2301 W. Big Beaver Rd., Ste. 900
Troy, MI   48084

Established in 2004 in MI.
Donors: Samuel Frankel; Jean Frankel.
Foundation type: Independent foundation.
Financial data (yr. ended 12/31/05): Assets, $107,606,020 (M); gifts received, $61,625,465; expenditures, $4,118,943; qualifying distributions, $3,953,500; giving activities include $3,953,500 for grants.
Fields of interest: Higher education; Theological school/education; Education; Jewish federated giving programs; Jewish agencies & temples.
Type of support: Program development; Endowments.
Limitations: Applications not accepted. Giving primarily in MI; giving also in New York, NY. No grants to individuals.
Application information: Contributes only to pre-selected organizations.
Officers and Trustees:* Samuel Frankel,* Pres.; Jean Frankel,* V.P.; Judith Frankel,* Secy.; Stanley Frankel,* Treas.
EIN: 300095016

4315
Fremont Area Community Foundation ▼
(formerly The Fremont Area Foundation)
4424 W. 48th St.
P.O. Box B
Fremont, MI   49412   (231) 924-5350
Contact: Elizabeth Cherin, C.E.O.; Gregory M. Zerlaut, C.F.O.
FAX: (231) 924-5391; E-mail: info@tfacf.org; Additional FAX: (231) 924-7637; Additional E-mails: echerin@tfacf.org and gzerlaut@tfacf.org; URL: http://www.tfacf.org

Incorporated in 1951 in MI.
Foundation type: Community foundation.
Financial data (yr. ended 12/31/05): Assets, $194,738,922 (M); gifts received, $3,086,579; expenditures, $11,557,038; giving activities include $9,386,427 for 825 grants (high: $1,100,000; low: $500), and $80,000 for 1 loan/program-related investment.
Purpose and activities: The foundation has established six broad funding categories: 1) Newaygo County Community Services: to sustain operations of this autonomous agency established for the delivery of general social welfare services and educational programs; 2) Community Development: to strengthen the municipal activities

of villages, cities, governmental units, and other related organizations; 3) Education: to augment and promote the special projects of schools, libraries, and other organizations for instruction and training, and for scholarships to promote higher education and learning in specialized programs; 4) Arts and Culture: to support activities that promote appreciation of and participation in artistic expression such as music, theater, dance, sculpture, and painting; 5) Human Services: to foster the delivery of services and the operation of programs to help meet basic human needs and to support the provision of rehabilitative services; and 6) Health Care: made to health care providers and other related organizations for activities designed to promote optimal well-being and to provide health-related education. The foundation is also interested in supporting programs that address the particular needs of youth and older (aged) adults.
Fields of interest: Visual arts; Performing arts; Arts; Libraries/library science; Education; Environment; Medical care, rehabilitation; Health care; Substance abuse, services; Health organizations, association; Recreation; Children/youth, services; Family services; Aging, centers/services; Human services; Community development; Government/public administration; Youth; Aging; Economically disadvantaged.
Type of support: General/operating support; Continuing support; Management development/capacity building; Capital campaigns; Building/renovation; Equipment; Endowments; Emergency funds; Program development; Conferences/seminars; Seed money; Curriculum development; Scholarship funds; Technical assistance; Consulting services; Program evaluation; Program-related investments/loans; Employee matching gifts; Scholarships—to individuals; Matching/challenge support.
Limitations: Giving primarily in Newaygo County, MI. No support for religious organizations for specific religions. No grants to individuals (except for scholarships), or for contingencies, reserves, services which are considered general government or school obligations, or deficit financing.
Publications: Application guidelines; Annual report; Financial statement; Grants list; Informational brochure; Newsletter.
Application information: Visit foundation Web site for application Cover Sheet and guidelines. Application form required.
   Initial approach: Letter or telephone to arrange interview
   Copies of proposal: 1
   Deadline(s): Feb. 15, May 15, and Sept. 15 for grants; Mar. 15 for scholarships
   Board meeting date(s): Bi-monthly
   Final notification: Within 3 months
Officers and Trustees:* Robert Johnson,* Chair.; Elizabeth Cherin, C.E.O. and Pres.; Gregory Zerlaut, C.O.O. and C.F.O.; Terry Sharp, Treas.; Richard Dunning; Peggy Gunnell; Duane Jones; Hendrick Jones; Danielle Merrill; Sheryl Meyer; Holly Moon; Liz Patterson; Lynne Robinson; Daniel Slate; Robert Wood; Kirk Wyers; Robert Zeldenrust.
Number of staff: 8 full-time professional; 6 full-time support.
EIN: 381443367
Selected grants: The following grants were reported in 2005.
$742,650 to Newaygo County Community Services, Fremont, MI. 2 grants: $712,650 (For operating and program support), $30,000 (For emergency heat and utility assistance).

$266,945 to Newaygo County Regional Educational Service Agency (RESA), Fremont, MI. For Fit for the Future, obesity prevention program, payable over 3 years.

$250,979 to Newaygo Public Schools, Newaygo, MI. 2 grants: $220,979 (For Newaygo County Even Start Family Literacy program), $30,000 (For Mini Grants for Educators and Special Projects program).

$228,000 to Arts Center for Newaygo County, Fremont, MI. For general operating support.

$200,000 to Baldwin Family Health Care, Baldwin, MI. For dental treatment rooms for Grant health care facility.

$135,510 to Newaygo County Economic Development Office, Fremont, MI. For expanded economic development programs.

$100,000 to Land Conservancy of West Michigan, Grand Rapids, MI. For land conservation project.

$17,000 to Newaygo County Council for the Arts, Fremont, MI. For general operating and program support.

4316
Frey Foundation ▼
40 Pearl St. N.W., Ste. 1100
Grand Rapids, MI 49503-3028 (616) 451-0303
Contact: Milton W. Rohwer, Pres.
FAX: (616) 451-8481; E-mail: contact@freyfdn.org;
URL: http://www.freyfdn.org

Established in 1974 in MI; endowed in 1988.
Donors: Edward J. Frey, Sr.†; Frances T. Frey‡.
Foundation type: Independent foundation.
Financial data (yr. ended 12/31/05): Assets, $131,802,000 (M); expenditures, $5,726,000; qualifying distributions, $5,726,000; giving activities include $4,847,000 for 68 grants (high: $750,000; low: $1,000; average: $10,000–$50,000).
Purpose and activities: Priorities include promoting healthy developmental outcomes for children in their early years (0-6 years); support for land use planning and growth management, and protection of natural resources; stimulating the vitality, effectiveness, and growth of community-based arts; encouraging civic progress and leadership; and strengthening philanthropy.
Fields of interest: Arts, cultural/ethnic awareness; Arts, folk arts; Arts education; Visual arts; Museums; Museums (art); Museums (children's); Museums (ethnic/folk arts); Museums (history); Museums (marine/maritime); Museums (natural history); Museums (science/technology); Museums (specialized); Performing arts; Performing arts centers; Performing arts, dance; Performing arts, ballet; Performing arts, theater; Performing arts, theater (musical); Performing arts, music; Performing arts, orchestra (symphony); Performing arts, opera; Performing arts, music (choral); Performing arts, music ensembles/groups; Performing arts, education; Historic preservation/historical societies; Arts; Education, reform; Education, early childhood education; Child development, education; Libraries (public); Environment, water pollution; Environment, natural resources; Environment, water resources; Environment, land resources; Botanical gardens; Environment, beautification programs; Environment; Animals/wildlife, preservation/protection; Animals/wildlife, fisheries; Zoos/zoological societies; Children/youth, services; Children, day care; Children, services; Child development, services;

Family services; Family services, parent education; Community development, neighborhood development; Community development, civic centers; Community development, public/private ventures; Urban/community development; Foundations (community); Philanthropy/voluntarism.
Type of support: Capital campaigns; Land acquisition; Program development; Seed money; Research; Technical assistance; Employee matching gifts.
Limitations: Giving primarily in Emmet, Charlevoix, and Kent counties, MI. No support for sectarian charitable activity. No grants to individuals, or for endowment funds, debt retirement, general operating expenses, scholarships, conferences, speakers, travel, or to cover routine, current, or emergency expenses.
Publications: Application guidelines; Annual report.
Application information: Application form required for all requests; online application available. Application form required.
  Initial approach: Letter of inquiry or telephone
  Copies of proposal: 1
  Deadline(s): Feb. 15, May 15, Aug. 15, and Nov. 15
  Board meeting date(s): Feb., May, Aug., and Nov.
Officers and Trustees:* David G. Frey,* Chair.; John M. Frey,* Vice-Chair.; Milton W. Rohwer, Pres.; Edward J. Frey, Jr.,* Secy.-Treas.; Mary Caroline "Twink" Frey, Tr. Emeritus.
Number of staff: 5 full-time professional; 1 full-time support.
EIN: 237094777
Selected grants: The following grants were reported in 2004.
$500,000 to Grand Rapids Community Foundation, Grand Rapids, MI. For Anonymous Advised Fund.
$500,000 to YMCA of Greater Grand Rapids, Grand Rapids, MI. For new David D. Hunting, Sr. YMCA facility.
$350,000 to Nature Conservancy, Michigan Chapter, Lansing, MI. For land purchase and protection in Upper Peninsula of Michigan.
$250,000 to University of Michigan, Gerald R. Ford School of Public Policy, Ann Arbor, MI. For new building.
$55,000 to Grand Action Foundation, Grand Rapids, MI. For economic analysis of proposed relocation of MSU's College of Human Medicine.
$50,000 to City Opera House Heritage Association, Traverse City, MI. For restoration of City Opera House and building for use as multipurpose meeting and performance facility.
$15,000 to Citizens Research Council of Michigan, Livonia, MI.
$5,000 to Land Conservancy of West Michigan, Grand Rapids, MI.
$3,000 to Santa Claus Girls of Kent County, Grand Rapids, MI.
$1,680 to United Way, Heart of West Michigan, Grand Rapids, MI.

4317
Warren E. & D. Lou Gast Charitable
  Foundation ✧ ☆
c/o 1st Source Bank
1600 Hilltop Rd.
St. Joseph, MI 49085

Established in 1996 in MI.
Donors: Warren E. Gast; D. Lou Gast.
Foundation type: Independent foundation.

Financial data (yr. ended 12/31/05): Assets, $1,525,882 (M); gifts received, $17,969; expenditures, $342,469; qualifying distributions, $336,108; giving activities include $330,500 for 4 grants (high: $260,000; low: $500).
Purpose and activities: Giving primarily for education and to Lutheran agencies and churches.
Fields of interest: Arts; Higher education; Education; Human services; Protestant agencies & churches.
Limitations: Applications not accepted. Giving in the U.S., with some emphasis on MI. No grants to individuals.
Application information: Contributes only to pre-selected organizations.
Trustees: D. Lou Gast; Warren E. Gast; 1st Source Bank.
EIN: 386676317
Selected grants: The following grants were reported in 2003.
$50,000 to Concordia University, Portland, OR. For capital support.
$8,000 to Island Lutheran Church, Hilton Head Island, SC. For general operating support.
$5,000 to Concordia University Foundation, Portland, OR. For capital support.
$5,000 to Curious Kids Museum, Saint Joseph, MI. For general operating support.
$5,000 to Fort Miami Heritage Society of Michigan, Saint Joseph, MI. For general operating support.
$5,000 to Maud Preston Palenske Memorial Library, Saint Joseph, MI. For general operating support.
$4,500 to Michigan Colleges Foundation, Southfield, MI. For general operating support.
$3,000 to Southwest Michigan Symphony Orchestra, Saint Joseph, MI. For general operating support.
$2,800 to Lakeshore Public Schools, Stevensville, MI. For band trip to Washington.
$1,750 to Fernwood Botanical Garden and Nature Preserve, Niles, MI. For general operating support.

4318
The Gayar Foundation ✧
26300 Telegraph Rd., 2nd Fl.
Southfield, MI 48034

Established in 1994 in MI.
Foundation type: Independent foundation.
Financial data (yr. ended 12/31/04): Assets, $2,364,605 (M); gifts received, $500,000; expenditures, $326,770; qualifying distributions, $324,648; giving activities include $324,650 for grants.
Purpose and activities: Giving to Islamic centers and medical centers.
Fields of interest: International relief; Islam.
International interests: Africa.
Limitations: Applications not accepted. Giving primarily in MI. No grants to individuals.
Application information: Unsolicited requests for funds not accepted.
Officer: Hesham E. Gayar, Pres.
EIN: 383176739

4319
General Motors Cancer Research Foundation, Inc. ✧

300 Renaissance Ctr., M.C. 482-C27-D76
Detroit, MI 48265-3000
Contact: Samuel A. Wells, Jr., M.D., Pres.
E-mail: gmcraward@mc.duke.edu; URL: http://www.gm.com/company/gmability/philanthropy/cancer_research/index.htm

Established in 1978 in MI.
Donors: General Motors Corp.; General Motors Foundation, Inc.
Foundation type: Company-sponsored foundation.
Financial data (yr. ended 12/31/04): Assets, $1,151,133 (M); gifts received, $2,830,000; expenditures, $2,926,130; qualifying distributions, $2,926,167; giving activities include $1,212,000 for 11 grants (high: $216,000; low: $24,000), and $750,000 for 4 grants to individuals (high: $250,000; low: $125,000).
Purpose and activities: The foundation supports programs designed to promote scientific research into the diagnosis, treatment, and prevention of cancer in its various forms and awards grants to individuals recognized for seminal contributions in cancer research.
Fields of interest: Cancer research.
Type of support: Research; Grants to individuals.
Limitations: Applications not accepted. Giving on a national and international basis. No grants for scholarships or fellowships; no loans.
Application information: Contributes only to pre-selected organizations and through an invitation only request for nomination process for grants to individuals.
Board meeting date(s): May
Officers and Trustees:* Harry J. Pearce, Jr.,* Chair.; Phillip A. Sharp, Ph.D.*, Chair., Awards Assembly; Samuel A. Wells, Jr., M.D.*, Pres.; James C. Cubbin, V.P.; Christopher C. Green, M.D., Ph.D., V.P.; Deborah I. Dingell, Secy.; Margreta D. Mobley, Treas.; Joseph G. Fortner, M.D.; Karen L. Katen; LaSalle D. Laffall, Jr., M.D.; John F. Smith, Jr.; Roger B. Smith; Louis W. Sullivan, M.D.
Number of staff: 1
EIN: 382219731
Selected grants: The following grants were reported in 2003.
$162,000 to Dartmouth College, Medical School, Hanover, NH. For cancer research scholars grant.
$108,000 to Johns Hopkins University, Baltimore, MD. For cancer research scholars grant.
$108,000 to University of Pittsburgh, Pittsburgh, PA. For cancer research scholars grant.
$54,000 to Dana-Farber Cancer Institute, Boston, MA. For cancer research scholars grant.
$54,000 to Memorial Sloan-Kettering Cancer Center, New York, NY. For cancer research scholars grant.
$54,000 to Northwestern University, Evanston, IL. For cancer research scholars grant.
$54,000 to Ohio State University, Columbus, OH. For cancer research scholars grant.
$54,000 to University of Alabama, Birmingham, AL. For cancer research scholars grant.
$54,000 to University of Pennsylvania Medical Center, Cancer Center, Philadelphia, PA. For research scholars grant.
$54,000 to University of Southern California, Cancer Center, Los Angeles, CA. For cancer research scholars grant.

4320
General Motors Foundation, Inc. ▼

(also known as GM Foundation)
300 Renaissance Ctr., M.C. 482-C27-D76
Detroit, MI 48265-3000 (313) 665-0824
URL: http://www.gm.com/company/gmability/community/index.html

Incorporated in 1976 in MI.
Donor: General Motors Corp.
Foundation type: Company-sponsored foundation.
Financial data (yr. ended 12/31/05): Assets, $225,608,246 (M); expenditures, $40,452,235; qualifying distributions, $39,507,551; giving activities include $39,338,242 for grants and $16,838,810 for set-asides.
Purpose and activities: The foundation supports organizations involved with arts and culture, education, the environment, health, cancer, cancer research, human services, community development, civic affairs, and minorities.
Fields of interest: Arts, public education; Arts, cultural/ethnic awareness; Arts education; Arts; Business school/education; Engineering school/education; Education; Environment, alliance; Environment, energy; Environment; Health care; Cancer; Cancer research; Human services; Community development, public education; Community development; Federated giving programs; Mathematics; Science; Public policy, research; Government/public administration; Public affairs; Minorities.
Type of support: General/operating support; Continuing support; Annual campaigns; Equipment; Emergency funds; Program development; Publication; Seed money; Research; Technical assistance; Employee matching gifts; Matching/challenge support.
Limitations: Giving primarily in areas of company operations; giving also to international organizations. No support for special interest groups, hospitals, religious organizations, political parties or candidates, or United Way-supported organizations. No grants to individuals, or for debt reduction, capital campaigns, conferences, workshops, or seminars not directly related to GM's business interests, or endowments; no loans.
Publications: Annual report (including application guidelines); Informational brochure.
Application information: Application form required.
Initial approach: Complete online application form
Deadline(s): None
Board meeting date(s): Quarterly
Final notification: 4 to 8 weeks
Officers and Trustees:* Roderick D. Gillum,* Chair.; Deborah I. Dingell,* Vice-Chair.; Karen A. Merkle, Secy.; Paul W. Schmidt, C.F.O.; William Wimsatt, Treas.
Number of staff: 4 full-time professional; 2 full-time support.
EIN: 382132136
Selected grants: The following grants were reported in 2004.
$2,165,050 to United Way for Southeastern Michigan, Detroit, MI. 3 grants: $785,050, $380,000, $1,000,000
$1,000,000 to National Safety Council, Itasca, IL. 2 grants: $500,000 each
$730,000 to Focus: Hope, Detroit, MI. 2 grants: $350,000, $380,000
$300,000 to American Red Cross, National Headquarters, DC.
$250,000 to Detroit Symphony Orchestra, Detroit, MI.

$250,000 to Hispanic Scholarship Fund, San Francisco, CA.

4321
The Gerber Foundation ▼

(formerly The Gerber Companies Foundation)
4747 W. 48th St., Ste. 153
Fremont, MI 49412-8119 (231) 924-3175
Contact: Catherine A. Obits, Prog. Mgr.
FAX: (231) 924-7906; E-mail: tgf@ncresa.org; Additional E-mail for Catherine A. Obits: cobits@ncresa.org; URL: http://www.gerberfoundation.org

Incorporated in 1952 in MI with funds from Gerber Products Co; in 1995 the foundation became independent from the company.
Foundation type: Independent foundation.
Financial data (yr. ended 12/31/05): Assets, $82,646,107 (M); expenditures, $5,141,405; qualifying distributions, $4,483,689; giving activities include $3,917,567 for 209 grants (high: $670,000; low: $150), $210,933 for 146 grants to individuals, and $148,500 for 137 employee matching gifts.
Purpose and activities: The foundation seeks to enhance the quality of life for infants and children by focusing on their nutrition, care, and development.
Fields of interest: Health care, infants; Health organizations, association; Pediatrics; Medical research, institute; Pediatrics research; Nutrition; Minorities.
Type of support: Seed money; Research; Scholarships—to individuals; Matching/challenge support.
Limitations: Giving on a national basis. No support for national child welfare or international based programs. No grants to individuals (except for scholarships), or for capital campaigns or operating support.
Publications: Application guidelines; Annual report (including application guidelines); Program policy statement.
Application information: The foundation prefers that applications be submitted only after receiving approval of a letter of inquiry. Application guidelines are available on foundation Web site. Application form required.
Initial approach: Letter of inquiry
Copies of proposal: 16
Deadline(s): Feb. 15 and Aug. 15; June 1 and Dec. 1 for letter of inquiry
Board meeting date(s): Feb., May, Aug., Nov.
Final notification: May and Nov.
Officers and Trustees:* Barbara J. Ivens,* Pres.; Fernando Flores-New,* V.P.; Tracy A. Baker,* Secy.; Stan M. VanderRoest,* Treas.; William L. Bush, M.D.; Ted C. Davis; Michael J. Ebert; John J. James, Esq.; Jane M. Jeannero; David C. Joslin; Carolyn R. Morby; Nancy Nevin-Folino; Steven W. Poole; Randy A. Puff; William B. Weil, Jr., M.D.
Number of staff: 1 full-time professional; 1 part-time support.
EIN: 386068090
Selected grants: The following grants were reported in 2004.
$1,022,827 to University of North Carolina, Chapel Hill, NC. To evaluate effects of chlorine supplementation on short term memory.
$844,397 to Yale University, New Haven, CT. For identification of biomarkers of calcium deficiency in young children.

$753,665 to Van Andel Research Institute, Grand Rapids, MI. For evaluation of congenital chromosomal abnormalities in newborns.

$625,150 to Cincinnati Childrens Hospital Medical Center, Cincinnati, OH. 2 grants: $377,819 (For evaluation of Interleukin-11 as preventive therapy against development of necrotizing entercolitis (NEC)), $247,331 (For evaluation of epidermal growth factor and maturation of the gastrointestinal tract in premature infants.)

$529,497 to Memorial Sloan-Kettering Cancer Center, New York, NY. For evaluation of oral beta-glucan therapy as a potential additive to cancer treatment.

$304,200 to Wayne State University, Detroit, MI. For evaluation of harmful effects of fatty acid supplementation on cognitive development.

$223,288 to University of Minnesota, Minneapolis, MN. For evaluation of the harmful effects of oxygen therapy given at birth.

$213,588 to Duke University Medical Center, Durham, NC. To evaluate current methods of diagnosis and treatment of gastroesophageal reflux disease in very low birth weight infants.

$139,668 to Childrens Memorial Hospital, Chicago, IL. For evaluation of risk factors for iron deficiency in Premature infants.

4322
The Rollin M. Gerstacker Foundation ▼
P.O. Box 1945
Midland, MI 48641-1945 (989) 631-6097
Contact: E.N. Brandt, V.P.

Incorporated in 1957 in MI.
Donors: Eda U. Gerstacker†; Carl A. Gerstacker†.
Foundation type: Independent foundation.
Financial data (yr. ended 12/31/05): Assets, $210,230,699 (M); expenditures, $11,554,220; qualifying distributions, $11,194,051; giving activities include $11,116,969 for 243 grants (high: $500,000; low: $500; average: $10,000–$100,000).
Purpose and activities: Giving to assist community projects, with emphasis on the aged and the youth; grants also for higher education, health care, medical research, and hospitals.
Fields of interest: Higher education; Hospitals (general); Health care; Mental health/crisis services; Health organizations, association; Human services; Children/youth, services; Aging, centers/services; Government/public administration; Aging.
Type of support: General/operating support; Continuing support; Annual campaigns; Capital campaigns; Building/renovation; Equipment; Land acquisition; Endowments; Emergency funds; Seed money; Research; Matching/challenge support.
Limitations: Giving primarily in MI; giving also in OH. No grants to individuals, or for scholarships or fellowships; no loans.
Publications: Annual report.
Application information: Application form not required.
Initial approach: Letter
Copies of proposal: 1
Deadline(s): Apr. 15, Aug. 15, and Nov. 15
Board meeting date(s): May, Sept., and Dec.
Final notification: 1 month
Officers and Trustees:* Gail E. Lanphear,* Pres.; Lisa J. Gerstacker,* V.P. and Secy.; Alan W. Ott,* V.P. and Treas.; E.N. Brandt,* V.P.; William D. Schuette,* V.P.; Alexio R. Baum; Frank Gerace;

Paula A. Liveris; Thomas L. Ludington; Paul F. Oreffice; William S. Stavropoulos.
EIN: 386060276
Selected grants: The following grants were reported in 2005.
$1,000,000 to Michigan State University, East Lansing, MI. 2 grants: $500,000 each
$400,000 to Nature Conservancy, Arlington, VA. 2 grants: $200,000 each
$400,000 to University of Michigan, Ann Arbor, MI.
$62,500 to Mid-Michigan Community Action Agency, Clare, MI.
$57,500 to Midland Community Center, Midland, MI.
$40,000 to Little Forks Conservancy, Midland, MI.
$30,000 to Southern University and A & M College, Baton Rouge, LA.
$18,000 to Council on Domestic Violence and Sexual Assault, Midland, MI.

4323
GII Charities ✧ ☆
3333 Evergreen Dr. N.E., Ste. 201
Grand Rapids, MI 49525 (616) 363-9209
Contact: Ronald K. Williams, Pres.

Established in 2002 in MI.
Donor: Gordon Food Service, Inc.
Foundation type: Independent foundation.
Financial data (yr. ended 12/31/03): Assets, $184,522 (M); gifts received, $2,000,000; expenditures, $1,878,467; qualifying distributions, $1,704,245; giving activities include $1,678,317 for 25 grants (high: $275,000; low: $5,000).
Purpose and activities: Giving limited to Christian non-profit organizations for effective evangelization activities emphasizing proclamation, church planting, discipleship, and leadership development.
Fields of interest: Christian agencies & churches.
Limitations: Giving on a worldwide basis. No grants to individuals.
Application information:
Initial approach: Letter
Officers: Ronald K. Williams, Pres.; James D. Gordon, V.P.; John M. Gordon, Jr., Secy.-Treas.
EIN: 300129615
Selected grants: The following grants were reported in 2003.
$200,000 to CURE International, Harrisburg, PA.
$140,000 to Trans World Radio, Cary, NC.
$100,000 to Bible League, Chicago, IL.
$50,000 to Beechpoint Christian Camp, Allegan, MI.
$50,000 to Citivision, New York, NY.
$50,000 to Focus on the Family, Colorado Springs, CO.
$50,000 to Fuller Theological Seminary, Pasadena, CA.
$50,000 to Global Mapping International, Colorado Springs, CO.
$50,000 to Partners International, Spokane, WA.
$10,000 to Calvin College, Grand Rapids, MI.

4324
Irving S. Gilmore Foundation ▼
136 E. Michigan Ave., Ste. 900
Kalamazoo, MI 49007 (269) 342-6411
Contact: Frederick W. Freund, C.E.O. and Exec. V.P.
FAX: (269) 342-6465; E-mail: fritz@isgilmore.org;
URL: http://www.isgilmore.org

Established in 1972 in MI.

Donor: Irving S. Gilmore†.
Foundation type: Independent foundation.
Financial data (yr. ended 12/31/05): Assets, $212,065,300 (M); expenditures, $11,353,748; qualifying distributions, $10,688,529; giving activities include $10,000,390 for grants.
Purpose and activities: The mission of the foundation is to support and enrich the cultural, social, and economic life of the greater Kalamazoo, MI, area. The priorities of the foundation are: 1) arts, culture, and humanities; 2) human services; 3) education and youth activities; 4) community development; and 5) health and well-being.
Fields of interest: Performing arts; Arts; Education; Health care; Youth development; Human services; Community development.
Type of support: General/operating support; Continuing support; Annual campaigns; Capital campaigns; Building/renovation; Equipment; Land acquisition; Debt reduction; Emergency funds; Program development; Conferences/seminars; Publication; Seed money; Scholarship funds; Technical assistance; Consulting services; Program evaluation; Employee matching gifts; Matching/challenge support.
Limitations: Giving primarily in the greater Kalamazoo, MI, area. No support for political organizations. No grants to individuals.
Publications: Annual report.
Application information: Please refer to foundation Web site for further guidelines and deadlines. Application form not required.
Initial approach: Unbound proposal including cover letter
Copies of proposal: 1
Deadline(s): 15th of Jan., Mar., May, July, Sept., and Nov.
Board meeting date(s): Jan., Mar., May, July, Sept., and Nov.
Final notification: Acknowledgement letter within 2 weeks
Officers and Trustees:* Richard M. Hughey, Sr.,* Chair. and Pres.; Floyd L. Parks,* Vice-Chair., 1st V.P., and Treas.; Frederick W. Freund,* C.E.O. and Exec. V.P.; Janice C. Elliott, V.P., Admin.; Richard M. Hughey, Jr., V.P., Prog.; Russell L. Gabier,* Secy.; Charles D. Wattles, Tr.
Number of staff: 3 full-time professional; 1 full-time support; 2 part-time support.
EIN: 237236057
Selected grants: The following grants were reported in 2004.
$1,000,000 to Kalamazoo Aviation History Museum, Air Zoo, Kalamazoo, MI. For Michigan Space and Science Center.
$1,000,000 to Western Michigan University Foundation, Kalamazoo, MI. For equipment.
$900,000 to Irving S. Gilmore International Keyboard Festival, Kalamazoo, MI. For operating support.
$500,000 to Kalamazoo Valley Community College Foundation, Kalamazoo, MI. To purchase and equip new media center.
$350,000 to Southwest Michigan First Corporation, Kalamazoo, MI. For operating support.
$100,000 to Community Advocates for Persons with Developmental Disabilities, Kalamazoo, MI. For Heersma Initiative programming.
$100,000 to Local Initiatives Support Corporation (LISC), Kalamazoo, MI. For local match funding.
$25,000 to Boys and Girls Club of Kalamazoo, Kalamazoo, MI. For Participating Arts program.
$20,000 to Kairos Dwelling, Kalamazoo, MI. For operating support.

$10,000 to Specialized Language Development (SLD) Learning Center, Kalamazoo, MI. For operating support.

4325
Grand Haven Area Community Foundation, Inc. ✧
1 S. Harbor Dr.
Grand Haven, MI   49417   (616) 842-6378
Contact: Ann Irish Tabor, Pres.; For grants: Carol Bedient, Dir., Grants and Progs.
FAX: (616) 842-9518; E-mail: info@ghacf.org; Grant application E-mail: cbedient@ghacf.org;
URL: http://www.ghacf.org

Incorporated in 1971 in MI.
Foundation type: Community foundation.
Financial data (yr. ended 3/31/04): Assets, $37,641,101 (M); gifts received, $1,928,451; expenditures, $2,763,806; giving activities include $2,385,118 for grants.
Purpose and activities: Primary areas of interest include: education (including technical training, mathematics, and business and accounting education), the environment, health, crime prevention, and community collaboration. Scholarship awards are limited to students of Grand Haven, Spring Lake, Holland Christian, Catholic Central, West Michigan Christian, West Ottawa, and Fruitport high schools, in MI.
Fields of interest: Vocational education, post-secondary; Business school/education; Environment; Health care; Crime/law enforcement; Community development; Mathematics.
Type of support: Land acquisition; Capital campaigns; Equipment; Program development; Seed money; Scholarship funds; Scholarships—to individuals; Matching/challenge support.
Limitations: Giving primarily in the MI Tri-Cities area. No support for profit-making organizations or religious programs that serve, or appear to serve, specific religious denominations. No grants to individuals (except for scholarships), or for annual campaigns, emergency or deficit financing, operating costs or ongoing operating support, fundraising events, or endowments.
Publications: Application guidelines; Annual report (including application guidelines); Financial statement; Informational brochure (including application guidelines); Newsletter; Program policy statement.
Application information: Visit foundation Web site for full application form and guidelines. Application form required.
Initial approach: Submit application form and attachments
Copies of proposal: 12
Deadline(s): Jan. 5, Apr. 2, and Sept. 29
Board meeting date(s): Distribution committee meets quarterly: Jan., Apr., July, and Oct.; board meetings are usually 2 weeks following the distribution committee meeting
Final notification: 1 week after board meeting
Officers and Trustees:* Jim MacLachlan,* Chair.; Don Anderson,* Vice-Chair.; Ann Irish Tabor, Pres.; Holly Johnson,* Secy.; Dennis Dornbush,* Treas.; Jeffrey Beswick; Melinda Brink; Mary Eagin; Mike McKeough; Darell Moreland; Shirley Poulton; L.J. Verplank.
Number of staff: 4 full-time professional.
EIN: 237108776

4326
Grand Rapids Community Foundation ▼
(formerly The Grand Rapids Foundation)
161 Ottawa Ave. N.W., Ste. 209-C
Grand Rapids, MI   49503-2757   (616) 454-1751
Contact: Diana R. Sieger, Pres.; For grant inquiries: Ann Puckett, Admin. Asst.
FAX: (616) 454-6455;
E-mail: grfound@grfoundation.org; Grant inquiry tel.: (616) 454-1751, ext. 123, and E-mail: apuckett@grfoundation.org; URL: http://www.grfoundation.org

Established in 1922 in MI by resolution and declaration of trust; Incorporated 1989.
Foundation type: Community foundation.
Financial data (yr. ended 6/30/05): Assets, $194,189,277 (M); gifts received, $8,515,770; expenditures, $10,829,473; giving activities include $7,824,644 for grants.
Purpose and activities: The foundation seeks to provide support for projects or causes designed to benefit the people and the quality of life in Grand Rapids, MI, and its surrounding communities through grants for social needs, youth agencies, cultural programs, health, recreation, neighborhood development, the environment, and education, including scholarships for Kent County residents to attend selected colleges. Grant decisions are made according to a project's fit with the following guiding principles: Accountability, Collaboration, Diversity, Justice, Prevention, Social Capital and Systems Approach.
Fields of interest: Museums; Performing arts; Performing arts, theater; Humanities; Arts; Higher education; Education, reading; Education; Environment; Health organizations, association; AIDS; Alcoholism; Employment; Nutrition; Housing/shelter, development; Recreation; Youth development, services; Children/youth, services; Family services; Aging, centers/services; Women, centers/services; Minorities/immigrants, centers/services; Human services; Civil rights, immigrants; Civil rights, minorities; Civil rights, disabled; Civil rights, women; Civil rights, aging; Civil rights, gays/lesbians; Civil rights, race/intergroup relations; Civil liberties, reproductive rights; Community development, neighborhood development; Community development; Voluntarism promotion; Leadership development; Aging; Disabilities, people with; Minorities; Asians/Pacific Islanders; African Americans/Blacks; Native Americans/American Indians; Women; LGBTQ; Immigrants/refugees; Economically disadvantaged; Homeless.
Type of support: Capital campaigns; Building/renovation; Land acquisition; Program development; Seed money; Scholarship funds; Technical assistance; Program-related investments/loans; Employee matching gifts; Employee-related scholarships; Scholarships—to individuals; Matching/challenge support.
Limitations: Giving limited to Kent County, MI. No support for religious programs, hospitals, child care centers, or nursing homes/retirement facilities. No grants to individuals (except for scholarships), or for continued operating support, annual campaigns, travel expenses, medical or scholarly research, deficit financing, endowment funds, computers, vehicles, films, videos, or conferences; no student loans; no venture capital for competitive profit-making activities.
Publications: Application guidelines; Annual report; Informational brochure; Newsletter.

Application information: Visit foundation Web site for letter of inquiry application, guidelines, and specific geographic fund deadlines. Faxed or e-mailed letters of inquiry are not accepted. The foundation will request a full proposal based on letter of inquiry. Application form required.
Initial approach: Submit online letter of inquiry (reviewed every 2 weeks)
Copies of proposal: 9
Deadline(s): Jan. 1 and Apr. 1
Board meeting date(s): 6 times a year (bimonthly)
Final notification: Within 30 days for letter of inquiry; June 16 for scholarships
Officers and Trustees:* Margaret Sellers-Walker,* Chair.; Marilyn A. Lankfer,* Vice-Chair.; Diana R. Sieger, Pres.; Lynne Black, V.P., Finance and Admin.; Roberta F. King, V.P., Public Rels. and Mktg.; Marcia Rapp, V.P., Progs.; Marilyn Zack, V.P., Devel.; Samuel M. Cummings; Paul Doyle; Cecile C. Fehsenfeld; Richard P. Haslinger; Joseph A. Medcalf; Mark Meijer; Bonnie K. Miller; Juan R. Olivarez; Thomas L. Stevens; Michelle Van Dyke.
Number of staff: 11 full-time professional; 1 part-time professional; 8 full-time support.
EIN: 382877959
Selected grants: The following grants were reported in 2005.
$1,000,000 to Grand Rapids Art Museum, Grand Rapids, MI.
$200,000 to Community Media Center, Grand Rapids, MI. To acquire Wealthy Theatre properties, equip with technology, and establish programs.
$183,000 to Grand Valley State University, Grand Rapids, MI. To operate and expand Community Research Institute capacity.
$150,000 to Dwelling Place of Grand Rapids, Grand Rapids, MI. To renovate buildings which currently comprise Dwelling Place Inn and construct new addition to increase both size of residential units and to increase number of units.
$150,000 to YMCA of Greater Grand Rapids, Grand Rapids, MI.
$145,000 to Lighthouse Communities, Grand Rapids, MI. For Healthy Neighborhoods model of neighborhood revitalization in central Grand Rapids neighborhoods.
$124,500 to Family Outreach Center, Grand Rapids, MI. To divert traditional foster care placements, by placing children at-risk of abuse and neglect with relatives.
$81,827 to Lowell Area Schools, Lowell, MI. To assure all children have opportunity to begin school healthy and ready to learn.
$75,000 to Alano Club of Kent County, Grand Rapids, MI. To renovate and expand current facility to meet needs of community.
$75,000 to Kent County Literacy Council, Grand Rapids, MI. To expand adult tutoring program and development and implementation of family literacy program.

4327
Grand Traverse Regional Community Foundation ✧
250 E. Front St., Ste. 310
Traverse City, MI   49684   (231) 935-4066
Contact: Jeanne Snow, Exec. Dir.
FAX: (231) 941-0021; E-mail: info@gtrcf.org;
URL: http://www.gtrcf.org

Established in 1992 in MI.
Foundation type: Community foundation.

Financial data (yr. ended 12/31/05): Assets, $24,244,902 (M); gifts received, $3,087,392; expenditures, $1,868,231; giving activities include $1,472,738 for grants.

Purpose and activities: The foundation seeks to enhance the quality of life and facilitate philanthropy in Antrim, Benzie, Grand Traverse, Kalkaska, and Leelanau counties, MI.

Fields of interest: Arts; Education; Environment; Community development; Youth.

Type of support: Building/renovation; Equipment; Endowments; Program development; Seed money; Curriculum development; Scholarship funds; Technical assistance; Scholarships—to individuals; Matching/challenge support.

Limitations: Giving limited to the counties of Antrim, Benzie, Grand Traverse, Kalkaska, and Leelanau, MI. No grants for routine training or professional conferences, annual events, budget shortfalls, or payroll or other general operating expenses.

Publications: Annual report; Informational brochure; Newsletter.

Application information: Visit foundation Web site for application form and guidelines. Applications can not be submitted without first setting an appointment with the foundation's Executive Director to discuss program in depth. Application form required.

Initial approach: Letter or telephone
Copies of proposal: 1
Deadline(s): Dec. 31 for MOD fund grants
Board meeting date(s): Quarterly

Officers and Directors:* Sydney McManus,* Chair.; Alan Olson,* Treas.; Jeanne Snow, Exec. Dir.; Truman Bicum; Gus Bishop; Lawrence Burks; Jerry Cannon; Bud Cline; Gail Dall'Olmo; Preston Dilts, Jr.; Gary Drew; Charlie Gilbert; John Hoagland; Stan Holzhauer; Dick Kennedy; Brenda Miller; Larry Miller; Jim Modrall; Joseph Muha; Clarine Olson; Peter Phinny; Al Potts; Bob Robbins; Louis H. Sanford; Donna Sowers; Toby Tull; Rob Turney; Suzanne Voltz; John Yeager.

Number of staff: 4 full-time professional; 1 part-time support.

EIN: 383056434

4328
Granger Foundation ◇

P.O. Box 22185
Lansing, MI 48909-7185 (517) 371-9765
Contact: Ray Easton
E-mail: elee@grangerconstruction.com; URL: http://www.grangerfoundation.org/

Established in 1978.

Donors: Granger Associates, Inc.; Granger Construction Co.; and members of the Granger family.

Foundation type: Independent foundation.

Financial data (yr. ended 12/31/04): Assets, $21,228,427 (M); gifts received, $540,500; expenditures, $1,362,605; qualifying distributions, $1,231,550; giving activities include $1,231,550 for 74 grants (high: $100,000; low: $500).

Purpose and activities: The foundation's primary mission is to support Christ-centered activities. It also supports efforts that enhance the lives of youth in the community.

Fields of interest: Youth development; Christian agencies & churches; Youth.

Type of support: Annual campaigns; Capital campaigns.

Limitations: Giving primarily in the greater Lansing and the Tri-County (Ingham, Eaton and Clinton counties), MI, areas. No grants to individuals, or for endowments, fundraising, social events, conferences, or exhibits; no grants for capital funds or improvements for churches or public schools.

Publications: Application guidelines; Annual report; Program policy statement.

Application information: Application form required.
Initial approach: Completed Request for Funding form
Copies of proposal: 4
Deadline(s): Apr. 15 and Oct. 15
Board meeting date(s): Semiannually

Trustees: Alton L. Granger; Donna Granger; Janice Granger; Jerry P. Granger; Lynne Granger; Ronald K. Granger.

EIN: 382251879

Selected grants: The following grants were reported in 2003.

$100,000 to Mission India, Grand Rapids, MI.
$50,000 to Teen Challenge, Lansing, Lansing, MI. For building upgrades.
$50,000 to Youth for Christ, Lansing, MI.
$44,000 to Eaton Community Hospice, Charlotte, MI.
$34,000 to Youth for Christ/USA, Wheaton, IL.
$30,000 to Ingham Regional Healthcare Foundation, Lansing, MI.
$25,000 to Cristo Rey Community Center, Lansing, MI. For capital campaign.
$25,000 to Highfields, Onondaga, MI. For Alternatives to Domestic Violence.
$25,000 to Salvation Army.
$16,000 to City Rescue Mission of Saginaw, Saginaw, MI. To purchase a refrigerated van or truck.

4329
Granger III Foundation, Inc. ◇

P.O. Box 27185
Lansing, MI 48909-7185 (571) 371-9717
Contact: Todd J. Granger, Treas.

Established in 2000 in OH.

Donors: Granger Electric; Granger Energy; Granger Associates, Inc.; Granger Holdings, LLC; Granger Energy of Decatur, LLC; Granger Energy of Honeybrook, LLC; Granger Meadows, LLC.

Foundation type: Independent foundation.

Financial data (yr. ended 12/31/05): Assets, $3,738,519 (M); gifts received, $1,012,000; expenditures, $771,795; qualifying distributions, $752,818; giving activities include $752,818 for 19 grants (high: $176,000; low: $1,500).

Purpose and activities: Giving primarily for a Christian school as well as for other Christian organizations; funding also for human services, education, volunteer organizations, and YMCAs.

Fields of interest: Theological school/education; Human services; YM/YWCAs & YM/YWHAs; Philanthropy/voluntarism; Christian agencies & churches.

Limitations: Giving primarily in MI. No grants to individuals.

Application information:
Initial approach: Letter
Deadline(s): None

Officers and Trustees:* Thomas D. Hofman,* Pres.; Ray A. Easton,* V.P.; Dawn M. Granger,* Secy.; Todd J. Granger,* Treas.; Keith L. Granger; Randy J. Russ; Joel M. Zylstra.

EIN: 383555568

4330
Great Lakes Capital Fund Nonprofit Housing Corporation ◇

(formerly Michigan Capital Fund for Non-Profit Housing Corporation)
1000 S. Washington Ave., Ste. 200
Lansing, MI 48910-1647

Foundation type: Operating foundation.

Financial data (yr. ended 12/31/04): Assets, $32,325,190 (M); expenditures, $8,306,644; qualifying distributions, $10,890,139; giving activities include $1,199,813 for 160 grants (high: $150,000; low: $50), $7,106,831 for foundation-administered programs and $2,639,766 for loans/program-related investments.

Purpose and activities: Giving primarily to the delivery of quality, affordable housing to the poor and underprivileged, the promotion of efforts to facilitate self-sufficiency and upward mobility of very-low and low-income households, and the preservation of social welfare through efforts to facilitate the construction and development of housing for very low-, low- and moderate-income households in a manner directed to eliminate prejudice and discrimination, lessen neighborhood tensions, and combat the deterioration of communities throughout MI.

Fields of interest: Housing/shelter; Economically disadvantaged.

Limitations: Applications not accepted. Giving primarily in MI.

Application information: Unsolicited requests for funds not accepted.

Officers: Mark McDaniel, C.E.O. and Pres.; Thomas Edmiston, C.O.O. and Sr. V.P.; Christopher Cox, C.F.O. and Sr. V.P.

Directors: Barbara Anderson; James Bernacki; Sally Harrison; Marsha Kreucher.

EIN: 383126310

4331
Greenville Area Community Foundation ☆

(formerly Greenville Area Foundation)
101 N. Lafayette St.
Greenville, MI 48838-1853 (616) 754-2640
Contact: Alison Barberi, C.E.O.
FAX: (616) 754-3174; E-mail: alison@gacfmi.org; URL: http://www.gacfmi.org

Established in 1989 in MI.

Foundation type: Community foundation.

Financial data (yr. ended 12/31/05): Assets, $11,579,845 (M); gifts received, $965,175; expenditures, $595,874; giving activities include $379,573 for grants.

Purpose and activities: The foundation seeks to enhance the quality of life in the Greenville area. Giving for education, health, the arts, the environment, recreation, youth services, and community development.

Fields of interest: Arts; Adult education—literacy, basic skills & GED; Education; Environment; Health care; Recreation; Children/youth, services; Community development; Government/public administration.

Type of support: Building/renovation; Capital campaigns; Equipment; Program development; Publication; Seed money; Scholarship funds; Matching/challenge support.

Limitations: Giving limited to Montcalm County, MI. No support for sectarian religious programs. No grants for general operating support, annual fundraising, or endowments (outside the foundation).

Publications: Application guidelines; Annual report; Financial statement; Grants list; Informational brochure; Informational brochure (including application guidelines); Newsletter.

Application information: Visit foundation Web site for grant information. Application forms are available at the foundation's office. Applicants are encouraged to call and set-up a visit to discuss proposal. Application form required.

Initial approach: Telephone
Copies of proposal: 16
Deadline(s): Late summer; Educational request, early spring
Board meeting date(s): Jan., Apr., June, Sept., Oct., and Nov.
Final notification: Dec. 1

Officers and Directors: * Peter Blinkilde,* Chair.; Charlotte Lothian,* Vice-Chair.; Alison Barberi, C.E.O. and Pres.; Christine Kohn,* Secy.-Treas.; Byron Cook,* Chair. Emeritus; Lemont Renterghem,* Chair. Emeritus; Jon Aylsworth; Bill Braman; Mike Devereaux; Dan Eagles; Richard Ellafrits; Jae Evans; Jelane Hamper; Eric Januzelli; John O'Donald, D.D.S.

Number of staff: 1 full-time professional; 2 part-time professional.

EIN: 382899657

4332
The Grosfeld Foundation ✧
2290 First National Bldg.
Detroit, MI   48226-3583

Established in 1984 in MI.

Donors: James Grosfeld; Nancy Grosfeld; Multivest.
Foundation type: Independent foundation.
Financial data (yr. ended 11/30/04): Assets, $3,080,085 (M); gifts received, $991,374; expenditures, $2,637,446; qualifying distributions, $2,618,086; giving activities include $2,615,231 for grants.
Purpose and activities: Giving primarily for colleges and universities and an employment service agency; support also for human services, including Jewish-affiliated organizations.
Fields of interest: Higher education; Hospitals (general); Employment, services; Human services; Jewish federated giving programs; Jewish agencies & temples.
Limitations: Applications not accepted. Giving primarily in MI. No grants to individuals.
Application information: Contributes only to pre-selected organizations.
Officers: James Grosfeld, Pres. and Treas.; Nancy Grosfeld, V.P. and Secy.
EIN: 382575307
Selected grants: The following grants were reported in 2003.
$456,800 to Jewish Federation of Metropolitan Detroit, Bloomfield Hills, MI. For unrestricted support.
$301,000 to Amherst College, Amherst, MA. For unrestricted support.
$250,000 to Anti-Defamation League of Bnai Brith, New York, NY. For unrestricted support.
$35,000 to Hillel Day School of Metropolitan Detroit, Farmington Hills, MI. For unrestricted support.
$20,000 to Columbia University, New York, NY. For unrestricted support.

$17,000 to Jewish Womens Foundation of Metropolitan Detroit, Bloomfield Hills, MI. For unrestricted support.
$10,000 to Jewish Vocational Service and Community Workshop, Southfield, MI. For unrestricted support.
$10,000 to Washington Institute for Near East Policy, DC. For unrestricted support.
$3,168 to United Jewish Foundation, Bloomfield Hills, MI. For unrestricted support.
$1,000 to Planned Parenthood of Southeast Michigan, Detroit, MI. For unrestricted support.

4333
Guardian Industries Educational Foundation ✧
2300 Harmon Rd.
Auburn Hills, MI   48326-1714

Established in 1986 in DE and MI.
Donor: Guardian Industries Corp.
Foundation type: Company-sponsored foundation.
Financial data (yr. ended 12/31/05): Assets, $36,862 (M); gifts received, $1,051,910; expenditures, $1,061,180; qualifying distributions, $1,061,180; giving activities include $1,011,123 for 265 grants to individuals (high: $4,000; low: $1,000).
Purpose and activities: The foundation awards college scholarships to children of full-time employees of Guardian Industries and its subsidiaries. The scholarship program is administered by Educational Testing Service.
Type of support: Employee-related scholarships.
Limitations: Applications not accepted. Giving primarily in areas of company operations. No loans or program-related investments.
Application information: Contributes only through employee-related scholarships.
Officers and Directors: * William Davidson,* Pres.; Bruce Cummings, V.P.; Ralph J. Gerson,* V.P.; Robert H. Gorlin, Secy.; Jeffrey A. Knight, Treas.
EIN: 382707035

4334
H.I.S. Foundation ✧ ☆
13919 S. West Bay Shore Dr., Ste. G-1
Traverse City, MI   49684
Contact: Dale M. Nielson, V.P.

Established in 1990 in MI.
Donors: Nielson Enterprises Corp.; Dale M. Nielson.
Foundation type: Independent foundation.
Financial data (yr. ended 12/31/05): Assets, $4,837 (M); gifts received, $510,928; expenditures, $422,907; qualifying distributions, $401,556; giving activities include $401,556 for 61 grants (high: $60,918; low: $100).
Purpose and activities: Giving primarily for Protestant and Roman Catholic agencies, as well as for Christian education, pro-life causes, conservative public policy, and entrepreneurship assistance.
Fields of interest: Education; Youth development, religion; Residential/custodial care, hospices; Civil liberties, right to life; Business/industry; Social sciences, public policy; Christian agencies & churches.
International interests: China; Mexico.
Type of support: Continuing support; Income development; Annual campaigns; Capital

campaigns; Building/renovation; Equipment; Land acquisition; Seed money; Fellowships; Scholarship funds; Matching/challenge support.
Limitations: Giving on a national and international basis, with emphasis on Antrim, Bonzie, Crawford, Grant Traverse, Kalkaska and Leelanau counties, MI, and China and Mexico. No support for liberal public policy, and religious organizations other than Christian.
Application information: Application form not required.
Initial approach: Letter
Copies of proposal: 1
Deadline(s): None
Board meeting date(s): Dec.
Officers and Directors: * Melvin K. Nielson,* Pres.; Dale M. Nielson,* V.P.; Barbara A. Nielson, Secy.; Ruth E. Nielson,* Treas.
EIN: 382953594

4335
William and Sharon Hahn Foundation, Inc. ✧
500 S. Opdyke Rd.
Pontiac, MI   48343-1046   (248) 332-9300
Contact: Sharon Hahn, Secy.

Established in 2000 in MI.
Donors: Sharon Hahn; William Hahn.
Foundation type: Independent foundation.
Financial data (yr. ended 12/31/05): Assets, $5,718 (M); gifts received, $370,000; expenditures, $370,248; qualifying distributions, $370,000; giving activities include $370,000 for 15 grants (high: $35,000; low: $10,000).
Purpose and activities: Giving primarily for family and other human services.
Fields of interest: Arts, association; Crime/violence prevention, child abuse; Human services; Children/ youth, services; Family services; Women, centers/ services; Federated giving programs.
Limitations: Giving primarily in MI, with emphasis on Pontiac. No grants to individuals.
Application information: Application form is currently in development.
Officers: William Hahn, Pres. and Treas.; Sharon Hahn, Secy.
EIN: 383549321
Selected grants: The following grants were reported in 2005.
$35,000 to Bound Together, Pontiac, MI.
$35,000 to Furniture Bank of Oakland County, Pontiac, MI.
$30,000 to Common Ground Sanctuary, Bloomfield Hills, MI.
$30,000 to Womens Survival Center of Oakland County, Bloomfield Hills, MI.
$25,000 to HAVEN, Bloomfield Hills, MI.
$25,000 to Oakland Livingston Human Service Agency, Pontiac, MI.
$25,000 to United Way, MI.
$20,000 to Baldwin Center, Pontiac, MI.
$20,000 to New Horizons Rehabilitation Services, Auburn Hills, MI.
$20,000 to Oakland Family Services, Pontiac, MI.

4336
Hampson Foundation ✧ ☆
800 W. Long Lake Rd., Ste. 210
Bloomfield Hills, MI   48302-2058
Contact: Robert J. Hampson, Pres.

Application address: P.O. Box 250614, Franklin, MI 48025, tel.: (248) 626-3264

Established in MI.
Donors: Robert J. Hampson; Sadie G. Hampson.
Foundation type: Independent foundation.
Financial data (yr. ended 12/31/05): Assets, $70,901 (M); expenditures, $1,148,204; qualifying distributions, $1,146,744; giving activities include $1,142,185 for 34 grants (high: $997,685; low: $500).
Purpose and activities: Giving primarily for education, particularly to a women's college; funding also for health associations and human services.
Fields of interest: Higher education; Education; Health organizations, association; Human services.
Type of support: General/operating support.
Limitations: Giving primarily in MI; some funding nationally.
Application information:
  Initial approach: Letter
  Deadline(s): Dec. 1
Officers: Robert J. Hampson, Pres. and Treas.; Jane J. Hampson Berca, V.P.; Sadie G. Hampson, V.P.
EIN: 386066115

4337
Charles Stewart Harding Foundation ✧
111 E. Court St., Ste. 3D
Flint, MI 48502-1649 (810) 767-0136
Contact: Frederick S. Kirkpatrick

Established in 1963 in MI.
Donors: C.S. Harding Mott†; C.S. Harding Mott II†; Claire Mott White.
Foundation type: Independent foundation.
Financial data (yr. ended 6/30/05): Assets, $12,853,818 (M); expenditures, $583,461; qualifying distributions, $531,670; giving activities include $527,000 for 16 grants (high: $250,000; low: $1,000).
Purpose and activities: Giving primarily for the arts.
Fields of interest: Media, television; Performing arts, music; Performing arts, orchestra (symphony); Arts; Human services.
Type of support: General/operating support; Continuing support; Annual campaigns; Scholarship funds.
Limitations: Giving primarily in Flint, MI. No grants to individuals.
Application information: Application form not required.
  Initial approach: Letter
  Deadline(s): None
  Board meeting date(s): Usually Oct.
  Final notification: Dec.
Officers and Trustees:* Claire Mott White,* Pres.; Paula M. Turrentine,* V.P.; C. Edward White, Jr., Secy.; William S. White,* Treas.
EIN: 386081208
Selected grants: The following grants were reported in 2005.
$250,000 to Saint Louis Symphony Orchestra, Saint Louis, MO.
$115,000 to Flint Institute of Arts, Flint, MI.
$50,000 to Flint Cultural Center Corporation, Flint, MI.
$50,000 to Flint Institute of Music, Flint, MI.
$11,000 to YWCA of Greater Flint, Flint, MI.
$5,000 to Flint Youth Theater, Flint, MI.
$5,000 to Greater Flint Arts Council, Flint, MI.
$1,000 to Holly, Village of, Holly, MI.

$1,000 to Whaley Childrens Center, Flint, MI.

4338
The Harding Foundation ✧
c/o MFO Management Co.
111 E. Court St., Ste. 3D
Flint, MI 48502-1649
Contact: Mark C. Turrentine, Exec. Dir.

Established in 1988 in MI.
Donor: C.S. Harding Mott Trust.
Foundation type: Independent foundation.
Financial data (yr. ended 6/30/05): Assets, $59,823,077 (M); gifts received, $30,000; expenditures, $2,657,016; qualifying distributions, $2,324,893; giving activities include $2,086,753 for 24 grants (high: $750,000; low: $4,570).
Purpose and activities: Giving primarily to organizations which are dedicated to supporting or contributing to the cause of Christian Science.
Fields of interest: Museums (history); Education, early childhood education; Christian agencies & churches.
Application information: Application form not required.
  Initial approach: Letter
  Copies of proposal: 1
  Deadline(s): None
Officers and Trustee:* Paula K. Turrentine, Chair. and Pres.; Paula M. Switzer, V.P. and Secy.; Milo I. Mott, V.P. and Treas.; Mark C. Turrentine,* Exec. Dir.
Number of staff: 1 full-time professional; 1 full-time support; 1 part-time support.
EIN: 382849003

4339
Hauenstein Foundation ✧
3739 Cook Valley Blvd. S.E.
Grand Rapids, MI 49548

Established in 1996 in MI.
Donors: Ralph Hauenstein; Karla Hauenstein; Mary Gerzanick†.
Foundation type: Independent foundation.
Financial data (yr. ended 12/31/05): Assets, $1,367,789 (M); expenditures, $425,546; qualifying distributions, $424,383; giving activities include $424,383 for 26 grants (high: $52,000; low: $1,000).
Fields of interest: Museums; Human services; Foundations (private grantmaking).
Limitations: Applications not accepted. Giving primarily in Grand Rapids, MI. No grants to individuals.
Application information: Contributes only to pre-selected organizations.
Officer: Ralph Hauenstein, Pres.
Director: William F. Roth.
EIN: 382898214
Selected grants: The following grants were reported in 2004.
$50,000 to Aquinas College, Grand Rapids, MI.
$50,000 to Grand Valley State University, Allendale, MI.
$50,000 to Van Andel Institute, Grand Rapids, MI.
$38,334 to Grand Rapids Art Museum, Grand Rapids, MI.
$30,000 to Davenport University Foundation, Grand Rapids, MI.

$30,000 to Michigan Military Preservation Society, Grand Rapids, MI.
$10,000 to American Heart Association, Grand Rapids, MI.
$10,000 to Arthritis Foundation, Grand Rapids, MI.
$6,000 to Gerald R. Ford Foundation, Grand Rapids, MI.
$1,000 to Parkinsons Association of West Michigan, Grand Rapids, MI.

4340
Heritage Mark Foundation ▼ ✧
P.O. Box 980
East Lansing, MI 48826-0980

Established in 1968 in MI.
Donors: David R. Foote; Frederick C. Foote; Shirley A. Foote; Kenneth J. Foote; Marnie Foote; Steven M. Foote; Lynne Foote; Cheryl F. Groenendyke; First National Bancshares, Inc.; 1889 Bankcorp, Inc.
Foundation type: Independent foundation.
Financial data (yr. ended 9/30/05): Assets, $55,360,390 (M); gifts received, $2,990,953; expenditures, $8,080,706; qualifying distributions, $7,897,888; giving activities include $7,681,917 for 136 grants (high: $3,200,500; low: $250; average: $1,000–$350,000).
Purpose and activities: Giving primarily for Christian agencies and churches, with emphasis on evangelism.
Fields of interest: Performing arts centers; Education, research; Health care, single organization support; Human services; Economics; Public policy, research; Christian agencies & churches.
Limitations: Applications not accepted. Giving on a national basis. No grants to individuals.
Application information: Contributes only to pre-selected organizations.
Officers: Shirley A. Foote, Chair.; Cheryl F. Groenendyke, Pres.; Barbara Shingleton, V.P.; Frederick C. Foote, Secy.-Treas.
Trustees: David R. Foote; Kenneth J. Foote; Steven M. Foote; Susan L. Foote; Rhonda F. Judy.
EIN: 237017100
Selected grants: The following grants were reported in 2005.
$3,200,500 to Cleveland Clinic Foundation, Cleveland, OH.
$694,845 to Rest Haven Homes, Grand Rapids, MI.
$455,000 to Boston Trinity Academy, Brookline, MA.
$353,000 to UPLOOK Ministries, Grand Rapids, MI.
$289,412 to Truth and Tidings Gospel Trust USA, Wadsworth, OH.
$231,372 to Christian Missions in Many Lands, Spring Lake, NJ.
$25,000 to Jewish Womens Archive, Brookline, MA.
$15,000 to New York City Ballet, New York, NY.
$10,000 to World Harvest Mission, Jenkintown, PA.
$5,000 to Marie Sandvik Center, Minneapolis, MN.

4341
Herrick Foundation ▼
150 W. Jefferson Ave., Ste. 2500
Detroit, MI 48226
Contact: Todd W. Herrick, Pres.

Incorporated in 1949 in MI.
Donors: Ray W. Herrick†; Hazel M. Herrick†.
Foundation type: Independent foundation.

Financial data (yr. ended 9/30/05): Assets, $178,431,140 (M); expenditures, $10,321,013; qualifying distributions, $9,295,006; giving activities include $9,167,959 for 37 grants (high: $2,000,000; low: $250; average: $5,000–$150,000).

Purpose and activities: Emphasis on higher education, including research grants, scholarship programs (made through college and postgraduate educational institutions, not individual scholarships), and capital funding; grants also for church support, youth, health and welfare agencies, hospitals, and libraries.

Fields of interest: Secondary school/education; Higher education; Hospitals (general); Health care; Human services; Children/youth, services; Aging, centers/services.

Type of support: General/operating support; Continuing support; Annual campaigns; Capital campaigns; Building/renovation; Equipment; Land acquisition; Endowments; Emergency funds; Program development; Professorships; Curriculum development; Scholarship funds; Research; Matching/challenge support.

Limitations: Giving primarily in MI; giving also in the New York Metropolitan area, Washington, DC, IN, MS, OH, OK, TN, and WI. No support for international organizations, or for domestic organizations for international programs. No grants to individuals.

Publications: Application guidelines.

Application information: Application form not required.

Initial approach: 1- to -3 page grant proposal letter
Copies of proposal: 1
Deadline(s): None
Board meeting date(s): Monthly
Final notification: By letter

Officers and Trustees:* Todd W. Herrick,* Chair., Pres. and Treas.; Kent B. Herrick,* V.P.; Michael A. Indenbaum,* Secy.

Number of staff: 1 part-time support.

EIN: 386041517

Selected grants: The following grants were reported in 2005.

$2,000,000 to Henry Ford Health System, Detroit, MI. 2 grants: $1,000,000 each (For Herrick Center for Translational Neuro-oncology and Neuroregeneration Research).

$2,000,000 to Heritage Foundation, DC. To establish Bernard and Barbara Lomas Fellow at Margaret Thatcher Center for Freedom.

$1,500,000 to Herrick Memorial Hospital Foundation, Tecumseh, MI. To renovate Herrick Birthing Center.

$1,000,000 to Chamber of Commerce of the United States, DC. For educational program, Creating a Competitive American Economy.

$1,000,000 to University of Michigan, Ann Arbor, MI. 2 grants: $500,000 to Kelsey Museum of Archeology (For National Endowment for Humanities Challenge Grant for Conservation Internship Program Endowment), $500,000 to Kelsey Museum of Archeology (For National Endowment for the Humanities Challenge Grant for Exhibits Preparator Endowment).

$250,000 to Clifford H Ted Rees Jr Scholarship Foundation, Arlington, VA. For Clifford H Ted Rees, Jr. Scholarship Fund.

$100,000 to Focus: Hope, Detroit, MI. For Machinist Training Institute program.

$100,000 to National Ovarian Cancer Coalition, Georgia Division, Buckhead, GA. For unrestricted support.

4342
HFF Foundation ✧
c/o Herman Frankel, Tr.
7214 Hidden Creek Ct.
West Bloomfield, MI 48322-5209

Established in 1993 in MI.

Donors: Simwood Co.; Herman Frankel; Suburban Communities, LLC.

Foundation type: Company-sponsored foundation.

Financial data (yr. ended 12/31/05): Assets, $3,588,700 (M); expenditures, $450,584; qualifying distributions, $448,686; giving activities include $448,686 for 17+ grants (high: $214,500).

Purpose and activities: The foundation supports organizations involved with arts and culture, health, and Judaism.

Fields of interest: Performing arts; Performing arts, orchestra (symphony); Performing arts, opera; Arts; Health care; Jewish federated giving programs; Jewish agencies & temples.

Limitations: Applications not accepted. Giving primarily in MI, with emphasis on Detroit. No grants to individuals.

Application information: Contributes only to pre-selected organizations.

Trustee: Herman Frankel.

EIN: 383149105

4343
Hudson-Webber Foundation ▼
333 W. Fort St., Ste. 1310
Detroit, MI 48226-3149 (313) 963-7777
Contact: David O. Egner, Pres.
FAX: (313) 963-2818;
E-mail: HWF@hudson-webber.org; URL: http://www.hudson-webber.org

Incorporated in 1943 in MI; on Jan. 1, 1984 absorbed the Richard H. and Eloise Jenks Webber Charitable Fund, Inc., and the Eloise and Richard Webber Foundation.

Donors: Eloise Webber†; Richard Webber†; The J.L. Hudson Co.; Mary Webber Parker; and members of the Webber family.

Foundation type: Independent foundation.

Financial data (yr. ended 12/31/05): Assets, $150,376,115 (M); gifts received, $654,322; expenditures, $8,608,489; qualifying distributions, $7,949,973; giving activities include $6,928,821 for 83+ grants (high: $1,000,000; average: $5,000–$250,000), $370,548 for 183 employee matching gifts, and $21,721 for 1 foundation-administered program.

Purpose and activities: Concentrates efforts and resources in support of projects within five program missions that impact the vitality and quality of life of the metropolitan Detroit, MI community: 1) growth and development of the Detroit Medical Center; 2) economic development of southeastern Michigan, with emphasis on assisting chronically unemployed Detroiters obtain and retain employment; 3) physical revitalization of the central city; 4) enhancement of major art and cultural resources in Detroit; and 5) reduction of crime in Detroit. The foundation also provides charitable assistance to qualified J.L. Hudson Co. employees or ex-employees needing help in overcoming personal crises and misfortunes.

Fields of interest: Arts; Crime/violence prevention; Urban/community development.

Type of support: General/operating support; Continuing support; Annual campaigns; Capital campaigns; Building/renovation; Program

development; Seed money; Consulting services; Program evaluation; Employee matching gifts; Matching/challenge support.

Limitations: Giving primarily in the city of Detroit, and the tri-county Wayne, Oakland, and Macomb area of southeastern MI. No support for educational institutions or neighborhood organizations (except for projects that fall within current program missions). No grants to individuals (except for J.L. Hudson Co. employees and their families), or for emergency funds, deficit financing, endowment funds, scholarships, fellowships, publications, conferences, fundraising, social events, or exhibits; no loans.

Publications: Biennial report (including application guidelines); Financial statement; Grants list.

Application information: Accepts CMF Common Grant Application Form. Application form not required.

Initial approach: Letter of request or proposal
Copies of proposal: 1
Deadline(s): Apr. 15, Aug. 15 (for July and Dec. meetings), and Dec. 15 (for meeting in Apr. of following year)
Board meeting date(s): Apr., July, and Dec.
Final notification: 1 week after board decision

Officers and Trustees:* Jennifer Hudson Parke,* Chair.; David O. Egner,* Pres.; Hudson Holland, Jr.,* Secy.; Alfred R. Glancy III,* Treas.; Matthew P. Cullen; Stephen R. D'Arcy; W. Frank Fountain; Frank M. Hennessey; Gilbert Hudson; Joseph L. Hudson, Jr.; Joseph L. Hudson IV; Reginald M. Turner; Amanda Van Dusen.

Number of staff: 2 full-time professional; 1 part-time professional; 1 full-time support; 1 part-time support.

EIN: 386052131

Selected grants: The following grants were reported in 2005.

$1,000,000 to Detroit Institute of Arts, Detroit, MI. For Campaign for Detroit Institute of Arts Transformation Initiative.

$620,000 to Detroit Symphony Orchestra, Detroit, MI. 2 grants: $20,000 to Detroit Symphony Orchestra Hall (For general program support), $600,000 to Detroit Symphony Orchestra Hall (For Summer in the City Programming Initiative).

$517,000 to Goodwill Industries of Greater Detroit, Detroit, MI. For Reducing Chronic Unemployment Initiative.

$500,000 to United Way for Southeastern Michigan, Detroit, MI. 2 grants: $200,000 (For Torch Drive), $300,000 (For 2-1-1 Call Center).

$300,000 to Habitat for Humanity of Metropolitan Detroit, Detroit, MI. For partnership to build capacity initiative.

$300,000 to Women A.R.I.S.E., Detroit, MI. For Women ARISE and Goodwill Industries collaborative.

$200,000 to Detroit Renaissance Foundation, Detroit, MI. For Super Bowl Downtown Improvement Plan Project.

$44,000 to New Detroit, Detroit, MI. For general program support.

4344
The Hurst Foundation ✧
675 Robinson Rd.
Jackson, MI 49203 (517) 788-8600

Trust established in 1955 in MI.

Donors: Peter F. Hurst†; Elizabeth S. Hurst†.

Foundation type: Independent foundation.

Financial data (yr. ended 12/31/04): Assets, $9,002,638 (M); expenditures, $330,099; qualifying distributions, $321,500; giving activities include $321,500 for 39 grants (high: $75,000; low: $1,000).

Fields of interest: Museums; Arts; Secondary school/education; Higher education; Human services; Youth, services; Community development; Protestant agencies & churches.

Type of support: General/operating support; Building/renovation; Equipment; Program development; Seed money.

Limitations: Giving primarily in Jackson County, MI. No grants to individuals, or for endowment funds, scholarships, fellowships, or matching gifts; no loans.

Application information: Application form not required.

  Initial approach: Letter
  Copies of proposal: 2
  Deadline(s): Oct. 1
  Board meeting date(s): Dec. and as necessary
  Final notification: Within 60 days for favorable decisions

Officer: Anthony P. Hurst, Pres.

EIN: 386089457

Selected grants: The following grants were reported in 2004.

$75,000 to Ella Sharp Museum, Jackson, MI.

$27,000 to Lily Missionary Baptist Church, Jackson, MI.

$26,000 to Lumen Christi High School, Jackson, MI.

$12,500 to Center for Family Health, Jackson, MI.

$12,000 to Jackson Friendly Home, Jackson, MI.

$10,000 to Michigan Coalition of Essential Schools, Jackson, MI.

$10,000 to Michigan Dyslexia Institute, Lansing, MI.

$7,500 to Building With Books, Stamford, CT.

$2,000 to Salvation Army, Port Huron, MI.

4345
ICN Foundation ◇
1 Riverfront Plz.
55 Campau N.W.
Grand Rapids, MI 49503 (616) 458-1150
Contact: Sidney J. Jansma, Jr., Pres.

Established in 1986.
Donors: Sidney J. Jansma, Jr.; Sidney J. Jansma III.
Foundation type: Independent foundation.
Financial data (yr. ended 12/31/05): Assets, $7,478,536 (M); gifts received, $25,000; expenditures, $1,221,388; qualifying distributions, $1,065,014; giving activities include $1,064,039 for 82 grants (high: $182,600; low: $25).

Purpose and activities: Giving primarily for evangelical Christian organizations and churches.

Fields of interest: Christian agencies & churches; Protestant agencies & churches.

Limitations: Giving primarily in MI. No grants to individuals.

Application information:
  Initial approach: Letter or proposal
  Deadline(s): None

Officers: Sidney J. Jansma, Jr., Pres. and Treas.; Joanne R. Jansma, V.P. and Secy.

EIN: 382638771

Selected grants: The following grants were reported in 2005.

$182,600 to International Aid, Spring Lake, MI.

$75,500 to Bible League, Chicago, IL.

$40,000 to Church Planters Training International, Grand Rapids, MI.

$31,000 to Grand Rapids Christian Schools, Grand Rapids, MI.

$24,000 to IDEA Ministries, Grand Rapids, MI.

$20,000 to Life International, Grand Rapids, MI.

$11,000 to Calvin Theological Seminary, Grand Rapids, MI.

$5,000 to Campus Crusade for Christ International, Orlando, FL.

$1,000 to Luke Society, Sioux Falls, SD.

$1,000 to Pregnancy Resource Center, Grand Rapids, MI.

4346
The Isabel Foundation ◇
111 E. Court St., Ste. 3D
Flint, MI 48502-1649 (810) 767-0136
Contact: C. Edward White, Jr.

Established in 1988 in MI.
Foundation type: Independent foundation.
Financial data (yr. ended 6/30/05): Assets, $59,112,952 (M); gifts received, $30,000; expenditures, $2,948,087; qualifying distributions, $2,711,761; giving activities include $2,665,580 for 52 grants (high: $300,000; low: $1,280).

Purpose and activities: Funding primarily for community foundations and to churches and other religious organizations dedicated to supporting or contributing to the cause of Christian Science.

Fields of interest: Recreation, camps; Foundations (community); Christian agencies & churches.

Type of support: Equipment; General/operating support; Continuing support; Annual campaigns.

Limitations: Giving in the U.S. No grants to individuals.

Application information: Application form not required.

  Initial approach: Letter
  Copies of proposal: 1
  Deadline(s): None
  Final notification: Grants are primarily made in June

Officers and Trustees:* Claire Mott White,* Chair. and Treas.; William S. White,* Pres. and Secy.; Tiffany W. Lovett; Ridgeway H. White.

EIN: 382853004

Selected grants: The following grants were reported in 2005.

$450,000 to Flint Institute of Arts, Flint, MI. 2 grants: $250,000, $200,000

$300,000 to Adventure Unlimited, Greenwood Village, CO.

$100,000 to Chestnut Hill Benevolent Association, Brookline, MA.

$50,000 to Camp Leelanau and Kohahna Foundation, Maple City, MI.

$50,000 to Morning Light Foundation, Atlanta, GA.

$50,000 to Peace Haven Association, Saint Louis, MO.

$50,000 to Sunrise Haven, Puyallup, WA.

$30,000 to Asher Student Foundation, Los Angeles, CA.

$20,000 to University of California, Davis, CA.

4347
The Jackson County Community Foundation ◇
(formerly The Jackson Community Foundation)
1 Jackson Sq., Ste. 110A
Jackson, MI 49201-1406 (517) 787-1321
Contact: Shelly Saines, C.E.O.; For grants: Jan Maino, V.P., Progs.
FAX: (517) 787-4333; E-mail: info@jacksoncf.org;
Additional E-mail: ssaines@jacksoncf.org;
URL: http://www.jacksoncf.org

Incorporated in 1948 in MI.
Foundation type: Community foundation.
Financial data (yr. ended 12/31/05): Assets, $18,768,103 (M); gifts received, $1,459,057; expenditures, $1,470,533; giving activities include $777,909 for grants, and $136,000 for grants to individuals.

Purpose and activities: The foundation seeks to improve the quality of life for the residents of Jackson County, MI.

Fields of interest: Humanities; Historic preservation/historical societies; Arts; Adult education—literacy, basic skills & GED; Education, reading; Education; Environment; Health care; Substance abuse, services; Recreation; Children/youth, services; Human services; Economic development; Community development.

Type of support: Scholarships—to individuals; Capital campaigns; Building/renovation; Equipment; Land acquisition; Program development; Seed money; Technical assistance; Consulting services; Program evaluation; Program-related investments/loans; Matching/challenge support.

Limitations: Giving limited to Jackson County, MI. No support for religious purposes. No grants to individuals (except for scholarships), or for endowment funds, debt retirement, fellowships, publications, or conferences.

Publications: Application guidelines; Annual report (including application guidelines); Newsletter.

Application information: Visit foundation Web site for application forms, guidelines, and specific deadlines. Grants over $5,000 require an approval based on letter of intent prior to full application submission. Application form required.

  Initial approach: Submit Community Partner grant application for grants less than $5,000; Letter of Intent for grants over $5,000
  Copies of proposal: 15
  Deadline(s): Varies
  Board meeting date(s): Jan., Mar., May, July, Sept., and Nov.
  Final notification: Within 14 days for Letter of Intent; 10 days after board meeting for grant determination

Officers and Trustees:* James S. Grace,* Chair.; Kevin T. Lavery, M.D.*, Incoming Chair.; Shelly Saines, C.E.O. and Pres.; Jan Maino, V.P., Progs.; Karen A. Brant; Anne E. Campau; Deborah Ann Craft; Carrie Glick; Dennis A. Hill; Miles E. Jones; Lt. Aaron B. Kantor; Carlene Walz Lefere, M.D.; Dennis E. Means, M.D.; R. Dale Moretz; Katherine Patrick; Dr. Daniel J. Phelan; John G. Russell; Ric Walton.

Number of staff: 4 full-time professional; 1 part-time professional.

EIN: 386070739

4348
JCT Foundation ◇
6812 Farrell Dr. N.E.
Rockford, MI 49341-9410
Contact: Jeff Power

Established in 1997 in MI.
Donors: William W. Idema; P. Craig Welch, Jr.
Foundation type: Independent foundation.
Financial data (yr. ended 12/31/05): Assets, $12,421,092 (M); gifts received, $68,400; expenditures, $413,701; qualifying distributions, $399,521; giving activities include $396,400 for 32 grants (high: $70,500; low: $2,500).
Purpose and activities: Giving primarily to Christian agencies and churches.
Limitations: Applications not accepted. Giving on a national basis.
Application information: Unsolicited requests for funds not accepted.
Officers and Trustees:* P. Craig Welch, Jr.,* Pres.; Mary K. Welch,* V.P.; Julie W. Regan; P. Craig Welch III; Thomas J. Welch.
EIN: 383386697
Selected grants: The following grants were reported in 2005.
$70,500 to North Hills Classical Academy, Grand Rapids, MI.
$50,000 to Gildas Club Grand Rapids, Grand Rapids, MI.
$20,000 to Leadership Foundation, Colorado Springs, CO.
$10,000 to Christian Counseling Center, Grand Rapids, MI.
$10,000 to Free Congress Research and Education Foundation, DC.
$10,000 to Michigan State University, East Lansing, MI.
$10,000 to Operation Mobilization, Tyrone, GA.
$10,000 to Potters House, Grand Rapids, MI.
$5,000 to Childhelp USA, Scottsdale, AZ.
$5,000 to YMCA, Lowell, Grand Rapids, MI.

4349
The Johnson Foundation ◇
225 Merrill St.
Birmingham, MI 48009

Established in 1986 in MI.
Donors: Paul H. Johnson; Pamela Callam; Scott A. Melby; Colleen M. Wolford; Kevin P. Johnson; Drew Wolford; Karen Melby; Lisa Johnson.
Foundation type: Independent foundation.
Financial data (yr. ended 11/30/05): Assets, $849,017 (M); gifts received, $795,267; expenditures, $770,563; qualifying distributions, $746,502; giving activities include $729,370 for 106 grants (high: $202,500; low: $100).
Purpose and activities: Giving primarily for Christian religious organizations including churches, schools, and missions.
Fields of interest: Education; Human services; Christian agencies & churches; Protestant agencies & churches.
Limitations: Applications not accepted. Giving on a national basis, with some emphasis on MI. No grants to individuals.
Application information: Contributes only to pre-selected organizations.
Officers: Paul H. Johnson, Pres.; Marilyn B. Johnson, V.P.; Kevin P. Johnson, Secy.
EIN: 382706960

Selected grants: The following grants were reported in 2004.
$192,000 to Walk Thru the Bible Ministries, Atlanta, GA.
$71,100 to Maranatha Bible and Missionary Conference, Muskegon, MI.
$60,000 to Crown Ministries, Longwood, FL.
$47,000 to OMS International, Greenwood, IN.
$35,000 to Highland Park Baptist Church, Southfield, MI.
$27,000 to Southfield Christian School, Southfield, MI.
$26,000 to Judson College, Elgin, IL.
$15,300 to Moody Bible Institute of Chicago, Chicago, IL.
$15,000 to Peter Deyneka Russian Ministries, Wheaton, IL.
$14,000 to Sanctuary Community Church, Greenwood, IN.

4350
Jim and Ginger Jurries Family Foundation ◇
c/o James Jurries
347 Settlers Rd., Ste. 120
Holland, MI 49423-3704

Established in 1997 in MI.
Donors: James Jurries; Virginia Jurries; E.I. Huizenga Foundation.
Foundation type: Independent foundation.
Financial data (yr. ended 12/31/04): Assets, $5,748,556 (M); gifts received, $419,563; expenditures, $541,431; qualifying distributions, $392,831; giving activities include $389,300 for 80 grants (high: $40,000; low: $1,000).
Purpose and activities: Giving to Christian schools, churches and organizations, higher education, and for boys and girls clubs.
Fields of interest: Higher education; Theological school/education; Education; Boys & girls clubs; Christian agencies & churches.
Type of support: Endowments; Capital campaigns; General/operating support.
Limitations: Applications not accepted. Giving in the U.S. primarily in MI, with emphasis on Grand Rapids and Holland. No grants to individuals.
Application information: Contributes only to pre-selected organizations.
Directors: James L. Jurries; Virginia L. Jurries.
EIN: 383342545
Selected grants: The following grants were reported in 2003.
$100,000 to Holland Christian Schools, Holland, MI. For general support.
$100,000 to Hope College, DeVos Fieldhouse, Holland, MI. For capital campaign.
$22,000 to Young Life, Holland, MI. For general support.
$5,000 to Boys and Girls Club of Greater Holland, Holland, MI. For general support.
$2,500 to Christian Schools International, Grand Rapids, MI. For general support.
$1,500 to Northwestern College, Orange City, IA. For general support.
$1,000 to Borculo Christian School, Zeeland, MI. For general support.
$1,000 to Christian Counseling Center, Grand Rapids, MI. For general support.
$1,000 to Grand Rapids Christian Schools, Grand Rapids, MI. For annual fund.
$1,000 to United Way, Greater Ottawa County, Holland, MI. For general support.

4351
The D. Dan and Betty Kahn Foundation ◇
(formerly Kahn Family Foundation)
8655 E. 8 Mile Rd.
Warren, MI 48089
Contact: David D. Kahn, Pres.

Established in 1986 in MI.
Donor: David D. Kahn.
Foundation type: Independent foundation.
Financial data (yr. ended 11/30/05): Assets, $3,290,191 (M); expenditures, $690,027; qualifying distributions, $685,783; giving activities include $685,763 for 12+ grants (high: $256,009).
Purpose and activities: Giving primarily for higher education as well as for Jewish organizations and Jewish federated giving programs; some funding for children and human services.
Fields of interest: Education; Health care; Human services; Children/youth, services; Jewish federated giving programs; Jewish agencies & temples.
Type of support: General/operating support; Building/renovation; Scholarship funds.
Limitations: Applications not accepted. Giving primarily in MI and NY. No grants to individuals.
Application information: Contributes only to pre-selected organizations.
Officers and Trustees:* David D. Kahn,* Pres.; Patrice Aaron, Secy.; Lawrence A. Wolfe,* Treas.
EIN: 382712361

4352
Kalamazoo Community Foundation ▼
(formerly Kalamazoo Foundation)
151 S. Rose St., Ste. 332
Kalamazoo, MI 49007-4775 (269) 381-4416
Contact: David D. Gardiner, V.P., Community Investment
FAX: (269) 381-3146; E-mail: info@kalfound.org; Additional E-mails: dgardiner@kalfound.org and sspringgate@kalfound.org; URL: http://www.kalfound.org

Established in 1925; incorporated in 1930 in MI.
Foundation type: Community foundation.
Financial data (yr. ended 12/31/05): Assets, $270,288,787 (M); gifts received, $10,446,200; expenditures, $18,229,359; giving activities include $12,956,552 for 457 grants (high: $600,000; low: $25), $1,462,068 for 500 grants to individuals (high: $7,500; low: $100), and $800,645 for 3 foundation-administered programs.
Purpose and activities: The foundation is dedicated to enhancing the spirit of the community and quality of life in the greater Kalamazoo area through its stewardship of permanently endowed funds. Primary areas of giving include: 1) economic development; 2) early childhood learning and school readiness; 3) community engagement and youth development; and 4) individuals and families. Grants largely for capital purposes and innovative programs.
Fields of interest: Education; Environment; Health care; Housing/shelter, development; Youth development; Family services; Economic development; Community development.
Type of support: General/operating support; Capital campaigns; Building/renovation; Equipment; Emergency funds; Program development; Seed money; Scholarship funds; Technical assistance; Program-related investments/loans; Employee matching gifts; Scholarships—to individuals; Matching/challenge support.

Limitations: Giving generally limited to Kalamazoo County, MI. No grants to individuals (except for scholarships), or for endowment funds.
Publications: Application guidelines; Annual report; Financial statement; Informational brochure; Informational brochure (including application guidelines); Newsletter; Quarterly report.
Application information: Visit foundation Web site for application information. Application form required.
  Initial approach: Telephone
  Copies of proposal: 1
  Deadline(s): Jan. and July for individuals and families, and economic development; Apr. and Oct. for early childhood learning and school readiness, and community engagement and youth development
  Board meeting date(s): Jan., Mar., June, Sept., Oct., Nov., and Dec.
  Final notification: 10 weeks
Officers and Distribution Committee:* Jeffrey L. DeNooyer,* Chair.; Marilyn J. Schlack,* Vice-Chair.; John E. "Jack" Hopkins, C.E.O., Pres. and Secy.-Treas.; Wesley Freeland, V.P., Donor Rels.; David D. Gardiner, V.P., Community Investment; Gloria Z. Royal, V.P., Mktg. Comms.; Susan Springgate, V.P., Finance and Admin.; Karen Racette, Cont.; J. Louis Felton; Barbara L. James; Judith L. Maze; Ronda E. Stryker; Donald J. Vander Kooy.
Custodian Bank: National City Bank.
Number of staff: 16 full-time professional; 3 part-time professional; 5 full-time support; 2 part-time support.
EIN: 383333202
Selected grants: The following grants were reported in 2005.
$200,000 to Southwest Michigan First Corporation, Kalamazoo, MI. For operational support.
$153,493 to Goodwill Industries of Southwestern Michigan, Kalamazoo, MI. For Literacy Together, intensive integration of literacy activities to promote school readiness and family literacy.
$150,000 to Family Health Center, Kalamazoo, MI. For capital campaign to construct larger, state-of-the-art medical facility to increase access to health care for uninsured and underinsured Kalamazoo area residents.
$150,000 to United Way, Greater Kalamazoo, Emergency Financial Assistance Network, Kalamazoo, MI. To ease individuals' or families' immediate emergency needs for housing, prescriptions, and utilities.
$100,000 to Big Brothers/Big Sisters of Greater Kalamazoo, Kalamazoo, MI. To assist with renovation of A Community of Caring, new Big Brothers Big Sisters Mentoring Center, with enough space to double number of children served.
$90,000 to Kalamazoo Area Housing Corporation, Kalamazoo, MI. To construct single-family homes for low- to moderate-income families in Rosewood Development.
$80,000 to Gull Lake Community Schools, Richland, MI. To continue Making Connections program, helping parents work with their children to ensure school readiness.
$40,000 to Edison Neighborhood Association, Kalamazoo, MI. To continue Edison Weed and Seed program after federal funding ends.
$35,000 to Kalamazoo Junior Girls, Kalamazoo, MI. To build organizational capacity.
$29,290 to Covenant Senior Day Program, Portage, MI. For kitchen and bathroom renovations.

4353
Ernest and Rosemarie Kanzler Foundation
1901 Saint Antoine St.
6th Fl. at Ford Field
Detroit, MI 48226 (313) 259-7777

Established in 2001 in MI.
Foundation type: Independent foundation.
Financial data (yr. ended 12/31/05): Assets, $7,035,093 (M); gifts received, $3,999,971; expenditures, $20,108,726; qualifying distributions, $20,039,500; giving activities include $20,000,000 for 1 grant.
Fields of interest: Arts; Education.
Limitations: Applications not accepted. Giving primarily in MI. No grants to individuals.
Application information: Contributes only to pre-selected organizations.
Officers and Directors:* Edsel B. Ford II,* Pres. and Treas.; David M. Hempstead, Secy.
EIN: 383624601
Selected grants: The following grants were reported in 2005.
$20,000,000 to Detroit Institute of Arts, Detroit, MI. For operating endowment.

4354
Helen L. Kay Charitable Trust ✧
(formerly Helen L. Kay Foundation)
c/o Comerica Bank
101 N. Main St., Ste. 100
Ann Arbor, MI 48104 (877) 405-1091
Contact: Scott Drogs, V.P., Comerica Charitable Services Group

Established in 2000 in MI.
Foundation type: Independent foundation.
Financial data (yr. ended 12/31/05): Assets, $8,758,586 (M); expenditures, $593,514; qualifying distributions, $484,335; giving activities include $465,000 for 7 grants (high: $100,000; low: $50,000).
Purpose and activities: Giving primarily to a school and a Presbyterian church.
Fields of interest: Elementary/secondary education; Hospitals (specialty); Goodwill Industries; Human services; Salvation Army; Protestant agencies & churches.
Limitations: Giving primarily in FL, MI, and PA. No grants to individuals.
Application information: Application form not required.
  Initial approach: Letter
  Deadline(s): None
Trustees: George D. Miller, Jr.; Comerica Bank.
EIN: 383047073

4355
The Keeler Foundation ✧
(formerly The Miner S. & Mary Ann Keeler Fund)
200 Monroe Ave. N.W., Ste. 240
Grand Rapids, MI 49503-2213
Contact: Mary Ann Keeler, Pres.

Incorporated in 1985 in MI as successor to the First Keeler Fund established in 1953, which transferred its assets to the new Keeler Fund in 1986.
Donors: Mary Ann Keeler; Miner S. Keeler II†; The Keeler Fund.
Foundation type: Independent foundation.

Financial data (yr. ended 7/31/05): Assets, $1,607,994 (M); expenditures, $734,532; qualifying distributions, $710,689; giving activities include $710,669 for 60 grants (high: $220,000; low: $25).
Purpose and activities: Giving primarily to organizations that are artistic or scholastic in nature.
Fields of interest: Museums (art); Performing arts; Arts; Secondary school/education; Higher education; Libraries (public); Environment; Health organizations, association; Human services; YM/YWCAs & YM/YWHAs; Christian agencies & churches.
Limitations: Giving primarily in MI, with emphasis on Grand Rapids; some giving in NY. No grants to individuals.
Application information:
  Initial approach: Letter
  Deadline(s): None
Officers: Mary Ann Keeler, Pres.; Isaac S. Keeler, V.P.; Rita L. Miller, Secy.-Treas.
Director: Donald Johnson.
EIN: 382625402
Selected grants: The following grants were reported in 2005.
$220,000 to Grand Rapids Art Museum, Grand Rapids, MI.
$82,500 to Frederik Meijer Gardens and Sculpture Park, Grand Rapids, MI.
$52,000 to YMCA of Greater Grand Rapids, Grand Rapids, MI.
$50,000 to East Grand Rapids Enhancement Fund, Grand Rapids, MI.
$26,000 to Baxter Community Center, Grand Rapids, MI.
$25,000 to Fountain Street Church, Grand Rapids, MI.
$22,500 to Grand Rapids Symphony, Grand Rapids, MI.
$16,000 to Opera Grand Rapids, Grand Rapids, MI.
$5,000 to Salvation Army.
$3,750 to Porter Hills Foundation, Grand Rapids, MI.

4356
Kellogg Company 25-Year Employees Fund, Inc. ✧
c/o Kellogg Co.
1 Kellogg Sq.
P.O. Box 3599
Battle Creek, MI 49016-3599 (269) 961-2000
Contact: Timothy S. Knowlton, Pres.
Application address: c/o Managing Decisions, 400 Orchard Ave., Battle Creek, MI 49017

Established in 1944 in MI.
Donor: W.K. Kellogg†.
Foundation type: Company-sponsored foundation.
Financial data (yr. ended 12/31/04): Assets, $61,365,510 (M); expenditures, $1,267,200; qualifying distributions, $1,246,443; giving activities include $1,105,899 for 166 grants to individuals (high: $35,500; low: $21).
Purpose and activities: The fund supports retiree associations and awards grants for living and medical expenses to current and former 25-year employees and the dependents of 25-year employees of Kellogg.
International interests: Canada; England; Mexico; South Africa.
Type of support: General/operating support; Grants to individuals.

Limitations: Giving primarily in areas of company operations, with emphasis on Battle Creek, MI; giving also in Canada, England, Mexico, and South Africa. Generally, no support for organizations. No grants to employees or dependents of employees not employed by Kellogg or a Kellogg subsidiary for at least 25 years or individuals with income greater than living expenses or liquid assets greater than $20,000 per couple or $15,000 per individual.

Application information: Application form not required.

Initial approach: Proposal

Board meeting date(s): Jan., Apr., July, and Oct.

Officers and Trustees:* Timothy S. Knowlton,* Pres.; J.W. Misner,* V.P.; D.M. Smith, Secy.; J. Wittenberg, Treas.; D.J. Banks; M.L. Bivens; C.A. Clark; G.A. Franklin; C.B. Hughes.

Number of staff: 1 full-time support.

EIN: 386039770

4357

W. K. Kellogg Foundation ▼

1 Michigan Ave. E.

Battle Creek, MI   49017-4058   (269) 968-1611

Contact: Debbie Rey, Supervisor of Proposal Processing

FAX: (269) 968-0413; URL: http://www.wkkf.org

Incorporated in 1930 in MI.

Donors: W.K. Kellogg‡; W.K. Kellogg Foundation Trust; Carrie Staines Kellogg Trust.

Foundation type: Independent foundation.

Financial data (yr. ended 8/31/06): Assets, $7,799,270,734 (M); expenditures, $406,541,671; qualifying distributions, $262,809,343; giving activities include $262,809,343 for grants.

Purpose and activities: The W.K. Kellogg Foundation was established in 1930 "to help people help themselves through the practical application of knowledge and resources to improve their quality of life and that of future generations." The foundation bases its programming on the following values: 1) The foundation believes all people have the inherent capacity to effect change in their lives, their organizations, and their communities. The foundation respects individuals and values their collective interests, strengths, and insights. 2) The foundation believes stewardship requires fidelity to the spirit and intent of the founder, and the wise use of resources. The foundation believes in being responsible, prudent, selfless, and exercising good judgment. 3) The foundation believes innovation of thought and action leads to enduring and positive change in both formal and informal systems. 4) The foundation values integrity of purpose and action and believes it is essential to all of its affairs. To achieve the greatest impact, the foundation targets its grants toward specific areas: health; food systems and rural development; youth and education; and philanthropy and volunteerism. Within these areas, attention is given to exploring learning opportunities in leadership; information and communication technology; capitalizing on diversity; and social and economic community development.

Fields of interest: Education, early childhood education; Elementary school/education; Secondary school/education; Adult/continuing education; Education; Health care, reform; Health care; Health organizations, association; Agriculture; Agriculture/food; Youth development, services; Youth, services; Minorities/immigrants, centers/

services; Community development, neighborhood development; Rural development; Community development; Voluntarism promotion; Leadership development; Minorities; African Americans/Blacks.

International interests: Botswana; Caribbean; Latin America; Lesotho; Malawi; Mozambique; South Africa; Swaziland; Zimbabwe.

Type of support: Program development; Seed money; Program evaluation; Employee matching gifts; Matching/challenge support.

Limitations: Giving primarily in the U.S., Latin America and the Caribbean, and the South African countries of Botswana, Lesotho, Malawi, South Africa, Swaziland, Zimbabwe and Mozambique. No support for religious purposes or for capital facilities. No grants to individuals (except through fellowship programs), or for endowment funds, development campaigns, films, equipment, publications, conferences, or radio and television programs unless they are an integral part of a project already being funded; no grants for operating budgets.

Publications: Application guidelines; Annual report (including application guidelines); Financial statement; Grants list; Informational brochure (including application guidelines); Newsletter; Occasional report; Program policy statement.

Application information: Proposals must conform to specified program priorities. Application form not required.

Initial approach: On-line application is preferred. Pre-proposal letter (1 to 2 pages) or letter of inquiry for those unable to access the web

Copies of proposal: 1

Deadline(s): None

Board meeting date(s): Monthly

Final notification: 3 months

Officers and Trustees:* Cynthia H. Milligan,* Chair.; Sterling Speirn, C.E.O. and Pres.; Gregory A. Lyman, Sr. V.P. and Corp. Secy.; James E. McHale, Sr. V.P., Progs.; La June Montgomery-Talley, V.P., Finance and Treas.; Richard M. Foster, V.P., Progs.; C. Patrick Babcock, V.P., Progs.; Paul J. Lawler, V.P. and C.I.O.; Robert F. Long, V.P., Progs.; Gail D. McClure, V.P., Progs.; Mary Carole Cotter, Genl. Counsel and Asst. Corp. Secy.; Shirley D. Bowser; Roderick D. Gillum; Dorothy A. Johnson; Fred P. Keller; Hanmin Liu; Wenda Weekes Moore; Joseph M. Stewart.

Number of staff: 115 full-time professional; 1 part-time professional; 73 full-time support; 2 part-time support.

EIN: 381359264

Selected grants: The following grants were reported in 2005.

$16,220,000 to Institute of American Indian Arts, Santa Fe, NM. To create home and place of permanency for learning for diverse tribal communities in U.S. and worldwide, payable over 4 years.

$6,800,000 to Great Lakes Center for Youth Development, Marquette, MI. To serve as catalyst for healthy development of youth in rural northern Michigan communities by establishing itself as resource to youth-serving organizations operating in state's Upper Peninsula and Lower Northern Region, payable over 5 years.

$6,000,000 to North Carolina Community Foundation, Raleigh, NC. To nurture and increase private giving for public good in North Carolina and strengthen organizations that support it, payable over 5 years.

$4,070,000 to Tides Center, San Francisco, CA. To provide projects and nonprofits with fiscal

sponsorship and affordable, quality management support services through developing shared standards, operating procedures, regional geographic centers, and technology infrastructure, payable over 3 years.

$4,000,000 to Battle Creek Community Foundation, Battle Creek, MI. To create endowed community-based, collaborative scholarship program to ensure that underserved, low-income, and minority students graduate from high school and successfully complete post-secondary education program.

$4,000,000 to Morehouse College, Atlanta, GA. To eliminate racial and ethnic health disparities by uniting communities, grassroots organizations, and students and faculty at Historically Black Colleges and Universities (HBCU) in Georgia through partnerships that effect sustainable community change, payable over 5 years.

$1,975,000 to Northeast-Midwest Institute, DC. To advance food and farm policy to enhance economic viability of farms, ranches, and rural communities, reward environmental stewardship, and increase access to healthy food, payable over 2.75 years.

$198,000 to Southern Africa Microfinance and Enterprise Enhancement Facility, Harare, Zimbabwe. To build capacity of Chimanimani Business Trust's mission as micro-finance and micro-enterprise development organization, payable over 2 years.

$195,000 to City at Peace, New York, NY. To strengthen capacity of current youth community engagement and service learning programs, enhance resource base for future, and improve management and organizational development effectiveness.

$109,260 to Center for Studies on Public Policies, Centro de Estudos de Politicas Publicas, Ipanema, Brazil. To strengthen arts and cultural component of development strategies in micro-regions of northeast Brazil.

4358

Kellogg's Corporate Citizenship Fund ▼ ✧

1 Kellogg Sq.

Battle Creek, MI   49016-3599   (616) 961-2000

Contact: Dawn M. Smith, Secy.

Established in 1994 in MI.

Donor: Kellogg Co.

Foundation type: Company-sponsored foundation.

Financial data (yr. ended 12/31/04): Assets, $14,881,783 (M); gifts received, $8,700,000; expenditures, $4,277,240; qualifying distributions, $4,260,148; giving activities include $3,557,810 for 102 grants (high: $971,459; low: $277), and $401,578 for 363 employee matching gifts.

Purpose and activities: The foundation supports organizations involved with arts and culture, education, wildlife preservation and protection, and human services.

Fields of interest: Arts; Elementary/secondary education; Higher education; Education; Animals/ wildlife, preservation/protection; Human services; Federated giving programs.

Type of support: General/operating support; Employee matching gifts.

Limitations: Giving primarily in areas of company operations.

Application information: Application form not required.

Initial approach: Proposal
  Deadline(s): None
Officers and Directors:* Celeste A. Clark,* Pres.; Gary Pilnick,* V.P.; Dawn M. Smith, Secy.; Janice L. Perkins,* Treas.; Timothy S. Knowlton,* Exec. Dir.; Carolee Deuel; Jeff Montle; Edward Moore.
EIN: 383167772
Selected grants: The following grants were reported in 2004.

$971,459 to United Way of Greater Battle Creek, Battle Creek, MI. For campaign support.

$250,000 to Heritage Center Foundation, Kelloggs Cereal City USA, Battle Creek, MI. For general support.

$250,000 to World of Children, Columbus, OH. For general support.

$151,257 to Baylor College of Medicine, Houston, TX. For program support.

$100,545 to United Way of the DuPage Area, Oak Brook, IL. For campaign support.

$99,750 to University of Kentucky, Lexington, KY. For program support.

$21,179 to United Way of the Central Savannah River Area, Augusta, GA. For campaign support.

$20,000 to Langston University National Alumni Association, Langston, OK. For program support.

$7,500 to Family Y Center of Battle Creek, Battle Creek, MI. For program support.

$3,070 to Music Center of South Central Michigan, Battle Creek, MI. For program support.

4359
The Kelly Services, Inc. Foundation ◇ ☆
999 W. Big Beaver Rd.
Troy, MI 48084
Contact: Kim Flowers, Admin.
FAX: (248) 244-5497;
E-mail: kim_flowers@kellyservices.com

Established in 1994 in MI.
Donor: Kelly Services, Inc.
Foundation type: Company-sponsored foundation.
Financial data (yr. ended 1/2/05): Assets, $73,417 (M); gifts received, $250,000; expenditures, $544,770; qualifying distributions, $550,840; giving activities include $550,840 for 456 grants (high: $200,000; low: $150).
Purpose and activities: The foundation supports organizations involved with arts and culture, education, health, employment, and children and youth.
Fields of interest: Arts; Higher education; Education; Hospitals (specialty); Health care; Employment; Children/youth, services; Federated giving programs.
Type of support: General/operating support; Continuing support; Annual campaigns; Emergency funds.
Limitations: Giving primarily in southeast MI. No grants to individuals.
Application information: Application form not required.
  Initial approach: Proposal
  Copies of proposal: 1
  Deadline(s): None
  Board meeting date(s): Semiannually
  Final notification: Within 1 month
Officers and Directors:* Terence E. Adderley,* Pres.; Carl T. Camden, V.P.; Michael Durik, Secy.; William Gerber, Treas.
EIN: 383207679
Selected grants: The following grants were reported in 2005.

$220,600 to Detroit Renaissance Foundation, Detroit, MI. 2 grants: $20,600, $200,000

$25,100 to United Way for Southeastern Michigan, Detroit, MI.

$2,500 to American Red Cross, Detroit, MI.

$2,500 to Michigan Womens Foundation, Livonia, MI.

$2,300 to Community House Association, Birmingham, MI.

$2,000 to HAVEN, Bloomfield Hills, MI.

$1,000 to Rochester Area Neighborhood House, Rochester, MI.

$250 to Ronald McDonald House, Corpus Christi, TX.

$250 to United Way of Greater Saint Louis, Saint Louis, MO.

4360
John C. & Nancy G. Kennedy Family Foundation ◇ ☆
4070 E. Paris Ave. S.E.
Kentwood, MI 49512-3909

Established in 1993 in MI.
Donors: John C. Kennedy; Nancy G. Kennedy.
Foundation type: Independent foundation.
Financial data (yr. ended 12/31/04): Assets, $1,279,179 (M); gifts received, $1,937,177; expenditures, $1,029,334; qualifying distributions, $1,029,334; giving activities include $1,029,334 for grants (high: $250,000).
Fields of interest: Elementary/secondary education; Higher education; Hospitals (general); Roman Catholic agencies & churches.
Type of support: General/operating support; Building/renovation; Program development.
Limitations: Applications not accepted. Giving primarily in Grand Rapids, MI. No grants to individuals.
Application information: Contributes only to pre-selected organizations.
Officers: John C. Kennedy, Pres.; Nancy G. Kennedy, V.P.
Director: Stuart F. Cheney.
EIN: 383099643

4361
Kiwanis of Michigan Foundation ◇
P.O. Box 572
Petoskey, MI 49770

Foundation type: Independent foundation.
Financial data (yr. ended 9/30/05): Assets, $674,346 (M); gifts received, $260,569; expenditures, $339,164; qualifying distributions, $336,272; giving activities include $325,833 for grants.
Purpose and activities: Support primarily for the C.S. Mott Hospital, Ann Arbor, MI.
Fields of interest: Hospitals (general); Children/youth, services.
Limitations: Applications not accepted. Giving limited to MI. No grants to individuals.
Application information: Contributes only to pre-selected organizations.
Officers and Trustees:* Thomas A. Mann,* Pres.; Allen J. LaFurgey,* 1st V.P.; Wendell Meyer,* 2nd V.P.; David L. Meyer,* Secy.-Treas.; Carl Romano; and 15 additional trustees.
EIN: 381723513

4362
Edward M. and Henrietta M. Knabusch Charitable Trust No. 1 ◇
c/o Monroe Bank & Trust
102 E. Front St.
Monroe, MI 48161

Established in 1994 in MI.
Donor: Edward M. Knabusch.
Foundation type: Independent foundation.
Financial data (yr. ended 12/31/05): Assets, $15,405,575 (M); expenditures, $2,560,672; qualifying distributions, $2,482,510; giving activities include $2,465,463 for 15 grants (high: $470,133; low: $14,702; average: $58,717–$117,435).
Purpose and activities: Giving primarily to Lutheran churches and organizations; support also for a YMCA.
Fields of interest: Historic preservation/historical societies; Higher education; Nursing home/convalescent facility; YM/YWCAs & YM/YWHAs; Children/youth, services; Protestant agencies & churches.
Type of support: General/operating support.
Limitations: Applications not accepted. Giving limited to Watertown, IA, Ann Arbor, Bay City, Detroit and Monroe, MI and St. Louis, MO. No grants to individuals.
Application information: Contributes only to pre-selected organizations.
Trustee: Monroe Bank & Trust.
EIN: 386643327
Selected grants: The following grants were reported in 2005.

$470,133 to YMCA of Monroe, Monroe, MI.

$404,739 to Salvation Army of Monroe, Monroe, MI.

$235,187 to American Red Cross, Monroe, MI.

$58,717 to Zion Lutheran Church, Monroe, MI.

$43,450 to Lutheran Home of Monroe, Monroe, MI.

$33,720 to Joslin Diabetes Foundation, Boston, MA.

4363
Edward M. and Henrietta M. Knabusch Charitable Trust No. 2 ☆
c/o Monroe Bank & Trust
102 E. Front St.
Monroe, MI 48161 (734) 242-2066
Contact: John F. Weaver, Tr.

Established in 1995 in MI.
Donor: Edward M. Knabusch Marital Trust.
Foundation type: Independent foundation.
Financial data (yr. ended 12/31/05): Assets, $10,733,308 (M); expenditures, $882,126; qualifying distributions, $839,707; giving activities include $817,000 for 34 grants (high: $50,000; low: $5,000).
Fields of interest: Performing arts centers; Higher education.
Limitations: Giving primarily in Monroe, MI, and High Point, NC. No grants to individuals.
Application information: Application form not required.
  Deadline(s): None
Trustees: John F. Weaver; Betty Lou White.
EIN: 386643328
Selected grants: The following grants were reported in 2005.

$50,000 to Philadelphia House, Monroe, MI.

$50,000 to Trinity Lutheran Church, Monroe, MI.

$30,000 to Trinity Lutheran School, Monroe, MI.
$25,000 to Camp Sunshine, Decatur, GA.
$25,000 to Grace Lutheran Church, Monroe, MI.
$25,000 to In the Image, Grand Rapids, MI.
$10,000 to Humane Society of Kent County, Grand Rapids, MI.
$10,000 to Paws With A Cause, Wayland, MI.

4364
James A. and Faith Knight Foundation ✧
180 Little Lake Dr., Ste. 6B
Ann Arbor, MI   48103   (734) 769-5653
Contact: Margaret A. Talburtt Ph.D., Exec. Dir.
FAX: (734) 769-8383;
E-mail: info@knightfoundationmi.org; URL: http://www.knightfoundationmi.org

Established in 1999 in MI.
Donor: James A. Knight Trust.
Foundation type: Independent foundation.
Financial data (yr. ended 12/31/05): Assets, $15,440,441 (M); gifts received, $81,106; expenditures, $803,069; qualifying distributions, $684,502; giving activities include $619,454 for 40 grants (high: $37,500; low: $1,434).
Purpose and activities: Primarily serving Jackson and Washtenaw counties, the foundation is dedicated to improving communities by providing grant support to qualified nonprofit organizations including, but not limited to, those that address the needs of women and girls, animals and the natural world, and internal capacity. Giving primarily for human services, including a neighborhood center, women's organizations, and family services; support also for nonprofit management, the United Way, housing, the arts, education, and environmental conservation.
Fields of interest: Performing arts, theater; Arts; Adult education—literacy, basic skills & GED; Education; Environment, natural resources; Housing/shelter, development; Human services; Neighborhood centers; Family services; Women, centers/services; Nonprofit management; Women.
Type of support: General/operating support; Capital campaigns; Building/renovation; Debt reduction; Program development.
Limitations: Giving limited to MI, with some emphasis on Ann Arbor and Jackson. No support for religious or political organizations. No grants to individuals, or for conferences or special events, or for annual campaigns.
Publications: Application guidelines; Grants list; Occasional report; Program policy statement.
Application information: Application form available on foundation Web site. Application form required.
  Initial approach: 2-page concept letter
  Copies of proposal: 3
  Deadline(s): Jan. 10 and Aug. 29
  Board meeting date(s): 10 times per year
  Final notification: Approximately 90 days
Officers: Carol Knight-Drain, Pres. and Secy.; David Knight, V.P.; Scott Drain, Treas.
Number of staff: 1 part-time professional.
EIN: 383465904

4365
Kogan Foundation ✧
c/o Kogan Co. Oakland Mall
39577 Woodward Ave., Ste. 110
Bloomfield Hills, MI   48304-5083

Established in 1943 in MI.
Donors: Jay Kogan; Oakland Mall Ltd.
Foundation type: Independent foundation.
Financial data (yr. ended 12/31/05): Assets, $2,712,052 (M); gifts received, $597,452; expenditures, $679,072; qualifying distributions, $678,922; giving activities include $673,132 for 12 + grants (high: $600,000).
Purpose and activities: Support primarily for Jewish federated giving programs and temples.
Fields of interest: Performing arts, orchestra (symphony); Human services; Jewish federated giving programs; Philanthropy/voluntarism; Jewish agencies & temples.
Limitations: Applications not accepted. Giving primarily in MI, with emphasis on Bloomfield Hills, Detroit, and Southfield; some funding nationally. No grants to individuals.
Application information: Contributes only to pre-selected organizations.
Officers: Lauren Daitch, Pres. and Treas.; Douglas Mossman, Secy.
EIN: 386064802
Selected grants: The following grants were reported in 2005.
$17,000 to Jewish Federation, MI.
$5,000 to Detroit Symphony Orchestra, Detroit, MI.
$5,000 to Wexner Center Foundation, Columbus, OH.
$4,600 to JARC, Farmington Hills, MI.
$4,597 to Congregation Shaarey Zedek, Southfield, MI.

4366
Jenny H. & Otto F. Krauss Charitable Foundation ✧ ☆
c/o Michael R. Ries, C.P.A.
409 Burrows Ave.
Roscommon, MI   48653

Donor: Otto F. Krauss.
Foundation type: Independent foundation.
Financial data (yr. ended 12/31/05): Assets, $6,325,152 (M); expenditures, $352,782; qualifying distributions, $321,205; giving activities include $315,060 for 25 grants (high: $35,000; low: $200).
Purpose and activities: Giving primarily to schools and churches.
Fields of interest: Higher education; Higher education, college; Christian agencies & churches; Protestant agencies & churches.
Type of support: General/operating support.
Limitations: Applications not accepted. Giving on a national basis, with some emphasis on MI. No grants to individuals.
Application information: Contributes only to pre-selected organizations.
Trustees: A.G. Edwards; Alan F. Krauss; Frederick G. Krauss.
EIN: 382837174

4367
The Kresge Foundation ▼ ✧
3215 W. Big Beaver Rd.
Troy, MI   48084   (248) 643-9630
Contact: Richard "Rip" Rapson, C.E.O. and Pres.
FAX: (248) 643-0588; E-mail: info@kresge.org;
URL: http://www.kresge.org

Incorporated in 1924 in MI.

Donor: Sebastian S. Kresge†.
Foundation type: Independent foundation.
Financial data (yr. ended 12/31/05): Assets, $3,032,422,497 (M); expenditures, $173,846,047; qualifying distributions, $255,657,516; giving activities include $148,651,561 for 221 grants (high: $20,000,000; low: $25,000; average: $100,000–$1,000,000), and $1,179,590 for employee matching gifts.
Purpose and activities: The foundation seeks to strengthen nonprofit organizations by catalyzing their growth, connecting them to their stake holders, and challenging greater support through grants. The foundation believes that strong, sustainable, high capacity organizations are positioned to achieve their missions and strengthen communities. Grants are awarded to nonprofit organizations operating in the fields of education, health and long-term care, human services, arts and humanities, public affairs, and science, nature, and the environment.
Fields of interest: Humanities; Arts; Higher education; Environment; Health care; Human services; Science; Public affairs.
Type of support: Capital campaigns; Building/renovation; Equipment; Land acquisition; Employee matching gifts; Matching/challenge support.
Limitations: No support for religious organizations, (unless applicant is operated by a religious organization and it serves secular needs and has financial and governing autonomy separate from the parent organization with space formally dedicated to its programs) community colleges, private foundations, or elementary or secondary schools (unless they predominantly serve individuals with physical and/or developmental disabilities). No grants to individuals, or for debt retirement or minor equipment, furnishings, operating/program support, or endowment funds by themselves; no loans.
Publications: Application guidelines; Annual report.
Application information: See foundation Web site for more application information. Application procedures vary for each foundation program area. Application form required.
  Initial approach: Letter or proposal
  Copies of proposal: 1
  Deadline(s): None
  Board meeting date(s): Mar., June, Sept., and Dec.
  Final notification: Generally within 4 to 6 months; decisions announced after each board meeting, applicants notified in writing
Officers and Trustees:* Irene Y. Hirano,* Chair.; Richard "Rip" Rapson, C.E.O. and Pres.; Edward M. Hunia, Sr. V.P. and Secy.-Treas.; Elizabeth C. Sullivan, V.P., Prog. and Admin.; Amy B. Coleman, Cont. and Dir., Finance; James L. Bildner; Lee C. Bollinger; Jane L. Delgado, Ph.D.; Steven K. Hamp; Paul C. Hillegonds; David W. Horvitz; Robert C. Larson; Katherine A. Lutey; Elaine D. Rosen; Nancy M. Schlichting; Robert D. Storey.
Number of staff: 23 full-time professional.
EIN: 381359217
Selected grants: The following grants were reported in 2005.
$3,000,000 to United Negro College Fund, Fairfax, VA. For challenge grant toward Phase I implementation of Historically Black Colleges and Universities (HBCU) Institutional Advancement Program as part of capacity-building initiative for selected HBCU's.
$2,500,000 to Detroit Educational Television Foundation-W T V S Channel 56, Detroit, MI. For challenge grant toward creation of classical

music station to be owned by Detroit Public Schools with studios in Detroit School of the Arts and managed by Detroit Public Television.

$2,000,000 to Minneapolis Institute of Arts, Minneapolis, MN. For challenge grant toward renovation and expansion of museum.

$2,000,000 to W G B H Educational Foundation, Boston, MA. For challenge grant toward purchase of property and renovation and construction of facilities.

$1,500,000 to Institute of Contemporary Art, Boston, MA. For challenge grant toward construction of museum.

$1,500,000 to Nashville Symphony Association, Nashville, TN. For challenge grant toward construction of replacement symphony hall.

$1,500,000 to University of Michigan, Ann Arbor, MI. For challenge grant toward renovation and expansion of Alumni Memorial Hall.

$1,500,000 to Virginia Museum of Fine Arts Foundation, Richmond, VA. For challenge grant toward museum's expansion and renovation.

$1,250,000 to Cleveland Institute of Music, Cleveland, OH. For challenge grant for renovation and expansion of conservatory.

$1,000,000 to Catholic Charities of the Archdiocese of Baltimore, Baltimore, MD. For challenge grant for renovation of Saint Vincent's Center, providing therapeutic care for emotionally and physically abused children.

4368
La-Z-Boy Foundation

(formerly La-Z-Boy Chair Foundation)
1284 N. Telegraph Rd.
Monroe, MI 48162-3390 (734) 242-1444
Contact: Donald E. Blohm, Admin.

Incorporated in 1953 in MI.

Donors: La-Z-Boy Chair Co.; La-Z-Boy Inc.; E.M. Knabusch†; Edwin J. Shoemaker†; H.F. Gertz†.
Foundation type: Company-sponsored foundation.
Financial data (yr. ended 12/31/05): Assets, $22,078,876 (M); expenditures, $1,278,780; qualifying distributions, $1,193,350; giving activities include $1,179,350 for 138 grants (high: $187,500; low: $500).
Purpose and activities: The foundation supports organizations involved with education, health, human services, and government and public administration.
Fields of interest: Education; Health care; Human services; Federated giving programs; Government/public administration.
Type of support: General/operating support; Building/renovation.
Limitations: Giving primarily in Siloam Springs, AR, Redlands, CA, Monroe, MI, Newton and Saltillo, MS, Neosho, MO, Greensboro, Hickory, Hudson, Lenoir, Lincolnton, North Wilkesboro, and Taylorsville, NC, Dayton and New Tazewell, TN, Tremonton, UT, and Bedford, VA. No support for religious or political organizations. No grants to individuals, or for travel or conferences or start-up needs; no loans.
Publications: Application guidelines; Annual report (including application guidelines).
Application information: Proposals should be brief. Additional information may be requested at a later date. Application form not required.
Initial approach: Proposal
Copies of proposal: 1
Deadline(s): Mar. 1, June 1, Sept. 1, and Dec. 1

Board meeting date(s): Mar., June, Sept., and Dec.
Final notification: 3 months
Officers and Directors:* P.H. Norton,* Chair.; K.L. Darrow,* C.E.O. and Pres.; David M. Risley,* Exec. V.P., Finance; J.H. Foss; D.K. Hehl; J.W. Johnston; H.G. Levy; R.E. Lipford; D.L. Mitchell; H.O. Petrauskas; J.L. Thompson.
Number of staff: 1 part-time support.
EIN: 386087673

4369
The Lachimi Foundation ◇

3270 W. Big Beaver Rd.
Troy, MI 48084

Established in 1998 in MI.
Donors: Madhava Reddy; HTC Global Svcs., Inc.
Foundation type: Independent foundation.
Financial data (yr. ended 12/31/05): Assets, $544,348 (M); gifts received, $2,200,000; expenditures, $2,134,026; qualifying distributions, $2,132,000; giving activities include $2,132,000 for 3 grants (high: $2,106,000; low: $1,000).
Purpose and activities: Giving primarily for the education and enhancement of knowledge and spirituality.
Fields of interest: Human services, mind/body enrichment; Spirituality.
Limitations: Applications not accepted. No grants to individuals.
Application information: Contributes only to pre-selected organizations.
Officer: Madhava G. Reddy, Pres.
Director: Sobha Reddy.
EIN: 383429963

4370
Patricia A. & William E. LaMothe
Foundation

620 Jennings Ln.
Battle Creek, MI 49015
Contact: Patricia A. LaMothe, Pres.

Established in 1986 in MI.
Donors: Patricia A. LaMothe; William E. LaMothe; Sydney McManus.
Foundation type: Independent foundation.
Financial data (yr. ended 12/31/05): Assets, $4,942,757 (M); gifts received, $35,358; expenditures, $423,883; qualifying distributions, $402,971; giving activities include $399,909 for 84 grants (high: $60,000; low: $50).
Purpose and activities: Giving primarily for higher education, Roman Catholic organizations, and conservation.
Fields of interest: Education; Environment, natural resources; Health organizations, association; Human services; Roman Catholic agencies & churches.
Limitations: Giving primarily in Battle Creek and Kalamazoo, MI.
Application information:
Initial approach: Letter
Deadline(s): None
Officers and Trustees:* Patricia A. LaMothe,* Pres.; Alexis LaMothe,* V.P.; Sydney McManus,* Secy.; William E. LaMothe,* Treas.
EIN: 386517929
Selected grants: The following grants were reported in 2004.

$60,000 to Hillsdale College, Hillsdale, MI.
$51,000 to Xavier High School, New York, NY.
$27,500 to YMCA.
$12,500 to Saint Joseph Catholic Church, Kalamazoo, MI.
$12,200 to Society of Saint Pius X, Kansas City, MO.
$11,000 to Acton Institute for the Study of Religion and Liberty, Grand Rapids, MI.
$10,000 to Conservation Fund, Arlington, VA.
$2,600 to Society of Saint John, Shohola, PA.
$1,044 to Kalamazoo College, Kalamazoo, MI.
$1,000 to Urban League, Southwestern Michigan, Battle Creek, MI.

4371
Arnold G. & Martha M. Langbo
Foundation ◇ ☆

20137 Evans Ct.
Beverly Hills, MI 48025
Application address: c/o Martha M. Langbo, 5606 Baltusrol Ct., Sanibel Island, FL 33957

Established in 1991 in MI.
Donors: Arnold G. Langbo; Martha M. Langbo.
Foundation type: Independent foundation.
Financial data (yr. ended 12/31/05): Assets, $919,258 (M); gifts received, $194,490; expenditures, $393,101; qualifying distributions, $388,719; giving activities include $386,216 for 64 grants (high: $250,041; low: $10).
Purpose and activities: Giving for education, human services, and Catholic organizations.
Fields of interest: Higher education; Human services; Federated giving programs; Roman Catholic agencies & churches.
Limitations: Giving limited to MI. No grants to individuals.
Application information:
Initial approach: Letter
Deadline(s): None
Officers: Martha M. Langbo, Pres. and Secy.-Treas.; Arnold G. Langbo, V.P.
Directors: Sharon A. Bateman; Maureen Langbo; Susan C. Maks.
EIN: 383026270
Selected grants: The following grants were reported in 2004.

$110,250 to Blessed Sacrament Church, Stowe, VT. For general operating support.
$28,000 to Saint Isabel Catholic Church, Sanibel, FL. For general operating support.
$12,500 to Lahey Clinic Hospital, Burlington, MA. For general operating support.
$10,000 to Our Lady of the Mississippi Abbey, Dubuque, IA. For general operating support.
$5,000 to Battle Creek Area Catholic Schools, Battle Creek, MI. For general operating support.
$5,000 to YMCA, Sherman Lake, Augusta, MI. For general operating support.
$250 to Christian Foundation for Children and Aging, Kansas City, KS. For general operating support.
$185 to Saint Lawrence Seminary High School, Mount Calvary, WI. For general operating support.
$150 to Mercy Home for Boys and Girls, Chicago, IL. For general operating support.
$100 to Helen Day Art Center, Stowe, VT. For general operating support.

4372

The Greater Lansing Foundation ✧

c/o National City Bank
120 N. Washington Sq., Ste. 650
Lansing, MI 48933-1619 (517) 334-5299
Contact: Steven J. Peters

Established as a community foundation in 1947 in MI; status changed in 1980 to independent foundation.
Foundation type: Independent foundation.
Financial data (yr. ended 12/31/05): Assets, $13,409,361 (M); expenditures, $687,832; qualifying distributions, $560,492; giving activities include $548,408 for 70 grants (high: $115,500; low: $95; average: $1,000–$25,000).
Purpose and activities: Support for charitable, public, or educational institutions, including support for health and the handicapped.
Fields of interest: Arts; Education; Health care; Health organizations, association; Disabilities, people with; Economically disadvantaged.
Type of support: Annual campaigns; Capital campaigns; Building/renovation; Equipment; Emergency funds; Program development; Conferences/seminars; Publication; Seed money; Scholarship funds; Research; Consulting services; Matching/challenge support.
Limitations: Giving limited to Ingham, Clinton, and Eaton counties, MI. No grants to individuals, or for operating budgets, endowment funds, continuing support, deficit financing, land acquisition, or technical assistance; no loans.
Application information: Unsolicited requests for funds not considered.
Initial approach: Letter
Deadline(s): Apr. 1
Board meeting date(s): May and Nov.
Trustee Bank: National City Bank.
EIN: 386057513
Selected grants: The following grants were reported in 2005.
$40,000 to American Red Cross.
$25,000 to Jupiter Medical Center, Jupiter, FL.
$25,000 to Stetson University, DeLand, FL.
$20,000 to Eles Place, Lansing, MI.
$9,485 to Humane Society.
$5,000 to American Diabetes Association, Alexandria, VA.
$5,000 to Scandia Village Good Samaritan, Sister Bay, WI.
$4,500 to Harbor Hall Fund, Harbor Springs, MI.
$4,000 to Library of Michigan Foundation, Lansing, MI.
$2,000 to Ingham Regional Healthcare Foundation, Lansing, MI.

4373

John C. Lasko Foundation ✧

c/o Charles Zimmerman
P.O. Box 339
Belleville, MI 48112-0339

Established in 1998 in MI.
Donors: John C. Lasko; Republic Die and Tool Co.
Foundation type: Independent foundation.
Financial data (yr. ended 12/31/05): Assets, $42,264,033 (M); gifts received, $6,310,563; expenditures, $1,972,967; qualifying distributions, $1,836,875; giving activities include $1,836,875 for 11 grants (high: $1,095,000; low: $200).
Purpose and activities: Giving primarily to Christian and Protestant churches.

Fields of interest: Christian agencies & churches; Protestant agencies & churches.
Limitations: Giving primarily in MI.
Application information:
Initial approach: Letter
Deadline(s): None
Officers: John C. Lasko, Pres.; William Kren, V.P.; Barbara T. Huston, Secy.; Charles Zimmerman, Treas.
Directors: Barton Bryant; Gordon Cook; Brian Eckhardt; Gary Lasko; James J. Walker.
EIN: 383440640

4374

Lear Corporation Charitable Foundation ✧ ☆

21557 Telegraph Rd.
Southfield, MI 48034

Established in 2003 in MI.
Donor: Lear Corp.
Foundation type: Company-sponsored foundation.
Financial data (yr. ended 12/31/05): Assets, $107,363 (M); gifts received, $1,000,000; expenditures, $1,725,577; qualifying distributions, $1,724,000; giving activities include $1,724,000 for 21 grants (high: $221,500; low: $20,000).
Purpose and activities: The foundation supports organizations involved with performing arts, higher education, and children and youth.
Fields of interest: Performing arts; Higher education; Children/youth, services; Federated giving programs.
Type of support: Capital campaigns.
Limitations: Applications not accepted. Giving primarily in MI, with emphasis on Detroit.
Application information: Contributes only to pre-selected organizations.
Trustees: Daniel A. Ninivaggi; Mel Stephens; James H. Vandenberghe.
EIN: 200302085

4375

The Legion Foundation ✧

1750 S. Telegraph Rd., Ste. 301
Bloomfield Hills, MI 48302
Contact: James E. Mulvoy, Tr.

Established in 1997 in MI.
Donors: The Thewes Charitable Annuity Lead Trust; The TT Charitable Annuity Lead Trust.
Foundation type: Independent foundation.
Financial data (yr. ended 12/31/05): Assets, $2,400,972 (M); gifts received, $1,498,400; expenditures, $574,751; qualifying distributions, $504,097; giving activities include $7,300 for 1 grant, and $471,563 for 43 grants to individuals (high: $49,120; low: $189).
Purpose and activities: Scholarships to individuals and grant awards to facilitate and encourage the study and maintenance of their Christian faith.
Fields of interest: Education; Christian agencies & churches.
Type of support: General/operating support; Scholarships—to individuals.
Limitations: Giving on a national basis.
Application information: Application form required.
Deadline(s): None
Trustee: James E. Mulvoy.
EIN: 383330588

4376

Lenawee Community Foundation

(formerly Tecumseh Community Fund Foundation)
603 N. Evans St.
P.O. Box 142
Tecumseh, MI 49286 (517) 423-1729
Contact: Suann Hammersmith, Exec. Dir.
FAX: (517) 424-6579; E-mail: info@lenaweecf.com; Grant request E-mail: shammersmith@ubat.com; URL: http://www.lenaweecf.com

Established in 1961 in MI.
Foundation type: Community foundation.
Financial data (yr. ended 9/30/05): Assets, $5,557,456 (M); gifts received, $998,797; expenditures, $628,358; giving activities include $370,113 for 248 grants (high: $16,000; low: $250; average: $250–$16,000), and $88,876 for 89 grants to individuals (high: $2,000; low: $250; average: $250–$2,000).
Purpose and activities: The mission of the foundation is to enhance the quality of life of the citizens of Lenawee County, Michigan by: 1) identifying and addressing current and anticipated community needs; and 2) raising, managing, and distributing funds for charitable purposes in the areas of civic, cultural, health, education, and social services with an emphasis on permanent endowments.
Fields of interest: Arts; Education; Health organizations, association; Human services; Community development; Youth.
Type of support: Capital campaigns; Building/renovation.
Limitations: Giving limited for the benefit of Lenawee County, MI. No support for religious purposes. No grants to individuals (except for scholarships), or for general operating expenses, fundraising, or construction or renovation of buildings.
Publications: Application guidelines; Annual report (including application guidelines); Grants list; Informational brochure.
Application information: Visit foundation Web site for application guidelines. Application form not required.
Initial approach: Inquiry by telephone or e-mail
Copies of proposal: 1
Deadline(s): Mar. 15, June 15, Sept. 15, and Dec. 15
Board meeting date(s): Quarterly, 4th Wed. of the month
Final notification: Feb. 28, May 30, Aug. 30, and Nov. 30
Officers and Directors:* David S. Hickman,* Pres. and Treas.; David E. Maxwell,* V.P.; Charles H. Gross,* Secy.; Suann D. Hammersmith,* Exec. Dir.; Merlyn H. Downing, Dir. Emeritus; Dr. Carlton Cook; Frank Dick; Christina Frost; Sue Goldsen; Scott Hill; Jim Kapnick; Kathryn Mohr; Breinne Reeder; Claude Rowley; W. Brett Shelton.
Number of staff: 1 full-time professional.
EIN: 386095474

4377

The Leppien Foundation ✧

815 N. State St.
Alma, MI 48801-1155

Established in 1987 in MI.
Donors: Cleo M. Leppien; John C. Leppien; Garr Tool Co.
Foundation type: Independent foundation.

Financial data (yr. ended 12/31/04): Assets, $0 (M); gifts received, $950,000; expenditures, $427,687; qualifying distributions, $420,000; giving activities include $420,000 for 14 grants (high: $75,000; low: $5,000).
Purpose and activities: Giving primarily for Christian organizations, and children and youth services.
Fields of interest: Higher education; Children/youth, services; Christian agencies & churches.
Limitations: Applications not accepted. Giving primarily in MI. No grants to individuals.
Application information: Contributes only to pre-selected organizations.
Trustees: Cleo M. Leppien; John C. Leppien.
EIN: 382692343

4378
Julie & Edward Levy, Jr. Foundation ✧
(formerly Edward C. Levy Foundation)
9300 Dix Ave.
Dearborn, MI 48120

Established in 1973 in MI.
Donors: Carol Levy; Ellen Levy; Edward C. Levy, Jr.; Edward C. Levy Co.; The Charitable Lead Trust.
Foundation type: Independent foundation.
Financial data (yr. ended 9/30/05): Assets, $17,177,472 (M); expenditures, $1,130,307; qualifying distributions, $1,046,776; giving activities include $1,044,626 for 54 grants (high: $250,226; low: $100).
Purpose and activities: Giving for health, education, and Jewish organizations.
Fields of interest: Higher education; Health care; Health organizations, association; Neuroscience; Cancer research; Jewish federated giving programs; Jewish agencies & temples.
Limitations: Applications not accepted. Giving primarily in MI, with emphasis on Detroit; some giving in Washington, DC, and Cambridge, MA. No grants to individuals.
Application information: Contributes only to pre-selected organizations.
Officer: Edward C. Levy, Jr., Pres.
Trustees: Patrick Duerr; Ellen Levy Horowitz; Carol Levy Johnstone.
EIN: 386091368

4379
Benard L. Maas Foundation ✧
715 Barclay Ct.
Ann Arbor, MI 48105

Established in 1942 in MI.
Donor: Benard L. Maas†.
Foundation type: Independent foundation.
Financial data (yr. ended 12/31/05): Assets, $7,928,130 (M); expenditures, $583,311; qualifying distributions, $380,680; giving activities include $380,680 for 98 grants (high: $43,000; low: $200).
Purpose and activities: Giving primarily for Jewish organizations.
Fields of interest: Performing arts; Law school/education; Hospitals (specialty); Health organizations, association; Human services; Children/youth, services; Jewish federated giving programs; Jewish agencies & temples.
Limitations: Applications not accepted. Giving primarily in MI. No grants to individuals.

Application information: Contributes only to pre-selected organizations. Unsolicited requests for funds not accepted.
Officers and Directors:* David E. Engelbert,* Pres. and Treas.; Matthew Engelbert,* V.P.; Lynn H. Engelbert,* Secy.
EIN: 386096405

4380
The Mackey Foundation ✧
(formerly The Harvey and Elizabeth Mackey Foundation)
c/o Bruce Mackey
3181 Tri-Park Dr.
Grand Blanc, MI 48439

Established in 1993 in MI.
Donor: Bruce B. Mackey.
Foundation type: Independent foundation.
Financial data (yr. ended 12/31/05): Assets, $3,355,542 (M); gifts received, $1,600,000; expenditures, $512,664; qualifying distributions, $510,000; giving activities include $510,000 for 12 grants (high: $100,000; low: $10,000).
Fields of interest: Housing/shelter, homeless; Boys & girls clubs; Human services; Homeless, human services; Christian agencies & churches; Protestant agencies & churches; Economically disadvantaged.
Limitations: Applications not accepted. Giving primarily in Flint, MI. No grants to individuals.
Application information: Contributes only to pre-selected organizations.
Officers: Marilyn Johnson, Pres.; Bruce B. Mackey, Secy.-Treas.
Trustee: Stanley D. Mackey.
Board Member: Robert B. Mackey.
EIN: 383134945
Selected grants: The following grants were reported in 2003.
$75,000 to Christ Episcopal Center, Flint, MI.
$70,000 to Young Life, Flint, MI.
$50,000 to Potters Clay Ministries, Hot Springs, AR.
$50,000 to Shelter of Flint, Flint, MI.
$40,000 to Boys and Girls Club of Greater Flint, Flint, MI.
$20,000 to Crossover Downtown Outreach Ministry, Flint, MI.
$20,000 to Saint Andrews Episcopal Church, Flint, MI.

4381
Manat Foundation ✧
26877 Northwestern Hwy., Ste. 413
Southfield, MI 48034

Established in 1986 in MI.
Donors: Manuel Charach; Natalie Charach; Jeffrey Charach; Michael Berman; Sherrill Berman.
Foundation type: Independent foundation.
Financial data (yr. ended 7/31/05): Assets, $4,341,598 (M); gifts received, $351,000; expenditures, $471,245; qualifying distributions, $389,370; giving activities include $389,370 for 39 grants (high: $250,000; low: $250).
Purpose and activities: Giving primarily for health associations, particularly a cancer institute, and to Jewish organizations; funding also for education, and children, youth and social services.
Fields of interest: Higher education; Hospitals (general); Health organizations, association; Cancer research; Human services; Children/youth,

services; Jewish federated giving programs; Jewish agencies & temples.
Limitations: Applications not accepted. Giving primarily in MI and NY. No grants to individuals.
Application information: Contributes only to pre-selected organizations.
Managers: Manuel Charach; Natalie Charach.
Trustees: Michael Berman; Joel Shulman.
EIN: 382710511

4382
Richard & Jane Manoogian Foundation ▼ ✧
21001 Van Born Rd.
Taylor, MI 48180-1300

Established in 1984 in MI.
Donors: Alex Manoogian†; Marie Manoogian.
Foundation type: Independent foundation.
Financial data (yr. ended 6/30/05): Assets, $228,638,216 (M); expenditures, $10,319,837; qualifying distributions, $38,213,301; giving activities include $8,334,005 for 48 grants (high: $6,079,140; low: $500; average: $5,000–$100,000).
Purpose and activities: Giving primarily for the arts, with emphasis on an art museum; funding also for education, health care, human services, community development, and federated giving programs.
Fields of interest: Museums; Performing arts; Performing arts, orchestra (symphony); Historic preservation/historical societies; Arts; Higher education; Education; Zoos/zoological societies; Health organizations, association; Human services; Children/youth, services; Community development; Foundations (private grantmaking); Foundations (community); Federated giving programs.
Type of support: General/operating support.
Limitations: Applications not accepted. Giving primarily in MI. No grants to individuals.
Application information: Contributes only to pre-selected organizations.
Officers: Richard A. Manoogian, Pres. and Treas.; Eugene A. Gargaro, Jr., Secy.
Director: Jane C. Manoogian.
EIN: 382531814
Selected grants: The following grants were reported in 2005.
$6,079,140 to Detroit Institute of Arts, Detroit, MI. For operating support.
$1,000,000 to College for Creative Studies, Detroit, MI. For operating support.
$225,000 to Detroit Symphony Orchestra, Detroit, MI. For operating support.
$125,000 to W T V S Detroit Educational Television, Detroit, MI. For operating support.
$50,000 to San Francisco Artspace, San Francisco, CA. For operating support.
$45,000 to University Cultural Center Association, Detroit, MI. 2 grants: $35,000 (For operating support), $10,000 (For operating support).
$25,000 to Detroit Artists Market, Detroit, MI. For operating support.
$12,500 to Jewish Ensemble Theater, West Bloomfield, MI. For operating support.
$10,000 to Crooked Tree Arts Council, Crooked Tree Arts Center, Petoskey, MI. For operating support.

4383
Manoogian Simone Foundation ▼ ✧
(formerly Louise Manoogian Simone Foundation)
21001 Van Born Rd.
Taylor, MI   48180

Established in 1962 in MI.
Donors: Alex Manoogian†; Marie Manoogian;
Masco Corp.
Foundation type: Independent foundation.
Financial data (yr. ended 12/31/05): Assets,
$169,166,081 (M); expenditures, $8,308,856;
qualifying distributions, $8,196,211; giving
activities include $8,194,600 for 25 grants (high:
$4,814,000; low: $1,000; average: $10,000–
$250,000).
Purpose and activities: Giving for Armenian
organizations, including Armenian churches and
cultural organizations, and education.
Fields of interest: Arts; Education; Orthodox
Catholic agencies & churches.
International interests: Armenia.
Limitations: Applications not accepted. Giving
primarily in CA, MI, NJ, and NY. No grants to
individuals.
Application information: Contributes only to
pre-selected organizations.
Officers and Directors:* Louise M. Simone,* Pres.;
David Simone,* V.P.; Christine M. Simone,
Secy.-Treas.; Mark Simone.
EIN: 381799107
Selected grants: The following grants were reported
in 2005.
$4,814,000 to Armenian General Benevolent
    Union, New York, NY. For operating support.
$1,000,000 to Armenia Fund USA, New York, NY.
    For operating support.
$1,000,000 to Habitat for Humanity International,
    Americus, GA. For operating support.
$500,000 to Friends of Holy Etchmiadzin, Mahwah,
    NJ. For operating support.
$250,000 to Children of Armenia Fund (COAF), New
    York, NY. For operating support.
$250,000 to Saint Leon Armenian Church, Fair
    Lawn, NJ. For operating support.
$5,000 to Armenian Missionary Association of
    America, Paramus, NJ.
$1,000 to Armenian Apostolic Society, Southfield,
    MI.

4384
Manthei Charitable Trust ✧
3996 U.S. 31 S.
Petoskey, MI   49770-9801

Established in 1960.
Donors: Theodore W. Manthei; Mary Manthei; Dan
Manthei; Tim Manthei.
Foundation type: Independent foundation.
Financial data (yr. ended 12/31/04): Assets,
$1,546,709 (M); gifts received, $309,787;
expenditures, $351,443; qualifying distributions,
$347,348; giving activities include $347,348 for 17
+ grants (high: $101,000).
Purpose and activities: Support for Christian
agencies and churches.
Fields of interest: Education; Christian agencies &
churches.
Type of support: General/operating support.
Limitations: Applications not accepted. Giving on a
national basis. No grants to individuals.
Application information: Contributes only to
pre-selected organizations.

Trustees: Daniel R. Manthei; Mark Manthei; Thomas
Manthei.
EIN: 381204856
Selected grants: The following grants were reported
in 2004.
$101,000 to Alliance Defense Fund, Scottsdale, AZ.
$58,250 to Campus Crusade for Christ. 2 grants:
    $41,500, $16,750
$12,000 to Thornston Educational Fund, Glendora,
    CA.
$10,000 to Asian Access Life Ministries, San
    Dimas, CA.
$6,000 to World Concern, Seattle, WA.

4385
Oliver Dewey Marcks Foundation ✧
645 Griswold St., Ste. 3180
Detroit, MI   48226-4250
Contact: John M. Chase, Jr., Pres.

Established in 1960.
Donors: Eula D. Marcks†; Oliver Dewey Marcks†.
Foundation type: Independent foundation.
Financial data (yr. ended 12/31/04): Assets,
$12,818,965 (M); expenditures, $582,436;
qualifying distributions, $553,742; giving activities
include $495,000 for 29 grants (high: $150,000;
low: $5,000).
Fields of interest: Arts; Education; Environment,
natural resources; Animal welfare.
Type of support: General/operating support;
Program development.
Limitations: Giving limited to Detroit, MI, and
surrounding communities. No grants to individuals.
Publications: Application guidelines.
Application information: Application form required.
    Initial approach: Letter, including a 1-page
        summary
    Copies of proposal: 4
    Board meeting date(s): May, July and Oct.
Officers and Board Members:* John M. Chase, Jr.,*
Pres.; Marion Valentine,* Secy.; Michael J.
Predhomme,* Treas.
EIN: 386081311

4386
Edward & Helen Mardigian Foundation ✧
c/o Comerica Bank
P.O. Box 75000, MC 3302
Detroit, MI   48275-3302   (248) 647-0077
Contact: Edward Mardigian, Jr.
Application address: 39400 N. Woodward Ave.,
Bloomfield Hills, MI 48304

Incorporated in 1955 in MI.
Donors: Edward S. Mardigian†; Helen Mardigian;
Arman Mardigian†.
Foundation type: Independent foundation.
Financial data (yr. ended 12/31/05): Assets,
$21,699,559 (M); gifts received, $350,000;
expenditures, $1,045,671; qualifying distributions,
$1,013,056; giving activities include $976,650 for
48 grants (high: $200,000; low: $100).
Purpose and activities: Giving primarily for
Armenian organizations and churches in the U.S.;
funding also for children, youth and social services,
and health associations.
Fields of interest: Arts; Higher education; Zoos/
zoological societies; Health organizations,
association; Human services; Children/youth,
services; Christian agencies & churches; Minorities.

Limitations: Giving in the U.S., primarily in MI. No
grants to individuals.
Application information:
    Initial approach: Letter
    Deadline(s): None
Officers: Helen Mardigian, Pres. and Secy.; Edward
S. Mardigian, V.P. and Treas.
Director: Robert D. Mardigian.
EIN: 386048886

4387
Masco Corporation Foundation
(formerly Masco Corporation Charitable Trust)
c/o Corp. Affairs
21001 Van Born Rd.
Taylor, MI   48180   (313) 274-7400
FAX: (313) 792-6262; *URL:* http://
www.masco.com/corporate_information/
citizenship/foundation/index.html

Trust established in 1952 in MI.
Donor: Masco Corp.
Foundation type: Company-sponsored foundation.
Financial data (yr. ended 12/31/05): Assets,
$8,204,339 (M); gifts received, $2,000,000;
expenditures, $5,687,612; qualifying distributions,
$5,599,327; giving activities include $5,596,950
for 128 grants (high: $980,000; low: $2,000).
Purpose and activities: The foundation supports
organizations involved with arts and culture outreach
for disadvantaged youth, human services, and civic
affairs. Special emphasis is directed toward
programs designed to promote decent housing
environments for disadvantaged, low-income
families.
Fields of interest: Arts; Housing/shelter; Human
services; Public affairs; Youth.
Type of support: General/operating support; Annual
campaigns; Capital campaigns; Building/
renovation; Matching/challenge support.
Limitations: Giving primarily in areas of company
operations, with emphasis on the greater Detroit,
MI, area. No support for discriminatory
organizations, political organizations or candidates
or lobbying organizations, athletic clubs, religious
organizations not of direct benefit to the entire
community, or organizations benefiting few people.
No grants to individuals, or for debt reduction,
endowments, sports programs or events or school
extracurricular activities, or conferences, travel,
seminars, or film or video projects; no loans.
Publications: Application guidelines; Annual report;
Corporate giving report.
Application information: Application form not
required.
    Initial approach: Letter of inquiry or telephone
    Copies of proposal: 1
    Deadline(s): None
    Board meeting date(s): Spring and fall
Officers and Trustees: Sharon Rothwell, Chair.;
Melonie B. Colaianne, Pres.; Eugene A. Gargaro, Jr.,
Secy.; Alan H. Barry; Richard A. Manoogian;
Comerica Bank.
Number of staff: 2 full-time professional; 1 full-time
support.
EIN: 386043605
Selected grants: The following grants were reported
in 2005.
$980,000 to Habitat for Humanity International,
    Americus, GA.
$465,000 to Detroit Institute of Arts, Detroit, MI.
$320,000 to Detroit Zoological Park, Royal Oak, MI.

$200,000 to Detroit Renaissance Foundation, Detroit, MI.

$100,000 to American Red Cross, Southeastern Michigan Chapter, Detroit, MI.

$90,000 to Detroit Zoological Society, Royal Oak, MI.

$50,000 to Arab Community Center for Economic and Social Services, Dearborn, MI.

$50,000 to Arts League of Michigan, Detroit, MI.

$25,000 to Coalition on Temporary Shelter (COTS), Detroit, MI.

$20,000 to Central Detroit Christian Community Development Corporation, Detroit, MI.

4388
McDonald Agape Foundation ✧
380 N. Old Woodward Ave., Ste. 314
Birmingham, MI 48009

Established in 1988 in MI.
Donor: Alonzo L. McDonald, Jr.
Foundation type: Independent foundation.
Financial data (yr. ended 12/31/04): Assets, $8,775,402 (M); gifts received, $129,460; expenditures, $1,249,245; qualifying distributions, $1,184,771; giving activities include $1,159,773 for 20 grants (high: $604,594; low: $500).
Purpose and activities: Giving primarily for Christian organizations and education.
Fields of interest: Higher education; Theological school/education; Human services; Children, services; Religious federated giving programs; Christian agencies & churches.
Limitations: Applications not accepted. Giving on a national basis. No grants to individuals.
Application information: Contributes only to pre-selected organizations.
Officers: Alonzo L. McDonald, Chair.; R. Jamison Williams, Secy.; Mark A. Maurice, Treas.
Trustees: Peter McDonald; Suzanne M. McDonald; Jennifer McDonald Peters; Robert M. Pool.
EIN: 382840692
Selected grants: The following grants were reported in 2003.
$247,987 to Emory University, Atlanta, GA.
$209,553 to Harvard University, Cambridge, MA. 2 grants: $194,553 (For chair endowment), $15,000.
$30,000 to Trinity Forum, Orlando, FL.
$12,120 to Young Life Ministries, Southfield, MI.
$9,686 to McLean Presbyterian Church, McLean, VA. For general support.
$7,732 to Our Lady of the Mississippi Abbey, Dubuque, IA.
$1,719 to Compassion International, Colorado Springs, CO.
$1,000 to International Justice Mission, Alexandria, VA.
$480 to Heifer Project International, Little Rock, AR.

4389
McGregor Fund ▼
333 W. Fort St., Ste. 2090
Detroit, MI 48226-3134   (313) 963-3495
Contact: C. David Campbell, Pres.
FAX: (313) 963-3512;
E-mail: info@mcgregorfund.org; URL: http://www.mcgregorfund.org

Incorporated in 1925 in MI.

Donors: Tracy W. McGregor‡; Katherine W. McGregor‡.
Foundation type: Independent foundation.
Financial data (yr. ended 6/30/05): Assets, $172,095,146 (M); expenditures, $11,229,395; qualifying distributions, $9,399,596; giving activities include $8,583,909 for 78 grants (high: $500,000; low: $4,500; average: $50,000–$100,000), and $189,272 for 82 employee matching gifts.
Purpose and activities: A private foundation organized to relieve misfortune and improve the well-being of people. The foundation provides grants to support activities in human services, education, health care, arts and culture, and public benefit.
Fields of interest: Arts; Higher education; Education; Medical care, in-patient care; Health organizations, association; Human services; Youth, services; Homeless.
Type of support: General/operating support; Continuing support; Capital campaigns; Building/renovation; Equipment; Program development; Seed money; Employee matching gifts.
Limitations: Giving primarily in the metropolitan Detroit, MI, area, including Wayne, Oakland, and Macomb counties. No support for disease-specific organizations (or their local affiliates). No grants to individuals, or for scholarships directly, fellowships, travel, workshops, seminars, special events, film or video projects, or conferences; no loans.
Publications: Application guidelines; Annual report (including application guidelines); Grants list.
Application information: Grantmaking guidelines and application procedures are available on the foundation's Web site. Potential applicants are encouraged to contact the foundation to discuss proposed projects before submitting a proposal. Organizations are limited to submitting one grant application per year. Application form required.
  Initial approach: Cover letter and proposal
  Copies of proposal: 1
  Deadline(s): Applicants are encouraged to submit proposals at least 3 months in advance of board meetings
  Board meeting date(s): Mar., June, Sept., and Dec.
  Final notification: 90 to 120 days
Officers and Trustees:* Eugene A. Miller,* Chair.; Ruth R. Glancy,* Vice-Chair.; C. David Campbell,* Pres. and Secy.; William W. Shelden, Jr.,* Treas.; Bruce W. Steinhauer, M.D.*, Tr. Emeritus; Dave Bing; Cynthia N. Ford; Ira J. Jaffe; James B. Nicholson; Susan Schooley, M.D.
Number of staff: 2 full-time professional; 1 part-time professional; 1 full-time support.
EIN: 380808800
Selected grants: The following grants were reported in 2005.
$2,000,000 to Detroit Institute of Arts, Detroit, MI. For Great Art-New Start, campaign to complete structural renovations, reinstall art, and carry on daily operation of museum, payable over 5 years.
$1,200,000 to Local Initiatives Support Corporation (LISC), New York, NY. To support Neighborhoods NOW, initiative of Detroit LISC, to encourage inter-neighborhood cooperation and collaboration between community development corporations, businesses, institutions, and residents to make impact on targeted neighborhoods within Detroit and inner-ring suburbs, payable over 3 years.
$900,000 to Starfish Family Services, Inkster, MI. For implementation of Family Success Model, to help families break cycle of intergenerational

poverty and achieve lasting success, payable over 3 years.
$500,000 to Community Health and Social Services Center, Detroit, MI. For capital campaign to build new facility in southwest Detroit, payable over 2 years.
$486,000 to University of Michigan, Ann Arbor, MI. For Geriatric Social Work Fellows Program and fieldwork in metropolitan Detroit, payable over 3 years.
$250,000 to Kenyon College, Gambier, OH. For Food for Thought, collaboration between students and faculty of college's Rural Life Center and local farmers to include applied student research across disciplines, aimed at raising consumer interest in locally produced foods.
$150,000 to Saint John Health System, Detroit, MI. To support renovation costs to prepare facility for operation as Northeast Health Center, Federally Qualified Health Center operated by Advantage Health in collaboration with Detroit Department of Health and Wellness Promotion and Saint John's Health.
$100,000 to Detroit Science Center, Detroit, MI. For program support.
$60,000 to Calvin College, Grand Rapids, MI. For trustee designated grant.
$50,000 to Volunteer Accounting Service Team of Michigan, Detroit, MI. To support Tax Assistance Program, providing volunteers to prepare and file tax returns for low-income residents of metropolitan Detroit.

4390
The Meijer Foundation ▼ ✧
c/o Fifth Third Bank
P.O. Box 3636
Grand Rapids, MI 49501-3636

Established in 1990 in MI.
Donors: Frederik G.H. Meijer; Meijer, Inc.; Lena Meijer.
Foundation type: Independent foundation.
Financial data (yr. ended 9/30/05): Assets, $81,359,690 (M); expenditures, $7,410,936; qualifying distributions, $6,906,785; giving activities include $6,906,785 for 47 grants (high: $1,510,000; low: $100; average: $25,000–$250,000).
Purpose and activities: Giving primarily to a horticultural society, and to a charitable trust; funding also for community foundations and an art museum. The foundation administers a donor-advised fund.
Fields of interest: Museums (art); Botanical gardens; Horticulture/garden clubs; Foundations (community).
Limitations: Applications not accepted. Giving primarily in Grand Rapids, MI, some giving also in Greenville, MI. No grants to individuals.
Application information: Contributes only to pre-selected organizations.
Trustee: Frederik G.H. Meijer.
EIN: 386575227
Selected grants: The following grants were reported in 2005.
$2,682,140 to Frederik Meijer Gardens and Sculpture Park, Grand Rapids, MI. 5 grants: $343,739 (For Degas sculpture), $669,734 (For general support), $532,167 (For matching grants), $986,500 (For Andy Goldsworthy sculpture), $150,000 (For The Fields sculpture).

$1,510,000 to Blodgett Butterworth Health Care Foundation, Grand Rapids, MI. For Heart Center.

$400,000 to Grand Rapids Art Museum, Grand Rapids, MI. 2 grants: $200,000 (For capital campaign), $200,000 (For purchase of Domestic Spider sculpture).

$35,000 to Labor Heritage Society of West Michigan, Grand Rapids, MI. For Spirit of Solidarity Campaign.

$30,000 to Saint Marys Doran Foundation, Grand Rapids, MI. For Hauenstein Neuroscience Center.

4391
Orville D. & Ruth A. Merillat Foundation ▼ ✧
1800 W. U.S. Hwy. 223
Adrian, MI   49221-8479

Established in 1983 in MI.
Donors: Orville D. Merillat†; Ruth A. Merillat.
Foundation type: Independent foundation.
Financial data (yr. ended 2/28/05): Assets, $82,292,161 (M); gifts received, $150,000; expenditures, $6,187,154; qualifying distributions, $5,508,152; giving activities include $5,508,132 for 90 grants (high: $2,698,000; low: $300; average: $3,000–$250,000).
Purpose and activities: Support primarily for churches and religious welfare.
Fields of interest: Elementary/secondary education; Human services; Religious federated giving programs; Religion.
Type of support: General/operating support; Building/renovation; Equipment.
Limitations: Applications not accepted. Giving primarily in MI. No grants to individuals.
Application information: Contributes only to pre-selected organizations.
Officers and Directors:* Ruth A. Merillat,* Pres. and Secy.; Richard D. Merillat,* V.P.; John D. Thurman, Treas.
EIN: 382476813
Selected grants: The following grants were reported in 2005.

$2,698,000 to Lenawee Christian Ministries, Adrian, MI. For operating support.

$1,083,333 to Huntington College, Huntington, IN. For operating support.

$250,000 to Emmanuel Community Church, Fort Wayne, IN. For building support.

$108,333 to Moody Bible Institute of Chicago, Chicago, IL. For operating support.

$100,000 to American Bible Society, New York, NY. For operating support.

$83,333 to Focus on the Family, Colorado Springs, CO. For operating support.

$25,000 to Adrian College, Adrian, MI. For building support.

$25,000 to Holy Cross Childrens Services, Clinton, MI. For operating support.

$15,000 to World Gospel Outreach, Humble, TX. For operating support.

$5,000 to Salvation Army of Adrian, Adrian, MI.

4392
Midland Area Community Foundation
(formerly Midland Foundation)
109 E. Main St.
P.O. Box 289
Midland, MI   48640-0289   (989) 839-9661
Contact: Nicole Charles, V.P.
FAX: (989) 839-9907;
E-mail: info@midlandfoundation.com; Additional tel: (800) 906-9661; URL: http://www.midlandfoundation.com

Established in 1973 in MI.
Foundation type: Community foundation.
Financial data (yr. ended 12/31/05): Assets, $55,817,605 (M); gifts received, $2,990,152; expenditures, $3,861,367; giving activities include $1,275,201 for 260 grants (high: $50,000; low: $100); and $191,932 for 105 grants to individuals (high: $5,000; low: $500).
Purpose and activities: The foundation seeks to promote and enable philanthropic giving to improve the quality of life for the people in the community.
Fields of interest: Humanities; Arts; Adult/continuing education; Education; Environment, energy; Environment; Health care; Recreation; Youth, services; Human services; Economic development; Community development.
Type of support: Building/renovation; Equipment; Seed money; Scholarship funds; Technical assistance; Consulting services; Matching/challenge support.
Limitations: Giving primarily in full support services to Midland and Gladwin counties, MI, and also Clare County through affiliate. No support for sectarian religious programs or basic governmental services. No grants to individuals (except for scholarships), or for operating budgets, continuing support, annual campaigns, deficit financing, endowment funds, or travel for groups such as school classes, clubs, or sports teams.
Publications: Application guidelines; Annual report; Grants list; Informational brochure; Newsletter.
Application information: Visit foundation Web site for application guidelines. Application form required.
   Initial approach: Telephone Prog. Off. to discuss project
   Copies of proposal: 3
   Deadline(s): Jan. 15, Apr. 15, July 15, and Oct. 15
   Board meeting date(s): 4th Mon. of every month
   Final notification: Early in Mar., June, Sept., and Dec.
Officers and Trustees:* Brian Rodgers,* Chair.; Maureen Donker,* Vice-Chair.; Janet McGuire, C.E.O. and Pres.; Nicole Charles, V.P. and C.F.O.; Marty McGuire,* Secy.; Chris Velasquez,* Treas.; Linda Cline; Carole Dennings; Richard Dolinski; Thomas Erickson; L. Scott Govitz; Bridgette Gransden; Kevin Guigou; Jim Hop; Cindy Newman; Linda Owen; Donna Rapp.
Number of staff: 4 full-time professional; 1 part-time professional; 2 full-time support; 1 part-time support.
EIN: 382023395

4393
Howard Miller Foundation ✧
860 E. Main Ave.
Zeeland, MI   49464-0301

Established in 1976 in MI.
Donors: Howard Miller Clock Co.; Herman Furniture Co.

Foundation type: Independent foundation.
Financial data (yr. ended 12/31/05): Assets, $14,036,428 (M); gifts received, $594,037; expenditures, $655,792; qualifying distributions, $598,140; giving activities include $567,000 for 45 grants (high: $52,500; low: $2,500), and $26,000 for 13 grants to individuals (high: $2,000; low: $2,000).
Purpose and activities: Giving primarily for education, Christian missionary work, the arts, health, and human services; also awards college scholarships.
Fields of interest: Arts; Higher education; Education; Hospitals (general); Health care; Mental health/crisis services; Human services; Christian agencies & churches.
Type of support: General/operating support; Scholarships—to individuals.
Limitations: Applications not accepted. Giving primarily in IA and MI.
Application information: Unsolicited requests for funds not accepted.
Officers: Philip D. Miller, Pres.; Jack H. Miller, V.P.; Howard J. Miller, Secy.-Treas.
EIN: 382137226

4394
The Miller Foundation
(formerly Albert L. and Louise B. Miller Foundation, Inc.)
310 WahWahTaySee Way
Battle Creek, MI   49015
Contact: Diane Thompson, Exec. Dir.
FAX: (269) 964-8455;
E-mail: dthompson@millerfdn.org; URL: http://www.willard.lib.mi.us/npa/miller

Incorporated in 1963 in MI.
Donors: Louise B. Miller†; Robert B. Miller†.
Foundation type: Independent foundation.
Financial data (yr. ended 12/31/05): Assets, $32,755,296 (M); expenditures, $1,703,280; qualifying distributions, $1,386,023; giving activities include $879,810 for 30 grants (high: $325,000; low: $500), and $52,820 for employee matching gifts.
Purpose and activities: Giving mainly to improve the quality of life in the Battle Creek, MI, community area by supporting local organizations and government agencies that provide for economic development, neighborhood improvement, improving educational outcomes for youth, and eliminating barriers to employment for all in Battle Creek, MI, and the surrounding area.
Fields of interest: Adult/continuing education; Human services; Children/youth, services; Community development, neighborhood development; Economic development.
Type of support: General/operating support; Annual campaigns; Capital campaigns; Building/renovation; Equipment; Emergency funds; Program development; Seed money; Consulting services; Program-related investments/loans; Matching/challenge support.
Limitations: Giving limited to the greater Battle Creek, MI, area. No support for religious or political organizations. No grants to individuals, or for endowments.
Publications: Application guidelines; Annual report.
Application information: Application guidelines available on foundation Web site. Application form required.
   Initial approach: Initial letter

Copies of proposal: 12

Deadline(s): Jan. 1, Mar. 1, May 1, July 1, Sept.
1, and Nov. 1

Board meeting date(s): Jan., Mar., May, July,
Sept., and Nov.

Final notification: 2 months

Officers and Trustees:* Barbara L. Comai,* Chair.;
Greg D. Dotson,* Vice-Chair.; Gloria J. Robertson,*
Secy.; John J. Gallagher,* Treas.; Arthur W. Angood;
Rance L. Leaders; Allen B. Miller; Robert B. Miller,
Jr.; Paul R. Ohm.

Number of staff: 1 full-time professional; 1 part-time
support.

EIN: 386064925

Selected grants: The following grants were reported
in 2005.

$175,000 to Miller College, Battle Creek, MI.
Toward initial funding for operations.

$100,000 to Family Health Center of Battle Creek,
Battle Creek, MI. For community obstetrics.

$75,000 to Battle Creek Health System, Battle
Creek, MI. For Cancer Care Center.

$75,000 to Lifespan, Battle Creek, MI. For capital
campaign.

$50,000 to Burnham Brook Center, Battle Creek,
MI. To support reorganization and development
plan.

$20,000 to SAFE Place, Battle Creek, MI. For shelter
case management.

$12,000 to KCC Foundation. For scholarships.

$10,000 to Big Brothers/Big Sisters, MI. For mentor
expansion program.

$9,010 to Seconds New Vision and Outreach
Ministries, Battle Creek, MI. For reading incentive
program.

$5,000 to Kingman Museum, Battle Creek, MI. For
Brain Matters exhibit.

4395
Molinello Family Foundation ◇

P.O. Box 721067

Berkley, MI 48072-0067   (248) 544-2775

Contact: Earl C. Bossenberry, Pres.

Established in 2000 in MI.

Donors: Richard Molinello Revocable Trust; John
Molinello Revocable Trust.

Foundation type: Independent foundation.

Financial data (yr. ended 12/31/05): Assets,
$16,751,432 (M); expenditures, $803,056;
qualifying distributions, $803,056; giving activities
include $664,690 for 26 grants (high: $47,130;
low: $2,000).

Fields of interest: Health care; Medical research,
institute; Human services; Christian agencies &
churches; Blind/visually impaired; Economically
disadvantaged.

Limitations: Giving primarily in MI.

Application information:

Initial approach: Letter

Deadline(s): None

Officers: Earl C. Bossenberry, Pres.; Rita Morelli,
V.P.

EIN: 383494266

Selected grants: The following grants were reported
in 2003.

$35,000 to National Shrine of the Little Flower
Catholic Church, Royal Oak, MI.

$24,576 to Barbara Ann Karmanos Cancer Institute,
Detroit, MI.

$24,576 to Capuchin Soup Kitchen, Detroit, MI.

$24,576 to Guest House, Lake Orion, MI. For
program support.

$24,576 to Leader Dogs for the Blind, Rochester,
MI.

$24,576 to Little Sisters of the Poor, Detroit, MI.

$24,576 to March of Dimes Birth Defects
Foundation, Southfield, MI.

$24,576 to Saint Jude Childrens Research Hospital,
Memphis, TN.

$24,576 to Saint Vincent de Paul Society, Detroit,
MI.

$2,000 to Angels Place, Southfield, MI.

4396
Monroe-Brown Foundation ◇

7950 Moorsbridge Rd.

Portage, MI 49024   (269) 324-5586

Contact: Jane Baker, Dir.

FAX: (269) 324-0686;

E-mail: info@monroebrown.org; *URL:* http://
www.monroebrown.org

Incorporated in 1983 in MI.

Donors: Albertine M. Brown†; Robert J. Brown†;
Robert M. Brown; Gail B. Kasdorf; Jane B. Todd;
Robert J. Brown Charitable Lead Trust.

Foundation type: Independent foundation.

Financial data (yr. ended 12/31/05): Assets,
$15,820,156 (M); gifts received, $153,562;
expenditures, $946,452; qualifying distributions,
$831,318; giving activities include $760,906 for 39
grants (high: $146,000; low: $100; average:
$1,000–$15,000).

Purpose and activities: Support primarily for
education and community improvement.

Fields of interest: Arts; Higher education;
Education; Human services; Urban/community
development; Foundations (community).

Type of support: Annual campaigns; Capital
campaigns; Building/renovation; Program
development; Matching/challenge support.

Limitations: Giving primarily in the Kalamazoo, MI
area. No grants to individuals.

Publications: Application guidelines.

Application information: Application guidelines and
form available on foundation Web site. Application
form required.

Initial approach: Letter

Copies of proposal: 7

Deadline(s): Mar. 31, June 30, Sept. 30, and Nov.
20

Board meeting date(s): Apr., July, Oct. and Dec.

Officers and Trustees:* Robert M. Brown,* Pres.;
Gail B. Kasdorf,* V.P.; Jane B. Todd,* Treas.;
Frederick O. Brown; Robert M. Brown, Jr.; A. John
Todd; John C. Wattles.

Director: Jane Baker.

Number of staff: 1 full-time professional.

EIN: 382513263

Selected grants: The following grants were reported
in 2004.

$192,486 to Western Michigan University
Foundation, Kalamazoo, MI. 2 grants: $82,486,
$110,000

$116,989 to Kalamazoo College, Kalamazoo, MI.

$57,200 to Kalamazoo Community Foundation,
Kalamazoo, MI. 2 grants: $57,000, $200

$31,133 to Kalamazoo Valley Community College,
Kalamazoo, MI.

$15,000 to Irving S. Gilmore International Keyboard
Festival, Kalamazoo, MI.

$10,000 to Kalamazoo Symphony Orchestra,
Kalamazoo, MI.

$2,900 to Western Michigan University, Kalamazoo,
MI.

$2,097 to Kalamazoo Institute of Arts, Kalamazoo,
MI.

4397
The Morey Foundation ◇ ☆

P.O. Box 1000

Winn, MI 48896

Contact: Lon Morey, Pres.

Established in 1990 in MI.

Donor: Norval Morey.

Foundation type: Independent foundation.

Financial data (yr. ended 12/31/05): Assets,
$37,432,216 (M); expenditures, $854,067;
qualifying distributions, $430,085; giving activities
include $422,564 for 15 grants (high: $100,000;
low: $810).

Fields of interest: Higher education; Education;
Human services.

Type of support: Scholarship funds.

Limitations: Giving primarily in MI. No grants to
individuals directly.

Application information: Application form required
for scholarship requests.

Initial approach: Letter

Deadline(s): Mar. 15 for Scholarships; none for
grants

Officers and Trustee:* Lon Morey,* Pres.; Jeffery
Power, Secy.; Larry H. Hoch, Treas.

Directors: Krista Morey; Terra Morey.

EIN: 382965346

4398
The Mosaic Foundation of R. & P.
Heydon ◇

2394 Winewood St.

P.O. Box 7801

Ann Arbor, MI 48107-7801

Established in 1990 in MI.

Donors: Kenneth F. Montgomery; Peter N. Heydon;
Henrietta M. Heydon.

Foundation type: Independent foundation.

Financial data (yr. ended 12/31/04): Assets,
$2,778,320 (M); expenditures, $400,809;
qualifying distributions, $366,984; giving activities
include $365,529 for 118 grants (high: $37,500;
low: $100), and $1,445 for 1 loan/program-related
investment.

Purpose and activities: Giving primarily for the arts
and education.

Fields of interest: Media, radio; Museums;
Performing arts; Arts; Elementary/secondary
education; Higher education; Environment;
Animals/wildlife; Human services.

Limitations: Applications not accepted. Giving in the
U.S., with emphasis on MI. No grants to individuals.

Application information: Contributes only to
pre-selected organizations.

Directors: James R. Beuche; Henrietta M. Heydon;
Peter N. Heydon.

EIN: 382910797

4399
Charles Stewart Mott Foundation ▼

c/o Office of Proposal Entry
Mott Foundation Bldg.
503 S. Saginaw St., Ste. 1200
Flint, MI 48502-1851 (810) 238-5651
FAX: (810) 766-1753; E-mail: info@mott.org;
Additional e-mail: publications@mott.org;
URL: http://www.mott.org

Incorporated in 1926 in MI.
Donors: Charles Stewart Mott‡; and family.
Foundation type: Independent foundation.
Financial data (yr. ended 12/31/05): Assets,
$2,480,562,766 (M); expenditures,
$137,952,616; qualifying distributions,
$126,989,113; giving activities include
$111,716,462 for grants, $1,036,470 for 688
employee matching gifts, and $581,449 for 12
foundation-administered programs.
Purpose and activities: To support efforts that
promote a just, equitable and sustainable society
with the primary focus on civil society, the
environment, the area of Flint, MI and poverty. The
foundation makes grants for a variety of purposes
within these program areas including: philanthropy
and voluntarism; assisting emerging civil societies
in Central/Eastern Europe, Russia and South Africa;
conservation of fresh water ecosystems in North
America; reform of international finance and trade;
improving the outcomes for children, youth and
families at risk of persistent poverty; education and
neighborhood and economic development. The
foundation also makes grants to strengthen the
capacity of local institutions in its home community
of Flint, MI.
Fields of interest: Education; Environment, pollution
control; Environment, natural resources; Human
services; Children, services; Child development,
services; Family services, parent education; Civil
rights, race/intergroup relations; Economic
development; Urban/community development;
Rural development; Community development;
Voluntarism promotion; Leadership development;
Minorities; Economically disadvantaged.
International interests: Eastern Europe; Latin
America; Russia; South Africa.
Type of support: General/operating support;
Continuing support; Program development;
Conferences/seminars; Seed money; Technical
assistance; Program evaluation; Employee
matching gifts; Matching/challenge support.
Limitations: Giving nationally and to emerging
countries in Central and Eastern Europe, Russia,
and South Africa. No support for religious
organizations for religious purposes. No grants to
individuals, or for building or endowment funds in
general or for research, film or video projects,
books, scholarships, or fellowships.
Publications: Annual report (including application
guidelines); Financial statement; Informational
brochure (including application guidelines);
Newsletter; Occasional report; Program policy
statement.
Application information: Applicants strongly
encouraged to submit proposals during first quarter
of the year. Application form not required.
Initial approach: Letter of inquiry or proposal
Copies of proposal: 1
Deadline(s): None; grants are determined by Aug.
31 of any given year
Board meeting date(s): Mar., June, Sept., and
Dec.
Final notification: 60 to 90 days

Officers and Trustees:* William S. White,* Chair.,
C.E.O. and Pres.; William H. Piper,* Vice-Chair.;
Maureen H. Smyth, Sr. V.P., Progs. and Comms.;
Phillip H. Peters, V.P., Admin. Group and
Secy.-Treas.; Michael J. Smith, V.P., Investments
and C.I.O.; Gavin T. Clabaugh, V.P., Inf. Svcs.;
Marilyn S. LeFeber, V.P., Comms.; A. Marshall Acuff,
Jr.; Rushworth M. Kidder; Tiffany W. Lovett; Webb F.
Martin; Olivia P. Maynard; John Morning; Maryanne
Mott; Douglas X. Patino; John W. Porter; Marise
M.M. Stewart; Claire M. White.
Number of staff: 60 full-time professional; 1
part-time professional; 26 full-time support.
EIN: 381211227
Selected grants: The following grants were reported
in 2005.
$2,500,000 to Foundations, Inc., Moorestown, NJ.
   For technical assistance for After-School
   Academies which will create system of services
   that enables after-school staff to design,
   implement, evaluate and manage programs that
   promote student success, payable over 3 years.
$2,500,000 to Nature Conservancy, Arlington, VA.
   For land acquisition as part of Northern Great
   Lakes Forest Project, payable over 6 years.
$1,500,000 to Foundation for the Uptown
   Reinvestment Corporation, Flint, MI. For mixed
   use development of three buildings in downtown
   Flint for use as office, restaurant and residential
   space adding jobs and redevelopment activity in
   Flint.
$1,225,000 to Collaborative Communications
   Group, DC. For Statewide After-School Network
   Meetings, initiative to promote learning and
   development for elementary school-age children
   through quality programs that provide safety and
   enrichment outside the traditional classroom,
   payable over 2 years.
$1,000,000 to Southern Education Foundation,
   Atlanta, GA. For regranting project which will
   establish Presidential Leadership Fund to benefit
   historically black Dillard and Xavier Universities
   which were forced to close due to Hurricane
   Katrina. Rebuilding efforts will include salaries
   for core administrators, faculty and staff and
   consulting support related to damage
   assessment and rebuilding and restoration of
   campus facilities.
$751,000 to Jobs for the Future, Boston, MA. For
   demonstration project/study to address
   challenges facing community colleges in helping
   low-income adults increase their skills and
   earnings. Study will identify better ways to move
   from adult basic education programs directly into
   college credit programs, and also try to identify
   effective strategies to enhance abilities of
   students in remedial programs to complete
   occupational certificates or associate degree
   programs.
$700,000 to Commonwealth Corporation, Boston,
   MA. For support for Diploma Plus, program that
   reconnects young people who have dropped out
   of school to the economy and higher education,
   payable over 3 years.
$652,000 to Tip of the Mitt Watershed Council,
   Petoskey, MI. For Great Lakes Aquatic Habitat
   Network and Fund, organization providing
   information and financial support to grassroots
   citizen initiatives working to protect and restore
   Great Lakes shorelines, inland lakes, rivers,
   wetlands, and other aquatic habitats in the Great
   Lakes Basin, payable over 2 years.
$600,000 to Center on Budget and Policy Priorities,
   DC. For continued support for State Fiscal

Project, effort to build state-based capacity to
   address issues of state budget priorities,
   revenue systems and program design and for
   State Low-Income Initiatives designed to meet
   challenges devolution poses by helping state
   organizations and policymakers develop policy
   options, analyze emerging proposals and
   consider promising new approaches to alleviating
   poverty, payable over 2 years.
$600,000 to Youth Law Center, San Francisco, CA.
   To expand policies for educational opportunities
   for vulnerable youth, payable over 3 years.

4400
Ruth Mott Foundation ▼ ✧

111 E. Court St., Ste. 3C
Flint, MI 48502-1649 (810) 233-0170
Contact: Joy Murray, Fdn. Secy.
FAX: (810) 233-7022; E-mail: rmf@rmfdn.org; E-mail
(for Joy Murray): jmurray@rmfdn.org; URL: http://
www.ruthmottfoundation.org

Established in 1989 in MI.
Donor: Ruth R. Mott‡.
Foundation type: Independent foundation.
Financial data (yr. ended 12/31/04): Assets,
$212,620,490 (M); gifts received, $400,000;
expenditures, $9,238,493; qualifying distributions,
$8,725,477; giving activities include $5,875,517
for 134 grants (high: $254,000; low: $136;
average: $25,000–$100,000), and $1,613,464 for
4 foundation-administered programs.
Purpose and activities: Giving primarily for
community arts, community health promotion, and
community beautification.
Fields of interest: Arts, cultural/ethnic awareness;
Arts; Higher education; Libraries (public); Education;
Health care; Youth development; Human services;
Children/youth, services; Community development;
Foundations (community); Federated giving
programs; Protestant agencies & churches.
Type of support: General/operating support;
Continuing support; Management development/
capacity building; Program development;
Scholarship funds; Technical assistance; Program
evaluation; Matching/challenge support.
Limitations: Giving primarily in Genesee County and
Flint, MI. No support for religious programs for
religious purposes. No grants to individuals.
Publications: Informational brochure (including
application guidelines).
Application information: Application form not
required.
Initial approach: Letter (2 - 3 pages)
Deadline(s): Jan. 15, Apr. 15, and Aug. 15
Board meeting date(s): Mar., June, and Oct.
Final notification: 1 month
Officers & Trustees: Susan S. Pool, C.O.O.;
Maryanne T. Mott, Pres.; Sandra K. Butler, Secy.;
Herman E. Warsh, Tr. Emeritus; Charles B. Webb,
Jr., Tr. Emeritus; Joseph R. Robinson; Virginia M.
Sullivan.
Number of staff: 9 full-time professional; 12 full-time
support; 4 part-time support.
EIN: 382876435
Selected grants: The following grants were reported
in 2004.
$284,360 to United Way of Genesee County, Flint,
   MI. 2 grants: $117,250 (For Keep Genesee
   County Beautiful program), $167,110 (For local
   child advocacy center).

$254,000 to Community Foundation of Greater Flint, Flint, MI. For downtown facade improvement.

$206,293 to Michigan Primary Care Association, Okemos, MI. For School-Community Health Alliance.

$184,475 to Mott Community College, Flint, MI. For Beecher Scholarship program.

$150,640 to Flint Institute of Arts, Flint, MI. For Lewandowski mosaic murals rescue.

$64,005 to Ready Set Grow Passport Initiative, Flint, MI.

$50,550 to Faith Access to Community Economic Development (FACED), Flint, MI. For faith-based health team initiative.

$25,000 to Greater Flint Arts Council, Flint, MI. For Flint Jazz Festival.

$21,565 to Council on Foundations, DC. For special initiatives, charitable programs.

4401
The Mozer Foundation ◇ ☆
500 Woodward Ave., Ste 2500
Detroit, MI 48226

Established in 2001 in MI.
Donor: Rudolf W. Mozer.
Foundation type: Independent foundation.
Financial data (yr. ended 12/31/05): Assets, $9,307 (M); expenditures, $527,964; qualifying distributions, $518,000; giving activities include $518,000 for grants.
Limitations: Applications not accepted.
Application information: Contributes only to pre-selected organizations.
Officers and Directors:* Rudolf W. Mozer,* Chair.; Eleanor M. Wagner,* Secy.; Karen M. Hoke,* Treas.; Eric Mozer.
EIN: 383573403

4402
David & Carol Myers Foundation ◇
(formerly David G. & Carol P. Myers Charitable Foundation)
c/o Carol P. Myers
109 W. 12th St.
Holland, MI 49423

Established in 1989 in MI.
Donors: David G. Myers; Carol P. Myers.
Foundation type: Independent foundation.
Financial data (yr. ended 12/31/05): Assets, $20,611,430 (M); expenditures, $1,035,546; qualifying distributions, $662,639; giving activities include $662,639 for grants.
Fields of interest: Higher education; Theological school/education; Human services; Religion.
Limitations: Applications not accepted. Giving on a national basis. No grants to individuals.
Application information: Contributes only to pre-selected organizations.
Board meeting date(s): Spring
Officers: Carol P. Myers, Pres.; David G. Myers, V.P.
EIN: 382884733

4403
The Nickless Family Charitable Foundation ◇ ☆
2121 University Park Dr., Ste. 150
Okemos, MI 48864
Application address: c/o James E. McCartney, Secy., P.O. Box 23125, Lansing, MI 48909-3125, tel.: (517) 347-5000

Established in 2000 in MI.
Foundation type: Independent foundation.
Financial data (yr. ended 12/31/05): Assets, $674,497 (M); gifts received, $959,502; expenditures, $504,280; qualifying distributions, $502,411; giving activities include $500,000 for 1 grant.
Purpose and activities: Giving primarily to a medical foundation for a volunteer clinic.
Fields of interest: Health organizations, association.
Limitations: Giving primarily in the Sun City West, AZ, and Bay City, MI, areas. No grants to individuals.
Application information: Application form not required.
Deadline(s): None
Officers: Arthur H. Nickless, Pres.; Judy N. Graham, V.P.; Joan N. Tankersley, V.P.; James E. McCartney, Secy.; Janet Royce, Treas.
EIN: 383501091

4404
The Nokomis Foundation ◇
161 Ottawa Ave. N.W., Ste. 305-C
Grand Rapids, MI 49503 (616) 451-0267
Contact: Kymberly Mulhern, C.E.O.
FAX: (616) 451-9914;
E-mail: info@nokomisfoundation.org; Additional E-mail for Kymberly Mulhern, C.E.O.: kmulhern@nokomisfoundation.org; URL: http://www.nokomisfoundation.org

Established in 1989 in MI.
Donor: Mary Caroline "Twink" Frey.
Foundation type: Independent foundation.
Financial data (yr. ended 12/31/05): Assets, $16,959,027 (M); expenditures, $1,379,263; qualifying distributions, $1,139,535; giving activities include $703,795 for 77 grants (high: $50,000; low: $250; average: $5,000–$20,000).
Purpose and activities: Giving to organizations whose efforts are directed primarily toward women and girls, and which are working in advocacy, community awareness and education, and public policy. Preference is given to social change efforts rather than to social services.
Fields of interest: Women, centers/services; Civil rights, advocacy; Community development, women's clubs; Women.
Type of support: General/operating support; Management development/capacity building; Program development; Seed money; Technical assistance; Program evaluation.
Limitations: Applications not accepted. Giving primarily in the greater Grand Rapids area and in Allegan, Kent, and Ottawa counties in western MI. No support for religious purposes. No grants to individuals, or for capital requests, endowments, equipment, renovations, medical research, fellowships, scholarships, or conferences.
Publications: Biennial report; Grants list; Informational brochure; Occasional report.

Application information: The foundation will not accept new unsolicited grant proposals while it undergoes a comprehensive planning and renewal process. The foundation will continue to award grants during this time, but such awards will be limited to pre-selected funding partners. See foundation Web site for periodic updates about the renewal process.
Board meeting date(s): Quarterly
Officers and Trustees:* Mary Caroline "Twink" Frey,* Chair.; Kymberly Mulhern,* C.E.O. and Pres.; James E. McKay,* Treas.; Patricia Oldt; Joel J. Orosz; Faye Richardson; Mary Alice Williams.
Number of staff: 2 full-time professional; 1 part-time professional; 2 part-time support.
EIN: 382882220

4405
Oleson Foundation ◇
6645 N. Long Lake Rd.
Traverse City, MI 49684-9607
Contact: John R. Spencer M.D., Dir.

Established in 1959 in MI.
Donors: Gerald W. Oleson†; Frances M. Oleson†.
Foundation type: Independent foundation.
Financial data (yr. ended 12/31/04): Assets, $17,299,255 (M); expenditures, $1,155,268; qualifying distributions, $835,900; giving activities include $833,046 for 77 grants (high: $75,000; low: $300).
Purpose and activities: Giving primarily for education and human services.
Fields of interest: Historic preservation/historical societies; Elementary/secondary education; Higher education; Environment; Health care; Youth development, centers/clubs; Human services; Federated giving programs; Christian agencies & churches.
Type of support: General/operating support; Continuing support; Annual campaigns; Capital campaigns; Building/renovation; Equipment; Land acquisition; Curriculum development; Matching/challenge support.
Limitations: Giving primarily in northwestern MI's Lower Peninsula region. No grants to individuals.
Application information: Application form required.
Initial approach: 1-page letter
Copies of proposal: 1
Deadline(s): Apr. 15
Board meeting date(s): June
Final notification: Usually in late June
Officers and Directors:* Donald W. Oleson,* Pres.; Gerald E. Oleson,* V.P.; Richard Ford,* Secy.-Treas.; John R. Spencer, M.D.; John Tobin.
Number of staff: 1 part-time professional.
EIN: 386083080
Selected grants: The following grants were reported in 2004.

$35,000 to Boy Scouts of America, Scenic Trails Council, Traverse City, MI.

$35,000 to Grand Traverse Regional Land Conservancy, Traverse City, MI.

$34,500 to Traverse City Area Public Schools, Traverse City, MI.

$25,000 to Inland Seas Education Association, Suttons Bay, MI.

$25,000 to Munson Healthcare Regional Foundation, Traverse City, MI.

$25,000 to Traverse Area District Library, Traverse City, MI.

$21,250 to Saint Marys School, Lake Leelanau, MI.

$20,000 to Michigan Community Blood Centers Foundation, Grand Rapids, MI.

$17,461 to Northwestern Michigan College, Traverse City, MI.

$17,000 to Mount Holiday, Traverse City, MI.

4406

Louis and Helen Padnos Foundation ✧ ☆

P.O. Box 1979
Holland, MI 49422-1979

Established in 1999 in MI.

Donors: Louis & Helen Padnos Foundation; Louis Padnos Iron and Metal Co.

Foundation type: Independent foundation.

Financial data (yr. ended 5/31/05): Assets, $7,008,757 (M); gifts received, $645,480; expenditures, $377,402; qualifying distributions, $360,342; giving activities include $358,726 for 121 grants (high: $91,000; low: $50).

Purpose and activities: Giving primarily to Jewish organizations and a community foundation; funding also for health care, education, youth and social services, and the arts.

Fields of interest: Museums; Arts; Education; Hospitals (general); Reproductive health, family planning; Cancer; Health organizations; Boys & girls clubs; Human services; Residential/custodial care, hospices; Jewish federated giving programs; Jewish agencies & temples.

Limitations: Applications not accepted. Giving primarily in MI, with emphasis on Grand Rapids and Holland. No grants to individuals.

Application information: Contributes only to pre-selected organizations.

Officers and Trustees:* Jeffrey S. Padnos,* Pres.; Shelley E. Padnos,* Secy.; Mitchell W. Padnos,* Treas.; Cynthia B. Padnos; Daniel P. Padnos; Douglas B. Padnos; William R. Padnos.

EIN: 383476218

Selected grants: The following grants were reported in 2005.

$25,000 to Black River Public School, Holland, MI.

$25,000 to Boys and Girls Club of Holland, Holland, NY.

$15,000 to Grand Rapids Art Museum, Grand Rapids, MI.

$10,000 to Childrens Hospital of Michigan, Detroit, MI.

$5,000 to Holland Area Arts Council, Holland, MI.

$5,000 to YWCA.

$2,500 to Holland Community Hospital Foundation, Holland, MI.

$1,000 to Michigan Military Preservation Society, Grand Rapids, MI.

$400 to Alternative House Highland Station, Lowell, MA.

$100 to Gerald R. Ford Foundation, Grand Rapids, MI.

4407

Elsa U. Pardee Foundation ▼

P.O. Box 2767
Midland, MI 48641-2767
Contact: James A. Kendall, Secy.
FAX: (989) 832-8842; *E-mail:* lucille@tm.net;
URL: http://www.pardeefoundation.org

Incorporated in 1944 in MI.
Donor: Elsa U. Pardee†.
Foundation type: Independent foundation.

Financial data (yr. ended 12/31/05): Assets, $106,019,850 (M); gifts received, $100; expenditures, $5,449,762; qualifying distributions, $5,153,240; giving activities include $5,100,135 for 48 grants (high: $247,122; low: $6,000; average: $50,000–$225,000).

Purpose and activities: Giving primarily to support: 1) research programs directed toward discovering new approaches for cancer treatment and cure; and 2) financial support for cancer treatment.

Fields of interest: Cancer; Medical research, institute; Cancer research.

Type of support: Research.

Application information: See website for application guidelines.

Initial approach: Online Application
Copies of proposal: 8
Deadline(s): None
Board meeting date(s): 3 times per year
Final notification: 4 to 6 months

Officers and Trustees:* Gail E. Lanphear,* Pres.; Lisa J. Gerstacker,* V.P.; James A. Kendall,* Secy.; Alan W. Ott,* Treas.; W. James Allen; Richard J. Kociba; Mary M. Neely; Patrick J. Oriel; William D. Schuette.

Number of staff: 1 part-time support.

EIN: 386065799

Selected grants: The following grants were reported in 2005.

$435,000 to Pardee Cancer Treatment Fund of Midland/Gladwin, Midland, MI. For cancer cure and control program.

$247,122 to Temple University, Philadelphia, PA. For study of BCR/ABL regulates Rad51 in recombination.

$225,000 to Pardee Cancer Treatment Fund of Isabella County, Mount Pleasant, MI. For cancer cure and control program.

$217,308 to Wayne State University, Detroit, MI. For study of identification of genes relevant to liver metastasis of pancreatic cancer.

$183,600 to Albert Einstein College of Medicine of Yeshiva University, Bronx, NY. For study of CAV-I in advanced prostate cancer and metastasis.

$176,072 to Boston Biomedical Research Institute, Boston, MA. For study of engineered superantigens for targeted tumor immunotherapy.

$175,000 to Pardee Cancer Treatment Fund of Bay County, Bay City, MI. For cancer cure and control program.

$164,355 to Wistar Institute of Anatomy and Biology, Philadelphia, PA. For study of identification of metastasis suppressor genes using functional genomics approach.

$150,000 to Pardee Cancer Treatment Fund of Clare County, Clare, MI. For cancer cure and control program.

$88,008 to Roswell Park Cancer Institute, Buffalo, NY. For study of estrogen receptor-tumor suppressor p53 interaction: How does it affect mammary tumorigenesis.

4408

Suzanne Upjohn Delano Parish Foundation ✧

(formerly Suzanne D. Parish Foundation)
100 W. Michigan Ave., Ste. 100
Kalamazoo, MI 49007 (269) 388-9800
Contact: Ronald N. Kilgore, V.P.

Established in MI.
Donor: Suzanne U.D. Parish.

Foundation type: Independent foundation.

Financial data (yr. ended 12/31/04): Assets, $7,582,816 (M); expenditures, $522,404; qualifying distributions, $508,105; giving activities include $500,000 for 1 grant.

Purpose and activities: Support primarily to an aviation history museum.

Fields of interest: Museums (history); Space/aviation.

Type of support: General/operating support.

Limitations: Giving primarily in Kalamazoo, MI. No grants to individuals; no loans.

Application information:

Initial approach: Letter
Deadline(s): None

Officers and Directors:* Suzanne U.D. Parish,* Pres. and Secy.; Ronald N. Kilgore,* V.P. and Treas.; Katharine P. Miller; Preston L. Parish.

EIN: 382484268

Selected grants: The following grants were reported in 2004.

$500,000 to Kalamazoo Aviation History Museum, Kalamazoo, MI.

4409

Anna Paulina Foundation ✧

3400 W. Bristol Rd.
Flint, MI 48507-3112
Contact: Albert J. Koegel, Treas.

Established in 1961 in MI.

Donors: Albert J. Koegel; Anne Rocco; Kathryn Koegel; Jane Koegel; John Koegel; Sunset Hills Assn.

Foundation type: Independent foundation.

Financial data (yr. ended 12/31/05): Assets, $12,024,605 (M); gifts received, $794,200; expenditures, $893,541; qualifying distributions, $893,541; giving activities include $877,891 for 98 grants (high: $500,000; low: $25).

Fields of interest: Arts; Education; Human services; YM/YWCAs & YM/YWHAs; Federated giving programs; Christian agencies & churches.

Limitations: Applications not accepted. Giving primarily in the Genesee County, MI, area. No grants to individuals.

Application information: Contributes only to pre-selected organizations. Unsolicited applications not considered.

Officers: Kathryn Koegel, Pres.; Elizabeth M. Neithercut, V.P.; Jeffry D. Rocco, Secy.; Albert J. Koegel, Treas.

Trustees: Barbara L. Koegel; Jane Koegel; John C. Koegel; Lisa A. Koegel; Edward J. Neithercut; Anne Koegel Rocco.

EIN: 386061335

Selected grants: The following grants were reported in 2004.

$502,950 to YMCA, Flint, Flint, MI.

$152,595 to Flint Institute of Arts, Flint, MI.

$100,375 to Boy Scouts of America, Flint, MI.

$60,000 to Culver Educational Foundation, Culver, IN.

$20,100 to Young Life, Flint, MI.

$11,000 to American Red Cross, Flint, MI.

$8,404 to Flint Community Players, Flint, MI.

$3,680 to Flint Institute of Music, Flint, MI.

$1,100 to Hillsdale College, Hillsdale, MI.

$500 to Urban League of Flint, Flint, MI.

4410
Perrigo Company Charitable Foundation ◇
515 Eastern Ave.
Allegan, MI 49010

Established in 2000 in MI.
Donor: L. Perrigo Co.
Foundation type: Company-sponsored foundation.
Financial data (yr. ended 6/30/05): Assets,
$781,028 (M); gifts received, $600,000;
expenditures, $994,557; qualifying distributions,
$995,282; giving activities include $995,282 for
129 grants (high: $200,000; low: $100).
Purpose and activities: The foundation supports
organizations involved with arts and culture,
education, health, medical research, youth
development, and human services.
Fields of interest: Arts; Elementary/secondary
education; Higher education; Education; Health
care; Cancer research; Medical research; Youth
development; Human services; Foundations
(community); Federated giving programs.
Type of support: Building/renovation; Program
development.
Limitations: Applications not accepted. Giving
primarily in MI. No grants to individuals.
Application information: Contributes only to
pre-selected organizations.
Officers: David T. Gibbons, Pres.; Douglas R.
Schrank, Exec. V.P. and C.F.O.; John T. Hendrickson,
Exec. V.P.; Todd W. Kingma, Secy.; James R.
Ondersma, Treas.
EIN: 383553518
Selected grants: The following grants were reported
in 2005.
$200,000 to University of Michigan, Ann Arbor, MI.
$150,841 to United Way, Allegan County, Allegan,
  MI.
$20,000 to Allegan Area Arts Council, Allegan, MI.
$20,000 to American Red Cross, Adrian, MI.
$8,000 to Allegan Public Schools, Allegan, MI.
$7,000 to Allegan County Community Foundation,
  Allegan, MI.
$5,000 to Grand Rapids Art Museum, Grand Rapids,
  MI.
$3,050 to Holy Cross Childrens Services, Clinton,
  MI.
$2,000 to Davenport University Foundation, Grand
  Rapids, MI.
$1,000 to Community Action House, Holland, MI.

4411
Dean & Diane Petitpren Family
Foundation ◇ ☆
44500 N. Groesbeck Hwy.
Clinton Township, MI 48036-1111

Established in 2003 in MI.
Donors: Dean Petitpren; Diane Petitpren.
Foundation type: Independent foundation.
Financial data (yr. ended 12/31/05): Assets,
$41,753 (M); gifts received, $350,000;
expenditures, $326,600; qualifying distributions,
$326,600; giving activities include $326,600 for 4
+ grants (high: $250,000).
Fields of interest: Arts; Education; Human services;
Federated giving programs.
Limitations: Applications not accepted. Giving
primarily in MI. No grants to individuals.
Application information: Contributes only to
pre-selected organizations.

Officers and Directors:* Dean Petitpren,* Pres.;
Diane Petitpren,* Secy.-Treas.
EIN: 200129571

4412
Petoskey-Harbor Springs Area Community
Foundation
616 Petoskey St., Ste. 100
Petoskey, MI 49770 (231) 348-5820
Contact: Maureen M. Nicholson, Exec. Dir.
FAX: (231) 348-5883; E-mail: info@phsacf.org;
Additional E-mails: mnicholson@phsacf.org and
lwendland@phsacf.org; URL: http://
www.petoskey-harborspringsfoundation.org

Established in 1991 in MI.
Foundation type: Community foundation.
Financial data (yr. ended 3/31/05): Assets,
$10,166,572 (M); gifts received, $1,090,124;
expenditures, $745,296; giving activities include
$409,144 for 103 grants (high: $28,224; low: $50;
average: $50–$15,000), and $32,000 for 18 grants
to individuals (high: $10,000; low: $500).
Purpose and activities: The foundation awards
grants to nonprofit organizations, schools, and
municipalities in Emmet County, MI or to those that
serve a significant number of Emmet County
residents.
Fields of interest: Historic preservation/historical
societies; Arts; Higher education; Education;
Environment; Health care; Recreation; Youth
development; Human services; Economic
development; Community development.
Type of support: Building/renovation; Equipment;
Program development; Seed money; Scholarship
funds; Technical assistance; Scholarships—to
individuals; Matching/challenge support.
Limitations: Giving limited to Emmet County, MI. No
support for sectarian religious purposes. No grants
to individuals (except for scholarships), or for
endowments, debt reduction, annual fundraising
drives, operational phases of established programs,
conferences, travel, or scholarly research; no loans.
Publications: Application guidelines; Annual report;
Financial statement; Informational brochure.
Application information: Potential applicants must
contact the foundation prior to submitting an
application to discuss their project. Visit foundation
Web site for application information. Application
form required.
  Initial approach: Telephone
  Copies of proposal: 30
  Deadline(s): Early Apr. and early Oct.
  Board meeting date(s): Monthly
  Final notification: Approx. 2 months
Officers and Directors:* James T. Ramer,* Pres.;
Louise T. Graham,* V.P.; David T. Buzzelli,* Secy.;
Maureen M. Nicholson, Exec. Dir.; Sandra T. Baker;
Lisa G. Blanchard; Kristin K. Clark; Jane T.
Damschroder; Michael FitzSimons; Charles H.
Gano; Charles W. Johnson; Kate Marshall; Virginia
B. McCoy; Philip H. Millard; Kyle Ronquist; Todd
Winnell.
Number of staff: 2 full-time professional; 1 full-time
support.
EIN: 383032185

4413
Murray C. and Ina C. Pitt Charitable
Trust ◇
2000 Town Ctr., Ste. 1350
Southfield, MI 48075

Established in 1995 in MI.
Donor: Murray C. Pitt.
Foundation type: Independent foundation.
Financial data (yr. ended 11/30/05): Assets,
$1,905,889 (M); expenditures, $630,699;
qualifying distributions, $551,008; giving activities
include $550,068 for 49 grants (high: $203,056;
low: $100).
Purpose and activities: Giving primarily to Jewish
agencies, temples, and federated giving programs;
funding also for education, health, and human
services.
Fields of interest: Arts; Higher education;
Education; Mental health/crisis services; Health
organizations; Cancer research; Human services;
Civil rights; Federated giving programs; Jewish
federated giving programs; Jewish agencies &
temples.
Limitations: Applications not accepted. Giving
primarily in MI; some funding in CO and NY. No
grants to individuals.
Application information: Contributes only to
pre-selected organizations.
Officers: Murray C. Pitt, Pres.; Ina C. Pitt, V.P.;
Carleen F. Lunsford, Secy.-Treas.
Directors: Erin R. Frankel; Jeffery S. Pitt.
EIN: 383268352

4414
Plym Foundation ◇
P.O. Box 906
Niles, MI 49120-0906
Application address: c/o Donald F. Walter, V.P., 423
Sycamore St., Ste. 101, Niles, MI 49120, tel.: (269)
684-3248

Incorporated in 1952 in MI.
Donor: Mrs. Francis J. Plym†.
Foundation type: Independent foundation.
Financial data (yr. ended 12/31/05): Assets,
$6,664,919 (M); expenditures, $549,711;
qualifying distributions, $446,650; giving activities
include $420,050 for 13+ grants (high: $75,000).
Purpose and activities: Giving primarily for higher
education and human services.
Fields of interest: Higher education; Education;
Human services.
Type of support: Building/renovation; Program
development; Matching/challenge support.
Limitations: Giving primarily in MI. No grants to
individuals.
Application information: Application form not
required.
  Initial approach: Letter or telephone
  Copies of proposal: 1
  Deadline(s): None
  Board meeting date(s): May
Officers and Trustees:* J. Eric Plym,* Pres.; Donald
F. Walter,* V.P. and Treas.; Sarah P. Campbell,*
V.P.; Andrew J. Plym,* V.P.; James F. Keenan, Secy.;
John M. Campbell; John E. Plym, Jr.
EIN: 386069680

4415
The Power Foundation ☆
c/o James C. Melvin, Secy.
136 E. Michigan Ave., Ste. 1201
Kalamazoo, MI 49007

Established in 1967 in MI.
Donors: Eugene B. Power†; Sadye H. Power†; Philip H. Power.
Foundation type: Independent foundation.
Financial data (yr. ended 12/31/05): Assets, $8,151,904 (M); gifts received, $858,846; expenditures, $441,481; qualifying distributions, $382,806; giving activities include $326,364 for 33 grants (high: $100,000; low: $500).
Purpose and activities: Giving for higher education, the arts, social services, and natural resource preservation and enhancement.
Fields of interest: Arts; Higher education; Education; Mental health/crisis services; Community development.
Type of support: General/operating support; Continuing support; Annual campaigns; Capital campaigns; Building/renovation; Research.
Limitations: Applications not accepted. Giving primarily in MI, with emphasis on Ann Arbor.
Application information: Unsolicited requests for funds not accepted.
Officers and Trustees:* Philip H. Power,* Pres.; Kathleen K. Power,* V.P.; James C. Melvin,* Secy.; James S. Hilboldt,* Treas.
EIN: 386119490
Selected grants: The following grants were reported in 2004.
$100,000 to Nature Conservancy, Lansing, MI.
$30,000 to University Musical Society, Ann Arbor, MI.
$28,600 to University of Michigan, Ann Arbor, MI.
$26,000 to Saint Andrews Episcopal Church, Ann Arbor, MI. 2 grants: $6,000, $20,000
$25,000 to Non-Profit Enterprise at Work, Ann Arbor, MI.
$2,000 to Huron Mountain Wildlife Foundation, Ann Arbor, MI.
$1,000 to Congregation Emanuel, Denver, CO.
$1,000 to United Negro College Fund, Detroit, MI.
$1,000 to University of Wisconsin Foundation, Madison, WI.

4416
Edgar and Elsa Prince Foundation ▼ ◇
(formerly Prince Foundation)
190 River Ave., Ste. 300
Holland, MI 49423 (616) 494-8143

Established in 1977.
Donors: Edgar D. Prince†; Elsa D. Prince; Prince Corp.
Foundation type: Independent foundation.
Financial data (yr. ended 6/30/05): Assets, $23,256,168 (M); expenditures, $5,365,145; qualifying distributions, $4,954,103; giving activities include $4,948,250 for 157 grants (high: $500,000; low: $250; average: $1,000–$100,000).
Purpose and activities: Giving to Christian organizations, churches, and schools and community activities.
Fields of interest: Elementary/secondary education; Health organizations, association; Family services; Aging, centers/services; Community development, neighborhood development; Christian agencies & churches; Aging.

Type of support: General/operating support.
Limitations: Applications not accepted. Giving primarily in MI. No grants to individuals.
Application information: Contributes only to pre-selected organizations.
Officers: Elsa D. Prince, Pres.; Elisabeth DeVos, V.P.; Eileen Ellens, V.P.; Erik D. Prince, V.P.; Emilie Wierda, V.P.; Robert Haveman, Secy.-Treas.
EIN: 382190330
Selected grants: The following grants were reported in 2005.
$500,000 to Haggai Institute for Advanced Leadership Training, Atlanta, GA.
$500,000 to Hope College, Holland, MI.
$500,000 to Ridge Point Community Church, Holland, MI.
$500,000 to Russian-American Christian University, Wheaton, MD.
$250,000 to Blodgett Butterworth Health Care Foundation, Grand Rapids, MI.
$64,000 to Focus on the Family, Colorado Springs, CO.
$25,000 to Christian Learning Center, Grand Rapids, MI.
$10,000 to Elim Christian Services, Palos Heights, IL.
$10,000 to Health Intervention Services, Grand Rapids, MI.
$10,000 to Worldwide Christian Schools, Grand Rapids, MI.

4417
Milton M. Ratner Foundation
P.O. Box 250628
Franklin, MI 48025-0628
Contact: Therese M. Thorn, Treas.
E-mail: ratner_foundation@sbcglobal.net

Incorporated in 1968 in MI.
Donor: Milton M. Ratner†.
Foundation type: Independent foundation.
Financial data (yr. ended 8/31/06): Assets, $8,268,541 (M); expenditures, $538,706; qualifying distributions, $473,366; giving activities include $421,800 for 48 grants (high: $20,000; low: $1,000).
Purpose and activities: Giving primarily for higher education, and health and human services for children, families, and the elderly. Giving also for research to fight heart disease, for aid and training for the blind, and to aid physically handicapped children.
Fields of interest: Higher education; Scholarships/financial aid; Hospitals (general); Health organizations, association; Medical research, institute; Heart & circulatory research; Blind/visually impaired.
Type of support: General/operating support; Continuing support; Building/renovation; Equipment; Endowments; Program development; Scholarship funds; Research; Matching/challenge support.
Limitations: Giving primarily in GA and MI. No grants to individuals.
Application information: Application form not required.
Initial approach: Letter no more than 3 pages
Copies of proposal: 1
Deadline(s): Aug. 31
Board meeting date(s): Oct.
Final notification: Dec. 31

Officers and Trustees:* Mary Jo Rossen,* Pres.; Charles R. McDonald,* V.P. and Secy.; Therese M. Thorn,* Treas.
Agent: Meadowbrook Investment Advisors.
EIN: 386160330

4418
The Ravitz Foundation ◇
P.O. Box 5058
Southfield, MI 48086-5058

Established in 2001 in MI.
Donor: The Edward Ravitz Revocable Living Trust.
Foundation type: Independent foundation.
Financial data (yr. ended 12/31/04): Assets, $21,867,435 (M); gifts received, $680,604; expenditures, $1,064,074; qualifying distributions, $1,064,074; giving activities include $798,600 for 12 grants (high: $250,000; low: $3,600).
Purpose and activities: Giving primarily for medical services and research.
Fields of interest: Dental school/education; Health care; Mental health, treatment; Cancer; Medical research; Boys & girls clubs; Residential/custodial care, hospices; Jewish agencies & temples.
Limitations: Applications not accepted. Giving primarily in MI; some funding also in New York, NY. No grants to individuals.
Application information: Contributes only to pre-selected organizations.
Directors: Bruce Gelbaugh; Burton R. Shifman; Neil Zales.
EIN: 383508943

4419
The Riley Foundation ◇
c/o Comerica Bank
P.O Box 75000, MC 3302
Detroit, MI 48275-3302
Application address: c/o Comerica Bank, P.O. Box 75000, MC 7806, Detroit, MI 48275

Established in 1998 in MI.
Donors: George Riley; Dolores Riley.
Foundation type: Independent foundation.
Financial data (yr. ended 9/30/05): Assets, $8,683,258 (M); expenditures, $1,292,211; qualifying distributions, $1,225,334; giving activities include $1,205,427 for 12 grants (high: $1,000,000; low: $300).
Purpose and activities: Giving primarily to a public television station, as well as for human services, community development, and to Roman Catholic organizations and churches.
Fields of interest: Media, television; Higher education; Human services; Community development; Roman Catholic agencies & churches.
Limitations: Giving primarily in MI, with emphasis on Detroit and Farmington. No grants to individuals; or for scholarships.
Application information: Application form not required.
Deadline(s): None
Board of Managers: Daniel G. Riley; George K. Riley; Michael J. Riley; William D. Riley.
Trustees: Kimberly A. Fouts; Comerica Bank.
EIN: 383439851

4420
RNR Foundation, Inc. ◈ ☆
3025 Exmoor Rd.
Ann Arbor, MI 48104

Established in 1994 in FL.
Donor: Rhoda Newberry Reed.
Foundation type: Independent foundation.
Financial data (yr. ended 7/31/05): Assets,
$8,927,554 (M); expenditures, $551,088;
qualifying distributions, $465,504; giving activities
include $424,504 for 5 grants (high: $197,231;
low: $570).
Purpose and activities: Giving primarily for
education and health and human services.
Fields of interest: Museums (art); Education; Health
care, EMS; Health care; Human services;
Foundations (community).
Limitations: Applications not accepted. Giving
primarily in FL and MI. No grants to individuals.
Application information: Contributes only to
pre-selected organizations.
Officers: David Lord, Pres.; Charles Lord, V.P.; Edith
Lord-Wolff, Secy.; Richard Lord, Treas.
EIN: 650539370
Selected grants: The following grants were reported
in 2004.
$202,094 to Morton Plant Mease Health Care
Foundation, Clearwater, FL. 3 grants: $107,211,
$94,425, $458
$40,209 to Rollins College, Winter Park, FL. 2
grants: $40,020 to Public Service Program,
$189 to Public Service Program
$15,417 to Jodi House, Santa Barbara, CA.
$15,255 to Ann Arbor Area Community Foundation,
Ann Arbor, MI.
$450 to Council on Foundations, DC.

4421
The Robideau Foundation, Inc. ◈ ☆
153 E. Maumee St.
Adrian, MI 49221-7882

Established in 1978 in MI.
Foundation type: Independent foundation.
Financial data (yr. ended 9/30/05): Assets,
$1,399,061 (M); gifts received, $100,000;
expenditures, $600,000; qualifying distributions,
$587,574; giving activities include $587,574 for 21
grants (high: $300,000; low: $300).
Purpose and activities: Giving primarily for Christian
churches, education, human services, and YMCAs.
Fields of interest: Arts; Education; Hospitals
(general); Human services; Christian agencies &
churches.
Limitations: Giving primarily in MI. No grants to
individuals.
Officers: James J. Robideau, Pres.; Gladys E.
Robideau, V.P. and Secy.; Jeffrey T. Robideau, V.P.;
Margaret Jeffery, Treas.
EIN: 382241755

4422
The Rodney Fund
19100 W. 8 Mile Rd.
Southfield, MI 48075-5726
Contact: James M. Rodney, Pres.

Established in 1992 in MI.
Donor: James M. Rodney.
Foundation type: Independent foundation.

Financial data (yr. ended 12/31/05): Assets,
$8,555,580 (M); gifts received, $1,007,551;
expenditures, $667,894; qualifying distributions,
$631,281; giving activities include $631,281 for 33
grants (high: $131,100; low: $1,000).
Purpose and activities: Giving primarily for public
affairs institutes and centers. The fund supports
libertarian principles: limited government, private
property, free markets, individual liberty, free trade,
and rule by law, as established by the U.S.
Constitution.
Fields of interest: Education, research; Higher
education; Education; Employment, public policy;
Human services; Federated giving programs; Social
sciences; Public affairs.
Limitations: Giving on a national basis.
Application information:
    Initial approach: Letter
    Deadline(s): None
Officer and Directors:* James M. Rodney,* Pres.;
Lawrence Reed; Leigh Rodney; Steven Thomas.
EIN: 383030437

4423
S. Dennis and Leslie L. Rogers Foundation Corporation ◈ ☆
32400 Telegraph Rd., No. 202
Bingham Farms, MI 48025-2460

Established in 1986 in MI.
Donors: S. Dennis Rogers; Leslie L. Rogers; Darryl
Rogers.
Foundation type: Independent foundation.
Financial data (yr. ended 12/31/05): Assets,
$540,570 (M); gifts received, $1,000,000;
expenditures, $1,013,127; qualifying distributions,
$1,009,327; giving activities include $1,008,787
for 31 grants (high: $1,000,000; low: $15).
Fields of interest: Arts; Higher education, university;
Education; Health organizations, association;
Cancer research; Human services; Children/youth,
services; Jewish agencies & temples.
Limitations: Applications not accepted. Giving
primarily in MI. No grants to individuals.
Application information: Contributes only to
pre-selected organizations.
Officers: S. Dennis Rogers, Pres. and Treas.; Leslie
L. Rogers, V.P. and Secy.
Directors: Darryl Rogers; Irvin Rogers.
EIN: 382710391

4424
The Rordor Foundation ◈
P.O. Box 202
Grand Rapids, MI 49501

Established in 1983 in MI.
Donors: Donald O. Roskam; Robert O. Roskam;
Harold Zeigler Chrysler; Don Roskam‡; Bakers Food.
Foundation type: Independent foundation.
Financial data (yr. ended 12/31/04): Assets,
$812,618 (M); gifts received, $525,469;
expenditures, $823,908; qualifying distributions,
$823,579; giving activities include $823,559 for 23
grants (high: $500,000; low: $1,000).
Purpose and activities: Giving primarily for health,
education, Christian organizations, and human
services.
Fields of interest: Higher education; Education;
Hospitals (general); Cancer; Health organizations;
Human services; Christian agencies & churches.

Limitations: Applications not accepted. Giving
limited to Grand Rapids, MI. No grants to individuals.
Application information: Contributes only to
pre-selected organizations.
Officers: Robert O. Roskam, Pres.
EIN: 382500050

4425
The Rosenzweig Coopersmith Foundation
c/o Vanderwerff Law Office PC, Robert VanDongen
2666 Capilano Dr., S.E.
Grand Rapids, MI 49546-5517

Established in 1997 in MI.
Donors: Dora Rosenzweig; Leonard Rosenzweig.
Foundation type: Independent foundation.
Financial data (yr. ended 12/31/05): Assets,
$11,243,644 (M); gifts received, $104,212;
expenditures, $653,212; qualifying distributions,
$620,072; giving activities include $547,000 for 21
grants (high: $85,000; low: $2,500; average:
$15,000–$40,000).
Purpose and activities: Support primarily for Jewish
organizations.
Fields of interest: Jewish federated giving programs;
Jewish agencies & temples.
Limitations: Applications not accepted. Giving on a
national basis. No grants to individuals.
Application information: Contributes only to
pre-selected organizations.
Officer: Robert Van Dongen, Mgr.
Trustees: Monica Armour; Suzanne Fenster; Harry
Rosenzweig; Herschel Rosenzweig; Joseph
Rosenzweig.
EIN: 383393545

4426
Saddle Foundation ◈
101 N. Main St., 7th Fl.
Ann Arbor, MI 48104-1400
Contact: Erik H. Serr, Dir.

Established in 1997 in MI.
Donor: Kathryn W. Holmes.
Foundation type: Independent foundation.
Financial data (yr. ended 12/31/05): Assets,
$7,227,516 (M); gifts received, $108,150;
expenditures, $502,026; qualifying distributions,
$486,415; giving activities include $480,000 for 8
grants (high: $110,000; low: $20,000; average:
$50,000–$90,000).
Purpose and activities: Giving primarily for the arts,
higher education, the environment, and human
services.
Fields of interest: Museums; Performing arts;
Higher education; Environment, natural resources;
Animals/wildlife, preservation/protection; Human
services; YM/YWCAs & YM/YWHAs.
Limitations: Applications not accepted. Giving
primarily in MI; some giving also in San Francisco,
CA. No grants to individuals.
Application information: Contributes only to
pre-selected organizations.
Officer: Kathryn W. Holmes, Pres. and Secy.-Treas.
Directors: Howard S. "Howdy" Holmes; Erik H. Serr.
EIN: 383347262

4427
Sage Foundation

P.O. Box 1919
Brighton, MI 48116
Contact: Melissa Sage Fadim, Chair.

Incorporated in 1954 in MI.
Donors: Charles F. Sage†; Effa L. Sage†.
Foundation type: Independent foundation.
Financial data (yr. ended 12/31/05): Assets, $56,855,247 (M); expenditures, $3,260,398; qualifying distributions, $2,921,307; giving activities include $2,696,150 for 124 grants (high: $225,000; low: $1,000).
Purpose and activities: Emphasis on higher and secondary education and hospitals; grants also for aid to the handicapped, Roman Catholic religious and charitable organizations, youth and child welfare agencies, church support, and cultural programs.
Fields of interest: Arts; Secondary school/education; Higher education; Hospitals (general); Human services; Children/youth, services; Roman Catholic federated giving programs; Roman Catholic agencies & churches; Disabilities, people with.
Type of support: General/operating support; Continuing support; Annual campaigns; Capital campaigns; Building/renovation; Equipment; Endowments; Program development; Scholarship funds; Research; Matching/challenge support.
Limitations: Giving on a national basis.
Application information: Application form not required.
  Initial approach: Letter
  Copies of proposal: 1
  Deadline(s): None
  Board meeting date(s): Quarterly
  Final notification: 12 weeks
Officers and Trustees:* Melissa Sage Fadim,* Chair., Pres., and Treas.; John J. Ayaub,* V.P. and Secy.; Anne Sage Price; James E. Van Doren.
Number of staff: 1 part-time professional.
EIN: 386041518
Selected grants: The following grants were reported in 2004.
$250,000 to Music Institute of Chicago, Winnetka, IL. 2 grants: $125,000 each
$50,000 to Big Shoulders Fund, Chicago, IL.
$50,000 to Bixby Community Health Foundation, Adrian, MI.
$50,000 to Cancer Support Center, Homewood, IL.
$25,000 to Lincoln Park Zoo, Chicago, IL.
$12,500 to Park Ridge Civic Orchestra, Rolling Meadows, IL.
$10,000 to Gildas Club New York City, New York, NY.
$10,000 to Herrick Memorial Hospital Foundation, Tecumseh, MI.
$10,000 to Saint Johns Jesuit High School, Toledo, OH.

4428
Saginaw Community Foundation ✧

100 S. Jefferson Ave., Ste. 201
Saginaw, MI 48607 (989) 755-0545
Contact: Renee S. Johnston, Pres.; For grants: Ken Horn, V.P., Progs. and Donor Svcs.
FAX: (989) 755-6524;
E-mail: info@saginawfoundation.org; Additional E-mail: Ken@saginawfoundation.org; URL: http://www.saginawfoundation.org

Incorporated in 1984 in MI.
Foundation type: Community foundation.

Financial data (yr. ended 12/31/05): Assets, $33,429,153 (M); gifts received, $4,989,493; expenditures, $1,934,559; giving activities include $680,194 for 195 grants (high: $67,481; low: $84).
Purpose and activities: Support for projects not currently being served by existing community resources and for projects providing leverage for generating other funds and community resources.
Fields of interest: Arts; Education; Environment; Health care; Recreation; Family services; Human services; Community development; General charitable giving; Youth; Aging.
Type of support: Building/renovation; Equipment; Emergency funds; Program development; Publication; Seed money; Scholarship funds; Technical assistance; Scholarships—to individuals; Matching/challenge support.
Limitations: Giving limited to Saginaw County, MI. No support for churches or sectarian religious programs. No grants to individuals (except for designated scholarship funds), or for operating budgets, endowment campaigns, debt reduction, travel, or basic municipal or educational services; generally no multi-year grants.
Publications: Application guidelines; Annual report (including application guidelines); Occasional report.
Application information: Visit foundation Web site for application cover form and guidelines. Application form required.
  Initial approach: Telephone
  Copies of proposal: 3
  Deadline(s): Feb. 1, May 1, Aug. 1, and Nov. 1
  Board meeting date(s): Monthly
  Final notification: 2 months after deadline
Officers and Directors:* Richard T. Watson,* Chair.; Joseph W. Madison,* Vice-Chair.; Renee S. Johnston, C.E.O. and Pres.; Ken Horn, V.P., Progs. and Donor Svcs.; Mark S. Flegenheimer,* Secy.; David J. Abbs,* Treas.; Raana Akbar, M.D.; Heidi A. Bolger; David R. Butts; David Carbajal; Bishop Robert J. Carlson; Paul Chaffee; Morrall M. Claramunt; Rev. Hurley J. Coleman, Jr.; Ellen E. Crane; JoAnn Crary; Desmon Daniel, Ph.D.; Craig C. Douglas, Ph.D.; James Fabiano II; Andrea L. Fisher; Frederick C. Gardner; Smallwood Holoman, Jr.; Deborah G. Kimble; Richard D. Lane; Timothy M. MacKay; Susan A. Pumford; Kala Kuru Ramasamy, M.D.; Ricardo Resio; Jerry L. Seese; Sam Shaheen, M.D.; James J. Shinners; Linda L. Sims; Martin H. Stark; Julie Case Swieczkowski; Mamie Thorns, Ph.D.; Jerry Ulrey.
Number of staff: 4 full-time professional.
EIN: 382474297

4429
The Shirley K. Schlafer Foundation ✧

1465 Clarendon Rd.
Bloomfield Hills, MI 48302-2604

Established in 1985 in MI.
Donors: Shirley K. Schlafer; Shirley K. Schlafer Trust.
Foundation type: Independent foundation.
Financial data (yr. ended 10/31/05): Assets, $9,183,157 (M); expenditures, $571,969; qualifying distributions, $505,529; giving activities include $505,529 for 40 grants (high: $200,000; low: $50).
Purpose and activities: Giving primarily for the arts, particularly to museums, including a folk art museum; some giving also for health care including hospitals, and education.

Fields of interest: Visual arts; Museums (art); Museums (ethnic/folk arts); Performing arts; Arts; Higher education; Education; Health care; Medical research, institute; Cancer research.
Limitations: Applications not accepted. Giving primarily in MI and in New York, NY. No grants to individuals.
Application information: Contributes only to pre-selected organizations.
Officers: Edith S. Briskin, Chair. and Treas.; Barry D. Briskin, Pres. and Secy.; Andrew Briskin, V.P.; Susannah M. Briskin, V.P.
EIN: 382637259
Selected grants: The following grants were reported in 2004.
$233,885 to American Folk Art Museum, New York, NY. 7 grants: $23,000, $1,300, $1,750, $2,460, $200,000, $1,250, $4,125
$200,000 to Michigan Opera Theater, Detroit, MI.
$30,000 to Detroit Symphony Orchestra, Detroit, MI.
$25,000 to Common Ground Sanctuary, Bloomfield Hills, MI.

4430
Sebastian Foundation ✧

3333 Evergreen Dr. N.E., Ste. 110
Grand Rapids, MI 49525-9756
Contact: David S. Sebastian, Exec. Dir.

Established in 1980 in MI.
Donors: Audrey M. Sebastian; James R. Sebastian.
Foundation type: Independent foundation.
Financial data (yr. ended 8/31/05): Assets, $25,810,757 (M); expenditures, $1,606,625; qualifying distributions, $1,423,797; giving activities include $1,345,100 for 62 grants (high: $150,000; low: $500).
Purpose and activities: Supports human services and public benefit organizations, education, and the arts.
Fields of interest: Arts; Education; Human services.
Limitations: Giving primarily in the Grand Rapids, MI, area. No support for religious programs. No grants to individuals.
Application information: Application form not required.
  Initial approach: Proposal
  Copies of proposal: 1
  Deadline(s): None
Officer: David S. Sebastian, Exec. Dir.
Trustees: Audrey M. Sebastian; John O. Sebastian.
Number of staff: 2 full-time support.
EIN: 382340219
Selected grants: The following grants were reported in 2005.
$150,000 to United Way, Heart of West Michigan, Grand Rapids, MI.
$135,000 to First United Methodist Church, Grand Rapids, MI.
$75,000 to Grand Rapids Childrens Museum, Grand Rapids, MI.
$62,500 to Grand Rapids Art Museum, Grand Rapids, MI.
$62,000 to Grand Valley University Foundation, Grand Rapids, MI.
$40,000 to Baxter Community Center, Grand Rapids, MI.
$25,000 to YMCA, Lowell, Grand Rapids, MI.
$15,000 to Grand Rapids Community College Foundation, Grand Rapids, MI.
$15,000 to Grand Rapids Community Foundation, Grand Rapids, MI.

$10,000 to Public Museum of Grand Rapids, Grand Rapids, MI.

4431

Secchia Family Foundation ✧

(formerly Peter F. Secchia Foundation)
c/o Universal Forest Products, Inc.
220 Lyon St. N.W., Ste. 510
Grand Rapids, MI 49503-2210

Established in 1985 in MI.
Donors: Peter F. Secchia; SIBSCO, LLC.
Foundation type: Independent foundation.
Financial data (yr. ended 12/31/05): Assets, $14,135,678 (M); gifts received, $1,050,000; expenditures, $536,928; qualifying distributions, $530,100; giving activities include $530,100 for 70 grants (high: $75,000; low: $100; average: $10,000–$25,000).
Purpose and activities: Giving for education, health associations, youth programs, and religion; some giving also in Italy.
Fields of interest: Education; Health organizations, association; Children/youth, services; Christian agencies & churches.
International interests: Italy.
Type of support: Building/renovation; Equipment; Scholarship funds.
Limitations: Applications not accepted. Giving on a national and international basis. No grants to individuals.
Application information: Contributes only to pre-selected organizations.
Officers: Peter F. Secchia, Pres.; Mark A. Schut, Treas.
Director: Sandra Secchia Aslanian.
EIN: 382641093
Selected grants: The following grants were reported in 2004.
$205,000 to Gerald R. Ford Foundation, Grand Rapids, MI. 2 grants: $5,000, $200,000
$200,000 to Grand Action Foundation, Grand Rapids, MI.
$1,000 to East Grand Rapids Schools Foundation, Grand Rapids, MI.
$500 to Hugh Michael Beahan Foundation, Grand Rapids, MI.

4432

The Sehn Foundation ✧

3515 Brookside Dr., Ste. A
Bloomfield Hills, MI 48302-1501

Established in 1968 in MI.
Donors: Francis J. Sehn; James T. Sehn.
Foundation type: Independent foundation.
Financial data (yr. ended 12/31/04): Assets, $6,363,854 (M); gifts received, $40,800; expenditures, $411,111; qualifying distributions, $331,470; giving activities include $331,450 for 15 + grants (high: $100,000).
Purpose and activities: Giving primarily for Roman Catholic organizations and education.
Fields of interest: Higher education; Education; Human services; Roman Catholic agencies & churches.
Type of support: General/operating support.
Limitations: Applications not accepted. Giving primarily in Detroit, MI. No grants to individuals.
Application information: Contributes only to pre-selected organizations.

Officers: Francis J. Sehn, Pres.; Barbara S. Day, Mgr.
EIN: 386160784
Selected grants: The following grants were reported in 2004.
$100,000 to Sacred Heart Seminary. For general support.
$50,000 to Saint Vincent de Paul Society. For general support.
$13,000 to Saint Hugo of the Hills Church, Bloomfield Hills, MI. For general support.
$5,000 to Equestrian Order of the Holy Sepulchre of Jerusalem. For general support.
$5,000 to Leukemia & Lymphoma Society, West Michigan Chapter, Grand Rapids, MI. For general support.
$4,000 to Saint Joseph Mercy Hospital, Ann Arbor, MI.
$2,000 to Michigan Catholic Radio, Troy, MI. For general support.
$2,000 to West Point Fund, West Point, NY. For general support.
$1,500 to University of Detroit Jesuit High School and Academy, Detroit, MI. For general support.
$1,400 to Middleburg Community Center, Middleburg, VA. For general support.

4433

The Seligman Family Foundation ✧

1 Towne Sq., Ste. 1913
Southfield, MI 48076

Established in 1991 in MI.
Donor: Irving Seligman.
Foundation type: Independent foundation.
Financial data (yr. ended 12/31/05): Assets, $2,491,290 (M); expenditures, $920,969; qualifying distributions, $919,951; giving activities include $919,951 for 43 grants (high: $300,000; low: $250; average: $5,000–$10,000).
Fields of interest: Arts; Higher education; Health organizations, association; Human services; Jewish federated giving programs; Jewish agencies & temples.
Limitations: Applications not accepted. Giving primarily in San Francisco, CA, and Detroit, MI. No grants to individuals.
Application information: Contributes only to pre-selected organizations.
Officers: Irving Seligman, Pres.; Mary K. Seligman, Secy.-Treas.
EIN: 382972397

4434

Elizabeth, Allan and Warren Shelden Fund

17152 Kercheval St.
Grosse Pointe Farms, MI 48230
Contact: William W. Shelden, Jr., Pres.

Incorporated in 1937 in MI.
Donors: Elizabeth Warren Shelden†; Allan Shelden III†; W. Warren Shelden†.
Foundation type: Independent foundation.
Financial data (yr. ended 12/31/05): Assets, $38,565,696 (M); gifts received, $237,083; expenditures, $2,173,939; qualifying distributions, $2,081,190; giving activities include $2,075,500 for grants (high: $700,000; low: $5,000; average: $5,000–$25,000).
Purpose and activities: Giving primarily for the arts, education, and health care.

Fields of interest: Performing arts, music; Arts; Higher education; Hospitals (general); Health care; Children/youth, services; Economically disadvantaged.
Type of support: General/operating support; Continuing support; Annual campaigns; Capital campaigns; Building/renovation; Equipment; Endowments; Research.
Limitations: Giving primarily in the metropolitan Detroit, MI, area. No grants to individuals, or for scholarships, fellowships, or matching gifts; no loans.
Publications: Annual report.
Application information: Application form not required.
   Initial approach: Proposal
   Copies of proposal: 1
   Deadline(s): Submit proposal preferably in Nov.; no set deadline
   Board meeting date(s): Nov. or Dec.
   Final notification: Positive replies only
Officers and Trustees: William W. Shelden, Jr.,* Pres. and Treas.; David M. Hempstead.
Number of staff: 1 part-time professional; 1 part-time support.
EIN: 386052198
Selected grants: The following grants were reported in 2004.
$810,000 to Childrens Hospital of Michigan, Detroit, MI.
$150,000 to University Liggett School, Grosse Pointe, MI.
$50,000 to Detroit Symphony Orchestra, Detroit, MI.
$40,000 to Salvation Army, Port Huron, MI.
$25,000 to Bon Secours Cottage Health Services Foundation, Grosse Pointe, MI.
$25,000 to Neighborhood Club, Grosse Pointe, MI.
$25,000 to Northern Michigan Hospital Foundation, Petoskey, MI.
$10,000 to Dominican High School, Detroit, MI.
$10,000 to Michigan Opera Theater, Detroit, MI.
$10,000 to New Common School Foundation, Detroit, MI.

4435

The Shepherd Foundation ✧

2967 Lakeshore Dr.
Holland, MI 49423
Contact: Max O. DePree, Dir.

Established in 1992 in MI.
Donors: Barbara DePree; Esther DePree; Kris DePree; Max O. DePree.
Foundation type: Independent foundation.
Financial data (yr. ended 12/31/05): Assets, $47,867 (M); gifts received, $55,868; expenditures, $6,276,319; qualifying distributions, $6,259,000; giving activities include $6,258,050 for 33 grants (high: $5,000,000; low: $1,000; average: $2,000–$5,000).
Purpose and activities: Giving primarily to Christian programs, including theological education and Christian youth groups.
Fields of interest: Theological school/education; Housing/shelter, services; Youth development; Human services; Christian agencies & churches.
Type of support: Capital campaigns; General/operating support.
Limitations: Giving in the U.S., primarily in MI.
Application information:
   Initial approach: Letter
   Deadline(s): None

Officers: Kris DePree, Pres. and Secy.; Jody VanDerwel, Treas.
Directors: Esther DePree; Max O. DePree.
EIN: 383046929
Selected grants: The following grants were reported in 2005.
$820,000 to Young Life, Colorado Springs, CO. 2 grants: $790,000, $30,000
$128,500 to Western Theological Seminary, Holland, MI.
$63,750 to Bethany Christian Services, Grand Rapids, MI.
$13,000 to Holland Christian Schools, Holland, MI.
$8,000 to Good Samaritan Ministries, Holland, MI.
$7,000 to Lakeshore Pregnancy Center, Holland, MI.
$5,000 to Holland Rescue Mission, Holland, MI.
$5,000 to Saint Petersburg Theological Seminary, Saint Petersburg, FL.
$2,000 to Boys and Girls Club of Greater Holland, Holland, MI.

4436
Edwin J. & Ruth M. Shoemaker Foundation ✧
214 E. Elm Ave., Ste. 100
Monroe, MI 48162

Established in 1998 in MI.
Donors: Edwin J. Shoemaker†; Dale Shoemaker.
Foundation type: Independent foundation.
Financial data (yr. ended 12/31/05): Assets, $16,038,543 (M); expenditures, $868,415; qualifying distributions, $816,872; giving activities include $772,500 for 24 grants (high: $150,000; low: $2,500).
Purpose and activities: The foundation supports organizations that pursue and further the tenets of the Christian faith.
Fields of interest: Civil liberties, right to life; Christian agencies & churches.
Limitations: Applications not accepted. Giving primarily in MI, NC, and TX.
Application information: Contributes only to pre-selected organizations.
Officers and Directors:* Robert L. Shoemaker,* Pres.; Dale A. Shoemaker,* V.P.; Mary Kaye Johnston,* Secy.-Treas.; David S. Johnston; Rocque E. Lipford; Erich C. Shoemaker.
EIN: 383137832

4437
Skilling and Andrews Foundation ☆
c/o Ann Skilling Andrews
11720 E. Shore Dr.
Whitmore Lake, MI 48189

Established in 1996 in MI.
Donors: Hazel D. Skilling†; Hugh H. Skilling Trust.
Foundation type: Independent foundation.
Financial data (yr. ended 12/31/05): Assets, $1 (M); expenditures, $471,276; qualifying distributions, $469,100; giving activities include $469,100 for 15 grants (high: $100,000; low: $500).
Purpose and activities: Giving primarily to aid new secondary schools; some support also for conservation.
Fields of interest: Secondary school/education; Environment, natural resources.

Limitations: Applications not accepted. Giving primarily in the central U.S. No grants to individuals.
Application information: Contributes only to pre-selected organizations.
Officers and Trustees:* Ann Skilling Andrews,* Pres. and Treas.; Kenneth Andrews,* V.P.; Steven Andrews,* Secy.
EIN: 383335356

4438
The Skillman Foundation ▼ ✧
100 Talon Centre Dr., Ste. 100
Detroit, MI 48207 (313) 393-1185
Contact: Prog. Off.
FAX: (313) 393-1187; E-mail: mailbox@skillman.org; URL: http://www.skillman.org

Incorporated in 1960 in MI.
Donor: Rose P. Skillman†.
Foundation type: Independent foundation.
Financial data (yr. ended 12/31/04): Assets, $507,839,550 (M); expenditures, $28,321,026; qualifying distributions, $24,895,508; giving activities include $21,092,046 for 150 grants (high: $1,200,000; low: $40), $496,567 for employee matching gifts, and $500,000 for loans/program-related investments.
Purpose and activities: The foundation is a resource for improving the lives of children in metropolitan Detroit, MI. Children in disadvantaged situations are of special concern. The foundation applies its resources to foster positive relationships between children and adults, support high quality learning opportunities and strengthen healthy, safe and supportive homes and communities.
Fields of interest: Visual arts; Performing arts; Arts; Education, early childhood education; Child development, education; Education, reading; Education; Health care; Substance abuse, services; Crime/violence prevention, youth; Food services; Recreation; Human services; Children/youth, services; Child development, services; Family services; Homeless, human services; Economically disadvantaged; Homeless.
Type of support: General/operating support; Program development; Seed money; Scholarship funds; Employee matching gifts.
Limitations: Giving primarily in southeastern MI, with emphasis on metropolitan Detroit, and Macomb, Oakland, and Wayne counties. No support for long-term projects not being aided by other sources, sectarian religious activities, political lobbying or legislative activities, or new organizations which do not have an operational and financial history. The foundation does not make grants to organizations that had public support and revenues of less than $100,000 for the preceding year. No grants to individuals, or for endowment funds, annual campaigns, purchase, construct or renovate facilities, basic research or deficit financing; no loans.
Publications: Application guidelines; Annual report; Informational brochure (including application guidelines); Newsletter; Occasional report; Program policy statement.
Application information: The foundation accepts grant applications online. Application form required.
   Initial approach: Letter of intent
   Copies of proposal: 1
   Deadline(s): None
   Board meeting date(s): Feb., Apr., June, Sept., and Nov.
   Final notification: 6 weeks after board meeting

Officers and Trustees:* Lillian Bauder,* Chair.; Stephen E. Ewing,* Vice-Chair.; Carol A. Goss, C.E.O. and Pres.; Andrea Cole, Treas. and Dir., Finance; Alan Harris, C.I.O.; Lizabeth Ardisana; Ralph W. Babb, Jr.; William M. Brodhead; Walter E. Douglas; Edsel B. Ford II; David Baker Lewis; Amyre Makupson; Robert S. Taubman; Jane R. Thomas.
Number of staff: 10 full-time professional; 5 full-time support.
EIN: 381675780
Selected grants: The following grants were reported in 2005.
$1,500,000 to Local Initiatives Support Corporation (LISC), New York, NY. For Neighborhoods NOW, effort to develop public safety, education, workforce development, child care, health care, business assistance and other community services, payable over 3 years.
$500,000 to Communication and Media Arts High School, Detroit, MI. To transform Communication and Media Arts High School into small high school model of success.
$500,000 to Michigan Womens Foundation, Livonia, MI. To expand Young Women for Change youth grantmaking program in four Detroit neighborhoods (Brightmoor, Cody/Rouge, Chadsey/Condon and Vernor), payable over 3 years.
$450,000 to Wayne State University, Detroit, MI. For evaluation of Good Schools Making the Grade Initiative, payable over 3 years.
$400,000 to High Tech High Foundation, San Diego, CA. To provide technical assistance to new urban High Tech High inspired school, payable over 3 years.
$380,000 to Marygrove College, Detroit, MI. To expand Marygrove College Technical Assistance Center for Good Schools Initiative.
$373,500 to Southwest Counseling and Development Services, Detroit, MI. To offer family literacy programs to low-income Latino families and build capacity of community to increase awareness and access to early childhood education programs, payable over 3 years.
$300,000 to Focus: Hope, Detroit, MI. To expand youth photography program and offer high school students opportunities to work with professional artists as instructors and mentors, payable over 3 years.
$300,000 to Michigans Children, Lansing, MI. To increase public awareness of public investments in children in state budget and to enhance ability of policymakers and public to be involved in budget advocacy, payable over 3 years.
$300,000 to Oakland Livingston Human Service Agency, Pontiac, MI. To align multiple social service agencies support systems for children of incarcerated and probationer parents, particularly fathers, payable over 3 years.

4439
Slikkers Foundation ✧
725 E. 40th St.
Holland, MI 49423

Established in 1998 in MI.
Donors: David A. Slikkers; Mary B. Slikkers; Leon R. Slikkers; Dolores E. Slikkers; Mark Ringwelski; Susan Ringwelski; S 2 Yachts; L&D Foundation; RBS Foundation.
Foundation type: Independent foundation.

Financial data (yr. ended 12/31/05): Assets, $2,185,210 (M); gifts received, $2,051,880; expenditures, $733,151; qualifying distributions, $731,848; giving activities include $731,848 for 24 + grants (high: $300,000).

Purpose and activities: Giving primarily to Seventh-day Adventist churches, agencies, and schools.

Fields of interest: Arts; Human services; Protestant agencies & churches.

Type of support: General/operating support.

Limitations: Applications not accepted. Giving in the U.S., with emphasis on in MI. No grants to individuals.

Application information: Contributes only to pre-selected organizations.

Officer and Trustees:* Robert L. Slikkers,* Pres. and Secy.; David A. Slikkers; Dolores E. Slikkers; Leon R. Slikkers; Thomas B. Slikkers; Susan K. Slikkers-Ringwelski.

EIN: 383431246

Selected grants: The following grants were reported in 2005.

$84,800 to Maranatha Volunteers International, Sacramento, CA.

$17,756 to American Red Cross, Holland, MI.

$13,500 to International Aid, Spring Lake, MI.

$2,500 to Great Lakes Adventist Academy, Cedar Lake, MI.

$2,000 to Community Action House, Holland, MI.

$1,500 to Adventist Frontier Missions, Berrien Springs, MI.

$1,250 to Bethany Christian Services, Holland, MI.

$1,000 to Center for Women in Transition, Holland, MI.

$1,000 to Hospice of Holland, Holland, MI.

$1,000 to Sponsors for Academic Talent, Jacksonville, NC.

4440
Arthur L. & Carra J. Smith Family Foundation ◇

428 Yale Ave.
Alma, MI 48801 (989) 463-3779
Contact: Karen L. Smith, Secy.-Treas.

Established in 2002 in MI.

Donors: Arthur L. Smith; Carra J. Smith.

Foundation type: Independent foundation.

Financial data (yr. ended 12/31/04): Assets, $2,702,383 (M); gifts received, $992,268; expenditures, $379,057; qualifying distributions, $378,859; giving activities include $378,859 for 1 grant.

Purpose and activities: Giving primarily to a liberal arts college.

Fields of interest: Higher education; American Red Cross.

Limitations: Giving primarily in MI.

Application information:

Initial approach: Letter

Deadline(s): None

Officers: Arthur L. Smith, Pres.; Carra J. Smith, V.P.; Karen L. Smith, Secy.-Treas.

EIN: 371451908

4441
William H. and Patricia M. Smith Foundation ◇ ☆

26479 Greythorne Trail
Farmington Hills, MI 48334

Established in 1994 in MI.

Donor: William H. Smith.

Foundation type: Independent foundation.

Financial data (yr. ended 6/30/06): Assets, $2,226,511 (M); gifts received, $193,551; expenditures, $672,921; qualifying distributions, $648,600; giving activities include $648,600 for 10 grants (high: $500,000; low: $600).

Fields of interest: Museums; Performing arts; Arts; General charitable giving.

Limitations: Applications not accepted. Giving primarily in Detroit, MI. No grants to individuals.

Application information: Contributes only to pre-selected organizations.

Officers and Trustees:* William H. Smith,* Pres.; Patricia M. Smith,* V.P.; Wendy A. Kubitskey, Secy.-Treas.; Kendall A. Smith; Scott D. Smith.

EIN: 383213042

4442
Southwest Michigan Rehab Foundation

100 Peet's Cove
Battle Creek, MI 49015
Contact: Cheryl Humbarger, Grant Coord.

Established in 1991 in MI.

Donor: Southwest Regional Rehabilitation Center.

Foundation type: Independent foundation.

Financial data (yr. ended 12/31/05): Assets, $1,973,342 (M); expenditures, $435,699; qualifying distributions, $433,801; giving activities include $404,871 for 4 grants (high: $400,000; low: $500), and $22,699 for 45 grants to individuals (high: $2,000; low: $30; average: $130–$1,000).

Purpose and activities: Aid to people with temporary or permanent conditions related to handicap, including prosthetics and equipment for home enablement.

Fields of interest: Physical therapy; Disabilities, people with.

Type of support: Equipment.

Limitations: Giving limited to residents of southwestern MI, with emphasis on the Battle Creek area, including Calhoun County.

Publications: Informational brochure.

Application information: Application form required.

Initial approach: Request application form

Copies of proposal: 1

Deadline(s): Fri. prior to board meetings

Board meeting date(s): 3rd Thurs. of each month

Final notification: 2 weeks after board meeting

Officers and Directors:* Carl F. Greene,* Pres.; Richard Allen, M.D.*, V.P.; Robert Humbarger,* Secy.; William Comai, M.D.*, Treas.; David Marousek; Roger Mattens; Marilyn Sharp; Jan Smith.

Number of staff: 1 part-time support.

EIN: 382939930

4443
John and Judy Spoelhof Foundation ◇

151 Central Ave., Ste. 200
Holland, MI 49423

Established in 1984 in MI.

Donors: John Spoelhof; Judy Spoelhof; Prince Holding Corp.; JJS Partnership.

Foundation type: Independent foundation.

Financial data (yr. ended 12/31/05): Assets, $20,881,863 (M); gifts received, $2,419,048;

expenditures, $1,117,852; qualifying distributions, $1,019,595; giving activities include $988,857 for 80 grants (high: $197,165; low: $500; average: $5,000–$50,000).

Purpose and activities: Support primarily for higher education, Christian schools and churches, and community foundations, and children, youth, families and social services.

Fields of interest: Performing arts; Arts; Elementary/secondary education; Higher education; Theological school/education; Youth development, religion; Human services; Children/youth, services; Family services; Christian agencies & churches.

Type of support: General/operating support; Building/renovation.

Limitations: Applications not accepted. Giving primarily in MI, with emphasis on Holland. No grants to individuals.

Application information: Contributes only to pre-selected organizations.

Officers: John Spoelhof, Pres.; Judith Spoelhof, Secy.

Trustee: Scott Spoelhof.

EIN: 382492821

Selected grants: The following grants were reported in 2005.

$207,111 to Christ Memorial Reformed Church, Holland, MI. 2 grants: $197,111, $10,000

$60,000 to Davenport University, Grand Rapids, MI. 2 grants: $10,000, $50,000

$60,000 to Luke Society, Sioux Falls, SD.

$50,000 to Geneva Camp and Retreat Center, Holland, MI.

$25,000 to Christian Learning Center, Grand Rapids, MI.

$20,000 to Family Research Council, DC.

$10,000 to Christian Reformed World Relief Committee, Grand Rapids, MI.

$8,895 to Hospice of Holland, Holland, MI.

4444
St. Deny's Foundation, Inc. ◇

(formerly Tremble Foundation, Inc.)
P.O. Box 704
Dowagiac, MI 49047
Contact: Kelly Deritter

Established in 1988 in MI.

Donor: Helen R. Tremble†.

Foundation type: Independent foundation.

Financial data (yr. ended 12/31/05): Assets, $7,137,323 (M); gifts received, $202,320; expenditures, $418,325; qualifying distributions, $316,250; giving activities include $316,250 for 41 grants (high: $40,000; low: $1,000).

Fields of interest: Higher education; Environment; Animal welfare.

Type of support: General/operating support; Program development; Scholarship funds.

Limitations: Giving primarily in MI, with emphasis on the Dowagiac area.

Application information: Application form not required.

Initial approach: Proposal

Copies of proposal: 1

Deadline(s): Feb. 1 and Aug. 1

Board meeting date(s): Spring and fall

Final notification: 6 months

Officers and Directors:* Thomas Dalton,* Pres.; Lynn Dalton, V.P.; Robert Sajdak, Secy.-Treas.; Cara Carrabine-Dalton; Dillon Dalton; Dusty Dalton; Jim McWilliams.

Trustee: Comerica Bank.
EIN: 382869889

4445
Mary G. Stange Charitable Trust ✧
201 W. Big Beaver Rd., Ste. 500
Troy, MI 48084

Established in 1999 in MI.
Donor: Mary G. Stange Trust.
Foundation type: Independent foundation.
Financial data (yr. ended 12/31/05): Assets, $14,229,712 (M); gifts received, $190,419; expenditures, $760,975; qualifying distributions, $685,099; giving activities include $618,300 for 15 grants (high: $155,000; low: $2,500; average: $10,000–$50,000).
Purpose and activities: Giving primarily for education.
Fields of interest: Elementary/secondary education; Higher education; Health care; Human services; Christian agencies & churches.
Limitations: Applications not accepted. Giving primarily in MI; some giving also in NC. No grants to individuals.
Application information: Contributes only to pre-selected organizations.
Trustee: David C. Stone.
EIN: 386739773

4446
Steelcase Foundation ▼
P.O. Box 1967, CH-4E
Grand Rapids, MI 49501-1967
Contact: Susan Broman, Exec. Dir.
FAX: (616) 475-2200;
E-mail: sbroman@steelcase.com; URL: http://www.steelcase.com/na/steelcase_foundation_ourcompany.aspx?f=18486

Established in 1951 in MI.
Donor: Steelcase Inc.
Foundation type: Company-sponsored foundation.
Financial data (yr. ended 11/30/05): Assets, $113,151,982 (M); gifts received, $336,862; expenditures, $7,930,027; qualifying distributions, $7,674,634; giving activities include $6,892,139 for 360 grants (high: $700,000), and $445,633 for employee matching gifts.
Purpose and activities: The foundation supports organizations involved with arts and culture, education, the environment, health, human services, and community development. Special emphasis is directed toward programs designed to assist youth, the elderly, disabled people, and economically disadvantaged people.
Fields of interest: Arts; Education; Environment; Health care; Human services; Economic development; Community development; Youth; Aging; Disabilities, people with; Economically disadvantaged.
International interests: Canada.
Type of support: Employee-related scholarships; General/operating support; Capital campaigns; Building/renovation; Equipment; Land acquisition; Program development; Seed money; Scholarship funds; Employee matching gifts; Matching/challenge support.
Limitations: Giving limited to areas of company operations, with emphasis on Athens, AL, City of Industry, CA, Grand Rapids, MI, and Markham,

Canada. No support for churches or religious organizations not of direct benefit to the entire community or discriminatory organizations. No grants to individuals (except for employee-related scholarships), or for endowments or conferences or seminars.
Publications: Application guidelines; Annual report (including application guidelines).
Application information: Application form required.
  Initial approach: Download application form
  Copies of proposal: 1
  Deadline(s): Quarterly
  Board meeting date(s): Quarterly
  Final notification: At least 90 days
Officers and Trustees:* Kate Pew Wolters,* Chair.; Susan Broman, Exec. Dir.; James P. Hackett; Earl D. Holton; David D. Hunting, Jr.; Mary Goodwillie Nelson; Robert C. Pew III; Peter M. Wege II; James C. Welch.
Number of staff: 1 full-time professional; 1 full-time support.
EIN: 386050470
Selected grants: The following grants were reported in 2005.
$1,000,000 to Aquinas College, Grand Rapids, MI.
$300,000 to Grand Rapids Ballet Company, Grand Rapids, MI.
$125,000 to Alano Club of Kent County, Grand Rapids, MI.
$100,000 to Kent County Parks Department, Grand Rapids, MI.
$35,000 to Public Park and Recreation Board of Limestone County, Athens, AL.
$22,500 to Specialized Language Development (SLD) Learning Center, Kalamazoo, MI.
$11,370 to Interfaith Assistance Ministry, Hendersonville, NC.
$10,000 to United Cerebral Palsy Association of Huntsville and Tennessee Valley, Huntsville, AL.

4447
Stoddard Family Foundation, Inc. ✧ ☆
29600 Southfield Rd.
Southfield, MI 48076-2039

Established in 2000 in MI.
Donor: Stanford C. Stoddard.
Foundation type: Independent foundation.
Financial data (yr. ended 12/31/05): Assets, $1,755,129 (M); gifts received, $292,210; expenditures, $409,106; qualifying distributions, $336,980; giving activities include $331,010 for 14 grants (high: $100,000; low: $200).
Purpose and activities: Support primarily for higher education.
Fields of interest: Museums; Arts; Higher education; Student services/organizations; Community development, business promotion.
Type of support: Program development; General/operating support.
Limitations: Applications not accepted. Giving in the U.S., with some emphasis on VA. No grants to individuals.
Application information: Contributes only to pre-selected organizations.
Officers and Director:* Stanford C. Stoddard,* Pres.; M. Richard Olson, Secy.-Treas.
EIN: 383539927

4448
The Vivian Vivio Stolaruk and Steve Stolaruk Foundation ✧
1928 Star Batt Dr., Ste. E
Rochester Hills, MI 48309-3722

Established in 2003 in MI.
Donor: Steve Stolaruk.
Foundation type: Independent foundation.
Financial data (yr. ended 12/31/05): Assets, $262,422 (M); gifts received, $160,000; expenditures, $395,660; qualifying distributions, $395,350; giving activities include $395,350 for 14 grants (high: $340,000; low: $200).
Fields of interest: Cancer; Human services; Roman Catholic agencies & churches.
Type of support: Building/renovation; General/operating support.
Limitations: Applications not accepted. Giving primarily in MI. No grants to individuals.
Application information: Contributes only to pre-selected organizations.
Officers: Steve Stolaruk, Pres.; Marc J. Stolaruk, Secy.-Treas.
EIN: 200515908

4449
Stonisch Foundation ✧
545 W. Brown St.
Birmingham, MI 48009-1458

Established in 1961 in MI.
Donor: Helen Stonisch.
Foundation type: Independent foundation.
Financial data (yr. ended 12/31/05): Assets, $21,700,530 (M); expenditures, $1,332,874; qualifying distributions, $865,000; giving activities include $865,000 for 8+ grants (high: $415,000).
Purpose and activities: Giving primarily for health care, education, and to Christian agencies and churches.
Fields of interest: Secondary school/education; Higher education; Cancer; Cancer research; Medical research; Children/youth, services; Christian agencies & churches.
Type of support: Research.
Limitations: Applications not accepted. Giving primarily in MI.
Application information: Contributes only to pre-selected organizations.
  Board meeting date(s): Nov.
Officers: Gail Riggs, Pres.; Rudy Stonisch, V.P.; Mary Sue Stonisch, Secy.
EIN: 386088638

4450
The Charles J. Strosacker Foundation ✧
P.O. Box 471
Midland, MI 48640-0471
Contact: Marian L. Cimbalik, Tr.

Incorporated in 1957 in MI.
Donors: Charles J. Strosacker†; Ula G. Shaffer Administration Trust.
Foundation type: Independent foundation.
Financial data (yr. ended 12/31/05): Assets, $61,186,503 (M); gifts received, $237,555; expenditures, $2,973,950; qualifying distributions, $2,796,070; giving activities include $2,741,450 for 109 grants (high: $225,000; low: $250).

Purpose and activities: Giving to assist and benefit political subdivisions of the state of Michigan, educational organizations, and social services.

Fields of interest: Performing arts; Education; Health organizations, association; Human services; Economic development; Engineering/technology; Science.

Type of support: Continuing support; Building/renovation; Equipment; Endowments; Program development; Seed money; Research.

Limitations: Giving primarily in MI, with emphasis on Midland County. No grants to individuals, or for matching gifts; no loans.

Publications: Annual report (including application guidelines).

Application information: Application form not required.

> *Initial approach:* Letter
> *Copies of proposal:* 1
> *Board meeting date(s):* May, Aug., and Nov.

Officers and Trustees:* David J. Arnold,* Chair.; Bobbie N. Arnold, C.E.O. and Pres.; Donna T. Morris,* V.P., Fin. and Secy.; Richard M. Reynolds, Treas.; Kimberlee K. Arnold; John N. Bartos; James L. Borin; Lawrence E. Burks; Marian L. Cimbalik; John S. Ludington; Charles J. Thrune; Charlie C. Thrune; Carolyn Thrune-Durand; Eugene C. Yehle.

Number of staff: 1 part-time support.

EIN: 386062787

Selected grants: The following grants were reported in 2005.

$225,000 to Midland Public Schools, Midland, MI.

$164,845 to Eagle Village, Hersey, MI.

$153,000 to Cleveland Manor, Midland, MI. 2 grants: $110,000, $43,000

$125,000 to Kalamazoo College, Kalamazoo, MI.

$100,000 to Boy Scouts of America, Auburn, MI.

$75,000 to Delta College Foundation, University Center, MI.

$50,000 to Gratiot Health System, Alma, MI.

$15,000 to Midland Area Homes, Midland, MI.

$8,000 to Meharry Medical College, Nashville, TN.

4451
The Ronda E. Stryker and William D. Johnston Foundation ✧

100 W. Michigan Ave., Ste. 100
Kalamazoo, MI   49007
Contact: William D. Johnston, Secy.-Treas.

Established in 1995 in MI.

Donors: Ronda E. Stryker; William Johnston.

Foundation type: Independent foundation.

Financial data (yr. ended 12/31/05): Assets, $14,799,653 (M); gifts received, $1,934,000; expenditures, $4,878,103; qualifying distributions, $4,688,764; giving activities include $4,687,824 for 35 grants (high: $700,000; low: $500; average: $1,000–$250,000).

Purpose and activities: Giving primarily for the arts, museums, higher education and human services.

Fields of interest: Museums; Arts; Higher education; Education; Human services; YM/YWCAs & YM/YWHAs; Community development; Foundations (community).

Limitations: Giving primarily in Kalamazoo, MI. No grants to individuals.

Application information:
> *Initial approach:* Letter
> *Deadline(s):* None

Officers: Ronda E. Stryker, Pres.; William D. Johnston, Secy.-Treas.

EIN: 383224966

Selected grants: The following grants were reported in 2005.

$800,000 to Western Michigan University Foundation, Kalamazoo, MI. 2 grants: $100,000 (For general support), $700,000 (For Partnering for Success: The Centennial Campaign for Western Michigan University).

$430,000 to Southwest Michigan First Corporation, Kalamazoo, MI. For general support.

$392,000 to Kalamazoo Institute of Arts, Kalamazoo, MI. For general support.

$200,000 to Kalamazoo College, Kalamazoo, MI. For Mary Jane Underwood Stryker Institute for Service Learning.

$110,000 to Kalamazoo Community Foundation, Kalamazoo, MI. For Community Redevelopment Fund.

$102,500 to Starr Commonwealth, Albion, MI. For general support.

$100,000 to American Red Cross, Kalamazoo, MI. For general support.

4452
Sturgis Area Community Foundation ✧ ☆

(formerly Sturgis Foundation)
310 N. Franks Ave.
Sturgis, MI   49091
FAX: (269) 659-8508; E-mail: stfound@i2k.com

Established in 1962 in MI.

Foundation type: Community foundation.

Financial data (yr. ended 3/31/05): Assets, $9,848,117 (M); gifts received, $700,681; expenditures, $596,844; giving activities include $410,045 for 30 grants (high: $169,500).

Purpose and activities: The foundation seeks to provide benefits to area community charitable organizations.

Fields of interest: Human services.

Type of support: General/operating support; Capital campaigns; Building/renovation; Equipment; Program development; Scholarship funds; Consulting services; Scholarships—to individuals; Matching/challenge support; Student loans—to individuals.

Limitations: Giving limited to the Sturgis, MI, area. No support for religious organizations. No grants for new business loans.

Publications: Application guidelines; Annual report; Financial statement; Grants list; Informational brochure; Informational brochure (including application guidelines).

Application information: Application form required.

> *Copies of proposal:* 10
> *Deadline(s):* May 1 and Nov. 1
> *Board meeting date(s):* Monthly
> *Final notification:* June 30 and Dec. 31

Officers and Trustees:* James Goethals,* Chair.; Laura Brothers,* Vice-Chair.; Mary Dresser, Co-Dir.; John Wiedlea, Co-Dir.; Tom Kool; LeeAnn McConnell; Kelly Murphy; Sheila Riley; John Svendsen; Philip Ward.

Number of staff: 1 full-time professional; 1 part-time support.

EIN: 383649922

4453
Tamer Foundation ✧

56 S. Groesbeck Hwy.
Clinton Township, MI   48036

Established in 1986 in MI.

Donors: James Tamer; James Tamer Restated Living Trust.

Foundation type: Independent foundation.

Financial data (yr. ended 4/30/05): Assets, $10,966,925 (M); expenditures, $617,831; qualifying distributions, $585,950; giving activities include $521,550 for 47 grants (high: $65,000; low: $500), and $64,400 for 24 grants to individuals (high: $6,008; low: $691).

Purpose and activities: Giving primarily for higher education, health and human services, and Christian organizations, primarily Maronite Catholic agencies and churches.

Fields of interest: Higher education; Hospitals (general); Health organizations, association; Food services; Human services; Christian agencies & churches.

Type of support: General/operating support; Scholarship funds; Scholarships—to individuals.

Limitations: Applications not accepted. Giving primarily in Detroit, MI.

Application information: Unsolicited requests for funds not considered.

Officer and Trustees:* Josephine Saigh,* Mgr.; James George; Joseph Thomas.

EIN: 382679633

4454
Tauber Family Foundation ✧

27777 Franklin Rd., Ste. 1630
Southfield, MI   48034

Established in 1993 in MI.

Donor: Joel D. Tauber.

Foundation type: Independent foundation.

Financial data (yr. ended 12/31/04): Assets, $3,167,667 (M); expenditures, $341,883; qualifying distributions, $331,168; giving activities include $334,190 for 30 grants (high: $91,000; low: $25).

Purpose and activities: Giving for education, medical education and research, federated giving programs and for Jewish organizations.

Fields of interest: Higher education; Medical school/education; Education; Human services; Federated giving programs; Jewish federated giving programs; Jewish agencies & temples.

Type of support: Scholarship funds; Building/renovation; General/operating support.

Limitations: Applications not accepted. Giving in the U.S., with emphasis on MI. No grants to individuals.

Application information: Contributes only to pre-selected organizations.

Officers: Joel D. Tauber, Chair. and Pres.; Julie T. McMahon, V.P.; Shelley J. Tauber, V.P.; Benjamin Brian Tauber, Secy.; Ellen T. Horing, Treas.

EIN: 383092417

Selected grants: The following grants were reported in 2003.

$200,000 to Jewish Federation of Metropolitan Detroit, Bloomfield Hills, MI. For unrestricted support.

$35,000 to American Friends of Shalom Hartman Institute, New York, NY. For unrestricted support.

$10,000 to Detroit Zoological Society, Royal Oak, MI. For unrestricted support.

$10,000 to Jewish Community Center of Metropolitan Detroit, West Bloomfield, MI.

$5,000 to Salk Institute for Biological Studies, San Diego, CA. For unrestricted support.

$2,000 to United Way for Southeastern Michigan, Detroit, MI. For capital campaign.

$1,865 to Temple Beth El of Marquette, Detroit, MI. For unrestricted support.

$1,500 to Aspen Music Festival, Aspen, CO. For unrestricted support.

$1,500 to Jewish Academy of Metropolitan Detroit, West Bloomfield, MI. For unrestricted support.

$1,000 to University of Michigan, Edward Ginsburg Center for Community Service Learning, Ann Arbor, MI. For unrestricted support.

4455
The Taubman Foundation ▼
200 E. Long Lake Rd., Ste. 180
Bloomfield Hills, MI 48304
Contact: Jeffrey M. Davidson
FAX: (248) 258-7684;
E-mail: jdavidson@taubman.com

Established in 1985 in MI.

Donor: A. Alfred Taubman.

Foundation type: Independent foundation.

Financial data (yr. ended 1/31/06): Assets, $347 (M); gifts received, $463,560; expenditures, $464,090; qualifying distributions, $464,089; giving activities include $461,150 for 10 grants (high: $250,000; low: $100; average: $500–$5,000).

Purpose and activities: Giving primarily for higher education.

Fields of interest: Higher education.

Limitations: Applications not accepted. Giving primarily in MI.

Application information: The foundation has suspended its new grantmaking, current commitments will be honored.

Officers and Trustees:* A. Alfred Taubman,* Chair., Pres., and Treas.; Jeffrey H. Miro,* Secy.

EIN: 382590369

Selected grants: The following grants were reported in 2005.

$5,010,000 to University of Michigan, Ann Arbor, MI. For general operating support.

$500,000 to Lawrence Technological University, Southfield, MI. For general operating support.

$10,000 to Tougaloo College, Tougaloo, MS. For general operating support.

4456
The Thomas Foundation ✧
201 W. Big Beaver Rd., Ste. 600
Troy, MI 48084-4161 (248) 528-1111
Contact: Jay Howard Brody, Dir.

Established in 1984 in MI.

Donor: Harriet Kay Thomas Revocable Trust.

Foundation type: Independent foundation.

Financial data (yr. ended 3/31/06): Assets, $11,033,766 (M); expenditures, $565,317; qualifying distributions, $333,808; giving activities include $333,808 for grants.

Purpose and activities: Giving primarily for medical research, particularly diabetes; funding also for children and youth services.

Fields of interest: Higher education; Medical school/education; Health organizations; Medical

research, institute; Diabetes research; Boys & girls clubs; Human services; Children/youth, services.

Limitations: Giving primarily in southeast MI.

Application information:
Initial approach: Letter
Deadline(s): None
Final notification: Within 60 days

Directors: Jay Howard Brody; Chester L. Uncapher.

EIN: 382510591

Selected grants: The following grants were reported in 2005.

$100,000 to Juvenile Diabetes Research Foundation International, Tulsa, OK.

$14,000 to Forgotten Harvest, Southfield, MI.

$10,000 to Detroit Institute for Children, Detroit, MI.

$10,000 to United Negro College Fund, Fairfax, VA.

$4,000 to Arthritis Foundation, Atlanta, GA.

$4,000 to Food Bank of Oakland County, Pontiac, MI.

$4,000 to Gleaners Community Food Bank, Detroit, MI.

$4,000 to YMCA.

$2,500 to Childrens Leukemia Foundation of Michigan, Southfield, MI.

$2,500 to Cystic Fibrosis Foundation, Bethesda, MD.

4457
Lucille S. Thompson Family Foundation ✧
c/o Comerica Bank
P.O. Box 75000 MC 3302
Detroit, MI 48275-3302
Contact: Mrs. Lila K. Pfleger, Exec. Dir.
Application address: 4823 Old Kingston Pike, Ste. 140, Knoxville, TN 37919, tel.: (865) 558-8654

Established in 1988 in TN.

Donor: Lucille S. Thompson.

Foundation type: Independent foundation.

Financial data (yr. ended 2/28/05): Assets, $19,173,961 (M); expenditures, $3,078,815; qualifying distributions, $2,751,650; giving activities include $2,564,922 for 174 grants (high: $200,000; low: $50).

Purpose and activities: Support primarily for human services, youth services, education, medical services, and arts and culture for individuals and families of the east TN region.

Fields of interest: Museums; Historic preservation/historical societies; Arts; Health care; Health organizations, association; Cancer; Cancer research; Human services; Children/youth, services.

Type of support: General/operating support; Equipment.

Limitations: Giving primarily in the east TN region. No grants to individuals or for endowment funds, or deficit operating budgets.

Application information: Application form required.
Initial approach: Letter or proposal
Deadline(s): Jan. 31, Apr. 30, July 31, and Oct. 31
Final notification: within 2 weeks after board meeting

Officer and Trust Committee:* Sandra K. Bishop,* Chair.; John W. Baker, Jr.; Archer W. Bishop III; Baker O'Neil Bishop; Sandra K. Bishop; Thompson A. Bishop; Kristin B. MacDermott; Lindsay Young.

Trustee: Comerica Bank.

EIN: 581788548

Selected grants: The following grants were reported in 2003.

$225,000 to Duke University, Durham, NC.

$200,000 to Episcopal Schools of Knoxville, Knoxville, TN.

$200,000 to Webb School of Knoxville, Knoxville, TN.

$118,750 to Music Associates of Aspen, Aspen, CO.

$100,000 to Child and Family, Knoxville, TN.

$100,000 to Knox Area Rescue Ministries, Knoxville, TN.

$100,000 to Maryville College, Maryville, TN.

$100,000 to Pellissippi State Technical Community College Foundation, Knoxville, TN.

$100,000 to West End Academy, Knoxville, TN.

$100,000 to YMCA of Knoxville, Knoxville, TN.

4458
Thompson Foundation ✧
(formerly Thompson-McCully Foundation)
c/o Bridget Makridakis
P.O. Box 6349
Plymouth, MI 48170
FAX: (734) 453-6475;
E-mail: bmakridakis@thompsonfdn.org; URL: http://www.thompsonfdn.org

Established in 1999 in MI.

Donors: Robert M. Thompson; Ellen Anne Thompson.

Foundation type: Independent foundation.

Financial data (yr. ended 12/31/05): Assets, $57,296,018 (M); expenditures, $3,533,659; qualifying distributions, $3,416,078; giving activities include $3,206,914 for 50 grants (high: $500,000; low: $500).

Purpose and activities: The foundation has narrowed its focus to a specific educational initiative.

Fields of interest: Elementary/secondary education; Higher education; Education.

Type of support: Program development; Scholarship funds.

Limitations: Applications not accepted. Giving in the metropolitan Detroit, MI, area. No grants to individuals.

Application information: Unsolicited requests for funds not accepted.
Board meeting date(s): Feb., Apr., June, Aug., Oct., Dec.

Officers and Trustees:* Robert M. Thompson,* Pres.; Ellen Anne Thompson,* V.P.; Joseph G. Horonzy; Edward M. Parks.

Number of staff: 1 full-time professional.

EIN: 383452577

Selected grants: The following grants were reported in 2003.

$745,000 to Salvation Army of Detroit, Detroit, MI. 2 grants: $735,000 (For purchase of Aurora facility to transfer Harbor Light and Booth operations), $10,000 (For Summer Day Camp program).

$600,000 to Focus: Hope, Detroit, MI. For Student Loan Fund.

$91,000 to Detroit Youth Foundation, Detroit, MI. For Detroit Parent Network.

$88,000 to Lighthouse of Oakland County, Pontiac, MI. For financial training and education program.

$60,000 to Southwest Counseling and Development Services, Detroit, MI. For Friends of the Homeless project.

$50,000 to Saint Patrick Senior Center, Detroit, MI. For general operating support.

$27,000 to Saint Rose Senior Citizens Center, Detroit, MI. For Project Aging Well Program.

4459
Michael T. & Nancy E. Timmis Foundation ◇
400 Talon Ctr.
Detroit, MI 48207-5037

Established in 1984 in MI.
Donor: Michael T. Timmis.
Foundation type: Independent foundation.
Financial data (yr. ended 12/31/04): Assets,
$5,038,536 (M); gifts received, $1,000;
expenditures, $1,456,293; qualifying distributions,
$1,317,345; giving activities include $1,316,345
for 57 grants (high: $457,195; low: $50), and
$1,000 for 1 grant to an individual.
Purpose and activities: Giving primarily to Roman
Catholic churches and organizations, and affiliated
programs.
Fields of interest: Education; Human services;
Children/youth, services; International affairs;
Federated giving programs; Roman Catholic
agencies & churches.
Type of support: General/operating support.
Limitations: Applications not accepted. Giving in the
U.S., primarily in Washington, DC, and MI.
Application information: Contributes only to
pre-selected organizations.
Officers: Michael T.O. Timmis, Pres.; Nancy E.
Timmis, V.P.; Justin P. Blomberg, Secy.-Treas.
EIN: 382519177
Selected grants: The following grants were reported
in 2003.
$397,960 to International Foundation, DC. For
general support.
$103,707 to Prison Fellowship International, DC.
For general support.
$75,000 to Cornerstone Schools, Detroit, MI. For
general support.
$32,500 to Navigators, The, Colorado Springs, CO.
For general support.
$31,000 to Wayne State University, Detroit, MI. For
general support.
$3,000 to Loyola High School, Detroit, MI. For
general support.
$1,000 to American Heart Association, Southfield,
MI. For general support.
$1,000 to Campus Crusade for Christ International,
Orlando, FL. For general support.
$500 to Franciscan University of Steubenville,
Steubenville, OH. For general support.
$200 to Childrens Home of Detroit, Grosse Pointe
Woods, MI. For general support.

4460
The Tiscornia Foundation, Inc. ◇ ☆
1010 Main St., Ste. A
St. Joseph, MI 49085 (269) 983-4711
Contact: Laurianne T. Davis, Pres.

Incorporated in 1942 in MI.
Donors: James W. Tiscornia†; Waldo V. Tiscornia†;
Auto Specialties Manufacturing Co.; Lambert Brake
Corp.
Foundation type: Independent foundation.
Financial data (yr. ended 12/31/05): Assets,
$3,673,100 (M); expenditures, $498,251;
qualifying distributions, $355,268; giving activities
include $355,268 for grants.
Fields of interest: Arts; Higher education;
Reproductive health, family planning; Health care;
Health organizations; Human services; Youth,
services.

Type of support: Continuing support; Capital
campaigns; Building/renovation; Equipment;
Emergency funds; Seed money; Scholarship funds;
Scholarships—to individuals.
Limitations: Giving limited to North Berrien County,
MI. No grants to individuals (except
committee-selected scholarship recipients), or for
research or matching gifts; no loans.
Publications: Annual report (including application
guidelines).
Application information: Scholarships only for
northern Berrien County high school seniors at the
following schools: St. Joseph, Benton Harbor,
Coloma, Watervliet, Lake Shore, Lake Michigan
Catholic, and Lake Michigan Lutheran. Application
form not required.
Initial approach: Letter or proposal
Copies of proposal: 1
Deadline(s): Apr. 1 for scholarships; Oct. 1 for
grants
Board meeting date(s): Jan.
Officers: Laurianne T. Davis, Pres. and Exec. Dir.;
Bernice Tiscornia, V.P.; James Tiscornia, V.P.; Lesli
D. Nadolski, Secy.; Henry Tippet, Treas.
Number of staff: 1 full-time professional; 1 part-time
support.
EIN: 381777343

4461
The Harry A. and Margaret D. Towsley Foundation
140 Ashman St.
P.O. Box 349
Midland, MI 48640 (989) 837-1100
Contact: Lynn T. White, Pres.

Incorporated in 1959 in MI.
Donor: Margaret D. Towsley†.
Foundation type: Independent foundation.
Financial data (yr. ended 12/31/05): Assets,
$69,709,596 (M); expenditures, $3,130,534;
qualifying distributions, $2,902,743; giving
activities include $2,808,843 for 49 grants (high:
$400,000; low: $500; average: $5,000–$50,000).
Purpose and activities: Support for medical and
preschool education, social services, and
continuing education and research in the health
sciences.
Fields of interest: Arts; Education, early childhood
education; Higher education; Medical school/
education; Education; Medical research, institute;
Human services.
Type of support: General/operating support;
Continuing support; Annual campaigns; Capital
campaigns; Building/renovation; Endowments;
Program development; Professorships; Seed
money; Research; Employee matching gifts;
Matching/challenge support.
Limitations: Giving limited to MI, primarily within Ann
Arbor and Washtenaw County. No grants to
individuals, or for travel, scholarships, fellowships,
conferences, books, publications, films, tapes,
audio-visual, or other communication media; no
loans.
Publications: Annual report (including application
guidelines).
Application information: Environmental Impact
Statement is required for all capital projects.
Application form not required.
Initial approach: Letter and proposal
Copies of proposal: 2
Deadline(s): Mar. 31

Board meeting date(s): Apr., July, Sept., and Dec.
Final notification: 60 to 90 days
Officers and Trustees:* Margaret Ann Riecker,*
Chair.; Lynn T. White,* Pres.; Judith D. Rumelhart,*
V.P.; John E. Riecker, Secy.; Wendell Dunbar,*
Treas.; Bruce Benner, Tr. Emeritus; David Inglish;
Jennifer R. Poteat-Flores; Steven Towsley Riecker;
Margaret E. Thompson, M.D.
Number of staff: 1 part-time support.
EIN: 386091798
Selected grants: The following grants were reported
in 2004.
$850,130 to University of Michigan, Ann Arbor, MI.
2 grants: $425,065 each
$212,365 to Saint Joseph Mercy Health System,
Ann Arbor, MI.
$200,000 to Kalamazoo College, Kalamazoo, MI.
$150,000 to Hope College, Holland, MI.
$125,000 to Culver Educational Foundation, Culver,
IN.
$50,000 to Catholic Social Services of Washtenaw
County, Ann Arbor, MI.
$50,000 to HelpSource, Ann Arbor, MI.
$50,000 to Hillsdale College, Hillsdale, MI.
$45,000 to West Midland Family Center, Shepherd,
MI.

4462
The Thomas J. Tracy Family Foundation ◇
38525 N. Woodward Ave., Ste. 1300
Bloomfield Hills, MI 48304-5089

Established in 1998 in MI.
Donors: Emmet and Frances Tracy Fund; Thomas J.
Tracy; Tracy Industries, Inc.
Foundation type: Independent foundation.
Financial data (yr. ended 12/31/04): Assets,
$1,769,142 (M); gifts received, $1,000,076;
expenditures, $614,905; qualifying distributions,
$610,640; giving activities include $610,640 for 31
grants (high: $120,000; low: $100), and $72,000
for foundation-administered programs.
Purpose and activities: Giving primarily for
education, hospitals and medical research, human
services, and Roman Catholic organizations.
Fields of interest: Higher education; Education;
Hospitals (general); Medical research, institute;
Human services; Federated giving programs; Roman
Catholic agencies & churches.
Limitations: Applications not accepted. Giving on a
national basis. No grants to individuals.
Application information: Contributes only to
pre-selected organizations.
Officers: Thomas J. Tracy, Pres.; Katherine
McCanna, V.P.; David M. Rosenberger, Secy.; Erma
Jean Tracy, Treas.
Trustee: Cynthia Tracy.
EIN: 383390017
Selected grants: The following grants were reported
in 2004.
$120,000 to Saint Joseph Hospital, Eureka, CA.
$100,000 to Catholic Charities, Arlington, VA.
$72,000 to Creighton University, Omaha, NE. 6
grants: $12,000 each
$25,000 to Orange Catholic Foundation, Orange,
CA.
$11,100 to Belvedere College, Dublin, Ireland. .

4463
Jerry L. & Marcia D. Tubergen Foundation
P.O. Box 230257
Grand Rapids, MI 49523-0257 (616) 643-4700
Contact: Ginny Vander Hart, Exec. Dir.

Established in 1996 in MI.
Donors: Jerry L. Tubergen; Helen J. DeVos.
Foundation type: Independent foundation.
Financial data (yr. ended 12/31/04): Assets, $18,927,220 (M); gifts received, $2,551,250; expenditures, $3,131,617; qualifying distributions, $2,858,975; giving activities include $2,856,500 for 43 grants (high: $1,900,000; low: $100).
Purpose and activities: Giving primarily for Christian-based programs and services.
Fields of interest: Medical care, rehabilitation; Human services; Christian agencies & churches.
Type of support: General/operating support; Annual campaigns; Capital campaigns.
Limitations: Applications not accepted. Giving primarily in the U.S., with emphasis on western MI; giving also internationally. No grants to individuals.
Application information: Contributes only to pre-selected organizations.
Officers: Jerry L. Tubergen, Pres. and Treas.; Marcia D. Tubergen, V.P and Secy.
EIN: 383297265
Selected grants: The following grants were reported in 2003.
$357,650 to Grand Rapids Baptist Schools, Grand Rapids, MI. For general support.
$25,000 to New Horizons Foundation, Colorado Springs, CO. For general support.
$20,000 to United Way, Heart of West Michigan, Grand Rapids, MI. For general support.
$17,200 to CURE International, Harrisburg, PA. For general support.
$4,000 to Education Freedom Fund, Grand Rapids, MI. For general support.
$2,500 to Indian Trails Camp, Grand Rapids, MI. For general support.
$2,500 to Stephens Children Foundation, Atlanta, GA. For general support.
$1,000 to Grand Action Foundation, Grand Rapids, MI. For general support.
$500 to Council of Michigan Foundations, Grand Haven, MI. For general support.
$200 to Oral Roberts University, Tulsa, OK. For general support.

4464
Jane Smith Turner Foundation, Inc. ✧
500 Woodward Ave., Ste. 2500
Detroit, MI 48226

Established in 1994 in MI.
Foundation type: Independent foundation.
Financial data (yr. ended 12/31/05): Assets, $9,540,523 (M); expenditures, $412,608; qualifying distributions, $364,527; giving activities include $348,500 for 54 grants (high: $20,000; low: $1,000).
Purpose and activities: Giving primarily to arts and cultural programs, education, wildlife preservation, health associations, and natural resource conservation.
Fields of interest: Arts; Education; Environment, natural resources; Animals/wildlife, preservation/protection; Hospitals (general); Health organizations, association; Children/youth, services; Protestant agencies & churches.

Limitations: Applications not accepted. Giving in the U.S., primarily in the South, with emphasis on GA and SC. No grants to individuals.
Application information: Contributes only to pre-selected organizations.
Officers and Directors:* Jane Smith Turner, Pres. and Secy.; David W. Laughlin,* Treas.; Sarah Jane Turner Garlington; Laura Turner Seydel; Reed Beauregard Turner; Rhett Lee Turner; Robert E. Turner IV; John Wilson.
EIN: 383199326
Selected grants: The following grants were reported in 2005.
$20,000 to Captain Planet Foundation, Atlanta, GA.
$15,000 to Robert W. Woodruff Arts Center, Atlanta, GA.
$10,000 to American Red Cross.
$10,000 to Baton Rouge Area Foundation, Baton Rouge, LA.
$10,000 to Brooks School, North Andover, MA.
$10,000 to Peregrine Fund, Boise, ID.
$10,000 to South Carolina Coastal Conservation League, Charleston, SC.
$5,000 to Central Kentucky Riding for Hope, Lexington, KY.
$5,000 to Fernbank Museum of Natural History, Atlanta, GA.
$5,000 to Rainforest Action Network, San Francisco, CA.

4465
Harold and Grace Upjohn Foundation
136 E. Michigan Ave., Ste. 9B
Kalamazoo, MI 49007 (269) 344-2818
Contact: Floyd L. Parks, Secy.-Treas.

Incorporated in 1958 in MI.
Donors: Grace G. Upjohn†; Edwin Meader; Mary Meader.
Foundation type: Independent foundation.
Financial data (yr. ended 10/31/05): Assets, $12,541,087 (M); gifts received, $195,962; expenditures, $651,696; qualifying distributions, $598,435; giving activities include $585,000 for 50 grants (high: $40,000; low: $500).
Purpose and activities: Grants primarily to promote scientific research for the alleviation of human suffering; to care for the sick, aged, and helpless whose private resources are inadequate; to conduct research for and otherwise assist in the improvement of living, moral and working conditions; to promote the spread of education and to provide scholarships for deserving young men and women; to promote and aid in the mental, moral, intellectual and physical improvement, assistance and relief of the poor, indigent or deserving inhabitants of the U.S., regardless of race, color or creed.
Fields of interest: Arts; Higher education; Environment; Family services; Aging, centers/services; Community development, neighborhood development; Christian agencies & churches.
Type of support: Program development; Seed money; Scholarship funds; Research.
Limitations: Giving limited to Kalamazoo, MI. No grants to individuals, or for operating budgets or annual campaigns.
Publications: Application guidelines; Annual report.
Application information: Application form required.
Initial approach: Call or write for application form and instructions
Copies of proposal: 6
Deadline(s): Apr. 1 and Sept. 1

Board meeting date(s): Spring and fall
Final notification: 30 days after board meeting
Officers and Trustees:* Janet J. Deal-Koestner,* Pres.; Jon L. Stryker,* V.P.; Floyd L. Parks,* Secy.-Treas.; Timothy Light; Mary U. Meader; Florence Upjohn Orosz.
EIN: 386052963
Selected grants: The following grants were reported in 2005.
$40,000 to Ministry with Community, Kalamazoo, MI.
$30,000 to Housing Resources, Kalamazoo, MI.
$25,000 to Goodwill Industries of Southwestern Michigan, Kalamazoo, MI.
$25,000 to Kalamazoo Civic Theater, Kalamazoo, MI.
$25,000 to Mount Zion Safe House, Kalamazoo, MI.
$25,000 to United Way, Greater Kalamazoo, Kalamazoo, MI.
$25,000 to University of Michigan, Ann Arbor, MI. For Radio Tower in Hastings, MI.
$23,000 to Kalamazoo Communities in Schools Foundation, Kalamazoo, MI.
$20,000 to Hispanic American Council, Kalamazoo, MI.
$20,000 to W. E. Upjohn Unemployment Trustee Corporation, Kalamazoo, MI.

4466
Frederick S. Upton Foundation
100 Ridgeway St.
St. Joseph, MI 49085-1047
Contact: Stephen E. Upton, Chair.
FAX: (269) 982-0323;
E-mail: fsuptonfdn@opexonline.com

Trust established in 1954 in IL.
Donor: Frederick S. Upton†.
Foundation type: Independent foundation.
Financial data (yr. ended 12/31/05): Assets, $37,985,021 (M); expenditures, $1,907,268; qualifying distributions, $1,666,726; giving activities include $1,593,377 for 183 grants (high: $100,000; low: $200).
Type of support: Research; Seed money; Management development/capacity building; General/operating support; Annual campaigns; Capital campaigns; Building/renovation; Equipment; Program development.
Limitations: Giving primarily in MI and SC.
Publications: Application guidelines.
Application information: Application form required.
Initial approach: Letter
Copies of proposal: 9
Deadline(s): Mar. 15, June 15, Aug. 15 and Oct. 15
Board meeting date(s): Varies
Final notification: All applicants will be notified
Officers and Trustees:* Stephen E. Upton,* Chair.; Sylvia Upton Wood,* Secy.; Priscilla Upton Byrns; Steven Byrns; Sarah duPont; Margaret Trumbull; David F. Upton; Michael Upton; JPMorgan Chase Bank, N.A.
Number of staff: 1 part-time professional.
EIN: 366013317
Selected grants: The following grants were reported in 2005.
$100,000 to Lakeland Health Foundation, Saint Joseph, MI.
$82,750 to Cornerstone Alliance, Benton Harbor, MI.
$74,000 to Salvation Army.

$50,000 to Western Michigan University, Kalamazoo, MI.

$47,500 to Sarett Nature Center, Benton Harbor, MI.

$40,500 to Fine Arts Center of Kershaw County, Camden, SC.

$15,000 to Berrien County Health Department, Benton Harbor, MI.

$10,000 to Infant Crisis Services, Oklahoma City, OK.

$3,200 to Greenhills School, Ann Arbor, MI.

$3,000 to Interlochen Center for the Arts, Interlochen, MI.

4467
Jay and Betty Van Andel Foundation ▼
3133 Orchard Vista Dr. S.E.
Grand Rapids, MI 49546
Contact: Casey Wondergern, Exec. Dir.

Established in 1963.
Donors: Jay Van Andel†; Betty Jean Van Andel†; Amway Corp.
Foundation type: Independent foundation.
Financial data (yr. ended 12/31/04): Assets, $137,756,955 (M); gifts received, $3,156,789; expenditures, $20,930,979; qualifying distributions, $18,294,313; giving activities include $18,294,313 for 126 grants (high: $11,752,180; low: $100; average: $2,500–$1,000,000).
Purpose and activities: Emphasis on Christian religious activities, including higher and secondary education; giving also for a museum foundation and other cultural programs.
Fields of interest: Museums; Arts; Secondary school/education; Higher education; Christian agencies & churches.
Limitations: Applications not accepted. Giving primarily in MI, with some emphasis on Grand Rapids. No grants to individuals.
Application information: Contributes only to pre-selected organizations.
Officers and Trustee:* David Van Andel, V.P.; James Rosloniec,* Secy.-Treas.; Mark Bugge, Cont.; Casey Wondergern, Exec. Dir.
Number of staff: 1 part-time professional.
EIN: 237066716
Selected grants: The following grants were reported in 2004.
$1,027,500 to Grand Rapids Art Museum, Grand Rapids, MI.
$250,000 to Grand Valley State University, Grand Rapids, MI.
$153,000 to Ada Christian School, Grand Rapids, MI.
$150,000 to Calvin Theological Seminary, Grand Rapids, MI.
$115,000 to Grand Rapids Symphony, Grand Rapids, MI.
$86,500 to LaGrave Avenue Christian Reformed Church, Grand Rapids, MI.
$75,000 to Public Museum of Grand Rapids, Grand Rapids, MI.
$65,000 to Hope College, Holland, MI.
$60,000 to Frederik Meijer Gardens and Sculpture Park, Grand Rapids, MI.
$50,000 to Creation Research Society, Chino Valley, AZ. For general support.

4468
Van Curler Foundation ◇
2008 Hogback Rd.
Ann Arbor, MI 48105

Established in 2000 in MI.
Donors: Donald E. Van Curler; Carol Van Curler.
Foundation type: Independent foundation.
Financial data (yr. ended 12/31/05): Assets, $732,562 (M); gifts received, $750,000; expenditures, $368,784; qualifying distributions, $353,050; giving activities include $344,050 for 6 grants (high: $311,000; low: $500), and $9,000 for 7 grants to individuals (high: $2,500; low: $500).
Fields of interest: Education; Christian agencies & churches.
Type of support: General/operating support; Scholarships—to individuals.
Limitations: Giving on a national basis.
Officers and Directors:* Donald E. Van Curler,* Pres. and Treas.; Carol Van Curler,* Secy.
EIN: 383529339

4469
Robert & Cheri Vanderweide Foundation
P.O. Box 230257
Grand Rapids, MI 49523 (616) 643-4700
Contact: Ginny Vander Hart, Exec. Dir.
FAX: (616) 774-0116; Application address: 126 Ottawa N.W., Ste. 500, Grand Rapids, MI 49503; E-mail (for Ginny Vander Hart): virginiav@rdvcorp.com

Established in 1992 in MI.
Donor: Suzanne DeVos Vanderweide.
Foundation type: Independent foundation.
Financial data (yr. ended 12/31/04): Assets, $2,115,343 (M); expenditures, $1,026,965; qualifying distributions, $1,005,714; giving activities include $970,034 for 45 grants (high: $130,000; low: $500).
Purpose and activities: The foundation seeks to create a legacy of caring and stewardship through their support of projects that build community and improve the quality of people's lives. To carry out this commitment, it focuses on organizations, projects, or programs that demonstrate Christian charity to meet both the spiritual and physical needs of people, which strengthen the bond of families and communities, and bring opportunity to disadvantaged persons. Giving primarily for Christian churches; giving also for education and human services.
Fields of interest: Education; Human services; Community development; Federated giving programs; Christian agencies & churches; Protestant agencies & churches.
Type of support: General/operating support; Continuing support; Annual campaigns; Capital campaigns; Building/renovation; Program development; Matching/challenge support.
Limitations: Giving primarily in west MI and central FL. No grants to individuals.
Publications: Application guidelines.
Application information: Application form not required.
  Initial approach: Letter or request application guidelines
  Copies of proposal: 1
  Deadline(s): 2 weeks prior to review
  Board meeting date(s): 3 times annually
  Final notification: 3 to 5 months

Officers: Suzanne C. Vanderweide, Pres.; Jerry L. Tubergen, C.O.O., V.P., and Secy.; Robert A. Vanderweide, V.P.; Robert H. Schierbeek, Treas.
Number of staff: 3 full-time professional.
EIN: 383035978
Selected grants: The following grants were reported in 2004.
$130,000 to Hope College, Holland, MI.
$125,000 to KeyStone Community Church, Grand Rapids, MI.
$104,280 to Grand Rapids Art Museum, Grand Rapids, MI.
$43,250 to Orlando Magic Youth Foundation, Orlando, FL.
$40,000 to Gospel Communications International, Muskegon, MI.
$25,000 to Blodgett Butterworth Health Care Foundation, Grand Rapids, MI.
$25,000 to Potters House, Grand Rapids, MI.
$12,500 to Grand Rapids Childrens Museum, Grand Rapids, MI.
$10,000 to Life International, Grand Rapids, MI.
$5,500 to Florida Hospital Foundation, Orlando, FL.

4470
The William and Katherine Vandomelen Foundation ◇ ☆
P.O. Box 20216
Kalamazoo, MI 49019

Established in 1992 in MI.
Donor: William F. Vandomelen.
Foundation type: Independent foundation.
Financial data (yr. ended 12/31/05): Assets, $6,762,154 (M); gifts received, $532,980; expenditures, $374,346; qualifying distributions, $372,100; giving activities include $372,100 for 14 grants (high: $125,000; low: $1,000).
Fields of interest: Education; Health care; Human services; Children/youth, services; Family services; Roman Catholic agencies & churches.
Limitations: Applications not accepted. Giving primarily in Kalamazoo, MI. No grants to individuals.
Application information: Contributes only to pre-selected organizations.
Officers and Directors:* William F. Vandomelen,* Pres.; Mark W. Vandomelen,* V.P.; Julia Vandomelen,* Secy.; Arthur E. Albin, Treas.; George Lennon.
EIN: 382916030
Selected grants: The following grants were reported in 2005.
$125,000 to Borgess Medical Center, Kalamazoo, MI.
$84,000 to Caring Network, Cape Town, South Africa. 2 grants: $42,000 each.
$35,000 to Habitat for Humanity International.
$23,100 to Hackett Catholic Central High School, Kalamazoo, MI.
$20,000 to International Aid, Spring Lake, MI.
$20,000 to National Alopecia Areata Foundation, San Rafael, CA.
$10,000 to Immokalee Foundation, Naples, FL.
$10,000 to Salvation Army.
$1,000 to Community Foundation of Collier County, Naples, FL.

4471
Vaughan Foundation ✧

c/o Erik H. Serr
101 N. Main St., 7th Fl.
Ann Arbor, MI 48104

Established in 1997 in MI.
Donor: Christine M. Holmes.
Foundation type: Independent foundation.
Financial data (yr. ended 12/31/05): Assets,
$6,418,529 (M); gifts received, $143,691;
expenditures, $373,458; qualifying distributions,
$360,000; giving activities include $360,000 for 23
grants (high: $40,000; low: $5,000).
Purpose and activities: Funding primarily for arts
and culture, human services, and animal welfare.
Fields of interest: Arts; Animal welfare; Human
services; American Red Cross.
Limitations: Applications not accepted. Giving
primarily in MI. No grants to individuals.
Application information: Contributes only to
pre-selected organizations.
Officer: Christine Holmes, Pres. and Secy.-Treas.
EIN: 383355160
Selected grants: The following grants were reported
in 2004.
$30,000 to Humane Society of Huron Valley, Ann
   Arbor, MI.
$30,000 to YMCA, Ann Arbor, Ann Arbor, MI.
$20,000 to Paws With A Cause, Wayland, MI.
$20,000 to Peace Neighborhood Center, Ann Arbor,
   MI.
$20,000 to Saint Louis Center, Chelsea, MI.
$20,000 to Washtenaw Literacy, Ypsilanti, MI.
$15,000 to American Red Cross, Ann Arbor, MI.
$15,000 to Great Lakes Rabbit Sanctuary,
   Whittaker, MI.
$15,000 to Horses Haven, South Lyon, MI.
$15,000 to Leader Dogs for the Blind, Rochester,
   MI.

4472
The Visteon Fund ✧

P.O. Box 850
Belleville, MI 48112-0850
URL: http://www.visteon.com/about/
community.shtml

Established in 1999 in MI.
Donor: Visteon Corp.
Foundation type: Company-sponsored foundation.
Financial data (yr. ended 12/31/04): Assets,
$2,009,718 (M); gifts received, $503,024;
expenditures, $1,335,572; qualifying distributions,
$1,330,161; giving activities include $1,328,918
for 198 grants (high: $100,000; low: $500).
Purpose and activities: The fund supports
museums and organizations involved with
education, the environment, health, hunger, youth
development, human services, and community
development. Special emphasis is directed toward
programs designed to enrich the lives of children;
and improve the environment.
Fields of interest: Museums; Elementary/
secondary education; Higher education; Education;
Environment, natural resources; Environment;
Hospitals (general); Health care; Food services;
Youth development, scouting agencies (general);
Youth development; Children/youth, services;
Family services; Human services; Community
development.
Type of support: General/operating support.

Limitations: Applications not accepted. Giving on a
national basis in areas of company operations, with
some emphasis on MI. No grants to individuals.
Application information: Contributes only to
pre-selected organizations.
Officers and Trustees:* Peter J. Pestillo,* Pres.;
Robert Marcin,* V.P.; Stacy L. Fox,* Secy.; Daniel
R. Coulson,* Treas.; Peter Look,* Treas.; Michael
Johnston.
EIN: 383566029
Selected grants: The following grants were reported
in 2004.
$100,000 to Edison Institute, Dearborn, MI.
$31,334 to Childrens Hospital of Michigan, Detroit,
   MI.
$30,000 to Focus: Hope, Detroit, MI.
$30,000 to United Negro College Fund, Fairfax, VA.
$15,000 to Girl Scouts of the U.S.A..
$5,000 to Boys Club.
$5,000 to George Washington Carver Community
   Center, Norristown, PA.
$5,000 to Greater Detroit Area Health Council,
   Detroit, MI.
$4,000 to Detroit Friendship House, Hamtramck,
   MI.
$2,500 to Niagara Frontier Radio Reading Service,
   Buffalo, NY.

4473
Volkswagen of America Foundation ✧

3800 Hamlin Rd.
Auburn Hills, MI 48326-2855

Established in 2001 in MI.
Donor: Volkswagen of America, Inc.
Foundation type: Company-sponsored foundation.
Financial data (yr. ended 12/31/05): Assets,
$1,596,719 (M); gifts received, $505;
expenditures, $562,500; qualifying distributions,
$562,500; giving activities include $500,000 for 1
grant, and $62,500 for 34 grants to individuals
(high: $3,000; low: $500).
Purpose and activities: The foundation supports
organizations involved with education and awards
disaster relief grants to individuals.
Fields of interest: Education; American Red Cross.
Type of support: General/operating support; Grants
to individuals.
Limitations: Applications not accepted. No grants to
individuals (except for disaster relief grants).
Application information: Contributes only to
pre-selected organizations and individuals.
Officers and Trustees:* Frank Witter,* Pres.;
Joseph S. Folz,* Secy.-Treas.; Steve Keyes.
EIN: 383628606

4474
Weatherwax Foundation ✧

P.O. Box 1111
Jackson, MI 49204
Application address: c/o Maria M. Dotterweich,
Exec. Dir., 245 W. Michigan Ave., 4th Fl., Jackson,
MI 49201-2265, tel.: (517) 787-2117

Established in 1981 in MI.
Donor: K.A. Weatherwax Trust I†.
Foundation type: Independent foundation.
Financial data (yr. ended 9/30/05): Assets,
$21,297,496 (M); expenditures, $1,553,796;
qualifying distributions, $1,400,445; giving
activities include $1,235,592 for 48 grants (high:

$125,000; low: $1,000), and $29,200 for 3
employee matching gifts.
Purpose and activities: Support primarily for arts
and culture, education, human services, and health
care.
Fields of interest: Museums; Performing arts,
orchestra (symphony); Arts; Higher education;
Education; Health care; Human services; Federated
giving programs.
Type of support: General/operating support; Annual
campaigns; Capital campaigns; Building/
renovation; Equipment; Emergency funds;
Conferences/seminars; Curriculum development;
Scholarship funds; Technical assistance;
Consulting services; Program evaluation; Matching/
challenge support.
Limitations: Giving primarily in Hillsdale, Lenawee,
and Jackson counties, MI. No grants to individuals,
or for computer purchases.
Publications: Application guidelines; Grants list.
Application information: Application form required.
   Initial approach: Proposal (not to exceed 2 pages)
   Copies of proposal: 3
   Deadline(s): None
   Board meeting date(s): Monthly
   Final notification: Acknowledgement within 60
   days
Officer: Maria Miceli Dotterweich, Exec. Dir.
Trustees: Lawrence Bullen; Comerica Bank.
Number of staff: 1 part-time professional.
EIN: 386439807
Selected grants: The following grants were reported
in 2005.
$154,447 to Artspace Projects, Minneapolis, MN. 2
   grants: $50,000, $104,447
$125,000 to Ella Sharp Museum, Jackson, MI.
$100,000 to Hillsdale College, Hillsdale, MI.
$75,000 to Lily Missions Center, Jackson, MI.
$50,000 to Albion College, Albion, MI.
$50,000 to Community Respite Center, Jackson,
   MI.
$35,000 to Disability Connections, Jackson, MI.
$25,000 to Michigan Shakespeare Festival,
   Jackson, MI.
$25,000 to Starr Commonwealth, Albion, MI.

4475
The Wayne and Joan Webber Foundation

c/o Gary Drainville, Genl. Mgr.
44710 Morley Dr.
Clinton Township, MI 48036

Established in 1998 in MI.
Donors: Joan Webber; Wayne Webber; Hanson
Aggregates West, Inc.; Southern Crushed Concrete,
Inc.
Foundation type: Independent foundation.
Financial data (yr. ended 12/31/04): Assets,
$5,538,762 (M); gifts received, $2,160,000;
expenditures, $1,055,477; qualifying distributions,
$1,050,047; giving activities include $1,038,546
for 7 grants (high: $328,571; low: $5,000).
Purpose and activities: Giving primarily for health
care, including to a cancer center, as well as for
education.
Fields of interest: Elementary/secondary
education; Hospitals (specialty); Health care;
Cancer; Human services.
Type of support: Capital campaigns.
Limitations: Applications not accepted. Giving
primarily in MI. No grants to individuals.
Application information: Contributes only to
pre-selected organizations.

Directors: Joan Webber; Wayne Webber.
EIN: 383390733
Selected grants: The following grants were reported in 2004.
$494,665 to Loyola High School, Detroit, MI.
$5,000 to Macomb County Child Advocacy Center, Mount Clemens, MI.

4476
Wege Foundation ▼
P.O. Box 6388
Grand Rapids, MI 49516-6388 (616) 957-0480
Contact: Ellen Satterlee, Treas. and Exec. Dir.

Established on July 13, 1967 in MI.
Donor: Peter M. Wege.
Foundation type: Independent foundation.
Financial data (yr. ended 12/31/04): Assets, $161,051,374 (M); expenditures, $17,490,860; qualifying distributions, $16,843,614; giving activities include $16,098,666 for 399 grants (high: $500,000; low: $400; average: $1,000–$50,000).
Purpose and activities: Giving primarily to museums, performing arts, health and human services, youth, Christian agencies, and education.
Fields of interest: Museums; Performing arts; Elementary/secondary education; Higher education; Environment, natural resources; Hospitals (general); Human services; Children/youth, services; Community development; Christian agencies & churches.
Type of support: Annual campaigns; Capital campaigns; Building/renovation; Equipment; Endowments; Program development; Curriculum development; Matching/challenge support.
Limitations: Giving primarily in greater Kent County, MI, with emphasis on the Grand Rapids area. No grants to individuals, or for operating budgets.
Publications: Application guidelines; Annual report.
Application information: Accepts CMF Common Grant Application Form. Application form not required.
   Initial approach: Proposal
   Copies of proposal: 1
   Deadline(s): Feb. 15 and Sept. 15
Officers and Directors:* Peter M. Wege,* Pres.; Terri McCarthy, V.P., Progs; Peter M. Wege II,* V.P.; W. Michael Van Haren,* Secy.; Ellen Satterlee, Treas. and Exec. Dir.; Mary Goodwillie Nelson; Christopher Wege; Diana Wege Sherogan; Jonathan C. Wege.
Number of staff: 3 full-time professional.
EIN: 386124363
Selected grants: The following grants were reported in 2005.
$550,000 to Saint Marys Mercy Medical Center, Grand Rapids, MI. 2 grants: $50,000, $500,000
$450,000 to Grand Rapids Art Museum, Grand Rapids, MI.
$166,668 to National Parks Conservation Association, DC.
$150,000 to Aquinas College, Grand Rapids, MI.
$50,000 to Catholic Social Services, Grand Rapids, MI.
$25,000 to Franciscan Life Process Child Development Center, Lowell, MI.
$25,000 to Grand Rapids Community College Foundation, Grand Rapids, MI.
$25,000 to Michigan Military Preservation Society, Grand Rapids, MI.
$25,000 to Muskegon River Watershed Assembly, Big Rapids, MI.

4477
Henry E. and Consuelo S. Wenger Foundation, Inc. ✧
8916 Gale Rd.
White Lake, MI 48386

Incorporated in 1959 in MI.
Donor: Consuelo S. Wenger.
Foundation type: Independent foundation.
Financial data (yr. ended 12/31/05): Assets, $14,586,816 (M); expenditures, $920,564; qualifying distributions, $888,045; giving activities include $884,805 for 81 grants (high: $125,000; low: $100).
Purpose and activities: Support for the arts, secondary and higher education, environmental preservation, hospitals, and Christian churches.
Fields of interest: Arts; Elementary/secondary education; Higher education; Environment; Hospitals (general); Health care; Youth development, centers/clubs; Human services; Christian agencies & churches.
Limitations: Applications not accepted. Giving primarily in FL, IL, MA, MI, NH, NY, and RI. No grants to individuals.
Application information: Contributes only to pre-selected organizations.
Officer: Diane Wenger Wilson, Pres.
EIN: 386077419

4478
Samuel L. Westerman Foundation
40700 N. Woodward Ave., Ste. A
Bloomfield Hills, MI 48304
Contact: Ruth R. LoPrete, Grant Off.
Application address: 2861 Masefield Dr., Bloomfield Hills, MI 48303, tel.: (248) 203-9343

Established in 1971 in MI.
Donor: Samuel L. Westerman†.
Foundation type: Independent foundation.
Financial data (yr. ended 12/31/05): Assets, $9,108,939 (M); expenditures, $489,223; qualifying distributions, $445,250; giving activities include $445,250 for 164 grants (high: $10,000; low: $40).
Purpose and activities: Giving primarily for education, youth services and religious programs.
Fields of interest: Performing arts, music; Arts; Higher education; Education; Hospitals (general); Health care; Health organizations, association; Human services; Children/youth, services; Religion.
Type of support: General/operating support; Continuing support; Endowments; Program development; Scholarship funds; Research.
Limitations: Giving primarily in MI. No grants to individuals.
Publications: Grants list.
Application information: Very limited funds available for new grants. Application form not required.
   Initial approach: Letter
   Copies of proposal: 1
   Deadline(s): None
   Board meeting date(s): Quarterly
   Final notification: Via letter
Officers and Trustees:* James H. LoPrete,* Pres.; Cameron K. Muir,* V.P. and Treas.; Ruth LoPrete, V.P. and Grant Off.; Kent G. LoPrete,* V.P., Investment Comm.; Gordon J. Muir, V.P., Investment

Comm.; Martha M. Muir,* V.P.; Mary M. Lyneus, Secy.
EIN: 237108795

4479
Wheeler Family Foundation, Inc. ✧
c/o TMW Enterprises, Inc.
2120 Austin Ave., Ste. 100
Rochester Hills, MI 48309-3667

Established in 1997 in DE.
Donor: Thomas M. Wheeler.
Foundation type: Independent foundation.
Financial data (yr. ended 6/30/05): Assets, $10,268,558 (M); expenditures, $576,061; qualifying distributions, $432,500; giving activities include $432,500 for 20 grants (high: $100,000; low: $400).
Purpose and activities: Giving primarily for elementary and secondary education, as well as for a Roman Catholic church; funding also for youth and social services.
Fields of interest: Elementary/secondary education; Human services; Salvation Army; Youth, services; Roman Catholic agencies & churches.
Limitations: Applications not accepted. Giving primarily in CO, FL, and MI. No grants to individuals.
Application information: Contributes only to pre-selected organizations.
Officers and Directors:* Michaleon A. Wright,* Pres.; Douglas S. Soifer,* Secy.; Paul Oster, Treas.; Lisa W. Huzella; Thomas M. Wheeler; Thomas R. Wheeler; Erin Wright; Morgan Wright.
EIN: 383392912

4480
Whirlpool Foundation ▼ ✧
2000 N. M-63
Benton Harbor, MI 49022-2692
(269) 923-5580
Contact: Barbara Hall, Exec. Dir.
FAX: (269) 925-0154; URL: http://whirlpoolcorp.com/social_responsibility/whirlpoolfoundation/default.asp

Incorporated in 1951 in MI.
Donor: Whirlpool Corp.
Foundation type: Company-sponsored foundation.
Financial data (yr. ended 3/31/04): Assets, $257,343 (M); gifts received, $9,086,000; expenditures, $8,902,630; qualifying distributions, $8,907,069; giving activities include $5,875,032 for 351 grants (high: $1,000,000; low: $100), $747,736 for 211 grants to individuals (high: $14,500; low: $900), and $1,863,232 for 668 employee matching gifts.
Purpose and activities: The foundation supports organizations involved with arts and culture, education, health, domestic violence, employment, human services, intergroup and race relations, and community development. Special emphasis is directed toward programs designed to promote lifelong learning, quality family life, and cultural diversity.
Fields of interest: Arts, cultural/ethnic awareness; Arts; Child development, education; Higher education; Adult/continuing education; Adult education—literacy, basic skills & GED; Education; Health care; Crime/violence prevention, domestic violence; Employment, services; Children, day care;

Family services; Human services; Civil rights, race/intergroup relations; Community development.
International interests: Asia.
Type of support: General/operating support; Continuing support; Program development; Scholarship funds; Research; Employee matching gifts; Employee-related scholarships; Matching/challenge support.
Limitations: Giving limited to Fort Smith, AR, Evansville and La Porte, IN, Benton Harbor, MI, Oxford, MS, Clyde, Findlay, Greenville, and Marion, OH, OK, and Knoxville and Lavergne, TN. No support for religious, theological, or other religion-related organizations training individuals for religious professions, social, labor, veterans', alumni, or fraternal organizations, athletic associations, or national organizations with local chapters already supported by Whirlpool. No grants to individuals (except for employee-related scholarships), or for conferences or seminars, political causes, capital campaigns or endowments, sporting events, goodwill advertisements for fundraising benefits or program books or tickets for testimonials or similar benefit events, or general operating support for United Way agencies.
Publications: Annual report (including application guidelines).
Application information: Application form required.
  Initial approach: Contact foundation for application form
  Copies of proposal: 1
  Deadline(s): Jan. 1, Apr. 1, July 1, and Oct. 1
  Board meeting date(s): Quarterly
  Final notification: 2 months
Officers and Trustees:* Daniel F. Hopp,* Chair. and Pres.; Frank J. Luongo, Secy.-Treas.; Barbara A. Hall, Exec. Dir.; John E. Alexander; Robert T. Kenagy; Kathryn L. Nelson; David Shellito; Thomas Welke.
Number of staff: 1 full-time professional; 1 full-time support.
EIN: 386077342
Selected grants: The following grants were reported in 2004.
$205,000 to Lake Michigan College Foundation, Benton Harbor, MI. For lifelong learning programs.
$150,000 to University of Notre Dame, Notre Dame, IN. For MBA Program's lifelong learning programs.
$50,000 to Boys and Girls Club of Benton Harbor, Benton Harbor, MI. For lifelong learning programs.
$50,000 to Montessori House of Children, Benton Harbor, MI. For lifelong learning programs.
$50,000 to University of Michigan, School of Business Administration, Ann Arbor, MI. For quality family life programs.
$44,350 to Michigan Tech Fund, Houghton, MI. For lifelong learning programs.
$44,200 to Matej Bel University, Banska Bystrica, Slovakia. For lifelong learning programs.
$31,300 to Inroads/Southwest Michigan, Grand Rapids, MI. For cultural diversity programs.
$30,000 to Benton Harbor Area Schools, Benton Harbor, MI. For lifelong learning programs.
$25,000 to Partners in Education, Marion Area, Marion, OH. For lifelong learning programs.

4481
The White Foundation ☆
c/o Glenn E. White
5530 Crabtree Rd.
Bloomfield Hills, MI   48301-1200

Established in 1945 in MI.
Donors: Glenn E. White; Ruth E. White; David B. White; Nancy White; Charles E. White; Carol L. White.
Foundation type: Independent foundation.
Financial data (yr. ended 12/31/05): Assets, $3,934,000 (M); gifts received, $136,000; expenditures, $453,000; qualifying distributions, $428,000; giving activities include $428,000 for 13 grants (high: $300,000; low: $500).
Purpose and activities: Grants primarily to organizations associated with the Free Methodist Church.
Fields of interest: Higher education; Christian agencies & churches.
Limitations: Applications not accepted. Giving primarily in MI. No grants to individuals.
Application information: Contributes only to pre-selected organizations.
Officers and Directors:* Glenn E. White,* Pres. and Treas.; Ruth E. White,* V.P.; Nancy Bergsma,* Secy.; Verlyn Beardslee; Charles E. White; David B. White.
EIN: 386054883
Selected grants: The following grants were reported in 2004.
$52,000 to Spring Arbor University, Spring Arbor, MI. For scholarships.
$37,000 to Ferndale Free Methodist Church, Ferndale, MI. For general support.
$10,000 to International Institute for Christian Studies, Overland Park, KS.
$10,000 to Somerset Beach Campground, Somerset, MI. For bath house.
$7,500 to Free Methodist Foundation, Spring Arbor, MI. For Hope Africa University dormatory.
$7,500 to Praying for You, Midlothian, TX. For general support.
$5,300 to Southfield Christian School, Southfield, MI. For library media, art, and chapel programs.
$5,000 to Greenville College, Greenville, IL. For comprehensive campaign.
$3,500 to Free Methodist Church of North America, Winona Lake, IN. For Operation Hope.
$1,000 to Rincon Mountain Presbyterian Church, Tucson, AZ. For Carl Woodson Mission.

4482
The Whiting Foundation ◇
G-9460 S. Saginaw St., Ste. A
Grand Blanc, MI   48439
Application address: c/o Donald E. Johnson, Jr., Pres., 901 Citizens Bank Bldg., Flint, MI 48502, tel.: (810) 767-3600

Incorporated in 1940 in MI.
Donor: Members of the Johnson family.
Foundation type: Independent foundation.
Financial data (yr. ended 6/30/05): Assets, $22,525,196 (M); expenditures, $908,392; qualifying distributions, $866,082; giving activities include $840,000 for 41 grants (high: $575,000; low: $500).
Purpose and activities: Giving primarily for cultural activities, and for basic needs for people who are underprivileged.
Fields of interest: Historic preservation/historical societies; Arts; Education; Cancer; Medical research, institute; Housing/shelter, development; Children/youth, services; Community development; Federated giving programs.
Type of support: General/operating support; Program development.

Limitations: Giving primarily in the Genesee County, MI, area, including the city of Flint.
Application information: Application form not required.
  Initial approach: Concise proposal
  Copies of proposal: 1
  Deadline(s): Apr. 30
Officers: Donald E. Johnson, Jr., Pres.; John T. Lindholm, Secy.-Treas.; Marsha A. Kump, Exec. Dir.
Trustees: Mary Alice J. Heaton; Linda J. Lemieux.
EIN: 386056693
Selected grants: The following grants were reported in 2005.
$575,000 to Flint Institute of Arts, Flint, MI.
$30,000 to Genesee County Historical Society, Flint, MI.
$11,000 to Flint Institute of Music, Flint, MI.
$2,500 to Greater Flint Arts Council, Flint, MI.

4483
Harvey Randall Wickes Foundation
Plaza N., Ste. 472
4800 Fashion Sq. Blvd.
Saginaw, MI   48604   (989) 799-1850
Contact: Hugo E. Braun, Jr., Pres.
FAX: (989) 799-3327;
E-mail: HRWickes@concentric.net

Incorporated in 1945 in MI.
Donors: Harvey Randall Wickes‡; members of the Wickes family.
Foundation type: Independent foundation.
Financial data (yr. ended 12/31/05): Assets, $43,166,791 (M); expenditures, $2,072,590; qualifying distributions, $1,838,697; giving activities include $1,750,003 for 54 grants (high: $500,000; low: $400).
Purpose and activities: Giving primarily for civic affairs groups, parks and recreation agencies; support also for a library, youth and social services, hospitals, and cultural programs, for the betterment of Saginaw County, MI.
Fields of interest: Arts; Libraries/library science; Education; Hospitals (general); Recreation; Human services; Children/youth, services.
Type of support: Annual campaigns; Building/renovation; Equipment; Seed money.
Limitations: Giving limited to the Saginaw, MI, area. No support for government where support is forth coming from tax dollars. No grants to individuals, or for endowments, travel, conferences, or film or video projects; no loans.
Publications: Application guidelines; Financial statement.
Application information: Application form not required.
  Initial approach: Letter followed by proposal
  Copies of proposal: 1
  Deadline(s): Submit proposal 2 weeks prior to meeting
  Board meeting date(s): Mar., June, Sept. and Dec.
  Final notification: 2 weeks following board meeting
Officers and Trustees:* Hugo E. Braun, Jr.,* Pres.; Craig W. Horn,* V.P.; Michele Pavlicek, Secy.; Lloyd J. Yeo,* Treas.; Mary Lou Case; Ellen Crane; Peter Ewend; William A. Hendrick; Richard Heuschele; Richard Katz.
Number of staff: 1 part-time professional; 1 part-time support.
EIN: 386061470
Selected grants: The following grants were reported in 2005.

$600,000 to Saginaw Valley State University Foundation, University Center, MI. 2 grants: $100,000, $500,000

$250,000 to Saginaw Childrens Zoo, Saginaw, MI.

$125,000 to Boys and Girls Club of Saginaw County, Saginaw, MI.

$75,000 to Saginaw Community Foundation, Saginaw, MI.

$70,000 to United Way of Saginaw County, Saginaw, MI. 2 grants: $20,000, $50,000

$50,000 to Saginaw Intermediate School District, Saginaw, MI.

$32,500 to Saginaw Valley Zoological Society, Saginaw, MI.

$13,000 to Junior Achievement.

4484
Ralph C. Wilson Foundation
99 Kercheval Ave.
Grosse Pointe Farms, MI   48236-3618

Established around 1954.
Donor: Ralph C. Wilson, Jr.
Foundation type: Independent foundation.
Financial data (yr. ended 10/31/05): Assets, $2,811,192 (M); gifts received, $50,000; expenditures, $970,963; qualifying distributions, $970,963; giving activities include $902,045 for 48 grants (high: $200,000; low: $50).
Purpose and activities: Giving primarily for education, health associations, social services, and federated giving programs.
Fields of interest: Higher education; Law school/ education; Education; Health organizations; Food banks; Human services; Children/youth, services; Residential/custodial care, hospices; Federated giving programs; Christian agencies & churches.
Type of support: General/operating support.
Limitations: Applications not accepted. Giving on a national basis, with emphasis on MI, NY, and OH. No grants to individuals.
Application information: Contributes only to pre-selected organizations.
Officers and Trustees:* Ralph C. Wilson, Jr.,* Pres.; Mary M. Owen, Secy.; Jeffrey C. Littmann,* Treas.; Eugene Driker; Mary M. Wilson.
EIN: 386091638

4485
Matilda R. Wilson Fund
1901 Saint Antoine St., 6th Fl.
Detroit, MI   48226   (313) 392-1040
Contact: David P. Larsen, Secy.
FAX: (313) 393-7579;
E-mail: roosterveen@bodmanllp.com

Incorporated in 1944 in MI.
Donors: Matilda R. Wilson†; Alfred G. Wilson†.
Foundation type: Independent foundation.
Financial data (yr. ended 12/31/05): Assets, $40,725,393 (M); expenditures, $4,135,811; qualifying distributions, $3,890,435; giving activities include $3,795,310 for 31 grants (high: $1,691,510; low: $5,000).
Purpose and activities: Support for the arts, youth agencies, higher education, and social services.
Fields of interest: Arts; Higher education; Hospitals (general); Human services; Youth, services.
Type of support: General/operating support; Building/renovation; Equipment; Endowments;

Program development; Scholarship funds; Research; Matching/challenge support.
Limitations: Giving primarily in southeast MI. No grants to individuals; no loans.
Application information: Application form not required.
Initial approach: Letter
Copies of proposal: 1
Deadline(s): None
Board meeting date(s): Apr., Aug., and Dec.
Officers and Trustees:* David M. Hempstead,* Pres.; David P. Larsen,* Secy.; David B. Stephens,* Treas.
EIN: 386087665
Selected grants: The following grants were reported in 2003.

$900,000 to Michigan State University, East Lansing, MI. 2 grants: $400,000 (For capital support), $500,000 (For capital support).

$350,000 to Detroit Symphony Orchestra, Detroit, MI. 2 grants: $250,000 to Detroit Symphony Orchestra Hall (For capital support), $100,000 (For operating support).

$200,000 to College for Creative Studies, Detroit, MI. 2 grants: $100,000 (For operating support), $100,000 (For capital support).

$150,000 to Oakland University, Rochester, MI. For capital and operating support.

$125,000 to Edison Institute, Dearborn, MI. For capital support.

$100,000 to New Detroit Science Center, Detroit, MI. For capital support.

$100,000 to Stratford Shakespearean Festival, Ontario, Canada. For capital support.

4486
Jean & Lewis Wolff Family Foundation ✧ ☆
c/o Comerica Bank
P.O. Box 75000, MC 3302
Detroit, MI   48275-3302
Application address: c/o Keith Wolff, 11828 La Grange Ave., Ste. 200, Los Angeles, CA 90025-5200

Established in 1998 in CA.
Donors: Jean Wolff; Lewis Wolff.
Foundation type: Independent foundation.
Financial data (yr. ended 5/31/06): Assets, $2,117,633 (M); gifts received, $742,311; expenditures, $808,744; qualifying distributions, $808,744; giving activities include $808,744 for grants.
Fields of interest: Museums (art); Education; Reproductive health, family planning; Health organizations, association; Human services; Children/youth, services; Jewish agencies & temples.
Limitations: Giving primarily in CA. No grants to individuals.
Application information: Application form not required.
Initial approach: Letter
Deadline(s): None
Officers: Lewis Wolff, Pres.; Jean Wolff, V.P.; Kevin Wolff, V.P.; Kari Wolff Goldstein, Secy.; Keith Wolff, C.F.O. and Treas.
EIN: 954679221

4487
Kate & Richard Wolters Foundation ✧
2260 Cascade Springs Dr. S.E.
Grand Rapids, MI   49546
Contact: Kate P. Wolters, Pres.

Established in 1997 in MI.
Donors: Kate Pew Wolters; Richard Wolters†.
Foundation type: Independent foundation.
Financial data (yr. ended 12/31/05): Assets, $9,394,424 (M); gifts received, $100,000; expenditures, $1,840,859; qualifying distributions, $1,767,445; giving activities include $1,762,500 for 42 grants (high: $270,000; low: $1,000).
Purpose and activities: Giving primarily for arts and culture, higher and other education, and human services.
Fields of interest: Museums (art); Performing arts, orchestra (symphony); Arts; Elementary/secondary education; Higher education; Human services; Children/youth, services; Christian agencies & churches.
Type of support: General/operating support; Capital campaigns; Program development.
Limitations: Giving primarily in Grand Rapids and Lansing, MI.
Application information:
Initial approach: Letter
Deadline(s): None
Officer and Trustee:* Kate Pew Wolters,* Pres. and Secy.-Treas.
EIN: 383384598

4488
Wolverine World Wide Foundation ✧
(formerly Wolverine Charitable Foundation)
9341 Courtland Dr. N.E.
Rockford, MI   49351   (616) 866-5500
Contact: Robert J. Sedrowski, Tr.
URL: http://www.wolverineworldwide.com/ main_foundation.asp

Trust established in 1959 in MI.
Donor: Wolverine World Wide, Inc.
Foundation type: Company-sponsored foundation.
Financial data (yr. ended 12/31/05): Assets, $0 (M); gifts received, $425,000; expenditures, $2,775,123; qualifying distributions, $2,768,891; giving activities include $2,768,891 for 116 grants (high: $2,373,616; low: $50).
Purpose and activities: The foundation supports organizations involved with arts and culture, higher education, health, children and youth, and minorities.
Fields of interest: Performing arts, music; Arts; Higher education; Health care; Children/youth, services; Federated giving programs; Minorities.
Type of support: General/operating support; Employee matching gifts.
Limitations: Giving primarily in Big Rapids, Grand Rapids, and Rockford, MI. No grants to individuals.
Application information: Application form not required.
Initial approach: Proposal
Copies of proposal: 1
Deadline(s): None
Trustees: Robert J. Sedrowski; UBS Financial Services Inc.
Officer: Christi Cowdin, V.P.
EIN: 383056939
Selected grants: The following grants were reported in 2004.

$150,000 to YMCA of Greater Grand Rapids, Grand Rapids, MI.

$14,500 to Junior Achievement.

$10,000 to Opera Grand Rapids, Grand Rapids, MI.

$10,000 to Valparaiso University, Valparaiso, IN.

$9,000 to United Way.

$2,000 to Boy Scouts of America, Anchorage, AK.

$2,000 to United Way of Montcalm County, Greenville, MI.

$1,500 to Urban Institute for Contemporary Arts, Grand Rapids, MI.

$1,000 to Hope Network, Grand Rapids, MI.

$400 to Calvin College, Grand Rapids, MI.

4489
World Heritage Foundation ◇
2675 W. Jefferson Ave.
Trenton, MI 48183

Established in 1985 in MI.
Donors: Heinz C. Prechter†; Thomas Denomme; Heinz C. Prechter Charitable Lead Trust.
Foundation type: Independent foundation.
Financial data (yr. ended 12/31/05): Assets, $9,122,051 (M); expenditures, $799,094; qualifying distributions, $642,600; giving activities include $642,600 for 50 grants (high: $333,334; low: $100; average: $1,000–$10,000).
Purpose and activities: Support primarily for a museum and for higher education.
Fields of interest: Museums; Arts; Higher education; Business school/education; Engineering school/education; Health care; Mental health,

depression; Medical research; Human services; Economic development.
Type of support: Capital campaigns; General/operating support; Program development.
Limitations: Giving primarily in MI; some giving also in Washington, DC. No grants to individuals.
Publications: Informational brochure (including application guidelines).
Application information: Application form required.
Initial approach: Letter
Deadline(s): None
Officers: Mrs. Waltraud Prechter, Pres.; Lori Koenig, V.P. and Secy.-Treas.; Paul Prechter, V.P.; Stephanie Prechter, V.P.
EIN: 382640416
Selected grants: The following grants were reported in 2003.

$1,640,514 to Heinz C. Prechter Bipolar Research Fund, Southgate, MI.

$333,333 to Edison Institute, Dearborn, MI.

$50,000 to Detroit Symphony Orchestra, Detroit, MI.

$50,000 to University of Michigan, Department of Engineering, Dearborn, MI.

$25,000 to Michigan Opera Theater, Detroit, MI.

$10,000 to Center for Creative Studies: Institute of Music and Dance, Detroit, MI.

$10,000 to Michigan State University, East Lansing, MI.

$3,000 to Downriver Council for the Arts, Taylor, MI.

$2,000 to Wayne State University, Detroit, MI.

$100 to Hutzel Hospital, Detroit, MI.

4490
Young Family Foundation ◇
P.O. Box 5430
Plymouth, MI 48170

Established in 2001 in MI.
Donors: William P. Young†; Plastipak Holdings, Inc.
Foundation type: Independent foundation.
Financial data (yr. ended 12/31/05): Assets, $2,803,721 (M); gifts received, $300,000; expenditures, $991,501; qualifying distributions, $978,483; giving activities include $965,465 for 12 grants (high: $300,000; low: $5,000; average: $50,000–$125,000).
Purpose and activities: Giving primarily to a Roman Catholic university, as well as for other education; some funding also for human services.
Fields of interest: Secondary school/education; Higher education; Scholarships/financial aid; Environment, natural resources; Animals/wildlife; Human services; American Red Cross; Roman Catholic agencies & churches.
Type of support: Building/renovation; Scholarship funds; General/operating support.
Limitations: Applications not accepted. Giving primarily in MI, with emphasis on Ann Arbor and Detroit. No grants to individuals.
Application information: Contributes only to pre-selected organizations.
Officers and Directors:* William C. Young,* Pres.; William Patrick Young,* V.P.; Tracey L. Deal,* Secy.; Amy L. Morgan,* Treas.
EIN: 300003762

MINNESOTA

4491
1988 Irrevocable Cochrane Memorial Trust ✧

c/o U.S. Bank, N.A., Tax Svcs. Dept.
P.O. Box 64713
St. Paul, MN 55164-0713
Application address: John L. Jerry, c/o U.S. Bank, 101 E. 5th St., St. Paul, MN 55101, tel.: (651) 466-8724

Established in 1989 in MN.
Foundation type: Independent foundation.
Financial data (yr. ended 12/31/04): Assets, $11,926,266 (M); expenditures, $681,944; qualifying distributions, $647,309; giving activities include $645,000 for 17 grants (high: $50,000; low: $25,000).
Purpose and activities: Giving primarily to Roman Catholic churches, schools, and federated giving programs.
Fields of interest: Secondary school/education; Legal services; Community development; Roman Catholic federated giving programs; Roman Catholic agencies & churches.
Type of support: General/operating support.
Limitations: Giving primarily in the Washington, DC, area, including MD. No grants to individuals.
Application information:
  Initial approach: Letter
  Deadline(s): None
Trustees: Mary McGahey Dwan; U.S. Bank, N.A.
EIN: 416309348

4492
3M Foundation ▼

(also known as Minnesota Mining and Manufacturing Foundation)
3M Ctr., Bldg. 225-1S-23
St. Paul, MN 55144-1000 (651) 733-0144
Contact: Cynthia F. Kleven, Secy.
FAX: (651) 737-3061; E-mail: cfkleven@mmm.com; URL: http://www.3Mgiving.com

Incorporated in 1953 in MN.
Donors: Minnesota Mining and Manufacturing Co.; 3M Co.
Foundation type: Company-sponsored foundation.
Financial data (yr. ended 12/31/04): Assets, $39,137,320 (M); gifts received, $40,000,000; expenditures, $19,978,313; qualifying distributions, $19,818,800; giving activities include $17,043,145 for 1,616 grants (high: $1,900,000; low: $105; average: $500–$10,000), and $1,698,611 for 630 employee matching gifts.
Purpose and activities: The foundation supports organizations involved with arts and culture, education, the environment, health, employment, youth development, human services, and minorities. Special emphasis is directed toward programs designed to help prepare individuals and families for success.
Fields of interest: Arts education; Arts; Elementary/ secondary education; Higher education; Business school/education; Education; Environment, natural resources; Environment; Health care; Employment, training; Employment; Youth development; Youth, services; Family services; Family services, parent

education; Human services; Science, formal/ general education; Mathematics; Engineering; Minorities.
Type of support: General/operating support; Capital campaigns; Building/renovation; Program development; Curriculum development; Employee matching gifts; In-kind gifts.
Limitations: Giving on a national and international basis in areas of company operations. No support for religious organizations, conduit agencies, political, fraternal, social, or veterans' organizations, hospitals, K-12 schools, or military organizations, animal-related organizations, or disease-specific organizations. No grants to individuals, or for endowments, emergency operating support, advocacy and lobbying efforts, fundraising events and associated advertising, travel, publications, start-up needs, non-3M equipment, debt reduction, conferences, athletic events, film or video production, or scholarship funds; no loans or investments.
Publications: Application guidelines; Corporate giving report (including application guidelines); Grants list; Informational brochure (including application guidelines).
Application information: The foundation utilizes an invitation only Request For Proposal (RFP) process for organizations located in Minneapolis and St. Paul, MN, and Austin, TX; unsolicited requests are not accepted. Application form not required.
  Initial approach: Letter of inquiry to nearest company facility
  Board meeting date(s): June and Dec.
Officers and Directors:* Robert D. MacDonald,* Pres.; A.C. Cirillo, Jr., V.P.; Cynthia F. Kleven, Secy.; J.L. Yeomans, Treas.; Thomas A. Boardman; Jay V. Ihlenfeld; Barbara W. Kaufmann; J.T. Mahan; W.J. Mahoney; R.M. Miller; K.E. Reed; J.B. Stake; S.K. Tokach.
EIN: 416038262
Selected grants: The following grants were reported in 2004.
$1,967,100 to University of Minnesota Foundation, Minneapolis, MN.
$160,000 to Childrens Theater Company and School, Minneapolis, MN.
$125,000 to Cornell University, Ithaca, NY.
$46,225 to Chamber of Commerce Foundation of Saint Paul, Saint Paul, MN.
$40,000 to Character Education Partnership, DC.
$25,000 to Arts Midwest, Minneapolis, MN.
$10,000 to Glenwood School for Boys, Glenwood, IL.
$5,000 to League Treatment Center, Brooklyn, NY.
$4,000 to Auburn University, Auburn, AL.
$3,000 to Michigan Performing Arts, Detroit, MI.

4493
A Better Place, Inc. ✧

3001 Hennepin Ave., Ste. D-210
Minneapolis, MN 55408

Established in 1999 in MN.
Donors: Stephen R. Sefton; Claudia Sefton.
Foundation type: Independent foundation.
Financial data (yr. ended 12/31/05): Assets, $15,055,520 (M); gifts received, $104,025; expenditures, $817,166; qualifying distributions, $698,525; giving activities include $694,500 for 23 grants (high: $350,500; low: $500; average: $5,000–$15,000).
Purpose and activities: Giving primarily for Roman Catholic education and programs.

Fields of interest: Higher education; Education; Human services; Roman Catholic agencies & churches.
Limitations: Applications not accepted. Giving on a national basis. No grants to individuals.
Application information: Contributes only to pre-selected organizations.
Officers: Stephen R. Sefton, Pres.; William L. Dietz, C.F.O.
EIN: 411955000
Selected grants: The following grants were reported in 2003.
$275,500 to Immaculate Heart of Mary Church, Saint Paul, MN.
$123,000 to School Sisters of Notre Dame, Mankato, MN.
$50,000 to CommonBond Communities, Saint Paul, MN.
$50,000 to Urban Ventures Leadership Foundation, Minneapolis, MN.
$35,000 to Saint Vincent de Paul Society, Minneapolis, MN.
$12,500 to Growing in Faith Capital Campaign, Saint Paul, MN.
$12,000 to Catholic Charities of the Archdiocese of Saint Paul and Minneapolis, Minneapolis, MN.
$12,000 to DeLaSalle High School, Minneapolis, MN.
$5,000 to Professional Association of Georgia Educators (PAGE) Foundation, Atlanta, GA.
$4,000 to Benilde-Saint Margarets High School, Saint Louis Park, MN.

4494
Acorn Foundation ✧

9475 Aspen Cir.
Eden Prairie, MN 55347 (612) 938-4811
Contact: Mark Hanson, V.P.
Application address: P.O. Box 5178, Hopkins, MN 55343

Established in 1997 in MN.
Donors: Mark Hanson; Shirly Hanson.
Foundation type: Independent foundation.
Financial data (yr. ended 12/31/05): Assets, $7,387,489 (M); gifts received, $1,564,108; expenditures, $519,822; qualifying distributions, $519,822; giving activities include $501,520 for 41 grants (high: $105,000; low: $2,080).
Fields of interest: Higher education; Protestant agencies & churches.
Limitations: Giving primarily in MN.
Application information:
  Initial approach: Letter
  Deadline(s): None
Officers: Phil Fandrei, Pres.; Mark Hanson, V.P.; Shirly Hanson, Secy.
EIN: 411891595
Selected grants: The following grants were reported in 2003.
$64,500 to Concordia University, Saint Paul, MN. For tuition reduction.
$35,000 to Pillsbury Baptist Bible College, Owatonna, MN. For tuition reduction.
$25,000 to Concordia College, Moorhead, MN. For tuition reduction.
$12,500 to Augsburg College, Minneapolis, MN. For tuition reduction.
$10,000 to Luther Seminary, Saint Paul, MN. For tuition reduction.
$7,500 to University of Saint Thomas, Saint Paul, MN. For tuition reduction.

$5,000 to Northwestern College, Saint Paul, MN. For tuition reduction.

$5,000 to Purdue University, West Lafayette, IN. For tuition reduction.

$5,000 to University of Minnesota, Minneapolis, MN. For tuition reduction.

$2,500 to Arizona State University, Tempe, AZ. For tuition reduction.

4495
Adams-Mastrovich Family Foundation
c/o Wells Fargo Bank Minnesota, N.A.
7900 Xerxes Ave. S., Ste. 203
Bloomington, MN 55431
Contact: Halsey H. Halls, V.P., Wells Fargo Bank Minnesota, N.A.
Additional tel.: (612) 667-9084

Established in 1957 in MN.
Donor: Mary Adams Balmat†.
Foundation type: Independent foundation.
Financial data (yr. ended 12/31/05): Assets, $27,508,231 (M); expenditures, $1,515,221; qualifying distributions, $1,299,552; giving activities include $1,238,000 for 30 grants (high: $335,000; low: $4,000; average: $10,000–$50,000).
Purpose and activities: Giving primarily for the arts, human services, and Roman Catholic agencies and churches.
Fields of interest: Performing arts; Performing arts, music; Arts; Higher education; Hospitals (general); Human services; Roman Catholic agencies & churches; Religion.
Type of support: General/operating support; Continuing support; Building/renovation; Equipment; Program development; Scholarship funds.
Limitations: Giving limited to Los Angeles County, CA, and SD. No grants to individuals.
Publications: Application guidelines; Informational brochure.
Application information: Application form required.
Copies of proposal: 2
Deadline(s): Aug. 1
Board meeting date(s): Sept.
Trustee: Wells Fargo Bank Minnesota, N.A.
EIN: 416014092
Selected grants: The following grants were reported in 2004.
$150,000 to University of Southern California, Los Angeles, CA. 3 grants: $50,000 each
$100,000 to Loyola Marymount University, Los Angeles, CA. 2 grants: $50,000 each
$60,000 to Young Musicians Foundation, Beverly Hills, CA.
$50,000 to Marycrest Manor, Culver City, CA.
$20,000 to Knights of Malta Free Clinic, Los Angeles, CA.
$15,000 to Downtown Womens Center, Los Angeles, CA.
$15,000 to Sisters of Social Service, Los Angeles, CA.

4496
ADC Foundation
P.O. Box 1101
Minneapolis, MN 55440-1101 (952) 917-0118
Contact: Glenda Schmitt, Grants Admin.

FAX: (952) 917-0965;
E-mail: glenda.schmitt@adc.com; URL: http://www.adc.com/aboutadc/adcfoundation/

Established in 1998 in MN.
Donors: ADC Telecommunications, Inc.; ADC Corp.
Foundation type: Company-sponsored foundation.
Financial data (yr. ended 10/31/05): Assets, $8,046,997 (M); gifts received, $2,275; expenditures, $1,463,810; qualifying distributions, $1,372,252; giving activities include $1,153,355 for grants.
Purpose and activities: The foundation supports organizations involved with K-12 and higher science, technology, engineering, and mathematics education and nonprofit access to technology.
Fields of interest: Elementary/secondary education; Higher education; Science, formal/general education; Mathematics; Engineering/technology; Science.
International interests: Australia; England; India; Mexico.
Type of support: Annual campaigns; Curriculum development; Scholarship funds; Employee matching gifts; Employee-related scholarships.
Limitations: Giving on a national and international basis, with emphasis on Marietta, GA, the Twin Cities, MN, metropolitan area, Santa Teresa, NM, and in Australia, India, Mexico, and the United Kingdom. No support for private primary or secondary schools or religious organizations not of direct benefit to the entire community. No grants to individuals (except for employee-related scholarships), or for environmental causes, health, general social services, general operating support, capital campaigns, or fundraising; no in-kind gifts.
Publications: Application guidelines; Annual report; IRS Form 990-PF.
Application information: Application form required.
Initial approach: Complete online application form
Board meeting date(s): Quarterly
Final notification: Quarterly
Officers: Robert E. Switz, Chair.; Laura N. Owen, Vice-Chair.; Jeffrey D. Pflaum, Secy.; Gokul V. Hemmady, Treas.; Bill Linder-Scholer, Exec. Dir.
Directors: Joanne M. Anderson; Mario Dena; Steve Mitchell; Jon Norton; Pat O'Brien; Mike Pratt; Mary Quay.
Number of staff: 2 full-time professional.
EIN: 311635636
Selected grants: The following grants were reported in 2005.
$5,000 to Bakken Library and Museum, Minneapolis, MN. For Science Education Program, to provide unique array of science resources and experiences that support young people in following educational path that draws out their spirit of inquiry and guides them to make innovative contributions to science that will benefit humanity.
$2,000 to Center for Homicide Research, Minneapolis, MN. For technology.
$2,000 to Child Care Works, Minneapolis, MN. To implement proposed technology upgrade projesct.
$1,000 to Century College Foundation, White Bear Lake, MN. For scholarships in Information and Telecommunication Technology.

4497
AHS Foundation ◇
90 S. 7th St., Ste. 5300
Minneapolis, MN 55402
Application address: c/o Thomas Wright, Secy.-Treas., Lowry Hill, MAC N9305-530, 6th & Marquette, Minneapolis, MN 55479

Established in 1968 in MN.
Donors: Arthur H. Schubert†; Leland Schubert; Helen D. Schubert†.
Foundation type: Independent foundation.
Financial data (yr. ended 6/30/05): Assets, $10,055,390 (M); expenditures, $572,231; qualifying distributions, $505,360; giving activities include $465,500 for 45 grants (high: $35,000; low: $3,000).
Purpose and activities: Support for the relief of poverty and the advancement of education, religion, and community issues.
Fields of interest: Arts; Health care; Human services; Federated giving programs; Christian agencies & churches; Religion, interfaith issues; Religion.
Type of support: General/operating support; Capital campaigns; Building/renovation; Endowments; Program development.
Limitations: Giving primarily in CA, HI, MN, NJ, and OH. No grants to individuals; no loans.
Application information: Application form not required.
Initial approach: Letter
Copies of proposal: 1
Deadline(s): None
Board meeting date(s): July
Final notification: 1 to 3 months
Officers: Leland W. Schubert, Pres.; John Dwan Schubert, 1st V.P.; Gage A. Schubert, 2nd V.P.; Thomas Wright, Secy.-Treas.
EIN: 410944654
Selected grants: The following grants were reported in 2005.
$35,000 to Slide Ranch, Muir Beach, CA.
$30,000 to District 202, Minneapolis, MN.
$27,000 to Hui Noeau Visual Arts Center, Makawao, HI.
$20,000 to Catholic Relief Services, Baltimore, MD.
$20,000 to Reconciling Ministries Network, Chicago, IL.
$16,750 to Bridge for Runaway Youth, Minneapolis, MN.
$16,750 to Eric Johnson House, Morristown, NJ.
$10,000 to Maui Arts and Cultural Center, Kahului, HI.
$10,000 to New Jersey Symphony Orchestra, Newark, NJ.
$8,000 to Full Circle Programs, San Rafael, CA.

4498
Alliss Educational Foundation ▼ ◇
(formerly Charles and Ellora Alliss Educational Foundation)
c/o U.S. Bank, N.A.
P.O. Box 64713
St. Paul, MN 55164-0713 (612) 303-3813
Contact: Joth Blodgett, Secy.
Application address: 800 Nicollet Mall, Minneapolis, MN 55402

Trust established in 1958 in MN.
Donors: Charles C. Alliss†; Ellora Martha Alliss†.
Foundation type: Independent foundation.

Financial data (yr. ended 12/31/05): Assets, $104,489,840 (M); expenditures, $5,429,546; qualifying distributions, $5,077,099; giving activities include $4,960,000 for 20 grants (high: $942,520; low: $60,326; average: $150,900–$325,000).
Purpose and activities: To further the education of young people by granting scholarships, fellowships, gifts, and awards; grants made in lump sums solely to institutions. Support of undergraduate aid programs administered by the grantee institutions and including the period of postgraduate study.
Fields of interest: Secondary school/education; Higher education; Higher education, college; Higher education, university; Graduate/professional education.
Type of support: Scholarship funds.
Limitations: Giving limited to MN educational institutions for scholarship programs for secondary, higher and postgraduate study. No grants to individuals directly.
Application information: Application form not required.
 Initial approach: Letter
 Copies of proposal: 1
 Deadline(s): None
 Board meeting date(s): Mar., June, Sept., and Dec.
 Final notification: 3 months
Officer: Joth Blodgett, Secy.
Trustees: Nina M. Archabal; Pamela J. Clarke; John B. Davis, Jr.; Anita Pampusch; Edward Stringer; Frederick T. Weyerhaeuser; U.S. Bank, N.A.
EIN: 416011054
Selected grants: The following grants were reported in 2004.
$966,494 to Minnesota State Colleges and Universities, Saint Paul, MN. For undergraduate scholarships.
$623,006 to University of Minnesota, Minneapolis, MN. For undergraduate scholarships.
$450,000 to Minnesota Independent School Forum, Saint Paul, MN. For campaign.
$431,456 to University of Saint Thomas, Saint Paul, MN. For undergraduate scholarships.
$272,454 to Saint Olaf College, Northfield, MN. For undergraduate scholarships.
$249,635 to Bethel University, Saint Paul, MN. For undergraduate scholarships.
$247,344 to Concordia College, Moorhead, MN. For undergraduate scholarships.
$229,016 to Gustavus Adolphus College, Saint Peter, MN. For undergraduate scholarships.
$180,809 to College of Saint Benedict, Saint Joseph, MN. For undergraduate scholarships.
$177,054 to Carleton College, Northfield, MN. For undergraduate scholarships.

4499
Marshall H. and Nellie Alworth Memorial Fund

402 Alworth Bldg.
306 W. Superior St., Ste. 402
Duluth, MN 55802
Contact: Patty Salow Downs, Exec. Dir.
FAX: (218) 529-3760;
E-mail: Alworth@cpinternet.com; *URL:* http://www.alworthscholarship.org/

Incorporated in 1949 by Marshall W. Alworth to honor parents who were early pioneers in northeastern MN.
Donor: Marshall W. Alworth†.

Foundation type: Independent foundation.
Financial data (yr. ended 12/31/05): Assets, $7,628,103 (M); gifts received, $1,320,897; expenditures, $2,423,884; qualifying distributions, $2,370,392; giving activities include $2,236,300 for 545 grants to individuals (high: $4,600; low: $2,150).
Purpose and activities: Scholarship grants are limited to students from northern MN, attending accredited colleges and universities of their choice, who are majoring in mathematics or one of the basic sciences, medicine or veterinary medicine, and can show evidence of need for financial assistance.
Fields of interest: Medical school/education; Engineering school/education; Pharmacy/prescriptions; Nursing care; Biomedicine; Medical research, institute; Physical/earth sciences; Chemistry; Mathematics; Physics; Engineering/technology; Engineering; Biological sciences; Science.
Type of support: Scholarships—to individuals.
Limitations: Giving limited to graduates of high schools in northern MN. No grants for building or endowment funds or matching gifts; no loans.
Publications: Application guidelines; Informational brochure; Informational brochure (including application guidelines).
Application information: Application form available from high school counselors in northern MN; application guidelines available on foundation Web site. Application form required.
 Initial approach: Letter
 Copies of proposal: 1
 Deadline(s): Jan. 15
 Board meeting date(s): Apr. and Oct.
 Final notification: May 1
Officers and Directors:* Cheryl Meese, Pres.; Nick Alworth,* Treas.; Patty Salo Downs, Exec. Dir.; James Abelsen; Carol Fryberger; Tere Ivanca; Peter J. Johnson; Deane Kischel; Lee Anne Lundgren.
Number of staff: 1 part-time professional; 1 part-time support.
EIN: 410797340

4500
Lloyd and Barbara Amundson Charity Foundation, Inc. ✧ ☆

100 E. Main St.
Sleepy Eye, MN 56085

Established in 1996 in MN.
Donors: Bank of Beulah; Lloyd Amundson.
Foundation type: Independent foundation.
Financial data (yr. ended 12/31/05): Assets, $605,348 (M); expenditures, $661,397; qualifying distributions, $660,551; giving activities include $660,251 for 28 grants (high: $489,363; low: $25).
Purpose and activities: Giving for hospitals, community services and foundations, youth services, education and religion.
Fields of interest: Scholarships/financial aid; Education; Health organizations, association; Human services; Youth, services; Community development; Foundations (community); Religion.
Limitations: Applications not accepted. Giving primarily in MN. No grants to individuals.
Application information: Contributes only to pre-selected organizations.
Officers and Directors:* L.A. Amundson,* Pres.; Barbara Amundson,* V.P.; Jane Harberts,* V.P.; A.R. Mixner,* Secy.-Treas.; Barbara Hegelund.
EIN: 411824559

4501
Fred C. and Katherine B. Andersen Foundation ▼

(formerly Andersen Foundation)
P.O. Box 80
Bayport, MN 55003
Contact: Mary Gillstrom, Dir.

Incorporated in 1959 in MN.
Donor: Fred C. Andersen†.
Foundation type: Independent foundation.
Financial data (yr. ended 12/31/05): Assets, $752,341,252 (M); expenditures, $26,523,203; qualifying distributions, $25,349,733; giving activities include $25,349,733 for 192 grants (high: $2,000,000; low: $1,000; average: $5,000–$250,000).
Purpose and activities: Focuses on higher education institutions that do not accept state or federal funding, youth, elderly and health programs in local areas.
Fields of interest: Arts; Higher education; Hospitals (general); Health care; Youth development; Aging, centers/services; Aging.
Type of support: General/operating support; Capital campaigns; Program development.
Limitations: Giving on a national basis for higher education, locally for all other areas. No support for federally funded colleges, universities, or endowment programs. No grants to individuals.
Application information: Proposals must be received in the foundation's office, not postmarked, on or before deadline date.
 Initial approach: Letter
 Copies of proposal: 1
 Deadline(s): Mar. 18, July 22, and Oct. 21
 Board meeting date(s): May, Sept., and Dec.
 Final notification: Varies
Officers and Directors:* Jerold W. Wulf,* Pres.; Alan H. Johnson,* V.P. and Secy.; Gregory L. Benson,* Treas.; David L. Croft; Mary Gillstrom; George O. Hoel; John D. Piepel.
Number of staff: 1 part-time professional.
EIN: 416020920
Selected grants: The following grants were reported in 2004.
$1,300,000 to Presbyterian Homes and Services, Roseville, MN.
$1,000,000 to Croixdale, Bayport, MN.
$780,000 to Gillette Childrens Specialty Healthcare, Saint Paul, MN.
$400,000 to American Swedish Institute, Minneapolis, MN.
$333,333 to Minnesota Medical Foundation, Minneapolis, MN.
$250,000 to Alice Lloyd College, Pippa Passes, KY.
$250,000 to Grand Canyon University, Phoenix, AZ.
$125,000 to Childrens Hospitals and Clinics Foundation, Roseville, MN.
$25,000 to Northeast Residence, Little Canada, MN.
$15,000 to Guthrie Theater, Minneapolis, MN.

4502
Hugh J. Andersen Foundation

White Pine Bldg.
342 5th Ave. N.
Bayport, MN 55003-1201 (651) 439-1557
Contact: Bradley E. Kruse, Prog. Dir.
FAX: (651) 439-9480; *E-mail:* hjafdn@srinc.biz;
Additional tel.: (888) 439-9508; *URL:* http://www.srinc.biz/hja/index.html

Established in 1962.
Donors: Hugh J. Andersen†; Jane K. Andersen†; Katherine B. Andersen†.
Foundation type: Independent foundation.
Financial data (yr. ended 2/28/06): Assets, $90,524,310 (M); expenditures, $4,166,350; qualifying distributions, $4,052,523; giving activities include $3,689,480 for 286 grants (high: $250,000; low: $500; average: $5,000–$55,000).
Purpose and activities: The foundation's mission is to give back to the community through focused efforts that foster inclusiveness, promote equality, and lead to increased human independence, self-sufficiency, and dignity. Emphasis on women and children's programs, community education and social issues, and general community health and medical services, including AIDS services.
Fields of interest: Humanities; Arts; Health care; Human services; Children/youth, services; Family services; Women; Economically disadvantaged; Homeless.
Type of support: General/operating support; Continuing support; Annual campaigns; Capital campaigns; Building/renovation; Program development.
Limitations: Giving primarily in St. Croix Valley-Washington County, MN, and Pierce, Polk, and St. Croix counties, WI, with a secondary interest in St. Paul, MN. No support for private foundations or schools, political or religious organizations, athletic teams, child care centers, civic action groups, business or economics education, or immigration and refugee issues and programming. No grants to individuals, or for fundraising dinners and events, travel, curriculum development, independent media productions, debt relief, scholarships, or fellowships; no loans.
Publications: Annual report (including application guidelines).
Application information: Accepts MN Common Grant Application Form (without modification) along with required grant proposal checklist and request cover sheet. Mass appeals or generic solicitations not considered. Faxed or E-mailed applications will not be considered. Application form required.
Initial approach: Letter or telephone requesting guidelines, requirements and cover sheet. Application cover forms can also be downloaded from foundation Web site
Copies of proposal: 1
Deadline(s): Mar. 15, June. 15 and Aug. 15
Board meeting date(s): Feb., June, Sept. and Nov.
Final notification: 4 weeks after board meeting
Officers and Trustees:* Sarah J. Andersen,* Pres.; Stephen S. Wolfson,* V.P.; William H. Rubenstein,* Secy.-Treas.; Christine E. Andersen, V.P.; Lisa W. Copeland.
EIN: 416020914
Selected grants: The following grants were reported in 2005.
$200,000 to Croixdale, Bayport, MN.
$120,000 to United States Fund for UNICEF, New York, NY.
$50,000 to Minnesota Public Radio, Saint Paul, MN.
$30,000 to Center for Victims of Torture, Minneapolis, MN.
$25,000 to Project for Pride in Living, Minneapolis, MN.
$25,000 to United Way of Saint Croix County, Hudson, WI.
$10,000 to Ain Dah Yung (Our Home) Shelter, Saint Paul, MN.
$10,000 to Amigos de las Americas, Minneapolis, MN.

$7,500 to Melpomene Institute for Womens Health Research, Saint Paul, MN.
$6,500 to Science Museum of Minnesota, Saint Paul, MN.

4503
L. & N. Andreas Foundation ◇ ☆
(formerly Cayman Conand Foundation)
c/o Andreas Office
P.O. Box 3584
Mankato, MN 56002-3584

Established in MN.
Donor: Lowell W. Andreas.
Foundation type: Independent foundation.
Financial data (yr. ended 12/31/05): Assets, $1,479,861 (M); gifts received, $1,142; expenditures, $3,054,821; qualifying distributions, $3,010,000; giving activities include $3,010,000 for 2 grants (high: $3,000,000; low: $10,000).
Purpose and activities: Giving primarily for a hospital foundation.
Fields of interest: Hospitals (general); Philanthropy/voluntarism.
Type of support: General/operating support.
Limitations: Applications not accepted. Giving primarily in MN; some funding on Grand Cayman in the Cayman Islands. No grants to individuals.
Application information: Contributes only to pre-selected organizations.
Officers: Lowell W. Andreas, Pres. and Secy.; David Andreas, V.P. and Treas.
Trustee: Andreas Lee.
EIN: 363382956

4504
The Andreas Foundation ◇
c/o Andreas Office
P.O. Box 3584
Mankato, MN 56002-3584

Incorporated in 1945 in IA.
Foundation type: Independent foundation.
Financial data (yr. ended 11/30/05): Assets, $70,193,104 (M); gifts received, $646; expenditures, $3,294,978; qualifying distributions, $2,256,996; giving activities include $2,256,996 for 109 grants (high: $342,000; low: $500).
Purpose and activities: Giving primarily for higher and secondary education, civil rights and economic opportunities for minority groups, and cultural programs; some support for hospitals, public policy research, churches, and youth agencies.
Fields of interest: Arts; Secondary school/education; Higher education; Hospitals (general); Youth, services; Minorities/immigrants, centers/services; Civil rights; Public policy, research; Religion; Minorities.
Limitations: Applications not accepted. Giving on a national basis. No grants to individuals.
Application information: Contributes only to pre-selected organizations.
Officers and Trustees:* Michael D. Andreas,* Pres. and Treas.; Dorothy Inez Andreas,* V.P. and Secy.; Terry Andreas,* V.P.; Sandra McMurtrie,* V.P.; D.O. Andreas.
EIN: 416017057

4505
Ankeny Foundation ◇
901 Marquette Ave., Ste. 2630
Minneapolis, MN 55402 (612) 596-3260
Contact: DeWalt H. Ankeny, Jr., Pres.

Established in 1963 in MN.
Donors: DeWalt H. Ankeny, Jr.; Sally A. Anson; Kendall A. Mix; Michael H. Ankeny.
Foundation type: Independent foundation.
Financial data (yr. ended 3/31/04): Assets, $2,051,490 (M); expenditures, $460,319; qualifying distributions, $438,510; giving activities include $438,510 for grants.
Purpose and activities: Giving primarily for the arts, education, and human services.
Fields of interest: Museums; Performing arts; Arts; Higher education; Libraries/library science; Scholarships/financial aid; Human services; YM/YWCAs & YM/YWHAs; Children/youth, services; Women, centers/services; Federated giving programs; Christian agencies & churches.
Type of support: General/operating support; Annual campaigns; Capital campaigns; Endowments; Program development.
Limitations: Applications not accepted. Giving primarily in MN, with emphasis on Minneapolis. No grants to individuals.
Application information: Unsolicited general requests for funding not considered; grants to new organizations seldom considered.
Officers and Trustees:* DeWalt H. Ankeny, Jr.,* Pres.; Sally A. Anson,* V.P.; Kendall A. Mix, Secy.; Michael H. Ankeny,* Treas.
Number of staff: 1 part-time support.
EIN: 416024188
Selected grants: The following grants were reported in 2003.
$35,789 to United Way, Greater Twin Cities, Minneapolis, MN.
$33,250 to Blake School, Minneapolis, MN.
$5,275 to Minnesota Orchestral Association, Minneapolis, MN.
$5,000 to Minneapolis Institute of Arts, Minneapolis, MN.
$3,500 to Project for Pride in Living, Minneapolis, MN.
$500 to Emergency Foodshelf Network, Saint Louis Park, MN.
$200 to Second Harvest Heartland, Saint Paul, MN.
$150 to Ballet Arts Minnesota, Minneapolis, MN.
$150 to Habitat for Humanity, Twin Cities, Minneapolis, MN.
$100 to Saint Paul Chamber Orchestra Society, Saint Paul, MN.

4506
Whitney Arcee Foundation ◇ ☆
c/o Wells Fargo Bank Minnesota, N.A.
90 S. 7th St., Ste. 5300
Minneapolis, MN 55402 (612) 667-1784
Contact: Thomas Wright

Established in 1995 in MN.
Foundation type: Independent foundation.
Financial data (yr. ended 12/31/05): Assets, $9,358,451 (M); gifts received, $6,147; expenditures, $992,060; qualifying distributions, $922,985; giving activities include $899,466 for 10 grants (high: $250,000; low: $10,000).
Purpose and activities: The foundation's primary interests are education, social services, humanities, and the arts in MN. Applications are

also accepted from individuals pursuing college or graduate school degrees or considering a religious career, and are in need of scholarship, fellowship, or loan assistance; fine arts and performing arts will also be considered.

Fields of interest: Education; Human services; Protestant agencies & churches.

Type of support: General/operating support; Scholarships—to individuals.

Limitations: Giving primarily in MN.

Application information:

Initial approach: Letter summary prior to proposal
Deadline(s): None
Board meeting date(s): Apr., Aug., and Nov.

Directors: Bradley Bakken; Constance L. Bakken; Jeffrey Bakken; Pamela C. Petersmeyer; Wendy K. Watson.

EIN: 411796283

Selected grants: The following grants were reported in 2003.

$155,583 to Hamline University, Law School, Saint Paul, MN.

$42,258 to First Lutheran Church, Saint Paul, MN. For roof repair.

$22,397 to Minnesota Medical Foundation, Minneapolis, MN. For general support for Bob Allison Ataxia Center.

4507
Asian Foundation ✦

790 Pleasant View Rd.
Chanhassen, MN 55317-9509

Established in 1998 in MN.

Donors: Gina Schmidt; Tom Schmidt.

Foundation type: Independent foundation.

Financial data (yr. ended 12/31/04): Assets, $338,637 (M); expenditures, $323,901; qualifying distributions, $323,901; giving activities include $323,901 for 17 grants (high: $176,000; low: $300).

Fields of interest: Higher education; Education; Health organizations, association; Human services; Christian agencies & churches.

Type of support: General/operating support.

Limitations: Applications not accepted. Giving primarily in the Minneapolis, MN, area. No grants to individuals.

Application information: Contributes only to pre-selected organizations.

Officers: Thomas A. Schmidt, Pres.; Gina M. Schmidt, V.P. and Secy.-Treas.

EIN: 411907847

Selected grants: The following grants were reported in 2004.

$35,000 to Wheaton College, Wheaton, IL.

$30,000 to Northwestern College, Saint Paul, MN.

$10,000 to Ducks Unlimited, Edina, MN.

4508
Athwin Foundation ✦

5200 Willson Rd., Ste. 307
Minneapolis, MN 55424   (952) 915-6165
Contact: Bruce W. Bean, Tr.

Trust established in 1956 in MN.

Donors: Atherton Bean†; Winifred W. Bean†.

Foundation type: Independent foundation.

Financial data (yr. ended 12/31/05): Assets, $10,213,515 (M); expenditures, $685,220; qualifying distributions, $639,512; giving activities

include $539,891 for 88 grants (high: $70,000; low: $1,000; average: $5,000–$20,000).

Purpose and activities: Giving primarily for arts and culture, church related projects, education, and social services.

Fields of interest: Visual arts; Performing arts; Arts; Education; Crime/law enforcement; Human services; Children/youth, services; Religion.

Type of support: General/operating support; Capital campaigns; Program development.

Limitations: Giving primarily in the Minneapolis-St. Paul, MN, area; some giving also in Claremont, CA. No grants to individuals, or for scholarships or fellowships; no loans.

Publications: Application guidelines.

Application information: The foundation prefers applicants to use the Minnesota Common Grant Application Form that can be obtained by calling the Minnesota Council on foundations (612) 338-1989 or by visiting their Web site: http://www.mcf.org and selecting Grant seeking in Minnesota. There is also a Minnesota Common Grant Report Form available which makes the reporting process more efficient and effective for nonprofits as well as for funders such as the Athwin Foundation. Application form required.

Initial approach: Letter of inquiry prior to submission of proposal (if invited)
Copies of proposal: 1
Deadline(s): Mar. 31 and Sept. 15
Board meeting date(s): Biannually
Final notification: 60 days

Trustees: Bruce W. Bean; Glen Atherton Bean; Mary F. Bean; Eleanor Nolan.

Number of staff: 1 full-time professional.

EIN: 416021773

4509
The ATK Foundation ✦

(formerly Alliant Techsystems Community Investment Foundation)
5050 Lincoln Dr., MN01-1030
Edina, MN 55436-1097
E-mail: karen.engelbret@atk.com

Established in 1990 in MN.

Donor: Alliant Techsystems Inc.

Foundation type: Company-sponsored foundation.

Financial data (yr. ended 3/31/06): Assets, $237,640 (M); gifts received, $1,560,000; expenditures, $1,346,382; qualifying distributions, $1,325,819.

Purpose and activities: The foundation supports organizations involved with community development and the military.

Fields of interest: Youth development; Community development; Federated giving programs; Military/veterans' organizations.

Type of support: Annual campaigns; Employee matching gifts; Employee-related scholarships.

Limitations: Applications not accepted. Giving primarily in areas of company operations. No support for religious organizations not of direct benefit to the entire community. No grants to individuals (except for employee-related scholarships), or for capital campaigns or endowments, travel, meetings, conferences or seminars, or advertising or printing.

Publications: Annual report.

Application information: Contributes only to pre-selected organizations.

Board meeting date(s): Quarterly

Officer and Board Members:* Rod Bitz,* Pres.; Caren Fitzgerald; Bob Gustafson; John Picek; Robert Shadley.

Number of staff: 1 part-time support.

EIN: 411683475

4510
Bailey Nurseries Foundation ✦ ☆

c/o John Bailey
1325 Bailey Rd.
Newport, MN 55055

Established in 1997 in MN.

Donor: Bailey Nurseries, Inc.

Foundation type: Company-sponsored foundation.

Financial data (yr. ended 12/31/05): Assets, $837,693 (M); gifts received, $220,000; expenditures, $395,736; qualifying distributions, $392,663; giving activities include $392,663 for grants.

Purpose and activities: The foundation supports organizations involved with arts and culture, education, horticulture, youth development, and community development.

Fields of interest: Arts; Education; Botanical/horticulture/landscape services; Youth development; Community development.

Limitations: Applications not accepted. Giving limited to MN. No grants to individuals.

Application information: Contributes only to pre-selected organizations.

Officers: Gordon J. Bailey, Chair.; Rodney P. Bailey, Pres.; John P. Bailey, Secy.; Theresa McEnaney, Treas.

EIN: 411890034

Selected grants: The following grants were reported in 2004.

$30,000 to Landscape Plant Development Center, Chanhassen, MN.

$16,000 to Saint Johns University, Collegeville, MN.

$10,000 to Great River Greening, Saint Paul, MN.

$10,000 to Iowa Arboretum, Madrid, IA.

$4,500 to Minneapolis Institute of Arts, Minneapolis, MN.

$3,000 to North Dakota State University, Fargo, ND.

$2,800 to South Washington County Schools Education Foundation, Woodbury, MN.

$2,000 to University of Minnesota, Saint Paul, MN.

$1,500 to Catholic Charities, MN.

$1,500 to Minnesota Orchestral Association, Minneapolis, MN.

4511
The Barry Foundation ✦

2104 Hastings Ave., Ste. 200
Newport, MN 55055

Established in 1986 in MN.

Donors: B. John Barry; Thomas J. Barry; Jessica M. Barry.

Foundation type: Independent foundation.

Financial data (yr. ended 12/31/05): Assets, $48,590,664 (M); gifts received, $12,662,772; expenditures, $1,379,885; qualifying distributions, $1,359,885; giving activities include $1,208,525 for 44 grants (high: $500,000; low: $100).

Purpose and activities: Giving primarily for higher education, to health associations, and to Roman Catholic agencies and churches.

Fields of interest: Education; Health organizations, association; Human services; Foundations (public); Roman Catholic agencies & churches.
Limitations: Applications not accepted. Giving primarily in MN. No grants to individuals.
Application information: Contributes only to pre-selected organizations; Unsolicited requests for funds not accepted.
Officers and Directors:* B. John Barry,* Chair; Dean C. Hoffrogge, Vice-Chair; Cheryl Sandeen,* Pres.; Jessica M. Barry,* Secy.; Pam Borgerding, Managing Dir.; Michael B. Barry; Thomas J. Barry.
EIN: 411571983

4512
The Bayport Foundation of Andersen Corporation

(formerly Bayport Foundation, Inc.)
White Pine Bldg.
342 5th Ave. N.
Bayport, MN 55003-1201 (651) 439-1557
Contact: Bradley E. Kruse, Prog. Dir.
FAX: (651) 439-9480; E-mail: bayportfdn@srinc.biz;
Additional tel.: (888) 439-9508; URL: http://www.srinc.biz/bp/index.html

Incorporated in 1941 in MN.
Donor: Andersen Corp.
Foundation type: Company-sponsored foundation.
Financial data (yr. ended 11/30/05): Assets, $49,352,626 (M); gifts received, $1,750,000; expenditures, $2,719,687; qualifying distributions, $2,496,475; giving activities include $2,341,445 for 152 grants (high: $200,000; low: $250), and $53,000 for employee matching gifts.
Purpose and activities: The foundation supports programs designed to provide community, social, and support services to better people's lives and strengthen communities.
Fields of interest: Human services; Community development.
Type of support: General/operating support; Capital campaigns; Program development; Employee matching gifts.
Limitations: Giving primarily in areas of company operations in the East Metro, MN, area and the St. Croix Valley, WI, area. No grants to individuals.
Publications: Application guidelines.
Application information: The Minnesota Common Grant Application Form is required. Application form required.
Initial approach: Download application form and mail proposal and application form to foundation
Copies of proposal: 1
Deadline(s): Apr. 15, July 15, Oct. 15, and Dec. 15
Board meeting date(s): Jan., Apr., July, and Nov.
Final notification: 10 working days
Officers and Directors: W.P. "Pat" Riley, Pres.; Keith D. Olson, Secy.-Treas.; Phil Donaldson; Donald L. Garofalo; Jim E. Humphrey; Jay Lund; Maureen E. McDonough; Julie Smith.
Number of staff: 1 full-time professional.
EIN: 416020912
Selected grants: The following grants were reported in 2005.
$75,000 to Oaklawn Harmony Center, Menomonie, WI.
$58,000 to Boy Scouts of America, Saint Paul, MN.
$50,000 to Bayport Public Library, Bayport, MN.

$50,000 to Gillette Childrens Hospital Foundation, Saint Paul, MN.
$50,000 to Minnesota Public Radio, Saint Paul, MN.
$12,000 to Phipps Center for the Arts, Hudson, WI.
$10,000 to Lakeview Memorial Hospital Association, Stillwater, MN.
$10,000 to Saint Croix Valley Teen Center, Stillwater, MN.
$10,000 to United Negro College Fund, Minneapolis, MN.
$7,000 to PACER Center, Minneapolis, MN.

4513
The Beim Foundation

3109 W. 50th St., No. 120
Minneapolis, MN 55410-2102 (612) 605-8192
Contact: Kerrie Blevins, Consultant; Mary Karen Lynn-Klimenko, Consultant
E-mail: contact@beimfoundation.org; URL: http://www.beimfoundation.org

Incorporated in 1947 in MN.
Donors: N.C. Beim†; Raymond N. Beim†.
Foundation type: Independent foundation.
Financial data (yr. ended 12/31/05): Assets, $11,000,441 (M); expenditures, $563,015; qualifying distributions, $540,808; giving activities include $458,042 for 61 grants (high: $25,000; low: $1,000).
Purpose and activities: Primary areas of interest are arts, education, environment, and human services.
Fields of interest: Arts; Education; Environment, natural resources; Environment; Human services; Women, centers/services; Women.
Type of support: Equipment; Program development; Program evaluation.
Limitations: Giving primarily in MN; some giving also in communities where directors live. No support for private foundations, or for political or religious organizations. No grants to individuals, or for deficit financing memberships, endowments, subscriptions, tickets, conferences, fundraisers, or annual campaigns, capital campaigns or for general operating support; no grants for building or equipment, except for equipment qualifying under small arts capital grants; no loans.
Application information: Minnesota Common Grant Application Form accepted. E-mailed proposals will not be accepted. Application form required.
Initial approach: Proposal
Copies of proposal: 1
Deadline(s): Application deadline available on foundation Web site
Board meeting date(s): Board meeting dates available on foundation Web site
Final notification: See foundation Web site
Officers: Carol Nulsen, Pres.; Beth Conover, Secy.; Margo Conover, Treas.
Directors: Patricia Arnold; Julie Packard; Allison Villani.
Number of staff: None.
EIN: 416022529

4514
James Ford Bell Foundation ◇

1818 Oliver Ave. S.
Minneapolis, MN 55405
Contact: Diane B. Neimann, Exec. Dir.
FAX: (612) 377-8407;
E-mail: general@fpadvisors.com; URL: http://

www.fpadvisors.com/jamesfordbell/jamesfordbell.htm

Established in 1955 in MN.
Donors: Charles H. Bell; James Ford Bell†.
Foundation type: Independent foundation.
Financial data (yr. ended 12/31/03): Assets, $13,068,318 (M); expenditures, $602,859; qualifying distributions, $597,213; giving activities include $431,931 for 17 grants (high: $200,000; low: $500), and $31,000 for 7 employee matching gifts.
Purpose and activities: Emphasis on cultural programs; support also for wildlife preservation and conservation, youth agencies, the environment, education, health and human services.
Fields of interest: Museums; Arts; Education, early childhood education; Child development, education; Higher education; Adult/continuing education; Adult education—literacy, basic skills & GED; Education, reading; Education; Environment, natural resources; Environment; Animals/wildlife, preservation/protection; Reproductive health, family planning; Human services; Children/youth, services; Child development, services; Family services; Civil liberties, reproductive rights; Urban/community development; Community development; Biological sciences; Population studies; Disabilities, people with; Minorities; Asians/Pacific Islanders; African Americans/Blacks; Hispanics/Latinos; Native Americans/American Indians; Women; Immigrants/refugees; Economically disadvantaged.
Type of support: General/operating support; Continuing support; Endowments; Program development; Seed money.
Limitations: Applications not accepted. Giving primarily in MN. No grants to individuals, or for fellowships, memberships, annual campaigns, or special events or fundraisers.
Publications: Annual report.
Application information: Unsolicited requests for funds not accepted.
Board meeting date(s): Spring and fall
Officers and Trustees:* Ford W. Bell,* Chair.; Diane B. Neimann, Exec. Dir.; Samuel H. Bell, Jr.; David B. Hartwell.
EIN: 416023099
Selected grants: The following grants were reported in 2003.
$200,000 to Minnesota Historical Society, Saint Paul, MN. For Saint Anthony Falls Historic Center capital campaign for restoration of Washburn-Crosby A Mill and construction of the Flour Tower Interpretive Center.
$50,000 to Minneapolis Institute of Arts, Minneapolis, MN.
$21,931 to Delta Waterfowl Foundation, Bismarck, ND. 2 grants: $18,122, $3,809 (For Sally Bell Perry Endowment).
$19,000 to Westminster Presbyterian Church of Minneapolis, Minneapolis, MN. For restoration of Heffelfinger window.
$7,000 to Connecticut College, New London, CT. For general operating support.
$5,000 to Belwin, Afton, MN. For outdoor education facility.
$5,000 to Minnesota Land Trust, Saint Paul, MN. For general operating support.
$1,200 to Saint Edwards School, Vero Beach, FL. For general operating support.
$1,000 to Greater Minneapolis Council of Churches, Minneapolis, MN. For Lighthouse Academy Project.

4515
Bemis Company Foundation

222 S. 9th St., No. 440
Minneapolis, MN 55402-3093 (612) 376-3093
Contact: Eugene H. Seashore, Jr., Tr.
E-mail: bemisfoundation@bemis.com; Additional
tel.: (612) 376-3007; URL: http://www.bemis.com/
corp_citizenship/community_relations.html

Trust established in 1959 in MO.
Donor: Bemis Co., Inc.
Foundation type: Company-sponsored foundation.
Financial data (yr. ended 12/31/05): Assets,
$23,133 (M); gifts received, $1,598,000;
expenditures, $2,002,388; qualifying distributions,
$1,953,237; giving activities include $1,514,690
for 154 grants (high: $653,590; low: $20), and
$438,547 for 759 employee matching gifts.
Purpose and activities: The foundation supports
food banks and organizations involved with arts and
culture, education, health, youth development,
human services, and civic affairs.
Fields of interest: Arts; Higher education;
Education; Hospitals (general); Health care; Food
banks; Youth development; Human services;
Federated giving programs; Government/public
administration; Public affairs.
Type of support: General/operating support;
Continuing support; Annual campaigns; Capital
campaigns; Building/renovation; Employee
matching gifts; Employee-related scholarships.
Limitations: Giving limited to areas of company
operations. No support for religious or political
organizations. No grants to individuals (except for
employee-related scholarships), or for endowments,
research, educational capital campaigns, or trips or
tours; no loans.
Publications: Application guidelines; Corporate
giving report (including application guidelines).
Application information: Application form not
required.
 Initial approach: Proposal
 Copies of proposal: 1
 Deadline(s): Mar. 15, June 15, Sept. 15, and Dec.
  15
 Board meeting date(s): Mar. 25, June 25, Sept.
  25, and Dec. 25
 Final notification: 1 week
Trustees: Stanley A. Jaffy; Melanie E.R. Miller;
Eugene H. Seashore, Jr.; Gene C. Wulf.
Number of staff: 2 part-time professional.
EIN: 416038616
Selected grants: The following grants were reported
in 2005.
$671,225 to Scholarship America, Saint Peter, MN.
  2 grants: $653,590, $17,635
$70,000 to United Way, WI.
$60,000 to United Way of the Wabash Valley, Terre
  Haute, IN.
$35,000 to Salvation Army, WI.
$12,100 to American Red Cross, Minneapolis, MN.
  2 grants: $12,000, $100
$10,000 to United Way of the Midlands, Omaha, NE.
$4,000 to Aquinas College, Grand Rapids, MI.
$400 to Worcester Polytechnic Institute, Worcester,
  MA.

4516
Best Buy Children's Foundation ▼ ◇

7601 Penn Ave. S.
Richfield, MN 55423-3645
FAX: (612) 292-4001; Application address: P.O. Box
9448, Minneapolis, MN 55440-9448; URL: http://
www.bestbuy.com/communityrelations

Established in 1994 in MN.
Donor: Best Buy Co., Inc.
Foundation type: Company-sponsored foundation.
Financial data (yr. ended 3/1/05): Assets,
$6,817,549 (M); gifts received, $9,118,439;
expenditures, $15,419,954; qualifying
distributions, $13,984,888; giving activities include
$13,984,888 for 370 grants (high: $2,285,000;
low: $16).
Purpose and activities: The foundation supports
programs designed to engage children through the
use of interactive technology.
Fields of interest: Education; Boys & girls clubs;
Children/youth, services.
Type of support: Capital campaigns; Program
development; Curriculum development; Scholarship
funds; Employee volunteer services; Scholarships—
to individuals.
Limitations: Giving on a national basis. No support
for labor organizations, fraternal organizations or
social clubs, religious organizations, or local
affiliates of national organizations. No grants to
individuals (except for scholarships), or for travel,
general operating support, or treatment or
residential programs; no in-kind gifts.
Publications: Application guidelines.
Application information: Application form required.
 Initial approach: Download application form and
  mail to foundation
 Copies of proposal: 1
 Deadline(s): Feb. 1, May 1, Aug. 1, and Nov. 1
 Board meeting date(s): Jan., Apr., July, and Oct.
 Final notification: 4 months
Officers and Directors:* Richard M. Schulze,*
Chair.; Susan S. Hoff,* Pres.; David P. Berg,* Secy.;
Bradbury H. Anderson; Ruby Anik; Allen U.
Lenzmeier; Tim D. McGeehan; John R. Thompson;
Barbara J. VanLoenen; Jack Welch.
Number of staff: 1 full-time professional.
EIN: 411784382
Selected grants: The following grants were reported
in 2005.
$2,360,000 to Scholarship America, Saint Peter,
  MN. 2 grants: $75,000 (For National Partnership
  Grant), $2,285,000 (For National Partnership
  Grant).
$1,324,026 to Junior Achievement, National,
  Colorado Springs, CO. For National Partnership
  Grant.
$750,000 to Ball State University, Muncie, IN. For
  National Partnership Grant.
$500,000 to American Red Cross, National
  Headquarters, DC. 2 grants: $100,000 (For
  Community Partnership Grant), $400,000 (For
  National Partnership Grant).
$250,000 to Marine Toys for Tots Foundation,
  Quantico, VA. For National Partnership Grant.
$220,000 to MOUSE, New York, NY. For National
  Partnership Grant.
$140,000 to Junior Achievement of New York, New
  York, NY. For National Partnership Grant.
$100,000 to Chicanos Latinos Unidos En Servicios
  (CLUES), Saint Paul, MN. For Twin City Metro
  Hometown grant.

4517
The Beverly Foundation ◇

(formerly The Beverly Deikel Foundation)
5354 Parkdale Dr., Ste. 310
Minneapolis, MN 55416 (952) 545-3000
Contact: Beverly Deikel, Pres. and Secy.-Treas.

Established in 1999 in MN.
Donor: Beverly Deikel.
Foundation type: Independent foundation.
Financial data (yr. ended 12/31/04): Assets,
$30,638,294 (M); gifts received, $1,000;
expenditures, $1,477,159; qualifying distributions,
$1,224,723; giving activities include $1,214,730
for 92 grants (high: $320,000; low: $25).
Fields of interest: Arts; Education; Environment;
Human services; Children/youth, services.
Type of support: General/operating support;
Management development/capacity building;
Capital campaigns; Building/renovation; Emergency
funds; Program development; Consulting services;
Program evaluation.
Limitations: Giving primarily in MN. No grants to
individuals.
Application information: Application form not
required.
 Initial approach: Letter or proposal
 Copies of proposal: 1
 Deadline(s): None
Officer: Beverly Deikel, Pres. and Secy.-Treas.
Number of staff: 1 part-time professional; 1
part-time support.
EIN: 411958161
Selected grants: The following grants were reported
in 2003.
$270,000 to Minneapolis Jewish Federation,
  Minnetonka, MN. For general operating support
  and capital campaign.
$105,000 to Wider Caribbean Sea Turtle
  Conservation Network (WIDECAST), Beaufort,
  NC. For ROSTI Project.
$48,863 to Aid to Southeast Asia, Minneapolis, MN.
  For general operating support.
$20,000 to Plymouth Christian Youth Center,
  Minneapolis, MN. For capital campaign.
$16,000 to Hand in Hand, American Friends of the
  Center for Jewish-Arab Education in Israel,
  Portland, OR. For general operating support.
$10,000 to HearthStone of Minnesota, South Saint
  Paul, MN. For Aftercare Program.
$5,000 to PACER Center, Minneapolis, MN. For
  general operating support and capital campaign.
$2,700 to Avenues for Homeless Youth,
  Minneapolis, MN. For general operating support.
$2,700 to Storefront Group, Richfield, MN. For
  general operating support.
$1,250 to Center for Science in the Public Interest,
  DC. For general operating support.

4518
The Bieber Family Foundation ◇

2600 Niagara Ln. N.
Plymouth, MN 55447-4718

Established in 1990.
Donor: members of the Bieber family.
Foundation type: Independent foundation.
Financial data (yr. ended 12/31/05): Assets,
$8,794,981 (M); expenditures, $483,249;
qualifying distributions, $433,158; giving activities
include $431,040 for 68 grants (high: $150,000;
low: $150).

Purpose and activities: Giving primarily for human services, with an emphasis on child welfare; support also for the arts and education.

Fields of interest: Arts; Education; Health care; Food services; Athletics/sports, Special Olympics; Human services; Youth, services; Developmentally disabled, centers & services; Federated giving programs; Christian agencies & churches; Disabilities, people with.

Limitations: Applications not accepted. Giving primarily in MN. No grants to individuals.

Application information: Contributes only to pre-selected organizations.

Officers and Directors:* William F. Bieber,* Pres.; Kathleen G. O'Connor,* V.P.; Christine Bieber Orris,* Secy.; Robert A. Levy, Treas.

EIN: 411679484

Selected grants: The following grants were reported in 2004.

$350,000 to Hammer Residences, Wayzata, MN. 2 grants: $150,000, $200,000

$1,000 to Childrens Home Society.

$1,000 to Mount Olivet Rolling Acres, Excelsior, MN.

$1,000 to PACER Center, Minneapolis, MN.

$1,000 to Reach for Resources, Hopkins, MN.

$1,000 to Ronald McDonald House.

4519

F. R. Bigelow Foundation ▼

600 5th St. Ctr.
55 E. 5th St.
St. Paul, MN   55101-1797   (651) 224-5463
Contact: Carleen K. Rhodes, Secy.
FAX: (651) 224-8123; E-mail: inbox@frbigelow.org;
URL: http://www.frbigelow.org

Trust established in 1934; incorporated in 1946 in MN.

Donors: Frederick Russell Bigelow‡; Eileen Bigelow‡; Sit Investments.

Foundation type: Independent foundation.

Financial data (yr. ended 12/31/05): Assets, $152,877,801 (M); gifts received, $23,851; expenditures, $7,474,111; qualifying distributions, $6,749,734; giving activities include $6,402,511 for 110 grants (high: $1,350,000; low: $1,000; average: $10,000–$200,000).

Purpose and activities: Established as a trust to promote the well-being of mankind and to support the civic, educational, religious, and other needs of the community.

Fields of interest: Humanities; Arts; Education, early childhood education; Child development, education; Elementary school/education; Secondary school/education; Higher education; Adult education—literacy, basic skills & GED; Education, reading; Human services; Child development, services; Economic development; Minorities; Economically disadvantaged.

Type of support: Capital campaigns; Building/renovation; Equipment; Program development; Seed money; Matching/challenge support.

Limitations: Giving limited to the Greater St. Paul, MN, metropolitan area, which includes; Ramsey, Washington, and Dakota counties, with a particular emphasis on serving people who live and work in the city of St. Paul. No support for sectarian religious programs. No grants to individuals, or for annual operating expenses, medical research, or ongoing, open-ended needs.

Publications: Application guidelines; Annual report (including application guidelines).

Application information: Application requirements are included in the foundation's application guidelines available on the foundation's Web site. Application form required.

Initial approach: Letter of inquiry or full proposal
Copies of proposal: 1
Deadline(s): Approximately 3 1/2 months prior to board meetings
Board meeting date(s): Apr., Aug., and Nov.
Final notification: 4 to 5 months

Officers and Trustees:* Jon A. Theobald,* Chair.; Carolyn J. Brusseau,* Vice-Chair.; Carleen K. Rhodes, Secy.; Elizabeth M. Kiernat,* Treas.; James H. Bradshaw; Joan L. Gardner; Louise G. Jones; Constance B. Kunin; Bert J. McKasy; Douglas D. McMillan; Sally D. Patterson; Edward Pendergast; John M. Scanlan, M.D.

Number of staff: None.

EIN: 510232651

Selected grants: The following grants were reported in 2005.

$600,000 to Saint Paul Riverfront Corporation, Saint Paul, MN. Toward operating support.

$285,000 to Saint Paul Foundation, Saint Paul, MN. Toward operating support for Words Work.

$250,000 to Jeremiah Program, Minneapolis, MN. For capital campaign to establish facility in Saint Paul.

$249,787 to United Way, Greater Twin Cities, Minneapolis, MN. For Annual Campaign.

$200,000 to Amherst H. Wilder Foundation, Saint Paul, MN. Toward expanding Achievement Plus Program to junior high schools in Saint Paul.

$175,000 to SteppingStone Theater, Saint Paul, MN. For Capital Campaign.

$75,000 to Metropolitan State University Foundation, Saint Paul, MN. Toward Health Partners Simulation Center for Patient Safety.

$40,000 to SPCPA Building Company, Saint Paul, MN. Toward capital improvements to Landmark Center.

$30,000 to American Indian Economic Development Fund, Saint Paul, MN. For start-up support for Business Incubator.

$15,000 to Lifeworks Services, Mendota Heights, MN. Toward Frameworks Project.

4520

The Blandin Foundation ▼ ✧

(formerly Charles K. Blandin Foundation)
100 N. Pokegama Ave.
Grand Rapids, MN   55744   (218) 326-0523
Contact: James Hoolihan, Pres.
FAX: (218) 327-1949;
E-mail: bfinfo@blandinfoundation.org; Additional tel.: (877) 882-2257; URL: http://www.blandinfoundation.org

Incorporated in 1941 in MN.

Donor: Charles K. Blandin‡.

Foundation type: Independent foundation.

Financial data (yr. ended 12/31/05): Assets, $423,323,009 (M); gifts received, $17,806,844; expenditures, $15,619,091; qualifying distributions, $15,417,367; giving activities include $8,249,021 for 166+ grants (high: $1,035,000; low: $200; average: $10,000–$100,000), $669,152 for 623 grants to individuals (high: $3,275; low: $250; average: $500–$2,075), $58,246 for 112 employee matching gifts, and $3,656,672 for foundation-administered programs.

Purpose and activities: Giving primarily in four areas for rural MN: 1) community leadership; 2) economic opportunity; 3) life-long learning; and 4) diversity.

Fields of interest: Higher education; Education; Economic development; Rural development; Community development; Leadership development.

Type of support: Employee matching gifts; General/operating support; Continuing support; Program development; Seed money; Scholarship funds; Technical assistance; Program-related investments/loans; Scholarships—to individuals; Matching/challenge support.

Limitations: Giving limited to rural areas of MN; scholarships limited to graduates of an Itasca County, Hill City, or Remer, Blackduck, or Northome, MN, high school. No support for religious activities or camping programs. No grants to individuals (except for Blandin Educational Awards), for operating budgets, annual campaigns, deficit financing, government services, capital funds (outside home community), endowments, publications, travel, medical research, films or videos, conferences, or seminars (outside of those sponsored by the foundation and related to its grantmaking).

Publications: Financial statement; Informational brochure (including application guidelines).

Application information: Scholarship applicants should call or write to the foundation for deadlines and other information. Foundation will accept the Minnesota Common Grant Application Form available on the foundation's Web site. Application form not required.

Initial approach: Letter or visit
Copies of proposal: 1
Deadline(s): Mar. 1, Sept. 1, and Dec. 1
Board meeting date(s): During the first 2 weeks of Mar., June, and Dec.
Final notification: 2 weeks after board meeting

Officers and Trustees:* George Thompson,* Chair.; James Hoolihan,* Pres.; Eugene Radecki,* Secy.; Jean M. Lane, Cont.; Marian Barcus; James Bensen; Timothy Bonner, M.D.; Karen Diver; Kris Ferraro; James Hamilton; Mike Johnson; Sandy Layman; Ken Lundcpen; Bruce Stender.

Number of staff: 12 full-time professional; 12 full-time support; 2 part-time support.

EIN: 416038619

Selected grants: The following grants were reported in 2005.

$350,000 to Independent School District No. 318, Grand Rapids, MN. For continued support for Baby Steps Boutique and Step Ahead parent education program, payable over 3 years.

$315,000 to Legal Aid Service of Northeastern Minnesota, Grand Rapids, MN. For continued operating support, payable over 3 years.

$313,000 to Itasca Community College, Grand Rapids, MN. For financial aid assistance for Itasca County students during school year.

$290,000 to Reif Arts Council, Grand Rapids, MN. For continued support to provide arts programming to residents in Itasca County and throughout rural Minnesota, payable over 2 years.

$134,000 to Bovey Coleraine Youth Center, Bovey, MN. For continued operating support.

$75,000 to Action Through Churches Together, Grand Rapids, MN. For project support to establish emergency shelter for homeless families and individuals and to advocate for needs of children who are homeless or at risk of becoming homeless in Itasca County, payable over 2 years.

$50,000 to Deer River Hired Hands, Deer River, MN. For project support to conduct feasbility study for diverting waste for use as biomass fuel and recycling in Itasca County.

$45,000 to First Call for Help of Itasca County, Grand Rapids, MN. For sustaining contribution for emergency, information and referral services in Itasca County.

$45,000 to Northern Community Radio, Grand Rapids, MN. For sustaining contribution for news programming throughout Itasca County area.

$40,000 to Itasca Orchestral Society, Grand Rapids, MN. For sustaining contribution to provide orchestral music opportunities for youth and adults in Itasca County area.

4521
Blue Cross and Blue Shield of Minnesota Foundation, Inc.

3535 Blue Cross Rd., Rte. M459
Eagan, MN 55122   (651) 662-3950
FAX: (651) 662-1361;
E-mail: foundation@bluecrossmn.com; Additional address: M459, P.O. Box 64560, St. Paul, MN 55164-0560; Additional tel.: (866) 812-1593; URL: http://www.bluecrossmn.com/public/foundation/index.html

Established in 1986 in MN.
Donors: Blue Cross and Blue Shield of Minnesota; American Healthways.
Foundation type: Company-sponsored foundation.
Financial data (yr. ended 12/31/05): Assets, $51,702,519 (M); gifts received, $14,000; expenditures, $3,118,849; qualifying distributions, $2,724,983; giving activities include $2,221,105 for 77 grants (high: $244,877; low: $596), and $116,544 for 4 foundation-administered programs.
Purpose and activities: The foundation supports organizations involved with children's health and the health of immigrants.
Fields of interest: Child development, education; Environment, toxics; Health care, equal rights; Health care; Mental health/crisis services; Housing/shelter; Children; Minorities; Asians/Pacific Islanders; Native Americans/American Indians; Immigrants/refugees; Economically disadvantaged.
Type of support: Continuing support; Program development; Technical assistance.
Limitations: Giving limited to MN; giving also to statewide and regional organizations. No support for athletic organizations. No grants to individuals, or for lobbying, political, or fraternal activities, sports events, religious activities, clinical quality improvement activities, biomedical research, capital campaigns, endowments, fundraising events, or development campaigns, debt reduction, the payment of services or benefits reimbursable from other sources, the supplanting of funds already secured for budgeted staff and/or services, or long-term support; no loans.
Publications: Application guidelines; Corporate giving report; Grants list; Informational brochure; Occasional report.
Application information: Support is limited to 1 contribution per organization during any given year. Application form not required.
   Initial approach: Telephone foundation; mail letter of inquiry to foundation
   Copies of proposal: 1

Deadline(s): Feb. 1 for Healthy Together: Creating Community with New Americans; Apr. 13 for Growing Up Healthy: Kids and Communities
Board meeting date(s): Mar., June, Sept., and Dec.
Officers and Directors:* Mark W. Banks, M.D.*, Chair.; Richard M. Niemiec,* Secy.-Treas.; Daniel Johnson, Exec. Dir.; Kathleen Annette, M.D.; Karen Bohn; William Collins, Jr.; Kathy Gaalswyk; Deborah B. Madson; Kathy Mock; Nancy Nelson; Timothy M. Peterson; Steven Richards, M.D.; Marsha Shotley; MaryAnn Stump, R.N.
Number of staff: 5 full-time professional; 2 part-time professional; 1 part-time support.
EIN: 363525653
Selected grants: The following grants were reported in 2005.
$150,000 to Centro Campesino, Owatonna, MN. To develop leadership among rural Latino youth and families and build organizational capacity, payable over 3 years.
$150,000 to Ready 4 K, Saint Paul, MN. To increase school readiness and improve early childhood development of Twin Cities Hmong preschoolers, payable over 3 years.
$89,000 to Centre for Asians and Pacific Islanders, Minneapolis, MN. To partner with Minneapolis public schools to improve mental health and education-related outcomes within North Minneapolis Hmong community, payable over 3 years.
$50,000 to Western Mental Health Center, Marshall, MN. To hire Community Health worker to provide mental health outreach, support and education to immigrants in greater Marshall Area, payable over 2 years.
$25,000 to Lutheran Social Service of Minnesota, Pelican Rapids, MN. To promote replication of their successful immigrant integration model into other communities.
$10,000 to Bosnian Womens Network, Brooklyn Park, MN. To assist in the development of board and staff that was established in 2000 to serve Bosnians living in the Twin Cities Metro area.
$10,000 to National Conference of State Legislatures, DC. For series of roundtable discussions between immigrants and policymakers.

4522
The Douglass Brandenborg Family Foundation ✧

1695 Hunter Dr.
Wayzata, MN 55391

Established in 1999 in MN.
Donors: John Brandenborg; Laurie Douglass Brandenborg.
Foundation type: Independent foundation.
Financial data (yr. ended 12/31/05): Assets, $36,344,484 (M); gifts received, $12,500,000; expenditures, $1,042,837; qualifying distributions, $905,000; giving activities include $905,000 for 10 grants (high: $525,000; low: $500).
Fields of interest: Higher education; Health organizations, association; Federated giving programs.
Limitations: Applications not accepted. Giving primarily in Denver, CO, Chicago, IL, and Minneapolis, MN. No grants to individuals.
Application information: Contributes only to pre-selected organizations.

Officers and Directors:* John Brandenborg,* Pres.; Laurie Douglass Brandenborg,* Secy.
EIN: 411958170
Selected grants: The following grants were reported in 2004.
$300,000 to University of Denver, Denver, CO.
$150,000 to Daniel Murphy Scholarship Foundation, Chicago, IL.
$90,000 to First Call for Help of the United Way of Minneapolis Area, Minneapolis, MN.
$250 to University of Wisconsin Foundation, Madison, WI.

4523
Otto Bremer Foundation ▼

445 Minnesota St., Ste. 2250
St. Paul, MN 55101-2107   (651) 227-8036
Contact: Viva Yang, Comms. Assoc.
FAX: (651) 312-3665; E-mail: obf@ottobremer.org; Additional tel.: (888) 291-1123; URL: http://www.ottobremer.org

Trust established in 1944 in MN.
Donor: Otto Bremer†.
Foundation type: Independent foundation.
Financial data (yr. ended 12/31/05): Assets, $535,178,874 (M); expenditures, $29,386,235; qualifying distributions, $30,120,161; giving activities include $26,968,819 for 807 grants (high: $500,000; low: $37,500; average: $1,000–$500,000), and $1,115,000 for 7 loans/program-related investments.
Purpose and activities: The mission of the foundation is to assist people in achieving full economic, civic and social participation in and for the betterment of their communities.
Fields of interest: Child development, education; Higher education; Libraries (public); Reproductive health, family planning; Health care; Mental health/crisis services; Health organizations, association; Crime/violence prevention, youth; Crime/violence prevention, domestic violence; Legal services; Nutrition; Housing/shelter, development; Youth development, citizenship; Human services; Children/youth, services; Child development, services; Residential/custodial care, hospices; Women, centers/services; Minorities/immigrants, centers/services; Homeless, human services; Civil rights, immigrants; Civil rights, minorities; Civil rights, disabled; Civil rights, women; Civil rights, aging; Civil rights, gays/lesbians; Civil rights, race/intergroup relations; Civil rights; Rural development; Community development; Voluntarism promotion; Public affairs, citizen participation; Aging; Disabilities, people with; Minorities; Asians/Pacific Islanders; African Americans/Blacks; Hispanics/Latinos; Native Americans/American Indians; Women; AIDS, people with; LGBTQ; Immigrants/refugees.
Type of support: Capital campaigns; General/operating support; Continuing support; Building/renovation; Equipment; Emergency funds; Program development; Conferences/seminars; Seed money; Internship funds; Technical assistance; Program evaluation; Program-related investments/loans; Matching/challenge support.
Limitations: Giving limited to organizations whose beneficiaries are residents of MN, MT, ND and WI with preference given to those in regions served by Bremer Banks. No support for economic development, or historic preservation, museums and interpretive centers, sporting activities. No grants to individuals, or for endowment funds,

medical research, professorships, annual fund drives, benefit events, camps, or artistic or media projects.

Publications: Annual report (including application guidelines); Grants list; Informational brochure (including application guidelines).

Application information: The Minnesota Common Grant Application is accepted by the foundation. Application form not required.

Initial approach: Letter or telephone
Copies of proposal: 1
Deadline(s): None
Board meeting date(s): Monthly
Final notification: 2-3 months

Officer: John Kostishack, Exec. Dir.

Trustees: Charlotte S. Johnson; William H. Lipschultz; Daniel C. Reardon.

Number of staff: 9 full-time professional; 1 part-time professional.

EIN: 416019050

Selected grants: The following grants were reported in 2004.

$200,000 to Red River Valley Community Action, Grand Forks, ND. For construction of transitional housing.

$160,000 to Community Homes and Resources in Service to Many (CHARISM), Fargo, ND. To expand nonprofit family resource center to an additional site.

$150,000 to Western Community Action, Marshall, MN. To support strategic planning process, assist in leadership development, and implement strategies.

$150,000 to YWCA of Saint Paul, Saint Paul, MN. For expansion.

$130,000 to Model Cities of Saint Paul, Saint Paul, MN. For Home Ownership Project, supportive housing program for single parent families.

$125,000 to Neighborhood House, Saint Paul, MN. To build new facility.

$122,500 to Minnesota Human Rights Department, Saint Paul, MN. For Educate to Eliminate program that focuses on activities that will promote human rights.

$100,000 to Cedar Riverside Peoples Center, Minneapolis, MN. To make improvements at community medical clinic.

$100,000 to Headwaters Foundation for Justice, Minneapolis, MN. For Democracy Fund, collaborative that works with foundations to support nonprofit advocacy.

$100,000 to Native American Community Clinic, Saint Paul, MN. For general operating support.

4524
Bush Foundation ▼

E-900 First National Bank Bldg.
332 Minnesota St.
St. Paul, MN 55101 (651) 227-0891
Contact: Anita M. Pampusch, Pres.
FAX: (651) 297-6485;
E-mail: info@bushfoundation.org; URL: http://www.bushfoundation.org

Incorporated in 1953 in MN.

Donors: Archibald Granville Bush†; Edyth Bassler Bush†.

Foundation type: Independent foundation.

Financial data (yr. ended 11/30/05): Assets, $796,152,567 (M); gifts received, $849,000; expenditures, $42,624,975; qualifying distributions, $34,604,887; giving activities include $27,731,321 for 277 grants (high: $2,000,000;

low: $5,000; average: $50,000–$200,000), and $2,632,396 for 48 grants to individuals (high: $136,400; low: $77,330).

Purpose and activities: To improve the quality of life in the geographic region of MN, ND, and SD through grantmaking that strives to help strengthen organizational, community and individual leadership.

Fields of interest: Media/communications; Visual arts; Museums; Performing arts; Performing arts, music; Humanities; Literature; Arts; Higher education; Education; Environment; Health care; Youth development, services; Human services; Children/youth; Minorities; Women; Immigrants/refugees.

Type of support: Management development/capacity building; Capital campaigns; Building/renovation; Program development; Fellowships; Matching/challenge support.

Limitations: Giving primarily in MN, ND, and SD. No support for private foundations or for organizations lacking 501c(3) status. No grants to individuals (except for fellowships), or for research in biomedical and health sciences. Generally, no grants for continuing operating support; construction of hospitals or medical facilities, church sanctuaries, individual day care centers, municipal buildings, or buildings in public colleges and universities; or for covering operating deficits or to retire mortgages or other debts; no loans.

Publications: Application guidelines; Annual report; Financial statement; Grants list; Informational brochure; Informational brochure (including application guidelines); Newsletter; Occasional report; Program policy statement.

Application information: Prefers use of foundation cover sheet.

Initial approach: Letter of inquiry required
Copies of proposal: 2
Deadline(s): For letter of inquiry: None; for proposal: Mar. 1, July 1, and Nov. 1
Board meeting date(s): Mar., July, and Nov.
Final notification: Letter of inquiry decision: 3 weeks; proposal decision: 10 days after board meetings

Officers and Directors:* William P. Pierskalla,* Chair.; Ivy S. Bernhardson,* 1st Vice-Chair.; L. Steven Goldstein,* 2nd Vice-Chair.; Anita M. Pampusch, Pres.; Dwight Gourneau,* Secy.; Esperanza Guerrero-Anderson,* Treas.; Terence Doyle, Genl. Counsel; Wilson G. Bradshaw; Dudley Cocke; Roxanne Givens Copeland; Robert J. Jones, Ph.D.; Jan K. Malcolm; Tim Mathern; Catherine V. Piersol; Gordon M. Sprenger; Kathryn H. Tunheim.

Number of staff: 15 full-time professional; 7 full-time support.

EIN: 416017815

Selected grants: The following grants were reported in 2006.

$2,000,000 to United Negro College Fund, Fairfax, VA. To develop and implement enrollment management program to increase enrollment and improve graduation rates at private historically black colleges and universities, payable over 3 years.

$1,500,000 to Northland Foundation, Duluth, MN. To implement early childhood mental health initiative in greater Minnesota, payable over 3 years.

$1,200,000 to Family Housing Fund, Minneapolis, MN. To continue development of system of supportive housing for children and families, especially in areas of asset management

practices and Healthy Families Network, payable over 3 years.

$1,162,131 to Village Family Service Center, Fargo, ND. To implement Family Group Decision Making in North Dakota, payable over 2 years.

$999,709 to Minnesota Historical Society, Saint Paul, MN. To expand technological infrastructure, payable over 3 years.

$526,000 to Migrant Health Service, Moorhead, MN. To link seventeen health clinics in northern Minnesota and to establish paperless charting system, payable over 2 years.

$400,000 to Northern Great Plains, Fargo, ND. To conduct Meadowlark Project, leadership laboratory on future of Northern Great Plains, payable over 2 years.

$345,000 to Indian Land Tenure Foundation, Little Canada, MN. For efforts to strengthen Indian land ownership and management in Minnesota and Dakotas through work of Institute for Indian Estate Planning and Probate, payable over 3 years.

$150,000 to Tougaloo College, Tougaloo, MS. For Historically Black College and University Faculty Development Network, payable over 3.25 years.

$90,000 to RESOURCE, Inc., Minneapolis, MN. For expansion of Young Dads program to Ramsey County, payable over 2 years.

4525
Patrick and Aimee Butler Family Foundation

332 Minnesota St., E-1420
St. Paul, MN 55101-1369 (651) 222-2565
Contact: Kerrie Blevins, Dir.
E-mail: info@butlerfamilyfoundation.org;
URL: http://www.butlerfamilyfoundation.org

Incorporated in 1951 in MN.

Donors: Patrick Butler†; Aimee Mott Butler†.

Foundation type: Independent foundation.

Financial data (yr. ended 12/31/05): Assets, $61,236,731 (M); expenditures, $2,623,087; qualifying distributions, $2,432,780; giving activities include $2,328,360 for 125 grants (high: $40,000; low: $2,500).

Purpose and activities: Primary areas of interest include the disadvantaged, women, family and other social services, and the environment.

Fields of interest: Museums; Humanities; Arts; Environment; Substance abuse, services; Housing/shelter, development; Human services; Family services; Women, centers/services.

Type of support: General/operating support; Continuing support; Annual campaigns; Program development; Consulting services.

Limitations: Giving primarily in the St. Paul and Minneapolis, MN, area. No support for criminal justice, secondary and elementary education, health or hospitals, employment or vocational programs, theater or dance programs, or economic education. No grants to individuals, or for medical research, films or videos, capital funds, endowment funds or events; no loans.

Publications: Annual report (including application guidelines); Grants list.

Application information: Applicant must submit Butler Family Foundation Application Form in addition to full proposal. Application form required.

Initial approach: See foundation Web site for guidelines
Copies of proposal: 1
Deadline(s): Check Web site

Board meeting date(s): July
Final notification: 3 months
Officers and Trustees:* Peter M. Butler,* Pres.;
Patrick Butler, Jr.,* V.P.; Shehla Tauscher, Secy.;
John K. Butler,* Treas.; Connie O'Brien, Cont.;
Brigid M. Butler; Catherine Butler; Cecelia M. Butler;
Patricia M. Butler; Paul S. Butler; Sandra K. Butler;
Suzanne A. LeFevour.
Director: Kerrie Blevins.
Number of staff: 2 part-time professional; 1
part-time support.
EIN: 416009902

4526
Buuck Family Foundation

c/o Lowry Hill
90 S. 7th St., Ste. 5300
Minneapolis, MN   55402
Contact: Robert E. Buuck, Pres.

Established in 1995 in MN.
Donors: Gail P. Buuck; Robert P. Buuck.
Foundation type: Independent foundation.
Financial data (yr. ended 12/31/05): Assets,
$10,249,069 (M); gifts received, $1,002,850;
expenditures, $769,630; qualifying distributions,
$669,153; giving activities include $660,000 for 92
grants (high: $60,000; low: $500).
Fields of interest: Arts; Education, early childhood
education; Scholarships/financial aid; Environment;
Community development.
Type of support: General/operating support;
Continuing support; Annual campaigns; Land
acquisition; Fellowships; Scholarship funds;
Research.
Limitations: Giving primarily in MN and AZ. No
support for religious or political organizations. No
grants to individuals.
Publications: Program policy statement.
Application information: Application form required.
Initial approach: Letter
Copies of proposal: 1
Deadline(s): None
Board meeting date(s): Quarterly
Final notification: 1 month
Officers: Robert E. Buuck, Pres.; David A. Buuck,
V.P. and Secy.; Gail P. Buuck, V.P. and Treas.; John
R. Buuck, V.P.; Katherine E. Fratzke, V.P.
Number of staff: 1 part-time support.
EIN: 411796911

4527
The Cafesjian Family Foundation, Inc. ✧

15 S. 5th St., Ste. 900
Minneapolis, MN   55402
Contact: Lou Ann Matossian, Prog. Officer
FAX: (941) 263-2952;
E-mail: LAMatossian@cafesjianfoundation.org;
Additional tel.: (612) 359-8991; FAX: (612)
359-8994; URL: http://
www.cafesjianfoundation.org

Established in 1996 in FL.
Donor: Gerard L. Cafesjian.
Foundation type: Independent foundation.
Financial data (yr. ended 12/31/04): Assets,
$44,138,570 (M); expenditures, $1,843,770;
qualifying distributions, $5,843,173; giving
activities include $1,212,323 for 31 grants (high:
$100,000; low: $600; average: $5,000–$10,000),

and $4,218,204 for 5 loans/program-related
investments.
Purpose and activities: Giving primarily for
economic development in the Republic of Armenia
and for US-Armenia friendship. Current interests are
to: 1) promote Armenia's energy independence; 2)
invest to support other economic development
initiatives in Armenia; 3) promote Armenia's
independent media sector, 4) giving for The
Cafesjian Museum Foundation to create an
international-caliber Center for the Arts in Armenia;
5) to bring new sources of debt and equity, capital,
and direct foreign investment to Armenia; and 6) to
build a stronger U.S.-Armenia relationship.
Fields of interest: Arts; Education; Health care;
Housing/shelter; Human services; Children,
services; International affairs; Community
development; Social sciences; Public affairs;
Orthodox Catholic agencies & churches.
International interests: Armenia.
Type of support: General/operating support; Annual
campaigns; Capital campaigns; Endowments;
Technical assistance; Program-related
investments/loans; Matching/challenge support.
Limitations: Applications not accepted. Giving
primarily in the Republics of Armenia and Nagorno
Karabakh; national funding in Washington, DC, and
New York, NY; some funding also in MN. No grants
to individuals.
Application information: Contributes only to
pre-selected organizations.
Officers and Directors:* Gerard L. Cafesjian,*
Pres.; Cleo T. Cafesjian,* V.P.; John Waters,*
Secy.-Treas.
EIN: 593417473

4528
Campbell Foundation ✧ ☆

c/o Wells Fargo Bank Minnesota, N.A.
90 S. 7th St., Ste. 5300
Minneapolis, MN   55402

Established in 2000 in MN.
Donor: James R. Campbell.
Foundation type: Independent foundation.
Financial data (yr. ended 12/31/05): Assets,
$9,389,697 (M); gifts received, $197,563;
expenditures, $663,404; qualifying distributions,
$627,513; giving activities include $618,386 for 40
grants (high: $323,036; low: $250).
Fields of interest: Hospitals (general); Christian
agencies & churches.
Limitations: Applications not accepted. No grants to
individuals.
Application information: Contributes only to
pre-selected organizations.
Officers and Directors:* Carmen D. Campbell,*
Pres.; James R. Campbell,* V.P.; Peter I.
Campbell,* V.P.; Kathryn A. Seguin,* V.P.; Laurie
Rivard, Secy.-Treas.
EIN: 411988560
Selected grants: The following grants were reported
in 2004.
$50,000 to University of Minnesota Foundation,
   Minneapolis, MN. For general support.
$20,000 to Minneapolis Heart Institute Foundation,
   Minneapolis, MN. For annual support.
$13,500 to Project for Pride in Living, Minneapolis,
   MN. For general support.
$8,000 to Minneapolis Institute of Arts,
   Minneapolis, MN. For general support.
$5,000 to Childrens Home Society and Family
   Services, Saint Paul, MN. For general support.

$3,500 to Abbott Northwestern Hospital,
   Minneapolis, MN. For general support.
$2,000 to Mentoring Partnership of Minnesota,
   Minneapolis, MN. For general support.
$1,000 to Leech Lake Area Watershed Foundation,
   Walker, MN. For general support.
$500 to Trust for Public Land, Midwest Field Office,
   Saint Paul, MN. For general support.
$250 to WomenVenture, Saint Paul, MN. For general
   support.

4529
Martin & Esther Capp Foundation ✧

7951 12th Ave. S.
Bloomington, MN   55425
Contact: Lisa Capp, Dir.

Established in 1961 in MN.
Foundation type: Independent foundation.
Financial data (yr. ended 12/31/05): Assets,
$1,876,120 (M); gifts received, $469,843;
expenditures, $401,858; qualifying distributions,
$384,854; giving activities include $382,960 for 45
grants (high: $200,000; low: $25).
Fields of interest: Environment; Jewish federated
giving programs; Jewish agencies & temples.
Type of support: General/operating support; Annual
campaigns; Capital campaigns; Building/
renovation; Endowments.
Limitations: Giving primarily in MN. No grants to
individuals.
Application information: Common Grant Application
Form accepted. Application form not required.
Initial approach: Letter or application form
Copies of proposal: 1
Officers: Martin Capp, Pres.; Esther Capp, V.P.;
Leonard Horowitz, Secy.-Treas.
Directors: Lisa Capp; Cynthia Rosenblatt.
EIN: 416038641
Selected grants: The following grants were reported
in 2005.
$80,000 to United Jewish Fund and Council, Saint
   Paul, MN.
$54,315 to Temple of Aaron, Saint Paul, MN. 2
   grants: $4,315, $50,000
$100 to Talmud Torah of Saint Paul, Saint Paul, MN.

4530
The Cargill Foundation ▼ ✧

P.O. Box 5626
Minneapolis, MN   55440-5626   (952) 742-4311
Contact: Stacy Smida, Admin., Grants
FAX: (952) 742-7224; URL: http://www.cargill.com/
about/citizenship/foundation.htm

Incorporated in 1952 in MN.
Donors: Cargill, Inc.; Cargill Charitable Trust.
Foundation type: Company-sponsored foundation.
Financial data (yr. ended 12/31/05): Assets,
$100,283,183 (M); gifts received, $25,000,000;
expenditures, $9,155,213; qualifying distributions,
$8,487,885; giving activities include $8,487,885
for 72 grants (high: $1,000,000; low: $1,500).
Purpose and activities: The foundation supports
programs designed to educate socio-economically
disadvantaged children and eliminate barriers to
their educational success.
Fields of interest: Elementary/secondary
education; Children; Economically disadvantaged.

Type of support: General/operating support; Continuing support; Capital campaigns; Program development.
Limitations: Giving primarily in Minneapolis, MN, and its western suburbs. No support for political, fraternal, veterans', or professional organizations or religious organizations not of direct benefit to the entire community. No grants to individuals, or for endowments, recognition or testimonial events, benefit fundraisers, travel, conferences, athletic scholarships, or projects at K-12 schools.
Publications: Application guidelines; Grants list; Informational brochure (including application guidelines).
Application information: A site visit may be requested. Application form required.
  Initial approach: Complete online application form
  Copies of proposal: 1
  Board meeting date(s): Apr., June, Sept., and Dec.
  Final notification: Within 3 to 4 weeks
Officers: Warren R. Staley, Pres.; Robbin S. Johnson, V.P.; Frank L. Sims, V.P.; Thomas O. Moe, Secy.; Katherine Kersten, Treas.; Mark Murphy, Exec. Dir.
Number of staff: 2 full-time professional; 1 full-time support.
EIN: 416020221

4531
Caridad Corporation ✧
2630 W. Lafayette Rd.
Excelsior, MN 55331-3016 (952) 470-3600
Contact: Thomas P. Lowe, Pres.

Established in 1987 in MN.
Donors: Margaret L. Lowe; Thomas P. Lowe; Morgan Arundel; Finley Bros. Enterprises.
Foundation type: Independent foundation.
Financial data (yr. ended 12/31/05): Assets, $2,917,683 (M); gifts received, $985,464; expenditures, $924,774; qualifying distributions, $873,799; giving activities include $873,799 for 126 grants (high: $101,000; low: $100).
Fields of interest: Arts; Education; Human services; Children/youth, services; Community development; Protestant agencies & churches.
Limitations: Giving primarily in Minneapolis, MN. No grants to individuals.
Application information:
  Initial approach: Letter
  Deadline(s): None
Officers: Thomas P. Lowe, Pres.; Margaret L. Lowe, V.P.; Thomas P. Lowe III, Treas.
EIN: 363505813

4532
The Curtis L. Carlson Foundation ✧
Carlson Pkwy.
P.O. Box 59159
Minneapolis, MN 55459-8250 (952) 404-5636
Contact: David Nelson
FAX: (952) 404-5051;
E-mail: david.nelson@carlson.com; Application address: c/o Donna Snyder, Secy., 301 Carlson Pkwy., Ste. 102, Minnetonka, MN 55305, tel.: (952) 404-5600; URL: http://www.clcfamilyfoundation.com

Incorporated in 1959 in MN, originally as The Curtis L. Carlson Foundation.

Donors: Curtis L. Carlson†; Arleen M. Carlson†; Glen D. Nelson; Marylyn C. Nelson; Arleen M. Carlson 2000 BCG Charitable Annuity Trust.
Foundation type: Independent foundation.
Financial data (yr. ended 12/31/03): Assets, $67,150,544 (M); gifts received, $5,371,752; expenditures, $3,065,759; qualifying distributions, $2,397,004; giving activities include $1,990,907 for 118 grants (high: $275,000; low: $25), and $116,408 for 114 employee matching gifts.
Purpose and activities: Giving primarily for children and mentoring and for education.
Fields of interest: Performing arts centers; Performing arts, theater; Arts; Education, association; Secondary school/education; Higher education; Scholarships/financial aid; Education; Medical research, association; Medical research, institute; Youth development, scouting agencies (general); Human services; Children/youth, services; Foundations (private grantmaking); Federated giving programs; Christian agencies & churches.
Limitations: Giving primarily in MN. No support for political activities or causes. No grants to individuals, (including scholarships), or for endowment funds, dinners, benefits, conferences, travel, athletic events, or endowments.
Application information: Application form available on foundation Web site. Application form required.
  Initial approach: Proposal; no telephone calls or personal visits to office
  Deadline(s): Jan. 15, Apr. 15, and Aug. 15
  Board meeting date(s): Mar., June, and Oct.
  Final notification: Following the board meeting
Officers: Barbara C. Gage, Pres.; Donna D. Snyder, Secy.
Trustees: Kelly K. Gage; Richard C. Gage; Scott C. Gage; Diana L. Nelson; Marilyn C. Nelson; Marjorie A. Nelson; Wendy M. Nelson.
EIN: 416028973
Selected grants: The following grants were reported in 2003.
$275,000 to Mayo Foundation, Rochester, MN. For transplantation medicine research.
$10,000 to Hands On Twin Cities, Minneapolis, MN. For general operating support.
$3,000 to Minneapolis Institute of Arts, Minneapolis, MN. For annual fund.
$3,000 to Minneapolis Public Library, Friends of the, Minneapolis, MN. For general operating support.
$3,000 to Minnesota Orchestral Association, Minneapolis, MN. For annual fund.
$3,000 to Walker Art Center, Minneapolis, MN. For annual fund.
$2,500 to YMCA of Metropolitan Minneapolis, Minneapolis, MN. For general operating support.
$1,000 to Boys and Girls Clubs, Hospitality House, Minneapolis, MN. For general operating support.
$1,000 to Page Education Foundation, Minneapolis, MN. For general operating support.
$500 to Access for All, Shoreview, MN. For general operating support.

4533
Carolyn Foundation
706 2nd Ave. S., Ste. 760
Minneapolis, MN 55402 (612) 596-3266
Contact: Cindy Mellin, Admin.
FAX: (612) 339-1951;
E-mail: cmellin@carolynfoundation.org; Rebecca L. "Becky" Erdahl, Exec. Dir., tel.: (612) 596-3279;
E-mail: berdahl@carolynfoundation.org; URL: http://www.carolynfoundation.org

Trust established in 1964 in MN.
Donor: Carolyn McKnight Christian†.
Foundation type: Independent foundation.
Financial data (yr. ended 12/31/05): Assets, $37,628,786 (M); gifts received, $20,000; expenditures, $2,006,944; qualifying distributions, $1,838,552; giving activities include $1,601,700 for 83 grants (high: $75,000; low: $5,000), and $28,636 for 63 employee matching gifts.
Purpose and activities: The mission of the Carolyn Foundation is to act with concern and compassion for communities and focus areas by supporting programs that make a meaningful difference now and in the future in community and environmental grantmaking in Minneapolis, MN and New Haven, CT.
Fields of interest: Arts; Environment; Youth development; Community development; Economically disadvantaged.
Type of support: General/operating support; Matching/challenge support.
Limitations: Giving limited to New Haven, CT, and Minneapolis, MN, and generally excluding suburbs. No support for political or veterans' groups, fraternal societies, umbrella organizations, or religious organizations for religious purposes. No grants to individuals, or for endowment funds, annual fund drives, conferences, seminars, fund raisers, deficit funding, costs of litigation, or continuing support; no loans.
Publications: Application guidelines; Annual report; Grants list.
Application information: Carolyn Foundation and Minnesota Common Grant Application Format preferred. Cover page required. Visit foundation Web site for updated application guidelines, download of application and cover sheet forms, and procedures. Cover sheet required. Grant requests not to exceed 6 pages. Application form required.
  Initial approach: Check foundation Web site
  Copies of proposal: 1
  Deadline(s): Jan. 15 and July 15
  Board meeting date(s): June and Dec.
  Final notification: June and Dec.
Officers and Trustees:* Charles C. Dobson,* Chair.; Anne T. Calabresi,* Vice-Chair.; Stewart F. Crosby,* Vice-Chair.; Rebecca L. Erdahl,* Secy. and Exec. Dir.; Edmund C. Graham III,* Treas.; Betsey Copp; Andrew Crosby; Edwin L. Crosby; Harriett Crosby; Sumner McK. Crosby III; Timothy B. Crosby; Jennifer Phelps; Eleanor Smith.
Number of staff: 1 full-time professional; 1 part-time support.
EIN: 416044416
Selected grants: The following grants were reported in 2005.
$40,000 to Sierra Club Foundation, San Francisco, CA. For Minnesota Clean Air Campaign.
$30,000 to New Haven Ecology Project, New Haven, CT. For Common Ground Seed-To-Table Initiative.
$25,000 to Youth Farm and Market Project, Minneapolis, MN. For general operating support.
$23,200 to Twin Cities International Elementary School, Saint Paul, MN. For family literacy resources.
$20,000 to Families in Crisis, Hartford, CT. For programs that benefit children of offenders.
$15,000 to Northwest Sustainable Energy for Economic Development (SEED), Seattle, WA. For general operating support.
$10,000 to MELD-Minnesota Early Learning Design, Minneapolis, MN.
$5,500 to American Composers Forum, Saint Paul, MN. For Lullaby Project.

$5,000 to Midtown Public Market, Minneapolis, MN. For community arts program.

4534
Central Minnesota Community Foundation

101 S. 7th Ave., Ste. 100
St. Cloud, MN 56301 (320) 253-4380
Contact: Steven R. Joul, Pres.; Greta Stark-Kraker, Office Mgr.
FAX: (320) 240-9215;
E-mail: gstark@communitygiving.org; Additional tel.: (877) 253-4380; E-mail for Susan Lorenz: slorenz@communitygiving.org; URL: http://www.communitygiving.org

Established in 1985 in MN.
Foundation type: Community foundation.
Financial data (yr. ended 6/30/05): Assets, $49,247,086 (M); gifts received, $5,217,308; expenditures, $4,152,124; giving activities include $3,088,230 for 833 grants (high: $100,000; low: $9), and $115,350 for 103 grants to individuals.
Purpose and activities: The foundation is a public charity that enables and promotes the abilities of individuals and organizations to make significant contributions that impact the needs of the region.
Fields of interest: Arts; Education; Environment; Health care; Youth development, services; Family services; Human services; Public affairs.
Type of support: Building/renovation; Equipment; Program development; Conferences/seminars; Seed money; Scholarship funds; Technical assistance; Program-related investments/loans; Scholarships—to individuals.
Limitations: Giving primarily in Benton, Sherburne, and Stearns counties, MN. No support for religious organizations for direct activities, or for fraternal organizations, societies, or orders. No grants to individuals (except for designated scholarship funds), or for medical research, general operating expenses, national fundraising, telephone solicitations, travel, capital campaigns, endowments, or debt retirement or deficit financing.
Publications: Application guidelines; Annual report; Informational brochure; Newsletter.
Application information: Visit foundation Web site for application guidelines, deadlines, and Minnesota Common Grant Application Form. Application form required.
Initial approach: Submit MN Common Grant Application Form and attachments
Copies of proposal: 10
Deadline(s): Varies
Board meeting date(s): 3rd Thurs. in Jan., Mar., May, July, and Oct.
Final notification: 2 months after deadline date
Officers and Directors:* Kevin Hughes,* Vice-Chair.; Shelly Bauerly Kopel,* Vice-Chair.; Steven R. Joul,* Pres.; Peter Hill,* Secy.; Loran Hall,* Treas.; Dean Anderson; Mimi Bitzan; Alex Didier; Keith Finstad; Dennis Gregory; Andy Hilger; Janet Knoblach; Gary Marsden; Asha Morgan Moran; Brian Myres; Brad Person; John Sullivan; Don Watkins.
Trustees: Bill Albrecht; Jack Amundson; Dean H. Anderson; Jason Bernick; Teresa Bohnen; John Brownson; Colette L. Carlson; Rob Cavanna; Dan Coborn; Alex Didier; Nancy Ehlen; Les Green; Dennis Gregory; Lee Hanson; Jack Happe; Colleen Hollinger-Petters; Keith Hughes; Jim Janochoski; Rev. Ben Johnson; Cindy Faye Johnson; Steve Laraway; John Leisen; Cheryl Lightle; Alan Marcyes; Dave Marquardt; Mary Mathews; Jerry McCarter;

Michelle Meyer; Jim Miller; David Noack; D. Michael Noonan; S. Colman O'Connell; Rev. Dee Pederson; Br. Dietrich Reinhart; Dennis Ringsmuth; Tom Schlough; Wayne Schluchter; Brian Schoenborn; Norman C. Skalicky; Jim Stigman; Shawn Teal; Marie Thompson; Leander Torborg; George Torrey; Ken Warner; Stanley Weinberger; John Weitzel; Clarence White.
Number of staff: 5 full-time professional; 3 full-time support.
EIN: 363412544
Selected grants: The following grants were reported in 2006.
$10,000 to Create CommUNITY, Saint Cloud, MN. For general operations.
$9,000 to American Red Cross, Saint Cloud, MN. For Train the Trainers.
$2,500 to United Way of Central Minnesota, Saint Cloud, MN. For proposal for the Center for Non-Profit Excellence Feasibility Study.
$2,000 to Minnesota Council on Foundations, Minneapolis, MN.
$1,500 to Good Samaritan Fund, Saint Cloud, MN. For staffing of cases for Good Samaritan Fund.
$1,000 to Neighbors for School Excellence, Waite Park, MN. For supporting ISD #742 school levy.
$500 to CentraCare Foundation, Saint Cloud, MN. For Coborn Cancer Center for Survivorship Program.

4535
Chadwick-Loher Foundation ✧

5140 Wells Fargo Ctr.
90 S. 7th St.
Minneapolis, MN 55402

Established in 1998 in MN.
Foundation type: Independent foundation.
Financial data (yr. ended 12/31/04): Assets, $9,709,342 (M); expenditures, $543,120; qualifying distributions, $454,445; giving activities include $447,135 for 18 grants (high: $100,000; low: $1,000).
Purpose and activities: Giving primarily for education, and the arts.
Fields of interest: Media, television; Media, radio; Museums (art); Performing arts centers; Performing arts, opera; Arts; Elementary/secondary education; Higher education; Education; Protestant agencies & churches.
Limitations: Applications not accepted. No grants to individuals.
Application information: Contributes only to pre-selected organizations.
Officers: John W. Dayton, Pres.; Arlene J. Dayton, Secy.-Treas.
Directors: Chadwick L. Dayton; Whitney L. Dayton.
EIN: 522390635

4536
Charity, Inc.

5786 118th Ave.
Clear Lake, MN 55319 (320) 743-5466
Contact: Deanna Hulme

Incorporated in 1962 in MN.
Donors: Rose W. Totino; Pillsbury Co.
Foundation type: Independent foundation.
Financial data (yr. ended 2/28/06): Assets, $8,630,851 (M); expenditures, $545,269;

qualifying distributions, $343,739; giving activities include $343,739 for 37+ grants (high: $156,799).
Purpose and activities: Primarily contributes to Christian religious and educational organizations.
Fields of interest: Elementary/secondary education; Higher education; Recreation, camps; Children/youth, services; Family services, domestic violence; Residential/custodial care; Roman Catholic agencies & churches.
Limitations: Giving primarily in the Minneapolis-St. Paul, MN, area. No grants to individuals.
Application information: Application form not required.
Initial approach: Letter
Deadline(s): None
Officers and Directors:* Joanne Elwell,* Pres. and Secy.- Treas.; Bonita Brenny,* V.P.; Donald Schwalm.
EIN: 410636273
Selected grants: The following grants were reported in 2004.
$156,799 to Totino-Grace High School, Fridley, MN. For building fund.
$100,000 to NET Ministries, West Saint Paul, MN. For general support.
$2,500 to Saint Olaf Catholic Church, Minneapolis, MN. For general support.
$2,000 to Home of the Good Shepherd, Saint Paul, MN. For general support.
$2,000 to Little Sisters of the Poor of Saint Paul, Saint Paul, MN. For general support.
$1,130 to Bridge for Runaway Youth, Minneapolis, MN. For general support.
$1,000 to Catholic Charities of the Archdiocese of Saint Paul and Minneapolis, Minneapolis, MN. For general support.
$1,000 to Catholic Eldercare, Minneapolis, MN. For general support.
$1,000 to Life Teen, Mesa, AZ. For general support.
$500 to Saint Davids School for Child Development and Family Services, Minnetonka, MN. For general support.

4537
Charlson Foundation

5275 Edina Industrial Blvd., Ste. 111
Edina, MN 55439-2902 (952) 938-6968
Contact: Karen McElrath, Pres.
FAX: (952) 938-0240;
E-mail: charlson@usinternet.com; URL: http://www.charlsonfoundation.org

Established in 1977 in MN.
Donor: Lynn L. Charlson.
Foundation type: Independent foundation.
Financial data (yr. ended 12/31/05): Assets, $13,918,529 (M); expenditures, $1,272,408; qualifying distributions, $1,116,603; giving activities include $1,095,420 for 63 grants (high: $250,000; low: $1,000).
Purpose and activities: The foundation invests in changing the lives and futures of high-risk youth and families. We do this by partnering with nonprofits that provide youth development services and supportive housing. Giving primarily for human services.
Fields of interest: Housing/shelter; Children/youth, services; Family services.
Type of support: General/operating support; Annual campaigns; Capital campaigns; Matching/challenge support.
Limitations: Giving limited to the Twin Cities area of Minneapolis and St. Paul, MN. No support for

organizations that use fiscal agents. No grants to individuals, or for scholarships, chemical dependency treatment, K-12 school programs, endowments, annual appeals, fundraisers, special events or memberships.

Publications: Application guidelines.

Application information: Full proposals are by invitation only. Unsolicited proposals will not be considered. There is a $10,000 limit for first-time requests. The foundation encourages applicants who are applying for renewal grants to use the Minnesota Common Report Form, which can be found at URL: http://www.mcf.org. If you are not invited to submit a full proposal, the foundation asks that you wait 3 years before submitting another letter of intent. The foundation accepts the Minnesota Council on Foundations' Common Grant Proposal form. Application form required.

> *Initial approach:* 2-page letter of intent
> *Copies of proposal:* 1
> *Deadline(s):* Mar. 2 and Aug. 2 for letters of intent; Apr. 1 and Sept. 1 for renewal grant proposals
> *Board meeting date(s):* Apr. and Oct.
> *Final notification:* Within 2 months of deadlines

Officers and Directors:* Karen K. McElrath,* Pres.; Mary L. Rippy,* Secy.; Leslie H. Stiles,* Treas.; Kim Herzog.

EIN: 411313302

Selected grants: The following grants were reported in 2004.

$250,000 to Arthritis Foundation, Denver, CO.
$80,000 to Jeremiah Program, Minneapolis, MN.
$50,000 to Courage Center, Golden Valley, MN.
$50,000 to Dakota Woodlands, Eagan, MN. 2 grants: $25,000 each
$30,000 to CommonBond Communities, Saint Paul, MN.
$20,000 to Youth Farm and Market Project, Minneapolis, MN.
$15,000 to Womens Cancer Resource Center, Minneapolis, MN.
$10,000 to Catholic Charities, Western Slope, Glenwood Springs, CO.
$10,000 to Youth Frontiers, Minneapolis, MN.

4538
Cherbec Advancement Foundation ✧

30 East 7th St., Ste. 2000
St. Paul, MN 55101-4930
Contact: Michele Bria, Sr. Fin. Consultant

Established in 1997 in MN.

Foundation type: Independent foundation.

Financial data (yr. ended 12/31/05): Assets, $768,727 (M); gifts received, $1,192,857; expenditures, $914,352; qualifying distributions, $911,725; giving activities include $911,725 for 44 grants (high: $130,000; low: $1,000).

Fields of interest: Human services.

Application information: Application form not required.

> *Initial approach:* Letter
> *Deadline(s):* None
> *Board meeting date(s):* 2 times per year
> *Final notification:* Following board meetings

Officers and Directors:* Carrie W. Farmer,* Pres.; Joseph S. Micallef, Secy.; Elizabeth W. Bentinck-Smith,* Treas.; Charles A. Weyerhaeuser; Henry G. Weyerhaeuser; Robert M. Weyerhaeuser.

EIN: 411906601

Selected grants: The following grants were reported in 2004.

$115,000 to Jonty Foundation for Research in Immuno Endocrine Neurological, Saint Paul, MN. For operating support.
$76,000 to Art Complex, Duxbury, MA. For operating support.
$63,000 to Animal Sanctuary of Saint Croix Valley, Stillwater, MN. For operating support.
$60,000 to Hill Monastic Manuscript Library, Collegeville, MN. For National Endowment for the Humanities.
$25,000 to American Composers Forum, Saint Paul, MN. For operating support.
$20,000 to Wildlands Trust of Southeastern Massachusetts, Duxbury, MA. For operating support.
$15,000 to High Street United Methodist Church, Franklin, VA. For Parsonage Fund.
$12,000 to Thalian Hall, Wilmington, NC. For Start-Up Fund.
$10,000 to Brimmer and May School, Chestnut Hill, MA. For operating support.
$10,000 to William Mitchell College of Law, Saint Paul, MN. For scholarship endowment.

4539
W. G. Christianson Foundation

8860 207th St. W.
Lakeville, MN 55044
Contact: Warren G. Christianson, Tr.

Established in 1992 in MN.

Donor: Warren G. Christianson.

Foundation type: Independent foundation.

Financial data (yr. ended 12/31/05): Assets, $10,357,917 (M); gifts received, $173,966; expenditures, $470,853; qualifying distributions, $394,925; giving activities include $394,900 for 45 grants (high: $50,000; low: $200).

Purpose and activities: Giving primarily to Roman Catholic churches and organizations.

Fields of interest: Health organizations, association; Human services; Children/youth, services; Civil liberties, right to life; Christian agencies & churches; Roman Catholic agencies & churches.

Type of support: General/operating support; Building/renovation; Scholarship funds.

Limitations: Applications not accepted. Giving primarily in MN; some funding nationally, particularly in CA. No grants to individuals.

Application information: Contributes only to pre-selected organizations.

Officers: Warren G. Christianson, Pres.; Theresa L. Christianson, Secy.

EIN: 411743109

4540
CHS Foundation

(formerly CHS Cooperatives Foundation)
5500 CENEX Dr., M.S. 407
Inver Grove Heights, MN 55077 (651) 355-5481
Contact: William J. Nelson, Pres.
FAX: (651) 355-5073;
E-mail: william.nelson@chsinc.com; URL: http://www.chsfoundation.org

Trust established in 1947 in MN.

Donors: Farmers Union Central Exchange, Inc.; CENEX, Inc.; Cenex Harvest States Cooperatives; CHS Inc.

Foundation type: Company-sponsored foundation.

Financial data (yr. ended 12/31/04): Assets, $25,935,541; gifts received, $1,004,434; expenditures, $1,486,126; qualifying distributions, $1,178,922; giving activities include $1,143,747 for 129 grants (high: $108,687; low: $500), and $35,175 for 11 grants to individuals (high: $6,000; low: $700).

Purpose and activities: The foundation supports organizations involved with higher education, agriculture, cooperative education, farm safety, rural youth leadership development, and children and youth.

Fields of interest: Higher education; Agriculture; Agriculture, farm cooperatives; Safety/disasters; Youth development, services; Children/youth, services.

Type of support: General/operating support; Program development; Scholarship funds; Program evaluation; Scholarships—to individuals.

Limitations: Giving limited to the Great Plains, upper Midwest, and Pacific Northwest. No grants for endowments.

Publications: Application guidelines; Informational brochure.

Application information: Application form required.

> *Initial approach:* Contact foundation for application form
> *Copies of proposal:* 1
> *Deadline(s):* None
> *Board meeting date(s):* Quarterly
> *Final notification:* 30 to 90 days

Officer and Trustees: William J. Nelson, Pres.; Bruce Anderson; Robert Bass; David Biernenberg; Dennis Carlson; Curt Eischens; Robert Elliott; Steve Fritel; Robert Grabarski; James Kile; Randy Knecht; Leonard Larsen; Richard Owen; Duane Stenzel; Michael Toelle; Merlin Van Walleghan; Elroy Webster.

Number of staff: 1 part-time professional; 1 part-time support.

EIN: 416025858

Selected grants: The following grants were reported in 2003.

$150,500 to North Dakota Farmers Union, ND.
$88,475 to South Dakota Farmers Union, SD.
$69,820 to Minnesota Farmers Union Foundation, Saint Paul, MN.
$63,790 to Wisconsin Farmers Union, WI.
$63,000 to Montana Farmers Union, MT.
$49,000 to Kansas Farmers Union, KS.
$30,000 to University of Wisconsin, Madison, WI. For Mueller Fellowship.
$25,800 to Rocky Mountain Farmers Union, Greenwood Village, CO.
$21,480 to Nebraska Farmers Union Foundation, Lincoln, NE.
$20,000 to University of Idaho, Moscow, ID.

4541
Cleveland Foundation ✧ ☆

c/o Fish Creek Ventures
120 S. 6th St., Ste. 801
Minneapolis, MN 55402

Established in NY.

Foundation type: Independent foundation.

Financial data (yr. ended 12/31/05): Assets, $588,437 (M); expenditures, $539,080; qualifying distributions, $533,779; giving activities include $533,779 for 8 grants (high: $486,979; low: $300).

Fields of interest: Performing arts; Arts; Education; Philanthropy/voluntarism.

Limitations: Applications not accepted. Giving primarily in Boston and Groton, MA, Minneapolis, MN, and Jackson Hole, WY. No grants to individuals.
Application information: Contributes only to pre-selected organizations.
Officer: Donald Thosett, C.F.O.
Trustees: Charles A. Cleveland, Sr.; John L. Cleveland.
EIN: 136037214

4542
Cloverfields Foundation ◇ ☆
c/o Dean Barr, Dorsey & Whitney, LLP
50 S. 6th St., Ste. 1500
Minneapolis, MN 55402-1498

Established in 2004 in MN.
Donors: Stephen J. Hemsley; Barbara K. Hemsley.
Foundation type: Independent foundation.
Financial data (yr. ended 12/31/05): Assets, $8,888,053 (M); expenditures, $1,740,449; qualifying distributions, $1,656,060; giving activities include $1,656,000 for 48 grants (high: $250,000; low: $500).
Fields of interest: Performing arts; Elementary/secondary education; Higher education; Medical school/education; Children/youth, services; Federated giving programs; Roman Catholic agencies & churches.
Limitations: Applications not accepted. No grants to individuals.
Application information: Contributes only to pre-selected organizations.
Officers and Directors:* Stephen J. Hemsley,* Pres. and Treas.; Barbara K. Hemsley,* Secy.; Matthew S. Hemsley.
EIN: 201919362

4543
Cox Family Fund ◇ ☆
1920 S. 1st St., Ste. 403
Minneapolis, MN 55454-1096

Incorporated in 1986 in MN.
Donors: David C. Cox; Vicki B. Cox.
Foundation type: Independent foundation.
Financial data (yr. ended 12/31/05): Assets, $4,887,797 (M); gifts received, $118,576; expenditures, $387,312; qualifying distributions, $385,237; giving activities include $385,212 for 43 grants (high: $75,576; low: $500).
Purpose and activities: Giving for arts and culture, education and the environment.
Fields of interest: Arts; Education; Environment; Human services.
Limitations: Applications not accepted. Giving primarily in MN. No grants to individuals.
Application information: Contributes only to pre-selected organizations.
Officers: David C. Cox, Pres. and Treas.; Vicki B. Cox, V.P. and Secy.
Director: Philip S. Sherburne.
EIN: 411570849

4544
Dr. C. C. and Mabel L. Criss Memorial Foundation ◇
c/o U.S. Bank, N.A.
P.O. Box 64713
St. Paul, MN 55164-0713

Trust established in 1978 in NE.
Donors: C.C. Criss, M.D.†; Mabel L. Criss†.
Foundation type: Independent foundation.
Financial data (yr. ended 2/28/06): Assets, $36,149,072 (M); expenditures, $2,612,881; qualifying distributions, $2,417,015; giving activities include $2,325,174 for 42 grants (high: $400,000; low: $2,500).
Purpose and activities: Support primarily for educational and scientific purposes, including a university; support also for education, including higher education, cultural agencies, youth and social service agencies, and a hospital.
Fields of interest: Arts; Higher education; Education; Human services; Children/youth, services.
Limitations: Applications not accepted. Giving limited to Omaha, NE. No grants to individuals.
Application information: Contributes only to pre-selected organizations.
 Board meeting date(s): Monthly
Trustees: M. Philip Crummer; Stanley Davis, M.D.; Donna Turner; John J. Vinardi; U.S. Bank, N.A.
EIN: 470601105
Selected grants: The following grants were reported in 2003.
$900,000 to Creighton University, Omaha, NE. 2 grants: $450,000 each (For general support).
$425,000 to College of Saint Mary, Omaha, NE. 3 grants: $50,000 (For general support), $250,000 (For residence halls renovation), $125,000 (For scholarships).
$400,000 to University of Nebraska Foundation, Omaha, NE. 2 grants: $200,000 each to Criss Library
$100,000 to Bellevue University, Bellevue, NE. For general support.
$100,000 to Holy Name Church and School, Omaha, NE. For general support.
$25,000 to Childrens Scholarship Fund, New York, NY. For general support.

4545
Meredyth Anne Dasburg Foundation ◇
2650 Marshland Rd.
Woodland, MN 55391

Established in 1989 in MN.
Donor: John H. Dasburg.
Foundation type: Independent foundation.
Financial data (yr. ended 12/31/04): Assets, $488,170 (M); gifts received, $602,442; expenditures, $467,453; qualifying distributions, $464,897; giving activities include $463,676 for 38 grants (high: $201,750; low: $100).
Fields of interest: Performing arts; Arts; Higher education; Education; Health care, association; Human services; Roman Catholic agencies & churches.
Type of support: Annual campaigns; Capital campaigns; Conferences/seminars; Scholarship funds.
Limitations: Applications not accepted. Giving in the U.S. primarily in FL and MN, with emphasis on the greater metropolitan Twin Cities area.
Application information: Contributes only to pre-selected organizations.
Trustees: John H. Dasburg; Mary Lou Dasburg.
EIN: 521608565
Selected grants: The following grants were reported in 2003.
$63,425 to Childrens Theater Company and School, Minneapolis, MN. For general operating support.

$55,000 to College of Saint Catherine, Saint Paul, MN. For annual support.
$53,965 to Blake School, Hopkins, MN. For annual fund.
$40,000 to University of Florida, Gainesville, FL. For general support.
$25,000 to Mayo Foundation, Rochester, MN. For general operating support.
$25,000 to World Conference of Religions for Peace, New York, NY. For general operating support.
$20,000 to Horatio Alger Association of Distinguished Americans, Alexandria, VA. For general operating support.
$10,000 to Church of Saint Patrick of Edina, Edina, MN. For general operating support.
$5,000 to Guthrie Theater Foundation, Minneapolis, MN. For general operating support.
$2,000 to Minnesota Orchestral Association, Minneapolis, MN. For general operating support.

4546
Edwin W. and Catherine M. Davis Foundation ◇
30 E. 7th St., Ste. 2000
St. Paul, MN 55101-1394 (651) 228-0935
Contact: Bette D. Moorman, Pres.; DeDe L. Connors, Grants Mgr.

Incorporated in 1956 in MN.
Donors: Samuel S. Davis†; Edwin W. Davis†; Frederick W. Davis†.
Foundation type: Independent foundation.
Financial data (yr. ended 12/31/04): Assets, $20,902,811 (M); gifts received, $40; expenditures, $796,883; qualifying distributions, $741,733; giving activities include $710,000 for 40 grants (high: $185,000; low: $1,000).
Purpose and activities: Concerned with the amelioration of social problems and increasing the opportunities available to disadvantaged people, with particular interest in the fields of education, social welfare, mental health, the arts, and environmental problems. Educational grants primarily for colleges and universities.
Fields of interest: Arts; Higher education; Environment, natural resources; Mental health/crisis services; Human services; Children/youth, services.
Type of support: General/operating support; Continuing support; Annual campaigns; Scholarship funds.
Limitations: Giving primarily in CA and WA. No grants to individuals, or for emergency funds, capital outlay, building funds or equipment, or endowments; no loans.
Publications: Annual report (including application guidelines).
Application information: Application form not required.
 Initial approach: Letter (no more than 3 pages)
 Copies of proposal: 1
 Deadline(s): None
 Board meeting date(s): May or June and as required
 Final notification: 4 to 6 weeks
Officers and Directors:* Bette D. Moorman,* Pres.; Mary E. Davis,* V.P.; Fred W. Davis II,* Secy.; Lisa M. Fremont.
EIN: 416012064

4547
Edward Dayton Family Fund ✧
5140 Wells Fargo Ctr.
90 S. 7th St.
Minneapolis, MN 55402

Established in 1998 in MN.
Foundation type: Independent foundation.
Financial data (yr. ended 12/31/04): Assets, $9,495,675 (M); expenditures, $726,775; qualifying distributions, $637,965; giving activities include $630,600 for 39 grants (high: $125,000; low: $1,500).
Fields of interest: Arts; Education; Environment, natural resources; Health care; Federated giving programs.
Limitations: Applications not accepted. No grants to individuals.
Application information: Contributes only to pre-selected organizations.
Officers: Edward N. Dayton, Pres.; Sherry Ann Dayton, Secy.-Treas.
Director: Risa Young.
EIN: 522390636

4548
The Deikel Family Foundation
(formerly The Ted Deikel Foundation)
4400 Baker Rd.
Minnetonka, MN 55343
Contact: Theodore Deikel, Pres.
FAX: (952) 975-4094;
E-mail: ted.deikel@pettersgroup.com

Established in 1989 in MN.
Donor: Theodore Deikel.
Foundation type: Independent foundation.
Financial data (yr. ended 12/31/05): Assets, $8,376,495 (M); expenditures, $514,789; qualifying distributions, $481,219; giving activities include $467,475 for 20 grants (high: $150,000; low: $150).
Purpose and activities: Giving primarily to Jewish organizations and human service organizations.
Fields of interest: Human services; Jewish federated giving programs; Jewish agencies & temples.
Type of support: General/operating support; Continuing support; Annual campaigns; Capital campaigns; Building/renovation; Equipment; Emergency funds; Program development; Seed money; Research; Consulting services; Matching/challenge support.
Limitations: Giving primarily in Minneapolis, MN. No grants to individuals.
Application information: The foundation requests that applicants limit their paper use and number of contacts. Application form not required.
　Initial approach: Letter
　Copies of proposal: 1
　Deadline(s): None
　Board meeting date(s): As needed
　Final notification: Varies
Officer: Theodore Deikel, Pres. and Secy.
Number of staff: 1 part-time professional.
EIN: 411651703
Selected grants: The following grants were reported in 2005.
$150,000 to Minneapolis Jewish Federation, Minnetonka, MN. 2 grants: $50,000, $100,000

4549
Deluxe Corporation Foundation ✧
(formerly Deluxe Check Printers Foundation)
P.O. Box 64235
St. Paul, MN 55164-0235
Contact: Jennifer A. Anderson, Secy.
URL: http://www.deluxe.com/dlxab/deluxe-foundation.jsp

Incorporated in 1952 in MN.
Donor: Deluxe Corp.
Foundation type: Company-sponsored foundation.
Financial data (yr. ended 12/31/04): Assets, $33,255,664 (M); gifts received, $1,100,000; expenditures, $2,141,464; qualifying distributions, $2,012,416; giving activities include $1,515,462 for 348 grants (high: $120,787; low: $100), and $381,824 for 638 employee matching gifts.
Purpose and activities: The foundation supports museums and organizations involved with performing arts, elementary and higher education, reading, domestic violence, human services, disabled people, senior citizens, and economically disadvantaged people.
Fields of interest: Museums; Performing arts; Elementary school/education; Higher education; Education, reading; Crime/violence prevention, domestic violence; Children/youth, services; Human services, emergency aid; Human services; Aging; Disabilities, people with; Economically disadvantaged.
Type of support: General/operating support; Annual campaigns; Capital campaigns; Building/renovation; Equipment; Emergency funds; Scholarship funds; Employee volunteer services; Employee matching gifts.
Limitations: Giving primarily in areas of company operations. No support for religious, political, civic, or national organizations, libraries, zoos, or community theater or music groups, or organizations associated with controversial issues. No grants to individuals, or for endowments, tours or travel, athletic events, sponsorships, research, seminars, conferences, workshops, fundraising, start-up needs, or long-term housing; no loans.
Publications: Application guidelines; Informational brochure.
Application information: Application form not required.
　Initial approach: Letter of inquiry to nearest company facility
　Copies of proposal: 1
　Deadline(s): Dec. 1
　Board meeting date(s): Feb.
　Final notification: 2 months
Officers and Directors:* Stuart Alexander,* Pres.; Lawrence J. Mosner,* V.P.; Jennifer A. Anderson,* Secy.; Ronald E. Eilers; Anthony C. Scarfone; Brett E. Scribner; Douglas J. Treff; Luann Widener.
Number of staff: 1 full-time professional; 1 full-time support.
EIN: 416034786
Selected grants: The following grants were reported in 2003.
$207,000 to United Way, Greater Twin Cities, Minneapolis, MN. For annual campaign.
$84,000 to Oil City Area School District, Oil City, PA. For general operating support.
$50,000 to Courage Center, Golden Valley, MN. For general operating support.
$25,000 to Childrens Home Society and Family Services, Saint Paul, MN. For program support.
$23,130 to United Way, Heart of America, Kansas City, MO. For general operating support.

$20,000 to Science Museum of Minnesota, Saint Paul, MN. For general operating support.
$17,000 to United Negro College Fund, Minneapolis, MN. For annual campaign.
$15,000 to A Chance to Grow, Minneapolis, MN. For general operating support.
$10,500 to Family Service, Saint Paul, MN. For general operating support.
$10,500 to Learning Disabilities Association, Minneapolis, MN. For capital support.

4550
John R. and Maryanne Dennis Foundation ✧ ☆
14 Bello Dr.
Edina, MN 55439-1658

Established in 1989 in MN and SD.
Donor: John R. Dennis.
Foundation type: Independent foundation.
Financial data (yr. ended 12/31/04): Assets, $286,731 (M); gifts received, $124,813; expenditures, $508,943; qualifying distributions, $504,084; giving activities include $502,800 for 8 grants (high: $495,000; low: $100).
Purpose and activities: Giving primarily to children and social services, and education.
Fields of interest: Arts; Elementary school/education; Nursing care; Health organizations, association; Boys & girls clubs; Human services; Children/youth, services.
Limitations: Applications not accepted. Giving primarily in Minneapolis, MN. No grants to individuals.
Application information: Contributes only to pre-selected organizations.
Officers: John R. Dennis, Pres.; Maryanne Dennis, V.P.
EIN: 363644050

4551
Desiring God Foundation ✧
1801 11th Ave. S.
Minneapolis, MN 55404

Established in 2001 in MN.
Donor: John Piper.
Foundation type: Independent foundation.
Financial data (yr. ended 12/31/04): Assets, $1,239,089 (M); gifts received, $368,835; expenditures, $430,617; qualifying distributions, $416,441; giving activities include $415,000 for 2 grants (high: $235,000; low: $180,000).
Fields of interest: Christian agencies & churches.
Limitations: Applications not accepted. Giving primarily in Minneapolis, MN. No grants to individuals.
Application information: Contributes only to pre-selected organizations.
Officers and Directors:* John Piper,* Pres.; Noel Piper,* Secy.; Justin Taylor,* Treas.
EIN: 412011129

4552
The Donaldson Foundation
P.O. Box 1299, M.S. 100
Minneapolis, MN 55440
Contact: Norman C. Linnell, Pres.
FAX: (952) 887-3005;
E-mail: nlinnell@mail.donaldson.com; Additional

E-mail: donaldsonfoundation@mail.donaldson.com;
URL: http://www.donaldson.com/en/about/
community/foundation.html

Established in 1966 in MN.
Donor: Donaldson Co., Inc.
Foundation type: Company-sponsored foundation.
Financial data (yr. ended 7/31/05): Assets,
$2,409,293 (M); expenditures, $874,744;
qualifying distributions, $834,687; giving activities
include $822,009 for 76 grants (high: $40,000;
low: $1,000), and $12,653 for employee matching
gifts.
Purpose and activities: The foundation supports
organizations involved with education and economic
self-sufficiency.
Fields of interest: Education; Economically
disadvantaged.
Type of support: Continuing support; Annual
campaigns; Capital campaigns; Building/
renovation; Scholarship funds; Employee matching
gifts; Employee-related scholarships.
Limitations: Giving on a national basis in areas of
company operations. No support for religious
organizations. No grants to individuals (except for
employee-related scholarships).
Publications: Application guidelines; Annual report
(including application guidelines); Informational
brochure (including application guidelines).
Application information: Application form not
required.
   Initial approach: Letter of inquiry
   Copies of proposal: 1
   Deadline(s): None
   Board meeting date(s): Feb., May, Aug., and Nov.
Officer and Directors: Norman C. Linnell,* Pres. and
Treas.; Jim Burrows; Becky Cahn; Karen Geronime;
Dennis Grigal; Jeff May; Darnell McElveen; Julie
O'Connor; Julie Rumsey; Chris Valle; Kristin Wendel.
EIN: 416052950

4553
Dorea Foundation ✧
P.O. Box 5628
Minneapolis, MN 55440

Established in 1991 in MN.
Donor: Members of the Keinath family.
Foundation type: Independent foundation.
Financial data (yr. ended 12/31/05): Assets,
$11,794,484 (M); expenditures, $1,422,405;
qualifying distributions, $1,270,000; giving
activities include $1,270,000 for 8 grants (high:
$250,000; low: $15,000).
Fields of interest: Christian agencies & churches.
Limitations: Applications not accepted. Giving
limited to MO. No grants to individuals.
Application information: Contributes only to
pre-selected organizations.
Officers: Warren G. Keinath, Jr., Pres.; Pauline M.
Keinath, V.P.; Steven A. Hornig, Secy.; Robert J.
Theiler, Treas.
EIN: 411703735

4554
Drew Foundation ✧
(formerly Jack, Helen, Louis & Jean Drew
Foundation)
P.O. Box 64713, Trust Tax Svcs.
St. Paul, MN 55164-0713
Application address: c/o Eleanor Swanson, 5439
Lafayette Ave., Omaha, NE 88132

Established in 1987.
Foundation type: Independent foundation.
Financial data (yr. ended 12/31/05): Assets,
$1,251,364 (M); expenditures, $646,314;
qualifying distributions, $635,111; giving activities
include $630,000 for 8 grants (high: $200,000;
low: $5,000).
Purpose and activities: The foundation supports
major artistic, cultural and performing arts
institutions and organizations, in the greater
Omaha, NE, metropolitan area.
Fields of interest: Media, radio; Museums (art);
Performing arts, theater; Performing arts, orchestra
(symphony); Performing arts, opera; Botanical
gardens.
Limitations: Giving primarily in Omaha, NE.
Application information:
   Deadline(s): None
Officers and Directors:* Eleanor K. Swanson,*
Pres.; Gary W. Radil,* V.P.; Linda Mattson
Anderson,* Secy.; Donald K. Engdahl,* Treas.;
Steven R. Brott; Jerry Pabst.
EIN: 470710311

4555
Driscoll Foundation ✧
200 Wells Fargo Pl.
30 E. 7th St.
St. Paul, MN 55101 (651) 228-0935
Contact: W. John Driscoll, Pres.

Incorporated in 1962 in MN.
Donor: Members of the Driscoll family.
Foundation type: Independent foundation.
Financial data (yr. ended 2/28/05): Assets,
$18,322,953 (M); gifts received, $1,001,105;
expenditures, $756,463; qualifying distributions,
$691,464; giving activities include $663,000 for 10
grants (high: $310,000; low: $2,000).
Fields of interest: Performing arts; Arts; Higher
education; Community development.
Type of support: General/operating support; Capital
campaigns.
Limitations: Giving primarily in the metropolitan
areas of St. Paul-Minneapolis, MN, and San
Francisco, CA. No grants to individuals, or for
scholarships, conferences, travel, publications, or
films.
Publications: Annual report (including application
guidelines).
Application information: Application form not
required.
   Initial approach: Proposal
   Copies of proposal: 1
   Deadline(s): None
   Board meeting date(s): Annually and as required
   Final notification: 3 to 4 weeks
Officers and Directors:* W. John Driscoll,* Pres.;
Michael J. Giefer, Secy.-Treas.; Elizabeth S. Driscoll.
EIN: 416012065
Selected grants: The following grants were reported
in 2003.
$150,000 to American University in Cairo, New
   York, NY. For Landscaping fund.

$150,000 to Vassar College, Poughkeepsie, NY. For
   Reunion Fund.
$100,000 to Yale University, New Haven, CT. For
   Davenport College renovation.
$80,000 to Minneapolis Institute of Arts,
   Minneapolis, MN. For endowment fund.
$50,000 to Shanti Project, San Francisco, CA. For
   Shanti endowment fund.
$50,000 to United Way, Greater Twin Cities,
   Minneapolis, MN.
$20,000 to Minnesota Landscape Arboretum
   Foundation, Chaska, MN. For Slade Perennial
   Gardens.
$20,000 to Saint Paul Academy and Summit
   School, Saint Paul, MN. For Driscoll Maintenance
   Fund.
$10,000 to Palo Alto Players, Palo Alto, CA. For
   operating support.
$5,000 to Neighborhood House, Saint Paul, MN. For
   operating support.

4556
**Duluth-Superior Area Community
   Foundation** ✧
Medical Arts Bldg.
324 W. Superior St., Ste. 212
Duluth, MN 55802-1707 (218) 726-0232
Contact: Holly C. Sampson, C.E.O.
FAX: (218) 726-0257;
E-mail: info@dsacommunityfoundation.com; Grant
application E-mail:
grantsinfo@dsacommunityfoundation.com;
URL: http://www.dsacommunityfoundation.com

Established in 1982 in MN.
Foundation type: Community foundation.
Financial data (yr. ended 12/31/05): Assets,
$43,064,025 (M); gifts received, $4,949,749;
expenditures, $2,737,314; giving activities include
$885,426 for 343 grants (high: $59,054; low:
$100), and $1,103,618 for 298 grants to
individuals (high: $5,000; low: $195).
Purpose and activities: The foundation supports a
wide variety of activities in five interest areas: Arts,
Community and Economic Development, Education,
Environment, and Human Services.
Fields of interest: Visual arts; Performing arts;
Performing arts, music; Arts; Child development,
education; Higher education; Education;
Environment; Animal welfare; Crime/violence
prevention; Employment; Food services; Housing/
shelter, development; Children/youth, services;
Child development, services; Family services;
Homeless, human services; Human services;
International affairs, goodwill promotion;
International peace/security; Civil rights, race/
intergroup relations; Economic development;
Community development; Government/public
administration; Disabilities, people with; Minorities;
Native Americans/American Indians; Women;
Economically disadvantaged; Homeless.
Type of support: General/operating support;
Emergency funds; Program development;
Publication; Seed money; Curriculum development;
Scholarship funds; Research; Technical assistance;
Consulting services; Program evaluation;
Scholarships—to individuals.
Limitations: Giving primarily in Bayfield and Douglas
counties, WI, and in Atkin, Carlton, Cook, Itasca,
Koochiching, Lake, and St. Louis counties in
northeastern MN. No support for religious
organizations for religious activities. No grants to
individuals (except for designated scholarship funds

---

or specialized one-time crisis programs), or for capital or annual campaigns, endowments, debt retirement, medical research, fundraising, continuing support, deficit financing, land acquisition, tickets for benefits, telephone solicitations, or for grants beyond single funding cycle; no loans.

Publications: Application guidelines; Annual report; Grants list; Informational brochure (including application guidelines); Newsletter.

Application information: Visit foundation Web site for application form, guidelines, and specific deadlines. Based on the outcome of the inquiry, an organization may be encouraged to submit a full proposal. Minnesota Common Grant Application Form required. Application form required.

Initial approach: Online funding inquiry form, letter, or telephone
Copies of proposal: 3
Deadline(s): Varies
Board meeting date(s): Monthly
Final notification: 60-90 days after deadline

Officers and Trustees:* Abbot G. Apter,* Chair.; Donald L. Wallgren,* Vice-Chair.; Holly C. Sampson, C.E.O. and Pres.;* Peter L. Boman,* Secy.; Helena E. Jackson,* Treas.; Paul R. Buckley; Jennifer L. Carey; Michael A. Cowles; Howard T. Klatzky; LeRoy T. Kolquist; John P. Lawien; Ilene F. Levin; Richard Loraas; Lyle W. Northey; Thomas B. Wheeler.

Number of staff: 3 full-time professional; 3 part-time professional; 1 full-time support.

EIN: 411429402

4557
Ecolab Foundation

370 Wabasha St.
St. Paul, MN   55102   (651) 293-2658
Contact: Kris J. Taylor, V.P.
E-mail: ecolabfoundation@ecolab.com; URL: http://www.ecolab.com/CompanyProfile/Foundation/default.asp

Established in 1982 in MN.
Donor: Ecolab Inc.
Foundation type: Company-sponsored foundation.
Financial data (yr. ended 12/31/04): Assets, $6,653,214 (M); gifts received, $4,045,897; expenditures, $3,433,859; qualifying distributions, $3,280,757; giving activities include $3,280,757 for 992 grants (high: $100,000; low: $15; average: $100–$10,000).

Purpose and activities: The foundation supports organizations involved with arts and culture, education, the environment, employment, hunger, housing, youth development, community development, civic affairs, and economically disadvantaged people.

Fields of interest: Arts; Elementary/secondary education; Education, reading; Education; Environment, natural resources; Environmental education; Environment; Employment; Food services; Housing/shelter; Youth development; Community development; Public affairs; Economically disadvantaged.

Type of support: Employee matching gifts; Program development; Grants to individuals; General/operating support.

Limitations: Giving primarily in City of Industry and San Jose, CA, McDonough, GA, Elk Grove Village and Joliet, IL, Huntington, IN, St. Paul, MN, Greensboro, NC, Grand Forks, ND, Hebron, OH, Garland, TX, Beloit, WI, and Martinsburg, WV. No support for sectarian or denominational religious organizations

not of direct benefit to the entire community, political or lobbying organizations, or disease-specific organizations. No grants to individuals (except for Visions for Learning), or for industry, trade, or professional association memberships, sports or athletic programs or facilities, or fundraising events or sponsorships; no loans or program-related investments.

Publications: Corporate giving report (including application guidelines).

Application information:

Initial approach: Complete online application form for organizations located in St. Paul, MN; telephone or E-mail foundation for application information for organizations located outside St. Paul, MN
Deadline(s): Sept. 22 for organizations located in St. Paul, MN
Board meeting date(s): Quarterly
Final notification: 3 to 4 months

Officers and Directors:* Allan L. Schuman,* Chair.; Michael J. Monahan,* Pres.; Lawrence T. Bell,* V.P.; John G. Forsythe, V.P.; Diana D. Lewis, V.P.; Thomas W. Schnack, V.P.; Kris J. Taylor, V.P.; David F. Duvick, Secy.; Thomas J. Hill, Treas.; Susan K. Nestegard.

Number of staff: 2 full-time professional.
EIN: 411372157

Selected grants: The following grants were reported in 2005.

$125,000 to American Red Cross. For disaster relief.

$25,000 to Minnesota Childrens Museum, Saint Paul, MN. For reduced admission for disadvantaged families.

$20,000 to Habitat for Humanity International. For affordable housing.

$15,000 to Big Brothers/Big Sisters. For operating support.

$15,000 to Chicanos Latinos Unidos En Servicios (CLUES), Saint Paul, MN. For work training and support services for Hispanic origin.

$10,000 to Childrens Theater Company and School, Minneapolis, MN. For school partnership program.

$7,500 to Northwoods Audubon Center, Sandstone, MN. For environment and science program for local students.

$5,000 to Admission Possible, Saint Paul, MN.

$5,000 to East Side Learning Center, Saint Paul, MN. For tutoring program for K-4th grade.

$5,000 to Ordway Center for the Performing Arts, Saint Paul, MN. For Asian theater group.

4558
Ecotrust Foundation

c/o Wells Fargo Bank Minnesota, N.A.
90 S. 7th St., Ste. 5300
Minneapolis, MN   55402

Established in 1992 in MN.
Donors: V. Wurtele; Peter Vaughan.
Foundation type: Independent foundation.
Financial data (yr. ended 12/31/05): Assets, $2,132,281 (M); gifts received, $50,000; expenditures, $428,458; qualifying distributions, $413,117; giving activities include $407,149 for 66 grants (high: $106,000; low: $100).

Purpose and activities: Giving primarily for environmental research, protection and conservation, including population control and family planning services.

Fields of interest: Environment, natural resources; Environment; Family services.

Limitations: Applications not accepted. No grants to individuals.

Application information: Contributes only to pre-selected organizations.

Officer: Peter Vaughan.
EIN: 411735062

Selected grants: The following grants were reported in 2005.

$106,000 to Nature Conservancy, Minneapolis, MN.

$20,000 to Greater Yellowstone Coalition, Bozeman, MT.

$15,000 to Minnesota Center for Environmental Advocacy, Saint Paul, MN.

$10,000 to Americans for UNFPA, New York, NY.

$10,000 to Environmental Defense, DC.

$10,000 to Pathfinder International, Watertown, MA.

$10,000 to Population Action International, DC.

$8,000 to International Projects Assistance Services (IPAS), Chapel Hill, NC.

$8,000 to Population Institute, DC.

$2,500 to Greenpeace Fund, DC.

4559
Edelstein Family Foundation ◇

c/o U.S. Trust
730 2nd Ave. S., Ste. 1400
Minneapolis, MN   55402

Established in 1954 in MN.
Donors: Ruth Easton Revocable Trust; David Edelstein†; Sparkle Sugar Corp.
Foundation type: Independent foundation.
Financial data (yr. ended 12/31/05): Assets, $38,283,822 (M); expenditures, $2,205,184; qualifying distributions, $1,980,438; giving activities include $1,717,238 for 16 grants (high: $261,045; low: $10,000).

Purpose and activities: Giving primarily for arts and cultural programs, education, with emphasis on secondary schools and higher education, health care, and Jewish agencies.

Fields of interest: Performing arts, theater; Secondary school/education; Higher education; Education; Health care; Jewish federated giving programs; Jewish agencies & temples.

Limitations: Applications not accepted. Giving primarily in St. Paul and Minneapolis, MN. No grants to individuals, or for loans or program-related investments.

Application information: Contributes only to pre-selected organizations.

Trustees: Thomas A. Keller III; U.S. Trust.
EIN: 416013675

Selected grants: The following grants were reported in 2004.

$298,682 to Brandeis University, Waltham, MA.

$298,682 to United Jewish Fund and Council, Saint Paul, MN.

$199,121 to National Jewish Medical and Research Center, Denver, CO.

$199,121 to Saint Paul Foundation, Saint Paul, MN.

$39,823 to Minnesota Masonic Home, Minneapolis, MN.

4560
Edina Realty Foundation ◇
6800 France Ave. S., Ste. 670
Edina, MN 55435-2017 (952) 928-5900
Contact: Susan Cowsert, Dir.
URL: http://www.edinarealty.com/Content/
Content.aspx?ContentID=187015

Established in 1996 in MN.
Donor: Edina Realty, Inc.
Foundation type: Company-sponsored foundation.
Financial data (yr. ended 9/30/04): Assets,
$648,158 (M); gifts received, $446,382;
expenditures, $462,141; qualifying distributions,
$462,141; giving activities include $457,412 for
115 grants (high: $29,412; low: $200).
Purpose and activities: The foundation supports
organizations involved with human services and
homeless people.
Fields of interest: Human services; Homeless.
Type of support: General/operating support; Capital
campaigns; Building/renovation; Emergency funds;
Program development; Curriculum development;
Research.
Limitations: Giving primarily in MN. No grants to
individuals.
Publications: Application guidelines; Occasional
report.
Application information: Application form required.
Initial approach: Download application form and
mail to nearest company facility
Copies of proposal: 1
Deadline(s): None
Board meeting date(s): Quarterly
Officer and Directors:* Michele Fremming,* V.P.
and C.F.O.; Mark Christopherson; Susan Cowsert;
Lori Day; Amy Kleinschmidt; Marc Kuhnley; Deb
Stumne.
Number of staff: 1 full-time support; 1 part-time
support.
EIN: 411826980
Selected grants: The following grants were reported
in 2005.
$28,336 to Bridging, Inc., Bloomington, MN.
$21,442 to Salvation Army.
$19,135 to American Red Cross.
$13,000 to Dakota Woodlands, Eagan, MN.
$12,289 to Habitat for Humanity International.
$7,000 to Simpson Housing Services, Minneapolis,
MN.
$6,500 to YMCA.
$6,480 to Cornerstone, DC.
$4,283 to Senior Housing, Saint Paul, MN.
$3,876 to Lutheran Social Services.

4561
Edwards Memorial Trust
c/o U.S. Bank, N.A.
101 E. 5th St., EP-MN-S12
St. Paul, MN 55101 (651) 466-8441
Contact: Jackie Copeland-Carson
Application address: c/o Cheryl Nelson, U.S. Bank,
N.A., P.O Box 64704, St. Paul, MN 55164

Established in 1961 in MN.
Donor: Ray Edwards‡.
Foundation type: Independent foundation.
Financial data (yr. ended 12/31/05): Assets,
$20,098,631 (M); expenditures, $935,838;
qualifying distributions, $823,178; giving activities
include $759,000 for 64 grants (high: $50,000;
low: $3,000).

Purpose and activities: Emphasis on public
hospitals, including the maintaining of free beds;
some support for social services and health
agencies, including those benefiting the
handicapped.
Fields of interest: Hospitals (general); Health care;
Mental health/crisis services; Human services;
Disabilities, people with.
Type of support: General/operating support; Capital
campaigns; Program development.
Limitations: Giving limited to the benefit of the East
Metro St. Paul, area, and in the counties of Ramsey,
Washington, and Dakota, MN. No grants to
individuals, or for endowments, research, film and
video production or travel.
Publications: Application guidelines.
Application information: MN Common Grant
Application Form (available on www.mcf.org) or PGG
Application Form required. Application form
required.
Initial approach: Letter
Copies of proposal: 1
Deadline(s): May 1 and Oct. 1
Board meeting date(s): May and Nov.
Final notification: 60 days
Trustee: U.S. Bank, N.A.
EIN: 416011292
Selected grants: The following grants were reported
in 2005.
$75,000 to Neighborhood Health Care Network,
Saint Paul, MN. 2 grants: $25,000, $50,000
$50,000 to Presbyterian Homes Foundation,
Roseville, MN.
$25,000 to Metropolitan State University, Saint
Paul, MN.
$25,000 to Regions Hospital Foundation, Saint
Paul, MN.
$20,000 to Childrens Health Care Foundation,
Minneapolis, MN.
$15,000 to American Cancer Society, Edina, MN.
$15,000 to Catholic Charities, MN.
$10,000 to Womens Cancer Resource Center,
Minneapolis, MN.
$7,500 to Northwest Youth and Family Services,
Shoreview, MN.

4562
The Emmerich Foundation Charitable Trust
7302 Claredon Dr.
Edina, MN 55439

Established in 1992 in MN.
Donors: Karol D. Emmerich; Richard J. Emmerich.
Foundation type: Independent foundation.
Financial data (yr. ended 12/31/05): Assets,
$4,326,025 (M); expenditures, $327,275;
qualifying distributions, $326,500; giving activities
include $325,750 for 30 grants (high: $68,000;
low: $100).
Purpose and activities: Support primarily for
evangelical Christian organizations.
Fields of interest: Christian agencies & churches.
Limitations: Applications not accepted. Giving on a
national basis. No grants to individuals.
Application information: Contributes only to
pre-selected organizations.
Trustees: Karol D. Emmerich; Richard J. Emmerich.
EIN: 411712553
Selected grants: The following grants were reported
in 2005.
$68,000 to Opportunity International, Oak Brook, IL.
$35,000 to Wooddale Church, Eden Prairie, MN.

$30,000 to Americans United for Life, Chicago, IL.
$25,000 to Jesus Film Project, Orlando, FL.
$18,000 to Pheasants Forever, Saint Paul, MN.
$15,000 to Northwestern College, Saint Paul, MN.
$10,000 to Minnehaha Academy, Minneapolis, MN.
$5,000 to Living Water International, Sugar Land,
TX.
$3,000 to World Vision, Tacoma, WA.
$2,000 to Gathering, The, Tyler, TX.

4563
Federated Insurance Foundation, Inc. ◇
121 E. Park Sq.
Owatonna, MN 55060 (507) 455-8906
Contact: Brian Brose, Admin.

Established in 1972 MN.
Donor: Federated Mutual Insurance Co.
Foundation type: Independent foundation.
Financial data (yr. ended 12/31/04): Assets,
$223,916 (M); gifts received, $35,629;
expenditures, $338,216; qualifying distributions,
$332,548; giving activities include $332,535 for
172 grants (high: $55,000; low: $75).
Purpose and activities: Giving primarily to education
and human services.
Fields of interest: Arts; Higher education; Libraries/
library science; Education; Environment; Animals/
wildlife, preservation/protection; Health
organizations, association; Children/youth,
services; Community development; Federated giving
programs.
Type of support: General/operating support.
Limitations: Giving primarily in MN.
Application information: Application form not
required.
Initial approach: Letter
Copies of proposal: 1
Deadline(s): None
Board meeting date(s): As needed
Officers: A.T. Annexstad, Pres.; H.J. Moret, V.P.;
A.D. Lewis, Secy.; R.R. Stawarz, Treas.
EIN: 237173646

4564
E. David Fischman Scholarship Fund
c/o U.S. Bank, N.A.
101 E. 5th St., EP-MN-S14
St. Paul, MN 55101
Contact: Cheryl Nelson

Established in 1998 in MN.
Donor: E. David Fischman‡.
Foundation type: Independent foundation.
Financial data (yr. ended 12/31/05): Assets,
$7,208,257 (M); expenditures, $412,157;
qualifying distributions, $362,472; giving activities
include $347,381 for 9 grants (high: $204,199;
low: $2,278).
Purpose and activities: Giving primarily for higher
education scholarships.
Fields of interest: Higher education, university;
Scholarships/financial aid.
Type of support: Scholarship funds.
Limitations: Applications not accepted. Giving
primarily in Boston, MA, and New York, NY. No
grants to individuals.
Application information: Contributes only to
pre-selected organizations. Unsolicited requests for
funds not accepted.

Trustee: U.S. Bank, N.A.
EIN: 416438510

4565

The Jack and Bessie Fiterman Foundation ✧

5600 N. Hwy. 169
Minneapolis, MN 55428 (763) 545-7213
Contact: Linda Fiterman, Treas.
Application address: P.O. Box 62053, St. Louis Park, MN 55426

Established in 1966 in MN.
Donors: Fidelity Products Co.; Liberty Carton Co.; Safco Products Co.; Shamrock Industries, Inc.; FLS Properties; B&B Lease Co.; Liberty Diversified Industries, Inc.
Foundation type: Company-sponsored foundation.
Financial data (yr. ended 5/31/05): Assets, $8,078,805 (M); gifts received, $2,450,000; expenditures, $637,358; qualifying distributions, $616,200; giving activities include $616,200 for 83 grants (high: $399,000; low: $100).
Purpose and activities: The foundation supports Jewish agencies and temples and organizations involved with arts and culture, health, children and youth, human services, and religion.
Fields of interest: Museums; Arts; Health care; Children/youth, services; Human services; Federated giving programs; Jewish agencies & temples; Religion.
Limitations: Giving primarily in MN. No support for lobbying or advocacy organizations. No grants to individuals.
Application information: Application form required.
  Initial approach: Contact foundation for application form
  Deadline(s): None
Officers: Michael Fiterman, Pres.; Ben Fiterman, V.P.; David Lenzen, Secy.; Linda Fiterman, Treas.
EIN: 416058465
Selected grants: The following grants were reported in 2004.
$470,000 to Minneapolis Jewish Federation, Minnetonka, MN.
$69,000 to United Way, Greater Twin Cities, Minneapolis, MN.
$25,000 to Minnesota Public Radio, Saint Paul, MN.
$19,400 to Jewish Community Center of Greater Minneapolis, Minneapolis, MN.
$10,000 to Jewish Family and Childrens Service of Minneapolis, Minnetonka, MN.
$4,500 to Family and Childrens Service, Minneapolis, MN.
$4,000 to United Way of Central Minnesota, Saint Cloud, MN.
$2,500 to Catholic Charities of the Archdiocese of Saint Paul and Minneapolis, Minneapolis, MN.
$2,500 to Sharing and Caring Hands, Minneapolis, MN.
$1,800 to Youth Frontiers, Minneapolis, MN.

4566

Frey Foundation

90 S. 7th St., Ste. 5000
Minneapolis, MN 55402 (612) 359-6200
Contact: JoAnn Gruesner
FAX: (612) 359-6210;
E-mail: joann@freyfoundationmn.org; URL: http://freyfoundationmn.org/

Established in 1988 in MN.
Foundation type: Independent foundation.
Financial data (yr. ended 6/30/05): Assets, $16,780,854 (M); gifts received, $1,250,000; expenditures, $778,650; qualifying distributions, $720,476; giving activities include $718,403 for 38 grants (high: $100,000; low: $100).
Purpose and activities: The foundation strives to be a catalyst in strengthening its community through effective, direct giving which promotes self-sufficiency and stimulates creative change, resulting in an improved quality of life for all.
Fields of interest: Higher education; Human services.
Type of support: General/operating support; Annual campaigns; Capital campaigns; Building/renovation; Program development; Matching/challenge support.
Limitations: Giving primarily in the Minneapolis-St. Paul, MN, area and in Naples, FL. No grants to individuals, including scholarships and tuition assistance, or for endowments.
Publications: Application guidelines; Annual report; Informational brochure.
Application information: Application form required.
  Initial approach: Letter of inquiry
  Copies of proposal: 1
  Deadline(s): Feb. 15, May 15, Aug. 15, and Nov. 15
  Board meeting date(s): Quarterly
  Final notification: 4 weeks
Officers and Directors: * Eugene U. Frey,* Chair.; Mary F. Frey,* Vice-Chair.; James R. Frey; John J. Frey; Mary W. Frey; Jane E. Letourneau; Carol F. Wolfe; Daniel T. Wolfe.
Number of staff: 2 full-time professional.
EIN: 363588505
Selected grants: The following grants were reported in 2005.
$100,000 to Hope Community, Minneapolis, MN.
$100,000 to Project for Pride in Living, Minneapolis, MN.
$50,000 to Risen Christ Catholic School, Minneapolis, MN.
$40,000 to Center for School Change, Minneapolis, MN.
$30,000 to Wilderness Inquiry, Minneapolis, MN.
$20,000 to Saint Johns University, Collegeville, MN.
$15,000 to A Chance to Grow, Minneapolis, MN.
$10,000 to Cabrini House, Minneapolis, MN.
$10,000 to Families Moving Forward, Minneapolis, MN.
$10,000 to Third Way Network, Minneapolis, MN.

4567

H. B. Fuller Company Foundation ✧

P.O. Box 64683
St. Paul, MN 55164-0683 (651) 236-5217
Contact: Christine Meyer, Community Affairs Asst.
FAX: (651) 236-5056

Established in 1986 in MN.
Donor: H.B. Fuller Co.
Foundation type: Company-sponsored foundation.
Financial data (yr. ended 11/30/04): Assets, $1,117,051 (M); gifts received, $157,896; expenditures, $470,205; qualifying distributions, $469,511; giving activities include $457,784 for 231 grants (high: $112,206; low: $25).
Purpose and activities: The foundation supports programs designed to involve youth in the arts; help families and communities provide economically for their children; provide programs in literacy and vocational training for youth with priority given to citizenship development and volunteer community service; promote local neighborhood environment improvement programs involving youth; and provide activities for disadvantaged children, engaging adults as volunteers in the development of healthy, nurtured children.
Fields of interest: Arts; Vocational education; Education, reading; Environment; Youth development, citizenship; Youth development; Voluntarism promotion; Children; Youth; Economically disadvantaged.
Type of support: General/operating support; Annual campaigns; Employee matching gifts.
Limitations: Giving primarily in areas of company operations in CA, FL, GA, IL, IN, KY, MI, MN, OH, TN, TX, and WA. No support for religious, fraternal, or veterans' organizations, national organizations, educational institutions, or disease-specific organizations. No grants to individuals, or for travel, basic or applied research, advertising, fundraising campaigns, capital campaigns, or endowments.
Publications: Corporate giving report.
Application information: Application form required.
  Initial approach: Contact foundation for application form
  Copies of proposal: 1
  Deadline(s): Feb., June, and Oct.
  Board meeting date(s): Feb., June, and Oct.
  Final notification: 2 weeks following board meetings
Officers and Directors: * Ann Wynia,* Pres.; Rich Kastner, Treas.; Karen P. Muller, Exec. Dir.; Reatha Clark King; Al Stroucken.
EIN: 363500811
Selected grants: The following grants were reported in 2003.
$100,437 to United Way, Greater Twin Cities, Minneapolis, MN. 2 grants: $80,437, $20,000
$50,000 to University of Minnesota Foundation, Minneapolis, MN. For Elmer L. Anderson Library Endowment for Special Collections.
$30,000 to Ready 4 K, Saint Paul, MN. For general operating support.
$20,000 to Lifetrack Resources, Saint Paul, MN. For Families Together Program.
$20,000 to Minnesota Humanities Commission, Saint Paul, MN. For Family Literacy Initiatives.
$15,000 to Lao Family Community of Minnesota, Saint Paul, MN. For English Education Program.
$10,250 to University of Minnesota, Minneapolis, MN. For HB Fuller McEvoy Lecture Series.
$10,000 to Mounds View Public Schools, Mounds View, MN. For Family Learning Program.
$4,000 to Ride to Walk, Granite Bay, CA. For general operating support.

4568

Janice Gardner Foundation ✧ ☆

11580 K-Tel Dr.
Minnetonka, MN 55343 (651) 714-2306
Contact: Elizabeth Glaeser, Secy.-Treas.

Established in 1987 in MN.
Donors: George J. Gardner; George W. Gardner; Susan M. Gardner; Packaging, Inc.
Foundation type: Independent foundation.
Financial data (yr. ended 12/31/05): Assets, $4,466,112 (M); expenditures, $480,055; qualifying distributions, $470,803; giving activities include $470,803 for grants.
Purpose and activities: Giving primarily for Roman Catholic education, organizations, and churches;

funding also for health associations, including services for people who are deaf, and social services.

Fields of interest: Elementary/secondary education; Higher education; Health organizations, association; Human services; Federated giving programs; Roman Catholic agencies & churches; Deaf/hearing impaired.

Limitations: Giving primarily in MN.

Application information: Application form not required.

Deadline(s): None

Board meeting date(s): Mar.

Officer: Elizabeth Glaeser, Secy.-Treas.

Directors: George W. Gardner; Jacqui Gardner; Susan M. Khaury.

EIN: 411603464

Selected grants: The following grants were reported in 2005.

$157,000 to World Vision, Federal Way, WA.

$40,000 to Park Nicollet Foundation, Saint Louis Park, MN.

$30,000 to Catholic Eldercare, Minneapolis, MN.

$25,000 to Basilica of Saint Mary, Minneapolis, MN.

$7,000 to Opportunity Partners, Minnetonka, MN.

$5,000 to NET Ministries, West Saint Paul, MN.

$2,500 to Catholic Charities.

$2,000 to American Red Cross, National Headquarters, DC.

$1,750 to Alzheimers Association, Chicago, IL.

4569
Garmar Foundation ◇

65742 State Hwy. 56
Dodge Center, MN 55927-7750
Contact: Garwin McNeilus, Pres.

Established in 1998 in MN.

Donors: Brandon McNeilus; Denzil McNeilus; Garwin McNeilus; Marilee McNeilus; GM, LLC; Bobilli Blind School; Ben Mallory; Don Kirkman; Ashlund Sams.

Foundation type: Independent foundation.

Financial data (yr. ended 6/30/05): Assets, $2,516,320 (M); gifts received, $772,508; expenditures, $1,038,287; qualifying distributions, $1,325,407; giving activities include $1,032,434 for 20 grants (high: $306,522; low: $100; average: $10,000–$141,046), and $287,124 for 1 foundation-administered program.

Purpose and activities: Giving primarily to the Minnesota Conference of Seventh Day Adventists, as well as for education and human services.

Fields of interest: Museums (science/technology); Libraries (public); Education; Human services; Protestant agencies & churches.

Limitations: Applications not accepted. Giving primarily in MN. No grants to individuals.

Application information: Contributes only to pre-selected organizations.

Officers: Garwin McNeilus, Pres.; Denzil McNeilus, V.P.; Marilee McNeilus, Secy.-Treas.

EIN: 411914753

Selected grants: The following grants were reported in 2004.

$1,420,247 to Outpost Centers, Apison, TN. For religious and missionary projects and roofs, missions and school.

$1,251,209 to Seventh-Day Adventist Church, Dhaka, Bangladesh. For religious and missionary projects, schools and missions, and orphanage and student support.

$1,250,297 to Maranatha Volunteers International, Sacramento, CA. For religious and missionary projects and orphans and school building.

$615,000 to Adventist-Laymens Services and Industries (ASI), Silver Spring, MD. For religious and missionary projects and for roofs, programs, and buildings.

$362,300 to Southern Asia Division of Seventh Day Adventists, Hosur, India. For religious and missionary projects and evangelism, eye equipment.

$304,467 to Global Mission, Silver Spring, MD. For religious and missionary projects, church and school.

$265,000 to Three Angels Broadcasting, West Frankfort, IL. For religious and missionary projects, satellite and programs.

$212,500 to Gospel Outreach, College Place, WA. For religious and missionary projects and outreach programs.

$170,000 to General Conference of Seventh-Day Adventists, Silver Spring, MD. For religious and missionary projects and seminary classroom.

$75,000 to Volunteers in Action, Petrie, Australia. For religious and missionary projects and church roofs.

4570
General Mills Foundation ▼

P.O. Box 1113
Minneapolis, MN 55440
Contact: Christina L. Shea, Pres.
FAX: (763) 764-4114; URL: http://www.generalmills.com/corporate/commitment/foundation.aspx

Incorporated in 1954 in MN.

Donor: General Mills, Inc.

Foundation type: Company-sponsored foundation.

Financial data (yr. ended 5/31/06): Assets, $30,353,622 (M); gifts received, $19,600,000; expenditures, $20,252,110; qualifying distributions, $20,203,452; giving activities include $13,581,433 for 707 grants (high: $500,000; low: $1,000), and $6,618,572 for 3,716 employee matching gifts.

Purpose and activities: The foundation supports organizations involved with arts and culture, education, hunger, youth nutrition and recreation, disaster relief, human services, and minorities.

Fields of interest: Visual arts; Performing arts; Arts; Elementary/secondary education; Education, reading; Education; Food services; Nutrition; Disasters, preparedness/services; Recreation; Human services; Children/youth; Minorities.

Type of support: General/operating support; Capital campaigns; Program development; Employee matching gifts; Employee-related scholarships; Scholarships—to individuals.

Limitations: Giving primarily in areas of major company operations. No support for religious, political, social, labor, veterans', alumni, or fraternal organizations, disease-specific organizations, or athletic associations. No grants to individuals (except for scholarships), or for endowments, research, publications, films, advertising, athletic events, testimonial dinners, workshops, symposia, travel, fundraising events, debt reduction, or recreation; no loans.

Publications: Application guidelines; Annual report; Corporate giving report (including application guidelines); Grants list; Informational brochure.

Application information: Telephone calls and personal visits are not encouraged. Requests may be submitted using the Minnesota Common Grant Application Form. Application form required.

Initial approach: Download application form and mail proposal and application form to nearest company facility; mail to foundation for organizations located in MN; complete online application form for Champions for Healthy Kids

Copies of proposal: 1

Deadline(s): Feb. 1 for Champions for Healthy Kids; Sept. 1 for Celebrating Communities of Color

Board meeting date(s): 4 times per year and as required

Final notification: 8 weeks

Officers and Trustees:* Stephen W. Sanger,* Chair.; Christina L. Shea,* Pres.; David B. Van Benschoten, Treas.; Ellen Luger, Exec. Dir.; Mark Belton; Randy G. Darcy; James A. Lawrence; Siri S. Marshall; Michael A. Peel; Kendall Powell; Jeff Rotsch.

Number of staff: 5 full-time professional; 4 full-time support.

EIN: 416018495

Selected grants: The following grants were reported in 2005.

$10,000 to Ballet Arts Minnesota, Minneapolis, MN. For City Children's Nutcracker Project.

$10,000 to Mesa Public Schools, Mesa, AZ. For Fitness Challenge and Nutrition Explosion, serving special education students in multi-cultural community.

$10,000 to Peta Wakan Tipi, Sacred Fire Lodge, Saint Paul, MN. For Dream of the Wild Health Network, cultural preservation project that brings Native American adults, elders and youth together to collect and grow indigenous, heirloom seeds as part of medicine garden used to teach young people about ancient traditions of American Indian medicine and gardening.

$10,000 to Tubman Family Alliance, Minneapolis, MN. For jobs, education, and training services.

$10,000 to Urban Resource Systems, San Francisco, CA. For Burbank Sprouts School Garden Program.

4571
Generations Health Care Initiatives, Inc. ◇

5 W. 1st St., Ste. 200
Duluth, MN 55802

Established in 2001 in MN.

Donors: U.S. Department of Health & Human Services; Minnesota Organization for Fetal Alcohol Syndrome.

Foundation type: Independent foundation.

Financial data (yr. ended 8/31/05): Assets, $13,298,465 (M); gifts received, $751,418; expenditures, $1,750,224; qualifying distributions, $710,652; giving activities include $368,075 for 4 grants (high: $300,112).

Fields of interest: Health care, clinics/centers; Health care; Health organizations, association.

Limitations: Applications not accepted. No grants to individuals.

Application information: Contributes only to pre-selected organizations.

Officers: Jack Schilling, Chair.; Steve Peterson, Vice-Chair.; Mary Nienaber, Secy.

Board Members: Henry Hanka; Bruce Hustad; Chris Maddy; Thomas Sailstad; Richard Ziegler.
EIN: 412000473

4572
George Family Foundation ✧
1818 Oliver Ave. S.
Minneapolis, MN 55405
Contact: Diane B. Neimann, Exec. Dir.
FAX: (612) 377-8407; URL: http://www.georgefamilyfoundation.org

Established in 1992 in MN.
Donors: Penny Pilgram George; William W. George.
Foundation type: Independent foundation.
Financial data (yr. ended 12/31/04): Assets, $39,770,736 (M); gifts received, $2,663,506; expenditures, $2,405,591; qualifying distributions, $2,164,086; giving activities include $1,706,183 for 52 grants (high: $251,000; low: $1,000).
Purpose and activities: The mission of the foundation is to foster human development, spiritual, intellectual, physical and psychological, and to enhance the work of people and organizations devoted to exemplary service in the community. Giving primarily for integrated healing, and education.
Fields of interest: Education; Health organizations, association; Leadership development; Religion.
Type of support: General/operating support; Continuing support; Program development.
Limitations: Applications not accepted. Giving primarily in the Twin Cities area, MN. No grants to individuals, or for endowments, capital campaigns, memberships, debt reduction, fundraisers, special events, or for operating expenses.
Publications: Annual report.
Application information: Unsolicited requests for funds not accepted.
Officers: Penny Pilgram George, Pres.; William W. George, V.P.; Diane B. Neimann, Exec. Dir.
Directors: Jeffrey Pilgram George; Jonathan Roulette George.
EIN: 411730855
Selected grants: The following grants were reported in 2004.
$249,000 to K T C A/K T C I Twin Cities Public Television, Saint Paul, MN.
$200,000 to Abbott Northwestern Hospital, Minneapolis, MN.
$150,000 to Sigma Chi Foundation, Evanston, IL.
$100,000 to Plymouth Congregational Church, Minneapolis, MN.
$55,000 to Commonweal, Bolinas, CA.
$48,333 to University of Saint Thomas, Saint Paul, MN.
$30,000 to Institute for Global Ethics, Camden, ME.
$20,000 to Opportunity International, Oak Brook, IL.
$15,000 to Macalester College, Saint Paul, MN.
$10,000 to Bakken, The, Minneapolis, MN.

4573
The Graco Foundation ✧
88 11th Ave. N.E.
Minneapolis, MN 55418 (612) 623-6684
Contact: Robert M. Mattison, Pres.
Application address: P.O. Box 1441, Minneapolis, MN 55440-1441; URL: http://www.graco.com/Internet/T_Corp.nsf/Webpages/Foundation2005?OpenDocument

Incorporated in 1956 in MN.
Donor: Graco Inc.
Foundation type: Company-sponsored foundation.
Financial data (yr. ended 12/31/04): Assets, $6,464,560 (M); gifts received, $3,700,100; expenditures, $1,467,659; qualifying distributions, $1,452,659; giving activities include $1,326,591 for 36 grants (high: $478,571; low: $1,000), and $78,433 for employee matching gifts.
Purpose and activities: The foundation supports organizations involved with ethics, education, human services, business awareness, and community development. Special emphasis is directed toward programs designed to help people become self-sufficient and more productive members of society.
Fields of interest: Philosophy/ethics; Education; Recreation; Youth development; Children/youth, services; Family services; Human services; Urban/community development; Business/industry; Community development.
Type of support: General/operating support; Continuing support; Capital campaigns; Building/renovation; Program development; Research; Employee matching gifts; Employee-related scholarships; Matching/challenge support.
Limitations: Giving primarily in areas of company operations, with emphasis on MN, including the northern and northeastern communities in Minneapolis, and Sioux Falls, SD. No support for political or religious organizations or fraternal organizations. No grants to individuals (except for employee-related scholarships), or for start-up needs, emergency needs, debt reduction, land acquisition, endowments, publications, fundraising, travel, or conferences; no loans.
Publications: Annual report (including application guidelines); Informational brochure (including application guidelines).
Application information: Proposals may be submitted using the Minnesota Common Grant Application Form or any other. Application form not required.
   Initial approach: Proposal
   Copies of proposal: 1
   Deadline(s): None
   Board meeting date(s): Quarterly
   Final notification: Quarterly
Officers and Directors:* Robert M. Mattison,* Pres.; Nancy Skaalrud, Secy.; Janel French, Treas.; Debra F. Hall; Dale D. Johnson; Patrick J. McHale; Fred A. Sutter; Brian F. Zumbolo.
Number of staff: None.
EIN: 416023537
Selected grants: The following grants were reported in 2004.
$150,000 to Opportunity Partners, Minnetonka, MN. For building improvements.
$150,000 to Seed Academy, Minneapolis, MN. For building renovation.
$100,000 to Opportunities Industrialization Center, Summit Academy, Minneapolis, MN. For hard hats painting program.
$100,000 to Sabathani Community Center, Minneapolis, MN. For Life Skills Center and capital projects.
$100,000 to Urban Ventures Leadership Foundation, Minneapolis, MN. For Colin Powell Youth Leadership Center.
$51,000 to A Chance to Grow, Minneapolis, MN. For kitchen and gymnasium renovations.
$50,000 to Bolder Options, Minneapolis, MN. For facilities improvements.
$50,000 to Project for Pride in Living, Minneapolis, MN. For facilities improvements.
$50,000 to YMCA, Sioux Falls Family, Sioux Falls, SD. For facilities improvements.
$40,000 to Minneapolis Park and Recreation Board, Minneapolis, MN. To add traveling teams to boys football and girls volleyball programs.

4574
Grand Rapids Area Community Foundation ✧
201 N.W. 4th St., Central Sq. Mall
Grand Rapids, MN 55744 (218) 327-8855
Contact: Wendy Roy, Exec. Dir.
FAX: (218) 327-8865; E-mail: info@gracf.org; Grant application E-mail: wroy@gracf.org; URL: http://www.gracf.org

Established in 1994 in MN.
Donors: Blandin Foundation; Itasca Medical Center Foundation; Larry Latterell.
Foundation type: Community foundation.
Financial data (yr. ended 12/31/04): Assets, $6,670,295 (L); gifts received, $2,903,689; expenditures, $1,992,371; giving activities include $1,682,645 for 556 grants (high: $435,641; low: $4), and $90,000 for 300 grants to individuals (high: $5,000; low: $50).
Purpose and activities: The foundation seeks to provide individuals and organizations opportunities to invest in their community to improve the quality of life.
Fields of interest: Humanities; Arts; Education; Environment; Health care; Recreation; Family services; Community development.
Type of support: Endowments; Emergency funds; Conferences/seminars; Curriculum development; Technical assistance; Scholarships—to individuals.
Limitations: Giving in the greater Itasca County, MN, area.
Publications: Application guidelines; Annual report; Informational brochure; Newsletter.
Application information: Contact foundation for pre-application information. Application form required.
   Initial approach: Telephone
   Copies of proposal: 1
   Deadline(s): Sept. 1
   Board meeting date(s): 1st Wed. of alternate months
   Final notification: 1 month
Officers and Directors:* Kris Ferraro,* Chair.; Larke Huntley,* 1st Vice-Chair.; Tom Fasteland,* 2nd Vice-Chair.; Cricket Guyer,* Secy.; Tom Karges,* Treas.; Wendy Roy, Exec. Dir.; Philip Anderson; Peggy Greenside; Kelly Hain; Tere Ivanca; Zona Kinn; Louise Koglin-Fideldy; Sue Mattson; Pat Medure; Michael Rourke; Ann Ryan; Rex Sala; Jeff Stampohar; Joe Stauffer; Elaine Yaggie.
Number of staff: 2 full-time professional; 1 full-time support.
EIN: 411761590

4575
Greycoach Foundation ✧
505 N. Highway 169, Ste. 595
Plymouth, MN 55441 (763) 417-2981
Contact: Sid Sehlin, Asst. Secy.
FAX: (763) 417-2984; E-mail: swaychoff@kochfamily.net

Established in 1974 in MN.
Donors: Barbara G. Koch; David A. Koch.
Foundation type: Independent foundation.
Financial data (yr. ended 12/31/05): Assets, $10,790,621 (M); expenditures, $1,164,016; qualifying distributions, $1,121,025; giving activities include $1,118,000 for 27 grants (high: $300,000; low: $2,500).
Purpose and activities: The foundation was established and is operated according to the basic truths and principles of the Roman Catholic church.
Fields of interest: Historic preservation/historical societies; Elementary school/education; Higher education; Theological school/education; Animal welfare; Girl scouts; Human services; Children/youth, services; Roman Catholic agencies & churches.
Type of support: General/operating support; Annual campaigns; Capital campaigns; Building/renovation; Endowments; Program development; Curriculum development; Program-related investments/loans.
Limitations: Giving primarily in the Twin Cities, MN, area. No grants to individuals.
Application information: Application form not required.
  Initial approach: Letter
  Copies of proposal: 1
  Deadline(s): None
Officers: David A. Koch, Pres.; Barbara G. Koch, V.P.; Paul M. Torgerson, Secy.
Trustee: Sidney R. Sehlin.
EIN: 237417559

4576
The Greystone Foundation
U.S. Trust Bldg.
730 2nd Ave. S., Ste. 1450
Minneapolis, MN 55402 (612) 752-1772

Established in 1948 in MN.
Donor: Members of the Paul A. Brooks family.
Foundation type: Independent foundation.
Financial data (yr. ended 12/31/05): Assets, $12,689,091 (M); gifts received, $136,528; expenditures, $2,130,513; qualifying distributions, $1,814,488; giving activities include $1,814,488 for 178 grants (high: $400,000; low: $250; average: $500–$50,000).
Purpose and activities: Giving for health and medical research, community funds, private secondary and higher education, and arts and cultural programs.
Fields of interest: Arts; Secondary school/education; Higher education; Hospitals (general); Health care; Medical research, institute; Human services; Federated giving programs.
Type of support: General/operating support; Continuing support; Annual campaigns; Building/renovation; Equipment; Land acquisition; Emergency funds; Program development; Conferences/seminars; Publication; Seed money; Research.
Limitations: Applications not accepted. Giving primarily in MN, with emphasis on the Twin Cities. No grants to individuals, or for endowment funds, matching gifts, scholarships, or fellowships; no loans.
Application information: Unsolicited requests for funds not accepted.
  Board meeting date(s): As required
Trustees: Michael P. Hollern; Katherine M. Leighton.
EIN: 416027765

Selected grants: The following grants were reported in 2004.
$403,000 to Abbott Northwestern Hospital, Minneapolis, MN. 2 grants: $3,000, $400,000
$275,000 to Project for Pride in Living, Minneapolis, MN. 2 grants: $75,000, $200,000
$55,000 to Cedars of Marin, Ross, CA.
$50,000 to Southside Family School, Minneapolis, MN. 2 grants: $25,000 each
$4,500 to Mayo Foundation, Rochester, MN.
$2,100 to Courage Center, Golden Valley, MN.
$1,500 to Chartwell School, Seaside, CA.

4577
Mary Livingston Griggs and Mary Griggs
Burke Foundation ◇
1400 5th St. Ctr.
55 E. 5th St.
St. Paul, MN 55101-1792
Contact: Marvin Pertzik, Secy.-Treas.

Established in 1966 in MN.
Donor: Mary L. Griggs†.
Foundation type: Independent foundation.
Financial data (yr. ended 6/30/05): Assets, $25,773,145 (M); expenditures, $1,685,777; qualifying distributions, $2,199,572; giving activities include $1,548,771 for 84 grants (high: $250,000; low: $450).
Purpose and activities: Giving primarily for arts and culture, and for social services.
Fields of interest: Museums (art); Performing arts; Performing arts, theater; Arts; Libraries (public); Animals/wildlife; Human services; Federated giving programs.
Type of support: General/operating support; Continuing support; Annual campaigns; Capital campaigns; Building/renovation; Endowments; Scholarship funds; Matching/challenge support.
Limitations: Giving primarily in St. Paul, MN, and New York, NY. No grants to individuals.
Application information: Application form not required.
  Initial approach: Letter
  Copies of proposal: 1
  Deadline(s): None
  Board meeting date(s): Semiannually
  Final notification: 10 days to 3 months
Officers: C.E. Bayliss Griggs, Pres.; Gale Lansing Davis, V.P.; Marvin Pertzik, Secy.-Treas.
Directors: Eleanor Briggs; Mary Griggs Burke.
EIN: 416052355
Selected grants: The following grants were reported in 2003.
$912,845 to Mary and Jackson Burke Foundation, Saint Paul, MN. 2 grants: $166,845 (For art acquisition), $746,000 (For general operating support)
$200,000 to Asia Society, New York, NY. For capital campaign.
$200,000 to International Crane Foundation, Baraboo, WI. For endowment.
$200,000 to Northland College, Ashland, WI. For science building.
$120,000 to Central Park Conservancy, New York, NY. For Shakespeare Garden.
$55,450 to Metropolitan Museum of Art, New York, NY. To purchase art.
$50,000 to Minneapolis Society of Fine Arts, Minneapolis, MN. For challenge grant.
$47,500 to Cable Natural History Museum, Cable, WI. For general operating support.

$40,000 to United Way, Greater Twin Cities, Minneapolis, MN. For general operating support.

4578
N. Bud and Beverly Grossman
Foundation ◇
(formerly N. Bud Grossman Foundation)
4670 Wells Fargo Ctr.
90 S. 7th St.
Minneapolis, MN 55402
Contact: Larry Waller

Incorporated in 1973 in MN as the Gelco Foundation; name changed to Boulevard Foundation in 1988; current name adopted in 1996.
Donors: N. Bud Grossman; BNG Management.
Foundation type: Independent foundation.
Financial data (yr. ended 12/31/04): Assets, $3,250,070 (M); gifts received, $1,141,130; expenditures, $1,670,934; qualifying distributions, $1,669,651; giving activities include $1,666,450 for 40 grants (high: $700,600; low: $35).
Purpose and activities: Giving primarily to the arts and Jewish organizations; funding also for a Lutheran church.
Fields of interest: Arts education; Performing arts, theater; Performing arts, orchestra (symphony); Arts; Higher education; Human services; Federated giving programs; Jewish federated giving programs; Protestant agencies & churches; Jewish agencies & temples.
Type of support: General/operating support; Annual campaigns; Program development.
Limitations: Giving primarily in MN, with emphasis on the Minneapolis-St. Paul area. No support for fraternal organizations or for religious organizations for sectarian purposes. No grants to individuals, or for scholarships, fellowships, fundraising events, medical research, or matching gifts; no loans.
Publications: Annual report.
Application information: Telephone solicitations and form letters will not be considered. Application form not required.
  Initial approach: Proposal
  Copies of proposal: 1
  Deadline(s): Apr. 15
  Board meeting date(s): Usually in Jan. and June
Officers: N. Bud Grossman, Pres. and Treas.; Beverly Grossman, V.P.
EIN: 237302799
Selected grants: The following grants were reported in 2004.
$700,600 to Minneapolis Institute of Arts, Minneapolis, MN. For general support.
$425,000 to Minneapolis Jewish Federation, Minnetonka, MN. For general support.
$121,500 to Minnesota Orchestral Association, Minneapolis, MN. For general support.
$102,500 to Childrens Theater Company and School, Minneapolis, MN. For general support.
$50,000 to Jewish Federation of Greater Phoenix, Phoenix, AZ. For general support.
$50,000 to University of Minnesota Foundation, Minneapolis, MN. For general support.
$47,400 to Adath Jeshurun Congregation, Minnetonka, MN. For general support.
$42,000 to Guthrie Theater, Minneapolis, MN. For general support.
$37,000 to Walker Art Center, Minneapolis, MN. For general support.
$27,000 to United Way, Greater Twin Cities, Minneapolis, MN. For general support.

4579
Grotto Foundation, Inc. ◇
5323 Lakeland Ave. N., Ste. 100
Minneapolis, MN 55429-3115 (763) 277-3434
Contact: Sarah Marquardt, Grants Mgr.
FAX: (763) 277-3444;
E-mail: info@grottofoundation.org; *URL:* http://
www.grottofoundation.org

Incorporated in 1964 in MN.
Donor: Louis W. Hill, Jr.‡.
Foundation type: Independent foundation.
Financial data (yr. ended 4/30/05): Assets,
$23,043,655 (M); gifts received, $12,000;
expenditures, $1,387,087; giving activities include
$840,121 for 63 grants (high: $100,000; low:
$2,500).
Purpose and activities: The mission of the Grotto
Foundation is to benefit society by improving the
education and the economic, physical and social
well-being of citizens with a special focus on families
and culturally diverse groups. The foundation is
further interested in increasing public understanding
of the American cultural heritage, the cultures of
nations and the individual's responsibility to fellow
human beings.
Fields of interest: Arts; Higher education; Human
services; Children/youth, services; Family services;
Civil rights; Minorities; Native Americans/American
Indians; LGBTQ; Immigrants/refugees;
Economically disadvantaged.
Type of support: General/operating support;
Program development.
Limitations: Giving primarily in MN. No support for
writing projects, non-operating foundations,
nonprofit organizations that re-grant, government
projects, or art programs. No grants to individuals,
or for capital or endowment funds or programs,
travel, operating budgets (except to aid in initiating
occasional programs), annual campaigns,
retroactive support, deficit financing, student
research, scholarships, fellowships, publications, or
conferences; no loans.
Publications: Annual report (including application
guidelines).
Application information: Minnesota Common Grant
Application Form accepted. See foundation Web site
for application guidelines. Application form not
required.
  Initial approach: 2- to 3-page proposal
  Copies of proposal: 1
  Deadline(s): Jan. 15, Mar. 15, July 15, and Nov.
  15
  Board meeting date(s): Apr., June, Oct., and Feb.
  Final notification: 1 week after board meeting
Officers and Directors:* Louis F. Hill,* Pres.;
Elizabeth Pegues-Smart,* 1st V.P.; Malcolm W.
McDonald,* 2nd V.P.; Ellis F. Bullock,* Secy. and
Exec. Dir.; Mary Manuel,* Treas.; Nancy Randall
Dana; Louis Shea Hill; Katherine E. Hill; Scott Hill;
Cris Stainbrook.
Number of staff: 3 full-time professional; 2 part-time
professional.
EIN: 416052604
Selected grants: The following grants were reported
in 2004.
$130,000 to University of Minnesota, Minneapolis,
  MN. 2 grants: $100,000 (For Louis W. Hill, Jr.
  fellowship), $30,000 to Department of American
  Indian Studies (For Minnesota Indigenous
  Language Symposium).
$55,000 to Waadookodaading, Hayward, WI. For
  salary of third grade teacher, the addition of

fourth-grade instruction, and curriculum
development.
$50,000 to Association on American Indian Affairs,
  Sisseton, SD. For implementation of a language
  nest for Dakota preschoolers, the Wakanheza kin
  Unspe (Teach the Children) project.
$45,000 to Fond du Lac Tribal and Community
  College, Cloquet, MN. For Ojibwe language skill
  development.
$30,000 to Na-Way-Ee, Minneapolis, MN. For
  continuation of its Native Language Program,
  now entitled the Positive Language environment
  program.
$25,000 to Alliance of Early Childhood
  Professionals, Minneapolis, MN. For Leaders
  Circle.
$20,000 to Circle Corporation, Minneapolis, MN.
  For new management to address financial
  issues.
$10,000 to Grand Excursion 2004, Saint Paul, MN.
  For full range of educational materials delivered
  to schools via Exploration Trunks.
$10,000 to Itasca Community College, Grand
  Rapids, MN. For Indigenous Language Quiz
  Bowls, as well as collaborative efforts related to
  secondary language instruction.

4580
Grundhofer Charitable Foundation ◇
800 Nicollet Mall, Ste. 2870
Minneapolis, MN 55402

Established in 1994 in MN.
Donors: John F. Grundhofer; Beverly J. Grundhofer.
Foundation type: Independent foundation.
Financial data (yr. ended 12/31/05): Assets,
$6,555,490 (M); expenditures, $605,875;
qualifying distributions, $486,753; giving activities
include $449,337 for 35 grants (high: $210,000;
low: $20).
Purpose and activities: Giving for Roman Catholic
agencies, education, eye disease research, higher
education, federated giving programs and the arts.
Fields of interest: Arts; Education; Health
organizations, association; Eye research; Federated
giving programs; Roman Catholic agencies &
churches.
Limitations: Applications not accepted. Giving
primarily in CA and MN. No grants to individuals.
Application information: Contributes only to
pre-selected organizations.
Officers and Directors:* John F. Grundhofer,* Pres.;
Beverly J. Grundhofer,* V.P. and Treas.; Lee E.
Johnson, Exec. Dir. and Secy.
EIN: 411805287

4581
E. W. Hallett Charitable Trust ◇
P.O. Box 39045
Edina, MN 55439-0045 (952) 946-1229
Contact: Margaret Poley

Established in 1984 in MN.
Foundation type: Independent foundation.
Financial data (yr. ended 11/30/05): Assets,
$15,471,097 (M); expenditures, $607,713;
qualifying distributions, $483,784; giving activities
include $415,805 for 14 grants (high: $130,000;
low: $1,800).

Fields of interest: Education; Hospitals (general);
Community development; Government/public
administration.
Limitations: Giving primarily in the Cuyuna Range
(Crosby, Ironton, Deerwood, etc.) MN, area. No
support for religious functions. No grants to
individuals.
Application information: The foundation uses the
Minnesota Common Grant Application Form.
Application form required.
  Initial approach: Letter
  Copies of proposal: 1
  Deadline(s): None
Officer: Margaret M. Poley, Exec. Dir.
Trustees: A.C. Jensen; N. Jean Rude; Paul
Schliesman; Kirk Springsted; U.S. Bank, N.A.
Number of staff: 1 part-time professional.
EIN: 416261160
Selected grants: The following grants were reported
in 2003.
$158,941 to Jessie F. Memorial Library, Crosby,
  MN. For operating support.
$122,293 to Hallett Community Center Foundation,
  Crosby, MN. 2 grants: $30,000 (For start-up fund
  for area Youth Teen Center), $92,293 (For
  general support).
$114,500 to Independent School District of
  Crosby-Ironton, Crosby, MN. 3 grants: $75,000
  (For new computers for teachers and staff),
  $34,500 (For scholarships), $5,000 (For
  satisfaction/attitude survey).
$40,000 to Cuyuna Range Medical Center, Crosby,
  MN. To purchase a care center van.
$25,000 to Advocates Against Domestic Abuse,
  Grand Rapids, MN. For operating support.
$25,000 to Crosby-Ironton Presbyterian Church,
  Crosby, MN. For operating support.
$5,000 to Minnesota Computers for Schools,
  Bayport, MN. For Minnesota High Technology
  Foundation.

4582
Jessie F. Hallett Charitable Trust ◇
(formerly Hallett Charitable Trust)
c/o U.S. Bank, N.A., Tax Svcs.
P.O. Box 64713
St. Paul, MN 55164-0713
Contact: Duane Faragen
Application address: c/o U.S. Bank, N.A., 155 1st
Ave. S.W., Rochester, MN 55902, tel.: (507)
285-7925

Established in 1984 in MN.
Donor: Jessie F. Hallett‡.
Foundation type: Independent foundation.
Financial data (yr. ended 11/30/05): Assets,
$10,485,372 (M); expenditures, $582,015;
qualifying distributions, $510,919; giving activities
include $450,064 for 16 grants (high: $67,097;
low: $250).
Purpose and activities: Giving for higher education
and Protestant agencies.
Fields of interest: Higher education; Theological
school/education; Protestant agencies & churches.
Limitations: Giving primarily in the Midwest, with
emphasis on MN. No grants to individuals.
Application information: Application form not
required.
  Initial approach: Letter
  Deadline(s): None
Officer: Paul Schliesman, Exec. Dir.

Trustees: A.C. Jensen; N. Jean Rude; Kirk Springsted; U.S. Bank, N.A.
EIN: 416211994
Selected grants: The following grants were reported in 2003.
$73,347 to Berea College, Berea, KY.
$73,347 to Bethel University, Saint Paul, MN.
$73,347 to Moody Bible Institute of Chicago, Chicago, IL.
$48,898 to Concordia College, Moorhead, MN.
$39,118 to McCormick Theological Seminary, Chicago, IL.
$24,449 to Christian Herald Association, New York, NY.
$24,449 to Luther College, Decorah, IA.
$24,449 to Presbyterian Church USA Foundation, Jeffersonville, IN.
$24,449 to Vision Loss Resources, Minneapolis, MN.
$7,707 to Crosby, City of, Crosby, MN. For Hallett Community Center.

4583
Hardenbergh Foundation
(formerly St. Croix Foundation)
c/o U.S. Bank, N.A.
101 E. 5th St., EP-MN-S14
St. Paul, MN 55101 (651) 466-8707
Contact: Jeffrey T. Peterson, Secy.

Established in 1950 in MN.
Donors: Ianthe B. Hardenbergh†; I. Hardenbergh Charitable Annuity Trust; Gabrielle Hardenbergh.
Foundation type: Independent foundation.
Financial data (yr. ended 12/31/05): Assets, $67,231,908 (M); gifts received, $18; expenditures, $2,928,580; qualifying distributions, $2,582,549; giving activities include $2,527,500 for 98 grants (high: $1,000,000; low: $1,000).
Purpose and activities: Giving for health organizations and hospitals, cultural programs, social service and youth agencies, and education; support also for churches.
Fields of interest: Arts; Education; Hospitals (general); Health care; Health organizations, association; Human services; Youth, services.
Type of support: General/operating support; Continuing support; Annual campaigns; Capital campaigns; Building/renovation; Equipment; Program development; Matching/challenge support.
Limitations: Giving limited to the Stillwater and St. Paul, MN, areas.
Application information: Common Grant Application Form accepted for full grant proposal. Application form not required.
   Initial approach: Letter
   Copies of proposal: 1
   Deadline(s): Nov. 1
   Board meeting date(s): Dec.
   Final notification: 6 weeks
Officers and Directors:* Robert S. Davis,* Pres.; Quentin O. Heimerman,* V.P.; Jeffrey T. Peterson,* Secy.; Edgerton Bronson,* Treas.; Jon A. Theobald.
EIN: 416011826

4584
Hersey Foundation
408 Saint Peter St., Rm. 434
St. Paul, MN 55102

Established about 1968 in MN.

Donor: William Hamm, Jr.†.
Foundation type: Independent foundation.
Financial data (yr. ended 12/31/05): Assets, $9,878,474 (M); expenditures, $498,040; qualifying distributions, $491,372; giving activities include $468,604 for 17 grants (high: $219,000; low: $1,000).
Purpose and activities: Giving primarily for higher education, human services and community development.
Fields of interest: Historic preservation/historical societies; Higher education; Children/youth, services; Community development; Public affairs; Christian agencies & churches.
Limitations: Applications not accepted. Giving primarily in FL, MN and NY. No grants to individuals.
Application information: Contributes only to pre-selected organizations.
Officers: Edward H. Hamm, Pres. and Treas.; Dean E. Busch, Secy.
EIN: 237001771

4585
Hiawatha Education Foundation ◇ ☆
360 Vila St.
Winona, MN 55987 (507) 453-5550
Contact: Patricia A. Knee, Managing Dir.
FAX: (507) 453-5553; E-mail: pknee@hefwinona.org

Established in 1987 in MN.
Donor: Robert A. Kierlin.
Foundation type: Independent foundation.
Financial data (yr. ended 12/31/05): Assets, $13,822,235 (M); gifts received, $650,716; expenditures, $614,800; qualifying distributions, $554,177; giving activities include $554,177 for grants.
Purpose and activities: Giving primarily for public and private tax-exempt Minnesota schools that are considering new/expanded preschool Montessori programs, particularly for children at-risk.
Fields of interest: Education, early childhood education.
Type of support: General/operating support; Scholarships—to individuals.
Limitations: Giving limited to MN.
Publications: Annual report.
Application information:
   Initial approach: Letter
   Copies of proposal: 1
   Deadline(s): June 1
   Board meeting date(s): As necessary
   Final notification: July 31
Directors: Laura Kierlin; Monique Kierlin; Robert A. Kierlin.
Number of staff: 1 full-time professional; 1 part-time professional.
EIN: 363537959
Selected grants: The following grants were reported in 2003.
$50,000 to University of Saint Thomas, Saint Paul, MN. For educational programs.
$25,000 to Schaeffer Academy, Rochester, MN. For educational programs.
$22,000 to Saint Marys University of Minnesota, Winona, MN. For educational programs.
$16,000 to Cotter High School, Winona, MN. For educational programs.

4586
Hillswood Foundation ◇ ☆
c/o James W. Emison
Cabriole Ctr.
9531 W. 78th St., Ste. 102
Eden Prairie, MN 55344

Established in 1999 in MN.
Donor: James W. Emison.
Foundation type: Independent foundation.
Financial data (yr. ended 12/31/05): Assets, $3,692,348 (M); gifts received, $35,792; expenditures, $628,597; qualifying distributions, $569,826; giving activities include $566,130 for 20 grants (high: $200,000; low: $100).
Fields of interest: Arts; Education; Human services; YM/YWCAs & YM/YWHAs.
Limitations: Applications not accepted. Giving primarily in IN and MN. No grants to individuals.
Application information: Contributes only to pre-selected organizations.
Officers: James W. Emison, Pres.; Jane B. Larson Emison, Secy.-Treas.
Directors: Elizabeth A. Emison; Thomas W. Emison; William A. Emison; Catherine Emison Stoick.
EIN: 411948564
Selected grants: The following grants were reported in 2005.
$128,965 to DePauw University, Greencastle, IN.
$25,000 to Boys and Girls Club of Valusia, Atlanta, GA.
$25,000 to Minneapolis Institute of Arts, Minneapolis, MN.
$10,000 to Indiana Historical Society, Indianapolis, IN.
$5,000 to Groves Academy, Saint Louis Park, MN.
$5,000 to KidsFirst Scholarship Fund of Minnesota, Minneapolis, MN.
$5,000 to Minnetonka Center for the Arts, Wayzata, MN.
$2,000 to Park Tudor School, Indianapolis, IN.
$500 to Madeline Island Music Camp, Minneapolis, MN.

4587
Homeownership Preservation Foundation ◇ ☆
8400 Normandale Lake Blvd., Ste. 250
Minneapolis, MN 55437-1059 (952) 857-8910
FAX: (952) 857-7535; E-mail: info@hpfonline.org;
URL: http://www.hpfonline.org/

Established in 2004 in MN.
Donor: Residential Funding Corp.
Foundation type: Independent foundation.
Financial data (yr. ended 12/31/05): Assets, $19,225,548 (M); expenditures, $1,456,857; qualifying distributions, $1,442,989; giving activities include $590,698 for 3 grants (high: $400,000; low: $90,698).
Purpose and activities: The foundation partners with local governments, other nonprofit organizations, borrowers and mortgage lenders/ servicers to deliver innovative homeownership preservation opportunities.
Fields of interest: Housing/shelter, owner/renter issues; Housing/shelter, services; Urban/ community development.
Type of support: General/operating support; Program development.
Limitations: Applications not accepted. Giving primarily for the benefit of U.S. citizens, including

military personnel overseas. No grants to individuals.

Application information: Contributes only to pre-selected organizations.

Officers: Michael Seats, Chair.; Walt Fricke, Pres. and Exec. Dir.; Jenneifer Bellini, Secy., Corp. Counsel, and Comm. Dir.; Nick Cucci, Treas.

Directors: William Apgar; Sharon Sayles Belton; Tom Jacob; Bruce Paradis.

EIN: 522403507

4588
Hormel Foods Corporation Charitable Trust ◇

1 Hormel Pl.
Austin, MN 55912

Established in 2003 in MN.

Donor: Hormel Foods Corp.

Foundation type: Company-sponsored foundation.

Financial data (yr. ended 12/31/03): Assets, $491,699 (M); gifts received, $1,570,000; expenditures, $1,080,858; qualifying distributions, $1,080,270; giving activities include $816,705 for 95 grants (high: $235,000; low: $50), and $263,565 for 201 employee matching gifts.

Purpose and activities: The foundation supports organizations involved with education, health, human services, and community development.

Fields of interest: Education; Health organizations, association; Human services; Community development.

Type of support: Employee matching gifts.

Limitations: Applications not accepted.

Application information: Contributes only to pre-selected organizations.

Officers: James A. Jorgenson, Pres.; Eric A. Brown, V.P.; Mahlon C. Schneider, Secy.; Michael J. McCoy, Treas.

Director: Julie H. Craven.

EIN: 010761416

4589
HRK Foundation

(formerly The MAHADH Foundation)
345 Saint Peter St., Ste. 1200
St. Paul, MN 55102
Contact: Kathleen Fluegel, Fdn. Dir.
FAX: (651) 298-0551;
E-mail: hrkadmin@hrkgroup.com; Toll-free tel.: (866) 342-5475; URL: http://www.hrkfoundation.org

Established in 1962 in MN.

Donors: Mary Andersen Hulings†; Albert D. Hulings†; Fred C. Andersen†; Katherine B. Andersen†; Katherine D. Rice; Katherine D.R. Hayes; Julia L. Hynnek; Frederick C. Kaemmer; Martha H. Kaemmer; Mary E. Rice; Mary H. Rice.

Foundation type: Independent foundation.

Financial data (yr. ended 12/31/05): Assets, $31,334,865 (M); gifts received, $1,448,941; expenditures, $2,915,867; qualifying distributions, $2,620,761; giving activities include $2,265,988 for 270 grants (high: $200,000; low: $100), and $20,000 for 3 employee matching gifts.

Purpose and activities: HRK Foundation is a family foundation defined and sustained by a sense of spirituality, creativity, and stewardship. Through quiet leadership and philanthropy, the board seeks to promote healthy families and communities, to enhance the quality of and access to education, and

to improve the fabric of society. Commitment and support for the arts, health, AIDS, community building, and education.

Fields of interest: Arts, single organization support; Arts, formal/general education; Arts, cultural/ethnic awareness; Child development, education; Education; Reproductive health, sexuality education; Health care, patient services; Health care; AIDS; Children/youth, services; Community development; AIDS, people with.

Type of support: General/operating support; Continuing support; Annual campaigns; Program development; Matching/challenge support.

Limitations: Giving primarily in MN, with emphasis on the metropolitan Twin Cities and St. Croix Valley areas, and in Ashland and Bayfield counties, WI. No grants to individuals, or for scholarships or fellowships; no loans.

Application information: Please see foundation Web site for application forms and guidelines. Application form required.

Initial approach: Telephone or e-mail to discuss request
Copies of proposal: 1
Deadline(s): Mar. 15 and Sept. 15
Board meeting date(s): Generally May., and Nov.
Final notification: 3 months

Officer and Directors:* Arthur W. Kaemmer, M.D.*, Chair.; James D. Hayes; Katherine D.R. Hayes; Eric M. Hynnek; Julia L. Hynnek; Frederick C. Kaemmer; Martha H. Kaemmer; Daniel Priebe; Mary H. Rice; Molly E. Rice; Katherine R. Tilney.

Number of staff: 1 full-time professional; 2 part-time professional.

EIN: 416020911

Selected grants: The following grants were reported in 2004.

$230,000 to Carleton College, Northfield, MN. 2 grants: $200,000, $30,000

$80,000 to Cathedral of Saint Paul, Saint Paul, MN.

$70,000 to VocalEssence, Minneapolis, MN.

$65,000 to Saint Paul Riverfront Corporation, Saint Paul, MN.

$50,000 to Guthrie Theater Foundation, Minneapolis, MN.

$50,000 to Lake Superior Big Top Chautauqua, Washburn, WI.

$15,000 to Saint Paul Area Council of Churches, Saint Paul, MN.

$5,000 to American Guild of Organists, New York, NY.

$2,000 to Independent School District No. 834, Stillwater, MN.

4590
The Hubbard Broadcasting Foundation ◇

(formerly The Hubbard Foundation)
3415 University Ave.
St. Paul, MN 55114 (651) 642-4305
Contact: Kathryn Hubbard Rominski, Exec. Dir.

Incorporated in 1958 in MN.

Donors: Hubbard Broadcasting, Inc.; KSTP, Inc.; Stanley E. Hubbard†.

Foundation type: Company-sponsored foundation.

Financial data (yr. ended 12/31/05): Assets, $20,293,637 (M); expenditures, $1,594,296; qualifying distributions, $1,279,985; giving activities include $1,165,496 for 251 grants (high: $200,000; low: $200).

Purpose and activities: The foundation supports organizations involved with arts and culture, K-12

and higher education, health, cancer research, human services, and Christianity.

Fields of interest: Museums; Performing arts; Arts; Elementary/secondary education; Higher education; Hospitals (general); Health care; Cancer research; Salvation Army; Children/youth, services; Human services; Christian agencies & churches.

Type of support: General/operating support; Capital campaigns.

Limitations: Giving primarily in MN. No grants to individuals.

Application information: Application form not required.

Initial approach: Proposal
Deadline(s): Nov. 30

Officers and Directors:* Stanley S. Hubbard,* Pres.; Karen H. Hubbard,* V.P.; Gerald D. Deeney, Secy.-Treas.; Kathryn Hubbard Rominski,* Exec. Dir.; Julia D. Coyte; Robert W. Hubbard; Stanley E. Hubbard; Virginia H. Morris.

EIN: 416022291

Selected grants: The following grants were reported in 2004.

$75,000 to Gillette Childrens Hospital Foundation, Saint Paul, MN.

$50,000 to Mounds Park Academy, Saint Paul, MN.

$20,000 to Ocean Reef Community Foundation, Key Largo, FL.

$10,000 to Minnesota Orchestra, Minneapolis, MN.

$10,000 to PACER Center, Minneapolis, MN.

$5,000 to Starkey Hearing Foundation, Eden Prairie, MN.

$2,500 to Alexandria Area Arts Association, Alexandria, MN.

$1,500 to Catching the Dream, Albuquerque, NM.

$1,000 to Child Haven, Las Vegas, NV.

$1,000 to United Way.

4591
Laura & Walter Hudson Foundation ◇ ☆

c/o Lowry Hill
90 S. 7th St., Ste. 5300
Minneapolis, MN 55402
Application address: Lilla A. Gidlow, Treas., 2526 Arcola Ln., Wayzata, MI, 55391

Established in 1961.

Foundation type: Independent foundation.

Financial data (yr. ended 12/31/05): Assets, $892,389 (M); expenditures, $330,539; qualifying distributions, $320,118; giving activities include $314,750 for 16 grants (high: $50,000; low: $250).

Purpose and activities: Preference given to MN institutions for education, health, and conservation.

Fields of interest: Arts; Higher education; Environment, natural resources; Hospitals (general); Cancer; Cancer research; Youth development, centers/clubs.

Type of support: General/operating support.

Limitations: Giving primarily in MN. No loans, or program-related investments.

Application information: The foundation is currently not accepting general applications for grants or scholarships.

Officers and Directors:* Laura A. Crosby,* Pres.; Laura Crosby Enebo, Secy.; Lilla A. Gidlow,* Treas.; Beth Emanuels; Jim Leslie, Jr.; Elise Kingman; Bill Patterson.

EIN: 416038634

Selected grants: The following grants were reported in 2005.

$40,000 to Minnesota Center for Photography, Minneapolis, MN.

$20,000 to Orono Alliance for Education, Long Lake, MN.

$17,500 to Alzheimers Association, Edina, MN.

$17,500 to Minneapolis Pathways, Minneapolis, MN.

$10,000 to Minnesota Public Radio, Saint Paul, MN.

$10,000 to Trust for Public Land, Saint Paul, MN.

$4,500 to Saint Alphonsus Foundation, Boise, ID.

4592
Huss Foundation

(formerly Alvin & Miriam Huss Foundation)
c/o A.J. Huss, Jr.
Park Towers
59 4th St. W., Apt. 23B
St. Paul, MN 55102-1636

Established in 1983 in WI.
Donor: Alvin J. Huss†.
Foundation type: Independent foundation.
Financial data (yr. ended 12/31/05): Assets, $12,677,331 (M); expenditures, $867,233; qualifying distributions, $796,192; giving activities include $792,000 for 36 grants (high: $100,000; low: $1,000).
Purpose and activities: To help make changes and break cycles of helplessness.
Fields of interest: Arts; Elementary school/ education; Higher education; Environment; Hospitals (general); Alcoholism; Human services; Aging, centers/services.
Type of support: General/operating support; Annual campaigns; Capital campaigns; Endowments; Research.
Limitations: Applications not accepted. Giving with an emphasis on the Midwest especially the Twin Cities, MN. No grants to individuals.
Application information: Contributes only to pre-selected organizations.
Board meeting date(s): As needed
Trustees: Alvin J. Huss, Jr.; Ruth S. Huss.
Number of staff: 1 part-time support.
EIN: 391474563

4593
Initiative Foundation ◇

(formerly Central Minnesota Initiative Fund)
405 1st St., S.E.
Little Falls, MN 56345 (320) 632-9255
Contact: Kathy Gaalswyk, Pres.
FAX: (320) 632-9258; E-mail: info@ifound.org; Additional tel: (877) 632-9255; Additional E-mail: Kgaalswyk@ifound.org; URL: http://www.ifound.org

Established in 1986 in MN.
Foundation type: Community foundation.
Financial data (yr. ended 6/30/04): Assets, $36,309,311 (L); gifts received, $3,264,564; expenditures, $3,118,067; giving activities include $725,403 for 149 grants (high: $50,000; low: $500), $44,455 for 57 grants to individuals (high: $2,000; low: $500), and $2,729,640 for 27 loans/ program-related investments (high: $250,000; low: $3,000).
Purpose and activities: The foundation awards grants and loans, pools resources, and creates partnerships to enhance the quality of life only in the 14-county area of central Minnesota. Primary areas of focus include strengthening children, youth, and families, preserving space, place and natural resources, promoting economic stability, embracing

diversity and reducing prejudice, increasing utilization of technology, and building capacity of nonprofit organizations.
Fields of interest: Environment, water pollution; Children/youth, services; Family services; Human services; Civil rights, race/intergroup relations; Community development, public/private ventures; Economic development; Nonprofit management; Community development.
Type of support: General/operating support; Program development; Seed money; Technical assistance; Program-related investments/loans; Scholarships—to individuals; Matching/challenge support.
Limitations: Giving limited to Benton, Cass, Chisago, Crow Wing, Isanti, Kanabec, Mille Lacs, Morrison, Pine, Sherburne, Stearns, Todd, Wadena, and Wright counties, MN. No support for religious programs, or arts or health. No grants to individuals (except for scholarships) or for continuing support, endowments, capital expenses, curriculum development, or video production.
Publications: Application guidelines; Annual report; Grants list; Informational brochure; Newsletter; Program policy statement.
Application information: Visit foundation Web site for application information. Contact John Kaliszewski, V.P., Economic Devel., for information concerning the foundation's business investment program. Application form required.
Initial approach: Complete online Letter of Inquiry for general grants
Deadline(s): Ongoing
Board meeting date(s): 4th Fri. of every month
Final notification: Within 90 days
Officers and Directors:* Patricia Spence,* Chair.; Warren Williams,* Vice-Chair.; Kathy Gaalswyk, Pres.; Curt Hanson, V.P., Donor Svcs.; John Kaliszewski, V.P., Economic Devel.; Karl Swamp, V.P., Community Initiatives; G. George Wallin, Ph.D.,* Secy.-Treas.; Barb Anderson; Barrett Colombo; Gloria Edin; Dave Gruenes; Janet Moran; William Scarince; John Schlagel; Mary Schwartz; Steve Shelley; Gene Waldorf.
Number of staff: 13 full-time professional; 1 part-time professional; 7 full-time support.
EIN: 363451562

4594
Jeffers Foundation ◇ ☆

P.O. Box 408
Wayzata, MN 55391

Established in 2005 in MN.
Foundation type: Operating foundation.
Financial data (yr. ended 12/31/05): Assets, $14,468,536 (M); gifts received, $8,351,832; expenditures, $377,355; qualifying distributions, $377,355; giving activities include $328,900 for 3 grants (high: $165,000; low: $3,414).
Fields of interest: Elementary/secondary education.
Limitations: Applications not accepted. Giving primarily in MN. No grants to individuals.
Application information: Unsolicited requests for funds not accepted.
Officers and Directors:* Paul W. Oberg,* C.E.O. and Treas.; Margaret A. T. Cronin,* Exec. Dir.; Darwin Fosse; James W. Krause; Fergus W. Woolley.
EIN: 202601947

4595
Jerome Foundation ▼

400 Sibley St., Ste. 125
St. Paul, MN 55101-1928 (651) 224-9431
Contact: Cynthia A. Gehrig, Pres.
FAX: (651) 224-3439; E-mail: info@jeromefdn.org; Toll-free tel.: (800) 995-3766 (MN and New York City only); URL: http://www.jeromefdn.org

Incorporated in 1964 in MN.
Donor: J. Jerome Hill†.
Foundation type: Independent foundation.
Financial data (yr. ended 4/30/06): Assets, $90,718,745 (M); gifts received, $57,500; expenditures, $4,599,655; qualifying distributions, $3,822,462; giving activities include $2,573,149 for 130 grants (high: $117,000; low: $750; average: $8,000–$80,000), $389,425 for 41 grants to individuals (high: $21,500; low: $1,152; average: $1,000–$30,000), and $158,767 for 3 foundation-administered programs.
Purpose and activities: Support for arts programs only, including dance, media arts, literature, music, theater, performance art, visual arts and arts criticism. The foundation is concerned primarily with providing financial assistance to emerging creative artists of promise, including choreographers, media artists, composers, literary and visual artists, playwrights, and multidisciplinary creators.
Fields of interest: Media/communications; Visual arts; Performing arts; Performing arts, dance; Performing arts, theater; Performing arts, music; Literature; Arts.
Type of support: General/operating support; Continuing support; Program development; Publication; Seed money; Fellowships; Research; Technical assistance; Program-related investments/loans; Grants to individuals.
Limitations: Giving limited to MN and New York, NY. No support for educational programs in the arts and humanities. No grants to individuals (except for Film and Video program, and Travel and Study Grant program) or for undergraduate or graduate student research projects, capital or endowment funds, equipment, scholarships, or matching gifts.
Publications: Application guidelines; Financial statement; Grants list; Informational brochure (including application guidelines).
Application information: Film and video artists and Travel and Study applications should apply as individuals directly to the foundation office in St. Paul, MN. Application form not required.
Initial approach: Letter or proposal, e-mail or telephone
Copies of proposal: 1
Deadline(s): See Web site
Board meeting date(s): 5 times per year
Final notification: 4 months
Officers and Directors:* Jessica Hagedorn, Chair.; Cynthia A. Gehrig, Pres.; Vickie Benson, V.P.; Libby Larsen,* Secy.; W. Andrew Boss, Tres.; Laurie Carlos; Seitu Jones*; Catherine Jordan; Cynthia Mayeda.
Number of staff: 3 full-time professional; 3 full-time support.
EIN: 416035163
Selected grants: The following grants were reported in 2005.
$234,000 to American Composers Forum, Saint Paul, MN. For Composers Commissioning Program and pilot program Subito.
$80,000 to New Dramatists, New York, NY. For Composer-Librettist Studio and new works development.

$77,000 to Franklin Furnace Archive, New York, NY. For Fund for Performance Art and The Future of the Present.

$65,000 to Forecast Public Artworks, Saint Paul, MN. For Public Art Affairs Program.

$57,000 to Red Eye Collaboration, Minneapolis, MN. For Isolated Acts and Works-in-Progress Series.

$55,000 to Danspace Project, New York, NY. For commissions for new choreographers.

$54,000 to Springboard for the Arts, Saint Paul, MN. For Artists Services Program.

$52,000 to Northern Clay Center, Minneapolis, MN. For Artists Project Grants Program.

$50,000 to Zenon Dance Company and School, Minneapolis, MN. For commissions of new works by emerging choreographers.

$21,000 to Southern Theater Foundation, Minneapolis, MN. For new work by Hijack.

4596
The Jostens Foundation, Inc. ✧
5501 American Blvd. W.
Minneapolis, MN 55437 (952) 830-3235
Contact: Mary Klimek, Dir. and Admin.
E-mail: foundation@jostens.com; URL: http://www.jostens.com/company/community/index.asp

Established in 1976 in MN.
Donor: Jostens, Inc.
Foundation type: Company-sponsored foundation.
Financial data (yr. ended 12/31/04): Assets, $72,651 (M); gifts received, $500,000; expenditures, $491,302; qualifying distributions, $489,427; giving activities include $479,427 for 469+ grants (high: $45,000).
Purpose and activities: The foundation supports organizations involved with education and youth development.
Fields of interest: Elementary/secondary education; Higher education; Education; Youth development.
Type of support: Employee volunteer services; Program development; Employee matching gifts; Employee-related scholarships; In-kind gifts.
Limitations: Giving primarily in areas of company operations. No support for schools, school districts, or school foundations, organizations involved with highly political or controversial issues, religious organizations, or fraternal, veterans', or professional organizations. No grants to individuals (except for employee-related scholarships), or for personal needs, political campaigns or political lobbying activities, benefit fundraising events or tickets to fundraisers, recognition or testimonial events, disease-specific fundraising campaigns, athletic scholarships or activities, advertising, endowments, or capital campaigns.
Publications: Application guidelines; Informational brochure (including application guidelines).
Application information: Requests may be submitted using the Minnesota Common Grant Form. Application form not required.
  Initial approach: Proposal
  Copies of proposal: 1
  Deadline(s): Mar. 9, June 8, Sept. 7, and Dec. 7
  Board meeting date(s): Mar., June, Sept., and Dec.
  Final notification: Within 1 month of board meetings
Officers: Bill Schlukebier, Pres.; Bill Sheehan, Secy.; Ron Somerville, Treas.
EIN: 411280587

Selected grants: The following grants were reported in 2003.

$45,000 to United Way, Greater Twin Cities, Minneapolis, MN.

$4,500 to YMCA of Metropolitan Minneapolis, Minneapolis, MN.

$4,000 to Girl Scouts of the U.S.A., Minneapolis, MN.

$3,500 to Safe Haven Shelter for Youth, Prior Lake, MN.

$3,000 to New Hope, Attleboro, MA.

$3,000 to Sounds of Hope, Saint Paul, MN.

$2,500 to Greater Minneapolis Crisis Nursery, Golden Valley, MN.

$2,000 to Boys and Girls Club of Elk River, Elk River, MN.

$2,000 to Bridge for Runaway Youth, Minneapolis, MN.

$1,000 to Big Brothers Big Sisters of the Greater Twin Cities, Saint Paul, MN.

4597
Margaret H. and James E. Kelley Foundation, Inc.
408 Saint Peter St., Ste. 425
St. Paul, MN 55102-1187 (651) 222-7463
Contact: Timothy J. Dwyer, Treas.

Established in 1960 in MN.
Foundation type: Independent foundation.
Financial data (yr. ended 11/30/05): Assets, $12,628,100 (M); expenditures, $695,081; qualifying distributions, $640,000; giving activities include $640,000 for grants.
Purpose and activities: Giving primarily for human rights, medical disciplines, family planning and social services; support also for higher education and a community fund.
Fields of interest: Arts; Law school/education; Hospitals (specialty); Reproductive health, family planning; Health care; Human services; Children/youth, services; International affairs; Civil liberties, advocacy; Federated giving programs; Disabilities, people with.
Type of support: General/operating support; Continuing support; Annual campaigns; Capital campaigns; Equipment; Program development; Professorships; Scholarship funds; Program-related investments/loans.
Limitations: Giving primarily in MN; some funding nationally. No grants to individuals.
Publications: Annual report (including application guidelines); Grants list.
Application information: Application form not required.
  Initial approach: Letter
  Copies of proposal: 1
  Deadline(s): Oct. 1
  Board meeting date(s): Varies
Officers and Directors:* James C. O'Neill,* Pres. and Secy.; Timothy J. Dwyer, Treas.; Hampton K. ONeill; Mrs. Hampton K. O'Neill; James W. O'Neill; Mrs. James W. O'Neill; Kelley O'Neill; Mrs. Kelley O'Neill.
Number of staff: 2 part-time professional.
EIN: 416017973

Selected grants: The following grants were reported in 2005.

$100,000 to Hamm Memorial Psychiatric Clinic, Saint Paul, MN.

$35,000 to William Mitchell College of Law, Saint Paul, MN.

$20,000 to Minnesota Medical Foundation, Minneapolis, MN.

$15,000 to International Rescue Committee, New York, NY.

$15,000 to Saint Paul Academy and Summit School, Saint Paul, MN.

$10,000 to Center for Reproductive Rights, New York, NY.

$8,000 to Saint Johns University, Collegeville, MN.

$7,500 to Bridge for Runaway Youth, Minneapolis, MN.

$7,500 to Childrens Hospitals and Clinics Foundation, Roseville, MN.

$7,500 to Oxfam America, Boston, MA.

4598
The Knowlton Foundation ✧ ☆
301 N. Main St.
Austin, MN 55912-3498

Established in 1997 in MN.
Donors: Nancy V. Knowlton; Richard L. Knowlton.
Foundation type: Independent foundation.
Financial data (yr. ended 12/31/05): Assets, $2,120,786 (M); gifts received, $13,200; expenditures, $438,403; qualifying distributions, $434,650; giving activities include $434,650 for grants.
Purpose and activities: Giving to human services.
Fields of interest: Education, public education; Higher education, university; Hospitals (general); Medical research; Human services; YM/YWCAs & YM/YWHAs; Federated giving programs; Christian agencies & churches.
Type of support: General/operating support.
Limitations: Applications not accepted. Giving primarily in Austin, MN. No grants to individuals.
Application information: Contributes only to pre-selected organizations.
Officers: Richard L. Knowlton, Pres. and Treas.; Nancy V. Knowlton, V.P. and Secy.
EIN: 411877113

Selected grants: The following grants were reported in 2005.

$5,500 to American Heart Association, Dallas, TX.

$5,000 to McCallum Theater, Palm Desert, CA.

$5,000 to United Way of Mower County, Austin, MN.

$3,000 to Salvation Army.

$2,000 to Vail Valley Medical Center Foundation, Vail, CO.

$500 to Invest in Kids, Denver, CO.

$300 to YMCA.

$200 to Planned Parenthood Federation of America, New York, NY.

$100 to Alzheimers Association, Chicago, IL.

$100 to American Cancer Society, Atlanta, GA.

4599
Kopp Family Foundation
(formerly Caring and Sharing Foundation, Inc.)
7701 France Ave. S., Ste. 500
Edina, MN 55435-3201 (952) 841-0438
Contact: Lindsey Lang, Admin.
FAX: (952) 841-0460;
E-mail: foundation@koppinvestments.com

Established in 1986 in MN.
Donors: LeRoy Kopp; Barbara Kopp.
Foundation type: Independent foundation.
Financial data (yr. ended 12/31/05): Assets, $38,352,000 (M); expenditures, $1,677,848;

giving activities include $1,676,740 for 482 grants (high: $50,000; low: $100).

Purpose and activities: Giving primarily for education and human services.

Fields of interest: Elementary/secondary education; Human services; Children/youth, services; Roman Catholic agencies & churches; Aging; Disabilities, people with.

Type of support: General/operating support; Annual campaigns; Capital campaigns; Emergency funds; Scholarship funds; Matching/challenge support.

Limitations: Giving primarily in MN. No grants to individuals.

Publications: Annual report (including application guidelines).

Application information: The foundation accepts the Minnesota Common Grant Application Form. Application form required.

  Initial approach: Letter of inquiry from a new organization
  Copies of proposal: 1
  Deadline(s): None
  Board meeting date(s): Every other month
  Final notification: Within 2 months

Directors: James Berbee; Barbara Kopp; Kristin Kopp; LeRoy Kopp.

Number of staff: 1 full-time professional.

EIN: 363485918

Selected grants: The following grants were reported in 2004.

$100,000 to Sisters of Saint Joseph of Carondelet Ministries Foundation, Saint Paul, MN.

$20,000 to Metropolitan State University, Saint Paul, MN.

$16,500 to Inver Hills Community College, Inver Grove Heights, MN.

$10,000 to Concordia University, Saint Paul, MN.

$5,000 to Eden Prairie High School, Eden Prairie, MN.

$2,000 to Owatonna High School, Owatonna, MN.

$1,000 to Childrens Chance, Hopkins, MN.

$1,000 to Learning Center for Homeless Families, Minneapolis, MN.

$500 to Hope House of Saint Croix Valley, Stillwater, MN.

$500 to Wayside House, Saint Louis Park, MN.

4600
Ida C. Koran Trust ✧

c/o U.S. Bank, N.A.
P.O. Box 64713
St. Paul, MN 55164-0704

Established around 1992.

Donor: Ida Koran‡.

Foundation type: Independent foundation.

Financial data (yr. ended 12/31/04): Assets, $39,764,035 (M); expenditures, $1,983,499; qualifying distributions, $2,202,671; giving activities include $32,000 for 1 grant, $1,635,266 for grants to individuals, and $339,654 for loans to individuals.

Fields of interest: Foundations (private grantmaking); Roman Catholic agencies & churches.

Type of support: General/operating support; Scholarship funds; Grants to individuals.

Limitations: Applications not accepted. Giving primarily in MN.

Application information: The scholarship award program has been discontinued. Only Ecolab, Inc., employees are eligible for grant awards.

Trustees: S. Bartley Osborn; Richard F. Rintelmann; U.S. Bank, N.A.

EIN: 416124022

Selected grants: The following grants were reported in 2003.

$1,323,700 to Scholarship America, Saint Peter, MN.

$217,614 to Ecolabs Foundation.

$125,000 to Archdiocese of Saint Paul and Minneapolis, Saint Paul, MN. For general support.

4601
Sharon and Joel Labovitz Foundation ✧ ☆

4750 London Rd.
Duluth, MN 55804

Established in 1986 in MN.

Donors: Sharon Labovitz; Joel Labovitz.

Foundation type: Independent foundation.

Financial data (yr. ended 12/31/05): Assets, $405,235 (M); gifts received, $419,120; expenditures, $408,545; qualifying distributions, $408,520; giving activities include $408,520 for grants.

Fields of interest: Performing arts, orchestra (symphony); Higher education; Federated giving programs; Christian agencies & churches.

Limitations: Applications not accepted. Giving primarily in La Jolla, CA and Duluth, MN. No grants to individuals.

Application information: Contributes only to pre-selected organizations.

Officers and Directors:* Sharon Labovitz,* Pres.; Joel Labovitz,* Secy.-Treas.

EIN: 363460105

Selected grants: The following grants were reported in 2003.

$200,000 to University of Minnesota, Duluth, MN. For capital support.

$3,500 to Duluth Superior Symphony Orchestra, Duluth, MN. For general support.

$1,000 to Congregational Church of La Jolla, La Jolla, CA. For general support.

$1,000 to Duluth Library Foundation, Duluth, MN. For general support.

$550 to Museum of Contemporary Art San Diego, La Jolla, CA. For general support.

4602
Land O'Lakes Foundation ✧

P.O. Box 64150
St. Paul, MN 55164-0150 (651) 481-2212
Contact for California Regions Grant Prog. and Mid-Atlantic Grants Prog.: Martha Atkins-Sakry, Exec. Asst., tel.: (651) 481-2470,
E-mail: mlatkins-sakry@landolakes.com;
URL: http://www.foundation.landolakes.com/

Established in 1996 in MN.

Donor: Land O'Lakes, Inc.

Foundation type: Company-sponsored foundation.

Financial data (yr. ended 12/31/05): Assets, $3,121,719 (M); gifts received, $1,250,000; expenditures, $1,207,918; qualifying distributions, $1,167,567; giving activities include $1,005,183 for 782 grants (high: $115,500).

Purpose and activities: The foundation supports organizations involved with arts and culture, K-12 education, soil and water preservation, hunger, human services, community development, and rural

leadership and awards graduate scholarships to graduate students studying the dairy sciences.

Fields of interest: Arts; Elementary/secondary education; Agriculture, soil/water issues; Food services; Youth development, services; Human services; Rural development; Community development; Leadership development.

Type of support: General/operating support; Capital campaigns; Building/renovation; Equipment; Seed money; Employee volunteer services; Employee matching gifts; Scholarships—to individuals; Matching/challenge support.

Limitations: Giving on a national basis in areas of company operations; giving also to statewide, regional, and national organizations. No support for lobbying or political organizations or religious organizations not of direct benefit to the entire community or veterans', fraternal, or labor organizations. No grants to individuals (except for scholarships), or for fundraising events, advertising, higher education capital campaigns or endowments, travel, racing or sports sponsorships, or disease or medical research or treatment.

Publications: Application guidelines; Annual report; Informational brochure (including application guidelines).

Application information: Community Grants have been allocated for 2006. Application form required.

  Initial approach: Contact Land O'Lakes dairy farmer for application form for California Regions Grants and Mid-Atlantic Grants
  Copies of proposal: 1
  Board meeting date(s): Feb., June, and Oct.
  Final notification: 2 to 4 weeks for California Regions Grants and Mid-Atlantic Grants

Officers and Directors:* Lawrence Hooks,* Treas.; Lydia Botham,* Exec. Dir.

Number of staff: 1 full-time professional; 1 full-time support.

EIN: 411864977

Selected grants: The following grants were reported in 2004.

$5,000 to Four-H Foundation, California, Davis, CA. For Western Regional leaders Forum.

$5,000 to Peta Wakan Tipi, Sacred Fire Lodge, Saint Paul, MN. For capital campaign.

$2,500 to North Dakota Museum of Art, Grand Forks, ND. For Lewis and Clark exhibition.

$2,500 to Northwest Cooperative Development Center, Olympia, WA. For operating support.

4603
Larson Foundation ☆

c/o Kenneth R. Larson
3060 Centerville Rd.
Little Canada, MN 55117-1100

Established in 1988 in MN.

Donors: Kenneth R. Larson; Slumberland, Inc.

Foundation type: Independent foundation.

Financial data (yr. ended 12/31/05): Assets, $1,301,665 (M); expenditures, $419,132; qualifying distributions, $418,000; giving activities include $418,000 for 13 grants (high: $250,000; low: $1,300).

Purpose and activities: Emphasis on Christian education and agencies.

Fields of interest: Christian agencies & churches.

Type of support: General/operating support; Fellowships.

Limitations: Applications not accepted. Giving on a national basis.

Application information: Unsolicited requests for funds not accepted.
Officers: Kenneth R. Larson, Pres. and Secy.; Barbara J. Larson, V.P.
EIN: 411605601
Selected grants: The following grants were reported in 2003.
$40,000 to Evangelical Free Church of America, Bloomington, MN. For general support.
$25,000 to Minnehaha Academy, Minneapolis, MN. For general support.
$25,000 to Northwestern College, Saint Paul, MN. For general support.
$17,000 to Mission America Coalition, Saint Paul, MN. For general support.
$15,000 to Jesus Film Project, San Clemente, CA. For general support.
$13,900 to American Leprosy Missions, Greenville, SC. For general support.
$12,000 to Healing Waters, Golden, CO. For general support.
$10,000 to House of Mercy. For general support.
$10,000 to Navigators, The, Colorado Springs, CO. For general support.
$10,000 to Wycliffe Associates, Orange, CA. For general support.

4604
The Leonard Street and Deinard Foundation
c/o Jill Weber
150 S. 5th St., Ste. 2300
Minneapolis, MN 55402
URL: http://www.leonard.com/about/foundation.aspx

Established in 1982 in MN.
Donor: Shareholders of Leonard Street and Deinard.
Foundation type: Independent foundation.
Financial data (yr. ended 12/31/05): Assets, $72,691 (M); gifts received, $388,218; expenditures, $388,641; qualifying distributions, $388,641; giving activities include $388,641 for 118 grants (high: $57,000; low: $100).
Purpose and activities: Support for major community institutions and legal organizations providing legal aid.
Fields of interest: Arts; Legal services; Crime/law enforcement; Community development.
Type of support: General/operating support; Annual campaigns; Program-related investments/loans.
Limitations: Applications not accepted. Giving primarily in IA, MN, ND, SD, and WI. No grants to individuals.
Application information: Contributes only to pre-selected organizations.
Director: Jill Weber.
EIN: 411446976
Selected grants: The following grants were reported in 2005.
$57,000 to First Call for Help of the United Way of Minneapolis Area, Minneapolis, MN.
$40,000 to William Mitchell College of Law, Saint Paul, MN.
$28,500 to Fund for the Legal Aid Society, Minneapolis, MN.
$12,500 to Minnesota Medical Foundation, Minneapolis, MN.
$5,000 to Southern Minnesota Regional Legal Services, Saint Paul, MN.
$3,000 to Walker Art Center, Minneapolis, MN.
$2,500 to Legal Rights Center, Minneapolis, MN.

$1,250 to Gustavus Adolphus College, Saint Peter, MN.
$1,000 to Park Square Theater, Saint Paul, MN.
$1,000 to Vietnamese Community of Minnesota, Minneapolis, MN.

4605
Steven C. Leuthold Family Foundation ◇
100 N. 6th St., Ste. 412A
Minneapolis, MN 55403
Application address: c/o Steven C. Leuthold, 412A Butler Sq., Minneapolis, MN 55403, tel. (612) 332-1567

Established in 1990 in MN.
Donor: Steven C. Leuthold.
Foundation type: Independent foundation.
Financial data (yr. ended 12/31/05): Assets, $21,760,325 (M); gifts received, $2,315,246; expenditures, $1,252,151; qualifying distributions, $1,050,500; giving activities include $1,004,000 for 123 grants (high: $63,000; low: $1,000).
Purpose and activities: Giving primarily for historical societies, education, nature conservation, animal welfare, children's and social services, and federated giving programs.
Fields of interest: Historic preservation/historical societies; Education; Environment, natural resources; Animal welfare; Hospitals (general); Human services; Salvation Army; Children/youth, services; Federated giving programs.
Limitations: Giving primarily in Washington, DC, ID, and MN, with emphasis on Minneapolis; some funding nationally.
Application information:
  Initial approach: Letter
  Deadline(s): None
Directors: Linda Leuthold Donerkiel; Kurt Leuthold; Michael Leuthold; Russell Leuthold; Steven C. Leuthold.
EIN: 411680986

4606
Richard Coyle Lilly Foundation ◇
c/o U.S. Bank, N.A.
101 E. 5th St., (EP-MN-514)
St. Paul, MN 55101
Contact: Jeffrey T. Peterson, Secy.

Incorporated in 1941 in MN.
Donor: Richard C. Lilly‡.
Foundation type: Independent foundation.
Financial data (yr. ended 12/31/05): Assets, $14,947,743 (M); expenditures, $747,845; qualifying distributions, $569,888; giving activities include $533,000 for 84 grants (high: $40,000; low: $500; average: $1,000–$25,000).
Purpose and activities: Emphasis on higher and environmental education, culture, youth, and social services.
Fields of interest: Arts; Higher education; Environment, natural resources; Environment; Human services; Children/youth, services.
Type of support: General/operating support; Continuing support; Annual campaigns; Building/renovation; Equipment; Land acquisition; Endowments; Program development; Publication; Seed money; Research; Matching/challenge support.

Limitations: Applications not accepted. Giving primarily in St. Paul, MN. No grants to individuals, or for fellowships or scholarships; no loans.
Application information: Unsolicited requests for funds not accepted.
  Board meeting date(s): Dec.
Officers: David M. Lilly, Pres.; Susanne Lilly Hutcheson, V.P.; David M. Lilly, Jr., V.P.; Jeffrey T. Peterson, Secy.; Bruce A. Lilly, Treas.
EIN: 416038717

4607
The Lyman Lumber Company Foundation ◇
c/o Lyman Lumber Co.
300 Morse Ave.
Excelsior, MN 55331

Established in 1997 in MN.
Donor: Lyman Lumber Co.
Foundation type: Company-sponsored foundation.
Financial data (yr. ended 12/31/05): Assets, $1,525,890 (M); gifts received, $867,430; expenditures, $547,674; qualifying distributions, $547,621; giving activities include $547,596 for grants.
Purpose and activities: The foundation supports organizations involved with housing and human services.
Fields of interest: Housing/shelter; Human services.
Limitations: Applications not accepted. Giving primarily in MN and WI. No grants to individuals.
Application information: Contributes only to pre-selected organizations.
Officers: Thomas P. Lowe, Pres.; John D. Gilpin, V.P.; James E. Hurd, V.P.; Jan M. Knott, Secy.; Brian C. Balcer, Treas.
Directors: Walter L. Bush, Jr.; Lyman Webb.
EIN: 411889416
Selected grants: The following grants were reported in 2004.
$100,000 to Habitat for Humanity, Twin Cities, Minneapolis, MN.
$100,000 to United Way, Greater Twin Cities, Minneapolis, MN.
$25,000 to Interfaith Outreach and Community Partners, Wayzata, MN.
$15,000 to Minneapolis Area Emergency Fund, Minneapolis, MN.
$10,000 to Dunwoody College of Technology, Minneapolis, MN.
$10,000 to Sharing and Caring Hands, Minneapolis, MN.
$10,000 to University of Minnesota Foundation, Minneapolis, MN.
$9,884 to Project for Pride in Living, Minneapolis, MN.
$2,500 to Episcopal Community Services, Minneapolis, MN.
$2,000 to Lawrence University, Appleton, WI.

4608
Maas Foundation ◇
4908 Lincoln Dr.
Edina, MN 55436

Established in 1986 in SD.
Donor: George E. Maas.
Foundation type: Independent foundation.

Financial data (yr. ended 12/31/05): Assets, $6,856,230 (M); expenditures, $595,890; qualifying distributions, $511,000; giving activities include $511,000 for 16 grants (high: $200,000; low: $1,000).

Fields of interest: Elementary/secondary education; Higher education; Health care; Human services; Roman Catholic agencies & churches.

Type of support: Annual campaigns; Building/renovation; Scholarship funds.

Limitations: Applications not accepted. Giving primarily in MN. No grants to individuals.

Application information: Contributes only to pre-selected organizations.

Officer and Trustees:* George E. Maas,* Pres.; Thomas K. Berg; Patricia A. Maas.

EIN: 460393558

Selected grants: The following grants were reported in 2003.

$340,000 to Spare Key Foundation, South Saint Paul, MN. For annual fund.

$330,000 to Scripps Foundation for Medicine and Science, San Diego, CA. For building fund.

$325,000 to N. C. Little Memorial Hospice, Edina, MN. For annual fund.

$320,000 to Watertown Hockey Association, Watertown, SD. For building fund.

$315,000 to Academy of Holy Angels, New Orleans, LA. For annual fund.

$305,000 to Benilde-Saint Margarets High School, Saint Louis Park, MN. For annual fund.

$295,000 to Archdiocese of Saint Paul and Minneapolis, Saint Paul, MN. For Growing in Faith Camp.

$95,000 to College of Saint Benedict, Saint Joseph, MN. For scholarship fund.

$70,000 to Risen Christ Catholic School, Minneapolis, MN. For annual fund.

$65,000 to NET Ministries, West Saint Paul, MN. For annual fund.

4609
Mahon Foundation ✧ ☆

c/o Peter M. Mahon, Jr.
3800 American Blvd. W., Ste. 990
Minneapolis, MN 55431

Established in 2005 in MN.

Donors: Peter M. Mahon, Jr.; Deborah P. Mahon.

Foundation type: Operating foundation.

Financial data (yr. ended 12/31/05): Assets, $1,713,841 (M); gifts received, $2,296,453; expenditures, $635,311; qualifying distributions, $634,800; giving activities include $634,800 for 21 grants (high: $298,000; low: $200).

Purpose and activities: Giving primarily for Protestant organizations and ministries, including a Baptist church.

Fields of interest: Human services; Protestant agencies & churches.

Limitations: Applications not accepted. Giving primarily in MN; some funding nationally. No grants to individuals.

Application information: Contributes only to pre-selected organizations.

Trustees: Deborah P. Mahon; Peter M. Mahon, Jr.

EIN: 416542523

4610
Manitou Fund ✧ ☆

c/o Space Center, Inc.
2501 Rosegate
St. Paul, MN 55113-2717 (651) 604-4200
Contact: Malcolm McDonald, Tr.

Established in 1966 in MN.

Donor: Donald G. McNeely.

Foundation type: Independent foundation.

Financial data (yr. ended 12/31/05): Assets, $12,509,025 (M); gifts received, $9,644,400; expenditures, $1,344,122; qualifying distributions, $1,061,035; giving activities include $1,061,035 for grants.

Fields of interest: Education; Community development, neighborhood development; Religion.

Limitations: Giving primarily in CA and MN. No grants to individuals.

Application information:

Initial approach: Letter
Deadline(s): None

Officers and Trustees:* Donald G. McNeely,* Chair.; J. Michael Miles,* Secy.; Paul Puerzer, Treas.; Cheryl Granlund; Malcolm McDonald; Gregory McNeely; Kevin McNeely; Nora McNeely; Mike Urbanos.

EIN: 416055113

Selected grants: The following grants were reported in 2005.

$26,000 to Catholic Charities, MN.

$10,000 to American Composers Forum, Saint Paul, MN.

$6,000 to Community Foundation for Monterey County, Monterey, CA.

$5,000 to Minneapolis Institute of Arts, Minneapolis, MN.

$5,000 to Minnesota Historical Society, Saint Paul, MN.

$5,000 to Santa Catalina School, Monterey, CA.

$3,500 to Claremont McKenna College, Claremont, CA.

$2,500 to Yale University, New Haven, CT.

$1,000 to Walker Art Center, Minneapolis, MN.

$500 to YMCA of Greater Saint Paul, Saint Paul, MN.

4611
Ted and Roberta Mann Foundation of Minnesota

19550 Cedarhurst St.
Wayzata, MN 55391-3010 (952) 475-2000
Contact: Roberta Mann, Pres.

Established in 2002 in MN.

Foundation type: Independent foundation.

Financial data (yr. ended 12/31/04): Assets, $42,361,907 (M); gifts received, $68,500; expenditures, $1,450,785; qualifying distributions, $1,775,795; giving activities include $1,775,795 for 110+ grants (high: $350,000).

Purpose and activities: The ongoing mission of the foundation is to make a difference principally in the areas of the arts, education, health, religion and social services.

Fields of interest: Arts; Education; Health care; Human services; Religion.

Type of support: Equipment; Scholarship funds.

Limitations: Giving primarily in Minneapolis and St. Paul, MN, and select areas. No grants to individuals or for capital and political campaigns.

Application information: Applicants must use the Minnesota Common Grant Form, available on

Minnesota Council on Foundations' Web site. Application form required.

Initial approach: Letter
Copies of proposal: 1
Deadline(s): Ongoing
Board meeting date(s): Quarterly
Final notification: 2 months

Officers: Roberta Mann, Pres.; Donald Benson, V.P.

Directors: Margaret Adams; Blythe Brenden; John Brenden; Tom Crosby; Michael F. Sullivan, Ph.D.

Number of staff: 1 full-time professional.

EIN: 412019561

Selected grants: The following grants were reported in 2004.

$350,000 to Minneapolis Jewish Federation, Minnetonka, MN. For general support.

$260,541 to Minneapolis Institute of Arts, Minneapolis, MN. For general support.

$250,200 to Minnesota Orchestral Association, Minneapolis, MN. For general support.

$100,000 to Saint Marys University of Minnesota, Winona, MN. For general support.

$100,000 to University of Minnesota Foundation, Minneapolis, MN. For general support.

$60,000 to University of Saint Thomas, Saint Paul, MN. For general support.

$50,000 to Mayo Clinic, Department of Dermatology, Rochester, MN. For general support.

$50,000 to Yale University, New Haven, CT. For general support.

$45,000 to Mount Olivet Lutheran Church, Minneapolis, MN. For general support.

$43,000 to Vanguard Charitable Endowment Program, Southeastern, PA. For general support.

4612
Marbrook Foundation

U.S. Trust Bldg.
730 2nd Ave. S., Ste. 1450
Minneapolis, MN 55402 (612) 752-1783
Contact: Julie S. Hara, Managing Dir.
FAX: (612) 752-1780;
E-mail: jhara@marbrookfoundation.org; URL: http://marbrookfoundation.org

Established in 1948 in MN.

Donors: Edward Brooks†; Markell C. Brooks†.

Foundation type: Independent foundation.

Financial data (yr. ended 12/31/05): Assets, $16,319,513 (M); expenditures, $1,027,055; qualifying distributions, $838,165; giving activities include $781,000 for 137 grants (high: $45,000; low: $1,500).

Purpose and activities: Primary areas of interest include education, the arts, the environment, social empowerment, health, and mind and spirit.

Fields of interest: Visual arts; Performing arts; Performing arts, theater; Historic preservation/historical societies; Arts; Elementary school/education; Education; Environment, natural resources; Environment; Health care; Health organizations, association; Employment; Housing/shelter; Human services; Children/youth, services; Community development.

Type of support: General/operating support; Continuing support; Annual campaigns; Capital campaigns; Building/renovation; Equipment; Land acquisition; Endowments; Program development; Professorships; Scholarship funds; Research; Matching/challenge support.

Limitations: Giving limited to the Minneapolis-St. Paul, MN, area. No support for political purposes, programs for the elderly, domestic abuse programs, disease-related organizations, or programs servicing the mentally or physically disabled. No grants to individuals, or for start-up organizations, conferences or events.

Publications: Annual report (including application guidelines); Financial statement; Grants list.

Application information: Accepts Minnesota Common Grant Form. Application form not required.

Initial approach: Proposal
Copies of proposal: 1
Deadline(s): June 1 and Dec. 1
Board meeting date(s): June and Dec.
Final notification: 1-2 weeks after meeting

Officer and Trustees:* Conley Brooks, Jr.,* Exec. Dir.; Conley Brooks; Markell C. Brooks; Stephen B. Brooks; Markell Kiefer; Katherine M. Leighton; Julie B. Zelle.

Number of staff: 1 part-time professional.
EIN: 416019899

Selected grants: The following grants were reported in 2005.

$20,000 to Minnesota Public Radio, Saint Paul, MN.
$20,000 to Project for Pride in Living, Minneapolis, MN.
$15,000 to First Call for Help of the United Way of Minneapolis Area, Minneapolis, MN.
$10,000 to Hazelden Foundation, Center City, MN.
$10,000 to Nature Conservancy, Minneapolis, MN.
$8,000 to Project SUCCESS, Minneapolis, MN.
$6,000 to Minneapolis Institute of Arts, Minneapolis, MN.
$5,000 to Admission Possible, Saint Paul, MN.
$5,000 to Friends of the Mississippi River, Saint Paul, MN.
$5,000 to Jeremiah Program, Minneapolis, MN.

4613
Mardag Foundation

55 5th St. E., Ste. 600
St. Paul, MN 55101-1797 (651) 224-5463
Contact: John G. Couchman, Admin. Dir.
FAX: (651) 224-8123; E-mail: inbox@mardag.org;
URL: http://www.mardag.org

Established in 1969 in MN.
Donor: Agnes E. Ober‡.
Foundation type: Independent foundation.
Financial data (yr. ended 12/31/05): Assets, $56,184,871 (M); expenditures, $2,816,363; qualifying distributions, $2,440,455; giving activities include $2,212,988 for 98 grants (high: $100,000; low: $200; average: $5,000–$100,000).

Purpose and activities: The foundation is committed to making grants to nonprofit organizations that improve the quality of life in Minnesota for children, seniors, and other at-risk populations and also for programs in education and the arts.

Fields of interest: Arts; Child development, education; Elementary school/education; Adult education—literacy, basic skills & GED; Education, reading; Education; Youth development; Human services; Children/youth, services; Child development, services; Aging, centers/services; Aging; Minorities.

Type of support: Capital campaigns; Building/renovation; Equipment; Program development; Seed money; Matching/challenge support.

Limitations: Giving primarily in the east metropolitan area of Ramsey, Washington, and Dakota counties, MN, and greater MN. No support for programs

serving Minneapolis, MN, and the surrounding west metropolitan area. No support for ongoing annual operating expenses, sectarian religious programs, medical research, federated campaigns, conservation or environmental programs, or for programs serving the physically, developmentally or mentally disabled. No grants or scholarships to individuals, or for events and conferences, capital campaigns of private secondary schools, or capital and endowment campaigns of private colleges and universities.

Publications: Application guidelines; Annual report (including application guidelines).

Application information: Application requirements are included in the foundation's guidelines, which are available on the foundation Web site. Application form required.

Initial approach: 2- to 3- page letter of inquiry or full proposal
Copies of proposal: 1
Deadline(s): Dec. 31 for Apr. meeting, May 1 for Aug. meeting, and Aug. 1 for Nov. meeting
Board meeting date(s): Apr., Aug., and Nov.
Final notification: 4-5 months

Officers and Directors:* Timothy M. Ober,* Pres.; Gayle M. Ober,* V.P.; Wilhelmina M. Wright,* Secy.; Richard B. Ober,* Treas.; Janice K. Angell; Gretchen D. Davidson; Cornelia Ober Eberhart; James R. Heltzer; Edward G. Pendergast.

EIN: 411698990

Selected grants: The following grants were reported in 2005.

$150,000 to Jeremiah Program, Minneapolis, MN. For capital campaign to establish Saint Paul campus.
$150,000 to SteppingStone Theater, Saint Paul, MN. For capital campaign.
$55,000 to Como Zoo and Conservatory Society, Saint Paul, MN. For operating support of Visitor Center.
$35,000 to Minnesota Humanities Commission, Saint Paul, MN. For Phase Two of Somali Bilingual Initiative.
$30,000 to Fergus Falls Community Child Care Center, Fergus Falls, MN. To expand the Center to include the addition of infant care services.
$20,000 to Hallock Area Senior Citizens Center, Hallock, MN. For construction of canopy for the entrance to the Center.
$20,000 to Human Services, Minneapolis, MN. For construction of SHARE Townhomes.
$20,000 to Penumbra Theater Company, Saint Paul, MN. For operating support of Four-Year Restructuring Project.
$15,000 to Roseville Living At Home Block Nurse Program, Roseville, MN. For Supportive Services Program.
$10,000 to Appletree Learning Center, MN. For Child Care Quality Improvement Project.

4614
McCarthy-Bjorklund Foundation ✧

336 Robert St. N., Ste. 1124
St. Paul, MN 55101

Established in 1994 in MN.
Donor: Alexandra O. Bjorklund.
Foundation type: Independent foundation.
Financial data (yr. ended 12/31/05): Assets, $15,721,859 (L); gifts received, $497,792; expenditures, $879,748; qualifying distributions, $790,655; giving activities include $789,275 for 71 grants (high: $115,500; low: $500).

Purpose and activities: Giving primarily for the arts, children's services, education, and human services.

Fields of interest: Museums (children's); Performing arts, theater; Arts; Education; Hospitals (general); Human services; YM/YWCAs & YM/YWHAs; Children/youth, services; Federated giving programs.

Type of support: General/operating support.

Limitations: Applications not accepted. Giving primarily in MN, with emphasis on St. Paul. No grants to individuals.

Application information: Contributes only to pre-selected organizations.

Officers: Alexandra O. Bjorklund, Pres.; Thomas O. McCarthy, Secy.; Edwin J. McCarthy, Treas.
Director: Kathryn M. Parsons.
EIN: 411794941

4615
The William W. and Nadine M. McGuire Family Foundation ▼ ✧

(formerly The William W. McGuire and Nadine M. McGuire Family Foundation)
c/o Dorsey & Whitney, LLP
50 S. 6th St., Ste. 1500
Minneapolis, MN 55402

Established in 1996 in MN.
Donors: William W. McGuire; Nadine M. McGuire.
Foundation type: Independent foundation.
Financial data (yr. ended 12/31/05): Assets, $6,760,320 (M); expenditures, $3,928,144; qualifying distributions, $3,860,000; giving activities include $3,860,000 for 9 grants (high: $1,000,000; low: $10,000; average: $50,000–$500,000).

Purpose and activities: Giving primarily for the arts and education.

Fields of interest: Arts; Higher education, university; Education; Zoos/zoological societies.

Limitations: Applications not accepted. Giving primarily in Gainesville, FL and MN. No grants to individuals.

Application information: Contributes only to pre-selected organizations.

Officers and Directors:* Nadine M. McGuire,* Pres.; William W. McGuire,* Secy.-Treas.
EIN: 411861103

Selected grants: The following grants were reported in 2004.

$3,000,000 to Amherst College, Amherst, MA. For operating support.
$2,814,200 to University of Florida, Gainesville, FL. For operating support.
$2,000,000 to Minnesota Medical Foundation, Minneapolis, MN. For operating support.
$1,015,000 to Walker Art Center, Minneapolis, MN. For operating support.
$1,012,000 to Guthrie Theater, Minneapolis, MN. For operating support.
$310,000 to Blake School, Hopkins, MN. For operating support.
$250,000 to Childrens Theater Company and School, Minneapolis, MN. For operating support.
$110,000 to Minneapolis Institute of Arts, Minneapolis, MN. For operating support.

4616
The McKnight Endowment Fund for Neuroscience ✧

710 2nd St. S., Ste. 400
Minneapolis, MN 55401 (612) 333-4220
Contact: Kathleen Rysted
FAX: (612) 332-2833; E-mail: info@mcknight.org;
URL: http://www.mcknight.org/neuroscience

Established in 1987 in MN.
Donor: The McKnight Foundation.
Foundation type: Independent foundation.
Financial data (yr. ended 12/31/04): Assets, $9,437 (M); gifts received, $4,250,000; expenditures, $4,244,615; qualifying distributions, $4,244,615; giving activities include $3,775,000 for 42 grants to individuals (high: $100,000; low: $75,000), and $225,382 for 1 foundation-administered program.
Purpose and activities: Awards grants for neuroscience research, especially as it pertains to memory and to a clearer understanding of diseases affecting memory and its biological substrates.
Fields of interest: Medical research, institute.
Type of support: Research.
Limitations: Giving limited to U.S. citizens or permanent residents.
Publications: Application guidelines.
Application information: Application form required.
Initial approach: Letter or telephone for application forms and guidelines; materials for Scholar Awards available after Sept. 15
Deadline(s): Jan. 3 for Scholar Awards; Dec. 1 for Technical Innovations; May 1 for Neuroscience of Brain Disorders Award
Board meeting date(s): Apr.
Final notification: May 15 for Scholar Awards; awards commence July 1; early June for Technical Innovations; awards commence Aug. 1; Dec. for Neuroscience of Brain Disorders Awards; awards commence Feb. 1
Officers and Directors:* Corey S. Goodman, Ph.D.*, Pres.; Carla J. Shatz, Ph.D.*, V.P.; Rip Rapson,* Secy.-Treas.; Patricia S. Binger; Thomas M. Jessell, Ph.D.; David Julius, Ph.D.; Eric Nestler, M.D., Ph.D.; Larry Squire, Ph.D.; Lubert Stryer, M.D.; David Tank, Ph.D.; Huda Yahya Zoghbi, M.D.
EIN: 411563321

4617
The McKnight Foundation ▼

710 S. 2nd St., Ste. 400
Minneapolis, MN 55401 (612) 333-4220
Contact: Kate Wolfard, Pres.
FAX: (612) 332-3833; E-mail: info@mcknight.org;
URL: http://www.mcknight.org

Incorporated in 1953 in MN.
Donors: William L. McKnight†; Maude L. McKnight†; Virginia M. Binger†; James H. Binger†.
Foundation type: Independent foundation.
Financial data (yr. ended 12/31/05): Assets, $2,050,595,000 (M); expenditures, $124,758,800; qualifying distributions, $97,877,000; giving activities include $90,552,788 for 673 grants (high: $6,500,000; low: $1,000), $115,000 for 11 grants to individuals, and $42,388 for 84 employee matching gifts.
Purpose and activities: Emphasis on grantmaking in the areas of human and social services; has multi-year comprehensive program in the arts,

environment, and housing; has multi-year program for support of projects in non-metropolitan areas of MN; supports nationwide scientific research programs in areas of: 1) neuroscience, particularly for research in memory and diseases affecting the memory; and 2) collaborative crop research, with support for basic and applied research aimed at improving food crops and agricultural systems in developing countries.
Fields of interest: Arts; Environment, energy; Environment; Neuroscience; Housing/shelter, development; Youth development; Children/youth, services; Child development, services; Family services; Family services, parent education; Rural development; Community development; Transportation.
International interests: Cambodia; Laos; Tanzania; Uganda; Vietnam.
Type of support: General/operating support; Capital campaigns; Building/renovation; Equipment; Program development; Fellowships; Technical assistance; Program evaluation; Program-related investments/loans; Employee matching gifts; Grants to individuals; Matching/challenge support.
Limitations: Giving limited to organizations in MN, especially the seven-county Twin Cities, MN, area, except for programs in the environment, international aid, or research. No support for religious organizations for religious purposes. No grants to individuals (except for the Virginia McKnight Binger Awards in Human Service), or for basic research in academic disciplines (except for defined programs in crop research and neuroscience) endowment funds, scholarships, fellowships, national fundraising campaigns, ticket sales, or conferences.
Publications: Application guidelines; Annual report; Financial statement; Grants list; Informational brochure; Newsletter; Occasional report.
Application information: Application form not required.
Initial approach: 2- to 4-page letter of inquiry
Copies of proposal: 3
Deadline(s): Feb. 15, May 15, Aug. 15, and Nov. 15 for children and families grants; Jan. 15, Apr. 15, July 15, and Oct. 15 for arts, environment, and region and communities
Board meeting date(s): Feb., May, Aug., Nov.
Final notification: 3 months
Officers and Directors:* Erika L. Binger,* Chair.; Kathryn Wolford, Pres.; Bernadette Christiansen, V.P., Human Resources and Admin.; Neal I. Cuthbert, V.P., Progs., and Prog. Dir.; Richard J. Scott, V.P., Finance and Compliance, and Secy.; Therese Simmons, Cont.; James M. Binger,* Treas.; Anne Binger; Benjamen M. Binger; Patricia S. Binger; Peggy J. Birk; Cynthia Binger Boynton; Meghan Binger Brown; Richard D. McFarland; Ted Staryk; Robert J. Struyk.
Number of staff: 22 full-time professional; 15 full-time support; 1 part-time support.
EIN: 410754835

4618
Richard F. McNamara Family Foundation ✧

7808 Creekridge Cir., Ste. 200
Minneapolis, MN 55439

Established in 1992 in MN.
Donor: Richard F. McNamara.
Foundation type: Independent foundation.

Financial data (yr. ended 12/31/04): Assets, $2,692,669 (M); expenditures, $1,360,455; qualifying distributions, $1,348,395; giving activities include $1,340,475 for 18 grants (high: $500,000; low: $100).
Purpose and activities: Giving primarily for education and the United Way.
Fields of interest: Elementary/secondary education; Higher education; Education; Youth development; Federated giving programs.
Limitations: Applications not accepted. Giving limited to MN. No grants to individuals.
Application information: Contributes only to pre-selected organizations.
Directors: Richard F. McNamara; James L. Reissner.
EIN: 411725127

4619
The McNeely Foundation ✧

444 Pine St.
St. Paul, MN 55101 (651) 228-4503
Contact: Karen M. Reynolds

Established in 1981 in MN.
Donor: Lee and Rose Warner Foundation.
Foundation type: Independent foundation.
Financial data (yr. ended 12/31/04): Assets, $19,189,341 (M); gifts received, $253,680; expenditures, $804,958; qualifying distributions, $789,381; giving activities include $713,584 for grants, and $59,182 for employee matching gifts.
Purpose and activities: Support for economics and business education; grants also for selected community projects, environmental programs and for arts education. Specific interest in funding projects that benefit the St. Paul area, especially the East Side neighborhoods.
Fields of interest: Arts education; Education; Environment; Human services; Children/youth, services; Community development.
Type of support: Endowments; Program development; Curriculum development; Program evaluation; Employee matching gifts.
Limitations: Giving primarily in the Minneapolis-St. Paul Metro area, especially in East Side St. Paul neighborhoods. No grants to individuals.
Publications: Application guidelines.
Application information: Accepts Minnesota Common Grant Application Form. Application form not required.
Initial approach: Proposal
Copies of proposal: 1
Deadline(s): Ongoing
Board meeting date(s): As necessary
Final notification: Average time is 180 days
Trustees: Armar A. Archbold; W.E. Barness; Gregory McNeely; Harry G. McNeely III; Kevin McNeely; Shannon McNeely Whitaker.
Number of staff: 1 part-time professional; 1 part-time support.
EIN: 411392221
Selected grants: The following grants were reported in 2004.
$75,000 to East Side Neighborhood Development Company, Saint Paul, MN. For Mainstream Program.
$35,000 to CommonBond Communities, Saint Paul, MN. For Westminster Place Advantage Center support.
$30,000 to Project SUCCESS, Minneapolis, MN. For Saint Paul expansion Wilson Middle School and Humboldt Jr. High School.

$25,000 to American Indian Family Center, Saint Paul, MN. For culturally based programming for youth and their Fathers and Women's Prenatal and Early Childhood Education.

$15,000 to East Side Learning Center, Saint Paul, MN. For Phase II support.

$15,000 to Saint Paul Area Council of Churches, Saint Paul, MN. For East Side Saint Paul Project and SPIRIT Site Support.

$10,000 to Childrens Safety Center Network, Saint Paul, MN. For program service support.

$10,000 to Community Design Center of Minnesota, Saint Paul, MN. For Youth Enterprise in Food and Ecology Program support.

$10,000 to Saint Paul Chamber Orchestra Society, Saint Paul, MN. For CONNECT Program.

$5,000 to Hmong American Partnership, Saint Paul, MN. For Struggle For Success Youth Program.

4620
McVay Foundation ✧
14820 Highway 7, Ste. 200
Minnetonka, MN 55345-3630

Established in 1984 in MN.
Donor: M.D. McVay.
Foundation type: Independent foundation.
Financial data (yr. ended 12/31/05): Assets, $11,917,742 (M); expenditures, $638,742; qualifying distributions, $563,984; giving activities include $558,062 for 85 grants (high: $75,000; low: $150).
Purpose and activities: Giving primarily for the arts, education, the environment, animals/wildlife, and children, youth, women, and social services.
Fields of interest: Arts education; Media, radio; Museums; Performing arts; Arts; Education, early childhood education; Higher education; Theological school/education; Education; Environment; Animals/wildlife, preservation/protection; Human services; American Red Cross; Children/youth, services; Federated giving programs; Christian agencies & churches; Women.
Type of support: General/operating support; Capital campaigns; Scholarship funds.
Limitations: Applications not accepted. Giving primarily in MN and the Midwest. No grants to individuals.
Application information: Contributes only to pre-selected organizations.
Officers: M.D. McVay, Pres.; Danita Greene, V.P. and Secy.; Mary McVay, Treas.
EIN: 363311833
Selected grants: The following grants were reported in 2005.
$69,700 to Hennepin Avenue United Methodist Church, Minneapolis, MN. 2 grants: $14,700, $55,000
$65,000 to Victory Gardens Theater, Chicago, IL.
$20,000 to Salvation Army.
$11,962 to Rust College, Holly Springs, MS.
$11,500 to Guthrie Theater Foundation, Minneapolis, MN.
$11,000 to Habitat for Humanity International.
$10,000 to Kansas State University, Manhattan, KS.
$4,000 to Minnesota Orchestra, Minneapolis, MN.
$2,000 to Childrens Home Society.

4621
Meadowood Foundation ✧
5140 Wells Fargo Ctr., Ste. 5140
Minneapolis, MN 55402-4139

Established in 1968 in MN.
Donor: Douglas J. Dayton.
Foundation type: Independent foundation.
Financial data (yr. ended 12/31/04): Assets, $11,802,536 (M); expenditures, $779,789; qualifying distributions, $659,941; giving activities include $650,752 for 66 grants (high: $105,000; low: $2).
Purpose and activities: Funding primarily for land and natural resource conservation, arts and culture, and human services.
Fields of interest: Arts; Education; Environment, natural resources; Hospitals (general); Human services; Community development.
Type of support: General/operating support; Building/renovation.
Limitations: Applications not accepted. Giving primarily in Minneapolis, MN. No grants to individuals.
Application information: Contributes only to pre-selected organizations.
Officers and Directors:* Douglas J. Dayton,* Pres. and Treas.; Wendy W. Dayton,* V.P.; James M. Karges, Secy.
EIN: 410943749

4622
The Medtronic Foundation ▼ ✧
710 Medtronic Pkwy.
Minneapolis, MN 55432-5604 (763) 505-2639
Contact: Deb Anderson, Grants Admin.
FAX: (763) 505-2648; URL: http://www.medtronic.com/foundation

Established in 1979 in MN.
Donors: Medtronic, Inc.; Georgia Institute of Technology.
Foundation type: Company-sponsored foundation.
Financial data (yr. ended 4/30/05): Assets, $3,712,390 (M); expenditures, $19,864,396; qualifying distributions, $19,845,818; giving activities include $17,638,115 for 961 grants (high: $1,799,409; low: $500), and $888,510 for 682 employee matching gifts.
Purpose and activities: The foundation supports organizations involved with arts and culture, education, health, human services, civic affairs, minorities, senior citizens, and economically disadvantaged people.
Fields of interest: Arts; Elementary/secondary education; Higher education; Education; Health care, alliance; Medicine/medical care, public education; Health care, patient services; Health care; Heart & circulatory diseases; Human services; Biological sciences; Public affairs; Aging; Minorities; Economically disadvantaged.
International interests: Asia; Canada; China; Europe; India; Mexico.
Type of support: Annual campaigns; Program development; Seed money; Scholarship funds; Employee volunteer services; Employee matching gifts.
Limitations: Giving primarily in areas of company operations, with emphasis on Phoenix and Tempe, AZ, Goleta, Northridge, Santa Ana, and Santa Rosa, CA, Louisville and Parker, CO, Warsaw, IN, Danvers and the Twin Cities-Seven County metro, MN, area, Humacao and Villalba, PR, Memphis, TN, and

Redmond, WA; giving also to national and international organizations active in areas of company operations. Generally, no support for social organizations, religious, political, or fraternal organizations, or United Way-supported organizations located in Minneapolis, Minnesota. No grants to individuals, or for debt reduction, capital campaigns, scientific research, travel, fundraising, general operating support, advertising, conferences, continuing support, reimbursable health treatment, or substance abuse programs.
Publications: Application guidelines; Annual report; Corporate giving report (including application guidelines); Grants list.
Application information: Application form required.
Initial approach: Complete online application form
Copies of proposal: 1
Deadline(s): Varies
Board meeting date(s): Varies
Final notification: At least 60 days
Officers and Directors:* Steve Mahle, Sr. V.P.; Penny A. Hunt, Secy. and Exec. Dir.; Jess Quam, Treas.; Arthur D. Collins, Jr.; Janet S. Fiola; Stephen Oesterle; Scott R. Ward.
Number of staff: 3 full-time professional; 1 part-time professional; 1 full-time support; 2 part-time support.
EIN: 411306950
Selected grants: The following grants were reported in 2005.
$1,799,409 to United Way, Greater Twin Cities, Minneapolis, MN. For Employee Campaign Support.
$520,325 to Scholarship America, Saint Peter, MN. For Medtronic Scholarships.
$500,000 to Indiana University Foundation, Bloomington, IN. For Douglas Zipes Medtronic Chair in Cardiology.
$425,000 to National Coalition for Women with Heart Disease, DC. For Science and Leadership Symposium.
$250,000 to Educational Broadcasting Corporation, New York, NY. For Sponsorship of Mysterious Human Heart.
$200,000 to Guthrie Theater, Minneapolis, MN. For Guthrie on the River Capital Campaign.
$150,000 to Regions Hospital Foundation, Saint Paul, MN. For Dissemination of Best Practices in Culturally Competent Health Care.
$40,000 to Hypertrophic Cardiomyopathy Association, Hibernia, NJ. For general support.
$39,308 to United Way of Kosciusko County, Warsaw, IN. For Employee Campaign.
$37,500 to Minnesota Childrens Museum, Saint Paul, MN. For Alice's Wonderland: A Most Curious Adventure.

4623
The Minneapolis Foundation ▼ ✧
800 IDS Ctr.
80 S. Eighth St.
Minneapolis, MN 55402 (612) 672-3878
Contact: Sandy Vargas, C.E.O.; For Connection Grants: Robert Hybben, Community Philanthropy Assoc.
FAX: (612) 672-3846;
E-mail: e-mail@mplsfoundation.org; Community grants E-mail: grants@mplsfoundation.org; Connection grants tel: (612) 672-3863, E-mail: rhybben@mplsfoundation.org; URL: http://www.MinneapolisFoundation.org
Additional URL: http://www.mplsfoundation.org

Incorporated in 1915 in MN.

Foundation type: Community foundation.

Financial data (yr. ended 3/31/06): Assets, $654,649,964 (M); gifts received, $21,777,780; expenditures, $46,465,712; giving activities include $37,154,937 for grants.

Purpose and activities: The foundation believes that the well-being of each citizen is connected to that of every other and that the vitality of any community is determined by the quality of those relationships. With this principle in mind, the foundation's purpose is to join with others to strengthen the community, in measurable and sustainable ways, for the benefit of all citizens, especially those who are disadvantaged. The foundation is committed to being an effective resource developer and a responsible steward of those resources, an active grantmaker and convener addressing crucial community needs, and a constructive catalyst, changing systems to serve people better.

Fields of interest: Education, early childhood education; Child development, education; Education; Health care; Crime/violence prevention, domestic violence; Housing/shelter; Disasters, Hurricane Katrina; Children/youth, services; Child development, services; Family services; Women, centers/services; Human services; Civil rights, immigrants; Civil rights, minorities; Civil rights, disabled; Civil rights, women; Civil rights, aging; Civil rights, race/intergroup relations; Civil rights; Economic development; Community development; Public policy, research; Aging; Disabilities, people with; Minorities; Asians/Pacific Islanders; African Americans/Blacks; Hispanics/Latinos; Native Americans/American Indians; Immigrants/ refugees; Economically disadvantaged; Homeless.

Type of support: General/operating support; Continuing support; Capital campaigns; Equipment; Program development; Seed money; Technical assistance; Program-related investments/loans.

Limitations: Giving limited to MN, with emphasis on organizations in the Twin Cities metropolitan region. No support for national campaigns, direct religious activities, veterans' or fraternal organizations, or organizations within umbrella organizations. No grants to individuals, or for annual campaigns, deficit financing, building or endowment funds, scholarships, fellowships, conferences, courtesy advertising, direct fundraising efforts, benefit tickets, telephone solicitations, or memberships.

Publications: Application guidelines; Annual report; Annual report (including application guidelines); Financial statement; Informational brochure; Newsletter.

Application information: Visit foundation Web site for additional guidelines per grant type or call to obtain the guidelines booklet. Minnesota Common Grant Application is required for community grants and can be found on the foundation's Web site. The letter of inquiry format for connection grants may also be found on the foundation's Web site; only one copy is required. The foundation hosts informational meetings for grantseekers every six months; visit Web site for dates and locations. Application form required.

Initial approach: Submit application form for community grants; submit letter of inquiry for connection grants

Copies of proposal: 2

Deadline(s): None

Board meeting date(s): Committee meets 4 times a year

Final notification: Approximately 4 to 6 months after receipt (initial response, 30 days) for community grants

Officers and Trustees:* Stephen Roszell,* Chair.; John F. Eisberg,* Vice-Chair.; Sandy Vargas,* C.E.O. and Pres.; Stuart Appelbaum, V.P., Devel.; Desiree Heller, V.P., Consulting Svcs.; Karen Kelley-Ariwoola, V.P., Community Philanthropy; Christelle Langer, V.P., Mktg. and Comms.; Marigrace Deters, Assoc. V.P. Community Philanthropy; Dorothy J. Bridges,* Secy.; Joan Anderson Growe,* Treas.; Hon. Pamela G. Alexander; Albert "Andy" Andrews, Jr.; Marshall J. Besikof; Lynn Casey; Mark Chronister; Jesse Bethke Gomez; Morris Goodwin, Jr.; Sima Griffith; Katherine Hadley; Patricia A. Harvey; Yvonne Cheung Ho; Eric J. Jolly, Ph.D.; John M. Lavander; Weiming Lu; Lee R. Mitau; Russell C. Nelson; James Pohlad; James W. Rockwell; Hussein Samator; Gerald Stenson.

Trustee Banks: U.S. Bank, N.A.; Wells Fargo Bank Minnesota, N.A.

Number of staff: 26 full-time professional; 2 part-time professional; 13 full-time support; 1 part-time support.

EIN: 416029402

Selected grants: The following grants were reported in 2006.

$1,515,000 to Abbott Northwestern Hospital Foundation, Minneapolis, MN. 2 grants: $1,500,000 (For technology and space needs for Virginia Piper Cancer Institute), $15,000 (For Virginia Piper Cancer Institute Gala).

$1,500,000 to Mayo Foundation, Rochester, MN. For general support.

$1,000,000 to Minnesota Medical Foundation, Minneapolis, MN. For Wurtele Family Professorship Endowment for Therapeutic Radiology-Radiation Oncology.

$1,000,000 to Walker Art Center, Minneapolis, MN. For capital support, payable over 3 years.

$590,449 to NorthWay Community Trust, Minneapolis, MN. For administrative and operating costs.

$500,000 to Dunwoody College of Technology, Minneapolis, MN. For general support, payable over 5 years.

$200,000 to Minnesota Coalition for Battered Women, Saint Paul, MN. For significant expansion of staffing to increase systems change capacity.

$100,000 to Calvary Lutheran Church, Golden Valley, MN. For building fund and general fund.

$14,000 to MacPhail Center for Music, Minneapolis, MN. For Annual Giving.

4624
Minnesota Community Foundation ◆

(formerly Minnesota Foundation)
55 5th St. E., Ste. 600
St. Paul, MN 55101-1797 (651) 224-0571
Contact: Judith H. Dutcher, Pres.
FAX: (651) 224-9502;
E-mail: inbox@mncommunityfoundation.org;
Additional tel.: (800) 875-6160; Additional E-mails: mco@mncommunityfoundation.org and jhd@mncommunityfoundation.org; URL: http://www.mncommunityfoundation.org

Incorporated in 1949 in MN; in 1984 became an affiliated organization of The Saint Paul Foundation.

Foundation type: Community foundation.

Financial data (yr. ended 12/31/04): Assets, $99,570,423 (M); gifts received, $9,920,052; expenditures, $10,442,982; giving activities include $7,755,831 for 1,173 grants (high: $1,200,000; low: $11), and $287,318 for foundation-administered programs.

Purpose and activities: The foundation seeks to assist individuals, organizations and communities statewide in developing local charitable trusts. Grants are made from these funds according to the recommendations and interests of donors and advisory boards.

Fields of interest: Humanities; Environment; Animal welfare; Health care; Youth development, services; Human services; Rural development; Community development; Federated giving programs; Leadership development.

Type of support: General/operating support; Continuing support; Endowments; Scholarships—to individuals.

Limitations: Giving limited to MN.

Publications: Annual report; Financial statement; Grants list; Informational brochure; Newsletter.

Application information: Visit foundation Web site for scholarship application information.

Board meeting date(s): Quarterly or as required

Officers and Trustees:* Ann Huntrods,* Chair.; Karen Bohn,* Vice-Chair.; Judith H. Dutcher, Pres.; John G. Couchman, V.P., Grants and Prog.; Jack H. Pohl, V.P., Finance; Diane K. Smith, V.P., Opers. and Admin.; Christine K. Searson, Cont.; Nancy Brataas; Robert L. Bullard; John Cowles III; Stephen J. Goodenow; Georgeanne B. Hilker; Joseph R. Kingman III; Thomas W. Kingston; Nancy E. Lindahl; John R. Ryan, Jr.; Louise K. Thoreson; Judith L. Titcomb; Emily Anne Tuttle; Leonard H. Wilkening; Mark Wilson.

EIN: 410832480

4625
Wildey H. Mitchell Family Foundation ◆

c/o Wells Fargo Bank, N.A.
230 W. Superior St., Ste. 400
Duluth, MN 55802

Established in 1979 in MN.

Donors: Wildey H. Mitchell‡; Margaret Mitchell‡.

Foundation type: Independent foundation.

Financial data (yr. ended 12/31/05): Assets, $7,919,642 (M); expenditures, $508,673; qualifying distributions, $458,461; giving activities include $450,000 for 47 grants (high: $60,000; low: $500).

Fields of interest: Arts; Education; Hospitals (general); Food services; Youth development, centers/clubs; Human services; Children/youth, services; Aging, centers/services; Federated giving programs.

Limitations: Applications not accepted. Giving primarily in Duluth, MN. No grants to individuals.

Application information: Contributes only to pre-selected organizations.

Directors: Michael S. Altman; Bruce W. Potter; Robert J. Zallar.

EIN: 416222997

Selected grants: The following grants were reported in 2003.

$60,000 to Boys and Girls Club of Duluth, Duluth, MN.

$30,000 to Duluth Superior Symphony Orchestra, Duluth, MN.

$25,000 to Bong P-38 Fund, Superior, WI.

$20,000 to American Red Cross, Duluth, MN.

$20,000 to Union Gospel Mission, Duluth, MN.

$15,000 to Benedictine Health Center, Duluth, MN.

$10,000 to Duluth Superior Symphony Association, Duluth, MN.

$10,000 to Scottish Rite Foundation of Duluth, Duluth, MN.

$10,000 to University of Minnesota, Duluth, MN.

$8,000 to Duluth Playhouse, Duluth, MN.

4626
Mithun Family Foundation ✧ ☆
90 S. 7th St., Ste. 5300
Minneapolis, MN 55402

Established in 1986 in MN.
Donors: Robert O. Mithun, Sr.; Doris B. Mithun; Doris Mithun Trust; Mithun Enterprises, Inc.
Foundation type: Independent foundation.
Financial data (yr. ended 12/31/05): Assets, $53,411,182 (M); gifts received, $43,373,777; expenditures, $729,353; qualifying distributions, $540,646; giving activities include $450,000 for 23 grants (high: $150,000; low: $1,000).
Fields of interest: Performing arts centers; Hospitals (general); Foundations (private grantmaking); Protestant agencies & churches.
Limitations: Applications not accepted. Giving primarily in Wayzata, MN. No grants to individuals.
Application information: Contributes only to pre-selected organizations.
Directors: John C. Mithun; Lewis M. Mithun; Raymond O. Mithun, Jr.
EIN: 363495071

4627
The Morning Foundation ✧
(formerly The Holman Charitable Trust)
85 Langford Park
St. Paul, MN 55108

Established in 1996 in MN & TX.
Donors: Thomas H. Holman, Jr.; Janelle Holman; Henry Holman.
Foundation type: Independent foundation.
Financial data (yr. ended 12/31/05): Assets, $7,578,354 (M); gifts received, $495,243; expenditures, $453,530; qualifying distributions, $453,501; giving activities include $452,246 for 11 grants (high: $264,323; low: $5,256), and $2,572 for 1 foundation-administered program.
Purpose and activities: Giving primarily for education and to the United Way.
Fields of interest: Elementary school/education; Business school/education; Health organizations; Human services; Children/youth, services; Christian agencies & churches; Roman Catholic agencies & churches.
Limitations: Applications not accepted. Giving primarily in MN. No grants to individuals.
Application information: Contributes only to pre-selected organizations.
Trustees: Kim D.L. Holman; Thomas H. Holman, Jr.
EIN: 742803921

4628
Kevin J. Mossier Foundation ✧ ☆
7201 Ohms Ln., No. 100
Edina, MN 55439-2148

Established in 1998 in MN.

Donor: Kevin J. Mossier.
Foundation type: Independent foundation.
Financial data (yr. ended 12/31/05): Assets, $6,635,789 (M); gifts received, $250,000; expenditures, $623,501; qualifying distributions, $538,550; giving activities include $538,550 for 12 grants (high: $100,000; low: $6,275).
Purpose and activities: Giving primarily to gay and lesbian organizations, and for youth services.
Fields of interest: Youth, services; LGBTQ.
Limitations: Applications not accepted. Giving primarily in Phoenix, AZ, Washington, DC, Minneapolis, MN, and New York, NY. No grants to individuals.
Application information: Contributes only to pre-selected organizations.
Trustees: Steve Brandwein; Larry Bye; Helen Dehner; Donald S. Ofstedal; Charles Rounds.
EIN: 411863691
Selected grants: The following grants were reported in 2003.

$60,000 to Gay, Lesbian and Straight Education Network (GLSEN), New York, NY. For general support.

$40,000 to Funders for Lesbian and Gay Issues, New York, NY. For general support.

$40,000 to Saint Paul Public Schools, Saint Paul, MN. For general support for Out for Equity.

$20,000 to Amnesty International USA, New York, NY. For Outfront Program.

$10,000 to American Civil Liberties Union (ACLU), New York, NY. For campus equality program.

$10,000 to Arizona Human Rights Funds, Phoenix, AZ. For program to change the climate in schools for GLBTQ youth.

$10,000 to Ballet of the Dolls, Minneapolis, MN. For general support.

$10,000 to Parents, Families and Friends of Lesbians and Gays, DC. For general support.

$5,984 to District 202, Minneapolis, MN. For capacity building.

$5,984 to Open Arms of Minnesota, Minneapolis, MN. For general support.

4629
The Laura Jane Musser Fund
(formerly The Musser Fund)
332 Minnesota St., No. E-1420
St. Paul, MN 55101 (651) 224-5209
Contact: Mary Karen Lynn-Klimenko, Managing Consultant
FAX: (651) 222-2566; E-mail: musser@visi.com; URL: http://www.musserfund.org/

Established in 1990 in MN.
Donor: Laura J. Musser‡.
Foundation type: Independent foundation.
Financial data (yr. ended 12/31/05): Assets, $18,293,382 (M); expenditures, $904,149; qualifying distributions, $1,004,980; giving activities include $515,662 for 80 grants (high: $35,000; low: $400).
Purpose and activities: Primary areas of interest include community-based approaches to solving environmental problems, smaller participatory arts programs, securing intercultural harmony and developing leadership in rural communities.
Fields of interest: Arts; Environment; Civil rights, race/intergroup relations; Rural development.
Type of support: Program development; Seed money.
Publications: Application guidelines; Program policy statement.

Application information: Application guidelines and procedures, and application form available on foundation Web site. Please note that granting in the Smaller Participatory Arts funding area has been suspended temporarily. Check the foundation Web site after Jan. 31, 2007 for any updates in this area. Application form required.
Initial approach: Proposal
Copies of proposal: 1
Deadline(s): Sept. 5 for Rural and Environmental Initiatives; Oct. 10 for Intercultural Harmony
Board meeting date(s): Biannually
Final notification: 3 months
Officer and Directors:* Joseph S. Micallef,* Pres.; Lisa Duke; Ivy Parish; Robert Strasburg; Jane Thronas; Drew Walker; Meg Walker.
Trustee: U.S. Bank, N.A.
Number of staff: 2 part-time professional.
EIN: 416334475
Selected grants: The following grants were reported in 2004.

$50,000 to Initiative Foundation, Little Falls, MN. 2 grants: $25,000 each

$36,000 to World Wildlife Fund, DC.

$35,000 to Colorado Working Landscapes, Denver, CO.

$20,000 to Community Design Center of Minnesota, Saint Paul, MN.

$12,500 to Saint Annes Episcopal School, Denver, CO.

$10,000 to Intercambio de Comunidades, Boulder, CO.

$10,000 to Kahilu Theater Foundation, Kamuela, HI.

$7,500 to Hana Arts, Hana, HI.

$5,000 to Gore Range Natural Science School, Red Cliff, CO.

4630
National Distillers Distributors Foundation ✧
100 Washington Ave. S., Ste. 1600
Minneapolis, MN 55401-2192

Established in 1959 as a publicly supported charity; reclassified as a private foundation in 1993.
Donors: Michael C. Carlos; Alfred A. Davis; A. Raymond Tye; B.L. Watson.
Foundation type: Independent foundation.
Financial data (yr. ended 2/28/05): Assets, $1,136,881 (M); expenditures, $558,655; qualifying distributions, $543,910; giving activities include $536,284 for 12 grants (high: $276,284; low: $5,000).
Purpose and activities: Giving limited to educational institutions for use as scholarships and student loans by children of current, retired, or deceased employees of a distributor who is a member of the National Distillers Distributors Foundation.
Fields of interest: Higher education.
Type of support: General/operating support; Scholarship funds.
Limitations: Applications not accepted. Giving primarily in GA, IL, MA, and MN. No grants to individuals.
Publications: Financial statement.
Application information: Contributes only to pre-selected organizations.
Officers: A. Raymond Tye, Pres.; B.L. Watson, 1st V.P.; Alfred A. Davis, V.P.; Edward Jay Phillips, V.P.; Simon Shlenker III, Secy.-Treas.

Directors: V. James Andretta, Jr.; Myron Feldman; Paul Fradin; Noland Glazer; Mervyn D. Lentz.
EIN: 416019579
Selected grants: The following grants were reported in 2005.
$276,284 to National Merit Scholarship Corporation, Evanston, IL.
$130,000 to Page Education Foundation, Minneapolis, MN.
$50,000 to Boston College, Chestnut Hill, MA.
$15,000 to Salve Regina University, Newport, RI.
$10,000 to Bridgewater State College, Bridgewater, MA.
$10,000 to Hampshire College, Amherst, MA.
$5,000 to Roxbury Community College Foundation, Boston, MA.
$5,000 to Saint Josephs College of Maine, Standish, ME.
$5,000 to Stonehill College, Easton, MA.
$5,000 to University of Massachusetts Medical School, Shrewsbury, MA.

4631
George W. Neilson Foundation

P.O. Box 692
Bemidji, MN   56619-0692   (218) 444-4963
Contact: Suzanne Liapis, Secy.
E-mail: sueliapis@excite.com; URL: http://www.gwnf.org

Trust established in 1962 in MN.
Donors: George W. Neilson†; Catherine Neilson Cram†.
Foundation type: Independent foundation.
Financial data (yr. ended 12/31/05): Assets, $25,611,402 (M); expenditures, $1,310,878; qualifying distributions, $1,217,026; giving activities include $1,148,536 for 26 grants (high: $400,000; low: $1,000).
Purpose and activities: Emphasis on matching funds for community needs, leadership, and rural and economic development in the Bemidji, MN, area.
Fields of interest: Arts; Human services; Children/youth, services; Community development.
Type of support: Building/renovation; Equipment; Program development; Matching/challenge support.
Limitations: Giving primarily in the Bemidji, MN, area. No support for religious activities or governmental services. No grants to individuals, or for endowment funds, scholarships, fellowships, or basic research.
Publications: Application guidelines; Grants list; Informational brochure (including application guidelines).
Application information: Accepts MN Common Grant Application Form; questions answered via telephone Wednesdays 12:30pm-4:30pm. Application form required.
  Initial approach: Letter (1-2 pages)
  Copies of proposal: 5
  Deadline(s): 2nd Wed. of each month
  Board meeting date(s): 3rd Tues. of each month
  Final notification: 1 week following board meeting
Officers and Trustees:* Lowell Gillett,* Chair.; Suzanne Liapis,* Secy.; Paul Welle,* Treas.; Charles Naylor; Marcus Wiechmann.
Number of staff: 1 part-time support.
EIN: 416022186

4632
The Nelson Family Foundation ◇

Carlson Pkwy.
P.O. Box 59159
Minneapolis, MN   55459-8250
Contact: Donna D. Snyder, Secy.
Application address: 301 Carlson Pkwy., Ste. 102, Minnetonka, MN 55305, tel.: (952) 404-5600

Established in 1997 in MN.
Donors: Glen D. Nelson; Marilyn C. Nelson.
Foundation type: Independent foundation.
Financial data (yr. ended 12/31/05): Assets, $1,039,675 (M); gifts received, $1,016,169; expenditures, $484,907; qualifying distributions, $483,872; giving activities include $483,847 for 11 grants (high: $299,847; low: $500).
Purpose and activities: Giving for children's education and cultural organizations, higher education, and for art organizations.
Fields of interest: Arts; Education, early childhood education; Higher education.
Type of support: General/operating support; Annual campaigns; Capital campaigns; Scholarship funds.
Limitations: Giving on a national basis, with emphasis on MN.
Application information:
  Initial approach: Proposal, including 3-year budget history
  Deadline(s): Mar. 1 and Sept. 1
Officers: Glen D. Nelson, Pres. and C.E.O.; Marilyn C. Nelson, V.P., Treas. and C.F.O.; Donna D. Snyder, Secy.
Directors: Daisy Mitchell; Curtis C. Nelson; Diana L. Nelson; Marjorie A. Nelson; Wendy M. Nelson.
EIN: 411876884

4633
NFC Foundation ◇ ☆

P.O. Box 355
Minneapolis, MN   55440   (952) 844-1201
Contact: Brian Numanville, Chair.

Established in 1997 in MN.
Donors: Nash Finch Co.; General Mills, Inc.
Foundation type: Company-sponsored foundation.
Financial data (yr. ended 12/31/05): Assets, $304,623 (M); gifts received, $378,618; expenditures, $438,880; qualifying distributions, $365,920; giving activities include $365,920 for grants.
Purpose and activities: The foundation supports food banks and organizations involved with arts and culture, higher education, health, human services, and children and youth.
Fields of interest: Arts; Higher education; Health care; Food banks; Children/youth, services; Human services; Federated giving programs.
Limitations: Giving primarily in MN. No grants to individuals.
Application information: Application form not required.
  Initial approach: Proposal
  Deadline(s): None
Officers and Directors:* Brian Numanville,* Chair.; Kathleen E. McDermott,* Secy.; Leanne M. Stewart,* Treas.; Ron Marshall.
EIN: 411878919
Selected grants: The following grants were reported in 2003.
$26,069 to United Way, Greater Twin Cities, Minneapolis, MN. For general support.

$25,000 to Loaves and Fishes Too, Minneapolis, MN. For general support.
$15,000 to Minnesota Orchestral Association, Minneapolis, MN. For community education.
$10,000 to Greater Minneapolis Crisis Nursery, Golden Valley, MN. For general support.
$5,000 to Juvenile Diabetes Research Foundation International, New York, NY. For health education.
$5,000 to Wright State University Foundation, Dayton, OH. For community support.
$4,950 to University of Minnesota Foundation, Minneapolis, MN. For community support.
$2,500 to Special Olympics of Minnesota, Minneapolis, MN. For community support.
$500 to American Heart Association, Dallas, TX. For health education.
$500 to Hope for Children Foundation, Toronto, Canada. For general support.

4634
Nicholson Family Foundation ☆

(formerly Richard H. and Nancy B. Nicholson Foundation)
c/o Kristine R. Johnston
336 Robert St. N., Ste. 1220
St. Paul, MN   55101-1506
FAX: (651) 290-0719; E-mail: krj@draftco.net

Established in 1986 in MN.
Donors: Richard H. Nicholson; Nancy B. Nicholson; David O. Nicholson; Ford J. Nicholson; Todd S. Nicholson.
Foundation type: Independent foundation.
Financial data (yr. ended 6/30/05): Assets, $8,827,926 (M); gifts received, $1,134,876; expenditures, $583,575; qualifying distributions, $462,416; giving activities include $459,170 for 151 grants (high: $53,790; low: $50).
Purpose and activities: Giving primarily for the arts, education, health, and human services.
Fields of interest: Arts; Education; Environment, natural resources; Health organizations, association; Human services; Christian agencies & churches.
Limitations: Applications not accepted. Giving primarily in MN. No grants to individuals.
Application information: Contributes only to pre-selected organizations. Unsolicited requests for funds not accepted.
Officers: Richard H. Nicholson, Pres.; Todd S. Nicholson, V.P. and Secy.; David O. Nicholson, V.P.; Ford J. Nicholson, Treas.
Number of staff: 1 part-time professional.
EIN: 411572346
Selected grants: The following grants were reported in 2004.
$20,400 to Mounds Park Academy, Saint Paul, MN.
$10,000 to Bethel University, Saint Paul, MN.
$10,000 to DePauw University, Greencastle, IN.
$10,000 to Park Square Theater, Saint Paul, MN.
$5,000 to Minnesota Medical Foundation, Minneapolis, MN.
$4,070 to Gillette Childrens Hospital Foundation, Saint Paul, MN.
$2,100 to Macalester College, Saint Paul, MN.
$1,000 to Minnesota Environmental Fund, Saint Paul, MN.
$250 to Eco Education, Saint Paul, MN.
$125 to Minneapolis Institute of Arts, Minneapolis, MN.

4635
Noreen Family Charitable Trust ✧

c/o U.S. Bank, N.A., Tax Dept.
P.O. Box 64713
St. Paul, MN 55164-0704
Application address: c/o Sally A. Mullen, Trust Off.,
U.S. Bank, N.A., 101 E. 5th St., St. Paul, MN 55101,
tel.: (651) 466-8444

Established in 1989 in MN.
Donor: Roger F. Noreen.
Foundation type: Independent foundation.
Financial data (yr. ended 12/31/05): Assets,
$7,061,710 (M); expenditures, $503,328;
qualifying distributions, $472,723; giving activities
include $465,000 for 16 grants (high: $150,000;
low: $2,000).
Purpose and activities: Giving primarily for human
services and to Christian agencies and churches.
Fields of interest: Education; Health care; Human
services; Religion.
Limitations: Giving primarily in the St. Paul, MN,
area. No grants to individuals.
Application information:
Initial approach: Letter
Deadline(s): None
Trustee: U.S. Bank, N.A.
EIN: 416309355
Selected grants: The following grants were reported
in 2004.
$150,000 to CAC Partners for Success, Saint Paul,
MN. For matching fund.
$100,000 to Childrens Theater Company and
School, Minneapolis, MN.
$50,000 to Presbyterian Homes and Services,
Roseville, MN. For annual fund.
$20,000 to Dakota Area Resources and
Transportation for Seniors (DARTS), Saint Paul,
MN.
$10,000 to Lutheran Social Service of Minnesota,
Saint Paul, MN. For homeless youth programs.
$5,000 to ACTS of Saint Paul, Saint Paul, MN. For
general support.
$5,000 to Catholic Charities of the Archdiocese of
Saint Paul and Minneapolis, Minneapolis, MN.
For Dorothy Day Center.
$5,000 to Loaves and Fishes Too, Minneapolis, MN.
For general support.
$3,000 to Face to Face Health and Counseling
Service, Saint Paul, MN. For general support.
$3,000 to Science Museum of Minnesota, Saint
Paul, MN. For general support.

4636
Northwest Area Foundation ▼

c/o Karl N. Stauber
60 Plato Blvd. E., Ste. 400
St. Paul, MN 55107   (651) 224-9635
FAX: (651) 225-7701; E-mail: info@nwaf.org;
URL: http://www.nwaf.org

Incorporated in 1934 in MN as Lexington
Foundation; name changed to Louis W. and Maud
Hill Family Foundation in 1950; present name
adopted 1975.
Donors: Louis W. Hill, Sr.†; Maud Hill†.
Foundation type: Independent foundation.
Financial data (yr. ended 3/31/06): Assets,
$483,308,560 (M); expenditures, $29,004,223;
qualifying distributions, $24,194,580; giving
activities include $15,881,274 for 199 grants (high:
$2,500,000; low: $200; average: $10,000–
$100,000), $2,160,769 for 3

foundation-administered programs and $735,427
for 3 loans/program-related investments (high:
$700,000; low: $5,427).
Purpose and activities: The foundation is seeking
to help communities in its eight-state region to
reduce poverty.
Fields of interest: Community development.
Type of support: Technical assistance;
Program-related investments/loans.
Limitations: Applications not accepted. Giving
limited to IA, ID, MN, MT, ND, OR, SD, and WA. No
support for lobbying activities. No grants to
individuals.
Publications: Annual report; Grants list;
Informational brochure; Occasional report; IRS Form
990-PF.
Application information: The foundation does not
accept proposals.
Board meeting date(s): Jan., Apr., July, and Oct.
Officers and Directors:* Cornelia Butler Flora,*
Chair.; Sandra Vargas,* Vice-Chair.; Karl N.
Stauber,* Pres. and Secy.-Treas.; Jean Adams, V.P.,
Opers.; Dorothy Bridges; Elouise Cobell; Humberto
Fuentes; Louis Fors Hill; Patricia A. Jensen; Daniel
Kemmis; Rev. Kevin M. McDonough; Elsie Meeks;
Nick Smith; Ted Strong; William Thorndike, Jr.
Trustees: James A. Dodge; Terrence Glarner; Linda
L. Hoeschler; Thomas J. Horak; Rodney W. Jordan.
Number of staff: 25 full-time professional; 1
part-time professional; 14 full-time support; 1
part-time support.
EIN: 410719221
Selected grants: The following grants were reported
in 2005.
$2,100,000 to Childrens Home Society of
Washington, Seattle, WA. For Central South King
County Venture Support.
$1,100,000 to Bear Paw Development Corporation
of Northern Montana, Havre, MT. For Ventures
Partnership Implementation.
$400,000 to Calvert Social Investment Foundation,
Bethesda, MD. For National Rural Funders
Collaborative Public Policy and Learning.
$352,000 to Salish Kootenai College, Pablo, MT.
For Horizons Delivery Organization.
$150,000 to Northwest Indian College, Bellingham,
WA. For tribal governance enhancement.
$40,000 to Amherst H. Wilder Foundation, Saint
Paul, MN. For Venture evaluation.
$40,000 to Cheyenne River Sioux Tribe, Eagle
Butte, SD. For Venture evaluation capacity
building.
$30,000 to Nonprofit Assistance Center, Seattle,
WA. For Community Outreach through informal
community leaders.
$15,000 to National Committee for Responsive
Philanthropy, DC.
$4,600 to Washington State University, Pullman,
WA. For playbook revision and Design Team
Video Conference.

4637
Northwest Minnesota Foundation (NWMF)

4225 Technology Dr. N.W.
Bemidji, MN 56601   (218) 759-2057
Contact: For grants: Jim Steenerson, Grants
Specialist; For grants: Peggy Crandall, Grants Svcs.
Assoc.
FAX: (218) 759-2328; E-mail: nwmf@nwmf.org;
Additional tel. for MN residents: (800) 659-7859;
Grant request E-mails: jims@nwmf.org and
peggyc@nwmf.org; URL: http://www.nwmf.org

Established in 1986 in MN.
Donors: The McKnight Foundation; The Bremer
Foundation; Blandin Foundation.
Foundation type: Community foundation.
Financial data (yr. ended 6/30/05): Assets,
$37,196,976 (M); gifts received, $3,138,040;
expenditures, $3,362,519; giving activities include
$1,015,101 for 177 grants (high: $40,000; low:
$52), $55,350 for 49 grants to individuals (high:
$5,000; low: $100), and $322,432 for 11
foundation-administered programs.
Purpose and activities: The foundation invests
resources, creates opportunities, and promotes
philanthropy to make the region a better place to live
and work.
Fields of interest: Arts; Education; Environment,
natural resources; Environment; Health care;
Housing/shelter; Recreation; Youth development;
Economic development; Community development,
business promotion; Leadership development;
Youth; Aging; Economically disadvantaged.
Type of support: Loans—to individuals; Emergency
funds; Program development; Conferences/
seminars; Seed money; Scholarship funds;
Research; Technical assistance; Consulting
services; Program evaluation; Program-related
investments/loans; Scholarships—to individuals;
Matching/challenge support.
Limitations: Giving limited to Beltrami, Clearwater,
Hubbard, Kittson, Lake of the Woods, Mahnomen,
Marshall, Norman, Pennington, Polk, Red Lake, and
Roseau counties, MN. No support for religious
activities. No grants to individuals (except for
scholarships), or for capital campaigns, major
equipment purchases, annual campaigns,
endowments, building construction, past operating
deficits, publicity or advertising, or general/
operating expenses.
Publications: Application guidelines; Annual report;
Grants list; Informational brochure; Newsletter.
Application information: The foundation strongly
encourages all potential applicants to contact the
foundation's staff before sending a pre-proposal. To
be considered for grant funding, a pre-proposal must
be submitted on the foundation's pre-proposal
application form; if a project is determined to be
eligible, a full application is invited. Visit foundation
Web site for pre-proposal form and guidelines.
Application form required.
Initial approach: Submit Pre-Proposal for Funding
form
Copies of proposal: 2
Deadline(s): Last Fri. of each month for
pre-proposal
Board meeting date(s): 3rd Fri. of each month
Final notification: 3 weeks for full proposal
determination
Officers and Directors:* Diane Blair,* Chair.; Anne
Sand,* Vice-Chair.; John Ostrem, Pres.; Ritchie
Houge, V.P., Philanthropic Svcs.; Marty Sieve, V.P.,
Progs.; Gary Purath,* Secy.; Dean Johnson,* Treas.;
Ann Beck; Eric Bergeson; David Bergman; Robert
Hager; Mark Hewitt; Roger Malm; Terri Anderson
Rothschadl; Kim Wilson.
Number of staff: 12 full-time professional; 4 full-time
support.
EIN: 411556013

4638
The Casey Albert T. O'Neil Foundation ✧
c/o U.S. Bank, N.A.
101 E. 5th St., EP-MN-514
St. Paul, MN 55101
Contact: Nancy Frankenberry
Application address: c/o U.S. Bank, N.A., P.O. Box
64704, St. Paul, MN 55164

Established in 1965 in MN.
Donor: Albert T. O'Neil†.
Foundation type: Independent foundation.
Financial data (yr. ended 6/30/05): Assets,
$16,054,597 (M); expenditures, $769,514;
qualifying distributions, $675,513; giving activities
include $632,000 for 97 grants.
Purpose and activities: Giving primarily for arts and
culture, and health associations; funding also for
education, children, youth, and social services,
federated giving programs, and religion.
Fields of interest: Museums (specialized); Historical
activities; Arts; Education; Hospitals (general);
Health care; Health organizations, association; Boys
& girls clubs; Human services; Children/youth,
services; Family services; Federated giving
programs; Roman Catholic agencies & churches;
Religion.
Type of support: General/operating support;
Continuing support; Annual campaigns; Emergency
funds; Seed money.
Limitations: Giving primarily in MN, with some
emphasis on St. Paul. No grants to individuals, or
for deficit financing, capital campaigns, endowment
or scholarship funds, matching gifts, research,
special projects, publications, or conferences; no
loans.
Application information: Application form required.
Initial approach: Letter
Copies of proposal: 1
Deadline(s): None
Board meeting date(s): As required
Final notification: 3 months
Trustees: Thomas Dwight; John Kelley; Casey Albert
O'Neil; U.S. Bank, N.A.
EIN: 416044079
Selected grants: The following grants were reported
in 2004.
$30,000 to Saint Johns Preparatory School,
Collegeville, MN. For general support.
$20,000 to Courage Center, Golden Valley, MN. For
general support.
$20,000 to Cystic Fibrosis Foundation, Saint Paul,
MN. For general support.
$18,000 to Minnesota Historical Society, Saint
Paul, MN. For general support.
$10,000 to American Diabetes Association of
Minnesota, Golden Valley, MN. For general
support.
$10,000 to Boys and Girls Clubs of the Twin Cities,
Saint Paul, MN. For general support.
$10,000 to Camphill Village Minnesota, Sauk
Centre, MN. For general support.
$10,000 to Saint Paul Chamber Orchestra Society,
Saint Paul, MN. For general support.
$10,000 to Salvation Army of Saint Paul, Saint Paul,
MN. For general support.
$10,000 to Science Museum of Minnesota, Saint
Paul, MN. For general support.

4639
I. A. O'Shaughnessy Foundation, Inc. ▼ ✧
332 Minnesota St., Ste. W 1271
St. Paul, MN 55101-1330 (651) 222-2323
Contact: Timothy J. O'Shaughnessy, Pres.
FAX: (651) 222-3638;
E-mail: iaoshaughnessyFD@Qwest.net; URL: http://
www.iaoshaughnessyfdn.org

Incorporated in 1941 in MN.
Donors: I.A. O'Shaughnessy†; John F.
O'Shaughnessy†; Globe Oil and Refining
Companies; Lario Oil and Gas Co.
Foundation type: Independent foundation.
Financial data (yr. ended 12/31/04): Assets,
$93,426,655 (M); expenditures, $5,013,278;
qualifying distributions, $4,135,162; giving
activities include $4,040,836 for 101 grants (high:
$200,000; low: $5,000; average: $10,000–
$50,000).
Purpose and activities: Giving for cultural programs,
secondary and higher education, social services,
Roman Catholic religious organizations, and youth
and children.
Fields of interest: Performing arts; Performing arts,
music; Arts; Secondary school/education; Higher
education; Human services; Roman Catholic
agencies & churches.
Type of support: General/operating support;
Continuing support; Annual campaigns; Capital
campaigns; Building/renovation; Equipment;
Endowments; Program development; Scholarship
funds; Research; Matching/challenge support.
Limitations: Giving limited to the U.S., with
emphasis on areas where foundation directors live.
No support for religious missions or individual
parishes, or for national fundraising organizations,
or political organizations. No grants to individuals,
or for operational dependence, lobbying, or capital
campaign gifts exceeding twenty percent of the
campaign goal; no loans.
Publications: Application guidelines; Grants list;
Program policy statement.
Application information: See foundation's Web site
for letter of inquiry form. Organizations should not
submit a full proposal unless invited to do so by the
foundation. Application form required.
Initial approach: Letter of inquiry
Copies of proposal: 1
Deadline(s): None
Board meeting date(s): Varies
Final notification: 1 week to 1 month
Officers and Directors:* Timothy J.
O'Shaughnessy,* Pres.; Eileen A. O'Shaughnessy,*
V.P. and Secy.; Teresa O'Shaugnessy Duggan, V.P.;
Kathleen O'Shaughnessy Hodge,* V.P.; Carol L.
Lyman,* V.P.; John F. O'Shaughnessy, Jr.,* V.P.;
Michael W. O'Shaughnessy,* V.P.; Terence P.
O'Shaughnessy,* V.P.; Timothy P.
O'Shaughnessy,* V.P.; Michele O'Shaughnessy
Traeger,* V.P.; Kathryn Lyman Wysong,* V.P.;
Michael F. Sullivan, Treas.; Lawrence M.
O'Shaugnessy, Pres. Emeritus; Barbara J.
O'Shaughnessy, Dir. Emeritus.
Number of staff: 1 part-time support.
EIN: 416011524
Selected grants: The following grants were reported
in 2004.
$200,000 to Cristo Rey Network, Chicago, IL. For
training and development programs for school
leaders, feasibility studies for new schools, and
development and implementation of common
learning outcomes model for Network schools.

$125,000 to Lyric Opera of Chicago, Chicago, IL. For
50th Anniversary of Aida as memorial to Marian
O'Shaughnessy Burke.
$100,000 to Childrens Hospital Foundation,
Denver, CO. To build new hospital at Fitzsimons
Biomedical Campus to incorporate latest
technology and emphasize family-centered care.
$100,000 to Church of Saint Michael, West Saint
Paul, MN. For renovation of John and Mary Youth
Center.
$100,000 to Growing in Faith Capital Campaign,
Saint Paul, MN. For capital campaign.
$100,000 to Misericordia Home, Chicago, IL. To
build chapel/multipurpose building.
$50,000 to Eternal Word Television Network,
Birmingham, AL. To produce new live television
show with Father Benedict Groeschel every
Sunday evening at ITV diocesan studios in
Yonkers, NY.
$30,000 to Kapaun-Mount Carmel High School,
Wichita, KS. For facility master plan for new
science and technology wing, renovation of
existing classroom wing.
$25,000 to Sunflower House - A Child Abuse
Prevention Center, Shawnee, KS. For Promise to
Protect Campaign.
$18,000 to Park City Performing Arts Foundation,
Park City, UT. Toward Thanksgiving weekend
performance of Forbidden Hollywood/Forbidden
Broadway.

4640
Earl B. Olson Foundation ✧
1516 Hansen Dr. S.W.
Willmar, MN 56201-2885

Established in 1988 in MN.
Donor: Earl B. Olson.
Foundation type: Independent foundation.
Financial data (yr. ended 12/31/04): Assets,
$3,269,445 (M); expenditures, $339,922;
qualifying distributions, $334,318; giving activities
include $338,300 for 7 grants (high: $300,000;
low: $100).
Purpose and activities: Giving primarily to a YMCA;
some funding for education, and to Lutheran
churches.
Fields of interest: Education; YM/YWCAs & YM/
YWHAs; Federated giving programs; Protestant
agencies & churches.
Limitations: Applications not accepted. Giving
primarily in MN. No grants to individuals.
Application information: Contributes only to
pre-selected organizations.
Trustee: Earl B. Olson.
EIN: 416315927
Selected grants: The following grants were reported
in 2003.
$300,000 to YMCA, Kandiyohi County Area Family,
Willmar, MN. For general support.
$1,000 to Boy Scouts of America, Viking Council,
Minneapolis, MN. For general support.
$1,000 to Historical Society of Kandiyohi County,
Willmar, MN. For general support.
$1,000 to Vinje Lutheran Church, Willmar, MN. For
general support.
$500 to Green Lake Lutheran Ministries, Spicer,
MN. For general support.

4641
The Dwight D. Opperman Foundation ✧
c/o Key Investment Inc.
601 2nd Ave. S., Ste. 5200
Minneapolis, MN 55402
Contact: Dwight D. Opperman, Pres.

Established in 1996 in MN.
Donor: Dwight D. Opperman.
Foundation type: Independent foundation.
Financial data (yr. ended 12/31/03): Assets,
$17,800,260 (L); expenditures, $894,527;
qualifying distributions, $889,083; giving activities
include $684,170 for 33 grants (high: $183,000;
low: $500).
Fields of interest: Performing arts; Performing arts,
orchestra (symphony); Historic preservation/
historical societies; Arts; Higher education;
Education; Courts/judicial administration; Human
services; Federated giving programs; Public affairs,
information services; Christian agencies &
churches.
Limitations: Giving primarily in MN, with emphasis
on Minneapolis and St. Paul; some giving also to
national organizations throughout the U.S. No grants
to individuals.
Application information: Application form not
required.
   Initial approach: Letter
   Deadline(s): None
Officer: Dwight D. Opperman, Pres.
Directors: Cathy Farrell; Fane W. Opperman; Vance
K. Opperman.
EIN: 411856258
Selected grants: The following grants were reported
in 2003.
$238,668 to American Judicature Society, Des
Moines, IA. 2 grants: $55,668 (For general
support), $183,000 (For general support).
$100,000 to Mayo Foundation, Rochester, MN. For
general support.
$100,000 to Minneapolis Medical Research
Foundation, Minneapolis, MN. For cardiac
research project.
$25,000 to Augsburg College, Minneapolis, MN. For
general support.
$25,000 to Gateway School. For general support.
$25,000 to PACER Center, Minneapolis, MN. For
general support.
$10,000 to Fork Union Military Academy, Fork
Union, VA. For general support.
$10,000 to Presbyterian Ear Institute Oral School,
Albuquerque, NM. For general support.
$10,000 to United Way, Greater Twin Cities,
Minneapolis, MN. For general support.

4642
Opus Foundation ✧
10350 Bren Rd. W., Tax Dept.
Minnetonka, MN 55343

Established in 2000 in MN.
Donors: Opus Corp.; Opus, LLC; North Star
Ventures.
Foundation type: Company-sponsored foundation.
Financial data (yr. ended 12/31/03): Assets,
$31,040,486 (M); gifts received, $7,658,370;
expenditures, $628,521; qualifying distributions,
$765,732; giving activities include $762,500 for 12
grants (high: $300,000; low: $5,000).
Purpose and activities: The foundation supports
Roman Catholic agencies and churches and

organizations involved with education, hunger, and
human services.
Fields of interest: Higher education; Education;
Hospitals (general); Food services; Human services;
Children/youth, services; Roman Catholic agencies
& churches.
Limitations: Applications not accepted. No grants to
individuals.
Application information: Contributes only to
pre-selected organizations.
Officers and Directors: * Mark Rauenhorst,* Pres.;
Keith P. Bednarowski, V.P. and Secy.; Luz Campa,
V.P. and Treas.; Don Neureuther, Secy. and Exec.
Dir.; Philip Goldman; John Solberg.
EIN: 411983284

4643
Ordean Foundation
501 Ordean Bldg.
Duluth, MN 55802 (218) 726-4788
Contact: Stephen A. Mangan, Exec. Dir.

Incorporated in 1933 in MN.
Donors: Albert L. Ordean†; Louise Ordean†.
Foundation type: Independent foundation.
Financial data (yr. ended 12/31/05): Assets,
$38,761,351 (M); gifts received, $155,000;
expenditures, $2,151,899; qualifying distributions,
$1,793,334; giving activities include $1,482,319
for 36+ grants (high: $150,000).
Purpose and activities: Giving primarily for the food,
clothing, shelter, physical and mental health care of
economically disadvantaged Duluthians, and for the
treatment, care, and rehabilitation of persons who
are chronically or temporarily mentally ill, or whose
physical capacity is impaired either by injury, illness,
birth defects, age, alcoholism or similar causes;
funding also for youth guidance programs designed
to avoid and prevent delinquency from lawful and
healthful pursuits by young citizens.
Fields of interest: Education; Medical care,
rehabilitation; Health care; Substance abuse,
services; Mental health/crisis services; Alcoholism;
Crime/violence prevention, youth; Food services;
Housing/shelter; Human services; YM/YWCAs &
YM/YWHAs; Children/youth, services; Family
services; Homeless, human services; Aging;
Disabilities, people with; Economically
disadvantaged.
Type of support: General/operating support;
Continuing support; Program development;
Scholarship funds; Program-related investments/
loans; Matching/challenge support.
Limitations: Applications not accepted. Giving
limited to Duluth and contiguous cities and
townships in St. Louis County, MN. No support for
direct religious purposes, or for political campaigns
or lobbying activities. No grants to individuals
(directly), or for endowment funds, travel,
conferences, seminars or workshops, telephone
solicitations, benefits, dinners, research, including
biomedical research, deficit financing, national
fundraising campaigns, or to supplant government
funding.
Application information: The foundation will not be
accepting unsolicited applications in 2007 and
2008. Accepts Minnesota Common Grant
Application Form. Scholarship applications are
available at the financial aid office of the College of
St. Scholastica and Lake Superior College.
   Board meeting date(s): 2nd Tues. of each month
Officers and Directors: * Mark Melhus,* Pres.;
JoAnn Hoag,* V.P.; Carol Person,* Secy.; Beth

Kelly,* Treas.; Stephen A. Mangan, Exec. Dir.; Larry
Fortner; Lauren Larsen; Mary Beth Santori; Lonnie
Swartz; Anntionette D. Thorstad.
Number of staff: 2 full-time professional; 1 part-time
support.
EIN: 410711611
Selected grants: The following grants were reported
in 2004.
$97,500 to YMCA. 2 grants: $47,500, $50,000
$76,888 to Lutheran Social Services. 3 grants:
   $15,000, $11,250, $50,638
$43,750 to Valley Youth Center, Santa Cruz, CA.
$42,500 to American Indian Community Housing
Organization, Duluth, MN.
$35,000 to Salvation Army.
$20,000 to United Way of Greater Duluth, Duluth,
MN.
$7,500 to Junior Achievement.

4644
Orson A. Hull & Minnie E. Hull Educational Foundation ✧
c/o Nancy Frankenberry
U.S. Bank, N.A., EP-MN-514
St. Paul, MN 55101
Application address: c/o Thomas Farrell, P.O. Box
18581, Minneapolis, MN 55418

Established in 1963 in MN.
Donors: Mrs. Orson A. Hull†; Orson A. Hull†.
Foundation type: Independent foundation.
Financial data (yr. ended 6/30/05): Assets,
$4,691,726 (M); expenditures, $488,871;
qualifying distributions, $441,538; giving activities
include $426,544 for 54 grants to individuals (high:
$11,723; low: $1,447).
Purpose and activities: Scholarships to graduating
seniors of Harding High School and Johnson High
School, in St. Paul, MN.
Type of support: Scholarships—to individuals.
Limitations: Applications not accepted. Giving
limited to residents of St. Paul, MN.
Application information: Scholarship applications
are submitted to school counselors on forms
prepared by the foundation.
Trustees: Gary R. Jernberg; Kirk H. Lindgren; Paul
Rhodes; Daniel Sorenson; U.S. Bank, N.A.
EIN: 416019516

4645
Oswald Family Foundation ✧
(formerly Oswald Charitable Foundation)
601 Carlson Pkwy., Ste. 1050
Minnetonka, MN 55305 (952) 475-6326
FAX: (952) 475-6327;
E-mail: scwilkes@adventuresingiving.com

Established in 1986 in MN.
Donor: Charles W. Oswald.
Foundation type: Independent foundation.
Financial data (yr. ended 12/31/05): Assets,
$17,705,510 (M); expenditures, $819,938;
qualifying distributions, $769,046; giving activities
include $589,600 for 77 grants (high: $30,000;
low: $1,000).
Purpose and activities: Giving primarily for the arts,
education, children, youth and social services,
international economic and community
development, leadership, and social
entrepreneurship.

Fields of interest: Arts; Education; Medical care, outpatient care; Mental health/crisis services; Human services; Children/youth, services; International affairs; Community development.
International interests: Bolivia; Kenya; Mexico; Tanzania.
Type of support: General/operating support; Continuing support; Program development; Seed money; Program-related investments/loans; Exchange programs; Matching/challenge support.
Limitations: Applications not accepted. Giving primarily in Minneapolis, MN, Troy, OH, Boston, MA, and San Diego, CA. No support for religious organizations. No grants to individuals.
Application information: Contributes only to pre-selected organizations, but will respond to inquiry by letter, telephone or e-mail.
  Board meeting date(s): Nov.
Officers: Julie Oswald, Pres.; David C. Oswald, Treas.
Board Members: Charles W. Oswald; Kathleen Oswald; Sara Oswald; Thomas Oswald; Carolyn Workman.
EIN: 363486546
Selected grants: The following grants were reported in 2005.
$20,000 to Lake Country School, Minneapolis, MN.
$20,000 to Nonviolent Peaceforce, Minneapolis, MN.
$20,000 to Pride Africa, Alexandria, VA.
$15,000 to Center for Independent Artists, Minneapolis, MN.
$15,000 to Minnesota Community Foundation, Saint Paul, MN.
$10,000 to Coalition for Womens Economic Development and Global Equality, DC.
$10,000 to Domestic Abuse Project, Minneapolis, MN.
$10,000 to HealthStore Foundation, Alexandria, VA.
$10,000 to Womens Educational Media, San Francisco, CA.
$5,000 to Minnehaha Academy, Minneapolis, MN.

4646
Pacific Foundation ◇ ☆
P.O. Box 408
Hibbing, MN   55746-0408

Established in 1957 in MN.
Donors: E.T. Binger; J.D. Boentje, Jr.
Foundation type: Operating foundation.
Financial data (yr. ended 3/31/05): Assets, $44,907 (M); gifts received, $148,750; expenditures, $715,322; qualifying distributions, $711,587; giving activities include $710,012 for 61 grants (high: $523,213; low: $100).
Purpose and activities: Giving for arts and culture, education, religion and human services.
Fields of interest: Performing arts, theater; Arts; Higher education; Health organizations, association; Disabilities, people with.
Type of support: General/operating support; Annual campaigns.
Limitations: Applications not accepted. Giving primarily in northeastern MN. No grants to individuals.
Application information: Contributes only to pre-selected organizations.
Officer and Directors:* Donald V. Larson,* Pres.; E.T. Binger.
Number of staff: 1 part-time professional.
EIN: 416033767

4647
Patterson Foundation ◇
(formerly Patterson Dental Foundation)
1031 Mendota Heights Rd.
St. Paul, MN   55120-1419   (651) 686-1600
Contact: R. Stephen Armstrong, Secy.-Treas.

Established in 2003 in MN.
Donors: Ronald Ezerski; Robert C. Clifford.
Foundation type: Independent foundation.
Financial data (yr. ended 12/31/05): Assets, $14,718,729 (M); gifts received, $12,383; expenditures, $1,103,426; qualifying distributions, $971,119; giving activities include $950,000 for 20 grants (high: $200,000; low: $5,000; average: $10,000–$100,000).
Purpose and activities: The foundation provides resources to programs and to nonprofit organizations in the areas of oral health, animal health, and occupational and physical rehabilitation. The foundation also supports educational programs, and programs for youth and for the economically disadvantaged. It also provides educational scholarships for dependents of Patterson Dental Co. employees.
Fields of interest: Museums (specialized); Business school/education; Education; Dental care; Physical therapy; Health care; Orthopedics; Human services; Children, services; Anatomy (human); Science; Disabilities, people with.
Type of support: General/operating support; Continuing support; Annual campaigns; Research; Employee-related scholarships.
Limitations: Giving on a national basis and in Canada. No support for religious, political or disease-specific organizations.
Publications: Application guidelines; Program policy statement.
Application information: Scholarships to dependents of Patterson Companies employees paid through Scholarship America. Application form required.
  Initial approach: Letter or telephone
  Copies of proposal: 3
  Deadline(s): Feb. 1, Mar. 1, May 1, Aug. 1, and Nov. 1
  Board meeting date(s): Mar., Jun., Sept., and Dec.
  Final notification: 3-6 months
Officers: Peter L. Frechette, Pres.; R. Stephen Armstrong, Secy.-Treas.
Directors: Robert C. Clifford; Ronald E. Ezerski; Scott R. Kabbes; Richard A. Kochmann; Matthew L. Levitt; David Sproat; Jeffrey H. Webster; James W. Wiltz.
EIN: 743076772

4648
Pax Christi Foundation ◇
c/o Hutterer & Krenn
7900 Xerxes Ave. S., Ste. 928
Minneapolis, MN   55431-1123

Established in 1987 in MN.
Donors: J.C. Pahl; J.M. Pahl.
Foundation type: Independent foundation.
Financial data (yr. ended 6/30/05): Assets, $9,003,319 (M); gifts received, $16,500; expenditures, $2,617,570; qualifying distributions, $2,544,631; giving activities include $2,527,750 for 74+ grants (high: $623,750; average: $10,000–$50,000).
Purpose and activities: Giving primarily to health associations, particularly an international medical

relief organization, and assistance to people with HIV/AIDS; funding also for youth, family and social services.
Fields of interest: Health organizations, association; AIDS; Housing/shelter, homeless; Human services; Youth, services; Family services; International relief; Hispanics/Latinos.
Limitations: Applications not accepted. Giving primarily in Mendota Heights and Minneapolis, MN. No grants to individuals.
Application information: Contributes only to pre-selected organizations.
Officers: J.C. Pahl, Pres.; J.M. Pahl, Secy.-Treas.; Vincent K. Hutterer, C.F.O.
EIN: 363550495
Selected grants: The following grants were reported in 2004.
$715,000 to Mano a Mano Medical Resources, Mendota Heights, MN. For international medical relief.
$110,000 to CARE, Minnetonka, MN. For international relief.
$100,000 to Feed My Starving Children (FMSC) Corporation, New Hope, MN. For child nutritional support.
$25,000 to Carmen Pampa Fund, Minneapolis, MN. For operating support of Unidad Academica Campesina.
$15,000 to Family and Youth Advancement Services, Saint Paul, MN. For operating support.
$10,000 to Christus Medicus Foundation, Bloomfield Hills, MI. For operating support.
$10,000 to Franciscan Brothers of Peace, Saint Paul, MN. For operating support of food shelf program.
$10,000 to Lakes Area Pregnancy Support Center, Brainerd, MN. For ultrasound machine.
$5,000 to Minnesota International Health Volunteers, Minneapolis, MN. For production of video.
$4,500 to Imani Family Services, Brooklyn Park, MN. For operational support and capacity building.

4649
The Pentair Foundation
5500 Wayzata Blvd., Ste. 800
Golden Valley, MN   55416-1259
Contact: Michelle R. Murphy, Admin.
FAX: (763) 656-5404;
E-mail: michelle.murphy@pentair.com; URL: http://www.pentair.com/foundation.html

Established in 1998 in MN.
Donor: Pentair, Inc.
Foundation type: Company-sponsored foundation.
Financial data (yr. ended 12/31/05): Assets, $3,540,953 (M); gifts received, $3,010,011; expenditures, $2,675,615; qualifying distributions, $2,665,774; giving activities include $2,496,952 for 147 grants (high: $244,000; low: $1,000), and $103,673 for 121 employee matching gifts.
Purpose and activities: The foundation supports organizations involved with arts and culture, education, housing, and human services.
Fields of interest: Arts, cultural/ethnic awareness; Arts; Vocational education; Education; Housing/shelter; Children/youth, services; Human services.
Type of support: General/operating support; Program development; Scholarship funds; Employee matching gifts.
Limitations: Giving on a national and international basis in areas of company operations. No support

for fraternal, political, or religious organizations. No grants to individuals, or for fundraising, sponsorships or advertising, or travel or tours.
Publications: Application guidelines; Grants list; Informational brochure.
Application information: Application form required.
Initial approach: Complete online application form
Deadline(s): Mar. 1, June 1, and Oct. 1
Board meeting date(s): Feb. and Aug.
Final notification: May 31, Sept. 30, and Dec. 31
Officer and Directors: Michael G. Meyer, Treas.; John Abbott; Judy Carle; Jeanne M. Gode; Susan Harrison; Randall J. Hogan; Frederick S. Koury; Lynn Sonterre; Joan Swartz; Gary S. Witt.
Number of staff: 1 full-time professional; 1 full-time support.
EIN: 411890149
Selected grants: The following grants were reported in 2004.
$80,000 to YMCA of the Triangle Area, Raleigh, NC.
$70,000 to First Call for Help of the United Way of Minneapolis Area, Minneapolis, MN.
$70,000 to Guthrie Theater Foundation, Minneapolis, MN.
$65,000 to Greater Minneapolis Crisis Nursery, Golden Valley, MN.
$25,000 to Jackson Symphony Association, Jackson, TN.
$20,000 to United Negro College Fund, Minneapolis, MN.
$18,000 to Ashland University, Ashland, OH.
$10,000 to Achieve Minneapolis, Minneapolis, MN.
$10,000 to S.E.T. Ministry, Milwaukee, WI.
$8,000 to Walker Art Center, Minneapolis, MN.

4650
People in Business Care, Inc. ◇
P.O. Box 977
Chanhassen, MN 55317

Established in 1983 in MN.
Donor: The Berquist Co.
Foundation type: Company-sponsored foundation.
Financial data (yr. ended 7/31/04): Assets, $1,682,128 (M); gifts received, $882,057; expenditures, $385,280; qualifying distributions, $385,280; giving activities include $384,754 for 308 grants (high: $16,200; low: $17).
Purpose and activities: The foundation supports organizations involved with health, children, human services, community development, and Christianity.
Fields of interest: Health care; Children, services; Human services; Community development; Christian agencies & churches.
Limitations: Giving primarily in MN and WI.
Application information: Application form not required.
Initial approach: Letter of inquiry
Copies of proposal: 1
Deadline(s): None
Board meeting date(s): Monthly
Officers: James Plewacki, Chair.; LeRoy Morgan, Secy.; Robert Hartline, Treas.
EIN: 363261419
Selected grants: The following grants were reported in 2004.
$15,000 to Campus Crusade for Christ International, Orlando, FL.
$12,000 to Banyan Foundation, Minneapolis, MN.
$7,200 to Christ Community Church, Nisswa, MN.
$6,300 to Navigators, The, Colorado Springs, CO.
$5,000 to Alliance Defense Fund, Scottsdale, AZ.

$4,000 to Cecil Newman Resource Center, Minneapolis, MN.
$3,000 to Safe Haven Shelter for Youth, Prior Lake, MN.
$1,800 to Northern Pines Mental Health Center, Little Falls, MN.
$1,000 to Minnesota Indian Womens Resource Center, Minneapolis, MN.
$1,000 to Washburn Child Guidance Center, Minneapolis, MN.

4651
Lawrence and Linda Perlman Family Foundation ☆
(formerly Perlman Family Foundation)
1818 Oliver Ave. S.
Minneapolis, MN 55405
Contact: Sara Barrow, Exec. Dir.

Established in 1997 in MN.
Donor: Lawrence Perlman.
Foundation type: Independent foundation.
Financial data (yr. ended 12/31/05): Assets, $1,318,799 (M); expenditures, $502,893; qualifying distributions, $477,302; giving activities include $477,302 for grants.
Fields of interest: Arts; Elementary/secondary education; Children/youth, services; Women.
Limitations: Applications not accepted. Giving primarily in MN. No grants to individuals.
Application information: Contributes only to pre-selected organizations.
Officers: Linda Peterson Perlman, Pres.; Justin Barrow, V.P.; David M. Perlman, V.P.; Lawrence Perlman, Secy.; Sara Perlman Barrow, Exec. Dir.
EIN: 411896827

4652
G. & D. Peterson Foundation ◇
c/o Barry Newman, Dorsey & Whitney
50 S. 6th St., Ste. 1500
Minneapolis, MN 55402

Established in 1997 in MN.
Donors: Gerald Peterson; Donna Peterson.
Foundation type: Independent foundation.
Financial data (yr. ended 12/31/03): Assets, $996,421 (M); gifts received, $39,267; expenditures, $343,126; qualifying distributions, $338,462; giving activities include $338,700 for 9 grants (high: $300,000; low: $1,000).
Purpose and activities: Giving primarily to a Lutheran church, as well as for higher education, and the performing arts.
Fields of interest: Performing arts; Higher education, university; Protestant agencies & churches.
Limitations: Applications not accepted. Giving primarily in MN. No grants to individuals.
Application information: Contributes only to pre-selected organizations.
Trustees: Barry Newman; Donna Peterson; Gerald Peterson.
EIN: 411866420
Selected grants: The following grants were reported in 2004.
$27,500 to Hamline University, Saint Paul, MN.
$1,200 to K T C A/K T C I Twin Cities Public Television, Saint Paul, MN.
$1,000 to Great American History Theater, Saint Paul, MN.

$1,000 to Lymphoma Research Foundation, New York, NY.
$1,000 to Ordway Center for the Performing Arts, Saint Paul, MN.

4653
Thomas J. Petters Family Foundation ◇
4400 Baker Rd.
Minnetonka, MN 55343 (952) 934-9918
Contact: Thomas J. Petters, Exec. Dir.

Established in 2002 in MN.
Donors: Thomas J. Petters; Thomas J. Petters Inc.
Foundation type: Independent foundation.
Financial data (yr. ended 12/31/05): Assets, $5,136 (M); gifts received, $1,383,000; expenditures, $1,384,200; qualifying distributions, $1,384,175; giving activities include $1,384,175 for 41 grants (high: $1,000,000; low: $100).
Purpose and activities: Giving primarily for higher and other education and Catholic churches and agencies.
Fields of interest: Elementary/secondary education; Higher education; Youth development; Roman Catholic agencies & churches.
Type of support: Scholarship funds; Program development; Building/renovation; Capital campaigns.
Application information:
Initial approach: Letter
Deadline(s): None
Officer: Thomas J. Petters, Exec. Dir.
Directors: Jennifer J. Petters; James C. Wehmhoff.
EIN: 412010037
Selected grants: The following grants were reported in 2004.
$1,250,000 to Miami University, Oxford, OH.
$1,000,000 to College of Saint Benedict, Saint Joseph, MN.
$10,000 to Saint Johns Preparatory School, Collegeville, MN.
$2,000 to Winona State University, Winona, MN.

4654
The Phileona Foundation ◇
2950 Dean Pkwy., Ste. 2501
Minneapolis, MN 55416

Established in 1993 in MN.
Donors: D.J. Miller; S.D. Miller; S.L. Miller; M.D. Miller.
Foundation type: Independent foundation.
Financial data (yr. ended 9/30/04): Assets, $32,085,413 (M); gifts received, $6,090,000; expenditures, $1,455,518; qualifying distributions, $1,432,044; giving activities include $1,427,044 for 45 grants (high: $400,000; low: $200).
Fields of interest: Human services; Community development; Roman Catholic federated giving programs; Jewish federated giving programs; Marine science; Jewish agencies & temples.
Limitations: Applications not accepted. Giving primarily in MN. No grants to individuals.
Application information: Contributes only to pre-selected organizations.
Officer and Directors:* M.D. Miller,* Chair.; D.J. Miller; M.J. Miller; S.D. Miller; S.L. Miller; T. Sledd.
EIN: 411763225
Selected grants: The following grants were reported in 2003.

$430,000 to Minneapolis Jewish Federation, Minnetonka, MN. For general support.

$275,000 to Ocean Conservancy, DC. For general support.

$60,661 to MELD-Minnesota Early Learning Design, Minneapolis, MN. For general support.

$52,500 to Temple Israel, Minneapolis, MN. For general support.

$37,315 to University of Minnesota, Minneapolis, MN. For general support.

$20,000 to Jane Goodall Institute for Wildlife Research, Education and Conservation, Arlington, VA. For general support.

$15,000 to Raincoast Conservation Foundation, Tofino, Canada. For general support.

$7,500 to Walker Art Center, Minneapolis, MN. For general support.

$5,500 to Lake Forest College, Lake Forest, IL. For general support.

$5,000 to United Way, Greater Twin Cities, Minneapolis, MN. For general support.

4655
The Jay and Rose Phillips Family Foundation ▼

(formerly The Phillips Foundation)
10 2nd St., N.E., Ste. 200
Minneapolis, MN 55413 (612) 623-1654
Contact: Amy K. Crawford, Exec. Dir.
FAX: (612) 623-1653;
E-mail: phillipsfnd@phillipsfnd.org; Additional tel. (for Dana Jensen, Grants Mgr.): (612) 623-1652;
URL: http://www.phillipsfnd.org

Incorporated in 1944 in MN.
Donor: Jay Phillips‡.
Foundation type: Independent foundation.
Financial data (yr. ended 12/31/05): Assets, $195,463,283 (M); expenditures, $11,904,294; qualifying distributions, $10,617,590; giving activities include $9,921,862 for 374 grants (high: $500,000; low: $1,000; average: $10,000–$50,000).
Purpose and activities: Giving primarily for health, human services, education, programs for people with disabilities and programs to combat discrimination. During times of severe economic hardship and financial distress, the foundation's primary concern is in providing support for projects that address unmet human and social needs. The foundation's preference is to support projects that represent new thinking about community needs and innovative efforts that have the potential for long-term solutions to the problems being addressed.
Fields of interest: Arts; Education; Health care; Health organizations, association; Crime/violence prevention, domestic violence; Human services; Family services; Civil rights, immigrants; Civil rights, minorities; Civil rights, disabled; Civil rights, women; Civil rights, aging; Civil rights, gays/lesbians; Civil liberties, reproductive rights; Jewish federated giving programs; Jewish agencies & temples; Aging; Disabilities, people with; Asians/Pacific Islanders; African Americans/Blacks; Hispanics/Latinos; Native Americans/American Indians; Women; AIDS, people with; LGBTQ; Immigrants/refugees; Economically disadvantaged; Homeless.
Type of support: Capital campaigns; Building/renovation; Equipment; Program development; Research; Technical assistance; Program evaluation; Matching/challenge support.

Limitations: Giving primarily in the Twin Cities metropolitan, MN, area. No support for political campaigns or lobbying efforts to influence legislation. No grants to individuals.
Publications: Application guidelines; Annual report (including application guidelines); Grants list.
Application information: The foundation has three grant rounds each year in Mar., July, and Nov. Unsolicited requests for funds not accepted from organizations outside of MN. Application form not required.
Initial approach: Letter or telephone; cover letter not required
Copies of proposal: 1
Deadline(s): Mar. 15, July 15 and Nov. 15
Board meeting date(s): Ongoing
Final notification: Up to six months
Officers and Trustees:* Paula P. Bernstein,* 1st Chair.; John P. Levin,* Co-Chair.; Edward J. Phillips, Co-Chair.; Amy K. Crawford, Secy. and Exec. Dir.; Erik P. Bernstein,* Treas.; Morton B. Phillips, Tr. Emeritus; Pauline Phillips, Tr. Emeritus; William E. Bernstein; Suzan Levin; Terryl A. Levin; Dean Phillips; Jeanne Phillips.
Number of staff: 3 full-time professional; 1 full-time support.
EIN: 416019578
Selected grants: The following grants were reported in 2004.

$2,500,000 to Sholom Community Alliance, Saint Louis Park, MN. For Roitenberg Family Assisted Living Residence at Sholom Community Alliance.

$532,000 to Jewish Family Service of Colorado, Denver, CO. 2 grants: $250,000 (For Reaching for the Future capital campaign), $282,000 (For Senior and Adult Services).

$297,250 to Minnesota Private College Fund, Saint Paul, MN. For Phillips Scholars program for next cohorts of scholars.

$250,000 to American Committee for Shaare Zedek Hospital in Jerusalem, Los Angeles, CA. For equipment for cardio thoracic surgery department.

$250,000 to Childrens Theater Company and School, Minneapolis, MN. For capital support.

$250,000 to Jewish Family and Childrens Services, San Francisco, CA. For Disability Project.

$250,000 to Minneapolis Public Library, Friends of the, Minneapolis, MN. For capital support for new Minneapolis Central Library, targeted to the New Citizens Center.

$250,000 to Stanford University, Stanford, CA. For the Campaign for Undergraduate Education.

$250,000 to United Jewish Fund and Council, Saint Paul, MN. For Preserving the Past, Focusing on the Future Capital Campaign, designated for Sholom Home East.

4656
Piper Jaffray Foundation ◇ ☆

800 Nicollet Mall, Ste. J13S25
Minneapolis, MN 55402
URL: http://www.piperjaffray.com/2col_largeright.aspx?id=127

Established in 2004 in MN.
Donor: Piper Jaffray & Co.
Foundation type: Company-sponsored foundation.
Financial data (yr. ended 12/31/04): Assets, $1,568,486 (M); gifts received, $2,364,994; expenditures, $862,201; qualifying distributions, $857,921; giving activities include $690,250 for 74

grants (high: $175,000; low: $1,000), and $167,671 for 361 employee matching gifts.
Type of support: Employee matching gifts.
Officers: Addison L. Piper, Pres.; R. Todd Firebaugh, V.P.; James L. Chosy, Secy.; Sandra G. Sponem, Treas.
EIN: 371478172

4657
Carl and Eloise Pohlad Family Foundation ▼ ◇

60 S. 6th St., Ste. 3900
Minneapolis, MN 55402 (612) 661-3910
Contact: Marina Munoz Lyon, V.P.
FAX: (612) 661-3715;
E-mail: info@pohladfamilygiving.org; Additional E-mail: rpeterson@pohladfamilygiving.org;
URL: http://www.pohladfamilygiving.org

Established in 1993 in MN.
Donors: Carl R. Pohlad; Eloise O. Pohlad‡; BP Corp.; Marquette Bancshares, Inc.
Foundation type: Independent foundation.
Financial data (yr. ended 12/31/05): Assets, $37,402,514 (M); gifts received, $844,025; expenditures, $8,436,084; qualifying distributions, $8,280,245; giving activities include $8,200,130 for 602 grants (high: $1,000,000; low: $50; average: $100–$15,000).
Purpose and activities: The mission of the foundation is to improve the lives of economically disadvantaged families and children, and also participate in projects that maintain or improve the quality of life in the Minneapolis/St. Paul metropolitan area.
Fields of interest: Education; Housing/shelter; Human services.
Type of support: General/operating support; Capital campaigns; Scholarship funds; Employee matching gifts.
Limitations: Giving primarily in Minneapolis and St. Paul, MN. No grants to individuals directly.
Publications: Annual report; Grants list.
Application information: Visit foundation's Web site for current Requests for Proposals (RFP).
Initial approach: See foundation's Web site
Officers and Directors:* William M. Pohlad,* Pres.; Marina Munoz Lyon,* V.P.; Pamela E. Omann,* Secy.-Treas.; Carl R. Pohlad; James O. Pohlad; Robert C. Pohlad.
Number of staff: 2 full-time professional; 1 full-time support.
EIN: 411768558
Selected grants: The following grants were reported in 2005.

$1,000,000 to Breck School, Minneapolis, MN. For capital support.

$600,000 to Abbott Northwestern Hospital Foundation, Minneapolis, MN. For capital support.

$500,000 to Guthrie Theater, Minneapolis, MN. For capital support.

$500,000 to Sisters of Saint Joseph of Carondelet Ministries Foundation, Saint Paul, MN. For capital support.

$250,000 to Neighborhood Development Center, Saint Paul, MN. For capital support.

$20,000 to Minnesota Twins Community Fund, Minneapolis, MN. For general operating support.

$5,000 to Theater de la Jeune Lune, Minneapolis, MN.

$1,000 to Project HOPE - People-to-People Health Foundation, Millwood, VA.

$1,000 to University of Wisconsin Foundation, Eau Claire, WI.

$250 to American Red Cross, Minneapolis, MN.

4658
Prophet Corporation Foundation ✧ ☆
220 24th Ave. N.W.
Owatonna, MN 55060 (507) 451-7470
Contact: Joel Jennings, Pres.

Donors: The Prophet Corp.; Joel Jennings; Mary Lee Jennings.
Foundation type: Company-sponsored foundation.
Financial data (yr. ended 12/31/05): Assets, $1,431,387 (M); gifts received, $1,349,200; expenditures, $331,783; qualifying distributions, $331,789; giving activities include $329,681 for 4 + grants (high: $50,000).
Purpose and activities: The foundation supports organizations involved with Alzheimer's disease, human services, Christianity, and economically disadvantaged people.
Fields of interest: Alzheimer's disease; Children/youth, services; Children, services; Family services; Human services; Christian agencies & churches; Economically disadvantaged.
Type of support: General/operating support.
Limitations: Giving primarily in MN.
Application information:
Initial approach: Contact foundation for application information
Deadline(s): None
Officer and Director: Joel Jennings, Pres.; Mary Lee Jennings.
EIN: 411765206
Selected grants: The following grants were reported in 2004.
$55,000 to National Center for Fathering, Kansas City, MO.
$50,000 to Kingdom Oil, Minneapolis, MN.
$35,000 to World Vision, Federal Way, WA.
$24,767 to Fellowship of Christian Athletes, Hills, MN.
$16,000 to Kenya Childrens Fund, Minneapolis, MN.
$10,000 to Alzheimers Association, Edina, MN.
$4,500 to American Cancer Society, Minneapolis, MN.
$500 to Big Brothers/Big Sisters of Owatonna, Owatonna, MN.

4659
Prospect Creek Foundation
4900 IDS Ctr.
80 S. 8th St.
Minneapolis, MN 55402
Contact: H.B. Atwater, Jr.

Established in 1993 in MN.
Donor: H. Brewster Atwater, Jr.
Foundation type: Independent foundation.
Financial data (yr. ended 12/31/04): Assets, $33,245,722 (M); gifts received, $1,463,702; expenditures, $1,392,562; qualifying distributions, $1,330,787; giving activities include $1,307,078 for 50 grants (high: $1,005,000; low: $100).
Fields of interest: Performing arts, theater; Arts; Education; Hospitals (general); Reproductive health, family planning; Health organizations, association;

Medical research, institute; Human services; Federated giving programs.
Limitations: Giving primarily in CA and MN. No grants to individuals.
Application information:
Initial approach: Proposal
Copies of proposal: 1
Deadline(s): None
Directors: H. Brewster Atwater, Jr.; Martha Clark Atwater; Elizabeth Atwater Connolly.
EIN: 411736420
Selected grants: The following grants were reported in 2003.
$415,000 to Schwab Fund for Charitable Giving, San Francisco, CA. For operating support.
$100,000 to Brentwood School, Los Angeles, CA. For operating support.
$45,000 to Saint Helena Hospital Foundation, Deer Park, CA. For operating support.
$41,000 to Guthrie Theater, Minneapolis, MN. For operating support.
$40,000 to San Francisco Museum of Modern Art, San Francisco, CA. For general support.
$28,500 to Walker Art Center, Minneapolis, MN. For operating support.
$14,000 to Fine Arts Museums of San Francisco, San Francisco, CA. For operating support.
$11,700 to Planned Parenthood of Los Angeles, Los Angeles, CA. For operating support.
$10,000 to Oxbow School, Napa, CA. For operating support.
$5,000 to Napa Valley Opera House, Napa, CA. For operating support.

4660
William D. Radichel Foundation ✧
145 Kingswood Dr.
P.O. Box 880
Mankato, MN 56002-0880

Established in 2000 in MN.
Donor: Radichel Family Intervivos Charitable Lead Trust.
Foundation type: Independent foundation.
Financial data (yr. ended 6/30/06): Assets, $169,750 (M); gifts received, $332,308; expenditures, $479,151; qualifying distributions, $456,000; giving activities include $456,000 for grants.
Fields of interest: Arts; Education; Boys & girls clubs; Boy scouts; Christian agencies & churches.
Limitations: Applications not accepted. Giving primarily in CO and MN. No grants to individuals.
Application information: Contributes only to pre-selected organizations.
Officers and Directors:* Brenda Radichel Quaye,* C.E.O. and Pres.; Bradley P. Radichel,* V.P.; Christina Radichel Caulkins,* Secy.-Treas.
EIN: 411944317
Selected grants: The following grants were reported in 2005.
$12,000 to Girl Scouts of the U.S.A.. 2 grants: $7,000, $5,000
$10,000 to Breck School, Minneapolis, MN.
$10,000 to Greater Minneapolis Crisis Nursery, Golden Valley, MN.
$10,000 to Minnesota International Center, Minneapolis, MN.
$10,000 to PRASAD Project, Hurleyville, NY.
$8,000 to Childrens Hospital.
$8,000 to Graland Country Day School, Denver, CO.
$5,000 to Minnesota Public Radio, Saint Paul, MN.
$5,000 to Nature Conservancy, Arlington, VA.

4661
RBC Dain Rauscher Foundation ✧ ☆
(formerly Dain Rauscher Foundation)
Dain Rauscher Plz., M.S. P20
60 S. 6th St.
Minneapolis, MN 55402 (612) 371-2936
Contact: Sherry Koster, Mgr.
FAX: (612) 371-7933;
E-mail: sherry.koster@rbcdain.com; Additional tel.: (612) 371-2765; URL: http://www.rbcdain.com/DRP_1.0/Public_Site/Common_Pages/DRP_1.0VSectionIndex/1,65489,4-3-2-0,00.html

Incorporated in 1960 in MN.
Donors: Dain Rauscher Inc.; RBC Dain Rauscher Corp.
Foundation type: Company-sponsored foundation.
Financial data (yr. ended 10/31/04): Assets, $282,716 (M); gifts received, $2,220,000; expenditures, $2,212,953; qualifying distributions, $2,212,953; giving activities include $1,752,000 for 439 grants, and $462,013 for 1,059 employee matching gifts.
Purpose and activities: The foundation supports organizations involved with arts and culture, K-12 education, human services, and economically disadvantaged people.
Fields of interest: Arts, cultural/ethnic awareness; Arts; Education, equal rights; Elementary/secondary education; Family services; Human services, financial counseling; Human services; Youth; Economically disadvantaged.
Type of support: General/operating support; Continuing support; Annual campaigns; Building/renovation; Program development; Employee volunteer services; Employee matching gifts.
Limitations: Giving primarily in areas of company operations. No support for religious, political, fraternal, or veterans' organizations, athletic teams, or hospitals, nursing homes, hospices, or daycare facilities. No grants to individuals, or for sponsorships, fundraising events, athletic events or scholarships, travel, academic, medical, or scientific research, recreational or athletic programs, audio or video recording projects, literary or media art projects, artist enrichment programs, medical, health, mental health, or disease-specific or disease-related services, senior citizen programs, or developmental disabilities or disorders, including deafness and blindness, non-K-12 educational programs, environmental education programs, or programs limited to special needs students.
Publications: Application guidelines.
Application information: Application form required.
Initial approach: Complete online application form
Deadline(s): Visit Web site for deadlines
Board meeting date(s): Feb., Mar., Aug., and Sept.
Final notification: Apr. and Sept. for organizations located in the Twin Cities, MN, metropolitan area; within 60 days following deadlines for organizations located outside the Twin Cities, MN, metropolitan area
Directors: Lisa Ferris; Charles Grose; Larry Holtz; Mike Kavanagh; Andre Lewis; John Taft; Irving Weiser.
Number of staff: 1 full-time professional; 1 full-time support.
EIN: 416030369
Selected grants: The following grants were reported in 2004.
$130,000 to United Way.
$50,000 to Minneapolis Institute of Arts, Minneapolis, MN.

$25,000 to Neighborhood Involvement Program, Minneapolis, MN.

$14,000 to Junior Achievement of the Upper Midwest, Maplewood, MN.

$12,500 to Minneapolis Community and Technical College Foundation, Minneapolis, MN.

$3,000 to Augsburg College, Minneapolis, MN.

$3,000 to Centers for Habilitation, Tempe, AZ.

$3,000 to Stages Theater Company, Hopkins, MN.

$2,854 to United Way of East Central Iowa, Cedar Rapids, IA.

$2,000 to Kinship of Greater Minneapolis, Minneapolis, MN.

4662
Horst M. Rechelbacher Foundation ✧ ☆
c/o Dennis Ritchie
220 S. 6th St., Ste. 300
Minneapolis, MN 55402

Established in 1999 in MN.
Donor: Horst Rechelbacher.
Foundation type: Independent foundation.
Financial data (yr. ended 12/31/05): Assets, $73,500 (M); gifts received, $403,915; expenditures, $364,615; qualifying distributions, $362,500; giving activities include $362,500 for grants.
Fields of interest: Arts; Education; Environment, natural resources; Medical care, in-patient care; Cancer.
Limitations: Applications not accepted. Giving on a national basis. No grants to individuals.
Application information: Contributes only to pre-selected organizations.
Officers: Horst Rechelbacher, Pres.; James Greupner, Secy.
Directors: Peter Rechelbacher; Nicole Thomas.
EIN: 411956679
Selected grants: The following grants were reported in 2004.
$50,000 to Cancer Prevention Coalition, Chicago, IL. For program support.
$15,000 to Minneapolis Heart Institute Foundation, Minneapolis, MN. For medical equipment.
$10,545 to Osceola High School, Kissimmee, FL. For marching band percussion.
$10,000 to American Botanical Council, Austin, TX. For ethnobotanical rainforest tours.
$10,000 to Continuum Center, Minneapolis, MN. For Discovery of Self Speaker series.
$10,000 to Greenpeace Fund, DC. For international ancient forests campaign.
$10,000 to Minnesota Dance Theater and School, Minneapolis, MN. For dance theater programs.
$10,000 to Youth for Environmental Sanity (YES), Soquel, CA.
$8,805 to Tibet House, New York, NY.
$3,000 to National Child Safety Council, Jackson, MI. For drug prevention education program.

4663
Red Wing Shoe Company Foundation ✧
314 Main St.
Red Wing, MN 55066
Contact: Stacy Crownhart, Secy.

Incorporated in 1955 in MN.
Donor: Red Wing Shoe Co., Inc.
Foundation type: Company-sponsored foundation.

Financial data (yr. ended 12/31/04): Assets, $166,805 (M); gifts received, $426,000; expenditures, $409,581; qualifying distributions, $409,555; giving activities include $337,898 for 64 grants (high: $235,000; low: $25), and $71,505 for 2 employee matching gifts.
Purpose and activities: The foundation supports organizations involved with arts and culture, education, health, youth development, and human services.
Fields of interest: Performing arts; Arts; Elementary/secondary education; Education; Health care; Youth development; YM/YWCAs & YM/YWHAs; Human services; Federated giving programs.
Type of support: Employee matching gifts; General/operating support; Continuing support; Capital campaigns; Program development; Scholarship funds; Matching/challenge support.
Limitations: Giving primarily in the Danville, KY, Red Wing, MN, and Potosi, MO, areas. No grants to individuals.
Publications: Annual report.
Application information: Application form not required.
  Initial approach: Proposal
  Deadline(s): None
Officers and Directors: William J. Sweasy, C.E.O.; Stacy Crownhart, Secy.; Suzanne Blue; Silas B. Foot III.
EIN: 416020177
Selected grants: The following grants were reported in 2005.
$51,200 to United Way. 2 grants: $50,000, $1,200
$11,500 to YMCA. 2 grants: $1,000, $10,500
$8,038 to American Red Cross.
$5,000 to Science Museum of Minnesota, Saint Paul, MN.
$1,000 to National Trust for Historic Preservation, DC.
$380 to Minnesota Public Radio, Saint Paul, MN. 2 grants: $300, $80
$250 to YMCA, Red Wing Family, Red Wing, MN.

4664
The Regis Foundation ✧
7201 Metro Blvd.
Minneapolis, MN 55439-2103 (952) 947-7777
Contact: Myron Kunin, Pres.

Established in 1981 in MN.
Donors: Regis Corp.; Regis, Inc.
Foundation type: Company-sponsored foundation.
Financial data (yr. ended 6/30/05): Assets, $1,434,166 (M); gifts received, $1,627,992; expenditures, $1,821,095; qualifying distributions, $1,807,460; giving activities include $1,807,460 for 21 grants (high: $650,000; low: $1,000).
Purpose and activities: The foundation supports organizations involved with arts and culture, education, human services, and Judaism.
Fields of interest: Arts; Elementary/secondary education; Higher education; Libraries (public); Education; Human services; Federated giving programs; Jewish federated giving programs; Jewish agencies & temples.
Type of support: Annual campaigns; Capital campaigns; General/operating support; Building/renovation; Scholarship funds.
Limitations: Giving primarily in the Minneapolis, MN, area.
Application information: Application form not required.

Initial approach: Proposal
Deadline(s): None
Officers and Directors:* Myron Kunin, Pres.; David B. Kunin,* V.P.; Eric Bakken, Secy.; Paul Finkelstein; Randy Pearce.
EIN: 411410790
Selected grants: The following grants were reported in 2005.
$650,000 to Minneapolis Jewish Federation, Minnetonka, MN.
$140,000 to Minneapolis Public Schools, Minneapolis, MN.
$62,000 to Minnesota Public Radio, Saint Paul, MN.
$56,000 to United Way.
$20,000 to American Jewish Committee, Chicago, IL.
$20,000 to Council on Crime and Justice, Minneapolis, MN.
$16,360 to Orange County Museum of Art, Newport Beach, CA.
$10,000 to Starlight Starbright Childrens Foundation, Los Angeles, CA.
$1,000 to K T C A/K T C I Twin Cities Public Television, Saint Paul, MN.

4665
Reimer Foundation ✧
8310 Creekside Cir., No. 820
Bloomington, MN 55437
Contact: William Reimer, Co-Chair.

Established in 1985 in MN.
Donor: William Reimer.
Foundation type: Independent foundation.
Financial data (yr. ended 11/30/05): Assets, $5,226,531 (M); gifts received, $5,000; expenditures, $637,231; qualifying distributions, $621,600; giving activities include $621,600 for 20 grants (high: $250,000; low: $100).
Purpose and activities: Giving for Christian organizations.
Fields of interest: Christian agencies & churches; Protestant agencies & churches.
Limitations: Giving primarily in Wheaton, IL, and MN.
Application information:
  Initial approach: Letter
  Deadline(s): None
Officers: Dolores Reimer, Co-Chair.; William Reimer, Co-Chair.
Directors: Barb Olson; Lynn Reimer; Michelle Vock.
EIN: 411557662

4666
Margaret Rivers Fund ✧
P.O. Box 197
Stillwater, MN 55082
Contact: David F. Pohl, Pres.

Incorporated in 1948 in MN.
Donor: Robert E. Slaughter†.
Foundation type: Independent foundation.
Financial data (yr. ended 12/31/05): Assets, $32,675,832 (M); expenditures, $5,798,550; qualifying distributions, $3,924,808; giving activities include $3,865,700 for 162 grants (high: $200,000; low: $500).
Purpose and activities: Grants primarily for hospitals, church support, youth agencies, aid to the handicapped, and care of the aged; support also for cultural programs and conservation.

Fields of interest: Arts; Environment, natural resources; Hospitals (general); Youth, services; Aging, centers/services; Christian agencies & churches; Aging; Disabilities, people with.

Type of support: General/operating support.

Limitations: Giving primarily in MN. No grants to individuals.

Application information: Application form not required.

Initial approach: Letter
Copies of proposal: 1
Deadline(s): None
Board meeting date(s): Monthly
Final notification: 30-60 days

Officers: David F. Pohl, Pres. and Treas.; Robert G. Briggs, V.P.; Lawrence Severson, Secy.

Director: Jean Berry.

EIN: 416017102

Selected grants: The following grants were reported in 2004.

$200,000 to Ascension Episcopal Church, Stillwater, MN.

$100,000 to FamilyMeans, Stillwater, MN.

$80,000 to Salvation Army of Saint Paul, Saint Paul, MN.

$74,000 to Community Volunteer Service, Stillwater, MN. 2 grants: $34,000, $40,000 (For building project).

$55,000 to Minnesota FoodShare, Minneapolis, MN.

$50,000 to Arcola Mills Historic Foundation, Stillwater, MN.

$37,000 to Boy Scouts of America, Indianhead Council, Saint Paul, MN.

$30,000 to Catholic Charities of the Archdiocese of Saint Paul and Minneapolis, Minneapolis, MN.

$30,000 to Courage Center, Golden Valley, MN.

4667
Robins, Kaplan, Miller & Ciresi Foundation ◇

800 LaSalle Ave., Ste. 2800
Minneapolis, MN 55402
Contact: Michael V. Ciresi, Pres.
Additional contact: Steven A. Schumeister, Dir.;
URL: http://www.rkmc.com/foundation.asp

Established in 1993 in MN.

Donor: Robins, Kaplan, Miller & Ciresi L.L.P.

Foundation type: Company-sponsored foundation.

Financial data (yr. ended 8/31/04): Assets, $2,040,925 (M); gifts received, $2,000,000; expenditures, $1,723,706; qualifying distributions, $1,709,289; giving activities include $1,675,155 for 250 grants (high: $300,000; low: $100).

Purpose and activities: The foundation supports organizations involved with arts and culture, education, health, legal services, human services, and community development.

Fields of interest: Arts; Higher education; Law school/education; Education; Health care; Health organizations; Legal services; Children, services; Human services; Community development; Federated giving programs; African Americans/Blacks.

Limitations: Giving on a national basis, with some emphasis on Minneapolis and St. Paul, MN. No grants to individuals.

Application information: Application form not required.

Initial approach: Proposal

Officer: Michael V. Ciresi, Chair.

Directors: Jan Conlin; B. Todd Jones; Steven A. Schumeister; Ronald Schutz; Roman Silberfeld; William Stanhope.

EIN: 411735325

Selected grants: The following grants were reported in 2004.

$300,000 to University of Minnesota Foundation, Minneapolis, MN.

$75,000 to Shakespeare Theater, DC.

$50,000 to Public Counsel, Los Angeles, CA.

$26,000 to Equal Justice Works, DC.

$25,875 to United Way, Greater Twin Cities, Minneapolis, MN.

$25,000 to Childrens Theater Company and School, Minneapolis, MN.

$25,000 to Guthrie Theater, Minneapolis, MN.

$25,000 to Mid-Minnesota Legal Assistance, Minneapolis, MN.

$25,000 to Minneapolis Institute of Arts, Minneapolis, MN.

$15,000 to Public Radio International, Minneapolis, MN.

4668
Rochester Area Foundation

2200 2nd St. S.W., Ste. 300
Rochester, MN 55902-4125 (507) 282-0203
Contact: Steve Thornton, Exec. Dir.; For grants: Jane Campion, Grants Admin.
FAX: (507) 282-4938;
E-mail: info@rochesterarea.org; Additional E-mail: steve@RochesterArea.org; URL: http://www.rochesterarea.org

Established in 1944 in MN by resolution of corporation.

Foundation type: Community foundation.

Financial data (yr. ended 12/31/05): Assets, $25,515,886 (M); gifts received, $3,003,050; expenditures, $1,373,940; giving activities include $649,598 for 145 grants (high: $42,000; low: $200), and $22,450 for 36 grants to individuals (high: $1,000; low: $250).

Purpose and activities: The foundation's mission is to help launch new projects which represent innovative approaches to community needs, support special purposes of established organizations, promote volunteer and citizen involvement in the community, respond to current human needs in the community, and support projects without other sources of support; giving in areas of health, education, human services, and development and assistance of community affairs.

Fields of interest: Arts; Child development, education; Higher education; Education; Environment; Health care; Housing/shelter, development; Recreation; Child development, services; Family services; Aging, centers/services; Minorities/immigrants, centers/services; Human services; Civil rights; Community development; Voluntarism promotion; Government/public administration; Public affairs; Aging; Disabilities, people with; Minorities.

Type of support: Management development/capacity building; Building/renovation; Emergency funds; Seed money; Technical assistance; Consulting services; Matching/challenge support.

Limitations: Giving limited to the greater Rochester, MN, area. No support for religious organizations for sectarian purposes. No grants to individuals (except for scholarships), or for endowment funds, annual campaigns, operating budgets, continuing support,

land acquisition, deficit financing, fellowships, or research.

Publications: Application guidelines; Annual report; Informational brochure (including application guidelines); Newsletter.

Application information: Visit foundation Web site for application forms and guidelines. If the foundation's Board of Trustees approves the applicant's pre-application for a grant, they will be notified and asked to submit a full application. Application form required.

Initial approach: Submit pre-application form
Copies of proposal: 7
Deadline(s): Jan. 1, May 1, and Sept. 1 for pre-application form; Mar. 1, July 3, and Nov. 1 for full application
Board meeting date(s): Jan., Feb., Apr., May, Aug., Sept., Oct., Nov., and Dec.
Final notification: Late Jan., late May, and late Sept. for pre-application determination; late Apr., late Aug., and late Dec. for grants

Officers and Trustees:* David Stenhaug,* Chair.; Michael McNeil,* Vice-Chair.; Craig Wendland,* Vice-Chair.; Carol Kamper,* Secy.; Charles Elliott,* Treas.; Steve Thornton, Exec. Dir.; Nancy Brubaker; Nancy Domaille; Joe Duffy; Paul Harkess; Leigh Johnson; Jean Locke; Jon Losness; Joe Powers; Alan Schafer; John Wade.

Number of staff: 5 full-time professional; 2 full-time support.

EIN: 416017740

4669
The Fran and Warren Rupp Foundation ◇ ☆

c/o Family Philanthropy Advisors
1818 Oliver Ave. S.
Minneapolis, MN 55404

Established in 1977 in OH.

Donors: Fran R. Christian; Warren Rupp‡; Suzanne R. Hartung.

Foundation type: Independent foundation.

Financial data (yr. ended 12/31/05): Assets, $21,113,398 (M); gifts received, $24,460; expenditures, $1,188,719; qualifying distributions, $711,500; giving activities include $711,500 for grants.

Fields of interest: Performing arts, theater; Arts; Scholarships/financial aid; Education; Environment, natural resources; Environment; Animal welfare; Crime/law enforcement; Housing/shelter, development; Human services.

Type of support: General/operating support; Capital campaigns; Building/renovation; Land acquisition; Endowments; Publication; Matching/challenge support.

Limitations: Applications not accepted. Giving primarily in Mansfield and Richland County, OH. No grants to individuals.

Application information: Contributes only to pre-selected organizations.

Board meeting date(s): May and Nov.

Officers: Sheron A. Rupp, Chair.; Suzanne R. Hartung, Pres.

Trustees: Stephen Frampton; Frederick Hartung.

EIN: 341230690

Selected grants: The following grants were reported in 2004.

$40,000 to Perry Mansfield Performing Arts Center, Steamboat Springs, CO. For general operating support.

$30,000 to Ohio State University, Columbus, OH. For scholarships.

$25,000 to Culliver Reading Center, Mansfield, OH. For program support.

$10,750 to Friendly House, Mansfield, OH. For program support.

$5,000 to Ashland University, Ashland, OH. For scholarships.

$5,000 to Bluffton College, Bluffton, OH. For scholarships.

$5,000 to Cedarville University, Cedarville, OH. For scholarships.

$5,000 to University of Akron, Akron, OH. For scholarships.

$2,400 to Renaissance Performing Arts, Mansfield, OH. For program support.

$1,500 to Richland County Childrens Services, Mansfield, OH. For program support.

4670

The Sabes Family Foundation ✧

(formerly The Moe and Esther Sabes Family Foundation)
c/o Steven Sabes
60 S. 6th St., Ste. 2540
Minneapolis, MN 55402

Established in 1991 in MN.
Donors: Moe Sabes; Esther Sabes; Robert Sabes; Janet Sabes; Steven Sabes; Amy Sabes.
Foundation type: Independent foundation.
Financial data (yr. ended 12/31/05): Assets, $46,174,815 (M); gifts received, $2,005,200; expenditures, $2,174,263; qualifying distributions, $1,869,370; giving activities include $1,796,215 for 45 grants (high: $1,495,000; low: $100).
Purpose and activities: Giving primarily for Jewish organizations and federated giving programs.
Fields of interest: Arts; Human services; Children/youth, services; Jewish federated giving programs; Jewish agencies & temples.
Limitations: Applications not accepted. Giving primarily in MN. No grants to individuals.
Application information: Contributes only to pre-selected organizations.
Trustees: Esther Sabes; Robert Sabes; Steven Sabes.
EIN: 411699714
Selected grants: The following grants were reported in 2003.
$430,000 to Minneapolis Jewish Federation, Minnetonka, MN. 3 grants: $125,000, $125,000, $180,000
$50,000 to Howard Pulley Basketball League, Minneapolis, MN. 2 grants: $25,000 each
$25,000 to Juvenile Diabetes Research Foundation International, Bloomington, MN.
$20,000 to Bnai Brith Foundation, Golden Valley, MN.
$10,000 to Jewish Family and Childrens Service of Minneapolis, Minnetonka, MN.
$10,000 to Trust for Public Land, Midwest Field Office, Saint Paul, MN.
$5,000 to University of Minnesota Foundation, Minneapolis, MN.

4671

The Saint Paul Foundation, Inc. ▼

55 5th St. E., Ste. 600
St. Paul, MN 55101-1797 (651) 224-5463
Contact: Carleen Rhodes, Pres.

FAX: (651) 224-8123;
E-mail: inbox@saintpaulfoundation.org; Additional tel.: (800) 875-6167; Additional E-mails: ckr@saintpaulfoundation.org and lmh@saintpaulfoundation.org; URL: http://saintpaulfoundation.org

Established in 1940 in MN by adoption of a plan; incorporated in 1964.
Foundation type: Community foundation.
Financial data (yr. ended 12/31/05): Assets, $617,910,511 (M); gifts received, $24,925,219; expenditures, $45,656,438; giving activities include $33,557,217 for 6,086 grants (high: $750,000; low: $25), and $1,118,489 for 1,939 grants to individuals (high: $40,623; low: $17).
Purpose and activities: The foundation actively serves the people of Saint Paul, MN, and the surrounding communities by building permanent charitable capital, making philanthropic grants, and providing services that contribute to the health and vitality of the community. This is done by working with donors to achieve their philanthropic goals; managing responsibly the foundation's assets; encouraging and participating in community initiatives and partnerships; broadening the base of effective leadership in the community; building awareness of the role of philanthropy in meeting the needs of the community; and providing services to other charitable organizations. The foundation pays special attention to helping achieve the following outcomes through its grants from unrestricted funds: an anti-racist community, economic development for disadvantaged people and communities, strong families that provide healthy beginnings for children and youth, and quality education for all.
Fields of interest: Humanities; Arts; Elementary/secondary education; Education, early childhood education; Higher education; Adult education—literacy, basic skills & GED; Education, reading; Education; Health care; Health organizations, association; Children/youth, services; Minorities/immigrants, centers/services; Human services; Civil rights, race/intergroup relations; Community development, neighborhood development; Economic development; Community development; Minorities.
Type of support: Capital campaigns; Building/renovation; Equipment; Program development; Seed money; Technical assistance; Matching/challenge support.
Limitations: Giving limited to Dakota, Ramsey, and Washington counties in the metropolitan Saint Paul, MN, area. No support for sectarian religious programs (except from designated funds). No grants to individuals (except from designated funds), or for ongoing annual operating budgets, agency endowment funds, and capital projects located outside the East Metro area.
Publications: Application guidelines; Financial statement; Grants list; Newsletter.
Application information: Prior to submitting a grant request, applicants should review the foundation's grant application cover sheet, proposal, and narrative guidelines. Copies of these forms can be obtained by telephone, e-mail, or by visiting foundation's Web site. Applicants who submit a letter of inquiry should only address information included in the Narrative Guidelines. Application form required.
Initial approach: Letter of inquiry (no more than 3 pages)
Copies of proposal: 1

Deadline(s): Approximately 3 1/2 months before next board meeting
Board meeting date(s): Apr., Aug., and Nov.
Final notification: Within 4 to 5 months
Officers and Directors:* Phyllis A. Rawls Goff,* Chair.; Jay Cowles III,* Vice-Chair.; Carleen K. Rhodes, Pres.; John G. Couchman, V.P., Grants and Progs.; Marcia E. Murray, V.P., Exec. Office; Jack H. Pohl, V.P., Finance; Diane K. Smith, V.P., Opers. and Admin.; Christine K. Searson, Cont.; Wilson G. Bradshaw; Mary K. Brainerd; Henry M. Buffalo, Jr.; Iris H. Cornelius, Ph.D.; Patrick J. Donovan; Robert A. Engebretsen; James R. Frey; Donald L. Garofalo; Joan A. Grzywinski; Robyn Hansen; R. Scott Jones; Susan Kimberly; Cynthia Lesher; Manuel Mariano Lopez; Wendy H. Rubin; L. Jim Schoenwetter; Cris E. Stainbrook; Jon A. Theobald; Elsa Vega-Perez.
Corporate Trustees: American National Bank; U.S. Bank, N.A.; U.S. Trust; Wells Fargo Bank Minnesota, N.A.
Number of staff: 38 full-time professional; 2 part-time professional; 19 full-time support.
EIN: 416031510
Selected grants: The following grants were reported in 2005.
$500,000 to Jeremiah Program, Minneapolis, MN. For capital campaign to establish Saint Paul campus.
$200,000 to Amherst H. Wilder Foundation, Saint Paul, MN. Toward financing budget for expanding Achievement Plus to junior high schools in Saint Paul.
$150,000 to Organizing Apprenticeship Project, Minneapolis, MN. Toward financing budget of Racial Justice Organizing Initiative.
$120,000 to Second Harvest Heartland, Saint Paul, MN. Toward financing budget for implementing Service Improvement Plan.
$60,000 to Greater Frogtown Community Development Corporation, Saint Paul, MN. Toward financing budget for organizing and coordinating Dale Street Corridor Plan.
$50,000 to Saint Paul Public Library, Friends of the, Saint Paul, MN. Toward operating budget of Homework Center at Rondo Library.
$25,000 to Childrens Dental Services, Minneapolis, MN. To start-up budget for program expansion in Saint Paul.
$25,000 to YWCA of Saint Paul, Saint Paul, MN. Toward financing budget of Lovin The Skin I'm in Youth Development Initiative.
$20,000 to Vietnamese Social Services of Minnesota, Saint Paul, MN. Toward financing budget of Karen Support Project.
$17,000 to Hmong Center, Minneapolis, MN. Toward financing budget for Refugee Youth Survival Skills Program.

4672

Sanger Family Foundation ✧

16588 Grays Bay Blvd.
Wayzata, MN 55391-2915

Established in 1996 in MN.
Donors: Stephen W. Sanger; Karen O. Sanger.
Foundation type: Independent foundation.
Financial data (yr. ended 12/31/05): Assets, $2,974,308 (M); gifts received, $897,345; expenditures, $760,251; qualifying distributions, $755,136; giving activities include $755,136 for 54 grants (high: $248,825; low: $100).
Fields of interest: Arts; Higher education; Education; Health organizations, association;

Human services; YM/YWCAs & YM/YWHAs; Children/youth, services; Federated giving programs.
Limitations: Applications not accepted. Giving primarily in MN, with some emphasis on the Minneapolis-St. Paul area; some giving nationally. No grants to individuals.
Application information: Contributes only to pre-selected organizations.
Officers and Directors: * Stephen W. Sanger,* Pres.; Karen O. Sanger,* V.P.
EIN: 411859638

4673
Carl and Verna Schmidt Foundation
P.O. Box 638
Rochester, MN 55903-0638
Contact: Alan C. Anderson, Tr.

Established in 1958 in MN.
Donors: Carl Schmidt‡; Verna Schmidt‡.
Foundation type: Independent foundation.
Financial data (yr. ended 12/31/05): Assets, $27,284,059 (M); expenditures, $1,377,733; qualifying distributions, $1,187,742; giving activities include $1,125,233 for 102 grants (high: $67,500; low: $250).
Purpose and activities: Giving primarily for public libraries, health associations, including a children's hospital, volunteer fire departments and human services; funding also for the arts, natural resource conservation, and animals and wildlife.
Fields of interest: Historic preservation/historical societies; Arts; Libraries (public); Environment, natural resources; Animals/wildlife; Hospitals (specialty); Health organizations, association; Housing/shelter, development; Disasters, fire prevention/control; Human services; Children, services.
Limitations: Giving primarily in MN. No grants to individuals.
Application information: Telephone applications not accepted. Application form required.
  Initial approach: Letter only
  Copies of proposal: 1
  Deadline(s): None
  Board meeting date(s): Monthly
  Final notification: 1 month from receipt of application
Trustees: Alan C. Anderson; Jonathan S. Anderson.
Number of staff: 1 part-time professional.
EIN: 237423942
Selected grants: The following grants were reported in 2004.
$200,000 to Saint Peter Community Hospital Foundation, Saint Peter, MN.
$100,100 to Minnesota Waterfowl Association, Minneapolis, MN.
$18,000 to Minnesota Department of Natural Resources, Saint Paul, MN.
$17,500 to Saint Peter Public Library, Saint Peter, MN.
$7,000 to Slayton Public Library, Slayton, MN.
$5,000 to Rochester Orchestra and Chorale, Rochester, MN.
$5,000 to Shriners Hospitals for Children, Minneapolis, MN.
$2,500 to Helping Paws of Minnesota, Minneapolis, MN.
$250 to Courage Center, Golden Valley, MN.
$250 to Union Gospel Mission Association of Saint Paul, Saint Paul, MN.

4674
Schoenecker Foundation ◇
c/o Guy Schoenecker
P.O. Box 1610
Minneapolis, MN 55440

Established in 1979 in MN.
Donor: Schoeneckers, Inc.
Foundation type: Company-sponsored foundation.
Financial data (yr. ended 9/30/05): Assets, $100,912 (M); gifts received, $500,000; expenditures, $561,596; qualifying distributions, $561,578; giving activities include $561,561 for 9 grants (high: $312,000; low: $100).
Purpose and activities: The foundation supports organizations involved with higher education and human services.
Fields of interest: Higher education; Human services.
Type of support: Continuing support; Capital campaigns.
Limitations: Applications not accepted. Giving primarily in MN. No grants to individuals.
Application information: Contributes only to pre-selected organizations.
Officers and Directors: * Guy Schoenecker, Pres. and Treas.; Larry Schoenecker,* V.P. and Secy.; James E. O'Brien; Barbara Schoenecker.
EIN: 411369001
Selected grants: The following grants were reported in 2003.
$400,000 to College of Saint Benedict, Saint Joseph, MN. For operating support.
$110,000 to University of Saint Thomas, Saint Paul, MN. For operating support.
$16,665 to Cheerful Givers. For operating support.
$3,623 to American Diabetes Association of Minnesota, Golden Valley, MN. For operating support.
$1,550 to Redeemer Lutheran Church, Wayzata, MN. For operating support.
$1,256 to Catholic Charities of the Archdiocese of Saint Paul and Minneapolis, Minneapolis, MN. For operating support.
$1,000 to Bridging, Inc., Bloomington, MN. For operating support.
$1,000 to United Way, Greater Twin Cities, Minneapolis, MN. For operating support.
$500 to Cystic Fibrosis Foundation, Grafton, WI. For operating support.
$200 to Eden Valley United Charities, Eden Valley, MN. For operating support.

4675
Richard M. Schulze Family Foundation ◇ ☆
8500 Normandale Lake Blvd., Rm. 1750
Minneapolis, MN 55437

Established in 2004 in MN.
Donor: Richard M. Schulze.
Foundation type: Independent foundation.
Financial data (yr. ended 12/31/05): Assets, $15,291,119 (M); gifts received, $7,600,031; expenditures, $790,891; qualifying distributions, $700,000; giving activities include $700,000 for 2 grants (high: $500,000; low: $200,000).
Fields of interest: Elementary/secondary education; Children/youth, services.
Limitations: Applications not accepted. Giving primarily in MN.
Application information: Contributes only to pre-selected organizations.

Director: Richard M. Schulze.
EIN: 200752440

4676
Schwan's Corporate Giving Foundation ◇
115 W. College Dr.
Marshall, MN 56258
Contact: David Paskach, Vice-Chair.

Established as a company-sponsored operating foundation in 2000 in MN.
Donors: Schwan's Sales Enterprises, Inc.; The Schwan Food Co., Inc.
Foundation type: Operating foundation.
Financial data (yr. ended 1/3/04): Assets, $4,576,382 (M); gifts received, $37,000; expenditures, $352,325; qualifying distributions, $350,000; giving activities include $350,000 for 3 grants (high: $200,000; low: $50,000).
Purpose and activities: The foundation supports organizations involved with higher education and community development.
Fields of interest: Higher education; Community development.
Type of support: Program development; Scholarship funds.
Limitations: Giving primarily in Marshall, MN.
Application information:
  Initial approach: Proposal
Officers: M. Lenny Pippin, Chair. and Pres.; David M. Paskach, Vice-Chair. and Secy.; Bernadette M. Kruk, Treas.
EIN: 411990835

4677
Securian Foundation ◇
(formerly Minnesota Mutual Foundation)
Minnesota Mutual Life Ctr.
400 N. Robert St.
St. Paul, MN 55101 (651) 665-3501
Contact: Lori J. Koutsky, Mgr.
FAX: (651) 665-3551;
E-mail: lori.koutsky@securian.com; *URL:* http://www.securian.com/About/community.asp

Established in 1988 in MN.
Donors: Minnesota Life Insurance Co.; Securian Holding Co.
Foundation type: Company-sponsored foundation.
Financial data (yr. ended 12/31/04): Assets, $34,139,775 (M); expenditures, $1,430,684; qualifying distributions, $1,387,252; giving activities include $1,185,625 for 93 grants (high: $360,000; low: $500), and $165,960 for 562 employee matching gifts.
Purpose and activities: The foundation supports organizations involved with arts and culture, education, employment, and human services.
Fields of interest: Arts; Higher education; Education; Employment; Human services; Federated giving programs.
Type of support: General/operating support; Annual campaigns; Capital campaigns; Program development; Employee matching gifts.
Limitations: Giving primarily in areas of company operations, with emphasis on the Twin Cities, MN, area. No support for political, lobbying, or fraternal organizations, international, veterans', or sports-related organizations, or religious organizations not of direct benefit to the entire community. No grants to individuals, or for

endowments, benefits, sponsorships, fundraising events, advertising, recreation, conferences, seminars, trips, or tours.
Publications: Application guidelines; Grants list; Informational brochure; Program policy statement.
Application information: Proposals should be no longer than 7 pages. Proposals may be submitted using the Minnesota Common Grant Application Form. Application form not required.
Initial approach: Proposal
Copies of proposal: 1
Deadline(s): Feb. 15, May 15, Aug. 15, and Nov. 15
Board meeting date(s): Mar. 15, June 15, Sept. 15, and Dec. 15
Final notification: Apr. 15, July 15, Oct. 15, and Jan. 15
Officers and Directors:* Robert L. Senkler,* Pres.; Keith M. Campbell,* V.P.; Dennis Prohofsky,* Secy.; Greg Strong, Treas.
Number of staff: 1 part-time professional; 1 part-time support.
EIN: 363608619
Selected grants: The following grants were reported in 2005.
$9,500 to Boys and Girls Clubs of the Twin Cities, Saint Paul, MN. For annual support.
$5,000 to Minnesota Minority Education Partnership, Minneapolis, MN.
$5,000 to Twin Cities RISE (TCR), Minneapolis, MN.
$4,000 to Minnesota Childrens Museum, Saint Paul, MN. For annual support.
$3,000 to Admission Possible, Saint Paul, MN.

4678
Sewell Family Foundation ☆
5200 W. 73rd St.
Minneapolis, MN 55439
Contact: Gloria Sewell, Pres.

Established in 1997 in MN.
Donors: Gloria Sewell; Frederick Sewell.
Foundation type: Independent foundation.
Financial data (yr. ended 12/31/05): Assets, $3,477,008 (M); expenditures, $344,654; qualifying distributions, $323,672; giving activities include $322,750 for 21 grants (high: $100,000; low: $400).
Purpose and activities: Giving primarily for the arts.
Fields of interest: Arts, multipurpose centers/ programs; Performing arts; Performing arts, theater.
Limitations: Giving primarily in MN.
Application information: Application form not required.
Initial approach: Letter
Copies of proposal: 1
Deadline(s): None
Board meeting date(s): Biannually
Officers: Gloria Sewell, Pres.; Frederick Sewell, V.P.; Kathleen Longo, C.F.O.
EIN: 411861892
Selected grants: The following grants were reported in 2004.
$170,000 to Ballet Works, Minneapolis, MN. 2 grants: $85,000 each
$115,000 to Saint Paul Chamber Orchestra Society, Saint Paul, MN.
$40,000 to Chamber Music America, New York, NY. 2 grants: $20,000 each
$22,000 to American Composers Forum, Saint Paul, MN. 2 grants: $11,000 each
$12,500 to MacPhail Center for Music, Minneapolis, MN.

$5,000 to Schubert Club, Saint Paul, MN.
$2,500 to Chamber Music Society of Minnesota, Saint Paul, MN.

4679
Sexton Foundation ✧
2225 Chelmsford Ln.
St. Cloud, MN 56301 (320) 230-9171
Contact: M. Yvonne Sexton, Pres.

Established in 1977.
Donors: American Trailers, Inc.; James Sexton.
Foundation type: Independent foundation.
Financial data (yr. ended 11/30/05): Assets, $9,146,577 (M); gifts received, $10,000; expenditures, $425,525; qualifying distributions, $425,380; giving activities include $425,380 for 42 grants (high: $102,880; low: $500).
Fields of interest: Elementary/secondary education; Environment, water pollution; Environment; Food services; Housing/shelter; Human services; Women; Economically disadvantaged.
Limitations: Giving primarily in MN. No support for private foundations. No grants to individuals.
Application information: Application form not required.
Initial approach: Letter
Deadline(s): None
Officers: M. Yvonne Sexton, Pres.; Thomas P. Sexton, V.P.; James Sexton, Secy.-Treas.
EIN: 411312086

4680
Shiebler Family Foundation ✧
12219 Wood Lake Dr.
Burnsville, MN 55337
Contact: William Perron, Tr.

Established in 1999 in MN.
Donors: William Shiebler; Joanne Shiebler.
Foundation type: Operating foundation.
Financial data (yr. ended 12/31/05): Assets, $1,320,996 (M); gifts received, $513,629; expenditures, $410,994; qualifying distributions, $409,469; giving activities include $409,469 for 17 grants (high: $305,219; low: $100).
Purpose and activities: Giving primarily for education, human services, and the arts, particularly the opera.
Fields of interest: Performing arts, opera; Arts; Higher education; Education; Health organizations, association; Human services.
Limitations: Giving primarily in UT; funding also nationally. No grants to individuals.
Application information: Application form not required.
Deadline(s): None
Trustees: William Perron; Christina Shiebler; Jason Shiebler; Joanne Shiebler; William Shiebler.
EIN: 411960074
Selected grants: The following grants were reported in 2003.
$62,650 to Utah Symphony and Opera, Salt Lake City, UT.
$51,200 to United States Ski Team Foundation, Park City, UT.
$28,300 to Cystic Fibrosis Foundation, New York, NY.
$25,000 to Oquirrh Institute, Salt Lake City, UT.

$5,000 to Christian Center of Park City, Park City, UT.
$5,000 to Nature Conservancy, Salt Lake City, UT.
$300 to Sharing and Caring Hands, Minneapolis, MN.
$250 to Childrens Hospital Trust, Boston, MA.
$250 to Ronald McDonald House Charities, Upper Midwest, Minneapolis, MN.
$250 to Salvation Army, Northern Division, Roseville, MN.

4681
Dan & Kay Shimek Family Foundation ✧ ☆
100 Washington Ave., Ste. 1600
Minneapolis, MN 55401

Established in 2002 in MN.
Donors: Dan Shimek; Kay Shimek.
Foundation type: Independent foundation.
Financial data (yr. ended 12/31/05): Assets, $31,855 (M); gifts received, $394,256; expenditures, $358,939; qualifying distributions, $358,354; giving activities include $358,354 for 16 grants (high: $100,000; low: $50).
Limitations: Applications not accepted. No grants to individuals.
Application information: Contributes only to pre-selected organizations.
Officers: Daniel C. Shimek, Pres. and Treas.; Kay N. Shimek, Exec. V.P.; Richard L. Ledin, V.P.
EIN: 270035772

4682
Sieben Foundation, Inc. ✧
c/o Adler Mgmt. LLC
10350 Bren Rd. W.
Minnetonka, MN 55343

Established in 1988 in MN.
Donor: Opus U.S. Corp.
Foundation type: Independent foundation.
Financial data (yr. ended 12/31/05): Assets, $16,322,951 (M); expenditures, $744,794; qualifying distributions, $700,840; giving activities include $652,390 for 13 grants (high: $250,000; low: $5,000).
Purpose and activities: Giving primarily for Roman Catholic education and for human services.
Fields of interest: Elementary school/education; Higher education; Substance abuse, treatment; Human services; Roman Catholic federated giving programs; Roman Catholic agencies & churches.
Type of support: Program-related investments/ loans.
Limitations: Applications not accepted. Giving primarily in MN; some giving nationally. No grants to individuals.
Application information: Contributes only to pre-selected organizations.
Officers and Directors:* Karen Rauenhorst,* Pres.; Luz Campa, V.P.; Don Neureuther, Secy.; Michael Rauenhorst,* Treas.; Loretta Rauenhorst; Jeffrey S. Turner.
EIN: 363608625

4683
The Eugene C. & Gail V. Sit Foundation ✧ ☆
80 S. 8th St., Rm. 3300
Minneapolis, MN 55402-4130

Established in 1986 in MN.
Donor: Eugene C. Sit.
Foundation type: Independent foundation.
Financial data (yr. ended 11/30/05): Assets, $7,048,411 (M); gifts received, $1,094,771; expenditures, $437,349; qualifying distributions, $395,175; giving activities include $395,175 for 15 grants (high: $250,000; low: $125).
Purpose and activities: Giving primarily for the arts, education, social services, and to a Presbyterian church.
Fields of interest: Performing arts, orchestra (symphony); Arts; Higher education; Boy scouts; Human services; Protestant agencies & churches.
Limitations: Applications not accepted. Giving primarily in MN, with emphasis on Minneapolis; some funding nationally, particularly in Chicago, IL. No grants to individuals.
Application information: Contributes only to pre-selected organizations.
Officers: Eugene C. Sit, Pres.; Ronald D. Sit, Secy.
EIN: 411572465
Selected grants: The following grants were reported in 2004.
$20,000 to Minneapolis Institute of Arts, Minneapolis, MN.
$5,000 to Carleton College, Northfield, MN.
$5,000 to DePaul University, Chicago, IL.
$5,000 to DePauw University, Greencastle, IN.
$2,500 to Minnesota Historical Society, Saint Paul, MN.
$2,000 to Minnesota Orchestral Association, Minneapolis, MN.
$1,000 to Boy Scouts of America, Minneapolis, MN.
$250 to Walker Art Center, Minneapolis, MN.

4684
Sit Investment Associates Foundation ◇
3300 IDS Ctr.
80 S. 8th St.
Minneapolis, MN 55402
Contact: Debra Beaudet

Established in 1984.
Donor: Sit Investment Associates, Inc.
Foundation type: Company-sponsored foundation.
Financial data (yr. ended 12/31/03): Assets, $15,345,641 (M); gifts received, $1,267,999; expenditures, $753,323; qualifying distributions, $728,508; giving activities include $728,508 for 140 grants (high: $300,000; low: $25).
Purpose and activities: The foundation supports food banks and organizations involved with arts and culture, higher education, health, housing, and human services.
Fields of interest: Arts; Higher education; Health care; Food banks; Housing/shelter; Children/youth, services; Human services; Federated giving programs.
Limitations: Applications not accepted. Giving on a national basis. No grants to individuals.
Application information: Contributes only to pre-selected organizations.
Directors: Debra Beaudet; Peter L. Mitchelson; Paul A. Rasmussen; Debra A. Sit; Eugene C. Sit.
EIN: 411468021

4685
Paul & Dawn Sjolund Foundation ◇
225 S. 6th St., Ste. 4390
Minneapolis, MN 55402

Established in 1997 in MN.
Donors: Dawn Sjolund; Paul Sjolund.
Foundation type: Independent foundation.
Financial data (yr. ended 12/31/05): Assets, $216,486 (M); gifts received, $400,283; expenditures, $762,021; qualifying distributions, $720,750; giving activities include $720,750 for 28 grants (high: $290,450; low: $500).
Purpose and activities: Giving for general funding.
Fields of interest: Family services; Christian agencies & churches.
Limitations: Applications not accepted. Giving primarily in MN. No grants to individuals.
Application information: Contributes only to pre-selected organizations.
Trustees: Dawn Sjolund; Paul Sjolund.
EIN: 416421780

4686
Slaggie Family Foundation ◇ ☆
1870 Ralph Scharmer Dr.
Winona, MN 55987
Contact: Stephen Slaggie, Pres.

Established in 1997 in MN.
Donor: Steve Slaggie.
Foundation type: Independent foundation.
Financial data (yr. ended 12/31/05): Assets, $10,222,713 (M); gifts received, $675,265; expenditures, $459,548; qualifying distributions, $398,909; giving activities include $398,909 for grants.
Purpose and activities: Giving primarily for education, human services, and religion.
Fields of interest: Museums; Secondary school/education; Higher education; Human services; Family services; Foundations (private independent).
Type of support: Capital campaigns; Debt reduction; Scholarship funds; Program-related investments/loans; Matching/challenge support.
Limitations: Giving primarily in MN. No grants to individuals.
Application information: Application form not required.
  Initial approach: Letter
  Copies of proposal: 1
  Deadline(s): None
  Board meeting date(s): Semiannually, or as needed
Officers: Stephen Slaggie, Pres.; Michael J. Slaggie, V.P.; Barbara J. Slaggie, Secy.-Treas.
EIN: 411878894
Selected grants: The following grants were reported in 2004.
$105,000 to Saint Johns University, Collegeville, MN.
$76,440 to Winona Health Foundation, Winona, MN.
$37,600 to Cotter High School, Winona, MN.
$25,000 to Rock Solid Youth Center, Winona, MN.
$5,000 to We Care Project, Morgan, MN.
$2,525 to Saint Annes Hospice, Winona, MN.
$1,000 to United Way of Greater Winona Area, Winona, MN.
$700 to Deer River HealthCare Center, Deer River, MN.

4687
Smikis Foundation ◇
Parkdale Plz., Ste. 426
1660 Hwy. 100 S.
St. Louis Park, MN 55416-1533
Contact: Linda Rees-Christianson

Established in 1993 in MN.
Foundation type: Independent foundation.
Financial data (yr. ended 12/31/05): Assets, $15,131,406 (M); gifts received, $3,143,192; expenditures, $671,191; qualifying distributions, $612,400; giving activities include $612,375 for 51 grants (high: $85,000; low: $500; average: $5,000–$25,000).
Fields of interest: Education; Environment; Housing/shelter, services; Youth development, services; Community development, neighborhood development.
Type of support: General/operating support; Capital campaigns; Program development; Seed money; Scholarship funds.
Limitations: Applications not accepted. Giving limited to MN, with emphasis on Minneapolis. No grants to individuals, or for membership drives.
Application information:
  Board meeting date(s): Monthly
Officer and Director:* Lucy B. Hartwell,* Pres.
EIN: 411742700
Selected grants: The following grants were reported in 2004.
$40,000 to Project for Pride in Living, Minneapolis, MN.
$22,000 to Nature Conservancy, Minneapolis, MN.
$20,000 to Bolder Options, Minneapolis, MN.
$16,000 to Colonial Church of Edina, Edina, MN.
$15,000 to Center for Victims of Torture, Minneapolis, MN.
$15,000 to Family Hope Services, Plymouth, MN.
$15,000 to Youth Frontiers, Minneapolis, MN.
$12,500 to Guthrie Theater, Minneapolis, MN.
$10,000 to Admission Possible, Saint Paul, MN.
$10,000 to Blake School, Hopkins, MN.

4688
The Southways Foundation ◇
c/o Sargent Mgmt. Co.
901 Marquette Ave., Ste. 2630
Minneapolis, MN 55402
Contact: Jon K. Crow, V.P.
FAX: (612) 338-2084

Incorporated in 1950 in MN.
Donors: John S. Pillsbury†; and family.
Foundation type: Independent foundation.
Financial data (yr. ended 12/31/04): Assets, $10,487,764 (M); expenditures, $808,893; qualifying distributions, $715,266; giving activities include $712,266 for 212 grants (high: $50,000; low: $100), and $3,000 for 3 employee matching gifts.
Purpose and activities: Giving primarily for education, and the arts; some giving also for health and social services.
Fields of interest: Visual arts; Performing arts; Performing arts, theater; Historic preservation/historical societies; Arts; Secondary school/education; Higher education; Health care; Human services; Children/youth, services; Family services; Federated giving programs; Christian agencies & churches.
Type of support: Annual campaigns; Capital campaigns; Building/renovation; Equipment; Land

acquisition; Endowments; Seed money; Employee matching gifts; Matching/challenge support.
Limitations: Giving primarily in MN; some giving nationally.
Application information: Application form not required.
 Initial approach: Proposal
 Copies of proposal: 1
 Deadline(s): None
 Board meeting date(s): 2 times a year
 Final notification: June and Dec.
Officers and Trustees:* Katharine P. Jose,* Pres.; Jon K. Crow, V.P.; Eleanor C. Winston,* Secy.; Priscilla P. Gaines; Lucy C. Mitchell; George S. Pillsbury, Jr.; John S. Pillsbury III.
EIN: 416018502
Selected grants: The following grants were reported in 2003.
$50,000 to Guthrie Theater, Minneapolis, MN. For capital support.
$50,000 to Minnesota Historical Society, Saint Paul, MN. For annual support.
$50,000 to Yale University, New Haven, CT. For Davenport Renovation JPR Advisor Fund.
$35,000 to United Way, Greater Twin Cities, Minneapolis, MN. For annual support.
$15,000 to Family and Childrens Service, Minneapolis, MN.
$15,000 to Minnesota Opera Company, Minneapolis, MN.
$10,000 to Blake School, Hopkins, MN.
$3,750 to Minneapolis College of Art and Design, Minneapolis, MN. For annual support.
$1,250 to Childrens Theater Company and School, Minneapolis, MN. For annual support.
$1,250 to Dunwoody College of Technology, Minneapolis, MN. For annual support.

4689
St. Jude Medical Foundation ◇
1 Lillehei Plz.
St. Paul, MN 55117

Established in 1997 in MN.
Donor: St. Jude Medical, Inc.
Foundation type: Company-sponsored foundation.
Financial data (yr. ended 12/31/05): Assets, $6,566,246 (M); gifts received, $6,000,000; expenditures, $6,039,179; qualifying distributions, $6,037,689; giving activities include $6,036,364 for 157 grants (high: $200,000; low: $500).
Purpose and activities: The foundation supports organizations involved with higher education, health, and medical research.
Fields of interest: Higher education; Health care; Medical research.
Limitations: Applications not accepted. Giving on a national basis, with some emphasis on MN. No grants to individuals.
Application information: Contributes only to pre-selected organizations.
Officer and Directors:* David Fetah,* Pres.; Robert Frenz; Kevin O'Malley.
Trustee: St. Jude Medical, Inc.
EIN: 411868372
Selected grants: The following grants were reported in 2004.
$150,000 to Institute for Medical Technology Innovation, DC.
$140,000 to University of California, Los Angeles, CA.
$100,000 to American Association for Thoracic Surgery, Beverly, MA.

$100,000 to Cleveland Clinic Foundation, Cleveland, OH.
$83,000 to Heart Rhythm Foundation, DC.
$75,000 to Johns Hopkins University, Baltimore, MD.
$50,000 to Loyola University of Chicago, Chicago, IL.
$50,000 to Texas Heart Institute, Houston, TX.
$50,000 to United Hospital Foundation, Saint Paul, MN.
$20,000 to Heartbeat International, Tampa, FL.

4690
St. Paul Travelers Foundation ▼
(formerly The St. Paul Companies, Inc. Foundation)
385 Washington St., M.C. 514D
St. Paul, MN 55102 (651) 310-7757
Contact: Mary Pickard, Pres. and Exec. Dir.
FAX: (651) 310-2327; Additional contact: Shary Kempainen, E-mail: shkempai@stpaultravelers.com; URL: http://www.stpaultravelers.com/about/community/index.html

Established in 1998 in MN.
Donors: The St. Paul Cos., Inc.; The St. Paul Travelers Cos., Inc.
Foundation type: Company-sponsored foundation.
Financial data (yr. ended 12/31/05): Assets, $520,717 (M); gifts received, $8,514,957; expenditures, $8,545,476; qualifying distributions, $8,545,331; giving activities include $7,359,400 for 293 grants (high: $450,000; low: $375), and $632,836 for 1,600 employee matching gifts.
Purpose and activities: The foundation supports organizations involved with arts and culture, education, housing, teacher diversity in urban schools, community development, leadership development, and economically disadvantaged people.
Fields of interest: Arts, equal rights; Arts education; Arts; Elementary/secondary education; Education; Housing/shelter, public policy; Housing/shelter; Civil rights, equal rights; Economic development; Community development; Leadership development; Economically disadvantaged.
Type of support: General/operating support; Capital campaigns; Program development; Employee volunteer services; Employee matching gifts.
Limitations: Giving primarily in areas of significant company operations, with emphasis on the Twin Cities, MN; giving also to national organizations. No support for discriminatory organizations, sectarian religious organizations, political, lobbying, veterans', or fraternal organizations, health or disease-specific organizations, or hospitals or other health services organizations generally supported by third-party reimbursement mechanisms. No grants to individuals, or for benefits, fundraisers, walk-a-thons, telethons, galas, or other revenue-generating events, advertising, health care or other health-related emergency assistance for individuals, direct delivery of health or medical services, medical research, medical equipment, or hospital capital campaigns or general operating support, replacement of government funding, start-up needs, capital campaigns, or general operating support for public or charter schools, human services such as counseling, chemical abuse services, or family programs, environmental programs, or special events not a key strategy in a continuum of efforts to achieve community goals in the foundation's priority areas.

Publications: Application guidelines; Grants list; Informational brochure.
Application information: Application form required.
 Initial approach: Complete online application form
 Deadline(s): Sept. 8
 Board meeting date(s): Every 6 weeks
 Final notification: 3 to 4 months
Officers and Trustees:* Andy Bessette, Vice-Chair.; Mary Pickard,* Pres. and Exec. Dir.; Mike Newman, V.P.; Kurt Schwartzkopf, Corp. Secy.; Bruce A. Backberg; Jay Benet; John Clifford; Ron James; Michael Klein; Michael Miller; Scott Rynda; Kenneth F. Spence III; Greg Vezzosi.
EIN: 411924256
Selected grants: The following grants were reported in 2005.
$450,000 to United Way, Greater Twin Cities, Minneapolis, MN. For operating support for annual campaign.
$201,000 to Minnesota Private College Fund, Saint Paul, MN. For project support for Urban Education Scholars program that provides support for low-income Minnesota students of color committed to careers in urban teaching.
$175,000 to Local Initiatives Support Corporation (LISC), Twin Cities, Saint Paul, MN. For operating support to promote affordable housing development and neighborhood revitalization in Minneapolis and Saint Paul.
$100,000 to Ordway Center for the Performing Arts, Saint Paul, MN. For project support for Bridge Fund.
$35,000 to East Side Neighborhood Development Company, Saint Paul, MN. For operating support.
$35,000 to Greater Metropolitan Housing Corporation-Twin Cities, Minneapolis, MN.
$20,000 to Hands On Twin Cities, Minneapolis, MN. For operating support.
$20,000 to Independent College Fund of Maryland, Baltimore, MD. For project support for Urban Teaching Scholarship Initiative, which provides scholarships to students of color pursuing urban teaching careers.
$15,000 to New Conservatory Theater Center, San Francisco, CA. For project support for YouthAware theatre-in-education program, which promotes understanding and respect by helping youth in Northern California understand impact of making right choices on tough issues through theater arts work.
$15,000 to Rondo Community Land Trust, Saint Paul, MN. For operating support.

4691
Star Tribune Foundation ◇
(formerly Cowles Media Foundation)
425 Portland Ave. S.
Minneapolis, MN 55488 (612) 673-7051
Contact: Sandra K. Fleitman, Mgr.
FAX: (612) 673-7307;
E-mail: sfleitman@startribune.com; URL: http://www.startribunecompany.com/140

Incorporated in 1945 in MN.
Donors: Cowles Media Co.; The Star Tribune Co.; The McClatchy Co.
Foundation type: Company-sponsored foundation.
Financial data (yr. ended 12/31/04): Assets, $13,626,294 (M); gifts received, $500,000; expenditures, $3,236,273; qualifying distributions, $3,114,912; giving activities include $2,782,108 for 136 grants (high: $370,000; low: $1,000), and $217,892 for 612 employee matching gifts.

Purpose and activities: The foundation supports organizations involved with arts and culture, education, employment, children and youth, and youth development. Special emphasis is directed toward programs designed to promote literacy, education, and journalism.

Fields of interest: Media, journalism/publishing; Arts; Elementary/secondary education; Education, reading; Education; Employment; Youth development; Children/youth, services.

Type of support: Continuing support; General/ operating support; Program development; Employee volunteer services; Employee matching gifts.

Limitations: Giving primarily in the Twin Cities, MN, area. No support for religious, international, political, lobbying, or advocacy organizations, organizations whose objectives are principally related to medicine, specific diseases, mental health, substance abuse, rehabilitation, or related research, adoption agencies, public broadcasting companies, or private foundations. No grants to individuals, or for transportation, busing, or travel, conventions, writing or performing, publications or films not related to a major interest of the foundation, sporting events, sponsorships, benefits, fundraisers, or recognition events, development of housing, foster care, or start-up needs.

Publications: Application guidelines; Annual report (including application guidelines); Newsletter; Program policy statement.

Application information: Multi-year funding is not automatic. Letters of inquiry and proposals should be no longer than 3 pages. Application form not required.

   Initial approach: Mail letter of inquiry or proposal to foundation

   Copies of proposal: 1

   Deadline(s): Mar.

   Board meeting date(s): Quarterly

Officer and Directors: Benjamin Taylor, Chair. and Sr. V.P.; Keith Moyer; Pat Talamantes; Robert J. Weil.

Number of staff: 1 full-time professional; 1 part-time support.

EIN: 416031373

4692
Stone Pier Foundation ✧
5140 Wells Fargo Center
90 S. 7th St.
Minneapolis, MN 55402

Established in 1998 in MN.

Foundation type: Independent foundation.

Financial data (yr. ended 12/31/04): Assets, $9,436,477 (M); expenditures, $609,713; qualifying distributions, $522,305; giving activities include $515,000 for 53 grants (high: $110,000; low: $500).

Fields of interest: Arts, multipurpose centers/ programs; Arts; Education; Environment, natural resources; Hospitals (general); Children/youth, services; Federated giving programs.

Limitations: Applications not accepted. Giving primarily in MN. No grants to individuals.

Application information: Contributes only to pre-selected organizations.

Officers: Robert J. Dayton, Pres.; Joan L. Dayton, V.P.; Megan M. Dayton, Secy.-Treas.

Directors: Ann C. Dayton; James G. Dayton; Mae F. Dayton; Scott N. Dayton; Tobin J. Dayton.

EIN: 522390637

4693
Sundance Pay It Forward Foundation ✧ ☆
3109 W. 50th St.
P.O. Box 129
Minneapolis, MN 55410 (612) 822-8580
Contact: Mary Karen Lynn-Klimenko
URL: http://www.sundancefamilyfoundation.org/about-pay.html

Established in 2004 in MN.

Donors: Mark Sandercott; Nancy Jacobs.

Foundation type: Independent foundation.

Financial data (yr. ended 12/31/05): Assets, $31,928 (M); gifts received, $315,000; expenditures, $445,006; qualifying distributions, $425,036; giving activities include $388,173 for 28 grants (high: $25,000; low: $400).

Fields of interest: Human services; Family services; International affairs.

Limitations: Giving primarily in MN.

Application information: See foundation Web site for application information and cover sheet. Application form required.

   Initial approach: Proposal

   Deadline(s): July 17

Officers: Nancy Jacobs, Pres.; Mark Sandercott, V.P.

Trustees: Tod Drescher; Dick Ericson; Verlene Grant; John Savereide; Kathleen Scherek.

EIN: 300276092

4694
Sundet Foundation ✧
7556 Washington Ave. S.
Eden Prairie, MN 55344

Established in 1980 in MN.

Donors: Lee Sundet; MDSC; Goodall; Mary, Inc.; Fountain Industries.

Foundation type: Independent foundation.

Financial data (yr. ended 12/31/05): Assets, $11,359,313 (M); gifts received, $292,606; expenditures, $664,763; qualifying distributions, $639,359; giving activities include $634,204 for 126 grants (high: $100,000; low: $50).

Purpose and activities: Giving primarily for education, and for Christian organizations, as well as Lutheran churches; funding also children, youth and social services, prison fellowships, medical research, and federated giving programs.

Fields of interest: Arts; Vocational education; Education; Cancer; Medical research, institute; Human services; Children/youth, services; Community development; Federated giving programs; Christian agencies & churches; Protestant agencies & churches.

Type of support: General/operating support.

Limitations: Applications not accepted. Giving primarily in MN. No grants to individuals directly.

Application information: Contributes only to pre-selected organizations.

Officers and Directors:* Leland N. Sundet,* Pres.; Louise C. Sundet,* V.P. and Secy.; Carol Meeker, V.P. and Treas.; Jim Dutscher.

EIN: 411378654

4695
SUPERVALU Foundation ✧
P.O. Box 990
Minneapolis, MN 55440 (952) 828-4000
Contact: James L. Stoffel, V.P.

URL: http://www.supervalu.com/sv-webapp/community/guidelines.jsp

Established in 1993 in MN.

Donor: SUPERVALU INC.

Foundation type: Company-sponsored foundation.

Financial data (yr. ended 2/25/06): Assets, $659,428 (M); gifts received, $1,656,072; expenditures, $1,578,680; qualifying distributions, $1,577,414; giving activities include $1,396,521 for 242 grants (high: $150,873; low: $20).

Purpose and activities: The foundation supports organizations involved with fine arts, education, employment, hunger, leadership development, disabled people, minorities, and economically disadvantaged people.

Fields of interest: Arts education; Visual arts; Education; Employment, training; Employment; Food services; Children, day care; Federated giving programs; Leadership development; Physically disabled; Minorities; Economically disadvantaged.

Type of support: Program development.

Limitations: Giving on a national basis, with emphasis on areas of company operations, including MN. No support for United Way-supported organizations (over 30 percent of budget) or veterans', fraternal, or labor organizations. No grants to individuals, or for travel or research expenses, fees for participation in competitive programs, or lobbying, political, or religious programs.

Application information: Requests may be submitted using the Minnesota Common Grant Application Form. Application form required.

   Initial approach: Download application form and mail to foundation

   Deadline(s): Feb. 15, May 15, Aug. 15, and Nov. 15

   Board meeting date(s): Quarterly

   Final notification: Within 90 days

Officers: John P. Breedlove, Pres.; David L. Boehnen, Exec. V.P.; Sherry M. Smith, Sr. V.P. and Treas.; Karen T. Borman, V.P.; James L. Stoffel, V.P.

EIN: 411752955

Selected grants: The following grants were reported in 2005.

$1,972,000 to Minneapolis Foundation, Minneapolis, MN.

$185,124 to United Way of Greater Saint Louis, Saint Louis, MO. 2 grants: $27,000, $158,124

$167,132 to United Way.

$25,000 to United Way, OH.

$22,028 to United Way of Westmoreland County, Greensburg, PA.

$15,063 to United Way of Central Georgia, Macon, GA.

$10,000 to United Way of Champaign County, Champaign, IL.

$10,000 to United Way of Spokane County, Spokane, WA.

$6,410 to United Way of Ashtabula County, Ashtabula, OH.

4696
Tankenoff Families Foundation ✧ ☆
2424 Kennedy St. N.E.
Minneapolis, MN 55413

Established in 1998 in MN.

Foundation type: Independent foundation.

Financial data (yr. ended 12/31/05): Assets, $6,043,491 (M); gifts received, $3,634,955; expenditures, $345,212; qualifying distributions,

$336,502; giving activities include $335,134 for 58 grants (high: $100,000; low: $100).

Purpose and activities: Giving for health associations, Jewish organizations, and human services.

Fields of interest: Health organizations, association; Human services; Jewish federated giving programs; Jewish agencies & temples.

Limitations: Applications not accepted. No grants to individuals.

Application information: Contributes only to pre-selected organizations.

Officers: Gary L. Tankenoff, Chair. and Pres.; Marsha J. Tankenoff, V.P. and Secy.; Leoda Swanson, V.P. and Treas.; Scott M. Tankenoff, V.P.

EIN: 411905115

Selected grants: The following grants were reported in 2004.

$97,500 to Minneapolis Jewish Federation, Minnetonka, MN.

$17,280 to Jewish Community Relations Council of Minnesota and the Dakotas, Minneapolis, MN.

$9,000 to Loft, Inc., Minneapolis, MN.

$7,090 to University Pediatrics Foundation, Louisville, KY.

$7,061 to Adath Jeshurun Congregation, Minnetonka, MN.

$5,050 to Planned Parenthood of Minnesota, North Dakota, South Dakota, Saint Paul, MN.

$5,000 to Sholom Foundation, Saint Paul, MN.

$5,000 to Sunstone Cancer Support Foundation, Tucson, AZ.

$4,000 to Hopkins Education Foundation, Hopkins, MN.

$3,396 to Temple of Aaron, Saint Paul, MN.

4697

Target Foundation ▼ ◇

(formerly Dayton Hudson Foundation)
1000 Nicollet Mall, TPS-3080
Minneapolis, MN 55403   (612) 696-6098
Contact: Jennifer Higgins
FAX: (612) 696-5088;
E-mail: community.relations@target.com;
URL: http://www.targetfoundation.org

Incorporated in 1918 in MN.

Donors: Dayton Hudson Corp.; Target Corp.

Foundation type: Company-sponsored foundation.

Financial data (yr. ended 1/29/05): Assets, $20,806,806 (M); expenditures, $9,513,397; qualifying distributions, $9,500,000; giving activities include $9,500,000 for 186 grants (high: $1,225,000; low: $3,000).

Purpose and activities: The foundation supports organizations involved with arts and culture, human services, and community development.

Fields of interest: Arts; Human services, emergency aid; Human services; Community development.

Type of support: General/operating support; Continuing support; Annual campaigns; Capital campaigns; Building/renovation; Endowments; Emergency funds; Program development; Seed money; Technical assistance; Program evaluation; In-kind gifts.

Limitations: Giving limited to the Minneapolis/St. Paul, MN, metropolitan area. No support for religious organizations not of direct benefit to the entire community; generally, no support for health organizations. No grants to individuals, or for national ceremonies, memorials, conferences, fundraising dinners, testimonials, or similar events,

recreation, therapeutic programs, living subsidies, or the care of disabled persons.

Publications: Application guidelines; Annual report; Informational brochure (including application guidelines).

Application information: Application form required.
Initial approach: Download application form and mail proposal and application form to foundation
Copies of proposal: 1
Deadline(s): Between Feb. and Nov. is preferred
Board meeting date(s): Varies
Final notification: Usually within 90 days

Officers and Trustees:* Robert J. Ulrich,* Chair.; Tim Baer,* Secy.; Todd Blackwell; Bart Butzer; Michael Francsis; John Griffith; Greg Steinhafel; Jerry Storch.

Director: Laysha Ward.

EIN: 416017088

Selected grants: The following grants were reported in 2004.

$1,452,548 to Minneapolis Institute of Arts, Minneapolis, MN. 2 grants: $191,000, $1,261,548

$660,000 to Guthrie Theater, Minneapolis, MN. 2 grants: $160,000, $500,000

$350,000 to Walker Art Center, Minneapolis, MN.

$250,000 to Catholic Charities of the Archdiocese of Saint Paul and Minneapolis, Minneapolis, MN.

$250,000 to Minnesota Orchestral Association, Minneapolis, MN.

$200,000 to Bridge for Runaway Youth, Minneapolis, MN.

$200,000 to People Serving People, Minneapolis, MN.

$200,000 to Sabathani Community Center, Minneapolis, MN.

4698

Glen A. Taylor Foundation ◇

1725 Roe Crest Dr.
North Mankato, MN 56003-1807
(507) 625-2828
Contact: Glen Taylor, Tr.

Established in 1992 in MN.

Donor: Taylor Corp.

Foundation type: Independent foundation.

Financial data (yr. ended 12/31/05): Assets, $2,785,619 (M); gifts received, $503,000; expenditures, $524,863; qualifying distributions, $524,114; giving activities include $523,764 for 10 grants (high: $266,667; low: $3,000).

Purpose and activities: Giving primarily for higher education and local community services.

Fields of interest: Higher education; Education; Human services.

Limitations: Giving primarily in MN.

Application information: Application form required.
Deadline(s): None

Trustees: Thomas Johnson; Bradley Schreier; Glen Taylor; Jean Taylor; Larry Taylor; Terri Taylor.

EIN: 411737411

Selected grants: The following grants were reported in 2003.

$337,979 to YMCA, Mankato Family, Mankato, MN. For operating support.

$200,000 to Augsburg College, Minneapolis, MN. For operating support.

$50,000 to Boy Scouts of America, Twin Valley Council, Mankato, MN. For operating support.

$20,000 to South Central Technical College, North Mankato, MN. For scholarships.

$12,150 to Mankato Area Public Schools, Mankato, MN. For operating support.

$10,000 to Chaminade College Preparatory School, Chatsworth, CA. For scholarships.

$10,000 to Friendship Ventures, Annandale, MN. For operating support.

$5,000 to Habitat for Humanity, South Central Minnesota, Mankato, MN. For operating support.

$3,000 to Minnesota State University, Mankato, MN. For scholarships.

$2,500 to Science Museum of Minnesota, Saint Paul, MN. For operating support.

4699

TCF Foundation

200 Lake St. E., M.C. EXO-02-C
Wayzata, MN 55391-1693
Contact: Denise Peterson, Community Affairs Off.
FAX: (952) 745-2775; E-mail: dpete@tcfbank.com; Additional application addresses: CO: TCF National Bank, CRA Off., 6400 S. Fiddler's Green Cir., Ste. 800, M.C. C00-00-0, Englewood, CO 80111, tel.: (720) 200-2469, IL, IN, and WI: TCF National Bank, V.P., Community Affairs, 800 Burr Ridge Pkwy., Burr Ridge, IL 60527, tel.: (630) 986-4920, MI: TCF National Bank, Dir., Community Affairs, 401 E. Liberty St., M.C. 604-05-E, Ann Arbor, MI 48104-2298, tel.: (800) 362-5555; URL: http://www.tcfbank.com/About/about_community_relations.jsp

Established in 1989 in MN.

Donors: TCF National Bank Minnesota; TCF National Bank.

Foundation type: Company-sponsored foundation.

Financial data (yr. ended 12/31/05): Assets, $61,989 (M); gifts received, $1,872,463; expenditures, $1,842,194; qualifying distributions, $1,847,684; giving activities include $1,452,804 for 200 grants (high: $100,000; low: $500), and $270,583 for 745 employee matching gifts.

Purpose and activities: The foundation supports organizations involved with arts and culture, education, health, housing, youth development, financial literacy, human services, economic development, community development, mentally and physically disabled people, and economically disadvantaged people.

Fields of interest: Performing arts; Arts; Education; Health care; Housing/shelter, rehabilitation; Housing/shelter; Youth development; Human services, financial counseling; Human services; Economic development; Community development, small businesses; Community development; Financial services; Disabilities, people with; Mentally disabled; Economically disadvantaged.

Type of support: General/operating support; Continuing support; Annual campaigns; Capital campaigns; Program development; Scholarship funds; Employee volunteer services; Loaned talent; Employee matching gifts; Employee-related scholarships.

Limitations: Giving primarily in areas of company operations in CO, MI, and MN, the greater Chicago, IL, area, northwest IN, and southeastern WI, including Kenosha, the greater Milwaukee area, and Racine; giving also to regional organizations. No support for political parties or candidates, religious organizations not of direct benefit to the entire community, lobbying organizations, or social organizations. No grants to individuals (except for employee-related scholarships), or for social events or advertising or publications.

Publications: Application guidelines; Annual report; Informational brochure.

Application information: The Minnesota Common Grant Application Form is recommended for organizations located in MN. Unsolicited requests from non-youth development arts and culture organizations located in IL, IN, and WI are not accepted. Unsolicited requests for capital campaign support from organizations located in IL, IN, and WI are not accepted. Support is limited to 3 years for organizations located in IL, IN, and WI. Multi-year funding is not automatic.

Initial approach: Mail cover letter and application form to foundation for organizations located in MN; visit Web site for application information for organizations located in CO, IL, IN, and WI; proposal to application address for organizations located in MI

Copies of proposal: 1

Deadline(s): Telephone foundation for deadlines for organizations located in CO and MN; visit Web site for deadlines for organizations located in IL, IN, and WI

Board meeting date(s): Telephone foundation for dates

Final notification: At least 2 months for organizations located in MN; visit Web site for dates for organizations located in IL, IN, and WI

Officers and Directors:* William A. Cooper,* Chair.; Gregory S. Pulles, Secy.; Neil W. Brown, Treas.; Mark L. Jeter; Jason E. Korstange.

Number of staff: 1 full-time professional.

EIN: 411659826

Selected grants: The following grants were reported in 2004.

$100,000 to University of Minnesota Foundation, Minneapolis, MN.

$50,000 to Courage Center, Golden Valley, MN.

$50,000 to Local Initiatives Support Corporation (LISC), Duluth, MN.

$50,000 to Taxpayers League Foundation, Plymouth, MN.

$30,000 to Acorn Housing Corporation, Saint Paul, MN.

$20,000 to Minnesota Orchestra, Minneapolis, MN.

$15,000 to CommonBond Communities, Saint Paul, MN.

$12,476 to Ascension School, Minneapolis, MN.

$10,000 to Artspace Projects, Minneapolis, MN.

$2,000 to Childrens Home Society and Family Services, Saint Paul, MN.

4700

Tennant Foundation ◇

(formerly Tennant Company Foundation)
P.O. Box 1452
Minneapolis, MN 55440   (763) 540-1209
Contact: Cheryl Timm, Secy. and Admin.

Established in 1973 in MN.

Donor: Tennant Co.

Foundation type: Company-sponsored foundation.

Financial data (yr. ended 12/31/03): Assets, $594,667 (M); gifts received, $200,000; expenditures, $352,953; qualifying distributions, $352,833; giving activities include $268,250 for 53 grants (high: $139,400; low: $550), and $54,671 for 23 employee matching gifts.

Purpose and activities: The foundation supports organizations involved with arts and culture, education, health, workforce readiness, safety, and human services. Special emphasis is directed toward organizations with which employees of

Tennant are involved and that have previously received support from the foundation.

Fields of interest: Arts; Education; Health care; Employment; Safety, education; Human services; Federated giving programs.

Type of support: General/operating support; Continuing support; Capital campaigns; Employee volunteer services; Employee matching gifts; Employee-related scholarships.

Limitations: Giving primarily in areas of company operations, with emphasis on the Minneapolis, MN, area and its western suburb. No support for United Way-supported organizations, umbrella organization-supported organizations, lobbying or political organizations, national organizations without active local chapters, religious organizations not of direct benefit to the entire community, or elementary or secondary schools. No grants to individuals (except for employee-related scholarships), or for trips or tours or tickets, tables, advertising, or benefit purposes.

Publications: Annual report (including application guidelines).

Application information: Proposals may be submitted using the Minnesota Common Grant Application Form. A site visit may be requested. Application form not required.

Initial approach: Proposal

Copies of proposal: 1

Deadline(s): 4 weeks prior to board meetings

Board meeting date(s): June 6 and Dec. 14

Officers and Directors:* Richard M. Adams, Pres.; Patricia A. Sellner, Treas.; Cheryl Timm, Secy. and Admin.; Thomas J. Dybsky.

Number of staff: 1 part-time professional; 1 part-time support.

EIN: 237297045

4701

James R. Thorpe Foundation

120 Broadway Ave. S., No. 100
Wayzata, MN 55391   (952) 476-0808
Contact: Edith D. Thorpe, Pres.
E-mail: jstamstad@jamesthorpefoundation.org; e-mail address for grant proposal submissions: application@jamesrthorpefoundation.org; URL: http://www.jamesrthorpefoundation.org

Incorporated in 1974 in MN.

Donor: James R. Thorpe‡.

Foundation type: Independent foundation.

Financial data (yr. ended 11/30/05): Assets, $9,084,842 (M); expenditures, $629,073; qualifying distributions, $566,606; giving activities include $500,350 for 67 grants (high: $35,000; low: $2,000).

Purpose and activities: Primary areas of interest include the disadvantaged, youth, the elderly, education, and cultural programs. Giving for social service agencies and higher and secondary education; support also for community health care.

Fields of interest: Performing arts; Performing arts, dance; Performing arts, ballet; Performing arts, orchestra (symphony); Arts; Education; Environment; Health care; Mental health/crisis services; Housing/shelter, development; Human services; Children/youth, services; Family services; Aging, centers/services; Homeless, human services; Disabilities, people with; Economically disadvantaged.

Type of support: General/operating support; Capital campaigns; Equipment; Program development; Internship funds; Scholarship funds.

Limitations: Giving limited to Minneapolis, MN; funding to a lesser extent in the western metropolitan suburbs. No support for organizations in the greater MN area, the east metro area, or outside of MN. No grants to individuals, or for continuing support, emergency or endowment funds, deficit financing, land acquisition, matching gifts, publications, seminars, tours, benefits, multi-year commitments, or conferences; no loans.

Publications: Annual report (including application guidelines).

Application information: Application guidelines available on foundation Web site. Minnesota Common Grant Application Form accepted, and is available through the Minnesota Council on Foundations Web site: http://www.mcf.org/mcf/grant/applicat.htm. Application form not required.

Initial approach: Telephone or letter of inquiry (no more than 10 pages)

Copies of proposal: 1

Deadline(s): Mar. 1 and Sept. 1. Hand-delivered proposals must arrive in the foundation's office by 4:30pm on deadline dates

Board meeting date(s): May, for Education and Arts proposals; Nov., for Social Services and Capital requests

Final notification: 1 week after grants meeting

Officers and Directors:* Edith D. Thorpe,* Pres.; Laura A. Thorpe,* Secy.; Robert C. Cote III,* Treas.; Jane M. Stamstad, Exec. Dir.; Mary C. Boos; Samuel C. Cote; Maragret T. Richards; Samuel S. Thorpe III; Timothy D. Thorpe.

Number of staff: 1 part-time professional.

EIN: 416175293

Selected grants: The following grants were reported in 2005.

$35,000 to Interfaith Outreach and Community Partners, Wayzata, MN.

$12,500 to District 202, Minneapolis, MN.

$10,000 to Childrens Law Center of Minnesota, Saint Paul, MN.

$10,000 to Migizi Communications, Minneapolis, MN.

$8,000 to Minnesota Independent School Forum, Saint Paul, MN.

$7,500 to Immigrant Law Center of Minnesota, Saint Paul, MN.

$7,500 to Kinship of Greater Minneapolis, Minneapolis, MN.

$5,000 to Ballet Arts Minnesota, Minneapolis, MN.

$5,000 to Teens Alone, Hopkins, MN.

$4,000 to Somali Education Center, Minneapolis, MN.

4702

The Toro Foundation ◇

8111 Lyndale Ave. S.
Bloomington, MN 55420-1196
Contact: Judson M. Tharin, Community Rels. Specialist
E-mail: judson.tharin@toro.com; URL: http://www.thetorocompany.com/community/foundation.html

Established in 1988 in MN.

Donor: The Toro Co.

Foundation type: Company-sponsored foundation.

Financial data (yr. ended 12/31/04): Assets, $1,620,500 (M); gifts received, $1,220,339; expenditures, $980,657; qualifying distributions, $965,496; giving activities include $963,313 for grants.

Purpose and activities: The foundation supports organizations involved with arts and culture, education, the environment, health, and human services.

Fields of interest: Performing arts; Arts; Secondary school/education; Higher education; Education; Environment; Hospitals (general); Health care; Boy scouts; Children/youth, services; Human services; Federated giving programs.

International interests: Australia; Mexico.

Type of support: Annual campaigns; Employee matching gifts; In-kind gifts; Matching/challenge support.

Limitations: Giving primarily in areas of company operations in El Cajon and Riverside, CA, Minneapolis and Windom, MN, Beatrice, NE, El Paso, TX, Tomah and western WI, and in Australia and Mexico. No support for political or religious organizations. No grants to individuals, or for capital campaigns.

Publications: Application guidelines; Corporate giving report.

Application information: The Minnesota Common Grant Application Form is accepted. Application form required.

  Initial approach: Letter of inquiry for application form
  Deadline(s): Jan., Apr., July, and Oct.
  Board meeting date(s): Quarterly
  Final notification: 3 months

Officers and Directors:* Stacy Bogart,* Pres.; Kathy Manson, Secy.; Blake Grams, Treas.; Tim Ford; Mike Hoffman; Larry McIntyre; Kendrick B. Melrose; Karen Meyer; Steve Wolfe.

Number of staff: 1 part-time professional; 1 full-time support; 1 part-time support.

EIN: 363593618

4703
Tozer Foundation, Inc.

P.O. Box 64713
St. Paul, MN 55164
Contact: Theodore O. Olsen
Application address for grants: c/o U.S. Bank, 101 E. 5th St., Saint Paul, MN 55101

Incorporated in 1946 in MN.

Donor: David Tozer‡.

Foundation type: Independent foundation.

Financial data (yr. ended 10/31/05): Assets, $27,025,995 (M); expenditures, $2,007,402; qualifying distributions, $1,677,482; giving activities include $1,539,500 for grants.

Purpose and activities: Giving primarily for scholarships to graduating high school students who are residents of Kanabec, Pine, or Washington counties in MN; support also for educational projects, cultural programs, community funds, and aid to the handicapped.

Fields of interest: Arts; Higher education; Education; Disabilities, people with.

Type of support: General/operating support; Continuing support; Annual campaigns; Capital campaigns; Building/renovation.

Limitations: Giving primarily in the St. Paul and Stillwater, MN, areas; scholarships limited to residents of Kanabec, Pine, and Washington counties, MN.

Application information: Candidates must apply for scholarships through selected high schools. Candidates must be residents of Washington, Pine or Kanabec County, MN. Application form not required.

Initial approach: Letter
Copies of proposal: 1
Deadline(s): Requests should be received prior to Apr. 20 and Sept. 20
Board meeting date(s): May and Oct.
Final notification: Immediately after board meeting

Officers and Directors:* Robert S. Davis,* Chair.; J. Thomas Simonet, Pres.; Jon A. Theobald, V.P.; Greg Benson; John F. Thoreen; David Wettergren.

EIN: 416011518

Selected grants: The following grants were reported in 2005.

$55,000 to United Way.
$35,600 to College of Saint Benedict, Saint Joseph, MN.
$29,000 to Boy Scouts of America.
$27,600 to Hamline University, Saint Paul, MN.
$26,400 to College of Saint Scholastica, Duluth, MN.
$20,000 to Minnesota Orchestra, Minneapolis, MN.
$15,000 to Saint Croix Valley Community Foundation, Hudson, WI.
$6,500 to Minnesota Public Radio, Saint Paul, MN.
$6,000 to Young Life.
$3,000 to Minnesota Council on Economic Education, Saint Paul, MN.

4704
U.S. Bancorp Foundation, Inc. ▼ ✧

(formerly First Bank System Foundation)
BC-MN-H21B
800 Nicollet Mall, 21st Fl.
Minneapolis, MN 55402 (612) 303-4000
Contact: Teresa Bonner
FAX: (612) 303-0787; *URL:* http://www.usbank.com/cgi_w/cfm/about/community_relations/charit_giving.cfm

Established in 1979.

Donors: First Bank System, Inc.; U.S. Bancorp; U.S. Bank, N.A.

Foundation type: Company-sponsored foundation.

Financial data (yr. ended 12/31/05): Assets, $52,818,986 (M); gifts received, $10,000,000; expenditures, $20,606,251; qualifying distributions, $20,405,927; giving activities include $20,271,339 for grants.

Purpose and activities: The foundation supports organizations involved with arts and culture, education, employment, housing, human services, and community development. Special emphasis is directed toward programs designed to improve the educational and economic opportunities of low- and moderate-income persons; and enhance the cultural and artistic life of communities.

Fields of interest: Arts; Elementary/secondary education; Education; Employment; Housing/shelter; Youth development; Human services; Community development; Federated giving programs.

Type of support: General/operating support; Capital campaigns; Program development; Scholarship funds; Sponsorships; Employee matching gifts; In-kind gifts.

Limitations: Giving primarily in AR, AZ, CA, CO, ID, IA, IL, IN, KS, KY, MN, MO, MT, ND, NE, NV, OH, OR, SD, TN, UT, WA, WI, and WY. No support for fraternal organizations, merchant associations, or 501(c)(4) or (6) organizations, pass-through organizations or private foundations, religious organizations, political organizations or lobbying organizations, United Way-supported organizations, or child care

---

providers. No grants to individuals, or for fundraising events or sponsorships, travel, endowments, debt reduction, or chamber memberships or programs.

Publications: Application guidelines; Annual report; Newsletter.

Application information: Proposals should be no longer than 1 page. Visit Web site application addresses. Application form required.

  Initial approach: Download application form and mail proposal and application form to nearest application address
  Copies of proposal: 1
  Board meeting date(s): Bi-monthly

Officers and Trustees:* Jerry A. Grundhofer,* Chair.; Lee R. Mitau,* Pres. and Secy.; Jennie Carlson; Andrew Cecere; Richard Davis; John Elmore; Joseph Hasten; Ralph Michael; Joseph M. Otting; Kent Stone.

EIN: 411359579

Selected grants: The following grants were reported in 2004.

$830,000 to United Way, Greater Twin Cities, Minneapolis, MN. For general operating support.
$175,000 to United Performing Arts Fund, Milwaukee, WI. For general operating support.
$100,000 to Oregon Childrens Foundation, Portland, OR. For program support.
$100,000 to Saint Louis University, Saint Louis, MO. For capital support.
$64,000 to Local Initiatives Support Corporation (LISC), Twin Cities, Saint Paul, MN. For general operating support.
$52,000 to Home Ownership Center, South Saint Paul, MN. For general operating support.
$22,000 to United Way of Salt Lake, Salt Lake City, UT. For general operating support.
$15,000 to Milwaukee Symphony Orchestra, Milwaukee, WI. For general operating support.
$12,500 to Hope Community, Minneapolis, MN. For capital support.
$12,000 to Missouri Western State College Foundation, Saint Joseph, MO. For program support.

4705
United Health Foundation ✧

9900 Bren Rd. E., MN008-W375
Minnetonka, MN 55343
Contact: Susan M. Hayes, Assoc. Dir.
URL: http://www.unitedhealthfoundation.org

Established in 1999 in MN.

Donors: United Healthcare Services, Inc.; UnitedHealth Group Inc.; Accenture, LLP.

Foundation type: Company-sponsored foundation.

Financial data (yr. ended 12/31/03): Assets, $24,709,886 (M); gifts received, $45,785; expenditures, $16,410,662; qualifying distributions, $16,532,091; giving activities include $1,655,691 for 28 grants (high: $266,000; low: $500), and $14,599,113 for foundation-administered programs.

Purpose and activities: The foundation supports programs designed to promote consumer and physician education and awareness programs; generate objective information that will contribute to improving health care delivery; and sponsor activities that improve the quality of life for all Americans.

Limitations: Giving limited to areas of company operations. No support for religious organizations not of direct benefit to the entire community, athletic associations, or fraternal, veterans', or professional

---

associations. No grants to individuals, or for scholarships, travel, or endowments, recognition or testimonial events, general operating support for educational institutions, conferences, advertising, recreational or sporting events, or civic organization or trade association memberships.

Publications: Application guidelines.

Application information: The Minnesota Common Grant Application Form is required for requests of over $5,000. Application form required.

  Initial approach: Contact foundation for application form

  Deadline(s): Jan. 15, Apr. 15, July 15, and Oct. 15

  Final notification: Mar. 15, June 15, Sept. 15, and Dec. 15

Officers: William W. McGuire, M.D., Chair. and Pres.; David J. Lubben, V.P. and Secy.; Reed V. Tuckson, V.P.; Patrick J. Erlandson, Treas.

Directors: Michael Kessler; William W. McGuire; Walter F. Mondale.

Number of staff: 1 full-time professional; 1 part-time support.

EIN: 411941615

Selected grants: The following grants were reported in 2004.

$2,000,000 to Volunteer Florida Foundation, Tallahassee, FL.

$500,000 to Childrens Health Fund, New York, NY. 2 grants: $250,000 each

$80,000 to Robert Wood Johnson Foundation, Princeton, NJ.

$50,000 to Institute of Medicine, DC.

$2,000 to Minnesota Department of Health, Saint Paul, MN.

$1,000 to Minnesota Public Health Association, Minneapolis, MN.

4706
The Valspar Foundation ◇
4900 IDS Ctr.
80 S. 8th St., Ste. 4900
Minneapolis, MN 55402-2226 (612) 337-5903
Contact: Gwen Leifeld, Mgr.

Established in 1979.

Donor: The Valspar Corp.

Foundation type: Company-sponsored foundation.

Financial data (yr. ended 9/30/05): Assets, $728,670 (M); gifts received, $1,046,787; expenditures, $951,326; qualifying distributions, $951,037; giving activities include $829,966 for 121 grants (high: $100,000; low: $10), and $121,071 for 82 grants to individuals (high: $1,500; low: $400).

Purpose and activities: The foundation supports organizations involved with arts and culture, education, and community housing restoration.

Fields of interest: Arts; Higher education; Education; Housing/shelter; Human services; Community development; Federated giving programs.

Type of support: General/operating support; Building/renovation; Employee-related scholarships; In-kind gifts.

Limitations: Giving limited to areas of company operations, with emphasis on the Twin Cities, MN, metropolitan area. No support for religious, ethnic, fraternal, labor, or veterans' organizations.

Publications: Application guidelines; Program policy statement.

Application information: Application form not required.

  Initial approach: Proposal

  Copies of proposal: 1

  Deadline(s): Nov. 1

  Board meeting date(s): As needed

Officers and Directors:* Richard M. Rompala, Pres.; Gary E. Gardner,* V.P.; Paul C. Reyelts,* V.P.; Richard M. Rompala, V.P.; R. Engh, Secy.; D.D. Weiss, Treas.

Number of staff: 1 full-time professional; 1 part-time support.

EIN: 411363847

4707
Frank W. Veden Charitable Trust ◇
c/o U.S. Bank, N.A.
P.O. Box 64713, Trust Tax Svcs.
St. Paul, MN 55164-0713

Established in 1997 in MN.

Donor: Frank Veden Trust.

Foundation type: Independent foundation.

Financial data (yr. ended 12/31/04): Assets, $10,471,816 (M); expenditures, $529,723; qualifying distributions, $465,173; giving activities include $427,860 for 26 grants (high: $80,000; low: $670).

Purpose and activities: Giving primarily for education, the arts, and human services, including a YMCA.

Fields of interest: Historic preservation/historical societies; Arts; Higher education; Education; Hospitals (general); Salvation Army; YM/YWCAs & YM/YWHAs; Community development; Federated giving programs; Christian agencies & churches.

Limitations: Applications not accepted. Giving primarily in MN, with emphasis on Fergus Falls. No grants to individuals.

Application information: Contributes only to pre-selected organizations.

Trustees: Kenneth Broin; Raymond Reister; U.S. Bank, N.A.

EIN: 416432193

4708
The Vest Foundation ◇
c/o Corporate Tax Dept.
1020 W. County Rd. F
St. Paul, MN 55126
Contact: Thomas Nitti

Donors: American Biosystems; Advanced Respiratory, Inc.

Foundation type: Operating foundation.

Financial data (yr. ended 12/31/04): Assets, $16,689 (M); gifts received, $3,471,023; expenditures, $3,473,278; qualifying distributions, $3,473,278; giving activities include $6,500 for 2 grants (high: $5,000; low: $1,500), and $3,466,200 for 218 grants to individuals.

Purpose and activities: The foundation donates products to individuals suffering from acute or chronic respiratory complications and supports organizations involved with lung diseases research.

Fields of interest: Lung diseases; Lung research.

Type of support: General/operating support; Research; Grants to individuals; Donated products.

Application information: Application form not required.

  Initial approach: Letter of inquiry

  Deadline(s): None

Officers and Directors:* Kathy Hohenberger,* Chair.; Rick Keller, Vice-Chair.; Larry V. Baker,*

Secy.; Mark R. Lanning, Treas.; Bill Hogan,* Exec. Dir.; Gregory N. Miller.

EIN: 411961092

4709
Vintage Foundation, Inc. ◇ ☆
(formerly Tamarack Foundation)
7550 France Ave. S.
Edina, MN 55435

Established in 1998 in MN.

Donor: Ralph W. Burnet.

Foundation type: Independent foundation.

Financial data (yr. ended 6/30/05): Assets, $503,233 (M); expenditures, $359,517; qualifying distributions, $351,714; giving activities include $351,714 for 2 grants (high: $311,714; low: $40,000).

Fields of interest: Arts, multipurpose centers/programs; Education.

Type of support: General/operating support.

Limitations: Applications not accepted. Giving primarily in Minneapolis, MN. No grants to individuals.

Application information: Contributes only to pre-selected organizations.

Officers: Ralph W. Burnet, Pres.; Kimberly Burnet, V.P.; Ryan W. Burnet, V.P.; Stephanie Burnet, V.P.; Peggy P. Burnet, Secy.-Treas.

EIN: 411925672

4710
W.M. Foundation ◇
1800 IDS Ctr., Rm. 1800
80 S. 8th St.
Minneapolis, MN 55402-4523

Established in MN.

Donors: Wallace C. Dayton; Mary Lee Dayton.

Foundation type: Independent foundation.

Financial data (yr. ended 12/31/05): Assets, $22,888,802 (M); expenditures, $1,522,685; qualifying distributions, $1,324,180; giving activities include $1,308,500 for 21 grants (high: $525,000; low: $3,000).

Purpose and activities: Giving primarily for the environment, and animal welfare and preservation; some funding also for the arts and education.

Fields of interest: Arts; Education; Environment, natural resources; Animals/wildlife, preservation/protection.

Limitations: Applications not accepted. Giving primarily in the Minneapolis-St. Paul, MN, area. No grants to individuals.

Application information: Contributes only to pre-selected organizations.

Officers: Mary L. Dayton, Pres. and Treas.; James M. Karges, Secy.

Directors: Sally D. Clement; Elizabeth D. Dovydenas; Katherine D. Nielsen; Ellen D. Sturgis.

EIN: 416080486

Selected grants: The following grants were reported in 2004.

$510,000 to Nature Conservancy, Arlington, VA.

$300,000 to Wilderness Society, DC.

$60,000 to Boundary Waters Wilderness Foundation, Minneapolis, MN.

$56,000 to Edith Wharton Restoration, Lenox, MA.

$50,000 to American Rivers, DC.

$35,000 to Milkweed Editions, Minneapolis, MN.

$35,000 to Walker Art Center, Minneapolis, MN.

4711
Archie D. and Bertha H. Walker Foundation

1121 Hennepin Ave.
Minneapolis, MN 55403-1785 (612) 332-3556
Contact: Joan Schoepke, Admin.

Incorporated in 1953 in MN.
Donors: Archie D. Walker†; Bertha H. Walker†.
Foundation type: Independent foundation.
Financial data (yr. ended 12/31/05): Assets, $6,957,146 (M); expenditures, $612,275; qualifying distributions, $545,063; giving activities include $468,708 for grants (high: $25,000; low: $25), and $66,182 for employee matching gifts.
Purpose and activities: Areas of major support include: 1) programs dealing with chemical dependency, chiefly alcoholism, and its effects on children and their development; 2) programs in the arts; and 3) programs addressing the treatment of racism, prejudice, and exclusivity. Within these 3 areas of primary interest, the foundation provides seed grants to pioneering programs. Also provides continued support of traditionally funded programs in conservation, education, and health. The foundation's preference is to fund organizations that operate without prejudice.
Fields of interest: Arts; Alcoholism; Civil rights, race/intergroup relations.
Type of support: General/operating support; Annual campaigns; Building/renovation; Land acquisition; Program development; Conferences/seminars; Publication; Seed money; Curriculum development; Research.
Limitations: Giving primarily in the seven-county Minneapolis-St. Paul, MN, metropolitan area. No support for private foundations. No grants to individuals, or for endowment funds.
Publications: Application guidelines; Annual report (including application guidelines); Grants list; Occasional report.
Application information: Application form required.
  Initial approach: Letter or telephone
  Copies of proposal: 1
  Deadline(s): Submit proposal by Dec. 1 or July 1
  Board meeting date(s): Mar. and Oct.
  Final notification: June and Dec.
Officers and Trustees:* James H. Heron,* Pres.; Teri M. Motley,* V.P.; Harriet W. Fitts, Secy.; Catherine L. Lamb,* Treas.; Susannah B. Dunlap; William S. Fitts; Bronwyn A.E. Griffith; Julia M. Lamb; Dana D. McCannel; Peter Money; Herbert J. Motley, Jr.; Sally L. Parker; Amy C. Walker; Elaine B. Walker; Alexa Griffith Winton.
Number of staff: 1 part-time professional.
EIN: 416022758

4712
Wallestad Foundation ◇

701 4th Ave. S., Ste. 700
Minneapolis, MN 55415-1812
Contact: Jay L. Bennett, Pres.

Established in 1986 in MN.
Donors: Phadoris Wallestad†; Cary Humphries; Jay L. Bennett; Stan Geyer; Bev Geyer; Fluoroware, Inc.; Entegris, Inc.; Youthworks!; Harvest Foundation.
Foundation type: Independent foundation.
Financial data (yr. ended 12/31/04): Assets, $9,271,118 (M); gifts received, $1,037,900; expenditures, $1,585,177; qualifying distributions, $1,931,033; giving activities include $1,353,489

for 49 grants (high: $388,500; low: $50), $35,000 for 2 employee matching gifts, and $393,396 for 5 loans/program-related investments.
Purpose and activities: Giving primarily to Christian agencies and churches.
Fields of interest: Human services; Children/youth, services; Family services; Religious federated giving programs; Christian agencies & churches.
Type of support: Program-related investments/loans; Employee matching gifts.
Limitations: Giving on a national and international basis, primarily in MN, particularly the Minneapolis area, and Africa. No grants to individuals.
Application information:
  Initial approach: Letter
  Deadline(s): None
Officer: Jay L. Bennett, C.E.O. and Pres.
Directors: Dan Quernemoen; Wayne Zitzloff.
EIN: 363485265
Selected grants: The following grants were reported in 2004.
$50,000 to Leadership Network, Dallas, TX.
$50,000 to Stairstep Foundation, Minneapolis, MN.
  2 grants: $25,000 each
$25,000 to Leadership Foundations of America, Pittsburgh, PA.
$25,000 to Total Victory Christian Center, Minneapolis, MN.
$10,460 to Search Ministries, Edina, MN.
$10,000 to Citysites Urban Media, Saint Paul, MN.
$10,000 to Harvest Evangelism, San Jose, CA.
$5,425 to Kingdom Oil, Minneapolis, MN.
$5,000 to New Salem Missionary Baptist Church, Minneapolis, MN.

4713
Phadoris Wallestad Foundation ◇

(formerly Luke Foundation)
701 4th Ave. S., Ste. 700
Minneapolis, MN 55415-1812 (612) 339-1290
Contact: Jay L. Bennett, Pres.

Established in 1992 in MN.
Foundation type: Independent foundation.
Financial data (yr. ended 12/31/03): Assets, $2,087,717 (M); expenditures, $506,316; qualifying distributions, $876,550; giving activities include $454,044 for 59 grants (high: $100,000; low: $50), and $375,000 for loans/program-related investments.
Purpose and activities: Giving primarily to Christian organizations and charities.
Fields of interest: Youth development, services; Children/youth, services; Family services; Christian agencies & churches.
Limitations: Giving primarily in MN. No grants to individuals.
Application information:
  Initial approach: Letter
  Deadline(s): None
Officers: Jay L. Bennett, Pres.; Wayne Zitzloff, V.P.
EIN: 411723942

4714
Wallin Foundation

2550 Metropolitan Ctr.
333 S. 7th St.
Minneapolis, MN 55402
FAX: (612) 338-0570;
E-mail: paula.deziel@wallinfoundation.org

Established in 1986 in MN.
Donors: Maxine H. Wallin; Winston R. Wallin.
Foundation type: Independent foundation.
Financial data (yr. ended 12/31/05): Assets, $24,204,893 (M); gifts received, $2,521,228; expenditures, $2,310,390; qualifying distributions, $2,055,479; giving activities include $1,744,212 for 104 grants (high: $629,375; low: $100).
Fields of interest: Arts; Higher education; Health care; Children/youth, services; Federated giving programs.
Limitations: Applications not accepted. Giving primarily in MN. No grants to individuals.
Application information: Contributes only to pre-selected organizations.
  Board meeting date(s): Quarterly
Officer: Paula DeZiel, Mgr.
Director: Rebecca L. Wallin.
Trustees: Maxine H. Wallin; Winston R. Wallin.
Number of staff: 2 full-time professional; 2 part-time professional.
EIN: 416283068
Selected grants: The following grants were reported in 2004.
$7,500 to Andrew Riverside Presbyterian Church, Minneapolis, MN.
$5,000 to Greater Minneapolis Council of Churches, Minneapolis, MN.
$5,000 to Minnesota International Center, Minneapolis, MN.
$2,500 to Minnesota Orchestra, Minneapolis, MN.
$2,000 to Nature Conservancy, Arlington, VA.
$1,000 to African American Family Services, Minneapolis, MN.
$800 to World Citizen, Saint Paul, MN.
$400 to National Trust for Historic Preservation, DC.
$225 to Salvation Army.
$200 to Minnesota Humanities Commission, Saint Paul, MN.

4715
Lee and Rose Warner Foundation ◇

2501 Rosegate
St. Paul, MN 55113-2717 (651) 604-4200
Contact: Michael A. Urbanos, Tr.

Incorporated in 1959 in MN.
Donor: Rose Warner†.
Foundation type: Independent foundation.
Financial data (yr. ended 12/31/05): Assets, $15,429,573 (M); gifts received, $9,644,400; expenditures, $1,089,357; qualifying distributions, $823,137; giving activities include $822,000 for 8 grants (high: $750,000; low: $500).
Purpose and activities: Giving primarily for education.
Fields of interest: Education; Environment.
Limitations: Giving primarily in MN. No grants to individuals, or for endowment funds, research programs, scholarships, or fellowships; no loans.
Application information: Application form not required.
  Initial approach: Letter
  Copies of proposal: 1
  Deadline(s): None
  Board meeting date(s): Sept. and Dec.
Officers and Trustees:* Donald G. McNeely,* Chair.; J. Michael Miles,* Secy.; Paul Puerzer,* Treas.; Chris Arend; Cheryl Granlund; Gregory McNeely; Kevin McNeely; Nora McNeely; Michael A. Urbanos.
EIN: 416011523

4716
The Wasie Foundation ✧

4999 France Ave. S., Ste. 250
Minneapolis, MN 55410-1711 (612) 455-6880
Contact: Jan Preble, Prog. Off.

Incorporated in 1966 in MN as the Wasie
Educational Foundation.
Donors: Donald A. Wasie†; Stanley L. Wasie†;
Marie F. Wasie†.
Foundation type: Independent foundation.
Financial data (yr. ended 12/31/04): Assets,
$49,509,288 (M); expenditures, $1,866,762;
qualifying distributions, $1,332,992; giving
activities include $753,448 for 17 grants (high:
$200,000; low: $2,000).
Purpose and activities: Giving primarily for the
education of students of Polish ancestry through the
establishment of endowed scholarship programs at
post secondary institutions; support also for
matters related to schizophrenia, cancer, arthritis,
and children's medical health.
Fields of interest: Higher education; Health care;
Mental health, schizophrenia; Cancer; Arthritis;
Children/youth, services.
Type of support: General/operating support; Capital
campaigns; Building/renovation; Equipment;
Program development; Scholarship funds;
Research; Matching/challenge support.
Limitations: Giving limited to FL and MN. No grants
to individuals; no loans.
Publications: Application guidelines; Informational
brochure.
Application information: Scholarship information
available from participating institution. Application
form not required.
  Initial approach: Telephone
  Copies of proposal: 1
  Deadline(s): Varies
  Board meeting date(s): Quarterly and as required
  Final notification: 30 days after board meetings
Officers and Directors:* Gregg D. Sjoquist,* C.E.O.,
Pres., and Treas.; Gary N. Berg,* V.P. and Secy.;
Andrew J. Leemhuis, M.D., Medical Dir.
Number of staff: 4 full-time professional.
EIN: 410911636
Selected grants: The following grants were reported
in 2003.
$200,000 to Jones-Harrison Residence,
  Minneapolis, MN. For capital improvements.
$145,000 to Stanford University, Stanford, CA. For
  research.
$100,000 to Fairview Foundation, Minneapolis, MN.
  For capital improvements.
$55,739 to University of Saint Thomas, Saint Paul,
  MN. For scholarship program.
$41,517 to College of Saint Scholastica, Duluth,
  MN. For scholarship program.
$32,500 to United Cerebral Palsy Association of
  Miami, Miami, FL. For general operating support.
$24,760 to Mayo Medical School and Mayo
  Graduate School of Medicine, Rochester, MN.
  For scholarship program.
$18,660 to Arthritis Foundation, Atlanta, GA. For
  research.
$15,500 to College of Saint Catherine, Saint Paul,
  MN. For scholarship program.
$10,000 to Association of Small Foundations, DC.
  For general operating support.

4717
Frederick O. Watson Foundation ✧

c/o Watson Ctrs., Inc.
3100 W. Lake St., Ste. 420
Minneapolis, MN 55416 (952) 920-4077
Contact: Douglas F. Watson, Pres.
FAX: (952) 920-5438

Established in 1989 in MN.
Donor: Frederick O. Watson†.
Foundation type: Independent foundation.
Financial data (yr. ended 12/31/05): Assets,
$1,940,534 (M); gifts received, $7,725;
expenditures, $585,002; qualifying distributions,
$581,500; giving activities include $581,500 for 59
grants (high: $100,000; low: $1,000).
Purpose and activities: Giving primarily for health
and human services.
Fields of interest: Arts; Education; Environment,
natural resources; Environment; Hospitals (general);
Cancer; Human services.
Limitations: Giving primarily in MN.
Application information: Application form not
required.
  Initial approach: Letter
  Copies of proposal: 1
  Deadline(s): None
  Board meeting date(s): Annually
Officers: Douglas F. Watson, Pres. and Treas.;
Stephen M. Watson, V.P. and Secy.
EIN: 411625546

4718
WCA Foundation

(formerly Woman's Christian Association)
10249 Yellow Circle Dr., Ste. 101
Minnetonka, MN 55343 (952) 932-9032
Contact: Karen Reamer, Exec. Dir.

Established in 1866 in MN.
Foundation type: Independent foundation.
Financial data (yr. ended 12/31/05): Assets,
$14,811,505 (M); gifts received, $10,178;
expenditures, $841,168; qualifying distributions,
$664,424; giving activities include $485,500 for 42
grants (high: $40,000; low: $5,000).
Purpose and activities: Primary area of interest is
in programs helping women achieve or sustain
self-sufficiency and general human services.
Fields of interest: Education; Employment, training;
Employment, retraining; Human services; Children/
youth, services; Family services; Aging, centers/
services; Women.
Type of support: General/operating support; Capital
campaigns; Building/renovation; Emergency funds;
Program development; Scholarship funds; Program
evaluation.
Limitations: Giving limited to MN. No support for
private foundations, political or veterans'
organizations, religious organizations for religious
purposes, national medical associations, pro-life/
pro-choice programs, or organizations affiliated with
the foundation. No grants to individuals, or for
annual fund drives for medical research, or for costs
of litigation or previously incurred deficits; no
organizations which require employees to raise
some or all of their own salaries in individual
fund-raising; no multi-year awards.
Publications: Application guidelines.
Application information: Application form required.
  Initial approach: Letter, fax or telephone to
    request application form
  Copies of proposal: 1

  Deadline(s): May 15 and Nov. 15
  Board meeting date(s): 1st Fri. of each month
  Final notification: 2 to 6 months following
    deadline dates
Officers and Directors:* Barbara Rose,* Pres.;
Helen Kuehn, 1st V.P.; Mary Galbraith,* 2nd V.P.;
Barbara Horton,* 3rd V.P.; Shirley Holt,* Secy.;
Carol Freeburg,* Treas.; Karen Reamer, Exec. Dir.
Number of staff: 1 full-time professional; 1 full-time
support.
EIN: 410694712

4719
J.A. Wedum Foundation ☆

2615 University Ave. S.E.
Minneapolis, MN 55414
Contact: Kathleen Hansen, Pres.
FAX: (612) 789-4044;
E-mail: kathleenhansen@wedum.org; URL: http://
www.wedum.org

Established in 1959 in MN.
Donors: Maynard C. Wedum†; John A. Wedum†.
Foundation type: Independent foundation.
Financial data (yr. ended 12/31/04): Assets,
$142,783,515 (L); gifts received, $156,600;
expenditures, $34,755,574; qualifying
distributions, $874,996; giving activities include
$874,996 for 21 grants (high: $721,057; low: $92).
Purpose and activities: Giving primarily for higher
education, including scholarships; support also for
social services.
Fields of interest: Business school/education;
Education, services; Education; Animals/wildlife,
preservation/protection; Health organizations,
association; Alcoholism; Human services; Youth,
services.
Type of support: Seed money; Program-related
investments/loans; Scholarships—to individuals;
Matching/challenge support.
Limitations: Giving primarily in MN.
Publications: Application guidelines; Annual report;
Informational brochure.
Application information: Student aid support
beyond existing programs available through local
Dollars for Scholars units. Application form required.
  Initial approach: Letter
  Copies of proposal: 1
  Deadline(s): None
  Board meeting date(s): Apr. and Sept.
  Final notification: Apr. and Sept.
Officers and Board Members:* Dale Vesledahl,*
Co-Chair.; Mary Beth Wedum, Co-Chair.; Kathleen
Hansen, Pres.; Gary Slette; Dayton Soby; Frank
Starke; John Wosepka.
Number of staff: 1 full-time professional; 1 part-time
professional.
EIN: 416025661

4720
Donald Weesner Charitable Trust

c/o U.S. Bank, N.A.
101 E. 5th St., EP-MN-S14
St. Paul, MN 55101 (651) 466-8441
Contact: Jackie Copeland-Carson; Cheryl L. Nelson,
V.P. and Trust Acct. Exec.

Established in 2000 in MN.
Foundation type: Independent foundation.
Financial data (yr. ended 12/31/05): Assets,
$13,484,649 (M); expenditures, $731,016;

qualifying distributions, $650,150; giving activities include $600,350 for 17 grants (high: $81,000; low: $5,000).

Purpose and activities: The foundation was established to promote the founder's lifelong commitment to preserving the Minnesota communities' natural ecosystems and historical legacy. It supports charitable organizations that preserve our natural environment and educate the public about the need for protection of our environmental resources. Well-established non-profit organizations with a long track record of successful environmental and wildlife preservation education programs will be given priority. The foundation has limited funds to support community groups.

Fields of interest: Museums (science/technology); Arts; Environment, natural resources; Zoos/zoological societies; Human services; Federated giving programs.

Limitations: Giving primarily in MN. No grants to individuals or for debt reduction, travel expenses or for general operating support.

Application information: Application form required.
Initial approach: Proposal
Copies of proposal: 1
Deadline(s): Mar. 31, for spring cycle and Aug. 15 for fall cycle
Final notification: 60 days
Trustee: U.S. Bank, N.A.
EIN: 416463406
Selected grants: The following grants were reported in 2005.
$59,410 to Courage Center, Golden Valley, MN.
$59,410 to Nature Conservancy, Minneapolis, MN.
$43,916 to Minnesota Zoo Foundation, Apple Valley, MN.
$29,705 to Minneapolis Institute of Arts, Minneapolis, MN.
$29,705 to Minnesota Orchestral Association, Minneapolis, MN.
$5,000 to Tree Trust, Saint Paul, MN.

4721
Wells Family Foundation Trust ✧
c/o Frederick B. Wells and John J. Knip, Jr.
100 Federal Dr.
St. Paul, MN 55111

Established in 1992 in MN.
Donor: Adele Roller.
Foundation type: Independent foundation.
Financial data (yr. ended 12/31/05): Assets, $6,368,948 (M); expenditures, $492,186; qualifying distributions, $377,000; giving activities include $377,000 for 16 grants (high: $87,000; low: $2,500).

Purpose and activities: Giving primarily for education and athletics, with emphasis on tennis; funding also for youth services and the arts.
Fields of interest: Performing arts, theater; Arts; Higher education; Education; Health care; Athletics/sports, racquet sports; Human services; Children/youth, services.
Type of support: General/operating support; Continuing support; Annual campaigns; Capital campaigns; Endowments.
Limitations: Applications not accepted. Giving primarily in MN. No grants to individuals.
Application information: Contributes only to pre-selected organizations.
Board meeting date(s): Varies

Trustees: Lee Booth; John J. Knip, Jr.; Frederick B. Wells.
Number of staff: 1 part-time professional; 2 part-time support.
EIN: 411732561

4722
WEM Foundation ▼ ✧
P.O. Box 5628
Minneapolis, MN 55440-9300 (952) 742-7544
Contact: Robert J. Theiler, Secy.-Treas.

Established in 1988 in MN.
Donor: Whitney MacMillan, Jr.
Foundation type: Independent foundation.
Financial data (yr. ended 12/31/05): Assets, $128,194,446 (M); gifts received, $6,737,327; expenditures, $6,037,415; qualifying distributions, $5,900,596; giving activities include $5,900,596 for 121 grants (high: $3,500,000; low: $100; average: $1,000–$100,000).

Purpose and activities: Giving primarily to arts and cultural programs, education, general hospitals, health associations, international affairs, and philanthropy.
Fields of interest: Arts; Education; Hospitals (general); Health organizations, association; International affairs, public policy; International relief; Foundations (community).
Limitations: Applications not accepted. Giving primarily in MN. No grants to individuals.
Application information: Contributes only to pre-selected organizations.
Officers and Directors:* Elizabeth S. MacMillan,* Chair.; Whitney MacMillan,* Vice-Chair.; Robert J. Theiler,* Secy.-Treas.; James Hield; Whitney MacMillan, Jr.; Harriet S. Norgren.
EIN: 411604640
Selected grants: The following grants were reported in 2005.
$3,500,000 to Yale University, Whitney and Betty MacMillan Center for International and Area Studies, New Haven, CT.
$1,025,000 to Smithsonian Institution, DC. 2 grants: $1,000,000 (For endowment for Director's Chair of NMAH), $25,000.
$110,000 to Riverside Theater, Vero Beach, FL.
$100,000 to Guthrie Theater, Minneapolis, MN.
$60,000 to George Washingtons Mount Vernon Estate and Gardens, Mount Vernon, VA. For Evans Mill.
$25,000 to Minneapolis Institute of Arts, Minneapolis, MN.
$25,000 to National Museum of American History, Kenneth E. Behring Center, DC.
$25,000 to University of Minnesota, Minneapolis, MN. For Minnesota History Project.
$25,000 to Walker Art Center, Minneapolis, MN.

4723
West Central Initiative
(formerly West Central Minnesota Initiative Fund)
1000 Western Ave.
Fergus Falls, MN 56537 (218) 739-2239
Contact: Nancy Straw, Pres.
FAX: (218) 739-5381; E-mail: grants@wcif.org;
Additional tel.: (800) 735-2239; URL: http://www.wcif.org

Established in 1986 in MN.
Foundation type: Community foundation.

Financial data (yr. ended 6/30/06): Assets, $40,401,138 (M); gifts received, $1,889,173; expenditures, $3,520,493; giving activities include $1,741,702 for 431 grants (high: $50,000; low: $500), and $1,575,667 for 23 loans/program-related investments.

Purpose and activities: The fund seeks to improve the region's economic and social viability by expanding quality employment opportunities, addressing shortages of skilled labor, strengthening families, addressing critical regional needs, and developing leadership capacity within local communities.

Fields of interest: Education; Employment, training; Employment; Youth development, services; Children/youth, services; Family services; Economic development; Nonprofit management; Community development; Leadership development.
Type of support: Income development; Program development; Seed money; Curriculum development; Scholarship funds; Research; Technical assistance; Program-related investments/loans.
Limitations: Giving limited to Becker, Clay, Douglas, Grant, Otter Tail, Pope, Stevens, Traverse, and Wilkin counties, MN. No support for religious activities, sports or recreational programs, arts, historical or cultural activities, or groups without physical presence in region. No grants to individuals.
Publications: Application guidelines; Annual report; Financial statement; Grants list; Informational brochure; Newsletter.
Application information: Visit foundation Web site for application form and guidelines per grant type. Application form required.
Initial approach: Telephone
Copies of proposal: 1
Deadline(s): Generally at least 6 weeks prior to planned commencement of project for grants exceeding $5,000; at least 3 weeks for grants less than $5,000
Board meeting date(s): Monthly
Final notification: 4 to 6 weeks for grants over $5,000; 2 to 3 weeks for less
Officers and Directors:* Paul Sukke,* Chair.; Ralph Lang,* Vice-Chair.; Nancy Straw, Pres.; Wes Binner, V.P., Devel.; Sandy King, V.P., Opers.; Thad Olsen, V.P., Prog.; Chere Rikimoto,* Secy.; Dave Weaklend,* Treas.; Jana Berndt; Ron Kirscht; Don Martodam; Jenny Nellis; Linda Roles; Sue Weber.
Number of staff: 11 full-time professional; 1 part-time professional; 2 full-time support; 1 part-time support.
EIN: 363453471
Selected grants: The following grants were reported in 2006.
$36,387 to Minnesota Technology, Minneapolis, MN. 3 grants: $7,387 (For worker training opportunities), $10,000 (For worker training at Portaco Industries), $19,000 (For worker training opportunities in the town of Starbuck to DyCast Specialties Corporation, in the areas of Training Within Industry, 5S Workplace Training, and Value Stream Mapping).
$25,000 to Pelican Rapids School District, Pelican Rapids, MN. For Early Childhood Initiative.
$20,000 to Brandon Public Schools, Brandon, MN. For Early Childhood Initiative.
$17,500 to Lakes and Prairies Community Action Partnership, Moorhead, MN. For Earned Income Tax Credit Opportunity.
$5,000 to West Central Minnesota Child Care Directors Association, Fergus Falls, MN.

4724
Westcliff Foundation ✧ ☆
730 2nd Ave. S, Ste. 1450
Minneapolis, MN 55402

Established in 2003 in MN.
Donor: Markell C. Brooks.
Foundation type: Independent foundation.
Financial data (yr. ended 12/31/05): Assets, $9,937 (M); gifts received, $325,000; expenditures, $328,472; qualifying distributions, $326,500; giving activities include $326,500 for grants.
Fields of interest: Education, PTA groups; Environment, air pollution; Environment, natural resources; Environment, water resources; Foundations (community).
Limitations: Applications not accepted. Giving primarily in CA, FL, and MN.
Application information: Contributes only to pre-selected organizations.
Officers and Director: * Markell C. Brooks, * Pres.; John Hinck, Secy.; Katherine Leighton, Treas.
EIN: 411999931

4725
Weyerhaeuser Family Foundation, Inc. ✧
(formerly Weyerhaeuser Foundation)
2000 Wells Fargo Pl.
30 E. 7th St.
St. Paul, MN 55101 (651) 215-4453
Contact: Peter Konrad, Prog. Consultant
E-mail: dlc@fidcouns.com; URL: http://www.wfamilyfoundation.org

Incorporated in 1950 in MN.
Donor: Members of the Weyerhaeuser family.
Foundation type: Independent foundation.
Financial data (yr. ended 12/31/04): Assets, $18,439,834 (M); gifts received, $184,311; expenditures, $730,308; qualifying distributions, $693,291; giving activities include $548,488 for 32 grants (high: $30,000; low: $1,000).
Purpose and activities: The Weyerhaeuser Family Foundation supports programs of national and international significance that promote the welfare of human and natural resources. These efforts will enhance the creativity, strengths and skills already possessed by those in need and reinforce the sustaining processes inherent in nature.
Fields of interest: Arts; Environment, natural resources; Environment; Health care; Mental health, treatment; Children, services; International development; International peace/security.
Type of support: Program development; Seed money.
Limitations: Giving for international programs only through U.S.-based organizations. No support for elementary or secondary education. No grants to individuals, or for building or endowment funds, annual campaigns, operating budgets, equipment, scholarships, fellowships, travel, or matching gifts; no loans.
Publications: Annual report (including application guidelines).
Application information: Application form required.
Initial approach: Letter of intent with coversheet
Copies of proposal: 1
Deadline(s): Submit proposal from Jan. through Apr.; deadline Apr. 1

Board meeting date(s): Program committee meets annually in early summer to review proposals; board usually meets in June and Nov.
Final notification: Notification on Letters of Intent after summer meeting. Notification on proposals in Nov.
Officers and Trustees: * Kathleen R. McGoldrick, * Pres.; Frederick W. Titcomb, V.P. and Secy.; Edward W. Phares, * Treas.; Susan Bonsall; Lisa M. Fremont; Peter E. Heymann; Brenda C. Jewett; Lucy R. Jones; Nathaniel J.W. Maher; Jane W. McFee; Samuel J. Pascoe; Charles W. Rasmussen; Thomas F. Rasmussen; Amy W. Stried; Megan L. Titcomb; Chrystal B. Vang; Justin H. Weyerhaeuser.
Number of staff: 1 part-time professional.
EIN: 416012062

4726
The Charles A. Weyerhaeuser Memorial Foundation ✧ ☆
2000 Wells Fargo Pl.
30 East 7th Pl.
St. Paul, MN 55101 (651) 228-0935
Contact: Lucy R. Jones, Pres.
FAX: (651) 228-0776

Incorporated in 1959 in MN.
Donors: Carl A. Weyerhaeuser Trusts; Sarah-Maud W. Sivertsen Trusts.
Foundation type: Independent foundation.
Financial data (yr. ended 2/28/06): Assets, $8,821,450 (M); gifts received, $61,503; expenditures, $409,071; qualifying distributions, $366,400; giving activities include $366,400 for grants.
Fields of interest: Arts; Higher education; Environment, natural resources.
Type of support: Continuing support; Annual campaigns.
Limitations: Giving primarily in MN. No grants to individuals.
Application information: Application form not required.
Initial approach: Letter
Copies of proposal: 1
Deadline(s): None
Board meeting date(s): As required
Final notification: 3 months
Officers and Directors: * Lucy R. Jones, * Pres.; Robert J. Sivertsen, * V.P.; Joseph S. Micallef, * Secy.-Treas.; Elise R. Donohue; Charles W. Rosenberry II.
EIN: 416012063
Selected grants: The following grants were reported in 2003.
$135,400 to Minnesota Public Radio, Saint Paul, MN. For capital campaign for opera underwriting.
$50,000 to Nature Conservancy, Minnesota Chapter, Minneapolis, MN. For Lake Alexander Endowment.
$25,000 to Planned Parenthood of Minnesota, North Dakota, South Dakota, Saint Paul, MN. For operating support.

4727
Weyerhaeuser/Day Foundation ✧ ☆
30 E. 7th St., Ste. 2000
St. Paul, MN 55101-4930 (651) 228-0935
Contact: Vivian W. Day, Pres.

Established in 1995 in MN.

Donors: Lynn Weyerhaeuser Day†; Stanley R. Stanley.
Foundation type: Independent foundation.
Financial data (yr. ended 12/31/05): Assets, $10,194,889 (M); expenditures, $457,714; qualifying distributions, $400,000; giving activities include $400,000 for grants.
Fields of interest: Higher education; Environment, natural resources; Health care.
Type of support: Continuing support.
Limitations: Giving primarily in MI.
Application information: Application form not required.
Initial approach: Proposal
Deadline(s): None
Officers and Directors: * Vivian W. Day, * Pres.; Lincoln W. Day, * V.P.; Stanley R. Day, Jr., * Secy.; Frederick W. Day, * Treas.; Stanley R. Day.
EIN: 411815686

4728
Whitney Foundation
1900 Foshay Twr.
821 Marquette Ave.
Minneapolis, MN 55402
Contact: Carol Van Ornum, Grant Admin.

Established in 1959 in MN.
Donors: Wheelock Whitney; and members of the Whitney family.
Foundation type: Independent foundation.
Financial data (yr. ended 12/31/04): Assets, $2,364,960 (M); gifts received, $950,118; expenditures, $755,271; qualifying distributions, $713,438; giving activities include $713,100 for 223 grants (high: $200,000; low: $25).
Purpose and activities: Giving primarily for education, substance abuse programs, and human services.
Fields of interest: Arts; Education; AIDS; Alcoholism; Human services; Children/youth, services.
Type of support: General/operating support; Continuing support; Annual campaigns.
Limitations: Giving limited to MN, with emphasis on Hennepin and Ramsey counties. No grants to individuals, or for publications, video productions, or trips.
Publications: Application guidelines.
Application information: The foundation does not consider unsolicited requests from organizations outside MN. Minnesota Common Grant Application Form is preferred. Application form not required.
Initial approach: Letter
Copies of proposal: 1
Deadline(s): 2 weeks prior to July and Oct. meetings
Board meeting date(s): Feb., July, and Oct.
Final notification: 1 month
Officers: Wheelock Whitney, Pres.; Wheelock Whitney III, V.P.; Joseph H. Whitney, Secy.
Director: Pennell Whitney.
Number of staff: 1 part-time support.
EIN: 416022514
Selected grants: The following grants were reported in 2003.
$50,400 to Minneapolis Community and Technical College, Minneapolis, MN.
$10,000 to Saint Cloud State University, Saint Cloud, MN.
$5,000 to Blake School, Minneapolis, MN.
$2,500 to Bailey House, New York, NY.
$2,000 to Macalester College, Saint Paul, MN.

$1,500 to Minneapolis Academy, Minneapolis, MN.

$1,000 to National Council on Alcoholism and Drug Dependence, New York, NY.

$750 to Carleton College, Northfield, MN.

$500 to Dunwoody College of Technology, Minneapolis, MN.

$250 to Mothers Against Drunk Driving (MADD) Minnesota, Saint Paul, MN.

4729
Winona Community Foundation ✧

(formerly Greater Winona Area Community Foundation)
51 E. 4th St., Ste. 314
Winona, MN 55987-6203 (507) 454-6511
Contact: Maggie Modjeski, Pres.
FAX: (507) 454-0441; E-mail: wincomf@hbci.com;
URL: http://www.winonacommunityfoundation.com

Established in 1987 in MN.
Foundation type: Community foundation.
Financial data (yr. ended 12/31/05): Assets, $9,187,317 (M); gifts received, $1,753,873; expenditures, $2,730,440; giving activities include $2,555,061 for 175+ grants (high: $1,212,289).
Purpose and activities: The foundation seeks, accepts, and administers contributions to meet the charitable needs of the Winona area community in MN. Preference is for organizations that have demonstrated actual and potential operating success.
Fields of interest: Arts, multipurpose centers/programs; Arts; Elementary/secondary education; Education; Environment; Health care; Recreation; Human services.
Type of support: Scholarships—to individuals; General/operating support; Continuing support; Annual campaigns; Equipment; Endowments; Program development; Conferences/seminars; Program-related investments/loans; Matching/challenge support.
Limitations: Giving primarily in Winona, MN, and its surrounding community. No support for religious programs or fraternal organizations, societies, or order. No grants to individuals (except for scholarships), or for ongoing program support, capital campaigns, endowments, debt retirements or debt financing, tickets for benefits, telephone solicitations, fundraising drives or activities, or travel.
Publications: Application guidelines; Annual report; Grants list; Informational brochure (including application guidelines); Newsletter.
Application information: Letters of inquiry are required to start the grant application process; proposals that are accepted will receive full application information by mail. Faxed or e-mailed letters are not accepted. Visit foundation Web site for application guidelines and next grant cycle information. Application form required.
  Initial approach: Letter of inquiry (no longer than 1 page)
  Copies of proposal: 6
  Deadline(s): Aug. 1 for letters of inquiry
  Board meeting date(s): 4th Tues. of each month
  Final notification: Sept. 1 for letter of inquiry determination; Nov. 1 for full applications
Officers and Directors:* William McNeil,* Chair.; Karen Fawcett,* Vice-Chair.; Maggie Modjeski, Pres.; Rev. William Flesch,* Secy.; Bud Nystrom,* Treas.; Chris Arnold; Bud Baechler; Mike Bernatz; Jan Brosnahan; David Bue; Margaret Shaw Johnson;

Dr. Darrell Krueger; Leone Mauszycki; Rod Nelson; Jack Richter; Judy Shepard.
Number of staff: 2 part-time professional; 1 part-time support.
EIN: 363500853

4730
Wolohan Family Foundation ✧

1705 Crosby Rd.
Wayzata, MN 55391

Established in 1986 in MI.
Donors: Richard V. Wolohan; Angela M. Wolohan; James L. Wolohan; Christine M. Wolohan.
Foundation type: Independent foundation.
Financial data (yr. ended 12/31/04): Assets, $15,281,028 (L); expenditures, $866,692; qualifying distributions, $650,279; giving activities include $647,250 for 32 grants (high: $101,000; low: $100).
Purpose and activities: Giving primarily to Roman Catholic organizations for education and human services.
Fields of interest: Higher education; Residential/custodial care; International development; Foundations (community); Roman Catholic agencies & churches.
Limitations: Applications not accepted. Giving primarily in MI. No grants to individuals.
Application information: Contributes only to pre-selected organizations.
Officers: Christine M. Wolohan, Pres.; James L. Wolohan, V.P. and Treas.; Michael J. Wolohan, Secy.
Directors: Mary K. Ness; Richard P. Wolohan; Sharon L. Wolohan.
EIN: 382700797

4731
Wood-Rill Foundation ▼ ✧

1800 Ids Ctr.
80 S. 8th St.
Minneapolis, MN 55402 (612) 339-7151

Established in 1967 in MN.
Donors: Bruce B. Dayton; Lucy B. Dayton.
Foundation type: Independent foundation.
Financial data (yr. ended 12/31/05): Assets, $1,364,167 (M); gifts received, $4,094,873; expenditures, $3,789,290; qualifying distributions, $3,776,525; giving activities include $3,776,235 for 60 grants (high: $2,515,000; low: $500; average: $1,000–$50,000).
Purpose and activities: Support primarily for the arts and cultural organizations, environmental associations, and education.
Fields of interest: Visual arts; Performing arts; Arts; Higher education; Biomedicine; Medical research, institute; Government/public administration.
Type of support: General/operating support.
Limitations: Applications not accepted. Giving on a national basis. No grants to individuals.
Application information: Contributes only to pre-selected organizations.
Officers and Directors:* Bruce B. Dayton,* Pres.; Ruth Ann Stricker, Exec. V.P.; Anne B. Dayton,* V.P.; Brandt N. Dayton,* V.P.; Lucy B. Dayton,* V.P.; Mark B. Dayton,* V.P.; James M. Karges, Secy.-Treas.
EIN: 416080487
Selected grants: The following grants were reported in 2004.

$3,590,000 to Minneapolis Institute of Arts, Minneapolis, MN. For unrestricted support.

$1,000,000 to Minneapolis Public Library, Minneapolis, MN. For unrestricted support.

$333,000 to Bravewell Collaborative, Minneapolis, MN. For unrestricted support.

$62,560 to Westminster Presbyterian Church of Minneapolis, Minneapolis, MN. For unrestricted support.

$50,000 to Macalester College, Saint Paul, MN. For unrestricted support.

$50,000 to William J. Clinton Presidential Foundation, Little Rock, AR. For unrestricted support.

$44,100 to University of Minnesota, Minneapolis, MN. For unrestricted support.

$25,200 to Groves Academy, Saint Louis Park, MN. For unrestricted support.

$25,000 to Positive Attitude Development Group, MN. For unrestricted support.

$25,000 to Trust for Public Land, San Francisco, CA. For unrestricted support.

4732
Xcel Energy Foundation ▼

414 Nicollet Mall
Minneapolis, MN 55401 (612) 215-5317
Contact: John Pacheco, Dir.
FAX: (612) 215-4522;
E-mail: john.pacheco-jr@xcelenergy.com; Additional E-mail: foundation@xcelenergy.com; URL: http://www.xcelenergy.com/XLWEB/CDA/0,3080,1-1-1_4359_4842-922-0_0_0-0,00.html

Established in 2001.
Donor: Xcel Energy Inc.
Foundation type: Company-sponsored foundation.
Financial data (yr. ended 12/31/05): Assets, $1,797,487 (M); gifts received, $7,030,160; expenditures, $6,996,961; qualifying distributions, $6,990,301; giving activities include $6,769,835 for 1,866 grants (high: $143,755).
Purpose and activities: The foundation supports organizations involved with arts and culture, education, the environment, animals and wildlife, employment, housing, financial counseling, diversity, community development, senior citizens, and economically disadvantaged people.
Fields of interest: Arts, equal rights; Arts education; Arts; Elementary/secondary education; Business school/education; Scholarships/financial aid; Education; Environment, alliance; Environment, public education; Environment, water resources; Environment, land resources; Environment, energy; Environment, beautification programs; Environmental education; Environment; Animals/wildlife, alliance; Animals/wildlife, public education; Animals/wildlife, preservation/protection; Employment; Housing/shelter, equal rights; Housing/shelter; Recreation, parks/playgrounds; Human services, financial counseling; Civil rights, equal rights; Economic development; Community development; Federated giving programs; Science, formal/general education; Mathematics; Aging; Economically disadvantaged.
Type of support: General/operating support; Program development; Employee volunteer services; Employee matching gifts.
Limitations: Giving limited to areas of company operations. No support for national organizations, government agencies, religious, political, veterans', or fraternal organizations not of direct benefit to the entire community or disease-specific organizations.

No grants to individuals, or for research programs, endowments, athletic or scholarship competitions, benefits or fundraising activities, sports or athletic programs, or capital campaigns.

Publications: Application guidelines; Grants list; Informational brochure.

Application information: Application form required.

Initial approach: Complete online application form

Deadline(s): Feb. 1 and Aug. 2 for Environment; Feb. 1 for Education; May 3 for Community Development; and Aug. 2 for Arts and Culture

Final notification: Within 3 weeks following deadlines

Officers and Directors: * Richard C. Kelly,* Chair.; Elizabeth A. Willis, Secy.; Cathy J. Hart, Treas.; Cynthia L. Lesher; Patricia K. Vincent.

EIN: 412007734

Selected grants: The following grants were reported in 2004.

$500,000 to University Enterprise Laboratories, Minneapolis, MN. For Biotech Center.

$125,007 to United Way, Greater Twin Cities, Minneapolis, MN. For corporate match.

$125,000 to Salvation Army, Northern Division, Roseville, MN.

$85,000 to Minnesota Private College Fund, Saint Paul, MN.

$40,000 to Greater Metropolitan Housing Corporation-Twin Cities, Minneapolis, MN.

$36,000 to Junior Achievement of the Upper Midwest, Maplewood, MN.

$35,000 to Globe-News Center for the Performing Arts, Amarillo, TX.

$22,946 to United Way of Pueblo County, Pueblo, CO. For corporate match.

$12,000 to Bridge for Runaway Youth, Minneapolis, MN.

$11,000 to Walker Art Center, Minneapolis, MN.

MISSISSIPPI

4733
AmSouth Foundation

(formerly Deposit Guaranty/First American
Foundation)
P.O. Box 13906
Jackson, MS 39236-3906
Contact: Sid Sims, Pres.

Incorporated in 1962 in MS.
Donors: Deposit Guaranty National Bank; First
American National Bank.
Foundation type: Company-sponsored foundation.
Financial data (yr. ended 12/31/04): Assets,
$14,187,945 (M); expenditures, $696,321;
qualifying distributions, $693,833; giving activities
include $647,500 for 25 grants (high: $100,000;
low: $10,000).
Purpose and activities: The foundation supports
hospitals and organizations involved with arts and
culture, education, youth development, human
services, and Christianity.
Fields of interest: Arts; Education; Hospitals
(general); Boys & girls clubs; Boy scouts; Youth
development; American Red Cross; Salvation Army;
YM/YWCAs & YM/YWHAs; Children/youth,
services; Human services; Christian agencies &
churches.
Type of support: General/operating support; Annual
campaigns; Capital campaigns; Scholarship funds;
Program-related investments/loans; Employee
matching gifts.
Limitations: Applications not accepted. Giving
limited to MS. No grants to individuals.
Application information: Contributes only to
pre-selected organizations.
  Board meeting date(s): Annually
Officers and Directors:* Charles L. Irby,* Chair.;
James W. Hood, Vice-Chair.; Sid Sims,* Pres.;
Debbie Purvis, Secy.-Treas.; Sharon S. Greener;
William R. James; B.T. Jones; Richard D. McRae, Jr.;
James L. Moore; W.R. Newman III; E.B. Robinson,
Jr.
EIN: 646026793

4734
The Armstrong Foundation

(formerly The Texas Educational Association)
P.O. Box 2299
Natchez, MS 39121-2299
Contact: Thomas K. Armstrong, Pres.
FAX: (601) 442-4716; E-mail: tka@natchez.net

Incorporated in 1949 in TX.
Donor: George W. Armstrong, Sr.†.
Foundation type: Independent foundation.
Financial data (yr. ended 12/31/04): Assets,
$18,613,741 (M); expenditures, $1,074,069;
qualifying distributions, $889,454; giving activities
include $801,281 for 134 grants (high: $50,000;
low: $141).
Purpose and activities: To support educational
undertakings through financial assistance to
schools, colleges, universities, and other
educational mediums advocating the perpetuation
of constitutional government. Grants only for
educational programs on American ideals and

traditional values; support for free market and free
enterprise educational programs.
Fields of interest: Education, research; Business/
industry; Economics; Government/public
administration.
Type of support: General/operating support;
Continuing support; Program development;
Conferences/seminars; Publication; Research.
Limitations: Giving on a national basis. No grants to
individuals, or for capital or endowment funds; no
loans.
Publications: Application guidelines.
Application information: Application form not
required.
  Initial approach: Proposal
  Copies of proposal: 1
  Deadline(s): None
  Board meeting date(s): Mar., June, Sept., and
    Dec.
  Final notification: 2 months
Officers and Directors:* Thomas K. Armstrong,*
Pres.; John H. James,* V.P. and Treas.; Allen L.
Armstrong,* V.P.; Thomas K. Armstrong, Jr.,* V.P.;
J. Hatcher James III,* V.P.; Laura J. Harrison,* Secy.
Number of staff: 1 part-time professional; 1 full-time
support; 1 part-time support.
EIN: 756003209
Selected grants: The following grants were reported
in 2004.
$45,000 to National Center for Policy Analysis,
  Dallas, TX.
$30,141 to Fort Worth Academy for the Education of
  Children and Youth, Fort Worth, TX. For program
  support.
$25,000 to Heritage Foundation, DC. For program
  support.
$25,000 to Media Research Center, Alexandria, VA.
  For Tell the Truth campaign.
$20,000 to Center for American Unity, Warrenton,
  VA. For program support.
$20,000 to Free Congress Research and Education
  Foundation, DC. For program support.
$20,000 to Mercatus Center, Arlington, VA. For
  program support.
$20,000 to National Right to Work Legal Defense
  and Education Foundation, Springfield, VA. For
  program support.
$15,000 to Students in Free Enterprise, Springfield,
  MO. For program support.
$10,000 to Young Americas Foundation, Herndon,
  VA. For program support.

4735
Asbury Foundation of Hattiesburg, Inc. ✧

P.O. Box 17797
Hattiesburg, MS 39404 (601) 296-3555
Application address: c/o William K. Ray, Board
Member, 201 Methodist Blvd., Hattiesburg, MS
39402

Established in 1989; converted from the sales of
Wesley Health System.
Foundation type: Independent foundation.
Financial data (yr. ended 3/31/06): Assets, $0 (M);
expenditures, $1,818,272; qualifying distributions,
$1,445,581; giving activities include $1,270,886
for 6 grants (high: $275,000; low: $114,346).
Purpose and activities: The foundation provides
support in areas of education and health to improve
the quality of life to other nonprofit organizations.
Fields of interest: Higher education; Health care.
Limitations: Giving limited to MS. No grants to
individuals.

Application information: Application form required.
  Initial approach: Letter
Board Members: Raymond Dearman; Hon. Richard
Foxworth; Glenn Galey; Rev. Keith Hagenson;
George Komp III; Harry McArthur; Doris Miller;
William K. Ray; Carey Revels; Tom Shows.
EIN: 640692161

4736
The Bower Foundation, Inc. ▼ ✧

(formerly Kidney Care, Inc.)
578 Highland Colony Pkwy., Ste. 120
Ridgeland, MS 39157 (601) 607-3163
FAX: (601) 607-3164;
E-mail: info@bowerfoundation.org; Additional e-mail
(for grant concept submissions):
atravis@bowerfoundation.org; URL: http://
www.bowerfoundation.org

Established in 1972 in MS.
Foundation type: Independent foundation.
Financial data (yr. ended 12/31/04): Assets,
$81,922,818 (M); expenditures, $3,608,280;
qualifying distributions, $3,354,725; giving
activities include $3,081,155 for 14 grants (high:
$750,000; low: $10,000; average: $100,000–
$750,000).
Purpose and activities: The foundation is
committed to the promotion of fundamental
improvements in the health status of all
Mississippians through the creation, expansion,
and support of quality healthcare initiatives. The
goals of the foundation are: 1) Access to health
care: All children and adults should have reasonable
access to health care services so that all citizens
have the opportunity to live healthy and productive
lives. 2) Health Care Services: To promote health,
prevent disease, and reduce health risks among
children, young adults, and the underserved. 3)
Health Policy and Education: To support approaches
that match the needs of the underserved with
existing public and private providers. 4) End Stage
Renal Disease: To improve the quality of life for
patients with End Stage Renal Disease.
Fields of interest: Health care; Kidney diseases.
Limitations: Giving primarily in MS. No grants to
individuals.
Publications: Grants list.
Application information: Nearly all the foundation's
grantmaking activities are pro-active. A small
percentage of grants develop from grant concepts
submitted by prospective grantees. The grant
concept can be mailed, faxed, or E-mailed to the
foundation.
  Initial approach: Grant concept proposal (no more
    than 2 pages)
  Deadline(s): None
Officers and Directors:* Anne Travis,* C.E.O. and
V.P.; John Bower, M.D., Pres.; James F. Dorris,
Secy.-Treas.; Ralph Didlake, M.D.; Kathy Ellis; Alan
Hull, M.D.; Walter Neely, Ph.D.; Dana Shires, M.D.
EIN: 640540635
Selected grants: The following grants were reported
in 2004.
$1,895,877 to University of Mississippi Medical
  Center, Jackson, MS. 5 grants: $405,421,
  $33,956, $696,500, $10,000, $750,000
$202,100 to Mississippi State Department of
  Health, Jackson, MS.
$55,000 to Mississippi Blood Services, Jackson,
  MS.
$55,000 to National Kidney Foundation, New York,
  NY.

$24,150 to Mississippi Primary Health Care Association, Jackson, MS.

4737
Community Foundation of Greater Jackson
(formerly Greater Jackson Foundation)
525 E. Capitol St., Ste. 5B
Jackson, MS 39201 (601) 974-6044
Contact: Linda Montgomery, Pres.
FAX: (601) 974-6045;
E-mail: info@cfgreaterjackson.org; URL: http://www.cfgreaterjackson.org

Established in 1994 in MS.
Foundation type: Community foundation.
Financial data (yr. ended 3/31/06): Assets, $15,945,105 (M); gifts received, $5,657,567; expenditures, $2,718,082; giving activities include $1,915,051 for 337 grants (high: $500,000; low: $100; average: $100–$500,000), and $274,506 for 203 grants to individuals (high: $5,000; low: $250; average: $250–$5,000).
Purpose and activities: The foundation helps charitable donors establish permanent giving funds that reflect individual philanthropic interests while also making a long term, positive impact on the community. Giving for the arts, education, health, families/children, environment, and community building.
Fields of interest: Museums; Performing arts; Arts; Elementary/secondary education; Higher education; Environment; Health organizations, association; Disasters, Hurricane Katrina; Children/youth, services; Family services; Community development, neighborhood development.
Type of support: General/operating support; Continuing support; Annual campaigns; Capital campaigns; Building/renovation; Endowments; Program development; Conferences/seminars; Professorships; Curriculum development; Scholarship funds; Scholarships—to individuals; Matching/challenge support.
Limitations: Giving primarily in Hinds, Madison, and Rankin counties, MS. No support for religious activities.
Publications: Application guidelines; Annual report; Informational brochure; Newsletter; Occasional report.
Application information: Visit foundation Web site for online application form and guidelines. Application form required.
Initial approach: E-mail application
Copies of proposal: 1
Deadline(s): Quarterly
Board meeting date(s): Feb., May, Aug., and Nov.
Final notification: 90 days
Officers and Trustees:* Con Maloney,* Chair.; Fred Banks,* Chair.-Elect; Linda Montgomery, Pres.; Denise Owens,* Secy.; Paul Varner,* Treas.; Jim Almas; Gary Anderson; Toni Cooley; Noel Daniels; Kane Ditto; Rick Fountain; Sonny Fountain; Monica Harrigill; Alferdteen Harrison; Jane Hiatt; Janet Hickson; David Hoster; Earle Jones; Susan Shands Jones; Ellen Leake; Mike McRee; Don Q. Mitchell; Dick Molpus; Billy Neville; John Newhouse; George Penick; Betty Lou Reeves; Carlton Reeves; Vonda Reeves-Darby; Asoka Srinivasan; Sylvia Stewart; Kimberly Noel Sweet; Stella Gray Bryant Sykes; Gwendolyn Taylor; Kathryn Wiener; J. Kelley Williams.
Number of staff: 3 full-time professional; 1 part-time professional; 1 full-time support.
EIN: 640845750

Selected grants: The following grants were reported in 2005.
$42,000 to Southside Assembly of God, Jackson, MS.
$10,000 to Congregation Beth Israel.
$5,000 to Country Oaks Recovery Center, Jackson, MS. For operating support.
$5,000 to Mississippi Opera Association, Jackson, MS. For operating support.
$3,200 to Family Support Center of Metro Jackson, Jackson, MS. For community-based parents' education.
$3,000 to Habitat for Humanity, Metro Jackson, Jackson, MS. For Project Nehemiah/Fences for Families.
$2,750 to Henley-Young Juvenile Justice Center, Jackson, MS. For Expressive Art Program.
$2,500 to Oak Forest Elementary School, Jackson, MS. For Hope, Heroes and the Blues.
$2,300 to Oaks House Museum, Jackson, MS. For Archaeological Testing and Archival Research.
$2,000 to Mississippi Center for Nonprofits, Jackson, MS. For Mississippi nonprofit sector report.
$1,000 to Gleaners, Jackson, MS. For operating support.
$500 to Junior Auxiliary of Clinton County, Clinton, MS. For Backpack Pals.

4738
The Community Foundation, Inc. ✧
P.O. Box 13328
Jackson, MS 39236-3328

Incorporated in 1963 in MS.
Donor: W.K. Paine.
Foundation type: Independent foundation.
Financial data (yr. ended 12/31/05): Assets, $43,320,871 (M); expenditures, $1,276,491; qualifying distributions, $1,085,450; giving activities include $1,085,000 for 9 grants (high: $250,000; low: $10,000).
Fields of interest: Higher education; Education; Human services; Family services.
Limitations: Applications not accepted. Giving primarily in MS. No grants to individuals.
Application information: Contributes only to pre-selected organizations.
Officers: W.K. Paine, Pres. and Treas.; Carolyn P. Davis, V.P.; Robert H. Paine, V.P.; Lucinda Fox, Secy.
EIN: 237033813
Selected grants: The following grants were reported in 2004.
$350,000 to Focus on the Family, Colorado Springs, CO.
$250,000 to Montreat College, Montreat, NC.
$100,000 to Baddour Center, Senatobia, MS.
$15,000 to Young Life, Colorado Springs, CO.
$5,000 to Gateway Rescue Mission, Jackson, MS.
$5,000 to Mustard Seed, Brandon, MS.

4739
The Carl and Virginia Day Trust ✧
125 E. Jefferson St.
Yazoo City, MS 39194-4552 (662) 746-4901
Contact: Carolyn Johnson

Trust established in 1948 in MS.
Donor: Carl Day, M.D.‡
Foundation type: Independent foundation.

Financial data (yr. ended 12/31/03): Assets, $3,271,954 (M); expenditures, $360,558; qualifying distributions, $343,248; giving activities include $320,750 for 187 loans to individuals (high: $2,500; low: $500).
Purpose and activities: Provides interest-free loans to MS residents under 25 years old who attend MS colleges.
Type of support: Student loans—to individuals.
Limitations: Giving limited to residents of MS.
Publications: Annual report; Financial statement.
Application information: Applications must include prior transcripts, state of residence, parent's financial statements, 4 references, and where you plan to attend school. Application form required.
Initial approach: Letter
Deadline(s): July 4 and Nov. 4
Trustees: Allen Bridgforth; Hugh Love, Jr.; Frank Patty, Jr.; Van Ray; Byron Seward.
Number of staff: 2 part-time professional.
EIN: 640386095

4740
Ergon Foundation, Inc. ✧
P.O. Drawer 1639
Jackson, MS 39215-1639

Established in 1980.
Donors: Diversified Technology, Inc.; Ergon Exploration, Inc.; Ergon Nonwovens, Inc.; Ergon Refining, Inc.; Ergon, Inc.; Magnolia Marine Transport Co.; Ergon Asphalt & Emulsions, Inc.; Ergon-West Virginia, Inc.
Foundation type: Company-sponsored foundation.
Financial data (yr. ended 6/30/05): Assets, $9,921,214 (M); gifts received, $1,500,000; expenditures, $729,131; qualifying distributions, $712,450; giving activities include $708,174 for 47 grants (high: $150,000; low: $1,000).
Purpose and activities: The foundation supports Christian agencies and churches, hospitals, and organizations involved with education, children and youth, and human services.
Fields of interest: Secondary school/education; Higher education; Education; Hospitals (general); YM/YWCAs & YM/YWHAs; Children/youth, services; Human services; Christian agencies & churches.
Type of support: General/operating support.
Limitations: Applications not accepted. Giving primarily in MS. No grants to individuals.
Application information: Contributes only to pre-selected organizations.
Officers and Directors:* Leslie B. Lampton,* Pres.; Dorothy Lee Lampton,* V.P.; Lee C. Lampton,* V.P.; Leslie B. Lampton III,* V.P.; Robert H. Lampton,* V.P.; William W. Lampton,* V.P.; Kathryn W. Stone,* Secy.-Treas.
EIN: 640656341
Selected grants: The following grants were reported in 2005.
$150,000 to University of Mississippi Medical Center, Jackson, MS.
$131,774 to Mississippi State University Foundation, Mississippi State, MS.
$55,000 to Salvation Army, Natchez, MS.
$32,000 to Southern Christian Services for Children and Youth, Jackson, MS.
$25,000 to French Camp Academy, French Camp, MS.
$20,500 to Jackson Preparatory School, Jackson, MS.

$20,000 to Saint Andrews Episcopal School, Jackson, MS.
$15,000 to Gateway Rescue Mission, Jackson, MS.
$12,500 to Holy Child Jesus School, Canton, MS.
$10,000 to Palmer Home for Children, Columbus, MS.

$4,000 to Palmer Home for Children, Columbus, MS. For general support.
$4,000 to Piney Woods School, Piney Woods, MS. For general support.
$4,000 to Southern Christian Services for Children and Youth, Jackson, MS. For general support.

4741
Feild Co-Operative Association, Inc. ◇
P.O. Box 5054
Jackson, MS 39225-5054 (601) 713-2312
Contact: Virginia G. Chill, Secy. and Dir. of Student Loans
FAX: (601) 713-2314; URL: http://www.feildstudentloans.org

Incorporated in 1919 in TN.
Donor: Sons of the late Dr. and Mrs. Monfort Jones.
Foundation type: Independent foundation.
Financial data (yr. ended 12/31/04): Assets, $17,228,810 (M); expenditures, $775,665; qualifying distributions, $685,506; giving activities include $109,500 for 36 grants (high: $10,000; low: $1,000), and $383,110 for loans to individuals.
Purpose and activities: Awards interest-bearing student loans to residents of MS, who are juniors or seniors in college, graduate and professional students, or students in special fields; some grants to local hospitals and social service agencies.
Fields of interest: Arts; Education; Hospitals (general); Health organizations; Human services; Children/youth, services.
Type of support: General/operating support; Student loans—to individuals.
Limitations: Giving limited to residents of MS. No grants for building or endowment funds, operating budgets, or for special projects.
Publications: Application guidelines; Informational brochure.
Application information: Application form and personal interview required for student loans. Student loan guidelines available on foundation Web site.
  Initial approach: Letter
  Copies of proposal: 1
  Deadline(s): 6 to 8 weeks before a semester begins
  Board meeting date(s): Annually
  Final notification: 4 to 6 weeks after applying
Officers and Directors:* Bernard B. Jones II,* Chair.; Hobson C. McGehee, Jr.,* Pres.; B. Bryan Jones III,* 1st V.P.; William M. Link, Jr.,* 2nd V.P.; Betty R. May,* 3rd V.P.; Virgina G. Chill, Secy.; Suzanne S. Neely, Treas.; Hobson C. McGehee III; Kirk Payne McGehee; Cynthia Jones Thompson.
Number of staff: 3
EIN: 640155700
Selected grants: The following grants were reported in 2003.
$25,000 to Glory of Baroque. For general support.
$10,000 to Belhaven College, Jackson, MS. For general support.
$6,000 to Mississippi Museum of Art, Jackson, MS. For general support.
$5,000 to Boy Scouts of America, Andrew Jackson Council, Jackson, MS. For general support.
$5,000 to Buckner Children and Family Services of North Texas, Dallas, TX. For general support.
$5,000 to Chamberlain-Hunt Academy, Port Gibson, MS. For general support.
$4,000 to Mississippi Opera Association, Jackson, MS. For general support.

4742
The Gertrude C. Ford Foundation, Inc. ◇
P.O. Box 13100
Jackson, MS 39236-3100
Contact: Anthony T. Papa, Mgr.
Application address: Lefleur Bluffs Twr., Ste. 410, Jackson, MS 39211, tel.: (601) 713-2300

Established in 1997 in MS.
Foundation type: Independent foundation.
Financial data (yr. ended 12/31/05): Assets, $57,905,841 (M); expenditures, $3,090,660; qualifying distributions, $2,736,686; giving activities include $2,584,276 for 77 grants (high: $1,347,676; low: $1,000).
Purpose and activities: Giving primarily to public schools, higher education, youth and children's services including children's hospitals, hospices, national health organizations, and Christian agencies and churches.
Fields of interest: Education, public education; Higher education; Hospitals (specialty); Health organizations; Children/youth, services; Residential/custodial care, hospices; Christian agencies & churches.
Type of support: Annual campaigns.
Limitations: Giving primarily in MS; limited funding nationally.
Application information:
  Initial approach: Letter
  Deadline(s): None
  Board meeting date(s): Tues. weekly
Managers: Leon E. Lewis, Jr.; Anthony T. Papa; Cheryle M. Sims.
EIN: 640804548
Selected grants: The following grants were reported in 2005.
$1,347,676 to University of Mississippi, University, MS. For Performing Arts Center.
$250,000 to Animal Rescue League of Mississippi, Jackson, MS. For facilities expansion.
$200,000 to Mississippi Museum of Art, Jackson, MS. For building fund.
$100,000 to Mississippi Ballet International, Jackson, MS. For operating support.
$75,000 to New Stage Theater, Jackson, MS. For operating support.
$17,500 to Mississippi Symphony Orchestra Association, Mississippi Symphony Orchestra, Jackson, MS. For musicians.
$15,000 to Mississippi Museum of Natural Science, Jackson, MS. For operating support.
$15,000 to Mississippi Opera, Jackson, MS. For operating support.
$15,000 to Tennessee Williams-New Orleans Literary Festival, New Orleans, LA. For Spring Festival.
$10,000 to Arts Alliance of Jackson and Hinds County, Jackson, MS. For operating support.

4743
Foundation for the Mid South ◇
134 E. Amite St.
Jackson, MS 39201 (601) 355-8167
Contact: Ivye L. Allen, Pres.; Christopher Crothers, Dir., Comms.; Dwanda Moore, Office Mgr.
FAX: (601) 355-6499;
E-mail: ccrothers@fndmidsouth.org; Additional E-mail: dlmoore@fndmidsouth.org; URL: http://www.fndmidsouth.org

Established in 1989 in MS.
Foundation type: Community foundation.
Financial data (yr. ended 12/31/04): Assets, $9,171,026 (M); gifts received, $1,295,626; expenditures, $4,380,129; giving activities include $866,798 for 70 grants (high: $70,000; low: $500), and $553,239 for loans/program-related investments.
Purpose and activities: The foundation makes grants in three program areas: Economic Development, to create an economy that works for all people; Education, to create a constituency for change at the local level; and Families and Children, to improve the quality of life for children and families of the mid-South.
Fields of interest: Education, early childhood education; Education; Disasters, Hurricane Katrina; Youth development, services; Children/youth, services; Family services; Minorities/immigrants, centers/services; Economic development; Community development; Leadership development; Religion; Minorities.
Type of support: General/operating support; Continuing support; Program development; Conferences/seminars; Curriculum development; Consulting services; Program-related investments/loans; Matching/challenge support.
Limitations: Giving limited to AR, LA, and MS.
Publications: Application guidelines; Annual report; Financial statement; Grants list; Informational brochure (including application guidelines); Multi-year report; Newsletter.
Application information: Visit foundation Web site for application information. Application form required.
  Initial approach: Contact program staff
  Copies of proposal: 1
  Deadline(s): Varies
  Board meeting date(s): Feb., June, and Oct.
Officers and Directors:* Beverly Wade Hogan,* Chair.; Diana Lewis,* Vice-Chair.; Ivye L. Allen, Pres.; Beverly Divers-White, V.P.; Gladys Whitney,* Secy.; Stephen Kuretich, C.F.O.; William J. "Bill" Bynum,* Treas.; Ted Kendall III, Dir. Emeritus; Don Munro, Dir. Emeritus; Pat Cooper; Curt L. Hebert, Jr.; Charles Victor McTeer; Nancy T. Montoya; Patrick C. Moore; Jennifer Eplett Reilly; Freddye Webb-Petett; Sherece West; Brad Williams; Michael Wilson; Hon. William Winter; Leila Clark Wynn.
Number of staff: 9 full-time professional; 8 full-time support.
EIN: 721151070

4744
Graeber Foundation ◇
P.O. Box 40
Marks, MS 38646-0040

Established in 1955 in MS.
Donors: James P. Graeber; Lewis A. Graeber, Jr.
Foundation type: Independent foundation.

Financial data (yr. ended 12/31/05): Assets, $9,867,989 (M); gifts received, $55,515; expenditures, $461,756; qualifying distributions, $456,562; giving activities include $456,562 for 59 grants (high: $139,356; low: $300).
Purpose and activities: Giving primarily to Christian organizations and educational foundations.
Fields of interest: Higher education; Education; Health organizations, association; Human services; Christian agencies & churches.
Limitations: Applications not accepted. Giving primarily in MS. No grants to individuals.
Application information: Contributes only to pre-selected organizations.
Trustees: James P. Graeber, Jr.; John C. Graeber; Lewis A. Graeber, Jr.; William M. Graeber.
EIN: 646023660

4745
Gulf Coast Community Foundation
P.O. Box 2984
Gulfport, MS 39505 (228) 897-4841
Contact: H. Rodger Wilder, Exec. Dir.; Rose Dellenger, Grants/Progs. Mgr.
FAX: (228) 897-4843; E-mail: rwilder@mgccf.org; Additional E-mail: rdellenger@mgccf.org; URL: http://www.mgccf.org

Established in 1989 in MS.
Foundation type: Community foundation.
Financial data (yr. ended 9/30/05): Assets, $4,607,526 (M); gifts received, $4,272,288; expenditures, $2,439,972; giving activities include $989,111 for grants, and $1,205,206 for grants to individuals.
Purpose and activities: The foundation is a public charity dedicated to the progressive development of worthy causes, providing donor services, and promoting and providing leadership in response to changing community needs. The foundation is a vehicle for charitable giving through which individuals, families, corporations, nonprofit organizations and private foundations can meet charitable objectives in the fields of education, arts and culture, historic preservation, neighborhood enrichment, and health and human services.
Fields of interest: Historic preservation/historical societies; Arts; Education; Health care; Disasters, Hurricane Katrina; Human services; Community development.
Type of support: General/operating support; Continuing support; Scholarship funds; Technical assistance; Matching/challenge support.
Limitations: Giving limited to George, Hancock, Harrison, Jackson, Pearl River, and Stone counties, MS. No support for governmental entities, private foundations, religious organizations or for religious purposes, athletic programs, or school band programs. No grants to individuals, or for capital or operating endowment drives.
Publications: Application guidelines; Annual report; Financial statement; Informational brochure; Newsletter; Occasional report.
Application information: Visit foundation Web site for application forms, guidelines, and specific deadlines. Application form required.
Initial approach: Complete Letter of Intent
Copies of proposal: 9
Deadline(s): Varies
Board meeting date(s): Bimonthly
Final notification: May and Dec.
Officers and Directors:* John M. Walton,* Pres.; Duncan McKenzie,* V.P.; Dorothy Roberts

McEwen,* Secy.; David Geiger,* Treas.; H. Rodger Wilder, Exec. Dir.; Wynn Alexander; Carlene Alfonso; Greg Cronin; Raymond L. Brown; Jane Dennis; Greg Descher; Ann Guice; Reed Guice; Ann Hairston; Rod Hartung; Bill McDonough; Gordon H. Myrick; Robert F. Neal; Jon E. Ritten; Leo W. Seal, Jr.; Chevis Swetman; Margaret Taylor; Barbara M. Thompson, Ph.D.; Anthony Topazi; David Treutel, Jr.; F. William Van Kirk, Jr.
Number of staff: 3 full-time professional.
EIN: 570908490

4746
L. D. Hancock Foundation, Inc. ◈ ☆
P.O. Box 2203
Tupelo, MS 38803 (662) 844-4080
Contact: Billy Haygood

Established in 1988 in MS.
Donor: L.D. Hancock.
Foundation type: Operating foundation.
Financial data (yr. ended 12/31/05): Assets, $8,079,662 (M); expenditures, $355,422; qualifying distributions, $316,300; giving activities include $316,300 for grants (high: $288,800; low: $27,500).
Purpose and activities: Giving primarily to Christian organizations.
Fields of interest: Theological school/education; Human services; Christian agencies & churches.
Limitations: Giving primarily in MS. No grants to individuals.
Application information: Application form supplied upon request.
Officers and Directors:* Elaine G. Hancock,* Pres.; Billy Haygood,* V.P. and Mgr.; Janice H. Allen,* V.P.; Doyce H. Deas,* V.P.; Lauren H. Patterson,* Treas.; Bill Deas; Larry G. Hancock; Sam G. Patterson.
EIN: 640582491
Selected grants: The following grants were reported in 2004.
$88,800 to Global Outreach International, Tupelo, MS.
$75,000 to Learning Skills Center, Tupelo, MS.
$20,000 to Link Center, Tupelo, MS.
$12,000 to CATCH Kids, Tupelo, MS.
$10,000 to Sanctuary Hospice House, Tupelo, MS.
$5,000 to Mission Mississippi, Jackson, MS.
$5,000 to Tupelo Skate Park, Tupelo, MS.

4747
Phil Hardin Foundation
1921 24th Ave.
Meridian, MS 39301 (601) 483-4282
Contact: C. Thompson Wacaster, V.P.
FAX: (601) 483-5665; E-mail: info@philhardin.org; URL: http://www.philhardin.org

Incorporated in 1964 in MS.
Donors: Philip Bernard Hardin†; Hardin's Bakeries Corp.
Foundation type: Independent foundation.
Financial data (yr. ended 12/31/05): Assets, $39,490,678 (M); expenditures, $1,855,468; qualifying distributions, $1,784,423; giving activities include $1,408,736 for 21 grants (high: $575,000; low: $500).
Purpose and activities: To improve teaching and learning for Mississippians from pre-kindergarten through the 12th grade.

Fields of interest: Education, association; Education, research; Education, early childhood education; Higher education; Education; Minorities.
Type of support: Building/renovation; Equipment; Endowments; Program development; Conferences/seminars; Professorships; Publication; Curriculum development; Fellowships; Research; Program-related investments/loans; Matching/challenge support.
Limitations: Giving primarily in MS; support also to out-of-state organizations for programs and projects benefiting the education of Mississippians. No grants to individuals, or for deficit financing or land acquisition.
Publications: Application guidelines; Grants list; Informational brochure (including application guidelines); Program policy statement.
Application information: Application guidelines and form available on foundation Web site. Priority is given to proposals solicited by the foundation. Application form required.
Initial approach: Telephone, letter, or proposal
Copies of proposal: 2
Deadline(s): None
Board meeting date(s): As required, usually at least every other month
Final notification: 3 months
Officers and Directors:* Robert F. Ward,* Pres.; Stephen O. Moore,* V.P.; C. Thompson Wacaster, V.P., Educational Progs. and Research; R.B. Deen, Jr.,* Secy.; Archie R. McDonnell,* Treas.; Joe S. Covington, M.D.; Edwin E. Downer; Lynne Taleff; Sarah W. Wile.
Number of staff: 1 full-time professional; 1 full-time support.
EIN: 646024940
Selected grants: The following grants were reported in 2005.
$575,000 to Millsaps College, Jackson, MS. For operating support and endowment.
$355,023 to Mississippi Center for Nonprofits, Jackson, MS. For Katrina Capacity Recovery Initiative for Licensed Day Care Centers on the Gulf Coast.
$150,000 to University of Mississippi Foundation, University, MS. For Endowment on the Future of the South.
$108,720 to Earthwatch Institute, Maynard, MA. For Rosenbaum Mississippi Teaching Fellows Program.
$60,000 to Public Education Forum of Mississippi, Jackson, MS. For Mississippi Scholars Program.
$36,600 to University of Mississippi, School of Education, University, MS. For planning grant.
$23,850 to Jackson State University, Jackson, MS. For Mississippi Learning Institute's 2005 Harvard Initiative.
$15,300 to Community of Hope, Meridian, MS. For tutors and scholarships.

4748
The Robert M. Hearin Foundation ◈
P.O. Box 16505
Jackson, MS 39236-6505 (601) 366-8363
Contact: Daisy S. Blackwell, Tr.

Established in 1965 in MS.
Donors: Robert M. Hearin, Sr.; Bay Street Corp.; Yazoo Investment Corp.
Foundation type: Independent foundation.
Financial data (yr. ended 11/30/05): Assets, $47,830,089 (M); expenditures, $2,586,785; qualifying distributions, $2,470,483; giving

activities include $2,305,271 for 9 grants (high: $500,000; low: $50,000).
Purpose and activities: Giving to 4-year colleges and graduate schools located in the state of Mississippi, and to other charities.
Fields of interest: Higher education.
Limitations: Giving primarily in MS. No grants to individuals.
Application information: Application form not required.
  Initial approach: Letter
  Deadline(s): None
Trustees: Daisy S. Blackwell; Robert M. Hearin, Jr.; Matthew L. Holleman III; E.E. Laird, Jr.; Laurie McRee; Alan W. Perry.
EIN: 646027443
Selected grants: The following grants were reported in 2005.
$500,000 to Mississippi State University, Mississippi State, MS.
$300,271 to Delta State University, Cleveland, MS.
$300,000 to Mississippi College, School of Law, Clinton, MS. For scholarships.
$300,000 to University of Mississippi Medical Center, Jackson, MS. For scholarships.
$300,000 to University of Southern Mississippi, Hattiesburg, MS.
$250,000 to University of Mississippi, Oxford, MS.
$205,000 to Jackson State University, Jackson, MS.
$100,000 to Tougaloo College, Tougaloo, MS. For scholarships.
$50,000 to Mississippi University for Women, Columbus, MS.

4749
Holloway Foundation, Inc. ✦ ☆
125 S. Congress St., Ste. 1200
Jackson, MS 39201-2706

Foundation type: Independent foundation.
Financial data (yr. ended 12/31/05): Assets, $22,413 (M); gifts received, $613,000; expenditures, $597,772; qualifying distributions, $597,682; giving activities include $597,682 for grants.
Fields of interest: Museums (sports/hobby).
Limitations: Applications not accepted. Giving primarily in Jackson, MS. No grants to individuals.
Application information: Contributes only to pre-selected organizations.
Officers and Directors:* J.L. Holloway,* Pres.; John G. Corlew,* V.P.; Max S. Bowman,* Secy.; A. Brent Saunders,* Treas.
EIN: 311617048

4750
Elizabeth M. Irby Foundation ✦
P.O. Box 1819
Jackson, MS 39215 (601) 989-1811
Contact: Stuart M. Irby, Pres.

Incorporated in 1952 in MS.
Donors: Stewart C. Irby, Jr.†; Irby Corp.; Stuart C. Irby Co.
Foundation type: Independent foundation.
Financial data (yr. ended 12/31/05): Assets, $782,302 (M); gifts received, $1,603,592; expenditures, $875,190; qualifying distributions, $871,410; giving activities include $867,610 for 65 grants (high: $400,000; low: $250).

Purpose and activities: Grants primarily for education, as well as support for churches and religious organizations.
Fields of interest: Arts; Education; Health organizations, association; Youth development, centers/clubs; Human services; Christian agencies & churches.
Type of support: General/operating support; Continuing support; Annual campaigns; Capital campaigns; Building/renovation; Endowments; Emergency funds; Program development; Scholarship funds; Research; Matching/challenge support.
Limitations: Giving primarily in MS. No grants to individuals.
Application information: Application form not required.
  Initial approach: Letter
  Deadline(s): None
Officers and Trustees:* Stuart M. Irby,* Pres.; Charles L. Irby,* V.P.; Debbie Purvis, Secy.-Treas.; Joseph A. Irby; Elizabeth Irby Milam.
EIN: 646020278
Selected grants: The following grants were reported in 2005.
$400,000 to Belhaven College, Jackson, MS.
$50,000 to Scholarship Fund for Inner-City Children, Newark, NJ.
$30,000 to Mississippi State University, Mississippi State, MS.
$25,000 to Young Life.
$21,250 to United Way. 2 grants: $20,000, $1,250
$20,000 to Mississippi Symphony Orchestra Association, Jackson, MS.
$13,200 to Boy Scouts of America.
$7,000 to Walter Anderson Museum of Art, Ocean Springs, MS.
$1,000 to Boys and Girls Club.

4751
Lower Pearl River Valley Foundation
505 Williams Ave.
Picayune, MS 39466 (601) 799-5353
Contact: Ted J. Alexander, C.E.O.
FAX: (601) 799-5116; E-mail: LPRVF@bellsouth.net

Established in 1998 in MS; converted from Crosby Memorial Hospital.
Foundation type: Independent foundation.
Financial data (yr. ended 9/30/05): Assets, $16,130,682 (M); expenditures, $650,959; qualifying distributions, $804,318; giving activities include $341,922 for 18 grants (high: $107,386; low: $525).
Fields of interest: Education; Health care; Community development, neighborhood development.
Type of support: Building/renovation; Seed money; Technical assistance; Consulting services; Matching/challenge support.
Limitations: Giving primarily in Pearl River County, MS, and its environs. No grants to individuals.
Publications: Application guidelines; Biennial report (including application guidelines).
Application information: Application form required.
  Initial approach: Letter on applicant's organizational letterhead, to request an application
  Copies of proposal: 10
  Deadline(s): 2 months prior to board meeting
  Board meeting date(s): Quarterly
  Final notification: Proposals are acknowledged the day they are received

Officers and Directors:* Ted J. Alexander, Ed.D.*, C.E.O.; Clyde Dease,* Pres.; Sidney Whitley,* V.P.; Pamela Thomas, Secy.; Rebecca Askew, Ph.D., Treas.; Tom Clark, Ed.D.; Martin Smith.
Number of staff: 2 full-time professional; 1 full-time support.
EIN: 640901092

4752
The Luckyday Foundation ▼ ✦
P.O. Box 22703
Jackson, MS 39225-2703
Contact: Holmes S. Adams, Chair.

Established in 1978 in MS.
Donor: Frank R. Day†.
Foundation type: Independent foundation.
Financial data (yr. ended 12/31/05): Assets, $107,878,417 (M); expenditures, $5,509,866; qualifying distributions, $4,903,539; giving activities include $4,785,946 for 15 grants (high: $2,939,000; low: $100; average: $10,000–$50,000).
Purpose and activities: Giving primarily for higher education.
Fields of interest: Higher education; Youth development; Protestant agencies & churches.
Limitations: Giving primarily in MS, with emphasis on Jackson. No grants to individuals.
Application information: Application form required.
  Initial approach: Letter
  Copies of proposal: 1
  Deadline(s): None
  Final notification: Usually within 3 months
Officer and Managers:* Holmes S. Adams,* Chair.; Patricia G. Smith, Exec. Dir.; Barbara Arnold Day; Roger P. Friou; Dean M. Miller; S. Griffin Norquist, Jr.
Number of staff: 1 full-time professional.
EIN: 640617746
Selected grants: The following grants were reported in 2004.
$2,015,000 to University of Mississippi Foundation, University, MS.
$1,250,000 to University of Mississippi, University, MS.
$847,390 to University of Southern Mississippi Foundation, Hattiesburg, MS. To provide support for public schools and higher education.
$25,000 to Hinds Community College Development Foundation, Raymond, MS. To promote higher education.
$10,000 to Parents for Public Schools, Jackson, MS. To promote public schools.

4753
Maddox Foundation ✦
180 W. Commerce St.
Hernando, MS 38632 (662) 449-3699
Contact: Michael C. Ward, Special Projects Dir.
FAX: (662) 449-3698;
E-mail: mward@maddoxfoundation.org; Application address: c/o Community Foundation of Middle Tennessee, 3833 Cleghorn Ave., No. 400, Nashville, TN 37215-2519, tel.: (615) 321-4939 or toll-free (888) 540-5200, e-mail: info@cfmt.org; URL: http://www.maddoxfoundation.org

Established in 1968 in TN.
Donors: Margaret Maddox Trust; Dan Maddox†; Margaret H. Maddox†; Margaret Energy, Inc.

Foundation type: Independent foundation.
Financial data (yr. ended 12/31/04): Assets, $111,062,028 (M); gifts received, $992,449; expenditures, $3,632,746; qualifying distributions, $2,879,214; giving activities include $1,211,556 for 27 grants (high: $600,500; low: $50).
Purpose and activities: Maddox serves as a catalyst for building strong and viable communities that meet the needs of their citizens through collaborative action and service. The foundation believes that successful communities must engage a diverse mix of human, social and economic assets in the process of defining and addressing community needs. The foundation encourages collaborative efforts that engage a wide range of public, corporate, private and other nonprofit partners as investors and service providers. Priority is given to investments that leverage additional support from other sources, and that serve as a channel for long-term strategic change in organizations and communities to better meet local needs. This includes supporting efforts to increase philanthropy in the region through the establishment and support of community foundations.
Fields of interest: Elementary/secondary education; Education, early childhood education; Higher education; Education, continuing education; Education; Environment, natural resources; Environment, plant conservation; Environment; Animal welfare; Health care; Human services; Children/youth, services; Aging, centers/services; Foundations (community); Religion.
Type of support: General/operating support; Capital campaigns; Building/renovation; Equipment; Land acquisition; Endowments; Program development; Conferences/seminars; Seed money; Scholarship funds; Technical assistance; Matching/challenge support.
Limitations: Applications not accepted. Giving primarily in northwest MS and middle TN. No grants to individuals, and generally no grants for annual campaigns or appeals, awards/prizes/competitions, start-up or expansion of businesses or other economic development ventures, debt reduction, emergency funds, loans or lines of credit, publications, public relations services, research, or travel to conferences or events.
Publications: Informational brochure; IRS Form 990-PF.
Application information: Unsolicited requests for funds not accepted.
  Board meeting date(s): Varies; meets as needed
Officers and Trustee:* Robin Grindstaff Costa,* Pres.; Paul T. Morris, Secy.; Suzie Browning, Treas.
Number of staff: 6 full-time professional; 2 full-time support.
EIN: 640917900
Selected grants: The following grants were reported in 2004.
$707,380 to Belmont University, Nashville, TN. 2 grants: $600,500 (For building fund), $106,880 (For Presidential Scholars).
$200,000 to YMCA of Nashville and Middle Tennessee, Nashville, TN.
$107,506 to Community Foundation of Northwest Mississippi, Hernando, MS. To assist donors with contributions to non-profits.
$40,000 to Vanderbilt University, Nashville, TN. For building fund.
$28,845 to University of Tennessee, Knoxville, TN.
$10,000 to DeSoto Sunrise, Southaven, MS. For after-school tutoring.

$5,000 to Community Foundation of Greater Memphis, Memphis, TN. To assist donors with contributions to non-profits.
$5,000 to Newspapers in Education, Southaven, MS.

4754
H. F. McCarty, Jr. Family Foundation ◇
6360 I-55 N., Ste. 480
Jackson, MS 39211

Established in 1995 in MS.
Donors: Allen Flynt; Katherine McCarty Flynt; Mary Helen McCarty Griffis; Angela Flynt Little; H.F. McCarty, Jr.; John R. McCarty; Mary Ann McCarty; Michael A. McCarty; Shellye S. McCarty; Elizabeth Stevens; Patti Stevens; William A. Stevens; Patti M. Sullivan; Ashley Wells; Leslie Wells; Marsha McCarty Wells.
Foundation type: Independent foundation.
Financial data (yr. ended 12/31/05): Assets, $65,709 (M); gifts received, $464,862; expenditures, $504,054; qualifying distributions, $490,216; giving activities include $490,216 for 30 grants (high: $100,000; low: $800).
Purpose and activities: Giving primarily for higher education, as well as for health associations, and social services.
Fields of interest: Higher education; Education; Health organizations, association; Human services; Children/youth, services; Foundations (public); Christian agencies & churches.
Limitations: Giving primarily in Jackson, MS.
Application information: Application form not required.
  Deadline(s): None
Officers: John R. McCarty, Pres.; Mary Ann McCarty, Secy.
Directors: Katherine McCarty Flynt; Patti M. Sullivan; Marsha McCarty Wells.
EIN: 640865125
Selected grants: The following grants were reported in 2003.
$176,000 to Millsaps College, Jackson, MS.
$166,000 to University of Mississippi Foundation, University, MS.
$50,000 to Wilson Research Foundation, Jackson, MS.
$40,000 to Rust College, Holly Springs, MS.
$20,000 to YMCA, Jackson Metropolitan, Jackson, MS.
$5,000 to Willowood Developmental Center, Jackson, MS.
$4,680 to Childrens Hospital, Friends of, Jackson, MS.
$2,500 to Mission Mississippi, Jackson, MS.
$1,000 to Multiple Sclerosis Society, National, Jackson, MS.
$1,000 to Public Education Forum of Mississippi, Jackson, MS.

4755
Selby and Richard McRae Foundation, Inc.
(formerly McRae Foundation)
P.O. Box 20080
Jackson, MS 39289-0080 (601) 968-4200
Contact: Contact for initial letter: Richard D. McRae Sr., Pres.
FAX: (601) 968-4354; Contact for information only: Renee Holm, Secy.

Established in 1965 in MS.
Donor: Richard McRae, Sr.
Foundation type: Independent foundation.
Financial data (yr. ended 1/31/05): Assets, $18,399,861 (M); gifts received, $250,401; expenditures, $1,042,432; qualifying distributions, $1,327,900; giving activities include $810,631 for 60 grants (high: $100,000; low: $500).
Purpose and activities: Grants primarily for social services, religion, and education; some support for cultural programs.
Fields of interest: Education; Human services; Christian agencies & churches.
Type of support: Continuing support; Annual campaigns; Capital campaigns; Scholarship funds.
Limitations: Giving primarily in MS. No grants to individuals.
Publications: Application guidelines; Financial statement; Program policy statement; Program policy statement (including application guidelines); Quarterly report.
Application information: Application form not required.
  Initial approach: Letter
  Copies of proposal: 1
  Deadline(s): None
  Board meeting date(s): Determined by board members
  Final notification: Varies
Officers and Directors:* Richard D. McRae, Sr.,* Pres.; Selby W. McRae,* V.P.; Renee Holm,* Secy.; Vaughan W. McRae,* Treas.; Richard D. McRae, Jr.; Susan M. Shanor.
EIN: 646026795
Selected grants: The following grants were reported in 2004.
$50,000 to Community Foundation for Greater Atlanta, Atlanta, GA.
$50,000 to Wilson Research Foundation, Jackson, MS.
$34,500 to Stewpot Community Services, Jackson, MS.
$25,000 to Rust College, Holly Springs, MS.
$22,500 to McCallie School, Chattanooga, TN.
$17,458 to Baddour Center, Senatobia, MS.
$10,000 to Clemson University, Clemson, SC.
$10,000 to Home Place, Chattanooga, TN.
$10,000 to Mississippi Sheriffs Boys and Girls Ranch, Columbus, MS.
$10,000 to Walter Anderson Museum of Art, Ocean Springs, MS.

4756
Mississippi Common Fund Trust
c/o Memory House
P.O. Box 249
University, MS 38677-0249

Established in 1996 in MS.
Donors: James L. Barksdale; Sally M. Barksdale†; Robert Seymour; R. Faser Triplett.
Foundation type: Independent foundation.
Financial data (yr. ended 6/30/05): Assets, $1,278,716 (M); gifts received, $3,615,883; expenditures, $6,022,023; qualifying distributions, $5,997,150; giving activities include $5,997,150 for 24 grants (high: $2,657,700; low: $5,000; average: $10,000–$50,000).
Purpose and activities: Giving primarily for education and human services.
Fields of interest: Higher education; Education; Human services; Protestant agencies & churches.

Limitations: Applications not accepted. Giving primarily in MS. No grants to individuals.
Application information: Contributes only to pre-selected organizations.
Officers: Don L. Fruge, Sr., C.E.O. and Pres.; Sandra M. Guest, Secy.-Treas.
Trustee: The University of Mississippi Foundation.
Number of staff: 7
EIN: 640875827
Selected grants: The following grants were reported in 2005.
$2,657,700 to University of Mississippi Foundation, University, MS.
$1,035,000 to National D-Day Museum Foundation, New Orleans, LA. For exhibitions.
$1,000,000 to Jackson State University Foundation, Jackson, MS.
$500,000 to King Hussein Foundation, Jordan. For programs promoting education.
$200,000 to Tulane University, New Orleans, LA.
$125,000 to Governors Mansion Foundation, Jackson, MS. For refurbishment and preservation.
$20,000 to University of Tennessee, Knoxville, TN.
$15,000 to Copiah Endowment Corporation, Hazlehurst, MS. For organizations in Copiah County.
$10,000 to Magnolia Speech School for the Deaf, Jackson, MS. For auditory-oral education.

4757
Mississippi Hospital Association Health, Research and Educational Foundation ◇
(formerly Mississippi Hospital Association Educational Foundation)
c/o Richard Grimes
P.O. Box 1909
Madison, MS 39130-1909 (601) 982-3251

Established in 1931 in MS.
Donors: Mississippi State Dept. of Health; Mississippi Development Authority; Mississippi Board of Nursing; Hinds County Workforce Investment Network.
Foundation type: Independent foundation.
Financial data (yr. ended 4/30/05): Assets, $2,578,642 (M); gifts received, $6,239,327; expenditures, $7,240,971; qualifying distributions, $5,254,462; giving activities include $5,254,462 for 2 grants (high: $5,224,462; low: $30,000).
Fields of interest: Hospitals (general); Public health, bioterrorism.
Type of support: Equipment; Scholarship funds.
Limitations: Giving primarily in MS.
Application information:
  Initial approach: Letter
  Deadline(s): None
Officers: William Oliver, Chair.; Gerald Wages, Chair.-Elect; Marcella McKay, Pres.
Board Members: Sam W. Cameron; Gerald Cotton; William Peaks; Harold H. Whitaker, Sr.; and 12 additional board members.
EIN: 237068714

4758
Mississippi Power Foundation, Inc. ◇
P.O. Box 4079
Gulfport, MS 39502 (228) 865-5925
Contact: Rebecca Montgomery
FAX: (228) 865-5876; Additional tel.: (228) 865-5909

Established in 1997 in MS.
Donor: Mississippi Power Co.
Foundation type: Company-sponsored foundation.
Financial data (yr. ended 12/31/04): Assets, $9,219,546 (M); gifts received, $471,302; expenditures, $485,697; qualifying distributions, $396,308; giving activities include $364,326 for 175 grants (high: $31,000; low: $48).
Purpose and activities: The foundation supports museums and organizations involved with arts and culture, health, children and youth, human services, and religion.
Fields of interest: Museums; Arts; Health care; Children/youth, services; Human services; Community development; Federated giving programs; Religion.
Type of support: Sponsorships; Capital campaigns; Employee matching gifts; General/operating support; Annual campaigns; Scholarship funds.
Limitations: Giving primarily in areas of company operations. No grants to individuals.
Application information: Application form required.
  Initial approach: Contact foundation for application form
  Deadline(s): Varies
Officers and Directors:* Don E. Mason,* Chair.; Vicki Pierce, Pres. and Treas.; Frances V. Turnage, Secy.; Michael G. Collins; Rex E. Kelly.
EIN: 721370746
Selected grants: The following grants were reported in 2003.
$133,814 to United Way of South Mississippi, Gulfport, MS. 3 grants: $42,508; $48,800; $42,506
$25,000 to Mississippi State University Foundation, Mississippi State, MS.
$25,000 to Ohr-OKeefe Museum of Art, Biloxi, MS.
$25,000 to Walter Anderson Museum of Art, Ocean Springs, MS.
$15,000 to Wolf River Conservancy, Memphis, TN.
$7,463 to United Way of Southeast Mississippi, Hattiesburg, MS.
$5,000 to Gulf Coast Symphony Orchestra, Gulfport, MS.
$4,200 to Center for the Prevention of Child Abuse, Baltimore, MD.

4759
Edwin E. & Ruby C. Morgan Foundation, Inc. ◇ ☆
1675 Lakeland Dr., Ste. 202
Jackson, MS 39216

Established in 1983 in MS.
Donors: Edwin E. Morgan; Ruby C. Morgan†; R. Miller Reid.
Foundation type: Independent foundation.
Financial data (yr. ended 12/31/05): Assets, $19,937,639 (M); expenditures, $1,089,133; qualifying distributions, $921,033; giving activities include $706,570 for 19 grants (high: $190,000; low: $3,000).
Purpose and activities: Giving for animal welfare, community and civic organizations, and human services.
Fields of interest: Animal welfare; Human services.
Limitations: Applications not accepted. Giving limited to CA and MS. No grants to individuals.
Application information: Contributes only to pre-selected organizations.

Officers and Directors:* R. Miller Reid,* Pres. and Treas.; Miller David Reid,* V.P. and Secy.; Philip L. Colson; G.E. Morgan; Karen M. Mogan.
EIN: 640667872
Selected grants: The following grants were reported in 2004.
$30,000 to Mustard Seed, Brandon, MS.
$30,000 to Salvation Army Divisional Headquarters, Jackson, MS.
$30,000 to Stewpot Community Services, Jackson, MS.
$20,000 to Mississippi Food Network, Jackson, MS.
$6,000 to Community Hospital Foundation, Monterey, CA.

4760
Oakwood Foundation Charitable Trust ◇
P.O. Box 4200
Tupelo, MS 38803 (662) 840-3322

Established in 1995 in MS.
Donors: Elizabeth Renee Grisham; John R. Grisham, Jr.
Foundation type: Independent foundation.
Financial data (yr. ended 12/31/04): Assets, $10,674 (M); gifts received, $945,000; expenditures, $1,518,858; qualifying distributions, $1,508,631; giving activities include $1,508,631 for 38 grants (high: $400,000; low: $500).
Fields of interest: Higher education; Education; Animal welfare; Health care; Housing/shelter, development; Recreation, parks/playgrounds; Human services; Foundations (private grantmaking); Christian agencies & churches.
Limitations: Applications not accepted. Giving primarily in MS.
Application information: Unsolicited requests for funds not accepted.
Officer: Robert E. McDade, Fin. Mgr.
Trustees: Elizabeth Renee Grisham; John R. Grisham.
EIN: 640858879
Selected grants: The following grants were reported in 2004.
$400,000 to Habitat for Humanity International, Charlottesville, VA.
$258,131 to Thomas Jefferson Memorial Foundation, Charlottesville, VA.
$170,000 to University of Mississippi, University, MS.
$100,000 to Animal Rescue League of Mississippi, Jackson, MS.
$80,000 to Brasil Project Charitable Trust, Tupelo, MS.
$60,000 to University Baptist Church, Charlottesville, VA.
$50,000 to National Law Center on Homelessness and Poverty, DC.
$50,000 to Tougaloo College, Tougaloo, MS.
$30,000 to Saint Annes Belfield School Foundation, Charlottesville, VA.
$10,000 to Eudora Welty Foundation, Jackson, MS.

4761
Peaster Foundation ◇
P.O. Box 1589
Yazoo City, MS 39194

Established in 2000 in MS.
Donor: Thomas G. Peaster.
Foundation type: Independent foundation.

Financial data (yr. ended 12/31/04): Assets, $705,114 (M); gifts received, $300,000; expenditures, $348,132; qualifying distributions, $345,862; giving activities include $345,975 for 4 grants (high: $139,461; low: $29,502).
Purpose and activities: Giving primarily to a Presbyterian church, and to Reformed and Presbyterian seminaries.
Fields of interest: Protestant agencies & churches.
Limitations: Applications not accepted. Giving primarily in MS. No grants to individuals.
Application information: Contributes only to pre-selected organizations.
Officers and Directors:* Thomas G. Peaster,* Pres. and Treas.; Linda Peaster,* V.P. and Secy.; Laura L. Peaster Nelson; Margaret M. Peaster.
EIN: 640926072

4762
Providence Foundation ✧
222 Ridge Dr.
Jackson, MS 39216

Established in 2000 in MS.
Donors: E.B. Martin, Jr.; Jamie Planck Martin.
Foundation type: Independent foundation.
Financial data (yr. ended 12/31/04): Assets, $2,571,107 (M); gifts received, $434,100; expenditures, $488,400; qualifying distributions, $414,733; giving activities include $414,733 for 22 grants (high: $250,000; low: $250).
Fields of interest: Arts; Education; Religion.
Limitations: Applications not accepted. Giving primarily in MS.
Application information: Contributes only to pre-selected organizations.
Directors: E.B. Martin, Jr.; Jamie Planck Martin.
EIN: 640934113

4763
The Riley Foundation ✧
4518 Poplar Springs Dr.
Meridian, MS 39305 (601) 481-1430
Contact: Becky G. Farley, Exec. Dir.
FAX: (601) 481-1434;
E-mail: info@rileyfoundation.org; URL: http://www.rileyfoundation.org

Established in 1998 in MS.
Foundation type: Independent foundation.
Financial data (yr. ended 12/31/05): Assets, $58,243,720 (M); expenditures, $8,283,310; qualifying distributions, $7,781,719; giving activities include $7,261,681 for 50 grants (high: $5,900,000; low: $200).
Purpose and activities: The foundation's purpose is to make grants, distributions, and/or loans to charitable and governmental organizations for charitable purposes, and to provide financial resources and assistance for community-wide projects and programs in health care, education, and the betterment of cultural, environmental, and economic conditions for the people of Meridian and Lauderdale County, MS.
Fields of interest: Arts; Education; Health care; Human services; Economic development; Community development.
Type of support: General/operating support; Continuing support; Building/renovation; Equipment; Endowments; Seed money; Technical

assistance; Consulting services; Program evaluation; Matching/challenge support.
Limitations: Giving limited to Meridian, and Lauderdale County, MS.
Publications: Application guidelines; Biennial report; Grants list.
Application information: E-mailed or faxed grant applications will not be accepted, and incomplete applications will be returned. Application guidelines and application forms available on foundation Web site. Application form required.
Copies of proposal: 1
Deadline(s): Feb. 15, May 15, Aug. 15, and Nov. 15
Board meeting date(s): Jan., Apr., July and Oct.
Final notification: 2 weeks after board meeting
Officers and Directors:* William G. Riley, M.D.*, Vice-Chair. and Pres.; R.B. Deen, Jr.,* V.P., Secy., and Genl. Counsel; I.A. Rosenbaum,* V.P., C.F.O., and Treas.; Becky G. Farley, Exec. Dir.; Marty Davidson; Edwin E. Downer; Tommy E. Dulaney; Malcolm Portera; Gail W. Riley; Mary Ann Riley; Richard F. Riley, Jr.
Number of staff: 5 full-time professional.
EIN: 640707746
Selected grants: The following grants were reported in 2005.
$5,900,000 to Mississippi State University, Mississippi State, MS. For Performing Arts Education Center.
$78,500 to Meridian Community College, Meridian, MS. For multimedia technology.
$10,000 to Meridian Little Theater, Meridian, MS.
$10,000 to Meridian Museum of Art, Meridian, MS.
$10,000 to Meridian Symphony Orchestra, Meridian, MS.
$10,000 to Upbeat Meridian Youth Symphony Association, Meridian, MS. For Music for All Ages program.

4764
Leo W. Seal, Jr. Family Foundation ✧
1 Hancock Plz.
Gulfport, MS 39501

Established in 1997 in MS.
Donors: Leo W. Seal, Jr.; Schooler Family Foundation.
Foundation type: Independent foundation.
Financial data (yr. ended 12/31/05): Assets, $9,988,910 (M); gifts received, $10,000; expenditures, $418,274; qualifying distributions, $409,970; giving activities include $409,970 for 300 grants (high: $25,200; low: $50).
Purpose and activities: Giving primarily for education, health organizations, and human services.
Fields of interest: Education; Health organizations; Human services; Children, services; Residential/custodial care; Christian agencies & churches.
Limitations: Applications not accepted. Giving on a national basis. No grants to individuals.
Application information: Contributes only to pre-selected organizations.
Officers: Leo W. Seal, Jr., Pres.; Leo W. Seal III, V.P.; W. Lee Seal, V.P.; Margie S. Johnson, Secy.
EIN: 721373522

4765
Homer Skelton Charitable Foundation ✧
4225 State Line Rd.
Olive Branch, MS 38654-7087
Contact: Homer D. Skelton, Tr.

Donor: Homer D. Skelton.
Foundation type: Independent foundation.
Financial data (yr. ended 12/31/04): Assets, $2,210,856 (M); gifts received, $800,000; expenditures, $1,059,423; qualifying distributions, $1,058,223; giving activities include $996,083 for 41 grants (high: $500,000; low: $200), and $62,140 for 16 grants to individuals (high: $13,528; low: $35).
Purpose and activities: Giving to Christian churches, including Christian schools and organizations as well as for children, youth, families, and social services; also awards educational scholarships to individuals, and grants to individuals.
Fields of interest: Elementary/secondary education; Higher education; Education; Hospitals (general); Crime/violence prevention, child abuse; Recreation, camps; Boys & girls clubs; Children, day care; Family services; Christian agencies & churches.
Type of support: Grants to individuals; Scholarships—to individuals.
Limitations: Giving primarily to residents of TN.
Application information:
Initial approach: Letter or proposal
Deadline(s): None
Trustees: Catherine M. Skelton; Homer D. Skelton.
EIN: 621578268
Selected grants: The following grants were reported in 2004.
$500,000 to Longview Heights Baptist Church, Olive Branch, MS.
$176,613 to Southern Baptist Educational Center of Whitehaven, Southaven, MS.
$102,160 to DeSoto County Schools, Hernando, MS.
$27,000 to Union University, Jackson, TN.

4766
The Algernon Sydney Sullivan Foundation
520 College Hill Rd.
P.O. Box 2286
Oxford, MS 38655 (662) 236-6335
Contact: Allan E. Strand, Pres.
FAX: (662) 236-0900;
E-mail: admin@sullivanfdn.org; URL: http://www.sullivanfdn.org

Incorporated in 1930 in NY.
Donors: Mrs. Algernon Sydney Sullivan†; George Hammond Sullivan†; Zilph P. Devereaux†; Charles Watson†.
Foundation type: Independent foundation.
Financial data (yr. ended 12/31/05): Assets, $16,944,068 (M); expenditures, $1,015,433; qualifying distributions, $962,801; giving activities include $900,000 for 32 grants (high: $40,000; low: $6,000).
Purpose and activities: Grants primarily to colleges and universities for scholarship funds.
Fields of interest: Higher education.
Type of support: General/operating support; Endowments; Scholarship funds.
Limitations: Applications not accepted. Giving primarily in the southeastern U.S. No grants to individuals, or for capital construction.

Application information: Unsolicited requests for funds not accepted.

Board meeting date(s): May and Nov.

Officers and Directors:* Allan E. Strand,* Pres.; Gray Williams, Jr.,* V.P.; Stephan L. McDavid,* Secy.-Treas.; William E. Bardusch, Jr., Pres. Emeritus.

Trustees: William Bruen, Jr.; David C. Farrand; Randolph V. Merrick, M.D.; Douglas M. Orr, Jr.; Thomas S. Rankin; Elizabeth H. Verner; Darla J. Wilkinson.

Number of staff: 1 part-time professional; 1 part-time support.

EIN: 136084596

Selected grants: The following grants were reported in 2004.

$51,000 to Warren Wilson College, Asheville, NC.

$40,500 to Lincoln Memorial University, Harrogate, TN.

$30,000 to Campbell University, Buies Creek, NC.

$30,000 to Coker College, Hartsville, SC.

$30,000 to Erskine College, Due West, SC.

$30,000 to Guilford College, Greensboro, NC.

$30,000 to Huntingdon College, Montgomery, AL.

$30,000 to Saint Andrews Presbyterian College, Laurinburg, NC.

$30,000 to Salem College, Winston-Salem, NC.

$30,000 to Shenandoah University, Winchester, VA.

4767

W. A. Taylor Foundation ✧ ☆

650 N. Church Ave.
Louisville, MS   39339-2033

Established in 1965.

Donors: W.A. Taylor, Jr.; The Taylor Group, Inc.; TEMTCO.

Foundation type: Independent foundation.

Financial data (yr. ended 9/30/05): Assets, $814,851 (M); gifts received, $852,000; expenditures, $500,464; qualifying distributions, $500,018; giving activities include $494,500 for 24 grants (high: $200,500; low: $100).

Purpose and activities: Giving for education, youth programs, and social services; funding also for Baptist churches, as well as to a Presbyterian church.

Fields of interest: Education; Boy scouts; Human services; Children/youth, services; Protestant agencies & churches.

Limitations: Applications not accepted. Giving primarily in MS. No grants to individuals.

Application information: Contributes only to pre-selected organizations.

Trustees: Pat Autry; W.A. Taylor, Jr.

EIN: 646028570

4768

Telos Foundation, Inc. ✧ ☆

P.O. Box 13362
Jackson, MS   39236-3362
Application address: c/o William M. Mounger II, 4400 Old Canton Rd., Ste. 310, Jackson, MS 39211-5982

Established in 1995.

Donor: William M. Mounger II.

Foundation type: Operating foundation.

Financial data (yr. ended 12/31/05): Assets, $7,653,587 (M); gifts received, $436,489; expenditures, $643,811; qualifying distributions, $502,575; giving activities include $502,575 for 23 grants (high: $100,000; low: $225).

Purpose and activities: Giving primarily for Christian preaching, teaching, and other religious activities.

Fields of interest: Education; Diabetes research; Human services; Children/youth, services; Christian agencies & churches.

International interests: Africa.

Limitations: Giving primarily in MS; some giving also in FL.

Application information: Needy persons should submit evidence as to the need for food, clothing, shelter and other items of basic sustenance. Requests for loans should contain evidence of an inability to obtain conventional financing.

Initial approach: Letter

Deadline(s): None

Final notification: 2 months after receipt

Officers: William M. Mounger II, Pres. and Secy.-Treas.; Callie Brandon Mounger, V.P.

EIN: 640854272

Selected grants: The following grants were reported in 2004.

$45,000 to Vanderbilt University, Nashville, TN.

$20,000 to Voice of Calvary Ministries, Jackson, MS. 2 grants: $5,000, $15,000

$10,000 to Mission to the World, Lawrenceville, GA.

$5,000 to Mississippi Commission for International Cultural Exchange, Jackson, MS.

$4,000 to Ole Miss Loyalty Foundation, Oxford, MS.

4769

Vicksburg Hospital Medical Foundation ✧

P.O. Box 1578
Vicksburg, MS   39180-1578   (601) 636-5514
Contact: Howell N. Gage, Chair.

Established in 1956 in MS.

Foundation type: Independent foundation.

Financial data (yr. ended 12/31/05): Assets, $12,940,203 (M); expenditures, $650,808; qualifying distributions, $543,985; giving activities include $530,000 for 10 grants (high: $150,000; low: $10,000).

Purpose and activities: Giving primarily for higher education scholarships.

Fields of interest: Higher education.

Type of support: Endowments; Scholarship funds.

Limitations: Applications not accepted. Giving primarily in MS. No grants to individuals.

Application information: Contributes only to pre-selected organizations.

Board meeting date(s): Quarterly

Officers: Howell N. Gage, Jr., Chair.; Robert K. Purks, Vice-Chair.; P.K. Watson, Secy.-Treas.

Trustees: Susan Chiarito; M.L. Davis.

Number of staff: 1 part-time professional; 1 part-time support.

EIN: 646025312

4770

Walker Foundation ✧

(formerly W. E. Walker Foundation)
2829 Lakeland Dr., Ste. 1600
Mirror Lake Plz.
Jackson, MS   39232-8880   (601) 939-3003
Contact: John S. Jenkins, Dir.

Established in 1972 in MS.

Donors: W.E. Walker, Jr.†; Gloria Walker; The Walker Cos.; His Way Homes.

Foundation type: Independent foundation.

Financial data (yr. ended 12/31/03): Assets, $9,296,426 (M); gifts received, $462,500; expenditures, $703,395; qualifying distributions, $562,101; giving activities include $560,000 for 4 grants (high: $548,000; low: $2,000).

Purpose and activities: Giving primarily to an educational foundation; funding also for children and youth services.

Fields of interest: Education; Children/youth, services; Christian agencies & churches.

Type of support: General/operating support; Annual campaigns; Capital campaigns.

Limitations: Giving primarily in MS. Generally no grants for deficit reduction, operating budgets, endowment programs, personnel costs, welfare agencies, physical plant construction, or individual scholarships.

Publications: Annual report.

Application information: Application form required for scholarships. Application form required.

Deadline(s): None

Board meeting date(s): As needed

Officers: James H. Daughdrill III, Pres.; Leigh B. Allen III, Secy.

Trustee: W.E. Walker III.

Director: John S. Jenkins.

Number of staff: 1 part-time professional.

EIN: 237279902

Selected grants: The following grants were reported in 2003.

$548,000 to Walker Education Foundation, Jackson, MS.

$5,000 to Mississippi Childrens Home Society and Family Service Association, Jackson, MS.

$5,000 to Renewed Life Ministries, Jackson, MS.

$2,000 to Inroads, Saint Louis, MO.

MISSOURI

4771
AJP Foundation ✧
7701 Forsyth Blvd., Ste. 1125
St. Louis, MO 63105-1828
Contact: Mark Gale, Tr.

Donor: David C. Pratt.
Foundation type: Independent foundation.
Financial data (yr. ended 11/30/04): Assets,
$10,331,911 (M); gifts received, $1,973,000;
expenditures, $1,972,751; qualifying distributions,
$1,972,751; giving activities include $1,971,601
for 8 grants (high: $1,200,000; low: $5,000).
Purpose and activities: Giving primarily to an animal
rescue foundation.
Fields of interest: Education; Animal welfare;
Human services.
Type of support: General/operating support; Capital
campaigns.
Limitations: Applications not accepted. Giving
primarily in MO. No grants to individuals.
Application information: Contributes only to
pre-selected organizations.
Trustee: Mark Gale.
EIN: 431420360

4772
Ameren Corporation Charitable Trust ▼
(formerly Union Electric Company Charitable Trust)
c/o Corp. Contribs., Ameren
P.O. Box 66149, M.C. 100
St. Louis, MO 63166-6149 (877) 426-3736,
ext. 46441
Contact: Otis Cowan, Mgr., Community Rels.
FAX: (314) 554-2888;
E-mail: ocowan@ameren.com; Application address
for organizations located in IL: Corp. Contribs.,
Ameren, 300 Liberty St., Peoria, IL 61602-1404,
tel.: (877) 426-3736, ext. 75001; Additional tel.:
(314) 554-6441; URL: http://www.ameren.com/
Community/ADC_CM_NonProfitGrants.asp

Trust established in 1944 in MO.
Donors: Union Electric Co.; Ameren Corp.
Foundation type: Company-sponsored foundation.
Financial data (yr. ended 12/31/05): Assets,
$4,941,303 (M); expenditures, $3,657,401;
qualifying distributions, $3,625,261; giving
activities include $3,583,308 for 74 grants (high:
$986,500; low: $25), and $37,478 for 49 employee
matching gifts.
Purpose and activities: The trust supports
organizations involved with arts and culture, human
services, and civic affairs. Special emphasis is
directed toward organizations involved with
education, the environment, youth, and senior
citizens.
Fields of interest: Arts; Education; Environment;
Youth, services; Human services; Public affairs;
Aging.
Type of support: General/operating support;
Continuing support; Annual campaigns; Capital
campaigns; Building/renovation; Equipment;
Emergency funds; Program development;
Scholarship funds; Employee matching gifts; In-kind
gifts; Matching/challenge support.

Limitations: Giving limited to areas of company
operations in IL and MO. No support for political
organizations or candidates or religious, fraternal,
veterans', social, or similar organizations. No grants
to individuals; no electric or natural gas service
donations.
Publications: Application guidelines; Annual report;
Corporate giving report.
Application information: Proposals should be
submitted using organization letterhead. Application
form not required.
Initial approach: Proposal to foundation for
organizations located in MO; proposal to
application address for organizations located
in IL; proposal to nearest company facility for
organizations located in outlying areas
Copies of proposal: 1
Deadline(s): None
Board meeting date(s): 2 or 3 times per year
Final notification: 2 to 6 months
Trustees: Gary L. Rainwater; Bank of America, N.A.
Number of staff: 2 full-time professional; 1 full-time
support.
EIN: 436022693
Selected grants: The following grants were reported
in 2004.
$986,500 to United Way of Greater Saint Louis,
Saint Louis, MO.
$200,000 to University of Missouri, Columbia, MO.
$75,000 to Arts and Education Council of Greater
Saint Louis, Saint Louis, MO.
$50,000 to Saint Louis University, Saint Louis, MO.
$50,000 to Wyman Center, Eureka, MO.
$29,000 to Junior Achievement of Mississippi
Valley, Chesterfield, MO.
$25,000 to Grand Center, Saint Louis, MO.
$25,000 to McKendree College, Lebanon, IL.
$10,000 to Saint Louis For Kids, Saint Louis, MO.
$8,000 to United Way, Callaway County, Fulton, MO.
$5,000 to Komen Saint Louis Race for the Cure,
Saint Louis, MO.

4773
American Century Companies
Foundation ✧
P.O. Box 418210
Kansas City, MO 64141-0210 (816) 531-5575
Contact: Mary Jo Browne
URL: http://www.americancentury.com/welcome/
community.jsp

Established in 2000 in MO.
Donor: American Century Cos., Inc.
Foundation type: Company-sponsored foundation.
Financial data (yr. ended 12/31/05): Assets,
$4,012,937 (M); gifts received, $1,000,000;
expenditures, $1,588,404; qualifying distributions,
$1,588,404; giving activities include $1,588,404
for 181 grants (high: $160,000; low: $500).
Purpose and activities: The foundation supports
organizations involved with arts and culture,
education, health, medical research, financial
education, human services, community
development, civic affairs, youth, senior citizens,
disabled people, and economically disadvantaged
people.
Fields of interest: Arts education; Visual arts;
Performing arts; Arts; Education; Health care;
Medical research; Human services, financial
counseling; Human services; Economic
development; Business/industry; Community
development; Public affairs; Youth; Aging;

Disabilities, people with; Economically
disadvantaged.
Limitations: Giving primarily in CO, KS, MO, and NY.
Application information:
Initial approach: Proposal
Deadline(s): None
Board meeting date(s): Quarterly
Officers and Directors:* William M. Lyons,* Pres.;
Jon W. Zindel,* V.P.; Wendy B. Welte, Secy.; Robert
T. Jackson,* Treas.
EIN: 431881225
Selected grants: The following grants were reported
in 2003.
$130,000 to United Way, Heart of America, Kansas
City, MO.
$75,000 to Friends of the Zoo, Kansas City, MO. For
capital support.
$70,500 to Salvation Army, Kansas City, MO. 2
grants: $20,500 (For operating support),
$50,000 (For capital campaign).
$50,000 to Liberty Memorial Association, Kansas
City, MO.
$50,000 to Ronald McDonald House Charities of
the Heart of America, Kansas City, MO. For
capital campaign.
$35,000 to Young Audiences, Kansas City, Kansas
City, MO. For operating support.
$25,000 to Charter School Partnership Fund,
Kansas City, MO. For operating support.
$25,000 to Rose Brooks Center, Kansas City, MO.
For Rose Brooks Center Cabaret.
$20,000 to Community School of Music and Arts,
Mountain View, CA. For capital campaign.

4774
Andrews McMeel Universal
Foundation ✧ ☆
(formerly Andrews & McMeel Foundation)
4520 Main St., Ste. 700
Kansas City, MO 64111
Contact: Kathleen W. Andrews, V.P. and Secy.

Established in 1991 in MO.
Donor: United Press Syndicate.
Foundation type: Company-sponsored foundation.
Financial data (yr. ended 12/31/05): Assets,
$4,315,130 (M); expenditures, $366,396;
qualifying distributions, $341,908; giving activities
include $341,908 for grants.
Purpose and activities: The foundation supports
organizations involved with arts and culture,
education, health, youth development, human
services, and community development.
Fields of interest: Media/communications;
Museums; Performing arts; Arts; Higher education;
Education; Health care; Youth development; Human
services; Community development.
Type of support: Employee matching gifts; General/
operating support.
Limitations: Giving primarily in KS and MO, with
emphasis on the bi-state Kansas City area.
Application information: Application form not
required.
Initial approach: Proposal
Deadline(s): None
Officers: John P. McMeel, Pres. and Treas.;
Kathleen W. Andrews, V.P. and Secy.
Directors: Hugh T. Andrews; James C. Andrews;
Elena Fallon; Suzanne E. McMeel Glynn; John T.
Howard; Maureen McMeel Jackoboice; Bridget J.
McMeel; Susan S. McMeel; Jeffrey F. Rayport;
Eugene L. Roberts, Jr.; Thomas N. Thornton.
EIN: 431570308

Selected grants: The following grants were reported in 2003.

$71,432 to University of Notre Dame, Notre Dame, IN.

$7,500 to Donnelly College, Kansas City, KS.

$5,000 to Rockhurst University, Kansas City, MO.

$3,500 to Kansas City Symphony, Kansas City, MO.

$2,750 to Boys and Girls Clubs of Greater Kansas City, Kansas City, MO.

$1,500 to Womens Employment Network, Kansas City, MO.

$500 to 18th and Vine Authority, American Jazz Museum, Kansas City, MO.

$300 to Rose Brooks Center, Kansas City, MO.

$250 to Kansas City Free Health Clinic, Kansas City, MO.

$100 to Pembroke Hill School, Kansas City, MO.

4775
William S. Anheuser Family Foundation ◇ ☆

4954 Lindell Blvd., No. W4E
St. Louis, MO 63108

Established in 2004 in MO.
Donor: William S. Anheuser.
Foundation type: Independent foundation.
Financial data (yr. ended 12/31/05): Assets, $103,620 (M); expenditures, $10,459,753; qualifying distributions, $10,158,103; giving activities include $10,148,575 for 9 grants (high: $9,348,369; low: $5,000).
Purpose and activities: Support primarily for a community foundation.
Fields of interest: American Red Cross; Salvation Army; Foundations (community); Christian agencies & churches.
Limitations: Applications not accepted. Giving primarily in St. Louis, MO. No grants to individuals.
Application information: Contributes only to pre-selected organizations.
Trustees: William S. Anheuser; Merrill Lynch Trust Co.
EIN: 226964985

4776
Anheuser-Busch Foundation ▼

c/o Anheuser-Busch Cos., Inc.
1 Busch Pl.
St. Louis, MO 63118
Contact: Judy Vonder Haar, Asst. Mgr., Charitable Contribs.
URL: http://www.anheuser-busch.com/ in_the_community/foundation.html

Established in 1975 in MO.
Donor: Anheuser-Busch Cos., Inc.
Foundation type: Company-sponsored foundation.
Financial data (yr. ended 12/31/05): Assets, $37,539,680 (M); gifts received, $5,000,000; expenditures, $13,571,748; qualifying distributions, $13,484,472; giving activities include $13,481,956 for 581 grants (high: $1,700,000).
Purpose and activities: The foundation supports organizations involved with arts and culture, education, the environment, health, youth development, human services, and minority development.
Fields of interest: Arts; Education; Environment; Health care; Youth development; Human services; Minorities.

Type of support: Continuing support; Capital campaigns; Building/renovation; Program development; Scholarship funds; Employee matching gifts; Matching/challenge support.
Limitations: Giving primarily in areas of company operations, with emphasis on Fairfield, Los Angeles, and San Diego, CA, Fort Collins, CO, Jacksonville, Orlando, and Tampa, FL, Cartersville, GA, St. Louis, MO, Merrimack, NH, Newark, NJ, Baldwinsville, NY, Columbus, OH, Houston and San Antonio, TX, and Williamsburg, VA. No support for political candidates or organizations, religious organizations, fraternal, social, or similar organizations, or athletic organizations. No grants to individuals, or for general operating support for hospitals.
Publications: Application guidelines; Informational brochure.
Application information: Video submissions are not encouraged. Application form not required.
Initial approach: Proposal
Copies of proposal: 1
Deadline(s): None
Board meeting date(s): Approximately every 3 months
Final notification: 6 to 8 weeks
Trustees: JoBeth G. Brown; August A. Busch III; John E. Jacob; U.S. Bank, N.A.
EIN: 510168084
Selected grants: The following grants were reported in 2005.

$1,000,000 to American Red Cross, Saint Louis, MO. For Hurricane Katrina disaster relief.

$1,000,000 to American Red Cross, National Headquarters, DC. For relief effort for Hurricane Katrina.

$1,000,000 to Saint Johns Mercy Health System, Saint Louis, MO. For endowment.

$1,000,000 to University of California at Davis Foundation, Davis, CA. For capital campaign.

$500,000 to Saint Louis University, Saint Louis, MO. For capital campaign.

$460,000 to Saint Louis Science Center, Saint Louis, MO. For capital campaign.

$400,000 to Barnes-Jewish Hospital Foundation, Saint Louis, MO. For project support.

$250,000 to Saint Louis Childrens Hospital, Saint Louis, MO. For capital campaign.

$240,000 to Washington University, Saint Louis, MO. For project support.

$237,500 to Saint Louis Regional Educational and Public Television Commission, Saint Louis, MO. For capital support.

4777
Apex Oil Company Charitable Foundation ◇

8235 Forsyth Blvd., Ste. 400
Clayton, MO 63105
Contact: Steven G. Twele, Treas.

Established in 2002 in MO.
Donors: Apex Oil Co., Inc.; Edgington Oil Co.
Foundation type: Company-sponsored foundation.
Financial data (yr. ended 12/31/05): Assets, $2,936,129 (M); gifts received, $4,800,000; expenditures, $4,052,734; qualifying distributions, $4,052,640; giving activities include $4,052,500 for 25 grants (high: $1,000,000; low: $500).
Purpose and activities: The foundation supports organizations involved with arts and culture, education, and health.
Fields of interest: Arts; Higher education; Education; Hospitals (general); Health care.

Application information: Application form not required.
Initial approach: Proposal
Deadline(s): None
Officers and Directors:* Paul A. Novelly,* Pres.; Douglas D. Hommert,* Secy.; Steven G. Twele,* Treas.
EIN: 710914470

4778
Arthur & Helen Baer Charitable Foundation ◇

c/o UHY Advisors Inc.
3117 S. Big Bend Blvd.
St. Louis, MO 63143

Established around 1984.
Donor: Helen K. Baer‡.
Foundation type: Independent foundation.
Financial data (yr. ended 12/31/05): Assets, $9,461,128 (M); expenditures, $614,115; qualifying distributions, $436,768; giving activities include $410,200 for 19 grants (high: $100,000; low: $1,500).
Purpose and activities: Support for museums and other cultural programs, human services, animal welfare, and education.
Fields of interest: Museums (art); Arts; Elementary/secondary education; Education; Animal welfare; Human services; Children/youth, services.
Type of support: Building/renovation; Equipment; Program development; Scholarship funds; Program-related investments/loans.
Limitations: Applications not accepted. Giving primarily in St. Louis, MO. No grants to individuals.
Application information: Contributes only to pre-selected organizations.
Officers: Richard T. Fisher, Pres.; Patrick E. Stark, Secy.-Treas.
Advisor: Mary Baer Fisher.
EIN: 431353474

4779
Sidney R. Baer Foundation

c/o U.S. Bank, N.A., Private Client Group
P.O. Box 387
St. Louis, MO 63166-0387
Contact: Ann Wells
URL: http://www.baerfoundation.org

Established in 1999 in MA.
Donor: Sidney R. Baer, Jr. Trust.
Foundation type: Independent foundation.
Financial data (yr. ended 6/30/05): Assets, $49,812,085 (M); gifts received, $11,309,353; expenditures, $2,559,357; qualifying distributions, $2,216,760; giving activities include $2,166,526 for 10 grants (high: $500,000; low: $50,000).
Purpose and activities: Giving to organizations that engage or are involved in mental health. The foundation's mission is to: 1) Provide preventive and early-intervention strategies, particularly those that work in tandem with educational programs; 2) Increase transitional and long term care for those sufferers of mental illness who cannot afford appropriate care; 3) Encourage and support research into the causes of, and cures for, mental illness; and 4) Provide public education for the wide dissemination of information about mental illness and those suffering from mental illness.
Fields of interest: Mental health, association.

Type of support: Program development; Research.
Limitations: Giving primarily in NY, Boston, MA and St. Louis, MO. No support for mental retardation, physical disability, drugs or alcohol addiction programs, or medical researchers. No grants to individuals, or for current operating funds, annual fund raising drives, endowments, international activities or foreign charitable institutions.
Publications: Application guidelines.
Application information: See foundation Web site for application guidelines and download of application form. Application form required.
  Initial approach: Complete grant application
  Copies of proposal: 3
  Deadline(s): Apr. 1 and Aug. 1
  Board meeting date(s): June and Oct.
Trustees: George B. Handran; U.S. Bank, N.A.
EIN: 436829338

4780
The Ballman Family Private Foundation ✧
c/o U.S. Bank, N.A.
P.O. Box 387
St. Louis, MO   63166
Contact: For Scholarship Awards: Mark Weaver, Trust Off., U.S. Bank, N.A.

Established in 1993 in MO.
Foundation type: Independent foundation.
Financial data (yr. ended 5/31/05): Assets, $27,608,293 (M); expenditures, $1,297,102; qualifying distributions, $1,256,589; giving activities include $1,119,250 for 26 grants (high: $90,750; low: $24,200), and $92,500 for 37 grants to individuals (high: $2,500; low: $2,500).
Purpose and activities: Giving for education, hospitals, and human services. Scholarships are awarded 1 time to female high school graduates from the St. Louis, MO, metropolitan area.
Fields of interest: Higher education; Nursing school/education; Education; Animal welfare; Hospitals (general); Food distribution, meals on wheels; Human services; Children/youth, services; Residential/custodial care.
Type of support: Scholarships—to individuals.
Limitations: Giving primarily in St. Louis, MO; scholarship awards limited to St. Louis, MO. No grants to individuals (except for designated scholarships).
Application information: Applications accepted for scholarship program only.
  Initial approach: Letter
Trustee: U.S. Bank, N.A.
EIN: 436466750
Selected grants: The following grants were reported in 2005.
$90,750 to Good Samaritan Home, Saint Louis, MO.
$60,500 to Childrens Home Society of Missouri, Saint Louis, MO.
$60,500 to Humane Society of Missouri, Saint Louis, MO.
$60,500 to Missouri Council of the Blind, Saint Louis, MO.
$60,500 to Ranken Technical College, Saint Louis, MO.
$60,500 to Saint Louis College of Pharmacy, Saint Louis, MO.
$60,500 to Salvation Army, Independence, MO.
$24,200 to Epworth Childrens Home, Saint Louis, MO.
$24,200 to Independence Center, Saint Louis, MO.
$2,500 to Truman State University, Kirksville, MO.

4781
Geraldine & R. A. Barrows Foundation ✧ ☆
c/o UMB Bank, N.A.
P.O. Box 419692, M.S. 1020305
Kansas City, MO   64141-6692
Contact: Jan Leonard
Application address: c/o UMB Bank, N.A., 1010 Grand Blvd., Kansas City, MO 64106

Established in 1979 in MO.
Donor: G.M. Barrows†.
Foundation type: Independent foundation.
Financial data (yr. ended 12/31/05): Assets, $7,231,263 (M); expenditures, $364,908; qualifying distributions, $338,148; giving activities include $315,000 for 11 grants (high: $150,000; low: $5,000).
Purpose and activities: Giving primarily for education and to benefit underprivileged children, including camps and clubs; support also for health associations, including cancer, and for the arts.
Fields of interest: Media, television; Performing arts, orchestra (symphony); Arts; Education; Health organizations, association; Cancer; Agriculture; Recreation, parks/playgrounds; Youth development; Children/youth, services.
Limitations: Giving limited to the greater Kansas City, MO, area.
Application information: Application form not required.
  Initial approach: Letter
  Deadline(s): None
Trustee: UMB Bank, N.A.
EIN: 431184875
Selected grants: The following grants were reported in 2003.
$125,000 to Agriculture Future of America, Kansas City, MO. For general support.
$25,000 to Bishop Spencer Place, Kansas City, MO.
$25,000 to Kansas City Symphony, Kansas City, MO. For general operating support.
$25,000 to Teel Institute for the Development of Integrity and Ethical Behavior, Kansas City, MO. For general support.
$10,000 to Boy Scouts of America, Heart of America Council, Kansas City, MO.
$10,000 to Lakemary Center, Paola, KS.
$10,000 to Salvation Army, Kansas City, MO.
$8,500 to WIN for KC, Kansas City, MO.
$5,000 to Boys and Girls Club of Greater Kansas City, Kansas City, KS. For general support.
$5,000 to Metropolitan Organization to Counter Sexual Assault, Kansas City, MO.

4782
The Bellwether Foundation, Inc. ✧
c/o University Club Twr.
1034 S. Brentwood Blvd., Ste. 850
St. Louis, MO   63117-1291
Contact: Robert B. Smith III, Pres.

Established in 1985 in MO.
Donors: Robert B. Smith†; Nancy M. Smith; Wallace H. Smith†.
Foundation type: Independent foundation.
Financial data (yr. ended 12/31/05): Assets, $18,519,748 (M); expenditures, $970,660; qualifying distributions, $842,911; giving activities include $770,000 for 18 grants (high: $250,000; low: $1,000).
Purpose and activities: Primarily supports projects which anticipate the future in the areas of the arts,

---

computer science, education, finance, health care, medicine, and the social sciences, including research in any of these areas.
Fields of interest: Arts; Higher education; Environment, natural resources; Botanical gardens; Medical research, institute.
Type of support: Program development; Research.
Limitations: Applications not accepted. Giving primarily in St. Louis, MO. No grants to individuals.
Application information: Contributes only to pre-selected organizations.
  Board meeting date(s): Apr. and Dec.
Officers and Trustees: * Sally Duffield,* Chair.; Robert B. Smith III,* Pres. and Secy.; Robert B. Smith II; John J. Wolfe.
EIN: 222635309
Selected grants: The following grants were reported in 2003.
$400,000 to Contemporary Art Museum Saint Louis, Saint Louis, MO.
$250,000 to Missouri Botanical Garden, Saint Louis, MO.
$92,500 to Crossroads School, Saint Louis, MO.
$50,000 to Sheldon Arts Foundation, Saint Louis, MO.
$10,000 to Covenant House Missouri, Saint Louis, MO.
$10,000 to Mayo Clinic Jacksonville, Jacksonville, FL.
$2,500 to Planned Parenthood of Saint Louis, Saint Louis, MO.
$2,500 to Saint Louis Zoo, Saint Louis, MO.
$2,500 to Salvation Army of Saint Louis, Saint Louis, MO.

4783
Gertrude and William A. Bernoudy Foundation
c/o Northern Trust Bank, N.A.
190 Carondelet Plz.
St. Louis, MO   63105   (314) 505-8318
Contact: Rita Mathews, V.P., Northern Trust Bank
FAX: (314) 505-8310; E-mail: rm18@ntrs.com;
Application address: c/o Northern Trust Bank, Attn.: Mark Rice, 50 S. LaSalle St., B-03, Chicago, IL 60675; tel.: (312) 444-7431

Established in 1994 in MO.
Donor: G. Bernoudy Interim Trust.
Foundation type: Independent foundation.
Financial data (yr. ended 11/30/05): Assets, $13,910,947 (M); gifts received, $466,177; expenditures, $1,293,955; qualifying distributions, $1,203,474; giving activities include $1,170,000 for 28 grants (high: $200,000; low: $5,000).
Purpose and activities: Giving primarily to animal welfare, architecture, art, civic projects, education, health services and human services.
Fields of interest: Performing arts; Historic preservation/historical societies; Higher education; Education; Health care; Children/youth, services; Civil rights, advocacy.
Type of support: General/operating support; Capital campaigns.
Limitations: Giving primarily in St. Louis, MO. No support for film/video (unless film is an integral part of the organization's activities). No grants for endowment scholarship funds, fundraising activities, loans, travel, medical research or to individuals.
Application information: Application form not required.
  Initial approach: Letter or proposal

Copies of proposal: 4
Deadline(s): None
Board meeting date(s): Spring and fall
Trustees: Edwin B. Meissner, Jr.; John D. Schaperkotter; Stuart Symington, Jr.; Northern Trust Bank, N.A.
EIN: 436512119
Selected grants: The following grants were reported in 2005.
$200,000 to Saint Louis Symphony Orchestra, Saint Louis, MO.
$125,000 to Humane Society of Missouri, Saint Louis, MO.
$50,000 to American Jewish Committee, New York, NY.
$50,000 to Central Institute for the Deaf, Saint Louis, MO.
$20,000 to Saint Louis Zoo, Saint Louis, MO.
$10,000 to Alzheimers Association, Chicago, IL.
$10,000 to Paraquad, Saint Louis, MO.
$10,000 to Springboard to Learning, Saint Louis, MO.
$5,000 to Arts and Education Council, Chattanooga, TN.

4784
Jack and Mary Jane Bodine Charitable Trust ◇ ☆
50 Creekwood Ln.
Ladue, MO 63124

Established in 1986 in MO.
Donors: Jack Bodine; Mary Jane Bodine.
Foundation type: Independent foundation.
Financial data (yr. ended 12/31/05): Assets, $278,162 (M); gifts received, $397,949; expenditures, $403,729; qualifying distributions, $400,702; giving activities include $399,762 for 20 grants (high: $275,300; low: $25).
Purpose and activities: Giving primarily for higher education.
Fields of interest: Performing arts, orchestra (symphony); Higher education; Medical research; Human services; Protestant agencies & churches.
Limitations: Applications not accepted. Giving primarily in Rolla and St. Louis, MO. No grants to individuals.
Application information: Contributes only to pre-selected organizations.
Trustees: Jack Bodine; Mary Jane Bodine.
EIN: 431435402
Selected grants: The following grants were reported in 2003.
$103,400 to Washington University, Saint Louis, MO. For general support.
$29,757 to Ladue Chapel, Saint Louis, MO. For general support.
$25,100 to Saint Louis Symphony Orchestra, Saint Louis, MO. For general support.
$11,500 to Foundry Educational Foundation, Des Plaines, IL. For general support.
$350 to University of Missouri, Rolla, MO. For general support.
$200 to American Parkinson Disease Association, Saint Louis, MO. For general support.
$200 to YMCA of the Ozarks, Potosi, MO. For general support.
$100 to American Cancer Society, Tampa, FL. For general support.
$100 to Multiple Sclerosis Society, National, Saint Louis, MO. For general support.
$100 to Salvation Army of Saint Louis, Saint Louis, MO. For general support.

4785
Boeing-McDonnell Foundation ▼ ◇
(formerly McDonnell Douglas Foundation)
P.O. Box 516, M.C. S100-3462
St. Louis, MO 63166
Contact: Evans Richardson, Pres.

Incorporated in 1947 in MO.
Donor: McDonnell Douglas Corp.
Foundation type: Company-sponsored foundation.
Financial data (yr. ended 12/31/05): Assets, $162,079 (M); expenditures, $4,398,362; qualifying distributions, $4,391,555; giving activities include $4,391,555 for 31 grants (high: $1,075,000; low: $2,000).
Purpose and activities: The foundation supports organizations involved with arts and culture, education, the environment, health, hunger, human services, community development, science, government and public administration, leadership development, minorities, and economically disadvantaged people.
Fields of interest: Arts councils; Arts; Elementary/secondary education; Higher education; Business school/education; Education; Environment, natural resources; Botanical gardens; Environment; Health care; Food services; Children/youth, services; Homeless, human services; Human services; Community development; Federated giving programs; Science, formal/general education; Mathematics; Engineering/technology; Science; Government/public administration; Leadership development; Minorities; Economically disadvantaged.
Type of support: General/operating support; Continuing support; Annual campaigns; Capital campaigns; Program development; Employee-related scholarships.
Limitations: Giving limited to the St. Louis, MO, area. No support for sectarian, denominational, fraternal, social, religious, or labor organizations. No grants to individuals (except for employee-related scholarships), or for advertising, fundraising, or sporting events or university, industry affiliate, or associates programs; no loans.
Publications: Application guidelines.
Application information: Application form required.
Initial approach: Contact foundation for application form
Copies of proposal: 1
Deadline(s): None
Board meeting date(s): Quarterly
Final notification: 2 to 3 months
Officers and Directors:* Norma Clayton,* Chair.; Evans Richardson, Pres.; Norma Bartlett; Patrick Finneran; Samuel Jenkins; Robert Krieger.
Number of staff: 1 full-time professional.
EIN: 431128093
Selected grants: The following grants were reported in 2003.
$1,105,000 to United Way of Greater Saint Louis, Saint Louis, MO. For general support.
$500,000 to Saint Louis Science Center Foundation, Saint Louis, MO. For general support.
$500,000 to Saint Louis University, Saint Louis, MO. For general support.
$200,000 to University of Missouri, Saint Louis, MO. For general support.
$111,446 to YWCA of Metropolitan Saint Louis, Saint Louis, MO.
$100,000 to Cardinal Ritter College Prep, Saint Louis, MO. For general support.

$80,000 to Independence Day Foundation, Saint Louis, MO. For general support.
$70,000 to Arts and Education Council of Greater Saint Louis, Saint Louis, MO. For general support.
$50,000 to Saint Louis Community College Foundation, Saint Louis, MO. For general support.
$37,500 to Missouri Historical Society, Saint Louis, MO. For general support.

4786
Boswell Foundation, Inc. ◇
1078 S. Jefferson
Lebanon, MO 65536
Contact: Paul Walker, Secy.

Established in 1985 in MO.
Donors: Independent Stave Co., Inc.; Amie Boswell Foundation; Joe Boswell Foundation; Johnathon Boswell Foundation; Julie Boswell Foundation; The Lois K. Boswell Charitable Lead Trust.
Foundation type: Company-sponsored foundation.
Financial data (yr. ended 11/30/03): Assets, $121,558 (M); gifts received, $1,113,012; expenditures, $1,066,524; qualifying distributions, $1,049,751; giving activities include $1,049,751 for 28 grants (high: $583,278; low: $75).
Purpose and activities: The foundation supports zoos and organizations involved with arts and culture, education, health, human services, and religion.
Fields of interest: Arts; Elementary/secondary education; Education; Zoos/zoological societies; Health organizations, association; Human services; Federated giving programs; Religion.
Type of support: Scholarship funds.
Limitations: Giving primarily in the Palm Beach, FL, area and Lebanon, MO. No grants to individuals.
Application information: Application form not required.
Initial approach: Proposal
Deadline(s): None
Final notification: Within 3 months
Officers: John J. Boswell, Pres.; Tiffany Boswell, V.P.; Paul Walker, Secy.
EIN: 431409051
Selected grants: The following grants were reported in 2003.
$108,253 to Chapel, The, Akron, OH.
$25,000 to Sky Ranch Foundation, Arlington, VA.
$10,000 to Chapel Haven, Westville, CT.
$5,000 to University of Pennsylvania, Philadelphia, PA.
$2,815 to American Heart Association, Dallas, TX.
$1,000 to Cystic Fibrosis Foundation, Bethesda, MD.
$1,000 to March of Dimes Birth Defects Foundation, White Plains, NY.
$1,000 to Urban Youth Impact, West Palm Beach, FL.
$500 to Multiple Sclerosis Society, Edmonton, Canada.
$100 to Humane Society.

4787
The Stephen F. and Camilla T. Brauer Charitable Trust
424 S. Woodsmill Rd., Rm. 325
Chesterfield, MO 63017

Established in 1997.
Donor: Stephen F. Brauer.
Foundation type: Independent foundation.
Financial data (yr. ended 12/31/05): Assets, $128,675 (M); gifts received, $667,677; expenditures, $561,940; qualifying distributions, $556,330; giving activities include $556,330 for 96 grants (high: $100,000; low: $100).
Purpose and activities: Giving for the arts and education.
Fields of interest: Museums (art); Arts; Higher education; Education; Environment; Zoos/zoological societies; Health organizations, association; Human services; Children/youth, services; Federated giving programs.
Limitations: Applications not accepted. Giving primarily in St. Louis, MO. No grants to individuals.
Application information: Contributes only to pre-selected organizations.
Trustees: Camilla Brauer; Stephen F. Brauer.
EIN: 311534822

4788
Dana Brown Charitable Trust ▼ ✧
c/o U.S. Bank, N.A.
P.O. Box 387
St. Louis, MO   63141-8695   (314) 418-2643
Application address: c/o Carol Eaves, U.S. Bank, N. A., P.O. Box 387 SL-MO-T14E, St. Louis, MO 63166

Established in 1994 in MO.
Donor: Dana Brown.
Foundation type: Independent foundation.
Financial data (yr. ended 6/30/05): Assets, $75,217,641 (M); expenditures, $3,850,718; qualifying distributions, $3,325,019; giving activities include $3,225,148 for 63 grants (high: $500,000; low: $5,000; average: $10,000–$60,000).
Purpose and activities: Giving primarily for health care and youth clubs; support also for the arts and human services in the St. Louis area.
Fields of interest: Education; Animals/wildlife, research; Animal welfare; Hospitals (specialty); Human services; Children/youth, services.
Type of support: General/operating support; Annual campaigns; Capital campaigns; Building/renovation; Equipment; Consulting services; Matching/challenge support.
Limitations: Giving primarily in the metropolitan St. Louis, MO, area. No grants to individuals.
Publications: Application guidelines; Program policy statement.
Application information: Application form required.
   Initial approach: Letter
   Deadline(s): Feb. 15, May 15, Aug. 15, and Nov. 15
   Board meeting date(s): Mar., June, Sept. and Dec.
Trustees: Lela G. Rice; U.S. Bank, N.A.
EIN: 436531876
Selected grants: The following grants were reported in 2005.
$500,000 to Cardinal Glennon Childrens Hospital Foundation, Saint Louis, MO. For renovation of and future expansion of neonatal intensive care unit.
$300,000 to K E T C-Channel 9, Saint Louis, MO. For 24-hour children's channel.
$225,125 to Saint Louis Childrens Hospital Foundation, Saint Louis, MO. For mobile intensive care unit vehicle.

$125,000 to Ranken Jordan Home for Convalescent Crippled Children, Saint Louis, MO. For pediatric hospital.
$100,000 to Catholic Charities of Saint Louis, Saint Louis, MO. For youth services.
$100,000 to Contemporary Art Museum Saint Louis, Saint Louis, MO. For educational resource center and peer-to-peer docent program.
$50,000 to Loyola Academy of Saint Louis, Saint Louis, MO. For endowment fund.
$33,000 to Central Institute for the Deaf, Saint Louis, MO. For early literacy program in pre-kindergarten department.
$25,000 to Center of Creative Arts, Saint Louis, MO. For Urban Arts Program in Saint Louis Public School Districts.
$25,000 to Foster Care Coalition of Greater Saint Louis, Saint Louis, MO. For recruitment/retention programs for foster and adoptive parents.

4789
Brown Shoe Company, Inc. Charitable Trust
(formerly Brown Group, Inc. Charitable Trust)
8300 Maryland Ave.
Clayton, MO   63105
Contact: Thomas G. Malecek, Secy.

Trust established in 1951 in MO.
Donors: Brown Group, Inc.; Brown Shoe Co., Inc.
Foundation type: Company-sponsored foundation.
Financial data (yr. ended 12/31/04): Assets, $5,124,284 (M); expenditures, $958,575; qualifying distributions, $934,047; giving activities include $919,900 for 114 grants (high: $223,500; low: $100).
Purpose and activities: The foundation supports organizations involved with arts and culture and education.
Fields of interest: Arts; Higher education; Education.
Type of support: General/operating support; Continuing support; Annual campaigns; Capital campaigns; Building/renovation; Equipment; Land acquisition; Emergency funds; Employee matching gifts.
Limitations: Giving limited to areas of major company operations, with emphasis on St. Louis, MO. No grants to individuals, or for endowments, special projects, research, publications, or conferences; no loans.
Application information: Application form not required.
   Initial approach: Proposal
   Copies of proposal: 1
   Deadline(s): None
   Board meeting date(s): As needed
   Final notification: 1 to 3 months
Control Committee and Trustees:* Ronald A. Fromm,* Chair.; Thomas G. Malecek, Secy.; Andrew M. Rosen.
Trustee Bank: SunTrust Banks, Inc.
EIN: 237443082
Selected grants: The following grants were reported in 2003.
$47,500 to Arts and Education Council of Greater Saint Louis, Saint Louis, MO. For general support.
$44,200 to Saint Louis Symphony Orchestra, Saint Louis, MO. For general support.
$27,540 to K E T C-Channel 9, Saint Louis, MO. For general support.

$25,318 to Saint Louis Science Center, Saint Louis, MO. For general support.
$15,800 to Missouri Botanical Garden, Saint Louis, MO. For general support.
$12,000 to Junior Achievement of Mississippi Valley, Chesterfield, MO. For general support.
$10,000 to Grand Center, Saint Louis, MO. For general support.
$8,670 to Saint Louis Art Museum, Saint Louis, MO. For general support.
$8,398 to Saint Louis Zoo, Saint Louis, MO. For general support.
$6,600 to Maryville University, Saint Louis, MO. For general support.

4790
Buckner Foundation ✧ ☆
P.O. Box 625
Marshall, MO   65340

Established in 2001 in MO.
Donor: Charles M. Buckner, Jr. Revocable Trust.
Foundation type: Operating foundation.
Financial data (yr. ended 6/30/05): Assets, $1,975,413 (M); expenditures, $355,743; qualifying distributions, $351,221; giving activities include $351,221 for 2 grants (high: $228,239; low: $122,982).
Purpose and activities: Giving primarily to a hospital and to a Baptist church.
Fields of interest: Hospitals (general); Protestant agencies & churches.
Limitations: Applications not accepted. Giving primarily in Marshall, MO. No grants to individuals.
Application information: Contributes only to pre-selected organizations.
Trustee: William Gordon Buckner.
Advisors: James Coe; Thomas B. Hall; William B. Kessinger; Charles D. Van Dyke.
EIN: 431933644

4791
The G. A., Jr. and Kathryn M. Buder Charitable Foundation ✧
c/o Jack Barsanti
1 Metropolitan Sq., Ste. 2600
St. Louis, MO   63102

Established in 1991 in MO.
Donor: Kathryn M. Buder.
Foundation type: Independent foundation.
Financial data (yr. ended 12/31/04): Assets, $15,244,394 (M); expenditures, $791,326; qualifying distributions, $746,300; giving activities include $746,300 for 9 grants (high: $591,000; low: $700).
Purpose and activities: Giving primarily to higher education for scholarships and music promotion.
Fields of interest: Performing arts, music; Performing arts, orchestra (symphony); Arts; Higher education; Education; Animal welfare; Hospitals (specialty); Health organizations, association; Human services; Christian agencies & churches.
Type of support: Scholarship funds.
Limitations: Applications not accepted. Giving primarily in MO. No grants to individuals.
Application information: Contributes only to pre-selected organizations.

Trustees: John R. Barsanti, Jr.; G.A. Buder IV; Marshall O. Buder; Theodore A. Buder; Rev. Robert Dorhauer; Shanti K. Khinduda.
EIN: 431582356
Selected grants: The following grants were reported in 2003.
$692,000 to Washington University, Saint Louis, MO. 2 grants: $591,000 to Burder Center (For scholarships and administration), $101,000 (For scholarship).
$25,000 to Archdiocesan Development Appeal, Department of Special Education, Saint Louis, MO.
$16,000 to University of Missouri, Columbia, MO.
$16,000 to Webster University, Saint Louis, MO.
$10,000 to Cardinal Glennon Childrens Hospital, Saint Louis, MO.
$10,000 to Saint Louis Childrens Hospital, Saint Louis, MO.
$10,000 to Shriners Hospitals for Children, Tampa, FL.
$6,000 to Southern Illinois University, Edwardsville, IL.
$2,300 to Music Institute of Chicago, Winnetka, IL.

4792
Bunge Corporation Foundation ◇
11720 Borman Dr.
St. Louis, MO 63146 (314) 292-2300
Contact: Philip W. Staggs, V.P.

Established in 1993 in MO.
Donor: Bunge North America, Inc.
Foundation type: Company-sponsored foundation.
Financial data (yr. ended 12/31/03): Assets, $85,990 (M); gifts received, $350,000; expenditures, $479,677; qualifying distributions, $479,675; giving activities include $479,522 for 172 grants (high: $139,547; low: $25).
Purpose and activities: The foundation supports organizations involved with arts and culture, education, and youth development.
Fields of interest: Performing arts; Arts; Higher education; Education; Youth development; Federated giving programs.
Application information:
Initial approach: Proposal
Deadline(s): Oct. 29
Officers: Carl L. Hausmann, Pres.; Michael M. Scharf, Sr. V.P.; Philip W. Staggs, V.P.; David G. Kabbes, Secy.; Francis X. Marchiony, Treas.; Karen D. Roebuck, Cont.
EIN: 431617648
Selected grants: The following grants were reported in 2003.
$139,547 to Harvard University, Cambridge, MA.
$30,550 to Wellesley College, Wellesley, MA.
$30,000 to Missouri Botanical Garden, Saint Louis, MO.
$25,545 to Metropolitan Museum of Art, New York, NY.
$21,300 to Saint Louis Science Center, Saint Louis, MO.
$16,500 to Pierpont Morgan Library, New York, NY.
$16,000 to New York Public Library, New York, NY.
$15,000 to Lincoln Center for the Performing Arts, New York, NY.
$12,225 to Child Center of Our Lady, Saint Louis, MO.
$10,000 to Characterplus, Saint Louis, MO.

4793
Butler Manufacturing Company Foundation ◇ ☆
P.O. Box 419917
Kansas City, MO 64141-0917 (816) 968-3208
Contact: Pamela Bird Yeater, Dir.
FAX: (816) 627-8946;
E-mail: psbirdyeater@butlermfg.com

Incorporated in 1952 in MO.
Donor: Butler Manufacturing Co.
Foundation type: Company-sponsored foundation.
Financial data (yr. ended 12/31/05): Assets, $6,223,673 (M); expenditures, $367,491; qualifying distributions, $328,440; giving activities include $293,550 for 70 grants (high: $62,500; low: $200), $2,000 for 1 grant to an individual, and $29,155 for 72 employee matching gifts.
Purpose and activities: The foundation supports organizations involved with arts and culture, education, health, employment, housing, youth development, community development, disabled people, minorities, women, and economically disadvantaged people.
Fields of interest: Arts; Elementary/secondary education; Higher education; Education; Hospitals (general); Health care; Employment, training; Employment; Housing/shelter; Youth development; Community development; Disabilities, people with; Minorities; Women; Economically disadvantaged.
Type of support: Seed money; Continuing support; Capital campaigns; General/operating support; Annual campaigns; Employee matching gifts; Employee-related scholarships; Grants to individuals.
Limitations: Giving primarily in areas of company operations, with emphasis on the greater Kansas City, MO, area. No support for political organizations, religious organizations not of direct benefit to the entire community, pre-K-12 educational institutions, fraternal or veterans' organizations, national health organizations, local or regional chapters of national health organizations, or grantmaking foundations. No grants to individuals (except for employee-related hardship grants and employee-related scholarships), or for tours, conferences, seminars, workshops, or similar events, fundraising, or endowments.
Publications: Application guidelines; Informational brochure (including application guidelines).
Application information: Application form not required.
Initial approach: Proposal to nearest company facility; proposal to foundation for organizations located in the greater Kansas City, MO, area
Copies of proposal: 1
Deadline(s): 2 months prior to board meetings
Board meeting date(s): Mar., June, Sept., and Dec.
Final notification: Following board meetings
Officers and Trustees:* John J. Holland,* Pres.; Ronald E. Rutledge,* V.P.; John W. Huey,* Secy.; Nanka A. Schneider, Treas.; David Goodwin; Thomas Harris.
Number of staff: 1 part-time support.
EIN: 440663648
Selected grants: The following grants were reported in 2003.
$83,000 to United Way, Heart of America, Kansas City, MO.
$20,000 to United Way of Knox County, Galesburg, IL.

$20,000 to United Way, Terrell/Kaufman County, Terrell, TX.
$20,000 to University of Missouri, Kansas City, MO.
$20,000 to Westside Agency Collaborative, Kansas City, MO.
$10,000 to Harvesters-The Community Food Network, Kansas City, MO.
$7,500 to United Way of Scotland County, Laurinburg, NC.
$7,000 to United Way of Hays County, San Marcos, TX.
$7,000 to United Way of Lebanon County, Lebanon, PA.
$4,000 to United Way of Greene County, Greeneville, TN.

4794
E. Kemper Carter and Anna Curry Carter Community Memorial Trust ◇
(formerly Carter Community Memorial Trust)
c/o UMB Bank, N.A.
P.O. Box 419692, M.S. 1020305
Kansas City, MO 64141-6692 (816) 860-7711
Contact: Jan B. Leonard, Trust Off., UMB Bank, N.A.

Established in 1993 in MO.
Foundation type: Independent foundation.
Financial data (yr. ended 12/31/05): Assets, $12,895,623 (M); expenditures, $634,797; qualifying distributions, $592,508; giving activities include $560,000 for 6 grants (high: $300,000; low: $10,000).
Purpose and activities: Giving primarily for higher education and agriculture; funding also for the arts, health care, children's services, and a YMCA.
Fields of interest: Media, television; Museums (art); Performing arts, orchestra (symphony); Higher education; Health care; Agriculture; YM/YWCAs & YM/YWHAs; Children, services.
Limitations: Giving limited to KS and MO, with emphasis on the Kansas City area.
Application information:
Initial approach: Letter
Deadline(s): None
Trustees: George R. Hayden, Jr.; Blackwell Sanders; UMB Bank, N.A.
EIN: 436483356
Selected grants: The following grants were reported in 2004.
$300,000 to Metropolitan Community Colleges, Kansas City, MO. For general support.
$150,000 to Agriculture Future of America, Kansas City, MO. For general support.
$50,000 to YMCA of Greater Kansas City, Kansas City, MO. For capital campaign.
$25,000 to Kansas City Symphony, Kansas City, MO. For general support.
$10,000 to Students in Free Enterprise, Springfield, MO.

4795
Jim Casey Youth Opportunities Initiative, Inc. ◇
222 S. Central Ave., Ste. 305
St. Louis, MO 63105 (314) 863-7000
FAX: (314) 863-7003; URL: http://www.jimcaseyyouth.org

Established in 2001 in DE.
Donors: Casey Family Grants Program; The Annie E. Casey Foundation.

Foundation type: Independent foundation.
Financial data (yr. ended 12/31/05): Assets, $8,130,659 (M); gifts received, $5,271,163; expenditures, $9,345,484; qualifying distributions, $9,391,155; giving activities include $4,739,536 for 20 grants (high: $815,000; low: $10,000).
Purpose and activities: The mission of the Jim Casey Youth Opportunities Initiative is to help youth in foster care make successful transitions to adulthood. It brings together the people and resources needed for youth to make the connections they need to education, employment, health care, housing, and supportive personal and community relationships.
Fields of interest: Children, foster care; Human services.
Limitations: Applications not accepted. No grants to individuals.
Application information: Contributes only to pre-selected organizations.
Officers: Douglas W. Nelson, Pres.; Kent C. Nelson, Secy.; Kathleen Lee, C.F.O.; Gary Stangler, Exec. Dir.
Directors: Dick Ford; Dennis Hightower; Ruth Massinga; Calvin Tyler.
EIN: 233081243
Selected grants: The following grants were reported in 2003.
$600,000 to Educational Broadcasting Corporation, New York, NY. For foster youth initiatives.
$594,458 to Michigan Family Independence Agency, Lansing, MI. For foster youth initiatives.
$404,330 to Community Foundation for Greater Atlanta, Atlanta, GA. For foster youth initiatives.
$401,456 to Child Welfare League of America, DC. For foster youth initiatives.
$399,905 to Child and Family Policy Center, Des Moines, IA. For foster youth initiatives.
$250,000 to Corporation for Enterprise Development (CFED), West, San Francisco, CA. For foster youth initiatives.
$244,029 to Center for the Study of Social Policy, DC. For foster youth initiatives.
$200,000 to Northwestern University, Evanston, IL. For foster youth initiatives for School of Law Children and Family Justice in Chicago.
$190,000 to Living in New Community (LINC), Kansas City, MO. For foster youth initiatives.
$150,000 to University of South Florida, Tampa, FL. For foster youth initiatives.

4796
The Centene Charitable Foundation ◇ ☆
Centene Pl.
7711 Carondelet Ave., Ste. 800
St. Louis, MO 63105

Established in 2005 in MO.
Donor: Centene Management Company, LLC.
Foundation type: Company-sponsored foundation.
Financial data (yr. ended 5/31/05): Assets, $37,568 (M); gifts received, $1,100,500; expenditures, $1,062,977; qualifying distributions, $1,062,477; giving activities include $1,062,477 for 42 grants (high: $137,500; low: $5,000).
Purpose and activities: The foundation supports organizations involved with arts and culture, education, and health.
Fields of interest: Performing arts, orchestra (symphony); Performing arts, opera; Arts; Education; Health care.
Limitations: Applications not accepted. Giving primarily in St. Louis, MO.

Application information: Contributes only to pre-selected organizations.
Officers: Michael F. Neidorff, Pres.; Karey L. Witty, Secy.; William N. Scheffel, Treas.
EIN: 201298192

4797
The Commerce Bancshares Foundation ◇
(formerly The Commerce Foundation)
922 Walnut, Ste. 200
Kansas City, MO 64106-1809
Contact: Michael D. Fields, Pres.

Incorporated in 1952 in MO.
Donor: Commerce Bancshares, Inc.
Foundation type: Company-sponsored foundation.
Financial data (yr. ended 12/31/04): Assets, $2,849,221 (M); gifts received, $348,851; expenditures, $1,303,783; qualifying distributions, $1,271,540; giving activities include $1,268,044 for 731 grants (high: $52,000; low: $50).
Purpose and activities: The foundation supports organizations involved with arts and culture, education, health, human services, and civic affairs.
Fields of interest: Arts; Education; Health care; Human services; Public affairs.
Type of support: General/operating support; Continuing support; Annual campaigns; Capital campaigns; Building/renovation; Equipment; Emergency funds; Program development; Conferences/seminars; Professorships; Seed money; Curriculum development.
Limitations: Giving primarily in west central IL, KS, and MO. No support for private foundations. No grants to individuals, or for general operating support; no loans; no matching gifts.
Application information: Application form not required.
Initial approach: Proposal to nearest company facility
Copies of proposal: 1
Deadline(s): None
Board meeting date(s): As required
Final notification: Varies
Officers and Directors:* Michael D. Fields,* Pres.; Edward J. Reardon II, V.P. and Treas.; Jonathan M. Kemper, V.P.; J. Daniel Stinnett, Secy.; Kevin G. Barth; David W. Kemper.
EIN: 446012453
Selected grants: The following grants were reported in 2005.
$53,000 to United Way of the Plains, Wichita, KS.
$50,120 to United Way of Greater Saint Louis, Saint Louis, MO.
$13,000 to Missouri Colleges Fund, Jefferson City, MO.
$10,000 to Saint Louis Symphony Orchestra, Saint Louis, MO.
$5,000 to Developmental Center of the Ozarks, Springfield, MO.
$5,000 to Kansas City Art Institute, Kansas City, MO.
$4,750 to United Way of Greater Saint Joseph, Saint Joseph, MO.
$1,500 to Negro Leagues Baseball Museum, Kansas City, MO.
$1,100 to Southwest Baptist University, Bolivar, MO.
$1,000 to Lees Summit Social Services, Lees Summit, MO.

4798
Community Foundation of the Ozarks
(formerly Community Foundation, Inc.)
425 E. Trafficway
Springfield, MO 65806 (417) 864-6199
Contact: Gary Funk, C.E.O.; Concept letter: Randy Russell, Sr. Prog. Off.; Concept letter: Gay Lynn Russell, Scholarship Coord.
FAX: (417) 864-8344; E-mail: gfunk@cfozarks.org; Additional tel.: (888) 266-6815; Concept letter E-mails: rrussell@cfozarks.org or grussell@cfozarks.org; URL: http://www.cfozarks.org

Incorporated in 1973 in MO.
Foundation type: Community foundation.
Financial data (yr. ended 6/30/05): Assets, $87,846,197 (M); gifts received, $13,201,804; expenditures, $6,190,741; giving activities include $4,614,480 for 612 grants (high: $257,335; low: $16).
Purpose and activities: The mission of the foundation is to enhance the quality of life for the citizens of southern Missouri, now and for future generations by building community endowments, meeting needs through grantmaking, providing leadership, and promoting collaboration on community issues.
Fields of interest: Arts; Education; Environment; Health care; Children, services; Human services; Civil rights; Community development; Aging.
Type of support: General/operating support; Continuing support; Annual campaigns; Building/renovation; Equipment; Endowments; Emergency funds; Program development; Conferences/seminars; Seed money; Curriculum development; Scholarship funds; Research; Technical assistance; Consulting services; Program evaluation; Program-related investments/loans; Matching/challenge support.
Limitations: Giving limited to southern MO.
Publications: Application guidelines; Annual report (including application guidelines); Informational brochure; Newsletter.
Application information: Visit foundation Web site for online application form and guidelines. Application form required.
Initial approach: Submit online grant application
Deadline(s): Feb. 10 for Education and Community Devel., Sept. 2 for Health and Social Svcs., and Oct. 7 for Arts and Culture and Environment
Board meeting date(s): 4th Wed. of most months
Final notification: Varied response
Officers and Directors:* Thomas D. Peebles, Jr.,* Chair.; Todd Parnell,* Chair.-Elect; Gary Funk,* C.E.O. and Pres.; Sally Baird,* Secy.; Ron Neville,* Treas.; James Anderson; Kevin Ausburn; Julie Brown; Margaret Carolla; James Leon Combs; John Cooper; Sharon Whitehill Gray; Susie Henry; Patti Holt; Jerry Jared; Lou Thelen Kemp; Yolanda Lorge; Lisa Officer; Dr. Nancy O'Reilly; Dr. Tom Prater; Maura Taylor; Robert Wheeler.
Number of staff: 7 full-time professional; 1 part-time professional; 3 full-time support.
EIN: 237290968

4799
The Floy L. and Paul F. Cornelsen Charitable Foundation ◇
P.O. Box 6488
Chesterfield, MO 63006-6488

Established in 1993 in MO.

Donors: Floy L. Cornelsen; Paul F. Cornelsen.

Foundation type: Independent foundation.

Financial data (yr. ended 6/30/05): Assets, $5,622,673 (M); expenditures, $950,383; qualifying distributions, $904,383; giving activities include $901,814 for 5 grants (high: $115,814; low: $3,000).

Purpose and activities: Giving primarily for Lutheran churches and schools.

Fields of interest: Theological school/education; Education; Children/youth, services; Family services; Protestant agencies & churches.

Limitations: Applications not accepted. Giving primarily in St. Louis, MO and Tacoma, WA. No grants to individuals.

Application information: Contributes only to pre-selected organizations.

Trustees: Barbara K. Cornelsen; Floy L. Cornelsen; Paul F. Cornelsen.

EIN: 431635732

Selected grants: The following grants were reported in 2004.

$500,000 to Lutheran School of Theology at Chicago, Chicago, IL. For general support.

$155,261 to Lutheran Family and Childrens Services of Missouri, Saint Louis, MO. For general support.

$50,000 to Christ Evangelical Lutheran Church, Webster Groves, MO. For general support.

$5,000 to Pacific Lutheran University, Tacoma, WA. For general support.

$3,500 to Lutheran Ministries Association, Saint Louis, MO. For general support.

4800
The E. L. Craig Foundation ✧
P.O. Box 1404
Joplin, MO   64802-1404

Incorporated in 1960 in MO.

Donors: Tamko Asphalt Products, Inc.; Royal Brand Roofing, Inc.

Foundation type: Independent foundation.

Financial data (yr. ended 7/31/05): Assets, $7,121,669 (M); expenditures, $377,369; qualifying distributions, $371,080; giving activities include $373,500 for 11 grants (high: $100,000; low: $3,500).

Fields of interest: Employment; Federated giving programs; Social sciences; Public affairs, research; Public policy, research.

Limitations: Applications not accepted. Giving on a national basis, with emphasis on Washington, DC, and VA. No grants to individuals, or for publicly funded groups.

Application information: Contributes only to pre-selected organizations.

Officers: Ethelmae C. Humphreys, Pres.; David C. Humphreys, V.P. and Secy.-Treas.; Sarah Humphreys Atkins, V.P.

EIN: 446015127

Selected grants: The following grants were reported in 2005.

$75,000 to Acton Institute for the Study of Religion and Liberty, Grand Rapids, MI.

$25,000 to Landmark Legal Foundation, Kansas City, MO.

$25,000 to Mercatus Center, Arlington, VA.

$25,000 to Reason Foundation, Los Angeles, CA.

$10,000 to Boy Scouts of America, Springfield, MO.

$5,000 to Heartland Institute, Chicago, IL.

4801
Cloud L. Cray Foundation
800 W. 47th St., Ste. 711
Kansas City, MO   64112   (816) 756-0600
Contact: Richard B. Cray, Tr.

Established in 1967 in MO.

Donor: Cloud L. Cray†.

Foundation type: Independent foundation.

Financial data (yr. ended 12/31/05): Assets, $10,800,172 (M); expenditures, $781,805; qualifying distributions, $653,669; giving activities include $626,450 for 32 grants (high: $233,500; low: $250).

Purpose and activities: Giving primarily for economic education.

Fields of interest: Higher education; Economics.

Type of support: General/operating support; Continuing support; Annual campaigns; Program development; Professorships.

Limitations: Applications not accepted. Giving primarily in KS and MO. No grants to individuals.

Application information: Contributes only to pre-selected organizations.

Trustees: Cloud L. Cray, Jr.; Richard B. Cray.

Trustee Banks: Bank of America, N.A.; UMB Bank, N.A.

EIN: 436077249

Selected grants: The following grants were reported in 2005.

$233,500 to University of Missouri, Kansas City, MO. 2 grants: $203,500 (For economic education), $30,000 to Bloch School (For general support).

$89,500 to Kansas University Endowment Association, Lawrence, KS. For economic education.

$65,000 to Genesis School, Kansas City, MO. For general support.

$50,000 to Center for Practical Bioethics, Kansas City, MO. For general support.

$25,000 to Kansas City Area Life Sciences Institute, Kansas City, MO. For general support.

$25,000 to Liberty Memorial Association, Kansas City, MO. For general support.

$20,000 to Habitat for Humanity International, Kansas City, MO. For general support.

$15,000 to Kansas City Community Gardens, Kansas City, MO. For general support.

$15,000 to Kansas Council on Economic Education, Wichita, KS. For general support.

4802
The Curry Family Foundation ✧
(formerly Mid-America Foundation)
800 W. 47th St., Ste. 601
Kansas City, MO   64112
Contact: Lee Curry, Secy.-Treas.

Established in 1986 in MO.

Donors: William H. Curry; Dorothy F. Curry.

Foundation type: Independent foundation.

Financial data (yr. ended 12/31/05): Assets, $11,459,188 (M); gifts received, $240,536; expenditures, $682,360; qualifying distributions, $620,267; giving activities include $474,750 for 54 grants (high: $25,000; low: $1,000; average: $10,000–$20,000).

Fields of interest: Performing arts; Elementary/secondary education; Housing/shelter, development; Family services; Federated giving programs.

Type of support: General/operating support; Continuing support; Capital campaigns; Building/renovation; Equipment; Endowments; Program development; Matching/challenge support.

Limitations: Giving primarily in Kansas City, MO. No grants to individuals.

Application information:

Initial approach: Letter; foundation will send application if interested

Deadline(s): Quarterly

Officers and Directors:* William H. Curry,* Pres.; Dorothy F. Curry,* V.P. and Secy.; Steven O'Neill,* V.P.; Lee Curry,* Secy.-Treas.; Jean Howard.

Number of staff: 2 full-time professional.

EIN: 431428340

4803
The Danforth Foundation ▼ ✧
1 Metropolitan Sq.
211 N. Broadway, Ste. 2390
St. Louis, MO   63102   (314) 588-1900
Contact: Peter Sortino, Pres.

Incorporated in 1927 in MO.

Donors: William H. Danforth, M.D.†; Mrs. William H. Danforth†.

Foundation type: Independent foundation.

Financial data (yr. ended 5/31/05): Assets, $229,013,462 (M); expenditures, $39,885,296; qualifying distributions, $36,384,596; giving activities include $35,749,768 for 24+ grants (high: $15,651,239; low: $1,000; average: $25,000–$895,483), $4,950 for employee matching gifts, and $513,653 for 5 foundation-administered programs.

Purpose and activities: The goal of the foundation is to help revitalize the St. Louis, MO region, making it one of the top metropolitan areas in America. To carry out its mission, the foundation concentrates its efforts on economic development with special interest in the plant and life sciences, neighborhood redevelopment, and downtown St. Louis revitalization. Because the foundation emphasizes excellence, it also supports unique projects which make outstanding contributions to the St. Louis area. In addition, special religious outreach activities and early childhood care and education projects are supported on occasion.

Fields of interest: Economic development; Community development.

Type of support: General/operating support; Capital campaigns; Program development; Program-related investments/loans; Employee matching gifts; Matching/challenge support.

Limitations: Applications not accepted. Giving limited to the metropolitan St. Louis, MO, area. No grants to individuals.

Publications: Annual report; Financial statement; Grants list.

Application information: With the exception of possible funding opportunities in the field of plant and life sciences, the board of trustees has put a hold on all grantmaking.

Board meeting date(s): May and Nov., and as required

Officers and Trustees:* Hon. John C. Danforth,* Chair.; James R. Compton,* Vice-Chair. and Secy.; William H. Danforth, M.D.*, Vice-Chair. and Acting Secy.; Peter G. Sortino,* Pres.; Melvin C. Bahle, Treas.; John H. Biggs; Virginia S. Brown; Walter L. Metcalfe, Jr.; P. Roy Vagelos.

Number of staff: 6 full-time professional; 2 full-time support.
EIN: 430653297
Selected grants: The following grants were reported in 2005.
$3,450,000 to Sustainable Neighborhoods Development Office (SNDO), Saint Louis, MO. Toward operating support and projects in selected neighborhoods.
$3,000,000 to Saint Louis Life Sciences Project, Saint Louis, MO. Toward management of Coalition for Plant and Life Sciences, committees, and projects.
$1,200,000 to Saint Louis University, Saint Louis, MO. To carry out process in which region's progress in meeting important community goals is measured, evaluated, and shared with public through RegionWise Initiative.
$760,000 to Regional Housing and Community Development Alliance, Saint Louis, MO. Toward Sustainable Neighborhoods Development Initiative to improve selected neighborhoods in Saint Louis region.
$750,000 to Faith Beyond Walls, Saint Louis, MO. To bring together people from different religions to work on community projects.
$498,844 to Vashon-Jeff Vanderlou Initiative, Saint Louis, MO. To provide administrative and program support for initiative to revitalize neighborhood surrounding Vashon High School.
$292,500 to Missouri Development Finance Board, Jefferson City, MO. For redevelopment of Old Post Office and revitalization of Downtown Saint Louis.
$33,000 to United Way of Greater Saint Louis, Saint Louis, MO. To carry out process in which region's progress in meeting important community goals is measured, evaluated, and shared with public through RegionWise Initiative.

4804
Deer Creek Foundation

720 Olive St., Ste. 1975
St. Louis, MO 63101 (314) 241-3228
Contact: Mary Stake Hawker, Dir.

Established in 1964 in MO.
Donors: Aaron Fischer†; Teresa M. Fischer†.
Foundation type: Independent foundation.
Financial data (yr. ended 12/31/05): Assets, $58,969,988 (M); expenditures, $3,495,844; qualifying distributions, $2,370,063; giving activities include $1,918,946 for 58 grants (high: $200,000; low: $107).
Purpose and activities: Support primarily for programs that preserve and advance our democratic system and government accountability, with civil liberties protection provided by the Constitution and the Bill of Rights, and to promote education about democracy; grants primarily to 'action programs' with promise of making a significant national or regional impact; some preference to projects in MO.
Fields of interest: Environment; Civil rights, race/intergroup relations; Civil liberties, advocacy; Civil liberties, reproductive rights; Civil rights; Public affairs, citizen participation; Public affairs; Minorities; Women.
Type of support: Program development; Seed money.
Limitations: Applications not accepted. Giving on a national basis, with some emphasis on MO. No grants to individuals, or for building or endowment funds, equipment, or operating budgets.

Publications: Informational brochure.
Application information: Unsolicited requests for funds not accepted.
Board meeting date(s): Apr. and Sept.
Officer and Trustees:* M. Peter Fischer,* Pres.; Lattie F. Coor; Lois B. De Fleur; Martha C. Fischer; Matthew A. Fischer; Michael P. Fischer; Margaret Mellon; Peter J. Rubin.
Director: Mary Stake Hawker.
Number of staff: 1 full-time professional; 1 full-time support; 1 part-time support.
EIN: 436052774
Selected grants: The following grants were reported in 2005.
$400,000 to American Constitution Society for Law and Policy, DC. To provide forum for discussion and debate on legal thought and to act as catalyst for a critical, broad rethinking of American jurisprudence commensurate with preservation of individual rights and liberties and protection of health and the environment.
$200,000 to Center for Investigative Reporting, Berkeley, CA. For reporting and public education on U.S. campaign finance system and need for its reform, and on government misconduct with respect to U.S. energy policy.
$200,000 to Western Environmental Law Center, Eugene, OR. To provide grassroots environmental organizations with pro bono legal services needed to protect the wildlands, wildlife, waters, and communities of the Western United States.
$150,000 to Center for Progressive Reform, Edgewater, MD. For research, monitoring, public education, and administrative agency work regarding the benefits of and threats to federal health, safety, and environmental regulations.
$74,912 to Citizenship Education Clearing House, Saint Louis, MO. For Saint Louis Region Kids Voting Project, which teaches students the importance of exercising their right to vote and of making their vote an informed one.
$50,000 to American Civil Liberties Union (ACLU), New York, NY. For public education and litigation to ensure that post-9/11 security measures taken by the government do not unduly intrude upon civil liberties.
$50,000 to Government Accountability Project (GAP), DC. For general support.
$25,000 to Verified Voting Foundation, San Francisco, CA. To educate state election administrators about dangers of paperless voting machines and to assist them in their procurement of voting machines that produce voter-verifiable ballot receipts.
$15,000 to Northern Plains Resource Council, Billings, MT. For public education and mobilization, administrative agency work, research, and litigation to ensure that environmental laws and regulations are enforced with respect to coal bed methane drilling in Montana.

4805
The Richard W. and Phyllis B. Duesenberg Foundation ◇

1 Indian Creek Ln.
St. Louis, MO 63131-3333
Contact: Richard W. Duesenberg, Tr.

Established in 1989 in MO.
Donors: Richard W. Duesenberg; Phyllis B. Duesenberg.

Foundation type: Independent foundation.
Financial data (yr. ended 12/31/05): Assets, $13,726,305 (M); gifts received, $350,000; expenditures, $660,000; qualifying distributions, $660,000; giving activities include $656,000 for 5 grants (high: $566,000; low: $10,000).
Purpose and activities: Giving generally limited to Lutheran musical and educational programs.
Fields of interest: Performing arts; Higher education; Education; Protestant agencies & churches.
Limitations: Giving primarily in IN, MN, and St. Louis, MO. No grants to individuals.
Application information: Generally contributes only to pre-selected organizations.
Trustees: Phyllis B. Duesenberg; Richard W. Duesenberg.
EIN: 431526439
Selected grants: The following grants were reported in 2003.
$554,000 to Valparaiso University, Valparaiso, IN.
$42,500 to Concordia Seminary, Saint Louis, MO.
$27,000 to Evangelical Lutheran Church of Saint Thomas, Leipzig, Germany. .
$25,000 to Lutheran Music Program, Minneapolis, MN.
$25,000 to Saint Louis Symphony Orchestra, Saint Louis, MO.
$5,500 to Opera Theater of Saint Louis, Saint Louis, MO.

4806
Caleb C. and Julia W. Dula Educational and Charitable Foundation ◇

112 S. Hanley Rd.
St. Louis, MO 63105-3418 (314) 726-2800
Contact: James F. Mauze

Established in 1995 in MO.
Foundation type: Independent foundation.
Financial data (yr. ended 12/31/05): Assets, $39,762,942 (M); expenditures, $2,430,521; qualifying distributions, $2,136,980; giving activities include $1,845,000 for 88 grants (high: $125,000; low: $5,000).
Purpose and activities: Grants to charities which the Dulas supported during their lifetime, with emphasis on education, hospitals, libraries, social service agencies, child welfare, church support, cultural programs, and historic preservation.
Fields of interest: Historic preservation/historical societies; Arts; Libraries/library science; Education; Environment; Health organizations, association; Human services.
Type of support: General/operating support.
Application information:
Initial approach: Letter
Deadline(s): Apr. 1 and Oct. 1
Trustees: Margaret W. Kobusch; Letitia W. Scott; Susan K. Werner; Orrin S. Wightman III.
EIN: 431716767
Selected grants: The following grants were reported in 2005.
$125,000 to Stages Saint Louis, Kirkwood, MO.
$100,000 to Brooks School, North Andover, MA.
$100,000 to Whitfield School, Saint Louis, MO.
$50,000 to Boca Grande Health Clinic Foundation, Boca Grande, FL.
$50,000 to Missouri Botanical Garden, Saint Louis, MO.
$45,000 to Child Center of Our Lady, Saint Louis, MO.
$30,000 to Brookwood School, Manchester, MA.

$25,000 to Center of Contemporary Arts, Saint Louis, MO.

$15,000 to Little Traverse Conservancy, Harbor Springs, MI.

$10,000 to Hospice of the North Shore, Danvers, MA.

4807
Harry Edison Foundation ✧
220 N. 4th St., Ste. A
St. Louis, MO 63102
Contact: Eric P. Newman, Pres.
Application address: 6450 Cecil Ave., St. Louis, MO 63105; FAX: (314) 331-6507

Incorporated in 1949 in IL.
Donor: Harry Edison†.
Foundation type: Independent foundation.
Financial data (yr. ended 12/31/05): Assets, $12,680,057 (M); expenditures, $804,612; qualifying distributions, $612,250; giving activities include $612,250 for 53 grants (high: $110,000; low: $100; average: $1,000–$5,000).
Purpose and activities: Support primarily for higher education, Jewish welfare funds, children's services, social services, cultural programs, hospitals, and medical research.
Fields of interest: Arts; Higher education; Medical school/education; Hospitals (general); Reproductive health, family planning; Medical research, institute; Human services; Youth, services; Jewish federated giving programs.
Type of support: Annual campaigns; Capital campaigns; Building/renovation; Professorships; Scholarship funds; Research.
Limitations: Giving primarily in St. Louis, MO. No grants to individuals.
Application information:
Copies of proposal: 1
Deadline(s): None
Board meeting date(s): As required
Officers and Directors:* Eric P. Newman,* Pres.; Bernard Edison,* V.P. and Secy.; Henry Kohn.
Number of staff: 2
EIN: 436027017

4808
Julian I. & Hope R. Edison Foundation, Inc. ✧
8 Saint Andrews Dr.
St. Louis, MO 63124-1622

Established in 1959.
Donor: Julian I. Edison.
Foundation type: Independent foundation.
Financial data (yr. ended 9/30/05): Assets, $8,341,497 (M); expenditures, $382,375; qualifying distributions, $372,326; giving activities include $369,580 for 71 grants (high: $130,000; low: $25).
Purpose and activities: Giving primarily for the arts, particularly to art museums, as well as for education, Jewish organizations, and health and human services.
Fields of interest: Museums (art); Performing arts; Arts; Elementary/secondary education; Higher education; Education; Hospitals (general); Health care; Health organizations, association; Human services; Foundations (community); Federated giving programs; Jewish federated giving programs; Jewish agencies & temples.

Limitations: Applications not accepted. Giving primarily in St. Louis, MO. No grants to individuals.
Application information: Contributes only to pre-selected organizations.
Officers: Julian I. Edison, Pres.; Hope R. Edison, V.P.; Evelyn E. Newman, Secy.
EIN: 436027034
Selected grants: The following grants were reported in 2005.
$150,000 to Saint Louis Art Museum, Saint Louis, MO. 2 grants: $20,000, $130,000
$60,000 to Jewish Federation of Saint Louis, Saint Louis, MO.
$50,000 to Brandeis University, Waltham, MA.
$30,000 to Saint Louis Symphony Orchestra, Saint Louis, MO.
$25,000 to Washington University, Saint Louis, MO.
$10,000 to Town School, New York, NY.
$10,000 to United Way of Greater Saint Louis, Saint Louis, MO.
$200 to American Antiquarian Society, Worcester, MA.
$100 to Community School, Saint Louis, MO.

4809
Emerson Charitable Trust ▼ ✧
8000 W. Florissant Ave.
P.O. Box 4100
St. Louis, MO 63136   (314) 553-2000
Contact: Robert M. Cox, Jr.

Established in 1944 in MO as Emerson Electric Manufacturing Company Charitable Trust; current name adopted in 1981.
Donors: Emerson Electric Co.; Daniel Industries, Inc.
Foundation type: Company-sponsored foundation.
Financial data (yr. ended 9/30/05): Assets, $29,618,173 (M); gifts received, $33,085,500; expenditures, $19,530,064; qualifying distributions, $19,416,514; giving activities include $19,249,259 for 2,491 grants (high: $1,240,000), and $165,750 for 218 grants to individuals (high: $1,500; low: $750).
Purpose and activities: The foundation supports organizations involved with arts and culture, education, health, recreation, and human services.
Fields of interest: Museums (science/technology); Performing arts, orchestra (symphony); Historical activities; Arts; Secondary school/education; Higher education; Education; Hospitals (general); Health care; Athletics/sports, golf; Recreation; Youth development, business; American Red Cross; Salvation Army; Youth, services; Residential/custodial care; Human services; Federated giving programs.
Type of support: General/operating support; Employee matching gifts; Employee-related scholarships.
Limitations: Giving primarily in areas of company operations.
Application information: Application form not required.
Initial approach: Proposal
Deadline(s): None
Board meeting date(s): 3 times per year
Trustees: Emerson Electric Co.; The Northern Trust Co.
EIN: 526200123
Selected grants: The following grants were reported in 2004.
$1,200,000 to United Way of Greater Saint Louis, Saint Louis, MO. For general support.

$1,074,250 to Washington University, Saint Louis, MO. 2 grants: $360,000 (For general support), $714,250 (For general support).
$600,000 to Saint Louis Symphony Orchestra, Saint Louis, MO. For general support.
$480,000 to Missouri Historical Society, Saint Louis, MO. For general support.
$300,000 to Harris-Stowe State College, Saint Louis, MO. For general support.
$300,000 to Interlochen Center for the Arts, Interlochen, MI. For general support.
$280,000 to Saint Louis Science Center, Saint Louis, MO. For general support.
$250,000 to Cornell University, Ithaca, NY. For general support.
$200,000 to Tulsa Boys Home, Tulsa, OK. For general support.

4810
Enterprise Rent-A-Car Foundation ▼ ✧
(formerly Enterprise Leasing Foundation)
600 Corporate Park Dr.
St. Louis, MO 63105   (314) 512-5000
Contact: Jo Ann Taylor Kindle, Pres.
FAX: (314) 512-4754; URL: http://aboutus.enterprise.com/what_we_believe/our_foundation.html

Established in 1982 in MO.
Donors: Enterprise Rent-A-Car Co.; Jack C. Taylor.
Foundation type: Company-sponsored foundation.
Financial data (yr. ended 7/31/05): Assets, $74,060,534 (M); gifts received, $14,822,804; expenditures, $9,339,977; qualifying distributions, $9,363,964; giving activities include $9,363,964 for 1,135+ grants (high: $935,209).
Purpose and activities: The foundation supports organizations involved with arts and culture, education, health, human services, public and society benefit, and disabled people.
Fields of interest: Arts; Education; Health care; Children/youth, services; Human services; Federated giving programs; Public affairs; Disabilities, people with.
International interests: Canada; United Kingdom.
Type of support: Research; Program development; Equipment; General/operating support; Annual campaigns; Capital campaigns; Building/renovation; Emergency funds; Scholarship funds; Employee matching gifts.
Limitations: Giving on a national and international basis in areas of company operations, including in Canada and the United Kingdom. No support for schools, churches, or sports teams. No vehicle or rental donations.
Application information: Support is limited to 1 contribution per organization during any given year. Unsolicited requests are accepted from Enterprise employees and customers on behalf of nonprofit organizations only. Application form not required.
Initial approach: Proposal to foundation for customers
Copies of proposal: 1
Deadline(s): 1 month prior to board meetings
Board meeting date(s): Jan., Apr., and Oct.
Final notification: 3 to 4 weeks following board meetings
Officers and Directors:* Jack C. Taylor,* Chair.; Jo Ann Taylor Kindle,* Pres.; Rick A. Short, V.P. and Treas.; Andrew C. Taylor, V.P.; William W. Snyder, Secy.; Marianne Knaup; Pamela M. Nicholson.
EIN: 431262762

Selected grants: The following grants were reported in 2005.

$935,209 to United Way, Inc., Los Angeles, CA.

$500,000 to Illinois State University Foundation, Normal, IL.

$477,704 to United Way of Greater Saint Louis, Saint Louis, MO.

$250,000 to American Red Cross, National Headquarters, DC.

$250,000 to Churchill Center and School for Learning Disabilities, Saint Louis, MO.

$178,813 to United Way of the Bay Area, San Francisco, CA.

$100,000 to Urban League, National, New York, NY.

$27,093 to United Way of the Midlands.

$10,000 to Ronald Reagan Presidential Foundation, Simi Valley, CA.

$10,000 to Urban League of Indianapolis, Indianapolis, IN.

4811
Express Scripts Foundation ✧
13900 Riverport Dr., Ste. 20S
Maryland Heights, MO   63043
URL: http://www.express-scripts.com/ourcompany/aboutus/foundation/

Established in 2002 in MO.
Donor: Express Scripts, Inc.
Foundation type: Company-sponsored foundation.
Financial data (yr. ended 12/31/03): Assets, $12,999,960 (M); gifts received, $943,400; expenditures, $1,022,414; qualifying distributions, $1,016,169; giving activities include $1,006,836 for 33 grants (high: $166,667; low: $1,000).
Purpose and activities: The foundation supports organizations involved with education, health, and youth development.
Fields of interest: Higher education; Education; Health organizations, association; Youth development.
Limitations: No support for political organizations or social clubs or athletic teams. No grants to individuals, or for endowments, capital campaigns, benefits, charitable dinners, galas, or athletic events.
Application information: Application form required.
Initial approach: Complete online application form
Deadline(s): None
Officers: Barrett A. Toan, Pres.; Thomas M. Boudreau, V.P.; Martin P. Akins, Secy.; Michael Salamone, Treas.
EIN: 020566229

4812
Fabick Charitable Trust, Inc. ✧ ☆
1 Fabick Dr.
Fenton, MO   63026-2928   (636) 343-5900
Contact: David Kramer

Incorporated in 1969 in MO.
Donor: John Fabick Tractor Co.
Foundation type: Company-sponsored foundation.
Financial data (yr. ended 12/31/05): Assets, $7,202 (M); gifts received, $341,000; expenditures, $335,100; qualifying distributions, $335,100; giving activities include $335,100 for grants.
Purpose and activities: The foundation supports organizations involved with education, human services, and Christianity.

Fields of interest: Education; Human services; Federated giving programs; Christian agencies & churches.
Limitations: Giving primarily in MO. No grants to individuals.
Application information: Application form not required.
Initial approach: Proposal
Copies of proposal: 1
Deadline(s): Oct. 15
Officers: Harry Fabick, Pres.; Scott Borlinghaus, Secy.
EIN: 237013262
Selected grants: The following grants were reported in 2004.

$100,000 to National Shrine of Mary, Mother of the Church, Laurie, MO. For general support.

$20,000 to Diocese of Belleville, Belleville, IL. For general support.

$20,000 to Saint Louis University, Saint Louis, MO. For general support.

$20,000 to Saint Patricks Center, Wilmington, DE. For general support.

$10,000 to Cardinal Glennon Childrens Hospital, Saint Louis, MO. For general support.

$10,000 to Cardinal Ritter College Prep, Saint Louis, MO. For general support.

$10,000 to Catholic Charities of Saint Louis, Saint Louis, MO. For general support.

$10,000 to Christian Brothers College High School, Saint Louis, MO. For general support.

$10,000 to Saint Louis Science Center, Saint Louis, MO. For general support.

$5,000 to MaryGrove Services, Florissant, MO. For general support.

4813
William Pablo Feraldo Memorial Fund ✧
c/o U.S. Bank, N.A.
P.O. Box 387
St. Louis, MO   63166
Contact: Angela Pearson

Foundation type: Independent foundation.
Financial data (yr. ended 12/31/05): Assets, $15,376,484 (M); expenditures, $728,108; qualifying distributions, $622,617; giving activities include $482,000 for 2 grants (high: $241,000; low: $241,000), and $119,800 for 45 grants to individuals.
Purpose and activities: Grants college scholarship aid for male applicants who have graduated or will graduate from an accredited secondary school.
Fields of interest: Higher education.
Type of support: Scholarships—to individuals.
Limitations: Giving primarily in MO.
Application information: Application forms are available at the high school counselors' offices in the metropolitan St. Louis, MO, area, and through the financial aid offices of St. Louis Univ. and Washington Univ. Application form required.
Deadline(s): Feb. 1
Final notification: Apr. 1
Trustee: U.S. Bank, N.A.
EIN: 436019398
Selected grants: The following grants were reported in 2003.

$227,518 to Saint Louis University, Saint Louis, MO. For scholarships.

$227,518 to Washington University, Saint Louis, MO. For scholarships.

4814
Forster-Powers Charitable Trust ✧
4635 Wyandotte, Ste. 206
Kansas City, MO   64112-1537   (816) 753-7777
Contact: Robert E. Turgeon, Tr.

Established in 1968 in MO.
Foundation type: Independent foundation.
Financial data (yr. ended 12/31/05): Assets, $9,043,141 (M); expenditures, $567,359; qualifying distributions, $417,069; giving activities include $417,069 for 33 grants (high: $100,000; low: $1,000; average: $5,000–$25,000).
Purpose and activities: Giving primarily to scholarship programs for higher and secondary education; support also for Roman Catholic churches and social services.
Fields of interest: Secondary school/education; Higher education; Human services; Federated giving programs; Roman Catholic agencies & churches.
Type of support: General/operating support; Building/renovation; Scholarship funds.
Limitations: Giving primarily in Kansas City, MO. No grants to individuals.
Application information: Application form not required.
Initial approach: Letter
Deadline(s): None
Trustees: Roger Fogelsong; John Gaughan; Gerard Meiners; Robert E. Turgeon.
EIN: 436110478
Selected grants: The following grants were reported in 2004.

$105,000 to Rockhurst High School, Kansas City, MO. 2 grants: $5,000, $100,000

$100,000 to Avila University, Kansas City, MO.

$25,000 to Benedictine College, Atchison, KS.

$25,000 to Vitae Caring Foundation, Jefferson City, MO.

$20,000 to Bishop Ward High School, Kansas City, KS. 2 grants: $10,000 each

$10,000 to Bishop Miege High School, Shawnee Mission, KS.

$10,000 to Donnelly College, Kansas City, KS.

$5,000 to Newman University, Wichita, KS.

4815
Fox Family Foundation
7701 Forsyth Blvd., Ste. 600
St. Louis, MO   63105   (314) 889-0890
Contact: Cheri Fox, Exec. Dir.
FAX: (314) 727-7314; *E-mail:* fff@harbourgroup.com

Established in 1986 in MO.
Donors: Marilyn Fox; Sam Fox.
Foundation type: Independent foundation.
Financial data (yr. ended 12/31/04): Assets, $27,543,013 (M); expenditures, $1,434,752; qualifying distributions, $1,183,760; giving activities include $1,045,084 for 211 grants (high: $300,000; low: $100).
Purpose and activities: The foundation is primarily interested in supporting projects which meet basic human needs, including food, shelter, basic adult education, job training, early childhood education for the poor, and independence for those dependent on others. In Israel, the foundation supports projects which address the issues of environmental protection, violence in Israeli society, and the full integration of the Ethiopian community.
Fields of interest: Education, early childhood education; Adult education—literacy, basic skills & GED; Employment, training; Housing/shelter;

Human services; Jewish agencies & temples; Economically disadvantaged; Homeless.

International interests: Israel.

Type of support: Program development; Seed money; Matching/challenge support.

Limitations: Giving primarily in St. Louis, MO; giving also in Israel. No grants to individuals, or for annual campaigns, endowment funds, deficit financing, or operating expenses.

Publications: Application guidelines.

Application information: Application form required.
  Initial approach: Letter requesting application form
  Copies of proposal: 2
  Deadline(s): Contact foundation for annual deadlines
  Board meeting date(s): Biannually
  Final notification: 3 months for preliminary applications; 6 months for formal applications if accepted for review

Officers and Directors:* Sam Fox,* Chair.; Marilyn Fox,* Vice-Chair.; Cheri Fox, Exec. Dir.; Gregory Fox; Jeffrey Fox; Steven Fox; Pamela Fox-Claman.

Number of staff: 2 full-time professional; 2 part-time support.

EIN: 431456258

Selected grants: The following grants were reported in 2003.

$300,000 to Jewish Federation of Saint Louis, Saint Louis, MO. For general support.

$100,000 to United Way of Greater Saint Louis, Saint Louis, MO. For annual campaign.

$35,000 to Webster University, Saint Louis, MO. For need-based scholarships.

$25,000 to Jewish Community Centers Association, Saint Louis, MO. For annual support.

$20,000 to Cardinal Ritter College Prep, Saint Louis, MO. For capital campaign.

$8,250 to University City Childrens Center, University City, MO. For scholarships.

$5,000 to Beyond Housing-Neighborhood Housing Services, Saint Louis, MO. For JETS Program.

$5,000 to Cornerstone Center for Early Learning, Saint Louis, MO. For Family Success Program: Enhancing Head Start.

$1,000 to Womens Support and Community Services, Saint Louis, MO. For 24-hour crisis line.

$350 to Jewish Family and Childrens Service of Saint Louis, Creve Coeur, MO. For food pantry.

4816
The Francis Family Foundation ◇
(formerly The Francis Families Foundation)
800 W. 47th St., Ste. 717
Kansas City, MO 64112 (816) 531-0077
Contact: Jerry Kitzi, Exec. Dir.; Lyn Knox, Prog. Off.
E-mail: info@francisfoundation.org; URL: http://www.francisfoundation.org/
Application address for fellowship program only: Dr. Joseph D. Brain, Dir., Parker B. Francis Fellowship Prog., Harvard School of Public Health, Rm. 1411, Bldg. 1, Harvard University, 665 Huntington Ave., Boston, MA 02115, tel.: (617) 432-1272

Established in 1989 in MO from the merger of the Parker B. Francis Foundation (established in 1951 in MO) and the Parker B. Francis III Foundation (established in 1962 in MO).

Donors: Parker B. Francis†; Mary B. Francis†; Parker B. Francis III†.

Foundation type: Independent foundation.

Financial data (yr. ended 12/31/04): Assets, $128,592,934 (M); expenditures, $6,874,079;

qualifying distributions, $5,655,442; giving activities include $5,076,625 for 165 grants (high: $989,490; low: $250; average: $1,000–$40,000), and $1,428 for in-kind gifts.

Purpose and activities: Giving primarily to fund post-doctoral fellowships in pulmonary research nationally, and in the metropolitan Kansas City area, to support child and youth development from early care through higher education and to support arts and cultural institutions.

Fields of interest: Arts; Education; Medical research, institute.

Type of support: General/operating support; Continuing support; Program development; Fellowships.

Limitations: Giving limited to a 60-mile radius of Kansas City, MO, for educational and arts and cultural institutions, and to the U.S. and Canada for pulmonary fellowships.

Publications: Informational brochure (including application guidelines).

Application information: Please visit foundation's Web site for the most current application requirements. Application form required for pulmonary fellowship program. Application form required.
  Initial approach: Letter
  Copies of proposal: 6
  Deadline(s): Aug. 1 for Kansas City education and arts and culture; Oct. for pulmonary research fellowships
  Board meeting date(s): Jan. and May
  Final notification: Feb.

Officers and Directors:* Ann Francis Barhoum,* Chair.; David V. Francis,* Vice-Chair.; Jerry Kitzi, Exec. Dir.; Peggy J. Dunn; J. Scott Francis; B. Spencer Heddens; Ramon Murguia.

Number of staff: 2 full-time professional; 2 part-time professional.

EIN: 431492132

4817
Gateway Foundation
720 Olive St., Ste. 1977
St. Louis, MO 63101 (314) 241-3337
Contact: Christy B. Fox, Admin.
FAX: (314) 241-3559;
E-mail: tsmith-gwfnd@sbcglobal.net; URL: http://www.gateway-foundation.org

Established in 1986 in MO under the EIN of 431420333; reincorporated in 2004 under the current EIN.

Foundation type: Independent foundation.

Financial data (yr. ended 12/31/04): Assets, $66,935,807 (M); gifts received, $300; expenditures, $1,996,466; qualifying distributions, $2,449,617; giving activities include $658,856 for 19 grants (high: $111,152; low: $27), and $375,466 for 2 foundation-administered programs.

Purpose and activities: Support for the arts and cultural projects and, on occasion, related educational activities. Priority given to acquisition, creation, or improvement of items of a physical, durable nature. Focus on enhancing the physical environment in the St. Louis, MO, metropolitan region.

Fields of interest: Visual arts; Visual arts, architecture; Museums; Performing arts; Arts; Recreation, parks/playgrounds; Recreation; Urban/community development.

Type of support: Building/renovation; Equipment; Land acquisition; Technical assistance; Matching/challenge support.

Limitations: Giving limited to the metropolitan St. Louis, MO, area. Generally no support for programmatic operating expenses or for endowments.

Publications: Application guidelines; Grants list; Informational brochure.

Application information: The foundation does not consider grant presentations. Written application is required. See foundation Web site for application guidelines, programs and procedures. Application form not required.
  Initial approach: Telephone
  Copies of proposal: 1
  Deadline(s): Feb. 1, May 1, Aug. 1 and Nov. 1
  Board meeting date(s): Quarterly
  Final notification: Mar., Jun., Sept., Dec.

Officers and Directors:* M. Peter Fischer,* Pres.; James D. Burke,* V.P.; Susan R. Rava,* Secy.-Treas.; Christy B. Fox, Admin.; Martha Fischer; Matthew G. Fischer; Michael P. Fischer; Paul Ha; David Mesker; Gyo Obata; Susan Philpott.

Number of staff: 1 full-time professional; 1 full-time support; 1 part-time support.

EIN: 206294706

Selected grants: The following grants were reported in 2003.

$271,519 to Urban Strategies, Saint Louis, MO. 2 grants: $17,404 (To develop fountain design for Adams Park), $254,115 (For construction of a water feature).

$124,826 to National Park Service. For electrical service and maintenance in connection with the lighting of the Arch.

$95,542 to Saint Louis Ambassadors Arts and Fountains Foundation, Saint Louis, MO. For exterior cleaning and outside work on Soldiers' Memorial.

$63,389 to Saint Louis Childrens Hospital, Saint Louis, MO. For playground.

$52,593 to Trailnet, Saint Louis, MO. For restoration of bridge for pedestrian use.

$24,224 to Frank Lloyd Wright Building Conservancy, Chicago, IL. To develop master plan to change Krause House into a cultural facility and to restore the motor court and fountains, brick exterior retaining walls, interior woodwork and concrete floors and complete one interior bath in the House.

$10,000 to Union Avenue Opera Theater, Saint Louis, MO. To purchase new lighting system.

$7,061 to Harris-Stowe State College, Saint Louis, MO. To illuminate the exterior of College's original building.

$5,000 to Saint Louis Ballet, Chesterfield, MO. For new dance floor.

4818
Gershman Foundation ◇
7 N. Bemiston Ave.
St. Louis, MO 63105-3303

Established in 1986 in MO.

Donors: Bettie Gershman; Gershman Investment Corp.

Foundation type: Independent foundation.

Financial data (yr. ended 11/30/05): Assets, $7,350,591 (M); gifts received, $6,000,000; expenditures, $330,755; qualifying distributions, $317,700; giving activities include $317,700 for 33 grants (high: $137,500; low: $1,000).

Purpose and activities: Giving primarily for Jewish federated giving programs, the arts, and medical research.

Fields of interest: Performing arts, orchestra (symphony); Hospitals (general); Medical research, institute; Human services; Jewish federated giving programs; Jewish agencies & temples.

Limitations: Applications not accepted. Giving primarily in St. Louis, MO. No grants to individuals.

Application information: Contributes only to pre-selected organizations.

Trustees: Bettie Gershman; Jeffrey S. Gershman; Diane L. Levine; Karen G. Stern.

EIN: 431431049

Selected grants: The following grants were reported in 2004.

$147,500 to Jewish Federation of Saint Louis, Saint Louis, MO.

$23,500 to Saint Louis Symphony Orchestra, Saint Louis, MO.

$15,000 to Alexis de Tocqueville Society, Kansas City, MO.

$13,400 to Doorways, Saint Louis, MO.

$5,000 to Craft Alliance, Saint Louis, MO.

$3,000 to Dance Saint Louis, Saint Louis, MO.

$1,250 to Opera Theater of Saint Louis, Saint Louis, MO.

$1,000 to Grand Center, Saint Louis, MO.

4819
The Goppert Foundation ◇

10401 Holmes Rd., Ste. 350
Kansas City, MO 64131 (816) 942-7595
Contact: Thomas A. Goppert, Secy.-Treas.

Incorporated in 1958 in MO.
Donor: Clarence H. Goppert†.
Foundation type: Independent foundation.
Financial data (yr. ended 10/31/05): Assets, $35,743,233 (M); gifts received, $4,212,348; expenditures, $1,437,952; qualifying distributions, $1,341,812; giving activities include $1,277,823 for 13 grants (high: $400,018; low: $500).
Fields of interest: Higher education; Education; Hospitals (general); Human services; Youth, services; Minorities; Economically disadvantaged.
Type of support: General/operating support; Capital campaigns; Building/renovation; Equipment; Endowments; Emergency funds; Program development; Scholarship funds; Matching/challenge support.
Limitations: Giving primarily in eastern KS and western MO. No grants to individuals.
Application information: Application form not required.
Initial approach: Letter
Copies of proposal: 1
Deadline(s): None
Board meeting date(s): Quarterly
Officers and Directors:* Richard D. Goppert,* Chair. and Pres.; M. Charles Kellogg, V.P.; Thomas A. Goppert,* Secy.-Treas.; Billy Campbell; David M. Christy; Carolyn Kellogg; Leon G. Kusnetzky.
EIN: 446013933

4820
Arvin Gottlieb Charitable Foundation ◇

c/o UMB Bank, N.A.
P.O. Box 419692
Kansas City, MO 64141-6692 (816) 860-7711
Contact: Jan B. Leonard, Trust Counsel, UMB Bank, N.A.

Established in 1990 in MO.
Foundation type: Independent foundation.
Financial data (yr. ended 12/31/05): Assets, $33,966,440 (M); expenditures, $1,370,351; qualifying distributions, $1,095,405; giving activities include $1,047,000 for 43 grants (high: $120,000; low: $1,000).
Purpose and activities: Giving primarily to arts and cultural programs, education, human services, housing development, and Jewish agencies.
Fields of interest: Museums; Arts; Higher education; Education; Housing/shelter, development; Human services; Jewish federated giving programs; Jewish agencies & temples.
Limitations: Giving primarily in Kansas City, MO.
Application information:
Initial approach: Typewritten letter
Deadline(s): None
Trustees: Peter Brown; Barton J. Cohen; UMB Bank, N.A.
EIN: 436380792
Selected grants: The following grants were reported in 2004.

$280,000 to Truman Medical Centers Charitable Foundation, Kansas City, MO. For general support.

$120,000 to Stanford University, For general support, Stanford, CA. For general support.

$100,000 to Kemper Museum of Contemporary Art and Design, Kansas City, MO. For general support.

$70,000 to Kansas City Art Institute, Kansas City, MO. For general support.

$70,000 to Kansas City Symphony, Kansas City, MO. For general support.

$55,000 to DeLaSalle Education Center, Kansas City, MO. For general support.

$50,000 to Johnson County Community College Foundation, Overland Park, KS.

$50,000 to Rose Brooks Center, Kansas City, MO. For general support.

$25,000 to Temple Bnai Jehudah, Overland Park, KS.

$22,000 to Kansas City Friends of Alvin Ailey, Kansas City, MO. For general support.

4821
Preston M. Green Charitable Foundation ◇

c/o Commerce Bank
P.O. Box 11356
Clayton, MO 63105
Contact: Dorothy Evers

Established in 2003 in MO.
Foundation type: Independent foundation.
Financial data (yr. ended 7/31/05): Assets, $15,741,090 (M); expenditures, $1,104,370; qualifying distributions, $1,041,221; giving activities include $1,000,000 for 1 grant.
Fields of interest: Higher education.
Type of support: Building/renovation.
Limitations: Giving primarily in the St. Louis, MO, area. No grants to individuals.
Application information:

Initial approach: Letter
Deadline(s): None
Trustee: Commerce Trust Co.
Directors: Nancy Green; Stephan A. Green, Jr.
EIN: 436911130

4822
Allen P. & Josephine B. Green Foundation

222 S. Jefferson, Rm. 108
P.O. Box 523
Mexico, MO 65265 (573) 581-5568
Contact: Walter G. Staley, Jr., Secy.-Treas.
FAX: (573) 581-1714;
E-mail: wstaley@greenfdn.org; Additional e-mail: nrcox@greenfdn.org; URL: http://www.greenfdn.org

Trust established in 1941 in MO.
Donors: Allen P. Green†; Josephine B. Green†.
Foundation type: Independent foundation.
Financial data (yr. ended 12/31/05): Assets, $12,485,225 (M); expenditures, $699,615; qualifying distributions, $585,283; giving activities include $539,581 for 47 grants (high: $50,000; low: $1,000; average: $5,000–$15,000), and $20,000 for 4 grants to individuals.
Purpose and activities: Giving for human services, with emphasis on child development and the family, women, and the elderly; health services, including rehabilitation programs for drug and alcohol abuse, cancer care, and nursing; arts and humanities, especially fine and performing arts groups and historic preservation; education, including early childhood, elementary and secondary, adult and vocational, theological and medical, and other higher educational institutions, and libraries; community development and civic affairs; and environmental conservation and animal welfare.
Fields of interest: Performing arts; History/archaeology; Historic preservation/historical societies; Arts; Education, early childhood education; Child development, education; Elementary school/education; Secondary school/education; Vocational education; Higher education; Theological school/education; Adult/continuing education; Adult education—literacy, basic skills & GED; Libraries/library science; Education, reading; Environment, natural resources; Environment; Animal welfare; Medical care, rehabilitation; Nursing care; Health care; Mental health/crisis services; Health organizations, association; Eye diseases; Crime/violence prevention, youth; Nutrition; Human services; Children/youth, services; Child development, services; Residential/custodial care, hospices; Aging, centers/services; Women, centers/services; Aging; Disabilities, people with; Women; Economically disadvantaged.
Type of support: Building/renovation; Equipment; Land acquisition; Endowments; Emergency funds; Program development; Conferences/seminars; Seed money; Curriculum development; Scholarship funds; Matching/challenge support.
Limitations: Giving primarily in MO, with special emphasis on the Mexico area; no giving outside the continental U.S. No grants for operating budgets; no loans.
Publications: Application guidelines; Annual report (including application guidelines); Grants list.
Application information: No grants to organizations in consecutive years. Application forms not required for organizations, but are required for scholarships. See foundation Web site for application information. Application form not required.
Initial approach: Letter, no more than 2 pages

Copies of proposal: 1

Deadline(s): Between Dec. 15 and Mar. 15 for consideration in May; June 15 and Sept. 15 for consideration in Nov. Scholarship application forms are available Sept. 15 at Mexico High School, and are due Jan. 15.

Board meeting date(s): May and Nov.

Final notification: 1 month for organizations; Mar. 15 for scholarships

Officers and Directors:* Nancy A. Ekern,* Pres.; Laura W. Erdel,* V.P.; Walter G. Staley, Jr.,* Secy.-Treas.; A.D. Bond III; Christopher S. Bond; Carl D. Fuemmeler; Robert E. McIntosh; Franklin E.W. Staley; Nancy White; John F. Wood; Robert A. Wood.

Number of staff: 1 part-time support.

EIN: 436030135

Selected grants: The following grants were reported in 2004.

$24,472 to Central Missouri Food Bank Network, Columbia, MO. For forklift and pallet jacks.

$20,000 to First Presbyterian Church, Mexico, MO. For scholarship.

$20,000 to Kings Daughters Home, Mexico, MO. For replacement windows and doors.

$15,000 to Rush Hill Community Christian Church, Rush Hill, MO. To construct and furnish areas of new multipurpose room.

$13,000 to William Woods University, Fulton, MO. To purchase and install interactive whiteboards.

$10,000 to Culver-Stockton College, Canton, MO. For computer laboratory in science center.

$10,000 to University of Missouri, Saint Louis, MO. For new preschooler playground.

$8,000 to Aim High Saint Louis, Saint Louis, MO. To sponsor students at summer program at Fontbonne.

$8,000 to Saint Vincent Home for Children, Saint Louis, MO. For upgrading science curriculum.

$7,000 to La Clinica-Latino Community Health Centers, Saint Louis, MO. For Pedatric Health and Nutrition Project.

$5,000 to Immacolata Manor, Liberty, MO. For wheelchair-accessible gliding swing.

$1,000 to Audrain County Area Literacy Council, Mexico, MO. For new materials and tutor training for literacy.

4823
The H & R Block Foundation ◇

1 H&R Block Way
Kansas City, MO 64105   (816) 932-8324
Contact: David P. Miles, Pres.
FAX: (816) 753-1585;
E-mail: foundation@hrblock.com; Additional tel.: (800) 869-9220, ext. 8324; URL: http://www.blockfoundation.org

Incorporated in 1974 in MO.

Donors: H&R Block, Inc.; HRB Management, Inc.; Frank and Sarah Salizzoni Foundation.

Foundation type: Company-sponsored foundation.

Financial data (yr. ended 12/31/04): Assets, $53,301,521 (M); gifts received, $2,049,500; expenditures, $3,041,143; qualifying distributions, $3,371,202; giving activities include $2,196,663 for 132 grants (high: $200,000; low: $100), and $201,435 for 316 employee matching gifts.

Purpose and activities: The foundation supports organizations involved with arts and culture, education, health, mental health, HIV/AIDS, housing, human services, community development, and homeless people.

Fields of interest: Visual arts; Museums; Performing arts; Performing arts, dance; Arts; Education, early childhood education; Child development, education; Secondary school/education; Vocational education; Higher education; Education; Health care; Mental health/crisis services; AIDS; Housing/shelter; Children/youth, services; Child development, services; Human services; Urban/community development; Community development; Homeless.

Type of support: General/operating support; Continuing support; Annual campaigns; Capital campaigns; Building/renovation; Equipment; Land acquisition; Emergency funds; Program development; Seed money; Curriculum development; Scholarship funds; Technical assistance; Consulting services; Employee volunteer services; Program evaluation; Employee matching gifts; Employee-related scholarships; Matching/challenge support.

Limitations: Giving primarily in Johnson and Wyandotte, KS, and Clay, Jackson, Kansas City, and Platte, MO. No support for religious organizations or disease-specific organizations. No grants to individuals (except for employee-related scholarships), or for endowments, travel, telethons, dinners, advertising, fundraising, research, demonstration projects, publications, conferences, or historic preservation projects; no loans.

Publications: Application guidelines; Financial statement; Grants list.

Application information: Application form required.

Initial approach: Download application form

Copies of proposal: 1

Deadline(s): Jan. 28, Apr. 29, July 29, and Oct. 14

Board meeting date(s): Quarterly

Final notification: 10 weeks following deadlines

Officers and Directors:* Henry W. Bloch,* Chair. and Treas.; Frank L. Salizzoni,* Vice-Chair.; David P. Miles, Pres.; Charles E. Curran; Mark A. Ernst; Edward T. Matheny, Jr.; Morton I. Sosland.

Number of staff: 3 full-time professional; 1 part-time professional; 1 full-time support; 1 part-time support.

EIN: 237378232

4824
Hall Family Foundation ▼

P.O. Box 419580, Dept. 323
Kansas City, MO 64141-6580
Contact: Tracy McFerrin Foster, V.P.; Jeanne Bates, V.P.; Sally Groves, Prog. Off.
FAX: (816) 274-8547; URL: http://www.hallfamilyfoundation.org

Hallmark Educational Foundation incorporated in 1943 in MO; Hallmark Educational Foundation of KS incorporated in 1954 in KS; combined funds formerly known as Hallmark Educational Foundations; current name adopted due to absorption of Hall Family Foundation of Kansas in 1993.

Donors: Hallmark Cards, Inc.; Joyce C. Hall‡; E.A. Hall‡; R.B. Hall‡.

Foundation type: Independent foundation.

Financial data (yr. ended 12/31/05): Assets, $814,088,561 (M); expenditures, $33,874,922; qualifying distributions, $29,628,310; giving activities include $29,628,310 for grants.

Purpose and activities: Giving within four main areas of interest: 1) the performing and visual arts; 2) education - all levels; 3) children, youth and families; and 4) community development.

Fields of interest: Performing arts; Arts; Education, early childhood education; Child development, education; Elementary school/education; Secondary school/education; Higher education; Education; Housing/shelter, development; Human services; Youth, services; Child development, services; Family services; Minorities/immigrants, centers/services; Homeless, human services; Urban/community development; Community development; Minorities; Homeless.

Type of support: General/operating support; Capital campaigns; Building/renovation; Equipment; Land acquisition; Emergency funds; Program development; Technical assistance; Program evaluation; Program-related investments/loans; Employee-related scholarships.

Limitations: Giving limited to greater Kansas City, MO. No support for international or religious organizations or for political purposes. No grants to individuals (except for employee-related scholarships), or for travel, operating deficits, conferences, scholarly or medical research, or fundraising campaigns or event promotion such as telethons, or for endowments.

Publications: Annual report; Grants list; Informational brochure (including application guidelines).

Application information: Scholarships are for the children and close relatives of Hallmark Cards employees only. Only eligible applicants should apply. Application form not required.

Initial approach: Letter

Copies of proposal: 1

Deadline(s): 6 weeks before board meetings

Board meeting date(s): Mar., June, Sept., and Dec.

Final notification: 6 to 8 weeks

Officers and Directors:* Donald J. Hall,* Chair.; William A. Hall, Pres.; John A. MacDonald, V.P. and Treas.; Jeanne Bates, V.P.; Tracy McFerrin Foster, V.P.; Terri Maybee, Secy.; Richard C. Green; Robert E. Hemenway; Irvine O. Hockaday, Jr.; Robert A. Kipp; Sandra A.J. Lawrence; Margaret Hall Pence; Morton I. Sosland.

Number of staff: 2 full-time professional; 1 part-time professional; 1 full-time support.

EIN: 446006291

Selected grants: The following grants were reported in 2005.

$8,460,815 to Nelson Gallery Foundation, Kansas City, MO. 2 grants: $2,460,815 (For donation of photography collection), $6,000,000 (For endowment).

$4,000,000 to Greater Kansas City Community Foundation, Kansas City, MO. For Center for Physical Activity, Nutrition, and Weight Management, payable over 3 years.

$2,572,316 to Kansas University Endowment Association, Lawrence, KS. For MD/PhD Program and Internal Research Programs, payable over 6 years.

$2,300,000 to Truman Medical Centers Charitable Foundation, Kansas City, MO. To upgrade women's health program and expand emergency department, payable over 3 years.

$2,000,000 to Kansas City Art Institute, Kansas City, MO. For Phase II of Capital Campaign, payable over 3 years.

$1,000,000 to City Union Mission, Kansas City, MO. For capital campaign, Building the Walls that Rebuild Lives.

$75,577 to Northwest Missouri State University, Maryville, MO. For residential internship program, payable over 4 years.

$50,000 to Niles Home for Children, Kansas City, MO. For operating support.

$40,000 to Harry S. Truman Library Institute for National and International Affairs, Independence, MO. For Churchill and the Great Republic exhibition.

4825
Hallmark Corporate Foundation
P.O. Box 419580, M.D. 323
Kansas City, MO 64141-6580
Contact: Karen Bartz, V.P.
URL: http://www.hallmark.com/webapp/wcs/ stores/servlet/article|10001|10051|/ HallmarkSite/AboutHallmark/ SupportingOurCommunity/

Established in 1983 in MO.
Donor: Hallmark Cards, Inc.
Foundation type: Company-sponsored foundation.
Financial data (yr. ended 12/31/05): Assets, $1,335,985 (M); gifts received, $2,694,059; expenditures, $2,792,668; qualifying distributions, $2,792,188; giving activities include $2,677,756 for grants.
Purpose and activities: The foundation supports organizations involved with arts and culture, education, and human services.
Fields of interest: Arts; Child development, education; Education; Children/youth, services; Human services.
Type of support: Employee volunteer services; General/operating support; Continuing support; Capital campaigns; Building/renovation; Equipment; Program development; Technical assistance; Program evaluation; Employee matching gifts.
Limitations: Giving limited to Enfield, CT, Columbus, GA, Metamora, IL, Lawrence, Leavenworth, and Topeka, KS, Liberty and the Kansas City, MO, area, and Center, TX. No support for religious, fraternal, political, international, or veterans' organizations, athletic or labor groups, social clubs, or disease-specific organizations. No grants to individuals, or for scholarships, endowments, debt reduction, travel, conferences, sponsorships, scholarly or health-related research, advertising, mass media campaigns, or fundraising.
Publications: Application guidelines; Grants list; Informational brochure (including application guidelines).
Application information: Additional information may be requested at a later date. A personal or telephone interview or site visit may be requested. Application form not required.
Initial approach: Letter of inquiry to foundation or nearest company facility
Copies of proposal: 1
Deadline(s): None
Board meeting date(s): Periodic
Final notification: 4 to 6 weeks
Officers and Directors:* Donald J. Hall, Sr.,* Chair.; William A. Hall, Pres.; Karen Bartz, V.P.; Terri R. Maybee, Secy.; John A. MacDonald, Treas.; David E. Hall; Donald J. Hall, Jr.
Number of staff: 3 full-time professional; 1 full-time support.
EIN: 431303258
Selected grants: The following grants were reported in 2005.
$1,226,400 to United Way, Heart of America, Kansas City, MO. For annual campaign.

$229,500 to Kansas City Symphony, Kansas City, MO. For general support.
$198,000 to Kansas City Repertory Theater, Kansas City, MO. For general support.
$123,500 to Kansas City Ballet Association, Kansas City, MO. For general support.
$69,000 to Lyric Opera of Kansas City, Kansas City, MO. For general support.
$17,000 to Friends of Chamber Music, Kansas City, MO. For general support.
$15,000 to University of Kansas, School of Fine Arts, Lawrence, KS. For annual symposium.

4826
John Q. Hammons Foundation, Inc. ◇
300 John Q. Hammons Pkwy., Ste. 900
Springfield, MO 65806
Contact: Jacqueline Dowdy, Secy.-Treas.

Established in 1990 in MO.
Foundation type: Independent foundation.
Financial data (yr. ended 12/31/05): Assets, $86,903 (M); expenditures, $2,301,132; qualifying distributions, $629,764; giving activities include $629,764 for 38 grants (high: $49,900; low: $2,228), and $1,671,368 for 1 foundation-administered program.
Purpose and activities: Giving for boys and girls clubs, athletics and recreation, children's services, and for health and medical services.
Fields of interest: Education; Health care, research; Health care; Boys & girls clubs; Federated giving programs.
Limitations: Giving primarily in southwest MO. No grants to individuals.
Application information:
Initial approach: Typed letter, not exceeding 4 pages
Deadline(s): None
Final notification: Usually within 2 months
Officers: John Q. Hammons, Pres.; Juanita K. Hammons, V.P.; Jacqueline Dowdy, Secy.-Treas.
EIN: 431521852
Selected grants: The following grants were reported in 2005.
$49,900 to Ronald McDonald House Charities of the Ozarks, Springfield, MO.
$48,242 to Good Samaritan Boys Ranch, Springfield, MO.
$24,643 to Childrens Miracle Network, Columbia, MO.
$22,380 to Special Olympics, Springfield, MO.
$19,618 to Fellowship of Christian Athletes, Springfield, MO.
$8,254 to AIDS Project of the Ozarks, Springfield, MO.
$8,172 to Barnabas Foundation, Purdy, MO.
$7,629 to American Diabetes Association, Saint Louis, MO.
$6,673 to YMCA, Springfield Family, Springfield, MO.
$3,675 to Family Violence Center, Springfield, MO.

4827
Hana Foundation ◇
c/o Robert B. Shapiro, PriceWaterhouseCoopers, LLP
800 Market St.
St. Louis, MO 63101

Established in 2000 in IL.

Donor: Robert B. Shapiro.
Foundation type: Independent foundation.
Financial data (yr. ended 12/31/04): Assets, $8,408,496 (M); gifts received, $150,000; expenditures, $956,192; qualifying distributions, $950,250; giving activities include $946,500 for 21 grants (high: $245,000; low: $1,000).
Purpose and activities: Support primarily for human services, with a focus on children and the disabled.
Fields of interest: Education, special; Down syndrome; Youth development; Human services; Children/youth, services; Human services, mind/ body enrichment; Jewish agencies & temples; Buddhism; Spirituality; Disabilities, people with.
Type of support: General/operating support.
Limitations: Applications not accepted. Giving on a national basis, with some emphasis on MO and IL.
Application information: Contributes only to pre-selected organizations.
Trustees: Kemery Bloom; Robert B. Shapiro.
EIN: 367323747

4828
Hauck Charitable Foundation ◇
999 Executive Pkwy., Ste. 202
St. Louis, MO 63141 (314) 628-6030

Established in 1987 in MO.
Donors: John M. Hauck; Steven J. Hauck; Ellen Hauck Smith; John C. Hauck; TSI Holding Co.
Foundation type: Independent foundation.
Financial data (yr. ended 12/31/05): Assets, $20,131,487 (M); gifts received, $26,602; expenditures, $1,509,598; qualifying distributions, $1,489,284; giving activities include $1,479,913 for 21 grants (high: $330,000; low: $500; average: $5,000–$200,000).
Purpose and activities: Giving primarily for education and human services.
Fields of interest: Arts; Education; Human services; Federated giving programs; Roman Catholic agencies & churches.
Limitations: Applications not accepted. Giving primarily in St. Louis, MO. No grants to individuals.
Application information: Contributes only to pre-selected organizations.
Officers and Directors:* John C. Hauck,* Pres.; Deborah Lohmuller,* V.P.; James A. Margon, Secy.-Treas.; Kathleen H. Alexander; Carolyn Gold; David P. Hauck; Steven J. Hauck; Ellen Hauck Smith.
EIN: 431467676
Selected grants: The following grants were reported in 2004.
$200,000 to United Way of Greater Saint Louis, Saint Louis, MO.
$31,966 to Cornerstone Center for Early Learning, Saint Louis, MO.
$20,000 to Catholic Charities of Saint Louis, Saint Louis, MO.
$10,000 to Grace Hill Neighborhood Services, Saint Louis, MO.
$5,000 to Barnes-Jewish Hospital Foundation, Saint Louis, MO.
$1,000 to Girl Scouts of the U.S.A., Glen Carbon, IL.
$1,000 to Saint Louis Science Center, Saint Louis, MO.
$720 to Junior Achievement of Mississippi Valley, Chesterfield, MO.
$500 to Boy Scouts of America, Saint Louis, MO.
$200 to Delta Gamma Center for Children with Visual Impairments, Saint Louis, MO.

4829
Shirley and Barnett Helzberg Foundation ◇
(formerly Helzberg Foundation)
American Century Twr. II
4520 Main St., Ste 1050
Kansas City, MO 64111

Established in 1982 in MO.

Donors: Barnett C. Helzberg, Jr.; National Indemnity Co.

Foundation type: Independent foundation.

Financial data (yr. ended 12/31/05): Assets, $19,766,411 (M); expenditures, $1,124,322; qualifying distributions, $839,453; giving activities include $696,602 for 33+ grants.

Purpose and activities: Giving primarily for education, Jewish and other federated giving programs, social services, and to a symphony orchestra.

Fields of interest: Performing arts, orchestra (symphony); Higher education; Education; Medical research, institute; Human services; Federated giving programs; Jewish federated giving programs.

Type of support: General/operating support; Annual campaigns; Capital campaigns; Building/renovation; Endowments.

Limitations: Applications not accepted. Giving primarily in Kansas City, MO. No grants to individuals.

Application information: Contributes only to pre-selected organizations.

Officers: Barnett C. Helzberg, Jr., Pres.; Shirley B. Helzberg, V.P. and Treas.; Peter Brown, Secy.

Directors: Barnett C. Helzberg III; Bush C. Helzberg.

EIN: 431265367

4830
Herschend Family Foundation ◇ ☆
c/o Jack R. Herschend
Silver Dollar City Inc.
100 Corporate Pl., Corp. Offices
Branson, MO 65616

Established in 1985 in MO.

Donor: Jack R. Herschend.

Foundation type: Independent foundation.

Financial data (yr. ended 12/31/05): Assets, $4,933,029 (M); gifts received, $1,496,878; expenditures, $389,740; qualifying distributions, $382,194; giving activities include $382,194 for grants.

Purpose and activities: Giving limited to Christian organizations, including churches and ministries to support family and social services, such as child welfare and development.

Fields of interest: Child development, education; Human services; Children/youth, services; Child development, services; Family services; Christian agencies & churches; Protestant agencies & churches; Economically disadvantaged.

Limitations: Applications not accepted. Giving limited to the Tri-Lakes area in southern MO, including Stone and Taney counties.

Application information: Unsolicited requests for funds will not be considered or acknowledged.

Board meeting date(s): 3rd Tues. of Jan. and Sept.

Officers and Directors:* Jack R. Herschend,* Pres.; Sherry J. Herschend,* Secy.; Dianna Herschend,* Treas.; Bruce Herschend; James R. Herschend; Ronald J. Herschend.

EIN: 431391940

Selected grants: The following grants were reported in 2005.

$17,720 to Salvation Army, Branson, MO.

$12,000 to Barnabas Foundation, Purdy, MO.

$10,000 to Focus on the Family, Colorado Springs, CO.

$10,000 to Presbyterian Childrens Services, Saint Louis, MO.

$10,000 to World Vision, Federal Way, WA.

$8,900 to College of the Ozarks, Point Lookout, MO.

$3,000 to Campus Crusade for Christ, Miami, FL.

$1,000 to Boys and Girls Club of the Ozarks, Branson, MO.

$100 to Muscular Dystrophy Association, Tucson, AZ.

4831
Hites Family Community College Scholarship Corporation ◇ ☆
1610 Des Peres Rd., Ste. 300
St. Louis, MO 63131-1891
Application address: c/o Ann Stillman, The Stolar Partnership LLP, 911 Washington Ave., St. Louis, MO 63101

Established in 1990 in MO.

Foundation type: Independent foundation.

Financial data (yr. ended 2/28/06): Assets, $2,686,080 (M); expenditures, $560,334; qualifying distributions, $550,000; giving activities include $550,000 for grants.

Purpose and activities: Grant awards for academic scholarships awarded to community college students with high academic achievement to enable them to complete their undergraduate degrees. Payment made in students' junior and/or senior years of study.

Fields of interest: Higher education, college.

Type of support: Scholarship funds.

Limitations: Applications not accepted.

Application information: Unsolicited requests for funds not considered.

Officers and Directors:* Raymond D. Hites,* Pres.; Raymond L. Kerlagon,* V.P.; Donald R. Davis,* Secy.; Thomas F. Hilgeman,* Treas.; Paul C. Gianini, Jr.

EIN: 431543776

Selected grants: The following grants were reported in 2006.

$100,000 to Saint Louis Community College, Saint Louis, MO.

4832
The Holekamp Foundation ◇
c/o William F. Holekamp
5 Barclay Woods
Ladue, MO 63124

Established in 1998 in MO.

Donors: Kerry L. Holekamp; William F. Holekamp.

Foundation type: Independent foundation.

Financial data (yr. ended 12/31/04): Assets, $7,574,054 (M); expenditures, $485,221; qualifying distributions, $419,189; giving activities include $417,975 for 53 grants (high: $50,000; low: $75).

Purpose and activities: Giving primarily for education, human services, and federated giving programs; funding also for a science center.

Fields of interest: Museums; Elementary/secondary education; Education; Botanical gardens;

Human services; Federated giving programs; Science, public education.

Limitations: Applications not accepted. Giving primarily in St. Louis, MO. No grants to individuals.

Application information: Contributes only to pre-selected organizations.

Managers: Kerry L. Holekamp; William F. Holekamp.

EIN: 436800541

4833
J. P. Humphreys Foundation ◇
P.O. Box 1404
Joplin, MO 64802-1404

Established in 1981 in MO.

Donors: Ethelmae Craig Humphreys; J.P. Humphreys†.

Foundation type: Independent foundation.

Financial data (yr. ended 7/31/05): Assets, $9,246,753 (M); expenditures, $483,838; qualifying distributions, $479,074; giving activities include $479,074 for 22 grants (high: $100,000; low: $200).

Purpose and activities: Giving for higher education and economic and social science research.

Fields of interest: Higher education; Education; Boy scouts; Civil rights; Social sciences, public policy; Economics; Public policy, research.

Limitations: Applications not accepted. Giving on a national basis. No grants to individuals.

Application information: Contributes only to pre-selected organizations.

Officers: Ethelmae C. Humphreys, Pres.; David C. Humphreys, V.P. and Secy.-Treas.; Sarah Humphreys Atkins, V.P.

EIN: 431244445

4834
Joe Ingram Trust ◇
c/o Bank of America, N.A.
211 South Broadway
Salisbury, MO 65281

Established in 1960 in MO.

Donor: Joe Ingram†.

Foundation type: Independent foundation.

Financial data (yr. ended 12/31/04): Assets, $14,270,352 (M); expenditures, $902,559; qualifying distributions, $902,559; giving activities include $21,010 for 13 grants (high: $5,208; low: $104), $32,759 for 61 grants to individuals (high: $1,000; low: $500), and $690,320 for 398 loans to individuals (high: $8,750; low: $261).

Purpose and activities: Giving primarily for student loans to residents of Chariton County MO, only; some support for local civic projects and valedictorian awards.

Fields of interest: Education; Community development; Government/public administration.

Type of support: General/operating support; Grants to individuals; Student loans—to individuals.

Limitations: Applications not accepted. Giving limited to residents of Chariton County, MO.

Application information: Inquiries outside Chariton County, MO, not considered or acknowledged as funding is limited. Chariton County residents should contact the foundation for information.

Board meeting date(s): 2nd Thur. of each month

Trustees: David Sturm; Bank of America, N.A.

Number of staff: 1 part-time professional; 1 part-time support.
EIN: 446006475

4835
Interco Inc. Charitable Trust ◇
c/o U.S. Bank, N.A.
P.O. Box 387
St. Louis, MO   63166-0387   (314) 863-1100
Contact: Michael Loynd, Admin.
FAX: (314) 863-5306; Application address: c/o Furniture Brands International, Inc., 101 S. Hanley Rd., Clayton, MO 63105

Trust established in 1944 in MO.
Donor: Furniture Brands International, Inc.
Foundation type: Company-sponsored foundation.
Financial data (yr. ended 12/31/03): Assets, $41,335,626 (M); expenditures, $2,250,532; qualifying distributions, $2,049,932; giving activities include $2,021,221 for 366 grants (high: $150,000; low: $200).
Purpose and activities: The foundation supports organizations involved with arts and culture, education, health, youth development, human services, science, and religion.
Fields of interest: Arts; Education; Health care; Youth development; Youth, services; Human services; Federated giving programs; Science; Religion.
Limitations: Giving primarily in St. Louis, MO. No grants to individuals.
Application information: Application form not required.
   Initial approach: Proposal
   Deadline(s): None
Trustees: Donald E. Lasater; Lee M. Liberman; Richard B. Loynd; Robert H. Quenon; U.S. Bank, N.A.
Number of staff: 1 full-time professional.
EIN: 311593436

4836
Mervyn W. Jenkins Foundation ☆
c/o Robert Cowherd
P.O. Box 228
Chillicothe, MO   64601
FAX: (660) 646-1105;
E-mail: rcowherd@ccttlaw.com

Established in 2000 in MO.
Donor: Mervyn W. Jenkins Trust.
Foundation type: Independent foundation.
Financial data (yr. ended 12/31/05): Assets, $8,854,208 (M); expenditures, $654,158; qualifying distributions, $593,260; giving activities include $593,260 for grants.
Fields of interest: Education; Human services; Christian agencies & churches.
Type of support: Matching/challenge support; Land acquisition; General/operating support; Equipment; Capital campaigns; Building/renovation.
Limitations: Applications not accepted. Giving limited to northern MO, with emphasis on Livingston County. No grants to individuals.
Application information: Contributes only to pre-selected organizations.
   Board meeting date(s): Quarterly
Officers: Robert Cowherd, Pres.; Gary Greener, V.P.; Beverly Childers, Secy.-Treas.
Directors: John Irvin; John Marcolla.
EIN: 431897857

Selected grants: The following grants were reported in 2005.
$366,000 to Grand River Entertainment, Chillicothe, MO.
$26,000 to Chillicothe Educational Foundation, Chillicothe, MO.
$10,550 to Fellowship of Christian Athletes, Chillicothe, MO.
$7,000 to Salvation Army, Independence, MO.
$1,500 to Americas Second Harvest of Greater Saint Joseph, Saint Joseph, MO.

4837
Jewish Heritage Foundation of Greater Kansas City ◇
1 Ward Pkwy., Ste. 234
Kansas City, MO   64112   (816) 561-0563
Contact: Steve Israelite, Exec. Dir.; Beth Gottstein, Sr. Prog. Off.
FAX: (816) 561-0687; URL: http://www.jhf-kc.org/

Established in 1994 MO.
Foundation type: Independent foundation.
Financial data (yr. ended 12/31/05): Assets, $47,881,061 (M); gifts received, $10; expenditures, $3,054,945; qualifying distributions, $2,615,808; giving activities include $2,359,693 for 162 grants (high: $300,000; low: $1,116; average: $5,000–$10,000).
Purpose and activities: The foundation's primary mission is to enhance health and human services within greater Kansas City, MO, with a priority to serve the Jewish community.
Fields of interest: Education; Health care; Health organizations, association; Human services; Children, services; Family services; Jewish federated giving programs; Jewish agencies & temples; Aging; Economically disadvantaged.
Type of support: General/operating support; Building/renovation; Equipment; Emergency funds; Publication; Technical assistance; Consulting services; Matching/challenge support.
Limitations: Giving limited to the greater bi-state Kansas City metropolitan area. No support for political activities or organizations lacking 501(c)(3) status. No grants to individuals, or generally for multi-year grants or for capital or construction purposes.
Publications: Application guidelines; Grants list; Multi-year report.
Application information: See foundation Web site for full guidelines and downloadable application forms. Applications submitted by e-mail or facsimile are not accepted. Application form required.
   Initial approach: Letter or telephone for guidelines
   Copies of proposal: 1
   Deadline(s): See Web site for deadline date cycles for Program Grants and Administrative Operations Grants
   Final notification: Dec. 31
Officers and Directors:* Daniel L. Scharf, M.D.*, Pres.; Sheryl T. Davidow,* Exec. V.P.; Merilyn Berenbom, V.P., Grants; Howard T. Jacobson,* V.P., Investments; James M. Klien,* Secy.; Steven A. Gershon,* Treas.; Joseph L. Hiersteiner; Jeanette Wishna; and 17 additional directors.
Number of staff: 2 full-time professional; 1 part-time support.
EIN: 431416766
Selected grants: The following grants were reported in 2004.
$125,000 to Village Shalom, Overland Park, KS.
$36,000 to Synergy Services, Parkville, MO.

$20,000 to Midwest WholeChild Development Group, Overland Park, KS.
$20,000 to Rehabilitation Institute, Kansas City, MO.
$15,000 to DeLaSalle Education Center, Kansas City, MO.
$10,950 to Hyman Brand Hebrew Academy, Overland Park, KS.
$10,000 to Center for Practical Bioethics, Kansas City, MO.
$10,000 to Kansas City Neighborhood Alliance, Kansas City, MO.
$10,000 to Shepherds Center of the Northland, Kansas City, MO.
$10,000 to University Academy, Kansas City, MO.

4838
The Edward D. Jones & Co. Foundation ◇
12555 Manchester Rd.
St. Louis, MO   63131

Established in 1991 in MO.
Donor: Edward D. Jones & Co., L.P.
Foundation type: Company-sponsored foundation.
Financial data (yr. ended 12/31/05): Assets, $15,908,524 (L); gifts received, $1,111,718; expenditures, $2,277,171; qualifying distributions, $2,277,171; giving activities include $2,277,171 for 2 grants (high: $1,500,000; low: $777,171).
Purpose and activities: The foundation supports Claremont Graduate University.
Fields of interest: Graduate/professional education.
Type of support: General/operating support.
Limitations: Applications not accepted. Giving primarily in Claremont, CA, and St. Louis, MO. No grants to individuals.
Application information: Contributes only to pre-selected organizations.
Officer: Douglas E. Hill, Chair.
Trustee: Norman L. Eaker; Steven Novik.
EIN: 431595600
Selected grants: The following grants were reported in 2004.
$1,500,000 to Claremont Graduate University, Claremont, CA.

4839
Dennis M. Jones Family Foundation ◇
(formerly Dennis & Judith Jones Charitable Foundation Trust)
1700 S. Warson Rd.
St. Louis, MO   63124
Contact: Dennis M. Jones

Established in 1998 in MO.
Donor: Dennis M. Jones.
Foundation type: Independent foundation.
Financial data (yr. ended 12/31/05): Assets, $42,687,443 (M); expenditures, $3,322,200; qualifying distributions, $2,956,750; giving activities include $2,956,750 for 25 grants (high: $1,010,000; low: $500).
Purpose and activities: Giving primarily for higher education; support also for youth services.
Fields of interest: Higher education; Education; Zoos/zoological societies; Human services; Youth, services.
Type of support: Scholarship funds.
Limitations: Giving primarily in MO, with emphasis on St. Louis. No grants to individuals.

Application information:
Initial approach: Letter on organization's letterhead
Deadline(s): None
Trustees: J. Denise Franz; Dennis M. Jones, Jr.; Judith A. Jones.
EIN: 436786094
Selected grants: The following grants were reported in 2005.
$1,010,000 to Saint Louis University, Saint Louis, MO.
$200,000 to Connections to Success, Saint Charles, MO.
$100,000 to American Red Cross, Saint Louis, MO.
$100,000 to Girls Inc., Saint Louis, MO.
$35,000 to Junior Achievement, Saint Louis, MO.
$12,000 to Oakland University, Rochester, MI.
$5,000 to Boys Hope Girls Hope, Bridgeton, MO.
$2,750 to Forest Park Forever, Saint Louis, MO.
$2,000 to Family Support Network, Saint Louis, MO.

4840
Mary Ranken Jordan and Ettie A. Jordan Charitable Foundation
c/o U.S. Bank, N.A.
P.O. Box 387
St. Louis, MO 63166 (314) 505-8203
Contact: Angela L. Pearson
Application address: c/o Fred E. Arnold, Advisory Committee, 1 U.S. Bank Plz., Ste. 3400, St. Louis, MO 63101, tel.: (314) 552-6000; E-mail: farnold@thompsoncoburn.com

Foundation established in 1957 in MO.
Donors: Mary Ranken Jordan†; Ettie A. Jordan†.
Foundation type: Independent foundation.
Financial data (yr. ended 12/31/05): Assets, $24,376,285 (M); expenditures, $1,347,798; qualifying distributions, $1,243,611; giving activities include $1,209,133 for 48 grants (high: $125,000; low: $2,000).
Purpose and activities: Giving limited to MO charitable and eleemosynary institutions, with emphasis on the arts, including a symphony orchestra, education, and children's health and welfare, including a pediatric rehabilitation center.
Fields of interest: Performing arts, orchestra (symphony); Arts; Higher education; Education; Botanical gardens; Children/youth, services; Family services.
Type of support: General/operating support; Continuing support; Capital campaigns; Building/renovation; Endowments.
Limitations: Giving limited to MO, with emphasis on the St. Louis area. No grants to individuals.
Application information: Application form not required.
Initial approach: Letter
Copies of proposal: 3
Deadline(s): Dec. 31
Board meeting date(s): Apr.
Advisory Board: Fred E. Arnold; W. Stanley Walch; David Wells.
Trustee: U.S. Bank, N.A.
EIN: 436020554
Selected grants: The following grants were reported in 2005.
$150,000 to Ranken Jordan Home for Convalescent Crippled Children, Saint Louis, MO.
$125,000 to Saint Louis Symphony Orchestra, Saint Louis, MO.

$100,000 to Washington University, Saint Louis, MO.
$50,000 to Missouri Botanical Garden, Saint Louis, MO.
$50,000 to Saint Louis Zoo Foundation, Saint Louis, MO.
$25,000 to Opera Theater of Saint Louis, Saint Louis, MO.

4841
The JSM Charitable Trust ▼
1034 S. Brentwood Blvd., Ste. 1860
St. Louis, MO 63117-1229
Contact: Jeffrey McDonnell, Tr.

Established in 1997.
Donors: James S. McDonnell Foundation; James S. McDonnell III; Jeffrey M. McDonnell; John F. McDonnell.
Foundation type: Independent foundation.
Financial data (yr. ended 12/31/05): Assets, $883 (M); gifts received, $10,226,172; expenditures, $10,232,492; qualifying distributions, $10,232,492; giving activities include $10,232,492 for 14 grants (high: $3,210,975; low: $2,049; average: $100,000–$400,000).
Purpose and activities: Giving primarily for higher education, civic and community, and cultural organizations.
Fields of interest: Arts; Higher education; Civil rights; Community development; Science, research.
Type of support: Research; Program development; Professorships; Matching/challenge support; Endowments; Capital campaigns; Building/renovation; Annual campaigns.
Limitations: Applications not accepted. Giving primarily in St. Louis, MO. No support for religious or political organizations. No grants to individuals.
Application information: Contributes only to pre-selected organizations.
Board meeting date(s): 3 times per year
Trustees: James S. McDonnell III; Jeffrey M. McDonnell.
EIN: 431769438
Selected grants: The following grants were reported in 2005.
$3,210,975 to Saint Louis Childrens Hospital Foundation, Saint Louis, MO. For Pediatric Brain Tumor Project.
$2,386,694 to Washington University, Saint Louis, MO. 3 grants: $578,469 to School of Medicine (For pediatrics building), $500,165 to School of Medicine (For capital campaign and unrestricted support), $1,308,060 to School of Medicine (For capital campaign and unrestricted support).
$2,253,196 to Smithsonian Institution, National Air and Space Museum, DC. For space hangar at Dulles Museum.
$980,042 to Bucknell University, Lewisburg, PA. For capital campaign.
$622,505 to Saint Louis Science Center Foundation, Saint Louis, MO. For refurbishment and renovation.
$273,910 to City Academy, Saint Louis, MO. For capital campaign.
$61,425 to John Burroughs School, Saint Louis, MO. For scholarship fund.
$29,445 to Character Education Partnership, DC. For operating support.

4842
Greater Kansas City Community Foundation ▼
(formerly The Greater Kansas City Community Foundation and Affiliated Trusts)
1055 Broadway, Ste. 130
Kansas City, MO 64105-1595 (816) 842-0944
Contact: Laura McKnight, C.E.O.
FAX: (816) 842-8079; E-mail: info@gkccf.org; Tel. for Donor Svcs. Ctr.: (816) 842-7444; URL: http://www.gkccf.org

Established in 1978 in MO.
Foundation type: Community foundation.
Financial data (yr. ended 12/31/05): Assets, $1,013,035,000 (M); gifts received, $157,300,000; expenditures, $146,402,000; giving activities include $140,702,000 for 10,500 grants.
Purpose and activities: The foundation seeks to improve the quality of life in Greater Kansas City by increasing charitable giving, connecting donors to the needs in the community they care about, and providing leadership on critical community issues.
Fields of interest: Arts; Health care; Children/youth, services; Family services; Civil rights, race/intergroup relations; Urban/community development; Community development; Biological sciences.
Type of support: General/operating support; Capital campaigns; Program development; Seed money; Scholarship funds; Research; Technical assistance; Program-related investments/loans; Employee matching gifts; Scholarships—to individuals; Matching/challenge support.
Limitations: Applications not accepted. Giving primarily in the bi-state greater Kansas City region. No grants to individuals (except through designated scholarship funds), or for deficit financing, endowments, or annual campaigns.
Publications: Annual report; Informational brochure; Newsletter.
Application information: The foundation does not currently accept unsolicited grant proposals. However, a few funds have competitive grant processes to which nonprofits can apply for grants. Visit foundation Web site for guidelines.
Board meeting date(s): Mar., June, Sept., and Dec.
Officers and Directors:* Sandra A.J. Lawrence,* Chair.; Thomas M. Bloch, Vice-Chair.; Ronald R. Pressman, Vice-Chair.; Laura McKnight,* C.E.O. and Pres.; George S. Bittner, Exec. V.P.; Brenda Chumley, Sr. V.P., Admin.; Larry Jacob, Sr. V.P., Community Investment; Roxie Jerde, Sr. V.P., Donor and Nonprofit Rels.; Brady Kelley, Sr. V.P., Finance; Peggy Dunn,* Secy.; Danley Sheldon,* Treas.; Jonathan E. Baum; William S. Berkley; Grant Burcham; Carl Chinnery; Byron Constance; E. Frank Ellis; Mark A. Ernst; G. David Gale; Rafael I. Garcia; Donald Hall, Jr.; Michael R. Haverty; Robert D. Regnier; Mac Tully; Deryl W. Wynn.
Number of staff: 30 full-time professional; 1 part-time professional; 10 full-time support; 3 part-time support.
EIN: 431152398
Selected grants: The following grants were reported in 2004.
$3,146,933 to Saint Lukes Hospital Foundation, Kansas City, MO.
$2,775,000 to Local Initiatives Support Corporation (LISC), Kansas City, MO.
$2,713,775 to Nelson Gallery Foundation, Kansas City, MO.

$1,990,425 to Union Station Kansas City, Kansas City, MO.

$1,866,784 to Northland Health Care Access, Kansas City, MO.

$1,206,336 to Kansas City Ballet Association, Kansas City, MO.

$662,678 to Missouri Development Finance Board, Jefferson City, MO.

$383,177 to Nelson-Atkins Museum of Art, Kansas City, MO.

$341,180 to Kansas City Symphony, Kansas City, MO.

$301,100 to Eisenhower Medical Center, Rancho Mirage, CA.

4843
Ewing Marion Kauffman Foundation ▼

4801 Rockhill Rd.
Kansas City, MO   64110-2046   (816) 932-1000
Contact: Joy Torchia, Comms. Mgr.
FAX: (816) 932-1100; E-mail: info@kauffman.org;
URL: http://www.kauffman.org

Established in 1966 in MO.
Donor: Ewing M. Kauffman†.
Foundation type: Independent foundation.
Financial data (yr. ended 6/30/05): Assets, $1,860,797,344 (M); gifts received, $15,000; expenditures, $101,798,347; qualifying distributions, $87,166,915; giving activities include $49,488,969 for 425 grants (high: $2,104,000; low: $100; average: $10,000–$100,000), $182,000 for 15 grants to individuals (high: $50,000; low: $3,000; average: $12,000–$12,000), $932,759 for 610 employee matching gifts, and $20,417,918 for 4 foundation-administered programs.
Purpose and activities: The foundation works with partners to encourage entrepreneurship across America and improve the education of children and youth. The foundation focuses its operations and grantmaking on two areas: entrepreneurship and education. The foundation strives to foster an environment nationwide in which entrepreneurs have the information and tools they need to succeed. In education, the foundation partners with others to improve the lives of children and their families to create an environment where they enter school prepared to succeed and, once in school, are able to prepare for life as productive, contributing citizens.
Fields of interest: Elementary/secondary education; Social entrepreneurship; Science; Mathematics.
Type of support: General/operating support; Emergency funds; Program development; Conferences/seminars; Seed money; Curriculum development; Fellowships; Scholarship funds; Research; Technical assistance; Consulting services; Program-related investments/loans; Employee matching gifts; Grants to individuals; Matching/challenge support.
Limitations: Giving limited to the U.S., with emphasis on the bi-state metropolitan Kansas City area (KS/MO) for K-12 education initiatives focused on math and science. No support for international programs, political, social, fraternal, or arts organizations, and capital campaigns or construction projects. No grants for fund endowments, or for special events.
Publications: Application guidelines; Annual report; Financial statement; Grants list; Informational

brochure (including application guidelines); Newsletter.
Application information: To receive a copy of the foundation's Guidelines for Grantseekers brochure, visit foundation's Web site or send a request via e-mail or by mail. Application form not required.
Initial approach: Letter of inquiry, less than 3 pages
Deadline(s): None
Board meeting date(s): Mar., June, Sept., and Dec.
Final notification: As soon as possible
Officers and Directors:* Thomas A. McDonnell, Chair.; Carl J. Schramm, Ph.D.*, C.E.O. and Pres.; Dennis W. Cheek, V.P., Education; Judith Cone, V.P., Entrepreneurship; Robert Litan, V.P., Research and Policy; Lesa Mitchell, V.P., Advancing Innovation; Paul Schofer, C.F.O.; John E. Tyler III, Genl. Counsel; Ramon de Oliveira; Thomas M. Hoenig, Ph.D.; John W. Jordan II; Anne Hodges Morgan, Ph.D.; Siobhan Nicolau; Thomas J. Rhone.
Number of staff: 45 full-time professional; 3 part-time professional; 36 full-time support; 2 part-time support.
EIN: 436064859
Selected grants: The following grants were reported in 2005.
$3,497,863 to National Council on Economic Education, New York, NY. To manage, operate, and disseminate Kauffman Foundation youth programs, Mini-Society, Making a Job and EntrePrep.
$2,500,000 to Greater Kansas City Community Foundation, Kansas City, MO. For Kauffman Fund to provide small grants to nonprofit agencies whose mission supports children, youth, and families.
$2,334,000 to Urban League, National, New York, NY. To create multiple entrepreneurial coaching centers around the country that will support creation and growth of minority firms.
$1,250,000 to Unified School District No. 500, Kansas City, KS. For transition support to complete Kansas City School District's First Things First school reform initiative.
$1,000,000 to Nelson Gallery Foundation, Kansas City, MO. For education initiative, including community and neighborhood outreach to low-income areas.
$800,000 to Education Trust, DC. To study effectiveness of middle school math teachers in Kansas City area schools.
$593,792 to University of Missouri, Columbia, MO. For Advancing Academic Research on Entrepreneurship, series of research projects conducted by interdisciplinary faculty team.
$60,000 to University of Illinois at Urbana-Champaign, College of Commerce and Business Administration, Urbana, IL. For Information Specialist for Academy for Entrepreneurial Leadership Development and Office for Strategic Business Initiatives Consulting to conduct research.
$50,000 to Distributive Education Clubs of America (DECA), Reston, VA. For events in entrepreneurship and professional development scholarships to teachers.
$30,000 to Skills USA - VICA, Youth Development Foundation, Jefferson City, MO. For Champions for Youth Development Campaign, supporting local KC Metro Schools Project and annual conference.

4844
Muriel McBrien Kauffman Foundation ▼ ✧

4801 Rockhill Rd.
Kansas City, MO   64110
Contact: Julia Irene Kauffman, Chair.

Established in 1987 in MO.
Donor: Muriel McBrien Kauffman†.
Foundation type: Independent foundation.
Financial data (yr. ended 12/31/04): Assets, $279,932,724 (M); gifts received, $328,562; expenditures, $13,338,695; qualifying distributions, $11,590,888; giving activities include $10,544,700 for 235 grants (high: $1,400,000; low: $250; average: $2,500–$50,000), and $17,400 for 24 employee matching gifts.
Purpose and activities: Primary fields of interest include the performing arts.
Fields of interest: Performing arts, dance; Performing arts, music; Arts.
Type of support: General/operating support; Program development; Employee matching gifts.
Limitations: Giving primarily in Kansas City, MO, and New York, NY. No support for religious or political organizations. No loans or program-related investments.
Application information: Application form not required.
Initial approach: Proposal
Copies of proposal: 1
Deadline(s): None
Board meeting date(s): Quarterly
Final notification: 1-2 months
Officers and Directors:* Julia Irene Kauffman,* Chair.; David Lady,* C.O.O. and Pres.; Sharon L. Blickensderfer, V.P., Finance; Cara Z. Newell; Julia Power Weld.
Number of staff: 3 full-time professional; 2 full-time support; 2 part-time support.
EIN: 431460787
Selected grants: The following grants were reported in 2004.
$1,600,000 to Nelson-Atkins Museum of Art, Kansas City, MO. 2 grants: $1,000,000 (For capital campaign), $600,000 (For Endowment Campaign).
$1,400,000 to Metropolitan Kansas City Performing Arts Center, Kansas City, MO. For grant to fund account.
$700,000 to Kansas City Symphony, Kansas City, MO. For annual operating season support.
$550,000 to Kansas City Ballet Association, Kansas City, MO. For general operating support for season.
$500,000 to Liberty Memorial Association, Kansas City, MO. For Liberty Memorial Museum.
$500,000 to Starlight Theater, Kansas City, MO. For Future Generations Campaign.
$350,000 to Lyric Opera of Kansas City, Kansas City, MO. For general operating support for season.
$300,000 to Metropolitan Arts Council of Greater Kansas City, Kansas City, MO. For general operating support.
$15,000 to Metropolitan Museum of Art, New York, NY. For Friends of the Costume Institute membership.

4845
The Kellwood Foundation ✧
P.O. Box 78039
St. Louis, MO 63178 (314) 576-3431
Contact: Teri Grandcolas
FAX: (314) 576-3439; Application address: 600
Kellwood Pkwy., Chesterfield, MO 63017

Established in 1965 in IL.
Donor: Kellwood Co.
Foundation type: Company-sponsored foundation.
Financial data (yr. ended 12/31/05): Assets,
$2,272,473 (M); gifts received, $515,178;
expenditures, $481,363; qualifying distributions,
$479,157; giving activities include $479,157 for
156 grants.
Purpose and activities: The foundation supports
organizations involved with arts and culture,
education, health, and human services.
Fields of interest: Arts; Education; Health care;
Cancer; Children/youth, services; Human services.
Type of support: General/operating support; Capital
campaigns; Program development; Employee
matching gifts.
Limitations: Giving primarily in the greater St. Louis,
MO, area. No grants to individuals.
Publications: Application guidelines.
Application information: Application form not
required.
  Initial approach: Proposal
  Copies of proposal: 1
  Deadline(s): Dec. 31
  Board meeting date(s): Mar., June, Sept., and
  Dec.
Directors: Gregory W. Kleffner; Thomas H. Pollihan;
Terri L. Wise.
EIN: 366141441

4846
R. C. Kemper Charitable Trust ✧
c/o UMB Bank, N.A.
P.O. Box 419692
Kansas City, MO 64141-6692
Contact: Jan Leonard

Established in 1953 in MO.
Donor: R. Crosby Kemper, Sr.†.
Foundation type: Independent foundation.
Financial data (yr. ended 12/31/05): Assets,
$24,811,558 (M); expenditures, $1,364,917;
qualifying distributions, $1,319,982; giving
activities include $1,261,860 for 25 grants (high:
$735,835; low: $2,500).
Purpose and activities: Giving primarily for
education and the arts.
Fields of interest: Arts; Secondary school/
education; Higher education; Agriculture;
Community development, neighborhood
development.
Type of support: General/operating support.
Limitations: Applications not accepted. Giving
primarily in MO. No grants to individuals.
Application information: Contributes only to
pre-selected organizations.
Trustees: Sheila Kemper Dietrich; John Mariner
Kemper; R. Crosby Kemper, Jr.; Rufus Crosby
Kemper III; UMB Bank, N.A.
EIN: 446010318
Selected grants: The following grants were reported
in 2003.
$612,910 to Kemper Museum of Contemporary Art
  and Design, Kansas City, MO.

$251,000 to American Royal Association, Kansas
  City, MO.
$50,000 to National Association of Intercollegiate
  Athletics, Olathe, KS.
$41,872 to Teel Institute for the Development of
  Integrity and Ethical Behavior, Kansas City, MO.
$25,000 to Saint Teresas Academy, Kansas City,
  MO.
$20,000 to Tower Grove Park, Saint Louis, MO.
$10,000 to Whitney Museum of American Art, New
  York, NY.
$9,000 to Smithsonian American Art Museum, DC.
$6,250 to University of Missouri Press, Columbia,
  MO.
$5,000 to Salvation Army, Kansas City, MO.

4847
William T. Kemper Charitable Trust ✧
c/o UMB Bank, N.A.
P.O. Box 419692
Kansas City, MO 64141-6692 (816) 860-7711
Contact: Jan Leonard

Established in 1989 in MO.
Foundation type: Independent foundation.
Financial data (yr. ended 12/31/05): Assets,
$51,647,020 (M); expenditures, $2,511,441;
qualifying distributions, $2,600,412; giving
activities include $2,286,723 for 37 grants (high:
$1,623,439; low: $500).
Purpose and activities: Giving primarily to art
institutes, museums, and other cultural programs.
Fields of interest: Visual arts; Museums; Performing
arts; Arts.
Limitations: Applications not accepted. Giving
primarily in Kansas City, MO. No grants to
individuals.
Application information: Contributes only to
pre-selected organizations.
Trustees: R. Crosby Kemper; UMB Bank, N.A.
EIN: 436362480
Selected grants: The following grants were reported
in 2005.
$205,000 to Kansas City Symphony, Kansas City,
  MO.
$75,000 to Students in Free Enterprise, Springfield,
  MO.
$25,000 to Florida Atlantic University Foundation,
  Boca Raton, FL.
$25,000 to Marillac Center for Children, Overland
  Park, KS.
$23,000 to American Royal Association, Kansas
  City, MO.
$20,500 to Cheyenne Mountain Zoological Society,
  Colorado Springs, CO.
$17,500 to Park University, Parkville, MO.
$10,000 to Wayside Waifs, Kansas City, MO.
$5,000 to DeLaSalle Education Center, Kansas
  City, MO.
$5,000 to Genesis School, Kansas City, MO.

4848
Enid and Crosby Kemper Foundation ✧
c/o UMB Bank, N.A.
P.O. Box 419692, M/S 1020305
Kansas City, MO 64141-6692
Contact: Jan Leonard

Established in 1972 in MO.
Donors: Enid J. Kemper; R. Crosby Kemper, Sr.†.
Foundation type: Independent foundation.

Financial data (yr. ended 12/31/05): Assets,
$43,463,579 (M); expenditures, $2,295,150;
qualifying distributions, $2,461,450; giving
activities include $2,095,460 for 7 grants (high:
$1,853,649; low: $1,000).
Purpose and activities: Emphasis on secondary
education and cultural programs, including
museums and the performing arts; some support
also for health and higher education.
Fields of interest: Museums; Performing arts; Arts;
Secondary school/education; Higher education;
Health care; Health organizations, association;
Human services.
Type of support: General/operating support.
Limitations: Applications not accepted. Giving
primarily in KS and MO. No support for medical
institutions. No grants to individuals, or for capital
funds.
Application information: Contributes only to
pre-selected organizations.
  Board meeting date(s): Quarterly and as needed
Trustees: Alexander C. Kemper; Mary S. Kemper; R.
Crosby Kemper, Jr.; UMB Bank, N.A.
EIN: 237279896
Selected grants: The following grants were reported
in 2003.
$1,421,378 to Kemper Museum of Contemporary
  Art and Design, Kansas City, MO.
$37,500 to Model Cities Health Corporation of
  Kansas City, Swope Health Services, Kansas
  City, MO.
$25,000 to Albrecht-Kemper Museum of Art, Saint
  Joseph, MO.
$20,000 to Cheyenne Mountain Zoological Society,
  Colorado Springs, CO.
$10,000 to Kappa Alpha Theta Foundation,
  Indianapolis, IN.
$10,000 to Westminster College, Fulton, MO.
$10,000 to YMCA, Grand River Area Family,
  Chillicothe, MO.
$5,000 to Saint Pauls Episcopal Day School, Waco,
  TX.
$5,000 to Strategic Leadership Institute, Seattle,
  WA.
$4,000 to Salvation Army of Saint Joseph, Saint
  Joseph, MO.

4849
William T. Kemper Foundation ▼ ✧
922 Walnut, Ste. 200
Kansas City, MO 64106-1809 (816) 234-2112
Contact: Michael D. Fields, Exec. Dir.

Established in 1989 in MO.
Donors: William T. Kemper†; William T. Kemper
Revocable Trust.
Foundation type: Independent foundation.
Financial data (yr. ended 10/31/05): Assets,
$257,711,150 (M); expenditures, $12,373,618;
qualifying distributions, $11,070,921; giving
activities include $10,489,199 for 310 grants (high:
$1,000,000; low: $500; average: $5,000–
$25,000).
Purpose and activities: Support primarily for arts,
civic improvements, education, health, and human
services.
Fields of interest: Arts; Education; Health care;
Human services; Community development.
Type of support: General/operating support;
Continuing support; Annual campaigns; Capital
campaigns; Building/renovation; Equipment;
Program development; Conferences/seminars;

Publication; Seed money; Curriculum development; Research; Technical assistance.

Limitations: Giving primarily in the Midwest with emphasis on MO and surrounding areas. No support for private foundations. No grants to individuals, or for tickets for dinners, benefits, exhibits, sports and other event activities, advertisements, endowment funds, or fundraising activities.

Publications: Informational brochure (including application guidelines).

Application information: Guidelines available upon request. Application form not required.

    Initial approach: Proposal with proof of nonprofit status

    Copies of proposal: 1

    Deadline(s): 3 weeks before board meetings

    Board meeting date(s): Quarterly

    Final notification: 2 - 4 months

Officer: Michael D. Fields, Exec. Dir.

Trustees: Jonathan M. Kemper, Member, Contribs. Comm.; Commerce Bank, N.A.

Contributions Committee: Laura Kemper Fields; Julie Kemper Foyer; David W. Kemper; James M. Kemper, Jr.

EIN: 436345116

Selected grants: The following grants were reported in 2005.

$1,009,150 to Nelson Gallery Foundation, Kansas City, MO. 2 grants: $1,000,000, $9,150

$950,000 to Missouri Botanical Garden, Saint Louis, MO.

$750,000 to Washington University, Saint Louis, MO.

$350,000 to Archdiocese of Saint Louis, Saint Louis, MO. For Kemper Donor-Advised Fund.

$333,333 to Saint Lukes Hospital Foundation, Kansas City, MO.

$90,000 to American Red Cross, Saint Louis, MO.

$11,450 to Bishop Spencer Place, Kansas City, MO.

$10,500 to Bishop Seabury Academy, Lawrence, KS.

$10,000 to Kansas City Community Gardens, Kansas City, MO.

4850
David Woods Kemper Memorial Foundation ✧

911 Main St., Ste. 100
Kansas City, MO 64105 (816) 374-0684
Contact: James M. Kemper, Jr., Pres.

Incorporated in 1946 in MO.

Donor: James M. Kemper, Jr.

Foundation type: Independent foundation.

Financial data (yr. ended 12/31/05): Assets, $15,109,912 (M); expenditures, $1,636,459; qualifying distributions, $1,618,503; giving activities include $1,616,609 for 88 grants (high: $257,150; low: $100).

Purpose and activities: Giving primarily for arts organizations, civic projects, education, health, and human services.

Fields of interest: Arts; Education; Health care; Human services; Community development; Public affairs.

Limitations: Applications not accepted. Giving primarily in Kansas City, MO. No grants to individuals.

Application information: Contributes only to pre-selected organizations.

Officers and Directors:* James M. Kemper, Jr.,* Pres.; David W. Kemper,* V.P.; Laura Kemper

Fields,* Secy.-Treas.; Julie Kemper Foyer; Jonathan M. Kemper.

Number of staff: 3

EIN: 446012535

Selected grants: The following grants were reported in 2004.

$250,000 to Downtown Kansas City Public Library Fund, Kansas City, MO.

$100,000 to Childrens Mercy Hospital, Kansas City, MO.

$100,000 to Mayo Foundation, Rochester, MN.

$100,000 to Nelson Gallery Foundation, Kansas City, MO.

$100,000 to Saint Lukes Hospital Foundation, Kansas City, MO.

$50,000 to University Leadership Academy, Kansas City, MO.

$25,000 to Barstow School, Kansas City, MO.

$10,000 to Friends of Chamber Music, Kansas City, MO.

$5,500 to Kansas City Art Institute, Kansas City, MO.

$3,500 to Chicago Symphony Orchestra, Chicago, IL.

4851
William Toben King Educational Trust ✧

c/o James Counts
320 Robidoux Ctr.
St. Joseph, MO 64501
Scholarship address: Julie Walker, c/o Commerce Bank, St. Joseph, P.O. Box 1119, St. Joseph, MO 64502, tel.: (816) 364-3131

Established in 1991 in MO.

Donor: William Toben King.

Foundation type: Independent foundation.

Financial data (yr. ended 9/30/05): Assets, $7,400,383 (M); expenditures, $418,549; qualifying distributions, $370,225; giving activities include $348,475 for grants to individuals.

Purpose and activities: Scholarships awarded to high school seniors of Buchanan and Andrew counties, MO, to obtain a college degree.

Type of support: Scholarships—to individuals.

Limitations: Giving limited to residents of Buchanan and Andrew counties, MO.

Application information: Application form required.

    Deadline(s): June 1

Trustees: Galen R. Bodenhausen; James Counts; Mark Hargens.

EIN: 431582893

4852
Laclede Gas Charitable Trust ✧

720 Olive St., Rm. 1517
St. Louis, MO 63101
Contact: Mary C. Kullman, Secy.

Established in 1966 in MO.

Donor: Laclede Gas Co.

Foundation type: Company-sponsored foundation.

Financial data (yr. ended 9/30/05): Assets, $3,873,106 (M); expenditures, $491,385; qualifying distributions, $489,210; giving activities include $489,210 for 32 grants (high: $254,250; low: $250).

Purpose and activities: The foundation supports organizations involved with arts and culture, education, health, and human services.

Fields of interest: Museums; Arts; Secondary school/education; Higher education; Education; Health care; Children/youth, services; Family services; Human services; Federated giving programs.

Type of support: General/operating support; Annual campaigns; Building/renovation; Equipment; Emergency funds; Program development; Employee matching gifts.

Limitations: Applications not accepted. Giving limited to areas of company operations in eastern MO. No support for religious or sectarian organizations or veterans' organizations. No grants to individuals.

Application information: Contributes only to pre-selected organizations.

    Board meeting date(s): Periodically as needed; at least quarterly

Officers and Trustees:* Douglas H. Yaeger,* Chair.; M.R. Spotanski,* Vice-Chair.; Mary C. Kullman,* Secy.; Ronald L. Krutzman, Treas.

EIN: 436068197

4853
The Lay Family Foundation ✧

(formerly Sister Mary Louis Foundation)
c/o Tod Moses, C.P.A.
10135 Manchester Rd., Ste. 206
St. Louis, MO 63122

Established in 1989 in MO.

Donor: Henry A. Lay‡.

Foundation type: Independent foundation.

Financial data (yr. ended 12/31/05): Assets, $22,034,049 (M); gifts received, $10,000; expenditures, $700,122; qualifying distributions, $616,724; giving activities include $595,066 for 21 grants (high: $175,502; low: $70; average: $1,000–$50,000).

Fields of interest: Arts education; Higher education, university; Education; Children, services; Christian agencies & churches.

Type of support: Endowments; Scholarship funds; General/operating support.

Limitations: Applications not accepted. Giving primarily in St. Louis, MO. No grants to individuals.

Application information: Contributes only to pre-selected organizations.

Officers: John E. Dooling, Jr., Chair.; Louis J. Garr, Jr., Pres.

EIN: 431510405

Selected grants: The following grants were reported in 2003.

$285,670 to Saint Louis University, Saint Louis, MO. 2 grants: $128,111 (For Lay Center for Education and the Arts Endowment), $157,559 (For general support).

$180,244 to Today and Tomorrow Educational Foundation, Saint Louis, MO. For children scholarships.

$13,600 to University of Connecticut Foundation, Storrs, CT. For scholarships.

$5,000 to Kilo Diabetes and Vascular Research Foundation, Saint Louis, MO.

$3,334 to Washington University, Saint Louis, MO. For general support.

$1,300 to Saint Louis Science Center, Saint Louis, MO.

$1,000 to Bishop Dubourg High School, Saint Louis, MO. For general support.

$1,000 to Saint John the Baptist College Preparatory High School, Saint Louis, MO. For scholarships.

$90 to Missouri Botanical Garden, Saint Louis, MO.

4854
Jean, Jack, & Mildred Lemons Charitable Trust ✧

P.O. Box 387, ML: SL-MO-T18S
St. Louis, MO   63166-0387

Established in 1987 in MO.
Foundation type: Independent foundation.
Financial data (yr. ended 6/30/05): Assets, $8,516,681 (M); expenditures, $510,447; qualifying distributions, $457,038; giving activities include $441,392 for 45 grants (high: $50,000; low: $880).
Purpose and activities: Giving primarily for education, health and human services, and youth groups.
Fields of interest: Arts; Elementary/secondary education; Education; Public health; Health care; Youth development; Human services; Children/youth, services; Protestant agencies & churches.
Limitations: Giving limited to MO, primarily in Joplin.
Trustee: U.S. Bank, N.A.
EIN: 436328116
Selected grants: The following grants were reported in 2004.
$50,000 to Joplin School District R-VIII, Joplin, MO. For general support.
$35,000 to Community Health Clinic of Joplin, Joplin, MO. For general support.
$25,000 to Mercy Regional Health Foundation, Joplin, MO. For general support.
$25,000 to Missouri Southern State University Foundation, Joplin, MO. For general support.
$20,000 to Salvation Army of Joplin, Joplin, MO. For general support.
$15,000 to United Way of Southwest Missouri, Joplin, MO. For general support.
$10,900 to College of the Ozarks, Point Lookout, MO. For general support.
$10,000 to American Cancer Society, Joplin, MO. For general support.
$4,000 to Joplin Area Catholic Schools, Joplin, MO. For general support.
$2,500 to Boy Scouts of America, Joplin, MO. For general support.

4855
David B. Lichtenstein Foundation ✧

(formerly Lichtenstein Foundation)
20 Country Aire Dr.
St. Louis, MO   63131-2318   (314) 872-3905
Contact: David B. Lichtenstein, Jr., Chair.
FAX: (314) 432-4704; E-mail: dblfound@aol.com

Established in 1947 in MO.
Donors: David B. Lichtenstein, Jr.; Doris Lichtenstein.
Foundation type: Independent foundation.
Financial data (yr. ended 12/31/05): Assets, $17,233,914 (M); expenditures, $1,127,321; qualifying distributions, $977,292; giving activities include $930,000 for 3 grants (high: $480,000; low: $150,000).
Fields of interest: Performing arts, opera; Botanical gardens; Zoos/zoological societies.
Type of support: Annual campaigns; Capital campaigns; Equipment; Matching/challenge support.

Limitations: Giving limited to MO. No support for for-profit organizations or organizations that contribute funds to a national organization.
Application information: Application form not required.
Deadline(s): None
Board meeting date(s): 4th Thurs. in Jan. and July; additional dates subject to call
Officers and Directors: * David B. Lichtenstein, Jr.,* Chair.; Doris Harris Lichtenstein,* Secy.; Davida Layer.
EIN: 436033786
Selected grants: The following grants were reported in 2003.
$265,000 to Saint Louis Zoo Foundation, Saint Louis, MO. For chimpanzee area, Puffin exhibit and benches.
$100,000 to Municipal Theater Association of Saint Louis, Saint Louis, MO.

4856
Litzsinger Road Ecology Foundation ✧

c/o John McFarland
1034 S. Brentwood Blvd., Ste. 1492
St. Louis, MO   63117

Established in 1990 in MO.
Foundation type: Independent foundation.
Financial data (yr. ended 12/31/04): Assets, $18,664,716 (M); gifts received, $18,363; expenditures, $812,801; qualifying distributions, $657,154; giving activities include $443,416 for 4 grants (high: $435,000; low: $54).
Fields of interest: Botanical gardens.
Type of support: General/operating support.
Limitations: Applications not accepted. Giving primarily in St. Louis, MO. No grants to individuals.
Application information: Contributes only to pre-selected organizations.
Officers and Directors: * M. Peter Fischer,* Pres.; G. Don Millar,* V.P.; Caroline M. Sant,* Secy.; Michael P. Fischer, Treas.
EIN: 431564336
Selected grants: The following grants were reported in 2004.
$435,000 to Missouri Botanical Garden, Saint Louis, MO.
$7,295 to Ladue School District, Saint Louis, MO.
$1,067 to Ladue, City of, Ladue, MO.

4857
Lockton Family Foundation ✧

444 W. 47th St., Ste. 900
Kansas City, MO   64112

Established in 2002 in MO.
Donors: Jack Lockton; Cheryl A. Lockton.
Foundation type: Independent foundation.
Financial data (yr. ended 12/31/05): Assets, $110,976 (M); gifts received, $100,160; expenditures, $1,636,081; qualifying distributions, $1,633,427; giving activities include $1,632,779 for 6 grants (high: $1,000,000; low: $5,000).
Purpose and activities: Support for medical research.
Fields of interest: Hospitals (specialty); Genetics/birth defects research; Cancer research; Biomedicine research; Medical research.
Limitations: Applications not accepted. Giving on a national basis. No grants to individuals.

Application information: Contributes only to pre-selected organizations.
Trustees: Cheryl A. Lockton; John T. Lockton III.
EIN: 481135485

4858
R. A. Long Foundation

600 Plaza W. Bldg.
4600 Madison Ave.
Kansas City, MO   64112-3012   (816) 410-4600
Contact: James H. Bernard, Jr., Dir.

Incorporated in 1958 in MO.
Donors: Loula Long Combs†; Sally Long Ellis†; R.A. Long Ellis†.
Foundation type: Independent foundation.
Financial data (yr. ended 11/30/05): Assets, $7,525,060 (M); expenditures, $464,574; qualifying distributions, $408,924; giving activities include $329,436 for grants.
Purpose and activities: Giving limited to services for youth, including the areas of child welfare, recreation, rehabilitation, and education, all of which must be in the greater Kansas City, MO, area.
Fields of interest: Elementary/secondary education; Youth development, centers/clubs; Youth development, services; Children/youth, services; Youth, services.
Type of support: General/operating support; Capital campaigns; Building/renovation; Equipment; Program development; Seed money; Consulting services.
Limitations: Giving limited to the greater Kansas City, MO, area. No grants to individuals, or for endowment funds, research programs, scholarships, or fellowships; no loans.
Publications: Application guidelines.
Application information: Application form not required.
Initial approach: Letter or telephone
Copies of proposal: 1
Deadline(s): Mar. 15 and Sept. 15
Board meeting date(s): Spring and fall
Final notification: Within 1 week of board meeting
Directors: James H. Bernard, Jr.; Enid Chetham; Hayne Ellis III; Long Ellis, Jr.; Linna Place; James Pyle; Ann J. Thompson.
EIN: 446014081
Selected grants: The following grants were reported in 2004.
$12,900 to Independence Boulevard Christian Church, Kansas City, MO.
$10,000 to Camp for Kids, Kansas City, MO.
$10,000 to Metropolitan Community Colleges Foundation, Kansas City, MO.
$10,000 to Planned Parenthood of Kansas and Mid-Missouri, Kansas City, MO.
$9,700 to Bishop Ward High School, Kansas City, KS.
$7,500 to Southwest Boulevard Family Health Care, Kansas City, KS.
$7,000 to Boys and Girls Club of Greater Kansas City, Kansas City, KS.
$7,000 to Operation Breakthrough, Kansas City, MO.
$5,000 to Donnelly College, Kansas City, KS.
$5,000 to YMCA of Greater Kansas City, Kansas City, MO.

4859
Stanley and Lucy Lopata Foundation ✧

c/o Lopata, Flegel & Co., LLP
600 Mason Ridge Ctr. Dr., Ste. 100
St. Louis, MO 63141

Established in 1968.
Donors: Stanley Lopata†; Lucy Lopata; Lopata Charitable Lead Trust No. 4.
Foundation type: Independent foundation.
Financial data (yr. ended 12/31/05): Assets, $9,281,918 (M); gifts received, $57,840; expenditures, $360,254; qualifying distributions, $319,857; giving activities include $315,919 for 194 grants (high: $50,000; low: $25; average: $1,000–$25,000).
Purpose and activities: Giving primarily to Jewish agencies and temples; support also for the arts, health associations, and for children, youth, and social services.
Fields of interest: Performing arts, theater; Performing arts, opera; Arts; Higher education; Education; Botanical gardens; Reproductive health, family planning; Health organizations, association; Human services; Children/youth, services; Federated giving programs; Jewish federated giving programs; Jewish agencies & temples; Disabilities, people with.
Type of support: General/operating support; Annual campaigns; Capital campaigns; Endowments; Emergency funds; Program development.
Limitations: Applications not accepted. Giving primarily in St. Louis, MO. No grants to individuals.
Application information: Contributes only to pre-selected organizations.
    Board meeting date(s): June 15, Dec. 15, and as needed
Trustees: James R. Lopata; Lucy Lopata.
EIN: 436099972
Selected grants: The following grants were reported in 2005.
$25,000 to Churchill School and Center for Learning Disabilities, New York, NY.
$16,000 to United Way.
$10,000 to Repertory Theater, Nashville, TN.
$2,500 to Center of Creative Arts, Saint Louis, MO.
$2,500 to International Institute, Akron, OH.
$1,000 to Missouri Historical Society, Saint Louis, MO.
$1,000 to Scholarship Foundation of Saint Louis, Saint Louis, MO.
$450 to Springboard to Learning, Saint Louis, MO.
$250 to Our Little Haven, Saint Louis, MO.
$250 to Scholarship Foundation, Cherry Hill, NJ.

4860
Edward Mallinckrodt, Jr. Foundation

8050 Watson Rd., No. 231
St. Louis, MO 63119
Contact: Oliver M. Langenberg, Chair. and Treas.
Application address: 1 N. Jefferson Ave., St. Louis, MO 63103-2205

Incorporated in 1953 in MO.
Donor: Edward Mallinckrodt, Jr.†
Foundation type: Independent foundation.
Financial data (yr. ended 9/30/06): Assets, $42,467,674 (M); expenditures, $3,580,307; qualifying distributions, $3,327,728; giving activities include $3,327,728 for grants (high: $75,000; low: $50,000).
Purpose and activities: Grants largely for domestic biomedical education and research.

Fields of interest: Medical research, institute.
Type of support: Annual campaigns; Capital campaigns; Conferences/seminars; Scholarship funds; Research.
Limitations: Giving on a national basis. No grants to individuals directly.
Publications: Annual report.
Application information: Applications received directly from medical schools. Application form required.
    Initial approach: Letter (2-4 typewritten pages)
    Copies of proposal: 7
    Deadline(s): None
    Board meeting date(s): Feb. or Mar., June, and Sept.
    Final notification: 3 to 6 weeks
Officers and Directors:* Oliver M. Langenberg,* Chair. and Treas.; Thomas F. Deuel, M.D., Pres.; Tom Cori,* V.P.; Charles C. Allen, Jr.,* Secy.; Spencer Burke; Philip R. Dodge, M.D.; Stuart A. Kornfeld, M.D.
EIN: 436030295

4861
The May Department Stores Foundation ▼

(formerly The May Department Stores Company Foundation, Inc.)
611 Olive St.
St. Louis, MO 63101   (314) 342-6299
Contact: Deidre Burke, Coord.
FAX: (314) 342-4461;
E-mail: mayfoundation@may-co.com; URL: http://www.fds.com/community/corpgiving.asp

Incorporated in 1945 in NY.
Donor: The May Department Stores Co.
Foundation type: Company-sponsored foundation.
Financial data (yr. ended 1/31/05): Assets, $28,654,589 (M); gifts received, $16,729,190; expenditures, $15,008,974; qualifying distributions, $14,739,050; giving activities include $14,739,050 for 8,213+ grants (high: $1,165,000).
Purpose and activities: The foundation supports organizations involved with arts and culture, education, health, human services, and civic affairs.
Fields of interest: Arts; Education; Health care; Human services; Federated giving programs; Public affairs.
Type of support: General/operating support; Employee matching gifts.
Limitations: Giving on a national basis in areas of company operations; giving also to national organizations. No grants to individuals.
Publications: Corporate giving report (including application guidelines); Grants list.
Application information: Proposals should be submitted using organization letterhead. Application form not required.
    Initial approach: Mail proposal to nearest company division; mail proposal to foundation for national organizations
    Deadline(s): None
    Final notification: 4 to 6 weeks
Officers and Directors:* John L. Dunham,* Pres.; Jan R. Kniffen,* V.P. and Secy.-Treas.; Thomas D. Fingleton,* V.P.; John A. Sztukowski.
EIN: 431728079
Selected grants: The following grants were reported in 2005.
$1,165,000 to United Way of Greater Saint Louis, Saint Louis, MO. For general support.

$881,950 to United Way of Eastern New England, Attleboro, MA. For general support.
$505,253 to OASIS Institute, Saint Louis, MO. 2 grants: $252,625 (For general support), $252,628 (For general support).
$318,330 to National Merit Scholarship Corporation, Evanston, IL. For general support.
$200,000 to Saint Louis Symphony Orchestra, Saint Louis, MO. For general support.
$35,000 to David May Employees Trust Fund, Saint Louis, MO. For general support.
$15,000 to Beta Theta Pi Foundation, Oxford, OH. For general support.
$15,000 to Pacific Symphony Association, Santa Ana, CA. For general support.
$13,000 to Delta Sigma Theta Life Development Center, Los Angeles, CA. For general support.

4862
McDavid Dental Educational Trust ✧

(formerly G. N. and Edna McDavid Dental Education Trust)
c/o U.S. Bank, N.A.
P.O. Box 387
St. Louis, MO 63166
Application address: c/o University of Missouri of Kansas City, 4825 Troost Ave., Kansas City, MO 64110, tel.: (816) 932-4422; c/o St. Louis University, 3556 Caroline Mall, St. Louis, MO 63104, tel.: (314) 577-8186

Established in 1975 in MO.
Donor: G.N. McDavid†.
Foundation type: Independent foundation.
Financial data (yr. ended 12/31/04): Assets, $2,072,151 (M); expenditures, $553,209; qualifying distributions, $961,294; giving activities include $455,605 for 2 grants to individuals (high: $284,105; low: $171,500), and $458,395 for 70 loans to individuals (high: $15,000; low: $3,500).
Purpose and activities: Loans to students at two accredited MO dental schools.
Fields of interest: Dental care.
Type of support: Scholarships—to individuals; Student loans—to individuals.
Limitations: Giving limited to residents of Madison County, MO.
Application information: Application form required.
    Deadline(s): None
Trustee: U.S. Bank, N.A.
EIN: 436192984

4863
McDonnell Foundation, Inc. ✧

4909 Sunset Dr.
Kansas City, MO 64112-2309

Established in 1986 in MO.
Donors: Tom McDonnell; Jean McDonnell.
Foundation type: Independent foundation.
Financial data (yr. ended 12/31/05): Assets, $21,710,729 (M); gifts received, $1,282,272; expenditures, $730,209; qualifying distributions, $719,435; giving activities include $719,435 for 51 grants (high: $150,000; low: $35; average: $5,000–$50,000).
Fields of interest: Secondary school/education; Education; Human services; Family services; Roman Catholic agencies & churches.
Limitations: Applications not accepted. Giving primarily in KS and MO. No grants to individuals.

Application information: Contributes only to pre-selected organizations.
Officer and Directors:* Jean McDonnell,* Pres.; Mary C. Fielder; Tom McDonnell.
EIN: 431439173

4864
James S. McDonnell Foundation ▼
1034 S. Brentwood Blvd., Ste. 1850
St. Louis, MO 63117-1229 (314) 721-1532
FAX: (314) 721-7421; E-mail: info@jsmf.org;
URL: http://www.jsmf.org

Established in MO.
Foundation type: Independent foundation.
Financial data (yr. ended 12/31/05): Assets, $501,441,160 (M); expenditures, $18,487,364; qualifying distributions, $17,023,503; giving activities include $15,815,410 for 82 grants (high: $2,196,067; low: $2,542; average: $119,755–$566,540).
Purpose and activities: The 21st Century Science Initiative, the foundation's revised program and funding strategy, will award two types of grants in three program areas. The three program areas are Bridging Brain, Mind, and Behavior; Brain Cancer Research; and Studying Complex Systems.
Fields of interest: Cancer research; Brain research; Medical research; Science, research; Science.
Type of support: Research.
Limitations: Giving on a national and international basis.
Publications: Financial statement.
Application information: See foundation's Web site for application information, all proposals accepted electronically only.
Board meeting date(s): Varies
Officers and Directors:* John T. Bruer, Ph.D, Pres.; Susan M. Fitzpatrick, Ph.D., V.P.; James S. McDonnell III,* Secy.; John F. McDonnell,* Treas.; Jeffrey M. McDonnell,* Secy.-Treas.; Marcella M. Stevens.
EIN: 542074788

4865
The McGee Foundation
709 W. 50th St.
Kansas City, MO 64112-2315 (816) 842-0944
FAX: (816) 627-3441; Application address: c/o Whitney Gee, Dir., Community Investment, Greater Kansas City Community Foundation & Affiliated Trusts, 1055 Broadway, Ste. 130, Kansas City, MO 64105-1595; tel.: (816) 627-3441; e-mail: grants@gkccf.org (include "McGee" in the subject line)

Incorporated in 1951 in MO.
Donors: Joseph J. McGee†; Mrs. Joseph J. McGee†; Frank McGee†; Mrs. Frank McGee†; Louis B. McGee†; Old American Insurance Co.; Thomas McGee and Sons; Joseph J. McGee, Jr.†; Julie McGee; David McGee; Simon McGee.
Foundation type: Independent foundation.
Financial data (yr. ended 12/31/05): Assets, $13,743,858 (M); expenditures, $731,008; qualifying distributions, $638,127; giving activities include $610,000 for 27 grants (high: $50,000; low: $2,500).
Purpose and activities: The foundation uses its funds primarily for education, health, charitable, and religious agencies and institutions operated,

supervised or controlled by or in connection with the Roman Catholic Church. This includes any Roman Catholic non-profit organization which qualifies for exemption from federal income tax under Section 501(c)(3) of the Internal Revenue Code to the United States Catholic Conference by virtue of its listing in the current official Catholic Directory.
Fields of interest: Education; Health care; Human services.
Type of support: Capital campaigns; Equipment; Debt reduction.
Limitations: Giving limited to the greater bi-state Kansas City area. No support for arts and cultural activities, or for charter schools, civic organizations, economic or neighborhood development, individual churches or diocesan schools, information/referral programs, local affiliates of national disease organizations, regranting organizations, historic preservation or for public schools or taxpayer supported institutions. No grants to individuals, or for annual campaigns, charitable advertising, compensation for specific positions, scholarly research, conferences and seminars, endowments, fund raisers, or for multi-year grants and United appeals.
Publications: Application guidelines.
Application information: Applications are available on http://www.gkccf.org in the "Grant Information" section. Application form required.
Initial approach: Via e-mail is preferable, otherwise by letter
Copies of proposal: 1
Deadline(s): Mar. 31 and Sept. 29
Board meeting date(s): June and Dec.
Final notification: Varies
Officers and Directors:* Thomas R. McGee, Jr.,* Pres.; Sheila M. Lillis,* V.P. and Secy.; Simon P. McGee,* V.P. and Treas.; Thomas F. McGee,* V.P.; Virginia L. Coppinger; B. Joseph Duffy III; Robert A. Long; John R. McGee; Clyde F. Wendel.
Number of staff: None.
EIN: 446006285

4866
MFA Foundation
201 Ray Young Dr.
Columbia, MO 65201
Contact: Larna Lavelle, Secy.-Treas.
URL: http://www.mfaincorporated.com/web/guest/youth/scholarships

Established in 1958 in MO.
Donors: Robert O. Wurmb; MFA Inc.; MFA Oil Co.
Foundation type: Company-sponsored foundation.
Financial data (yr. ended 6/30/06): Assets, $12,486,544 (M); gifts received, $237,132; expenditures, $536,642; qualifying distributions, $536,642; giving activities include $58,900 for 22 grants (high: $5,000; low: $1,000), and $426,410 for 295 grants to individuals (high: $1,500; low: $100).
Purpose and activities: The foundation supports organizations involved with higher education, youth, and senior citizens and awards college scholarships to high school seniors.
Fields of interest: Higher education; Youth development.
Type of support: General/operating support; Scholarships—to individuals.
Limitations: Giving primarily in areas of company operations, with emphasis on MO.
Publications: Financial statement; Informational brochure.

Application information: Unsolicited requests for grants are not accepted.
Initial approach: Contact high school guidance counselor for application form for scholarships
Deadline(s): Mar. 15 for scholarships
Board meeting date(s): June and Nov.
Officers and Directors:* Don Copenhaver,* Pres.; Jerry Taylor, V.P.; Larna Lavelle, Secy.-Treas.; Ken Caspall; Dale Creach; J. Brian Griffith; John Percival; Phil Perkins; Janice Schuerman; Bill Streeter; Ernie Verslues.
EIN: 436026877

4867
Millstone Foundation ◇
7701 Forsyth Blvd., Ste. 925
St. Louis, MO 63105-1842
Contact: I.E. Millstone, Pres; Colleen Millstone, Dir.

Incorporated in 1955 in MO.
Donors: I.E. Millstone; Goldie G. Millstone†.
Foundation type: Independent foundation.
Financial data (yr. ended 5/31/05): Assets, $15,671,294 (M); expenditures, $1,205,993; qualifying distributions, $1,143,036; giving activities include $1,121,524 for 158 grants (high: $216,800; low: $100).
Purpose and activities: Giving primarily for higher education and to Jewish organizations. Most giving is in the form of on-going support. Limited new grantmaking.
Fields of interest: Higher education; Education; Human services; Jewish federated giving programs; Jewish agencies & temples.
International interests: Israel.
Type of support: General/operating support; Continuing support; Annual campaigns; Emergency funds; Scholarship funds; Research.
Limitations: Giving primarily in St. Louis, MO. No grants to individuals; no loans.
Application information: Funds for new grantmaking are extremely limited. Application form not required.
Initial approach: Letter
Copies of proposal: 1
Deadline(s): None
Board meeting date(s): Monthly
Final notification: Within 6-8 weeks
Officers and Directors:* I.E. Millstone,* Pres.; Robert Millstone,* V.P. and Secy.; Thomas E. Kuhn, V.P. and Treas.; Colleen Millstone.
Number of staff: 2 part-time professional.
EIN: 436027373
Selected grants: The following grants were reported in 2004.
$269,167 to Jewish Federation of Saint Louis, Saint Louis, MO.
$100,200 to United Hebrew Congregation, Saint Louis, MO.
$61,666 to American Friends of the Hebrew University, New York, NY.
$50,000 to Hebrew Union College-Jewish Institute of Religion, Cincinnati, OH.
$36,750 to United Way of Greater Saint Louis, Saint Louis, MO.
$29,000 to Saint Louis Science Center, Saint Louis, MO.
$22,000 to Contemporary Art Museum Saint Louis, Saint Louis, MO.
$10,000 to Saint Louis Symphony Orchestra, Saint Louis, MO.
$5,000 to Citizens for Home Rule, Saint Louis, MO.
$2,100 to American Jewish Committee, Saint Louis, MO.

4868
Monsanto Fund ▼ ◆
800 N. Lindbergh Blvd.
St. Louis, MO 63167 (314) 694-4391
Contact: Deborah J. Patterson, Pres.
FAX: (314) 694-7658;
E-mail: monsanto.fund@monsanto.com; Additional contacts: Augusta, GA: Robert E. Ford, E-mail: robert.e.ford@monsanto.com, Soda Springs, ID: Trent L. Clark, E-mail: trent.l.clark@monsanto.com, Muscatine, IA: Christina L. Boar, E-mail: christina.l.boar@monsanto.com, Luling, LA: Dione A. Davenport, E-mail: dione.a.davenport@monsanto.com; Application address for equipment donations: Lisa Bannon-Bergmann, Mgr., Contribs., 800 N. Lindbergh, A2SA, St. Louis, MO 63167, FAX: (314) 694-7658; URL: http://www.monsantofund.org/

Incorporated in 1964 in MO as successor to the Monsanto Charitable Trust.
Donors: Monsanto Co.; Olympia Industries, Inc.
Foundation type: Company-sponsored foundation.
Financial data (yr. ended 12/31/05): Assets, $3,471,805 (M); gifts received, $1,366,588; expenditures, $13,510,112; qualifying distributions, $13,482,820; giving activities include $12,571,307 for 218 grants (high: $1,325,018; low: $200), and $812,534 for 4,550 employee matching gifts.
Purpose and activities: The fund supports fire departments and organizations involved with arts and culture, education, the environment, animals and wildlife, agriculture, nutrition, ag safety for young people, human services, and economically disadvantaged children.
Fields of interest: Arts education; Arts; Elementary/secondary education; Education; Environment, public education; Environment, water pollution; Environment, natural resources; Environment, land resources; Environmental education; Environment; Animals/wildlife, preservation/protection; Agriculture/food, research; Agriculture/food, public education; Agriculture; Nutrition; Disasters, fire prevention/control; Safety, education; Human services; Science, formal/general education; Children; Youth; Economically disadvantaged.
International interests: Africa; Asia; Brazil; Canada; Europe; Latin America; Mexico; Oceania.
Type of support: Equipment; Program development; Conferences/seminars; Curriculum development; Research; Program evaluation; Employee matching gifts; Donated equipment; In-kind gifts; Matching/challenge support.
Limitations: Giving on a national and international basis in areas of company operations, with emphasis on Augusta, GA, Soda Springs, ID, Muscatine, IA, Luling, LA, and the greater St. Louis, MO, area and in Africa, Asia, Brazil, Canada, Europe, Latin America, Mexico, and Oceania; giving also to statewide, regional, national, and international organizations. No support for start-up organizations, fraternal, labor, or veterans' organizations not of direct benefit to the entire community, religious, politically partisan, or similar organizations, or discriminatory organizations. No grants to individuals, or for debt reduction, benefits, dinners, or advertisements, endowments, marketing, or projects in which Monsanto Company has a financial interest or could derive a financial benefit through cash or rights to intellectual property; no donations of printers, computer software, copiers, scanners, or computers.
Publications: Application guidelines; Grants list.

Application information: Proposals for national organizations and organizations located in the greater St. Louis, MO, area should be no longer than 2 to 3 double-spaced, single-sided pages. Proposals for U.S.-based organizations located outside Augusta, GA, Soda Springs, ID, Muscatine, IA, Luling, LA, and the greater St. Louis, MO, area should be no longer than 5 double-spaced, single-sided pages. Proposals for U.S.-based international organizations and organizations located outside the U.S. should be no longer than 6 single-sided pages. Extraneous proposal materials are not encouraged. An application form will be sent following receipt of an eligible proposal for national organizations and organizations located in the greater St. Louis, MO, area. Contributions to U.S.-based organizations located outside Augusta, GA, Soda Springs, ID, Muscatine, IA, Luling, LA, and the greater St. Louis, MO, area generally do not exceed $20,000. Unsolicited requests for equipment donations from organizations located outside the greater St. Louis, MO, area are not accepted. Equipment donations are limited to 8 items per organization. Proposals for equipment donations should be submitted using organization letterhead. Visit Web site for nearest application address for U.S.-based international organizations and organizations located outside the U.S. Unsolicited requests from human services organizations located in the U.S. are not accepted. An application form is required for organizations located outside the U.S.
Initial approach: Mail proposal to fund for national organizations and organizations located in the greater St. Louis, MO, area; contact nearest company facility for application information for organizations in Augusta, GA, Soda Springs, ID, Muscatine, IA, and Luling, LA
Copies of proposal: 1
Deadline(s): Jan. 1 for June and July 1 for Dec. for national organizations and organizations located in the greater St. Louis, MO, area
Board meeting date(s): Twice per year
Final notification: 4 to 8 weeks for national organizations and organizations located in the greater St. Louis, MO, area; June or July and Dec. or Jan. for U.S.-based international organizations and organizations located outside the U.S.
Officers and Directors:* Carl M. Casale,* Chair.; Deborah J. Patterson, Pres.; Sonya Meyers Davis, Secy.; Robert A. Paley, Treas.; Brett D. Begemann; Janet Holloway; Kathleen L. Klepfer; Gerald A. Steiner.
Number of staff: 1 full-time professional; 1 part-time professional; 1 full-time support; 1 part-time support.
EIN: 436044736
Selected grants: The following grants were reported in 2005.
$1,325,018 to Donald Danforth Plant Science Center, Saint Louis, MO.
$1,000,000 to Friends of the World Food Programme, DC.
$861,582 to Washington University, Saint Louis, MO.
$750,000 to American Red Cross, Saint Louis, MO.
$415,000 to United Way of Greater Saint Louis, Saint Louis, MO.
$407,000 to Audubon Society, National, Ivyland, PA.
$300,000 to Saint Louis Symphony Orchestra, Saint Louis, MO.

$62,500 to European Development Corporation, Amsterdam, Netherlands. .
$52,266 to Centro Educacional de Tecnologia em Administracao (CETEAD), Brazil. .
$37,080 to Academy of Science of Saint Louis, Saint Louis, MO.

4869
Johnny Morris Foundation ◆
c/o Sportsman Park Ctr.
2500 E. Kearney St.
Springfield, MO 65803-5048

Established in MO.
Donors: Johnny L. Morris; Bass Pro Trademark, LP; Bass Pro, Inc.
Foundation type: Independent foundation.
Financial data (yr. ended 12/31/05): Assets, $29,552 (M); gifts received, $1,765,996; expenditures, $1,986,435; qualifying distributions, $1,985,000; giving activities include $1,985,000 for grants.
Purpose and activities: Giving primarily for wildlife and the environment; support also for youth services.
Fields of interest: Animals/wildlife, preservation/protection; Youth, services.
Limitations: Applications not accepted. Giving on a national basis, with some emphasis on Washington, DC, IN, MO, and VA. No grants to individuals.
Application information: Contributes only to pre-selected organizations.
Officers: Johnny L. Morris, Pres.; Susie Henry, V.P.; Joe C. Greene, Secy.
EIN: 431512191

4870
Musgrave Foundation
1 Corporate Centre
1949 E. Sunshine St., Ste. 1-130
Springfield, MO 65804-1602 (417) 841-4698
Contact: Jerry L. Redfern, Mgr.
FAX: (417) 882-2529;
E-mail: jredfern@musgravefoundation.org; Additional tel.: (417) 882-9090; URL: http://www.musgravefoundation.org

Established in 1983 in MO.
Donor: Jeannette Musgrave.
Foundation type: Independent foundation.
Financial data (yr. ended 6/30/05): Assets, $13,154,927 (M); expenditures, $933,803; qualifying distributions, $652,300; giving activities include $652,300 for 46 grants (high: $50,000; low: $500).
Purpose and activities: Giving primarily for human services.
Fields of interest: Arts; Education, fund raising/fund distribution; Higher education; Nursing school/education; Nursing care; Boys & girls clubs; Boy scouts; Human services; Salvation Army; Children/youth, services; Community development; Christian agencies & churches; Economically disadvantaged.
Type of support: Program development; General/operating support; Continuing support; Annual campaigns; Capital campaigns; Building/renovation; Equipment; Scholarship funds; Matching/challenge support.
Limitations: Giving limited to the greater Springfield, MO, area. No grants to individuals.

Application information: See foundation Web site for application information and application form. Application form required.

Initial approach: Contact foundation offices for submission form
Copies of proposal: 5
Deadline(s): May 31
Board meeting date(s): Quarterly, with budget meeting in June
Final notification: Spring & fall

Officers: Charles Fuller, Chair.; Jerry L. Redfern, Mgr.

Grant Committee Members: Rob Baird; Junior Cline; Tom Slaight; Neil Wortley.

Trustee: U.S. Bank, N.A.

Number of staff: 1 part-time professional.

EIN: 431304514

Selected grants: The following grants were reported in 2004.

$52,000 to Springfield Community Center, Springfield, MO.

$30,000 to Kitchen, Inc., Springfield, MO. For general operating support.

$22,500 to Boys and Girls Town of Missouri, Springfield, MO.

$12,500 to Drury University, Springfield, MO. For capital improvements.

$8,000 to Developmental Center of the Ozarks, Springfield, MO.

$7,000 to Special Olympics, Springfield, MO.

$5,300 to Big Brothers/Big Sisters of Springfield, Springfield, MO. For general operating support.

$5,000 to Child Advocacy Center, Springfield, MO.

$3,500 to American Red Cross, Springfield, MO.

$2,500 to Girl Scouts of the U.S.A., Springfield, MO.

4871
Margaret Irene Taylor Nelson and Mary Nelson Family Foundation, Inc. ✧ ☆

P.O. Box 6045
Chesterfield, MO 63006 (314) 542-9660
Contact: Herm Shields, Secy.-Treas.

Established in 1999 in MO.
Foundation type: Independent foundation.
Financial data (yr. ended 9/30/05): Assets, $1,507,546 (M); expenditures, $365,846; qualifying distributions, $362,600; giving activities include $362,600 for grants.
Purpose and activities: Giving primarily for evangelism.
Fields of interest: Hospitals (general); Christian agencies & churches.
Limitations: Giving in the U.S., with emphasis on the greater St. Louis, MO, area.
Application information:
Initial approach: Letter
Deadline(s): June 30
Officers and Board Members:* Barclay Nelson, Chair. and Pres.; Herm Shields,* Secy.-Treas.; Susan Nelson.
EIN: 431864378

4872
Nestle Purina PetCare Trust Fund ✧

(formerly Ralston Purina Trust Fund)
c/o Nestle Purina PetCare Community Affairs
Checkerboard Sq., 1C
St. Louis, MO 63164 (314) 982-1607
Contact: Kasey Bergh, Mgr., Community Affairs

E-mail: donations@purina.com; URL: http://www.purina.com/company/CommunityInv/Index.aspx

Trust established in 1951 in MO.
Donors: Ralston Purina Co.; Nestle Purina PetCare Co.
Foundation type: Company-sponsored foundation.
Financial data (yr. ended 12/31/05): Assets, $16,731,167 (M); expenditures, $959,816; qualifying distributions, $901,200; giving activities include $901,200 for 27 grants (high: $540,000; low: $2,500).
Purpose and activities: The foundation supports organizations involved with arts and culture, education, health, and human services.
Fields of interest: Elementary/secondary education; Animal welfare; Health care; Children; Youth; Economically disadvantaged.
Type of support: General/operating support; Continuing support; Annual campaigns; Capital campaigns; Building/renovation; Emergency funds; Program development; Employee matching gifts.
Limitations: Giving primarily in Flagstaff, AZ, Maricopa, CA, Denver, CO, Atlanta, GA, Clinton, Davenport, and Fort Dodge, IA, Bloomfield, Cape Girardeau, Springfield, St. Joseph, and the greater St. Louis, MO, area, Crete, NE, Dunkirk, NY, Zanesville, OH, Oklahoma City, OK, Allentown and Mechanicsburg, PA, King William, VA, Hager City and Jefferson, WI, and Wierton, WV, with emphasis on the greater St. Louis area. No support for veterans' or fraternal organizations not of direct benefit to the entire community. No grants to individuals, or for religious or politically partisan purposes, investment funds, tickets for dinners, benefits, exhibits, conferences, sports events, or other short-term activities, advertisements, debt reduction, or post-event support; no loans.
Publications: Application guidelines.
Application information: Application form not required.
Initial approach: Proposal to foundation for organizations located in the greater St. Louis, MO, area; proposal to nearest company facility for organizations located outside the greater St. Louis, MO, area
Copies of proposal: 1
Deadline(s): None
Board meeting date(s): Quarterly
Final notification: Up to 2 to 3 months
Trustees: Kevin Berryman; Susan Denigan; James Ryan.
Number of staff: 1 part-time professional; 1 part-time support.
EIN: 431209652
Selected grants: The following grants were reported in 2003.
$175,000 to Tony La Russas Animal Rescue Foundation, Walnut Creek, CA.
$127,500 to United Way of Greater Saint Louis, Saint Louis, MO.
$50,000 to Cardinal Ritter College Prep, Saint Louis, MO.
$10,000 to Magic House, Saint Louis, MO.
$8,250 to Girls Inc., Saint Louis, MO.
$7,500 to Mentor Saint Louis, Saint Louis, MO.
$7,500 to YMCA of Greater Saint Louis, Saint Louis, MO.
$5,000 to American Red Cross, Saint Louis, MO.
$5,000 to Brooks Memorial Hospital, Dunkirk, NY.
$2,500 to Franciscan University of Steubenville, Steubenville, OH.

4873
Miller Nichols Charitable Foundation ✧

400 W. 49th Terr., Ste. 2176
Kansas City, MO 64112

Established in 1960.
Donor: Miller Nichols†.
Foundation type: Independent foundation.
Financial data (yr. ended 12/31/05): Assets, $22,870,155 (M); expenditures, $1,394,563; qualifying distributions, $1,311,405; giving activities include $1,279,100 for 44 grants (high: $125,000; low: $500).
Purpose and activities: Giving primarily for hospitals, federated giving programs and arts and cultural programs.
Fields of interest: Museums; Performing arts, theater; Performing arts, orchestra (symphony); Hospitals (general); Federated giving programs.
Limitations: Applications not accepted. Giving primarily in Kansas City, MO. No grants to individuals.
Application information: Contributes only to pre-selected organizations.
Officers: Jeannette Nichols, Pres.; Kay Callison, V.P.; Terrence P. Dunn, Secy.
EIN: 431567351
Selected grants: The following grants were reported in 2003.
$857,295 to Nelson-Atkins Museum of Art, Kansas City, MO. 3 grants: $282,551 (For grant made in form of stock), $498,584 (For grant made in form of stock), $76,160 (For grant made in form of stock).
$500,000 to Liberty Memorial Association, Kansas City, MO.
$478,210 to Childrens Mercy Hospital, Kansas City, MO. 2 grants: $216,573, $261,637 (For grant made in form of stock).
$222,643 to Saint Lukes Hospital Foundation, Kansas City, MO. 2 grants: $125,000, $97,643 (For grant made in form of stock).
$100,000 to Kansas City Art Institute, Kansas City, MO.
$95,234 to Kansas City Ballet Association, Kansas City, MO. For grant made in form of stock.

4874
The Oceanic Heritage Foundation ✧

211 N. Broadway, Ste. 3600
St. Louis, MO 63102-2750

Established in 1998 in DE and MO.
Foundation type: Independent foundation.
Financial data (yr. ended 12/31/05): Assets, $7,817,321 (M); gifts received, $650,000; expenditures, $694,455; qualifying distributions, $540,346; giving activities include $505,768 for 47 grants (high: $50,000; low: $1,500).
Purpose and activities: Giving only to organizations deemed worthy by the foundation.
Fields of interest: Arts; Higher education.
Limitations: Applications not accepted. Giving primarily on a national basis. No grants to individuals.
Application information: Contributes only to pre-selected organizations.
EIN: 431836518

4875
Tom W. and Jeanne H. Olofson Foundation ◇
400 W. 49th Terr., Ste. 2136
Kansas City, MO 64112

Established in 2001 in MO.
Donors: Tom H. Olofson; Jeanne H. Olofson.
Foundation type: Independent foundation.
Financial data (yr. ended 12/31/05): Assets, $1,962,360 (M); gifts received, $855,000; expenditures, $851,478; qualifying distributions, $850,822; giving activities include $850,000 for 2 grants (high: $600,000; low: $250,000).
Fields of interest: Higher education, university; Protestant agencies & churches.
Limitations: Applications not accepted. Giving on a national basis. No grants to individuals.
Application information: Contributes only to pre-selected organizations.
Officers: Tom W. Olofson, Chair.; Jeanne H. Olofson, Pres.
Directors: Christopher E. Olofson; Scott W. Olofson.
EIN: 431945167

4876
Oppenstein Brothers Foundation ◇
922 Walnut St., Ste. 200
Kansas City, MO 64106-1809 (816) 234-8671
Contact: Sheila K. Rice, Prog. Off.

Established in 1975 in MO.
Donor: Michael Oppenstein†.
Foundation type: Independent foundation.
Financial data (yr. ended 3/31/05): Assets, $33,392,608 (M); expenditures, $1,349,949; qualifying distributions, $1,158,351; giving activities include $1,111,400 for 82 grants (high: $75,000; low: $2,000).
Purpose and activities: Grants primarily for education (excluding scholarship assistance), arts (primarily educational programming for children), health services (programs that promote wellness), and social services.
Fields of interest: Arts; Education; Health care; Human services.
Type of support: General/operating support; Capital campaigns; Building/renovation; Equipment; Emergency funds; Program development; Seed money; Curriculum development; Technical assistance.
Limitations: Giving limited to the 5-county metropolitan Kansas City, MO, area only. No grants to individuals, or for annual campaigns, building funds or expansion.
Publications: Informational brochure (including application guidelines); Multi-year report.
Application information: Application guidelines available on request. Application form not required.
Initial approach: Telephone or letter
Copies of proposal: 1
Deadline(s): 3 weeks prior to board meetings
Board meeting date(s): Every other month
Final notification: 2 to 4 months
Disbursement Committee: Warren W. Weaver, Chair.; Mary Bloch; Laura Kemper Fields; Roger T. Hurwitz; Estelle Sosland.
Trustee: Commerce Bank, N.A.
EIN: 436203035
Selected grants: The following grants were reported in 2006.

$100,000 to Jewish Federation of Greater Kansas City, Overland Park, KS. 2 grants: $50,000 each
$75,000 to Saint Lukes Hospital Foundation, Kansas City, MO.
$30,000 to Kansas City Repertory Theater, Kansas City, MO.
$29,000 to Southwest Boulevard Family Health Care, Kansas City, KS.
$25,000 to Central City School Fund, Kansas City, MO.
$25,000 to Child Advocacy Services Center, Kansas City, MO.
$12,000 to Kansas City Art Institute, Kansas City, MO.
$10,000 to Jewish Family and Childrens Services, Overland Park, KS.
$10,000 to Youth Symphony Association of Kansas City, Prairie Village, KS.

4877
Orscheln Industries Foundation, Inc. ◇
P.O. Box 280
Moberly, MO 65270 (660) 263-4377
Contact: R. Brent Bradshaw

Established in 1968 in MO.
Donors: ADEO, LLC; AGAO, LLC; Orscheln Co.
Foundation type: Company-sponsored foundation.
Financial data (yr. ended 9/30/05): Assets, $17,476,639 (M); gifts received, $4,517,416; expenditures, $1,026,008; qualifying distributions, $948,731; giving activities include $828,103 for 111+ grants (high: $88,119), and $120,028 for grants to individuals.
Purpose and activities: The foundation supports organizations involved with arts and culture, education, health, cancer research, human services, community development, and Catholicism.
Fields of interest: Performing arts, theater; Arts; Secondary school/education; Higher education; Education; Health care; Cancer research; Boys & girls clubs; Children/youth, services; Human services; Community development; Federated giving programs; Roman Catholic agencies & churches.
Type of support: General/operating support; Continuing support; Annual campaigns; Building/ renovation; Employee-related scholarships.
Limitations: Giving primarily in MO.
Publications: Application guidelines; Informational brochure; Program policy statement.
Application information: Application form required.
Initial approach: Contact foundation for application form
Officers and Directors:* W.L. Orscheln,* Chair., V.P., and Treas.; D.W. Orscheln,* Pres.; James L. O'Loughlin, Sr. V.P., Secy., and Genl. Counsel; Linda M. Mustoe, V.P. and Genl. Counsel; Brian K. Habermehl, V.P.; Phillip A. Orscheln,* V.P.; Barbara A. Westhues,* Exec. Dir.; W.C. Orscheln.
EIN: 237115623

4878
The William R. Orthwein, Jr. & Laura Rand Orthwein Foundation ◇ ☆
c/o U.S. Bank N.A.
P.O. Box 387
St. Louis, MO 63166

Donors: William R. Orthwein; Laura R. Orthwein.
Foundation type: Independent foundation.

Financial data (yr. ended 11/30/05): Assets, $35,276,222 (M); gifts received, $98,082; expenditures, $1,694,516; qualifying distributions, $1,474,061; giving activities include $1,450,000 for 23 grants (high: $315,000; low: $4,350).
Fields of interest: Elementary/secondary education; Higher education; Hospitals (general).
Limitations: Applications not accepted. Giving primarily in St. Louis, MO. No grants to individuals.
Application information: Contributes only to pre-selected organizations.
Trustees: Nettie Orthwein Dodge; Nina Orthwein Durham; Stephen C. Jones; U.S. Bank, N.A.
EIN: 200257512

4879
The Pearl Foundation ◇
P.O. Box 4572
Springfield, MO 65808-4572

Established in 2000.
Donor: Eddina F. Mackey.
Foundation type: Independent foundation.
Financial data (yr. ended 3/31/06): Assets, $6,642,010 (M); expenditures, $349,376; qualifying distributions, $323,669; giving activities include $323,669 for 48 grants (high: $50,000; low: $100).
Purpose and activities: Giving primarily for human services, and to Christian and Protestant churches.
Fields of interest: Health organizations, association; Human services; Children/youth, services; Federated giving programs; Christian agencies & churches; Protestant agencies & churches.
Limitations: Giving primarily in Monett, MO.
Trustees: Robert J. Helm; Dayton Mackey; Eddina F. Mackey.
EIN: 431889713
Selected grants: The following grants were reported in 2003.
$50,000 to Boys and Girls Clubs of Springfield, Springfield, MO.
$30,000 to Kitchen, Inc., Springfield, MO.
$25,000 to Fellowship of Christian Athletes, Springfield, MO. 2 grants: $15,000 (For summer camps), $10,000.
$20,383 to Make-A-Wish Foundation of Missouri, Springfield, MO. 2 grants: $12,000, $8,383 (For summer wishes).
$5,000 to Convoy of Hope, Springfield, MO. For operating support.
$5,000 to Crosslines, Monett, MO.
$5,000 to Springfield Public Schools Foundation, Springfield, MO. For operating support.
$1,086 to Lester E. Cox Medical Centers, Springfield, MO.

4880
Pershing Charitable Trust ◇
6419 Ellenwood Ave.
St. Louis, MO 63105-2228
Contact: Oliver M. Langenberg, Pres.

Established in 1968 in MO.
Donors: Oliver M. Langenberg; Mary B. Langenberg.
Foundation type: Independent foundation.
Financial data (yr. ended 9/30/05): Assets, $9,668,446 (M); expenditures, $490,895; qualifying distributions, $481,500; giving activities

include $481,500 for 57 grants (high: $50,000; low: $1,000).

Purpose and activities: Giving primarily for education, and human services; funding also for a botanical garden.

Fields of interest: Media/communications; Arts; Elementary/secondary education; Higher education; Botanical gardens; Human services; Children/youth, services.

Type of support: General/operating support; Annual campaigns; Capital campaigns; Emergency funds; Program development; Seed money; Curriculum development; Scholarship funds; Research; Scholarships—to individuals.

Limitations: Giving primarily in St. Louis, MO.

Application information: Application form not required.

   Initial approach: Letter
   Copies of proposal: 1
   Deadline(s): None

Officers: Oliver M. Langenberg, Pres.; Mary B. Langenberg, Treas.

EIN: 436103545

Selected grants: The following grants were reported in 2005.

$50,000 to Missouri Botanical Garden, Saint Louis, MO.

$50,000 to Princeton University, Princeton, NJ.

$25,000 to Loyola Academy of Saint Louis, Saint Louis, MO.

$16,000 to United Way of Greater Saint Louis, Saint Louis, MO.

$15,000 to American Red Cross.

$15,000 to Chautauqua Foundation, Chautauqua, NY.

$10,000 to Salvation Army.

$10,000 to Scholarship Foundation, Cherry Hill, NJ.

$5,000 to Saint Patrick Center, Saint Louis, MO.

$3,500 to Crossroads School, Saint Louis, MO.

4881
Pershing Place Foundation ✧

c/o William Jochens, Greensfelder, Hemker & Gale
10 S. Broadway
St. Louis, MO   63102

Established in 1998 in MO.

Donor: John D. Weil.

Foundation type: Independent foundation.

Financial data (yr. ended 12/31/05): Assets, $8,868,006 (M); expenditures, $438,970; qualifying distributions, $416,640; giving activities include $416,640 for 26 grants (high: $149,800; low: $40; average: $1,000–$50,000).

Fields of interest: Museums (art); Performing arts, theater; Arts; Elementary/secondary education; Education, special; Higher education, college; Environment, natural resources; Reproductive health, family planning; Human services; Federated giving programs; Jewish agencies & temples.

Limitations: Applications not accepted. Giving primarily in St. Louis, MO. No grants to individuals.

Application information: Contributes only to pre-selected organizations.

Director: William Jochens.

Trustees: Anabeth Calkins; Joseph D. Lehrer; John D. Weil.

EIN: 436795985

Selected grants: The following grants were reported in 2004.

$129,200 to Washington University, Saint Louis, MO.

$109,217 to Saint Louis Art Museum, Saint Louis, MO.

$55,100 to Metro Theater Company, Saint Louis, MO.

$50,000 to Central Institute for the Deaf, Saint Louis, MO.

$5,000 to New City School, Saint Louis, MO.

$4,500 to Contemporary Art Museum Saint Louis, Saint Louis, MO.

$1,000 to Amherst College, Amherst, MA.

$1,000 to Missouri Historical Society, Saint Louis, MO.

$500 to American Federation of Arts, New York, NY.

$150 to Craft Alliance, Saint Louis, MO.

4882
Pettus Foundation

(formerly James T. Pettus, Jr. Foundation)
c/o Finch Assocs.
1175 Mill Crossing Dr., No. 100
Creve Coeur, MO   63141   (314) 605-6430
Contact: James A. Finch III, Managing Tr.
E-mail: jimfinch@finchassociates.net

Established in 1960 in MO.

Donor: James T. Pettus Jr. Rev. Trust.

Foundation type: Independent foundation.

Financial data (yr. ended 12/31/05): Assets, $20,469,740 (M); expenditures, $1,252,658; qualifying distributions, $1,167,655; giving activities include $1,085,000 for 122 grants (high: $55,000; low: $1,000).

Purpose and activities: Giving primarily for children at risk, and training and support for under or unemployed.

Fields of interest: Child development, education; Education; Employment; Human services; Children/youth, services; Child development, services; Disabilities, people with.

Type of support: General/operating support; Continuing support; Scholarship funds.

Limitations: Giving primarily in HI and St. Louis, MO. No grants for capital campaigns.

Application information: Rarely funds new applicants; all new applications limited to HI and St. Louis MO. Application form not required.

   Initial approach: Letter
   Copies of proposal: 2
   Deadline(s): None
   Final notification: Within 90 days

Trustees: James A. Finch III, Managing Tr.; Lisa Hamilton; The Northern Trust Co.

Number of staff: 1 part-time professional.

EIN: 436029569

Selected grants: The following grants were reported in 2004.

$35,500 to Saint Louis Public Schools Foundation, Saint Louis, MO.

$30,000 to Holy Nativity School, Honolulu, HI.

$20,500 to Palama Settlement, Honolulu, HI.

$15,000 to Paraquad, Saint Louis, MO.

$15,000 to Planned Parenthood of Saint Louis, Saint Louis, MO.

$10,000 to Barnes-Jewish Hospital Foundation, Saint Louis, MO.

$10,000 to Bridges Project for Education, Taos, NM.

$10,000 to Cardinal Glennon Childrens Hospital, Saint Louis, MO.

$10,000 to Family Support Network, Saint Louis, MO.

$8,500 to Brother Benno Foundation, Oceanside, CA.

4883
Ed and H. Pillsbury Foundation ✧

10702 Manchester Rd., Ste. 10
St. Louis, MO   63122
Contact: Mr. Joyce S. Pillsbury, Pres.

Established in 1995 in MO.

Foundation type: Independent foundation.

Financial data (yr. ended 12/31/03): Assets, $6,380,737 (M); expenditures, $479,466; qualifying distributions, $458,087; giving activities include $449,060 for 19 grants (high: $255,000; low: $280).

Fields of interest: Arts; Higher education; Human services; Christian agencies & churches.

Type of support: General/operating support; Continuing support; Emergency funds; Matching/challenge support.

Limitations: Applications not accepted. Giving on a national basis. No grants to individuals.

Application information: Contributes only to pre-selected organizations.

   Board meeting date(s): Jan.

Officers and Board Members:* Mr. Joyce S. Pillsbury,* Pres.; William E. Pillsbury,* V.P.; Linda Roos,* Secy.-Treas.; Ruth Lister; John Pillsbury; Nancy Pillsbury Shirley; Mary Pillsbury Wainwright.

EIN: 431699917

Selected grants: The following grants were reported in 2003.

$255,000 to Missouri Baptist College, Saint Louis, MO.

$50,000 to Missouri Baptist Childrens Home, Bridgeton, MO.

$40,000 to Third Baptist Church, Saint Louis, MO.

$11,000 to North Side Team Ministry of Saint Louis, Saint Louis, MO.

$10,375 to Leukemia & Lymphoma Society, Saint Louis, MO.

$8,840 to National Right to Work Legal Defense and Education Foundation, Springfield, VA.

$5,340 to World Bible Translation Center, Fort Worth, TX.

$5,000 to Saint Louis Art Museum, Saint Louis, MO.

$3,000 to Navigators, The, Colorado Springs, CO.

$2,950 to Missouri Mansion Preservation, Jefferson City, MO.

4884
Harriet Pillsbury Foundation ✧

(formerly William Pillsbury Foundation)
10702 Manchester Rd., Ste. 10
St. Louis, MO   63122

Established in MO in 1995.

Foundation type: Independent foundation.

Financial data (yr. ended 12/31/03): Assets, $10,220,969 (M); expenditures, $621,599; qualifying distributions, $586,790; giving activities include $571,700 for 17 grants (high: $345,000; low: $200).

Fields of interest: Higher education, college; Christian agencies & churches.

Type of support: General/operating support; Continuing support; Capital campaigns; Building/renovation; Program development.

Limitations: Applications not accepted. Giving primarily in MO. No grants to individuals.

Application information: Contributes only to pre-selected organizations. Unsolicited requests for funds not accepted.

   Board meeting date(s): Jan.

Officers and Board Members:* Mr. Joyce S. Pillsbury,* V.P.; Linda Roos,* Secy.-Treas.; Douglas Copeland; John Pillsbury; Ruth Pillsbury; Arthur D. Wainwright.
EIN: 431699919

4885
PMJ Foundation ◇ ☆
720 Olive St., 24th Fl.
St. Louis, MO 63101-2313

Established in 1986 in MO.
Foundation type: Independent foundation.
Financial data (yr. ended 7/31/05): Assets, $748,543 (M); gifts received, $46,883; expenditures, $1,028,360; qualifying distributions, $727,594; giving activities include $1,017,540 for 62 grants (high: $280,000; low: $100).
Fields of interest: Arts; Higher education; Education; Federated giving programs; Christian agencies & churches; Protestant agencies & churches.
Type of support: General/operating support.
Limitations: Applications not accepted. Giving primarily in St. Louis, MO. No grants to individuals.
Application information: Contributes only to pre-selected organizations.
Officers: Matthew G. Perlow, Pres.; Douglas L. Kelly, V.P.; Warren R. Maichel, Secy.
EIN: 431418697
Selected grants: The following grants were reported in 2003.
$50,000 to Saint Louis Abbey, Saint Louis, MO. For endowment.
$40,000 to Covenant Presbyterian Church of Naples, Naples, FL. For general support.
$30,000 to Washington University, Saint Louis, MO. 3 grants: $10,000 each to School of Law.
$25,000 to Saint Patrick Center, Saint Louis, MO. For general support.
$5,000 to Archdiocesan Development Appeal, Saint Louis, MO. For general support.
$5,000 to Covenant Theological Seminary, Saint Louis, MO. For general support.
$3,500 to Humane Society of Missouri, Saint Louis, MO. For general support.
$3,000 to Saint Louis University, Saint Louis, MO. For general support.

4886
Herman T. & Phenie R. Pott Foundation ◇
c/o U.S. Bank, N.A.
P.O. Box 387
St. Louis, MO 63166 (314) 418-4907
Contact: Cathy Meeks

Trust established in 1963 in MO.
Foundation type: Independent foundation.
Financial data (yr. ended 12/31/05): Assets, $28,828,810 (M); expenditures, $1,723,463; qualifying distributions, $1,631,639; giving activities include $1,539,000 for 125 grants (high: $120,000; low: $1,000).
Purpose and activities: Support primarily for health organizations, human services, education, youth development, housing, and employment.
Fields of interest: Education; Health care; Mental health/crisis services; Human services; Children/youth, services; Family services; Homeless, human services; Federated giving programs; Disabilities, people with; Homeless.

Type of support: General/operating support; Continuing support; Annual campaigns; Scholarship funds.
Limitations: Giving primarily in MO, particularly the St. Louis area. No grants to individuals.
Publications: Application guidelines.
Application information: Application form not required.
 Initial approach: Letter (no more than 2 pages)
 Copies of proposal: 1
 Deadline(s): None
 Board meeting date(s): Late spring and fall
Trustee: U.S. Bank, N.A.
Advisory Committee: Kristine E. Collins; Roy T. Collins; Thomas R. Corbet; John F. Fechter; Mary Jane King; Richard D. Rogers.
Number of staff: 1 part-time professional.
EIN: 436041541
Selected grants: The following grants were reported in 2005.
$120,000 to Family Resource Center, Saint Louis, MO.
$85,000 to Saint Louis Mercantile Library Association, Saint Louis, MO.
$75,000 to Grace Hill Settlement House, Saint Louis, MO.
$75,000 to Washington University, Saint Louis, MO.
$35,000 to American Lung Association of Eastern Missouri, Saint Louis, MO.
$35,000 to Ranken Jordan Home for Convalescent Crippled Children, Saint Louis, MO.
$15,000 to American Heart Association, Saint Louis, MO.
$10,000 to Saint Louis Childrens Hospital, Saint Louis, MO.
$7,500 to Cornerstone Center for Early Learning, Saint Louis, MO.
$7,500 to Saint Joseph Institute for the Deaf, Saint Louis, MO.

4887
Powell Crown Foundation ◇
2405 Grand Blvd., Ste. 1040
Kansas City, MO 64108
Contact: Randi Romans, Office Mgr.

Established in 1997 in MO.
Donor: Marilyn Powell Rinker.
Foundation type: Independent foundation.
Financial data (yr. ended 12/31/05): Assets, $4,551,321 (M); expenditures, $405,913; qualifying distributions, $374,800; giving activities include $374,800 for 15 grants (high: $149,000; low: $2,000; average: $3,000–$6,500).
Purpose and activities: Giving to organizations that support or directly administer charitable activities of the Christian Science Church.
Fields of interest: Christian agencies & churches.
Type of support: General/operating support.
Limitations: Applications not accepted. No grants to individuals.
Application information: Contributes only to pre-selected organizations.
Officers: Marilyn Powell Rinker, Chair.; Laura Marilyn Hanser, Vice-Chair.; Leslie A. Bishop, Secy.-Treas.
EIN: 431787126
Selected grants: The following grants were reported in 2003.
$180,000 to Principle Foundation, Kansas City, MO.
$31,000 to First Church of Christ Scientist, Boston, MA.
$28,500 to Camps Leelanau and Kohahna, Maple City, MI.

$11,000 to Mary Baker Eddy Library for the Betterment of Humanity, Boston, MA.
$6,000 to Adventure Unlimited, Greenwood Village, CO.
$6,000 to Camps Newfound Owatonna, Harrison, ME.
$6,000 to Cedars Camps, Manchester, MO.
$6,000 to Crystal Lake Camps, Hughesville, PA.
$5,000 to Longyear Museum and Historical Society, Chestnut Hill, MA.
$3,000 to Peace Haven Association, Saint Louis, MO.

4888
Carol Swanson Price Foundation ◇
7 W. Armour Blvd., Ste 300
Kansas City, MO 64112 (816) 360-6174
Contact: Carol Swanson Price, Tr.

Established in 1969 in MO.
Foundation type: Independent foundation.
Financial data (yr. ended 12/31/05): Assets, $4,401,714 (M); expenditures, $427,089; qualifying distributions, $396,705; giving activities include $388,130 for 39 grants (high: $160,000; low: $450; average: $1,000–$20,000).
Purpose and activities: Giving primarily for arts and culture, particularly museums, as well as for human services and children's organizations, and for hospitals, including children's hospitals.
Fields of interest: Museums; Arts; Health care; Human services; Children, services.
Application information:
 Initial approach: Letter
 Deadline(s): None
Trustees: Carol Swanson Price.
EIN: 431781880
Selected grants: The following grants were reported in 2005.
$166,000 to Eisenhower Medical Center, Rancho Mirage, CA. 2 grants: $6,000, $160,000
$50,000 to Mayo Foundation, Rochester, MN.
$25,000 to Salvation Army, Rockland, ME.
$15,000 to Library of Congress, DC.
$15,000 to McCallum Theater, Palm Desert, CA.
$10,000 to Stanford University, Stanford, CA.
$5,000 to American Red Cross, Kansas City, MO.
$1,700 to Nelson Gallery Foundation, Kansas City, MO.
$1,000 to Santa Clara University, Santa Clara, CA.

4889
The Ceil & Michael E. Pulitzer Foundation, Inc. ◇
(formerly The Michael E. Pulitzer Foundation, Inc.)
c/o James V. Maloney
P.O. Box 23368
St. Louis, MO 63156 (314) 398-1396
Contact: Michael E. Pulitzer, Pres.

Established in 1993 in MO.
Donors: Michael E. Pulitzer; Ceil Pulitzer.
Foundation type: Independent foundation.
Financial data (yr. ended 10/31/05): Assets, $9,379,414 (M); gifts received, $15; expenditures, $741,227; qualifying distributions, $565,942; giving activities include $558,717 for 28 grants (high: $125,000; low: $500).
Purpose and activities: Giving primarily for the arts and children's services.

Fields of interest: Museums; Performing arts; Arts; Higher education; Children/youth, services; Human services.
Limitations: Giving on a national basis.
Application information:
Initial approach: Letter
Deadline(s): None
Officers: Michael E. Pulitzer, Pres.; James V. Maloney, V.P. and Secy.; Christina H. Eisenbeis, V.P.; Ceil Pulitzer, V.P.
EIN: 431659437
Selected grants: The following grants were reported in 2005.
$180,000 to Los Angeles Opera Company, Los Angeles, CA. 2 grants: $55,000, $125,000
$108,517 to Saint Louis Abbey, Saint Louis, MO.
$30,000 to Center for Independent Documentary, Sharon, MA.
$20,000 to Saint Louis Psychoanalytic Institute, Saint Louis, MO.
$20,000 to Santa Barbara Center for the Performing Arts, Santa Barbara, CA.
$10,000 to Los Angeles County Museum of Art, Los Angeles, CA.
$10,000 to Los Angeles Philharmonic Association, Los Angeles, CA.
$5,000 to Hazelden Foundation, Center City, MN.
$1,000 to Santa Barbara Maritime Museum, Santa Barbara, CA.

4890
Reding Family Foundation ✧ ☆
c/o Nicholas L. Reding
10045 Litzsinger Rd.
St. Louis, MO 63124

Established in 2004 in MO.
Donor: Nicholas L. Reding.
Foundation type: Independent foundation.
Financial data (yr. ended 12/31/05): Assets, $767,153 (M); gifts received, $428,400; expenditures, $448,532; qualifying distributions, $423,852; giving activities include $423,852 for 9 grants (high: $100,000; low: $5,000).
Purpose and activities: Givign primarily for Protestant churches and universities; support also for a symphony, a zoo,and a botanical garden.
Fields of interest: Performing arts, orchestra (symphony); Higher education; Botanical gardens; Zoos/zoological societies; Protestant agencies & churches.
Type of support: Endowments; Annual campaigns; General/operating support.
Limitations: Applications not accepted. Giving primarily in MO, with emphasis on St. Louis. No grants to individuals.
Application information: Contributes only to pre-selected organizations.
Trustees: Nancy Reding Breckenridge; Nicholas L. Reding; Patricia J. Reding; S. Nicholas Reding.
EIN: 330993783

4891
Remington Family Foundation ✧ ☆
P.O. Box 6007
St. Joseph, MO 64506

Established in 2002.
Donors: C. Wesley Remington; Patricia Remington; Stephanie Remington; Scott Remington; Lee A. Swartz; Gay L. Barwald.

Foundation type: Independent foundation.
Financial data (yr. ended 12/31/05): Assets, $1,078,070 (M); gifts received, $1,000,000; expenditures, $1,041,587; qualifying distributions, $1,031,000; giving activities include $1,031,000 for 5 grants (high: $1,000,000; low: $5,000).
Fields of interest: Boy scouts; Human services; Federated giving programs.
Limitations: Applications not accepted. Giving primarily in MO. No grants to individuals.
Application information: Contributes only to pre-selected organizations.
Director: C. Wesley Remington.
EIN: 046990614

4892
The J. B. Reynolds Foundation ✧
P.O. Box 219139
Kansas City, MO 64141-9139

Incorporated in 1961 in MO.
Donors: Walter Edwin Bixby, Sr.; Pearl G. Reynolds†.
Foundation type: Independent foundation.
Financial data (yr. ended 12/31/05): Assets, $15,170,232 (M); expenditures, $785,300; qualifying distributions, $785,300; giving activities include $785,300 for 84 grants (high: $40,000; low: $500).
Purpose and activities: Giving primarily for the arts, education, and for health and human services.
Fields of interest: Museums; Performing arts; Education; Health organizations, association; Medical research, institute; Youth development; Human services; Children/youth, services; Government/public administration.
Type of support: General/operating support; Continuing support; Annual campaigns; Capital campaigns; Building/renovation; Equipment; Land acquisition; Endowments; Emergency funds; Publication; Research.
Limitations: Applications not accepted. Giving primarily within a 150-mile radius of Kansas City, MO. No grants to individuals.
Application information: Contributes only to pre-selected organizations.
Officers: R. Philip Bixby, Pres. and V.P.; Richard L. Finn, Secy.-Treas.
EIN: 446014359
Selected grants: The following grants were reported in 2005.
$25,000 to Kansas City Art Institute, Kansas City, MO.
$25,000 to Lyric Opera of Kansas City, Kansas City, MO.
$25,000 to Research Foundation, Kansas City, MO.
$20,000 to Kansas City Symphony, Kansas City, MO.
$15,000 to Childrens Mercy Hospital, Kansas City, MO.
$15,000 to Marian Clinic, Topeka, KS.
$15,000 to Redemptorist Center, Kansas City, MO.
$10,000 to Victory Junction Gang Camp, Randleman, NC.
$7,500 to Central City School Fund, Kansas City, MO.
$7,500 to Child Advocacy Services Center, Kansas City, MO.

4893
Joseph H. and Florence A. Roblee Foundation
c/o Bank of America, N.A., attn.: Peggy Thomas
P.O. Box 14737
St. Louis, MO 63178-9802 (314) 963-7713
Contact: Kathy Doellefeld-Clancy, Exec. Dir.
FAX: (314) 963-7716;
E-mail: kathydc@robleefoundation.org

Trust established in 1971 in MO.
Donors: Louise Roblee McCarthy†; Florence Roblee Trust.
Foundation type: Independent foundation.
Financial data (yr. ended 12/31/05): Assets, $17,383,823 (M); expenditures, $1,019,159; qualifying distributions, $903,740; giving activities include $773,371 for 86 grants (high: $25,000; low: $1,000; average: $5,000–$10,000).
Purpose and activities: Grants to enable organizations to promote change by addressing significant social issues in order to improve the quality of life and help fulfill the potential of individuals. The foundation arises out of a Christian framework, and values ecumenical endeavors. The foundation particularly supports programs which work to break down cultural, racial, and ethnic barriers. Organizations and churches are encouraged to collaborate in achieving positive change through advocacy, prevention, and systemic improvements.
Fields of interest: Education, reform; Teacher school/education; Substance abuse, prevention; Crime/violence prevention; Crime/violence prevention, domestic violence; Housing/shelter; Youth development, citizenship; Children/youth, services; Youth, pregnancy prevention; Family services; Women, centers/services; Civil rights, race/intergroup relations; Civil liberties, reproductive rights; Public affairs, citizen participation; Women; Economically disadvantaged; Homeless.
Type of support: Technical assistance.
Limitations: Giving limited to the greater bi-state St. Louis region, and Miami/Dade, FL. No grants to individuals, or for annual campaigns; no loans.
Publications: Application guidelines.
Application information: First time applicants are encouraged to contact the Executive Director prior to developing proposal. Grantseekers from Miami/Dade FL are required to submit 3 additional copies of the proposal to Miami. Application form required.
Initial approach: Obtain application guidelines from foundation
Copies of proposal: 3
Deadline(s): Jan. 15 and June 15
Board meeting date(s): June and Dec.
Officer and Trustees:* Jeffrey Von Arx,* Pres.; Kathy Doellefeld-Clancy, Exec. Dir.; Carol M. Duhme; Carol Von Arx; Bank of America, N.A.
Number of staff: 1 full-time professional.
EIN: 436109579
Selected grants: The following grants were reported in 2003.
$20,000 to Off the Cuff Productions, Saint Louis, MO.
$15,000 to YWCA of Metropolitan Saint Louis, Saint Louis, MO.
$14,000 to Rescue Missions Ministries, Durham, NC.
$14,000 to Social Capital, Woburn, MA.
$12,000 to Genesis Home, Durham, NC.
$11,500 to Housing for New Hope, Durham, NC.
$10,000 to Generations, Boston, MA.

$10,000 to Legal Services of Eastern Missouri, Saint Louis, MO.

$10,000 to Newton Symphony Orchestra, Newton, MA.

$10,000 to Saint Louis Public Schools Foundation, Saint Louis, MO.

4894

Rosewood Foundation ◇

(formerly Hardin T. & Katie McClendon Foundation)
c/o The Guaranty Trust Co. of Missouri
7733 Forsyth Blvd., Ste. 900
Clayton, MO 63105
Contact: Roy Blair

Established in 1988 in MO.
Donor: Katie Rose McClendon Revocable Trust.
Foundation type: Independent foundation.
Financial data (yr. ended 6/30/05): Assets, $7,111,298 (M); gifts received, $1,000,000; expenditures, $1,105,092; qualifying distributions, $1,076,850; giving activities include $1,074,000 for 43 grants (high: $100,000; low: $3,000).
Purpose and activities: Giving primarily for education, health care and medical research, and to Protestant ministries and organizations including education, and for children, youth, and social services.
Fields of interest: Elementary school/education; Secondary school/education; Higher education; Theological school/education; Education; Hospitals (specialty); Health organizations, association; Medical research, association; Medical research, institute; Human services; American Red Cross; International relief; Federated giving programs; Protestant agencies & churches.
Limitations: Giving primarily in Hattiesburg and Jackson, MS; some giving nationally. No grants to individuals.
Application information: Application form not required.
Deadline(s): None
Trustees: Katie Rose W. McClendon; The Guaranty Trust Co. of Missouri.
EIN: 436348906

4895

The Saigh Foundation

7777 Bonhomme Ave., Ste. 2007
St. Louis, MO 63105 (314) 862-3055
Contact: JoAnn Hejna, Exec. Dir.
FAX: (314) 862-9288;
E-mail: joann@thesaighfoundation.org; URL: http://www.thesaighfoundation.org/

Established in 1998 in NY.
Donor: Fred M. Saigh†.
Foundation type: Independent foundation.
Financial data (yr. ended 3/31/06): Assets, $68,528,408 (M); gifts received, $25; expenditures, $3,521,663; qualifying distributions, $3,160,569; giving activities include $2,651,250 for 83 grants (high: $235,000; low: $5,000).
Purpose and activities: Supports funding for St. Louis, MO, area organizations benefiting children and youth in the areas of education and health care.
Fields of interest: Education; Health care; Children/youth, services.
Type of support: Program development; Scholarship funds; Research; Matching/challenge support.

Limitations: Giving limited to St. Louis, MO. No grants for capital campaigns, annual appeals, dinner functions, fundraising events, or for films and travel; no loans.
Application information: Proposals may be submitted by mail or fax. Application form required.
Initial approach: Letter
Copies of proposal: 1
Deadline(s): At least 3 months before next board meeting
Board meeting date(s): Feb., May, Aug., and Nov.
Final notification: 2 days after quarterly mtg.
Trustees: JoAnn Hejna; Heidi Veron; Franklin F. Wallis; Fidicuary Trust Co., Int'l.
Number of staff: 2 full-time professional.
EIN: 516511117
Selected grants: The following grants were reported in 2005.
$100,000 to Scholarship Foundation of Saint Louis, Saint Louis, MO. For tuition support.
$50,000 to Saint Louis For Kids, Saint Louis, MO. For general support.
$50,000 to Voices for Children, Saint Louis, MO. For foster care program.
$35,000 to AmeriCorps Saint Louis, Saint Louis, MO.
$35,000 to Saint Vincent Home for Children, Saint Louis, MO. For counseling program.
$25,000 to Boys and Girls Club, Herbert Hoover, Saint Louis, MO. For childrens dental program.
$25,000 to Nurses for Newborns Foundation, Saint Louis, MO. For general support.
$12,000 to Ready Readers, Saint Louis, MO.
$10,000 to Aim High Saint Louis, Saint Louis, MO. For summer enrichment program.
$10,000 to Delta Gamma Center for Children with Visual Impairments, Saint Louis, MO. For general support.
$10,000 to Shakespeare Festival of Saint Louis, Saint Louis, MO. For general support.

4896

Greater Saint Louis Community Foundation

(formerly St. Louis Community Foundation)
319 N. 4th St., Ste. 300
St. Louis, MO 63102 (314) 588-8200
Contact: David R. Luckes, C.E.O.; For grants: Linda S. Aitch, Dir., Community Investment
FAX: (314) 588-8088; E-mail: info@gstlcf.org;
Additional E-mail: david@stlcf.org; Grant application E-mail: linda@stlcf.org; URL: http://www.gstlcf.org

Established in 1915 in MO.
Foundation type: Community foundation.
Financial data (yr. ended 12/31/04): Assets, $93,843,900 (M); gifts received, $8,533,693; expenditures, $10,473,958; giving activities include $8,930,898 for 1,248 grants (high: $1,044,800; low: $50).
Purpose and activities: The foundation seeks to improve the quality of life in the greater St. Louis metropolitan area by facilitating the philanthropy of individuals, families and businesses in, but not limited to, the areas of arts and culture, community building, education, environment, health, and human services.
Fields of interest: Arts; Education; Environment; Health care; Human services; Nonprofit management; Community development; Philanthropy/voluntarism; Government/public administration.

Type of support: General/operating support; Management development/capacity building; Program development; Seed money; Scholarship funds; Technical assistance; Consulting services; Program-related investments/loans; Matching/challenge support.
Limitations: Giving primarily in IL, and the metropolitan St. Louis, MO, area. No grants to individuals (except through scholarship funds), or for deficit financing, or endowment or building funds; grants for operating expenses only during an organization's start-up.
Publications: Application guidelines; Annual report; Informational brochure; Newsletter.
Application information: Contact foundation for specific guidelines and special grant initiative guidelines. Application form required.
Initial approach: Letter of inquiry
Deadline(s): Applications accepted throughout the year. Deadlines and application criteria for special grant initiatives vary depending on grant program or individual fund specifications
Board meeting date(s): Mar., June, Sept., and Dec.
Final notification: Within 2 weeks of board meetings
Officers and Directors:* Lester J. Buechele,* Chair.; David R. Luckes, C.E.O. and Pres.; Albert E. Suter,* V.P.; Kathryn S. Bader,* Secy.; Dwight D. Canning, C.F.O.; Parker Condie,* Treas.; Clifton D. Berry; William H.T. Bush; Gretta Forrester; Terry L. Franc; Laurna Godwin; Frank J. Guyol III; Frederick O. Hanser; John M. Hillhouse; Bruce B. Holland; Dennis J. Jacknewitz; Stephen C. Jones; Bruce A. Olson; Derek K. Rapp; Mark J. Schnuck; Anne T. Shapleigh; Leslie A. Small; James M. Snowden.
Trustee Banks: Commerce Bank, N.A.; A.G. Edwards Trust Co.; The Guaranty Trust Co. of Missouri; U.S. Bank, N.A.; Merrill Lynch Trust Co.; Bank of America, N.A.; Union Planters Trust.
Number of staff: 7 full-time professional; 2 full-time support.
EIN: 436023126

4897

Sayler-Hawkins Foundation ◇ ☆

1588 S. Lindbergh Blvd., Ste. 205
St. Louis, MO 63131 (314) 997-8080
Contact: John R. Woods, Dir.

Established in 1984 in MO.
Donors: Marjorie Hankins; John R. Woods.
Foundation type: Independent foundation.
Financial data (yr. ended 12/31/04): Assets, $3,869,556 (M); gifts received, $50,000; expenditures, $382,832; qualifying distributions, $320,700; giving activities include $320,700 for 15 grants (high: $140,000; low: $1,000).
Purpose and activities: Giving primarily to an advocacy group promoting firearms safety and for Protestant churches; some support also for museums.
Fields of interest: Museums; Athletics/sports, fishing/hunting; Civil liberties, advocacy; Protestant agencies & churches; General charitable giving.
Limitations: Giving on a national basis.
Application information: Application form not required.
Initial approach: Proposal
Copies of proposal: 1
Deadline(s): None
Board meeting date(s): Dec.

Directors: Elizabeth Bradbury; Marjorie Hankins; John R. Woods; John R. Woods, Jr.
EIN: 431347116
Selected grants: The following grants were reported in 2004.
$140,000 to NRA Foundation, Fairfax, VA.
$5,000 to Museum of the American West, Lander, WY.
$500 to Richard L. Hoffman Foundation, Mars Hill, NC.

4898
A. J. Schwartze Community Foundation ✧

c/o Central Bank
238 Madison St.
Jefferson City, MO 65101-3230 (573) 634-1221
Contact: Michael W. Prenger, Trust Off., Central Bank

Established in 1976 in MO.
Donor: A.J. Schwartze.
Foundation type: Independent foundation.
Financial data (yr. ended 11/30/05): Assets, $43,855,714 (M); gifts received, $12,526; expenditures, $2,201,546; qualifying distributions, $2,024,468; giving activities include $2,022,806 for 101 grants (high: $325,000; low: $500).
Purpose and activities: Giving exclusively for charitable, religious, scientific, literary or educational purposes primarily to promote the well-being of inhabitants of Westphalia, MO and its vicinity, including Osage County. Giving primarily to local fire departments, Roman Catholic churches and for Roman Catholic education.
Fields of interest: Elementary/secondary education; Disasters, fire prevention/control; Community development; Government/public administration; Roman Catholic agencies & churches.
Type of support: General/operating support.
Limitations: Giving primarily in the Westphalia, MO, area, including Osage County. No grants to individuals.
Application information:
  Initial approach: Letter or proposal
  Deadline(s): Feb.
  Board meeting date(s): Mar.
Distribution Committee: Gary Boes; Gilbert Hilkemeyer; Emil Schwartz; Charles Schwartze; Elizabeth Sestak; Fred Wieberg; Julie Wieberg.
Trustee: Central Bank.
EIN: 431092255
Selected grants: The following grants were reported in 2005.
$317,611 to Saint Marys Health Center, Saint Louis, MO.
$45,000 to Sacred Heart School, Sedalia, MO. 2 grants: $40,000, $5,000
$45,000 to Saint Joseph School, Sainte Genevieve, MO. 2 grants: $5,000, $40,000
$25,000 to Holy Family Church, Saint Louis, MO.
$25,000 to Saint Louis Church, Saint Louis, MO.
$25,000 to Visitation Church, Kansas City, MO.
$20,000 to School Sisters of Notre Dame, Saint Louis, MO.
$5,000 to Missouri River Regional Library, Jefferson City, MO.

4899
The Schweppe Foundation ✧

1127 S. Mason Rd.
St. Louis, MO 63131 (314) 878-5805
Contact: Gary H. Kline, Treas.
FAX: (314) 878-5807;
E-mail: schweppefnd@aol.com; URL: http://www.schweppefoundation.org

Established in 1947 in IL.
Donors: John S. Schweppe; Lydia E. Schweppe.
Foundation type: Independent foundation.
Financial data (yr. ended 12/31/05): Assets, $12,554,284 (M); expenditures, $704,084; qualifying distributions, $614,997; giving activities include $489,000 for 22 grants (high: $50,000; low: $1,000; average: $5,000–$50,000).
Purpose and activities: Awards medical research fellowships for training at Chicago, IL, area medical schools or university-affiliated hospitals.
Fields of interest: Education, research; Medical school/education; Education; Biomedicine; Medical research, institute; Biological sciences.
Type of support: Fellowships.
Limitations: Giving limited to the Chicago, IL, area.
Publications: Application guidelines; Grants list; Informational brochure.
Application information: Fellowships are granted to institutions on behalf of individuals. See foundation Web site for application guidelines. Application form required.
  Initial approach: Letter
  Deadline(s): Sept. 1
Officers: David P. Schweppe, Pres.; Thomas A. Polachek, Secy.; Gary H. Kline, Treas.
Directors: Marjorie A. Ariana, Ph.D.; Donald Bellgrau, Ph.D.; Richard V. Benya; Joel A. Block; Alfred P. Buettner; Charles H. Schweppe; and 16 additional directors.
EIN: 366014667

4900
Seaworld & Busch Gardens Conservation Fund ✧ ☆

231 S. Bemiston Ave., Ste. 600
Clayton, MO 63105 (314) 613-6081
E-mail: mail@swbgfund.org; Additional E-mail: mailbox@swbgfund.org; URL: http://www.swbg-conservationfund.org/default.htm

Established in 2003 in DE and MO.
Donor: Busch Entertainment Corp.
Foundation type: Company-sponsored foundation.
Financial data (yr. ended 12/31/05): Assets, $390,672 (M); gifts received, $867,196; expenditures, $656,295; qualifying distributions, $654,045; giving activities include $643,180 for 68 grants (high: $20,000; low: $2,500).
Purpose and activities: The fund supports organizations involved with K-12 environmental education and wildlife conservation and awards grants to K-12 educators.
Fields of interest: Elementary/secondary education; Environmental education; Animals/wildlife, research; Animals/wildlife, public education; Animal welfare; Animals/wildlife, preservation/protection; Animals/wildlife.
Type of support: General/operating support; Program development; Research; Grants to individuals.
Publications: Newsletter.
Application information: Application form required.

Initial approach: Download application form and mail in CD format to foundation or E-mail to foundation
Deadline(s): June 1 and Dec. 1
Board meeting date(s): Twice per year
Officers and Directors: * Virginia M. Busch,* Pres.; Brad Andrews,* V.P.; David Grabe, Treas.; Jack Hanna; Laura H. Reeves; Julie Scardina; Hugh Share; Sheila Sullivan Voss; Glenn Yoy.
EIN: 113692807

4901
Arch W. Shaw Foundation

HC3, Box 60-B
Birch Tree, MO 65438
Contact: William W. Shaw, Tr.

Trust established in 1949 in IL.
Donor: Arch W. Shaw†.
Foundation type: Independent foundation.
Financial data (yr. ended 12/31/05): Assets, $15,198,240 (M); expenditures, $765,300; qualifying distributions, $750,076; giving activities include $750,000 for 90 grants (high: $50,000; low: $1,000).
Fields of interest: Museums; Arts; Education, fund raising/fund distribution; Higher education; Business school/education; Libraries/library science; Hospitals (general); Health care; Medical research, institute; Residential/custodial care, hospices.
Type of support: General/operating support; Continuing support; Annual campaigns; Capital campaigns; Building/renovation; Equipment; Endowments; Emergency funds; Program development; Seed money; Scholarship funds; Research.
Limitations: Giving primarily in IL, MA, MO, NY, and WI. No support for private foundations. No grants to individuals.
Publications: Financial statement.
Application information: Application form not required.
  Initial approach: Letter
  Copies of proposal: 1
  Deadline(s): None
  Board meeting date(s): Dec.
Trustees: Arch W. Shaw II; Bruce P. Shaw; Roger D. Shaw, Jr.; William W. Shaw.
EIN: 366055262

4902
Shelter Insurance Foundation ✧

1817 W. Broadway
Columbia, MO 65218 (573) 214-4290
Contact: Raymond E. Jones, Secy.

Established in 1981 in MO.
Donor: Shelter Mutual Insurance Co.
Foundation type: Company-sponsored foundation.
Financial data (yr. ended 6/30/05): Assets, $8,395,112 (M); gifts received, $3,100,475; expenditures, $583,182; qualifying distributions, $576,760; giving activities include $113,260 for 63 grants (high: $14,905; low: $20), and $463,500 for grants to individuals.
Purpose and activities: The foundation supports organizations involved with education, health, safety, human services, and children and youth.
Fields of interest: Higher education; Education; Health care; Food banks; Housing/shelter, aging;

Safety/disasters; Children/youth, services; Human services.
Type of support: General/operating support; Scholarship funds; Scholarships—to individuals.
Limitations: Giving primarily in areas of company operations in AR, CO, IA, IL, IN, KS, KY, LA, MO, MS, NE, OK, and TN.
Application information: Application form required.
  Initial approach: Contact foundation for application form; contact high school for application form for scholarships
  Deadline(s): None
Officers and Directors:* J. Donald Duello,* Pres.; Raymond E. Jones,* V.P. and Secy.; Jerry L. French, Treas.; Max Dills; Don A. McCubbin; Rick L. Means; Joe L. Moseley; Gary L. Myers; James A. Offutt.
EIN: 431224155
Selected grants: The following grants were reported in 2003.
$13,643 to University of Missouri, Columbia, MO.
$7,500 to Columbia College, Columbia, MO.
$5,000 to Ellis Fischel State Cancer Center, Columbia, MO.
$2,500 to Boy Scouts of America, Great Rivers Council, Columbia, MO.
$1,100 to Mississippi State University, Mississippi State, MS.
$1,000 to United Way, Columbia Area, Columbia, MO.
$840 to Central Missouri State University, Warrensburg, MO.
$400 to Advent Enterprises, Columbia, MO.
$300 to Boys and Girls Club of the Columbia Area, Columbia, MO.
$200 to University of Tulsa, Tulsa, OK.

4903
Mildred, Herbert and Julian Simon Foundation ☆
P.O. Box 78544
St. Louis, MO   63178
Contact: Charles Baron, Chair., Steering Comm.
FAX: (314) 241-1588;
E-mail: mrosen@mersgoodwill.org

Established in 1993 in MO.
Donors: Herbert Simon†; Julian Simon†; Mildred Simon†.
Foundation type: Independent foundation.
Financial data (yr. ended 9/30/05): Assets, $14,455,796 (M); gifts received, $758,991; expenditures, $669,729; qualifying distributions, $616,907; giving activities include $490,781 for 39 grants (high: $50,000; low: $1,000).
Purpose and activities: The foundation is interested in developing projects which will have a significant impact on the St. Louis area. It seeks concept papers concerning programs that will meet unique specific community needs and seeks the appropriate organizations to best implement them. The primary focus includes but is not limited to programs which enhance the quality of life of senior citizens and children, with primary consideration given to the needs of the St. Louis Jewish community.
Fields of interest: Elementary/secondary education; Higher education; Employment, services; Neighborhood centers; Children, services; Jewish agencies & temples; Aging.
International interests: Israel; Middle East.
Type of support: Program development; Seed money; Scholarship funds.

Limitations: Giving primarily in St. Louis, MO. No grants to individuals or for capital campaigns.
Application information: Concepts preferred to grant applications. Application form not required.
  Initial approach: Letter/concept paper
  Copies of proposal: 1
  Board meeting date(s): Monthly
  Final notification: 1-6 months
Officers and Steering Committee:* Charles B. Baron,* Chair.; Lewis Chartock,* Vice-Chair.; Martin M. Rosen,* Exec. Dir.; Joan M. Newman; Rabbi Alvan D. Rubin.
Trustee: U.S. Bank, N.A.
Number of staff: 1 part-time professional; 1 part-time support.
EIN: 436498119

4904
Singing for Change ✧
(also known as SFC Charitable Foundation)
P.O. Box 7210
Kansas City, MO   64113   (816) 363-8132
Contact: Judith Ranger Smith, Exec. Dir.
FAX: (816) 363-1290;
E-mail: info@singingforchange.com; Additional E-mail: sfc@kc.rr.com; URL: http://margaritaville.com/SFC.php

Established in 1995.
Donor: Jimmy Buffett.
Foundation type: Independent foundation.
Financial data (yr. ended 12/31/04): Assets, $367,366 (M); gifts received, $590,249; expenditures, $670,477; qualifying distributions, $551,500; giving activities include $551,500 for 29 grants (high: $66,849; low: $50).
Purpose and activities: Funding primarily for human services.
Fields of interest: Education; Environmental education; Human services; Children/youth, services.
Type of support: General/operating support; Continuing support.
Limitations: Applications not accepted. Giving on a national basis. No support for religious organizations, or other grant-making operations. No grants to individuals, or for art, music, or recreational purposes.
Publications: Annual report.
Application information: Proposals are by invitation only. The foundation does not accept unsolicited requests. See foundation Web site for two-stage application process.
  Board meeting date(s): Quarterly
Officers and Trustees:* Howard Kaufman,* Pres.; Joel A. Katz,* Secy.; Irwin L. Rennert,* Treas.; Sunshine Smith.
Number of staff: 1 full-time professional.
EIN: 650565248
Selected grants: The following grants were reported in 2003.
$100,000 to Hands On Network, Atlanta, GA.
$50,000 to Second Harvest Food Bank of Nashville, Nashville, TN.
$10,000 to Appalachian Mountain Club, Boston, MA.
$10,000 to Carolina Farm Stewardship Association, Pittsboro, NC.
$10,000 to Educated Eats, Chicago, IL.
$10,000 to Hands On Atlanta, Atlanta, GA.
$10,000 to Hands On Miami, Miami, FL.
$10,000 to Ohio Environmental Council, Columbus, OH.

$10,000 to Park Pride Atlanta, Atlanta, GA.
$10,000 to Philadelphia Cares, Philadelphia, PA.

4905
The Smith Foundation ✧ ☆
P.O. Box 801
Chesterfield, MO   63006

Established in 2000 in MO.
Donor: E. Smith.
Foundation type: Independent foundation.
Financial data (yr. ended 12/31/05): Assets, $9,979,860 (M); gifts received, $2,000,000; expenditures, $439,454; qualifying distributions, $402,326; giving activities include $402,326 for 53 grants (high: $50,000; low: $1,000).
Fields of interest: Education; Animal welfare; Hospitals (general); Hospitals (specialty); Optometry/vision screening; Food banks; Boys & girls clubs; American Red Cross; Family services.
Limitations: Applications not accepted. No grants to individuals.
Application information: Contributes only to pre-selected organizations.
Trustee: Ed Smith.
EIN: 436855044
Selected grants: The following grants were reported in 2003.
$10,000 to Chesterfield Day School, Chesterfield, MO.
$10,000 to Family Resource Center.
$10,000 to Junior Achievement of Southern California, Los Angeles, CA.
$10,000 to LensCrafters Foundation, Mason, OH.
$5,000 to American Heart Association, Dallas, TX.
$5,000 to American Lung Association of Eastern Missouri, Saint Louis, MO.
$5,000 to Marian Middle School, Saint Louis, MO.
$5,000 to United Negro College Fund, Fairfax, VA.
$3,000 to Saint Louis Childrens Hospital, Saint Louis, MO.
$3,000 to Saint Louis Crisis Nursery, Saint Louis, MO.

4906
Smurfit-Stone Container Corporation Charitable Fund ✧
(formerly Jefferson Smurfit Charitable Corporation)
8182 Maryland Ave.
St. Louis, MO   63105
Contact: Mary Duda
Application address: P.O. Box 66820, St. Louis, MO 52166, tel.: (314) 746-1100

Donors: Jefferson Smurfit Corp. (U.S.); Smurfit-Stone Container Enterprises, Inc.
Foundation type: Company-sponsored foundation.
Financial data (yr. ended 12/31/05): Assets, $438,775 (M); gifts received, $1,450,000; expenditures, $1,232,392; qualifying distributions, $1,232,392; giving activities include $1,232,392 for 104 grants (high: $125,000; low: $50).
Purpose and activities: The foundation supports organizations involved with education, health, youth development, human services, and community development.
Fields of interest: Education; Health care; Athletics/sports, Special Olympics; Youth development; Human services; Community development; Federated giving programs.
Type of support: General/operating support.

Limitations: Giving primarily in Chicago, IL, and St. Louis, MO.
Application information: Application form not required.
Initial approach: Proposal
Deadline(s): None
Officers and Directors:* Mr. Patrick Moore,* Pres.; Mr. Craig Hunt,* Secy.; Mr. Charles Hinrichs,* Treas.
EIN: 431776694

4907
Solutia Fund ◇
575 Maryville Centre Dr., Mail Zone 3N
P.O. Box 66760
St. Louis, MO 63166-6760 (314) 674-3083
Contact: Liesl M. Livingston, Pres.
FAX: (314) 674-1585; URL: http://www.solutia.com/pages/corporate/about/outreach.asp

Established in 1997 in MO.
Donor: Solutia Inc.
Foundation type: Company-sponsored foundation.
Financial data (yr. ended 12/31/03): Assets, $233,721 (M); gifts received, $620,779; expenditures, $613,089; qualifying distributions, $613,029; giving activities include $613,029 for 141 grants (high: $50,000; low: $250).
Purpose and activities: The fund supports organizations involved with arts and culture, education, the environment, human services, and science and technology.
Fields of interest: Arts; Education; Health care; Human services; Science; General charitable giving.
Limitations: Giving primarily in areas of company operations. No support for advocacy groups or religious, fraternal, social, veterans', or military organizations. No grants to individuals, or for lobbying, endowments, or travel.
Application information: Application form not required.
Initial approach: Proposal
Copies of proposal: 1
Deadline(s): None
Final notification: 2 to 3 weeks
Officers:* Glenn S. Ruskin, Chair.; Liesl M. Livingston, Pres.; Rosemary Klein, Secy.
EIN: 431796473
Selected grants: The following grants were reported in 2004.
$35,000 to United Way of Escambia County, Pensacola, FL.
$20,000 to United Way of South Baldwin County, Foley, AL.
$15,000 to United Way of Santa Rosa County, Milton, FL.

4908
The Sosland Foundation
4800 Main St., Ste. 100
Kansas City, MO 64112
Contact: Debbie Sosland-Edelman Ph.D., Exec. Dir.
FAX: (816) 756-0494; E-mail: debbie@sosland.com; URL: http://www.soslandfoundation.org

Incorporated in 1955 in MO.
Donor: Members of the Sosland family.
Foundation type: Independent foundation.
Financial data (yr. ended 12/31/04): Assets, $22,569,119 (M); expenditures, $3,039,325;

qualifying distributions, $2,587,059; giving activities include $2,522,614 for 231 grants (high: $249,632; low: $100).
Purpose and activities: Giving to Jewish and social welfare funds, higher and secondary education, the arts, and health organizations.
Fields of interest: Performing arts; Performing arts, theater; Performing arts, music; Arts; Secondary school/education; Higher education; Health care; Health organizations, association; Human services; Jewish federated giving programs; Government/public administration; Jewish agencies & temples.
Type of support: Fellowships; Professorships; General/operating support; Continuing support; Annual campaigns; Capital campaigns; Building/renovation; Equipment; Endowments; Program development; Curriculum development; Scholarship funds; Research; Program evaluation; Employee matching gifts.
Limitations: Giving primarily in the metropolitan bi-state Kansas City area. No grants to individuals, or for publications or conferences.
Publications: Application guidelines.
Application information: See Web site for grant guidelines. Application form not required.
Initial approach: Letter
Copies of proposal: 1
Deadline(s): None
Board meeting date(s): Mar., June, Sept., and Dec.
Final notification: 3 months
Officers and Directors:* Morton I. Sosland,* Pres.; Neil Sosland,* V.P.; Charles Sosland, Secy.; L. Joshua Sosland,* Treas.; Debbie Sosland-Edelman, Ph.D., Exec. Dir.
Number of staff: 2 part-time professional; 2 part-time support.
EIN: 446007129
Selected grants: The following grants were reported in 2004.
$449,632 to Jewish Federation. 2 grants: $200,000, $249,632
$125,000 to Pembroke Hill School, Kansas City, MO. For general support.
$110,000 to Childrens Mercy Hospital, Kansas City, MO.
$100,000 to Kansas State University, Manhattan, KS.
$100,000 to Nelson Gallery Foundation, Kansas City, MO.
$100,000 to United States Holocaust Memorial Museum, DC.
$100,000 to Village Shalom, Overland Park, KS. For capital campaign.
$89,043 to Congregation Beth Shalom, Kansas City, MO.
$50,000 to Hyman Brand Hebrew Academy, Overland Park, KS.

4909
Richard J. Stern Foundation for the Arts ◇
922 Walnut St., Ste. 200
Kansas City, MO 64106-1809
Contact: Michael D. Fields, Chair.

Established in 1986 in MO.
Foundation type: Independent foundation.
Financial data (yr. ended 6/30/05): Assets, $48,358,572 (M); expenditures, $2,403,472; qualifying distributions, $2,124,430; giving activities include $2,091,509 for 69 grants (high: $250,000; low: $1,000).

Purpose and activities: Giving only to organizations engaged in supporting the arts in the 5-county, metropolitan Kansas City, MO, area, including the performing arts and art education.
Fields of interest: Performing arts; Performing arts, music; Arts.
Type of support: General/operating support; Continuing support; Capital campaigns; Building/renovation; Equipment; Emergency funds; Program development.
Limitations: Giving limited to the 5-county, metropolitan Kansas City, MO, area only. No support for private foundations. No grants to individuals.
Publications: Informational brochure (including application guidelines).
Application information: Application form not required.
Initial approach: Request guidelines
Copies of proposal: 1
Deadline(s): 3 weeks prior to meeting
Board meeting date(s): Quarterly
Final notification: 2-4 months
Contributions Committee: Michael D. Fields, Chair.; Jonathan M. Kemper; John A. Ovel.
Trustee: Commerce Bank, N.A.
EIN: 436313811
Selected grants: The following grants were reported in 2005.
$390,000 to Kansas City Symphony, Kansas City, MO. 2 grants: $250,000, $140,000
$250,000 to Lyric Opera of Kansas City, Kansas City, MO. 2 grants: $125,000 each
$100,000 to Kansas City Art Institute, Kansas City, MO.
$26,551 to Kansas City Public Library, Kansas City, MO.
$25,000 to Saint Teresas Academy, Kansas City, MO.
$17,500 to K C P T-Kansas City Public Television Channel 19, Kansas City, MO.
$10,000 to Avila University, Kansas City, MO.
$10,000 to Hyman Brand Hebrew Academy, Overland Park, KS.

4910
Stupp Bros. Bridge & Iron Company Foundation ◇
3800 Weber Rd.
St. Louis, MO 63125

Trust established about 1952 in MO.
Donors: Stupp Bros. Bridge & Iron Co.; Stupp Bridge Co.
Foundation type: Company-sponsored foundation.
Financial data (yr. ended 10/31/05): Assets, $8,635,846 (M); expenditures, $541,725; qualifying distributions, $480,003; giving activities include $480,003 for 148 grants (high: $38,000; low: $100).
Purpose and activities: The foundation supports organizations involved with arts and culture, education, health, parks and playgrounds, youth development, human services, and religion.
Fields of interest: Arts; Elementary school/education; Higher education; Education; Hospitals (general); Health care; Recreation, parks/playgrounds; Youth development; Human services; Federated giving programs; Religion.
Limitations: Applications not accepted. Giving primarily in MO. No grants to individuals.
Application information: Contributes only to pre-selected organizations.

Trustees: John P. Stupp, Jr.; Robert P. Stupp.
EIN: 237412437

4911
Norman J. Stupp Foundation
c/o Commerce Bank, N.A.
8000 Forsyth Blvd.
St. Louis, MO 63105 (314) 746-8940
Contact: Cynthia Crim, Grants Mgr.
FAX: (314) 746-3907;
E-mail: susan.muse@commercebank.com

Established in 1952 in MO.
Donor: Norman J. Stupp†.
Foundation type: Independent foundation.
Financial data (yr. ended 6/30/06): Assets,
$20,148,972 (M); expenditures, $1,137,673;
qualifying distributions, $1,074,330; giving
activities include $977,934 for 74 grants (high:
$50,000; low: $2,500).
Purpose and activities: The foundation focus is
within three categories: Strengthening the Region;
Building Strong Communities and Neighborhoods;
and Helping Youth Succeed. The mission is to
enhance the lives of residents in the metropolitan
St. Louis area.
Fields of interest: Arts; Education; Botanical/
horticulture/landscape services; Housing/shelter;
Youth development; Human services; Children/
youth, services; Community development.
Type of support: Capital campaigns; Building/
renovation; Equipment; Program development;
Research; Technical assistance; Matching/
challenge support.
Limitations: Giving primarily in the metropolitan St.
Louis, MO, area. No grants to individuals.
Publications: Application guidelines.
Application information: Requests from
organizations outside the St. Louis, MO, area not
usually considered. Use of application forms
preferred. Potential applicants are encouraged to
contact the foundation for information on current
funding priorities before submitting letters of intent
or full applications. Application form not required.
Initial approach: Telephone and letter of intent
Copies of proposal: 1
Deadline(s): Mar. 1, July 1, Nov. 1
Board meeting date(s): Jan., May, Sept.
Final notification: 60-90 days
Trustee: Commerce Bank, N.A.
EIN: 436027433
Selected grants: The following grants were reported
in 2005.
$20,000 to Big Brothers/Big Sisters of Eastern
Missouri, Saint Louis, MO.
$12,500 to Saint Louis Symphony Orchestra, Saint
Louis, MO.
$10,000 to De La Salle Middle School at Saint
Matthews, Saint Louis, MO.
$5,000 to College Summit, DC.
$3,000 to Friedens Haus, Saint Louis, MO.

4912
John J. Sullivan, Jr. Foundation ✧
c/o J. Houlehan and M. Henke
11914 Summit
Kansas City, MO 64145

Established in 1997 in MO.
Donor: John J. Sullivan, Jr.
Foundation type: Independent foundation.

Financial data (yr. ended 12/31/05): Assets,
$6,534,422 (M); expenditures, $486,234;
qualifying distributions, $406,874; giving activities
include $369,180 for 55 grants (high: $60,000;
low: $250; average: $1,000–$10,000).
Purpose and activities: Giving primarily to Catholic
agencies and churches, and for education.
Fields of interest: Secondary school/education;
Higher education; Roman Catholic agencies &
churches.
Limitations: Applications not accepted. Giving
primarily in KS and MO. No grants to individuals.
Application information: Contributes only to
pre-selected organizations.
Trustees: Mark Henke; John Houlehan.
EIN: 742815203
Selected grants: The following grants were reported
in 2004.
$32,000 to Rockhurst High School, Kansas City,
MO.
$11,700 to Saint Teresas Academy, Kansas City,
MO.
$8,000 to DeLaSalle Education Center, Kansas
City, MO.
$5,850 to Bishop Ward High School, Kansas City,
KS.
$3,000 to Bishop Sullivan Center, Kansas City, MO.
$2,000 to Donnelly College, Kansas City, KS.
$1,000 to Horizon Academy, Overland Park, KS.
$1,000 to Little Sisters of the Poor, Kansas City,
MO.
$900 to Benedictine College, Atchison, KS.
$500 to Sunflower House - A Child Abuse Prevention
Center, Shawnee, KS.

4913
Sunnen Foundation
7910 Manchester Ave.
St. Louis, MO 63143
Contact: Kurt J. Kallaus, Pres.

Incorporated in 1953 in MO.
Donors: Joseph Sunnen†; Helen Sly; Sunnen
Products Company.
Foundation type: Independent foundation.
Financial data (yr. ended 12/31/05): Assets,
$14,623,035 (M); gifts received, $97,500;
expenditures, $613,609; qualifying distributions,
$536,400; giving activities include $531,900 for 22
grants (high: $104,400; low: $1,000).
Purpose and activities: Specific goal-oriented
projects for protection of reproductive and First
Amendment rights, educational opportunities for the
economically or physically disadvantaged and for
youth and family services.
Fields of interest: Child development, education;
Reproductive health, family planning; Children/
youth, services; Child development, services; Family
services; Civil liberties, reproductive rights.
Type of support: Capital campaigns; Program
development; Matching/challenge support.
Limitations: Giving primarily in MO, with emphasis
on the metropolitan St. Louis area. No support for
educational institutions, environmental
organizations, hospitals or medical charities, the
arts or private day care centers. Generally no
support for charities with broad-based public appeal,
or religious bodies. No grants to individuals, or for
scholarships, general operating costs, or research
projects.
Publications: Informational brochure (including
application guidelines).

Application information: Proposals submitted in
notebooks, binders or plastic folders are not
accepted. Application form not required.
Initial approach: Proposal, not to exceed 10
pages
Copies of proposal: 6
Deadline(s): Proposal due June or July; final
deadline is Aug. 1
Board meeting date(s): Generally in Dec.
Officers and Directors:* Kurt J. Kallaus,* Pres.;
Matthew S. Kreider,* V.P.; Ruth Cardinale,* Secy.;
Susan S. Brasel,* Treas.; Helen S. Sly.
EIN: 436029156
Selected grants: The following grants were reported
in 2003.
$95,865 to YMCA of the Ozarks, Potosi, MO.
$75,000 to Court Appointed Special Advocates
(CASA) of Saint Louis County, Saint Louis, MO.
$55,000 to Planned Parenthood of Saint Louis,
Saint Louis, MO.
$50,000 to Missouri Historical Society, Saint Louis,
MO.
$50,000 to Museum of Transportation, Brookline,
MA.
$35,000 to Religious Coalition for Reproductive
Choice, Missouri, Saint Louis, MO.
$32,000 to Planned Parenthood of Alabama,
Birmingham, AL.
$25,000 to Boy Scouts of America, Greater Saint
Louis Council, Saint Louis, MO.
$20,000 to Operation Food Search, Saint Louis,
MO.
$15,000 to Our Little Haven, Saint Louis, MO.

4914
W. Clarke Swanson, Jr. Foundation ✧ ☆
1 W. Armour Blvd., Ste. 300
Kansas City, MO 64111 (816) 360-6174
Contact: W. Clarke Swanson, Jr., Dir.

Established in 1998 in MO.
Foundation type: Independent foundation.
Financial data (yr. ended 12/31/05): Assets,
$1,885,712 (M); expenditures, $882,841;
qualifying distributions, $870,245; giving activities
include $869,500 for 8 grants (high: $642,500;
low: $2,000).
Purpose and activities: Giving primarily to the arts,
and education.
Fields of interest: Arts; Education; Health care.
Limitations: Giving primarily in CA; some funding
nationally.
Application information: Application form not
required.
Initial approach: Letter
Deadline(s): None
Directors: Alexis Swanson; Elizabeth Swanson; W.
Clarke Swanson, Jr.
EIN: 311530763

4915
Sycamore Tree Trust ✧
P.O. Box 66734
St. Louis, MO 63166

Trust established about 1953 in MO.
Donors: Adelaide Schlafly; Maria Bryne Schlafly;
Theresa Bryne Schlafly; Thomas F. Schlafly
Charitable Lead Trust; Daniel Schlafly; Mrs. Daniel
Schlafly; Thomas Schlafly; Mrs. Thomas Schlafly.
Foundation type: Independent foundation.

Financial data (yr. ended 12/31/05): Assets, $126,800 (M); gifts received, $337,366; expenditures, $656,901; qualifying distributions, $649,704; giving activities include $649,704 for 57 grants (high: $129,890; low: $100).

Purpose and activities: Giving to Roman Catholic churches and organizations, education, arts & culture, and human service organizations.

Fields of interest: Arts; Elementary/secondary education; Higher education; Human services; Christian agencies & churches; Roman Catholic agencies & churches.

Type of support: Continuing support; Annual campaigns; Professorships.

Limitations: Applications not accepted. Giving primarily in MO. No grants to individuals, or for scholarships or fellowships; no loans.

Application information: Contributes only to pre-selected organizations.

Board meeting date(s): Monthly

Trustee: A.G. Edwards Trust Co.

EIN: 436026719

4916

The Crawford Taylor Foundation ▼

600 Corporate Park Dr.
Clayton, MO 63105
Contact: Jo Ann Kindle, V.P. and Secy.

Established in 1997 in MO.

Donor: Jack C. Taylor.

Foundation type: Independent foundation.

Financial data (yr. ended 12/31/05): Assets, $11,070,508 (M); gifts received, $10,000,000; expenditures, $7,326,354; qualifying distributions, $7,291,455; giving activities include $7,291,455 for 23 grants (high: $7,086,955; low: $1,000; average: $5,000–$50,000).

Purpose and activities: Support primarily for charitable and educational organizations.

Fields of interest: Performing arts, orchestra (symphony); Higher education; Health care, association; Human services.

Limitations: Giving primarily in St. Louis, MO.

Application information:

Initial approach: Proposal

Deadline(s): None

Board meeting date(s): July and Dec.

Final notification: Within 3 months of application

Officers and Directors:* Jack C. Taylor,* Pres.; Jo Ann Kindle,* V.P. and Secy.; Andrew C. Taylor,* V.P. and Treas.

Number of staff: 1 part-time professional; 1 part-time support.

EIN: 431790817

Selected grants: The following grants were reported in 2005.

$7,086,955 to Saint Louis Symphony Endowment Trust, Saint Louis, MO.

$50,000 to Magic House, Saint Louis Childrens Museum, Saint Louis, MO.

4917

The Tilles Fund

(formerly Rosalie Tilles Nonsectarian Charity Fund)
c/o U.S. Bank, N.A.
SL-MO-T14E, Private Client Group
P.O. Box 387
St. Louis, MO 63166
Contact: Garth Silvey, V.P.
URL: http://www.thetillesfund.org

Trust established in 1926 in MO.

Donor: Cap Andrew Tilles†.

Foundation type: Independent foundation.

Financial data (yr. ended 6/30/05): Assets, $13,223,494 (M); gifts received, $180; expenditures, $703,957; qualifying distributions, $605,620; giving activities include $210,000 for 13 grants (high: $40,000; low: $400), and $375,817 for 52 grants to individuals (high: $14,850; low: $734).

Purpose and activities: The foundation awards scholarships to recent high school graduates who are residents of the City or County of St. Louis, MO, to attend any Missouri university or college. The fund also solicits grant requests annually from St. Louis area organizations for a one-year period that provide services for the special needs of children with physical and/or mental disabilities.

Fields of interest: Children/youth, services.

Type of support: Scholarship funds.

Limitations: Giving limited to the city of St. Louis and St. Louis County, MO. No grants to individuals directly; or for political causes and candidates, for-profit entities, operating costs, fundraising dinners, courtesy advertising or other benefits and endowment projects.

Publications: Application guidelines.

Application information: Nominations for scholarships are only accepted from the scholarship coordinator at a Missouri college or university. Scholarships are not paid directly to individuals. The foundation generally does not accept unsolicited applications. Please see foundation Web site for Phase 1 of the funding process. Application form not required.

Initial approach: 1-page concept paper

Copies of proposal: 7

Deadline(s): Aug. 15th for grants; May 1 for scholarships

Board meeting date(s): Monthly

Officer: Garth Silvey, V.P.

Number of staff: 1 part-time professional; 1 part-time support.

EIN: 436020833

4918

Trio Foundation of St. Louis

(formerly Trio Foundation)
8029 Forsyth Blvd., No. 201
St. Louis, MO 63105 (314) 725-3040
Contact: Wendy Jaffe, Exec. Dir.
FAX: (314) 725-2603; E-mail: trio@triostl.org

Established in 1990 in MO.

Donor: Dorothy Moog.

Foundation type: Independent foundation.

Financial data (yr. ended 12/31/05): Assets, $10,561,362 (M); expenditures, $901,161; qualifying distributions, $829,063; giving activities include $769,000 for 91 grants (high: $25,000; low: $1,000).

Fields of interest: Arts; Education; Environment; Youth development; Human services; Jewish agencies & temples; Women.

Type of support: General/operating support; Capital campaigns; Program development; Seed money.

Limitations: Giving primarily in St. Louis, MO. No grants to individuals, or for medical/science research; generally not interested in supporting the production of videos, CD-ROMs, conferences, seminars, feasibility studies, the development of strategic plans, or for the purchase of computer hardware or software.

Publications: Application guidelines.

Application information: Contact staff for most current application forms. Application form required.

Initial approach: Telephone or E-mail for guidelines

Copies of proposal: 3

Deadline(s): Sept. 1

Final notification: Dec.

Officers and Directors:* Donna L. Moog,* Pres.; James R. Moog,* V.P. and Secy.; Thomas H. Moog,* Treas.; Wendy Jaffe, Exec. Dir.; Terri Mason; Mary Moog.

Number of staff: 1 part-time professional.

EIN: 431553538

Selected grants: The following grants were reported in 2003.

$50,000 to Contemporary Art Museum Saint Louis, Saint Louis, MO. For operating support.

$25,000 to Center of Creative Arts, Saint Louis, MO. For capital campaign.

$25,000 to National Conference for Community and Justice, Saint Louis, MO.

$25,000 to Nurses for Newborns Foundation, Saint Louis, MO. For general operating support.

$20,000 to Racine Heritage Museum, Racine, WI. For Double Vision/Single Focus Capital campaign.

$20,000 to Ranken Technical College, Saint Louis, MO. For Centennial Campaign.

$20,000 to Saint Louis Zoo, Saint Louis, MO. For Gateway to the Animal World.

$20,000 to Scholarship Foundation of Saint Louis, Saint Louis, MO. For Bravo Fund Grant Program.

$15,000 to Forest Park Forever, Saint Louis, MO. For Voyage of Learning Teacher's Academy.

$10,000 to Grand Center, Saint Louis, MO. For general operating support.

4919

Truman Heartland Community Foundation

(formerly Independence Community Foundation)
Commerce Bank Bldg.
300 N. Osage St.
Independence, MO 64050 (816) 836-8189
Contact: Paul M. Thomson Ph.D., C.E.O.
FAX: (816) 836-8898; E-mail: thomson@thcf.org;
Additional E-mail: mcclure@thcf.org; URL: http://www.thcf.org

Incorporated in 1982 in MO; received assets converted from merger of Independence Community Foundation with Independence Regional Health Center Foundation in 1994.

Foundation type: Community foundation.

Financial data (yr. ended 12/31/04): Assets, $22,548,476 (M); gifts received, $2,247,142; expenditures, $2,174,892; giving activities include $1,576,713 for 574 grants (high: $115,800; low: $100).

Purpose and activities: The foundation primarily provides support for arts, culture, and historic preservation, stronger neighborhoods, education, community spirit, health, leadership development, seniors, youth development, transportation, and violence prevention.

Fields of interest: Historic preservation/historical societies; Arts; Adult/continuing education; Education; Health care; Crime/violence prevention; Employment, services; Employment, training; Housing/shelter, development; Youth development; Children/youth, services; Family services, domestic violence; Aging, centers/services; Human services; Community development; Transportation; Aging.

Type of support: General/operating support; Continuing support; Program development; Seed money; Scholarship funds; In-kind gifts; Matching/challenge support.

Limitations: Giving limited to Eastern Jackson County, MO. No support for religious purposes. No grants to individuals (except for scholarships).

Publications: Application guidelines; Annual report; Informational brochure; Newsletter.

Application information: Visit foundation Web site for application forms, guidelines, and specific deadlines. Organizations whose letters of interest show the greatest potential for serving or strengthening the community will be invited to submit full applications. Application form required.

Initial approach: Letter (no more than 2 pages) on letterhead
Copies of proposal: 12
Deadline(s): Varies
Board meeting date(s): Quarterly
Final notification: Varies

Officers and Directors:* R. James Stilley, Jr.,* Chair.; Allen Lefko,* Vice-Chair.; Paul M. Thomson, Ph.D., C.E.O. and Pres.; Roberta Coker,* Secy.; G.L. "Tom" Thomas,* Treas.; Ron Bruch; Vicki Digby; Randall Ferguson; Colleen Foudree; Steven W. Gildehaus; Dr. Fred Hahn; Doug Hammer; Joy Hobick; Lydia Jeter; Nancy C. Kimak; Judy Ness; James Pryde; Carson Ross; Dr. Steve Silverstein; Freddye Smith.

Number of staff: 2 full-time professional; 2 full-time support; 1 part-time support.

EIN: 431482136

4920
John W. Uhlmann Foundation ✧
c/o UMB Bank, N.A.
P.O. Box 419692
Kansas City, MO 64141-6692
Application address: c/o John Uhlmann Co., P.O. Box 410, Kansas City, MO 64141

Established in 1976 in MO.

Donor: John W. Uhlmann.

Foundation type: Independent foundation.

Financial data (yr. ended 6/30/05): Assets, $1,213,453 (M); expenditures, $1,207,356; qualifying distributions, $1,195,666; giving activities include $1,192,617 for 21 grants (high: $900,000; low: $250).

Purpose and activities: Giving primarily for Jewish education.

Fields of interest: Museums (history); Arts; Education; Civil rights; Jewish federated giving programs; Jewish agencies & temples.

Limitations: Giving primarily in the metropolitan Kansas City, MO, area.

Application information: Application form required.

Initial approach: Letter
Deadline(s): None
Final notification: Usually within 2 months

Officers: John H. Uhlmann, Pres.; Patricia W. Uhlmann, V.P.

Director: Robert Uhlmann.

Agent: UMB Bank, N.A.

EIN: 431113857

Selected grants: The following grants were reported in 2004.

$100,000 to Hyman Brand Hebrew Academy, Overland Park, KS.

$82,500 to Jewish Federation of Greater Kansas City, Overland Park, KS.

$25,000 to Right to Life Committee Educational Trust Fund, National, DC.

$20,000 to Voices United for Israel, Shawnee Mission, KS.

$15,100 to Americans for Tax Reform Foundation, DC.

$12,000 to Coalition on Urban Renewal and Education (CURE), DC.

$10,000 to Jewish Institute for National Security Affairs, DC.

$1,800 to Jewish Community Center of Greater Kansas City, Overland Park, KS.

$1,000 to Congregation BIAV (Beth Israel Abraham and Voliner), Kansas City, MO.

$1,000 to University Academy, Kansas City, MO.

4921
Vatterott Foundation ☆
10449 St. Charles Rock Rd., Ste. 200
St. Ann, MO 63074 (314) 427-4000, ext. 304
Contact: Marilyn Haggerty, Admin.

Established in 1948 in MO.

Donors: William H. Erker; Charles F. Vatterott, Jr.†; John Harvey Vatterott†; Joseph A. Vatterott†; Mary Patricia Vatterott†; John C. Vatterott.

Foundation type: Independent foundation.

Financial data (yr. ended 5/31/05): Assets, $3,107,601 (M); gifts received, $510,000; expenditures, $458,178; qualifying distributions, $396,762; giving activities include $396,762 for 38 grants (high: $150,000; low: $500).

Purpose and activities: Giving primarily for elementary and secondary education for economically disadvantaged youngsters, programs that serve minority populations and enhance racial equality, and to Roman Catholic organizations and human service agencies that serve the poor.

Fields of interest: Elementary/secondary education; Education, early childhood education; Education; Human services; Christian agencies & churches; Roman Catholic agencies & churches; Religion; Minorities; Economically disadvantaged.

Type of support: General/operating support; Continuing support; Capital campaigns; Seed money.

Limitations: Giving primarily in St. Louis, MO. No grants to individuals.

Application information:

Initial approach: Letter
Deadline(s): None
Board meeting date(s): Quarterly

Trustees: William H. Erker; Louise Hart; Claire Vatterott Hundelt; Ed Kelley; Leo Kennedy; Charles Riley; Daniel Vatterott; Frank J. Vatterott; Glennon R. Vatterott, Jr.; John C. Vatterott; Paul B. Vatterott, Jr., M.D.

Number of staff: 1 part-time professional.

EIN: 436031155

Selected grants: The following grants were reported in 2004.

$30,000 to Continuum of Life Care Center, East Saint Louis, IL.

$25,000 to Cardinal Ritter College Prep, Saint Louis, MO.

$5,000 to Saint Elizabeth Academy, Saint Louis, MO.

$3,250 to City Academy, Saint Louis, MO.

$2,500 to Child Center of Our Lady, Saint Louis, MO.

$2,500 to Lutheran Family and Childrens Services Foundation, Saint Louis, MO.

$1,000 to Franciscan Connection, Saint Louis, MO.

$1,000 to Saint Margaret of Scotland Church, Saint Louis, MO.

$1,000 to School Sisters of Notre Dame, Saint Louis, MO.

$1,000 to Society of the Sacred Heart, Saint Louis, MO.

4922
The Earl E. Walker and Myrtle E. Walker Foundation ✧
c/o Earl E. Walker
12071 Carberry Pl.
St. Louis, MO 63131-3123

Established in 1987 in MO.

Donors: Earl E. Walker; Myrtle E. Walker; CARR Lane Manufacturing; Walker Family Trust; W & W, Inc.; Home Towne Suites - Bowling Green LLC; Home Towne Suites - Clarksville LLC; All American Products.

Foundation type: Independent foundation.

Financial data (yr. ended 12/31/05): Assets, $8,886,006 (M); gifts received, $1,907,000; expenditures, $1,803,242; qualifying distributions, $1,752,593; giving activities include $1,752,593 for 27 grants (high: $1,000,000; low: $910).

Purpose and activities: Giving primarily for education and health services.

Fields of interest: Elementary/secondary education; Higher education, university; Health care; Human services; Children/youth, services.

Type of support: General/operating support; Building/renovation; Endowments; Scholarships—to individuals.

Limitations: Applications not accepted. Giving primarily in MO.

Application information: Contributes only to pre-selected organizations and individuals.

Trustees: Earl E. Walker; Myrtle E. Walker.

EIN: 431466121

Selected grants: The following grants were reported in 2004.

$1,002,000 to Washington University, Saint Louis, MO. 2 grants: $2,000, $1,000,000

$10,000 to KidSmart, Bridgeton, MO.

$4,000 to Saint Louis University, Saint Louis, MO.

$3,900 to Kansas City Art Institute, Kansas City, MO.

$2,699 to Southern Illinois University, Carbondale, IL.

$2,000 to Pennsylvania State University, Philadelphia, PA.

$2,000 to Southeast Missouri State University, Cape Girardeau, MO.

$2,000 to Southwest Baptist University, Bolivar, MO.

$2,000 to University of Oregon, Eugene, OR.

4923
The Wampus Beth Zion Trust ✧ ☆
(formerly The Wampus Fund)
c/o David Krauss
911 Washington Ave., 7th Fl.
St. Louis, MO 63101-1290 (314) 259-2000

Established in 1997 in MO.

Donors: Sue Fischlowitz; David Roberts.

Foundation type: Independent foundation.

Financial data (yr. ended 12/31/04): Assets, $3,447,174 (M); expenditures, $443,035; qualifying distributions, $352,468; giving activities

include $352,468 for 32 grants (high: $156,000; low: $150).

Purpose and activities: Giving primarily to Jewish organizations and temples, and for Jewish education; funding also for the arts, and human services.

Fields of interest: Arts; Education; Human services; Jewish federated giving programs; Jewish agencies & temples.

Limitations: Applications not accepted. Giving on a national basis, with emphasis on St. Louis, MO. No grants to individuals.

Application information: Contributes only to pre-selected organizations.

Trustees: Sue Fischlowitz; David Roberts.

EIN: 436763559

Selected grants: The following grants were reported in 2004.

$156,000 to Jewish Federation of Saint Louis, Saint Louis, MO.

$8,700 to Compassion Over Killing, DC.

$7,200 to New Israel Fund, DC.

$5,000 to United Way of Greater Saint Louis, Saint Louis, MO.

$2,500 to Tribe of Heart, Ithaca, NY.

$1,968 to Truman State University, Kirksville, MO.

$1,000 to Shakespeare Festival of Saint Louis, Saint Louis, MO.

$360 to Shefa Fund, Philadelphia, PA.

$150 to Saint Louis Rabbinical Association, Saint Louis, MO.

4924
Louis L. & Adelaide C. Ward Foundation ✧
(formerly Ward Foundation)
P.O. Box 30480
Kansas City, MO 64112-0480

Established in 1966 in MO.

Donor: Members of the Ward Family.

Foundation type: Independent foundation.

Financial data (yr. ended 12/31/04): Assets, $33,292,946 (M); gifts received, $3,500,000; expenditures, $1,425,861; qualifying distributions, $1,402,132; giving activities include $1,397,500 for 6 grants (high: $1,200,000; low: $37,500).

Purpose and activities: Support primarily for health and culture; some support for education.

Fields of interest: Elementary/secondary education; Recreation, parks/playgrounds.

Type of support: Annual campaigns; Capital campaigns; Endowments.

Limitations: Applications not accepted. Giving limited to KS and MO. No grants to individuals.

Application information: Unsolicited requests for funds not accepted.

Officers: Adelaide C. Ward, V.P. and Treas.; Scott H. Ward, Secy.

EIN: 436064548

4925
James L. & Nellie M. Westlake Scholarship Fund ✧
c/o U.S. Bank, N.A.
P.O. Box 387
St. Louis, MO 63166
Contact: Angela Pearson
Scholarship application address: c/o Scholarship Management Svcs., 1 Scholarship Way, P.O. Box 297, St. Peter, MN 56082

Established in 1981 in MO.

Donors: James L. Westlake†; Nellie M. Westlake.

Foundation type: Independent foundation.

Financial data (yr. ended 6/30/05): Assets, $22,092,420 (M); expenditures, $996,939; qualifying distributions, $963,116; giving activities include $867,220 for 73 grants to individuals (high: $30,200; low: $3,800).

Purpose and activities: Awards scholarships to graduates of Missouri high schools, based on need and scholastic achievement, for higher education scholarships.

Type of support: Scholarships—to individuals.

Limitations: Giving limited to high school graduates who are residents of MO. No loans or program-related investments.

Publications: Application guidelines.

Application information: Application form required.
  Initial approach: Applications are available from high school counseling offices
  Deadline(s): Feb. 28
  Final notification: May 1

Trustee: U.S. Bank, N.A.

EIN: 436248269

4926
Whitaker Foundation
(also known as Lyndon C. and Mae M. Whitaker Charitable Foundation)
308 N. 21st St., Ste. 400
St. Louis, MO 63103   (314) 241-4352
Contact: Christy E. Gray, Exec. Dir.
FAX: (314) 241-4381;
E-mail: cgray@thewhitakerfoundation.org;
URL: http://www.thewhitakerfoundation.org

Trust established in 1975 in MO.

Donor: Mae M. Whitaker†.

Foundation type: Independent foundation.

Financial data (yr. ended 4/30/06): Assets, $31,407,283 (M); expenditures, $2,101,887; qualifying distributions, $1,727,433; giving activities include $1,567,326 for 43 grants (high: $200,000; low: $1,200).

Purpose and activities: Giving primarily to strengthen arts organizations and local park preservation and use.

Fields of interest: Arts; Recreation, parks/playgrounds.

Type of support: Capital campaigns; Building/renovation; Program development.

Limitations: Giving in the metropolitan St. Louis, MO, area. No grants to individuals, or for galas, tournaments, or other social events.

Application information: Contact foundation for application materials. Prefer project-specific requests. Do not fax or e-mail proposal, or submit in notebooks, binders or plastic folders. Application form required.
  Initial approach: Telephone call
  Copies of proposal: 1
  Deadline(s): Aug. 1, Nov. 1, Feb. 1
  Board meeting date(s): Jan., Apr., July and Oct.
  Final notification: Oct., Jan. and Apr.

Officer: Christy E. Gray, Exec. Dir.

Trustees: John Capps; Clark Davis; Shaun Hayes; Marylen Mann.

Number of staff: 1 full-time professional; 1 part-time support.

EIN: 510173109

Selected grants: The following grants were reported in 2005.

$550,000 to Saint Louis Symphony Orchestra, Saint Louis, MO.

$184,000 to Opera Theater of Saint Louis, Saint Louis, MO. 2 grants: $84,000, $100,000

$100,000 to Forest Park Forever, Saint Louis, MO.

$90,000 to Missouri Botanical Garden, Saint Louis, MO.

$75,000 to Repertory Theater of Saint Louis, Saint Louis, MO.

$75,000 to Sheldon Arts Foundation, Saint Louis, MO.

$70,000 to Contemporary Art Museum Saint Louis, Saint Louis, MO.

$37,500 to Gateway Greening, Saint Louis, MO.

$33,000 to Saint Louis Black Repertory Company, Saint Louis, MO.

4927
Wolff Foundation No. 2 ✧ ☆
c/o U.S. Bank, N.A.
P.O. Box 387
St. Louis, MO 63166
Application address: c/o Edith Wolff, 724 Audubon Dr., St. Louis, MO 63105

Established in 1993 in MO.

Donors: Edith Wolff; The Wolff Foundation.

Foundation type: Independent foundation.

Financial data (yr. ended 9/30/05): Assets, $665,185 (M); gifts received, $900,000; expenditures, $951,357; qualifying distributions, $949,064; giving activities include $945,845 for 16 grants (high: $200,000; low: $530).

Purpose and activities: Giving primarily for education, health, and Jewish agencies.

Fields of interest: Higher education; Education; Health care; Jewish agencies & temples.

Limitations: Giving limited to St. Louis, MO. No grants to individuals.

Application information:
  Initial approach: Letter
  Deadline(s): None

Advisory Committee: James Fogle; Edith Wolff.

Trustee: U.S. Bank, N.A.

EIN: 436498120

4928
James H. Woods Foundation ✧
1588 S. Lindbergh Blvd., Ste. 205
St. Louis, MO 63131   (314) 997-8088
Contact: Becky Power
FAX: (314) 567-9798;
E-mail: becky_power@stoutmarketing.com

Trust established in 1958 in MO.

Donor: James H. Woods†.

Foundation type: Independent foundation.

Financial data (yr. ended 11/30/05): Assets, $17,731,974 (M); expenditures, $664,654; qualifying distributions, $434,569; giving activities include $373,000 for 11 grants (high: $200,000; low: $1,000).

Purpose and activities: Funding primarily for education, federated giving programs, and human services.

Fields of interest: Elementary/secondary education; Education; Environment, natural resources; Animal welfare; Health care; Human services; Children/youth, services; Federated giving programs.

Type of support: General/operating support; Building/renovation; Endowments; Seed money; Scholarship funds.
Limitations: Giving on a national basis with emphasis on MO.
Application information:
 Deadline(s): None
Trustees: Elizabeth Woods Bradbury; James H. Woods, Jr.; John R. Woods; Bank of America, N.A.
EIN: 436024866

4929
Kearney Wornall Charitable Foundation ◇
(formerly Kearney Wornall Charitable Trust & Foundation)
c/o UMB Bank, N.A.
P.O. Box 419692
Kansas City, MO 64141-6692
Contact: Jan Leonard

Established in 1954 in MO.
Donor: Kearney Wornall†.
Foundation type: Independent foundation.
Financial data (yr. ended 12/31/05): Assets, $12,585,276 (M); expenditures, $631,280; qualifying distributions, $606,185; giving activities include $580,500 for 23 grants (high: $175,000; low: $2,500; average: $10,000–$25,000).
Fields of interest: Museums; Performing arts; Arts; Education; Human services; Federated giving programs.
Type of support: General/operating support.
Limitations: Applications not accepted. Giving primarily in the Kansas City, MO, area. No grants to individuals.

Application information: Contributes only to pre-selected organizations.
Trustees: Paul L. Skahan; UMB Bank, N.A.
EIN: 446013874
Selected grants: The following grants were reported in 2004.
$225,000 to Agriculture Future of America, Kansas City, MO. For general support.
$90,000 to Kansas City Symphony, Kansas City, MO. For general support.
$40,000 to Kemper Museum of Contemporary Art and Design, Kansas City, MO. For general support.
$37,500 to Archdiocese of Kansas City, Kansas City, KS. For general support.
$30,000 to Students in Free Enterprise, Springfield, MO.
$25,000 to Harvesters-The Community Food Network, Kansas City, MO. For general support.
$10,000 to American Royal Association, Kansas City, MO. For general support.
$10,000 to Boys Hope Girls Hope, Bridgeton, MO.
$10,000 to Donnelly College, Kansas City, KS.
$5,000 to DeLaSalle Education Center, Kansas City, MO. For general support.

4930
Wyeth Pharmaceutical Assistance Foundation ◇ ☆
c/o Patient Assistance Prog.
P.O. Box 66762
St. Louis, MO 63166-6762 (800) 568-9938
Contact: Lewis Adams, Pres.

Additional tel.: (866) 590-5885; URL: http://www.wyeth.com/patientassistance

Established as a company-sponsored operating foundation in 2002 in DE.
Donor: Wyeth.
Foundation type: Operating foundation.
Financial data (yr. ended 12/31/05): Assets, $0 (M); gifts received, $247,184,612; expenditures, $247,184,612; qualifying distributions, $247,184,612; giving activities include $247,184,612 for grants to individuals.
Purpose and activities: The foundation provides Wyeth medication to economically disadvantaged individuals lacking prescription drug coverage.
Fields of interest: Economically disadvantaged.
Type of support: Donated products; Grants to individuals.
Limitations: Giving on a national basis and in Puerto Rico.
Application information: Application form required.
 Initial approach: Download application form and mail to foundation
 Copies of proposal: 1
 Deadline(s): None
 Final notification: 5 to 7 business days
Officers: Lewis Adams, Pres.; Constance Kossally, Secy.; Alfred Demola, Treas.
Directors: John M. Alvernini; Lucinda E. Long; Lee Mathias; Christina Morrison; Michael J. Sinapi.
EIN: 300089114

MONTANA

4931
Charles M. Bair Memorial Trust ✧
c/o U.S. Bank, N.A.
P.O. Box 30678
Billings, MT   59115   (406) 657-8134

Established in 1978 in MT.
Donors: Marguerite B. Lamb†; Bair Ranch Foundation.
Foundation type: Independent foundation.
Financial data (yr. ended 1/31/05): Assets, $50,498,124 (M); gifts received, $1,999,591; expenditures, $1,959,871; qualifying distributions, $1,888,897; giving activities include $1,515,000 for 4 grants (high: $740,000; low: $125,000), and $366,814 for grants to individuals.
Purpose and activities: Giving restricted to educational institutions, hospitals, and health-related organizations, and to cultural civic service, and human service organizations; scholarships limited to graduates or seniors of Harlowton and White Sulphur Springs high schools, and to graduates or seniors of high schools in Meagher and Wheatland counties in MT.
Fields of interest: Higher education; Hospitals (general); Protestant agencies & churches.
Type of support: General/operating support; Scholarships—to individuals.
Limitations: Giving limited to MT, with preference given to applicants from Yellowstone, Meagher, and Wheatland counties.
Application information: Applications may be obtained from the high schools in Harlowton, White Sulphur Springs and Judith Gap, MT, or from U.S. Bank, N.A. Application form required.
  Initial approach: Letter requesting application
  Deadline(s): Mar. 1 for organizations; Apr. 15 for scholarships
  Final notification: Within 60-90 days of the grant application cycle deadline
Advisory Committee: Louise Galt; Wayne Hirsch; Allan Murphy; Gerald B. Murphy; James P. Roscoe.
Trustee: U.S. Bank, N.A.
EIN: 810370774
Selected grants: The following grants were reported in 2005.
$740,000 to Deaconess Billings Clinic Foundation, Billings, MT. For capital support.
$325,000 to Mountainview Memorial Hospital, White Sulphur Springs, MT. For capital support.
$325,000 to Wheatland Memorial Hospital and Nursing Home, Harlowton, MT. For capital support.
$125,000 to First Church of Christ Scientist, Billings, MT. For capital support.

4932
The Bair Ranch Foundation ✧
P.O. Box 30678
Billings, MT   59103

Established in 1998 in MT.
Foundation type: Independent foundation.
Financial data (yr. ended 12/31/03): Assets, $86,460,638 (M); expenditures, $3,778,889; qualifying distributions, $3,061,214; giving

activities include $2,516,992 for 3 grants (high: $1,007,954; low: $501,084).
Purpose and activities: The foundation was created for the purpose of owning and operating a working ranch that will be used for scientific research, experimentation, and educational programs to be conducted in conjunction with local universities.
Fields of interest: Higher education; Science.
Limitations: Applications not accepted. No grants to individuals.
Application information: Contributes only to pre-selected organizations.
Officers: Wayne Hirsch, Pres.; John T. Garcia, Jr., V.P.; Marie R. Dawson, Secy.
Board Member: Richard Spong.
EIN: 810108184
Selected grants: The following grants were reported in 2003.
$2,015,908 to Charles M. Bair Family Trust Fund, Billings, MT. 2 grants: $1,007,954 (For general operating support), $1,007,954 (For scholarships).
$501,084 to Montana State University, Bozeman, MT.

4933
Browning-Kimball Foundation ✧
P.O. Box 375
Great Falls, MT   59403-0375   (406) 454-1449
Contact: William S. MacFadden, Admin.

Established in 1981 in UT.
Donors: Barbara K. Browning; Barbara Browning Cowan; Matt S. Browning.
Foundation type: Independent foundation.
Financial data (yr. ended 12/31/05): Assets, $15,448,586 (M); expenditures, $494,904; qualifying distributions, $400,000; giving activities include $400,000 for 27 grants (high: $50,000; low: $1,000).
Purpose and activities: Giving primarily for health care including mental health associations, and for children, youth, and social services.
Fields of interest: Museums; Libraries (public); Education; Environment; Animals/wildlife; Mental health, association; Medical research, association; Human services; Children/youth, services; Community development; Christian agencies & churches; Roman Catholic agencies & churches.
Limitations: Giving primarily in MT and Ogden, UT. No grants to individuals.
Application information:
  Initial approach: Request application package
  Deadline(s): None
Officer: Barbara Cowan, Pres.
Directors: Lisa Cowan; William Cowan; William B. Cowan.
Administrator: William S. MacFadden.
EIN: 942766079
Selected grants: The following grants were reported in 2005.
$50,000 to Mental Health Association of Montana, Helena, MT. For unrestricted support.
$40,194 to Youth Impact, Ogden, UT. For unrestricted support.
$40,000 to Eagle Mount Great Falls, Great Falls, MT. For unrestricted support.
$40,000 to Golden Triangle Mental Health Center Foundation, Great Falls, MT. For unrestricted support.
$35,000 to Trigg-C. M. Russell Foundation, Great Falls, MT. For unrestricted support.

$30,000 to Ursuline Historical Foundation, Great Falls, MT. For capital campaign.
$30,000 to Your Community Connection of Ogden/ Northern Utah, Ogden, UT. For unrestricted support.
$25,000 to Northern Montana Youth Ranch, Whitewater, MT. For unrestricted support.
$10,000 to Great Falls Childrens Receiving Home, Great Falls, MT. For unrestricted support.
$5,000 to Union Station Foundation, Ogden, UT.

4934
The Chutney Foundation, Inc. ✧
P.O. Box 8688
Missoula, MT   59807-8688

Established in 1991 in MI.
Donor: Cora Buhl Barbour.
Foundation type: Independent foundation.
Financial data (yr. ended 12/31/04): Assets, $2,045,411 (M); expenditures, $348,359; qualifying distributions, $346,869; giving activities include $345,757 for 14 grants (high: $145,000; low: $3,500).
Fields of interest: Education; Environment; Health care; Youth, services; Philanthropy/voluntarism; Aging.
Limitations: Giving limited to the upper Blackfoot Valley area of western MT. No grants to individuals.
Publications: Informational brochure (including application guidelines).
Application information:
  Initial approach: Letter
  Deadline(s): May 15 (letter of inquiry); Aug. 15 (invited applications)
Officers: William A. Reynolds, M.D., Pres.; John O. Mudd, V.P.
Directors: Thomas C. Barbour; Lawrence D. Buhl, Jr.; Elizabeth B. Cocchiarella; Land M. Lindbergh.
EIN: 810468460
Selected grants: The following grants were reported in 2004.
$145,000 to Blackfoot Challenge, Helena, MT. For stream restoration and reclamation, conservation, education, and weed control projects.
$50,000 to Partnership Health Center, Missoula, MT. For dental health education and prevention.
$30,000 to Saint Patrick Hospital and Health Foundation, Missoula, MT. For diabetes education, and mammogram scholarships.
$25,000 to Five Valleys Land Trust, Missoula, MT. Toward ranch conservation.
$25,000 to Rocky Mountain Partnership for Children, Missoula, MT. For facility improvement and adoptive family recruitment.
$15,000 to Saint Thomas the Apostle Parish, Helmville, MT. For building remodeling and addition.
$13,007 to Cooperative Health Center, Helena, MT. For remodeling costs and x-ray developer for Park Medical Clinic in Lincoln, MT.
$10,000 to Childrens Oncology Camp Foundation, Camp Mak-A-Dream, Missoula, MT. For scholarships.
$10,000 to Raptors of the Rockies, Florence, MT. For educational projects.

4935
The Cinnabar Foundation ☆
219 Vawter St.
Helena, MT 59601 (406) 449-2795
Contact: James Posewitz, V.P.
FAX: (406) 449-2795;
E-mail: cinnabar@bresnan.net

Established in 1982 in MT.
Donors: Leonard Sargent†; members of the Kelsey family.
Foundation type: Independent foundation.
Financial data (yr. ended 12/31/05): Assets, $9,693,196 (M); expenditures, $542,169; qualifying distributions, $528,291; giving activities include $489,000 for 67 grants (high: $34,000; low: $1,000).
Purpose and activities: Giving primarily to promote environmental protection and fish and wildlife conservation in MT and the greater Yellowstone ecosystem.
Fields of interest: Environment, natural resources; Environment; Animals/wildlife, management/ technical aid; Animals/wildlife, preservation/ protection; Animals/wildlife, fisheries.
Type of support: General/operating support; Land acquisition; Conferences/seminars; Research; Scholarships—to individuals; Matching/challenge support.
Limitations: Giving limited to MT and the Yellowstone area.
Publications: Annual report; Annual report (including application guidelines).
Application information: Application form required.
Initial approach: Proposal (no more than 2 pages)
Copies of proposal: 1
Deadline(s): Generally, Mar. 15
Board meeting date(s): Semiannually
Final notification: May 31
Officers and Directors:* Robin Tawney,* Pres.; James Posewitz,* V.P.; Rick Hubbard-Sargent, Secy.; Ernest J. Turner,* Treas.
Member: William Madden.
Number of staff: 1 part-time professional.
EIN: 810415045
Selected grants: The following grants were reported in 2004.
$10,000 to Clark Fork Coalition, Missoula, MT.
$10,000 to Five Valleys Land Trust, Missoula, MT.
$10,000 to Montana Wilderness Association, Helena, MT.
$10,000 to Northern Plains Resource Council, Billings, MT.
$10,000 to Prickly Pear Land Trust, Helena, MT.
$10,000 to Rocky Mountain Elk Foundation, Missoula, MT.
$8,000 to Trout Unlimited, Helena, MT.
$7,000 to Montana Land Reliance, Helena, MT.
$5,000 to Friends of the Wild Swan, Swan Lake, MT.
$5,000 to Montana Wildlife Federation, Helena, MT.

4936
O. P. and W. E. Edwards Foundation, Inc. ▼
c/o Jo Ann Eder
P.O. Box 2445
Red Lodge, MT 59068 (406) 446-1077
FAX: (406) 446-1363; E-mail: joeder@mac.com;
URL: http://foundationcenter.org/grantmaker/ edwards/

Incorporated in 1962 in NY.

Donors: William E. Edwards†; J.N. Edwards†; Harriet E. Gamper; David E. Gamper; Jo Ann Eder.
Foundation type: Independent foundation.
Financial data (yr. ended 8/31/05): Assets, $13,386,089 (M); gifts received, $200,000; expenditures, $6,794,052; qualifying distributions, $5,664,547; giving activities include $5,642,787 for 80 grants (high: $722,700; low: $1,000; average: $5,000–$100,000).
Purpose and activities: Major interest in programs helping economically disadvantaged young people become able to survive and thrive on their own, with preference to smaller, comprehensive programs that are integral parts of their communities' networks of services.
Fields of interest: Visual arts; Performing arts; Human services; Children/youth, services; Family services; Community development; Astronomy; Economically disadvantaged.
International interests: Developing countries.
Type of support: General/operating support; Continuing support; Debt reduction; Emergency funds; Program development; Seed money; Scholarship funds; Program-related investments/ loans; Matching/challenge support.
Limitations: Applications not accepted. Giving on a national basis; some interest also in Third World countries. No grants to individuals.
Publications: Grants list.
Application information: Unsolicited requests for funding not considered. The foundation requests proposals from organizations about which the trustees are personally and directly knowledgeable.
Board meeting date(s): As required
Officers and Trustees:* Jo Ann Eder,* Pres. and Treas.; Harriet E. Gamper,* V.P.; David E. Gamper,* Secy.; Mark D. Eder; Christopher E. Gamper.
EIN: 136100965
Selected grants: The following grants were reported in 2005.
$722,700 to United Methodist Church of Leipsic, Leipsic, OH. For grant made through W.E. Edwards Fund.
$481,800 to Asbury College, Wilmore, KY. For grant made through W.E. Edwards Fund.
$481,800 to Twin Towers, Home on College Hill, Cincinnati, OH. For grant made through W.E. Edwards Fund.
$481,800 to Wesley Hall, Cincinnati, OH. For grant made through W.E. Edwards Fund.
$240,900 to Leipsic Board of Education, Leipsic, OH. For grant made through W.E. Edwards Fund.
$65,000 to Friendship House, Billings, MT.
$60,000 to Center for Creative Education, Stone Ridge, NY.
$50,000 to Langberg Foundation, Evergreen, CO.
$48,200 to Wycliffe Bible Translators, Santa Ana, CA. For grant made through W.E. Edwards Fund.
$10,000 to Maine Humanities Council, Portland, ME. For grant made through Art Fund.

4937
First Interstate BancSystem Foundation, Inc. ◇
490 N. 31st St., Ste. 300
Billings, MT 59101 (406) 255-5393
Contact: James Scott, Pres.

Established in 1990 in MT.
Donors: First Interstate Bank of Commerce; Wells Fargo Bank, N.A.; First Interstate Bank.
Foundation type: Company-sponsored foundation.

Financial data (yr. ended 12/31/03): Assets, $610,504 (M); gifts received, $933,000; expenditures, $860,206; qualifying distributions, $857,539; giving activities include $632,409 for 328 grants, and $188,158 for 353 employee matching gifts.
Purpose and activities: The foundation supports organizations involved with arts and culture, education, health, human services, community development, and government and public administration.
Fields of interest: Arts; Secondary school/ education; Higher education; Education; Health care; Human services; Community development; Government/public administration.
Limitations: Giving primarily in areas of company operations in MT and WY. No support for sectarian or religious organizations not of direct benefit to the entire community. No grants for general operating support for established organizations or discriminatory programs.
Application information: Application form required.
Initial approach: Contact foundation for application form
Officer and Directors:* James Scott,* Pres.; Elouise Cobell; Gary Crum; John Heyneman; Lyle Knight; Homer Scott, Jr.; Randy Scott; Thomas Scott; Sandy Suzor.
Trustee Bank: Wells Fargo Bank, N.A.
EIN: 810465899
Selected grants: The following grants were reported in 2004.
$50,000 to Montana State University Foundation, Billings, MT. For People, Pride and Promise Campaign.
$40,000 to Boy Scouts of America, Montana Council, Great Falls, MT. For Reservation Scouting Project.
$20,000 to Rocky Mountain Elk Foundation, Missoula, MT. For Building for the Future.
$16,500 to Livingston-Park County Library, Friends of the, Livingston, MT. For Library Expansion Campaign.
$15,000 to Montana State University, Billings, MT. For Montana Chamber Foundation Leadership Montana program.
$15,000 to Whitefish Community Aquatic and Health Center, Whitefish, MT. For cardio-fitness equipment.
$15,000 to Wyoming Heritage Foundation, Casper, WY. For Leadership Wyoming.
$14,000 to United Way of Yellowstone County, Billings, MT.
$12,500 to Art Museum of Missoula, Missoula, MT. For Renaissance Renewal and Renovation Project.
$12,500 to Habitat for Humanity, Mid-Yellowstone Valley, Billings, MT. For home construction.

4938
Gilhousen Family Foundation ◇
599 Hightower Rd.
Bozeman, MT 59718 (406) 586-2517
Contact: Patti A. Guptill, Admin.
E-mail: foundation.admin@gilhousen.net; Tel. for Patti A. Guptill: (503) 643-4183

Established in 1999 in MT.
Donor: Gilhousen Investments, LP.
Foundation type: Independent foundation.
Financial data (yr. ended 12/31/05): Assets, $7,063,253 (M); expenditures, $1,684,441; qualifying distributions, $1,888,580; giving

activities include $1,598,911 for 61 grants (high: $510,000; low: $100), and $252,005 for loans/program-related investments.

Purpose and activities: Giving primarily for higher education, Christian agencies and churches, and a museum; funding also for children and youth services, and for emergency assistance.

Fields of interest: Higher education; Human services; Children/youth, services; Christian agencies & churches.

Limitations: Giving primarily in Gallatin County, MT. No grants to individuals.

Application information: Contributes only to pre-selected organizations outside of MT. Application form not required.

> *Initial approach:* 1-page letter of inquiry
> *Copies of proposal:* 1
> *Deadline(s):* Mar. 31, June 30, Sept. 30 and Dec. 31
> *Board meeting date(s):* Jan., Apr., July and Oct.
> *Final notification:* 2-4 months

Officers and Director:* Klein Gilhousen, Pres.; Karen M. Gilhousen, V.P.; Patricia A. Guptill,* Admin.

Number of staff: 1 part-time professional.

EIN: 742938609

Selected grants: The following grants were reported in 2005.

$510,000 to Montana TheaterWorks, Bozeman, MT. For preservation of historic theater.

$238,331 to Reaching Our Community Kids (ROCK), Midland, MI. For building.

$70,000 to Intermountain Childrens Home, Helena, MT. For development of parent training materials and general after-school programs.

$60,000 to American Baptist Churches of the Northwest, Post Falls, ID. For Leader Learning Communities.

$35,000 to Gallatin County Love, Bozeman, MT. For general support.

$30,000 to Campus Crusade for Christ. For missionary support in Albania and Irktusk.

$30,000 to Network Against Sexual and Domestic Abuse, Bozeman, MT. For general support.

$25,750 to American Red Cross, Great Falls, MT. For general support.

$20,000 to Four-H Club, Bozeman, Bozeman, MT. For after-school programs.

$10,000 to English Language Institute in China, San Dimas, CA. For missionary support in Mongolia.

4939

Montana Community Foundation ✧

101 N. Last Chance Gulch, Ste. 211
Helena, MT 59601 (406) 443-8313
Contact: Linda E. Reed, Exec. Dir.
FAX: (406) 442-0482; *E-mail:* mtcf@mt.net;
Additional E-mails: lindareed@mtcf.org and mgorsich@mtcf.org; *URL:* http://www.mtcf.org

Incorporated in 1988 in MT.

Foundation type: Community foundation.

Financial data (yr. ended 6/30/05): Assets, $49,909,125 (M); gifts received, $1,141,706; expenditures, $3,287,614; giving activities include $1,734,972 for grants.

Purpose and activities: The foundation is a philanthropic services organization offering donor services, endowment building, and philanthropic advocacy.

Fields of interest: Arts; Education; Environment, natural resources; Human services; Economic development.

Type of support: Grants to individuals.

Limitations: Giving limited to MT. No support for religious purposes. No grants for annual or capital campaigns, endowment funds, or generally for debt retirement.

Publications: Annual report; Newsletter.

Application information: Visit foundation Web site for Application Cover Sheet and application guidelines. Application form required.

> *Initial approach:* Submit Application Cover Sheet with proposal
> *Deadline(s):* Varies
> *Board meeting date(s):* Quarterly
> *Final notification:* Within 30 days

Officers and Directors:* Harvey Stewart,* Chair.; Joan Bennett,* Vice-Chair.; Marie Nopper,* Vice-Chair.; Carolyn Colman,* Secy.; Mary Ann Gorsich, C.F.O.; Obert Undem,* Treas.; Bill Kearns,* Treas.-Elect; Linda E. Reed, Exec. Dir.; Randal Hanson; Melvin McNea; Jack Nickels.

Number of staff: 5 full-time professional; 1 part-time professional; 1 full-time support.

EIN: 810450150

Selected grants: The following grants were reported in 2006.

$6,000 to Bridger Clinic, Bozeman, MT. For marketing campaign for family planning services for young women to reduce teen pregnancy.

$5,000 to Holter Museum of Art, Helena, MT. For Bridging the Divide, intergeneraitonal, oral history and photography project promoting self-awareness among Caucasian and Native American youth.

$5,000 to YWCA of Great Falls, Great Falls, MT. To hire coordinator for TechGyrls program.

$3,500 to Montana Natural History Center, Missoula, MT.

$3,000 to Child Care Resources, Missoula, MT. For child care scholarships.

$3,000 to Family Service, Billings, MT. For rent, utilities, and mortgage.

$3,000 to Planned Parenthood Affiliates of Montana, Billings, MT. For teen education.

$2,000 to Barrett Memorial Hospital Foundation, Dillon, MT. For operating support for family planning programs.

$2,000 to Montana Outdoor Science School (MOSS), Bozeman, MT. For education program.

$1,700 to Sunburst Community Service Foundation, Eureka, MT. For music outreach for schools.

4940

The Sample Foundation, Inc.

14 N. 24th St., Fargo Hotel Bldg.
P.O. Box 279
Billings, MT 59103 (406) 245-6342
Contact: Miriam T. Sample, Pres.

Incorporated in 1954 in FL.

Donors: Helen S. Sample†; John Glen Sample†; Joseph S. Sample; Miriam T. Sample; Michael S. Sample; David F. Sample; Patrick G. Sample.

Foundation type: Independent foundation.

Financial data (yr. ended 10/31/05): Assets, $6,794,305 (M); gifts received, $112,413; expenditures, $344,696; qualifying distributions, $328,000; giving activities include $328,000 for 47 grants (high: $29,000; low: $1,000).

Purpose and activities: Grants for services for the disadvantaged. Grant support primarily for capital outlays or to assist in initiating a particular project.

Fields of interest: Human services.

Type of support: Capital campaigns; Equipment; Land acquisition.

Limitations: Giving primarily in Collier County, FL, and MT. No grants to individuals, or for scholarships, operating budgets, or duplication of services.

Publications: Application guidelines; Annual report; Grants list; Informational brochure (including application guidelines); Program policy statement.

Application information: Application form required.

> *Initial approach:* Letter
> *Copies of proposal:* 1
> *Deadline(s):* Sept. 1
> *Board meeting date(s):* Oct.
> *Final notification:* Before Oct. 31

Officers and Trustees:* Joseph S. Sample,* Chair.; Miriam T. Sample,* Pres.; Michael S. Sample,* V.P.; T.A. Cox,* Treas.; David F. Sample; Patrick G. Sample.

Number of staff: None.

EIN: 596138602

Selected grants: The following grants were reported in 2005.

$29,000 to Saint Vincent Hospital and Health Center, Billings, MT.

$27,650 to Childrens Oncology Camp Foundation, Missoula, MT.

$15,000 to Fun Time Nursery, Naples, FL.

$12,500 to United Way of Yellowstone County, Billings, MT.

$10,600 to Boys and Girls Club of Yellowstone County, Billings, MT.

$10,000 to Benefis Healthcare Foundation, Great Falls, MT.

$10,000 to Big Sky Elementary School Parent-Teacher Association, Billings, MT.

$10,000 to Guadalupe Center, Immokalee, FL.

$10,000 to Yellowstone Association, Yellowstone National Park, WY.

$7,500 to Rocky Mountain College, Billings, MT.

4941

Dennis & Phyllis Washington Foundation, Inc. ✧

(formerly Dennis R. Washington Foundation, Inc.)
P.O. Box 16630
Missoula, MT 59808-6630 (406) 523-1325
Contact: Mike Halligan, Exec. Dir.
E-mail address for Horatio Alger Montana Scholarships: horatioalger@act.org; *URL:* http://www.dpwfoundation.org/home.htm

Established in 1988 in MT.

Donors: Washington Corporations; Montana Rail Link, Inc.; Montana Resources, Inc.; Dennis Washington; Phyllis Washington.

Foundation type: Company-sponsored foundation.

Financial data (yr. ended 12/31/04): Assets, $15,436,662 (M); gifts received, $1,691,683; expenditures, $771,555; qualifying distributions, $743,024; giving activities include $669,195 for 94 grants (high: $50,000; low: $500).

Purpose and activities: The foundation supports organizations involved with arts and culture, education, health, human services, and community development and awards college scholarships to Montana high school seniors planning to attend the University of Montana. Special emphasis is directed toward programs designed to provide a direct service to economically and socially disadvantaged youth and their families, at-risk or troubled youth, and individuals with special needs.

Fields of interest: Arts; Education; Health care; Youth development; Human services; Community development; Youth; Economically disadvantaged.
Type of support: Program development; Scholarship funds; Scholarships—to individuals.
Limitations: Giving primarily in MT and areas of company operations. No support for discriminatory organizations, sectarian or religious organizations not of direct benefit to the entire community, veterans' or fraternal organizations not of direct benefit to the entire community, private or public foundations, or political action or legislative advocacy groups. No grants to individuals (except for scholarships), or for debt reduction, general operating support, travel expenses or trips, endowments, sponsorships, curriculum development for educational institutions, or motor vehicle or other transportation equipment purchases; generally, no grants for capital campaigns; no loans.

Publications: Application guidelines; Grants list.
Application information: Application form required.
Initial approach: Complete online application form
Deadline(s): Oct. 30 for Horatio Alger Montana Scholarships
Final notification: Within 45 days; after May 1 for Horatio Alger Montana Scholarships
Officers and Directors:* Phyllis J. Washington,* Chair.; Russell J. Ritter,* Pres.; Larry Simkins, V.P.; Brian Sheridan, Secy.; Deborah M. Brown, Treas.; Mike Halligan, Exec. Dir.; William H. Brodsky; Helen Miller; Terry Payne; Mike Stevenson.
EIN: 363606913
Selected grants: The following grants were reported in 2004.
$70,000 to Horatio Alger Association of Distinguished Americans, Alexandria, VA. 2 grants: $50,000 (For awards table at awards banquet), $20,000 (For Montana program).

$40,000 to Association for the Cure of Cancer of the Prostate (CaP CURE), Santa Monica, CA. For Indian Wells Tennis Tournament Sponsorship.
$30,000 to Special Olympics of Montana, Billings, MT. For Premiere Sponsor of 2004 Summer Games.
$25,000 to Butte Center for the Performing Arts, Butte, MT. For drama program and endowment.
$25,000 to Flagship Program, Missoula, MT.
$25,000 to Missoula Childrens Theater, Missoula, MT. For scholarships.
$25,000 to Young Life, Colorado Springs, CO. For Jubilee Fund.
$20,000 to Saint Patrick Hospital and Health Foundation, Missoula, MT. For rural connection via telemedicine for cardiac patients.
$15,000 to Boy Scouts of America, Longhorn Council, Fort Worth, TX.

NEBRASKA

4942
Ethel S. Abbott Charitable Foundation ✧
P.O. Box 81407
Lincoln, NE 68501-1407 (402) 435-4369
Contact: Del Lienemann Sr., Pres.

Established in 1989 in NE.
Donor: Ethel S. Abbott†.
Foundation type: Independent foundation.
Financial data (yr. ended 9/30/05): Assets,
$21,899,316 (M); expenditures, $829,487;
qualifying distributions, $828,503; giving activities
include $628,445 for 33 grants (high: $105,000;
low: $200).
Purpose and activities: Giving for arts and culture,
education, health, federated giving programs and
human services.
Fields of interest: Arts; Higher education; Botanical
gardens; Hospitals (general); Health organizations,
association; Human services; Community
development; Foundations (community); Federated
giving programs.
Limitations: Giving primarily in NE, with emphasis on
Lincoln and Omaha. No grants to individuals.
Application information: Application form required.
Initial approach: Letter or telephone requesting
application form
Deadline(s): Within 90 days after contacting the
Fdn. Mgr.
Officers: Del Lienemann, Sr., Pres.; Denise Scholz,
1st V.P.; Daniel Lienemann, 2nd V.P.; Ruth
Cummings, Secy.; Del Lienemann, Jr., Treas.
EIN: 237265876
Selected grants: The following grants were reported
in 2004.
$100,000 to Omaha Botanical Center, Omaha, NE.
For Ethel S. Abbott Great Hall in visitor's center.
$25,000 to American Red Cross, Lincoln, NE. For
endowment.
$10,000 to University of Nebraska Foundation,
Lincoln, NE. For scholarships.
$2,500 to Childrens Hospital, Omaha, NE. For
research.
$2,500 to Lienemann Charitable Foundation,
Lincoln, NE. For general support.
$2,500 to Special Olympics Nebraska, Omaha, NE.
For general support.
$2,000 to Doane College, Crete, NE. For
scholarships.
$2,000 to Grant County Historical Society, Hyannis,
NE. For educational support.
$2,000 to Hastings College, Hastings, NE. For
scholarships.
$1,000 to Creighton University, Omaha, NE. For
scholarships.

4943
Fred G. Arkoosh, Jr. Foundation ✧ ☆
1700 Farnam St., Ste. 1500
Omaha, NE 68102-2002

Established in 1999 in NE.
Foundation type: Independent foundation.
Financial data (yr. ended 12/31/05): Assets,
$942,458 (M); gifts received, $5,000;
expenditures, $600,461; qualifying distributions,

$597,630; giving activities include $592,500 for 5
grants (high: $300,000; low: $2,500).
Fields of interest: Secondary school/education;
Education; Boys & girls clubs; Human services;
Salvation Army.
Type of support: General/operating support.
Limitations: Applications not accepted. Giving
primarily in Omaha, NE. No grants to individuals.
Application information: Contributes only to
pre-selected organizations.
Directors: William G. Dittrick; Michael L. Sullivan.
EIN: 470814938

4944
Alan and Marcia Baer Foundation ✧ ☆
1001 Fort Crook Rd., Ste. 140
Bellevue, NE 68005
Contact: Marcia Baer, Pres.

Established in 1950 in NE and OK.
Donor: E. John Brandeis†.
Foundation type: Independent foundation.
Financial data (yr. ended 6/30/05): Assets,
$7,228,583 (M); expenditures, $436,631;
qualifying distributions, $315,350; giving activities
include $315,350 for 75 grants (high: $52,500;
low: $275).
Purpose and activities: Giving primarily for religious
organizations, schools and charities.
Fields of interest: Arts; Higher education;
Education; Health organizations, association; AIDS;
Children/youth, services; Religion.
Type of support: General/operating support.
Limitations: Giving primarily in Omaha, NE. No
grants to individuals.
Application information: Application form not
required.
Deadline(s): At least 30 days before grant is
required
Officers: Marcia Baer, Pres.; Theodore Baer, V.P.;
Kathy Baer, Secy.
EIN: 476032560
Selected grants: The following grants were reported
in 2004.
$67,500 to University of Nebraska Foundation,
Lincoln, NE. For operating support.
$10,000 to Nebraska AIDS Project (NAP), Omaha,
NE. For operating support.
$5,000 to Iowa Western Community College,
Council Bluffs, IA. For operating support.
$2,000 to All Our Kids, Omaha, NE. For operating
support.
$2,000 to American Heart Association, Omaha, NE.
For operating support.
$1,500 to Saint Richards School, Omaha, NE. For
operating support.
$750 to Childrens Hospital Foundation, Omaha, NE.
For operating support.
$750 to Omaha Community Playhouse, Omaha, NE.
For operating support.
$500 to Nebraska Childrens Home Society, Omaha,
NE. For operating support.
$200 to Creighton University, Omaha, NE. For
operating support.

4945
Hollis and Helen Baright Foundation ✧
6015 N.W. Radial Hwy.
Omaha, NE 68104
Contact: Thomas V. Van Robays

Established in 1995 in NE.
Donor: Hollis I. Baright†.
Foundation type: Independent foundation.
Financial data (yr. ended 12/31/05): Assets,
$3,939,230 (M); expenditures, $375,888;
qualifying distributions, $346,500; giving activities
include $346,500 for 5 grants (high: $250,000;
low: $1,500).
Fields of interest: Education; Zoos/zoological
societies; Health care; Human services; Homeless,
human services.
Type of support: Building/renovation; Scholarships
—to individuals.
Limitations: Giving primarily in Omaha, NE. No
grants for operating expenses.
Application information: Application form not
required.
Initial approach: Proposal
Copies of proposal: 3
Deadline(s): None
Trustees: Ralph W. Palmer; Nick R. Taylor; Great
Western Bank.
EIN: 470789577
Selected grants: The following grants were reported
in 2004.
$212,500 to Omaha Zoo Foundation, Omaha, NE.
$25,000 to University of Nebraska Foundation,
Omaha, NE.
$900 to Ralston, City of, Ralston, NE.

4946
Bishop Clarkson Episcopal Foundation ✧
109 N. 18th St.
Omaha, NE 68102-4903

Established in 1999 in NE.
Foundation type: Independent foundation.
Financial data (yr. ended 12/31/04): Assets,
$14,166,453 (M); expenditures, $626,445;
qualifying distributions, $541,199; giving activities
include $541,199 for 17 grants (high: $189,649;
low: $2,500).
Purpose and activities: Giving primarily to Episcopal
churches, as well as for health care.
Fields of interest: Health care; Children/youth,
services; Protestant agencies & churches.
Limitations: Applications not accepted. Giving
primarily in Omaha, NE. No grants to individuals.
Application information: Contributes only to
pre-selected organizations.
Directors: Dana Bradford; Bishop Joe G. Burnett;
Todd Engle; Bruce R. Lauritzen.
EIN: 470824591

4947
Thomas D. Buckley Trust ✧
P.O. Box 647
Chappell, NE 69129-0647 (308) 874-2212
Contact: Dwight E. Smith, Tr.

Established about 1980 in NE.
Donor: Thomas D. Buckley†.
Foundation type: Independent foundation.
Financial data (yr. ended 5/31/05): Assets,
$11,467,097 (M); expenditures, $732,128;
qualifying distributions, $662,254; giving activities
include $585,515 for 115 grants (high: $50,000;
low: $25).
Purpose and activities: Giving primarily for social
services, health care, and community development,
and to Lutheran, Roman Catholic and United

Methodist churches; funding also for scholarship programs.

Fields of interest: Elementary/secondary education; Education; Hospitals (general); Health care; Human services; Children/youth, services; Community development; Protestant agencies & churches; Roman Catholic agencies & churches.

Type of support: General/operating support; Continuing support; Capital campaigns; Building/ renovation; Equipment; Emergency funds; Seed money; Scholarship funds.

Limitations: Giving primarily in NE, with emphasis on Chappell and surrounding counties. No grants to individuals directly.

Application information: Scholarships administered through established programs at local schools. Application form required.

Initial approach: Letter requesting application form

Copies of proposal: 1

Deadline(s): None

Board meeting date(s): 2nd Wed. of each month

Final notification: 2 weeks after meeting

Trustees: Bill M. Hughes; D. Francis Kripal; Dwight E. Smith.

Number of staff: 1 part-time support.

EIN: 476121041

Selected grants: The following grants were reported in 2005.

$50,000 to Sedgwick County Health Center, Julesburg, CO.

$25,000 to Nebraska Lutheran Outdoor Ministries, Ashland, NE.

$10,000 to Legal Aid of Nebraska, Omaha, NE.

$2,500 to Western Nebraska Community College, Scottsbluff, NE.

$2,000 to First United Methodist Church, Norfolk, NE.

$2,000 to Fort Sedgwick Historical Society, Julesburg, CO.

$2,000 to Hospice of the Plains, Wray, CO.

4948
Buffett Early Childhood Fund ✧ ☆
7914 W. Dodge Rd., Ste. 291
Omaha, NE 68114

Established in 2005 in NE.

Donors: Susan A. Buffett Foundation; Novo Foundation.

Foundation type: Independent foundation.

Financial data (yr. ended 12/31/05): Assets, $1,687,794 (M); gifts received, $6,000,000; expenditures, $4,329,725; qualifying distributions, $4,329,594; giving activities include $4,178,461 for 20 grants (high: $1,046,715; low: $25,000; average: $75,000–$200,000).

Purpose and activities: Support for education.

Fields of interest: Education.

Limitations: Applications not accepted.

Application information: Contributes only to pre-selected organizations.

Directors: Peter Buffett; Susan Buffett; Daniel Pederson.

EIN: 201768874

4949
The Susan A. Buffett Foundation ▼
1440 Kiewet Plz.
Omaha, NE 68131
Contact: Dan Pedersen, Pres.

Established in 1999 in NE.

Donor: Warren E. Buffett.

Foundation type: Independent foundation.

Financial data (yr. ended 12/31/04): Assets, $80,741,033 (M); gifts received, $10,020; expenditures, $6,539,486; qualifying distributions, $6,426,209; giving activities include $6,025,183 for 196 grants (high: $1,000,000; low: $50).

Purpose and activities: Giving primarily for early childhood education in low income neighborhoods.

Fields of interest: Performing arts, theater; Arts; Higher education, college; Girls clubs; Human services; Children/youth, services; Federated giving programs.

Limitations: Applications not accepted. Giving primarily in Omaha, NE.

Application information: Unsolicited requests for funds not accepted.

Officers: Daniel Pedersen, Pres.; Susan A. Buffett, V.P. and Secy.

Directors: Brenda Council; Wallace Weitz.

Number of staff: 1 full-time professional; 1 part-time professional; 2 part-time support.

EIN: 470824755

Selected grants: The following grants were reported in 2003.

$750,000 to Educare of Omaha, Omaha, NE. For capital campaign.

$50,000 to University of Kansas Medical Center, Kansas City, KS. For educare facility.

$30,000 to College of Saint Mary, Omaha, NE. For general support.

$22,000 to Countryside Community Church, Omaha, NE. For capital and general support.

$20,000 to Jesuit Middle School, Omaha, NE. For general support.

$20,000 to Morehouse College, Atlanta, GA. For capital and operating support.

$15,000 to Omaha Theater Company for Young People, Omaha, NE. For operating support.

$12,000 to Girls Inc. of Omaha, Omaha, NE. For general support.

$10,000 to Habitat for Humanity of Omaha, Omaha, NE. For general support.

$10,000 to National Conference for Community and Justice, New York, NY. For general support.

4950
The Susan Thompson Buffett Foundation ▼
(formerly The Buffett Foundation)
222 Kiewit Plz.
Omaha, NE 68131
Contact: Allen Greenberg, Pres.
E-mail: scholarships@stbfoundation.org; Tel. for scholarship information: (402) 943-1383

Incorporated in 1964 in NE. In 2006, Warren Buffett pledged almost $3 billion worth of his Berkshire-Hathaway, Inc. stock to the foundation to be paid out over time. As a result, the Susan Thompson Buffett Foundation's annual giving is expected to rise sharply in the immediate future.

Donors: Warren E. Buffett; Susan T. Buffett†; Berkshire Hathaway Inc.

Foundation type: Independent foundation.

Financial data (yr. ended 12/31/05): Assets, $318,521,200 (M); gifts received, $383,873,299; expenditures, $61,222,850; qualifying distributions, $61,122,823; giving activities include $59,533,343 for 113 grants (high: $10,000,000; low: $195; average: $10,000–$1,000,000), and

$150,000 for 15 grants to individuals (high: $10,000; low: $10,000).

Purpose and activities: Grants primarily for family planning programs, and scholarships to residents of Nebraska attending Nebraska public colleges or universities.

Fields of interest: Reproductive health, family planning; Civil liberties, reproductive rights.

Type of support: General/operating support; Scholarships—to individuals.

Limitations: Giving on a national basis; scholarships awarded only to residents in NE. No grant to individuals (except for Teacher Awards).

Application information: Unsolicited requests for funds not accepted, with the exception of scholarship applications.

Initial approach: Application form required for scholarship program only

Deadline(s): Request application by Mar. 1, submit application by Apr. 10 (for scholarships)

Officers and Directors:* Susan A. Buffett,* Chair. and Treas.; Allen Greenberg, Pres.; Melissa How, Secy.; Peter A. Buffett; Geoffrey Cowan; Carol Loomis; Patti Matson.

Number of staff: 3 full-time professional; 1 part-time professional; 1 full-time support.

EIN: 476032365

Selected grants: The following grants were reported in 2005.

$10,000,000 to Save the Children Federation, Westport, CT. For general support.

$7,270,000 to International Projects Assistance Services (IPAS), Chapel Hill, NC. For project support.

$7,000,000 to Nuclear Threat Initiative, DC. For general support.

$2,965,218 to Willows Foundation, McLean, VA. For support for programs in Istanbul, Turkey.

$2,256,723 to University of California, San Francisco, CA. For project support.

$2,243,595 to Family Health International, Research Triangle Park, NC. For research.

$1,250,000 to Religious Coalition for Reproductive Choice, DC. For project support.

$300,000 to Physicians for Reproductive Choice and Health, New York, NY. For general support.

$176,297 to Planned Parenthood of Wisconsin, Madison, WI. For project support.

$84,000 to University of Montreal, Montreal, Canada. For fellowships.

4951
Commercial Federal Charitable Foundation ✧
13220 California St., 2nd Fl.
Omaha, NE 68154-5225

Established in 2001 in NE.

Donor: Commercial Federal Bank, FSB.

Foundation type: Company-sponsored foundation.

Financial data (yr. ended 12/31/04): Assets, $2,311,147 (M); gifts received, $105,000; expenditures, $483,637; qualifying distributions, $483,637; giving activities include $462,200 for 40 grants (high: $50,000; low: $1,000).

Purpose and activities: The foundation supports organizations involved with arts and culture, education, health, housing, human services, and community development.

Fields of interest: Arts; Education; Hospitals (general); Health care; Housing/shelter; Children/youth, services; Human services; Community development.

Type of support: General/operating support; Annual campaigns; Capital campaigns; Building/renovation; Scholarship funds.

Limitations: Applications not accepted. Giving limited to areas of company operations. No grants to individuals.

Application information: Contributes only to pre-selected organizations.

Trustees: William A. Fitzgerald; John J. Griffith; Roger L. Lewis.

EIN: 396765096

4952
ConAgra Foods Feeding Children Better Foundation ◇

1 ConAgra Dr.
Omaha, NE 68102-5001
E-mail: feedingchildrenbetter@congrafoods.com;
URL: http://www.feedingchildrenbetter.org

Established in 1999 in NE.
Donors: ConAgra, Inc.; ConAgra Foods, Inc.
Foundation type: Company-sponsored foundation.
Financial data (yr. ended 5/28/06): Assets, $244,347 (M); gifts received, $2,361,566; expenditures, $2,355,450; qualifying distributions, $2,355,450; giving activities include $2,323,000 for 13 grants (high: $192,334; low: $15,000).
Purpose and activities: The foundation supports organizations involved with child hunger.
Fields of interest: Food services; Children.
Limitations: Applications not accepted. Giving on a national basis. No support for fraternal or religious organizations. No grants to individuals, or for fundraising, travel, or advertising.
Application information: Contributes only to pre-selected organizations.
Officers: Bruce Rohde, Chair.; Anita Wheeler, Pres. and Secy.; Mike Fernandez, Treas.
EIN: 470824577
Selected grants: The following grants were reported in 2005.
$1,538,668 to Americas Second Harvest, Chicago, IL. 8 grants: $192,334, $192,333, $192,333, $192,333, $192,333, $192,334, $192,334, $192,334
$500,533 to ConAgra Foods Foundation, Omaha, NE.
$200,000 to Brandeis University, Waltham, MA.

4953
ConAgra Foods Foundation ▼ ◇

(formerly The ConAgra Foundation, Inc.)
1 ConAgra Dr., CC-304
Omaha, NE 68102-5001
Contact: Anita Wheeler, Pres.
URL: http://www.conagrafoods.com/company/corporate_responsibility/foundation/index.jsp

Established in 1980.
Donors: ConAgra, Inc.; ConAgra Foods, Inc.
Foundation type: Company-sponsored foundation.
Financial data (yr. ended 5/30/05): Assets, $2,237,226 (M); gifts received, $6,370,442; expenditures, $4,970,884; qualifying distributions, $4,970,884; giving activities include $4,911,980 for 148 grants (high: $1,000,000; low: $200), and $38,978 for 111 employee matching gifts.
Purpose and activities: The foundation supports organizations involved with arts and culture, education, health, nutrition and hunger, human

services, children and youth, and community development.
Fields of interest: Arts; Higher education; Education; Health care; Agriculture/food, ethics; Food services; Nutrition; Agriculture/food; Children/youth, services; Human services; Community development; Federated giving programs.
Type of support: Grants to individuals; General/operating support; Continuing support; Annual campaigns; Capital campaigns; Building/renovation; Program development; Curriculum development; Scholarship funds; Employee matching gifts; Employee-related scholarships; Matching/challenge support.
Limitations: Giving on a national basis in areas of company operations, with emphasis on NE. No support for religious organizations not of direct benefit to the entire community, clubs, fraternal or social organizations, grantmaking organizations, public or private K-12 schools, or athletic teams. No grants to individuals (except for scholarships), or for fundraising or testimonial events or dinners, travel or tours, advertising, endowments, conferences, seminars, workshops, symposia, or publication of proceedings, radio or television programming underwriting, emergency needs, or athletic events; no product donations or in-kind gifts; no grants totaling more than 10 percent of an organization's campaign goal or budget.
Publications: Application guidelines; Informational brochure (including application guidelines).
Application information: Support is limited to 3 years in length. Telephone calls, faxes, and E-mail messages are not encouraged. Application form not required.
Initial approach: Proposal
Copies of proposal: 1
Deadline(s): Last working day of Jan., Apr., July, and Oct.
Final notification: 8 to 10 weeks following deadlines
Officers and Director:* Bruce Rohde,* Chair.; Anita Wheeler, Pres.; Mike Fernandez, Treas.
Number of staff: 2 full-time professional; 1 full-time support.
EIN: 362899320
Selected grants: The following grants were reported in 2005.
$1,000,000 to Donors Trust, Omaha, NE.
$800,000 to Heritage Services, Omaha, NE. For performing arts.
$271,480 to Scholarship America, Saint Peter, MN. For scholarships.
$200,000 to American Red Cross, National Headquarters, DC. For disaster relief.
$100,000 to United Service Organization, DC.
$25,000 to Omaha Community Foundation, Omaha, NE.
$20,000 to American Red Cross, Heartland Chapter, Omaha, NE. For disaster relief.
$15,000 to Childrens Museum of Eau Claire, Eau Claire, WI.
$10,000 to CityTeam Ministries, San Jose, CA. For community service awards.
$10,000 to Indiana University Foundation, Bloomington, IN.

4954
Cooper Foundation

304 Cooper Plz.
211 N. 12th St.
Lincoln, NE 68508-1411   (402) 476-7571
Contact: E. Arthur Thompson, Pres.

FAX: (402) 476-2356;
E-mail: info@cooperfoundation.org; URL: http://www.cooperfoundation.org/

Incorporated in 1934 in NE.
Donor: Joseph H. Cooper‡.
Foundation type: Independent foundation.
Financial data (yr. ended 12/31/05): Assets, $21,142,689 (M); expenditures, $1,063,550; qualifying distributions, $1,013,947; giving activities include $728,885 for grants.
Purpose and activities: The mission of the foundation is to invest in support of people living in NE, with the majority living in Lincoln and Lancaster County, through education, human services, the arts and humanities, and the environment.
Fields of interest: Humanities; Arts; Education; Environment; Human services.
Type of support: General/operating support; Program development; Seed money; Technical assistance; Program-related investments/loans; Matching/challenge support.
Limitations: Giving limited to NE, with emphasis on Lincoln and Lancaster County. No support for religious or health purposes, private foundations, businesses, or travel. No grants to individuals, or for memberships, travel or endowment funds; generally no loans.
Publications: Application guidelines; Biennial report; Financial statement; Grants list.
Application information: Lincoln/Lancaster Grantmakers Common Grant Application Form required only by invitation after having met foundation objectives. See foundation Web site for application guidelines and procedures. Application form required.
Initial approach: Contact foundation in person, or via telephone, letter, fax, or e-mail
Copies of proposal: 1
Deadline(s): Jan 1, Apr 1, Aug 1, and Oct 1
Board meeting date(s): Quarterly
Final notification: 2 months
Officers and Trustees:* Jack D. Campbell,* Chair.; Norton E. Warner,* Vice-Chair.; E. Arthur Thompson,* Pres.; Victoria Kovar,* Secy.; Richard J. Vierk,* Treas.; Richard Knudsen, Genl. Counsel; Kathryn Druliner; Jane Renner Hood; Brad Korell; Robert Nefsky; John W. White, Jr.
Number of staff: 2 full-time professional; 1 part-time professional.
EIN: 470401230
Selected grants: The following grants were reported in 2006.
$60,000 to Malone Community Center, Lincoln, NE. For Executive Director's salary, payable over 2 years.
$42,164 to University of Nebraska, Lincoln, NE. 2 grants: $14,389 to Nebraska Center for Research on Children, Youth, Families and Schools (For Project TEAMS for students at-risk of dropping out of high school, payable over 2 years), $27,775 to Public Policy Center (For Nebraska Integrated Information and Referral Project).
$32,328 to Hispanic Community Center, Lincoln, NE. For operating expenses for rent and accounting.
$27,050 to Sunrise Communications, Lincoln, NE. For RadioActive Theater Project.
$25,000 to Center for Rural Affairs, Lyons, NE. For REAP Hispanic Rural Business Center.
$17,500 to Prairie Plains Resource Institute, Aurora, NE. For second year funding for

Development Coordinator/Office Manager position.

$15,000 to Mid-America Arts Alliance, Kansas City, MO. For programming support for Nebraska events.

$15,000 to Nature Conservancy, Omaha, NE. For staffing for Rulo Bluffs Preserve.

$10,000 to Nebraska Community Foundation, Lincoln, NE. For Women's Economic Empowerment Fund.

4955
Ron and Carol Cope Foundation ✧
c/o Wells Fargo Bank Nebraska, N.A., Trust Dept.
P.O. Box 1768
Grand Island, NE 68802
Contact: Lynne Werner

Established in 1990 in NE.
Donor: Carol I. Cope.
Foundation type: Independent foundation.
Financial data (yr. ended 12/31/05): Assets, $12,048,054 (M); expenditures, $617,333; qualifying distributions, $572,053; giving activities include $560,065 for 12 grants (high: $125,000; low: $5,000; average: $10,000–$100,000).
Fields of interest: Higher education; Education; Roman Catholic agencies & churches.
Type of support: Capital campaigns; Building/renovation.
Limitations: Applications not accepted. Giving limited to Buffalo County, NE, with emphasis on Kearney. No grants to individuals.
Application information: Contributes only to pre-selected organizations.
Board meeting date(s): Quarterly
Trustees: Carol I. Cope; Larry Jepson; Alan Oldfather; Wells Fargo Bank Nebraska, N.A.
EIN: 363693227
Selected grants: The following grants were reported in 2004.
$160,000 to University of Nebraska Foundation, Lincoln, NE. 2 grants: $10,000, $150,000 (For Safety Center Building).
$100,000 to American Red Cross, Kearney, NE.
$100,000 to Good Samaritan Hospital, Kearney, NE. For Healthy Living Center.
$100,000 to Kearney Public Schools Foundation, Kearney, NE.
$75,000 to Kearney Area Community Foundation, Kearney, NE. 2 grants: $25,000 (For Legacy Builder Project fund), $50,000 (For Kearney Area Humane Society).
$25,000 to Buffalo County Citizen Advocacy, Kearney, NE.
$5,000 to Kearney Catholic High School Foundation, Kearney, NE.
$5,000 to Nebraska Art Collection Foundation, Kearney, NE.

4956
Dillon Foundation ✧
P.O. Box 6368
Lincoln, NE 68506
Contact: Joseph Kerrigan, Pres.

Established in 1997.
Donor: Donald F. Dillon.
Foundation type: Independent foundation.
Financial data (yr. ended 12/31/05): Assets, $28,591,476 (M); expenditures, $1,407,540;

qualifying distributions, $1,327,699; giving activities include $1,309,199 for 87 grants (high: $125,000; low: $250).
Purpose and activities: Giving primarily to Roman Catholic agencies, churches, and schools; funding also for higher education, the arts, and human services.
Fields of interest: Arts; Secondary school/education; Higher education; Education; Youth development, services; Human services; Community development; Federated giving programs; Roman Catholic agencies & churches.
Limitations: Giving primarily in NE, with emphasis on Lincoln. No grants to individuals.
Application information: Application form required.
Initial approach: Letter requesting application
Deadline(s): None
Officers and Directors:* Joseph Kerrigan, Pres. and Treas.; Patrick J. Kerrigan,* V.P. and Secy.; Donald F. Dillon; David B. Policky.
EIN: 911805591
Selected grants: The following grants were reported in 2004.
$50,000 to Doane College, Crete, NE.
$25,000 to Catholic Bishop of Lincoln, Lincoln, NE.
$25,000 to Christian Heritage Childrens Home, Hickman, NE.
$25,000 to Food Bank of Lincoln, Lincoln, NE.
$20,000 to Lincoln Childrens Museum, Lincoln, NE.
$20,000 to Saint Elizabeth Foundation, Lincoln, NE.
$10,000 to American Red Cross, Lincoln, NE.
$10,000 to Bright Lights, Lincoln, NE.
$7,000 to Cathedral of the Risen Christ, Lincoln, NE.
$4,670 to Nebraska Humanities Council, Lincoln, NE.

4957
Dinsdale Family Foundation, Inc. ✧ ☆
P.O. Box 275
Central City, NE 68826

Established in 2003 in NE.
Donor: Pinnacle Bancorp, Inc.
Foundation type: Independent foundation.
Financial data (yr. ended 12/31/05): Assets, $260,134 (M); gifts received, $422,600; expenditures, $395,505; qualifying distributions, $394,000; giving activities include $394,000 for 985 grants to individuals (high: $400; low: $400).
Purpose and activities: Giving grants to families of active duty soldiers in the Army National Guard, or the Army Reserves.
Type of support: Grants to individuals.
Limitations: Giving primarily in NE.
Application information: Application form required.
Deadline(s): None
Directors: Jack Dinsdale; Roy Dinsdale.
EIN: 201292494

4958
Rupert Dunklau Foundation, Inc.
2948 Deer Run
Fremont, NE 68025-6489
Contact: Rupert Dunklau, Pres.
FAX: (402) 721-6231; Application address: P.O. Box 1558, Fremont, NE 68026

Established in 1968 in NE.
Donor: Rupert Dunklau.
Foundation type: Independent foundation.

Financial data (yr. ended 12/31/05): Assets, $13,604,288 (M); expenditures, $661,345; qualifying distributions, $639,350; giving activities include $639,350 for 32 grants (high: $80,000; low: $2,000; average: $500–$100,000).
Purpose and activities: In this constantly changing world, the foundation exists to glorify God and serve His gracious will by providing financial resources for the varied ministries related to the Lutheran tradition, especially the Lutheran Church-Missouri Synod, and to consider appropriate projects that promote the welfare of mankind.
Fields of interest: Higher education; Family services; Foundations (private grantmaking); Protestant agencies & churches.
Type of support: Annual campaigns; Capital campaigns; Building/renovation; Conferences/seminars; Scholarship funds; Matching/challenge support.
Limitations: Giving primarily in NE. No grants to individuals.
Publications: Application guidelines; Informational brochure (including application guidelines).
Application information: Application form required.
Copies of proposal: 4
Deadline(s): Mar. 31 and Sept. 30
Board meeting date(s): Twice per year
Final notification: Varies
Officer and Directors:* Rupert Dunklau,* Pres.; Paul Dunklau; Larry R. Larson; Rev. Donald Levenhagen; Janet R. Love; Lloyd Probasco; Larry Shepard; Del Toebben.
EIN: 476059030
Selected grants: The following grants were reported in 2003.
$101,000 to Trinity Lutheran Church, Fremont, NE. For general operating support.
$35,000 to Lutheran Family Services, Lincoln, NE. For building projects.
$25,000 to Concordia University, Seward, NE. For general operating support.
$25,000 to Valparaiso University, Valparaiso, IN. For general operating support.
$25,000 to Wheat Ridge Ministries, Itasca, IL. For general operating support.
$20,000 to Pastoral Leadership Institute, Santa Ana, CA. For general operating support.
$15,000 to Wider Omaha Lutheran School Association, Omaha, NE. For general operating support.
$10,000 to Concordia Seminary, Saint Louis, MO. For general operating support.
$10,000 to Concordia University, Saint Paul, MN. For general operating support.
$10,000 to Midland Lutheran College, Fremont, NE. For general operating support.

4959
Durham Foundation ▼ ✧
8401 W. Dodge Rd., Ste. 100
Omaha, NE 68114 (402) 390-2450
Contact: Charles W. Durham, Chair.

Established in 1990 in NE.
Donors: Charles W. Durham; Margre H. Durham.
Foundation type: Independent foundation.
Financial data (yr. ended 12/31/05): Assets, $18,370,616 (M); expenditures, $3,141,604; qualifying distributions, $3,075,480; giving activities include $3,063,438 for 98 grants (high: $500,000; low: $250; average: $5,000–$50,000).

Purpose and activities: Giving primarily for museums, higher education, and general charitable giving.
Fields of interest: Museums (art); Higher education; General charitable giving.
Type of support: General/operating support.
Limitations: Applications not accepted. Giving primarily in Omaha, NE. No grants to individuals.
Application information: Contributes only to pre-selected organizations.
Officers and Directors:* Charles W. Durham,* Chair.; John K. Wilson, V.P. and Secy.-Treas.; Scott Wallace,* V.P.
EIN: 363752053
Selected grants: The following grants were reported in 2004.
$707,000 to Durham Western Heritage Foundation, Omaha, NE. 3 grants: $200,000 (For general operating support), $400,000 (For general operating support), $107,000 (For general operating support).
$500,000 to University of Nebraska Foundation, Omaha, NE. For capital improvements.
$425,000 to Durham Western Heritage Museum, Omaha, NE. 3 grants: $150,000 (For general operating support), $150,000 (For general operating support), $125,000 (For general operating support).
$250,000 to Omaha Performing Arts Society, Omaha, NE. For capital improvements.
$100,000 to Dana College, Blair, NE. For general operating support.
$100,000 to Joslyn Art Museum, Omaha, NE. For general operating support.

4960
Eagle Foundation ◇
1125 S. 103rd St., No. 800
Omaha, NE 68124-1079
Contact: Paul C. Jessen, Asst. Secy.

Established in 1993 in NE.
Donor: James W. Cabela.
Foundation type: Independent foundation.
Financial data (yr. ended 12/31/05): Assets, $74,138,467 (M); expenditures, $3,156,803; qualifying distributions, $2,700,000; giving activities include $2,700,000 for 7 grants (high: $1,384,000; low: $5,000).
Purpose and activities: Giving primarily to Roman Catholic agencies and churches.
Fields of interest: Human services; Roman Catholic agencies & churches.
Type of support: General/operating support.
Limitations: Applications not accepted. Giving primarily in NE; some giving in MD. No grants to individuals.
Application information: Contributes only to pre-selected organizations.
Officers and Directors:* James W. Cabela,* Pres. and Treas.; Richard N. Cabela,* V.P.; Gerald Matzke,* Secy.
EIN: 470773892
Selected grants: The following grants were reported in 2005.
$1,384,000 to Catholic Relief Services, Baltimore, MD.
$1,000,000 to Diocese of Grand Island, Grand Island, NE.
$200,000 to Cross International Catholic Outreach, Boca Raton, FL.
$100,000 to National Religious Retirement Office, DC.

$5,000 to Pope Paul VI Institute for the Study of Human Reproduction, Omaha, NE.

4961
Virgil Eihusen Foundation, Inc. ◇ ☆
(formerly Eihusen-Chief Foundation, Inc.)
4100 W. Husker Hwy.
Grand Island, NE 68803-6539 (308) 389-3300

Established in 1988 in NE.
Donors: Chief Industries, Inc.; Virgil Eihusen Estate.
Foundation type: Company-sponsored foundation.
Financial data (yr. ended 6/30/05): Assets, $3,979,999 (M); gifts received, $1,794,362; expenditures, $461,862; qualifying distributions, $456,750; giving activities include $456,750 for 7 grants (high: $400,000; low: $1,000).
Purpose and activities: The foundation supports Christian agencies and churches, museums, and organizations involved with historic preservation, higher education, human services, youth, and community development.
Fields of interest: Museums; Historic preservation/historical societies; Higher education; Business school/education; YM/YWCAs & YM/YWHAs; Youth, services; Human services; Community development; Federated giving programs; Christian agencies & churches.
Type of support: Scholarship funds; Capital campaigns.
Limitations: Giving primarily in Grand Island, NE. No grants to individuals.
Application information: Application form not required.
Initial approach: Proposal
Deadline(s): None
Officers and Directors:* Marilyn Eihusen,* Pres.; Jack Henry,* V.P.; Jill Fargo,* Secy.
EIN: 363661287

4962
Fremont Area Community Foundation ◇
605 N. Broad St.
P.O. Box 182
Fremont, NE 68025 (402) 721-4252
Contact: Elizabeth Mulliken, Exec. Dir.
FAX: (402) 721-9359;
E-mail: inquire@facfoundation.org; *URL:* http://www.facfoundation.org

Established in 1980 in NE.
Foundation type: Community foundation.
Financial data (yr. ended 6/30/05): Assets, $7,383,381 (M); gifts received, $4,977,004; expenditures, $548,101; giving activities include $433,021 for grants (high: $100,000; low: $300; average: $300–$100,000), and $21,250 for 37 grants to individuals (high: $2,500; low: $100; average: $1,000–$2,500).
Purpose and activities: The foundation seeks to improve the quality of life by connecting donor interests with community needs. Grantmaking primarily for civic, health, human services, cultural and educational purposes.
Fields of interest: Arts; Education; Health care; Recreation; Human services; Government/public administration.
Type of support: Capital campaigns; Building/renovation; Equipment; Program development; Seed money; Scholarships—to individuals; In-kind gifts; Matching/challenge support.

Limitations: Giving limited to the Fremont and Dodge County, NE, area. No support for religious organizations for religious purposes. No grants to individuals (except for designated scholarship funds).
Publications: Application guidelines; Annual report; Informational brochure (including application guidelines); Newsletter.
Application information: Visit foundation Web site for application information and specific deadlines. Application form required.
Initial approach: Contact foundation
Copies of proposal: 1
Deadline(s): Bimonthly
Board meeting date(s): Monthly. Grant committee meets bimonthly
Final notification: Within 2 months
Officers and Directors:* Linda Chapman,* Pres.; Katherine Rhea,* Pres.-Elect; Tom Thomsen,* V.P.; Steve Navarrette,* Secy.-Treas.; Elizabeth Mulliken, Exec. Dir.; Stan Darling; Hazel Dillon; Don Dolejs; Bill Dugan; Larry Flamme; Cherry Gocken; Robert Hillis; Dave Hingst; Paul D. Johnson; Cyndy Koerber; Howard Krasne; Dale Olson; Leona Paden; Russ Peterson, Jr.; Steve Pribnow; Bart Qualsett; Marianne Simmons; Abe Tamayo; Joanne Thietje; Beth Vech; Tom Waring; Marvin G. Welstead.
Number of staff: 1 part-time professional; 2 part-time support.
EIN: 470629642

4963
Friedland Family Foundation ◇ ☆
(formerly David & Nancy Friedland Foundation)
4320 S. 94th St.
Omaha, NE 68127
Contact: David L. Friedland, Secy.-Treas.

Established in 1985 in NE.
Donors: United Distillers Products Co.; Paula Friedland Boggust; David L. Friedland; Edward Friedland; Nancy B. Friedland; Melissa Friedland Steiner.
Foundation type: Independent foundation.
Financial data (yr. ended 12/31/05): Assets, $2,024,583 (M); gifts received, $99,648; expenditures, $317,420; qualifying distributions, $315,435; giving activities include $315,435 for grants.
Purpose and activities: Giving primarily for Nebraska charities, with emphasis on medical needs for children.
Fields of interest: Arts; Higher education; Education; Health care; Jewish federated giving programs.
Type of support: General/operating support; Capital campaigns; Building/renovation; Endowments.
Limitations: Applications not accepted. Giving primarily in Omaha, NE. No grants to individuals.
Application information: Contributes only to pre-selected organizations. Unsolicited applications not considered or acknowledged.
Board meeting date(s): May and Nov.
Officers: Nancy B. Friedland, Pres.; Edward Friedland, V.P.; Melissa R. Friedland, V.P.; Paula Friedland Boggust, V.P.; David L. Friedland, Secy.-Treas.
EIN: 363354408
Selected grants: The following grants were reported in 2004.
$53,200 to Jewish Federation of Omaha, Omaha, NE.

$20,000 to Omaha Performing Arts Society, Omaha, NE.

$5,000 to Child Saving Institute, Omaha, NE.

$1,000 to Colorado State University Foundation, Fort Collins, CO.

$1,000 to Omaha Symphony Association, Omaha, NE.

$1,000 to Opera Omaha, Omaha, NE.

$500 to Childrens Respite Care Center, Omaha, NE.

$500 to Joslyn Art Museum, Omaha, NE.

$500 to Omaha Public Library, Friends of the, Omaha, NE.

$250 to Omaha Childrens Museum, Omaha, NE.

4964
Fulk Family Foundation, Inc. ✧

1221 N St., Ste. 600
Lincoln, NE 68508
Application address: c/o Robert W. Fulk, 150 S. Wacker Dr., Ste. 740, Chicago, IL 60606, tel.: (312) 236-2233

Established in 1989 in NE.
Donors: Wilma B. Fulk†; Robert W. Fulk; Fulk Farms, Inc.
Foundation type: Independent foundation.
Financial data (yr. ended 7/31/05): Assets, $14,722,021 (M); gifts received, $1,771; expenditures, $594,294; qualifying distributions, $571,682; giving activities include $566,710 for 32 grants (high: $160,000; low: $710).
Purpose and activities: Giving primarily for education, the arts, health, human services, and federated giving programs.
Fields of interest: Arts education; Humanities; Arts; Education; Reproductive health, family planning; Health care; Human services; Federated giving programs.
Limitations: Giving primarily in Chicago, IL; some funding nationally.
Application information:
Initial approach: Letter
Deadline(s): Dec. 1
Final notification: Dec. 31
Officer and Directors:* Robert W. Fulk,* Pres. and Treas.; Alice Brunner; Marcia Coffman; N. Jane Morrison.
EIN: 470732237
Selected grants: The following grants were reported in 2004.
$155,000 to Lincoln Community Foundation, Lincoln, NE. For general operating support.
$25,000 to School of the Art Institute of Chicago, Chicago, IL. For general operating support.
$20,000 to Thresholds, Chicago, IL. For general operating support.
$5,000 to Association House of Chicago, Chicago, IL. For general operating support.
$5,000 to Cornell University, Ithaca, NY. For general operating support.
$3,000 to Chicago Symphony Orchestra, Chicago, IL. For general operating support.
$3,000 to Field Museum of Natural History, Chicago, IL. For general operating support.
$2,000 to Joyce Theater, New York, NY. For general operating support.
$1,000 to Memorial Sloan-Kettering Cancer Center, New York, NY. For general operating support.
$1,000 to Ragdale Foundation, Lake Forest, IL. For general operating support.

4965
Gardner Foundation ✧

307 Main St.
Wakefield, NE 68784
Contact: Board of Trustees
Application address: P.O. Box 629, Wakefield, NE 68784, tel.: (402) 287-2538

Established in 1990 in NE.
Donors: David J. Gardner; Kirk N. Gardner; Leslie A. Bebee.
Foundation type: Independent foundation.
Financial data (yr. ended 12/31/04): Assets, $23,983,043 (M); expenditures, $2,144,202; qualifying distributions, $1,055,296; giving activities include $1,055,296 for 34 grants.
Purpose and activities: Giving primarily for education and the arts.
Fields of interest: Performing arts, theater; Performing arts, orchestra (symphony); Education, fund raising/fund distribution; Higher education; Health care; Aging, centers/services; Community development.
Type of support: Capital campaigns; Building/renovation; Equipment; Endowments; Seed money.
Limitations: Giving primarily in NE, with emphasis on the 75-mile radius of Wakefield, NE. No support for private, non-operating foundations. No grants to individuals.
Publications: Program policy statement.
Application information: Application form required.
Initial approach: Letter
Copies of proposal: 1
Deadline(s): 75 days before board meeting
Board meeting date(s): Mar., June, Sept., and Dec.
Final notification: 90 days
Officers: Jeanne M. Gardner, Pres. and Treas.; Leslie A. Bebee, V.P. and Secy.
Trustees: David J. Gardner; Kirk N. Gardner.
EIN: 363705723
Selected grants: The following grants were reported in 2004.
$474,000 to Little Red Hen Theater, Wakefield, NE. 7 grants: $15,000, $30,000, $15,000, $20,000, $80,000, $114,000, $200,000
$200,000 to Better Ponca Foundation, Ponca, NE.
$52,000 to Dana College, Blair, NE. 2 grants: $25,000, $27,000

4966
The GFH & SAH Foundation ✧

7411 Madison St.
Omaha, NE 68127
Contact: George F. Haddix, Chair.

Established in 1998 in NE.
Donor: George F. Haddix.
Foundation type: Independent foundation.
Financial data (yr. ended 12/31/05): Assets, $8,925,121 (M); expenditures, $428,460; qualifying distributions, $360,000; giving activities include $360,000 for 4 grants (high: $250,000; low: $5,000).
Purpose and activities: Giving for education and youth services.
Fields of interest: Museums; Higher education; Health organizations, association.
Limitations: Giving primarily in NE.
Application information:
Initial approach: Letter
Deadline(s): None

Officer and Trustees:* George F. Haddix,* Chair.; Sally A. Haddix.
EIN: 470816444
Selected grants: The following grants were reported in 2003.
$200,000 to Fontenelle Nature Association, Bellevue, NE.
$75,000 to University of Nebraska, Omaha, NE. For scholarship fund.
$50,000 to Boy Scouts of America, Mid-America Council, Omaha, NE.
$50,000 to Doane College, Crete, NE.
$5,000 to Cancer Research and Prevention Foundation, Alexandria, VA.
$3,500 to Salvation Army of Omaha, Omaha, NE.
$2,000 to Girls Inc. of Omaha, Omaha, NE.
$2,000 to Nebraska Childrens Home Society, Omaha, NE.

4967
Global Quest Foundation ✧

(formerly Vinod Gupta Charitable Foundation)
P.O. Box 27395
Omaha, NE 68127

Established in 1992 in NE.
Donors: Vinod Gupta; Sullivan Properties, Inc.
Foundation type: Independent foundation.
Financial data (yr. ended 12/31/04): Assets, $1,109 (M); gifts received, $512,100; expenditures, $505,408; qualifying distributions, $481,286; giving activities include $481,286 for 6 grants (high: $300,000; low: $7,897).
Purpose and activities: Giving primarily for higher education, with emphasis on women's education in India.
Fields of interest: Higher education; Education; Federated giving programs; Women.
International interests: India.
Type of support: General/operating support; Annual campaigns; Capital campaigns; Building/renovation; Endowments; Curriculum development.
Limitations: Applications not accepted. Giving in the U.S. and India.
Application information: Contributes only to pre-selected organizations.
Directors: Laurel Gottesman; Benjamin Gupta; Jess Gupta; Vinod Gupta; Fred Vakili.
Number of staff: 1 part-time professional.
EIN: 470747228

4968
Hamilton Community Foundation, Inc. ✧

1216 L St.
P.O. Box 283
Aurora, NE 68818 (402) 694-3200
Contact: Sidney L. Widga, Exec. Secy.

Incorporated in 1965 in NE.
Foundation type: Community foundation.
Financial data (yr. ended 12/31/05): Assets, $4,012,010 (M); gifts received, $733,571; expenditures, $462,164; giving activities include $292,233 for 81 grants (high: $63,714; low: $36), and $139,680 for 93 grants to individuals.
Purpose and activities: The foundation seeks to meet local community needs for all manner of civic, charitable, educational, cultural, health, recreational, and humanitarian purposes.
Fields of interest: Arts; Higher education; Education; Health care; Recreation; Human

services; Community development; Christian agencies & churches; Aging.

Type of support: Scholarships—to individuals; Equipment; Scholarship funds.

Limitations: Giving limited to Hamilton County, NE. No grants for operating expenses, deficit financing, or fund demonstration.

Publications: Annual report.

Application information:

Initial approach: Letter

Board meeting date(s): Quarterly and as necessary

Officers and Directors:* Audrey Vaught,* Pres.; John Ferguson,* V.P.; Sidney L. Widga, Exec. Secy.-Treas.; Rita Petersen,* Secy.; Shirley Barnell; Dick Carlson; Sue Dallegge; Rachel George; Larry Hansen; Robin Hansen; Jerry Hinrichs; Jim Johnson; Jennie Akerlund Keuhner; Marlene Mersch; Rev. Paul Nauman; Bob Person; Pat Phillips; Terry Rieke; Scott Simonsen; Judy Sullivan; Ila Wedeking; Lila Wolff.

EIN: 476038289

4969

The Harper Family Foundation ◇

(formerly M & J Foundation)

6625 State St.

Omaha, NE 68152-1633

Contact: Charles M. Harper, Jr., Chair.

FAX: (402) 571-2151;

E-mail: 104041.2012@compuserve.com

Established in 1992 in NE.

Foundation type: Independent foundation.

Financial data (yr. ended 12/31/04): Assets, $38,214,341 (M); expenditures, $1,664,733; qualifying distributions, $1,449,250; giving activities include $1,420,000 for 60 grants (high: $1,000,000; low: $500).

Fields of interest: Elementary/secondary education; Higher education; Cancer research; Recreation; Youth development; Federated giving programs.

Limitations: Giving primarily in NE. No grants to individuals.

Application information: Application form not required.

Initial approach: Proposal

Copies of proposal: 1

Deadline(s): None

Board meeting date(s): Fall

Final notification: 1 week from receipt

Officers and Directors:* Charles M. Harper, Jr.,* Chair.; Kathleen S. Wenngatz,* Vice-Chair.; Carolyn J. Harper,* Secy.; Chris J. Murphy,* Treas.; Mary Robbins,* Exec. Dir.; Charles M. Harper; Halbert Wenngatz.

Number of staff: 1 part-time support.

EIN: 470761456

Selected grants: The following grants were reported in 2004.

$1,000,000 to Nebraska Methodist College of Nursing and Allied Health, Omaha, NE. For general operating support.

$110,000 to Vanguard Charitable Endowment Program, Southeastern, PA. For general operating support.

$25,000 to Alexis de Tocqueville Society, Alexandria, VA. For general operating support.

$25,000 to Hospice House, Omaha, NE. For general operating support.

$20,000 to Annandale High School, Annandale, MN. For general operating support.

$15,000 to Father Flanagans Boys Town, Lake Forest, CA. For general operating support.

$11,000 to Saint Wenceslaus Parish, Saint Louis, MO. For general operating support.

$10,000 to Amherst College, Amherst, MA. For general operating support.

$10,000 to Mayo Foundation, Rochester, MN. For general operating support.

$10,000 to Nebraska Childrens Home Society, Omaha, NE. For general operating support.

4970

Hawkins Charitable Trust ◇

2516 Deer Park Blvd.

Omaha, NE 68105-3771 (402) 342-1607

Contact: Fred Hawkins Sr., Tr.

Established in 1964 in NE.

Donor: Hawkins Construction Co.

Foundation type: Independent foundation.

Financial data (yr. ended 12/31/05): Assets, $4,497,473 (M); gifts received, $350,000; expenditures, $497,133; qualifying distributions, $442,633; giving activities include $442,633 for 34 grants (high: $60,000; low: $50).

Fields of interest: Arts; Education; Health care; Agriculture; Youth, services; Federated giving programs.

Type of support: Annual campaigns; Building/renovation; Scholarship funds.

Limitations: Giving primarily in NE. No grants to individuals.

Application information: Application form not required.

Initial approach: Proposal

Deadline(s): None

Trustees: Fred Hawkins, Sr.; Fred Hawkins, Jr.; Kim Hawkins.

EIN: 476041927

4971

The Hawks Foundation ◇

1044 N. 115th St., Ste. 400

Omaha, NE 68154 (402) 691-9500

Contact: Rhonda Hawks, Tr.

Established in 1994.

Donors: Tom Hawks; McCarthy Group, Inc.

Foundation type: Independent foundation.

Financial data (yr. ended 12/31/05): Assets, $19,475,795 (M); gifts received, $6,827,854; expenditures, $1,286,817; qualifying distributions, $1,168,495; giving activities include $1,087,826 for grants, and $46,877 for grants to individuals.

Purpose and activities: Giving primarily for higher education and to Lutheran churches and organizations; funding also for health associations, children, youth and social services, and the arts, and Christian organizations and churches.

Fields of interest: Arts; Higher education; Education; Health organizations, association; Youth development; Human services; Children/youth, services; Family services; Christian agencies & churches; Protestant agencies & churches.

Type of support: Scholarships—to individuals.

Limitations: Giving primarily in Lincoln and Omaha, NE.

Application information: Application form required for scholarships.

Deadline(s): None

Trustees: Heather L. Hawks; Howard L. Hawks; Neal H. Hawks; Rhonda A. Hawks; Troy T. Hawks.

EIN: 476194021

4972

The Charles and Mary Heider Family Foundation ◇ ☆

9409 Westchester Ln.

Omaha, NE 68114

Established in 1998 in NE.

Donor: Charles F. Heider.

Foundation type: Independent foundation.

Financial data (yr. ended 12/31/05): Assets, $7,653,382 (M); expenditures, $418,473; qualifying distributions, $390,000; giving activities include $390,000 for 54 grants (high: $25,000; low: $800).

Fields of interest: Education; Human services; Christian agencies & churches.

Limitations: Giving primarily in NE.

Officers and Directors:* Charles F. Heider,* Pres. and Treas.; Mary C. Heider,* V.P. and Secy.; Mark J. Heider; Scott C. Heider.

EIN: 470810266

4973

B. Keith & Norma F. Heuermann Foundation

(formerly Bernard K. & Norma F. Heuermann Foundation)

c/o Law Offices, Professional Bldg.

P.O. Box 228

Aurora, NE 68818-0228

Contact: Charles L. Whitney, Secy.-Treas.

Established in 1991 in NE.

Donors: B. Keith Heuermann; Norma F. Heuermann.

Foundation type: Independent foundation.

Financial data (yr. ended 7/31/05): Assets, $9,545,814 (M); expenditures, $499,980; qualifying distributions, $441,399; giving activities include $437,527 for 47 grants (high: $115,577; low: $200).

Purpose and activities: Giving primarily for children, education and for learning disabilities; funding also for hospitals, Christian schools, community foundations, and libraries.

Fields of interest: Education; Hospitals (general); Children, services; Aging, centers/services; Developmentally disabled, centers & services; Foundations (community); Christian agencies & churches.

Type of support: Program development; Land acquisition; Capital campaigns; Annual campaigns; General/operating support; Building/renovation; Equipment; Endowments; Emergency funds; Fellowships; Research; Matching/challenge support.

Limitations: Giving primarily in NE, with emphasis on rural areas. No grants to individuals; no loans or non-monetary contributions.

Publications: Application guidelines.

Application information: If unfamiliar with the foundation, request guidelines. Application form not required.

Initial approach: 2-page proposal

Copies of proposal: 4

Deadline(s): None

Board meeting date(s): Summer, fall, and spring

Final notification: Varies

Officers and Directors: Bernard K. Heuermann,* Pres.; Norma F. Heuermann,* V.P.; Charles L. Whitney,* Secy.-Treas.
EIN: 470748466
Selected grants: The following grants were reported in 2005.
$115,577 to Hamilton Community Foundation, Hamilton, OH.
$59,350 to Nebraska Wesleyan University, Lincoln, NE.
$25,000 to Hastings College Foundation, Hastings, NE.
$5,000 to Randolph Public Library, Randolph, NE.
$5,000 to Stromsburg Public Library, Stromsburg, NE.
$3,000 to Nebraska Independent College Foundation, Omaha, NE.

4974
Hirschfeld Family Foundation, Inc. ✧
P.O. Box 1060
Kearney, NE 68848-1060
Contact: Jeffrey Orr

Established in 1992 in NE.
Donor: Daniel J. Hirschfeld.
Foundation type: Independent foundation.
Financial data (yr. ended 8/31/05): Assets, $12,082,539 (M); expenditures, $560,996; qualifying distributions, $469,275; giving activities include $469,275 for 35 grants (high: $111,000; low: $1,000).
Purpose and activities: Giving primarily for education and for human services.
Fields of interest: Museums; Elementary/secondary education; Higher education; Hospitals (general); Human services; YM/YWCAs & YM/YWHAs; Aging, centers/services.
Type of support: General/operating support; Capital campaigns; Building/renovation; Equipment; Land acquisition; Emergency funds; Program development; Professorships; Seed money; Curriculum development; Scholarship funds; Matching/challenge support.
Limitations: Giving primarily in NE. No grants to individuals.
Application information: Application form required.
Initial approach: Letter requesting application form
Copies of proposal: 1
Deadline(s): None
Board meeting date(s): As needed
Final notification: 1 month
Officers and Directors: Daniel J. Hirschfeld,* Pres. and Treas.; Benjamin G. Hirschfeld, V.P.; Letitia A. Spencer, V.P.; Monya A. Hirschfeld,* Secy.
EIN: 470762188
Selected grants: The following grants were reported in 2004.
$118,000 to Humane Society of Kearney, Kearney, NE.
$50,000 to Kearney Public Schools, Kearney, NE.
$45,000 to Good Samaritan Hospital Foundation, Kearney, NE.
$11,000 to York College, York, NE.
$9,900 to Hastings College, Hastings, NE.
$7,500 to Saint Lukes Good Samaritan Village, Kearney, NE.
$5,000 to Concordia University, Seward, NE.
$5,000 to Girl Scouts of the U.S.A., Goldenrod Council, Kearney, NE.
$5,000 to Museum of Nebraska Art, Kearney, NE.

$5,000 to Stromsburg Public Library, Stromsburg, NE.

4975
Gilbert M. and Martha H. Hitchcock Foundation ✧
1755 E. Locust St.
Omaha, NE 68110 (402) 345-0043
Contact: Neely Kountze, Pres.

Incorporated in 1943 in NE.
Donor: Martha H. Hitchcock‡.
Foundation type: Independent foundation.
Financial data (yr. ended 12/31/05): Assets, $15,832,686 (M); expenditures, $924,474; qualifying distributions, $826,870; giving activities include $826,870 for 37 grants (high: $250,000; low: $750).
Purpose and activities: Support for private education; support also for the arts and social service agencies; sponsors scholarship program for Omaha World-Herald newspaper carriers.
Fields of interest: Performing arts centers; Arts; Higher education; Education; Human services.
Type of support: General/operating support; Capital campaigns; Building/renovation; Endowments; Scholarship funds; Matching/challenge support.
Limitations: Giving limited to western IA, and to NE. No grants to individuals.
Publications: Application guidelines.
Application information: Application form not required.
Initial approach: Proposal or letter
Copies of proposal: 8
Deadline(s): Dec. 31 for grants
Board meeting date(s): Annually
Final notification: Following board meeting
Officers and Directors: Neely Kountze,* Pres.; Mary L. Kountze,* V.P.; Tyler B. Gaines,* Secy.; John W. Webster,* Treas.; W. Russell Bowie III; John C. Burke; Charles Denman Kountze.
EIN: 476025723

4976
Hofer Family Foundation ✧ ☆
3645 Hidden Acres Ln.
Fort Calhoun, NE 68023

Donors: Curtis Hofer; Linda Hofer.
Foundation type: Independent foundation.
Financial data (yr. ended 12/31/05): Assets, $46,863 (M); gifts received, $295,000; expenditures, $402,923; qualifying distributions, $387,298; giving activities include $387,298 for 27 grants (high: $150,000; low: $1,000).
Fields of interest: Human services; Christian agencies & churches.
Limitations: Applications not accepted. Giving primarily in NE. No grants to individuals.
Application information: Contributes only to pre-selected organizations.
Trustees: Curtis L. Hofer; Linda M. Hofer.
EIN: 436901598

4977
The Holland Foundation ▼ ✧
1501 S. 80th St.
Omaha, NE 68124 (402) 397-5500
Contact: Richard D. Holland, Pres.

Established in 1996 in NE.
Donors: Marilyn M. Holland; Richard D. Holland.
Foundation type: Independent foundation.
Financial data (yr. ended 12/31/05): Assets, $66,300,322 (M); gifts received, $31,875,900; expenditures, $9,610,541; qualifying distributions, $9,425,871; giving activities include $9,425,871 for 39 grants (high: $6,684,031; low: $5,000; average: $10,000–$100,000).
Purpose and activities: Giving primarily for youth services, and arts and culture.
Fields of interest: Performing arts, opera; Arts; Education, early childhood education; Education; Zoos/zoological societies; Children/youth, services; Religion.
Limitations: Giving primarily in NE. No grants to individuals.
Application information:
Initial approach: Proposal
Deadline(s): None
Officers: Richard D. Holland, Pres.; Marilyn M. Holland, V.P.; Thomas R. Pansing, Secy.
Director: Wallace R. Weitz.
Number of staff: 1 part-time support.
EIN: 470804949
Selected grants: The following grants were reported in 2005.
$7,500,631 to Omaha Performing Arts Society, Omaha, NE. 2 grants: $816,600 (For capital support), $6,684,031 (For capital support).
$400,000 to Opera Omaha, Omaha, NE. 4 grants: $100,000 each (For operating support).
$195,000 to Omaha Symphony, Omaha, NE. 2 grants: $100,000 (For operating support), $95,000 (For operating support).
$50,000 to Joslyn Art Museum, Omaha, NE. For operating support.
$30,000 to Omaha Area Youth Orchestra, Omaha, NE. For operating support.

4978
The Theodore F. and Claire M. Hubbard Family Foundation ✧
1005 Meadow Rd.
Omaha, NE 68154-3434
Contact: Claire M. Hubbard, V.P.

Established in 1995 in NE.
Donor: Claire M. Hubbard.
Foundation type: Independent foundation.
Financial data (yr. ended 11/30/05): Assets, $21,132,986 (M); gifts received, $4,321,000; expenditures, $1,274,170; qualifying distributions, $1,274,170; giving activities include $1,213,544 for 3 grants.
Fields of interest: Performing arts, opera; Zoos/zoological societies; Human services.
Limitations: Giving primarily in Omaha, NE. No grants to individuals.
Application information: Application form not required.
Initial approach: Letter
Officers and Directors: Theodore F. Hubbard, Jr.,* Pres.; Claire M. Hubbard,* V.P.; Anne M. Hubbard.
EIN: 476205113

4979
Hubbell-Waterman Foundation ✧
c/o Wells Fargo Bank Nebrsaka, N.A.
1248 O St., 4th Fl.
Lincoln, NE 68508

Established in 1971 in IA.
Donor: Mary Waterman.
Foundation type: Independent foundation.
Financial data (yr. ended 12/31/05): Assets,
$28,880,024 (M); gifts received, $15,919,312;
expenditures, $657,371; qualifying distributions,
$611,566; giving activities include $600,500 for 26
grants (high: $100,000; low: $1,000).
Purpose and activities: Giving primarily for the arts,
with emphasis on museums, as well as for human
services.
Fields of interest: Museums (natural history);
Historic preservation/historical societies; Arts;
Education; Environment, natural resources; Human
services; Foundations (community).
Limitations: Applications not accepted. Giving
primarily in Davenport, IA. No grants to individuals.
Application Information: Contributes only to
pre-selected organizations.
Trustee: Wells Fargo Bank Nebraska, N.A.
EIN: 426126467

4980
Lawrence R. & Jeanette James Foundation ✧ ☆
9974 Bloomfield Dr.
Omaha, NE 68114
Application address: c/o Lawrence R. James, 11550
W. Dodge Rd., Omaha, NE 68114, tel.: (402)
496-9600

Established in 1966 in NE.
Donors: Sweetbriar Syndicate; Jeannette James;
Lawrence James.
Foundation type: Independent foundation.
Financial data (yr. ended 6/30/06): Assets,
$4,831,239 (M); gifts received, $200,000;
expenditures, $354,168; qualifying distributions,
$354,168; giving activities include $354,168 for
grants.
Fields of interest: Museums; Performing arts;
Higher education; Environment; Zoos/zoological
societies; Health organizations, association;
Salvation Army; Children/youth, services; Federated
giving programs; Christian agencies & churches.
Type of support: General/operating support.
Limitations: Giving primarily in Omaha, NE. No
grants to individuals.
Application Information:
 Initial approach: Letter
 Deadline(s): None
Officer: Lawrence R. James, Pres.
EIN: 476040364
Selected grants: The following grants were reported
in 2005.
$105,000 to Omaha Zoological Society, Omaha,
 NE.
$10,500 to Joslyn Art Museum, Omaha, NE.
$10,000 to United Way of the Midlands, Omaha, NE.
$2,600 to Fontenelle Nature Association, Bellevue,
 NE.
$2,500 to Arts on the Green, Omaha, NE.
$2,500 to Boys and Girls Clubs of Omaha, Omaha,
 NE.
$1,600 to Salvation Army of Omaha, Omaha, NE.
$1,500 to Catholic Charities of the Archdiocese of
 Omaha, Omaha, NE.
$1,000 to Big Brothers/Big Sisters of the Midlands,
 Omaha, NE.
$1,000 to University of Nebraska Foundation,
 Lincoln, NE.

4981
Robert and Carole Julian Foundation ✧
500 Energy Plz., 409 S. 17th St.
Omaha, NE 68102

Established in 1996 in NE.
Donors: Carole Julian; Robert E. Julian.
Foundation type: Independent foundation.
Financial data (yr. ended 12/31/03): Assets,
$1,483,753 (M); expenditures, $962,426;
qualifying distributions, $958,145; giving activities
include $958,145 for 31 grants (high: $795,000;
low: $100).
Fields of interest: Arts; Education; Health care;
Human services; Children/youth, services.
Limitations: Applications not accepted. Giving
primarily in Omaha, NE. No grants to individuals.
Application information: Contributes only to
pre-selected organizations.
Trustees: Carole Julian; Robert E. Julian; Elizabeth
Shults; Robert Shults.
EIN: 470800777

4982
Kawasaki Good Times Foundation ✧ ☆
P.O. Box 81469
Lincoln, NE 68501-1469
Contact: Rob Fairchild

Established in 1993 in NE.
Donors: Kawasaki Motors Manufacturing Corp.,
U.S.A.; Kawasaki Heavy Industries (USA), Inc.;
Kawasaki Motors Corp., U.S.A.; Kawasaki Rail Car,
Inc.
Foundation type: Company-sponsored foundation.
Financial data (yr. ended 12/31/05): Assets,
$3,075,522 (M); gifts received, $264,482;
expenditures, $344,190; qualifying distributions,
$321,500; giving activities include $321,500 for
grants.
Purpose and activities: The foundation supports
organizations involved with arts and culture, higher
education, and health.
Fields of interest: Museums; Arts; Higher
education; Medical care, in-patient care; Health
care; Federated giving programs.
Limitations: Giving primarily in Lincoln, NE, and the
New York, NY, area.
Application information: Application form not
required.
 Initial approach: Proposal
 Deadline(s): None
Officers and Directors:* Yuichi Yamamoto,* Pres.;
Kazuo Ohta, V.P.; Yasuhiro Mori, Secy.-Treas.;
Shigeru Hamada; Shoichi Tamba.
EIN: 363879896
Selected grants: The following grants were reported
in 2005.
$200,000 to American Red Cross in Greater New
 York, New York, NY.
$20,000 to Metropolitan Museum of Art, New York,
 NY.
$15,000 to New York Transit Museum, New York,
 NY.
$4,000 to United Way, MI.

4983
Kiewit Companies Foundation ▼
(formerly The Peter Kiewit Sons', Inc. Foundation)
1000 Kiewit Plz.
Omaha, NE 68131 (402) 342-2052
Contact: Mike Faust
FAX: (402) 943-1302;
E-mail: mike.faust@kiewit.com

Established in 1963 in NE.
Donors: Peter Kiewit Sons', Inc.; Wytana, Inc.; Big
Horn Coal Co.; Kiewit Construction Group Inc.; Kiewit
Diversified Group Inc.; Peter Kiewit & Sons Co.
Foundation type: Company-sponsored foundation.
Financial data (yr. ended 12/31/05): Assets,
$6,070,533 (M); gifts received, $3,000,000;
expenditures, $3,680,018; qualifying distributions,
$3,655,292; giving activities include $3,649,748
for 238 grants (high: $700,000; low: $100).
Purpose and activities: The foundation supports
organizations involved with arts and culture, higher
education, youth development, human services, and
community development.
Fields of interest: Arts; Higher education; Youth
development; Human services; Community
development.
Type of support: General/operating support; Annual
campaigns; Capital campaigns; Building/
renovation; Scholarship funds.
Limitations: Giving primarily in areas of company
operations, with emphasis on Omaha, NE. No
support for elementary or secondary schools or
individual churches or similar religious groups. No
grants to individuals, or for endowments.
Publications: Annual report (including application
guidelines).
Application information: Application form not
required.
 Initial approach: Letter of inquiry
 Copies of proposal: 1
 Deadline(s): None
 Board meeting date(s): As needed
 Final notification: 1 to 3 months
Trustee: U.S. Bank, N.A.
EIN: 476029996
Selected grants: The following grants were reported
in 2005.
$300,000 to University of Nebraska Foundation,
 Omaha, NE. To help establish School of
 Architectural Engineering and Construction.
$100,000 to American Red Cross, Heartland
 Chapter, Omaha, NE. For hurricane relief.
$65,000 to Omaha Symphony Association, Omaha,
 NE.
$25,000 to Omaha Theater Company for Young
 People, Omaha, NE.
$25,000 to Salvation Army of Omaha, Omaha, NE.
 For Tree of Lights Campaign.
$25,000 to United Way of the Midlands, Omaha, NE.
 For facility repair and renovation project.

4984
Peter Kiewit Foundation ▼
8805 Indian Hills Dr., Ste. 225
Omaha, NE 68114 (402) 344-7890
Contact: Lyn Wallin Ziegenbein, Secy.

Established in 1975 in NE.
Donor: Peter Kiewit†.
Foundation type: Independent foundation.
Financial data (yr. ended 6/30/05): Assets,
$380,416,544 (M); expenditures, $20,101,243;
qualifying distributions, $18,315,342; giving

activities include $13,596,049 for 148 grants (high: $3,500,000; low: $400), $3,244,323 for grants to individuals, and $280,375 for 4 foundation-administered programs.

Purpose and activities: Giving primarily for cultural programs, including the arts, civic affairs, community development, higher and other education, health and social service agencies, and youth programs. Contributions almost always made as challenge or matching grants.

Fields of interest: Arts; Higher education; Education; Health care; Human services; Youth, services; Rural development; Community development; Government/public administration.

Type of support: General/operating support; Capital campaigns; Building/renovation; Equipment; Land acquisition; Program development; Seed money; Program-related investments/loans; Scholarships —to individuals; Matching/challenge support.

Limitations: Giving limited to Rancho Mirage, CA, western IA, NE, and Sheridan, WY; college scholarships available to graduating seniors in NE. No support for elementary or secondary schools, churches, or religious groups. No grants to individuals (except for scholarships), or for endowment funds or annual campaigns.

Publications: Application guidelines; Annual report; Informational brochure (including application guidelines).

Application information: Application form required.

Initial approach: Letter or telephone
Copies of proposal: 4
Deadline(s): Jan. 1 for scholarships; Jan. 15, Apr. 15, July 15, and Oct. 15 for grants
Board meeting date(s): Mar., June, Sept., and Dec.
Final notification: Within quarter submitted

Officers and Trustees:* Eva-Alta D. Kiewit,* Chair.; G. Richard Russell,* Vice-Chair.; Lyn Wallin Ziegenbein,* Secy.; Mogens C. Bay; Michael L. Gallagher; John W. Hancock; U.S. Bank, N.A.

Number of staff: 3 full-time professional; 3 full-time support.

EIN: 476098282

Selected grants: The following grants were reported in 2005.

$3,500,000 to University of Nebraska Foundation, Lincoln, NE. Toward construction of new Biomedical Research Center on campus of University of Nebraska Medical Center.

$1,000,000 to Omaha Performing Arts Society, Omaha, NE. Toward construction of planned new Performing Arts Center in downtown Omaha.

$1,000,000 to Omaha Zoological Society, Omaha, NE. For Hubbard Gorilla Valley Complex.

$500,000 to Creighton University, Omaha, NE. Toward construction of new soccer stadium.

$500,000 to Joslyn Art Museum, Omaha, NE. For expansion and redevelopment of campus facilities at Joslyn, Creighton and Central High School.

$500,000 to Missouri River Basin Lewis and Clark Interpretative Trail and Visitor Center, Nebraska City, NE. Toward construction of new visitor center facility.

$500,000 to OneWorld Community Health Center, Omaha, NE. Toward furnishings and equipment for new health care clinic facility.

$70,000 to Visiting Nurse Health Services, Omaha, NE. For program support.

$50,000 to Omaha Sports Commission, Omaha, NE. For program support.

$9,231 to Hartington, City of, Hartington, NE. For Lewis and Clark Initiative.

4985

E. H. Kilbourne Residuary Charitable Trust ✧

c/o Wells Fargo Bank Indiana, N.A.
1919 Douglas St., 2nd Fl.
Omaha, NE 68102-1310 (260) 461-6451
Contact: Jennifer King, V.P., Wells Fargo Bank Indiana, N.A.

Trust established in 1978 in IN.
Donor: Edgar Kilbourne†.
Foundation type: Independent foundation.
Financial data (yr. ended 11/30/05): Assets, $10,458,538 (M); expenditures, $545,549; qualifying distributions, $508,638; giving activities include $470,393 for 170 grants (high: $19,366; low: $200).

Purpose and activities: Giving for higher education, including scholarships for graduating high school seniors in Allen County, IN. Support also for youth agencies, health and social services, and the arts.

Fields of interest: Arts; Higher education; Education; Human services; Children/youth, services.

Type of support: General/operating support; Continuing support; Annual campaigns; Equipment; Scholarship funds; Matching/challenge support.

Limitations: Giving limited to Allen County, IN. No grants to individuals (except for scholarships), or for endowment funds, research, publications, or conferences; no loans.

Application information: Scholarship awards paid directly to colleges; obtain applications from high schools. Application form required.

Initial approach: Letter
Deadline(s): Apr. 15 for scholarships
Board meeting date(s): May for scholarships; quarterly for other grants
Final notification: 6 weeks

Trustee: Wells Fargo Bank Indiana, N.A.
EIN: 356332820

4986

Lexington Community Foundation

607 N. Washington St.
P.O. Box 422
Lexington, NE 68850 (308) 324-6704
Contact: Jacqueline Berke, Exec. Dir.
E-mail: lexfoundation@alltel.net; URL: http://www.lexfoundation.org

Established in 1982 in NE.
Foundation type: Community foundation.
Financial data (yr. ended 12/31/05): Assets, $2,235,855 (M); gifts received, $890,656; expenditures, $1,987,240; giving activities include $1,770,061 for grants, and $48,990 for grants to individuals.

Purpose and activities: The foundation seeks to encourage and strengthen philanthropy in order to provide a permanent source of funding for opportunities to improve the quality of life, strengthen the sense of community, and benefit future generations in Lexington, NE.

Fields of interest: Arts; Education; Health care; Recreation, camps; Recreation; Children/youth, services; Human services; Community development, neighborhood development; Community development.

Type of support: Capital campaigns; Building/renovation; Equipment; Program development; Seed money; Technical assistance; Scholarships—to individuals; Matching/challenge support.

Limitations: Giving limited to the Lexington, NE, area. No support for religious activities (unless non-denominational and serving a brand segment of the population). No grants to individuals directly, or for operational expenses, debt servicing, trips, tours, camps, or endowment funds.

Publications: Application guidelines; Annual report; Financial statement; Grants list; Newsletter; Program policy statement.

Application information: Visit foundation Web site for application form and guidelines. Application form required.

Initial approach: Contact foundation
Copies of proposal: 1
Deadline(s): None
Board meeting date(s): 4th Mon. in Jan., Mar., May, July, Sept., and Nov.
Final notification: 1 to 2 months

Officers and Directors:* W. Wes Lubberstedt,* Pres.; Patty Mandelko,* V.P.; Bill Orthman,* Secy.-Treas.; Jacqueline Berke, Exec. Dir.; Rob Anderson; Mary Barmore; Bill Barrett; Ed Bennett; Amy Biehl-Owens; Jerry Brown; Stephanie Buell; Dan Clark; Ed Darby; Tom Fagot; David Fairbanks; Tom Feltes; Ernie French; Mogen Knudsen; Tod McKeone; Linda Miller; Bill Ohlmann; Ray Otero; Mark Sarratt; Rusty Sutton; Gail Wightman; John Wightman.

Number of staff: 1 full-time professional; 1 part-time support.

EIN: 470794760

Selected grants: The following grants were reported in 2006.

$75,000 to Optimist International, Lexington, NE. For Hitting Facility Matching Grant.

$40,000 to Grand Generation Center, Lexington, NE.

$2,500 to Lexington Public Schools, Lexington, MA. For Dual Language program.

$2,000 to EGP, Lexington, NE. 2 grants: $1,000 (For Pershing Horizontal Climbing Wall), $1,000 (For Opera Omaha).

$1,500 to Operation Santa Claus, Lincoln, NE.

$1,000 to Music and Fine Arts Association, Lexington, NE. For portable risers.

$1,000 to Plum Creek Community Players, Lexington, NE. For South Pacific performance.

4987

Lincoln Community Foundation, Inc.

(formerly Lincoln Foundation, Inc.)
215 Centennial Mall S., Ste. 100
Lincoln, NE 68508-1813 (402) 474-2345
Contact: Debra Shoemaker, Dir., Prog. and Dist.
FAX: (402) 476-8523; E-mail: lcf@lcf.org; Additional
E-mail: debs@lcf.org; URL: http://www.lcf.org

Incorporated in 1955 in NE.
Foundation type: Community foundation.
Financial data (yr. ended 12/31/05): Assets, $59,869,692 (M); gifts received, $12,818,393; expenditures, $4,114,232; giving activities include $2,771,726 for 1,674 grants (high: $71,000; low: $25).

Purpose and activities: The foundation seeks to enrich the quality of life in the greater Lincoln, NE, area by responding to emerging and changing needs and sustaining existing organizations and institutions through grants for education, arts and culture, health, social services, economic development, and civic affairs in Lincoln/Lancaster

County, NE. Primary areas of interest include family issues, children's issues, older adults, environmental enhancement, higher education, and basic needs.

Fields of interest: Arts, cultural/ethnic awareness; Museums (marine/maritime); Arts; Child development, education; Higher education; Environment; Health care; Child development, services; Family services; Aging, centers/services; Human services; Economic development; Public affairs; Aging.

Type of support: General/operating support; Management development/capacity building; Capital campaigns; Building/renovation; Equipment; Land acquisition; Emergency funds; Program development; Seed money; Scholarship funds; Research; Technical assistance; Consulting services; Program evaluation; Employee matching gifts; Matching/challenge support.

Limitations: Giving limited to the Lincoln-Lancaster County, NE, area. No support for religious purposes. No grants to individuals (except for scholarships), or for endowments, large capital expenditures, budget deficits, or projects with long future commitments.

Publications: Application guidelines; Annual report; Grants list; Informational brochure (including application guidelines); Newsletter; Program policy statement.

Application information: Visit foundation Web site for application forms and guidelines. Application form required.

Initial approach: Contact foundation
Copies of proposal: 15
Deadline(s): June 1 and Dec. 1 for program grants; Sept. 1 for capital improvement grants
Board meeting date(s): 3rd Thurs. of Feb., May, Aug., and Nov.
Final notification: Following board meeting

Officers and Directors:* Ron Ecklund,* Chair.; Jeff Peetz,* Vice-Chair.; Dawson Dowty, Pres.; Chandler Tyrrell II, V.P.; Christie Schwartzkopf Schroff,* Secy.; Gretchen Thornburg, C.F.O.; Lori McClurg,* Treas.; Patrick E. Beans; Nina M. Beck; Loel P. Brooks; Rich Claussen; Dale E. Gruntorad; Nancy Haessler; Marilyn Harris, Ph.D.; Tom Henning; Orville Jones III; Kathy LeBaron; David G. Livingston; Vann Price; Sue Quambusch; Kim M. Robak; Will Scott; Lawrence D. Small; Nana G.H. Smith; Jose J. Soto; Cori Sampson Vokoun; Donna W. Woods.

Number of staff: 4 full-time professional; 4 full-time support; 1 part-time support.

EIN: 470458128

Selected grants: The following grants were reported in 2005.

$20,000 to Lincoln Public Schools, Lincoln, NE. For media literacy education at local elementary school.

$20,000 to Peoples City Mission, Lincoln, NE. For the MIRROR project, a program for women and children fleeing from violence or domestic abuse.

$15,000 to Lincoln Action Program, Lincoln, NE. For financial literacy workshops for low-income families.

$10,000 to Goodwill Industries of Lincoln, Lincoln, NE. For purchasing computers and software for computer lab to assist job seekers.

$10,000 to Lincoln Arts Council, Lincoln, NE. For Stories of Home, a community arts project that celebrates diversity and family.

$10,000 to Nebraska Art Association, Lincoln, NE. For development of a strategic plan for the Sheldon Memorial Art Gallery/Nebraska Art Association through 2010.

$10,000 to South Salt Creek Community Organization, Lincoln, NE. For playground equipment to be installed at a local park.

$8,000 to Lincoln Literacy Council, Lincoln, NE. For the Sudanese Womens Group.

$5,120 to Lancaster County Youth Intervention Center, Lincoln, NE. For developing horticulture program for at-risk youth.

$5,000 to Audubon Nebraska, Denton, NE. For program costs at Spring Creek Prairie for six low-income schools, including transportation.

4988
Lozier Foundation ▼

c/o Barbara Molck
6336 Pershing Dr.
Omaha, NE 68110-1100 (402) 457-8160
E-mail: bob.braun@lozier.biz

Established in 1986 in WA.
Donor: Allan Lozier.
Foundation type: Independent foundation.
Financial data (yr. ended 12/31/05): Assets, $169,298,452 (M); gifts received, $6,896,873; expenditures, $8,314,162; qualifying distributions, $7,995,761; giving activities include $7,995,761 for 145 grants (high: $2,020,223; low: $50; average: $1,000–$100,000).
Purpose and activities: Giving primarily for higher education, domestic violence prevention, human and youth services, women centers, homeless, minorities, and economically disadvantaged.
Fields of interest: Higher education; Crime/violence prevention, domestic violence; Human services; Youth, services; Women, centers/services; Homeless, human services; Minorities; Women; Economically disadvantaged; Homeless.
Type of support: General/operating support; Continuing support; Annual campaigns; Capital campaigns; Building/renovation; Employee matching gifts; Matching/challenge support.
Limitations: Applications not accepted. Giving primarily in the immediate Omaha, NE area. No grants to individuals.
Application information: Contributes only to pre-selected organizations.
Trustees: Sheri Andrews; Vickey Kleinsmith; Allan Lozier; Dianne Lozier.
EIN: 943027928

Selected grants: The following grants were reported in 2004.

$500,000 to College of Saint Mary, Omaha, NE. For general operating support for Walsh Hall Capital Campaign.

$250,000 to Project Harmony, Omaha, NE. For general operating support.

$180,000 to Childrens Scholarship Fund of Omaha, Omaha, NE. 2 grants: $60,000 (For general operating support), $120,000 (For general operating support).

$125,000 to Mercy High School, Omaha, NE. For general operating support.

$100,000 to Family Housing Advisory Services, Omaha, NE. For general operating support.

$100,000 to Omaha Schools Foundation, Omaha, NE. For general operating support for Educare of Omaha.

$100,000 to Salvation Army of Omaha, Omaha, NE. For general operating support.

$50,000 to Childrens Respite Care Center, Omaha, NE. For general operating support.

$45,000 to Omaha Police Foundation, Omaha, NE. For general operating support.

4989
Armstrong McDonald Foundation ✧

1221 N St., Ste. 600
Lincoln, NE 68508
Contact: Laurie L. Bouchard, Pres.
Application address: P.O. Box 900, Cortaro, AZ 85652-0900, tel.: (520) 878-9627; FAX: (520) 797-3866; E-mail: armmcdfdn@aol.com

Established in 1987 in NE.
Donor: J.M. McDonald, Sr.†.
Foundation type: Independent foundation.
Financial data (yr. ended 12/31/05): Assets, $18,163,772 (M); expenditures, $943,262; giving activities include $849,400 for 32 grants (high: $100,000; low: $2,500).
Purpose and activities: Giving primarily for health education, handicapped, and human services; giving also for religious organizations and child welfare.
Fields of interest: Higher education; Animal welfare; Animals/wildlife, endangered species; Health care; Health organizations, association; Human services; Children/youth, services; Disabilities, people with.
Type of support: General/operating support; Continuing support; Building/renovation; Equipment; Program development; Research.
Limitations: Giving to states west of the Mississippi River. No grants to individuals, or for salaries or capital campaigns.
Publications: Application guidelines.
Application information: Application form not required.
Initial approach: Proposal
Copies of proposal: 1
Deadline(s): Sept. 30
Board meeting date(s): Oct.
Officers: Laurie L. Bouchard, Pres.; Ryan M. Bouchard, V.P.; James M. McDonald IV, V.P.; Michael J. Bouchard, Secy.-Treas.
EIN: 363458711

Selected grants: The following grants were reported in 2005.

$100,000 to College of the Ozarks, Point Lookout, MO.

$64,000 to College of Saint Mary, Omaha, NE.

$50,000 to Hastings College Foundation, Hastings, NE.

$50,000 to Mosaic, Omaha, NE.

$36,000 to Bellevue University, Bellevue, NE.

$26,000 to Arizona Childrens Foundation, Tucson, AZ.

$25,000 to Primavera Foundation, Tucson, AZ.

$25,000 to Scripps Research Institute, La Jolla, CA.

$20,000 to Casa de los Ninos, Tucson, AZ.

$17,500 to Omaha Street School, Omaha, NE.

4990
Merrick Foundation, Inc. ✧

1530 17th Ave.
Central City, NE 68826 (308) 946-3707
FAX: (308) 946-3049;
E-mail: merrickf@hamilton.net; URL: http://www.merrick-foundation.org

Established in 1960 in NE.
Foundation type: Community foundation.
Financial data (yr. ended 10/31/04): Assets, $9,528,126 (M); gifts received, $737,947; expenditures, $449,150; giving activities include $308,505 for 38+ grants, and $56,543 for grants to individuals.

Purpose and activities: The foundation seeks to contribute to the growth of the quality of life in Merrick County by directing charitable funds to achieve the maximum benefits for the community's residents.

Fields of interest: Arts; Education; Environment; Health care; Recreation; Human services; Community development; Public affairs.

Type of support: Scholarships—to individuals; Endowments.

Limitations: Giving limited to Merrick County, NE. No support for religious purposes. No grants to individuals (except for scholarships).

Application information: Visit foundation Web site for application form and guidelines. Application form required.

Initial approach: Submit application form and attachments
Copies of proposal: 7
Deadline(s): 1st Mon. of every month, except Dec.
Board meeting date(s): 4th Mon. of every month, except Dec.
Final notification: Within 1 month

Officers and Board Members:* Ed Detweiler,* Pres.; Roxanne Brandes, Secy.; Marla Ortegren,* Exec. Dir.; Richard Chochon; Kristy Clarke; Vance Condon; Steve Curry; Don Daberkaw; John Ellefson; Dean Hartwig; Kurt Kuhn; Mary McHargue; Genie Solt; Randy Stewart; Kim Szatko; Carol Wegner.

EIN: 476024770

4991
Mid-Nebraska Community Foundation, Inc.
120 N. Dewey
P.O. Box 1321
North Platte, NE 69103 (308) 534-3315
Contact: Eric Seacrest, Exec. Dir.
FAX: (308) 534-6117; E-mail: mncf@hamilton.net;
URL: http://www.midnebraskafoundation.org

Established in 1978 in NE.
Foundation type: Community foundation.
Financial data (yr. ended 5/31/05): Assets, $13,856,112 (M); gifts received, $866,781; expenditures, $596,971; giving activities include $353,009 for 68 grants (high: $212,925; low: $152), and $94,060 for grants to individuals.

Purpose and activities: The foundation seeks to enhance the quality of life in the mid-Nebraska area by providing a vehicle for the pooling of financial resources and wisely managing those resources to allow the making of grants for present and future charitable purposes. The foundation is interested in supporting innovative solutions to community problems, including collaborative efforts.

Fields of interest: Arts; Elementary/secondary education; Education; Environment; Health care; Human services; Community development.

Type of support: Capital campaigns; Building/ renovation; Equipment; Land acquisition; Program development; Conferences/seminars; Seed money; Curriculum development; Scholarship funds.

Limitations: Giving limited to Custer, Dawson, Frontier, Hayes, Keith, Lincoln, Logan, McPherson and Perkins counties, NE. No support for religious organizations for religious activities, or for-profit organizations. No grants to individuals (except through designated scholarship funds), or for current operating budgets or deficit financing.

Publications: Annual report; Biennial report; Informational brochure; Occasional report.

Application information: Visit foundation Web site for application information. Scholarship applications generally available only through area school counselors, except for non-traditional students or for college students from the North Platte area. Application form required.

Initial approach: 1-page letter of inquiry or telephone for grants; complete current application form for scholarships
Copies of proposal: 5
Deadline(s): Jan. 15, Apr. 15, July 15, and Oct. 15
Board meeting date(s): Quarterly
Final notification: Approx. 45 days

Officers and Directors:* Kim Baxter,* Pres.; Alan Erickson,* V.P.; Jean States,* Secy.; Glenn Van Velson,* Treas.; Eric Seacrest, Exec. Dir.; Mitch Bean; Janet Bernard, M.D.; Stephanie J. Branch; John Childears; Pat Gale; Julie J. Jacobson; Don Kilgore; DiAnn Kolkman; Nancy Macke; Irene Mattox; Todd R. McWha; Jean A. Niedan; Lynda Perry; Margene Phares; Brenda Robinson; Rob Stefka; Kim Steger; Darlene Stewart; Larry Stobbs; Glen Waltemath.

Number of staff: 2 full-time professional.
EIN: 470604965

4992
G. Robert Muchemore Foundation ✧
c/o First National Bank of Omaha
1620 Dodge St.
Omaha, NE 68197-1081

Established in 1998 in NE.
Donor: Agnes B. Muchemore†.
Foundation type: Independent foundation.
Financial data (yr. ended 12/31/05): Assets, $12,096,476 (M); expenditures, $592,104; qualifying distributions, $536,757; giving activities include $530,608 for 5 grants (high: $287,986; low: $6,690).

Purpose and activities: Giving primarily to universities for scholarship funds.

Fields of interest: Higher education; Scholarships/ financial aid; Boys & girls clubs.

Type of support: Scholarship funds.

Limitations: Applications not accepted. Giving primarily in IA and Omaha, NE. No grants to individuals.

Application information: Contributes only to pre-selected organizations.

Officers: Harold Kosowsky, Pres.; John Maginn, V.P.; Kathy Callahan, Secy.-Treas.

Trustee: First National Bank of Omaha.

EIN: 911781660

Selected grants: The following grants were reported in 2003.

$348,666 to Creighton University, Omaha, NE. For scholarship program.
$250,758 to University of Nebraska Foundation, Omaha, NE. For scholarship program.
$39,102 to Iowa State University Foundation, Ames, IA. For scholarship program.
$24,568 to Iowa Law School Foundation, Iowa City, IA. For scholarship program.
$14,579 to Boys and Girls Clubs of Omaha, Omaha, NE. For general support.

4993
Mutual of Omaha Foundation ✧ ☆
Mutual of Omaha Plz.
Omaha, NE 68175
Contact: Christine D. Johnson, Pres.
URL: http://www.mutualofomaha.com/about/ mutual_of_omaha_foundation/index.html

Donor: Mutual of Omaha Insurance Co.
Foundation type: Independent foundation.
Financial data (yr. ended 12/31/05): Assets, $3,221,707 (M); gifts received, $3,900,000; expenditures, $921,000; qualifying distributions, $921,000; giving activities include $921,000 for grants.

Purpose and activities: The foundation is committed to providing financial assistance to programs that directly impact families with the greatest needs in order to help them overcome obstacles such as substance abuse, domestic violence, obesity in children and illiteracy.

Fields of interest: Education; Human services; Family services.

Limitations: Giving primarily in areas of company operations in Omaha, NE and Western IA, or in cities where Mutual of Omaha has a significant presence. No support for religious or sectarian organizations, social clubs or fraternal organizations. No grants to individuals, or for tickets or tables, endowment funds, travel, team sponsorships, advertising, festivals, monuments or memorials.

Application information: See foundation Web site prior to submitting application. Application form required.

Initial approach: Via online application form
Deadline(s): Dec. 1, Mar. 1, June 1 or Sept.1

Officers and Directors:* Christine D. Johnson,* Pres.; Richard A. Witt,* V.P.; Susan S. Lebens,* Secy.; Michael J. Jareske, Treas.; Daniel P. Martin; Michael C. Weekly*.

EIN: 202176636

4994
Omaha Community Foundation ▼
302 S. 36th St., Ste. 100
Omaha, NE 68131 (402) 342-3458
Contact: Michael E. Leighton, C.E.O.; For grants: Patrick McNamara, Dir., Philanthropic Svcs.
FAX: (402) 342-3582;
E-mail: sara@omahafoundation.org; Grant inquiry
E-mail: patrick@omahafoundation.org; URL: http:// www.omahafoundation.org

Established in 1982 in NE.
Foundation type: Community foundation.
Financial data (yr. ended 12/31/05): Assets, $393,005,266 (M); gifts received, $53,617,510; expenditures, $59,705,519; giving activities include $53,598,735 for grants.

Purpose and activities: The foundation seeks to build enduring charitable partnerships that make the community better. Support primarily for cultural programs, education, neighborhood development, civic affairs, health, and social services, programs for women.

Fields of interest: Arts; Education; Health care; Health organizations, association; Children/youth, services; Human services; Community development; Government/public administration; General charitable giving.

Type of support: Continuing support; Building/ renovation; Equipment; Emergency funds; Program development; Conferences/seminars; Publication;

Seed money; Scholarship funds; Technical assistance; Matching/challenge support.

Limitations: Giving primarily in the metropolitan Omaha, NE, area including southwest IA. No support for tax-supported institutions, religious organizations for religious purposes, organizations funded by the United Way, arts groups, social clubs, or veterans', labor, or fraternal organizations. No grants to individuals, or for endowments, capital campaigns, deficit financing, annual fund drives, fundraising events, dinners, or tickets.

Publications: Application guidelines; Annual report (including application guidelines); Grants list; Informational brochure; Newsletter.

Application information: Visit foundation Web site for application form and guidelines. Handwritten grant applications are not accepted. Application form required.

> *Initial approach:* Contact foundation
> *Copies of proposal:* 1
> *Deadline(s):* Mar. 1 and Sept.1
> *Board meeting date(s):* Mar., June, Sept., and Dec.
> *Final notification:* May and Nov.

Officers and Directors:* Michael McCarthy,* Chair.; John Scott,* Vice-Chair.; Michael E. Leighton, C.E.O. and Pres.; Sara Russell Boyd, V.P.; James A. Timmerman,* Secy.; John Maginn,* Treas.; Thomas R. Pansing, Jr.,* Legal Counsel; Jerry M. Bartee; David Catalan; Carol Gendler; Deryl F. Hamann; John W. Hancock; J. Terrance Haney; Paul C. Jessen; Richard W. Kelley; Sandra Parker; Thomas L. Schmitt; Todd D. Simon; Maria Vazquez; Mark Weber; M. Jane Weekley.

Number of staff: 8 full-time professional; 1 part-time professional; 6 full-time support.

EIN: 470645958

Selected grants: The following grants were reported in 2005.

$175,000 to Intercessors of the Lamb, Omaha, NE.
$160,000 to Heartland Family Service, Omaha, NE. 2 grants: $150,000, $10,000
$120,000 to Omaha Performing Arts Society, Omaha, NE. 2 grants: $20,000, $100,000
$60,000 to Saint Pius X/Saint Leo School, Omaha, NE.
$50,000 to Anti-Defamation League of Bnai Brith, Omaha, NE.
$20,000 to National Conference for Community and Justice, Omaha, NE.
$15,000 to King of Kings Lutheran Church, Omaha, NE.
$10,000 to Jesuit Middle School, Omaha, NE.

4995
The Omaha World-Herald Foundation ◇

c/o Omaha World-Herald Co.
1334 Dodge St.
World Herald Sq.
Omaha, NE 68102-1138 (402) 444-1000
Contact: John Gottschalk, Pres.

Trust established in 1968 in NE.
Donors: Omaha World-Herald Co.; Omaha World Herald Branching Out.
Foundation type: Company-sponsored foundation.
Financial data (yr. ended 12/31/05): Assets, $51,157 (M); gifts received, $1,294,070; expenditures, $1,404,747; qualifying distributions, $1,403,651; giving activities include $1,401,833 for 36 grants (high: $234,000; low: $1,000).

Purpose and activities: The foundation supports organizations involved with arts and culture, education, natural resources, and youth.

Fields of interest: Media, journalism/publishing; Historic preservation/historical societies; Arts; Education; Environment, natural resources; Youth, services.

Type of support: Building/renovation; Equipment; Program development; Seed money; Internship funds; Scholarship funds; Matching/challenge support.

Limitations: Giving limited to western IA and NE. No grants to individuals, or for endowments, research, seminars, or dinners.

Application information: Application form not required.

> *Initial approach:* Proposal
> *Copies of proposal:* 1
> *Deadline(s):* None
> *Board meeting date(s):* As required
> *Final notification:* 2 months

Officer and Distribution Committee:* John Gottschalk,* Pres.; A. William Kernen.
Trustee: Wells Fargo Bank Nebraska, N.A.
EIN: 476058691

Selected grants: The following grants were reported in 2004.

$250,000 to Omaha Performing Arts Society, Omaha, NE.
$125,000 to Chamber Foundation, Greater Omaha, Omaha, NE. 2 grants: $62,500 each
$75,000 to Creighton University, Omaha, NE.
$50,000 to College of Saint Mary, Omaha, NE.
$50,000 to Omaha Community Foundation, Omaha, NE.
$50,000 to Omaha Symphony, Omaha, NE.
$35,721 to United Way of the Midlands, Omaha, NE.
$30,000 to Opera Omaha, Omaha, NE.
$25,000 to Hastings College Foundation, Hastings, NE.

4996
Kitty M. Perkins Foundation

c/o J. Richard Shoemaker
304 Nelson St.
Cambridge, NE 69022 (308) 697-4721
FAX: (308) 697-4101; *URL:* http://www.kmpfoundation.com

Incorporated in 1966 in IL.
Donor: Kitty M. Perkins†.
Foundation type: Independent foundation.
Financial data (yr. ended 12/31/04): Assets, $8,834,836 (M); expenditures, $392,875; qualifying distributions, $381,117; giving activities include $381,117 for 26 grants (high: $150,000; low: $617).

Purpose and activities: Grants for higher education, rural libraries, medical research, and rural community hospitals.

Fields of interest: Higher education; Libraries/library science; Hospitals (general); Medical research, institute.

Type of support: General/operating support; Continuing support; Annual campaigns; Capital campaigns; Building/renovation; Equipment; Program development; Professorships; Research.

Limitations: Giving primarily in NE. No grants to individuals, or for matching gifts; no loans.

Publications: Application guidelines.

Application information: Application guidelines and form available on foundation Web site. Application form required.

> *Copies of proposal:* 2
> *Board meeting date(s):* As required

Officers and Directors:* J. Richard Shoemaker,* Pres.; Don C. Shoemaker,* Secy.; William Shoemaker,* Treas.; Kathryn Heitmann; George Franklin Shoemaker.
EIN: 366154399

Selected grants: The following grants were reported in 2004.

$170,000 to Cambridge, City of, Cambridge, NE. 2 grants: $150,000, $20,000
$10,000 to Doane College, Crete, NE.
$10,000 to Loft at the Mill, Lincoln, NE.
$10,000 to Nebraska Humanities Council, Lincoln, NE.
$10,000 to YMCA.
$5,000 to Lincoln Orchestra Association, Lincoln, NE.
$1,000 to Hastings College, Hastings, NE.

4997
Edgar & Frances Reynolds Foundation, Inc. ◇

(formerly Edgar Reynolds Foundation, Inc.)
P.O. Box 1492
Grand Island, NE 68802 (308) 384-0957
Contact: Fred Glade, Tr.
E-mail: lawyer@lauritsenlaw.com

Established in 1977 in NE.
Donors: Edgar Reynolds†; Frances Reynolds†.
Foundation type: Independent foundation.
Financial data (yr. ended 12/31/05): Assets, $9,023,724 (M); expenditures, $586,938; qualifying distributions, $465,535; giving activities include $454,357 for 17 grants (high: $142,857; low: $1,000).

Purpose and activities: Giving primarily for higher education and human services.

Fields of interest: Higher education; Human services; Community development.

Type of support: Building/renovation; Scholarship funds; Matching/challenge support.

Limitations: Giving primarily in central NE. No grants to individuals.

Publications: Application guidelines.

Application information: Application form required.

> *Initial approach:* Letter requesting application form
> *Copies of proposal:* 6
> *Deadline(s):* None
> *Board meeting date(s):* Varies

Trustees: Kent Coen; Carolyn Glade; Fred Glade; Gordon Glade; Sarah Glade; Susan Glade; Don Jelinek.
EIN: 470589941

4998
Morrison Roberts Foundation ◇

12th and Brentwood
P.O. Box 609
Hastings, NE 68902-0609
Contact: Susan M. Morrison Roberts, Secy.-Treas.

Established around 1994 in NE.
Donor: Kenneth Morrison.
Foundation type: Independent foundation.
Financial data (yr. ended 8/31/05): Assets, $1,910,273 (M); gifts received, $1,500,000; expenditures, $1,291,181; qualifying distributions,

$1,290,000; giving activities include $1,290,000 for 8 grants (high: $1,000,000; low: $2,500).
Purpose and activities: Giving to colleges and their foundations, animal welfare organizations and human service organizations.
Fields of interest: Elementary/secondary education; Higher education; Animal welfare; Human services; Foundations (community).
Limitations: Giving primarily in Adams County, NE. No grants to individuals.
Application information: Preference given to organizations recommended by the officers and directors. Application form not required.
  Deadline(s): None
Officers: Kenneth Morrison, Pres.; Susan M. Morrison Roberts, Secy.-Treas.
Director: Gretchen Roberts.
EIN: 363988367

4999

Rogers Foundation ◇
1311 M St., Ste. A
Lincoln, NE 68508-2539 (402) 477-3725
Contact: Richard W. Agee, Pres. and Treas.

Established in 1954 in NE.
Donor: Richard H. Rogers†.
Foundation type: Independent foundation.
Financial data (yr. ended 12/31/05): Assets, $10,677,548 (M); expenditures, $501,403; qualifying distributions, $464,146; giving activities include $447,014 for 47 grants (high: $45,000; low: $14).
Purpose and activities: Giving primarily for programs that fulfill immediate and practical needs of the community.
Fields of interest: Performing arts; Animals/wildlife, preservation/protection; Health care; Human services; Children/youth, services; Youth, services; Community development.
Limitations: Giving primarily in Lincoln and Lancaster County, NE. No support for religious activities, national organizations, or organizations supported by government agencies. No grants to individuals, or for fundraising benefits, program advertising, endowments, or continuing support; no loans.
Publications: Application guidelines.
Application information:
  Initial approach: Proposal
  Deadline(s): None
Officers: Richard W. Agee, Pres. and Treas.; Eloise R. Agee, V.P. and Secy.; Rex Marquart, V.P.
EIN: 476026897
Selected grants: The following grants were reported in 2004.
$40,000 to Madonna Foundation, Lincoln, NE.
$30,000 to Nebraska Wesleyan University, Lincoln, NE.
$25,000 to Bright Lights, Lincoln, NE.
$25,000 to BryanLGH Medical Center, School of Nursing, Lincoln, NE.
$15,000 to American Red Cross, Lincoln, NE. f.
$15,000 to Groundwater Foundation, Lincoln, NE.
$15,000 to Humane Society of Nebraska-Capitol, Lincoln, NE.
$11,000 to Lighthouse, Lincoln, NE.
$10,000 to Tabitha Foundation, Lincoln, NE.
$5,000 to Salvation Army of Lincoln, Lincoln, NE.

5000

The Ryan Foundation ◇
P.O. Box 45625
Omaha, NE 68145 (402) 333-1982
Contact: Wayne L. Ryan, Dir.

Established in 1990 in NE.
Donors: Wayne L. Ryan; Eileen Ryan.
Foundation type: Independent foundation.
Financial data (yr. ended 12/31/04): Assets, $4,901,195 (M); gifts received, $1,874,353; expenditures, $356,382; qualifying distributions, $343,950; giving activities include $343,950 for 45 grants.
Purpose and activities: Giving primarily to educational institutions.
Fields of interest: Higher education; Education; Human services; Christian agencies & churches.
Type of support: Scholarships—to individuals.
Limitations: Giving primarily in NE.
Application information:
  Initial approach: Proposal
  Deadline(s): None
Directors: Carol Ryan; Constance Ryan; Eileen Ryan; Stacy Ryan; Steve Ryan; Tim Ryan; Wayne L. Ryan.
EIN: 363755606

5001

Phillip and Terri Schrager Foundation ◇
(formerly Phillip Schrager Foundation)
4405 S. 96 St.
Omaha, NE 68127-1283

Established in 1972 in NE.
Donors: Phillip G. Schrager; The Pacesetter Corp.
Foundation type: Independent foundation.
Financial data (yr. ended 12/31/05): Assets, $9,700,609 (M); expenditures, $403,806; qualifying distributions, $393,321; giving activities include $393,321 for 39 grants (high: $188,751; low: $50).
Purpose and activities: Funding primarily for education, the arts, particularly to art museums and for opera, human services, Jewish agencies and organizations.
Fields of interest: Museums; Arts; Education; Hospitals (general); Human services; Youth, services; Federated giving programs; Jewish federated giving programs; Jewish agencies & temples.
Limitations: Applications not accepted. Giving primarily in Omaha, NE. No grants to individuals.
Application information: Contributes only to pre-selected organizations.
Officers and Directors:* Phillip G. Schrager,* Pres.; Terri L. Schrager, V.P.; Richard A. Schrager,* Secy.; Harley Schrager,* Treas.; David Gilinsky; Timothy Schrager; Todd Simon; John Vann; Rosie Zweiback.
EIN: 237184025
Selected grants: The following grants were reported in 2005.
$63,915 to Joslyn Art Museum, Omaha, NE.
$50,000 to Jewish Federation of Omaha, Omaha, NE.
$14,446 to Temple Israel, Omaha, NE.
$8,333 to Project Harmony, Omaha, NE.
$6,667 to Beth El Synagogue, Omaha, NE.
$2,500 to Aspen Theater in the Park, Aspen, CO.
$1,000 to Durham Western Heritage Museum, Omaha, NE.

5002

Simon Charitable Foundation ◇ ☆
442 S. 82nd St.
Omaha, NE 68114-4408

Established in 1988 in NE.
Donor: Frederick J. Simon.
Foundation type: Independent foundation.
Financial data (yr. ended 12/31/05): Assets, $11,820 (M); gifts received, $385,000; expenditures, $401,286; qualifying distributions, $400,310; giving activities include $400,310 for grants.
Purpose and activities: Giving primarily for arts and culture, education and Jewish organizations.
Fields of interest: Performing arts; Performing arts, opera; Arts; Education; Jewish agencies & temples.
Limitations: Applications not accepted. Giving primarily in the Omaha, NE, area. No grants to individuals.
Application information: Contributes only to pre-selected organizations.
Officers: Frederick J. Simon, Pres. and Treas.; Eve B. Simon, V.P. and Secy.
EIN: 363585646

5003

Slosburg Family Charitable Trust ◇
10040 Regency Cir., Ste. 200
Omaha, NE 68114 (402) 391-7900
Contact: D. David Slosburg, Tr.

Established in 1996 in NE.
Foundation type: Independent foundation.
Financial data (yr. ended 12/31/05): Assets, $587,551 (M); expenditures, $863,155; qualifying distributions, $862,268; giving activities include $862,261 for 57 grants (high: $625,000; low: $35).
Purpose and activities: Giving for Jewish agencies, medical and health agencies, art and education.
Fields of interest: Arts; Higher education; Alzheimer's disease; Christian agencies & churches; Roman Catholic agencies & churches; Jewish agencies & temples.
Limitations: Giving on a national basis.
Application information:
  Initial approach: Letter or telephone
  Deadline(s): None
Trustees: D. David Slosburg; Richard H. Slosburg.
EIN: 470798965

5004

Frank L. and Laura L. Smock Foundation ◇
c/o Wells Fargo Bank Indiana, N.A.
4707 S. 96th St.
Omaha, NE 68127

Established in 1953 in IN.
Donor: Laura L. Smock†.
Foundation type: Independent foundation.
Financial data (yr. ended 12/31/05): Assets, $16,586,080 (M); expenditures, $735,645; qualifying distributions, $677,073; giving activities include $371,784 for 4 grants (high: $174,527; low: $15,000), and $272,434 for grants to individuals (high: $46,446).
Purpose and activities: To promote the health, welfare and happiness of poor and elderly men and women of the Presbyterian faith throughout the state of IN.

Fields of interest: Aging, centers/services; Protestant agencies & churches.
Type of support: Grants to individuals.
Limitations: Applications not accepted. Giving limited to IN. No grants for general or operating support, capital campaigns, building or endowment funds.
Application information: Unsolicited requests for funds not accepted.
   Board meeting date(s): Monthly
Trustee: Wells Fargo Bank Indiana, N.A.
EIN: 356011335

5005
The Steinhart Foundation, Inc. ✧
P.O. Box 640
1901 1st Ave.
Nebraska City, NE 68410-2359 (402) 873-3285
Contact: Leta Harshman, Pres.
Application address: 1901 Central Ave., Nebraska City, NE 68410-2359

Incorporated in 1954 in NE.
Donors: Morton Steinhart†; Ella S. Steinhart†; Ella Steinhart Charitable Remainder Unitrust.
Foundation type: Independent foundation.
Financial data (yr. ended 12/31/05): Assets, $9,023,827 (L); expenditures, $628,307; qualifying distributions, $517,745; giving activities include $517,745 for 40 grants (high: $150,000; low: $500).
Fields of interest: Historic preservation/historical societies; Arts; Elementary/secondary education; Higher education; Education; Mental health/crisis services; Food banks; Safety/disasters, volunteer services; Human services; Children/youth, services; Family services; Foundations (community); Government/public administration; Christian agencies & churches.
Type of support: Scholarships—to individuals.
Limitations: Giving primarily in Nebraska City, NE, and the immediate surrounding area.
Application information: Funds presently committed. Application form required.
   Initial approach: Proposal
   Copies of proposal: 1
   Deadline(s): Mar. 15 and Sept. 15
   Board meeting date(s): Annually
Officers: Leta Harshman, Pres.; John James, V.P.; George T. Blazek, Secy.-Treas.
Directors: Garry Ailes; Mary Ellen Bosworth; Deroy Harshman; Henry Schwake; Nancy Weldon.
EIN: 476025185
Selected grants: The following grants were reported in 2004.
$100,000 to Hastings College, Hastings, NE.
$76,000 to Nebraska Community Foundation, Lincoln, NE. 3 grants: $6,000, $60,000, $10,000
$26,000 to Nebraska City, City of, Nebraska City, NE.
$10,000 to Nebraska City Public Schools Foundation, Nebraska City, NE.
$2,500 to Creighton University, Omaha, NE.
$2,500 to Missouri Western State College, Saint Joseph, MO.
$2,500 to Peru State College, Peru, NE.
$2,000 to Nebraska City Cares, Nebraska City, NE.

5006
Robert Herman Storz Foundation
8805 Indian Hills Dr., Ste. 175
Omaha, NE 68114
Contact: Herbert A. Engdahl, Tr.

Established in 1957.
Donor: Robert Herman Storz†.
Foundation type: Independent foundation.
Financial data (yr. ended 12/31/05): Assets, $7,185,617 (M); expenditures, $453,712; qualifying distributions, $427,252; giving activities include $427,252 for 33 grants (high: $58,090; low: $500).
Fields of interest: Arts; Human services.
Type of support: Annual campaigns; Capital campaigns; Building/renovation; Matching/challenge support.
Limitations: Giving primarily in the immediate Omaha, NE, area. No grants to individuals.
Application information: Application form not required.
   Initial approach: Letter
   Copies of proposal: 1
   Board meeting date(s): 2nd Mon. in May, Sept., and Dec.
   Final notification: If approved, applicants will be notified after Board meeting
Trustees: Susan Storz Butler; Herbert A. Engdahl; Robert S. Howard.
Number of staff: 1 full-time professional.
EIN: 476025980
Selected grants: The following grants were reported in 2005.
$65,000 to Omaha Performing Arts Society, Omaha, NE.
$35,000 to Joslyn Art Museum, Omaha, NE.
$25,000 to Alexis de Tocqueville Society, Alexandria, VA.
$25,000 to Bellevue University, Bellevue, NE.
$25,000 to Durham Western Heritage Museum, Omaha, NE.
$25,000 to Strategic Air and Space Museum, Ashland, NE.
$20,000 to Lauritzen Gardens, Omaha, NE.
$16,000 to Omaha Symphony, Omaha, NE.
$10,000 to Child Saving Institute, Omaha, NE.
$1,660 to American Red Cross.

5007
Sunshine Foundation Trust ✧ ☆
14301 FNB Pkwy., Rm. 115
Omaha, NE 68154 (402) 496-7200
Contact: Gail Werner-Robertson, Tr.

Established in 1997 in NE.
Foundation type: Independent foundation.
Financial data (yr. ended 12/31/05): Assets, $1,338,894 (M); gifts received, $368,166; expenditures, $578,218; qualifying distributions, $439,140; giving activities include $439,140 for grants.
Fields of interest: Arts; Hospitals (general); Youth, services; Roman Catholic agencies & churches.
Limitations: Giving primarily in Omaha, NE.
Application information:
   Initial approach: Letter
Trustee: Gail Werner-Robertson.
Directors: Scott Robertson; Gloria Werner; and 4 additional directors.
EIN: 911816672

5008
Gretchen Swanson Family Foundation, Inc. ✧ ☆
4935 Battlefield Ave.
Omaha, NE 68152 (402) 453-7500
Contact: Kurt S. Bucholz, Pres.

Established in 1960.
Donors: Frederick S. Bucholz; Kurt S. Bucholz; Gretchen Swanson Velde†.
Foundation type: Independent foundation.
Financial data (yr. ended 12/31/05): Assets, $19,280,810 (M); expenditures, $653,930; qualifying distributions, $537,832; giving activities include $535,000 for 3 grants (high: $500,000; low: $10,000).
Purpose and activities: Giving primarily for a community center; some funding also for a museum, and social services for diaster relief.
Fields of interest: Museums (art); Human services.
Limitations: Giving primarily in Omaha, NE.
Application information: Application form not required.
   Deadline(s): None
Officers and Directors:* Kurt S. Bucholz,* Pres.; Michael Jones, Secy.; Edward J. Fitzpatrick, Treas.; Frederick S. Bucholz; Laura S. Bucholz.
EIN: 476024650

5009
Carl and Caroline Swanson Foundation, Inc. ✧ ☆
4935 Battlefield Dr.
Omaha, NE 68152 (402) 453-7500
Contact: Frederick S. Bucholz, Pres.

Trust established in 1945; incorporated in 1953 in NE.
Donors: Kurt S. Bucholz; Frederick S. Bucholz; Gretchen Swanson Velde†; members of the Carl A. Swanson family.
Foundation type: Independent foundation.
Financial data (yr. ended 12/31/05): Assets, $19,258,043 (M); expenditures, $724,773; qualifying distributions, $528,555; giving activities include $526,000 for 6 grants (high: $350,000; low: $10,000).
Fields of interest: Higher education; Environment, land resources; Environmental education; Animals/wildlife; Health care; Agriculture, farmlands; Athletics/sports, equestrianism; Human services.
Type of support: General/operating support.
Limitations: Giving primarily in NE, TX, and CO. No grants to individuals.
Application information: Application form not required.
   Deadline(s): None
   Board meeting date(s): Quarterly
Officers: Frederick S. Bucholz, Pres.; Michael Jones, Secy.; Edward J. Fitzpatrick, Treas.
Directors: Kurt S. Bucholz; Lori Bucholz.
EIN: 476024644
Selected grants: The following grants were reported in 2005.
$75,000 to University of Nebraska Foundation, Lincoln, NE.
$50,000 to Breckenridge Outdoor Education Center, Breckenridge, CO.
$31,000 to Center for Human Nutrition, Omaha, NE.
$10,000 to Divers Alert Network, Durham, NC.

5010
TierOne Charitable Foundation ✧

1235 N St.
Lincoln, NE 68508
Application address: c/o Pat Young, P.O. Box 83009, Lincoln, NE 68501

Established in 2003 in DE and NE.
Donor: TierOne Corp.
Foundation type: Company-sponsored foundation.
Financial data (yr. ended 12/31/05): Assets, $12,586,044 (M); expenditures, $767,452; qualifying distributions, $761,820; giving activities include $760,278 for 151 grants (high: $30,000; low: $300).
Purpose and activities: The foundation supports orchestras and organizations involved with higher education, health, housing, parks and playgrounds, and human services.
Fields of interest: Performing arts, orchestra (symphony); Higher education; Health care; Housing/shelter; Recreation, parks/playgrounds; Children/youth, services; Family services; Human services; Federated giving programs.
Limitations: Giving limited to areas of company operations. No support for religious organizations or lobbying organizations. No grants to individuals, or for advertising, publications, brochures, books, or newsletters.
Application information: An application form is required for requests of less than $2,500. Support is limited to 1 year. Letters of inquiry should be no longer than 2 pages.
  Initial approach: Letter of inquiry; contact foundation for application form for requests of less than $2,500
  Board meeting date(s): Jan., Apr., July, and Oct.
  Final notification: Within 4 weeks
Officers: Gilbert G. Lundstrom, Chair.; James A. Laphen, Pres. and Treas.; Roger R. Ludemann, Secy.
Board Member: Thomas C. Woods III.
EIN: 050532793

5011
Stanley M. Truhlsen Family Foundation, Inc. ✧

c/o Michael D. Jones
8805 Indian Hills Dr., Ste. 280
Omaha, NE 68114

Established in 1997 in NE.
Donor: Stanley M. Truhlsen.
Foundation type: Independent foundation.
Financial data (yr. ended 12/31/05): Assets, $1,644,846 (M); gifts received, $681,600; expenditures, $595,326; qualifying distributions, $555,600; giving activities include $555,600 for 36 grants (high: $500,000; low: $200).
Fields of interest: Elementary/secondary education; Education; Human services; Children/youth, services.
Limitations: Applications not accepted. Giving primarily in NE. No grants to individuals.
Application information: Contributes only to pre-selected organizations.
Officers and Directors:* Stanley M. Truhlsen,* Pres.; William C. Truhlsen,* V.P.; Dorothy D. Truhlsen,* Secy.; Michael D. Jones,* Treas.; Nancy Brager, Barbara Truhlsen; Stanley M. Truhlsen, Jr.
EIN: 311525292

5012
Union Pacific Foundation ▼

1400 Douglas St., Stop 1560
Omaha, NE 68179 (402) 544-5600
Contact: Darlynn Herweg, Dir.
E-mail: upf@up.com; *URL:* http://www.up.com/found

Incorporated in 1959 in UT.
Donor: Union Pacific Corp.
Foundation type: Company-sponsored foundation.
Financial data (yr. ended 12/31/04): Assets, $19,531 (M); gifts received, $7,621,400; expenditures, $8,779,411; qualifying distributions, $8,643,517; giving activities include $8,643,517 for 525 grants (high: $383,333; low: $300).
Purpose and activities: The foundation supports libraries and organizations involved with arts and culture, the environment, health, at-risk youth, human services, and community development.
Fields of interest: Museums; Historic preservation/historical societies; Arts; Libraries/library science; Environment, natural resources; Environment; Hospitals (general); Medical care, rehabilitation; Health care; Youth development; Human services; Community development.
Type of support: General/operating support; Capital campaigns; Building/renovation; Equipment; Program development.
Limitations: Giving on a national basis in areas of company operations. No support for specialized national health and welfare organizations, religious or labor organizations, social clubs, or fraternal or veterans' organizations. No grants to individuals, or for sponsorship of dinners, benefits, seminars, or other special events or non-capital support for United Way-supported organizations.
Publications: Application guidelines.
Application information: Application form required.
  Initial approach: Complete online application form
  Deadline(s): Aug. 15
  Board meeting date(s): Late Jan.
  Final notification: Feb. through Apr.
Officers and Trustees:* Richard K. Davidson,* Chair.; R.W. Turner,* Pres.; Robert M. Knight, Jr.,* V.P., Finance; J. Michael Hemmer,* Genl. Counsel; Barbara W. Schaefer; James R. Young.
Number of staff: 1 full-time professional.
EIN: 136406825
Selected grants: The following grants were reported in 2004.
$1,383,332 to Educational Partnerships, Fairfield, CT. 4 grants: $333,333, $333,333, $333,333, $383,333
$277,000 to United Way of the Midlands, Omaha, NE.
$100,000 to United Way of Greater Saint Louis, Saint Louis, MO.
$100,000 to United Way of Metropolitan Chicago, Chicago, IL.
$65,000 to United Way, Mid-Plains, North Platte, NE.
$20,000 to Clark Atlanta University, Atlanta, GA.
$15,000 to United Way of the Columbia-Willamette, Portland, OR.

5013
The Valmont Foundation

c/o Valmont Industries, Inc.
1 Valmont Plz., 6th Fl.
Omaha, NE 68154-5215
Contact: Ed Burchfield, Exec. Secy.

FAX: (402) 963-1095;
E-mail: ed.burchfield@valmont.com

Established in 1976.
Donor: Valmont Industries, Inc.
Foundation type: Company-sponsored foundation.
Financial data (yr. ended 2/28/06): Assets, $71,440 (M); gifts received, $900,002; expenditures, $917,353; qualifying distributions, $917,351; giving activities include $917,351 for 147 grants (high: $125,000; low: $25).
Purpose and activities: The foundation supports organizations involved with arts and culture, K-12 and higher education, health, and human services.
Fields of interest: Arts; Elementary/secondary education; Higher education; Health care; Children/youth, services; Family services; Human services.
Limitations: Giving primarily in NE.
Application information: Application form not required.
  Initial approach: Proposal
  Copies of proposal: 1
  Deadline(s): None
  Board meeting date(s): Varies
  Final notification: Varies
Directors: Mogens C. Bay; Terry J. McClain.
EIN: 362895245
Selected grants: The following grants were reported in 2005.
$128,000 to United Way.
$75,000 to Omaha Performing Arts Society, Omaha, NE.
$44,000 to Knights of Ak-Sar-Ben Foundation, Omaha, NE.
$27,500 to Strategic Air and Space Museum, Ashland, NE.
$25,000 to American Red Cross.
$17,000 to Salvation Army.
$14,250 to Omaha Symphony Association, Omaha, NE.
$11,000 to Opera Omaha, Omaha, NE.
$10,000 to Joslyn Art Museum, Omaha, NE.
$5,000 to YMCA.

5014
Vetter Foundation ✧

c/o Jack Vetter
5020 S. 118th St.
Omaha, NE 68137

Established in NE.
Donors: Vetter Holding, Inc; Heritage Partners.
Foundation type: Independent foundation.
Financial data (yr. ended 6/30/05): Assets, $1,140,662 (M); gifts received, $265,265; expenditures, $634,796; qualifying distributions, $620,844; giving activities include $555,184 for grants, and $65,660 for foundation-administered programs.
Fields of interest: Nursing care; Nursing home/convalescent facility; Health care.
Limitations: Applications not accepted. No grants to individuals.
Application information: Contributes only to pre-selected organizations.
Officers: Jack D. Vetter,* Pres.; Eldora D. Vetter, V.P.
Directors: Vicki Cates; Dennith D. Vetter; Todd Vetter.
EIN: 470762483

5015
Terry K. Watanabe Charitable Trust ✧
P.O. Box 3737
Omaha, NE 68108 (402) 955-2837
Contact: Shannon Leather

Established in 1992 in NE.
Donors: Terry K. Watanabe; Joy Watanabe.
Foundation type: Independent foundation.
Financial data (yr. ended 12/31/05): Assets, $6,098,303 (M); gifts received, $52,769; expenditures, $869,546; qualifying distributions, $835,141; giving activities include $800,732 for 57 grants (high: $375,000; low: $100).
Purpose and activities: Giving primarily for education, human rights, and healthcare issues, such as teen pregnancy, substance abuse, teen violence, domestic abuse, HIV/AIDS, and for programs which promote human rights, encourage diversity in all facets of community life, and fight bias, bigotry, racism, and discrimination of all kinds.
Fields of interest: Education; AIDS; Human services.
Application information: Application form not required.
Initial approach: Letter
Copies of proposal: 1
Final notification: Within 90 days
Trustee: Terry K. Watanabe.
EIN: 363839201
Selected grants: The following grants were reported in 2004.
$152,500 to Beth Israel Deaconess Medical Center, Boston, MA.
$35,000 to Thresholds, Chicago, IL.
$30,000 to Stonewall Community Foundation, New York, NY.
$27,290 to National Conference for Community and Justice, New York, NY.
$6,000 to Bone Marrow Buddies, Independence, OH.
$2,500 to American Red Cross.
$2,500 to Ollie Webb Center, Omaha, NE.
$1,000 to Human Rights Campaign, DC.

5016
Weitz Family Foundation ✧
1610 S. 91st Ave.
Omaha, NE 68124
Contact: Wallace R. Weitz, Pres. and Treas.
Application address: 1 Pacific Pl., Ste. 600, 1125 S. 103rd St., Omaha, NE 68124

Established in 1999 in NE.
Donors: Wallace R. Weitz; Barbara V. Weitz; Roger Weitz.
Foundation type: Independent foundation.
Financial data (yr. ended 8/31/05): Assets, $25,503,411 (M); gifts received, $3,875,929; expenditures, $1,371,786; qualifying distributions, $1,326,436; giving activities include $1,326,436 for 46 grants (high: $150,000; low: $850).
Purpose and activities: Giving primarily for higher education, the arts, federated giving programs, and children, youth, family and social services.
Fields of interest: Media, television; Media, radio; Performing arts; Arts; Education; Housing/shelter, development; Housing/shelter; Human services; American Red Cross; Community development; Economically disadvantaged.
Type of support: General/operating support; Continuing support; Professorships; Seed money; Research.

Limitations: Giving primarily in Chicago, IL, Minneapolis, MN and Omaha, NE.
Application information:
Initial approach: Letter
Deadline(s): None
Board meeting date(s): Apr., Oct. and Dec.
Officers: Wallace R. Weitz, Pres. and Treas.; Barbara V. Weitz, V.P. and Secy.
Directors: Andrew S. Weitz; Roger T. Weitz; Kathryn W. White; Watie White.
Number of staff: 1 part-time support.
EIN: 470834133
Selected grants: The following grants were reported in 2004.
$500,000 to Family Housing Advisory Services, Omaha, NE. For general operating support.
$500,000 to Project Harmony, Omaha, NE. For general operating support.
$200,000 to New Community Development Corporation, Omaha, NE. 2 grants: $150,000 (For grant made to Miami Heights Development for general operating support), $50,000 (For general operating support).
$177,750 to Omaha Community Foundation, Omaha, NE. For general operating support.
$100,000 to Camp Fire USA, Council of the Midlands, Omaha, NE. For general operating support.
$82,000 to University of Nebraska Foundation, Lincoln, NE. For general operating support for Service Learning Academy Project.
$75,000 to Winners Circle Education Foundation, Omaha, NE. For general operating support.
$50,000 to Carleton College, Northfield, MN. For general operating support.
$50,000 to Chicago Opera Theater, Chicago, IL. For general operating support.

5017
Wiebe Charitable Foundation ✧
3626 S. 149th St.
Omaha, NE 68144
Contact: Kenneth Patry, Treas.
FAX: (402) 392-2251;
E-mail: Kpatry@patryassociates.com

Established in 1990 in NE.
Donors: John A. Wiebe; Harriet K. Wiebe.
Foundation type: Independent foundation.
Financial data (yr. ended 9/30/05): Assets, $10,344,146 (L); gifts received, $136,307; expenditures, $572,203; qualifying distributions, $484,500; giving activities include $484,500 for 98 grants (high: $25,000; low: $1,000).
Purpose and activities: Giving primarily for children and youth services, including children's hospitals and other healthcare facilities for children, health associations, education, family and social services, and Christian and Lutheran organizations.
Fields of interest: Performing arts; Higher education; Education; Hospitals (specialty); Health organizations, association; Boys & girls clubs; Human services; Children/youth, services; Family services; Christian agencies & churches; Protestant agencies & churches.
Type of support: General/operating support; Scholarship funds.
Limitations: Applications not accepted. Giving primarily in NE; some funding also nationally. No grants to individuals.
Application information: Contributes only to pre-selected organizations.
Board meeting date(s): Sept.

Officers: Harriet K. Wiebe, Chair.; Barbara Heikel, Pres.; Linda Fauss, V.P.; Gary Radil, Secy.; Kenneth Patry, Treas.
Directors: John O'Gara; Denese Stalnaker; Patrick Tucker.
Number of staff: 1 part-time support.
EIN: 470731612
Selected grants: The following grants were reported in 2005.
$10,000 to Nebraska Childrens Home Society, Omaha, NE.
$10,000 to Wings of Hope, Chesterfield, MO.
$7,500 to Shriners Hospitals for Children, Tampa, FL.
$7,000 to National Challenged Homeschoolers Associated Network, Porthill, ID.
$5,000 to American Heritage Girls, Cincinnati, OH.
$5,000 to Council on Child Abuse of Southern Ohio, Cincinnati, OH.
$5,000 to Good News Ministries, Austin, IN.
$5,000 to National Center for Family Literacy, Louisville, KY.
$5,000 to Strategic Air and Space Museum, Ashland, NE.
$4,000 to Child Saving Institute, Omaha, NE.

5018
Woods Charitable Fund, Inc.
1440 M St.
P.O. Box 81309
Lincoln, NE 68501 (402) 436-5971
Contact: Pam Baker, Secy. and Exec. Dir.; Tom Woods, Prog. off.; Angie Zmarzly, Prog. Assoc.
FAX: (402) 436-4128;
E-mail: pbaker@woodscharitable.org; Additional e-mails: twoods@woodscharitable.org or azmarzly@woodscharitable.org; URL: http://www.woodscharitable.org

Incorporated in 1941 in NE.
Donors: Frank H. Woods†; Nelle C. Woods†; Frank H. Woods, Jr.†; Thomas C. Woods, Jr.†; Henry C. Woods†; Sahara Coal Co., Inc.
Foundation type: Independent foundation.
Financial data (yr. ended 12/31/05): Assets, $36,153,479 (M); gifts received, $200; expenditures, $1,732,804; qualifying distributions, $1,679,751; giving activities include $1,353,740 for 62 grants (high: $200,000; low: $1,200).
Purpose and activities: Grants primarily to nonprofit organizations working to build a stronger community. Particular interest in projects that benefit children, young people, families, community development and housing, education, and the arts and humanities.
Fields of interest: Visual arts; Performing arts; Humanities; Arts; Elementary school/education; Education; Crime/violence prevention, domestic violence; Housing/shelter, development; Human services; Children/youth, services; Family services; Community development; Immigrants/refugees.
Type of support: Program-related investments/loans; General/operating support; Continuing support; Program development; Seed money; Technical assistance; Consulting services; Matching/challenge support.
Limitations: Giving primarily in Lincoln, NE. No support for religious activities, or college or university programs that do not involve students and/or faculty in projects of benefit to the Lincoln, NE, area, or for environmental programs or residential care and medical clinics. No grants to individuals, or for endowments, scholarships,

fellowships, fundraising benefits, program advertising, medical or scientific research, recreation programs, individual school programs, or capital projects in healthcare institutions.

Publications: Application guidelines; Annual report (including application guidelines).

Application information: If a full proposal is requested, include a completed copy of the Lincoln-Lancaster County Grantmakers Common Application Form. The proposal itself should not exceed 10 pages. Application form required.

Initial approach: Telephone or 2-page letter of intent prior to submitting application
Copies of proposal: 1
Deadline(s): Mar. 1, July 1, and Nov. 1
Board meeting date(s): Mar., June, and Nov.
Final notification: 1 week after board meeting

Officers and Directors:* Michael J. Tavlin,* Pres.; Donna W. Woods,* V.P.; Pam Baker,* Secy. and Exec. Dir.; Lynn Roper,* Treas.; Ann Chang-Barnes; Nelle Woods Jamison; Hank Woods; Jose J. Soto.

Number of staff: 3 full-time professional; 1 part-time professional.

EIN: 476032847

Selected grants: The following grants were reported in 2006.

$116,076 to University of Nebraska, Lincoln, NE. 2 grants: $36,076 to Department of Educational Psychology, Counseling Psychology Program (For renewal of Target Bully project), $80,000 to Nebraska Center for Research on Children, Youth, Families and Schools (For renewal of Project Transition, Education, Attendance and Motivation to Succeed (TEAMS), mentoring program to increase graduation rate and reduce recidivism rate for at-risk youth, particularly those from racial/ethnic minority groups, payable over 2 years).

$100,000 to Fresh Start, Lincoln, NE. For capital grant to purchase/renovate transitional group home.

$91,257 to Lincoln Literacy Council, Lincoln, NE. For ESL Academy project.

$80,000 to Center for People in Need, Lincoln, NE. For construction of warehouse to operate its shared programs, payable over 2 years.

$75,000 to Community Development Resources, Lincoln, NE. For general operating support.

$30,000 to Madonna Foundation, Lincoln, NE. For expansion of on-site children's learning center, payable over 2 years.

$30,000 to Northeast Family Resource Center, Lincoln, NE. For general operating and planning.

$25,000 to Lied Center for the Performing Arts, Lincoln, NE. For production of Train.

$20,000 to Big Brothers/Big Sisters of the Heartland, Lincoln, NE. For staff support.

5019

J. A. Woollam Foundation ✧
c/o D.R. Stogsdill
233 S. 13th St., Ste. 1900
Lincoln, NE 68508-2095

Established in 2001 in NE.

Donors: John A. Woollam; John A. Woollam Co., Inc.

Foundation type: Operating foundation.

Financial data (yr. ended 12/31/05): Assets, $7,375,657 (M); gifts received, $2,813,056; expenditures, $437,282; qualifying distributions, $2,024,616; giving activities include $378,616 for 24 grants (high: $150,000; low: $49), and $1,619,622 for 2 foundation-administered programs.

Fields of interest: Environment, natural resources.

Limitations: Applications not accepted. Giving primarily in MI and NE; some funding also in CA. No grants to individuals.

Application information: Contributes only to pre-selected organizations.

Trustee: John A. Woollam.

EIN: 470812219

5020

Zollner Foundation ✧
c/o Wells Fargo Bank, N.A.
4707 S. 96th St.
Omaha, NE 68127 (260) 461-6451
Contact: Alice Kopfer, V.P., Wells Fargo Bank Indiana, N.A.
Application address: c/o Wells Fargo Bank, N.A., P.O. Box 960, Fort Wayne, IN 46802

Established in 1983 in IN.

Donor: Fred Zollner‡.

Foundation type: Independent foundation.

Financial data (yr. ended 12/31/05): Assets, $11,077,738 (M); expenditures, $585,957; qualifying distributions, $548,431; giving activities include $512,961 for 22 grants (high: $61,065; low: $5,000).

Purpose and activities: Giving primarily for education.

Fields of interest: Higher education; Education; Children/youth, services; Federated giving programs.

Type of support: General/operating support; Continuing support; Annual campaigns; Capital campaigns; Building/renovation; Equipment.

Limitations: Giving primarily in Allen County, IN. No grants to individuals.

Application information:
Initial approach: Letter
Board meeting date(s): June

Trustee: Wells Fargo Bank Indiana, N.A.

EIN: 356381471

NEVADA

5021
The Bennett Foundation ◇ ☆
2535 S. Las Vegas Blvd., Exec. Offices
Las Vegas, NV 89109
Contact: Lynn M. Bennett, Pres.

Established in 1994 in NV.
Donors: Lynn M. Bennett; William G. Bennett.
Foundation type: Independent foundation.
Financial data (yr. ended 12/31/05): Assets, $3,397,700 (M); expenditures, $352,579; qualifying distributions, $323,566; giving activities include $323,566 for 8 grants (high: $236,000; low: $100).
Purpose and activities: Giving primarily for health and human services and to Jewish agencies and temples.
Fields of interest: Higher education; Health care, patient services; Health organizations, association; Cancer research; Children, services; Residential/custodial care, hospices; Science; Mathematics; Roman Catholic agencies & churches; Jewish agencies & temples.
Limitations: Giving primarily in CA and Las Vegas, NV.
Application information:
  Initial approach: Letter of inquiry
  Deadline(s): None
Officer and Director:* Lynn M. Bennett,* Pres.
EIN: 943189650

5022
Bing Fund Corporation ▼ ◇
990 N. Sierra St.
Reno, NV 89503
Contact: Peter S. Bing, Pres.

Established in 1920 in NY; incorporated in 1978 in NV as partial successor to Bing Fund, Inc.
Donors: Leo S. Bing‡; Anna Bing Arnold; Peter S. Bing.
Foundation type: Independent foundation.
Financial data (yr. ended 5/31/05): Assets, $48,782,501 (M); expenditures, $4,779,606; qualifying distributions, $4,659,278; giving activities include $4,649,000 for 45 grants (high: $1,000,000; low: $5,000; average: $25,000–$100,000).
Purpose and activities: Giving primarily for higher education, museums, the arts, secondary education, hospitals, and family planning.
Fields of interest: Museums; Arts; Secondary school/education; Higher education; Hospitals (general); Reproductive health, family planning.
Limitations: Applications not accepted. Giving on a national basis. No grants to individuals.
Application information: Contributes only to pre-selected organizations.
Officers and Trustee:* Peter S. Bing,* Pres. and Treas.; William Stinehart, Jr., Secy.
EIN: 942476169
Selected grants: The following grants were reported in 2005.
$1,000,000 to Dana-Farber Cancer Institute, Boston, MA. For Waldenstrom's Research.
$1,000,000 to Monterey Bay Aquarium, Monterey, CA. For general support.

$250,000 to University of California, School of Medicine, Los Angeles, CA. For digestive diseases.
$150,000 to House Ear Institute, Los Angeles, CA. For general support.
$150,000 to Smithsonian American Art Museum, DC. For Quilt Show support.
$100,000 to Digestive Disease Research Foundation, Encino, CA. For general support.
$100,000 to Oregon Shakespeare Festival, Oregon Shakespeare Festival Association, Ashland, OR. For general support.
$100,000 to University of Southern California, Los Angeles, CA. For Franklin Endowed Fellowship.
$50,000 to K C E T Community Television of Southern California, Los Angeles, CA. For general support.
$50,000 to Library Foundation of Los Angeles, Los Angeles, CA. For David Macaulay exhibition.

5023
The Boyd Foundation ◇ ☆
2950 S. Industrial Rd.
Las Vegas, NV 89109-1100 (702) 233-0186
Contact: William S. Boyd, Pres.

Established in 1986 in NV.
Donors: Sam A. Boyd; William S. Boyd.
Foundation type: Operating foundation.
Financial data (yr. ended 12/31/05): Assets, $23,063,430 (M); expenditures, $470,132; qualifying distributions, $417,821; giving activities include $375,174 for 21 grants (high: $205,000; low: $250).
Purpose and activities: Giving limited to those purposes which are charitable, religious, scientific, testing for public safety, literary, educational, fostering national or international amateur sports competitions, or for the prevention of cruelty to children or animals.
Fields of interest: Museums; Higher education; Law school/education; Hospitals (general); Medical research, institute; Youth development, services; Human services; Roman Catholic agencies & churches.
Limitations: Giving primarily in Las Vegas, NV. No support for national or international amateur sports competitions, whose activities involve the provision of athletic facilities or equipment. No grants to individuals.
Application information: Application form required.
  Initial approach: Letter or telephone requesting application form
  Deadline(s): None
Officer: William S. Boyd, Pres.
Trustees: Samuel J. Boyd; William R. Boyd; Marianne E. Boyd Johnson; Bruno Mark.
EIN: 880220082
Selected grants: The following grants were reported in 2003.
$120,000 to University of Nevada, Las Vegas, NV. 2 grants: $100,000 to Law School (For unrestricted support), $20,000 (For unrestricted support for scholarship fund).
$50,000 to Saint Rose Dominican Hospital, Henderson, NV. For unrestricted support.
$25,000 to Holy Family Catholic Church, Las Vegas, NV. For unrestricted support.
$6,000 to Alexander Dawson School, Las Vegas, NV. For unrestricted support.
$5,000 to Las Vegas Natural History Museum, Las Vegas, NV. For unrestricted support.

$5,000 to Reach Out, Las Vegas, NV. For unrestricted support.
$4,100 to Boys and Girls Clubs of Las Vegas, Las Vegas, NV. For unrestricted support.
$2,500 to Lied Discovery Childrens Museum, Las Vegas, NV. For unrestricted support.
$1,000 to House Ear Institute, Los Angeles, CA. For unrestricted support.

5024
The Bretzlaff Foundation, Inc. ◇
165 W. Liberty St.
Reno, NV 89501 (775) 333-0330
Contact: Michael J. Melarkey, Secy.

Established in 1988 in NV.
Donors: Hazel C. Van Allen; Hazel Van Allen Marital Trust.
Foundation type: Independent foundation.
Financial data (yr. ended 6/30/05): Assets, $17,939,495 (M); gifts received, $54,059; expenditures, $1,067,571; qualifying distributions, $959,996; giving activities include $925,544 for 42 grants (high: $200,000; low: $5,000).
Purpose and activities: Primary interests are (in this order): higher education, youth, the arts, health care, and the environment.
Fields of interest: Arts; Higher education; Environment; Health care; Youth, services.
Type of support: General/operating support; Building/renovation; Equipment; Endowments; Scholarship funds.
Limitations: Giving primarily in Honolulu, HI and Reno, NV. No grants to individuals.
Application information:
  Initial approach: Letter
  Board meeting date(s): Apr., July, and Oct.
Officers and Directors:* Richard Gilbert,* Pres.; Michael J. Melarkey,* Secy.
EIN: 880241424
Selected grants: The following grants were reported in 2004.
$200,000 to Hawaii Justice Foundation, Honolulu, HI. For social service endowment.
$57,627 to University of Nevada Reno Foundation, Reno, NV. For scholarship endowments.
$55,000 to Boys and Girls Club of Truckee Meadows, Reno, NV. For youth programs.
$50,000 to Nature Conservancy, Reno, NV. For conservation programs.
$20,000 to Reno Philharmonic, Reno, NV. For operating support.
$10,000 to American Cancer Society, Honolulu, HI. For childhood cancer programs.
$10,000 to Honolulu Symphony, Honolulu, HI. For music education program.
$10,000 to Reno Cancer Foundation, Reno, NV. For patient aid program.
$10,000 to Washoe Medical Foundation, Reno, NV. For Washoe Cancer Center.
$10,000 to Western Folklife Center, Elko, NV. For education programs.

5025
Carol Franc Buck Foundation
(formerly Carol Buck Sells Foundation)
P.O. Drawer 6085
Incline Village, NV 89450
Contact: Marya A. Beam, Admin. Dir.
Tel. and fax: (775) 831-6366

Incorporated in 1979 in NV.
Donor: Carol B. Sells.
Foundation type: Independent foundation.
Financial data (yr. ended 11/30/05): Assets, $13,735,140 (M); expenditures, $1,765,155; qualifying distributions, $1,687,155; giving activities include $1,546,450 for 26 grants (high: $684,025; low: $2,500; average: $25,000–$50,000).
Purpose and activities: Support for visual and performing arts, especially music, and for education in arts.
Fields of interest: Performing arts; Performing arts, ballet; Performing arts, music; Performing arts, orchestra (symphony); Performing arts, opera; Arts.
Type of support: General/operating support; Continuing support; Equipment; Endowments; Program development; Matching/challenge support.
Limitations: Giving primarily in the western U.S. No grants to individuals, or for emergency funds, deficit financing, capital campaigns, renovations, scholarships, fellowships, research, publications, or conferences; no loans.
Publications: Application guidelines.
Application information: Application form not required.
 Initial approach: Letter or telephone
 Copies of proposal: 1
 Deadline(s): Mar. 15 - Sept. 15
 Board meeting date(s): Jan., Apr., July, and Oct.
 Final notification: 3 months
Trustees: Carol Franc Buck; Christian P. Erdman; Helen I. O'Hanlon.
Number of staff: 2 full-time professional.
EIN: 880163505
Selected grants: The following grants were reported in 2004.
$75,000 to Nevada Opera Theater, Las Vegas, NV.
$25,000 to Chamber Music San Francisco, San Francisco, CA.
$25,000 to Smuin Ballets/SF, San Francisco, CA.
$15,000 to Chanticleer Theater, Council Bluffs, IA.
$15,000 to Nevada Ballet Theater, Las Vegas, NV.
$11,000 to K U N R-FM Public Radio, Reno, NV.
$10,000 to Central City Opera House Association, Denver, CO.
$10,000 to Orchestra of Santa Fe, Santa Fe, NM.
$10,000 to Reno Philharmonic, Reno, NV.
$3,000 to Sierra Nevada Chorale, Reno, NV.

5026
Christian Missionary Scholarship Foundation ◇
3441 W. Sahara Ave., Ste. B7
Las Vegas, NV   89102

Established in MI.
Donors: Stanley Van Reken; Randall S. Van Reken; Capital Ventures of NV.
Foundation type: Independent foundation.
Financial data (yr. ended 12/31/05): Assets, $6,863,209 (M); gifts received, $79,048; expenditures, $338,216; qualifying distributions, $332,830; giving activities include $332,830 for 8 grants (high: $212,450; low: $1,000).
Purpose and activities: Scholarship awards paid directly to college or university for children of missionaries families of specific Christian organizations.
Fields of interest: Theological school/education; Christian agencies & churches.
Type of support: Scholarship funds.

Limitations: Applications not accepted. Giving primarily in MI and IL; some giving on a national basis and in Dublin, Ireland. No grants to individuals.
Application information: Unsolicited request for funds not accepted.
Officers: Gaylen Byker, Pres.; Stanley R. Van Reken, Pres.; Randall Van Reken, Treas.
Directors: Tom Dykstra; Marge Hoogeboom; Walter Olsson; Thomas Stuit; Calvin P. Van Reken; Scott Wolterink.
EIN: 363553749

5027
James H. Clark Charitable Foundation ▼ ◇
5441 Kietzke Ln., 2nd Fl.
Reno, NV   89511

Established in 1999 in NV.
Donors: James H. Clark; Monaco Partners, LP; James K. Clark.
Foundation type: Independent foundation.
Financial data (yr. ended 3/31/06): Assets, $61,912,372 (M); expenditures, $8,587,186; qualifying distributions, $8,097,605; giving activities include $8,070,634 for 8 grants (high: $6,000,000; low: $22,720; average: $94,000–$500,000).
Purpose and activities: Giving primarily for higher education.
Fields of interest: Higher education.
Limitations: Applications not accepted. Giving primarily in CA. No grants to individuals.
Application information: Contributes only to pre-selected organizations.
Officer and Director: * Harvey L. Armstrong, * Secy.
EIN: 943346273
Selected grants: The following grants were reported in 2006.
$6,000,000 to Tulane University, New Orleans, LA. For general support.
$1,000,000 to Oceanic Preservation Society, Boulder, CO. For general support.
$500,000 to University of Utah, College of Engineering, Salt Lake City, UT. For general support.
$249,466 to Philharmonic-Symphony Society of New York, New York, NY. For general support.
$150,000 to Fidelity Investments Charitable Gift Fund, Boston, MA. For general support.
$94,000 to Give2Asia, San Francisco, CA. For general support.
$54,448 to Ogden Museum of Southern Art, New Orleans, LA. For general support.
$22,720 to Perlman Music Program, New York, NY. For general support.

5028
Community Foundation of Western Nevada ◇
1885 S. Arlington Ave., Ste. 103
Reno, NV   89509   (775) 333-5499
Contact: Christopher Askin, Exec. Dir.
FAX: (775) 333-5487; E-mail: info@cfwnv.org;
Additional E-mail: caskin@cfwnv.org; URL: http://www.cfwnv.org

Established in 1998 in NV.
Foundation type: Community foundation.

Financial data (yr. ended 12/31/04): Assets, $22,342,933 (M); gifts received, $2,496,076; expenditures, $5,026,567; giving activities include $4,641,443 for 174 grants (high: $1,000,000; low: $50).
Purpose and activities: The foundation seeks to create a permanent community resource of charitable funds, to be administered in a spirit of public responsibility.
Fields of interest: Arts; Higher education; Education; Environment; Health care; Human services; Community development; Federated giving programs.
Type of support: General/operating support; Management development/capacity building; Program development; Scholarship funds; Scholarships—to individuals.
Limitations: Giving primarily in Carson City, Reno, Sparks, and rural western NV. No support for religious purposes (unless from a donor-advised or organizational endowment fund). No grants to individuals (except scholarships), or for tickets for benefits, capital outlay or capital campaigns, debt retirement, or endowment.
Publications: Annual report; Newsletter.
Application information: The foundation is not currently accepting grant applications. Visit foundation Web site for updates.
 Board meeting date(s): Quarterly
Officers and Directors: * Jennifer A. Satre, * Pres.; Sally Armstrong, * V.P.; John Mulligan, * Secy.; Richard Barnard, * Treas.; Christopher Askin, Exec. Dir.; Kathie Bartlett; Fred Boyd; Kathie Dees; Mendy Elliot; Brian Kennedy; Diana Kern; Linda Smith; James Webster III; Norma Webster.
Number of staff: 1 full-time professional; 1 part-time professional; 2 part-time support.
EIN: 880370179

5029
The Cord Foundation ▼
(also known as The E. L. Cord Foundation)
418 Flint St.
Reno, NV   89501
Contact: William O. Bradley, Tr.

Established in 1962 in NV.
Donor: E.L. Cord†.
Foundation type: Independent foundation.
Financial data (yr. ended 12/31/04): Assets, $99,073,012 (M); expenditures, $5,631,272; qualifying distributions, $4,918,666; giving activities include $4,892,095 for 157 grants (high: $250,000; low: $1,000; average: $10,000–$100,000).
Purpose and activities: Support primarily for secondary and higher education, including colleges and universities, social services and youth organizations, and for cultural organizations.
Fields of interest: Secondary school/education; Higher education; Human services; Youth, services.
Type of support: General/operating support; Building/renovation; Equipment; Emergency funds; Program development; Scholarship funds; Research; Matching/challenge support.
Limitations: Giving primarily in northern NV and the rural counties of NV. No support for religious organizations for sectarian purposes. No grants to individuals, or for continuing support.
Publications: Application guidelines; Informational brochure.
Application information: All grants are restricted to and are to be used only for the purposes set forth in

the respective grant proposals. Administrative fees, grant writer fees and other indirect costs shall not be included in grant proposals. Application form not required.

Initial approach: Write for brochure
Copies of proposal: 1
Board meeting date(s): Monthly (if schedules permit)
Final notification: 1 week after board meeting
Trustees: Bill Bradley; Joseph S. Bradley; William O. Bradley; Robert L. Sims.
Number of staff: 1 full-time professional; 1 part-time professional.
EIN: 366072793
Selected grants: The following grants were reported in 2004.
$500,000 to University of Nevada Reno Foundation, Reno, NV. 2 grants: $250,000 each (For Knowledge Center UNR Campus).
$100,000 to Reno, City of, Reno, NV. For construction of Reno-Sparks Gospel Mission at homeless shelter.
$91,200 to Northern Nevada Center for Independent Living, Reno, NV. 2 grants: $50,000 (For Minor Home Modification Program), $41,200 (For autism pilot project).
$50,000 to Grizzly Sports Complex, Reno, NV. For all weather track surface at Galena High School.
$50,000 to National Judicial College, Reno, NV. For equipment for technology learning center.
$45,000 to Reno High School, Reno, NV. To build girl's softball facility.
$45,000 to Washoe Library Foundation, Reno, NV. For Spanish Springs library meeting room.
$40,000 to Special Advocates for Elders (SAFE), Reno, NV. For operating support.

5030
Crescere Foundation ✧
5836 S. Pecos Rd.
Las Vegas, NV   89120

Established in 1997 in NV.
Donors: Beverly O. Hamman; Stephen R. Hamman.
Foundation type: Independent foundation.
Financial data (yr. ended 12/31/05): Assets, $608,958 (M); gifts received, $550,000; expenditures, $482,788; qualifying distributions, $471,923; giving activities include $467,500 for 10 grants (high: $125,000; low: $2,500).
Purpose and activities: Giving primarily for wildlife preservation, veterans, and to Christian agencies and churches.
Fields of interest: Animals/wildlife, preservation/ protection; Christian agencies & churches.
Limitations: Applications not accepted. Giving primarily in Las Vegas, NV. No grants to individuals.
Application information: Contributes only to pre-selected organizations.
Officer: Beverly L. Ozmun, Pres.
EIN: 860877267
Selected grants: The following grants were reported in 2003.
$300,000 to Calvary Chapel of Green Valley, Henderson, NV.
$50,000 to United States Veterans Initiative, Inglewood, CA.
$25,000 to National Geographic Society, DC.
$25,000 to Salvation Army of Las Vegas, Las Vegas, NV.
$25,000 to Young Life, Las Vegas, NV.
$15,000 to Ducks Unlimited, Memphis, TN.
$1,000 to Best Friends Animal Society, Kanab, UT.

$1,000 to Career Resource Center, Lake Forest, IL.
$1,000 to Chinese Mutual Aid Association, Chicago, IL.
$1,000 to Ragdale Foundation, Lake Forest, IL.

5031
Engelstad Family Foundation ✧
P.O. Box 97979
Las Vegas, NV   89193-7979

Established in 2002 in NV.
Donors: Richard A. Clyne; Ralph Engelstad; Ralph and Betty Engelstad Trust.
Foundation type: Independent foundation.
Financial data (yr. ended 12/31/04): Assets, $7,885,137 (M); gifts received, $4,256,136; expenditures, $1,914,331; qualifying distributions, $1,910,300; giving activities include $1,910,300 for 27 grants (high: $1,200,000; low: $500).
Purpose and activities: Giving primarily to Roman Catholic schools, organizations and churches; funding also for human services.
Fields of interest: Education; Human services; Roman Catholic agencies & churches.
Limitations: Applications not accepted. Giving primarily in NV. No grants to individuals.
Application information: Contributes only to pre-selected organizations.
Officers and Trustees:* Betty Engelstad,* V.P.; Owen Nitz,* Secy.; Jeffrey Cooper, Treas.
EIN: 806008137

5032
The Fairweather Foundation
(formerly The Hall Family Foundation)
P.O. Box 1479
Minden, NV   89423-1479
Contact: Joanne Hall, Secy.-Treas.

Established in 1983 in NV.
Donor: Joanne Hall.
Foundation type: Independent foundation.
Financial data (yr. ended 12/31/05): Assets, $21,904,078 (M); expenditures, $905,145; qualifying distributions, $840,945; giving activities include $822,500 for grants.
Purpose and activities: Giving primarily for higher education, conservation of wilderness areas, cancer research and a facility that provides temporary lodging for families of cancer patients on a cost-free basis, and a child welfare organization; support also for health, including medical education, and the biological sciences, and nursing.
Fields of interest: Performing arts; Performing arts, music; Arts; Higher education; Education; Environment, natural resources; Environment; Hospitals (general); Reproductive health, family planning; Speech/hearing centers; Nursing care; Health care; Substance abuse, services; Health organizations, association; Cancer; Heart & circulatory diseases; AIDS; Alcoholism; Biomedicine; Medical research, institute; Cancer research; Heart & circulatory research; AIDS research; Human services; Children/youth, services; Aging, centers/services; Biological sciences; Aging; Disabilities, people with; Economically disadvantaged.
Type of support: General/operating support; Continuing support; Capital campaigns; Building/ renovation; Emergency funds; Research; Matching/ challenge support.

Limitations: Applications not accepted. Giving primarily in CA and NV. No grants to individuals.
Application information: Contributes only to pre-selected organizations.
Board meeting date(s): Fall
Officers and Directors:* Arthur E. Hall,* Chair.; Joanne Hall,* Secy.-Treas.; William H.T. Bush.
Number of staff: None.
EIN: 880193741

5033
Frank and Victoria Fertitta Foundation, Ltd. ✧
2960 W. Sahara Ave., Ste. 200
Las Vegas, NV   89102   (702) 221-4700

Established in 1994 in NV.
Donors: Frank J. Fertitta, Jr.; Victoria Fertitta.
Foundation type: Independent foundation.
Financial data (yr. ended 12/31/05): Assets, $2,178,519 (M); expenditures, $913,187; qualifying distributions, $909,500; giving activities include $909,500 for 19 grants (high: $250,000; low: $1,000).
Purpose and activities: Support primarily for Roman Catholic organizations, and health associations; funding also for human services, and arts and culture.
Fields of interest: Performing arts, dance; Performing arts, ballet; Elementary/secondary education; Health organizations, association; Cancer; Liver disorders; Medical research, institute; Ear & throat research; Human services; Children/ youth, services; Roman Catholic federated giving programs; Roman Catholic agencies & churches.
Limitations: Giving primarily in Las Vegas, NV.
Application information: Application form not required.
Initial approach: Letter
Deadline(s): None
Trustees: Frank J. Fertitta III; Lorenzo J. Fertitta; Delise F. Santini.
EIN: 880313659
Selected grants: The following grants were reported in 2003.
$500,000 to Bishop Gorman High School, Las Vegas, NV.
$100,000 to Catholic Charities of Southern Nevada, Las Vegas, NV.
$100,000 to Salvation Army of Las Vegas, Las Vegas, NV.
$30,000 to Andre Agassi Charitable Foundation, Las Vegas, NV.
$20,000 to Meadows School, Las Vegas, NV.
$20,000 to Nevada Ballet Theater, Las Vegas, NV.
$15,000 to New Horizons Academy, Las Vegas, NV.
$12,000 to Make-A-Wish Foundation of Southern Nevada, Las Vegas, NV.
$10,000 to United Way of Southern Nevada, Las Vegas, NV.
$10,000 to YMCA of Southern Nevada, Las Vegas, NV.

5034
Greenspun Family Foundation ✧
901 N. Green Valley Pkwy., Ste. 210
Henderson, NV   89074
Contact: Screening Comm.

Established in 1989 in NV.

Donors: Jane T. Greenspun Gale; American Nevada Corp.; G.C. Investments.
Foundation type: Independent foundation.
Financial data (yr. ended 12/31/04): Assets, $79,727,990 (M); gifts received, $84,969; expenditures, $8,834,493; qualifying distributions, $3,491,126; giving activities include $3,491,126 for 31 grants (high: $1,000,000; low: $500).
Purpose and activities: Giving for children's services, higher education, the physically and mentally challenged, and to churches and synagogues that provide for the homeless.
Fields of interest: Higher education; Education; Cancer research; Youth, services; Jewish agencies & temples; Disabilities, people with.
Limitations: Giving primarily in the Las Vegas, NV, area. No grants to individuals.
Application information: Application form not required.
   Initial approach: Letter
   Deadline(s): None
Officers and Director:* Barbara Greenspun, Pres.; Jane T. Greenspun Gale,* V.P.; Brian L. Greenspun, V.P.; Daniel A. Greenspun, Secy.; Susan Greenspun Fine, Treas.
Number of staff: 1 part-time support.
EIN: 880254521
Selected grants: The following grants were reported in 2004.
$1,000,000 to Nevada Cancer Institute, Las Vegas, NV.
$100,000 to Teach for America, New York, NY.
$25,750 to Opportunity Village Foundation, Las Vegas, NV. 2 grants: $25,000, $750
$23,950 to Simon Wiesenthal Center, Los Angeles, CA.
$22,000 to Andre Agassi Charitable Foundation, Las Vegas, NV.
$12,350 to Keep Memory Alive, Las Vegas, NV.
$10,700 to Clark County Public Education Foundation, Las Vegas, NV. 2 grants: $10,000, $700
$1,800 to American Friends of the Hebrew University, New York, NY.

5035
Richard V. Harris Foundation ✧ ☆
974 Third Green Ct.
P.O. Box 6474
Incline Village, NV 89450

Established in 1986 in CA.
Donors: Richard V. Harris; Trina B. Harris.
Foundation type: Independent foundation.
Financial data (yr. ended 12/31/05): Assets, $1,862,153 (M); gifts received, $907,612; expenditures, $422,830; qualifying distributions, $421,250; giving activities include $421,250 for grants.
Purpose and activities: Giving primarily for a Christian church.
Fields of interest: Higher education, university; Boy scouts; Christian agencies & churches.
Limitations: Applications not accepted. No grants to individuals.
Application information: Contributes only to pre-selected organizations.
Trustees: Richard V. Harris; Trina B. Harris.
EIN: 680153093
Selected grants: The following grants were reported in 2004.
$204,148 to Church of Jesus Christ of Latter Day Saints.

$500 to Boy Scouts of America, San Rafael, CA.
$400 to Huntsman Cancer Institute, Salt Lake City, UT.

5036
Robert Z. Hawkins Foundation
1 E. Liberty St., Ste. 509
Reno, NV 89501
Contact: William H. Wallace, Chair.

Established in 1980 in NV.
Donors: Kathryn Ackley Hawkins Trust; Robert Z. Hawkins†.
Foundation type: Independent foundation.
Financial data (yr. ended 12/31/05): Assets, $23,086,864 (M); expenditures, $1,006,381; qualifying distributions, $958,110; giving activities include $846,822 for 81 grants (high: $50,000; low: $300).
Purpose and activities: Giving primarily to charitable and social services in northern NV.
Fields of interest: Media/communications; Museums (art); Performing arts; Performing arts, orchestra (symphony); Arts; Higher education; Education; Animal welfare; Health care; Human services; Children/youth, services; Roman Catholic agencies & churches.
Type of support: Building/renovation; Equipment; Program development; Scholarship funds; Matching/challenge support.
Limitations: Giving limited to NV, particularly in or near northern NV. No grants to individuals.
Publications: Informational brochure (including application guidelines).
Application information: Requests for application form may be obtained by calling (775) 786-1105. This telephone line is solely for application form requests, regarding grants in northern NV only. Application form required.
   Initial approach: Proposal
   Copies of proposal: 6
   Deadline(s): None
   Board meeting date(s): 2nd Tues. of every month
Officer and Trustees:* William H. Wallace,* Chair.; Carolyn K. Bernard; Prince A. Hawkins; Bill A. Ligon, Jr.; Roy Powers.
Number of staff: 1 full-time support.
EIN: 880162645

5037
Conrad N. Hilton Foundation ▼
100 W. Liberty St., Ste. 840
Reno, NV 89501
Contact: Steven M. Hilton, C.E.O. and Pres.
FAX: (310) 556-2301;
E-mail: cnhf@hiltonfoundation.org; Additional address (Los Angeles office): 10100 Santa Monica Blvd., No. 1000, Los Angeles, CA 90067;
URL: http://www.hiltonfoundation.org

Established in 1944; incorporated in 1950 in CA; incorporated in 1989 in NV.
Donor: Conrad N. Hilton†.
Foundation type: Independent foundation.
Financial data (yr. ended 2/28/06): Assets, $889,768,444 (M); gifts received, $31,921,686; expenditures, $45,602,774; qualifying distributions, $42,707,215; giving activities include $38,108,321 for 256 grants (high: $3,475,000; low: $100; average: $5,000–$200,000), $613,064

for 1 foundation-administered program and $1,000,000 for 1 loan/program-related investment.
Purpose and activities: The greater part of the foundation's giving is devoted to several major long-term projects which include multi-year/long-term grants; funding for smaller scale miscellaneous grants is very limited. Special areas of interest are: 1) Works of Catholic Sisters funded through Conrad N. Hilton Fund for Sisters; 2) Substance abuse prevention education funded through the BEST Foundation for a Drug-Free Tomorrow; 3) Multi-handicapped blind services funded through Perkins School for the Blind; and 4) Water development in West Africa, funded through World Vision and multiple entities.
Fields of interest: Environment, water resources; Substance abuse, prevention; Eye diseases; Children/youth, services.
International interests: Africa; Asia; South America.
Type of support: General/operating support; Continuing support; Capital campaigns; Building/renovation; Equipment; Endowments; Program development; Publication; Seed money; Curriculum development; Scholarship funds; Research; Technical assistance; Program evaluation; Program-related investments/loans; Employee matching gifts; Matching/challenge support.
Limitations: Applications not accepted. No support for political organizations. No grants to individuals, or for fundraising events.
Publications: Annual report.
Application information: The foundation accepts applications primarily from its specified beneficiaries; unsolicited proposals generally not considered. If application is invited, information will be requested.
   Board meeting date(s): Quarterly
Officers and Directors:* Steven M. Hilton,* Chair., C.E.O., and Pres.; Patrick J. Modugno, V.P., Admin. and C.F.O.; Judy M. Miller, V.P. and Dir., Humanitarian Prize; Edmund J. Cain,* V.P., Grant Progs.; Marcia Trujillo-Penman, Corp. Secy.; Donald H. Hubbs, Dir. Emeritus; Robert Buckley, M.D.; Gregory R. Dillon; James R. Galbraith; Barron Hilton; Conrad N. Hilton III; Eric M. Hilton; William B. Hilton, Jr.; Hawley Hilton McAuliffe; John L. Notter; William G. Ouchi.
Number of staff: 9 full-time professional; 3 full-time support; 2 part-time support.
EIN: 943100217
Selected grants: The following grants were reported in 2006.
$3,475,000 to BEST Foundation for a Drug Free Tomorrow, Sherman Oaks, CA.
$2,975,000 to World Vision, Federal Way, WA. For water development program and blindness prevention and treatment.
$2,035,660 to Perkins School for the Blind, Watertown, MA. For blindness prevention and treatment.
$1,685,000 to Sonoma State University, California Institute on Human Services, Rohnert Park, CA. For Early Childhood Development program.
$1,362,500 to Carter Center, Atlanta, GA. For blindness prevention and treatment health programs.
$1,130,000 to UNICEF, New York, NY. For Water Development program.
$861,865 to University of Houston-University Park, Conrad N. Hilton College of Hotel and Restaurant Management, Houston, TX.
$750,000 to Corporation for Supportive Housing, Oakland, CA.

$750,000 to Mayo Foundation, Rochester, MN. For multiple sclerosis research and treatment.

$271,911 to Desert Research Institute, Reno, NV. For water development.

5038
Houssels Family Foundation
Corporation ✧ ☆
2580 Sorrel St.
Las Vegas, NV 89146

Established in 1998 in NV.
Donor: J.K. Houssels.
Foundation type: Independent foundation.
Financial data (yr. ended 12/31/05): Assets, $419,528 (M); gifts received, $52,042; expenditures, $325,010; qualifying distributions, $320,440; giving activities include $320,440 for grants.
Fields of interest: Performing arts; Performing arts, ballet; Performing arts, orchestra (symphony); Higher education.
Limitations: Applications not accepted. Giving primarily in Las Vegas, NV. No grants to individuals.
Application information: Contributes only to pre-selected organizations.
Trustees: J.K. Houssels; Nancy C. Houssels.
EIN: 880411205
Selected grants: The following grants were reported in 2004.
$146,872 to Nevada Ballet Theater, Las Vegas, NV.
$5,000 to Meadows School, Las Vegas, NV.
$3,000 to Las Vegas Philharmonic, Las Vegas, NV.
$2,800 to Keep Memory Alive, Las Vegas, NV.
$1,000 to Foundation for an Independent Tomorrow, Las Vegas, NV.
$1,000 to Hour of Power, Garden Grove, CA.
$300 to Nathan Adelson Hospice, Las Vegas, NV.

5039
The Robert S. & Dorothy J. Keyser
Foundation ✧ ☆
4795 Caughlin Pkwy., Ste. 100
Reno, NV 89509

Established in 1996 in NV.
Donor: The Charlene King Trust.
Foundation type: Independent foundation.
Financial data (yr. ended 12/31/05): Assets, $16,602,719 (M); gifts received, $203,209; expenditures, $761,674; qualifying distributions, $638,246; giving activities include $580,000 for 13 grants (high: $125,000; low: $5,000).
Fields of interest: Museums (art); Historic preservation/historical societies; Elementary school/education; Secondary school/education; Higher education; Cancer; Youth development; Human services.
Limitations: Applications not accepted. Giving primarily in NV. No grants to individuals.
Application information: Contributes only to pre-selected organizations.
Trustees: Timothy Cashman; Mike Melarkey; G. Blake Smith.
EIN: 880346537

5040
The Lemelson Foundation ▼
930 Tahoe Blvd., No. 802, PMB 363
Incline Village, NV 89451
URL: http://www.lemelson.org/

Established in 1994 in NV.
Donors: Dorothy Lemelson; Eric Lemelson; Robert B. Lemelson.
Foundation type: Independent foundation.
Financial data (yr. ended 12/31/04): Assets, $311,885,533 (M); expenditures, $13,655,587; qualifying distributions, $12,200,319; giving activities include $10,973,883 for 84 grants (high: $2,920,000; low: $5,000; average: $10,000–$100,000), and $100,825 for 1 loan/program-related investment.
Purpose and activities: The foundation celebrates and supports inventors and entrepreneurs in order to strengthen social and economic life in the United States and developing countries. The foundation is a private philanthropy established by U.S. inventor Jerome Lemelson, and his family. It uses its resources to inspire, encourage and recognize inventors, innovators and entrepreneurs, with a growing emphasis on those who harness invention for sustainable development where the needs are the greatest.
Fields of interest: Higher education; Economic development; Business/industry; Engineering/technology.
Type of support: Program-related investments/loans.
Limitations: Applications not accepted. Giving primarily in the United States and internationally in Africa, Asia and Latin America. No grants to individuals.
Application information: Contributes only to pre-selected organizations.
Officers and Directors:* Dorothy Lemelson,* Chair and Pres.; Robert Lemelson, Ph.D.*, V.P. and Secy.; Eric Lemelson,* V.P. and Treas.; Julia Nova-Hildesley, Exec. Dir.; Jennifer Bruml Lemelson; Susan Morse.
EIN: 880391959
Selected grants: The following grants were reported in 2004.
$4,100,000 to Massachusetts Institute of Technology, Cambridge, MA. 2 grants: $2,600,000 (For Lemelson-MIT Program), $1,500,000 (For endowment funds for Lemelson Foundation Mite2s fellowships, minority engineering fellowships, Project-Based Student Machine Shop, and Lemelson Technology Research Ignition Fund).
$3,379,200 to Smithsonian Institution, DC. 3 grants: $150,000 (For National Museum of American History's Hands on Science Center), $309,200 (For continuing research, documentation, education, and outreach activities of Jerome and Dorothy Lemelson Center for Invention and Innovation at National Museum of American History), $2,920,000 (To endow Jerome and Dorothy Lemelson Center for Invention and Innovation).
$1,043,145 to Five Colleges, Amherst, MA. For National Collegiate Inventors and Innovators Alliance.
$517,200 to Hampshire College, Amherst, MA. For Lemelson Assistive Technology Development Center.
$107,530 to EARTH University Foundation, Atlanta, GA. For planning for pilot implementation of

premier center for inventors and innovators in Latin America.
$100,000 to Oregon Museum of Science and Industry, Portland, OR. For renovation of Museum's Technology Hall.
$16,400 to Finlandia University, Hancock, MI. For Global Design Solutions.

5041
Lied Foundation Trust ▼ ✧
3907 W. Charleston Blvd.
Las Vegas, NV 89102 (702) 878-1559
Contact: Christina M. Hixson, Tr.

Established in 1972 in NE.
Donor: Ernst F. Lied†.
Foundation type: Independent foundation.
Financial data (yr. ended 12/31/05): Assets, $76,732,679 (M); expenditures, $12,589,147; qualifying distributions, $11,885,507; giving activities include $11,821,098 for 17 grants (high: $5,000,000; low: $450; average: $50,000–$1,000,000).
Purpose and activities: Giving primarily for youth organizations and higher education.
Fields of interest: Arts; Higher education; Youth development, services; Children/youth, services.
Limitations: Giving primarily in NE and Las Vegas, NV.
Application information: Application form not required.
Deadline(s): None
Trustee: Christina M. Hixson.
EIN: 237282946
Selected grants: The following grants were reported in 2005.
$5,000,000 to University of Nebraska Foundation, Lincoln, NE. For construction of Clinical Excellence Building.
$3,000,000 to Creighton University, Omaha, NE. For Hixson Lied Science Building.
$1,165,626 to Salvation Army of Las Vegas, Las Vegas, NV. 2 grants: $1,150,626 (For construction of dining facility), $15,000 (For meals).
$980,805 to Iowa State University Foundation, Ames, IA. 2 grants: $50,000 (For Hixson Opportunity Awards), $930,805 (For construction of Student Success Center).
$238,691 to Imperial Library Foundation, Imperial, NE. For construction of library.
$50,000 to Irwin, City of, Irwin, IA. To complete interior construction of library.
$15,000 to Catholic Charities of Southern Nevada, Las Vegas, NV. For food for Lied Dining Room.

5042
Lifestyle Homes Foundation ✧
(formerly Pioneer Foundation)
P.O. Box 7548
Reno, NV 89510-7548

Established in 1987 in NV.
Donors: R.J. Lissner; Woodland Village North, LLC; Elaine Lissner.
Foundation type: Independent foundation.
Financial data (yr. ended 12/31/05): Assets, $0 (M); gifts received, $374,100; expenditures, $440,468; qualifying distributions, $440,464; giving activities include $438,153 for 7+ grants (high: $219,346).

Fields of interest: Education; Medical research, institute.
Type of support: Research.
Limitations: Applications not accepted. Giving primarily in NV. No grants to individuals.
Application information: Contributes only to pre-selected organizations.
Directors: A.P. Harris; R.J. Lissner; J.A. Quinn.
EIN: 880230583

5043
Mallory Foundation ✧ ☆
223 S. Division St.
Carson City, NV 89703

Established in 1991 in NV.
Donor: Jean L. Mallory.
Foundation type: Independent foundation.
Financial data (yr. ended 12/31/05): Assets, $14,652,063 (M); gifts received, $95,074; expenditures, $907,339; qualifying distributions, $600,000; giving activities include $600,000 for grants.
Fields of interest: Arts; Higher education; Human services.
Limitations: Applications not accepted. Giving primarily in NV. No grants to individuals.
Application information: Contributes only to pre-selected organizations.
Officers: Riley Beckett, Chair.; Ellen Shock, Secy.; Tom Cook, Treas.
EIN: 880272695

5044
The Marnell Foundation ✧
222 Via Marnell Way
Las Vegas, NV 89119
Contact: Board of Trustees

Established in 1996 in NV.
Donor: Anthony A. Marnell II.
Foundation type: Independent foundation.
Financial data (yr. ended 12/31/04): Assets, $6,902,858 (L); gifts received, $2,800,000; expenditures, $957,439; qualifying distributions, $944,625; giving activities include $944,625 for 19 grants (high: $510,000; low: $1,000).
Purpose and activities: Funding primarily for education and human services.
Fields of interest: Higher education; Cancer; Human services; Federated giving programs.
Limitations: Giving primarily in Las Vegas, NV. No grants to individuals.
Application information: Application form required.
Initial approach: Letter requesting application
Deadline(s): None
Officers and Trustees: Anthony A. Marnell II,* Pres.; James A. Barrett, Jr.,* Treas.; Meredith C. Ellis; Alisa A. Marnell; Anthony A. Marnell III.
EIN: 943252819
Selected grants: The following grants were reported in 2003.
$200,000 to Keep Memory Alive, Las Vegas, NV. For program support.
$100,000 to Stephen A Wynn and Elaine P Wynn Foundation, Las Vegas, NV. For program support.
$25,000 to National Italian American Foundation, DC. For program support.
$15,000 to Nevada Cancer Institute, Las Vegas, NV. For program support.

$10,000 to Boys and Girls Clubs of Las Vegas, Las Vegas, NV. For program support.
$10,000 to Greater Las Vegas Inner City Games, Las Vegas, NV. For program support.
$5,000 to Daly Mansion Preservation Trust, Hamilton, MT. For program support.
$5,000 to Lied Discovery Childrens Museum, Las Vegas, NV. For program support.
$5,000 to Make-A-Wish Foundation of Southern Nevada, Las Vegas, NV. For program support.
$1,000 to Susan G. Komen Breast Cancer Foundation, Grand Rapids, MI. For program support.

5045
Charles N. Mathewson Foundation ✧
165 W. Liberty St., Ste. 210
Reno, NV 89501
Application address: c/o Charles N. Mathewson, Pres., 9295 Prototype Dr., Reno, NV 89511, tel.: (775) 448-0641

Established in 1993.
Donor: Charles N. Mathewson.
Foundation type: Independent foundation.
Financial data (yr. ended 12/31/05): Assets, $23,955,300 (M); expenditures, $958,620; qualifying distributions, $958,620; giving activities include $932,009 for 59 grants (high: $165,000; low: $35).
Purpose and activities: Giving primarily for education; funding also for health associations, and the arts.
Fields of interest: Arts; Education; Health organizations, association; Youth development.
Limitations: Giving primarily in CA and NV; funding also in NY.
Application information: Application form required.
Deadline(s): None
Officers and Trustees:* Charles N. Mathewson,* Pres. and Secy.; Ann Mathewson, Exec. V.P.; Curtis N. Mathewson, V.P.; Raymond Zimmerman, Treas.; Charlton Reed Bingham; John Russell.
EIN: 943179777
Selected grants: The following grants were reported in 2004.
$217,500 to Andre Agassi Charitable Foundation, Las Vegas, NV.
$109,000 to Keep Memory Alive, Las Vegas, NV.
$50,000 to Nevada Museum of Art, Reno, NV.
$42,500 to Prostate Cancer Foundation, Santa Monica, CA. 2 grants: $5,000, $37,500
$15,000 to American Cinematheque, Hollywood, CA.
$5,000 to Joslin Diabetes Center, Boston, MA.
$2,000 to Capital Public Radio, Sacramento, CA.
$200 to Muscular Dystrophy Association, Las Vegas, NV.

5046
Wilbur May Foundation ✧
c/o Suellen Fulstone
6100 Neil Rd., Ste. 500
Reno, NV 89511

Established in 1992 as successor to the Wilbur D. May Foundation.
Donor: Wilbur May†.
Foundation type: Independent foundation.
Financial data (yr. ended 5/31/05): Assets, $48,099,507 (M); expenditures, $2,694,997;

qualifying distributions, $2,242,661; giving activities include $2,242,661 for 50 grants (high: $274,661; low: $500).
Purpose and activities: Giving primarily to a parks and recreation department, and to an art museum; funding also for higher and other education, arts and culture, AIDS services and other healthcare organizations, and children, youth and social services including a camp for deaf children, and services for visually impaired children.
Fields of interest: Museums (art); Arts; Higher education; Education; Health care; Health organizations, association; AIDS; Eye research; Recreation, parks/playgrounds; Boys & girls clubs; Human services; Children/youth, services.
Limitations: Applications not accepted. Giving primarily in CA and NV. No grants to individuals.
Application information: Contributes only to pre-selected organizations.
Officers: Anita May Rosenstein, Chair. and Pres.; Amanda May Stefan, Vice-Chair. and V.P.; Dorothy Duffy May, V.P. and Secy.; Dixie May, V.P. and Treas.; Kathy May Fritz, V.P.; Suellen Fulstone, V.P.; Alysia May, V.P.; Brian Rosenstein, V.P.
EIN: 943126741
Selected grants: The following grants were reported in 2005.
$500,000 to Los Angeles Educational Alliance for Restructuring Now (LEARN), Los Angeles, CA. 2 grants: $250,000 each.
$274,661 to Washoe County Department of Parks and Recreation, Reno, NV.
$250,000 to Nevada Museum of Art, Reno, NV.
$225,000 to University of Nevada Reno Foundation, Reno, NV.
$165,000 to AIDS Services Foundation Orange County, Irvine, CA. 2 grants: $75,000 (For children's camp), $90,000.
$150,000 to Friends of the Center, Redding, CA.
$100,000 to University of California, Jules Stein Eye Institute, Los Angeles, CA.
$65,000 to Childrens Cabinet-A Child and Family Resource, Reno, NV.

5047
Nevada Community Foundation, Inc. ✧
300 S. Fourth St., Ste. 1009
Las Vegas, NV 89101 (702) 892-2326
Contact: Bret Bicoy, Pres.
FAX: (702) 892-8580; E-mail: info@nevadacf.org;
URL: http://www.nevadacf.org

Established in 1988 in NV.
Foundation type: Community foundation.
Financial data (yr. ended 6/30/05): Assets, $29,613,699 (M); gifts received, $2,022,513; expenditures, $3,247,372; giving activities include $2,592,011 for grants.
Purpose and activities: The foundation is committed to improving the lives of southern Nevadans today and for future generations by matching acts of caring to the many needs in the community. It strives to: encourage philanthropy at all levels; provide leadership in building a lasting source of funds; sustain nonprofit organizations through grants now and forever; provide citizens with new and meaningful ways to act on their charitable objectives; serve as a leader, resource, catalyst, convener and partner; and respond to changing community needs and opportunities.
Fields of interest: Arts; Adult/continuing education; Adult education—literacy, basic skills & GED; Education, reading; Education; Environment; Animal

welfare; Medical care, rehabilitation; Health care; Substance abuse, services; Mental health/crisis services; Health organizations, association; Cancer; Heart & circulatory diseases; AIDS; Cancer research; Heart & circulatory research; AIDS research; Food services; Youth development, citizenship; Children/youth, services; Family services; Aging, centers/services; Women, centers/services; Minorities/immigrants, centers/services; Homeless, human services; Human services; Economic development; Community development; Federated giving programs; Government/public administration; Public affairs, citizen participation; Aging; Disabilities, people with; Minorities; Women; Economically disadvantaged; Homeless.

Type of support: General/operating support; Capital campaigns; Equipment; Emergency funds; Program development; Conferences/seminars; Publication; Seed money; Scholarship funds; Technical assistance; Matching/challenge support.

Limitations: Giving limited to Nevada, with an overwhelming emphasis on the southern communities around greater Las Vegas. No support for religious purposes. No grants for capital campaigns, annual campaigns, or fundraising events.

Publications: Application guidelines; Annual report; Financial statement.

Application information: Visit foundation Web site for application form and guidelines. Faxed applications are not accepted. Application form required.

  Initial approach: Telephone
  Copies of proposal: 2
  Deadline(s): Last Friday in Feb. and Aug.
  Board meeting date(s): Quarterly

Officers and Directors:* Elaine Roesener,* Chair.; Maureen Peckman,* Vice-Chair.; Bret Bicoy, Pres.; Leah Benjamin,* Secy.; Larry Carter,* Treas.; Douglas Beckley; Richard H. Bryan; Douglas Carson; Robert E. Clark; Darlene Ensign; Sherman Frederick; Randy Garcia; Carlene Gaydosh; Dara J. Goldsmith; Dan Goulet; Duncan Lee; Mike Morrissey; Ralph Piercy; Don Pitchford; Mujahid Ramadan.

Number of staff: 3 full-time professional; 1 part-time professional; 1 part-time support.

EIN: 880241420

5048
Nevada Partners, Inc. ✦ ☆
710 W. Lake Mead Blvd.
North Las Vegas, NV 89030

Donors: Lincy Foundation; Clark County Nevada; United Way of Southern Nevada.

Foundation type: Independent foundation.

Financial data (yr. ended 12/31/04): Assets, $2,860,959 (M); gifts received, $4,403,738; expenditures, $4,504,023; qualifying distributions, $1,065,470; giving activities include $1,065,470 for 2 grants (high: $1,000,000; low: $65,470), and $4,320,609 for 2 foundation-administered programs.

Purpose and activities: Giving primarily for job readiness training and placement, including computer training, and to a culinary training academy; funding also for gym equipment and the provision of a workout area and boxing training for NV individuals.

Fields of interest: Employment, training; Athletics/sports, training.

Limitations: Giving limited to NV.

Officers: Geoconda Arguello-Kline, Chair.; Anthony F. Santo, Vice-Chair.; Jan Laverty Jones, Sr. V.P., Comm.; Danny Thompson, Exec. Secy.-Treas.

Board Members: D. Taylor, Secy.-Treas.; Steven Horsford, Board Advisor.

Trustees: Rose McKinney James; Tony F. Sanchez.

EIN: 880291463

5049
Michael A. O'Bannon Foundation ✦
2275 E. Desert Inn Rd.
Las Vegas, NV 89109-3216

Established in 1995 in NV.

Foundation type: Independent foundation.

Financial data (yr. ended 12/31/05): Assets, $10,668,244 (M); expenditures, $558,821; qualifying distributions, $485,654; giving activities include $412,148 for 9 grants (high: $266,241; low: $907).

Purpose and activities: Giving primarily for cancer research, and for children and youth services.

Fields of interest: Reproductive health, family planning; Cancer research; Human services; Children/youth, services; Family services.

Limitations: Applications not accepted. Giving primarily in AZ and NV. No grants to individuals.

Application information: Contributes only to pre-selected organizations.

Officer and Trustees:* Kay F. Alchu,* Grants Mgr. and Invest. Mgr.; Ryan Lawrence; Mark McElroy.

EIN: 943216555

5050
The Omega Foundation ✦ ☆
P.O. Box 7565
Incline Village, NV 89452

Established in 1997 in NV.

Donor: Robert C. Elias.

Foundation type: Independent foundation.

Financial data (yr. ended 12/31/05): Assets, $4,701,664 (M); expenditures, $421,007; qualifying distributions, $370,055; giving activities include $370,055 for grants.

Fields of interest: Education; Breast cancer research; Disasters, search/rescue; Athletics/sports, Special Olympics.

International interests: Nepal.

Type of support: General/operating support.

Limitations: Applications not accepted. Giving on a national and international basis. No grants to individuals.

Application information: Contributes only to pre-selected organizations.

Officer and Trustee:* Robert C. Elias,* Pres. and Secy.-Treas.

EIN: 880379653

5051
Parasol Foundation, Inc. ✦
(formerly Parasol Community Foundation, Inc.)
948 Incline Way
Incline Village, NV 89451 (775) 298-0100
FAX: (775) 298-0099; E-mail: info@parasol.org
Additional E-mail: RaineH@parasol.org; URL: http://www.parasol.org

Established in 1996 in NV.

Foundation type: Community foundation.

Financial data (yr. ended 6/30/05): Assets, $26,064,353 (M); gifts received, $1,680,389; expenditures, $2,083,962; giving activities include $986,175 for grants, and $29,795 for grants to individuals.

Purpose and activities: The foundation seeks to serve as a catalyst for a new nonprofit model that will better serve the community.

Fields of interest: Arts; Education; Environment; Human services; Community development.

Type of support: General/operating support; Annual campaigns; Endowments; In-kind gifts.

Limitations: Applications not accepted. Giving limited to Incline Village, Crystal Bay, and Kings Beach, NV.

Publications: Annual report; Newsletter.

Officers and Directors:* Dean Meiling,* Chair.; Ed Boleky,* Vice-Chair.; Gerry Eick, C.F.O.; David Williams,* Treas.; Howard Thomas, Exec. Dir.; Jan Clark; David Hardie; Howard Marguleas; Roger W. Norman; Rod Smallwood; Stuart Yount.

Number of staff: 2 full-time professional; 3 part-time professional.

EIN: 880362053

5052
Parks Education Foundation ✦ ☆
c/o Loren E. Parks
1131 Geneva Ave.
Henderson, NV 89015-4750

Established in 2003 in NV.

Donor: Loren E. Parks.

Foundation type: Independent foundation.

Financial data (yr. ended 8/31/05): Assets, $4,307,990 (M); expenditures, $484,526; qualifying distributions, $476,963; giving activities include $437,244 for 12 grants (high: $128,799; low: $365).

Fields of interest: Education; Animals/wildlife; Cancer research; Public affairs, election regulation; Public affairs.

Limitations: Applications not accepted. Giving on a national basis, primarily in CA, CO, Washington, DC, and OR.

Application information: Contributes only to pre-selected organizations.

Officers: Loren E. Parks, Pres.; Gary Parks, Secy.-Treas.

Director: Ray Parks.

EIN: 200423537

5053
William N. and Myriam Pennington Foundation ✦
(formerly William N. Pennington Foundation)
550 W. Plumb Ln.
P.O. Box 512
Reno, NV 89509 (775) 333-9100
Contact: Kent Green, Cont.

Established in 1989 in NV.

Donor: William N. Pennington.

Foundation type: Independent foundation.

Financial data (yr. ended 12/31/05): Assets, $12,836,274 (M); expenditures, $711,140; qualifying distributions, $645,041; giving activities include $617,500 for 19 grants (high: $150,000; low: $2,000).

Purpose and activities: Giving limited to education, health, and medical research.

Fields of interest: Higher education; Medical school/education; Hospitals (general); Medical care, rehabilitation; Cancer; Medical research, institute; Human services; Children/youth, services; Aging; Disabilities, people with; Economically disadvantaged.

Type of support: General/operating support; Building/renovation; Equipment; Scholarships—to individuals.

Limitations: Giving primarily in NV.

Publications: Financial statement.

Application information: Applications are reviewed semiannually. Application form not required.

> *Initial approach:* Proposal
> *Copies of proposal:* 1
> *Deadline(s):* Applications are accepted on a continual basis, but reviewed only twice during the year
> *Board meeting date(s):* Nov. or Dec.

Officers: William N. Pennington, Chair.; Richard P. Banis, Secy.-Treas.; Kent Green, Cont.

Trustees: Donald L. Carano; John Mackell; Fred Scarpello.

EIN: 943096845

Selected grants: The following grants were reported in 2005.

$110,000 to Boys and Girls Club of Truckee Meadows, Reno, NV. 2 grants: $50,000, $60,000

$70,000 to University of Nevada Reno Foundation, Reno, NV. 2 grants: $40,000, $30,000

$50,000 to Care Chest of Sierra Nevada, Reno, NV.

$30,000 to Assistance League of Reno-Sparks, Reno, NV.

$20,000 to Foster Grandparent Program, Sparks, NV.

$20,000 to Senior Companion Program, Sparks, NV.

$20,000 to YMCA of the Sierra, Reno, NV.

$10,000 to Make-A-Wish Foundation, Reno, NV.

5054
Wayne L. Prim Foundation ✧

P.O. Box 12219
Zephyr Cove, NV 89448-4219 (775) 588-7300
Contact: Wayne L. Prim, Tr.

Established in 1990 in NV.
Donors: Wayne L. Prim; Prim Ventures, Inc.
Foundation type: Independent foundation.
Financial data (yr. ended 12/31/05): Assets, $28,061,905 (M); expenditures, $1,343,976; qualifying distributions, $1,219,182; giving activities include $1,219,084 for 23 grants (high: $1,097,550; low: $30).

Purpose and activities: Giving primarily for education.

Fields of interest: Museums (art); Performing arts, theater; Education; Crime/violence prevention, youth; Crime/violence prevention, abuse prevention; Human services.

Limitations: Giving primarily in CA and NV. No grants to individuals.

Application information: Application form not required.

> *Initial approach:* Letter
> *Deadline(s):* None

Trustees: K. Marshall Matzinger; Wayne L. Prim; Wayne L. Prim, Jr.

EIN: 880265893

Selected grants: The following grants were reported in 2005.

$1,097,550 to Sierra Nevada College, Incline Village, NV. For student library.

$50,000 to Eisenhower Medical Center, Rancho Mirage, CA. For expansion of Emergency Department.

$20,560 to Parasol Foundation, Incline Village, NV. For community collaboration.

$16,000 to Nevada Museum of Art, Reno, NV. For programs and exhibitions.

$10,000 to Habitat for Humanity International, Americus, GA. For home ownership for low-income families.

5055
Nell J. Redfield Foundation

1755 E. Plumb Ln., Ste. 212
Reno, NV 89502 (775) 323-1373
Contact: Gerald C. Smith, Dir.
FAX: (775) 323-4476; Application address: P.O. Box 61, Reno, NV 89504

Established in 1982 in NV.
Donors: Nell J. Redfield†; Nell J. Redfield Trust.
Foundation type: Independent foundation.
Financial data (yr. ended 12/31/04): Assets, $47,799,021 (M); gifts received, $13,879,219; expenditures, $2,354,954; qualifying distributions, $2,211,665; giving activities include $2,211,665 for 55 grants (high: $500,000; low: $1,000).

Purpose and activities: Support primarily for the advancement of health care, medical research, and the care of handicapped children; support also for the aged, education, and religion.

Fields of interest: Higher education; Education; Health care; Health organizations, association; Medical research, institute; Human services; Aging, centers/services; Women, centers/services; Christian agencies & churches; Aging; Disabilities, people with.

Type of support: Building/renovation; Equipment; Endowments; Scholarship funds.

Limitations: Giving primarily in northern NV.

Publications: Application guidelines; Annual report.

Application information: Application form not required.

> *Initial approach:* Letter
> *Copies of proposal:* 1
> *Deadline(s):* Jan. 15 through June 1
> *Board meeting date(s):* Quarterly
> *Final notification:* Usually within 3 months

Directors: Helen Jeane Jones; Gerald C. Smith; Kenneth G. Walker.

Trustee: Farmers & Merchants Trust Co.

Number of staff: 1 full-time professional; 4 part-time support.

EIN: 237399910

Selected grants: The following grants were reported in 2004.

$525,000 to University of Nevada Reno Foundation, Reno, NV. 2 grants: $500,000 (For Nell J. Redfield campus building), $25,000 (For upgrades to learning center).

$300,000 to Saint Marys Foundation, Reno, NV. For Sun Valley Clinic expansion program and operating support.

$283,333 to Boys and Girls Club of Truckee Meadows, Reno, NV. For building expansion program.

$125,000 to Truckee Meadows Community College, Reno, NV. For renovation of Keystone Theater.

$100,833 to Washoe Library Foundation, Reno, NV. For Young People's Library.

$50,000 to YMCA of the Sierra, Reno, NV. For construction of new youth center.

$30,564 to Jerry Whitehead Elementary School, Sparks, NV. For medical and dental equipment for low income individuals.

$25,000 to K N P B Channel 5 Public Broadcasting, Reno, NV. Toward program.

$20,000 to Committee to Aid Abused Women, Reno, NV. For Thanksgiving and Christmas family certificates.

5056
Donald W. Reynolds Foundation ▼

1701 Village Center Cir.
Las Vegas, NV 89134 (702) 804-6000
FAX: (702) 804-6099;
E-mail: generalquestions@dwrf.org; URL: http://www.dwreynolds.org

Incorporated in 1954 in NV.
Donor: Donald W. Reynolds†.
Foundation type: Independent foundation.
Financial data (yr. ended 12/31/05): Assets, $1,204,806,991 (M); expenditures, $68,044,720; qualifying distributions, $73,182,328; giving activities include $69,058,172 for 160 grants (high: $10,239,487; low: $1,000; average: $10,000–$1,500,000), and $145,192 for 42 employee matching gifts.

Purpose and activities: The foundation seeks to honor the memory of its benefactor, for whom it is named, by filling unmet needs and attempting to gain an immediate, transformational impact in four principal areas of interest: 1) Meeting the greatest needs of communities in Arkansas, Nevada and Oklahoma, primarily through improved facilities for their outstanding local nonprofit organizations; 2) Accelerating the fight against atherosclerosis and atherosclerotic heart disease through cutting-edge, translational research; 3) Improving the quality of life of America's growing elderly population through better training of physicians in geriatrics; and 4) Enhancing the quality and integrity of journalism, focusing particularly on better training of journalists who serve smaller communities and on business journalism. The foundation remains open to consideration of special opportunities in other areas that are consistent with its broad goals. In pursuing its goals, the foundation is committed to the support of nonprofit organizations and institutions that demonstrate sound financial management, efficient operation, program integrity and an entrepreneurial spirit.

Fields of interest: Arts; Higher education; Health care; Medical research, institute; Human services; Public affairs.

Type of support: Building/renovation; Equipment; Program development; Research; Employee matching gifts.

Limitations: Giving primarily in AR, NV, and OK for capital and planning grants. Giving nationally for cardiovascular clinic research and geriatrics training of physicians, and business journalism. No support for elementary or secondary education, or religious institutions or hospitals. No grants to individuals, or for continuing support, program or operating support, or endowment funds.

Publications: Application guidelines; Financial statement; Grants list.

Application information: Request guidelines before submitting proposal or visit the foundation's Web site. Proposals sent by fax or E-mail not considered. Applicants are encouraged to discuss projects/

requests with foundation staff by telephone or in writing. Application form not required.

Initial approach: Letter (1-2 pages)

Deadline(s): Varies by program, contact the foundation or visit foundation Web site

Board meeting date(s): Jan., May, and Oct.

Officers and Trustees:* Fred W. Smith,* Chair.; Steven L. Anderson, Pres.; Lynn Mosier, Exec. V.P. and C.F.O.; William L. Winter, Ph.D., V.P., Programs; Keith G. Boman, M.D.; Barbara Smith Campbell; Barbara H. Hanna; Debby Smith Magness; Neal R. Pendergraft; Donald E. Pray; John V. Schlereth; Robert E. Slater; Jonathan Smith, O.D.; Wes Smith.

Number of staff: 16 full-time professional; 4 full-time support; 1 part-time support.

EIN: 716053383

Selected grants: The following grants were reported in 2004.

$31,000,000 to University of Missouri, Columbia, MO. 2 grants: $18,565,831 to Columbia School of Journalism (For construction and renovation of building to house Donald W. Reynolds Journalism Institute), $12,434,169 to Columbia School of Journalism (For program support for Donald W. Reynolds Journalism Institute).

$12,000,000 to University of Texas Southwestern Medical Center, Dallas, TX. For additional support for cardiovascular clinical research center and symposium.

$6,000,000 to Stanford University, Stanford, CA. For additional support for cardiovascular clinical research center and symposium.

$3,009,689 to Capital Resource Corporation, Little Rock, AR. For Donald W. Reynolds Governors Cup Business Plan Competitions in AR, NV and OK.

$3,000,000 to Duke University Medical Center, Durham, NC. For D.W. Reynolds Consortium, to strengthen faculty expertise in geriatrics in U.S. academic health center.

$3,000,000 to Johns Hopkins University, Baltimore, MD. For D.W. Reynolds, to strengthen faculty expertise in geriatrics in U.S. academic health centers.

$3,000,000 to Mount Sinai School of Medicine of New York University, New York, NY. For D.W. Reynolds, to strengthen faculty expertise in geriatrics in U.S. academic health centers.

$3,000,000 to University of California, Los Angeles, CA. For D.W. Reynolds, to strengthen faculty expertise in geriatrics in U.S. academic health centers.

$1,652,189 to National Judicial College, Reno, NV. For program support for DWR Center for the Courts and Media and for state-by-state workshops and national conference.

5057

Abraham and Sonia Rochlin Foundation ✧

275 Hill St., Ste. 250

Reno, NV 89501

Contact: Heidemarie Rochlin, Pres.

Established in 1969 in CA.

Donors: Abraham Rochlin†; Sonia Rochlin.

Foundation type: Independent foundation.

Financial data (yr. ended 12/31/03): Assets, $36,544,647 (M); gifts received, $20,000; expenditures, $2,090,906; qualifying distributions, $1,943,940; giving activities include $1,813,353 for 22 grants (high: $771,000; low: $2).

Purpose and activities: Grants primarily for Jewish organizations, including welfare funds and higher educational institutions.

Fields of interest: Higher education; Human services; Jewish federated giving programs; Jewish agencies & temples.

Limitations: Applications not accepted. Giving primarily in CA, NV, and NY. No grants to individuals.

Publications: Annual report.

Application information: Contributes only to pre-selected organizations.

Officers: Heidemarie Rochlin, Pres.; Joseph Schonwald, V.P.

EIN: 941696244

Selected grants: The following grants were reported in 2003.

$863,000 to P.E.F. Israel Endowment Funds, New York, NY. 2 grants: $771,000, $92,000

$450,000 to American Jewish Joint Distribution Committee, New York, NY.

$80,000 to American Committee for the Weizmann Institute of Science, New York, NY.

$50,000 to American Associates, Ben-Gurion University of the Negev, New York, NY.

$50,000 to Hadassah, The Womens Zionist Organization of America, New York, NY.

$35,000 to American Friends of the Open University of Israel, New York, NY.

$35,000 to American Society for Technion-Israel Institute of Technology, New York, NY.

$30,000 to Organization for Rehabilitation through Training (ORT), Jerusalem, Israel. .

$30,000 to Temple Emanu-El, Reno, NV.

5058

Raymond C. Rude Foundation, Inc. ✧ ☆

160 Wunotoo Rd.

Sparks, NV 89434-6608

Established in 2002 in NV.

Foundation type: Independent foundation.

Financial data (yr. ended 12/31/05): Assets, $2,376,164 (M); gifts received, $316,000; expenditures, $471,964; qualifying distributions, $455,000; giving activities include $455,000 for grants.

Fields of interest: Athletics/sports, water sports.

Limitations: Applications not accepted. Giving primarily in IN. No grants to individuals.

Application information: Contributes only to pre-selected organizations.

Officers: Thomas E. Gompf, Pres.; Janice R. Rude, V.P. and Secy.-Treas.

Directors: Steve McFarland; James L. Pfrommer.

EIN: 880502059

5059

Archibald C. and Frances F. Rufty Foundation ✧

209 Canyon Dr.

Las Vegas, NV 89107-3221

Established in 1994 in NV.

Donors: Archibald C. Rufty; Frances F. Rufty.

Foundation type: Independent foundation.

Financial data (yr. ended 6/30/06): Assets, $1,965,806 (M); expenditures, $669,684; qualifying distributions, $663,750; giving activities include $663,750 for grants.

Purpose and activities: Giving primarily for historical activities, higher education, human services and Protestant churches and agencies.

Fields of interest: Historical activities; Higher education; Law school/education; Health

organizations, association; Human services; Protestant agencies & churches.

Limitations: Applications not accepted. Giving primarily in NC and Las Vegas, NV. No grants to individuals.

Application information: Contributes only to pre-selected organizations.

Officers: Archibald C. Rufty, Jr., Pres.; Frances F. Rufty, Secy.

Directors: Frances R. Parkton; Diane B. Rufty.

EIN: 880321645

Selected grants: The following grants were reported in 2004.

$375,000 to Duke University, Durham, NC. 2 grants: $250,000 to Law School (For general support), $125,000 (For general support).

$20,000 to Rufty-Holmes Senior Center, Salisbury, NC. For general support.

$6,000 to Salvation Army of Las Vegas, Las Vegas, NV. For general support.

$5,000 to Meadows School, Las Vegas, NV. For general support.

$5,000 to Opportunity Village, Las Vegas, NV. For general support.

$4,000 to Las Vegas Rescue Mission, Las Vegas, NV. For general support.

$1,000 to American Institute for Cancer Research, DC. For general support.

$1,000 to Catawba College, Salisbury, NC. For general support.

$1,000 to Habitat for Humanity International, Americus, GA. For general support.

5060

The Ruvo Family Foundation ✧ ☆

24 Sawgrass Ct.

Las Vegas, NV 89113

Contact: Camille Ruvo, Dir.

Donors: Larry Ruvo; Camille Ruvo.

Foundation type: Operating foundation.

Financial data (yr. ended 11/30/05): Assets, $1,279,577 (M); gifts received, $222,494; expenditures, $769,983; qualifying distributions, $765,084; giving activities include $765,084 for 70 grants (high: $160,000; low: $50).

Fields of interest: Cancer research; Roman Catholic federated giving programs; Roman Catholic agencies & churches.

Application information:

Initial approach: Letter

Deadline(s): None

Director: Camille Ruvo.

EIN: 731688102

5061

The Sawyer Family Foundation ✧ ☆

2654 W. Horizon Ridge Pkwy., Ste. B-5

PMB176

Henderson, NV 89052 (702) 796-9991

Contact: Gail L. Sawyer, Pres.

Established in 2004 in NV.

Donor: Gail L. Sawyer.

Foundation type: Independent foundation.

Financial data (yr. ended 12/31/05): Assets, $7,605,890 (M); gifts received, $7,040,511; expenditures, $589,349; qualifying distributions, $524,120; giving activities include $524,120 for 4 grants (high: $360,000; low: $120).

Fields of interest: Animal welfare; Human services; Children/youth, services.
Limitations: Giving primarily in Las Vegas, NV.
Application information:
Initial approach: Letter
Deadline(s): None
Officer: Gail L. Sawyer, Pres.
EIN: 680559353

5062
The SFO Foundation ◇
P.O. Box 4913
Stateline, NV   89449

Established in 2000 in CA.
Donor: Edward W. Scott, Jr.
Foundation type: Independent foundation.
Financial data (yr. ended 8/31/05): Assets, $11,175,975 (M); gifts received, $1,420,000; expenditures, $1,618,517; qualifying distributions, $1,607,738; giving activities include $1,416,300 for 13 grants (high: $375,000; low: $5,000).
Fields of interest: Education; Human services; International development; International economic development; Christian agencies & churches.
Limitations: Applications not accepted. Giving primarily in the U.S.; also some giving internationally. No grants to individuals.
Application information: Contributes only to pre-selected organizations.
Officers and Directors:* Edward W. Scott, Jr.,* Pres.; Barbara Carlisle,* Secy.; Kenneth M. Morris.
EIN: 770554313
Selected grants: The following grants were reported in 2005.
$750,000 to Center for Global Development, DC. 2 grants: $375,000 each
$295,700 to Metropole Film Board, New York, NY. 2 grants: $140,700, $155,000
$100,000 to American Friends of University College Oxford, Ashland, KY.
$5,000 to Holy Trinity Episcopal Academy, Melbourne, FL.

5063
The David and Linda Shaheen Foundation, Inc. ◇
P.O. Box 973
Crystal Bay, NV   89402
Contact: David M. Shaheen, Chair.
E-mail: s@eatyourpeas.org; *URL:* http://www.eatyourpeas.org

Established in 2001 in NV.
Donors: David M. Shaheen; Linda F. Shaheen.
Foundation type: Operating foundation.
Financial data (yr. ended 12/31/05): Assets, $11,547,100 (M); expenditures, $693,406; qualifying distributions, $693,406; giving activities include $594,750 for 19 grants (high: $115,000; low: $10,000).
Purpose and activities: Giving primarily for the education of economically repressed children, and for health research.
Fields of interest: Higher education; Education; Health care; Human services.
Limitations: Giving primarily in CA and GA. No grants to individuals.
Application information: Application information available on foundation Web site.

Initial approach: E-mail
Deadline(s): None
Officers and Directors:* David M. Shaheen,* Chair.; Del Martin; Linda F. Shaheen.
EIN: 582493866

5064
Sierra Pacific Resources Charitable Foundation ◇
c/o Admin.
P.O. Box 30150
Reno, NV   89520-3150   (775) 834-5741
URL: http://www.sierrapacific.com/comenv/comrel/foundation/

Established in 1987 in NV.
Donor: Sierra Pacific Resources.
Foundation type: Company-sponsored foundation.
Financial data (yr. ended 12/31/04): Assets, $289,900 (M); gifts received, $532,000; expenditures, $446,847; qualifying distributions, $446,847; giving activities include $446,847 for 163 grants (high: $50,000; low: $40).
Purpose and activities: The foundation supports organizations involved with arts and culture, education, the environment, health, youth, human services, and civic affairs. Special emphasis is directed toward programs designed to target at risk youth, seniors, disabled people, and multicultural groups; and support workforce development, rural economic development, the enhancement of educational opportunity, the preservation of the natural environment, and the implementation of conservation initiatives that will return long term utility cost savings to organizations.
Fields of interest: Arts; Education; Environment; Youth development; Youth, services; Human services; Community development; Federated giving programs; Government/public administration; Aging; Disabilities, people with; Minorities.
Type of support: Employee matching gifts; General/operating support; Continuing support; Capital campaigns; Program development.
Limitations: Giving limited to areas of company operations in northeastern CA and northern NV. No support for religious organizations, foundations, political organizations, or sports leagues. No grants to individuals, or for tickets for contests, raffles, or other activities with prizes, film, television, or video productions, advertising, debt reduction, sports events or tournaments, trips or tours, talent or beauty contests, or conferences.
Publications: Application guidelines.
Application information: Application form not required.
Initial approach: Proposal
Copies of proposal: 1
Deadline(s): None
Board meeting date(s): Bi-monthly
Final notification: 60 days
Officers and Directors: Jeff Ceccarelli, Chair.; Karen C. Foster, Secy.-Treas.; Lisa Harris, Admin.; Bob Balzar; Clyyne Cook; Linda Galli; Greg Lambert; Stephanie McCaffrey; Mary Simmons.
Number of staff: 1 part-time professional; 1 part-time support.
EIN: 880244735
Selected grants: The following grants were reported in 2003.
$55,000 to United Way of Southern Nevada, Las Vegas, NV.

$50,000 to University of Nevada Reno Foundation, Reno, NV.
$25,000 to United Way of Northern Nevada and the Sierra, Reno, NV.
$15,000 to Desert Research Institute, Reno, NV.
$8,500 to Sierra Nevada College, Incline Village, NV.
$5,000 to Western Nevada Community College, Carson City, NV.
$2,500 to Nature Conservancy, Reno, NV.
$1,000 to University of Nevada, Las Vegas, NV.
$350 to Girl Scouts of the U.S.A., Las Vegas, NV.
$200 to YMCA of the Sierra, Reno, NV.

5065
Morris S. Smith Foundation ◇
c/o Alvin Hicks
P.O. Box 2670
Reno, NV   89505-2670

Established in 1993 in NE.
Foundation type: Independent foundation.
Financial data (yr. ended 9/30/04): Assets, $0 (M); expenditures, $1,040,427; qualifying distributions, $923,807; giving activities include $815,850 for grants.
Purpose and activities: Giving primarily for higher education, and family planning services.
Fields of interest: Higher education; Education; Reproductive health, family planning; Health organizations, association; Human services.
Type of support: Annual campaigns; Endowments; Scholarship funds.
Limitations: Applications not accepted. Giving primarily in the greater Los Angeles, CA, area. No grants to individuals.
Application information: Contributes only to pre-selected organizations.
Trustees: Carl M. Franklin; Larry Franklin; Sterling C. Franklin.
EIN: 954452450
Selected grants: The following grants were reported in 2003.
$475,000 to University of Southern California, Los Angeles, CA. 4 grants: $100,000 to School of Education (For Doris T. Westcott Scholarship), $50,000 (For scholarships), $25,000 (For Mary Ryan Scholarship Fund), $300,000.
$43,000 to Planned Parenthood of Maryland, Baltimore, MD. 3 grants: $13,000 (For unrestricted support), $15,000 (For unrestricted support), $15,000 (For training project).
$25,000 to Eisenhower Medical Center Foundation, Rancho Mirage, CA. For capital campaign.
$10,000 to Blind Childrens Center, Los Angeles, CA. For unrestricted support.
$10,000 to Planned Parenthood of Pasadena, Pasadena, CA. For equipment.

5066
The Southwest Gas Corporation Foundation
P.O. Box 98510
Las Vegas, NV   89193-8510   (702) 876-7247
Contact: Suzanne Farinas

Established in 1985 in NV.
Donor: Southwest Gas Corp.
Foundation type: Company-sponsored foundation.
Financial data (yr. ended 12/31/05): Assets, $470,925 (M); gifts received, $784,593;

expenditures, $570,365; qualifying distributions, $570,101; giving activities include $570,101 for 305 grants (high: $50,000; low: $25).

Purpose and activities: The foundation supports organizations involved with arts and culture, education, the environment, health, and human services.

Fields of interest: Arts; Education; Environment; Health care; Children/youth, services; Human services.

Type of support: General/operating support; Continuing support; Annual campaigns; Capital campaigns; Building/renovation; Emergency funds; Program development; Research; Employee matching gifts.

Limitations: Giving limited to areas of company operations in AZ, San Bernardino County, CA, and NV. No support for religious organizations. No grants to individuals.

Publications: Application guidelines; Informational brochure (including application guidelines).

Application information: Application form required.

Initial approach: Contact foundation for application form

Copies of proposal: 1

Deadline(s): None

Board meeting date(s): As needed

Final notification: Approximately 4 to 6 weeks

Directors: George C. Biehl; Jeffrey W. Shaw; Thomas R. Sheets.

EIN: 942988564

5067
The Spector Family Foundation ◇ ☆
801 S. Rampart Blvd., Ste. 200
Las Vegas, NV 89145

Established in 2004 in NV.

Donor: Arthur Spector.

Foundation type: Independent foundation.

Financial data (yr. ended 12/31/05): Assets, $529,308 (M); gifts received, $1,510,000; expenditures, $1,538,483; qualifying distributions, $1,535,437; giving activities include $1,529,410 for 7 grants (high: $1,020,000; low: $100).

Fields of interest: Medical research, association; Medical research, institute; Cancer research; Alzheimer's disease research; Human services.

Limitations: Applications not accepted. Giving primarily in Las Vegas, NV. No grants to individuals.

Application information: Contributes only to pre-selected organizations.

Trustees: Kenneth Chupinsky; Arthur Spector; Todd Spector.

EIN: 202059717

5068
Charles H. Stout Foundation
P.O. Box 20733
Reno, NV 89515-0733
Contact: Richard M. Stout, Pres.
E-mail: richardmstout@earthlink.net; URL: http://www.chstoutfoundation.org

Established in 1982 in NV.

Foundation type: Independent foundation.

Financial data (yr. ended 6/30/05): Assets, $7,591,711 (M); expenditures, $401,244; qualifying distributions, $372,223; giving activities include $372,550 for 42 grants (high: $20,000; low: $500).

Fields of interest: Arts; Higher education; Education; Health care; Human services.

Limitations: Giving primarily in Siloam Springs, AR, Del Mar, CA, Reno, NV, New York, NY, or in communities where foundation trustees live or visit regularly. No grants to individuals; no loans.

Publications: Application guidelines; Informational brochure (including application guidelines).

Application information: Application form required.

Copies of proposal: 1

Deadline(s): June 15

Board meeting date(s): Sept. or Oct.

Final notification: Within one month following board meeting

Officers: Richard M. Stout, Pres.; Martha Stout Gilweit, V.P.; Douglas B. McDonald, Secy.; Ross B. Stout, Treas.

Trustee: Katherine Gilweit Cartiglia.

EIN: 942797249

Selected grants: The following grants were reported in 2005.

$20,000 to ArtWatch International, New York, NY.

$20,000 to Barnard College, New York, NY.

$20,000 to Cookson Hills Christian School, Kansas, OK.

$20,000 to Life Styles, Fayetteville, AR.

$20,000 to Mamas Kitchen, San Diego, CA.

$15,000 to Desert Home Care, Borrego Springs, CA.

$15,000 to Nevada Womens Fund, Reno, NV.

$10,000 to National Council of Juvenile and Family Court Judges, Reno, NV.

$10,000 to University of Nevada Reno Foundation, Reno, NV.

$1,000 to Reno Philharmonic, Reno, NV.

5069
Terri and Roland Sturm Family Foundation ◇ ☆
6680 Rebecca Rd.
Las Vegas, NV 89131

Established in 2002 in NV.

Foundation type: Independent foundation.

Financial data (yr. ended 12/31/04): Assets, $1,727,643 (M); gifts received, $1,500,000; expenditures, $415,081; qualifying distributions, $412,950; giving activities include $412,950 for 11 grants (high: $350,000; low: $500).

Fields of interest: Arts; Elementary/secondary education; Human services.

Limitations: Applications not accepted. Giving primarily in Las Vegas, NV. No grants to individuals.

Application information: Contributes only to pre-selected organizations.

Officers: Roland Sturm, Pres.; Terri Sturm, V.P.

EIN: 880479977

5070
Michael Sweig Foundation ◇
1306 Hwy. 50
P.O. Box 10769
Zephyr Cove, NV 89448

Established in 2000 in IL.

Donor: Michael Sweig.

Foundation type: Independent foundation.

Financial data (yr. ended 12/31/05): Assets, $2,770,621 (M); gifts received, $100,000; expenditures, $835,539; qualifying distributions, $832,707; giving activities include $832,692 for 14 grants (high: $208,000; low: $1,000).

Fields of interest: Cancer research; Cancer, leukemia research; Human services; American Red Cross.

Limitations: Applications not accepted. Giving primarily in Chicago, IL; some funding nationally. No grants to individuals.

Application information: Contributes only to pre-selected organizations.

Trustee: Michael Sweig.

EIN: 367333404

5071
Donald and Jean Tang Family Foundation ◇ ☆
3773 Howard Hughes Pkwy., Ste. 350N
Las Vegas, NV 89109

Established in 1999 in IL.

Donor: Donald Tang.

Foundation type: Independent foundation.

Financial data (yr. ended 12/31/05): Assets, $640,095 (M); gifts received, $251,039; expenditures, $441,431; qualifying distributions, $434,700; giving activities include $434,700 for grants.

Fields of interest: Human services.

Limitations: Applications not accepted. Giving primarily in Chicago, IL and CA. No grants to individuals.

Application information: Contributes only to pre-selected organizations.

Trustees: Donald Tang; Zhen Jean Tang.

EIN: 946740588

5072
Cyrus Tang Foundation ◇
(formerly Tang Family Foundation)
8960 Spanish Ridge Ave.
Las Vegas, NV 89148   (702) 734-3700
Contact: Stella Liang, Treas.
FAX: (702) 734-6766; URL: http://www.tangfoundation.org

Established in 1996 in NV.

Donors: Cyrus Tang; Tang Industries, Inc.

Foundation type: Independent foundation.

Financial data (yr. ended 12/31/03): Assets, $51,217,710 (M); gifts received, $3,845,656; expenditures, $1,465,051; qualifying distributions, $1,288,156; giving activities include $1,280,880 for 21 grants (high: $530,939; low: $2,904; average: $25,000–$150,000).

Purpose and activities: Giving primarily to support new and established educational institutions in China.

Fields of interest: Higher education; Scholarships/financial aid; Education; Human services.

International interests: China.

Type of support: Building/renovation; Scholarship funds; Matching/challenge support.

Limitations: Applications not accepted. Giving primarily in China. No grants to individuals.

Application information: Contributes only to pre-selected organizations. Applications are by invitation only, as well as those applications are accepted in either traditional or simplified Chinese.

Officers and Directors:* Cyrus Tang,* Pres.; Michael Tang,* V.P.; Vytas Ambutas, Secy.; Stella Liang,* Treas.

Number of staff: 3 full-time professional.

EIN: 880361180

Selected grants: The following grants were reported in 2003.

$530,939 to Soochow University, Suzhou, China. For annual support.

$79,857 to Fudan University, Shanghai, China. 2 grants: $36,298 (For scholarships), $43,559 (For scholarships).

$78,407 to Tsinghua University, Beijing, China. For scholarships.

$39,203 to Nanjing University, Nanjing, China. For scholarships.

$39,082 to Chongqing University, Chongqing, China. For scholarships.

$39,081 to Sichuan University, Chengdu, China. For scholarships.

$38,720 to Zhejiang University, Hangzhou, China. For scholarships.

$38,718 to Beijing University, Beijing, China. For scholarships.

$37,266 to Beijing Normal University, Beijing, China. For scholarships.

5073
The Trans-Atlantic Foundation ✧ ☆
c/o Christian Alpers
774 Mays Blvd., Ste.10-300
Incline Village, NV 89451

Established in 2002 in NV.
Donor: Christian Alpers.
Foundation type: Independent foundation.
Financial data (yr. ended 12/31/05): Assets, $1,449,597 (M); gifts received, $377,190; expenditures, $807,527; qualifying distributions, $750,000; giving activities include $750,000 for grants.
Fields of interest: Athletics/sports, amateur leagues; Athletics/sports, amateur competition; Christian agencies & churches.
Limitations: Applications not accepted. No grants to individuals.
Application information: Contributes only to pre-selected organizations.
Officer and Director:* Christian Alpers,* Pres. and Secy.
EIN: 710914811

5074
Tuscany Research Institute ✧
222 Via Marnell Way
Las Vegas, NV 89119-3522
Contact: Robert C. Anderson, Tr.

Established in 1986 in NV.
Donors: CCRC Farms; Anthony A. Marnell II; Rombauer Vineyards, Inc.; Club & Restaurant Wines, Inc.; James A. Barrett, Jr.
Foundation type: Operating foundation.
Financial data (yr. ended 12/31/05): Assets, $21,100,380 (M); expenditures, $1,329,275; qualifying distributions, $1,276,719; giving activities include $325,000 for 3 grants (high: $200,000; low: $5,000), and $951,719 for 1 foundation-administered program.
Purpose and activities: Giving to protect and enhance waterfowl habitats.
Fields of interest: Environment, water resources; Animals/wildlife, preservation/protection.
Type of support: Research.
Limitations: Giving primarily in CA. No grants to individuals.

Application information: Application form required.
Initial approach: Letter requesting application
Copies of proposal: 8
Deadline(s): None
Board meeting date(s): Dec.
Final notification: June
Trustees: Robert C. Anderson; James A. Barrett, Jr.; Christopher L. Kaempfer; Anthony A. Marnell II; Anthony A. Marnell III; John Stuart; Gregory Wells; Alisa M. Wilson.
EIN: 943025713

5075
The Dale & Edna Walsh Foundation ✧
(also known as D.E.W. Foundation)
P.O. Box 7796
Incline Village, NV 89452-7796
Contact: Shai B. Edberg, Dir.
FAX: (775) 831-7132;
E-mail: mail@dewfoundation.org; *URL:* http://www.dewfoundation.org

Established in 1994 in IL.
Donors: Dale Walsh; Edna Walsh.
Foundation type: Independent foundation.
Financial data (yr. ended 12/31/05): Assets, $21,815,453 (M); gifts received, $145,000; expenditures, $886,923; qualifying distributions, $760,538; giving activities include $603,960 for 73 grants (high: $50,000; low: $200).
Purpose and activities: The foundation joins hands with effective charitable organizations to meet human need and to promote the common good world-wide, encouraging and empowering the foundation family's personal involvement.
Fields of interest: Arts; Higher education; Environment; Health organizations, association; Human services; Children, services; Family services; International affairs; Foundations (community).
Type of support: General/operating support; Continuing support; Income development; Management development/capacity building; Capital campaigns; Building/renovation; Equipment; Land acquisition; Emergency funds; Program development; Conferences/seminars; Publication; Seed money; Curriculum development; Research; Technical assistance; Consulting services; Program evaluation; Employee matching gifts; Matching/challenge support; Student loans—to individuals.
Limitations: Giving in the U.S. only, including organizations benefiting international programs. No support for church operations, or political organizations.
Application information: Application form not required.
Initial approach: 1-2 page letter with general information about the organization
Copies of proposal: 1
Deadline(s): Sept. 30
Board meeting date(s): Spring and fall
Officers: Dale Walsh, Chair.; Edna Walsh, Secy.; Patricia Walsh, Treas.
Director: Shai B. Edberg.
Board Members: Jennifer Connell; Darin Walsh; Mark Walsh.
Number of staff: 1 full-time professional.
EIN: 363994121
Selected grants: The following grants were reported in 2005.
$50,000 to Saint Jude Childrens Research Hospital, Memphis, TN.

$42,400 to Chaddock School, Quincy, IL.
$30,000 to Lake Tahoe Shakespeare Festival, Incline Village, NV.
$20,000 to Green Isle Childrens Ranch, Clermont, FL.
$15,000 to Alliance for School Choice, Phoenix, AZ.
$15,000 to Chicago Womens Health Center, Chicago, IL.
$15,000 to Experimental Sound Studio, Chicago, IL.
$10,000 to Christian Service Center for Central Florida, Orlando, FL.
$10,000 to Edgewood Childrens Ranch, Orlando, FL.
$10,000 to Focus on the Family, Colorado Springs, CO.

5076
Wendy's of Montana Foundation, Inc. ✧ ☆
1349 Galleria Dr.
Henderson, NV 89014
Contact: Sam E. McDonald, Jr., Dir.

Established in 1998 in NV.
Donor: Wendy's of Montana, Inc.
Foundation type: Company-sponsored foundation.
Financial data (yr. ended 12/31/05): Assets, $124,870 (M); gifts received, $338,000; expenditures, $398,740; qualifying distributions, $394,168; giving activities include $394,168 for grants.
Purpose and activities: The foundation supports organizations involved with arts and culture, education, and veterinary medicine.
Fields of interest: Museums (art); Arts; Elementary/secondary education; Higher education; Scholarships/financial aid; Education; Veterinary medicine; YM/YWCAs & YM/YWHAs.
Type of support: General/operating support; Equipment; Program development; Scholarship funds.
Limitations: Giving primarily in MT.
Application information:
Initial approach: Letter
Deadline(s): None
Directors: Deborah V. McDonald, Exec. Dir.; Gregory C. McDonald; Judith C. McDonald; Sam E. McDonald, Jr.
EIN: 880393923
Selected grants: The following grants were reported in 2004.
$147,500 to Montana State University, Bozeman, MT. 2 grants: $7,500, $140,000
$75,000 to Boys and Girls Club of Yellowstone County, Billings, MT.
$30,000 to Rocky Mountain College, Billings, MT. 2 grants: $15,000 each
$10,000 to Yellowstone Art Museum, Billings, MT.
$10,000 to ZooMontana, Billings, MT. 2 grants: $5,000 each
$7,500 to University of Montana, Missoula, MT.
$4,000 to Western Heritage Center, Billings, MT.

5077
E. L. Wiegand Foundation ▼
Wiegand Ctr.
165 W. Liberty St., Ste. 200
Reno, NV 89501 (775) 333-0310
Contact: Kristen A. Avansino, Pres. and Exec. Dir.

Established in 1982 in NV.
Donors: Ann K. Wiegand†; Edwin L. Wiegand†.

Foundation type: Independent foundation.
Financial data (yr. ended 10/31/05): Assets, $121,646,706 (M); gifts received, $25,188; expenditures, $7,856,295; qualifying distributions, $7,394,890; giving activities include $6,625,338 for 63 grants (high: $1,000,000; low: $200; average: $10,000–$200,000).
Purpose and activities: The foundation makes grants primarily to develop and strengthen programs and projects: at educational institutions in the academic areas of science, business, fine arts, law, and medicine; and at health institutions in the areas of heart, eye, and cancer surgery, treatment and research, with priority given to programs and projects that benefit children. Emphasis on Roman Catholic institutions.
Fields of interest: Visual arts; Museums; Performing arts; Performing arts, theater; Performing arts, music; Arts; Elementary school/education; Secondary school/education; Higher education; Business school/education; Law school/education; Medical school/education; Education; Hospitals (general); Health care; Health organizations, association; Cancer; Eye diseases; Heart & circulatory diseases; Medical research, institute; Cancer research; Eye research; Heart & circulatory research; Chemistry; Physics; Biological sciences; Public affairs; Roman Catholic agencies & churches.
Type of support: Equipment; Program development.
Limitations: Giving primarily in NV and adjoining western states, including AZ, ID, OR, UT and WA; public affairs grants given primarily in Washington, DC, and New York, NY. No support for organizations receiving significant support from the United Way or public tax funds; organizations with beneficiaries of their own choosing; or federal, state, or local government agencies or institutions. No grants to individuals, or for endowment funds, fundraising campaigns, debt reductions, emergency funding, film or media presentations, or operating funds; no loans.
Publications: Informational brochure (including application guidelines).
Application information: An informational booklet outlining the foundation's grant criteria is available on request. Application form required.
  Initial approach: Letter of inquiry with precise description of request. If proposal complies with staff review, a numbered Application for Grant form shall be forwarded to the applicant

Copies of proposal: 1
Deadline(s): None
Board meeting date(s): Feb., June, and Oct.
Final notification: Within 15 days of meeting at which application is reviewed
Officers and Trustees:* Raymond C. Avansino, Jr.,* Chair.; Kristen A. Avansino, Pres. and Exec. Dir.; James T. Carrico, Treas.; Frank J. Fahrenkopf, Jr.; Harvey C. Fruehauf, Jr.; William J. Raggio, Esq.; Jones Vargas.
EIN: 942839372
Selected grants: The following grants were reported in 2004.
$1,000,000 to Bishop Manogue High School, Reno, NV. For Science and Math Technology.
$300,000 to University of San Francisco, San Francisco, CA. For moot court room.
$220,000 to Roger Williams University, Bristol, RI. For center for financial services.
$208,199 to Sisters of Our Lady of Mount Carmel, Reno, NV. For library.
$200,000 to Basque Museum and Cultural Center, Boise, ID. For building restoration.
$162,283 to Saint Theresa School, South Lake Tahoe, CA. For science and technology.
$158,400 to Pacific Lutheran University, Tacoma, WA. For multimedia lab.
$119,697 to Saint Pauls Catholic School, Nampa, ID. For science lab equipment.
$96,536 to Christ the King School, Mesa, AZ. For technology and playground equipment.
$20,000 to Uptown Downtown Artown, Reno, NV. For Joffery Ballet trip to Reno.

5078
The Williams Foundation ✧
5755 S. Sandhill Rd., Ste. B
Las Vegas, NV 89120

Established in 1994 in NV.
Donor: Claudine B. Williams.
Foundation type: Independent foundation.
Financial data (yr. ended 10/31/05): Assets, $6,929,516 (L); expenditures, $1,360,525; qualifying distributions, $1,359,250; giving activities include $1,358,000 for 29 grants (high: $1,000,000; low: $500).

Purpose and activities: Giving primarily for education, based on academic achievements.
Fields of interest: Education; Big Brothers/Big Sisters.
Limitations: Giving primarily in Las Vegas, NV. No grants to individuals.
Application information: Scholarship applicants telephone for information.
  Initial approach: Proposal, transcripts, SAT, and ACT scores
  Deadline(s): None
Officers: Claudine B. Williams, Pres. and Secy.-Treas.; Michael S. Williams, V.P.
EIN: 880329401
Selected grants: The following grants were reported in 2005.
$1,000,000 to Community Foundation of Western Nevada, Reno, NV.
$250,000 to University of Nevada Reno Foundation, Reno, NV.
$10,000 to Clark County Public Education Foundation, Las Vegas, NV. 2 grants: $5,000 each

5079
The Severin Wunderman Family Foundation ✧
1645 Village Center Cir., Ste. 60
Las Vegas, NV 89134

Established in 1985.
Donor: Severin Wunderman.
Foundation type: Independent foundation.
Financial data (yr. ended 12/31/05): Assets, $7,458,347 (M); gifts received, $7,000,000; expenditures, $3,254,821; qualifying distributions, $3,050,000; giving activities include $3,050,000 for grants.
Purpose and activities: Giving primarily for the study of cancer.
Fields of interest: Cancer.
Limitations: Applications not accepted. Giving primarily in CA. No grants to individuals.
Application information: Contributes only to pre-selected organizations.
Officers: Lawrence P. Edelman, Pres.; Richard E. Tomlin, Secy. and C.F.O.
Number of staff: 2 full-time professional.
EIN: 330642389

NEW HAMPSHIRE

5080
Norwin S. and Elizabeth N. Bean Foundation
c/o New Hampshire Charitable Foundation
37 Pleasant St.
Concord, NH   03301-4005
Contact: Donna V. Dunlop, Sr. Prog. Off.
FAX: (603) 225-1700; E-mail: dvd@nhcf.org;
URL: http://www.nhcf.org

Trust established in 1957 in NH; later became an affiliated trust of the New Hampshire Charitable Foundation.
Donors: Norwin S. Bean†; Elizabeth N. Bean†.
Foundation type: Independent foundation.
Financial data (yr. ended 12/31/04): Assets, $13,188,923 (M); expenditures, $751,005; qualifying distributions, $722,049; giving activities include $696,914 for 39 grants (high: $85,000; low: $1,575).
Purpose and activities: Giving primarily for human services, including low-income housing programs and youth; support also for education, health associations, the arts, and environment.
Fields of interest: Arts; Education; Health care; Health organizations, association; Housing/shelter, development; Human services; Youth, services.
Type of support: General/operating support; Capital campaigns; Building/renovation; Equipment; Program development; Conferences/seminars; Seed money; Consulting services; Program evaluation; Matching/challenge support.
Limitations: Giving limited to Amherst and Manchester, NH. No grants to individuals, or for scholarships, fellowships, operating budgets, deficit financing, or endowment funds.
Publications: Application guidelines; Annual report (including application guidelines); Informational brochure (including application guidelines).
Application information: Application form required.
Initial approach: Letter or telephone
Copies of proposal: 2
Deadline(s): Apr. 1, Sept. 1, and Dec. 1
Board meeting date(s): Feb., June, and Oct.
Final notification: 2-3 months
Trustees: Kathleen Cook; Thomas J. Donovan; Christopher Emerson; Lisa Di Brigida; William G. Steele; Sally Wilkins.
Number of staff: 1 part-time professional.
EIN: 026013381
Selected grants: The following grants were reported in 2004.
$85,000 to Palace Theater Trust, Manchester, NH. For capital campaign to complete Athens building office space and infrastructure improvements.
$50,000 to Families in Transition, Manchester, NH. 2 grants: $25,000 (For development of historic mill), $25,000 (For core support and to expand fundraising and development functions).
$50,000 to Manchester, City of, Department of Health, Manchester, NH. For Adolescent Pregnancy Prevention program.
$40,000 to Child Health Services, Manchester, NH. For transportation and other services that provide access to health care.
$36,318 to Boys and Girls Club of Souhegan Valley, Milford, NH. For after-school and enrichment program at Amherst Middle School.

$36,000 to New Hampshire Charitable Foundation, Concord, NH. For professional and administrative services to non-profit sector.
$24,686 to Makin It Happen Coalition for Resilient Youth, Manchester, NH. For training, technical assistance and assessment services provided to youth service groups.
$10,000 to Manchester Community Resource Center, Manchester, NH. For start-up support of new drop-in-child care center.
$6,000 to Amherst Historical Society and Sandstone Museum Center, Amherst, OH. For repairs to roof of chapel museum that houses collection.

5081
The Byrne Foundation, Inc. ▼ ✧
3 Laramie Rd.
P.O. Box 599
Etna, NH   03750   (603) 643-4555
Contact: Dorothy M. Byrne, Pres.

Established in 1994.
Donors: John J. Byrne; Harleysville Insurance.
Foundation type: Independent foundation.
Financial data (yr. ended 12/31/05): Assets, $15,598,230 (M); expenditures, $6,613,549; qualifying distributions, $6,572,523; giving activities include $6,323,685 for 369 grants (high: $880,000; low: $65; average: $1,000–$100,000).
Purpose and activities: Support for the Dartmouth College community, cancer research, and general philanthropy; the majority of this will be directed to the upper valley of NH and VT, and other communities in which the directors reside or have a strong historical interest.
Fields of interest: Higher education; Cancer; Philanthropy/voluntarism.
Limitations: Giving primarily in NH, NY, and VT. No grants to individuals.
Application information:
Initial approach: Letter via mail
Deadline(s): None
Officers: Dorothy M. Byrne, Pres.; Robert E. Snyder, Secy.-Treas.
Directors: John J. Byrne III; Mark J. Byrne; Patrick M. Byrne.
EIN: 020462931
Selected grants: The following grants were reported in 2004.
$800,000 to Dartmouth College, Hanover, NH. For general/operating support.
$700,000 to Dartmouth-Hitchcock Medical Center, Norris Cotton Cancer Center, Lebanon, NH. For general/operating support.
$106,000 to Visiting Nurse Alliance of Vermont and New Hampshire, White River Junction, VT. For general/operating support.
$91,000 to Upper Valley Haven, White River Junction, VT. For general/operating support.
$80,000 to Milton and Rose D. Friedman Foundation, Indianapolis, IN. For general/operating support.
$65,000 to Upper Valley Teacher Institute, Lebanon, NH. For general/operating support.
$53,000 to Fannie Clac, Lebanon, NH. For general/operating support.
$30,000 to Dartmouth-Hitchcock Corner Medical, Lyndonville, VT. For annual fund.
$25,000 to Davids House, Lebanon, NH. For general/operating support.
$20,000 to Hanover High School, Crew Club, Hanover, NH. For program support.

5082
Chesterfield Charitable Foundation ✧
P.O. Box 177
Chesterfield, NH   03443   (603) 256-8045
Contact: Caren B. Foisie, Dir.
FAX: (860) 388-3077;
E-mail: info@chesterfieldfoundation.com;
URL: http://www.chesterfieldfoundation.com

Established in 2000 in NH.
Donor: Saybrook Charitable Trust.
Foundation type: Independent foundation.
Financial data (yr. ended 12/31/05): Assets, $302,722 (M); gifts received, $485,000; expenditures, $655,665; qualifying distributions, $654,190; giving activities include $62,000 for 11 grants (high: $17,500; low: $500), and $592,190 for 109 grants to individuals (high: $10,000; low: $1,000).
Purpose and activities: The foundation is dedicated to assisting high school seniors and full-time college undergraduates in furthering their education toward a bachelor's degree in the field of engineering, technology, science or education at accredited colleges and universities through the award of annual scholarships. Applicants must be residents of or attending school in Hartford or Middlesex County, Connecticut, Cheshire County, New Hampshire or Windham County, VT. They must exhibit the following: strong moral and ethical character, a financial need, strong academic achievement, service to school and community, evidence of part-time work and/or extra-curricular activities/sports.
Fields of interest: Higher education.
Type of support: Scholarships—to individuals.
Limitations: Giving primarily in CT, NH and VT.
Application information: Applications are available in high school guidance departments or online.
Deadline(s): Mar. 31
Final notification: May 15
Officers: Robert M. Rubin, Pres. and Secy.; G. Tyler Henshaw, Treas.; Thomas E. Cross, Mgr.
Directors: Caren B. Foisie; Jeanmarie Foisie; Lauren F. Glennon.
EIN: 020533669

5083
Taylor Christian Foundation ✧
P.O. Box 457
Wolfeboro Falls, NH   03896

Established in 2000 in NH.
Foundation type: Independent foundation.
Financial data (yr. ended 9/30/05): Assets, $8,913,873 (M); expenditures, $576,882; qualifying distributions, $408,051; giving activities include $408,051 for 14 grants (high: $225,000; low: $1,000).
Fields of interest: Children/youth, services; Christian agencies & churches.
Limitations: Applications not accepted. Giving on a national basis. No grants to individuals.
Application information: Contributes only to pre-selected organizations.
Trustees: G. Robert Lockhart; Romona Lockhart.
EIN: 311745034

5084

Cogswell Benevolent Trust ✧

1001 Elm St.
Manchester, NH 03101-1828 (603) 622-4013

Trust established in 1929 in NH.
Donor: Leander A. Cogswell†.
Foundation type: Independent foundation.
Financial data (yr. ended 12/31/05): Assets, $28,286,061 (M); expenditures, $1,392,289; qualifying distributions, $1,338,754; giving activities include $1,195,462 for 88 grants (high: $75,000; low: $500).
Purpose and activities: Giving primarily for human services and housing services; funding also for health care, YMCAs, and federated giving programs.
Fields of interest: Education; Health care; Housing/shelter; Human services; American Red Cross; YM/YWCAs & YM/YWHAs; Children/youth, services; Federated giving programs.
Limitations: Giving primarily in NH (90 percent of funding limited to NH). No grants to individuals, or for endowment funds, operating budgets, or deficit financing.
Application information: The foundation no longer gives scholarships or loans to individuals; scholarship funds have been donated to the New Hampshire Charitable Foundation Student Aid Program. Application form not required.
  Initial approach: Letter
  Copies of proposal: 1
  Deadline(s): None
  Board meeting date(s): Usually monthly and as required
  Final notification: 30 days
Trustees: David Goodwin; Mark Northridge; Theodore Wadleigh.
Number of staff: 1 part-time support.
EIN: 020235690
Selected grants: The following grants were reported in 2005.
$75,000 to Gibson Center for Senior Services, Conway, NH. To purchase Silver Lake Landing in Madison, NH for senior housing.
$50,000 to Easter Seals New Hampshire, Manchester, NH. For comprehensive autism diagnostic and treatment clinic.
$50,000 to YMCA, Greater Manchester Family, Manchester, NH. For Step-Up for Kids capital program.
$40,000 to United Way, Heritage, Manchester, NH. For annual campaign.
$35,000 to Wentworth-Douglass Hospital, Dover, NH. For community dental program.
$31,379 to Camp Allen, Bedford, NH. For camp repairs and safety upgrades.
$25,000 to Catholic Medical Center, Manchester Dental Alliance, Manchester, NH. For specialty dental care for children and to cover costs of services not covered by insurance or Medicare system.
$25,000 to Hannah House, Lebanon, NH. For coordinator for vocational program.
$25,000 to Manchester City Library, Manchester, NH. To purchase books and audio books.
$5,000 to Caregivers, Bedford, NH.

5085

The Couch Family Foundation ✧

c/o Richard W. Couch
P.O. Box 5010
Hanover, NH 03755

Established in 2001 in MA.
Donor: Richard W. Couch, Jr.
Foundation type: Independent foundation.
Financial data (yr. ended 12/31/04): Assets, $782,108 (M); expenditures, $393,798; qualifying distributions, $386,161; giving activities include $386,870 for 5 grants (high: $285,000; low: $1,000).
Fields of interest: Higher education.
Limitations: Applications not accepted. Giving primarily in NH. No grants to individuals.
Application information: Contributes only to pre-selected organizations.
Trustees: Barbara J. Couch; Richard W. Couch.
EIN: 100000573

5086

Dorr Foundation ✧

84 Hillside Dr.
Portsmouth, NH 03801 (603) 433-6438
Contact: Barbara McMillan, Chair.

Trust established in 1940 in CT.
Donor: John Dorr‡.
Foundation type: Independent foundation.
Financial data (yr. ended 12/31/05): Assets, $6,778,190 (M); expenditures, $397,039; qualifying distributions, $342,494; giving activities include $332,100 for 15 grants (high: $35,000; low: $1,500).
Purpose and activities: Grants are made primarily for programs designed to develop new and innovative science curricula at grade levels 6 through college. Support is also given to special education projects for youth relating to conservation and the environment especially if they involve the school's science curriculum.
Fields of interest: Science; Physical/earth sciences; Chemistry; Engineering; Biological sciences.
Type of support: Equipment; Emergency funds; Program development; Seed money; Curriculum development; Scholarship funds; Research; Matching/challenge support.
Limitations: Giving on a national basis, with limited international grants. No grants to individuals, or for annual campaigns, conferences and seminars, or fellowships; no loans.
Application information: Foundation does not respond to requests for guidelines or annual reports, except by telephone. Application form not required.
  Initial approach: Telephone contact required
  Copies of proposal: 8
  Deadline(s): None
  Board meeting date(s): Apr. and Nov.
  Final notification: 2 months
Officer and Trustees:* Barbara McMillan,* Chair.; Allen Hardon; Roger Hardon; Virginia Maxwell; Peter McMillan; Kenneth Punzeit; Shirley M. Punzeit; Gina Sessler.
EIN: 136017294

5087

Alexander Eastman Foundation

c/o New Hampshire Charitable Foundation
37 Pleasant St.
Concord, NH 03301-4005 (603) 225-6641
Contact: Donna V. Dunlop, Sr. Prog. Off.

Established in 1983 in NH.

Foundation type: Independent foundation.
Financial data (yr. ended 9/30/05): Assets, $11,283,574 (M); gifts received, $76,219; expenditures, $491,301; qualifying distributions, $450,968; giving activities include $390,443 for 15 grants (high: $210,000; low: $1,000), and $21,000 for 11 grants to individuals (high: $2,500; low: $500).
Purpose and activities: Awards grants to improve the quality and availability of health care and to promote good health and well-being for residents of the Derry, Londonderry, Windham, Chester, Hampstead, and Sandown, NH, area; giving also includes scholarship assistance for area residents working in the health care field.
Fields of interest: Education; Health care; Human services; Family services.
Type of support: General/operating support; Continuing support; Capital campaigns; Building/renovation; Equipment; Program development; Conferences/seminars; Scholarship funds; Technical assistance; Consulting services; Program evaluation; Scholarships—to individuals.
Limitations: Giving limited to Derry, Londonderry, Windham, Chester, Hampstead, and Sandown, NH. No grants to individuals (except for designated scholarship funds).
Publications: Application guidelines; Annual report; Informational brochure (including application guidelines).
Application information: Application form not required.
  Initial approach: Proposal
  Copies of proposal: 1
  Deadline(s): May 1 and Nov. 1
  Board meeting date(s): Mar., June, Sept., and Dec.
  Final notification: 8 weeks
Officers and Trustees:* Joel C. Olbricht,* Chair.; Barbara Coish,* Vice-Chair.; Laurie Warnock,* Clerk; James Rausch,* Treas.; Barbara Brundage; Marjorie Giannetti; Gordon Graham; Frank Landino; Carol Mack; Mary Louise McLean; Bruce Moeckel; Ann Sweet.
Number of staff: 1 part-time professional; 1 part-time support.
EIN: 020222124
Selected grants: The following grants were reported in 2005.
$65,950 to Greater Derry Community Health Services, Derry, NH.
$18,631 to Londonderry School District, Londonderry, NH.
$12,500 to Upper Room Education for Parenting, Derry, NH.
$10,000 to Rockingham Community Action, Portsmouth, NH.
$9,000 to Community Caregivers of Greater Derry, Derry, NH.
$5,000 to YMCA, Greater Manchester Family, Manchester, NH.

5088

Endowment for Health, Inc.

14 South St.
Concord, NH 03301 (603) 228-2448
FAX: (603) 228-1304;
E-mail: info@endowmentforhealth.org; URL: http://www.endowmentforhealth.org

Established in 1999 in NH; converted from Blue Cross/Blue Shield.
Foundation type: Independent foundation.

Financial data (yr. ended 9/30/05): Assets, $92,865,590 (M); expenditures, $2,551,623; qualifying distributions, $4,356,371; giving activities include $921,293 for 40 grants (high: $263,050; low: $495).

Purpose and activities: The mission of the endowment is to improve the health and reduce the burden of illness of the people of New Hampshire. Giving for oral health, and reducing social-cultural, geographic, and economic barriers to receiving health care.

Type of support: Emergency funds; Program development; Conferences/seminars; Research; Technical assistance.

Limitations: Giving primarily limited to NH. No support for biomedical research organizations, or for out of state projects. No grants for capital campaigns, lobbying efforts, expensed already incurred, fundraisers, or ongoing expenses.

Publications: Application guidelines; Annual report; Annual report (including application guidelines); Financial statement; Grants list; Informational brochure (including application guidelines); Newsletter; Program policy statement.

Application information: Application form available on foundation Web site. Application form required.

Deadline(s): Dec. 31, Mar. 31, June 30 and Sept. 30

Board meeting date(s): Quarterly

Final notification: Mar. 31, June 30, Sept. 30, and Dec. 31

Officers and Directors:* Susan R. Chollet,* Chair.; Cynthia Dokmo,* Vice-Chair.; James W. Squires, M.D., Pres.; Mary Vallier-Kaplan, V.P., Prog.; Mike Coughlin, Secy.; Harvey Hill,* Treas.; Sanders Burstein, M.D.; Dick Chevrefils; Sylvio Dupuis; Art Froburg; Deanna Howard; Margaret McClellan; Greg McConahey; Jane A. Nisbet, Ph.D.; Ann Peters; Trinidad Tellez, M.D.; Martha Van Oot; Bill Walker.

Number of staff: 5 full-time professional; 3 part-time professional; 1 full-time support.

EIN: 020512290

Selected grants: The following grants were reported in 2005.

$263,050 to New Hampshire Public Health Association, Concord, NH. For Watch Your Mouth.

$66,920 to Dartmouth College, Hanover, NH. 2 grants: $24,651 (For Using Clinical Process Cost Analysis to Eliminate Waste in Health Care), $42,269 (For It's Your Life, Reducing Barriers to medical care for low-income older adult).

$65,309 to Bi-State Primary Care Association, Concord, NH. To improve New Hampshire Health Centers Financial Sustainability.

$63,388 to New Hampshire Center for Public Policy Studies, Durham, NH. For Workforce Health Insurance in New Hampshire.

$53,633 to Avis Goodwin Community Health Center, Dover, NH. For Dental Care of Strafford County.

$48,940 to JSI Research and Training Institute, Boston, MA. For New Hampshire HIV/AIDS Care Service.

$32,900 to New Hampshire Department of Health and Human Services, Concord, NH. For New Hampshire Statewide Sealant Project.

$29,735 to Lutheran Community Services of New Hampshire, Concord, NH. For Language Bank II.

$7,500 to American Red Cross, Keene, NH.

5089
Foundation for Seacoast Health

100 Campus Dr., Ste. 1
Portsmouth, NH   03801   (603) 422-8200
Contact: Susan Bunting, C.E.O.
FAX: (603) 422-8207;
E-mail: ffsh@communitycampus.org; URL: http://www.ffsh.org

Incorporated in 1984 in NH as the Portsmouth Hospital Foundation; converted from the proceeds of the sale of Portsmouth Hospital to Hospital Corporation of America. Name changed in 1986 to Foundation for Seacoast Health.

Foundation type: Independent foundation.

Financial data (yr. ended 12/31/05): Assets, $70,554,388 (M); gifts received, $31,459; expenditures, $4,057,679; qualifying distributions, $2,941,010; giving activities include $1,034,545 for 19 grants (high: $475,000; low: $170), and $10,000 for 2 grants to individuals (high: $5,000; low: $5,000).

Purpose and activities: The foundation invests its resources to improve the health and well being of Seacoast citizens. Funding particularly for affordable mental health services, preventative and restorative dental services, affordable child care and after school care, affordable primary medical care, and coordination and dissemination of health information related to identified priority needs.

Type of support: General/operating support; Program development; Technical assistance; Scholarships—to individuals; Matching/challenge support.

Limitations: Giving limited to Kittery, Eliot, and York, ME and Portsmouth, Rye, New Castle, Greenland, Newington, and North Hampton, NH. No support for political activities. No grants to individuals (except through the foundation scholarship program), bricks and mortar, deficit financing, travel, lodging, or conferences.

Publications: Application guidelines; Annual report; Annual report (including application guidelines); Financial statement; Newsletter; Occasional report.

Application information: The foundation only considers new grant initiatives through the Partnership for Effective Nonprofits (PEN). (URL:http://www.partnershipforeffectivenonprofits.org). Funding requests may not exceed one-third of the submitting agency's operating budget. See foundation Web site for details. Application form required.

Initial approach: Letter (no more than 2 pages)

Copies of proposal: 2

Deadline(s): Feb. 1 for scholarships; Mar. 1 for infant/child/adolescent health; June 1 for health and preventing disease

Board meeting date(s): 3rd Tues. of Jan., Mar., May, Aug., Sept., Oct., and Nov.; annual meeting, 3rd Tues. in Apr.

Final notification: Mar. for scholarships; May for infant/child/adolescent health; Aug. for general health

Officers and Trustees:* Timothy J. Connors,* Chair.; Daniel C. Hoefle,* Vice-Chair.; Susan R. Bunting,* C.E.O. and Pres.; Nancy L. Cutter,* Secy.; Patricia A. Barbour,* Treas.; Donavon Albertson, M.D.; Richard Chace, M.D.; Timothy Driscoll; Wendy J. Frosh; Peter Loughlin; J. Gregg Sanborn; Sharon R. Weston.

Number of staff: 2 full-time professional; 3 full-time support; 1 part-time support.

EIN: 020386319

Selected grants: The following grants were reported in 2005.

$475,000 to Seacoast Mental Health Center, Portsmouth, NH. For programs for children and youth.

$400,000 to Families First of the Greater Seacoast, Portsmouth, NH. For medical financial assistance.

$70,999 to Community Child Care Center, Portsmouth, NH. 2 grants: $10,999, $60,000

$55,000 to Lamprey Health Care, Newmarket, NH. For medical financial assistance.

$12,076 to New Hampshire Healthy Schools Coalition, Action for Healthy Kids, Durham, NH.

$5,000 to Krempels Foundation, Portsmouth, NH.

$2,500 to Sexual Assault Support Services, Portsmouth, NH.

5090
The Fuller Foundation, Inc. ✧

P.O. Box 479
Rye Beach, NH   03871   (603) 964-6998
Contact: John T. Bottomley, Exec. Dir.
E-mail: ATfuller@aol.com; URL: http://www.fullerfoundation.org

Incorporated in 1938 in MA.

Donor: Alvan T. Fuller, Sr.‡.

Foundation type: Independent foundation.

Financial data (yr. ended 12/31/05): Assets, $15,619,561 (M); expenditures, $893,903; qualifying distributions, $667,789; giving activities include $569,412 for 6 grants (high: $245,112; low: $31,300).

Purpose and activities: The purpose of the foundation is to support non-profit agencies which improve the quality of life for people, animals, and the environment. The Foundation also funds the Fuller Foundation of New Hampshire, which supports horticultural and educational programs for the public at Fuller Gardens.

Fields of interest: Arts education; Museums; Performing arts; Arts; Education; Environment, natural resources; Animals/wildlife, preservation/protection; Substance abuse, services; Youth development.

Type of support: General/operating support; Continuing support; Land acquisition; Emergency funds; Program development; Seed money; Scholarship funds; Matching/challenge support.

Limitations: Giving primarily in the greater Boston, MA, area (inside Rte. 128), and the immediate seacoast area of NH. No grants to individuals or for capital projects, or conferences; no loans.

Publications: Application guidelines.

Application information: Contact foundation for current guidelines; Faxed requests not accepted. The Associated Grantmakers of Massachusetts, Inc. Common Proposal Format is accepted, and can be downloaded via foundation Web site. Application form required.

Initial approach: Proposal

Copies of proposal: 1

Deadline(s): Jan. 15 and June 15

Board meeting date(s): May and Oct.

Final notification: 30 to 60 days

Officers and Trustees:* Peter D. Fuller, Jr.,* Pres.; James O. Henderson II,* Treas.; John T. Bottomley,* Exec. Dir.; Miranda Fuller Bocko; Peter Fuller; James D. Henderson II; Corey Fuller MacDonald; Melinda Fuller vanden Heuvel.

Number of staff: 1 full-time professional; 1 full-time support.
EIN: 042241130

5091

Mary Gale Foundation, Inc. ◇ ☆
c/o Wadleigh, Starr & Peters, PLLC
95 Market St.
Manchester, NH 03101
Contact: Kathleen Sullivan, Pres.

Foundation type: Independent foundation.
Financial data (yr. ended 2/28/05): Assets, $10,036,795 (M); gifts received, $833; expenditures, $558,294; qualifying distributions, $494,620; giving activities include $489,800 for 8 grants (high: $150,000; low: $9,600).
Purpose and activities: Giving to organizations which provide housing and healthcare services which benefit women over age 65 in the greater Manchester, NH, area.
Fields of interest: Nursing care; Health care, home services; Health care; Health organizations, association; Housing/shelter, aging; Human services; Children/youth, services; Family services; Aging, centers/services; Women, centers/services; Roman Catholic agencies & churches.
Limitations: Giving primarily in Manchester, NH.
Application information:
Deadline(s): None
Officers: Kathleen Sullivan, Pres.; Theodore Wadleigh, Secy.
Directors: Eleanor Bruso; Carol Cuzo; Jeffrey Hickok; Genevieve T. Merrill; Douglas Tilson; Dorothy Wageman.
EIN: 571171038

5092

HNHfoundation
(formerly Healthy New Hampshire Foundation, Inc.)
14 Dixon Ave.
Concord, NH 03301   (603) 229-3260
Contact: Sandi Van Scoyoc, Pres.
FAX: (603) 229-3259;
E-mail: info@hnhfoundation.org; *URL:* http://www.hnhfoundation.org

Established in 1997 in NH, as a result of the merger of the Matthew Thornton Health Plan and Blue Cross/Blue Shield of New Hampshire.
Donor: Matthew Thornton, Inc.
Foundation type: Independent foundation.
Financial data (yr. ended 12/31/05): Assets, $23,869,873 (M); gifts received, $3,545,470; expenditures, $836,248; qualifying distributions, $766,574; giving activities include $588,448 for 39 grants (high: $250,000; low: $1,000).
Purpose and activities: The mission of the foundation is evaluating and promoting access to healthcare insurance and promoting healthy life styles for the residents of New Hampshire.
Fields of interest: Health care, insurance; Health care; Children/youth, services.
Type of support: Program development; Matching/challenge support.
Limitations: Giving limited to NH. No support for sectarian or religious programs. No grants to individuals, or for capital campaigns or expenditures, fundraisers, or bricks and mortar.
Publications: Annual report; Financial statement; Grants list.

Application information: Application form not required.
Initial approach: Telephone
Copies of proposal: 1
Deadline(s): None
Board meeting date(s): Jan. 24, Mar. 28, Apr. 25, May 16, June 27, Sept. 26, Oct. 24 and Nov. 28
Final notification: 1-2 months
Officers and Directors:* Harry A. Schibanoff,* Chair.; Molly Kelly,* Vice-Chair. and Treas.; Sandra M. Van Scoyoc, Pres.; Karen Reed,* Secy.; Sr. Carol Descoteaux; Todd Fahey; Retha Fielding; David Freeman-Woolpert; Valerie Long; Alida Millham; Barbara Reid; Barbara Walters.
Number of staff: 1 part-time professional; 1 part-time support.
EIN: 020497577
Selected grants: The following grants were reported in 2004.
$250,000 to New Hampshire Department of Health and Human Services, Concord, NH. For health benefits to uninsured children.
$100,433 to White Mountain Community Health Center, Conway, NH. 3 grants: $11,197 (To implement strategies to enroll kids in New Hampshire Healthy Kids Program), $56,442 (To implement strategies to enroll kids in New Hampshire Healthy Kids Program), $32,794 (For Carroll County Health Insurance Program for children).
$75,000 to FrameWorks Institute, DC. For strategies to solve New Hampshire Health Insurance.
$30,000 to New Hampshire Public Radio, Concord, NH. To increase amount of health reporting.
$20,000 to Child Health Services, Manchester, NH. For outreach and coordination for children's health insurance needs.
$20,000 to HUB Family Support Center, Dover, NH. For outreach and coordination for rural areas for health insurance.
$10,000 to Childrens Alliance of New Hampshire, Concord, NH. For outreach and coordination for children's health insurance needs.
$10,000 to New Hampshire Healthy Kids Corporation, Concord, NH. For efforts to assist with database.

5093

Samuel P. Hunt Foundation ◇
Wall St. Twr.
555 Canal St., Ste. 710
Manchester, NH 03101-1517   (603) 627-1121
Contact: Janet P. Magee, Asst. to Trustees
FAX: (603) 627-2845; *E-mail:* FDTN555@aol.com

Trust established in 1951 in NH.
Donor: Samuel P. Hunt†.
Foundation type: Independent foundation.
Financial data (yr. ended 9/30/05): Assets, $12,280,009 (M); expenditures, $617,062; qualifying distributions, $574,793; giving activities include $548,122 for 47 grants (high: $26,667; low: $1,000).
Purpose and activities: Giving primarily for human services.
Fields of interest: Arts; Education; Health care; Human services; Children/youth, services; Christian agencies & churches.
Type of support: General/operating support; Continuing support; Annual campaigns; Capital campaigns; Building/renovation; Equipment; Land

acquisition; Emergency funds; Program development; Conferences/seminars; Publication; Seed money; Research; Matching/challenge support.
Limitations: Giving limited to NH. No support for public schools. No grants to individuals; no loans.
Publications: Application guidelines.
Application information: Guidelines and applications are available via e-mail. Application form required.
Initial approach: Letter
Copies of proposal: 3
Deadline(s): Feb. 15 and Aug. 15
Board meeting date(s): Mar. and Sept.
Final notification: Within 90 days after meeting
Trustees: Douglas A. McIninch; James C. Tyrie; Citizens Bank.
Number of staff: 1 part-time support.
EIN: 026004471
Selected grants: The following grants were reported in 2004.
$30,000 to Police Athletic League of Manchester, Manchester, NH. For rehabilitation of Saint Cecilia's Hall.
$26,000 to Unitarian Universalist Church of Manchester, Manchester, NH. For repairs and renovations.
$25,000 to Avis Goodwin Community Health Center, Dover, NH. For equipment.
$25,000 to Families in Transition, Manchester, NH. For building development.
$25,000 to Girls Inc. of New Hampshire, Manchester, NH. For firebox.
$25,000 to Manchester Community Health Center, Manchester, NH. For Healthy Kids program.
$25,000 to New Hampshire Public Television, Durham, NH. For transition to digital technology.
$21,000 to New Hampshire Humanities Council, Concord, NH. For BlackBaud Raiser's Edge software.
$20,000 to Green Mountain Conservation Group, Effingham, NH. For acquisition and stewardship of Trout Pond.
$20,000 to Home Health and Hospice Care, Nashua, NH. For telemedicine project.

5094

Caroline C. Levine Charitable Trust ◇
146 Main St.
Nashua, NH 03060   (603) 964-3922
Additional address: P.O. Box 120, Rye, NH 03870

Established in 1994 in NH.
Donor: Caroline C. Levine.
Foundation type: Independent foundation.
Financial data (yr. ended 12/31/05): Assets, $7,402,111 (M); expenditures, $718,361; qualifying distributions, $631,500; giving activities include $631,500 for 14 grants (high: $250,000; low: $1,000).
Purpose and activities: Giving primarily for education, health associations, particularly a children's hospital and an ear institute; funding also for children, youth, and social services, and to an inter-denominational church.
Fields of interest: Elementary/secondary education; Education; Hospitals (specialty); Health organizations, association; Human services; Children/youth, services; Religion, interfaith issues.
Limitations: Giving primarily in NH. No grants to individuals.
Application information:

Initial approach: Letter
Deadline(s): None
Trustees: Joseph M. Kerrigan; Caroline C. Levine.
EIN: 026101659
Selected grants: The following grants were reported in 2004.
$250,000 to Childrens Hospital Corporation, Boston, MA. For general operating support.
$250,000 to House Ear Institute, Los Angeles, CA. For general operating support.
$125,000 to Chapel Hill-Chauncy Hall School, Waltham, MA. For general operating support.
$17,500 to Michael J. Fox Foundation for Parkinsons Research, New York, NY. For general operating support.
$15,000 to Beaver Country Day School, Chestnut Hill, MA. For general operating support.
$10,500 to Bethany Church, Greenland, NH. For general operating support.
$10,000 to Cameron M. Neely Foundation for Cancer Care, Boston, MA. For general operating support.
$10,000 to Seacoast Repertory Theater, Portsmouth, NH. For general operating support.

5095

Agnes M. Lindsay Trust ✧

660 Chestnut St.
Manchester, NH 03104 (603) 669-1366
Contact: Susan Bouchard, Admin. Dir.
FAX: (603) 665-8114;
E-mail: admin@lindsaytrust.org; Additional tel.: (866) 669-1366; URL: http://www.Lindsaytrust.org

Trust established in 1939 in NH.
Donor: Agnes M. Lindsay‡.
Foundation type: Independent foundation.
Financial data (yr. ended 12/31/05): Assets, $29,621,608 (M); expenditures, $1,935,043; qualifying distributions, $1,819,610; giving activities include $1,634,163 for 342 grants (high: $40,000; low: $950).
Purpose and activities: Giving for child welfare and the education of poor and deserving students from rural areas; support largely for higher education, capital needs to health agencies, agencies for the handicapped, health and welfare institutions, youth services and camperships.
Fields of interest: Higher education; Education; Health care; Human services; Children/youth, services; Disabilities, people with.
Type of support: Capital campaigns; Building/renovation; Equipment; Program development; Scholarship funds; Matching/challenge support.
Limitations: Giving limited to MA, ME, NH, and VT. No support for municipalities, public entities, sectarian organizations, or for colleges, universities or private schools. No grants to individuals or for endowments.
Publications: Application guidelines; Annual report; Grants list.
Application information: Proposal summary form available on foundation Web site. Application form required.
Initial approach: Proposal
Copies of proposal: 1
Deadline(s): None
Board meeting date(s): Monthly
Final notification: 2 months
Trustees: Robert L. Chiesa; Ernest E. Dion; Alan G. Lampert.
Number of staff: 1 full-time professional.
EIN: 026004971

Selected grants: The following grants were reported in 2005.
$40,000 to Vermont State Colleges, Waterbury, VT. For annual scholarship.
$30,000 to Massachusetts Board of Higher Education, Boston, MA. For annual scholarship.
$10,000 to Colby-Sawyer College, New London, NH. For annual scholarship.
$10,000 to YMCA of Maine, State, Winthrop, ME.
$5,500 to Abused Womens Advocacy Project, Auburn, ME.
$5,000 to Big Brothers Big Sisters Of The Greater Seacoast, Dover, NH.
$5,000 to Cedarcrest Foundation, Keene, NH.
$5,000 to Community Service Care, Jamaica Plain, MA.
$3,000 to Boys and Girls Club of Concord, Concord, NH.
$2,500 to Henry C. Nevins Home for the Aged and Incurable, Methuen, MA.

5096

Linnell Foundation

39 Wentworth Rd.
P.O. Box 192
New Castle, NH 03854-0192
Contact: Russell N. Cox, Tr.

Established in 1977 in MA.
Donor: Robert C. Linnell‡.
Foundation type: Independent foundation.
Financial data (yr. ended 12/31/04): Assets, $8,505,814 (M); expenditures, $409,902; qualifying distributions, $355,987; giving activities include $333,310 for 6 grants (high: $317,000; low: $310).
Fields of interest: Substance abuse, services; Crime/law enforcement; Public policy, research.
Type of support: Continuing support.
Limitations: Applications not accepted. Giving on a national basis.
Application information: Unsolicited requests for funds not accepted.
Board meeting date(s): Mar., June, Sept., and Dec.
Trustees: Russell N. Cox; Renee Linnell; Robert J. Richards; Robert C. Silver; Eric Sterling.
EIN: 042625173
Selected grants: The following grants were reported in 2003.
$256,000 to Criminal Justice Policy Foundation, Silver Spring, MD.
$25,000 to Newton-Wellesley Hospital Charitable Foundation, Newton, MA.
$10,000 to United Service Organization World Headquarters, Arlington, VA.
$2,000 to SurfAid International USA, Encinitas, CA.

5097

James G. Martin Memorial Trust ✧ ☆

20 Church Rd.
Rye Beach, NH 03871
Contact: M. Martin

Established in 1977.
Donor: G. Martin.
Foundation type: Independent foundation.
Financial data (yr. ended 3/31/05): Assets, $3,627,450 (M); expenditures, $612,121; qualifying distributions, $537,130; giving activities

include $317,000 for 11 grants (high: $100,000; low: $1,000).
Purpose and activities: Giving primarily for education, health and human services.
Fields of interest: Elementary school/education; Higher education, college; Theological school/education; Education; Hospitals (general); Cancer, leukemia; AIDS; Roman Catholic agencies & churches.
Type of support: Research.
Application information: Application form required for scholarship applicants. Application form required.
Deadline(s): None
Officer: Marianne Burke, Exec. Dir.
Trustees: G. Martin; K. Martin; R. Solano.
EIN: 042613244
Selected grants: The following grants were reported in 2005.
$110,000 to Newton Country Day School of the Sacred Heart, Newton, MA. 2 grants: $100,000, $10,000
$100,000 to Boston College, Chestnut Hill, MA.
$50,000 to Immigrant Learning Center, Malden, MA.
$25,000 to Caritas Good Samaritan Hospice, Friends of, Brighton, MA.
$11,000 to Crohns and Colitis Foundation of America, Needham, MA. 2 grants: $5,000, $6,000
$10,000 to Wang Center for the Performing Arts, Boston, MA.
$5,000 to Leukemia & Lymphoma Society, Framingham, MA.
$5,000 to Saint Anselm College, Manchester, NH.

5098

The New Hampshire Charitable Foundation ▼

37 Pleasant St.
Concord, NH 03301-4005 (603) 225-6641, ext. 229
Contact: Racheal Stuart, V.P., Progs.; For grant inquiries: Lorraine Albanese, Prog. Asst.
FAX: (603) 225-1700; E-mail: info@nhcf.org; Grant inquiry E-mail: grants_info@nhcf.org; NHCF-Piscataqua Region application address: 446 Market St., Portsmouth, NH 03801; NHCF-Upper Valley Region application address: 16 Buck Rd., Hanover, NH 03755-2700; URL: http://www.nhcf.org

Incorporated in 1962 in NH.
Foundation type: Community foundation.
Financial data (yr. ended 12/31/05): Assets, $344,269,144 (M); gifts received, $18,919,762; expenditures, $31,187,329; giving activities include $25,528,024 for 2,900 grants, and $75,000 for 1 loan/program-related investment.
Purpose and activities: The foundation seeks to improve the quality of life in New Hampshire. Giving for charitable and educational purposes including the arts, humanities, the environment and conservation, health, and social and community services; grants primarily to inaugurate new programs and strengthen existing charitable organizations, with emphasis on programs rather than capital needs; support also for college scholarships.
Fields of interest: Humanities; Arts; Education; Environment, natural resources; Environment; Health care; Health organizations, association; Disasters, Hurricane Katrina; Human services.

Type of support: General/operating support; Income development; Management development/capacity building; Program development; Seed money; Fellowships; Scholarship funds; Technical assistance; Consulting services; Program-related investments/loans; Scholarships—to individuals; Student loans—to individuals.

Limitations: Giving in the Lakes, Manchester, Monadnock, Nashua, North Country, Piscataqua, and Upper Valley regions in NH. No support for sectarian or religious purposes. No grants to individuals (except for student aid and special awards); generally no grants for building funds, endowments, deficit financing, capital campaigns for acquisition of land or renovations to facilities, purchase of major equipment, academic research, travel, or to replace public funding or for purposes which are a public responsibility.

Publications: Application guidelines; Annual report; Financial statement; Grants list; Informational brochure; Informational brochure (including application guidelines); Newsletter; Program policy statement.

Application information: Visit foundation Web site for application Coversheet and guidelines. Application form required.

Initial approach: Telephone
Copies of proposal: 2
Deadline(s): Mar. 1 and Sept. 1 for community grants; and 3rd Friday in Apr. for student aid applicants for upcoming school year
Board meeting date(s): Feb., June, Nov., and Dec.
Final notification: 6 to 12 weeks

Officers and Directors:* Barry L. Brensinger,* Chair.; James W. Varnum,* Vice-Chair.; Lewis M. Feldstein,* Pres.; Helen Goodman, C.O.O. and V.P.; Thomas Deans, Sr. V.P.; Peter Lamb, V.P., Philanthropic Svcs.; Racheal Stuart, V.P., Progs.; Michael J. Wilson, C.F.O.; Jameson S. French,* Treas.; Rebecca Carr, Cont.; Patience Chamberlin; Ann McLane Kuster; Philip McLaughlin; J. Bonnie Newman; Dan A. Prior; James A. Putnam; Donna Sytek.

Number of staff: 23 full-time professional; 4 part-time professional; 8 full-time support; 4 part-time support.

EIN: 026005625

Selected grants: The following grants were reported in 2005.

$1,904,873 to Vermont Community Foundation, Middlebury, VT.

$470,500 to Passumpsic Valley Land Trust, Saint Johnsbury, VT.

$465,596 to New Futures, Portsmouth, NH. 2 grants: $364,293, $101,303

$169,727 to New Hampshire Symphony, Manchester, NH.

$160,834 to Familystrength, Inc., Concord, NH.

$124,099 to North Country Community Recreation Center, Colebrook, NH.

$75,000 to Crotched Mountain Foundation, Greenfield, NH.

$20,000 to Essex County Community Foundation, Danvers, MA.

$20,000 to Rainforest Alliance, New York, NY.

5099
The Penates Foundation ✧
1 Liberty Ln.
Hampton, NH 03842 (603) 926-5911
Contact: Michele M. Cogan, V.P.

Established in 1984 in NH.

Donors: Paul M. Montrone; Sandra G. Montrone; Prestolite Wire Corp.; Latona Associates Inc.; Chatam, Inc.; Winthrop, Inc.; The Oxford League, Inc.

Foundation type: Independent foundation.

Financial data (yr. ended 8/31/04): Assets, $19,987,628 (M); gifts received, $471,000; expenditures, $1,263,440; qualifying distributions, $1,073,197; giving activities include $1,021,700 for 50 grants.

Fields of interest: Arts; Secondary school/education; Higher education; Education; Environment, natural resources; Environment; Medical research, institute; Human services; Residential/custodial care, hospices; Roman Catholic agencies & churches; Economically disadvantaged.

Type of support: Continuing support; Annual campaigns; Capital campaigns; Building/renovation; Land acquisition; Emergency funds; Scholarship funds.

Limitations: Giving on a national basis. No grants to individuals.

Application information: Application form not required.

Initial approach: Letter
Copies of proposal: 1
Deadline(s): None
Board meeting date(s): Nov.

Officers and Directors:* Sandra G. Montrone,* Pres.; Michele M. Cogan,* V.P. and Secy.-Treas.; Kevin Clark; Matthew Friel; Theodore Kurz; Paul Meister; Angelo Montrone; Jerome Montrone; Paul M. Montrone.

EIN: 222536075

Selected grants: The following grants were reported in 2004.

$314,500 to Metropolitan Opera, Lincoln Center, New York, NY.

$250,000 to Columbia University, Business School, New York, NY.

$86,000 to University of Scranton, Scranton, PA.

$30,000 to New England Conservatory of Music, Boston, MA.

$25,000 to Lakes Region Conservation Trust, Meredith, NH.

$25,000 to National Institutes of Health, Foundation for the, Bethesda, MD.

$25,000 to Saint Katharine Drexel Parish, Wolfeboro, NH.

$20,000 to Roger Williams University, Bristol, RI.

$20,000 to Wolfeboro Area Childrens Center, Wolfeboro, NH.

$16,700 to Richard Tucker Music Foundation, New York, NY.

5100
Putnam Foundation
P.O. Box 323
Keene, NH 03431-0323 (603) 352-2448
Contact: Rosamond P. Delori, Secy.

Trust established in 1952 in NH.

Donor: David F. Putnam‡.

Foundation type: Independent foundation.

Financial data (yr. ended 10/31/05): Assets, $8,440,333 (M); gifts received, $30,107; expenditures, $513,738; qualifying distributions, $443,675; giving activities include $443,675 for 71 grants (high: $100,000; low: $250).

Purpose and activities: The Putnam Foundation's mandate and purpose are to provide funds on a regional basis in New Hampshire, and, in particular,

the Monadnock Region for historic preservation, cultural enhancement, and ecological maintenance.

Fields of interest: Historic preservation/historical societies; Arts; Education; Environment; Children/youth, services; Government/public administration.

Type of support: General/operating support; Capital campaigns; Endowments.

Limitations: Giving limited to NH. No grants to individuals or for scholarships.

Publications: Application guidelines.

Application information: Application form not required.

Initial approach: Letter
Copies of proposal: 1
Deadline(s): None
Board meeting date(s): Monthly

Officer: Rosamond P. Delori, Secy.

Trustees: James A. Putnam; Rosamond P. Putnam; Thomas P. Putnam.

EIN: 026011388

5101
The Smith Family Foundation ✧
c/o McLane, Graf, Raulerson & Middleton
900 Elm St.
Manchester, NH 03105-5650

Established in 1989 in NH.

Donor: Robert F. Smith.

Foundation type: Independent foundation.

Financial data (yr. ended 12/31/04): Assets, $936,256 (M); expenditures, $503,601; qualifying distributions, $500,000; giving activities include $500,000 for 2 grants (high: $250,000; low: $250,000).

Fields of interest: Higher education, college.

Limitations: Applications not accepted. Giving primarily in NH. No grants to individuals.

Application information: Contributes only to pre-selected organizations.

Directors: Miriam D. Smith; Robert F. Smith; Robert F. Smith, Jr.; Brenda M. Stowe.

EIN: 020437015

5102
Treat Foundation ✧
P.O. Box 800
Stratham, NH 03885-0800

Established in NH.

Donor: William W. Treat.

Foundation type: Independent foundation.

Financial data (yr. ended 12/31/04): Assets, $625,904 (M); expenditures, $333,763; qualifying distributions, $327,555; giving activities include $327,660 for 31 grants (high: $300,000; low: $50).

Fields of interest: Museums; Education; Human services.

Limitations: Giving primarily in FL, MA, and NH.

Application information: Application form not required.

Deadline(s): None

Officer: William W. Treat, Mgr.

EIN: 026013780

Selected grants: The following grants were reported in 2005.

$8,500 to New England Historic Genealogical Society, Boston, MA.

$4,350 to Massachusetts Historical Society, Boston, MA.

$3,870 to New Hampshire Humanities Council, Concord, NH.

$1,000 to Philharmonic Center for the Arts, Naples, FL.

$500 to American Independence Museum, Exeter, NH.

$500 to Strawbery Banke, Portsmouth, NH.

$200 to Naples Players, Naples, FL.

$200 to Portsmouth Athenaeum, Portsmouth, NH.

$140 to New Hampshire Historical Society, Concord, NH.

$100 to New Hampshire Public Television, Durham, NH.

5103
The Trust Family Foundation ✧
1 Stiles Rd., Ste. 202
Salem, NH 03079-4844 (603) 898-6670

Established in 1986 in NH.
Donors: Diane Trust; Martin Trust.
Foundation type: Independent foundation.
Financial data (yr. ended 12/31/04): Assets, $22,786,691 (M); expenditures, $1,345,681; qualifying distributions, $1,275,438; giving activities include $1,243,317 for 28 grants (high: $404,000; low: $100).
Purpose and activities: Giving primarily for the arts, education, medical technology, and Jewish philanthropies.
Fields of interest: Visual arts; Performing arts; Humanities; Arts; Education; Medical research, institute; Jewish agencies & temples.
Type of support: Program development.
Limitations: Giving primarily in New England, with emphasis on MA and NH. No grants to individuals, including scholarships, or for capital campaigns, operating budgets, or endowments.
Publications: Annual report (including application guidelines).
Application information: Request annual report for application guidelines. Application form not required.
  Initial approach: Various
  Copies of proposal: 4
  Deadline(s): Feb. 15, Apr. 30, July 15, and Oct. 30
  Board meeting date(s): Mar., June, Sept., and Dec.
  Final notification: Varies
Trustees: David Trust; Diane Trust; Laura Trust; Martin Trust.
Number of staff: None.
EIN: 026070843

Selected grants: The following grants were reported in 2004.
$404,000 to New England Aquarium, Boston, MA.
$135,000 to Temple Adath Yeshurun.
$100,000 to Barnard College, New York, NY.
$36,000 to Beth Israel Hospital.
$10,000 to Brookline Foundation, Brookline, MA.
$500 to Middlebury College, Middlebury, VT.

5104
Madelaine G. von Weber Trust ✧
95 Market St.
Manchester, NH 03101-1933 (603) 669-4140
Contact: Theodore Wadleigh, Tr.

Established in 1990 in NH.
Donor: Madelaine G. von Weber†.
Foundation type: Independent foundation.
Financial data (yr. ended 12/31/05): Assets, $9,212,790 (M); expenditures, $378,979; qualifying distributions, $352,000; giving activities include $329,500 for 24 grants (high: $25,000; low: $2,500).
Purpose and activities: Giving primarily for children and family services, arts and culture, and human services; funding also for hospitals, community housing, and community development.
Fields of interest: Arts; Hospitals (general); Housing/shelter; Human services; Children, services; Family services; Community development.
Limitations: Giving primarily in NH, with emphasis on Manchester. No grants to individuals.
Application information: Application form not required.
  Deadline(s): None
Trustee: Theodore Wadleigh.
EIN: 046055699
Selected grants: The following grants were reported in 2004.
$25,000 to Boston Symphony Orchestra, Boston, MA.
$25,000 to Child Health Services, Manchester, NH.
$25,000 to Manchester Community Music School, Manchester, NH.
$15,000 to Salvation Army, Laconia, NH.
$10,000 to Handel and Haydn Society, Boston, MA.
$10,000 to Odyssey House, Hampton, NH.
$10,000 to Webster House, Manchester, NH.
$6,000 to Circle Program, Plymouth, NH.
$5,000 to Marguerites Place, Nashua, NH.
$5,000 to Ozanam Place, Laconia, NH.

5105
Winthrop, Inc. ✧
Liberty Ln.
Hampton, NH 03842
Contact: Mary Damas, Pres. and Secy.
Application address: 12625 High Bluff Dr., Ste. 215, San Diego, CA 92130, tel.: (858) 793-2554

Incorporated in 1992 in NH.
Donors: Chatam, Inc.; Fisher Scientific International Inc.
Foundation type: Company-sponsored foundation.
Financial data (yr. ended 5/31/05): Assets, $5,535,856 (M); gifts received, $6,500,000; expenditures, $1,349,566; qualifying distributions, $1,344,893; giving activities include $1,298,498 for 343+ grants (high: $60,000).
Purpose and activities: The foundation supports organizations involved with arts and culture, education, health, recreation, and human services.
Fields of interest: Arts; Higher education; Education; Health care; Recreation; Human services; Economics.
Type of support: General/operating support; Employee matching gifts.
Limitations: Giving on a national basis. No grants to individuals.
Application information: Application form not required.
  Initial approach: Proposal
  Deadline(s): None
Officers and Directors: Mary Damas, Pres. and Secy.; Paul M. Meister,* V.P. and Treas.; Michael Dingman; Paul M. Montrone.
EIN: 020453999
Selected grants: The following grants were reported in 2005.
$60,000 to Phillips Exeter Academy, Exeter, NH.
$50,000 to Berwick Academy, South Berwick, ME.
$50,000 to Boston Medical Center, Boston, MA. 2 grants: $25,000 each.
$50,000 to University of Michigan, Ann Arbor, MI.
$36,000 to Boston Symphony Orchestra, Boston, MA.
$25,000 to Boston College, Chestnut Hill, MA. For fundraiser.
$25,000 to Columbia University, Business School, New York, NY.
$25,000 to Dana-Farber Cancer Institute, Boston, MA.
$25,000 to Governor Dummer Academy, Byfield, MA.

NEW JERSEY

5106
1772 Foundation, Inc. ✧
P.O. Box 1
Elizabeth, NJ 07207

Established in 1985 in NJ.
Donor: Stewart B. Kean†.
Foundation type: Independent foundation.
Financial data (yr. ended 12/31/04): Assets, $62,227,563 (M); gifts received, $28,563,317; expenditures, $2,420,060; qualifying distributions, $1,865,710; giving activities include $1,856,195 for 62 grants (high: $125,000; low: $250), and $36,000 for 1 employee matching gift.
Purpose and activities: Giving for historical preservation and museums.
Fields of interest: Museums (history); Museums (science/technology); Museums (specialized); Historic preservation/historical societies.
Type of support: Building/renovation.
Limitations: Applications not accepted. Giving primarily on the East Coast, with emphasis on NJ; some funding nationally. No grants to individuals.
Application information: Contributes only to pre-selected organizations.
Officers and Trustees:* G. Stanton Geary,* Pres.; John R. Livesey, Secy.; J. David Schardien, Treas.; B. Danforth Ely; Robert Raynolds.
EIN: 222578377
Selected grants: The following grants were reported in 2003.
$300,000 to Liberty Hall Museum, Union, NJ. For Stewart B. Kean Memorial Firehouse.
$11,000 to Ralston Cider Mill, Morristown, NJ. For mill restorations.
$10,000 to Herreshoff Marine Museum, Bristol, RI. For vessel restoration.
$10,000 to Howell Living History Farm, Titusville, NJ.
$10,000 to Museum of the American West, Lander, WY. For Pioneer Cabin Museum.
$6,500 to New Hampshire Farm Museum, Milton, NH. For general support.
$3,100 to Connecticut Audubon Society, Fairfield, CT. For land acquisition fund.
$2,000 to Dinosaur Ridge, Friends of, Morrison, CO. For general support.
$1,000 to Kings College, Wilkes Barre, PA. For general support.
$1,000 to Upper Raritan Watershed Association, Gladstone, NJ. For general support.

5107
Abar Foundation ✧
c/o Merrill Lynch Trust Co.
P.O. Box 1525, Ste. MSC 06-03
Pennington, NJ 08534

Established in 2000 in NJ.
Donors: Robert A. Hoff; Mrs. Robert A. Hoff.
Foundation type: Independent foundation.
Financial data (yr. ended 7/31/05): Assets, $24,705,786 (M); gifts received, $204,333; expenditures, $1,136,062; qualifying distributions, $922,009; giving activities include $897,500 for 9 grants (high: $500,000; low: $10,000; average: $20,000–$100,000).

Fields of interest: Athletics/sports, winter sports; Human services; Children/youth, services; Foundations (private grantmaking); Foundations (community).
Limitations: Applications not accepted. Giving primarily in CA. No grants to individuals.
Application information: Contributes only to pre-selected organizations.
Officers: Robert A. Hoff, Pres. and C.F.O.; Ann W. Hoff, Secy.
EIN: 330928475
Selected grants: The following grants were reported in 2004.
$466,666 to Mater Dei High School, Santa Ana, CA. For general support.
$168,350 to United States Ski and Snowboard Association, Park City, UT. For general support.
$50,000 to Bucknell University, Lewisburg, PA. For general support.
$50,000 to Orangewood Childrens Foundation, Santa Ana, CA. For general support.
$30,000 to Make-A-Wish Foundation of Orange County, Tustin, CA. For general support.
$20,000 to First Presbyterian Church of Boulder, Boulder, CO. For general support.
$20,000 to Olive Crest Homes and Services for Abused Children, Santa Ana, CA. For general support.
$10,000 to California Community Foundation, Los Angeles, CA. For general support.
$10,000 to Human Options, Irvine, CA. For general support.
$10,000 to Marys Shelter, Santa Ana, CA. For general support.

5108
Adelson Family Foundation ✧
44 Buckingham Rd.
Tenafly, NJ 07670

Established in 2000 in NY.
Donors: Andrew Adelson; Nancy Adelson.
Foundation type: Independent foundation.
Financial data (yr. ended 12/31/05): Assets, $9,729,902 (M); gifts received, $500,000; expenditures, $422,476; qualifying distributions, $379,300; giving activities include $379,300 for 35 grants (high: $161,000; low: $1,000; average: $5,000–$10,000).
Fields of interest: Education; Human services; Jewish federated giving programs; Jewish agencies & temples.
Limitations: Applications not accepted. Giving primarily in NY. No grants to individuals.
Application information: Contributes only to pre-selected organizations.
Trustees: Andrew Adelson; Nancy Adelson.
EIN: 223769645
Selected grants: The following grants were reported in 2005.
$10,000 to Architecture for Humanity, Sausalito, CA.
$10,000 to East Harlem Tutorial Program, New York, NY.
$10,000 to Hastings Center, Garrison, NY.
$10,000 to Jewish Home at Rockleigh, Rockleigh, NJ.
$5,000 to City Harvest, New York, NY.
$5,000 to Conservation Fund, Arlington, VA.
$5,000 to Habitat for Humanity International.
$5,000 to Link Community School, Newark, NJ.
$5,000 to Student Conservation Association, Charlestown, NH.

$1,000 to United Negro College Fund, Fairfax, VA.

5109
Aicher Family Foundation, Inc. ✧
8 Random Rd.
Princeton, NJ 08540

Established in 1997 in CT.
Donors: Paul J. Aicher; The Paul J. Aicher Trust.
Foundation type: Independent foundation.
Financial data (yr. ended 12/31/05): Assets, $217,360 (M); gifts received, $1,150,000; expenditures, $1,143,528; qualifying distributions, $1,142,341; giving activities include $1,140,000 for 3 grants (high: $1,100,000; low: $15,000).
Fields of interest: Humanities; Foundations (private operating); Public policy, research.
Limitations: Giving primarily in CT, ME, and New York, NY.
Officers: Kathryn Aicher Slawson, Pres.; Diana Johnson, V.P.; Peter Aicher, Secy.; Bradford Sparrow, Treas.
EIN: 061398331

5110
Alcatel-Lucent Foundation ▼
(formerly Lucent Technologies Foundation)
600 Mountain Ave., Rm. 6F4
Murray Hill, NJ 07974 (908) 582-7906
Contact: Michele Donato, Mgr., Finance and Opers.
E-mail: foundation@lucent.com; Tel. for Conqueror of the Hill: (908) 582-7436; E-mail for Conqueror of the Hill: lucentcoh@alcatel-lucent.com; E-mail for Graduate Research Fellowships: coopgraduate@alcatel-lucent.com

Established in 1996.
Donor: Lucent Technologies Inc.
Foundation type: Company-sponsored foundation.
Financial data (yr. ended 9/30/05): Assets, $929,640 (M); gifts received, $6,418,500; expenditures, $6,551,188; qualifying distributions, $6,522,667; giving activities include $5,666,045 for 162 grants (high: $1,550,000; low: $250), and $285,600 for 84 grants to individuals (high: $5,000; low: $50).
Purpose and activities: The foundation supports organizations involved with cultural diversity, education, health, employment training, and youth development and awards fellowships to female, African American, Native American, and Hispanic college seniors and first-year graduate students.
Fields of interest: Arts, cultural/ethnic awareness; Elementary/secondary education; Education; Health care; Employment, training; Youth development; Science, formal/general education; Mathematics; African Americans/Blacks; Hispanics/Latinos; Native Americans/American Indians; Women.
Type of support: Scholarships—to individuals; General/operating support; Continuing support; Program development; Seed money; Fellowships; Employee volunteer services; Program evaluation; Grants to individuals.
Application information: Unsolicited requests for grants are not accepted in 2007. The Bell Labs Graduate Research Fellowship Program has been suspended for the 2007-2008 academic year.
Initial approach: Complete online application form for Conqueror of the Hill

Deadline(s): Mar. 7 for Conqueror of the Hill in NJ; Feb. 21 for Conqueror of the Hill in IL

Board meeting date(s): Quarterly

Officers and Trustees:* Patricia F. Russo, Chair.; Christine Park, Pres.; Beatrice Tassot, Secy.; Frank A. D'Amelio,* Treas.; Mary Lou Ambrus; William R. Carapezzi, Jr.; John Giere; John A. Kritzmacher; Vincent Molinaro.

EIN: 223480423

Selected grants: The following grants were reported in 2005.

$1,550,000 to Scholarship America, Saint Peter, MN.

$1,400,000 to International Youth Foundation, Baltimore, MD.

$570,000 to Institute of International Education, New York, NY.

$100,000 to National Science Resources Center, DC.

$90,000 to New Community Corporation, Newark, NJ. 2 grants: $60,000, $30,000

$80,000 to Edison Township Public Schools, Edison, NJ.

$80,000 to Trenton Public Schools, Trenton, NJ.

$60,000 to Greater Newark Conservancy, Newark, NJ.

$60,000 to La Casa de Don Pedro, Newark, NJ.

$60,000 to North Ward Center, Newark, NJ.

$30,000 to Catholic Charities of the Archdiocese of Newark, Newark, NJ.

$30,000 to Young Science Achievers Program, North Branch, NJ.

$22,000 to Plainfield Public Schools, Plainfield, NJ.

5111

Rita Allen Foundation, Inc.

96 Hun Rd.
Princeton, NJ 08540
Contact: Moore Gates, Jr., Pres.

Incorporated in 1953 in NY.

Donor: Rita Allen Cassel†.

Foundation type: Independent foundation.

Financial data (yr. ended 12/31/05): Assets, $19,775,161; expenditures, $1,238,554; qualifying distributions, $1,095,824; giving activities include $1,028,522 for 31 grants (high: $149,015; low: $2,000).

Purpose and activities: Giving primarily for medical grants, with emphasis on research in the fields of cancer, multiple sclerosis, cerebral palsy, and euphorics and analgesics related to the terminally ill; some support for recognized welfare and religious organizations.

Fields of interest: Higher education; Medical research, institute; Jewish federated giving programs; Biological sciences.

Type of support: Fellowships; Scholarship funds; Research.

Limitations: Applications not accepted. Giving on a national basis. No grants to individuals (except university research scientists), or for building funds.

Application information: Unsolicited requests for funds not accepted.

Board meeting date(s): Annually and as required

Officers and Directors:* Moore Gates, Jr.,* Pres.; Anne O'Neill Gates,* Secy.; Henry H. Hitch,* Treas.; William Gadsden; Aristides Georgantas.

EIN: 136116429

Selected grants: The following grants were reported in 2004.

$148,380 to Brandeis University, Waltham, MA.

$74,190 to United Jewish Appeal, New York, NY.

$50,000 to Baylor College of Medicine, Houston, TX.

$50,000 to Cold Spring Harbor Laboratory, Cold Spring Harbor, NY.

$50,000 to Rockefeller University, New York, NY.

$50,000 to Stanford University Hospital, Stanford, CA.

$15,000 to South Kent School, South Kent, CT.

$10,000 to Kent Place School, Summit, NJ.

$5,000 to Norwalk Community College, Norwalk, CT.

$5,000 to Princeton Area Community Foundation, Lawrenceville, NJ.

5112

The Amboy Foundation, Inc.

c/o Amboy National Bank
3590 U.S. Hwy. 9
Old Bridge, NJ 08857-2837 (732) 591-8700
Contact: Karen A. Mlynarski
URL: http://www.amboybank.com/bank/foundation.html

Established in 1996 in NJ.

Donor: Amboy National Bank.

Foundation type: Company-sponsored foundation.

Financial data (yr. ended 12/31/04): Assets, $5,082,231 (M); expenditures, $321,160; qualifying distributions, $315,300; giving activities include $315,300 for 26 grants (high: $100,000; low: $2,000).

Purpose and activities: The foundation supports organizations involved with health, housing, human services, and women.

Fields of interest: Health care; Housing/shelter; Human services; Women.

Limitations: Giving primarily in central NJ. No support for private clubs or fraternal organizations, labor groups, or pass-through organizations. No grants to individuals.

Application information: Support is limited to 1 contribution per organization during any given year. Application form not required.

Initial approach: Mail proposal to foundation

Copies of proposal: 1

Deadline(s): None

Board meeting date(s): Quarterly

Final notification: 15 days following board meetings

Officers and Trustees:* Patricia M. Keys,* Secy.; George G. Brennan,* Treas.; Marguerite DiSepio; George E. Scharpf.

EIN: 223484075

Selected grants: The following grants were reported in 2003.

$250,000 to University of Notre Dame, Notre Dame, IN.

$12,500 to Habitat for Humanity, Raritan Valley, Bridgewater, NJ.

$10,000 to Housing Coalition of Central Jersey, New Brunswick, NJ.

$7,500 to Family and Childrens Service of Monmouth County, Oakhurst, NJ.

$7,500 to Somerset Home for Temporarily Displaced Children, Bridgewater, NJ.

$7,000 to Manna House, Cliffwood, NJ.

$7,000 to Resource Center for Women and Their Families, Hillsborough, NJ.

$5,000 to Crawford House, Skillman, NJ.

$5,000 to Women Helping Women, Metuchen, NJ.

$4,000 to Mercy Center Corporation, Asbury Park, NJ.

5113

American Standard Foundation ◇

1 Centennial Ave.
P.O. Box 6820
Piscataway, NJ 08855-6820 (732) 980-6000
Contact: G. Peter D'Aloia, Pres.

Trust established in 1952 in PA as Westinghouse Air Brake Foundation; name changed in 1977.

Donors: American Standard Inc.; American Standard Cos., Inc.

Foundation type: Company-sponsored foundation.

Financial data (yr. ended 12/31/05): Assets, $739,914 (M); gifts received, $2,606,153; expenditures, $2,311,729; qualifying distributions, $2,311,729; giving activities include $1,658,179 for 64 grants (high: $254,380; low: $48), and $653,550 for 440 employee matching gifts.

Purpose and activities: The foundation supports organizations involved with education.

Fields of interest: Higher education; Education; Federated giving programs.

Type of support: Employee matching gifts; Employee-related scholarships.

Limitations: Giving primarily in areas of significant company operations.

Publications: Program policy statement.

Application information: Application form not required.

Initial approach: Proposal

Deadline(s): None

Officers and Directors:* G. Peter D'Aloia,* Pres.; J. Paul McGrath,* V.P. and Secy.; R. Scott Massengil,* V.P. and Treas.; Lawrence B. Costello,* V.P.

EIN: 256018911

5114

Hossein Amirsaleh Foundation Trust ◇ ☆

25 Enterprise Ave.
Secaucus, NJ 07094

Established in 2000 in NJ.

Donors: Mahyar Amirsaleh; Child Foundation; Encyclopedia Iranica; New York University; Kharizak Foundation; Earthquake Prevention Program.

Foundation type: Independent foundation.

Financial data (yr. ended 11/30/05): Assets, $1,112,935 (M); gifts received, $200,000; expenditures, $453,250; qualifying distributions, $453,250; giving activities include $453,250 for 9 grants (high: $400,000; low: $500).

Purpose and activities: Giving primarily for a scholarship fund for undergraduate Iranian students attending business school, and for an art museum.

Fields of interest: Museums (art); Business school/education; Human services.

Type of support: General/operating support; Scholarship funds.

Trustees: Fran Amirsaleh; Mahyar Amirsaleh; Mehrdad Amirsaleh; Morad Amirsaleh.

EIN: 226831721

Selected grants: The following grants were reported in 2005.

$400,000 to New York University, New York, NY.

$1,500 to Hudson Cradle, Jersey City, NJ.

$1,000 to Horace Mann School, Riverdale, NY.

5115
Anderson Foundation ✧
c/o Thomas Anderson
31 Roebling Rd.
Bernardsville, NJ 07924-1409

Established in 1981 in NJ.
Donors: Thomas Anderson; Bear Stearns & Co.
Foundation type: Independent foundation.
Financial data (yr. ended 11/30/04): Assets,
$11,313,924 (M); gifts received, $43,457;
expenditures, $495,393; qualifying distributions,
$487,894; giving activities include $441,001 for 14
grants (high: $100,000; low: $1), and $43,457 for
1 foundation-administered program.
Purpose and activities: Giving primarily to Christian
causes.
Fields of interest: Higher education; Family
services; Residential/custodial care; Civil liberties,
right to life; Christian agencies & churches.
Limitations: Giving on a national basis, with some
emphasis on NJ and NY. No grants to individuals.
Trustee: Thomas Anderson.
EIN: 222393971
Selected grants: The following grants were reported
in 2004.
$100,000 to Walter Hoving Home, Garrison, NY.
$50,000 to Focus on the Family, Colorado Springs,
CO.
$5,000 to Life Issues Institute, Cincinnati, OH.
$5,000 to Wycliffe Bible Translators, Huntington
Beach, CA.

5116
Armour-Lewis Family Foundation ✧
c/o McElroy, Deutsch, Mulvaney & Carpenter
3 Gateway Ctr.
100 Mulberry St.
Newark, NJ 07102-4079

Established in 1998 in NJ.
Donor: Robert L. Armour Revocable Trust.
Foundation type: Independent foundation.
Financial data (yr. ended 12/31/05): Assets,
$6,069,962 (M); expenditures, $411,822;
qualifying distributions, $348,000; giving activities
include $348,000 for 5 grants (high: $98,000; low:
$55,000).
Fields of interest: Higher education; Engineering
school/education; Theological school/education.
Limitations: Applications not accepted. Giving
primarily in NJ, NY, and PA. No grants to individuals.
Application information: Contributes only to
pre-selected organizations.
Trustees: Tara L. Fallon; Warren Lloyd Lewis; Louise
Ouellette.
EIN: 223476006

5117
Arnold Foundation, Inc. ✧
c/o Lowenstein Sandler
65 Livingston Ave.
Roseland, NJ 07068

Established in 2002 in NJ.
Donor: Erica Enterprises, LLC.
Foundation type: Independent foundation.
Financial data (yr. ended 11/30/04): Assets,
$48,205,393 (M); expenditures, $3,095,550;
qualifying distributions, $3,000,000; giving
activities include $3,000,000 for 1 grant.

Purpose and activities: Support primarily for a
community foundation.
Fields of interest: Foundations (community).
Type of support: General/operating support.
Limitations: Applications not accepted. Giving
primarily in CA. No grants to individuals.
Application information: Contributes only to
pre-selected organizations.
Officers and Trustees:* Kenneth J. Slutsky,* Pres.
and Treas.; Allen Levithan,* V.P. and Secy.; John L.
Berger,* V.P. and Treas.
EIN: 223885473

5118
Aspen Foundation, Inc. ▼ ✧
c/o Attn: Ken Slutsky, Lowenstein Sandler
65 Livingston Ave.
Roseland, NJ 07068

Established in 2000 in NJ.
Donors: ANFA Co., LLC; Western Birch Co., LLC.
Foundation type: Independent foundation.
Financial data (yr. ended 11/30/05): Assets,
$47,597,199 (M); gifts received, $1,500,000;
expenditures, $32,233,470; qualifying
distributions, $32,218,455; giving activities include
$32,218,455 for 2 grants (high: $30,066,470; low:
$2,151,985).
Purpose and activities: Giving primarily for
philanthropy management.
Fields of interest: Philanthropy/voluntarism,
management/technical aid; Philanthropy/
voluntarism; Philanthropy/voluntarism.
Limitations: Applications not accepted. Giving on a
national basis. No grants to individuals.
Application information: Contributes only to
pre-selected organizations.
Officers: Kenneth J. Slutsky, Pres. and Treas.; Allen
Levithan, V.P. and Secy.; John L. Berger, V.P.
Board Member: ANFA Co., LLC.
EIN: 223768991
Selected grants: The following grants were reported
in 2004.
$48,494,381 to Vanguard Charitable Endowment
Program, Southeastern, PA. 2 grants:
$20,000,000 (For general support),
$28,494,381 (For general support).

5119
The David R. and Patricia D. Atkinson
Foundation
100 Overlook Ctr., 2nd Fl.
Princeton, NJ 08540
Contact: Steven Atkinson, Tr.

Established in 2000 in NJ.
Donors: David R. Atkinson; Patricia D. Atkinson.
Foundation type: Independent foundation.
Financial data (yr. ended 8/31/05): Assets,
$14,755,126 (M); gifts received, $2,849,581;
expenditures, $491,438; qualifying distributions,
$431,100; giving activities include $431,100 for 56
grants (high: $82,000; low: $1,000).
Purpose and activities: Giving primarily for health
associations and human services, including
services for people who are blind; funding also for
children and youth services.
Fields of interest: Education; Health organizations,
association; Alzheimer's disease research; Human
services; Salvation Army; Children/youth, services;
Blind/visually impaired.

Limitations: Applications not accepted. Giving
primarily in NJ; some funding nationally, particularly
in NY and PA. No grants to individuals.
Application information: Contributes only to
pre-selected organizations.
Trustees: David R. Atkinson; Patricia D. Atkinson;
Paul D. Atkinson; Steven R. Atkinson.
EIN: 223753685
Selected grants: The following grants were reported
in 2005.
$82,000 to CARE, Narberth, PA.
$28,000 to Salvation Army. 2 grants: $18,000,
$10,000
$25,000 to Alzheimers Association, Chicago, IL.
$18,000 to Nature Conservancy, Conshohocken,
PA.
$12,000 to Trenton Area Soup Kitchen, Trenton, NJ.
$10,000 to Meals on Wheels, Quakertown, NJ.
$7,000 to Seeing Eye, Morristown, NJ.
$6,000 to American Cancer Society, Morristown, NJ.
$3,000 to Make-A-Wish Foundation, Mount Kisco,
NY.

5120
Aventis Pharmaceuticals Foundation
(formerly Hoechst Marion Roussel Foundation)
400 Somerset Corporate Blvd.
Bridgewater, NJ 08807 (908) 243-6777
Contact: Evelyn Seif, Treas.

Established in 1988 in MO.
Donors: Marion Merrell Dow Inc.; Hoechst Marion
Roussel, Inc.
Foundation type: Company-sponsored foundation.
Financial data (yr. ended 6/30/05): Assets,
$3,452,617 (M); expenditures, $2,510,138;
qualifying distributions, $2,509,964; giving
activities include $2,462,914 for 89 grants (high:
$500,000).
Purpose and activities: The foundation supports
organizations involved with medical and nursing
education, disease, medical research, children, and
senior citizens.
Fields of interest: Medical school/education;
Nursing school/education; Cancer; Lung diseases;
Asthma; Diabetes; Medical research; Children,
services; Aging.
Type of support: Program development.
Limitations: Giving primarily in Kansas City, MO, and
NJ. No support for political, religious, or veterans'
organizations, service clubs, professional
associations, or organizations posing a conflict of
interest with Aventis' goals or products. No grants
to individuals or groups of individuals, or for travel,
scholarships or memorials, marathons, runs, or
walks, capital campaigns or endowments, school
advertising, or symposiums or conferences.
Publications: Application guidelines; Informational
brochure (including application guidelines).
Application information: Proposals should be no
longer than 1 to 2 pages. Application form not
required.
Initial approach: Proposal
Copies of proposal: 1
Deadline(s): None
Final notification: 15 to 21 days
Officers and Trustees:* Charles F. Rouse III, Pres.;
Evelyn Self, Treas.; Timothy Rothwell.
Number of staff: 3 full-time professional.
EIN: 431503440
Selected grants: The following grants were reported
in 2004.

$500,000 to Somerset Medical Center Foundation, Somerville, NJ.

$250,000 to Society for Womens Health Research, DC.

$23,000 to Truman Medical Centers, Kansas City, MO.

5121

Aventis Pharmaceuticals Health Care Foundation ▼ ◇

(formerly Hoechst Marion Roussel Health Care Foundation for the III)
400 Somerset Corp. Blvd.
P.O. Box 6912
Bridgewater, NJ 08807

Established in 1992.
Donors: Marion Merrell Dow Inc.; Hoechst Marion Roussel, Inc.; Aventis Pharmaceuticals Inc.
Foundation type: Company-sponsored foundation.
Financial data (yr. ended 12/31/05): Assets, $0; gifts received, $217,845,821; expenditures, $217,845,821; qualifying distributions, $217,845,821; giving activities include $217,845,821 for grants to individuals.
Purpose and activities: The foundation provides medication for patients who are below the federal poverty level and who are not eligible for any third-party medication payments.
Fields of interest: Economically disadvantaged.
Type of support: Grants to individuals; Donated products.
Application information: Application form required.
 Initial approach: Letter of inquiry for application form
 Deadline(s): None
Officers and Trustees: Charles F. Rouse III,* Pres.; Evelyn Self, Treas.
EIN: 431614543

5122

Matan B'Seter Foundation, Inc. ◇

65 Livingston Ave.
Roseland, NJ 07068
Contact: Kenneth J. Slutsky, Pres.

Established in 1998 in NJ.
Donors: BLTN, LLC; BLTN Holdings, LLP.
Foundation type: Independent foundation.
Financial data (yr. ended 11/30/05): Assets, $58,003,459 (M); gifts received, $34,500,000; expenditures, $17,227,977; qualifying distributions, $17,212,006; giving activities include $15,000,000 for 1 grant.
Fields of interest: Children/youth, services.
Limitations: Applications not accepted. Giving primarily in PA. No grants to individuals.
Application information: Contributes only to pre-selected organizations.
Officers and Trustees:* Kenneth J. Slutsky,* Pres. and Treas.; Allen Levithan,* V.P. and Secy.; John L. Berger,* V.P.; BLTN Holdings, LLC.
EIN: 223692921
Selected grants: The following grants were reported in 2003.
$10,407,600 to Fidelity Investments Charitable Gift Fund, Boston, MA. For general support.
$3,398,400 to Vanguard Charitable Endowment Program, Southeastern, PA. For general support.

5123

Thomas E. and Linda O. Baker Family Foundation ◇

17 Glennon Farm Ln.
Lebanon, NJ 08833 (908) 832-2505
Contact: Cecile McKenzie, Prog. Dir.
FAX: (908) 832-2772;
E-mail: info@bakerfamilyfoundation.org; Additional tel. in Florida: (239) 481-5821; URL: http://www.bakerfamilyfoundation.org

Established in 1999 in NJ.
Donor: Thomas E. Baker.
Foundation type: Independent foundation.
Financial data (yr. ended 12/31/05): Assets, $5,106,543 (M); expenditures, $592,846; qualifying distributions, $588,704; giving activities include $476,429 for grants to individuals.
Purpose and activities: Scholarships awarded for undergraduate education to individuals with financial need, and qualifying academic records.
Fields of interest: Higher education; Scholarships/financial aid.
Type of support: General/operating support; Scholarships—to individuals.
Limitations: Giving primarily in the NJ and NY area.
Application information: Application guidelines and form available on foundation Web site. Application form required.
 Initial approach: Letter
 Deadline(s): None, although applicants are encouraged to apply as soon after the first of the new year as possible
Trustees: Linda O. Baker; Thomas E. Baker.
Number of staff: 1 full-time professional.
EIN: 256611063

5124

Bernice Barbour Foundation, Inc.

130 Main St.
Hackensack, NJ 07601-7152
Contact: Eve Lloyd Thompson, Secy.-Treas.
E-mail: eve@bernicebarbour.org; Application address: 14434 Laurel Trail, Wellington, FL 33414, tel.: (561) 791-0861, FAX: (561) 753-9153; URL: http://www.bernicebarbour.org

Established in 1987 in NJ; funded in 1990.
Donor: Bernice Barbour‡.
Foundation type: Independent foundation.
Financial data (yr. ended 12/31/05): Assets, $23,659,010 (M); expenditures, $1,706,123; qualifying distributions, $1,240,911; giving activities include $1,202,200 for 153 grants.
Purpose and activities: Giving primarily for the preservation and care of animals and for the prevention of cruelty to animals in the United States.
Fields of interest: Animals/wildlife.
Type of support: General/operating support; Continuing support; Building/renovation; Equipment; Program development; Fellowships; Research; Technical assistance; Matching/challenge support.
Limitations: Giving on a national basis. No support for organizations that do not spay/neuter animals before adopting them out. No grants to individuals, or for indirect costs, litigation, or for costs relating to animals which are not indigenous to the United States, or land acquisition.
Publications: Application guidelines; Informational brochure; Program policy statement (including application guidelines).

Application information: Application guidelines and form available on foundation Web site. Application form required.
 Initial approach: Application form
 Copies of proposal: 2
 Deadline(s): Aug. 10
 Board meeting date(s): Mar., June, Oct. and Nov.
 Final notification: After Dec. 1
Officers and Trustees:* Frank V.D. Lloyd,* Pres.; Gregory Little,* V.P.; Eve Lloyd Thompson,* Secy.-Treas.; Judith Little; Jacqueline Little; Karen Lloyd; Kristina Lloyd Sample; Henry Turmon.
Number of staff: 2 full-time professional.
EIN: 222779967

5125

C. R. Bard Foundation, Inc.

730 Central Ave.
New Providence, NJ 07974
Contact: Linda Hrevnack
FAX: (908) 277-8098; URL: http://www.crbard.com/about/com_relations/foundations/index.cfm

Established in 1987 in NY.
Donor: C.R. Bard, Inc.
Foundation type: Company-sponsored foundation.
Financial data (yr. ended 12/31/05): Assets, $1,258,034 (M); gifts received, $2,550,000; expenditures, $2,190,122; qualifying distributions, $2,182,702; giving activities include $1,869,956 for grants, and $312,746 for 606 employee matching gifts.
Purpose and activities: The foundation supports organizations involved with higher education, health, and human services.
Fields of interest: Higher education; Health care; Human services; Federated giving programs.
Type of support: Research; Fellowships; General/operating support; Program development; Scholarship funds; Employee matching gifts.
Limitations: Applications not accepted. Giving primarily in areas of company operations. No support for religious or political organizations. No grants to individuals, or for capital campaigns.
Application information: Contributes only to pre-selected organizations.
 Board meeting date(s): Quarterly
Officers: Timothy M. Ring, Pres.; Scott T. Lowry, V.P. and Treas.; John H. Weiland, V.P.; Bronwen Kelly, Secy.
EIN: 222840708

5126

The Bendheim Foundation, Inc. ◇

(formerly Siegfried & Nannette Bendheim Foundation, Inc.)
65 Challenger Rd., 3rd Fl.
Ridgefield Park, NJ 07660-2104
(201) 329-7300
Contact: Jack C. Bendheim, Pres.

Established around 1949.
Donors: Jack C. Bendheim; Stuart Tauber; Daniel M. Bendheim; Gail B. Bendheim; Shulamit Y. Bendheim; Yonina B. Jacobson; Phibro Animal Health Corp.; Charles & Els Bendheim Foundation, Inc.; Phillip Brothers Chemicals, Inc.; The Packer Family Foundation.
Foundation type: Independent foundation.

Financial data (yr. ended 12/31/05): Assets, $558,995 (M); gifts received, $700,000; expenditures, $1,033,235; qualifying distributions, $1,029,023; giving activities include $1,020,200 for 121 grants (high: $50,000; low: $25).

Purpose and activities: Giving primarily to Jewish organizations, temples and schools.

Fields of interest: Elementary/secondary education; Human services; Jewish federated giving programs; Jewish agencies & temples.

International interests: Israel.

Limitations: Giving primarily in New York, NY; some funding also in Israel. No grants to individuals.

Application information:
Initial approach: Letter
Deadline(s): None

Officers: Jack C. Bendheim, Pres. and Treas.; Gail B. Bendheim, V.P.; Peggy Hagel, Secy.

Directors: Daniel M. Bendheim; Shulamit Y. Bendheim; Yonina B. Jacobson.

EIN: 136103768

5127
The Elizabeth and Barets O. Benjamin Charitable Foundation, Inc. ✦ ☆

c/o Mary R. Lasser
P.O. Box 258
Pottersville, NJ 07979

Established in 1995 in NJ.

Donor: Elizabeth Benjamin.

Foundation type: Independent foundation.

Financial data (yr. ended 12/31/05): Assets, $11,261,480 (M); expenditures, $572,088; qualifying distributions, $499,886; giving activities include $475,000 for 7 grants (high: $263,000; low: $2,000).

Fields of interest: Health organizations, association; Cancer.

Limitations: Applications not accepted. Giving primarily in NJ and NY. No grants to individuals.

Application information: Contributes only to pre-selected organizations.

Officers and Trustees:* Mary R. Lasser,* Pres.; Peter Lasser,* V.P. and Treas.; Andrew Stamelman, Secy.

EIN: 223390586

5128
Sol and Margaret Berger Foundation ✦

140 Hepburn Rd.
Clifton, NJ 07012 (973) 777-1400

Established in 1962 in NY.

Donor: Sol Berger.

Foundation type: Independent foundation.

Financial data (yr. ended 4/30/05): Assets, $15,938,692 (M); expenditures, $849,634; qualifying distributions, $803,560; giving activities include $707,741 for grants.

Purpose and activities: Giving primarily for health, education, and human services.

Fields of interest: Arts; Elementary/secondary education; Higher education; Medical school/education; Education; Hospitals (general); Health organizations, association; Cancer; Cancer research; Children/youth, services; Jewish agencies & temples; Disabilities, people with; Minorities.

Type of support: Scholarship funds.

Limitations: Applications not accepted. Giving primarily in NJ and NY. No grants to individuals.

Application information: Unsolicited requests for funds not accepted.
Board meeting date(s): Mar.

Trustees: Sandye Aidner; Renee Berger; Sol Berger.

EIN: 136118516

5129
The Berlind Foundation ✦ ☆

c/o Michael Schwartzbard & Assocs.
101 Eisenhower Pkwy.
Roseland, NJ 07068-1032

Established in 1994 in NY.

Donor: Roger Berlind.

Foundation type: Independent foundation.

Financial data (yr. ended 12/31/05): Assets, $1,973,301 (M); gifts received, $899,851; expenditures, $333,170; qualifying distributions, $324,501; giving activities include $324,000 for 64 + grants (high: $62,000).

Purpose and activities: Giving for the arts, higher education, and federated giving programs.

Fields of interest: Museums (art); Arts; Higher education; Higher education, university; Federated giving programs.

Limitations: Applications not accepted. Giving primarily in New York, NY. No grants to individuals.

Application information: Contributes only to pre-selected organizations.

Director: Roger Berlind.

EIN: 133800078

Selected grants: The following grants were reported in 2003.

$25,000 to Franklin and Eleanor Roosevelt Institute (FERI), Hyde Park, NY. For general support.

$14,500 to Museum of Modern Art, New York, NY. For general support.

$14,500 to Princeton University, Princeton, NJ. For general support.

$12,400 to World Monuments Fund, New York, NY. For general support.

$10,000 to New York City Opera, New York, NY. For general support.

$8,500 to Metropolitan Museum of Art, New York, NY. For general support.

$7,500 to Brooklyn Academy of Music, Brooklyn, NY. For general support.

$2,500 to Shakespeare Society, New York, NY. For general support.

$1,000 to Solomon R. Guggenheim Museum, New York, NY. For general support.

$1,000 to Whitney Museum of American Art, New York, NY. For general support.

5130
The Russell Berrie Foundation ▼ ✦

300 Frank W. Burr Blvd., Bldg. E., 7th Fl.
Teaneck, NJ 07666-6704 (201) 928-1880
Contact: Robert Gordon, C.F.O.
URL: http://www.russberrie.com

Established in 1985 in NJ.

Donor: Russell Berrie†.

Foundation type: Independent foundation.

Financial data (yr. ended 12/31/04): Assets, $162,574,934 (M); gifts received, $38,966,338; expenditures, $24,483,654; qualifying distributions, $23,014,833; giving activities include $21,384,480 for 95 grants (high: $4,029,617; low: $75; average: $10,000–$100,000), and $150,000

for 19 grants to individuals (high: $50,000; low: $25,000).

Purpose and activities: Giving primarily to arts/cultural programs, higher education, human services, Jewish federated giving programs and Jewish agencies and temples.

Fields of interest: Arts; Higher education; Hospitals (general); Health organizations, association; Human services; Jewish federated giving programs; Jewish agencies & temples.

Type of support: Grants to individuals.

Limitations: Applications not accepted. Giving on a national basis, with emphasis on NJ and NY.

Application information: Unsolicited requests for funds not accepted.

Officers: Angelica Berrie, Pres.; Scott Berrie, V.P.; Ilan Kaufthal, V.P.; Myron Rosner, Secy.; Robert Gordon, C.F.O.; Paul Rovinsky, Exec. Dir.

EIN: 222620908

Selected grants: The following grants were reported in 2004.

$900,000 to UJA Federation of Northern New Jersey, River Edge, NJ. 2 grants: $600,000 (For annual campaign), $300,000 (For Young Leadership Initiative, program to prepare people ages 36-49 for leadership roles in UJA).

$200,000 to American Friends of Shalom Hartman Institute, New York, NY. For general support.

$168,038 to Jewish Community Center on the Palisades, Tenafly, NJ. 2 grants: $67,256 (For 21st Century Endowment), $100,782 (For challenge grant for Scholarship Fund).

$104,000 to Boys Town Jerusalem Foundation of America, New York, NY. For general support.

$100,000 to Arnold P. Gold Foundation, Englewood Cliffs, NJ. For annual grant.

$100,000 to New Jersey Symphony Orchestra, Newark, NJ. For general support.

$70,000 to Caucus Educational Corporation, Montclair, NJ. For general support for Families in Focus, television series that examines issues confronting the modern American Family.

$50,000 to Metropolitan Opera Association, New York, NY. For general support.

5131
David & Susan Bershad Foundation, Inc. ✦ ☆

c/o David J. Bershad
2 Stonebridge Rd.
Montclair, NJ 07042

Established in 1997 in NJ.

Donors: David J. Bershad; Susan G. Bershad.

Foundation type: Independent foundation.

Financial data (yr. ended 11/30/05): Assets, $4,396,161 (M); gifts received, $3,547,524; expenditures, $3,534,817; qualifying distributions, $849,680; giving activities include $849,680 for 93 grants (high: $250,000; low: $36).

Purpose and activities: Giving for the arts, education, and Jewish organizations.

Fields of interest: Arts; Libraries (public); Education; Jewish agencies & temples.

Limitations: Applications not accepted. Giving primarily in Montclair, NJ and New York, NY. No grants to individuals.

Application information: Contributes only to pre-selected organizations.

Officers: David J. Bershad, Pres.; Susan V. Bershad, Secy.

Directors: Jeffrey Bershad; William Bershad; Carrie Dubow.
EIN: 226711103
Selected grants: The following grants were reported in 2003.
$71,250 to Cornell University, Ithaca, NY.
$36,000 to UJA-Federation of New York, New York, NY.
$10,000 to Gates of Israel Foundation, South Orange, NJ.
$10,000 to Montclair Kimberley Academy, Montclair, NJ.
$5,000 to Montclair Art Museum, Montclair, NJ.
$2,000 to Hunter College of the City University of New York Foundation, New York, NY.
$1,000 to Parsons Dance Foundation, New York, NY.
$300 to Temple Sharey Tefilo, East Orange, NJ.
$150 to W L I W-Channel 21 Public Television, Garden City, NY.
$100 to Montclair Historical Society, Montclair, NJ.

5132
Bestfoods Educational Foundation
(formerly CPC Educational Foundation)
P.O. Box 131
Mountain Lakes, NJ   07046   (973) 541-9150
Contact: Richard Bergeman, Pres.

Established in 1961 in NJ.
Foundation type: Independent foundation.
Financial data (yr. ended 11/30/05): Assets, $11,681,215 (M); expenditures, $1,511,110; qualifying distributions, $1,388,000; giving activities include $1,388,000 for 11 grants (high: $500,000; low: $25,000).
Purpose and activities: The foundation supports organizations involved with education.
Fields of interest: Education.
Type of support: Income development.
Limitations: Applications not accepted. Giving on a national basis.
Application information: Contributes only through employee-related scholarships and to pre-selected organizations.
Officers and Director: Richard P. Bergeman,* Chair.; Luis Schuchinski, V.P.; Gale L. Griffen, Secy.; Rainer H. Mimberg, Treas.; Philip Braverman, Genl. Counsel.
EIN: 136103949
Selected grants: The following grants were reported in 2005.
$150,000 to Bloomfield College, Bloomfield, NJ.
$125,000 to America SCORES, New York, NY.
$100,000 to Project Acorn, Morris Plains, NJ. 3 grants: $30,000, $50,000, $20,000.
$90,000 to Dalton Schools, New York, NY.
$60,000 to Montclair Fund for Educational Excellence, Montclair, NJ.
$2,000 to Bucknell University, Lewisburg, PA.
$2,000 to De La Salle University, Manila, Philippines. .
$2,000 to University of Central Florida, Orlando, FL.

5133
Bildner Family Foundation ✧
(formerly KSM Foundation)
293 Eisenhower Pkwy., Ste. 150
Livingston, NJ   07039
Contact: Patti DelPriore

Established in 1983 in NJ.
Donors: Allen Bildner; Joan Bildner.
Foundation type: Independent foundation.
Financial data (yr. ended 6/30/05): Assets, $1,557,155 (M); expenditures, $2,630,582; qualifying distributions, $2,367,522; giving activities include $2,367,522 for 53 grants (high: $300,000; low: $2,000).
Purpose and activities: Giving primarily for higher education, the arts and Jewish organizations; funding also for health associations and human services.
Fields of interest: Performing arts centers; Performing arts, theater; Arts; Education; Health organizations, association; Human services; Children/youth, services; Foundations (community); Jewish federated giving programs; Jewish agencies & temples.
Type of support: Continuing support.
Limitations: Giving primarily in NJ and NY. No support for private foundations. No grants to individuals.
Application information:
   Initial approach: Letter
   Deadline(s): None
Officers: Allen Bildner, Pres.; Joan Bildner, V.P.
EIN: 222541254
Selected grants: The following grants were reported in 2005.
$250,000 to Dartmouth College, Hanover, NH.
$75,711 to Rowan University, Glassboro, NJ.
$57,090 to Richard Stockton College of New Jersey, Pomona, NJ.
$55,000 to Bloomfield College, Bloomfield, NJ.
$50,000 to Foundation for Jewish Camping, New York, NY.
$30,000 to Yale University, New Haven, CT.
$29,000 to Bergen Community College, Paramus, NJ.
$25,000 to Boston Symphony Orchestra, Boston, MA.
$20,000 to Paper Mill Playhouse, Millburn, NJ.
$16,000 to New Jersey Historical Society, Newark, NJ.

5134
The Paul and Irene Bogoni Operating Foundation ✧ ☆
P.O. Box 26
Midland Park, NJ   07432

Donors: Paul Bogoni; Irene Bogoni.
Foundation type: Operating foundation.
Financial data (yr. ended 12/31/04): Assets, $26,857 (M); gifts received, $640,000; expenditures, $648,143; qualifying distributions, $648,143; giving activities include $601,560 for 4 grants (high: $500,000; low: $25,000).
Fields of interest: Religion, research; Religion, formal/general education.
Limitations: Applications not accepted. Giving on a national and international basis, particularly in NY and Vicenza, Italy. No grants to individuals.
Application information: Contributes only to pre-selected organizations.
Officers and Directors: Paul Bogoni, Pres.; Irene Bogoni, V.P. and Secy.; Joan M. Fisher,* Treas.; Br. Edward Coughlin, OFM; Fr. Alcuin Coyle; Ira J. Kaltman.
EIN: 161635037

5135
Bohnert Foundation, Inc. ✧ ☆
P.O. Box 565
New Vernon, NJ   07976

Established in 2002 in NJ.
Donor: Robert Manzo.
Foundation type: Independent foundation.
Financial data (yr. ended 12/31/05): Assets, $1,032,740 (M); expenditures, $321,098; qualifying distributions, $316,848; giving activities include $316,848 for 11 grants (high: $192,267; low: $100).
Fields of interest: Education.
Limitations: Giving primarily in NJ.
Officers: Robert Manzo, Pres.; Cynthia Manzo, V.P.
Trustee: Ellen Jacob Wraith.
EIN: 542072845
Selected grants: The following grants were reported in 2004.
$14,400 to Peck School, Morristown, NJ.
$3,500 to Family Service of Morris County, Morristown, NJ.
$2,500 to Happiness Unlimited, Morristown, NJ.
$2,500 to Special Friends Foundation, Millington, NJ.
$1,000 to Monmouth University, West Long Branch, NJ.
$950 to Cancer Hope Network, Chester, NJ.
$100 to CaringBridge, Eagan, MN.

5136
Bolger Foundation ✧
79 Chestnut St.
Ridgewood, NJ   07450-2533

Established in 1964.
Donor: David F. Bolger.
Foundation type: Independent foundation.
Financial data (yr. ended 12/31/05): Assets, $1,855,101 (M); gifts received, $2,276,000; expenditures, $1,249,955; qualifying distributions, $1,227,293; giving activities include $1,226,403 for 28 grants (high: $360,000; low: $500).
Purpose and activities: Giving to mental health organizations, relief services, public charities, and a Presbyterian church.
Fields of interest: Elementary school/education; Hospitals (general); Protestant agencies & churches.
Type of support: General/operating support.
Limitations: Applications not accepted. Giving primarily in NJ; some funding also in IA. No grants to individuals.
Application information: Contributes only to pre-selected organizations.
Officers: David F. Bolger, Pres.; John G. Bolger, V.P.; Thomas Wells, V.P.
EIN: 237418090

5137
The Corella & Bertram F. Bonner Foundation, Inc. ▼ ✧
10 Mercer St.
Princeton, NJ   08540   (609) 924-6663
Contact: Wayne Meisel, Pres.
FAX: (609) 683-4626; E-mail: info@bonner.org
URL: http://www.bonner.org

Established in 1981 in NJ; reactivated in 1989.
Donors: Bertram F. Bonner†; Corella A. Bonner†.

Foundation type: Independent foundation.
Financial data (yr. ended 6/30/05): Assets, $107,479,136 (M); gifts received, $1,138,534; expenditures, $5,476,903; qualifying distributions, $4,130,437; giving activities include $3,680,888 for 163 grants (high: $122,200; low: $131; average: $5,000–$25,000), $12,000 for 4 grants to individuals (high: $3,000; low: $3,000), and $437,549 for foundation-administered programs.
Purpose and activities: Through sustained partnerships with colleges and congregations, the foundation seeks to improve the lives of individuals and communities by helping meet the basic needs of nutrition and educational opportunity. Support primarily for higher and other education, including educational programs for minorities; religious organizations, including those operating missionary programs, and welfare programs; social services and hunger programs; and hospitals, medical research, and ophthalmology.
Fields of interest: Higher education; Education; Food services; Human services; Religious federated giving programs; Christian agencies & churches; Religion; Minorities.
Type of support: Continuing support; Scholarship funds.
Limitations: Giving limited to domestic programs in the U.S. No grants for capital improvements, endowments, operating budgets, building funds, or renovations.
Publications: Informational brochure.
Application information: See foundation's Web site for applications and proposal guidelines. Application form required.

  Initial approach: Telephone
  Copies of proposal: 1
  Deadline(s): None
  Board meeting date(s): Mar., June, Sept., and Dec.

Officers and Trustees:* Kenneth F. Kunzman,* Chair.; Wayne Meisel,* Pres.; Robert Hackett, V.P.; William Bush; Carol Clark; Edward R. Farley, Jr.; Charles C. Goodfellow; Rev. Dr. John Kuykendall.
Number of staff: 2 full-time professional; 8 full-time support.
EIN: 222316452
Selected grants: The following grants were reported in 2005.
$122,200 to Morehouse College, Atlanta, GA. For Bonner Scholars Program, which provides four-year community service scholarships for students with demonstrated financial need and willing to engage in ongoing service work.
$116,507 to Wofford College, Spartanburg, SC. For Bonner Scholars Program, which provides four-year community service scholarships for students with demonstrated financial need and willing to engage in ongoing service work.
$113,534 to Waynesburg College, Waynesburg, PA. For Bonner Scholars Program, which provides four-year community service scholarships for students with demonstrated financial need and willing to engage in ongoing service work.
$111,900 to Carson-Newman College, Jefferson City, TN. For Bonner Scholars Program, which provides four-year community service scholarships for students with demonstrated financial need and willing to engage in ongoing service work.
$104,875 to Guilford College, Greensboro, NC. For Bonner Scholars Program, which provides four-year community service scholarships for students with demonstrated financial need and willing to engage in ongoing service work.

$52,875 to Maryville College, Maryville, TN. For Bonner Scholars Program, which provides four-year community service scholarships for students with demonstrated financial need and willing to engage in ongoing service work.
$25,000 to Church of the Holy Apostles, Soup Kitchen, New York, NY. For Crisis Ministry Program, community-based hunger relief program providing food for the hungry while encouraging congregations to build community relationships and strengthen their outreach programs.
$25,000 to Crisis Ministry of Princeton and Trenton, Princeton, NJ. For Crisis Ministry Program, community-based hunger relief program providing food for the hungry while encouraging congregations to build community relationships and strengthen their outreach programs.
$15,000 to Appalachian Community Development Association, Cincinnati, OH. For Crisis Ministry Program, community-based hunger relief program providing food for the hungry while encouraging congregations to build community relationships and strengthen their outreach programs.
$15,000 to Big Creek People in Action, Caretta, WV. For Crisis Ministry Program, community-based hunger relief program providing food for the hungry while encouraging congregations to build community relationships and strengthen their outreach programs.

5138
The Mary Owen Borden Memorial Foundation ✧
4 Blackpoint Horseshoe
Rumson, NJ   07760   (732) 741-4645
Contact: Quinn McKean, Exec. Dir.
FAX: (732) 741-2542; E-mail: qmckean@aol.com; URL: http://foundationcenter.org/grantmaker/borden/

Incorporated in 1934 in NJ.
Donors: Bertram H. Borden†; Victory Memorial Park Foundation.
Foundation type: Independent foundation.
Financial data (yr. ended 12/31/04): Assets, $14,737,173 (M); expenditures, $868,403; qualifying distributions, $777,533; giving activities include $774,200 for 59 grants (high: $50,000; low: $200; average: $5,000–$20,000).
Purpose and activities: The foundation's special focus will be on programs in New Jersey's Mercer and Monmouth counties, addressing the needs of economically disadvantaged youth and their families. This will include health, family planning, education, counseling, child care, substance abuse, and delinquency. Other areas of interest include affordable housing, conservation and the environment, and the arts.
Fields of interest: Arts; Education, early childhood education; Child development, education; Education; Environment, natural resources; Environment; Reproductive health, family planning; Health care; Substance abuse, services; Mental health/crisis services; Health organizations, association; Alcoholism; Crime/violence prevention, youth; Housing/shelter, development; Human services; Children/youth, services; Child development, services; Family services; Women, centers/services; Homeless, human services; Women; Economically disadvantaged; Homeless.
Type of support: General/operating support; Continuing support; Capital campaigns; Building/renovation; Equipment; Program development; Seed

money; Program-related investments/loans; Matching/challenge support.
Limitations: Giving limited to Monmouth and Mercer counties, NJ. No grants to individuals, or for scholarships, fellowships, or multi-year grants.
Publications: Application guidelines; Annual report (including application guidelines).
Application information: Maximum grant award is $25,000, unless trustees determine circumstances warrant larger award for program with a projected major impact in the foundation's area of interest. See Web site for application guidelines. Application form required.

  Initial approach: Write for application form; if request meets foundation guidelines and funds are available, application will be sent. Express or certified mail will not be accepted
  Copies of proposal: 1
  Deadline(s): Mar. 15 and Sept. 15
  Board meeting date(s): June and Dec.
  Final notification: 2-3 months

Officers and Trustees:* Linda B. McKean,* Pres.; Lois Broder,* V.P.; John C. Borden, Jr.,* Secy.; Quincy A.S. McKean III,* Exec. Dir.; Thomas A. Borden; Gordon N. Litwin; Jerri L. Morrison.
Number of staff: 1 part-time professional.
EIN: 136137137
Selected grants: The following grants were reported in 2003.
$50,000 to Council of New Jersey Grantmakers, Trenton, NJ.
$22,500 to Planned Parenthood of Central New Jersey, Shrewsbury, NJ.
$20,000 to Boys and Girls Club of Monmouth County, Asbury Park, NJ.
$20,000 to Princeton Friends School, Princeton, NJ.
$20,000 to Young Scholars Institute, Trenton, NJ.
$16,500 to Monmouth Housing Alliance, Red Bank, NJ.
$10,000 to Family Guidance Center, Princeton, NJ.
$8,000 to Brookdale Community College, Lincroft, NJ.
$7,500 to Big Brothers Big Sisters of Monmouth County, Eatontown, NJ.
$7,500 to Childrens Home Society of New Jersey, Trenton, NJ.

5139
The Nicholas J. and Anna K. Bouras Foundation, Inc. ✧
112 Beekman Rd.
Summit, NJ   07901

Established in 1998 in NJ.
Donors: Nicholas J. Bouras; United Steel Deck, Inc.
Foundation type: Independent foundation.
Financial data (yr. ended 12/31/05): Assets, $1,002,066 (M); gifts received, $2,000,000; expenditures, $1,436,058; qualifying distributions, $1,432,914; giving activities include $1,426,781 for 10 grants (high: $500,000; low: $5,000).
Purpose and activities: Giving primarily to Greek Orthodox agencies and churches, to human service organizations which support Greek people, and for higher education and the elderly.
Fields of interest: Arts; Higher education; Human services.
Limitations: Applications not accepted. Giving primarily in NJ, and New York, NY; some funding nationally. No grants to individuals.
Application information: Contributes only to pre-selected organizations.

Officers and Trustees:* Nicholas J. Bouras,* Pres.; William S. Crane,* Secy.-Treas.; Andrew J. Stamelman.

EIN: 223591803

Selected grants: The following grants were reported in 2003.

$341,961 to Greek Orthodox Archdiocese of North and South America, New York, NY.

$100,000 to Hellenic College/Holy Cross, Brookline, MA.

$78,900 to Holy Trinity Greek Church, Westfield, NJ.

$55,000 to Greek Orthodox Church, New York, NY.

$25,000 to Orthodox Christian Mission Center, Saint Augustine, FL.

$10,000 to Museum of Fine Arts, Boston, MA.

$8,000 to Overlook Hospital Foundation, Summit, NJ.

$5,000 to Boy Scouts of America, Greater New York Council, New York, NY.

$5,000 to YMCA of Summit, Summit, NJ.

$1,000 to Philadelphia International Foundation, Wilmore, KY. For medical relief fund.

5140
The Boye Foundation, Inc. ✧

575 Curran Pl.
Franklin Lakes, NJ 07417

Established in 2000 in NJ.

Donor: William E. Boye, Jr.†

Foundation type: Independent foundation.

Financial data (yr. ended 12/31/05): Assets, $26,243,694 (M); expenditures, $1,265,005; qualifying distributions, $1,255,826; giving activities include $1,253,000 for 41 grants (high: $125,000; low: $2,000).

Fields of interest: Arts; Human services.

Limitations: Applications not accepted. Giving primarily in NJ. No grants to individuals.

Application information: Contributes only to pre-selected organizations.

Officers: Nancy R. Boye, Pres.; Robert B. Boye, V.P.; Melinda L. Nolan-Boye, V.P.; Robert R. Boye, Secy.; William D. Boye, Treas.

EIN: 223769157

Selected grants: The following grants were reported in 2004.

$100,000 to YMCA, Wyckoff Family, Wyckoff, NJ.

$75,000 to Visiting Nurse Association of Somerset Hills, Bernardsville, NJ.

$50,000 to Christian Health Care Center, Wyckoff, NJ.

$50,000 to University of Arizona, Optical Sciences Center, Tucson, AZ.

$31,000 to Homeless Solutions, Morristown, NJ.

$30,000 to Soch Foundation, Manahawkin, NJ.

$25,000 to Habitat for Humanity of Paterson, Paterson, NJ.

$20,000 to University of Medicine and Dentistry, School of Osteopathic Medicine Alumni Association, Stratford, NJ.

$15,000 to Covenant House New Jersey, Newark, NJ.

$15,000 to Evas Kitchen and Sheltering Programs, Paterson, NJ.

5141
Brady Foundation ☆

P.O. Box 351
Gladstone, NJ 07934 (908) 439-9941
Contact: James C. Brady, Pres.

Incorporated in 1953 in NJ.

Donors: Helen M. Cutting†; Nicholas Brady.

Foundation type: Independent foundation.

Financial data (yr. ended 12/31/05): Assets, $6,341,332 (M); expenditures, $1,983,906; qualifying distributions, $1,795,450; giving activities include $1,795,450 for 31 grants (high: $1,500,000; low: $450), and $107,713 for foundation-administered programs.

Purpose and activities: Giving for arts, education, children and youth services, and religion.

Fields of interest: Museums; Arts; Education; Hospitals (general); Children/youth, services; Federated giving programs; Religion.

Type of support: General/operating support.

Limitations: Giving primarily in NJ.

Publications: Financial statement.

Application information: Application form not required.

Initial approach: Letter
Copies of proposal: 1
Deadline(s): None
Board meeting date(s): Annually
Final notification: 3-4 weeks

Officers and Trustees:* James C. Brady,* Pres. and Treas.; Elizabeth Brady Richards,* V.P.; Karen Z. Wisnosky, Secy.; Eliot Brady Stewart.

EIN: 136167209

Selected grants: The following grants were reported in 2003.

$50,000 to Nature Conservancy, Pottersville, NJ.

$50,000 to New Jersey Performing Arts Center, Newark, NJ.

$22,400 to Boys and Girls Clubs of Newark, Newark, NJ.

$20,000 to Boston University, School of Medicine, Boston, MA.

$20,000 to Skowhegan School of Painting and Sculpture, Skowhegan, ME.

$11,227 to Morristown-Beard School, Morristown, NJ.

$5,000 to National Museum of Racing, Saratoga Springs, NY.

$5,000 to New Jersey SEEDS (Scholars, Educators, Excellence, Dedication, Success), Newark, NJ.

$5,000 to YMCA of Somerset Valley, Somerville, NJ.

$1,000 to Somerset Art Association, Bedminster, NJ.

5142
Branfman Family Foundation

100 Springdale Rd., A-3 No. 180
Cherry Hill, NJ 08003

Established in 2002 in NJ.

Donors: Alan R. Branfman; Mrs. Alan R. Branfman.

Foundation type: Independent foundation.

Financial data (yr. ended 12/31/04): Assets, $14,668 (M); gifts received, $300,669; expenditures, $322,035; qualifying distributions, $319,230; giving activities include $319,230 for 2 grants (high: $214,230; low: $105,000).

Purpose and activities: Giving for basic research into Parkinson's Disease.

Fields of interest: Brain research; Nerve, muscle & bone research.

Limitations: Applications not accepted. Giving primarily in CA, IL, and MA.

Application information: Unsolicited requests for funds not accepted.

Trustees: Alan R. Branfman; Joyce Branfman; Michael Wolk.

EIN: 020628229

5143
The Bristol-Myers Squibb Patient Assistance Foundation, Inc. ✧

777 Scudders Mill Rd., M.S. P25-37
Plainsboro, NJ 08536 (800) 736-0003
Application address for individuals: c/o McKesson, P.O. Box 52112, Phoenix, AZ, 85072-2112

Established in 1999 in NJ as a company-sponsored operating foundation.

Donors: E.R. Squibb & Sons, Inc.; E.R. Squibb & Sons, L.L.C.; Bristol-Myers Squibb Co.

Foundation type: Operating foundation.

Financial data (yr. ended 12/31/05): Assets, $2,208,209 (M); gifts received, $591,331,609; expenditures, $591,331,609; qualifying distributions, $591,010,199; giving activities include $582,106,194 for grants to individuals.

Purpose and activities: The foundation provides prescription medicines to patients with financial hardships who have no private prescription drug insurance and are not eligible for prescription drug coverage through Medicaid or other government programs.

Fields of interest: Economically disadvantaged.

Type of support: Donated products.

Limitations: Giving on a national basis.

Application information: Application form required.

Initial approach: Telephone foundation for application form
Deadline(s): 1 month prior to need

Officers: John L. Damonti, Pres.; James Prazak, V.P.; Margaret Yonco-Haines, V.P.; Sandra Leung, Secy.; Harrison M. Bains, Jr., Treas.

Trustee: Freda Lewis-Hall.

EIN: 223622487

5144
Sophie & Arthur Brody Foundation ✧

c/o Lowenstein, Sandler, et al.
65 Livingston Ave.
Roseland, NJ 07068-1725

Established in NJ.

Donors: Arthur Brody; Sophie Brody.

Foundation type: Independent foundation.

Financial data (yr. ended 12/31/05): Assets, $10,547,593 (M); gifts received, $342,072; expenditures, $522,862; qualifying distributions, $478,084; giving activities include $475,839 for 42 grants (high: $286,005; low: $25).

Purpose and activities: Giving primarily for higher education as well as for medical research, a retirement community, children and youth services, and the arts.

Fields of interest: Museums (art); Performing arts; Elementary/secondary education; Higher education; Education; Health organizations, association; Medical research, institute; Human services; Children/youth, services; Jewish federated giving programs; Jewish agencies & temples.

Limitations: Applications not accepted. Giving primarily in CA; some funding nationally. No grants to individuals.

Application information: Contributes only to pre-selected organizations.

Officers: Arthur Brody, Pres.; Janice Brody, Secy.; Donald Brody, Treas.

EIN: 226097164

Selected grants: The following grants were reported in 2004.

$135,250 to University of California at San Diego Foundation, La Jolla, CA.

$30,000 to University of California at San Francisco Foundation, San Francisco, CA.

$21,947 to Jewish Community Federation, CA.

$15,000 to San Diego Opera Association, San Diego, CA.

$10,000 to Jewish Family and Childrens Services, Long Beach, CA.

$2,500 to Salvation Army, Redding, CA.

$2,500 to San Diego Museum of Art, San Diego, CA.

$610 to Head-Royce School, Oakland, CA.

$250 to Guiding Eyes for the Blind, Yorktown Heights, NY.

$100 to United Jewish Appeal, West Orange, NJ.

5145
Fred J. Brotherton Charitable Foundation
(formerly Fred J. Brotherton Foundation, Inc.)
1141 Greenwood Lake Tpke., Ste. C-6
Ringwood, NJ   07456   (973) 728-6100
Contact: Maribeth A. Ligus, Admin. Dir.
FAX: (973) 728-6060;
E-mail: brothertonfoundation@yahoo.com;
URL: http://foundationcenter.org/grantmaker/brotherton/

Established in 1995.
Donor: Fred J. Brotherton†.
Foundation type: Independent foundation.
Financial data (yr. ended 9/30/06): Assets, $14,137,868 (M); expenditures, $835,387; qualifying distributions, $651,754; giving activities include $629,763 for 26 grants (high: $50,000; low: $9,000; average: $10,000–$25,000).
Purpose and activities: The foundation's major areas of interest are: 1) Educational programs and/or institutions (primarily schools and colleges), with emphasis on, but not limited to, educational programs providing assistance to the needy or disabled; 2) Religion-based programs and/or institutions, with an emphasis on, but not limited to, providing assistance to the needy or disabled, or to benefit a local church in a capital program; 3) Historic Preservation programs and/or institutions (including "societies"); and 4) Medical and/or Scientific programs and/or their affiliated institutions.
Fields of interest: Historic preservation/historical societies; Education; Medical research; Human services; Children/youth, services; Science, research; Religion; Disabilities, people with; Economically disadvantaged.
Limitations: Giving primarily in NJ and NY.
Application information: When an organization receives an invitation to submit a full grant proposal, then the full grant proposal guidelines will be provided.
Initial approach: Letter of Inquiry (2 to 3 pages)
Deadline(s): LOI, none; June 15 and Dec. 15 for full grant proposals
Board meeting date(s): June 15 and Dec. 15
Final notification: Aug. (June 15 cycle); Feb. (Dec. 15 cycle)
Trustees: Wayne A. Brotherton; William P. Brotherton, M.D.
Board of Advisors: Nancy S. Bowser; Glen Brotherton; Gary Jannarone; J. Andrew Lark; Robert H. Neth, Jr.; William Rahal.
EIN: 650774706
Selected grants: The following grants were reported in 2004.

$55,000 to Ringwood Christian Fellowship, West Milford, NJ.

$50,000 to Foundation for Anesthesia Education and Research, Rochester, MN.

$50,000 to Society of the Four Arts, Palm Beach, FL.

$43,341 to Albert Einstein College of Medicine of Yeshiva University, Bronx, NY.

$42,000 to Moody Bible Institute of Chicago, Chicago, IL.

$35,000 to Centenary College, Hackettstown, NJ.

$30,000 to Ringwood Christian School, Ringwood, NJ.

$25,000 to Henry Morrison Flagler Museum, Palm Beach, FL.

$25,000 to Opus 118 Harlem School of Music, New York, NY.

$20,000 to Paper Mill Playhouse, Millburn, NJ.

5146
Emil Buehler Perpetual Trust ◇
c/o Boyle & Co., PA
113 Johnson Ave.
Hackensack, NJ   07601
Application address: c/o Grants Admin., 115 W. Century Rd., Paramus, NJ 07652

Established in 1984 in NJ.
Donor: Emil Buehler†.
Foundation type: Independent foundation.
Financial data (yr. ended 11/30/05): Assets, $57,313,700 (M); expenditures, $4,866,035; qualifying distributions, $2,010,302; giving activities include $1,231,222 for 8 grants (high: $415,450; low: $20,000).
Purpose and activities: Giving limited to the research, development, improvement, and promotion of aviation science and technology.
Fields of interest: Museums (science/technology); Space/aviation; Engineering/technology; Science.
Type of support: Building/renovation; Equipment; Internship funds; Research; Matching/challenge support.
Limitations: Giving primarily in southern FL, and NJ.
Publications: Informational brochure (including application guidelines).
Application information: Application form required.
Initial approach: Letter of inquiry
Copies of proposal: 1
Deadline(s): None
Board meeting date(s): Monthly
Trustees: Robert D. Boyle; John Payne; George Weaver.
EIN: 226395303

5147
Louise and Arde Bulova Fund, Inc. ◇
c/o Maurice Silberman
403 Blanketflower Ln.
West Windsor, NJ   08550

Established in 1987 in NY.
Donors: Louise B. Guilden†; Paul B. Guilden.
Foundation type: Independent foundation.
Financial data (yr. ended 9/30/05): Assets, $10,066,908 (M); expenditures, $553,595; qualifying distributions, $487,599; giving activities include $436,015 for 65 grants (high: $40,000; low: $100).
Fields of interest: Performing arts; Human services.
Type of support: General/operating support.

Limitations: Applications not accepted. Giving primarily in NY. No grants to individuals.
Application information: Contributes only to pre-selected organizations.
Officers and Directors:* Paul B. Guilden,* Chair. and Secy.; Stephen Becker,* Pres.; Phillip Li,* Treas.; Linda Ardigo; Sonya Cooper; Alisa Feinstein Swidler.
EIN: 133470502

5148
The Bunbury Company ◇
2 Railroad Pl.
Hopewell, NJ   08525   (609) 333-8800
Contact: Garth J. Allen, Grants Mgr.
FAX: (609) 333-8900; E-mail: bunburyco@aol.com;
URL: http://www.bunburycompany.org

Incorporated in 1952 in NY.
Donor: Dean Mathey†.
Foundation type: Independent foundation.
Financial data (yr. ended 12/31/05): Assets, $25,397,205 (M); expenditures, $1,490,880; qualifying distributions, $1,205,239; giving activities include $1,031,432 for 123 grants (high: $40,000; low: $500).
Purpose and activities: Grants primarily for disadvantaged youth and families, ecology and the natural world, education in the broadest sense, and promotion of the arts.
Fields of interest: Performing arts, music; Arts; Education; Environment; Children/youth, services; Family services.
Type of support: General/operating support; Capital campaigns; Endowments; Program development; Matching/challenge support.
Limitations: Giving limited to NJ, with emphasis on Mercer County, as well as Burlington, Camden, Hunterdon, Middlesex, Monmouth, Ocean, and Somerset counties. No grants to individuals, or for building funds or fellowships; no loans.
Publications: Application guidelines; Annual report; Grants list.
Application information: Please follow submission requirements as outlined in guidelines. Application guidelines and forms available on foundation Web site. Faxed or e-mailed applications are not accepted. Application form required.
Initial approach: 1-page letter (prior to submitting a formal application)
Copies of proposal: 7
Deadline(s): Mar. 3, May 5, and Aug. 4
Board meeting date(s): Jan., May, July, and Oct.
Final notification: 8-10 weeks after deadline
Officers and Directors:* Jamie Kyte Sapoch,* Pres.; Edward J. Zuccaro,* V.P.; Elizabeth Bankowski,* Secy.; Samuel W. Lambert III,* Treas.; William Bruett; William A. Gilbert; Stephan A. Morse; Robert M. Olmsted.
Number of staff: 1 full-time professional; 8 part-time professional.
EIN: 136066172
Selected grants: The following grants were reported in 2004.

$50,000 to Council of New Jersey Grantmakers, Trenton, NJ.

$50,000 to New Jersey Conservation Foundation, Far Hills, NJ.

$40,000 to Windham Foundation, Windham, NY.

$25,000 to Elijahs Promise, New Brunswick, NJ.

$25,000 to Historic Morven, Princeton, NJ.

$20,000 to Young Scholars Institute, Trenton, NJ.

$10,000 to Goodrich Memorial Library, Newport, VT.

$10,000 to Perkins Center for the Arts, Moorestown, NJ.

$8,300 to Rescue Mission of Trenton, Trenton, NJ.

$2,000 to Center for Woodlands Education, Corinth, VT.

5149
James E. and Diane W. Burke Foundation, Inc. ◈

(formerly James E. Burke Foundation)
c/o R.E. Ingram
410 George St.
New Brunswick, NJ 08901

Established in 1988 in NJ.
Donor: James E. Burke.
Foundation type: Independent foundation.
Financial data (yr. ended 11/30/05): Assets, $16,484,727 (M); expenditures, $2,474,172; qualifying distributions, $2,455,202; giving activities include $2,436,602 for 24 grants (high: $1,099,111; low: $100).
Purpose and activities: Giving primarily for programs that benefit children and youth; funding also for a cancer center and drug prevention programs.
Fields of interest: Arts; Education; Hospitals (general); Hospitals (specialty); Substance abuse, prevention; Human services; Children/youth, services.
Limitations: Applications not accepted. Giving primarily in NJ and NY. No grants to individuals.
Application information: Contributes only to pre-selected organizations.
Officers and Trustees:* James E. Burke,* Pres.; Richard E. Ingram,* Secy.-Treas.; Diane W. Burke; James C.E. Burke.
EIN: 521632596
Selected grants: The following grants were reported in 2005.
$3,000 to Bruce Museum, Greenwich, CT.
$2,000 to Coalition for a Drug-Free Greater Cincinnati, Cincinnati, OH.
$2,000 to Girls Choir of Harlem, New York, NY.
$2,000 to Hastings Center, Garrison, NY.
$2,000 to Matheny School and Hospital, Peapack, NJ.
$1,200 to Bay Street Theater Festival, Sag Harbor, NY.
$1,000 to Garrison Art Center, Garrison, NY.
$1,000 to Salvation Army.
$500 to Xeroderma Pigmentosum Society, Craryville, NY.
$100 to New England Kurn Hattin Homes, Westminster, VT.

5150
C Funding ◈

348 Jones Rd.
Englewood, NJ 07631
Contact: David Fishel, Tr.

Established in 2000 in NJ.
Donor: David Fishel.
Foundation type: Independent foundation.
Financial data (yr. ended 12/31/04): Assets, $1,885,465 (M); gifts received, $1,400,000; expenditures, $534,879; qualifying distributions, $534,879; giving activities include $534,879 for 36 + grants (high: $185,000).

Purpose and activities: Giving primarily to Jewish agencies, temples and schools.
Fields of interest: Education; Human services; Jewish agencies & temples.
Limitations: Applications not accepted. No grants to individuals.
Application information: Contributes only to pre-selected organizations.
Trustee: David Fishel.
EIN: 223769647

5151
Campbell Soup Foundation ◈

(formerly Campbell Soup Fund)
1 Campbell Pl.
Camden, NJ 08103-1799   (856) 342-4800
Contact: J.S. Buckley, Chair.
URL: http://www.campbellsoupcompany.com/community_center.asp

Incorporated in 1953 in NJ.
Donor: Campbell Soup Co.
Foundation type: Company-sponsored foundation.
Financial data (yr. ended 6/30/04): Assets, $19,799,887 (M); expenditures, $1,600,181; qualifying distributions, $1,457,438; giving activities include $1,299,170 for 102 grants (high: $304,000; low: $34), and $158,267 for 262 employee matching gifts.
Purpose and activities: The foundation supports organizations involved with arts and culture, health, nutrition, children and youth, community development, and minorities.
Fields of interest: Arts; Health care; Nutrition; Children/youth, services; Community development; Voluntarism promotion; Minorities.
Type of support: Program development; Seed money; Employee matching gifts; Employee-related scholarships; Matching/challenge support.
Limitations: Giving primarily in areas of company operations, with emphasis on Camden, NJ. No grants to individuals (except for employee-related scholarships), or for general operating support, continuing support, annual campaigns, emergency needs, debt reduction, land acquisition, endowment funds, equipment, or scholarships or fellowships; no loans.
Publications: Annual report (including application guidelines).
Application information: Application form required.
  Initial approach: Contact foundation for application form
  Copies of proposal: 1
  Deadline(s): None
  Board meeting date(s): As required
  Final notification: 4 to 8 weeks
Officers and Trustees:* J.S. Buckley,* Chair.; C. Del Sol,* Vice-Chair.; W. Milanese, Secy.; W.J. O'Shea, Treas.; G.S. Lord, Cont.; A.F. George; Jerry S. Buckley; S. Jander; K. Lewis; M. Linder.
Number of staff: 1 part-time professional; 1 part-time support.
EIN: 216019196
Selected grants: The following grants were reported in 2005.
$250,000 to United Way.
$115,000 to Saint Josephs Carpenter Society, Camden, NJ.
$40,160 to United Way of Norwalk and Wilton, Norwalk, CT.
$25,000 to Neighborhood Center, Camden, NJ.
$23,000 to Perkins Center for the Arts, Moorestown, NJ.

$16,280 to United Way of Berks County, Reading, PA.
$12,000 to American Red Cross.
$5,000 to Habitat for Humanity of Cache Valley, Logan, UT.
$5,000 to Housing Hope, Everett, WA.
$5,000 to Mann Center for the Performing Arts, Philadelphia, PA.

5152
Cantor Foundation ◈

c/o Nemiroff
611 Rte. 46
Hasbrouck Heights, NJ 07604

Established around 1995 in NY.
Donor: Richard Cantor.
Foundation type: Independent foundation.
Financial data (yr. ended 10/31/05): Assets, $5,981,956 (M); expenditures, $818,040; qualifying distributions, $817,750; giving activities include $817,750 for 34 grants (high: $200,000; low: $250).
Purpose and activities: Giving primarily for education and the arts and for children's mental health.
Fields of interest: Performing arts; Performing arts, opera; Arts; Education; Legal services; Human services; Jewish federated giving programs.
Limitations: Applications not accepted. Giving primarily in NY. No grants to individuals.
Application information: Contributes only to pre-selected organizations.
Officer: Richard Cantor, Pres.
EIN: 133745664

5153
Cape Branch Foundation ◈

P.O. Box 86
Oldwick, NJ 08858

Established in 1964 in NJ.
Foundation type: Independent foundation.
Financial data (yr. ended 12/31/04): Assets, $23,431,781 (M); expenditures, $2,169,783; qualifying distributions, $965,001; giving activities include $2,005,338 for 20 grants (high: $370,000; low: $1,000).
Purpose and activities: Support for secondary education, conservation, museums, and a university.
Fields of interest: Museums; Secondary school/education; Education; Environment, natural resources.
Type of support: General/operating support; Building/renovation; Land acquisition; Scholarship funds; Research.
Limitations: Giving primarily in NJ. No grants to individuals.
Application information: Application form not required.
  Initial approach: Brief letter
  Deadline(s): None
  Board meeting date(s): Annually
Directors: Gretchen W. Johnson; James L. Johnson.
Trustees: G.O. Danser; F.J. Hoenemeyer; S.G. Snow-Johnson.
EIN: 226054886
Selected grants: The following grants were reported in 2003.

$733,593 to Willow School, Gladstone, NJ. For general support.

$335,000 to Pingry School, Martinsville, NJ. For general support.

$175,000 to Edison Wetlands Association, Edison, NJ. For Raritan River Project.

$100,000 to Benjamin School, North Palm Beach, FL. For general support.

$75,000 to Institute for Democracy Studies, New York, NY. For general support.

$28,572 to Rutgers, The State University of New Jersey, Graduate School of Applied and Professional Psychology, New Brunswick, NJ. For general support.

$20,000 to Somerset Art Association, Bedminster, NJ. For general support.

$10,000 to Boomer Esiason Foundation, New York, NY. For general support.

$10,000 to Olana Partnership, Hudson, NY. For general support.

$5,000 to Batoto Yetu, New York, NY. For general support.

5154
Emil R. Capita Charitable Foundation ◇ ☆

c/o Denise Meroni
88 Passaic Valley Rd.
Montville, NJ 07045-9675

Established in 1984 in NJ.
Donor: Emil R. Capita.
Foundation type: Independent foundation.
Financial data (yr. ended 9/30/05): Assets, $1,324,316 (M); expenditures, $1,499,341; qualifying distributions, $1,466,606; giving activities include $1,466,606 for grants.
Purpose and activities: Grant recipients must be scientists affiliated with Columbia University engaged in hearing research.
Fields of interest: Higher education, university; Hospitals (general); Medical research, institute; Biological sciences.
Type of support: Research.
Limitations: Giving limited to NY.
Officers: Denise Meroni, Pres.; Robert Capita, V.P.; Paul Meroni, Secy.; Marianna Capita, Treas.
Trustees: Shyam Khanna; Bart S. Ziegler.
EIN: 222593954

5155
Carlson Family Foundation, Inc. ◇

240 W. Crescent Ave.
Allendale, NJ 07401
Contact: Michael A. Norton, Secy.

Established in 2000 in NJ.
Foundation type: Independent foundation.
Financial data (yr. ended 12/31/04): Assets, $17,320,499 (M); expenditures, $758,558; qualifying distributions, $628,228; giving activities include $500,430 for grants.
Fields of interest: Education; Environment, natural resources; Cancer research; Children/youth, services; Family services.
International interests: Peru; Spain.
Type of support: General/operating support; Capital campaigns; Matching/challenge support.
Limitations: Applications not accepted. Giving on a national and international basis.
Application information: Unsolicited requests for funds not accepted.

Officers: John A. Norton, Pres.; Michael A. Norton, Secy.; Thomas A. Norton, Treas.
Directors: Elaine Boylen; John Lont; James M. Norton; Lenore C. Norton; Lenore "Trilby" Norton; Mary T. Norton; Paul S. Norton.
EIN: 311678303

5156
Tina and Richard V. Carolan Foundation, Inc. ◇

88 E. Main St., Ste. 507
Mendham, NJ 07945

Established in 1990 in NJ.
Donors: Richard V. Carolan; Tina Carolan.
Foundation type: Independent foundation.
Financial data (yr. ended 11/30/05): Assets, $11,193,901 (M); expenditures, $590,727; qualifying distributions, $516,888; giving activities include $473,900 for 13 grants (high: $100,000; low: $5,000).
Purpose and activities: Giving primarily for the arts, education, and human services.
Fields of interest: Arts, cultural/ethnic awareness; Medical research, institute; Prostate cancer research; Children/youth, services; Community development; Biological sciences; Christian agencies & churches; Native Americans/American Indians.
Type of support: Emergency funds; Program development; Research; Matching/challenge support.
Limitations: Giving on a national basis with emphasis on CA. No grants to individuals.
Application information:
   Initial approach: Letter
   Deadline(s): None
Officers: Tina Carolan, Pres.; Kimberly M. Carolan-Faga, V.P. and Secy.; Richard C. Carolan, V.P. and Treas.
EIN: 223085237
Selected grants: The following grants were reported in 2004.
$175,000 to Memorial Sloan-Kettering Cancer Center, New York, NY.
$50,000 to Armenian Cultural Foundation, Glendale, CA.
$25,000 to Calvary Community Church, Westlake Village, CA.
$25,000 to Cleveland Clinic Foundation, Cleveland, OH.
$25,000 to Dream Center, Los Angeles, CA.

5157
The Cendant Charitable Foundation ◇

c/o Cendant Corp.
1 Campus Dr., M.S. 1C3-100
Parsippany, NJ 07054 (973) 428-9700
Contact: Lynn A. Feldman, V.P. and Secy.

Established in 2001 in DE.
Donors: Cendant Corp.; First American Real Estate Tax Svcs.
Foundation type: Company-sponsored foundation.
Financial data (yr. ended 12/31/04): Assets, $3,602,073 (M); gifts received, $1,000,000; expenditures, $1,142,560; qualifying distributions, $1,130,881; giving activities include $1,082,740 for 73 grants (high: $116,230; low: $150).

Purpose and activities: The foundation supports organizations involved with arts and culture, education, health, and human services.
Fields of interest: Museums (art); Arts; Education; Health care; Children/youth, services; Human services; Federated giving programs.
Limitations: Giving primarily in NJ and NY.
Application information: Application form required.
   Initial approach: Contact foundation for application form
   Deadline(s): None
Officers: Ray B. Shepard,* Chair. and Pres.; Lynn A. Feldman, V.P. and Secy.; Eric J. Bock, V.P.; Terence P. Conley, V.P.; David K. Kelley, V.P.; Richard S. Meisner, V.P.; Vincent Ventura, Treas.
EIN: 223758292
Selected grants: The following grants were reported in 2003.
$150,000 to Whitney Museum of American Art, New York, NY.
$25,000 to Breast Cancer Research Foundation, New York, NY.
$10,000 to Canine Assistants, Alpharetta, GA.
$10,000 to Homeless Solutions, Morristown, NJ.
$10,000 to Manhattan Theater Source, New York, NY.
$5,000 to Jersey Battered Womens Service, Morristown, NJ.
$5,000 to Metropolitan Opera, New York, NY.
$3,000 to Intrepid Museum Foundation, New York, NY.
$2,000 to Families of Spinal Muscular Atrophy (FSMA), Libertyville, IL.
$1,000 to Memorial Sloan-Kettering Cancer Center, New York, NY.

5158
Ceres Foundation ◇

c/o Merrill Lynch Trust Co.
P.O. Box 1525, MSC 06-03
Pennington, NJ 08534-1525
E-mail: ceresmd@comcast.net; Application address: 18606 Reliant Dr., Gaithersburg, MD 20879; URL: http://foundationcenter.org/grantmaker/ceres/

Established in 2000 in MD.
Donor: Donald B. Milder.
Foundation type: Independent foundation.
Financial data (yr. ended 11/30/04): Assets, $26,065,224 (M); expenditures, $1,358,440; qualifying distributions, $1,058,120; giving activities include $1,032,500 for 15 grants (high: $100,000; low: $2,500).
Purpose and activities: The foundation's mission is to provide the catalyst needed to mobilize human energies and talents that lie dormant. The foundation will focus on programs that aim to produce permanent improvements in peoples' lives by means of short-term interventions. The foundation will favor applicants who can best demonstrate a tangible, direct connection between the services their programs provide and the positive shifts that take place in individuals' lives.
Fields of interest: Secondary school/education; Higher education, university; Youth development; Family services; Women, centers/services.
Limitations: Giving restricted to the West Coast or the Eastern Seaboard. No support for foreign organizations, or to organizations that promote religious doctrines. No grants to individuals.

Application information: WG Common Grant Application Form required. Application form required.

Initial approach: Send application
Copies of proposal: 2
Deadline(s): None
Board meeting date(s): Nov.

Officers: Daniel C. Milder, Pres.; Terri L. Milder, Secy.; Donald B. Milder, C.F.O.

EIN: 912170962

5159
The Cesatam Foundation, Inc. ✧ ☆
P.O. Box 690
Morgan Dr.
New Vernon, NJ 07976

Established in 1999 in NJ.
Donors: Raul E. Cesan; Liliana C. Cesan.
Foundation type: Operating foundation.
Financial data (yr. ended 12/31/05): Assets, $8,032,768 (M); expenditures, $345,302; qualifying distributions, $329,350; giving activities include $326,600 for 8 grants (high: $230,000; low: $1,000).
Fields of interest: Higher education; Education.
Limitations: Applications not accepted. Giving primarily in MD and NJ. No grants to individuals.
Application information: Contributes only to pre-selected organizations.
Officers: Raul E. Cesan, Pres. and Treas.; Liliana C. Cesan, V.P.; Thomas C. Lauda, Secy.
EIN: 223692117

5160
Robert N. Chang Foundation ✧
P.O. Box 1525
Pennington, NJ 08534-1525
Contact: Allan Liu, Pres.
Application address: 737 Rustic Ln., Mountain View, CA 94040

Established in 2000 in CA.
Donor: Robert N. Chang†.
Foundation type: Independent foundation.
Financial data (yr. ended 8/31/05): Assets, $8,810,211 (M); expenditures, $604,837; qualifying distributions, $431,105; giving activities include $409,700 for 8 grants (high: $120,000; low: $10,000).
Fields of interest: Higher education; Education; Human services.
Limitations: Giving primarily in CA.
Application information:
Initial approach: Letter
Deadline(s): None
Officers: Allan Liu, Pres.; Stephen Liu, Secy.; Zhoe Yu "Frank" Tung, Treas.
EIN: 770550139

5161
Charles Foundation, Inc.
c/o Robert C. Rooke
668 Spring Valley Rd.
Morristown, NJ 07960

Established in 1994 in NJ.
Donors: Robert C. Rooke; Robert L. Rooke†.
Foundation type: Independent foundation.

Financial data (yr. ended 12/31/05): Assets, $35,093,274 (M); expenditures, $1,761,555; qualifying distributions, $1,699,112; giving activities include $1,696,579 for 39 grants (high: $265,000; low: $1,000).
Purpose and activities: Giving for education and health care.
Fields of interest: Higher education; Education; Hospitals (general).
Type of support: Capital campaigns; Building/renovation; Equipment; Land acquisition; Endowments; Scholarship funds.
Limitations: Applications not accepted. Giving primarily in NH and NJ. No grants to individuals.
Application information: Contributes only to pre-selected organizations.
Board meeting date(s): Varies
Officers and Directors:* Robert C. Rooke,* Pres. and Treas.; Natalie D. Rooke,* V.P.; Robert C. Rooke, Jr.,* Secy.
Number of staff: None.
EIN: 223292066
Selected grants: The following grants were reported in 2005.
$175,000 to Colby-Sawyer College, New London, NH.
$160,579 to Bucknell University, Lewisburg, PA.
$152,000 to Delbarton School, Morristown, NJ.
$150,000 to Proctor Academy, Andover, NH.
$106,000 to Morristown Memorial Health Foundation, Morristown, NJ.
$100,000 to Overlook Hospital Foundation, Summit, NJ.
$100,000 to Susquehanna University, Selinsgrove, PA.
$8,000 to Dartmouth College, Hanover, NH.
$5,000 to Babson College, Babson Park, MA.
$2,000 to Villa Walsh Academy, Morristown, NJ.

5162
The Chubb Foundation ✧
15 Mountain View Rd.
Warren, NJ 07059 (908) 903-3580
Contact: Roger Lehecka
Scholarship address: c/o R & R Consultants, P.O. Box 250861, Columbia University Station, New York, NY 10025

Established in 1953 in NJ.
Donor: Hendon Chubb†.
Foundation type: Independent foundation.
Financial data (yr. ended 12/31/05): Assets, $19,030,021 (M); expenditures, $1,075,878; qualifying distributions, $1,019,878; giving activities include $960,488 for 357 grants to individuals (high: $6,000; low: $500).
Purpose and activities: Support for employee-related academic scholarships for undergraduate studies.
Type of support: Employee-related scholarships.
Limitations: Giving limited to Chubb Group employees and dependents worldwide.
Application information: Application information available from all branches and affiliated companies. Application form required.
Deadline(s): Dec. 31 for return of formal application; Feb. 24 for financial statement; Mar. 1 for Secondary School Report
Board meeting date(s): Apr. or May
Officers and Trustees:* Percy Chubb III,* Chair.; Brice R. Gamber,* Pres.; Kathleen B. Travinsky, Secy.; Philip J. Sempier,* Treas.; William J. Falsone;

Elizabeth R. Lynn; William C. McGlynn; Gerald A. Navratil; Marjorie D. Raines; Marjorie L. Smith.
EIN: 226058567

5163
Civitas Foundation ✧
(formerly Quigley Family Foundation)
P.O. Box 1525
Pennington, NJ 08534-1525

Established in 1998 in NJ.
Donors: John G. Quigley; Quigley Family Partners, LP.
Foundation type: Operating foundation.
Financial data (yr. ended 12/31/05): Assets, $1,548,397 (M); gifts received, $24,415; expenditures, $592,644; qualifying distributions, $559,722; giving activities include $555,300 for grants.
Purpose and activities: Giving primarily for higher and other education.
Fields of interest: Elementary/secondary education; Higher education; Law school/education; Education; Health care.
Limitations: Applications not accepted. Giving primarily in Washington, DC, NJ, and NY. No grants to individuals.
Application information: Contributes only to pre-selected organizations.
Officers: John G. Quigley, Pres. and Treas.; Kathryn Quigley, V.P. and Secy.
EIN: 223594586
Selected grants: The following grants were reported in 2004.
$215,000 to Princeton University, Princeton, NJ. For general operating support.
$152,500 to Stanford University, Stanford, CA. 2 grants: $150,000 to School of Law (For general operating support), $2,500 (For general operating support).
$123,000 to Georgetown University, DC. For building fund.
$50,000 to FeldenEducational Foundation, Portland, OR. For general support.
$15,000 to Washington Jesuit Academy, DC. For general support.
$10,000 to Saint Benedicts Preparatory School, Newark, NJ. For general operating support.
$3,000 to Johns Hopkins University, Baltimore, MD. For general operating support.
$2,200 to Princeton Day School, Princeton, NJ. For general support.
$2,000 to New York University, New York, NY. For general support.

5164
David R. Clare & Margaret C. Clare Foundation ✧
c/o R.E. Ingram
410 George St.
New Brunswick, NJ 08901

Established in 1991 in FL.
Donor: David R. Clare.
Foundation type: Independent foundation.
Financial data (yr. ended 10/31/05): Assets, $12,533,993 (M); gifts received, $405,031; expenditures, $541,487; qualifying distributions, $536,062; giving activities include $534,000 for 33 grants (high: $50,000; low: $2,500).

Purpose and activities: Giving primarily to Roman Catholic churches, schools, and federated giving programs.

Fields of interest: Elementary/secondary education; Higher education; Education; Hospitals (general); Federated giving programs; Roman Catholic federated giving programs; Roman Catholic agencies & churches.

Type of support: Building/renovation; Conferences/seminars; Consulting services; Employee matching gifts; In-kind gifts; Matching/challenge support.

Limitations: Applications not accepted. Giving on a national basis. No grants to individuals.

Application information: Contributes only to pre-selected organizations.

Trustees: David R. Clare; Margaret C. Clare.

EIN: 650300004

Selected grants: The following grants were reported in 2004.

$50,000 to Massachusetts Institute of Technology, Cambridge, MA.

$35,000 to Lost Tree Village Charitable Foundation, North Palm Beach, FL.

$25,000 to Hope Rural School, Indiantown, FL.

$20,000 to Overlook Hospital, Summit, NJ.

$15,000 to United Way of Palm Beach County, Boynton Beach, FL.

$10,000 to Catholic Charities.

$10,000 to United Fund of Westfield, Westfield, NJ.

$5,000 to Colonial Williamsburg Foundation, Williamsburg, VA.

$5,000 to Norton Museum of Art, West Palm Beach, FL.

$500 to Middlesex County College Foundation, Edison, NJ.

5165
Codispoti Foundation ◇ ☆

(formerly The Burfeind-Codispoti Foundation, Inc.)
P.O. Box 79
Red Bank, NJ   07701
E-mail: ncodispoti@comcast.net

Established in 1996 in NJ.

Donor: Henry F. Burfeind.

Foundation type: Independent foundation.

Financial data (yr. ended 12/31/05): Assets, $14,262,241 (M); expenditures, $1,063,640; qualifying distributions, $552,412; giving activities include $552,412 for grants.

Purpose and activities: Giving for preservation of historical buildings, to secondary high schools, health related issues and public charities.

Limitations: Applications not accepted. Giving primarily in NJ. No grants to individuals.

Application information: Contributes only to pre-selected organizations.

Trustees: Joyce Codispoti; Nicholas Codispoti.

EIN: 223361120

Selected grants: The following grants were reported in 2003.

$40,000 to Colonial Williamsburg Foundation, Williamsburg, VA. 2 grants: $20,000 each

$25,000 to Riverview Medical Center, Red Bank, NJ.

$10,000 to Gift of Life, Madison, NJ.

$5,000 to Johns Hopkins Medical Institutions, Baltimore, MD.

$1,000 to Jasons Dreams for Kids, Red Bank, NJ.

$1,000 to Jersey Shore University Medical Center, Neptune, NJ.

$500 to Habitat for Humanity International, Americus, GA.

$200 to Saint Jude Childrens Research Hospital, Memphis, TN.

$100 to Memorial Sloan-Kettering Cancer Center, New York, NY.

5166
Karen B. Cohen Foundation, Inc. ◇

c/o Herrick Feinstein
40 Carnegie Ctr.
Princeton, NJ   08540

Donor: Karen B. Cohen.

Foundation type: Independent foundation.

Financial data (yr. ended 12/31/05): Assets, $5,869 (M); gifts received, $405,000; expenditures, $404,517; qualifying distributions, $404,449; giving activities include $404,380 for 34 grants (high: $116,000; low: $100).

Fields of interest: Museums (art); Arts; Libraries/library science; Education; Health organizations, association; Jewish agencies & temples.

Limitations: Applications not accepted. Giving primarily in New York, NY. No grants to individuals.

Application information: Contributes only to pre-selected organizations.

Officer: Karen B. Cohen, Pres.

EIN: 133833164

Selected grants: The following grants were reported in 2005.

$116,000 to Metropolitan Museum of Art, New York, NY.

$51,830 to Master Drawings Association, New York, NY.

$20,000 to Pierpont Morgan Library, New York, NY.

$10,000 to Katonah Museum of Art, Katonah, NY.

$10,000 to New York City Ballet, New York, NY.

$5,000 to School of American Ballet, New York, NY.

$1,500 to Actors Fund of America, New York, NY.

$1,500 to Frick Collection, New York, NY.

5167
Community Foundation of New Jersey ▼

35 Knox Hill Rd.
P.O. Box 338
Morristown, NJ   07963-0338   (973) 267-5533
Contact: Hans Dekker, C.E.O.
FAX: (973) 267-2903; *E-mail:* info@cfnj.org;
Additional Tel: (800) 659-5533; Additional E-mail:
hdekker@cfnj.org; URL: http://www.cfnj.org

Incorporated in 1979 in NJ.

Foundation type: Community foundation.

Financial data (yr. ended 12/31/05): Assets, $153,164,235 (M); gifts received, $33,285,003; expenditures, $14,966,926; giving activities include $13,119,158 for 2,438 grants (high: $700,000; low: $10).

Purpose and activities: The foundation promotes and champions the betterment of New Jersey and the quality of life for its citizens by helping donors to fulfill their philanthropic goals.

Fields of interest: Arts; Education; Environment; Youth development, services; Family services; Human services; Urban/community development; Community development; Leadership development; Public affairs; Economically disadvantaged.

Type of support: Program development; Scholarship funds; Program-related investments/loans.

Limitations: Giving on a national basis for the benefit of NJ. No grants to individuals (except for

scholarships), or for continuing support, emergency funds, or deficit financing.

Publications: Annual report; Informational brochure; Newsletter.

Application information: Visit foundation Web site for scholarship and NLI Fellow information. The foundation does not accept unsolicited grant proposals.

Board meeting date(s): 4 times per year

Officers and Trustees:* Stephen A. Tyler,* Chair.; Hans Dekker,* C.E.O. and Pres.; Faith A. Krueger, C.O.O.; Susan I. Soldivieri, C.P.A., C.F.O.; Scot R. Guempel,* Treas.; Thomas W. Berry; James H. Caulfield; Nancy G. Farese; Michael M. Horn; Julane W. Miller-Armbrister; Ingrid W. Reed; Peter S. Reinhart; Richard D. Urfer; Robert J. Vogel.

Number of staff: 6 full-time professional.

EIN: 222281783

Selected grants: The following grants were reported in 2005.

$700,000 to Seton Hall Preparatory School, West Orange, NJ.

$346,707 to United Way of King County, Seattle, WA.

$272,300 to Homeless Solutions, Morristown, NJ.

$267,747 to Baton Rouge Area Foundation, Baton Rouge, LA.

$206,000 to Diocese of Paterson, Paterson, NJ.

$185,828 to New Jersey SEEDS (Scholars, Educators, Excellence, Dedication, Success), Newark, NJ.

$180,100 to Plaid House, Morristown, NJ.

$160,757 to Seton Hall University, South Orange, NJ.

$156,612 to American Red Cross, National Headquarters, DC.

$147,325 to Visiting Nurse Association of Central Jersey, Red Bank, NJ.

5168
The Leon and Toby Cooperman Family Foundation ▼ ◇

(formerly Leon & Toby Cooperman Foundation)
c/o Gittelman & Co., PC
P.O. Box 2369
Clifton, NJ   07015-2369

Established in 1981.

Donors: Leon G. Cooperman; Toby F. Cooperman.

Foundation type: Independent foundation.

Financial data (yr. ended 1/31/06): Assets, $105,914,878 (M); gifts received, $19,061,467; expenditures, $5,488,468; qualifying distributions, $5,345,400; giving activities include $5,345,400 for 138 grants (high: $900,000; low: $20; average: $1,000–$10,000).

Purpose and activities: Giving primarily for Jewish organizations, education, and human services. Some funding also for arts and culture.

Fields of interest: Arts; Higher education; Hospitals (general); Health organizations, association; Human services; Jewish federated giving programs; Jewish agencies & temples.

Type of support: General/operating support.

Limitations: Applications not accepted. Giving primarily in NJ and New York, NY. No grants to individuals.

Application information: Currently contributes only to pre-selected organizations.

Trustees: Leon G. Cooperman; Michael S. Cooperman; Toby F. Cooperman; Wayne M. Cooperman.

EIN: 133102941

Selected grants: The following grants were reported in 2006.

$1,750,000 to Seton Hall University, South Orange, NJ. 3 grants: $500,000, $500,000, $750,000

$1,000,000 to Crohns and Colitis Foundation of America, New York, NY. 2 grants: $200,000, $800,000

$1,000,000 to International Rescue Committee, New York, NY. 2 grants: $100,000, $900,000

$530,000 to United Jewish Communities of MetroWest, Whippany, NJ. 2 grants: $380,000, $150,000

$25,000 to Columbia University, Business School, New York, NY.

5169

The Copper Beech Foundation ✧

244 Highland Ave.
Ridgewood, NJ 07450
Contact: Susan Snyder, Pres.
Application address: P.O. Box 597, Ridgewood, NJ 07450

Established in 2001 in NJ.

Donors: Charles Snyder; Sue Snyder.

Foundation type: Independent foundation.

Financial data (yr. ended 12/31/05): Assets, $8,315,706 (M); gifts received, $2,154,720; expenditures, $959,076; qualifying distributions, $907,431; giving activities include $904,600 for 21 grants (high: $130,000; low: $2,000).

Purpose and activities: The Copper Beech Foundation seeks to support deserving organizations which work to improve quality of life for all people through education, social services and the arts. Special consideration will be given to those projects that encourage recipients to work toward self-sufficiency.

Fields of interest: Human services.

Type of support: Continuing support.

Limitations: Applications not accepted. Giving primarily in NJ. No grants to individuals.

Application information: Contributes only to pre-selected organizations.

Officer and Trustees:* Susan Snyder,* Pres.; Ann Marie Snyder; Charles Snyder.

EIN: 223793126

Selected grants: The following grants were reported in 2004.

$150,000 to West Bergen Mental Health Center, Ridgewood, NJ.

$125,000 to Saint Pauls Community Development Corporation, Paterson, NJ.

$102,500 to Saint Philips Academy, Newark, NJ.

$100,000 to Pember Museum of Natural History, Granville, NY.

$75,000 to Childrens Aid and Family Services, Paramus, NJ.

$75,000 to Village School for Children, Waldwick, NJ.

$55,000 to Youth Consultation Service, Newark, NJ.

$50,000 to Animal Rescue League of Southern Rhode Island, Wakefield, RI.

$20,000 to Valley Hospital Foundation, Ridgewood, NJ.

$10,000 to Friends of the Hermitage, Ho Ho Kus, NJ.

5170

The Cowles Charitable Trust ✧

P.O. Box 219
Rumson, NJ 07760 (732) 936-9826
Contact: Gardner Cowles, III, Pres.

Trust established in 1948 in NY.

Donor: Gardner Cowles†.

Foundation type: Independent foundation.

Financial data (yr. ended 12/31/04): Assets, $22,323,584 (M); expenditures, $1,351,353; qualifying distributions, $1,164,256; giving activities include $1,088,000 for 155 grants (high: $40,000; low: $500).

Purpose and activities: Grants largely for arts and culture, including museums and the performing arts, education, including early childhood, higher, and secondary, hospitals and AIDS programs, social services, including family planning, and community funds.

Fields of interest: Visual arts; Museums; Performing arts; Performing arts, dance; Performing arts, theater; Performing arts, music; Historic preservation/historical societies; Arts; Education, research; Education, fund raising/fund distribution; Education, early childhood education; Child development, education; Secondary school/education; Higher education; Medical school/education; Adult/continuing education; Adult education—literacy, basic skills & GED; Libraries/library science; Education, reading; Education; Environment, natural resources; Environment; Animal welfare; Hospitals (general); Reproductive health, family planning; Health care; Substance abuse, services; Mental health/crisis services; Health organizations, association; Cancer; AIDS; Medical research, institute; Cancer research; AIDS research; Food services; Youth development, services; Human services; Children/youth, services; Child development, services; Family services; Residential/custodial care, hospices; Aging, centers/services; Women, centers/services; Minorities/immigrants, centers/services; Homeless, human services; Civil rights, race/intergroup relations; Civil rights; Federated giving programs; Population studies; Leadership development; General charitable giving; Aging; Disabilities, people with; Minorities; Women; Homeless.

Type of support: General/operating support; Continuing support; Annual campaigns; Capital campaigns; Building/renovation; Equipment; Endowments; Emergency funds; Program development; Professorships; Seed money; Matching/challenge support.

Limitations: Giving primarily along the Eastern Seaboard, with emphasis on FL and NY. No grants to individuals; no loans.

Publications: Application guidelines; Annual report.

Application information: Applications from any organizations submitted more than once every 12 months not considered. Telephone inquiries not considered. Proposals must be sent by USPS First Class or Priority Mail. Application form required.

Initial approach: Letter requesting proposal cover sheet and guidelines
Copies of proposal: 8
Deadline(s): Dec. 1, Mar. 1, June 1, and Sept. 1
Board meeting date(s): Jan., Apr., July, and Oct.
Final notification: Within 2 weeks of board meeting

Officers and Trustees:* Gardner Cowles III,* Pres.; Mary Croft, Secy.-Treas.; Charles Cowles; Jan Cowles; Lois Cowles Harrison; Lois Eleanor

Harrison; Kate Cowles Nichols; Virginia Cowles Schroth.

Number of staff: 1 full-time professional.

EIN: 136090295

5171

J. Fletcher Creamer Foundation ✧

101 E. Broadway
Hackensack, NJ 07601-6851 (201) 488-9800
Contact: J. Fletcher Creamer, Tr.

Established in 1980 in NJ.

Donor: J. Fletcher Creamer & Son, Inc.

Foundation type: Independent foundation.

Financial data (yr. ended 3/31/06): Assets, $666,294 (M); gifts received, $250,000; expenditures, $1,130,114; qualifying distributions, $1,126,117; giving activities include $1,126,117 for grants.

Purpose and activities: Giving primarily for higher education, and human services, and to hospitals, and Roman Catholic agencies and churches.

Fields of interest: Higher education; Hospitals (general); Human services; Roman Catholic agencies & churches.

Limitations: Giving primarily in NJ. No grants to individuals.

Application information: Application form not required.

Deadline(s): None

Trustees: Dale A. Creamer; J. Fletcher Creamer; J. Fletcher Creamer, Jr.

EIN: 222335557

Selected grants: The following grants were reported in 2005.

$25,000 to Jersey Shore University Medical Center, Neptune, NJ.

$3,000 to Bergen Community College Foundation, Paramus, NJ.

$2,500 to Dwight School Foundation, New York, NY.

$2,000 to American Diabetes Association, Somerset, NJ.

$1,500 to YMCA of Ridgewood, Ridgewood, NJ.

$1,000 to American Cancer Society, Hackensack, NJ.

$1,000 to Scleroderma Foundation of the Delaware Valley, Spring Lake, NJ.

$500 to Stevens Institute of Technology, Hoboken, NJ.

$350 to Holiday Express, Sea Bright, NJ.

$100 to Fox Chase Cancer Center, Philadelphia, PA.

5172

Edward L. Croman Foundation ✧

395 Pleasant Valley Way
West Orange, NJ 07052 (973) 736-4500
Contact: Edward L. Croman, Tr.

Established in 1989 in NJ.

Donor: Edward L. Croman.

Foundation type: Independent foundation.

Financial data (yr. ended 12/31/04): Assets, $1,356,228 (M); gifts received, $450,000; expenditures, $579,726; qualifying distributions, $579,540; giving activities include $579,540 for 18 grants (high: $316,000; low: $90).

Purpose and activities: Giving primarily to Jewish organizations, schools, and temples.

Fields of interest: Elementary/secondary education; Higher education; Jewish federated giving programs; Jewish agencies & temples.

Limitations: Giving primarily in NJ and NY. No grants to individuals.
Application information:
Initial approach: Proposal
Deadline(s): None
Trustees: Edward L. Croman; Rita Nadler; Edward M. Schotz.
EIN: 223044476

5173
Cyh Foundation ◇ ☆
P.O. Box 517
Lakewood, NJ 08701

Established in 2003 in NJ.
Foundation type: Independent foundation.
Financial data (yr. ended 12/31/05): Assets, $718,482 (M); expenditures, $413,668; qualifying distributions, $413,358; giving activities include $413,358 for 92 grants (high: $360,000; low: $18).
Fields of interest: Jewish agencies & temples.
Trustee: Jacob Halper.
EIN: 593769177

5174
D & K Charitable Foundation ◇ ☆
485 Sylvan Ave.
Englewood Cliffs, NJ 07632

Established in 1997 in NJ.
Donors: Daniel Borislow; George P. Farley.
Foundation type: Operating foundation.
Financial data (yr. ended 12/31/05): Assets, $2,063,908 (M); expenditures, $1,530,454; qualifying distributions, $1,348,506; giving activities include $496,995 for grants.
Purpose and activities: Giving primarily to a performing arts center, as well as to a college.
Fields of interest: Performing arts; Health care; Health organizations, association; Jewish agencies & temples.
Limitations: Applications not accepted. Giving primarily in New York, NY, and Philadelphia, PA. No grants to individuals.
Application information: Contributes only to pre-selected organizations.
Officers: Daniel Borislow, C.E.O. and Pres.; George P. Farley, Secy. and C.F.O.
Director: Michele Borislow.
EIN: 232928907

5175
D'Angelo Foundation ◇
731 Alexander Rd.
Princeton Plz., Bldg. 2
Princeton, NJ 08540

Established in 1997 in NY and DE.
Donors: Peter P. D'Angelo; Margaret A. D'Angelo.
Foundation type: Independent foundation.
Financial data (yr. ended 12/31/04): Assets, $7,276,002 (M); gifts received, $1,000,000; expenditures, $592,682; qualifying distributions, $520,000; giving activities include $520,000 for 14 grants (high: $175,000; low: $5,000).
Purpose and activities: Giving primarily for human services, health care, children and youth services, and to a Roman Catholic church.
Fields of interest: Higher education; Health care; Food services; Housing/shelter, development;

Human services; Children/youth, services; Roman Catholic agencies & churches.
Limitations: Applications not accepted. Giving primarily in New York, NY. No grants to individuals.
Application information: Contributes only to pre-selected organizations.
Officers and Directors:* Peter P. D'Angelo,* Pres.; Margaret A. D'Angelo,* Secy.-Treas.
EIN: 223555150

5176
The Dagish Charitable Foundation Trust ◇
c/o X-L Plastics
220 Clifton Blvd.
Clifton, NJ 07011-3645

Established in 1999 in NY.
Donors: Arnold Fischman; Melvin Fischman.
Foundation type: Independent foundation.
Financial data (yr. ended 12/31/05): Assets, $380,715 (M); expenditures, $959,487; qualifying distributions, $959,487; giving activities include $959,400 for 45 grants (high: $100,000; low: $1,400; average: $8,500–$25,000).
Purpose and activities: Giving primarily to Jewish organizations.
Fields of interest: Education; Jewish agencies & temples.
Type of support: General/operating support.
Application information:
Initial approach: Typed letter stating reason and intended use
Trustees: Arnold Fischman; Melvin Fischman.
EIN: 116509168
Selected grants: The following grants were reported in 2003.
$50,000 to Yeshiva Beth Hillel. 3 grants: $10,000, $30,000, $10,000
$40,000 to Yeshiva Toldos Hillel. 2 grants: $20,000 each
$28,500 to Yeshiva of Kasho, Bedford Hills, NY. 2 grants: $20,000, $8,500
$20,000 to Yeshiva Beth Hillel of Krasna, Brooklyn, NY. 2 grants: $10,000 each
$10,000 to Mosdos Nadvorna.

5177
Danellie Foundation
P.O. Box 375/376
Marlton, NJ 08053 (856) 810-8320
Contact: Daniel L. Cheney, Pres.
E-mail: danelliefoundation@verizon.net

Established in 1988 in NJ.
Donor: Daniel L. Cheney.
Foundation type: Independent foundation.
Financial data (yr. ended 12/31/05): Assets, $15,099,596 (M); expenditures, $2,409,679; qualifying distributions, $2,334,259; giving activities include $2,333,924 for 133 grants (high: $180,000; low: $1,500; average: $5,000–$20,000).
Purpose and activities: Primary areas of interest include services for the disadvantaged, including housing and social services.
Fields of interest: Education; AIDS; Employment, training; Housing/shelter, development; Human services; Children/youth, services; Residential/custodial care, hospices; Homeless, human services; International relief; Community

development; Christian agencies & churches; Economically disadvantaged; Homeless.
Type of support: Scholarship funds; General/operating support; Continuing support; Capital campaigns; Building/renovation; Program development; Sponsorships.
Limitations: Giving primarily in southern NJ (including Mercer and Monmouth counties), the Delaware Valley area, and Baltimore, MD. No support for political organizations or professional sports, libraries or museums. No grants to individuals, or for endowments or radio and television.
Publications: Application guidelines.
Application information: Contact foundation for application guidelines. Application form required.
Initial approach: Proposal
Copies of proposal: 2
Deadline(s): 3 weeks prior to meetings
Board meeting date(s): Varies
Final notification: 2 weeks after board meeting
Officers and Trustees:* Daniel L. Cheney,* Pres.; Eleanora L. Cheney,* Secy.-Treas.; Nancy L. Dinsmore,* Exec. Dir.; Julia Carleton Barlow; Richard D. Dinsmore; Keith A. Walter; Patricia E. Walter.
Number of staff: 1 part-time professional.
EIN: 222935245

5178
The Dealessandro Foundation ◇ ☆
77-55 Schanck Rd., Ste. B-15
Freehold, NJ 07728

Established in 2003 in NJ.
Donor: Joseph P. Dealessandro†.
Foundation type: Independent foundation.
Financial data (yr. ended 12/31/05): Assets, $16,501,135 (M); gifts received, $250,000; expenditures, $834,225; qualifying distributions, $547,000; giving activities include $547,000 for grants.
Fields of interest: Performing arts, orchestra (symphony); Roman Catholic federated giving programs; Roman Catholic agencies & churches.
Limitations: Applications not accepted. Giving primarily in NJ. No grants to individuals.
Application information: Contributes only to pre-selected organizations.
Officer: Frank J. Dealessandro, Chair.
Trustees: Barbara M. Dealessandro; Joseph P. Dealessandro; Joan F. Orlick.
EIN: 566594082

5179
Marion & Silfred Dephillips Foundation ◇ ☆
c/o David F. Bolger
79 Chestnut St.
Ridgewood, NJ 07450

Established in 2000 in NJ.
Donor: Helene Arlene DePhillips Trust.
Foundation type: Independent foundation.
Financial data (yr. ended 12/31/05): Assets, $1,071,575 (M); gifts received, $1,632,931; expenditures, $687,070; qualifying distributions, $686,610; giving activities include $686,150 for 16 grants (high: $100,000; low: $600).

Fields of interest: Hospitals (general); Mental health/crisis services; Human services; Protestant agencies & churches.
Limitations: Applications not accepted. Giving primarily in Ridgewood, NJ. No grants to individuals.
Application information: Contributes only to pre-selected organizations.
Officers: David F. Bolger, Pres.; John Kandravy, V.P.; Thomas M. Wells, V.P.
EIN: 223747579

5180
Robert and Joan Dircks Foundation, Inc. ◇
(formerly Joan M. Dircks Foundation, Inc.)
P.O. Box 6
Mountain Lakes, NJ 07046
Contact: Joan Dircks Walsh, Pres.
E-mail: grants@dircksfoundation.org; PA tel.: (610) 925-3713; MA tel.: (978) 449-0072; URL: http://www.dircksfoundation.org

Established in 1991 in NJ.
Donor: Robert J. Dircks†.
Foundation type: Independent foundation.
Financial data (yr. ended 12/31/04): Assets, $10,542,074 (M); expenditures, $509,181; qualifying distributions, $470,694; giving activities include $434,400 for 51 grants (high: $20,000; low: $1,000; average: $1,000–$15,000).
Purpose and activities: The mission is to support small non-profit organizations that enrich and improve the quality of life for individuals primarily located in NJ. The focus is to encourage innovative programs and projects that benefit and improve the lives of children and individuals who are physically, mentally, or economically disadvantaged.
Fields of interest: Education; Health care; Children/youth, services.
Type of support: Management development/capacity building; Program development; Publication; Curriculum development; Scholarship funds; Research; Technical assistance; Program evaluation.
Limitations: Giving primarily in NJ. No support for environmental or cultural organizations, or for programs of national or international scope. No grants to individuals, or for capital or annual campaigns, endowments, operating budgets, deficit/debt reduction, or for housing projects; no loans.
Publications: Application guidelines.
Application information: Application form available on foundation Web site. Application form required.
Initial approach: Online
Copies of proposal: 1
Deadline(s): None
Board meeting date(s): 6 times per year
Final notification: By mail or via Web site
Officers and Trustees:* Joan D. Walsh,* Pres.; Carolyn D. Van Riper,* Secy.; Thomas C. Dircks,* Treas.; Robert E. Dircks; William C. Dircks.
Number of staff: 2 part-time professional.
EIN: 223135737
Selected grants: The following grants were reported in 2004.
$20,000 to Cancer Hope Network, Chester, NJ. For salary of Patient Service Coordinator.
$10,000 to Oasis Haven for Women and Children, Paterson, NJ. For food program.
$10,000 to Quest Therapeutic Services, West Chester, PA. For clinical affiliation and staff training program for pediatric therapy and hippotherapy.

$5,000 to Winston School, Short Hills, NJ. For purchase of computers.

5181
Geraldine R. Dodge Foundation, Inc. ▼
163 Madison Ave., 6th Fl.
P.O. Box 1239
Morristown, NJ 07962-1239 (973) 540-8442
Contact: David Grant, C.E.O. and Pres.
FAX: (973) 540-1211; E-mail: info@grdodge.org; URL: http://www.grdodge.org

Incorporated in 1974 in NJ.
Donor: Geraldine R. Dodge†.
Foundation type: Independent foundation.
Financial data (yr. ended 12/31/04): Assets, $295,393,959 (M); gifts received, $812,712; expenditures, $25,288,384; qualifying distributions, $23,775,173; giving activities include $18,537,375 for 499 grants (high: $500,000; low: $500; average: $30,000–$50,000); $438,310 for grants to individuals; $28,862 for 118 employee matching gifts, and $2,021,309 for 10 foundation-administered programs.
Purpose and activities: The mission of the foundation is to support and encourage those educational, cultural, social and environmental values that contribute to making our society more humane and our world more livable.
Fields of interest: Media/communications; Visual arts; Museums; Performing arts; Performing arts, dance; Performing arts, theater; Performing arts, music; Humanities; Language/linguistics; Literature; Arts; Elementary school/education; Secondary school/education; Education; Environment, natural resources; Environment; Animal welfare; Animals/wildlife, preservation/protection; Leadership development.
Type of support: Program-related investments/loans; General/operating support; Continuing support; Management development/capacity building; Program development; Conferences/seminars; Publication; Seed money; Curriculum development; Research; Technical assistance; Program evaluation; Employee matching gifts; Grants to individuals; Matching/challenge support.
Limitations: Giving primarily in NJ, with support for the arts and local humane groups limited to NJ, and support for other local projects limited to the Morristown-Madison area; some giving to national organizations. No support for religious, higher education, health, or conduit organizations. No grants for capital projects, equipment purchases, indirect costs, endowment funds, deficit financing, or scholarships.
Publications: Application guidelines; Annual report (including application guidelines); Grants list.
Application information: Letters of inquiry can be sent via standard mail, submitted online, or E-mailed to the foundation. Proposal limited to 6 pages plus attachments specified (two-sided copying preferred). Binders not accepted; accepts the NYRAG Common Application Form. Proposal via fax or E-mail not considered. Application form required.
Initial approach: Letter of inquiry (one page)
Copies of proposal: 2
Deadline(s): Jan. 20 for Welfare of Animals; Mar. 1 for Arts; May 1 for Morris County; June 1 for Environment; and Nov. 1 for Education

Board meeting date(s): mid-Mar.- Precollegiate Educ.; mid-June- Arts/Animal Welfare; mid-Sept.- Morris County; mid-Nov.- Envir.
Final notification: End of months in which board meets
Officers and Trustees:* Robert LeBuhn,* Chair.; Christopher J. Elliman,* Vice-Chair.; David Grant, C.E.O. and Pres.; Cynthia Sherwood Evans, C.F.O.; Preston D. Pinkett III, Treas.; J. Lloyd Huck, Tr. Emeritus; Nancy D. Lindsay, Tr. Emeritus; Paul J. O'Donnell, Tr. Emeritus; Walter J. Neppl, Tr. Emeritus; Brenda S. Davis; Barbara Knowles Debs; Elizabeth A. Duffy; Betsy S. Michel; Clement A. Price, Ph.D.; James W. Stevens.
Number of staff: 9 full-time professional; 1 part-time professional; 10 full-time support; 2 part-time support.
EIN: 237406010
Selected grants: The following grants were reported in 2005.
$250,000 to Association of New Jersey Environmental Commissions, Mendham, NJ. For Smart Growth Planning Grants to NJ municipalities.
$200,000 to New Jersey Symphony Orchestra, Newark, NJ. For general operating support.
$200,000 to Newark Museum, Newark, NJ. For general operating support of exhibitions and education initiatives.
$175,000 to Eastern Environmental Law Center, Newark, NJ. For general operating support.
$175,000 to George Street Playhouse, New Brunswick, NJ. For general operating support.
$150,000 to Communities in Schools of New Jersey, Newark, NJ. For programs.
$150,000 to Johns Hopkins University, Baltimore, MD. For participation of Newark Middle School students in Center for Talented Youth summer program.
$50,000 to Living Classrooms Foundation, Baltimore, MD. For environmental programs serving Paterson, NJ, public school students.
$40,000 to Pennsylvania State University, University Park, PA. For general operating support.
$36,700 to Young Audiences of New Jersey, Princeton, NJ. For Creative Beginnings program for Head Start teachers.

5182
The Doherty Foundation ◇ ☆
41 Post Rd.
Bernardsville, NJ 07924-1512

Established in 1994 in DE.
Donor: Robert K. Doherty.
Foundation type: Independent foundation.
Financial data (yr. ended 12/31/05): Assets, $262,248 (M); gifts received, $150,000; expenditures, $386,519; qualifying distributions, $383,950; giving activities include $383,950 for grants.
Purpose and activities: Giving primarily for higher education.
Fields of interest: Performing arts, education; Higher education; Education.
Limitations: Applications not accepted. No grants to individuals.
Application information: Contributes only to pre-selected organizations.
Officers: Robert K. Doherty, Pres.; Susan O'Connell Doherty, V.P.

Director: Jack D. Gunther, Jr.
EIN: 223309349

5183

The Dow Foundation ✧ ☆

2719 Main St.
Lawrenceville, NJ 08648

Foundation type: Independent foundation.
Financial data (yr. ended 11/30/05): Assets, $21,998,375 (M); gifts received, $17,995,691; expenditures, $1,062,341; qualifying distributions, $1,051,086; giving activities include $1,036,118 for 24 grants (high: $490,000; low: $150).
Fields of interest: Elementary/secondary education; Environment; Community development.
Limitations: Applications not accepted. Giving primarily in NY. No grants for indivduals.
Application information: Contributes only to pre-selected organizations.
Trustees: Christina Seix Dow; Robert S. Dow.
EIN: 136877648

5184

Dow Jones Newspaper Fund, Inc. ✧

P.O. Box 300
Princeton, NJ 08543-0300 (609) 452-2820
Contact: Richard S. Holden, Exec. Dir.
FAX: (609) 520-5804;
E-mail: newsfund@wsj.dowjones.com; Street address: 4300 Rte. 1 N., South Brunswick, NJ 08852; URL: http://djnewspaperfund.dowjones.com

Incorporated in 1958 in DE.
Donors: Dow Jones Foundation; and other news companies.
Foundation type: Independent foundation.
Financial data (yr. ended 12/31/03): Assets, $492,975 (M); gifts received, $533,458; expenditures, $551,507; qualifying distributions, $551,097; giving activities include $232,200 for 110 grants (high: $27,000; low: $500), and $243,214 for 13 grants to individuals (high: $38,245; low: $167).
Purpose and activities: Programs include editing internships (up to 100) for upper-level and graduate college students; reporting internships (up to 10) for sophomore and junior minority college students; grants to colleges and universities supporting workshops for high school minority students; grants to colleges and universities operating workshops for high school journalism teachers and publications advisers; selection of the National High School Journalism Teacher of the Year; and journalism career guides.
Fields of interest: Media/communications; Minorities.
Type of support: Fellowships; Internship funds.
Limitations: Giving on a national basis. No grants for building or endowment funds, research, publications, or conferences and seminars; no loans.
Publications: Application guidelines; Annual report; Grants list.
Application information: Guidelines available for programs listed in the fund's annual report and on foundation Web site. Unsolicited proposals are welcome as long as they directly relate to students' pursuit of careers in journalism. Application form required.

Initial approach: Letter and telephone
Copies of proposal: 1
Deadline(s): Submit proposal preferably in Sept.; deadline Oct. 1. See Web site for various program deadlines
Board meeting date(s): May and Nov.
Final notification: Dec. 1
Officers and Directors:* Barney Colame, Pres.; Barbara Martinez,* Secy.; Thomas W. McGuirl,* Treas.; Richard S. Holden,* Exec. Dir.; Vickee Adams; Thomas E. Engleman; Peter Kann; Melanie Kirkpatrick; Laurence J. O'Donnell; Reginald Owens; Robin Gibson Sawyer; Russell G. Todd.
Number of staff: 3 full-time professional; 1 full-time support; 1 part-time support.
EIN: 136021439

5185

Drapkin Family Charitable Foundation ✧

Rio Vista Dr.
P.O. Box 1040
Alpine, NJ 07620
NY tel.: (212) 755-0070

Established in 1994 in NJ.
Donor: Donald Drapkin.
Foundation type: Independent foundation.
Financial data (yr. ended 12/31/05): Assets, $1,777,059 (M); expenditures, $671,500; qualifying distributions, $669,500; giving activities include $669,500 for 22 grants (high: $100,000; low: $5,000; average: $10,000–$25,000).
Fields of interest: Performing arts; Higher education; Jewish agencies & temples.
Limitations: Giving primarily in New York, NY.
Application information: Application form not required.
Initial approach: Letter
Deadline(s): None
Officer: Donald Drapkin, Pres.
EIN: 223326491
Selected grants: The following grants were reported in 2005.
$100,000 to Brandeis University, Waltham, MA.
$100,000 to Princeton University, Princeton, NJ.
$66,667 to Dwight-Englewood School, Englewood, NJ.
$65,000 to Vivian Beaumont Theater, New York, NY.
$50,000 to Elisabeth Morrow School, Englewood, NJ.
$33,333 to Bergen Performing Arts Center, Englewood, NJ.
$25,000 to University of Pennsylvania, Philadelphia, PA.
$5,000 to Center for Jewish History, New York, NY.

5186

Charles Edison Fund ✧

1 Riverfront Plz., 4th Fl.
Newark, NJ 07102-5401 (973) 648-0500
Contact: John P. Keegan, Pres.

Incorporated in 1948 in DE.
Donors: Charles Edison†; and others.
Foundation type: Independent foundation.
Financial data (yr. ended 12/31/05): Assets, $31,799,920 (M); gifts received, $10,706; expenditures, $3,108,606; qualifying distributions, $2,675,183; giving activities include $1,187,234 for 22 grants (high: $916,250; low: $250).

Purpose and activities: Grants largely for historic preservation, with emphasis on the homes of Thomas Alva Edison, and for education, medical research, and hospitals. Support also for foundation-sponsored exhibits at over 80 museums throughout the U.S., for science education teaching kits in over 60,000 classrooms, and for cassette re-recording of antique phonograph records for schools and museums.
Fields of interest: Museums; Historic preservation/historical societies; Arts; Education; Hospitals (general); Medical research; Engineering/technology; Science.
Type of support: General/operating support; Continuing support; Equipment; Program development; Seed money; Research.
Limitations: Giving on a national basis. No grants to individuals; no loans.
Publications: Informational brochure (including application guidelines).
Application information: Application form not required.
Initial approach: Letter or proposal
Copies of proposal: 1
Deadline(s): None
Board meeting date(s): Mar., June, Sept., and Dec.
Officers and Trustees:* John P. Keegan,* Pres. and Treas.; Robert E. Murray,* V.P.; Alberta Ench, Secy.; James E. Howe; John N. Schullinger, M.D.
Number of staff: 7 full-time professional.
EIN: 221514861
Selected grants: The following grants were reported in 2005.
$24,158 to Princeton Academy of the Sacred Heart, Princeton, NJ.
$23,475 to Saint Francis Cathedral School, Santa Fe, NM.
$20,000 to College of Saint Elizabeth, Morristown, NJ.
$20,000 to New Jersey Historical Society, Newark, NJ.
$10,000 to Thomas G. Labrecque Foundation, New York, NY.
$8,000 to Newark Boys Chorus School, Newark, NJ.
$3,400 to Council on Foundations, DC.
$2,500 to National Trust for Historic Preservation, DC.

5187

Mitzi & Warren Eisenberg Family Foundation, Inc. ▼ ✧

c/o Rockdale Capital
650 Liberty Ave.
Union, NJ 07083

Established in 1992 in NJ.
Donors: Warren Eisenberg; Bed Bath & Beyond, Inc.
Foundation type: Independent foundation.
Financial data (yr. ended 6/30/05): Assets, $95,248,127 (M); expenditures, $4,336,415; qualifying distributions, $4,106,963; giving activities include $4,097,999 for 174 grants (high: $1,200,000; low: $24; average: $1,000–$50,000).
Purpose and activities: Giving primarily to Jewish organizations and temples; giving also for the arts, medical research, and human services.
Fields of interest: Arts; Environment; Medical research, institute; Human services; Jewish agencies & temples.
Limitations: Applications not accepted. Giving primarily in NJ and NY. No grants to individuals.

Application information: Contributes only to pre-selected organizations.
Officers: Warren Eisenberg, Pres.; Maxine Eisenberg, Secy.; Ronald Eisenberg, Treas.
EIN: 521798583
Selected grants: The following grants were reported in 2004.
$800,000 to New Museum of Contemporary Art, New York, NY. 2 grants: $400,000 each (For general support).
$500,000 to I. H. Schwartz Childrens Rehabilitation Center, New Bedford, MA. For general support.
$300,000 to Jewish Federation of Central New Jersey, Scotch Plains, NJ. For general support.
$200,000 to Friends of the Israel Defense Forces, New York, NY. For general support.
$200,000 to Yeshiva University, New York, NY. For general support.
$100,000 to Childrens Hospital Foundation at Westchester Medical Center, Valhalla, NY. For general support.
$100,000 to Temple Emanu-El, Westfield, NJ. For general support.
$50,000 to Mount Sinai School of Medicine of New York University, New York, NY. For general support.
$50,000 to P.E.F. Israel Endowment Funds, New York, NY. For general support.

5188

Elizabethtown Healthcare Foundation

P.O. Box 259
Elizabeth, NJ   07207-0259   (908) 994-8065
Contact: David A. Fletcher, Pres.

Established in 2002 in NJ.
Foundation type: Independent foundation.
Financial data (yr. ended 12/31/05): Assets, $7,959,278 (M); expenditures, $834,311; qualifying distributions, $511,730; giving activities include $495,000 for 15 grants (high: $100,000; low: $5,000).
Purpose and activities: Giving to strengthen existing and/or seed innovative initiatives that address health care and related needs in Elizabeth, NJ, and surrounding communities. Funding priorities include services for women and children, and mental health.
Fields of interest: Health care.
Type of support: Equipment; Program development; Seed money; Curriculum development.
Limitations: Giving limited to Elizabeth, NJ, and surrounding communities. No support for lobbying activities or religious activities. No grants to individuals, or for budget deficits or general operating expenses, endowments, lending, research, annual appeals, fundraising dinners or journals, scholarships, attendance at workshops, or for conferences.
Publications: Application guidelines.
Application information: Application form not required.
Initial approach: Proposal (letter form, no more than 4 pages)
Copies of proposal: 2
Deadline(s): Apr. 10 or Oct. 10
Board meeting date(s): May and Nov.
Final notification: 60 days
Officers and Directors:* Richard English,* Chair.; Andrew Campbell,* Vice-Chair.; David A. Fletcher,* Pres.; Alice A. Holzapfel,* Secy.; Mortimer Gershman,* Treas.; Kathleen Leifeste, R.N.; Victor Richel; Richard Width.

Number of staff: 1 part-time professional.
EIN: 222473474
Selected grants: The following grants were reported in 2005.
$320,000 to Trinitas Health Foundation, Elizabeth, NJ. 5 grants: $100,000, $100,000, $50,000, $20,000, $50,000
$35,000 to YWCA of Eastern Union County, Elizabeth, NJ.
$25,000 to Bridgeway, Lakewood, CO.
$20,000 to Elizabethport Presbyterian Center, Elizabeth, NJ.
$15,000 to Community Access Unlimited, Elizabeth, NJ.
$10,000 to Saint Joseph Social Service Center, Elizabeth, NJ.

5189

The Lester M. and Sally Entin Foundation ◇

c/o Marc J. Lenner
P.O. Box 2189
Clifton, NJ   07015-2189

Established in 1997 in DE and NJ.
Foundation type: Independent foundation.
Financial data (yr. ended 12/31/05): Assets, $10,892,165 (M); expenditures, $617,666; qualifying distributions, $498,545; giving activities include $498,545 for 38 grants (high: $100,000; low: $120).
Purpose and activities: Giving primarily to Jewish organizations; funding also for health care, education, and human services.
Fields of interest: Education; Health care; Health organizations, association; Human services; Jewish federated giving programs; Jewish agencies & temples.
Limitations: Applications not accepted. Giving primarily in NJ, and NY. No grants to individuals.
Application information: Contributes only to pre-selected organizations.
Officers and Directors:* Marc J. Lenner,* Pres. and Treas.; Robert A. Hoberman,* V.P. and Secy.
EIN: 650758118

5190

Eshet Chayil Foundation ◇ ☆

1640 Vauxhall Rd., Ste. 2A
Union, NJ   07083   (908) 851-0778
Contact: Susan Roth, Tr.

Established in 1998 in NJ.
Donors: Michael Roth; Susan Roth.
Foundation type: Independent foundation.
Financial data (yr. ended 10/31/05): Assets, $31,590 (M); gifts received, $320,059; expenditures, $448,954; qualifying distributions, $448,954; giving activities include $330,201 for 30 grants (high: $100,000; low: $200).
Purpose and activities: Giving to a food program for needy Israelis, as well as for breast cancer prevention for Israeli women, a facility to assist mentally incapacitated Holocaust victims in Israel, and Jewish education, organizations and synagogues.
Fields of interest: Education; Jewish agencies & temples.
International interests: Israel.

Type of support: General/operating support; Continuing support; Conferences/seminars; Seed money; Internship funds.
Limitations: Giving primarily to organizations assisting Israeli individuals and agencies. No grants to individuals.
Application information:
Initial approach: Letter
Trustees: Sylvia Blitz; Susan Roth; Dianne Roth-Medina.
Number of staff: 1 full-time professional; 1 part-time professional.
EIN: 223621981

5191

Family Development Center, Inc. ◇ ☆

50 Smith Rd.
Denville, NJ   07834-9405   (973) 328-0303
Contact: Bob Howitt, Chair.

Foundation type: Operating foundation.
Financial data (yr. ended 6/30/05): Assets, $191,086 (M); gifts received, $100,340; expenditures, $431,067; qualifying distributions, $429,279; giving activities include $353,744 for grants, and $75,535 for 1 foundation-administered program.
Purpose and activities: Giving primarily for education and financially disadvantaged students.
Fields of interest: Education; Economically disadvantaged.
Application information:
Initial approach: Paper
Deadline(s): None
Officer and Trustee:* Robert Howitt,* Chair.
EIN: 223760128

5192

The Fanwood Foundation ◇

P.O. Box 5244
Plainfield, NJ   07061   (908) 756-7804
Contact: Victor E. King
E-mail: victore@eclipse.net

Trust established in 1940 in NJ.
Donor: Dorothy W. Stevens.
Foundation type: Independent foundation.
Financial data (yr. ended 12/31/04): Assets, $11,302,588 (M); expenditures, $821,595; qualifying distributions, $626,111; giving activities include $622,425 for 180 grants (high: $30,000; low: $250).
Fields of interest: Education; Environment, natural resources; Environment; Animals/wildlife; Hospitals (general).
Type of support: Land acquisition; General/operating support; Annual campaigns; Endowments.
Limitations: Giving on a national basis, with emphasis on MT, NJ and NY. No support for religious or political organizations. No grants to individuals.
Publications: Annual report.
Application information: Application form not required.
Initial approach: Letter
Copies of proposal: 1
Deadline(s): Varies
Board meeting date(s): Various
Final notification: Varies
Trustees: Victor E.D. King; J. Whitney Stevens; Robert T. Stevens, Jr.; Whitney Stevens.
EIN: 136051922

5193
Fenwick Foundation ◇ ☆
(formerly Phoenix Family Foundation)
P.O. Box 1525
Pennington, NJ 08534-1525

Established in 1999 in NC.
Donors: Anne Phoenix; Anne & Julius Phoenix Charitable Trust.
Foundation type: Independent foundation.
Financial data (yr. ended 4/30/06): Assets, $7,277,749 (M); gifts received, $2,191,871; expenditures, $451,642; qualifying distributions, $367,888; giving activities include $367,888 for grants.
Purpose and activities: Giving primarily for education and children's services.
Fields of interest: Education; Human services; Children/youth, services; Community development.
Limitations: Applications not accepted. Giving primarily in CA and NC. No grants to individuals.
Application information: Contributes only to pre-selected organizations.
Officers: Frank J. Phoenix, Pres.; James E. Phoenix, Secy.; J. Staurt Phoenix, Treas.
EIN: 562150323
Selected grants: The following grants were reported in 2005.
$25,000 to Mary Baldwin College, Staunton, VA. For general operating support.
$15,000 to Planned Parenthood of Central North Carolina, Chapel Hill, NC. For general operating support.
$13,000 to Nonviolent Peaceforce, Minneapolis, MN. For general operating support.
$10,800 to Sunny Hills Childrens Garden, San Anselmo, CA. For general operating support.
$10,000 to Blue Mountain Center of Meditation, Tomales, CA. For general operating support.
$10,000 to Youth in Arts, San Rafael, CA. For general operating support.
$5,000 to Public Allies North Carolina, Durham, NC. For general operating support.
$3,000 to Center for Child and Family Health - North Carolina, Durham, NC. For general operating support.
$2,500 to AmeriCares, Stamford, CT. For general operating support.
$2,000 to Duke School for Children, Durham, NC. For general operating support.

5194
First Brokers Good Samaritan Fund ◇
Harborside Financial Ctr.
Plz. 5, Ste. 1500
Jersey City, NJ 07311

Established in 2001 in NY.
Donors: Kevin Boyle; Richard Bonanno; Nicholas Garofolo; Andrew O'Keefe; First Brokers Securities, Inc.; Scott Dudley; Perry DeVitto; Kevin Gilligan; Michael Tomczyk; Val Cihak; Nicholas Algiero; Anthony Bonanno, Jr.; Thomas Carroll; Jean Colin; Robert F. Cudequest; John Cuzzocrea; Robert Dennis, Sr.; Robert Dennis, Jr.; Peter Dwyer; Peter Garofolo; Richard Graham; Jon Greenburg; Gerri Grena Daneman; Robert Haverlin; Nunzio Innucci; Vincent Irwin; Paul Karpowich; Kenneth O. Kunz; Louis LoPresti; Timothy Lucas; Michael Malamed; Owen McVeigh; David Mindnich; Frank Morretti III; Dennis Newman, Jr.; George Olvanny; Augustine Ortiz; Richard Palmer; Michael Phillips, Jr.; Edward

Preato; Kevin Pryor; Robert Spellman; Darrell Spinner; W. DeWees Yeager III; Anthony Zuzio.
Foundation type: Operating foundation.
Financial data (yr. ended 12/31/05): Assets, $525,742 (M); gifts received, $243,484; expenditures, $334,032; qualifying distributions, $328,000; giving activities include $280,000 for 12 grants (high: $50,000; low: $10,000), and $48,000 for 7 grants to individuals (high: $20,000; low: $1,000).
Fields of interest: Safety/disasters; Human services; Economically disadvantaged.
Type of support: Grants to individuals.
Trustees: John J. Corcoran; Robert F. Cudequest; Scott Dudley; Dee Lipka Jones; Timothy E. Lane; Frank Moretti; Andrew J. O'Keefe.
EIN: 137298341

5195
Fishoff Family Foundation ◇
300-2C Rte. 17, S.
Lodi, NJ 07644   (973) 458-8070
Contact: Benjamin Fishoff, Pres.

Established in 1982.
Donors: Benjamin Fishoff; Marilyn Fishoff‡; Donald Fishoff; Henry M. Shapiro; Avi Fishoff; Meryl Gross; Saul D. Levy; Interocean Industries, Inc.
Foundation type: Independent foundation.
Financial data (yr. ended 7/31/05): Assets, $7,183,307 (M); gifts received, $129,200; expenditures, $792,775; qualifying distributions, $761,233; giving activities include $761,233 for 430 grants (high: $101,080; low: $25).
Purpose and activities: Support primarily for Jewish organizations, temples, and yeshivas.
Fields of interest: Elementary/secondary education; Hospitals (general); Human services; Jewish agencies & temples.
Limitations: Giving primarily in New York, NY. No grants to individuals.
Application information: Application form not required.
   Initial approach: Letter
   Deadline(s): None
Officer: Benjamin Fishoff, Pres.
Directors: Abraham Fishoff; Donald Fishoff; Barbara Gold; Meryl Gross; Regina Weinstock.
EIN: 133076576

5196
Samuel J. & Connie M. Frankino Charitable Foundation ◇
c/o Preziosi & Assocs.
3071 E. Chestnut Ave., Ste. E-13
Vineland, NJ 08361-7847   (856) 794-8400
Contact: Connie M. Frankino, Tr.

Established in 1988 in OH.
Donors: Connie M. Frankino; Samuel J. Frankino.
Foundation type: Independent foundation.
Financial data (yr. ended 3/31/05): Assets, $32,936,640 (M); expenditures, $1,597,805; qualifying distributions, $1,440,416; giving activities include $1,432,315 for 83 grants (high: $125,000; low: $100).
Purpose and activities: Giving primarily for education, children, youth and social services; funding also for health care.
Fields of interest: Arts; Elementary/secondary education; Higher education; Education; Hospitals

(specialty); Health care; Cancer; Health organizations; Human services; Children/youth, services; Family services; Foundations (private grantmaking).
Type of support: General/operating support; Building/renovation; Research.
Limitations: Giving on a national basis. No grants to individuals.
Application information: Application form not required.
   Initial approach: Letter
   Deadline(s): Jan. 1
Trustees: Connie M. Frankino; Samuel J. Frankino.
EIN: 341577766
Selected grants: The following grants were reported in 2004.
$125,000 to American Cancer Society, Tampa, FL. For ROCK Camp.
$125,000 to Cleveland Clinic Foundation, Cleveland, OH. For general support.
$100,000 to Prestons Hope, Chagrin Falls, OH. For general support.
$80,000 to KidSanctuary, Loxahatchee, FL. For general support.
$75,000 to Center For Family Services. For general support.
$25,000 to Jupiter Medical Center Foundation, Jupiter, FL. For general support.
$25,000 to Middle School of the Arts Foundation, West Palm Beach, FL. For general support.
$25,000 to Ohio University, Athens, OH. For general support.
$25,000 to Playhouse Square Foundation, Cleveland, OH. For general support.
$25,000 to South Florida Science Museum, West Palm Beach, FL. For general support.

5197
Carl & Sylvia Freyer Family Foundation, Inc. ◇
302 Fountain Rd.
Englewood, NJ 07631

Established in 1989 in NJ.
Donors: Carl J. Freyer; Edco Supply Corp.
Foundation type: Independent foundation.
Financial data (yr. ended 3/31/06): Assets, $80,991 (M); gifts received, $455,275; expenditures, $662,447; qualifying distributions, $659,710; giving activities include $659,710 for 31 grants (high: $366,005; low: $10).
Purpose and activities: Funding primarily for Jewish temples and agencies.
Fields of interest: Human services; Jewish federated giving programs; Jewish agencies & temples.
Limitations: Applications not accepted. Giving on a national and international basis, primarily in NJ and NY, and in Jerusalem, Israel. No grants to individuals.
Application information: Contributes only to pre-selected organizations.
Officers: Carl J. Freyer, Pres. and Treas.; Sylvia Freyer, V.P. and Secy.
Directors: Maura Ruskin; Louisa Susman.
EIN: 223000538

5198

The Fund for Children of the Americas ✧
c/o William S. Villafranco
577 Chestnut Ridge Rd.
Woodcliff Lake, NJ 07677

Classified as a private operating foundation in 1995.
Donors: Roy M. Adams; Virginia Toulmin.
Foundation type: Operating foundation.
Financial data (yr. ended 6/30/05): Assets, $314,263 (M); gifts received, $793,440; expenditures, $873,338; qualifying distributions, $800,676; giving activities include $800,676 for grants.
Fields of interest: Education; Human services.
Limitations: Applications not accepted. No grants to individuals.
Application information: Contributes only to pre-selected organizations.
Officers: John Brandt, Pres.; Daniel Adams, Secy.-Treas.
Directors: Roy M. Adams; Virginia Toulmin.
EIN: 363993358

5199

The Fund for New Jersey ▼ ✧
94 Church St., Ste. 303
New Brunswick, NJ 08901 (732) 220-8656
Contact: Mark M. Murphy, Exec. Dir.
FAX: (732) 220-8654; E-mail: info@fundfornj.org;
URL: http://www.fundfornj.org

Incorporated in 1969 in NJ as successor to The Florence Murray Wallace Fund established in 1958.
Donors: Charles F. Wallace†; and members of his family.
Foundation type: Independent foundation.
Financial data (yr. ended 12/31/05): Assets, $70,050,826 (M); expenditures, $4,056,320; qualifying distributions, $3,722,236; giving activities include $3,175,000 for 64 grants (high: $150,000; low: $500; average: $15,000–$50,000).
Purpose and activities: Emphasis on projects which provide the basis for public action on state or local problems by way of research, litigation, citizen action, or supervision of government in the areas of social and economic opportunity, environment and land use, and public policy in New Jersey.
Fields of interest: Education; Environment, land resources; Environment; AIDS; Minorities/immigrants, centers/services; Community development; Public policy, research; Government/public administration; Public affairs; Minorities.
Type of support: General/operating support; Continuing support; Program development; Conferences/seminars; Publication; Seed money; Research; Matching/challenge support.
Limitations: Giving primarily in NJ or to regional programs that benefit NJ. No support for day care centers, drug treatment programs, health care delivery, or arts programs. No grants to individuals, or for capital projects, equipment, scholarships.
Publications: Annual report (including application guidelines); Grants list.
Application information: Proposals are not accepted via e-mail. Application form not required.
  Initial approach: Proposal
  Copies of proposal: 1
  Deadline(s): 7 weeks prior to board meeting

Board meeting date(s): Mar., June, Sept., and Dec.
Final notification: 2 weeks after board meeting
Officers and Trustees: * Leonard Lieberman,* Chair.; Candace McKee Ashmun,* Vice-Chair.; Joseph C. Cornwall, Chair. Emeritus; Mark M. Murphy, Pres., Secy., and Exec. Dir.; Jane W. Thorne, Tr. Emeritus; Ernestine Schlant Bradley, Ph.D.; Brendan Thomas Byme, Jr.; John W. Cornwall, M.D.; Hon. Dickinson R. Debevoise; Linda Dennery; Susan H. Fuhrman; Hon. John J. Gibbons; Gustav Heninburg; Edward Lloyd; Lawrence S. Lustberg; Clement A. Price; Richard J. Sullivan; Gary D. Rose; Richard L. Wright.
Number of staff: 2 full-time professional; 1 part-time professional; 1 full-time support.
EIN: 221895028
Selected grants: The following grants were reported in 2005.
$150,000 to Housing and Community Development Network of New Jersey, Trenton, NJ. For public policy work with community development sector advocating for affordable housing.
$150,000 to New Jersey Policy Perspective, Trenton, NJ. To continue public policy advocacy and to advance progressive agenda in New Jersey through production and dissemination of timely, targeted reports and analyses.
$125,000 to Eastern Environmental Law Center, Newark, NJ. To continue to represent New Jersey's environmental community and promote environmental regulations, remediation of contaminated waste sites, and smart growth alternatives in New Jersey.
$100,000 to CityWorks, Trenton, NJ. For renewed operating support for redevelopment efforts in Trenton and Neptune.
$95,000 to Legal Services of New Jersey, Edison, NJ. For renewed operating support for Poverty Research Institute and for coordination of Anti-Poverty Network.
$85,000 to New Jersey Citizen Action Education Fund, Hackensack, NJ. For public education activities to support first round of publicly financed legislative elections in New Jersey, following state's adoption of Fair and Clean Elections Pilot Program.
$75,000 to Leadership Newark, Newark, NJ. For implementation of second year of Community Leadership Initiative and leadership training programs with hands-on experience to address public policy issues.
$75,000 to Princeton University, Woodrow Wilson School, Princeton, NJ. To engage public and private sector leaders to discuss best practices, create regional website on public policy research and develop database to policymakers through Policy Research Institute for the Region.
$70,000 to Association of New Jersey Environmental Commissions, Mendham, NJ. To continue technical assistance to environment commissions and municipalities to transfer development rights programs in helping balance preservation with growth.
$60,000 to New Jersey Work Environment Council, Trenton, NJ. For research, preparation and dissemination of Action Steps for Chemical Security in N.J., blueprint for disaster preparedness and prevention.

5200

Gabelli Foundation, Inc. ✧
c/o Angelo & O'Brien, PA
340 North Ave. E.
Cranford, NJ 07016-2461

Established in 1985 in NV.
Donor: Mario J. Gabelli.
Foundation type: Independent foundation.
Financial data (yr. ended 3/31/05): Assets, $35,174,819 (M); gifts received, $4,648,435; expenditures, $1,698,793; qualifying distributions, $1,470,065; giving activities include $1,432,500 for 28 grants (high: $600,000; low: $500).
Purpose and activities: Giving primarily for secondary and higher education.
Fields of interest: Secondary school/education; Higher education; Human services.
Type of support: General/operating support; Building/renovation.
Limitations: Applications not accepted. Giving primarily in NY; some giving in Chestnut Hill, MA, Bristol, RI and NV, with emphasis on Reno. No grants to individuals.
Application information: Contributes only to pre-selected organizations.
Officer: Mario J. Gabelli, Pres.
Trustees: Marc J. Gabelli; Matthew R. Gabelli; Michael Gabelli; Mary Mazzolla; Elisa Gabelli Wilson.
EIN: 942975159
Selected grants: The following grants were reported in 2005.
$600,000 to Boston College, Chestnut Hill, MA.
$250,000 to Roger Williams University, Bristol, RI.
$160,000 to Fordham Preparatory School, Bronx, NY.
$51,000 to Ursuline School, New Rochelle, NY.
$20,000 to Saint Aloysius School, New York, NY.
$1,000 to Bishop Manogue High School, Reno, NV.
$1,000 to Sacred Heart School, Bronx, NY.
$500 to Bishop Gorman High School, Las Vegas, NV.

5201

The Lois & Neil Gagnon Foundation, Inc. ✧
P.O. Box 691
Bernardsville, NJ 07924

Established in 1994 in NJ.
Donor: Neil J. Gagnon.
Foundation type: Independent foundation.
Financial data (yr. ended 11/30/03): Assets, $15,937,608 (M); expenditures, $1,138,926; qualifying distributions, $1,060,635; giving activities include $1,060,635 for 24 grants (high: $500,000; low: $25).
Purpose and activities: Giving primarily for higher education and to a hospital.
Fields of interest: Elementary/secondary education; Education; Hospitals (general); Human services.
Limitations: Applications not accepted. Giving primarily in NJ and NY. No grants to individuals.
Application information: Contributes only to pre-selected organizations.
Officers: Neil J. Gagnon, Pres.; Lois E. Gagnon, Secy.
Director: Brian Gagnon.
EIN: 521868735
Selected grants: The following grants were reported in 2003.
$500,000 to Lafayette College, Easton, PA. For Gen Quasi Endowment Fund.

$200,000 to Morristown Memorial Hospital, Morristown, NJ. For children's center.

$200,000 to Seton Hall Preparatory School, West Orange, NJ.

$10,000 to Bonnie Brae, Liberty Corner, NJ.

$10,000 to Lee David Pesky Center for Learning Enrichment, Boise, ID.

$5,000 to Visiting Nurse Association of Somerset Hills, Bernardsville, NJ.

$3,200 to YMCA, Somerset Hills, Basking Ridge, NJ.

$2,800 to Saint Anthonys High School, South Huntington, NY.

$1,810 to Cancer Hope Network, Chester, NJ.

$1,000 to Leukemia & Lymphoma Society, White Plains, NY.

5202
Galanta Foundation, Inc. ✧ ☆

c/o Royal Wine Corp.
63 Lefante Ln.
Bayonne, NJ 07002

Established in 2003 in NY.
Donor: Royal Wine Corp.
Foundation type: Company-sponsored foundation.
Financial data (yr. ended 12/31/05): Assets, $200,472 (M); gifts received, $101; expenditures, $324,353; qualifying distributions, $324,110; giving activities include $324,110 for grants.
Purpose and activities: The foundation supports Jewish agencies and temples.
Fields of interest: Jewish agencies & temples.
Limitations: Applications not accepted. Giving limited to NY. No grants to individuals.
Application information: Contributes only to pre-selected organizations.
Officers and Directors:* David Herzog,* Pres.; Eli Herzog, V.P.; Gary Herzog, V.P.; Herman Herzog, V.P.; Joseph Herzog, V.P.; Joseph Herzog, V.P.; Judith Buchler, V.P.; Michael Herzog,* V.P.; Michael B. Herzog, V.P.; Mordechai Herzog, V.P.; Morris Herzog, V.P.; Nathan Herzog,* V.P.; Phillip Herzog, V.P.; Robert Herzog, V.P.; Aaron Herzog,* Secy.-Treas.
EIN: 030533223

5203
The Jose M. Garcia Foundation, Inc. ✧

851 Franklin Lakes Rd.
Franklin Lakes, NJ 07417
Contact: Donald Quinn, Pres.

Foundation type: Independent foundation.
Financial data (yr. ended 10/31/04): Assets, $7,810,283 (M); expenditures, $477,862; qualifying distributions, $377,000; giving activities include $377,000 for 15 grants (high: $150,800; low: $2,000).
Purpose and activities: Giving primarily to Christian and Lutheran churches and organizations, as well as to other religious organizations; funding also for children, youth and social services.
Fields of interest: Human services; Children/youth, services; Philanthropy/voluntarism; Christian agencies & churches; Religion.
Application information:
Initial approach: Letter
Deadline(s): Oct. 31 through Dec. 31

Officer and Trustees:* Donald Quinn,* Pres.; Jorge Corominal; Laura Figueroa; Ella Glover; Roswitha Klahn.
EIN: 223369956

5204
The Geier Foundation ✧

c/o Joseph E. Hanlon
358 Wall St.
Princeton, NJ 08540-1517

Established in 1997 in NY.
Donor: Philip H. Geier, Jr.
Foundation type: Independent foundation.
Financial data (yr. ended 3/31/05): Assets, $7,243,018 (M); gifts received, $1,126,200; expenditures, $565,100; qualifying distributions, $560,190; giving activities include $489,250 for 6 grants (high: $300,000; low: $1,000).
Fields of interest: Museums (art); Performing arts centers; Secondary school/education; Education; Hospitals (general); Cancer; Autism research; Children, services.
Limitations: Applications not accepted. Giving primarily in the metropolitan New York, NY, area. No grants to individuals.
Application information: Contributes only to pre-selected organizations.
Trustees: Faith Geier; Johanna Geier Howard; Hope Smith.
EIN: 227311735
Selected grants: The following grants were reported in 2004.
$84,515 to Whitney Museum of American Art, New York, NY. 2 grants: $75,000 (For software program), $9,515 (For print committee).
$50,000 to Save the Children Federation, Westport, CT. For general support.
$18,000 to Lenox Hill Hospital, Tropical Disease Center, New York, NY. For general support.
$10,000 to Multiple Sclerosis Society, National, New York, NY. For general support.
$5,000 to American Red Cross, Westport, CT. For capital campaign.
$5,000 to Metropolitan Opera, New York, NY. For national council education fund.
$5,000 to SASS Foundation for Medical Research, Roslyn, NY. For general support.
$4,700 to Ronald McDonald House of New York, New York, NY. For general support.

5205
Geiger Foundation, Inc. ✧ ☆

c/o Wiss & Co., LLP
354 Eisenhower Pkwy.
Livingston, NJ 07039

Established in 1989 in NJ.
Donor: Ralph G. Geiger.
Foundation type: Independent foundation.
Financial data (yr. ended 6/30/05): Assets, $1,149,584 (M); expenditures, $1,053,743; qualifying distributions, $1,052,910; giving activities include $1,050,000 for 2 grants (high: $1,000,000; low: $50,000).
Purpose and activities: Giving primarily to higher education.
Fields of interest: Higher education, university; Hospitals (general); Residential/custodial care, hospices.
Type of support: Scholarship funds.

Limitations: Applications not accepted. Giving primarily in NJ. No grants to individuals.
Application information: Contributes only to pre-selected organizations.
Trustees: Ralph G. Geiger; Stuart A. Rosenblatt.
EIN: 222999899
Selected grants: The following grants were reported in 2005.
$1,000,000 to Rutgers, The State University of New Jersey, New Brunswick, NJ.

5206
Joel and Elaine Gershman Foundation ✧

(formerly Joel Gershman Foundation)
c/o Jager Mgmt., Inc.
2000 Maplewood Dr.
Maple Shade, NJ 08052

Established in 1984.
Donors: Joel Gershman; Elaine Gershman.
Foundation type: Independent foundation.
Financial data (yr. ended 11/30/05): Assets, $3,730,104 (M); expenditures, $398,452; qualifying distributions, $376,557; giving activities include $376,557 for 46 grants (high: $125,000; low: $10).
Purpose and activities: Giving primarily to the arts, including a performing arts center and for education, including an arts university. Some giving to Jewish organizations and for health care and social services.
Fields of interest: Arts; Higher education; Education; Hospitals (general); Health organizations, association; Medical research, association; Human services; Federated giving programs; Jewish agencies & temples; Religion, interfaith issues.
Type of support: Research.
Limitations: Applications not accepted. Giving primarily in Philadelphia, PA. No grants to individuals.
Application information: Unsolicited requests for funds not accepted.
Officers: Joel Gershman, Pres.; Sylvan Cohen, V.P.; Elaine Levitt Gershman, Secy.-Treas.
Directors: J. David Levitt; William J. Levitt III.
EIN: 222529629
Selected grants: The following grants were reported in 2005.
$125,000 to University of the Arts, Philadelphia, PA.
$50,000 to Kimmel Center for the Performing Arts, Philadelphia, PA.
$15,000 to Womens Way, Philadelphia, PA.
$10,000 to Philadelphia Museum of Art, Philadelphia, PA.
$5,000 to Friends of Rittenhouse Square, Philadelphia, PA.
$2,100 to Philadelphia Art Alliance, Philadelphia, PA.
$2,000 to Philadelphia Orchestra Association, Philadelphia, PA.
$1,325 to Free Library of Philadelphia, Philadelphia, PA.
$600 to Curtis Institute of Music, Philadelphia, PA.
$500 to National Constitution Center, Philadelphia, PA.

5207
GHH Foundation, Inc. ✧ ☆

401 Cooper Landing Rd., Rm. C-12
Cherry Hill, NJ 08002

Established in 2005 in NJ.
Foundation type: Independent foundation.
Financial data (yr. ended 12/31/05): Assets, $4,623,695 (M); gifts received, $4,599; expenditures, $438,902; qualifying distributions, $394,325; giving activities include $382,000 for 7 grants (high: $247,000; low: $5,000).
Fields of interest: Residential/custodial care, hospices; Residential/custodial care, senior continuing care; Aging, centers/services; Aging.
Limitations: Applications not accepted. Giving on a national basis. No grants to individuals.
Application information: Contributes only to pre-selected organizations.
Officers: William Oliver, Pres.; Alexander Higgins, 1st V.P.; Robert Rexon, Secy.; T. Edgar Chambers, Treas.
Trustees: Harold Clark; J. Wilbur Coleman; John Coleman; Piaw Haun.
EIN: 210735044

5208
Gibson Family Foundation, Inc. ✧ ☆
58 Lyons Pl.
Basking Ridge, NJ 07920

Established in 1993 in NJ.
Donor: James G. Gibson.
Foundation type: Independent foundation.
Financial data (yr. ended 12/31/05): Assets, $3,360,231 (M); expenditures, $376,249; qualifying distributions, $332,476; giving activities include $332,476 for grants.
Purpose and activities: Giving for environmental conservation, higher education, and human services.
Fields of interest: Higher education; Environment, natural resources; Housing/shelter, development; General charitable giving.
Limitations: Applications not accepted. Giving primarily in NJ. No grants to individuals.
Application information: Contributes only to pre-selected organizations.
Officers and Trustees:* James G. Gibson,* Pres.; Jill R. Gibson,* Secy.
EIN: 223197727
Selected grants: The following grants were reported in 2004.
$25,000 to Lehigh University, Bethlehem, PA.
$20,000 to Brand New Day, Elizabeth, NJ.
$15,000 to Wilderness Society, DC.
$10,000 to Cornell University, Ithaca, NY.
$10,000 to University of Tennessee, Knoxville, TN.
$5,000 to Natural Resources Defense Council, New York, NY.
$5,000 to W N Y C Radio, New York, NY.
$3,000 to Museum of Modern Art, New York, NY.
$2,500 to Union County College Foundation, Cranford, NJ.
$2,500 to W N E T Channel 13, New York, NY.

5209
Arthur M. Goldberg and Veronica Goldberg Foundation, Inc. ☆
(formerly Arthur M. Goldberg Foundation, Inc.)
P.O. Box 266
Sergeantsville, NJ 08557-0226

Established in 1986 in NJ.
Foundation type: Independent foundation.

Financial data (yr. ended 12/31/05): Assets, $8,099,261 (M); expenditures, $458,368; qualifying distributions, $367,146; giving activities include $367,146 for grants.
Fields of interest: Higher education; Graduate/professional education; Hospitals (general); Cancer; Medical research, institute; Human services; Children/youth, services; Roman Catholic agencies & churches.
Type of support: General/operating support; Annual campaigns; Research.
Limitations: Applications not accepted. Giving primarily in MD and NJ. No grants to individuals.
Application information: Contributes only to pre-selected organizations.
Trustees: Veronica Goldberg; Richard B. Neff.
EIN: 222779193
Selected grants: The following grants were reported in 2003.
$98,590 to Villanova University, Villanova, PA. 2 grants: $73,940 to School of Law (For Albert W Goldberg Scholarship Fund), $24,650 to School of Law (For Arthur M Goldberg Scholarship Fund).
$50,000 to Archdiocese of Newark, Newark, NJ. For general support.
$7,000 to New Jersey Conservation Foundation, Far Hills, NJ. For Bamboo Brook.
$5,000 to Boston College, Chestnut Hill, MA. For William J Flynn Scholarship Fund.
$5,000 to Duke University, Durham, NC. For Trinity College Annual Fund.
$5,000 to Project Pride, Newark, NJ. For general support.
$1,500 to Columbia University, School of Business, New York, NY. For annual fund.
$1,000 to Save a Heart Foundation, Pikesville, MD. For general support.
$500 to Pingry School, Martinsville, NJ. For general support.

5210
The Goldring Family Foundation, Inc. ✧
51 J.F.K. Pkwy., 4th Fl.
Short Hills, NJ 07078

Established in 1995 in NJ.
Donors: Education for Youth Society; Gary F. Goldring.
Foundation type: Independent foundation.
Financial data (yr. ended 9/30/05): Assets, $16,419,157 (M); expenditures, $840,588; qualifying distributions, $828,995; giving activities include $713,694 for 63 grants (high: $108,308; low: $100).
Purpose and activities: Giving primarily for education, community, children and Jewish organizations.
Fields of interest: Higher education; Graduate/professional education; Environment, land resources; Hospitals (general); Recreation, formal/general education; Recreation, camps; Children/youth, services; Foundations (community); Jewish agencies & temples.
Limitations: Applications not accepted. Giving primarily in NJ and NY. No grants to individuals.
Application information: Contributes only to pre-selected organizations.
Officers: Gary F. Goldring, Pres. and Treas.; Paul Wolanksy, V.P. and Secy.
EIN: 223407792
Selected grants: The following grants were reported in 2005.
$108,308 to Earthwatch Institute, Maynard, MA.

$58,000 to Zoological Society.
$25,000 to Overcoming Obstacles, Indianapolis, IN.
$25,000 to Saint Barnabas Hospital, Bronx, NY.
$10,000 to Adaptive Sports Foundation, Windham, NY.
$10,000 to Music Center, Providence, RI.
$6,100 to New Jersey Center for Visual Arts, Summit, NJ.
$5,000 to Delaware Valley Friends School, Bryn Mawr, PA.
$5,000 to New Milford Hospital, New Milford, CT.
$5,000 to Special Olympics-Egypt, Egypt. .

5211
Goldstein Charity Fund, Inc. ✧ ☆
1423 Cedar Row
Lakewood, NJ 08701 (732) 370-1141
Contact: Joshua Goldstein, Tr.

Established in 2000 in NJ.
Donor: Joshua Goldstein.
Foundation type: Operating foundation.
Financial data (yr. ended 12/31/04): Assets, $0 (M); gifts received, $20,000; expenditures, $341,687; qualifying distributions, $339,351; giving activities include $339,351 for grants.
Fields of interest: Jewish agencies & temples.
Application information:
Initial approach: Letter
Deadline(s): None
Trustees: Joshua Goldstein; Morris Silberberg; Joseph Singer.
EIN: 223711451
Selected grants: The following grants were reported in 2003.
$100,000 to Chesed Avraham, Brooklyn, NY. 4 grants: $25,000 each
$700 to Chicago Chesed Fund, Chicago, IL.
$500 to Congregation Zichron Schneur, Brooklyn, NY.
$360 to Chai Lifeline, New York, NY.
$180 to Yeshiva Mkor Chaim, Brooklyn, NY.
$100 to Sinai Academy, Brooklyn, NY.
$25 to Tzedakah Vchesed, Brooklyn, NY.

5212
Melvin R. Goodes Family Foundation, Inc. ✧ ☆
12 Thackery Ln.
Mendham, NJ 07945
Application address: c/o Melvin R. Goodes, 640 Ocean Rd., Vero Beach, FL 32963

Established in 1997 in NJ.
Donor: Melvin R. Goodes.
Foundation type: Independent foundation.
Financial data (yr. ended 12/31/05): Assets, $13,048,289 (M); gifts received, $10,087,986; expenditures, $578,924; qualifying distributions, $560,000; giving activities include $560,000 for 12 grants (high: $250,000; low: $2,500).
Purpose and activities: Giving primarily for higher education.
Fields of interest: Higher education.
International interests: Canada.
Type of support: Building/renovation.
Limitations: Giving in the U.S. and Canada. No support for private foundations. No grants to individuals.
Application information:

Initial approach: Letter
Deadline(s): None
Officers: Melvin R. Goodes, Pres.; Melanie G. Caceres, V.P.; Michelle R. Goodes, Secy.; David R. Goodes, Treas.
EIN: 223513671
Selected grants: The following grants were reported in 2003.
$240,000 to U.S. Foundation for Queens University at Kingston, School of Business, Kingston, Canada. .
$10,000 to The Edward W and Betty Knight Scripps Foundation, Charlottesville, VA. For general support.
$5,000 to Saint Johns Episcopal School, Olney, MD. For general support.
$2,500 to Jasons Dreams for Kids, Red Bank, NJ. For general support.

5213
E. J. Grassmann Trust ◇
P.O. Box 4470
Warren, NJ   07059   (908) 753-2440
Contact: William V. Engel, Exec. Dir.

Trust established in 1979 in NJ.
Donor: Edward J. Grassmann†.
Foundation type: Independent foundation.
Financial data (yr. ended 12/31/05): Assets, $33,031,697 (M); expenditures, $1,863,953; qualifying distributions, $1,790,501; giving activities include $1,691,900 for 184 grants (high: $75,000; low: $1,900).
Purpose and activities: Grants for educational institutions, local hospitals and health organizations, organizations engaged in ecological endeavors, and social welfare organizations, particularly those helping children. Preference given to organizations with low administration costs, and which show efforts to achieve a broad funding base.
Fields of interest: Historic preservation/historical societies; Education, fund raising/fund distribution; Secondary school/education; Higher education; Education; Environment, natural resources; Environment; Hospitals (general); Health care; Health organizations, association; Human services; Children/youth, services.
Type of support: Capital campaigns; Building/ renovation; Equipment; Land acquisition; Endowments.
Limitations: Giving primarily in GA, particularly middle GA, and in NJ, with emphasis on Union County. No grants to individuals, or for operating expenses, current scholarship funds, conferences, or workshops.
Publications: Application guidelines.
Application information: Application form not required.
Initial approach: Letter, no more than 4 pages
Copies of proposal: 1
Deadline(s): Apr. 20 and Oct. 15
Board meeting date(s): May or June and Nov.
Final notification: After May or June meeting by July 31; after Nov. meeting by Dec. 31
Officer and Trustees:* William V. Engel,* Exec. Dir.; Hunter W. Corbin; Suzanne B. Engel; Haydn H. Murray; Anita Spivey.
Number of staff: 1 part-time professional; 2 part-time support.
EIN: 226326539
Selected grants: The following grants were reported in 2005.

$75,000 to Trinitas Health Foundation, Elizabeth, NJ.
$50,000 to YMCA of Eastern Union County, Elizabeth, NJ.
$30,000 to Nature Conservancy, Chester, NJ.
$20,000 to Saint Peter Claver School, Macon, GA.
$17,500 to Paper Mill Playhouse, Millburn, NJ.
$12,500 to Trust for Public Land, Morristown, NJ.
$11,295 to Planned Parenthood of Greater Northern New Jersey, Morristown, NJ.
$10,000 to Saint Philips Academy, Newark, NJ.
$7,500 to New York City Relief, New York, NY.
$7,500 to Save Ellis Island, Gladstone, NJ.

5214
The Graymer Foundation ◇
P.O. Box 251
Madison, NJ   07940-2714

Established in 2000 in NJ.
Donor: C. Graydon Rogers.
Foundation type: Independent foundation.
Financial data (yr. ended 12/31/05): Assets, $7,558,197 (M); expenditures, $413,189; qualifying distributions, $408,047; giving activities include $405,000 for grants.
Fields of interest: Human services.
Limitations: Applications not accepted. No grants to individuals.
Application information: Contributes only to pre-selected organizations.
Officers: C. Graydon Rogers, Pres.; Mary Elizabeth Rogers, V.P.; Stacy Rogers Golding, Secy.-Treas.
Trustees: Ann Bronwyn Rogers; David S. Rogers; Stuart G. Rogers.
EIN: 226798520

5215
The Howard L. Green Foundation ◇ ☆
1100 Willowdale Dr.
Cherry Hill, NJ   08003-2835

Established in NJ.
Donor: Howard L. Green†.
Foundation type: Independent foundation.
Financial data (yr. ended 12/31/05): Assets, $17,669,421 (M); gifts received, $99,861; expenditures, $789,087; qualifying distributions, $690,482; giving activities include $596,100 for 50 grants (high: $140,000; low: $675).
Fields of interest: Performing arts, theater; Performing arts, music; Arts; Higher education, college; Education; Cancer, leukemia; Human services; Salvation Army; Christian agencies & churches.
Limitations: Applications not accepted. No grants to individuals.
Application information: Contributes only to pre-selected organizations.
Trustees: Calvin Green; Donald J. Green; Ivor Rich; Richard S. Scolaro.
EIN: 556151985

5216
The Frank J. Guarini Foundation, Inc. ◇ ☆
c/o Mandel, Fekete & Bloom, C.P.A.
30 Montgomery St., Ste. 685
Jersey City, NJ   07302

Established in 1999 in NJ.

Donor: Frank J. Guarini.
Foundation type: Independent foundation.
Financial data (yr. ended 12/31/05): Assets, $4,957,967 (M); expenditures, $1,247,799; qualifying distributions, $1,244,533; giving activities include $1,244,533 for grants.
Fields of interest: Higher education; Foundations (public); Foundations (community).
Limitations: Applications not accepted. No grants to individuals.
Application information: Contributes only to pre-selected organizations.
Officers: Frank J. Guarini, Pres.; Caroline M. Mangin, V.P.; Frank L. Fekete, Secy.-Treas.
Trustees: Marie L. Garibaldi; Carol A. Mangin.
EIN: 223677856
Selected grants: The following grants were reported in 2003.
$20,000 to New Jersey City University Foundation, Jersey City, NJ. 2 grants: $10,000 each (For unrestricted support).
$20,000 to New York University, New York, NY. 2 grants: $10,000 each (For unrestricted support).
$11,000 to National Italian American Foundation, DC. For program support.
$10,000 to John Cabot University, Rockville, MD. For unrestricted support.
$10,000 to Saint Peters College, Jersey City, NJ. For Guarini Oratorical Contest.
$3,000 to Dartmouth College, Hanover, NH.
$1,000 to California Community Foundation, Los Angeles, CA. For Dean F. Johnson Alzheimer's.
$1,000 to Jersey City Museum, Jersey City, NJ. For unrestricted support.

5217
Gulton Foundation, Inc. ◇
c/o Raia, Bredefeld and Assocs., PC
163 Washington Valley Rd., Ste. 103
Warren, NJ   07059

Incorporated in 1961 in NY.
Donors: Leslie K. Gulton†; Marian G. Malcolm; Edith Gulton.
Foundation type: Independent foundation.
Financial data (yr. ended 10/31/05): Assets, $8,792,440 (M); expenditures, $691,974; qualifying distributions, $666,882; giving activities include $645,445 for 45 grants (high: $225,000; low: $45).
Purpose and activities: Grants for higher education, and to an art museum; funding also for the arts, and human services.
Fields of interest: Media/communications; Museums (art); Arts; Higher education; Human services; Federated giving programs.
Limitations: Applications not accepted. Giving primarily on the East Coast. No grants to individuals.
Application information: Contributes only to pre-selected organizations.
Officers: Marian G. Malcolm, Pres.; Daniel Malcolm, V.P.; John Malcolm, Secy.
EIN: 136105207
Selected grants: The following grants were reported in 2005.
$50,000 to Metropolitan Museum of Art, New York, NY.
$20,000 to Columbus Community Center, Columbus, GA. 2 grants: $10,000 each
$20,000 to W N E T Channel 13, New York, NY.
$2,200 to American Red Cross. 2 grants: $2,000, $200
$2,000 to New York City Ballet Guild, New York, NY.

5218
The Gordon and Llura Gund Foundation ▼ ✧
14 Nassau St.
Princeton, NJ 08542-0449
Contact: Gordon Gund, Tr.

Established in 1989 in NJ.
Foundation type: Independent foundation.
Financial data (yr. ended 12/31/04): Assets, $67,034,058 (M); expenditures, $6,263,969; qualifying distributions, $5,963,403; giving activities include $5,963,403 for 185 grants (high: $2,012,618; low: $125; average: $1,000–$25,000).
Purpose and activities: Giving primarily to organizations fighting blindness and to services for people who are blind; funding also for arts and culture, education, health associations and medical research, youth development, human services, and federated giving programs.
Fields of interest: Arts; Education; Health care; Health organizations, association; Eye diseases; Medical research, institute; Youth development, services; Human services; Foundations (community); Federated giving programs.
Limitations: Applications not accepted. Giving in the U.S., with emphasis on Washington, DC, MA, MD, NJ, and NY. No grants to individuals.
Application information: Contributes only to pre-selected organizations.
Trustees: Gordon Gund; Llura A. Gund.
EIN: 222987293
Selected grants: The following grants were reported in 2004.
$2,800,858 to Foundation Fighting Blindness, Owings Mills, MD. 3 grants: $200,000 to National Neurovision Research Institute (NNRI), $588,240 (For grant made in form of stock), $2,012,618 (For grant made in form of stock).
$753,600 to Groton School, Groton, MA. For grant made in form of stock.
$565,200 to Northwestern University, Kellogg Graduate School of Management, Evanston, IL. For grant made in form of stock.
$489,840 to Harvard University, Cambridge, MA. For grant made in form of stock.
$149,433 to Princeton Area Community Foundation, Lawrenceville, NJ. 2 grants: $36,393, $113,040 (For grant made in form of stock).
$97,968 to Tregoe Education Forum, Princeton, NJ. For grant made in form of stock.
$65,000 to Museum of Modern Art, New York, NY.

5219
The Hackett Foundation, Inc.
P.O. Box 693
Pittstown, NJ 08867 (908) 238-9444
Contact: Maggie Hackett, Grant Prog. Off.
URL: http://foundationcenter.org/grantmaker/hackett/

Incorporated in 1975 in NY.
Donor: William J. Hackett†.
Foundation type: Independent foundation.
Financial data (yr. ended 12/31/05): Assets, $16,751,100 (M); expenditures, $1,070,836; qualifying distributions, $901,374; giving activities include $634,661 for 66 grants (high: $20,080; low: $500).
Purpose and activities: Giving to provide assistance primarily to Roman Catholic organizations, including Roman Catholic missions and agencies, which

promote the health, welfare, education, and independence of individuals; funding also for schools for people who are handicapped and disabled including the physically, emotionally, and developmentally disabled.
Fields of interest: Human services; Developmentally disabled, centers & services; Roman Catholic agencies & churches; Disabilities, people with.
International interests: Developing countries.
Type of support: Equipment.
Limitations: Giving primarily in NJ, NY, and PA. No grants to individuals, or for endowment funds, scholarships, fellowships, demonstration projects, salaries, conferences, or administrative expenses; no loans.
Publications: Application guidelines; Grants list.
Application information: See foundation Web site for application guidelines and procedures. Typically grants range from $1,000 to $20,000, or at the discretion of the Board of Directors. Application form required.
> *Initial approach:* Letter requesting guidelines and application form
> *Copies of proposal:* 1
> *Deadline(s):* 5th of every month, or as indicated by Grant Prog. Off. on application form
> *Board meeting date(s):* 2nd Tues. of every month
> *Final notification:* 30 days
Officers and Trustees:* R. Kevin Hackett,* Pres. and Treas.; Maggie Hackett,* Secy. and Grant Prog. Off.; Colleen Hackett; Kerri Smith.
Number of staff: 2 full-time professional.
EIN: 132840750
Selected grants: The following grants were reported in 2004.
$33,000 to Little Sisters of the Poor, Bronx, NY.
$21,990 to Capuchin Franciscans, New York, NY.
$20,000 to Catholic Home Bureau, New York, NY.
$20,000 to Catholic Medical Mission Board, New York, NY.
$19,000 to De La Salle Blackfeet Middle School, Browning, MT.
$18,601 to Jewish Board of Family and Childrens Services, New York, NY.
$18,112 to Paulist National Catholic Evangelization Association, DC.
$14,200 to Saint Vincents Services, Brooklyn, NY.
$13,637 to Bernardine Franciscan Sisters, King of Prussia, PA.
$12,366 to Little Sisters of the Poor, Totowa, NJ.

5220
Arie and Eva Halpern Family Foundation, Inc. ✧
1163 Rte. 22 E.
Mountainside, NJ 07092

Established in 1986 in NJ.
Donor: Arie Halpern.
Foundation type: Independent foundation.
Financial data (yr. ended 12/31/05): Assets, $7,630,938 (M); gifts received, $745,000; expenditures, $737,340; qualifying distributions, $731,500; giving activities include $731,500 for 28 grants (high: $190,000; low: $1,000).
Purpose and activities: Giving primarily to Jewish agencies.
Fields of interest: Jewish federated giving programs; Jewish agencies & temples.
Limitations: Applications not accepted. Giving primarily in New York, NY. No grants to individuals.

Application information: Contributes only to pre-selected organizations.
Trustees: Arie Halpern; Eva Halpern; Henry Stein.
EIN: 222764210

5221
Sam Halpern Family Foundation, Inc. ✧
1163 Rte. 22 E.
Mountainside, NJ 07092

Established in 1986 in NJ.
Donors: Sam Halpern; Gladys Halpern.
Foundation type: Independent foundation.
Financial data (yr. ended 12/31/05): Assets, $8,863,321 (M); gifts received, $588,000; expenditures, $450,867; qualifying distributions, $445,000; giving activities include $445,000 for 9 grants (high: $130,000; low: $500).
Fields of interest: Higher education; Jewish federated giving programs.
Type of support: General/operating support.
Limitations: Applications not accepted. Giving primarily in NY; some giving in NJ. No grants to individuals.
Application information: Contributes only to pre-selected organizations.
Trustees: Gladys Halpern; Sam Halpern.
EIN: 222707942

5222
Ralph J. Harary Foundation, Inc. ✧
12 Lady Bess Dr.
Deal, NJ 07723
Contact: Ralph J. Harary, Mgr.

Established in 1984 in NJ.
Donors: Ralph J. Harary; Joseph Harary; Jacques Moret, Inc.; SBH Intimates Inc.
Foundation type: Independent foundation.
Financial data (yr. ended 12/31/04): Assets, $821,866 (M); gifts received, $500,000; expenditures, $1,587,373; qualifying distributions, $1,558,412; giving activities include $1,558,412 for 531 grants (high: $183,027; low: $10).
Purpose and activities: Funding primarily for Jewish organizations, temples, schools, and federated giving programs.
Fields of interest: Elementary/secondary education; Human services; Jewish federated giving programs; Jewish agencies & temples.
Limitations: Giving primarily in New York, NY. No grants to individuals.
Application information:
> *Initial approach:* Proposal
> *Deadline(s):* None
Officers: Joseph Harary, C.F.O.; Ralph J. Harary, Mgr.
Trustee: Gloria Harary.
EIN: 222457455

5223
Harbourton Foundation ✧
47 Hulfish St., Ste. 305
Princeton, NJ 08542
Contact: Amy H. Regan, V.P.

Established in 1982 in NJ.
Donor: James S. Regan.
Foundation type: Independent foundation.

Financial data (yr. ended 6/30/05): Assets, $12,772,903 (M); gifts received, $7,000,000; expenditures, $801,125; qualifying distributions, $790,070; giving activities include $788,545 for 33 grants (high: $234,395; low: $750).

Purpose and activities: Support for educational associations, including those seeking to identify learning disabilities of economically disadvantaged children.

Fields of interest: Education, association; Environment, natural resources; Children/youth, services.

Type of support: Technical assistance; Program development; Capital campaigns; General/operating support.

Limitations: Applications not accepted. Giving primarily in NJ. No grants to individuals.

Application information: Contributes only to pre-selected organizations.

Officers: James S. Regan, Pres.; Amy H. Regan, V.P.; Steven Smotrich, V.P.

EIN: 222436112

Selected grants: The following grants were reported in 2003.

$151,191 to Young Scholars Institute, Trenton, NJ.

$55,370 to Council of New Jersey Grantmakers, Trenton, NJ.

$50,000 to Woods Hole Research Center, Woods Hole, MA.

$25,000 to Recording for the Blind and Dyslexic, Princeton, NJ.

$20,000 to New Jersey SEEDS (Scholars, Educators, Excellence, Dedication, Success), Newark, NJ.

$15,000 to Princeton Area Community Foundation, Lawrenceville, NJ.

$15,000 to Women in Need (WIN), New York, NY.

$14,000 to HiTOPS (Health Interested Teens Own Program on Sexuality), Princeton, NJ.

$12,500 to Youth Foundation, Edwards, CO.

$10,000 to Partnership for New Jersey, New Brunswick, NJ.

5224
The Robinson Harris Foundation, Inc. ✧ ☆
71 South Orange Ave., Ste. 385
South Orange, NJ 07079

Established in 2003 in NJ.

Donors: Malcom Ari Robinson; Tamara Leona Robinson.

Foundation type: Independent foundation.

Financial data (yr. ended 12/31/05): Assets, $12,637,264 (M); gifts received, $3,449,000; expenditures, $762,320; qualifying distributions, $575,420; giving activities include $337,500 for 5 grants (high: $150,000; low: $30,000).

Fields of interest: Scholarships/financial aid; Education; African Americans/Blacks.

Limitations: Applications not accepted. No grants to individuals.

Application information: Contributes only to pre-selected organizations.

Officers and Trustees:* Tamara Leona Robinson,* Pres.; M. Bruce Robinson; Malcom Ari Robinson.

EIN: 200518403

5225
Mortimer J. Harrison Article 11(A) Trust ✧
c/o Gregory E. Mulroy
48 Hillside Rd.
Elizabeth, NJ 07208
Contact: Arthur E. Lashinsky, Tr.

Established in 1996 in NY.

Donor: Mortimer J. Harrison‡.

Foundation type: Independent foundation.

Financial data (yr. ended 12/31/03): Assets, $7,451,750 (M); expenditures, $457,473; qualifying distributions, $418,370; giving activities include $418,370 for 3 grants (high: $362,970; low: $5,400).

Purpose and activities: Giving primarily to finance costs of corrective facial surgery.

Fields of interest: Hospitals (specialty); Surgery; Human services.

Limitations: Giving primarily in NY.

Trustee: Arthur E. Lashinsky.

EIN: 137075860

5226
Gates Helms Hawn Foundation ✧
c/o Cappiccille
615 W. Mt. Pleasant Ave.
Livingston, NJ 07039

Established in 1990 in NY.

Donor: Gates Helms Hawn.

Foundation type: Independent foundation.

Financial data (yr. ended 12/31/05): Assets, $2,342,416 (M); expenditures, $582,347; qualifying distributions, $565,000; giving activities include $565,000 for 9 grants (high: $250,000; low: $3,000).

Fields of interest: Elementary/secondary education; Higher education; Hospitals (general).

Limitations: Applications not accepted. Giving primarily in MA and NJ. No grants to individuals.

Application information: Contributes only to pre-selected organizations.

Trustee: Gates Helms Hawn.

EIN: 136939318

5227
The Healey Family Foundation ✧
c/o Thomas & Margaret Healey
310 South St., 2nd Fl.
Morristown, NJ 07960

Established in 1989 in NJ.

Donor: Thomas J. Healey.

Foundation type: Independent foundation.

Financial data (yr. ended 4/30/05): Assets, $14,702,226 (M); gifts received, $3,026,300; expenditures, $787,010; qualifying distributions, $688,613; giving activities include $624,370 for 120 grants (high: $125,000; low: $171).

Purpose and activities: Giving for education, health, medical and human services, and for religion.

Fields of interest: Arts; Higher education, university; Education; Health care; Health organizations, association; Youth development; Human services; Community development; Roman Catholic agencies & churches; Women.

Limitations: Applications not accepted. Giving primarily in Washington, DC, NJ, and NY. No grants to individuals.

Application information: Contributes only to pre-selected organizations.

Trustees: Megan H. Hagerty; Margaret S. Healey; Thomas J. Healey; Thomas Jeremiah Healey.

EIN: 133531967

5228
The Healthcare Foundation of New Jersey ▼ ✧
(formerly NBI Healthcare Foundation, Inc.)
60 E. Willaw St. 2nd Fl.
Livingston, NJ 07039 (973) 921-1210
Contact: Ellen W. Kramer-Lambert, Exec. Dir.
FAX: (973) 921-1274; E-mail: info@hfnj.org; URL: http://www.hfnj.org/

Established in 1996 in NJ; converted from the sale of the assets of the Newark Beth Israel Medical Center.

Foundation type: Independent foundation.

Financial data (yr. ended 12/31/05): Assets, $161,199,337 (M); expenditures, $9,028,405; qualifying distributions, $7,507,178; giving activities include $6,787,112 for 168 grants (high: $500,000; low: $150; average: $1,000–$150,000).

Purpose and activities: The foundation's grantmaking is focused on: 1) serving the healthcare needs of the vulnerable population of Newark, NJ; 2) serving the healthcare needs of the MetroWest Jewish community of northern New Jersey; and 3) clinical medical research and medical education, particularly, programs that positively impact the foundation's targeted communities. The foundation has an interest in innovative health-related programs for vulnerable communities and medically underserved populations. The foundation supports efforts to improve humanism in medicine, especially programs that support compassion and sensitivity in direct patient care.

Fields of interest: Medical school/education; Hospitals (specialty); Medical care, bioethics; Health organizations, association; Biomedicine; Geriatrics; Health organizations; Medical research, institute; Crime/violence prevention; Crime/violence prevention, abuse prevention; Human services; Family services, domestic violence; Aging, centers/services; Jewish agencies & temples; African Americans/Blacks.

Type of support: Capital campaigns; Building/renovation; Equipment; Program development; Seed money; Research.

Limitations: Giving primarily in NJ, with emphasis on Newark and Essex, Morris, and Union counties. No support for political campaigns. No grants to individuals (except for scholarships), or for deficit retirement, ongoing general operating expenses, endowments, or fundraising campaigns.

Publications: Annual report (including application guidelines).

Application information: Grant proposals should be submitted using the NY/NJ Common Application Form. See foundation's Web site for downloadable form. Application form required.

Initial approach: 5-page proposal
Copies of proposal: 1
Deadline(s): Rolling basis
Board meeting date(s): Mar. and Sept.
Final notification: 4 months

Officers and Trustees:* Lester Z. Lieberman,* Chair.; Beth Levithan, Ph.D.*, 1st Vice-Chair.; Lester M. Bornstein,* Vice-Chair.; Steven E. Gross,*

Application information: Contributes only to pre-selected organizations.

Vice-Chair.; Sima K. Jelin,* Vice-Chair.; John H. Reichman,* Secy.; Carolyn M. Weiss, C.F.O.; Ellen R. Wagenberg,* Treas.; Robert Hypler, Ph.D., Exec. Dir.; Gary O. Aidekman; Richard L. Amster; Philip M. Berman; Jay Blumenfeld; Eric S. Bodner; Lawrence R. Buchalter; Michael Francis; Amy Reisen Freundlich; Suzanne J. Groisser; Alan Helfman, M.D.; Kenneth Heyman; Kenneth Jaffe; Steven R. Kamen; Nancy Kridel; Lionel M. Levey; Jerome S. Lieb; Carol P. Marcus; Adam Perlman, M.D.; Jaime B. Ploscowe; Selma Rosen; Bruce Shoulson; Joanne Weinbach; Gary Wingens.

Number of staff: 6 full-time professional.
EIN: 223451664
Selected grants: The following grants were reported in 2003.
$3,390,000 to University of Medicine and Dentistry of New Jersey, Newark, NJ. 2 grants: $3,200,000 to Center for Humanistic Medicine (To establish first national center to train physicians in humanistic practice), $190,000 (To test use of dietary potassium to prevent strokes among African Americans, a group at disproportionate risk).
$492,342 to Newark Beth Israel Medical Center, Newark, NJ. 2 grants: $225,000 to Children's Hospital of New Jersey (For school-based full-service dental care to Newark public school children), $267,342 (To upgrade emergency room with state of the art cardiac telemetry and bedside ultrasound and to support related Physician training).
$126,170 to Programs for Parents, Newark, NJ. To produce video, Identifying the Red Flags of Child Abuse and Neglect, and conduct related training for Essex County Day Care providers.
$117,000 to Daughters of Israel Geriatric Center, West Orange, NJ. To plan and pilot MetroWest Transportation Program which provides medical and essential transportation to elderly in Morris and Essex counties.
$100,000 to Jespy House, South Orange, NJ. For Comprehensive Day Program, structured daily activities and life skills for developmentally disabled adults.
$85,000 to Family Connections, Orange, NJ. For on-site mental health therapy, teacher training and parenting skills to Newark preschool programs.
$75,000 to New Community Corporation, Newark, NJ. For School of Practical Nursing, increasing pool of practical nurses from Newark area.
$69,489 to Jewish Family Service of Metrowest, Florham Park, NJ. To establish pyramid of services that educates and trains youth professionals about eating disorders and how to identify and address young people at risk.
$50,000 to Association of Community Organizations for Reform Now (ACORN), Newark, NJ. To assist Newark immigrants to access and retain health care services.
$50,000 to Hyacinth AIDS Foundation, New Brunswick, NJ. For The Wellness Community initiative in Newark which provides health services and counseling to individuals living with HIV/AIDS.
$38,470 to New Jersey Coalition Against Sexual Assault (NJ CASA), Trenton, NJ. To educate and develop materials for physicians and health professionals on how to screen for and address sexual assault.

5229
Heart Institute of Southern New Jersey ✧
1400 E. Rte. 70
Cherry Hill, NJ 08034-2230

Established in 1999 in NJ.
Foundation type: Independent foundation.
Financial data (yr. ended 6/30/05): Assets, $9,367,468 (M); expenditures, $866,256; qualifying distributions, $402,649; giving activities include $402,649 for 2+ grants (high: $271,200).
Fields of interest: Medical research, association; Heart & circulatory research.
Limitations: Applications not accepted. No grants to individuals.
Application information: Contributes only to pre-selected organizations.
Officers and Board Members:* Harvey L. Waxman, M.D.*, Pres. and Treas.; William J. Untereker, M.D.*, V.P.; Terry D. Friedman, M.D.
EIN: 222574758
Selected grants: The following grants were reported in 2004.
$405,000 to University of Pennsylvania Medical Center, Philadelphia, PA. For cardiology research and education.

5230
The Helm Foundation
c/o John R. Helm
49 Glenwood Rd.
Upper Montclair, NJ 07043

Donor: Harold Helm†.
Foundation type: Independent foundation.
Financial data (yr. ended 12/31/04): Assets, $265,308 (M); expenditures, $501,230; qualifying distributions, $488,658; giving activities include $483,750 for 18 grants (high: $201,500; low: $500), and $1,000 for 1 grant to an individual.
Fields of interest: Education; Human services.
Type of support: General/operating support; Capital campaigns.
Limitations: Applications not accepted. Giving primarily in MA and NJ. No grants for direct charitable activities; no program-related investments.
Application information: Contributes only to pre-selected organizations.
Trustees: Aubin Z. Ames; Henry Bessire; Grant M. Gille; John R. Helm; Eleanor Ketcham; John Ketcham.
EIN: 226041312

5231
Hess Foundation, Inc. ▼ ✧
75 Eisenhower Pkwy.
Roseland, NJ 07068
Contact: Norma Hess, Pres.

Incorporated in 1954 in DE.
Donor: Leon Hess†.
Foundation type: Independent foundation.
Financial data (yr. ended 11/30/04): Assets, $303,111,395 (M); gifts received, $32,321,166; expenditures, $10,620,558; qualifying distributions, $10,004,821; giving activities include $9,673,267 for 234 grants (high: $660,000; low: $200; average: $1,000–$50,000).
Purpose and activities: Emphasis on higher education and hospitals; grants also for performing arts and cultural organizations, synagogues, and human services.
Fields of interest: Performing arts; Higher education; Hospitals (general); Human services; Jewish agencies & temples.
Limitations: Applications not accepted. Giving on a national basis, with some emphasis on NY. No grants to individuals.
Application information: Contributes only to pre-selected organizations.
Board meeting date(s): As required
Officers and Directors:* Norma Hess,* Pres.; John B. Hess,* Exec. V.P.; Marlene Hess,* V.P.; Constance Hess Williams,* V.P.; John Y. Schreyer,* Secy.; Burton Lefkowitz,* Treas.; Eugene W. Goodwillie, Jr.
Number of staff: 1 full-time professional.
EIN: 221713046
Selected grants: The following grants were reported in 2004.
$660,000 to American Museum of Natural History, New York, NY. For unrestricted support.
$505,000 to Lincoln Center Theater, New York, NY. For unrestricted support.
$425,000 to Columbia University, New York, NY. For unrestricted support.
$400,000 to Wellesley College, Wellesley, MA. For unrestricted support.
$375,000 to Metropolitan Opera, New York, NY. For unrestricted support.
$308,000 to Museum of Modern Art, New York, NY. For unrestricted support.
$225,000 to Brown University, Providence, RI. For unrestricted support.
$201,000 to Harvard University, Cambridge, MA. For unrestricted support.
$200,000 to Archdiocese of Washington, DC. For unrestricted support.
$200,000 to Deerfield Academy, Deerfield, MA. For unrestricted support.

5232
Hickory Foundation ✧
P.O. Box 281
Lambertville, NJ 08530

Established in 1997 in NY.
Donor: Virginia Manheimer.
Foundation type: Independent foundation.
Financial data (yr. ended 12/31/03): Assets, $14,195,550 (M); gifts received, $508,155; expenditures, $1,357,837; qualifying distributions, $1,339,035; giving activities include $1,333,900 for 57 grants (high: $525,000; low: $250; average: $1,000–$100,000).
Purpose and activities: Giving primarily for education, federated giving programs, and public affairs.
Fields of interest: Media/communications; Historic preservation/historical societies; Arts; Education; Environment; Hospitals (general); Human services; Children, services; Federated giving programs; Social sciences, public policy; Public affairs.
Limitations: Applications not accepted. Giving primarily in NY.
Application information: Contributes only to pre-selected organizations.
Officer: Virginia Manheimer, Pres.
EIN: 223472805
Selected grants: The following grants were reported in 2003.
$525,000 to Brighter Choice Foundation, Clifton Park, NY. For general support.

$65,000 to Fund for Educational Reform, Chicago, IL. For general support.

$60,000 to Center for Equal Opportunity, Sterling, VA. For general support.

$50,000 to American Civil Rights Institute, Sacramento, CA. For general support.

$50,000 to Friends of Czech Greenways, New York, NY. For general support.

$50,000 to Institute for Justice, DC. For general support.

$50,000 to Institute of World Politics, DC. For general support.

$25,000 to Becket Fund for Religious Liberty, DC. For general support.

$20,000 to National Center for Neighborhood Enterprise, DC. For general support.

$20,000 to Saint Lukes Chamber Ensemble, New York, NY. For general support.

5233
Hidden Pond Foundation ✧ ☆
310 South St.
P.O. Box 1913
Morristown, NJ 07960-1913
Contact: J. Peter Simon, Tr.

Established in 1994 in NJ.
Donor: J. Peter Simon.
Foundation type: Independent foundation.
Financial data (yr. ended 12/31/05): Assets, $328,595 (M); gifts received, $325,000; expenditures, $465,797; qualifying distributions, $461,710; giving activities include $461,710 for 274 grants (high: $50,000; low: $50).
Purpose and activities: Giving to education, Roman Catholic churches, community foundations, and public charities.
Fields of interest: Arts; Education; Medical research; Civil liberties, right to life; Community development; Roman Catholic federated giving programs; Government/public administration; Roman Catholic agencies & churches.
Type of support: General/operating support; Continuing support; Annual campaigns; Emergency funds; Program development; Curriculum development.
Limitations: Giving primarily in NJ.
Publications: Financial statement.
Application information:
   Initial approach: Letter
   Deadline(s): None
Trustee: J. Peter Simon.
EIN: 223338066
Selected grants: The following grants were reported in 2004.
$55,000 to Delbarton School, Morristown, NJ. 2 grants: $5,000, $50,000
$25,250 to Covenant House New Jersey, Newark, NJ. 2 grants: $250, $25,000
$10,000 to Union Hospital Foundation, Union, NJ.
$6,000 to Morristown-Beard School, Morristown, NJ. 2 grants: $5,000, $1,000
$450 to Church of Christ the King, New Vernon, NJ. 2 grants: $200, $250
$250 to Birth Haven, Newton, NJ.

5234
The High Q Foundation, Inc. ✧
c/o Kenneth J. Slutsky, Lowenstein Sandler
65 Livingston Ave.
Roseland, NJ 07068

Established in 2002 in NJ.
Donor: Triplet Investment Company, LLC.
Foundation type: Independent foundation.
Financial data (yr. ended 11/30/05): Assets, $44,084,763 (M); gifts received, $2,000,000; expenditures, $23,055,016; qualifying distributions, $23,015,316; giving activities include $4,859,508 for 9 grants (high: $3,552,000; low: $8,800), and $17,817,575 for 1 foundation-administered program.
Fields of interest: Higher education; Medical research.
Limitations: Applications not accepted. Giving on a national basis. No grants to individuals.
Application information: Contributes only to pre-selected organizations.
Officers and Trustees:* Kenneth J. Slutsky,* Pres. and Treas.; Allen Levithan,* V.P. and Secy.; John L. Berger,* V.P.
EIN: 020537670

5235
The Hilfiger Family Foundation, Inc. ✧ ☆
c/o Graham, Curtin & Sheridan
P.O. Box 1991
Morristown, NJ 07962-1991

Established in 1999 in CT.
Donors: Thomas J. Hilfiger; Susan D. Hilfiger.
Foundation type: Independent foundation.
Financial data (yr. ended 12/31/05): Assets, $1,075 (M); gifts received, $322,000; expenditures, $323,244; qualifying distributions, $321,000; giving activities include $321,000 for 4 grants (high: $200,000; low: $1,000).
Purpose and activities: Giving primarily for natural resource conservation.
Fields of interest: Environment, natural resources; Human services; Federated giving programs.
Limitations: Giving primarily in NY. No grants to individuals.
Officers and Directors:* Thomas R. Curtin,* Pres.; Susan D. Hilfiger,* Secy.; Joseph M. Lamastra,* Treas.; Thomas J. Hilfiger.
EIN: 223626164
Selected grants: The following grants were reported in 2003.
$100,000 to Eagle Hill Foundation, Greenwich, CT.
$10,000 to Professional Childrens School, New York, NY.
$10,000 to United Way of the Southern Tier, Corning, NY.
$5,000 to American Red Cross.
$1,000 to Western Wish List.
$950 to Silver Shield Association, Greenwich, CT.

5236
The Hill Family Foundation, Inc. ✧ ☆
c/o Vernon W. Hill, II, Commerce Bank, N.A.
1701 Rte. 70 E.
Cherry Hill, NJ 08034

Established in 1999 in NJ.
Donors: Vernon W. Hill II; Shirley Hill.
Foundation type: Independent foundation.
Financial data (yr. ended 9/30/05): Assets, $9,953,281 (M); gifts received, $1,661,126; expenditures, $604,438; qualifying distributions, $604,438; giving activities include $602,329 for 4 grants (high: $290,400; low: $10,000).

Fields of interest: Elementary/secondary education; Education, early childhood education; Education; Boys & girls clubs.
Limitations: Applications not accepted. Giving primarily in NJ and PA. No grants to individuals.
Application information: Contributes only to pre-selected organizations.
Officers: Vernon W. Hill II, Pres.; Shirley Hill, Secy.; Susan Singer, Treas.
EIN: 223714460

5237
The Hiller Family Foundation, Inc. ✧
7 Willow Woods Trail
Warren, NJ 07059

Established in 2004 in NJ.
Donors: Anatol Hiller; Pnina Hiller.
Foundation type: Independent foundation.
Financial data (yr. ended 12/31/05): Assets, $599,115 (M); gifts received, $1,200,013; expenditures, $606,137; qualifying distributions, $606,125; giving activities include $604,475 for 14 grants (high: $500,000; low: $250).
Purpose and activities: Giving primarily for higher education, particularly to a law school, as well as to Jewish organizations, temples and schools.
Fields of interest: Elementary/secondary education; Higher education; Law school/ education; Human services; Jewish federated giving programs; Jewish agencies & temples.
Limitations: Applications not accepted. Giving primarily in NJ; some funding in New York, NY. No grants to individuals.
Application information: Contributes only to pre-selected organizations.
Trustees: Anatol Hiller; Pnina Hiller; Fay Hiller Verbel.
EIN: 200849460

5238
Richard H. Holzer Memorial Foundation
c/o Chick Master
25 Rockwood Pl.
Englewood, NJ 07631
Contact: Vivian Holzer, Pres.

Established in 1969 in NJ.
Donor: Erich Holzer†.
Foundation type: Independent foundation.
Financial data (yr. ended 12/31/04): Assets, $7,678,833 (L); gifts received, $79,030; expenditures, $420,965; qualifying distributions, $340,916; giving activities include $314,800 for 56 grants (high: $50,000; low: $100).
Purpose and activities: Giving primarily for the arts.
Fields of interest: Performing arts; Performing arts, music; Arts; Higher education; Jewish agencies & temples.
Type of support: Continuing support; Annual campaigns; Endowments.
Limitations: Giving primarily in northern NJ.
Application information: Application form not required.
   Initial approach: Letter
   Deadline(s): None
Officers and Directors:* Vivian Holzer,* Pres.; Robert Holzer,* V.P. and Treas.; Waltraud Dietl, Secy.
Number of staff: 2 part-time professional.
EIN: 237014880

Selected grants: The following grants were reported in 2004.
$50,000 to Metropolitan Opera, New York, NY.
$20,000 to Solomon Schechter Day School, NJ.
$15,000 to Lincoln Center for the Performing Arts, New York, NY.
$15,000 to Pascack Valley Hospital Foundation, Westwood, NJ.
$10,000 to Metropolitan Museum of Art, New York, NY.
$10,000 to New Jersey Symphony Orchestra, Newark, NJ.
$5,500 to Philadelphia Orchestra Association, Philadelphia, PA.
$5,000 to Cornell University, Ithaca, NY.
$5,000 to Jewish Museum, New York, NY.
$2,500 to Medina General Hospital, Medina, OH.

5239

The Honickman Charitable Fund ✧
8275 Rte. 130
Pennsauken, NJ 08110-1435

Established in 1998 in PA.
Donor: Pepsi-Cola & National Brand Beverages, Ltd.
Foundation type: Company-sponsored foundation.
Financial data (yr. ended 12/31/05): Assets, $2,942,377 (M); gifts received, $3,016,871; expenditures, $398,700; qualifying distributions, $398,700; giving activities include $398,700 for grants.
Purpose and activities: The foundation supports organizations involved with arts and culture, education, and health.
Fields of interest: Museums; Arts; Higher education; Education; Health care.
Limitations: Applications not accepted. No grants to individuals.
Application information: Contributes only to pre-selected organizations.
Trustees: Harold Honickman; Jeffrey Honickman; Walter Wilkinson.
EIN: 256612575

5240

Horizon Charitable Foundation, Inc. ✧ ☆
(doing business as The Horizon Foundation for New Jersey)
3 Penn Plz. E., PP-15V
Newark, NJ 07105-2200
Contact: Susan Austin, Prog. Off.; Jonathan Pearson
E-mail: foundation_info@horizonblue.com;
URL: http://www.horizonblue.com/foundation

Established in 2003 in NJ.
Donor: Horizon Healthcare Services, Inc.
Foundation type: Company-sponsored foundation.
Financial data (yr. ended 12/31/04): Assets, $10,000,312 (M); expenditures, $803,245; qualifying distributions, $658,100; giving activities include $650,000 for 24 grants (high: $135,000; low: $5,000), and $8,100 for employee matching gifts.
Purpose and activities: The foundation supports organizations involved with arts and culture, education, and health.
Fields of interest: Arts; Education; Health care.
Type of support: Continuing support; General/operating support; Capital campaigns; Endowments; Research; Technical assistance; Employee matching gifts.

Limitations: Giving limited to NJ. No support for political organizations or candidates. No grants to individuals.
Application information: Support is limited to 1 contribution per organization during any given year. Multi-year funding is not automatic. Application form required.
Initial approach: Complete online application form
Copies of proposal: 1
Deadline(s): From Jan. 1 to Oct. 31
Final notification: 120 days
Officers and Directors:* William J. Marino,* Chair. and Pres.; Robert A. Marino,* V.P.; John W. Campbell,* Secy.; Robert J. Pures,* Treas.; Lawrence B. Altman, Exec. Dir.; Christy W. Bell; Clive S. Cummis; Rocco J. Marano.
Number of staff: None.
EIN: 200252405

5241

Hirair and Anna Hovnanian Foundation, Inc. ✧
4000 Rte. 66, 4th Fl.
Tinton Falls, NJ 07753 (732) 922-6100
Contact: Hirair Hovnanian, Chair.

Established in 1986 in FL.
Donors: Hirair Hovnanian; Anna Hovnanian.
Foundation type: Independent foundation.
Financial data (yr. ended 12/31/04): Assets, $54,241,218 (M); expenditures, $2,086,579; qualifying distributions, $1,953,601; giving activities include $1,948,350 for 18 grants (high: $610,000).
Purpose and activities: Giving primarily for Armenian culture, and education.
Fields of interest: Education; International affairs.
International interests: Armenia.
Limitations: Giving on a national and international basis. No grants to individuals.
Application information:
Initial approach: Letter
Deadline(s): None
Officers: Hirair Hovnanian, Chair.; Anna Hovnanian, Pres.; Edele Hovnanian, V.P. and Treas.; Armen Hovnanian, V.P.; Leela Hovnanian, V.P.; Siran Sahakian, V.P.; Tanya Hovnanian, Secy.
EIN: 592714390
Selected grants: The following grants were reported in 2003.
$622,285 to Armenian Assembly of America, DC. For general support.
$300,000 to Armenia Fund USA, New York, NY. For general support.
$10,000 to Diocese of the Armenian Church, New York, NY. For general support.
$10,000 to Georgian Court University, Lakewood, NJ. For general support.
$10,000 to Monmouth Medical Center Foundation, Long Branch, NJ. For general support.
$5,000 to Junior Achievement, National, Colorado Springs, CO. For general support.

5242

The Kevork and Sirwart Hovnanian Foundation ✧ ☆
110 W. Front St.
Red Bank, NJ 07701

Established in 2002.
Donors: Sirwart K. Hovnanian; Kevork S. Hovnanian.

Foundation type: Independent foundation.
Financial data (yr. ended 12/31/05): Assets, $18,461,268 (M); expenditures, $1,060,799; qualifying distributions, $1,048,700; giving activities include $1,048,700 for grants.
Fields of interest: Higher education; Education; Human services.
Limitations: Applications not accepted. Giving primarily in NJ. No grants to individuals.
Application information: Unsolicited requests for funds not accepted.
Trustees: Kevork S. Hovnanian; Sirwart K. Hovnanian.
EIN: 050562489

5243

The Wesley J. Howe Family Foundation, Inc. ✧
c/o Duncan Financial Group
1200 E. Ridgewood Ave., Ste. 300W
Ridgewood, NJ 07450
Contact: Jock Duncan, Secy.-Treas.

Established in 1997 in NJ.
Donors: Suzanne R. Howe; Jack Howe; Wesley J. Howe.
Foundation type: Independent foundation.
Financial data (yr. ended 12/31/03): Assets, $3,012,143 (M); gifts received, $1,383; expenditures, $1,165,810; qualifying distributions, $1,115,000; giving activities include $1,115,000 for 4 grants (high: $600,000; low: $5,000).
Purpose and activities: Giving primarily for higher education.
Fields of interest: Higher education; Education.
Limitations: Applications not accepted. Giving primarily in New York, NY. No grants to individuals.
Application information: Contributes only to pre-selected organizations.
Officers: Wesley J. Howe, Pres.; Richard Comerford, V.P.; Suzanne R. Howe, V.P.; Jock Duncan, Secy.-Treas.
EIN: 223479643

5244

The Huber Foundation
P.O. Box 277
Rumson, NJ 07760 (732) 933-7700
Contact: Lorraine Barnhart, V.P. and Exec. Dir.

Incorporated in 1949 in NJ.
Donor: Members of the Huber and Mertens families.
Foundation type: Independent foundation.
Financial data (yr. ended 12/31/05): Assets, $47,189,359 (M); expenditures, $2,481,905; qualifying distributions, $2,230,125; giving activities include $2,097,000 for 30 grants (high: $200,000; low: $2,000).
Purpose and activities: Grants primarily to organizations working in the areas of family planning and reproductive rights.
Fields of interest: Reproductive health, family planning; Civil liberties, reproductive rights.
Type of support: General/operating support; Continuing support; Annual campaigns; Program development; Publication; Seed money.
Limitations: Giving limited to the U.S. No support for foreign organizations, international projects, or projects that are local or regional in scope. No grants to individuals, or for scholarships, fellowships,

research, building endowment funds, capital campaigns or film production; no loans.
Publications: Annual report (including application guidelines).
Application information: Application form not required.
Initial approach: Proposal
Copies of proposal: 1
Deadline(s): None
Board meeting date(s): Quarterly; dates not fixed
Final notification: 3 months
Officers and Trustees:* Hans A. Huber,* Pres.; Lorraine Barnhart,* V.P. and Exec. Dir.; Michael W. Huber,* Secy.; Julia Ann Nagy, Treas.; Jennifer Currie; Lisa Goodspeed; Laurel D. Huber; Christopher W. Seely; Catherine Weiss.
Number of staff: 1 part-time professional.
EIN: 210737062
Selected grants: The following grants were reported in 2005.
$225,000 to Planned Parenthood Federation of America, New York, NY.
$200,000 to American Civil Liberties Union Foundation, New York, NY.
$200,000 to Center for Reproductive Rights, New York, NY.
$150,000 to NARAL Pro-Choice America Foundation, DC.
$100,000 to People for the American Way Foundation, DC.
$60,000 to Advocates for Youth, DC.
$60,000 to National Abortion Federation, DC.
$60,000 to National Family Planning and Reproductive Health Association, DC.
$40,000 to Planned Parenthood of New York City, New York, NY.
$40,000 to Planned Parenthood of Northern New England, Williston, VT.

5245
Hugin Family Foundation, Inc. ✧ ☆
19 Essex Rd.
Summit, NJ 07901

Established in 2001 in NJ.
Donor: Robert J. Hugin.
Foundation type: Independent foundation.
Financial data (yr. ended 12/31/04): Assets, $941,060 (M); gifts received, $134,000; expenditures, $343,967; qualifying distributions, $343,967; giving activities include $343,792 for 8 grants (high: $119,868; low: $2,854).
Fields of interest: Higher education; Education; Hospitals (general); Foundations (private grantmaking); Protestant agencies & churches.
Limitations: Applications not accepted. Giving primarily in NJ. No grants to individuals.
Application information: Contributes only to pre-selected organizations.
Officers: Robert J. Hugin, Pres. and Treas.; Kathleen M. Hugin, Secy.
Director: James R. Swenson.
EIN: 030374762

5246
Huntsman Family Foundation ✧
P.O. Box 1525
Pennington, NJ 08534-1525

Established in 1998 in VA.
Donor: Kenneth A. Huntsman.

Foundation type: Independent foundation.
Financial data (yr. ended 5/31/05): Assets, $3,107,508 (M); expenditures, $692,754; qualifying distributions, $666,164; giving activities include $665,000 for 6 grants (high: $250,000; low: $20,000).
Purpose and activities: Giving primarily for education and to a United Methodist church.
Fields of interest: Performing arts, music; Education; Recreation, association; Recreation, parks/playgrounds; Youth, services; Christian agencies & churches; Protestant agencies & churches.
Limitations: Applications not accepted. Giving on a national basis. No grants to individuals.
Application information: Contributes only to pre-selected organizations.
Officers: Kenneth A. Huntsman, Pres.; Marcia K. Huntsman, Secy.
Director: M. Pauline Huntsman.
EIN: 541913075
Selected grants: The following grants were reported in 2003.
$425,000 to Northern Bedford Community Athletic Association, Loysburg, PA. For general operating support.
$267,765 to Village at Morrisons Cove, Martinsburg, PA. For general operating support.
$75,000 to Centreville United Methodist Church, Centreville, VA. For general operating support.
$46,000 to Wesley Theological Seminary, DC. For general operating support.
$20,000 to InterVarsity Christian Fellowship/USA, Madison, WI. For general operating support.
$20,000 to Strings in the Mountains, Steamboat Springs, CO. For general operating support.

5247
The Hyde and Watson Foundation ▼
31-F Mountain Blvd.
Warren, NJ 07059 (908) 753-3700
Contact: Hunter W. Corbin, Pres.
FAX: (908) 753-0004;
E-mail: hydeandwatson@yahoo.com; URL: http://foundationcenter.org/grantmaker/hydeandwatson

The Lillia Babbitt Hyde Foundation incorporated in 1924 in NY; The John Jay and Eliza Jane Watson Foundation incorporated in 1949; consolidation of two foundations into Hyde and Watson Foundation in 1983.
Donors: Lillia Babbitt Hyde†; Eliza Jane Watson†.
Foundation type: Independent foundation.
Financial data (yr. ended 12/31/05): Assets, $118,332,308 (M); expenditures, $5,778,312; qualifying distributions, $5,979,313; giving activities include $4,510,950 for 324 grants (high: $125,000; low: $3,000; average: $5,000–$25,000).
Purpose and activities: Support for capital projects such as hard costs related to purchase or relocation of facilities, and/or building improvements, purchase of capital equipment, one-time capital seeds, and limited medical research areas. Broad fields include health, education, religion, social services, arts, and humanities.
Fields of interest: Performing arts; Humanities; Arts; Education, early childhood education; Child development, education; Elementary school/education; Secondary school/education; Medical school/education; Education; Environment, natural resources; Environment; Hospitals (general); Medical care, rehabilitation; Health care; Substance

abuse, services; Mental health/crisis services; Health organizations, association; Cancer; Medical research, institute; Cancer research; AIDS research; Human services; Children/youth, services; Child development, services; Family services; Aging, centers/services; Minorities/immigrants, centers/services; Homeless, human services; Religion; Aging; Disabilities, people with; Minorities; Economically disadvantaged; Homeless.
Type of support: Capital campaigns; Building/renovation; Equipment; Land acquisition; Debt reduction; Emergency funds; Research; Matching/challenge support.
Limitations: Giving is focused in the five boroughs of New York, NY, and Essex, Union and Morris counties in NJ. No giving outside the U.S. No grants for endowments, operating support, benefit fundraisers, annual fund appears, or scholarships or from fiscal agents.
Publications: Application guidelines; Annual report (including application guidelines); Financial statement; Grants list.
Application information: Supplemental information may be required if proposal is considered by grants committee. The foundation also accepts the New York/New Jersey Area Common Application Form but prefers its own application procedure. Application form required.
Initial approach: Letter with grant application form, which is available by fax or at the foundation's Web site, and attachments
Copies of proposal: 1
Deadline(s): No later than Feb. 15 and Sept. 15
Board meeting date(s): Apr./May and Nov./Dec.
Final notification: After grant or board meeting or preliminary review
Officers and Directors:* John W. Holman, Jr.,* Chair.; Hunter W. Corbin,* Pres.; William V. Engel,* Sr. V.P. and Secy.; Brunilda Moriarty, V.P. and Grants Admin.; Thomas W. Berry,* Treas.; G. Morrison Hubbard, Jr., Dir. Emeritus; Elizabeth R. Curry; H. Corbin Day; Jennifer Chandler Hauge; John W. Holman III; Robert W. Parsons, Jr.; Roger B. Parsons; Kate B. Wood.
Number of staff: 6 full-time professional.
EIN: 222425725
Selected grants: The following grants were reported in 2005.
$250,000 to Kent Place School, Summit, NJ. For facility renovations and improvements.
$250,000 to YMCA of Frost Valley, Claryville, NY. For facility improvements and expansion.
$200,000 to Family Service of Morris County, Morristown, NJ. For construction of new facility.
$200,000 to Saint Philips Academy, Newark, NJ. For support of Securing Excellence campaign.
$150,000 to Muhlenberg Hospital Foundation, Plainfield, NJ. For construction of new facility.
$100,000 to Delbarton School, Morristown, NJ. For construction of fine arts building.
$15,000 to Kids Corporation, Newark, NJ. For transportation vehicle.
$15,000 to Overlook Hospital Foundation, Summit, NJ. For equipment for Family Practice Center.
$10,000 to SAGE Eldercare, Summit, NJ. For computer equipment and software.
$10,000 to TADA! Theater and Dance Alliance, New York, NY. For specialized equipment.

5248
The IDT Charitable Foundation ▼ ✧
520 Broad St.
Newark, NJ 07102

Established in 2001 as a company-sponsored operating foundation.
Donor: IDT Corp.
Foundation type: Operating foundation.
Financial data (yr. ended 12/31/05): Assets, $12,981,303 (M); expenditures, $8,195,466; qualifying distributions, $12,870,259; giving activities include $8,175,259 for grants.
Purpose and activities: The foundation supports Jewish agencies and temples and organizations involved with arts and culture, education, the environment, health, and children and youth.
Fields of interest: Arts; Education; Environment; Health care; Athletics/sports, Olympics; Children/youth, services; Jewish agencies & temples.
Limitations: Applications not accepted. Giving on a national and international basis. No grants to individuals.
Application information: Contributes only to pre-selected organizations.
Directors: James Courter; Ira Greenstein; Joyce Mason.
EIN: 364450442
Selected grants: The following grants were reported in 2004.
$1,750,000 to New York City Host Committee, New York, NY.
$250,000 to Chai Lifeline, New York, NY.
$240,125 to Yeshiva Bais Tzvi Yaakov Institute, Newark, NJ.
$100,000 to American Israel Education Foundation (AIEF), DC.
$75,000 to Hebrew Institute of Riverdale, Bronx, NY.
$25,000 to United Jewish Community Gemach, Lawrence, NY.
$20,000 to Chabad of Argentina Relief Appeal, New York, NY.
$18,000 to American Friends of Yad Eliezer, Brooklyn, NY.
$15,000 to William Annin Middle School Parent-Teacher Organization, Basking Ridge, NJ.
$12,500 to Young Israel of Riverdale, Bronx, NY.

5249
The Imada Foundation ✧ ☆
Witherspoon St.
Princeton, NJ 08542

Established in 2004 in NJ.
Foundation type: Independent foundation.
Financial data (yr. ended 12/31/05): Assets, $6,321,695 (M); expenditures, $362,634; qualifying distributions, $356,579; giving activities include $356,579 for 35 grants (high: $82,221; low: $180).
Fields of interest: Higher education; Health care.
Limitations: Applications not accepted. Giving primarily in NJ. No grants to individuals.
Application information: Contributes only to pre-selected organizations.
Officer and Directors:* Ivy Lewis Powell,* Pres.; Marc Powell.
EIN: 201422978

5250
Indian Trail Charitable Foundation, Inc. ✧
c/o Konner & Harbus
80 E. Rte. 4, Ste. 408
Paramus, NJ 07652 (201) 816-0088

Established in 1986 in DE.
Donors: Edna Askwith; Patricia Kenner; Bertram J. Askwith; Kathy Franklin.
Foundation type: Independent foundation.
Financial data (yr. ended 11/30/04): Assets, $11,848,207 (M); gifts received, $150,000; expenditures, $1,038,909; qualifying distributions, $1,007,483; giving activities include $1,007,483 for 14 grants (high: $453,333; low: $1,000).
Purpose and activities: Giving primarily for higher education, and to Jewish organizations, including a Jewish museum; funding also for other educational organizations, including a girls' school, health associations, and for food allergy research.
Fields of interest: Museums (ethnic/folk arts); Education, alliance; Elementary/secondary education; Higher education; Health organizations, association; Agriculture/food, research; Federated giving programs; Jewish agencies & temples.
Limitations: Giving primarily in Harrison and New York, NY; funding also in Cambridge, MA, and Pittsburgh, PA.
Application information:
Initial approach: Letter
Deadline(s): Sept. 30
Trustee: Bertram J. Askwith.
EIN: 222769941
Selected grants: The following grants were reported in 2003.
$321,000 to Harvard University, Cambridge, MA. For general support.
$210,000 to Carnegie Mellon University, Pittsburgh, PA. For general support.
$25,000 to United Way of Harrison, Harrison, NY. For general support.
$15,000 to University of Michigan, Ann Arbor, MI. 2 grants: $5,000 (For general support), $10,000 (For general support).
$11,000 to Food Allergy Initiative, New York, NY. For general support.
$10,000 to Educational Alliance, New York, NY. For general support.
$2,000 to Nightingale-Bamford School, New York, NY. For general support.
$1,000 to American Jewish Committee, New York, NY. For general support.
$1,000 to Chemotherapy Foundation, New York, NY. For general support.

5251
The Integra Foundation, Inc.
311 Enterprise Dr.
Plainsboro, NJ 08536 (609) 936-2494
Contact: Gianna Sabella, Exec. Dir.
FAX: (609) 799-3297;
E-mail: gsabella@integra-ls.com; Additional E-mail: info@integra-foundation.org; URL: http://www.integra-foundation.org

Established in 2002 in NJ.
Donor: Integra LifeSciences Corp.
Foundation type: Company-sponsored foundation.
Financial data (yr. ended 12/31/04): Assets, $1,645,265 (M); expenditures, $414,519; qualifying distributions, $378,891; giving activities include $378,891 for 45 grants (high: $93,188; low: $500).
Purpose and activities: The foundation supports programs designed to advance innovative medical and health care research and education, primarily in the areas of neurosurgery, reconstructive surgery, and general surgery, to improve the outcome and quality of life for patients and their communities.

Fields of interest: Medical school/education; Neuroscience research; Medical research; Surgery research.
Limitations: No support for political, fraternal, social, veterans', or religious organizations. No grants to individuals, or for programs that directly support marketing or sales objectives of Integra LifeSciences.
Application information: Application form required.
Initial approach: Download application form and mail or fax to foundation
Copies of proposal: 1
Deadline(s): None
Board meeting date(s): Feb., May, Aug., and Nov.
Officers: Linda Littlejohns, Pres.; Simon Archibald, V.P.; Zeev Hadass, V.P.; Wilma Davis, Treas.; Gianna Sabella, Exec. Dir.
Trustees: Stuart Essig; Jack Henneman; Judith O'Grady.
Number of staff: 1 part-time professional.
EIN: 522388679
Selected grants: The following grants were reported in 2004.
$93,188 to University of Washington Foundation, Seattle, WA.
$35,000 to Plastic Surgery Educational Foundation, Arlington Heights, IL.
$20,503 to Brain Trauma Foundation, New York, NY.
$15,000 to Angels of the OR, Baltimore, MD.
$12,000 to Hydrocephalus Association, San Francisco, CA.
$5,000 to Methodist Healthcare Foundation, Memphis, TN.
$5,000 to TIRR Foundation, Houston, TX.
$2,500 to Oregon Health and Science University Foundation, Portland, OR.
$2,000 to Interplast, Mountain View, CA.
$1,000 to Brain Injury Association of New Jersey, Edison, NJ.

5252
The International Foundation ✧
271 Rte. 46 W., Bldg. G, Apt. 110
Fairfield, NJ 07004 (973) 227-6107
Contact: Edward A. Holmes, Grants Chair.
FAX: (973) 227-6821;
E-mail: kgaiser@carricocpa.net; Additional tel.: (973) 227-6618

Incorporated in 1948 in DE.
Foundation type: Independent foundation.
Financial data (yr. ended 12/31/04): Assets, $29,589,924 (M); expenditures, $1,609,610; qualifying distributions, $1,236,872; giving activities include $935,100 for 89 grants (high: $25,000; low: $3,000).
Purpose and activities: Giving to help people of developing nations in their endeavors to solve some of their problems, to attain a better standard of living, and to obtain a reasonable degree of self-sufficiency. Grants are made in the following general areas: 1) Agriculture: research and production, 2) Health: medical, nutrition, and water, 3) Education: formal at all levels research, 4) Social Development: cultural, economic, community, and entrepreneurial activity, and some aid to refugees, and grants for population planning are given, and 5) Environment.
Fields of interest: Arts; Libraries/library science; Education; Environment, natural resources; Environment; Hospitals (general); Medical care, rehabilitation; Health care; Health organizations, association; AIDS; Biomedicine; Medical research,

institute; AIDS research; Agriculture; Food services; Human services; International economic development; Urban/community development; Rural development; Voluntarism promotion; Marine science; Engineering/technology; Science; Roman Catholic agencies & churches.

International interests: Caribbean; Latin America; Middle East; Oceania; Philippines; Southern Africa.

Type of support: Building/renovation; Equipment; Emergency funds; Program development; Seed money; Matching/challenge support.

Limitations: Giving primarily in Asia, the Caribbean, Latin America, the Middle East, the Philippines, the South Pacific, and Southern Africa through U.S.-based philanthropies. No grants to individuals, or for endowment funds, operating budgets, scholarships, fellowships, matching gifts, video productions, or conferences; no loans.

Publications: Informational brochure (including application guidelines).

Application information: Application should include a SASE for reply. Application form not required.

  Initial approach: Letter requesting descriptive brochure
  Copies of proposal: 1
  Deadline(s): None
  Board meeting date(s): Jan., Apr., July, and Oct.
  Final notification: 6 months; grants paid in Dec.

Officers and Trustees:* Edward A. Holmes,* Grants Chair.; Gary Dicovitsky,* Fin. Chair.; Frank Madden,* Pres.; David S. Bate,* V.P.; John D. Carrico,* Secy.-Treas.; Duncan W. Clark, M.D.; William McCormack, M.D.

Number of staff: 1 part-time professional; 1 part-time support.

EIN: 131962255

Selected grants: The following grants were reported in 2003.

$75,000 to Concern/America, Santa Ana, CA. For health and technology in Chiapas, payable over 3 years.

$25,000 to Healing the Children, Spokane, WA. For stateside foreign program for surgery and medical care for children from overseas.

$15,000 to Africare, DC. For HIV/AIDS Liberia Volunteer Service Corps in Nimba County.

$15,000 to American Leprosy Missions, Greenville, SC. For sustainable food sources for three leprosy centers in Thailand.

$15,000 to Global Links, Pittsburgh, PA. For Suture Donation Program.

$10,000 to American Friends Service Committee, New York, NY. For Haiti Integrated Community Development Program.

$9,000 to Consolata Society for Foreign Missions, Somerset, NJ. For purchase of 10 cows for rural families in San Vicente, Colombia.

$7,000 to ARADO International, Shepherdstown, WV. For strategic agricultural practices in Lake Titicaca Basin of Peru.

$7,000 to Guatemala Human Rights Commission/USA, DC. For Puentes de Paz mental health program.

$5,000 to Catholic Relief Services, Baltimore, MD. For emergency aid for Liberia.

5253
Isermann Family Foundation, Inc. ✧
c/o Conroy, Smith & Co.
385 Prospect Ave.
Hackensack, NJ 07601

Established in 1985 in NJ.

Donor: Howard Isermann.

Foundation type: Independent foundation.

Financial data (yr. ended 12/31/05): Assets, $7,958,728 (M); gifts received, $1,000,000; expenditures, $365,227; qualifying distributions, $334,250; giving activities include $328,500 for 40 grants (high: $50,000; low: $200).

Fields of interest: Arts; Higher education; Health care; Health organizations, association; Human services; Jewish federated giving programs; Jewish agencies & temples.

Type of support: General/operating support; Capital campaigns; Scholarship funds.

Limitations: Applications not accepted. Giving primarily in FL, NJ, and NY. No grants to individuals.

Application information: Contributes only to pre-selected organizations.

Officers: Howard Isermann, Pres. and Treas.; Betty Isermann, V.P.; Carol Isermann, V.P.; Frederick Petermann, Secy.

EIN: 222615361

Selected grants: The following grants were reported in 2004.

$50,000 to Newark Beth Israel Medical Center, Newark, NJ. For Development Fund.

$50,000 to Rensselaer Polytechnic Institute, Troy, NY. For Biotechnology Center.

$25,000 to Jewish Community Center of Metropolitan New Jersey, West Orange, NJ. For scholarship fund.

$25,000 to Jewish Family Service of Metrowest, Florham Park, NJ. For learning disabilities service.

$25,000 to Saint Barnabas Development Foundation, Livingston, NJ. For general support.

$20,000 to Sarasota Memorial Hospital Foundation, Sarasota, FL. For general support.

$10,200 to New College of the University of South Florida Foundation, Sarasota, FL. For general support.

$10,000 to Jewish Federation, Sarasota-Manatee, Sarasota, FL. For general support.

$10,000 to NARSAD Research Institute, Great Neck, NY. For general support.

$10,000 to United Way of Sarasota County, Sarasota, FL. For general support.

5254
The James Family Charitable Foundation ✧
c/o Cappiccille
615 W. Mount Pleasant Ave.
Livingston, NJ 07039
Contact: Mike Cappiccille

Established in 1994 in DE and NY.

Donors: Amabel B. James; Hamilton E. James.

Foundation type: Independent foundation.

Financial data (yr. ended 12/31/03): Assets, $17,441,030 (M); gifts received, $5,257,969; expenditures, $692,136; qualifying distributions, $639,453; giving activities include $639,453 for 61 grants (high: $66,500; low: $50).

Fields of interest: Secondary school/education; Animals/wildlife, preservation/protection; Hospitals (general); Diabetes research; Boys clubs; Boy scouts; Christian agencies & churches.

Limitations: Applications not accepted. Giving on a national basis, with emphasis along the East Coast. No grants to individuals.

Application information: Contributes only to pre-selected organizations.

Officers: Hamilton E. James, Pres. and Treas.; Amabel B. James, V.P. and Secy.

EIN: 137051493

5255
Janssen Ortho Patient Assistance Foundation, Inc. ✧
1 Johnson & Johnson Plz.
New Brunswick, NJ 08933   (800) 652-6227

Established as a company-sponsored operating foundation in 1998 in NJ.

Donors: Janssen Pharmaceutica Inc.; Johnson & Johnson; Ortho Biotech Inc.; Ortho-McNeil Pharmaceutical, Inc.

Foundation type: Operating foundation.

Financial data (yr. ended 12/31/05): Assets, $5,858,833 (M); gifts received, $426,510,118; expenditures, $426,510,118; qualifying distributions, $387,671,696; giving activities include $387,671,696 for grants.

Purpose and activities: The foundation distributes pharmaceutical products to needy persons on a non-discriminatory basis without charge.

Type of support: Donated products; Grants to individuals.

Limitations: Giving on a national basis.

Application information: Application form required.

  Initial approach: Contact foundation for application form
  Deadline(s): None

Officers: David Martin, Pres.; Denise Sitarik, V.P.; Michael B. McCulley, Secy.; Gary Fair, Treas.

Directors: Mary Beth Callan; Irene Infanti; Binyah Kesselly; Chris Panarites; Conrad Person; Stacey Ross; Mona Terrell; Louise Weingrod.

EIN: 311520982

5256
Jaqua Foundation ✧
100 Campus Dr.
P.O. Box 944
Florham Park, NJ 07932-0944   (973) 593-7000
Contact: Eli Hoffman, Chair.
URL: http://foundationcenter.org/grantmaker/jaqua/

Established in 1977.

Donor: George R. Jaqua†.

Foundation type: Independent foundation.

Financial data (yr. ended 12/31/05): Assets, $4,110,079 (M); expenditures, $1,070,915; qualifying distributions, $1,010,331; giving activities include $999,333 for 53 grants (high: $250,000; low: $500).

Purpose and activities: Giving primarily for the arts and for education.

Fields of interest: Performing arts; Elementary/secondary education; Higher education; Animal welfare; Health care.

Limitations: Giving primarily in New Jersey. No support for private foundations. No grants to individuals.

Application information: Application form not required.

  Initial approach: Letter
  Deadline(s): None
  Board meeting date(s): Quarterly

Officers: Eli Hoffman, Chair.; W. Fletcher Hock, Jr., Secy.

Number of staff: 1 part-time support.
EIN: 222086399
Selected grants: The following grants were reported in 2004.
$215,000 to Valley Hospital, Ridgewood, NJ.
$100,000 to Animal Medical Center, New York, NY.
$100,000 to New Jersey Performing Arts Center, Newark, NJ.
$100,000 to Saint Barnabas Medical Center, Livingston, NJ.
$83,666 to Newark Museum, Newark, NJ.
$35,000 to Cornell University, Ithaca, NY.
$35,000 to Lafayette College, Easton, PA.
$33,333 to Pi Lambda Phi Educational Foundation, Danbury, CT.
$25,000 to New Jersey State Opera, Newark, NJ.
$10,000 to Middlebury College, Middlebury, VT.

5257
Clara L. D. Jeffery Charitable Trust
c/o Bank of America, N.A., NJ6-219-02-03
P.O. Box 441
Ridgefield Park, NJ 07660-9984
(908) 253-4863
Contact: Cindy Leip

Trust established in 1969.
Donor: Clara L.D. Jeffery†.
Foundation type: Independent foundation.
Financial data (yr. ended 12/31/05): Assets, $8,092,447 (M); expenditures, $435,480; qualifying distributions, $417,326; giving activities include $390,000 for 36 grants (high: $55,000; low: $2,000).
Purpose and activities: Giving primarily for education, conservation, and animal welfare.
Fields of interest: Education; Environment, natural resources; Animals/wildlife.
Limitations: Giving on a national basis. No grants to individuals.
Publications: Application guidelines.
Application information: Application form required.
  Initial approach: Letter
  Copies of proposal: 3
  Deadline(s): None
  Board meeting date(s): Dec.
  Final notification: Varies
Trustees: Coleman P. Burke, Jr.; Daniel Burke II; Mary B. Partridge; Bank of America, N.A.
EIN: 226138410

5258
Jensam Foundation, Inc. ✧ ☆
c/o M. Schwartzbard & Assoc.
101 Eisenhower Pkwy., 3rd Fl.
Roseland, NJ 07068

Established in 1997 in NJ.
Foundation type: Independent foundation.
Financial data (yr. ended 12/31/04): Assets, $3,155,262 (M); gifts received, $8,000; expenditures, $513,457; qualifying distributions, $500,000; giving activities include $500,000 for 1 grant.
Fields of interest: Foundations (private operating).
Limitations: Applications not accepted. Giving primarily in Roseland, NJ. No grants to individuals.
Application information: Contributes only to pre-selected organizations.

Officers: Herbert Kayden, Pres.; David S. Kayden, V.P.; Joelle Kayden-Killian, V.P.; Michael Schwartzbard, V.P.; Gabrielle Reem Kayden, Secy.
EIN: 223523249

5259
JHJ Foundation, Inc. ▼ ✧
c/o Ken Slutsky, Tax Exempt Inst. Group
65 Livingston Ave.
Roseland, NJ 07068

Established in 2002 in NJ.
Donor: Marital Holdings, LLC.
Foundation type: Independent foundation.
Financial data (yr. ended 11/30/04): Assets, $18,839,469 (M); gifts received, $20,000,000; expenditures, $14,709,525; qualifying distributions, $14,700,000; giving activities include $14,700,000 for grants.
Purpose and activities: Giving primarily for promotion of philanthropy.
Fields of interest: Philanthropy/voluntarism.
Limitations: Applications not accepted. Giving primarily in PA. No grants to individuals.
Application information: Contributes only to pre-selected organizations.
Officers and Trustees:* Kenneth J. Slutsky,* Pres.; Allen Levithan,* V.P. and Secy.; John L. Berger,* V.P. and Treas.; Marital Holdings, LLC.
EIN: 113665718
Selected grants: The following grants were reported in 2004.
$14,700,000 to Vanguard Charitable Endowment Program, Southeastern, PA. For general support.

5260
The Jockey Hollow Foundation, Inc. ✧
P.O. Box 462
Bernardsville, NJ 07924 (973) 425-3212
Contact: Betsy S. Michel, Tr.

Incorporated in 1960 in NJ.
Donors: Carl Shirley†; Mrs. Carl Shirley.
Foundation type: Independent foundation.
Financial data (yr. ended 3/31/05): Assets, $25,706,973 (M); expenditures, $1,808,839; qualifying distributions, $1,649,554; giving activities include $1,644,685 for 169 grants (high: $175,000; low: $35).
Purpose and activities: Giving primarily for the arts, education, and health, and to community programs.
Fields of interest: Museums; Performing arts; Historic preservation/historical societies; Arts; Elementary/secondary education; Higher education; Law school/education; Libraries/library science; Education; Environment, natural resources; Hospitals (general); Reproductive health, family planning; Health organizations, association; Human services; Children/youth, services; Family services; Community development, neighborhood development; Community development; Christian agencies & churches.
Limitations: Giving primarily in MA, NJ, and New York, NY; some funding in Islesboro, ME, and also nationally. No grants to individuals.
Application information: Application form not required.
  Initial approach: Proposal
  Copies of proposal: 1
  Deadline(s): None
  Board meeting date(s): Feb. and June

Trustees: Joanne S. Gill; Thomas Gill; Betsy S. Michel.
EIN: 221724138
Selected grants: The following grants were reported in 2005.
$175,000 to Bernards Area Scholarship Assistance, Bernardsville, NJ.
$155,000 to Morristown Neighborhood House Association, Morristown, NJ.
$135,000 to Yale University, Beinecke Rare Book and Library, New Haven, CT.
$125,000 to Boston Lyric Opera Company, Boston, MA.
$100,000 to Visiting Nurse Association of Somerset Hills, Bernardsville, NJ.
$40,000 to Big Tree Boating Association, Islesboro, ME.
$30,000 to Matheny School and Hospital, Peapack, NJ.
$30,000 to Morristown Memorial Health Foundation, Morristown, NJ.
$22,125 to Peck School, Morristown, NJ.
$20,000 to Essex County College, Newark, NJ.

5261
Johnson & Johnson Family of Companies Contribution Fund ▼ ✧
1 Johnson & Johnson Plz.
New Brunswick, NJ 08933 (732) 524-3255
URL: http://www.jnj.com/community/contributions/index.htm

Incorporated in 1953 in NJ.
Donor: Johnson & Johnson.
Foundation type: Company-sponsored foundation.
Financial data (yr. ended 12/31/05): Assets, $74,824,234 (M); gifts received, $95,948,368; expenditures, $59,408,177; qualifying distributions, $59,408,178; giving activities include $48,443,901 for grants, and $10,955,424 for employee matching gifts.
Purpose and activities: The foundation supports organizations involved with arts and culture, education, health, mental health, HIV/AIDS, human services, senior citizens, and disabled people.
Fields of interest: Arts; Education; Hospitals (general); Public health; Health care; Mental health/crisis services; AIDS; Human services; Federated giving programs; Aging; Disabilities, people with.
Type of support: General/operating support; Continuing support; Annual campaigns; Program development; Fellowships; Scholarship funds; Sponsorships; Employee matching gifts.
Limitations: Applications not accepted. No support for fraternal, political, religious, or athletic organizations. No grants to individuals, or for debt reduction, trips, tours, capital campaigns or endowments, or publications; no loans.
Publications: Corporate giving report.
Application information: Contributes only to pre-selected organizations.
  Board meeting date(s): Mar., June, Sept., and Dec.
Officers: B.D. Perkins, Pres.; A.T. Mays, V.P.; M.H. Ullmann, Secy.; J.A. Papa, Treas.
EIN: 226062811
Selected grants: The following grants were reported in 2004.
$2,000,000 to American Red Cross, National Headquarters, DC. For Hurricane Relief Fund and Caribbean relief.

$898,313 to Dartmouth-Hitchcock Medical Center, Lebanon, NH. For Johnson & Johnson Community Mental Health Project.

$625,000 to Rutgers, The State University of New Jersey Foundation, New Brunswick, NJ. For programs in Newark, Camden, and New Brunswick in areas of research, student support, and community outreach.

$500,000 to New Brunswick Cultural Center, New Brunswick, NJ. To revitalize and enhance New Brunswick's urban core through arts.

$495,000 to Elizabeth Glaser Pediatric AIDS Foundation, Santa Monica, CA. For Call to Action program, preventing mother-to-child transmission of HIV/AIDS.

$375,000 to UCLA Foundation, Los Angeles, CA. For Health Literacy Program.

$364,000 to Georgia Southwestern State University, Americus, GA. For staffing, selection panel, Web site, and grant screening of Rosalynn Carter Institute Caregivers Program.

$100,000 to National Council of La Raza, DC. For Florida Hurricane Relief Fund.

$25,400 to International Management Education Foundation (INSEAD), New York, NY. For Corporate Affiliation Program.

$25,000 to La Fondita de Jesus, San Juan, PR. For San Juan Health Partnership for Homeless.

5262
Johnson Art and Education Foundation ◇
14 Fairgrounds Rd., Ste. A
Hamilton, NJ 08619-3447

Established in 2001 in NJ.
Foundation type: Independent foundation.
Financial data (yr. ended 6/30/05): Assets, $144,121,184 (M); expenditures, $4,398,811; qualifying distributions, $2,695,268; giving activities include $1,741,000 for 2 grants (high: $1,700,000; low: $41,000).
Purpose and activities: Giving primarily to a public art foundation, as well as for educational programs in arts organizations.
Fields of interest: Arts, management/technical aid; Arts, formal/general education.
Type of support: Building/renovation.
Limitations: Applications not accepted. Giving primarily in NY and NJ. No grants to individuals.
Application information: Contributes only to pre-selected organizations.
  Board meeting date(s): May and Nov.
Officer: Louis Hewitt, C.F.O.
Trustees: Michael Greenleaf; J.S. Johnson, Jr.; J.S. Johnson III.
Number of staff: None.
EIN: 223808507

5263
Barbara Piasecka Johnson Foundation ◇
c/o Danser Balaam & Frank
5 Independence Way
Princeton, NJ 08540 (609) 688-1030
Contact: Beata Piasecka, Tr.

Established in 1976 in DE.
Donors: Barbara Piasecka Johnson; J. Seward Johnson, Sr.‡
Foundation type: Independent foundation.
Financial data (yr. ended 12/31/04): Assets, $3,686,906 (M); gifts received, $1,036,752;

expenditures, $850,256; qualifying distributions, $815,972; giving activities include $713,259 for 14 grants (high: $553,778; low: $500), and $82,737 for 16 grants to individuals (high: $20,000; low: $300).
Purpose and activities: To support institutions which promote human rights in Poland, promote institutions of Polish character in the U.S. and abroad, and support artists and scientists, primarily those who are Polish or of Polish extraction, and institutions which support such individuals.
Fields of interest: Media, journalism/publishing; Visual arts; Museums; Performing arts; Language/ linguistics; Literature; Arts; Higher education; Medical school/education; Adult/continuing education; Libraries/library science; Education; Environment, natural resources; Environment; Heart & circulatory diseases; Medical research, institute; Heart & circulatory research; International human rights; International affairs; Civil rights; Engineering/ technology; Biological sciences; Science; International studies; Religion; Economically disadvantaged.
International interests: Monaco; Poland.
Limitations: Giving limited for the benefit of Poland.
Publications: Application guidelines.
Application information: Contributes generally only to pre-selected organizations. Scholarships and fellowships are for graduate, doctoral and postgraduate education only; no undergraduate programs considered. Application form required.
  Initial approach: Letter or telephone
  Copies of proposal: 1
  Deadline(s): Mar. 30 and Sept. 1; all considered within 3-month basis
  Board meeting date(s): July
Trustees: Barbara Piasecka Johnson; Beata P. Piasecka; Christopher Piasecki; Gregory Piasecki; Wojciech Piasecki.
Number of staff: 1 part-time professional; 1 part-time support.
EIN: 510201795

5264
The Joyce and Seward Johnson Foundation, Inc. ◇
P.O. Box 369
Hopewell, NJ 08525
Contact: J. Seward Johnson, Jr., Pres.
Application address: c/o Matthews & Co., 331 Madison Ave., New York, NY 10017

Established in 1990 in NJ.
Donors: J. Seward Johnson, Jr.; J. Seward Johnson, Jr. Charitable Annuity Lead Trust.
Foundation type: Independent foundation.
Financial data (yr. ended 12/31/05): Assets, $2,986,678 (M); gifts received, $330,184; expenditures, $537,650; qualifying distributions, $507,034; giving activities include $506,959 for 47 grants (high: $91,357; low: $100).
Purpose and activities: Giving primarily for education and the arts.
Fields of interest: Performing arts, theater; Arts; Higher education; Education; Environment, natural resources; Hospitals (general).
Limitations: Giving primarily in Key West, FL, Nantucket, MA, and New York, NY. No grants to individuals.
Application information: Application form not required.
  Deadline(s): None

Officers: J. Seward Johnson, Jr., Pres. and Treas.; Joyce H. Johnson, V.P. and Secy.
Trustees: Garrett M. Heher; Robert S. Matthews.
EIN: 223048720
Selected grants: The following grants were reported in 2004.
$121,174 to Artists Association of Nantucket, Nantucket, MA.
$66,000 to Nantucket Land Council, Nantucket, MA.
$58,333 to Key West Film Society, Key West, FL.
$50,000 to Film Society of Lincoln Center, New York, NY.
$25,000 to Nantucket Film Festival, New York, NY.
$10,000 to Bay Street Theater Festival, Sag Harbor, NY.
$10,000 to Reef Relief, Key West, FL.
$5,000 to Lincoln Center Theater, New York, NY.
$4,200 to Theater for the New City, New York, NY.
  2 grants: $3,600, $600

5265
The Robert Wood Johnson Foundation ▼
College Rd. E. and Rte. 1
P.O. Box 2316
Princeton, NJ 08543-2316 (888) 631-9989
Contact: Richard J. Toth, Dir., Office of Proposal Mgmt.
E-mail: mail@rwjf.org; URL: http://www.rwjf.org

Incorporated in 1936 in NJ; became a national philanthropy in 1972.
Donor: Robert Wood Johnson‡.
Foundation type: Independent foundation.
Financial data (yr. ended 12/31/05): Assets, $9,359,361,000 (M); expenditures, $451,091,000; qualifying distributions, $372,500,000; giving activities include $372,500,000 for grants.
Purpose and activities: The foundation is devoted exclusively to health and health care and concentrates its grantmaking in four areas: assuring access to quality health services for all Americans at reasonable cost; improving quality of care and support for people with chronic health conditions; promoting healthy communities and lifestyles; and reducing the harm caused by substance abuse - tobacco, alcohol, and illicit drugs.
Fields of interest: Child development, education; Medical school/education; Hospitals (general); Health care, insurance; Health care, cost containment; Nursing care; Health care; Substance abuse, services; Mental health, smoking; Mental health/crisis services; Health organizations, association; Children/youth, services; Child development, services; Family services; Residential/custodial care, hospices; Aging, centers/services; Homeless, human services; Voluntarism promotion; Aging; Disabilities, people with; Minorities; Native Americans/American Indians; Homeless.
Type of support: Program development; Seed money; Research; Technical assistance; Program evaluation; Program-related investments/loans; Employee matching gifts; Matching/challenge support.
Limitations: Giving limited to the U.S. No support for political organizations, international activities, programs or institutions concerned solely with a specific disease or basic biomedical research. No grants to individuals, or for ongoing general operating expenses, endowment funds, capital costs, including construction, renovation, or

equipment, or research on unapproved drug therapies or devices.

Publications: Application guidelines; Annual report (including application guidelines); Grants list; Informational brochure; Newsletter; Occasional report.

Application information: As of Jan. 2007, RWJF issues Open Calls for Proposals periodically for eight of its 11 Interest Areas: Addiction Prevention & Treatment, Childhood Obesity, Disparities, Health Insurance Coverage, Nursing, Public Health, Quality and Tobacco. As a result of this change, RWJF does not accept unsolicited proposals in these eight Interest Areas after Dec. 31, 2006. RWJF will continue to accept unsolicited proposals for the remaining three Interest Areas: Building Human Capital, Pioneer and Vulnerable Populations. Check website for Open Calls for Proposals. Application form required.

> *Initial approach:* Electronic brief proposal
> *Deadline(s):* None
> *Board meeting date(s):* Quarterly
> *Final notification:* 6 to 12 months

Officers and Trustees: * Hon. Thomas H. Kean,* Chair.; Risa Lavizzo-Mourey, M.D.*, C.E.O. and Pres.; Calvin Bland, Chief of Staff; John R. Lumpkin, M.D., Sr. V.P. and Dir., Health Care Group; James S. Marks, Sr. V.P. and Dir., Health Group; Katherine Hatton, V.P., Secy., and Genl. Counsel; Peter Goodwin, V.P., National Prog. Affairs; David J. Morse, V.P., Comms.; Albert O. Shar, Ph.D., V.P., Inf. Tech.; David L. Waldman, V.P., Human Resources and Admin.; Brian S. O'Neil, C.I.O.; Margaret H. Einhorn, C.F.O. and Treas.; Mary E. Castria, Cont.; Robert E. Campbell; Nancy-Ann DeParle; George S. Frazza; James R. Gavin III, M.D., Ph.D.; Linda Griego; Wendy W. Hagen; Edward J. Hartnett; Robert Wood Johnson IV; Ralph S. Larsen; Edward E. Matthews; William L. Roper, M.D.; Marla E. Salmon; Richard B. Worley.

Number of staff: 134 full-time professional; 8 part-time professional; 86 full-time support; 3 part-time support.

EIN: 226029397

Selected grants: The following grants were reported in 2005.

$20,000,000 to University of Medicine and Dentistry of New Jersey, Foundation of the, New Brunswick, NJ. 2 grants: $10,000,000 (For institutional and infrastructure building at Cardiovascular Institute of New Jersey, payable over 4 years), $10,000,000 (For general support for Child Health Institute of New Jersey, payable over 4 years).

$10,000,000 to Rutgers, The State University of New Jersey Foundation, New Brunswick, NJ. To establish Health Sciences Center, payable over 5 years.

$9,584,202 to NCB Development Corporation, Oakland, CA. For communications and program support in effort to develop replication strategy for Green House Project, initiative to develop small community homes as nursing home alternatives, payable over 5 years.

$8,300,000 to University of California, Center for the Health Professions, San Francisco, CA. For technical assistance, direction and training for Health Policy Fellowships Program, to help extend public policy horizons of health professional schools in the U.S. and improve capabilities of their faculty to study health policy and assume leadership roles in health activities at all levels, payable over 6 years.

$5,000,000 to Princeton Healthcare System Foundation, Princeton, NJ. To replace and relocate University Medical Center at Princeton.

$5,000,000 to Robert Wood Johnson University Hospital Foundation, New Brunswick, NJ. For positive identification and enhanced clinical documentation of Patient Safety Initiative, payable over 5 years.

$4,941,400 to National Hospice and Palliative Care Organization, Alexandria, VA. For Caring Connections: Initiative to Promote and Expand Consumer Engagement in End-of-Life Care, payable over 2 years.

$3,838,995 to Trust for Americas Health, DC. For research and conferences to help build sustainable advocacy capacity for improving nation's public health system, payable over 2.50 years.

$3,604,306 to Boston University, School of Public Health, Boston, MA. For program support and technical assistance for new initiative, Join Together: Advancing Effective Alcohol and Drug Policy, Prevention and Treatment, resource for improving addiction treatment quality, payable over 1.75 years.

5266
The Jonas Foundation ▼ ✧
c/o Ann Burke, IDT Corp.
520 Broad St., 10th Fl.
Newark, NJ 07102
Contact: Howard Jonas, Tr.

Established in 1997 in NY.
Donors: Howard Jonas; IDT Corp.
Foundation type: Independent foundation.
Financial data (yr. ended 7/31/05): Assets, $18,820,898 (M); gifts received, $8,585; expenditures, $7,347,640; qualifying distributions, $8,123,430; giving activities include $7,344,930 for 131+ grants (high: $1,177,000; low: $360; average: $5,000–$200,000), and $778,500 for 2 loans/program-related investments.
Purpose and activities: Giving preference is for education and human rights.
Fields of interest: Education; Human services; International affairs, equal rights.
Type of support: Program-related investments/loans.
Application information:
> *Initial approach:* Letter (1 or 2 pages)
> *Deadline(s):* None

Officer: Miriam Gonzales, Secy.
Trustees: Debbie Jonas; Howard Jonas.
EIN: 223592322

5267
JSY Foundation, Inc. ✧
c/o Lowenstein Sandler
65 Livingston Ave.
Roseland, NJ 07068

Established in 1998 in NJ.
Donor: Rhonda Management, LLC.
Foundation type: Independent foundation.
Financial data (yr. ended 11/30/04): Assets, $60,165,689 (M); gifts received, $7,000,000; expenditures, $3,117,387; qualifying distributions, $3,018,150; giving activities include $3,018,150 for 1 grant.
Fields of interest: Environment.

Limitations: Applications not accepted. Giving primarily in Oak Glen, CA. No grants to individuals.
Application information: Contributes only to pre-selected organizations.
Officers and Trustees: * Kenneth J. Slutsky,* Pres. and Treas.; Allen Levithan,* V.P. and Secy.; John L. Berger, V.P.
EIN: 223692917

5268
The Kaplen Foundation ▼ ✧
P.O. Box 792
Tenafly, NJ 07670
Contact: Margaret R. Kaplen, Admin.

Established about 1963.
Donor: Wilson R. Kaplen.
Foundation type: Independent foundation.
Financial data (yr. ended 7/31/05): Assets, $134,021,216 (M); expenditures, $7,371,975; qualifying distributions, $6,583,208; giving activities include $6,202,263 for 113 grants (high: $1,000,000; low: $51; average: $10,000–$250,000).
Purpose and activities: Giving primarily for hospitals and health associations and cultural organizations, including the performing arts.
Fields of interest: Higher education; Education; Hospitals (general); Health organizations, association; Human services; Jewish agencies & temples.
Limitations: Giving primarily in NJ, with some emphasis on Englewood. Some giving also in NY. No grants to individuals.
Application information: Application form not required.
> *Initial approach:* Letter
> *Copies of proposal:* 1
> *Deadline(s):* None
> *Board meeting date(s):* Quarterly

Officer and Trustees: * Margaret R. Kaplen,* Admin.; Alexander Kaplen; Lawrence Kaplen; Wilson R. Kaplen; Andrew V. Schnurr, Jr.
Number of staff: 1 part-time support.
EIN: 226048152
Selected grants: The following grants were reported in 2005.

$1,000,000 to Jewish Home at Rockleigh, Rockleigh, NJ. For general support.

$830,000 to Roundabout Theater Company, New York, NY. For general support.

$750,000 to W N Y C Radio, New York, NY. For general support.

$400,200 to United Jewish Community of Bergen County, River Edge, NJ. For general support.

$250,000 to American Jewish Committee, New York, NY. For general support.

$250,000 to Solomon Schechter Regional High School, Teaneck, NJ. For general support.

$173,250 to Englewood Hospital and Medical Center Foundation, Englewood, NJ. For general support.

$75,000 to Museum of the City of New York, New York, NY. For general support.

$50,000 to Jewish Theological Seminary of America, New York, NY. For general support.

$21,750 to Jewish Community Center on the Palisades, Tenafly, NJ. For general support.

5269
Karma Foundation ✧
140 Arreton Rd.
Princeton, NJ 08540 (609) 924-5939
Contact: Dina Elkins, Exec. Dir.
FAX: (609) 924-2714;
E-mail: info@karmafoundation.org; URL: http://
www.karmafoundation.org/

Established in 1996 in NJ.
Donors: Sharon Karmazin; Sharon Karmazin
Charitable Lead Annuity Trust.
Foundation type: Independent foundation.
Financial data (yr. ended 12/31/03): Assets,
$11,769,232 (M); gifts received, $136,080;
expenditures, $1,087,119; qualifying distributions,
$1,064,841; giving activities include $986,442 for
207 grants (high: $50,000; low: $50).
Purpose and activities: Giving primarily for arts
and culture, health and human services, education,
literacy, public libraries in NJ, and the enrichment of
Jewish life.
Fields of interest: Arts; Education; Health care;
Human services; Jewish agencies & temples.
Type of support: General/operating support; Annual
campaigns; Capital campaigns; Building/
renovation; Equipment; Emergency funds; Program
development; Seed money; Scholarship funds;
Research; Technical assistance; Program
evaluation.
Limitations: Giving limited to NJ, with emphasis on
Middlesex, Union, Somerset and Mercer counties,
and parts of WI. No support for charter schools. No
grants to individuals, or for travel expenses,
advertising, fundraising or litigation; no loans.
Publications: Application guidelines.
Application information: Proposals submitted by
E-mail or fax are not accepted. Application
information is available on foundation's Web site.
Application form not required.
Initial approach: Telephone call or 1-2 page letter
of inquiry (letter, fax or E-mail acceptable)
Copies of proposal: 2
Deadline(s): None
Board meeting date(s): Monthly
Final notification: Within 1 month
Officers: Sharon Karmazin, Pres.; Craig Karmazin,
Secy.; Dina Karmazin Elkins, Treas. and Exec. Dir.
Number of staff: 1 full-time professional.
EIN: 223478433
Selected grants: The following grants were reported
in 2003.
$50,000 to George Street Playhouse, New
Brunswick, NJ.
$25,000 to Memorial Sloan-Kettering Cancer
Center, New York, NY.
$7,500 to Appel Farm Arts and Music Center, Elmer,
NJ.
$5,000 to Doctors Without Borders USA, New York,
NY.
$3,500 to Lincoln Center Theater, New York, NY.
$2,500 to Cumberland County Library, Bridgeton,
NJ.
$2,250 to Museum of Arts and Design, New York,
NY.
$2,000 to Broadway Cares/Equity Fights AIDS, New
York, NY.
$1,000 to Women Aware, New Brunswick, NJ.
$100 to Rutgers, The State University of New Jersey,
New Brunswick, NJ.

5270
Katz Foundation ✧
c/o Lewis Katz
905 N. Kings Hwy.
Cherry Hill, NJ 08034

Established in 1994 in NJ.
Donor: Lewis Katz.
Foundation type: Independent foundation.
Financial data (yr. ended 12/31/05): Assets,
$68,543 (M); gifts received, $1,024,478;
expenditures, $945,184; qualifying distributions,
$941,615; giving activities include $939,625 for 41
grants (high: $200,000; low: $150).
Purpose and activities: Giving primarily for higher
education and to a Roman Catholic diocese.
Fields of interest: Higher education; Roman
Catholic agencies & churches.
Limitations: Applications not accepted. Giving
primarily in NJ and NY. No grants to individuals.
Application information: Contributes only to
pre-selected organizations.
Director: Lewis Katz.
EIN: 223336393
Selected grants: The following grants were reported
in 2004.
$247,702 to Jewish Community Center of Atlantic
County, Margate, NJ. 2 grants: $200,000,
$47,702
$170,000 to Boys and Girls Clubs of Camden
County, Camden, NJ.
$100,000 to William J. Clinton Presidential
Foundation, New York, NY.
$75,000 to Columbia University, New York, NY.
$75,000 to Sisters of Mercy, Watchung, NJ.
$50,000 to Greater Camden Partnership, Camden,
NJ.
$40,000 to Naismith Memorial Basketball Hall of
Fame, Springfield, MA.
$28,900 to Jewish Federation of Southern New
Jersey, Cherry Hill, NJ.
$15,000 to Womens American ORT, New York, NY.

5271
M. D. Katz Foundation, Inc. ✧
300 E. Linden Ave.
Englewood, NJ 07631-3719

Established in 1960 in NY.
Donors: Monique C. Katz; Mordecai D. Katz.
Foundation type: Independent foundation.
Financial data (yr. ended 7/31/05): Assets,
$30,326,572 (M); gifts received, $380,000;
expenditures, $1,166,283; qualifying distributions,
$1,099,684; giving activities include $1,098,765
for 25 grants (high: $842,200; low: $5).
Purpose and activities: Support for higher
education, Jewish organizations, including welfare
funds, religious associations, and yeshivas.
Fields of interest: Elementary/secondary
education; Higher education; Human services;
Jewish federated giving programs; Jewish agencies
& temples.
Limitations: Applications not accepted. Giving
primarily in NJ and NY. No grants to individuals.
Application information: Contributes only to
pre-selected organizations.
Officers: Mordecai D. Katz, Pres. and Treas.;
Monique C. Katz, V.P. and Secy.
EIN: 116035541
Selected grants: The following grants were reported
in 2004.

$736,319 to Bar-Ilan University in Israel, New York,
NY. For general support.
$26,000 to Ohr Torah Stone Colleges and Graduate
Programs, New York, NY. For general support.
$10,072 to Orthodox Union - Union of Orthodox
Jewish Congregations of America, New York, NY.
For general support.
$4,000 to Rabbinical Seminary of America, Forest
Hills, NY. For general support.
$450 to P.E.F. Israel Endowment Funds, New York,
NY. For general support.
$110 to Anti-Defamation League of Bnai Brith, New
York, NY. For general support.
$106 to AMIT Women, New York, NY. For general
support.
$50 to Simon Wiesenthal Center, Los Angeles, CA.
For general support.
$50 to World Jewish Congress American Section,
New York, NY. For general support.
$36 to Yeshiva Gedola of Passaic-Talmudic
Research Center, Passaic, NJ. For general
support.

5272
**The Fritz and Adelaide Kauffmann
Foundation, Inc.** ✧
6 Oxford Pl.
Cresskill, NJ 07626-1625 (212) 269-8628
Contact: Bernard Turner, Treas.

Established in 1999 in NJ.
Donors: Fritz Kauffman†; Adelaide Kauffman†.
Foundation type: Independent foundation.
Financial data (yr. ended 6/30/06): Assets,
$11,182,880 (M); expenditures, $847,378;
qualifying distributions, $744,000; giving activities
include $733,000 for 36 grants (high: $100,000;
low: $5,000).
Purpose and activities: Giving primarily to hospitals
and for medical research.
Fields of interest: Museums; Education; Hospitals
(general); Hospitals (specialty); Health care; Health
organizations, association; Orthopedics; Cancer
research; Parkinson's disease research;
Neuroscience research; Human services; Children/
youth, services; Jewish federated giving programs;
Military/veterans.
Limitations: Giving primarily in NJ and NY. No grants
to individuals.
Application information:
Initial approach: Letter
Deadline(s): None
Officers: Elliot M. Hershberg, Pres.; Theodore N.
Mirvis, Secy.; Bernard Turner, Treas.
EIN: 223689518
Selected grants: The following grants were reported
in 2004.
$50,000 to Memorial Sloan-Kettering Cancer
Center, New York, NY. For research.
$50,000 to Montefiore Medical Center, Bronx, NY.
For general support.
$40,000 to Yeshiva University Museum, New York,
NY. For general support.
$20,000 to Albert Einstein College of Medicine of
Yeshiva University, Bronx, NY. For cancer center.
$12,500 to Mount Sinai Hospital, New York, NY. For
neurology research fund.
$10,000 to Holy Name Hospital, Teaneck, NJ. For
oncology center.
$10,000 to Marilyn Horne Foundation, New York,
NY. For scholarships.
$10,000 to Prep for Prep, New York, NY. For general
support.

$10,000 to Weill Medical College of Cornell University, New York, NY. For general support.
$5,000 to Beth Israel Medical Center, New York, NY. For general support.

5273
KDK Charitable Trust ✧
c/o Untracht Early & Assocs., LLC
325 Columbia Tpke.
Florham Park, NJ   07932

Established in 1997 in CT.
Donor: Dennis J. Keegan.
Foundation type: Independent foundation.
Financial data (yr. ended 12/31/05): Assets, $5,101,808 (M); expenditures, $609,182; qualifying distributions, $586,460; giving activities include $583,160 for 29 grants (high: $200,000; low: $25).
Purpose and activities: Giving primarily for education, health associations and human services.
Fields of interest: Higher education; Education; Health organizations; Human services; Family services; Public policy, research; Roman Catholic agencies & churches.
Type of support: General/operating support.
Limitations: Applications not accepted. Giving primarily in CT. No grants to individuals.
Application information: Contributes only to pre-selected organizations.
Trustees: Dennis J. Keegan; Karen S. Keegan.
EIN: 066455317
Selected grants: The following grants were reported in 2003.
$250,650 to Greenwich Academy, Greenwich, CT. For general support.
$25,000 to Cato Institute, DC. For general support.
$20,600 to Brunswick School, Greenwich, CT. For general support.
$15,000 to Family Centers, Greenwich, CT. For general support.
$10,000 to Saint Michaels Church, Greenwich, CT. For general support.
$10,000 to Student Sponsor Partners, New York, NY. For general support.
$10,000 to Time for Lyme, Greenwich, CT. For general support.
$5,145 to Audubon Society of Greenwich, Greenwich, CT. For general support.
$5,000 to UCLA Foundation, Los Angeles, CA. For general support.
$1,500 to United Way of Greenwich, Greenwich, CT. For general support.

5274
Stewart B. Kean Revocable Trust ✧
P.O. Box 1
Elizabeth, NJ   07207

Established in 2003 in NJ.
Foundation type: Independent foundation.
Financial data (yr. ended 12/31/04): Assets, $12,472,422 (M); expenditures, $28,577,973; qualifying distributions, $28,563,317; giving activities include $28,563,317 for 1 grant.
Fields of interest: Human services; Philanthropy/voluntarism.
Limitations: Applications not accepted. Giving primarily in NJ. No grants to individuals.
Application information: Contributes only to pre-selected organizations.

Trustees: Robert Raynolds; J. David Schardien.
EIN: 226924083

5275
The Kemmerer Family Foundation, Inc. ✧
c/o Kemmerer Resources Corp.
323 Main St.
Chatham, NJ   07928

Established in 2000 in NJ.
Foundation type: Independent foundation.
Financial data (yr. ended 12/31/05): Assets, $48,541,737 (M); expenditures, $2,678,172; qualifying distributions, $2,470,000; giving activities include $2,450,000 for 32 grants (high: $500,000; low: $10,000).
Fields of interest: Higher education; Higher education, university; Education; Environment, natural resources; Hospitals (general); Foundations (community); Christian agencies & churches; Protestant agencies & churches.
Limitations: Applications not accepted. Giving primarily in NJ and WY; some giving nationally. No grants to individuals.
Application information: Contributes only to pre-selected organizations.
Officers: John L. Kemmerer, III, Pres.; Peter F. Nejes, Secy.-Treas.
EIN: 223706044
Selected grants: The following grants were reported in 2005.
$900,000 to YMCA, Wood River Community, Ketchum, ID. 2 grants: $500,000, $400,000
$335,000 to Saint Johns Medical Center, Jackson, WY. 2 grants: $35,000, $300,000
$125,000 to Teton Science School, Kelly, WY.
$100,000 to Paper Mill Playhouse, Millburn, NJ.
$50,000 to Family Promise, Summit, NJ.
$25,000 to International Medical Corps, Santa Monica, CA.
$25,000 to Market Street Mission, Morristown, NJ.
$15,000 to New Jersey Family Policy Council, Parsippany, NJ.

5276
Quentin J. Kennedy Foundation, Inc. ✧
22 Old Smith Rd.
Tenafly, NJ   07670

Established in 1986 in NJ.
Donor: Quentin J. Kennedy.
Foundation type: Independent foundation.
Financial data (yr. ended 12/31/05): Assets, $15,057,768 (M); expenditures, $974,597; qualifying distributions, $720,000; giving activities include $720,000 for 26 grants (high: $250,000; low: $1,000).
Purpose and activities: Giving primarily to a hospital, and for Catholic organizations, including welfare agencies; support also for health and child welfare.
Fields of interest: Higher education; Hospitals (general); Health care; Medical research, institute; Human services; Children/youth, services; Residential/custodial care; Roman Catholic federated giving programs; Roman Catholic agencies & churches.
Limitations: Applications not accepted. Giving primarily in NJ and NY. No grants to individuals.
Application information: Contributes only to pre-selected organizations.

Officers: Quentin J. Kennedy, Pres. and Treas.; Mary E. Kennedy, V.P.; Quentin J. Kennedy, Jr., Secy.
EIN: 222653050

5277
The Keren Yitzchak Foundation, Inc. ✧ ☆
c/o Mironov, Sloan & Parziale, LLC
146 Route 1 N.
Edison, NJ   08817

Established in 2000 in NJ.
Donors: David Kahane; Leon Kreisler; Stephanie Pomerantz.
Foundation type: Independent foundation.
Financial data (yr. ended 12/31/05): Assets, $2,240,608 (M); gifts received, $238,000; expenditures, $434,383; qualifying distributions, $429,788; giving activities include $429,788 for grants.
Fields of interest: Children/youth, services; Jewish federated giving programs; Jewish agencies & temples.
Limitations: Giving primarily in NJ. No grants to individuals.
Application information:
Initial approach: Letter
Trustees: Batya Kahane; Claire Kahane; David Kahane; Stephanie Pomerantz.
EIN: 223741992
Selected grants: The following grants were reported in 2004.
$142,000 to Jewish Education Center.
$26,822 to Bris Avrohom, Jersey City, NJ.
$11,800 to Yeshivat Ben Yitzchak.
$5,600 to Ben Porat Yosef, Leonia, NJ.
$4,000 to YM-YWHA of Union County, Union, NJ.
$2,124 to Shermni Torah Ohel Yosef.
$2,000 to Congregation Ansche Chesed, New York, NY.
$1,922 to Congregation Shomrei Torah, Hillside, NJ.
$1,800 to East Hill Synagogue, Englewood, NJ.
$1,598 to Chedin Yaliber Menscher.

5278
The William A. Kerr Foundation ✧
P.O. Box 1525
Pennington, NJ   08534-1525

Established in 1998 in WA.
Foundation type: Independent foundation.
Financial data (yr. ended 12/31/05): Assets, $16,266,538 (M); expenditures, $1,102,132; qualifying distributions, $1,049,461; giving activities include $663,350 for 18 grants (high: $250,000; low: $1,000).
Purpose and activities: Support primarily for the fine and performing arts, Jewish synagogues and other religious organizations, mental health services, and higher education, including medical schools; giving also for community services and recreation.
Fields of interest: Museums; Performing arts; Performing arts, theater; Arts; Higher education; Medical school/education; Environment, natural resources; Animals/wildlife, preservation/ protection; Jewish agencies & temples.
Type of support: General/operating support.
Limitations: Applications not accepted. Giving primarily in CA and MO, with emphasis on Walnut Creek and St. Louis. No grants to individuals.
Application information: Contributes only to pre-selected organizations.

Trustees: John H.K. Sweet; William R. Sweet.
EIN: 431770857

5279
F. M. Kirby Foundation, Inc. ▼
17 DeHart St.
P.O. Box 151
Morristown, NJ 07963-0151 (973) 538-4800
Contact: For application procedure questions: S.
Dillard Kirby, Exec. V.P. and Exec. Dir.
URL: http://www.foundationcenter.org/
grantmaker/kirby

Incorporated in 1931 in DE.
Donors: F.M. Kirby†; Allan P. Kirby, Sr.†.
Foundation type: Independent foundation.
Financial data (yr. ended 12/31/05): Assets,
$484,579,224 (M); expenditures, $25,631,854;
qualifying distributions, $22,738,500; giving
activities include $22,438,950 for 363 grants (high:
$1,200,000; low: $500; average: $17,500–
$100,000).
Purpose and activities: Support for community
programs, the arts, historic preservation, social
services, conservation, public policy and education
organizations, and family planning. Grants are
generally limited to organizations associated with
the personal interests of present or former family
members. Requests to support churches, hospitals,
schools and colleges, other than ones attended by
or used by members of the family, are not likely to
receive favorable consideration.
Fields of interest: Performing arts; Humanities;
Historic preservation/historical societies; Arts;
Environment, natural resources; Biomedicine;
Medical research, institute; AIDS research;
Recreation; Youth development, services; Youth,
services; Economics; Public policy, research;
Government/public administration; Leadership
development.
Type of support: General/operating support;
Continuing support; Annual campaigns; Capital
campaigns; Building/renovation; Equipment;
Endowments; Emergency funds; Program
development; Conferences/seminars; Seed money;
Research.
Limitations: Giving primarily in Raleigh-Durham, NC,
Morris County, NJ, and eastern PA. Generally no
support for churches, hospitals, schools and
colleges, other than ones attended by or used by
members of the family. No grants to individuals, or
for fundraising benefits, dinners, theater, or sporting
events; no loans or pledges.
Publications: Informational brochure (including
application guidelines).
Application information: No solicitations by
telephone, fax or E-mail are accepted. Application
form not required.
 Initial approach: Proposal with cover letter;
  telephone solicitations not considered
 Copies of proposal: 1
 Deadline(s): Proposals received throughout the
  year; requests received after Oct. 31 are held
  over to the following year
 Board meeting date(s): Three times per year
 Final notification: Monthly for positive responses
  only
Officers and Directors:* F.M. Kirby,* Pres.; S.
Dillard Kirby,* Exec. V.P. and Exec. Dir.; Walker D.
Kirby,* V.P.; Thomas J. Bianchini, Secy.-Treas.; Alice
Kirby Horton; Jefferson W. Kirby; Laura H. Virkler.

Number of staff: 2 full-time professional; 1 part-time
professional; 1 full-time support; 1 part-time
support.
EIN: 516017929
Selected grants: The following grants were reported
in 2005.
$800,000 to Kennedy Krieger Institute, Baltimore,
 MD. Toward upgrade of research facilities to help
 advance pediatric brain imaging research
 programs in autism and spinal cord injury.
$235,000 to Community Theater, Morristown, NJ. 2
 grants: $150,000 (For capital support fulfilling
 challenge grant), $85,000 (For general operating
 support).
$215,000 to F. M. Kirby Center for the Performing
 Arts, Wilkes Barre, PA. For Children's Cultural
 Education Endowment Fund, and general
 operating support.
$210,000 to Family Service of Morris County,
 Morristown, NJ. Toward Building a New Home for
 Families and Community capital campaign.
$120,000 to Morris Museum, Morristown, NJ.
 Toward new wing to be built for Guinness
 Collection.
$115,000 to Shakespeare Theater of New Jersey,
 Madison, NJ. For S. Dillard Kirby Endowment
 Fund and general operating support.
$115,000 to State Theater Center for the Arts,
 Easton, PA. For general operating support and
 F.M. Kirby Endowment Fund.
$100,000 to Mount Vernon Ladies Association,
 Mount Vernon, VA. For creation of traveling
 exhibition commemorating 250th Anniversary of
 Lafayette's birth.
$80,000 to American Red Cross, Morristown, NJ.
 Toward disaster relief and blood donor programs
 in Morris County.

5280
A. P. Kirby, Jr. Foundation, Inc. ✧
c/o Allan P. Kirby, Jr.
14 E. Main St.
P.O. Box 90
Mendham, NJ 07945

Established in 1988 in NJ.
Donor: Allan P. Kirby, Jr.
Foundation type: Independent foundation.
Financial data (yr. ended 12/31/05): Assets,
$12,823,367 (M); gifts received, $1,000,000;
expenditures, $544,483; qualifying distributions,
$495,073; giving activities include $489,000 for 64
grants (high: $50,000; low: $500).
Purpose and activities: Giving primarily to support
public policy, free enterprise, entrepreneurship,
historical preservation, medical research, and
education.
Fields of interest: Historical activities; Education;
Medical research, institute; Public affairs.
Limitations: Giving primarily in NJ and PA. No grants
to individuals.
Application information: Application form required.
 Initial approach: Letter
 Deadline(s): None
Officers: Allan P. Kirby, Jr., Chair.; Milan S. Kirby,
Pres.; Coray S. Kirby, Secy.; Slater B. Kirby, Treas.
EIN: 222922817

5281
Faith & James Knight Foundation, Inc. ☆
c/o R.J. Gaughran
P.O. Box 143
Middletown, NJ 07748

Established in 1999 in NJ.
Donor: J.A. Knight†.
Foundation type: Independent foundation.
Financial data (yr. ended 6/30/05): Assets,
$5,582,100 (M); gifts received, $40,553;
expenditures, $511,352; qualifying distributions,
$450,945; giving activities include $426,200 for 13
grants (high: $129,000; low: $500).
Purpose and activities: Giving primarily for women's
issues, as well as for animal issues, education, and
health care.
Fields of interest: Education; Animal welfare; Health
care; Women, centers/services; Women.
Limitations: Applications not accepted. Giving
primarily in NJ. No grants to individuals.
Application information: Contributes only to
pre-selected organizations.
Trustees: Donna Balon; Cheryl Bliss; Robert J.
Gaughran; Lisa Knight Giuliani; Frances Lobl; Margot
R. McCord.
Number of staff: None.
EIN: 223656542
Selected grants: The following grants were reported
in 2005.
$129,000 to 180, Turning Lives Around, Hazlet, NJ.
$60,000 to Girl Scouts of the U.S.A., Farmingdale,
 NJ.
$30,000 to American Heart Association, North
 Brunswick, NJ.
$5,000 to Parkinsons Disease Foundation, New
 York, NY.
$500 to Providence Presbyterian Church, West
 Columbia, SC.

5282
Fanny and Svante Knistrom Foundation ✧
229 Main St.
Chatham, NJ 07928 (973) 635-5200
Contact: Carl A. Frahn, Secy.

Established in 1972 in NJ.
Donors: Svante Knistrom†; Fanny Knistrom†.
Foundation type: Independent foundation.
Financial data (yr. ended 5/31/05): Assets,
$9,444,251 (M); expenditures, $680,624;
qualifying distributions, $551,616; giving activities
include $535,500 for 50 grants (high: $25,000;
low: $2,500).
Purpose and activities: Emphasis on health,
education, and human rights, especially of marginal
groups such as battered women, homeless families,
and disabled persons.
Fields of interest: Education; Health care; Crime/
violence prevention, abuse prevention; Children/
youth, services; Youth, pregnancy prevention;
International human rights; Disabilities, people with;
Minorities.
International interests: Mexico.
Type of support: General/operating support; Capital
campaigns; Seed money; Matching/challenge
support.
Limitations: Applications not accepted. Giving
primarily in CA, NH, NJ, and SC. No support for
political or religious purposes. No grants to
individuals.

Application information: Contributes only to pre-selected organizations.

Board meeting date(s): Apr. and Oct.

Officers and Trustees:* Virginia Kreuzberger,* Pres.; Gregory P. Buesing,* V.P. and Treas.; Carl A. Frahn,* Secy.; Donna Barrett; Guy K. Buesing; Jean Buesing; Donald Kreuzberger; Douglas Kreuzberger; Kurt Kreuzberger; Karen Turner.

EIN: 222011417

Selected grants: The following grants were reported in 2004.

$30,000 to P. F. Bresee Foundation, Los Angeles, CA. For after-school programs for at-risk youth.

$15,000 to Basic Adult Spanish Education, Canoga Park, CA. To teach elder care to low-income, Spanish-speaking people.

$15,000 to Cheshire Home, Florham Park, NJ. For operating support at home for physically disabled.

$15,000 to Haven Hills, Canoga Park, CA. For day care subsidies.

$15,000 to Museum of Early Trades and Crafts, Madison, NJ. For general support.

$15,000 to Tierra del Sol Center for the Handicapped Foundation, Sunland, CA. To train developmentally disabled people.

$10,000 to Inside Out Community Arts, Venice, CA. For after-school arts program.

$10,000 to Interfaith Council for the Homeless of Union County, Plainfield, NJ. For scholarships to day care and summer camp.

$10,000 to San Fernando Valley Interfaith Council, Chatsworth, CA. For general support for food pantries.

$10,000 to Santa Clarita Valley Youth Project, Santa Clarita, CA. To link at-risk youth to social services.

5283
Janet H. and C. Harry Knowles Foundation, Inc.
1000 N. Church St.
Moorestown, NJ   08057   (856) 608-0001
Contact: Angelo Collins Ph.D., Exec. Dir
FAX: (856) 608-0008; E-mail: info@kstf.org;
URL: http://www.kstf.org

Established in NJ in 1999.

Donors: Janet H. Knowles; C. Harry Knowles.

Foundation type: Operating foundation.

Financial data (yr. ended 12/31/05): Assets, $30,456,209 (M); gifts received, $224,418; expenditures, $1,458,831; qualifying distributions, $1,447,335; giving activities include $75,000 for 3 grants (high: $37,500; low: $10,000), $337,442 for 48 grants to individuals, and $332,716 for foundation-administered programs.

Purpose and activities: To enhance the quantity of high school science and mathematics teachers.

Fields of interest: Secondary school/education; Higher education; Teacher school/education; Education; Science; Mathematics.

Type of support: Continuing support; Conferences/seminars; Seed money; Fellowships; Research; Grants to individuals; Scholarships—to individuals.

Limitations: Applications not accepted. No support for religious or political organizations, schools or universities. No grants for second career or advanced degrees in any discipline other than education.

Publications: Annual report; Informational brochure; Occasional report.

Application information: Unsolicited requests for funds not accepted.

Board meeting date(s): Three times a year

Officers and Trustees:* C. Harry Knowles,* Pres.; Janet H. Knowles,* Secy.-Treas.; Angelo Collins, Ph.D., Exec. Dir.; Scott McVay.

Number of staff: 5 full-time professional; 1 part-time professional; 3 full-time support; 2 part-time support.

EIN: 010485964

5284
The Leo Koguan Foundation ✧
c/o SHI
2 Riverview Dr.
Somerset, NJ   08873

Established in 2002 in NJ.

Foundation type: Independent foundation.

Financial data (yr. ended 12/31/05): Assets, $1,010,126 (M); gifts received, $2,550,000; expenditures, $1,582,135; qualifying distributions, $1,581,560; giving activities include $1,581,100 for 2 grants (high: $1,531,100; low: $50,000).

Fields of interest: Arts, cultural/ethnic awareness; Higher education, university.

Limitations: Applications not accepted. Giving primarily in CA and NY. No grants to individuals.

Application information: Contributes only to pre-selected organizations.

Trustees: Leo Koguan; Fred Teng.

EIN: 320065960

Selected grants: The following grants were reported in 2003.

$500,000 to Asia Society, New York, NY. For unrestricted support.

5285
Kolatch Family Foundation ✧ ☆
910 Sylvan Ave., Ste. 130
Englewood Cliffs, NJ   07632

Established in 1996 in NJ.

Donor: Jonathan L. Kolatch.

Foundation type: Independent foundation.

Financial data (yr. ended 10/31/05): Assets, $6,324,630 (M); gifts received, $281,007; expenditures, $529,628; qualifying distributions, $443,173; giving activities include $443,173 for grants.

Fields of interest: Education; Jewish agencies & temples.

Limitations: Applications not accepted. Giving primarily in MA, NJ, and NY. No grants to individuals.

Application information: Contributes only to pre-selected organizations.

Trustees: Jonathan L. Kolatch; Mindy S. Kolatch.

EIN: 133918276

Selected grants: The following grants were reported in 2004.

$33,000 to Congregation Ahavath Torah, Englewood, NJ.

$10,000 to Moriah School of Englewood, Englewood, NJ.

$2,500 to Yad Avraham Institute, New York, NY.

$1,000 to David Project, Newtonville, MA.

$1,000 to Harvard University, Business School, Cambridge, MA.

$500 to American Committee for Shaare Zedek Hospital in Jerusalem, New York, NY.

$500 to Yeshiva Ohr Hatalmud of Englewood, Englewood, NJ.

$500 to Yeshivat Har Etzion, Alon Shevut, Israel. .

$150 to Ramaz School, New York, NY.

$126 to AMIT Women, New York, NY.

5286
The Arthur Kontos Foundation, Inc. ✧ ☆
1702 Channel Club Dr.
Monmouth Beach, NJ   07750
Contact: Joseph De Maio

Established in 1985 in NY and DE.

Donor: Arthur Kontos.

Foundation type: Independent foundation.

Financial data (yr. ended 11/30/04): Assets, $7,657,100 (M); gifts received, $1,020,000; expenditures, $367,314; qualifying distributions, $332,304; giving activities include $332,000 for 19 grants (high: $100,000; low: $1,000).

Fields of interest: Higher education; Hospitals (general); Health organizations, association; Athletics/sports, winter sports; Human services.

Limitations: Applications not accepted. Giving on a national basis. No grants to individuals.

Application information: Contributes only to pre-selected organizations.

Officers: Arthur Kontos, Pres.; James Kontos, V.P. and Secy.; Michael Kontos, V.P. and Treas.

EIN: 133339956

Selected grants: The following grants were reported in 2004.

$100,000 to First Reformed Church, Lynden, WA.

$15,000 to Catskill Mountain Foundation, Hunter, NY.

$10,000 to Clean Ocean Action, Highlands, NJ.

$5,000 to American Red Cross.

$1,000 to W N E T Channel 13, New York, NY.

5287
The Kovner Foundation ▼ ✧
Princeton Plz., Bldg. 2
731 Alexander Rd.
Princeton, NJ   08540

Established in 1986.

Donor: Bruce S. Kovner.

Foundation type: Independent foundation.

Financial data (yr. ended 12/31/04): Assets, $20,144,797 (M); expenditures, $6,190,236; qualifying distributions, $5,864,301; giving activities include $5,864,301 for 17 grants (high: $2,750,000; low: $25,000; average: $50,000–$100,000).

Purpose and activities: Giving primarily for education.

Fields of interest: Higher education; Education; Public policy, research.

Limitations: Applications not accepted. Giving primarily in New York, NY. No grants to individuals.

Application information: Contributes only to pre-selected organizations.

Officers and Directors:* Bruce S. Kovner,* Pres.; Scott B. Bernstein, Secy.; Peter P. D'Angelo,* Treas.; Frank Wohl.

EIN: 223468030

Selected grants: The following grants were reported in 2004.

$2,750,000 to Juilliard School, New York, NY. For program support.

$1,299,301 to American Enterprise Institute for Public Policy Research, DC. For general support.

$600,000 to Bronx Preparatory Charter School, Friends of, Bronx, NY.

$200,000 to Brooklyn Academy of Music, Brooklyn, NY.

$200,000 to Foundation for Education Reform and Accountability, Clifton Park, NY. For education reform.

$110,000 to Beginning with Children Foundation, New York, NY.

$100,000 to American Friends of the Israel Museum, New York, NY. For museum acquisitions.

$100,000 to Brighter Choice Foundation, Clifton Park, NY.

$100,000 to Childrens Progress Unlimited, Hazlet, NJ. For support of disadvantaged preschoolers.

$50,000 to School Choice Scholarships Foundation, Clifton Park, NY.

5288

The KPMG Foundation ▼

(formerly The KPMG Peat Marwick Foundation)
3 Chestnut Ridge Rd.
Montvale, NJ 07645 (201) 307-7932
Contact: Tara Perino, Assoc. Dir.
FAX: (201) 307-7093; E-mail: tperino@kpmg.com;
Additional E-mail: kpmgfoundation-gm@kpmg.com;
URL: http://www.kpmgfoundation.org
Application address for Minority Accounting Doctoral Scholarships: KPMG Foundation Doctoral Scholarship Prog., c/o Tara Perino, Assoc. Dir., The KPMG Foundation, 3 Chestnut Ridge Rd., Montvale, NJ 07645, FAX: (201) 307-7093

Trust established in 1968 in NY.
Donors: KPMG Peat Marwick LLP; KPMG LLP.
Foundation type: Company-sponsored foundation.
Financial data (yr. ended 6/30/05): Assets, $1,966,794 (M); gifts received, $9,343,027; expenditures, $9,030,963; qualifying distributions, $8,800,369; giving activities include $1,383,610 for 48 grants (high: $250,000; low: $1,000), $480,000 for 50 grants to individuals (high: $10,000; low: $5,000), and $4,331,851 for 427 employee matching gifts.
Purpose and activities: The foundation supports organizations involved with higher education, business education, and volunteerism and awards graduate scholarships to minority doctoral accounting students.
Fields of interest: Higher education; Business school/education; Voluntarism promotion; Minorities; African Americans/Blacks; Hispanics/Latinos; Native Americans/American Indians.
Type of support: Continuing support; Seed money; Employee matching gifts; Scholarships—to individuals.
Limitations: Giving on a national basis.
Publications: Annual report.
Application information: An application form is required for Minority Accounting Doctoral Scholarships. Cover letters for Minority Accounting Doctoral Scholarships should be brief. Unsolicited requests for grants are not accepted.
  Initial approach: Download application form and mail or fax to application address for Minority Accounting Doctoral Scholarships
  Deadline(s): May 1 for Minority Accounting Doctoral Scholarships
  Board meeting date(s): May

Officers and Trustees:* Michael J. Nolan,* Chair.; Bernard J. Milano,* Pres.; Kapila Anand; Melisa A. Denis; Manuel J. Fernandez; David M. Fowler; Robert P. Garrett; Kathy A.H. Hannan; Teresa Iannaconi; Bruce Pfau; Reginald C. Reed; Scott D. Showalter; Edward F. Silicani.
Number of staff: 2 full-time professional; 6 full-time support.
EIN: 136262199
Selected grants: The following grants were reported in 2004.
$60,000 to Beta Alpha Psi, New York, NY.
$33,333 to Texas A & M University, College Station, TX. For professorships.
$30,000 to University of Notre Dame, Notre Dame, IN.
$25,000 to AACSB International-The Association to Advance Collegiate Schools of Business, Saint Louis, MO.
$25,000 to Baylor University, Waco, TX.
$25,000 to Campus Compact, Providence, RI.
$25,000 to Howard University, DC.
$25,000 to North Carolina A & T State University, Greensboro, NC.
$25,000 to University of North Carolina, Chapel Hill, NC.
$15,000 to New York University, New York, NY.

5289

The Kreitchman Family Foundation, Inc. ✧

62 Crest Dr.
South Orange, NJ 07079
Contact: Lilyan G. Kreitchman, Pres.

Established in 1997 in NJ.
Donor: Lilyan G. Kreitchman.
Foundation type: Independent foundation.
Financial data (yr. ended 12/31/05): Assets, $7,044,160 (M); expenditures, $379,631; qualifying distributions, $379,240; giving activities include $379,240 for 26 grants (high: $170,000; low: $25).
Purpose and activities: Giving primarily for higher education, Jewish organizations, and hospitals.
Fields of interest: Higher education; Hospitals (general); Health organizations, association; Jewish federated giving programs; Jewish agencies & temples.
Limitations: Giving primarily in NJ and NY. No grants to individuals.
Application information: Application form not required.
  Deadline(s): None
Officers and Trustees:* Lilyan G. Kreitchman,* Pres.; Lori K. Klinghoffer,* V.P.; Steven Klinghoffer, V.P.; Robin K. Walters,* V.P.
EIN: 223518906

5290

Krieger Charitable Trust ✧

11 Brook Ridge Ct.
Cedar Grove, NJ 07009
Contact: Jacqueline Klein, Tr.

Established in 1986 in NJ.
Foundation type: Independent foundation.
Financial data (yr. ended 12/31/05): Assets, $7,977,934 (M); expenditures, $441,166; qualifying distributions, $441,166; giving activities include $407,508 for 96 grants (high: $55,086; low: $18).

Purpose and activities: Giving primarily to Jewish organizations.
Fields of interest: Higher education; Human services; Federated giving programs; Jewish agencies & temples.
Type of support: Scholarship funds; Endowments; General/operating support; Continuing support; Annual campaigns; Capital campaigns.
Limitations: Applications not accepted. Giving primarily in northern NJ. No grants to individuals; no loans.
Application information: Contributes only to pre-selected organizations.
Trustee: Jacqueline Klein.
Board Member: Marian S. Filan.
EIN: 226374448
Selected grants: The following grants were reported in 2004.
$81,075 to Rutgers, The State University of New Jersey Foundation, New Brunswick, NJ.
$80,000 to Jewish Federation of Greater Clifton-Passaic, Clifton, NJ.
$25,150 to Wellesley College, Wellesley, MA.
$20,000 to Harvard University, School of Law, Cambridge, MA.
$9,778 to Montclair Art Museum, Montclair, NJ.
$5,000 to American Society for Technion-Israel Institute of Technology, New York, NY.
$5,000 to Birthright Israel North America, New York, NY.
$5,000 to Washington Institute for Near East Policy, DC.
$3,041 to Daughters of Miriam Center, Clifton, NJ.
$1,500 to Israel Project, DC.

5291

The Kurr Foundation ✧

c/o Norma R. Pane
P.O. Box 143
Middletown, NJ 07748

Established in 1992 in NJ.
Donor: Sara Zock.
Foundation type: Independent foundation.
Financial data (yr. ended 12/31/05): Assets, $17,131,890 (M); expenditures, $1,089,578; qualifying distributions, $904,438; giving activities include $777,725 for 51 grants (high: $60,000; low: $500).
Purpose and activities: Giving primarily to education.
Fields of interest: Elementary/secondary education; Higher education; Cancer; Heart & circulatory diseases; Salvation Army; Foundations (community); Protestant agencies & churches.
Limitations: Applications not accepted. Giving primarily in PA. No grants to individuals.
Application information: Contributes only to pre-selected organizations.
Officers and Trustees:* John H. Rogicki,* Pres.; Robert J. Gaughran,* Secy.; Norma R. Pane,* Treas.
EIN: 223176150

5292

The L.A.W. Foundation, Inc. ✧

1163 Rte. 22 E.
Mountainside, NJ 07092

Established in 1990 in NJ.
Donors: Leonard A. Wilf; Jenna Wilf Charitable Lead Trust; Judith Wilf Charitable Lead Trust; Harley Ryan

Wilf Charitable Lead Trust; Harrison Wilf Charitable Lead Trust; Alex H. Wilf Charitable Lead Trust.
Foundation type: Independent foundation.
Financial data (yr. ended 12/31/05): Assets, $53,301,080 (M); gifts received, $6,454,017; expenditures, $2,308,156; qualifying distributions, $2,278,070; giving activities include $2,278,070 for 41 grants (high: $1,305,000; low: $100).
Purpose and activities: Giving primarily for Jewish organizations; support also for the arts, education, and community improvement.
Fields of interest: Museums (art); Law school/education; Education; Hospitals (general); Human services; Jewish federated giving programs; Jewish agencies & temples.
Limitations: Applications not accepted. Giving primarily in NY. No grants to individuals.
Application information: Contributes only to pre-selected organizations.
Trustees: Beth Wilf; Leonard A. Wilf.
EIN: 223074635
Selected grants: The following grants were reported in 2003.
$550,000 to New York University, New York, NY. 2 grants: $500,000 to School of Law (For general support), $50,000 (For general support).
$210,000 to UJA-Federation of New York, New York, NY. For general support.
$200,000 to United States Holocaust Memorial Museum, DC. For general support.
$120,000 to Jerusalem Foundation, New York, NY. For general support.
$117,000 to Allen-Stevenson School, New York, NY. For general support.
$100,000 to Hun School of Princeton, Princeton, NJ. For general support.
$50,000 to Memorial Sloan-Kettering Cancer Center, New York, NY. For general support.
$40,000 to Metropolitan Golf Association Foundation, Elmsford, NY. For general support.
$20,000 to Birch Wathen School, New York, NY. For general support.

5293
The Charles Lafitte Foundation ✧
818 Linden Ln.
Brielle, NJ 08730-1714
Contact: Jennifer Vertetis, Pres.
E-mail: jennifer@charleslafitte.org; Application address: 29520 2nd Ave. S.W., Federal Way, WA 98023; URL: http://www.charleslafitte.org/

Established in 1999 in NY.
Donors: Jeffrey Adam Citron; Suzanne Lyman Citron.
Foundation type: Independent foundation.
Financial data (yr. ended 6/30/05): Assets, $3,589,917 (M); expenditures, $580,596; qualifying distributions, $547,563; giving activities include $382,067 for 39 grants (high: $100,000; low: $500), and $13,096 for foundation-administered programs.
Purpose and activities: The foundation is committed to helping groups and individuals foster lasting improvement on the human condition by providing support to education, children's advocacy, medical research and the arts.
Fields of interest: Arts education; Arts; Education; Health care; Cancer; Cancer research; Medical research; Youth development; Children/youth, services; Civil rights, advocacy.
Limitations: Giving on a national basis. No support for organizations lacking 501(c)(3) status, political

initiatives, studies by groups advocating for a political or public policy perspective, or projects whose purpose would benefit principally the members of sectarian or religious organizations. No grants to individuals.
Publications: Application guidelines.
Application information: Submit proposals by E-mail. The foundation will reply to inquiries which fit within the current goals and budget of the foundation. See foundation Web site for full application guidelines. Application form not required.
Initial approach: Brief letter of inquiry (no more than 10 double-spaced pages)
Deadline(s): None
Officer: Jennifer Vertetis, Pres.
Board Members: Jeffrey Adam Citron; Suzanne Lyman Citron; Joseph Patrick Woods.
EIN: 134034999
Selected grants: The following grants were reported in 2005.
$100,000 to American Cancer Society, Atlanta, GA.
$45,800 to Montclair Art Museum, Montclair, NJ. 3 grants: $5,500, $2,800, $37,500
$25,000 to Several Sources Foundation, Ramsey, NJ.
$10,000 to United Neighbors of East Midtown, New York, NY.
$5,000 to Celiac Disease Foundation, Studio City, CA.
$1,000 to Whitney Museum of American Art, New York, NY.

5294
Lanza Family Foundation ✧
c/o Lisa Zangara, Merrill Lynch Trust Co.
P.O. Box 1525
Pennington, NJ 08534-1525

Established in 1996 in NY.
Donors: Frank Lanza†; The Lanza Family Foundation.
Foundation type: Independent foundation.
Financial data (yr. ended 6/30/05): Assets, $2,941,676 (M); gifts received, $800,000; expenditures, $1,245,606; qualifying distributions, $1,213,515; giving activities include $1,210,200 for 36 grants (high: $250,000; low: $5,000).
Purpose and activities: Giving primarily to help minorities overcome financial impediments in order to have equal opportunities.
Fields of interest: Education; Housing/shelter, development; Human services; Christian agencies & churches.
Type of support: Scholarship funds.
Limitations: Applications not accepted. Giving primarily in Westchester County, NY. No support for New York City (except Manhattan or Brooklyn), or for CT and NJ. No grants to individuals directly.
Application information: Unsolicited requests for funds not accepted.
Board meeting date(s): Apr. 1
Officer: Patricia Lanza, Pres. and Secy.
EIN: 133922706
Selected grants: The following grants were reported in 2004.
$100,000 to Childrens Village, Dobbs Ferry, NY. For general operating support.
$100,000 to Habitat for Humanity of Westchester, New Rochelle, NY. For general operating support.
$100,000 to Wheelchair Classics Charities, Jackson Heights, NY. For general operating support.

$40,000 to Womens Research and Education Fund of the Westchester County Office for Women, White Plains, NY. For general operating support.
$25,000 to Borough of Manhattan Community College of the City University of New York, New York, NY. For general operating support.
$25,000 to Saint Vincents Services, Brooklyn, NY. For general operating support.
$15,000 to College Careers Fund of Westchester, White Plains, NY. For general operating support.
$5,000 to Covenant House, New York, NY. For general operating support.
$5,000 to Literacy Volunteers of Rochester, Rochester, NY. For general operating support.
$5,000 to Todays Students, Tomorrows Teachers, Elmsford, NY. For general operating support.

5295
The Large Foundation ✧
171 Main St.
Flemington, NJ 08822-1607 (908) 782-5315
Contact: C. Gregory Watts, Pres.

Incorporated in 1957 in NJ.
Donors: George K. Large†; Edwin J.S. Anderson†; and members of the Large family.
Foundation type: Independent foundation.
Financial data (yr. ended 12/31/05): Assets, $11,561,781 (M); expenditures, $573,163; qualifying distributions, $545,036; giving activities include $526,736 for 59 grants (high: $95,148; low: $500).
Purpose and activities: Emphasis on health services and agencies; grants also for social services, youth agencies, and community development.
Fields of interest: Education; Medical care, community health systems; Health care; Health organizations, association; Food distribution, groceries on wheels; Human services; YM/YWCAs & YM/YWHAs; Children/youth, services; Community development.
Limitations: Giving primarily in Hunterdon County, NJ. No grants to individuals.
Application information: Application form not required.
Initial approach: Letter
Deadline(s): None
Board meeting date(s): Oct.
Officers: C. Gregory Watts, Pres.; Cheryl Copeland, V.P.; Richard L. Tice, Secy.; Paul C. Sauerland, Jr., Treas.
Trustees: Franklin H. Barlow; J. Kirby Fowler; Teresa H. Martin; Charles J. Scammell; Anne M. Thomas.
EIN: 226049246

5296
Larsen Foundation, Inc. ✧
c/o Richard E. Ingram
410 George St.
New Brunswick, NJ 08901

Established in 1996 in NJ.
Donor: Ralph S. Larsen.
Foundation type: Independent foundation.
Financial data (yr. ended 9/30/05): Assets, $15,066,700 (M); expenditures, $1,103,209; qualifying distributions, $1,097,917; giving activities include $1,094,089 for 17 grants (high: $499,589; low: $500).

Purpose and activities: Giving for Christian organizations and for Christian education.
Fields of interest: Higher education; Federated giving programs; Christian agencies & churches.
Limitations: Applications not accepted. No grants to individuals.
Application information: Contributes only to pre-selected organizations.
Officers and Trustees:* Ralph S. Larsen,* Pres.; Dorothy M. Larsen,* Secy.-Treas.; Kristen Larsen Dries; Garret W. Larsen; Karen Larsen Verblaauw.
EIN: 311482756

5297
Blanche & Irving Laurie Foundation, Inc.
P.O. Box 53
Roseland, NJ 07068-5788
Contact: Gene R. Korf, Exec. Dir.

Established in 1983 in NJ.
Donor: Irving Laurie†.
Foundation type: Independent foundation.
Financial data (yr. ended 9/30/05): Assets, $62,967,330 (M); gifts received, $29,406; expenditures, $4,167,017; qualifying distributions, $3,561,286; giving activities include $3,303,620 for 118 grants (high: $265,000; low: $475; average: $1,000–$50,000).
Purpose and activities: Support for Jewish social services, secondary schools, and cultural organizations; the arts, particularly for theater; also for medical and health centers.
Fields of interest: Performing arts, theater; Arts; Children/youth, services; Aging, centers/services; Jewish agencies & temples; Aging.
Type of support: Capital campaigns; Building/ renovation; Equipment; Program development.
Limitations: Giving primarily in NJ. No support for medical research.
Publications: Application guidelines; Informational brochure (including application guidelines).
Application information: Application form not required.
  Initial approach: Proposal
  Copies of proposal: 7
  Deadline(s): None
  Board meeting date(s): Quarterly
  Final notification: 3-4 months
Officers and Trustees:* Adelaide Marcus Zagoren,* Pres.; Gene R. Korf,* Exec. Dir.; Scott Korf; Ruth Marcus Patt; Harvey S. Rich; Laura Master Zagoren.
EIN: 222489725

5298
The Lautenberg Foundation ◇
(formerly The L. Family Foundation)
P.O. Box 960
Cliffside Park, NJ 07010
Contact: E. Rigolosi, Asst. Secy.

Established in 1967 in NJ.
Donor: Frank R. Lautenberg Charitable Trusts.
Foundation type: Independent foundation.
Financial data (yr. ended 12/31/05): Assets, $13,089,617 (M); expenditures, $753,813; qualifying distributions, $719,513; giving activities include $672,324 for 110 grants (high: $217,861; low: $500).
Purpose and activities: Grants largely for Jewish welfare funds, education, and cultural programs

locally; some support also for educational and cultural institutions in Israel.
Fields of interest: Media, television; Museums; Arts; Higher education; Education; Environment; Animals/wildlife, preservation/protection; Hospitals (general); Cancer; Medical research, institute; Cancer research; Human services; Minorities/immigrants, centers/services; Jewish federated giving programs; Jewish agencies & temples; Minorities.
International interests: Israel.
Type of support: Annual campaigns; Capital campaigns; Building/renovation; Endowments; Emergency funds; Program development; Scholarship funds; Research.
Limitations: Applications not accepted. Giving on a national basis, with some emphasis on the greater metropolitan New York, NY, area, including NJ. No grants to individuals.
Application information: Contributes only to pre-selected organizations.
Officers: Frank R. Lautenberg, Pres.; Lois Lautenberg, V.P.; Fred S. Lafer, Secy.
Number of staff: 1 part-time support.
EIN: 226102734
Selected grants: The following grants were reported in 2004.
$100,000 to Salvation Army.
$97,000 to Columbia University, New York, NY.
$30,600 to John F. Kennedy Center for the Performing Arts, DC.
$25,000 to Yeshiva University, New York, NY.
$5,000 to Newark Academy, Livingston, NJ.
$5,000 to Newark Museum, Newark, NJ.
$3,000 to Jazz at Lincoln Center, New York, NY.
$2,200 to Metropolitan Museum of Art, New York, NY.
$2,000 to Boys Town Jerusalem, Jerusalem, Israel. .
$2,000 to Jewish Family and Career Services, Atlanta, GA.

5299
The Lazarus Charitable Trust ◇
(formerly The Helen and Charles Lazarus Charitable Trust)
c/o Toys R Us
1 Geoffrey Way, Lake Bldg.
Wayne, NJ 07470-2030
Contact: Charles Lazarus, Tr.

Established in 1986 in NJ.
Donor: Charles Lazarus.
Foundation type: Independent foundation.
Financial data (yr. ended 5/31/05): Assets, $4,627,605 (M); gifts received, $406,501; expenditures, $370,099; qualifying distributions, $361,048; giving activities include $361,048 for 42 grants (high: $200,000; low: $25).
Purpose and activities: Giving primarily for the arts, education, and health and human services.
Fields of interest: Museums; Arts; Education; Hospitals (general); Health organizations, association; Cancer; Medical research, institute; Cancer research; Human services.
Limitations: Giving primarily in New York, NY.
Application information:
  Initial approach: Letter
  Deadline(s): None
Officer: Charles Lazarus, Pres.
EIN: 133360876

5300
The Frances Lear Foundation ◇
c/o Conroy, Smith & Co.
385 Prospect Ave.
Hackensack, NJ 07601

Established in 2000 in DE.
Foundation type: Independent foundation.
Financial data (yr. ended 12/31/03): Assets, $10,342,934 (M); expenditures, $539,687; qualifying distributions, $481,026; giving activities include $480,120 for 30 grants (high: $30,000; low: $5,000).
Fields of interest: Performing arts, ballet; Elementary school/education; Environment, forests; Hospitals (general); Legal services; Girls clubs; Children/youth, services; Public affairs; Women.
Limitations: Applications not accepted. Giving primarily in NY. No grants to individuals.
Application information: Contributes only to pre-selected organizations.
Officer: Thomas R. Asher, Secy.
Directors: Daniel R. Katz; Jonathan LaPook; Kate Breckir Lear; Maggie Lear.
EIN: 043489966
Selected grants: The following grants were reported in 2003.
$30,000 to Women at Risk, Los Angeles, CA. For general support.
$25,000 to Girls Inc., New York, NY. For general support.
$25,000 to People for the American Way Foundation, New York, NY. For general support.
$25,000 to Rainforest Alliance, New York, NY. For general support.
$21,800 to Ballet Hispanico of New York, New York, NY. For general support.
$20,000 to DreamYard Drama Project, New York, NY. For general support.
$20,000 to Interfaith Neighbors, New York, NY. For general support.
$20,000 to Rockefeller Philanthropy Advisors, Philanthropic Collaborative, New York, NY. For general support.
$20,000 to Urban Justice Center, New York, NY. For general support.
$15,000 to New York Civil Liberties Union, New York, NY. For general support.

5301
The Lebensfeld Foundation ◇
c/o UIS, Inc.
15 Exchange Pl.
Jersey City, NJ 07302-3912
Contact: Joseph F. Arrigo, Secy.-Treas.

Incorporated in 1959 in NY.
Donor: Harry Lebensfeld Revocable Trust.
Foundation type: Independent foundation.
Financial data (yr. ended 8/31/05): Assets, $35,022,576 (M); expenditures, $3,617,858; qualifying distributions, $3,612,300; giving activities include $3,607,500 for 71 grants (high: $1,500,000; low: $1,000).
Purpose and activities: Giving primarily for health care and to health associations.
Fields of interest: Arts; Elementary/secondary education; Higher education; Libraries/library science; Education; Hospitals (general); Health organizations, association; Federated giving programs; Roman Catholic agencies & churches.

Limitations: Giving primarily in NY and PA. No grants to individuals.
Application information: Application form not required.
Deadline(s): None
Officers and Directors:* Andrew G. Pietrini,* Pres.; Robert J. Giuffra, Jr.,* V.P.; Joseph F. Arrigo,* Secy.-Treas.
EIN: 136086169
Selected grants: The following grants were reported in 2005.
$200,000 to Salk Institute for Biological Studies, San Diego, CA.
$100,000 to Bon Secours New Jersey Health System, Jersey City, NJ.
$100,000 to Ramaz School, New York, NY.
$50,000 to American Ballet Theater, New York, NY.
$50,000 to Barth Syndrome Foundation, Lincoln, NE.
$25,000 to Memorial Hospital Foundation, Oconomowoc, WI.
$25,000 to Metropolitan Museum of Art, New York, NY.
$20,000 to New York Public Library, New York, NY.
$10,000 to Childrens Blood Foundation, New York, NY.
$10,000 to Muscular Dystrophy Association, Maywood, NJ.

5302
Chaim Leib & Chaya Sara Kahan Memorial ✧
c/o Omni Asset Mgmt. LLC
26 Journal Sq., 16th Fl.
Jersey City, NJ 07306-4105

Established in 1999 in NY.
Donors: Michael Silberberg; Mifal Ezra Zichron Yehida; Western Environmental Solutions, LLC; Future Care; Hospitality Consulting and Supply; Comprehensive Cleaning Co., Inc.; Hersh Foundation; Confidence Services.
Foundation type: Operating foundation.
Financial data (yr. ended 12/31/04): Assets, $400,560 (M); gifts received, $478,989; expenditures, $599,343; qualifying distributions, $597,569; giving activities include $597,069 for 147 grants (high: $108,700; low: $36).
Fields of interest: Human services; Jewish agencies & temples.
Type of support: General/operating support; Grants to individuals.
Limitations: Applications not accepted. Giving primarily in NY.
Application information: Unsolicited requests for funds not accepted.
Officers: Simon Perlmutter, Pres.; Michael Silberberg, V.P. and Treas.; Joseph Zelmanowitz, Secy.
Directors: Avery Eisenreich; Rabbi Krupenia; Rabbi Perl; Max Stern; Sam Stern; Tzirel Stern; Channa Tauber.
EIN: 134057201

5303
Leitner Family Foundation, Inc. ✧
Janice Brennan-Falcon Mgmt. Corp.
400 W. Main St.
Wyckoff, NJ 07481

Established in 2002 in NJ.

Donor: James Leitner.
Foundation type: Independent foundation.
Financial data (yr. ended 12/31/05): Assets, $32,472,427 (L); expenditures, $2,236,053; qualifying distributions, $1,592,799; giving activities include $1,587,135 for grants.
Fields of interest: Safety/disasters; Human services; Christian agencies & churches.
Limitations: Applications not accepted. Giving primarily in NJ. No grants to individuals.
Application information: Contributes only to pre-selected organizations.
Officers and Trustees:* James Leitner,* Pres.; Sandra Leitner,* Secy.; Janice Brennan, Treas.; Allegra Leitner.
EIN: 043726988
Selected grants: The following grants were reported in 2005.
$325,600 to Saint Leon Armenian Church, Fair Lawn, NJ. 5 grants: $25,000, $50,000, $200,000, $600, $50,000

5304
The Philip & Janice Levin Foundation ✧
893 Rte. 22
North Plainfield, NJ 07060 (908) 755-2401

Incorporated in 1963 in NJ.
Donors: Janice H. Levin†; Philip J. Levin†; Adam Corp.
Foundation type: Independent foundation.
Financial data (yr. ended 8/31/05): Assets, $40,111,272 (M); gifts received, $82,414; expenditures, $604,020; qualifying distributions, $549,700; giving activities include $549,700 for 18 grants (high: $125,000; low: $5,000).
Purpose and activities: Giving primarily for the arts, particularly to art museums, as well as for higher education and health associations.
Fields of interest: Museums; Museums (art); Museums (specialized); Performing arts centers; Arts; Higher education; Medical school/education; Health organizations, association; Human services; Jewish federated giving programs.
Limitations: Giving primarily in NJ and New York, NY. No grants to individuals.
Application information: Application form not required.
Initial approach: Letter
Deadline(s): None
Officers: Adam Levin, Pres.; Paul Skwiersky, V.P. and Treas.; William A. Farber, V.P.; Maureen Mooney, Secy.
EIN: 226075837
Selected grants: The following grants were reported in 2003.
$300,000 to New York University, School of Medicine, New York, NY.
$250,000 to Foundation for Art and Preservation in Embassies, DC.
$100,000 to Metropolitan Museum of Art, New York, NY.
$82,000 to W N E T Channel 13, New York, NY.
$50,000 to Juilliard School, New York, NY.
$50,000 to Rutgers, The State University of New Jersey, New Brunswick, NJ.
$50,000 to Rutgers, The State University of New Jersey Foundation, School of Law, New Brunswick, NJ.
$40,000 to School of American Ballet, New York, NY.
$20,000 to Guild Hall of East Hampton, East Hampton, NY.

$15,000 to Metropolitan Opera, New York, NY.

5305
Mortimer Levitt Foundation, Inc. ✧
c/o Levitt Properties
100 Quarry Rd., Ste. 2
Hamburg, NJ 07419
Application address: 10 E. 82nd St., New York, NY 10028

Established in 1966 in NY.
Donors: Mortimer Levitt†; The Custom Shops.
Foundation type: Independent foundation.
Financial data (yr. ended 2/28/03): Assets, $20,254,648 (M); expenditures, $1,158,987; qualifying distributions, $840,734; giving activities include $833,326 for 245 grants (high: $100,000; low: $50).
Fields of interest: Museums (specialized); Performing arts; Performing arts, ballet; Performing arts, theater; Performing arts, opera; Historic preservation/historical societies; Arts; Higher education; Health organizations, association; Cancer research; Human services; Children/youth, services; Community development; Foundations (community); Jewish federated giving programs.
Limitations: Giving primarily in New York, NY. No grants to individuals.
Application information:
Initial approach: Letter
Deadline(s): None
Officers: AnneMarie Levitt, V.P.; Estelle Rubenstein, Secy.-Treas.
EIN: 136204678

5306
The Ken and Laurie Levy Family Foundation, Inc. ✧
312 Boulevard
Mountain Lakes, NJ 07046-1501

Established in 2002 in NJ.
Donor: Kenneth Levy.
Foundation type: Independent foundation.
Financial data (yr. ended 12/31/05): Assets, $9,157,242 (M); expenditures, $326,847; qualifying distributions, $317,000; giving activities include $317,000 for 13 grants (high: $100,000; low: $1,000; average: $1,000–$40,000).
Fields of interest: Elementary/secondary education; Education; Civil rights; Jewish federated giving programs; Public policy, research; Jewish agencies & temples.
Limitations: Applications not accepted. Giving primarily in NJ and NY.
Application information: Contributes only to pre-selected organizations.
Officers: Kenneth Levy, Pres.; Laurie Levy, V.P.
Director: Kara Levy.
EIN: 030438401

5307
The George Link, Jr. Charitable Trust ✧
P.O. Box 160
Milltown, NJ 08850-0160
Contact: Michael J. Catanzaro, Tr.

Established in 1999 in NJ.
Donor: Eleanor I. Link.
Foundation type: Independent foundation.

Financial data (yr. ended 12/31/05): Assets, $28,015,538 (M); expenditures, $1,485,349; qualifying distributions, $1,250,279; giving activities include $1,157,200 for 86 grants (high: $55,000; low: $500).

Purpose and activities: Giving primarily for education, hospitals and health associations, Roman Catholic churches, social services, and community programs.

Fields of interest: Arts; Elementary/secondary education; Higher education; Hospitals (general); Health organizations, association; Cancer research; Human services; Children/youth, services; Community development.

Limitations: Giving primarily in NY, with emphasis on the metropolitan New York, NY, area, and NJ; some funding also nationally.

Application information:
  Initial approach: Letter
  Deadline(s): None

Trustees: Michael J. Catanzaro; Bernard F. Joyce; Robert Emmet Link.

EIN: 226799699

Selected grants: The following grants were reported in 2005.

$55,000 to Bishop George Ahr High School, Edison, NJ.

$55,000 to Saint Dominics Church, Oyster Bay, NY.

$50,000 to Christian Blind Mission International, Greenville, SC.

$35,000 to Calvary Hospital, Bronx, NY.

$20,000 to Deborah Hospital Foundation, Browns Mills, NJ.

$20,000 to Several Sources Foundation, Ramsey, NJ.

$10,000 to Cerebral Palsy Association of Middlesex County, Edison, NJ.

$10,000 to Life Experience and Faith Sharing Association, New York, NY.

$10,000 to Sisters of Saint Joseph, Brentwood, NY.

$10,000 to Wake Forest University, Winston-Salem, NC.

5308

The Lipper Family Charitable Foundation ◇

c/o A. Michael Lipper
85 Hobart Ave.
Summit, NJ 07901

Established in 1999 in NJ.

Donors: A. Michael Lipper; Ruth C. Lipper.

Foundation type: Independent foundation.

Financial data (yr. ended 11/30/04): Assets, $98,090 (M); gifts received, $100,000; expenditures, $449,032; qualifying distributions, $448,868; giving activities include $448,868 for 80 grants (high: $65,000; low: $10).

Purpose and activities: Giving primarily for the arts, particularly the symphony, education, human services, health associations, and to Episcopal churches.

Fields of interest: Museums (art); Performing arts centers; Elementary/secondary education; Higher education; Health organizations, association; Human services; Protestant agencies & churches.

Limitations: Applications not accepted. Giving primarily in NJ. No grants to individuals.

Application information: Contributes only to pre-selected organizations.

Trustees: A. Michael Lipper; Ruth C. Lipper.

EIN: 137152755

Selected grants: The following grants were reported in 2004.

$100,000 to New Jersey Symphony Orchestra, Newark, NJ. 3 grants: $25,000, $25,000, $50,000

$95,000 to New Jersey Performing Arts Center, Newark, NJ. 2 grants: $65,000, $30,000

$50,000 to Mount Vernon.

$25,000 to Drew University, Madison, NJ.

$25,000 to Newark Museum, Newark, NJ.

$1,200 to University of California at San Diego, La Jolla, CA.

$100 to Summit Speech School, New Providence, NJ.

5309

The Lissak Foundation, Inc. ◇

465 South St.
Morristown, NJ 07960 (973) 898-9494
Contact: Kenneth Lissak, Mgr.

Established in 1996 in CT.

Donors: Kenneth Lissak; Miriam Lissak.

Foundation type: Independent foundation.

Financial data (yr. ended 11/30/05): Assets, $10,947 (L); gifts received, $538,509; expenditures, $574,772; qualifying distributions, $574,672; giving activities include $569,672 for 35 grants (high: $100,000; low: $2,165), and $5,000 for 1 grant to an individual.

Purpose and activities: Giving primarily for education, health care, and human services.

Fields of interest: Arts; Education; Hospitals (general); Health organizations, association; Human services; Religion.

Limitations: Giving primarily in CT and NY.

Application information: Application form not required.

  Initial approach: Letter or telephone
  Deadline(s): None

Officer: Kenneth Lissak, Mgr.

EIN: 061468915

Selected grants: The following grants were reported in 2005.

$100,000 to Saint Raymond Community Outreach, Bronx, NY.

$75,000 to Temple Emanuel, Paterson, NJ.

$22,000 to Mount Sinai Hospital, New York, NY. 2 grants: $11,000 each

$5,000 to Shul of New York, New York, NY.

5310

The Long Bay Charitable Foundation ◇

(formerly The David & Lois Shakarian Foundation)
c/o Windels Marx Lane & Mittendorf, LLP
325 Columbia Tpke.
Florham Park, NJ 07932-1212

Established in 1986 in DE.

Donors: Lois V. Shakarian Blackburn†; Linda Lucas; Louise Urleja; David Lucas; Michael Urleja; Brian Lucas; Melinda Lucas.

Foundation type: Independent foundation.

Financial data (yr. ended 12/31/05): Assets, $7,800,191 (M); expenditures, $1,268,537; qualifying distributions, $1,218,000; giving activities include $1,218,000 for 10 grants (high: $400,000; low: $1,000).

Fields of interest: Theological school/education; Education; Christian agencies & churches.

Limitations: Applications not accepted. Giving primarily in CA and FL. No grants to individuals.

Application information: Contributes only to pre-selected organizations.

Officers: P. Michael Ukleja, Chair. and Pres.; David Lucas, V.P. and Treas.; Linda S. Lucas, V.P.; Louise Ukleja, V.P.; Edward Beimfohr, Secy.

EIN: 133047543

5311

The John Victor Machuga Foundation, Inc. ◇

P.O. Box 738
Totowa, NJ 07511-0738

Established in 1994 in NJ.

Donor: John Victor Machuga†.

Foundation type: Independent foundation.

Financial data (yr. ended 12/31/05): Assets, $5,220,552 (M); expenditures, $562,328; qualifying distributions, $518,518; giving activities include $435,818 for 29 grants (high: $169,593; low: $100).

Purpose and activities: Giving primarily for higher education and hospitals.

Fields of interest: Elementary/secondary education; Higher education; Hospitals (general); Health organizations, association; Human services.

Type of support: Capital campaigns; Equipment; Program development; Matching/challenge support.

Limitations: Giving primarily in northern NJ. No grants to individuals, or for salaries or construction.

Publications: Application guidelines.

Application information: Application form not required.

  Initial approach: Letter
  Copies of proposal: 3
  Deadline(s): None
  Board meeting date(s): 1st Tues. of each month
  Final notification: 1 to 2 months

Trustees: Joseph M. Makoujy; Bruce Waldman.

EIN: 223162765

Selected grants: The following grants were reported in 2005.

$50,000 to Hackensack University Medical Center, Hackensack, NJ.

$25,000 to Fairleigh Dickinson University, Teaneck, NJ.

$25,000 to Saint Josephs Hospital and Medical Center, Paterson, NJ.

$17,000 to Montclair State University, Montclair, NJ.

$10,000 to Phoenix Center, Little Falls, NJ.

$9,000 to New Jersey Institute of Technology, Newark, NJ.

$8,500 to New Jersey City University, Jersey City, NJ.

$4,500 to Childrens Specialized Hospital, Mountainside, NJ.

$2,000 to Valley Home Care, Paramus, NJ.

5312

The David & Sondra Mack Family Foundation, Inc. ◇ ☆

2115 Linwood Ave., Rm. 110
Fort Lee, NJ 07024 (201) 346-5400

Established in 1998.

Donor: David Mack.

Foundation type: Independent foundation.

Financial data (yr. ended 12/31/04): Assets, $13,493,305 (M); gifts received, $5,100,000; expenditures, $1,553,757; qualifying distributions, $1,553,706; giving activities include $1,553,706 for 230 grants (high: $250,000; low: $12).
Fields of interest: Performing arts; Education; Health care; Cancer; Human services; Jewish agencies & temples.
Limitations: Applications not accepted. Giving primarily in NY. No grants to individuals.
Application information: Contributes only to pre-selected organizations.
Trustee: David Mack.
EIN: 223632663
Selected grants: The following grants were reported in 2004.
$250,000 to Jewish Institute for National Security Affairs, DC.
$113,000 to Temple Israel of Great Neck, Great Neck, NY. 2 grants: $100,000, $13,000
$25,000 to Hofstra University, Hempstead, NY.
$15,000 to Pratt Institute, Brooklyn, NY.
$10,000 to Norton Museum of Art, West Palm Beach, FL.
$5,500 to Jewish Museum, New York, NY.
$2,000 to Lincoln Center Theater, New York, NY.
$2,000 to Rabbi Arthur Schneier Park East Day School, New York, NY.
$1,000 to Livnot ULehibanot, Safed, Israel. .

5313
The William & Phyllis Mack Family Foundation, Inc. ✧
2115 Linwood Ave., Ste. 110
Fort Lee, NJ   07024

Established in 1997 in NJ.
Donor: William Mack.
Foundation type: Independent foundation.
Financial data (yr. ended 12/31/04): Assets, $4,667,826 (M); gifts received, $2,416,655; expenditures, $5,010,356; qualifying distributions, $4,973,563; giving activities include $4,973,563 for 106 grants (high: $1,017,000; low: $100).
Purpose and activities: Giving primarily for higher education, Jewish organizations and federated giving programs, and human services.
Fields of interest: Higher education; Hospitals (general); Human services; Jewish federated giving programs; Jewish agencies & temples.
Limitations: Applications not accepted. Giving on a national basis. No grants to individuals.
Application information: Contributes only to pre-selected organizations.
Trustee: William Mack.
EIN: 223512719

5314
The Earle I. Mack Foundation, Inc. ✧ ☆
c/o M. Schwartzbard
101 Eisenhower Pkwy., 3rd Fl.
Roseland, NJ   07068

Established in 2002 in NJ.
Donor: Earle I. Mack.
Foundation type: Independent foundation.
Financial data (yr. ended 12/31/04): Assets, $4,342,346 (M); gifts received, $1,715,053; expenditures, $692,487; qualifying distributions, $684,983; giving activities include $684,983 for 39 + grants.

Fields of interest: Arts; Health organizations, association; Human services; Jewish agencies & temples.
Officer: Earle I. Mack, Pres.
EIN: 911981393

5315
Makk Charitable Foundation ✧
96 Rte. 23
Little Falls, NJ   07424-1106

Donors: Agnes Varis; Karl Leichtman; Agvar Chemicals, Inc.
Foundation type: Independent foundation.
Financial data (yr. ended 12/31/05): Assets, $57,667 (M); gifts received, $130,000; expenditures, $1,588,075; qualifying distributions, $1,587,500; giving activities include $1,587,500 for 12 grants (high: $1,000,000; low: $5,000).
Fields of interest: Performing arts centers; Performing arts, music; Performing arts, opera; Arts; Medical research, institute.
Limitations: Applications not accepted. Giving primarily in New York, NY. No grants to individuals.
Application information: Contributes only to pre-selected organizations.
Officers and Directors: * Agnes Varis,* Pres. and Treas.; Karl Leichtman,* V.P. and Secy.
EIN: 223588549
Selected grants: The following grants were reported in 2003.
$500,000 to Jazz at Lincoln Center, New York, NY.
$250,000 to Lincoln Center Consolidated Corporate Fund, New York, NY. For Golden Circle Agvar Fund.
$250,000 to Lincoln Center for the Performing Arts, New York, NY.
$250,000 to Metropolitan Opera, New York, NY.
$150,000 to BMA Medical Foundation, Flushing, NY. For Infectious Disease Laboratory.
$100,000 to Bide-A-Wee Home Association, New York, NY. For general support.
$25,000 to Hope Enterprises, Williamsport, PA. For general support.

5316
Mamiye Foundation ✧
180 Raritan Center Pkwy., Ste. 11
Edison, NJ   08837
Contact: Charles M. Mamiye, Tr.
Application address: P.O. Box 320, Keasbey, NJ 08832

Incorporated in 1982 in NJ.
Donors: Mamiye Brothers, Inc.; MB Kids Clothes LLC.
Foundation type: Company-sponsored foundation.
Financial data (yr. ended 12/31/03): Assets, $308,639 (M); gifts received, $693,450; expenditures, $385,749; qualifying distributions, $385,650; giving activities include $385,650 for 63 grants (high: $82,000; low: $100).
Purpose and activities: The foundation supports Jewish agencies and temples and organizations involved with health and human services.
Fields of interest: Theological school/education; Health care; Children/youth, services; Human services; Jewish federated giving programs; Jewish agencies & temples.

Limitations: Giving primarily in NJ and the greater metropolitan New York, NY, area. No grants to individuals.
Application information:
Initial approach: Proposal
Deadline(s): None
Trustees: Charles D. Mamiye; Charles M. Mamiye.
EIN: 222471712
Selected grants: The following grants were reported in 2004.
$116,000 to Magen David Yeshiva, Brooklyn, NY. 2 grants: $40,000, $76,000
$35,000 to Sephardic Bikur Holim, Brooklyn, NY. 2 grants: $30,000, $5,000
$30,000 to Hillel Yeshiva, Ocean, NJ. 2 grants: $20,000, $10,000
$25,000 to Sephardic Community Center, Brooklyn, NY. 2 grants: $20,000, $5,000
$15,000 to Ann Schreiber Ovarian Cancer Research Fund, New York, NY.
$6,000 to Chai Lifeline, New York, NY.

5317
Marcon Foundation, Inc. ✧ ☆
79 Chestnut St., Ste. 101
Ridgewood, NJ   07450

Established in 2003 in NJ.
Donors: Fred R. Marcon; Natalie Marcon.
Foundation type: Independent foundation.
Financial data (yr. ended 12/31/05): Assets, $1,065,245 (M); gifts received, $610,192; expenditures, $466,492; qualifying distributions, $459,500; giving activities include $459,500 for grants.
Fields of interest: Animal welfare; Human services; Roman Catholic agencies & churches.
Limitations: Applications not accepted. Giving on a national basis. No grants to individuals.
Application information: Contributes only to pre-selected organizations.
Trustees: Alison M. Marcon; Anthony G. Marcon; Fred R. Marcon; Mark C. Marcon; Michael C. Marcon; Michelle G. Marcon; Natalie Marcon.
EIN: 571167051

5318
The Marianthi Foundation, Inc. ✧
82 Mosle Rd.
Far Hills, NJ   07931

Established in 1993 in NJ.
Donor: P. Roy Vagelos.
Foundation type: Independent foundation.
Financial data (yr. ended 12/31/04): Assets, $60,106,446 (M); gifts received, $298,986; expenditures, $2,975,087; qualifying distributions, $2,478,612; giving activities include $2,478,612 for 17 grants (high: $600,000; low: $5,000).
Purpose and activities: Giving primarily for higher education; funding also for the arts.
Fields of interest: Museums; Performing arts centers; Performing arts, orchestra (symphony); Arts; Secondary school/education; Higher education.
Limitations: Applications not accepted. Giving primarily in NJ and PA; some funding also in NY. No grants to individuals.
Application information: Contributes only to pre-selected organizations.

Officers and Director:* P. Roy Vagelos,* Pres.; Diana T. Vagelos, V.P. and Treas.

EIN: 226616473

Selected grants: The following grants were reported in 2004.

$600,000 to Barnard College, New York, NY.

$508,224 to Columbia University, New York, NY.

$421,900 to University of Pennsylvania, Philadelphia, PA.

$258,000 to New Jersey Symphony Orchestra, Newark, NJ.

$257,000 to New Jersey Performing Arts Center, Newark, NJ.

$50,000 to Newark Museum, Newark, NJ.

$33,333 to National Constitution Center, Philadelphia, PA.

$25,000 to American Philosophical Society, Philadelphia, PA.

$10,000 to Brown University, Providence, RI.

5319

Nicholas Martini Foundation ◇

777 Passaic Ave.

Clifton, NJ   07012   (973) 594-1899

Contact: George J. Homcy, Exec Dir.

Established in 1986 in NJ.

Donor: Nicholas Martini‡.

Foundation type: Independent foundation.

Financial data (yr. ended 12/31/04): Assets, $13,589,546 (M); expenditures, $784,373; qualifying distributions, $667,220; giving activities include $526,500 for 93 grants (high: $75,000; low: $500).

Purpose and activities: The foundation supports programs in the fields of youth and education, public health and welfare, community development, and arts and humanities programs.

Fields of interest: Arts; Secondary school/ education; Higher education; Libraries/library science; Hospitals (general); Youth development, services; Human services; Children/youth, services.

Type of support: General/operating support; Matching/challenge support.

Limitations: Giving primarily in Bergen, Essex, and Passaic counties, NJ. No grants to individuals.

Publications: Application guidelines; Annual report.

Application information: Application form required.

Initial approach: Letter requesting application form on organization letterhead; phone requests not accepted

Copies of proposal: 1

Deadline(s): Varies

Board meeting date(s): Varies; 2 to 3 meetings per year

Final notification: Varies

Officer: William J. Martini, Pres.

Trustees: Fannie Rosta; Marie Salanitri.

Number of staff: 1 part-time professional.

EIN: 222756049

5320

Martinson Family Foundation, Inc. ◇

1009 Lenox Dr., Ste. 4

Lawrenceville, NJ   08648

Established in 1999 in NJ.

Donor: John H. Martinson.

Foundation type: Independent foundation.

Financial data (yr. ended 11/30/05): Assets, $7,437,201 (M); expenditures, $441,410;

qualifying distributions, $429,100; giving activities include $429,100 for 11 grants (high: $100,000; low: $100).

Fields of interest: Higher education; Education.

Limitations: Applications not accepted. Giving primarily in NJ. No grants to individuals.

Application information: Contributes only to pre-selected organizations.

Officers and Trustees:* John H. Martinson,* Chair., V.P. and Secy.; Margaret M. Martinson,* Pres. and Treas.; Ross T. Martinson.

EIN: 223695793

Selected grants: The following grants were reported in 2004.

$100,000 to Rutgers, The State University of New Jersey Foundation, New Brunswick, NJ. For Math and Science lab.

$50,000 to New Jersey Institute of Technology Foundation, Newark, NJ. For technology curriculum for secondary schools.

$50,000 to Technology Educators Association of New Jersey, Fair Lawn, NJ. For innovative teacher awards.

$41,000 to Thomas A. Edison State College, Trenton, NJ. For on-line class curriculum.

$39,000 to Montclair State University, Montclair, NJ. For Prism Program.

$10,000 to Fairleigh Dickinson University, Rothman Institute of Entrepreneurial Studies, Madison, NJ. For collegiate entrepreneur awards.

$6,000 to New Jersey Technology Council Education Foundation, Princeton, NJ. For NJBIZ NEXT, high school publication.

$1,000 to Multiple Sclerosis Society of Delaware, Wilmington, DE. For Innphase and Luehr Bike Event.

$750 to Boys and Girls Club of the Delaware Valley, Trenton, NJ. For Greg Olsen event.

$500 to Purdue Foundation, West Lafayette, IN. For President's Council.

5321

Helen and William Mazer Foundation

P.O. Box 542

Berkeley Heights, NJ   07922

Contact: Leonard Berkowitz, Treas.

Established in 1999 in DE.

Foundation type: Independent foundation.

Financial data (yr. ended 9/30/05): Assets, $12,216,477 (M); expenditures, $655,861; qualifying distributions, $567,286; giving activities include $558,220 for 104 grants (high: $40,000; low: $20).

Fields of interest: Arts; Education; Environment; Health organizations, association; Community development.

Limitations: Applications not accepted. No grants to individuals.

Application information: Unsolicited requests for funds not accepted.

Board meeting date(s): As needed

Officers: Linda Berkowitz, Pres.; Steven Bercu, Secy.; Leonard Berkowitz, Treas.

Directors: Alan Berkowitz; David Berkowitz.

EIN: 020511160

5322

The McCutchen Foundation ◇

c/o PNC Advisors

454 Rte. 28

Bridgewater, NJ   08807

Application address: c/o Charles W. McCutchen, Tr., 209 W. 2nd St., Plainfield, NJ 07061, tel.: (908) 756-0042

Trust established in 1956 in NJ.

Donors: Brunson S. McCutchen; Charles W. McCutchen; Margaret W. McCutchen.

Foundation type: Independent foundation.

Financial data (yr. ended 12/31/05): Assets, $19,839,292 (M); gifts received, $291,221; expenditures, $1,098,062; qualifying distributions, $770,625; giving activities include $770,000 for 51 grants (high: $100,000; low: $1,000).

Purpose and activities: Giving primarily for education, human services, and health associations.

Fields of interest: Performing arts, orchestra (symphony); Arts; Higher education; Education; Animal welfare; Hospitals (general); Health organizations, association; Human services; Residential/custodial care, hospices.

Limitations: Giving primarily in NJ and NY; some funding nationally. No grants to individuals.

Application information:

Initial approach: Letter

Deadline(s): Dec. 1

Trustees: Ben Chapman; Charles W. McCutchen; Anne Terry.

EIN: 226050116

5323

The Curtis W. McGraw Foundation

c/o Drinker, Biddle & Reath, LLP

P.O. Box 627

Princeton, NJ   08542-0627   (609) 716-6511

Contact: Samuel W. Lambert III, Secy.-Treas.

Established in 1964 in NJ.

Donor: Elizabeth McGraw Webster.

Foundation type: Independent foundation.

Financial data (yr. ended 12/31/05): Assets, $22,700,771 (M); expenditures, $1,547,806; qualifying distributions, $1,336,218; giving activities include $1,327,500 for 135 grants (high: $100,000; low: $1,000).

Purpose and activities: Support primarily for hospitals, mental health, AIDS research, elementary and other educational institutions, the arts, social services, and churches. Grants usually made to charities which are of interest to the officers.

Fields of interest: Performing arts; Arts; Elementary school/education; Education; Environment, natural resources; Environment; Hospitals (general); Substance abuse, services; Mental health/crisis services; AIDS; AIDS research; Human services; Religion.

Type of support: General/operating support; Continuing support; Annual campaigns.

Limitations: Giving limited to the Vail, CO, Sun Valley, ID, and Princeton, NJ, areas. No grants to individuals, or for endowment funds, research, scholarships, fellowships, or matching gifts; no loans.

Publications: Annual report.

Application information: Application form not required.

Initial approach: Letter

Copies of proposal: 1

Deadline(s): Oct. 15
Board meeting date(s): Nov. or Dec., and as required
Final notification: By Dec. 31

Officers and Trustees: * Elizabeth McGraw Webster,* Pres.; Curtis M. Webster,* Exec. V.P.; Lisette S. Edmond,* V.P.; Mariana S. Paen,* V.P.; Theo M. Webster,* V.P.; Samuel W. Lambert III,* Secy.-Treas.

EIN: 221761678

Selected grants: The following grants were reported in 2004.

$1,000,000 to Princeton Regional Scholarship Foundation, Princeton, NJ.

$115,000 to TASIS Foundation, DC.

$30,000 to Lawrenceville School, Lawrenceville, NJ.

$30,000 to Princeton Friends School, Princeton, NJ.

$25,000 to Metropolitan Opera, New York, NY.

$20,000 to American Boychoir School, Princeton, NJ.

$20,000 to Frick Collection, New York, NY.

$20,000 to Historic Morven, Princeton, NJ.

$10,000 to Drumthwacket Foundation, Princeton, NJ.

$5,000 to A Better Chance, New York, NY.

5324
The MCJ Foundation ▼ ✧

310 South St.
Morristown, NJ 07960 (973) 540-1946
Contact: Suzanne M. Spero, Exec. Dir.

Established in 1983 in NJ.
Donors: Raymond G. Chambers; Kurt T. Borowsky; Harding Service, LLC.
Foundation type: Independent foundation.
Financial data (yr. ended 12/31/04): Assets, $129,330,266 (M); gifts received, $6,529; expenditures, $7,369,897; qualifying distributions, $6,902,617; giving activities include $6,248,772 for 476 grants (high: $500,000; low: $25; average: $1,000–$50,000).
Purpose and activities: Giving primarily for mentoring and youth initiatives.
Fields of interest: Education, early childhood education; Child development, education; Elementary school/education; Education; Health organizations, association; Crime/violence prevention, gun control; Crime/violence prevention, domestic violence; Human services; Children/ youth, services; Youth, pregnancy prevention; Child development, services; Community development; Federated giving programs; Disabilities, people with; Minorities; Women; AIDS, people with; Economically disadvantaged; Homeless.
Type of support: General/operating support; Seed money; Technical assistance; Matching/challenge support.
Limitations: Applications not accepted.
Application information: Contributes only to pre-selected organizations.
Officers and Directors: * Christine Chambers Gilfillan,* Pres.; Donald R. Smith, Secy.; Anthony J. Romano, Treas.; Suzanne M. Spero,* Exec. Dir.; Jennifer G. Chambers; Michael J. Chambers; Patricia A. Chambers; Raymond G. Chambers; Tina Brown Chambers; Barbara B. Coleman; Michael Gilfillan; Joseph Walsh.
Number of staff: 2 full-time professional; 1 full-time support.
EIN: 222497895
Selected grants: The following grants were reported in 2004.

$500,000 to Communities in Schools, Alexandria, VA. General operating support.

$332,800 to Newark Alliance, Newark, NJ. 2 grants: $284,000 (For general operating support), $48,800 (For general operating support).

$250,000 to National Mentoring Partnership, Alexandria, VA. For general operating support.

$250,000 to New Jersey Symphony Orchestra, Newark, NJ. For general operating support.

$125,000 to Green Chimneys Childrens Services, Brewster, NY. For general operating support.

$48,150 to Burden Center for the Aging, New York, NY. For general operating support.

$25,000 to American Museum of Natural History, New York, NY. For general operating support.

$25,000 to Big Brothers Big Sisters of America, Philadelphia, PA. For general operating support.

$20,000 to Newark Boys Chorus School, Newark, NJ. For general operating support.

5325
McMullen Family Foundation

26 Park St.
Montclair, NJ 07042
Contact: Linda M. Drasheff, Secy.
FAX: (973) 744-4428;
E-mail: lindamdrasheff@aol.com

Established in 1993 in NY.
Donor: John J. McMullen, Sr.‡.
Foundation type: Independent foundation.
Financial data (yr. ended 5/31/05): Assets, $16,361,932 (M); expenditures, $2,699,237; qualifying distributions, $2,545,082; giving activities include $2,544,083 for 25+ grants (high: $1,000,000).
Purpose and activities: Giving primarily for higher education; funding also for human services.
Fields of interest: Museums (art); Elementary/ secondary education; Higher education; Human services; Foundations (private grantmaking).
International interests: Ireland.
Type of support: General/operating support; Continuing support; Capital campaigns; Endowments; Professorships; Fellowships; Scholarship funds; Exchange programs.
Limitations: Applications not accepted. Giving primarily in NJ, with emphasis on Montclair. No grants to individuals.
Application information: Contributes only to pre-selected organizations.
Officers: Catherine McMullen, Pres.; John J. McMullen, Jr., V.P.; Linda M. Drasheff, Secy.; Peter McMullen, Treas.
Directors: Patrick Gilmartin; Jacqueline McMullen; John J. McMullen, Sr.; Sanford E. Moore.
EIN: 133721747
Selected grants: The following grants were reported in 2004.

$230,000 to Montclair Art Museum, Montclair, NJ. For general support.

$55,000 to Saint Barnabas Medical Center, Livingston, NJ. For general support.

$50,000 to Montclair Fund for Educational Excellence, Montclair, NJ. For general support.

$40,000 to United Way of North Essex, Montclair, NJ. For general support.

$33,333 to Seton Hall University, South Orange, NJ. For general support.

$25,000 to Boys and Girls Clubs of Newark, Newark, NJ. For general support.

$20,000 to Montclair Foundation, Montclair, NJ. For general support.

$20,000 to Webb Institute of Naval Architecture, Glen Cove, NY. For general support.

$18,000 to Delbarton School, Morristown, NJ. For general support.

$2,500 to Lupus Research Institute, New York, NY. For general support.

5326
The Merck Company Foundation ▼ ✧

1 Merck Dr., WS 1A-17
P.O. Box 100
Whitehouse Station, NJ 08889-0100
(908) 423-2042
Contact: Christine Funk, Assoc. Mgr., Corp. Contribs.
FAX: (908) 423-1987; Contact for PPPI: Patricia Fricke, Coord., tel.: (908) 423-1539; URL: http:// www.merck.com/cr/company_profile/ philanthropy_at_merck/ the_merck_company_foundation/home.html

Incorporated in 1957 in NJ.
Donor: Merck & Co., Inc.
Foundation type: Company-sponsored foundation.
Financial data (yr. ended 12/31/05): Assets, $124,449,548 (M); gifts received, $53,177; expenditures, $42,871,877; qualifying distributions, $42,440,881; giving activities include $41,596,594 for grants.
Purpose and activities: The foundation supports programs designed to improve access to quality health care and promote the appropriate use of medicines and vaccines; build capacity in the biomedical and health sciences; promote environments that support innovation, economic growth, and development in an ethical and fair context; and support communities where employees of Merck work and live.
Fields of interest: Philosophy/ethics; Environment, natural resources; Environmental education; Environment; Health care, public policy; Health care, equal rights; Public health; Health care; Medical research; Human services.
Type of support: General/operating support; Program development; Seed money; Research; Technical assistance; Employee volunteer services; Employee matching gifts.
Limitations: Applications not accepted. Giving on a national and international basis in areas of company operations. No support for political organizations, fraternal, labor, or veterans' organizations, religious organizations not of direct benefit to the entire community, or discriminatory organizations. No grants to individuals, or for political campaigns or activities, fundraising, capital campaigns, non-public broadcasting media productions, basic or clinical research projects, direct medical care or the purchase of medications, devices, or biologics, meetings, conferences, symposia, or workshops, fellowships or scholarships for training purposes intended for a specific individual or institution, debt reduction, beauty or talent contests, or programs directly supporting marketing or sales objectives of Merck.
Publications: Annual report; Corporate giving report.
Application information: Contributes only to pre-selected organizations.
Board meeting date(s): Semiannually and as required
Officers and Directors: * Joan Wainwright,* Pres.; Brenda Colatrella, V.P.; Leslie M. Hardy, V.P.; David Ruth, V.P.; Celia A. Colbert, Secy.; Caroline Dorsa, Treas.; Lawrence A. Bossidy; William G. Bowen, Ph.D.; Johnnetta B. Cole, Ph.D.; William B. Harrison,

Jr.; William H. Kelley, M.D.; Rochelle B. Lazarus; Thomas E. Shenk, Ph.D.; Anne M. Tatlock; Samuel O. Thier, M.D.; Wendell P. Weeks; Peter C. Wendell.
EIN: 226028476
Selected grants: The following grants were reported in 2004.
$9,816,126 to African Comprehensive HIV/AIDS Partnerships, Dover, DE.
$3,679,648 to JK Group, Plainsboro, NJ.
$2,882,138 to Merck Institute for Science Education, Rahway, NJ.
$1,325,000 to United Negro College Fund, Fairfax, VA.
$500,000 to Regional Performing Arts Center, Philadelphia, PA.
$71,553 to Fondos Unidos de Puerto Rico, San Juan, PR.
$50,000 to Flint RiverCenter Partners, Albany, GA.
$40,000 to Hyacinth AIDS Foundation, New Brunswick, NJ.
$25,000 to American Heart Association, San Juan, PR.
$20,000 to University of Wisconsin, Eau Claire, WI.

5327
Merck Institute for Science Education, Inc. ✧
P.O. Box 100, WS2F-96
Whitehouse Station, NJ 08889-0100
Contact: Carlo Parravano, Exec. V.P.
URL: http://www.mise.org

Established in 1992 in NJ.
Donor: Merck & Co., Inc.
Foundation type: Company-sponsored foundation.
Financial data (yr. ended 12/31/03): Assets, $0; gifts received, $3,054,468; expenditures, $3,054,468; giving activities include $1,060,150 for 40 grants (high: $182,100; low: $500), and $271,750 for 630 grants to individuals (high: $40,000; low: $50).
Purpose and activities: The institute supports organizations involved with K-12 and higher science education.
Fields of interest: Elementary/secondary education; Higher education; Science.
Limitations: Applications not accepted. Giving primarily in NJ and PA.
Application information: Contributes only to pre-selected organizations.
Officers and Trustees:* Raymond V. Gilmartin,* Chair.; Kenneth C. Frazier,* Pres.; Carlo Parravano, Ph.D., Exec. V.P. and Dir.; John R. Taylor, V.P.; Celia A. Colbert,* Secy.; Caroline Dorsa, Treas.; Judy C. Lewent.
EIN: 223208944

5328
Merck Patient Assistance Program, Inc. ✧
1 Merck Dr.
P.O. Box 100, Ste. WSF-96
Whitehouse Station, NJ 08889-0100
(800) 727-5400
Application address: P.O. Box 690, Horsham, PA 19044-9979; URL: http://www.merck.com/pap/pap/consumer/index.jsp

Established in 2001 in New Jersey as a company-sponsored operating foundation.
Donor: Merck & Co., Inc.

Foundation type: Operating foundation.
Financial data (yr. ended 12/31/05): Assets, $0; gifts received, $533,118,219; expenditures, $533,118,219; qualifying distributions, $533,118,219; giving activities include $533,118,219 for grants to individuals.
Purpose and activities: The foundation provides Merck medication to economically disadvantaged individuals lacking prescription drug coverage.
Fields of interest: Economically disadvantaged.
Type of support: Grants to individuals; Donated products.
Limitations: Giving on a national basis and in Guam, Puerto Rico, and the U.S. Virgin Islands.
Application information: Application form required.
Initial approach: Download application form, complete online application form, or telephone foundation for application form
Officers: Michael E. Doodson, Pres.; Nancy Wicks, Exec. V.P.; Denise Von Dohren, Secy.; Cheryl L. Dobleske, Treas.
EIN: 010575520

5329
Merck-Schering Plough Patient Assistance Program ✧ ☆
1 Merck Dr., P.O. Box 100, WS2F96
Whitehouse Station, NJ 08889-0100
Application address: Merck-Schering Plough Patient Assistance Prog., P.O. Box 365, Horsham, PA 19044-0365

Established as a company-sponsored operating foundation in 2003.
Donor: MSP Distribution Services LLC.
Foundation type: Operating foundation.
Financial data (yr. ended 12/31/05): Assets, $0 (M); gifts received, $50,464,494; expenditures, $50,464,494; qualifying distributions, $50,464,494; giving activities include $48,702,436 for grants to individuals.
Purpose and activities: The foundation provides Zetia/Vytorin prescription medicine to low-income individuals and families.
Type of support: Grants to individuals; Donated products.
Application information: Application form required.
Initial approach: Contact foundation for application form
Deadline(s): None
Officers: Robert A. McMahon, Pres.; Arthur J. Hirt, Exec. V.P.; Patrick Magri, Exec. V.P.; Celia A. Colbert, Secy.; Caroline Dorsa, Treas.
EIN: 030500536

5330
Richard D. & Lynette S. Merillat Private Foundation ✧
c/o Merrill Lynch Trust Co.
P.O. Box 1525
Pennington, NJ 08534
Application address: c/o Richard D. Merillat, Pres., 2600 Gordon Dr., Naples, FL 34102

Established in 1993 in MI.
Donors: Richard D. Merillat; Lynette S. Merillat.
Foundation type: Independent foundation.
Financial data (yr. ended 6/30/05): Assets, $22,952,079 (M); gifts received, $50,000; expenditures, $1,729,789; qualifying distributions,

$1,332,520; giving activities include $1,328,000 for 44 grants (high: $200,000; low: $1,000).
Purpose and activities: Grants primarily to organizations promoting Christian values.
Fields of interest: Higher education; Human services; Family services; Christian agencies & churches.
Limitations: Giving primarily in Adrian, MI; some giving nationally. No grants to individuals.
Application information:
Initial approach: Letter
Deadline(s): None
Officers and Trustees:* Richard D. Merillat,* Pres.; Lynette S. Merillat,* Secy.
EIN: 383148627

5331
Leib and Hermann Merkin Foundation, Inc. ✧
c/o Leib Merkin Inc.
910 Sylvan Ave.
Englewood Cliffs, NJ 07632

Incorporated in 1950 in NY.
Donors: Leib Merkin†; Hermann Merkin†; Ursula Merkin†.
Foundation type: Independent foundation.
Financial data (yr. ended 6/30/05): Assets, $128,334 (M); gifts received, $295,950; expenditures, $383,118; qualifying distributions, $379,490; giving activities include $379,490 for 77 grants (high: $200,000; low: $18).
Purpose and activities: Giving primarily to Jewish organizations, education, and human services.
Fields of interest: Arts; Elementary/secondary education; Higher education; Hospitals (general); Human services; Jewish federated giving programs; Jewish agencies & temples.
Type of support: Continuing support.
Limitations: Applications not accepted. Giving primarily in New York, NY. No grants to individuals.
Application information: Contributes only to pre-selected organizations.
Officers: Solomon N. Merkin, V.P.; Andrew J. Mendes, Secy.
EIN: 136093666
Selected grants: The following grants were reported in 2005.
$1,800 to Manhattan High School for Girls, New York, NY.
$1,800 to National Society for Hebrew Day Schools - Torah Umesorah, New York, NY.
$1,000 to MATAN: The Gift of Jewish Learning for Every Child, New York, NY.
$500 to Jewish Childrens Learning Lab, New York, NY.
$500 to Upper East Side Hatzolah, New York, NY.
$500 to Yeshiva University, New York, NY.
$375 to American Friends of Shalva, New York, NY.
$250 to Mount Sinai Childrens Center Foundation, New York, NY.
$180 to Dorot, New York, NY.
$100 to PTACH, Brooklyn, NY.

5332
Milstein Foundation, Inc. ✧
c/o Lowenstein Sandler
65 Livingston Ave.
Roseland, NJ 07068

Established in 2002 in NJ.

Donor: LVB Funding, Inc.
Foundation type: Independent foundation.
Financial data (yr. ended 11/30/04): Assets, $59,561,832 (M); gifts received, $30,500,000; expenditures, $1,411,740; qualifying distributions, $1,400,000; giving activities include $1,400,000 for 1 grant.
Fields of interest: Higher education, university.
Limitations: Applications not accepted. Giving primarily in Baltimore, MD. No grants to individuals.
Application information: Contributes only to pre-selected organizations.
Officers: Kenneth J. Slustky, Pres.; Allen Levithan, V.P. and Secy.; John L. Berger, V.P. and Treas.
Member: Malden Management, LLC.
EIN: 043726873

5333
A. M. Monius Institute, Inc. ✧ ☆

P.O. Box 1412
Princeton, NJ   08542
E-mail: rd@ammonius.org; *URL:* http://www.ammonius.org
Application address for Young Scholar Prize: Oxford Studies in Metaphysics, Philosophy Dept., Rutgers University, Davison Hall, Douglass Campus, New Brunswick, NJ 08903

Established in 2001 in NJ.
Donor: Marc Sanders.
Foundation type: Independent foundation.
Financial data (yr. ended 12/31/05): Assets, $875,227 (M); gifts received, $1,150,000; expenditures, $882,514; qualifying distributions, $752,736; giving activities include $569,000 for 10 grants to individuals (high: $297,000; low: $400).
Purpose and activities: Grant awards to established scholars and annual prizes to younger scholars for essays in metaphysics.
Fields of interest: Science.
Type of support: Grants to individuals.
Trustees: Jeffrey I. Pasek; Elina Sanders; Marc Sanders.
EIN: 223840808

5334
Mushett Family Foundation, Inc. ✧

c/o PGB Investments
P.O. Box 178
Gladstone, NJ   07934

Established in 1998 in NJ.
Donors: Charles Mushett†; The Mushett Estate.
Foundation type: Independent foundation.
Financial data (yr. ended 5/31/06): Assets, $13,408,541 (M); expenditures, $799,847; qualifying distributions, $670,437; giving activities include $600,661 for 12 grants (high: $200,000; low: $2,800).
Purpose and activities: Giving primarily for human services, health care, particularly a cancer hospital, and for animal/wildlife preservation, and environmental conservation.
Fields of interest: Higher education; Environment; Animals/wildlife, preservation/protection; Hospitals (specialty); Health care; Health organizations, association; Human services.
Limitations: Applications not accepted. Giving primarily in NJ and New York, NY. No grants to individuals.

Application information: Contributes only to pre-selected organizations.
Officer: Henry J. Daaleman, Chair.
Trustees: Timothy P. Daaleman; John E. Engelhart; Rev. Jack Martin.
EIN: 223614593
Selected grants: The following grants were reported in 2006.
$50,000 to New York Academy of Sciences, New York, NY.
$25,000 to Nature Conservancy, Chester, NJ.
$15,000 to Raritan BayKeeper, Raritan, NJ.
$10,000 to American Littoral Society, Highlands, NJ.

5335
National Starch and Chemical Foundation, Inc. ✧

c/o ICI Tax Dept.
10 Finderne Ave.
Bridgewater, NJ   08807   (908) 685-5201
Contact: Carmen M. Ortiz

Incorporated in 1968 in NY.
Donor: National Starch and Chemical Co.
Foundation type: Company-sponsored foundation.
Financial data (yr. ended 12/31/03): Assets, $47,608 (M); gifts received, $1,864,660; expenditures, $1,877,600; qualifying distributions, $1,877,600; giving activities include $1,875,664 for 900+ grants (high: $272,298).
Purpose and activities: The foundation supports hospitals and organizations involved with higher education and youth.
Fields of interest: Higher education; Hospitals (general); Youth, services; Federated giving programs.
Type of support: General/operating support; Continuing support; Employee matching gifts; Employee-related scholarships.
Limitations: Giving limited to areas of company operations in CA, IL, IN, MA, ME, MI, MN, MO, NC, NJ, PA, SC, TN, and VA.
Application information: Application form required.
   Initial approach: Telephone foundation for application form
   Copies of proposal: 1
   Deadline(s): Dec. 31
Officers and Directors: M.J. Torbert,* Chair.; C.E. Montgomery,* Pres.; P.C. Maloff, Secy.; R.J. Forrest,* Treas.; L.J. Berlik; R.W. Buchan; C.F. Knott; W.H. Powell; P.A. Salit; W.F. Schlauch.
EIN: 237010264
Selected grants: The following grants were reported in 2003.
$272,298 to United Way of Somerset County, Bridgewater, NJ.
$80,000 to Somerset Medical Center, Somerville, NJ. 3 grants: $30,000, $20,000 (For Breaking New Ground), $30,000.
$67,192 to United Way of Central Indiana, Indianapolis, IN.
$60,207 to National Merit Scholarship Corporation, Evanston, IL.
$51,960 to United Way of the Piedmont, Spartanburg, SC.
$33,559 to United Way, Heart of America, Kansas City, MO.
$25,000 to State Theater Regional Arts Center at New Brunswick, New Brunswick, NJ.
$20,000 to Hunterdon Medical Center Foundation, Flemington, NJ.

5336
New Jersey Natural Gas Foundation ✧
(formerly New Jersey Resources Foundation, Inc.)
P.O. Box 1468
Wall, NJ   07719   (732) 938-1134
Contact: Thomas J. Kononowitz, V.P.
Application address: P.O. Box 1464, Wall, NJ 07719

Established in 1987 in NJ.
Donors: New Jersey Resources Corp.; New Jersey Natural Gas Co.
Foundation type: Company-sponsored foundation.
Financial data (yr. ended 9/30/03): Assets, $732,400 (M); gifts received, $1,330,932; expenditures, $647,182; qualifying distributions, $647,182; giving activities include $647,182 for grants.
Purpose and activities: The foundation supports organizations involved with education, health, civic affairs, and human services.
Fields of interest: Education; Hospitals (general); Health care; Health organizations, association; Human services; Civil rights, minorities; Federated giving programs; Government/public administration; General charitable giving.
Limitations: Giving limited to NJ. No grants to individuals.
Application information: Application form not required.
   Initial approach: Proposal
   Deadline(s): None
Officers and Trustees: Laurence M. Downes,* Pres.; Thomas J. Kononowitz,* V.P.; Oleta J. Harden, Secy.; Glenn C. Lockwood, Treas.; Thomas E. Hayes.
EIN: 222835065

5337
New Jersey Nets and Devils Foundation ✧
(formerly New Jersey Nets Foundation, Inc.)
50 Rte. 120 N.
East Rutherford, NJ   07073   (201) 635-3140
Contact: Shane Harris, Exec. Dir.
FAX: (201) 935-8140; *URL:* http://www.nba.com/nets/foundation/index.html

Established in 1993 in NJ.
Donors: Lewis Katz; MCJ Foundation.
Foundation type: Company-sponsored foundation.
Financial data (yr. ended 12/31/03): Assets, $579,236 (M); gifts received, $1,038,116; expenditures, $784,706; qualifying distributions, $752,306; giving activities include $670,260 for 34 grants (high: $150,000; low: $1,000), and $7,500 for 3 grants to individuals (high: $2,500; low: $2,500).
Purpose and activities: The foundation supports programs designed to revitalize and rebuild underprivileged communities in New Jersey by investing in underserved youth by providing them with access to five essential building blocks of development: a caring adult; a healthy start; safe and structured environments; effective education for marketable skills; and opportunities to serve their communities.
Fields of interest: Youth development.
Type of support: Scholarship funds; Scholarships—to individuals.
Limitations: Giving limited to NJ.
Application information: Application form required.
   Initial approach: Contact foundation for application form
   Deadline(s): None

Officers and Trustees:* Alan Aufzien,* Pres.; Jerry Cohen,* V.P.; David Gerstein,* Secy.-Treas.; Shane Harris, Exec. Dir.

EIN: 521815967

Selected grants: The following grants were reported in 2003.

$150,000 to Seton Hall University, South Orange, NJ. For general support.

$100,000 to Boys and Girls Club of America, New Jersey Area Council, Madison, NJ. For general support.

$66,747 to William Paterson University of New Jersey, Wayne, NJ. For general support.

$45,000 to Jewish Adoption and Foster Care Options, Fort Lauderdale, FL. For general support.

$40,000 to UJA-Federation of New York, New York, NY. For general support.

$33,000 to UJA Federation of Northern New Jersey, Wayne, NJ. For general support.

$18,000 to New Jersey City University, Jersey City, NJ. For scholarships.

$17,500 to Boys and Girls Clubs of Camden County, Camden, NJ. For general support.

$17,000 to Rutgers, The State University of New Jersey, Newark, NJ. For scholarships.

$15,000 to Rider University, Lawrenceville, NJ. For scholarships.

5338

The Charlotte W. Newcombe Foundation

35 Park Pl.

Princeton, NJ 08542-6918 (609) 924-7022

Contact: Janet A. Fearon, Exec. Dir.

FAX: (609) 252-1773; E-mail: cwnf@patmedia.net

URL: http://www.newcombefoundation.org

Fellowship application address: Newcombe Fellowships, Woodrow Wilson National Fellowship Foundation, CN 5281, Princeton, NJ 08543; tel.: (609) 452-7007 or (800) 899-9963; FAX: (609) 452-7828; E-mail: charlotte@woodrow.org; URL: http://www.woodrow.org/newcombe/newcombe_about_newcombe_founda.html

Trust established in 1979 in PA.

Donor: Charlotte W. Newcombe‡.

Foundation type: Independent foundation.

Financial data (yr. ended 12/31/05): Assets, $48,456,195 (M); expenditures, $2,538,392; qualifying distributions, $2,301,501; giving activities include $2,085,580 for 41 grants (high: $715,650; low: $2,000).

Purpose and activities: Grants available to colleges and universities for scholarship or fellowship aid only in four programs: 1) doctoral dissertation fellowships awarded annually for degree candidates in the humanities and social sciences whose work focuses on ethics and religion (national selection process administered by Woodrow Wilson National Fellowship Foundation); 2) scholarships for students with disabilities, restricted to four-year colleges and universities in Washington, DC, DE, MD, NJ, New York, NY, and PA; 3) scholarships for mature second-career women in the same states with no grants made in this program to two-year colleges, professional schools, or theological seminaries; and 4) scholarships for economically disadvantaged or minority students attending colleges affiliated with the Presbyterian Church (U.S.A.). Scholarships for undergraduate and graduate students only; no aid available for post-doctoral fellowships. Selection of student recipients and scholarship administration are the responsibility of the academic institution.

The following information is applicable to programs 2, 3 and 4 as described above. The foundation makes grants to colleges and universities for current-year scholarship aid. Once accepted into one of these programs a college or university is likely to receive multi-year funding. The foundation requests that a portion of each year's grant be matched with funds from other donors to create and augment a Charlotte W. Newcombe Scholarship Endowment.

Fields of interest: Humanities; Higher education; Adult/continuing education; Disabilities, people with; Minorities; African Americans/Blacks; Native Americans/American Indians; Women; Economically disadvantaged.

Type of support: Endowments; Fellowships; Internship funds; Scholarship funds; Matching/challenge support.

Limitations: Giving on a national basis, except for scholarship programs for mature women and students with disabilities which are limited to colleges in Washington, DC, DE, MD, NJ, New York, NY, and PA. No support for colleges (except for scholarship and fellowship programs); within the scholarships for physically disabled students, no grants to publicly supported two-year colleges; within the scholarship program for mature women students, no grants to two-year colleges or professional schools, including theological schools and schools of nursing. No grants to individuals, or for staffing, program development, postdoctoral fellowships, or building funds; scholarships to institutions only; no loans.

Publications: Application guidelines; Annual report (including application guidelines); Grants list; Informational brochure (including application guidelines).

Application information: Unsolicited requests for funds are not accepted. Application materials available from mid-June through Sept. 5 for physically disabled students and mature women students; Presbyterian college scholarships have no application materials, colleges should inquire to the foundation regarding these scholarships; fellowship applicants should request applications by Nov. 15 from the Woodrow Wilson National Fellowship Foundation at the address given above.

   Initial approach: Interested colleges and universities should contact the foundation to discuss prior to requesting application materials

   Board meeting date(s): Feb., Apr., June, Oct., and Dec.

Officer and Trustees:* Janet A. Fearon,* Exec. Dir.; Robert M. Adams; Elizabeth T. Frank; Aaron E. Gast; J. Barton Luedeke.

Number of staff: 2 full-time professional; 1 part-time support.

EIN: 232120614

Selected grants: The following grants were reported in 2006.

$55,000 to Pennsylvania State University, University Park, PA. For Newcombe scholarships for students with disabilities.

$53,000 to Temple University, Philadelphia, PA. For Newcombe scholarships for students with disabilities.

$50,000 to Columbia University, School of General Studies, New York, NY. For Newcombe scholarships for mature women students.

$50,000 to Gallaudet University, DC. For Newcombe scholarships for students with disabilities.

$50,000 to Jamestown College, Jamestown, ND. For all Newcombe scholarships for

disadvantaged minority students at Presbyterian Colleges.

$48,000 to New York University, New York, NY. For Newcombe scholarships for students with disabilities.

$45,000 to Fordham University, College of Liberal Studies, New York, NY. For Newcombe scholarships for mature women students.

$45,000 to Towson University Foundation, Towson, MD. For Newcombe scholarships for mature women students.

$25,000 to Warren Wilson College, Asheville, NC. For all Newcombe scholarships for disadvantaged minority students at Presbyterian Colleges.

5339

The Nicolais Foundation, Inc. ◇ ☆

26 Chandler Rd.

Chatham, NJ 07928-1842

Established in 1994.

Donors: Michael A. Nicolais; Margaret Nicolais.

Foundation type: Independent foundation.

Financial data (yr. ended 3/31/05): Assets, $4,668,020 (M); expenditures, $1,373,317; qualifying distributions, $1,356,265; giving activities include $1,355,700 for 16 grants (high: $1,000,000; low: $1,000).

Purpose and activities: Giving primarily for higher and other education.

Fields of interest: Museums; Elementary/secondary education; Higher education; Libraries (public); Environment, natural resources; Recreation, parks/playgrounds; Protestant agencies & churches.

Limitations: Applications not accepted. Giving primarily in NY, NJ, and CT. No grants to individuals.

Application information: Contributes only to pre-selected organizations.

Officers: Michael A. Nicolais, Pres.; Margaret M. Nicolais, V.P.

EIN: 223269467

Selected grants: The following grants were reported in 2005.

$1,000,000 to Wagner College, Staten Island, NY.

$140,000 to Morris Museum, Morristown, NJ.

$100,000 to Central Park Conservancy, New York, NY.

$20,000 to Greenhill School, Addison, TX.

$10,000 to Darien Library, Darien, CT.

$10,000 to Partnership in Philanthropy, Chatham, NJ.

$10,000 to Pathfinder Village, Edmeston, NY.

$10,000 to Saint Lawrence University, Canton, NY.

$1,000 to Family Promise, Summit, NJ.

$1,000 to Salvation Army, Salem, NJ.

5340

NSN Foundation, Inc. ◇

c/o Ken Slutsky, Tax Exempt Institute Group

65 Livingston Ave.

Roseland, NJ 07068

Established in 2000 in NJ.

Donors: Nison Management, LLC; Stepansky Co., LLC.

Foundation type: Independent foundation.

Financial data (yr. ended 11/30/04): Assets, $58,151,868 (M); expenditures, $2,025,551;

qualifying distributions, $2,000,000; giving activities include $2,000,000 for grants.

Purpose and activities: Giving primarily for Jewish programs.

Fields of interest: Jewish federated giving programs; Jewish agencies & temples.

Limitations: Applications not accepted. Giving primarily in NJ. No grants to individuals.

Application information: Contributes only to pre-selected organizations.

Officers: Kenneth J. Slutsky, Pres. and Treas.; Allen Levithan, V.P. and Secy.; John L. Berger, V.P.

EIN: 223769097

Selected grants: The following grants were reported in 2003.

$3,988,000 to United Jewish Communities, New York, NY. For general support for Overseas Supplemental Giving Fund.

5341

OceanFirst Foundation

(formerly Ocean Federal Foundation)
1415 Hooper Ave., Ste. 304
Toms River, NJ 08753 (732) 341-4676
Contact: Katherine B. Durante, Secy. and Exec. Dir.
FAX: (732) 473-9641;
E-mail: kdurante@oceanfirstfdn.org; *URL:* http://www.oceanfirstfdn.org

Established in 1996 in NJ.

Donors: Ocean Financial Corp.; OceanFirst Financial Corp.; Ocean Federal Savings Bank; OceanFirst Bank.

Foundation type: Company-sponsored foundation.

Financial data (yr. ended 12/31/04): Assets, $40,246,415 (M); expenditures, $2,393,973; qualifying distributions, $2,337,968; giving activities include $2,188,021 for 341 grants (high: $125,000; low: $100).

Purpose and activities: The foundation supports school libraries, food banks, and organizations involved with arts and culture, education, the environment, health, mental health, employment training, housing, youth development, human services, disabled people, and domestic violence victims.

Fields of interest: Museums; Performing arts, theater; Performing arts, music; Arts; Elementary/secondary education; Libraries (school); Education; Environment, water resources; Environment; Health care, equal rights; Medical care, in-patient care; Health care; Mental health/crisis services; Employment, training; Food banks; Housing/shelter, homeless; Housing/shelter; Youth development, adult & child programs; Youth development; Aging, centers/services; Homeless, human services; Human services; Children; Disabilities, people with; Crime/abuse victims.

Type of support: Continuing support; Annual campaigns; Capital campaigns; Building/renovation; Equipment; Program development; Seed money; Sponsorships; Matching/challenge support.

Limitations: Giving primarily in Monroe Township, southern and western Monmouth County, and Ocean County, NJ. No support for religious congregations, political candidates or organizations, or lobbying organizations; no support for preschools, childcare centers, or adult schools for School Library Enhancement Grants. No grants to individuals, or for research or political causes or campaigns; no grants for the replacement of regular school library funding, personnel expenses, building campaigns or

improvements, or start-up needs for School Library Enhancement Grants.

Publications: Application guidelines; Informational brochure.

Application information: Small Grants are grants less than $3,500; Major Grants are grants greater than $3,500. An application form is required for Major Grants and School Library Enhancement Grants. Organizations receiving Major Grants and School Library Enhancement Grants are asked to provide a final report. A site visit may be requested for School Library Enhancement Grants. Support for School Library Enhancement Grants of over $3,500 is limited to 1 contribution per organization during any given two-year period.

Initial approach: Telephone foundation and complete online application form for Major Grants; mail proposal to foundation for Small Grants; complete online application form for School Library Enhancement Grants

Copies of proposal: 1

Deadline(s): Rolling for Major Grants; 2 months prior to need for Small Grants; Apr. 1 for School Library Enhancement Grants

Board meeting date(s): 1st, 2nd, and 4th quarters for Major Grants; 3rd quarter for School Library Enhancement Grants

Final notification: 2 weeks following board meetings for Major Grants; Sept. for School Library Enhancement Grants

Officers and Directors:* John R. Garbarino,* Pres.; Katherine B. Durante,* Secy. and Exec. Dir.; Michael J. Fitzpatrick, Treas.; Joseph J. Burke; Angelo Catania; John W. Chadwick; Anthony J. DiCroce II; Carl Feltz, Jr.; Anita M. Kneeley; Msgr. Casimir H. Ladzinski; Amy W. Lotano; Donald E. McLaughlin; Samuel T. Melillo; Diane F. Rhine; James T. Snyder; John E. Walsh; David C. Wintrode; David T. Wolfe.

Number of staff: 1 full-time professional; 1 part-time support.

EIN: 223465454

Selected grants: The following grants were reported in 2004.

$125,000 to Ocean Medical Center Foundation, Neptune, NJ. To establish Oncology Navigator Program.

$100,000 to United Way of Ocean County, Toms River, NJ.

$91,206 to Twenty-One Plus, Toms River, NJ. For improvements of residential and work environments.

$75,000 to Deborah Hospital Foundation, Browns Mills, NJ. To purchase of Electro Anatomical Navigation System.

$75,000 to Long Beach Island Community Center, Brant Beach, NJ. To rebuild outdoor swimming pool.

$75,000 to Ocean County Library Foundation, Toms River, NJ. For Youth Services Area Expansion.

$70,000 to Community Medical Center Foundation, Toms River, NJ. For expansion of emergency department.

$62,503 to Georgian Court University, Lakewood, NJ. For creation of Fitness Center.

$50,000 to Jersey Shore Animal Center, Brick, NJ. For building renovation and expansion.

$45,000 to Monmouth Medical Center Foundation, Long Branch, NJ. For Cystic Fibrosis Center.

5342

The Olsen Foundation, a New Jersey Nonprofit Corporation ✧

66 Witherspoon, Ste. 272
Princeton, NJ 08542 (609) 466-4661
Contact: Gregory H. Olsen, Tr.

Donor: Gregory H. Olsen.

Foundation type: Independent foundation.

Financial data (yr. ended 12/31/05): Assets, $3,428,847 (M); gifts received, $1,046,370; expenditures, $374,872; qualifying distributions, $368,105; giving activities include $365,800 for 13 grants (high: $140,000; low: $1,000).

Fields of interest: Higher education; Libraries/library science; Foundations (community); Roman Catholic federated giving programs; Roman Catholic agencies & churches.

Limitations: Giving primarily in NJ.

Application information:

Initial approach: Letter

Deadline(s): None

Trustees: Krista J. Dibsie; Kimberly A. Lapadula; Gregory H. Olsen.

EIN: 260029441

Selected grants: The following grants were reported in 2004.

$140,000 to Educational Industries Scholarship Fund, Flushing, NY. For scholarships for children of union.

$50,000 to Boys and Girls Club of the Delaware Valley, Trenton, NJ. For Alma Hill LIFT grants and dinner.

$50,000 to Princeton Public Library, Princeton, NJ. For Olsen Tech Center.

$50,000 to Trenton Area Soup Kitchen, Trenton, NJ. For Alma Hill LIFT grants and dinner.

$25,000 to Fairleigh Dickinson University, Teaneck, NJ. For faculty development, and scholarships.

$25,000 to Prince of Peace Church, Princeton, NJ. For adopted family and general support.

$12,500 to Georgia College and State University, Milledgeville, GA. For Paul D. Coverdell Leadership Endowment.

$10,000 to Phillips Collection, DC.

$5,775 to Spina Bifida Association of the Tri-State Region, Flemington, NJ.

$5,100 to Eden Institute, Princeton, NJ. For charity dinner to benefit autisitc adults and children.

5343

The Orange Orphan Society ✧

c/o Barbara Murray
11 Schindler Ct.
Chatham, NJ 07928

Established in 1855 in NJ.

Foundation type: Independent foundation.

Financial data (yr. ended 12/31/05): Assets, $11,939,722 (M); expenditures, $735,306; qualifying distributions, $636,000; giving activities include $636,000 for grants.

Purpose and activities: Giving primarily to agencies that benefit needy residents of the Oranges and Maplewood, NJ, who are under 19 years of age.

Fields of interest: Education; Pediatrics; Youth development, scouting agencies (general); Human services; YM/YWCAs & YM/YWHAs; Children/youth, services; Family services; Homeless.

Type of support: General/operating support; Capital campaigns; Equipment; Program development.

Limitations: Giving limited to Maplewood and the Orange, NJ, area in Essex County. No support for religious institutions. No grants to individuals.
Publications: Application guidelines.
Application information: Application form required.
  Initial approach: Letter
  Copies of proposal: 2
  Deadline(s): None
  Board meeting date(s): Jan., Apr., and Dec.
  Final notification: Open
Officers and Trustees:* Barbara B. Murray,* Pres.; Jacques Silva, V.P.; Rebecca Linn Rebhorn,* Secy.; Kristen Paulos, Treas.; Ernest Booker; Betty Debraun; Richard Dutton; Gates McG Helms; Geraldine Livengood; Curtis Pew; Anne Stone; Paula Stuart; Barbara Van Doren; Scott Walker; Byron Yake.
EIN: 221711513

5344
Henry and Carolyn Sue Orenstein Foundation, Inc. ✧
c/o Henry Orenstein
35 Smull Ave.
Caldwell, NJ 07006

Established in 1986 in NJ.
Donors: Carolyn Sue Orenstein; Henry Orenstein.
Foundation type: Independent foundation.
Financial data (yr. ended 12/31/05): Assets, $990,562 (M); expenditures, $350,407; qualifying distributions, $340,908; giving activities include $303,753 for 15 grants (high: $240,000; low: $100), $37,080 for 2 grants to individuals, and $75 for 1 foundation-administered program.
Purpose and activities: Grants primarily for Jewish organizations, including support for elderly survivors of the Holocaust, and for other welfare programs, and educational activities; giving also for medical research.
Fields of interest: Arts; Hospitals (general); Medical research, institute; Human services; International development; Jewish agencies & temples.
Type of support: Grants to individuals.
Limitations: Applications not accepted. Giving primarily in New York, NY.
Application information: Unsolicited requests for funds not accepted.
Trustees: Carolyn Sue Orenstein; Frederick Orenstein; Henry Orenstein.
EIN: 222806030

5345
Alfiero and Lucia Palestroni Foundation, Inc. ✧
333 Sylvan Ave.
Englewood Cliffs, NJ 07632

Donor: Alfiero Palestroni†.
Foundation type: Independent foundation.
Financial data (yr. ended 6/30/05): Assets, $0 (M); expenditures, $1,999,440; qualifying distributions, $1,999,440; giving activities include $1,771,200 for 41 grants (high: $1,000,000; low: $350).
Fields of interest: Education; Human services; Children/youth, services; Christian agencies & churches.
Limitations: Applications not accepted. Giving primarily in NJ and NY. No grants to individuals.
Application information: Contributes only to pre-selected organizations.

Officers: Lucia Palestroni, Pres.; Frank Lloyd, Treas.
Trustees: Joseph Della Monica; Msgr. John J. Gilchrist; Kristine Sayrafe.
EIN: 223452466
Selected grants: The following grants were reported in 2003.
$250,000 to Church of Saint Ann, Hoboken, NJ. For repairs and general support.
$210,000 to Redemptoris Seminary, Newark, NJ. For general suppport.
$21,000 to Make-A-Wish Foundation of New Jersey, Union, NJ. For general support.
$20,000 to Catholic Community Services, Newark, NJ.
$12,000 to Elaine Kaufman Cultural Center, New York, NY. For general support.
$5,000 to Englewood Community Foundation, Englewood, NJ. For general support.
$5,000 to United Cerebral Palsy of Hudson County, North Bergen, NJ. For general support.
$2,500 to Center for Food Action in New Jersey, Englewood, NJ. For general support.
$2,500 to Community Chest of Englewood, Englewood, NJ.
$2,000 to University of Medicine and Dentistry of New Jersey, Piscataway, NJ. For general support.

5346
Parker Family Foundation ✧
P.O. Box 1525
Pennington, NJ 08534-1525

Established in 2000 in MA.
Donors: Faith K.P. Parker; Glen P. Parker.
Foundation type: Independent foundation.
Financial data (yr. ended 7/31/05): Assets, $8,520,546 (M); expenditures, $444,452; qualifying distributions, $396,257; giving activities include $390,000 for 7 grants (high: $80,000; low: $30,000).
Fields of interest: Arts; Education; Human services.
Limitations: Applications not accepted. Giving in the U.S., with emphasis on MA.
Application information: Contributes only to pre-selected organizations.
Trustees: Faith K.P. Parker; Glen P. Parker.
EIN: 043542674
Selected grants: The following grants were reported in 2005.
$50,000 to DeCordova Museum and Sculpture Park, Lincoln, MA.

5347
Parnassus Foundation ✧
25 N. Murray Ave.
Ridgewood, NJ 07450

Established in 1986 in DE.
Donor: Raphael Bernstein.
Foundation type: Operating foundation.
Financial data (yr. ended 11/30/05): Assets, $899,371 (M); gifts received, $160,569; expenditures, $427,005; qualifying distributions, $409,504; giving activities include $391,340 for 25 grants (high: $170,765; low: $150).
Purpose and activities: Provides support for museum exhibitions and related catalogues, and educational programs.
Fields of interest: Museums (art); Higher education; Education.
International interests: Canada; England.

Limitations: Applications not accepted. Giving on a national and international basis, with emphasis on Hanover, NH, New York, NY, Canada, and London, England. No grants to individuals.
Application information: Contributes only to pre-selected organizations.
Officers: Raphael Bernstein, Pres. and Treas.; Jane Bernstein, V.P.; Carol Boulanger, Secy.
Trustees: Daniel S. Bernstein; John M. Bernstein.
EIN: 521491214
Selected grants: The following grants were reported in 2004.
$194,398 to Stratford Festival, Stratford, CT.

5348
E. & H. Parnes Foundation, Inc. ✧
P.O. Box 703
Edison, NJ 08818
Contact: Herschel Parnes, Mgr.

Established in 1971 in NY.
Donors: Emanuel Parnes; Herschel Parnes.
Foundation type: Independent foundation.
Financial data (yr. ended 6/30/05): Assets, $5,851,755 (L); expenditures, $953,064; qualifying distributions, $952,696; giving activities include $950,500 for 40 grants (high: $250,000; low: $100).
Purpose and activities: Funding primarily for Jewish agencies, temples, yeshivas, and seminaries.
Fields of interest: Elementary/secondary education; Jewish agencies & temples.
Limitations: Applications not accepted. Giving primarily in NY. No grants to individuals.
Application information: Contributes only to pre-selected organizations.
Managers: Emanuel Parnes; Herschel Parnes.
EIN: 237237932

5349
Pascale/Sykes Foundation, Inc. ✧
P.O. Box 3085
Sea Bright, NJ 07760-3085 (732) 747-2807
Contact: Frances P. Sykes, Pres.
FAX: (732) 747-2691;
E-mail: pascalesykes@aol.com

Established in 1992 in NJ.
Donors: Donald M. Sykes; Frances P. Sykes; Tiernan E. Sykes.
Foundation type: Independent foundation.
Financial data (yr. ended 12/31/05): Assets, $4,565,178 (M); gifts received, $1,116,464; expenditures, $759,255; qualifying distributions, $742,022; giving activities include $742,022 for 11 grants (high: $125,000; low: $31,500).
Purpose and activities: Support given to innovative, flexible, holistic, long-range umbrella programs targeting working low-income families that promote the independence, well-being, and the integrity of the entire family unit, with emphasis on projects using integrated services and interagency linkages; the foundation also encourages programs with volunteers, neighborhood workers, interagency cooperation and marriage strengthening.
Fields of interest: Health care; Human services; Family services; Community development, neighborhood development; Economically disadvantaged.
Type of support: Continuing support; Emergency funds; Program development; Seed money;

Research; Consulting services; Program evaluation; Program-related investments/loans; Matching/challenge support.
Limitations: Giving limited to NJ and parts of New York, NY, that are within the Red Bank, NJ, vicinity. No grants to individuals.
Publications: Annual report; Grants list; Informational brochure; Program policy statement.
Application information: Site visit and preliminary evaluation of project required before proposal will be considered; telephone for complete guidelines. Application form required.
  Initial approach: Telephone call
  Copies of proposal: 7
  Deadline(s): Apr. 5
  Board meeting date(s): Jan. and May
  Final notification: 30 days
Officers and Trustees:* Frances P. Sykes,* Pres.; Thomas F. Anderson,* Co-Secy.; William H. Hyatt, Jr.,* Co-Secy.; William J. Leahey,* Co-Treas.; Donald M. Sykes,* Co-Treas.; Elaine Bradford; Robert Liversidge, Jr.
Number of staff: None.
EIN: 223161324
Selected grants: The following grants were reported in 2003.
$125,000 to Grand Street Settlement, New York, NY. For counseling for teens and parents.
$90,000 to Our Lady of Lourdes Medical Center, Camden, NJ.
$75,000 to Jewish Board of Family and Childrens Services, Asbury Park, NJ.
$40,350 to Youth on the Move, Camden, NJ. For life skills training.
$40,000 to Family Promise, Summit, NJ. For family mentoring.
$40,000 to Jewish Family and Vocational Services of Louisville, Louisville, KY.
$35,000 to Highbridge Community Life Center, Bronx, NY. For community newspaper.
$32,450 to Saint Marys Hospital, Passaic, NJ. For ESL family literacy.
$30,000 to Catholic Charities, New Brunswick, NJ. For physician's assistant.

5350
The Perrin Foundation ✧
926 Coolidge St.
Westfield, NJ 07090 (908) 232-8315
Contact: John G. Jeffers, Pres.

Established in 1928 in NY.
Donor: Mary Ricks†.
Foundation type: Independent foundation.
Financial data (yr. ended 12/31/05): Assets, $20,185,946 (M); gifts received, $5,500,000; expenditures, $1,477,921; qualifying distributions, $1,458,000; giving activities include $1,458,000 for 2 grants (high: $1,060,000; low: $398,000).
Purpose and activities: Giving limited to Christian organizations, including churches, missionary programs, and schools.
Fields of interest: Elementary/secondary education; Christian agencies & churches; Religion.
Type of support: General/operating support.
Limitations: Giving primarily in NJ. No grants to individuals.
Application information: Application form not required.
  Deadline(s): None
Officers: John G. Jeffers, Pres.; Robert Q. Bennett, V.P.; David C. Wohlgemuth, Secy.

Directors: Robert Dadd; George MacKenzie.
EIN: 226049335

5351
Gustavus and Louise Pfeiffer Research Foundation
89 Diamond Spring Rd.
Denville, NJ 07834 (973) 983-0480
Contact: Matthew G. Herold, Jr., Secy.
FAX: (973) 586-3456; *URL:* http://foundationcenter.org/grantmaker/pfeiffer/

Incorporated in 1942 in NY.
Donors: Gustavus A. Pfeiffer†; Louise F. Pfeiffer†.
Foundation type: Independent foundation.
Financial data (yr. ended 12/31/05): Assets, $25,359,904 (M); expenditures, $1,627,607; qualifying distributions, $1,542,662; giving activities include $1,401,984 for 17 grants (high: $400,000; low: $23,000).
Purpose and activities: The improvement of public health through the advancement of medicine and pharmacy; grants for biomedical research limited to prostate, ovarian, and breast cancer.
Fields of interest: Medical research, institute; Cancer research.
Type of support: Seed money; Fellowships; Scholarship funds; Research.
Limitations: Giving limited to the U.S. No support for national fundraising organizations or publicly financed projects, or for projects involving vivisection or other experiments on animal subjects. No grants to individuals, or for building or endowment funds, supplies, equipment, travel, conferences, exhibits, seminars, lectures, workshops, surveys or general purposes, delivery of healthcare services, sabbatical leave, indirect costs, or fund raising; no loans.
Publications: Application guidelines; Biennial report (including application guidelines).
Application information: Only 1 grant per organization per year will be made. Call, write or see foundation Web site for complete application guidelines and procedures. Application form required.
  Initial approach: Letter of inquiry (not to exceed 2 pages)
  Copies of proposal: 10
  Deadline(s): Jan. 8 and July 25 for initial inquiry; for formal application, deadline to be advised
  Board meeting date(s): Apr. and Oct.
  Final notification: 2 weeks after meeting
Officers and Directors:* H. Robert Herold II,* Pres.; Robert H. Pfeiffer,* V.P.; Matthew G. Herold, Jr.,* Secy.; Anne Herold Keeney, Treas.; Kimberly Herold Bakaly; Lise P. Chapman; Matthew Mayro Keeney; Patricia Herold Nagle.
Number of staff: 4 part-time support.
EIN: 136086299
Selected grants: The following grants were reported in 2004.
$100,000 to Pfeiffer University, Misenheimer, NC. For Gustavus and Louise Pfeiffer Research Foundation Program.
$75,000 to Harvard University, Medical School, Cambridge, MA. For Pfeiffer Minority Students Research Careers Program.
$75,000 to New Jersey Institute of Technology, Newark, NJ. For Biomechanical Mediated Computer Recognition and Translation of Sign Language program.

$74,910 to Arizona State University, Tempe, AZ. For project on The Role of Insulin Sensitivity in the Success of Weight Loss Diets.
$74,327 to Purdue University, West Lafayette, IN. For project on Prevention of Atrial Fibrillation after Open Chest Surgery.
$71,688 to University of Texas Health Science Center, Houston, TX. For project on Microarray Identification of Mutations Causing Retinitis Pigmentosa.
$68,770 to State University of New York at Buffalo, Buffalo, NY. For project on Diagnostic Imaging for the Early Detection of Vascular Dementia of the Brain.
$66,567 to Frazier Rehabilitation Center, Louisville, KY. For Pediatric Neuropsychological Laboratory.
$50,000 to Johns Hopkins University, Baltimore, MD. For Pfeiffer Scholars in Pharmacology and Molecular Science.
$35,000 to Duke University Medical Center, Durham, NC. For Role of Monocyte Activation in the Heparin-Induced Thrombocytopenia and Thrombosis project.

5352
Howard Phipps Foundation ✧
c/o Bessemer Trust Co., N.A.
100 Woodbridge Ctr. Dr.
Woodbridge, NJ 07095-0983

Established in 1967 in NJ.
Donor: Harriet Phipps†.
Foundation type: Independent foundation.
Financial data (yr. ended 6/30/05): Assets, $8,964,284 (M); expenditures, $1,626,449; qualifying distributions, $1,569,950; giving activities include $1,566,500 for 41 grants (high: $1,000,000; low: $1,000).
Purpose and activities: Giving primarily for museums, education, the environment, and human services.
Fields of interest: Museums (natural history); Education; Environment, natural resources; Animals/wildlife, preservation/protection; Girl scouts; Human services; Community development; Christian agencies & churches.
Limitations: Applications not accepted. Giving primarily in NY. No grants to individuals.
Application information: Contributes only to pre-selected organizations.
Trustees: Howard Phipps, Jr.; Anne P. Sidamon-Eristoff; Bessemer Trust Co., N.A.
EIN: 226095226
Selected grants: The following grants were reported in 2004.
$325,000 to American Museum of Natural History, New York, NY.
$75,000 to Audubon New York, Albany, NY. 2 grants: $25,000, $50,000
$50,000 to Bryn Mawr College, Bryn Mawr, PA.
$50,000 to Old Westbury Gardens, Old Westbury, NY.
$25,000 to Rockefeller University, New York, NY.
$10,000 to American Farmland Trust, DC.
$10,000 to Eaglebrook School, Deerfield, MA.
$10,000 to Millbrook School, Millbrook, NY.
$10,000 to Westbury Friends School, Westbury, NY.

5353
Point Gammon Foundation ✧
c/o Paseornek & Stimola
140 Rte. 17 N., Ste. 206
Paramus, NJ 07652

Established in 1994 in DE.
Foundation type: Independent foundation.
Financial data (yr. ended 12/31/03): Assets, $11,874,115 (M); expenditures, $499,426; qualifying distributions, $485,321; giving activities include $485,321 for 62 grants (high: $100,000; low: $100).
Purpose and activities: Giving primarily for the arts, higher education, including design schools, hospitals, human services, and religious purposes.
Fields of interest: Visual arts, design; Museums (art); Performing arts; Performing arts, ballet; Performing arts, theater; Higher education; Hospitals (general); Human services; Protestant agencies & churches.
Limitations: Applications not accepted. Giving primarily in New York, NY, and RI.
Application information: Unsolicited requests for funds not accepted.
Director: Jane Carroll.
EIN: 134049057
Selected grants: The following grants were reported in 2003.
$100,000 to J. P. Morgan Chase Foundation, New York, NY. For unrestricted support.
$49,125 to Metropolitan Museum of Art, New York, NY. For unrestricted support.
$25,000 to New York City Ballet, New York, NY. For unrestricted support.
$13,500 to New York Botanical Garden, Bronx, NY. For unrestricted support.
$10,000 to Skowhegan School of Painting and Sculpture, New York, NY. For unrestricted support.
$6,000 to Saint James Church, New York, NY. For unrestricted support.
$3,500 to Saint Timothys School, Stevenson, MD. For unrestricted support.
$3,000 to Smith College, Museum of Art, Northampton, MA. For unrestricted support.
$2,000 to Cape Cod Hospital Foundation, Hyannis, MA. For unrestricted support.
$1,000 to United Hospital Fund of New York, New York, NY. For unrestricted support.

5354
The Poses Family Foundation ✧ ☆
c/o Robert J. Diquollo
175 S. St., Ste. 200
Morristown, NJ 07960

Established in 2004 in NJ.
Donor: Frederic Poses.
Foundation type: Independent foundation.
Financial data (yr. ended 12/31/05): Assets, $7,112,813 (M); gifts received, $3,567,275; expenditures, $1,542,793; qualifying distributions, $1,538,750; giving activities include $1,535,000 for 24 grants (high: $500,000; low: $500).
Purpose and activities: Giving primarily for education; funding also for children and youth services, and health associations.
Fields of interest: Elementary/secondary education; Higher education; Education; Health organizations, association; Children/youth, services; Jewish agencies & temples.

Limitations: Applications not accepted. Giving primarily in New York, NY. No grants to individuals.
Application information: Contributes only to pre-selected organizations.
Trustees: Robert J. Diquollo; Frederic Poses; Nancy Poses.
EIN: 206375470

5355
John A. & Margaret Post Foundation ✧ ☆
P.O. Box 24
Tranquility, NJ 07879

Established in 1997 in NJ.
Donors: John A. Post; Margaret Post.
Foundation type: Independent foundation.
Financial data (yr. ended 12/31/05): Assets, $12,834,073 (M); gifts received, $2,022,531; expenditures, $469,249; qualifying distributions, $411,600; giving activities include $411,600 for grants.
Purpose and activities: Giving primarily to Roman Catholic schools and churches, as well as to human services, and federated giving programs.
Fields of interest: Arts; Education; Human services; Federated giving programs; Roman Catholic agencies & churches.
Limitations: Applications not accepted. Giving primarily in NJ, with emphasis on Newton and Sparta. No grants to individuals.
Application information: Contributes only to pre-selected organizations.
Trustees: John A. Post; Margaret Post; Wachovia Bank, N.A.
EIN: 223401833
Selected grants: The following grants were reported in 2005.
$100,000 to Pope John XXIII High School, Sparta, NJ. 2 grants: $50,000 each
$25,000 to Christian Health Care Center, Wyckoff, NJ.
$25,000 to Greater Newark Conservancy, Newark, NJ.
$25,000 to Hackettstown Community Hospital, Hackettstown, NJ.
$25,000 to Newton Memorial Hospital Foundation, Newton, NJ.
$25,000 to Saint Clares Foundation, Denville, NJ.
$20,000 to United Way of Sussex County, Newton, NJ.
$15,000 to Montclair State University Foundation, Montclair, NJ.
$10,000 to Salvation Army.

5356
Michael F. Price Foundation, Inc. ▼ ✧
51 JFK Pkwy.
Short Hills, NJ 07078
Contact: Michael F. Price, Mgr.

Established in 1997 in NJ.
Donor: Michael F. Price.
Foundation type: Independent foundation.
Financial data (yr. ended 11/30/05): Assets, $36,586,048 (M); gifts received, $3,380,748; expenditures, $9,469,694; qualifying distributions, $9,217,229; giving activities include $9,149,900 for 50 grants (high: $1,250,000; low: $250; average: $5,000–$250,000).

Purpose and activities: Giving primarily for higher education, children's services, and health associations.
Fields of interest: Higher education; Health organizations, association; Children/youth, services.
Limitations: Applications not accepted. Giving primarily in NJ. No grants to individuals.
Application information: Contributes only to pre-selected organizations.
Officer: Michael F. Price, Mgr.
Trustees: Martin Bernstein; Claudia Forbs; Jordan M. Price.
EIN: 223483367
Selected grants: The following grants were reported in 2005.
$5,000,000 to Albert Einstein College of Medicine of Yeshiva University, Bronx, NY. 4 grants: $1,250,000 each (For general operating support).
$720,000 to University of Oklahoma, Norman, OK. For general operating support.
$720,000 to University of Oklahoma Foundation, Oklahoma City, OK. For general operating support.
$505,000 to American Jewish Committee, New York, NY. 3 grants: $5,000 (For general operating support), $250,000 (For general operating support), $250,000 (For general operating support).
$195,483 to AVID Center, San Diego, CA. For general operating support for programs in New Jersey.

5357
Princeton Area Community Foundation, Inc.
(formerly The Princeton Area Foundation, Inc.)
15 Princess Rd.
Lawrenceville, NJ 08648 (609) 219-1800
Contact: Nancy W. Kieling, Pres.
FAX: (609) 219-1850; E-mail: info@pacf.org;
URL: http://www.pacf.org

Established in 1991 in NJ.
Foundation type: Community foundation.
Financial data (yr. ended 12/31/05): Assets, $40,518,340 (M); gifts received, $5,820,589; expenditures, $3,000,036; giving activities include $2,395,698 for 225 grants (high: $591,968; low: $100), and $53,800 for 29 grants to individuals (high: $5,000; low: $250).
Purpose and activities: The foundation seeks to promote philanthropy across central New Jersey by managing charitable funds created by members of the community, providing competitive discretionary grants to nonprofits, and by making advised grants to nonprofits after consultation with individuals or groups of donors. The foundation also serves as a convener and catalyst, leveraging new funds, and creating partnerships to enable residents to solve community problems.
Fields of interest: Education; Health care; Substance abuse, services; Minorities/immigrants, centers/services; Human services; Community development; Minorities; Economically disadvantaged.
Type of support: Technical assistance; Program development; General/operating support; Continuing support; Emergency funds; Seed money; Curriculum development; Scholarship funds.

Limitations: Giving limited to Mercer County, NJ and surrounding communities in Hunterdon, Somerset, Middlesex, Monmouth and Burlington counties.
Publications: Application guidelines; Annual report; Grants list; Informational brochure; Newsletter.
Application information: Visit foundation Web site for application forms and information. Application form required.

> *Initial approach:* The foundation recommends attending a grant information session before applying for a grant
> *Copies of proposal:* 1
> *Deadline(s):* Varies
> *Board meeting date(s):* Quarterly
> *Final notification:* 2 to 3 months

Officers and Trustees:* William P. Burks, M.D.*, Chair.; Andrew K. Golden,* Chair., Investments; Debra A. D'Arcangelo,* Co-Chair., Devel.; Van Zandt Williams, Jr.,* Co-Chair., Devel.; Eleanor Horne,* Vice-Chair.; Nancy W. Kieling, Pres. and Exec. Dir.; Joan Hollendonner, V.P., Progs.; Ralph Serpe, V.P.; John P. Hall,* Secy.; Maria Santisi, C.F.O.; Thomas B. Harvey,* Treas.; Ted Boyer; Ken Field; Melinda Green; Ramon Kapur; Yuki Moore Laurenti; Robin V. Levy; Christine Lokhammer; Michele Minter; Marguerite Mount; Barbara Rambo; Ann Reichelderfer; David R. Scott; John D. Wallace; Susan N. Wilson.
Number of staff: 5 full-time professional; 2 part-time professional; 2 full-time support.
EIN: 521746234

5358
The Providence Charitable Foundation, Inc. ✧
c/o Schiff Foods
7401 W. Side Ave.
North Bergen, NJ   07047-6430   (201) 868-6800
Contact: David Deutscher, Tr.

Established in 1999 in NY.
Donor: Schiff Food Products Co.
Foundation type: Independent foundation.
Financial data (yr. ended 11/30/05): Assets, $117,500 (M); gifts received, $450,000; expenditures, $369,495; qualifying distributions, $369,376; giving activities include $369,376 for grants.
Fields of interest: Education; Health organizations, association; Jewish agencies & temples.
Limitations: Giving primarily in NJ and NY.
Application information:

> *Initial approach:* Letter
> *Deadline(s):* None

Trustee: David Deutscher.
EIN: 134037405
Selected grants: The following grants were reported in 2005.
$30,000 to Mesorah Heritage Foundation, Brooklyn, NY.
$4,840 to Tomche Shabbos of Rockland County, Monsey, NY.
$1,180 to Yeshiva Machzikei Hadas, Brooklyn, NY.
$461 to Congregation Ohr Yitzchok, Monsey, NY.
$452 to Congregation Shaarei Chesed, Monsey, NY.
$252 to Hatzoloh EMS, Monsey, NY.
$180 to Jewish Childrens Museum, New York, NY.
$101 to Bais Medrash Elyon, Monsey, NY.
$50 to Stam Gemilas Chesed Fund, Lakewood, NJ.
$15 to Bonei Olam, Brooklyn, NY.

5359
The Provident Bank Foundation ✧ ☆
830 Bergen Ave.
Jersey City, NJ   07306   (201) 915-5434
Contact: Angel R. Denis, Treas.
FAX: (866) 353-3172;
E-mail: foundation@providentnj.com; URL: http://www.providentnjfoundation.org

Established in 2003 in NJ.
Donor: Provident Financial Services, Inc.
Foundation type: Company-sponsored foundation.
Financial data (yr. ended 12/31/04): Assets, $38,429,416 (M); expenditures, $2,546,160; qualifying distributions, $2,497,505; giving activities include $2,332,905 for 394 grants (high: $200,000; low: $100).
Purpose and activities: The foundation supports organizations involved with arts and culture, education, health, recreation, and human services.
Fields of interest: Arts; Education; Health care; Recreation; Human services.
Type of support: Scholarship funds; Building/renovation; Equipment; Program development; Sponsorships; Capital campaigns; General/operating support.
Limitations: Giving primarily in areas of company operations in NJ. No support for political organizations or religious organizations not of direct benefit to the entire community.
Publications: Application guidelines.
Application information: An application form is required for requests of over $5,000.

> *Initial approach:* Mail or fax proposal to foundation for requests of under $5,000; download application form and mail or fax to foundation for requests of over $5,000
> *Deadline(s):* Jan. 1 to Apr. 30 for requests of over $10,000; 2 months prior to need for sponsorships
> *Final notification:* On or before July 30 for grant of over $10,000

Officers and Directors: Paul M. Pantozzi, Pres.; Gregory French, V.P.; Freeman P. Ingram, V.P.; Christopher Martin, V.P.; Michael Revesz, V.P.; Kevin J. Ward, V.P.; John F. Kuntz, Secy.; Angel R. Denis, Treas.; Carlos Hernandez; Karen McMullen; Thomas E. Sheenan.
EIN: 043739441

5360
The Prudential Foundation ▼ ✧
Prudential Plz.
751 Broad St., 15th Fl.
Newark, NJ   07102-3777   (973) 802-4791
Contact: Lata N. Reddy, V.P. and Secy.
E-mail: community.resources@prudential.com;
URL: http://www.prudential.com/productsAndServices/0,1474,intPageID%253D1440%2526blnPrinterFriendly%253D0,00.html

Incorporated in 1977 in NJ.
Donor: The Prudential Insurance Co. of America.
Foundation type: Company-sponsored foundation.
Financial data (yr. ended 12/31/04): Assets, $104,122,812 (M); gifts received, $37,979,734; expenditures, $23,033,783; qualifying distributions, $28,707,643; giving activities include $14,595,510 for 1,183 grants (high: $1,000,000; low: $250), $7,222,520 for 8,522 employee matching gifts, and $6,641,818 for 20 loans/program-related investments.

Purpose and activities: The foundation supports organizations involved with arts and culture, education, HIV/AIDS, employment, housing, recreation, youth development, human services, community development, and leadership development.
Fields of interest: Arts; Education, reform; Elementary/secondary education; Education, early childhood education; Higher education; Education, reading; Education; AIDS; Employment, services; Employment; Housing/shelter; Recreation; Youth development; Children/youth, services; Family services; Human services, financial counseling; Human services; Economic development; Community development; Leadership development.
Type of support: Employee volunteer services; General/operating support; Program development; Seed money; Curriculum development; Technical assistance; Program-related investments/loans; Employee matching gifts; Employee-related scholarships.
Limitations: Giving primarily in areas of company operations, with emphasis on Phoenix, AZ, Los Angeles, CA, Jacksonville, FL, Atlanta, GA, Minneapolis, MN, Newark, NJ, Philadelphia, PA, and Houston, TX. No support for veterans', labor, religious, fraternal, or athletic organizations. No grants to individuals (except for employee-related scholarships), or for advertising, fundraising , or disease-specific general operating support.
Publications: Annual report (including application guidelines); Corporate giving report; Financial statement.
Application information: The New York Area Common Application Form is accepted. Additional information may be requested at a later date. Application form required.

> *Initial approach:* Download application form and mail to foundation
> *Copies of proposal:* 1
> *Deadline(s):* None
> *Board meeting date(s):* Feb., June, and Oct.
> *Final notification:* Within 60 days

Officers and Trustees:* Sharon C. Taylor,* Chair.; Gabriella E. Morris, Pres.; Lata N. Reddy, V.P. and Secy.; Charles E. Chaplin, Treas.; Dennis G. Sullivan, Compt.; Gilbert F. Casellas; Robert C. Golden; Jon F. Hanson; Constance J. Horner; Arthur F. Ryan; John R. Strangfeld, Jr.
Number of staff: 5 full-time professional; 4 full-time support.
EIN: 222175290
Selected grants: The following grants were reported in 2004.
$650,000 to United Way of Essex and West Hudson, Newark, NJ. For Success By Six Initiative, collaborative project providing HIV/AIDS prevention services targeting single mothers and children, and training and technical assistance to grantees and partners of Prudential Neighborhood Partnership initiative.
$500,000 to Urban League, National, New York, NY. For Opportunity Works project.
$450,000 to Child Welfare League of America, DC. For Creating Parenting-Rich Communities, and Prudential Positive Parenting Programs.
$335,000 to Childrens Defense Fund, DC. For Children and Working Families Benefits Initiative, and building leadership for expanded child and early education programs.
$250,000 to Princeton Area Community Foundation, Lawrenceville, NJ. For New Jersey AIDS Partnership and Safe Child Fund.

$200,000 to La Casa de Don Pedro, Newark, NJ. For partnership with Fannie Mae Foundation localizing Building Neighborhood Assets (BNA) initiative.

$150,000 to Episcopal Community Development, Newark, NJ. For YouthBuild Newark.

$150,000 to New Jersey Institute for Social Justice, Newark, NJ. For Newark-Essex County Construction Careers and associated programs.

$110,000 to Aspira of New Jersey, Newark, NJ. For summer employment, including Elizabeth, Jersey City, Paterson, and other programs.

$100,000 to Community Loan Fund of New Jersey, Trenton, NJ. To implement Newark Lighthouse Initiative.

5361
PSEG Foundation, Inc.
(formerly Public Service Electric and Gas Company Foundation, Inc.)
80 Park Plz., T-10
Newark, NJ 07101 (973) 430-7842
Contact: Marion C. O'Neill
Additional tel.: (973) 430-5763; URL: http://www.pseg.com/community

Established in 1991 in NJ.
Donors: Public Service Electric and Gas Co.; Public Service Enterprise Group, Inc.
Foundation type: Company-sponsored foundation.
Financial data (yr. ended 12/31/05): Assets, $13,675,494 (M); gifts received, $14,185,752; expenditures, $9,491,222; qualifying distributions, $4,055,722; giving activities include $3,681,126 for grants, and $374,596 for 1,300 employee matching gifts.
Purpose and activities: The foundation supports organizations involved with K-12 education, early childhood education, drop-out prevention, literacy, pollution, natural resources, energy, environmental education, substance abuse prevention, housing, youth leadership development, day care, community economic development, and children.
Fields of interest: Elementary/secondary education; Education, early childhood education; Education, drop-out prevention; Education, reading; Environment, pollution control; Environment, natural resources; Environment, energy; Environmental education; Substance abuse, prevention; Housing/shelter; Youth development, services; Children, day care; Urban/community development; Science, formal/general education; Mathematics; Engineering/technology; Children.
Type of support: Continuing support; Annual campaigns; Capital campaigns; Program development; Employee matching gifts.
Limitations: Giving primarily in areas of company operations in NJ. No support for religious, political, athletic, labor, or fraternal organizations or disease-specific organizations. No grants for endowments.
Publications: Application guidelines; Corporate giving report; Multi-year report; Newsletter.
Application information: Multi-year funding is not automatic. Application form required.
  Initial approach: Complete online application form
  Deadline(s): Oct. 30
  Board meeting date(s): Nov.
  Final notification: 3 to 6 months
Officers and Trustees:* John R. Smith,* Pres.; Edward J. Biggins, Jr., Secy.; Morton A. Plawner, Treas.; Patricia A. Rado,* Cont.; James Foran, Genl. Counsel; Frank Cassidy; Frederick D. DeSanti;

Robert J. Dougherty, Jr.; Ralph Izzo, Ph.D.; Mark G. Kahrer; Robert C. Murray; Thomas M. O'Flynn; Ardeshir Rostami; R. Edwin Selover.
EIN: 223125880

5362
Puffin Foundation, Ltd. ✧
20 E. Oakdene Ave.
Teaneck, NJ 07666
Contact: Gladys Miller-Rosenstein, Exec. Dir.
FAX: (201) 836-1734;
E-mail: puffingrant@mindspring.com; URL: http://www.puffinfoundation.org

Established in 1985 in NY.
Donors: Perry Rosenstein; Brighton-Best Socket Screw Manufacturing, Inc.
Foundation type: Independent foundation.
Financial data (yr. ended 12/31/03): Assets, $14,421,182 (M); gifts received, $947,295; expenditures, $946,545; qualifying distributions, $719,899; giving activities include $354,221 for grants, and $1,454,050 for foundation-administered programs.
Purpose and activities: The Puffin Foundation continues to make grants that encourage emerging artists in the fields of art, music, theater and literature whose works, due to their genre and/or social philosophy might have difficulty being aired. The foundation seeks to open the doors of artistic expression by providing grants to artists and art organizations who are often excluded from mainstream opportunities.
Fields of interest: Media, film/video; Visual arts, photography; Performing arts; Performing arts, dance; Performing arts, theater; Performing arts, music; Arts.
Type of support: Publication; Seed money; Fellowships; Scholarship funds; Research; Grants to individuals.
Limitations: Giving on a national basis. No support for religious organizations. No grants for travel, general living expenses, continuing education, or publications.
Publications: Application guidelines; Informational brochure.
Application information: Application information available on foundation Web site. Application form required.
  Initial approach: Letter of request
  Copies of proposal: 1
  Deadline(s): Oct. 1 through Dec. 31
  Board meeting date(s): Annually
Officers and Directors:* Perry Rosenstein,* Pres.; Gladys Miller-Rosenstein, Exec. Dir; Judith Kitrick; Carl Rosenstein; Neal Rosenstein.
Number of staff: 6
EIN: 133155489

5363
The Quercus Fund, Inc. ✧
c/o Dudley & Shanley, LLC
130 Maple Ave., Ste. EB2
Red Bank, NJ 07701-1735

Established in CT.
Foundation type: Independent foundation.
Financial data (yr. ended 7/31/05): Assets, $9,290,274 (M); expenditures, $454,117; qualifying distributions, $400,000; giving activities include $400,000 for 1 grant.

Purpose and activities: Giving primarily to a private foundation for the operation of an arboretum.
Fields of interest: Botanical gardens.
Limitations: Applications not accepted. Giving primarily in CT. No grants to individuals.
Application information: Contributes only to pre-selected organizations.
Officers: Elisabeth C. Dudley, Pres.; Henry C. Dudley, V.P. and Treas.; Jane C. Dudley, V.P.; Sarah Dudley Plimpton, V.P.; Paul R. Brenner, Secy.
EIN: 134156738

5364
Ravi and Pratibha Reddy Foundation, Inc. ✧ ☆
200 Lanidex Plz., 2nd Fl.
Parsippany, NJ 07054

Established in 1997 in DE and NJ.
Foundation type: Independent foundation.
Financial data (yr. ended 11/30/05): Assets, $6,182,489 (M); expenditures, $410,741; qualifying distributions, $359,134; giving activities include $345,050 for 20 grants (high: $100,000; low: $350).
Purpose and activities: Giving primarily for education, human services, and for the relief of poverty.
Fields of interest: Arts, cultural/ethnic awareness; Historic preservation/historical societies; Elementary/secondary education; Hospitals (general); Health care; Housing/shelter; Human services; International development; Federated giving programs; Economically disadvantaged.
Limitations: Applications not accepted. Giving in the U.S., primarily in NJ. No grants to individuals.
Application information: Contributes only to pre-selected organizations.
Trustees: Pratibha B. Reddy; Ravi B. Reddy.
EIN: 223531803

5365
The Reeves Foundation, Inc. ✧
115 Summit Ave.
Summit, NJ 07901-2899

Established in 1988 as successor foundation to The Reeves Brothers Foundation, Inc.
Donor: Margie Hall.
Foundation type: Independent foundation.
Financial data (yr. ended 6/30/05): Assets, $25,842,612 (M); expenditures, $1,484,687; qualifying distributions, $1,170,518; giving activities include $918,267 for 13 grants (high: $250,000; low: $1,000).
Fields of interest: Higher education; Hospitals (general); Medical research, institute; Boy scouts; Girl scouts; Children/youth, services.
Type of support: Capital campaigns.
Limitations: Applications not accepted. Giving primarily on the East Coast, with emphasis on NJ and NY, and in the South, with emphasis on NC and SC. No grants to individuals.
Application information: Contributes only to pre-selected organizations. Unsolicited requests for funds not considered or acknowledged.
Officers: J.E. Reeves, Jr., Pres. and Treas.; Caroline Strong, Secy.
EIN: 581792933
Selected grants: The following grants were reported in 2004.

$250,000 to Wofford College, Spartanburg, SC.

$125,000 to Overlook Hospital Foundation, Summit, NJ.

$95,833 to Boy Scouts of America, New York, NY. 2 grants: $12,500, $83,333

$40,000 to Fauquier Hospital Foundation, Warrenton, VA.

$25,000 to Carolinas HealthCare Foundation, Charlotte, NC.

$25,000 to Wingate University, Wingate, NC.

$25,000 to YMCA, Spartanburg Family Center, Spartanburg, SC.

$23,650 to Girl Scouts of the U.S.A..

5366

Rheuminations, Inc. ✧

47 Hulfish St., Ste. 442
Princeton, NJ 08540

Established in 2000 in NJ.

Donors: Arnold H. Snider; Katherine M. Snider; Snider Holdings, LLC.

Foundation type: Independent foundation.

Financial data (yr. ended 12/31/05): Assets, $19,206,711 (M); gifts received, $3,500,000; expenditures, $11,932,868; qualifying distributions, $11,938,914; giving activities include $5,363,069 for 5 grants (high: $3,400,000; low: $52,000), and $6,073,199 for foundation-administered programs.

Fields of interest: Hospitals (general); Hospitals (specialty); Lupus; Lupus research.

Limitations: Applications not accepted. Giving primarily in NY. No grants to individuals.

Application information: Contributes only to pre-selected organizations.

Officers and Trustees:* Katherine M. Snider,* Pres.; Arnold H. Snider,* V.P. and Treas.; Nancy S. Hearne,* Secy.; Gina DelGivdice, M.D.

EIN: 223723547

5367

Rigorous Educational Assistance for Deserving Youth Foundation, Inc. ✧

(also known as READY Foundation, Inc.)
310 South St.
P.O. Box 1975
Morristown, NJ 07962-1975
Contact: Donald R. Smith

Established in 1987 in NJ.

Donors: Raymond G. Chambers; Pepsi Cola, Inc.; Ready Charitable Fund.

Foundation type: Independent foundation.

Financial data (yr. ended 9/30/05): Assets, $79,942 (M); gifts received, $1,051,400; expenditures, $1,012,444; qualifying distributions, $441,293; giving activities include $441,293 for grants.

Purpose and activities: Provides tuition assistance for post-secondary training for students.

Fields of interest: Education; Children/youth, services.

Type of support: General/operating support; Scholarship funds.

Limitations: Applications not accepted. Giving primarily in Essex County, NJ.

Application information: Unsolicited requests for funding not considered.

Officer: Charles Rubin, Chair and Pres.; Barbara Bell Coleman, V.P.; Anthony Romano, Secy. and Treas.; Edith Minnicks, Exec. Dir.

EIN: 222815535

5368

Fannie E. Rippel Foundation ✧

180 Mount Airy Rd., Ste. 200
Basking Ridge, NJ 07920-2021 (908) 766-0404
Contact: Barbara Vanderkolk Gardner, C.E.O. and Pres.
FAX: (908) 766-0527; E-mail: rippel@attglobal.net; URL: http://foundationcenter.org/grantmaker/rippel

Incorporated in 1953 in NJ.

Donor: Julius S. Rippel†.

Foundation type: Independent foundation.

Financial data (yr. ended 4/30/05): Assets, $76,549,415 (M); expenditures, $2,945,111; qualifying distributions, $2,183,919; giving activities include $1,340,000 for 8 grants (high: $500,000; low: $25,000; average: $75,000–$150,000).

Purpose and activities: The foundation's activities are legally restricted to the support of hospitals, organizations involved in treatment of and/or research concerning cancer or heart disease and for organizations addressing the needs of the elderly and women of all ages and related activities. Within these purposes the foundation is also interested in projects which: 1) develop effective strategies to reach underserved rural and urban populations; 2) address issues related to women's health; 3) emphasize strategies to change or modify the wellness behavior of populations including research and access to preventive care; and 4) focus on humanistic medicine and mind-body-spirit connections including the importance of belief, support, communications and relationships on healing of diseases.

Fields of interest: Health care, ethics; Medical care, community health systems; Hospitals (general); Hospitals (specialty); Health care, rural areas; Cancer; Heart & circulatory diseases; Geriatrics; Cancer research; Heart & circulatory research; Geriatrics research; Human services, mind/body enrichment; Gerontology; Aging; Women.

Type of support: Management development/capacity building; Building/renovation; Equipment; Program development; Seed money; Fellowships; Research; Program evaluation; Matching/challenge support.

Limitations: Giving primarily in NJ, as well as in the Northeast and middle Atlantic states. No grants to individuals, or for general purposes, operating budgets, continuing support, annual campaigns, deficit financing, scholarships, indirect costs, or building funds, no loans.

Publications: Financial statement; Grants list.

Application information: Application guidelines available on foundation Web site. Application form not required.

  Initial approach: Letter of inquiry
  Copies of proposal: 1
  Deadline(s): None
  Board meeting date(s): Approximately 5 times a year
  Final notification: Varies

Officers and Trustees:* Edward W. Probert,* Chair.; Laura K. Landy, Acting Pres.; Chana Fitton, Treas.; S. Jervis Brinton, Jr., Emeritus; Bruce N. Bensley; John D. Campbell; Albert L. Strunk, M.D.

Number of staff: 3 full-time professional; 1 full-time support.

EIN: 221559427

Selected grants: The following grants were reported in 2005.

$150,000 to Canton-Potsdam Hospital, Potsdam, NY. For personnel and operating support for Mobile Mammography Program being instituted in North Country with partnering organizations.

$100,000 to Prostate Net, Guttenberg, NJ. 2 grants: $25,000 (For The Barbershop Initiative to assist in community marketing efforts to reach target populations and to encourage funders to support important effort), $75,000 (For The Barbershop Initiative to assist in community marketing efforts to reach target populations and to encourage funders to support important effort).

5369

Philip W. Riskin Charitable Foundation, Inc. ✧

c/o SGA, PC
1199 Raritan Rd.
Clark, NJ 07066

Established in 1993 in NJ.

Donor: Philip W. Riskin.

Foundation type: Operating foundation.

Financial data (yr. ended 12/31/05): Assets, $8,632,247 (M); expenditures, $369,027; qualifying distributions, $369,027; giving activities include $332,000 for 64 grants (high: $15,000; low: $1,500).

Fields of interest: Media, television; Media, radio; Museums (art); Performing arts; Hospitals (general); Reproductive health, family planning; Health organizations, association; Cancer research; Human services; Jewish federated giving programs.

Limitations: Applications not accepted. Giving primarily in NJ, and New York, NY. No grants to individuals.

Application information: Contributes only to pre-selected organizations.

Officers and Trustees:* Jane Riskin Bean,* Pres.; Francesca Liechenstein,* Secy.; George Bean; Michael Liechenstein.

EIN: 223265173

Selected grants: The following grants were reported in 2005.

$10,000 to Deborah Hospital Foundation, Browns Mills, NJ.

$10,000 to W N E T Channel 13, New York, NY.

$8,500 to Jewish Family Services, Roseland, NJ.

$7,500 to Gildas Club Worldwide, New York, NY.

$7,500 to Ronald McDonald House of New York, New York, NY.

$5,000 to Carnegie Hall Society, New York, NY.

$5,000 to Museum of Modern Art, New York, NY.

$5,000 to New Jersey Symphony Orchestra, Newark, NJ.

$2,500 to Childrens Defense Fund, DC.

$2,500 to NAACP, Baltimore, MD.

5370

The Gareth and Gwenna Roberts Foundation ✧

P.O. Box 1525
Pennington, NJ 08534-1525

Donors: Gareth Roberts; Gwenna Roberts.

Foundation type: Independent foundation.

Financial data (yr. ended 11/30/05): Assets, $79,077 (M); expenditures, $476,160; qualifying distributions, $444,731; giving activities include $443,107 for 1 grant.

Fields of interest: Higher education; Health care; Health organizations, research.

Limitations: Applications not accepted. Giving primarily on a national basis. No grants to individuals.

Application information: Contributes only to pre-selected organizations.

Officers and Directors:* Gareth Roberts,* Pres.; Gwenna Roberts,* V.P. and Secy.-Treas.; Mary Jane Roberts.

EIN: 752738828

5371
The Norman and Bettina Roberts Foundation, Inc. ✧

11 Kiel Ave
Kinnelon, NJ 07405
Contact: David McIntee, Treas.

Established in 1992 in NY.

Donors: Norman Roberts†; Bettina Roberts†.

Foundation type: Independent foundation.

Financial data (yr. ended 12/31/05): Assets, $16,932,457 (M); gifts received, $1,500,000; expenditures, $1,370,640; qualifying distributions, $1,370,640; giving activities include $1,330,262 for grants.

Purpose and activities: Giving for emergency services, human services, and education.

Fields of interest: Education; Youth development; Human services.

Type of support: Matching/challenge support; Emergency funds; Continuing support; General/operating support.

Limitations: Giving primarily in NJ and NY. No grants to individuals, or for administrative expenses.

Application information: Application form not required.

Initial approach: Proposal
Copies of proposal: 1
Deadline(s): Rolling
Board meeting date(s): Various
Final notification: Varies

Officers: Joseph R. Canciglia, Pres.; Lawrence Magid, Secy.; David McIntee, Treas.

EIN: 133702467

5372
The Roche Patient Assistance Foundation ✧

340 Kingsland St.
Nutley, NJ 07110 (973) 235-5000
Contact: Joann Hanley
Additional tel.: (877) 757-6243; URL: http://www.rocheusa.com/programs/patientassist.asp

Established in 2002 in DE.

Donor: Roche Laboratories Inc.

Foundation type: Operating foundation.

Financial data (yr. ended 12/31/05): Assets, $0 (M); gifts received, $174,463,465; expenditures, $174,463,465; qualifying distributions, $174,463,465; giving activities include $174,463,465 for grants to individuals.

Purpose and activities: The foundation provides pharmaceutical products to economically disadvantaged patients.

Fields of interest: Economically disadvantaged.

Type of support: Grants to individuals; Donated products.

Application information: Application form required.

Initial approach: Contact foundation for application form
Deadline(s): None

Officers and Directors:* Kevin O'Leary, V.P.; Frederick C. Kentz III,* Secy.; David McDede, Treas.

EIN: 300058986

5373
The Rose Foundation ✧

P.O. Box 359
Elmwood Park, NJ 07407

Established in 1990 in NJ.

Donor: Martin J. Wygod.

Foundation type: Independent foundation.

Financial data (yr. ended 11/30/05): Assets, $976,543 (M); expenditures, $963,998; qualifying distributions, $940,482; giving activities include $823,243 for 28 grants (high: $333,333; low: $375).

Fields of interest: Education; Health care; Health organizations, association; Medical research, institute.

Limitations: Applications not accepted. Giving primarily in CA, NJ, and NY. No grants to individuals.

Publications: Occasional report.

Application information: Contributes only to pre-selected organizations.

Officers and Directors:* Pamela Wygod,* Pres.; Frank J. Failla, Jr., V.P.; Charles A. Mele,* V.P.; Martin J. Wygod,* Secy.-Treas.

Number of staff: 2 part-time professional.

EIN: 223088744

Selected grants: The following grants were reported in 2004.

$433,333 to Francis Parker School, San Diego, CA. 2 grants: $333,333, $100,000

$22,050 to Grayson-Jockey Club Research Foundation, New York, NY.

$20,000 to Boys and Girls Club of West San Gabriel Valley, Monterey Park, CA. 2 grants: $10,000 each

$12,500 to Clemson University Foundation, Clemson, SC.

$7,500 to San Diego Opera Association, San Diego, CA.

$5,000 to YMCA, CA.

$3,846 to Casa de Amparo, Oceanside, CA.

$1,000 to San Diego Youth and Community Services, San Diego, CA.

5374
Meyer Rosenbaum Family Foundation I ✧

1125 Ocean Ave.
Lakewood, NJ 08701

Established in 2000 in NJ.

Foundation type: Independent foundation.

Financial data (yr. ended 12/31/05): Assets, $278,504 (M); gifts received, $1,751,828; expenditures, $1,460,873; qualifying distributions, $1,460,873; giving activities include $1,457,598 for 974 grants.

Fields of interest: Jewish agencies & temples.

Limitations: Giving primarily in NJ and NY. No grants to individuals.

Application information:

Initial approach: Letter or telephone
Deadline(s): None

Trustees: David Rosenbaum; Dovid Rosenbaum; Joseph Rosenbaum; Moshe Rosenbaum.

EIN: 223718432

5375
Eric F. Ross Foundation ✧

80 Main St., 5th Fl.
West Orange, NJ 07052-5414

Established in 1986 in NJ.

Donor: Eric F. Ross.

Foundation type: Independent foundation.

Financial data (yr. ended 12/31/04): Assets, $1,770,497 (M); expenditures, $571,773; qualifying distributions, $537,625; giving activities include $506,816 for 41 grants (high: $280,116; low: $100).

Purpose and activities: Giving primarily to the arts and to Jewish organizations, temples, and schools.

Fields of interest: Arts; Education; Jewish federated giving programs; Jewish agencies & temples.

Type of support: Building/renovation; Research.

Limitations: Applications not accepted. Giving primarily in NJ and NY; some funding nationally. No grants to individuals.

Application information: Contributes only to pre-selected organizations.

Trustees: Eric F. Ross; Lore Ross.

EIN: 133383843

5376
E. Burke Ross, Jr. Charitable Foundation, Inc. ✧

P.O. Box 1975
Morristown, NJ 07962

Incorporated in 1987 in NJ.

Donor: E. Burke Ross, Jr.

Foundation type: Independent foundation.

Financial data (yr. ended 11/30/04): Assets, $340,999 (M); gifts received, $899,497; expenditures, $564,164; qualifying distributions, $562,362; giving activities include $562,362 for 33 grants (high: $276,487; low: $500).

Purpose and activities: Giving primarily for education as well as for health and social services.

Fields of interest: Arts; Education; Hospitals (general); Health organizations, association; Boys & girls clubs; Human services; Children/youth, services; Family services; Federated giving programs.

Limitations: Applications not accepted. Giving primarily in FL and NJ. No grants to individuals.

Application information: Contributes only to pre-selected organizations.

Officers: E. Burke Ross, Jr., Pres.; Benson T. Ross, V.P.; Amory Ross, Treas.

EIN: 521578961

Selected grants: The following grants were reported in 2004.

$276,487 to Saint Pauls School.

$99,400 to Boston College, Chestnut Hill, MA.

$50,000 to Morristown Memorial Hospital, Morristown, NJ.

$22,500 to Eaglebrook School, Deerfield, MA.

$5,000 to Princeton University, Princeton, NJ.

$2,000 to University of Chicago, Chicago, IL.

$1,000 to Marthas Vineyard Hospital, Oak Bluffs, MA.

$500 to Sewickley Valley Hospital, Sewickley, PA.

5377
Daryl & Steven Roth Foundation ◇
c/o Interstate Properties
210 Rte. 4E
Paramus, NJ   07652

Established in 1994 in NJ.
Donor: Steven Roth.
Foundation type: Independent foundation.
Financial data (yr. ended 12/31/05): Assets, $1,327,173 (M); expenditures, $2,113,856; qualifying distributions, $2,095,121; giving activities include $2,095,121 for 150 grants (high: $175,000; low: $100).
Purpose and activities: Giving primarily for Jewish agencies and temples, Jewish federated giving programs, education, the arts, and health and human services.
Fields of interest: Museums; Museums (specialized); Performing arts; Arts; Higher education; Medical school/education; Theological school/education; Education; Animal welfare; Health care; Human services; Jewish federated giving programs; Jewish agencies & temples.
Limitations: Applications not accepted. Giving primarily in NJ and NY. No grants to individuals.
Application information: Contributes only to pre-selected organizations.
Trustee: Steven Roth.
EIN: 223339611
Selected grants: The following grants were reported in 2005.
$130,000 to Horace Mann School, Riverdale, NY. 2 grants: $30,000, $100,000
$100,000 to Dartmouth College, Hanover, NH.
$100,000 to Lincoln Center Theater, New York, NY.
$100,000 to NYU Hospitals Center, New York, NY.
$100,000 to Outward Bound, Garrison, NY.
$30,000 to New York Shakespeare Festival, New York, NY.
$25,000 to Museum of Jewish Heritage, New York, NY.
$25,000 to New York University Medical Center, New York, NY.
$3,000 to Guild Hall, New York, NY.

5378
Henry M. Rowan Family Foundation ◇
P.O. Box 157
Rancocas, NJ   08073
Contact: Henry M. Rowan, Pres.
Application address: 10 Indel Ave., Rancocas, NJ 08073

Established in 1999 in NJ.
Donor: Henry M. Rowan.
Foundation type: Independent foundation.
Financial data (yr. ended 12/31/04): Assets, $13,222,345 (M); expenditures, $664,318; qualifying distributions, $581,000; giving activities include $581,000 for 30 grants (high: $50,000; low: $5,000).
Fields of interest: Scholarships/financial aid; Education; Human services.
Application information: Application form not required.
Initial approach: Letter
Deadline(s): None

Officers and Directors:* Henry M. Rowan,* Pres.; Virginia Rowan Smith,* V.P.; Manning J. Smith III,* Secy.-Treas.; John Scott Boyer; Gilbert A. Gehin-Scott.
EIN: 223655770

5379
The Fred C. Rummel Foundation ◇
316 Lenox Ave., Ste. 2C
Westfield, NJ   07090   (908) 317-8600
Contact: Annmarie Puleio, Exec. Dir.

Established in 1997 in NJ.
Foundation type: Independent foundation.
Financial data (yr. ended 12/31/04): Assets, $10,219,298 (M); expenditures, $518,494; qualifying distributions, $485,440; giving activities include $419,000 for 81 grants (high: $25,000; low: $200).
Purpose and activities: Grant support for children, elderly, human services, and health programs.
Fields of interest: Education; Health organizations, association; Youth development; Human services.
Limitations: Giving limited to NJ. No grants for operating capital.
Publications: Application guidelines.
Application information: Application form required.
Initial approach: Letter or telephone for guidelines
Copies of proposal: 5
Deadline(s): Mar. 31 or Sept. 30
Board meeting date(s): June and Dec.
Final notification: 3 months
Officer: Annmarie Puleio, Exec. Dir.
Trustees: Patricia Burch Byers; Robert W. Cockren; Bank of America, N.A.
Number of staff: 1 part-time professional.
EIN: 226703253

5380
The RuthMarc Foundation, Inc. ◇
37 Hageman Ln.
Princeton, NJ   08540

Established in 2000 in NJ.
Donor: Andrew M. Okun.
Foundation type: Independent foundation.
Financial data (yr. ended 3/31/06): Assets, $2,279,474 (M); expenditures, $370,114; qualifying distributions, $369,000; giving activities include $369,000 for 14 grants (high: $125,000; low: $1,000).
Fields of interest: Elementary/secondary education; Higher education; Legal services, public interest law; Public policy, research.
Limitations: Applications not accepted. Giving primarily in Princeton, NJ, and Washington, DC; some funding nationally. No grants to individuals.
Application information: Contributes only to pre-selected organizations.
Officers: Andrew M. Okun, Pres. and Treas.; Laurie R. Okun, V.P. and Secy.
EIN: 061580750
Selected grants: The following grants were reported in 2006.
$125,000 to Princeton Junior School, Princeton, NJ.
$50,000 to Institute for Justice, DC.
$30,000 to University of Pennsylvania, Philadelphia, PA.
$25,000 to Cato Institute, DC.
$20,000 to ALS Therapy Development Foundation, Cambridge, MA.

$20,000 to Reason Foundation, Los Angeles, CA.
$5,000 to Drug Policy Alliance, New York, NY.
$2,000 to Competitive Enterprise Institute, DC.
$1,000 to Arts Council of Princeton, Princeton, NJ.
$1,000 to Liberty Foundation, Port Townsend, WA.

5381
The Sagner Family Foundation ◇
293 Eisenhower Pkwy.
Livingston, NJ   07039
Contact: Alan Sagner, Chair.

Established in 1961 in NJ.
Donors: Ruth Levin Sagner; Alan Sagner.
Foundation type: Independent foundation.
Financial data (yr. ended 12/31/04): Assets, $8,879,702 (M); gifts received, $806,380; expenditures, $1,083,294; qualifying distributions, $895,731; giving activities include $895,731 for 66 grants (high: $358,566; low: $100).
Purpose and activities: Giving primarily for the arts, and to Jewish organizations.
Fields of interest: Performing arts; Performing arts centers; Performing arts, ballet; Arts; Family services; Jewish federated giving programs.
Limitations: Giving primarily in NJ, and New York, NY. No grants to individuals.
Application information: Application form not required.
Initial approach: Letter
Deadline(s): None
Officers: Alan Sagner, Chair.; Deborah Sagner, Pres.; Mary Baltycki, Secy.-Treas.
Trustee: Rachel Buurma.
EIN: 221711646

5382
George H. and Estelle M. Sands Foundation ◇ ☆
c/o Jeffrey H. Sands
194 Nassau St.
Princeton, NJ   08542

Established in 1996.
Donors: George H. Sands; Estelle M. Sands.
Foundation type: Independent foundation.
Financial data (yr. ended 12/31/05): Assets, $11,335,657 (M); gifts received, $1,922,000; expenditures, $484,706; qualifying distributions, $446,019; giving activities include $446,019 for grants.
Purpose and activities: Giving for education.
Fields of interest: Arts; Libraries (public); Education; Human services.
Limitations: Applications not accepted. Giving primarily in NJ. No grants to individuals.
Application information: Contributes only to pre-selected organizations.
Trustee: Jeffrey H. Sands.
EIN: 223483828
Selected grants: The following grants were reported in 2004.
$10,000 to Lost Tree Village Charitable Foundation, North Palm Beach, FL.
$3,000 to Lawrenceville School, Lawrenceville, NJ.
$1,300 to Arts Council of Princeton, Princeton, NJ.
$1,000 to Delaware and Raritan Greenway, Princeton, NJ.
$500 to YMCA.
$100 to Drumthwacket Foundation, Princeton, NJ.
$100 to Society of the Four Arts, Palm Beach, FL.

5383
Sandy Hill Foundation ✧
330 South St.
P.O. Box 1975
Morristown, NJ 07962-1975

Incorporated in 1985 in NJ.
Donor: Frank E. Walsh, Jr.
Foundation type: Independent foundation.
Financial data (yr. ended 12/31/03): Assets, $31,904,176 (M); expenditures, $1,163,683; qualifying distributions, $1,096,010; giving activities include $977,525 for 76 grants (high: $50,000; low: $500).
Purpose and activities: Support primarily for education, particularly higher education; support also for social services and health.
Fields of interest: Higher education; Education; Health care; Health organizations, association; Human services.
Limitations: Applications not accepted. Giving primarily in NJ, NY, and PA. No grants to individuals.
Application information: Unsolicited requests for funds not considered or acknowledged.
Officers and Director:* Frank E. Walsh, Jr.,* Chair.; Joseph Walsh, Pres.; Jeffrey R. Walsh, V.P. and Treas.; Frank E. Walsh III, V.P.; Meghan Walsh, V.P.; Mary D. Walsh, Secy.
EIN: 222668774
Selected grants: The following grants were reported in 2003.
$389,260 to University of Vermont, Burlington, VT. For general support.
$10,000 to Memorial Sloan-Kettering Cancer Center, New York, NY. For general support.
$8,200 to Boys and Girls Clubs of Newark, Newark, NJ. For general support.
$1,000 to Arthritis Foundation, Iselin, NJ. For general support.
$1,000 to Family Resource Associates, Shrewsbury, NJ. For general support.
$1,000 to Immaculata University, Immaculata, PA. For general support.
$1,000 to Lehigh University, Bethlehem, PA. For general support.
$1,000 to National Down Syndrome Society, New York, NY. For general support.
$1,000 to Seton Hall University, South Orange, NJ. For general support.
$500 to Multiple Sclerosis Society, National, Mid Jersey Chapter, Oakhurst, NJ. For general support.

5384
Sato Foundation ✧
P.O. Box 1525
Pennington, NJ 08534-1525

Established in 2000 in CA.
Donors: Kozo Sato; Nieves Sato; Sato Lead Trust 80C-74C03; Sato Lead Trust 80C-7C04.
Foundation type: Independent foundation.
Financial data (yr. ended 12/31/05): Assets, $11,703,959 (M); gifts received, $1,635,116; expenditures, $492,652; qualifying distributions, $442,780; giving activities include $430,389 for 16 grants (high: $104,689; low: $2,700).
Fields of interest: Arts; Education.
Limitations: Applications not accepted. Giving primarily in the San Francisco Bay Area, CA. No grants to individuals.
Application information: Contributes only to pre-selected organizations.

Officers: Kozo Sato, Pres.; Nieves Sato, Secy.-Treas.
Directors: Kate Sato Burton; Sonia Sato.
EIN: 943356933

5385
The Schecter Family Foundation, Inc. ✧ ☆
55 Passaic Ave.
Kearny, NJ 07032

Foundation type: Independent foundation.
Financial data (yr. ended 12/31/05): Assets, $14,957,265 (M); gifts received, $9,100,000; expenditures, $599,240; qualifying distributions, $489,200; giving activities include $489,200 for grants.
Fields of interest: Historic preservation/historical societies; Medical school/education; Education; Human services; Federated giving programs; Jewish agencies & temples.
Limitations: Giving primarily in FL, MA, and NY.
Officers: Leroy Schecter, Pres.; Beth Semel, V.P.; Carleton Semel, V.P.; Shoshana Schecter, Secy.
EIN: 300134495

5386
L. P. Schenck Fund
c/o PNC Wealth Management
265 Millburn Ave.
Millburn, NJ 07041-1703 (973) 218-2102
Contact: Claudia LaTorre, V.P., PNC Wealth Management
FAX: (973) 218-2222;
E-mail: claudia.latorre@pnc.com

Established in 1960 in NJ.
Donor: Lillian Pitkin Schenck†.
Foundation type: Independent foundation.
Financial data (yr. ended 8/31/05): Assets, $10,419,902 (M); expenditures, $574,726; qualifying distributions, $485,625; giving activities include $485,000 for 65 grants (high: $70,000; low: $500).
Purpose and activities: Grants restricted to institutions in the NJ area, including support for youth, social service and mental health agencies, and cultural programs.
Fields of interest: Performing arts, theater; Arts; Mental health/crisis services; Human services; Children/youth, services.
Type of support: General/operating support; Building/renovation; Equipment; Program development; Curriculum development.
Limitations: Giving limited to NJ. No grants to individuals, or for endowment funds.
Application information: Application form not required.
 Initial approach: Proposal
 Copies of proposal: 3
 Deadline(s): Aug. 1
 Board meeting date(s): Oct.
Trustees: Marguerite Logan; Susan C. Madden; PNC Bank, N.A.
EIN: 226040581
Selected grants: The following grants were reported in 2005.
$30,000 to Englewood Hospital and Medical Center, Englewood, NJ.
$29,000 to Volunteer Center of Bergen County, Hackensack, NJ.

$20,000 to Van Ost Institute for Family Living, Englewood, NJ.
$8,000 to Shelter Our Sisters, Hackensack, NJ.
$8,000 to Southeast Senior Center for Independent Living, Englewood, NJ.
$7,500 to Habitat for Humanity, Millville, NJ.
$5,000 to Hudson Cradle, Jersey City, NJ.
$5,000 to Valley Home Care, Paramus, NJ.
$3,000 to Arts Power, Ridgewood, NJ.
$2,500 to Nai-Ni Chen Dance Company, Fort Lee, NJ.

5387
Schering-Plough Foundation, Inc. ✧
2000 Galloping Hill Rd.
Kenilworth, NJ 07033-0530 (908) 298-7232
Contact: Christine A. Fahey, V.P.
FAX: (908) 298-7349; URL: http://www.sgp.com/schering_plough/corp/sp_foundation.jsp

Incorporated in 1955 in NJ.
Donor: Schering-Plough Corp.
Foundation type: Company-sponsored foundation.
Financial data (yr. ended 12/31/05): Assets, $10,178,133 (M); gifts received, $2,080,000; expenditures, $3,304,414; qualifying distributions, $3,281,772; giving activities include $1,865,899 for 65 grants (high: $200,000; low: $2,500), and $400,783 for employee matching gifts.
Purpose and activities: The foundation supports organizations involved with arts and culture, education, the environment, health, legal services, mentoring, civic affairs, minorities, and women.
Fields of interest: Arts; Elementary/secondary education; Secondary school/education; Higher education; Education; Environment; Hospitals (general); Health care; Legal services; Youth development, adult & child programs; Science, formal/general education; Public affairs; Minorities; Women.
International interests: Ireland.
Type of support: General/operating support; Annual campaigns; Capital campaigns; Building/renovation; Endowments; Program development; Fellowships; Internship funds; Scholarship funds; Sponsorships; Employee matching gifts.
Limitations: Giving primarily in areas of company operations, with emphasis on NJ, PR, and TN. No support for religious organizations not of direct benefit to the entire community, discriminatory organizations, or political candidates. No grants to individuals, or for political causes or campaigns.
Publications: Application guidelines; Corporate giving report; Program policy statement.
Application information: An interview or site visit may be requested. Application form required.
 Initial approach: Complete online application form
 Deadline(s): None
 Board meeting date(s): Fall
 Final notification: Within 60 days
Officers and Trustees: Joseph P. Starkey, Pres.; Christine A. Fahey, V.P.; E. Kevin Moore, Treas.; Robert Bertolini; C. Ron Cheeley; Thomas Sabatino.
Number of staff: 1 full-time professional; 3 part-time professional; 1 part-time support.
EIN: 221711047
Selected grants: The following grants were reported in 2004.
$100,000 to Trinitas Hospital, Elizabeth, NJ.
$60,000 to Pharmaceutical Research and Manufacturers of America Foundation, DC.
$50,000 to Caucus Educational Corporation, Montclair, NJ.

$50,000 to Overlook Hospital Foundation, Summit, NJ.

$37,500 to United Negro College Fund, Fairfax, VA.

$25,000 to ECLC of New Jersey, Morristown, NJ.

$25,000 to New Jersey Performing Arts Center, Newark, NJ.

$25,000 to Newark Museum, Newark, NJ.

$23,600 to Newark Beth Israel Medical Center Foundation, Newark, NJ.

$10,000 to Newark Academy, Livingston, NJ.

5388

The Scholarship Foundation ✧

307 Provincetown Rd.
Cherry Hill, NJ 08034 (856) 573-9400
Contact: Bernard T. Cote, Pres.

Established in 1988.

Foundation type: Independent foundation.

Financial data (yr. ended 12/31/05): Assets, $202,773 (M); gifts received, $2,235,670; expenditures, $2,289,770; qualifying distributions, $2,158,670; giving activities include $2,158,670 for 836 grants to individuals.

Purpose and activities: The foundation administers several scholarship programs including: The Lukens Foundation Scholarship Program and the Robert J. Moonan, Jr. Scholarship Program.

Fields of interest: Education.

Type of support: Employee matching gifts; Scholarships—to individuals.

Limitations: Applications not accepted. Giving on a national basis.

Application information: Unsolicited requests for funds not accepted.

Board meeting date(s): Fall

Officers and Directors:* Susan Watson,* Chair.; Bernard T. Cote,* Pres. and Treas.; Ann Ostrosky,* Secy.; Gina Amodio-DeMartis; Conrad Berthiaume; Jennifer Figueroa.

EIN: 521560429

5389

The Schreyer Foundation ✧

(formerly The William A. & Joan L. Schreyer Foundation)
117 Mercer St.
Princeton, NJ 08540-6809

Established in 1985.

Donors: William A. Schreyer; Joan L. Schreyer; Kelly A. Frazier Charitable Lead Trust; Charles Frazier Charitable Lead Trust.

Foundation type: Independent foundation.

Financial data (yr. ended 11/30/05): Assets, $17,153,198 (M); gifts received, $4,072,204; expenditures, $1,736,230; qualifying distributions, $1,543,141; giving activities include $1,543,141 for 125 grants (high: $100,000; low: $100).

Purpose and activities: Giving primarily for education, as well as for hospitals and health associations, and social services, including an outpatient substance abuse program.

Fields of interest: Education, early childhood education; Elementary school/education; Higher education; Medical school/education; Hospitals (general); Health care; Substance abuse, treatment; Lupus research; Human services; American Red Cross; Children/youth, services; Christian agencies & churches.

Limitations: Applications not accepted. Giving primarily in the northeastern U.S., including MD, NJ, NY and PA. No grants to individuals.

Application information: Contributes only to pre-selected organizations.

Trustee: William A. Schreyer.

EIN: 222671777

5390

The Schumann Center for Media and Democracy, Inc. ▼ ✧

(formerly The Florence and John Schumann Foundation)
33 Park St.
Montclair, NJ 07042 (973) 783-6660
Contact: Lynn C. Welhorsky, V.P., Admin.

Incorporated in 1961 in NJ.

Donors: Florence F. Schumann†; John J. Schumann, Jr.‡.

Foundation type: Independent foundation.

Financial data (yr. ended 12/31/05): Assets, $60,402,551 (M); expenditures, $7,560,462; qualifying distributions, $7,079,012; giving activities include $6,313,895 for 26 grants (high: $1,100,000; low: $4,500; average: $15,000–$140,000).

Purpose and activities: Grants for programs in effective governance and the environment.

Fields of interest: Media/communications; Public affairs, citizen participation.

Type of support: General/operating support; Continuing support; Program development; Matching/challenge support.

Limitations: Giving on a national basis. No grants to individuals, or for annual campaigns, capital campaigns, deficit financing, equipment and materials, land acquisition, or endowment funds; no loans.

Publications: Application guidelines.

Application information: Application form not required.

Initial approach: Letter of inquiry (1 - 2 pages)
Copies of proposal: 1
Board meeting date(s): Feb., June, and Oct.
Final notification: 2 to 3 months

Officers and Trustees:* Robert F. Schumann,* Co-Chair.; W. Ford Schumann,* Co-Chair.; Bill D. Moyers,* Pres.; Lynn C. Welhorsky, V.P., Admin.; Michael J. Johnston,* V.P.; David S. Bate,* Secy.-Treas.; Joan Konner; William McKibben; Margaret Schumann.

Number of staff: 2 full-time professional.

EIN: 226044214

Selected grants: The following grants were reported in 2005.

$1,100,000 to Business Leaders for Sensible Priorities, True Majority, New York, NY. For Win Without Wars, national education campaign on foreign policy to be coordinated in Washington, DC.

$600,000 to Free Press, Northampton, MA. For challenge grant for work to advance citizen action on media reform.

$500,000 to American Prospect, Boston, MA. For general support.

$500,000 to Center for Public Integrity, DC. For general support.

$500,000 to Institute for Americas Future, DC. For challenge grant for work to support Contract with America effort to engage progressive activists to define issues and ideas for political debate and for challenge grant for general support.

$420,000 to National Security Archive Fund, DC. Toward Iraq War Media Project.

$155,000 to Institute for Public Affairs, Chicago, IL. Toward journalism fellowships for In These Times magazine.

$140,000 to Global Exchange, San Francisco, CA. Toward public education efforts on United Nations efforts to improve global, social, economic and on-line reporting of environmental issues.

$100,000 to Foundation for National Progress, San Francisco, CA. Toward Media Consortium's multi-organizational editorial collaboration in reshaping terrain of independent media.

$75,000 to Sierra Club Foundation, San Francisco, CA. For activities of Environmental Litigation Meeting.

5391

The Schumann Fund for New Jersey, Inc.

21 Van Vleck St.
Montclair, NJ 07042 (973) 509-9883
Contact: Barbara Reisman, Exec. Dir.
URL: http://foundationcenter.org/grantmaker/schumann/

Established in 1988 in NJ.

Donors: Florence Schumann†; John Schumann†; Florence and John Schumann Foundation.

Foundation type: Independent foundation.

Financial data (yr. ended 12/31/06): Assets, $32,085,791 (M); expenditures, $2,517,452; qualifying distributions, $2,056,813; giving activities include $1,743,314 for 97 grants (high: $50,000; low: $2,500).

Purpose and activities: Support primarily for 1) early childhood development; 2) environmental protection; 3) school innovation; and 4) local activities directed at solving community problems within Essex County.

Fields of interest: Education, early childhood education; Education; Environment; Human services; Children/youth, services; Public affairs.

Type of support: General/operating support; Continuing support; Program development; Seed money.

Limitations: Giving limited to NJ, with emphasis on Essex County. No grants to individuals, or for capital campaigns, annual giving, or endowments.

Publications: Application guidelines; Annual report; Grants list.

Application information: NY/NJ Common Application Form is accepted. Program guidelines available on foundation Web site. Application form not required.

Initial approach: Proposal
Copies of proposal: 1
Deadline(s): Jan. 15, Apr. 15, July 15, and Oct. 15
Board meeting date(s): Mar., June, Sept., and Dec.
Final notification: 4 to 8 weeks

Officers and Trustees:* Leonard S. Coleman, Jr.,* Chair.; Andrew C. Halvorsen, Vice-Chair. and Treas.; John F. Noonan, Secy.; Barbara Reisman, Exec. Dir.; Aubin Z. Ames; Christopher J. Daggett.

Number of staff: 2 full-time professional.

EIN: 521556076

Selected grants: The following grants were reported in 2003.

$75,000 to Bloomfield College, Bloomfield, NJ. For development of Early Childhood concentration.

$50,000 to Chad School Foundation, Newark, NJ.
For operating support.
$30,000 to Hackensack Riverkeeper, Hackensack,
NJ. For operating support.
$30,000 to Youth Development Clinic of Newark,
Newark, NJ. For operating support.
$25,000 to Citizens for Better Schools, Newark, NJ.
For operating support.
$25,000 to Link Community School, Newark, NJ. For
operating support.
$25,000 to New Jersey Charter Public Schools
Association, Trenton, NJ. For operating support.
$25,000 to Newark Emergency Services for
Families, Newark, NJ. For operating support.
$12,500 to Eastern Environmental Law Center,
Newark, NJ. For operating support.
$1,500 to Council of New Jersey Grantmakers,
Trenton, NJ. For general support.

5392
Alvin & Dorothy Schwartz Foundation ✧
c/o M. Schwartzbard
101 Eisenhower Pkwy.
Roseland, NJ 07068

Established in 1966 in NY.
Donors: Alvin Schwartz; Amy Speilman; Thomas
Schwartz; Jane Stein.
Foundation type: Independent foundation.
Financial data (yr. ended 12/31/03): Assets,
$3,951,129 (M); gifts received, $229,000;
expenditures, $359,719; qualifying distributions,
$356,171; giving activities include $358,019 for 39
grants (high: $106,700; low: $100).
Purpose and activities: Giving primarily to Jewish
agencies, temples, and federated giving programs.
Fields of interest: Jewish federated giving programs;
Jewish agencies & temples.
Limitations: Applications not accepted. Giving
primarily in the greater metropolitan New York, NY,
area. No support for private foundations. No grants
to individuals.
Application information: Contributes only to
pre-selected organizations.
Officers and Directors:* Amy Speilman,* Pres.;
Jane Stein,* V.P.; Thomas Schwartz,* Secy.-Treas.
EIN: 116112410
Selected grants: The following grants were reported
in 2003.
$106,700 to Temple Beth-El of Great Neck, Great
Neck, NY.
$100,000 to North Shore-Long Island Jewish Health
System Foundation, Great Neck, NY.
$35,000 to Juvenile Diabetes Research Foundation
International, New York, NY.
$15,000 to National Jewish Medical and Research
Center, New York, NY.
$10,000 to Jewish Family Services.
$10,000 to Lawrence Family Jewish Community
Center of San Diego County, La Jolla, CA.
$10,000 to Meals on Wheels of Greater San Diego,
San Diego, CA.
$10,000 to Scripps Foundation for Medicine and
Science, San Diego, CA.
$5,000 to New York Foundling Hospital, New York,
NY.
$2,500 to Rensselaer Polytechnic Institute, Troy,
NY.

5393
The Schwartz Foundation, Inc. ✧
(formerly The Bernard Schwartz and Robert Schwartz
Foundation)
821 E. Gate Dr.
Mount Laurel, NJ 08054

Established in 1983 in PA.
Donors: Bernard Schwartz; Robert S. Schwartz.
Foundation type: Independent foundation.
Financial data (yr. ended 8/31/05): Assets,
$21,443,311 (M); gifts received, $70,000;
expenditures, $1,114,780; qualifying distributions,
$1,060,979; giving activities include $1,057,041
for 21 grants (high: $777,511; low: $1,000).
Purpose and activities: Giving primarily for the arts,
human services and to Jewish agencies and
temples.
Fields of interest: Arts; Education; Human services;
Jewish federated giving programs; Philanthropy/
voluntarism; Jewish agencies & temples.
Limitations: Applications not accepted. Giving
primarily in NJ and Philadelphia, PA. No grants to
individuals.
Application information: Contributes only to
pre-selected organizations.
Officer: Robert Schwartz, Chair.
Directors: Rhonda H. Lauer; Bernard Schwartz; Erika
Schwartz; Lois Schwartz; Michael Schwartz.
EIN: 232267403
Selected grants: The following grants were reported
in 2005.
$777,511 to Foundations, Inc., Moorestown, NJ.
$110,000 to American Friends of the Jaffa Institute,
Flushing, NY.
$40,000 to Friends of Yemin Orde, DC.
$10,000 to Jewish Community Center, Scranton,
PA.
$5,805 to Auerbach Central Agency for Jewish
Education, Melrose Park, PA.
$5,000 to Greater Philadelphia Urban Affairs
Coalition, Philadelphia, PA.
$5,000 to Jewish Federation of Southern New
Jersey, Cherry Hill, NJ.
$1,000 to Gesu School, Philadelphia, PA.
$1,000 to Jewish Employment and Vocational
Service, Philadelphia, PA.
$1,000 to W H Y Y, Philadelphia, PA.

5394
Schwarz Foundation ✧
1163 Rte. 22 E.
Mountainside, NJ 07092

Established in 1982 in NJ.
Donors: Steven Schwarz; Henryk Schwarz;
Brooklawn Gardens, Inc.; East Rock Village, Inc.;
Hensyn, Inc.; Greenwood Gardens, Inc.; Oakwood
Homes, Inc.; Woodcliff, Inc.
Foundation type: Independent foundation.
Financial data (yr. ended 6/30/06): Assets,
$13,289,281 (L); gifts received, $490,000;
expenditures, $748,359; qualifying distributions,
$747,250; giving activities include $747,250 for 12
grants (high: $400,000; low: $250).
Purpose and activities: Giving primarily to Jewish
organizations, and federated giving programs.
Fields of interest: Museums (ethnic/folk arts);
Family services; Jewish federated giving programs;
Jewish agencies & temples.
Limitations: Applications not accepted. Giving
primarily in Washington, DC, NJ, and NY. No grants
to individuals.

Application information: Contributes only to
pre-selected organizations.
Officers: Steven Schwarz, Pres.; Henryk Schwarz,
Secy.
EIN: 222430208
Selected grants: The following grants were reported
in 2003.
$200,000 to American Society for Yad Vashem,
New York, NY. For unrestricted support.
$115,000 to UJA-Federation of New York, New York,
NY. For unrestricted support.
$60,000 to P.E.F. Israel Endowment Funds, New
York, NY. For unrestricted support.
$50,000 to American Friends of the Open University
of Israel, New York, NY. For unrestricted support.
$30,000 to United States Holocaust Memorial
Council, DC. For unrestricted support.
$2,000 to Anti-Defamation League of Bnai Brith,
New York, NY. For unrestricted support.
$2,000 to Simon Wiesenthal Center, New York, NY.
For unrestricted support.
$2,000 to World Jewish Congress American
Section, New York, NY. For unrestricted support.
$1,000 to Bnai Brith, New York, NY. For unrestricted
support.
$1,000 to Holocaust Resource Foundation, Short
Hills, NJ. For unrestricted support.

5395
George & Helen Segal Foundation ✧
136 Davidson's Mill Rd.
North Brunswick, NJ 08902
Contact: Susan Kutliroff, Secy.-Treas.
FAX: (732) 821-5877;
E-mail: segalfoundation@comcast.net; URL: http://
www.segalfoundation.org

Established in 2000 in NJ.
Donor: George Segal.
Foundation type: Independent foundation.
Financial data (yr. ended 6/30/05): Assets,
$15,007,274 (M); gifts received, $500;
expenditures, $944,713; qualifying distributions,
$713,000; giving activities include $663,000 for 2
grants (high: $650,000; low: $13,000), and
$50,000 for 10 grants to individuals (high: $5,000;
low: $5,000).
Purpose and activities: Giving to exhibit and display
the works of George Segal, and to award grants to
artists for the pursuit of their artistic endeavors.
Fields of interest: Museums (art).
Type of support: Grants to individuals.
Publications: Grants list; Informational brochure.
Application information:
Initial approach: Letter
Deadline(s): None
Board meeting date(s): Monthly
Officers: Helen Segal, Pres.; Rena Segal, V.P.;
Susan Kutliroff, Secy.-Treas.
Number of staff: 2 full-time professional.
EIN: 223744151
Selected grants: The following grants were reported
in 2003.
$650,000 to Jane Voorhees Zimmerli Art Museum,
New Brunswick, NJ.

5396
Norman and Barbara Seiden Foundation ✧
c/o Norman Seiden
1095 Cranbury S. River Rd., Ste. 18
Jamesburg, NJ 08831-3411

Established in 1973 in NJ.
Donors: Norman Seiden; Barbara Seiden; Mark Seiden.
Foundation type: Independent foundation.
Financial data (yr. ended 12/31/05): Assets, $11,037,937 (M); gifts received, $7,153; expenditures, $528,546; qualifying distributions, $447,150; giving activities include $447,150 for grants.
Purpose and activities: Giving primarily to Jewish agencies and temples; funding also for arts and culture, education, health associations, and human services.
Fields of interest: Arts; Education; Hospitals (general); Health organizations, association; Human services; Jewish federated giving programs; Jewish agencies & temples.
Limitations: Applications not accepted. Giving primarily in NJ and NY; some giving nationally. No grants to individuals.
Application information: Contributes only to pre-selected organizations.
Officers and Trustees: Norman Seiden,* Pres. and Treas.; Barbara Seiden,* V.P.; Mark Seiden,* V.P.; Stephen Seiden,* Secy.; Mildred Graye; Charles Klatskin; Pearl Seiden.
EIN: 237351938

5397
Thomas & Ruth Sharkey Family Foundation ✧
14 Commerce Dr.
Cranford, NJ 07016

Established in 2000 in NJ.
Donor: Bloody Forland, LP.
Foundation type: Independent foundation.
Financial data (yr. ended 12/31/04): Assets, $1,487,224 (M); expenditures, $446,306; qualifying distributions, $440,395; giving activities include $440,395 for 35 grants (high: $104,200; low: $100).
Fields of interest: Higher education; Education; Hospitals (general); Human services.
Limitations: Applications not accepted. Giving primarily in NJ. No grants to individuals.
Application information: Contributes only to pre-selected organizations.
Trustees: Ellen Delmauro; Ann McCormick; Edward D. Sharkey; Ruth Sharkey; Thomas J. Sharkey, Sr.; Thomas J. Sharkey, Jr.
EIN: 223693578

5398
The Shen Family Foundation ✧
c/o Cappiccille & Co.
615 W. Mt. Pleasant Ave.
Livingston, NJ 07039-1620

Established around 1994 in NY.
Donors: Theodore P. Shen; The Shen Family 2003 Charitable Lead Trust.
Foundation type: Independent foundation.
Financial data (yr. ended 12/31/05): Assets, $18,789,837 (M); gifts received, $1,505,000; expenditures, $814,205; qualifying distributions, $719,500; giving activities include $719,500 for 21 grants (high: $150,000; low: $1,000).
Purpose and activities: Giving primarily for the arts, and for education.

Fields of interest: Museums (art); Performing arts; Higher education; Education.
Limitations: Applications not accepted. Giving primarily in the New York, NY, area. No grants to individuals.
Application information: Contributes only to pre-selected organizations.
Trustees: Carla Shen; Theodore P. Shen.
EIN: 226627837

5399
Shepherd Foundation ✧
70 Grand Ave., Ste. 100
River Edge, NJ 07661

Established in 1988 in NJ.
Donor: Charles V. Schaefer, Jr.
Foundation type: Independent foundation.
Financial data (yr. ended 12/31/05): Assets, $25,746,450 (L); expenditures, $1,659,786; qualifying distributions, $1,186,900; giving activities include $1,186,900 for 88 grants (high: $225,000; low: $250).
Fields of interest: Performing arts; Higher education; Health care; Human services.
Limitations: Applications not accepted. Giving primarily in NJ; some funding nationally, particularly in New York, NY. No grants to individuals.
Application information: Contributes only to pre-selected organizations.
Officer and Trustees: Richard B. Passen,* Mgr.; Lynn S. Bovenizer; Charles V. Schaefer III.
EIN: 226460210
Selected grants: The following grants were reported in 2003.
$335,000 to Stevens Institute of Technology, Hoboken, NJ. 2 grants: $135,000, $200,000
$118,000 to Federation of Jewish Communities of the CIS and Baltic States, New York, NY. 2 grants: $75,000, $43,000
$70,000 to Lehigh University, Bethlehem, PA. 2 grants: $50,000, $20,000
$50,000 to Yale University, New Haven, CT.
$25,000 to Philharmonic-Symphony Society of New York, New York, NY.
$16,000 to Ramapo College Foundation, Mahwah, NJ.
$15,000 to Metropolitan Opera, New York, NY.

5400
Siemens Foundation ✧
170 Wood Ave. S.
Iselin, NJ 08830 (877) 822-5233
FAX: (732) 603-5890;
E-mail: foundation@sc.siemens.com; URL: http://www.siemens-foundation.org

Established in 1998 in NY.
Donor: Siemens Corp.
Foundation type: Company-sponsored foundation.
Financial data (yr. ended 9/30/03): Assets, $6,284,407 (L); gifts received, $3,782,333; expenditures, $3,766,058; qualifying distributions, $3,536,662; giving activities include $210,120 for 36 grants (high: $50,000; low: $1,000), and $452,676 for 120 grants to individuals (high: $103,000; low: $166).
Purpose and activities: The foundation supports programs designed to enhance secondary school math and science education.

Fields of interest: Secondary school/education; Mathematics; Science.
Limitations: Giving on a national basis.
Application information: Telephone calls, faxes, and E-mail messages are not encouraged. Application form required.
  Initial approach: Contact foundation for application form
  Deadline(s): Mar. 1
  Final notification: May 1
Officers and Directors: Albert Hoser,* Chair. and C.E.O.; Jack Bergen,* Pres.; Herb Carter, Exec. V.P.; Kevin Royer, Secy.; Klaus Stegemann, C.F.O.; Norbert Gaus; Oliver Hauck; Klaus Kleinfeld; Stan Kunka; Aubert Martin; Thomas N. McCausland; George Nolen; Roland Orchard; John Sanderson; Peter von Siemens; Randy Zwirn.
EIN: 522136074
Selected grants: The following grants were reported in 2003.
$50,000 to Center for Excellence in Education, Vienna, VA.
$36,330 to National Merit Scholarship Corporation, Evanston, IL.
$25,000 to Smithsonian Institution, DC.
$20,000 to Notre Dame University, Philippines. .
$15,950 to Carnegie Mellon University, Pittsburgh, PA.
$15,000 to Georgia Institute of Technology, Atlanta, GA.
$15,000 to Texas State University, San Marcos, TX.
$12,000 to University of Texas, Austin, TX.
$11,120 to Massachusetts Institute of Technology, Cambridge, MA.
$7,000 to Partnership for Americas Future, Akron, OH.

5401
Sierra Foundation, Inc. ✧
(formerly S. T. Grim Foundation)
33 Witherspoon St., 3rd Fl.
Princeton, NJ 08542
Contact: Martin J. Deitchman, Tr.

Established in 1994 in NJ.
Donors: Sierra Enterprises Group LLC; Andrew J. Schechtel; C. Fred Taylor.
Foundation type: Independent foundation.
Financial data (yr. ended 10/31/05): Assets, $13,587,455 (M); expenditures, $507,253; qualifying distributions, $462,200; giving activities include $462,200 for 10 grants (high: $175,000; low: $1,000; average: $1,000–$25,000).
Purpose and activities: Giving primarily for educational purposes, as well as to Jewish organizations.
Fields of interest: Education; Human services; Jewish agencies & temples.
Limitations: Applications not accepted. Giving primarily in NJ and NY. No grants to individuals.
Application information: Contributes only to pre-selected organizations.
Trustees: Martin J. Deitchman; Andrew J. Schechtel; Raquel Shechtel.
EIN: 223331554
Selected grants: The following grants were reported in 2003.
$2,500,000 to AISH New York, New York, NY. For general support.
$1,500,000 to Stanford University, Stanford, CA. For general support.
$180,000 to Johns Hopkins University, Baltimore, MD. For general support.

$25,000 to Yeshiva University, New York, NY. For general support.

5402
Curt C. & Else Silberman Foundation ✧
c/o Meisel & Tuteur
101 Eisenhower Pkwy.
Roseland, NJ 07068

Donor: Curt C. Silberman.
Foundation type: Independent foundation.
Financial data (yr. ended 6/30/05): Assets, $4,827,400 (M); gifts received, $705,487; expenditures, $3,695,887; qualifying distributions, $3,688,091; giving activities include $3,600,000 for 1 grant.
Fields of interest: Federated giving programs.
Limitations: Applications not accepted. Giving primarily in NJ and NY. No grants to individuals.
Application information: Unsolicited requests for funds not requested.
Officers and Trustees: * Peter Friedmann, Pres.; Evi Meinhardt,* Secy.; Herbert Tuteur,* Treas.; Debbie Friedmann; Edward Meinhardt.
EIN: 226065494

5403
The Rosanne H. Silbermann Foundation, Inc. ✧
23 Camelot Dr.
Livingston, NJ 07039
Contact: M. Steven Silbermann, Secy.-Treas.

Established in 1997 in NJ.
Donor: Rosanne H. Silbermann.
Foundation type: Independent foundation.
Financial data (yr. ended 12/31/05): Assets, $8,437,814 (M); expenditures, $415,767; qualifying distributions, $400,000; giving activities include $400,000 for 4 grants (high: $100,000; low: $100,000).
Purpose and activities: Giving for medical research.
Fields of interest: Hospitals (general).
Type of support: Grants to individuals; Continuing support; Research.
Limitations: Applications not accepted.
Officers: Rosanne H. Silbermann, Pres.; S. David Silbermann, V.P.; M. Steven Silbermann, Secy.-Treas.
EIN: 223578791
Selected grants: The following grants were reported in 2004.
$172,500 to Memorial Sloan-Kettering Cancer Center, New York, NY. 2 grants: $72,500 (For research), $100,000 (For research).
$100,000 to Albert Einstein College of Medicine of Yeshiva University, Bronx, NY. For research.
$100,000 to University of Pennsylvania, Philadelphia, PA. For research.
$100,000 to Weill Medical College of Cornell University, New York, NY. For research.
$50,000 to New York-Presbyterian Hospital, New York, NY. For building fund.

5404
Silver Mountain Foundation for the Arts ✧ ☆
c/o William E. Simon & Sons, Inc., LLC
P.O. Box 1913
Morristown, NJ 07962-1913
Contact: Donald Gummer, Tr.; M.S. Gummer, Tr.

Established in 1983.
Donors: Donald Gummer; Meryl S. Gummer.
Foundation type: Independent foundation.
Financial data (yr. ended 12/31/05): Assets, $3,315,248 (M); gifts received, $2,005,000; expenditures, $677,320; qualifying distributions, $666,000; giving activities include $666,000 for grants.
Purpose and activities: Giving primarily for the performing arts, environmental conservation and education.
Fields of interest: Performing arts; Performing arts, theater; Education; Environment, natural resources; Housing/shelter, development; International relief.
Limitations: Giving primarily in CT and NY. No loans or program-related investments.
Application information:
  Initial approach: Letter
  Deadline(s): None
Trustees: Donald Gummer; Meryl S. Gummer.
EIN: 133157286
Selected grants: The following grants were reported in 2004.
$30,000 to Poly Prep Country Day School, Brooklyn, NY.
$15,000 to Northwestern University, Evanston, IL.
$10,000 to Indiana University Foundation, Bloomington, IN.
$10,000 to Juvenile Diabetes Research Foundation International, New York, NY.
$10,000 to Massachusetts Museum of Contemporary Art, North Adams, MA.
$10,000 to Scenic Hudson, Poughkeepsie, NY.
$10,000 to Vassar College, Poughkeepsie, NY.
$5,000 to Museum of Fine Arts, Boston, MA.
$5,000 to New York Stage and Film, New York, NY.
$1,000 to Salisbury Association, Salisbury, CT.

5405
Cynthia L. & William E. Simon, Jr. Foundation ✧ ☆
310 South St.
P.O. Box 1913
Morristown, NJ 07962-1913
Application address: c/o William E. Simon and Sons, 10990 Wilshire Blvd., Ste. 500, Los Angeles, CA 90024

Established in 1994 in NJ.
Donor: William E. Simon Foundation, Inc.
Foundation type: Independent foundation.
Financial data (yr. ended 12/31/05): Assets, $243,628 (M); gifts received, $556,348; expenditures, $613,710; qualifying distributions, $527,178; giving activities include $527,178 for 51 grants (high: $50,000; low: $100).
Fields of interest: Human services; Children/youth, services; Christian agencies & churches; Roman Catholic agencies & churches.
Limitations: Giving primarily in CA.
Application information:
  Initial approach: Letter
  Deadline(s): None

Officer and Trustees: * Cynthia Simon,* Pres.; William E. Simon, Jr.
EIN: 133799555

5406
Herbert Smilowitz Private Foundation ✧
P.O. Box 511
East Rutherford, NJ 07073

Established in 1998 in NJ.
Donors: Herbert Smilowitz; Marilyn Smilowitz.
Foundation type: Independent foundation.
Financial data (yr. ended 12/31/04): Assets, $2,335,997 (M); gifts received, $423,900; expenditures, $348,731; qualifying distributions, $348,592; giving activities include $345,903 for 112 grants (high: $40,000; low: $20).
Fields of interest: Education; Human services; Jewish federated giving programs; Jewish agencies & temples.
Type of support: General/operating support.
Limitations: Applications not accepted. Giving primarily in NJ. No grants to individuals.
Application information: Contributes only to pre-selected organizations.
Trustees: Herbert Smilowitz; Marilyn Smilowitz.
EIN: 137171363
Selected grants: The following grants were reported in 2004.
$105,000 to Jewish Educational Center, Elizabeth, NJ. 2 grants: $100,000, $5,000
$40,000 to United Jewish Appeal, New York, NY.
$36,000 to Etzion Foundation, New York, NY.
$7,500 to Rabbinical Council of America, New York, NY. 2 grants: $5,000, $2,500
$5,000 to Rabbinical College of America, Morristown, NJ.
$500 to Mesivta of North Jersey, Newark, NJ.
$500 to YUSSR, New York, NY.
$100 to Tzedakah Vchesed, Brooklyn, NY.

5407
The Ian & Margaret Smith Family Foundation, Inc. ✧ ☆
c/o Merrill Lynch Trust Co.
P.O. Box 1525, MSC 06-03
Pennington, NJ 08534-1525

Established in 2001 in NY.
Donors: Ian Smith; A.J.C. Smith.
Foundation type: Independent foundation.
Financial data (yr. ended 12/31/05): Assets, $1,958,937 (M); expenditures, $511,643; qualifying distributions, $500,000; giving activities include $500,000 for grants.
Fields of interest: Museums (specialized); Performing arts, music.
Limitations: Applications not accepted. Giving primarily in New York, NY. No grants to individuals.
Application information: Contributes only to pre-selected organizations.
Officers: Ian Smith, Pres. and Treas.; Margaret Smith, V.P. and Secy.
Director: Joseph D. Salerno.
EIN: 134201730
Selected grants: The following grants were reported in 2004.
$50,000 to Charities Aid Foundation (CAF) America, Alexandria, VA. For general support.
$30,000 to Central Park Conservancy, New York, NY. For general support.

$25,000 to Museum of Scotland and Heritage Trust Foundation, New York, NY. For general support.

$25,000 to W N E T Channel 13, New York, NY. For general support.

5408

The Winthrop H. & Margaret D. Smith Family Foundation, Inc. ✧

(formerly The Winthrop H. Smith Family Foundation, Inc.)

c/o Merrill Lynch & Co., Inc.
100 Union Ave.
Cresskill, NJ 07626

Established in 1993 in DE.
Donor: Winthrop H. Smith, Jr.
Foundation type: Independent foundation.
Financial data (yr. ended 12/31/03): Assets, $5,758,407 (M); expenditures, $735,259; qualifying distributions, $696,806; giving activities include $684,750 for 26 grants (high: $210,000; low: $50; average: $100–$5,000).
Purpose and activities: Giving limited to the education of employees of Merrill Lynch & Co.
Fields of interest: Elementary/secondary education; Elementary school/education; Higher education.
Limitations: Applications not accepted. Giving primarily in CT, MA, NJ, and NY. No grants to individuals.
Application information: Contributes only to pre-selected organizations. Unsolicited requests for funds not accepted.
Officers: Winthrop H. Smith, Pres. and Treas.; Margaret D. Smith, V.P. and Secy.
EIN: 223267556
Selected grants: The following grants were reported in 2003.
$210,000 to Brunswick School, Greenwich, CT. For general operating support.
$165,000 to Deerfield Academy, Deerfield, MA. For general operating support.
$20,000 to Japan Society, New York, NY. For general operating support.
$20,000 to Wheaton College, Norton, MA. For general operating support.
$17,500 to Warren Education Fund, Warren, VT. For general operating support.
$5,000 to Amherst College, Amherst, MA. For general operating support.
$5,000 to Greenwich Teen Center, Greenwich, CT. For general operating support.
$5,000 to Vermont Ski Museum, Stowe, VT. For general operating support.
$1,000 to Vermont Land Trust, Montpelier, VT. For general operating support.
$500 to Greenwich Library, Greenwich, CT. For general operating support.

5409

The Matthew J. & Anne B. Smith Foundation ✧ ☆

P.O. Box 1525
Pennington, NJ 08534-1525

Established in 2001 in FL.
Donor: Matthew J. Smith.
Foundation type: Independent foundation.
Financial data (yr. ended 2/28/06): Assets, $4,775,235 (M); expenditures, $475,755;

qualifying distributions, $415,000; giving activities include $415,000 for grants.
Fields of interest: Human services; Residential/custodial care; hospices; Federated giving programs; Roman Catholic agencies & churches.
Type of support: General/operating support.
Limitations: Applications not accepted. Giving primarily in Vero Beach, FL. No grants to individuals.
Application information: Contributes only to pre-selected organizations.
Directors: Bryon T. Cooskey; Anne B. Smith; Matthew J. Smith; Regina Ward.
EIN: 020536250
Selected grants: The following grants were reported in 2006.
$50,000 to Hillsdale College, Hillsdale, MI.
$50,000 to Indian River Community College Foundation, Fort Pierce, FL.
$25,000 to Environmental Learning Center, Vero Beach, FL.
$20,000 to Hibiscus Childrens Center, Jensen Beach, FL.

5410

ST2 Foundation, Inc. ✧

33 Witherspoon St., 3rd Fl.
Princeton, NJ 08542

Established in 2000 in NJ.
Donor: Sierra Enterprises Group LLC.
Foundation type: Independent foundation.
Financial data (yr. ended 11/30/04): Assets, $29,773,755 (M); expenditures, $1,683,060; qualifying distributions, $1,680,000; giving activities include $1,680,000 for 4 grants (high: $1,000,000; low: $180,000).
Fields of interest: Law school/education; Jewish agencies & temples.
Limitations: Applications not accepted. Giving primarily in CA, and New York, NY. No grants to individuals.
Application information: Contributes only to pre-selected organizations.
Officers and Trustees:* Andrew J. Shechtel,* Pres.; Martin J. Deitchman, Secy.-Treas.; Raquel Shechtel.
EIN: 223766419
Selected grants: The following grants were reported in 2003.
$750,000 to UJA-Federation of New York, New York, NY. For general support.
$500,000 to American Committee for the Weizmann Institute of Science, New York, NY. For general support.
$200,000 to University of California at Santa Cruz Foundation, Santa Cruz, CA. For general support.
$50,000 to Legal Aid Society of San Mateo County, San Mateo, CA. For general support.
$50,000 to Quest Scholars Program, Palo Alto, CA. For general support.
$25,000 to FOCUS Hispanic Center for Community Development, Newark, NJ. For general support.
$15,000 to Businesses United in Investing, Lending and Development (BUILD), Menlo Park, CA. For general support.

5411

The David S. and Sylvia Steiner Charitable Trust ✧

75 Eisenhower Pkwy.
Roseland, NJ 07068-1697 (973) 228-5800
Contact: David S. Steiner, Tr.

Established in 1986 in NJ.
Donor: David S. Steiner.
Foundation type: Independent foundation.
Financial data (yr. ended 12/31/05): Assets, $1,156,434 (M); expenditures, $810,626; qualifying distributions, $787,958; giving activities include $786,208 for 128 grants (high: $203,250; low: $20).
Fields of interest: Higher education; Jewish agencies & temples.
Limitations: Giving primarily in Washington, DC, NJ, and New York, NY. No grants to individuals.
Application information:
Initial approach: Brief proposal
Deadline(s): None
Trustees: David S. Steiner; Sylvia Steiner.
EIN: 226423709
Selected grants: The following grants were reported in 2004.
$200,000 to National Yiddish Book Center, Amherst, MA. For unrestricted support.
$125,100 to American Israel Education Foundation (AIEF), DC. For unrestricted support.
$122,150 to United Jewish Appeal of Metrowest, Whippany, NJ. For unrestricted support.
$100,000 to Brooklyn Academy of Music, Brooklyn, NY. For unrestricted support.
$50,000 to Progressive Policy Institute, DC. For unrestricted support.
$50,000 to William J. Clinton Presidential Foundation, New York, NY. For unrestricted support.
$25,250 to New Jersey Performing Arts Center, Newark, NJ. For unrestricted support.
$18,000 to Israel Policy Forum, New York, NY. For unrestricted support.
$15,000 to Actors Fund of America, New York, NY. For unrestricted support.
$2,500 to Paper Mill Playhouse, Millburn, NJ. For unrestricted support.

5412

The Stern Family Foundation ✧

1000 E. Park Blvd.
Cranbury, NJ 08512-3507
Contact: A. Joseph Stern, Pres.

Established in 1983 in NJ.
Donors: A. Joseph Stern; Eli Stern; Feldberg Family Foundation; Frieda Stern.
Foundation type: Independent foundation.
Financial data (yr. ended 12/31/05): Assets, $11,818 (M); gifts received, $2,915,860; expenditures, $2,822,755; qualifying distributions, $2,821,360; giving activities include $2,821,360 for 175 grants (high: $478,400; low: $100).
Purpose and activities: Giving primarily to Jewish agencies and temples and yeshivas.
Fields of interest: Elementary/secondary education; Jewish federated giving programs; Jewish agencies & temples.
Application information:
Initial approach: Letter
Deadline(s): None
Trustee: A. Joseph Stern.
EIN: 222495169
Selected grants: The following grants were reported in 2003.
$475,800 to Bais Medrash.
$10,000 to Bais Medrash Ateres Yisroel, Lawrence, NY.
$9,000 to Talmudical Yeshiva of Philadelphia, Philadelphia, PA.

$1,800 to Keren Aniyim, Brooklyn, NY.

$1,800 to Ner Israel Rabbinical College, Baltimore, MD.

$1,800 to Yeshiva Tiferes Boruch, New York, NY.

$1,300 to Yeshiva Gedola of Passaic-Talmudic Research Center, Passaic, NJ.

$500 to Young Israel of West Hempstead, West Hempstead, NY.

$250 to Congregation Ohr Torah, Monsey, NY.

$180 to Yad Yisroel, Brooklyn, NY.

5413

The Daniel E. and Joyce G. Straus Family Foundation ✧

(formerly The Daniel E. Straus Family Foundation)
173 Bridge Plaza N.
Fort Lee, NJ 07024

Established in 1996 in NJ.
Donors: Daniel E. Straus; Joyce G. Straus.
Foundation type: Independent foundation.
Financial data (yr. ended 9/30/05): Assets, $5,056,089 (M); gifts received, $2,500,000; expenditures, $434,780; qualifying distributions, $414,419; giving activities include $412,627 for 45 grants (high: $200,000; low: $50).
Purpose and activities: Giving primarily to Jewish agencies; funding also for higher education, including a law school.
Fields of interest: Higher education; Law school/education; Education; Human services; Jewish federated giving programs; Jewish agencies & temples.
Limitations: Applications not accepted. No grants to individuals.
Application information: Contributes only to pre-selected organizations.
Officers and Director:* Daniel E. Straus,* Pres.; Joyce G. Straus, V.P.; Moshael J. Straus, Secy.-Treas.
EIN: 133913231
Selected grants: The following grants were reported in 2005.
$12,500 to EDAH, New York, NY.
$10,000 to Yad Eliezer, Brooklyn, NY.
$2,500 to Jewish Family Services.
$1,800 to National Jewish Outreach Program, New York, NY.
$1,800 to Sinai Special Needs Institute, Teaneck, NJ.
$1,000 to American Friends of Nishmat, New York, NY.
$1,000 to Frisch School, Paramus, NJ.
$850 to Institute for Educational Advancement, South Pasadena, CA.
$750 to Etzion Foundation, New York, NY.
$500 to Torah Academy of Bergen County, Teaneck, NJ.

5414

The Zahava and Moshael J. Straus Family Foundation ✧

173 Bridge Plaza N.
Fort Lee, NJ 07024

Established in 1996 in NJ.
Donors: Moshael J. Straus; Zahava Straus.
Foundation type: Independent foundation.
Financial data (yr. ended 9/30/05): Assets, $2,035,280 (L); gifts received, $500,000; expenditures, $770,943; qualifying distributions,

$763,517; giving activities include $761,830 for 29 grants (high: $225,000; low: $500).
Purpose and activities: Giving primarily to Jewish higher education, and to Jewish agencies and temples.
Fields of interest: Elementary/secondary education; Higher education, university; Jewish agencies & temples.
Limitations: Applications not accepted. Giving primarily in NJ and NY. No grants to individuals.
Application information: Contributes only to pre-selected organizations.
Officers and Director:* Moshael J. Straus,* Pres.; Zahava Straus, V.P.; Daniel E. Straus, Secy.-Treas.
EIN: 133913229
Selected grants: The following grants were reported in 2005.
$225,000 to Yeshiva University, New York, NY.
$37,500 to Barnard College, New York, NY.
$36,800 to Mesorah Heritage Foundation, Brooklyn, NY.
$18,000 to Moriah School of Englewood, Englewood, NJ.
$15,000 to Riverdale Jewish Center, Bronx, NY.
$12,000 to Orthodox Caucus, Cedarhurst, NY.
$6,250 to EDAH, New York, NY.
$1,000 to Etzion Foundation, New York, NY.
$1,000 to Yeshiva Ohr Hatalmud of Englewood, Englewood, NJ.
$500 to Young Israel of West Hempstead, West Hempstead, NY.

5415

Subaru of America Foundation, Inc. ✧

c/o Mgr.
P.O. Box 6000
Cherry Hill, NJ 08034-6000 (856) 488-5099
E-mail: foundation@subaru.com; URL: http://www.subaru.com/common/about/community/index.jsp

Established in 1984 in NJ.
Donor: Subaru of America, Inc.
Foundation type: Company-sponsored foundation.
Financial data (yr. ended 12/31/05): Assets, $1,891,423 (M); gifts received, $300,000; expenditures, $434,887; qualifying distributions, $434,494; giving activities include $386,215 for 29 grants (high: $100,000; low: $1,000), and $48,279 for 395 employee matching gifts.
Purpose and activities: The foundation supports K-12 programs designed to promote positive attitudes toward learning; encourage development of skills that will help children and youth succeed in school; promote positive attitudes, understanding, and appreciation for the diverse society in which we live; and provide professional training and development for teachers.
Fields of interest: Elementary/secondary education.
Type of support: General/operating support; Program development; Employee matching gifts; Employee-related scholarships.
Limitations: Giving limited to areas of company operations, with emphasis on the Aurora, CO, Austell, GA, Itasca, IL, Cherry Hill and Westhampton, NJ, and Portland, OR, areas. No support for organizations with fund balances exceeding $5 million, veterans', fraternal, or labor organizations, government agencies, churches or religious or sectarian organizations, social, membership, or other organizations not of direct benefit to the entire community, political organizations, discriminatory

organizations, or national organizations. No grants to individuals (except for employee-related scholarships), or for advertising, special events sponsorships, tables or athletic campaigns, or capital campaigns; no vehicle donations.
Publications: Application guidelines.
Application information: Application form not required.
   Initial approach: Letter of inquiry or complete online application form
   Deadline(s): Jan. 31 and Aug. 31
   Board meeting date(s): Twice per year
   Final notification: May and Dec.
Officers and Trustees:* Kunio Ishigami,* Pres.; Joseph T. Scharff,* Secy.-Treas.; Daniel Dalton; Thomas Doll; Sheila Galluci-Davis; Hidetoshi Kobayashi.
EIN: 222531774

5416

The Sudler Foundation ✧

(formerly The Samuel and Claire Sudler Charitable Trust)
1 Morris Corporate Ctr.
300 Interpace Pkwy., Bldg. C
Parsippany, NJ 07054-1100 (973) 257-0700
Contact: Claire Sudler, Tr.

Established in 1986 in NJ.
Donors: Samuel Sudler†; Claire E. Sudler.
Foundation type: Independent foundation.
Financial data (yr. ended 12/31/05): Assets, $1,692,001 (M); gifts received, $408,000; expenditures, $558,079; qualifying distributions, $556,600; giving activities include $555,800 for 21 grants (high: $270,000; low: $100).
Fields of interest: Higher education; Law school/education; Health care; Human services; Jewish federated giving programs.
Type of support: Continuing support; Annual campaigns; Building/renovation; Equipment; Emergency funds; Research; Program-related investments/loans.
Limitations: Giving primarily in NJ and NY. No support for private foundations. No grants to individuals; or for administrative expenses.
Application information: Application form not required.
   Initial approach: Proposal
   Copies of proposal: 1
   Deadline(s): None
Trustees: Claire Sudler; Peter Sudler.
EIN: 226423710

5417

The Summit Area Public Foundation

P.O. Box 867
Summit, NJ 07902-0867 (908) 277-1422
Contact: For grants: Joanne McDonough, Dir.
FAX: (908) 277-3043; E-mail: barbunt@aol.com; Grant information E-mail: Joanne.MCD@att.net

Established in 1972 in NJ.
Foundation type: Community foundation.
Financial data (yr. ended 12/31/04): Assets, $10,050,038 (M); gifts received, $274,969; expenditures, $775,300; giving activities include $709,411 for 189 grants (high: $100,000; low: $32).
Purpose and activities: The foundation seeks to assist, encourage, and promote well-being of

mankind, and to benefit the inhabitants of Summit, NJ, and the surrounding area.

Fields of interest: Education; Cancer research; Children, services; Community development; Disabilities, people with.

Type of support: Emergency funds; Conferences/seminars; Building/renovation; Equipment; Program development; Seed money; Scholarship funds; Technical assistance; Employee matching gifts; Matching/challenge support.

Limitations: Giving limited to the Summit, NJ, area. No support for religious organizations. No grants to individuals (except for scholarships).

Publications: Application guidelines; Informational brochure.

Application information: Application form required.

Initial approach: Letter
Copies of proposal: 10
Deadline(s): Feb. 15 and Sept. 15
Board meeting date(s): Quarterly
Final notification: June and Dec.

Officers and Directors:* John W. Cooper,* Pres.; Alexander F. Wilhelm,* V.P.; Lyle Brehm,* Secy.; Barbara E. Bunting,* Treas.; Steve Ford; Eugene Fox; Wendy Graeb; Linda B. Hander; Cary Hardy; Michael Helmer; Thomas Inglesby; Virginia Jordan; Julie Keenan; Joanne McDonough; Henry M. Ogden; Sarah Rosen; Christina Whitman.

EIN: 221948007

5418

Sunfield Foundation, Inc. ✦

P.O. Box 845
Red Bank, NJ   07701   (732) 219-8686
Contact: Linda Wiseman, Pres.
FAX: (732) 219-8648; *E-mail:* sunfieldfdn@usa.net

Incorporated in 1992 in NJ.

Foundation type: Independent foundation.

Financial data (yr. ended 12/31/05): Assets, $3,736,941 (M); expenditures, $1,141,392; qualifying distributions, $1,084,337; giving activities include $1,084,337 for 46 grants (high: $67,838; low: $4,135).

Purpose and activities: To further the availability of education, to enhance the lives of others through human service organizations, and to support and encourage interest in the arts and historic preservation.

Fields of interest: Museums; Performing arts, theater; Performing arts, music; Historic preservation/historical societies; Arts; Education; Health care; Human services.

Type of support: Building/renovation; Equipment; Program development; Matching/challenge support.

Limitations: Giving limited to Barnstable, Middlesex, and Suffolk counties, MA, and Monmouth and Ocean counties, NJ. No grants for general capital campaigns, continuing operating support, operating deficits, or for mortgages or debt retirement; no loans and no multi-year funding.

Publications: Application guidelines; Program policy statement.

Application information: Application form required.

Initial approach: Letter, telephone or e-mail
Copies of proposal: 1
Deadline(s): May 1 and Nov. 1
Board meeting date(s): May and Nov.
Final notification: 10 days following board meeting; funding starts 3 weeks after notification

Officers and Directors:* Linda Wiseman,* Pres.; William H. White,* Treas.; Ann B. White; William F. Wiseman.

EIN: 521800049

Selected grants: The following grants were reported in 2003.

$50,000 to Boston Urban Youth Foundation, Boston, MA. For two vans.

$35,320 to Aslan Youth Ministries, Red Bank, NJ. For computers.

$30,000 to Red Bank Charter School, Red Bank, NJ. For science lab equipment.

$22,325 to Recording for the Blind and Dyslexic, Cambridge, MA. For digital audio textbook for schools.

$20,000 to New Jersey Repertory Company, Long Branch, NJ. For equipment.

$19,750 to Monmouth University, West Long Branch, NJ. For theater upgrades.

$19,500 to Family Resource Associates, Shrewsbury, NJ. For equipment.

$17,800 to Emmanuel Gospel Center, Boston, MA. For capital campaign.

$13,000 to West Side Community Center, Asbury Park, NJ. For equipment and field trips.

$11,000 to Boston Chinatown Neighborhood Center, Boston, MA. For furnishings for two classrooms.

5419

Sunup Foundation, Inc. ✦ ☆

c/o J.H. Cohn, LLP
997 Lenox Dr., Bldg. 3
Lawrenceville, NJ   08648
Application address: c/o Edward C. Taylor, Pres., 288 Western Way, Princeton, NJ 08540

Established in 1999 in NJ.

Donors: Edward C. Taylor; Virginia C. Taylor.

Foundation type: Operating foundation.

Financial data (yr. ended 12/31/05): Assets, $329,340 (M); gifts received, $800,000; expenditures, $504,840; qualifying distributions, $502,500; giving activities include $502,500 for 3 grants (high: $400,000; low: $2,500).

Fields of interest: Media, radio; Environment.

Type of support: General/operating support.

Limitations: Giving primarily in WA and VT. No grants to individuals.

Application information:

Initial approach: Letter
Deadline(s): None

Officers: Edward C. Taylor, Pres.; Virginia C. Taylor, Treas.

Directors: Richard Spielman; Susan Spielman; Connie Taylor; Edward N. Taylor.

EIN: 223693832

5420

The Joseph & Eileen Sutton Foundation, Inc. ✦

115 Kennedy Dr.
Sayreville, NJ   08872

Established in 1999 in NJ.

Donors: E.S. Sutton, Inc.; Sutton Warehousing, Inc.; Hi-Rollers Sportswear; Extra Sportswear; E.S. Sutton Sales Corp.

Foundation type: Independent foundation.

Financial data (yr. ended 12/31/03): Assets, $4,059,292 (M); gifts received, $675,000;

expenditures, $326,808; qualifying distributions, $326,808; giving activities include $324,863 for 57 grants (high: $50,000; low: $25).

Purpose and activities: Giving primarily for Jewish agencies, temples, and yeshivas.

Fields of interest: Elementary/secondary education; Jewish agencies & temples.

Limitations: Applications not accepted. Giving primarily in NJ and NY. No grants to individuals.

Application information: Contributes only to pre-selected organizations.

Officer: Joseph Sutton, Chair.

Trustees: Albert J. Sutton; Eileen Sutton.

EIN: 223556524

Selected grants: The following grants were reported in 2004.

$48,418 to Yeshiva of Flatbush, Brooklyn, NY. 2 grants: $7,000, $41,418

$25,000 to Yeshiva Ktana of Passaic, Passaic, NJ. 2 grants: $10,000, $15,000

$10,000 to Mesivta of Long Beach, Long Beach, NY.

$10,000 to Yeshiva Ohr Hatalmud of Englewood, Englewood, NJ.

$7,500 to Bais Yaakov Academy.

$1,000 to Sephardic Bikur Holim, Brooklyn, NY.

$301 to Ohel Yaacob Congregation, Deal, NJ.

$100 to Colel Chabad, Brooklyn, NY.

5421

Sweetfeet Foundation, Inc. ✦

c/o Kenneth J. Slutsky
65 Livingston Ave.
Roseland, NJ   07068

Established in 1993 in NJ.

Donors: Andrew J. Shechtel; Stone Holdings LLC.

Foundation type: Independent foundation.

Financial data (yr. ended 11/30/04): Assets, $26,344,795 (M); expenditures, $1,288,400; qualifying distributions, $1,282,320; giving activities include $1,282,320 for 6 grants (high: $500,000; low: $100,000).

Fields of interest: Media/communications; Education; International affairs, goodwill promotion; International conflict resolution; Jewish agencies & temples.

International interests: Israel; Middle East.

Limitations: Applications not accepted. Giving primarily in Washington, DC; giving also in New York, NY and in PA. No grants to individuals.

Application information: Contributes only to pre-selected organizations.

Officers and Trustees:* Kenneth J. Slutsky,* Pres. and Treas.; Allen Levithan,* V.P. and Secy.; John L. Berger,* V.P.; Stone Holdings LLC.

EIN: 223271692

Selected grants: The following grants were reported in 2003.

$635,000 to The Israel Project, Arlington, VA. For general support.

$450,000 to Auerbach Central Agency for Jewish Education, Melrose Park, PA. For general support.

$250,000 to Tel Aviv University, Tel Aviv, Israel. For general support.

5422

Sy Syms Foundation ✦

Syms Way
Secaucus, NJ   07094

Established in 1985 in NJ.
Donor: Sy Syms.
Foundation type: Independent foundation.
Financial data (yr. ended 4/30/05): Assets, $30,149,098 (M); expenditures, $1,612,970; qualifying distributions, $1,488,450; giving activities include $1,488,400 for 151 grants (high: $500,000; low: $500).
Purpose and activities: Support for Jewish welfare and other Jewish organizations, including those in Israel; grants also for higher education.
Fields of interest: Arts; Higher education; Education; Human services; Jewish federated giving programs; Jewish agencies & temples.
International interests: Israel.
Type of support: General/operating support; Scholarship funds.
Limitations: Applications not accepted. Giving primarily in the U.S.; some giving also in Israel. No grants to individuals.
Application information: Contributes only to pre-selected organizations.
Trustees: Marcy Syms Merns; Sy Syms.
EIN: 222617727

5423
Jane and Tom Tang Foundation for Education, Inc. ✧ ☆
c/o Tom Tang
800 Palisades Ave., Ste. 23C
Fort Lee, NJ   07024

Established in 2000 in NJ.
Donor: Tom Y.C. Tang.
Foundation type: Operating foundation.
Financial data (yr. ended 12/31/05): Assets, $54,974 (M); gifts received, $44,960; expenditures, $394,800; qualifying distributions, $394,800; giving activities include $323,610 for 10 grants (high: $209,100; low: $500), and $65,311 for 3 grants to individuals (high: $27,918; low: $13,393).
Fields of interest: Higher education.
International interests: China.
Type of support: Program development; Scholarship funds.
Limitations: Applications not accepted. Giving primarily in China; giving also in the U.S.
Application information: Contributes only to pre-selected organizations.
Trustees: Edwin C. Landis, Jr.; Carl Schwartz; Jane Y. Tang; Tom Y.C. Tang.
EIN: 223693816

5424
The Henry and Marilyn Taub Foundation ▼ ✧
c/o Wiss & Co., LLP
354 Eisenhower Pkwy.
Livingston, NJ   07039

Established in 1967 in DE.
Donors: Henry Taub; Endowment Foundation of UJA Federation of Bergen County & North Hudson.
Foundation type: Independent foundation.
Financial data (yr. ended 12/31/04): Assets, $137,829,372 (M); gifts received, $4,700,000; expenditures, $6,979,523; qualifying distributions, $5,939,285; giving activities include $5,819,880 for 137 grants (high: $1,515,000; low: $10; average: $100–$500,000).

Purpose and activities: Grants largely for Jewish welfare funds; some support for higher and other education, social service and youth agencies, and hospitals.
Fields of interest: Higher education; Education; Hospitals (general); Human services; Children/youth, services; Jewish federated giving programs; Jewish agencies & temples.
Limitations: Applications not accepted. Giving primarily in NJ. No grants to individuals.
Application information: Contributes only to pre-selected organizations.
Officers and Directors:* Henry Taub,* Chair.; Fred S. Lafer,* Pres. and Treas.; Marilyn Taub,* V.P. and Secy.; Judith Gold; Ira Taub; Steven Taub.
EIN: 226100525
Selected grants: The following grants were reported in 2004.
$1,515,000 to American Society for Technion-Israel Institute of Technology, New York, NY.
$1,170,000 to Columbia University, College of Physicians and Surgeons, New York, NY.
$1,035,000 to American Jewish Joint Distribution Committee, New York, NY.
$787,000 to New York University, New York, NY. 3 grants: $175,000 to Skirball Department of Hebrew and Judiac Studies, $537,000 to Taub Center for Israeli Studies, $75,000 to Taub Urban Research Center
$500,000 to Jewish Community Center on the Palisades, Tenafly, NJ. For auditorium project.
$92,442 to William Paterson University of New Jersey, Wayne, NJ. For Teachers for Tomorrow.
$70,000 to American Friends of Bar-Ilan University, New York, NY.
$10,000 to Washington Institute for Near East Policy, DC.

5425
Joseph and Arlene Taub Foundation ✧
c/o Wiss & Co., LLP
354 Eisenhower Pkwy.
Livingston, NJ   07039

Established in 1968 in DE.
Donors: Joseph Taub; Sylvia Gorelick†.
Foundation type: Independent foundation.
Financial data (yr. ended 12/31/05): Assets, $14,619,258 (M); gifts received, $1,000,000; expenditures, $869,891; qualifying distributions, $566,554; giving activities include $554,304 for 41 + grants (high: $146,200).
Purpose and activities: Primary support for Jewish welfare funds and temple support, and health care.
Fields of interest: Education; Hospitals (specialty); Health organizations, association; Medical research, institute; Human services; Jewish federated giving programs; Jewish agencies & temples.
Type of support: General/operating support; Endowments.
Limitations: Applications not accepted. Giving primarily in NJ, and New York, NY. No grants to individuals.
Application information: Contributes only to pre-selected organizations.
Officers and Directors:* Joseph Taub,* Pres.; Fred S. Lafer, Secy.-Treas.; Arlene Taub,* Treas.
EIN: 226104545
Selected grants: The following grants were reported in 2005.
$30,000 to United Jewish Appeal, New York, NY.

$10,000 to Hospital for Special Surgery, New York, NY.
$10,000 to Project Pride, Newark, NJ.
$2,425 to Chemotherapy Foundation, New York, NY.
$1,000 to American Friends of the Hebrew University, New York, NY.
$1,000 to American Jewish Committee, New York, NY.
$1,000 to Childrens Blood Foundation, New York, NY.
$394 to Museum of Modern Art, New York, NY.
$335 to Jewish Guild for the Blind, New York, NY.

5426
Tavitian Foundation, Inc. ✧
c/o Syncsort Inc.
50 Tice Blvd.
Woodcliff Lake, NJ   07677

Established in 1995 in NJ.
Donor: Assadour Tavitian.
Foundation type: Independent foundation.
Financial data (yr. ended 12/31/05): Assets, $27,772,616 (M); gifts received, $15,000,000; expenditures, $726,887; qualifying distributions, $658,096; giving activities include $267,170 for 31 grants (high: $62,000; low: $100), and $383,345 for 12 grants to individuals (high: $103,474; low: $6,000).
Purpose and activities: Giving primarily for higher education, including scholarships, with a preference given to persons of Armenian and Eastern European descent; some support also for the arts.
Fields of interest: Arts; Higher education.
Type of support: Program development; Scholarship funds; Research; Scholarships—to individuals.
Limitations: Applications not accepted. Giving on a national and international basis.
Application information: Foundation approaches potential awardees through contact with professors who recommend a recipient.
Officers: Assadour Tavitian, Pres.; Joyce Barsam, V.P.; David Oifer, Secy.
EIN: 521939275
Selected grants: The following grants were reported in 2003.
$262,080 to Austin Riggs Center, Stockbridge, MA.
$64,500 to Berkshire Theater Festival, Stockbridge, MA.
$7,500 to Berkshire Opera Company, Pittsfield, MA.
$5,000 to Berkshire South Regional Community Center, Stockbridge, MA.
$2,500 to Trustees of Reservations, Beverly, MA. For Charles Eliot Society.
$1,500 to Chesterwood, Stockbridge, MA.
$1,500 to Close Encounters with Music, Great Barrington, MA.
$1,000 to Barrington Stage Company, Sheffield, MA.
$100 to Berkshire County Historical Society, Herman Melvilles Arrowhead, Pittsfield, MA.

5427
The Thomas Charitable Foundation ✧ ☆
c/o John C. Pretto & Karen Kriendler Nelson
P.O. Box 93
Berkeley Heights, NJ   07922

Established in 1997 in CT.
Donor: Wilmer J. Thomas, Jr.
Foundation type: Independent foundation.

Financial data (yr. ended 12/31/05): Assets, $715,050 (M); gifts received, $1,750; expenditures, $571,918; qualifying distributions, $548,075; giving activities include $548,075 for 40 grants (high: $250,000; low: $50).
Purpose and activities: Giving primarily for the arts, including the enrichment and encouragement of promising careers of exceptionally talented native-born or naturalized American opera singers; funding also for cancer research.
Fields of interest: Performing arts centers; Performing arts, opera; Arts; Environment, natural resources; Cancer research.
Type of support: General/operating support; Grants to individuals.
Limitations: Applications not accepted. Giving primarily in New York, NY; some funding nationally.
Application information: Unsolicited requests for funds not accepted.
Officer: Karen Kriendler Nelson, Exec. Dir.
Trustees: William D. Porteous; Douglas D. Thomas; Wilmer J. Thomas, Jr.
Number of staff: 1 full-time professional; 1 part-time professional.
EIN: 066444610
Selected grants: The following grants were reported in 2004.
$350,000 to Metropolitan Opera Association, New York, NY. 2 grants: $300,000, $50,000
$250,000 to Santa Fe Opera, Santa Fe, NM. 2 grants: $200,000, $50,000
$50,000 to Seattle Opera, Seattle, WA.
$20,000 to Boston Symphony Orchestra, Boston, MA.
$20,000 to Lady Bird Johnson Wildflower Center, Austin, TX. 2 grants: $10,000 each
$12,500 to Scenic Hudson, Poughkeepsie, NY.
$10,000 to Garden Conservancy, Cold Spring, NY.

5428
Gary & Tamar Tolchin Foundation, Inc. ✧ ☆
c/o Gary Tolchin
10 Black Walnut Way
Marlboro, NJ 07746

Established in 1997 in NJ.
Donor: Gary Tolchin.
Foundation type: Independent foundation.
Financial data (yr. ended 9/30/05): Assets, $2,079,842 (M); expenditures, $399,248; qualifying distributions, $378,937; giving activities include $373,712 for 156 grants (high: $75,000; low: $20).
Fields of interest: Performing arts, theater; Arts; Education, early childhood education; Environment; Health care; Substance abuse, treatment; Cancer research; Food banks; Human services; Jewish federated giving programs; Jewish agencies & temples.
Limitations: Applications not accepted. Giving primarily in NY and NJ. No grants to individuals.
Application information: Contributes only to pre-selected organizations.
Officers: Gary Tolchin, Pres. and Treas.; Tamar Tolchin, V.P. and Secy.; Sam Tolchin, V.P.
EIN: 133986712

5429
The Tuchman Foundation, Inc. ✧
211 College Rd. E., 3rd Fl.
Princeton, NJ 08540-6623

Established in 1996 in NJ.
Donor: Martin Tuchman.
Foundation type: Independent foundation.
Financial data (yr. ended 12/31/04): Assets, $1,397,287 (M); gifts received, $313,970; expenditures, $351,289; qualifying distributions, $345,376; giving activities include $339,484 for 8 + grants (high: $269,890).
Purpose and activities: Giving primarily for health associations.
Fields of interest: Health organizations, association; Medical research, institute; Science.
Type of support: General/operating support.
Officer: Martin Tuchman, Mgr.
Trustees: Herbert Tuchman; Margaret Tuchman.
EIN: 226682754

5430
The Turock Family Foundation ✧ ☆
P.O. Box 244
Cedar Grove, NJ 07009
Contact: David L. Turock, Tr.

Established in 1998 in NJ.
Foundation type: Independent foundation.
Financial data (yr. ended 12/31/04): Assets, $4,938,453 (M); expenditures, $333,559; qualifying distributions, $340,880; giving activities include $338,207 for 15 grants (high: $124,827; low: $932).
Fields of interest: Libraries (public); Education; Cancer; Human services; Christian agencies & churches.
Application information: Application form required.
Initial approach: Letter
Deadline(s): None
Trustees: David L. Turock; Nancy G. Turock.
EIN: 223758083
Selected grants: The following grants were reported in 2004.
$30,000 to Keystone College, La Plume, PA.
$14,448 to Children, Inc., Richmond, VA.
$2,000 to Children International, Kansas City, MO.
$1,000 to Fountain House, New York, NY.
$1,000 to University of Pennsylvania, Philadelphia, PA.
$932 to Compassion International, Colorado Springs, CO.

5431
Turrell Fund ▼
21 Van Vleck St.
Montclair, NJ 07042-2358 (973) 783-9358
Contact: Curtland E. Fields, Exec. Dir.
FAX: (973) 783-9283; E-mail: turrell@turrellfund.org;
URL: http://foundationcenter.org/grantmaker/turrell/

Incorporated in 1935 in NJ.
Donors: Herbert Turrell†; Margaret Turrell†.
Foundation type: Independent foundation.
Financial data (yr. ended 12/31/05): Assets, $128,974,219 (M); expenditures, $9,896,278; qualifying distributions, $9,313,582; giving activities include $8,335,442 for 309 grants (high:

$350,000; low: $1,000; average: $5,000–$50,000).
Purpose and activities: Grants to organizations dedicated to service or care of children and youth under 12 years of age, with emphasis on the needy, and the disadvantaged.
Fields of interest: Education, early childhood education; Education; Crime/violence prevention, youth; Human services; Children/youth, services; Economically disadvantaged.
Type of support: General/operating support; Continuing support; Capital campaigns; Building/renovation; Equipment; Program development; Seed money; Scholarship funds; Matching/challenge support.
Limitations: Giving limited to Essex, Union, Hudson and Passaic counties, NJ, and VT. No support for advocacy work, most hospital work, or health delivery services; generally no support for cultural activities. No grants to individuals, or for endowment funds, conferences, or research; no loans.
Publications: Annual report (including application guidelines); Financial statement; Grants list.
Application information: No proposals are to be faxed or sent by e-mail. Organizations applying to the fund for the first time should submit written travel instructions (or a map) along with the proposal in order to facilitate a possible site visit. Application form not required.
Initial approach: Proposal
Copies of proposal: 1
Deadline(s): Feb. 1 and Aug. 1.
Board meeting date(s): May and Nov. and/or Dec.
Final notification: Late June and Dec.
Officers and Trustees:* S. Lawrence Prendergast,* Chair.; Curtland E. Fields, Secy. and Exec. Dir.; Sonyia Woloshyn, Treas.; Robert E. Angelica; Elizabeth W. Christie; Ann G. Dinse; Rev. William S. Gannon; Julia A. Miller; Rev. John P. Mitchell; E. Belvin Williams, Ph.D.
Number of staff: 2 full-time professional; 2 full-time support.
EIN: 221551936
Selected grants: The following grants were reported in 2005.
$250,000 to North Ward Center, Newark, NJ. For capital support for the Fine Arts Pavilion.
$250,000 to YMCA of Montclair, Montclair, NJ. For capital support for family center.
$200,000 to Saint Philips Academy, Newark, NJ. For capital support.
$175,000 to Saint Benedicts Preparatory School, Newark, NJ. For financial aid and operating support.
$100,000 to New Jersey Performing Arts Center, Newark, NJ. For summer youth programs.
$75,000 to Boys and Girls Clubs of Newark, Newark, NJ. For program support.
$25,000 to Ironbound Community Corporation, Newark, NJ. For after-school and enrichment programs.
$25,000 to Princeton-Blairstown Center, Princeton, NJ. For program support for Essex County students.
$23,000 to Orchard Valley School, East Montpelier, VT. For program and capital support.
$15,000 to New Jersey Historical Society, Newark, NJ. For trustee grant for general operating support.

5432

Twin Chimney, Inc. ✧
80 Westcott Rd.
Princeton, NJ 08540

Established in 1986 in NJ.

Donors: F. Helmut Weymar; Caroline Weymar.
Foundation type: Independent foundation.
Financial data (yr. ended 11/30/05): Assets,
$5,358,574 (M); gifts received, $201,542;
expenditures, $405,597; qualifying distributions,
$2,876,649; giving activities include $393,324 for
76 grants (high: $91,444; low: $150).
Purpose and activities: Giving primarily for
education.
Fields of interest: Arts; Elementary/secondary
education; Higher education; Animals/wildlife;
Health organizations, association; Human services;
Foundations (private grantmaking); Protestant
agencies & churches.
Limitations: Applications not accepted. Giving
primarily in MA, NJ, NY, and PA. No grants to
individuals.
Application information: Contributes only to
pre-selected organizations.
Officers: F. Helmut Weymar, Pres.; Caroline
Weymar, Secy.
Trustees: Emily Weymar Vandixhoorn; Mathew
Weymar.
EIN: 222787076

5433

UBS Foundation U.S.A. ▼ ✧
(formerly PaineWebber Foundation)
800 Harbor Blvd.
Weehawken, NJ 07086

Established in 1973 in NY.

Donors: PaineWebber Inc.; UBS PaineWebber Inc.;
UBS Financial Services Inc.; Charles H. Putney.
Foundation type: Company-sponsored foundation.
Financial data (yr. ended 12/31/04): Assets,
$28,157,759 (M); gifts received, $161,844;
expenditures, $8,595,035; qualifying distributions,
$8,559,979; giving activities include $7,645,644
for 355 grants, and $914,335 for employee
matching gifts.
Purpose and activities: The foundation supports
cancer centers and hospitals and organizations
involved with arts and culture, education, health,
youth development, human services, and homeless
people.
Fields of interest: Arts; Education; Hospitals
(general); Health care; Cancer; Youth development;
Human services; Homeless.
Type of support: Employee matching gifts.
Limitations: Applications not accepted. Giving
primarily in NY. No grants to individuals.
Application information: Contributes only to
pre-selected organizations.
Trustees: Mike Davis; Matthew Levitan; Bob Silver;
Mark Sutton.
EIN: 046032804
Selected grants: The following grants were reported
in 2004.
$580,237 to Joseph J. Grano Jr. Scholarship
  Foundation, New York, NY.
$287,500 to Memorial Sloan-Kettering Cancer
  Center, New York, NY.
$250,000 to New York City Leadership Academy,
  New York, NY. For grant made through New York
  City Partnership Foundation.
$187,500 to Museum of Modern Art, New York, NY.

$81,000 to Habitat for Humanity of Metropolitan
  Detroit, Detroit, MI.
$16,000 to University Neighborhood Partners, Salt
  Lake City, UT.
$13,000 to Connecticut Childrens Medical Center
  Foundation, Hartford, CT.
$10,500 to United Way, Heart of America, Kansas
  City, MO.

5434

Unilever United States Foundation ▼ ✧
c/o Unilever United States, Inc., Tax Dept.
700 Sylvan Ave.
Englewood Cliffs, NJ 07632 (201) 894-2236
Contact: Deirdre Gann

Incorporated in 1952 in NY.

Donors: Unilever United States, Inc.; Lever Bros.
Co.; Van den Bergh Foods Co.; Unilever Research.
Foundation type: Company-sponsored foundation.
Financial data (yr. ended 12/31/04): Assets,
$9,662,130 (L); gifts received, $12,814,852;
expenditures, $4,906,451; qualifying distributions,
$4,735,679; giving activities include $3,689,773
for 357 grants (high: $400,000; low: $150), and
$1,045,906 for employee matching gifts.
Purpose and activities: The foundation supports
organizations involved with arts and culture,
education, the environment, health, disease,
housing, children and youth, human services,
community development, minorities, and homeless
people.
Fields of interest: Arts; Education, early childhood
education; Elementary school/education;
Education; Environment; Health care; Housing/
shelter; Children/youth, services; Human services;
Community development; Minorities; Homeless.
Type of support: General/operating support;
Employee matching gifts; Employee-related
scholarships; In-kind gifts.
Limitations: Giving primarily in areas of company
operations. No support for religious, labor, political,
or veterans' organizations. No grants to individuals
(except for employee-related scholarships), or for
goodwill advertising, fundraising events or
testimonial dinners, or capital campaigns; no loans.
Application information: Application form not
required.
  Initial approach: Proposal
  Copies of proposal: 1
  Deadline(s): None
  Board meeting date(s): May, Oct., and Dec.
  Final notification: 1 month following board
    meetings
Officers and Directors:* John W. Rice,* Pres.; Fiona
C. Laird,* V.P.; Ronald M. Soiefer,* Secy.; Paul
McMahon, Treas.; Alan C. Jope.
Number of staff: 1 part-time professional.
EIN: 136122117
Selected grants: The following grants were reported
in 2004.
$850,000 to Girl Scouts of the U.S.A., New York,
  NY. 3 grants: $400,000, $50,000, $400,000
$333,333 to National Park Foundation, DC.
$209,750 to Jackie Robinson Foundation, New
  York, NY. 2 grants: $72,000, $137,750
$174,193 to National Merit Scholarship
  Corporation, Evanston, IL.
$73,000 to Kids Across America Foundation,
  Branson, MO.
$61,000 to Children First Fund: The Chicago Public
  Schools Foundation, Chicago, IL.
$12,000 to Columbia University, New York, NY.

5435

Union Foundation ✧
P.O. Box 4470
Warren, NJ 07059-0470 (908) 753-2440
Contact: William V. Engel, Pres.

Incorporated in 1951 in NJ.

Donor: Edward J. Grassmann†.
Foundation type: Independent foundation.
Financial data (yr. ended 11/30/05): Assets,
$14,880,995 (M); expenditures, $792,760;
qualifying distributions, $774,219; giving activities
include $720,090 for 93 grants (high: $25,000;
low: $3,000).
Purpose and activities: Grants to local hospitals
and health organizations, organizations engaged in
ecological endeavors, educational institutions,
especially privately supported ones, organizations
that help the needy, particularly children, and
religious organizations. Preference given to
organizations with low administrative expenses that
show efforts to encourage individuals to help
themselves, and which make efforts to achieve a
broad base of funding.
Fields of interest: Arts; Higher education;
Education; Environment; Hospitals (general);
Reproductive health, family planning; Health
organizations; Boys & girls clubs; Human services;
YM/YWCAs & YM/YWHAs; Children/youth,
services; Foundations (community); Roman Catholic
agencies & churches.
Type of support: Capital campaigns; Building/
renovation; Equipment; Land acquisition;
Endowments.
Limitations: Giving primarily in Union County, NJ. No
grants to individuals, or for operating budgets.
Publications: Application guidelines.
Application information: Application form not
required.
  Initial approach: Proposal (less than 4 pages)
  Copies of proposal: 1
  Deadline(s): Oct. 15
  Board meeting date(s): Nov.
  Final notification: Nov.
Officers: William V. Engel, Pres.; Edward S. Atwater
IV, V.P.; Suzanne B. Engel, V.P.; Harold W. Borden,
Jr., Secy.; Thomas H. Campbell, Treas.
Trustee: Haydn H. Murray.
Number of staff: 1 part-time professional; 2
part-time support.
EIN: 226046454

5436

**Lucy and Eleanor S. Upton Charitable
  Foundation** ✧ ☆
c/o McElroy, Deutsch, Mulvaney & Carpenter, LLP
3 Gateway Ctr.
100 Mulberry St.
Newark, NJ 07102-4079 (973) 622-7711
Contact: Francis X. O'Brien, Tr.

Established in 1965 in NJ.

Donor: Eleanor S. Upton†.
Foundation type: Independent foundation.
Financial data (yr. ended 12/31/05): Assets,
$7,486,789 (M); expenditures, $370,659;
qualifying distributions, $315,000; giving activities
include $315,000 for 23 grants (high: $70,000;
low: $1,000).
Fields of interest: Performing arts, orchestra
(symphony); Arts; Education; Hospitals (specialty);

Human services; Children/youth, services; Christian agencies & churches.
Type of support: General/operating support; Fellowships; Research.
Limitations: Giving primarily in NJ. No grants to individuals.
Application information: Application form not required.
Deadline(s): None
Board meeting date(s): Nov.
Trustees: William B. Cater; Francis X. O'Brien.
EIN: 226074947
Selected grants: The following grants were reported in 2005.
$70,000 to New Jersey Symphony Orchestra, Newark, NJ.
$30,000 to Newark Museum, Newark, NJ.
$30,000 to Saint Philips Academy, Newark, NJ.
$25,000 to Memorial Sloan-Kettering Cancer Center, New York, NY.
$20,000 to Isaiah House, Orange, NJ.
$12,000 to Chad School, Newark, NJ.
$12,000 to Saint Benedicts Preparatory School, Newark, NJ.
$10,000 to Childrens Specialized Hospital Foundation, Mountainside, NJ.
$10,000 to Christ Hospital Foundation, Jersey City, NJ.
$7,500 to Newark Boys Chorus School, Newark, NJ.

5437
The Emet V'Emunah Foundation, Inc. ✧
c/o Sam Sasson
130 Roseld Ave.
Deal, NJ 07723

Established in 2001 in NJ.
Donors: Sam N. Sasson; Samantha Sasson.
Foundation type: Independent foundation.
Financial data (yr. ended 12/31/04): Assets, $0 (M); expenditures, $638,030; qualifying distributions, $637,746; giving activities include $637,476 for grants.
Fields of interest: Jewish agencies & temples.
Limitations: Applications not accepted. No grants to individuals.
Application information: Contributes only to pre-selected organizations.
Trustees: Albert Sasson; Sam N. Sasson; Samantha Sasson.
EIN: 311814428

5438
The Valley Foundation, Inc. ✧ ☆
c/o Valley National Bank
1195 Hamburg Tpke.
Wayne, NJ 07470-0933

Established in 1996 in NJ.
Donor: Valley National Bancorp.
Foundation type: Company-sponsored foundation.
Financial data (yr. ended 12/31/05): Assets, $407,369 (M); expenditures, $325,400; qualifying distributions, $325,520; giving activities include $325,520 for grants.
Purpose and activities: The foundation supports organizations involved with housing.
Fields of interest: Housing/shelter; Boys & girls clubs; YM/YWCAs & YM/YWHAs; Federated giving programs.
Type of support: General/operating support.

Limitations: Applications not accepted. Giving limited to NJ.
Publications: Annual report.
Application information: Contributes only to pre-selected organizations.
Officers and Directors:* Gerald H. Lipkin,* Pres.; Garret Nieuwenhuis,* V.P.; Jack Blackin, Secy.; Alan Eskow,* Treas.
EIN: 223473532

5439
Verizon Foundation ▼
(formerly Bell Atlantic Foundation)
1 Verizon Way
Basking Ridge, NJ 07920
Contact: Joseph E. Scaccia, Dir., Finance and Opers.
FAX: (212) 840-6988;
E-mail: verizon.foundation@verizon.com;
URL: http://foundation.verizon.com

Established in 1985 in NY; name changed to Bell Atlantic Foundation in Feb. 1998 following the merger of NYNEX Foundation with Bell Atlantic Charitable Foundation; current name adopted in June 2000.
Donors: NYNEX Corp.; Bell Atlantic Corp.; Verizon Communications Inc.
Foundation type: Company-sponsored foundation.
Financial data (yr. ended 12/31/05): Assets, $382,799,097 (M); gifts received, $50,334; expenditures, $67,483,146; qualifying distributions, $63,976,206; giving activities include $61,834,820 for grants.
Purpose and activities: The foundation supports organizations involved with arts and culture, literacy, employment, domestic violence, and community development.
Fields of interest: Humanities; Arts; Education, reading; Employment; Family services, domestic violence; Community development.
International interests: Dominican Republic; Venezuela.
Type of support: Equipment; Scholarship funds; Technical assistance; Employee volunteer services; Employee matching gifts; Scholarships—to individuals.
Limitations: Giving on a national basis and in PR, the Dominican Republic, and Venezuela. No support for religious organizations not of direct benefit to the entire community, religious organizations duplicating the work of other organizations in the same community, political organizations or candidates, discriminatory organizations, lobbying organizations, or organizations that duplicate or significantly overlap the work of public agencies on the local, state, or federal level. No grants to individuals (except for scholarships), or for political causes or campaigns, endowments or capital campaigns, film, music, television, video, or media production or broadcast underwriting, research studies not related to projects already being supported by the Verizon Foundation, sports sponsorships, performing arts tours, or association memberships.
Publications: Application guidelines; Informational brochure (including application guidelines).
Application information: Support is limited to 3 years in length. Application form required.
Initial approach: Complete online application form
Deadline(s): Nov. 30
Board meeting date(s): Annually
Officers and Directors:* Ivan G. Seidenberg,* Chair.; Thomas J. Tauke,* Vice-Chair. and Secy.;

Patrick R. Gaston, Pres.; Neil D. Olson, V.P. and Treas.; Michael Morrell, V.P. and Cont.; T. Britton Harris IV, C.I.O.; Katherine J. Harless; Doreen A. Toben.
Number of staff: 8 full-time professional.
EIN: 133319048
Selected grants: The following grants were reported in 2004.
$4,958,535 to Scholarship America, Saint Peter, MN. For unrestricted support.
$1,025,885 to Stevens Institute of Technology, Hoboken, NJ. For unrestricted support.
$500,000 to United Ways of New England, Boston, MA. For unrestricted support.
$333,483 to Childrens Museum of Los Angeles, Los Angeles, CA. For unrestricted support.
$253,500 to Urban League, National, New York, NY. For unrestricted support.
$200,000 to American Foundation for the Blind, New York, NY. For unrestricted support.
$20,000 to MELMAC Education Foundation, Augusta, ME. For unrestricted support.
$17,850 to Citadel Foundation, Charleston, SC. For unrestricted support.
$15,000 to Family Service League of Suffolk County, Huntington, NY. For unrestricted support.
$15,000 to Santa Barbara Museum of Natural History, Santa Barbara, CA. For unrestricted support.

5440
Victoria Foundation, Inc. ▼
946 Bloomfield Ave., 2nd Fl.
Glen Ridge, NJ 07028 (973) 748-5300
Contact: Irene Cooper-Basch, Exec. Off.
FAX: (973) 748-0016;
E-mail: info@victoriafoundation.org; URL: http://www.victoriafoundation.org

Incorporated in 1924 in NJ.
Donor: Hendon Chubb†.
Foundation type: Independent foundation.
Financial data (yr. ended 12/31/05): Assets, $221,479,980 (M); gifts received, $1,079,026; expenditures, $10,647,353; qualifying distributions, $10,143,996; giving activities include $9,208,358 for 140 grants (high: $525,000; low: $5,000; average: $10,000–$200,000).
Purpose and activities: Within Newark, NJ, grants primarily for urban activities and education programs, including early childhood and elementary education; support also for urban problems, leadership development, youth agencies, and certain statewide environmental projects.
Fields of interest: Arts education; Education, early childhood education; Elementary school/education; Education; Environment; Reproductive health, family planning; Crime/violence prevention, youth; Crime/violence prevention, domestic violence; Housing/shelter, development; Youth development, services; Human services; Children/youth, services; Minorities/immigrants, centers/services; Civil rights, minorities; Urban/community development; Community development; Leadership development; Public affairs; Minorities; African Americans/Blacks; Hispanics/Latinos; Immigrants/refugees; Economically disadvantaged; Homeless.
Type of support: Management development/capacity building; General/operating support; Continuing support; Capital campaigns; Building/renovation; Land acquisition; Emergency funds; Program development; Seed money; Curriculum development; Scholarship funds; Technical

assistance; Consulting services; Program-related investments/loans; Matching/challenge support.

Limitations: Giving limited to greater Newark, NJ; environmental grants limited to NJ. No support for organizations dealing with specific diseases or afflictions, geriatric needs, or day care. No grants to individuals, or for publications or conferences.

Publications: Application guidelines; Annual report; Grants list.

Application information: Request application guidelines or visit the foundation's Web site for application information. Application form required.

Initial approach: Proposal or 2-page letter of introduction
Copies of proposal: 1
Deadline(s): Submit proposal prior to Feb. 1 or Aug. 1; Mar. 1 for schools only; Sept. 1 for summer camps and summer programs only
Board meeting date(s): June and Dec.
Final notification: Within 3 weeks after board meeting if accepted

Officers and Trustees:* Percy Chubb III,* Pres.; Margaret H. Parker,* V.P.; Kevin Shanley,* Treas.; Charles M. Chapin III; Sally Chubb; Charles E. Hance; Gordon A. Millspaugh, Jr.; Franklin E. Parker IV; John F. Parker; Helen Frye Parr; Sarah Chubb Sauvayre; A. Zachary Yamba.

Number of staff: 4 full-time professional; 3 full-time support.

EIN: 221554541

Selected grants: The following grants were reported in 2006.

$200,000 to La Casa de Don Pedro, Newark, NJ. For general operating support.

$110,000 to Ironbound Community Corporation, Newark, NJ. For general operating support.

$95,000 to Friendly Fuld Neighborhood Centers, Newark, NJ. For after-school program, summer day camp, mentoring, and sports leagues.

$75,000 to Greater Newark Conservancy, Newark, NJ. For educational programs and the Outdoor Learning Center.

$50,000 to Helen Keller International, New York, NY. For ChildSight Program.

$40,000 to Rutgers, The State University of New Jersey, Abbott Leadership Institute, Newark, NJ. For general operating support.

$35,000 to Hackensack Riverkeeper, Hackensack, NJ. For general operating support.

$25,000 to New Jersey Highlands Coalition, NJ. For general operating support.

$15,000 to GlassRoots, Newark, NJ. For general operating support.

5441
Frank Visceglia Foundation ◇
300 Raritan Ctr. Pkwy.
Edison, NJ   08818

Established in 1976 in NJ.
Donor: Peter C. Visceglia.
Foundation type: Independent foundation.
Financial data (yr. ended 12/31/05): Assets, $5,306,013 (M); gifts received, $5,000; expenditures, $1,292,295; qualifying distributions, $1,283,295; giving activities include $1,268,295 for 57 grants (high: $1,000,000; low: $25).
Purpose and activities: Support primarily for Roman Catholic schools, colleges, churches and religious orders.
Fields of interest: Elementary/secondary education; Higher education; Hospitals (general); Health organizations, association; Disasters, fire

prevention/control; Christian agencies & churches; Roman Catholic agencies & churches; Religion.
Limitations: Applications not accepted. Giving primarily in NJ; some giving also in CA.
Application information: Contributes only to pre-selected organizations.
Trustee: Peter C. Visceglia.
EIN: 510174975

5442
Vision of Hope Foundation ◇
(formerly The Bob Rohrman Autombile Dealership Foundation, Inc.)
c/o Merrill Lynch Trust Co.
P.O. Box 1525, MSC 06-03
Pennington, NJ   08534-1525

Established in 1986 in IN.
Foundation type: Independent foundation.
Financial data (yr. ended 9/30/05): Assets, $8,314,626 (M); expenditures, $752,872; qualifying distributions, $676,297; giving activities include $667,521 for 24 grants (high: $106,665; low: $1,000).
Purpose and activities: Giving primarily for Baptist organizations and churches; funding also for human services and education.
Fields of interest: Education; Mental health/crisis services; Human services; Children/youth, services; Christian agencies & churches.
Limitations: Applications not accepted. Giving primarily in Lafayette, IN. No grants to individuals.
Application information: Contributes only to pre-selected organizations.
Officer: Linda Rohrman, Pres.
EIN: 311195123
Selected grants: The following grants were reported in 2003.

$87,192 to Hanna Community Center, Lafayette, IN. For general operating support.

$64,474 to Community of Hope, Lafayette, IN. For general operating support.

$61,495 to Evangelical Baptist Missions, Kokomo, IN. For general operating support.

$50,000 to Vision for Youth, Clarks Summit, PA. For general operating support.

$30,000 to Faith Christian School, Lafayette, IN. For general operating support.

$30,000 to Kossuth Baptist Church, Lafayette, IN. For general operating support.

$30,000 to Kossuth Street Baptist Church, Lafayette, IN. For general operating support.

$25,000 to International Orphanage Relief, Newburg, IN. For general operating support.

$22,500 to Campus Crusade for Christ, West Lafayette, IN. For general operating support.

$9,100 to Calvary Chapel Church, Lafayette, IN. For general operating support.

5443
Vollmer Foundation, Inc. ◇
c/o Albert L. Ennist
P.O. Box 704
Butler, NJ   07405

Incorporated in 1965 in NY.
Donor: Alberto F. Vollmer‡.
Foundation type: Independent foundation.
Financial data (yr. ended 12/31/05): Assets, $27,753,596 (M); expenditures, $1,575,907;

qualifying distributions, $1,458,267; giving activities include $1,339,747 for grants.
Purpose and activities: Emphasis on health, and higher and other education in Venezuela; support also for Roman Catholic churches in Venezuela.
Fields of interest: Higher education; Education; Health care; Youth development; Children/youth, services; Community development; Science, research; Roman Catholic agencies & churches.
International interests: Venezuela.
Type of support: General/operating support; Continuing support; Research.
Limitations: Applications not accepted. Giving limited to Venezuela. No grants to individuals, or for building funds or matching gifts; no loans.
Application information: Contributes only to pre-selected organizations. Unsolicited requests for funds not considered.
Board meeting date(s): As required
Officers and Directors:* Gustavo J. Vollmer,* Pres.; Ana Luisa Wallis,* V.P. and Treas.; Carolina V. De Eseverri, Secy.; Gustavo A. Vollmer.
Number of staff: 1 full-time professional; 1 part-time professional.
EIN: 132620718

5444
Vopicka Family Foundation, Inc. ◇ ☆
c/o Robert J. Gaughran
P.O. Box 4151
Middletown, NJ   07748
Application address: c/o Ellen Vopicka, 5 Circle Dr., Rumson, NJ 07760

Established in 2003.
Donors: Carolina Vopicka‡; Ellen Vopicka.
Foundation type: Independent foundation.
Financial data (yr. ended 9/30/05): Assets, $1,980,998 (M); gifts received, $208,451; expenditures, $356,670; qualifying distributions, $356,670; giving activities include $356,670 for 4 grants (high: $200,000; low: $6,670).
Fields of interest: Human services; Children/youth, services.
Limitations: Giving primarily in NJ.
Application information:
Initial approach: Letter
Deadline(s): None
Officers: Ellen Vopicka, Pres.; Robert Gaughran, Secy.; James D. Carroll, Jr., Treas.
EIN: 010683241

5445
Vance Wall Foundation, Inc. ◇
c/o Carol Wall
160 Lloyd Rd.
Montclair, NJ   07042

Established in 1990 in NJ.
Donor: Terence D. Wall.
Foundation type: Independent foundation.
Financial data (yr. ended 12/31/05): Assets, $1,011,885 (M); gifts received, $8,296; expenditures, $372,345; qualifying distributions, $366,315; giving activities include $365,900 for 20 grants (high: $135,000; low: $500).
Fields of interest: Education; Cancer; Breast cancer; Recreation, parks/playgrounds; Human services; YM/YWCAs & YM/YWHAs; Women, centers/services.

Limitations: Applications not accepted. Giving on a national basis, with some emphasis on Montclair, NJ. No grants to individuals.
Application information: Contributes only to pre-selected organizations.
Trustees: Carol Vance Wall; Douglas V. Wall; Terence D. Wall.
EIN: 521739419
Selected grants: The following grants were reported in 2003.
$225,000 to Center for Social and Emotional Education, New York, NY. For general operating support.
$104,975 to National Breast Cancer Coalition, DC. For general operating support.
$29,000 to Skating Association for the Blind and Handicapped (SABAH), West Seneca, NY. For general operating support.
$12,000 to Craig School, Boonton, NJ. For general operating support.
$8,000 to Central Park Conservancy, New York, NY. For general operating support.
$5,000 to Junior League of Montclair-Newark, Montclair, NJ. For general operating support.
$4,000 to Yogi Berra Museum, Little Falls, NJ. For general operating support.
$2,000 to National Alliance for Autism Research, Princeton, NJ. For general operating support.
$1,000 to American Sudden Infant Death Syndrome (SIDS) Institute, Marietta, GA. For general operating support.
$1,000 to Boston University, Boston, MA. For general operating support.

5446
Wallerstein Foundation for Geriatric Life Improvement

200 Executive Dr., Ste. 100
West Orange, NJ 07052 (973) 731-2500
Contact: Melvin J. Wallerstein, Pres.
FAX: (973) 731-0163; *E-mail:* mjwpaesq@aol.com

Established in 1956 in NJ.
Donor: Julian W. Wallerstein†.
Foundation type: Independent foundation.
Financial data (yr. ended 6/30/05): Assets, $14,198,280 (M); gifts received, $5,000; expenditures, $1,051,965; qualifying distributions, $811,729; giving activities include $811,729 for 120 grants (high: $123,530; low: $15).
Purpose and activities: Grants primarily for health, and human service organizations for the aged.
Fields of interest: Health care; Health organizations, association; Aging, centers/services; Aging.
Type of support: Program development; Seed money.
Limitations: Giving primarily in NJ and NY. No grants to individuals.
Application information: Contributes only to established organizations. Application form not required.
Initial approach: Simple 3-page letter
Copies of proposal: 1
Deadline(s): None
Board meeting date(s): Varies
Officers and Trustees:* Melvin J. Wallerstein,* Pres.; Mitchel B. Wallerstein,* V.P.; Rita Wallerstein,* Secy.
Number of staff: 1 part-time professional; 2 part-time support.
EIN: 223052726

5447
Johanette Wallerstein Institute

Llewellyn Park
1 Elm Court Way
West Orange, NJ 07052 (973) 731-1394
Contact: Bernard Wallerstein, Pres.
E-mail: bwallerstein@comcast.net

Established in 1967 in NJ.
Donors: Julian Wallerstein†; Jane Wallerstein; Bernard Wallerstein.
Foundation type: Independent foundation.
Financial data (yr. ended 6/30/05): Assets, $10,335,960 (M); gifts received, $49,300; expenditures, $617,169; qualifying distributions, $601,570; giving activities include $601,570 for 49 grants (high: $77,000; low: $500).
Purpose and activities: Primary interests are the environment and environmental justice.
Fields of interest: Environment.
Type of support: Annual campaigns; Building/renovation; Publication; Seed money; Research; Program evaluation; Matching/challenge support.
Limitations: Giving primarily in northern NJ. No grants for endowment campaigns.
Publications: Informational brochure (including application guidelines); Program policy statement.
Application information: Application form not required.
Initial approach: Letter
Copies of proposal: 4
Deadline(s): None
Board meeting date(s): July
Final notification: Varies
Officers and Trustee:* Bernard Wallerstein,* Pres.; Jane Wallerstein, V.P. and Secy.
EIN: 226042908
Selected grants: The following grants were reported in 2004.
$85,000 to Vanguard Charitable Endowment Program, Southeastern, PA.
$50,000 to Riverkeeper, Tarrytown, NY. For operating support.
$22,760 to Audubon Society, New Jersey, Bernardsville, NJ. For operating support.
$20,000 to Natural Resources Defense Council, New York, NY. For operating support.
$20,000 to New York Botanical Garden, Bronx, NY. For operating support.
$20,000 to Rocky Mountain Institute, Snowmass, CO. For operating support.
$15,000 to Greater Newark Conservancy, Newark, NJ. For operating support.
$15,000 to Worldwatch Institute, DC. For operating support.
$10,000 to Black United Fund, National, Newark, NJ. For educational program.
$10,000 to New Jersey Future, Trenton, NJ. For operating support.

5448
Charles B. Wang Foundation ▼ ✧

Park 80 W., Plz. 2
Saddle Brook, NJ 07663
Contact: Robert T. Bell, Dir.

Established in 1999 in NY, NJ and DE.
Foundation type: Independent foundation.
Financial data (yr. ended 11/30/05): Assets, $4,395,411 (M); expenditures, $1,747,551; qualifying distributions, $1,263,044; giving activities include $1,092,529 for 31 grants (high: $215,000; low: $100).

Purpose and activities: Giving primarily for children's health and education programs.
Fields of interest: Education; Children, services; Foundations (private operating).
Limitations: Giving primarily in NY. No grants to individuals.
Application information:
Copies of proposal: 1
Deadline(s): None
Directors: Robert T. Bell; Judy Cedeno; Charles B. Wang; Kimberly Wang; Nancy Li Wang.
EIN: 113461453
Selected grants: The following grants were reported in 2004.
$2,899,120 to Soochow University, Suzhou, China. For program support.
$200,000 to Cultural Development Center, Plainview, NY. For program support.
$100,000 to Friends Academy, Locust Valley, NY. For program support.
$100,000 to Queens Library Foundation, Jamaica, NY. For program support.
$12,667 to Childrens Museum of Manhattan, New York, NY. For program support.
$12,500 to Transfiguration School, New York, NY. For program support.
$12,000 to Incarnation, Queens Village, NY. For program support.
$3,000 to New York Chinese Cultural Center, New York, NY. For program support.
$2,500 to Assets School, Honolulu, HI. For program support.
$2,000 to Chinese Center on Long Island, West Hempstead, NY. For program support.

5449
Jack Weisberg Charitable Foundation ✧

c/o SJM & Assoc.
14 Ridgedale Ave., Ste. 255
Cedar Knolls, NJ 07927
Application address: c/o Jack Weisberg, Pres., 173 Franklin St., New York, NY 10013, tel.: (212) 431-7466

Established in 2000 in NY.
Donor: Jack Weisberg.
Foundation type: Independent foundation.
Financial data (yr. ended 12/31/05): Assets, $1,699,382 (M); expenditures, $395,939; qualifying distributions, $317,000; giving activities include $317,000 for 1 grant.
Purpose and activities: Giving primarily to an organization which provides performance space and assists artists for presentation of music art; funding also for international medical relief.
Fields of interest: Arts, single organization support; International affairs.
Limitations: Giving primarily in New York, NY.
Application information:
Initial approach: Letter
Deadline(s): None
Officers: Jack Weisberg, Pres.; John Bennett, Secy.; Arthur Weisberg, Treas.
EIN: 223771411

5450
Frank X. Weny & Mary Ethel Weny Charitable Trust ✧

2035 E. Hamburg Tpke.
Wayne, NJ 07470 (973) 831-8700
Contact: William C. Hanse, Tr.

Established in 2000 in NJ.
Donor: Frank X. Weny†.
Foundation type: Independent foundation.
Financial data (yr. ended 12/31/05): Assets, $14,237,439 (M); expenditures, $879,130; qualifying distributions, $705,000; giving activities include $705,000 for 23 grants (high: $110,000; low: $600).
Purpose and activities: Giving primarily for a museum of fine arts, a boys and girls club, Christian organizations; funding also for health and social programs, and a YMCA.
Fields of interest: Museums (art); Hospitals (general); Health care; Boys & girls clubs; Human services; YM/YWCAs & YM/YWHAs; Foundations (community); Christian agencies & churches.
Limitations: Giving primarily in MA and NJ. No grants to individuals.
Application information: Application form not required.
  Deadline(s): None
  Final notification: Within 3 months
Trustees: William C. Hanse; Roger W. Ludwig.
EIN: 316636669
Selected grants: The following grants were reported in 2004.
$110,000 to YMCA of Cape Cod, Hyannis, MA.
$107,500 to Boys and Girls Club of Morris County, Pequannock, NJ.
$75,000 to Cape Museum of Fine Arts, Dennis, MA.
$60,000 to West Side Presbyterian Church, Ridgewood, NJ.
$57,500 to Diabetes Education and Support Center of Southern Colorado, Colorado Springs, CO.
$55,000 to Cape Cod Foundation, Yarmouth Port, MA.
$50,000 to Heritage Plantation of Sandwich, Sandwich, MA.
$50,000 to Ron Hutchcraft Ministries, Wayne, NJ.

5451
The Werdiger Family Foundation ✧ ☆
900 Hart St.
Rahway, NJ   07065
Contact: Jonah Blumenfrucht, Secy.-Treas.

Established in 1989 in NY.
Donors: Outerstuff, Ltd.; Solomon Werdiger.
Foundation type: Independent foundation.
Financial data (yr. ended 11/30/05): Assets, $5,598,530 (M); gifts received, $3,252,000; expenditures, $430,049; qualifying distributions, $424,551; giving activities include $424,551 for grants.
Fields of interest: Jewish agencies & temples.
Application information:
  Initial approach: Letter or proposal
  Deadline(s): None
Officers: Solomon Werdiger, Pres.; Esther Werdiger, V.P.; Jonah Blumenfrucht, Secy.-Treas.
EIN: 133505439
Selected grants: The following grants were reported in 2005.
$30,000 to Mesorah Heritage Foundation, Brooklyn, NY. 2 grants: $20,000, $10,000
$25,150 to Agudath Israel of America, New York, NY. 3 grants: $150, $10,000, $15,000
$5,000 to Congregation Adath Jacob, Brooklyn, NY.
$25 to Ateret Torah Center, Brooklyn, NY.

5452
Josh & Judy Weston Family Foundation ✧
217 Christopher St.
Montclair, NJ   07042

Established in 1992 in NJ.
Donor: Josh S. Weston.
Foundation type: Operating foundation.
Financial data (yr. ended 12/31/05): Assets, $11,255,000 (M); expenditures, $2,401,000; qualifying distributions, $2,401,000; giving activities include $2,379,000 for 56 grants (high: $500,000; low: $2,000).
Purpose and activities: Giving primarily for arts and culture, education, including Jewish education, and social services.
Fields of interest: Museums; Arts; Higher education; Education; Human services.
Type of support: Emergency funds; Program development.
Limitations: Applications not accepted. Giving primarily in NJ and New York, NY. No grants to individuals.
Application information: Contributes only to pre-selected organizations.
Officers: Josh S. Weston, Pres.; Heather Weston, V.P.; Judy Weston, Treas.
Director: Eric Weston.
EIN: 521798616

5453
Wicks Chapin, Inc. ✧
855 Centennial Ave.
Piscataway, NJ   08855   (732) 885-5555
Contact: Edward J. Foley III, Tr.

Established in 1985 in NJ.
Donors: Edward J. Foley III; Joan Foley†; John C. Foley.
Foundation type: Independent foundation.
Financial data (yr. ended 12/31/04): Assets, $4,403,734 (M); expenditures, $355,099; qualifying distributions, $355,956; giving activities include $326,500 for 6 grants (high: $300,000; low: $500).
Fields of interest: Arts; Elementary/secondary education; Higher education; Health care; Human services.
Limitations: Applications not accepted. Giving primarily in NJ. No grants to individuals.
Application information: Unsolicited requests for funds not accepted.
Officers and Trustees:* Edward J. Foley III,* Co-Pres.; John C. Foley,* Co-Pres.
EIN: 222691706
Selected grants: The following grants were reported in 2005.
$169,000 to Bancroft School, Worcester, MA. 3 grants: $22,000, $125,000, $22,000
$160,000 to Morristown Memorial Health Foundation, Morristown, NJ. 3 grants: $5,000, $150,000, $5,000
$3,000 to Peck School, Morristown, NJ. 2 grants: $1,500 each

5454
The Wight Foundation, Inc. ✧
60 Park Pl., 17th Fl.
Newark, NJ   07102   (973) 824-1195
Contact: Rhonda Auguste, Exec. Dir.

FAX: (973) 824-1199; E-mail: wightfdn@aol.com; URL: http://www.wightfoundation.org

Incorporated in 1986 in NJ.
Donor: Russell Wight, Jr.
Foundation type: Independent foundation.
Financial data (yr. ended 12/31/05): Assets, $13,513,415 (M); gifts received, $938,940; expenditures, $1,103,977; qualifying distributions, $1,122,490; giving activities include $70,000 for 6 grants (high: $25,000; low: $2,500), and $330,281 for grants to individuals.
Purpose and activities: Awards scholarships only to seventh-grade students, primarily economically disadvantaged, who attend school in the greater Newark, NJ, area.
Fields of interest: Education.
Type of support: Scholarships—to individuals.
Limitations: Giving limited to the greater Newark, NJ, area.
Publications: Informational brochure (including application guidelines); Newsletter.
Application information: Application forms and guidelines available on foundation Web site. Application form required.
  Initial approach: Complete preliminary application form
  Deadline(s): Nov. 15 for priority consideration, Jan. 30 for regular admissions
  Board meeting date(s): Bimonthly
Officers and Trustees:* Russell Wight, Jr.,* Pres.; Rhonda Auguste,* Exec. Dir.; LaToya Battle-Brown; Sheila Boyd; Bruce Byrne; Yvonne Goyins; Milton Harrison; Alfred Woods.
Number of staff: 1 full-time professional; 2 full-time support.
EIN: 222743349

5455
Wilf Family Foundation ▼ ✧
820 Morris Tpke.
Short Hills, NJ   07078
Contact: Joseph Wilf, Tr.

Established in 1964.
Donors: Harry Wilf†; Joseph Wilf.
Foundation type: Independent foundation.
Financial data (yr. ended 10/31/05): Assets, $105,950,078 (M); gifts received, $2,021,335; expenditures, $7,290,842; qualifying distributions, $7,219,826; giving activities include $7,219,826 for 107 grants (high: $2,200,000; low: $200; average: $5,000–$100,000).
Purpose and activities: Grants for Jewish welfare funds, including educational programs, and temple support; giving also for educational institutions.
Fields of interest: Elementary/secondary education; Higher education; Education; Human services; Jewish federated giving programs; Jewish agencies & temples; Religion.
Type of support: Annual campaigns; Capital campaigns; Building/renovation; Endowments; Scholarship funds.
Limitations: Applications not accepted. Giving on a national basis.
Publications: Annual report.
Application information: Unsolicited requests for funds not considered.
Trustees: Joseph Wilf; Judith Wilf; Leonard Wilf; Zygmunt Wilf.
EIN: 226075840
Selected grants: The following grants were reported in 2005.

$2,200,000 to New York University, New York, NY. For unrestricted support.

$1,000,000 to Yeshiva University, New York, NY. For unrestricted support.

$865,202 to Jewish Federation of Central New Jersey, Scotch Plains, NJ. For unrestricted support.

$454,836 to UJA-Federation of New York, New York, NY. For unrestricted support.

$430,000 to American Society for Yad Vashem, New York, NY. For unrestricted support.

$300,000 to Central New Jersey Jewish Home for the Aged, Somerset, NJ. For unrestricted support.

$20,000 to Jewish Federation of Greater Monmouth County, Deal, NJ. For unrestricted support.

$10,000 to American Friends of Melitz, Baltimore, MD. For unrestricted support.

$5,000 to Aleh Foundation, Brooklyn, NY. For unrestricted support.

$5,000 to Christian Arts and Theater of Corona, Corona, CA. For unrestricted support.

5456
Z. S. & M. Wilf Foundation, Inc. ✧
(formerly Z & M Foundation, Inc.)
1163 Rte. 22 E.
Mountainside, NJ   07092

Established in 1997 in NJ.
Donors: Mark Wilf; Zygmunt Wilf; Joseph Wilf.
Foundation type: Independent foundation.
Financial data (yr. ended 12/31/05): Assets, $61,004,389 (M); gifts received, $10,057,220; expenditures, $2,073,980; qualifying distributions, $2,051,085; giving activities include $2,051,085 for grants.
Purpose and activities: Giving primarily for Jewish agencies and temples, and Jewish federated giving programs; funding also for education and health associations.
Fields of interest: Education; Health care; Health organizations, association; Human services; Jewish federated giving programs; Jewish agencies & temples.
Limitations: Applications not accepted. Giving primarily in NY, with some giving in NJ. No grants to individuals.
Application information: Contributes only to pre-selected organizations.
Trustees: Jeffrey Wilf; Mark Wilf; Zygmunt Wilf.
EIN: 223553441
Selected grants: The following grants were reported in 2003.
$200,000 to University of Pennsylvania, Philadelphia, PA. For general support.
$52,500 to Pingry School, Martinsville, NJ. For general support.
$50,000 to Center for Jewish Life, Princeton, NJ. For general support.
$17,000 to United Jewish Appeal of Metrowest, Whippany, NJ. For general support.
$16,000 to Anti-Defamation League of Bnai Brith, New York, NY. For general support.
$10,000 to Jewish National Fund, New York, NY. For general support.
$10,000 to Princeton University, Princeton, NJ. For general support.
$10,000 to Solomon Schechter Day School of Essex and Union, West Orange, NJ. For general support.
$7,500 to Jewish Telegraphic Agency, New York, NY. For general support.

$5,000 to Shoah Foundation, Philadelphia, PA. For general support.

5457
The Willits Foundation
730 Central Ave.
New Providence, NJ   07974

Incorporated in 1963 in NJ.
Donors: Harris L. Willits†; John H. Evans; members of the Willits family.
Foundation type: Independent foundation.
Financial data (yr. ended 11/30/05): Assets, $12,909,455 (M); expenditures, $648,592; qualifying distributions, $539,964; giving activities include $531,000 for 111 grants.
Purpose and activities: Emphasis on grants to higher educational institutions for scholarships for the children of employees at C.R. Bard, Inc. only; some support for hospitals and social service agencies.
Fields of interest: Higher education; Hospitals (general); Human services.
Type of support: General/operating support; Scholarships—to individuals.
Limitations: Applications not accepted. Giving primarily in NJ. No grants to individuals (except for scholarships).
Application information: Unsolicited requests for funds not accepted.
   Board meeting date(s): Nov. and as required
Officers and Trustees:* John H. Evans,* Chair.; Caroline Jones, Pres.; Barbara W. Evans,* V.P.; Laura Evans,* Secy.; Geoffrey Jones, Treas.; Christopher W. Jones; George T. Maloney; Robert H. McCaffrey; John F. Willits.
Number of staff: None.
EIN: 226063106
Selected grants: The following grants were reported in 2004.
$50,000 to Presbyterian Church, Westfield, NJ.
$30,000 to Peck School, Morristown, NJ.
$25,000 to Childrens Specialized Hospital Foundation, Mountainside, NJ.
$25,000 to Indian River Hospital Foundation, Vero Beach, FL.
$25,000 to Morristown Memorial Health Foundation, Morristown, NJ.
$25,000 to Overlook Hospital Foundation, Summit, NJ.
$25,000 to Wayside House, Delray Beach, FL.
$15,000 to Saint Jude Childrens Research Hospital, Memphis, TN.
$10,000 to Blair Academy, Blairstown, NJ.
$2,500 to Adirondack Community College, Glens Falls, NY.

5458
Withington Foundation, Inc.
c/o William W. Rooke
175 South St.
Morristown, NJ   07960

Established in 1994 in NJ.
Donors: William W. Rooke; Robert L. Rooke†.
Foundation type: Independent foundation.
Financial data (yr. ended 12/31/04): Assets, $23,206,858 (M); expenditures, $1,075,003; qualifying distributions, $954,092; giving activities include $842,000 for 25 grants (high: $125,000; low: $2,000).

Purpose and activities: Funding primarily for education. Funding also for health care, human services, and religious organizations.
Fields of interest: Education; Hospitals (general); Medical research, institute; Human services; Religion.
Type of support: Continuing support; Capital campaigns.
Limitations: Applications not accepted. No grants to individuals.
Application information: Contributes only to pre-selected organizations.
   Board meeting date(s): Nov.
Officers: William W. Rooke, Pres.; Andrew K. Rooke, V.P.; Charles C. Rooke, Secy.-Treas.
EIN: 223291812

5459
WKBJ Partnership Foundation
(formerly The Made in Dover Foundation)
50 Smith Rd.
Denville, NJ   07834-9405   (973) 328-0303
Contact: Bob Howitt, Exec. Dir.

Established in 1990 in NJ.
Donors: Joan S. Howitt; Robert M. Howitt.
Foundation type: Operating foundation.
Financial data (yr. ended 12/31/05): Assets, $5,603,655 (M); gifts received, $1,472; expenditures, $1,373,867; qualifying distributions, $1,329,547; giving activities include $1,014,000 for 22 grants (high: $550,000; low: $500), $65,300 for 27 grants to individuals (high: $7,949; low: $200), and $250,247 for 1 foundation-administered program.
Purpose and activities: Giving primarily for education, particularly financially disadvantaged students.
Fields of interest: Education.
Type of support: General/operating support; Capital campaigns; Conferences/seminars; Seed money; Curriculum development; Scholarship funds; Technical assistance.
Limitations: Giving limited to the northeastern U.S.
Application information: Application should also include nature of school program.
   Initial approach: Letter
   Deadline(s): None
Officer and Trustees: Robert M. Howitt,* Exec. Dir.; Norman Atkins; Ismael Irada; Brett Peiser; Dasha Perez.
Number of staff: 1 full-time professional.
EIN: 223000244

5460
Woolley-Clifford Foundation ✧
c/o Gerald A. Wolf
15 Engle St., Ste. 104
Englewood, NJ   07631

Incorporated in 1953 in DE.
Donors: Cornelia W. Clifford; Stewart B. Clifford.
Foundation type: Independent foundation.
Financial data (yr. ended 12/31/05): Assets, $1,780,465 (M); gifts received, $400,103; expenditures, $422,112; qualifying distributions, $422,112; giving activities include $410,100 for grants.
Purpose and activities: Giving primarily for the arts and education.

Fields of interest: Arts; Elementary/secondary education; Higher education; Human services.
Limitations: Applications not accepted. Giving primarily in NY. No grants to individuals.
Application information: Contributes only to pre-selected organizations.
Officers and Trustees:* Stewart B. Clifford,* Pres.; Cornelia W. Clifford,* V.P.; J.L.C. Danner,* Secy.; C.L.C. Wareham,* Treas.
EIN: 136100412

5461
YPI Charitable Trust ✧
c/o J. Harvey
6 Revere Ct.
Princeton Junction, NJ 08550

Established in 1991.
Donors: John T. Dorrance III; Charles A. Dorrance.
Foundation type: Independent foundation.
Financial data (yr. ended 5/31/05): Assets, $0 (M); expenditures, $631,253; qualifying distributions, $559,597; giving activities include $559,597 for 31 grants (high: $137,500; low: $500).
Purpose and activities: Giving primarily for human services, conservation, education, and health associations, including associations for dyslexia.
Fields of interest: Arts; Education; Environment, natural resources; Animals/wildlife; Health organizations, association; Human services; Foundations (private grantmaking).
International interests: Bahamas; England; Ireland.
Limitations: Applications not accepted. Giving in the U.S., the Bahamas, England, and Ireland. No grants to individuals.
Application information: Contributes only to pre-selected organizations.
Trustees: Charles A. Dorrance; Gunda S. Dorrance; John T. Dorrance III; John T. Dorrance IV.
EIN: 237675355
Selected grants: The following grants were reported in 2005.
$70,000 to Ducks Unlimited, Memphis, TN.
$25,000 to Jackson Memorial Foundation, Miami, FL.
$20,000 to Versailles Foundation, New York, NY.
$10,000 to Brandywine Conservancy, Chadds Ford, PA.
$10,000 to Cate School, Carpinteria, CA.
$5,000 to Garden Conservancy, Cold Spring, NY.
$5,000 to Sand County Foundation, Madison, WI.
$5,000 to Vanderbilt University, Nashville, TN.

5462
Zayat Foundation, Inc. ✧ ☆
598 Warwick Ave.
Teaneck, NJ 07666-2927

Donors: Ahmed Zayat; Joanne Zayat.
Foundation type: Independent foundation.
Financial data (yr. ended 12/31/05): Assets, $1,060,496 (M); gifts received, $500,000; expenditures, $490,333; qualifying distributions, $480,804; giving activities include $480,804 for 40 grants (high: $150,000; low: $100).

Purpose and activities: Giving primarily to Jewish agencies, temples, and schools.
Fields of interest: Education; Jewish federated giving programs; Jewish agencies & temples.
Limitations: Applications not accepted. No grants to individuals.
Application information: Contributes only to pre-selected organizations.
Officers: Ahmed Zayat, Pres.; Joanne El Zayat, Treas.
EIN: 522387634

5463
The Zimmer Family Foundation, Inc. ✧ ☆
c/o Jennifer Zimmer
101 Chestnut Ridge
Saddle River, NJ 07458

Donor: Stuart Zimmer.
Foundation type: Independent foundation.
Financial data (yr. ended 12/31/04): Assets, $2,390,324 (M); gifts received, $750,000; expenditures, $590,400; qualifying distributions, $590,350; giving activities include $590,350 for 5 grants (high: $355,350; low: $5,000).
Fields of interest: Jewish agencies & temples.
Limitations: Applications not accepted.
Application information: Contributes only to pre-selected organizations.
EIN: 810586837

5464
Zobel Foundation, Inc. ✧
c/o Zager, Fuchs & Ambrose
268 Broad St.
Red Bank, NJ 07701
Contact: Lawrence M. Fuchs, Pres.
Additional address: P.O. Box 489, Red Bank, NJ 07701

Established in 2000 in NJ.
Foundation type: Independent foundation.
Financial data (yr. ended 10/31/05): Assets, $581,115 (M); expenditures, $539,176; qualifying distributions, $513,597; giving activities include $382,621 for grants.
Purpose and activities: To provide aid to worthy and deserving educational, religious, medical and community projects and charities.
Fields of interest: Performing arts; Elementary/secondary education; Adult education—literacy, basic skills & GED; Scholarships/financial aid; Cancer; Medical research, institute; Human services; Christian agencies & churches; Jewish agencies & temples.
Type of support: General/operating support; Continuing support; Program development; Fellowships; Scholarship funds; Research.
Limitations: Applications not accepted. Giving primarily in Red Bank and Monmouth County, NJ and Cleveland, OH. No grants to individuals.
Application information: Contributes only to pre-selected organizations.

Officers: Lawrence M. Fuchs, Pres. and Treas.; Franklyn Ellis, V.P.; Lavina Ellis, V.P.; Madeline R. Ottino, Secy.
Number of staff: 3 part-time professional; 3 part-time support.
EIN: 223764673
Selected grants: The following grants were reported in 2005.
$35,000 to Riverview Medical Center, Red Bank, NJ.
$30,000 to Childrens Specialized Hospital, Mountainside, NJ.
$13,638 to Red Bank Charter School, Red Bank, NJ. 2 grants: $3,638, $10,000
$5,500 to YMCA.
$5,000 to Clarke School for the Deaf, Northampton, MA.
$5,000 to Gift of Life Bone Marrow Foundation, Boca Raton, FL.
$5,000 to Jewish Family and Childrens Service.
$1,000 to Childrens Hospital.
$1,000 to Smile Train, New York, NY.

5465
The Zodiac Fund, Inc. ▼ ✧
211 McClees Rd.
Red Bank, NJ 07701

Established in 1999 in DE and NJ.
Donors: Joan Rechnitz; Robert Heilbrunn.
Foundation type: Independent foundation.
Financial data (yr. ended 12/31/04): Assets, $67,396,072 (M); expenditures, $4,070,109; qualifying distributions, $4,063,617; giving activities include $3,884,047 for 30 grants (high: $2,028,000; low: $300; average: $1,000–$100,000).
Purpose and activities: Giving primarily for arts, higher education, human services, Jewish federated giving programs, and Jewish agencies and temples.
Fields of interest: Arts; Higher education; Human services; Jewish federated giving programs; Jewish agencies & temples.
Limitations: Applications not accepted. Giving primarily in NJ. No grants to individuals.
Application information: Contributes only to pre-selected organizations.
Officers: Joan Rechnitz, Pres.; Robert Rechnitz, Secy.-Treas.
EIN: 223683214
Selected grants: The following grants were reported in 2004.
$2,134,400 to Two River Theater Company, Red Bank, NJ. 2 grants: $106,400, $2,028,000 (For non-cash grant).
$1,000,000 to Rockefeller University, New York, NY. 2 grants: $22,155, $977,845 (For non-cash grant).
$150,000 to Monmouth Conservatory, Red Bank, NJ.
$100,000 to Long Island University, C.W. Post Center, Brookville, NY.
$25,000 to Algonquin Arts, Manasquan, NJ.
$25,000 to New York University, New York, NY.
$18,800 to Count Basie Theater, Red Bank, NJ.
$10,000 to Columbia University, New York, NY.

NEW MEXICO

5466
Albuquerque Community Foundation
3301 Menaul Blvd. N.E., Ste. 2
P.O. Box 36960
Albuquerque, NM 87176-6960 (505) 883-6240
Contact: For grants: Nancy Johnson, Prog. Dir.
FAX: (505) 883-3629;
E-mail: foundation@albuquerquefoundation.org;
Additional E-mail:
njohnson@albuquerquefoundation.org; URL: http://
www.albuquerquefoundation.org

Established in 1981 in NM.
Foundation type: Community foundation.
Financial data (yr. ended 6/30/05): Assets,
$39,283,237 (M); gifts received, $5,528,146;
expenditures, $2,338,653; giving activities include
$1,749,258 for 282 grants, and $100,400 for 130
grants to individuals.
Purpose and activities: Giving primarily from a pool
of charitable funds whose income is used to benefit
the community in grants to local nonprofits.
Fields of interest: Historic preservation/historical
societies; Arts; Education; Environment, natural
resources; Environment; Health care; Children/
youth, services; Human services; Children/youth.
Type of support: Continuing support; Program
development; Publication; Seed money; Scholarship
funds; Technical assistance; Scholarships—to
individuals.
Limitations: Giving primarily in the greater
Albuquerque, NM, area. No support for religious
purposes, private foundations, or for grantmaking
organizations. Generally, no grants to individuals
(except for scholarship funds), or for debt
retirement, annual campaigns, endowments,
conferences or symposia, emergency funding or
interest or tax payments; no multi-year grants.
Publications: Annual report (including application
guidelines); Financial statement; Newsletter.
Application information: Visit foundation Web site
for the online Nonprofit Information form, application
guidelines, and scholarship deadlines. Faxed
applications are not accepted. Application form not
required.
　Initial approach: Complete Nonprofit Information
　　form (for applicants completely new to ACF);
　　submit proposal (for returning applicants)
　Copies of proposal: 8
　Deadline(s): Varies
　Board meeting date(s): Quarterly
　Final notification: Within 3 months
Officers and Trustees:* Barry Ramo, M.D.*, Pres.;
Victor Chavez,* V.P.; Barbara H. Trythall,* Secy.; S.
Michael Walker,* Treas.; R. Randall Royster, Exec.
Dir.; Suzanne Barker; Julie Bowdich; Douglas M.
Brown; Susanne B. Brown; Don Chalmers; Robert M.
Goodman; Mark Gorham; Courtney Jackson; James
N. King; Larry Lujan; Beth Moise; Kim Nunley; Diane
Harrison Ogawa; Ann Rhoades; John P. Salazar;
Jeffry E. Sterba.
Number of staff: 2 full-time professional; 2 part-time
professional; 1 full-time support.
EIN: 850295444
Selected grants: The following grants were reported
in 2006.
$16,500 to ENLACE Comunitario, Albuquerque, NM.
$10,000 to Adelante Development Center,
　Albuquerque, NM.

$10,000 to Albuquerque Health Care for the
　Homeless, Albuquerque, NM. For continued
　development of ArtStreet initiative for children.
$10,000 to Keshet Dance Company, Albuquerque,
　NM. For Outreach Program to incarcerated teens
　at the New Mexico Youth Diagnostic and
　Development Center.
$10,000 to New Mexico Center on Law and Poverty,
　Albuquerque, NM. For project to expand
　healthcare services.
$10,000 to New Mexico Teen Pregnancy Coalition:
　Prevention and Parenting, Albuquerque, NM. For
　training young fathers and enhancement of
　evaluation component.
$10,000 to Roadrunner Food Bank, Albuquerque,
　NM. For Food for Kids, a school-based program
　that provides take-home food in backpacks.
$8,000 to Albuquerque Youth Symphony Program,
　Albuquerque, NM. For Bach to Basics weeklong
　summer music camp.
$6,000 to Cornerstones Community Partnerships,
　Santa Fe, NM. For Youth Applied Learning
　Program.
$5,000 to Tree New Mexico, Albuquerque, NM. For
　collaboration with Albuquerque Tree Initiative to
　plant trees and conduct tree care workshops.
$2,000 to Human Rights Advocacy, Crossroads,
　Albuquerque, NM. For supporting vocational
　coordinator and direct client expenses.

5467
The Hugh Bancroft, Jr. Foundation ✧
c/o Ronnie L. Hemphill
1035 Mechem Dr.
Ruidoso, NM 88345

Established in 1960 in CO.
Donors: Jacqueline E. Spencer; Jacqueline Spencer
Morgan Trust.
Foundation type: Independent foundation.
Financial data (yr. ended 12/31/04): Assets,
$5,512,020 (M); gifts received, $5,047,980;
expenditures, $599,923; qualifying distributions,
$502,898; giving activities include $469,978 for 1
grant.
Fields of interest: Performing arts centers; Arts.
Type of support: General/operating support;
Continuing support.
Limitations: Applications not accepted. Giving
primarily in Alto, NM. No grants to individuals.
Application information: Contributes only to
pre-selected organizations.
Trustees: Hugh Bancroft III; Ronnie L. Hemphill;
Michael S. Line.
EIN: 846020971

5468
Brindle Foundation
P.O. Box 31696
Santa Fe, NM 87594-1696
Contact: Kim Straus, Admin.

Established in 2002 in DE.
Donor: Martha Healy.
Foundation type: Independent foundation.
Financial data (yr. ended 12/31/04): Assets,
$11,801,034 (M); gifts received, $2; expenditures,
$398,814; qualifying distributions, $368,224;
giving activities include $364,900 for 31 grants
(high: $50,000; low: $2,500).

Purpose and activities: Giving primarily for early
childhood development and literacy.
Fields of interest: Arts; Environment, legal rights;
Environment, formal/general education; Animal
welfare; Family services.
Limitations: Applications not accepted. Giving
primarily in NM. No grants to individuals.
Application information: Contributes only to
pre-selected organizations.
　Board meeting date(s): Annually
Officers: Nancy Healy Schwanfelder, Pres.; Kevin
Schwanfelder, V.P.; Craig Schwanfelder,
Secy.-Treas.
Director: Martha A. Healy.
Number of staff: 1 part-time professional; 1
part-time support.
EIN: 030466957
Selected grants: The following grants were reported
in 2004.
$35,000 to Santa Fe Community Foundation, Santa
　Fe, NM.
$30,000 to New Mexico Environmental Law Center,
　Santa Fe, NM.
$25,000 to Santa Fe Rape Crisis Center, Santa Fe,
　NM.
$25,000 to Youth Shelters and Family Services,
　Santa Fe, NM.
$15,000 to La Familia Medical Center, Santa Fe,
　NM.
$15,000 to Santa Fe Preparatory School, Santa Fe,
　NM.
$10,000 to Museum of New Mexico Foundation,
　Santa Fe, NM.
$10,000 to Santa Fe Conservation Trust, Santa Fe,
　NM.
$8,000 to Pink Church Art Center, Santa Fe, NM.
$3,000 to New Mexico Association of Grantmakers,
　Santa Fe, NM.

5469
Carlsbad Foundation, Inc. ✧
116 S. Canyon St.
Carlsbad, NM 88220 (505) 887-1131
Contact: Jim Harrison, Exec. Dir.

Incorporated in 1977 in NM.
Foundation type: Community foundation.
Financial data (yr. ended 6/30/05): Assets,
$19,668,552 (M); gifts received, $200,909;
expenditures, $760,828; giving activities include
$368,255 for grants, and $112,449 for grants to
individuals.
Purpose and activities: The foundation exists to
improve the quality of life for the people of Carlsbad
and South Eddy County, NM. The foundation
provides leadership for local charitable
organizations by building and preserving permanent
funds for the support of arts and humanities,
community development, education, environmental
needs, health and human services, and law and
protection.
Fields of interest: Arts; Education; Environment;
Health care; Mental health/crisis services; Health
organizations, association; Crime/law enforcement;
Food services; Human services; Community
development; General charitable giving.
Type of support: General/operating support;
Continuing support; Building/renovation;
Equipment; Emergency funds; Program
development; Conferences/seminars; Publication;
Seed money; Scholarship funds; Technical
assistance; Consulting services; Program-related
investments/loans; Scholarships—to individuals;

Matching/challenge support; Student loans—to individuals.

Limitations: Giving limited to South Eddy County, NM, with emphasis on Carlsbad. No grants for annual campaigns.

Publications: Annual report (including application guidelines); Newsletter.

Application information: Grants to individuals are by nomination only. Application form not required.

  Initial approach: Letter
  Copies of proposal: 1
  Deadline(s): 1 week in advance of board meetings for organizations; nominations for individuals accepted throughout the year
  Board meeting date(s): Monthly
  Final notification: Individual recipients announced at Sept. meeting

Officers and Directors:* Vicki Moutray,* Pres.; Dale Janway,* Secy.; Craig Stephens,* Treas.; Jim Harrison, Exec. Dir.; Neal Dungan; Robert Murray II; Mario Salinas; Julia Williams.

Number of staff: 1 full-time professional; 1 full-time support; 1 part-time support.

EIN: 850206472

5470

Coleman Family Foundation ◇ ☆

P.O. Drawer 3337
Farmington, NM 87499-3337 (505) 327-0356
Contact: George E. Coleman, Pres.

Established in 2004 in NM.

Foundation type: Independent foundation.

Financial data (yr. ended 12/31/05): Assets, $1,070,752 (M); gifts received, $1,000,000; expenditures, $733,605; qualifying distributions, $733,240; giving activities include $733,240 for grants.

Fields of interest: Housing/shelter, homeless; Human services; American Red Cross; Family services; Roman Catholic agencies & churches.

Limitations: Giving primarily in NM.

Application information:

  Initial approach: Letter
  Deadline(s): None

Officers and Directors:* George E. Coleman,* Pres.; Barbara Mary Coleman,* Secy.; Jeffrey E. Coleman.

EIN: 201716049

5471

Con Alma Health Foundation, Inc. ◇

144 Park Ave.
Santa Fe, NM 87501 (505) 438-0776
FAX: (505) 438-6223; E-mail: staff@conalma.org;
URL: http://www.conalma.org

In 2001, converted from sale of BC/BS to Health Care Corp. In 2003, assumed management of conversion fund from the sale of Banner to Province.

Foundation type: Independent foundation.

Financial data (yr. ended 12/31/05): Assets, $28,861,350 (M); gifts received, $182,614; expenditures, $1,680,290; qualifying distributions, $1,550,984; giving activities include $885,388 for 35 grants (high: $140,000; low: $3,000; average: $10,000–$25,000).

Purpose and activities: The foundation is organized to be aware of and respond to the health rights and needs of culturally and demographically diverse peoples and communities of New Mexico.

Fields of interest: Health care.

Type of support: Seed money; Program evaluation; Program development; Conferences/seminars.

Limitations: Giving limited to NM. No grants to individuals, for scholarships/fellowships, or for bricks, mortar, or property.

Publications: Application guidelines; Annual report; Informational brochure.

Application information: Application form available on foundation Web site. See foundation Web site for guidelines and requirements.

  Initial approach: Letter of intent; full proposals upon invitation only
  Board meeting date(s): Aug.

Officers: Eric P. Sena, Pres.; Deborah Hartz, V.P.; Richard Carpenter, Treas.

Trustees: Mike Anaya; Elizabeth Bernal; Jim Harrison; Arturo Jaramillo; and 10 additional trustees.

Number of staff: 3 part-time professional; 1 full-time support.

EIN: 850484396

Selected grants: The following grants were reported in 2005.

$50,000 to New Mexico Voices for Children, Albuquerque, NM. For Covering Kids and Families.

$50,000 to Reach 2000, Roswell, NM. For Chaves County Community Pharmacy Program.

$50,000 to University of New Mexico Foundation, Envision NM, Albuquerque, NM. For Initiative for Child Healthcare Quality.

$40,000 to Las Cumbres Learning Services, Los Alamos, NM. For Northern New Mexico Community Infant Program.

$40,000 to National Dance Institute New Mexico, Santa Fe, NM. For Program Evaluation, Phase II.

$30,000 to Dona Ana County (DAC) Advocates for Children and Families, Las Cruces, NM. For Intergenerational Training and Research.

$30,000 to New Mexico Coalition Against Domestic Violence, Albuquerque, NM. For Puppets are Life Savers (PALS) program, puppet show program in public schools used to teach children about the nature of violence among peers.

$25,000 to Center of Protective Environment (COPE), Alamogordo, NM. For Our Children Are Watching.

$25,000 to P B and J Family Services, Albuquerque, NM. For Teletherapeutic Visits for Children of Prisoners.

$20,000 to New Mexico Public Health Association, Albuquerque, NM. For Policy and Media Advocacy for Pre-Adolescent Programs.

5472

Cudd Foundation ◇

P.O. Box 1890
Santa Fe, NM 87592-1980

Established in 1987 in LA.

Donors: Carol D. Cudd; Robert C. Cudd III.

Foundation type: Independent foundation.

Financial data (yr. ended 12/31/05): Assets, $3,088,119 (M); gifts received, $17,034; expenditures, $341,143; qualifying distributions, $325,662; giving activities include $310,679 for 40 grants (high: $211,089; low: $90; average: $1,000–$5,000).

Purpose and activities: Giving primarily for children's organizations.

Fields of interest: Performing arts, music; Education; Health care; Human services.

Type of support: Continuing support; Endowments; Emergency funds; Program development; Curriculum development; Scholarship funds.

Limitations: Applications not accepted. Giving primarily in New Orleans, LA, and Santa Fe and Taos, NM. No grants to individuals.

Application information: Contributes only to pre-selected organizations.

  Board meeting date(s): June

Officers and Directors:* Robert C. Cudd III,* Pres.; Carol D. Cudd,* V.P.; Leslie Hale,* Secy.; Blair Naylor,* Treas.; Amanda Stuermer,* Exec. Dir.; Linda Miller, Regional Adv.

Number of staff: 1 part-time professional.

EIN: 721101712

Selected grants: The following grants were reported in 2005.

$211,089 to Tulane University, New Orleans, LA.

$10,300 to New Orleans Museum of Art, New Orleans, LA.

$10,000 to Santa Fe Childrens Museum, Santa Fe, NM.

$7,500 to Millicent Rogers Museum, Taos, NM.

$5,000 to National D-Day Museum, New Orleans, LA.

$2,500 to Keyes Foundation, New Orleans, LA.

$2,500 to Louisiana Museum Foundation, New Orleans, LA.

$1,000 to Taos Art Museum, Taos, NM.

5473

The Edgar Foster Daniels Foundation ◇

c/o Jane Douthitt
200 W. DeVarges, Ste. 1-A
Santa Fe, NM 87501

Established in 1995 in NM.

Donor: Edgar Foster Daniels.

Foundation type: Independent foundation.

Financial data (yr. ended 12/31/05): Assets, $4,399 (M); gifts received, $208,975; expenditures, $401,972; qualifying distributions, $398,798; giving activities include $375,309 for 6 grants (high: $250,000; low: $2,500).

Purpose and activities: Giving limited to major operas.

Fields of interest: Performing arts, opera; Higher education.

Limitations: Applications not accepted. Giving on a national basis. No grants to individuals.

Application information: Contributes only to pre-selected organizations. Unsolicited requests for funds not considered.

Officers and Directors:* Edgar Foster Daniels,* Pres.; Jane Douthitt,* Secy.-Treas. and Exec. Dir.; Kurt Sommer.

EIN: 850435024

Selected grants: The following grants were reported in 2004.

$476,910 to Metropolitan Opera Association, New York, NY.

$400,000 to Washington Opera, DC.

$300,000 to Houston Grand Opera, Houston, TX.

$250,000 to Lyric Opera of Chicago, Chicago, IL.

$150,000 to Santa Fe Opera, Santa Fe, NM.

$100,000 to Saint Vincent Hospital Foundation, Santa Fe, NM.

$50,000 to International Festival Society, Santa Monica, CA.

$3,000 to Lensic Performing Arts Center, Santa Fe, NM.

$2,500 to Spoleto Festival USA, Charleston, SC.

$2,000 to New York City Opera, New York, NY.

5474
The Delle Foundation ☆
721 42nd St.
Los Alamos, NM 87544-1804

Established in 2004 in NM.
Donors: George A. Cowan; Helen Dunham Cowan.
Foundation type: Independent foundation.
Financial data (yr. ended 12/31/05): Assets, $9,437,365 (M); expenditures, $614,202; qualifying distributions, $605,100; giving activities include $605,100 for grants.
Fields of interest: Museums (children's); Performing arts, dance; Higher education, university; Human services.
Application information: Application form not required.
 Initial approach: Letter
 Copies of proposal: 1
 Deadline(s): None
 Board meeting date(s): Quarterly
 Final notification: One month
Officers: George A. Cowan, Pres.; Helen Dunham Cowan, V.P.; William C. Enloe, Secy.-Treas.
Number of staff: None.
EIN: 201247630

5475
The Domanica Foundation ☆
c/o Linda Anderson, Exec. Dir.
P.O. Box 1987
Las Vegas, NM 87701 (505) 425-0936
E-mail: lindatanderson@domanicafoundation.org;
URL: http://www.domanicafoundation.org

Established in 1994 in CO.
Donors: Donald V. Berlanti; McKenna L. Berlanti; Matthew D. Berlanti; Karen L. Berlanti.
Foundation type: Independent foundation.
Financial data (yr. ended 12/31/05): Assets, $5,719,277 (M); gifts received, $2,766,028; expenditures, $509,560; qualifying distributions, $390,630; giving activities include $390,630 for 27 grants (high: $50,000; low: $1,000).
Purpose and activities: To promote the welfare of the people of New Mexico through programs that enhance and enrich their lives.
Fields of interest: Education; Homeless, human services.
Type of support: General/operating support; Emergency funds; Program development; Curriculum development; Scholarship funds.
Limitations: Giving primarily in NM. No support for fraternal, veterans or labor organizations, or for athletic organizations, international organizations, national health and disease organizations, or for private foundations. No grants to individuals, or for capital fund drives (for colleges).
Publications: Application guidelines; Grants list; Program policy statement (including application guidelines).
Application information: Contributes only to pre-selected organizations. See foundation Web site for application information.
 Board meeting date(s): Quarterly
Officers: Donald V. Berlanti, Pres.; Karen L. Berlanti, V.P.; McKenna L. Berlanti, Secy.; Matthew D. Berlanti, Treas.; John P. Hill, Admin.; Karina VanCamp.
Number of staff: 1 full-time professional.
EIN: 521906206
Selected grants: The following grants were reported in 2005.

$25,000 to Amy Biehl High School, Albuquerque, NM.
$15,000 to Literacy Volunteers of Santa Fe, Santa Fe, NM.
$15,000 to New Vistas, Santa Fe, NM.
$12,000 to Las Cumbres Learning Services, Los Alamos, NM.
$5,000 to Lensic Performing Arts Center, Santa Fe, NM.
$5,000 to Santa Fe Childrens Museum, Santa Fe, NM.
$1,200 to Think New Mexico, Santa Fe, NM.
$500 to American Association of Suicidology, DC.

5476
The Frost Foundation, Ltd. ◇
511 Armijo St., Ste. A
Santa Fe, NM 87501 (505) 986-0208
Contact: Mary Amelia Whited-Howell, Pres.
E-mail: info@frostfound.org; Louisiana grant request
Fax: (505) 986-0430; URL: http://www.frostfound.org

Incorporated in 1959 in LA.
Donor: Virginia C. Frost†.
Foundation type: Independent foundation.
Financial data (yr. ended 12/31/04): Assets, $39,705,779 (M); expenditures, $2,613,885; qualifying distributions, $2,271,824; giving activities include $2,148,348 for grants.
Purpose and activities: Focus on the following areas: 1) Social service and humanitarian needs including, but not limited to, violence in the streets, domestic violence, child abuse, specific public health issues such as alcohol and drug abuse, homelessness, and problems of the elderly; 2) Environment - consideration given to programs in research, education, and action to conserve and protect the environment for the well-being and safety of plants, animals, and human beings; and 3) Education - focus on new, innovative, creative, practical programs to address students' and society's needs today, and which recognize our changing sociological structure and concerns.
Fields of interest: Higher education; Business school/education; Education; Environment, natural resources; Environment; Animal welfare; Health care; Substance abuse, services; Mental health/crisis services; Health organizations, association; AIDS; AIDS research; Food services; Human services; Children/youth, services; Family services; Residential/custodial care, hospices; Aging, centers/services; Women, centers/services; Minorities/immigrants, centers/services; Homeless, human services; Aging; Minorities; Native Americans/American Indians; Women; Homeless.
Type of support: Continuing support; Capital campaigns; Equipment; Program development; Conferences/seminars; Publication; Seed money; Curriculum development; Fellowships; Technical assistance; Matching/challenge support.
Limitations: Giving primarily in LA; some giving in NM. No support for animal experimentation. No grants to individuals, or for building funds, sponsorships for special events, endowment funds, medical research, or scholarships; no loans.
Publications: Application guidelines; Biennial report.
Application information: See foundation Web site for application guidelines and procedures. Faxed submissions are not accepted. Application form not required.

 Initial approach: 1-page letter; full proposal at foundation's request
 Copies of proposal: 5
 Deadline(s): Dec. 1, for consideration at Mar. meeting, and June 1, for consideration at Sept. meeting
 Board meeting date(s): Mar. and Sept.
 Final notification: 7 to 10 days
Officers and Directors:* Mary Amelia Whited-Howell,* Pres.; Philip B. Howell,* Exec. V.P. and Treas.; Taylor Frost Moore,* Secy.; Ann Rogers Gerber; John A. LeVan; Edwin Frost Whited; Mitchal R. Woodard.
Number of staff: 1 full-time professional; 1 part-time professional; 1 full-time support.
EIN: 720520342
Selected grants: The following grants were reported in 2004.

$500,000 to Tulane University, New Orleans, LA.
$157,857 to Centenary College of Louisiana, Shreveport, LA.
$40,000 to Volunteers of America, Alexandria, VA.
$30,000 to Northern New Mexico Animal Protection Society, Espanola, NM.
$30,000 to Wildlife Center, Espanola, NM.
$22,500 to University of New Mexico Foundation, Albuquerque, NM.
$20,000 to Canones Early Childhood Center, Canones, NM.
$20,000 to Cuidando Los Ninos, Albuquerque, NM.
$20,000 to Esperanza Shelter for Battered Families, Santa Fe, NM.
$20,000 to Northern New Mexico Family Crisis Center, Espanola, NM.

5477
Garfield Street Foundation ◇
330 Garfield St.
Santa Fe, NM 87501

Established in 1999 in NM.
Donors: Edward M. Gilbert; BGK Equities II, LLC.
Foundation type: Independent foundation.
Financial data (yr. ended 6/30/05): Assets, $0 (M); gifts received, $372,780; expenditures, $357,105; qualifying distributions, $357,012; giving activities include $357,012 for grants.
Fields of interest: Human services.
Limitations: Applications not accepted.
Application information: Unsolicited requests for funds not accepted.
Directors: Edward Gilbert; Sandra L. Osterman; Pamela Porter; Robin Smith; Alexandra Ward.
EIN: 752830956

5478
Frank D. Gorham, Jr., and Marie K. Gorham Charitable Foundation ◇
P.O. Box 451
Albuquerque, NM 87103-0451

Established in 1998 in NM.
Donors: Frank D. Gorham, Jr.†; Marie K. Gorham.
Foundation type: Independent foundation.
Financial data (yr. ended 12/31/05): Assets, $9,108,511 (M); expenditures, $719,222; qualifying distributions, $635,000; giving activities include $635,000 for 20 grants (high: $150,000; low: $5,000).
Fields of interest: Arts; Education; Boy scouts; YM/YWCAs & YM/YWHAs.

Type of support: General/operating support.
Limitations: Applications not accepted. Giving limited to the Southwest. No grants to individuals.
Application information: Contributes only to pre-selected organizations.
Trustees: Daniel K. Gorham; Frank D. Gorham III; Mark L. Gorham; Robert H. Gorham II; Timothy W. Gorham.
EIN: 850453092

5479
The Healy Foundation ✧ ☆
c/o Edmond Healy
P.O. Box 767
Taos, NM 87571

Established in 2002 in NM.
Donor: M.A. Healy Family Foundation, Inc.
Foundation type: Independent foundation.
Financial data (yr. ended 12/31/05): Assets, $13,974,451 (M); gifts received, $989,215; expenditures, $595,547; qualifying distributions, $377,000; giving activities include $377,000 for grants.
Fields of interest: Arts; Environment, natural resources; Zoos/zoological societies; Animals/wildlife.
Limitations: Applications not accepted. No grants to individuals.
Application information: Contributes only to pre-selected organizations.
Advisors: Edmund Healy; Wilmington Trust Co.
EIN: 030466977
Selected grants: The following grants were reported in 2004.
$25,000 to National Zoological Park, DC. For general support.
$15,000 to Chesapeake Wildlife Heritage, Easton, MD. For general support.
$10,000 to Amigos Bravos, Taos, NM. For general support.
$10,000 to Potomac Conservancy, Silver Spring, MD. For general support.
$10,000 to Taos Valley Acequia Association, Taos, NM. For general support.
$7,500 to Rocky Mountain Youth Corps, Ranchos de Taos, NM. For general support.
$7,000 to Rio Grande Restoration, El Prado, NM. For general support.
$5,000 to Museum of New Mexico Foundation, Santa Fe, NM. For general support.
$2,500 to Greater Ogden Community Nature Center, Ogden, UT. For general support.
$2,000 to La Jicarita News, Chamisal, NM. For general support.

5480
William Knox Holt Foundation ✧
300 W. Aztec Ave., Ste. 200
Gallup, NM 87301
Contact: George M. Malti, Pres. and Treas.

Established in 1967.
Donor: William Knox Holt†.
Foundation type: Independent foundation.
Financial data (yr. ended 12/31/04): Assets, $11,138,267 (M); expenditures, $693,569; qualifying distributions, $536,062; giving activities include $385,643 for 22 grants (high: $40,000; low: $1,193).

Purpose and activities: Giving primarily for higher and secondary education in the field of science; some support also for museums.
Fields of interest: Museums; Secondary school/education; Higher education; Engineering/technology; Science.
Type of support: Program development; Fellowships; Scholarship funds; Research; Matching/challenge support.
Limitations: Giving primarily in northern CA and southern TX. No grants for general support, operating budgets, continuing support, annual campaigns, emergency funds, deficit financing, equipment, land acquisition, or endowment funds; no loans.
Application information: Application form not required.
  Initial approach: Letter
  Copies of proposal: 1
  Deadline(s): Submit proposal in Jan. or Feb.; deadline Feb. 15
  Board meeting date(s): Quarterly
  Final notification: 3 months
Officers and Directors:* George M. Malti,* Pres. and Treas.; Geary Atherton, Secy.; Holt Atherton; Richard Perkins; Roberta Plummer.
EIN: 746084245
Selected grants: The following grants were reported in 2004.
$29,450 to Crime Prevention Institute, Austin, TX.
$20,000 to Childrens Museum of the Brazos Valley, Bryan, TX.
$20,000 to Helping Hand Home for Children, Austin, TX.
$20,000 to Safe Place, Dumas, TX.
$20,000 to Western Health Foundation, Gallup, NM.
$10,000 to Monterey Bay Aquarium, Monterey, CA.
$10,000 to Stanford University, Stanford, CA.
$10,000 to University of Southern California, Los Angeles, CA.
$5,000 to Hospice Brazos Valley, Bryan, TX.

5481
The R. D. & Joan Dale Hubbard Foundation ✧
P.O. Box 2498
Ruidoso, NM 88345 (505) 258-5919
Contact: James A. Stoddard, Exec. Dir.

Established in 1986 in CA as the R. Dee Hubbard Foundation, reincorporated in 1989 in TX.
Donor: R.D. Hubbard.
Foundation type: Independent foundation.
Financial data (yr. ended 12/31/03): Assets, $36,686,063 (M); expenditures, $1,038,801; qualifying distributions, $1,143,128; giving activities include $933,898 for 112 grants (high: $350,000; low: $215).
Purpose and activities: Primary areas of interest include early childhood, elementary, secondary, and higher education, museums, and other cultural programs.
Fields of interest: Museums; Arts; Education, early childhood education; Elementary school/education; Secondary school/education; Higher education; Business school/education; Education; Cancer; Cancer research; Human services.
Type of support: Annual campaigns; Building/renovation; Endowments; Professorships; Scholarship funds; Scholarships—to individuals; Matching/challenge support.

Limitations: Giving primarily in CA, KS, NM, OK, and TX. No grants to individuals (except from designated scholarship funds).
Publications: Application guidelines; Annual report; Program policy statement.
Application information: Application form not required.
  Initial approach: Letter
  Copies of proposal: 1
  Deadline(s): None
  Board meeting date(s): Varies
Officers and Directors:* R.D. Hubbard,* Pres.; Joan Dale Hubbard,* V.P.; Edward A. Burger,* Secy.-Treas.; James A. Stoddard, Exec. Dir.; Jennings J. Newcom.
Number of staff: 1 full-time professional; 1 part-time support.
EIN: 752266308
Selected grants: The following grants were reported in 2004.
$1,050,000 to Hubbard Museum of the American West, Ruidoso Downs, NM. 2 grants: $750,000 (For public parking lot), $300,000 (For arts education program).
$100,000 to Scripps Foundation for Medicine and Science, San Diego, CA. For research.
$73,000 to Butler County Community College, El Dorado, KS. For training center.
$60,000 to Ivy Hall Academy of Provo, Provo, UT.
$30,000 to Smith Center Public Schools, Smith Center, KS. For scholarships.
$25,000 to University of Kentucky, Lexington, KY. For library endowment fund.
$20,000 to Fairweather Communities, Hot Springs, AR. For dental program.
$15,000 to New Mexico State University, Las Cruces, NM. For scholarships.
$14,000 to University of San Diego, San Diego, CA. For scholarships.

5482
Johns Family Foundation
(formerly La Vida Foundation)
1311 Tijeras Ave. N.W.
Albuquerque, NM 87102 (505) 281-1011
Contact: Virgil Dugan, Admin.
FAX: (505) 224-9001; E-mail: vdugan@tijeras.org

Established in 1985 in NM.
Donors: Kenneth E. Johns; Cynthia Johns; Julie Johns Taylor; Jeffrey Johns.
Foundation type: Independent foundation.
Financial data (yr. ended 10/31/05): Assets, $13,402,994 (M); gifts received, $30,500; expenditures, $781,450; qualifying distributions, $695,785; giving activities include $687,300 for 62 grants (high: $130,000; low: $50).
Purpose and activities: Giving for communications and Christian organizations.
Fields of interest: Media/communications; Christian agencies & churches; Protestant agencies & churches.
Type of support: Program development; Matching/challenge support.
Limitations: Applications not accepted. Giving on a national and international basis. No support for political organizations, or to programs antithetical to Christian values. No grants to individuals.
Application information: Contributes only to pre-selected organizations. Unsolicited requests for funds not accepted.

Officers and Directors:* Kenneth E. Johns, Chair. and Pres.; Cynthia Johns,* V.P.; Don Miller, Secy.-Treas.; Jeffrey Johns; Julie Johns Felty.
Number of staff: None.
EIN: 850348850
Selected grants: The following grants were reported in 2005.
$39,500 to Navigators, The, Colorado Springs, CO.
$25,000 to Educate New Mexico, Albuquerque, NM.
$10,000 to Discovery Institute, Seattle, WA.
$10,000 to Evangelism Explosion International, Fort Lauderdale, FL.
$10,000 to New Song Community Church, New York, NY.
$6,000 to International Cooperating Ministries, Hampton, VA.
$5,000 to Bosque Preparatory School, Albuquerque, NM.
$5,000 to Gathering, The, Tyler, TX.
$5,000 to Haggai Institute for Advanced Leadership Training, Atlanta, GA.
$3,500 to Bible Study Fellowship, San Antonio, TX.

5483
The Kind World Foundation ✧
P.O. Box 32927
Santa Fe, NM 87594 (505) 982-1034
Contact: Lee Lysne, Exec. Dir.

Established in 1991 in SD.
Donor: Norman W. Waitt, Jr.
Foundation type: Independent foundation.
Financial data (yr. ended 12/31/04): Assets, $24,803,548 (M); expenditures, $1,321,178; qualifying distributions, $1,072,023; giving activities include $891,370 for 38 grants (high: $250,000; low: $1,000).
Purpose and activities: Giving primarily for the environment, education and human services.
Fields of interest: Arts; Education; Environment, natural resources; Children/youth, services; Family services.
Type of support: General/operating support; Continuing support; Annual campaigns; Capital campaigns; Building/renovation; Equipment; Land acquisition; Endowments; Program development; Scholarship funds; Research; Consulting services; Matching/challenge support.
Limitations: Applications not accepted. Giving primarily in Santa Barbara, CA, Sioux City, IA, and nationally for overseas relief programs and projects.
Application information: Foundation is in transition, and revised giving procedures are undetermined as of this time. Unsolicited proposals will not be accepted. Those seeking funding in the Midwest should contact the Siouxland Community Foundation.
Officer: Lee Lysne,* Exec. Dir.
Directors: Cindy Waitt; Norman W. Waitt, Jr.
Number of staff: 1 full-time professional; 1 part-time professional; 1 part-time support.
EIN: 363776553
Selected grants: The following grants were reported in 2003.
$260,000 to Morningside College, Sioux City, IA. 2 grants: $250,000 (For Residence Hall Project), $10,000 (For scholarships).
$75,000 to Sioux City Community School District, Sioux City, IA. For instrumental music proposal.
$50,000 to Childrens Home Society of South Dakota, Sioux Falls, SD. For endowment.
$50,000 to Shattuck-Saint Marys School, Faribault, MN. For choral/music facility renovation.

$25,000 to TeamMates Mentoring Program, Lincoln, NE.
$15,000 to Briar Cliff University, Sioux City, IA. For scholarship program.
$15,000 to Mary J. Treglia Community House, Sioux City, IA. For nurturing children and youth programs.

5484
Lannan Foundation ▼ ✧
313 Read St.
Santa Fe, NM 87501-2628 (505) 986-8160
Contact: Ruth Simms, Cont.
FAX: (505) 986-8195; E-mail: info@lannan.org;
Additional contact information (for Ruth Simms): FAX: (505) 954-5143, E-mail: ruth@lannan.org;
URL: http://www.lannan.org

Established in 1960 in IL.
Donors: J. Patrick Lannan†; James Turrell; Thomas Joshua Cooper; Jean-Luc Telliez; Mylene Birembaut; Sebastio Salgado; Chuck Close.
Foundation type: Independent foundation.
Financial data (yr. ended 12/31/04): Assets, $241,070,074 (M); gifts received, $211,350; expenditures, $17,103,550; qualifying distributions, $16,139,540; giving activities include $9,559,712 for 194 grants (high: $1,000,000; low: $50; average: $5,000–$50,000), $1,068,250 for 23 grants to individuals (high: $125,000; low: $10,000; average: $25,000–$50,000), $689,228 for 3 foundation-administered programs and $25,000 for 1 loan/program-related investment.
Purpose and activities: The foundation is a family foundation dedicated to cultural freedom, diversity and creativity through projects which support exceptional contemporary artists and writers, as well as inspired Native activists in rural indigenous communities. The foundation recognizes the profound and often unquantifiable value of the creative process and is willing to take risks and make substantial investments in ambitious and experimental thinking. Understanding that globalization threatens all cultures and ecosystems, the foundation is particularly interested in projects that encourage freedom of inquiry, imagination, and expression. The foundation supports this mission with long-term special projects requiring multi-year commitments of funding and technical assistance in the areas of contemporary visual art, literature, indigenous communities, and issues of cultural freedom.
Fields of interest: Visual arts; Museums; Literature; Historic preservation/historical societies; Arts; Native Americans/American Indians.
Type of support: In-kind gifts; General/operating support; Building/renovation; Equipment; Land acquisition; Endowments; Publication; Fellowships; Technical assistance; Program-related investments/loans; Employee matching gifts; Grants to individuals; Matching/challenge support.
Limitations: Giving on a national basis. No grants to individuals (except for Lannan Literary Awards and certain fellowships in the Literary and Cultural Freedom program areas).
Application information: If a letter of inquiry is of interest to the foundation, program staff will then contact selected organizations with an invitation to apply for funding by writing a full proposal. Funding in each program is highly competitive, however. Please be aware that the foundation rarely awards funding for unsolicited requests. Letters of inquiry submitted via fax or E-mail are not accepted.

Initial approach: Letter of inquiry
Board meeting date(s): Three times per year
Officers and Directors:* J. Patrick Lannan, Jr.,* Pres.; Frank C. Lawler,* V.P. and Dir., Opers.; Marian P. Day; Sharon A. Ferrill; Karen Hetherington; William E. Johnston; Sharron Lannan Korybut; John J. Lannan; John R. Lannan; Lawrence P. Lannan, Jr.; Mary M. Plauche.
Number of staff: 1 part-time support.
EIN: 366062451
Selected grants: The following grants were reported in 2005.
$2,242,484 to Dia Center for the Arts, New York, NY. For construction at Roden Crater.
$560,000 to Universidad Iberoamericana, Mexico. For construction.
$500,000 to Blackfeet Reservation Development Fund, Browning, MT. For public relations campaign.
$500,000 to Dia Art Foundation, New York, NY. For City construction.
$500,000 to Environmental-Aboriginal Guardianship through Law and Education (EAGLE), Canada. For challenge grant and legal services.
$300,000 to Democracy Now Productions, New York, NY.
$125,000 to Foundation for National Progress, San Francisco, CA. To expand investigative journalism project.
$55,000 to Intertribal Sinkyone Wilderness Council, Ukiah, CA. For legal services for Four Corners.
$25,000 to California Indian Basketweavers Association, Woodland, CA. For resource protection program.
$17,700 to Texas State University, San Marcos, TX.

5485
The Allene & Jerome Lapides Foundation, Inc. ✧ ☆
19 Double Arrow Rd.
Santa Fe, NM 87505
Contact: Allene Lapides, V.P.

Established around 1943.
Foundation type: Independent foundation.
Financial data (yr. ended 12/31/05): Assets, $566,865 (M); gifts received, $500,000; expenditures, $338,052; qualifying distributions, $328,650; giving activities include $328,650 for grants.
Purpose and activities: Giving for community development, animal welfare, and the environment.
Fields of interest: Environment, natural resources; Animal welfare; Animals/wildlife, preservation/protection; Community development.
Limitations: Giving primarily in Washington, DC, Annapolis and Baltimore, MD, and Santa Fe, NM. No grants to individuals.
Application information:
Initial approach: Letter
Deadline(s): None
Officers: Jerome Lapides, Pres. and Treas.; Allene Lapides, V.P.; Robert Goldman, Secy.
EIN: 237418069
Selected grants: The following grants were reported in 2004.
$20,000 to Espanola Animal Shelter, Espanola, NM. For general support.
$14,000 to Primarily Primates, San Antonio, TX. For general support.
$11,500 to College of the Christian Brothers of New Mexico, Santa Fe, NM. For general support.

$10,000 to AmeriCares, Stamford, CT. For general support.
$8,000 to Farm Sanctuary, Watkins Glen, NY. For general support.
$5,000 to Heart and Soul Animal Sanctuary, Santa Fe, NM. For general support.
$2,500 to Defenders of Animal Rights, Phoenix, MD. For general support.
$2,500 to Island Institute, Rockland, ME. For general support.
$2,500 to Lensic Performing Arts Center, Santa Fe, NM. For general support.
$2,000 to Habitat for Humanity International, Santa Fe, NM. For general support.

5486
Max and Anna Levinson Foundation ◇ ☆
P.O. Box 6309
Santa Fe, NM 87502-6309 (505) 995-8802
Contact: Charlotte Talberth, V.P.
FAX: (505) 995-8982;
E-mail: info@levinsonfoundation.org; URL: http://www.levinsonfoundation.org

Incorporated in 1956 in DE.
Donors: Max Levinson†; Carl A. Levinson.
Foundation type: Independent foundation.
Financial data (yr. ended 5/31/05): Assets, $17,607,739 (M); expenditures, $1,329,685; qualifying distributions, $985,697; giving activities include $985,697 for grants.
Purpose and activities: Funding is allocated among three categories: 1) Environment - including preservation of ecosystems and biological diversity, alternative energy and efficiency; toxins, alternative agriculture, environmental restoration, natural resource conservation, and sustainable communities; 2) Social - including urban and rural community economic development, multiculturalism, human rights, youth leadership and empowerment, conflict resolution, and aid to survivors of violence, and health care; and 3) Jewish/Israel - including Jewish culture and spirituality, history and education, eastern and world Jewry, the Israeli peace movement, and social and environmental issues in Israel. Whatever the specific area of interest, the foundation encourages projects which are concerned with promoting community, social justice, a healthy environment and a sustainable economy, either by developing alternatives to the status quo or by responsibly modifying existing systems, institutions, conditions, and attitudes which block promising innovation. Support for large organizations given a lower priority.
Fields of interest: Environment; International human rights; Jewish agencies & temples.
International interests: Israel.
Type of support: General/operating support; Equipment; Program development; Conferences/seminars; Publication; Seed money; Grants to individuals.
Limitations: Giving on a national basis. No support for projects of primary local community significance. No grants for capital or endowment funds, building programs, travel, expansion of existing services, matching gifts, scholarships, or fellowships; no loans.
Publications: Application guidelines; Grants list; Informational brochure (including application guidelines).
Application information: Application form available on foundation Web site; applications sent via fax

FedEx, Express Mail, or overnight mail will not be accepted. Application form required.
Initial approach: Letter of inquiry or proposal (2-to 6-pages)
Copies of proposal: 1
Deadline(s): Apr. 1; however, proposals may be submitted at any time
Board meeting date(s): Varies
Final notification: 2 weeks after board meeting
Officers: Carl A. Levinson, Pres.; Charlotte Talberth, V.P.; Helen Doroshow, Secy.; Carol Doroshow, Treas.
Directors: Robin Beck; James Doroshow; Douglas Levinson; Julian Levinson.
Number of staff: 1 full-time professional.
EIN: 236282844

5487
J. F Maddox Foundation ▼
220 W. Broadway, Ste. 200
P.O. Box 2588
Hobbs, NM 88241-2588 (505) 393-6338
Contact: Robert J. Reid, Secy. and Exec. Dir.
FAX: (505) 397-7266; E-mail: bobreid@leaco.net;
URL: http://www.jfmaddox.org/
Tel. and e-mail for Cassie Ater: (505) 393-6338, ext. 26, cater@leaco.net

Established in 1963 in NM.
Donors: J.F Maddox†; Mabel S. Maddox†.
Foundation type: Independent foundation.
Financial data (yr. ended 12/31/05): Assets, $177,948,913 (M); expenditures, $12,105,319; qualifying distributions, $8,529,589; giving activities include $6,695,841 for 175 grants, $195,071 for 32 grants to individuals, $108,413 for 2 foundation-administered programs and $40,314 for 1 loan/program-related investment.
Purpose and activities: The mission of the J.F Maddox Foundation is to significantly improve the quality of life in southeastern New Mexico by investing in education, community development, and other social programs. The foundation particularly supports initiatives driven by innovative leadership, designed for substantial impact, and committed to lasting value.
Fields of interest: Performing arts; Elementary/secondary school reform; Higher education; Education; Environment, beautification programs; Substance abuse, services; Youth development; Human services; Children/youth, services; Aging, centers/services; Economic development; Aging.
Type of support: Curriculum development; General/operating support; Capital campaigns; Building/renovation; Equipment; Program development; Program-related investments/loans; Scholarships—to individuals; Matching/challenge support.
Limitations: Giving primarily in southeast NM; scholarships limited to Lea County, NM, residents. No support for private foundations or political organizations. No grants to individuals (except for scholarships), or for operating budgets, or endowment funds.
Publications: Grants list.
Application information: Application form required for scholarships. Refer to foundation Web site for full application guidelines and requirements. Application form not required.
Initial approach: Letter; telephone for recommended proposal outline
Copies of proposal: 1
Deadline(s): None

Board meeting date(s): Quarterly
Final notification: Varies
Officers and Directors:* James M. Maddox,* Pres.; Don Maddox,* V.P.; Patty Robbins,* V.P., Finance and Treas.; Dennis M. Holmberg,* V.P., Admin. and Off., Special Projects; Robert J. Reid,* Secy. and Exec. Dir.; Harry H. Lynch; Benjamin W. Maddox; Catherine M. Maddox; John L. Maddox; Thomas M. Maddox; Ann M. Utterback.
Number of staff: 5 full-time professional; 3 full-time support.
EIN: 756023767
Selected grants: The following grants were reported in 2004.
$3,421,543 to College of the Southwest, Hobbs, NM. 3 grants: $56,543 (For general operating support for Distinguished Lecture Series), $1,865,000 (For general operating support), $1,500,000 (For property and improvements).
$657,077 to Hobbs Municipal Schools, Hobbs, NM. 3 grants: $512,262 (For general operating support), $120,434 (For general operating support), $24,381 (For general operating support).
$50,000 to Texas Tech University, Lubbock, TX. For general operating support.
$43,000 to Greensboro College Foundation, Greensboro, NC. For general operating support.
$36,537 to New Mexico Junior College, Hobbs, NM. For general operating support.
$30,000 to Tatum Municipal Schools, Tatum, NM. For general operating support.

5488
McCune Charitable Foundation ▼ ◇
(formerly Marshall L. & Perrine D. McCune Charitable Foundation)
345 E. Alameda St.
Santa Fe, NM 87501-2229
Contact: Wendy Lewis, Grants and Office Admin.
FAX: (505) 983-7887; E-mail: info@nmmccune.org;
URL: http://www.nmmccune.org

Established in 1992 in NM.
Donors: Perrine Dixon McCune†; Marshall L. McCune†.
Foundation type: Independent foundation.
Financial data (yr. ended 12/31/04): Assets, $132,740,488 (M); expenditures, $8,741,342; qualifying distributions, $7,856,598; giving activities include $6,090,550 for 322 grants (high: $100,000; low: $1,000; average: $5,000–$50,000), and $248,231 for 1 loan/program-related investment.
Purpose and activities: The mission of the foundation is to memorialize its benefactors through grants which enrich the cultural life, health, education, environment, and spiritual life of the citizens of New Mexico. The Foundation supports philanthropic programs which are responsive, flexible, and may be proven effective at aiding the people of New Mexico to reach their full human and spiritual potential. Primary areas of interest include the arts, education, youth, health, social services and environment.
Fields of interest: Visual arts; Museums; Performing arts; Performing arts, dance; Performing arts, theater; Performing arts, music; History/archaeology; Historic preservation/historical societies; Arts; Education, early childhood education; Child development, education; Elementary school/education; Secondary school/education; Vocational education; Higher education;

Adult/continuing education; Adult education—literacy, basic skills & GED; Libraries/library science; Education, reading; Education; Environment, natural resources; Environment; Animal welfare; Animals/wildlife, preservation/protection; Hospitals (general); Reproductive health, family planning; Medical care, rehabilitation; Health care; Substance abuse, services; Mental health/crisis services; Health organizations, association; Cancer; Heart & circulatory diseases; AIDS; Alcoholism; Crime/violence prevention, youth; Crime/law enforcement; Employment; Agriculture; Food services; Nutrition; Housing/shelter, development; Youth development, services; Youth development, citizenship; Human services; Children/youth, services; Child development, services; Family services; Residential/custodial care, hospices; Aging, centers/services; Women, centers/services; Minorities/immigrants, centers/services; Homeless, human services; Rural development; Community development; Federated giving programs; Public affairs, citizen participation; Leadership development; Public affairs; Aging; Disabilities, people with; Minorities; Native Americans/American Indians; Women; LGBTQ; Economically disadvantaged; Homeless.

Type of support: General/operating support; Continuing support; Annual campaigns; Building/renovation; Equipment; Emergency funds; Program development; Conferences/seminars; Seed money; Scholarship funds; Technical assistance; Program-related investments/loans; Matching/challenge support.

Limitations: Giving limited to NM. No grants to individuals, or for endowments, research, operating or capital expenses, voter registration drives, or to cover deficits.

Publications: Application guidelines; Biennial report.

Application information: See Web site for current cycle dates for initial approach and deadlines; submissions received by fax not accepted. Application form not required.

Initial approach: Online application only
Copies of proposal: 1
Deadline(s): July 1 through Oct. 31 for 2007 funding
Board meeting date(s): Changes annually
Final notification: Changes annually

Officers and Directors:* Sarah McCune Losinger,* Chair.; Owen M. Lopez, Exec. Dir.; James M. Edwards; John R. McCune VI.

Number of staff: 1 full-time professional; 5 full-time support.

EIN: 850429439

Selected grants: The following grants were reported in 2004.

$200,000 to New Mexico Community Foundation, Santa Fe, NM. 2 grants: $100,000 (For general operating support for Alliance for Rio Grande Heritage), $100,000 (For Forum for Youth in Community project).

$150,000 to Lensic Performing Arts Center, Santa Fe, NM. For operating support of Community Box Office.

$100,000 to Coordinated Systems of Care, Albuquerque, NM. For demonstrating value and effectiveness of expanded case management program for high risk clients.

$100,000 to Council for Educational Improvement, Santa Fe, NM. For general operating support.

$100,000 to EDO Foundation, Albuquerque, NM. For holding charrette concerning downtown Albuquerque.

$100,000 to Homeless Advocacy Coalition, Albuquerque, NM. To develop system of care for homeless in Albuquerque.

$50,000 to New Mexico Tax Research Institute, Albuquerque, NM. For general operating support.

$25,000 to Outpost Productions, Albuquerque, NM. For challenge match for capital campaign.

$20,000 to Southwest Environmental Center, Las Cruces, NM. For general operating support.

5489
Messengers of Healing Winds Foundation

P.O. Box 32360
Santa Fe, NM 87594-2360 (505) 954-4702
Contact: Steven Rasmussen, Exec. Dir.
FAX: (505) 954-4762;
E-mail: srasmussen@mhw-foundation.org

Established in 1998 in DE and NM.
Donors: Andrea Waitt Carlton; Norman W. Waitt; Kind World Foundation; Goldman Sachs & Co.
Foundation type: Independent foundation.
Financial data (yr. ended 12/31/05): Assets, $43,361,316 (M); gifts received, $406,469; expenditures, $3,182,069; qualifying distributions, $2,618,753; giving activities include $2,541,700 for 114 grants (high: $520,000; low: $100).
Purpose and activities: Giving primarily in four major areas: 1) environmental concerns, with emphasis on programs that strive to preserve the land and educate our children on the importance of protecting and caring for our natural heritage; 2) animal welfare, with emphasis on the protection and humane treatment of both wild and domestic animals; 3) social concerns, with emphasis on helping Native Americans help themselves; and 4) the fine arts, with emphasis on renovation. The foundation may also fund other charitable organizations or programs as deemed appropriate by the board of directors.
Fields of interest: Performing arts centers; Environment, natural resources; Environmental education; Animal welfare; Animals/wildlife, preservation/protection; Zoos/zoological societies.
Type of support: Land acquisition; Annual campaigns; Capital campaigns; Building/renovation; Endowments; Program development; Matching/challenge support.
Limitations: Giving primarily in the lake region of northwest IA, FL, SD, Santa Fe, NM, and the Southwest. Giving on a national basis for environmental concerns. No grants to individuals.
Application information: It is suggested that prior to submitting a formal grant application, the organization contact the foundation office on a more informal basis, which will help both the foundation and the applicant assess interest in the proposal and prepare a more concise application. Application form not required.

Initial approach: Telephone and/or letter
Copies of proposal: 4
Deadline(s): Varies
Board meeting date(s): 5 times per year
Final notification: Within 90 days of receipt of proposal

Officers and Directors:* Andrea Waitt Carlton,* Pres.; Donald Poppen,* V.P.; Jennifer Kronebusch,* Secy.-Treas.; Steven Rasmussen, Exec. Dir.; Charles Mosley.
Number of staff: 1 full-time professional; 1 part-time support.
EIN: 860910220

Selected grants: The following grants were reported in 2003.

$100,000 to Center for Captive Chimpanzee Care, Fort Pierce, FL.

$100,000 to Santa Fe Animal Shelter and Humane Society, Santa Fe, NM. For construction.

$80,000 to Institute of Range and American Mustang, Hot Springs, SD. For land acquisition.

$75,000 to Northern New Mexico Animal Protection Society, Espanola, NM. For operating support and endowment fund.

$62,500 to Santa Fe Community Foundation, Santa Fe, NM. For Santa Fe Plaza Bandstand Program and endowment fund.

$60,000 to Animal Alliance, Santa Fe, NM. For sea turtle spay/neuter program.

$45,000 to Wildlife Center, Espanola, NM. For supplies and endowment fund.

$30,000 to International Center for Gibbon Studies, Santa Clarita, CA. For nutritional needs and facility supervisor.

$30,000 to Santa Fe Mountain Center, Santa Fe, NM. For Cochiti Pueblo Youth Program.

$27,000 to Clinic for the Rehabilitation of Wildlife (CROW), Sanibel, FL. For new mammal compound.

5490
New Cycle Foundation

c/o Peregrine Financial Corp.
51 Jack Rabbit Ln.
Santa Fe, NM 87505

Established in 1985 in NY.
Donor: Michael Currier†.
Foundation type: Independent foundation.
Financial data (yr. ended 12/31/04): Assets, $13,005,063 (M); expenditures, $631,707; qualifying distributions, $626,707; giving activities include $549,000 for 29 grants (high: $150,000; low: $1,000).
Fields of interest: Higher education; Education; Environment; Human services.
Type of support: Program development.
Limitations: Applications not accepted. Giving primarily in NM. No support for religious organizations. No grants to individuals.
Application information: Contributes only to pre-selected organizations.
Officer: Nicholas Noon, Pres.
Trustee: Karin A. Griscom.
Number of staff: 1 part-time professional.
EIN: 133260471

Selected grants: The following grants were reported in 2004.

$150,000 to Conservation Fund, Arlington, VA.

$45,000 to Amigos Bravos, Taos, NM.

$45,000 to Santa Fe Waldorf School, Santa Fe, NM.

$25,000 to Regional Development Corporation, Santa Fe, NM.

$10,000 to Concerned Citizens for Nuclear Safety, Santa Fe, NM.

$10,000 to Institute for Energy and Environmental Research, Takoma Park, MD.

$5,000 to Forest Guardians, Santa Fe, NM.

$2,500 to Wild Angels, Santa Fe, NM.

5491
The New Mexico Community Foundation ◇

343 E. Alameda St.
Santa Fe, NM 87501 (505) 820-6860
Contact: Robert H. Stark, Exec. Dir.
FAX: (505) 820-7860; E-mail: nmcf@nmcf.org;
Additional address: 303 Roma N.W., Ste. 400,
Albuquerque, NM 87102, tel.: (505) 821-6735;
URL: http://www.nmcf.org

Incorporated in 1983 in NM.
Foundation type: Community foundation.
Financial data (yr. ended 12/31/04): Assets,
$18,549,931 (M); gifts received, $7,978,698;
expenditures, $4,791,313; giving activities include
$2,962,063 for 166 grants (high: $234,000; low:
$100).
Purpose and activities: Giving primarily to build
community resources and relationships, with
special emphasis on rural communities, and issues
important to communities such as water, kids,
health, families, elderly, education, hardship, and
livelihoods.
Fields of interest: Education; Health care; Health
organizations, association; AIDS; Child
development, services; Family services; Rural
development; Aging; Native Americans/American
Indians.
Type of support: General/operating support;
Continuing support; Annual campaigns;
Endowments; Program development; Conferences/
seminars; Publication; Seed money; Internship
funds; Scholarship funds; Technical assistance;
In-kind gifts; Matching/challenge support.
Limitations: Giving limited to NM, with emphasis on
rural communities. No support for religious
purposes or the United Way or other federated giving
organizations. No grants for endowment funds.
Publications: Annual report; Newsletter; Occasional
report.
Application information: Unsolicited requests for
funds not accepted.
 Board meeting date(s): Quarterly
Officers and Directors:* John P. Ulrich,* Chair.;
Gilbert Sanchez,* Secy.; Rebeca Romero Rainey,*
Treas.; Robert H. Stark, Exec. Dir.; Michael
Chamberlain, C.O.O.; Suzanne Barker; Marty Cope;
Deborah Gallegos; Sarah Alley Manges; Bruce
Newman; Jay Rosenblum.
Number of staff: 6 full-time professional; 2 part-time
professional.
EIN: 850311210
Selected grants: The following grants were reported
in 2004.
$52,220 to Community Action Agency of Southern
 New Mexico, Las Cruces, NM.
$47,553 to Border Area Mental Health Services,
 Silver City, NM.
$45,600 to Laguna Rainbow Corporation, Casa
 Blanca, NM.
$44,862 to Hidalgo Medical Services, Lordsburg,
 NM.
$42,433 to Self Help, Los Alamos, NM.
$40,550 to Concerned Citizens for Nuclear Safety,
 Santa Fe, NM.
$40,000 to Santa Fe Art Institute, Santa Fe, NM.
$32,750 to Amigos Bravos, Taos, NM.
$28,084 to P B and J Family Services, Albuquerque,
 NM.
$26,659 to New Mexico Forum for Youth in
 Community, Albuquerque, NM.

5492
Waite and Genevieve Phillips Foundation ◇

P.O. Box 5726
Santa Fe, NM 87502-5726

Established in 1986 in NM.
Donors: Genevieve Phillips; Waite and Genevieve
Phillips Charitable Trust.
Foundation type: Independent foundation.
Financial data (yr. ended 5/31/05): Assets,
$12,044,455 (M); expenditures, $1,128,403;
qualifying distributions, $986,193; giving activities
include $891,560 for 34 grants (high: $750,275;
low: $250).
Fields of interest: Museums (art); Arts; Education;
Hospitals (general); Health care; Health
organizations, association; Human services;
Children/youth, services; Federated giving
programs.
Limitations: Applications not accepted. Giving
primarily in NM, OK, and TX. No grants to individuals.
Application information: Contributes only to
pre-selected organizations.
Officers: Julie Phillips Puckett, Chair. and Pres.;
Elliott W. Phillips, Vice-Chair. and Sr. V.P.; Tom
Coker, V.P.; Addie Jo Iversen, V.P.; Virginia Phillips,
Secy.-Treas.
EIN: 850335071
Selected grants: The following grants were reported
in 2004.
$300,275 to Philbrook Museum of Art, Tulsa, OK.
 For general support.
$70,000 to Saint Andrews Episcopal School,
 Amarillo, TX. For general support.
$25,000 to Globe-News Center for the Performing
 Arts, Amarillo, TX. For general support.
$20,000 to Seymour Hospital Foundation, Seymour,
 TX. For general support.
$5,000 to Albuquerque Academy, Albuquerque, NM.
 For general support.
$5,000 to Don and Sybil Harrington Regional
 Medical Center, Amarillo, TX. For general
 support.
$5,000 to Panhandle-Plains Historical Society,
 Canyon, TX. For general support.
$5,000 to Texas Tech University Health Sciences
 Center, Amarillo, TX. For general support.
$5,000 to University of Texas M. D. Anderson
 Cancer Center, Houston, TX. For general support.
$2,000 to Amarillo Museum of Art, Amarillo, TX. For
 general support.

5493
PNM Foundation, Inc. ◇

Alvarado Sq., M.S. 1225
Albuquerque, NM 87158-1225
E-mail: fund@pnm.com; For PNM Partnership Grants
and Earth Study Grants: Catherine Conran, tel.:
(505) 241-2284; For PNM Classroom Innovation
Grants: Monica Hussey, tel.: (505) 241-2207;
URL: http://www.pnmfoundation.org

Incorporated in 1983 in NM.
Donor: Public Service Co. of New Mexico.
Foundation type: Company-sponsored foundation.
Financial data (yr. ended 12/31/04): Assets,
$11,869,199 (M); expenditures, $597,662;
qualifying distributions, $539,217; giving activities
include $422,280 for 121 grants (high: $40,000;
low: $250), and $76,516 for 139 employee
matching gifts.

Purpose and activities: The foundation supports
organizations involved with education, the
environment, and economic vitality.
Fields of interest: Education; Environment;
Economic development.
Type of support: Building/renovation; Equipment;
Program development; Publication; Seed money;
Research; Employee matching gifts.
Limitations: Giving primarily in NM. No support for
discriminatory organizations, sectarian or religious
organizations, veterans', labor, or political
organizations, fraternal, athletic, or social clubs, or
municipalities. No grants to individuals, or for
testimonial dinners, fundraising events, or
advertising, debt reduction, special events, annual
events, or one-time only events, endowments,
capital campaigns, administrative or overhead
costs, documentaries or film production, or
programs or projects that duplicate existing services
and/or programs.
Publications: Application guidelines; Grants list.
Application information: Application form required.
 Initial approach: Complete online application form
 Deadline(s): July 15 for Partnership Grants
 Board meeting date(s): 3 times per year
Officers and Directors: Edward Padilla, Jr., Pres.;
Ramon Gonzales, V.P.; Shirley Ragin, Secy.-Treas.;
Barbara Barsky; Deborah Brunt; Pat Ortiz; Carol
Radosevich; Bill Real.
Number of staff: 1 full-time professional; 1 full-time
support.
EIN: 850309005
Selected grants: The following grants were reported
in 2003.
$100,000 to New Mexico State University
 Foundation, Las Cruces, NM.
$7,500 to Southwestern College, Santa Fe, NM.
$5,000 to Embudo Valley Library and Community
 Center, Dixon, NM.
$2,000 to Cimarron Elementary School, Cimarron,
 NM.
$2,000 to Deming Public Schools, Deming, NM.
$2,000 to Golden Apple Foundation of New Mexico,
 Albuquerque, NM.
$1,600 to Challenge New Mexico, Santa Fe, NM.
$1,500 to Agua Fria Elementary School, Santa Fe,
 NM.
$1,000 to New Mexico AIDS Services, Albuquerque,
 NM.
$1,000 to YWCA of the Middle Rio Grande,
 Albuquerque, NM.

5494
Pond Foundation ◇

1447 Seville Rd.
Santa Fe, NM 87505-4647

Established in 1997 in NM.
Donors: Georgia Lloyd; Lola Maverick Berndt.
Foundation type: Independent foundation.
Financial data (yr. ended 12/31/05): Assets,
$3,429,291 (M); gifts received, $2,500;
expenditures, $1,886,797; qualifying distributions,
$1,661,111; giving activities include $1,402,059
for 47 grants (high: $225,720; low: $252).
Purpose and activities: Giving primarily for
international affairs, with emphasis on peace and
security; the environment; and civil rights.
Fields of interest: Environment; Animal welfare;
Animals/wildlife, preservation/protection; Food
services; Housing/shelter, development;
International peace/security; Civil rights.

Limitations: Applications not accepted. Giving on a national basis. No grants to individuals.
Application information: Contributes only to pre-selected organizations.
Officers and Directors: Lola Maverick Berndt,* Pres.; Frederick S. Brown,* V.P. and Treas.; Robert Allen Rikoon,* Secy.; Sandra Ingerman.
EIN: 860892601
Selected grants: The following grants were reported in 2005.
$225,720 to Peace Development Fund, Amherst, MA. For project support.
$144,582 to Collective Heritage Institute, Lamy, NM. For project support.
$97,956 to Grassroots International, Boston, MA. For project support.
$90,000 to Equality Now, New York, NY. For project support.
$90,000 to Permacultura America Latina, Santa Fe, NM. For project support.
$72,000 to Santa Fe Rape Crisis Center, Santa Fe, NM. For project support.
$54,000 to Wildlife Center, Espanola, NM. For project support.
$36,000 to Animal Protection of New Mexico, Albuquerque, NM. For project support.
$36,000 to Physicians for Human Rights, Cambridge, MA. For project support.
$18,000 to Newtown Florist Club, Gainesville, GA. For project support.

5495
Proteus Foundation ✧
960 Old Santa Fe Trail
Santa Fe, NM   87505-0369   (505) 983-1274
Contact: Celia W. Rutt, Dir.

Established in 2000 in VI.
Donors: Celia W. Rutt; James P. Rutt.
Foundation type: Independent foundation.
Financial data (yr. ended 9/30/05): Assets, $10,626,822 (L); expenditures, $532,837; qualifying distributions, $468,840; giving activities include $468,840 for 16 grants (high: $78,340; low: $2,000).
Purpose and activities: Giving primarily for scientific research in areas of environmental science and complex adaptive systems, preservation of historically or scientifically important documents and artifacts, environmental protection, preservation and enhancement.
Fields of interest: Historical activities; Elementary/secondary education; Graduate/professional education; Environment; Hospitals (general); Neighborhood centers; Civil liberties, advocacy; Civil rights; Community development; Social sciences, interdisciplinary studies.
Limitations: Giving primarily in NM and VA; some giving also in Washington, DC. No grants to individuals.
Application information:
Initial approach: Letter
Deadline(s): None
Directors: Celia W. Rutt; James P. Rutt.
EIN: 542013543

5496
Santa Fe Community Foundation
516 Alto St.
Santa Fe, NM   87501   (505) 988-9715
Contact: Billie Blair, Pres.; For grants: Amy S. Duggan, Prog. Off.
FAX: (505) 988-1829;
E-mail: foundation@santafecf.org; Additional E-mail: info@santafecf.org; Application address: P.O. Box 1827, Santa Fe, NM 87504-1827; Grant application E-mail: aduggan@santafecf.org; Workshop registration E-mail: workshops@santafecf.org; URL: http://www.santafecf.org

Incorporated in 1981 in NM.
Foundation type: Community foundation.
Financial data (yr. ended 12/31/05): Assets, $22,062,611 (M); gifts received, $5,938,227; expenditures, $3,026,446; giving activities include $2,184,704 for 300 grants (high: $115,000; low: $19), and $8,480 for 8 grants to individuals (high: $3,587; low: $342).
Purpose and activities: The foundation improves the quality of life for people in Santa Fe and Northern New Mexico, now and for future generations, by: 1) building and managing endowment funds in order to award grants; 2) helping nonprofits operate more effectively; 3) convening area residents to discuss issues of critical importance to the community; and 4) providing leadership for key community initiatives.
Fields of interest: Arts education; Visual arts; Performing arts; Performing arts, music; Humanities; Arts; Education, public education; Child development, education; Elementary school/education; Adult education—literacy, basic skills & GED; Education, drop-out prevention; Education; Environment, natural resources; Environment; Animals/wildlife, preservation/protection; Health care; Substance abuse, prevention; Mental health/crisis services; Health organizations, association; Cancer; AIDS; Alcoholism; Crime/violence prevention, domestic violence; Food services; Housing/shelter; Children/youth, services; Child development, services; Family services, domestic violence; Family services, adolescent parents; Aging, centers/services; Homeless, human services; Human services; Civil rights, immigrants; Civil rights, minorities; Civil rights, disabled; Civil rights, women; Civil rights, aging; Civil rights, gays/lesbians; Civil rights, race/intergroup relations; Community development, citizen coalitions; Economic development; Nonprofit management; Community development; Science; Public affairs, citizen participation; Public affairs; Aging; Disabilities, people with; Minorities; Asians/Pacific Islanders; African Americans/Blacks; Hispanics/Latinos; Native Americans/American Indians; Women; AIDS, people with; LGBTQ; Immigrants/refugees; Economically disadvantaged; Homeless.
Type of support: General/operating support; Continuing support; Management development/capacity building; Annual campaigns; Emergency funds; Program development; Publication; Seed money; Scholarship funds; Technical assistance; Matching/challenge support.
Limitations: Giving limited to northern NM counties, including Los Alamos, Mora, Rio Arriba, San Miguel, and Taos. No support for religious purposes. No grants for capital campaigns, endowments, or technical assistance grants for travel, conferences, start-up costs, or staff salaries or functions.
Publications: Annual report; Informational brochure (including application guidelines); Newsletter.

Application information: Visit foundation Web site for online application and guidelines. Free pre-proposal workshops are offered to assist perspective applicants with information on proposal guidelines and the application/grant process for the foundation's grant cycles; telephone or e-mail to register. Faxed proposals are not accepted. Application form required.
Initial approach: Complete online application
Copies of proposal: 1
Deadline(s): June 30
Board meeting date(s): Bimonthly
Final notification: Mid-Oct.
Officers and Directors: Felice Gonzales,* Chair.; Alexis K. Girard,* Vice-Chair.; Patricia A. McFate,* Vice-Chair.; Billie Blair, Pres.; Jerry G. Jones,* Secy.; Sarah Sawtell, C.F.O.; Stephen G. Gaber,* Treas.; Bill Belzner; Jeffrey P. Branch; Sally Corning Buchanan; Thomas Bustamante; Randy Chitto; James Duncan, Jr.; Alex J. Gancarz, Jr.; Barbara Gudwin; Richard Hertz; Patricia Salazar Ives; Nancy Lang; Cindy Lovato-Farmer; Francie Gomez Miles; Ruth Ortega; Sheila M. Paterson; Carol Romero-Wirth; Liz Stefanics, Ph.D.; Stephen E. Stork; John Vazquez.
Number of staff: 5 full-time professional; 3 part-time professional; 1 full-time support.
EIN: 850303044

5497
Stockman Family Foundation Trust ✧
1041 Matador Ave. S.E.
Albuquerque, NM   87123   (505) 296-7057
Contact: Sarah A. Stockman, Chair.

Established in 1990 in NM.
Donors: Hervey S. Stockman; Sarah A. Stockman; Sally Stockman.
Foundation type: Independent foundation.
Financial data (yr. ended 11/30/05): Assets, $18,888,573 (M); gifts received, $300,000; expenditures, $1,064,011; qualifying distributions, $952,767; giving activities include $933,790 for 18 grants (high: $100,000; low: $5,000).
Purpose and activities: Grants are made to organizations to advance the knowledge and practice of conservation of historic and artistic property in the museum and university domain.
Fields of interest: Museums; Historic preservation/historical societies; Education.
International interests: United Kingdom.
Limitations: Giving primarily in NM. No grants to individuals.
Application information:
Initial approach: Typewritten letter or proposal
Deadline(s): None
Officers: Sarah A. Stockman, Chair. and Secy.; Hervey S. Stockman, Jr., Pres.; Hervey S. Stockman, V.P.; Karl W. Gustafson, Treas.
Trustee: Bankers Trust Co.
EIN: 856104630
Selected grants: The following grants were reported in 2004.
$150,000 to Walters Art Museum, Baltimore, MD.
$77,000 to Wheelwright Museum of the American Indian, Santa Fe, NM.
$75,000 to New Mexico State University, Las Cruces, NM.
$65,000 to University College London, London, England. .
$50,000 to Baltimore Museum of Art, Baltimore, MD.

$40,000 to Williamstown Art Conservation Center, Williamstown, MA.
$30,000 to Crocker Art Museum, Sacramento, CA.
$30,000 to Museum of New Mexico, Santa Fe, NM.
$12,000 to Canajoharie Library and Art Gallery, Canajoharie, NY.
$10,000 to Vassar College, Poughkeepsie, NY.

5498
Taos Community Foundation

229A Camino de la Placita
P.O. Box 1925
Taos, NM 87571 (505) 737-9300
Contact: Elizabeth Crittenden-Palacios, Exec. Dir.;
For grants: Sharon Pomerang, Prog. Off.
FAX: (505) 751-7130;
E-mail: ecrittenden@taoscf.org; Additional E-mail:
grantsofficer@taoscf.org; Grant application E-mail:
grantapplication@taoscf.org; Grant writing workshop
registration E-mail: admintcf@taoscf.org;
URL: http://www.taoscf.org

Established in 1998 in NM.
Foundation type: Community foundation.
Financial data (yr. ended 6/30/05): Assets,
$3,246,336 (M); gifts received, $609,092;
expenditures, $810,845; giving activities include
$518,101 for 58 grants (high: $116,397; low: $76),
and $10,000 for 6 grants to individuals (high:
$4,000; low: $1,000).
Purpose and activities: The mission of the
foundation is to enhance the quality of life in the
communities served by encouraging permanent
charitable giving for present and future generations.
Giving primarily in the areas of health and human
services; education and activities for youth; visual,
literary, and performing arts; community and
economic development; natural environment; and
historic preservation.
Fields of interest: Visual arts; Performing arts,
music; Historic preservation/historical societies;
Arts; Education; Environment, natural resources;
Environment; Health care; Children/youth, services;
Family services; Human services; Economic
development; Community development; Children.
Type of support: General/operating support;
Continuing support; Management development/
capacity building; Annual campaigns; Capital
campaigns; Building/renovation; Equipment; Land
acquisition; Endowments; Emergency funds;
Program development; Publication; Seed money;
Curriculum development; Scholarship funds;
Program evaluation; Program-related investments/
loans; Scholarships—to individuals; In-kind gifts;
Matching/challenge support; Student loans—to
individuals.
Limitations: Giving limited to Taos and western
Colfax counties, NM. No support for religious
purposes, or government agencies. No grants to
individuals (except for scholarships).
Publications: Application guidelines; Annual report;
Financial statement; Grants list; Informational
brochure.
Application information: Visit foundation Web site
for application form and guidelines. Applicants are
strongly encouraged to attend one of the
foundation's grant writing workshops; e-mail
foundation to sign-up. Application form required.
Initial approach: Telephone
Copies of proposal: 1
Deadline(s): Apr. 10
Board meeting date(s): Feb.
Final notification: June 30

Officers and Directors:* John Speirs,* Chair.; Wes
Patterson,* Vice-Chair.; Maggie Evans-Rael,* Secy.;
Angel Reyes,* Treas.; Elizabeth Crittenden-Palacios,
Exec. Dir.; Edy Anderson; Betty Backer; Barney
Berkowitz; B.T. Coleman; Leslee Peterson; Eleanor
Romero; Arthur Sargent; Fred Winter.
Number of staff: 1 full-time professional; 2 part-time
professional; 1 full-time support.
EIN: 850425147

5499
Eugene Victor Thaw Art Foundation ✧

553 Canyon Rd.
P.O. Box 2422
Santa Fe, NM 87501

Donors: Eugene V. Thaw; Clare E. Thaw.
Foundation type: Operating foundation.
Financial data (yr. ended 12/31/05): Assets,
$2,197,084 (M); gifts received, $1,310,000;
expenditures, $674,633; qualifying distributions,
$1,890,985; giving activities include $672,030 for
2 grants (high: $650,000; low: $22,030).
Purpose and activities: Giving for the preservation
of artwork, including the catalogued collection of
drawings owned by Eugene V. Thaw and Clare E.
Thaw, which shall be transferred to the corporation,
and to facilitate the display of such works through
an active program of loans of artwork to museums
and other nonprofit charitable or educational
institutions. Funding also to improve education
relating to the visual arts.
Fields of interest: Museums (art); Historic
preservation/historical societies.
Limitations: Applications not accepted. Giving
primarily in New York, NY. No grants to individuals.
Application information: Contributes only to
pre-selected organizations.
Officers: Eugene V. Thaw, Pres.; Clare E. Thaw, V.P.
and Secy.
Directors: William Acquavella; Charles Ryscamp;
Nicholas E. Thaw.
EIN: 850418029

5500
Eugene V. & Clare E. Thaw Charitable
Trust ▼ ✧

P.O. Box 2422
Santa Fe, NM 87504-2422 (505) 982-7023
Contact: Sherry Thompson, Exec. Dir.
FAX: (505) 982-7027; E-mail (for Sherry Thompson):
sherryt@thawtrust.org

Established in 1981 in NY as a private operating
foundation; status changed to an independent
grantmaking foundation in 1994 in NM.
Donors: Eugene Victor Thaw; Clare Eddy Thaw.
Foundation type: Independent foundation.
Financial data (yr. ended 12/31/05): Assets,
$43,354,592 (M); expenditures, $3,842,228;
qualifying distributions, $3,678,469; giving
activities include $3,311,845 for 98 grants (high:
$500,000; low: $1,000; average: $5,000–
$50,000).
Purpose and activities: Support for the arts, ecology
and the environment, and animal rights and
protection. The trust prefers to make challenge
grants that are conditional on recipients matching
the funds in an agreed-upon proportion.
Fields of interest: Arts; Environment; Animal
welfare.

International interests: Russia; United Kingdom.
Type of support: Program development;
Conferences/seminars; Publication; Seed money;
Research; Technical assistance; Matching/
challenge support.
Limitations: Applications not accepted. Giving on a
national basis. No grants to individuals or for
operating support.
Publications: Biennial report.
Application information: Contributes only to
pre-selected organizations.
Board meeting date(s): Fall
Officers and Directors:* Eugene Victor Thaw,*
Pres.; Sherry Thompson, Exec. Dir.; William
Acquavella; Jeffrey L. Fornaciari; Patricia Tang; Clare
Eddy Thaw; Nicholas Thaw.
Number of staff: 2 full-time professional.
EIN: 133081491
Selected grants: The following grants were reported
in 2004.
$520,000 to Pierpont Morgan Library, New York, NY.
2 grants: $20,000 (For annual support of
Director's Roundtable), $500,000 (Toward
capital campaign).
$200,000 to Museum of Modern Art, New York, NY.
Toward capital campaign.
$150,000 to Santa Fe Animal Shelter and Humane
Society, Santa Fe, NM. For capital campaign.
$100,000 to Cornell University, Baker Institute for
Animal Health, Ithaca, NY. Toward construction
of new auditorium.
$100,000 to Museum of Indian Arts and Culture,
Santa Fe, NM. Toward design and construction of
Masterpieces Gallery.
$75,000 to Quivira Coalition, Santa Fe, NM. For
general operating support and New Ranch
Campaign.
$31,500 to Colorados Helping Hands Foundation,
Denver, CO. For lameness evaluation laboratory.
$25,000 to Metropolitan Opera, New York, NY. For
annual support for President's Circle.
$20,000 to Think New Mexico, Santa Fe, NM. For
challenge grant toward strategic water reserve for
New Mexico.

5501
Thornburg Charitable Foundation ✧

(formerly Garrett Thornburg Foundation)
369 Montezuma Ave., Ste. 508
Santa Fe, NM 87501
Contact: Garrett H. Thornburg, Chair.

Established in 1998 in NM.
Donor: Garrett Thornburg.
Foundation type: Independent foundation.
Financial data (yr. ended 12/31/05): Assets,
$10,777,878 (M); gifts received, $3,005,951;
expenditures, $722,980; qualifying distributions,
$684,800; giving activities include $684,800 for 37
grants (high: $250,000; low: $1,000).
Purpose and activities: Giving primarily to foster
human development by providing support to a variety
of nonprofit organizations locally, nationally, and
internationally.
Fields of interest: Performing arts; Youth
development; Child development, services; Family
services.
Type of support: General/operating support;
Continuing support; Program development.
Limitations: Applications not accepted. Giving
primarily in NM. No support for political or religious
organizations, animal rights, or large scale medical

programs. No grants to individuals, or for debt retirement or endowment campaigns.
Application information: Contributes only to pre-selected organizations.
Officers and Directors:* Garrett H. Thornburg,* Chair.; Catherine Oppenheimer, Vice-Chair.; Beckie Hanttula,* Secy.-Treas.; Lloyd J. Thornburg.
Number of staff: 1 part-time professional.
EIN: 850457010

5502
J. E. & Lillian Tipton Foundation ◇
324 Paseo De Peralta
Santa Fe, NM   87501

Established in 1997.
Donor: J.E. Tipton.
Foundation type: Independent foundation.
Financial data (yr. ended 12/31/05): Assets, $5,395,866 (M); expenditures, $541,992; qualifying distributions, $375,000; giving activities include $375,000 for 3 grants (high: $300,000; low: $25,000).
Fields of interest: Higher education.
Limitations: Applications not accepted. Giving primarily in CA. No grants to individuals.
Application information: Contributes only to pre-selected organizations.
Officers: J.E. Tipton, Chair.; Joseph Byrne, Pres.; Nancy J. Byrne, V.P.; L. Nelle Byrne, Secy.-Treas.
EIN: 911868563

Selected grants: The following grants were reported in 2004.
$400,000 to University of California at Santa Barbara Foundation, Santa Barbara, CA.
$143,224 to University of California, Regents, Oakland, CA.
$125,000 to Capuchin Franciscan Order, Burlingame, CA.
$80,000 to Santa Barbara Museum of Natural History, Santa Barbara, CA.
$50,000 to Direct Relief International, Santa Barbara, CA.
$30,000 to Dunn School, Los Olivos, CA.
$20,000 to Wilding Museum, Santa Barbara, CA.
$10,000 to Catholic Charities, Santa Barbara, CA.

5503
Doris Goodwin Walbridge Foundation ◇
P.O. Box 32196
Santa Fe, NM   87594
Application address: c/o Ryann Whalen, Secy., Harris, Kessler and Goldstein, 640 N. LaSalle St., No. 590, Chicago, IL 60610, tel.: (312) 280-0111

Established in 2001 in WI.
Foundation type: Independent foundation.
Financial data (yr. ended 12/31/05): Assets, $8,060,778 (M); expenditures, $459,477; qualifying distributions, $398,480; giving activities include $398,480 for 32 grants (high: $35,000; low: $4,576).

Fields of interest: Higher education; Scholarships/financial aid; American Red Cross; Foundations (community); Protestant agencies & churches.
Limitations: Giving primarily in IL, NM and WI.
Application information:
  Initial approach: Letter
  Deadline(s): None
Officers and Directors:* Stephen Gaber,* Pres.; Ryann Whalen,* Secy.; David Gaber.
EIN: 391999473
Selected grants: The following grants were reported in 2004.
$50,000 to Santa Fe Community Foundation, Santa Fe, NM. 2 grants: $25,000 each
$30,000 to Alverno College, Milwaukee, WI.
$20,000 to Saint Matthias Episcopal Church, Minocqua, WI.
$15,000 to Fine Arts for Children and Teens, Santa Fe, NM.
$15,000 to Mentoring New Mexico, Santa Fe, NM.
$15,000 to Music Theater Workshop, Chicago, IL.
$15,000 to Outside In, Santa Fe, NM.
$10,000 to Food for Santa Fe, Santa Fe, NM.
$10,000 to Self Help, Los Alamos, NM.

NEW YORK

5504
1101 Foundation ✧
c/o Hodgson, Russ, Andrews, Woods & Goodyear
1 M&T Plz., Ste. 200
Buffalo, NY 14203

Established in 1995 in NY.
Donors: Donald L. Meyer; American Lumber, LP; Baillie Properties; Baillie Lumber; DLM Holdings, Inc.
Foundation type: Independent foundation.
Financial data (yr. ended 12/31/05): Assets, $2,120,816 (M); gifts received, $200,864; expenditures, $923,878; qualifying distributions, $900,000; giving activities include $900,000 for 2 grants (high: $700,000; low: $200,000).
Fields of interest: Human services; Protestant agencies & churches.
Limitations: Applications not accepted. Giving primarily in upstate, NY. No grants to individuals.
Application information: Contributes only to pre-selected organizations.
Trustees: Donald L. Meyer; Doris C. Meyer.
EIN: 161478622

5505
291 Foundation
291 Church St.
New York, NY 10013

Established in 2001 in NY.
Donor: Nancy L. Wender.
Foundation type: Independent foundation.
Financial data (yr. ended 10/31/05): Assets, $4,174,947 (M); expenditures, $478,068; qualifying distributions, $453,585; giving activities include $452,065 for 35 grants (high: $75,000; low: $15).
Purpose and activities: Giving primarily to an art curatorial fund, as well as for human services.
Fields of interest: Arts, single organization support; Housing/shelter, development; Human services.
Limitations: Applications not accepted. Giving primarily in CT and NY. No grants to individuals.
Application information: Contributes only to pre-selected organizations.
Trustee: Nancy L. Wender.
EIN: 137298760
Selected grants: The following grants were reported in 2005.
$25,000 to Geisinger Health System, Danville, PA.
$8,000 to New York University, New York, NY. 2 grants: $500, $7,500
$5,000 to Southern Connecticut State University, New Haven, CT.
$2,500 to Roxbury Land Trust, Roxbury, CT.
$500 to Minor Memorial Library, Roxbury, CT. 2 grants: $250 each
$500 to Roxbury Ambulance Association, Roxbury, CT. 2 grants: $250 each

5506
A.E. Charitable Foundation ✧
c/o U.S. Trust
114 W. 47th St., TAX KJM
New York, NY 10036 (212) 649-5971

Established in 1986 in NY.
Donors: Anthony B. Evnin; Judith W. Evnin.
Foundation type: Independent foundation.
Financial data (yr. ended 12/31/05): Assets, $8,303,709 (M); gifts received, $1,369,730; expenditures, $472,785; qualifying distributions, $462,849; giving activities include $459,450 for 84 grants (high: $100,000; low: $250).
Purpose and activities: Giving primarily for the arts and to health organizations.
Fields of interest: Museums (art); Performing arts centers; Performing arts, music; Arts; Education; Health organizations.
Type of support: Annual campaigns; Capital campaigns; Endowments.
Limitations: Giving primarily in Westchester County and New York, NY.
Application information: Application form not required.
Initial approach: Letter
Deadline(s): None
Officers: Anthony B. Evnin, Pres.; Judith W. Evnin, Secy.
EIN: 133317246
Selected grants: The following grants were reported in 2004.
$25,000 to Metropolitan Opera Association, New York, NY.
$11,750 to Carnegie Hall Society, New York, NY. 2 grants: $10,000, $1,750
$5,000 to Greenwich Hospital, Greenwich, CT.
$5,000 to Teach America, Chicago, IL.
$5,000 to Whitney Museum of American Art, New York, NY.
$3,500 to Metropolitan College of New York, New York, NY.
$2,500 to Bruce Museum, Greenwich, CT.
$2,500 to Storm King Art Center, Mountainville, NY.
$1,500 to Montefiore Hospital, Pittsburgh, PA.

5507
A.R. & M.G.R. Charitable Foundation, Inc. ✧ ☆
276 Riverside Dr.
New York, NY 10025

Established in 2002 in NY.
Donors: Abraham Reiss; Marie Reiss.
Foundation type: Independent foundation.
Financial data (yr. ended 12/31/05): Assets, $2,444,090 (M); expenditures, $770,162; qualifying distributions, $740,750; giving activities include $740,500 for grants.
Fields of interest: Jewish agencies & temples.
Limitations: Applications not accepted. No grants to individuals.
Application information: Contributes only to pre-selected organizations.
Officers: Abraham Reiss, Pres.; Marie Reiss, V.P.; Jacob Weinreb, Secy.-Treas.
EIN: 010719924

5508
The Abelard Foundation, Inc. ✧
c/o White & Case
1155 Ave. of the Americas
New York, NY 10036
URL: http://foundationcenter.org/grantmaker/abelardeast

Incorporated in 1958 in NY as successor to Albert B. Wells Charitable Trust established in 1950 in MA.
Donor: Members of the Wells family.
Foundation type: Independent foundation.
Financial data (yr. ended 12/31/03): Assets, $6,202,156 (M); gifts received, $252,000; expenditures, $651,376; qualifying distributions, $575,123; giving activities include $453,500 for 45 grants (high: $10,000; low: $8,750).
Purpose and activities: Giving especially for seed money to new organizations and model projects, with emphasis on protection of civil rights and civil liberties; support for programs designed to achieve social, political, and economic equality for urban and rural poor, including giving them a voice in decisions about their environment.
Fields of interest: Environment, natural resources; Crime/law enforcement; Employment, labor unions/organizations; Human services; Women, centers/services; Minorities/immigrants, centers/services; International human rights; Civil rights, advocacy; Civil liberties, advocacy; Urban/community development; Rural development; Public policy, research; Public affairs; Minorities; Native Americans/American Indians; Women; Immigrants/refugees; Economically disadvantaged.
Type of support: General/operating support; Program development; Publication; Seed money; Technical assistance; Matching/challenge support.
Limitations: Giving limited to New York, NY, the western states, and the southern states, including the Appalachia region. No support for medical, educational, cultural institutions, or government sponsored programs. No grants to individuals, or for building or endowment funds, continuing support, annual campaigns, emergency funds, scholarships, fellowships, research, or video or film production; no loans.
Publications: Grants list; Informational brochure (including application guidelines).
Application information: Application form not required.
Initial approach: Letter
Copies of proposal: 1
Deadline(s): None
Board meeting date(s): May and Nov.
Final notification: Immediately following board meeting
Officers and Trustee: * Susan Collins, Pres.; Steven Bernhard, V.P.; Melissa Blessing, V.P.; Charles Schreck, V.P.; George B. Wells II, V.P.; Malcolm J. Edgerton, Jr.,* Secy.; Charles R. Schreck, Treas.
Number of staff: 1 part-time professional; 2 part-time support.
EIN: 136064580

5509
Joseph & Sophia Abeles Foundation, Inc. ✧
1055 Bedford Rd.
Pleasantville, NY 10570-3907

Established in 1960 in NY.
Donors: Joseph C. Abeles; Sophia Abeles‡.
Foundation type: Independent foundation.
Financial data (yr. ended 12/31/05): Assets, $6,238,145 (M); expenditures, $552,012; qualifying distributions, $479,500; giving activities include $479,250 for 64 grants (high: $28,000; low: $250).
Fields of interest: Museums (art); Performing arts; Arts; Higher education; Hospitals (general); Human services.

Type of support: General/operating support; Annual campaigns; Emergency funds; Program development.
Limitations: Applications not accepted. Giving primarily in New York, NY, and Westchester County, NY. No grants to individuals.
Application information: Contributes only to pre-selected organizations.
Officers: Joseph C. Abeles, Pres.; Lucille Werlinich, V.P.
Number of staff: 2 part-time professional; 1 part-time support.
EIN: 136259577

5510
The Alexander Abraham Foundation ◇ ☆
c/o B. Strauss Assoc. LTD.
307 5th Ave., 8th Fl.
New York, NY   10016-6517

Established in 2002 in DE.
Donors: Nancy Abraham; Tiger Conservation Fund.
Foundation type: Independent foundation.
Financial data (yr. ended 11/30/05): Assets, $961,695 (M); gifts received, $474,361; expenditures, $693,913; qualifying distributions, $685,655; giving activities include $622,522 for 45 grants (high: $173,948; low: $250; average: $1,000–$10,000).
Fields of interest: Animal welfare; Animals/wildlife; Human services.
Limitations: Applications not accepted.
Application information: Contributes only to pre-selected organizations.
Officers and Directors:* Nancy Abraham,* Pres.; Antonia Abraham,* Secy.; Arnold Moss,* Treas.
EIN: 300139596

5511
Louis and Anne Abrons Foundation, Inc. ▼
437 Madison Ave.
New York, NY   10017   (212) 756-3376
Contact: Richard Abrons, Pres.

Incorporated in 1950 in NY.
Donors: Anne S. Abrons†; Louis Abrons†.
Foundation type: Independent foundation.
Financial data (yr. ended 12/31/05): Assets, $91,643,404 (M); expenditures, $4,426,413; qualifying distributions, $4,249,001; giving activities include $4,234,600 for 195 grants (high: $300,000; low: $1,000; average: $5,000–$50,000).
Purpose and activities: Giving primarily to social welfare agencies, Jewish charities, major New York, NY, institutions, civic improvement programs, education, and environmental and cultural projects.
Fields of interest: Museums; Arts; Libraries/library science; Education; Environment; Hospitals (general); Reproductive health, family planning; Legal services; Employment; Human services; Children/youth, services; Family services; Aging, centers/services; Minorities/immigrants, centers/services; Community development; Jewish agencies & temples; Aging; African Americans/Blacks; Economically disadvantaged; Homeless.
Type of support: Continuing support; Annual campaigns; Building/renovation; Program development; Scholarship funds; Research; Technical assistance; Consulting services.

Limitations: Applications not accepted. Giving primarily in the metropolitan New York, NY, area. No grants to individuals.
Application information: Contributes only to pre-selected organizations. Telephone calls not accepted. Unsolicited applications not considered or acknowledged.
Board meeting date(s): Feb., June, and Oct.
Officers and Directors:* Richard Abrons,* Pres.; Rita Aranow,* V.P.; Anne S. Abrons,* Secy.-Treas.; Adam Abrons; Alix Abrons; Eleanor Abrons; Henry Abrons; John Abrons; Leslie Abrons; Peter Abrons; Judith Aranow; Stephanie DeChristina; Vicki Feiner; Jennifer Schwartz.
EIN: 136061329
Selected grants: The following grants were reported in 2005.
$300,000 to Henry Street Settlement, New York, NY. For scholarship fund.
$160,000 to UJA-Federation of New York, New York, NY.
$125,000 to Council on the Environment, New York, NY.
$100,000 to Northern Westchester Hospital Center, Mount Kisco, NY.
$50,000 to Albany Park Theater Project, Chicago, IL.
$50,000 to We Can, New York, NY.
$40,000 to Public School 42, Benjamin Altman School, New York, NY.
$20,000 to Hudson Guild, New York, NY.
$20,000 to New York Botanical Garden, Bronx, NY.
$17,500 to Poets and Writers, New York, NY.

5512
The Richard & Iris Abrons Foundation, Inc. ☆
(formerly The Richard & Mimi Abrons Foundation)
c/o Richard Abrons
437 Madison Ave.
New York, NY   10017
Contact: Richard Abrons, Pres.

Established in 1964 in NY.
Donors: Richard Abrons; Iris Abrons.
Foundation type: Independent foundation.
Financial data (yr. ended 12/31/05): Assets, $1,277,193 (M); gifts received, $125,738; expenditures, $395,218; qualifying distributions, $392,140; giving activities include $391,750 for 82 grants (high: $50,000; low: $150).
Fields of interest: Performing arts, theater; Arts; Reproductive health, family planning; Human services; Jewish agencies & temples.
Type of support: General/operating support; Continuing support; Annual campaigns; Program development; Research.
Limitations: Applications not accepted. Giving primarily in New York, NY. No grants to individuals.
Application information: Contributes only to pre-selected organizations.
Officers and Directors:* Richard Abrons,* Pres.; Iris Abrons,* Secy.; John Abrons; Leslie Abrons; Peter Abrons.
EIN: 136184029
Selected grants: The following grants were reported in 2005.
$130,000 to We Can, New York, NY. 3 grants: $50,000, $50,000, $30,000
$25,400 to Henry Street Settlement, New York, NY. 3 grants: $20,000, $2,500, $2,900
$15,000 to Lenox Hill Hospital, New York, NY.
$5,000 to New Alternatives for Children, New York, NY.

$2,400 to Planned Parenthood Hudson Peconic, Hawthorne, NY.
$1,000 to East Hampton Healthcare Center, East Hampton, NY.

5513
The Achelis Foundation
767 3rd Ave., 4th Fl.
New York, NY   10017   (212) 644-0322
Contact: Joseph S. Dolan, Secy.
FAX: (212) 759-6510;
E-mail: main@achelis-bodman-fnds.org;
URL: http://foundationcenter.org/grantmaker/achelis-bodman/

Incorporated in 1940 in NY.
Donor: Elisabeth Achelis†.
Foundation type: Independent foundation.
Financial data (yr. ended 12/31/05): Assets, $40,386,945 (M); gifts received, $5,500; expenditures, $2,005,079; qualifying distributions, $1,677,016; giving activities include $1,471,060 for grants.
Purpose and activities: Giving for social services, including child welfare and youth, the disabled, and issues of health, including hospitals, medical research, drug abuse, and rehabilitation programs, literacy projects and other educational agencies, with preference for school reforms, school choice, and charter school projects rather than nonprofits that provide direct services in public schools, and the arts, culture, and the media. Other interests include voluntarism, entrepreneurship, strengthening the two-parent family, fatherhood (and father absence), private sector job placement, self-help and self-reliance, economic development, promoting the institution of marriage, faith-based programs, and prevention and early intervention. The foundation prefers programs that emphasize measurable participant outcomes and program results, innovations and new cost-saving approaches, consumer choice, and parental involvement.
Fields of interest: Humanities; Arts; Education, reform; Elementary/secondary school reform; Higher education reform; Adult education—literacy, basic skills & GED; Education; Medical care, rehabilitation; Health care, cost containment; Health care; Substance abuse, prevention; Alcoholism; Medical research, institute; Crime/violence prevention, youth; Offenders/ex-offenders, prison alternatives; Employment; Children/youth, services; Children, adoption; Family services; Public policy, research; Welfare policy/reform; Religion; Disabilities, people with; Homeless.
Type of support: General/operating support; Equipment; Program development; Conferences/seminars; Publication; Seed money; Curriculum development; Fellowships; Internship funds; Scholarship funds; Research; Technical assistance; Program evaluation; Matching/challenge support.
Limitations: Giving primarily in the New York, NY, area. Generally, no support for colleges and universities, small art, dance, music, or theater groups, national health or mental health organizations, housing, international projects, government agencies, public schools (except charter schools), or nonprofit programs and services significantly funded or wholly reimbursed by the government. No grants to individuals, or for annual appeals, dinner functions, fundraising events, capital campaigns, deficit financing, or film or travel; no loans.

Publications: Application guidelines; Biennial report (including application guidelines); Financial statement; Grants list.
Application information: Do not send CDs, DVDs, discs or tapes, or proposals through the internet unless requested; see foundation Web site for application guidelines and procedures. Application form not required.
Initial approach: Letter or short proposal
Copies of proposal: 1
Deadline(s): None
Board meeting date(s): Usually in May, Sept., and Dec.
Final notification: 3 to 4 weeks
Officers and Trustees:* John N. Irwin III,* Chair. and C.E.O.; Russell P. Pennoyer,* Pres.; Peter Frelinghuysen,* V.P.; Mary S. Phipps,* V.P.; Joseph S. Dolan, Secy. and Exec. Dir.; Horace I. Crary, Jr., Treas.; Hon. Walter J.P. Curley; Anthony Drexel Duke; Leslie Lenkowsky.
Number of staff: 2 full-time professional; 1 part-time support.
EIN: 136022018
Selected grants: The following grants were reported in 2005.
$100,000 to Manhattan Institute for Policy Research, New York, NY. For Temporary Assistance to Parolees in Need initiative.
$75,000 to Baruch College of the City University of New York, Zicklin School of Business, Center for the Study of Business and Government, New York, NY. For Health Policy Research and Uninsured.
$50,000 to Bronx Charter School for Excellence, Bronx, NY. For renovation and start-up expenses at new building, payable over 1.50 years.
$50,000 to KIPP (Knowledge is Power Program) Academy, Bronx, NY. For start-up expenses of KIPP AMP Charter School.
$50,000 to Syracuse University, Maxwell School of Citizenship and Public Affairs, Alan K. Campbell Public Affairs Institute, Syracuse, NY. For new book, Charity and Selfishness: Truth About Who Gives in America and the World.
$30,000 to Hope Program, Brooklyn, NY. For Probationer Employment Project.
$25,000 to Abraham House, Bronx, NY. For Healthy Family Workshops, payable over 1.50 years.
$25,000 to Achievement First, New Haven, CT. For start-up support and first-year support for Achievement First East New York Charter Elementary School.
$25,000 to Girls Preparatory Charter School, New York, NY. For start-up and first-year expenses of Girls Preparatory Charter School.
$25,000 to New York Society for the Prevention of Cruelty to Children, New York, NY. Toward Positive Parenting Plus Initiative, payable over 1.50 years.

5514
The Edith & F. M. Achilles Memorial Fund ✧
c/o JPMorgan Chase Bank, N.A.
345 Park Ave., 4th Fl.
New York, NY 10154 (212) 464-2441
Contact: Edward L. Jones, V.P.
FAX: (212) 464-2305;
E-mail: jones_ed_1@jpmorgan.com

Established in 1996 in NY.
Foundation type: Independent foundation.

Financial data (yr. ended 12/31/05): Assets, $13,689,399 (M); expenditures, $804,312; qualifying distributions, $668,463; giving activities include $640,000 for 5 grants (high: $275,000; low: $50,000).
Purpose and activities: Giving to schools, libraries, museums, and related organizations having education as their principal purpose.
Fields of interest: Museums (art); Higher education.
Limitations: Applications not accepted. Giving primarily in the metropolitan New York, NY, area, and NC. No grants to individuals.
Publications: Grants list; Informational brochure.
Application information: Contributes only to pre-selected organizations.
Trustee: JPMorgan Chase Bank, N.A.
EIN: 137102170

5515
Acorn Foundation, Inc. ✧ ☆
c/o The Bank of New York, Tax Dep't.
1 Wall St., 28th Fl.
New York, NY 10286

Established in 1992 in NJ.
Donors: Grace K. Culbertson; John H. Culbertson, Jr.; Marian V.C. Hvolbeck; Katherine C. Prentice.
Foundation type: Independent foundation.
Financial data (yr. ended 12/31/05): Assets, $8,381,696 (M); gifts received, $2,649,094; expenditures, $406,580; qualifying distributions, $365,208; giving activities include $365,208 for grants.
Purpose and activities: Giving primarily for the arts, education, particularly to schools of medicine, the environment, youth, family and social services, health associations, and to Episcopal organizations.
Fields of interest: Museums (art); Performing arts; Arts; Higher education; Medical school/education; Education; Environment, natural resources; Botanical gardens; Hospitals (general); Health care; Health organizations, association; Cancer research; Human services; Children/youth, services; Family services; Protestant agencies & churches.
Limitations: Applications not accepted. Giving primarily in NJ, and New York, NY. No grants to individuals.
Application information: Contributes only to pre-selected organizations.
Officers: Grace K. Culbertson, Pres.; Marian V.C. Hvolbeck, V.P.; Katherine C. Prentice, Secy.; John H. Culbertson, Jr., Treas.
Trustee: The Bank of New York.
EIN: 223079659
Selected grants: The following grants were reported in 2004.
$20,000 to Lawrenceville School, Lawrenceville, NJ.
$5,000 to Family Service of Morris County, Morristown, NJ.
$5,000 to Planned Parenthood of Metropolitan New Jersey, Newark, NJ.
$5,000 to Wilkes University, Wilkes Barre, PA.
$3,000 to Hospice of Morris County, Morristown, NJ.
$2,000 to American Museum of Natural History, New York, NY.
$2,000 to Central Park Conservancy, New York, NY.
$1,000 to Citymeals-on-Wheels, New York, NY.
$1,000 to Emory University, School of Medicine, Atlanta, GA.
$1,000 to New-York Historical Society, New York, NY.

5516
Joan & Alan Ades-Taub Foundation, Inc. ✧ ☆
575 Madison Ave., Ste. 1006
New York, NY 10022

Established in 1997.
Donor: Alan M. Ades.
Foundation type: Independent foundation.
Financial data (yr. ended 12/31/05): Assets, $4,372,543 (M); gifts received, $4,501,687; expenditures, $329,074; qualifying distributions, $329,074; giving activities include $326,675 for 9 grants (high: $50,000; low: $25).
Purpose and activities: Giving for the arts, health, and religious organizations.
Fields of interest: Performing arts, opera; Arts; Medical care, in-patient care; Health care; Religion, association; Christian agencies & churches; Jewish agencies & temples.
Limitations: Applications not accepted. Giving on a national basis, with emphasis on NY.
Application information: Unsolicited requests for funds not accepted.
Officers: Joan Ades, Pres.; Alan M. Ades, V.P.
EIN: 113293314

5517
Adirondack Community Trust
2284 Saranac Ave.
Lake Placid, NY 12946 (518) 523-9904
Contact: Cali Brooks, Exec. Dir.
FAX: (518) 523-9905; E-mail: info@generousact.org;
URL: http://www.generousact.org

Established in 1997 in NY.
Foundation type: Community foundation.
Financial data (yr. ended 6/30/05): Assets, $7,250,103 (M); gifts received, $1,973,146; expenditures, $1,499,560; giving activities include $1,203,137 for 315 grants.
Purpose and activities: The foundation seeks to unite donors' charitable interests with the needs of the Adirondack region by: 1) building a permanent and flexible endowment that can respond to the most pressing current, and future, needs of the region; 2) working with donors and their advisors to design named endowments that meet the unique and individual charitable objectives of the donor; 3) administering a creative program of grantmaking to give maximum benefit to charitable needs within the area and carry out the wishes of donors; 4) being a prudent manager and faithful steward of philanthropic assets; 5) and being a leader and catalyst focusing attention on the needs of the region.
Fields of interest: Historic preservation/historical societies; Arts; Libraries/library science; Education; Environment; Animal welfare; Health care; Recreation; Children/youth, services; Human services; Community development.
Type of support: General/operating support; Continuing support; Annual campaigns; Capital campaigns; Building/renovation; Land acquisition; Endowments; Program development; Publication; Seed money; Curriculum development; Scholarship funds; Technical assistance; Scholarships—to individuals; Matching/challenge support.
Limitations: Giving limited to the Adirondack region of NY.
Publications: Annual report; Financial statement; Grants list; Informational brochure; Newsletter.

Application information: Visit foundation Web site for scholarship applications and information.

Board meeting date(s): Jan., May, July, and Oct.

Officers and Trustees:* Meredith Prime,* Chair.; David Johnson,* Vice-Chair.; Ann Merkel,* Secy.; Roderic G. Giltz,* Treas.; Cali Brooks, Exec. Dir.; Gary Benware; Adele Connors; Carol Ann Inserra; John Lansing; Vincent McCelland; Michael O'Connor; Peter Paine; Glenn Pearsall; Craig Randall.

Number of staff: 2 full-time professional; 1 part-time professional.

EIN: 161535724

5518
Jack Adjmi Family Foundation, Inc. ◇
500 7th Ave., 16th Fl.
New York, NY 10018 (212) 239-8615
Contact: Eric Adjmi, Dir.

Established in 1983 in NY.

Donors: Eric Adjmi; Jack Adjmi†; Mark Adjmi; Ronald Adjmi; Joey Dewk; Kim Dabah; Rachel Adjmi; Solomon Dabah; Elliott Mahana; Joy Mahana; Beluga, Inc.; Consolidated Childrens Apparel; IFG Corp.; Popsicle Playwear, Ltd.; Blue School; Congregation Z.Y.C.; Klatskin Assocs.; Adjmi Dwek Foundation.

Foundation type: Independent foundation.

Financial data (yr. ended 11/30/05): Assets, $64,735 (M); gifts received, $4,723,422; expenditures, $4,609,796; qualifying distributions, $4,609,796; giving activities include $4,609,666 for 631 grants (high: $627,912; low: $18; average: $1,000–$50,000).

Purpose and activities: Giving primarily to Jewish organizations including education, medical, and human services.

Fields of interest: Elementary/secondary education; Hospitals (general); Human services; Jewish federated giving programs; Jewish agencies & temples.

Limitations: Giving primarily in NY. No grants to individuals.

Application information: Application form not required.

Initial approach: Proposal
Deadline(s): None

Officer and Directors: Eli Seruya, Mgr.; Eric Adjmi; Rachel Adjmi.

EIN: 133202295

5519
Lillian Adjmi Foundation ◇
1407 Broadway, 32nd Fl.
New York, NY 10018

Established in 1999 in NY.

Donors: Harry Adjmi; One Step Up.

Foundation type: Independent foundation.

Financial data (yr. ended 7/31/05): Assets, $0 (M); gifts received, $643,279; expenditures, $748,338; qualifying distributions, $748,338; giving activities include $746,031 for 171 grants (high: $62,100; low: $40; average: $1,000–$25,000).

Purpose and activities: Giving primarily for Jewish education, temples and organizations.

Fields of interest: Education; Human services; Children/youth, services; Jewish agencies & temples.

Limitations: Applications not accepted. Giving primarily in NY. No grants to individuals.

Application information: Contributes only to pre-selected organizations.

Trustee: Harry Adjmi.

EIN: 061532888

5520
The Adjmi-Dwek Family Foundation, Inc. ◇
c/o Eli Seruya
500 7th Ave., 16th Fl.
New York, NY 10018 (212) 239-8615
Contact: Joseph Dwek, Dir.

Established in 1994 in NY.

Donors: Joseph Dwek; Sister Sister, Inc.; Sports Products of America, LLC.

Foundation type: Independent foundation.

Financial data (yr. ended 12/31/04): Assets, $1,536 (M); gifts received, $4,446,600; expenditures, $4,436,195; qualifying distributions, $4,436,195; giving activities include $4,436,195 for 332 grants (high: $310,400; low: $10).

Purpose and activities: Support primarily for Jewish agencies and temples, and secondary education.

Fields of interest: Secondary school/education; Jewish agencies & temples.

Limitations: Giving on a national and international basis.

Application information:

Initial approach: Letter
Deadline(s): None

Directors: Jack Adjmi; Joseph Dwek; Terry Dwek.

EIN: 133782816

Selected grants: The following grants were reported in 2003.

$455,000 to Deal Yeshiva, Deal, NJ.

$33,000 to Ichud Mosdos Hachinuch in Brooklyn, Brooklyn, NY.

$26,000 to Yad Eliezer, Brooklyn, NY.

$21,893 to Magen Israel Society, Brooklyn, NY.

$17,000 to Sephardic Bikur Holim, Brooklyn, NY.

$15,000 to Yeshiva Shaare Torah, Brooklyn, NY.

$3,600 to Ilan High School, Long Branch, NJ.

$1,800 to Ner Israel Rabbinical College, Baltimore, MD.

$500 to Diaspora Yeshiva Toras Yisrael, Jerusalem, Israel. .

$500 to Knesset Yehuda, Spring Valley, NY.

5521
Adler Foundation, Inc. ◇
c/o Helen A. Potter
6 Windward Ln.
Scarsdale, NY 10583

Incorporated in 1951 in NY.

Donors: Morton M. Adler†; Helen R. Adler†; Harry Rosenthal†; John Adler.

Foundation type: Independent foundation.

Financial data (yr. ended 9/30/05): Assets, $2,361,953 (M); expenditures, $552,233; qualifying distributions, $528,866; giving activities include $506,375 for 13 grants (high: $80,000; low: $125).

Purpose and activities: Grants limited to medical research.

Fields of interest: Medical research, institute.

Type of support: Conferences/seminars; Seed money; Research.

Limitations: Applications not accepted. Giving on a national basis. No grants to individuals.

Application information: Contributes only to pre-selected organizations.

Officers: John Adler, Pres.; Joel I. Berson, Secy.; Helen A. Potter, Treas.

EIN: 136087869

5522
Adnim Foundation ◇ ☆
c/o Stanley Fleishman
98 Rye Ridge Rd.
Harrison, NY 10528

Established in 2002 in NY.

Donor: Stanley Fleishman.

Foundation type: Independent foundation.

Financial data (yr. ended 9/30/05): Assets, $237,825 (M); gifts received, $311,720; expenditures, $517,510; qualifying distributions, $517,497; giving activities include $517,497 for grants.

Fields of interest: Health care; Jewish federated giving programs; Jewish agencies & temples.

Limitations: Applications not accepted. Giving primarily in NY, with emphasis on the greater metropolitan New York City region. No grants to individuals.

Application information: Contributes only to pre-selected organizations.

Officers and Directors:* Stanley Fleishman,* Pres.; Richard Kirschner,* Secy.; Martine Fleishman,* Treas.

EIN: 542067979

5523
The Aeneas Capital Management Foundation ◇
100 S. Bedford Rd., Ste. 240
Mount Kisco, NY 10549

Established in 2000 in NY.

Donors: Thomas Grossman; Aeneas Capital Management, LP; Jason Konidaris.

Foundation type: Company-sponsored foundation.

Financial data (yr. ended 12/31/04): Assets, $1,059,340 (M); gifts received, $250,000; expenditures, $347,093; qualifying distributions, $317,232; giving activities include $317,232 for 12 grants (high: $150,000; low: $1,000).

Purpose and activities: The foundation supports organizations involved with education and youth development.

Fields of interest: Education; Big Brothers/Big Sisters; Youth development.

Type of support: General/operating support.

Limitations: Giving primarily in NY.

Trustees: Thomas Grossman; John Suglia.

EIN: 137232145

Selected grants: The following grants were reported in 2004.

$150,000 to Lehigh University, Bethlehem, PA.

$66,332 to Hackley School, Tarrytown, NY.

$15,000 to Boys and Girls Clubs of Boston, Boston, MA.

$12,500 to Greenpeace Fund, DC.

$5,000 to Goshen Historic Track, Goshen, NY.

$3,000 to Standardbred Retirement Foundation, Blairstown, NJ.

$2,500 to Albany Law School, Albany, NY.

5524
Aequus Institute ✧
P.O. Box 3485
Elmira, NY 14905
Contact: Larry P. Arnn Ph.D., Exec. Dir.

Established in 1990 in CA as successor to Aequus
Institute.
Foundation type: Independent foundation.
Financial data (yr. ended 12/31/05): Assets,
$5,565,684 (M); gifts received, $158;
expenditures, $562,593; qualifying distributions,
$476,374; giving activities include $324,000 for 50
grants (high: $100,000; low: $1,000; average:
$2,500–$10,000).
Purpose and activities: To promote the teaching of
Mary Baker Eddy and the Christian Science Church,
and the free market economic system.
Fields of interest: Economics; Political science;
Public policy, research; Government/public
administration.
Publications: Informational brochure (including
application guidelines).
Application information:
Initial approach: Letter
Deadline(s): None
Officers and Directors:* Patrick Parker,* Pres.;
David Keyston,* V.P.; Edwin Feulner, Jr., Ph.D.*,
Secy.; Larry Arnn, Ph.D.*, Exec. Dir.
Number of staff: 2
EIN: 521620982

5525
The Afognak Foundation ✧
c/o U.S. Trust Co.
114 W. 47th St.
New York, NY 10036
Contact: Linda Franciscovich, Managing Dir.;
Christine O'Donnell, Asst. V.P., U.S. Trust Co.

Established in 1998 in MA.
Foundation type: Independent foundation.
Financial data (yr. ended 12/31/05): Assets,
$19,420,495 (M); expenditures, $944,301;
qualifying distributions, $918,475; giving activities
include $910,000 for 20 grants (high: $100,000;
low: $5,000; average: $25,000–$40,000).
Fields of interest: Arts; Environment, natural
resources; Science, formal/general education.
Limitations: Applications not accepted. No grants to
individuals.
Application information: Contributes only to
pre-selected organizations.
EIN: 061521981

5526
Ahava Foundation ✧
200 W. 57th St., Ste. 1005
New York, NY 10019

Established in 1998 in NY.
Donors: Tamar Abraham Wolchok; Carey Wolchok;
Netanya Endeavors, LLC.
Foundation type: Independent foundation.
Financial data (yr. ended 6/30/05): Assets,
$93,162 (M); gifts received, $717,689;
expenditures, $1,128,706; qualifying distributions,
$1,114,447; giving activities include $1,114,252
for 34 grants (high: $310,000; low: $136).
Purpose and activities: Giving primarily for Jewish
organizations.

Fields of interest: Recreation; Human services;
Jewish agencies & temples.
Limitations: Applications not accepted. Giving
primarily in NY; some funding nationally. No grants
to individuals.
Application information: Contributes only to
pre-selected organizations.
Director: Tamar Abraham Wolchok.
EIN: 133990332

5527
Ahavas Chesed Charitable Trust ✧
c/o Abraham Trusts
1325 Ave. of the Americas, 20th Fl.
New York, NY 10019

Established in 1995 in NY.
Donors: Simona Abraham Ganz; Lionel "Aryeh"
Ganz; Joshua Teitelbaum; Helene Teitelbaum;
Yehuda Scharf; Cheryl Scharf; Reiss Charity
Account; P & L Charity Foundation.
Foundation type: Independent foundation.
Financial data (yr. ended 6/30/05): Assets,
$71,598 (M); gifts received, $51,050;
expenditures, $703,374; qualifying distributions,
$703,300; giving activities include $703,300 for 13
grants (high: $600,000; low: $200).
Fields of interest: Jewish federated giving programs;
Jewish agencies & temples.
Type of support: General/operating support.
Limitations: Applications not accepted. Giving
primarily in New York, NY. No grants to individuals.
Application information: Contributes only to
pre-selected organizations.
Trustees: Estanne Abraham; Lionel "Aryeh" Ganz;
Simona Abraham Ganz; Hirschell E. Levine.
EIN: 133780739
Selected grants: The following grants were reported
in 2004.
$250,000 to P.E.F. Israel Endowment Funds, New
York, NY. For general support.
$30,000 to Yeshivas Mir Yerushalayim. For general
support.
$25,000 to Kiryat Chinuch Lebanim-Ashdod,
American Friends of, New York, NY. For general
support.
$15,000 to Agudath Israel of America, New York,
NY. For general support.
$10,000 to Ezras Torah Fund, New York, NY. For
general support.
$10,000 to Yeshivas L'Zeirim Manchester. For
general support.
$6,000 to Yeshiva Imrei Shefer, NY. For general
support.
$5,000 to Tree of Life Congregation, Spring Valley,
NY. For general support.
$3,000 to Congregation Shaarei Tefillah, Newton,
MA. For general support.
$2,500 to American Friends of Yad Kliezer,
Brooklyn, NY. For general support.

5528
AHBA, Inc. ✧
c/o Hertz, Herson & Co., LLP
2 Park Ave., Ste. 1500
New York, NY 10016

Established in 1998 in DE and NY.
Donors: Bella Wexner Charitable Remainder
Unitrust; Susan Wexner Revocable Trust.
Foundation type: Independent foundation.

Financial data (yr. ended 3/31/05): Assets,
$39,785,135 (M); expenditures, $1,613,394;
qualifying distributions, $1,339,093; giving
activities include $1,285,000 for 1 grant.
Purpose and activities: Giving primarily to a
charitable endowment program.
Fields of interest: Philanthropy/voluntarism.
Limitations: Applications not accepted. Giving
primarily in Southeastern, PA. No grants to
individuals.
Application information: Contributes only to
pre-selected organizations.
Officer and Directors:* Susan R. Wexner,* Pres.
and Secy.-Treas.; Bertrand Agus.
EIN: 133997367

5529
AIG Disaster Relief Fund-New York ✧ ☆
70 Pine St., 53rd Fl.
New York, NY 10270

Established in 2003 in NY.
Donor: Starr Foundation.
Foundation type: Independent foundation.
Financial data (yr. ended 12/31/05): Assets,
$1,538,758 (M); gifts received, $8,632,050;
expenditures, $7,668,210; qualifying distributions,
$7,666,627; giving activities include $7,642,038
for 15 grants (high: $2,456,136; low: $100,000).
Fields of interest: Disasters, preparedness/
services; Disasters, floods; Disasters, Hurricane
Katrina; Disasters, domestic resettlement; Safety/
disasters; Human services.
Limitations: Applications not accepted. Giving on a
national basis. No grants to individuals.
Application information: Contributes only to
pre-selected organizations.
Officers: Martin J. Sullivan, Chair.; Alex I. Freudman,
Vice-Chair.; Frank G. Wisner, Vice-Chair.; Edward T.
Cloonan, Pres.; Robert A. Gender, Treas.; Kathleen
E. Shannon, Secy.
EIN: 743085338

5530
Alavi Foundation ✧
500 5th Ave., Ste. 2320
New York, NY 10110-0397 (212) 944-8333
FAX: (212) 921-0325; URL: http://
www.alavifoundation.org

Incorporated in 1973 in NY.
Foundation type: Independent foundation.
Financial data (yr. ended 3/31/05): Assets,
$84,071,238 (M); gifts received, $10,849;
expenditures, $4,200,870; qualifying distributions,
$2,797,420; giving activities include $2,797,420
for 53 grants (high: $1,000,000; low: $1,000), and
$80,000 for 2 loans/program-related investments.
Purpose and activities: A primary aim of the
foundation is to promote harmony and
understanding among people of different religions.
Another of its basic aims is to promote the study of
the humanities, arts, and pure and applied
sciences. It also gives to organizations that are
involved in the teaching of Islamic culture and the
Persian language.
Fields of interest: Arts; Education; Islam.
Type of support: Continuing support; Building/
renovation; Student loans—to individuals.
Limitations: Applications not accepted. Giving on a
national basis.

Publications: Grants list; IRS Form 990-PF.
Application information: Student scholarship program has been suspended.
Board meeting date(s): Annually
Officers and Directors:* Mohammad Geramian, Pres.; Alireza Ebrahimi,* Secy.; Abbas Mirakhor,* Treas.; Hoshang Ahmadi; Mehdi Hodjat; Mohammad Pirayandeh.
Number of staff: 3 full-time professional; 2 full-time support.
EIN: 237345978
Selected grants: The following grants were reported in 2005.
$1,000,000 to Mercy Corps, Portland, OR.
$224,000 to Muslim Community School, Potomac, MD. 2 grants: $25,000, $199,000
$98,191 to Islamic Institute of New York, Woodside, NY.
$75,000 to Catholic University of America, DC.
$50,000 to Columbia University, New York, NY.
$41,000 to Harvard University, Cambridge, MA.
$30,000 to Islamic Message Group, Memphis, TN.
$26,700 to Pars Academy, Arlington, TX.
$20,000 to Noor Center Corporation, Medford, NJ.

5531
The Frances Alexander Foundation ✧
(formerly The Ann F. Kaplan & Robert Fippinger Foundation)
c/o Anchin, Block, & Anchin, LLP
1375 Broadway, 18th Fl.
New York, NY   10018

Established in 1991 in NY.
Donor: Ann F. Kaplan.
Foundation type: Independent foundation.
Financial data (yr. ended 4/30/05): Assets, $4,450,349 (M); expenditures, $957,955; qualifying distributions, $944,027; giving activities include $940,229 for 56 grants (high: $250,000; low: $250).
Purpose and activities: Giving primarily for higher education.
Fields of interest: Higher education.
Type of support: Scholarship funds.
Limitations: Applications not accepted. Giving primarily in MA and NY. No grants to individuals.
Application information: Contributes only to pre-selected organizations.
Trustees: Robert A. Fippinger; Ann F. Kaplan.
EIN: 133638507

5532
Joseph Alexander Foundation, Inc. ✧
400 Madison Ave., Ste. 906
New York, NY   10017   (212) 355-3688
Contact: Robert Weintraub, Pres.

Established in 1960 in NY.
Donor: Joseph Alexander†.
Foundation type: Independent foundation.
Financial data (yr. ended 10/31/05): Assets, $16,875,730 (M); expenditures, $871,875; qualifying distributions, $828,033; giving activities include $686,000 for 68 grants (high: $50,000; low: $1,000).
Purpose and activities: Giving primarily for Jewish organizations, as well as for education and health associations; funding also for social services.
Fields of interest: Museums; Arts; Higher education; Health organizations; Medical research,

institute; Human services; Jewish agencies & temples.
Type of support: General/operating support; Annual campaigns; Capital campaigns; Building/renovation; Equipment; Endowments; Program development; Conferences/seminars; Curriculum development; Scholarship funds; Research; Exchange programs.
Limitations: Giving primarily in New York, NY. No grants to individuals.
Publications: Financial statement.
Application information: Application form not required.
Initial approach: Proposal
Copies of proposal: 1
Deadline(s): None
Board meeting date(s): Jan., Apr., July, and Oct.
Officers and Directors:* Robert Weintraub,* Pres.; Helen Mackler,* Secy.; Harvey Mackler; Randi Windheim.
EIN: 510175951

5533
Alff Aid, Inc. ✧ ☆
1402 59th St.
Brooklyn, NY   11219

Established in 1999 in NY.
Donor: Mayer Laufer.
Foundation type: Independent foundation.
Financial data (yr. ended 12/31/05): Assets, $5,398,918 (M); gifts received, $1,575,000; expenditures, $378,117; qualifying distributions, $365,610; giving activities include $365,610 for grants.
Fields of interest: Jewish agencies & temples.
Limitations: Applications not accepted. Giving primarily in NY. No grants to individuals.
Application information: Contributes only to pre-selected organizations.
Officers: Mayer Laufer, Pres.; Doris Laufer, V.P.
EIN: 113145407

5534
Alfiero Family Charitable Foundation ✧
2150 Elmwood Ave.
Buffalo, NY   14207   (716) 876-9855
Contact: Salvatore H. Alfiero, Chair.

Established in 1989 in NY.
Donor: Salvatore H. Alfiero.
Foundation type: Independent foundation.
Financial data (yr. ended 12/31/04): Assets, $7,590,931 (M); expenditures, $584,683; qualifying distributions, $575,250; giving activities include $575,250 for 13 grants (high: $333,333; low: $1,000).
Purpose and activities: Giving primarily for education, and to children, youth and social services.
Fields of interest: Higher education; Environment, forests; Human services; Children/youth, services; Foundations (private grantmaking).
Type of support: General/operating support.
Limitations: Giving limited to NY.
Application information:
Initial approach: Proposal
Deadline(s): Nov. 30

Officers: Salvatore H. Alfiero, Chair.; Victor S. Alfiero, Pres.; Charles C. Alfiero, V.P.; James J. Alfiero, Secy.
EIN: 110036051

5535
Alison Foundation ✧ ☆
5 Taylor's Rise
Rochester, NY   14618-4800

Established in 2004 in NY.
Donors: Ronald Fielding; Donna M. Fielding.
Foundation type: Independent foundation.
Financial data (yr. ended 12/31/05): Assets, $7,368,409 (M); expenditures, $585,104; qualifying distributions, $580,680; giving activities include $580,000 for 4 grants (high: $557,000; low: $1,000).
Purpose and activities: Giving primarily to a college.
Fields of interest: Media, film/video; Higher education, college.
Limitations: Applications not accepted. Giving primarily in Annapolis, MD. No grants to individuals.
Application information: Contributes only to pre-selected organizations.
Trustees: Donna M. Fielding; Ronald H. Fielding.
EIN: 200226054

5536
The Herbert Allen Foundation ✧
711 5th Ave.
New York, NY   10022-3194
Contact: Howard Felson, Asst. Treas.

Established in 1994 in NY.
Foundation type: Independent foundation.
Financial data (yr. ended 12/31/05): Assets, $13,032,103 (M); expenditures, $645,003; qualifying distributions, $645,003; giving activities include $644,000 for 26 grants (high: $200,000; low: $1,000).
Purpose and activities: Funding primarily for education, human services, and the environment.
Fields of interest: Elementary/secondary education; Medical school/education; Education; Environment, natural resources; Human services.
Type of support: General/operating support.
Limitations: Applications not accepted. Giving primarily in New York, NY. No grants to individuals.
Application information: Contributes only to pre-selected organizations.
Officers and Directors:* Susan K. Allen, Pres.; Bradley A. Roberts,* V.P. and Secy.; Herbert A. Allen III,* V.P. and Treas.
EIN: 133791176
Selected grants: The following grants were reported in 2004.
$200,000 to Hackley School, Tarrytown, NY.
$110,000 to Prep for Prep, New York, NY.
$25,000 to Acumen Fund, New York, NY.
$20,000 to New York Times Neediest Cases Fund, New York, NY.
$15,000 to City Harvest, New York, NY.
$10,000 to Central Park Conservancy, New York, NY.
$10,000 to Conservation International, DC.
$10,000 to Fresh Air Fund, New York, NY.
$7,000 to Doe Fund, New York, NY.

5537
The Allison Family Foundation, Inc. ◇
50 Butler Rd.
Scarsdale, NY 10583-2238

Established in 1998 in NY.
Donor: Herbert M. Allison, Jr.
Foundation type: Independent foundation.
Financial data (yr. ended 5/31/05): Assets,
$3,354,319 (M); gifts received, $513,953;
expenditures, $526,584; qualifying distributions,
$509,989; giving activities include $502,997 for 1
grant.
Purpose and activities: Giving primarily to a dance
theater foundation.
Fields of interest: Performing arts, dance.
Type of support: General/operating support.
Limitations: Applications not accepted. Giving
primarily in NY. No grants to individuals.
Application information: Contributes only to
pre-selected organizations.
Officers: Simin Nazemi Allison, Pres.; Herbert M.
Allison, Jr., V.P.
EIN: 134011223
Selected grants: The following grants were reported
in 2004.
$999,878 to Yale University, New Haven, CT. 4
   grants: $499,841 (For general support),
   $199,972 (For general support), $250,037 (For
   general support), $50,028 (For general support).
$751,292 to Alliance for Lifelong Learning, New
   York, NY. 3 grants: $250,000 (For general
   support), $249,720 (For general support),
   $251,572 (For general support).
$511,883 to Alvin Ailey American Dance Theater,
   New York, NY. 3 grants: $200,634 (For general
   support), $261,883 (For general support),
   $49,366 (For general support).

5538
The Allwin Family Foundation ◇
c/o Aetos Capital, LLC
875 Park Ave.
New York, NY 10022

Established in 1997 in NY.
Donor: James M. Allwin.
Foundation type: Independent foundation.
Financial data (yr. ended 12/31/05): Assets,
$314,584 (M); gifts received, $5,620,654;
expenditures, $5,907,226; qualifying distributions,
$5,893,411; giving activities include $5,888,761
for 26 grants (high: $2,026,250; low: $250;
average: $10,000–$200,000).
Purpose and activities: Giving primarily for
education and the arts.
Fields of interest: Visual arts; Museums (art);
Performing arts, opera; Secondary school/
education; Higher education; Education; Human
services; Children/youth, services.
Limitations: Applications not accepted. Giving on a
national basis, with emphasis on CT, NH, and NY.
Application information: Contributes only to
pre-selected organizations.
Advisory Committee: Maria Allwin.
Trustees: James M. Allwin; Robert F. Larson.
EIN: 137088461
Selected grants: The following grants were reported
in 2004.
$526,000 to Yale University, New Haven, CT.
$210,000 to Museum of Modern Art, New York, NY.
$200,000 to Greenwich Hospital, Greenwich, CT.
$125,000 to Brunswick School, Greenwich, CT.

$100,000 to Communities in Schools, Alexandria,
   VA.
$55,000 to Greenwich Academy, Greenwich, CT.
$33,000 to Bard College, Annandale on Hudson,
   NY.
$19,900 to Metropolitan Opera Association, New
   York, NY.
$4,000 to Waterside School, Stamford, CT.
$3,000 to Spoleto Festival USA, Charleston, SC.

5539
Allyn Foundation, Inc. ◇
P.O. Box 22
Skaneateles, NY 13152
Contact: Meg M. O'Connell, Exec. Dir.

Incorporated in 1956 in NY.
Donors: William N. Allyn†; Welch Allyn, Inc.
Foundation type: Independent foundation.
Financial data (yr. ended 12/31/05): Assets,
$11,186,267 (M); expenditures, $610,562;
qualifying distributions, $581,697; giving activities
include $563,196 for 76 grants (high: $27,000;
low: $375).
Purpose and activities: Emphasis on higher and
other education; support also for general charitable
purposes, including youth and social service
agencies, hospitals, and community development in
the central NY area.
Fields of interest: Adult education—literacy, basic
skills & GED; Education, reading; Education;
Hospitals (general); Reproductive health, family
planning; Medical research, institute; Human
services; Children/youth, services; General
charitable giving; Minorities.
Type of support: Capital campaigns; Building/
renovation; Equipment; Seed money; Scholarship
funds; Matching/challenge support.
Limitations: Giving limited to Onondaga and Cayuga
counties in NY. No support for religious programs.
No grants to individuals, or for endowment funds; no
loans.
Publications: Application guidelines.
Application information: Application form required.
   Initial approach: Letter
   Copies of proposal: 1
   Deadline(s): None
   Board meeting date(s): 2 times per year
Officers: William F. Allyn, Pres.; Lew F. Allyn, V.P.;
Dawn N. Allyn, Secy.; Elsa A. Soderberg, Treas.; Meg
O'Connell, Exec. Dir.
Directors: Amy Allyn; David Allyn; Eric R. Allyn; Janet
J. Allyn; Scott Allyn, M.D.; Donald Nelson; Jon
Soderberg; Libby Soderberg; Peer Soderberg; Peter
Soderberg; Robert Soderberg; Wilbur Townsend;
Charles S. Tracy; Sonya Weinfeld.
Number of staff: 1 part-time professional.
EIN: 156017723

5540
Alpern Family Foundation, Inc. ◇
c/o Weitzman & Rubin, PC
400 Jericho Tpke., Ste. 205
Jericho, NY 11753

Established in 1952.
Donor: Bernard E. Alpern†.
Foundation type: Independent foundation.
Financial data (yr. ended 12/31/03): Assets,
$11,456,203 (M); gifts received, $594,500;
expenditures, $710,332; qualifying distributions,

$581,677; giving activities include $495,500 for 33
grants (high: $250,000; low: $1,000).
Purpose and activities: Support for medical
research, including cancer and cerebral palsy, as
well as to hospitals and health associations, and for
children and youth services.
Fields of interest: Medical school/education;
Environment; Hospitals (general); Cancer; Medical
research, institute; Cerebral palsy research; Cancer
research; Human services; Children/youth,
services; Federated giving programs.
Type of support: Research.
Limitations: Applications not accepted. Giving
primarily in New York, NY. No grants to individuals.
Application information: Contributes only to
pre-selected organizations.
Officers and Directors:* Martin H. Schneider,*
Pres.; Rochelle A. Rubin,* V.P. and Secy.; Steven I.
Rubin,* Treas.
EIN: 136100302
Selected grants: The following grants were reported
in 2004.
$250,000 to Albert Einstein College of Medicine of
   Yeshiva University, Bronx, NY. For biomedical
   cerebral palsy research.
$30,000 to Michigan Land Use Institute, Beulah,
   MI.
$25,000 to Chemotherapy Foundation, New York,
   NY. For cancer research.
$25,000 to Childrens Hospital Corporation, Boston,
   MA. For Dr. Robert Rosenthal Children's Cerebral
   Palsy Fund.
$25,000 to Jewish Museum, New York, NY. For
   Children's Education Fund.
$20,000 to Harvard University, Cambridge, MA. For
   Loan Fund for Law School students.
$20,000 to National Council of Jewish Women, New
   York, NY. For general support.
$10,000 to Ann Schreiber Ovarian Cancer Research
   Fund, New York, NY.
$10,000 to Gildas Club Worldwide, New York, NY.
$10,000 to Make-A-Wish Foundation, Suffolk
   County, Ronkonkoma, NY.

5541
The Alpert Family Foundation, Inc. ◇
17 Linden Dr.
Purchase, NY 10577-1438

Established in 1995 in NY.
Donor: Norman W. Alpert.
Foundation type: Independent foundation.
Financial data (yr. ended 11/30/05): Assets,
$281,814 (M); gifts received, $654,994;
expenditures, $955,890; qualifying distributions,
$940,195; giving activities include $940,195 for 73
grants (high: $285,000; low: $25).
Purpose and activities: Giving primarily for
education, and to Jewish organizations.
Fields of interest: Arts; Education; Hospitals
(general); Health care; Health organizations,
association; Jewish federated giving programs;
Jewish agencies & temples.
Limitations: Applications not accepted. Giving
primarily in MA and RI. No grants to individuals.
Application information: Contributes only to
pre-selected organizations.
Officers: Norman W. Alpert,* Pres.; Jane Alpert,*
V.P.
Director: William Goldberg.
EIN: 133745910
Selected grants: The following grants were reported
in 2005.

$285,000 to Brown University, Providence, RI.
$7,500 to Rye Country Day School, Rye, NY.
$500 to Gordon A. Rich Memorial Foundation, New York, NY.

5542
Altman Foundation ▼
521 5th Ave., 35th Fl.
New York, NY 10175 (212) 682-0970
Contact: Karen L. Rosa, V.P. and Exec. Dir.
FAX: (212) 682-1648; URL: http://www.altmanfoundation.org

Incorporated in 1913 in NY.
Donors: Benjamin Altman†; Col. Michael Friedsam†.
Foundation type: Independent foundation.
Financial data (yr. ended 12/31/05): Assets, $257,195,714 (M); expenditures, $14,615,065; qualifying distributions, $12,480,265; giving activities include $11,163,875 for 165 grants (high: $300,000; low: $2,000; average: $10,000–$100,000), and $96,318 for employee matching gifts.
Purpose and activities: The foundation's mission is to support programs and institutions that enrich the quality of life in New York City, NY, with a particular focus on initiatives that help individuals, families and communities benefit from the services and opportunities that will enable them to achieve their full potential.
Fields of interest: Arts; Education, early childhood education; Elementary school/education; Secondary school/education; Education; Health care; Mental health/crisis services; Health organizations; Employment; Housing/shelter, development; Human services; Youth, services; Family services; Aging, centers/services; Aging; Minorities; Economically disadvantaged.
Type of support: Program development; Employee matching gifts.
Limitations: Giving limited to NY, with emphasis on the boroughs of New York City. No grants to individuals, or for building funds, or capital equipment.
Publications: Annual report (including application guidelines).
Application information: Accepts but does not require NYRAG Common Application Form. Application form not required.
  Initial approach: Proposal (no longer than 5 pages)
  Copies of proposal: 1
  Deadline(s): None
  Board meeting date(s): 6 times per year
  Final notification: Several weeks
Officers and Trustees:* Jane B. O'Connell,* Pres.; Karen L. Rosa, V.P. and Exec. Dir.; John W. Townsend IV,* V.P.; Julia V. Shea,* Secy.; John P. Casey, Treas.; Thomas C. Burke, Tr. Emeritus; James M. Burke; Bernard Finkelstein; Sharon B. King; Maurice A. Selinger, Jr.; Patricia J. Volland.
Number of staff: 3 full-time professional; 2 part-time professional; 4 full-time support.
EIN: 131623879
Selected grants: The following grants were reported in 2005.
$600,000 to Fund for the City of New York, New York, NY. To help support Youth Development Institute's Young Adult Literacy Initiative, payable over 3 years.
$600,000 to Structured Employment Economic Development Corporation (SEEDCO), New York,

NY. To help support major expansion of EarnFair Alliance, payable over 3 years.
$450,000 to New York Botanical Garden, Bronx, NY. To renew support for Children's Education program, payable over 3 years.
$300,000 to Saint Vincents Hospital and Medical Center of New York, New York, NY. To help support Section of Palliative Medicine and help move program toward self-sufficiency.
$300,000 to United Hospital Fund of New York, New York, NY. For The Family Caregiving Impact Initiative: Improving Transitions in the Health Care System, payable over 2 years.
$174,000 to Museum of the City of New York, New York, NY. To build staff capacity and help launch strategic marketing campaign to increase outreach to and attendance by visitors from underrepresented communities, payable over 2 years.
$127,550 to What To Expect Foundation, New York, NY. To help expand Baby Basics prenatal health literacy pilot program in Jamaica, Queens and plan for citywide replication.
$50,000 to Childrens Storefront Foundation, New York, NY. To renew support for Support Services Program.
$50,000 to Lincoln Center for the Performing Arts, New York, NY. To support planning initiative to revitalize Harmony Atrium.
$50,000 to Little Sisters of the Assumption Family Health Service, New York, NY. For final grant for Community Life Program.

5543
The Jeffrey A. Altman Foundation, Inc. ✧ ☆
c/o Jeffrey A. Altman
205 E. 22nd St., Ste. 420
New York, NY 10010

Established in 1997 in NY.
Donor: Jeffrey A. Altman.
Foundation type: Independent foundation.
Financial data (yr. ended 11/30/05): Assets, $414,041 (M); gifts received, $674,117; expenditures, $676,287; qualifying distributions, $676,287; giving activities include $596,657 for 41 grants (high: $117,500; low: $300).
Fields of interest: Hospitals (general); Health organizations, association; Cystic fibrosis; Athletics/sports, golf; Human services; Children/youth, services; Jewish federated giving programs; Jewish agencies & temples.
Type of support: General/operating support.
Limitations: Applications not accepted. No grants to individuals.
Application information: Contributes only to pre-selected organizations.
Directors: Georgia Altman; Jeffrey A. Altman; Lawrence Altman.
EIN: 133979282
Selected grants: The following grants were reported in 2004.
$77,650 to Cystic Fibrosis Foundation, New York, NY.
$15,000 to Project ALS, New York, NY.
$10,500 to UJA-Federation of New York, New York, NY.
$10,000 to Northside Center for Child Development, New York, NY.
$10,000 to Samuel Waxman Cancer Research Foundation, New York, NY.

$5,000 to Friends of the Israel Defense Forces, New York, NY.
$5,000 to Love Heals, New York, NY.
$4,500 to Tomorrows Childrens Fund, Hackensack, NJ.
$2,500 to Buddy Program, Aspen, CO.
$600 to American Jewish Committee, New York, NY.

5544
Altman/Kazickas Foundation ✧
c/o Dorian A. Vergos & Co., LLC
592 5th Ave., 2nd Fl.
New York, NY 10036

Established in 1996 in NY.
Donors: Robert C. Altman; Roger C. Altman.
Foundation type: Independent foundation.
Financial data (yr. ended 4/30/05): Assets, $2,415,598 (M); gifts received, $1,872,664; expenditures, $1,476,841; qualifying distributions, $1,448,544; giving activities include $1,448,294 for 90 grants (high: $140,000; low: $50).
Purpose and activities: Giving primarily for arts and cultural programs, education, and human services.
Fields of interest: Museums (natural history); Arts; Education; Health organizations; Heart & circulatory research; Human services; Children/youth, services; Community development; Federated giving programs; Roman Catholic agencies & churches.
Limitations: Applications not accepted. Giving on a national basis. No grants to individuals.
Application information: Contributes only to pre-selected organizations.
Trustees: Richard M. Altman; Roger C. Altman; Jurate Kazickas.
EIN: 133944577
Selected grants: The following grants were reported in 2005.
$140,000 to Brookings Institution, DC.
$140,000 to Saint Anns Church of Morrisania, Bronx, NY.
$100,000 to Columbia University, New York, NY.
$100,000 to Wesleyan University, Middletown, CT.
$90,000 to American Museum of Natural History, New York, NY.
$75,000 to East Side House, Bronx, NY.
$51,350 to Womens Commission for Refugee Women and Children, New York, NY.
$15,000 to Roxbury Latin School, West Roxbury, MA.
$10,000 to Lenox Hill Neighborhood House, New York, NY.
$5,000 to Playwrights Horizons, New York, NY.

5545
Altria Fund, Inc. ✧
(formerly Philip Morris Fund, Inc.)
120 Park Ave.
New York, NY 10017-5592 (917) 663-4000

Established in 1998 in NY.
Donors: Philip Morris Cos. Inc.; Altria Group, Inc.
Foundation type: Company-sponsored foundation.
Financial data (yr. ended 12/31/03): Assets, $310,000 (M); gifts received, $1,282,000; expenditures, $1,282,000; qualifying distributions, $1,282,000; giving activities include $1,282,000 for 36 grants (high: $100,000; low: $10,000).
Purpose and activities: The foundation supports organizations involved with arts and culture,

education, health, human services, and international affairs.

Fields of interest: Arts; Education; Health organizations, association; Food banks; Human services; International development; International affairs.

Limitations: Applications not accepted. Giving on a national and international basis.

Application information: Contributes only to pre-selected organizations.

Officers: Louis C. Camilleri, Chair.; Dinyar S. Devitre, Vice-Chair.; Steven C. Parrish, Vice-Chair.; Jennifer Goodale, Secy.; Thomas J. Collamore, Treas.

EIN: 133896922

Selected grants: The following grants were reported in 2004.

$151,000 to Learning Through Landscapes, United Kingdom. .

$150,000 to Innovation and Development Centre, Kiev, Ukraine. .

$119,000 to Civil Society Initiative Fund, Japan. .

$115,000 to Business in the Community, London, England. .

$100,000 to Berliner Initiative gegen Gewalt gegen Frauen eV, Germany. .

$100,000 to SeSoBel Foyer Notre Dame de LEsperance Ain El Rihani Kesrouan, Lebanon. .

$80,000 to Hong Kong Arts Festival Society, Hong Kong. .

$61,000 to Casa di Accoglienza delle Donne Maltrattate di Milano, Milano, Italy. .

$60,000 to Modern Womens Foundation, Taipei, Taiwan. .

$25,000 to Frauenschmiede eV, Berlin, Germany. .

5546
The Altschul Foundation

c/o Holland & Knight, LLP
195 Broadway
New York, NY 10007
Contact: Sergio Stifelman, Legal Asst.

Incorporated in 1941 in NY.
Donors: Louis Altschul†; Jeanette Cohen Altschul‡.
Foundation type: Independent foundation.
Financial data (yr. ended 6/30/05): Assets, $12,874,892 (M); expenditures, $881,842; qualifying distributions, $702,560; giving activities include $700,000 for 36 grants (high: $115,000; low: $1,000).
Fields of interest: Arts; Education; Health care; Human services; Jewish agencies & temples.
Type of support: General/operating support; Continuing support; Research.
Limitations: Applications not accepted. Giving primarily in FL, New York, NY, and UT. No grants to individuals.
Application information: Contributes only to pre-selected organizations.
  Board meeting date(s): 3 times per year
Officers and Trustees:* Susan Rothstein-Schwimmer,* Pres.; William Rothstein,* V.P. and Secy.; Seth Schapiro,* Treas.; Daniel L. Kurtz.
EIN: 136400009

5547
The Altus One Fund, Inc. ✧

c/o Randall R. Weisenburger
437 Madison Ave., 9th Fl.
New York, NY 10022-7001 (212) 415-3393

Established in 1999 in NY.
Donor: Orchard, Stanwich & Pierce Trusts.
Foundation type: Independent foundation.
Financial data (yr. ended 12/31/05): Assets, $37,792,006 (M); expenditures, $3,135,761; qualifying distributions, $2,644,850; giving activities include $2,644,850 for 48 grants (high: $525,000; low: $1,000; average: $5,000–$50,000).
Purpose and activities: Giving primarily for the arts, education, including a high school sports foundation, health care and medical research, particularly for cancer, hospitals, social services, Jewish and other religious organizations, an Olympic ski and snowboard team foundation, and to a YWCA.
Fields of interest: Arts, cultural/ethnic awareness; Museums (specialized); Performing arts; Arts; Secondary school/education; Higher education; Hospitals (general); Health care; Health organizations, association; Medical research, institute; Cancer research; Athletics/sports, school programs; Athletics/sports, Olympics; Human services; YM/YWCAs & YM/YWHAs; Children, services; Jewish agencies & temples; Religion.
Limitations: Applications not accepted. Giving primarily in NY. No grants to individuals.
Application information: Contributes only to pre-selected organizations.
Officers: Randall R. Weisenburger, Pres. and Secy.; John Wren, V.P.
EIN: 510388792
Selected grants: The following grants were reported in 2004.

$250,000 to Delaware Valley College, Doylestown, PA.

$100,000 to Lincoln Center for the Performing Arts, New York, NY.

$95,000 to University of Pennsylvania, Philadelphia, PA.

$75,175 to New York Academy of Medicine, New York, NY.

$50,500 to Arthur Ashe Institute for Urban Health, Brooklyn, NY.

$50,000 to Catholic Charities.

$25,000 to Bank Street College of Education, New York, NY.

$25,000 to Big Apple Circus, New York, NY.

$25,000 to New Visions for Public Schools, New York, NY.

$5,000 to Urban League.

5548
American Academy of Arts and Letters ✧

(formerly American Academy & Institute of Arts and Letters)
633 W. 155th St.
New York, NY 10032-7501 (212) 368-5900
Contact: Virginia Dajani, Exec. Dir.

Established in 1898 as the National Institute of Arts and Letters. The American Academy of Arts and Letters was founded in 1904. In 1976 the two merged into The American Academy and Institute of Arts and Letters. In 1993, name changed to American Academy of Arts and Letters.
Donors: Mildred B. Strauss†; Channing Pollock†; Archer M. Huntington†; Charles Ives†; Katharine Lane Weems†.
Foundation type: Operating foundation.
Financial data (yr. ended 12/31/05): Assets, $64,482,804 (M); expenditures, $2,581,984; qualifying distributions, $2,466,653; giving activities include $876,240 for grants to individuals,

and $2,466,653 for foundation-administered programs.
Purpose and activities: A private operating foundation. Awards by nomination only to individuals for extraordinary achievement in literature, music, and the fine arts.
Limitations: Giving on a national basis. No support for the performing arts (except for Richard Rodgers Awards for Musical Theater) or photography.
Publications: Informational brochure.
Application information: Applications accepted only for the Richard Rodgers Awards for the Musical Theater. Applications for other prizes not accepted under any circumstances. Award nominations made by membership recommendations only. The Academy will not respond to unsolicited requests for nomination consideration from individuals or organizations. Application form required.
  Initial approach: Send SASE for application form for Richard Rodgers Awards for the Musical Theater
  Deadline(s): Nov. 1
  Final notification: Mar.
Officers and Directors:* Ned Rorem,* Pres.; Will Barnet,* V.P., Art; Varujan Boghosian,* V.P., Art; Jane Wilson,* V.P., Art; Shirley Hazzard, V.P., Literature; Alison Lurie,* V.P., Literature; Leon Kirchner,* V.P., Music; Ezra Laderman,* V.P., Music; John Hollander,* Secy.; Henry N. Cobb,* Treas.; Virginia Dajani, Exec. Dir.
Number of staff: 8 full-time professional.
EIN: 130429640

5549
The American Art Foundation, Inc. ▼ ✧

(also known as The American Contemporary Art Foundation, Inc.)
c/o Joan Krupskas
767 5th Ave., 40th Fl.
New York, NY 10153

Established in 1999 in DE and NY.
Donors: Leonard A. Lauder; Estee Lauder†.
Foundation type: Operating foundation.
Financial data (yr. ended 6/30/05): Assets, $77,107,944 (M); expenditures, $4,337,095; qualifying distributions, $4,646,294; giving activities include $4,100,000 for grants, and $544,769 for 1 foundation-administered program.
Purpose and activities: The foundation acquires, preserves, loans and donates works of art to public museums, libraries, universities, galleries and other institutions for public display and education.
Fields of interest: Museums (art).
Limitations: Applications not accepted. Giving primarily in New York, NY. No grants to individuals.
Application information: Contributes only to pre-selected organizations.
Officers: Leonard A. Lauder, Pres.; Carol Boulanger, V.P.; Meredith Edwards, Secy.; Joan Krupskas, Treas.
Trustee: William Lauder.
EIN: 134069969
Selected grants: The following grants were reported in 2004.

$4,900,000 to Whitney Museum of American Art, New York, NY.

5550
American Center Foundation
Church St. Station
P.O. Box 765
New York, NY   10008-0765

Established in DE.
Foundation type: Independent foundation.
Financial data (yr. ended 8/31/05): Assets, $19,922,890 (M); expenditures, $772,366; qualifying distributions, $629,640; giving activities include $310,950 for 10 grants (high: $129,950; low: $10,000), and $100,000 for 20 grants to individuals (high: $5,000; low: $5,000).
Fields of interest: Arts, research; Arts.
Limitations: Applications not accepted. Giving primarily on a national and international basis.
Application information: Contributes only to pre-selected organizations.
Officers: Frederick B. Henry, Chair. and Treas.; Marie-Claude Beaud, Vice.-Chair.; Kynaston McShine, Vice.-Chair.; Joan Weakley, Secy.
Board Members: Manuel J. Borja-Villel; Robert Fitzpatrick; Christophe Girard; Vasif Kortun; Herve Mikaeloff; Ann Philbin.
EIN: 986000319

5551
American Conservation Association, Inc. ✧ ☆
30 Rockefeller Plz., Rm. 5600
New York, NY   10112
Contact: Charles M. Clusen, Exec. Dir.

Incorporated in 1958 in NY.
Donors: Laurance S. Rockefeller‡; Laurance Rockefeller; Rockefeller Brothers Fund; Jackson Hole Preserve, Inc.
Foundation type: Operating foundation.
Financial data (yr. ended 12/31/05): Assets, $692,373 (M); gifts received, $1,000,000; expenditures, $867,670; qualifying distributions, $860,617; giving activities include $445,500 for 28 grants (high: $250,000; low: $1,000), and $142,972 for 4 foundation-administered programs.
Purpose and activities: A private operating foundation organized to advance knowledge and understanding of conservation; to preserve the beauty of the landscape and the natural and living resources in areas of the U.S. and elsewhere; and to educate the public in the proper use of such areas.
Fields of interest: Environment, natural resources.
Type of support: General/operating support; Continuing support; Program development; Conferences/seminars; Publication; Technical assistance; Consulting services; Program-related investments/loans.
Limitations: Giving on a national basis, with emphasis on Washington, DC. No grants to individuals, or for building funds, endowments, scholarships, or fellowships.
Application information: Application form not required.
   Initial approach: Letter or proposal
   Copies of proposal: 1
   Deadline(s): None
   Board meeting date(s): Sept. or Oct.; Executive Committee meets as necessary
   Final notification: Varies
Officers and Trustees:* Laurance Rockefeller,* Pres.; R. Scott Greathead,* Secy.; Carmen Reyes,

Treas.; Charles M. Clusen, Exec. Dir.; John H. Adams; Frances G. Beinecke; Nash Castro; William G. Conway; Henry L. Diamond; Fred I. Kent III; W. Barnabas McHenry; Patrick F. Noonan; Story Clark Resor; David S. Sampson; Cathleen Douglas Stone.
Number of staff: 2 part-time professional; 2 part-time support.
EIN: 131874023
Selected grants: The following grants were reported in 2004.
$50,000 to Natural Resources Defense Council, New York, NY. For Public Lands Program.
$20,000 to Catskill Center for Conservation and Development, Arkville, NY. 2 grants: $10,000 (For general support), $10,000 (For conservation and planning assistance programs with emphasis on water and land protection).
$15,000 to New York League of Conservation Voters Education Fund, New York, NY. For general support.
$10,000 to Alaska Conservation Foundation, Anchorage, AK. For general support.
$10,000 to League of Conservation Voters Education Fund, DC. For general support.
$10,000 to Open Space Institute, New York, NY. For general support.
$10,000 to Scenic Hudson, Poughkeepsie, NY. For general support.
$5,000 to Wildlife Conservation Society, Bronx, NY. For general support.
$2,500 to World Wildlife Fund, DC. For general support.

5552
American Dream Foundation, Inc. ✧
c/o Schiff Hardin LLP
623 5th Ave.
New York, NY   10022
Contact: John D. Dadakis, Secy.

Established in 2003 in NY.
Donor: Richard A. Grasso.
Foundation type: Independent foundation.
Financial data (yr. ended 12/31/05): Assets, $3,617,124 (M); expenditures, $1,193,446; qualifying distributions, $1,173,408; giving activities include $1,170,000 for 27 grants (high: $225,000; low: $5,000).
Fields of interest: Higher education; Business school/education; Education; Health organizations, association; Crime/law enforcement, police agencies; Disasters, fire prevention/control; Human services.
Limitations: Giving primarily in NY.
Application information:
   Initial approach: Letter
   Deadline(s): None
Officers and Directors:* Richard A. Grasso, Pres.; John D. Dadakis,* Secy.; Lorraine P. Grasso,* Treas.
EIN: 200363876

5553
American Express Foundation ▼ ✧
World Financial Ctr.
200 Vesey St., 48th Fl.
New York, NY   10285-4804   (212) 640-5661
Contact: For organizations located outside the U.S.: Cornelia W. Higginson, V.P., Intl. Prog., and Secy.
Application addresses: Greensboro, NC: Laura T. Rhodes, Sr. Community Affairs Specialist,

Philanthropy and Media, M.C. NC-06-03-10, American Express Svc. Ctr., 7701 Airport Center Dr., Greensboro, NC 27409, Cultural Heritage: Cheryl G. Rosario, Mgr., Philanthropic Prog., M.C. NY-01-48-04, American Express Co., 3 World Financial Ctr., New York, NY 10285, Economic Independence: Terry Savage, Dir., Philanthropic Prog., M.C. NY-01-48-04 American Express Co., 3 World Financial Ctr., New York, NY 10285, Community Service: Angela C. Woods, Dir., Philanthropic Prog., M.C. NY-01-48-04, American Express Co., 3 World Financial Ctr., New York, NY 10285, Phoenix, AZ: JoEllen L. Lynn, Mgr., Community Affairs, M.C. AZ-08-01-08, American Express Svc. Ctr., 20022 N. 31st Ave., Phoenix, AZ 85027, Salt Lake City, UT: Dorothy Anderson, Mgr., Community Affairs, M.C. UT-02-03-10, American Express Svc. Ctr., 4315 S. 2700 W., Salt Lake City, UT 84184, South FL (Ft. Lauderdale and Miami): Stacey L. Orange, Dir., Public Affairs and Comms., M.C. FL-05-02-16A, American Express Svc. Ctr., 777 American Expwy., Fort Lauderdale, FL 33337; URL: http://home3.americanexpress.com/corp/giving_back.asp

Incorporated in 1954 in NY.
Donor: American Express Co.
Foundation type: Company-sponsored foundation.
Financial data (yr. ended 12/31/04): Assets, $10,565,668 (M); gifts received, $22,399,910; expenditures, $20,610,016; qualifying distributions, $20,046,545; giving activities include $15,402,327 for 853 grants (high: $614,000; low: $400), and $4,644,218 for 7,757 employee matching gifts.
Purpose and activities: The foundation supports organizations involved with arts and culture, the environment, employment training, disaster relief, youth development, financial counseling, and entrepreneurism.
Fields of interest: Arts, cultural/ethnic awareness; Visual arts; Performing arts; Historic preservation/historical societies; Arts; Environment, public education; Environment; Employment, public education; Employment, training; Disasters, preparedness/services; Youth development; American Red Cross; Human services, financial counseling; Business/industry.
International interests: Africa; Asia; Australia; Canada; Caribbean; Europe; Japan; Latin America; Middle East.
Type of support: General/operating support; Annual campaigns; Emergency funds; Program development; Seed money; Curriculum development; Employee matching gifts; Employee-related scholarships.
Limitations: Giving on a national and international basis, including in Asia, Canada, the Caribbean, Europe, and Latin America, with emphasis on Phoenix, AZ, South FL, New York, NY, Greensboro, NC, and Salt Lake City, UT. No support for discriminatory organizations, religious organizations not of direct benefit to the entire community, or political organizations. No grants to individuals (except for employee-related scholarships), or for fundraising, goodwill advertising, souvenir journals, or dinner programs, travel, books, magazines, or articles in professional journals, endowments or capital campaigns, traveling exhibitions, or sports sponsorships.
Publications: Grants list.
Application information: Application form required.
   Initial approach: Download application form and mail to nearest application address

Copies of proposal: 1
Board meeting date(s): Biannually
Final notification: 3 to 4 months
Officers and Trustees:* Thomas Schick,* Chair.;
Timothy McClimon, Pres.; Cornelia W. Higginson,
V.P., Intl. Prog., and Secy.; Gary Crittenden, Treas.;
Kenneth I. Chenault; Jon S. Linen.
EIN: 136123529
Selected grants: The following grants were reported
in 2004.
$100,000 to Kurogane Kosakusho Limited, Osaka,
   Japan. .
$100,000 to September 11th Families Association,
   New York, NY.
$75,000 to New York City Partnership Foundation,
   New York, NY.
$50,000 to Count Me In for Womens Economic
   Independence, New York, NY.
$50,000 to National Council of La Raza, DC.
$50,000 to Wall Street Rising Corporation, New
   York, NY.
$30,000 to Asian Art Options, Singapore. .
$30,000 to Community Partners, Los Angeles, CA.
$30,000 to ISED Solutions, DC.
$30,000 to New Visions, New Ventures, Richmond,
   VA.

5554
American Friends of Binyan-Av
Foundation, Inc. ✧
1466 Broadway, Ste. 607
New York, NY   10036

Established in 1999 in NY.
Donors: David Kattan; Morris Sabaa; Joe Tina
Carey; Frida Jack Sardar; Isaac Assa; Jackob
Kassin; Ventura Ent; Eli Shalam; Elliott Kattan;
Hagai Laniado; Kambiz Babaoff; Solomon Dwek;
Steve Kattan; Better Choice Development; Joseph
Jack Sitt Foundation; Gabriel & Sara Bildirici Hesed
Foundation; Jane & Sam Sutton Family Foundation;
Marvin Azrak & Sons Foundation; Ralph Friedland &
Bros., Inc.; Ralph Tawil Foundation; Regal Home
Collections; Textile From Europe; Top Choice
Development; Y&S Nazarian Family Foundation.
Foundation type: Independent foundation.
Financial data (yr. ended 12/31/04): Assets,
$21,802 (M); gifts received, $493,848;
expenditures, $731,966; qualifying distributions,
$731,172; giving activities include $726,000 for 1
grant.
Purpose and activities: Giving primarily for a
rabbinical college in Israel.
Fields of interest: Theological school/education.
International interests: Israel.
Limitations: Applications not accepted. Giving
limited to Jerusalem, Israel. No grants to individuals.
Application information: Contributes only to
pre-selected organizations.
Officer and Directors:* Victor Kameo,* Pres.; Julie
Levy; Eli Shalam.
EIN: 113472950
Selected grants: The following grants were reported
in 2003.
$740,500 to Yeshivat Binyan Av Rabbinical College,
   Jerusalem, Israel. For unrestricted support.
$61,476 to Yad Lebaal Hatshuva, Jerusalem, Israel.
   For unrestricted support.

5555
The American Friends of the Hebrew
University Charitable Common Fund,
Inc. ✧
1 Battery Park Plz., 25th Fl.
New York, NY   10004

Established in 1989 in NY.
Donors: Ernest Bogan; Stanley Bogan; Robert
Savin; John Steinhardt.
Foundation type: Independent foundation.
Financial data (yr. ended 9/30/05): Assets,
$2,236,125 (M); gifts received, $912,666;
expenditures, $1,675,227; qualifying distributions,
$1,674,217; giving activities include $1,674,217
for 171 grants (high: $232,309; low: $200).
Purpose and activities: Support for Jewish
agencies, temples, and federated giving programs,
the arts, education, and health.
Fields of interest: Arts; Education; Hospitals
(general); Medical research, institute; Jewish
federated giving programs; Jewish agencies &
temples.
Type of support: Continuing support.
Limitations: Applications not accepted. Giving
primarily in New York, NY. No grants to individuals.
Application information: Contributes only to
pre-selected organizations.
Trustees: Stanley Bogen; Keith Sachs; Ira Lee
Sorkin; Peter Willner.
EIN: 133525587
Selected grants: The following grants were reported
in 2004.
$200,000 to Hackley School, Tarrytown, NY.
$67,500 to Washington Institute, DC.
$51,000 to Polytechnic Preparatory Country Day
   School, Brooklyn, NY.
$25,000 to United Way International, Alexandria,
   VA.
$16,668 to United Jewish Appeal, Deerfield Beach,
   FL.
$11,000 to Jewish Federation of Palm Beach
   County, West Palm Beach, FL.
$8,500 to Manhattan Institute for Policy Research,
   New York, NY.
$7,000 to Metropolitan Opera, New York, NY.
$2,000 to Philharmonic-Symphony Society of New
   York, New York, NY.
$1,800 to American Friends of MaTaN, Levittown,
   PA.

5556
American Friends of Torah Umesorah of
Latino America ✧
16 Cameo Ridge Rd.
Monsey, NY   10952-2513   (845) 356-9243
Contact: David Ehrman, Pres.

Established in NY.
Foundation type: Independent foundation.
Financial data (yr. ended 8/31/05): Assets,
$17,091 (M); gifts received, $340,268;
expenditures, $351,620; qualifying distributions,
$351,000; giving activities include $351,000 for 2
grants (high: $277,000; low: $74,000).
Fields of interest: Jewish agencies & temples.
Limitations: Giving primarily in Argentina.
Application information:
   Initial approach: Letter
   Deadline(s): None

Officers: David Ehrman, Pres.; Ruth Ehrman, V.P.;
Daniel Kugielsky, Treas.
EIN: 133752354

5557
Amicus Foundation, Inc. ✧
c/o Philip Mintz
29 W. 38th St.
New York, NY   10018

Established in 1976.
Foundation type: Independent foundation.
Financial data (yr. ended 10/31/05): Assets,
$10,653,743 (M); expenditures, $603,869;
qualifying distributions, $582,065; giving activities
include $560,000 for 11 grants (high: $200,000;
low: $4,000).
Purpose and activities: Giving primarily for the
performing arts, education, a film society, human
services, and children's services.
Fields of interest: Museums; Performing arts,
ballet; Performing arts, theater; Arts; Education;
Children, services; Federated giving programs.
Limitations: Applications not accepted. Giving
primarily in FL, NH, and NY. No grants to individuals.
Application information: Contributes only to
pre-selected organizations.
Officers and Directors:* Leigh Weiner,* Pres.;
Sharyn Weiner, V.P.; Theodore Schiffman,* Treas.
EIN: 136075489

5558
The G. C. Andersen Family Foundation ✧
c/o Sung Andersen
1050 5th Ave., Apt. 8F
New York, NY   10028-0140

Established in 1996 in DE and NJ.
Donor: G. Chris Andersen.
Foundation type: Independent foundation.
Financial data (yr. ended 12/31/03): Assets,
$3,402,931 (M); expenditures, $876,357;
qualifying distributions, $834,132; giving activities
include $832,075 for 7 grants (high: $800,000;
low: $200).
Purpose and activities: Giving primarily for
environmental studies as well as for higher
education, and prostate cancer research.
Fields of interest: Higher education; Environment;
Cancer research.
Limitations: Applications not accepted. Giving on a
national basis, with emphasis on New York, NY. No
grants to individuals.
Application information: Contributes only to
pre-selected organizations.
Officers: G. Chris Andersen, Chair.; Sung Han
Andersen, Pres. and Secy.
EIN: 133921968
Selected grants: The following grants were reported
in 2004.
$541,885 to Manhattan School of Music, New York,
   NY. For general support.
$16,667 to Philharmonic-Symphony Society of New
   York, New York, NY. For general support.
$5,000 to Joyce Theater Foundation, New York, NY.
   For general support.
$1,200 to New York Public Library, New York, NY.
   For general support.
$1,000 to E. Monte Motion Dance Company, New
   York, NY. For general support.

5559
The Frank J. Antun Foundation ✧
100 Crossways Park W., Ste. 205
Woodbury, NY 11797
Contact: Josephine Alex, Mgr.

Established in 1986 in NY.
Donor: Frank J. Antun†.
Foundation type: Independent foundation.
Financial data (yr. ended 8/31/05): Assets, $12,462,946 (M); expenditures, $796,896; qualifying distributions, $727,963; giving activities include $630,000 for 66 grants (high: $25,000; low: $2,000).
Purpose and activities: Giving primarily for children and youth services, as well as for health associations; funding also for social services, including services for people who are blind or hard of hearing.
Fields of interest: Health organizations, association; Human services; Children/youth, services.
Limitations: Giving primarily in the greater New York, NY, area. No grants to individuals.
Application information: Application form required.
Initial approach: Request application form
Deadline(s): None
Officer: Josephine Alex, Mgr.
Trustees: I.J. LaSurdo; Joseph P. Scanlon.
EIN: 112822395

5560
The Antz Foundation ✧
c/o BCRS Group/Marcum & Kliegman, LLP
635 3rd Ave.
New York, NY 10017

Established in 1989 in NY.
Donor: John A. Thain.
Foundation type: Independent foundation.
Financial data (yr. ended 1/31/05): Assets, $16,234,534 (M); expenditures, $353,245; qualifying distributions, $349,895; giving activities include $346,800 for 33 grants (high: $50,000; low: $250).
Purpose and activities: Giving primarily for education with emphasis on a private day school, as well as for health care including a children's hospital; some giving also for the arts with emphasis on art museums.
Fields of interest: Museums (art); Performing arts, circus arts; Elementary/secondary education; Higher education; Education; Environment, beautification programs; Health organizations, association; Cancer; Human services; Children/youth, services.
Type of support: General/operating support.
Limitations: Applications not accepted. Giving primarily in New York and Rye, NY. No grants to individuals, or scholarships; no loans.
Application information: Contributes only to pre-selected organizations.
Trustees: David Blood; Richard W. Sabo; Barry Zubrow.
EIN: 133536523
Selected grants: The following grants were reported in 2005.
$50,000 to Big Apple Circus, New York, NY.
$50,000 to Haverford College, Haverford, PA.
$10,000 to New York Restoration Project, New York, NY.
$10,000 to Whitney Museum of American Art, New York, NY.

$7,500 to Prep for Prep, New York, NY. 2 grants: $5,000, $2,500
$500 to Jay Heritage Center, Rye, NY.
$500 to Yale University, New Haven, CT.

5561
Apfelbaum Family Foundation ✧
c/o McLaughlin & Stern, LLP
260 Madison Ave.
New York, NY 10016

Established in 1996 in NY.
Donors: Bonnie Apfelbaum; William Apfelbaum.
Foundation type: Independent foundation.
Financial data (yr. ended 12/31/05): Assets, $2,915,958 (M); expenditures, $362,684; qualifying distributions, $359,048; giving activities include $359,048 for 45 grants (high: $100,000; low: $100).
Fields of interest: Media, film/video; Visual arts, photography; Performing arts, theater; Arts; Hospitals (general); Health organizations, association; Cancer; Human services; Jewish federated giving programs; Jewish agencies & temples.
Limitations: Applications not accepted. Giving primarily in NY. No grants to individuals.
Application information: Contributes only to pre-selected organizations.
Officers: William Apfelbaum, Pres. and Treas.; Bonnie Apfelbaum, V.P.; Geoffry Handler, Secy.
EIN: 133907687

5562
The Appleman Foundation, Inc. ✧
c/o Bessemer Trust Co.
630 5th Ave.
New York, NY 10111 (212) 708-9216
Application address: 222 Royal Palm Way, Palm Beach, FL 33480; tel.: (561) 655-4030

Incorporated in 1952 in DE.
Donors: Nathan Appleman†; and members of the Appleman family; Appleman Charitable Trust.
Foundation type: Independent foundation.
Financial data (yr. ended 12/31/03): Assets, $23,988,662 (M); gifts received, $3,063,620; expenditures, $2,556,980; qualifying distributions, $2,410,145; giving activities include $2,345,670 for 77 grants (high: $400,000; low: $100).
Purpose and activities: Giving for Jewish welfare funds, higher education, including a Jewish theological seminary, hospitals, social services, and temple support.
Fields of interest: Higher education; Hospitals (general); Human services; Jewish federated giving programs; Jewish agencies & temples.
Type of support: Research.
Limitations: Giving primarily in Palm Beach, FL, and NY.
Application information:
Initial approach: Letter
Deadline(s): None
Officers: David Roberts, Pres.; Susan A. Unterberg, V.P.
Directors: Ellen Unterberg Celli; Jill A. Roberts.
EIN: 136154978
Selected grants: The following grants were reported in 2003.
$400,000 to New York-Presbyterian Hospital, New York, NY.

$250,000 to Weill Medical College of Cornell University, New York, NY.
$100,000 to University of Pennsylvania, Philadelphia, PA.
$20,000 to Riverdale Country School, Bronx, NY.
$10,000 to Jewish Museum, New York, NY.
$5,000 to Hineni, New York, NY.
$5,000 to Sarah Lawrence College, Bronxville, NY.
$5,000 to Yeshiva Ateres Yisroel, Brooklyn, NY.
$3,000 to Hobart and William Smith Colleges, Geneva, NY.
$1,000 to Brearley School, New York, NY. For annual fund.

5563
Adrian & Jessie Archbold Charitable Trust
401 E. 60th St., Ste. 36B
New York, NY 10022
Contact: Arthur J. Mahon, Tr.

Trust established in 1976 in NY.
Donor: Jessie Archbold†.
Foundation type: Independent foundation.
Financial data (yr. ended 11/30/05): Assets, $27,048,535 (M); expenditures, $2,765,350; qualifying distributions, $2,639,470; giving activities include $2,528,500 for 113 grants (high: $1,000,000; low: $1,500).
Purpose and activities: Grants primarily for the medical sciences; support also for hospitals, (including the Archbold Hospital, Thomasville, GA), and health-related organizations, child welfare and youth programs, and social service agencies.
Fields of interest: Education; Hospitals (general); Health care; Health organizations, association; Biomedicine; Medical research, institute; Human services; Children/youth, services; Biological sciences.
Type of support: General/operating support; Continuing support; Program development; Research.
Limitations: Giving primarily in the northeastern U.S.; some giving in GA. No support for political organizations. No grants to individuals, or for endowment and/or building funds; no loans.
Application information: Unsolicited proposals not encouraged. Application form not required.
Initial approach: Letter
Copies of proposal: 1
Deadline(s): None
Board meeting date(s): As required
Final notification: 1-3 months
Trustees: Arthur J. Mahon; JPMorgan Chase Bank, N.A.
Number of staff: 1 part-time professional; 1 part-time support.
EIN: 510179829
Selected grants: The following grants were reported in 2005.
$1,000,000 to Weill Medical College of Cornell University, New York, NY.
$60,000 to Alvin Ailey Dance Foundation, New York, NY. 2 grants: $10,000, $50,000
$25,000 to Catholic Charities.
$15,000 to Philharmonic-Symphony Society of New York, New York, NY.
$12,500 to Student Sponsor Partners, New York, NY.
$10,000 to Mercy College, Dobbs Ferry, NY.
$7,500 to Good Shepherd Services, New York, NY.
$5,000 to Choate Rosemary Hall, Wallingford, CT.
$5,000 to East Side Settlement House, New York, NY.

5564
The Area Fund
(doing business as The Community Foundation of Dutchess County)
80 Washington St., Ste. 201
Poughkeepsie, NY 12601 (845) 452-3077
Contact: Andrea L. Reynolds, C.E.O.
FAX: (845) 452-3083; E-mail: cfdc@cfdcny.org;
Additional E-mail: areynolds@cfdcny.org;
URL: http://www.cfdcny.org

Established in 1969 in NY.
Donors: McCann Foundation; Lester Freer†.
Foundation type: Community foundation.
Financial data (yr. ended 6/30/05): Assets, $22,819,139 (M); gifts received, $3,309,796; expenditures, $2,373,800; giving activities include $659,579 for 235 grants (high: $65,506; low: $100), and $187,478 for 296 grants to individuals (high: $6,000; low: $10).
Purpose and activities: The foundation strengthens the community by offering donors the means to establish charitable legacies, by making grants, and by providing leadership to address community needs.
Fields of interest: Arts; Education, early childhood education; Elementary school/education; Secondary school/education; Education; Human services; Nonprofit management.
Type of support: Seed money; Management development/capacity building; Equipment; Program development; Scholarship funds.
Limitations: Giving primarily in Dutchess and Ulster counties, NY. No grants to individuals (except through The Area Fund Partnership in Education Grants Program), or for endowment funds, capital campaigns, building funds, land acquisition, matching gifts, deficit financing, operating budgets, or where amount of grant will not make a significant impact on a project; no loans.
Publications: Application guidelines; Annual report; Newsletter.
Application information: Visit foundation Web site for application information. Application form required.
  Initial approach: Letter
  Copies of proposal: 1
  Deadline(s): Feb. 28 and Sept. 29
  Board meeting date(s): Jan., Mar., May, Sept., and Nov.
  Final notification: Late May and Nov.
Officers and Trustees:* Wayne L. Nussbickel,* Chair.; Timothy Dean, Vice-Chair., Planning & Grants; Arthur DeDominicis, Vice-Chair., Audit; Barbara M. Murphy,* Vice-Chair., Governance; Steven Tinkelman,* Vice-Chair., Devel. & Mktg.; Andrea L. Reynolds, C.E.O. and Pres.; David J. Ringwood, V.P., Devel.; Nevill Smythe, V.P., Progs.; J. Joseph McGowan,* Secy.; John Cina,* Treas.; Patrick Adams; Elizabeth Peale Allen; Joseph A. Bonura, Jr.; Robert R. Butts; Thomas R.B. Campbell; Joel Canter, M.D.; Stephen E. Diamond; Ira Effron; Richard E. Fisher; John Gifford; Sue Hartshorn; Sunil Khurana, M.D.; Bonnie Meagher; Pari Forood; Jeffrey C. Richards; Niloufer Rodrigues, M.D.; Michael J. Tomkovitch.
Number of staff: 3 full-time professional; 1 full-time support; 1 part-time support.
EIN: 237026859

5565
Arkell Hall Foundation, Inc.
P.O. Box 240
Canajoharie, NY 13317-0240
Contact: Joseph A. Santangelo, Pres.

Incorporated in 1948 in NY.
Donor: Mrs. F.E. Barbour†.
Foundation type: Independent foundation.
Financial data (yr. ended 11/30/05): Assets, $55,518,999 (M); expenditures, $2,937,125; qualifying distributions, $2,338,810; giving activities include $1,385,325 for 52 grants (high: $1,015,000; low: $200), and $920,395 for 1 foundation-administered program.
Purpose and activities: The foundation maintains multi-purpose senior citizen residential and service facilities in Canajoharie, NY; it also does general local giving, with emphasis on higher education, including scholarship funds, hospitals, and health and social services, including youth agencies.
Fields of interest: Higher education; Medical school/education; Adult education—literacy, basic skills & GED; Education, reading; Education; Hospitals (general); Health care; Health organizations, association; Human services; Children/youth, services; Family services; Disabilities, people with.
Type of support: Building/renovation; Equipment; Scholarship funds.
Limitations: Giving limited to Canajoharie, NY. No grants to individuals, or for multi-year commitments, travel, conferences or other personal expenses; no loans.
Publications: Application guidelines.
Application information: Application form not required.
  Initial approach: 1-to 3-page proposal
  Copies of proposal: 1
  Deadline(s): Oct. 1
  Board meeting date(s): Feb., May, Aug., and Oct.
  Final notification: Dec. 1
Officers and Trustees:* Joseph A. Santangelo,* Pres.; Ferdinand C. Kaiser,* V.P. and Secy.; Charles Tallent, Treas.; Joyce G. Dresser; Edward W. Shineman, Jr.; Robert H. Wille.
Number of staff: 2 full-time professional; 1 part-time professional; 2 full-time support.
EIN: 141343077
Selected grants: The following grants were reported in 2005.
$1,015,000 to Canajoharie Library and Art Gallery, Canajoharie, NY.
$10,000 to American Red Cross, Albany, NY.
$10,000 to Siena College, Loudonville, NY.
$3,000 to American Cancer Society, New York, NY.
$3,000 to American Heart Association, Albany, NY.
$3,000 to Church of the Good Shepherd, Buffalo, NY.
$1,000 to Joslin Diabetes Center, Boston, MA.
$200 to Mountain Valley Hospice, Gloversville, NY.

5566
Arm Foundation ✧ ☆
c/o A. Miller
14 Manor Dr.
Monsey, NY 10952

Established in 2005 in NY.
Donors: Abraham Miller; Ruth Miller; Mike Kohn.
Foundation type: Independent foundation.
Financial data (yr. ended 3/31/06): Assets, $142,356 (M); gifts received, $485,000;
expenditures, $366,075; qualifying distributions, $363,454; giving activities include $363,454 for grants.
Fields of interest: Federated giving programs; Jewish agencies & temples.
Limitations: Giving primarily in NY.
Application information:
  Deadline(s): None
Officers: Abraham Miller, Pres.; Ruth Miller, Secy.-Treas.
EIN: 201056342

5567
Louis Armstrong Educational Foundation, Inc. ✧
c/o Present, Cohen, et al.
40 Cuttermill Rd., Ste. 305
Great Neck, NY 11021-3213

Established in 1988 in NY.
Foundation type: Independent foundation.
Financial data (yr. ended 6/30/05): Assets, $4,297,001 (M); expenditures, $1,341,532; qualifying distributions, $1,205,481; giving activities include $1,103,542 for 20 grants (high: $250,000; low: $1,000; average: $5,000–$75,000).
Purpose and activities: Giving primarily for education and the musical arts.
Fields of interest: Performing arts centers; Performing arts, music; Arts; Higher education; Education; Hospitals (general).
Limitations: Applications not accepted. Giving primarily in the greater metropolitan New York, NY, area. No grants to individuals.
Application information: Contributes only to pre-selected organizations.
Trustees: David Gold; Phoebe Jacobs.
EIN: 132659286
Selected grants: The following grants were reported in 2004.
$179,500 to Columbia University, New York, NY.
$75,000 to American Society of Composers, Authors and Publishers (ASCAP) Foundation, New York, NY.
$75,000 to Beth Israel Medical Center Foundation, New York, NY.
$65,996 to University of New Orleans, New Orleans, LA.
$35,000 to French Quarter Festival, New Orleans, LA.
$15,000 to North General Hospital, New York, NY.
$10,000 to Boys Choir of Harlem, New York, NY.
$5,000 to Harlem School of the Arts, New York, NY.
$5,000 to Queens Library Foundation, Jamaica, NY.
$2,500 to Flushing Council on Culture and the Arts, Flushing, NY.

5568
Arnhold Foundation, Inc. ✧
c/o Joel E. Sammet & Co.
60 Broad St., Ste. 3600
New York, NY 10004-2338

Established in 1988 in NY.
Donors: Henry H. Arnhold; John P. Arnhold; Bruder-Stiftung; Clarisse Arnhold; Michele Arnhold.
Foundation type: Independent foundation.
Financial data (yr. ended 12/31/04): Assets, $26,068,607 (M); gifts received, $961,508; expenditures, $4,016,964; qualifying distributions,

$3,888,821; giving activities include $3,889,351 for 236 grants (high: $748,500; low: $100).
Purpose and activities: Giving primarily to arts and cultural programs, education, natural resource conservation and protection, animal welfare and human services.
Fields of interest: Museums; Performing arts; Arts; Education; Environment, natural resources; Animal welfare; Human services.
Limitations: Applications not accepted. Giving primarily in New York, NY. No grants to individuals.
Application information: Contributes only to pre-selected organizations.
Officers: Henry H. Arnhold, Pres.; John P. Arnhold, Secy.-Treas.
EIN: 133456684
Selected grants: The following grants were reported in 2003.
$400,000 to Conservation International, DC. For general support.
$17,000 to Juilliard School, New York, NY. For general support.
$10,000 to Ballet Hispanico of New York, New York, NY. For general support.
$3,000 to New York City Opera, New York, NY. For general support.
$2,500 to Equus Foundation, Westport, CT. For general support.
$1,500 to Discovery Creek Childrens Museum of Washington, DC. For general support.
$1,000 to American Society for the Prevention of Cruelty to Animals, New York, NY. For general support.
$500 to Animal Cancer Foundation, New York, NY. For general support.
$500 to Western Connecticut State University, Danbury, CT. For general support.
$100 to Pegasus Therapeutic Riding, Stamford, CT. For general support.

5569

J. Aron Charitable Foundation, Inc. ▼ ✧
126 E. 56th St., Ste. 2300
New York, NY 10022 (212) 832-3405
Contact: Peter A. Aron, Pres.

Incorporated in 1934 in NY.
Donor: Members of the Aron family.
Foundation type: Independent foundation.
Financial data (yr. ended 12/31/05): Assets, $27,171,472 (M); expenditures, $4,064,769; qualifying distributions, $3,805,200; giving activities include $3,559,806 for 137 grants (high: $300,000; low: $100; average: $1,000–$100,000).
Purpose and activities: Giving primarily for hospitals and health associations, cultural programs, social service and youth agencies, Jewish welfare funds, and education, including medical schools.
Fields of interest: Museums; Historic preservation/historical societies; Arts; Medical school/education; Education; Hospitals (general); Health organizations, association; Medical research, institute; Human services; Youth, services; Jewish federated giving programs.
Type of support: General/operating support; Annual campaigns; Capital campaigns; Building/renovation; Program development; Research.
Limitations: Applications not accepted. Giving in the U.S., with emphasis on CT, New Orleans, LA, and New York, NY. No grants to individuals.

Application information: Contributes only to pre-selected organizations.
Board meeting date(s): Apr., July, Sept., and Dec.
Officers and Directors:* Peter A. Aron,* Pres. and Exec. Dir.; Robert Aron,* V.P.; Hans G. Jepson,* Secy.-Treas.; Ronald Stein; Martha Ward.
Number of staff: 2 full-time professional; 1 full-time support; 1 part-time support.
EIN: 136068230
Selected grants: The following grants were reported in 2004.
$1,000,000 to Avon Old Farms School, Avon, CT. For Building Fund.
$910,000 to South Street Seaport Museum, New York, NY. 4 grants: $500,000 (For Building Fund), $200,000 (For general support), $25,000 (For general support), $185,000 (For general support).
$335,000 to Tulane University, New Orleans, LA. 2 grants: $300,000 (For general support), $35,000 (For general support).
$225,000 to Woods Hole Oceanographic Institution, Woods Hole, MA. 2 grants: $200,000 (For general support), $25,000 (For general support).
$200,000 to Marymount School, New York, NY. For Building Fund.

5570

The Arrison Family Charitable Foundation ✧ ☆
35 Lincoln Pkwy.
Buffalo, NY 14222
Contact: Clement R. Arrison, Dir.

Established in 1989 in NY.
Foundation type: Independent foundation.
Financial data (yr. ended 12/31/05): Assets, $4,410,251 (M); expenditures, $537,262; qualifying distributions, $530,463; giving activities include $530,463 for grants.
Purpose and activities: Giving primarily for art and culture, religion, and human services.
Fields of interest: Performing arts, theater; Performing arts, music; Higher education; Animal welfare; Youth, services; Federated giving programs; Christian agencies & churches.
Limitations: Giving primarily in Buffalo, NY.
Trustees: Clement R. Arrison; Graig Arrison; Karen Arrison; Barbara Regan.
EIN: 223021980
Selected grants: The following grants were reported in 2005.
$75,000 to Buffalo Philharmonic Orchestra, Buffalo, NY.
$20,000 to Moving Miracles, Buffalo, NY.
$20,000 to Suburban Adult Services, Sardinia, NY.
$250 to Interlochen Center for the Arts, Interlochen, MI.
$25 to March of Dimes Birth Defects Foundation, White Plains, NY.

5571

The ASDA Foundation ✧
c/o First Spring Corp.
499 Park Ave., 26th Fl.
New York, NY 10022

Established in 1983 in NY.
Foundation type: Independent foundation.

Financial data (yr. ended 12/31/05): Assets, $434,265 (M); expenditures, $6,823,971; qualifying distributions, $6,767,126; giving activities include $6,766,776 for grants.
Fields of interest: Higher education.
Type of support: General/operating support; Research.
Limitations: Applications not accepted. Giving primarily in Cambridge, MA. No grants to individuals.
Application information: Contributes only to pre-selected organizations.
Officers: Guido Goldman, Pres.; Ken Musen, Secy.; Mark O'Donnell, Treas.
Directors: Stanley N. Bergman; Charles De Gunzburg; Jean De Gunzburg; Leonard M. Nelson.
EIN: 521319624

5572

Jack H. Ashkenazie Foundation, Inc. ✧
31 W. 34th St., 8th Fl.
New York, NY 10001

Established in 2001 in NY.
Donor: Almar Sales Co. Inc.
Foundation type: Company-sponsored foundation.
Financial data (yr. ended 12/31/03): Assets, $0 (M); gifts received, $372,191; expenditures, $365,166; qualifying distributions, $364,952; giving activities include $364,952 for 244 grants (high: $57,404; low: $18).
Purpose and activities: The foundation supports organizations involved with K-12 education and Judaism.
Fields of interest: Elementary/secondary education; Jewish agencies & temples.
Limitations: Applications not accepted. No grants to individuals.
Application information: Contributes only to pre-selected organizations.
Officer: Jack R. Ashkenazie, Treas.
Directors: Harry J. Ashkenazie; Raymond J. Ashkenazie.
EIN: 134161819

5573

Ashner Family Evergreen Foundation ☆
2 Jericho Plz., Wing A, Ste. 111
Jericho, NY 11753-1681
E-mail: mla@wfzjericho.com

Established in 2003 in NY.
Donors: Michael Ashner; Susan Ashner.
Foundation type: Independent foundation.
Financial data (yr. ended 12/31/05): Assets, $2,611,196 (M); gifts received, $698,881; expenditures, $699,605; qualifying distributions, $699,056; giving activities include $699,056 for 22 grants (high: $359,764; low: $50).
Fields of interest: Hospitals (general); Human services; Jewish federated giving programs.
Limitations: Giving primarily in NY. No grants to individuals.
Application information: Application form not required.
Initial approach: E-mail
Copies of proposal: 1
Officers: Susan Ashner, Pres.; Michael Ashner, Secy.-Treas.
Number of staff: 1 part-time support.
EIN: 010772925

5574
The Atlantic Foundation of New York ▼ ✧
125 Park Ave., 21st Fl.
New York, NY 10017-5581 (212) 916-7300
FAX: (212) 922-0360;
E-mail: USA@atlanticphilanthropies.org;
URL: http://www.atlanticphilanthropies.org

Established in 1989 in NY.
Donors: Atlan Management Corp.; Interpacific Holdings, Inc.; General Atlantic Corp.
Foundation type: Independent foundation.
Financial data (yr. ended 12/31/05): Assets, $13,377,570 (M); expenditures, $6,664,140; qualifying distributions, $6,644,833; giving activities include $6,643,545 for 29 grants (high: $800,000; low: $3,700; average: $75,000–$400,000).
Purpose and activities: The purpose of the foundation is to bring about lasting changes that will improve the lives of disadvantaged and vulnerable people.
Fields of interest: Health care; Children, services; Aging, centers/services; International affairs, goodwill promotion; Aging; Economically disadvantaged.
Type of support: Program-related investments/loans.
Limitations: Applications not accepted. Giving on a national basis. No grants to individuals.
Publications: Financial statement.
Application information: Contributes only to pre-selected organizations.
Officers and Directors:* Frank H.T. Rhodes,* Chair.; John R. Healy,* C.E.O. and Pres.; Gara LaMarche, C.E.O. and Pres-Elect.; Colin McCrea, Sr. V.P., Progs.; Deborah R. Phillips, Sr. V.P., Group Svcs. and Eval.; Philip Coates, C.I.O.; David Sternlieb, Genl. Counsel; Harvey P. Dale; Christine V. Downton; Charles F. Feeney; Sara Lawrence-Lightfoot; Elizabeth J. McCormack; Thomas N. Mitchell; Frederick A.O. Schwarz, Jr.; Peter Smitham; Michael I. Sovern; Cummings V. Zuill.
EIN: 133562971
Selected grants: The following grants were reported in 2004.
$300,000 to Brennan Center for Justice, New York, NY. For Liberty and National Security project.

5575
Atran Foundation, Inc. ✧
23-25 E. 21st St., 3rd Fl.
New York, NY 10010 (212) 505-9677
Contact: Diane Fischer, Pres.

Incorporated in 1945 in NY.
Donor: Frank Z. Atran†.
Foundation type: Independent foundation.
Financial data (yr. ended 11/30/05): Assets, $15,597,132 (M); expenditures, $766,805; qualifying distributions, $733,623; giving activities include $574,796 for 34 grants (high: $120,000; low: $250).
Purpose and activities: Support for research relating to labor and labor relations, art, science, literature, economics, and sociology; support of publications furthering these purposes; and endowment for chairs of learning in these fields.
Fields of interest: Arts, cultural/ethnic awareness; History/archaeology; Medical school/education; Employment, labor unions/organizations; Jewish federated giving programs; International studies.

Type of support: General/operating support; Continuing support; Annual campaigns; Endowments; Program development; Conferences/seminars; Professorships; Publication; Scholarship funds; Research; Exchange programs.
Limitations: Giving on a national basis. No grants to individuals.
Publications: Application guidelines.
Application information: Application form not required.
Initial approach: Proposal
Copies of proposal: 1
Deadline(s): Sept. 30
Board meeting date(s): Between Nov. and Feb. and as required
Final notification: Positive references only
Officers and Trustees:* Diane Fischer,* Pres.; Emanuel Muravchik, V.P.; George Fraenkel,* Treas.
Number of staff: 1 full-time professional; 1 part-time support.
EIN: 135566548

5576
The Atticus Foundation ✧
c/o Atticus Capital LLC
152 W. 57th St.
New York, NY 10019 (212) 373-0800
Contact: Timothy R. Barakett, Tr.

Established in 1997 in NY.
Donors: Timothy R. Barakett; Nathaniel Rothschild; Atticus Capital LLC.
Foundation type: Independent foundation.
Financial data (yr. ended 12/31/05): Assets, $2,150,833 (M); gifts received, $3,911,097; expenditures, $2,231,881; qualifying distributions, $2,223,973; giving activities include $2,223,973 for 33 grants (high: $1,128,000; low: $500).
Fields of interest: Higher education, university; Education; Hospitals (general); Health organizations, association; Children, services; Human services, emergency aid; Aging, centers/services; Jewish agencies & temples.
Type of support: General/operating support.
Limitations: Giving primarily in NY. No grants to individuals.
Application information: Application form not required.
Initial approach: Letter
Deadline(s): None
Trustees: Peter Barakett; Timothy R. Barakett.
EIN: 133981257
Selected grants: The following grants were reported in 2005.
$100,000 to Lincoln Center Hedge Fund Council, New York, NY.
$50,000 to Prep for Prep, New York, NY.
$50,000 to Robin Hood Foundation, New York, NY.
$35,000 to Childrens Museum of the East End, Bridgehampton, NY.
$14,567 to Sun Valley Writers Conference, Ketchum, ID.
$10,000 to American Friends of the Israel Museum, New York, NY.
$10,000 to League for the Hard of Hearing, New York, NY.
$5,000 to Beth Israel Medical Center Foundation, New York, NY.
$1,000 to Cystic Fibrosis Foundation, Bethesda, MD.
$500 to New York Foundling Hospital, New York, NY.

5577
Lily Auchincloss Foundation, Inc.
16 E. 79th St., Ste. 31
New York, NY 10021 (212) 737-9533
Contact: Alexandra A. Herzan, Pres.
FAX: (212) 737-9578; E-mail: info@lilyauch.org;
URL: http://www.lilyauch.org

Established in 1985 in NY; incorporated in 1997.
Donors: Lily Auchincloss†; Hedwig A. van Ameringen†; Lily Auchincloss Foundation.
Foundation type: Independent foundation.
Financial data (yr. ended 12/31/04): Assets, $56,659,103 (M); expenditures, $3,233,222; qualifying distributions, $2,963,413; giving activities include $2,724,717 for 140 grants (high: $400,000; low: $2,500).
Purpose and activities: Supports visual contemporary arts, preservation, and community programs that serve to enrich the lives of the people of the New York City area.
Fields of interest: Historic preservation/historical societies; Arts; Youth development; Human services; Aging, centers/services.
Type of support: General/operating support; Capital campaigns; Program development; Matching/challenge support.
Limitations: Giving limited to New York, NY and its surrounding boroughs. No support for hospitals, nursing homes, substance abuse programs, mental health programs, or private schools. No grants to individuals, or for research projects or dance, film, music or theater programs.
Publications: Application guidelines; Grants list; Program policy statement (including application guidelines).
Application information: Do not send applications by registered mail or other delivery service requiring a signature. A complete list of grants awarded is available on foundation Web site. Foundation publications are available on Web site only. Application form not required.
Initial approach: Proposal with cover letter or E-mail
Copies of proposal: 1
Deadline(s): Mar. 15, Aug. 15, and Dec. 15
Board meeting date(s): Mar., June, and Nov.
Final notification: Mar., June, and Nov.
Officers and Directors:* Alexandra A. Herzan,* Pres. and Treas.; Paul K. Herzan,* V.P.; Steadman H. Westergaard,* Secy.; Lynne Harlow, Foundation Mgr.; James Gara; Janet Levoff; Lee Auchincloss Link.
Number of staff: 1 part-time professional.
EIN: 133935995

5578
The Neil and Judith Auerbach Foundation, Inc. ✧ ☆
15 Langeries Dr.
Monsey, NY 10952-1907

Established in 1999 in NY.
Donors: Neil Auerbach; Judith Auerbach.
Foundation type: Independent foundation.
Financial data (yr. ended 12/31/04): Assets, $284,267 (M); gifts received, $719,645; expenditures, $429,380; qualifying distributions, $425,486; giving activities include $425,486 for 135 grants (high: $170,000; low: $10).
Fields of interest: Jewish agencies & temples.

Limitations: Applications not accepted. Giving primarily in NY. No grants to individuals.
Application information: Contributes only to pre-selected organizations.
Directors: Judith Auerbach; Neil Auerbach; Michael Kutzin.
EIN: 134088697

5579
Avalon Foundation ✧
c/o BCRS Assocs., LLC
100 Wall St., 11th Fl.
New York, NY   10005

Established in 1987 in NY.
Donor: Michael D. McCarthy.
Foundation type: Independent foundation.
Financial data (yr. ended 1/31/05): Assets, $13,187,786 (M); expenditures, $642,031; qualifying distributions, $584,345; giving activities include $583,500 for 9 grants (high: $200,000; low: $1,000).
Fields of interest: Education; Foundations (private operating).
Limitations: Applications not accepted. Giving primarily in New York, NY. No grants to individuals; no loans.
Application information: Contributes only to pre-selected organizations.
Trustees: Jonathan L. Cohen; Deborah Berg McCarthy; Michael D. McCarthy.
EIN: 133437931
Selected grants: The following grants were reported in 2004.
$902,000 to Eureka Foundation, DC. 5 grants: $250,000, $100,000, $100,000, $300,000, $152,000
$10,000 to Challenge Aspen, Aspen, CO.
$1,000 to La Salle College High School, Wyndmoor, PA.

5580
Avanessians Family Foundation ✧ ☆
c/o Goldman Sachs Family Office
1 New York Plz., 40th Fl.
New York, NY   10004

Established in 1995 in NY.
Donors: Armen Avanessians; Goldman Sachs & Co.
Foundation type: Independent foundation.
Financial data (yr. ended 2/28/06): Assets, $5,402,918 (M); expenditures, $698,438; qualifying distributions, $698,100; giving activities include $698,100 for grants.
Purpose and activities: Giving primarily for higher education.
Fields of interest: Elementary/secondary education; Higher education; Roman Catholic agencies & churches.
Limitations: Applications not accepted. Giving primarily in New York, NY; some giving in MA and TX. No grants to individuals; no loans.
Application information: Contributes only to pre-selected organizations.
Trustees: Armen Avanessians; Janette Avanessians.
EIN: 133862934
Selected grants: The following grants were reported in 2005.
$75,000 to Oregon Public Broadcasting, Portland, OR.

$54,000 to Columbia University, New York, NY. 2 grants: $4,000, $50,000
$30,000 to FJC-A Foundation of Donor-Advised Funds, New York, NY. 2 grants: $25,000, $5,000
$10,000 to Oxfam America, Boston, MA.
$10,000 to Robin Hood Foundation, New York, NY.
$4,000 to Our Lady of Solace, Brooklyn, NY.
$1,000 to Fund for Park Avenue, New York, NY.

5581
Milton and Sally Avery Arts Foundation
c/o Radin, Glass & Co., LLP
360 Lexington Ave.
New York, NY   10017
Contact: March A. Cavanaugh, Pres.
FAX: (212) 595-2840; Application address: 300 Central Park W., Apt. 16J, New York, NY 10024

Established in 1983 in NY.
Donor: Sally M. Avery‡.
Foundation type: Independent foundation.
Financial data (yr. ended 12/31/05): Assets, $4,420,396 (M); expenditures, $479,984; qualifying distributions, $389,300; giving activities include $389,300 for 118 grants (high: $30,000; low: $1,000; average: $2,000–$5,000).
Purpose and activities: Awards restricted to art education, with emphasis on the visual arts, and to further the development of artists through nonprofit institutions, and to artists' communities and residency programs.
Fields of interest: Arts education; Visual arts, sculpture; Visual arts, painting; Arts; Elementary/secondary education; Higher education.
Type of support: Professorships; Fellowships; Internship funds; Scholarship funds.
Limitations: Giving primarily in NY. No support for religious or political organizations. No grants to individuals.
Publications: Annual report.
Application information: Application form not required.
    Initial approach: Letter
    Copies of proposal: 1
    Deadline(s): None
    Board meeting date(s): Jan. 9
Officers: March A. Cavanaugh, Pres.; Sean A. Cavanaugh, V.P.; Harvey S. Miller, Secy.; Philip G. Cavanaugh, Treas.
EIN: 133093638
Selected grants: The following grants were reported in 2004.
$19,000 to Yaddo, Saratoga Springs, NY.
$6,000 to Sculpture Space, Utica, NY.
$5,000 to Artists Space, New York, NY.
$5,000 to Bard College, Annandale on Hudson, NY.
$5,000 to Catching the Dream, Albuquerque, NM.
$5,000 to College Art Association, New York, NY.
$5,000 to Frick Collection, New York, NY.
$5,000 to Green Guerillas, New York, NY.
$2,000 to Symphony Space, New York, NY.
$2,000 to Wave Hill, Bronx, NY.

5582
The AVI CHAI Foundation ▼ ✧
(formerly AVI CHAI - A Philanthropic Foundation)
1015 Park Ave.
New York, NY   10028   (212) 396-8850
Contact: Yossi Prager, Exec. Dir., North America
FAX: (212) 396-8833; E-mail: info@avichaina.org;
Additional address (Israel office): 31 Hanevlim,

95103 Jerusalem, tel.: (02) 624-3330, FAX: (02) 624-3310, E-mail: office@avichai.org.il; URL: http://www.avichai.org

Established in 1984 in NY.
Donor: Zalman Chaim Bernstein‡.
Foundation type: Independent foundation.
Financial data (yr. ended 12/31/05): Assets, $653,609,340 (M); gifts received, $7,000,000; expenditures, $35,761,750; qualifying distributions, $43,393,346; giving activities include $30,655,330 for 206 grants (high: $10,135,000; low: $1,000; average: $6,000–$1,038,542), $801,300 for 4 foundation-administered programs and $8,250,000 for 10 loans/program-related investments (high: $1,000,000; low: $230,000).
Purpose and activities: The foundation is committed to the perpetuation of the Jewish people, Judaism, and the centrality of the state of Israel to the Jewish people. The objectives of the foundation are to encourage those of the Jewish faith towards greater commitment to Jewish observance and lifestyle by increasing their understanding, appreciation, and practice of Jewish traditions, customs, and laws; and to encourage mutual understanding and sensitivity among Jews of different religious backgrounds and commitments to observance.
Fields of interest: Education; Human services; Youth, services; Jewish federated giving programs.
International interests: Israel.
Type of support: Program development; Conferences/seminars; Curriculum development; Research; Program-related investments/loans.
Limitations: Applications not accepted. Giving primarily in North America and Israel. No grants for building projects or deficits.
Publications: Annual report.
Application information:
    Board meeting date(s): 3 times a year
Officers and Trustees:* Arthur W. Fried,* Chair.; Azriel Novick, C.F.O.; Yossi Prager, Exec. Dir., North America; Eli Silver, Exec. Dir., Israel; Henry Taub, Tr. Emeritus; Mem Dryan Bernstein; Meir Buzaglo; Avital Darmon; Alan R. Feld; Lauren K. Merkin; George Rohr; Lief D. Rosenblatt; David E. Tadmor; Ruth R. Wisse.
Number of staff: 7 full-time professional; 4 full-time support.
EIN: 133252800
Selected grants: The following grants were reported in 2005.
$10,135,000 to Avi Chai, Israel. For general support.
$2,974,334 to Jewish Funders Network, New York, NY. For general support.
$1,966,492 to Hebrew College, Newton Centre, MA. For general support.
$1,477,333 to BabagaNewz, Newton, MA. For general support.
$1,178,433 to American Jewish Joint Distribution Committee, New York, NY. For general support.
$480,780 to Jewish Agency for Israel, New York, NY. For general support.
$330,750 to Ohr Avner Foundation, New York, NY. For general support.
$60,716 to Partnership for Excellence in Jewish Education, Boston, MA. For general support.
$30,000 to Conference of Presidents of Major American Jewish Organizations, New York, NY. For general support.
$6,000 to Yeshiva Rambam, Brooklyn, NY. For general support.

5583
Avon Foundation ▼

(formerly Avon Products Foundation, Inc.)
1345 Ave. of the Americas
New York, NY 10105-0196 (212) 282-5000
Contact: Denise L.C. Yap, Mgr., Grants and Progs.
FAX: (212) 282-6049;
E-mail: info@avonfoundation.org; Application
address for Breast Care Fund: 505 8th Ave., Ste.
1601, New York, NY 10018, tel.: (212) 244-5368,
FAX: (212) 695-3081; Contact for Safety Net
Program and Breast Cancer Prevention Research
Initiative: Marc Hulbert, E-mail:
marc.hulbert@avonfoundation.org; Additional tel.:
(866) 505-2866; URL: http://
www.avonfoundation.org

Incorporated in 1955 in NY.
Donor: Avon Products, Inc.
Foundation type: Company-sponsored foundation.
Financial data (yr. ended 12/31/05): Assets,
$52,373,251 (M); gifts received, $50,928,931;
expenditures, $73,076,415; qualifying
distributions, $72,860,936; giving activities include
$45,674,226 for 193 grants (high: $5,500,000;
low: $1,000), and $300,455 for employee matching
gifts.
Purpose and activities: The foundation supports
organizations involved with breast cancer and
domestic violence.
Fields of interest: Hospitals (general); Breast
cancer; Breast cancer research; Children, services;
Family services, domestic violence.
Type of support: General/operating support;
Continuing support; Program development;
Research; Employee matching gifts;
Employee-related scholarships.
Limitations: Giving on a national and international
basis. No support for political, religious, veterans',
or fraternal organizations. No grants to individuals
(except for employee-related scholarships), or for
endowments, fundraising events, telethons,
marathons, races, benefits, courtesy advertising, or
films; no loans.
Publications: Annual report; Financial statement;
Grants list; Newsletter; IRS Form 990-PF.
Application information: Application form required.
Initial approach: Visit Web site for application
information
Deadline(s): Sept. 1 for Breast Care Fund; Mar. 1
and June 1 for Safety Net Program; July 15 for
Breast Cancer Prevention Research Initiative;
Aug. 1 for Local and Regional Domestic
Violence; and Apr. 1 for Helping Children of
Domestic Violence
Board meeting date(s): 3 times per year
Officers and Directors:* Robert Corti,* Chair.; Brian
Connolly,* V.P.; Nancy Glaser,* V.P.; Carol Kurzig,*
V.P. and Exec. Dir.; Richard C. Matthews,* Secy.;
Pauline Brown,* Treas.; Mary Quinn.
Number of staff: 2 full-time professional; 1 full-time
support; 1 part-time support.
EIN: 136128447
Selected grants: The following grants were reported
in 2004.
$5,596,306 to National Cancer Institute, Bethesda,
MD. For Avon-NCI Progress for Patients Awards
Program, public-private initiative in early phase
clinical interventions in breast cancer.
$5,542,000 to Cicatelli Associates, New York, NY.
2 grants: $542,000 (To provide grants through
Avon Foundation Breast Care Fund Coordinating
Center to community-based organizations that
conduct breast health outreach and patient

navigation services), $5,000,000 (To provide
grants through Avon Foundation Breast Care
Fund Coordinating Center to community-based
organizations that conduct breast health
outreach and patient navigation services).
$2,148,266 to Johns Hopkins Hospital, Sidney
Kimmel Comprehensive Cancer Center,
Baltimore, MD. To establish Avon Foundation
Comprehensive Breast Center, for innovative
prevention research project focused on
estrogen-negative breast tumors, and for clinical
care programs for underserved, primarily
African-American populations.
$2,013,495 to University of California,
Comprehensive Cancer Center, San Francisco,
CA. To continue basic and translational research
in breast cancer biology, recruit additional faculty
to expand clinical trials program and establish
comprehensive breast cancer screening and
treatment program with San Francisco General
Hospital.
$833,333 to Y-ME National Breast Cancer
Organization, Chicago, IL. For Women's Test
programs, patient navigators, addition of
translation services in Mandarin Chinese and
Vietnamese to Y-Me hotline, and expansion of
teen program.
$600,000 to Cancer Care, New York, NY. For
nationwide Avon Cares Program for medically
underserved women, providing breast cancer
patients with transportation to and from
appointments and child or elder care while they
undergo treatment.
$500,000 to Georgetown University Medical Center,
Vincent T. Lombardi Cancer Research Center,
DC. For operating support of Capital Breast Care
Center and for community health advisors, nurse
practitioner/supervisor, medical and
administration staff and local transportation
costs for women.
$500,000 to John Wayne Cancer Institute, Santa
Monica, CA. For collaboration with Center for
Healthy Aging, focusing on breast cancer
education, outreach, screening, diagnostic and
treatment services for women over 65.
$500,000 to National Breast Cancer Coalition Fund,
DC. For continued support for expanded Project
LEAD Program, which provides medical education
and advocacy training, to include advanced
session on clinical trials and web-based
component.

5584
AXA Foundation, Inc. ▼ ◇

(formerly The Equitable Foundation, Inc.)
1290 Ave. of the Americas, 7th Fl.
New York, NY 10104 (212) 314-3662
Contact: Faith Frank, C.E.O. and Pres.
FAX: (212) 314-4480; Application address for AXA
Achievement Scholarship: AXA Achievement
Scholarship, Scholarship Management Svcs.,
Scholarship America, Inc., 1 Scholarship Way, P.O.
Box 297, St. Peter, MN 56082, tel.: (800)
537-4180, E-mail:
axaachievement@scholarshipamerica.org;
URL: http://www.axaonline.com/axafoundation

Established in 1986 in NY.
Donors: The Equitable Cos. Inc.; The Equitable Life
Assurance Society of the U.S.; AXA Financial, Inc.;
The MONY Group, Inc.
Foundation type: Company-sponsored foundation.

Financial data (yr. ended 9/30/05): Assets,
$43,064,664 (M); gifts received, $4,907,892;
expenditures, $6,449,832; qualifying distributions,
$5,620,917; giving activities include $3,327,974
for 73 grants (high: $500,000; low: $750), and
$1,842,711 for 3,208 employee matching gifts.
Purpose and activities: The foundation supports
organizations involved with arts and culture,
education, human services, and community
development and awards college scholarships.
Fields of interest: Performing arts, theater; Arts;
Secondary school/education; Higher education;
Education; American Red Cross; Children/youth,
services; Human services; Community
development; Federated giving programs.
Type of support: Annual campaigns; Program
development; Scholarship funds; Sponsorships;
Employee matching gifts; Employee-related
scholarships; Scholarships—to individuals.
Limitations: Giving on a national basis. No support
for private foundations, United Way member
agencies, or religious or international organizations.
No grants to individuals (except for scholarships), or
for capital campaigns, medical research, or
media-related projects.
Publications: Application guidelines; Informational
brochure; Program policy statement.
Application information: Unsolicited requests for
non-AXA Achievement scholarships are not
accepted.
Initial approach: Download application form and
mail to application address for AXA
Achievement Scholarships; contact nearest
AXA Advisors branch office for application form
for AXA Achievement Community Scholarships
Deadline(s): Dec. 15 for AXA Achievement
Scholarships; Feb. 17 for AXA Achievement
Community Scholarships
Board meeting date(s): As needed
Final notification: Mid-Mar. for AXA Achievement
Scholarships
Officers and Directors:* Jane C. Mahoney, Chair.;
Faith Frank, C.E.O. and Pres.; Jan Goldstein,* V.P.
and Secy.; John C. Taroni, V.P. and Treas.;
Christiann M. Bishop, V.P. and Cont.; Christopher M.
Condron; Stanley B. Tulin.
Number of staff: 6 full-time professional; 1 full-time
support.
EIN: 131340512
Selected grants: The following grants were reported
in 2004.
$2,895,581 to Scholarship America, Saint Peter,
MN. 8 grants: $65,000 (For Month Info Kit),
$200,000 (For month sponsorship), $63,581
(For management fee), $100,000 (For program
support), $335,000 (For awards), $335,000 (For
awards), $297,000 (For program awards),
$1,500,000 (For scholarships. Grant made
through 9/11 Relief Fund).
$50,000 to Inner-City Scholarship Fund, New York,
NY. For endowment.
$50,000 to Lycee Francais de New York, New York,
NY. For scholarships.

5585
Marvin Azrak and Sons Foundation ◇

10 W. 33rd St., Rm. 516
New York, NY 10001

Established in 1994 in NY.
Donors: Marvin Azrak; members of the Azrak family.
Foundation type: Independent foundation.

Financial data (yr. ended 12/31/05): Assets, $2,136,306 (M); gifts received, $1,641,200; expenditures, $810,145; qualifying distributions, $808,893; giving activities include $808,893 for 109 grants (high: $84,905; low: $10).
Purpose and activities: Giving primarily for Jewish agencies and temples.
Fields of interest: Health organizations, association; Cancer; Jewish federated giving programs; Jewish agencies & temples.
Limitations: Applications not accepted. Giving primarily in NJ, and New York, NY. No grants to individuals.
Application information: Contributes only to pre-selected organizations.
Officer: Marvin Azrak, Mgr.
Trustees: Adam Azrak; Elliot Azrak; Victor Azrak.
EIN: 133771410

5586
Babbitt Family Charitable Trust ◇
c/o Davis & Graber
150 E. 58th St., 22nd Fl.
New York, NY 10155

Established in 1991 in NY.
Donor: Edward Babbitt.
Foundation type: Independent foundation.
Financial data (yr. ended 6/30/06): Assets, $5,778,152 (M); gifts received, $85,000; expenditures, $370,718; qualifying distributions, $365,775; giving activities include $362,000 for 39 grants (high: $200,000; low: $500).
Purpose and activities: Funding primarily for arts and culture, human services, health associations, and federated giving programs.
Fields of interest: Performing arts; Performing arts, theater; Arts; Education; Environment; Animal welfare; Health organizations, association; Disasters, 9/11/01; Human services; Children/youth, services; Federated giving programs; Economically disadvantaged.
Limitations: Applications not accepted. Giving primarily in NY. No grants to individuals.
Application information: Contributes only to pre-selected organizations.
Trustee: Susan Babbitt.
EIN: 136975951
Selected grants: The following grants were reported in 2004.
$200,000 to Loomis Chaffee School, Windsor, CT.
$5,000 to Childrens Aid Society, New York, NY.
$5,000 to New York City Ballet Guild, New York, NY.
$5,000 to Phoenix House, New York, NY.
$5,000 to Robin Hood Foundation, New York, NY.
$3,000 to Hazelden Foundation, New York, NY.
$3,000 to Roundabout Theater Company, New York, NY.
$2,000 to Citymeals-on-Wheels, New York, NY.
$2,000 to Jazz at Lincoln Center, New York, NY.
$100 to Leukemia & Lymphoma Society, New York, NY.

5587
The Bachmann Strauss Family Fund ◇
(formerly The Bachmann Foundation)
c/o Stephen M. Cutting, The Ayco Company, L.P.
P.O. Box 860
Saratoga Springs, NY 12866-0860

Incorporated in 1949 in NY.

Donors: Louis Bachmann†; Thomas W. Strauss; B. Bachmann; GST Charitable Lead Trust.
Foundation type: Independent foundation.
Financial data (yr. ended 12/31/04): Assets, $9,710,329 (M); gifts received, $472,653; expenditures, $616,768; qualifying distributions, $532,416; giving activities include $532,416 for 129 grants (high: $105,450; low: $100).
Fields of interest: Museums (art); Performing arts; Arts; Education; Hospitals (general); Health organizations, association; Medical research, institute; Boys & girls clubs; Human services; Children, services; Jewish federated giving programs; Jewish agencies & temples.
Limitations: Applications not accepted. Giving primarily in New York, NY. No grants to individuals.
Application information: Contributes only to pre-selected organizations.
Officers: Barbara Bachmann Strauss, Pres.; Thomas W. Strauss, V.P. and Treas.; Richard M. Danziger, Secy.
EIN: 136043497
Selected grants: The following grants were reported in 2004.
$105,450 to American Folk Art Museum, New York, NY.
$53,300 to New York City Ballet, New York, NY.
$42,350 to Bachmann-Strauss Dystonia and Parkinson Foundation, New York, NY.
$25,380 to Dystonia Medical Research Foundation, Chicago, IL.
$19,050 to Mount Sinai Hospital, New York, NY.
$10,000 to Prep for Prep, New York, NY.
$2,500 to Memorial Sloan-Kettering Cancer Center, New York, NY.
$2,000 to Center for Educational Innovation-Public Education Association (CEI-PEA), New York, NY.
$1,350 to Metropolitan Museum of Art, New York, NY.
$1,000 to American Lung Association, New York, NY.

5588
Rose M. Badgeley Residuary Charitable Trust ◇
c/o HSBC Bank USA
452 5th Ave., 17th Fl.
New York, NY 10018-2706 (212) 525-2418
Contact: Marianne Caskran, Grants Admin.
FAX: (212) 525-2395;
E-mail: marianne.caskran@hsbcpb.com

Trust established in 1976 in NY.
Donor: Rose Badgeley†.
Foundation type: Independent foundation.
Financial data (yr. ended 1/31/05): Assets, $25,468,097 (M); expenditures, $1,634,271; qualifying distributions, $1,531,148; giving activities include $1,492,500 for 83 grants (high: $125,000; low: $5,000; average: $5,000–$50,000).
Purpose and activities: The Badgeley Trust provides support to a variety of nonprofit organizations. The scope of the trust's distributions includes support for the benefit of religious, charitable, scientific, literary, or educational purposes, or to such corporations or other organizations having such purposes, which HSBC, the trustee, in its sole discretion, may select. Such selections and appointments shall include purposes that are for the benefit and cure of alcoholism, general education, medical and scientific research and education, or medical and hospital care.

Type of support: General/operating support; Continuing support; Equipment; Program development; Research; Technical assistance.
Limitations: Giving limited to the greater metropolitan New York, NY, area. No grants to individuals or for capital campaigns.
Publications: Application guidelines.
Application information: Contact foundation for application and application guidelines. Application form required.
   Initial approach: Telephone or letter
   Copies of proposal: 1
   Deadline(s): Submit proposal postmarked no earlier than Dec. 1 and no later than Mar. 15
   Board meeting date(s): June
   Final notification: Usually within a month after grant committee meeting if approved
Trustee: HSBC Bank USA.
EIN: 136744781
Selected grants: The following grants were reported in 2005.
$125,000 to Samuel Waxman Cancer Research Foundation, New York, NY.
$50,000 to Roundabout Theater Company, New York, NY.
$30,000 to Federation of Protestant Welfare Agencies, New York, NY.
$25,000 to Bedford Stuyvesant Restoration Corporation, Brooklyn, NY.
$25,000 to Junior Achievement of New York, New York, NY.
$25,000 to Lenox Hill Hospital, New York, NY.
$25,000 to Saint Josephs College, Brooklyn, NY.
$20,000 to Good Shepherd Services, New York, NY.
$15,000 to Brooklyn Youth Chorus Academy, Brooklyn, NY.
$15,000 to Henry Street Settlement, New York, NY.

5589
The Bahnik Foundation, Inc. ◇
190 Pine Hollow Rd.
Oyster Bay, NY 11771
Contact: Roger L. Bahnik, Pres.

Established in 1994 in NY.
Donors: Roger L. Bahnik; Lore Bahnik.
Foundation type: Independent foundation.
Financial data (yr. ended 4/30/05): Assets, $12,146,695 (M); gifts received, $311,615; expenditures, $678,422; qualifying distributions, $591,150; giving activities include $591,150 for 43 grants (high: $250,000; low: $750).
Purpose and activities: Giving primarily for education, community development and human services.
Fields of interest: Higher education; Human services; Children/youth, services; Family services.
Type of support: Continuing support; Annual campaigns; Capital campaigns; Scholarship funds.
Limitations: Applications not accepted. Giving primarily on Long Island, NY. No grants to individuals.
Application information: Contributes only to pre-selected organizations.
   Board meeting date(s): Nov.
Officers: Roger L. Bahnik, Pres.; Claude Bahnik, V.P.; Michele Bahnik Mercier, V.P.; Lore Bahnik, Secy.
EIN: 113216930
Selected grants: The following grants were reported in 2004.
$78,500 to Institute for Student Achievement, Lake Success, NY. For general support.

$58,500 to Portledge School, Locust Valley, NY. For general support.

$45,000 to Boys and Girls Club of Oyster Bay, East Norwich, NY. For general support.

$14,000 to SCO Family of Services, Glen Cove, NY. For general support.

$12,500 to Saint Francis Hospital, Roslyn, NY. For general support.

$10,000 to Cold Spring Harbor Laboratory, Cold Spring Harbor, NY. For general support.

$10,000 to Doubleday Babcock Senior Center, Oyster Bay, NY. For general support.

$10,000 to Family and Childrens Association, Mineola, NY. For general support.

$5,000 to Community Foundation of Oyster Bay, Oyster Bay, NY. For general support.

$5,000 to Planting Fields Foundation, Oyster Bay, NY. For general support.

5590
Marie Baier Foundation, Inc. ✧
6 E. 87th St.
New York, NY 10128
Contact: John Baier

Established about 1967.
Donor: John F. Baier†.
Foundation type: Independent foundation.
Financial data (yr. ended 12/31/05): Assets, $12,669,348 (M); expenditures, $970,146; qualifying distributions, $905,731; giving activities include $632,000 for 13 grants (high: $150,000; low: $10,000).
Purpose and activities: Grants primarily for higher education and the performing arts; support also for German-American organizations.
Fields of interest: Performing arts; Higher education.
International interests: Germany.
Limitations: Giving primarily in New York, NY. No grants to individuals.
Application information:
    Initial approach: Letter
    Deadline(s): None
Officers and Directors:* John F. Baier, Jr.,* Pres.; Karin Gerbavsits, V.P. and Secy.; Berteline Baier Dale,* V.P.; Guenter F. Metsch*; Sidney Sirkin.
EIN: 136267032
Selected grants: The following grants were reported in 2004.
$150,000 to Metropolitan Opera Association, New York, NY.
$75,000 to Los Angeles Philharmonic Association, Los Angeles, CA.
$40,000 to Carnegie Hall Corporation, New York, NY.
$20,000 to Liederkranz Foundation, New York, NY.
$20,000 to Viewpoint Educational Foundation, Calabasas, CA.
$15,700 to Wagner College, Staten Island, NY.
$15,000 to Tufts University, Medford, MA.
$10,000 to Tuxedo Park School, Tuxedo Park, NY.

5591
The Cameron Baird Foundation ✧
726 Exchange St., Ste. 800
Buffalo, NY 14202
Contact: Brian D. Baird, Tr.

Trust established in 1960 in NY.
Donor: Members of the family of Cameron Baird.

Foundation type: Independent foundation.
Financial data (yr. ended 12/31/05): Assets, $61,194,864 (M); expenditures, $3,233,972; qualifying distributions, $3,170,903; giving activities include $3,156,219 for 100 grants (high: $750,000; low: $3,000; average: $5,000–$50,000).
Purpose and activities: Emphasis on music and cultural programs, higher and secondary education, social services, family planning, conservation, and civil rights.
Fields of interest: Performing arts, music; Arts; Secondary school/education; Higher education; Environment, natural resources; Reproductive health, family planning; Civil rights.
Limitations: Applications not accepted. Giving primarily in the Buffalo, NY, area. No support for religious organizations. No grants to individuals.
Application information: Contributes only to pre-selected organizations. Unsolicited requests for funds not considered or acknowledged.
    Board meeting date(s): Annually
Trustees: Brian D. Baird; Bridget B. Baird; Bruce C. Baird; Jane D. Baird; Peter C. Clauson; Brenda Baird Senturia.
EIN: 166029481
Selected grants: The following grants were reported in 2005.
$750,000 to Buffalo Philharmonic Orchestra Society, Buffalo, NY.
$120,000 to Planned Parenthood Federation of America, New York, NY. 2 grants: $45,000, $75,000
$85,000 to NAACP Legal Defense and Educational Fund, New York, NY.
$85,000 to Sierra Club Foundation, San Francisco, CA.
$68,218 to Community Foundation for Greater Buffalo, Buffalo, NY.
$65,000 to Bryn Mawr College, Bryn Mawr, PA.
$25,000 to Women for Human Rights and Dignity, Buffalo, NY.
$15,000 to Buffalo Prep, Buffalo, NY.
$10,000 to Young Audiences of Connecticut, Hamden, CT.

5592
The Baird Foundation
11 Summer St., 4th Fl.
Buffalo, NY 14209 (716) 883-2429
Contact: Catherine F. Schweitzer, Exec. Dir.
Application address: P.O. Box 1210, Ellicott Sta., Buffalo, NY 14205

Trust established in 1947 in NY.
Donors: Flora M. Baird†; Frank B. Baird, Jr.†; Cameron Baird†; William C. Baird†.
Foundation type: Independent foundation.
Financial data (yr. ended 12/31/05): Assets, $11,690,204 (M); expenditures, $949,836; qualifying distributions, $906,966; giving activities include $777,145 for 82 grants (high: $50,000; low: $100).
Purpose and activities: Giving primarily for the arts, children, youth and social services, and medical research.
Fields of interest: Museums; Performing arts; Performing arts, orchestra (symphony); Historic preservation/historical societies; Arts; Education; Environment; Animal welfare; Hospitals (general); Boys & girls clubs; Human services; Children/youth, services; Disabilities, people with; Economically disadvantaged.

International interests: South Africa.
Type of support: General/operating support; Capital campaigns; Equipment; Research; Matching/challenge support.
Limitations: Giving primarily in the western NY area. No grants to individuals.
Publications: Grants list.
Application information: Application form not required.
    Initial approach: Letter
    Copies of proposal: 5
    Deadline(s): None
    Board meeting date(s): About 3 times a year
    Final notification: Variable
Officer: Catherine F. Schweitzer, Exec. Dir.
Trustees: Arthur W. Cryer; Robert J.A. Irwin; William B. Irwin.
Number of staff: 1 full-time professional; 1 part-time support.
EIN: 166023080

5593
Mr. and Mrs. Robert C. Baker Family Foundation ✧
c/o National Realty and Development Corp.
3 Manhattanville Rd.
Purchase, NY 10577-2116 (914) 694-4444
Contact: Robert C. Baker, Pres.

Established in 1995 in NY.
Donor: Robert C. Baker.
Foundation type: Independent foundation.
Financial data (yr. ended 12/31/05): Assets, $1,029,040 (M); gifts received, $1,493,164; expenditures, $1,924,381; qualifying distributions, $1,875,410; giving activities include $1,875,410 for 86 grants (high: $1,000,000; low: $100).
Purpose and activities: Giving for Jewish federated giving programs, art and cultural programs, and higher education.
Fields of interest: Museums (art); Performing arts, opera; Arts; Higher education; Medical school/education; Education; Health care; Health organizations, association; Cancer research; Human services; Children/youth, services; Jewish federated giving programs; Jewish agencies & temples.
Limitations: Giving on a national basis, with some emphasis on the greater metropolitan New York, NY, area. No grants to individuals.
Application information: Application form not required.
    Initial approach: Letter or telephone
    Deadline(s): None
Officer: Robert C. Baker, Pres.
EIN: 133798665

5594
The George F. Baker Trust ✧
477 Madison Ave., Ste. 1650
New York, NY 10022 (212) 755-1890
Contact: Miss. Rocio Suarez, Exec. Dir.
FAX: (212) 319-6316; E-mail: rocio@bakernye.com

Trust established in 1937 in NY.
Donor: George F. Baker†.
Foundation type: Independent foundation.
Financial data (yr. ended 12/31/04): Assets, $13,713,673 (M); expenditures, $2,788,125; qualifying distributions, $2,406,593; giving

activities include $2,183,954 for 53 grants (high: $500,000; low: $5,000).

Purpose and activities: Giving primarily for higher and secondary education, hospitals, social services, civic affairs, and religious and international affairs.

Fields of interest: Secondary school/education; Higher education; Environment, natural resources; Hospitals (general); Human services; International affairs; Government/public administration; Religion.

Type of support: General/operating support; Matching/challenge support.

Limitations: Giving primarily in the eastern U.S., with some emphasis on the New York, NY, area. No grants to individuals, or for scholarships; no loans.

Publications: Annual report.

Application information: Application form not required.

  Initial approach: Letter with brief outline of proposal

  Copies of proposal: 1

  Deadline(s): None

  Board meeting date(s): June and Nov.

  Final notification: Up to 6 months

Officer: Rocio Suarez, Exec. Dir.

Trustees: Anthony K. Baker; Kane K. Baker.

Number of staff: 1 full-time professional.

EIN: 136056818

Selected grants: The following grants were reported in 2003.

$397,590 to Aiken Preparatory School, Aiken, SC. For general support.

$200,000 to Harvard University, Cambridge, MA. For general support.

$200,000 to Salisbury School, Salisbury, CT. For general support.

$100,000 to New York-Presbyterian Hospital, New York, NY. For general support.

$75,000 to YMCA of the Palm Beaches, West Palm Beach, FL. For general support.

$50,000 to Nantucket Cottage Hospital, Nantucket, MA. For capital campaign.

$10,000 to Human Rights First, New York, NY. For general support.

$5,000 to Emma Willard School, Troy, NY. For general support.

$5,000 to Place of Hope, Palm Beach Gardens, FL. For general support.

$2,500 to Rosarian Academy, West Palm Beach, FL. For general support.

5595
The David M. & Barbara Baldwin Foundation, Inc. ◇

c/o McGrath, Doyle & Phair
150 Broadway
New York, NY 10038

Established in 1986 in NJ.

Donor: David M. Baldwin.

Foundation type: Independent foundation.

Financial data (yr. ended 11/30/05): Assets, $5,082,938 (M); expenditures, $467,982; qualifying distributions, $436,955; giving activities include $416,355 for 54 grants (high: $250,038; low: $62).

Purpose and activities: Giving primarily for hospitals and health associations; funding also for education.

Fields of interest: Performing arts, theater; Higher education; Environment; Hospitals (general); Health organizations, association.

Limitations: Applications not accepted. Giving primarily in NJ and NY. No grants to individuals.

Application information: Contributes only to pre-selected organizations.

Officers: David M. Baldwin, Pres.; Barbara Baldwin, V.P.; Charles J. Gengler, V.P.; Nicholas Jacangelo, Secy.-Treas.

EIN: 133391384

Selected grants: The following grants were reported in 2004.

$121,500 to Riverside Theater, Vero Beach, FL.

$117,590 to Pingry School, Martinsville, NJ.

$26,050 to Paper Mill Playhouse, Millburn, NJ.

$25,950 to Skidmore College, Saratoga Springs, NY.

$25,500 to Christopher Reeve Paralysis Foundation, Springfield, NJ.

$20,000 to Johns Island Foundation, Indian River Shores, FL.

$10,500 to Southampton Hospital Foundation, Southampton, NY.

$10,000 to Rockefeller University, New York, NY. For annual fund.

$5,000 to Boy Scouts of America, Patriots Path Council, Florham Park, NJ.

$5,000 to Lehigh University, Bethlehem, PA.

5596
The Balm Foundation, Inc.

c/o Janet Stein
P.O. Box 5015
Southampton, NY 11968-5015

Established in 1993 in NY.

Donor: Howard Stein.

Foundation type: Independent foundation.

Financial data (yr. ended 11/30/05): Assets, $8,948,638 (M); expenditures, $665,157; qualifying distributions, $657,951; giving activities include $545,227 for 38 grants (high: $55,000; low: $1,000).

Purpose and activities: Giving primarily for education, the arts and health.

Fields of interest: Performing arts; Historical activities; Elementary/secondary education; Higher education; Hospitals (general); Human services.

Limitations: Applications not accepted. Giving primarily in CA and NY. No grants to individuals.

Application information: Contributes only to pre-selected organizations.

Officer and Directors:* Janet Stein,* Pres.; Peggy Davis; Vincent McGee.

Number of staff: 1 part-time professional.

EIN: 133746421

Selected grants: The following grants were reported in 2004.

$88,370 to Healing Opportunities, Santa Barbara, CA.

$55,000 to National Dance Institute, New York, NY.

$29,200 to New York University Medical Center, New York, NY.

$22,000 to Lineage Project, Bronx, NY.

$15,000 to Sound Portraits Productions, Brooklyn, NY.

$15,000 to Triform Camphill Community, Hudson, NY.

$13,560 to Los Angeles Free Clinic, Los Angeles, CA.

$12,500 to Mercy Center, Bronx, NY.

$10,000 to Projectile Arts, Brooklyn, NY.

$9,692 to Youth Consultation Service, Newark, NJ.

5597
The Banfi Vintners Foundation

(formerly The Villa Banfi Foundation)
1111 Cedar Swamp Rd.
Glen Head, NY 11545
Contact: Philip D. Calderone, Exec. Dir.

Established in 1982 in NY.

Donor: Banfi Products Corp.

Foundation type: Independent foundation.

Financial data (yr. ended 12/31/05): Assets, $13,022,005 (M); expenditures, $705,534; qualifying distributions, $682,397; giving activities include $630,843 for 82 grants (high: $45,000; low: $100).

Fields of interest: Higher education; Hospitals (general); Food services; International affairs, goodwill promotion; Civil rights, race/intergroup relations.

Limitations: Giving primarily in, but not limited to, MA and NY.

Application information:

  Board meeting date(s): Nov.

Officers and Directors:* Joan C. Rupp, Secy.; Frank Savino, Treas.; Philip D. Calderone,* Exec. Dir.; Cristina Mariani-May; Harry F. Mariani; James W. Mariani; John Mariani.

EIN: 112622792

Selected grants: The following grants were reported in 2004.

$60,000 to Cornell University, Ithaca, NY. 2 grants: $25,000, $35,000

$45,000 to Pasadena Hospital Association, Pasadena, CA.

$30,000 to De La Salle School, Freeport, NY.

$25,000 to Culinary Institute of America, Hyde Park, NY.

$25,000 to University of Denver, Denver, CO.

$20,000 to Society of Wine Educators, DC.

$20,000 to Sons of Italy Foundation, DC.

$10,000 to Huntington Hospital Association, Huntington, NY.

$1,000 to Visiting Nurse Association of Long Island, Garden City, NY.

5598
The Bank of New York Foundation ◇

c/o The Bank of New York, Tax Dept.
1 Wall St., 28th Fl.
New York, NY 10286

Established in 1997 in NY.

Donors: The Bank of New York; BNY Capital Corp.

Foundation type: Company-sponsored foundation.

Financial data (yr. ended 12/31/05): Assets, $1,948 (M); gifts received, $871,300; expenditures, $1,219,453; qualifying distributions, $1,219,453; giving activities include $1,219,453 for 910 employee matching gifts.

Purpose and activities: The foundation matches contributions made by employees and retirees of Bank of New York to educational institutions.

Type of support: Employee matching gifts.

Limitations: Applications not accepted. No grants to individuals.

Application information: Contributes only through employee matching gifts.

Officers and Directors:* J. Michael Shepard,* Chair.; John De Rosa, V.P. and Treas.; Patricia A. Bicket; John S. Lipori.

EIN: 311605320

5599
J. M. R. Barker Foundation
c/o Gagnon Securities
1370 Ave. of the Americas
New York, NY 10019 (212) 554-5064
Contact: Maureen Hopkins, Secy.
FAX: (212) 265-6417;
E-mail: mhopkins@gagnonsec.com

Established in 1968 in NY.
Donors: James M. Barker‡; Margaret R. Barker‡; Robert R. Barker.
Foundation type: Independent foundation.
Financial data (yr. ended 12/31/05): Assets, $49,905,980 (M); expenditures, $3,003,382; qualifying distributions, $2,658,292; giving activities include $2,658,292 for 27 grants.
Purpose and activities: Support primarily for organizations that are well-known to one or more directors, with some emphasis on the areas of higher education, cultural programs, and scientific research.
Fields of interest: Arts; Higher education; Education; Environment, natural resources; Science.
Type of support: General/operating support; Continuing support; Annual campaigns; Capital campaigns; Building/renovation; Endowments; Program development; Seed money; Research; Matching/challenge support.
Limitations: Applications not accepted. Giving primarily in the greater Boston, MA, area, and the greater New York, NY, area. No grants to individuals, or for scholarships, fellowships, or matching gifts; no loans.
Application information: Unsolicited requests for funds not accepted.
Board meeting date(s): June and Dec.
Officers and Directors: Margaret B. Clark,* Pres.; James R. Barker,* V.P. and C.I.O.; W.B. Barker,* V.P.; Maureen A. Hopkins, Secy. and Admin.; Robert P. Connor,* Treas.; Margaret S. Barker; William S. Barker; John W. Holman, Jr.; Richard D. Kahn; Troy Y. Murray.
Number of staff: 1 part-time support.
EIN: 136268289
Selected grants: The following grants were reported in 2005.
$200,000 to Amazon Conservation Team, Arlington, VA.
$105,000 to Poets and Writers, New York, NY.
$60,000 to Grammar School, Putney, VT.
$29,352 to Kimball Union Academy, Meriden, NH.
$25,000 to Saint Anselm College, Manchester, NH.
$10,000 to Concerned Citizens of Montauk, Montauk, NY.
$10,000 to Group for the South Fork, Bridgehampton, NY.
$10,000 to North Shore Music Theater, Beverly, MA.
$5,000 to Nature Museum at Grafton, Grafton, VT.

5600
The Barker Welfare Foundation ✧
P.O. Box 2
Glen Head, NY 11545 (516) 759-5592
Contact: Sarane H. Ross, Pres.
FAX: (516) 759-5497; E-mail: BarkerSMD@aol.com;
URL: http://www.barkerwelfare.org

Incorporated in 1934 in IL.
Donor: Mrs. Charles V. Hickox‡.
Foundation type: Independent foundation.

Financial data (yr. ended 9/30/05): Assets, $68,936,542 (M); expenditures, $3,401,795; qualifying distributions, $3,000,678; giving activities include $2,699,718 for 234 grants (high: $79,588; low: $500).
Purpose and activities: The mission of the Barker Welfare Foundation is to make grants to qualified charitable organizations whose initiatives improve the quality of life, with an emphasis on strengthening youth and families and to reflect the philosophy of Catherine B. Hickox, the Founder. Grants to established organizations and charitable institutions, with emphasis on youth and families, museums and the fine and performing arts, child welfare and youth agencies, health services and rehabilitation, welfare, aid to the handicapped, family planning, libraries, the environment, recreation, and programs for the elderly.
Fields of interest: Visual arts; Museums; Arts; Libraries/library science; Environment; Health care; Mental health/crisis services; Recreation; Human services; Children/youth, services; Disabilities, people with.
Type of support: General/operating support; Continuing support; Annual campaigns; Capital campaigns; Building/renovation; Equipment.
Limitations: Giving primarily in Chicago, IL, Michigan City, IN, and New York, NY. No support for political activities, start-up organizations, national health, welfare, or education agencies, institutions or funds. No grants to individuals, or for endowment funds, seed money, emergency funds, deficit financing, scholarships, fellowships, medical or scientific research, films or videos, or conferences; no loans.
Publications: Application guidelines; Annual report (including application guidelines).
Application information: Proposals must be completed according to the foundation's guidelines and grants process in order to be considered for funding. Grants to Chicago agencies are by invitation only. Proposals sent by fax not considered. Application information available on foundation Web site. Application form required.
Initial approach: 2- to 3-page letter of inquiry
Copies of proposal: 2
Deadline(s): Feb. 1 and Aug. 1
Board meeting date(s): May and Oct.
Final notification: After board meeting for positive responses; any time for negative responses
Officers and Directors:* Sarane H. Ross,* Pres.; Katrina H. Becker,* V.P. and Secy.; Thomas P. McCormick,* Treas.; Diane Curtis; Danielle A. Hickox; John B. Hickox; Mary Lou Linnen; Alline Matheson; Sarane R. O'Connor; Alexander B. Ross.
Number of staff: 2 full-time professional; 1 part-time support.
EIN: 366018526

5601
Lawrence and Isabel Barnett Charitable Foundation ✧
c/o Ezkr, LLP
120 Bloomingdale Rd.
White Plains, NY 10605

Established in 1986 in CA.
Donor: Lawrence R. Barnett.
Foundation type: Independent foundation.
Financial data (yr. ended 9/30/05): Assets, $25,134,479 (M); gifts received, $3,411,440; expenditures, $2,022,945; qualifying distributions,

$1,933,375; giving activities include $1,933,375 for 30 grants (high: $1,000,000; low: $100).
Purpose and activities: Giving primarily for higher education, community economic development and to a medical center; funding also for health organizations, a theater and for education.
Fields of interest: Performing arts, theater; Arts; Higher education; Education; Hospitals (general); Health organizations; Alzheimer's disease research; Children, services; Community development; Federated giving programs.
Limitations: Applications not accepted. Giving on a national basis. No grants to individuals.
Application information: Contributes only to pre-selected organizations.
Officers and Directors:* Lawrence R. Barnett,* Pres.; Lawrence R. Barnett, Jr., V.P. and Secy.; Isabel Barnett,* V.P.; James Joseph Barnett, V.P.; Laurey J. Barnett, V.P.
EIN: 943031397
Selected grants: The following grants were reported in 2003.
$500,000 to Ohio State University Development Fund, Columbus, OH. For unrestricted support.
$450,000 to Eisenhower Medical Center, Rancho Mirage, CA. 2 grants: $250,000 (For unrestricted support), $200,000 (For unrestricted support).
$100,000 to Alzheimers Association, Chicago, IL. For unrestricted support.
$25,000 to Le Lycee Francais School, Los Angeles, CA. For unrestricted support.
$25,000 to McCallum Theater, Palm Desert, CA. For unrestricted support.
$20,000 to Stanford University, Stanford, CA. 2 grants: $10,000 each (For unrestricted support).
$15,000 to Cedars-Sinai Medical Center, Los Angeles, CA. For unrestricted support.
$10,000 to Phillips Brooks School, Menlo Park, CA. For unrestricted support.

5602
The Barrington Foundation, Inc.
7-11 S. Broadway, Ste. 200
White Plains, NY 10601
Application address: c/o David H. Strassler, P.O. Box 750, Great Barrington, MA 01230

Established in 1978 in DE.
Donors: Samuel A. Strassler‡; David Strassler; Lorna Strassler; Robert Strassler; Abbie Strassler; Gary Strassler; Alan Strassler; Matthew Strassler; Karen Strassler.
Foundation type: Independent foundation.
Financial data (yr. ended 12/31/05): Assets, $2,575,872 (M); gifts received, $1,025,950; expenditures, $1,010,995; qualifying distributions, $1,009,150; giving activities include $1,009,150 for 121 grants (high: $85,000; low: $500).
Purpose and activities: Giving primarily to music, arts and cultural programs, higher education, human services, Jewish federated giving programs and Jewish agencies and temples.
Fields of interest: Performing arts, music; Arts; Higher education; Human services; Jewish federated giving programs; Jewish agencies & temples.
Type of support: Annual campaigns; Capital campaigns; Endowments; Scholarship funds.
Limitations: Applications not accepted. Giving primarily in MA. No grants to individuals.
Application information: Unsolicited requests for funds not accepted.

Officers: David H. Strassler, Pres.; Robert B. Strassler, Secy.-Treas.
EIN: 132930849
Selected grants: The following grants were reported in 2005.
$58,000 to Simons Rock College of Bard, Great Barrington, MA.
$55,000 to ACCION International, Boston, MA.
$35,000 to Shakespeare and Company, Lenox, MA.
$30,000 to Berkshire Country Day School, Lenox, MA.
$25,000 to National Humanities Center, Research Triangle Park, NC.
$16,000 to Baton Rouge Area Foundation, Baton Rouge, LA.
$5,000 to Jewish Partisan Educational Foundation, San Francisco, CA.
$4,000 to Jewish Foundation for the Righteous, New York, NY.
$2,500 to Boston Athenaeum, Boston, MA.
$2,500 to United Way, Berkshire, Pittsfield, MA.

5603
Theodore H. Barth Foundation, Inc. ✧
45 Rockefeller Plz., 20th Fl., Ste. 2006
New York, NY 10111 (212) 332-3466
Contact: Ellen S. Berelson, Pres.
E-mail: barthfoundation@earthlink.net

Incorporated in 1953 in DE.
Donor: Theodore H. Barth†.
Foundation type: Independent foundation.
Financial data (yr. ended 12/31/03): Assets, $27,719,003 (M); expenditures, $1,497,921; qualifying distributions, $1,316,093; giving activities include $1,206,000 for 85 grants (high: $100,000; low: $750).
Purpose and activities: Grants for higher education, health, the performing and other arts, cultural organizations, and social services; support also for aid to the handicapped and conservation.
Fields of interest: Performing arts; Arts; Higher education; Environment; Health care; Human services; Disabilities, people with.
Type of support: General/operating support; Continuing support; Annual campaigns; Endowments; Program development; Seed money.
Limitations: Giving limited to the northeastern U.S. and to MD, NJ, PA, and VA. No grants to individuals, or for capital projects.
Publications: Application guidelines.
Application information: Telephone inquiries will not be accepted. Application form not required.
  Initial approach: Letter
  Copies of proposal: 1
  Deadline(s): None
  Final notification: Dec.
Officers and Directors:* Ellen S. Berelson,* Pres. and Treas.; Lois Herrmann, V.P.; Lawrence Franks,* Secy.
EIN: 136103401
Selected grants: The following grants were reported in 2003.
$260,000 to League for the Hard of Hearing, New York, NY.
$100,000 to Metropolitan Opera Association, New York, NY.
$15,000 to Brooklyn Botanic Garden, Brooklyn, NY.
$15,000 to New York Public Library, New York, NY.
$10,000 to New York Cares, New York, NY.
$10,000 to Wildlife Conservation Society, Bronx, NY.

$5,000 to Educational Broadcasting Corporation, New York, NY.
$5,000 to Guiding Eyes for the Blind, Yorktown Heights, NY.
$2,500 to Smith College, Northampton, MA.
$2,500 to University of Vermont, Burlington, VT.

5604
Sandra Atlas Bass & Edythe & Sol G. Atlas Fund, Inc. ▼ ✧
185 Great Neck Rd.
Great Neck, NY 11021

Established in 1962 in NY.
Donors: Sol G. Atlas; Sandra Atlas Bass.
Foundation type: Independent foundation.
Financial data (yr. ended 12/31/05): Assets, $4,021,705 (M); gifts received, $524,480; expenditures, $4,159,043; qualifying distributions, $4,152,550; giving activities include $4,150,800 for 160 grants (high: $2,025,000; low: $500; average: $10,000–$25,000).
Purpose and activities: Giving primarily for health associations, and animal welfare; funding also for higher education, children, youth and social services, including services for people who are blind; funding as well for Jewish organizations.
Fields of interest: Higher education; Animal welfare; Hospitals (general); Cancer; Health organizations; Human services; Children/youth, services; Jewish federated giving programs; Jewish agencies & temples.
Limitations: Applications not accepted. Giving primarily in the metropolitan New York, NY, area, with emphasis on Long Island.
Application information: Unsolicited requests for funds not accepted.
Officers: Sandra Atlas Bass, Pres.; Morton Bass, V.P.; Robert Zabelle, Secy.; Lincoln Page, Treas.
EIN: 116036928
Selected grants: The following grants were reported in 2005.
$2,025,000 to North Shore University Hospital, Manhasset, NY.
$94,500 to Canine Companions for Independence, Santa Rosa, CA.
$50,000 to Muscular Dystrophy Association, New York, NY.
$36,500 to Vivisection Investigation League, Canaan, CT.
$35,000 to Kent Animal Shelter, Carmel, NY.
$25,000 to Saint Francis Hospital, Roslyn, NY.
$24,000 to Fidelco Guide Dog Foundation, Bloomfield, CT.
$18,000 to National Burn Victim Foundation, Basking Ridge, NJ.
$16,500 to Humane Society of Washington, DC.
$12,500 to American Kidney Fund, Rockville, MD.

5605
Bausch & Lomb Foundation, Inc. ✧
c/o Bausch & Lomb Inc.
1 Bausch & Lomb Pl.
Rochester, NY 14604-2701 (585) 338-6000
Contact: Barbara M. Kelley, V.P.

Incorporated in 1927 in NY.
Donor: Bausch & Lomb Inc.
Foundation type: Company-sponsored foundation.
Financial data (yr. ended 12/31/05): Assets, $3,065,404 (M); gifts received, $1,000,000;

expenditures, $552,973; qualifying distributions, $550,000; giving activities include $550,000 for grants.
Purpose and activities: The foundation supports organizations involved with arts and culture, education, health, human services, and community development.
Fields of interest: Arts; Education; Health care; Human services; Community development.
Type of support: Program development; Program evaluation.
Limitations: Giving primarily in Rochester, NY. No grants to individuals.
Application information: Application form not required.
  Initial approach: Proposal
  Copies of proposal: 1
  Deadline(s): None
Officers and Directors:* Stephen C. McCluski,* Pres.; Barbara M. Kelley,* V.P.; Jean F. Geisel, Secy.; Efrain Rivera,* Treas.; Robert Stiles.
Number of staff: 1 full-time professional.
EIN: 166039442

5606
The Bay and Paul Foundations, Inc.
(formerly Josephine Bay Paul and C. Michael Paul Foundation, Inc.)
17 W. 94th St., 1st Fl.
New York, NY 10025 (212) 663-1115
Contact: Frederick Bay, Exec. Dir.
FAX: (212) 932-0316;
E-mail: info@bayandpaulfoundations.org;
URL: http://www.bayandpaulfoundations.org

Established in 2005 in NY.
Donors: Josephine Bay Paul†; Charles Ulrick Bay†.
Foundation type: Independent foundation.
Financial data (yr. ended 12/31/04): Assets, $73,879,324 (M); expenditures, $3,841,382; qualifying distributions, $3,360,726; giving activities include $2,348,817 for 152 grants (high: $350,000; low: $50; average: $1,000–$100,000), and $300,000 for 6 grants to individuals (high: $60,000; low: $30,000; average: $30,000–$60,000).
Purpose and activities: Support for organizations demonstrating or developing pre-collegiate educational restructuring; support projects which reinforce the centrality of the arts in pre-collegiate curricula. The foundation also has an interest in projects seeking to sustain the earth's biodiversity. K-12 math and science, arts-in-education: first time grants are limited to the New York, NY, metropolitan area.
Fields of interest: Arts education; Education, research; Elementary school/education; Secondary school/education; Education; Environment.
Type of support: General/operating support; Continuing support; Program development; Conferences/seminars; Seed money; Research; Technical assistance; Matching/challenge support.
Limitations: Giving on a national basis. No support for sectarian religious programs, or to other than publicly recognized charities. No grants to individuals (other than the Bio diversity Leadership Awards) or for building campaigns.
Application information: Application guidelines available on foundation Web site. The foundation accepts the New York/New Jersey Area Common Application Form which can also be downloaded from Web site. Application form not required.
  Initial approach: Proposal

Copies of proposal: 1
Deadline(s): Postmarked Mar. 1, Sept. 1, and
   Dec. 1
Board meeting date(s): Feb., May, and Oct.
Final notification: Within 30 days following board
   meeting
Officers and Directors:* Robert Ashton,* Chair.;
Synnova B. Hayes,* Pres. and Treas.; Corinne Steel,
Secy.; Frederick Bay,* Exec. Dir.; Rebecca
Adamson; David Bury; Kenneth D. Hurwitz.
Number of staff: 2 full-time professional; 2 part-time
professional; 2 full-time support.
EIN: 131991717
Selected grants: The following grants were reported
in 2004.
$300,000 to Harmony School, Bloomington, IN.
$130,000 to First Nations Development Institute,
   Fredericksburg, VA.
$75,000 to Symphony Space, New York, NY.
$41,000 to Shelburne Farms, Shelburne, VT. 2
   grants: $40,000, $1,000
$40,000 to Kinhaven Music School, Bethlehem, PA.
$40,000 to Vermont Community Works, South
   Burlington, VT.
$40,000 to Vermont Rural Education Collaborative,
   Cabot, VT.
$25,000 to National Center for Fair and Open
   Testing, Cambridge, MA.
$5,000 to Brooklyn Arts Exchange, Brooklyn, NY.

5607
The Howard Bayne Fund ✧
c/o Simpson Thacher & Bartlett
425 Lexington Ave.
New York, NY   10017-3909

Incorporated in 1960 in NY.
Donor: Louise Van Beuren Bayne Trust.
Foundation type: Independent foundation.
Financial data (yr. ended 12/31/05): Assets,
$16,450,750 (M); expenditures, $968,236;
qualifying distributions, $789,194; giving activities
include $760,000 for 143 grants (high: $34,500;
low: $500).
Purpose and activities: Giving primarily for
education and the arts.
Fields of interest: Museums; Museums (art);
Performing arts, theater; Performing arts, music;
Performing arts, orchestra (symphony); Historic
preservation/historical societies; Arts; Higher
education; Education; Environment, natural
resources; Hospitals (general); Human services;
Family services; Federated giving programs;
Religion.
Type of support: Annual campaigns; Capital
campaigns.
Limitations: Applications not accepted. Giving
primarily in CT, FL, NJ, and NY, with some emphasis
on the New York, NY, area. No grants to individuals.
Application information: Contributes only to
pre-selected organizations.
Officers and Directors:* Gurdon B. Wattles,* Pres.;
Daisy Paradis,* V.P.; Victoria Bjorklund,
Secy.-Treas.; Diana de Vegh; Pierre J. de Vegh;
Alexander B. Wattles; Gurdon S. Wattles; Elizabeth
W. Wilkes.
EIN: 136100680

5608
BCHB, Inc. ✧
c/o Hertz, Herson & Co., LLP
2 Park Ave., Ste. 1500
New York, NY   10016

Established in 1997 in DE and NY.
Donors: Bella Wexner Charitable Remainder
Unitrust; Susan Wexner Revocable Trust.
Foundation type: Independent foundation.
Financial data (yr. ended 3/31/05): Assets,
$37,725,388 (M); expenditures, $1,594,371;
qualifying distributions, $1,398,823; giving
activities include $1,345,000 for 1 grant.
Fields of interest: Philanthropy/voluntarism.
Limitations: Applications not accepted. Giving
primarily in Southeastern, PA. No grants to
individuals.
Application information: Contributes only to
pre-selected organizations.
Officer and Directors:* Susan R. Wexner,* Pres.
and Secy.-Treas.; Bertrand Agus.
EIN: 133997366
Selected grants: The following grants were reported
in 2004.
$1,850,000 to Vanguard Charitable Endowment
   Program, Southeastern, PA.

5609
Bear Stearns Charitable Foundation,
Inc. ✧
383 Madison Ave.
New York, NY   10179

Established in 2001 in NY.
Donors: Employees of The Bear Stearns Cos. Inc.;
The Bear Stearns Cos. Inc.
Foundation type: Company-sponsored foundation.
Financial data (yr. ended 12/31/03): Assets,
$2,047,999 (M); expenditures, $578,250;
qualifying distributions, $578,250; giving activities
include $578,250 for 5 grants (high: $298,250;
low: $10,000).
Purpose and activities: The foundation supports
organizations assisting individuals and families who
suffered loss, injury, property damage, or financial
hardship as a result of the September 11th terrorist
attacks.
Fields of interest: Disasters, 9/11/01.
Limitations: Applications not accepted. Giving
primarily in NY. No grants to individuals.
Application information: Contributes only to
pre-selected organizations.
Officers and Trustees:* Samuel L. Molinaro, Jr.,*
Pres.; Arnold F. Kananck,* V.P.; Kenneth L. Edlow,*
Secy.; Marshall J. Levinson,* Treas. and Cont.
EIN: 311802175

5610
Beaverkill Foundation, Inc. ✧ ☆
P.O. Box 311
Liberty, NY   12754   (845) 295-2400
Contact: Darrell Supak

Established in 1998 in DE and NY.
Donors: Sandra Gerry; The 1997 Liberty Trust.
Foundation type: Independent foundation.
Financial data (yr. ended 10/31/05): Assets,
$1,674,390 (M); gifts received, $58,811;
expenditures, $396,094; qualifying distributions,

$358,876; giving activities include $358,876 for
grants.
Purpose and activities: Giving primarily for human
services, education, and health associations.
Fields of interest: Arts; Education; Health
organizations, association; Human services;
Federated giving programs.
Type of support: General/operating support.
Limitations: Giving primarily in NY. No grants to
individuals.
Application information:
   Initial approach: Letter
   Deadline(s): None
Officers and Directors:* Sandra Gerry,* Pres.;
Jonathan Drapkin, V.P.; Christopher Grillo, V.P.;
Louis J. Boyd, Secy.-Treas.; Adam Gerry; Robyn
Gerry; Annelise Melchick.
EIN: 141800129
Selected grants: The following grants were reported
in 2004.
$103,500 to Sullivan First, Liberty, NY.
$25,250 to Hebrew Day School of Sullivan County,
   Liberty, NY.
$15,000 to American Friends of the Hebrew
   University, New York, NY.
$12,000 to Court Appointed Special Advocates
   (CASA) of Sullivan County, Monticello, NY.
$10,000 to Metropolitan Foundation, New York, NY.
$5,000 to Amyotrophic Lateral Sclerosis (ALS)
   Association, New York, NY.
$5,000 to Audubon New York, Albany, NY.
$5,000 to Saint Johns University, Jamaica, NY.
$3,600 to Mid-Hudson Pattern for Progress,
   Newburgh, NY.
$2,500 to National Actors Theater, New York, NY.

5611
The Bedminster Fund, Inc. ✧
1330 Ave. of the Americas, 27th Fl.
New York, NY   10019-5490

Incorporated in 1948 in NY.
Foundation type: Independent foundation.
Financial data (yr. ended 6/30/05): Assets,
$11,604,123 (M); expenditures, $536,452;
qualifying distributions, $506,911; giving activities
include $490,000 for 35 grants (high: $100,000;
low: $500).
Purpose and activities: Giving primarily for
education, hospitals, the arts, and welfare
agencies. Grants only to present beneficiary
organizations and to special proposals developed by
the directors; additional requests seldom
considered.
Fields of interest: Arts; Elementary/secondary
education; Education; Environment; Hospitals
(general); Human services.
Type of support: General/operating support;
Continuing support; Annual campaigns; Capital
campaigns; Building/renovation; Conferences/
seminars.
Limitations: Applications not accepted. Giving
primarily in MA, ME, NJ, and NY; some funding also
in FL. No grants to individuals; no loans.
Application information: Contributes only to
pre-selected organizations.
   Board meeting date(s): Nov. and as required
Officers and Directors:* Philip D. Allen,* Pres.;
Christine Allen,* V.P.; Martin C. Zetterberg,* V.P.;
Eileen B. Kane, Secy.; James J. Ruddy, Treas.;
Alexandra F. Allen; Andrew D. Allen; Christopher D.
Allen; Douglas E. Allen; Elisabeth F. Allen; Nicholas

E. Allen; Dorothy D. Caplow; Theodore Caplow;
Judith S. Leonard.
Number of staff: 1 part-time professional.
EIN: 136083684
Selected grants: The following grants were reported
in 2005.
$60,000 to Groton School, Groton, MA.
$30,000 to Massachusetts General Hospital,
  Boston, MA.
$16,000 to Saint Lukes Episcopal Church,
  Gladstone, NJ.
$5,000 to Advanced Medical Research Foundation,
  Boston, MA.
$5,000 to Citizens Advice Bureau, Bronx, NY.
$5,000 to Far Hills Country Day School, Far Hills, NJ.
$2,500 to Rollins College, Winter Park, FL.
$1,000 to City Harvest, New York, NY.
$500 to Foxcroft School, Middleburg, VA.

5612
The Mary Taylor Behrens and Christopher C. Behrens Foundation, Inc. ✦ ☆
303 Pondfield Rd.
Bronxville, NY   10708-4936

Established in 2005 in NY.
Donors: Mary Taylor Behrens; Christopher C.
Behrens.
Foundation type: Independent foundation.
Financial data (yr. ended 6/30/06): Assets,
$114,703 (M); gifts received, $515,042;
expenditures, $520,800; qualifying distributions,
$512,900; giving activities include $512,900 for
grants.
Fields of interest: Higher education, university;
Education; Medical research; Human services; YM/
YWCAs & YM/YWHAs.
Limitations: Applications not accepted. No grants to
individuals.
Application information: Contributes only to
pre-selected organizations.
Officers and Directors:* Mary Taylor Behrens,*
Pres.; Christopher C. Behrens,* V.P. and Treas.;
John D. Dadakis,* Secy.
EIN: 202271170

5613
The Beker Foundation ✦
c/o The Millburn Corp.
1270 Ave. of the Americas, 11th Fl.
New York, NY   10020

Established in 1984 in NY.
Donor: Harvey Beker.
Foundation type: Independent foundation.
Financial data (yr. ended 12/31/04): Assets,
$28,903,677 (M); gifts received, $903,968;
expenditures, $1,516,821; qualifying distributions,
$1,370,800; giving activities include $1,370,800
for 84 grants (high: $315,400; low: $360).
Purpose and activities: Giving primarily for Jewish
education and Jewish organizations.
Fields of interest: Arts; Elementary/secondary
education; Education; Human services; Children/
youth, services; Jewish federated giving programs;
Jewish agencies & temples.
Limitations: Applications not accepted. Giving
primarily in New York, NY; some funding nationally,
particularly in MA and NJ. No grants to individuals.
Application information: Contributes only to
pre-selected organizations.

Officers: Harvey Beker, Pres.; Jayne Beker, Secy.
Director: George E. Crapple.
EIN: 133249239
Selected grants: The following grants were reported
in 2004.
$315,400 to SAR Academy, Bronx, NY.
$125,000 to Yeshiva University, New York, NY.
$96,410 to Hebrew Institute of Riverdale, Bronx,
  NY.
$60,000 to Hillel: The Foundation for Jewish
  Campus Life, DC.
$20,000 to Ramaz School, New York, NY.
$11,180 to Maimonides School, Brookline, MA.
$5,000 to Sinai Special Needs Institute, Teaneck,
  NJ.
$5,000 to Yavneh Academy, Paramus, NJ.
$5,000 to Young Israel of Riverdale, Bronx, NY.
$1,000 to Galilee Foundation, New York, NY.

5614
Beldon Fund ▼
(also known as Beldon II Fund)
99 Madison Ave., 8th Fl.
New York, NY   10016   (800) 591-9595
Contact: Holeri Faruolo, Grants Mgr.
FAX: (212) 616-5656; *E-mail:* info@beldon.org;
Additional tel.: (212) 616-5600; URL: http://
www.beldon.org

Established in 1987 in MI.
Donor: John R. Hunting.
Foundation type: Independent foundation.
Financial data (yr. ended 12/31/04): Assets,
$58,633,508 (M); expenditures, $16,991,633;
qualifying distributions, $16,341,432; giving
activities include $14,208,041 for 166+ grants
(high: $555,556; average: $25,000–$200,000).
Purpose and activities: By supporting effective
nonprofit advocacy organizations, the Beldon Fund
seeks to build a national consensus to achieve and
sustain a healthy planet. To attain this goal, the fund
plans to invest its entire principal and earnings by
2009. The fund focuses support in two programs:
Human Health and the Environment, and Key
States.
Fields of interest: Environment, management/
technical aid; Environment, toxics.
Type of support: General/operating support;
Program development; Conferences/seminars;
Technical assistance; Consulting services;
Employee matching gifts.
Limitations: Giving on a national basis. No support
for forest, wildlife habitat/refuges, land, marine,
river, lake, wilderness preservation, protection or
restoration, arts and culture, international
programs, service delivery programs, academic or
university projects, school- or classroom-based
environmental education. No grants to individuals,
or for land acquisition, endowment or capital
campaigns, scholarships, research, film, video and
radio projects, publications, deficit reduction, or
museums or collections acquisitions.
Application information: Applications submitted
through Beldon Fund; the foundation encourages
applicants to use environmentally sensitive
applications. See program guidelines and grant
application procedures posted on Web site.
Application form not required.
  Initial approach: Letter of inquiry (see letter of
    inquiry checklist posted on Web site)
  Copies of proposal: 2
  Deadline(s): Due dates posted on Web site and
    updated regularly

Board meeting date(s): Winter, spring, and fall
Final notification: Approximately one month after
  application deadline
Officers and Trustees:* John R. Hunting,* Chair.
and Treas.; Azade Ardali, C.O.O.; William J. Roberts,
Pres. and Exec. Dir.; Holly Schadler,* Secy. and
Genl. Counsel; Patricia Bauman; Wade Greene; Ruth
G. Henning; Gene Karpinski; Lael Stegall; Ann
Fowler Wallace.
Number of staff: 7 full-time professional; 2 full-time
support.
EIN: 382756784
Selected grants: The following grants were reported
in 2004.
$1,400,750 to Michigan Environmental Council,
  Lansing, MI. 2 grants: $735,500 (For
  Environmental Communications and Community
  Organizing Initiative (ECCO), collaborative of
  twelve organizations working to increase impact
  of environmental and conservation advocates in
  Michigan, payable over 3 years), $665,250 (For
  general support of various programs, including
  Environmental Communications Organizing
  Initiative to increase impact of environmental
  conservation advocates in Michigan, payable
  over 3 years).
$600,000 to League of Conservation Voters
  Education Fund, DC. For general support to
  strengthen state environmental movements and
  increase participation of environmental
  supporters.
$550,000 to Partnership Project, DC. For general
  support to coordinate activities of its member
  groups in defense of environmental protections.
$505,000 to Minnesota Environmental Partnership,
  Saint Paul, MN. For general support field efforts
  of collaborative of environmental and
  conservation groups in Minnesota working to
  increase support for strong public policies to
  protect the environment at state and national
  level, payable over 3 years.
$400,000 to Earth Day Network, DC. For
  Communities Project to mobilize
  underrepresented populations using
  environmental health themes.
$375,000 to Environmental Support Center, DC. For
  general support to help grassroots and
  state-based advocacy organizations in Key
  States and Human Health and the Environment
  programs build capacity and strengthen
  leadership, payable over 2 years.
$325,000 to Breast Cancer Fund, San Francisco,
  CA. For Campaign for Safe Cosmetics.
$275,000 to Clean Water Fund, DC. For ongoing
  grassroots organizing and outreach program in
  Florida to strengthen its capacity to educate and
  mobilize the public around environmental issues.
$200,000 to Environmental Working Group, DC. For
  Toxics and Health Program to demonstrate link
  between chemical exposure and health using
  body burden and monitoring data.

5615
Robert A. and Renee E. Belfer Family Foundation ✦
c/o Belfer Mgmt., LLC
767 5th Ave., 46th Fl.
New York, NY   10153
Contact: Robert A. Belfer, Pres.

Established in 1990 in NY.
Donors: Robert A. Belfer; Jack Resnick & Sons, Inc.
Foundation type: Independent foundation.

Financial data (yr. ended 12/31/04): Assets, $33,020,065 (M); expenditures, $897,768; qualifying distributions, $601,838; giving activities include $601,838 for 121 grants (high: $100,000; low: $50).

Purpose and activities: Giving primarily for the arts, education and Jewish causes.

Fields of interest: Museums (art); Museums (ethnic/folk arts); Performing arts centers; Performing arts, opera; Arts; Higher education; Medical school/education; Environment, natural resources; Hospitals (general); Health organizations; Jewish federated giving programs; Jewish agencies & temples; Economically disadvantaged.

Limitations: Giving primarily in NY. No grants to individuals.

Application information:
Deadline(s): None

Officer: Robert A. Belfer, Pres. and Secy.

Trustees: Laurence D. Belfer; Renee E. Belfer.

EIN: 136935616

Selected grants: The following grants were reported in 2003.

$400,000 to Weill Medical College of Cornell University, New York, NY. For general support.

$200,000 to American Jewish Committee, New York, NY. For general support.

$25,000 to Lincoln Center for the Performing Arts, New York, NY. For general support.

$22,850 to American Friends of the Israel Museum, New York, NY. For general support.

$20,000 to Dalton Schools, New York, NY. For general support.

$18,000 to Central Synagogue, New York, NY. For general support.

$15,000 to Natural Resources Defense Council, New York, NY. For general support.

$10,000 to Metropolitan Museum of Art, New York, NY. For general support.

$10,000 to Sutton Place Synagogue, New York, NY. For general support.

$10,000 to Washington Institute, DC. For general support.

5616

The Arthur and Rochelle Belfer Foundation, Inc. ▼ ✧

(formerly The Belfer Foundation, Inc.)
c/o Belfer Mgmt., LLC
767 5th Ave., 46th Fl.
New York, NY 10153
Contact: Robert A. Belfer, V.P.

Incorporated in 1951 in NY.

Donors: Members of the Belfer family; Belfer Corp.

Foundation type: Independent foundation.

Financial data (yr. ended 12/31/04): Assets, $12,001,769 (M); expenditures, $3,868,223; qualifying distributions, $3,801,900; giving activities include $3,801,900 for 22 grants (high: $1,000,000; low: $900; average: $25,000–$200,000).

Purpose and activities: Emphasis on health agencies, higher education, Jewish welfare funds, and religious organizations; also some giving for cultural organizations.

Fields of interest: Higher education; Health care; Health organizations, association; Human services; Jewish federated giving programs; Jewish agencies & temples.

Limitations: Applications not accepted. Giving primarily in NY. No grants to individuals.

Application information: Contributes only to pre-selected organizations.

Officers and Directors:* Robert A. Belfer,* V.P.; Lawrence Ruben, V.P.; Laurence D. Belfer,* Secy.; Norman Belfer; Renee E. Belfer; Richard Ruben; Jack Saltz; Leonard Saltz.

EIN: 136086711

Selected grants: The following grants were reported in 2004.

$2,100,000 to American Jewish Committee, New York, NY. 3 grants: $100,000 (For general support), $1,000,000 (For general support), $1,000,000 (For general support).

$800,000 to Hillel: The Foundation for Jewish Campus Life, New York, NY. For general support.

$400,000 to Breast Cancer Research Foundation, New York, NY. 2 grants: $200,000 each (For general support).

$125,000 to Lincoln Center for the Performing Arts, New York, NY. For general support.

$100,000 to Juvenile Diabetes Research Foundation International, New York, NY. For general support.

$7,000 to Metropolitan Museum of Art, New York, NY. For general support.

$900 to Central Synagogue, New York, NY. For general support.

5617

The Avi & Jody Ben-Haim Family Foundation ✧

511 Ave. T
Brooklyn, NY 11223

Established in 2003 in NJ.

Donors: Zvi Ben-Haim; Jody Ben-Haim; Jerry Harary; Michael Harary; Edward Baranoff.

Foundation type: Independent foundation.

Financial data (yr. ended 1/31/05): Assets, $5,712 (M); gifts received, $763,500; expenditures, $953,544; qualifying distributions, $953,544; giving activities include $948,102 for 57 grants (high: $195,952; low: $60).

Fields of interest: Education; Human services; Jewish federated giving programs; Jewish agencies & temples.

Limitations: Applications not accepted. Giving primarily in NJ. No grants to individuals.

Application information: Contributes only to pre-selected organizations.

Officers: Zvi Ben-Haim, Pres.; Jody Ben-Haim, V.P.; Jennifer Bawabeh, Secy.; Solar Bawabeh, Treas.

Director: Michael Harary.

EIN: 251902663

5618

Helen Andrus Benedict Foundation, Inc.

c/o The Philanthropic Group
630 5th Ave., 20th Fl.
New York, NY 10111 (212) 501-7785
Contact: Barbara R. Greenberg, Staff Consultant
FAX: (212) 501-7788;
E-mail: BGreenberg@philanthropicgroup.com;
URL: http://foundationcenter.org/grantmaker/benedict/

Established in 1997 in NY.

Donor: John E. Andrus Memorial, Inc.

Foundation type: Independent foundation.

Financial data (yr. ended 12/31/04): Assets, $44,137,467 (M); expenditures, $1,158,827;

qualifying distributions, $2,104,635; giving activities include $841,240 for 23 grants (high: $110,000; low: $2,000), and $1,033,152 for 1 loan/program-related investment.

Purpose and activities: The foundation is committed to creating good places for people to grow old while maintaining the maximum possible levels of independence. An important component of such an elder-friendly community is the opportunity for older people to remain actively engaged in the life of their communities.

Fields of interest: Residential/custodial care, senior continuing care; Aging, centers/services; Jewish agencies & temples.

Limitations: Applications not accepted. Giving primarily in Westchester County, NY, with emphasis on the city of Yonkers. No grants to individuals.

Application information: Grants are made by invitation only.

Officers and Directors:* Kate Downes,* Chair.; John J. Lynagh, Secy.; Josephine B. Lowman,* Treas.; Colby L. Andrus, Jr.; Carol M. Cardon; Marc de Venoge; McCain McMurray; Frederick F. Moon III; Michael S. Spensley; Samuel S. Thorpe III.

EIN: 133940833

5619

Dr. William O. Benenson Family Foundation ✧ ☆

(formerly Benenson Family Foundation)
35-15 Parsons Blvd.
Flushing, NY 11354-4236

Established in 1996 in NY.

Donors: Esther Benenson; Michael Benenson.

Foundation type: Independent foundation.

Financial data (yr. ended 6/30/05): Assets, $0 (M); gifts received, $240,619; expenditures, $932,813; qualifying distributions, $932,644; giving activities include $932,644 for 81 grants (high: $300,000; low: $10).

Purpose and activities: Giving primarily to Jewish organizations.

Fields of interest: Education; Hospitals (general); Health organizations, association; Human services; Jewish agencies & temples.

Limitations: Applications not accepted. Giving primarily in NY. No grants to individuals.

Application information: Contributes only to pre-selected organizations.

Officers: Esther Benenson, Pres.; Amy Benenson, V.P.; Michael Benenson, V.P.; Sharon Benenson Sydney, V.P.; Blanche Benenson, Secy.

EIN: 113352088

Selected grants: The following grants were reported in 2004.

$58,334 to Temple Shearith Israel, Ridgefield, CT.

$10,000 to New York-Presbyterian Hospital, New York, NY.

$5,000 to Jewish Childrens Museum, New York, NY.

$5,000 to P.E.F. Israel Endowment Funds, New York, NY.

$3,000 to Saint Francis Preparatory School, Fresh Meadows, NY.

$2,500 to Dalton Schools, New York, NY.

$100 to Guide Dog Foundation for the Blind, Smithtown, NY.

$50 to New York Public Library, New York, NY.

$32 to National Kidney Foundation, New York, NY.

$25 to Christopher Reeve Paralysis Foundation, Springfield, NJ.

5620
Frances & Benjamin Benenson Foundation, Inc. ✧
708 3rd Ave., 28th Fl.
New York, NY 10017 (212) 867-0990
Contact: Bruce W. Benenson, V.P.

Established in 1983 in NY.
Donors: Charles B. Benenson†; Marx Realty & Improvement Co., Inc.
Foundation type: Independent foundation.
Financial data (yr. ended 11/30/05): Assets, $42,648,353 (M); gifts received, $250,000; expenditures, $2,473,501; qualifying distributions, $1,857,502; giving activities include $1,857,502 for 173 grants (high: $550,000; low: $50).
Purpose and activities: Support primarily for human services, arts and culture, education, health care, and community development.
Fields of interest: Museums; Arts; Elementary/ secondary education; Higher education; Education; Health care; Health organizations, association; Human services; Jewish agencies & temples.
Type of support: Continuing support; Endowments.
Application information: Application form not required.
Initial approach: Letter
Deadline(s): None
Officers: Bruce W. Benenson, V.P.; Richard Kessler, Secy.; Lloyd Stabner, Treas.
Directors: Frederick C. Benenson; Lawrence B. Benenson.
EIN: 133267113
Selected grants: The following grants were reported in 2005.
$5,048,346 to Aish HaTorah. 2 grants: $48,346, $5,000,000
$2,400,000 to Duke University, Durham, NC.
$50,000 to Purchase College Foundation, Purchase, NY.
$25,000 to New York University, New York, NY.
$10,000 to Buffalo Inner-City Scholarship Opportunity Network (BISON), Buffalo, NY.
$10,000 to Wildwood School, Los Angeles, CA.
$5,000 to Library Foundation of Los Angeles, Los Angeles, CA.
$1,000 to Jewish Outreach Institute, New York, NY.
$100 to Trinity Fund, Tallahassee, FL.

5621
The David Berg Foundation, Inc.
16 E. 73rd St.
New York, NY 10021 (212) 517-8634
Contact: Michele Tocci, Pres.
E-mail: mtocci@bergfoundation.org; FAX: (212) 517-8636; E-mail: mtocci@bergfoundation.org

Established in 1994 in NY.
Donor: David Berg Settlor Trust.
Foundation type: Independent foundation.
Financial data (yr. ended 12/31/04): Assets, $470,699 (M); gifts received, $1,980,000; expenditures, $1,768,869; qualifying distributions, $1,549,725; giving activities include $1,059,650 for 35 grants (high: $95,000; low: $5,000).
Fields of interest: Museums; Law school/ education; Legal services; Jewish agencies & temples.
International interests: England; Israel.
Type of support: General/operating support; Continuing support; Annual campaigns; Equipment; Program development; Conferences/seminars;

Professorships; Publication; Curriculum development; Fellowships; Scholarship funds; Research; Exchange programs.
Limitations: Giving primarily in New York, NY. No grants to individuals.
Publications: Application guidelines; Grants list.
Application information: Application form not required.
Initial approach: Proposal
Copies of proposal: 1
Board meeting date(s): June, Oct., and Feb.
Officers: Michele Tocci, Pres.; William D. Zabel, V.P.; Jerome Zoffer, Secy.-Treas.
Number of staff: 1 full-time professional; 1 part-time support.
EIN: 133753217
Selected grants: The following grants were reported in 2004.
$95,000 to Center for Jewish History, New York, NY.
$75,000 to American Miklat Committee, New York, NY.
$75,000 to Human Rights First, New York, NY.
$58,100 to Metropolitan Museum of Art, New York, NY.
$50,000 to New York Legal Assistance Group, New York, NY.
$25,000 to Eldridge Street Project, New York, NY.
$25,000 to Museum of the City of New York, New York, NY.
$25,000 to New Israel Fund, New York, NY.
$20,000 to Jewish Community Center in Manhattan, New York, NY.
$15,000 to Folksbiene Yiddish Theater, New York, NY.

5622
The Judy & Howard Berkowitz Foundation ✧
c/o Dan Curran, The Ayco Co., LP
P.O. Box 860
Saratoga Springs, NY 12866-0860

Established in 1987 in NY.
Donors: Howard P. Berkowitz; Judith R. Berkowitz.
Foundation type: Independent foundation.
Financial data (yr. ended 3/31/05): Assets, $93,410 (M); gifts received, $675,717; expenditures, $832,435; qualifying distributions, $824,651; giving activities include $824,651 for 95 grants (high: $200,000; low: $20).
Purpose and activities: Giving primarily for the arts, particularly the performing arts, as well as for education, health and human services, and Jewish agencies.
Fields of interest: Performing arts, orchestra (symphony); Arts; Higher education, university; Education; Hospitals (general); Health organizations, association; Human services; Children/youth, services; International affairs; Jewish federated giving programs; Jewish agencies & temples.
Limitations: Applications not accepted. Giving primarily in NY. No grants to individuals.
Application information: Contributes only to pre-selected organizations.
Trustees: Howard P. Berkowitz; Judith R. Berkowitz; Roger S. Berkowitz; Sandra L. Berkowitz.
EIN: 133371065

5623
The Berlys Foundation ✧
c/o Coblence & Assocs.
200 Park Ave. S., Ste. 910
New York, NY 10003 (212) 593-9191
Contact: Alain Coblence, Secy.

Established in 2000 in NY.
Donors: The Mach Foundation; Yves Saint Laurent; The Crest Foundation.
Foundation type: Independent foundation.
Financial data (yr. ended 12/31/05): Assets, $11,643 (M); gifts received, $325,000; expenditures, $359,392; qualifying distributions, $359,365; giving activities include $354,150 for 6 grants (high: $150,000; low: $33,125).
Purpose and activities: The foundation supports humanitarian causes, and medical and scientific research and charitable organizations providing care and shelter to those with severe illnesses.
Fields of interest: Arts; Education; Health care; Medical research, institute; Human services.
International interests: France; Morocco.
Limitations: Giving in New York, NY; funding also in Paris, France, and Tangier, Morocco.
Application information:
Initial approach: Proposal
Deadline(s): None
Officers: Connie Uzzo, Pres.; Alain Coblence, Secy.
Directors: Etienne Boillot; Jean Francis Bretelle.
EIN: 134086223

5624
The Arnold Bernhard Foundation, Inc. ✧
220 E. 42nd St., 6th Fl.
New York, NY 10017-5891
Contact: Jean B. Buttner, Pres.

Established in 1976.
Donors: Arnold Bernhard†; Arnold Bernhard Charitable Annuity Trust I; Arnold Bernhard Charitable Annuity Trust II.
Foundation type: Independent foundation.
Financial data (yr. ended 12/31/05): Assets, $6,284,609 (M); expenditures, $582,084; qualifying distributions, $579,688; giving activities include $579,663 for 6 grants (high: $288,663; low: $1,000).
Purpose and activities: Giving primarily for education, with emphasis on a private secondary school; funding also for a psychiatric medical research hospital facility, including a drug and alcohol abuse program.
Fields of interest: Secondary school/education; Higher education; Hospitals (psychiatric); Protestant agencies & churches.
Type of support: General/operating support; Annual campaigns; Capital campaigns; Building/ renovation; Professorships; Scholarship funds.
Limitations: Giving primarily in Wallingford, CT, and Belmont and Cambridge, MA.
Application information:
Initial approach: Letter
Deadline(s): None
Final notification: Nov. or Dec.
Officers and Directors:* Jean B. Buttner,* Pres.; Howard A. Brecher,* V.P.; David T. Henigson,* V.P.
EIN: 136100457

5625
The Stanley & Vivian Bernstein Foundation ✧ ☆
300 Trenor Dr.
New Rochelle, NY 10804

Established in 1997 in NY.
Donors: Stanley Bernstein; Vivian Bernstein.
Foundation type: Operating foundation.
Financial data (yr. ended 12/31/04): Assets, $1,652,204 (M); gifts received, $175,000; expenditures, $665,711; qualifying distributions, $665,650; giving activities include $665,650 for 17 grants (high: $600,000; low: $500).
Purpose and activities: Giving primarily to Jewish organizations; support also for education.
Fields of interest: Education; Foundations (private independent); Jewish agencies & temples.
Limitations: Applications not accepted. Giving primarily in New York, NY. No grants to individuals.
Application information: Contributes only to pre-selected organizations.
Trustees: Stanley Bernstein; Vivian Bernstein.
EIN: 137104060

5626
Theresa A. and Thomas W. Berry Foundation ✧ ☆
c/o BCRS Assocs., LLC
100 Wall St., 11th Fl.
New York, NY 10005

Established in 1987 in NJ.
Donor: Thomas W. Berry.
Foundation type: Independent foundation.
Financial data (yr. ended 3/31/06): Assets, $612,312 (M); gifts received, $133,800; expenditures, $431,101; qualifying distributions, $427,272; giving activities include $421,455 for 52 grants (high: $144,255; low: $25).
Purpose and activities: Giving primarily for higher education; funding also for health associations, children, youth and social services, and services for seniors.
Fields of interest: Historic preservation/historical societies; Arts; Higher education; Health organizations, association; Human services; Children/youth, services; Aging, centers/services.
Limitations: Applications not accepted. Giving primarily in NJ, and Providence, RI; some funding nationally, particularly in New York, NY. No grants to individuals, or for scholarships; no loans.
Application information: Contributes only to pre-selected organizations.
Trustees: Theresa A. Berry; Thomas W. Berry; Barrie A. Wigmore.
EIN: 133437930
Selected grants: The following grants were reported in 2005.
$159,865 to Brown University, Providence, RI. 2 grants: $102,500, $57,365
$43,000 to New Jersey Historical Society, Newark, NJ. 3 grants: $3,000, $20,000, $20,000
$10,000 to YMCA, Frost Valley, Montclair, NJ.
$5,000 to Partnership in Philanthropy, Chatham, NJ.
$2,500 to New Jersey Foundation for Aging, Trenton, NJ.
$2,500 to Rosemont College, Rosemont, PA.
$1,000 to Truckee Tahoe Community Foundation, Truckee, CA.

5627
Sol E. Betesh & Sons Foundation, Inc. ✧
c/o Mitzi International
1 E. 33rd St., 10th Fl.
New York, NY 10016-5011

Established in 1988 in NY.
Donors: Sol E. Betesh; Norma Betesh; Elliot Betesh; Michael Betesh; Steven Betesh; Baby Boom Consumer; Betgold; Steven's Baby Boom, Ltd.
Foundation type: Independent foundation.
Financial data (yr. ended 12/31/04): Assets, $476,193 (M); gifts received, $524,420; expenditures, $526,936; qualifying distributions, $522,714; giving activities include $522,714 for 21 + grants (high: $506,920).
Purpose and activities: Giving primarily to yeshivas and other Jewish agencies and temples.
Fields of interest: Elementary/secondary education; Human services; Jewish federated giving programs; Jewish agencies & temples.
Limitations: Applications not accepted. Giving primarily in New York City, with emphasis on Brooklyn, NY. No grants to individuals.
Application information: Contributes only to pre-selected organizations.
Officers: Sol E. Betesh, Pres.; Elliot Betesh, V.P.; Michael Betesh, V.P.; Norma Betesh, Secy.
EIN: 133479984
Selected grants: The following grants were reported in 2003.
$302,700 to Jewish Communal Fund of New York, New York, NY.
$5,101 to Deal Yeshiva, Deal, NJ.
$5,063 to Sephardic Community Center, Brooklyn, NY.
$5,000 to Hillel Yeshiva, Brooklyn, NY.
$5,000 to Torah Academy High School of Brooklyn, Brooklyn, NY.
$1,800 to Yeshiva of Kings Bay, Brooklyn, NY.
$1,500 to Porat Yosef Foundation, Brooklyn, NY.
$1,500 to Torah Academy of Monmouth County, Deal, NJ.
$1,253 to Magen Israel Society, Brooklyn, NY.
$1,000 to Yeshiva Mikdash Melech, Brooklyn, NY.

5628
The Eddie and Rachelle Betesh Family Foundation, Inc. ✧
c/o Saramax Apparel
1372 Broadway, 7th Fl.
New York, NY 10018

Established in 1998 in DE and NY.
Donors: Eddie Betesh; Rachelle Betesh.
Foundation type: Independent foundation.
Financial data (yr. ended 12/31/03): Assets, $74,874 (M); gifts received, $1,521,050; expenditures, $1,468,525; qualifying distributions, $1,468,426; giving activities include $1,468,401 for 292 grants (high: $254,500; low: $18).
Purpose and activities: Giving primarily for Jewish agencies, temples, and schools.
Fields of interest: Education; Jewish federated giving programs; Jewish agencies & temples.
Limitations: Applications not accepted. Giving primarily in NY. No grants to individuals.
Application information: Contributes only to pre-selected organizations.
Officers: Eddie Betesh, Pres.; Rachelle Betesh, Treas.
EIN: 133981963

Selected grants: The following grants were reported in 2003.
$254,500 to Medrash Emek Hatorah, New York, NY.
$73,000 to Mesivta of Long Beach, Long Beach, NY.
$55,992 to Beth Medrash Govoha, Brooklyn, NY.
$26,120 to Yeshivat Ohel Torah, Brooklyn, NY.
$24,251 to Deal Yeshiva, Deal, NJ.
$14,000 to Agudath Israel of America, New York, NY.
$11,200 to Sephardic Food Fund, New York, NY.
$11,000 to Friends of Arachim, Spring Valley, NY.
$10,000 to Vaad L Hatzolas Nidchei Yisroel, Brooklyn, NY.
$10,000 to Yeshiva of Brooklyn, Brooklyn, NY.

5629
Bialkin Family Foundation ✧
c/o Skadden, Arps, Slate, Megher & Flom
4 Times Sq.
New York, NY 10036

Established in 1968 in NY.
Donors: Kenneth J. Bialkin; Ann E. Bialkin.
Foundation type: Independent foundation.
Financial data (yr. ended 12/31/03): Assets, $12,706,839 (M); expenditures, $470,298; qualifying distributions, $426,163; giving activities include $421,005 for grants.
Purpose and activities: Giving primarily to Jewish causes.
Fields of interest: Elementary/secondary education; Human services; Jewish federated giving programs; Jewish agencies & temples.
Limitations: Applications not accepted. Giving primarily in New York, NY. No grants to individuals.
Application information: Contributes only to pre-selected organizations.
Officers and Directors:* Kenneth J. Bialkin,* Pres.; Ann E. Bialkin,* Sr. V.P.; Johanna Bialkin, V.P.; Lisa Bialkin, V.P.; Jonathan L. Koslow, Secy.
EIN: 237003181

5630
Gabriel and Sara Bildirici Hesed Foundation ✧ ☆
12 E. 37th St.
New York, NY 10016
Application address: c/o David Bildirici, 12 E. 37th St., New York NY 10016, tel.: (212) 447-6848

Foundation type: Independent foundation.
Financial data (yr. ended 12/31/05): Assets, $0 (M); gifts received, $465,332; expenditures, $435,273; qualifying distributions, $432,090; giving activities include $432,090 for grants.
Fields of interest: Jewish agencies & temples.
Limitations: Giving primarily in NY.
Officers: Moris Antebi, Pres.; Albert Antebi, Secy.; Sam Massry, Treas.
EIN: 134149144

5631
William Bingham 2nd Betterment Fund ✧
c/o U.S. Trust
114 W. 47th St.
New York, NY 10036 (212) 852-3388
Contact: Christine O'Donnell, Asst. V.P., U.S. Trust
FAX: (212) 852-3377;
E-mail: betterment@ustrust.com; URL: http://www.megrants.org/betterment.htm

Foundation type: Independent foundation.
Financial data (yr. ended 12/31/03): Assets, $38,285,500 (M); expenditures, $2,605,249; qualifying distributions, $2,446,481; giving activities include $2,081,510 for grants.
Purpose and activities: Giving primarily for the advancement of medicine in the state of ME.
Fields of interest: Education; Environment; Health care; Philanthropy/voluntarism.
Type of support: General/operating support; Capital campaigns; Scholarship funds.
Limitations: Giving limited to ME. No support for religious activities or programs. No grants to individuals.
Publications: Application guidelines; Grants list.
Application information: Only full proposals accepted for review. No letters of inquiry or pre-submission proposal review. Application cover sheet and guidelines available on foundation Web site. Application form required.
  Initial approach: Proposal
  Copies of proposal: 7
  Deadline(s): Jan. 31. Apr. 30, July 31 and Oct. 31
  Board meeting date(s): Mar., June, Sept. and Dec.
  Final notification: 2 months
Trustees: William P. Clough III; Carol Berg Geist; Martin Grohman; Andrew Tansey; William Winship; Carolyn S. Wollen; U.S. Trust.
EIN: 136072625
Selected grants: The following grants were reported in 2003.
$113,600 to Maine School Administrative District No. 44, Bethel, ME.
$50,000 to Forest Society of Maine, Bangor, ME.
$50,000 to Nature Conservancy, Arlington, VA.
$30,000 to Maine Sea Coast Missionary Society, Bar Harbor, ME.
$20,000 to Maine Childrens Alliance, Augusta, ME.
$20,000 to Maine Development Foundation, Augusta, ME.
$16,815 to Healthy Community Coalition, Farmington, ME.
$15,000 to Maine Initiatives, Augusta, ME.
$10,000 to Board Network, Portland, ME.
$10,000 to Conservation Law Foundation, Boston, MA.

5632
The Birkelund Fund ✧
c/o Barry M. Strauss Assocs., Ltd.
307 5th Ave., 8th Fl.
New York, NY 10016-6517

Established in 1989 in DE and NY.
Donor: John P. Birkelund.
Foundation type: Independent foundation.
Financial data (yr. ended 4/30/05): Assets, $12,890,038 (M); gifts received, $1,650,050; expenditures, $589,794; qualifying distributions, $537,145; giving activities include $536,090 for 32 grants (high: $330,000; low: $40).
Purpose and activities: Giving primarily for education, particularly to a public library; some giving also for the arts, and health and human services.
Fields of interest: Museums (art); Higher education; Libraries (public); Education; Health care; Human services; International affairs.
Limitations: Applications not accepted. Giving primarily in CT, NJ, NY, and RI. No grants to individuals.
Application information: Contributes only to pre-selected organizations.

Officer: John P. Birkelund, Pres.
Director: Immanuel Kohn.
EIN: 133539224
Selected grants: The following grants were reported in 2004.
$330,000 to New York Public Library, New York, NY. For general support.
$40,000 to Brown University, Providence, RI. For general support.
$21,350 to Metropolitan Museum of Art, New York, NY. For general support.
$10,000 to Columbia University, New York, NY. For general support.
$10,000 to Council on Foreign Relations, New York, NY. For general support.
$10,000 to Our Lady Queen of Angels. For general support.
$5,000 to Manhattan Institute for Policy Research, New York, NY. For general support.
$5,000 to United Way. For general support.
$3,000 to Horizons Student Enrichment Program, New Canaan, CT. For general support.
$2,000 to Greenwich Hospital, Greenwich, CT. For general support.

5633
Mona Bismarck Charitable Trust ✧
1133 Ave. of the Americas
New York, NY 10036-6710

Established in 1986 in NY.
Donor: Mona Bismarck†.
Foundation type: Independent foundation.
Financial data (yr. ended 12/31/04): Assets, $16,091,898 (M); expenditures, $1,003,529; qualifying distributions, $907,477; giving activities include $870,000 for 11 grants.
Purpose and activities: Giving primarily to an affiliated private foundation which operates a cultural center in Paris, France; some support for higher education and cultural institutions with the aim to enhance Franco-American friendships.
Fields of interest: Arts; Education; International affairs, goodwill promotion; Civil rights, race/intergroup relations.
International interests: France.
Type of support: General/operating support.
Limitations: Applications not accepted. Giving primarily in Paris, France; some funding also in the U.S., particularly in New York, NY, and San Diego, CA. No grants to individuals.
Application information: Contributes only to pre-selected organizations.
Trustee: Russell M. Porter.
EIN: 133244269
Selected grants: The following grants were reported in 2003.
$900,000 to Mona Bismark Foundation, Paris, France. .
$20,000 to Lafayette Escadrille Memorial Foundation, New York, NY.
$3,000 to American Library in Paris, Paris, France. For purchase of books.

5634
Laszlo Bito and Olivia Carino Foundation, Inc. ✧
c/o R. Braunschweig
350 Fifth Ave., Ste. 1000
New York, NY 10118-1099

Established in 2002 in NY.
Donors: Olivia Carino; Laszlo Bito.
Foundation type: Independent foundation.
Financial data (yr. ended 12/31/04): Assets, $1,772,333 (M); gifts received, $1,500,000; expenditures, $844,820; qualifying distributions, $837,750; giving activities include $837,750 for 10 grants (high: $200,000; low: $15,000).
Fields of interest: Higher education; Human services; International development.
International interests: Hungary.
Limitations: Giving in the U.S. and Budapest, Hungary.
Application information:
  Initial approach: Letter
  Deadline(s): None
Officer and Directors:* Laszlo Bito,* Pres.; Olivia Carino.
EIN: 223863244

5635
Robert Black Charitable Foundation ✧
c/o U.S. Trust
P.O. Box 2004
New York, NY 10109-1910
Application address: c/o U.S. Trust Co. of NY, 114 W. 47th St., New York, NY 10036-1510

Established in 1998 in NY.
Donor: Robert Black†.
Foundation type: Independent foundation.
Financial data (yr. ended 12/31/05): Assets, $8,253,437 (M); expenditures, $482,839; qualifying distributions, $429,015; giving activities include $396,346 for 9 grants (high: $57,000; low: $25,929).
Purpose and activities: Grants limited to medical research preferably for lung, pancreatic, and liver cancers, and gastrointestinal problems.
Fields of interest: Cancer research; Digestive disorders research.
Type of support: Research.
Limitations: Applications not accepted. Giving on a national basis. No grants to individuals.
Application information: Unsolicited requests for funds not accepted. Grants are awarded based on the recommendations of Damon Runyon Cancer Research Foundation, which also manages the Robert Black Charitable Foundation's RFP process.
Trustee: U.S. Trust.
Number of staff: 1 part-time professional.
EIN: 137174452

5636
Leon Black Family Foundation, Inc. ✧
9 W. 57th St., 43rd Fl.
New York, NY 10019

Established in 1997 in DE and NY.
Donor: Leon D. Black.
Foundation type: Independent foundation.
Financial data (yr. ended 12/31/05): Assets, $464,649 (M); gifts received, $5,876,000; expenditures, $5,924,315; qualifying distributions, $5,924,000; giving activities include $5,924,000 for 9 grants (high: $5,676,000; low: $5,000).
Purpose and activities: Giving primarily for arts and culture, museums, secondary education, human services, and youth development.
Fields of interest: Museums; Performing arts centers; Historical activities; Arts; Libraries/library

science; Education; Animals/wildlife, preservation/ protection; Hospitals (specialty); Boy scouts; Youth development; Children, services; Residential/ custodial care; Federated giving programs.
Limitations: Applications not accepted. Giving primarily in New York, NY. No grants to individuals.
Application information: Contributes only to pre-selected organizations.
Officers: Leon D. Black, Pres. and Treas.; Debra R. Black, V.P. and Secy.
Director: Jeffrey Epstein.
EIN: 133947890
Selected grants: The following grants were reported in 2004.
$2,882,142 to Museum of Modern Art, New York, NY.
$275,000 to Trinity School, New York, NY. 2 grants: $200,000, $75,000
$274,168 to Dartmouth College, Hanover, NH.
$100,000 to Prep for Prep, New York, NY.
$60,000 to Jewish Childrens Museum, New York, NY.
$50,000 to American Ballet Theater, New York, NY.
$33,000 to Brown University, Providence, RI.
$30,000 to Jewish Museum, New York, NY.
$25,000 to Public Theater, New York, NY.

5637
The Lloyd and Laura Blankfein Foundation ◇
c/o Goldman Sachs Family Office
1 New York Plz., 40th Fl.
New York, NY   10004

Established in 1989 in NY.
Donor: Lloyd C. Blankfein.
Foundation type: Independent foundation.
Financial data (yr. ended 1/31/06): Assets, $5,537,482 (M); gifts received, $2,890,506; expenditures, $1,175,350; qualifying distributions, $1,168,000; giving activities include $1,168,000 for 31 grants (high: $350,000; low: $500).
Purpose and activities: Funding for education with emphasis on an Ethical Culture school, Jewish organizations, and social services.
Fields of interest: Elementary/secondary education; Education, early childhood education; Higher education; Health organizations, association; Human services; Children/youth, services; Jewish federated giving programs; Jewish agencies & temples.
Limitations: Applications not accepted. Giving primarily in New York, NY. No grants to individuals.
Application information: Contributes only to pre-selected organizations.
Trustees: Laura Blankfein; Lloyd C. Blankfein; Gregory P. Ho.
EIN: 133557478

5638
Adele and Leonard Block Foundation, Inc. ◇
499 7th Ave., 21st Fl., South Tower
New York, NY   10018-6803   (917) 339-0344
Contact: Thomas Block, V.P.

Established in 1945 in NJ.
Donors: Leonard N. Block; Adele Block.
Foundation type: Independent foundation.
Financial data (yr. ended 11/30/05): Assets, $3,645,713 (L); gifts received, $1,300,000;

expenditures, $1,244,835; qualifying distributions, $1,239,514; giving activities include $1,239,514 for 81 grants (high: $150,000; low: $50).
Fields of interest: Arts; Higher education; Medical school/education; Reproductive health, family planning; Health care; Food distribution, meals on wheels.
Type of support: General/operating support.
Limitations: Giving primarily in NJ and NY.
Application information:
   Initial approach: Letter
   Deadline(s): None
Officers and Directors:* Peggy Block Danziger,* Pres.; Adele G. Block,* V.P.; Thomas Block,* V.P.; Robert Heun, Secy.; Gordon J. Girvin, Treas.
EIN: 226026000
Selected grants: The following grants were reported in 2005.
$150,000 to Lincoln Center Theater, New York, NY.
$100,000 to Dalton Schools, New York, NY.
$100,000 to Planned Parenthood of New York City, New York, NY.
$100,000 to Steppingstone Foundation, Boston, MA.
$50,000 to Mount Sinai Medical Center, New York, NY.
$49,755 to American Museum of Natural History, New York, NY.
$44,562 to Museum of Modern Art, New York, NY.
$25,000 to Two River Theater Company, Red Bank, NJ.
$10,000 to New York Public Library, New York, NY.
$5,000 to Philharmonic-Symphony Society of New York, New York, NY.

5639
The Blood Family Foundation ◇
c/o Goldman Sachs & Co., Family Office
1 New York Plz., 40th Fl.
New York, NY   10004

Established in 1996 in NY.
Donor: David W. Blood.
Foundation type: Independent foundation.
Financial data (yr. ended 3/31/06): Assets, $10,717,681 (M); gifts received, $260,000; expenditures, $2,748,972; qualifying distributions, $2,735,000; giving activities include $2,735,000 for 7 grants (high: $1,000,000; low: $10,000).
Purpose and activities: Giving primarily for education.
Fields of interest: Higher education; Education; Human services; Federated giving programs.
Limitations: Applications not accepted. Giving on a national and international basis, particularly in Washington, DC, MA, NY, and London, England. No grants to individuals.
Application information: Contributes only to pre-selected organizations.
Trustees: Alison Blood; David W. Blood.
EIN: 133919765

5640
Blue Ridge Foundation New York ◇
(formerly Rubicon Foundation)
150 Court St., 2nd Fl.
Brooklyn, NY   11201   (718) 923-1400
Contact: Matthew Klein, Exec. Dir.
FAX: (718) 923-2869; E-mail: info@brfny.org;
URL: http://www.brfny.org

Established in 1993 in NY.
Donor: John A. Griffin.
Foundation type: Independent foundation.
Financial data (yr. ended 11/30/03): Assets, $8,788,018 (M); gifts received, $242,579; expenditures, $1,533,567; qualifying distributions, $747,989; giving activities include $720,700 for 23 grants (high: $390,000; low: $500).
Purpose and activities: Supports social change strategies that operate in high poverty communities and connect people to the opportunities, resources and support they need to fulfill their full potential. The foundation supports start-up organizations in New York City only, helping to develop organizations by providing opportunities for capacity development.
Fields of interest: Education; Youth development; Children/youth, services; Community development; Venture philanthropy.
Type of support: Management development/ capacity building.
Limitations: Giving limited to New York, NY.
Application information: Application information available on foundation Web site.
   Initial approach: Letter (not to exceed 2 pages)
   Deadline(s): Letters of inquiry received in the First Quarter from Jan. 15-Mar. 15, the Second Quarter from Apr. 15-June 15, the Third Quarter from Jul. 15-Sept. 15, and the Fourth Quarter from Oct. 15-Dec. 15
   Final notification: Apr. 15, Jul. 15, Oct. 15, and Jan. 15
Trustee: John A. Griffin.
EIN: 137029270

5641
Blue Star Foundation, Inc. ◇ ☆
825 3rd Ave., 14th Fl.
New York, NY   10022

Established in 2005 in NY.
Donor: David Grin.
Foundation type: Operating foundation.
Financial data (yr. ended 6/30/05): Assets, $83,509 (M); gifts received, $2,780,000; expenditures, $2,704,558; qualifying distributions, $2,703,200; giving activities include $2,703,200 for 12 grants (high: $500,000; low: $500).
Purpose and activities: Giving primarily for Jewish agencies, temples, and schools.
Fields of interest: Elementary/secondary education; Jewish agencies & temples.
Officer: David Grin, Pres.
EIN: 201450579

5642
Charles G. & Yvette Bluhdorn Charitable Trust ◇
c/o HRR, LLP
1430 Broadway, 17th Fl.
New York, NY   10018

Established in 1967 in NY.
Donor: Paul Bluhdorn.
Foundation type: Independent foundation.
Financial data (yr. ended 12/31/04): Assets, $4,752,731 (M); expenditures, $1,052,350; qualifying distributions, $1,001,531; giving activities include $880,000 for 16 grants (high: $400,000; low: $2,000).
Purpose and activities: Giving primarily for cultural programs, child welfare and social services, animal

welfare and education, the environment, and hospitals and medical research.

Fields of interest: Arts; Higher education; Hospitals (general); Health organizations, association; Medical research, institute; Human services; Children/youth, services.

Type of support: General/operating support; Program development; Scholarship funds.

Limitations: Applications not accepted. Giving primarily in NY, with emphasis on the greater metropolitan New York, NY, area; some giving nationally. No grants to individuals.

Application information: Contributes only to pre-selected organizations.

Trustees: Dominique Bluhdorn; Paul Bluhdorn; Yvette Bluhdorn.

Number of staff: 1 full-time professional.

EIN: 136256769

Selected grants: The following grants were reported in 2004.

$10,000 to Doctors Without Borders USA, New York, NY.

$5,000 to Saint James Church, New York, NY.

$5,000 to Salvation Army of Greater New York, New York, NY.

$5,000 to Trinity School, New York, NY.

$2,000 to Coalition for the Homeless, DC.

5643

Edith C. Blum Foundation, Inc. ✧

c/o Eisner, LLP
750 3rd Ave.
New York, NY 10017
Application address: Frances M. Friedman, Pres., c/o Roberts & Holland, LLP, 825 8th Ave., 37th Fl., New York, NY 10019-7416

Established in 1990 in NY as successor to the Edith C. Blum Foundation.

Donor: Edith C. Blum Foundation.

Foundation type: Independent foundation.

Financial data (yr. ended 9/30/05): Assets, $15,245,528 (M); expenditures, $735,836; qualifying distributions, $643,883; giving activities include $521,600 for 149 grants (high: $80,000; low: $100).

Purpose and activities: Giving primarily for arts and culture, particularly to an organization dealing with history and archeology, as well as to an art museum, federated giving programs, Jewish organizations, and for medical research and human services.

Fields of interest: Arts; Medical research, institute; Human services; Federated giving programs; Jewish agencies & temples.

Limitations: Giving primarily in New York, NY. No grants to individuals.

Application information: Application form not required.

Deadline(s): None

Officers: Frances M. Friedman, Pres.; Wilbur H. Friedman, Secy.-Treas.

Director: Lionel Etra.

EIN: 133564317

5644

Blythmour Corporation ✧ ☆

c/o Winston & Strawn LLP
200 Park Ave.
New York, NY 10166-4193 (212) 294-6700
Contact: David F. Kroenlein, Secy.-Treas.

Established in 1951 in NY.

Donor: Lloyd S. Gilmour, Jr.

Foundation type: Independent foundation.

Financial data (yr. ended 12/31/05): Assets, $0 (M); expenditures, $357,725; qualifying distributions, $342,880; giving activities include $334,500 for 38 grants (high: $50,000; low: $2,000).

Purpose and activities: Giving primarily for medical purposes, youth, and human services.

Fields of interest: Arts; Libraries (public); Education; Animal welfare; Zoos/zoological societies; Hospitals (general); Medical care, rehabilitation; Medical research; Human services; American Red Cross; Salvation Army; Religion.

Limitations: Giving primarily in NY. No grants to individuals.

Application information: Application form not required.

Initial approach: Letter
Deadline(s): Aug. 31

Officers and Directors:* Blyth G. Gilmour,* Co-Pres.; Katherine G. Gilmour,* Co-Pres.; David F. Kroenlein, Secy.-Treas.

EIN: 136157750

Selected grants: The following grants were reported in 2005.

$50,000 to Boca Raton Community Hospital, Boca Raton, FL.

$20,000 to Humane Society.

$20,000 to Zoological Society of the Palm Beaches, West Palm Beach, FL.

$10,000 to Canine Companions for Independence.

$10,000 to Hospice by the Sea, Boca Raton, FL.

$7,500 to American Red Cross.

$7,000 to Learning Leaders, New York, NY.

$4,000 to Cape Cod Chamber Music Festival, North Chatham, MA.

$4,000 to Dalton Schools, New York, NY.

$4,000 to Wellfleet Harbor Actors Theater, Wellfleet, MA.

5645

The Bobolink Foundation ▼ ✧

(formerly Henry M. & Wendy J. Paulson, Jr. Foundation)
c/o Goldman Sachs & Co.
1 New York Plz., 40th Fl.
New York, NY 10004

Established in 1985 in IL.

Donors: Henry M. Paulson, Jr.; Goldman Sachs & Co.

Foundation type: Independent foundation.

Financial data (yr. ended 3/31/05): Assets, $26,771,488 (M); gifts received, $6,282,913; expenditures, $5,246,590; qualifying distributions, $5,004,506; giving activities include $5,004,506 for 67 grants (high: $1,000,000; low: $500; average: $10,000–$100,000).

Purpose and activities: Support primarily for Christian Science churches, environmental conservation and wildlife preservation, and higher education.

Fields of interest: Higher education; Business school/education; Environment, natural resources; Animals/wildlife, preservation/protection; Children, services; Protestant agencies & churches.

Limitations: Applications not accepted. Giving on a national basis, with some emphasis on New York, NY, Washington, DC, Arlington, VA, Boston, MA, and Hanover, NH. No grants to individuals; no loans.

Application information: Contributes only to pre-selected organizations.

Trustees: Amanda Clark Paulson; Henry M. Paulson, Jr.; Henry Merritt Paulson III; Wendy J. Paulson.

EIN: 942988627

Selected grants: The following grants were reported in 2005.

$1,000,000 to First Church of Christ Scientist, Boston, MA. For general support.

$1,000,000 to Mother Church, Boston, MA. For general support.

$450,000 to Dartmouth College, Hanover, NH. For general support.

$450,000 to Wellesley College, Wellesley, MA. For general support.

$350,000 to Cornell University, Laboratory of Ornithology, Ithaca, NY. For general support.

$350,000 to RARE Center for Tropical Conservation, Arlington, VA. 2 grants: $250,000 (For general support), $100,000 (For general support).

$100,000 to Nature Conservancy, New York, NY. For general support.

$25,000 to Harvard University, Cambridge, MA. For general support for School of Business in Boston.

$10,000 to Citizens for Conservation, Barrington, IL. For general support.

5646

Elmer and Mamdouha Bobst Foundation, Inc. ✧

c/o Mamdouha S. Bobst
70 Washington Sq. S., Ste. 1209
New York, NY 10012

Incorporated in 1968 in NY.

Donor: Elmer H. Bobst†.

Foundation type: Independent foundation.

Financial data (yr. ended 12/31/05): Assets, $47,705,072 (M); expenditures, $1,747,666; qualifying distributions, $1,519,509; giving activities include $1,475,150 for 21 grants (high: $1,000,000; low: $500).

Purpose and activities: Emphasis on the promotion of health and medical research services, higher education, children, youth and social services, and international affairs.

Fields of interest: Higher education; Animal welfare; Hospitals (general); Health care; Health organizations, association; Human services; Children/youth, services; International affairs.

Limitations: Applications not accepted. Giving on a national basis, with emphasis on New York, NY, and NJ.

Publications: Annual report; Informational brochure.

Application information: Contributes only to pre-selected organizations.

Officer: Mamdouha S. Bobst, Pres. and Treas.

Directors: Farouk As-Sayed; Patricia Nixon Cox; Charles Goodfellow; Robert Task.

EIN: 132616114

5647

The Bodman Foundation

767 3rd Ave., 4th Fl.
New York, NY 10017-2023 (212) 644-0322
Contact: Joseph S. Dolan, Secy. and Exec. Dir.
FAX: (212) 759-6510;
E-mail: main@achelis-bodman-fnds.org;
URL: http://www.foundationcenter.org/grantmaker/achelis-bodman/

Incorporated in 1945 in NJ.
Donors: George M. Bodman†; Louise C. Bodman†.
Foundation type: Independent foundation.
Financial data (yr. ended 12/31/04): Assets, $66,268,355 (M); expenditures, $4,102,391; qualifying distributions, $3,296,273; giving activities include $2,779,500 for 63 grants (high: $250,000; low: $10,000), and $147,140 for 77 employee matching gifts.
Purpose and activities: Support largely for youth; social service agencies; educational agencies, with preference for school reform projects, charter schools, and school choice programs rather than nonprofits that provide direct services in public schools; cultural programs; health; including medical research, and rehabilitation programs. Other interests include voluntarism, entrepreneurship, strengthening the two-parent family, fatherhood (and father absence), promoting the institution of marriage, placement into private sector jobs, faith-based programs, prevention and earlier intervention, and measurable participant outcomes and program results, parent involvement, consumer choice, and innovation and cost-saving approaches.
Fields of interest: Humanities; Arts; Education, reform; Elementary/secondary education; Elementary/secondary school reform; Medical care, rehabilitation; Health care, cost containment; Substance abuse, prevention; Medical research, institute; Crime/violence prevention, youth; Employment, services; Children/youth, services; Children, adoption; Family services; Family services, adolescent parents; Homeless, human services; Public policy, research; Disabilities, people with; Offenders/ex-offenders.
Type of support: General/operating support; Equipment; Program development; Conferences/seminars; Publication; Seed money; Curriculum development; Fellowships; Internship funds; Scholarship funds; Research; Technical assistance; Program evaluation; Matching/challenge support.
Limitations: Giving primarily in northern NJ and New York, NY. Generally, no support for colleges or universities, international projects, government agencies, public schools, (except charter schools), nonprofit programs and services mostly funded or wholly reimbursed by government, small performing arts groups, or national health or mental health organizations. No grants to individuals; generally no grants for travel, endowments, capital campaigns, housing, annual appeals, dinner functions, fundraising events, deficit financing, or films; no loans.
Publications: Biennial report (including application guidelines); Financial statement; Grants list.
Application information: Unless requested, do not send CDs, DVDs, discs, tapes, or proposals through the internet. Application guidelines and procedures are available on foundation Web site. Application form not required.
  Initial approach: Letter or short proposal
  Copies of proposal: 1
  Deadline(s): None
  Board meeting date(s): May, Sept., Dec., and as needed
  Final notification: 3 to 4 weeks
Officers and Trustees:* John N. Irwin III,* Chair. and C.E.O.; Russell P. Pennoyer,* Pres.; Peter Frelinghuysen,* V.P.; Mary S. Phipps,* V.P.; Joseph S. Dolan, Secy. and Exec. Dir.; Horace I. Crary, Jr., Treas.; Hon. Walter J.P. Curley; Anthony Drexel Duke; Leslie Lenkowsky.

Number of staff: 2 full-time professional; 1 part-time support.
EIN: 136022016
Selected grants: The following grants were reported in 2005.
$150,000 to Rockefeller University, New York, NY. For Bio-Imaging Resource Center.
$100,000 to Manhattan Institute for Policy Research, New York, NY. For Temporary Assistance to Needy Parolees initiative.
$75,000 to Baruch College of the City University of New York, New York, NY. For Free Institutions program under Professor Robert David Johnson.
$75,000 to Village Academies Network, New York, NY. For Leadership Village Academy Charter School.
$50,000 to Achievement First, New Haven, CT. For start-up and first-year expenses of Achievement First Crown Heights Charter School.
$50,000 to Bronx Charter School for Excellence, Bronx, NY. For renovation and start-up expenses at new building, payable over 1.50 years.
$50,000 to Excellent Education for Everyone, Newark, NJ. For New Jersey Charter School Advocacy Project.
$50,000 to KIPP (Knowledge is Power Program) Academy, Bronx, NY. For start-up expenses of KIPP Infinity Charter School.
$50,000 to Scholarship Fund for Inner-City Children, Newark, NJ. For scholarships from Newark Group I Program, payable over 1.50 years.
$25,000 to Center of the American Experiment, Minneapolis, MN. For conference and book, Bringing It Home: Todays Public Debates on Fatherhood and Marriage, payable over 1.50 years.

5648
Bodner Family Foundation, Inc. ◇
152 W. 57th St.
New York, NY   10019
Contact: David Bodner, Pres.

Established in 1999 in NY.
Foundation type: Independent foundation.
Financial data (yr. ended 12/31/04): Assets, $10,668,827 (M); gifts received, $1,400,000; expenditures, $2,644,905; qualifying distributions, $2,640,000; giving activities include $2,640,000 for 2 grants (high: $2,140,000; low: $500,000).
Fields of interest: Jewish agencies & temples.
Limitations: Giving primarily in New York, NY.
Application information:
  Initial approach: Letter
  Deadline(s): None
Officers and Directors:* David Bodner,* Pres.; Naomi Bodner,* Secy.-Treas.; Moishe Bodner.
EIN: 134042545
Selected grants: The following grants were reported in 2003.
$2,100,000 to Kollel Meor Yitzchok, Monsey, NY.
$1,255,000 to Congregation Ahavas Tzdokah V Chesed, Brooklyn, NY.
$100,000 to Beth Hammedrash Sharrie Yosher.
$100,000 to Yeshiva Mir Yerushalayim, Brooklyn, NY.
$100,000 to Yeshiva Shaarei Yosher, Brooklyn, NY.
$36,000 to Kollel Emes Vermunah Viznur, Monsey, NY.
$36,000 to Mechon L Hoyroa, Monsey, NY.
$25,000 to Congregation Kahal Mekor Chaim, Monsey, NY.
$25,000 to Yeshiva of South Monsey, Monsey, NY.

$10,000 to Congregation Shaarei Tefillah, Newton, MA.

5649
John and Linda Bohlsen Family Foundation ◇ ☆
c/o North Fork Bank
275 Broadhollow Rd., 4th Fl.
Melville, NY   11747

Foundation type: Independent foundation.
Financial data (yr. ended 12/31/05): Assets, $1,987,182 (M); expenditures, $440,444; qualifying distributions, $428,750; giving activities include $428,750 for grants.
Fields of interest: Hospitals (general); Human services; Children/youth, services; Family services.
Limitations: Applications not accepted. Giving primarily in CT and NY. No grants to individuals.
Application information: Contributes only to pre-selected organizations.
Officers: John Bohlsen, Pres.; Linda Bohlsen, Secy.
Directors: Kurt Bohlsen; Michael Bohlsen.
EIN: 113440712
Selected grants: The following grants were reported in 2004.
$5,000 to Brookhaven Memorial Hospital Medical Center, Patchogue, NY.
$5,000 to Family Service.
$3,000 to YMCA.
$1,500 to American Cancer Society, Atlanta, GA.
$1,000 to Hope House Ministries, Port Jefferson, NY.
$1,000 to Hospice Care Network, Woodbury, NY.
$1,000 to World Wildlife Fund, DC.
$100 to Humane Society.

5650
The Boisi Family Foundation ◇
c/o Bisys Private Equity Svcs., Inc.
245 5th Ave., 16th Fl.
New York, NY   10016

Established in 1983 in NY.
Donors: Geoffrey T. Boisi; Norine I. Boisi.
Foundation type: Independent foundation.
Financial data (yr. ended 2/28/05): Assets, $4,750,241 (M); gifts received, $705,000; expenditures, $692,276; qualifying distributions, $683,241; giving activities include $619,848 for grants.
Purpose and activities: Giving primarily for education, human services, and community development.
Fields of interest: Arts; Education; Medical research, association; Human services; Community development, neighborhood development.
Limitations: Applications not accepted. Giving primarily in NY. No grants to individuals, or for scholarships; no loans.
Application information: Contributes only to pre-selected organizations.
Trustees: Geoffrey T. Boisi; Norine I. Boisi.
EIN: 133165815
Selected grants: The following grants were reported in 2004.
$262,500 to Chaminade Development Fund, Mineola, NY. 2 grants: $12,500, $250,000
$145,000 to National Mentoring Partnership, Alexandria, VA. 3 grants: $20,000, $100,000, $25,000

$50,000 to Boston College, Chestnut Hill, MA.
$50,000 to Seton Hall University, South Orange, NJ.
$15,000 to Knights Trust, Bronxville, NY.
$15,000 to Sesame Workshop, New York, NY.
$10,000 to Inner-City Scholarship Fund, New York, NY.

5651
Booth Ferris Foundation ▼
c/o JPMorgan Chase Bank, N.A.
345 Park Ave., 4th Fl., NY1-N040
New York, NY 10154 (212) 464-2487
Contact: Edward L. Jones, Prog. Off.
FAX: (212) 464-2305; URL: http://foundationcenter.org/grantmaker/boothferris/

Trusts established in 1957 and 1958 in NY; merged in 1964.
Donors: Chancie Ferris Booth†; Willis H. Booth†.
Foundation type: Independent foundation.
Financial data (yr. ended 12/31/05): Assets, $226,734,766 (M); expenditures, $12,700,198; qualifying distributions, $11,826,358; giving activities include $11,307,000 for 115 grants (high: $200,000; low: $10,000; average: $50,000–$100,000).
Purpose and activities: Grants primarily for education, smaller colleges, and independent secondary schools; limited support also for urban programs, social service agencies, and cultural activities.
Fields of interest: Museums; Arts; Education, association; Secondary school/education; Higher education; Adult education—literacy, basic skills & GED; Education, reading; Education; Human services; Children/youth, services; Community development; Government/public administration; Public affairs.
Type of support: Annual campaigns; Capital campaigns; Building/renovation; Equipment; Program development; Curriculum development; Matching/challenge support.
Limitations: Giving limited to the New York, NY, metropolitan area for the arts, K-12 education, and civic and urban affairs; a broader geographic scope for higher education. No support for federated campaigns, community chests, social services and cultural institutions from outside the New York metropolitan area, or for work with specific diseases or disabilities. No grants to individuals, or for research; generally no grants to educational institutions for scholarships, fellowships, or unrestricted endowments; no loans.
Publications: Annual report; Annual report (including application guidelines).
Application information: Application form not required.
  Initial approach: Proposal
  Copies of proposal: 1
  Deadline(s): None
  Board meeting date(s): Approximately 4 times per year
  Final notification: 4 months
Trustee: JPMorgan Chase Bank, N.A.
Number of staff: None.
EIN: 136170340
Selected grants: The following grants were reported in 2005.
$300,000 to Legal Services for New York City, New York, NY. To establish a new development department.
$250,000 to Urban Assembly, New York, NY. To strengthen evaluation infrastructure.

$200,000 to Big Apple Circus, New York, NY. To purchase two new big top performance tents.
$200,000 to Educators for Social Responsibility Metropolitan Area, New York, NY. For 4rs Research Project.
$200,000 to Fund for the City of New York, New York, NY. For Agenda for Children Tomorrow for One City/One Community project.
$150,000 to Bates College, Lewiston, ME. To establish new Imaging and Computing Center.
$150,000 to Hobart and William Smith Colleges, Geneva, NY. For capital support.
$150,000 to National Dance Institute, New York, NY. To implement strategic plan.
$150,000 to New Partners for Community Revitalization, Great Neck, NY. For Brownfields START-UP Pool and for program support.
$120,000 to Project Reach Youth, Brooklyn, NY. For volunteer coordinator and development consultant.

5652
Borderline Personality Disorder Research Foundation ✧
(formerly Personality Disorder Research Corp.)
650 Madison Ave., 18th Fl.
New York, NY 10022-1029 (212) 937-1955
Contact: Marco Stoffel M.D., Pres.
FAX: (212) 937-1956;
E-mail: BPDRF.USA@Verizon.net; URL: http://www.borderlineresearch.org

Established in 1999 in NY.
Donors: Maytown Universal, S.A.; Rainer Blickle; Colleen Investments, LLC.
Foundation type: Independent foundation.
Financial data (yr. ended 12/31/03): Assets, $1,486,193 (M); gifts received, $5,769,430; expenditures, $1,212,066; qualifying distributions, $1,152,021; giving activities include $1,000,977 for 21 grants (high: $150,000; low: $5,000).
Purpose and activities: Funding for research into the treatment of personality disorders.
Fields of interest: Higher education; Mental health, association; Medical research.
Limitations: Applications not accepted. Giving on a national basis, with emphasis on New York, NY; also giving in Australia, and Europe, with emphasis on Germany, the Netherlands, and the United Kingdom. No grants to individuals.
Application information: Contributes only to pre-selected organizations.
Officers: Marco Stoffel, M.D., Pres.; Raymond Merritt, Secy.; David Jones, Treas.
Directors: Max M. Burger, M.D.; Paul Greengard, Ph.D.; Fritz Henn, Ph.D.; Steven Hyman, Ph.D.; Judith Rapoport.
Scientific Advisory Board: Andrew Skodol, Chair.
EIN: 134069081
Selected grants: The following grants were reported in 2003.
$150,000 to Rockefeller University, New York, NY. For research and treatment for personality disorders.
$75,000 to Harvard University, Cambridge, MA. For research project.
$62,393 to Queensland Institute of Medical Research, Brisbane, Australia. For research project.
$60,370 to Vrije Universiteit, Amsterdam, Netherlands. For research project.

$50,000 to Mount Sinai School of Medicine of New York University, New York, NY. For research project.
$50,000 to University of Michigan, Ann Arbor, MI. For research project.
$37,500 to Duke University Medical Center, Durham, NC. For research project.
$37,500 to University of Fribourg, Fribourg, Switzerland. For research project.
$37,500 to Weill Medical College of Cornell University, New York, NY. For research project.
$37,464 to Barnard College, New York, NY. For research project.

5653
Botwinick-Wolfensohn Foundation, Inc. ☆
c/o Bridget Batson
1350 Ave. of the Americas, Ste. 2900
New York, NY 10019

Established in 1952 in NY.
Donors: James D. Wolfensohn; Benjamin Botwinick†; Edward Botwinick; Bessie Botwinick†.
Foundation type: Independent foundation.
Financial data (yr. ended 12/31/05): Assets, $15,767,116 (M); gifts received, $1,369,074; expenditures, $623,991; qualifying distributions, $621,354; giving activities include $604,000 for 12 grants (high: $330,000; low: $1,000).
Purpose and activities: Emphasis on Israeli and Jewish interests, music education, medical research, and social services.
Fields of interest: Performing arts, music; Education; Medical research, institute; Human services; Jewish agencies & temples.
International interests: Israel.
Type of support: General/operating support; Continuing support; Annual campaigns; Capital campaigns; Building/renovation; Program development; Seed money; Scholarship funds; Research.
Limitations: Applications not accepted. Giving primarily in New York, NY. No grants to individuals.
Application information: Unsolicited requests for funds not accepted.
Officers: James D. Wolfensohn, Chair.; Edward Botwinick, Pres.; Adam Wolfensohn, V.P.; Elaine R. Wolfensohn, V.P.; Andrew Botwinick, Secy.; Sara R. Wolfensohn, Secy.; Naomi R. Wolfensohn, Treas.
Number of staff: 1 part-time professional.
EIN: 136111833

5654
The Bovin Family Foundation ✧ ☆
c/o Clearly, Gottlieb, Steen & Hamilton
1 Liberty Plz.
New York, NY 10006

Established in 2000 in NY.
Donors: Denis A. Bovin; Steven M. Loeb.
Foundation type: Independent foundation.
Financial data (yr. ended 12/31/05): Assets, $173,638 (M); gifts received, $324,421; expenditures, $486,225; qualifying distributions, $486,162; giving activities include $482,112 for 78 grants (high: $120,000; low: $25).
Fields of interest: Museums (marine/maritime); Higher education, university; Hospitals (general); Cancer research; Human services; International affairs; Jewish agencies & temples.

Limitations: Applications not accepted. Giving primarily in NJ and NY. No grants to individuals.
Application information: Contributes only to pre-selected organizations.
Trustees: Denis A. Bovin; Steven M. Loeb.
EIN: 134107990
Selected grants: The following grants were reported in 2005.
$105,000 to Intrepid Museum Foundation, New York, NY.
$25,000 to Temple University, Philadelphia, PA.
$25,000 to Tides Foundation, San Francisco, CA.
$15,000 to Marine Corps Scholarship Foundation, Alexandria, VA.
$10,000 to Massachusetts Institute of Technology, Cambridge, MA.
$10,000 to Santa Barbara Museum of Natural History, Santa Barbara, CA.
$3,300 to Joslyn Art Museum, Omaha, NE.
$1,250 to Jewish Museum, New York, NY.
$1,000 to Prep for Prep, New York, NY.
$1,000 to Robin Hood Foundation, New York, NY.

5655
The Robert Bowne Foundation, Inc. ✧
c/o Bowne & Co., Inc.
55 Water St.
New York, NY   10041-0006   (212) 229-7223
Contact: Anne Lawrence, Prog. Off.
FAX: (212) 658-5876;
E-mail: alawrence@robertbownefoundation.org;
Additional tels.: for Lena Townsend, Exec. Dir.: (212) 658-5873; for Anne Lawrence, Prog. Off. (212) 658-5874; for Sara Hill, Research Off. (212) 658-5875; URL: http://www.robertbownefoundation.org

Incorporated in 1968 in NY.
Donors: Edmund A. Stanley, Jr.; Thomas O. Stanley; Bowne & Co., Inc.; and members of the Stanley family.
Foundation type: Independent foundation.
Financial data (yr. ended 12/31/05): Assets, $15,943,279 (M); gifts received, $51,000; expenditures, $1,585,916; qualifying distributions, $1,458,681; giving activities include $1,037,250 for 43 grants (high: $55,000; low: $2,500), and $12,025 for 20 grants to individuals (high: $2,500; low: $300).
Purpose and activities: The foundation supports the development of quality programs that offer literacy education to children and youth of New York City, in the out-of-school hours, especially those living in economically disadvantaged neighborhoods.
Fields of interest: Education, services; Education, reading; Education, community/cooperative; Youth development, services; Family services, parent education.
Type of support: General/operating support; Continuing support; Program development; Conferences/seminars; Seed money; Curriculum development; Research; Technical assistance; Program evaluation; Matching/challenge support.
Limitations: Giving limited to the New York, NY, area. No support for religious organizations, primary or secondary schools, colleges, or universities, except when some aspect of their work is an integral part of a program supported by the foundation. No grants for capital campaigns or endowments.
Publications: Grants list; Informational brochure (including application guidelines); Occasional report.

Application information: Currently, the foundation is not accepting proposals. See Web site for updates. Application form required.
Initial approach: Letter of inquiry
Copies of proposal: 1
Board meeting date(s): Varies
Officers and Trustees:* Jennifer Stanley,* Chair. and Pres.; Suzanne C. Carothers, Ph.D.*, V.P.; Susan Cummiskey,* Secy.-Treas.; Dianne Kangisser; Jane Quinn; Edmund A. Stanley, Jr.; Ernest Tollerson; Franz VonZiegesar.
Number of staff: 3 full-time professional.
EIN: 132620393

5656
The Boxer Foundation
c/o George Rothkopf
366 N. Broadway, Ste. 410
Jericho, NY   11753-2000

Established in 1985 in NY.
Donor: Leonard Boxer.
Foundation type: Independent foundation.
Financial data (yr. ended 11/30/05): Assets, $7,378,236 (M); expenditures, $572,643; qualifying distributions, $539,625; giving activities include $515,021 for 99 grants (high: $200,000; low: $36).
Purpose and activities: Funding primarily for hospitals and health care, and for Jewish agencies and temples.
Fields of interest: Arts; Higher education; Education; Hospitals (general); Health organizations, association; Human services; Jewish agencies & temples.
Type of support: General/operating support.
Limitations: Applications not accepted. Giving primarily in the greater metropolitan New York, NY, area, including Long Island. No grants to individuals.
Application information: Contributes only to pre-selected organizations.
Officer: Leonard Boxer, Mgr.
Trustee: Steven E. Boxer.
EIN: 133345823
Selected grants: The following grants were reported in 2004.
$53,000 to UJA-Federation of New York, New York, NY. For general support.
$30,000 to Jewish Federation of Palm Beach County, West Palm Beach, FL. For general support.
$21,030 to Memorial Sloan-Kettering Cancer Center, New York, NY. For general support.
$20,000 to Lekotek of Georgia, Atlanta, GA. For general support.
$17,850 to Alzheimers Association, New York, NY. For general support.
$14,150 to American Cancer Society, New York, NY. For general support.
$13,100 to Jewish Guild for the Blind, Palm Beach, FL. For general support.
$11,000 to Southampton Hospital Association, Southampton, NY. For general support.
$10,000 to Raymond F. Kravis Center for the Performing Arts, West Palm Beach, FL. For general support.
$2,750 to Juvenile Diabetes Research Foundation International, New York, NY. For general support.

5657
Brach Family Foundation, Inc. ✧
1600 63rd St.
Brooklyn, NY   11204-2713
Contact: Zigmond Brach, Pres.

Established in 1991 in NY.
Donors: Zigmond Brach; Sound Around, Corp.; United Talmudical Academy.
Foundation type: Independent foundation.
Financial data (yr. ended 12/31/03): Assets, $4,553,951 (M); gifts received, $1,557,000; expenditures, $315,045; qualifying distributions, $315,045; giving activities include $315,045 for 98 grants (high: $25,000; low: $100).
Purpose and activities: Giving primarily to a Jewish organizations.
Fields of interest: Jewish agencies & temples.
Type of support: General/operating support; Research.
Limitations: Giving primarily in Brooklyn, NY.
Application information: Application form not required.
Initial approach: Proposal
Deadline(s): None
Final notification: 2 months
Officer: Zigmond Brach, Pres.
EIN: 113067698
Selected grants: The following grants were reported in 2004.
$14,800 to Congregation Vayoel Moshe, Monsey, NY. 3 grants: $5,000, $1,800, $8,000
$1,000 to Congregation Ohel Torah, Brooklyn, NY.
$500 to Beth Jacob Seminary, Brooklyn, NY.

5658
The Brand Foundation ✧ ☆
51 Lee Ave.
Brooklyn, NY   11211
Contact: Lipot Brand, Dir.

Established in 2002 in NY.
Donor: Lipot Brand.
Foundation type: Independent foundation.
Financial data (yr. ended 12/31/05): Assets, $6,214,339 (M); gifts received, $400,000; expenditures, $340,735; qualifying distributions, $339,299; giving activities include $339,299 for grants.
Fields of interest: Education; Jewish agencies & temples.
Type of support: Grants to individuals.
Limitations: Giving primarily in NY.
Application information:
Initial approach: Letter
Deadline(s): None
Directors: Lipot Brand; Rachel Brand; Raizi Klein.
EIN: 043598347
Selected grants: The following grants were reported in 2003.
$100,000 to United Talmudical Academy of Borough Park, Brooklyn, NY.
$75,180 to Kollel Shomrei Hachomos, Brooklyn, NY.
$4,175 to Congregation Yetev Lev D Jerusalem, Brooklyn, NY. For operating support.
$3,600 to Yeshiva Tzoin Yosef Pupa, Spring Valley, NY.
$1,000 to Kollel Chafets Tashbar, NY.
$1,000 to Zichron Tzvi Charitable Foundation, Brooklyn, NY.
$500 to Kollel Soro BOhel, Brooklyn, NY.
$200 to Kollel Avreichim of Brooklyn, Brooklyn, NY.

$200 to Yeshivat Makowa, Brooklyn, NY.
$180 to Congregation Khal Tzemach Tzadik Viznitz, Brooklyn, NY.

5659
Branta Foundation, Inc. ✧
c/o Perelson Weiner
1 Dag Hammarskjold Plz., 42nd Fl.
New York, NY 10017-2286

Established in 1955 in NY.
Donor: Harvey Picker.
Foundation type: Independent foundation.
Financial data (yr. ended 5/31/05): Assets, $14,076,062 (M); expenditures, $1,716,560; qualifying distributions, $1,642,323; giving activities include $1,603,000 for 3 grants (high: $1,570,000; low: $10,000).
Fields of interest: Arts; Higher education; Education.
Type of support: General/operating support.
Limitations: Applications not accepted. Giving primarily along the East Coast, with some preference for NY and the New England region. No grants to individuals.
Application information: Contributes only to pre-selected organizations.
Officers and Directors:* Harvey Picker,* Pres. and Treas.; Christine Beshar,* V.P. and Secy.
EIN: 136130955
Selected grants: The following grants were reported in 2004.
$495,000 to Picker Institute, Boston, MA. For general support.
$100,000 to Boston University, Boston, MA. For general support.
$51,000 to Westchester Community College, Valhalla, NY. For general support.
$50,000 to Henry Ford Health System, Detroit, MI. For general support.
$50,000 to On the Rise, Cambridge, MA. For general support.
$15,000 to Bay Chamber Concerts, Rockport, ME. For general support.
$5,000 to Maine Public Broadcasting Corporation, Lewiston, ME. For general support.
$5,000 to University of New England, Biddeford, ME. For general support.
$1,000 to Council on Foreign Relations, New York, NY. For general support.
$1,000 to Maine Coast Artists, Rockport, ME. For general support.

5660
Daniel L. Nir & Jill E. Braufman Family Foundation, Inc. ✧ ☆
10 Gracie Sq., Ste. 4A
New York, NY 10028

Donors: Daniel L. Nir; Jill E. Braufman; Daniel L. Nir and Jill E. Braufman Family.
Foundation type: Independent foundation.
Financial data (yr. ended 12/31/05): Assets, $1,207,043 (M); gifts received, $2,122,024; expenditures, $888,268; qualifying distributions, $888,243; giving activities include $888,243 for 114 grants (high: $115,000; low: $125).
Fields of interest: Arts; Education; Hospitals (general); Health organizations, association; Food distribution, meals on wheels; Human services;

Jewish federated giving programs; Jewish agencies & temples.
Limitations: Applications not accepted. Giving primarily in NY.
Application information: Contributes only to pre-selected organizations.
Officers: Jill E. Braufman, Pres.; Barry S. Berger, Secy.; Daniel L. Nir, Treas.
EIN: 300218951

5661
The L. Bravmann Foundation, Inc. ✧
3333-B Henry Hudson Pkwy., Apt. 6E
Riverdale, NY 10463-3241

Established in 1964 in NY.
Donors: Ludwig Bravmann; Lotte Bravmann.
Foundation type: Independent foundation.
Financial data (yr. ended 6/30/05): Assets, $21,354,576 (M); gifts received, $1,090,670; expenditures, $937,925; qualifying distributions, $894,150; giving activities include $887,400 for 36 grants (high: $832,518; low: $18).
Purpose and activities: Giving primarily for Jewish welfare and Jewish agencies.
Fields of interest: Education; Human services; Jewish federated giving programs; Jewish agencies & temples.
Type of support: Capital campaigns; Building/renovation; Emergency funds; Scholarship funds.
Limitations: Applications not accepted. Giving primarily in New York, NY. No grants to individuals.
Application information: Contributes only to pre-selected organizations.
Officers and Directors:* Ludwig Bravmann,* Pres.; Lotte Bravmann,* Secy.-Treas.; Carol Bravmann; Judith E. Kaufthal; Matthew Maryles; Jack Nash; Shimon Wolf.
EIN: 136168525
Selected grants: The following grants were reported in 2004.
$715,000 to Jewish Communal Fund of New York, New York, NY.
$50,000 to UJA-Federation of New York, New York, NY.
$1,000 to Lincoln Center for the Performing Arts, New York, NY.
$260 to Yeshiva University, New York, NY.
$210 to Young Israel of Riverdale, Bronx, NY.
$180 to American Committee for Shaare Zedek Hospital in Jerusalem, New York, NY.
$180 to Bay Terrace Jewish Center, Bayside, NY.
$180 to Wall Street Synagogue, New York, NY.
$175 to Museum of Modern Art, New York, NY.
$100 to Arthritis Foundation, Melville, NY.

5662
Deborah L. Brice Foundation ✧
c/o John A. Levin & Co., Inc.
1 Rockefeller Plz., 25th Fl.
New York, NY 10020

Donor: Deborah L. Brice.
Foundation type: Independent foundation.
Financial data (yr. ended 12/31/04): Assets, $26,556,859 (M); gifts received, $1,000,000; expenditures, $1,241,317; qualifying distributions, $1,196,220; giving activities include $1,119,375 for 21 grants (high: $500,000; low: $250).

Purpose and activities: Giving primarily for art museums and education, particularly to an all-girls college preparatory boarding and day school.
Fields of interest: Museums (art); Arts; Elementary/secondary education; Higher education; Education.
Limitations: Applications not accepted. Giving on a national basis. No grants to individuals.
Application information: Contributes only to pre-selected organizations.
Trustees: Deborah L. Brice; Taran Davies; John A. Levin; Jerome A. Manning.
EIN: 237065499

5663
Peter and Devon Briger Foundation ✧
c/o BCRS Assocs.
100 Wall St., 11th Fl.
New York, NY 10005

Established in 1997 in NY.
Donor: Peter L. Briger, Jr.
Foundation type: Independent foundation.
Financial data (yr. ended 12/31/05): Assets, $1,220,732 (M); gifts received, $1,000,000; expenditures, $1,045,870; qualifying distributions, $1,018,552; giving activities include $1,018,202 for 70 grants (high: $100,000; low: $500).
Fields of interest: Arts; Higher education; Education; Health care; Human services.
Type of support: General/operating support.
Limitations: Applications not accepted. Giving primarily in MA, NJ, and NY. No grants to individuals.
Application information: Contributes only to pre-selected organizations.
Trustees: Peter L. Briger, Jr.; Devon Elizabeth Fenton.
EIN: 133939006
Selected grants: The following grants were reported in 2004.
$100,000 to Brookings Institution, DC.
$50,000 to Acumen Fund, New York, NY.
$25,000 to Episcopal School in the City of New York, New York, NY.
$25,000 to Trinity School, New York, NY.
$25,000 to Wildlife Conservation Society, Bronx, NY.
$10,000 to American Museum of Natural History, New York, NY.
$10,000 to Childrens Museum of the East End, Bridgehampton, NY.
$10,000 to School for Strings, New York, NY.
$5,000 to Teach for America, New York, NY.
$2,000 to Common Cents New York, New York, NY.

5664
Bright Horizon Foundation ✧
c/o Kleinberg, Kaplan, Wolff & Cohen
551 5th Ave.
New York, NY 10176

Established in 2000 in DE and NY.
Donor: Louis Salkind.
Foundation type: Independent foundation.
Financial data (yr. ended 12/31/04): Assets, $20,299,002 (M); gifts received, $3,279,535; expenditures, $885,793; qualifying distributions, $873,052; giving activities include $870,000 for 8 grants (high: $250,000; low: $10,000).
Purpose and activities: Support primarily for environmental conservation.

Fields of interest: Environment, natural resources; Human services; Foundations (community); Science; Public policy, research.

Type of support: General/operating support.

Limitations: Applications not accepted. Giving to national organizations located in the metropolitan New York, NY, area, MA, CA, and GA. No grants to individuals.

Application information: Contributes only to pre-selected organizations.

Director: Louis Salkind.

EIN: 134121003

Selected grants: The following grants were reported in 2003.

$250,000 to Robin Hood Foundation, New York, NY. 2 grants: $100,000 (For general support), $150,000 (For general support).

$200,000 to Community Foundation of Santa Cruz County, Soquel, CA. For general support.

$150,000 to Union of Concerned Scientists, Cambridge, MA. 2 grants: $100,000 (For general support), $50,000 (For general support).

$20,000 to Conservation Fund, Arlington, VA. For general support.

$10,000 to Trust for Public Land, San Francisco, CA. For general support.

$5,000 to American Indian College Fund, Denver, CO. For general support.

5665

The Brine Family Charitable Trust ✧

(formerly Madeline and Kevin Brine Charitable Trust)
433 W. 14th St., 3rd Fl.
New York, NY 10012
Contact: Kevin R. Brine, Tr.

Established in 1989 in NY.

Donors: Madeline Brine; Kevin R. Brine.

Foundation type: Independent foundation.

Financial data (yr. ended 12/31/05): Assets, $9,010 (M); gifts received, $675,949; expenditures, $705,247; qualifying distributions, $703,810; giving activities include $638,000 for 20 grants (high: $170,000; low: $1,000).

Purpose and activities: Giving primarily for education as well as for the arts, including art museums, art education, and a music festival.

Fields of interest: Arts, alliance; Arts, research; Arts, formal/general education; Museums (art); Historic preservation/historical societies; Elementary/secondary education; Higher education; Libraries/library science; Human services; Children, services.

Limitations: Applications not accepted. Giving primarily in New York, NY. No grants to individuals.

Application information: Contributes only to pre-selected organizations.

Trustees: Kevin R. Brine; Madeline Brine.

EIN: 133549098

Selected grants: The following grants were reported in 2004.

$825,000 to Whitney Museum of American Art, New York, NY.

$501,000 to New York University, New York, NY.

$125,000 to New York Studio School of Drawing, Painting and Sculpture, New York, NY.

$100,000 to University of Pennsylvania, Philadelphia, PA.

$55,000 to American Academy in Rome, New York, NY.

$51,200 to World Monuments Fund, New York, NY.

$50,000 to Metropolitan Museum of Art, New York, NY.

$50,000 to New York Public Library, New York, NY.

$30,000 to American Council for Cultural Policy, New York, NY.

$25,000 to Shelter Island Historical Society, Shelter Island, NY.

5666

The Bristol-Myers Squibb Foundation, Inc. ▼ ✧

(formerly The Bristol-Myers Fund, Inc.)
c/o Fdn. Coord.
345 Park Ave., 43rd Fl.
New York, NY 10154
E-mail for Distinguished Achievement Awards: daa_admin@bms.com; URL: http://www.bms.com/aboutbms/founda/data

Incorporated in 1982 in FL as successor to a foundation established in 1953.

Donor: Bristol-Myers Squibb Co.

Foundation type: Company-sponsored foundation.

Financial data (yr. ended 12/31/05): Assets, $24,312,468 (M); gifts received, $14,000,000; expenditures, $23,022,545; qualifying distributions, $23,009,097; giving activities include $23,009,097 for grants.

Purpose and activities: The foundation supports organizations involved with education, health, medical research, community development, civic affairs, minorities, and women and awards grants to scientists conducting medical research.

Fields of interest: Elementary/secondary education; Higher education; Education; Health care; Cancer research; Heart & circulatory research; Neuroscience research; Medical research; Children/youth, services; Human services; Community development; Public affairs; Minorities; African Americans/Blacks; Hispanics/Latinos; Native Americans/American Indians; Women.

International interests: Africa.

Type of support: General/operating support; Management development/capacity building; Program development; Curriculum development; Research; Employee volunteer services; Program evaluation; Employee matching gifts; Employee-related scholarships; Grants to individuals; In-kind gifts.

Limitations: Giving on a national and international basis, including in Africa, with emphasis on Wallingford, CT, Evansville, IN, New Brunswick, Princeton, and Skillman, NJ, and Buffalo and Syracuse, NY. No support for political, fraternal, social, or veterans' organizations, religious or sectarian organizations not of direct benefit to the entire community, or federated campaign-supported organizations. No grants to individuals (except for Distinguished Achievement Awards and employee-related scholarships), or for endowments, conferences, sponsorships or independent medical research, or specific public broadcasting or films; no loans.

Publications: Corporate giving report.

Application information: Unsolicited requests for Biomedical Research Grants are not accepted.

Initial approach: Proposal; complete online nomination form for Distinguished Achievement Awards

Deadline(s): Oct. 1; preferred between Feb. and Sept.; Oct. 31 for Distinguished Achievement Awards for cancer, Dec. 5 for cardiovascular, Feb. 27 for metabolic diseases, Jan. 13 for nutrition, Mar. 13 for neuroscience, and Apr. 13 for infectious diseases

Board meeting date(s): Dec. and as needed

Final notification: 2 to 3 months

Officers and Directors:* Peter R. Dolan, Chair.; John L. Damonti,* Pres.; Sandra Leung, Secy.; Steve Bear; John McGoldrick; Laurie Smaldone; Richard Thompson; Robert Zito.

Number of staff: 6 full-time professional; 4 full-time support.

EIN: 133127947

Selected grants: The following grants were reported in 2004.

$2,750,000 to United Way of Tri-State, New York, NY.

$2,000,000 to Baylor College of Medicine, Houston, TX. For South Africa Secure the Future, program providing care and support for women and children with HIV/AIDS in Western Africa.

$1,000,000 to American Red Cross, National Headquarters, DC. For tsunami disaster relief.

$428,609 to National Merit Scholarship Corporation, Evanston, IL.

$202,327 to Guangxi Center for Disease Prevention and Control, Nanning, China. .

$100,000 to Flanders Interuniversity Institute for Biotechnology, Ghent, Belgium. For Cardiovascular Research Program.

$58,400 to Irvington Institute for Immunological Research, New York, NY.

$51,000 to Life Sciences Research Foundation, Baltimore, MD. Grant made through Secure the Future program.

$48,975 to Botswana Christian AIDS Intervention Programme, Gaborone, Botswana. For grant made through Secure the Future, program providing care and support for women and children with HIV/AIDS in Western Africa.

$25,000 to Columbia University, Graduate School of Business, New York, NY.

5667

Muriel and Bert Brodsky Family Foundation ✧

(formerly Port Charitable Foundation)
26 Harbor Park Dr.
Port Washington, NY 11050 (516) 484-4400
Contact: Bert Brodsky

Established in 1997 in NY.

Donors: Bert Brodsky; National Health Mgmt. Svcs.; Lee Brodsky; David Brodsky.

Foundation type: Independent foundation.

Financial data (yr. ended 12/31/05): Assets, $742,621 (M); gifts received, $1,101,022; expenditures, $555,316; qualifying distributions, $554,897; giving activities include $554,476 for 85 grants (high: $236,300; low: $25).

Purpose and activities: Giving primarily for Jewish organizations.

Fields of interest: Education; Health organizations, association; Human services; Jewish federated giving programs; Jewish agencies & temples.

Limitations: Giving primarily in NY.

Application information:

Initial approach: Letter

Deadline(s): None

Officers: Jessica Miller, Pres.; David Brodsky, V.P.; Jeffrey Brodsky, Secy.

EIN: 113298376

Selected grants: The following grants were reported in 2003.

$175,000 to Crohns and Colitis Foundation of America, New York, NY. For general support.

$2,080 to Jewish Center of the Hamptons, East Hampton, NY. For general support.

$2,000 to Lauri Strauss Leukemia Foundation, New York, NY. For general support.

$975 to American Jewish Committee, New York, NY. For general support.

$750 to Institute for Student Achievement, Lake Success, NY. For general support.

$500 to Morrys Camp, White Plains, NY. For general support.

$318 to Jewish Museum, New York, NY. For general support.

$300 to Outreach Project, Richmond Hill, NY. For general support.

$250 to North Shore Child and Family Guidance Center, Roslyn Heights, NY. For general support.

$100 to City College Fund, New York, NY. For general support.

5668

The Brodsky Family Foundation ◇
400 W. 59th St.
New York, NY 10019 (212) 315-5555

Established in 1984 in NY.
Donor: Nathan Brodsky†.
Foundation type: Independent foundation.
Financial data (yr. ended 12/31/04): Assets, $3,100,062 (M); gifts received, $600,000; expenditures, $340,736; qualifying distributions, $339,033; giving activities include $339,033 for 47 grants (high: $40,000; low: $200).
Purpose and activities: Giving primarily for medical research; some funding also for the arts and education.
Fields of interest: Arts; Health care; Health organizations; Medical research, institute.
Type of support: General/operating support; Seed money.
Limitations: Giving primarily in NY.
Application information: Application form not required.
  Initial approach: Letter or proposal
  Copies of proposal: 3
  Deadline(s): Varies
Trustees: Hady Amro; Daniel Brodsky; Katherine Brodsky; Shirley Brodsky.
EIN: 133236064
Selected grants: The following grants were reported in 2004.
$40,000 to Lenox Hill Hospital, New York, NY.
$33,333 to Philharmonic-Symphony Society of New York, New York, NY.
$15,000 to Macula Foundation, New York, NY.
$12,000 to Carnegie Hall Society, New York, NY.
$10,000 to Alzheimers Disease and Related Disorders, Nacogdoches, TX.
$10,000 to Central Park Conservancy, New York, NY.
$10,000 to El Museo del Barrio, New York, NY.
$10,000 to Princeton University, Princeton, NJ.
$6,000 to Center for American Progress, DC.
$4,000 to Recording for the Blind and Dyslexic, Princeton, NJ.

5669

Daniel J. and Estrellita Brodsky Foundation ◇
400 W. 59th St., 3rd Fl.
New York, NY 10019-1105 (212) 315-5555
Contact: Daniel Brodsky, Tr.

Established in 1999 in NY.
Donor: Daniel Brodsky.
Foundation type: Independent foundation.
Financial data (yr. ended 12/31/05): Assets, $1,820,062 (M); gifts received, $1,000,000; expenditures, $746,704; qualifying distributions, $746,704; giving activities include $746,317 for 60 grants (high: $200,000; low: $400).
Purpose and activities: Giving primarily for arts and culture, particularly to museums and Hispanic cultural organizations; funding also for education, health associations, and social services.
Fields of interest: Museums; Museums (art); Museums (ethnic/folk arts); Arts; Elementary/secondary education; Higher education; Health organizations, association; Human services; Jewish agencies & temples.
Limitations: Giving primarily in New York, NY.
Application information:
  Initial approach: Letter
  Deadline(s): Nov. 15
Trustees: Daniel Brodsky; Estrellita Brodsky.
EIN: 134065150

5670

Brokaw Family Foundation ◇
c/o Starr & Co.
850 3rd Ave.
New York, NY 10022

Established in 1990 in NY.
Donors: Thomas J. Brokaw; Fast Track Productions, Inc.
Foundation type: Independent foundation.
Financial data (yr. ended 12/31/05): Assets, $50,042 (M); gifts received, $685,000; expenditures, $692,733; qualifying distributions, $692,050; giving activities include $692,000 for 68 grants (high: $50,000; low: $250).
Purpose and activities: Giving primarily for environmental conservation as well as for wildlife; funding also for health associations, and for health and human services.
Fields of interest: Museums (natural history); Arts; Education; Environment, natural resources; Cancer research; Human services.
Limitations: Applications not accepted. Giving on a national basis, with emphasis on NY and SD. No grants to individuals.
Application information: Contributes only to pre-selected organizations.
Trustee: Thomas J. Brokaw.
EIN: 133594435
Selected grants: The following grants were reported in 2004.
$125,000 to Committee to Protect Journalists, New York, NY. 3 grants: $60,000, $40,000, $25,000
$75,000 to American Museum of Natural History, New York, NY. 3 grants: $25,000 each
$55,000 to Conservation International, DC. 2 grants: $30,000, $25,000
$25,000 to Robin Hood Foundation, New York, NY.
$5,000 to City Lights Youth Theater, New York, NY.

5671

The Andrea and Charles Bronfman Foundation, Inc. ◇
110 E. 59th St., 26th Fl.
New York, NY 10022

Established in 1998 in DE and NY.

Donors: Charles R. Bronfman; Stepworth Holdings, Inc.
Foundation type: Independent foundation.
Financial data (yr. ended 12/31/04): Assets, $44,176 (M); expenditures, $2,030,132; qualifying distributions, $2,030,132; giving activities include $2,025,000 for 1 grant.
Fields of interest: Education; Human services; Religion.
Limitations: Applications not accepted. Giving on a national basis. No grants to individuals.
Application information: Contributes only to pre-selected organizations.
Officers and Directors:* Charles R. Bronfman,* Chair. and V.P.; Jeffrey Solomon,* Pres.; Geri Craig, Secy.; Andrew Parsons, Treas.
EIN: 133999708

5672

The Samuel Bronfman Foundation ◇
(formerly The Edgar M. Bronfman Family Foundation, Inc.)
c/o Reminick, Aaron, & Co., LLP
1430 Broadway
New York, NY 10018

Re-established in 2005 in DE; originally established in 1995 in NY.
Donor: Edgar M. Bronfman.
Foundation type: Independent foundation.
Financial data (yr. ended 12/31/05): Assets, $225,099 (M); gifts received, $1,906,726; expenditures, $1,718,939; qualifying distributions, $1,637,697; giving activities include $1,177,334 for 15 grants (high: $344,334; low: $1,000; average: $4,000–$150,000).
Purpose and activities: Giving primarily for education and to Jewish organizations.
Fields of interest: Elementary/secondary education; Higher education; Jewish federated giving programs; Jewish agencies & temples.
Type of support: General/operating support.
Limitations: Applications not accepted. Giving primarily in North America. No grants to individuals.
Application information: Contributes only to pre-selected organizations.
Officers and Directors:* Edgar M. Bronfman,* Pres.; Adam R. Bronfman,* Managing Dir.; Clare W. Bronfman; Edgar M. Bronfman, Jr.; Matthew Bronfman; Samuel Bronfman II; Sara R. Bronfman; Holly Bronfman Lev.
EIN: 141918185
Selected grants: The following grants were reported in 2003.
$1,500,000 to Bronfman Youth Fellowships in Israel, Delmar, NY. For general support.
$1,250,000 to World Jewish Congress American Section, New York, NY. For general support.
$1,020,214 to Hebrew College, Newton Centre, MA. For general support.
$581,765 to Hillel: The Foundation for Jewish Campus Life, DC. For general support.
$500,000 to American Friends of Shalom Hartman Institute, New York, NY. For general support.
$312,500 to Synagogue Transformation and Renewal (STAR), Chicago, IL. For general support for work in Minneapolis, MN.
$300,000 to Partnership for Excellence in Jewish Education, Boston, MA. For general support.
$250,000 to Bnai Brith Youth Organization, DC. For general support.
$250,000 to Foundation for the Defense of Democracies, DC. For general support.

$230,000 to New York University, New York, NY. For general support.

5673
The Andrea and Charles Bronfman Philanthropies, Inc. ◇
110 E. 59th St., 26th Fl.
New York, NY 10022 (212) 931-0100

Established in 1998 in DE and NY.
Donors: Charles R. Bronfman; Andrea M. Bronfman†.
Foundation type: Independent foundation.
Financial data (yr. ended 12/31/04): Assets, $19,262,411 (M); gifts received, $23,397,790; expenditures, $11,442,373; qualifying distributions, $11,063,363; giving activities include $4,859,823 for 31+ grants (high: $3,170,000), and $9,732,181 for foundation-administered programs.
Purpose and activities: The foundation's mission is to encourage young people to strengthen their knowledge and appreciation of their history, heritage and cultural identity. The foundation has four program areas: 1) Jewish Peoplehood- a range of initiatives from travel to exchange programs designed to support the shared Jewish identity; 2) Project Involvement- an educational reform program in Israel; 3) Education for the Environment- support to research a variety of community initiatives to raise Israelis' knowledge of environmental issues; 4) Education for Co-operation and Co-existence- encourages greater knowledge and understanding between Israelis and Palestinians.
Fields of interest: Education; Human services; Jewish agencies & temples.
International interests: Israel.
Type of support: General/operating support; Program development; Conferences/seminars; Seed money; Curriculum development; Research; Technical assistance; Consulting services; Employee matching gifts.
Limitations: Applications not accepted. Giving in the U.S. and Israel. No grants to individuals.
Application information: Contributes only to pre-selected organizations.
Officers and Directors:* Charles R. Bronfman,* Chair. and V.P.; Jeffrey Solomon,* Pres.; Karen Adler, Sr. V.P., Admin.; Janet Aviad, Sr. V.P., Israel Prog.; Roger Bennett, V.P., Strategic Initiatives; Simon Klarfeld, V.P.; Johanne McDonald, Secy.; Ehud Afek, C.F.O.; Andrew Parsons, Treas.
Number of staff: 50
EIN: 133984936
Selected grants: The following grants were reported in 2004.
$50,000 to Foundation for Jewish Camping, New York, NY.
$43,334 to Birthright Israel Foundation, New York, NY. 2 grants: $18,334, $25,000
$25,000 to Hillel: The Foundation for Jewish Campus Life, DC.
$25,000 to New Foundation for Excellence in the Arts, Ramat Efal, Israel. .
$15,000 to Friends of the Israel Defense Forces, New York, NY.
$13,000 to San Francisco Jewish Film Festival, San Francisco, CA.
$7,000 to National Foundation for Jewish Culture, New York, NY.
$3,000 to Tawonga Jewish Community Corporation, San Francisco, CA.

5674
Gladys Brooks Foundation ◇
630 W. 168th St.
New York, NY 10032
Contact: Jessica L. Rutledge
Mailing address: 1055 Franklin Ave., Ste. 102, Garden City, NY 11530, tel.: (516) 746-6103;
URL: http://www.gladysbrooksfoundation.org

Established in 1981 in NY.
Donor: Gladys Brooks Thayer†.
Foundation type: Independent foundation.
Financial data (yr. ended 12/31/05): Assets, $36,175,371 (M); expenditures, $2,007,578; qualifying distributions, $1,771,218; giving activities include $1,592,230 for 23 grants (high: $350,000; low: $200).
Purpose and activities: The foundation's primary purpose is to provide for the intellectual, moral, and physical welfare of the people of this country by establishing and supporting nonprofit libraries, educational institutions, hospitals, and clinics.
Fields of interest: Higher education; Libraries/library science; Hospitals (general); Health care.
Type of support: Building/renovation; Equipment; Endowments; Scholarship funds.
Limitations: Giving limited to CT, Washington, DC, DE, IN, MA, MD, ME, NH, NJ, NY, OH, PA, RI, TN, VA, VT, and WV. No grants to individuals, or for research.
Publications: Application guidelines; Annual report; Annual report (including application guidelines); Grants list; Program policy statement.
Application information: Application form available on Web site. Application form required.
    Initial approach: Letter, (Electronic submissions are not accepted)
    Copies of proposal: 2
    Deadline(s): June 1
    Board meeting date(s): Monthly
    Final notification: Dec.
Officers and Governors:* James J. Daly,* Chair.; Thomas Q. Morris, M.D.*, Secy.; Christopher R. Hawkins; U.S. Trust.
Number of staff: 1 full-time professional.
EIN: 132955337
Selected grants: The following grants were reported in 2004.
$150,000 to Winthrop-University Hospital, Mineola, NY.
$100,000 to American University of Beirut, New York, NY.
$100,000 to Columbia University, New York, NY.
$100,000 to Friends of Weeks Memorial Library, Lancaster, NH.
$100,000 to Helen Keller Services for the Blind, Brooklyn, NY.
$100,000 to Indian River Hospital Foundation, Vero Beach, FL.
$100,000 to Manhattan Institute for Cancer Research, New York, NY.
$100,000 to New York-Presbyterian Hospital, New York, NY.
$100,000 to Pennsylvania Hospital of the University of Pennsylvania Health System, Philadelphia, PA.
$100,000 to Saint Ignatius Academy, Bronx, NY.
$100,000 to University of Notre Dame, Notre Dame, IN.
$100,000 to Vermont Law School, South Royalton, VT.
$92,750 to Mount Washington Observatory, Gorham, NH.
$50,000 to Currier Museum of Art, Manchester, NH.

5675
William Gundry Broughton Charitable Private Foundation, Inc.
133 Saratoga Rd., Ste. 6
Glenville, NY 12302-4162
Contact: Shirley M. Vogt, Pres.

Established in 1995 in NY.
Donor: William Broughton Charitable Remainder Unitrust.
Foundation type: Independent foundation.
Financial data (yr. ended 12/31/05): Assets, $9,445,151 (M); expenditures, $476,934; qualifying distributions, $417,281; giving activities include $405,110 for 34 grants (high: $25,000; low: $1,000).
Fields of interest: Education; Youth development; Human services.
Limitations: Giving primarily in Schenectady County, NY. No support for non 501(c)(3) organizations. No grants to individuals.
Publications: Application guidelines.
Application information: Application form not required.
    Initial approach: Proposal
    Copies of proposal: 1
    Deadline(s): None
    Board meeting date(s): 5 times per year
    Final notification: After review by trustees
Officers and Trustees:* Shirley M. Vogt,* Pres.; Ronald L. Lagasse,* V.P.; Grace E. Golden,* Secy.; Phyllis Mrozkowski,* Treas.
EIN: 223122633

5676
The Robin Brown and Charles Seelig Family Foundation ◇ ☆
c/o BCRS Assocs., LLC
100 Wall St., 11th Fl.
New York, NY 10005

Established in 1993 in NY.
Donor: Charles B. Seelig, Jr.
Foundation type: Independent foundation.
Financial data (yr. ended 5/31/06): Assets, $548,316 (M); gifts received, $25,000; expenditures, $510,450; qualifying distributions, $504,500; giving activities include $504,500 for grants.
Fields of interest: Arts; Higher education; Health organizations, association; Multiple sclerosis; AIDS; Athletics/sports, soccer; Human services.
Type of support: General/operating support.
Limitations: Applications not accepted. Giving primarily in NY. No grants to individuals.
Application information: Contributes only to pre-selected organizations.
Trustees: Robin D. Brown; Charles B. Seelig, Jr.
EIN: 133748044
Selected grants: The following grants were reported in 2004.
$76,000 to National Architectural Trust, DC. For general support.
$61,000 to Roundabout Theater Company, New York, NY. 2 grants: $48,500 (For general support), $12,500 (For general support).
$50,000 to America SCORES, New York, NY. For general support.
$48,000 to Prep for Prep, New York, NY. For general support.

$32,000 to Endeavor Global, New York, NY. 2 grants: $25,000 (For general support), $7,000 (For general support).

$25,000 to Ethical Culture Fieldston Schools, New York, NY. For general support.

$25,000 to Public Theater, New York, NY. For general support.

$10,000 to LAByrinth, Inc., LAByrinth Theater Company, New York, NY. For general support.

5677
The Brownington Foundation ✧
c/o Morris & McVeigh LLP
767 3rd Ave.
New York, NY 10017

Established about 1970 in NY.
Donor: Mary J. Tweedy†.
Foundation type: Independent foundation.
Financial data (yr. ended 12/31/04): Assets, $17,460,238 (M); expenditures, $1,229,532; qualifying distributions, $1,160,318; giving activities include $1,141,750 for 159 grants (high: $75,000; low: $1,000; average: $1,000–$25,000).
Purpose and activities: Giving primarily for secondary and higher education; support also for civic and general charitable organizations, conservation and cultural organizations.
Fields of interest: Arts; Secondary school/education; Higher education; Health organizations, association.
Limitations: Applications not accepted. Giving primarily in NY. No grants to individuals.
Application information: Contributes only to pre-selected organizations.
Officers: Ann T. Savage, Pres.; Margot T. Egan, V.P.; Leonard B. Boehner, Secy.; Clare T. McMorris, Treas.
EIN: 237043230
Selected grants: The following grants were reported in 2004.
$50,000 to Asia Society, New York, NY.
$50,000 to Middlebury College, Middlebury, VT.
$10,000 to Brearley School, New York, NY.
$10,000 to China Institute in America, New York, NY.
$10,000 to Metropolitan Museum of Art, New York, NY.
$10,000 to Recording for the Blind and Dyslexic, Princeton, NJ.
$10,000 to Sierra Club, San Francisco, CA.
$5,000 to Shakespeare and Company, Lenox, MA.
$3,000 to Friends of the Earth, DC.
$2,500 to Childrens Aid Society.

5678
The Brunckhorst Foundation ✧
24 Rock St.
Brooklyn, NY 11206-3886

Established in 1968.
Donor: Barbara Brunckhorst.
Foundation type: Independent foundation.
Financial data (yr. ended 12/31/05): Assets, $39,198,893 (M); gifts received, $7,500,000; expenditures, $1,441,238; qualifying distributions, $1,370,848; giving activities include $1,370,000 for 15 grants (high: $300,000; low: $25,000).
Purpose and activities: Giving primarily for environmental conservation.

Fields of interest: Education; Environment, natural resources; Animal welfare; Animals/wildlife, preservation/protection.
Limitations: Applications not accepted. Giving primarily in NY. No grants to individuals.
Application information: Contributes only to pre-selected organizations.
Trustees: Barbara Brunckhorst; Frank Brunckhorst III; Richard Todd Stravitz.
EIN: 237000850
Selected grants: The following grants were reported in 2003.
$200,000 to Sierra Club Foundation, San Francisco, CA. For general support.
$160,000 to Conservation Fund, Arlington, VA. For general support.
$150,000 to Chesapeake Bay Foundation, Richmond, VA. For general support.
$150,000 to Southern Environmental Law Center, Charlottesville, VA. For general support.
$100,000 to Environmental Defense, New York, NY. For general support.
$75,000 to World Wildlife Fund, DC. For general support.
$50,000 to Nature Conservancy, Arlington, VA. For general support.
$50,000 to Riverside School, Richmond, VA. For general support.
$30,000 to Humane Society of Sarasota, Sarasota, FL. For general support.
$30,000 to Planned Parenthood Federation of America, New York, NY. For general support.

5679
Jean I. & Charles H. Brunie Foundation ✧
21 Elm Rock Rd.
Bronxville, NY 10708

Established in 1986 in NY.
Donors: Charles H. Brunie; Jean I. Brunie.
Foundation type: Independent foundation.
Financial data (yr. ended 6/30/05): Assets, $386,883 (M); gifts received, $605,975; expenditures, $328,432; qualifying distributions, $319,242; giving activities include $317,250 for 25 grants (high: $100,000; low: $250).
Purpose and activities: Support for education, health associations, human services, and federated giving programs.
Fields of interest: Education; Health organizations, association; Human services; Children, services; Federated giving programs; Public policy, research.
Limitations: Applications not accepted. Giving on a national basis. No grants to individuals.
Application information: Contributes only to pre-selected organizations.
Trustees: Charles H. Brunie; Jean I. Brunie.
EIN: 133384777
Selected grants: The following grants were reported in 2005.
$50,000 to Amherst College, Amherst, MA.
$30,000 to National Center for Policy Analysis, Dallas, TX.
$25,000 to Cato Institute, DC.
$10,000 to American Council on Science and Health, New York, NY.
$10,000 to Competitive Enterprise Institute, DC.
$10,000 to Fabretto Childrens Foundation, Evanston, IL. 2 grants: $5,000 each
$10,000 to Hudson Institute, Indianapolis, IN.
$5,000 to CERGE-EI Foundation, Teaneck, NJ.
$2,000 to Mont Pelerin Society, Alexandria, VA.

5680
The 1994 Sheila Johnson Brutsch Charitable Trust ✧
c/o The Johnson Co., Inc.
630 5th Ave., Ste. 1510
New York, NY 10111

Established in 1994 in NY.
Donor: Betty W. Johnson.
Foundation type: Independent foundation.
Financial data (yr. ended 12/31/05): Assets, $5,128,607 (M); expenditures, $385,314; qualifying distributions, $377,850; giving activities include $377,600 for 8 grants (high: $102,600; low: $10,000).
Fields of interest: Media/communications; Higher education; Environment, natural resources; Animals/wildlife, preservation/protection; International relief.
Limitations: Applications not accepted. Giving primarily in FL. No grants to individuals.
Application information: Contributes only to pre-selected organizations.
Trustees: Sheila Johnson Brutsch; Betty W. Johnson.
EIN: 137046312
Selected grants: The following grants were reported in 2003.
$75,000 to World Wildlife Fund, New York, NY. For unrestricted support.
$56,200 to Direct Relief International, Santa Barbara, CA. 2 grants: $30,000 (To provide medical supplies in Bulgaria), $26,200 (For scholarships).
$50,000 to Alliance for Lupus Research, New York, NY. For unrestricted support.
$25,000 to Harbor Branch Oceanographic Institution, Fort Pierce, FL.
$25,000 to Planned Parenthood Association of the Mercer Area, Trenton, NJ. For unrestricted support.
$20,000 to Historic Morven, Princeton, NJ. For unrestricted support.
$15,000 to Sarah Lawrence College, Bronxville, NY. For unrestricted support.
$10,000 to Educational Broadcasting Corporation, New York, NY. For unrestricted support.

5681
The Josef Buchmann Charitable Foundation ✧
c/o Meltzer, Lippe, Goldstein & Schlissel LLP
190 Willis Ave.
Mineola, NY 11501

Established in 2001 in NY.
Donors: Lodz Properties, L.P.; JB 680 5th Avenue Associates LP.
Foundation type: Company-sponsored foundation.
Financial data (yr. ended 12/31/04): Assets, $1,511,088 (M); gifts received, $100,000; expenditures, $577,548; qualifying distributions, $560,000; giving activities include $560,000 for 4 grants (high: $200,000; low: $10,000).
Purpose and activities: The foundation supports orchestras, Jewish agencies and temples, and organizations involved with higher education.
Fields of interest: Performing arts, orchestra (symphony); Higher education; Jewish agencies & temples.
International interests: Germany.

Limitations: Applications not accepted. Giving primarily in New York, NY; some giving in Germany.
Application information: Contributes only to pre-selected organizations.
Trustees: Stephan M. Breitstone; Josef Buchmann; Ted Haft.
EIN: 116569821

5682
The Peter and Carmen Lucia Buck Foundation ☆

177 E. 87th St., St. 306
New York, NY 10128
Contact: Francesca Burack
E-mail: manager@PCLBFoundation.org

Established in 1999 in CT.
Foundation type: Independent foundation.
Financial data (yr. ended 6/30/05): Assets, $31,096,256 (M); gifts received, $20,000,000; expenditures, $378,514; qualifying distributions, $373,483; giving activities include $337,569 for 29 grants (high: $45,264; low: $1,973).
Purpose and activities: The foundation considers a wide range of proposals within the following areas: summer program for city youths, land conservation/sprawl prevention, and health care.
Fields of interest: Environment, land resources; Health care, volunteer services; Boy scouts; Girl scouts; Salvation Army.
Type of support: General/operating support; Land acquisition; Program development.
Limitations: Giving primarily in CT and NY. No grants to individuals, or for annual campaigns, endowments, other private foundations, dinners, balls or other ticketed events.
Publications: Application guidelines.
Application information: Application form required.
  Initial approach: Letter
  Copies of proposal: 3
  Deadline(s): Feb. 28
  Board meeting date(s): May
  Final notification: Late May
Officers: Vera Lourenco, Chair.; Christopher Buck, Pres. and Treas.; Michael Buck, Secy.
Number of staff: 2 part-time professional; 1 part-time support.
EIN: 061547852
Selected grants: The following grants were reported in 2005.
$45,264 to Nature Conservancy, New York, NY.
$25,000 to Boy Scouts of America, Portland, ME.
$25,000 to Salvation Army of Greater New York, New York, NY.
$25,000 to Scenic Hudson, Poughkeepsie, NY.
$20,000 to SEE International, Santa Barbara, CA.
$20,000 to Smile Train, New York, NY.
$15,000 to Yale University, New Haven, CT.
$10,000 to Boy Scouts of America, New York, NY.
$10,000 to Boy Scouts of America, Milford, CT.
$10,000 to Boy Scouts of America, East Hartford, CT.

5683
Henrietta B. & Frederick H. Bugher Foundation ◇

(also known as Bugher Foundation)
c/o The Daniel Adams Co.
P.O. Box 555
Barneveld, NY 13304
Contact: Daniel N. Adams, Tr.

E-mail: dan@bugher.org

Established in 1961 in DC.
Donor: Frederick McLean Bugher†.
Foundation type: Independent foundation.
Financial data (yr. ended 8/31/05): Assets, $35,024,895 (M); expenditures, $1,882,475; qualifying distributions, $1,414,099; giving activities include $1,274,800 for 3 grants (high: $1,200,000; low: $10,000).
Purpose and activities: Giving is focused on cardiovascular research and treatment. Within these areas, the foundation seeks to fund seminal projects- those judged to be both important and unique which otherwise might have difficulty finding initial funding. The foundation works at the leading edge of this research, funding innovative projects under the highest quality investigators and institutions.
Fields of interest: Heart & circulatory research.
Type of support: Research.
Limitations: Giving on a worldwide basis. No grants to individuals, or for general funding, equipment, facilities, or indirect expenses over 10 percent.
Application information: Full applications by invitation only. Applications should follow the format of the application used by the National Institute of Health. Application form not required.
  Initial approach: E-mail only
  Deadline(s): None
  Board meeting date(s): Quarterly
Trustees: Camilla Adams; D. Nelson Adams; Daniel N. Adams, Jr.; Robert A. Robinson; Gayllis Ward.
EIN: 526034266
Selected grants: The following grants were reported in 2003.
$1,406,250 to American Heart Association, Dallas, TX. 2 grants: $1,206,250 (For cardiovascular research), $200,000 (For cardiovascular research).
$163,015 to Tsinghua University, Beijing, China. For cardiovascular research.

5684
The Buhl Foundation, Inc. ◇

(formerly The Buhl Family Foundation, Inc.)
c/o Fulvio & Associates, LLP
60 E. 42nd St., Ste. 1313
New York, NY 10165-0006

Established in 1989 in FL.
Donors: Henry M. Buhl; Bruce M. Kaplan.
Foundation type: Independent foundation.
Financial data (yr. ended 9/30/05): Assets, $8,423,186 (M); gifts received, $487,846; expenditures, $973,245; qualifying distributions, $936,169; giving activities include $655,952 for 58 grants (high: $25,000; low: $250).
Purpose and activities: Giving primarily for human services, arts and culture, and youth services.
Fields of interest: Arts; Human services; Children/youth, services; Homeless.
Type of support: General/operating support; Continuing support; Annual campaigns; Capital campaigns; Publication.
Limitations: Applications not accepted. Giving primarily in NJ and NY. No grants to individuals.
Application information: Contributes only to pre-selected organizations.
  Board meeting date(s): 3 times a year
Officers: Henry M. Buhl, Pres.; Raymond W. Merritt, V.P.; Kenneth Klein, Treas.

Number of staff: 1 full-time professional.
EIN: 136937849

5685
Bukkyo Dendo Kyokai America, Inc. ◇

(formerly Buddha Dharma Kyokai (Society), Inc.)
c/o K. William Kolbe, Thelen, Reid, & Priest
875 3rd Ave.
New York, NY 10022-6225

Established in 1997 in NJ.
Foundation type: Independent foundation.
Financial data (yr. ended 12/31/04): Assets, $10,879,165 (L); gifts received, $65,971; expenditures, $1,574,726; qualifying distributions, $1,513,518; giving activities include $1,047,694 for 14 grants (high: $530,283; low: $200).
Purpose and activities: Giving primarily for Buddhist studies.
Fields of interest: Education; Buddhism.
Limitations: Applications not accepted. Giving primarily in CA. No grants to individuals.
Application information: Contributes only to pre-selected organizations. Unsolicited requests for funds not accepted.
Officers: Rev. Masahiro Takahaski, Pres.; K. William Kolbe, Secy.; Rev. Brian Kensho Nagata, Treas.
Trustees: Rev. Takamaro Shigaragi; Norio Takatsuji; Bishop Hirofumi Watanabe.
EIN: 222706437

5686
The Burch Foundation ☆

(also known as The Burch Family Foundation)
c/o Robert L. Burch, III
1 Rockefeller Plz.
New York, NY 10020

Established in 2000 in NY.
Donors: Robert L. Burch III; Jonathan Manufacture Corp.
Foundation type: Independent foundation.
Financial data (yr. ended 12/31/05): Assets, $17,918,054 (M); gifts received, $4,188,740; expenditures, $503,292; qualifying distributions, $440,810; giving activities include $439,060 for 24 grants (high: $100,000; low: $500).
Fields of interest: Education; Eye diseases; Eye research; Christian agencies & churches.
Type of support: Research.
Limitations: Applications not accepted. Giving primarily in MD and NY. No grants to individuals.
Application information: Contributes only to pre-selected organizations.
  Board meeting date(s): Jan. 1
Directors: Catherine C. Burch; Dale J. Burch; Robert L. Burch III; Robert L. Burch IV.
Number of staff: None.
EIN: 134144134
Selected grants: The following grants were reported in 2004.
$250,000 to Columbia University, New York, NY.
$25,000 to Foundation Fighting Blindness, Owings Mills, MD.
$25,000 to Lighthouse International, New York, NY.
$15,000 to Cate School, Carpinteria, CA.
$6,750 to University of Southern California, Los Angeles, CA.
$6,000 to Salvation Army of Greater New York, New York, NY.

$500 to American Heart Association, Watertown, NY.

$500 to University School of Milwaukee, Milwaukee, WI.

5687
Florence V. Burden Foundation ✧
c/o Marjorie Lipkin
10 E. 53rd St., 32nd Fl.
New York, NY 10022 (212) 872-1122
William Gould tel.:(212) 872-1150

Incorporated in 1967 in NY.
Donors: Florence V. Burden†; and members of her family.
Foundation type: Independent foundation.
Financial data (yr. ended 12/31/04): Assets, $14,393,878 (M); expenditures, $975,800; qualifying distributions, $760,834; giving activities include $609,800 for 92 grants (high: $37,000; low: $300).
Purpose and activities: The foundation focuses on three fields: Aging, Children and Youth, and Criminal Justice. Aging programs seek to support aging programs in general, family caregivers, both those caring for frail elders, as well as elders caring for grandchildren, and to benefit elders and children, families and communities through intergenerational programs. Children and youth programs seek to assist children living in poverty, to intervene early in children's lives, to build their self-esteem and socialization skills, and to prevent abuse and violence against children, including both physical and sexual abuse. The criminal justice programs seek to address the needs of children, families and elderly whose lives may be affected by encounters with the criminal justice system.
Fields of interest: Education; Crime/violence prevention, abuse prevention; Crime/violence prevention, child abuse; Children/youth, services; Family services; Aging; Economically disadvantaged.
Type of support: Program development; Publication; Seed money; Curriculum development; Research; Technical assistance.
Limitations: Applications not accepted. Giving primarily in New England, Washington, DC, NJ, NY, and PA. No grants to individuals, or for capital or endowment funds, operating expenses, annual campaigns, emergency funds, deficit financing, scholarships, fellowships, or matching gifts; no loans.
Application information: Unsolicited requests for funds not accepted.
Board meeting date(s): Biannually
Officers and Directors:* Edward P.H. Burden,* Co-Chair.; Margaret Burden Childs,* Co-Chair.; Ordway P. Burden,* V.P.; Susan L. Burden,* Secy.-Treas.; Marjorie Lipkin, Exec. Dir.; Charmaine S. Burden; Jean E.P. Burden; Wendy L. Burden; Beatrice I. Childs; Jean A.R. Childs; Flobelle Burden Davis.
Number of staff: 1 part-time professional.
EIN: 136224125
Selected grants: The following grants were reported in 2004.
$37,000 to Girls Inc. of New Hampshire, Manchester, NH. For Southern Maine Expansion.
$35,000 to Village Academies Network, New York, NY. For Principal Mentoring Program.
$30,000 to radKIDS, South Dennis, MA. For Train the Trainer Project.
$25,000 to America SCORES, Urban Teachers Training Corps, New York, NY.

$24,400 to Lionheart Foundation, Boston, MA. For production of two Power Source videos.
$18,000 to Westchester Mediation Center, NY. For Truancy Mediation Program.

5688
Helen Keeler Burke Charitable Foundation ✧ ☆
c/o Brown Brothers Harriman Trust Co., LLC
140 Broadway, 4th Fl.
New York, NY 10005

Established in IL.
Foundation type: Independent foundation.
Financial data (yr. ended 12/31/05): Assets, $1,615,470 (M); expenditures, $505,935; qualifying distributions, $488,928; giving activities include $480,000 for 19 grants (high: $100,000; low: $10,000).
Fields of interest: Arts; Higher education; Environment, natural resources; Environment, land resources.
Type of support: General/operating support.
Limitations: Applications not accepted. Giving on a national basis, with emphasis on New York, NY. No grants to individuals.
Application information: Contributes only pre-selected organizations.
Trustee: Keeler G. Thompson.
EIN: 363233157

5689
Jacob Burns Foundation, Inc. ✧
c/o Barry Shenkman
427 Bedford Rd., Ste. 170
Pleasantville, NY 10570 (914) 769-3600

Incorporated in 1957 in NY.
Donors: Mary Elizabeth Hood†; Jacob Burns†; Rosalie A. Goldberg.
Foundation type: Independent foundation.
Financial data (yr. ended 12/31/05): Assets, $32,493,994 (M); gifts received, $240,000; expenditures, $1,811,841; qualifying distributions, $1,331,742; giving activities include $1,091,500 for 155 grants (high: $150,000; low: $100).
Purpose and activities: Giving primarily for Jewish organizations, including welfare funds and a yeshiva university, and cultural programs, especially an opera association and a public broadcasting network; minor support also for hospitals.
Fields of interest: Media/communications; Performing arts, music; Arts; Higher education; Hospitals (general); Human services; Jewish federated giving programs; Jewish agencies & temples.
Type of support: Annual campaigns; Capital campaigns; Program development; Conferences/ seminars; Curriculum development.
Limitations: Applications not accepted. Giving primarily in NY. No grants to individuals.
Application information: Contributes only to pre-selected organizations.
Board meeting date(s): 4 times per year
Officers: Barry A. Shenkman, Pres.; Rosalie A. Goldberg, V.P.; Jamie Shenkman, Secy.
Number of staff: 1 full-time professional; 1 part-time support.
EIN: 136114245
Selected grants: The following grants were reported in 2004.

$200,000 to W N E T Channel 13, New York, NY.
$91,667 to George Washington University, DC. 2 grants: $25,000, $66,667
$50,000 to Jacob Burns Film Center, Pleasantville, NY.
$50,000 to Westchester Arts Council, White Plains, NY.
$30,000 to Opera Company of Philadelphia, Philadelphia, PA.
$20,000 to University of Georgia, Athens, GA.
$3,000 to Yale University, New Haven, CT.
$2,500 to Alumnae Association of Smith College, Northampton, MA.
$1,100 to Academy of Vocal Arts, Philadelphia, PA.

5690
The Burpee Foundation ✧
c/o Brauner Baron Rosenzweig & Klein, LLP
61 Broadway, 18th Fl.
New York, NY 10006
Contact: Mel P. Barkan, V.P.

Established in 2002 in NY.
Donor: George C. Ball, Jr.
Foundation type: Independent foundation.
Financial data (yr. ended 12/31/05): Assets, $7,587,111 (M); expenditures, $539,625; qualifying distributions, $453,025; giving activities include $408,400 for 9 grants (high: $103,900; low: $2,000).
Fields of interest: Horticulture/garden clubs; Animals/wildlife, bird preserves; Substance abuse, treatment; International relief; Protestant agencies & churches.
Limitations: Giving on a national basis. No grants to individuals.
Application information: Application form required.
Initial approach: Completed New York/New Jersey Area Common Application Form
Deadline(s): None
Officers and Trustees:* George C. Ball, Jr.,* Pres. and Treas.; Mel P. Barkan,* V.P.; David Brauner,* Secy.
EIN: 743047509

5691
Gilbert & Ildiko Butler Foundation, Inc. ✧
(formerly Butler Foundation, Inc.)
c/o Butler Capital Corp.
745 5th Ave., Ste. 1702
New York, NY 10151-1706

Established in 1988 in MA.
Donors: Gilbert Butler; Butler Capital Corp.
Foundation type: Company-sponsored foundation.
Financial data (yr. ended 12/31/04): Assets, $65,263,276 (M); gifts received, $13,385,703; expenditures, $2,816,020; qualifying distributions, $2,352,273; giving activities include $2,352,273 for 83+ grants (high: $430,000).
Purpose and activities: The foundation supports organizations involved with arts and culture, education, the environment, animals and wildlife, health, and human services.
Fields of interest: Museums; Performing arts, theater (playwriting); Performing arts, opera; Historic preservation/historical societies; Arts; Higher education; Education; Environment, natural resources; Botanical gardens; Environment; Animals/wildlife; Health care; Eye diseases; Human services; Federated giving programs.

Type of support: General/operating support; Capital campaigns; Research.
Limitations: Applications not accepted. Giving on a national basis, with emphasis on NY and New England, primarily MA and ME.
Application information: Contributes only to pre-selected organizations.
Officers and Directors:* Gilbert Butler,* Pres. and Treas.; Jill Bauer, V.P., Finance; R. Bradford Malt,* V.P.; Henry R. Breck; Ildiko Butler; Christopher J. Elliman; Emily Rafferty.
EIN: 043032409
Selected grants: The following grants were reported in 2003.
$350,000 to NARSAD Research Institute, Great Neck, NY.
$100,000 to New York Botanical Garden, Bronx, NY.
$30,000 to Columbia University, School of Business, New York, NY.
$15,000 to Glimmerglass Opera, Cooperstown, NY.
$10,000 to Memorial Sloan-Kettering Cancer Center, New York, NY.
$10,000 to Wildlife Conservation Society, Bronx, NY.
$5,000 to Central Park Conservancy, New York, NY.
$3,557 to Syracuse University, Syracuse, NY.
$239 to New York City Ballet, New York, NY.
$200 to Frick Collection, New York, NY.

5692
J. E. & Z. B. Butler Foundation, Inc. ▼
825 3rd Ave., 40th Fl.
New York, NY   10022

Established in 1958.
Donors: Zella B. Butler†; Jack E. Butler†.
Foundation type: Independent foundation.
Financial data (yr. ended 12/31/05): Assets, $100,522,107 (M); expenditures, $6,053,641; qualifying distributions, $4,952,581; giving activities include $4,623,400 for 80 grants (high: $255,000; low: $2,500; average: $10,000–$75,000).
Purpose and activities: Giving primarily for Jewish welfare, direct service programs in community based organizations, programming for people with special needs, including after school and summer programming and youth development, including workforce development.
Fields of interest: Education, special; Learning disorders; Crime/violence prevention, child abuse; Employment; Youth development, intergenerational programs; Youth development; Human services; Children/youth, services; Family services; Family services, adolescent parents; Family services, counseling; Community development, public/private ventures; Jewish agencies & temples; Youth; Disabilities, people with; Physically disabled; Mentally disabled.
Limitations: Applications not accepted. Giving primarily in New York, NY. No grants to individuals.
Application information: Contributes only to pre-selected organizations.
Board meeting date(s): Apr., Sept., and Dec.
Officers and Directors:* Ruth B. Pearson,* Co-Chair. and V.P.; Beatrice B. Doniger,* Co-Chair.; Bruce Doniger,* C.E.O. and Pres.; Carol Parrish,* V.P.; Patricia Goldman,* Secy.
EIN: 136082916
Selected grants: The following grants were reported in 2005.
$255,000 to Board of Jewish Education, New York, NY.

$255,000 to New York Legal Assistance Group, New York, NY.
$234,000 to YM-YWHA, Samuel Field, Little Neck, NY.
$182,500 to Federation Employment and Guidance Service, New York, NY.
$175,000 to Mayors Fund to Advance New York City, Urban Park Rangers, New York, NY.
$100,000 to Childrens Health Fund, New York, NY.
$50,000 to Blythedale Childrens Hospital, Valhalla, NY.
$50,000 to Dorot, New York, NY.
$25,000 to Citizen Schools, Boston, MA.
$25,000 to StreetSquash, New York, NY.

5693
Catherine & Paul Buttenwieser Foundation ◇
c/o Barry M. Strauss Assocs., Ltd.
307 5th Ave., 8th Fl.
New York, NY   10016-6517

Established in 1993 in MA.
Donor: Paul A. Buttenwieser.
Foundation type: Independent foundation.
Financial data (yr. ended 9/30/05): Assets, $424,814 (M); gifts received, $598,035; expenditures, $533,451; qualifying distributions, $527,756; giving activities include $526,256 for 140 grants (high: $60,000; low: $50).
Fields of interest: Museums (art); Performing arts, ballet; Performing arts, theater; Performing arts, music; Performing arts, orchestra (symphony); Performing arts, opera; Arts; Education; Health care; Health organizations; Human services; Federated giving programs.
Limitations: Applications not accepted. Giving primarily in Boston, MA. No grants to individuals.
Application information: Contributes only to pre-selected organizations.
Trustees: Catherine F. Buttenwieser; Paul A. Buttenwieser.
EIN: 043216632
Selected grants: The following grants were reported in 2005.
$40,000 to Partners in Health, Boston, MA.
$25,100 to Harvard University, Cambridge, MA.
$25,000 to Boston Ballet, Boston, MA.
$20,000 to Family-to-Family Project, Somerville, MA.
$20,000 to Neptune Foundation, New York, NY.
$15,000 to United Way of Massachusetts Bay, Boston, MA.
$14,000 to American Repertory Theater, Cambridge, MA.
$1,000 to Berklee College of Music, Boston, MA.
$1,000 to Cantata Singers, Cambridge, MA.
$150 to Health Care for All, Boston, MA.

5694
The Bydale Foundation ◇
c/o U.S. Trust Co.
114 W. 47th St.
New York, NY   10036   (212) 852-3629
Contact: Linda R. Franciscovich, Mng. Dir.

Incorporated in 1965 in DE.
Donor: James P. Warburg†.
Foundation type: Independent foundation.
Financial data (yr. ended 12/31/05): Assets, $12,696,143 (M); expenditures, $883,639; qualifying distributions, $827,110; giving activities

include $764,500 for 69 grants (high: $35,000; low: $1,000).
Purpose and activities: Emphasis on international understanding, public policy research, the environment, cultural programs, the law and civil rights, social services, higher education, and economics.
Fields of interest: Arts; Higher education; Environment, natural resources; Environment; Crime/violence prevention, gun control; Crime/law enforcement; Human services; International affairs; Civil rights, women; Civil liberties, reproductive rights; Civil rights; Economics; Political science; Public policy, research; African Americans/Blacks; Women; Economically disadvantaged.
Type of support: General/operating support; Continuing support; Program development; Conferences/seminars; Publication; Seed money; Research; Matching/challenge support.
Limitations: Applications not accepted. Giving on a national basis. No grants to individuals, or for annual campaigns, emergency funds, deficit financing, endowment funds, demonstration projects, capital funds, scholarships, or fellowships; no loans.
Publications: Annual report.
Application information: Unsolicited requests for funds not accepted.
Board meeting date(s): Dec.
Officers and Trustees:* Joan M. Warburg,* Pres.; Frank J. Kick, Treas.; Sarah W. Bliumis-Dunn; James P. Warburg, Jr.; Jennifer Warburg; Philip N. Warburg.
Number of staff: 1 part-time professional; 1 part-time support.
EIN: 136195286
Selected grants: The following grants were reported in 2004.
$50,000 to Foundation on Economic Trends, DC.
$20,000 to Commonwealth Education Project, Boston, MA.
$20,000 to Planned Parenthood League of Connecticut, Hartford, CT.
$20,000 to Poets House, New York, NY.
$15,000 to Institute for Public Accuracy, San Francisco, CA.
$15,000 to Social Agenda, New York, NY.
$10,000 to Center for War/Peace Studies, New York, NY.
$10,000 to Choice USA, DC.
$10,000 to Poets and Writers, New York, NY.
$5,000 to Amnesty International USA, DC.

5695
The C.O.U.Q. Foundation, Inc. ◇
c/o George V. Delson Assocs.
110 E. 59th St.
New York, NY   10022

Established in 1998 in NY.
Donors: Jeffrey E. Epstein; The Leslie H. Wexner Charitable Fund.
Foundation type: Independent foundation.
Financial data (yr. ended 2/29/04): Assets, $20,391,162 (M); gifts received, $10,000,000; expenditures, $1,041,848; qualifying distributions, $1,041,560; giving activities include $1,008,203 for 37 grants (high: $120,000; low: $1,798).
Purpose and activities: Giving primarily for higher education, and international affairs; funding also for the arts, particularly the performing arts.
Fields of interest: Performing arts; Performing arts, ballet; Arts; Higher education; Cancer research;

International affairs, research; International peace/ security; International affairs.
Type of support: Scholarship funds; General/ operating support.
Limitations: Applications not accepted. Giving on a national and international basis. No grants to individuals.
Application information: Contributes only to pre-selected organizations.
Officers and Directors:* Jeffrey E. Epstein,* Pres.; Darren K. Indyke,* V.P.; Ghislaine Maxwell, Treas.
EIN: 133996471
Selected grants: The following grants were reported in 2003.
$310,000 to Harvard University, Cambridge, MA. 2 grants: $200,000, $110,000
$250,000 to Neurosciences Research Foundation, San Diego, CA.
$150,000 to Santa Fe Institute, Santa Fe, NM. 2 grants: $50,000, $100,000
$100,000 to Massachusetts Institute of Technology, Cambridge, MA.
$75,000 to Dalton Schools, New York, NY.
$25,000 to Council on Foreign Relations, New York, NY.
$25,000 to Stockholm School of Economics, Stockholm, Sweden. .
$15,000 to Ballet Florida, West Palm Beach, FL.

5696
The Andrew Cader Foundation, Inc. ◇
70 Meetinghouse Rd.
Bedford Corners, NY   10549

Established in 2002 in NY.
Donor: Andrew Cader.
Foundation type: Independent foundation.
Financial data (yr. ended 11/30/05): Assets, $17,933,260 (M); expenditures, $1,193,294; qualifying distributions, $892,720; giving activities include $886,833 for 32 grants (high: $175,000; low: $500).
Fields of interest: Arts; Education; Health care; Athletics/sports, winter sports.
Limitations: Applications not accepted. Giving on a national basis. No grants to individuals.
Application information: Contributes only to pre-selected organizations.
Officers and Directors:* Andrew Cader,* Pres. and Treas.; Michael Cader,* Secy.; Seth J. Lapidow.
EIN: 030497916

5697
The Cain Brothers Foundation ◇ ☆
360 Madison Ave., 5th Fl.
New York, NY   10017   (212) 869-5600

Established around 1993.
Donor: Daniel M. Cain.
Foundation type: Independent foundation.
Financial data (yr. ended 12/31/04): Assets, $1,586,206 (M); gifts received, $320,306; expenditures, $502,631; qualifying distributions, $502,631; giving activities include $502,631 for 12 grants (high: $300,000; low: $500).
Fields of interest: Higher education, university; Business school/education; Human services.
Type of support: Scholarship funds.
Limitations: Applications not accepted. Giving primarily in MA and NY. No grants to individuals.

Application information: Contributes only to pre-selected organizations.
Directors: Daniel M. Cain; James E. Cain; William M. Cain.
EIN: 133692990

5698
The John Calicchio Family Foundation ◇ ☆
140 Franklin St.
New York, NY   10013

Established in 2005 in NY.
Foundation type: Independent foundation.
Financial data (yr. ended 12/31/05): Assets, $34,634 (M); gifts received, $620,000; expenditures, $585,496; qualifying distributions, $585,496; giving activities include $577,675 for 26 grants (high: $375,285; low: $600).
Fields of interest: Museums; Performing arts; Arts; Higher education.
Limitations: Applications not accepted. Giving primarily in NY. No grants to individuals.
Application information: Contributes only to pre-selected organizations.
Officers: John Calicchio, Pres. and Treas.; Lisa Jackson, V.P. and Secy.
EIN: 202831864

5699
The Cambr Charitable Foundation Trust ◇
c/o George V. Delson Assocs.
110 E. 59th St.
New York, NY   10022

Established in 1996 in NY.
Donors: Allen Skolnick; Connie Skolnick; CAMBR Co.; CAMBR Labs.
Foundation type: Independent foundation.
Financial data (yr. ended 1/31/05): Assets, $12,674,253 (M); gifts received, $107,613; expenditures, $629,442; qualifying distributions, $610,381; giving activities include $604,905 for 39 grants (high: $75,000; low: $72).
Fields of interest: Jewish agencies & temples.
Limitations: Applications not accepted. Giving primarily in NY. No grants to individuals.
Application information: Contributes only to pre-selected organizations.
Trustees: Allen Skolnick; Connie Skolnick.
EIN: 116462058

5700
Ruth Camp Campbell Charitable Trust ◇
(formerly Ruth Camp McDougall Charitable Trust)
c/o Brown Brothers Harriman Trust Co.
140 Broadway, 4th Fl.
New York, NY   10005
Application address: c/o Vince Tran, Brown Brothers Harriman Trust Co., 240 Royal Palm Way, Palm Beach, FL 33480

Established in 1976 in VA.
Donor: Ruth Camp McDougall†.
Foundation type: Independent foundation.
Financial data (yr. ended 12/31/05): Assets, $11,186,292 (M); expenditures, $478,421; qualifying distributions, $381,579; giving activities include $375,878 for 130 grants (high: $22,500; low: $1,000).

Purpose and activities: Giving primarily for education as well as for the arts; funding also for health care including a children's hospital and a visiting nurse service, Christian churches, schools, and organizations, and children, youth, families, and social services including services for the blind.
Fields of interest: Museums; Performing arts; Historic preservation/historical societies; Arts; Higher education; Education; Hospitals (general); Health organizations, association; Cancer; Disasters, fire prevention/control; Human services; Children/youth, services; Family services; Christian agencies & churches; Protestant agencies & churches.
Type of support: Grants to individuals.
Limitations: Giving in the U.S., with emphasis on VA.
Application information:
  Initial approach: Letter
  Deadline(s): None
Directors: John M. Camp, Jr.; Paul D. Camp III; Paul Camp Marks; Harry W. Walker.
Trustee: Brown Brothers Harriman Trust Co.
EIN: 546162697
Selected grants: The following grants were reported in 2004.
$70,000 to Southampton Academy, Courtland, VA. 3 grants: $25,000, $20,000, $25,000
$12,500 to Carolina Ballet, Raleigh, NC.
$12,500 to North Carolina Museum of Art, Raleigh, NC.
$4,000 to Virginia Holocaust Museum, Richmond, VA.
$4,000 to Woods Services Foundation, Langhorne, PA.
$3,000 to American Red Cross, Richmond, VA.
$2,500 to Hibiscus Childrens Center, Jensen Beach, FL.
$2,000 to Saint Catherines School, Richmond, VA.

5701
The Canaday Family Charitable Trust ◇
(formerly Canaday Educational and Charitable Trust)
c/o U.S. Trust Co.
114 W. 47th St.
New York, NY   10036   (212) 852-3629
Contact: Linda R. Franciscovich, Managing Dir.
FAX: (212) 852-3377;
E-mail: canaday@ustrust.com; URL: http:// www.canadayfamily.org/

Trust established in 1945 in OH.
Donors: Ward M. Canaday†; Mariam C. Canaday†.
Foundation type: Independent foundation.
Financial data (yr. ended 12/31/04): Assets, $577,384 (M); expenditures, $701,384; qualifying distributions, $680,194; giving activities include $653,070 for 12 grants (high: $568,500; low: $12,500).
Purpose and activities: Giving primarily to organizations that work in Vermont to improve the lives of children and families, promote environmental education and conservation, and preserve the environment.
Fields of interest: Environment, natural resources; Environmental education; Children/youth, services; Family services.
Limitations: Giving primarily in VT. No support for private foundation or organizations lacking 501(c)(3) status. No grants to individuals, or for capital campaigns or endowments.
Application information: Organizations in which the foundation is interested will be contacted and invited to submit a formal grant proposal.

Initial approach: Letter or inquiry, no more than 3 pages; may be submitted in writing or by e-mail
Deadline(s): Feb. 1 for letters of inquiry
Board meeting date(s): Annually
Final notification: July
Trustee: U.S. Trust Co.
EIN: 346523619
Selected grants: The following grants were reported in 2004.
$125,333 to Vermont Institute of Natural Science, Woodstock, VT. For general support.
$107,000 to Vermont Humanities Council, Morrisville, VT. For general support.
$75,000 to Conservation Law Foundation, Montpelier, VT. For general support.
$75,000 to National Wildlife Federation, Montpelier, VT. For general support.
$75,000 to Vermont Natural Resources Council, Montpelier, VT. For general support.
$72,000 to Altai Conservancy, Woodstock, VT. For general support.
$66,047 to NorthWoods Stewardship Center, East Charleston, VT. For general support.
$18,000 to Vermont State Mathematics Coalition, Essex Junction, VT. For general support.
$12,000 to Focusing Institute, Spring Valley, NY. For general support.

5702

The Canary Charitable Foundation ✧
c/o First Spring Corp.
499 Park Ave., 26th Fl.
New York, NY 10022
Contact: Guido Goldman, V.P.

Established in 1998 in DE.
Donors: Charles De Gunzburg; Carob Trust.
Foundation type: Independent foundation.
Financial data (yr. ended 12/31/03): Assets, $13,994,261 (M); gifts received, $2,378,600; expenditures, $933,574; qualifying distributions, $879,968; giving activities include $878,964 for 26 grants (high: $225,000; low: $1,000).
Fields of interest: Media, television; Museums (art); Museums (ethnic/folk arts); Museums (specialized); Hospitals (general); Health organizations, association; Disasters, 9/11/01; Jewish federated giving programs; Jewish agencies & temples.
Limitations: Giving primarily in MA and NY.
Application information: Application form not required.
Deadline(s): None
Officers and Directors:* Charles De Gunzburg,* Pres.; Guido Goldman,* V.P.; Susan Shehan, Secy.-Treas.; Nathalie Cohen; Leonard M. Nelson.
EIN: 134005475

5703

The Louis R. Cappelli Foundation, Inc. ✧
115 Stevens Ave.
Valhalla, NY 10595 (914) 769-6500
Contact: Denise Groneman, Exec. Dir.
FAX: (914) 747-9268;
E-mail: jfevola@cappelli-inc.com; URL: http://www.cappelli-inc.com/lrc.shtml

Established in 1999 in NY.
Donor: Louis R. Cappelli.
Foundation type: Independent foundation.

Financial data (yr. ended 12/31/03): Assets, $4,372 (L); gifts received, $361,000; expenditures, $366,965; qualifying distributions, $362,765; giving activities include $362,765 for 68 grants (high: $50,000; low: $250).
Purpose and activities: Giving primarily to organizations addressing the needs of at-risk youth; funding also for the arts, education, health associations and hospitals, including children's hospitals, social services, community development, federated giving programs, and Jewish organizations.
Fields of interest: Arts councils; Arts; Education; Hospitals (general); Hospitals (specialty); Health organizations, association; Human services; YM/YWCAs & YM/YWHAs; Children/youth, services; Family services; Community development; Federated giving programs; Jewish agencies & temples.
Limitations: Giving primarily in NY.
Application information: Application form required.
Initial approach: Letter requesting application via E-mail or surface mail
Officers and Directors:* Louis R. Cappelli,* Pres.; Russell Cooper, Treas.; Celia Clark; Richard Ferrucci; Margaret Schneider.
EIN: 134048754
Selected grants: The following grants were reported in 2003.
$50,000 to New Rochelle, City of, New Rochelle, NY. For general support.
$10,000 to Child Care Council of Westchester, White Plains, NY. For general support.
$10,000 to Grace Church Community Center, White Plains, NY. For general support.
$5,000 to Arthritis Foundation, New York, NY. For general support.
$5,000 to Mount Kisco Day Care Centers, Mount Kisco, NY. For general support.
$5,000 to Salvation Army of Greater New York, New York, NY. For general support.
$5,000 to Westchester Medical Center Foundation, Valhalla, NY. For general support.
$5,000 to Youth Theater Interactions, Yonkers, NY. For general support.
$2,500 to White Plains Library Foundation, White Plains, NY. For general support.
$1,500 to Westchester Fund for Women and Girls, Westchester, NY. For general support.

5704

W. P. Carey Foundation
50 Rockefeller Plz.
New York, NY 10020

Established in 1991 in PA.
Donor: William P. Carey.
Foundation type: Independent foundation.
Financial data (yr. ended 12/31/05): Assets, $15,818,320 (M); gifts received, $3,001,000; expenditures, $3,042,500; qualifying distributions, $3,017,294; giving activities include $2,970,097 for 116 grants (high: $502,500; low: $150).
Purpose and activities: Giving primarily for international relief and education.
Fields of interest: Museums; Higher education; Education; International relief; Christian agencies & churches.
Limitations: Applications not accepted. Giving on a national basis. No grants to individuals.
Application information: Contributes only to pre-selected organizations.

Officers and Trustees:* William P. Carey,* Chair.; Francis J. Carey,* Pres.; Elizabeth P. Carey,* V.P.; Claude Fernandez,* Treas.; William R. Polk, Sr. Dir.; Juliana K. Harris, Exec. Dir.; J. Samuel Armstrong IV; Gwendolyn G. Bond; H. Augustus Carey; Francis J. Carey III; Gordon F. Dugan; Jan F. Karst; Lawrence R. Klein; Edward V. Lapuma; Zachary J. Pack; A. Patterson Pendleton III; George E. Stoddard; Anne Coolidge Taylor; Elizabeth Shaw Wills.
EIN: 133597510
Selected grants: The following grants were reported in 2005.
$502,500 to Calvert School, Baltimore, MD.
$125,500 to Springside School, Philadelphia, PA.
$79,942 to American Red Cross.
$61,329 to University of Pennsylvania, Philadelphia, PA.
$45,000 to Baltimore School for the Arts Foundation, Baltimore, MD.
$25,000 to American Philosophical Society, Philadelphia, PA.
$25,000 to Brigham Young University, Provo, UT.
$10,000 to Robert E. Lee Memorial Association, Stratford, VA.
$1,500 to University of Virginia Fund, Charlottesville, VA.
$925 to On Your Mark, Staten Island, NY.

5705

The Carmel Hill Fund
(formerly Ruane Family Fund)
767 5th Ave., Ste. 4701
New York, NY 10153-4798

Established in 1986 in NY.
Donors: William J. Ruane†; The Riordan Fund.
Foundation type: Independent foundation.
Financial data (yr. ended 12/31/04): Assets, $65,438,328 (M); gifts received, $8,545,426; expenditures, $3,576,035; qualifying distributions, $3,564,652; giving activities include $3,368,675 for 56 grants (high: $696,863; low: $1,000; average: $5,000–$50,000).
Purpose and activities: Giving primarily for education, human services, and arts and cultural organizations. Major funding for an organization that strives to eradicate the abuse of drugs in the United States.
Fields of interest: Arts; Education; Substance abuse, prevention; Human services; Youth, services.
Limitations: Applications not accepted. Giving primarily in NY. No grants to individuals.
Application information: Contributes only to pre-selected organizations.
Trustees: George J. Gillespie, III; Robert D. Goldfarb.
Number of staff: 7 full-time professional; 3 part-time support.
EIN: 136881103
Selected grants: The following grants were reported in 2004.
$405,593 to Childrens Aid Society.
$175,000 to Fund for Public Schools, New York, NY.
$109,945 to Mount Carmel Holy Rosary School, New York, NY.
$100,000 to Specialist School.
$68,767 to Monroe School District, Monroe, WA.
$27,500 to Shelburne Museum, Shelburne, VT.
$25,000 to New York Theater Workshop, New York, NY.
$6,000 to Burlington City Arts, Burlington, VT.
$5,000 to Philharmonic-Symphony Society of New York, New York, NY.

5706
Carnahan-Jackson Foundation
13 E. 4th St.
Jamestown, NY 14701
Contact: Stephen E. Sellstrom, Exec. Secy.
Application address: P.O. Box 3326, Jamestown, NY
14702-3326

Trust established in 1972 in NY.
Donor: Katharine J. Carnahan†.
Foundation type: Independent foundation.
Financial data (yr. ended 7/31/05): Assets,
$11,898,282 (M); expenditures, $662,091;
qualifying distributions, $581,971; giving activities
include $479,825 for 18 grants (high: $100,000;
low: $2,500).
Purpose and activities: Primary areas of interest
include higher and other education, libraries,
hospitals, and youth; support also for the
handicapped, drug abuse programs, ecology,
housing, community development, dance and other
performing arts groups, and church support; some
support for certain prior interests of the donor.
Fields of interest: Performing arts; Higher
education; Education; Hospitals (general); Human
services; Children/youth, services; Christian
agencies & churches.
Type of support: General/operating support;
Continuing support; Capital campaigns; Building/
renovation; Equipment; Program development; Seed
money; Curriculum development; Scholarship funds;
Matching/challenge support.
Limitations: Giving primarily in Chautauqua County,
NY, particularly in the Jamestown area. No grants to
individuals.
Publications: Application guidelines; Grants list.
Application information: Application form not
required.
  Initial approach: Letter outlining needs and use of
    grant per guidelines
  Copies of proposal: 8
  Deadline(s): Apr. 30 and Oct. 31
  Board meeting date(s): June and Dec.
  Final notification: July and Dec./Jan.
Trustee: Bank of America, N.A.
Number of staff: 2 part-time professional; 1
part-time support.
EIN: 166151608

5707
Carnegie Corporation of New York ▼
437 Madison Ave.
New York, NY 10022 (212) 371-3200
Contact: Rikard Treiber, Assoc. Corp. Secy. and Dir.,
Grants Management
FAX: (212) 754-4073; URL: http://
www.carnegie.org

Incorporated in 1911 in NY.
Donors: Andrew Carnegie†; Michael R. Bloomberg;
The Bill and Melinda Gates Foundation.
Foundation type: Independent foundation.
Financial data (yr. ended 9/30/05): Assets,
$2,244,208,247 (M); gifts received, $21,164,624;
expenditures, $114,160,539; qualifying
distributions, $105,310,789; giving activities
include $83,582,366 for 842 grants (high:
$4,500,000; low: $975; average: $25,000–
$500,000), $1,277,958 for 31 grants to
individuals, $397,701 for employee matching gifts,
and $5,795,464 for foundation-administered
programs.

Purpose and activities: As a grantmaking
foundation, Carnegie Corporation of New York seeks
to carry out Andrew Carnegie's vision of
philanthropy, which he said should aim "to do real
and permanent good in this world." Currently the
foundation's work is focused on four program areas:
Education, International Development, International
Peace and Security and Strengthening U.S.
Democracy.
Fields of interest: Education, reform; Higher
education; Higher education, university; Teacher
school/education; Libraries, archives; Education,
reading; Youth development, citizenship;
International peace/security; International affairs,
arms control; International affairs, national security;
International conflict resolution; Civil rights,
immigrants; Civil rights, voter education; Campaign
finance reform; Adults, women.
International interests: Africa; Russia; Sub-Saharan
Africa.
Type of support: General/operating support;
Continuing support; Program development;
Conferences/seminars; Publication; Curriculum
development; Research; Technical assistance;
Program evaluation; Employee matching gifts.
Limitations: Giving primarily for U.S. projects,
although some grants are made to selected
countries in Sub-Saharan Africa through the
International Development Program. No support for
libraries, cultural institutions, programs or facilities
of community-based educational or human services
institutions. No grants for scholarships, fellowships
(except the Carnegie Scholars Program), travel,
capital campaigns, endowments or program-related
investments.
Publications: Annual report; Grants list;
Informational brochure (including application
guidelines); Occasional report.
Application information: Application form required.
  Initial approach: Letter
  Copies of proposal: 2
  Deadline(s): None
  Board meeting date(s): Mar., June, and Sept., and
    Dec.
  Final notification: 4-6 months
Officers and Trustees:* Helene L. Kaplan,* Chair.;
Martin L. Leibowitz,* Vice-Chair.; Vartan Gregorian,*
Pres.; Edward M. Sermier, V.P., C.A.O., and Corp.
Secy.; D. Ellen Shuman, V.P. and C.I.O.; Neil
Grabois, V.P. and Dir., Strategic Planning and Prog.
Coord.; Susan Robinson King, V.P., Public Affairs;
David A. Hamburg, Pres. Emeritus; Bruce Alberts;
Pedro Aspe; Geoffrey T. Boisi; Richard H. Brodhead;
Fiona Druckenmiller; Amy Gutmann; Susan
Hockfield; James B. Hunt; Thomas H. Kean; Olara A.
Otunnu; William A. Owens; Ana Palacio; Norman
Pearlstine; Amb. Thomas R. Pickering; Richard W.
Riley; Janet L. Robinson; Raymond W. Smith.
Number of staff: 39 full-time professional; 1
part-time professional; 29 full-time support; 4
part-time support.
EIN: 131628151
Selected grants: The following grants were reported
in 2004.
$12,559,600 to Academy for Educational
  Development, DC. Toward Teachers for a New
  Era, initiative to reform and improve education of
  teachers, payable over 3 years.
$5,068,300 to University of Dar es Salaam, Dar es
  Salaam, Tanzania. 2 grants: $2,968,300 (To
  implement institutional transformation, payable
  over 3 years), $2,100,000 (For scholarship
  program for undergraduate women, payable over
  3 years).

$5,020,400 to Makerere University, Kampala,
  Uganda. 2 grants: $2,020,500 (For scholarship
  program for undergraduate women, payable over
  3 years), $2,999,900 (For institutional
  development, payable over 3 years).
$2,028,600 to Msunduzi, Municipality of,
  Pietermaritzburg, South Africa. Toward creation
  of model junior reference library in
  Pietermaritzburg, payable over 3 years.
$2,000,000 to Ahmadu Bello University, Zaria,
  Nigeria. Toward support of institutional
  strengthening including gender equity projects,
  payable over 3 years.
$2,000,000 to Cape Town, City of, Cape Town,
  South Africa. Toward creation of model reference
  library in Cape Town, payable over 3 years.
$1,686,000 to University of Education, Winneba,
  Winneba, Ghana. Toward distance education,
  student internship and graduate studies
  programs, payable over 3 years.
$1,637,300 to University of Ghana, Accra, Ghana.
  To leverage comparative strengths and
  competencies in University of Ghana through
  information and communication technology,
  payable over 3 years.

5708
The Kristen Ann Carr Fund
39 W. 32nd St., Ste. 1403
New York, NY 10001 (212) 501-0748
FAX: (212) 268-3544; E-mail: info@sarcoma.com;
URL: http://www.sarcoma.com/

Established in 1994 in NY.
Donors: Shelley Lazar; Robert Muller; T.J. Martell
Foundation; Sony Music Entertainment; May Ellen &
Gerald Ritter Foundation; Bob Benjamin (School
House); Rock-It-Cargo; Kaplan, Inc.
Foundation type: Independent foundation.
Financial data (yr. ended 12/31/05): Assets,
$2,964,511 (M); gifts received, $714,443;
expenditures, $463,099; qualifying distributions,
$321,000; giving activities include $321,000 for 7
grants (high: $280,000; low: $1,000).
Purpose and activities: Giving for the prevention
and treatment of cancer and sarcomas, and for
psychological services for teen and young adult
cancer patients.
Fields of interest: Cancer.
Type of support: Fellowships.
Limitations: Applications not accepted. Giving
primarily in New York, NY. No grants to individuals.
Application information: Contributes only to
pre-selected organizations.
Trustees: Barbara Carr; Sasha Carr; David Marsh.
EIN: 133800442

5709
The Carson Family Charitable Trust ▼ ✧
c/o U.S. Trust
114 W. 47th St.
New York, NY 10036

Established in 1990 in NY.
Donors: Russell L. Carson; Judith M. Carson.
Foundation type: Independent foundation.
Financial data (yr. ended 12/31/04): Assets,
$25,217,062 (M); expenditures, $23,810,284;
qualifying distributions, $23,610,345; giving
activities include $23,585,500 for 95 grants (high:

$5,000,000; low: $1,000; average: $25,000–$100,000).

Purpose and activities: Funding primarily for poverty relief and community development in New York City.

Fields of interest: Museums (art); Higher education; Environment, natural resources; Public health; Human services; Community development.

Type of support: General/operating support; Capital campaigns.

Limitations: Applications not accepted. Giving primarily in New York, NY. No grants to individuals.

Application information: Contributes only to pre-selected organizations.

Trustees: Cecily M. Carson; Edward S. Carson; Judith M. Carson; Russell L. Carson; U.S. Trust.

EIN: 136957038

Selected grants: The following grants were reported in 2004.

$5,000,000 to Dartmouth College, Hanover, NH. For construction.

$3,000,000 to Rockefeller University, New York, NY.

$2,500,000 to Metropolitan Museum of Art, New York, NY. 2 grants: $2,400,000 (Toward Egyptian exhibit), $100,000.

$2,000,000 to Columbia University, Business School, New York, NY.

$1,000,000 to Inner-City Scholarship Fund, New York, NY.

$250,000 to New-York Historical Society, New York, NY.

$100,000 to Metropolitan Opera Guild, New York, NY. Toward radio broadcasts.

$100,000 to Notre Dame School, New York, NY. For tuition.

$50,000 to Metropolitan Opera, New York, NY.

5710
The Thomas & Agnes Carvel Foundation

35 E. Grassy Sprain Rd.
Yonkers, NY 10710 (914) 793-7300
Contact: William E. Griffin, Pres.

Established in 1976 in NY.

Donors: Thomas Carvel‡; Agnes Carvel‡; The Agnes Carvel 1991 Trust; Thomas Carvel Unitrust Remainderman.

Foundation type: Independent foundation.

Financial data (yr. ended 11/30/05): Assets, $34,671,718 (M); gifts received, $70,000; expenditures, $2,151,803; qualifying distributions, $1,267,718; giving activities include $1,148,290 for 52 grants (high: $200,000; low: $200).

Purpose and activities: Giving primarily for health care, including hospitals and children's hospitals, funding also for the arts, and children, youth and social services, and for higher education.

Fields of interest: Performing arts, music; Arts; Secondary school/education; Higher education; Hospitals (general); Hospitals (specialty); Health care; Cancer; Human services; Children/youth, services.

Type of support: Scholarship funds; Program development; Building/renovation; Research; Matching/challenge support.

Limitations: Giving primarily in Westchester County, NY. No support for political and international organizations.

Application information: Application form not required.

Initial approach: Letter
Copies of proposal: 1
Deadline(s): None

Board meeting date(s): Jan., Mar., May, July, and Nov.

Final notification: 2 months

Officers: William E. Griffin, Pres.; Salvador Molella, V.P.; Marie Holcombe, Treas.

Director: Brendan Byrne.

Number of staff: 2 part-time professional; 2 full-time support.

EIN: 132879673

Selected grants: The following grants were reported in 2005.

$150,000 to Saint Johns Riverside Hospital, Yonkers, NY.

$75,000 to Richmond Childrens Center, Yonkers, NY.

$60,000 to Garden State Cancer Center, Belleville, NJ.

$25,000 to Saint Barnabas Church, Greenwich, CT.

$25,000 to Seton Hall University, South Orange, NJ.

$15,000 to Cerebral Palsy of North Jersey, Maplewood, NJ.

$12,000 to Midnight Run, Dobbs Ferry, NY.

$10,000 to Manhattan College, Riverdale, NY.

$10,000 to United Spinal Association, Jackson Heights, NY.

$5,000 to Guiding Eyes for the Blind.

5711
The Carwill Foundation ◇

c/o BCRS Assocs., LLC
100 Wall St., 11th Fl.
New York, NY 10005
Contact: William C. Stutt, Tr.

Established in 1985 in NY.

Donor: William C. Stutt.

Foundation type: Independent foundation.

Financial data (yr. ended 8/31/05): Assets, $632,766 (M); gifts received, $414,586; expenditures, $395,789; qualifying distributions, $391,060; giving activities include $385,645 for 98 grants (high: $100,000; low: $25).

Purpose and activities: Support primarily for education, including a naval academy.

Fields of interest: Arts; Elementary/secondary education; Higher education; Hospitals (general); Health organizations, association; Human services; Children/youth, services.

Type of support: Annual campaigns; Capital campaigns; Endowments; Professorships; Scholarship funds; Research.

Limitations: Applications not accepted. Giving primarily in FL, MD, and NY. No grants to individuals.

Application information: Contributes only to pre-selected organizations.

Trustees: Carolyn Stutt; David S. Stutt; William C. Stutt.

EIN: 133318130

Selected grants: The following grants were reported in 2004.

$106,000 to Packer Collegiate Institute, Brooklyn, NY. 3 grants: $100,000, $1,000, $5,000

$26,000 to Trinity Episcopal Church, Vero Beach, FL. 2 grants: $6,000, $20,000

$1,000 to Maple Street School, Manchester Center, VT.

$1,000 to Northfield Mount Hermon School, Northfield, MA.

$1,000 to Stratton Mountain School, Stratton Mountain, VT.

$500 to Eaglebrook School, Deerfield, MA.

$500 to Prep for Prep, New York, NY.

5712
Mary Flagler Cary Charitable Trust ▼

122 E. 42nd St., Rm. 3505
New York, NY 10168 (212) 953-7700
Contact: Edward A. Ames, Tr. and Prog. Dir., Conservation; Gayle Morgan, Prog. Dir., Music
FAX: (212) 953-7720; URL: http://www.carytrust.org/

Trust established in 1968 in NY.

Donor: Mary Flagler Cary‡.

Foundation type: Independent foundation.

Financial data (yr. ended 6/30/05): Assets, $111,234,009 (M); expenditures, $6,292,783; qualifying distributions, $5,772,900; giving activities include $4,741,159 for 74 grants (high: $2,486,159; low: $5,000).

Purpose and activities: The trust considers grant proposals in two areas: for music in New York City (directed toward community music schools and small- to medium-sized professional music institutions, with an emphasis on the commissioning, performance, and recording of contemporary music); and for the conservation of natural resources (focused on the preservation of coastal wetlands and estuaries in the southern states from Maryland to Florida, primarily for programs to protect selected regional ecosystems). The balance of the trust's grant budget is devoted to special commitments undertaken for reasons relating to its history and origin, but no additional, unrelated support is offered in these fields. These include support for the Institute of Ecosystem Studies, Inc. at the Mary Flagler Cary Arboretum in Millbrook, NY; The Rockefeller University Field Research Center for Ecology and Ethnology in Millbrook, NY; and the Rochester Institute of Technology School of Printing.

Fields of interest: Performing arts; Performing arts, music; Environment, reform; Environment, natural resources; Environment.

Type of support: General/operating support; Continuing support; Land acquisition; Program development; Matching/challenge support.

Limitations: Giving limited to New York, NY, for music; and the southeastern coastal states for conservation. No support for private foundations, hospitals, religious organizations, primary or secondary schools, colleges and universities, libraries, or museums. No grants to individuals, or for scholarships, fellowships, capital funds, annual campaigns, seed money, emergency funds, deficit financing, or endowment funds; no loans to individuals.

Publications: Application guidelines; Annual report; Grants list.

Application information: Due to the trust's plan to terminate in 2009, very few new grants will be considered. If further consideration is appropriate, a formal proposal will be requested. Application form not required.

Initial approach: Letter of inquiry with brief proposal; foundation only accepts proposals for their music program
Copies of proposal: 1
Deadline(s): None
Board meeting date(s): Monthly
Final notification: 2 months

Trustees: Edward A. Ames, Prog. Dir., Conservation; Paul B. Guenther; Phyllis J. Mills.

Number of staff: 1 full-time professional; 2 full-time support.

EIN: 136266964

Selected grants: The following grants were reported in 2005.

$10,458,477 to Institute of Ecosystem Studies, Millbrook, NY. For general support and stewardship of Mary Flagler Cary Arboretum, payable over 3 years.

$200,000 to Nature Conservancy, Arlington, VA. For protection of South Carolina coastal ecosystems, payable over 2 years.

$50,000 to Chesapeake Bay Foundation, Annapolis, MD. For conservation of natural resources on Eastern Shore of Maryland.

$50,000 to Citizens for a Better Eastern Shore, Eastville, VA. For general support, payable over 1.50 years.

$30,000 to South Carolina Environmental Law Project, Pawleys Island, SC. To help provide legal representation for environmental groups working to protect coastal resources in South Carolina.

$25,000 to American Composers Orchestra, New York, NY. For general support.

$25,000 to American Music Center, New York, NY. For Live Music for Dance program.

$25,000 to Bronx Opera Company, Bronx, NY. For general support.

$25,000 to Brooklyn Philharmonic Symphony Orchestra, Brooklyn, NY. For general support.

$15,000 to Brooklyn Music School, Brooklyn, NY. For general support.

5713
Case Family Foundation ✧ ☆
44 W. 77th St., Apt. 7E
New York, NY   10024

Established in 1997 in NY.
Donor: Robert A. Case.
Foundation type: Independent foundation.
Financial data (yr. ended 12/31/05): Assets, $2,467,218 (M); gifts received, $47,600; expenditures, $525,117; qualifying distributions, $512,500; giving activities include $512,500 for 7 grants (high: $400,000; low: $1,000).
Fields of interest: Higher education, university; Christian agencies & churches; Protestant agencies & churches.
Limitations: Applications not accepted. No grants to individuals.
Application information: Contributes only to pre-selected organizations.
Trustees: Robert A. Case; Suzanne P. Case.
EIN: 137105895

5714
Sophia & William Casey Foundation ✧
c/o Steven T. Rosenberg
201 Moreland Rd., Ste. 6
Hauppauge, NY   11788
Application address: c/o Bernadette Casey-Smith, 12 Glenwood Rd., Roslyn Harbor, NY 11576

Established in 1974 in NY.
Donors: William J. Casey†; Sophia B. Casey†.
Foundation type: Independent foundation.
Financial data (yr. ended 11/30/05): Assets, $2,295,710 (M); gifts received, $2,400,000; expenditures, $343,939; qualifying distributions, $327,100; giving activities include $327,100 for 32 grants (high: $100,000; low: $150).
Fields of interest: Higher education; Education; Human services; International studies; Christian

agencies & churches; Roman Catholic agencies & churches.
Limitations: Giving primarily in the greater metropolitan Washington, DC, including portions of MD and VA, and the metropolitan New York, NY, areas; some funding nationally. No grants to individuals.
Application information:
Initial approach: Letter
Deadline(s): None
Officer: Bernadette Casey-Smith, Pres. and Secy.
EIN: 510153218

5715
Castelnau Foundation ✧
(formerly John Michael Evans Foundation)
c/o Goldman Sachs - Family Office
1 New York Plz., 40th Fl.
New York, NY   10004

Donors: John Michael Evans; Goldman Sachs & Co.
Foundation type: Independent foundation.
Financial data (yr. ended 5/31/05): Assets, $7,533,069 (M); expenditures, $510,052; qualifying distributions, $388,334; giving activities include $388,334 for 19 grants (high: $100,000; low: $500).
Purpose and activities: Giving primarily for higher education; funding also for human services, as well as for a community arts center.
Fields of interest: Arts, multipurpose centers/programs; Arts; Elementary/secondary education; Higher education; Environment; Human services; Foundations (private grantmaking).
Limitations: Applications not accepted. Giving primarily in DE, with emphasis on Wilmington; some funding nationally. No grants to individuals; no loans or scholarships.
Application information: Contributes only to pre-selected organizations.
Trustees: Heather Richards Evans; John Michael Evans.
EIN: 133933323
Selected grants: The following grants were reported in 2005.

$100,000 to Brandywine Conservancy, Chadds Ford, PA.

$60,000 to Tower Hill School, Wilmington, DE. 2 grants: $10,000, $50,000

$35,000 to Princeton University, Princeton, NJ. 2 grants: $25,000, $10,000

$25,000 to Robin Hood Foundation, New York, NY.

$25,000 to Ronald McDonald House, Buffalo, NY.

$7,000 to Friends of Winterthur, Winterthur, DE.

$5,000 to Northeast Harbor Library, Northeast Harbor, ME.

$1,500 to Delaware Theater Company, Wilmington, DE.

5716
Castle Foundation ✧
500 Mamaroneck Ave.
Harrison, NY   10528

Established in 1989 in NY.
Donors: Castle Oil Corp.; Rom Terminals, Ltd.
Foundation type: Independent foundation.
Financial data (yr. ended 12/31/04): Assets, $63,403 (M); gifts received, $445,000; expenditures, $395,052; qualifying distributions,

$395,000; giving activities include $395,000 for 4 grants (high: $125,000; low: $20,000).
Purpose and activities: Giving primarily for education.
Fields of interest: Law school/education; Education.
Limitations: Applications not accepted. Giving primarily in NY. No grants to individuals.
Application information: Contributes only to pre-selected organizations.
Trustees: Camille Romita; Mauro C. Romita; Michael Romita.
EIN: 133490144
Selected grants: The following grants were reported in 2004.

$150,000 to Ursuline School, New Rochelle, NY.

$100,000 to Iona College, New Rochelle, NY.

5717
The James E. and Patricia D. Cayne Charitable Trust ✧
383 Madison Ave.
New York, NY   10179

Established in 1996 in NY.
Donor: James E. Cayne.
Foundation type: Independent foundation.
Financial data (yr. ended 5/31/05): Assets, $20,750,658 (M); expenditures, $2,164,597; qualifying distributions, $2,106,675; giving activities include $2,104,080 for 67 grants (high: $300,000; low: $180).
Purpose and activities: Giving primarily to Jewish organizations and charities; funding also for health services.
Fields of interest: Education; Hospitals (general); Health organizations, association; Foundations (private grantmaking); Jewish federated giving programs; Jewish agencies & temples.
Limitations: Applications not accepted. Giving on a national basis, with emphasis on New York, NY. No grants to individuals.
Application information: Contributes only to pre-selected organizations.
Trustees: James E. Cayne; Patricia Cayne.
EIN: 137100859
Selected grants: The following grants were reported in 2005.

$207,000 to Hineni, New York, NY.

$200,000 to Gillen Brewer School, New York, NY.

$200,000 to Jewish Federation of Greater Monmouth County, Deal, NJ.

$60,000 to Yeshiva Ateres Yisroel, Brooklyn, NY.

$50,000 to Mount Sinai Hospital, New York, NY.

$25,000 to Riverdale Country School, Bronx, NY.

$20,000 to Saint Johns University, Jamaica, NY.

$10,000 to Congregation Kehilath Jeshurun, New York, NY.

$10,000 to Gift of Life Bone Marrow Foundation, Boca Raton, FL.

$5,000 to Yeshiva University High School, New York, NY.

5718
The Joseph & Trina Cayre Foundation, Inc. ✧
(formerly Jack & Grace Cayre Foundation)
417 5th Ave.
New York, NY   10016
Contact: Joseph Cayre, Pres.

Established in 1988 in DE.
Donors: Joseph Cayre; Kenneth Cayre; Stanley Cayre.
Foundation type: Independent foundation.
Financial data (yr. ended 12/31/05): Assets, $5,254,619 (M); gifts received, $1,592,348; expenditures, $2,662,735; qualifying distributions, $2,623,206; giving activities include $2,623,206 for grants.
Purpose and activities: Giving primarily to Jewish agencies and temples and for Jewish education.
Fields of interest: Education; Human services; Jewish federated giving programs; Jewish agencies & temples.
Limitations: Giving primarily in NY, with strong emphasis on Brooklyn. No grants to individuals.
Application information: Application form not required.
Initial approach: Letter
Deadline(s): None
Officers: Joseph Cayre, Pres.; Trina Cayre, V.P.
EIN: 133494146
Selected grants: The following grants were reported in 2004.
$165,000 to Magen David Yeshiva, Brooklyn, NY.
$125,500 to Sephardic Bikur Holim, Brooklyn, NY. 3 grants: $100,000, $6,000, $19,500
$60,000 to Yismach Moshe, Beverly Hills, CA.
$27,200 to Southwest Creations Collaborative, Albuquerque, NM. 2 grants: $22,000, $5,200
$20,000 to Safe and Fear-Free Environment, Dillingham, AK.
$20,000 to Shaare Torah.
$10,000 to Baruch College Fund, New York, NY.

5719
The Kenneth & Lillian Cayre Foundation, Inc. ✧
417 5th Ave., 9th Fl.
New York, NY 10016
Contact: Kenneth Cayre, Pres.

Established in 1993 in DE.
Donors: Jack Cayre; Kenneth Cayre; Nathan Cayre; Grace K. Cayre; Michelle Cayre; Raquel Cayre; Lillian Cayre.
Foundation type: Independent foundation.
Financial data (yr. ended 12/31/04): Assets, $6,773,200 (M); gifts received, $330,000; expenditures, $1,824,593; qualifying distributions, $1,760,584; giving activities include $1,760,584 for 160 grants (high: $100,000; low: $100).
Fields of interest: Education; Jewish agencies & temples.
Limitations: Giving on a national basis. No grants to individuals.
Application information:
Initial approach: Letter
Deadline(s): None
Officers: Kenneth Cayre, Pres.; Lillian Cayre, V.P.
EIN: 133746793
Selected grants: The following grants were reported in 2003.
$36,000 to Congregation Ohel Eliahu, Deal, NJ. For general support.
$36,000 to Hillel Yeshiva, Brooklyn, NY. For general support.
$10,000 to Shaare Torah. For general support.
$7,500 to Sephardic Bikur Holim, Brooklyn, NY. For general support.
$5,200 to Torah Academy High School of Brooklyn, Brooklyn, NY. For general support.

$1,800 to American Friends of Yad Eliezer, Brooklyn, NY. For general support.
$1,000 to Sephardic Community Center, Brooklyn, NY. For general support.
$1,000 to Sephardic Food Fund, New York, NY. For general support.
$501 to Chabad of Great Neck, Great Neck, NY. For general support.
$500 to Beth Medrash Govoha, Brooklyn, NY. For general support.

5720
The Stanley & Frieda Cayre Foundation, Inc. ✧
c/o The Cayre Group
1407 Broadway, 41st Fl.
New York, NY 10018   (212) 789-7200
Contact: Stanley Cayre, Pres.

Established in 1993 in DE.
Donors: Stanley Cayre; Grace S. Cayre; Aurora Capital Assocs., LLC.
Foundation type: Independent foundation.
Financial data (yr. ended 12/31/04): Assets, $12,317,120 (M); gifts received, $368,410; expenditures, $693,268; qualifying distributions, $585,508; giving activities include $585,508 for 128 grants (high: $56,000; low: $36).
Purpose and activities: Giving primarily to Jewish agencies, temples, and yeshivas.
Fields of interest: Elementary/secondary education; Jewish agencies & temples.
Limitations: Giving primarily in NY.
Application information:
Initial approach: Letter
Deadline(s): None
Officers: Stanley Cayre, Pres.; Frieda Cayre, V.P.
EIN: 133746789
Selected grants: The following grants were reported in 2004.
$56,000 to Sephardic Bikur Holim, Brooklyn, NY. 2 grants: $50,000, $6,000
$25,000 to Ohel Yaacob Congregation, Deal, NJ.
$6,500 to University of Hartford, West Hartford, CT.
$5,000 to Central Fund of Israel, New York, NY.
$1,800 to Ilan High School, Long Branch, NJ.
$1,800 to Yeshivat Or Hatorah, Brooklyn, NY.
$1,300 to Nefesh Academy, Brooklyn, NY.
$1,000 to Chabad of Great Neck, Great Neck, NY.
$1,000 to Friends of the Israel Defense Forces, New York, NY.

5721
Cedar Fund, Inc. ✧
(formerly Hochschild Fund, Inc.)
c/o Anchin, Block & Anchin, LLP
1375 Broadway
New York, NY 10018

Incorporated in 1948 in NY as Hochschild Fund, Inc.; reorganized and renamed in 1985.
Foundation type: Independent foundation.
Financial data (yr. ended 12/31/05): Assets, $2,844,009 (M); expenditures, $1,546,496; qualifying distributions, $1,519,110; giving activities include $1,513,554 for 16 grants (high: $1,264,605; low: $1,000).
Fields of interest: Arts, multipurpose centers/programs; Arts; Health care; General charitable giving.

Limitations: Applications not accepted. Giving limited to NY. No grants to individuals, or for endowment funds, scholarships, fellowships, or research; no loans.
Application information: Contributes only to pre-selected organizations.
Officers and Directors:* Adam Hochschild,* Pres.; Kira Sergievsky,* V.P.; Alan D. Spiegel,* Secy.-Treas.; Nicholas Boillot; Lisa Labalme; Ann H. Poole.
EIN: 136091737
Selected grants: The following grants were reported in 2005.
$175,949 to Foundation for National Progress, San Francisco, CA.
$15,000 to Long Lake, Town of, Long Lake, NY.
$5,000 to American Red Cross, National Headquarters, DC.
$3,000 to Brearley School, New York, NY.
$2,000 to Adirondack Lakes Center for the Arts, Blue Mountain Lake, NY.
$2,000 to Residents Committee to Protect the Adirondacks, North Creek, NY.
$1,500 to Adirondack Council, Elizabethtown, NY.
$1,500 to Adirondack Museum, Blue Mountain Lake, NY.
$1,000 to Natural History Museum of the Adirondacks, Tupper Lake, NY.

5722
Centennial Foundation ✧
c/o Joel E. Sammet & Co.
60 Broad St., Ste. 3600
New York, NY 10004

Incorporated in 1965 in NY.
Donors: Henry H. Arnhold; Arnhold Ceramics, Inc.; A.M. & S.M. Kellen Foundation; Arnhold Foundation; A. Bleichroeder; S. Bleichroeder; Stephen M. Kellen.
Foundation type: Independent foundation.
Financial data (yr. ended 12/31/05): Assets, $4,309,297 (M); gifts received, $660,428; expenditures, $1,126,915; qualifying distributions, $1,120,520; giving activities include $1,114,125 for 46 grants (high: $250,000; low: $1,000; average: $5,000–$25,000).
Purpose and activities: Giving primarily for the arts, higher education, children, youth and social services, health, international affairs and relations, and Jewish organizations.
Fields of interest: Media, television; Museums (art); Performing arts centers; Arts; Higher education; Health organizations, association; Human services; Children/youth, services; International affairs, goodwill promotion; International affairs, foreign policy; International affairs; Federated giving programs; Jewish federated giving programs; Jewish agencies & temples; Economically disadvantaged.
Limitations: Applications not accepted. Giving primarily in New York, NY. No grants to individuals.
Application information: Contributes only to pre-selected organizations.
Officers and Trustees:* Henry H. Arnhold,* Pres.; Michael Kellen,* Treas.; John P. Arnhold.
Number of staff: 1 part-time support.
EIN: 136189397
Selected grants: The following grants were reported in 2004.
$500,000 to American Academy in Berlin, New York, NY. For general support.
$60,000 to UJA-Federation of New York, New York, NY. For general support.

$48,750 to Conservation International, DC. For general support.

$38,500 to Young Audiences (YA), New York, NY. For general support.

$30,000 to American Council on Germany, New York, NY. For general support.

$25,000 to Leo Baeck Institute, New York, NY. For general support.

$25,000 to Philharmonic-Symphony Society of New York, New York, NY. For general support.

$22,500 to Juvenile Diabetes Research Foundation International, New York, NY. For general support.

$15,000 to Council on Foreign Relations, New York, NY. For general support.

$15,000 to W N E T Channel 13, New York, NY. For general support.

5723
The Central National-Gottesman Foundation ✧
3 Manhattanville Rd.
Purchase, NY 10577-2110

Established in 1981 in NY.
Donor: Central National-Gottesman, Inc.
Foundation type: Company-sponsored foundation.
Financial data (yr. ended 12/31/04): Assets, $23,021,293 (M); expenditures, $1,186,253; qualifying distributions, $869,861; giving activities include $625,050 for 74 grants (high: $50,000; low: $250), and $138,733 for 21 grants to individuals (high: $13,705; low: $934).
Purpose and activities: The foundation supports Jewish agencies and temples, hospitals, and organizations involved with literature, higher education, health, food services, human services, and international affairs.
Fields of interest: Literature; Higher education; Hospitals (general); Health care; Food services; Human services; International affairs, U.N.; Jewish agencies & temples.
Type of support: General/operating support; Employee-related scholarships.
Limitations: Giving primarily in New York, NY. No grants to individuals (except for employee-related scholarships).
Application information:
Initial approach: Contact foundation for application information
Officers: Kenneth L. Wallach, Pres; Ira D. Wallach, Exec. V.P.; Peter Sigefried, Secy.; Steven Eigen, Treas.
EIN: 133047546
Selected grants: The following grants were reported in 2004.
$50,000 to City Harvest, New York, NY.
$50,000 to People for the American Way Foundation, DC.
$50,000 to United Nations Association of the United States of America, New York, NY.
$37,000 to National Book Foundation, New York, NY.
$36,000 to American Jewish Committee, New York, NY.
$26,200 to New York Public Library, New York, NY.
$25,000 to American Museum of Natural History, New York, NY.
$25,000 to White Plains Hospital Center, White Plains, NY.
$10,000 to Poets and Writers, New York, NY.
$10,000 to Student Sponsor Partners, New York, NY.

5724
Central New York Community Foundation, Inc. ▼
500 S. Salina St., Ste. 428
Syracuse, NY 13202 (315) 422-9538
Contact: Margaret G. "Peggy" Ogden, C.E.O.
FAX: (315) 471-6031; E-mail: peggy@cnycf.org;
URL: http://www.cnycf.org

Incorporated in 1927 in NY; reorganized in 1951.
Foundation type: Community foundation.
Financial data (yr. ended 3/31/05): Assets, $96,146,225 (M); gifts received, $6,835,313; expenditures, $6,800,033; giving activities include $5,070,139 for 1,231 grants (high: $295,000; low: $30), and $189,660 for 132 grants to individuals.
Purpose and activities: The mission of the foundation is to enhance the quality of life for those who live and work within the community by: 1) encouraging the growth of a permanent charitable endowment to meet the community's changing opportunities and needs; 2) providing donors and their diverse philanthropic interests with vehicles to make giving easy, personally satisfying and effective; 3) serving as a catalyst, neutral convener, and facilitator, stimulating and promoting collaborations among various organizations to accomplish common objectives; and 4) carrying out a strategic grant making program that is flexible, visionary, and inclusive.
Fields of interest: Humanities; Historic preservation/historical societies; Arts; Child development, education; Education; Environment; Health care; Disasters, Hurricane Katrina; Recreation; Child development, services; Homeless, human services; Human services; Community development; Homeless.
Type of support: Management development/capacity building; Capital campaigns; Building/renovation; Equipment; Program development; Publication; Seed money; Scholarship funds; Research; Technical assistance; Scholarships—to individuals; Matching/challenge support.
Limitations: Giving limited to Onondaga and Madison counties, NY, for general grants; giving in a wider area for Donor-Advised funds. No support for religious purposes. No grants to individuals (except for scholarships), or for conferences and seminars, deficit financing, consulting services, endowment funds, fellowships, operating budgets, medical or academic research (except where directed by a donor), or travel expenses; no loans.
Publications: Annual report (including application guidelines); Informational brochure (including application guidelines); Newsletter.
Application information: Visit foundation Web site for application form and guidelines. Faxed applications are not accepted. Application form required.
Initial approach: Letter or telephone
Copies of proposal: 1
Deadline(s): Feb. 10, Apr. 14, and Aug. 11
Board meeting date(s): Mar., May, Sept., and Dec.
Final notification: Immediately following board meetings
Officers and Directors:* Michael E. O'Connor,* Chair.; Margaret G. "Peggy" Ogden, C.E.O. and Pres.; Mary C. Meyer, V.P., Finance and Admin.; Kimberly S. Scott, V.P., Progs.; Dirk E. Sonneborn,* V.P., Devel. and Mktg.; Edward J. Audi; Vicki Brakens; Michael J. Connor; Christine Woodcock Dettor; Ray T. Forbes, M.D.; Gary R. Germain; H. Baird Hansen; Gloria Hooper-Rasberry; Anne Messenger; Paul Nojaim; Sybil Ridings Oakes;

Marilyn L. Pinsky; Jeffrey M. Rubenstein; Mansukh J. Shah; Mary Ann Shaw; Barry L. Wells.
Number of staff: 11 full-time professional; 2 full-time support.
EIN: 150626910
Selected grants: The following grants were reported in 2005.
$100,000 to Discovery Center of Science and Technology, Syracuse, NY. For final design phase of Making More of the MOST capital project.
$100,000 to Salvation Army of Syracuse, Syracuse, NY. For Prevention Services Partnership with Dunbar Association and Huntington Family Centers, which will support joint provision of mandated case services for families at-risk of child abuse and neglect.
$60,000 to Boys and Girls Club of Syracuse, Syracuse, NY. For revenue action plan.
$27,500 to Loretto Independent Living Services, Syracuse, NY. To expand and upgrade McAuliffe Day Center for frail elderly.
$25,000 to Manlius Library, Manlius, NY. For renovation and expansion of library.
$25,000 to Syracuse City School District Educational Foundation, Syracuse, NY. For Syracuse Middle School Choice, a mentoring project.
$20,000 to Legal Aid Society of Oneida County, Utica, NY. To create central New York Legal Helpline for low-income individuals needing legal assistance.
$18,000 to On Point for College, Syracuse, NY. To develop renewable and multi-year sources of funding for long-term sustainability.
$15,640 to DeRuyter Central School, DeRuyter, NY. To create after-school program for latchkey children in DeRuyter community.
$11,500 to ThINC: The Institution of A Now Culture, Syracuse, NY. For Gallery without Walls exhibition, creation of catalog and other educational programming.

5725
Century 21 Associates Foundation, Inc. ✧
(formerly Gindi Associates Foundation, Inc.)
22 Cortlandt St.
New York, NY 10007

Established in 1982 in NJ.
Donor: Century 21, Inc.
Foundation type: Company-sponsored foundation.
Financial data (yr. ended 5/31/04): Assets, $2,258,096 (L); gifts received, $2,000,000; expenditures, $1,734,684; qualifying distributions, $1,734,566; giving activities include $1,732,966 for 274 grants (high: $166,667; low: $100).
Purpose and activities: The foundation supports hospitals and organizations involved with education, human services, and Judaism.
Fields of interest: Elementary/secondary education; Education; Hospitals (general); Human services; Federated giving programs; Jewish federated giving programs; Jewish agencies & temples.
Limitations: Applications not accepted. Giving primarily in NJ and Brooklyn and New York, NY. No grants to individuals.
Application information: Contributes only to pre-selected organizations.
Trustees: Abraham Gindi; Raymond Gindi; Sam Gindi.
EIN: 212412138

5726
Dorothy Jordan Chadwick Fund ✧
c/o U.S. Trust, Tax Dept.
114 W. 47th St., 7th Fl.
New York, NY 10036

Trust established in 1957 in NY.
Donors: Dorothy J. Chadwick†; Dorothy R. Kidder†.
Foundation type: Independent foundation.
Financial data (yr. ended 5/31/06): Assets,
$21,002,953 (M); expenditures, $1,576,335;
qualifying distributions, $1,490,159; giving
activities include $1,407,200 for 29 grants (high:
$200,000; low: $5,000).
Purpose and activities: Giving primarily to
organizations of interest to the family, with
emphasis on purposes initiated by the fund. These
interests include environmental and wildlife
conservation, and non-traditional developmental
education.
Fields of interest: Performing arts, education; Arts;
Elementary/secondary education; Education;
Environment; Animals/wildlife, preservation/
protection; Health care; Human services.
Type of support: General/operating support;
Continuing support; Capital campaigns; Building/
renovation; Program development; Seed money;
Research.
Limitations: Giving primarily along the Eastern
Seaboard (Boston, MA to Washington, DC). No
grants to individuals.
Publications: Application guidelines.
Application information: Application form not
required.
   Initial approach: Letter
   Copies of proposal: 1
   Deadline(s): None
   Board meeting date(s): As required
   Final notification: May or June
Trustees: Katherine K. Hildner; Randolph K. Luskey;
U.S. Trust.
EIN: 136069950
Selected grants: The following grants were reported
in 2004.
$300,000 to New England Conservatory of Music,
   Boston, MA.
$125,600 to Proctor Academy, Andover, NH.
$25,000 to Childrens Storefront, New York, NY.
$22,500 to Institute of Contemporary Art, Boston,
   MA.
$15,000 to City Kids to Wilderness Project,
   Jackson, WY.
$15,000 to Food and Friends, DC.
$10,000 to Reach Out and Read, Somerville, MA.
$10,000 to University of Vermont, Burlington, VT.
$10,000 to Washington College, Chestertown, MD.
$5,000 to Darien Nature Center, Darien, CT.

5727
Chai X Four Charitable Trust ✧
c/o Abraham Trusts
200 W. 57th St., Ste. 1005
New York, NY 10019

Established in 1990 in NY.
Donors: Rebecca Abraham Gridish; Tamar A.
Wolchok; Simona Abraham Ganz; Laurie Abraham
Pinck; Martin Fawer; Estanne Abraham; Stephen
Rudin.
Foundation type: Independent foundation.
Financial data (yr. ended 10/31/05): Assets,
$10,743 (M); gifts received, $942,581;
expenditures, $995,003; qualifying distributions,

$994,795; giving activities include $994,795 for 43
grants (high: $713,000; low: $75).
Purpose and activities: Giving primarily to Jewish
charities and organizations.
Fields of interest: Human services; Jewish agencies
& temples.
Type of support: General/operating support.
Limitations: Applications not accepted. Giving
primarily in New York, NY. No grants to individuals.
Application information: Contributes only to
pre-selected organizations.
Trustees: Estanne Abraham; Simona Abraham
Ganz; Rebecca Abraham Gridish; Hirschell E. Levine;
Laurie A. Pinck; Richard A. Sauer; Tamar A. Wolchok.
EIN: 136963182

5728
Chaim Foundation ✧
c/o HIS
1310 48th St., Rm. 1
Brooklyn, NY 11219
Contact: Harry Silber, Pres.

Donor: Harry Silber.
Foundation type: Operating foundation.
Financial data (yr. ended 12/31/05): Assets,
$66,627 (M); gifts received, $1,295,900;
expenditures, $1,260,429; qualifying distributions,
$1,260,429; giving activities include $1,260,429
for 46+ grants (high: $299,000).
Purpose and activities: Giving primarily to Jewish
agencies, temples, and schools.
Fields of interest: Education; Human services;
Jewish agencies & temples.
Limitations: Applications not accepted. Giving
primarily in NY. No grants to individuals.
Application information: Contributes only to
pre-selected organizations.
Officers: Harry Silber, Pres.; Eva Silber, Secy.
EIN: 113247210
Selected grants: The following grants were reported
in 2004.
$41,640 to Tzedakah Vchesed, Brooklyn, NY.
$30,910 to Bais Yaakov Academy.
$15,300 to Jewish Center for Special Education,
   Brooklyn, NY.
$14,500 to Keren Aniyim, Brooklyn, NY.
$12,500 to Young Israel of Teaneck, Teaneck, NJ.
$7,200 to Yeshiva Torah Vodaath, Brooklyn, NY.
$7,000 to Yad Eliezer, Brooklyn, NY.
$5,860 to Sinai Academy, Brooklyn, NY.

5729
Chana Sasha Foundation, Inc. ✧
1 State St. Plz., 29th Fl.
New York, NY 10004 (212) 344-5210
Contact: Morris Wolfson, Pres.

Established in 1995 in NY.
Foundation type: Independent foundation.
Financial data (yr. ended 8/31/05): Assets,
$1,914,922 (M); gifts received, $391,603;
expenditures, $400,431; qualifying distributions,
$400,431; giving activities include $373,644 for
grants.
Limitations: Giving primarily in NY. No grants to
individuals.
Application information:
   Deadline(s): None
Officer: Morris Wolfson, Pres.
EIN: 133739189

5730
**Marcy and Leona Chanin Foundation,
Inc.** ✧
50 E. 77th St., Ste. 11B
New York, NY 10021

Established in 1972.
Foundation type: Independent foundation.
Financial data (yr. ended 12/31/05): Assets,
$6,213,148 (M); expenditures, $368,341;
qualifying distributions, $358,941; giving activities
include $319,253 for 122 grants (high: $50,000;
low: $25).
Purpose and activities: Giving primarily for Jewish
religious, educational, and welfare organizations;
support also for health associations, the arts, and
higher education.
Fields of interest: Museums; Performing arts; Arts;
Higher education; Medical school/education;
Education; Health organizations, association;
Neuroscience research; Human services; Jewish
agencies & temples.
Type of support: General/operating support.
Limitations: Applications not accepted. Giving
primarily in New York, NY. No grants to individuals.
Application information: Contributes only to
pre-selected organizations.
Officer: Leona Chanin, Pres.
EIN: 237156719

5731
Charina Foundation, Inc.
85 Broad St.
New York, NY 10004
Contact: Richard L. Menschel, Pres.

Incorporated in 1980 in NY.
Donors: Richard L. Menschel; The Menschel
Foundation.
Foundation type: Independent foundation.
Financial data (yr. ended 8/31/05): Assets,
$25,504,771 (M); expenditures, $1,086,747;
qualifying distributions, $1,069,423; giving
activities include $1,061,103 for 311 grants (high:
$250,000; low: $100).
Purpose and activities: Emphasis on arts and
culture, including museums; support also for health
services, medical research, and hospitals; higher
and other education; Jewish organizations, including
welfare funds; recreation; and community
development.
Fields of interest: Museums; Arts; Higher
education; Business school/education; Medical
school/education; Education; Hospitals (general);
Medical care, rehabilitation; Health care; Medical
research, institute; Legal services; Recreation;
Community development; Jewish agencies &
temples.
Type of support: Continuing support; Annual
campaigns; Capital campaigns; Building/
renovation; Equipment; Endowments;
Professorships; Seed money; Curriculum
development; Scholarship funds; Research;
Matching/challenge support.
Limitations: Applications not accepted. Giving
primarily in NY. No grants to individuals.
Application information: Contributes only to
pre-selected organizations.
Officers and Directors: * Richard L. Menschel,*
Pres. and Treas.; Ronay Menschel,* Secy.; Eugene
P. Polk.
Number of staff: None.
EIN: 133050294

Selected grants: The following grants were reported in 2005.

$250,000 to Schwab Fund for Charitable Giving, San Francisco, CA.

$25,000 to Metropolitan Museum of Art, New York, NY.

$15,000 to Syracuse University, Syracuse, NY.

$10,000 to Socrates Sculpture Park, Long Island City, NY.

$9,100 to Storm King Art Center, Mountainville, NY.

$5,000 to Cornell University, Ithaca, NY.

$3,000 to United Way, NY.

$2,500 to Baruch College Fund, New York, NY.

$1,500 to Aperture Foundation, New York, NY.

$1,000 to Jewish Womens Foundation of New York, New York, NY.

5732
Charitable Leadership Foundation ▼ ✧
747 Pierce Rd.
Clifton Park, NY   12065   (518) 877-6701
Contact: Eliza McKinney, Prog. Off., MTAP
FAX: (518) 877-6546;
E-mail: info@charitableleadership.org; URL: http://www.charitableleadership.org/

Established in 1997 in NY.
Donor: Isabel Liebich.
Foundation type: Independent foundation.
Financial data (yr. ended 12/31/05): Assets, $25,434,751 (M); expenditures, $10,042,896; qualifying distributions, $9,518,425; giving activities include $8,519,308 for 21 grants (high: $6,477,450; low: $10,000; average: $34,051–$100,000), and $165,470 for 1 foundation-administered program.
Purpose and activities: Giving primarily in the areas of education, housing, job skills, and economic opportunities for the low-income population; support also for initiatives in medicine and medical research.
Fields of interest: Education; Community development; Foundations (community).
Type of support: Program development; Technical assistance; Program-related investments/loans.
Limitations: Giving primarily in upstate NY. Generally, no support for arts and cultural organizations, or religious organizations for sectarian purposes. No grants to individuals.
Application information: See foundation Web site for application guidelines.
 Initial approach: Letter of inquiry, no more than 2 pages
 Deadline(s): None
Officers and Trustee:* Richard C. Liebich,* C.E.O. and Pres.; Jennifer L. Cornell, Secy.-Treas., Prog. Off., Medical Affairs, and Admin. Mgr.; L. James Miller, C.I.O.; Rosemary Weaver McKenna, Genl. Counsel and Prog. Off., Ed.
EIN: 161514887
Selected grants: The following grants were reported in 2004.
$1,914,564 to Project Lead the Way, Clifton Park, NY. For educational program.
$118,224 to Habitat for Humanity, Capital District, Albany, NY. For North Albany Neighborhood Revitalization Project.
$89,010 to Rensselaer City School District, Rensselaer, NY. To improve literacy.
$86,235 to Research Foundation of the State University of New York, Albany, NY. For housing expansion.

$51,338 to Middleburgh Central School District, Middleburgh, NY. To improve literacy.

$37,842 to Greater Amsterdam School District, Amsterdam, NY. To improve literacy.

$35,000 to College of Saint Rose, Albany, NY. For problem-based learning and teaching in science and math.

$34,396 to Russell Sage College, Troy, NY. For Girls Excited about Engineering, Mathematics, and Computer Science.

$34,215 to Albany School District, Albany, NY. To improve literacy.

$25,000 to State University of New York Empire State College, Saratoga Springs, NY. For master of arts in teaching.

5733
Charitable Trust dated 4/28/83 ✧
c/o Cravath, Swaine & Moore
P.O. Box 825
New York, NY   10101-0825

Established in 1983 in NY.
Donor: George J. Gillespie III.
Foundation type: Independent foundation.
Financial data (yr. ended 3/31/06): Assets, $2,642,351 (M); gifts received, $902,150; expenditures, $341,690; qualifying distributions, $341,440; giving activities include $341,440 for 33 grants (high: $177,200; low: $1,000).
Purpose and activities: Giving primarily to hospitals, as well as for museums, including a media broadcast museum; funding also for higher education, health associations, boys and girls clubs, and social services.
Fields of interest: Museums (art); Museums (specialized); Historic preservation/historical societies; Higher education; Libraries/library science; Education; Hospitals (general); Multiple sclerosis; Boys & girls clubs; Human services; Children/youth, services.
Type of support: General/operating support.
Limitations: Applications not accepted. Giving primarily in the greater New York, NY, area; some funding also in CT. No grants to individuals.
Application information: Contributes only to pre-selected organizations.
Trustee: George J. Gillespie III.
EIN: 133183734
Selected grants: The following grants were reported in 2006.
$11,000 to Convent of the Sacred Heart, Greenwich, CT. 2 grants: $10,000, $1,000
$10,000 to National Trust for Historic Preservation, DC.
$5,000 to Greenwich Hospital, Greenwich, CT.
$5,000 to Millbrook School, Millbrook, NY.
$5,000 to Pomfret School, Pomfret, CT.
$2,500 to Frick Collection, New York, NY. 2 grants: $1,000, $1,500
$1,000 to Muscular Dystrophy Association, Tucson, AZ.
$1,000 to Pregnancy Care Center, New Rochelle, NY.

5734
Charitable Venture Foundation ✧
747 Pierce Rd.
Clifton Park, NY   12065   (518) 877-8454
Contact: William Dessingue, Exec. Dir.

Established in 1992 in NY.
Donors: Herbert K. Liebich†; Isabel C. Liebich.
Foundation type: Independent foundation.
Financial data (yr. ended 12/31/04): Assets, $4,264,551 (M); expenditures, $580,437; qualifying distributions, $544,970; giving activities include $490,915 for 15 grants (high: $130,000; low: $2,698).
Purpose and activities: Giving primarily for education.
Fields of interest: Education; Housing/shelter, development; Human services; Community development.
Type of support: Program development; Seed money.
Limitations: Giving primarily in the Albany, NY, area. No support for religious organizations for religious purposes, or for arts or cultural organizations. No grants to individuals, or for capital projects or operating budgets.
Publications: Program policy statement.
Application information: Application form required.
 Initial approach: 1- to 2-page letter of inquiry
 Deadline(s): None
Trustees: Arthur Bates; Donald Liebich; Kurt Liebich; Richard C. Liebich; Daniel P. Nolan.
Number of staff: 1 part-time support.
EIN: 141751211

5735
Chasanoff Foundation, Inc. ✧
c/o Michael J. Chasanoff
2 Jericho Plz.
Jericho, NY   11753-1658

Established in 1989 in NY.
Donors: Chasco Co.; Hubspot Co.; Allan Chasanoff; Michael J. Chasanoff; Nancy Chasanoff; Robert Chasanoff; Judith Chasanoff; Stephen Chasanoff.
Foundation type: Independent foundation.
Financial data (yr. ended 6/30/05): Assets, $9,807 (M); gifts received, $631,500; expenditures, $626,118; qualifying distributions, $626,118; giving activities include $597,180 for 120 grants (high: $100,000; low: $50).
Purpose and activities: Giving primarily to art and cultural programs, education, hospitals and health associations, and Jewish agencies and temples.
Fields of interest: Museums; Performing arts, theater; Arts; Higher education; Education; Hospitals (general); Health organizations, association; Heart & circulatory research; Jewish agencies & temples.
Limitations: Applications not accepted. Giving primarily in NY. No grants to individuals.
Application information: Contributes only to pre-selected organizations.
Officers and Directors:* Michael J. Chasanoff,* Pres.; Nancy Chasanoff Butler,* V.P.; Judith Chasanoff,* V.P.; Robert Chasanoff,* V.P.; Stephen Chasanoff,* V.P.; Allan Chasanoff,* Secy.-Treas.
EIN: 112978524

5736
The Chasdei Yisroel Charitable Trust ✧
P.O. Box 190-312
Brooklyn, NY   11219
Application address: c/o Dov Rabinowitz, Tr., 1446 42nd St., Brooklyn, NY 11219, tel.: (718) 972-2440

Established in 2000 in NY.

Donors: Strand Hill; Island Gardens; RL Assocs.; Sunrise Apartments LLC; 30 Bay Apartments; 7101 Colonial; 800 Ocean Apartments; 8320 Apartments.
Foundation type: Independent foundation.
Financial data (yr. ended 10/31/05): Assets, $549,604 (M); gifts received, $1,883,000; expenditures, $1,899,490; qualifying distributions, $1,891,000; giving activities include $1,891,000 for 54 grants (high: $125,000; low: $500).
Fields of interest: Jewish agencies & temples.
Limitations: Giving primarily in NY. No grants to individuals.
Application information:
  Initial approach: Letter
  Deadline(s): None
Trustees: Dov Rabinowitz; Goldy Rabinowitz.
EIN: 116552381

5737
Chatterjee Charitable Foundation ◇
888 7th Ave., Ste. 3000
New York, NY   10106

Established in 1995 in NY.
Donors: Purnendu Chatterjee; Sidhartha Maitra; Subir K. Sanyal.
Foundation type: Independent foundation.
Financial data (yr. ended 11/30/03): Assets, $15,612,066 (M); expenditures, $847,521; qualifying distributions, $835,514; giving activities include $831,757 for 14 grants (high: $610,000; low: $250).
Purpose and activities: Giving primarily to an institute of molecular medicine, as well as for higher education and federated giving programs; funding also for children, youth and social services.
Fields of interest: Higher education; Biomedicine; Human services; Children/youth, services; Federated giving programs; Science, research.
International interests: India.
Limitations: Applications not accepted. Giving on a national basis. No grants to individuals.
Application information: Contributes only to pre-selected organizations.
Director: Purnendu Chatterjee.
EIN: 137072667
Selected grants: The following grants were reported in 2003.
$610,000 to Institute of Molecular Medicine, Kolkata, India. .
$100,000 to Asia Society, New York, NY. For International Asian Art Fair.
$53,407 to University of California, School of Journalism, Berkeley, CA. For Nirupama Chatterjee Teaching.
$11,500 to Brearley School, New York, NY. For unrestricted support.
$5,000 to Student/Partner Alliance, Millburn, NJ. For unrestricted support.
$1,600 to Central Park Conservancy, New York, NY. For unrestricted support.
$1,000 to Abraham Lincoln School for Boys, New York, NY. For unrestricted support.
$1,000 to Cheetah Conservation Fund, Cincinnati, OH. For unrestricted support.
$1,000 to Dr. William Bissell Fund for Hospital Aid, Lakeville, CT. For general support.
$1,000 to Teach for America, New York, NY. For unrestricted support.

5738
**Chautauqua Region Community
  Foundation, Inc.**
418 Spring St.
Jamestown, NY   14701   (716) 661-3390
Contact: Randall J. Sweeney, Exec. Dir.; For grant inquiries: June C. Diethrick, Grants Coord.; For scholarship inquiries: Lisa W. Lynde, Scholarship Coord.
FAX: (716) 488-0387; *E-mail:* crcf@crcfonline.org; Grant inquiries tel.: (716) 661-3392 and E-mail: jdiethrick@crcfonline.org; URL: http://www.crcfonline.org
Scholarship inquiries E-mail: llynde@crcfonline.org; Kids First Mini-Grants E-mail: ccy@crcfonline.org

Incorporated in 1978 in NY.
Foundation type: Community foundation.
Financial data (yr. ended 12/31/05): Assets, $51,307,520 (M); gifts received, $1,560,491; expenditures, $2,748,500; giving activities include $1,385,419 for 474 grants (high: $75,000; low: $100), and $626,139 for 813 grants to individuals (high: $3,500; low: $100).
Purpose and activities: The foundation seeks to enrich the quality of life in the Chautauqua region.
Fields of interest: Arts; Libraries/library science; Education; Housing/shelter, development; Children/youth, services; Human services; Community development; Government/public administration.
Type of support: Program development; General/operating support; Continuing support; Building/renovation; Equipment; Emergency funds; Conferences/seminars; Publication; Seed money; Scholarships—to individuals; Matching/challenge support.
Limitations: Giving limited to the southern Chautauqua County, NY, area. No support for religious purposes (excluding church related requests supported by the Karl Peterson Fund only). No grants to individuals (except for scholarship grants), or for debt retirement.
Publications: Application guidelines; Annual report (including application guidelines); Informational brochure; Newsletter.
Application information: Visit foundation Web site for application forms and additional guidelines per grant type. Kids First Mini-Grants range from $100 to $500. Application form required.
  Initial approach: Submit application form and attachments
  Copies of proposal: 16
  Deadline(s): Jan. 1 to Jan. 31 for Karl Peterson grants; Jan. 15 to Feb. 28 for Kids First Mini-Grants; Sept. 1 to Oct. 31 for Community Service grants; and the last Fri. of each month for Fields-of-Interest grants
  Board meeting date(s): Monthly
  Final notification: Within 1 month for Field-of-Interest grants; 3 to 4 months for others
Officers and Directors:* Michael D. Metzger,* Pres.; Lyman A. Buck III,* V.P.; Cristie L. Herbst,* Secy.; Paul H. Hedberg,* Treas.; Randall J. Sweeney, Exec. Dir.; Daniel A. Black; Hon. Stephen W. Cass; Anna Marie Jochum; Bridget B. Johnson; Melsetta H. McFadden; Max R. Pickard; Kristy B. Zabrodsky.
Number of staff: 7 full-time professional.
EIN: 161116837

5739
The Chazen Foundation ◇
c/o Nathan Berkman & Co., Inc.
29 Broadway, Ste. 2900
New York, NY   10006
Application address: 767 5th Ave., 26th Fl., New York, NY 10153

Established in 1985 in NY.
Donors: Jerome Chazen; Simona Chazen.
Foundation type: Independent foundation.
Financial data (yr. ended 12/31/04): Assets, $37,576,834 (M); gifts received, $1,764,500; expenditures, $2,308,522; qualifying distributions, $1,963,075; giving activities include $1,779,436 for 102+ grants (high: $532,200; low: $300), and $137,000 for 49 grants to individuals (high: $5,000; low: $500).
Purpose and activities: Support for social services, higher education, music, museums, and medical needs.
Fields of interest: Museums; Performing arts, music; Arts; Higher education; Business school/education; Hospitals (general); Human services; Jewish federated giving programs; Jewish agencies & temples.
International interests: Israel.
Type of support: General/operating support; Capital campaigns; Building/renovation; Professorships; Scholarship funds; Grants to individuals; Scholarships—to individuals.
Limitations: Giving primarily in the northeastern U.S.; education grants limited to students in the Rockland County, NY, area.
Publications: Application guidelines; Informational brochure.
Application information:
  Initial approach: Letter
  Deadline(s): None
Trustees: Jerome Chazen; Simona Chazen.
Number of staff: 1 part-time professional; 1 part-time support.
EIN: 133229474
Selected grants: The following grants were reported in 2003.
$203,080 to Museum of Arts and Design, New York, NY.
$101,125 to Volunteer Counseling Service of Rockland County, New City, NY.
$16,500 to Columbia University, New York, NY.
$6,959 to Metropolitan Opera, New York, NY.
$5,000 to University of Scranton, Scranton, PA.
$3,400 to Museum of Modern Art, New York, NY.
$2,000 to Harvard University, Medical School, Cambridge, MA.
$2,000 to Phoenix House Development Fund, New York, NY.
$500 to Memorial Sloan-Kettering Cancer Center, New York, NY.
$500 to National Marfan Foundation, Port Washington, NY.

5740
Chehebar Family Foundation, Inc. ◇
1000 Pennsylvania Ave.
Brooklyn, NY   11207-8417

Incorporated in 1985 in NY.
Donors: Albert Chehebar; Isaac Chehebar; Jack Chehebar; Joseph Chehebar; Rainbow Store, Inc.; Rainbow Apparel Companies; Baraka Realty; Skiva International; Joseph Chehebar Family Foundation; Middlegate Securities, Ltd.; Ahaba Ve Ahva

Congregation; Charles Kushner; Ike Rudy; Magen Israel Society.
Foundation type: Independent foundation.
Financial data (yr. ended 8/31/05): Assets, $3,264,096 (M); gifts received, $3,902,101; expenditures, $2,088,933; qualifying distributions, $2,086,970; giving activities include $2,086,970 for 1,462 grants (high: $250,000; low: $18).
Purpose and activities: Giving primarily to Jewish temples and agencies.
Fields of interest: Elementary/secondary education; Jewish federated giving programs; Jewish agencies & temples.
Limitations: Applications not accepted. Giving primarily in the greater metropolitan New York, NY, area, with emphasis on Brooklyn. No grants to individuals.
Application information: Unsolicited requests for funds not accepted.
Directors: Albert Chehebar; Jack Chehebar; Joseph Chehebar; Isaac Shehebar.
EIN: 133178015

5741
Joseph Chehebar Family Foundation ✧
1000 Pennsylvania Ave.
Brooklyn, NY 11207

Established in 1998 in NY.
Donors: Joseph Chehebar; Middlegate Securities, Ltd.
Foundation type: Independent foundation.
Financial data (yr. ended 12/31/05): Assets, $33,410 (M); gifts received, $1,080,000; expenditures, $1,209,250; qualifying distributions, $1,209,158; giving activities include $1,209,158 for 177 grants (high: $175,000; low: $5).
Purpose and activities: Giving primarily for Jewish organizations.
Fields of interest: Theological school/education; Jewish agencies & temples.
Limitations: Applications not accepted. Giving primarily in NY. No grants to individuals.
Application information: Contributes only to pre-selected organizations.
Officer: Joseph Chehebar, Mgr.
EIN: 113388342

5742
Chencinski Brothers Charitable Foundation, Inc. ✧ ☆
c/o Issac Gottesman
1879 48th St.
Brooklyn, NY 11204-1239

Established in 1994.
Donors: Isaac Chencinski; Moses Chencinski.
Foundation type: Independent foundation.
Financial data (yr. ended 12/31/05): Assets, $276,685 (M); gifts received, $927,835; expenditures, $1,001,419; qualifying distributions, $1,000,100; giving activities include $1,000,100 for grants.
Purpose and activities: Giving for Jewish educational activities.
Fields of interest: Jewish federated giving programs; Jewish agencies & temples.
Limitations: Applications not accepted. Giving primarily in Brooklyn, NY. No grants to individuals.
Application information: Contributes only to pre-selected organizations.

Officers: Moses Chencinski, Pres.; Isaac Chencinski, Secy.-Treas.
EIN: 521892265

5743
The Chernin Family Foundation, Inc. ✧ ☆
c/o Executive Monetary Mgmt.
220 E. 42nd St., 32nd Fl.
New York, NY 10017

Established in 2000 in DE.
Donors: Peter Chernin; Megan Chernin.
Foundation type: Independent foundation.
Financial data (yr. ended 12/31/05): Assets, $381,986 (M); gifts received, $300,801; expenditures, $390,929; qualifying distributions, $383,550; giving activities include $383,550 for 20 grants (high: $100,000; low: $100).
Fields of interest: Arts; Education; Environment; Hospitals (general); Human services; Children/youth, services.
Limitations: Applications not accepted. Giving on a national basis. No grants to individuals.
Application information: Contributes only to pre-selected organizations.
Officers and Director: * Peter Chernin, Pres.; Megan Chernin, V.P. and Treas.; John D. Dadakis,* Secy.
EIN: 522281012
Selected grants: The following grants were reported in 2003.
$55,000 to Fulfillment Fund, Los Angeles, CA.
$50,000 to Brown University, Providence, RI.
$50,000 to Harvard-Westlake School, North Hollywood, CA.
$25,000 to Community Partners, Los Angeles, CA.
$15,000 to Music Center Foundation, Los Angeles, CA.
$10,000 to PXE International, DC.
$2,500 to Manhattanville College, Purchase, NY.
$2,150 to AIDS Project Los Angeles (APLA), Los Angeles, CA.
$1,000 to Marthas Vineyard Hospital, Oak Bluffs, MA.
$1,000 to Spoken Interludes, Los Angeles, CA.

5744
Michael Chernow Trust 2 ✧ ☆
P.O. Box 197
Larchmont, NY 10538-0197 (914) 834-1900
Contact: Gordon S. Oppenheimer

Established in 1968 in NY.
Foundation type: Independent foundation.
Financial data (yr. ended 6/30/05): Assets, $1,545,867 (M); expenditures, $506,729; qualifying distributions, $469,971; giving activities include $445,500 for 26 grants (high: $300,000; low: $500).
Fields of interest: Performing arts, music; Performing arts, opera; Higher education; Health organizations, association; Jewish agencies & temples.
Limitations: Giving primarily in New York, NY.
Application information: Application form not required.
Deadline(s): None
Trustees: Albert Krassner; Martin P. Krassner; Lynn Streim.
EIN: 136758228

5745
Michael Chernow Trust ✧
P.O. Box 197
Larchmont, NY 10538-0197 (914) 834-1900
Contact: Gordon S. Oppenheimer

Established in 1975 in NY.
Foundation type: Independent foundation.
Financial data (yr. ended 6/30/05): Assets, $6,758,275 (M); expenditures, $563,115; qualifying distributions, $480,218; giving activities include $453,000 for 14 grants (high: $302,000; low: $1,000).
Fields of interest: Performing arts, opera; Hospitals (general); Eye diseases; Breast cancer research; Human services; Jewish federated giving programs; Biological sciences; Jewish agencies & temples; Economically disadvantaged.
Type of support: General/operating support; Continuing support; Research.
Limitations: Giving primarily in NY. No grants to individuals.
Application information: Application form not required.
Deadline(s): None
Trustees: Martin P. Krasner; Edward Streim; Lynn Streim.
EIN: 136758226
Selected grants: The following grants were reported in 2005.
$302,000 to Salk Institute for Biological Studies, San Diego, CA. For general support.
$56,000 to North Shore University Hospital, Manhasset, NY. For general support.
$18,000 to Temple Emanuel of Great Neck, Great Neck, NY. For general support.
$15,000 to Macula Foundation, New York, NY. For general support.
$15,000 to New Israel Fund, New York, NY. For general support.
$12,500 to Metropolitan Opera Association, New York, NY. For general support.
$10,000 to Union for Reform Judaism, New York, NY. For general support.
$7,000 to Ice Hockey in Harlem, New York, NY. For general support.
$5,000 to United States Holocaust Memorial Museum, DC. For general support.
$4,000 to City of Hope, New York, NY. For general support.

5746
Chesed Foundation ✧ ☆
3920 Cypress Ave.
Brooklyn, NY 11224

Established in 1997 in NY.
Donors: Michael Weiss; Michael Weiss Trust; Pelstate Trust; Idy Weiss Irrevocable Trust.
Foundation type: Independent foundation.
Financial data (yr. ended 12/31/05): Assets, $1,579,909 (M); gifts received, $940,321; expenditures, $579,398; qualifying distributions, $576,235; giving activities include $576,235 for 8 grants (high: $212,000; low: $14,235).
Fields of interest: Jewish agencies & temples.
Limitations: Applications not accepted. Giving primarily in Brooklyn, NY. No grants to individuals.
Application information: Contributes only to pre-selected organizations.
Trustee: Michael Weiss.
EIN: 113364001

5747
Chesed Foundation of America ✧
59 Maiden Ln., Plaza Level
New York, NY 10038
Contact: Henry Reinhold

Donors: George Karfunkel; Michael Karfunkel; Karfunkel Family Foundation.
Foundation type: Independent foundation.
Financial data (yr. ended 6/30/04): Assets, $28,368,406 (M); gifts received, $1,201,139; expenditures, $918,798; qualifying distributions, $700,540; giving activities include $700,540 for 118 grants (high: $200,000; low: $250).
Purpose and activities: Giving primarily to cover operating expenses for schools and synagogues, as well as for educational scholarships and assistance for the needy.
Fields of interest: Elementary/secondary education; Jewish federated giving programs; Jewish agencies & temples.
Application information:
   Initial approach: Letter
   Deadline(s): None
Officers: George Karfunkel, Pres.; Rene Karfunkel, V.P.
Trustee: Ann Karfunkel.
EIN: 133922068

5748
Judith L. Chiara Charitable Fund, Inc. ✧
c/o Loeb Partners Corp.
61 Broadway, Ste. 2400
New York, NY 10006

Established in 1997 in NY.
Foundation type: Independent foundation.
Financial data (yr. ended 10/31/05): Assets, $15,919,382 (M); expenditures, $1,127,808; qualifying distributions, $1,034,145; giving activities include $1,034,145 for grants.
Fields of interest: Arts; Education; Health organizations, association; Human services; Children/youth, services.
Limitations: Applications not accepted. Giving primarily in NY. No grants to individuals.
Application information: Contributes only to pre-selected organizations.
Trustees: John T. Beaty, Jr.; Judith L. Chiara; Jerome Manning.
EIN: 311577990
Selected grants: The following grants were reported in 2003.
$350,000 to Exponents, New York, NY. For unrestricted support.
$100,000 to Lyford Cay Foundation, New York, NY. For unrestricted support.
$75,000 to Catalog for Giving, New York, NY. For unrestricted support.
$75,000 to Children of Bellevue, New York, NY. 2 grants: $50,000 (For unrestricted support), $25,000 (For unrestricted support).
$50,000 to Council on Hemispheric Affairs, DC. For unrestricted support.
$50,000 to Madeira School, McLean, VA. For unrestricted support.
$25,000 to Villa I Tatti, Florence, Italy. For unrestricted support.
$20,000 to Center for Mind-Body Medicine, DC. For unrestricted support.
$20,000 to Handel House Foundation of America, New York, NY. For unrestricted support.

5749
The Children's Investment Fund Foundation ✧
(formerly Cooper-Hohn Family Foundation)
c/o Perlman & Perlman
41 Madison Ave., Ste. 40
New York, NY 10010-2202

Established in 2002 in NY.
Donors: Perry Capital Corp.; The Children's Investment Fund, Ltd.; The Children's Investment Fund, LP; TCIF Fund.
Foundation type: Independent foundation.
Financial data (yr. ended 12/31/05): Assets, $65,898,688 (M); gifts received, $30,374,811; expenditures, $2,480,297; qualifying distributions, $2,477,671; giving activities include $2,250,529 for 10 grants (high: $766,584; low: $14,650).
Purpose and activities: Support for organizations benefiting children in developing countries.
Fields of interest: Education; Youth development; International development; International economic development.
International interests: Developing countries.
Limitations: Applications not accepted. Giving on a national and international basis for the benefit of developing countries. No grants to individuals.
Application information: Contributes only to pre-selected organizations.
Trustees: Phyllis Kurlander Constanza; Jamie Cooper-Hohn; Peter McDermott.
EIN: 043632641

5750
China Medical Board of New York, Inc. ▼ ✧
750 3rd Ave., 23rd Fl.
New York, NY 10017-2701   (212) 682-8000
Contact: M. Roy Schwarz M.D., Pres.

Incorporated in 1928 in NY.
Donor: The Rockefeller Foundation.
Foundation type: Independent foundation.
Financial data (yr. ended 6/30/05): Assets, $223,771,873 (M); expenditures, $10,964,956; qualifying distributions, $10,252,472; giving activities include $7,702,703 for 26 grants (high: $1,012,000; low: $25,000; average: $100,000–$300,000), and $584,633 for 2 foundation-administered programs.
Purpose and activities: Grantmaking is aimed at institutions that are leading resources in their countries. The board is especially interested in grants to advance the recipient's pursuit of excellence and to enhance the academic and professional infrastructure of the institution. It also has special interest in innovative efforts designed to meet the needs of underserved areas. The board makes grants almost exclusively to institutions in East and Southeast Asia.
Fields of interest: Medical school/education; Libraries/library science; Nursing care; Health care; Health organizations, association; Medical research, institute.
International interests: Asia; China & Mongolia; Hong Kong; Indonesia; Korea; Malaysia; Philippines; Singapore; Southeast Asia; Taiwan; Thailand.
Type of support: Endowments; Program development; Conferences/seminars; Publication; Fellowships; Scholarship funds; Research; Technical assistance.
Limitations: Applications not accepted. Giving limited to East and Southeast Asia, including the People's Republic of China, Hong Kong, Indonesia, Korea, Malaysia, the Philippines, Singapore, Taiwan, and Thailand. No support for professional or scientific societies, or research institutes not directly under medical school control. No grants to individuals (except for scholarships and fellowships), or for capital projects.
Publications: Annual report.
Application information: Submit request through Dean's office of Asian institution in which foundation has a program of support.
   Board meeting date(s): June and Dec.
Officers and Trustees:* Mary Brown Bullock, Ph.D.*, Chair.; M. Roy Schwarz, M.D.*, Pres.; Jean Hogan, V.P., Admin.; Laura E. Butzel, Secy. and Genl. Counsel; Michael A. Duffy, Ph.D.*, Treas.; Jordan J. Cohen, M.D.; Jane E. Henney, M.D.; Thomas S. Inui, M.D.; Tom G. Kessinger, Ph.D.; Peter J. Robbins; Anthony J. Saich; Gloria H. Spivak.
Number of staff: 2 full-time professional; 3 full-time support.
EIN: 131659619
Selected grants: The following grants were reported in 2005.
$1,465,000 to Sun Yat-Sen University of Medical Sciences, Guangzhou, China. 2 grants: $815,000 to School of Nursing (For faculty and doctoral student training at four U.S. schools of nursing, extending earlier project creating new blueprint for nursing education in China), $650,000 (For state-of-the-art, simulation-based clinical skills learning center to train medical undergraduate students, graduate and postgraduate students, residents, fellows, practicing physicians, and nurses).
$1,082,000 to Central South University, Xiangya School of Medicine, Changsha, China. To establish South China Center for Medical Education, Research, and Development in south central China, in affiliation with University of Washington School of Medicine, which will train Chinese faculty and guide program initiation.
$861,600 to Peking Union Medical College, Beijing, China. 2 grants: $497,000 (For small grants program to improve quality and implementation of research projects about suicide in China through nationwide network of researchers from multiple disciplines to work with government and other stakeholders), $364,600 (For continuation of project with Chinese Academy of Medical Sciences, Institute of Medical Biology, to study genetic diversity among minority populations of China, create cell-DNA bank of Chinese minority groups, and study disease-related genes).
$660,200 to Fudan University, Shanghai, China. 2 grants: $310,200 to Shanghai Medical College (For two-year project to strengthen capacity of institutions to teach preventive medicine to medical students, promoting integrated preventive and medical services in clinical practice), $350,000 to Shanghai Medical College (For prevention of high-risk pregnancy and birth through establishment of training center at Women's and Children's Hospitals, emphasizing training practitioners from regions with significant rural populations).
$565,000 to Harbin Medical University, Harbin, China. For reform of medical education curriculum in accordance with international standards, and for training medical professionals to implement program.

$314,000 to Beijing University, Health Science Center, Beijing, China. For initiative to bring medicine and public health together in medical education through workshops and through team effort to study and modify medical school curricula.

$300,000 to Sichuan University, West China School of Public Health and West China Center of Medical Sciences, Chengdu, China. For initiative to formulate essential requirements for public health education, reform existing educational model of public health in China, and train qualified public health professionals.

5751
The William Chinnick Charitable Foundation ✧

c/o The Ayco Co., LP
P.O. Box 860
Saratoga Springs, NY 12866-0860
Contact: Nancy Furnari

Established in 1992 in FL.
Donor: William C. Swaney.
Foundation type: Independent foundation.
Financial data (yr. ended 12/31/04): Assets, $10,919,507 (M); expenditures, $817,324; qualifying distributions, $793,594; giving activities include $793,594 for 30 grants (high: $243,143; low: $1,000).
Purpose and activities: Giving primarily for Episcopal church support, and primary and secondary education, including an Episcopal school; support also for health care.
Fields of interest: Education; Health care; Health organizations; Human services; Residential/custodial care, hospices; Protestant agencies & churches.
Limitations: Applications not accepted. Giving on a national basis, with some emphasis on FL. No grants to individuals.
Application information: Contributes only to pre-selected organizations.
Officers: William C. Swaney, Pres. and Treas.; Nancy C. Swaney, V.P.; Richard G. Swaney, Secy.
EIN: 650377446
Selected grants: The following grants were reported in 2003.
$579,244 to Saint Josephs Episcopal School, Boynton Beach, FL. For general support.
$500,000 to YMCA of Greater Grand Rapids, Grand Rapids, MI. For general support.
$103,100 to Community Child Care Center of Delray Beach, Delray Beach, FL. For general support.
$10,000 to Bethesda Hospital Foundation, Boynton Beach, FL. For general support.
$10,000 to CRC Recovery Foundation, Delray Beach, FL. For general support.
$7,500 to Young Life, Holland, MI. For general support.
$5,000 to Memorial Sloan-Kettering Cancer Center, New York, NY. For general support.
$5,000 to Saint Lukes Wood River Foundation, Ketchum, ID. For general support.
$2,500 to Hospice of Palm Beach County, West Palm Beach, FL. For general support.
$1,500 to Lupus Foundation of America, Newton, MA. For general support.

5752
M. A. Chisholm Charitable Trust ✧

P.O. Box 2004
New York, NY 10109-1910
Application address: c/o U.S. Trust, 114 W. 47th St., New York, NY 10036

Established in 1991 in NY.
Donors: E.G. Chisholm; M.A. Chisholm.
Foundation type: Independent foundation.
Financial data (yr. ended 11/30/03): Assets, $15,486,521 (M); expenditures, $728,896; qualifying distributions, $706,127; giving activities include $677,200 for 72 grants (high: $50,000; low: $1,000).
Fields of interest: Museums; Performing arts; Arts; Higher education; Medical school/education; Christian agencies & churches.
Limitations: Giving primarily in NY. No grants to individuals.
Application information:
  Initial approach: Letter
  Deadline(s): None
Trustee: U.S. Trust.
EIN: 136984354
Selected grants: The following grants were reported in 2003.
$50,000 to Little School, San Francisco, CA. For capital campaign.
$50,000 to Smith College, Northampton, MA. To establish JGC Lindsey Faculty Fellowship Fund.
$25,000 to Alvin Ailey Dance Foundation, New York, NY.
$25,000 to American Ballet Theater, New York, NY. For studio scholarships.
$25,000 to Grameen Foundation USA, DC. For India Initiative.
$25,000 to Harlem Educational Activities Fund, New York, NY.
$25,000 to Metropolitan Opera Guild, New York, NY.
$10,000 to Mabel Mercer Foundation, New York, NY.
$10,000 to Roundabout Theater Company, New York, NY.
$10,000 to University of Southern Mississippi Foundation, Center for Gifted Studies, Hattiesburg, MS. For summer scholarships.

5753
The Chisholm Foundation ✧

c/o U.S. Trust
114 W. 47th St.
New York, NY 10036

Established in 1960 in MS.
Donor: A.F. Chisholm†.
Foundation type: Independent foundation.
Financial data (yr. ended 12/31/04): Assets, $26,216,695 (M); expenditures, $1,433,625; qualifying distributions, $1,177,851; giving activities include $1,122,670 for 80 grants (high: $60,000; low: $1,000).
Purpose and activities: Giving primarily for higher and regular education, including a school of architecture; funding also for the arts, health care, and human services.
Fields of interest: Visual arts, architecture; Museums (art); Arts; Higher education; Education; Health care; Human services.
Type of support: General/operating support; Endowments; Program development; Matching/challenge support.

Limitations: Applications not accepted. Giving primarily in MS, and New York, NY. No grants to individuals.
Application information: Contributes only to pre-selected organizations. Unsolicited requests for funds not accepted.
Officers and Trustees:* John L. Lindsey,* Pres.; Alexander C. Lindsey,* Secy.; Nathan E. Saint-Amand, Treas.; Julia V. Lindsey; Alexander Saint-Amand; Lynn M. Lindsey; Cynthia C. Saint-Amand.
EIN: 646014272
Selected grants: The following grants were reported in 2004.
$151,500 to Pierpont Morgan Library, New York, NY.
$100,000 to Memorial Sloan-Kettering Cancer Center, New York, NY.
$85,000 to Manhattan Institute for Policy Research, New York, NY.
$50,000 to Columbia University, New York, NY.
$50,000 to National Center for Policy Analysis, Dallas, TX.
$40,000 to Childhaven, Seattle, WA.
$25,000 to Eudora Welty Foundation, Jackson, MS.
$25,000 to University of the South, Sewanee, TN.
$23,500 to Burden Center for the Aging, New York, NY.
$2,500 to Apollo Theater Foundation, New York, NY.

5754
The Gina and David Chu Foundation ✧

c/o Wai G. Eng, CPA
800 2nd Ave., 8th Fl.
New York, NY 10017

Established in 2001 in DE.
Donor: David Chu.
Foundation type: Independent foundation.
Financial data (yr. ended 6/30/05): Assets, $636,012 (M); expenditures, $409,735; qualifying distributions, $409,701; giving activities include $401,093 for 7 grants (high: $125,000; low: $10,000).
Purpose and activities: Giving primarily to an Asian cultural organization.
Fields of interest: Arts, multipurpose centers/programs; Health care, alliance; Human services; Roman Catholic agencies & churches.
Limitations: Applications not accepted. Giving primarily in New York, NY. No grants to individuals.
Application information: Contributes only to pre-selected organizations.
Officers: David Chu, Pres.; Gina Lin Chu, Treas.
EIN: 311816440
Selected grants: The following grants were reported in 2004.
$200,000 to Asia Society, New York, NY. 3 grants: $125,000 (For Asia 21 Campaign Fund), $25,000 (For annual support), $50,000 (For Nicholas Platt Endowment Fund).
$125,000 to Nature Conservancy, Hong Kong. .
$100,000 to Committee of 100, New York, NY. For growth campaign fund.
$100,000 to Convent of the Sacred Heart, New York, NY. For capital campaign.
$10,000 to Sesame Workshop, New York, NY. For Aids in China Project.
$2,000 to China Institute in America, New York, NY. For Renwen Society Program.

5755
Citigroup Foundation ▼
(formerly Citicorp Foundation)
850 3rd Ave., 13th Fl.
New York, NY 10022-6211 (212) 559-9163
Contact: Alan Okada, C.O.O.
FAX: (212) 793-5944;
E-mail: citigroupfoundation@citigroup.com;
URL: http://www.citigroupfoundation.org

Established in 1994 in NY.
Donors: Citicorp; Citibank, N.A.; Citigroup Inc.;
Citigroup Venture Capital Ltd.
Foundation type: Company-sponsored foundation.
Financial data (yr. ended 12/31/04): Assets,
$64,789,440 (M); gifts received, $1,882,656;
expenditures, $70,303,661; qualifying
distributions, $69,025,772; giving activities include
$67,389,779 for 2,937+ grants, and $1,046,240
for employee matching gifts.
Purpose and activities: The foundation supports
organizations involved with education, health,
employment, housing, disaster relief, financial
counseling, human services, community
development, and economically disadvantaged
people.
Fields of interest: Arts education; Elementary/
secondary education; Education, early childhood
education; Higher education; Graduate/
professional education; Business school/
education; Education, reading; Education; Health
care; Employment; Housing/shelter; Disasters,
preparedness/services; Children, day care; Human
services, financial counseling; Human services;
Community development, management/technical
aid; Economic development; Business/industry;
Community development; Youth; Minorities;
Women; Economically disadvantaged.
Type of support: General/operating support;
Continuing support; Income development;
Management development/capacity building;
Emergency funds; Program development; Seed
money; Curriculum development; Scholarship funds;
Technical assistance; Employee volunteer services;
Employee matching gifts.
Limitations: Giving on a national and international
basis, with emphasis on areas of company
operations. No support for political candidates or
religious, veterans', or fraternal organizations not of
direct benefit to the entire community. No grants to
individuals, or for political causes, fundraising
events, telethons, marathons, races, or benefits,
advertising, sponsorships, dinners or luncheons, or
membership fees.
Publications: Annual report; Grants list.
Application information: Visit Web site for nearest
company facility. Application form required.
Initial approach: Contact nearest company facility
for application form
Officers and Directors:* Lewis B. Kaden,* Chair.;
Alan Okada, C.O.O.; Ajay Banga; Sir Winfried F.W.
Bischoff; Michael A. Carpenter; Robert Druskin;
Stephen J. Freiberg; Sallie L. Krawcheck; Stephen H.
Long; Manuel Medina-Mora; Michael Schlein; Todd
S. Thomson.
Number of staff: 11 full-time professional; 3 full-time
support; 3 part-time support.
EIN: 133781879
Selected grants: The following grants were reported
in 2005.
$600,000 to American Museum of Natural History,
New York, NY. For Structures and Culture
Moveable Museum.

$100,000 to New York Hall of Science, Corona, NY.
For Citigroup Early Childhood Fellows Program.
$75,000 to New York Botanical Garden, Bronx, NY.
For teacher training program.
$25,000 to YM-YWHA, 92nd Street, New York, NY.
For poetry center schools project.
$20,000 to American Ballet Theater, New York, NY.
For young people's ballet workshops.
$20,000 to Lincoln Center Theater, New York, NY.
For Open Stages Program.
$15,000 to Brooklyn Academy of Music, Brooklyn,
NY. For Generation BAM.
$15,000 to Brooklyn Childrens Museum, Brooklyn,
NY. For community access program.
$10,000 to Nassau County Museum of Art, Roslyn,
NY. For Museum as Classroom Program.
$10,000 to Snug Harbor Cultural Center, Staten
Island, NY. For young audience series.

5756
CJM Foundation ◇
c/o Constance Milstein
390 Park Ave., Ste. 600
New York, NY 10022

Established in 1996 in NY.
Donors: Seymour Milstein†; Vivian Milstein.
Foundation type: Independent foundation.
Financial data (yr. ended 12/31/05): Assets,
$2,669,798 (M); gifts received, $1,129,684;
expenditures, $932,712; qualifying distributions,
$932,454; giving activities include $931,580 for 12
grants (high: $500,000; low: $1,000).
Purpose and activities: Giving primarily for human
services, particularly an organization which
addresses world-wide international problems,
hospitals, particularly a hospital for women, the
arts, education, and volunteer fire departments.
Fields of interest: Museums; Performing arts,
opera; Education; Hospitals (general); Hospitals
(specialty); Disasters, fire prevention/control;
Human services; International affairs; Jewish
agencies & temples.
Limitations: Applications not accepted. Giving
primarily in NY. No grants to individuals.
Application information: Contributes only to
pre-selected organizations.
Trustees: Abigail Black Elbaum; Constance Milstein;
Joanna Milstein.
EIN: 137105559
Selected grants: The following grants were reported
in 2003.
$225,000 to Humpty Dumpty Institute, New York,
NY.
$200,000 to American Hospital of Paris Foundation,
New York, NY.
$100,000 to Refugees International, DC.
$100,000 to Statue of Liberty-Ellis Island
Foundation, New York, NY.
$50,000 to American Jewish Joint Distribution
Committee, New York, NY.
$50,000 to City Parks Foundation, New York, NY.
$50,000 to National Democratic Institute for
International Affairs, DC.
$50,000 to UJA-Federation of New York, New York,
NY.
$25,000 to Columbia University, New York, NY. For
Caring at Columbia.
$25,000 to Columbia University Foundation, New
York, NY.

5757
**Liz Claiborne & Art Ortenberg
Foundation** ◇
(formerly The Ortenberg Foundation)
650 5th Ave., 15th Fl.
New York, NY 10019 (212) 333-2536
Contact: James Murtaugh, Prog. Dir.
FAX: (212) 956-3531; E-mail: lcaof@lcaof.org;
URL: http://www.lcaof.org/home.html

Established in 1984 in NY.
Donors: Arthur Ortenberg; Elisabeth Claiborne
Ortenberg.
Foundation type: Independent foundation.
Financial data (yr. ended 12/31/05): Assets,
$41,507,553 (M); gifts received, $2,447,881;
expenditures, $4,475,140; qualifying distributions,
$4,387,694; giving activities include $3,658,150
for 108 grants (high: $411,960; low: $400;
average: $1,000–$25,000), and $82,726 for 1
foundation-administered program.
Purpose and activities: The board of directors has
identified two primary program interests for the
foundation: 1) Mitigation of conflict between the
land and resource needs of rural communities and
conservation of biological diversity; and 2)
Implementation of field-based scientific, technical
and practical training programs in conservation
biology for local people. The foundation typically
funds modest, carefully designed field activities—
primarily in developing countries and in the northern
Rocky Mountains region of the United States—in
which local communities have substantial
proprietary interest.
Fields of interest: Environment, natural resources;
Animals/wildlife, preservation/protection.
International interests: Africa; Asia; Central
America; Developing countries; Oceania; South
America.
Type of support: Continuing support; Seed money;
Matching/challenge support.
Limitations: Giving primarily in Third World countries
in the Tropics and in the Interior West region of the
U.S. No grants for general support, or for
underwriting of overhead.
Publications: Grants list; Informational brochure
(including application guidelines).
Application information: Application form not
required.
Initial approach: Letter
Copies of proposal: 1
Deadline(s): None
Board meeting date(s): Spring and fall
Final notification: As soon as possible
Directors: William Conway; William DeBuys; Robert
Dewar; Arthur Ortenberg; Elisabeth Claiborne
Ortenberg; Alison Richard; David Western.
Number of staff: 3 full-time professional.
EIN: 133200329
Selected grants: The following grants were reported
in 2005.
$422,615 to Wildlife Conservation Society, Bronx,
NY. 2 grants: $186,665, $235,950
$411,960 to Montana Historical Society, Helena,
MT.
$259,500 to Conservation Fund, Arlington, VA. 2
grants: $142,500, $117,000
$100,000 to Oxfam America, Boston, MA.
$100,000 to Save the Children Federation,
Westport, CT.
$38,000 to Grounded Eagle Foundation, Seeley
Lake, MT.
$15,000 to Big Sky Conservation Institute,
Missoula, MT.

$5,000 to Yellowstone Art Museum, Billings, MT.

5758
Liz Claiborne Foundation ✧
1441 Broadway
New York, NY 10018 (212) 626-5704
Contact: Melanie Lyons, V.P., Philanthropic Progs.
FAX: (212) 626-5304; URL: http://
www.lizclaiborneinc.com/foundation/default.asp

Established in 1981 in NY.
Donor: Liz Claiborne, Inc.
Foundation type: Company-sponsored foundation.
Financial data (yr. ended 12/31/03): Assets,
$25,973,562 (M); expenditures, $1,432,649;
qualifying distributions, $1,317,136; giving
activities include $1,317,136 for grants (high:
$65,000).
Purpose and activities: The foundation supports
organizations involved with HIV/AIDS, domestic
violence, human services, economic development,
minorities, women, and economically disadvantaged
people.
Fields of interest: AIDS; Children/youth, services;
Family services, domestic violence; Human
services; Economic development; Minorities;
Women; Economically disadvantaged.
Type of support: General/operating support;
Continuing support; Annual campaigns; Program
development; Employee matching gifts; Matching/
challenge support.
Limitations: Giving limited to Montgomery, AL,
Hudson County, NJ, New York, NY, and Mount
Pocono, PA. No support for disease-specific
organizations or religious, fraternal, or veterans'
organizations. No grants to individuals, or for capital
campaigns, equipment, conferences or symposia,
endowments, research, technical assistance,
media projects, fundraising events, sponsorships,
or journal advertisements.
Publications: Application guidelines.
Application information: Application form not
required.
> *Initial approach:* Proposal
> *Copies of proposal:* 1
> *Deadline(s):* None
> *Board meeting date(s):* Approximately every 10
> weeks
> *Final notification:* 5 days following board meetings
Trustees: Paul R. Charron; Robert McKean; Michael
Scarpa; Robert Vill.
Number of staff: 2 full-time professional; 1 full-time
support; 1 part-time support.
EIN: 133060673

5759
Frank E. Clark Charitable Trust ✧
(formerly Clark Charitable Fund)
c/o JPMorgan Chase Bank, N.A., Global
Foundations Group
345 Park Ave., 4th Fl.
New York, NY 10154 (212) 464-2443
Contact: Monica J. Neal, V.P. and Trust Off.,
JPMorgan Chase Bank, N.A.
FAX: (212) 464-2305;
E-mail: neal_monica@jpmorgan.com; URL: http://
foundationcenter.org/grantmaker/feclark/

Trust established in 1936 in NY.
Donor: Frank E. Clark†.
Foundation type: Independent foundation.

Financial data (yr. ended 12/31/05): Assets,
$6,890,098 (M); expenditures, $408,621;
qualifying distributions, $333,219; giving activities
include $326,000 for 7 grants (high: $75,000; low:
$25,000).
Purpose and activities: Giving primarily (through
regional and national denominational bodies) for
small churches and services for very low-income
adults, including people who are homeless.
Fields of interest: Religion; Economically
disadvantaged; Homeless.
Type of support: General/operating support;
Building/renovation; Program development.
Limitations: Giving limited to New York, NY, for
programs serving homeless adults; giving on a
national basis for small churches. No support for
private foundations. No grants to individuals or
matching gifts; no loans.
Publications: Application guidelines; Grants list.
Application information: Support for small churches
is provided via regional and national denominational
bodies; proposals from individual congregations are
not considered. Application form not required.
> *Initial approach:* Proposal
> *Copies of proposal:* 1
> *Deadline(s):* July 1
> *Board meeting date(s):* Oct.
> *Final notification:* Dec. 31
Trustee: JPMorgan Chase Bank, N.A.
Number of staff: None.
EIN: 136049032
Selected grants: The following grants were reported
in 2004.
$75,000 to Episcopal Diocese of New York, New
York, NY.
$75,000 to United Methodist City Society, New
York, NY.
$75,000 to Upstate New York Synod of the
Evangelical Lutheran Church in America,
Syracuse, NY.
$30,000 to Project Renewal, New York, NY.
$25,000 to Bridge, The, New York, NY. To upgrade
technology.
$25,000 to Providence House, Brooklyn, NY. For
housing readiness program.

5760
The Edna McConnell Clark Foundation ▼
415 Madison Ave., 10th Fl.
New York, NY 10017 (212) 551-9100
Contact: Albert Chung, Comms. Assoc.
FAX: (212) 421-9325; E-mail: info@emcf.org;
Additional E-mail (for Albert Chung):
achung@emcf.org; URL: http://www.emcf.org

Incorporated in 1950 in NY and 1969 in DE; the NY
corporation merged into the DE corporation in 1974.
Donors: Edna McConnell Clark†; W. Van Alan
Clark†.
Foundation type: Independent foundation.
Financial data (yr. ended 9/30/05): Assets,
$808,121,944 (M); expenditures, $40,766,838;
qualifying distributions, $37,595,125; giving
activities include $30,805,999 for 52 grants (high:
$4,500,000; low: $8,000; average: $25,000–
$500,000), and $369,455 for 2
foundation-administered programs.
Purpose and activities: The foundation focuses on
strengthening nonprofit youth development
organizations so they can better serve more young
people with high-quality programs. The foundation's
approach to grantmaking is primarily focused on
individual institutions. Key to the foundation's

approach is a comprehensive, multistage process
used to identify promising youth development
organizations, assess their overall capabilities, and
subsequently invest in the growth of those
organizations most capable of benefiting from this
kind of support.
Fields of interest: Youth development, services;
Youth development; Youth, services.
Type of support: General/operating support;
Continuing support; Program development;
Technical assistance; Consulting services; Program
evaluation.
Limitations: Applications not accepted. Giving on a
national basis. No grants to individuals, or for capital
funds, construction and equipment, endowments,
scholarships, fellowships, annual appeals, deficit
financing, or matching gifts; no loans to individuals.
Publications: Annual report; Grants list;
Informational brochure; Newsletter; Occasional
report.
Application information: The foundation is not
actively seeking or accepting unsolicited proposals.
Direct-service youth organizations working with
youth during non-school hours are invited to share
some information about their organizations by
completing an online form on the foundation's Web
site. Proposals will be invited by the foundation if
there is a potential match.
> *Board meeting date(s):* Mar., June, Sept., and
> Dec.
Officers and Trustees: * James McConnell Clark,
Jr.,* Chair.; Nancy Roob, Pres.; Ralph Stefano, V.P.,
Finance and Admin.; Hays Clark, Tr. Emeritus;
James McConnell Clark, Tr. Emeritus; Patricia C.
Barron; H. Lawrence Clark; Alice F. Emerson; Janice
C. Kreamer; Theodore E. Martin; James E. Moltz;
James E. Preston.
Number of staff: 15 full-time professional; 4 full-time
support.
EIN: 237047034
Selected grants: The following grants were reported
in 2005.
$8,000,000 to Boys and Girls Clubs of America,
Atlanta, GA. To accelerate and expand
implementation throughout network of quality
improvement initiative, Project Upward Bound,
and develop management and capacity-building
skills of executive directors of local BGCA
organizations.
$8,000,000 to Nurse-Family Partnership, Denver,
CO. For continued implementation of business
plan.
$6,000,000 to Center for Employment
Opportunities, New York, NY. To support
implementation of business plan.
$6,000,000 to Youth Villages, Arlington, TN. For
implementation of business plan.
$2,500,000 to Our Piece of the Pie, Hartford, CT.
For implementation of business plan.
$2,000,000 to Green Dot Education Project, Venice,
CA. To implement already existing business plan.
$1,320,000 to Bridgespan Group, Boston, MA. For
business planning support to grantees,
knowledge development projects, and general
advisory support for Foundation staff.
$1,250,000 to Good Shepherd Services, New York,
NY. For general operating support and toward
program expansion and new performance and
outcomes tracking system.
$750,000 to Big Sister Association of Greater
Boston, Boston, MA. To strengthen marketing
and communications capacity, do more research
to show whether girl-only mentoring produces

positive outcomes, and improve prospects for future financial sustainability.

$500,000 to Childrens Aid Society, New York, NY. For general operating support, including help to defray costs associated with time that staff will spend on business planning.

5761
Robert Sterling Clark Foundation, Inc. ▼ ✧

135 E. 64th St.
New York, NY 10021 (212) 288-8900
Contact: Margaret C. Ayers, Exec. Dir.
FAX: (212) 288-1033; URL: http://www.rsclark.org

Incorporated in 1952 in NY.
Donor: Robert Sterling Clark‡.
Foundation type: Independent foundation.
Financial data (yr. ended 10/31/05): Assets, $108,146,871 (M); expenditures, $5,984,011; qualifying distributions, $4,947,031; giving activities include $4,310,200 for 103 grants (high: $160,000; low: $1,000; average: $20,000–$100,000), and $8,188 for employee matching gifts.
Purpose and activities: The foundation supports projects that: 1) strengthen cultural institutions in New York City; 2) support arts advocacy; 3) ensure the effectiveness and accountability of public agencies in New York City and State; and 4) ensure access to comprehensive reproductive health information and services.
Fields of interest: Visual arts; Museums; Performing arts; Performing arts, dance; Performing arts, theater; Performing arts, music; Arts; Education; Environment; Reproductive health, family planning; Human services; Family services; Civil liberties, reproductive rights; Urban/community development; Community development; Public policy, research; Government/public administration; Public affairs; Aging; Economically disadvantaged; Homeless.
Type of support: Management development/capacity building; General/operating support; Continuing support; Income development; Program development; Publication; Research; Technical assistance; Consulting services; Employee matching gifts.
Limitations: Giving primarily in New York State for the Public Institutions Program and in New York City for the Cultural Program; giving nationally for reproductive freedom and arts advocacy projects. No grants to individuals, or for annual campaigns, seed money, emergency funds, deficit financing, capital or endowment funds, scholarships, fellowships, conferences, or films.
Publications: Application guidelines; Annual report (including application guidelines).
Application information: Application form not required.
  Initial approach: Proposal (not exceeding 15 pages) and a one-page proposal summary
  Copies of proposal: 1
  Deadline(s): None
  Board meeting date(s): Jan., Apr., July, and Oct.
  Final notification: 1 to 6 months
Officers and Directors:* Winthrop R. Munyan,* Pres.; Miner D. Crary, Jr.,* Secy.; Clara Miller,* Treas.; Margaret C. Ayers, Exec. Dir.; Virginia Hayes Sibbison; James Allen Smith; John Hoyt Stookey*; Joanna D. Underwood.

Number of staff: 3 full-time professional; 1 full-time support.
EIN: 131957792
Selected grants: The following grants were reported in 2005.
$160,000 to Planned Parenthood Federation of America, New York, NY. For public policy advocacy, organizing, and assistance to affiliates to preserve and expand access to abortion and family planning services.
$150,000 to NARAL Pro-Choice America, DC. For continued updating and expansion of database of reproductive rights, related legislation and court decisions, analysis of data, and publication of report, Who Decides: A State-by-State Review of Abortion and Reproductive Rights.
$75,000 to Welfare Law Center, Project Fair Play, New York, NY. For litigation, monitoring of government performance and client data, and assistance to government officials to ensure access to public assistance benefits and safeguard rights of recipients and applicants, including those with disabilities.
$70,000 to Pro-Choice Public Education Project, New York, NY. To develop and disseminate pro-choice media messages directed at young women, and to help other organizations engage young people in reproductive rights movement. Grant made through Tides Center.
$65,000 to Americans for the Arts, DC. For overall arts advocacy efforts that include coordinating Arts Advocacy Day, educating the nation's elected and appointed officials about the value of the arts; and the building of the state-level arts advocacy infra-structure.
$60,000 to Environmental Defense, New York, NY. In support of Solid Waste Project.
$50,000 to Citizens Environmental Coalition, Albany, NY. To enhance and publicize Web site that maps polluted sites; to produce reports on chemical spills and releases of bioaccumulative toxins and relationship between cancer incidence and locations of toxic sites; and to publicize local pollution problems.
$50,000 to Community Catalyst, MergerWatch, Boston, MA. To publicize and counter religious efforts to restrict access to contraception, and to develop and disseminate a model protocol to guide drug stores whose pharmacists refuse to dispense contraceptives.
$45,000 to Hunger Action Network of New York State, Albany, NY. For education and organizing around state budget and tax policy, job creation, and health care access issues, and to assist local coalitions that monitor county Social Services agencies.
$40,000 to Dance Theater Workshop, New York, NY. For support of work with consultant to develop press materials and story ideas, and to solicit media coverage of artists.

5762
The Clark Foundation ▼ ✧

1 Rockefeller Plz., 31st Fl.
New York, NY 10020-2102
Contact: Charles H. Hamilton, Exec. Dir.

Incorporated in 1931 in NY; merged with Scriven Foundation, Inc. in 1973.
Donor: Members of the Clark family.
Foundation type: Independent foundation.
Financial data (yr. ended 6/30/05): Assets, $544,631,091 (M); gifts received, $300;

expenditures, $28,821,942; qualifying distributions, $25,692,919; giving activities include $19,822,838 for 157 grants (high: $1,000,000; low: $2,000; average: $20,000–$200,000), $37,462 for 4 grants to individuals (high: $18,600; low: $262), $1,743,056 for 1 foundation-administered program and $1,000,000 for 1 loan/program-related investment.
Purpose and activities: Support for a hospital and museums in Cooperstown, NY; grants also for charitable and educational purposes, including undergraduate scholarships to students residing in the Cooperstown area. The foundation owns and supports the Clark Sports Center, which is located in Cooperstown, NY. Support also for educational, youth, cultural, and community organizations and institutions in New York City, NY.
Fields of interest: Museums; Education; Employment; Human services; Children/youth, services; Economically disadvantaged.
Type of support: Program-related investments/loans; General/operating support; Continuing support; Capital campaigns; Building/renovation; Program development; Seed money; Technical assistance; Scholarships—to individuals.
Limitations: Giving primarily in Cooperstown, NY and New York City; scholarships restricted to students residing in the Cooperstown, NY, area. No grants to individuals (except as specified in restricted funds), or for deficit financing or matching gifts.
Publications: Application guidelines; Program policy statement.
Application information: Accepts NYRAG Common Application Form. Application form not required.
  Initial approach: Letter
  Copies of proposal: 1
  Deadline(s): Jan. 1, Apr. 1, July 15, and Oct. 1
  Board meeting date(s): Mar., June, Oct., and Dec.
  Final notification: 2 to 6 months
Officers and Directors:* Jane Forbes Clark,* Pres.; Alexander F. Treadwell,* V.P.; Charles H. Hamilton, Secy. and Exec. Dir.; Kevin S. Moore,* Treas.; Kent L. Barwick; Felicia H. Blum; William M. Evarts; Gates Helms Hawn; Archie F. MacAllaster; Thomas Q. Morris, M.D.; Anne L. Peretz; John Hoyt Stookey; Edward W. Stack; Clifton R. Wharton, Jr.
Number of staff: 4 full-time professional; 3 part-time professional; 43 full-time support; 20 part-time support.
EIN: 135616528
Selected grants: The following grants were reported in 2006.
$1,000,000 to Good Shepherd Services, New York, NY.
$800,000 to East Harlem Employment Services, Project STRIVE, New York, NY.
$700,000 to Clara Welch Thanksgiving Home, Cooperstown, NY.
$700,000 to Fund for the City of New York, New York, NY. 2 grants: $100,000, $600,000
$311,000 to Brookwood School, Cooperstown, NY.
$250,000 to Civic Builders, New York, NY.
$150,000 to Vocational Foundation, Brooklyn, NY.
$100,000 to Hope Program, Brooklyn, NY.
$75,000 to George Jackson Academy, New York, NY.

5763
The Clinton Family Foundation ✧ ☆

P.O. Box 937
Chappaqua, NY 10514

Established in 2001 in NY.

Donors: William Jefferson Clinton; Hillary Rodham Clinton.
Foundation type: Independent foundation.
Financial data (yr. ended 12/31/05): Assets, $3,967,622 (M); gifts received, $1,755,453; expenditures, $551,758; qualifying distributions, $549,000; giving activities include $549,000 for grants.
Fields of interest: Historical activities; Higher education; Education; Health organizations; Human services.
Limitations: Applications not accepted. Giving primarily in AR and NY. No grants to individuals.
Application information: Contributes only to pre-selected organizations.
Officers: William Jefferson Clinton, Pres.; Hillary Rodham Clinton, Secy.-Treas.
Director: Chelsea V. Clinton.
EIN: 300048438
Selected grants: The following grants were reported in 2004.
$75,000 to THEA Foundation, North Little Rock, AR. For general support.
$25,000 to Drew University, Madison, NJ. For general support.
$25,000 to Immanuel Baptist Church, Little Rock, AR. For general support.
$25,000 to New Jobs for New York, New York, NY. For general support.
$25,000 to Vital Voices Global Partnership, DC. For general support.
$10,000 to Amnesty International USA, New York, NY. For general support.
$5,000 to American Battle Monuments Commission, Arlington, VA. For general support.
$5,000 to University of Arkansas, Little Rock, AR. For general support.
$1,000 to Arkansas Community Foundation, Little Rock, AR. For general support.
$100 to American Heart Association, Dallas, TX. For general support.

5764
Cloud Mountain Foundation ◇ ☆
c/o Louis Sternbach & Co.
1333 Broadway, Ste. 516
New York, NY   10018

Established in 1999 in MA.
Donor: Benjamin Friedman.
Foundation type: Independent foundation.
Financial data (yr. ended 12/31/05): Assets, $12,723,996 (M); gifts received, $1,613,970; expenditures, $425,332; qualifying distributions, $380,500; giving activities include $380,500 for 32 grants (high: $60,000; low: $2,500).
Fields of interest: Arts; Environment.
Limitations: Applications not accepted. No grants to individuals.
Application information: Contributes only to pre-selected organizations.
Officer: Benjamin Friedman, Pres.
EIN: 043493352
Selected grants: The following grants were reported in 2003.
$52,500 to New England Grassroots Environment Fund, Montpelier, VT.
$15,000 to Environmental Research Foundation, New Brunswick, NJ.
$12,500 to Global Exchange, San Francisco, CA.
$10,000 to Deep Dish T.V. Network, New York, NY.
$10,000 to Earth Island Institute, San Francisco, CA.

$9,500 to Center for Media and Democracy, Madison, WI.
$5,000 to Center for Ecological Technology, Pittsfield, MA.
$5,000 to Clean Water Fund, DC.
$5,000 to Independent Media Institute, San Francisco, CA.
$5,000 to Pacifica Foundation, Berkeley, CA.

5765
CLRC, Inc. ◇
c/o Hertz, Herson & Co., LLP
2 Park Ave., Ste. 1500
New York, NY   10016

Established in 1998 in DE and NY.
Donors: Bella Wexner Charitable Remainder Unitrust; Susan Wexner Revocable Trust.
Foundation type: Independent foundation.
Financial data (yr. ended 3/31/05): Assets, $34,606,461 (M); expenditures, $1,528,055; qualifying distributions, $1,286,555; giving activities include $1,240,000 for 1 grant.
Fields of interest: Philanthropy/voluntarism.
Limitations: Applications not accepted. Giving on a national basis. No grants to individuals.
Application information: Contributes only to pre-selected organizations.
Officer and Directors:* Susan R. Wexner,* Pres. and Secy.-Treas.; Bertrand Agus.
EIN: 133997365
Selected grants: The following grants were reported in 2004.
$1,505,000 to Vanguard Charitable Endowment Program, Southeastern, PA.

5766
The Craig & Deborah Cogut Foundation, Inc. ◇
c/o L.H. Frishkoff & Co.
529 5th Ave.
New York, NY   10017

Established in 1993 in DE and NY.
Donors: Craig Cogut; Deborah Cogut.
Foundation type: Independent foundation.
Financial data (yr. ended 12/31/05): Assets, $3,991,611 (M); expenditures, $4,782,057; qualifying distributions, $4,751,200; giving activities include $4,751,200 for 11 grants (high: $4,100,000; low: $500).
Fields of interest: Elementary/secondary education; Higher education; Health care; Civil rights; Jewish agencies & temples.
Limitations: Applications not accepted. Giving on a national basis, including the greater metropolitan New York, NY, area and Washington, DC. No grants to individuals.
Application information: Contributes only to pre-selected organizations.
Officers: Craig Cogut, Pres.; Deborah Cogut, Secy.-Treas.
EIN: 133746440
Selected grants: The following grants were reported in 2004.
$125,000 to Brown University, Providence, RI.
$125,000 to Greenwich Hospital, Greenwich, CT.
$100,000 to Horace Mann School, Riverdale, NY.
$25,000 to Human Rights First, New York, NY.
$10,000 to Washington Institute for Near East Policy, DC.

$5,198 to Temple Sholom, Greenwich, CT.
$1,850 to American Jewish Committee, New York, NY.

5767
The Abby and David Cohen Family Foundation ◇ ☆
c/o Goldman Sachs & Co.
1 New York Plz., 40th Fl.
New York, NY   10004

Established in 1999 in NY.
Donor: Abby J. Cohen.
Foundation type: Independent foundation.
Financial data (yr. ended 3/31/06): Assets, $5,992,796 (M); expenditures, $392,550; qualifying distributions, $378,200; giving activities include $378,200 for grants.
Fields of interest: Museums; Secondary school/education; Higher education; Theological school/education; Health care; Human services; Jewish federated giving programs; Jewish agencies & temples.
Limitations: Applications not accepted. Giving primarily in Ithaca and New York, NY. No grants to individuals.
Application information: Contributes only to pre-selected organizations.
Trustees: Abby J. Cohen; David M. Cohen; Ellen M. Cohen.
EIN: 134090442
Selected grants: The following grants were reported in 2006.
$75,000 to Jewish Theological Seminary of America, New York, NY. 2 grants: $50,000, $25,000
$45,000 to American Jewish Committee, New York, NY. 3 grants: $25,000, $10,000, $10,000
$10,000 to American Museum of Natural History, New York, NY.
$10,000 to Legal Momentum, New York, NY.
$10,000 to Museum of Modern Art, New York, NY.
$5,000 to American Friends of the Israel Museum, New York, NY.
$5,000 to YIVO Institute for Jewish Research, New York, NY.

5768
The Michele and Martin Cohen Family Foundation ◇
16 E. 64th St.
New York, NY   10021

Established in 1995 in NY.
Donors: Martin Cohen; Michele Cohen.
Foundation type: Independent foundation.
Financial data (yr. ended 12/31/05): Assets, $1,094,150 (M); gifts received, $36,664; expenditures, $756,942; qualifying distributions, $756,942; giving activities include $743,424 for 68 grants (high: $200,000; low: $100).
Purpose and activities: Giving for Jewish organizations, higher education, and human services.
Fields of interest: Education; Health organizations, association; Housing/shelter; Community development; Jewish federated giving programs; Jewish agencies & temples; Disabilities, people with.
Limitations: Applications not accepted. Giving primarily in NY. No grants to individuals.

Application information: Contributes only to pre-selected organizations.
Trustees: Martin Cohen; Michele Cohen.
EIN: 133863473

5769
Abraham and Yvonne Cohen Family, Inc. ◇
100 United Nations Plz., Ste. 44A
New York, NY 10017-1713

Established in 2000 in NY.
Donor: Abraham E. Cohen.
Foundation type: Independent foundation.
Financial data (yr. ended 11/30/05): Assets, $358,159 (M); gifts received, $303,358; expenditures, $580,071; qualifying distributions, $562,050; giving activities include $562,050 for 57 grants (high: $50,000; low: $100).
Purpose and activities: Giving primarily for health, the arts, and Jewish causes.
Fields of interest: Museums (specialized); Arts; Higher education; Hospitals (general); Jewish federated giving programs; Jewish agencies & temples.
Type of support: General/operating support.
Limitations: Applications not accepted. Giving primarily in New York, NY. No grants to individuals.
Application information: Contributes only to pre-selected organizations.
Officers: Yvette C. Pomerantz, Pres.; Denise A. Cohen, Secy.; Daniel H. Cohen, Treas.
EIN: 522283127
Selected grants: The following grants were reported in 2005.
$65,000 to American Friends of Rabin Medical Center, New York, NY. 3 grants: $5,000, $50,000, $10,000
$52,000 to International Sephardic Education Foundation (ISEF), New York, NY. 2 grants: $40,000, $12,000
$25,000 to Congregation Shearith Israel, New York, NY.
$25,000 to Richard Tucker Music Foundation, New York, NY.
$10,500 to Philharmonic-Symphony Society of New York, New York, NY.
$5,000 to American Friends of Keshet Eilon, New York, NY.
$3,000 to Bnos Malka Academy, Flushing, NY.

5770
Joseph M. & Barbara Cohen Foundation, Inc. ◇
410 E. 57th St.
New York, NY 10022

Established in 1990 in NY.
Donor: Joseph M. Cohen.
Foundation type: Independent foundation.
Financial data (yr. ended 10/31/05): Assets, $887,738 (M); gifts received, $1,281,509; expenditures, $569,941; qualifying distributions, $568,815; giving activities include $567,700 for 36 grants (high: $107,500; low: $500).
Purpose and activities: Giving primarily for art and cultural programs, higher education, health services, and Jewish organizations.
Fields of interest: Museums; Museums (art); Performing arts, opera; Arts; Higher education; Health care; Medical research, institute; Cancer

research; Eye research; Food distribution, meals on wheels; Human services; Jewish agencies & temples.
Limitations: Applications not accepted. Giving primarily in New York, NY. No grants to individuals.
Application information: Contributes only to pre-selected organizations.
Officers: Joseph M. Cohen, Pres.; Jarrod Cohen, Secy.; Raymond Merritt, Treas.
EIN: 133636511
Selected grants: The following grants were reported in 2005.
$107,500 to Metropolitan Museum of Art, New York, NY.
$100,000 to Citymeals-on-Wheels, New York, NY.
$25,000 to Glaucoma Foundation, New York, NY.
$25,000 to Manhattan Institute for Cancer Research, New York, NY.
$25,000 to Metropolitan Opera, New York, NY.
$15,000 to Jackson Laboratory, Bar Harbor, ME.
$15,000 to National Gallery of Art, DC.
$10,000 to American Cancer Society, Atlanta, GA.
$10,000 to Philharmonic-Symphony Society of New York, New York, NY.
$7,500 to Norton Museum of Art, West Palm Beach, FL.

5771
Jack D. Cohen Foundation ◇
505 Park Ave., 5th Fl.
New York, NY 10022

Established in 1984 in NY.
Donors: Jack D. Cohen; Abraham J. Cohen; David J. Cohen; Albert Dweck; Francine Dweck; First American Title Ins. Co.; Monbruk Abstract Co.; Lori Cohen Trust; Rochelle Beyda Trust.
Foundation type: Independent foundation.
Financial data (yr. ended 10/31/05): Assets, $290,137 (M); gifts received, $941,000; expenditures, $790,305; qualifying distributions, $790,305; giving activities include $790,305 for 212 grants (high: $250,000; low: $18).
Purpose and activities: Giving primarily for Jewish agencies, temples, and schools.
Fields of interest: Elementary/secondary education; Human services; Jewish federated giving programs; Jewish agencies & temples.
Limitations: Applications not accepted. Giving primarily in New York, NY. No grants to individuals.
Application information: Contributes only to pre-selected organizations.
Officer: Jack D. Cohen, Pres.
EIN: 112715275

5772
Cohen LD Family Foundation, Inc. ◇ ☆
c/o Steinmetz Brothers Inc.
18 W. 33rd St.
New York, NY 10001 (212) 563-5737
Contact: Bernat Steinmetz

Foundation type: Independent foundation.
Financial data (yr. ended 6/30/06): Assets, $3,074,809 (M); gifts received, $183,600; expenditures, $355,158; qualifying distributions, $353,663; giving activities include $353,663 for grants.
Fields of interest: Jewish federated giving programs; Jewish agencies & temples.

Application information: Application form not required.
Deadline(s): None
Trustees: Bernat Steinmetz; Michael Steinmetz; Abraham Weingarten; Fay Weingarten.
EIN: 300082673

5773
Jacques & Emy Cohenca Foundation, Inc. ◇ ☆
550 Park Ave.
New York, NY 10021

Established in 1979 in NY.
Donors: Emy Cohenca; Jacques Cohenca†; Jason Industrial, Inc.; TBMC, Inc.
Foundation type: Independent foundation.
Financial data (yr. ended 12/31/05): Assets, $3,643,576 (M); gifts received, $20,000; expenditures, $363,972; qualifying distributions, $327,459; giving activities include $327,459 for grants.
Purpose and activities: Giving for the arts, health, and Jewish organizations.
Fields of interest: Museums; Arts; Hospitals (general); Health organizations, association; Human services; Jewish federated giving programs; Jewish agencies & temples.
Limitations: Applications not accepted. Giving primarily in the greater metropolitan New York, NY, area. No grants to individuals.
Application information: Contributes only to pre-selected organizations.
Officers: Emy Cohenca, Pres.; Philip Cohenca, Treas.
Director: Nevine Michaan.
EIN: 133022911
Selected grants: The following grants were reported in 2003.
$78,700 to Congregation Shearith Israel, New York, NY.
$60,000 to Weill Medical College of Cornell University, New York, NY.
$16,250 to Metropolitan Opera, New York, NY.
$15,000 to Peter Westbrook Foundation, New York, NY.
$10,500 to UJA-Federation of New York, New York, NY.
$5,000 to Tulane University, School of Law, New Orleans, LA.
$3,500 to Metropolitan Museum of Art, New York, NY.
$3,000 to Harvey School, Katonah, NY.
$2,195 to Westchester Reform Temple, Scarsdale, NY.
$1,600 to Brooklyn Museum, Brooklyn, NY.

5774
Kenneth Cole Foundation ◇
c/o TAG Assocs.
75 Rockefeller Plz., Ste. 900
New York, NY 10019

Established in 1994 in NY.
Donor: Kenneth Cole.
Foundation type: Independent foundation.
Financial data (yr. ended 4/30/05): Assets, $4,499,241 (M); expenditures, $775,385; qualifying distributions, $772,210; giving activities include $771,960 for 40 grants (high: $200,000; low: $400).

Purpose and activities: Giving primarily for higher education, as well as for hospitals and health associations, and to Jewish agencies and temples.
Fields of interest: Arts; Elementary/secondary education; Higher education; Education; Botanical gardens; Hospitals (general); Health organizations, association; AIDS research; Crime/violence prevention, gun control; Human services; Philanthropy/voluntarism; Jewish agencies & temples.
Limitations: Applications not accepted. Giving primarily in NY; funding also in Atlanta, GA. No grants to individuals.
Application information: Contributes only to pre-selected organizations.
Trustees: Kenneth Cole; Maria Cuomo Cole.
EIN: 133799161
Selected grants: The following grants were reported in 2004.
$200,000 to American Foundation for AIDS Research (AMFAR), New York, NY.
$100,000 to Emory University, Atlanta, GA.
$75,000 to Aish HaTorah, Brooklyn, NY.
$50,000 to Rye Country Day School, Rye, NY.
$10,000 to Aging in America, Bronx, NY.
$10,000 to V-Day New York, Pelham, NY.
$9,620 to Anti-Defamation League of Bnai Brith, New York, NY.
$5,000 to Jacob Burns Film Center, Pleasantville, NY.
$2,000 to UJA-Federation of New York, New York, NY.
$1,500 to Hope and Heroes Childrens Cancer Fund, New York, NY.

5775
Coles Family Foundation ✧
c/o BCRS Associates, LLC
100 Wall St., 11th Fl.
New York, NY 10005

Established in 1980 in NY.
Donors: Michael H. Coles; Joan C. Coles‡.
Foundation type: Independent foundation.
Financial data (yr. ended 3/31/05): Assets, $2,108,039 (M); expenditures, $837,028; qualifying distributions, $799,671; giving activities include $787,275 for 89 grants (high: $40,600; low: $250).
Purpose and activities: Giving primarily for higher and other education, arts and cultural programs, the environment, Christian organizations and churches, and children, youth, and social services.
Fields of interest: Museums; Performing arts, theater; Arts; Elementary/secondary education; Higher education; Education; Environment, natural resources; Hospitals (general); Children/youth, services; International affairs, foreign policy; Christian agencies & churches.
Type of support: General/operating support; Endowments.
Limitations: Applications not accepted. Giving primarily in the greater metropolitan New York, NY, area, as well as Long Island, particularly Shelter Island. No grants to individuals.
Application information: Contributes only to pre-selected organizations.
Trustees: Alison Aldredge; Isobel Coles; Michael C. Coles; Michael H. Coles; Richard Coles; Caroline Scudder; Roy C. Smith.
Number of staff: 1 part-time support.
EIN: 133050747

Selected grants: The following grants were reported in 2005.
$353,600 to Manhattan Theater Club, New York, NY. 3 grants: $28,600 (For general support), $75,000 (For general support), $250,000 (For general support).
$40,000 to Hospital for Special Surgery, New York, NY. 2 grants: $20,000 each (For general support).
$40,000 to Inner-City Scholarship Fund, New York, NY. 2 grants: $20,000 each (For general support).
$25,000 to Foreign Policy Association, New York, NY. For general support.
$25,000 to Peconic Land Trust, Southampton, NY. For general support.
$15,000 to Enterprise Community Partners, Columbia, MD. For general support.

5776
Simon and Eve Colin Foundation ✧
1520 Northern Blvd.
Manhasset, NY 11030-3006
Contact: Fred Colin, Dir.

Established in 1984 in NY.
Donors: Fred Colin; Stephen Colin; Star Enterprises.
Foundation type: Independent foundation.
Financial data (yr. ended 10/31/05): Assets, $14,970,209 (L); gifts received, $407,571; expenditures, $746,145; qualifying distributions, $699,345; giving activities include $697,250 for 104 grants (high: $380,000; low: $50).
Purpose and activities: Giving primarily to Jewish agencies and temples, as well as for arts and culture, education, health associations, and human services.
Fields of interest: Arts; Higher education; Hospitals (general); Health organizations, association; Human services; Jewish federated giving programs; Jewish agencies & temples.
Limitations: Giving primarily in the greater metropolitan New York, NY, area, including Long Island.
Application information: Application form not required.
    Deadline(s): None
Directors: Barbara Colin; Fred Colin; Rebecca Colin; Samuel F. Colin; Eva Usdan.
EIN: 112676434

5777
Joseph Collins Foundation ✧
c/o Willkie Farr & Gallagher
787 7th Ave., Rm. 3950
New York, NY 10019-6099
Contact: Augusta L. Packer, Secy.-Treas.

Incorporated in 1951 in NY.
Donor: Joseph Collins, M.D.‡.
Foundation type: Independent foundation.
Financial data (yr. ended 6/30/05): Assets, $25,781,264 (M); expenditures, $1,487,651; qualifying distributions, $1,278,773; giving activities include $1,160,000 for 116 grants (high: $10,000; low: $10,000).
Purpose and activities: The foundation makes annual grants only to students with inadequate resources, in attendance at medical schools in states east of or contiguous to the Mississippi River, in sums not exceeding $10,000. Grants for tuition

to needy second through fourth year undergraduate medical students on the recommendation of medical school authorities. Students must have outside cultural interests.
Fields of interest: Medical school/education.
Type of support: Grants to individuals.
Limitations: Giving limited to students attending accredited medical schools located east of the Mississippi River. No grants for pre-medical or postgraduate medical students.
Publications: Application guidelines; Annual report; Program policy statement.
Application information: Telephone inquiries are not accepted. Application forms should be obtained from and submitted by medical schools on behalf of the students. Application form required.
    Initial approach: Full proposal
    Copies of proposal: 1
    Deadline(s): Jan. 15 for application requests; Mar. 1 for filing
    Board meeting date(s): Nov. and as required
Officers and Trustees:* Jack H. Nusbaum,* Pres.; Mark F. Hughes, Jr.,* V.P.; W. Graham Knox, M.D.*, V.P.; Nora Ann Wallace,* V.P.; Augusta L. Packer,* Secy.-Treas.
EIN: 136404527

5778
P. & C. Collins Fund ✧
c/o U.S. Trust
114 W. 47th St.
New York, NY 10036

Established in 2000 in DE.
Donor: Paul J. Collins.
Foundation type: Independent foundation.
Financial data (yr. ended 12/31/03): Assets, $9,857,039 (M); gifts received, $614,828; expenditures, $338,113; qualifying distributions, $320,917; giving activities include $315,750 for 27 grants (high: $100,000; low: $1,000).
Fields of interest: Arts; Education; Environment, natural resources.
Limitations: Applications not accepted. No grants to individuals.
Directors: Carol H. Collins; Julia D. Collins; Paul J. Collins; Roland A. Collins.
EIN: 134112988
Selected grants: The following grants were reported in 2003.
$100,000 to Nature Conservancy, Boston, MA.
$100,000 to University of Wisconsin Foundation, Madison, WI.
$20,000 to Sheffield Land Trust, Sheffield, MA.
$10,000 to Central Park Conservancy, New York, NY.
$10,000 to Mount Holyoke College, South Hadley, MA.
$7,500 to Northfield Mount Hermon School, Northfield, MA.
$6,500 to Philharmonic-Symphony Society of New York, New York Philharmonic, New York, NY.
$4,500 to Loomis Chaffee School, Windsor, CT.
$2,500 to Trustees of Reservations, Beverly, MA.
$1,000 to Georgetown University, DC.

5779
The Commonwealth Fund ▼ ✧
1 E. 75th St.
New York, NY 10021-2692 (212) 606-3800
Contact: Andrea C. Landes, Dir., Grants Mgmt.

FAX: (212) 606-3500; E-mail: cmwf@cmwf.org;
URL: http://www.cmwf.org

Incorporated in 1918 in NY.
Donors: Mrs. Stephen V. Harkness†; Edward S.
Harkness†; Mrs. Edward S. Harkness†.
Foundation type: Independent foundation.
Financial data (yr. ended 6/30/05): Assets,
$634,403,522 (M); gifts received, $251;
expenditures, $29,386,113; qualifying
distributions, $24,720,763; giving activities include
$13,437,426 for 259 grants (high: $368,239; low:
$1,000; average: $10,000–$100,000),
$1,114,242 for grants to individuals, $403,243 for
60 employee matching gifts, $274,402 for 6
foundation-administered programs and $100,000
for 1 loan/program-related investment.
Purpose and activities: The mission of the fund is
to promote a high performing healthcare system that
achieves better access, improved quality, and
greater efficiency, particularly for society's most
vulnerable, including low-income people, the
uninsured, minority Americans, young children, and
elderly adults. The fund carries out this mandate by
supporting independent research on health care
issues and making grants to improve healthcare
practice and policy.
Fields of interest: Health care, insurance; Health
care.
International interests: Australia; Canada; New
Zealand; United Kingdom.
Type of support: Program development;
Fellowships; Research; Program evaluation;
Employee matching gifts.
Limitations: Giving on a national basis. No support
for religious organizations for religious purposes, or
basic biomedical research. No grants to individuals
(except through the Commonwealth Fund's
fellowship programs), or for scholarships, general
planning or ongoing activities, existing deficits,
endowment or capital costs, construction,
renovation, equipment, conferences, symposia,
major media projects, or documentaries (unless
they are an out growth of one of the fund's
programs).
Publications: Annual report (including application
guidelines); Financial statement; Grants list;
Informational brochure; Newsletter; Occasional
report; Program policy statement.
Application information: The fund strongly prefers
grant applicants submit letters of inquiry using the
online application form, however, letters submitted
via regular mail or fax will be accepted. The fund
acknowledges letters on receipt; applicants are
typically advised of results of initial staff review
within two months. Application form not required.
  Initial approach: Letter of inquiry
  Copies of proposal: 1
  Deadline(s): None
  Board meeting date(s): Apr., July, and Nov.
  Final notification: 4-6 weeks
Officers and Directors:* Samuel O. Thier, M.D.*,
Chair.; Christine Russell,* Vice-Chair.; John E. Craig,
Jr., C.O.O. and Exec. V.P.; Karen Davis, Ph.D.*,
Pres.; Stephen C. Schoenbaum, M.D., Exec. V.P.,
Progs.; Cathy Schoen, Sr. V.P., Research and Eval.;
Bill Silberg, Sr. V.P., Comms. and Publishing; Robin
Osborn, V.P., and Dir., International Prog., Health
Policy; Anne-Marie J. Audet, V.P.; Edward L. Schor,
V.P.; Gary M. Stehr, Cont.; William R. Brody, M.D.;
Benjamin K. Chu, M.D.; Samuel C. Fleming; Jane E.
Henney, M.D.; Walter E. Massey; Robert C. Pozen;
James R. Tallon, Jr.; William Y. Yun.

Number of staff: 28 full-time professional; 21
full-time support.
EIN: 131635260
Selected grants: The following grants were reported
in 2005.
$800,000 to Harvard University, Cambridge, MA.
  For Commonwealth Fund/Harvard University
  Fellowship in Minority Health Policy: Support for
  Program Direction and Fellowships at Medical
  School in Boston.
$623,102 to Health Research and Educational
  Trust, Chicago, IL. 2 grants: $323,136 (For
  Assessing and Improving Patient Safety in
  Ambulatory Care, payable over 1.75 years),
  $299,966 (For Linking Race and Ethnicity Data
  with Inpatient Quality-of-Care Measures in Private
  Hospitals, payable over 2 years).
$472,759 to Massachusetts General Hospital,
  Boston, MA. For Commonwealth Fund Quality
  Improvement Colloquia, Series III.
$350,000 to Harris Interactive, New York, NY. For
  International Health Policy Survey.
$348,710 to American Institutes for Research in the
  Behavioral Sciences, DC. For Critical Issues for
  Medicare's Future.
$332,939 to Childrens Hospital and Research
  Center at Oakland, Oakland, CA. For Rethinking
  Well Child Care, payable over 2 years.
$320,810 to University of Rochester, Rochester,
  NY. For Developing Manual for Pediatric
  Preventive Services: Bright Futures in Practice,
  payable over 2 years.
$313,249 to Center for Health Policy Development,
  Portland, ME. For Building State Medicaid
  Capacity to Support Children's Healthy Mental
  Development, Phase 2.
$300,716 to National Committee for Quality
  Assurance, DC. For Enhancing Patient-Centered
  Care in Office Practice, payable over 1.50 years.

5780
Community Foundation for Greater
Buffalo ▼ ✧
(formerly The Buffalo Foundation)
712 Main St.
Buffalo, NY 14202-1720 (716) 852-2857
Contact: Myra S. Lawrence, V.P., Finance and Admin.
FAX: (716) 852-2861; E-mail: mail@cfgb.org;
URL: http://www.cfgb.org

Established in 1919 in NY by resolution and
declaration of trust; corporate version established in
1985.
Foundation type: Community foundation.
Financial data (yr. ended 12/31/04): Assets,
$90,204,606 (M); gifts received, $448,870;
expenditures, $5,108,123; giving activities include
$3,541,193 for 2,389 grants (high: $380,000; low:
$1).
Purpose and activities: The foundation seeks to
support creative and innovative responses to
existing or emerging community problems; and to
support efforts that recognize and build on the
community's strengths and assets.
Fields of interest: Arts; Education; Environment;
Animal welfare; Hospitals (general); Health care;
AIDS; Medical research, institute; AIDS research;
Disasters, Hurricane Katrina; Children/youth,
services; Family services; Human services;
Community development; Science; Leadership
development.
Type of support: Building/renovation; Equipment;
Emergency funds; Program development;

Conferences/seminars; Seed money; Scholarship
funds; Research; Technical assistance; Program
evaluation; Scholarships—to individuals; Matching/
challenge support.
Limitations: Giving limited to Western NY;
scholarships awarded to students primarily from
Erie County. No support for religious purposes or
schools not registered with the State Education
Department. No grants to individuals (except from
designated scholarship funds), or for annual events
or festivals, fundraising events, activities that have
not yet occurred, after-the-fact funding (except in
extraordinary cases), or endowments; no loans.
Publications: Application guidelines; Annual report
(including application guidelines); Informational
brochure; Newsletter; Program policy statement.
Application information: Visit foundation Web site
for application form and guidelines. The foundation
will host brief sessions to assist organizations in the
application process 2-6 weeks prior to each
application; call to register. Application forms
required for scholarships, and must be requested in
writing between Mar. 1 and May 1 and include a
SASE. Application form required.
  Initial approach: Telephone or letter
  Deadline(s): Feb. 1 for arts, animals, civic needs,
    community devel., education and environment
    & science; Aug. 1 for health and human
    services
  Board meeting date(s): Mar., May, Aug., and Nov.
  Final notification: Within 2 weeks of meeting
Officers and Directors:* Robert D. Gioia,* Chair.;
Joseph J. Castiglia,* Vice-Chair.; Gail E. Johnstone,
C.E.O. and Pres.; Clotilde Perez-Bode Dedecker,
V.P., Prog.; Finley Greene, V.P., Philanthropic Svcs.;
Myra S. Lawrence, V.P., Finance and Admin.;
Anthony J. Colucci, Jr.,* Treas.; Kathryn L. Chatmon,
Compt.; Charles Balbach; Betty Calvo-Torres;
Kathleen Doucet-Miller; Gayle L. Eagan; Reginald
Melson; John A. Mitchell; Andrew J. Rudnick, Ph.D.;
Anne Saldanha, M.D.; Katie Schneider; Hon. Hugh
B. Scott; Leslie Zemsky.
Trustee Banks: Bank of America, N.A.; HSBC Bank
USA; KeyBank N.A.; M&T Bank.
Number of staff: 9 full-time professional; 2 part-time
professional; 4 full-time support.
EIN: 160743935
Selected grants: The following grants were reported
in 2004.
$898,963 to Roswell Park Alliance Foundation,
  Buffalo, NY.
$370,150 to Western New York Rural Area Health
  Education Center, Batavia, NY.
$46,746 to Church Mission of Help of Western New
  York, Buffalo, NY.
$42,500 to Pursuing Perfection Collaborative of
  Western New York, Williamsville, NY.
$25,878 to Medical Media Associates, Buffalo, NY.
$25,123 to American Red Cross, Buffalo Chapter,
  Buffalo, NY.
$25,051 to DYouville College, Buffalo, NY.
$25,000 to Western New York Independent Living
  Project, Buffalo, NY.
$21,350 to Literacy Volunteers of America, Buffalo,
  NY. For Buffalo and Erie counties.
$20,254 to Neglia Ballet Artists, Ballet Artists of
  WNY, Buffalo, NY.

5781
The Community Foundation for South Central New York, Inc.

70 Front St.
Binghamton, NY 13905 (607) 772-6773
FAX: (607) 722-6752; E-mail: cfscny@stny.rr.com;
URL: http://www.cfscny.org

Established in 1997 in NY.
Foundation type: Community foundation.
Financial data (yr. ended 12/31/05): Assets, $34,329,498 (M); gifts received, $1,366,935; expenditures, $1,936,884; giving activities include $1,473,869 for 92+ grants.
Purpose and activities: The purpose of the foundation is to establish and maintain charitable endowments, donor-advised funds and restricted funds for charitable grants and scholarships in Broome, Chenango, Cortland, Delaware and Tioga Counties.
Fields of interest: Humanities; Arts; Higher education; Education; Hospitals (general); Health care; Youth development; Human services; Community development; Youth; Aging; Disabilities, people with.
Type of support: Capital campaigns; Building/renovation; Equipment; Emergency funds; Program development; Conferences/seminars; Seed money; Curriculum development; Technical assistance; Consulting services; Program-related investments/loans; Matching/challenge support.
Limitations: Giving limited to Broome, Chenango, Cortland, Delaware and Tioga counties, NY. No support for religious purposes. No grants to individuals (except for scholarships), or for operating or program deficits, mortgage payments, operating funds, special events, or individual musical theatre productions or performances.
Publications: Application guidelines; Annual report; Financial statement; Grants list; Informational brochure; Newsletter.
Application information: Visit foundation Web site for application forms and guidelines. Number of copies vary per application attachment. Application form required.
  Initial approach: Telephone to confirm project eligibility
  Copies of proposal: 12
  Deadline(s): Mar. 1 and Sept. 1
  Board meeting date(s): Apr. and Oct.
  Final notification: Approx. 8 weeks
Officers and Directors:* Stephen P. Feehan,* Chair.; Jeffrey A. Loew,* Vice-Chair.; Natalie Thompson,* Secy.; Kent Turner,* Treas.; Diane L. Brown,* Exec. Dir.; George Akel; Keith Chadwick; J. Richard Cunningham, M.D.; John W. Foley; Deborah A. Gouldin; David Hall; John F. Russell.
Number of staff: 4 full-time professional.
EIN: 161512085

5782
The Community Foundation for the Capital Region, Inc.

6 Tower Pl.
Albany, NY 12203 (518) 446-9638
Contact: E. Kristen Frederick, C.E.O.
FAX: (518) 446-9708; E-mail: info@cfcr.org;
URL: http://www.cfcr.org

Incorporated in 1968 in NY.
Foundation type: Community foundation.

Financial data (yr. ended 12/31/05): Assets, $33,854,605 (M); gifts received, $2,084,299; expenditures, $2,749,141; giving activities include $1,810,024 for 378 grants (high: $51,200; low: $25).
Purpose and activities: The general policy of the foundation is to make grants to innovative, creative projects and programs that are responsive to changing community needs. The purpose of the foundation is to use, apply and devote the foundation's properties and funds exclusively for charitable, scientific, cultural and educational purposes, through the making of grants or otherwise extending financial assistance and support to duly authorized persons, institutions and organizations.
Fields of interest: Adult education—literacy, basic skills & GED; Environment; Art & music therapy; Health care; AIDS; Crime/violence prevention, abuse prevention; Employment; Children/youth, services; Aging, centers/services; Homeless, human services; Disabilities, people with; Blind/visually impaired; Deaf/hearing impaired.
Type of support: General/operating support; Income development; Management development/capacity building; Program development; Seed money; Technical assistance; Employee-related scholarships.
Limitations: Giving primarily in the Capital Area region, including Albany, Renssealar, Saratoga, and Schenectady, NY. No support for sectarian religious purposes. No grants to individuals (except for scholarships), or for endowments or foundations, deficit financing, consulting services, continuing support, emergency funds, land acquisition, annual campaigns, research, capital campaigns or equipment, travel, conferences, advertisements, fundraising events, annual appeals, membership contributions, or fellowships; no loans.
Publications: Application guidelines; Annual report; Financial statement; Informational brochure; Newsletter.
Application information: Visit foundation Web site for application guidelines. Based on letter of inquiry, the applicant organization will be screened for eligibility and will either be notified of the reason for ineligibility or will be invited to submit an application; the applicant will be supplied with a grant application form and the deadline for submission. Application form required.
  Initial approach: Letter of inquiry (not exceeding 2 pages)
  Copies of proposal: 1
  Deadline(s): Feb. 13 and Aug. 31 for full applications
  Board meeting date(s): Bimonthly
  Final notification: June and Dec.
Officers and Directors:* James E. Prout,* Chair.; John H. Lavelle,* 1st Vice-Chair.; Robert F. Kopp,* 2nd Vice-Chair.; E. Kristen Frederick, C.E.O and Pres.; Roy M. Hershey,* Secy.; Sheridan C. Biggs,* Treas.; Judith Lyons, Exec. Dir; Steven B. Bouchey; Anthony Capobianco; Cristine Cioffi; Robert G. Dollar; Barbara L. Glaser; Barbara K. Hoehn; Paul M. Hohenberg; Nancy E. Hoffman; Frank M. Lasch; Steven E. Lobel; John MacAffer; J. Briggs McAndrews; Marcus Pryor; Maggie Vinciguerra; C. Wayne Williams.
Number of staff: 5 full-time professional; 2 part-time professional.
EIN: 141505623
Selected grants: The following grants were reported in 2006.
$30,000 to Whitney M. Young Jr. Health Center, Albany, NY. For Dental Capital Project.

$20,000 to Northeast Parent and Child, Schenectady, NY. For intensive therapeutic program.
$20,000 to Sunnyview Hospital and Rehabilitation Center Foundation, Schenectady, NY. For Brainstem Auditory Evoked Response (BSER).
$15,000 to Saratoga Therapeutic Equestrian Program, Waterford, NY. For Therapeutic Indoor Riding Ring.
$7,500 to AIDS Council of Northeastern New York, Albany, NY. For Targeted Outreach kits.
$5,000 to Arthritis Foundation, New York, NY. For Life Improvement Program.
$5,000 to Capital Region Center for Arts in Education, Albany, NY. For dance at Roessleville School.
$4,450 to New York State Historical Association, Cooperstown, NY. For the Fenimore Museum's Grandma Moses Exhibit.
$3,900 to Shaker Heritage Society, Albany, NY. For Communications Technology Project.
$3,000 to Peppertree Rescue, Albany, NY. For Serve a Senior by Saving a Senior.

5783
The Community Foundation of Herkimer & Oneida Counties, Inc.

(formerly Utica Foundation, Inc.)
1222 State St.
Utica, NY 13502 (315) 735-8212
Contact: Peggy O'Shea, C.E.O.
FAX: (315) 735-9363;
E-mail: info@foundationhoc.org; URL: http://www.foundationhoc.org

Incorporated in 1952 in NY.
Foundation type: Community foundation.
Financial data (yr. ended 12/31/05): Assets, $65,630,601 (M); gifts received, $2,000,069; expenditures, $3,542,336; giving activities include $2,387,951 for 445 grants.
Purpose and activities: The foundation provides support for programs and projects that: offer the greatest opportunity for positive and significant change in the community; identify and enhance local strengths to address and provide creative solutions for important existing or emerging community issues; develop organizational and/or individual self-sufficiency; focus on identifiable outcomes that will make a difference; leverage investment of other community resources; and improve the quality or scope of charitable works in the community.
Fields of interest: Arts; Higher education; Libraries/library science; Education; Environment; Hospitals (general); Health care; Children/youth, services; Family services; Aging, centers/services; Human services; Public affairs; Aging; Disabilities, people with.
Type of support: Scholarships—to individuals; Program evaluation; Curriculum development; Conferences/seminars; Capital campaigns; Building/renovation; Equipment; Land acquisition; Endowments; Emergency funds; Program development; Seed money; Fellowships; Scholarship funds; Technical assistance; Consulting services; Program-related investments/loans; Matching/challenge support.
Limitations: Giving limited to Herkimer and Oneida counties, NY. No support for religious purposes. No grants to individuals (except for scholarships), or for ongoing operating support, or requests that exceed $100,000; no loans to individuals.

Publications: Application guidelines; Annual report; Newsletter.
Application information: Visit foundation Web site for application cover sheet and guidelines. Application form required.
  Initial approach: Telephone
  Copies of proposal: 19
  Deadline(s): None
  Board meeting date(s): Grants committee meets 5 to 6 times per year
  Final notification: 4 to 8 weeks
Officers and Directors:* Camille T. Kahler,* Chair.; John Livingston,* Chair.-Elect; Rudy D'Amico,* Vice-Chair.; Harrison Hummel III,* Vice-Chair.; Georgiana Roberts Ide,* Vice-Chair.; Albert Mazloom,* Vice-Chair.; Mary F. Morse,* Vice-Chair.; William R. Stevens,* Vice-Chair.; Richard Zick, Vice-Chair.; Peggy O'Shea, C.E.O. and Pres.; Timothy Foley,* Secy.-Treas.; George F. Aney; Milton J. Bloch; Lauren Bull; Don Carbone; Hon. Robert Julian; Linda Macartney; Theodore Max, M.D.; Anthony Paolozzi; Faye Short; Sheila Smith.
Trustee Banks: Bank of America, N.A.; HSBC Bank USA.
Number of staff: 6 full-time professional; 1 full-time support; 1 part-time support.
EIN: 156016932

5784
The Community Foundation of the Elmira-Corning Area
(formerly The Community Foundation of the Chemung County Area and Corning Community Foundation)
307B E. Water St.
Elmira, NY 14901-3402 (607) 734-6412
Contact: For grant applications: Suzanne Lee, Pres.; Randi Hewit, V.P., Grants and Initiatives
FAX: (607) 734-7335;
E-mail: shl@communityfund.org; E-mail for grant applications: rlh@communityfund.org; URL: http://www.communityfund.org

Established in 1977 in NY as Chemung County; Corning established in 1972 in NY; reincorporated in 1993 under current name after merger of Community Foundation of Chemung County Area and Corning Community Foundation.
Foundation type: Community foundation.
Financial data (yr. ended 6/30/05): Assets, $15,720,450 (M); gifts received, $929,121; expenditures, $1,253,662; giving activities include $807,579 for 202 grants (high: $56,000; low: $15); and $90,150 for 47 grants to individuals (high: $14,000; low: $150).
Purpose and activities: The foundation's unrestricted endowment supports organizations that benefit the Chemung and southeastern Steuben counties, NY, as a whole, especially those that need seed money for pilot projects and innovative solutions to problems, and which promote self-help for individuals and groups.
Fields of interest: Humanities; Arts; Education; Environment; Animal welfare; Health care; Youth development; Human services; Community development, neighborhood development.
Type of support: Program evaluation; General/operating support; Management development/capacity building; Building/renovation; Equipment; Endowments; Program development; Conferences/seminars; Publication; Seed money; Curriculum development; Scholarship funds; Research; Technical assistance; Consulting services;

Employee-related scholarships; Scholarships—to individuals; Matching/challenge support.
Limitations: Giving only in Chemung, Schuyler, Yates, and southeastern Steuben counties, NY. No support for religious purposes. No grants to individuals (except for scholarships), or for annual campaigns, special event fundraisers, sponsorships, trips, or deficit funding or debt retirement; no loans.
Publications: Application guidelines; Annual report (including application guidelines); Financial statement; Newsletter.
Application information: Visit foundation Web site for application forms and guidelines. Organizations submitting a proposal for $5,000 or more are required to submit a letter of intent. The foundation will hold a series of workshops to explain how grants are reviewed and selected, as well as the role of site visit in the application process; attendance at one of the workshops is mandatory. Scholarship applications and guidelines (for residents of Chemung and southeastern Steuben counties only) available each year on Dec. 15; other grant applications available on Aug. 15. Application form required.
  Initial approach: Attend grant application workshop
  Copies of proposal: 5
  Deadline(s): Mar. 17 and Aug. 2 for Letter of Intent; Apr. 17 and Sept. 9 for grant application; Feb. 24 for scholarships
  Board meeting date(s): Varies
  Final notification: Mid-Jun. and mid-Oct.
Officers and Trustees:* George Welch,* Chair.; Carl T. Hayden,* Vice-Chair.; Suzanne Lee, Pres.; Randi Hewit, V.P., Grants and Initiatives; Clover M. Drinkwater,* Secy.; Robert Grassi,* Treas.; John Brand III; Daniel Burke; Shelley Dugas-Thomas; James B. Flaws; John Gough; Linda J. Gudas; Michael Hosey; Donald B. Keck; Judith McIntosh; Richard Niles; John Peck; Richard Rossettie; Ginger Schirmer; Thomas G. Snow; Robert Spooner.
Number of staff: 4 full-time professional.
EIN: 161100837

5785
Community Health Foundation of Western & Central New York, Inc.
11 Summer St., 3rd Fl.
Buffalo, NY 14209 (716) 881-5600
Contact: Ann F. Monroe, Pres.
FAX: (716) 881-0520; E-mail: info@chfwcny.org;
URL: http://www.chfwcny.org

Established in 2001 in NY.
Donors: Univera Heathcare- CNY, Inc.; Genesee Valley Group Health Assoc.
Foundation type: Independent foundation.
Financial data (yr. ended 12/31/05): Assets, $102,502,032 (M); gifts received, $1,623,565; expenditures, $3,219,875; qualifying distributions, $2,897,007; giving activities include $1,840,319 for 41 grants (high: $150,000; low: $1,200; average: $25,000–$50,000), and $315,036 for 4 foundation-administered programs.
Purpose and activities: The Community Health Foundation of Western and Central New York is dedicated to improving the health and health care of the people and communities of western and central New York. Frail elders and children in communities of poverty are the current priority focus areas.

Fields of interest: Medical care, community health systems; Health care; Foundations (community); Children; Aging; Economically disadvantaged.
Type of support: Building/renovation; Program development; Conferences/seminars; Fellowships; Scholarship funds; Technical assistance; Consulting services; Program evaluation; Matching/challenge support.
Limitations: Giving limited to select counties in western and central NY.
Publications: Application guidelines; Grants list; Newsletter.
Application information: Check foundation Web site for current Requests for Proposals. Application form not required.
  Initial approach: Telephone call, letter of intent or e-mail
  Board meeting date(s): Bimonthly
Officers: Robert M. Bennett, Chair.; George S. Deptula, Vice-Chair.; Ann F. Monroe, Pres.; James H. Abbott, Secy.; Stephen C. Ames, Treas.
Directors: Marilyn J. Baader; Louis P. Dudek; Catherine A. Gale; Angel (Lito) Guttierez; June W. Hoefich; James E. Intone; Robert A. Ludwig; James L. Magayern; Edward J. Marine, M.D.; James P. Nolan; Peter J. O'Neill; Margaret W. Paroski; Kathryn H. Ruscitto; Stephen J. Suhowatsky; Maurizio Treusan; Thomas L. Wolff.
Number of staff: 2 full-time professional; 1 part-time professional; 1 full-time support; 2 part-time support.
EIN: 223804398
Selected grants: The following grants were reported in 2004.
$125,000 to Community Foundation for Greater Buffalo, Buffalo, NY.
$100,000 to Northwest Buffalo Community Health Care Center, Buffalo, NY.
$100,000 to Resource Center, Jamestown, NY.
$98,895 to Research Center for Stroke and Heart Disease, Buffalo, NY.
$84,868 to UB Foundation Services, Buffalo, NY.
$80,000 to Research Foundation of the State University of New York, Syracuse, NY.
$71,500 to Research Foundation of the State University of New York, Amherst, NY.
$53,515 to Center for Health Improvement, Sacramento, CA.
$50,500 to Ithaca Breast Cancer Alliance, Ithaca, NY.
$2,500 to Grantmakers in Health, DC.

5786
ContiGroup Companies Foundation ◇
(formerly Continental Grain Foundation)
277 Park Ave., 50th Fl.
New York, NY 10172-0003 (212) 207-5879
Contact: Susan McIntyre, Asst. Secy.
URL: http://www.contigroup.com/2004_about_found.html

Incorporated in 1961 in NY.
Donors: Continental Grain Co.; ContiGroup Cos., Inc.
Foundation type: Company-sponsored foundation.
Financial data (yr. ended 1/31/04): Assets, $192 (M); gifts received, $383,971; expenditures, $384,086; qualifying distributions, $384,086; giving activities include $383,971 for 59 grants (high: $25,000; low: $100).
Purpose and activities: The foundation supports organizations involved with arts and culture, education, health, and youth development.

Fields of interest: Arts; Education; Health care; Youth development, centers/clubs; Youth development.
Limitations: Applications not accepted. Giving primarily in NY.
Application information: Contributes only to pre-selected organizations.
Officers: Paul J. Fribourg, Pres.; Richard Anderson, Treas.
Director: Teresa E. McCaslin.
EIN: 136160912
Selected grants: The following grants were reported in 2004.
$25,000 to Appeal of Conscience Foundation, New York, NY.
$25,000 to Brooklyn Bridge Park Conservancy, Brooklyn, NY.
$25,000 to Endeavor Global, New York, NY.
$25,000 to Jewish Theological Seminary of America, New York, NY.
$25,000 to YMCA of Greater New York, New York, NY.
$20,000 to Library of Congress, DC.
$15,000 to Museum of Modern Art, New York, NY.
$10,000 to Conservation International, DC.
$10,000 to Prep for Prep, New York, NY.
$10,000 to Young Audiences (YA), New York, NY.

5787
The Robert M. Conway Foundation ✧ ☆
(formerly Robert M. & Lois Conway Foundation)
c/o BCRS Group Associates, LLC
100 Wall St., 11th Fl.
New York, NY 10005

Established in 1982 in NY.
Donor: Robert M. Conway.
Foundation type: Independent foundation.
Financial data (yr. ended 9/30/05): Assets, $3,816,279 (M); gifts received, $1,804,875; expenditures, $422,983; qualifying distributions, $417,155; giving activities include $416,805 for 8 grants (high: $355,455; low: $500).
Purpose and activities: Giving primarily for higher education and the arts.
Fields of interest: Performing arts, ballet; Performing arts, orchestra (symphony); Higher education.
International interests: England.
Limitations: Applications not accepted. Giving in the U.S. and England. No grants to individuals, or for scholarships; no loans.
Application information: Contributes only to pre-selected organizations.
Trustees: Robert M. Conway; Robert J. Hurst.
EIN: 133153721

5788
The Cooper Family Foundation, Inc. ✧
(formerly Milton Cooper Foundation)
3333 New Hyde Park Rd., No. 100
New Hyde Park, NY 11042-0020

Established in 1987 in NY.
Donors: Milton Cooper; Martin S. Kimmel.
Foundation type: Independent foundation.
Financial data (yr. ended 12/31/05): Assets, $13,904,277 (M); gifts received, $375,500; expenditures, $1,880,653; qualifying distributions, $1,858,416; giving activities include $1,857,605 for 90 grants (high: $1,093,820; low: $300).

Fields of interest: Arts; Higher education; Education; Health care; Health organizations, association; Human services; Jewish federated giving programs; Jewish agencies & temples.
Limitations: Applications not accepted. Giving primarily in New York, NY. No grants to individuals.
Application information: Contributes only to pre-selected organizations.
Officers: Milton Cooper, Pres.; Arthur Friedman, Secy.; Todd Cooper, Treas.
EIN: 112831400
Selected grants: The following grants were reported in 2005.
$1,093,820 to American Jewish Committee, New York, NY.
$256,000 to UJA-Federation of New York, New York, NY.
$36,500 to Long Island University, Brookville, NY.
$25,000 to Teach for America, New York, NY.
$23,500 to Yeshiva University, New York, NY.
$20,000 to University of Michigan, Ann Arbor, MI.
$12,010 to Building With Books, Stamford, CT.
$10,000 to Abrams Hebrew Academy, Yardley, PA.
$2,600 to Hofstra University, Hempstead, NY.
$1,000 to Variety Child Learning Center, Syosset, NY.

5789
The Aaron Copland Fund for Music, Inc. ✧
c/o Brown Raysman LLP
900 3rd Ave., 23rd Fl.
New York, NY 10022 (212) 895-2367
Contact: James M. Kendrick, Secy.
FAX: (212) 366-5265; Application address: c/o American Music Ctr., 30 W. 26th St., Ste. 1001, New York, NY 10010-2011, tel.: (212) 366-5260 (for performing ensemble and recording programs); URL: http://www.amc.net/resources/grants

Established in 1991 in NY; funded in 1992.
Donors: Aaron Copland†; Sylvia Goldstein†; Robert Eugene Helps†.
Foundation type: Independent foundation.
Financial data (yr. ended 6/30/05): Assets, $17,197,426 (M); expenditures, $1,948,653; qualifying distributions, $1,805,987; giving activities include $1,429,000 for 154 grants (high: $50,000; low: $1,000).
Purpose and activities: Giving to encourage and improve public knowledge and appreciation for contemporary American music. The fund has established the Performing Ensembles Program, which awards grants to performing organizations with a commitment for contemporary American music, and the Recording Program to support recordings, as well as a Supplemental Program for service organizations and others.
Fields of interest: Performing arts, music.
Type of support: General/operating support; Program development.
Limitations: Giving on a national basis. No grants to individuals.
Publications: Application guidelines; Informational brochure (including application guidelines).
Application information: Visit Web site of American Music Center for grant guidelines. Application form required.
  Initial approach: Completed application form with all supporting materials
  Copies of proposal: 1

Deadline(s): June 30 for performing organizations; Jan. 15 for recording program; Sept. 15 for Supplemental Program
Final notification: In or about Nov. for performing organizations; June for recording program; Dec. for supplemental program
Officers and Directors:* John Harbison,* Pres.; Vivian Perlis,* V.P.; James M. Kendrick, Secy.; Norman Feit, Treas.; Elliot Carter; John Corigliano; David Del Tredici; Lukas Foss; Ursula Oppens; Christopher Rouse; Ellen Taaffe Zwilich.
EIN: 133620909
Selected grants: The following grants were reported in 2005.
$500,000 to American Music Center, New York, NY.
$55,000 to Albany Symphony Orchestra, Albany, NY.
$50,000 to American Symphony Orchestra League, New York, NY.
$40,000 to Meet the Composer, New York, NY.
$35,000 to American Composers Orchestra, New York, NY.
$35,000 to Bang On A Can, New York, NY.
$35,000 to Boston Modern Orchestra Project, Roslindale, MA.
$35,000 to Recorded Anthology of American Music, New York, NY.
$30,500 to Copland House, Cortlandt Manor, NY.
$10,000 to Chicago Classical Recording Foundation, Chicago, IL.

5790
Cordelia Corp. ✧
c/o Citibank, N.A.
153 E. 53rd St., 23rd Fl.
New York, NY 10022-0000

Established in 1994 in NV.
Donors: Mary A. Bing; R.D. Burch.
Foundation type: Independent foundation.
Financial data (yr. ended 5/31/05): Assets, $29,678,526 (M); gifts received, $1; expenditures, $1,948,360; qualifying distributions, $1,617,086; giving activities include $1,543,180 for 9 grants (high: $607,180; low: $1,000).
Purpose and activities: Giving primarily for higher education, and for the arts, particularly the performing arts.
Fields of interest: Media, film/video; Performing arts centers; Performing arts, dance; Performing arts, ballet; Arts; Higher education; Education.
Limitations: Applications not accepted. Giving in the U.S., with emphasis on New Haven, CT and New York, NY. No grants to individuals.
Application information: Contributes only to pre-selected organizations.
Officers and Directors:* Mary A. Bing,* Pres.; William Stinehart, Jr.,* Secy.; Douglas Ellis,* Treas.
Trustee: Citibank, N.A.
EIN: 880326514
Selected grants: The following grants were reported in 2005.
$607,180 to Yale University, New Haven, CT.
$50,000 to Moving Image, New York, NY.
$25,000 to Ballet Tech Foundation, New York, NY.

5791
The Corey Foundation ✧
c/o M. Corey
2 Columbus Ave., Ste. 35A
New York, NY 10023-6933

Established in 1998 in NY.
Donors: Emilie Corey; Michael Corey.
Foundation type: Independent foundation.
Financial data (yr. ended 12/31/04): Assets, $23,414,002 (M); gifts received, $574,700; expenditures, $1,238,047; qualifying distributions, $1,179,250; giving activities include $1,177,750 for 32 grants (high: $500,000; low: $1,000).
Fields of interest: Performing arts, opera; Arts; Education; Human services; Aging.
Limitations: Applications not accepted. Giving primarily in NY. No grants to individuals.
Application information: Contributes only to pre-selected organizations.
Trustees: Emilie Corey; Michael Corey.
EIN: 113453820
Selected grants: The following grants were reported in 2004.
$510,000 to Polytechnic University, Brooklyn, NY. 2 grants: $10,000, $500,000
$378,350 to New York City Opera, New York, NY. 2 grants: $125,000, $253,350
$25,000 to Brooklyn Bureau of Community Service, Brooklyn, NY.
$25,000 to Jazz at Lincoln Center, New York, NY.
$25,000 to Park Slope Geriatric Day Center, Brooklyn, NY.
$25,000 to Simmons College, Boston, MA.
$20,000 to East End Hospice, Westhampton Beach, NY.
$20,000 to Westhampton Beach Performing Arts Center, Westhampton Beach, NY.

5792
The Henry Cornell Foundation ◇
c/o Goldman Sachs Family Office
1 New York Plz., 40th Fl.
New York, NY   10004

Established in 1996 in NY.
Donor: Henry Cornell.
Foundation type: Independent foundation.
Financial data (yr. ended 8/31/05): Assets, $4,891,066 (M); gifts received, $3,219,950; expenditures, $952,433; qualifying distributions, $919,251; giving activities include $919,251 for 31 grants (high: $200,000; low: $500).
Fields of interest: Museums (art); Performing arts, opera; Arts; Higher education.
Limitations: Applications not accepted. Giving primarily in NY. No grants to individuals.
Application information: Contributes only to pre-selected organizations.
Trustee: Henry Cornell.
EIN: 133921374
Selected grants: The following grants were reported in 2003.
$150,000 to Asia Society, New York, NY. 2 grants: $100,000 (For general support), $50,000 (For general support).
$100,000 to Grinnell College, Grinnell, IA. For general support.
$65,000 to Whitney Museum of American Art, New York, NY. For general support.
$50,000 to Asian Art Museum of San Francisco, San Francisco, CA. For general support.
$35,000 to Citizens Committee for Children of New York, New York, NY. 2 grants: $25,000 (For general support), $10,000 (For general support).
$25,000 to Council on Foreign Relations, New York, NY. For general support.
$6,000 to Catie Hoch Foundation, Ballston Lake, NY. For general support.

$5,000 to Mount Sinai Hospital and Medical Center Foundation, New York, NY. For general support.

5793
The Joseph and Robert Cornell Memorial Foundation ◇ ☆
c/o RSM Mcgladrey, Inc.
1185 6th Ave.
New York, NY   10036-2602

Donor: Joseph Cornell‡.
Foundation type: Independent foundation.
Financial data (yr. ended 12/31/05): Assets, $71,418,045 (M); expenditures, $4,392,023; qualifying distributions, $4,071,223; giving activities include $3,852,500 for 12 grants (high: $1,000,000; low: $95,000).
Purpose and activities: Giving primarily for art museums.
Fields of interest: Museums (art); Higher education; Hospitals (general).
Type of support: Program development.
Limitations: Applications not accepted. Giving nationally, with some emphasis on Washington, DC, MD, and VA. No grants to individuals.
Application information: Contributes only to pre-selected organizations.
Trustees: Richard M. Ader; Donald Windham.
EIN: 133097502

5794
Corning Incorporated Foundation ▼
(formerly Corning Glass Works Foundation)
MP-BH-07
Corning, NY   14831   (607) 974-8489
Contact: Karen C. Martin, Assoc. Dir.
FAX: (607) 974-4756;
E-mail: martinkc@corning.com; URL: http://www.corning.com/inside_corning/our_commitment/community.aspx

Incorporated in 1952 in NY.
Donor: Corning Inc.
Foundation type: Company-sponsored foundation.
Financial data (yr. ended 12/31/05): Assets, $9,878,295 (M); gifts received, $498,262; expenditures, $4,380,392; qualifying distributions, $4,356,918; giving activities include $3,274,839 for 191 grants (high: $209,000; low: $68), and $499,979 for 1,546 employee matching gifts.
Purpose and activities: The foundation supports hospitals and hospices and organizations involved with arts and culture, education, and human services.
Fields of interest: Media/communications; Museums; Arts; Elementary/secondary education; Higher education; Libraries/library science; Education; Hospitals (general); YM/YWCAs & YM/YWHAs; Youth, services; Residential/custodial care, hospices; Women, centers/services; Human services; Foundations (community); Federated giving programs.
Type of support: Management development/capacity building; General/operating support; Fellowships; Capital campaigns; Building/renovation; Equipment; Program development; Seed money; Curriculum development; Technical assistance; Program evaluation; Employee matching gifts; Matching/challenge support.
Limitations: Giving primarily in Harrodsburg, KY, Kennebunk, ME, Canton, Oneonta, and the greater

Corning-Elmira, NY, area, Hickory and Wilmington, NC, and Blacksburg and Danville, VA; giving also to national and international organizations. No support for political parties, labor or veterans' organizations, religious or fraternal organizations, or volunteer emergency squads. No grants to individuals, or for political campaigns or causes, athletic activities, advertising, or fundraising.
Publications: Biennial report (including application guidelines); Grants list.
Application information: Letters of inquiry should be no longer than 2 to 3 pages. Application form not required.
Initial approach: Letter of inquiry
Copies of proposal: 1
Deadline(s): None
Board meeting date(s): Mar., June, Sept., and Nov.
Final notification: 6 weeks
Officers and Trustees:* E. Marie McKee,* Chair.; Kristin A. Swain, Pres.; Denise A. Hauselt, Secy.; Mark S. Rogus,* Treas.; Katherine A. Asbeck; Thomas S. Buechner; William D. Eggers; James B. Flaws; Kirk P. Gregg; James R. Houghton; Joseph A. Miller; Pamela C. Schneider; Peter F. Volanakis; Wendell P. Weeks.
Number of staff: 2 full-time professional; 1 full-time support.
EIN: 166051394
Selected grants: The following grants were reported in 2005.
$659,000 to Corning City School District, Painted Post, NY. 2 grants: $489,000 (For curriculum and staff development), $170,000 (For International Baccalaureate Program).
$420,077 to American Red Cross, National Headquarters, DC. 2 grants: $366,902 (For Hurricane Katrina disaster relief efforts), $53,175 (For Tsunami disaster relief efforts).
$350,000 to United Way of the Southern Tier, Corning, NY.
$260,000 to One Seventy One Cedar, Corning, NY. For general operating support.
$10,000 to Corning-Painted Post Civic Music Association, Corning, NY. For concert series.
$5,513 to United Way of York County, Kennebunk, ME.
$5,000 to Dartmouth College, Hanover, NH.
$5,000 to Executive Council on Diplomacy, DC.

5795
Cornpauw Foundation, Ltd. ◇ ☆
c/o Barry M. Strauss Assocs., Ltd.
307 5th Ave., 8th Fl.
New York, NY   10016-6517

Established in 1986 in NY.
Donor: Nelson Schaenen, Jr.
Foundation type: Independent foundation.
Financial data (yr. ended 3/31/06): Assets, $1,216,291 (M); gifts received, $253,378; expenditures, $396,011; qualifying distributions, $393,429; giving activities include $391,130 for 38 grants (high: $76,100; low: $1,000).
Purpose and activities: Giving primarily to higher education; funding also for the arts, particularly museums, health care and hospitals, a YMCA, and human services.
Fields of interest: Museums; Arts; Higher education; Education; Hospitals (general); Health care; Human services; YM/YWCAs & YM/YWHAs.
Limitations: Applications not accepted. Giving primarily in NJ and NY. No grants to individuals.

Application information: Contributes only to pre-selected organizations.
Officers: Nelson Schaenen, Jr., Pres. and Treas.; Nancy Schaenen, V.P. and Secy.; Douglas K. Schaenen, V.P.
EIN: 133387939

5796
The Corrigan Foundation ✧
c/o Goldman Sachs & Co.
1 New York Plz., 40th Fl.
New York, NY 10004

Established in 1996 in NY.
Donors: E. Gerald Corrigan; Goldman Sachs & Co.
Foundation type: Independent foundation.
Financial data (yr. ended 7/31/05): Assets, $11,756,262 (M); gifts received, $3,125,125; expenditures, $728,000; qualifying distributions, $650,250; giving activities include $650,250 for 69 grants (high: $200,000; low: $250).
Purpose and activities: Giving primarily for education, particularly higher education, and to university funds; funding also for the arts, human services, health associations, environmental conservation, and for research in international economics and finance.
Fields of interest: Museums (natural history); Historic preservation/historical societies; Arts; Elementary/secondary education; Higher education; Environment; Animals/wildlife; Health organizations, association; Human services; Economics.
Type of support: General/operating support.
Limitations: Applications not accepted. Giving primarily in CT, MA, and NY. No grants to individuals.
Application information: Contributes only to pre-selected organizations.
Trustees: E. Gerald Corrigan; Elizabeth A. Corrigan; Karen B. Corrigan; Cathy E. Minehan.
EIN: 137109402
Selected grants: The following grants were reported in 2004.
$1,250,000 to Fairfield University, Fairfield, CT. 3 grants: $500,000 (For general support), $500,000 (For general support), $250,000 (For general support).
$200,000 to Fordham University, Bronx, NY. For general support.
$100,000 to University of Rochester, Rochester, NY. For general support.
$70,000 to Episcopal Academy, Merion, PA. For general support.
$25,000 to American Museum of Natural History, New York, NY. For general support.
$25,000 to Environmental Defense, New York, NY. For general support.
$10,000 to Bretton Woods Committee, DC. For general support.
$10,000 to National Committee on American Foreign Policy, New York, NY. For general support.

5797
The Joanne D. Corzine Foundation ✧
c/o The Ayco Co.
321 Broadway
P.O. Box 860
Saratoga Springs, NY 12866-0860

Established in 2002 in NJ.

Donors: The Jon and Joanne Corzine Foundation; Joanne D. Corzine.
Foundation type: Independent foundation.
Financial data (yr. ended 12/31/05): Assets, $5,969,720 (M); gifts received, $2,815; expenditures, $1,990,881; qualifying distributions, $1,941,000; giving activities include $1,941,000 for 15 grants (high: $510,000; low: $1,000).
Purpose and activities: Giving primarily for the arts, education, and human services.
Fields of interest: Performing arts; Arts; Education; Human services.
Limitations: Applications not accepted. Giving primarily in NJ. No grants to individuals.
Application information: Contributes only to pre-selected organizations.
Officer and Trustees:* John Barry,* V.P.; Joanne D. Corzine.
EIN: 306034293
Selected grants: The following grants were reported in 2003.
$500,000 to New Jersey Performing Arts Center, Newark, NJ. For cultural programs.
$500,000 to Overlook Hospital Foundation, Summit, NJ. For medical programs.
$500,000 to Pomfret School, Pomfret, CT. For educational programs.
$500,000 to University of Chicago, Chicago, IL. For educational programs.
$250,000 to SAGE Eldercare, Summit, NJ. For elderly support.
$250,000 to University of Illinois at Urbana-Champaign, Urbana, IL. For educational programs.
$125,000 to Seton Hall University, South Orange, NJ. For educational services.
$83,534 to Chad School Foundation, Newark, NJ. For educational programs.
$80,000 to Patrons Program, New York, NY. For educational programs.
$50,000 to Telluride Foundation, Telluride, CO. For community support.

5798
The Jon S. Corzine Foundation ▼ ✧
c/o BCRS Assocs., LLC
100 Wall St., 11th Fl.
New York, NY 10017

Established in 2002 in NJ.
Donors: The Jon and Joanne Corzine Foundation; Jon S. Corzine; The Corzine Blind Trust.
Foundation type: Independent foundation.
Financial data (yr. ended 12/31/04): Assets, $20,748,951 (M); gifts received, $2,000,839; expenditures, $6,755,581; qualifying distributions, $4,906,615; giving activities include $4,906,565 for 134 grants (high: $500,000; low: $200; average: $5,000–$50,000).
Purpose and activities: Giving primarily for education, health care, and religious organizations.
Fields of interest: Education; Reproductive health, family planning; Health care; Human services; Christian agencies & churches; Jewish agencies & temples.
Limitations: Applications not accepted. Giving primarily in NJ. No grants to individuals.
Application information: Contributes only to pre-selected organizations.
Trustee: Jon S. Corzine.
EIN: 306034295
Selected grants: The following grants were reported in 2004.

$500,000 to New Jersey Performing Arts Center, Newark, NJ. For general support.
$500,000 to Pomfret School, Pomfret, CT. For general support.
$463,884 to University of Chicago, Chicago, IL. For general support.
$250,000 to GAVI Fund, DC. For general support.
$250,000 to Nation Institute, New York, NY. For general support.
$100,000 to John F. Kennedy Center for the Performing Arts, DC. For general support.
$25,000 to Planned Parenthood of Greater Northern New Jersey, Morristown, NJ. For general support.
$20,200 to American Jewish Congress, New York, NY. For general support.
$15,000 to Saint Benedicts Preparatory School, Newark, NJ. For general support.
$10,000 to Ballet Theater Foundation, New York, NY. For general support.

5799
The Frank L. and Sarah Miller Coulson Foundation ✧
c/o Goldman Sachs Family Office
1 New York Plz., 40th Fl.
New York, NY 10004

Established in 2000 in PA.
Donor: Frank L. Coulson, Jr.
Foundation type: Independent foundation.
Financial data (yr. ended 10/31/05): Assets, $7,354,939 (M); expenditures, $562,774; qualifying distributions, $538,884; giving activities include $538,884 for 38 grants (high: $200,000; low: $500).
Purpose and activities: Giving primarily for higher education, and to performing arts centers.
Fields of interest: Performing arts centers; Arts; Higher education; Education; Animals/wildlife; Philanthropy/voluntarism.
Limitations: Applications not accepted. Giving primarily in New York, NY and Philadelphia, PA. No grants to individuals or for scholarships; no loans.
Application information: Contributes only to pre-selected organizations.
Trustees: Frank L. Coulson, Jr.; Sarah Miller Coulson.
EIN: 134148044

5800
The Countess Moira Charitable Foundation ✧ ☆
c/o Analytic Asset Mgmt., Inc.
600 3rd Ave., 17th Fl.
New York, NY 10016

Established in 2000 in NY.
Donors: Moira Rossi; Edward W.T. Gray III; Moira Forbes.
Foundation type: Independent foundation.
Financial data (yr. ended 6/30/05): Assets, $34,791,089 (M); gifts received, $31,682,360; expenditures, $845,744; qualifying distributions, $608,707; giving activities include $605,000 for 13 grants (high: $450,000; low: $5,000).
Purpose and activities: Giving to organizations that provide medical, nutritional and educational programs for children.
Fields of interest: Education; Medical care, in-patient care; Children.
Type of support: General/operating support.

Limitations: Applications not accepted. Giving primarily in NY. No grants to individuals.
Application information: Contributes only to pre-selected organizations.
Officers: Edward W.T. Gray III, Chair.; Michele J. Le Moal-Gray, Vice-Chair.; Carolyn B. Gray, Pres.; Peter G. Gray, V.P. and Secy.; Taylor T. Gray, V.P. and Treas.
Trustee: Moira Forbes.
EIN: 113551993

5801
Randolph L. Cowen & Phyllis Green Foundation ◇
c/o Goldman Sachs
1 New York Plz., 40th Fl.
New York, NY 10004

Established in 1996 in NY.
Donor: Randolph L. Cowen.
Foundation type: Independent foundation.
Financial data (yr. ended 5/31/05): Assets, $3,323,383 (M); gifts received, $990,803; expenditures, $786,410; qualifying distributions, $736,500; giving activities include $736,500 for 6 grants (high: $500,000; low: $1,500).
Fields of interest: Higher education.
Type of support: General/operating support.
Limitations: Applications not accepted. Giving primarily in NY. No grants to individuals.
Application information: Contributes only to pre-selected organizations.
Trustees: Randolph L. Cowen; Phyllis Green.
EIN: 137109419

5802
The Joyce and Daniel Cowin Foundation, Inc. ◇ ☆
640 Park Ave.
New York, NY 10021
Contact: Joyce B. Cowin, Pres.

Established in 1957 in NY.
Donors: Sylvia J. Berger; Daniel Cowin; Joyce B. Cowin.
Foundation type: Independent foundation.
Financial data (yr. ended 12/31/05): Assets, $7,501,723 (M); gifts received, $302,513; expenditures, $423,343; qualifying distributions, $417,975; giving activities include $413,000 for 3 grants (high: $300,000; low: $13,000).
Purpose and activities: Giving primarily for the arts, and to Jewish and other human service organizations.
Fields of interest: Museums (art); Arts; Human services; Jewish agencies & temples.
Limitations: Applications not accepted. Giving primarily in New York, NY.
Application information: Contributes only to pre-selected organizations.
Officer: Joyce B. Cowin, Pres.
EIN: 136154142

5803
The Donald & Maria Cox Trust ◇ ☆
c/o Fiduciary Trust Co. International
600 5th Ave.
New York, NY 10020 (212) 632-3000

Established in 1985 in NY.

Donor: Donald M. Cox†.
Foundation type: Independent foundation.
Financial data (yr. ended 12/31/05): Assets, $2,150,109 (M); expenditures, $346,306; qualifying distributions, $327,000; giving activities include $327,000 for grants.
Purpose and activities: The foundation primarily supports Roman Catholic agencies and churches, and organizations involved with arts and culture, health, and human services.
Fields of interest: Museums (art); Arts; Health organizations, association; Human services; Roman Catholic agencies & churches.
Limitations: Giving primarily in New York, NY. No grants to individuals.
Application information:
 Initial approach: Letter
 Deadline(s): None
Trustee: Maria R. Cox.
EIN: 136864749
Selected grants: The following grants were reported in 2004.
$65,500 to American Federation of Arts, New York, NY.
$52,500 to Cornell University, Ithaca, NY.
$20,000 to Polytechnic University, Brooklyn, NY.
$11,330 to Our Lady Star of the Sea, Staten Island, NY.
$5,000 to Museum of Modern Art, New York, NY.
$5,000 to Virginia Polytechnic Institute and State University, Blacksburg, VA.
$1,500 to Jacksonville Museum of Modern Art, Jacksonville, FL.
$1,350 to Metropolitan Museum of Art, New York, NY.
$1,000 to Inner-City Scholarship Fund, New York, NY.
$1,000 to Whitney Museum of American Art, New York, NY.

5804
Gerald B. Cramer Family Foundation, Inc. ◇
c/o Cramer Rosenthal McGlynn
707 Westchester Ave., Ste. 405
White Plains, NY 10604

Established in 1993 in NY.
Donors: Gerald Cramer; Daphna Cramer; Members of the Cramer family.
Foundation type: Independent foundation.
Financial data (yr. ended 12/31/04): Assets, $4,707,396 (M); gifts received, $493,200; expenditures, $540,323; qualifying distributions, $484,764; giving activities include $484,764 for grants.
Purpose and activities: Giving primarily for higher education and the arts.
Fields of interest: Museums; Arts; Higher education; Jewish agencies & temples.
Limitations: Applications not accepted. Giving primarily in NY. No grants to individuals.
Application information: Contributes only to pre-selected organizations.
Officers: Gerald B. Cramer, Pres.; Camille Parisi, V.P. and Secy.-Treas.
Directors: Daphna Cramer; Douglas Cramer; Kimberly Cramer; Lauren Cramer; Thomas Cramer; Roy Raskin; Shelley Raskin.
EIN: 133749869

5805
Cranaleith Foundation, Inc. ◇
c/o M. Mullaney, BDO Seidman
330 Madison Ave.
New York, NY 10017

Established in 1993 in PA.
Donors: Francis H. Trainer, Jr.; Jeanne A. Trainer.
Foundation type: Independent foundation.
Financial data (yr. ended 12/31/05): Assets, $16,774,520 (M); gifts received, $550,000; expenditures, $789,637; qualifying distributions, $742,829; giving activities include $741,500 for 22 grants (high: $200,000; low: $1,000).
Purpose and activities: Giving primarily for children's services, particularly to a shelter for homeless children; funding also for higher education, and human services, including an organization for people who are developmentally disabled.
Fields of interest: Higher education; Environment, natural resources; Human services; Children, services; Developmentally disabled, centers & services.
Limitations: Applications not accepted. Giving on a national basis. No grants to individuals.
Application information: Contributes only to pre-selected organizations.
Officers: Francis H. Trainer, Jr., Pres.; Jeanne A. Trainer, V.P.
EIN: 232726952
Selected grants: The following grants were reported in 2005.
$200,000 to Saint Josephs University, Philadelphia, PA.
$100,000 to Covenant House, New York, NY.
$60,000 to Hastings Center, Garrison, NY.
$50,000 to Cranaleith Spiritual Center, Philadelphia, PA.
$50,000 to Nature Conservancy, Chester, NJ.
$30,000 to Friends of the Americas, Baton Rouge, LA. 2 grants: $10,000, $20,000
$5,000 to Berea College, Berea, KY.
$5,000 to Fund for Peace, DC.

5806
Bruce L. Crary Foundation, Inc. ◇
c/o Hand House, River St.
P.O. Box 396
Elizabethtown, NY 12932 (518) 873-6496
Contact: Hanna Kissam, Exec. Dir.

Incorporated in 1973 in NY.
Donors: Crary Public Trust; Bruce L. Crary†.
Foundation type: Independent foundation.
Financial data (yr. ended 6/30/05): Assets, $8,536,502 (M); gifts received, $2,835; expenditures, $493,675; qualifying distributions, $443,386; giving activities include $5,250 for 10 grants (high: $1,000; low: $100), and $329,430 for 473 grants to individuals (high: $5,000; low: $125).
Purpose and activities: Giving primarily to scholarship aid for post-secondary education with minor support for educational and social service agencies.
Fields of interest: Higher education; Human services.
Type of support: Scholarships—to individuals.
Limitations: Giving limited to Clinton, Essex, Franklin, Hamilton, and Warren counties, NY, for undergraduate scholarships, and to Essex County, NY, for educational and social service agencies.

Application information: Scholarship application form is available through high school guidance offices in Clinton, Essex, Franklin, Hamilton, and Warren counties, NY. Application form required.

Initial approach: Letter or telephone
Copies of proposal: 1
Deadline(s): Apr. 15 for scholarships
Board meeting date(s): Quarterly
Final notification: 60 to 90 days for grants; scholarships awarded in early July

Officers and Governors:* Euphemia V. Hall,* Pres.; Arthur V. Savage,* V.P.; Meredith Prime,* Secy.-Treas.; Mary E. Bell, Exec. Dir.; Janet Decker; Steven Engelhart; Sue Reaser; Gail Rogers-Rice.
Number of staff: 1 full-time professional; 2 part-time professional.
EIN: 237366844

5807
Credit Suisse Americas Foundation ▼ ◈
(formerly Credit Suisse First Boston Foundation Trust)
1 Madison Ave., 6th Fl.
New York, NY 10010-3629 (212) 325-2389
Contact: Anne Marie Fell, Prog. Off.
E-mail: annemarie.fell@csfb.com; Additional tel.: (212) 325-2000; URL: http://www.csfb.com/about_csfb/company_information/foundation/index.shtml

Trust established in 1959 in MA.
Donors: Credit Suisse First Boston Corp.; Credit Suisse First Boston LLC.
Foundation type: Company-sponsored foundation.
Financial data (yr. ended 12/31/04): Assets, $29,868,664 (M); gifts received, $435,777; expenditures, $4,370,197; qualifying distributions, $4,194,565; giving activities include $4,194,565 for 235 grants (high: $658,537; low: $250).
Purpose and activities: The foundation supports organizations involved with arts and culture, education, health, youth development, and human services.
Fields of interest: Arts; Higher education; Education; Health care; Youth development; Human services; Federated giving programs.
Type of support: General/operating support; Continuing support; Annual campaigns.
Limitations: Giving primarily in areas of company operations, with emphasis on New York, NY. No support for religious organizations not of direct benefit to the entire community, veterans', fraternal, or political organizations, or public or private schools. No grants to individuals, or for scholarships, capital campaigns, endowments, dinners or events, or medical research; no matching gifts.
Publications: Application guidelines; Corporate giving report; Informational brochure.
Application information: Unsolicited requests for non-renewal contributions are not accepted. Application form not required.

Initial approach: Letter of inquiry
Copies of proposal: 1
Deadline(s): None
Board meeting date(s): Quarterly
Final notification: 90 days

Trustees: Liza Bailey; Michael Clark; Gates Hawn; Grace Koo; Christopher Lawrence; Elizabeth Millard; Rodney Miller; Tom Nides; Robert O'Brien; Douglas L. Paul; G.T. Sweeney; Simon Yates.

Number of staff: 3 full-time professional; 1 full-time support.
EIN: 046059692
Selected grants: The following grants were reported in 2004.
$991,870 to Robin Hood Foundation, New York, NY. 2 grants: $658,537, $333,333
$251,000 to Good Shepherd Services, New York, NY.
$200,000 to Habitat for Humanity International.
$135,000 to Prep for Prep, New York, NY.
$100,000 to CityKids Foundation, New York, NY.
$75,000 to New York Cares, New York, NY.
$25,000 to Inwood House, New York, NY.
$15,000 to Fulfillment Fund, Los Angeles, CA.
$15,000 to iMentor, New York, NY.

5808
The Cricket Island Foundation ◈
780 3rd Ave., Ste. 3400
New York, NY 10017 (212) 842-5732
Contact: Julie F. Simpson, Exec. Dir.
E-mail: info@cricketisland.org; URL: http://www.cricketisland.org

Established in 2000 in NY.
Donors: David K. Welles; Georgia E. Welles; Jeffrey F. Welles; David K. Welles, Jr.; Peter C. Welles; Christopher S. Welles; Virginia W. Jordan.
Foundation type: Independent foundation.
Financial data (yr. ended 12/31/04): Assets, $40,708,603 (M); expenditures, $2,113,275; qualifying distributions, $1,672,409; giving activities include $1,250,000 for 27 grants (high: $90,000; low: $10,000).
Purpose and activities: The mission of the foundation is to develop the capacity and commitment of young people to improve their lives, communities and the world around them. We support organizations that offer meaningful opportunities for youth to contribute to contribute to positive societal change.
Fields of interest: Children/youth, services.
Type of support: General/operating support; Continuing support; Management development/capacity building; Program development; Conferences/seminars; Publication; Seed money; Research; Technical assistance; Consulting services; Program evaluation; Program-related investments/loans.
Limitations: Giving primarily in New York, NY, San Francisco, CA, and Chicago, IL. No support for general recreational activities or organizations, academic and classroom based training programs, tutoring or job training programs, or for groups that don't involve youth in community change. No grants for scholarships, internships, direct school-based support, individual fellowships, or capital campaigns.
Publications: Grants list.
Application information: Application form required.

Initial approach: Letter of inquiry
Copies of proposal: 2
Deadline(s): Apr. 15 and Nov. 15
Board meeting date(s): Apr. and Nov.
Final notification: 2-3 weeks after submission

Officers and Directors:* Jeffrey F. Welles,* Pres.; Georgia E. Welles,* V.P.; Peter C. Welles,* Secy.; Christopher S. Welles,* Treas.; Roger Jordan; Taylor Jordan; Virginia W. Jordan; David E. Welles; David K. Welles; David K. Welles, Jr.; Hope Welles IV; Hope V. Welles; Kathrene Welles; Maud Welles.

Number of staff: 2 full-time professional; 1 part-time support.
EIN: 341925915
Selected grants: The following grants were reported in 2003.
$80,000 to Alternatives in Action, Oakland, CA.
$70,000 to Youth in Focus, Davis, CA.
$60,000 to El Puente de Williamsburg, Brooklyn, NY.
$60,000 to Youth Ministries for Peace and Justice, Bronx, NY.
$50,000 to CityKids Foundation, New York, NY.
$50,000 to Fresh Youth Initiatives, New York, NY.
$50,000 to Leadership Excellence, Oakland, CA.
$50,000 to Pacific News Service, San Francisco, CA.
$50,000 to Project Reach Youth, Brooklyn, NY.
$40,000 to Power of Hope, Bellingham, WA.

5809
The Crisp Family Foundation ◈
(formerly The Peter O. Crisp Fund)
c/o U.S. Trust
114 W. 47th St.
New York, NY 10036
Contact: Peter O. Crisp, Tr.; Carolyn Larke, V.P., U.S. Trust
FAX: (212) 852-3377

Established in 1993 in NY.
Donor: Peter O. Crisp.
Foundation type: Independent foundation.
Financial data (yr. ended 12/31/05): Assets, $5,976,170 (M); gifts received, $885,740; expenditures, $1,253,024; qualifying distributions, $1,233,100; giving activities include $1,233,100 for 66 grants (high: $25,000; low: $100).
Purpose and activities: Giving primarily for health and human services.
Fields of interest: Elementary/secondary education; Education; Health care; Cancer; Children/youth, services; Community development.
Limitations: Applications not accepted. Giving primarily in NY. No grants to individuals.
Application information: Contributes only to pre-selected organizations.
Trustee: Peter O. Crisp.
EIN: 137028080
Selected grants: The following grants were reported in 2003.
$1,000,000 to North Shore-Long Island Jewish Health System Foundation, Great Neck, NY. 3 grants: $100,000, $400,000, $500,000
$100,000 to Memorial Sloan-Kettering Cancer Center, New York, NY.
$25,000 to Walsh Park Benevolent Corporation, Fishers Island, NY.
$5,000 to Fishers Island Fire Department, Fishers Island, NY.
$5,000 to Island Health Project, Fishers Island, NY.
$1,500 to Miss Porters School, Farmington, CT.
$1,000 to Community Chest, Hobe Sound, Hobe Sound, FL.
$1,000 to Vassar College, Poughkeepsie, NY.

5810
Irma L. & Abram S. Croll Charitable Trust ◈
c/o Lehman Brothers Trust Co., N.A.
605 3rd Ave., 44th Fl.
New York, NY 10158-3698

Established in 2001 in NY.
Foundation type: Independent foundation.
Financial data (yr. ended 9/30/05): Assets, $21,552,591 (M); expenditures, $2,286,377; qualifying distributions, $2,146,890; giving activities include $2,130,000 for 5 grants (high: $1,450,000; low: $20,000).
Purpose and activities: Giving primarily to an institute for Jewish religious and scholarly learning; funding also for health associations and hospitals.
Fields of interest: Higher education; Hospitals (general); Health organizations, association; Jewish agencies & temples.
Limitations: Applications not accepted. No grants to individuals.
Application information: Contributes only to pre-selected organizations.
Trustees: Edward S. Schlesinger; Lehman Brothers Trust Co.
EIN: 137312974

5811
Lewis B. & Dorothy Cullman Foundation, Inc. ▼
c/o Lewis B. Cullman
767 3rd Ave., 36th Fl.
New York, NY   10017   (212) 751-6655

Established in 1958 in NY.
Donors: Dorothy F. Cullman; Lewis B. Cullman.
Foundation type: Independent foundation.
Financial data (yr. ended 11/30/05): Assets, $44,691,303 (M); expenditures, $16,970,445; qualifying distributions, $16,507,936; giving activities include $16,371,481 for 77 grants (high: $5,000,000; low: $650; average: $10,000–$1,000,000).
Purpose and activities: Giving primarily for the arts.
Fields of interest: Museums; Performing arts; Arts.
Limitations: Applications not accepted. Giving primarily in NY. No grants to individuals.
Application information: Contributes only to pre-selected organizations.
Officers and Directors:* Lewis B. Cullman,* Pres.; Dorothy F. Cullman,* V.P.; John C. Emmert, Treas.; Edgar M. Cullman, Jr.; Joseph P. Kramer.
Number of staff: 1 part-time professional; 1 full-time support.
EIN: 510243747
Selected grants: The following grants were reported in 2005.
$5,000,000 to Museum of Modern Art, New York, NY. For general support.
$2,759,010 to Neurosciences Research Foundation, San Diego, CA. 2 grants: $297,335 (For general support), $2,461,675 (For general support. Grant made in the form of stock).
$1,799,000 to New York Public Library, New York, NY. 2 grants: $1,751,000 (For general support), $48,000 (For general support).
$1,108,250 to Chess in the Schools, New York, NY. 2 grants: $1,000,000 (For general support), $108,250 (For general support).
$1,000,000 to W N E T Channel 13, New York, NY. For general support.
$500,000 to Metropolitan Museum of Art, New York, NY. For general support.
$27,588 to Lincoln Center Theater, New York, NY. For general support.

5812
Louise B. & Edgar M. Cullman Foundation ◇
641 Lexington Ave., 29th Fl.
New York, NY   10022-4599   (212) 838-0211
Application address: c/o Edgar M. Cullman Sr., 387 Park Ave. S., New York, NY 10016

Established in 1956 in NY.
Donor: Edgar M. Cullman.
Foundation type: Independent foundation.
Financial data (yr. ended 12/31/04): Assets, $18,060,693 (M); gifts received, $252,833; expenditures, $2,588,395; qualifying distributions, $2,534,189; giving activities include $2,533,344 for 84 grants (high: $1,005,085; low: $200; average: $1,000–$25,000).
Fields of interest: Museums; Arts; Higher education; Education; Animals/wildlife, preservation/protection; Hospitals (general); Health care; Human services.
Type of support: Annual campaigns; Capital campaigns; Professorships.
Limitations: Giving primarily in CT and NY. No grants to individuals.
Application information: Application form required.
Copies of proposal: 1
Deadline(s): None
Board meeting date(s): Dec.
Officers: Edgar M. Cullman, Sr., Chair.; Louise B. Cullman, V.P.
Number of staff: 1 part-time professional; 1 part-time support.
EIN: 136100041
Selected grants: The following grants were reported in 2003.
$2,100,000 to Mount Sinai School of Medicine of New York University, New York, NY. 3 grants: $1,000,000, $1,000,000, $100,000
$1,075,000 to Mount Sinai Hospital, New York, NY.
$245,288 to Yale University, New Haven, CT.
$216,425 to Hotchkiss School, Lakeville, CT. 2 grants: $20,000, $196,425
$25,000 to Manhattan Theater Club, New York, NY.
$20,000 to Crohns and Colitis Foundation of America, New York, NY.
$19,739 to New York City Outward Bound Center, Long Island City, NY.

5813
James H. Cummings Foundation, Inc.
1807 Elmwood Ave., Rm. 112
Buffalo, NY   14207
Contact: William J. McFarland, Exec. Dir.
E-mail: cummings.foundation@verizon.net; Tel./FAX: (716) 874-0040

Incorporated in 1962 in NY.
Donor: James H. Cummings†.
Foundation type: Independent foundation.
Financial data (yr. ended 5/31/06): Assets, $36,975,360 (M); expenditures, $2,067,148; qualifying distributions, $1,819,472; giving activities include $1,745,505 for 40 grants (high: $250,000; low: $1,500).
Purpose and activities: Giving exclusively for charitable purposes in advancing medical science, research, and education in selected cities in the U.S. and Canada, and for charitable work among underprivileged boys and girls, and aged and infirm persons in designated areas. Priority is given to medical proposals.

Fields of interest: Medical school/education; Hospitals (general); Biomedicine; Medical research, institute; Human services; Children/youth, services; Aging, centers/services; Aging; Economically disadvantaged.
International interests: Canada.
Type of support: Capital campaigns; Building/renovation; Equipment; Land acquisition; Seed money; Research; Matching/challenge support.
Limitations: Giving limited to Toronto, Ontario, Canada, and to Hendersonville, NC, and Buffalo, NY. No support for national health organizations. No grants to individuals, or for annual campaigns, program support, endowment funds, operating budgets, program costs, emergency funds, deficit financing, scholarships, fellowships, publications, conferences, contingency reserves, or continuing support; no loans.
Publications: Annual report (including application guidelines).
Application information: In addition to the signature of C.E.O., the signature of Board Chair. is also required. Application form not required.
Initial approach: Preliminary letter (no more than 2 pages) or telephone inquiry is encouraged
Copies of proposal: 8
Deadline(s): 4 weeks prior to board meetings
Board meeting date(s): Quarterly
Final notification: 1 to 4 weeks
Officers and Directors:* John N. Walsh, Jr.,* Pres.; John P. Naughton, M.D.*, V.P.; William J. McFarland, Secy. and Exec. Dir.; Robert J.A. Irwin,* Treas.; Richard C. Bryan, Jr.; Charles F. Kreiner, Jr.; Theodore I. Putnam, M.D.
Number of staff: 1 part-time professional; 1 part-time support.
EIN: 160864200
Selected grants: The following grants were reported in 2004.
$250,000 to State University of New York at Buffalo, Buffalo, NY. To purchase new camera.
$100,000 to Niagara Aerospace Museum, Niagara Falls, NY. For displays, attractions and museum quality.
$83,333 to Buffalo Seminary, Buffalo, NY. For renovation of biology, chemistry, and physics labs.
$74,000 to United Way of Buffalo and Erie County, Buffalo, NY. For annual campaign.
$66,667 to YMCA of Greater Buffalo, Buffalo, NY. For capital campaign.
$50,000 to Hospice Foundation of Western New York, Cheektowaga, NY. For renovation of inpatient unit and residence.
$50,000 to Saint Michaels Hospital, Toronto, Canada. For construction of a Heart Health Center.
$38,705 to Hospital for Sick Children, Toronto, Canada. To purchase equipment.
$30,000 to Canisius College, Buffalo, NY. To purchase equipment for biology laboratory.
$25,000 to Alcohol and Drug Dependency Services Foundation, Buffalo, NY. For Renaissance campus construction.

5814
The Nathan Cummings Foundation ▼ ◇
475 10th Ave., 14th Fl.
New York, NY   10018   (212) 787-7300
Contact: Lance E. Lindblom, C.E.O. and Pres.
FAX: (212) 787-7377;
E-mail: info@nathancummings.org; URL: http://www.nathancummings.org

Established in 1949 in IL.
Donor: Nathan Cummings†.
Foundation type: Independent foundation.
Financial data (yr. ended 12/31/05): Assets, $480,924,387 (M); expenditures, $21,395,907; qualifying distributions, $17,371,600; giving activities include $16,857,000 for 250 grants (high: $990,000; low: $800; average: $10,000–$100,000).

Purpose and activities: The foundation is rooted in the Jewish tradition and committed to democratic values and social justice, including fairness, diversity, and community. It seeks to build a socially and economically just society that values and protects the ecological balance for future generations; promotes humane health care; and fosters arts and culture that enriches communities.

Fields of interest: Arts; Environment; Health care; Health organizations, association; Human services; Jewish agencies & temples.

International interests: Israel.

Type of support: General/operating support; Continuing support; Program development; Seed money; Research; Program evaluation; In-kind gifts.

Limitations: Giving primarily in the U.S. and Israel. No support for specific diseases, general support for Jewish education, Holocaust-related projects, foreign-based organizations, or local synagogues or institutions with local projects. No grants to individuals, scholarships, sponsorships, projects with no plans for replication, endowments or capital campaigns.

Publications: Application guidelines; Annual report; Financial statement; Grants list.

Application information: Application form required.
   Initial approach: 2- to 3-page letter of inquiry
   Copies of proposal: 1
   Deadline(s): None
   Board meeting date(s): Spring and fall
   Final notification: 60 days

Officers and Trustees:* Adam N. Cummings,* Chair.; Ernest Tollerson,* Vice-Chair.; Lance E. Lindblom,* C.E.O. and Pres.; Leisle Lin, V.P., Finance and Admin.; James K. Cummings,* Secy.; Robert N. Mayer,* Treas.; Roberta Friedman Cummings; Sonia Simon Cummings; Rachel Durchslag; Stephen P. Durchslag; Andrew Golden; Sara Horowitz; Andrew Lee; Beatrice Cummings Mayer; Ruth Cummings Sorensen; Debra Weese-Mayer.

Number of staff: 9 full-time professional; 12 full-time support; 1 part-time support.

EIN: 237093201

Selected grants: The following grants were reported in 2005.
$990,000 to New Israel Fund, DC.
$500,000 to Rockefeller Philanthropy Advisors, Philanthropic Collaborative, New York, NY.
$475,000 to Union for Reform Judaism, New York, NY.
$403,000 to American Institute for Social Justice, New Orleans, LA.
$400,000 to Center for American Progress, DC.
$350,000 to Earthjustice, Oakland, CA.
$265,000 to National Womens Law Center, DC.
$250,000 to Research Foundation of the City University of New York, New York, NY.
$245,000 to Community Catalyst, Boston, MA.
$200,000 to Bread and Roses Cultural Project, New York, NY.

5815
The Frances L. & Edwin L. Cummings Memorial Fund ✧
501 5th Ave., Ste. 708
New York, NY   10017   (212) 286-1778
Contact: Elizabeth Costas, Exec. Dir.

Established in 1982 in NY.
Donors: Edwin L. Cummings†; Frances L. Cummings†.
Foundation type: Independent foundation.
Financial data (yr. ended 7/31/05): Assets, $36,156,571 (M); expenditures, $2,209,283; qualifying distributions, $2,015,351; giving activities include $1,802,500 for 49 grants (high: $100,000; low: $500).

Purpose and activities: The foundation's primary interest is in the piloting or expansion of new, innovative programs of organizations operating in New York, NY, and its more urbanized surrounding areas in northeastern NJ. The fund has a particular interest in programs serving young people and on institutions serving economically and socially disadvantaged populations. Funding interests include education, especially programs that serve public school children from disadvantaged backgrounds, social welfare concerns, which focus on programs addressing issues including child abuse, parent education, juvenile delinquency, teenage pregnancy, youth employment and job training. Also focuses on education- a focus on efforts to reform the public education system or programs that serve public school children from disadvantaged backgrounds.

Fields of interest: Elementary/secondary education; Elementary/secondary school reform; Vocational education; Higher education; Adult education—literacy, basic skills & GED; Hospitals (general); Medical care, rehabilitation; Health care; Mental health/crisis services; Cancer; AIDS; Crime/violence prevention, youth; Crime/violence prevention, child abuse; Employment, services; Human services; Children/youth, services; Youth, pregnancy prevention; Child development, services; Family services, parent education; Minorities; Economically disadvantaged; Homeless.

Type of support: Endowments; Program development; Seed money; Technical assistance; Consulting services; Matching/challenge support.

Limitations: Giving primarily in New York, NY and its more urbanized surrounding areas in northeastern NJ (including Bergen, Essex, Hudson, Passaic, and Union counties). No support for the cultural arts, alcoholism or drug addiction treatment programs, camping programs, day care programs, environmental programs, private elementary and secondary schools, programs for senior citizens, public policy and/or lobbying groups, well-endowed institutions, private institutions, or legal aid programs. No grants to individuals, or for capital building campaigns, general operating support, moving expenses, conferences, media projects, scholarships, public opinion polls and surveys, annual fundraising campaigns, or research conducted by individuals, soup kitchens and/or food banks, or for equipment.

Publications: Biennial report (including application guidelines).

Application information: Proposals received by fax or e-mail not accepted. Application form not required.
   Initial approach: Proposal, preferably no more than 7 pages
   Copies of proposal: 3

   Deadline(s): Apr. 1 or Oct. 1
   Board meeting date(s): June and Dec.
   Final notification: 10 days following board meeting

Trustees: J. Andrew Lark; The Bank of New York.

Board of Advisors: Sean Delany; Felton Johnson; Anne Nordeman; Sarah Rosen.

Number of staff: 1 full-time professional; 1 full-time support.

EIN: 136814491

Selected grants: The following grants were reported in 2005.
$100,000 to Cancer Research Institute, New York, NY.
$100,000 to Lawyers Alliance for New York, New York, NY.
$90,000 to East Side House, Bronx, NY.
$83,000 to Boys and Girls Clubs of Union County, Union, NJ.
$50,000 to Coalition of Voluntary Mental Health Agencies, New York, NY.
$50,000 to Future Leaders Institute, New York, NY.
$50,000 to Highbridge Community Life Center, Bronx, NY.
$50,000 to South Bronx Overall Economic Development Corporation, Bronx, NY.
$32,000 to Resources for Children with Special Needs, New York, NY.
$30,000 to iMentor, New York, NY.

5816
The John P. & Constance A. Curran Charitable Foundation ✧
101 Park Ave., 23rd Fl.
New York, NY   10178   (212) 251-3880
Contact: John Curran, Tr.
Application address: 100 Scarborough Station Rd., Scarborough, NY 10510

Established in 1997 in NY.
Foundation type: Independent foundation.
Financial data (yr. ended 12/31/05): Assets, $6,661,444 (M); expenditures, $468,780; qualifying distributions, $464,549; giving activities include $461,000 for 15 grants (high: $132,000; low: $1,000).

Purpose and activities: Giving primarily for education, health, the arts, and church organizations.

Fields of interest: Education; Health care.

International interests: Ireland.

Type of support: General/operating support; Continuing support; Annual campaigns; Capital campaigns; Building/renovation; Program development; Curriculum development; Scholarship funds; Research.

Limitations: Giving primarily in NY, especially New York, NY, with other areas of donor interest in Ossining and Briarcliff Manor. No grants to individuals; the arts, debt reduction, travel or for groups.

Publications: Application guidelines.

Application information: On site visit required. Application form required.
   Initial approach: Cover letter
   Copies of proposal: 6
   Deadline(s): May 1 and Nov. 1
   Board meeting date(s): As needed

Trustees: Constance A. Curran, Admin.; John P. Curran, Prog. Dir.; Sean Curran; Michael Hartigan; Anthony Rauhut; Meredith Rauhut.

EIN: 133923928

5817
Ravenel B. Curry III Foundation ✧
435 E. 52nd St., Ste. 4C
New York, NY 10022

Established in 1974 in NY.
Donors: Elizabeth R. Curry; Ravenel B. Curry III.
Foundation type: Independent foundation.
Financial data (yr. ended 11/30/05): Assets, $8,987,020 (M); gifts received, $1,879,138; expenditures, $484,419; qualifying distributions, $483,419; giving activities include $460,775 for 41 grants (high: $225,000; low: $150).
Purpose and activities: Giving primarily for education, art, culture, religion, and human services.
Fields of interest: Museums (art); Arts; Higher education, college; Education; Hospitals (specialty); Human services.
Limitations: Applications not accepted. Giving primarily in New York, NY. No grants to individuals.
Application information: Contributes only to pre-selected organizations.
Officers: Ravenel B. Curry III, Pres.; Elizabeth R. Curry, V.P. and Secy.
EIN: 237411083
Selected grants: The following grants were reported in 2004.
$79,830 to Furman University, Greenville, SC.
$51,000 to New York Hall of Science, Corona, NY.
$35,000 to Manhattan Institute for Policy Research, New York, NY.
$25,000 to Cato Institute, DC.
$20,000 to Womens Law Initiative, Brooklyn, NY.
$5,000 to Doe Fund, New York, NY.
$5,000 to Excellent Education for Everyone, Newark, NJ.
$5,000 to Manhattan Theater Club, New York, NY.
$5,000 to New-York Historical Society, New York, NY.
$2,500 to Rockefeller University, New York, NY.

5818
Filomena M. D'Agostino Foundation ✧
950 3rd Ave., 32nd Fl.
New York, NY 10022 (212) 486-8615
Contact: David Malkin, V.P.

Established in 1990 in NY.
Donor: Filomena M. D'Agostino Greenberg.
Foundation type: Independent foundation.
Financial data (yr. ended 2/28/06): Assets, $28,520,221 (M); expenditures, $1,502,479; qualifying distributions, $1,400,000; giving activities include $1,400,000 for 27 grants.
Purpose and activities: Giving primarily for the arts, particularly to museums, as well as for higher education, health associations and medical research, and children, youth, and social services including recordings and services for the blind.
Fields of interest: Media, television; Museums (natural history); Arts; Higher education; Law school/education; Hospitals (general); Health organizations, association; Eye diseases; Breast cancer research; Alzheimer's disease research; Human services; Children/youth, services; Blind/visually impaired.
Limitations: Giving primarily in New York, NY. No grants to individuals.
Application information: Application form not required.
Deadline(s): None

Officers and Directors:* Max D'Agostino,* V.P.; David Malkin,* V.P.; Lorene A. Corrado; Jessica A. Malkin.
EIN: 133548660
Selected grants: The following grants were reported in 2006.
$100,000 to American Museum of Natural History, New York, NY.
$100,000 to Metropolitan Museum of Art, New York, NY.
$35,000 to Mount Sinai Hospital, New York, NY.
$25,000 to American Society for the Prevention of Cruelty to Animals, New York, NY.
$25,000 to Cancer Care, New York, NY.
$25,000 to Childrens Aid Society, New York, NY.
$25,000 to Childrens Defense Fund, DC.
$25,000 to Macula Foundation, New York, NY.
$20,000 to Doe Fund, New York, NY.
$10,000 to Salvation Army, Yonkers, NY.

5819
Ezra & Renee Dabah Charitable Foundation, Inc. ✧
c/o Krusch & Modell
10 Rockefeller Plz., Ste. 710
New York, NY 10020

Established in 1998 in NY.
Donor: Ezra Dabah.
Foundation type: Independent foundation.
Financial data (yr. ended 12/31/05): Assets, $660,929 (M); gifts received, $1,572,636; expenditures, $1,213,814; qualifying distributions, $1,162,498; giving activities include $1,162,498 for 450 grants (high: $192,934; low: $18).
Purpose and activities: Giving primarily to Jewish organizations, temples, and schools; funding also for health associations, and children, youth and social services.
Fields of interest: Health organizations, association; Human services; Children/youth, services; Jewish federated giving programs; Jewish agencies & temples.
Limitations: Applications not accepted. Giving on a national and international basis. No grants to individuals.
Application information: Contributes only to pre-selected organizations.
Officers: Ezra Dabah, Pres.; Eva Dabah, V.P.; Renee Dabah, Secy.-Treas.
EIN: 133986707
Selected grants: The following grants were reported in 2005.
$58,600 to Chabads Children of Chernobyl, New York, NY.
$28,600 to Aleh Foundation, Brooklyn, NY. 2 grants: $2,600, $26,000
$26,250 to Sephardic Bikur Holim, Brooklyn, NY.
$18,000 to International Sephardic Education Foundation (ISEF), New York, NY.
$4,000 to Shalva, Chicago, IL.
$1,800 to Hebron Fund, Brooklyn, NY.
$1,200 to American Friends of Bet El Yeshiva Center, Hempstead, NY.
$1,002 to Colel Chabad, Brooklyn, NY.
$400 to Bailey House, New York, NY.

5820
Barbara & Haim Dabah Family Foundation, Inc. ✧ ☆
c/o Hecht and Co., P.C.
111 W. 40th St.
New York, NY 10018

Donors: Haim Dabah; Barbara Dabah.
Foundation type: Independent foundation.
Financial data (yr. ended 12/31/04): Assets, $386,416 (M); gifts received, $517,850; expenditures, $369,624; qualifying distributions, $366,917; giving activities include $366,817 for 49 grants (high: $46,220; low: $260).
Purpose and activities: Giving primarily for Jewish organizations, temples, and schools.
Fields of interest: Education; Medical research, association; Human services; Neighborhood centers; Children/youth, services; Jewish agencies & temples.
Limitations: Applications not accepted. Giving primarily in the metropolitan New York, NY, area.
Application information: Unsolicited requests for funds not accepted.
Officers and Directors:* Haim Dabah,* Pres.; Barbara Dabah,* Secy.-Treas.; Morris Dabah, Jr.
EIN: 300138485

5821
Daedalus Foundation, Inc. ✧ ☆
c/o Starr & Co.
350 Park Ave.
New York, NY 10022

Established in 1988 in NY.
Donors: L. Diane Sawyer; Mike Nichols.
Foundation type: Independent foundation.
Financial data (yr. ended 12/31/04): Assets, $13,706 (M); gifts received, $377,550; expenditures, $366,589; qualifying distributions, $366,589; giving activities include $366,400 for grants.
Purpose and activities: Giving primarily for children and social services; funding also for the arts, and health associations.
Fields of interest: Arts; Health organizations, association; Human services; Children/youth, services; International development; International affairs; Economically disadvantaged.
Limitations: Applications not accepted. Giving on a national basis. No grants to individuals.
Application information: Contributes only to pre-selected organizations.
Officers: Mike Nichols, Chair.; L. Diane Sawyer, Pres.; Ed Bradley, Treas.
EIN: 133489057
Selected grants: The following grants were reported in 2003.
$60,000 to Friends in Deed, New York, NY.
$25,000 to ActionAid USA, DC.
$5,000 to Michael J. Fox Foundation for Parkinsons Research, New York, NY.
$5,000 to Sesame Workshop, New York, NY.
$2,500 to Phoenix House, New York, NY.
$2,000 to Ballet Theater Foundation, New York, NY.
$1,000 to Drug Strategies, DC.
$1,000 to Leukemia & Lymphoma Society, Atlanta, GA.
$1,000 to Marthas Vineyard Hospital, Oak Bluffs, MA.
$1,000 to New York Landmarks Conservancy, New York, NY.

5822
The Damaris Foundation ✧
c/o U.S. Trust
114 W. 47th. St., 7th Fl.
New York, NY 10036

Established in 1992 in NY.
Donor: Gretchen K. Finch.
Foundation type: Independent foundation.
Financial data (yr. ended 12/31/05): Assets, $1,578,951 (M); expenditures, $683,679; qualifying distributions, $674,122; giving activities include $671,000 for 34 grants (high: $200,000; low: $3,000).
Fields of interest: Christian agencies & churches.
Limitations: Applications not accepted. Giving on a national basis. No grants to individuals.
Application information: Contributes only to pre-selected organizations.
Trustee: U.S. Trust.
EIN: 133709363
Selected grants: The following grants were reported in 2003.
$200,000 to Elim Bible Institute, Lima, NY.
$125,000 to Promise Keepers, Denver, CO.
$50,000 to Elim Fellowship, Lima, NY. 2 grants: $20,000, $30,000
$20,000 to Abundant Lifestyle Ministries, Canandaigua, NY.
$20,000 to Scripture Ministries of India.
$20,000 to Vino Nuevo, El Paso, TX.
$20,000 to Walter Hoving Home, Garrison, NY.
$15,000 to New Covenant Fellowship.
$10,000 to Missionary Revival Crusade, Cedar Hill, TX.

5823
The Damial Foundation, Inc. ✧
c/o Mark J. Krinsky, C.P.A.
655 Madison Ave., 19th Fl.
New York, NY 10021

Established in 1992 in NY and DE.
Donors: Laurence A. Tisch†; Daniel R. Tisch.
Foundation type: Independent foundation.
Financial data (yr. ended 12/31/05): Assets, $14,231,432 (M); gifts received, $1,342,275; expenditures, $979,604; qualifying distributions, $950,810; giving activities include $947,216 for 28 grants (high: $250,000; low: $125).
Purpose and activities: Giving primarily for education and to Jewish organizations.
Fields of interest: Education; Hospitals (general); Health organizations, association; Human services; Jewish federated giving programs; Jewish agencies & temples.
Limitations: Applications not accepted. Giving primarily in NY. No grants to individuals.
Application information: Contributes only to pre-selected organizations.
Officers: Thomas M. Steinberg, V.P. and Secy.; Mark J. Krinsky, Treas.
EIN: 133693581
Selected grants: The following grants were reported in 2005.
$162,500 to Suffield Academy, Suffield, CT.
$100,000 to New York University, New York, NY.
$75,000 to Montefiore Medical Center, Bronx, NY.
$50,000 to Birthright Israel Foundation, New York, NY.
$30,000 to Congregation Kol Ami, White Plains, NY.
$12,415 to Memorial Sloan-Kettering Cancer Center, New York, NY.

$2,500 to Educational Foundation for the Fashion Industries, New York, NY.
$1,000 to Union for Reform Judaism, New York, NY.
$360 to Larchmont Temple, Larchmont, NY.

5824
The Dammann Fund, Inc.
521 5th Ave., 31st Fl.
New York, NY 10175
Contact: Penelope Johnston, Pres.
FAX: (212) 262-9321;
E-mail: df@engelanddavis.com; URL: http://www.thedammannfund.com

Incorporated in 1946 in NY.
Donor: Members of the Dammann family.
Foundation type: Independent foundation.
Financial data (yr. ended 11/30/05): Assets, $7,123,499 (M); expenditures, $458,094; qualifying distributions, $405,479; giving activities include $357,025 for 146 grants (high: $40,000; low: $250).
Purpose and activities: Supporting teen parenthood programs and programs to foster independent living skills for the mentally ill.
Fields of interest: Mental health/crisis services; Children/youth, services; Family services.
Type of support: General/operating support; Continuing support; Program development; Seed money.
Limitations: Giving primarily in the greater metropolitan New York, NY, area, including southern Fairfield County, CT; giving also in Charlottesville, VA. No grants to individuals, or for scholarships, fellowships, or matching gifts; no loans.
Application information: Application form required.
   Initial approach: Letter
   Copies of proposal: 1
   Deadline(s): July 1 for Joint Gifts program
   Board meeting date(s): May, July and Nov.
   Final notification: Nov. 30
Officers and Directors:* Penelope Johnston,* Pres.; Christopher M. Kramer,* V.P.; Daniel R. Kramer, V.P.; John P. Engel, Secy.; Lorraine M. Callaghan, Treas.; Katherine S. Penna.
EIN: 136089896
Selected grants: The following grants were reported in 2005.
$40,000 to Skidmore College, Saratoga Springs, NY.
$33,000 to Family Services of Westchester, Port Chester, NY.
$17,000 to Mount Sinai Medical Center, New York, NY. 2 grants: $2,000, $15,000
$15,000 to Human Development Services of Westchester, Mamaroneck, NY.
$15,000 to Inwood House, New York, NY.
$5,000 to Advocates for Children of New York, New York, NY.
$1,500 to Henry Street Settlement, New York, NY.
$1,500 to New York Public Library, New York, NY.
$500 to Charlottesville Free Clinic, Charlottesville, VA.

5825
Dana Alliance for Brain Initiatives, Inc.
745 5th Ave., Ste. 900
New York, NY 10151
Contact: Burton M. Mirsky, Treas.
FAX: (212) 317-8721; E-mail: dabiinfo@dana.org;
URL: http://www.dana.org

Established in 1993 in CT as a private operating foundation.
Donor: The Dana Foundation.
Foundation type: Operating foundation.
Financial data (yr. ended 12/31/05): Assets, $1,405,380 (M); gifts received, $3,892,195; expenditures, $3,897,122; qualifying distributions, $3,825,997; giving activities include $438,765 for 1 grant, and $3,458,357 for 4 foundation-administered programs.
Purpose and activities: Giving to educate and inform the general public and interested professionals about human brain research and development of new treatments of brain diseases.
Fields of interest: Brain disorders; Brain research.
International interests: Europe.
Type of support: Research.
Limitations: Applications not accepted. No grants to individuals.
Publications: Annual report; Informational brochure; Newsletter; Occasional report.
Application information: Unsolicited requests for funds not accepted.
   Board meeting date(s): Sept.
Officers and Directors:* William L. Safire,* Chair.; Edward F. Rover,* Pres.; Barbara E. Gill, V.P.; Rosemary Shields, Secy.; Burton M. Mirsky, Treas.; Lasalle D. Leffall, Jr.
Number of staff: 3 full-time professional; 5 full-time support.
EIN: 061360140
Selected grants: The following grants were reported in 2003.
$317,195 to University of Lausanne, Lausanne, Switzerland. .

5826
Eleanor Naylor Dana Charitable Trust ✧
c/o J. Signorile
10 Park Ave.
New York, NY 10016
Application address: c/o The Trustees, P.O. Box 1803, Murray Hill Station, New York, NY 10156

Established in 1979 in CT.
Donor: Eleanor Naylor Dana†.
Foundation type: Independent foundation.
Financial data (yr. ended 5/31/05): Assets, $5,061,002 (M); expenditures, $1,854,267; qualifying distributions, $1,808,191; giving activities include $1,648,194 for 80 grants (high: $600,000; low: $694).
Purpose and activities: Grants are given mainly to foster and finance progress and the pursuit of excellence in two areas: 1) biomedical research, to support clinical investigations by established scientists in qualified institutions in the U.S. to pursue innovative projects designed to improve medical practice or prevent disease; and 2) the performing arts, to assist the various performing arts fields in ways that could be of substantial import to the grantees and the artists and the public which they serve.
Fields of interest: Performing arts; Higher education; Health care; Health organizations, association; Medical research, institute; Biological sciences.
Type of support: Program development; Research.
Limitations: Giving primarily in areas east of the Mississippi River. No grants to individuals, or for instrumentation other than that required for a specific project, large-scale field studies of a therapeutic or epidemiological nature, or

conferences (in biomedical research); or for deficit financing, exhibits, publications, or conclaves (in the arts).

Publications: Informational brochure.
Application information: Application form not required.

Initial approach: Letter of intent not exceeding 1,000 words
Copies of proposal: 6
Deadline(s): Feb. 1, May 1, Sept. 1, and Nov. 1
Board meeting date(s): Mar., June, Oct., and Dec.
Final notification: Following board meetings

Trustees: Wallace L. Cook; Carlos Moseley; A.J. Signorile; Stephen A. Signorile; Robert E. Wise, M.D.
Number of staff: 1 full-time professional; 1 part-time support.
EIN: 132992855
Selected grants: The following grants were reported in 2005.
$600,000 to Vanguard Charitable Endowment Program, Southeastern, PA.
$166,000 to Lahey Clinic Foundation, Burlington, MA. 2 grants: $96,000, $70,000
$50,000 to Metropolitan Opera Association, New York, NY.
$40,000 to Lincoln Center Theater, New York, NY.
$40,000 to New York City Opera, New York, NY.
$35,000 to Lincoln Center for the Performing Arts, New York, NY.
$35,000 to Roundabout Theater Company, New York, NY.
$30,000 to Young Concert Artists, New York, NY.
$5,000 to Cunningham Dance Foundation, New York, NY.

5827
The Dana Foundation ▼ ✧
(formerly The Charles A. Dana Foundation, Inc.)
745 5th Ave., Ste. 900
New York, NY 10151-0799 (212) 223-4040
Contact: Burton M. Mirsky, V.P., Finance
FAX: (212) 317-8721; E-mail: danainfo@dana.org;
URL: http://www.dana.org

Incorporated in 1950 in CT.
Donors: Charles A. Dana†; Eleanor Naylor Dana†.
Foundation type: Independent foundation.
Financial data (yr. ended 12/31/05): Assets, $317,717,289 (M); expenditures, $26,084,864; qualifying distributions, $23,813,969; giving activities include $16,820,559 for 185 grants (high: $3,892,094; low: $100; average: $5,000–$300,000), and $6,519,861 for 4 foundation-administered programs.
Purpose and activities: Principal interests are in education and health, particularly neuroscience and immunology.
Fields of interest: Arts education; Education; Medical research, institute.
Type of support: General/operating support; Research; Employee matching gifts; Matching/challenge support.
Limitations: Giving on a national basis. No support for professional organizations, or for organizations outside the U.S. No grants to individuals, or for annual operating costs, deficit reduction, capital campaigns, or individual sabbaticals.
Publications: Application guidelines; Annual report (including application guidelines); Financial statement; Informational brochure (including application guidelines); Newsletter; Occasional report.

Application information: Letter of intent may be submitted online via the foundation's Web site for the arts education grants. Application form not required.

Initial approach: Letter of intent
Copies of proposal: 1
Deadline(s): None
Board meeting date(s): Apr., June, Oct., and Dec.
Final notification: 2 to 3 months

Officers and Directors:* William L. Safire,* Chair.; Edward F. Rover,* Pres.; Barbara Rich, Ed.D., V.P. News and Internet; Barbara E. Gill, V.P., Public Affairs; Burton M. Mirsky, V.P., Finance; Jane Nevins, V.P.; Brigida C. Gay, Cont.; Edward Bleier; Wallace L. Cook; Charles A. Dana III; Steven E. Hyman, M.D.; Ann McLaughlin Korologos; LaSalle D. Leffall, M.D.; Hildegarde E. Mahoney; Donald B. Marron; L. Guy Palmer II; Herbert J. Siegel.
Number of staff: 10 full-time professional; 18 full-time support.
EIN: 066036761
Selected grants: The following grants were reported in 2005.
$3,892,094 to Dana Alliance for Brain Initiatives, New York, NY. For public education campaign on neuroscience research.
$600,000 to Mayo Clinic, Rochester, MN. For human immunology.
$600,000 to Tel Aviv University: American Council, New York, NY. For Neuroimmunology Research.
$600,000 to Weill Medical College of Cornell University, New York, NY. For neuroimmunology.
$200,000 to Johns Hopkins University, Baltimore, MD. For brain and immuno-imaging.
$105,000 to Lincoln Center Institute, New York, NY. For arts education.
$75,000 to Shakespeare Theater, DC. For arts education.
$75,000 to University of California at San Diego, La Jolla, CA. For ArtsBridge America.
$70,000 to Education Through Music, New York, NY. For arts education.
$50,000 to ArtsLab, Astoria, NY. For arts education.

5828
Dancing Tides Foundation, Inc. ✧ ☆
c/o Seth Starr, Frankel Loughran Starr & Vallone
404 Park Ave. S., 6th Fl.
New York, NY 10016

Established in 2001 in NJ.
Donor: Peter Muller.
Foundation type: Independent foundation.
Financial data (yr. ended 12/31/05): Assets, $13,491,863 (M); gifts received, $1,712,375; expenditures, $655,617; qualifying distributions, $647,143; giving activities include $640,333 for 23 grants (high: $483,333; low: $1,500).
Fields of interest: Community development; Economically disadvantaged.
Limitations: Applications not accepted. Giving primarily in NY. No grants to individuals.
Application information: Unsolicited requests for funds not accepted.
Trustees: Nathan E. Arnell; Peter Muller; Seth Starr.
EIN: 010553351
Selected grants: The following grants were reported in 2005.
$483,333 to Robin Hood Foundation, New York, NY.
$15,000 to Trust for Public Land, San Francisco, CA.
$10,000 to Surfrider Foundation, San Clemente, CA.
$5,000 to Aspetuck Land Trust, Westport, CT.

$5,000 to Sierra Club, San Francisco, CA.
$2,500 to Salmon River Restoration Council, Sawyers Bar, CA.

5829
The Gloria & Sidney Danziger Foundation ✧
c/o Wolf, Block, Schorr, et al.
250 Park Ave.
New York, NY 10177

Established in 1959 in NY.
Donor: Sidney Danziger†.
Foundation type: Independent foundation.
Financial data (yr. ended 12/31/05): Assets, $4,174,422 (M); expenditures, $694,936; qualifying distributions, $597,316; giving activities include $519,600 for 187 grants (high: $40,000; low: $100; average: $1,000–$10,000).
Purpose and activities: Giving primarily to Jewish agencies, temples, and federated giving programs; funding also for the arts, health care and medical research.
Fields of interest: Museums (ethnic/folk arts); Arts; Education; Health organizations; Cancer research; Human services; Children, services; Federated giving programs; Jewish federated giving programs; Jewish agencies & temples.
Limitations: Applications not accepted. No grants to individuals; no loans.
Application information: Contributes only to pre-selected organizations.
Officer: Rabbi B. Kreitman, Pres.
Director: Stanley T. Miller.
EIN: 136124448
Selected grants: The following grants were reported in 2003.
$75,000 to Neve Hanna for Children in Israel. For general support.
$40,000 to Lymphoma Research Foundation, New York, NY. For general support.
$40,000 to Samuel Waxman Cancer Research Foundation, New York, NY. For general support.
$35,000 to Memorial Sloan-Kettering Cancer Center, New York, NY. For general support.
$30,000 to Jewish Museum, New York, NY. For general support.
$25,000 to Winston Preparatory School, New York, NY. For general support.
$20,000 to Jewish Federation of South Palm Beach County, Boca Raton, FL. For general support.
$20,000 to Museum of Jewish Heritage, New York, NY. For general support.
$17,000 to Churchill School and Center for Learning Disabilities, New York, NY. For general support.
$17,000 to Community Synagogue. For general support.

5830
The Daphne Foundation ☆
79 5th Ave., 4th Fl.
New York, NY 10003 (212) 337-0160
Contact: Yvonne L. Moore, Exec. Dir.
FAX: (212) 337-0908;
E-mail: info@daphnefoundation.org; URL: http://www.daphnefoundation.org

Established in 1990 in CA and NY.
Donors: Abigail E. Disney; Pierre Hauser II.
Foundation type: Independent foundation.

Financial data (yr. ended 6/30/05): Assets, $11,472,623 (M); gifts received, $790,449; expenditures, $832,101; qualifying distributions, $713,731; giving activities include $713,731 for 28 grants (high: $30,000; low: $5,000).

Purpose and activities: The foundation funds programs that confront the causes and consequences of poverty in the 5 boroughs of New York City. The foundation has a particular interest in grassroots and emerging organizations which engage their members in the creation and implementation of long-term solutions to intractable social problems. The foundation believes it should fund in a manner that reinforces and facilitates the work of the programs it funds and that the most inventive and humane solutions to social problems often come from the people most affected by those problems. The foundation gives preference to organizations that: 1) focus on historically underfunded areas, such as women's issues 2) are grassroots organizations with little or no funding from traditional sources; 3) address the effects of poverty on families, youth and children; 4) include their participants in management, planning and/or staffing; 5) build upon the pre-existing strengths of communities; 6) promote the self-sufficiency of their participants; and 7) build evaluation practices into their programming.

Fields of interest: Education, reading; AIDS; Legal services; Children/youth, services; Family services; Women; Economically disadvantaged.

Type of support: General/operating support; Continuing support.

Limitations: Giving limited to the five boroughs of New York City. No grants to individuals, or for capital campaigns.

Application information:
   Initial approach: Visit foundation Web site for application instructions

Officers and Directors:* Abigail E. Disney,* Pres.; Pierre Hauser II,* V.P. and Treas.; Leah F. Doyle,* Secy.; Deborah Howes.

Number of staff: 1 full-time professional.

EIN: 954288541

Selected grants: The following grants were reported in 2005.

$30,000 to Abraham House, Bronx, NY.

$30,000 to Amethyst Womens Project, Brooklyn, NY.

$30,000 to Dome Project, New York, NY.

$30,000 to Fresh Youth Initiatives, New York, NY.

$30,000 to Haitian Womens Program, Brooklyn, NY.

$30,000 to Hour Children, Long Island City, NY.

$30,000 to Korean-American Family Service Center, Flushing, NY.

$30,000 to Make the Road By Walking, Brooklyn, NY.

$30,000 to Mercy Center, Bronx, NY.

$30,000 to Mothers on the Move, Bronx, NY.

5831

The Darivoff Family Foundation ◇

c/o Goldman Sachs & Co.
1 New York Plz., 40th Fl.
New York, NY   10004

Established in 1999 in NJ.

Donors: Philip M. Darivoff; Goldman Sachs & Co.

Foundation type: Independent foundation.

Financial data (yr. ended 11/30/05): Assets, $2,609,799 (M); gifts received, $2,081,000; expenditures, $1,195,077; qualifying distributions,

$1,155,037; giving activities include $1,155,037 for 68 grants (high: $655,126; low: $25).

Purpose and activities: Giving primarily for higher education, and to Jewish organizations and temples.

Fields of interest: Higher education; Health organizations, association; Human services; Jewish agencies & temples; Women.

Limitations: Applications not accepted. Giving primarily in NY, NJ and PA. No grants to individuals.

Application information: Contributes only to pre-selected organizations.

Trustees: Betsy S. Darivoff; Philip M. Darivoff.

EIN: 134039056

Selected grants: The following grants were reported in 2005.

$655,126 to University of Pennsylvania, Philadelphia, PA.

$100,000 to Hannah Peretsman Breene Foundation, South Orange, NJ.

$613 to Solomon Schechter Day School, NJ.

5832

E. S. P. Das Educational Foundation, Inc. ◇

c/o Gerald Desroches, WTAS
452 5th Ave., 23rd Fl.
New York, NY   10018

Established in 1994 in NJ.

Donor: E.S.P. Das.

Foundation type: Operating foundation.

Financial data (yr. ended 12/31/05): Assets, $2,105,653 (M); gifts received, $2,250; expenditures, $353,900; qualifying distributions, $351,900; giving activities include $351,500 for 10 grants (high: $200,000; low: $1,000).

Fields of interest: Elementary/secondary education; Education; Hospitals (specialty); Human services; Children/youth, services; Foundations (private grantmaking).

Limitations: Applications not accepted. Giving on a national basis. No grants to individuals.

Application information: Contributes only to pre-selected organizations.

Officers: E.S.P. Das, Pres. and Treas.; Kuntala Das, Secy.

EIN: 223346203

5833

The Davenport-Hatch Foundation

P.O. Box 124
Penfield, NY   14526
Contact: Tom Hildebrandt, Dir.
Application address: c/o Bank of America, N.A., Attn.: Bill McKee, 1 East Ave., Rochester, NY 14638

Incorporated in 1952 in NY.

Donor: Augustus Hatch†.

Foundation type: Independent foundation.

Financial data (yr. ended 5/31/05): Assets, $36,434,702 (M); expenditures, $2,068,340; qualifying distributions, $1,968,835; giving activities include $1,906,050 for 99 grants (high: $125,000; low: $1,000).

Purpose and activities: Giving primarily for the arts, health associations and medical research, children, youth and social services, and Christian ministries and organizations.

Fields of interest: Media/communications; Museums; Performing arts; Arts; Higher education; Education; Hospitals (general); Health

organizations, association; Medical research, institute; Human services; YM/YWCAs & YM/YWHAs; Children/youth, services; Christian agencies & churches; Jewish agencies & temples.

Type of support: Capital campaigns; Building/renovation; Equipment; Seed money; Scholarship funds.

Limitations: Giving primarily in the greater Rochester, NY, area. No grants to individuals.

Application information: Application form not required.

   Initial approach: Letter
   Copies of proposal: 1
   Deadline(s): None
   Board meeting date(s): Approximately the 15th of Apr., June, Sept., and Dec.
   Final notification: 3 weeks after board meeting; positive responses only

Officer: Austin E. Hildebrandt, Pres.

Directors: Robert J. Brinkman; William L. Ely; A. Thomas Hildebrandt; Mary Hildebrandt; William T. Knoble; David H. Taylor; Douglas F. Taylor; Shirley Warren.

Trustee: Bank of America, N.A.

EIN: 166027105

Selected grants: The following grants were reported in 2005.

$125,000 to Unity Health System Foundation, Rochester, NY. For renovation and expansion.

$75,000 to Hillside Childrens Center Foundation, Rochester, NY. For renovation and equipment of Campus Center Monroe Avenue.

$75,000 to Rochester Institute of Technology, Rochester, NY. For construction of new Women's Center.

$75,000 to Saint John Fisher College, Rochester, NY. For building Campus Center.

$65,000 to GeVa Theater, Rochester, NY. For program support.

$60,000 to Genesee Country Museum, Mumford, NY. For barn maintenance and renovation.

$60,000 to State University of New York at Albany, Albany, NY. For Presidents Fund.

$50,000 to University of Rochester Medical Center, Rochester, NY. For Health-E-Access Program.

$31,000 to Family Service of Rochester, Rochester, NY. For annual support.

$25,000 to Boys and Girls Club of Rochester, Rochester, NY. For building upgrade and repair.

5834

The Davidowitz Family Foundation ◇

1439 E. 21st St.
Brooklyn, NY   11210

Established in 1999 in NY.

Donor: Jacob Davidowitz.

Foundation type: Independent foundation.

Financial data (yr. ended 6/30/05): Assets, $248,544 (M); gifts received, $400,000; expenditures, $430,847; qualifying distributions, $427,910; giving activities include $427,910 for 62 grants (high: $75,000; low: $180).

Fields of interest: Jewish agencies & temples.

Limitations: Applications not accepted. Giving primarily in Brooklyn, NY. No grants to individuals.

Application information: Contributes only to pre-selected organizations.

Officers: Jacob Davidowitz, Pres.; Leah Davidowitz, V.P.; Tova Rubin, Secy.

EIN: 113517517

Selected grants: The following grants were reported in 2005.

$50,000 to American Friends of Kesher, Brooklyn, NY.

$22,500 to Mirrer Yeshiva Central Institute, Brooklyn, NY. 2 grants: $15,000, $7,500

$7,000 to Yad Eliezer, Brooklyn, NY. 2 grants: $5,000, $2,000

$2,500 to Sinai Academy, Brooklyn, NY.

$1,000 to Haazinu Charitable Foundation, Brooklyn, NY.

5835
The Marvin H. Davidson Foundation, Inc. ✧
c/o M.H. Davidson & Co.
65 E. 55th St., 19th Fl.
New York, NY 10022

Established in 1967 in NY.
Donors: Marvin H. Davidson; Scott Davidson; Davidson Kempner Advisors, Inc.
Foundation type: Independent foundation.
Financial data (yr. ended 12/31/05): Assets, $11,306,510 (M); gifts received, $445,405; expenditures, $1,694,760; qualifying distributions, $396,513; giving activities include $392,068 for 84 grants (high: $28,500; low: $60).
Fields of interest: Media, television; Arts; Elementary/secondary education; Botanical gardens; Hospitals (general); Health organizations, association; Cancer; Human services; Residential/custodial care; Federated giving programs; Jewish agencies & temples.
Limitations: Applications not accepted. Giving primarily in NY. No grants to individuals.
Application information: Contributes only to pre-selected organizations.
Officers and Directors:* Marvin H. Davidson,* Pres.; Scott Davidson,* Secy.; Seymour Hertz.
EIN: 136217756
Selected grants: The following grants were reported in 2003.
$165,000 to Foundation for United Hospital, Port Chester, NY.
$50,000 to Museum of the City of New York, New York, NY.
$32,500 to Memorial Sloan-Kettering Cancer Center, New York, NY. 2 grants: $10,000 (For annual support), $22,500.
$15,000 to Hackley School, Tarrytown, NY.
$13,500 to New York Botanical Garden, Bronx, NY.
$11,250 to Nantucket Cottage Hospital, Nantucket, MA.
$10,000 to United Way of Westchester and Putnam, White Plains, NY.
$10,000 to W N E T Channel 13, New York, NY.
$10,000 to Woods Hole Oceanographic Institution, Woods Hole, MA.

5836
Clive J. Davis Foundation ✧
c/o Executive Monetary Mgmt.
220 E. 42nd St., 32nd Fl.
New York, NY 10017

Established in 1995 in NY.
Donors: Clive J. Davis; The Learning Annex of New York.
Foundation type: Independent foundation.
Financial data (yr. ended 12/31/04): Assets, $1,109,138 (M); gifts received, $989,471; expenditures, $1,036,401; qualifying distributions,

$1,011,075; giving activities include $1,011,075 for 17 grants (high: $979,471; low: $100).
Purpose and activities: Giving primarily for higher education and human services.
Fields of interest: Higher education; Education; Hospitals (general); Human services.
Limitations: Applications not accepted. Giving primarily in NY. No grants to individuals.
Application information: Contributes only to pre-selected organizations.
Trustee: Clive J. Davis.
EIN: 137079336

5837
M. G. Davis Trust ✧ ☆
c/o U.S. Trust Co.
114 W. 47th St., 7th Fl.
New York, NY 10036

Donor: M.G. Davis Trust.
Foundation type: Independent foundation.
Financial data (yr. ended 12/31/04): Assets, $43,536,088 (M); expenditures, $1,890,813; qualifying distributions, $1,832,424; giving activities include $1,800,000 for 1 grant.
Fields of interest: Foundations (private grantmaking).
Limitations: Giving primarily in New York, NY.
Trustee: U.S. Trust Co.
EIN: 136138067

5838
DBID, Inc. ✧
c/o Hertz, Herson & Co., LLP
2 Park Ave., Ste. 1500
New York, NY 10016

Established in 1998 in DE and NY.
Donors: Bella Wexner Charitable Remainder Unitrust; Susan Wexner Revocable Trust.
Foundation type: Independent foundation.
Financial data (yr. ended 3/31/05): Assets, $33,492,452 (M); expenditures, $1,456,761; qualifying distributions, $1,272,725; giving activities include $1,225,000 for 1 grant.
Fields of interest: Philanthropy/voluntarism.
Limitations: Applications not accepted. Giving primarily in Southeastern, PA. No grants to individuals.
Application information: Contributes only to pre-selected organizations.
Officer and Directors:* Susan R. Wexner,* Pres. and Secy.-Treas.; Bertrand Agus.
EIN: 133997364
Selected grants: The following grants were reported in 2004.
$1,580,000 to Vanguard Charitable Endowment Program, Southeastern, PA.

5839
Sarah K. de Coizart Article TENTH Perpetual Charitable Trust
(formerly Sarah K. de Coizart Perpetual Charitable Trust)
c/o JPMorgan Chase Bank, N.A.
345 Park Ave., 4th Fl.
New York, NY 10154
Contact: Jacqueline Elias, V.P. and Trust Off., JPMorgan Chase Bank, N.A.

URL: http://foundationcenter.org/grantmaker/decoizart/

Established in 1992 in NY.
Foundation type: Independent foundation.
Financial data (yr. ended 1/31/06): Assets, $35,132,525 (M); expenditures, $1,307,578; qualifying distributions, $1,126,216; giving activities include $930,000 for 42 grants (high: $70,000; low: $10,000; average: $20,000–$40,000).
Purpose and activities: Giving primarily for the environment, including conservation, research, and education; and for blindness-related services and research.
Fields of interest: Environment, natural resources; Environmental education; Eye diseases; Eye research.
Type of support: Research; Program development.
Limitations: Giving limited to the metropolitan New York, NY, area, for blindness funding; giving primarily in NY and the Northeast for the environment. No support for organizations lacking 501(c)(3) status. No grants to individuals, or for matching gifts; no loans.
Publications: Application guidelines; Grants list.
Application information: Grants range in size from $25,000 to $100,000 per year. See foundation Web site for application guidelines and requirements. Application form required.
Initial approach: Proposal
Copies of proposal: 1
Deadline(s): Apr. 30 and Sept. 30
Board meeting date(s): July and Dec.
Final notification: Jan. and July
Trustees: Carl S. Forsythe III; JPMorgan Chase Bank, N.A.
EIN: 137046581
Selected grants: The following grants were reported in 2005.
$75,000 to Natural Resources Defense Council, New York, NY.
$75,000 to Trust for Public Land, San Francisco, CA.
$60,000 to Bronx River Alliance, Bronx, NY.
$45,000 to Metropolitan Museum of Art, New York, NY.
$45,000 to Student Conservation Association, Charlestown, NH.
$40,000 to Bruce Museum, Greenwich, CT.
$35,000 to Boy Scouts of America, Greenwich, CT.
$25,000 to American Red Cross, Greenwich, CT.
$23,500 to Breast Cancer Alliance, Greenwich, CT.
$20,000 to Boys Club of Greenwich, Greenwich, CT.

5840
The Baron de Hirsch Fund ✧
130 E. 59th St., 12th Fl.
New York, NY 10022
Contact: Lauren Katzowitz Shenfield, Managing Dir.

Incorporated in 1891 in NY.
Donors: Baron Maurice de Hirsch†; Baroness Clara de Hirsch†.
Foundation type: Independent foundation.
Financial data (yr. ended 8/31/05): Assets, $6,279,416 (M); gifts received, $2,500; expenditures, $811,903; qualifying distributions, $736,195; giving activities include $564,290 for 24 grants (high: $40,690; low: $2,000).
Purpose and activities: Giving to provide resettlement assistance to Jewish immigrants in the U.S. and Israel; also awards fellowships to Israeli agriculturists.

Fields of interest: Vocational education; Agriculture; Jewish agencies & temples; Immigrants/refugees.
International interests: Israel.
Type of support: General/operating support; Continuing support; Program development; Seed money; Scholarship funds.
Limitations: Applications not accepted. Giving on a national basis, with emphasis on the New York, NY area; support also in Israel. No grants to individuals (other than fellowships to Israeli agriculturalists), or for annual campaigns, deficit financing, capital or endowment funds, matching gifts, or publications.
Application information:
Board meeting date(s): Jan.
Officers and Trustees:* Jenny Morgenthau,* Pres.; Linda Gerstel,* V.P.; Mikhail Ratner,* Secy.; Edwin H. Stern III,* Treas.; James A. Block; Valerie Block; Beverly S. Coleman; William M. Heineman; Abby Knopp; Ezra P. Mager; Ellen Merlo; George W. Naumburg, Jr.; Laura Scheuer; Christopher C. Schwabacher; Arthur D. Sporn; Seymour Zises.
EIN: 135562971

5841
The de Kay Foundation
c/o JPMorgan Chase Bank, N.A.
345 Park Ave., 4th Fl.
New York, NY   10154
Contact: Yvette Boisnier MSW, Prog. Dir.
Application address: c/o United Neighborhood Houses, 70 W. 30th St., 14th Fl., New York, NY 10018-8007

Established in 1967 in CT.
Donor: Helen M. de Kay‡.
Foundation type: Independent foundation.
Financial data (yr. ended 2/28/06): Assets, $37,727,954 (M); expenditures, $2,232,612; qualifying distributions, $2,054,075; giving activities include $1,785,029 for grants.
Purpose and activities: The foundation traditionally awards monthly stipends directly to elderly individuals and couples to help them remain in their home in safety and comfort, to protect their dignity and individuality, and to encourage them to continue contributing to their community. Stipendiary program applicants must be 65 years of age or older and must be referred by social service agencies and have an assigned social worker. Applicants must demonstrate a history of self-sufficiency and minimal dependence on private charitable or government assistance. Individuals should also demonstrate a history of volunteering or engaging in civic or cultural activities. Applicants may have assets up to $25,000, excluding their primary residence.
Type of support: Grants to individuals.
Limitations: Giving limited to the New York, NY metropolitan area, including the five boroughs of New York City, Westchester, Rockland, and Nassau counties, NY, Fairfield County, CT, and Essex, Bergen, Hudson, and Passaic counties, NJ. No grants for building or endowment funds, scholarships, fellowships, or matching gifts; no loans.
Publications: Application guidelines.
Application information: Monthly stipends range from $150-$1,000. Application form required.
Initial approach: Application form
Copies of proposal: 1
Deadline(s): Mar., June, Sept., Dec.
Board meeting date(s): Quarterly
Final notification: 3 months

Trustees: JPMorgan Chase Bank, N.A.
EIN: 136203234

5842
De La Cour Family Foundation ✧
P.O. Box 94
Glen Cove, NY   11542

Established in 1999 in DE.
Donor: Willis S. De La Cour‡.
Foundation type: Independent foundation.
Financial data (yr. ended 12/31/05): Assets, $7,619,500 (M); expenditures, $480,033; qualifying distributions, $423,650; giving activities include $421,000 for 94 grants (high: $50,000; low: $200).
Fields of interest: Education; Health care; Housing/shelter; Youth development; Human services; YM/YWCAs & YM/YWHAs; Children/youth, services; Federated giving programs.
Limitations: Applications not accepted. Giving in the U.S., with emphasis on local and national organizations in NY and MA. No grants to individuals.
Application information: Contributes only to pre-selected organizations.
Directors: Edmund P. De La Cour; Eleanor P. De La Cour; Lea De La Cour; Willis S. De La Cour, Jr.
EIN: 233025610

5843
The Edmond de Rothschild
Foundation ▼ ✧
c/o Proskauer Rose LLP
1585 Broadway
New York, NY   10036
Contact: Paul H. Epstein, Pres.

Incorporated in 1963 in NY.
Donor: Edmond de Rothschild‡.
Foundation type: Independent foundation.
Financial data (yr. ended 12/31/05): Assets, $62,256,955 (M); expenditures, $4,020,939; qualifying distributions, $3,877,955; giving activities include $3,638,460 for 22 grants (high: $1,750,000; low: $5,000; average: $10,000–$100,000).
Purpose and activities: Grants largely for Jewish welfare funds, higher education, and organizations concerned with Israeli affairs in the U.S. and abroad; support also for cultural programs, hospitals, and scientific research.
Fields of interest: Arts; Education; Biomedicine; Medical research, institute.
International interests: France; Israel.
Limitations: Applications not accepted. Giving primarily in New York, NY. No grants to individuals.
Application information: Contributes only to pre-selected organizations.
Board meeting date(s): As required
Officers and Directors:* Benjamin de Rothschild,* Chair.; Gabriel Brack,* Pres.; Paul H. Epstein,* V.P.; Georges C. Karlweis,* V.P.; Stanley Komaroff,* V.P.; Philip M. Susswein, Secy.; Nadine de Rothschild.
Number of staff: 1 part-time professional.
EIN: 136119422
Selected grants: The following grants were reported in 2004.
$260,000 to American Friends of the Open University of Israel, New York, NY.

$37,500 to Cornell University, School of Law, Ithaca, NY.
$35,000 to Harvard University, Cambridge, MA. 2 grants: $25,000 to Harvard University Library, $10,000 (For Theater Collection).
$10,000 to Medical Education for South African Blacks, DC.

5844
The Debs Foundation ✧
1 Beekman Pl., Apt. 7A
New York, NY   10022

Established in 1991 in DE and CT.
Donor: Richard A. Debs.
Foundation type: Independent foundation.
Financial data (yr. ended 12/31/05): Assets, $4,517,071 (M); expenditures, $955,108; qualifying distributions, $927,193; giving activities include $914,575 for 77 grants (high: $200,000; low: $100; average: $1,000–$10,000).
Purpose and activities: Giving primarily to cultural, historical, and educational institutions.
Fields of interest: Museums (art); Performing arts; Historic preservation/historical societies; Arts; Higher education; Human services.
Limitations: Applications not accepted. Giving primarily in New York, NY. No grants to individuals.
Application information: Contributes only to pre-selected organizations.
Officers: Richard A. Debs, Pres.; Barbara K. Debs, V.P.
Directors: Elizabeth A. Debs; Nicholas A. Debs.
EIN: 133639449

5845
The Ira W. DeCamp Foundation ▼ ✧
c/o JPMorgan Private Bank, Global Foundations Group
345 Park Ave., 4th Fl.
New York, NY   10154
Contact: Lisa Philp, V.P., JPMorgan Private Bank
FAX: (212) 464-2305; E-mail (for Lisa Philp): Philp_lisa@jpmorgan.com; URL: http://foundationcenter.org/grantmaker/decamp/

Trust established in 1970 in NY.
Donor: Elizabeth DeCamp McInerny‡.
Foundation type: Independent foundation.
Financial data (yr. ended 10/31/05): Assets, $79,552,268 (M); expenditures, $4,402,019; qualifying distributions, $4,037,829; giving activities include $3,712,500 for 42 grants (high: $190,000; low: $20,000; average: $50,000–$100,000).
Purpose and activities: Grants for community-based health care, foster care, and workforce development.
Fields of interest: Health care; Employment; Children, foster care.
Type of support: Building/renovation; Equipment; Program development; Seed money; Research.
Limitations: Giving primarily in the New York City metropolitan area. No support for private foundations. No grants to individuals, or for general support, land acquisition, matching gifts, publications, conferences, endowment funds, operating budgets, continuing support, annual campaigns, emergency funds, scholarships, fellowships, or deficit financing; no loans.
Publications: Application guidelines; Grants list.

Application information: See foundation Web site for full application requirements. Application form not required.
Initial approach: Proposal
Copies of proposal: 1
Deadline(s): Mar. 15 and July 15
Board meeting date(s): July and Oct.
Final notification: 3 to 6 months
Trustee: JPMorgan Chase & Co.
EIN: 510138577
Selected grants: The following grants were reported in 2005.
$190,000 to Lutheran Medical Center, Brooklyn, NY. To expand and modernize dental facilities in Lutheran Family Health Center Network.
$160,000 to New Alternatives for Children, New York, NY. To hire clinic administrator/nursing director for new health center.
$150,000 to Community Funds, New York, NY. For New York City Workforce Development Funders Group to support technical assistance and program development.
$150,000 to Montefiore Medical Center, Bronx, NY. To expand Practice Redesign Initiative.
$137,500 to Fund for the City of New York, New York, NY. For Agenda for Children Tomorrow, for project to foster and sustain neighborhood-based networks; and for Bushwick network liaison staff member.
$100,000 to Binding Together, New York, NY. For program development.
$100,000 to Opportunities for a Better Tomorrow, Brooklyn, NY. For computers and related equipment.
$75,000 to New York Community Trust, New York, NY. For Partnership for Family Supports and Justice.
$60,000 to Horticultural Society of New York, New York, NY. To hire additional project manager and provide drivers education and training in pesticide application, all in connection with expanding Green Team program.
$50,000 to Good Shepherd Services, New York, NY. For Project Success.

5846
Dr. G. Clifford & Florence B. Decker Foundation ◇
8 Riverside Dr.
Binghamton, NY 13905 (607) 722-0211
Contact: Gerald E. Putman, Exec. Dir.
E-mail: deckerfn@pronetisp.net; URL: http://www.pronetisp.net/~deckerfn/index.html

Established in 1979 in NY.
Donor: G. Clifford Decker, M.D.†.
Foundation type: Independent foundation.
Financial data (yr. ended 12/31/05): Assets, $33,231,416 (M); expenditures, $1,817,428; qualifying distributions, $1,686,540; giving activities include $1,545,660 for 22 grants (high: $500,000; low: $427).
Purpose and activities: The purpose of the foundation is to assist bona fide charitable organizations, focusing primarily on educational, medical and medical research institutions, and cultural and human service organizations providing principal service to residents of Broome County, NY. This assistance is in the form of grants that may be used for capital projects or new and innovative projects and programs. Efforts are directed toward helping organizations provide programs to earn income and thus become more self-sufficient.

Fields of interest: Arts; Education; Health care; Medical research, institute; Human services.
Type of support: Capital campaigns; Building/renovation; Equipment; Program development.
Limitations: Giving limited to Broome County, NY. No support for religious organizations for religious purposes. No grants to individuals, or for endowments, operating expenses, continuing support, or for travel and trips.
Publications: Annual report (including application guidelines).
Application information: Submission of 1 copy of proposal required for funding requests under $5,000. Application form required.
Initial approach: Letter or telephone for application form; meeting required prior to receipt of application form
Copies of proposal: 7
Deadline(s): Mar. 1, May 1, Sept. 1, and Nov. 1
Board meeting date(s): Apr., June, Oct., and Dec.
Final notification: Within 45 business days
Officers and Trustees:* Ferris G. Akel,* Chair.; Alice A. Wales,* Vice-Chair.; Mary Lou Faust, Secy.; Douglas R. Johnson,* Treas.; Gerald E. Putman, Exec. Dir.; James A. Carrigg; John T. Fitzsimmons.
Number of staff: 1 full-time professional; 1 part-time support.
EIN: 161131704
Selected grants: The following grants were reported in 2005.
$250,000 to Lourdes Hospital Foundation, Binghamton, NY.
$250,000 to United Health Services Foundation, Binghamton, NY.
$156,402 to Broome Community College Foundation, Binghamton, NY. 2 grants: $111,402, $45,000
$110,376 to Roberson Memorial, Binghamton, NY. 3 grants: $36,791, $36,791, $36,794
$63,000 to United Way of Broome County, Binghamton, NY.
$38,000 to Broome County Arts Council, Binghamton, NY.
$10,000 to Community Foundation for South Central New York, Binghamton, NY.

5847
Dedalus Foundation, Inc. ◇
(formerly Motherwell Foundation, Inc.)
555 W. 57th St., Ste. 1222
New York, NY 10019
Contact: Richard Rubin, Chair.

Established in 1981.
Donor: Robert Motherwell†.
Foundation type: Operating foundation.
Financial data (yr. ended 12/31/03): Assets, $48,106,632 (M); expenditures, $3,067,651; qualifying distributions, $2,670,890; giving activities include $626,679 for 23 grants (high: $257,500; low: $250), $114,000 for 9 grants to individuals (high: $30,000; low: $1,000), and $1,930,211 for foundation-administered programs.
Purpose and activities: The foundation seeks to educate the public about modern art and modernism, and the art of Robert Motherwell.
Fields of interest: Arts education.
Type of support: Conferences/seminars; Publication; Seed money; Fellowships; Internship funds; Scholarship funds; Research; Grants to individuals; In-kind gifts.
Limitations: Giving on a national basis. No grants to individuals (except for fellowships).

Publications: Informational brochure (including application guidelines).
Application information: Contributes to mostly to pre-selected organizations, but has 3 separate grant programs offered to individuals: Senior Fellowship Program, Ph.D. Dissertation Fellowship, and M.F.A. Fellowship. Application form required.
Initial approach: Letter of request
Copies of proposal: 7
Deadline(s): Oct. 1 for Senior Fellowship Program, Dec. 1 for Ph.D. Dissertation Fellowship, and July 1 for M.F.A. Fellowship
Officers: Richard Rubin, Chair.; Jack Flam, Pres.; Joan Banach, Secy.; Morgan Spangle, Exec. Dir.
Directors: Dore Ashton; John Elderfield; David Rosand.
Number of staff: 4 full-time professional; 1 part-time professional.
EIN: 133091704
Selected grants: The following grants were reported in 2003.
$257,500 to Judith Rothschild Foundation, New York, NY. To educate public about art of Robert Motherwell and modernism.
$79,811 to Walker Art Center, Minneapolis, MN. For printing of new Robert Motherwell prints catalogue raisonne.
$25,000 to Modern Art Museum of Fort Worth, Fort Worth, TX. For Anselm Kiefer retrospective exhibition.
$25,000 to Young Audiences (YA), New York, NY. For Breaking the Rules project.
$15,000 to Harlem School of the Arts, New York, NY. For Opportunities for Learning program.
$15,000 to New York University, New York, NY. For Dedalus Foundation Fellow in Conservation at Institute of Fine Arts.
$10,000 to ABC No Rio, New York, NY. For renovation of facility at Rivington Street.
$10,000 to National Academy of Design, New York, NY. For exhibition catalogue, Surrealism in America.
$10,000 to Studio Museum in Harlem, New York, NY. For Arts-in-Residence program.
$1,000 to Asian American Arts Center, New York, NY. For exhibitions programs for young Asian artists.

5848
Lawrence J. & Florence A. DeGeorge Charitable Trust ◇
c/o Deutsche Bank Trust Co. of NY
P.O. Box 1297, Church St. Sta.
New York, NY 10008 (212) 454-3931

Established in 1994 in FL.
Donors: Lawrence J. DeGeorge; Florence A. DeGeorge.
Foundation type: Independent foundation.
Financial data (yr. ended 1/31/06): Assets, $57,510,293 (M); expenditures, $3,007,055; qualifying distributions, $2,809,361; giving activities include $2,787,395 for 190 grants (high: $500,000; low: $25; average: $1,000–$50,000).
Purpose and activities: Giving primarily for health associations, medical research, and children and youth services.
Fields of interest: Health organizations, association; Medical research, institute; Boys & girls clubs; Children/youth, services; Philanthropy/voluntarism.
Limitations: Applications not accepted. Giving primarily in FL. No grants to individuals.

Application information: Contributes only to pre-selected organizations.
Trustees: Florence A. DeGeorge; Lawrence J. DeGeorge; Deutsche Bank Trust Co. of NY.
EIN: 137053836
Selected grants: The following grants were reported in 2005.
$700,000 to Juvenile Diabetes Research Foundation International, New York, NY. 3 grants: $100,000, $100,000, $500,000
$548,000 to Boggy Creek Gang-A Hole in the Wall Gang Camp, Eustis, FL. 4 grants: $100,000, $98,000, $150,000, $200,000
$500,000 to Juvenile Diabetes Research Foundation International, Palm Beach, FL.
$250,000 to American Red Cross.
$104,875 to Boys and Girls Clubs of Broward County, Fort Lauderdale, FL.

5849

The Delancey Foundation ✧ ☆
c/o Transammonia, Inc.
350 Park Ave.
New York, NY   10022

Established in 1990 in NY as a private operating foundation.
Donor: Ronald P. Stanton.
Foundation type: Operating foundation.
Financial data (yr. ended 12/31/04): Assets, $363 (M); gifts received, $1,860,000; expenditures, $1,860,025; qualifying distributions, $1,860,025; giving activities include $1,860,000 for grants.
Fields of interest: Libraries/library science; Education; Jewish federated giving programs; Jewish agencies & temples.
Type of support: Building/renovation.
Limitations: Applications not accepted. Giving primarily in NJ and NY. No grants to individuals.
Application information: Contributes only to pre-selected organizations.
Officers: Ronald P. Stanton, Pres.; Fred M. Lowenfels, Secy.; Edward G. Weiner, Treas.
Director: Oliver K. Stanton.
EIN: 133576731
Selected grants: The following grants were reported in 2003.
$400,000 to Yeshiva University, New York, NY.
$30,000 to Ruth Keeler Memorial Library, North Salem, NY.

5850

The Gladys Krieble Delmas Foundation
521 5th Ave., Ste. 1612
New York, NY   10175-1699   (212) 687-0011
Contact: Shirley Lockwood, Fdn. Admin.
FAX: (212) 687-8877; *E-mail:* info@delmas.org;
URL: http://www.delmas.org

Established in 1976 in NY.
Donors: Gladys V.K. Delmas†; Jean Paul Delmas†.
Foundation type: Independent foundation.
Financial data (yr. ended 12/31/04): Assets, $55,554,542 (M); expenditures, $3,337,924; qualifying distributions, $2,768,817; giving activities include $2,274,809 for 141 grants (high: $123,000; low: $500), $131,620 for 24 grants to individuals, and $64,000 for 3 employee matching gifts.
Purpose and activities: The foundation supports the humanities, research libraries, and New York City

performing arts organizations, and has a particular interest in encouraging Venetian scholarship.
Fields of interest: Performing arts; Humanities; Libraries/library science.
International interests: Italy.
Type of support: General/operating support; Research; Grants to individuals.
Limitations: Giving on a national basis to organizations, but only in New York, NY, for performing arts grants; giving for individual research projects conducted in Venice or the Veneto, Italy. Research libraries primarily directed toward European and American letters. No grants to individuals (except for advanced research in Venice and the Veneto), or for building campaigns; no loans.
Publications: Application guidelines; Financial statement; Grants list; Informational brochure.
Application information: Application form required for grants for independent research on Venetian history and culture. Application form not required.
  Initial approach: Letter, not exceeding 2 pages
  Copies of proposal: 1
  Deadline(s): Dec. 15 for grants for independent research on Venetian history and culture
  Board meeting date(s): Varies
  Final notification: Apr. 1 for grants for independent research on Venetian history and culture
Trustees: George Labalme, Jr.; Joseph C. Mitchell; David H. Stam.
Number of staff: 1 full-time professional; 1 full-time support.
EIN: 510193884
Selected grants: The following grants were reported in 2004.
$25,000 to University of Toronto, Center for Medieval Studies, Toronto, Canada. Toward publication of the Dictionary of Old English.
$20,000 to National Gallery of Canada, Ottawa, Canada. Toward preparation of Index to National Gallery Exhibition Catalogues.
$18,000 to University of Texas, Harry Ransom Humanities Research Center, Austin, TX. Toward Samuel Beckett web-based exhibition.
$15,000 to Martha Graham Center of Contemporary Dance, New York, NY. Toward New York City Center.
$15,000 to Saint Lukes Chamber Ensemble, New York, NY. Toward 30th Anniversary of New Music Initiative.
$12,500 to CSC Repertory, Classic Stage Company, New York, NY. For general support.
$12,000 to University of Notre Dame, Notre Dame, IN. Toward publication of papers on an international symposium, Academia Eolia Revisited.
$10,000 to Save Venice, New York, NY. Toward exhibition at the Isabella Stewart Gardner Museum titled Gondola Days: Isabella Stewart Gardner and the Palazzo Barbaro Circle.
$10,000 to University of Connecticut, Storrs, CT. Toward national conference on emerging image coding systems for libraries and archives.
$5,000 to Cave Canem Foundation, New York, NY. Toward Summer Workshop and Retreat for African American Poets.

5851

Demartini Family Foundation ✧
8 Elm Rock Rd.
Bronxville, NY   10708

Established in 2001 in NY.
Donor: Richard M. Demartini.
Foundation type: Independent foundation.
Financial data (yr. ended 9/30/05): Assets, $5,487,958 (M); gifts received, $8,665; expenditures, $478,283; qualifying distributions, $443,586; giving activities include $439,254 for 50 grants (high: $100,000; low: $200).
Purpose and activities: Giving primarily for education.
Fields of interest: Arts; Education; Animals/wildlife, preservation/protection; Health care; Cancer; Human services.
Limitations: Applications not accepted. Giving primarily in CA, CT and NY. No grants to individuals.
Application information: Contributes only to pre-selected organizations.
Trustees: Jennifer L. Brorsen; Richard M. Demartini.
EIN: 946781245
Selected grants: The following grants were reported in 2004.
$110,000 to Vermont Academy, Saxtons River, VT. 2 grants: $10,000, $100,000
$32,200 to Cancer Research Institute, New York, NY. 2 grants: $27,500, $4,700
$26,000 to Eagle Hill School, Greenwich, CT. 2 grants: $1,000, $25,000
$25,000 to United Way, NY.
$17,500 to Lawrence Hospital, Bronxville, NY. 2 grants: $5,000, $12,500
$2,000 to San Diego State University, San Diego, CA.

5852

Frederick and Nancy DeMatteis Family Charitable Trust
(also known as The DeMatteis Family Foundation)
c/o The DeMatteis Family Foundation
P.O. Box 25
Glen Head, NY   11545   (516) 705-4974
Contact: Robert F. Vizza Ph.D., Pres.
URL: http://foundationcenter.org/grantmaker/dematteis/

Established in 2001 in NY.
Donors: Frederick DeMatteis; Nancy DeMatteis; 2001 Frederick DeMatteis Revocable Trust.
Foundation type: Independent foundation.
Financial data (yr. ended 12/31/04): Assets, $40,165,936 (M); expenditures, $1,964,978; qualifying distributions, $1,570,979; giving activities include $1,333,500 for 17 grants (high: $268,000; low: $500).
Purpose and activities: The mission of the foundation is to make life better by serving human needs through support of institutions involved in education, health, human services, medical research, social services, and the arts.
Fields of interest: Arts; Education; Health care; Medical research, institute; Human services.
Type of support: Building/renovation; Equipment; Program development; Research; Matching/challenge support.
Limitations: Giving primarily in the metropolitan New York, NY, area. No grants to individuals, or for operating deficits, general operating support, endowments, unrestricted funds, or annual appeals; no loans.
Publications: Application guidelines; Informational brochure.
Application information: See foundation Web site for full application requirements. Application form required.

Initial approach: 1-page letter of inquiry
Copies of proposal: 1
Deadline(s): 1 month prior to quarterly board meeting
Board meeting date(s): Quarterly
Final notification: 1 week after board meeting
Officers and Trustees:* Nancy DeMatteis,* Chair.; Robert F. Vizza, Ph.D., Pres.; Richard F. DeMatteis; Scott L. DeMatteis; Linda Langer; Donald M. Schaeffer; Tracey Serko; Stanley Sirote.
Number of staff: 1 part-time professional; 1 full-time support.
EIN: 137294014
Selected grants: The following grants were reported in 2003.
$560,000 to Saint Francis Research and Educational Corporation, Old Brookville, NY. For MRI research project.
$250,000 to Chaminade High School, Mineola, NY. For field turf project.
$150,000 to Saint Vincents Services, Brooklyn, NY. For The American Dream program.
$100,000 to Wheelchair Classics Charities, Jackson Heights, NY. For general support.
$50,000 to Association for the Help of Retarded Children, New York, NY. For Pearl and Jack Ain Diagnostic Treatment Center.
$50,000 to Greenvale School, Glen Head, NY. For Harris Theater renovation project.
$50,000 to North Shore Child and Family Guidance Center, Roslyn Heights, NY. For bereavement and trauma center.
$15,000 to Childrens Village, Dobbs Ferry, NY. Toward new group home.
$15,000 to Friends of the Arts, Locust Valley, NY. For outreach program.
$5,000 to National Theater Workshop of the Handicapped, New York, NY. For general support.

5853
The Daniele Agostino Derossi Foundation, Inc.
(formerly The Daniele Agostino Foundation, Inc.)
870 United Nations Plz., No. 35C
New York, NY 10017
Contact: Flavia Robinson, Pres.
FAX: (212) 752-1668; *E-mail:* da.found@verizon.net;
URL: http://www.dafound.org

Established in 1992 in NY.
Donor: Flavia D. Robinson.
Foundation type: Independent foundation.
Financial data (yr. ended 6/30/05): Assets, $2,936,306 (M); expenditures, $821,528; qualifying distributions, $732,353; giving activities include $732,353 for 54 grants (high: $125,546; low: $100).
Purpose and activities: Support primarily for the welfare of women and children in the indigenous communities, mainly Mayan, of Guatemala and Mexico. Occasionally support is given for projects of special merit in photography and social welfare in New York, NY.
Fields of interest: Education; Health care; Women.
International interests: Guatemala; Mexico.
Type of support: General/operating support; Scholarship funds.
Limitations: Giving primarily in Guatemala and Mexico; some giving also in New York, NY. No support for political organizations. No grants to individuals or building construction.
Publications: Application guidelines; Informational brochure; Occasional report.

Application information: Application guidelines available on foundation Web site. Application form not required.
Initial approach: Proposal
Copies of proposal: 1
Deadline(s): None
Board meeting date(s): July and Dec.
Final notification: Within 10 weeks
Officers and Directors:* Flavia Robinson,* Pres.; Lorna Opatow,* Secy.-Treas.; Peter De Janosi; Daniele Derossi; David Pollock.
Number of staff: None.
EIN: 133636541

5854
Deutsche Bank Americas Foundation ▼ ✧
(formerly BT Foundation)
60 Wall St., NYC60-2110
New York, NY 10005-2858 (212) 250-0555
Contact: Gary S. Hatten, Pres.
URL: http://www.community.db.com/

Established as the BT Foundation in 1986 in NY; changed name to Deutsche Bank Americas Foundation in 1999.
Donors: Bankers Trust Co.; BT Capital Corp.; Deutsche Bank Americas Holding Corp.
Foundation type: Company-sponsored foundation.
Financial data (yr. ended 12/31/04): Assets, $13,199,430 (M); gifts received, $19,345,829; expenditures, $12,263,021; qualifying distributions, $14,992,612; giving activities include $8,636,504 for 422 grants (high: $250,000; low: $100), $3,626,109 for employee matching gifts, and $2,729,841 for loans/program-related investments.
Purpose and activities: The foundation supports organizations involved with arts and culture, education, housing, human services, community development, economically disadvantaged people, and homeless people.
Fields of interest: Arts education; Arts; Education; Employment; Housing/shelter, development; Housing/shelter; Human services; Community development; Economically disadvantaged; Homeless.
International interests: Canada; Latin America.
Type of support: General/operating support; Continuing support; Program development; Internship funds; Technical assistance; Program-related investments/loans; Employee matching gifts.
Limitations: Giving on a national basis in areas of company operations and in Canada and Latin America. No support for political parties or candidates, or for legal advocacy, religious purposes, veterans', military, or fraternal organizations, United Way agencies (except for those providing a fundraising waiver), or professional or trade associations. No grants to individuals, or for endowments, or capital campaigns.
Publications: Application guidelines; Annual report; Corporate giving report; Grants list; Newsletter.
Application information: Support is limited to 3 years. Letters of inquiry should be no longer than 3 pages. Application form not required.
Initial approach: Letter of inquiry
Deadline(s): None
Officer and Directors:* Gary S. Hattem, Pres.; Alessandra Digiusto, Secy.-Treas. and C.A.O.; Jorge Calderon; Robert Cotter; Hanns Michael Hoelz; Thomas J. Hughes; Miguel Noriega.

Number of staff: 3 full-time professional; 3 full-time support.
EIN: 133321736
Selected grants: The following grants were reported in 2004.
$350,000 to Charities Aid Foundation (CAF) America, Alexandria, VA. 2 grants: $250,000 (For Donor Advised Fund), $100,000 (For Donor Advised Fund).
$250,000 to Neighborhood Opportunities Fund, New York, NY. For general operating support.
$250,000 to New York City Host Committee, New York, NY. For New York City Republican Convention.
$142,500 to Common Ground Community Housing Development Fund Corporation, New York, NY. For DB SHARE (Supportive Housing Acquisition and Rehabilitation Effort).
$125,000 to Metropolitan Opera Association, New York, NY. For Opening Nights at the Met.
$125,000 to Sponsors for Educational Opportunity, New York, NY. For career program.
$25,000 to Community Resource Exchange, New York, NY. For general operating support.
$25,000 to Lantern Group, New York, NY. For DB SHARE (Supportive Housing Acquisition and Rehabilitation Effort).
$24,300 to New York Foundation for the Arts, New York, NY. For Inspiration Awards.

5855
The Devlin Foundation ✧
c/o Bessemer Trust
730 5th Ave., Ste. 2102
New York, NY 10019
Contact: Erin Devlin, Exec. V.P.

Established in 1998 in TX.
Donors: Robert M. Devlin; Katharine B. Devlin.
Foundation type: Independent foundation.
Financial data (yr. ended 12/31/04): Assets, $21,738,383 (M); expenditures, $1,223,342; qualifying distributions, $1,065,708; giving activities include $1,004,225 for 46 grants (high: $253,000; low: $150).
Purpose and activities: Giving primarily for education and the arts.
Fields of interest: Museums; Performing arts, theater; Arts; Higher education, college; Education; Human services; Foundations (private grantmaking).
Type of support: General/operating support; Scholarship funds.
Limitations: Giving primarily in CT and NY; some funding nationally.
Application information:
Initial approach: Letter
Officers: Katharine B. Devlin, Pres.; Erin C. Devlin, Exec. V.P.; Matthew B. Devlin, V.P.; Michael Devlin, V.P.; Robert M. Devlin, V.P.
EIN: 760574063

5856
The Dewar Foundation, Inc. ✧
16 Dietz St.
Oneonta, NY 13820
Contact: Sidney Levine, Pres.

Incorporated in 1947 in NY.
Donors: Jessie Smith Dewar†; James A. Dewar†; Frank Getman.
Foundation type: Independent foundation.

Financial data (yr. ended 12/31/05): Assets, $11,457,661 (M); expenditures, $852,637; qualifying distributions, $564,500; giving activities include $564,500 for 78 grants (high: $137,500; low: $1,000).

Purpose and activities: Giving primarily for the arts, education, and Christian agencies and churches.

Fields of interest: Arts; Higher education; Hospitals (general); Health organizations, association; Human services; Children/youth, services; Protestant agencies & churches; Roman Catholic agencies & churches.

Type of support: Continuing support; Annual campaigns; Building/renovation; Endowments; Program development; Scholarship funds.

Limitations: Giving limited to the greater Oneonta, NY, area. No grants to individuals.

Application information: Application form not required.

Initial approach: Letter
Deadline(s): None

Officers and Directors:* Sidney Levine, Pres.; Michael F. Getman,* Secy.-Treas.; James F. Lettis; John M. Pontius; Geoffrey A. Smith.

EIN: 166054329

Selected grants: The following grants were reported in 2005.

$35,000 to Hartwick College, Oneonta, NY.
$25,000 to Saint Marys School, Ticonderoga, NY.
$20,000 to Opportunities for Otsego, Oneonta, NY.
$20,000 to State University of New York College at Oneonta Foundation, Oneonta, NY.
$14,000 to YMCA of Oneonta, Oneonta, NY.
$5,000 to Catholic Charities of Delaware and Otsego Counties, Oneonta, NY.
$5,000 to First Baptist Church, Owego, NY.
$5,000 to First United Methodist Church, Akron, NY.
$5,000 to Glimmerglass Opera, Cooperstown, NY.
$5,000 to Salvation Army, Yonkers, NY.

5857
Miriam and Arthur Diamond Charitable Trust ✧
c/o Cadwalader
1 World Financial Ctr.
New York, NY   10281-0006   (212) 504-5558
Contact: Jay H. McDowell, Tr.; Jack Adelman, Tr.

Established in 1996 in NY.
Foundation type: Independent foundation.
Financial data (yr. ended 12/31/05): Assets, $40,701,003 (M); expenditures, $2,130,959; qualifying distributions, $2,096,043; giving activities include $1,850,000 for 21 grants (high: $500,000; low: $5,000; average: $10,000–$100,000).

Purpose and activities: Giving primarily for higher education, including law schools, as well as for the arts, hospitals including medical research, and health and human services.

Fields of interest: Performing arts; Performing arts centers; Arts; Higher education; Law school/education; Hospitals (general); Medical research, institute; Genetics/birth defects research; Cancer research; Neuroscience research; Human services; American Red Cross; Jewish federated giving programs.

Limitations: Giving primarily in New York, NY; some funding nationally. No grants to individuals.

Application information:

Initial approach: Letter
Deadline(s): None

Trustees: Jack Adelman; Jay H. McDowell.
EIN: 137093689
Selected grants: The following grants were reported in 2004.
$500,000 to Dorot, New York, NY.
$500,000 to Lenox Hill Hospital, New York, NY.
$125,000 to United Jewish Appeal, New York, NY.

5858
The Robert & Jennifer Diamond Family Foundation ☆
c/o Clarfeld Financial Advisors, Inc.
560 White Plains Rd., 5th Fl.
Tarrytown, NY   10591
Contact: Carole Pipolo, Dir.
E-mail: carole@clarfeld.com

Established in 2003 in DE.
Donor: Robert E. Diamond, Jr.
Foundation type: Independent foundation.
Financial data (yr. ended 3/31/06): Assets, $3,687,454 (M); gifts received, $2,389,098; expenditures, $2,980,247; qualifying distributions, $2,938,957; giving activities include $2,938,957 for 5 grants (high: $2,649,980; low: $8,977).

Fields of interest: Higher education, university; Scholarships/financial aid; Education.

Type of support: Continuing support; Annual campaigns; Capital campaigns; Building/renovation; Fellowships; Scholarship funds.

Limitations: Applications not accepted. Giving primarily in the United States and the United Kingdom. No grants to individuals.

Application information: Contributes only to pre-selected organizations.

Directors: Jennifer Diamond; Robert E. Diamond; Robert E. Diamond III; Carole Pipolo; Teresa Jane Taylor; Paul Wrobleski.

EIN: 200618456

5859
Diamond Foundation ✧ ☆
59 Olympia Ln.
Monsey, NY   10952-2829

Established in 2003 in NY.
Donor: Morria Lichtenstein.
Foundation type: Independent foundation.
Financial data (yr. ended 11/30/05): Assets, $651,000 (M); gifts received, $651,000; expenditures, $349,804; qualifying distributions, $343,904; giving activities include $343,904 for grants.

Fields of interest: Jewish agencies & temples.

Trustees: Devora Shoshana Lichtenstein; Morris Lichtenstein.

EIN: 020657867

Selected grants: The following grants were reported in 2004.
$5,000 to Yeshiva of Spring Valley, Monsey, NY.
$3,000 to Exploited Childrens Help Organization, Louisville, KY.
$2,500 to Bais Yaakov.
$1,500 to Areivim, Brooklyn, NY.

5860
Irene Diamond Fund ▼
800 3rd Ave., Ste. 2700
New York, NY   10022
Contact: Jane Silver, Pres.

Established in 1994 in NY.
Donor: Irene Diamond†.
Foundation type: Independent foundation.
Financial data (yr. ended 12/31/04): Assets, $83,845,674 (M); gifts received, $12,384,908; expenditures, $19,741,842; qualifying distributions, $16,789,863; giving activities include $14,975,495 for grants (high: $3,173,756; low: $5,000).

Purpose and activities: Giving for pre-determined projects in New York, NY, for medical research on HIV/AIDS and immunology, human rights and for the performing arts.

Fields of interest: Arts; Medical research; International human rights.

Limitations: Applications not accepted. Giving primarily in NY. No grants to individuals; no loans.

Application information: Contributes only to pre-selected organizations.

Officers and Board Members:* Jane Silver,* Pres.; Joseph Polisi,* V.P.; Yvette Neier,* Secy.; Peter Kimmelman,* Treas.; Ann Gebhardt, C.F.O.

Number of staff: 2 full-time professional; 3 full-time support.

EIN: 132678431

5861
Dickler Family Foundation, Inc.
(formerly Ruth & Gerald Dickler Foundation, Inc.)
c/o TCC Group, Inc.
50 E. 42nd St., 19th Fl.
New York, NY   10017   (212) 949-0990, ext. 225
Contact: Carol Gallo, Admin.

Established in 1995 in DE and MA.
Donor: Gerald Dickler.
Foundation type: Independent foundation.
Financial data (yr. ended 12/31/05): Assets, $11,094,022 (M); expenditures, $935,944; qualifying distributions, $758,769; giving activities include $636,600 for 88 grants (high: $40,000; low: $500).

Purpose and activities: Giving primarily for education, and to family planning and reproductive health services.

Fields of interest: Education; Reproductive health; Reproductive health, family planning.

Type of support: General/operating support; Continuing support; Annual campaigns; Capital campaigns; Endowments; Research.

Limitations: Giving primarily in New York, NY.

Application information: New York/New Jersey Common Application Form accepted. Application form required.

Initial approach: Letter
Copies of proposal: 3
Deadline(s): Feb. 1, Sept. 1
Board meeting date(s): May and Dec.
Final notification: June, Dec.

Officers: Ruth Dickler, Pres.; Susan Dickler, Exec. V.P.; Jane Lebow, V.P.; Abby Pratt, V.P.; Andrew Lawrence, Secy.; Lawrence Pratt, Treas.

EIN: 133864553

5862
Valerie & Charles Diker Fund, Inc. ✧
c/o Eisner LLP
750 3rd Ave.
New York, NY   10017

Established in 1961 in NY.

Donors: Charles Diker; Valerie Diker.
Foundation type: Independent foundation.
Financial data (yr. ended 11/30/04): Assets, $6,025,705 (M); gifts received, $17,865; expenditures, $853,589; qualifying distributions, $780,291; giving activities include $762,051 for 101 grants (high: $149,887).
Purpose and activities: Giving primarily to Jewish organizations and temples, and for education, and the arts.
Fields of interest: Museums; Museums (art); Performing arts centers; Performing arts, dance; Arts; Elementary school/education; Higher education; Cancer research; Children/youth, services; Federated giving programs; Jewish federated giving programs; Jewish agencies & temples.
Limitations: Applications not accepted. Giving primarily in New York, NY; some funding also in Santa Fe, NM. No grants to individuals.
Application information: Contributes only to pre-selected organizations.
Directors: Charles Diker; Valerie Diker.
EIN: 136075504
Selected grants: The following grants were reported in 2003.
$142,857 to National Museum of the American Indian, New York, NY. For general support.
$100,000 to National Dance Institute New Mexico, Santa Fe, NM. For general support.
$100,000 to UJA-Federation of New York, New York, NY. For general support.
$50,000 to Whitney Museum of American Art, New York, NY. For general support.
$35,000 to Polytechnic Preparatory Country Day School, Brooklyn, NY. For general support.
$20,000 to Legal Services for Children, New York, NY. For general support.
$5,000 to American Folk Art Museum, New York, NY. For general support.
$3,000 to Saint Johns College, Santa Fe, NM. For general support.
$2,000 to American Museum of the Moving Image, Astoria, NY. For general support.
$2,000 to Breast Cancer Research Foundation, New York, NY. For general support.

5863
The Diller-von Furstenberg Family Foundation ✧
(also known as The Diller Foundation)
c/o Sarah Knutson, Interactive Corp.
152 W. 57th St., 42nd Fl.
New York, NY 10019

Established in 1986 in CA.
Donors: Barry Diller; Ranger Investments, L.P.
Foundation type: Independent foundation.
Financial data (yr. ended 12/31/05): Assets, $11,945,215 (M); expenditures, $1,893,942; qualifying distributions, $1,891,065; giving activities include $1,891,065 for 102 grants (high: $200,000; low: $250).
Purpose and activities: Giving primarily for health care and health associations, as well as to hospitals, including children's hospitals; funding also for education, the arts, and children, youth and social services.
Fields of interest: Arts, alliance; Media/communications; Performing arts, theater; Arts; Elementary/secondary education; Higher education; Education (general); Health care; Health organizations, association; Cancer; AIDS; Cancer,

leukemia research; Human services; Children/youth, services; Foundations (private grantmaking).
Type of support: Research.
Limitations: Applications not accepted. Giving primarily in CA and New York, NY. No grants to individuals.
Application information: Contributes only to pre-selected organizations.
Officer: Barry Diller, Pres.
EIN: 954081892

5864
The James & Judith K. Dimon Foundation ✧
c/o J. Popper
192 Lexington Ave., 11th Fl.
New York, NY 10016

Established in 1996 in NY.
Donors: James Dimon; Judith K. Dimon.
Foundation type: Independent foundation.
Financial data (yr. ended 11/30/03): Assets, $3,937,190 (M); gifts received, $13,901; expenditures, $2,018,837; qualifying distributions, $2,013,187; giving activities include $1,995,615 for 84 grants (high: $1,200,000; low: $25).
Purpose and activities: Funding primarily for arts and culture and youth services.
Fields of interest: Arts; Higher education; Boys clubs; Big Brothers/Big Sisters; Boy scouts; Youth development, services; Federated giving programs; Jewish agencies & temples.
Limitations: Applications not accepted. No grants to individuals.
Application information: Contributes only to pre-selected organizations.
Officers: James Dimon, Pres.; Theodore Dimon, Secy.; Judith K. Dimon, Treas.
EIN: 133922199
Selected grants: The following grants were reported in 2003.
$1,200,000 to 5-11 Club, Chicago, IL.
$25,000 to Chicago Symphony Orchestra, Chicago, IL.
$12,000 to Dance Theater Workshop, New York, NY.
$9,821 to Whitney Museum of American Art, New York, NY.
$5,000 to Junior Achievement of Chicago, Chicago, IL.
$2,500 to Museum of Contemporary Art, Chicago, IL.
$1,000 to Childrens Museum of Manhattan, New York, NY.
$1,000 to Fresh Air Fund, New York, NY.
$1,000 to Merit School of Music, Chicago, IL.
$1,000 to Philadelphia Futures for Youth, Philadelphia, PA.

5865
Ditmars Foundation, Inc. ✧
c/o Irwin Kalmanowitz & Lee, PLLC, C.P.A.s
462 7th Ave., 6th Fl.
New York, NY 10018-7439

Established in 1995 in NY.
Donors: Tibor Klein; York Home Care, LLC; Skatz Realty Corp.; Gershon Klein.
Foundation type: Independent foundation.
Financial data (yr. ended 12/31/05): Assets, $61,257 (M); gifts received, $993,000;

expenditures, $970,325; qualifying distributions, $970,325; giving activities include $968,000 for 90 grants (high: $356,250; low: $300).
Fields of interest: Jewish federated giving programs; Jewish agencies & temples.
Limitations: Applications not accepted. Giving primarily in NY. No grants to individuals.
Application information: Contributes only to pre-selected organizations.
Officers: Tibor Klein, Pres.; Chaim Klein, V.P.; Gershon Klein, V.P.; Miriam Klein, Secy.-Treas.
EIN: 133861379
Selected grants: The following grants were reported in 2004.
$7,800 to Ohr Chadash, Fresh Meadows, NY.
$5,400 to Pesach Tikvah - Hope Development, Brooklyn, NY.
$1,750 to American Friends of Ramot Torah Schools, Brooklyn, NY.
$1,000 to Orthodox Council of Jerusalem, Jerusalem, Israel. .
$1,000 to Tifrach Torah Center, Brooklyn, NY.
$260 to PTACH, Brooklyn, NY.
$26 to Lev LAchim, Brooklyn, NY.
$26 to Yeshiva Darchei Torah, Far Rockaway, NY.
$26 to Yeshiva Toras Emes.
$26 to Yeshiva Zichron Yaakov, Spring Valley, NY.

5866
Dobkin Family Foundation ✧
c/o BCRS Associates LLC
100 Wall St., 11th Fl.
New York, NY 10005

Established in 1984 in NY.
Donors: Eric S. Dobkin; Barbara Dobkin.
Foundation type: Independent foundation.
Financial data (yr. ended 3/31/05): Assets, $25,427,193 (M); gifts received, $6,025,850; expenditures, $4,513,166; qualifying distributions, $3,608,577; giving activities include $3,187,102 for 139+ grants (high: $344,000).
Purpose and activities: Giving primarily to Jewish organizations and for human services.
Fields of interest: Museums; Arts; Higher education; Health organizations, association; Human services; Women, centers/services; Jewish federated giving programs; Jewish agencies & temples; Women.
International interests: Israel.
Type of support: General/operating support.
Limitations: Applications not accepted. Giving primarily in New York, NY. No grants to individuals.
Application information: Contributes only to pre-selected organizations.
Trustees: Barbara Dobkin; Eric S. Dobkin; Rachel L. Dobkin.
EIN: 133248042

5867
Cleveland H. Dodge Foundation, Inc.
670 W. 247th St.
Bronx, NY 10471 (718) 543-1220
Contact: Phyllis M. Criscuoli, Exec. Dir.
FAX: (718) 543-0737;
E-mail: info@chdodgefoundation.org; URL: http://www.chdodgefoundation.org

Incorporated in 1917 in NY.
Donor: Cleveland H. Dodge†.
Foundation type: Independent foundation.

Financial data (yr. ended 12/31/05): Assets, $44,985,159 (M); expenditures, $2,186,572; qualifying distributions, $2,306,753; giving activities include $1,151,380 for grants, and $345,820 for employee matching gifts.

Purpose and activities: The purpose of the foundation is to promote the well-being of mankind throughout the world. Grants for a selected list of international organizations in the Near East, including those working toward reversing global overpopulation; grants also to a selected few national agencies in the U.S., the balance directed to organizations located in New York City. Most grants in the U.S. for higher and secondary education, youth agencies and child welfare, and cultural programs.

Fields of interest: Arts; Secondary school/education; Higher education; Children/youth, services; Population studies.

International interests: Middle East.

Type of support: Building/renovation; Equipment; Endowments; Employee matching gifts; Matching/challenge support.

Limitations: Giving primarily in New York, NY, the Near East, and to national organizations. No support for health care, or schools, colleges, and universities, except those that the foundation has consistently supported. No grants to individuals, including scholarships and fellowships, or for general purposes, medical and other research; no loans.

Publications: Annual report; Grants list; Program policy statement.

Application information: Application form not required.

    Initial approach: Letter
    Copies of proposal: 1
    Deadline(s): Submit letter prior to the 15th of Jan., Apr., and Sept.
    Board meeting date(s): 3 times a year
    Final notification: Within 3 months of submitting the proposal

Officers and Directors:* Cleveland E. Dodge, Jr.,* Chair.; William Dodge Rueckert,* Pres.; Bayard Dodge, V.P.; Louis E. Black,* Secy.; Phyllis M. Criscuoli, Treas. and Exec. Dir.; David S. Dodge; Robert Garrett; Alfred H. Howell, Jr.,* Catherine Kerr; Sally Dodge Mole; Bayard D. Rea; Elizabeth Tebbe; Ingrid R. Warren.

Number of staff: 1 full-time professional.

EIN: 136015087

5868

The Henry L. and Grace Doherty Charitable Foundation, Inc. ✧

c/o McGrath, Doyle & Phair
150 Broadway
New York, NY 10038 (212) 571-2300
Contact: Walter R. Brown, Pres.

Incorporated in 1947 in DE.

Donors: Mrs. Henry L. Doherty†; Helen Lee Lassen†.

Foundation type: Independent foundation.

Financial data (yr. ended 12/31/05): Assets, $22,506,761 (M); expenditures, $1,190,473; qualifying distributions, $1,045,772; giving activities include $952,250 for 65 grants (high: $200,000; low: $100).

Purpose and activities: Primarily to promote research in the marine sciences, and to assist institutions engaged in oceanographic activities.

Only limited expansion of activities is anticipated in the foreseeable future.

Fields of interest: Higher education; Human services; Marine science.

Type of support: Seed money; Research; Matching/challenge support.

Limitations: Giving on a national basis, with some emphasis on MA and NY institutions. No grants to individuals, or for building funds or construction equipment.

Application information: Application form not required.

    Initial approach: Letter
    Copies of proposal: 1
    Deadline(s): None
    Board meeting date(s): As required

Officers and Directors:* Walter R. Brown,* Pres.; James R. Billingsley,* V.P. and Treas.; James R. Billingsley, Jr.,* Secy.; Helen Lee Billingsley; Kiyoko O. Brown; Hugh Barr Rardin; Jacob C. Rardin IV.

EIN: 136401292

5869

Dolan Family Foundation ☆

c/o William A. Frewin, Jr.
340 Crossways Park Dr.
Woodbury, NY 11797 (516) 803-9210
Contact: Marianne E. Weber, Pres.

Established in 1987 in NY.

Donors: Charles F. Dolan; Helen A. Dolan.

Foundation type: Independent foundation.

Financial data (yr. ended 11/30/05): Assets, $28,715,782 (M); gifts received, $90,000; expenditures, $1,843,863; qualifying distributions, $1,829,865; giving activities include $1,816,618 for 7 grants (high: $1,000,000; low: $15,000).

Purpose and activities: Giving primarily for education and human services, as well as for a public television station, and to an organization which provides help for children born with a cleft lip and palate.

Fields of interest: Education; Health care; Human services; Children/youth, services.

Type of support: Research; Program development; Matching/challenge support; Equipment; Building/renovation.

Limitations: Giving primarily in the greater metropolitan New York, NY, area, including Long Island. No grants to individuals.

Publications: Application guidelines; Informational brochure.

Application information:

    Initial approach: Brief summary
    Deadline(s): None

Officers and Director:* Marianne E. Weber,* Pres.; William A. Frewin, Jr.,* V.P.

EIN: 113129948

5870

The Katherine and Peter Dolan Family Foundation ✧ ☆

c/o Ayco Company, L.P., Tax Dept.
P.O. Box 15014
Albany, NY 12212-5014

Established in 2001 in NY.

Donors: Peter R. Dolan; Katherine L. Dolan.

Foundation type: Independent foundation.

Financial data (yr. ended 12/31/05): Assets, $429,389 (M); gifts received, $291,289;

expenditures, $456,429; qualifying distributions, $454,988; giving activities include $454,988 for 33 grants (high: $106,803; low: $85; average: $1,000–$10,000).

Fields of interest: Higher education; Environment.

Limitations: Applications not accepted. Giving in the U.S., primarily in NY, the Washington, DC, area, and the New England region in CT, MA, NH, and VT. No grants to individuals.

Application information: Contributes only to pre-selected organizations.

Officers: Katherine L. Dolan, Pres.; Peter R. Dolan, V.P.

EIN: 470846774

5871

Oliver S. and Jennie R. Donaldson Charitable Trust ✧

c/o U.S. Trust
114 W. 47th St.
New York, NY 10036-1530
Contact: Carolyn L. Larke, V.P., U.S. Trust

Established in 1969 in NY.

Donor: Oliver S. Donaldson†.

Foundation type: Independent foundation.

Financial data (yr. ended 12/31/05): Assets, $32,969,997 (M); expenditures, $1,561,522; qualifying distributions, $1,493,478; giving activities include $1,434,000 for 56 grants (high: $100,000; low: $2,000; average: $10,000–$25,000).

Purpose and activities: Interests include cancer research and treatment, child welfare and youth agencies, hospitals and health agencies, elementary, secondary, and higher education; support also for wildlife preservation, and the town of Pawling, NY; 11 named institutions are given first consideration.

Fields of interest: Elementary school/education; Secondary school/education; Higher education; Animals/wildlife, preservation/protection; Hospitals (general); Health care; Cancer; Medical research, institute; Cancer research; Children/youth, services.

Limitations: Giving primarily in the Northeast, with emphasis on MA and NY. No grants to individuals.

Application information: NY/NJ Area Common Application Form required. Application form required.

    Initial approach: Proposal
    Copies of proposal: 1
    Deadline(s): Rolling
    Board meeting date(s): Semiannually

Trustees: Marjorie Atwood; Mark A. Lawrence; Priscilla A. Lawrence; Robert P. Lawrence; William E. Murray; Pamela C. Smith; U.S. Trust.

EIN: 046229044

Selected grants: The following grants were reported in 2003.

$200,000 to Spoleto Festival USA, Charleston, SC.

$100,000 to Medical University of South Carolina (MUSC), Charleston, SC.

$100,000 to Saint Annes Hospital, Fall River, MA.

$50,000 to Columbia University, School of Nursing, New York, NY.

$25,000 to Marymount Manhattan College, New York, NY.

$25,000 to Rosemont College, Rosemont, PA.

$25,000 to Salvation Army of Greater New York, New York, NY.

$15,000 to Tufts University, School of Veterinary Medicine, Medford, MA.

$10,000 to Childrens Storefront, New York, NY.
$10,000 to StreetSquash, New York, NY.

5872
Angelo Donghia Foundation, Inc. ✧
c/o Levy Sonet & Siegel, LLP
630 3rd Ave., 23rd Fl.
New York, NY   10017

Established in 2001 in NY.
Donor: Angelo Donghia‡.
Foundation type: Independent foundation.
Financial data (yr. ended 12/31/05): Assets,
$22,813,866 (M); expenditures, $852,457;
qualifying distributions, $743,292; giving activities
include $660,442 for 13 grants (high: $200,000;
low: $2,500).
Purpose and activities: Giving primarily for
scholarship funds for interior design students;
funding also for AIDS research.
Fields of interest: Visual arts, design; Hospitals
(general); AIDS research.
Type of support: Scholarship funds.
Limitations: Applications not accepted. Giving on a
national basis, with some emphasis on CA, NY and
Washington, DC.
Application information: Unsolicited requests for
funds not accepted.
Officers and Trustees:* Jerrold M. Sonet,* Pres.;
Alan M. Siegel,* Secy.; Steven G. Sonet,* Treas.
EIN: 133523056

5873
The William H. Donner Foundation ▼ ✧
60 E. 42nd St., Ste. 1560
New York, NY   10165   (212) 949-0404
Contact: Rachel Gregg, Prog. Mgr.
FAX: (212) 949-6022; E-mail: dfeeney@donner.org;
Additional tel.: (212) 949-5213; URL: http://
www.donner.org

Incorporated in 1961 in DC.
Donor: William H. Donner‡.
Foundation type: Independent foundation.
Financial data (yr. ended 10/31/05): Assets,
$128,803,437 (M); expenditures, $7,238,108;
qualifying distributions, $5,614,779; giving
activities include $4,996,013 for 166 grants (high:
$233,901; low: $2,000; average: $5,000–
$501,000).
Purpose and activities: Giving primarily for
international development and relief services,
education, arts and culture, and public affairs.
Fields of interest: Arts; Elementary/secondary
education; Education; Animals/wildlife; Human
services; International development; International
relief; International affairs; Philanthropy/
voluntarism; Public affairs.
Type of support: General/operating support;
Program development.
Limitations: Applications not accepted. Giving on a
national basis.
Application information: Only applications invited by
the foundation will be considered.
 Board meeting date(s): Sept.
Officers and Trustees:* Robert D. Spencer,* Pres.;
Stephanie K. Hanson,* V.P.; Anita Winsor
Edwards,* Secy.; Daniel W. Donner,* Treas.;
Alexander B. Donner; Joseph W. Donner III; Robert
Donner, Jr.; Deborah Donner*; Timothy E. Donner;
Michael Hunter Spencer; William M. Spencer III;

Cristina Winsor; Hon. Curtin Winsor, Jr.; Curtin
Winsor III; Monica Winsor; Rebecca Winsor.
Number of staff: 1 full-time professional; 3 part-time
professional; 1 full-time support; 1 part-time
support.
EIN: 231611346

5874
Donovan Foundation ✧
c/o Michael Donovan
1040 5th Ave., Ste. 2A
New York, NY   10028-0137

Established in 1999 in NY.
Donor: Michael D.S. Donovan.
Foundation type: Independent foundation.
Financial data (yr. ended 12/31/04): Assets,
$3,041,126 (M); gifts received, $900,000;
expenditures, $596,866; qualifying distributions,
$595,036; giving activities include $576,276 for 15
grants (high: $200,000; low: $10,000).
Purpose and activities: Giving primarily for higher
education.
Fields of interest: Higher education; Education;
Federated giving programs.
Limitations: Applications not accepted. Giving
primarily in NY and VA; some funding also in
Washington, DC. No grants to individuals.
Application information: Contributes only to
pre-selected organizations. Unsolicited requests for
funds not accepted.
Trustees: Stephen Briganti; Linda Ramsey Donovan;
Michael D.S. Donovan.
Number of staff: 1 part-time professional.
EIN: 137205869
Selected grants: The following grants were reported
in 2004.
$200,000 to Lynchburg College, Lynchburg, VA.
$45,000 to Jefferson Area Board for Aging,
 Charlottesville, VA.
$40,000 to Yale University, New Haven, CT.
$15,000 to Nelson County Community Development
 Foundation, Lovingston, VA.
$15,000 to PAX, New York, NY.
$10,000 to Central Park Conservancy, New York,
 NY.
$10,000 to Doe Fund, New York, NY.
$10,000 to Statue of Liberty-Ellis Island Foundation,
 New York, NY.

5875
Doran Family Charitable Trust ✧
c/o U.S. Trust, Tax Dept.
114 W. 47th St.
New York, NY   10036

Established in 1986 in MA.
Donor: Robert W. Doran.
Foundation type: Independent foundation.
Financial data (yr. ended 12/31/05): Assets,
$5,112,840 (M); gifts received, $273,324;
expenditures, $1,036,533; qualifying distributions,
$984,897; giving activities include $973,567 for
2 employee matching gifts.
Purpose and activities: Giving primarily for
education, the environment, the arts, and health
and human services.
Fields of interest: Museums; Arts; Elementary/
secondary education; Higher education; Education;

Botanical gardens; Environment; Hospitals
(general); Human services.
Limitations: Applications not accepted. Giving
primarily in MA. No grants to individuals.
Application information: Contributes only to
pre-selected organizations.
Trustees: Evelyn H. Doran; Robert W. Doran.
EIN: 226424850

5876
The Double H Foundation, Inc. ✧
c/o Muchnick, Golieb & Golieb
200 Park Ave. S., Ste. 1700
New York, NY   10003

Established in 2001 in NY.
Donor: Harvey M. Krueger.
Foundation type: Independent foundation.
Financial data (yr. ended 12/31/05): Assets,
$1,235,559 (M); gifts received, $2,345,684;
expenditures, $1,753,161; qualifying distributions,
$1,737,150; giving activities include $1,736,700
for 40 grants (high: $200,000; low: $5,000;
average: $10,000–$100,000).
Fields of interest: Museums; Higher education;
Hospitals (general); Human services; Jewish
agencies & temples.
Limitations: Applications not accepted. No grants to
individuals.
Application information: Contributes only to
pre-selected organizations.
Officers and Directors:* Harvey M. Krueger,* Pres.;
John A. Golieb,* Secy.-Treas.; Constance A.
Krueger.
EIN: 134134703

5877
Dove Givings Foundation ✧
222 Purchase St.
P.O. Box 316
Rye, NY   10580   (914) 460-4040
Contact: Rich Cayne

Established in 1995 in NY.
Donor: Kevin J. Heneghan.
Foundation type: Independent foundation.
Financial data (yr. ended 12/31/04): Assets,
$3,331,005 (M); gifts received, $251,000;
expenditures, $790,462; qualifying distributions,
$790,462; giving activities include $779,253 for
grants.
Purpose and activities: Giving primarily for needy
children and families, and to Christian causes.
Fields of interest: Higher education, university; Food
services; Family services, single parents; Christian
agencies & churches.
Type of support: Grants to individuals.
Limitations: Applications not accepted.
Application information: Unsolicited requests for
funds not accepted.
Officers: John A. Heneghan, Pres.; Bartly Heneghan,
V.P.; Kevin J. Heneghan, Secy.-Treas.
EIN: 133795957
Selected grants: The following grants were reported
in 2004.
$50,000 to Habitat for Humanity International.
$25,000 to Anthony House, Zellwood, FL.
$25,000 to Gordon College, Wenham, MA.
$10,000 to Apostolic Connections, New Canaan,
 CT.
$5,000 to New York University, New York, NY.

$5,000 to Samaritan Health and Living Center, Elkhart, IN.

$2,500 to Iona College, New Rochelle, NY.

$1,000 to Capital City Rescue Mission, Albany, NY.

$1,000 to Family Service.

$1,000 to Mission to the World, Lawrenceville, GA.

5878
Dove Givings Foundation II ✧
222 Purchase St.
P.O. Box 316
Rye, NY   10580   (914) 460-4040
Contact: Rich Cayne, Asst. Secy.-Treas.

Established in 2001 in NY.
Donors: Kevin Heneghan; EH Limited Partnership.
Foundation type: Operating foundation.
Financial data (yr. ended 12/31/03): Assets, $2,430,390 (M); gifts received, $1,330,078; expenditures, $596,347; qualifying distributions, $593,482; giving activities include $593,405 for 75 grants (high: $155,000; low: $200).
Purpose and activities: Giving primarily to Christian organizations and churches, as well as for education and human services.
Fields of interest: Education; Housing/shelter, development; Human services; Children/youth, services; Family services; Christian agencies & churches.
Limitations: Applications not accepted. Giving primarily in NY. No grants to individuals.
Application information: Contributes only to pre-selected organizations.
Officers: Kevin J. Heneghan, Pres.; Eileen Heneghan, V.P.
EIN: 134188889
Selected grants: The following grants were reported in 2004.
$202,200 to Young Life.
$160,000 to World Vision, Federal Way, WA.
$110,000 to Focus on the Family, Colorado Springs, CO.
$81,000 to Habitat for Humanity International.
$50,000 to Institute for Student Achievement, Lake Success, NY.
$30,000 to Global Action, Colorado Springs, CO.
$28,500 to Making Headway, Eureka, CA.
$10,000 to Apostolic Connections, New Canaan, CT.
$5,000 to Compassion International, Colorado Springs, CO.
$5,000 to World Help, Forest, VA.

5879
Dow Jones Foundation
c/o U.S. Trust Corp.
114 W. 47th St.
New York, NY   10036
Contact: Christine O'Donnell, Asst. V.P.
FAX: (212) 852-3377; Application address: P.O. Box 300, Princeton, NJ 08543, tel.: (609) 520-5146

Established in 1954 in NY.
Donor: Dow Jones & Co., Inc.
Foundation type: Company-sponsored foundation.
Financial data (yr. ended 12/31/03): Assets, $1,391,391 (M); gifts received, $902,150; expenditures, $897,444; qualifying distributions, $897,144; giving activities include $893,810 for 80 grants (high: $325,000; low: $200).

Purpose and activities: The foundation supports organizations involved with journalism and higher education.
Fields of interest: Media, journalism/publishing; Higher education; Federated giving programs.
Type of support: General/operating support; Continuing support; Annual campaigns; Internship funds; Scholarship funds.
Limitations: Applications not accepted. Giving primarily in areas of company operations. No grants to individuals, or for medical or scientific research.
Application information: Contributes only to pre-selected organizations.
  Board meeting date(s): Usually in the last quarter
Advisory Committee: Nicole Bourgois; Peter R. Kann; Jane MacElree; Thomas McGuirl; James H. Ottaway, Jr.; Elizabeth Steele.
Trustee: U.S. Trust Corp.
EIN: 136070158
Selected grants: The following grants were reported in 2003.
$325,000 to Dow Jones Newspaper Fund, Princeton, NJ.
$270,410 to National Merit Scholarship Corporation, Evanston, IL.
$25,000 to Childrens Home Society of New Jersey, Trenton, NJ.
$20,000 to United Way of Pioneer Valley, Springfield, MA.
$17,100 to Institute of International Education, New York, NY.
$10,000 to Arthur F. Burns Fellowship Program, Reston, VA.
$10,000 to Committee to Protect Journalists, New York, NY.
$10,000 to Online News Association, New York, NY.
$6,500 to National Association of Black Journalists, Adelphi, MD.
$5,000 to Freedom House, DC.

5880
William C. Dowling Jr. Foundation ✧ ☆
c/o Belair & Evans
61 Broadway
New York, NY   10006   (212) 344-3900
Contact: John T. Evans, Tr.

Established in 2003 in NY.
Foundation type: Independent foundation.
Financial data (yr. ended 12/31/05): Assets, $22,299,617 (M); gifts received, $50,000; expenditures, $1,718,544; qualifying distributions, $1,066,907; giving activities include $1,066,907 for grants.
Fields of interest: Higher education; Medical research; Human services; Roman Catholic agencies & churches.
Limitations: Giving in the U.S., primarily in Baltimore, MD, New York, NY, and Hartford, WI.
Application information:
  Initial approach: Letter
  Deadline(s): None
Trustees: John T. Evans; Marie Evans.
EIN: 470933520

5881
Robert N. & Nancy A. Downey Foundation ✧
c/o BCRS Assocs., LLC
100 Wall St., 11th Fl.
New York, NY   10005

Established in 1982 in NY.
Donor: Robert N. Downey.
Foundation type: Independent foundation.
Financial data (yr. ended 1/31/06): Assets, $119,795 (M); gifts received, $315,000; expenditures, $339,215; qualifying distributions, $336,665; giving activities include $334,906 for 86 grants (high: $105,000; low: $100).
Purpose and activities: Giving primarily to private higher, secondary, and elementary educational institutions; support also for health associations.
Fields of interest: Arts; Elementary/secondary education; Higher education; Hospitals (general); Health organizations, association; Human services.
Limitations: Applications not accepted. Giving primarily in New York, NY; funding also in CT, Hanover, NH, and VT. No grants to individuals; no loans or program-related investments.
Application information: Contributes only to pre-selected organizations.
Trustees: Nancy A. Downey; Robert N. Downey.
EIN: 133103213
Selected grants: The following grants were reported in 2005.
$125,000 to Dartmouth College, Hanover, NH. For general support.
$46,850 to Lenox Hill Hospital, New York, NY. For general support.
$20,000 to Taft School, Watertown, CT. For general support.
$10,000 to Brick Church School, New York, NY. For general support.
$10,000 to Keystone Center, Keystone, CO. For general support.
$8,800 to American Cancer Society, New York, NY. For general support.
$8,790 to Reach the World Company, New York, NY. For general support.
$8,321 to Lincoln Center Theater, New York, NY. For general support.
$8,150 to International Tennis Hall of Fame, New York, NY. For general support.
$6,000 to Hole in the Wall Gang Fund, New Haven, CT. For general support.

5882
Doreen Downs Miller Foundation, Inc. ✧ ☆
c/o Doreen D. Miller
105 Rockaway Ave.
Garden City, NY   11530

Foundation type: Independent foundation.
Financial data (yr. ended 6/30/05): Assets, $1,252,634 (M); gifts received, $1,530,900; expenditures, $671,478; qualifying distributions, $632,954; giving activities include $619,050 for 24 grants (high: $250,000; low: $100).
Fields of interest: Media/communications; Higher education.
Limitations: Applications not accepted. Giving primarily in New York, NY. No grants to individuals.
Application information: Unsolicited requests for funds not accepted.
Officer and Director:* Doreen D. Miller,* Pres. and Treas.
EIN: 743116739

5883
Dramatists Guild Fund, Inc. ☆
1501 Broadway
New York, NY 10036 (212) 391-8384
Contact: Susan Drury
FAX: (212) 944-0420;
E-mail: sdrury@dramaguild.com; URL: http://
www.dramaguild.com

Established in 1962 in NY.
Donors: Charlotte Kesselring†; Sidney S. Kingsley
Fund; James Kirkwood†; Lowe Foundation;
Lindsay†; Flora Roberts Foundation.
Foundation type: Independent foundation.
Financial data (yr. ended 12/31/05): Assets,
$3,335,568 (M); gifts received, $309,564;
expenditures, $460,525; qualifying distributions,
$320,350; giving activities include $320,350 for
grants.
Purpose and activities: Support for theater
companies and workshops producing new works;
also provides loans-in-aid to support playwrights
who have had their work produced or published.
Fields of interest: Performing arts, theater;
Economically disadvantaged.
Type of support: General/operating support;
Emergency funds.
Limitations: Giving on a national basis.
Application information: Application form required.
  Initial approach: Letter or telephone
  Copies of proposal: 1
  Deadline(s): None for individual loans; Oct. 31 for
    theater grants
  Board meeting date(s): Apr.
  Final notification: 2 weeks for individual loans
Officers and Directors:* Gretchen Cryer, Pres.;
Carol Hall,* V.P.; Tina Howe,* Secy.; Paula Wilson,*
Treas.; Lee Adams; Susan Birkeuhead; Kirsten
Childs; Betty Comden; Sheldon Harnick; Shirley
Lauro; Herbert Mitgang; Peter Ratray.
Number of staff: 1 full-time professional.
EIN: 136144932
Selected grants: The following grants were reported
in 2004.
$7,500 to Vineyard Theater and Workshop Center,
  New York, NY.
$5,000 to Culture Project, New York, NY.
$5,000 to Magic Theater, San Francisco, CA.
$5,000 to New Theater, Boston, MA.
$5,000 to New York Shakespeare Festival, New
  York, NY.
$5,000 to New York Theater Workshop, New York,
  NY.
$5,000 to Prospect Theater Company, New York,
  NY.
$5,000 to Signature Theater Company, New York,
  NY.
$5,000 to Tectonic Theater Project, New York, NY.
$2,500 to Dixon Place, New York, NY.

5884
The Dreitzer Foundation, Inc. ◇
60 E. 42nd St., No. 38
New York, NY 10165 (212) 557-7700
Contact: Alan D. Seget, Secy.

Established in 1958 in NY.
Donors: Albert J. Dreitzer†; Mildred H. Dreitzer†.
Foundation type: Independent foundation.
Financial data (yr. ended 12/31/05): Assets,
$10,130,276 (M); expenditures, $738,442;
qualifying distributions, $640,000; giving activities

include $640,000 for 27 grants (high: $65,000;
low: $10,000).
Purpose and activities: Support for youth, social
services, social action, the arts, health, the
homeless, and nonsectarian organizations.
Fields of interest: Arts; Health care; Health
organizations, association; Human services;
Children/youth, services; Homeless, human
services; Homeless.
Type of support: General/operating support.
Limitations: Giving primarily in New York, NY.
Publications: Application guidelines.
Application information: Application form not
required.
  Initial approach: Letter or fax requesting
    guidelines; telephone requests will not be
    accepted
  Copies of proposal: 1
  Deadline(s): July 1
  Board meeting date(s): July 31
  Final notification: Sept. 30
Officers: Judith Wallach, Pres.; Steven Halpern,
V.P.; Amy Laff, V.P.; Sylvan Wallach, V.P.; Alan D.
Seget, Secy.
EIN: 136162509
Selected grants: The following grants were reported
in 2005.
$65,000 to Equality Now, New York, NY.
$40,000 to Partnership for the Homeless, New
  York, NY.
$20,000 to Feminist Majority Foundation, Arlington,
  VA.
$15,000 to Fountain House, New York, NY.
$15,000 to Lawyers Alliance for New York, New
  York, NY.
$10,000 to Calvary Hospital, Bronx, NY.
$10,000 to Lawyers for Children, New York, NY.
$10,000 to Raynault Foundation, Englewood, NJ.

5885
Peggy and Millard Drexler Foundation ◇
770 Broadway, 12th Fl.
New York, NY 10003-9512

Established in 1998 in CA.
Donors: Millard S. Drexler; Peggy Drexler.
Foundation type: Independent foundation.
Financial data (yr. ended 12/31/05): Assets,
$4,931,998 (M); expenditures, $606,038;
qualifying distributions, $572,292; giving activities
include $572,292 for 37 grants (high: $210,000;
low: $18).
Purpose and activities: Giving primarily for
education, youth-related causes, human services,
and environmental preservation.
Fields of interest: Child development, education;
Education; Environment, natural resources;
Hospitals (general); Health organizations,
association; Human services; Jewish federated
giving programs; Jewish agencies & temples.
Limitations: Applications not accepted. Giving
primarily in CA, NY, and MA. No grants to individuals.
Application information: Contributes only to
pre-selected organizations.
Officers: Millard S. Drexler, Chair. and Treas.; Peggy
F. Drexler, Pres.; Hume Steyer, Secy.
EIN: 522106490

5886
**The Camille and Henry Dreyfus
  Foundation, Inc.** ▼
555 Madison Ave., 20th Fl.
New York, NY 10022-3301 (212) 753-1760
Contact: Mark J. Cardillo Ph.D., Exec. Dir.
E-mail: admin@dreyfus.org; URL: http://
www.dreyfus.org

Incorporated in 1946 in NY.
Donor: Camille Dreyfus†.
Foundation type: Independent foundation.
Financial data (yr. ended 12/31/04): Assets,
$119,790,088 (M); expenditures, $6,987,634;
qualifying distributions, $6,120,447; giving
activities include $1,359,035 for 41 grants (high:
$175,000; low: $5,500; average: $10,500–
$35,000), and $3,636,000 for grants to individuals.
Purpose and activities: To advance the sciences of
chemistry, biochemistry, chemical engineering, and
related sciences as a means of improving human
relations and circumstances. The foundation
assists organizations which afford facilities for the
production, collection, or dissemination of scientific
information; support mainly for postsecondary
academic institutions through sponsorship of
Dreyfus New Faculty in Chemistry Program, the
Dreyfus Teacher-Scholar Awards Programs, the
Dreyfus Special Grant Program in the Chemical
Sciences, the Dreyfus Faculty Start-Up Grant
Program for Undergraduate Institutions, and the
Dreyfus Postdoctoral Program in Environmental
Chemistry.
Fields of interest: Engineering school/education;
Chemistry; Science.
Type of support: Equipment; Program development;
Seed money; Fellowships; Research.
Limitations: Giving only on a national basis. No
grants to individuals who are not sponsored or
nominated by a nonprofit or educational institution,
or for specific research projects, emergency funds,
deficit financing, land acquisition, endowments,
capital construction, or renovation; no loans.
Application information: Candidates for awards
must be nominated by applying academic
institution; individual applications not accepted;
nomination forms required for all programs.
Application form required.
  Initial approach: Preliminary letter for Special
    Grant Program in the Chemical Sciences
  Copies of proposal: 5
  Deadline(s): Current information available on
    foundation's Web site; Nov. 15th for complete
    proposals
  Board meeting date(s): Jan., Apr., July, and Oct.
  Final notification: 4 to 5 months
Officers and Directors:* Dorothy Dinsmoor,* Pres.;
John R.H. Blum,* V.P.; Edward A. Reilly,* Secy.;
Henry C. Walter, Treas.; Mark J. Cardillo, Ph.D.,
Exec. Dir.; John I. Brauman; Marye Anne Fox, Ph.D.;
Joshua Lederberg, Ph.D.; H. Marshall Schwarz;
Harry H. Wasserman, Ph.D.
Number of staff: 2 full-time professional; 1 full-time
support.
EIN: 135570117
Selected grants: The following grants were reported
in 2004.
$350,000 to Massachusetts Institute of
  Technology, Cambridge, MA. 2 grants: $175,000
  each to Department of Chemistry (For Special
  Grant Program in the Chemical Sciences).
$128,789 to Princeton University, Department of
  Chemistry, Princeton, NJ. For Special Grant
  Program in the Chemical Sciences.

$62,500 to University of California, Department of Chemical Engineering, Berkeley, CA. For Special Grant Program in the Chemical Sciences.

$60,000 to Vassar College, Department of Chemistry, Poughkeepsie, NY. For Special Grant Program in the Chemical Sciences.

$58,500 to University of Illinois at Urbana-Champaign, Department of Chemistry, Urbana, IL. For Special Grant Program in the Chemical Sciences.

$56,776 to Earth and Sky, Austin, TX. For Special Grant Program in the Chemical Sciences.

$54,000 to American Chemical Society, DC. For Special Grant Program in the Chemical Sciences.

$50,000 to American Friends of the Royal Institution, DC. For Special Grant Program in the Chemical Sciences.

$13,246 to North Carolina State University, Department of Chemical Engineering, Raleigh, NC. For Special Grant Program in the Chemical Sciences, as part of Wake Educational Partnership.

5887
Jean and Louis Dreyfus Foundation, Inc. ✧
420 Lexington Ave., Ste. 626
New York, NY 10170 (212) 599-1931
Contact: Ms. Edmee de M. Firth, Exec. Dir.
FAX: (212) 599-2956;
E-mail: jldreyfusfdtn@hotmail.com; URL: http://foundationcenter.org/grantmaker/dreyfus/

Incorporated about 1979 in NY.
Donor: Louis Dreyfus†.
Foundation type: Independent foundation.
Financial data (yr. ended 12/31/04): Assets, $20,527,080 (M); expenditures, $1,547,038; qualifying distributions, $1,445,684; giving activities include $1,322,500 for 91 grants (high: $20,000; low: $5,000).
Purpose and activities: Grants primarily to established institutions of the arts; some support also for health and social services, including youth agencies, women, and the elderly, and education, including literacy.
Fields of interest: Arts; Adult education—literacy, basic skills & GED; Education, reading; Education; Health care; Health organizations, association; Employment, training; Housing/shelter, homeless; Human services; Children/youth, services; Aging, centers/services; Women, centers/services; Aging, Women.
Type of support: General/operating support; Capital campaigns; Program development; Seed money; Matching/challenge support.
Limitations: Giving limited within the five boroughs of New York, NY. No grants to individuals.
Publications: Application guidelines; Annual report; Grants list.
Application information: New letters of inquiry will not be accepted until 2007. The foundation uses its own application form provided at its discretion; NYRAG Common Application Form is not accepted. Letters of inquiry sent after deadline will be held until next grant cycle. See foundation Web site for application guidelines and procedures. Application form required.
 Initial approach: Letter of inquiry (2 pages)
 Copies of proposal: 1
 Deadline(s): Between Dec. and Jan. Feb. 1 is final deadline
 Board meeting date(s): June and Dec.
 Final notification: 1 month

Officers and Directors:* Nicholas L.D. Firth,* Pres.; Katherine V. Firth,* V.P.; Thomas J. Hubbard,* Secy.; Thomas J. Sweeney,* Treas.; Edmee de M. Firth,* Exec. Dir.
Number of staff: 1 part-time professional; 1 full-time support.
EIN: 132947180

5888
The Max and Victoria Dreyfus Foundation, Inc.
50 Main St., Ste. 1000
White Plains, NY 10606 (914) 682-2008
Contact: Lucy Gioia, Office Admin.

Incorporated in 1965 in NY.
Donors: Victoria Dreyfus†; Max Dreyfus†.
Foundation type: Independent foundation.
Financial data (yr. ended 12/31/04): Assets, $67,729,433 (M); expenditures, $4,112,766; qualifying distributions, $3,536,052; giving activities include $2,974,315 for 383 grants (high: $45,000; low: $1,000; average: $5,000–$20,000).
Purpose and activities: Support for museums, cultural, performing, and visual arts programs, schools, hospitals, educational and skills training projects, and programs for youth, seniors, and people who are handicapped.
Fields of interest: Performing arts; Arts; Education; Hospitals (general); Health care; Medical research, institute; Human services.
Limitations: Giving on a national basis. No support for foreign charitable organizations. No grants to individuals.
Publications: Application guidelines.
Application information: Application guidelines available from the foundation. Application form required.
 Initial approach: Letter, not exceeding 3 pages
 Copies of proposal: 1
 Deadline(s): Post marked by Mar. 10, July 10, and Nov. 10
 Board meeting date(s): Mar., June, and Oct.
 Final notification: Notification made by mail, approximately 8 weeks after respective deadlines dates
Officers and Directors:* Winifred Riggs Portenoy,* Chair.; Mary P. Surrey,* Pres.; Norman S. Portenoy,* Sr. V.P.; Elizabeth Brown,* V.P.; Nancy E. Oddo,* V.P.; Sara R. Surrey,* Secy.-Treas.
Number of staff: 1 full-time support; 2 part-time support.
EIN: 131687573
Selected grants: The following grants were reported in 2004.
$45,000 to For Love of Children (FLOC), DC.
$42,500 to Our House, Ellicott City, MD.
$30,000 to Groundwork, Brooklyn, NY.
$20,000 to Childrens Museum of San Diego/Museo de los Ninos, San Diego, CA. For Museum Without Walls Outreach Program.
$20,000 to Loyola University Medical Center, Maywood, IL. For Pediatric Mobile Health Unit.
$15,000 to Chatham Historical Society, Chatham, MA. For Atwood House Museum Campaign.
$10,000 to Alzheimers Disease Resource Agency of Alaska, Anchorage, AK. For education programs.
$10,000 to Bonner General Hospital, Sandpoint, ID. For general support.
$10,000 to Hospice of the Foothills Foundation, Seneca, SC.
$2,000 to Ballet Concerto, Fort Worth, TX. For Summer Dance Concert.

5889
Druckenmiller Foundation ✧ ☆
c/o Duquesne Capital Mgmt.
40 W. 57th St., 25th Fl.
New York, NY 10019

Established in 1993 in NY.
Donor: Stanley F. Druckenmiller.
Foundation type: Independent foundation.
Financial data (yr. ended 11/30/05): Assets, $5,076,611 (M); gifts received, $1,500; expenditures, $374,290; qualifying distributions, $370,000; giving activities include $370,000 for grants to individuals.
Purpose and activities: Giving primarily for universities and international human rights.
Fields of interest: Higher education, university; Scholarships/financial aid.
Type of support: Scholarships—to individuals.
Limitations: Giving primarily in NY and PA.
Application information: Scholarship applicant must supply transcript and letters of recommendation. Application form required.
 Deadline(s): July 1
Trustees: Fiona Druckenmiller; Stanley F. Druckenmiller.
EIN: 133735187

5890
The Drukier Foundation, Inc. ✧ ☆
60 E. 54th St.
New York, NY 10022 (212) 753-1066
Contact: Ira Drukier, Pres.

Established in 1998 in NY.
Donors: Charles Drukier†; Ira Drukier.
Foundation type: Independent foundation.
Financial data (yr. ended 12/31/04): Assets, $856,042 (M); gifts received, $356,000; expenditures, $535,894; qualifying distributions, $532,650; giving activities include $532,650 for 19 grants (high: $175,000; low: $100).
Purpose and activities: Giving primarily to Jewish organizations and temples; funding also for higher education, and human services.
Fields of interest: Museums (art); Higher education; Human services; Jewish federated giving programs; Jewish agencies & temples.
Limitations: Giving primarily in NY.
Application information:
 Initial approach: Letter
 Deadline(s): None
Officer: Ira Drukier, Pres.
Directors: Gale Drukier; Jennifer Drukier.
EIN: 134018561
Selected grants: The following grants were reported in 2004.
$175,000 to American Society for Yad Vashem, New York, NY.
$75,000 to Cornell University, Ithaca, NY.
$7,000 to Jewish Partisan Educational Foundation, San Francisco, CA.
$5,000 to Museum of Jewish Heritage, New York, NY.
$5,000 to Museum of Modern Art, New York, NY.
$4,500 to Parrish Art Museum, Southampton, NY.
$2,500 to Metropolitan Museum of Art, New York, NY.
$250 to Institute for Educational Achievement, New Milford, NJ.

5891
G. & E. Dubin Family Foundation ✧
c/o BCRS Group/Marcum Kleigman LLP
100 Wall St., 11th Fl.
New York, NY 10005

Foundation type: Independent foundation.
Financial data (yr. ended 12/31/05): Assets,
$9,653,671 (M); gifts received, $50,850;
expenditures, $8,225,906; qualifying distributions,
$8,066,945; giving activities include $8,064,345
for 40 grants (high: $3,000,000; low: $500;
average: $10,000–$200,000).
Fields of interest: Education; Environment; Human
services; Jewish agencies & temples.
Limitations: Applications not accepted. Giving
primarily in NY. No grants to individuals, or for
scholarships; no loans.
Application information: Unsolicited requests for
funds not accepted.
Trustees: Eva Andersson Dubin; Glenn R. Dubin.
EIN: 137265141
Selected grants: The following grants were reported
in 2004.
$420,000 to Robin Hood Foundation, New York, NY.
    2 grants: $320,000, $100,000
$200,000 to Stony Brook Foundation, Stony Brook,
    NY.
$10,000 to GRADS Foundation, Jamaica, NY.
$5,000 to Spence School, New York, NY.

5892
Doris Duke Charitable Foundation ▼
650 5th Ave., 19th Fl.
New York, NY 10019 (212) 974-7000
Contact: Betsy Fader, Dir., Strategy and Planning
FAX: (212) 974-7590; *Additional tel.:* (212)
974-7100; *URL:* http://www.ddcf.org

Established in 1996 in NY.
Donor: Doris Duke†.
Foundation type: Independent foundation.
Financial data (yr. ended 12/31/05): Assets,
$1,920,145,122 (M); expenditures, $98,191,911;
qualifying distributions, $62,691,247; giving
activities include $62,691,247 for grants.
Purpose and activities: The mission of the
foundation is to improve the quality of people's lives
through grants supporting the performing arts,
wildlife conservation, medical research and the
prevention of child maltreatment. In addition to its
grantmaking activities, the foundation will support
three affiliated operating foundations: Duke Farms
Foundation, the Doris Duke Foundation for Islamic
Art, and the Newport Restoration Foundation.
Fields of interest: Performing arts; Environment,
natural resources; Medical research, institute;
Crime/violence prevention, child abuse.
Type of support: Employee matching gifts.
Limitations: Giving on a national basis. No support
for water or aquatic issues, air or climate change
issues, toxic issues, litigation, the visual arts,
museums or galleries, or arts programs for
rehabilitative or therapeutic purposes. No grants to
individuals (except through special foundation
programs), or for conferences or publications.
Application information: The foundation staff
responds to all letters of inquiry, however, it should
be noted that very few grants result from unsolicited
letters of inquiry. Do not send binders, books, CDs,
videotapes, or audiotapes.
    Initial approach: Letter of inquiry (2 pages)
    Final notification: 2 months for letter of inquiry

Officers and Trustees: * Nannerl O. Keohane,*
Chair.; John J. Mack,* Vice-Chair.; Joan E. Spero,*
Pres.; Eileen Oberlander, Cont. and Dir., Finance;
Rita Berkowitz, Genl. Counsel; William Barnet III;
Marion Oates Charles; Harry B. Demopoulos, M.D.;
Anthony S. Fauci, M.D.; James F. Gill; Anne Hawley;
John H.T. Wilson.
EIN: 137043679
Selected grants: The following grants were reported
in 2005.
$7,650,000 to Nonprofit Finance Fund, New York,
    NY. To launch and administer Mid-Sized
    Presenting Organizations Initiative, providing
    re-grants and customized technical assistance to
    mid-sized presenters selected to participate in
    initiative through national competition, payable
    over 5.25 years.
$3,999,642 to Nature Conservancy, Arlington, VA.
    For Conservation Finance Initiative, to research
    and identify potential sources of public funding
    for implementation of strategies identified in
    state Comprehensive Wildlife Conservation
    Strategies, payable over 4 years.
$3,034,885 to CDC Foundation, Division of
    Violence Prevention, Atlanta, GA. For re-granting
    program to develop uses of technology in existing
    child abuse prevention programs, payable over
    4.75 years.
$2,250,000 to Johns Hopkins University, Baltimore,
    MD. For Clinical Interfaces Award for research
    project, Development of the First Test for
    Common Cancer Risk in the General Population,
    payable over 5 years.
$1,248,260 to Michigan Childrens Trust Fund,
    Lansing, MI. For Early Childhood Initiative of
    National Alliance of Children's Trust and
    Prevention Funds, to implement alliance's new
    Early Childhood Initiative by holding regional
    training institutes to educate trust fund staff on
    integrating prevention techniques and strategies
    into early education and child care centers, and
    administering matching grants competition to
    award seed funding to trust funds for
    programming that promotes child abuse
    prevention in early education settings, payable
    over 3 years.
$904,248 to National Wildlife Federation, Reston,
    VA. To promote implementation of wildlife action
    plans in Georgia, Massachusetts, Montana,
    North Carolina, and Wisconsin by working with
    affiliates in each state to reinvigorate
    state-based Teaming With Wildlife Coalitions
    around shared agenda for implementation of
    action plans; identify best opportunities within
    action plans for proactive, incentive-based
    habitat conservation; implement high-priority
    conservation actions from action plans; and
    disseminate lessons learned, best practices and
    success stories to other states, payable over 3
    years.
$500,000 to Jazz at Lincoln Center, New York, NY.
    For Higher Ground Hurricane Relief Fund,
    assisting New Orleans-based musicians,
    nonprofit music enterprises, and other
    performing artists and performing arts
    organizations affected by Hurricane Katrina
    through regranting for immediate concerns and
    long-term goals.
$405,000 to Brigham and Womens Hospital,
    Boston, MA. For Clinical Scientist Development
    Award for research, Black Women's Health Study
    and Cardiovascular Risk, payable over 3 years.
$200,000 to Northwestern University, Evanston, IL.
    For research, Directly Observed,

Community-based Treatment in Nigeria, to
increase antiretroviral therapy adherence in HIV
patients, payable over 2 years.
$50,000 to American Medical Informatics
    Association, Bethesda, MD. For planning phase
    of Global Trial Bank, public register of
    computable peer-reviewed results from clinical
    trials conducted worldwide.

5893
The Dun & Bradstreet Corporation
Foundation ✧
512 7th Ave.
New York, NY 10018 (973) 921-6080
Contact: Yvette Rudich, Dir.
FAX: (866) 810-7132; *E-mail:* rudichy@dnb.com;
Application address: 103 JFK Pkwy., Short Hills, NJ
07078

Incorporated in 1953 in DE.
Donor: The Dun & Bradstreet Corp.
Foundation type: Company-sponsored foundation.
Financial data (yr. ended 12/31/04): Assets,
$553,315 (M); gifts received, $449,066;
expenditures, $336,619; qualifying distributions,
$329,819; giving activities include $217,930 for
grants, and $111,889 for employee matching gifts.
Purpose and activities: The foundation supports
organizations involved with disadvantaged youth.
Special emphasis is directed toward organizations
with which D&B employees are involved.
Fields of interest: Youth development.
Type of support: General/operating support;
Continuing support; Annual campaigns; Employee
matching gifts.
Limitations: Giving on a national basis. No support
for religious organizations, political organizations, or
K-12 school organizations. No grants to individuals,
or for building or endowments or research; no loans.
Application information: Application form not
required.
    Initial approach: Proposal
    Deadline(s): None
    Board meeting date(s): Semiannually
    Final notification: Within 2 weeks
Officers and Trustee: * David J. Lewinter,* Pres.;
David J. Slobodein, Secy.
Number of staff: 2
EIN: 136148188

5894
Clarence and Anne Dillon Dunwalke
Trust ✧
1330 Ave. of the Americas, 27th Fl.
New York, NY 10019

Trust established in 1969 in NY.
Donor: Clarence Dillon†.
Foundation type: Independent foundation.
Financial data (yr. ended 6/30/05): Assets,
$36,069,299 (M); expenditures, $1,779,090;
qualifying distributions, $1,469,418; giving
activities include $1,440,177 for 68 grants (high:
$537,177; low: $1,000).
Purpose and activities: Emphasis on hospitals,
education, public affairs, the arts, and community
funds. Grants primarily to present beneficiary
organizations and for special proposals developed
by the trustees.
Fields of interest: Arts; Higher education;
Education; Environment, natural resources;

Hospitals (general); Medical research, institute; Boys & girls clubs; Children/youth, services; Federated giving programs; Public policy, research.
Type of support: General/operating support; Continuing support; Annual campaigns; Capital campaigns; Building/renovation; Endowments; Fellowships; Research.
Limitations: Applications not accepted. Giving primarily in FL, ME, NJ and NY. No grants to individuals; no loans.
Application information: Contributes only to pre-selected organizations.
Board meeting date(s): Nov. and as required
Officers and Trustees: Phyllis Dillon Collins,* Chair.; Eileen Kane, Secy.; James J. Ruddy,* Treas.; Alexandra F. Allen; Andrew D. Allen; Christine Allen; Christopher D. Allen; Nicholas E. Allen; Philip D. Allen; Sophie Bryan; Theodore Caplow, Jr.; Douglas Collins; Frances Collins; Mark M. Collins, Jr.; Joan M. Frost; Robert Luxembourg; Crosby R. Smith; Katherine Stillman; Martin C. Zetterberg.
Number of staff: 1 part-time professional.
EIN: 237043773
Selected grants: The following grants were reported in 2004.
$80,000 to Middlebury College, Middlebury, VT. For Dillon Dunwalke Overseas Internships Program.
$25,000 to Boys and Girls Club of Martin County, Hobe Sound, FL. For capital campaign.
$10,000 to Groton School, Groton, MA. For capital campaign.
$10,000 to Jemicy School, Owings Mills, MD. For general support.
$5,000 to Boys and Girls Clubs of Newark, Newark, NJ. For general support.
$5,000 to University of Denver, Denver, CO. For capital campaign.
$2,500 to New Jersey Ballet Company, Livingston, NJ. For annual support.
$1,000 to City Harvest, New York, NY. For general support.
$1,000 to Phillips Academy, Andover, MA. For general support.
$1,000 to Robin Hood Foundation, New York, NY. For general support.

5895
The Durst Family Foundation ◇
1155 Ave. of the Americas
New York, NY 10036

Established in 2000 in NY.
Foundation type: Independent foundation.
Financial data (yr. ended 12/31/05): Assets, $12,240,648 (M); expenditures, $646,884; qualifying distributions, $640,433; giving activities include $555,000 for 28 grants (high: $25,000; low: $10,000).
Fields of interest: Education; Agriculture/food; Human services.
Limitations: Applications not accepted. Giving primarily in New York, NY. No grants to individuals.
Application information: Contributes only to pre-selected organizations.
Officers and Directors: Wendy Durst Kreeger,* Pres.; Leslie B. Durst,* V.P.; Nan Rothschild Cooper,* Secy.; Laurel Durst Strong,* Treas.; Anita Durst; Keith Kreeger; Emily Rothchild.
EIN: 522262647
Selected grants: The following grants were reported in 2004.
$29,000 to New York Public Library, New York, NY.
$25,000 to Advocates for Children, Aurora, CO.

$25,000 to International Center in New York, New York, NY.
$25,000 to Just Food, New York, NY.
$25,000 to Per Scholas, Bronx, NY.
$25,000 to Womens Housing and Economic Development Corporation, Bronx, NY.
$20,000 to City Harvest, New York, NY.
$15,000 to Bridge Fund of New York, New York, NY.
$15,000 to Community Access, New York, NY.
$15,000 to We Can, New York, NY.

5896
Susan & Morris E. Dweck Foundation ◇ ☆
c/o Ambras Fine Jewelry
469 7th Ave., 7th Fl.
New York, NY 10018

Established in 1988 in DE.
Donor: Morris E. Dweck.
Foundation type: Independent foundation.
Financial data (yr. ended 12/31/05): Assets, $3,598,252 (M); gifts received, $500,000; expenditures, $316,232; qualifying distributions, $315,660; giving activities include $315,660 for 15 + grants (high: $65,600).
Purpose and activities: Giving primarily for Jewish organizations.
Fields of interest: Education; Human services; Jewish federated giving programs; Jewish agencies & temples.
Limitations: Applications not accepted. Giving primarily in NJ and NY. No grants to individuals.
Application information: Contributes only to pre-selected organizations.
Officers: Morris E. Dweck, Pres.; Susan Dweck, V.P.
EIN: 133496732

5897
Dynamic Strategies Research Foundation, Inc. ◇
c/o Landau, Arnold Laufer & Company LLP
85 E. Hoffman Ave.
Lindenhurst, NY 11757-5010

Established in 1967 in NY.
Donor: Ethel R. Wells.
Foundation type: Independent foundation.
Financial data (yr. ended 8/31/05): Assets, $4,424,797 (M); expenditures, $705,738; qualifying distributions, $695,100; giving activities include $695,100 for 3+ grants (high: $475,000).
Purpose and activities: Giving primarily for public health and to peace foundations focused on nuclear policy.
Fields of interest: Public health; Mental health, smoking; International peace/security.
Limitations: Applications not accepted. Giving on a national basis. No grants to individuals.
Publications: Annual report; Financial statement.
Application information: Contributes only to pre-selected organizations.
Trustee: Ethel R. Wells.
EIN: 116103324
Selected grants: The following grants were reported in 2004.
$528,600 to Nuclear Age Peace Foundation, Santa Barbara, CA.

5898
Dyson Foundation ▼
25 Halcyon Rd.
Millbrook, NY 12545   (845) 677-0644
Contact: Diana M. Gurieva, Exec. V.P.
FAX: (845) 677-0650; E-mail: info@dyson.org;
URL: http://www.dysonfoundation.org

Trust established in 1956 in NY; incorporated in 1957 in DE.
Donors: Charles H. Dyson†; Margaret M. Dyson†.
Foundation type: Independent foundation.
Financial data (yr. ended 12/31/05): Assets, $322,654,083 (M); expenditures, $18,348,849; qualifying distributions, $15,800,497; giving activities include $14,399,624 for 278 grants (high: $1,500,000; low: $190; average: $10,000–$200,000), and $20,000 for 3 loans/program-related investments.
Purpose and activities: The foundation supports nonprofit organizations in the Mid-Hudson Valley of NY in a variety of fields. The foundation has a national program in community pediatrics training; and makes grants that are linked to the interests of the family of the president, Robert R. Dyson.
Fields of interest: Arts; Education; Health care; Human services; Children/youth, services; Philanthropy/voluntarism, management/technical aid; Economically disadvantaged.
Type of support: General/operating support; Continuing support; Income development; Management development/capacity building; Annual campaigns; Capital campaigns; Building/renovation; Equipment; Program development; Conferences/seminars; Professorships; Seed money; Fellowships; Scholarship funds; Technical assistance; Consulting services; Program evaluation; Program-related investments/loans; Matching/challenge support.
Limitations: Giving primarily in Dutchess County, NY, and organizations providing services in Dutchess County; limited grants to other Mid-Hudson Valley counties. National and other grants on a solicited basis. No support for international organizations. No grants to individuals, or for debt reduction, direct mail campaign or fundraising events.
Publications: Annual report (including application guidelines); Grants list.
Application information: Applicants should visit the foundation Web site for full grantmaking guidelines and eligibility questionnaire. After submitting LOI, if a project appears to address key foundation interests, the applicant will be invited to submit additional information or a fully developed proposal. Application form required.
Initial approach: Submit letter of inquiry either online or via postal mail
Copies of proposal: 1
Deadline(s): None
Board meeting date(s): Quarterly
Final notification: Three to six months
Officers and Directors: Robert R. Dyson,* Pres.; Diana M. Gurieva, Exec. V.P.; John S. FitzSimmons, Secy.; Marc Feldman, Treas.; Janet Van Why, Cont.; Raymond A. Lamontagne; Timmian C. Massie; Michael P. Murphy; David G. Nathan, M.D.
Number of staff: 4 full-time professional; 1 part-time professional; 5 full-time support.
EIN: 136084888
Selected grants: The following grants were reported in 2005.
$750,000 to Dana-Farber Cancer Institute, Boston, MA. For multi-year funding to support work of

Director of Breast Oncology Center and senior clinician in Women's Cancers Program, payable over 3 years.

$300,000 to Gateway to Entrepreneurial Tomorrows (GET), Poughkeepsie, NY. For general operating support, payable over 2 years.

$225,000 to Eleanor Roosevelt Center at Val-Kill, Hyde Park, NY. For multi-year support for Girls' Leadership Workshop programming, payable over 3 years.

$112,800 to AIDS-Related Community Services, Newburgh, NY. To present HIV/AIDS prevention play, Between Seams, to middle and high schools students in Mid-Hudson Valley, payable over 2 years.

$100,000 to Media Matters for America, DC. Toward update and redesign of website.

$100,000 to Third Way Foundation, DC. Toward policy research and communications projects to develop and support progressive public policy.

$65,000 to Planned Parenthood of the Mid-Hudson Valley, Poughkeepsie, NY. For general operating support.

$50,000 to Miles of Hope Breast Cancer Foundation, LaGrangeville, NY. For Gap Care Fund, which provides funds for life emergencies and expenses not covered by health insurance for those undergoing treatment for breast cancer in Mid-Hudson Valley.

$50,000 to Workers Rights Law Center of New York, Kingston, NY. For general operating support.

$37,000 to Mediation Center of Dutchess County, Poughkeepsie, NY. For Domestic Violence and Mediation Safety Project, to increase safety for victims of domestic violence who are referred to mediation.

$10,000 to Highland Cultural Center, Highland, NY. Toward organizational assessment and planning as part of Foundation's Strategic Restructuring Initiative.

$9,000 to Resource Center for Accessible Living, Kingston, NY. For mini-grant for strategic planning and board development.

5899
E & WG Foundation ◇ ☆
(formerly Eleanor and Wilson Greatbatch Foundation)
8975 Main St.
Clarence, NY 14031
Contact: Richard K. Milewicz, Secy.

Donor: Wilson Greatbatch.
Foundation type: Independent foundation.
Financial data (yr. ended 12/31/05): Assets, $642,436 (M); expenditures, $1,217,638; qualifying distributions, $1,216,011; giving activities include $1,203,940 for 12 grants (high: $1,000,000; low: $100).
Fields of interest: Medical research, institute; Medical research.
Limitations: Giving primarily in western NY.
Application information:
Initial approach: Letter
Copies of proposal: 6
Deadline(s): None
Officers and Directors: * Wilson Greatbatch,* Pres. and Treas.; Eleanor Greatbatch,* V.P.; Richard K. Milewicz,* Secy.; Mary Ann Pula; Jane Sweet; Keith Zehr.
EIN: 161065309

5900
Sarita Kenedy East Foundation, Inc. ◇
P.O. Box 604138
Bayside, NY 11360-4138
Contact: Margaret Devine

Established in 1962 in NY.
Donor: Sarita Kenedy East†.
Foundation type: Independent foundation.
Financial data (yr. ended 12/31/04): Assets, $19,512,528 (M); expenditures, $853,502; qualifying distributions, $760,660; giving activities include $743,500 for 50 grants (high: $50,000; low: $2,500).
Purpose and activities: Giving primarily to Roman Catholic organizations.
Fields of interest: Roman Catholic agencies & churches; Economically disadvantaged.
Type of support: General/operating support; Continuing support; Seed money.
Limitations: Giving on a national basis. No grants to individuals.
Application information: Contributes primarily to pre-selected organizations. Application form not required.
Initial approach: Letter
Copies of proposal: 1
Deadline(s): Sept. 1
Board meeting date(s): As necessary
Final notification: Dec.
Officers and Directors: * Margaret F. Grace,* Pres.; Patrick P. Grace,* V.P. and Secy.-Treas.; Justine M. Carr; Thomas M. Doyle; Theresa G. Sears.
Number of staff: 1 part-time support.
EIN: 136116447
Selected grants: The following grants were reported in 2004.
$50,000 to Holy Cross Abbey, Berryville, VA.
$50,000 to Holy Family Medical Center, Des Plaines, IL.
$20,000 to Abraham House, Bronx, NY.
$20,000 to Our Lady of Angels, Burlingame, CA.
$16,000 to Big Brothers.
$15,000 to Catholic Home Bureau, New York, NY.
$15,000 to Saint Jude Media Ministry, Passaic, NJ.
$10,000 to Association for Cultural Interchange, Princeton, NJ.
$10,000 to Cistercian Publications, Kalamazoo, MI.
$10,000 to Hour Children, Long Island City, NY.

5901
East Hill Foundation ◇
6500 Main St., Ste. 6
Williamsville, NY 14221-5836 (716) 204-0204
Contact: Michele R. Schmidt, Grants Dir.
E-mail: info@easthillfdn.org; URL: http://www.easthillfdn.org

Established in 1986 in NY.
Donors: Eleanor Greatbatch; Warren Greatbatch.
Foundation type: Independent foundation.
Financial data (yr. ended 12/31/05): Assets, $20,718,043 (M); gifts received, $1,000; expenditures, $1,056,846; qualifying distributions, $1,214,945; giving activities include $634,537 for 48 grants (high: $50,000; low: $500).
Purpose and activities: Giving for community needs and opportunities, social services, arts and culture, education, and health and social needs.
Fields of interest: Arts, multipurpose centers/programs; Education; Animal welfare; Health care; Youth development.

Type of support: Building/renovation; Equipment; Program development.
Limitations: Giving primarily in western NY. No support for religious organizations for direct religious purposes. No grants to individuals.
Publications: Grants list; Informational brochure (including application guidelines).
Application information: Application and grant guidelines available on foundation Web site. Only 1 application per grant cycle. Application form required.
Initial approach: Visit Web site or telephone
Copies of proposal: 2
Deadline(s): Aug. 7
Board meeting date(s): Semiannually
Final notification: By letter
Directors: Warren D. Greatbatch,* Pres.; Ami Greatbatch,* V.P.; John E. Siegel,* Secy.-Treas.; Michele R. Schmidt, Grants Dir.; Eleanor Greatbatch, Dir. Emerita; Stanton H. Hudson, Jr.
Number of staff: 1 full-time professional.
EIN: 161441497

5902
Eastern Star Hall and Home Foundation, Inc. ◇
c/o Lois M. Carlsen, Grand Chapter, O.E.S.
1400 Utica St., P.O. Box 106
Oriskany, NY 13424
Contact: Mrs. Pounder

Established in 1986 in NY.
Donors: Tucker Anthony; Elia Juchter†; Gladys Hart†; Ann Alsheimen†; John Cole†; J. Bleich Kolhmeir; Hilda Brooks†; Mildred Niley†; Althea Julson†; Geraldine Bear†.
Foundation type: Independent foundation.
Financial data (yr. ended 6/30/05): Assets, $14,649,967 (M); gifts received, $578,958; expenditures, $2,248,306; qualifying distributions, $2,066,825; giving activities include $2,066,825 for 4 grants (high: $1,500,000; low: $14,000).
Purpose and activities: Giving for social services.
Fields of interest: Human services; Children, day care.
Type of support: Endowments.
Limitations: Giving primarily in NY. No grants to individuals.
Publications: Annual report.
Application information:
Initial approach: Letter
Copies of proposal: 1
Board meeting date(s): Apr., July, Oct., and Dec.
Directors: Lois Carlsen; Peggy Grupp; Adelbert Hall; Janet Johnson; Everett Vail.
EIN: 133458370

5903
Fred Ebb Foundation ◇ ☆
40 W. 20th St., 11 Fl.
New York, NY 10011
Contact: Mitchell Bernard

Established in 2005 in NY.
Donor: Fred Ebb.
Foundation type: Operating foundation.
Financial data (yr. ended 12/31/05): Assets, $12,823,933 (M); gifts received, $10,255,500; expenditures, $426,879; qualifying distributions, $426,879; giving activities include $300,000 for 1 grant, and $50,000 for 1 grant to an individual.

Purpose and activities: The foundation provides an annual award to one of more persons working in the field of musical theater as composers or lyricists.
Fields of interest: Performing arts, theater; AIDS.
Type of support: Grants to individuals.
Limitations: Giving primarily in New York.
Application information: Applications only accepted for theater award. Contibutes to pre-selected organizations.
  Initial approach: Letter
Officer: Mitchell Bernard, Pres.
EIN: 202184998

5904
Eberstadt-Kuffner Fund, Inc. ✧
(formerly The Vera and Walter Eberstadt Foundation)
c/o Anchin, Block and Anchin, LLP
1375 Broadway
New York, NY 10018

Established in 1967 in NY.
Donors: Vera Eberstadt; Walter Eberstadt; Helene Kuffner†.
Foundation type: Independent foundation.
Financial data (yr. ended 12/31/05): Assets, $10,266,563 (M); gifts received, $116,130; expenditures, $446,189; qualifying distributions, $372,678; giving activities include $372,428 for 65 grants (high: $86,300; low: $100).
Purpose and activities: Giving primarily for the arts, education, health, and children's services.
Fields of interest: Media, television; Arts; Higher education; Hospitals (general); Health care; Health organizations, association; Human services; Child development, services; Jewish federated giving programs.
Limitations: Applications not accepted. Giving primarily in NY. No grants to individuals.
Application information: Contributes only to pre-selected organizations.
Officer: Alan D. Spiegel, Treas.
Directors: Vera Eberstadt; Walter Eberstadt; Daniel L. Mosley.
EIN: 136225395

5905
Echoing Green ✧
(formerly Echoing Green Foundation)
60 E. 42nd St., Ste. 520
New York, NY 10165 (212) 689-1165
Contact: Cheryl L. Dorsey, Pres.
FAX: (212) 689-9010;
E-mail: info@echoinggreen.org; URL: http://www.echoinggreen.org

Established in 1987 in DE.
Donors: David Hodgson; Laurie Hodgson; Steve Denning; Roberta Denning; Peter Bloom; Bill Ford; Charlotte Ford; William Grabe; Rene Kern; Marie-France Kern; Amy Berkower; Daniel Weiss; Michael Loeb; Michele Snyder; Phil Trahanas; General Atlantic LLC; Oak Foundation; Advance Magazine Group; Ford Foundation, The; Morino Institute; Paul, Weiss, Rifkind, Wharton & Garrison LLP; The Porter Revocable Trust; The Robert Wood Johnson Foundation; The Spirit Foundation; Flora Family Foundation; Friedman French Foundation; PricewaterhouseCoopers, LLP; Calvert Group; The Price Family Foundation.
Foundation type: Operating foundation.

Financial data (yr. ended 6/30/05): Assets, $859,626 (M); gifts received, $2,032,733; expenditures, $1,943,981; giving activities include $544,718 for 28 grants (high: $59,718; low: $5,000), $165,000 for 6 grants to individuals (high: $30,000; low: $22,500), and $2,019,400 for 2 foundation-administered programs.
Purpose and activities: The Echoing Green offers fellowships to individuals. Through Echoing Green's Public Service Fellowship, seed money and technical support are provided to social entrepreneurs starting innovative public service organizations and projects that seek to catalyze positive social change. Echoing Green invests in entrepreneurs' organizations and projects at an early stage, before most funders are willing to do so, and then provides them with support to help them grow beyond start-up. The Echoing Green network currently includes over 350 fellows working domestically and internationally in a wide range of issue areas, including human rights, the environment, the arts, education, criminal justice, and community development.
Fields of interest: Education; Environment; Health care; Housing/shelter; Children/youth, services; International economic development; International relief; International human rights; Civil rights; Economic development; Community development; Public affairs.
Type of support: Technical assistance; Fellowships; Seed money.
Limitations: Giving on a national and international basis. No support for faith-based initiatives, or for the expansion of existing project or recipients of prior Echoing Green funding. No grants for lobbying or research.
Publications: Application guidelines; Grants list.
Application information: Initial application and guidelines are available on the Web site in early fall, Sept./Oct. annually. Faxed applications are not accepted. Only on-line submissions will be considered. Application guidelines are available on foundation Web site. Application form required.
  Initial approach: Submit application form online
  Copies of proposal: 1
  Deadline(s): Beginning of Dec.; check Web site for dates
  Final notification: Applicants will be notified to submit full proposals, final selection takes place in May
Officer and Directors:* David C. Hodgson, Chair.; Maya Ajmera; Carter Bales; Peter Campbell; Betsy Fader; William Ford; Adam Janovic; Billy Shore; Bill Shutkin; Anthony So; Reggie Stanley; Esther Benjamin.
Number of staff: 9 full-time professional; 1 part-time support.
EIN: 133424419

5906
Edelman Family Foundation, Inc. ✧
49 Lawrence Ave.
Lawrence, NY 11559

Established in 1998.
Donors: Alex Edelman; Susan Edelman.
Foundation type: Independent foundation.
Financial data (yr. ended 12/31/05): Assets, $321,077 (M); gifts received, $800,000; expenditures, $592,913; qualifying distributions, $592,913; giving activities include $590,953 for 117 grants (high: $145,750; low: $75; average: $250–$1,000).

Fields of interest: Jewish agencies & temples.
Limitations: Applications not accepted. Giving primarily in NY. No grants to individuals.
Application information: Contributes only to pre-selected organizations.
Officers: Alex Edelman, Pres.; Jeffrey Edelman, V.P.; Fay Greenberg, V.P.; Susan Edelman, Secy.-Treas.
EIN: 113455820
Selected grants: The following grants were reported in 2003.
$114,000 to American Friends of College Rabbinique de Montreal, New York, NY. For general support.
$90,500 to Bnos Bais Yaakov of Far Rockaway, Far Rockaway, NY. For general support.
$46,000 to Netzach Yisrael School, Petach Tikva, Israel. For general support.
$40,885 to Agudath Israel of Long Island, Far Rockaway, NY. For general support.
$40,000 to P.E.F. Israel Endowment Funds, New York, NY. For general support.
$14,500 to Bais Medrash Ateres Yisroel, Lawrence, NY. For general support.
$3,600 to Chesed Avraham, Brooklyn, NY. For general support.
$2,900 to Keren Aniyim, Brooklyn, NY. For general support.
$2,000 to Mesivta Bvet Chazon Ish. For general support.
$1,800 to Agudath Israel of America, New York, NY. For general support.

5907
The Sidney and Mildred Edelstein Foundation ✧
(formerly The Sidney M. Edelstein Foundation)
c/o American Express Tax & Business Svcs. of NY, Inc.
1185 Ave. of the Americas
New York, NY 10036

Established in 1986 in NY.
Donors: Sidney M. Edelstein†; Mildred Edelstein†.
Foundation type: Independent foundation.
Financial data (yr. ended 12/31/03): Assets, $632,414 (M); gifts received, $23,146; expenditures, $335,190; qualifying distributions, $331,287; giving activities include $331,500 for 5 grants (high: $155,000; low: $1,500).
Purpose and activities: Giving primarily for higher education and Jewish agencies and temples.
Fields of interest: Higher education; Jewish agencies & temples.
Limitations: Applications not accepted. Giving primarily in New York, NY. No grants to individuals.
Application information: Contributes only to pre-selected organizations.
Directors: Richard Finkelstein; Leo Goldberg; Jeffrey Grossman; Roy Jacobs; Harvey Reich.
EIN: 133347784
Selected grants: The following grants were reported in 2003.
$155,000 to Hebrew University of Jerusalem, Jerusalem, Israel. .
$75,000 to Chemical Heritage Foundation, Philadelphia, PA.
$65,000 to American Committee for Shenkar College in Israel, New York, NY.
$35,000 to P.E.F. Israel Endowment Funds, New York, NY.
$1,500 to Lubavitch Center of Essex County, West Orange, NJ.

5908
Edelweiss Foundation ✧
c/o Griffin, Coogan, & Veneruso, PC
51 Pondfield Rd.
Bronxville, NY 10708

Established in 1999 in NY.
Donor: Robert H. Abplanalp.
Foundation type: Independent foundation.
Financial data (yr. ended 12/31/05): Assets,
$4,199,492 (M); expenditures, $390,181;
qualifying distributions, $379,833; giving activities
include $379,833 for 12 grants (high: $100,000;
low: $4,000; average: $10,000–$50,000).
Fields of interest: Hospitals (general); Cancer;
Federated giving programs; Christian agencies &
churches.
Limitations: Applications not accepted. Giving
primarily in NY. No grants to individuals.
Application information: Contributes only to
pre-selected organizations.
Directors: John Abplanalp; Josephine Abplanalp;
Marie Holcombe.
EIN: 134090193

5909
The Edouard Foundation, Inc. ✧
c/o Phillips Nizer, LLP
666 5th Ave., 28th Fl.
New York, NY 10103-0084 (212) 977-9700
Contact: Morton Freilicher, Treas.

Established in 1987 in NY.
Foundation type: Independent foundation.
Financial data (yr. ended 12/31/05): Assets,
$8,943,470 (M); gifts received, $15,196;
expenditures, $608,143; qualifying distributions,
$489,000; giving activities include $489,000 for 61
grants (high: $35,000; low: $1,000).
Purpose and activities: The foundation is
committed to funding programs which improve the
quality of life primarily in the communities in which
the directors reside. The funding is focused in the
areas of human services, education, health care,
art, animal welfare, environmental protection, and
disaster relief.
Fields of interest: Health care; Health
organizations, association; Food services; Human
services; Children/youth, services; International
relief; International human rights; Federated giving
programs; Disabilities, people with; Native
Americans/American Indians.
Type of support: General/operating support;
Emergency funds; Program development; Research.
Limitations: Applications not accepted. Giving on a
national basis. No grants to individuals.
Application information: Contributes only to
pre-selected organizations.
Board meeting date(s): Nov.
Officers and Directors:* Sandra Finch-Nguyen,*
Pres.; Christopher Finch,* V.P.; Ronald Finch,* V.P.;
Edwin A. Margolius,* Secy.; Morton Freilicher,*
Treas.
EIN: 133446831

5910
Educational Support Foundation, Inc. ✧ ☆
(formerly Leon & Irene Scharf Foundation, Inc.)
800 West End Ave.
New York, NY 10025

Established in 1963 in NY.
Donors: Leon Scharf; Irene Scharf; S. Schoferig;
Chada Foundation; Franconia Foundation; Scharf,
Scharf, & Beer; Weinreb Management; Nazel Family
Trust.
Foundation type: Independent foundation.
Financial data (yr. ended 5/31/05): Assets,
$14,036,332 (M); gifts received, $105,000;
expenditures, $969,586; qualifying distributions,
$773,045; giving activities include $766,660 for
258 grants (high: $100,000; low: $18).
Purpose and activities: Giving primarily to Jewish
agencies and temples and to yeshivas.
Fields of interest: Elementary/secondary
education; Jewish agencies & temples.
Limitations: Applications not accepted. Giving
primarily in NY. No grants to individuals.
Application information: Contributes only to
pre-selected organizations.
Managers: Irene Scharf; Leon Scharf.
EIN: 136159760
Selected grants: The following grants were reported
in 2004.
$50,000 to Kedushat Zion, Brooklyn, NY.
$1,000 to Bayith Lepleitot, Brooklyn, NY.
$500 to Beth Medrash Govoha, Brooklyn, NY.
$500 to Congregation Zichron Shlomo, Monsey, NY.
$200 to PTACH, Brooklyn, NY.
$100 to Bobover Yeshiva Bnei Zion, Brooklyn, NY.
$50 to Jewish Renaissance Center, New York, NY.
$50 to Yeshiva Ketana of Manhattan, New York, NY.
$36 to Yeshiva Mkor Chaim, Brooklyn, NY.
$18 to Bikur Cholim of Manhattan, New York, NY.

5911
The Craig Effron Family Foundation ✧ ☆
129 E. 73rd St.
New York, NY 10021
Contact: Craig Effron, Dir.

Established in 2002 in NY.
Donor: Craig Effron.
Foundation type: Independent foundation.
Financial data (yr. ended 12/31/05): Assets,
$918,589 (M); gifts received, $208,450;
expenditures, $452,077; qualifying distributions,
$430,910; giving activities include $430,910 for 64
grants (high: $55,500; low: $25).
Fields of interest: Education; Nerve, muscle & bone
diseases; Jewish federated giving programs; Jewish
agencies & temples.
Application information:
Initial approach: Letter
Deadline(s): None
Directors: Blair Effron; Caryn Effron; Craig Effron;
Drew Effron.
EIN: 030415243

5912
EHA Foundation, Inc. ✧
c/o Kelley Drye & Warren, LLP
101 Park Ave., 30th Fl.
New York, NY 10178
Contact: Christina M. Mason, Secy.

Established in 1996 in NY.
Donors: Ruth Uris†; Linda M. Sanger.
Foundation type: Independent foundation.
Financial data (yr. ended 1/31/05): Assets,
$30,725,198 (M); expenditures, $1,331,961;
qualifying distributions, $1,073,982; giving

activities include $1,068,000 for 20 grants (high:
$250,000; low: $6,000).
Fields of interest: Performing arts, dance; Arts;
Elementary/secondary education; Higher education;
Mental health/crisis services; Children/youth,
services; Jewish agencies & temples.
Type of support: General/operating support;
Continuing support; Building/renovation; Program
development; Seed money; Fellowships;
Scholarship funds; Matching/challenge support.
Limitations: Applications not accepted. Giving on a
national and international basis. No grants to
individuals.
Application information: Contributes only to
pre-selected organizations. Unsolicited requests for
funds not accepted.
Officers: Linda M. Sanger, Pres.; Abbie W. Sanger,
V.P.; Terence D. Sanger, V.P.; Victoria Sanger, V.P.;
Christina M. Mason, Secy.; Michael S. Insel, Treas.
EIN: 133898642
Selected grants: The following grants were reported
in 2003.
$200,000 to Mental Health Association, National,
Alexandria, VA. For general support.
$200,000 to New York Public Library, New York, NY.
For general support.
$150,000 to Palo Alto Public Library, Friends of the,
Palo Alto, CA. For general support.
$75,000 to Teachers and Writers Collaborative,
New York, NY. For general support.
$67,200 to Churchill School and Center for Learning
Disabilities, New York, NY. For general support.
$50,000 to Kinhaven Music School, Bethlehem, PA.
For general support.
$35,000 to Grand Street Settlement, New York, NY.
For general support.
$30,000 to W G B H Educational Foundation,
Boston, MA. For general support.
$26,000 to American Repertory Theater Company,
New York, NY. For general support.
$25,000 to Metropolitan Museum of Art, New York,
NY. For general support.

5913
Ehrenkranz Family Foundation ✧
c/o Joel S. Ehrenkranz
375 Park Ave., Ste. 2800
New York, NY 10152

Established in 1997 in NY.
Donor: Joel S. Ehrenkranz.
Foundation type: Independent foundation.
Financial data (yr. ended 12/31/05): Assets,
$6,704,439 (M); gifts received, $3,132,991;
expenditures, $2,307,921; qualifying distributions,
$2,258,444; giving activities include $2,253,194
for 73 grants (high: $525,000; low: $100).
Purpose and activities: Giving primarily for higher
education and the arts; funding for Jewish
organizations and social services.
Fields of interest: Museums; Performing arts
centers; Arts; Higher education; Education;
Hospitals (general); Human services; Jewish
agencies & temples.
Limitations: Applications not accepted. Giving
primarily in New York, NY. No grants to individuals.
Application information: Contributes only to
pre-selected organizations.
Trustees: Anne B. Ehrenkranz; Joel S. Ehrenkranz.
EIN: 133977888
Selected grants: The following grants were reported
in 2005.
$525,000 to New York University, New York, NY.

$360,000 to Lincoln Center for the Performing Arts, New York, NY.

$248,000 to Mount Sinai Medical Center, New York, NY.

$114,089 to Whitney Museum of American Art, New York, NY.

$100,000 to North Salem Open Land Foundation, North Salem, NY.

$50,000 to Hospital for Special Surgery, New York, NY.

$25,000 to New York Public Library, New York, NY.

$1,750 to Conservation International, DC.

$1,700 to Lincoln Center Theater, New York, NY.

$1,500 to California Institute of the Arts, Valencia, CA.

5914
The Eig Family Foundation, Inc. ✧
c/o ROJ, Inc.
888 7th Ave., 40th Fl.
New York, NY 10019
Contact: Norman Eig, Pres.

Established in 1986 in NY.
Donors: Norman Eig; Barbara Eig.
Foundation type: Independent foundation.
Financial data (yr. ended 9/30/05): Assets, $1,542,201 (M); expenditures, $508,698; qualifying distributions, $503,483; giving activities include $503,133 for 34 grants (high: $200,000; low: $100).
Fields of interest: Business school/education; Education; Cancer; Cancer research; Youth development; Human services; Jewish agencies & temples.
Limitations: Giving primarily in NJ and NY. No grants to individuals.
Application information:
 Initial approach: Letter
 Deadline(s): None
Officers and Directors:* Norman Eig,* Pres.; Barbara Eig,* V.P.; Charles W. Steiglitz,* Secy.-Treas.
EIN: 133384957

5915
Einhorn Family Charitable Trust ✧
c/o David Einhorn
140 E. 45th St., 24th Fl.
New York, NY 10017

Established in 2002 in NY.
Donors: David Einhorn; Cheryl Einhorn.
Foundation type: Independent foundation.
Financial data (yr. ended 12/31/03): Assets, $352,389 (M); gifts received, $350,000; expenditures, $355,325; qualifying distributions, $354,650; giving activities include $354,650 for 11 grants (high: $250,000; low: $100).
Fields of interest: Arts; Higher education; Human services; Community development; Jewish agencies & temples.
Limitations: Applications not accepted. Giving primarily in NY. No grants to individuals.
Application information: Contributes only to pre-selected organizations.
Trustees: Cheryl Einhorn; David Einhorn.
EIN: 226921358
Selected grants: The following grants were reported in 2004.
$125,000 to Cornell University, Ithaca, NY.

$100,000 to Robin Hood Foundation, New York, NY.

$54,500 to Community Synagogue of Rye, Rye, NY.

$48,000 to Gift of Life Bone Marrow Foundation, Boca Raton, FL.

$20,000 to Math for America, New York, NY.

$10,000 to United Cerebral Palsy Association of Westchester County, Rye, NY.

$5,000 to Multiple Sclerosis Society, National, New York, NY.

$2,500 to Sallie Foundation, New York, NY.

$1,000 to American Cancer Society, New York, NY.

$1,000 to Chai Lifeline, New York, NY.

5916
The Einhorn Family Foundation ✧
c/o BCRS Group/Marcum & Kliegman, LLP
100 Wall St., 11th Fl.
New York, NY 10005

Established in 1989 in NJ.
Donor: Steven G. Einhorn.
Foundation type: Independent foundation.
Financial data (yr. ended 1/31/06): Assets, $3,125,724 (M); gifts received, $2,039,520; expenditures, $1,224,262; qualifying distributions, $1,196,650; giving activities include $1,194,900 for 35 grants (high: $500,000; low: $500).
Fields of interest: Arts; Higher education; Health care; Human services; Jewish federated giving programs; Jewish agencies & temples.
Limitations: Applications not accepted. Giving primarily in NY. No grants to individuals.
Application information: Contributes only to pre-selected organizations.
Trustees: Shelley Einhorn; Steven G. Einhorn.
EIN: 133531970
Selected grants: The following grants were reported in 2006.
$56,250 to Abraham Joshua Heschel School, New York, NY. 2 grants: $25,000, $31,250

$50,000 to Glaucoma Foundation, New York, NY.

$50,000 to New York City Opera, New York, NY. 3 grants: $25,000, $15,000, $10,000

$25,000 to Gotham Chamber Opera, New York, NY.

$25,000 to New York Eye and Ear Infirmary, New York, NY.

$10,000 to Philharmonic-Symphony Society of New York, New York, NY.

$7,500 to American Friends of the Israel Museum, New York, NY.

5917
The Eisenreich Family Foundation ✧
c/o Avery Eisenreich
3269 Bedford Ave.
Brooklyn, NY 11210

Established in 1997 in NY.
Donors: Commercial Security Mortgage Credit, Inc.; Avery Eisenreich.
Foundation type: Independent foundation.
Financial data (yr. ended 12/31/04): Assets, $2,803,881 (M); gifts received, $215,000; expenditures, $354,147; qualifying distributions, $347,671; giving activities include $348,470 for 13 grants (high: $200,000; low: $180).
Purpose and activities: Funding primarily for Jewish agencies and temples; some support also for yeshivas.
Fields of interest: Elementary/secondary education; Jewish agencies & temples.

Limitations: Applications not accepted. Giving primarily in NJ and NY. No grants to individuals.
Application information: Contributes only to pre-selected organizations.
Trustees: Avery Eisenreich; Toby Eisenreich.
EIN: 137118478

5918
Elbogen Family Charitable Trust ✧
1650 49th St.
Brooklyn, NY 11204

Established in 2000 in NY.
Donor: Aaron Elbogen.
Foundation type: Independent foundation.
Financial data (yr. ended 12/31/04): Assets, $7,713,532 (M); expenditures, $441,322; qualifying distributions, $428,022; giving activities include $425,949 for 63 grants (high: $189,534; low: $36).
Purpose and activities: Giving primarily for Jewish causes.
Fields of interest: Jewish agencies & temples.
Limitations: Applications not accepted. No grants to individuals.
Application information: Contributes only to pre-selected organizations.
Trustees: Aaron Elbogen; Chaya Elbogen; Naftali Manela.
EIN: 116552018

5919
Baisley Powell Elebash Fund ✧
c/o JPMorgan Chase Bank, N.A.
345 Park Ave., 4th Fl.
New York, NY 10154 (212) 464-2441
Contact: Edward L. Jones, V.P., JPMorgan Chase Bank, N.A.
FAX: (212) 464-2305;
E-mail: jones_ed_l@JPMorgan.com

Established in 1997.
Foundation type: Independent foundation.
Financial data (yr. ended 10/31/05): Assets, $8,774,959 (M); expenditures, $903,274; qualifying distributions, $727,296; giving activities include $700,000 for 11 grants (high: $125,000; low: $25,000).
Purpose and activities: Giving primarily for music, and health care for low-income adults.
Fields of interest: Performing arts, music; Health care.
Limitations: Applications not accepted. Giving primarily in AL, AZ, and NY. No grants to individuals.
Publications: Grants list; Informational brochure.
Application information: Contributes only to pre-selected organizations.
Trustee: JPMorgan Chase Bank, N.A.
EIN: 137125140
Selected grants: The following grants were reported in 2004.
$180,000 to New York Immigration Coalition, New York, NY. For general support.

$125,000 to Graduate Center, City University of New York, New York, NY. For general support.

$50,000 to Medicare Rights Center, New York, NY. For general support.

$40,000 to University of Alabama, Tuscaloosa, AL. For general support.

$35,000 to Cathedral Church of Saint John the Divine, New York, NY. For general support.

$35,000 to Research Foundation of the City University of New York, New York, NY. For general support.

$35,000 to Trinity Church, New York, NY. For general support.

$30,000 to Manhattan School of Music, New York, NY. For general support.

$30,000 to Mannes College of Music, New York, NY. For general support.

$25,000 to New York Philomusica Chamber Ensemble, New York, NY. For general support.

5920
The Elias Foundation ◇ ☆
c/o U.S. Trust Co. of NY
114 W. 47th St., TAXRGR
New York, NY   10036
E-mail: info@eliasfoundation.org; *URL:* http://www.eliasfoundation.org

Established in 1999 in DE.
Donors: Jacqueline Mann; James E. Mann.
Foundation type: Independent foundation.
Financial data (yr. ended 12/31/05): Assets, $5,318,591 (M); gifts received, $1,060,125; expenditures, $624,131; qualifying distributions, $590,251; giving activities include $547,758 for 75 grants (high: $100,000; low: $100).
Purpose and activities: The foundation seeks to promote a more equitable and progressive society by supporting projects that mobilize community leadership and create networks for community change. The foundation values the pursuit of economic equity and social justice, self-directed change led by the experience and wisdom of local communities, community advocacy as a fundamental strategy for progressive action, and community leaders as catalysts, guiding and inspiring future generations.
Fields of interest: Civil rights, advocacy; Civil rights, minorities; Civil rights; Community development; Economically disadvantaged.
Type of support: General/operating support; Management development/capacity building; Research.
Limitations: Giving primarily in Westchester County, NY. No grants to individuals.
Application information: Full proposals will be accepted only following approval of Letter of Intent. Unsolicited full proposals will not be accepted. Guidelines available on foundation Web site.
  Initial approach: Letter of Intent
  Deadline(s): None
Officers: Jacqueline Mann, Pres.; Alison Mann, V.P.; Anastasia Mann, V.P.; James E. Mann, Secy.; Eldar Shafir, Treas.
EIN: 134092287
Selected grants: The following grants were reported in 2004.
$10,000 to Insight Arts, Chicago, IL.
$10,000 to Jews for Racial and Economic Justice, New York, NY.
$10,000 to Mount Vernon United Tenants, Mount Vernon, NY.
$10,000 to People for the American Way, DC.
$10,000 to Voices Unbroken, Bronx, NY.
$5,000 to Princeton Regional Scholarship Foundation, Princeton, NJ.
$1,000 to W N Y C Radio, New York, NY.
$750 to National Coalition to Abolish the Death Penalty, DC.
$100 to Lenox Library Association, Lenox, MA.

5921
The Elishis Family Foundation ◇
c/o Oracle Svcs., Inc.
211 Madison Ave., Ste. 20B
New York, NY   10016

Established in 1999 in NY.
Donors: Isser Elishis; Brenda Elishis; David Elishis†; Tony Inder Reiden.
Foundation type: Independent foundation.
Financial data (yr. ended 12/31/05): Assets, $0 (M); gifts received, $558,600; expenditures, $673,962; qualifying distributions, $673,738; giving activities include $671,723 for 104 grants (high: $347,200; low: $18).
Purpose and activities: Giving primarily to Jewish agencies, temples, schools and Jewish youth programs; some funding for national health associations.
Fields of interest: Health organizations, association; Cancer; Diabetes; Youth development, religion; Jewish agencies & temples.
Limitations: Applications not accepted. Giving primarily in Brooklyn and New York, NY. No grants to individuals.
Application information: Contributes only to pre-selected organizations.
Officers and Directors:* Brenda Elishis,* Pres.; Isser Elishis,* V.P.
EIN: 113502742
Selected grants: The following grants were reported in 2003.
$265,572 to Colel Chabad, Brooklyn, NY. For general support.
$70,000 to Gmach Chemed Shlomo Tenka, Brooklyn, NY. For general support.
$36,000 to Chabad, New York, NY. For general support.
$30,000 to Congregation Tiferes of Nadverna, Brooklyn, NY. For general support.
$18,000 to Congregation Beni Asher, Brooklyn, NY. For general support.
$16,100 to Congregation LMan Achai, Brooklyn, NY. For general support.
$15,000 to Chevra Tzedoka V Chesed, Brooklyn, NY. For general support.
$12,200 to Congregation Yeshiva Chunah David, Brooklyn, NY. For general support.
$10,000 to Hebrew Institute of Riverdale, Bronx, NY. For general support.
$10,000 to Romemah Institute of Rabbinics, Brooklyn, NY. For general support.

5922
The Elkes Foundation ◇
12 Trails End
Rye, NY   10580   (914) 381-5350

Established in 1989 in NY.
Foundation type: Operating foundation.
Financial data (yr. ended 11/30/04): Assets, $6,045,928 (M); expenditures, $526,194; qualifying distributions, $511,450; giving activities include $511,450 for 27 grants (high: $250,000; low: $100).
Purpose and activities: Giving primarily for higher education, with emphasis on a law school; some funding also to Jewish organizations and education.
Fields of interest: Arts; Higher education; Law school/education; Education; Medical care, in-patient care; Human services; Jewish agencies & temples.

Limitations: Applications not accepted. Giving primarily in Ann Arbor, MI and NY. No grants to individuals.
Application information: Contributes only to pre-selected organizations.
Trustees: Ruth F. Elkes; Terrence A. Elkes.
EIN: 133497016
Selected grants: The following grants were reported in 2003.
$250,000 to University of Michigan, Law School, Ann Arbor, MI.
$105,000 to Jewish Outreach Institute, Center for Jewish Studies, New York, NY.
$5,000 to American Ireland Fund, Boston, MA.
$5,000 to Jewish Educational Ventures, DC.
$5,000 to Middle East Forum, Philadelphia, PA.
$3,000 to Connecticut College, Development Office, New London, CT.
$2,500 to Grinnell College, Grinnell, IA.
$2,000 to Philharmonic-Symphony Society of New York, New York, NY.
$1,000 to Emelin Theater, Mamaroneck, NY.
$1,000 to Horace Mann School, Riverdale, NY.

5923
Joseph H. & Barbara I. Ellis Foundation ◇
c/o BCRS Group/Marcum & Kliegman, LLP
100 Wall St., 11th Fl.
New York, NY   10005

Established in 1987 in NY.
Donor: Joseph H. Ellis.
Foundation type: Independent foundation.
Financial data (yr. ended 6/30/05): Assets, $4,396,007 (M); gifts received, $900,000; expenditures, $1,377,896; qualifying distributions, $1,374,996; giving activities include $1,373,346 for 49 grants (high: $250,000; low: $100).
Purpose and activities: Giving primarily for environmental conservation, higher education, Jewish organizations, and community services.
Fields of interest: Higher education; Education; Environment, plant conservation; Environment; Animals/wildlife, preservation/protection; Food services; Human services; Jewish federated giving programs; Jewish agencies & temples.
Type of support: General/operating support.
Limitations: Applications not accepted. Giving primarily in New York, NY; some funding also in Cornwall, CT. No grants to individuals.
Application information: Contributes only to pre-selected organizations.
Trustees: Leon Cooperman; Barbara I. Ellis; Joseph H. Ellis.
EIN: 133437916
Selected grants: The following grants were reported in 2005.
$300,000 to CARE, New York, NY. 2 grants: $100,000, $200,000
$287,500 to RARE Center for Tropical Conservation, Arlington, VA. 2 grants: $250,000, $37,500
$150,000 to Nature Conservancy, New York, NY.
$145,000 to Barnard College, New York, NY. 2 grants: $25,000, $120,000
$75,000 to Dorot, New York, NY.
$50,000 to Coalition for the Homeless, New York, NY.
$25,000 to Cornwall Conservation Trust, West Cornwall, CT.

5924
Victor Elmaleh Foundation ✧
c/o World Wide Holdings Corp.
150 E. 58th St.
New York, NY 10155-0002

Established about 1962 in NY.
Donors: Victor Elmaleh; World-Wide Volkswagen Corp.
Foundation type: Independent foundation.
Financial data (yr. ended 12/31/04): Assets, $3,910,320 (M); gifts received, $1,005,256; expenditures, $503,439; qualifying distributions, $475,760; giving activities include $473,843 for grants.
Purpose and activities: Giving primarily for the arts, education, and human services.
Fields of interest: Arts, multipurpose centers/programs; Performing arts, dance; Education; Human services; Children/youth, services.
Limitations: Applications not accepted. Giving primarily in NY. No grants to individuals.
Application information: Contributes only to pre-selected organizations.
Trustees: Ernest Alson; Antonio Elmaleh; Niko Elmaleh; Sono Elmaleh; Victor Elmaleh.
EIN: 136075674
Selected grants: The following grants were reported in 2003.
$300,000 to University of Virginia, School of Architecture, Charlottesville, VA.
$25,000 to Concert Artists Guild, New York, NY.
$2,000 to Ballet Tech, New York, NY.
$1,150 to Huggy Bears, New York, NY.
$150 to Metropolitan Museum of Art, New York, NY.
$100 to Amnesty International USA, New York, NY.
$100 to Citymeals-on-Wheels, New York, NY.
$50 to American Civil Liberties Union Foundation, New York, NY.
$25 to Freedom Guide Dogs for the Blind, Cassville, NY.
$25 to Habitat for Humanity International, Americus, GA.

5925
Thomas and Jeanne Elmezzi Private Foundation
(also known as The Jet Foundation)
185 Great Neck Rd., Ste. 410
Great Neck, NY 11021-3312
Contact: Lynn Grossman, Pres.; Pooja Joshi, Prog. Officer
FAX: (516) 498-2859;
E-mail: info@jetfoundation.org; URL: http://www.jetfoundation.org

Established in 1996 in NY.
Donors: Thomas Elmezzi†; Jeanne Elmezzi†.
Foundation type: Independent foundation.
Financial data (yr. ended 12/31/05): Assets, $4,698,786 (M); gifts received, $38,991; expenditures, $845,284; qualifying distributions, $785,102; giving activities include $634,050 for 9 grants (high: $256,050; low: $25,000).
Fields of interest: Education; Geriatrics; Medical research; Children/youth, services.
Type of support: Endowments; General/operating support; Program development.
Limitations: Applications not accepted. Giving primarily in the New York tri-state region, with emphasis on New York City. Limited international giving primarily for disaster relief. No support for housing, international organizations (except for

some disasters) and foreign travel or study. No grants for individuals, annual appeals, dinners, fundraising events, capital campaigns, loans and deficit financing.
Publications: Grants list; Occasional report.
Application information: Contributes only to pre-selected organizations.
Board meeting date(s): Ongoing
Officers and Trustees:* Jose Rivero,* Chair.; Lynn Grossman,* Pres.; Stephen J. Saft,* Secy.; Alfred LaRosa, Treas.; Dominick Fortino; Allen Freed; Nivia Pedroza; Jack Sollazzo.
Number of staff: 1 full-time professional; 1 part-time professional.
EIN: 113343740

5926
Emerald Foundation, Inc. ✧
c/o Solomon Pearl Blum Heymann & Stich
40 Wall St., 35th Fl.
New York, NY 10001

Established in 1998 in NY.
Foundation type: Independent foundation.
Financial data (yr. ended 12/31/05): Assets, $18,493,611 (M); expenditures, $1,269,022; qualifying distributions, $1,125,033; giving activities include $850,000 for 17 grants to individuals (high: $50,000; low: $50,000).
Purpose and activities: Giving primarily to medical research.
Fields of interest: Higher education; Hospitals (general); Medical research, institute.
Limitations: Applications not accepted. Giving primarily in Boston, MA and New York, NY; some funding nationally. No grants to individuals.
Application information: Contributes only to pre-selected organizations.
Officers and Directors:* Olivia Flatto, Pres.; Andrew W. Heymann,* V.P.; Robert A. Ladislaw, Treas.; Donna R. Kesselman.
EIN: 133912580

5927
Fred L. Emerson Foundation, Inc. ▼ ✧
P.O. Box 276
Auburn, NY 13021 (315) 253-9621
Contact: Ronald D. West, Exec. Dir.

Incorporated in 1943 in DE.
Donor: Fred L. Emerson†.
Foundation type: Independent foundation.
Financial data (yr. ended 12/31/05): Assets, $77,678,099 (M); expenditures, $4,120,540; qualifying distributions, $3,586,288; giving activities include $3,471,816 for 54 grants (high: $500,000; low: $250; average: $2,500–$25,000).
Purpose and activities: Giving to private colleges and universities, community funds, and a library; grants also for youth and social service agencies and cultural programs.
Fields of interest: Arts; Higher education; Libraries/library science; Human services; Children/youth, services; Federated giving programs.
Type of support: Annual campaigns; Capital campaigns; Building/renovation; Equipment; Endowments; Emergency funds; Program development; Internship funds; Scholarship funds; Research; Matching/challenge support.
Limitations: Giving primarily in Auburn, Cayuga County, and upstate NY. No grants to individuals, or

for deficit financing; no loans. Support for operating budgets is discouraged.
Publications: Application guidelines.
Application information: Application form not required.
Initial approach: Letter, telephone, or proposal
Copies of proposal: 1
Deadline(s): May 1 and Nov. 1
Board meeting date(s): June and Dec.
Final notification: 2 to 3 weeks after board meetings (positive replies only)
Officers and Directors:* David L. Emerson,* Pres.; Anthony D. Franceschelli,* V.P.; Ronald D. West,* Secy. and Exec. Dir.; J. David Hammond,* Treas.; Christopher S. Emerson; Heather A. Emerson; Peter J. Emerson; W. Gary Emerson; Lori E. Robinson; Kristen E. Rubacka; Sally E. Wagner.
Number of staff: 1 full-time professional; 1 full-time support.
EIN: 156017650
Selected grants: The following grants were reported in 2003.
$280,500 to Auburn Hospital System Foundation, Auburn, NY. For nursing scholarship and permanently restricted endowment.
$251,000 to Ithaca College, Ithaca, NY. For permanently restricted endowment.
$250,000 to Russell Sage College, Troy, NY. For Bush Memorial Center renovations.
$194,500 to Cayuga County Community College Foundation, Auburn, NY. For alumni appeal, sports, child care facility and restricted endowment.
$171,666 to Hamilton College, Clinton, NY. For chair and curricular reform.
$165,500 to Foundation Historical Association, Auburn, NY. For capital initiatives operating budget.
$134,830 to United Way of Cayuga County, Auburn, NY. For annual campaign and unrestricted support.
$125,000 to University of New England, Biddeford, ME. For smart classroom project.
$120,000 to Union College, Schenectady, NY. For North Colonnade Arts Complex renovations.
$100,000 to Merry-Go-Round Playhouse, Auburn, NY. For Renaissance campaign.

5928
Emes Foundation Inc. ✧
5018 Old New Utrecht Rd.
Brooklyn, NY 11204

Established in 2001 in NY.
Donors: Emunah Trust; Manuel Scharf; Educational Support Foundation.
Foundation type: Independent foundation.
Financial data (yr. ended 9/30/05): Assets, $1,266,470 (M); gifts received, $10,000; expenditures, $758,144; qualifying distributions, $629,032; giving activities include $628,230 for 71 grants (high: $100,000; low: $180).
Fields of interest: Jewish agencies & temples.
Limitations: Applications not accepted. No grants to individuals.
Application information: Contributes only to pre-selected organizations.
Officers and Directors:* Maurice Meisels,* Pres.; Rabbi Solomon Herbst,* V.P.; Alfred I. Scherzer,* Secy.-Treas.
EIN: 113640577
Selected grants: The following grants were reported in 2005.

$100,000 to Yeshiva Machzikei Hadas, Brooklyn, NY.

$42,000 to Bobover Yeshiva Bnei Zion, Brooklyn, NY.

$27,500 to Kedushat Zion, Brooklyn, NY. 2 grants: $25,000, $2,500

$5,000 to Congregation Beth Medrash Govoha, Miami, FL.

$5,000 to Keren Zichron Pesach Moshe Zvi, Brooklyn, NY.

$5,000 to Kolel Chibas Jerusalem, Brooklyn, NY.

$3,000 to ZAKA, Brooklyn, NY.

$360 to Beth Medrash Govoha, Brooklyn, NY.

$250 to Yeshiva Darchei Torah, Far Rockaway, NY.

5929
EMLE, Inc. ✧
c/o Hertz, Herson & Co., LLP
2 Park Ave., Ste. 1500
New York, NY 10016

Established in 1998 in DE and NY.
Donors: Bella Wexner Charitable Remainder Unitrust; Susan Wexner Revocable Trust.
Foundation type: Independent foundation.
Financial data (yr. ended 3/31/05): Assets, $29,438,623 (M); expenditures, $1,282,281; qualifying distributions, $1,124,581; giving activities include $1,080,000 for 1 grant.
Fields of interest: Philanthropy/voluntarism.
Limitations: Applications not accepted. Giving primarily in Southeastern, PA. No grants to individuals.
Application information: Contributes only to pre-selected organizations.
Officer and Directors:* Susan R. Wexner,* Pres. and Secy.-Treas.; Bertrand Agus.
EIN: 133997362
Selected grants: The following grants were reported in 2004.
$1,510,000 to Vanguard Charitable Endowment Program, Southeastern, PA.

5930
Emwiga Foundation ✧
(formerly Overlock Family Foundation)
c/o BCRS Group/Marcum & Kliegman, LLP
100 Wall St., 11th Fl.
New York, NY 10005

Established in 1984 in NY.
Donor: Willard J. Overlock.
Foundation type: Independent foundation.
Financial data (yr. ended 2/28/05): Assets, $6,318,665 (M); gifts received, $1,177,586; expenditures, $1,581,607; qualifying distributions, $1,498,145; giving activities include $1,495,750 for 116 grants (high: $200,000; low: $50).
Purpose and activities: Giving primarily for education, health associations, particularly for juvenile diabetes research, the arts, and children, youth and social services.
Fields of interest: Museums; Performing arts, theater; Arts; Higher education; Business school/education; Education; Environment, natural resources; Hospitals (general); Health organizations, association; Diabetes research; Human services; Children/youth, services; Philanthropy/voluntarism.

Limitations: Applications not accepted. Giving primarily in CT, MA, NH and New York, NY. No grants to individuals, or for scholarships; no loans.
Application information: Contributes only to pre-selected organizations.
Trustees: James G. Kenan III; Emily Phelps Overlock; Katharine Overlock; Willard J. Overlock, Jr.; William J. Overlock III.
EIN: 133247601
Selected grants: The following grants were reported in 2003.
$400,000 to Juvenile Diabetes Research Foundation International, New York, NY. For general support.
$200,000 to University of North Carolina, Chapel Hill, NC. For general support.
$150,000 to Columbia University, New York, NY. 2 grants: $100,000 to Columbia Business School (For general support), $50,000 to School of General Studies (For general support).
$150,000 to Prep for Prep, New York, NY. For general support.
$100,000 to Brunswick School, Greenwich, CT.
$50,000 to Conservation International, DC. For general support.
$25,000 to Dartmouth College, Hanover, NH. For general support.
$25,000 to Urban Education Exchange, New York, NY. For general support.
$10,000 to Alliance for Lupus Research, New York, NY. For general support.

5931
The Endowment for Vietnamese Education, Inc. ✧ ☆
(formerly The Stewart Family Foundation)
c/o Michele Stewart
527 Madison Ave., Ste. 24
New York, NY 10022-4304

Established in 1991 in DE.
Donors: William P. Stewart; Barbara Stewart; Michele Stewart; Lisa Stewart Trust; Gregory Stewart Trust; Jeffrey Stewart Trust; William P. Stewart III Trust.
Foundation type: Independent foundation.
Financial data (yr. ended 12/31/04): Assets, $24,103 (M); gifts received, $707,500; expenditures, $709,292; qualifying distributions, $705,871; giving activities include $317,620 for 2 grants (high: $300,000; low: $17,620).
Purpose and activities: Giving for development projects in Vietnam.
Fields of interest: International affairs, formal/general education; International economic development.
International interests: Vietnam.
Type of support: General/operating support.
Limitations: Applications not accepted. Giving limited to Vietnam. No grants to individuals.
Application information: Contributes only to pre-selected organizations.
Officer and Directors:* Michele Stewart,* V.P.; Barbara Stewart.
EIN: 133292282

5932
The Charles Engelhard Foundation ▼ ✧
c/o Engelhard Hanovia, Inc.
Olympic Twrs.
645 5th Ave., Ste. 712
New York, NY 10022 (212) 935-2433
Contact: Mary Ogorzaly, Secy.

Incorporated in 1940 in NJ.
Donors: Charles Engelhard†; Engelhard Hanovia, Inc.; and others.
Foundation type: Independent foundation.
Financial data (yr. ended 12/31/05): Assets, $120,224,067 (M); expenditures, $10,669,398; qualifying distributions, $9,741,592; giving activities include $9,486,577 for 220 grants (high: $895,000; low: $500; average: $10,000–$200,000).
Purpose and activities: Emphasis on higher and secondary education, and cultural, medical, religious, wildlife, and conservation organizations.
Fields of interest: Arts; Secondary school/education; Higher education; Environment, natural resources; Animals/wildlife, preservation/protection; Biomedicine; Medical research, institute; Religion.
Type of support: General/operating support; Continuing support; Annual campaigns; Capital campaigns; Building/renovation; Endowments; Program development; Conferences/seminars; Publication; Research; Matching/challenge support.
Limitations: Applications not accepted. Giving primarily on a national basis. No grants to individuals.
Application information: Giving only to organizations known to the trustees. Unsolicited requests for funds not considered.
Board meeting date(s): Quarterly
Officers: Mary Ogorzaly, Secy.; Edward G. Beimfohr, Treas.
Trustees: Sophie Engelhard Craighead; Anne E. de la Renta; Charlene B. Engelhard; Susan O'Connor; Sally E. Pingree.
Number of staff: 1 full-time professional; 2 part-time professional.
EIN: 226063032
Selected grants: The following grants were reported in 2004.
$400,000 to Boston College, Chestnut Hill, MA.
$200,000 to Community Center for the Arts, Jackson, WY.
$200,000 to Delta Society, Renton, WA.
$200,000 to Monastery of Christ in the Desert, Abiquiu, NM.
$100,000 to American Prairie Foundation, Bozeman, MT.
$100,000 to Families First Missoula, Missoula, MT.
$100,000 to San Francisco Society for the Prevention of Cruelty to Animals, San Francisco, CA.
$10,000 to Midland School.
$10,000 to Premiere Commission, New York, NY.
$10,000 to Saint Marys Church.

5933
Englander Foundation, Inc. ▼ ✧
740 Park Ave.
New York, NY 10021 (212) 841-4148

Established in 1991 in NY.
Donors: Israel A. Englander; Englander Capital Corp.
Foundation type: Independent foundation.

Financial data (yr. ended 11/30/05): Assets, $7,578,961 (M); gifts received, $11,960,350; expenditures, $9,784,262; qualifying distributions, $9,780,262; giving activities include $9,774,709 for 163 grants (high: $2,094,000; low: $250; average: $1,000–$210,000).
Purpose and activities: Giving primarily for Jewish agencies and temples; some funding for education, health care, and human services.
Fields of interest: Elementary/secondary education; Theological school/education; Hospitals (general); Human services; Jewish federated giving programs; Jewish agencies & temples.
International interests: Israel.
Type of support: General/operating support; Continuing support; Annual campaigns; Capital campaigns; Building/renovation.
Limitations: Applications not accepted. Giving primarily in the metropolitan New York, NY, area. No grants to individuals.
Publications: Financial statement; Grants list.
Application information: Contributes only to pre-selected organizations.
Officers: Israel A. Englander, Pres.; Caryl S. Englander, V.P.; Allan S. Sexter, Secy.; Steven C. Weidman, Treas.
EIN: 133640833
Selected grants: The following grants were reported in 2005.
$2,094,000 to Congregation Yaldai Zion, Brooklyn, NY.
$1,878,500 to Mesivta Yeshiva Rabbi Chaim Berlin, Brooklyn, NY.
$1,000,000 to Yeshiva University, New York, NY.
$680,000 to Chabad, Upper East Side, New York, NY.
$297,500 to Bobover Yeshiva Bnei Zion, Brooklyn, NY.
$289,000 to Ramaz School, New York, NY.
$280,000 to M.Y. Keren Hashluchim, Brooklyn, NY.
$275,800 to Congregation Shaarei Zion of Bobov, Brooklyn, NY.
$32,000 to Yeshiva Mesivtah of Tucson, Tucson, AZ.
$28,594 to Congregation Kehilath Jeshurun, New York, NY.

5934
Epstein Philanthropies ✧
666 5th Ave., 14th Fl.
New York, NY 10103
Contact: Milton S. Teicher, Pres.

Established in 1977 in NY.
Donors: Thomas Epstein†; William A. Epstein†; Florence E. Teicher†.
Foundation type: Independent foundation.
Financial data (yr. ended 12/31/04): Assets, $13,015,015 (M); gifts received, $9,748,267; expenditures, $385,423; qualifying distributions, $325,000; giving activities include $325,000 for 45 grants (high: $55,000; low: $1,000).
Purpose and activities: Giving primarily for the arts, education, and human rights and poverty issues.
Fields of interest: Museums; Arts; Education; Health organizations, association; Human services; International human rights.
Limitations: Giving primarily in New York, NY. No support for religious or political organizations. No grants to individuals.
Application information: Application form not required.
Initial approach: Letter

Copies of proposal: 1
Deadline(s): None
Officers: Milton S. Teicher, Pres.; Vincent McGee, V.P.; James Mulcahy, Treas.
EIN: 132902852

5935
Equinox Foundation, Inc. ✧ ☆
c/o M.R. Weiser & Co.
20 Corporate Woods Blvd., Rm. 600
Albany, NY 12211

Established in 1990 in NY.
Donors: John D. Picotte; KMP Trust I; KMP Trust V.
Foundation type: Independent foundation.
Financial data (yr. ended 12/31/05): Assets, $11,919,404 (M); gifts received, $347,911; expenditures, $619,502; qualifying distributions, $511,293; giving activities include $463,133 for 36 grants (high: $150,000; low: $400).
Purpose and activities: Giving primarily for education and human services.
Fields of interest: Education; Boys & girls clubs; Human services; Roman Catholic agencies & churches.
Type of support: Annual campaigns.
Limitations: Applications not accepted. Giving primarily in NY. No grants to individuals.
Officers: John D. Picotte, Pres.; Michelle R. Leclair, Secy.; Margaret P. MacClarence, Treas.
Directors: Brooke A. Picotte; John D. Picotte, Jr.; Jeffrey P. Resnick.
EIN: 223109260
Selected grants: The following grants were reported in 2004.
$12,000 to Hope House, Albany, NY.
$10,000 to Capital City Rescue Mission, Albany, NY.
$2,000 to Adirondack Museum, Blue Mountain Lake, NY.
$2,000 to Mystic Seaport Museum, Mystic, CT.
$2,000 to Save the Bay, Providence, RI.
$2,000 to Village Community School, New York, NY.
$2,000 to Xavier High School, New York, NY.

5936
The Equipart Foundation ✧
2323 Eastchester Rd.
Bronx, NY 10469-5910

Established in 1986 in NY.
Donors: Arnold Berkowitz; Joseph Brachfeld; Isaac Goldbrenner; Israel Hartman; Equipart Assocs.; BHC Co.
Foundation type: Independent foundation.
Financial data (yr. ended 6/30/05): Assets, $12,923 (M); gifts received, $287,055; expenditures, $346,780; qualifying distributions, $346,463; giving activities include $346,463 for grants.
Purpose and activities: Giving primarily for Jewish organizations.
Fields of interest: Elementary/secondary education; Human services; Jewish agencies & temples.
Type of support: General/operating support.
Limitations: Applications not accepted. Giving primarily in NY. No grants to individuals.
Application information: Contributes only to pre-selected organizations.

Directors: Joseph Brachfeld; Isaac Goldbrenner; Israel Hartman.
EIN: 133355056
Selected grants: The following grants were reported in 2005.
$2,435 to Congregation Shaarei Chesed, Monsey, NY.
$1,600 to Congregation BMG.
$1,500 to Congregation Yismach Moshe, Brooklyn, NY.
$1,200 to Tomchei Shabbos, Monsey, NY.
$1,000 to Yad Eliezer, Brooklyn, NY.

5937
The Armand G. Erpf Fund, Inc. ✧
c/o Condon, O'Meara, McGinty, and Donnelly, LLP
3 New York Plz., 18th Fl.
New York, NY 10004
Application address: c/o Grant Admin., 640 Park Ave., New York, NY 10021, tel.: (212) 535-6678

Incorporated in 1951 in NY.
Donors: Armand G. Erpf†; Erpf Charitable Trust.
Foundation type: Independent foundation.
Financial data (yr. ended 11/30/05): Assets, $11,872,718 (M); gifts received, $183,398; expenditures, $671,273; qualifying distributions, $551,201; giving activities include $375,728 for 97 grants (high: $25,000; low: $65).
Purpose and activities: Giving primarily for conservation and the environment, including wildlife conservation. Giving also for arts and culture, education, human services, and health associations.
Fields of interest: Museums; Museums (art); Performing arts; Arts; Higher education; Education; Environment, natural resources; Animals/wildlife, preservation/protection; Health organizations, association; Human services.
Limitations: Giving primarily in New York, NY; funding also in DE, Washington, DC, and NJ. No grants to individuals, or for endowment funds.
Application information: Application form not required.
Initial approach: Proposal
Copies of proposal: 1
Deadline(s): None
Board meeting date(s): Quarterly
Officers: Sue Erpf Van de Bovenkamp, Pres.; Roger D. Stone, V.P.; Gina Caimi, Secy.; Armand B. Erpf, Treas.
Directors: Louis Auchincloss; Cornelia A. Erpf; Robert B. Oxnam; Sophie Marr Veronis.
EIN: 136085594

5938
Essel Foundation, Inc. ▼ ✧
2500 Westchester Ave.
Purchase, NY 10577 (914) 698-7133
Contact: Constance Lieber, Pres.

Established in 1966.
Donors: Stephen Lieber; Constance Lieber.
Foundation type: Independent foundation.
Financial data (yr. ended 11/30/05): Assets, $135,554,427 (M); gifts received, $3,697,220; expenditures, $5,633,565; qualifying distributions, $5,548,915; giving activities include $5,545,915 for 2 grants (high: $4,556,915; low: $989,000).

Purpose and activities: Support for research in neuroscience, biological psychiatry, and higher education.

Fields of interest: Higher education; Neuroscience research.

Type of support: General/operating support; Research.

Limitations: Applications not accepted. Giving on a national basis. No grants to individuals.

Application information: Contributes only to pre-selected organizations.

Officers: Constance Lieber, Pres.; Samuel Lieber, Secy.-Treas.

Trustee: Janice Lieber.

EIN: 136191234

Selected grants: The following grants were reported in 2005.

$4,556,915 to NARSAD Research Institute, Great Neck, NY. For unrestricted support.

5939
The Eunice Foundation ✧ ☆
c/o Ronald Berman
150 W. 56th St., Ste. 6703
New York, NY 10019

Established in 2000 in DE.

Donor: Ronald Berman.

Foundation type: Independent foundation.

Financial data (yr. ended 12/31/05): Assets, $199 (M); gifts received, $452,752; expenditures, $800,000; qualifying distributions, $800,000; giving activities include $800,000 for grants.

Purpose and activities: Giving primarily to a cancer hospital.

Fields of interest: Hospitals (specialty); Medical research, single organization support; Cancer research.

Limitations: Applications not accepted. Giving primarily in New York, NY. No grants to individuals.

Application information: Contributes only to pre-selected organizations.

Officer: Ronald Berman, Pres.

EIN: 134108529

5940
R. S. Evans Foundation, Inc. ✧
(formerly Evans Family Foundation, Inc.)
c/o Deutsche Bank Trust Co. of NY
P.O. Box 1297
Church St. Sta.
New York, NY 10008

Established in 1997 in CT.

Donor: Robert S. Evans.

Foundation type: Independent foundation.

Financial data (yr. ended 12/31/05): Assets, $7,913,473 (M); expenditures, $432,546; qualifying distributions, $373,525; giving activities include $361,000 for 26 grants (high: $50,000; low: $1,000).

Purpose and activities: Giving primarily for education, including higher education and business schools.

Fields of interest: Higher education; Business school/education; Education; Environment.

Limitations: Applications not accepted. No grants to individuals.

Application information: Contributes only to pre-selected organizations.

Officers: Robert S. Evans, Pres.; Susan C. Evans, Secy.

Directors: Ashley Reid Evans; Jonathan Perry Evans; Michael Robinson.

Agent: Deutsche Bank Trust Co. of NY.

EIN: 061480414

Selected grants: The following grants were reported in 2003.

$195,000 to Afghanistan Foundation, DC. For general support.

$25,000 to Babson College, School of Business, Babson Park, MA. For general support.

$25,000 to Eaglebrook School, Deerfield, MA. For general support.

$20,000 to Hebron Academy, Hebron, ME. For general support.

$10,000 to Grayson-Jockey Club Research Foundation, Lexington, KY. For general support.

$10,000 to Weill Medical College of Cornell University, New York, NY. For general support.

$5,000 to National Public Radio, DC. For general support.

$5,000 to Thoroughbred Retirement Foundation, Shrewsbury, NJ. For general support.

$5,000 to Trickle Up Program, New York, NY. For general support.

$5,000 to World Wildlife Fund, New York, NY. For general support.

5941
Everett Foundation ✧
150 E. 69th St.
New York, NY 10021
Contact: Edith B. Everett, Pres.

Incorporated in 1957 in NY.

Donors: Henry Everett‡; Edith B. Everett.

Foundation type: Independent foundation.

Financial data (yr. ended 12/31/04): Assets, $28,388,242 (M); expenditures, $4,308,814; qualifying distributions, $3,266,623; giving activities include $3,265,678 for 48 grants (high: $2,150,000; low: $100).

Purpose and activities: Giving for Jewish welfare and cultural organizations, including those in Israel; support for museums, botanical gardens, and other cultural programs; all levels of education; the disadvantaged, including issues of employment, hunger, and youth opportunities; the environment; areas of public interest, including citizenship, civic affairs groups, and advocacy; history and sociology, and public service internship programs.

Fields of interest: Media/communications; Museums; Historic preservation/historical societies; Arts; Education, association; Education, research; Elementary school/education; Vocational education; Higher education; Business school/education; Education; Employment; Youth development, citizenship; Human services; Youth, services; Voluntarism promotion; Jewish federated giving programs; Anthropology/sociology; Government/public administration; Public affairs, citizen participation; Economically disadvantaged.

International interests: Israel.

Limitations: Applications not accepted. Giving primarily in the metropolitan New York, NY, area. No support for hospitals, motion pictures, videos, or theatrical plays. No grants to individuals, or for capital campaigns, conferences, annual campaigns, endowments, and operating support.

Application information: Contributes only to pre-selected organizations.

Officers and Directors:* Edith B. Everett,* Pres.; Carolyn Everett,* Secy; David F. Everett.

EIN: 116038040

Selected grants: The following grants were reported in 2003.

$2,045,000 to FJC-A Foundation of Donor-Advised Funds, Everett Philanthropic Fund, New York, NY.

$50,200 to Jewish Community Center in Manhattan, New York, NY.

$11,000 to American Jewish World Service, New York, NY.

$10,080 to Columbia University, New York, NY.

$10,000 to American Museum of Natural History, New York, NY.

$10,000 to New York Botanical Garden, Bronx, NY.

$8,000 to Museum of Modern Art, New York, NY.

$2,000 to Harlem Educational Activities Fund, New York, NY.

$1,000 to Everybody Wins Foundation, New York, NY.

$1,000 to Manhattan Institute for Policy Research, New York, NY.

5942
F. & J.S. Fund, Inc. ✧
c/o Mac Corkindale
3960 Merrick Rd.
Seaford, NY 11783

Established in 1969.

Donor: David W. and Sadie Klau Foundation.

Foundation type: Independent foundation.

Financial data (yr. ended 12/31/05): Assets, $10,927,615 (M); gifts received, $154,500; expenditures, $738,719; qualifying distributions, $605,959; giving activities include $575,322 for 122 grants (high: $100,000; low: $100).

Purpose and activities: Giving primarily for education and health care.

Fields of interest: Higher education; Law school/education; Animals/wildlife, fisheries; Hospitals (general).

Limitations: Applications not accepted. Giving primarily in NY. No grants to individuals.

Application information: Contributes only to pre-selected organizations.

Officers: Felice K. Shea, Pres. and Treas.; Andrew B. Shea, V.P.; Steven J.C. Shea, V.P.; Sandra S. Weiskner, Secy.

EIN: 237042425

5943
Falconwood Foundation, Inc. ✧
67 Irving Pl., 12th Fl.
New York, NY 10023 (212) 984-1444
Contact: Stanley Lefkowitz, V.P.

Established in 1987 in NY.

Donor: Henry G. Jarecki.

Foundation type: Independent foundation.

Financial data (yr. ended 12/31/04): Assets, $225,303 (M); gifts received, $583,290; expenditures, $694,737; qualifying distributions, $694,699; giving activities include $694,175 for 50 grants (high: $108,800; low: $25).

Purpose and activities: Giving primarily for education and conservation.

Fields of interest: Higher education; Education; Environment, natural resources; Philanthropy/voluntarism.

Limitations: Giving on a national basis.

Application information: Application form not required.

Initial approach: Proposal

Deadline(s): None

Officers and Directors:* Henry G. Jarecki,* Pres. and Treas.; Stanley Lefkowitz, V.P. and Secy.; Thomas A. Russo.

EIN: 133456475

5944
Michael David Falk Foundation, Inc. ✧
Canal St. Station
P.O. Box 483
New York, NY 10013

Established in 1968 in NY.

Donor: Isidore Falk.

Foundation type: Independent foundation.

Financial data (yr. ended 12/31/05): Assets, $5,598,501 (M); expenditures, $2,208,739; qualifying distributions, $2,200,000; giving activities include $2,200,000 for 1 grant.

Fields of interest: Hospitals (general).

Limitations: Applications not accepted. Giving primarily in New York, NY. No grants to individuals.

Application information: Contributes only to pre-selected organizations.

Manager: Maurice B. Falk.

EIN: 136265854

5945
The Howard and Barbara Farkas Foundation ✧
c/o Gasser & Hayes
106-19 Metropolitan Ave.
Forest Hills, NY 11375-6739

Donor: Barbara Farkas†.

Foundation type: Independent foundation.

Financial data (yr. ended 12/31/03): Assets, $6,128,465 (M); gifts received, $572,543; expenditures, $400,083; qualifying distributions, $395,455; giving activities include $390,500 for 54 grants (high: $30,000; low: $500).

Fields of interest: Education; Food banks; Christian agencies & churches.

Limitations: Applications not accepted. Giving limited to NY. No grants to individuals.

Application information: Contributes only to pre-selected organizations.

Officers: John C. Crabill, Pres. and Treas.; James A. Beha, V.P.; Macy Ann Beha, Secy.

EIN: 133107852

Selected grants: The following grants were reported in 2004.

$20,000 to CARE, New York, NY.

$15,000 to Food Bank.

$15,000 to Fund for Public Schools, New York, NY.

$15,000 to Loyola School, New York, NY.

$10,000 to Holy Apostles Soup Kitchen, New York, NY.

$7,500 to Adaptive Sports Foundation, Windham, NY.

$5,025 to Saint John the Baptist Church, New York, NY.

$5,000 to Catholic Relief Services, New York, NY.

5946
The Fascitelli Family Foundation ✧
c/o Elizabeth Cogan
25 East End Ave., Ste. 11G
New York, NY 10028

Established in 1993 in NY.

Donors: Michael D. Fascitelli; Elizabeth Cogan Fascitelli.

Foundation type: Independent foundation.

Financial data (yr. ended 1/31/06): Assets, $538,705 (M); expenditures, $548,232; qualifying distributions, $537,200; giving activities include $537,200 for 68 grants (high: $200,000; low: $100; average: $1,000–$10,000).

Purpose and activities: Giving primarily for education, hospitals, and health associations.

Fields of interest: Museums (history); Higher education; Scholarships/financial aid; Hospitals (general); Health organizations, association; Jewish federated giving programs.

Limitations: Applications not accepted. Giving primarily in New York, NY. No grants to individuals.

Application information: Contributes only to pre-selected organizations.

Officers: Elizabeth Cogan Fascitelli, Treas.; Michael D. Fascitelli, Mgr.

EIN: 133748071

Selected grants: The following grants were reported in 2006.

$200,000 to Dartmouth College, Hanover, NH.

$27,000 to Columbia Grammar and Preparatory School, New York, NY. 2 grants: $2,000, $25,000

$25,000 to Rockefeller University, New York, NY.

$20,000 to Phillips Academy, Andover, MA.

$10,000 to Jewish Childrens Learning Lab, New York, NY.

$5,000 to Manhattan Theater Club, New York, NY.

$1,000 to Jazz at Lincoln Center, New York, NY.

$1,000 to Teach for America, New York, NY.

$250 to Alliance for Young Artists and Writers, New York, NY.

5947
The Fatta Foundation, Inc.
70 W. Chippewa St., Ste. 500
Buffalo, NY 14202-2013 (716) 566-2924

Established in 1998 in NY.

Donors: Angelo M. Fatta; Carol A. Fatta.

Foundation type: Independent foundation.

Financial data (yr. ended 12/31/05): Assets, $8,879,700 (M); expenditures, $556,767; qualifying distributions, $487,219; giving activities include $473,710 for 69 grants (high: $69,380; low: $50).

Purpose and activities: Giving primarily for the arts, education, and human services including a camp for handicapped children.

Fields of interest: Performing arts; Historic preservation/historical societies; Arts; Secondary school/education; Higher education; Education; Health care; Health organizations, association; Boys & girls clubs; Human services; Children/youth, services; Federated giving programs; Roman Catholic agencies & churches.

Limitations: Applications not accepted. Giving primarily in Buffalo, NY. No grants to individuals.

Application information: Contributes only to pre-selected organizations.

Board meeting date(s): Dec., annually

Officers and Directors:* Carol A. Fatta,* Pres.; Angelo M. Fatta,* Secy.-Treas.; John D. Fatta; Suzanne E. Fatta.

Number of staff: 1 full-time support.

EIN: 311617296

Selected grants: The following grants were reported in 2005.

$103,000 to Nardin Academy, Buffalo, NY.

$69,380 to Buffalo Philharmonic Orchestra, Buffalo, NY.

$30,250 to Buffalo Inner-City Scholarship Opportunity Network (BISON), Buffalo, NY.

$30,000 to Canisius College, Buffalo, NY.

$18,500 to Sisters Hospital Foundation, Buffalo, NY.

$15,200 to Roswell Park Cancer Institute, Buffalo, NY.

$15,000 to Artpark and Company, Lewiston, NY.

$8,500 to Buffalo Prep, Buffalo, NY.

$5,000 to Sheas Performing Arts Center, Buffalo, NY.

$1,845 to Burchfield-Penney Art Center, Buffalo, NY.

5948
Marianne G. Faulkner Trust
(formerly Marianne Galliard Faulkner Trust)
c/o JPMorgan Chase Bank, N.A.
345 Park Ave., 4th Fl., N41-N040
New York, NY 10154
Contact: Ed Jones, V.P., JPMorgan Chase Bank, N.A.

Trust established in 1959 in VT.

Donor: Marianne Gaillard Faulkner†.

Foundation type: Independent foundation.

Financial data (yr. ended 12/31/05): Assets, $10,152,979 (M); expenditures, $544,430; qualifying distributions, $461,100; giving activities include $437,625 for 2 grants.

Purpose and activities: Annual funding for groups identified by the donor; limited funding available to other groups primarily near or in Woodstock, VT within program areas.

Fields of interest: Education; Environment; Aging, centers/services.

Type of support: Building/renovation; General/operating support; Program development.

Limitations: Giving primarily in the Woodstock, VT, area, with emphasis on organizations identified by the donor. No grants to individuals, or for endowment funds.

Publications: Application guidelines; Grants list.

Application information: Prefer matching or 1-time grants.

Initial approach: Proposal

Copies of proposal: 1

Deadline(s): June 1

Board meeting date(s): As required

Final notification: Dec. 31

Trustee: JPMorgan Chase Bank, N.A.

Number of staff: None.

EIN: 136047458

5949
The Feil Family Foundation ✧
(formerly Louis & Gertrude Feil Foundation, Inc.)
370 7th Ave., Ste. 618
New York, NY 10001 (212) 563-6557

Established in 1977 in NY.

Donors: Louis Feil†; Gertrude Feil†.

Foundation type: Independent foundation.

Financial data (yr. ended 6/30/05): Assets, $1,530,485 (M); gifts received, $1,750,000; expenditures, $1,323,389; qualifying distributions, $1,323,139; giving activities include $1,321,805 for 69 grants (high: $501,500; low: $200).
Purpose and activities: Giving primarily for health and human services, and to Jewish agencies and temples.
Fields of interest: Higher education; Medical school/education; Hospitals (general); Health organizations, association; Human services; Jewish federated giving programs; Jewish agencies & temples.
Limitations: Applications not accepted. Giving primarily in NY.
Application information: Contributes only to pre-selected organizations.
Officers: Jeffrey Feil, Pres.; Carole Feil, V.P. and Secy.; Jay Anderson, Treas.
EIN: 132958414
Selected grants: The following grants were reported in 2004.
$1,000,000 to New York-Presbyterian Hospital, New York, NY.
$83,333 to American Jewish Joint Distribution Committee, New York, NY.
$25,000 to Graduate Center, City University of New York, New York, NY.
$25,000 to Hampton Synagogue, Hampton, NY.
$25,000 to Lower East Side Conservancy, New York, NY.
$15,900 to Jewish National Fund, New York, NY.
$10,000 to Crohns and Colitis Foundation of America, New York, NY.
$10,000 to Jewish Association for Services for the Aged, New York, NY.
$10,000 to Jewish Theological Seminary of America, New York, NY.
$10,000 to Weill Medical College of Cornell University, New York, NY.

5950
Jac & Eva Feinberg Foundation, Inc. ✧ ☆
c/o Schneider & Abrams
1333 Broadway, Rm. 516
New York, NY   10018

Established around 1946.
Donors: Elmsmere Assocs.; Abraham Feinberg†.
Foundation type: Independent foundation.
Financial data (yr. ended 8/31/05): Assets, $3,820 (M); gifts received, $2,250,000; expenditures, $2,253,483; qualifying distributions, $2,253,482; giving activities include $2,250,000 for 1 grant.
Fields of interest: Higher education; Medical research, institute.
Type of support: Research.
Limitations: Applications not accepted. Giving primarily in Waltham, MA; some giving also in New York, NY and Tel Aviv, Israel. No grants to individuals.
Publications: Annual report.
Application information: Contributes only to pre-selected organizations.
Officers: Norbert Weissberg, Pres.; Stephen R. Abrams, Secy.-Treas.
EIN: 136103597
Selected grants: The following grants were reported in 2003.
$625,000 to Brandeis University, Waltham, MA. For Center for Ethics Justice and Public Life.

$200,000 to Albert Einstein College of Medicine of Yeshiva University, Bronx, NY. For Feinberg chair.
$181,500 to Medical Development for Israel, New York, NY. For Schneider Medical Center.

5951
Susan & Leonard Feinstein Foundation ▼ ✧
(formerly Feinstein Family Foundation)
c/o Bed Bath & Beyond
110 Bi-County Blvd., Ste. 114
Farmingdale, NY   11735

Established in 1992.
Donors: Leonard Feinstein; Amy Feinstein.
Foundation type: Independent foundation.
Financial data (yr. ended 6/30/05): Assets, $94,124,027 (M); gifts received, $41,410; expenditures, $4,671,494; qualifying distributions, $4,450,769; giving activities include $4,442,522 for 123 grants (high: $2,000,000; low: $100; average: $1,000–$100,000).
Purpose and activities: Giving primarily for the arts, health care, and to Jewish agencies and temples.
Fields of interest: Arts; Hospitals (general); Health care; Health organizations, association; Jewish federated giving programs; Jewish agencies & temples.
Limitations: Applications not accepted. Giving primarily in NY. No grants to individuals.
Application information: Contributes only to pre-selected organizations.
Officers: Susan Feinstein, Vice-Chair.; Leonard Feinstein, Pres.; Amy Feinstein, Secy.
EIN: 113131761
Selected grants: The following grants were reported in 2005.
$2,000,000 to North Shore-Long Island Jewish Health System Foundation, Great Neck, NY. For general support.
$350,000 to UJA-Federation of New York, New York, NY. For general support for UJA-Federation of Long Island.
$225,000 to New York Institute of Technology, Old Westbury, NY. For general support.
$200,000 to Friends Academy, Locust Valley, NY. For general support.
$100,000 to American Friends of Shalva, New York, NY. For general support.
$100,000 to Friends of the Israel Defense Forces, New York, NY. For general support.
$100,000 to Hospital for Special Surgery, New York, NY. For general support.
$25,000 to Seeds of Peace, New York, NY. For general support.
$24,000 to National Jewish Medical And Research Center, Boca Raton, FL. For general support.
$20,000 to Project Renewal, New York, NY. For general support.

5952
Fernleigh Foundation ✧
1 Rockefeller Plz., 31st Fl.
New York, NY   10020
Contact: Charles H. Hamilton, Secy.

Established in 1993.
Donor: Jane F. Clark.
Foundation type: Independent foundation.
Financial data (yr. ended 12/31/04): Assets, $16,226,928 (M); expenditures, $767,752;

qualifying distributions, $675,850; giving activities include $675,850 for 16 grants (high: $100,000; low: $1,000).
Fields of interest: Arts; Education; Hospitals (general); Athletics/sports, equestrianism; Christian agencies & churches.
Limitations: Applications not accepted. Giving on a national basis.
Application information: Unsolicited requests for funds not accepted.
Officers and Directors: Jane F. Clark,* Pres.; Edward W. Stack,* V.P.; Charles H. Hamilton,* Secy.; Kevin S. Moore,* Treas.
EIN: 137027378
Selected grants: The following grants were reported in 2003.
$150,000 to United States Equestrian Team, Gladstone, NJ.
$100,000 to Clara Welch Thanksgiving Home, Cooperstown, NY.
$100,000 to Mary Imogene Bassett Hospital and Clinics, Cooperstown, NY.
$40,000 to National Baseball Hall of Fame and Museum, Cooperstown, NY.
$13,500 to Boys Club of New York, New York, NY.
$10,000 to Brookwood School, Cooperstown, NY.
$10,000 to Cooperstown Fire Department, Cooperstown, NY.
$10,000 to Society for the Prevention of Cruelty to Animals of Susquehanna, Susquehanna, PA.
$5,000 to Leatherstocking Theater Company, Cooperstown, NY.
$1,000 to FDNY Foundation, Brooklyn, NY.

5953
Andrew U. Ferrari Foundation ✧ ☆
c/o Anchin, Block & Anchin, LLP
1375 Broadway
New York, NY   10018

Donors: Andrew U. Ferrari; Barbara Ferrari.
Foundation type: Independent foundation.
Financial data (yr. ended 12/31/05): Assets, $1,084,055 (M); gifts received, $5,000; expenditures, $357,875; qualifying distributions, $345,735; giving activities include $345,735 for 39 grants (high: $250,000; low: $35).
Purpose and activities: Giving primarily for higher education as well as for social services for children, and families, and for housing and shelter, and health services.
Fields of interest: Museums; Performing arts centers; Arts; Elementary/secondary education; Higher education; Education; Human services; Children/youth, services; Family services.
Limitations: Applications not accepted.
Application information: Unsolicited requests for funds not accepted.
Trustees: Andrew U. Ferrari; Barbara Q. Ferrari.
EIN: 206084198

5954
The Ferriday Fund Charitable Trust ✧
c/o The Bank of New York, Tax Dept.
1 Wall St., 28th Fl.
New York, NY   10286
Application address: c/o Douglas J. Boyle, The Bank of New York, 1290 Ave. of Americas, 5th Fl., New York, NY 10104

Established in 1991 in NY.

Donor: Carolyn Ferriday†.
Foundation type: Independent foundation.
Financial data (yr. ended 7/31/05): Assets, $10,202,458 (M); expenditures $543,149; qualifying distributions, $498,635; giving activities include $475,230 for grants.
Purpose and activities: Giving primarily for education and historic preservation.
Fields of interest: Historic preservation/historical societies; Higher education; Education; Hospitals (general); Human services.
Limitations: Giving primarily in CT. No grants to individuals.
Application information:
Initial approach: Letter
Deadline(s): None
Trustees: Richard J. Carter, Jr.; The Bank of New York.
EIN: 136967609

5955
Eugene V. Fife Family Foundation ✧
c/o BCRS Group/Marcum & Kliegman, LLP
100 Wall St., 11th Fl.
New York, NY   10005
Contact: Eugene V. Fife, Tr.

Established in 1982 in CA.
Donor: Eugene V. Fife.
Foundation type: Independent foundation.
Financial data (yr. ended 1/31/05): Assets, $5,921,114 (M); expenditures, $404,771; qualifying distributions, $351,489; giving activities include $347,379 for 59 grants (high: $100,000; low: $500).
Purpose and activities: Giving primarily for higher education.
Fields of interest: Higher education; Education; Philanthropy/voluntarism; Protestant agencies & churches.
Type of support: General/operating support; Endowments.
Limitations: Applications not accepted. Giving primarily in VA and WV. No grants to individuals; no loans.
Application information: Contributes only to pre-selected organizations.
Trustees: Jonathan L. Cohen; Amy S. Fife; David Fife; Eugene V. Fife.
EIN: 133153715
Selected grants: The following grants were reported in 2004.
$100,832 to San Francisco Theological Seminary, San Anselmo, CA.
$50,000 to Berea College, Berea, KY.
$50,000 to Court Appointed Special Advocates (CASA), Piedmont, Charlottesville, VA.
$50,000 to Miller Center Foundation, Charlottesville, VA.
$13,000 to Thomas Jefferson Memorial Foundation, Charlottesville, VA.
$10,000 to Elon University, Elon College, NC.
$10,000 to Emory and Henry College, Emory, VA.
$10,000 to Jackson Hole Land Trust, Jackson, WY.
$2,000 to Mountain State University, Beckley, WV.
$1,000 to Legal Aid Justice Center, Charlottesville, VA.

5956
FIMF, Inc. ✧
c/o Hertz, Herson & Co., LLP
2 Park Ave., Ste. 1500
New York, NY   10016

Established in 1995 in DE and NY.
Foundation type: Independent foundation.
Financial data (yr. ended 12/31/05): Assets, $29,286,640 (M); expenditures, $1,106,719; qualifying distributions, $1,125,450; giving activities include $1,115,000 for 4 grants (high: $950,000; low: $10,000).
Purpose and activities: Giving primarily through a national donor-advised fund; support also to Jewish organizations and medical education.
Fields of interest: Medical school/education; Philanthropy/voluntarism; Jewish agencies & temples.
Limitations: Applications not accepted. Giving primarily in New York, NY. No grants to individuals.
Application information: Contributes only to pre-selected organizations.
Officer and Directors:* Susan Wexner,* Pres. and Secy.-Treas.; Bernard Agus.
EIN: 134072661

5957
Francis Finlay Foundation ✧
200 Park Ave.
New York, NY   10166

Established in 1997 in NY.
Donor: Francis Finlay.
Foundation type: Independent foundation.
Financial data (yr. ended 12/31/05): Assets, $2,737,445 (M); expenditures, $612,551; qualifying distributions, $612,551; giving activities include $611,931 for 14 grants (high: $181,950; low: $2,000; average: $10,000–$100,000).
Purpose and activities: Giving primarily for higher education.
Fields of interest: Arts; Higher education; Medical research, association.
Limitations: Applications not accepted. No grants to individuals.
Application information: Contributes only to pre-selected organizations.
Officers: Francis Finlay, Pres.; Robert Wessley, Secy.
EIN: 133922229

5958
First Niagara Bank Foundation
(formerly Lockport Savings Bank Foundation)
6950 S. Transit Rd.
P.O. Box 514
Lockport, NY   14095-0514   (716) 625-7002
Contact: Helen Tederous, Mgr., Corp. Affairs
FAX: (716) 625-8681;
E-mail: helen.tederous@fnfg.com; E-mail for Mentoring Matters: Central NY: mentoringcny@fnfg.com, Eastern NY: mentoringeny@fnfg.com, the Rochester, NY, area: mentoringroch@fnfg.com, Western NY: mentoringwng@fnfg.com; URL: http://www.fnfg.com/basetemp.asp?pID=aboutus&sID=foundation

Established in 1998 in NY.

Donors: Niagara Bancorp, Inc.; First Niagara Financial Group, Inc.; Lockport Savings Bank; First Niagra Bank.
Foundation type: Company-sponsored foundation.
Financial data (yr. ended 3/31/04): Assets, $14,417,902 (M); expenditures, $479,605; qualifying distributions, $451,422; giving activities include $446,800 for 23 grants (high: $80,800; low: $4,000).
Purpose and activities: The foundation supports organizations involved with mentoring and children and youth.
Fields of interest: Youth development, adult & child programs; Children/youth, services.
Type of support: Capital campaigns; Building/renovation; Equipment; Program development; Scholarship funds; Employee volunteer services.
Limitations: Giving primarily in areas of company operations in NY. No support for organizations not of direct benefit to the entire community, political organizations or candidates, or national or international organizations without significant local impact. No grants to individuals, or for lobbying efforts or golf tournaments; no grants for travel, administrative activities, or miscellaneous spending for Mentoring Matters.
Publications: Application guidelines.
Application information: Support is limited to 1 contribution per organization during any given year. Proposals should be no longer than 2,600 words for Mentoring Matters. Extraneous proposal materials are not encouraged for Mentoring Matters. Organizations receiving Mentoring Matters grants are asked to provide a final report. Proposals should be submitted in PDF format for Mentoring Matters.
Initial approach: Download application form and deliver proposal and application form to nearest bank branch; E-mail proposal for Mentoring Matters
Copies of proposal: 1
Deadline(s): None; Jan. 12 for Mentoring Matters
Board meeting date(s): Monthly
Final notification: Mar. 5 to Nov. 16 for Mentoring Matters
Officers: Dan Cantara, Pres.; James Miklinski, V.P.; Ann Segarra, Treas.; John J. Bisgrove; Sharon Randaccio; Ann Swan; Louise Woerner.
EIN: 161549641

5959
Harry and Jane Fischel Foundation ✧
60 E. 42nd St., Ste. 1419
New York, NY   10165

Incorporated in 1932 in NY.
Donor: Harry Fischel†.
Foundation type: Independent foundation.
Financial data (yr. ended 12/31/05): Assets, $9,280,135 (M); expenditures, $960,193; qualifying distributions, $516,281; giving activities include $344,832 for 10 grants (high: $281,000; low: $350).
Purpose and activities: Organized to develop Talmudic research to aid Jewish knowledge and present the Orthodox Jewish contributions to civilization. Funding also to an institute which includes a school for training judges for religious courts, publishes tracts in the field of religious law, researches and republishes Talmudic commentary in new editions utilizing heretofore unknown manuscripts, as well as to Jewish education and temples.

Fields of interest: Education; Jewish agencies & temples.
International interests: Israel.
Type of support: General/operating support.
Limitations: Applications not accepted. Giving primarily in Jerusalem, Israel; some giving also in Brooklyn and New York, NY. No grants to individuals.
Application information: Contributes only to pre-selected organizations.
Officers and Directors:* Chief Rabbi S.Y. Cohen,* Chair.; Rabbi O. Asher Reichel,* Pres.; Michael Jaspan, V.P. and Exec. Dir.; Ronald Jaspan,* Secy.; Frederic Goldstein,* Treas.; Seth M. Goldstein; Simeon H.F. Goldstein; Steven Jaspan; Rabbi Aaron Reichel; Rabbi Hillel Reichel; Jay Stepelman.
Number of staff: 1 part-time professional; 2 part-time support.
EIN: 135677832

5960
The Alan & Laraine Fischer Foundation ✧
28 Pryer Ln.
Larchmont, NY   10538

Established in 1984 in NY.
Donors: Alan A. Fischer; Laraine Fischer.
Foundation type: Independent foundation.
Financial data (yr. ended 5/31/04): Assets, $213,799 (M); gifts received, $558,000; expenditures, $349,185; qualifying distributions, $348,332; giving activities include $348,332 for 18 grants (high: $232,067; low: $10).
Purpose and activities: Giving for Jewish organizations.
Fields of interest: Human services; Jewish agencies & temples; Religion.
Type of support: General/operating support; Capital campaigns.
Limitations: Applications not accepted. Giving primarily in the greater New York, NY, area. No grants to individuals.
Application information: Contributes only to pre-selected organizations.
Officers and Directors:* Alan A. Fischer,* Pres.; Laraine Fischer,* Secy.-Treas.; Bernard Mindich.
EIN: 133235209
Selected grants: The following grants were reported in 2004.
$8,180 to Westchester Jewish Center, Mamaroneck, NY.
$4,000 to Film Society of Lincoln Center, New York, NY.
$3,000 to American Museum of Natural History, New York, NY.
$2,000 to National Actors Theater, New York, NY.
$2,000 to Variety Childrens Lifeline, Solana Beach, CA.
$1,100 to Emelin Theater, Mamaroneck, NY.
$100 to Larchmont Manor Park Society, Larchmont, NY.

5961
The Fisher Brothers Foundation, Inc. ✧
c/o Fisher Brothers
299 Park Ave.
New York, NY   10017

Established in 1981 in NY.
Donors: Fisher Brothers; Fisher Park Lane Co.; Fisher Capital Assets; 1345 Cleaning Service Co. II LP; 299 Cleaning Service Co. II LP; Plaza Cleaning Service Co. II LP.
Foundation type: Company-sponsored foundation.
Financial data (yr. ended 12/31/04): Assets, $908,529 (M); gifts received, $1,575,000; expenditures, $1,853,838; qualifying distributions, $1,839,838; giving activities include $1,829,084 for 31 grants (high: $750,000; low: $250).
Purpose and activities: The foundation supports Jewish agencies and temples and organizations involved with arts and culture, health, human services, and veterans.
Fields of interest: Arts; Health care; Human services; Federated giving programs; Jewish federated giving programs; Military/veterans' organizations; Jewish agencies & temples; Military/veterans.
Limitations: Applications not accepted. Giving primarily in New York, NY. No grants to individuals.
Application information: Contributes only to pre-selected organizations.
Directors: Arnold Fisher; Richard Fisher.
EIN: 133118286
Selected grants: The following grants were reported in 2003.
$800,000 to UJA-Federation of New York, New York, NY.
$750,000 to Intrepid Museum Foundation, New York, NY.
$105,000 to Temple Israel of the City of New York, New York, NY.
$50,000 to Anti-Defamation League of Bnai Brith, New York, NY.
$30,990 to Metropolitan Opera, New York, NY.
$25,000 to New York University, Child Study Center, New York, NY.
$10,000 to Settlement Housing Fund, New York, NY.
$6,000 to Metropolitan Museum of Art, New York, NY.
$5,000 to Lincoln Center for the Performing Arts, New York, NY.
$3,500 to Jackie Robinson Foundation, New York, NY.

5962
Zachary and Elizabeth Fisher Charitable Trust ✧ ☆
c/o Fisher Brothers
299 Park Ave.
New York, NY   10171

Established in 2004 in NY.
Donor: The Elizabeth Fisher Trust.
Foundation type: Independent foundation.
Financial data (yr. ended 12/31/05): Assets, $104,610 (M); gifts received, $13,500,000; expenditures, $14,013,248; qualifying distributions, $14,013,148; giving activities include $14,000,000 for 2 grants (high: $12,000,000; low: $2,000,000).
Fields of interest: Museums; Medical research.
Limitations: Applications not accepted. Giving primarily in NY. No grants to individuals.
Application information: Contributes only to pre-selected organizations.
Trustees: Martin L. Edelman; Arnold Fisher; Richard L. Fisher.
EIN: 047004908

5963
Louis & Gloria Flanzer Charitable Trust ✧
c/o E. Kaplan
335 Madison Ave., Ste. 1500
New York, NY   10017

Established in 1996 in FL.
Donors: Louis Flanzer; Gloria Flanzer.
Foundation type: Independent foundation.
Financial data (yr. ended 12/31/05): Assets, $7,468,216 (M); expenditures, $698,893; qualifying distributions, $698,150; giving activities include $698,150 for 10 grants (high: $501,500; low: $350).
Fields of interest: Higher education; Hospitals (general); Jewish agencies & temples.
Limitations: Applications not accepted. Giving primarily in NY. No grants to individuals.
Application information: Contributes only to pre-selected organizations.
Trustees: Gloria Flanzer; Louis Flanzer.
EIN: 137080259

5964
Fludzinski Foundation ✧
c/o Thales
140 Broadway, 45th Fl.
New York, NY   10005

Established in NY.
Donor: Marek T. Fludzinski.
Foundation type: Independent foundation.
Financial data (yr. ended 12/31/05): Assets, $1,027,839 (M); gifts received, $800,000; expenditures, $482,140; qualifying distributions, $470,135; giving activities include $470,035 for 20 grants (high: $150,000; low: $35).
Purpose and activities: Giving primarily for international relief, as well as for the training and use of assistance dogs; funding also for social services and wildlife.
Fields of interest: Animals/wildlife, preservation/protection; Animals/wildlife; Disasters, search/rescue; Youth development; Human services; International relief.
Limitations: Applications not accepted. Giving primarily in CA and NY; some funding nationally.
Application information: Contributes only to pre-selected organizations.
Trustees: Marek T. Fludzinski; Laurel G. Philippakos.
EIN: 134147622
Selected grants: The following grants were reported in 2004.
$100,000 to Doctors Without Borders USA, New York, NY.
$50,000 to Family Center, New York, NY.
$10,000 to Friends of Green Chimneys, Brewster, NY.
$3,000 to Farm Sanctuary, Watkins Glen, NY.
$3,000 to West Side Rowing Club, Buffalo, NY.

5965
The Aaron and Esther Fogel Foundation, Inc. ✧
c/o Bridgeview Nursing Home
143-10 20th Ave.
Whitestone, NY   11357

Established in 1998 in NY.

Donors: Aaron Fogel; Max Karfiol; Wolf Karfiol; Esther Fugel; Pearl Altman; Chaim Cohen; Nechama Cohen; BMG Charitable Foundation.
Foundation type: Independent foundation.
Financial data (yr. ended 7/31/04): Assets, $1,142,766 (M); gifts received, $463,355; expenditures, $508,181; qualifying distributions, $503,220; giving activities include $503,220 for 7 + grants (high: $475,000).
Fields of interest: Human services; Jewish agencies & temples.
Limitations: Giving primarily in Brooklyn and Far Rockaway, NY.
Directors: Aaron Fogel; Frady Kalter.
Board Members: Esther Fogel; Moshe Kalter.
EIN: 113459020

5966
Herman Forbes Charitable Trust ◇
c/o JPMorgan Chase Bank, N.A.
345 Park Ave., 4th Fl.
New York, NY 10154
Contact: Jacqueline Elias, V.P., JPMorgan Private Bank

Incorporated in 1982 in NY.
Donor: Herman Forbes†.
Foundation type: Independent foundation.
Financial data (yr. ended 3/31/05): Assets, $8,211,062 (M); expenditures, $488,385; qualifying distributions, $414,652; giving activities include $360,000 for 23 grants (high: $51,000; low: $4,000).
Purpose and activities: Giving primarily to Jewish organizations.
Limitations: Applications not accepted. Giving primarily in FL and New York, NY. No grants to individuals or for matching gifts or loans.
Publications: Grants list.
Application information: Unsolicited requests for funds not accepted.
Board meeting date(s): Mar. and Dec.
Trustees: William H. Fleece; JPMorgan Chase Bank, N.A.
EIN: 136814404

5967
Forbes Foundation ◇
c/o Forbes Inc.
60 5th Ave.
New York, NY 10011 (212) 620-2248

Established in 1979 in NJ.
Donors: Forbes Inc.; Forbes Family Holdings, Inc.
Foundation type: Company-sponsored foundation.
Financial data (yr. ended 12/31/05): Assets, $754 (M); gifts received, $1,878,779; expenditures, $1,879,052; qualifying distributions, $1,878,547; giving activities include $1,878,547 for 224 grants (high: $1,000,000; low: $100).
Purpose and activities: The foundation supports hospitals and organizations involved with arts and culture, education, health, and human services.
Fields of interest: Museums; Arts; Secondary school/education; Higher education; Education; Hospitals (general); Health care; Human services.
Type of support: General/operating support; Building/renovation; Endowments.
Limitations: Applications not accepted. Giving on a national basis. No grants to individuals; no loans; no matching gifts.

Application information: Contributes only to pre-selected organizations.
Board meeting date(s): As required
Officers and Director: Timothy C. Forbes, Pres.; Malcolm S. Forbes, Jr., V.P.; Christopher Forbes, Secy.-Treas.; Robert L. Forbes.
EIN: 237037319
Selected grants: The following grants were reported in 2004.
$1,000,000 to Princeton University, Princeton, NJ.
$500,000 to Brown University, Providence, RI.
$103,000 to Saint Marks School, San Rafael, CA. 2 grants: $3,000, $100,000
$50,000 to Portland Art Museum, Portland, OR.
$50,000 to Prince of Wales Foundation, DC.
$25,000 to American Friends of Versailles, Chicago, IL.
$25,000 to National Museum of Women in the Arts, DC.
$20,000 to Phillips Exeter Academy, Exeter, NH.
$1,000 to Frick Collection, New York, NY.

5968
Leo and Julia Forchheimer Foundation
(formerly The Forchheimer Foundation)
c/o Golenbock, Eiseman, Assor, Bell & Peskoe, LLP
437 Madison Ave., 35th Fl.
New York, NY 10022
Contact: Donald Hamburg

Established about 1957 in NY.
Donor: Leo Forchheimer†.
Foundation type: Independent foundation.
Financial data (yr. ended 12/31/04): Assets, $6,361,829 (M); expenditures, $1,636,583; qualifying distributions, $1,559,795; giving activities include $1,559,450 for 38 grants (high: $300,000; low: $200; average: $10,000–$50,000).
Purpose and activities: Giving primarily for hospitals, health agencies, higher education, including medical and technical education, Jewish welfare funds, museums, and social services.
Fields of interest: Museums; Higher education; Medical school/education; Hospitals (general); Health care; Health organizations, association; Human services; Jewish federated giving programs.
International interests: Israel.
Limitations: Applications not accepted. Giving primarily in New York, NY; giving also in Israel.
Application information: Contributes only to pre-selected charitable organizations.
Officers and Directors:* Rudolph Forchheimer,* Pres.; Barbara Kamen,* V.P.; Michael Jesselson,* Secy.-Treas.
Number of staff: None.
EIN: 136075112
Selected grants: The following grants were reported in 2003.
$1,750,000 to UJA-Federation of New York, New York, NY. 2 grants: $1,500,000, $250,000
$500,000 to Abraham Joshua Heschel School, New York, NY.
$500,000 to Hebrew Home for the Aged at Riverdale, Riverdale, NY.
$66,000 to AKIM, Israel-National Association for the Rehabilitation of the Mentally Handicapped, Tel Aviv, Israel. .
$50,000 to ELEM Youth in Distress, New York, NY.
$50,000 to Jewish Museum, New York, NY.
$30,000 to Yeshiva University Museum, New York, NY.
$25,000 to Dorot, New York, NY.

$25,000 to Leo Baeck Education Center Foundation, Houston, TX.

5969
The Ford Family Foundation ◇
(formerly The David B. & Virginia M. Ford Foundation)
c/o BCRS Assocs., LLC
100 Wall St., 11th Fl.
New York, NY 10005

Established in 1986 in PA.
Donor: David B. Ford.
Foundation type: Independent foundation.
Financial data (yr. ended 6/30/05): Assets, $19,671,879 (M); gifts received, $393,414; expenditures, $633,212; qualifying distributions, $582,018; giving activities include $581,018 for 54 grants (high: $343,720; low: $250).
Purpose and activities: Giving primarily for education, health associations, human services, and Christian agencies and churches.
Fields of interest: Elementary/secondary education; Higher education, university; Education; Health organizations, association; Human services; Christian agencies & churches.
Limitations: Applications not accepted. Giving primarily in PA. No grants to individuals; no loans.
Application information: Contributes only to pre-selected organizations.
Trustees: David B. Ford; David B. Ford, Jr.; James M. Ford; Virginia M. Ford.
EIN: 133385063

5970
The Ford Foundation ▼
320 E. 43rd St.
New York, NY 10017 (212) 573-5000
Contact: Secy.
FAX: (212) 351-3677;
E-mail: office-secretary@fordfound.org; URL: http://www.fordfound.org

Incorporated in 1936 in MI.
Donors: Henry Ford†; Edsel Ford†.
Foundation type: Independent foundation.
Financial data (yr. ended 9/30/05): Assets, $11,615,906,693 (M); expenditures, $663,979,509; qualifying distributions, $621,924,695; giving activities include $515,157,652 for 3,034 grants (high: $15,814,025; low: $2; average: $100,000–$250,000), $619,169 for 12 grants to individuals (high: $100,000; low: $503; average: $5,000–$25,000), $1,130,356 for employee matching gifts, $5,919,996 for 4 foundation-administered programs and $15,672,579 for loans/program-related investments.
Purpose and activities: The foundation's mission is to serve as a resource for innovative people and institutions worldwide. Its goals are to: strengthen democratic values, reduce poverty and injustice, promote international cooperation, and advance human achievement. Grants are made primarily within three broad categories: (1) asset building and community development; (2) knowledge, creativity, and freedom; and (3) peace and social justice. Local needs and priorities, within these subject areas, determine program activities in individual countries.
Fields of interest: Media/communications; Media, film/video; Museums; Performing arts; Performing arts, dance; Performing arts, theater; Performing

arts, music; Arts; Education, research; Education, early childhood education; Elementary school/ education; Secondary school/education; Higher education; Education; Environment, natural resources; Environment; Reproductive health; Reproductive health, sexuality education; Public health, STDs; AIDS; Crime/violence prevention, abuse prevention; Legal services; Employment; Agriculture; Housing/shelter, development; Youth development; Human services; Women, centers/ services; Minorities/immigrants, centers/services; International economic development; International affairs, arms control; International affairs, foreign policy; International human rights; International affairs; Civil rights, race/intergroup relations; Civil rights; Urban/community development; Rural development; Community development; Philanthropy/voluntarism; Social sciences; Economics; Law/international law; International studies; Public policy, research; Government/public administration; Public affairs, citizen participation; Leadership development; Religion, interfaith issues; Minorities; Women; Immigrants/refugees; Economically disadvantaged.

International interests: Africa; Asia; Latin America; Middle East; Russia; Southeast Asia.

Type of support: Management development/ capacity building; Income development; General/ operating support; Continuing support; Endowments; Program development; Conferences/ seminars; Film/video/radio; Publication; Seed money; Curriculum development; Fellowships; Research; Technical assistance; Consulting services; Program evaluation; Program-related investments/loans; Employee matching gifts; Grants to individuals; Matching/challenge support.

Limitations: Giving on an international basis, including the U.S., Africa and the Middle East, Asia, Russia, Latin America and the Caribbean. No support for programs for which substantial support from government or other sources is readily available, or for religious sectarian activities. No grants for routine operating costs, construction or maintenance of buildings, or undergraduate scholarships; graduate fellowships generally channeled through grants to universities or other organizations; no grants for purely personal or local needs.

Publications: Application guidelines; Annual report (including application guidelines); Informational brochure (including application guidelines); Newsletter; Occasional report.

Application information: Prospective applicants are advised to review the foundation's Web site for information or current funding guidelines. Foreign applicants should contact foundation for addresses of its overseas offices, through which they must apply. Application form not required.

Initial approach: Brief letter of inquiry
Copies of proposal: 1
Deadline(s): None
Board meeting date(s): Jan., May, and Sept.
Final notification: Initial indication as to whether proposal falls within program interests within 6 weeks

Officers and Trustees:* Kathryn S. Fuller,* Chair.; Susan V. Berresford,* Pres.; Barron M. Tenny, Exec. V.P., Secy., and Genl. Counsel; Linda B. Strumpf, V.P. and C.I.O.; Alison R. Bernstein, V.P., Knowledge, Creativity, and Freedom; Pablo J. Farias, V.P., Asset Building and Community Devel.; Mary E. McClymont, V.P.. Peace and Social Justice; Marta L. Tellado, V.P., Comms.; Nicholas M. Gabriel, Treas. and Dir., Financial Svcs.; Nancy P. Feller, Assoc.

Genl. Counsel; Afsaneh M. Beschloss; Anke A. Ehrhardt; Juliet V. Garcia; Irene Y. Hirano; J. Clifford Hudson; Wilmot G. James; Yolanda Kakabadse; Thurgood Marshall, Jr.; Richard Moe; Yolanda T. Moses; Carl B. Weisbrod; W. Richard West.

Number of staff: 281 full-time professional; 220 full-time support; 3 part-time support.

EIN: 131684331

Selected grants: The following grants were reported in 2005.

$3,500,000 to International Center for Transitional Justice, New York, NY. Toward general support for activities to help countries respond to legacy of human rights abuse, to advance accountability, respond to needs of victims, and to prevent recurrence of such violence.

$1,270,000 to African Virtual University, Nairobi, Kenya. To secure and oversee delivery of low-cost bandwidth for research and scholarly activities to consortium comprising Association of African Universities and 33 universities, payable over 3 years.

$1,100,000 to Anti-Defamation League of Bnai Brith, New York, NY. For on-line platform to deliver teacher education programs for A World of Difference Institute.

$800,000 to Public Radio Capital, Englewood, CO. For general support to expand choices for public radio programming in United States by protecting and expanding public radio's scarce broadcast assets, payable over 2 years.

$605,000 to University of Michigan, Ann Arbor, MI. To evaluate effectiveness of student dialogues for bridging inter-group differences in ten universities, payable over 3 years.

$600,000 to National Commission on Violence Against Women, Jakarta, Indonesia. For work to rebuild women's human rights and promote women's legal and economic empowerment in post-tsunami Aceh, payable over 2 years.

$300,000 to Advancement Project, DC. For Voter Protection Program to coordinate nonpartisan efforts to educate public about voting rights policies to ensure that all eligible Americans participate in democratic process.

$260,000 to Charities Aid Foundation (UK), West Malling, England. For small grants competitions and technical assistance to build capacity of self-help groups of people living with HIV-AIDS across Russia, payable over 2 years.

$225,000 to Centre for Research and Innovation in Social Policy and Practice (CENTRIS), Newcastle Upon Thyme, England. To evaluate International Initiative to Strengthen Philanthropy, payable over 2.50 years.

$200,000 to Watershed Research and Training Center, Hayfork, CA. To undertake regional organizing and training for community-based forestry groups, payable over 1.50 years.

5971
Foundation for Child Development

145 E. 32nd St., 14th Fl.
New York, NY 10016-6055
Contact: Mark Bogosian, Comms. and Grants Assoc.
FAX: (212) 213-5897;
E-mail: inforequest@fcd-us.org; URL: http://www.fcd-us.org

Incorporated as a voluntary agency in 1900 in NY and established as the Association for the Aid of Crippled Children in 1908; current name adopted in 1972, affirming a broader focus on children at risk.

Donors: Milo M. Belding†; Annie K. Belding†; and others.

Foundation type: Independent foundation.

Financial data (yr. ended 3/31/06): Assets, $114,164,869 (M); gifts received, $17,595; expenditures, $5,212,741; qualifying distributions, $4,685,039; giving activities include $2,981,203 for 29+ grants (high: $354,333), and $1,055,383 for foundation-administered programs.

Purpose and activities: The Foundation for Child Development (FCD) is a national, private philanthropy dedicated to the principle that all families should have the social and material resources to raise their children to be healthy, educated and productive members of their communities. The foundation seeks to understand children, particularly the disadvantaged, and to promote their well-being. The foundation believes that families, schools, nonprofit organizations, businesses and government at all levels share complementary responsibilities in the critical task of raising new generations.

Fields of interest: Education, reform; Education, early childhood education; Public policy, research; Children; Immigrants/refugees.

Type of support: Fellowships; Endowments; General/operating support; Continuing support; Program development; Conferences/seminars; Publication; Seed money; Research; Technical assistance.

Limitations: Applications not accepted. Giving limited to research and policy grants related to foundation focus and restricted to the U.S. No support for the direct provision of pre-kindergarten education, child care, or health care. No grants for capital campaigns, endowments, or for the purchase, construction, or renovation of buildings.

Publications: Annual report; Grants list; Informational brochure; Newsletter; Occasional report; Program policy statement.

Application information: Unsolicited requests for funds not accepted.

Board meeting date(s): Mar., June, and Oct.

Officers and Directors:* P. Lindsay Chase-Lansdale, Ph.D.*, Chair.; Ruby Takanishi, Ph.D.*, Pres.; Arthur Greenberg, V.P., Strategic Partnerships, Institute for Student Achievement; Margarita Rosa,* Secy.; John L. Furth, Treas.; Michael Cohen; Anthony J. Colon; Nancy Folbre; Barbara Doran; Ellen Berland Gibbs; Karen Hill-Scott; Christopher Knowlton; David Lawrence; Julius B. Richmond; Barbara Paul Robinson; Margaret Beale Spencer, Ph.D.

Number of staff: 5 full-time professional; 1 part-time professional; 1 part-time support.

EIN: 131623901

Selected grants: The following grants were reported in 2005.

$403,999 to Georgetown University, DC. For continuing longitudinal study of impact of Tulsa Universal Pre-Kindergarten program on children from PreK-3.

$300,000 to Center for Law and Social Policy, DC. For documentation of uses of Title I funds for early education, including policy options to serve PreK, kindergarten and early elementary education needs of newcomer children and families.

$250,000 to University of Maryland-College Park Foundation, College Park, MD. For continuing support for Journalism Fellowships in Child and Family Policy.

$200,000 to Pew Charitable Trusts, Philadelphia, PA. To develop guide and model procedures for states to establish accountability systems for state PreK programs, and to connect them to K-12 assessment systems.

$169,594 to Yale University, New Haven, CT. For analysis of topics related to PreK-3 from National Pre-Kindergarten Study.

$150,000 to American Forum, DC. For locally authored opinion pieces, press releases, and public service announcements on PreK-3 for key state-based media.

$120,750 to Harvard University, Cambridge, MA. For series of articles in the Harvard Education Letter on effective ways to educate children from PreK-3.

$104,479 to NEA Foundation for the Improvement of Education, DC. For identification and promotion of provisions in collective bargaining agreements that support well-aligned system of PreK-3 instruction.

$65,000 to Minnesota Public Radio, Saint Paul, MN. For Work and Family Desk to cover early childhood education, immigrant children, and topics related to the FCD index of Child Well-Being.

$65,000 to New School, New York, NY. For feature article and series of op-eds related to FCDs PreK-3 initiative.

5972
Franconia Foundation, Inc. ◇
c/o Eli Robins
1333 Broadway, Ste. 730
New York, NY 10018

Established in 1991 in NY.
Donors: Willy Beer; Rachel Beer.
Foundation type: Independent foundation.
Financial data (yr. ended 10/31/05): Assets, $1,931,145 (M); expenditures, $748,364; qualifying distributions, $690,086; giving activities include $689,236 for 299 grants (high: $125,000; low: $18).
Purpose and activities: Giving primarily to Jewish agencies and temples, and for education.
Fields of interest: Elementary/secondary education; Human services; Jewish federated giving programs; Jewish agencies & temples.
Limitations: Applications not accepted. Giving primarily in NY. No grants to individuals.
Application information: Contributes only to pre-selected organizations.
Officers: Elliot Beer, V.P.; Rachel Beer, Secy.
Director: Henri Beer.
Manager: Willy Beer.
EIN: 133646294

5973
Francqui Foundation ◇ ☆
(formerly Foundation Francqui Belgium)
c/o Lutz and Carr
300 E. 42nd St.
New York, NY 10017 (212) 697-2299

Established in Belgium.
Foundation type: Independent foundation.
Financial data (yr. ended 12/31/05): Assets, $53,570,838 (M); expenditures, $1,652,811; qualifying distributions, $1,559,200; giving activities include $846,860 for 4 grants (high: $283,266; low: $128,310).

Purpose and activities: Giving primarily for Belgian scholars and education.
Fields of interest: Higher education.
International interests: Belgium.
Limitations: Applications not accepted. Giving limited to Belgium. No grants to individuals.
Application information: Contributes only to pre-selected organizations.
Officers: Mark Eyskens, Chair.; Herman Balthazar, Vice-Chair.; Viscount Emile Davignon, Vice-Chair.; Luc Eyckmans, Exec. Dir.
Directors: Thierry Boon; Sir. Emile Boulpaep; Sir. Jacques Brotchi; Desire Collen; Count Claude d'Aspremont-Lynden; Baron Paul deMeester; Baroness Janine Delruelle; Count Frederic Francqui; Baron Daniel Janssen; Regine Kurgan-Van Hentenryk; Guy Quaden; Niceas Schamp; Alexander Sevrin; Baroness Greta Suetens-Bourgeois; Anton van Rossum; Baron Piet Van Waeyenberge.
EIN: 986001286

5974
Ernst & Elfriede Frank Foundation, Inc ◇
112-01 Queens Blvd., Apt. 11C
Forest Hills, NY 11375

Established around 1962.
Donor: Ernst L. Frank.
Foundation type: Independent foundation.
Financial data (yr. ended 8/31/05): Assets, $8,064,347 (M); expenditures, $372,776; qualifying distributions, $368,553; giving activities include $363,898 for 143 grants (high: $20,000; low: $100).
Purpose and activities: Giving primarily for the arts, health, and human services.
Fields of interest: Arts; Education; Health care; Health organizations, association; Human services; Religion.
International interests: Canada; South America.
Limitations: Applications not accepted. Giving on a national and international basis, with emphasis on Washington, DC, MA, and NY; some funding also in Canada and South America. No grants to individuals.
Application information: Contributes only to pre-selected organizations.
Officers: Sybil Ann Brennan, V.P.; Ernst H. Frank, V.P.; Eva-Maria Tausig, V.P.
EIN: 136106471

5975
Sidney E. Frank Foundation ◇ ☆
20 Cedar St.
New Rochelle, NY 10801

Established in 2004 in NY.
Donor: Sidney E. Frank†.
Foundation type: Independent foundation.
Financial data (yr. ended 12/31/05): Assets, $12,942,622 (M); gifts received, $4,663,079; expenditures, $27,576,245; qualifying distributions, $27,188,074; giving activities include $27,188,074 for 36+ grants.
Fields of interest: Higher education; Education; Hospitals (general); Cancer; Human services.
Limitations: Applications not accepted. Giving primarily in NY. No grants to individuals.
Application information: Contributes only to pre-selected organizations.

Director: Cathy Halstead.
EIN: 206383779

5976
Evan Frankel Foundation
c/o Nancy Wendell
P.O. Box 5072
East Hampton, NY 11937 (631) 329-2833
FAX: (631) 329-7102;
E-mail: frankelfound@hamptons.com

Established in 1978.
Donor: Evan M. Frankel†.
Foundation type: Independent foundation.
Financial data (yr. ended 9/30/05): Assets, $2,335,483 (M); expenditures, $626,477; qualifying distributions, $554,168; giving activities include $457,695 for 62 grants (high: $100,000; low: $250).
Purpose and activities: Giving primarily for higher education in the humanities and the environment.
Fields of interest: Humanities; Higher education; Environment, land resources; Environment.
Type of support: General/operating support; Continuing support; Annual campaigns; Capital campaigns; Building/renovation; Equipment; Land acquisition; Endowments; Professorships; Fellowships; Scholarship funds; Research; Matching/challenge support.
Limitations: Applications not accepted. Giving primarily in Manhattan and Suffolk County, NY and Los Angeles, CA. No grants to individuals.
Application information: Unsolicited requests for funds not accepted.
Board meeting date(s): Varies
Officers and Directors:* Ernest Frankel,* Pres.; C. Leonard Gordon,* Secy.; Andrew E. Sabin,* Treas.; Nancy Wendell, Exec. Dir.
Number of staff: 1 full-time professional.
EIN: 132998402

5977
The Regina Bauer Frankenberg Foundation
c/o JPMorgan Chase Bank, N.A.
345 Park Ave., 4th Fl., N41-N040
New York, NY 10154
Contact: Megan Watkins, Prog. Off., JPMorgan Chase Bank, N.A.
FAX: (212) 464-2305;
E-mail: sara.j.rosen@jpmchase.com; URL: http://foundationcenter.org/grantmaker/frankenberg/

Established in 1994 in NY.
Donor: Regina Bauer Frankenberg†.
Foundation type: Independent foundation.
Financial data (yr. ended 12/31/05): Assets, $23,971,109 (M); expenditures, $1,346,907; qualifying distributions, $1,142,648; giving activities include $1,120,000 for 16 grants (high: $150,000; low: $15,000).
Purpose and activities: Giving exclusively for animal welfare, particularly for the protection of endangered wild animals or threatened species by supporting conservation and research, and for strengthening the capacity of organizations working to reduce the homelessness, mistreatment and euthanasia of companion animals through adoption, training, spaying/neutering, and other programs.
Fields of interest: Animal welfare; Animals/wildlife, preservation/protection.

Type of support: Capital campaigns; Building/renovation; Program development.
Limitations: Giving for companion animals limited to New York, NY; giving for wildlife on a national and international scope. No grants to individuals; no loans.
Publications: Application guidelines; Grants list.
Application information: Application form not required.

Initial approach: Proposal
Copies of proposal: 1
Deadline(s): July 1
Board meeting date(s): Nov.
Final notification: Dec. 31

Trustee: JPMorgan Chase Bank, N.A.
Number of staff: None.
EIN: 133741659
Selected grants: The following grants were reported in 2004.
$100,000 to Friends of Animals, Darien, CT. For Spay and Neuter project.
$100,000 to Fund for Public Health in New York, New York, NY. For pilot program to address animal hoarding in New York City.
$75,000 to Animal Haven, Flushing, NY. For hiring development director.
$75,000 to Johns Hopkins University, Baltimore, MD. For Altweb project of Center for Alternatives to Animal Testing.
$60,000 to Farm Sanctuary, Watkins Glen, NY. For capital support to complete Emergency Rescue and Rehabilitation Center in New York.
$50,000 to American Littoral Society, Highlands, NJ.
$50,000 to Audubon Society, National, New York, NY. For Seabird Restoration Project.
$50,000 to Earth Island Institute, San Francisco, CA. For Dolphin Safe Tuna Label Campaign.
$50,000 to Humane Society of the United States, DC. For Humane Society University.
$50,000 to Predator Conservation Alliance, Bozeman, MT. For Northern Great Plains Prairie Dog Ecosystem Restoration.

5978
Julie and Martin Franklin Charitable Foundation, Inc. ✧
555 Theodore Fremd Ave., Ste. B-302
Rye, NY 10580

Established in 1994.
Donors: Julie Franklin; Martin E. Franklin.
Foundation type: Independent foundation.
Financial data (yr. ended 10/31/05): Assets, $1,232,029 (M); gifts received, $944,750; expenditures, $460,874; qualifying distributions, $419,905; giving activities include $419,905 for 57 grants (high: $100,000; low: $180).
Purpose and activities: Giving primarily to Jewish organizations, youth services, and medical centers.
Fields of interest: Hospitals (general); Medical research; Human services; Jewish agencies & temples.
Limitations: Applications not accepted. Giving primarily in NY. No grants to individuals.
Application information: Contributes only to pre-selected organizations.
Officers: Martin E. Franklin, Pres. and Treas.; Julie Franklin, V.P. and Secy.
Director: Ian Ashken.
EIN: 133800643

5979
Herman Frasch Foundation for Chemical Research ✧
c/o U.S. Trust
114 W. 47th St.
New York, NY 10036-1532
Contact: Andrew Lane, V.P.
FAX: (212) 852-3377; Address for requesting application forms: c/o American Chemical Society, 1155 16th St. N.W., Washington, DC 20036, tel.: (202) 872-4487

Trust established in 1924 in NY.
Donor: Elizabeth Blee Frasch‡.
Foundation type: Independent foundation.
Financial data (yr. ended 12/31/05): Assets, $10,645,368 (M); expenditures, $797,731; qualifying distributions, $743,606; giving activities include $680,000 for 18 grants (high: $40,000; low: $10,978).
Purpose and activities: Grants for research in agricultural chemistry made for 5-year periods to nonprofit incorporated institutions in the U.S., selected with the advice of the American Chemical Society as well as Frasch committee members.
Fields of interest: Agriculture; Chemistry.
Type of support: Research.
Limitations: Applications not accepted. Giving limited to the U.S. No grants to individuals, or for endowment funds, building funds, operating budgets, scholarships, fellowships, or matching gifts; no loans.
Application information: Grants are awarded in five-year cycles. The next cycle will begin in 2007. An RFP will be issued by the American Chemical Society sometime in 2006. No applications will be reviewed until then.
Trustee: U.S. Trust.
Number of staff: 1 part-time professional.
EIN: 136073145

5980
Samuel Freeman Charitable Trust ✧
c/o U.S. Trust
114 W. 47th St.
New York, NY 10036-1532
Contact: Linda R. Franciscovich, Managing Dir., U.S. Trust; Carolyn L. Larke, V.P., U.S. Trust
FAX: (212) 852-3377

Established in 1981 in NY.
Donor: Samuel Freeman‡.
Foundation type: Independent foundation.
Financial data (yr. ended 12/31/05): Assets, $44,111,852 (M); expenditures, $1,513,147; qualifying distributions, $1,286,310; giving activities include $1,086,500 for grants.
Purpose and activities: Preferred consideration is given to cancer research and treatment; the preservation, exhibition, and operation of historical railway equipment; and secondary schools and universities.
Fields of interest: Historic preservation/historical societies; Secondary school/education; Higher education; Cancer; Cancer research.
Type of support: General/operating support; Continuing support; Annual campaigns; Seed money.
Limitations: Applications not accepted. Giving on a national basis. No grants to individuals or private foundations.

Application information: Proposals are accepted by invitation only. Therefore, the trust is unable to consider or respond to unsolicited proposals.
Trustees: Daniel P. Kelly; William E. Murray; Hilton C. Smith, Jr.; Pamela Stack; U.S. Trust.
EIN: 136803465
Selected grants: The following grants were reported in 2003.
$150,000 to Health Sciences Foundation of the Medical University of South Carolina, Charleston, SC.
$30,000 to Marymount Manhattan College, New York, NY.
$25,000 to South Carolina Aquarium, Charleston, SC.
$20,000 to College of Charleston Foundation, Charleston, SC.
$15,000 to EastWest Institute, New York, NY.
$10,000 to American Friends of the State Hermitage Museum, New York, NY.
$10,000 to Spoleto Festival USA, Charleston, SC.
$5,000 to Furman University, Greenville, SC.
$5,000 to Madeira School, McLean, VA.
$1,000 to Leukemia & Lymphoma Society, White Plains, NY.

5981
Freeman Foundation ▼
c/o The Rockefeller Trust Company
30 Rockefeller Plz.
New York, NY 10112 (212) 649-5853
Contact: George S. Tsandikos
E-mail: freemanfoundation@hjsimmons.com;
Application address: 499 Tabor Hill Road, Stowe, VT 05672

Established in 1978 in VT.
Donors: Houghton Freeman; Mansfield Freeman‡; members of the Freeman family.
Foundation type: Independent foundation.
Financial data (yr. ended 12/31/05): Assets, $1,105,466,120 (M); expenditures, $44,172,936; qualifying distributions, $43,956,856; giving activities include $42,067,148 for 175 grants (high: $8,300,000; low: $1,000; average: $10,000–$100,000).
Purpose and activities: Support primarily for the promotion of international understanding and farmland preservation projects in the state of VT.
Fields of interest: Education, public education; Environment, natural resources; International affairs, goodwill promotion; International studies.
International interests: Asia.
Type of support: Research; Scholarship funds; Curriculum development; Professorships; General/operating support; Land acquisition; Program development; Fellowships; Exchange programs; Matching/challenge support.
Limitations: Giving primarily in VT for conservation and environment grants; Asian studies grants are awarded nationally. No grants to individuals, or for endowments or capital campaigns.
Publications: Annual report.
Application information: Application form not required.

Initial approach: Letter
Copies of proposal: 6
Deadline(s): One month before meetings
Board meeting date(s): Quarterly

Officer: Graeme Freeman, Exec. Dir.
Trustees: Doreen Freeman; Houghton Freeman; George B. Snell.

Number of staff: 1
EIN: 132965090
Selected grants: The following grants were reported in 2005.

$8,300,000 to Wesleyan University, Middletown, CT. For Freeman Asian Scholars Program.

$2,460,239 to Vermont Land Trust, Montpelier, VT. For farm and land conservation projects and for general support.

$2,000,000 to University of Vermont, Burlington, VT. For Freeman Medical Scholars Program.

$1,795,500 to Institute of International Education, New York, NY. For tsunami relief education projects in Thailand, and Aceh, Indonesia.

$497,000 to Preservation Trust of Vermont, Burlington, VT. For historic conservation projects and for general support.

$339,250 to Shelburne Farms, Shelburne, VT. For Phase Two renovations of Farm Barn.

$120,000 to Associated Kyoto Program, Northampton, MA. For scholarships for Smith College students participating in Program.

$100,000 to United Board for Christian Higher Education in Asia, New York, NY. For Faculty Fellowships.

$100,000 to University of Kansas, Lawrence, KS. For National Consortium for Teaching about Asia (NCTA), multi-year initiative to encourage and facilitate teaching and learning about Asia in world history, geography, social studies, and literature courses.

$75,000 to Northeast Cultural Coop, Amherst, NH. For East by Northeast, public program on Southeast Asia.

5982
Tom and Kathy Freston Foundation ✦ ☆
57 E. 66th St.
New York, NY   10021

Established in 2003 in NY.
Donors: Thomas E. Freston; Kathleen L. Freston.
Foundation type: Independent foundation.
Financial data (yr. ended 12/31/05): Assets, $1,706,508 (M); gifts received, $484,643; expenditures, $383,370; qualifying distributions, $361,219; giving activities include $348,688 for 20 grants (high: $86,750; low: $250).
Fields of interest: Museums (natural history); Animal welfare; Children, services; Family services; Federated giving programs.
Limitations: Applications not accepted. No grants to individuals.
Application information: Contributes only to pre-selected organizations.
Trustees: Andrew Freston; Kathleen L. Freston; Thomas E. Freston.
EIN: 736350005

5983
Frey Family Foundation, Inc. ✦ ☆
98 Cliff Rd.
Port Jefferson, NY   11777

Donor: Robert Frey.
Foundation type: Operating foundation.
Financial data (yr. ended 12/31/05): Assets, $11,203,907 (M); gifts received, $3,000,000; expenditures, $657,902; qualifying distributions, $607,877; giving activities include $602,240 for grants.

Fields of interest: Education; Religion.
Limitations: Applications not accepted.
Application information: Contributes only to pre-selected organizations.
Officers: Robert Frey, Pres.; Stephen Rizzo, Secy.; Kathryn Frey, Treas.
EIN: 113640474

5984
Fribourg Family Foundation ✦
277 Park Ave., 50th Fl.
New York, NY   10172

Established in 2000 in NY.
Donor: Michel Fribourg‡.
Foundation type: Independent foundation.
Financial data (yr. ended 12/31/05): Assets, $731,395 (M); gifts received, $1,145,597; expenditures, $1,728,304; qualifying distributions, $1,722,274; giving activities include $1,721,924 for 118 grants (high: $500,000; low: $200).
Purpose and activities: Giving primarily to Jewish agencies and schools, the arts, higher education, hospitals and youth development.
Fields of interest: Arts; Higher education, university; Hospitals (general); Human services; Children/youth, services; Jewish federated giving programs; Jewish agencies & temples.
Limitations: Applications not accepted. Giving primarily in NY. No grants to individuals.
Application information: Contributes only to pre-selected organizations.
Trustees: William Cafarella; Charles Fribourg; Mary-Ann Fribourg; Paul Jules Fribourg; Teresa E. McCaslin; Susan McIntyre.
EIN: 134148779
Selected grants: The following grants were reported in 2004.

$200,000 to New York University, New York, NY.
$25,000 to Human Rights Watch, New York, NY.
$25,000 to Lincoln Center Theater, New York, NY.
$25,000 to National Dance Institute, New York, NY.
$25,000 to Nightingale-Bamford School, New York, NY.
$25,000 to School of American Ballet, New York, NY.
$20,000 to Browning School, New York, NY.
$7,500 to Trinity School, New York, NY.
$5,000 to International Rescue Committee, New York, NY.
$2,500 to Young Concert Artists, New York, NY.

5985
The Barry Friedberg and Charlotte Moss Family Foundation ✦
c/o Merrill Lynch Trust Co.
2 World Financial Ctr., 38th Fl.
New York, NY   10281-6100

Established in 1998 in NY.
Donor: Barry S. Friedberg.
Foundation type: Independent foundation.
Financial data (yr. ended 5/31/06): Assets, $1,135,062 (M); gifts received, $140,200; expenditures, $888,397; qualifying distributions, $885,075; giving activities include $885,075 for 125 grants (high: $200,000; low: $100).
Purpose and activities: Giving primarily for the performing arts, education, children, youth and social services, health associations, and Jewish organizations.

Fields of interest: Performing arts; Performing arts, ballet; Historic preservation/historical societies; Arts; Education; Hospitals (general); Health organizations, association; Human services; Children/youth, services; Jewish agencies & temples.
Limitations: Applications not accepted. Giving primarily in New York, NY. No grants to individuals.
Application information: Contributes only to pre-selected organizations.
Trustees: Barry S. Friedberg; Charlotte A. Moss.
EIN: 137154197

5986
Friedman Family Foundation ▼ ✦
(formerly Stephen & Barbara Friedman Foundation)
c/o BCRS
100 Wall St., 11th Fl.
New York, NY   10005   (212) 440-0800

Established in 1979 in NY.
Donors: Stephen B. Friedman; Barbara Friedman.
Foundation type: Independent foundation.
Financial data (yr. ended 7/31/05): Assets, $20,803,330 (M); expenditures, $4,035,966; qualifying distributions, $3,781,195; giving activities include $3,780,250 for 60 grants (high: $1,250,000; low: $200; average: $5,000–$50,000).
Purpose and activities: Giving primarily for higher education. Some support for health organizations and for various Jewish organizations.
Fields of interest: Higher education; Human services; Jewish federated giving programs; Jewish agencies & temples; General charitable giving.
Limitations: Applications not accepted. Giving primarily in NY. No grants to individuals.
Application information: Contributes only to pre-selected organizations.
Trustees: David Cohen; Suzy Cohen; David Friedman; Caroline Levy.
EIN: 133025979
Selected grants: The following grants were reported in 2005.

$1,250,000 to Weill Medical College of Cornell University, New York, NY. For general support.

$1,000,000 to Memorial Sloan-Kettering Cancer Center, New York, NY. For general support.

$500,000 to Hebrew Union College-Jewish Institute of Religion, New York, NY. For general support.

$275,000 to Jewish Braille Institute of America, New York, NY. 2 grants: $75,000 (For general support), $200,000 (For general support).

$270,000 to Columbia University, New York, NY. 2 grants: $250,000 (For general support), $20,000 to School of Law (For general support).

$200,000 to UJA-Federation of New York, New York, NY. 2 grants: $50,000 (For general support), $150,000 (For general support).

$10,000 to Georgetown Day School, DC. For general support.

5987
Richard A. and Susan P. Friedman Family Foundation ✦
c/o Goldman Sachs Family Office
1 New York Plz., 40th Fl.
New York, NY   10004

Established in 1991 in NY.
Donors: Richard A. Friedman; Goldman Sachs & Co.

Foundation type: Independent foundation.
Financial data (yr. ended 6/30/06): Assets, $11,745,594 (M); gifts received, $3,090,287; expenditures, $4,339,002; qualifying distributions, $4,253,364; giving activities include $4,253,364 for 67 grants (high: $1,200,000; low: $50).
Purpose and activities: Giving primarily for education, including a co-educational college preparatory day school from K to 12th grade, as well as to a school of medicine; funding also for hospitals, health associations, youth services, and Jewish organizations.
Fields of interest: Arts; Elementary/secondary education; Higher education; Education; Hospitals (general); Health organizations, association; Recreation; Human services; Children/youth, services; Federated giving programs; Jewish federated giving programs; Jewish agencies & temples.
Limitations: Applications not accepted. Giving primarily in the metropolitan New York, NY, area. No grants to individuals.
Application information: Contributes only to pre-selected organizations.
Trustee: Richard A. Friedman.
EIN: 133634385
Selected grants: The following grants were reported in 2005.
$175,000 to Horace Mann School, Riverdale, NY.
$136,000 to Central Synagogue, New York, NY. 3 grants: $18,000, $100,000, $18,000
$30,000 to New York Yankees Foundation, Bronx, NY.
$27,000 to Hewitt School, New York, NY. 2 grants: $25,000, $2,000
$5,000 to Prep for Prep, New York, NY.
$2,955 to Park Avenue Synagogue, New York, NY.
$1,000 to Special Olympics of New York, New York, NY.

5988
The Gerald J. & Dorothy R. Friedman New York Foundation for Medical Research ✧

c/o RSM McGladrey
1185 Ave. of the Americas
New York, NY 10036

Established in 1999 in NY.
Donors: Dorothy Friedman; Gerald J. Friedman†.
Foundation type: Independent foundation.
Financial data (yr. ended 2/28/05): Assets, $38,592,030 (M); expenditures, $1,987,052; qualifying distributions, $1,782,632; giving activities include $1,705,000 for 17 grants (high: $750,000; low: $5,000).
Purpose and activities: Giving primarily to organizations involved in medical research.
Fields of interest: Medical school/education; Education; Health care; Health organizations, research; Medical research, institute.
Limitations: Applications not accepted. Giving on a national basis, with emphasis on New York, NY. No grants to individuals.
Application information: Contributes only to pre-selected organizations.
Officers and Directors:* Dorothy Friedman, Pres.; Jane Friedman,* Secy.; Peter Schmidt,* Treas.
EIN: 134034562

5989
Friends of China Heritage Fund, Ltd. ✧ ☆

c/o Diane Woo
440 West End Ave.
New York, NY 10024

Donors: Thierry G. Porte; ChevronTexaco Corporation.
Foundation type: Independent foundation.
Financial data (yr. ended 9/30/05): Assets, $178,827 (M); gifts received, $15,000; expenditures, $834,150; qualifying distributions, $820,000; giving activities include $820,000 for 1 grant.
Purpose and activities: Giving for the restoration of Chinese historical sites.
Limitations: Applications not accepted.
Application information: Contributes only to pre-selected organizations.
Officers: Barbara Bush, Chair.; Ronnie Chan, Pres.; Diane T. Woo, Secy.-Treas.
Director: Nicolas Platt.
EIN: 133973817

5990
Friends of the Congressional Glaucoma Caucus Foundation, Inc.

1983 Marcus Ave., Ste. 111
Lake Success, NY 11042 (516) 327-2236
Contact: S.J. "Bud" Grant, C.E.O
FAX: (516) 327-0260;
E-mail: budgrant@glaucomacongress.org;
URL: http://glaucomacongress.org

Established in 2000 in NY.
Donors: Pharmacia & Upjohn, Inc.; Pfizer Inc.; Allergan, Inc.; CDC of Health and Human Services Dept.
Foundation type: Operating foundation.
Financial data (yr. ended 12/31/04): Assets, $427,825 (M); gifts received, $4,698,611; expenditures, $4,759,361; qualifying distributions, $1,504,760; giving activities include $1,504,760 for 29 grants (high: $191,155; low: $7,525), and $4,337,582 for 1 foundation-administered program.
Purpose and activities: The foundation is dedicated to supporting the activities of the Congressional Glaucoma Caucus, a group of United States Congress members who are dedicated to helping all Americans fight the scourge of glaucoma and other eye diseases. The foundation awards grants to organizations to provide diagnostic screening opportunities and follow up for high risk glaucoma population groups in their home districts across the nation.
Fields of interest: Health care, rural areas; Public health; Eye diseases.
Type of support: Consulting services; Fellowships; Curriculum development; General/operating support.
Limitations: Giving on a national basis. No grants to individuals.
Application information: See foundation Web site for downloading of the Medical School Student Sight Saver Program application form. Application form not required.
Initial approach: Letter or telephone Brian Quinn, Grants Officer
Copies of proposal: 1
Deadline(s): None
Board meeting date(s): Quarterly
Final notification: 3 months

Officers: Anthony M. Pisacano, M.D., Chair.; S.J. "Bud" Grant, C.E.O.; Randall D. Bloomfield, M.D., Secy.; Robert J. Bishop, Treas.
EIN: 134098767

5991
Friends of Toras Simcha ✧

200 W. 57th St., Ste. 1005
New York, NY 10019-3211

Established in 1996 in NY.
Donors: Laurie Abraham Pinck; Mandalor II LLC; Reliable Health Systems, Inc.
Foundation type: Independent foundation.
Financial data (yr. ended 8/31/05): Assets, $40,364 (M); gifts received, $315,750; expenditures, $367,152; qualifying distributions, $367,150; giving activities include $367,000 for 1 grant.
Fields of interest: Theological school/education; Jewish agencies & temples.
International interests: Israel.
Limitations: Applications not accepted. Giving primarily in Jerusalem, Israel. No grants to individuals.
Application information: Contributes only to pre-selected organizations.
Directors: Hirschell E. Levine; Menachem Pinck; Rabbi Nate Siegel.
EIN: 133913533

5992
The Frog Rock Foundation

P.O. Box 865
Chappaqua, NY 10514 (914) 273-1375
Contact: Libbie Naman Poppick, Exec. Dir.
FAX: (914) 273-5056;
E-mail: info@frogrockfoundation.org; *URL:* http://www.frogrockfoundation.org

Established in 2000 in NY.
Foundation type: Independent foundation.
Financial data (yr. ended 12/31/05): Assets, $16,857,915 (M); gifts received, $9,999,561; expenditures, $714,917; qualifying distributions, $645,268; giving activities include $600,300 for 20 grants (high: $125,000; low: $10,000).
Purpose and activities: Funding for programs and projects benefiting disadvantaged children in Westchester County, NY.
Fields of interest: Children/youth, services.
Type of support: Program development; Seed money; Curriculum development; Program evaluation.
Limitations: Giving limited to Westchester County, NY. No support for religious organizations. No grants to individuals, or for endowments or scholarships. Very limited consideration for capital campaigns.
Application information: Application information available on foundation Web site. Application form not required.
Initial approach: Letter of inquiry, no more than 2 pages
Copies of proposal: 2
Deadline(s): Rolling, for letters of inquiry. Deadlines for full proposals: Feb. 1, May 1, Sept. 1 and Nov. 1
Board meeting date(s): Quarterly
Officer and Trustees:* Libbie Naman Poppick,* Exec. Dir.; Janet Inskeep Benton; Gretchen Haury Reison.

Number of staff: 1 part-time professional.
EIN: 134127228

5993
Paul & Maxine Frohring Foundation, Inc. ✧

c/o U.S. Trust
114 W. 47th St., TaxVas
New York, NY 10036-1510
Contact: Andrew D. Lane

Established in 1958 in OH.
Donors: Paul R. Frohring†; Maxine A. Frohring†.
Foundation type: Independent foundation.
Financial data (yr. ended 12/31/05): Assets, $22,183,261 (M); expenditures, $1,200,761; qualifying distributions, $1,031,268; giving activities include $990,000 for 13 grants (high: $525,000; low: $5,000).
Purpose and activities: Support primarily for higher and secondary education; support also for health and social service agencies.
Fields of interest: Secondary school/education; Higher education; Human services.
Type of support: General/operating support; Building/renovation; Equipment; Scholarship funds.
Limitations: Applications not accepted. Giving primarily in MD and OH. No grants to individuals; no loans or program-related investments.
Application information: Unsolicited requests for funds not accepted.
Officer and Trustees:* Paula Frohring Kushlan,* Pres.; William W. Falsgraf,* Secy.-Treas.; Jeffrey Larich; Adele Wick.
EIN: 346513729
Selected grants: The following grants were reported in 2005.
$525,000 to Hiram College, Hiram, OH.
$250,000 to HealthSpace Cleveland, Cleveland, OH.
$30,000 to South River Federation, Annapolis, MD.
$25,000 to Habitat for Humanity International.
$20,000 to University of Richmond, Richmond, VA.
$15,000 to Maryland Therapeutic Riding, Annapolis, MD.

5994
Saul Fromkes Foundation, Inc. ✧ ☆

c/o Richenthal, Abrams & Moss
122 E. 42nd St., Ste. 4400
New York, NY 10168
Contact: Arthur Richenthal, Dir.

Established in 1993 in NY.
Foundation type: Independent foundation.
Financial data (yr. ended 12/31/05): Assets, $700,000 (M); expenditures, $534,259; qualifying distributions, $533,275; giving activities include $533,275 for 1 grant.
Fields of interest: Arts; Youth development.
Limitations: Giving primarily in NY. No grants to individuals.
Application information:
    Initial approach: Letter
    Deadline(s): None
Director: Arthur Richenthal.
EIN: 133682406

5995
The Alex & Ruth Fruchthandler Foundation, Inc. ✧

111 Broadway, 20th Fl.
New York, NY 10006

Established in 1945 in NY.
Donors: Olympia & York Financial Co.; Fruchthandler Bros. Enterprises; Abraham H. Fruchthandler.
Foundation type: Independent foundation.
Financial data (yr. ended 12/31/03): Assets, $8,567,334 (M); gifts received, $1,112,000; expenditures, $1,509,163; qualifying distributions, $1,489,578; giving activities include $1,489,578 for 668 grants (high: $70,000; low: $10).
Purpose and activities: Support primarily for Jewish organizations, including yeshivas.
Fields of interest: Elementary/secondary education; Jewish agencies & temples.
Limitations: Applications not accepted. Giving on a national basis. No grants to individuals.
Application information: Contributes only to pre-selected organizations.
Officers: Abraham Fruchthandler, Pres.; Zachary Fruchthandler, Secy.-Treas.
Directors: Joseph Fruchthandler; Solomon Fruchthandler.
EIN: 136156031

5996
Shmuel Fuchs Foundation, Inc. ✧

1271 60th St.
Brooklyn, NY 11219

Established in 1997 in NY.
Donors: Bernard Fuchs; Morris Fuchs.
Foundation type: Independent foundation.
Financial data (yr. ended 12/31/05): Assets, $53,945 (M); gifts received, $560,016; expenditures, $568,848; qualifying distributions, $568,848; giving activities include $566,662 for 324 grants (high: $82,400; low: $50; average: $500–$3,000).
Purpose and activities: Giving primarily to Jewish organizations, temples and yeshivas.
Fields of interest: Hospitals (general); Human services; Jewish federated giving programs; Jewish agencies & temples.
Limitations: Applications not accepted. Giving primarily in NY. No grants to individuals.
Application information: Contributes only to pre-selected organizations.
Officers: Bernard Fuchs, Pres.; Morris Fuchs, Treas.
Director: Serena Fuchs.
EIN: 113372438

5997
Fuchsberg Family Foundation, Inc. ✧

49 E. 86th St., Apt. 18B
New York, NY 10028
Contact: Peter Levine, Exec. Dir.

Incorporated in 1954 in NY.
Donors: Jacob D. Fuchsberg†; Abraham Fuchsberg; Shirley Fuchsberg; Fuchsberg & Fuchsberg.
Foundation type: Independent foundation.
Financial data (yr. ended 12/31/05): Assets, $6,385,629 (M); expenditures, $1,090,410; qualifying distributions, $1,065,447; giving activities include $1,057,762 for 44 grants (high:

$313,226; low: $100; average: $5,000–$100,000).
Purpose and activities: To engage in research and promote the study, analysis, and interpretation of legal systems and concepts in order to improve the judicial procedures and techniques of trials in the courts of New York State and the U.S.; support also for Jewish welfare funds and higher education.
Fields of interest: Arts; Education; Human services; Jewish federated giving programs; Jewish agencies & temples.
Limitations: Giving primarily in NY. No grants to individuals.
Application information: Application form not required.
    Initial approach: Proposal
    Deadline(s): None
Officers: Rosalind F. Kaufman, Pres.; Susan C. Raphaelson, V.P.; Alan L. Fuchsberg, Secy.; Janet Levine, Treas.; Peter Levine, Exec. Dir.
EIN: 136165600

5998
Abraham Fuchsberg Family Foundation, Inc. ✧

29 Broadway, No. 2410
New York, NY 10006 (212) 480-4240
Contact: Jonathan Minkoff, Pres.

Established in 1978.
Donors: Abraham Fuchsberg; Seymour Fuchsberg; Ira Kessler; Ronnie Kessler; Fuchsberg & Fuchsberg; Fuchsberg Family Foundation.
Foundation type: Independent foundation.
Financial data (yr. ended 10/31/05): Assets, $6,138,494 (M); expenditures, $329,895; qualifying distributions, $314,735; giving activities include $314,735 for 50 grants (high: $100,000; low: $200; average: $1,000–$5,000).
Purpose and activities: Giving primarily for public interest groups and legal services; support also for Jewish welfare funds.
Fields of interest: Medical research, institute; Courts/judicial administration; Legal services; Human services; Civil rights; Jewish federated giving programs; Public affairs; Jewish agencies & temples.
Limitations: Giving on a national basis, with emphasis on New York, NY. No grants to individuals.
Application information: Application form not required.
    Initial approach: Proposal
    Deadline(s): Applications submitted in the late spring and summer are preferred
Officers: Jonathan Minkoff, Pres.; Irene Minkoff, V.P.
EIN: 132966385
Selected grants: The following grants were reported in 2005.
$30,000 to American Civil Liberties Union (ACLU), New York, NY.
$25,000 to United Jewish Appeal, New York, NY.
$15,000 to American Ballet Theater, New York, NY.
$10,000 to Feed the Children, Oklahoma City, OK.
$10,000 to Southern Poverty Law Center, Montgomery, AL.
$5,000 to National Public Radio, DC.

5999
Helene Fuld Health Trust ▼ ✧
c/o HSBC Bank USA
452 5th Ave., 17th Fl.
New York, NY 10018 (212) 525-2418
Contact: Marianne Caskran, Grants Admin.
FAX: (212) 525-2395; E-mail:
marianne.caskran@hsbcpb.com; URL: http://
www.fuld.org

Trust established in 1951 in NJ; activated in 1969
as successor to Helene Fuld Health Foundation;
incorporated in 1935.
Donors: Leonhard Felix Fuld†; Florentine M. Fuld†.
Foundation type: Independent foundation.
Financial data (yr. ended 9/30/05): Assets,
$131,835,084 (M); expenditures, $6,307,811;
qualifying distributions, $5,853,536; giving
activities include $5,733,000 for 17 grants (high:
$1,200,000; low: $8,000; average: $165,000–
$500,000).
Purpose and activities: The primary mission of the
trust is to support and promote the health, welfare,
and education of student nurses. The first priority of
the trust is financial aid to nursing students.
Acknowledging the increased complexity of and
sophisticated knowledge required for health care
delivery, the trust will give preference to programs
that offer BSN degrees and higher. The trust will
seek opportunities to establish endowed
scholarships for students in baccalaureate
programs at selected nursing schools through an
invitational process. The trust will continue to award
grants to leading nursing schools and other
organizations which undertake innovative programs
designed to develop and expand the professional
and leadership skills of nursing students, faculty,
and administration.
Fields of interest: Nursing school/education;
Education; Nursing care.
Type of support: Program development; Curriculum
development; Scholarship funds.
Limitations: Applications not accepted. Giving on a
national basis. No grants to individuals; no loans.
Application information: Contributes only to
pre-selected organizations.
Trustee: HSBC Bank USA.
EIN: 136309307
Selected grants: The following grants were reported
in 2005.
$1,200,000 to Duke University, Durham, NC. To
  promote programs and study in the nursing field.
$1,000,000 to Emory University, Nell Hodgson
  Woodruff School of Nursing, Atlanta, GA. To
  promote programs and study in the nursing field.
$800,000 to New York University, Division of
  Nursing, New York, NY. To promote programs and
  study in the nursing field.
$500,000 to Foundation of National Student Nurses
  Association, Brooklyn, NY. To promote programs
  and study in the nursing field.
$500,000 to Johns Hopkins University, School of
  Nursing, Baltimore, MD. To promote programs
  and study in the nursing field.
$165,000 to Alverno College, Milwaukee, WI. To
  promote programs and study in the nursing field.
$165,000 to Hunter College of the City University of
  New York Foundation, New York, NY. To promote
  programs and study in the nursing field.
$165,000 to University of Buffalo Foundation,
  School of Nursing, Buffalo, NY. To promote
  programs and study in the nursing field.
$165,000 to University of North Carolina at Chapel
  Hill School of Nursing Foundation, Chapel Hill,

NC. To promote programs and study in the
nursing field.
$165,000 to University of Texas Health Science
  Center, Houston, TX. To promote programs and
  study in the nursing field.

6000
**Kathy and Richard S. Fuld, Jr. Family
Foundation, Inc.** ✧
(formerly Richard S. Fuld, Jr. Foundation, Inc.)
P.O. Box 3977
Albany, NY 12203
Contact: W. Michael Reickert

Established in 1994.
Donor: Richard S. Fuld, Jr.
Foundation type: Independent foundation.
Financial data (yr. ended 12/31/05): Assets,
$1,519,767 (M); gifts received, $5,575,350;
expenditures, $5,308,116; qualifying distributions,
$5,260,407; giving activities include $5,260,407
for 79 grants (high: $1,005,401; low: $200;
average: $1,000–$100,000).
Purpose and activities: Funding primarily for Jewish
federated giving programs, education, and health
and human services.
Fields of interest: Museums; Education; Hospitals
(general); Health care; Health organizations,
association; Jewish federated giving programs;
Jewish agencies & temples.
Limitations: Applications not accepted. Giving
primarily in CT and NY. No grants to individuals.
Application information: Contributes only to
pre-selected organizations.
Officers: Richard S. Fuld, Pres. and Treas.; Kathleen
Bailey Fuld, V.P. and Secy.
EIN: 137042848
Selected grants: The following grants were reported
in 2004.
$150,000 to Lehman Brothers Foundation, New
  York, NY.
$80,000 to Prep for Prep, New York, NY.
$50,000 to Charities Aid Foundation (CAF) America,
  Alexandria, VA.
$50,000 to Greenwich Hospital, Greenwich, CT.
$40,000 to Metropolitan Council on Jewish Poverty,
  New York, NY.
$25,000 to Bruce Museum, Greenwich, CT.
$25,000 to Ronald McDonald House.
$10,000 to Drawing Center, New York, NY.
$10,000 to Massachusetts General Hospital,
  Boston, MA.
$5,000 to Juilliard School, New York, NY.

6001
Fund for Life Foundation, Inc. ✧
1428 36th St., Ste. 200
Brooklyn, NY 11218

Established in 1996 in NY.
Donor: Harry Reichman.
Foundation type: Independent foundation.
Financial data (yr. ended 12/31/04): Assets,
$12,008,784 (M); gifts received, $3,265,796;
expenditures, $601,768; qualifying distributions,
$562,510; giving activities include $551,840 for
186 grants (high: $100,000; low: $18).
Purpose and activities: Giving primarily for
education and Jewish organizations.
Fields of interest: Education; Jewish agencies &
temples.

Limitations: Giving primarily in Brooklyn, NY. No
grants to individuals.
Officers: Harry Reichman, Pres.; Joshua Assaf,
Secy.; Chaya Reichman, Treas.
EIN: 113239215
Selected grants: The following grants were reported
in 2003.
$100,000 to United Sanz International Institutions,
  Brooklyn, NY.
$53,950 to Press Foundation of America, Brooklyn,
  NY.
$39,372 to Yeshiva Shearith Hapleth, Brooklyn, NY.
$18,000 to Bnos Bais Yaakov of Far Rockaway, Far
  Rockaway, NY.
$17,690 to Yeshiva Toras Chesed, Brooklyn, NY.
$13,600 to Congregation Arugath Habosem,
  Brooklyn, NY.
$12,175 to Congregation Sanz Klausenberg,
  Brooklyn, NY.
$10,036 to Kollel Shomrei Hachomos, Brooklyn,
  NY.
$1,400 to Keren Hachesed, Monsey, NY.
$1,000 to Beth Chana School and High School for
  Girls, Brooklyn, NY.

6002
Furman Foundation, Inc. ✧
151 E. 83rd St., Ste. 1A
New York, NY 10028
Contact: Gail Furman, Pres.

Established in 2000 in NY.
Donors: Jason Furman; Gail Furman; Jay Furman.
Foundation type: Independent foundation.
Financial data (yr. ended 12/31/04): Assets,
$1,094,281 (M); gifts received, $624,000;
expenditures, $359,939; qualifying distributions,
$357,655; giving activities include $357,460 for 29
grants (high: $50,000; low: $250).
Fields of interest: Performing arts centers;
Education; Human services; Children/youth,
services; International affairs.
Limitations: Giving primarily in NY.
Application information: Application form not
required.
  Deadline(s): None
Officers: Gail Furman, Pres.; Ariela Dubler, V.P.;
Jason Furman, Secy.; Jesse Furman, Treas.
Directors: Eve Gerber; Roger Ratner.
EIN: 134094739
Selected grants: The following grants were reported
in 2003.
$52,500 to Auburn Theological Seminary, New York,
  NY. 2 grants: $2,500, $50,000
$50,000 to Tides Center, DC. 2 grants: $25,000
  each
$15,000 to Bay Street Theater Festival, Sag Harbor,
  NY.
$10,000 to Council on Foreign Relations, New York,
  NY.
$5,000 to Cambodian Health Committee, Boston,
  MA.
$2,500 to National Museum of Women in the Arts,
  DC.
$250 to PEN American Center, New York, NY.

6003
Frieda & Roy Furman Foundation, Inc. ✧
770 Park Ave., Ste. 15D
New York, NY 10021
Contact: John G. McColskey

Established in 1997 in NY.
Donor: Roy L. Furman.
Foundation type: Independent foundation.
Financial data (yr. ended 12/31/05): Assets, $2,540,502 (M); gifts received, $202,042; expenditures, $345,382; qualifying distributions, $329,500; giving activities include $329,500 for grants.
Fields of interest: Performing arts, theater; Performing arts, opera; Arts; Higher education; Education; Jewish federated giving programs; Jewish agencies & temples.
Limitations: Applications not accepted. Giving primarily in New York, NY. No grants to individuals.
Application information: Contributes only to pre-selected organizations.
Officers: Frieda Furman, Pres.; Roy L. Furman, Secy.-Treas.
EIN: 133970732
Selected grants: The following grants were reported in 2004.
$29,800 to American Friends of the Israel Museum, New York, NY.
$10,000 to Brooklyn College Foundation, Brooklyn, NY.
$6,000 to Lincoln Center Theater, New York, NY.
$5,000 to Jewish Center of the Hamptons, East Hampton, NY.
$2,750 to Central Synagogue, New York, NY.
$1,000 to Childrens Defense Fund, DC.
$500 to Cunningham Dance Foundation, New York, NY.
$500 to Graduate Center Foundation, New York, NY.
$100 to Fund for Park Avenue, New York, NY.

6004
The Furth Family Foundation ✧
c/o Klingenstein, Fields & Co., LLC
787 7th Ave.
New York, NY   10019

Established in 1986 in NY.
Donor: John L. Furth.
Foundation type: Independent foundation.
Financial data (yr. ended 11/30/05): Assets, $4,223,353 (M); gifts received, $1,070,292; expenditures, $953,653; qualifying distributions, $913,637; giving activities include $910,575 for 96 grants (high: $200,000; low: $100).
Purpose and activities: Giving for higher education, human service and community healthcare organizations, including a neurology department of a hospital, Jewish federated giving programs, and cultural institutions.
Fields of interest: Museums; Arts; Higher education; Libraries (public); Libraries (special); Education; Hospitals (general); Hospitals (specialty); Health organizations, association; Human services; Neighborhood centers; Jewish federated giving programs.
Limitations: Applications not accepted. Giving primarily in CT and New York, NY. No grants to individuals.
Application information: Contributes only to pre-selected organizations.
Trustees: Hope L. Furth; John L. Furth.
EIN: 133401839
Selected grants: The following grants were reported in 2005.
$250,000 to Yale University, New Haven, CT. 2 grants: $50,000, $200,000
$200,000 to Barnard College, New York, NY.

$95,000 to Blythedale Childrens Hospital, Valhalla, NY. 3 grants: $20,000, $15,000, $60,000
$36,000 to Grand Street Settlement, New York, NY. 2 grants: $25,000, $11,000
$2,500 to Mercy College, Dobbs Ferry, NY.
$1,000 to Chapel Haven, Westville, CT.

6005
Galasso Foundation ✧
74 N. Aurora St.
Lancaster, NY   14086
E-mail: galasso@rdinet.net

Established in 1963 in NY.
Donors: Susquehanna Motel Corp.; August J. Galasso.
Foundation type: Independent foundation.
Financial data (yr. ended 12/31/05): Assets, $10,187,586 (M); expenditures, $591,095; qualifying distributions, $441,083; giving activities include $417,355 for 49 grants (high: $51,000; low: $50).
Purpose and activities: Primary areas of interest include education, health services, and family services.
Fields of interest: Education; Health care; Family services; Public affairs; Christian agencies & churches.
Type of support: General/operating support; Continuing support; Annual campaigns; Capital campaigns; Building/renovation; Scholarship funds; Employee matching gifts; Matching/challenge support.
Limitations: Applications not accepted. Giving primarily in upstate NY. No grants to individuals.
Application information: Contributes only to pre-selected organizations.
Board meeting date(s): May and Sept.
Trustees: Emil J. Galasso; Martin A. Galasso; August J. Gillon; Paul M. Gonzalez; J. Michael Kelleher.
Number of staff: 1 part-time professional.
EIN: 166031447
Selected grants: The following grants were reported in 2004.
$100,000 to Saint Bonaventure University, Saint Bonaventure, NY. 2 grants: $50,000 each
$50,000 to Our Lady of Pompeii Church, New York, NY. 2 grants: $25,000 each
$50,000 to Sisters of Saint Francis, Williamsville, NY.
$30,000 to Christ the King Seminary, East Aurora, NY. 2 grants: $15,000 each
$5,000 to Canisius College, Buffalo, NY.
$5,000 to Corpus Christi Church, Port Chester, NY.
$2,500 to Schoharie Free Library, Schoharie, NY.

6006
The Gant Family Foundation ✧
(formerly Donald R. & Jane T. Gant Foundation)
c/o Behan, Ling, and Ruta
475 Park Ave. S., 31st Fl.
New York, NY   10016

Established in 1968 in NY.
Donors: Donald R. Gant; Alison A. Grant.
Foundation type: Independent foundation.
Financial data (yr. ended 5/31/06): Assets, $7,825,779 (M); expenditures, $378,854; qualifying distributions, $366,775; giving activities include $366,775 for grants.

Purpose and activities: Giving primarily for a federated giving program, and higher education.
Fields of interest: Museums (history); Higher education; Education; Human services; Community development; Federated giving programs; Protestant agencies & churches.
Limitations: Applications not accepted. Giving primarily in NJ and NY. No grants to individuals.
Application information: Contributes only to pre-selected organizations.
Trustees: Alison A. Gant; Christopher T. Gant; Donald R. Gant; Jane T. Gant; Laura G. Lilienfield; Sarah G. Mandanis.
EIN: 237015091
Selected grants: The following grants were reported in 2005.
$20,000 to Haverford College, Haverford, PA.
$15,000 to Presbyterian Church, Westfield, NJ.
$9,000 to Kent Place School, Summit, NJ.
$5,000 to Delbarton School, Morristown, NJ.
$5,000 to New Jersey Historical Society, Newark, NJ.
$2,000 to San Francisco State University Foundation, San Francisco, CA.
$1,000 to Central Moravian Church, Bethlehem, PA.
$1,000 to Creative Alternatives of New York, New York, NY.
$1,000 to First Presbyterian Church, Westfield, NJ.
$1,000 to MacCulloch Hall Historical Museum, Morristown, NJ.

6007
The Joseph & Susan Gatto Foundation ✧
c/o BCRS Group/Marcum & Kleigman, LLP
100 Wall St., 11th Fl.
New York, NY   10005

Established in 1996 in CT.
Donor: Joseph D. Gatto.
Foundation type: Independent foundation.
Financial data (yr. ended 9/30/05): Assets, $7,636,735 (M); expenditures, $391,316; qualifying distributions, $355,316; giving activities include $355,316 for grants.
Fields of interest: Higher education; Education; Human services; Religion.
Limitations: Applications not accepted. Giving primarily in NY. No grants to individuals; no loans or scholarships.
Application information: Contributes only to pre-selected organizations.
Trustees: Joseph D. Gatto; Susan Gatto.
EIN: 133921102

6008
GBRG, Inc. ✧
c/o Hertz, Herson & Company, LLP
2 Park Ave., Ste. 1500
New York, NY   10016

Established in 1995 in DE and NY.
Foundation type: Independent foundation.
Financial data (yr. ended 12/31/05): Assets, $29,420,329 (M); expenditures, $1,190,479; qualifying distributions, $1,215,450; giving activities include $1,205,000 for 22 grants (high: $275,000; low: $2,000).
Fields of interest: International affairs; Jewish federated giving programs; Jewish agencies & temples.
International interests: Israel.

Type of support: General/operating support.
Limitations: Applications not accepted. Giving primarily to national organizations in New York, NY, and Washington, DC. No grants to individuals.
Application information: Contributes only to pre-selected organizations.
Officer and Directors:* Susan Wexner,* Pres. and Secy.-Treas.; Bernard Agus.
EIN: 134072646

6009
Gebbie Foundation, Inc.

Furniture Mart Bldg.
111 W. 2nd St., Ste. 1100
Jamestown, NY 14701 (716) 487-1062
Contact: John C. Merino, Exec. Dir.
FAX: (716) 484-6401; E-mail: info@gebbie.org;
URL: http://www.gebbie.org

Incorporated in 1964 in NY.
Donors: Marion B. Gebbie†; Geraldine G. Bellinger†.
Foundation type: Independent foundation.
Financial data (yr. ended 9/30/05): Assets, $76,738,858 (M); expenditures, $3,905,258; qualifying distributions, $3,511,500; giving activities include $3,195,030 for 30 grants (high: $1,921,925; low: $250; average: $10,000–$100,000).
Purpose and activities: Grants primarily for the arts, children and youth services, community development, education, and human services. The strategic focus of 2006 is to rejuvenate downtown Jamestown, NY, through economic development.
Fields of interest: Arts; Education; Human services; Children/youth, services; Community development.
Type of support: General/operating support; Continuing support; Annual campaigns; Capital campaigns; Building/renovation; Equipment; Endowments; Seed money; Scholarship funds; Matching/challenge support.
Limitations: Giving primarily in Chautauqua County in western NY, especially the Jamestown, NY, area. No support for sectarian or religious organizations or United Way. No grants to individuals.
Publications: Application guidelines; Grants list.
Application information: Applicants will be contacted for further information after review of letter of inquiry. A signed grant agreement is required before approval of the grant. Application guidelines and procedures available on foundation Web site. Application form not required.
   Initial approach: Letter of inquiry
   Copies of proposal: 1
   Deadline(s): None
   Board meeting date(s): Quarterly
   Final notification: 1 to 4 months
Officers and Directors:* Linda V. Swanson III,* Pres.; Daniel E. Kathman,* V.P.; Martin A. Coyle,* Secy.; Kristy Zabrodsky,* Treas.; John C. Merino, Exec. Dir.; Nancy Gleason; Charles T. Hall; Rhoe B. Henderson III; John Lloyd; Lillian Vitanza Ney; Bertram B. Parker.
Number of staff: 1 full-time professional; 3 full-time support.
EIN: 166050287

6010
Geds Help Fund Foundation ◇ ☆

225 Broadhollow Rd., CS 5341
Melville, NY 11747
Contact: Scott Rechler, Dir.

Established in 2001 in NY.
Donors: Scott Rechler; Deborah Rechler.
Foundation type: Independent foundation.
Financial data (yr. ended 12/31/05): Assets, $539,207 (M); gifts received, $1,054,775; expenditures, $597,567; qualifying distributions, $585,881; giving activities include $581,978 for 25 grants (high: $303,678; low: $500).
Fields of interest: Museums (children's); Higher education; Human services; Family services; Family services, counseling.
Limitations: Giving primarily in NY.
Application information: Application form not required.
Directors: Jordan Heller; Deborah Rechler; Scott Rechler.
EIN: 113613923
Selected grants: The following grants were reported in 2005.
$303,678 to Friends Academy, Locust Valley, NY.
$50,000 to Long Island Childrens Museum, Garden City, NY.
$10,000 to Long Island Head Injury Association, Commack, NY.
$5,000 to Huntington Hospital, Huntington, NY.
$5,000 to Washington Center for Internships and Academic Seminars, DC.
$2,500 to Diabetes Research Institute, Miami, FL.
$750 to Habitat for Humanity International, SD.
$500 to Saint Jude School, New York, NY.

6011
Lawrence M. Gelb Foundation, Inc.

1585 Broadway, 22nd Fl.
New York, NY 10036-8299
Contact: Robert M. Kaufman, Secy.-Treas.

Established in 1957 in NY.
Donors: Lawrence M. Gelb†; Richard L. Gelb†; Bruce S. Gelb; Lawrence N. Gelb.
Foundation type: Independent foundation.
Financial data (yr. ended 12/31/05): Assets, $4,519,876 (M); gifts received, $395,778; expenditures, $1,700,919; qualifying distributions, $1,665,149; giving activities include $1,659,600 for 96 grants (high: $361,000; low: $500).
Purpose and activities: Support primarily for private secondary and higher education; some support also for cultural programs and hospitals.
Fields of interest: Arts; Secondary school/education; Higher education; Hospitals (general).
Limitations: Giving on a national basis. No grants to individuals.
Application information: Application form not required.
   Initial approach: Letter
   Deadline(s): None
   Board meeting date(s): Various
Officers and Directors:* Bruce S. Gelb,* Chair.; Phyllis N. Gelb,* Pres.; Robert M. Kaufman, Secy.-Treas.; Wilbur H. Friedman; John T. Gelb; Lawrence N. Gelb.
EIN: 136113586
Selected grants: The following grants were reported in 2004.
$303,000 to Choate Rosemary Hall, Wallingford, CT.

$100,000 to Cleveland Clinic, Cleveland, OH.
$50,000 to Hospital for Special Surgery, New York, NY.
$50,000 to Metropolitan Museum of Art, New York, NY.
$50,000 to North Haven Arts and Enrichment, North Haven, ME.
$50,000 to Walnut Hill School, Natick, MA.
$18,000 to Yale University, New Haven, CT.
$10,000 to National Constitution Center, Philadelphia, PA.
$6,000 to Classroom, Inc., New York, NY.
$3,000 to Doctors Without Borders USA, New York, NY.

6012
Michael E. Gellert Trust ◇

122 E. 42nd St., 34th Fl.
New York, NY 10168-0001

Established in 1962 in NY.
Donor: Michael E. Gellert.
Foundation type: Independent foundation.
Financial data (yr. ended 6/30/05): Assets, $6,609,742 (M); expenditures, $1,763,423; qualifying distributions, $1,753,923; giving activities include $1,753,923 for 59 grants (high: $600,000; low: $100).
Purpose and activities: Giving primarily for education and the arts.
Fields of interest: Performing arts; Performing arts centers; Performing arts, music; Arts; Higher education; Education; Hospitals (general); Health organizations, association; Civil rights.
Limitations: Applications not accepted. Giving primarily in CT and NY. No grants to individuals.
Application information: Contributes only to pre-selected organizations.
Trustees: David B. Spohn Gellert; Michael E. Gellert; Robert J. Gellert; Hugh McLoughlin.
EIN: 136093842
Selected grants: The following grants were reported in 2004.
$583,500 to New School, New York, NY.
$24,210 to Lincoln Center for the Performing Arts, New York, NY.
$6,546 to Metropolitan Museum of Art, New York, NY.
$3,500 to Metropolitan Opera, New York, NY.
$2,500 to Harvard University, Cambridge, MA.
$523 to Museum of Modern Art, New York, NY.
$500 to Connecticut Grand Opera and Orchestra, Stamford, CT.
$300 to Brooklyn Academy of Music, Brooklyn, NY.
$300 to Greenwich Choral Society, Greenwich, CT.
$250 to Rye Country Day School, Rye, NY.

6013
The Gellman Foundation ◇ ☆

4053 Maple Rd.
Amherst, NY 14226

Established in 1988 in FL.
Donors: Jack E. Gellman†; Jack E. Gellman Family Trust; Members of the Gellman family.
Foundation type: Independent foundation.
Financial data (yr. ended 12/31/05): Assets, $1,207,915 (M); gifts received, $21,525; expenditures, $485,653; qualifying distributions, $477,900; giving activities include $477,900 for 14 grants (high: $401,000; low: $400).

Fields of interest: YM/YWCAs & YM/YWHAs; Foundations (private grantmaking); Federated giving programs; Jewish federated giving programs.
Limitations: Applications not accepted. Giving primarily in NY, with emphasis on Buffalo. No grants to individuals.
Application information: Contributes only to pre-selected organizations.
Trustees: Arthur M. Gellman; George I. Gellman; Deborah Gellman Zaretsky.
EIN: 581765283

6014
Jacques and Natasha Gelman Trust ◇
c/o McLaughlin & Stern, LLP
260 Madison Ave., 18th Fl.
New York, NY   10016-2401   (212) 448-1100
Contact: Janet C. Neschis, Tr.

Established in 1998 in NY.
Foundation type: Independent foundation.
Financial data (yr. ended 11/30/04): Assets, $31,669,103 (M); expenditures, $2,348,019; qualifying distributions, $1,670,180; giving activities include $1,600,000 for 9 grants (high: $600,000; low: $10,000).
Purpose and activities: Giving primarily for the arts, including art schools, museums and arts alliances.
Fields of interest: Arts education; Museums (art); Arts, services; Arts.
Application information:
  Initial approach: Letter
Trustees: Marylin G. Diamond; Janet C. Neschis.
EIN: 137166150
Selected grants: The following grants were reported in 2003.
$775,000 to Rhode Island School of Design, Providence, RI.
$165,000 to Cooper Union for the Advancement of Science and Art, New York, NY.
$135,600 to Carnegie Mellon University, School of Art, Pittsburgh, PA.
$125,000 to Maryland Institute College of Art, Baltimore, MD.
$100,000 to El Museo del Barrio, New York, NY.
$100,000 to National Foundation for Advancement in the Arts, New York, NY.
$50,000 to Alliance for Young Artists and Writers, New York, NY.
$35,000 to Art in General, New York, NY.
$20,000 to Fideicomiso para la Cultural Mexico - Estados Unidos, Mexico. .
$20,000 to Savannah College of Art and Design, Savannah, GA.

6015
The Peter and Kristen Gerhard Foundation ◇
c/o Goldman Sachs- Family Office
1 New York Plz., 40th Fl.
New York, NY   10004

Donor: Peter C. Gerhard.
Foundation type: Independent foundation.
Financial data (yr. ended 8/31/05): Assets, $3,331,677 (M); expenditures, $633,996; qualifying distributions, $616,881; giving activities include $616,881 for 57 grants (high: $200,000; low: $50).
Purpose and activities: Giving primarily for higher education, as well as to a medical center; funding

also for social services and federated giving programs.
Fields of interest: Higher education; Hospitals (general); Health organizations, association; Big Brothers/Big Sisters; Human services; Children, services; Federated giving programs; Protestant agencies & churches.
Limitations: Applications not accepted. Giving primarily in NJ, with some emphasis on Hackensack, and New York, NY. No grants to individuals, or for scholarships; no loans.
Application information: Contributes only to pre-selected organizations.
Trustees: Kristen Gerhard; Peter C. Gerhard.
EIN: 133921375

6016
Gerry Charitable Trust ◇
(also known as Perry N. & Robert G. Gerry Charitable Trust)
c/o McLauglin & Stern, LLP
260 Madison Ave.
New York, NY   10016
Contact: Huyler C. Held, Tr.
FAX: (212) 448-6260;
E-mail: hheld@mclaughlinstern.com

Established in NY in 1978.
Donors: Roger G. Gerry‡; Peggy N. Gerry‡.
Foundation type: Independent foundation.
Financial data (yr. ended 12/31/04): Assets, $19,414,517 (M); gifts received, $6,566,822; expenditures, $782,660; qualifying distributions, $705,283; giving activities include $633,937 for 10 grants (high: $268,750; low: $5,350).
Fields of interest: Performing arts, music; Historic preservation/historical societies; Arts; Higher education; Higher education, college (community/junior); Botanical gardens; Botany.
Limitations: Applications not accepted. Giving primarily in Long Island, NY; some giving elsewhere in NY. No grants to individuals.
Application information: Unsolicited requests for funds strongly discouraged.
Trustees and Advisory Committee:* Huyler C. Held*; Robert B. Mackay; Theodore S. Wickersham; The Bank of New York.
EIN: 136753033

6017
Gerry Foundation, Inc. ◇
P.O. Box 311
Liberty, NY   12754   (845) 295-2400
Contact: Darrell Supak

Established in 1997 in NY.
Donors: Alan Gerry; Empire State Development Corp.
Foundation type: Operating foundation.
Financial data (yr. ended 10/31/05): Assets, $166,190,382 (M); gifts received, $9,216,094; expenditures, $3,923,900; qualifying distributions, $28,106,337; giving activities include $845,100 for 8+ grants (high: $350,000), $25,427,829 for foundation-administered programs and $395,022 for loans/program-related investments.
Purpose and activities: Emphasis on higher education, medical institutes, and community development.

Fields of interest: Museums; Performing arts; Education; Hospitals (general); Community development.
Type of support: Program-related investments/loans.
Limitations: Giving primarily in Sullivan County, NY.
Application information:
  Initial approach: Letter
  Deadline(s): None
Officers and Directors:* Alan Gerry,* Pres.; Jonathan Drapkin, V.P.; Christopher Grillo, V.P.; Louis J. Boyd, Secy.-Treas.; Adam Gerry; Annelise Gerry; Robyn Gerry; Sandra Gerry.
EIN: 141798234

6018
Laurent and Alberta Gerschel Foundation ◇
P.O. Box 42, Planetarium Sta.
New York, NY   10024
Contact: Laurent Gerschel, Pres.

Established in 1981 in NY.
Donor: Laurent Gerschel.
Foundation type: Independent foundation.
Financial data (yr. ended 12/31/04): Assets, $3,888,420 (M); expenditures, $1,215,249; qualifying distributions, $1,123,143; giving activities include $775,225 for 8 grants (high: $461,250; low: $125).
Purpose and activities: Giving primarily for a zoo; funding also for Jewish agencies and temples.
Fields of interest: Museums (ethnic/folk arts); Environment; Zoos/zoological societies; Jewish federated giving programs; Jewish agencies & temples.
Limitations: Giving primarily in MD and New York, NY. No grants to individuals.
Application information:
  Initial approach: Proposal
  Deadline(s): None
Officers: Laurent Gerschel, Pres.; Alberta Gerschel, V.P.; Allan Eagleshan, Mgr.
EIN: 133098507
Selected grants: The following grants were reported in 2003.
$300,000 to American Zoo and Aquarium Association, Silver Spring, MD.
$100,000 to Weill Medical College of Cornell University, New York, NY.
$65,000 to UJA-Federation of New York, New York, NY.
$10,050 to American Jewish Committee, New York, NY.
$10,000 to Gateway School of New York, New York, NY.
$6,045 to Park East Synagogue, New York, NY.
$3,000 to Hineni, New York, NY.
$2,500 to Childrens Aid Society, New York, NY.
$100 to United Cerebral Palsy, DC.
$50 to New York Road Runners Club, New York, NY.

6019
Patrick A. Gerschel Foundation ◇
600 Madison Ave., 16th Fl.
New York, NY   10022-1615   (212) 399-4278

Established in 1986 in NY.
Donor: Patrick A. Gerschel.
Foundation type: Independent foundation.

Financial data (yr. ended 12/31/04): Assets, $5,914,987 (M); expenditures, $388,225; qualifying distributions, $345,900; giving activities include $345,000 for 5 grants (high: $240,000; low: $5,000).
Purpose and activities: Giving primarily to a university.
Fields of interest: Museums (art); Historic preservation/historical societies; Arts; Higher education; Environment, natural resources; Botanical gardens; International affairs, goodwill promotion; International affairs.
Type of support: Research.
Limitations: Applications not accepted. Giving primarily in the New York, NY, area. No grants to individuals.
Application information: Unsolicited requests for funds not accepted.
Officer and Director:* Patrick A. Gerschel,* Pres.
EIN: 133317180

6020
The Gershwind Family Foundation ✧
152 W. 57th St., 56th Fl.
New York, NY   10019

Established in 1998 in NY.
Donor: Marjorie Gershwind.
Foundation type: Independent foundation.
Financial data (yr. ended 12/31/04): Assets, $17,161,228 (M); gifts received, $5,110,000; expenditures, $782,702; qualifying distributions, $520,430; giving activities include $517,895 for 22 grants (high: $211,020; low: $250).
Purpose and activities: Support for a Jewish temple, Jewish federated giving programs and health care.
Fields of interest: Hospitals (general); Jewish federated giving programs; Jewish agencies & temples.
Limitations: Applications not accepted. Giving primarily in NY. No grants to individuals.
Application information: Contributes only to pre-selected organizations.
Officers and Directors:* Marjorie Gershwind,* Pres.; Mark Gershwind,* V.P. and Secy.; Erik Gershwind.
EIN: 113359917
Selected grants: The following grants were reported in 2004.
$211,020 to Temple Beth-El of Great Neck, Great Neck, NY.
$100,000 to Sid Jacobson Jewish Community Center, East Hills, NY.
$8,000 to University of Pennsylvania, Philadelphia, PA.
$1,000 to American Friends of Migdal Ohr, New York, NY.
$1,000 to American Jewish Committee, New York, NY.
$675 to American Cancer Society, Atlanta, GA.

6021
Gerson Family Foundation, Inc. ✧ ☆
19 W. 95th St.
New York, NY   10025

Established in 1993 in NY.
Donors: James Gerson; Ruth Joffe†; Barbara N. Gerson.
Foundation type: Independent foundation.

Financial data (yr. ended 9/30/05): Assets, $10,476,972 (M); gifts received, $180,000; expenditures, $483,251; qualifying distributions, $429,930; giving activities include $422,000 for 29 grants (high: $238,000; low: $200).
Fields of interest: Children/youth, services; Jewish agencies & temples.
Limitations: Applications not accepted. Giving primarily in CT, MA, and NY. No grants to individuals.
Application information: Contributes only to pre-selected organizations.
Officer: James Gerson, Pres.
Directors: Barbara N. Gerson; Richard A. Krantz.
EIN: 133750336
Selected grants: The following grants were reported in 2004.
$25,000 to Congregation Rodeph Sholom.
$5,000 to National Council of Jewish Women, New York, NY.
$5,000 to Smith College, Northampton, MA.
$2,500 to Bowdoin College, Brunswick, ME.
$2,500 to United Way of New York City, New York, NY.
$1,000 to Center for Reproductive Rights, New York, NY.
$1,000 to Hopkins School, New Haven, CT.
$1,000 to Trevor Day School, New York, NY.
$500 to City Harvest, New York, NY.
$500 to City Year New York, New York, NY.

6022
Charlotte Geyer Foundation
P.O. Box 1276
Williamsville, NY   14231-1276   (716) 632-6448
Contact: Nancy Falletta, Exec. Dir.
FAX: (716) 632-6098; Courier address: 9 Clarion Ct., Williamsville, NY 14221; URL: http://www.charlottegeyer.org

Established in 1991 in FL.
Donor: Paul F. Eckel.
Foundation type: Independent foundation.
Financial data (yr. ended 12/31/05): Assets, $6,116 (M); gifts received, $980,660; expenditures, $1,101,550; qualifying distributions, $1,100,890; giving activities include $994,800 for 18 grants (high: $169,000; low: $16,600).
Purpose and activities: The foundation's principal area of activity is to work in conjunction with the National Institutes of Health/National Cancer Institute to provide funding for cancer research.
Fields of interest: Cancer; Cancer research.
Type of support: Research.
Limitations: Giving on a national basis. No grants to individuals.
Application information: See foundation Web site for application guidelines and procedures. Application form not required.
Copies of proposal: 4
Deadline(s): Feb. 1, June 1, and Oct. 1
Board meeting date(s): 30 days following deadline
Final notification: 30 days following deadline
Officer and Trustees:* Nancy E. Falletta,* Exec. Dir.; Charlotte E. Blaney; Joyce A. Eckel; Paul F. Eckel.
Number of staff: 1 full-time professional.
EIN: 650281614
Selected grants: The following grants were reported in 2004.
$83,300 to University of Alabama, Birmingham, AL.
$66,700 to Ludwig Institute for Cancer Research, La Jolla, CA.
$58,500 to University of Chicago, Chicago, IL.

$58,500 to Yale University, New Haven, CT.
$56,000 to Greenville Hospital System, Greenville, SC.
$50,000 to Duke University, Durham, NC.
$50,000 to Fred Hutchinson Cancer Research Center, Seattle, WA.
$50,000 to University of California, San Francisco, CA.
$50,000 to University of Michigan, Ann Arbor, MI.
$25,000 to Roswell Park Cancer Institute, Buffalo, NY.

6023
The Giant Steps Foundation ✧
c/o Miller Ellin & Co., LLP
750 Lexington Ave.
New York, NY   10022
E-mail: gsf@giantsteps.org; URL: http://www.giantsteps.org

Established in 1997 in CA and DE.
Donors: Jennifer Leeds; Tides Foundation.
Foundation type: Independent foundation.
Financial data (yr. ended 11/30/05): Assets, $11,330,923 (M); expenditures, $656,926; qualifying distributions, $651,926; giving activities include $577,450 for 56 grants (high: $50,000; low: $2,750).
Purpose and activities: The foundation's mission is to promote and support healthy lifestyles, holistic health practices, and participation is sports and fitness activities. The foundation is particularly interested in encouraging women's and girls' participation in these approaches. Secondary aims are to protect and preserve the environment, animals, and wildlife, and to further educational and gender equality.
Fields of interest: Environment; Animal welfare; Human services.
Limitations: Applications not accepted. Giving primarily in CA, with some emphasis on San Francisco; some funding nationally. No grants to individuals.
Application information: Contributes only to pre-selected organizations.
Officers and Directors:* Jennifer Leeds,* Pres.; Richard L. Braunstein, Secy.; Jeffrey J. Sundheim,* Treas.; Lilo J. Leeds.
EIN: 522069841

6024
Malcolm Gibbs Foundation, Inc. ✧
14 E. 60th St., No. 702
New York, NY   10022

Established in 1999 in NY.
Donor: The Green Fund, Inc.
Foundation type: Independent foundation.
Financial data (yr. ended 1/31/06): Assets, $13,786,819 (M); gifts received, $113,371; expenditures, $519,464; qualifying distributions, $444,317; giving activities include $374,877 for 81 grants (high: $111,477; low: $100).
Purpose and activities: Giving primarily to a hospital, the arts, education, and human services.
Fields of interest: Arts education; Performing arts, dance; Performing arts, opera; Arts; Education; Hospitals (general); Housing/shelter, development; Human services; Children/youth, services; Family services; Jewish agencies & temples.

Limitations: Applications not accepted. Giving primarily in NY. No grants to individuals.
Application information: Contributes only to pre-selected organizations.
Officers: Ann Colin Herbst, Chair.; Laura Colin Klein, Pres.
EIN: 134041340

6025

The Gibson Family Foundation ✧ ☆
(formerly Nancy & Craig Gibson Charitable Trust)
c/o Montrose Accounting
505 Park Ave., 20th Fl.
New York, NY 10022-1106

Established in 1997 in NY.
Donors: Nancy Quick Gibson; Craig Gibson.
Foundation type: Independent foundation.
Financial data (yr. ended 12/31/05): Assets, $179,621 (M); gifts received, $3,138; expenditures, $638,268; qualifying distributions, $630,120; giving activities include $630,120 for grants.
Fields of interest: Performing arts, ballet; Elementary/secondary education; Education; Human services; Christian agencies & churches.
Type of support: General/operating support.
Limitations: Applications not accepted. Giving primarily in MA; some giving also in FL. No grants to individuals.
Application information: Contributes only to pre-selected organizations.
Trustees: Craig B. Gibson; Nancy Quick Gibson.
EIN: 043410276
Selected grants: The following grants were reported in 2004.
$25,000 to Winchester Hospital Foundation, Winchester, MA.
$22,500 to Arthritis Foundation, West Palm Beach, FL.
$20,000 to Boston Ballet, Boston, MA.
$20,000 to Inner-City Scholarship Fund, New York, NY.
$10,000 to Babson College, Babson Park, MA.
$8,300 to Little Sisters of the Poor, Totowa, NJ.
$7,500 to Pine Manor College, Chestnut Hill, MA.
$7,500 to University of Chicago, Chicago, IL.
$5,000 to Eagle Hill School, Greenwich, CT.
$1,000 to Max Warburg Courage Curriculum, Boston, MA.

6026

The Rosamond Gifford Charitable Corporation ✧
126 N. Salina St., 3rd Fl.
100 Clinton Sq.
Syracuse, NY 13202 (315) 474-2489
Contact: Kathy Goldfarb, Exec. Dir.
FAX: (315) 475-4983; URL: http://www.giffordfd.org

Incorporated in 1954 in NY.
Donor: Rosamond Gifford†.
Foundation type: Independent foundation.
Financial data (yr. ended 12/31/05): Assets, $27,437,148 (M); gifts received, $381,370; expenditures, $2,584,721; qualifying distributions, $2,363,294; giving activities include $1,492,708 for 85 grants (high: $177,483; low: $1,000).
Purpose and activities: Giving support for educational, scientific, social, and religious needs in Onondaga, Oswego, and Madison, counties, NY.

Particular interest in issues around youth violence, employment for youth, and neighborhood revitalization.
Fields of interest: Arts; Higher education; Hospitals (general); Crime/violence prevention; Youth development; Human services; Children/youth, services; Aging, centers/services.
Type of support: General/operating support; Capital campaigns; Building/renovation; Equipment; Land acquisition; Emergency funds; Program development; Conferences/seminars; Seed money; Curriculum development; Research; Technical assistance; Program evaluation; Matching/ challenge support.
Limitations: Giving limited to organizations located within and serving the residents of the town of Syracuse, and Onondaga, Oswego, and Madison counties, NY. No grants to individuals, or for endowment funds, continuing support.
Publications: Application guidelines; Annual report; Program policy statement.
Application information: Application guidelines available on Web site. E-mailed or faxed applications not accepted. Application form not required.
  Initial approach: Letter or telephone. Telephone call is encouraged in advance to discuss proposal concepts
  Copies of proposal: 1
  Deadline(s): Feb. 1, May 1, and Oct. 1; no deadline for grants $10,000 or less
  Board meeting date(s): Monthly
  Final notification: 2-3 months
Officers and Trustees:* Judith Mower,* Pres.; Patrick Mannion,* V.P.; Linda M. Hall,* Secy.; Edward S. Green,* Treas.; Kathy Goldfarb, Exec. Dir.; Richard G. Case; Charles A. Chappell, Jr.; Patricia T. Civil; Robert F. Dewey; Bethaida C. Gonzalez; Amelia Greiner; Billy Harper; Mark D. Muhammad, Minister; Sharon C. Northrup; Kathleen O'Connell; M. Catherine Richardson; Jack H. Webb.
Number of staff: 5 full-time professional; 1 full-time support.
EIN: 150572881
Selected grants: The following grants were reported in 2005.
$177,483 to Neighborhood Initiative, New Haven, CT.
$125,000 to United Way of Central New York, Syracuse, NY.
$53,000 to Boys and Girls Club.
$30,000 to Habitat for Humanity International. 2 grants: $20,000, $10,000
$20,000 to Syracuse City School District, Syracuse, NY. 2 grants: $15,000, $5,000
$20,000 to Tully Free Library, Tully, NY.
$15,000 to Jowonio School, Syracuse, NY.
$5,000 to Syracuse University, Syracuse, NY.

6027

Gifford Family Foundation ✧
(formerly The Cody Foundation)
c/o Hinman Straub, PC
121 State St.
Albany, NY 12207 (518) 436-0751
Contact: Debra Hamway
E-mail: JohnA@HSPM.com; Additional e-mail: DebraH@HSPM.com

Established in 1992 in NY.
Foundation type: Independent foundation.
Financial data (yr. ended 12/31/05): Assets, $1,961,085 (M); gifts received, $2,950; expenditures, $414,758; qualifying distributions,

$395,000; giving activities include $395,000 for 10 grants (high: $200,000; low: $5,000).
Purpose and activities: Giving primarily for youth organizations; funding also for health associations.
Fields of interest: Health organizations, association; Human services; Children/youth, services.
Limitations: Applications not accepted. Giving limited to CT and NY. No grants to individuals.
Application information: Contributes only to pre-selected organizations.
Trustees: Frank Gifford; Kathie Lee Gifford.
EIN: 136992402

6028

Lewis D. & John J. Gilbert Foundation ✧ ☆
c/o Lewis D. Gilbert
333 W. Hoffman Ave., Ste. A
Lindenhurst, NY 11757-4028

Established in 1992 in NY.
Donors: John J. Gilbert; Lewis D. Gilbert†; Corporate Democracy.
Foundation type: Independent foundation.
Financial data (yr. ended 12/31/05): Assets, $640,085 (M); expenditures, $353,027; qualifying distributions, $322,254; giving activities include $322,254 for grants.
Fields of interest: Museums; Performing arts; Arts; Higher education; Health organizations, association; Medical research, institute; Jewish federated giving programs; Jewish agencies & temples.
Limitations: Applications not accepted. Giving on a national basis. No grants to individuals.
Application information: Contributes only to pre-selected organizations.
Trustees: David Brown; M. Allan Frank; Margot R. Gilbert; Bernadette Liberti; Valerie Roberts; Sandi Rosenthal; Lisa Tharpe.
EIN: 133648972
Selected grants: The following grants were reported in 2003.
$111,501 to University of Denver, Denver, CO.
$40,532 to Denver Center for the Performing Arts, Denver, CO.
$30,000 to Junior Achievement, National, Colorado Springs, CO.
$13,100 to American Heart Association, Dallas, TX.
$5,000 to Volunteers of America, Alexandria, VA.
$3,000 to GRADS Foundation, Jamaica, NY.
$2,500 to Childrens Hospital Foundation, Denver, CO.
$1,350 to Metropolitan Museum of Art, New York, NY.
$1,000 to Colorado Symphony Association, Denver, CO.
$1,000 to Kempe Childrens Foundation, Denver, CO.

6029

Gilder Foundation, Inc. ▼ ✧
1775 Broadway
New York, NY 10019
Contact: Daniella Muhling, Grants Admin.

Established in 1965 in NY.
Donors: Richard Gilder; Great Circle Trust.
Foundation type: Independent foundation.
Financial data (yr. ended 12/31/04): Assets, $30,653,779 (M); gifts received, $4,624,580;

expenditures, $16,413,580; qualifying distributions, $16,374,977; giving activities include $16,289,060 for 244 grants (high: $6,066,000; low: $500; average: $1,000–$25,000).

Purpose and activities: Support for libraries, scholarship funds, and secondary education; support also for recreational programs, public affairs organizations, and cultural groups.

Fields of interest: Arts; Education; Recreation; Economic development; Public affairs, association.

Type of support: General/operating support; Continuing support; Annual campaigns; Capital campaigns; Endowments; Fellowships; Scholarship funds.

Limitations: Applications not accepted. Giving primarily in NY. No grants to individuals.

Application information: Contributes only to pre-selected organizations.

Officers: Richard Gilder, Jr., Pres.; Virginia Anne Gilder, V.P.; Howard Rothman, Secy.; Richard Schneidman, Treas.

Trustee: Joseph J. Pinto.

Number of staff: 2 part-time professional; 1 part-time support.

EIN: 136176041

Selected grants: The following grants were reported in 2004.

$6,066,000 to Gilder Lehrman Institute of American History, New York, NY.

$1,580,000 to American Museum of Natural History, New York, NY.

$1,088,290 to Pierpont Morgan Library, New York, NY.

$711,950 to New-York Historical Society, New York, NY.

$508,000 to Yale University, New Haven, CT.

$300,000 to Mount Vernon Ladies Association, Mount Vernon, VA.

$225,000 to Thomas Jefferson Memorial Foundation, Charlottesville, VA.

$200,000 to Brighter Choice Foundation, Clifton Park, NY.

$200,000 to Foundation for Education Reform and Accountability, Clifton Park, NY.

$193,340 to Inner-City Scholarship Fund, New York, NY.

6030
The Gilder Lehrman Institute of American History ✧

19 W. 44th St.
New York, NY 10036

Classified as a private operating foundation in 1995.

Donors: Gilder Foundation; John M. Olen Foundation; The Lynde and Harry Bradley Foundation, Inc.

Foundation type: Operating foundation.

Financial data (yr. ended 6/30/05): Assets, $2,256,802 (M); gifts received, $8,848,789; expenditures, $8,131,427; qualifying distributions, $7,790,944; giving activities include $616,779 for 20 grants (high: $200,000; low: $5,000), and $5,309,877 for foundation-administered programs.

Fields of interest: Museums (history); Historic preservation/historical societies; Higher education; Libraries (public).

Limitations: Applications not accepted. Giving on a national basis. No grants to individuals.

Application information: Contributes only to pre-selected organizations.

Officers and Trustees:* James Basker, Pres.; Lewis E. Lehrman,* Exec. V.P.; Howard Rothman,* Secy.; Richard S. Gilder, Treas.; Lesley S. Herrmann, Exec. Dir.

EIN: 133795391

Selected grants: The following grants were reported in 2005.

$200,000 to Oxford University Press, New York, NY.

$80,000 to Organization of American Historians, Bloomington, IN.

$50,000 to New York Public Library, New York, NY.

$23,000 to Columbia University, New York, NY.

$21,087 to American Antiquarian Society, Worcester, MA.

$15,000 to American Historical Association, DC.

$15,000 to George Washington University, DC.

$10,000 to National History Day, College Park, MD.

$5,000 to Bill of Rights Institute, Arlington, VA.

$5,000 to New Bedford Whaling Museum, New Bedford, MA.

6031
The Deane A. and John D. Gilliam Foundation ✧

(formerly John D. Gilliam Foundation)
c/o BCRS Group/Marcum & Kliegman, LLP
100 Wall St., 11th Fl.
New York, NY 10005

Established in 1978 in NY.

Donors: John D. Gilliam; Deane A. Gilliam.

Foundation type: Independent foundation.

Financial data (yr. ended 3/31/06): Assets, $5,385,145 (M); expenditures, $368,496; qualifying distributions, $335,111; giving activities include $329,515 for 70 grants (high: $50,000; low: $50).

Purpose and activities: Giving primarily for health care, human services, and arts and culture, with emphasis on a NY theater.

Fields of interest: Performing arts, theater; Arts; Education; Hospitals (general); Health care; Human services; Federated giving programs; Protestant agencies & churches.

Type of support: Annual campaigns; Capital campaigns; Endowments; Professorships; Fellowships.

Limitations: Applications not accepted. Giving primarily in the Mount Kisco and New York, NY areas; some funding nationally. No grants to individuals, or for scholarships; no loans.

Application information: Contributes only to pre-selected organizations.

Trustees: Peter M. Fahey; Deane A. Gilliam; John D. Gilliam; Donald R. Grant; Stephanae D. Lariviere.

EIN: 132967490

Selected grants: The following grants were reported in 2006.

$32,500 to Cleveland Institute of Music, Cleveland, OH. 2 grants: $2,500, $30,000

$25,000 to Single Parent Resource Center, New York, NY.

$20,000 to Manhattan Theater Club, New York, NY.

$17,000 to Wellesley College, Wellesley, MA.

$15,000 to Ravinia Festival Association, Highland Park, IL.

$15,000 to Walton Arts Center, Fayetteville, AR.

$5,000 to Ronald McDonald House Charities, Oak Brook, IL.

$1,500 to Museum of Modern Art, New York, NY.

$500 to Jewish Board of Family and Childrens Services, New York, NY.

6032
Howard Gilman Foundation, Inc. ✧

111 W. 50th St., 40th Fl.
New York, NY 10020 (212) 307-1073
Contact: Harry Brown, Prog. Assoc.
FAX: (212) 262-4108; E-mail: hfbrown@gilman.com

Incorporated in 1981 in DE.

Donors: Gilman Investment Co.; Gilman Paper Co.; Gilman Securities Corp.; Howard Gilman†; Sylvia P. Gilman†.

Foundation type: Independent foundation.

Financial data (yr. ended 12/31/03): Assets, $87,289,852 (M); gifts received, $6,150,000; expenditures, $13,107,500; qualifying distributions, $8,476,106; giving activities include $2,904,650 for 40 grants (high: $480,000; low: $1,000; average: $1,000–$100,000).

Purpose and activities: The mission of the foundation is to preserve the legacy of Howard Gilman by supporting philanthropic programs in his primary areas of interest: performing arts, wildlife conservation and cardiovascular diseases. The foundation accomplishes its mission through three major activities: 1) managing White Oak Plantation as a refuge for wildlife conservation and a center for residencies by performing artists, and a conference facility for professionals to explore critical issues in the foundation's fields of interest; 2) awarding grants to support creative talent and leadership in the performing arts in New York City; and 3) sustaining research at the Howard Gilman Institute for Valvular Heart Diseases at Weill Medical College of Cornell University.

Fields of interest: Performing arts; Performing arts, dance; Performing arts, theater; Animals/wildlife, preservation/protection; Medical research, institute; AIDS research; Family services.

Type of support: General/operating support; Continuing support; Building/renovation; Program development; Seed money; Curriculum development; Fellowships; Internship funds; Research; Matching/challenge support.

Limitations: Applications not accepted. Giving primarily in the metropolitan New York, NY, area with emphasis on the performing arts. No support for political or religious organizations. No grants to individuals, capital investments, scholarships, or deficit operations.

Publications: Informational brochure; Program policy statement.

Application information: The foundation has suspended all new grantmaking for the foreseeable future. It will continue to meet its present commitments.

Officers and Directors:* Jeffrey S. Borer, M.D.*, V.P.; Stephen W. Cropper,* V.P.; Pierre Apraxine; Bernard D. Bergreen; Donald Bruce; John Lukas; Natalie P. Moody.

Number of staff: 1 part-time support.

EIN: 133097486

6033
Sondra & Charles Gilman, Jr. Foundation, Inc.

109 E. 64th St.
New York, NY 10021
Contact: Sondra Gilman Gonzalez-Falla, Chair.
FAX: (212) 734-9606; Application address: 140 Lake Blvd., Ste. A, Kingsland, CA 31548

Established in NY in 1981 as a successor to the Gilman Foundation.

Foundation type: Independent foundation.
Financial data (yr. ended 4/30/06): Assets, $7,564,614 (M); expenditures, $937,856; qualifying distributions, $559,878; giving activities include $377,841 for 39 grants (high: $314,775; low: $50).
Purpose and activities: Giving primarily to organizations that are involved in contemporary art and theater.
Fields of interest: Visual arts; Museums (art); Arts; Education; Health care; Health organizations, association; Jewish agencies & temples.
Type of support: General/operating support; Continuing support; Endowments; Program development.
Limitations: Applications not accepted. Giving on a national basis, with some emphasis on GA, New York, NY, and TX. No grants to individuals.
Publications: Program policy statement.
Application information:
  Board meeting date(s): Quarterly
Officers: Sondra Gilman Gonzalez-Falla, Chair.; Celso M. Gonzalez-Falla, Pres.; Jack Friedland, V.P.; Walter Bauer, Treas.
Directors: Charles Gilman III; Myrna Schatz.
EIN: 133097485
Selected grants: The following grants were reported in 2004.
$342,924 to Whitney Museum of American Art, New York, NY.
$10,000 to Memorial Sloan-Kettering Cancer Center, New York, NY.
$5,000 to Aperture Foundation, New York, NY.
$3,700 to Richard J. Caron Foundation New York Regional Office, New York, NY.
$3,000 to South Texas Institute for the Arts, Corpus Christi, TX.
$2,500 to Henry Street Settlement, New York, NY.
$1,500 to Lenox Hill Hospital, New York, NY.
$1,000 to Big Apple Circus, New York, NY.
$1,000 to Breast Cancer Research Foundation, New York, NY.
$1,000 to Institute for the Study of Aging, New York, NY.

6034

Bernard F. and Alva B. Gimbel Foundation, Inc.

271 Madison Ave., Ste. 605
New York, NY   10016   (212) 895-8050
Contact: Leslie Gimbel, Exec. Dir.
FAX: (212) 895-8052; URL: http://www.gimbelfoundation.org

Incorporated in 1943 in NY.
Donors: Bernard F. Gimbel†; Alva B. Gimbel†.
Foundation type: Independent foundation.
Financial data (yr. ended 12/31/05): Assets, $72,578,186 (M); expenditures, $6,091,697; qualifying distributions, $4,469,374; giving activities include $4,173,650 for 119 grants (high: $100,000; low: $500; average: $50,000–$75,000).
Purpose and activities: Support for education, workforce/economic development, criminal justice, civil legal services, reproductive rights, the environment, and for advocacy in these areas.
Fields of interest: Elementary/secondary education; Environment; Offenders/ex-offenders, prison alternatives; Courts/judicial administration; Employment, services; Housing/shelter; Children, day care; Civil liberties, reproductive rights;

Community development, neighborhood development; Economic development; Homeless.
Type of support: General/operating support; Continuing support; Program development.
Limitations: Giving primarily in New York, NY for direct services; nationally for some advocacy grants. No support for individual schools, short-term educational programs or workshops, or mentoring, after-school, summer, or youth development programs. No grants to individuals.
Application information: Accepts NY/NJ Area Common Application Form or similar format. The foundation does accept unsolicited proposals for the environment program area. The foundation does not accept proposals or letters of inquiry by fax. Applicants with questions regarding funding guidelines or the application process are encouraged to call. Application form not required.
  Initial approach: Letter of inquiry (2-3 pages)
  Copies of proposal: 1
  Deadline(s): Jan. 26 and July 31 for invited proposals
  Board meeting date(s): June and Dec.
  Final notification: Varies
Officers and Directors:* Caral G. Lebworth,* Hon. Chair.; Hope G. Solinger,* Hon. Chair.; Leslie Gimbel,* Pres. and Exec. Dir.; Lynn S. Stern,* V.P.; Stephen D. Greenberg,* Treas.; Judy Mendelsund; Nicholas S.G. Stern.
Number of staff: 2 full-time professional; 1 full-time support.
EIN: 136090843

6035

Gimprich Family Foundation, Inc.

1 W. 4th St.
New York, NY   10012   (212) 824-2208
Contact: Zelda Goldsmith, Exec. Admin.

Established in 1975.
Donor: Marvin Gimprich†.
Foundation type: Independent foundation.
Financial data (yr. ended 5/31/05): Assets, $7,831,055 (M); expenditures, $957,414; qualifying distributions, $957,414; giving activities include $854,660 for 82 grants (high: $125,000; low: $2,500).
Purpose and activities: Giving primarily for Jewish projects and programs in Israel.
Fields of interest: Human services; Children/youth, services; Civil liberties, advocacy; Jewish agencies & temples.
International interests: Israel.
Type of support: Seed money.
Limitations: Giving in the U.S. and internationally, primarily in Israel. No grants to individuals, or for building.
Application information: Application form required.
  Initial approach: Letter
  Copies of proposal: 12
  Deadline(s): Feb. 1 and July 15
  Final notification: Within 4 months
Officers: David M. Fishman, Pres.; Lila Gimprich d'Adolf, V.P.; Rosalie Dolmatch, Recording Secy.; Eric S. Wittstein, Treas.
Directors: Leora Fishman; Jeremy Nussbaum; Max Nussbaum; Michael Schmidt; Steven Windmueller.
Number of staff: 1 part-time professional.
EIN: 510147095
Selected grants: The following grants were reported in 2005.
$125,000 to Dorot, New York, NY.

$25,000 to American Jewish Joint Distribution Committee, New York, NY.
$15,000 to Children of the Night, Van Nuys, CA.
$10,000 to Israel Guide Dog Center for the Blind, Warrington, PA.
$10,000 to Keren Klita, Jerusalem, Israel. .
$10,000 to King Street Youth Center, Burlington, VT.
$10,000 to Melitz Centers for Jewish Zionist Education, Jerusalem, Israel. .
$10,000 to Shekel, Jerusalem, Israel. .
$8,000 to Society for the Advancement of Education in Israel, Lod, Israel. .
$5,000 to Erin Gruwell Education Project, Long Beach, CA.

6036

The Ralph S. Gindi Private Foundation ✧

c/o Jeff Gindi, LLC
2089 E. 3rd St.
Brooklyn, NY   11223

Established in 1998 in NY.
Donors: Jeffrey Gindi; Eli Gindi; Irwin Gindi.
Foundation type: Independent foundation.
Financial data (yr. ended 12/31/04): Assets, $617,416 (M); gifts received, $829,150; expenditures, $628,847; qualifying distributions, $626,844; giving activities include $625,394 for 32 grants (high: $65,563; low: $18).
Fields of interest: Jewish federated giving programs; Jewish agencies & temples.
Limitations: Applications not accepted. Giving primarily in New York, NY. No grants to individuals.
Application information: Contributes only to pre-selected organizations.
Officers: Jeffrey Gindi, Pres.; Irwin Gindi, V.P.; Eli Gindi, Secy.
EIN: 113431763

6037

The Glades Foundation ✧

c/o Sullivan & Cromwell
125 Broad St.
New York, NY   10004

Established in 1991 in NY.
Donors: Mark F. Dalton; Paul T. Jones II.
Foundation type: Independent foundation.
Financial data (yr. ended 12/31/05): Assets, $6,047,974 (M); gifts received, $250,000; expenditures, $765,680; qualifying distributions, $765,350; giving activities include $765,000 for 32 grants (high: $225,000; low: $2,000).
Purpose and activities: Giving primarily for higher education, youth and social services, and the arts.
Fields of interest: Arts; Higher education, university; Human services; Children/youth, services; Foundations (private grantmaking).
Limitations: Applications not accepted. Giving on a national and international basis, primarily in the U.S., with emphasis on the Northeast; some funding also in Geneva, Switzerland. No grants to individuals.
Application information: Contributes only to pre-selected organizations.
Trustees: James I. Black III; Mark F. Dalton.
EIN: 136986506
Selected grants: The following grants were reported in 2003.

$125,000 to Sheridan Arts Foundation, Telluride, CO. For unrestricted support.

$25,000 to Americas Foundation for Chess, Seattle, WA. For unrestricted support.

$25,000 to Big Brothers of Massachusetts Bay, Boston, MA.

$5,000 to Health Sciences Foundation of the Medical University of South Carolina, Charleston, SC. For unrestricted support.

$5,000 to National Outdoor Leadership School, Lander, WY. For unrestricted support.

$2,500 to Riverkeeper, Tarrytown, NY. For unrestricted support.

$2,000 to American Geographical Society of New York, New York, NY. For unrestricted support.

$2,000 to Childrens Village, Dobbs Ferry, NY.

$2,000 to Creative Alternatives of New York, New York, NY. For unrestricted support.

$2,000 to Walter Hoving Home, Garrison, NY. For unrestricted support.

6038
The Anne and Eric Gleacher Foundation ✧
c/o Gleacher & Co., LLC
660 Madison Ave.
New York, NY 10021
Contact: Eric J. Gleacher, Pres.

Established in 1990 in DE and NY.
Donor: Eric J. Gleacher.
Foundation type: Independent foundation.
Financial data (yr. ended 12/31/05): Assets, $8,499,088 (M); expenditures, $1,492,097; qualifying distributions, $1,446,049; giving activities include $1,444,865 for 48 grants (high: $600,000; low: $500).
Purpose and activities: Giving primarily for secondary and higher education, for health services including family planning, and for social services.
Fields of interest: Elementary/secondary education; Higher education; Environment; Hospitals (general); Reproductive health; Human services; Children/youth, services.
Limitations: Giving primarily in NY. No grants to individuals.
Application information: Application form not required.
  Initial approach: Letter
  Deadline(s): None
Officers: Eric J. Gleacher, Pres.; Anne G. Gleacher, V.P.
EIN: 133597695
Selected grants: The following grants were reported in 2005.
$600,000 to Prep for Prep, New York, NY.
$321,565 to Northwestern University, Evanston, IL.
$250,000 to University of Pennsylvania, Philadelphia, PA.
$30,000 to University of Chicago, Chicago, IL. 2 grants: $25,000, $5,000
$15,000 to Millbrook School, Millbrook, NY.
$10,000 to Marine Corps Scholarship Foundation, Princeton, NJ.
$5,000 to Choate Rosemary Hall, Wallingford, CT.
$3,000 to Student Advocacy, Elmsford, NY.
$1,000 to Brick Church School, New York, NY.

6039
Gleason Foundation ▼ ✧
(formerly Gleason Memorial Fund, Inc.)
P.O. Box 22970
Rochester, NY 14692-2970 (585) 241-4030
Contact: Ralph E. Harper, Secy.-Treas.
FAX: (585) 241-4099;
E-mail: gf@gleasonfoundation.org

Incorporated in 1959 in NY.
Foundation type: Independent foundation.
Financial data (yr. ended 12/31/04): Assets, $137,707,254 (M); expenditures, $6,761,406; qualifying distributions, $6,089,077; giving activities include $5,608,565 for 55+ grants (high: $1,250,000; average: $10,000–$125,000).
Purpose and activities: Emphasis on education, including research and technology; support also for community funds, youth, and social service agencies, public interest and civic affairs groups, and cultural activities.
Fields of interest: Arts; Education, research; Higher education; Education; Human services; Children/youth, services; Community development; Public affairs.
Type of support: General/operating support; Annual campaigns; Capital campaigns; Building/renovation; Equipment; Professorships; Curriculum development; Scholarship funds; Research; Technical assistance.
Limitations: Giving primarily in Monroe County, NY. No support for United Way-supported agencies. No grants to individuals.
Application information: Application form required.
  Initial approach: Letter and application
  Copies of proposal: 1
  Deadline(s): None
  Board meeting date(s): Quarterly
  Final notification: 1 to 2 weeks after board meetings
Officers and Directors:* James S. Gleason,* Chair.; Tracy Gleason,* Pres.; Gary Kimmet,* V.P.; Ralph Harper,* Secy.-Treas.; Edward Atwater; Janis F. Gleason; Albert Moore.
Number of staff: 1 part-time professional; 1 full-time support.
EIN: 166023235
Selected grants: The following grants were reported in 2004.
$1,250,000 to Rochester Institute of Technology, Kate Gleason College of Engineering, Rochester, NY.
$1,000,000 to University of Rochester, River Campus Library, Rochester, NY.
$280,000 to United Way of Greater Rochester, Rochester, NY.
$150,000 to Strong Museum, Rochester, NY.
$146,500 to Center for Governmental Research, Rochester, NY.
$100,000 to McQuaid Jesuit High School, Rochester, NY.
$63,890 to Gleason Fund Inc. Life Benefit Plan, Rochester, NY.
$40,000 to Pacific Research Institute for Public Policy, San Francisco, CA.
$35,000 to WZL Forum GmbH, Aachen, Germany.
$30,000 to GeVa Theater, Rochester, NY.

6040
Joseph & Carson Gleberman Foundation ✧
c/o Goldman Sachs & Co.
1 New York Plz., 40th Fl.
New York, NY 10004

Established in 1991 in NY.
Donor: Joseph H. Gleberman.
Foundation type: Independent foundation.
Financial data (yr. ended 3/31/06): Assets, $17,510,869 (M); gifts received, $1,922,250; expenditures, $423,996; qualifying distributions, $370,360; giving activities include $370,360 for 70 grants (high: $50,000; low: $250).
Purpose and activities: Giving primarily for arts and cultural programs, education, natural resource conservation and protection, health associations, and human services.
Fields of interest: Arts; Education; Environment, natural resources; Health organizations, association; Human services; Jewish agencies & temples.
Limitations: Applications not accepted. Giving on a national basis, with emphasis on New York, NY. No grants to individuals.
Application information: Contributes only to pre-selected organizations.
Trustees: Carson Gleberman; Joseph H. Gleberman.
EIN: 133632753
Selected grants: The following grants were reported in 2004.
$275,000 to Manhattan Theater Club, New York, NY.
$100,000 to Yale University, New Haven, CT.
$30,000 to Stanford University, Stanford, CA.
$10,000 to Nature Conservancy, New York, NY.
$3,000 to Robin Hood Foundation, New York, NY.
$2,500 to Public Art Fund, New York, NY.
$2,000 to Riverkeeper, Tarrytown, NY.
$1,000 to National Mentoring Partnership, Alexandria, VA.
$500 to City Harvest, New York, NY.
$500 to New York City Ballet, New York, NY.

6041
The Glens Falls Foundation ✧
16 Maple St.
Glens Falls, NY 12801 (518) 761-7350
Contact: John G. Zeis, Admin.

Established in 1939 in NY by declaration of trust.
Foundation type: Community foundation.
Financial data (yr. ended 12/31/05): Assets, $11,549,872 (M); gifts received, $59,666; expenditures, $405,702; giving activities include $170,959 for 32 grants (high: $25,000; low: $474; and $158,982 for 118 grants to individuals (high: $12,000; low: $75).
Purpose and activities: Giving solely to promote the mental, moral, and physical improvement of the people of Glens Falls and environs. Direct financial aid to individuals limited to scholarships to medical students and to students at Dartmouth and Harvard colleges. All other scholarships are awarded through area institutions.
Fields of interest: Human services; Community development.
Type of support: Capital campaigns; Building/renovation; Equipment; Land acquisition; Emergency funds; Program development; Conferences/seminars; Seed money; Research; Scholarships—to individuals; Matching/challenge support.

Limitations: Giving limited to Warren, Washington, and northern Saratoga counties, NY. No grants for annual campaigns, continuing support, or endowment funds; no loans; no direct scholarship grants (except for medical students and students at Dartmouth and Harvard colleges).

Publications: Application guidelines; Annual report; Informational brochure.

Application information: The foundation does not participate in the selection process for scholarship awards, except for scholarships to medical students. Application form not required.

Initial approach: Letter or telephone
Copies of proposal: 8
Deadline(s): Mar. 20, June 20, Sept. 20, or Dec. 20
Board meeting date(s): 2nd Wed. in Jan., Apr., July, and Oct.
Final notification: 4 business days after quarterly meetings

Officers and Distribution Committee:* Marilyn Cohen,* Chair.; John G. Zeis, Admin.; Katherine M. Barton; Thomas H. Lapham; Donald A. Metivier; Kathryn O'Keeffe, M.D.; Floyd H. Rourke; Thomas R. Yole.

Trustee: TD Banknorth Wealth Management Group.

EIN: 146036390

6042

The Glickenhaus Foundation ✧

100 Dorchester Rd.
Scarsdale, NY   10583
Contact: Maddy Wehle

Incorporated in 1960 in NY.

Donors: Seth M. Glickenhaus; Sarah Glickenhaus.

Foundation type: Independent foundation.

Financial data (yr. ended 11/30/05): Assets, $21,400,157 (M); gifts received, $2,000,000; expenditures, $3,958,925; qualifying distributions, $3,829,098; giving activities include $3,829,098 for 565 grants (high: $2,000,000; low: $20).

Purpose and activities: Support for general charitable activities.

Fields of interest: Humanities; Arts; Education, association; Child development, education; Education; Environment, natural resources; Environment; Hospitals (general); Reproductive health, family planning; Health care; Substance abuse, services; Mental health/crisis services; Cancer; AIDS; Biomedicine; Medical research, institute; Cancer research; AIDS research; Crime/violence prevention, youth; Human services; Children/youth, services; Child development, services; Family services; Aging, centers/services; International affairs, arms control; Civil rights; Community development; Jewish agencies & temples; Aging; Disabilities, people with; Minorities.

Type of support: Endowments; Emergency funds; Research.

Limitations: Giving primarily in the greater metropolitan New York, NY, area, including Westchester County.

Application information:
Initial approach: Letter

Officers: Nancy G. Pier, Pres.; James Glickenhaus, V.P.; Alfred Feinman, Secy.-Treas.

Number of staff: 1 full-time support.

EIN: 136160941

Selected grants: The following grants were reported in 2004.

$100,000 to UJA-Federation of New York, New York, NY.

$85,000 to Harvard University, Cambridge, MA.
$50,000 to Planned Parenthood Hudson Peconic, Hawthorne, NY.
$25,000 to Museum of Arts and Design, New York, NY.
$25,000 to P.E.F. Israel Endowment Funds, New York, NY.
$5,000 to FJC-A Foundation of Donor-Advised Funds, New York, NY.
$5,000 to Hudson Guild, New York, NY.
$1,492 to Lincoln Center Theater, New York, NY.
$1,000 to Teach for America, New York, NY.
$1,000 to United Hebrew Geriatric Center, New Rochelle, NY.

6043

Global Resource Action Center for the Environment, Inc. ✧

(also known as GRACE)
215 Lexington Ave., Ste. 1001
New York, NY   10016
E-mail: info@gracelinks.org; *URL:* http://www.gracelinks.org/

Established in 1997 in NY.

Donors: Helaine Lerner; Berkshire Hathaway Inc.; Heilbrunn Foundation; W. Alton Jones Foundation; The Tamarind Foundation.

Foundation type: Operating foundation.

Financial data (yr. ended 12/31/04): Assets, $173,756 (M); gifts received, $2,639,293; expenditures, $2,968,997; qualifying distributions, $2,915,950; giving activities include $1,265,035 for 11 grants (high: $879,035; low: $5,000), and $717,715 for foundation-administered programs.

Purpose and activities: GRACE works to form new links with the research, policy and grassroots communities to preserve the future of the planet and protect the quality of the environment.

Fields of interest: Environment, pollution control; Environment, natural resources; Agriculture/food; International affairs; Public affairs, research; Public policy, research; Consumer protection.

Type of support: General/operating support; Program development.

Limitations: Applications not accepted. Giving on a national and international basis. No grants to individuals.

Application information: Contributes only to pre-selected organizations.

Officers: Helaine Lerner, Chair.; Alice Slater, Pres.

EIN: 113332888

6044

The Godinger Lefkowitz Memorial Foundation, Inc. ✧

63-15 Traffic Ave.
Ridgewood, NY   11385
Contact: William Lefkowitz, V.P.

Donors: Arnold Godinger; William Lefkowitz; Godindger Silver Art, Ltd.

Foundation type: Independent foundation.

Financial data (yr. ended 11/30/05): Assets, $54,449 (M); gifts received, $1,290,000; expenditures, $1,243,590; qualifying distributions, $1,243,439; giving activities include $1,243,439 for grants.

Purpose and activities: Giving primarily to Jewish agencies, temples, and schools.

Fields of interest: Education; Jewish federated giving programs; Jewish agencies & temples.

Application information:
Initial approach: Letter
Deadline(s): None

Officers: Arnold Godinger, Pres.; William Lefkowitz, V.P.; Rita Godinger, Secy.

EIN: 133800381

6045

Goldberg/Nash Family Foundation ✧

(formerly Beth Nash & Joshua Nash Charitable Trust)
c/o Ulysses Partners, LP
280 Park Ave., 21st Fl.
New York, NY   10017

Established in 1989 in NY.

Donor: Joshua Nash.

Foundation type: Independent foundation.

Financial data (yr. ended 6/30/05): Assets, $747,238 (M); expenditures, $595,028; qualifying distributions, $507,376; giving activities include $503,612 for 135 grants (high: $60,000; low: $20).

Fields of interest: Arts, association; Museums; Museums (ethnic/folk arts); Arts; Higher education; Education; Hospitals (general); Health organizations, association; Human services; Jewish federated giving programs; Jewish agencies & temples.

Limitations: Applications not accepted. Giving primarily in New York, NY. No grants to individuals.

Application information: Contributes only to pre-selected organizations.

Trustees: Beth Nash; Joshua Nash.

EIN: 133560261

Selected grants: The following grants were reported in 2005.

$127,309 to Congregation Or Zarua, New York, NY. 3 grants: $65,000, $2,309, $60,000
$39,700 to Jewish Museum, New York, NY. 2 grants: $9,700, $30,000
$5,000 to American Friends of the Jaffa Institute, Flushing, NY.
$5,000 to Perlman Music Program, New York, NY.
$5,000 to Stanley M. Isaacs Neighborhood Center, New York, NY.
$1,800 to Chamah, New York, NY.
$1,000 to Independent Curators International, New York, NY.

6046

Golden Family Foundation

500 5th Ave., 50th Fl.
New York, NY   10110
Contact: William T. Golden, Pres.

Incorporated in 1952 in NY.

Donors: William T. Golden; Sibyl L. Golden†.

Foundation type: Independent foundation.

Financial data (yr. ended 12/31/05): Assets, $50,527,738 (M); expenditures, $2,506,077; qualifying distributions, $2,094,017; giving activities include $2,094,017 for 180 grants (high: $400,000), and $1,539,207 for 16 loans/program-related investments (low: $1,813).

Purpose and activities: Support for a broad range of programs in higher education, science, public affairs, and cultural areas.

Fields of interest: Arts; Higher education; Engineering/technology; Science; Public policy, research.
Type of support: General/operating support; Annual campaigns; Capital campaigns; Building/renovation; Program-related investments/loans; Matching/challenge support.
Limitations: Applications not accepted. Giving primarily in NY. No grants to individuals.
Application information: Contributes only to pre-selected organizations.
  Board meeting date(s): Jan. and as required
Officers and Directors: * William T. Golden,* Pres.; Sibyl R. Golden,* V.P.; Helene L. Kaplan,* Secy.; Ralph E. Hansmann,* Treas.; Pamela P. Golden, M.D.
EIN: 237423802
Selected grants: The following grants were reported in 2003.
$5,271,390 to American Association for the Advancement of Science, DC.
$1,379,780 to American Museum of Natural History, New York, NY.
$100,050 to New York Academy of Sciences, New York, NY.
$100,000 to After-School Corporation, New York, NY.
$100,000 to Carnegie Institution of Washington, DC.
$55,000 to Princeton University, Princeton, NJ.
$50,500 to American Academy of Arts and Sciences, Cambridge, MA.
$25,000 to National Museum of the American Indian, DC.
$25,000 to University of Wisconsin, Madison, WI.
$16,000 to Mount Sinai School of Medicine of New York University, New York, NY.

6047
Goldenson-Arbus Foundation, Inc. ◇
(formerly The Isabelle and Leonard Goldenson Association, Inc.)
35 Underhill St.
Tuckahoe, NY 10707

Established in 1946 in NY.
Foundation type: Independent foundation.
Financial data (yr. ended 12/31/04): Assets, $13,992,922 (M); expenditures, $1,072,393; qualifying distributions, $830,539; giving activities include $830,539 for 36 grants (high: $542,014; low: $96).
Purpose and activities: Giving primarily for medical research and health care; funding also for education, including educational programs at a film institute, and to women's organizations.
Fields of interest: Media, film/video; Education; Health care; Medical research, institute; Cerebral palsy research; Cancer research; Women.
Limitations: Applications not accepted. Giving primarily in CA; some giving also in NY. No grants to individuals.
Application information: Contributes only to pre-selected organizations.
Officers: Martin Pompadur, Chair.; Loreen J. Arbus, Pres.; Maxine W. Goldenson, V.P.; Maryellen Mastrogiorgio, Secy.
EIN: 136115597
Selected grants: The following grants were reported in 2003.
$193,135 to Museum of Television and Radio, Beverly Hills, CA.

$84,000 to United Cerebral Palsy of New York City, New York, NY.
$50,125 to WOMEN of Washington, DC.
$20,000 to Israel Cancer Research Fund, Los Angeles, CA.
$20,000 to Women Incorporated, Los Angeles, CA.
$10,000 to Harvard University, Cambridge, MA.
$10,000 to Los Angeles Womens Foundation, Los Angeles, CA.
$7,000 to Servite High School, Anaheim, CA. For scholarships.
$250 to Volunteers of America of Los Angeles, Los Angeles, CA.
$125 to EngenderHealth, New York, NY.

6048
The Lionel Goldfrank III Foundation ◇
667 Madison Ave., 20th Fl.
New York, NY 10021-8029

Established in 1999 in NY.
Donor: Lionel Goldfrank III.
Foundation type: Independent foundation.
Financial data (yr. ended 4/30/04): Assets, $281,721 (M); gifts received, $1,082,000; expenditures, $865,130; qualifying distributions, $860,000; giving activities include $860,000 for 5 grants (high: $350,000; low: $5,000).
Fields of interest: Higher education; Environment, natural resources; Botanical gardens.
Type of support: General/operating support.
Limitations: Applications not accepted. Giving primarily in CT and NY. No grants to individuals.
Application information: Contributes only to pre-selected organizations.
Officer: Lionel Goldfrank III, Pres.
EIN: 316623852
Selected grants: The following grants were reported in 2003.
$300,000 to Yale University, New Haven, CT. 2 grants: $250,000, $50,000 to Art Gallery
$275,000 to New York Botanical Garden, Bronx, NY.
$50,000 to Preservation League of New York State, Albany, NY.
$20,000 to Museum of the City of New York, New York, NY.

6049
The Goldie-Anna Charitable Trust ◇
5 Woods Witch Lake
Chappaqua, NY 10514
Contact: Kenneth L. Stein, Tr.

Established about 1977 in NY.
Foundation type: Independent foundation.
Financial data (yr. ended 12/31/04): Assets, $24,902,155 (M); expenditures, $1,157,799; qualifying distributions, $1,020,864; giving activities include $995,765 for 124 grants (high: $236,600; low: $250).
Purpose and activities: Emphasis on higher education, including some support in Israel, medical research, hospitals, Jewish giving, cultural organizations, and the elderly and disadvantaged.
Fields of interest: Arts; Higher education; Human services; Jewish agencies & temples; Economically disadvantaged.
International interests: Israel.
Limitations: Applications not accepted. Giving primarily in the metropolitan New York, NY, area.

Application information: Unsolicited requests for funds not accepted.
Trustees: Julius Greenfield; Kenneth L. Stein.
EIN: 132897474
Selected grants: The following grants were reported in 2003.
$136,500 to American Friends of the Hebrew University, New York, NY.
$100,000 to Columbia University, School of Law, New York, NY.
$25,000 to Mount Kisco Day Care Centers, Mount Kisco, NY.
$21,000 to UJA-Federation of New York, New York, NY.
$10,000 to Central Park Conservancy, New York, NY.
$10,000 to Citymeals-on-Wheels, New York, NY.
$10,000 to Inner-City Scholarship Fund, New York, NY.
$10,000 to Northern Westchester Hospital Center, Mount Kisco, NY.
$10,000 to PeaceWorks Foundation, OneVoice-Silent No Longer, New York, NY.
$10,000 to Shield Institute for Retarded Children, Flushing, NY.

6050
The Lillian Goldman Charitable Trust ◇
c/o Anchin, Block & Anchin LLP
1375 Broadway, 18th Fl.
New York, NY 10018

Established in 1995 in NY.
Donors: Sol Goldman†; The Sol Goldman Charitable Trust.
Foundation type: Independent foundation.
Financial data (yr. ended 4/30/05): Assets, $42,007,515 (M); expenditures, $3,350,088; qualifying distributions, $3,132,319; giving activities include $3,086,200 for 23 grants (high: $1,000,000; low: $5,000).
Fields of interest: Arts; Law school/education; Health organizations, association; Human services.
Limitations: Applications not accepted. Giving primarily in CT and New York, NY. No grants to individuals.
Application information: Contributes only to pre-selected organizations.
Trustee: Amy Goldman.
EIN: 137048279
Selected grants: The following grants were reported in 2005.
$300,000 to New York Restoration Project, New York, NY.
$300,000 to Seed Savers Exchange, Decorah, IA.
$200,000 to Center for Jewish History, New York, NY.
$200,000 to Planned Parenthood Federation of America, New York, NY.
$200,000 to W N E T Channel 13, New York, NY.
$50,000 to PEN American Center, New York, NY.
$50,000 to Women Make Movies, New York, NY.
$30,000 to Open Space Institute, New York, NY.
$25,000 to American Friends of the Israel Museum, New York, NY.
$10,000 to Garden Conservancy, Cold Spring, NY.

6051
The Sol Goldman Charitable Trust ▼ ✧
640 5th Ave., 3rd Fl.
New York, NY 10019
Contact: Jane H. Goldman, Tr.

Established in 1988 in NY; funded in 1990.
Donor: Sol Goldman†.
Foundation type: Independent foundation.
Financial data (yr. ended 1/31/05): Assets,
$126,675,868 (M); expenditures, $6,709,266;
qualifying distributions, $6,414,426; giving
activities include $6,395,100 for 70 grants (high:
$2,000,000; low: $1,000; average: $5,000–
$25,000).
Purpose and activities: Giving primarily to Jewish
organizations, health organizations, and education.
Fields of interest: Education; Health organizations,
association; Human services; YM/YWCAs & YM/
YWHAs; Jewish agencies & temples.
Limitations: Giving primarily in New York, NY. No
grants to individuals.
Application information: Application form not
required.
  Initial approach: Proposal
  Deadline(s): None
Trustees: Allan H. Goldman; Jane H. Goldman;
Louisa Little.
EIN: 133577310
Selected grants: The following grants were reported
in 2005.
$2,000,000 to Johns Hopkins University, Baltimore,
  MD.
$2,000,000 to Lighthouse International, New York,
  NY.
$500,000 to Yale University, Law School, New
  Haven, CT.
$350,000 to Congregation Emanu-El of the City of
  New York, New York, NY.
$300,000 to Johns Hopkins Medical Institutions,
  Baltimore, MD.
$20,000 to Ramaz School, New York, NY.
$15,000 to Jewish Family and Childrens Service,
  Waltham, MA.
$15,000 to New York-Presbyterian Hospital, New
  York, NY.
$10,000 to Well Spouse Foundation, New York, NY.
$5,000 to Congregation Orach Chaim, Brooklyn, NY.

6052
Joyce and Irving Goldman Family Foundation ✧
(formerly Irving Goldman Foundation, Inc.)
52 Vanderbilt Ave., 16th Fl.
New York, NY 10017 (212) 624-4300
Contact: Robyn Calisti, Exec. Dir.

Established in 1984 in NY.
Donors: Goldman Children Trust; Goldman
Grandchildren Trust.
Foundation type: Independent foundation.
Financial data (yr. ended 12/31/04): Assets,
$197,328,797 (M); gifts received, $30,688,064;
expenditures, $4,109,238; qualifying distributions,
$3,209,345; giving activities include $3,141,167
for 62 grants (high: $1,500,000; low: $1,000;
average: $1,000–$50,000).
Purpose and activities: Giving primarily for public
health education, Jewish continuity, and breast
cancer research and advocacy.
Fields of interest: Medical research; Jewish
federated giving programs; Jewish agencies &
temples.

Type of support: General/operating support;
Program development; Conferences/seminars;
Seed money; Fellowships; Research.
Limitations: Giving primarily in the U.S. No grants to
individuals, or for capital requests.
Application information: Application form not
required.
  Initial approach: Letter of inquiry
  Copies of proposal: 1
  Deadline(s): None
  Board meeting date(s): Ongoing
  Final notification: Acknowledgment of application
  immediately; decision within 3-9 months
Officers and Director:* Dorian Goldman,* Pres.;
Robyn Calisti, Exec. Dir.
Number of staff: 1 full-time professional.
EIN: 133216152

6053
Herman Goldman Foundation
61 Broadway, 18th Fl.
New York, NY 10006 (212) 797-9090
Contact: Richard K. Baron, Exec. Dir.

Incorporated in 1943 in NY.
Donor: Herman Goldman†.
Foundation type: Independent foundation.
Financial data (yr. ended 2/28/05): Assets,
$26,290,162 (M); expenditures, $2,168,627;
qualifying distributions, $1,949,659; giving
activities include $1,357,363 for 137 grants (high:
$75,000; low: $1,000).
Purpose and activities: Emphasis on enhancing the
quality of life through innovative grants in four main
areas: 1) Health - to achieve effective delivery of
physical and mental health care services; 2) Social
Justice - to develop organizational, social, and legal
approaches to aid deprived or handicapped people;
3) Education - for new or improved counseling for
effective preschool, vocational and
paraprofessional training; and 4) the Arts - to
increase opportunities for talented youth to receive
training and for less affluent individuals to attend
quality presentations; some aid for programs
relating to nationwide problems.
Fields of interest: Performing arts; Education, early
childhood education; Vocational education;
Education; Health care; Mental health/crisis
services; Health organizations, association; Crime/
law enforcement; Human services; Disabilities,
people with; Economically disadvantaged.
Type of support: General/operating support;
Continuing support; Annual campaigns; Capital
campaigns; Building/renovation; Endowments;
Program development; Seed money; Fellowships;
Internship funds; Scholarship funds; Research.
Limitations: Giving primarily in the metropolitan New
York, NY, area. No support for religious
organizations. No grants to individuals, or for
emergency funds.
Publications: Annual report (including application
guidelines).
Application information: Accepts the NY/NJ Area
Common Application Form. Application form not
required.
  Initial approach: Proposal
  Copies of proposal: 1
  Deadline(s): Middle of month preceding board
  meeting
  Board meeting date(s): Monthly; grants
  considered in Apr., July, and Nov.
  Final notification: 2 to 3 months

Officers and Directors:* Alan Nisselson,* Pres.;
David A. Brauner,* V.P.; Christopher C.
Schwabacher,* V.P.; Mel P. Barkan,* Secy.; Howard
L. Simon,* Treas.; Richard K. Baron, Exec. Dir.;
Jules M. Baron; Michael F. Clain; Charles A. Damato;
John H.F. Enteman; Donald Gibson; Michael L.
Goldstein; David R. Kay; Alan Michigan; Roy M.
Sparber.
Number of staff: 2 full-time professional.
EIN: 136066039
Selected grants: The following grants were reported
in 2005.
$75,000 to United Jewish Appeal, New York, NY.
$25,000 to New York Shakespeare Festival, New
  York, NY.
$25,000 to Philharmonic-Symphony Society of New
  York, New York, NY.
$25,000 to Stanley M. Klein Foundation, New York,
  NY.
$25,000 to Williams College, Williamstown, MA.
$22,500 to Seamens Church Institute of New York
  and New Jersey, New York, NY.
$20,000 to Bucknell University, Lewisburg, PA.
$10,000 to American Museum of Natural History,
  New York, NY.
$10,000 to Parents Foundation for Transitional
  Living, New Haven, CT.
$7,500 to Teachers Network, New York, NY.

6054
Robert I. Goldman Foundation ✧ ☆
c/o Richard Rothberg, Kronish, Lieb at al.
1114 6th Ave.
New York, NY 10036-7798

Established in 2005 in NY.
Donor: Robert I. Goldman†.
Foundation type: Independent foundation.
Financial data (yr. ended 12/31/05): Assets,
$9,889,934 (M); gifts received, $10,428,000;
expenditures, $538,066; qualifying distributions,
$538,066; giving activities include $525,000 for 12
grants (high: $175,000; low: $15,000).
Fields of interest: Museums (history); Human
services; American Red Cross.
Limitations: Giving on a national basis.
Application information:
  Initial approach: Letter
  Deadline(s): None
Directors: Melva Bucksbaum; Olexa Celine; Richard
S. Rothberg; Walter H. Weiner.
EIN: 202371917

6055
Goldman Sachs Charitable Fund ✧
c/o Goldman, Sachs & Co.
10 Hanover Sq., 22nd Fl.
New York, NY 10005

Established in 1999 in NY.
Donors: Goldman, Sachs & Co.; MTGLQ Investors,
L.P.
Foundation type: Company-sponsored foundation.
Financial data (yr. ended 6/30/03): Assets,
$21,581 (L); gifts received, $135,000;
expenditures, $340,250; qualifying distributions,
$340,250; giving activities include $340,250 for 74
grants to individuals (high: $7,500; low: $2,500).
Purpose and activities: The fund awards college and
graduate scholarships to employees and the

children and spouses of employees of Goldman, Sachs.

Type of support: Employee-related scholarships.
Limitations: Applications not accepted.
Application information: Contributes only through employee-related scholarships.
Officers: Esta E. Stecher, Pres.; Robert J. Katz, V.P.; Gregory K. Palm, V.P.; David Viniar, Treas.
EIN: 311678646

6056

The Goldman Sachs Foundation ▼ ✧
(formerly Goldman Sachs Fund)
85 Broad St., 22nd Fl.
New York, NY 10004 (212) 902-5402
Contact: Eileen M. Scott, Treas. and C.F.O.
FAX: (212) 888-9482; URL: http://www.gs.com/foundation

Established in 1968 in NY.
Donors: Goldman, Sachs & Co.; Semlitz/Glaser Foundation; Stephen and Ruth Hendel Foundation; The Goldman Sachs Group, Inc.
Foundation type: Company-sponsored foundation.
Financial data (yr. ended 11/30/05): Assets, $257,385,951 (M); gifts received, $48,000,000; expenditures, $15,641,006; qualifying distributions, $12,052,263; giving activities include $10,911,037 for grants.
Purpose and activities: The foundation supports organizations involved with education, youth business development, and entrepreneurship.
Fields of interest: Education, reform; Secondary school/education; Education; Youth development, business; Community development, small businesses.
International interests: China; Europe.
Type of support: General/operating support; Continuing support; Management development/capacity building; Program development; Seed money; Curriculum development; Program evaluation; Program-related investments/loans; Matching/challenge support.
Limitations: Giving on a national basis. No support for advocacy groups or religious, fraternal, or political organizations. No grants to individuals, or for fundraising events.
Publications: Annual report; Informational brochure; Newsletter; Occasional report.
Application information: Letters of inquiry should be no longer than 2 pages. Application form not required.
  Initial approach: Letter of inquiry
  Board meeting date(s): Quarterly
  Final notification: Approximately 2 months
Officers and Directors: * John C. Whitehead,* Chair.; Stephanie Bell-Rose, Pres.; Richard A. Brown, Secy.; Eileen M. Scott, Treas. and C.F.O.; Josef Joffe; Suzanne Nora Johnson; Thomas W. Payzant; Frank H.T. Rhodes; John F.W. Rogers; Stuart Rothenberg; Neil L. Rudenstine.
Number of staff: 5 full-time professional; 2 full-time support.
EIN: 237000346
Selected grants: The following grants were reported in 2004.
$1,250,000 to Institute of International Education, New York, NY. For Goldman Sachs Leaders Program, competition held annually at college campuses worldwide.
$785,000 to Johns Hopkins University, Baltimore, MD. To launch Next Generation Venture Fund and to conduct additional outreach activities.

$640,000 to Public Education Network, DC. To implement public engagement strategies aimed at improving teacher quality policies and practices, and increase student achievement, in model districts Durham, NC, Mobile, AL and Portland, OR.
$600,000 to Bank Street College of Education, New York, NY. To continue Goldman Sachs Scholars Institute for Leadership, Excellence, and Academic Development, which provides talented New York City parochial school students with individualized academic enrichment services through Saturday and summer programs exposure to arts and entrepreneurship, and standardized test preparation.
$385,000 to National Foundation for Teaching Entrepreneurship, New York, NY. To expand entrepreneurial education programs in China and Germany and training for students in conjunction with Center for Talented Youth in Los Angeles, New York, and San Francisco.
$334,000 to Asia Society, New York, NY. To initiate and administer international education awards program.
$332,500 to United Nations Association of the United States of America, New York, NY. To expand Global Classrooms Model UN program in selected cities around the world and increase number of urban and international public high school students to participate and develop skills.
$200,000 to World Links for Development (WorLD), DC. To engage Brazilian and Chinese students and teachers in international online collaborative learning projects.
$120,000 to Prep for Prep, New York, NY. To implement New York Metro Region Leadership Academy and to continue Goldman Sachs Institute for Entrepreneurship, which helps students improve their entrepreneurship, communications and leadership skills.
$100,000 to Teachers College Columbia University, New York, NY. To develop and implement new field model to define school admissions criteria appropriate for young children from low-income backgrounds.

6057

The Joseph G. Goldring Foundation ✧
100 Crossways Park W., Rm. 306
Woodbury, NY 11797-2084

Established about 1970 in NY.
Donors: Overseas Military Sales Corp.; Military Car Sales, Inc.; Chrysler Military Sales Corp.; Allen A. Goldring.
Foundation type: Independent foundation.
Financial data (yr. ended 6/30/05): Assets, $386,274 (M); gifts received, $658,000; expenditures, $731,294; qualifying distributions, $728,600; giving activities include $728,600 for 37 grants (high: $180,000; low: $150).
Purpose and activities: Giving primarily for arts, health and human services.
Fields of interest: Museums; Performing arts; Education; Hospitals (general); Human services; Jewish federated giving programs.
Limitations: Applications not accepted. Giving primarily in the metropolitan New York, NY, area, including the North Shore of Long Island. No grants to individuals.
Application information: Contributes only to pre-selected organizations. Unsolicited requests for funds not accepted.

Officers: Allen A. Goldring, Pres.; Lola A. Goldring, V.P.; Norman Rosenberg, Treas.
EIN: 116084103
Selected grants: The following grants were reported in 2004.
$210,000 to New Museum of Contemporary Art, New York, NY.
$180,000 to Syracuse University, Syracuse, NY.
$110,000 to United Jewish Appeal, New York, NY.
$60,500 to Cold Spring Harbor Laboratory, Cold Spring Harbor, NY.
$6,500 to Ballet Theater Foundation, New York, NY.
$5,000 to John F. Kennedy Center for the Performing Arts, DC.
$5,000 to Sidwell Friends School, DC.
$2,500 to School of American Ballet, New York, NY.
$2,500 to Washington Opera, DC.
$1,500 to Great Neck United Community Fund, Great Neck, NY.

6058

Louis Callmann Goldschmidt Family Foundation, Inc. ✧ ☆
900 Park Ave., No. 3D
New York, NY 10021-0213

Established in 1992 in NY.
Donor: Clifford H. Goldsmith.
Foundation type: Independent foundation.
Financial data (yr. ended 12/31/05): Assets, $1,842,502 (M); gifts received, $598,024; expenditures, $376,107; qualifying distributions, $322,641; giving activities include $322,641 for grants.
Purpose and activities: Giving primarily for education, human services, health associations, and Jewish agencies and temples.
Fields of interest: Arts; Higher education; Medical school/education; Hospitals (general); Health organizations, association; Multiple sclerosis; Boys & girls clubs; Human services; Children/youth, services; Jewish federated giving programs; Jewish agencies & temples.
Limitations: Applications not accepted. Giving primarily in NY. No grants to individuals.
Application information: Contributes only to pre-selected organizations.
Directors: Alexandra Fallon; Clifford H. Goldsmith; Katherine W. Goldsmith; Audrey Kubie; James W. Shea.
EIN: 133691057
Selected grants: The following grants were reported in 2003.
$50,000 to Jewish Communal Fund of New York, New York, NY.
$25,000 to Polytechnic University, Brooklyn, NY.
$15,000 to Boys and Girls Club, Madison Square, New York, NY.
$15,000 to Multiple Sclerosis Society, National, New York, NY.
$12,036 to Temple Shaaray Tefila, New York, NY.
$2,500 to Leo Baeck Institute, New York, NY.
$2,500 to United Neighborhood Houses of New York, New York, NY.
$1,800 to Lincoln Center Theater, New York, NY.
$1,000 to Medical College of Virginia Foundation, Richmond, VA.
$1,000 to UJA-Federation of New York, New York, NY.

6059
Barbara Lubin Goldsmith Foundation ◈
(formerly Goldsmith-Perry Philanthropies, Inc.)
c/o Hecht and Co., PC
111 W. 40th St.
New York, NY 10018

Established in 1969 in NY.
Donors: Joseph I. Lubin†; Barbara Lubin Goldsmith Charitable Trust.
Foundation type: Independent foundation.
Financial data (yr. ended 12/31/04): Assets, $9,793,745 (M); expenditures, $1,252,170; qualifying distributions, $1,153,850; giving activities include $992,166 for 125 grants (high: $102,500; low: $35).
Purpose and activities: Support primarily for Jewish giving, a public library, higher education, and cultural programs.
Fields of interest: Museums; Arts; Higher education; Libraries/library science; Children/youth, services; Jewish agencies & temples.
Limitations: Applications not accepted. Giving primarily in New York, NY. No grants to individuals.
Application information: Contributes only to pre-selected organizations.
Officers and Directors:* Barbara L. Goldsmith,* Pres.; Alice Elgart,* Secy.
Number of staff: 1
EIN: 237031986
Selected grants: The following grants were reported in 2004.
$102,500 to Wellesley College, Wellesley, MA.
$50,000 to Curtis School, Los Angeles, CA.
$50,000 to New York Public Library, New York, NY.
$42,000 to PEN American Center, New York, NY.
$38,500 to Aspen Institute, DC.
$25,000 to Anderson Ranch Arts Center, Snowmass Village, CO.
$25,000 to Music Festival of the Hamptons, Amagansett, NY.
$10,000 to American Academy of Arts and Sciences, Cambridge, MA.
$5,000 to ArtsConnection, New York, NY.
$5,000 to Northeast Harbor Library, Northeast Harbor, ME.

6060
Horace W. Goldsmith Foundation ▼
375 Park Ave., Ste. 1602
New York, NY 10152
Contact: James C. Slaughter, C.E.O.

Incorporated in 1955 in NY.
Donor: Horace W. Goldsmith†.
Foundation type: Independent foundation.
Financial data (yr. ended 12/31/05): Assets, $788,615,258 (M); expenditures, $40,192,664; qualifying distributions, $38,613,965; giving activities include $37,495,001 for 449 grants (high: $750,000; low: $5,000; average: $25,000–$100,000).
Purpose and activities: Support for cultural programs, including the performing arts and museums; Jewish welfare funds and temple support; hospitals and a geriatric center; and education, especially higher education.
Fields of interest: Visual arts; Museums; Performing arts; Performing arts, dance; Performing arts, theater; Performing arts, music; Arts; Education, research; Higher education; Business school/education; Libraries/library science; Education; Environment, natural resources; Hospitals (general);

Reproductive health, family planning; Medical care, rehabilitation; Cancer; AIDS; Medical research, institute; Cancer research; AIDS research; Crime/law enforcement; Human services; Aging, centers/services; Homeless, human services; International relief; Jewish federated giving programs; Jewish agencies & temples; Aging; Disabilities, people with; Homeless.
International interests: Israel.
Type of support: Program evaluation; Program development; General/operating support; Continuing support; Capital campaigns; Building/renovation; Endowments; Scholarship funds; Research; Matching/challenge support.
Limitations: Applications not accepted. Giving primarily in AZ, MA, and New York, NY. No grants to individuals.
Application information: Foundation depends almost exclusively on internally initiated grants.
Board meeting date(s): 6 times a year
Officer and Managing Directors:* James C. Slaughter,* C.E.O.; Richard L. Menschel; Robert B. Menschel; Thomas R. Slaughter; William A. Slaughter.
Number of staff: 1 full-time professional; 1 full-time support.
EIN: 136107758
Selected grants: The following grants were reported in 2005.
$3,000,000 to Cornell University, Ithaca, NY.
$1,300,000 to New York City Opera, New York, NY.
$1,000,000 to American Society for Technion-Israel Institute of Technology, New York, NY.
$1,000,000 to Kimmel Center for the Performing Arts, Philadelphia, PA.
$750,000 to Museum of Modern Art, New York, NY.
$300,000 to Academy of Natural Sciences of Philadelphia, Philadelphia, PA.
$300,000 to Kivel Geriatric Center, Phoenix, AZ.
$250,000 to Memorial Sloan-Kettering Cancer Center, New York, NY. For Lacher Fellows.
$100,000 to American Society for Yad Vashem, New York, NY.
$100,000 to Israel Childrens Centers, New York, NY.

6061
Goldstein Family Foundation ◈ ☆
6 Vincent Rd.
Spring Valley, NY 10977 (212) 239-7500

Established in 2002.
Donors: Sam Goldstein; Exacta Sweaters.
Foundation type: Independent foundation.
Financial data (yr. ended 12/31/05): Assets, $1,190,635 (M); gifts received, $915,436; expenditures, $322,633; qualifying distributions, $322,146; giving activities include $322,146 for 7 grants (high: $262,500; low: $5,000).
Fields of interest: Jewish agencies & temples.
Type of support: General/operating support.
Limitations: Applications not accepted.
Application information: Unsolicited requests for fund not accepted.
Officers: Sam Goldstein, Pres.; Miriam Goldstein, V.P.
EIN: 020581239

6062
Arnold & Arlene Goldstein Family Foundation ◈
c/o Samson Mgmt.
97-77 Queens Blvd., Ste. 710
Rego Park, NY 11374

Established in 1996 in NY.
Donor: Arnold Goldstein.
Foundation type: Independent foundation.
Financial data (yr. ended 12/31/04): Assets, $8,873,542 (M); gifts received, $253,000; expenditures, $1,405,318; qualifying distributions, $1,292,212; giving activities include $1,292,212 for 57 grants (high: $300,000; low: $25).
Purpose and activities: Giving for Jewish federated giving programs and other Jewish organizations, as well as for health associations and hospitals, particularly a children's hospital, and for human services.
Fields of interest: Museums; Arts; Hospitals (general); Health organizations; Human services; Children, services; Jewish federated giving programs; Jewish agencies & temples.
Limitations: Applications not accepted. Giving primarily in NY. No grants to individuals.
Application information: Contributes only to pre-selected organizations.
Trustees: Arlene Goldstein; Arnold Goldstein.
EIN: 137091014
Selected grants: The following grants were reported in 2003.
$350,000 to Childrens Hospital Foundation at Westchester Medical Center, Valhalla, NY.
$129,000 to UJA-Federation of New York, New York, NY.
$60,000 to Anti-Defamation League of Bnai Brith, New York, NY.
$50,000 to Montefiore Medical Center, Bronx, NY.
$25,000 to American Liver Foundation, New York, NY.
$10,000 to Jewish National Fund, New York, NY.
$6,000 to P.E.F. Israel Endowment Funds, New York, NY.
$3,550 to National Kidney Foundation, New York, NY.
$800 to Doctors Without Borders USA, New York, NY.
$96 to Crohns and Colitis Foundation of America, New York, NY.

6063
The Goldstein Family Foundation ◈
383 Madison Ave., 36th Fl.
New York, NY 10179
Contact: Jerome Goldstein, Pres.

Established in 1984 in NY.
Donor: Jerome Goldstein.
Foundation type: Independent foundation.
Financial data (yr. ended 11/30/05): Assets, $15,131,664 (M); expenditures, $712,931; qualifying distributions, $636,710; giving activities include $631,121 for 76 grants (high: $151,446; low: $200).
Fields of interest: Arts; Higher education; Education; Environment; Hospitals (general); Jewish federated giving programs; Jewish agencies & temples.
Limitations: Applications not accepted. Giving primarily in New York, NY. No grants to individuals.
Application information: Contributes only to pre-selected organizations.

Officers and Directors:* Jerome Goldstein,* Pres.; Dorothy Goldstein,* V.P.; Susan Hounsell, Secy.; Bettina Decker, Treas.

EIN: 133192220

Selected grants: The following grants were reported in 2005.

$151,446 to Dartmouth College, Hanover, NH.

$78,025 to Westchester Land Trust, Bedford Hills, NY.

$50,000 to American Jewish Committee, New York, NY.

$30,000 to Barnard College, New York, NY.

$25,000 to Rutgers, The State University of New Jersey Foundation, New Brunswick, NJ.

$10,000 to Wilkes University, Wilkes Barre, PA.

$2,900 to New York Botanical Garden, Bronx, NY.

$2,500 to Chapin School, New York, NY.

$2,000 to New York Public Library, New York, NY.

$1,000 to Center for Jewish History, New York, NY.

6064
The Leslie & Roslyn Goldstein Foundation ◇

c/o Nathan Berkman & Co., Inc.
29 Broadway, Rm. 2900
New York, NY 10006-3296

Established in 1980 in CT.

Donors: Leslie Goldstein; Roslyn Goldstein.

Foundation type: Independent foundation.

Financial data (yr. ended 11/30/04): Assets, $28,643,062 (M); expenditures, $1,275,259; qualifying distributions, $1,214,420; giving activities include $1,205,600 for 43+ grants (high: $601,000).

Purpose and activities: Giving primarily for the arts, health, human services, and to Jewish organizations.

Fields of interest: Museums (art); Museums (ethnic/folk arts); Arts; Health care; Cancer research; Human services; Federated giving programs; Jewish federated giving programs; Jewish agencies & temples.

Type of support: Annual campaigns; Capital campaigns; Building/renovation; Program-related investments/loans.

Limitations: Applications not accepted. Giving primarily in Stamford, CT and New York, NY. No grants to individuals.

Application information: Contributes only to pre-selected organizations.

Board meeting date(s): Varies

Trustees: Leslie Goldstein; Roslyn Goldstein.

EIN: 061035614

Selected grants: The following grants were reported in 2004.

$160,000 to Jewish Museum, New York, NY.

$50,000 to Montefiore Medical Center, Bronx, NY.

$15,000 to Israel Philharmonic Orchestra, Israel. .

$6,500 to Katonah Museum of Art, Katonah, NY.

$2,000 to Metropolitan Museum of Art, New York, NY.

$2,000 to Orpheus Chamber Orchestra, New York, NY.

$1,500 to American Ballet Theater, New York, NY.

6065
The Goldstone Family Foundation ◇

570 Lexington Ave., 37th Fl.
New York, NY 10022-6860

Established in 2000 in NY and DE.

Donors: Steven F. Goldstone; Elizabeth Goldstone.

Foundation type: Independent foundation.

Financial data (yr. ended 12/31/04): Assets, $24,097,097 (M); expenditures, $1,274,719; qualifying distributions, $967,229; giving activities include $965,925 for 29+ grants (high: $405,500).

Fields of interest: Museums; Arts; Education.

Limitations: Applications not accepted. No grants to individuals.

Application information: Contributes only to pre-selected organizations.

Officers and Directors:* Steven F. Goldstone,* Pres. and Treas.; Elizabeth Goldstone,* V.P. and Secy.

EIN: 061596255

Selected grants: The following grants were reported in 2003.

$180,000 to Founders Hall Foundation, Ridgefield, CT. For general support.

$96,150 to Roundabout Theater Company, New York, NY. For general support.

$25,000 to Saint Anns School. For general support.

$5,000 to Groove With Me, New York, NY. For general support.

$5,000 to Saint Lukes School. For general support.

$5,000 to University of Pennsylvania, Philadelphia, PA. For general support.

$1,000 to Boys and Girls Club of Ridgefield, Ridgefield, CT. For general support.

$500 to Ridgefield Library and Historical Association, Ridgefield, CT. For general support.

$250 to Big Brothers Big Sisters of Southwestern Connecticut, Bridgeport, CT. For general support.

$200 to Drama League, New York, NY. For general support.

6066
The Jonathan Plutzik & Lesley Goldwasser Family Foundation ◇

1841 Broadway
New York, NY 10023

Established in 2003 in NY.

Donors: Johnathan Plutzik; Lesley Goldwasser Plutzik.

Foundation type: Independent foundation.

Financial data (yr. ended 11/30/05): Assets, $3,040,855 (M); gifts received, $922,159; expenditures, $463,665; qualifying distributions, $463,665; giving activities include $448,498 for 33 grants (high: $105,400; low: $300).

Limitations: Applications not accepted.

Application information: Contributes only to pre-selected organizations.

Officers and Directors:* Johnathan Plutzik, Pres. and Treas.; Deborah Plutzik Briggs,* V.P.; Lesley Goldwasser Plutzik,* Secy.; Neil Baldwin.

EIN: 710927327

6067
The B. Thomas Golisano Foundation

c/o Fishers Asset Mgmt.
1 Fishers Rd.
Pittsford, NY 14534 (585) 340-1203

Contact: Ann M. Costello, Dir.

FAX: (585) 340-1204;

E-mail: info@GolisanoFoundation.org; *URL:* http://www.golisanofoundation.org

Established in 1985 in NY.

Donor: B. Thomas Golisano.

Foundation type: Independent foundation.

Financial data (yr. ended 10/31/05): Assets, $25,411,874 (M); expenditures, $1,262,803; qualifying distributions, $971,429; giving activities include $862,916 for 47 grants (high: $150,000; low: $2,500; average: $10,000–$30,000).

Purpose and activities: Support for programs that create opportunities for people with developmental disabilities to achieve maximum potential and be active in their communities.

Type of support: General/operating support; Capital campaigns; Building/renovation; Equipment; Seed money; Program evaluation; Matching/challenge support.

Limitations: Giving limited to the greater Rochester, NY area. No support for municipal programs. No grants to individuals, or for fund-raising events, medical research, or for endowments.

Publications: Application guidelines; Annual report; Grants list; Program policy statement.

Application information: Use the Common Application Form developed by the Rochester Grantmakers Forum. See foundation Web site for application procedures. Application form required.

Initial approach: Telephone or letter of inquiry with application

Copies of proposal: 2

Deadline(s): 4 weeks prior to board meeting

Board meeting date(s): Quarterly; usually 4th Wed. of Jan., Apr., July and Oct.

Final notification: Within 2 weeks after board meeting

Director: Ann M. Costello.

Trustees: Gloria Austin; G. Thomas Clark; B. Thomas Golisano; Nancy N. Koch; Patricia Malgieri; James D. Murray.

Number of staff: 1 part-time professional.

EIN: 222692938

Selected grants: The following grants were reported in 2003.

$200,000 to Heritage Christian Home, East Rochester, NY. 2 grants: $100,000 each (For Springdale Farm capital expansion project for the disabled).

$200,000 to Lifespan of Greater Rochester, Rochester, NY. 2 grants: $100,000 each

$100,000 to Association for Retarded Children, Canandaigua, NY. For facility renovation.

$25,000 to East House Properties, Rochester, NY. For job employment program for disabled.

$25,000 to Rochester Rehabilitation Center, Rochester, NY. For SportsNet, a sports and recreation program for disabled.

$25,000 to YMCA of Greater Rochester, Rochester, NY. For facility renovation to expand programs for the disabled.

$20,000 to Stepping Stones Learning Center, Rochester, NY. For support groups for families of children with Autism.

$20,000 to Urban League of Rochester, Rochester, NY. For housing support program for the disabled.

6068
Perry & Donna Golkin Family Foundation ◇ ☆

c/o Kohlberg Kravis Roberts & Co.
9 W. 57th St.
New York, NY 10019

Established in 1997 in NY.

Donor: Perry Golkin.

Foundation type: Independent foundation.
Financial data (yr. ended 11/30/05): Assets, $2,800,086 (M); gifts received, $742,090; expenditures, $565,249; qualifying distributions, $563,249; giving activities include $543,557 for 44 grants (high: $400,000; low: $75).
Purpose and activities: Giving primarily for higher education and the arts.
Fields of interest: Arts; Higher education; Human services; Christian agencies & churches.
Limitations: Applications not accepted. No grants to individuals.
Application information: Contributes only to pre-selected organizations.
Officers: Perry Golkin, Pres. and Treas.; Donna Golkin, V.P.
EIN: 133928587
Selected grants: The following grants were reported in 2005.
$400,000 to University of Pennsylvania, Philadelphia, PA.
$15,000 to Princeton University, Princeton, NJ.
$1,000 to New Visions for Public Schools, New York, NY.
$250 to Spence School, New York, NY.

6069
The Gollust Foundation ✧
500 Park Ave., 5th Fl.
New York, NY   10022

Established in 1989 in NY.
Donor: Keith R. Gollust.
Foundation type: Independent foundation.
Financial data (yr. ended 12/31/03): Assets, $1,450,091 (M); expenditures, $353,409; qualifying distributions, $343,749; giving activities include $344,519 for 7 grants (high: $180,000; low: $19).
Fields of interest: Arts education; Performing arts, ballet; Education; Human services.
Limitations: Applications not accepted. Giving primarily in NJ and NY. No grants to individuals.
Application information: Contributes only to pre-selected organizations.
Trustee: Keith R. Gollust.
EIN: 136935600

6070
The William and Estelle Golub Foundation, Inc. ✧
501 Duanesburg Rd.
Schenectady, NY   12306-1058

Established in 1986 in NY.
Donors: William Golub†; Estelle Golub†.
Foundation type: Independent foundation.
Financial data (yr. ended 12/31/05): Assets, $17,138,733 (M); gifts received, $492,062; expenditures, $1,423,015; qualifying distributions, $1,312,711; giving activities include $1,311,619 for 27 grants (high: $295,000; low: $500).
Purpose and activities: Giving primarily for health associations, including camps for children with illnesses; funding also for Jewish organizations, children, youth, and social services, and for the arts.
Fields of interest: Arts; Higher education; Education; Hospitals (general); Health organizations, association; Recreation, camps; Human services; Children/youth, services;

Federated giving programs; Jewish federated giving programs; Jewish agencies & temples.
Type of support: General/operating support.
Limitations: Applications not accepted. Giving primarily in Albany and Schenectady, NY. No grants to individuals.
Application information: Contributes only to pre-selected organizations.
Officers and Trustees:* Neil M. Golub,* Pres. and Treas.; Mona Golub, Secy.; Jane Golub.
EIN: 222809785

6071
Sidney E. and Amy O. Goodfriend Foundation ✧ ☆
c/o U.S. Trust
114 W. 47th St., TAXRGR
New York, NY   10036

Established in 1999 in NY.
Donors: Amy O. Goodfriend; Sidney E. Goodfriend.
Foundation type: Independent foundation.
Financial data (yr. ended 12/31/05): Assets, $1,946,482 (M); gifts received, $544,344; expenditures, $469,905; qualifying distributions, $464,905; giving activities include $461,605 for 38 grants (high: $200,000; low: $250).
Purpose and activities: Giving primarily for education.
Fields of interest: Secondary school/education; Higher education; Education; Human services.
Limitations: Applications not accepted. Giving primarily in NY. No grants to individuals.
Application information: Unsolicited requests for funds are not accepted.
Trustees: Amy O. Goodfriend; Sidney E. Goodfriend.
EIN: 134082157

6072
The Goodman Family Foundation ✧
1035 5th Ave.
New York, NY   10028
Contact: Roy M. Goodman, Tr.

Trust established in 1970 in NY as one of two successor trusts to the Matz Foundation.
Donor: Israel Matz†.
Foundation type: Independent foundation.
Financial data (yr. ended 6/30/05): Assets, $4,382,506 (M); expenditures, $432,530; qualifying distributions, $372,868; giving activities include $362,209 for 95 grants (high: $54,900; low: $25).
Purpose and activities: Giving primarily for education, the arts, and Jewish agencies and temples; funding also for health, human services, and federated giving programs.
Fields of interest: Performing arts; Arts; Higher education; Education; Health organizations, association; Medical research, institute; Recreation, parks/playgrounds; Human services; Federated giving programs; Jewish agencies & temples.
Limitations: Giving primarily in New York, NY. No grants to individuals.
Application information: Application form required.
Initial approach: Letter
Deadline(s): None
Final notification: Within 6 months of application
Trustees: Barbara F. Goodman; Roy M. Goodman.
EIN: 136355553

6073
Joseph C. and Clare F. Goodman Memorial Foundation, Inc. ✧
c/o Lipsky Goodkin & Co.
120 W. 45th St., 7th Fl.
New York, NY   10036

Incorporated in 1969 in NY.
Donor: Clare F. Goodman†.
Foundation type: Independent foundation.
Financial data (yr. ended 9/30/05): Assets, $5,551,667 (M); expenditures, $395,976; qualifying distributions, $354,106; giving activities include $340,000 for 31 grants (high: $38,000; low: $1,500).
Purpose and activities: Giving primarily for arts and education.
Fields of interest: Arts; Education; Hospitals (general); Health organizations, association; Human services; Christian agencies & churches.
Limitations: Applications not accepted. Giving primarily in New York, NY. No grants to individuals.
Application information: Contributes only to pre-selected organizations.
Officers: Joyce N. Eichenberg, Pres.; Joseph F. Seminara, V.P.
EIN: 237039999
Selected grants: The following grants were reported in 2005.
$17,000 to Childrens Health Fund, New York, NY.
$15,000 to Childrens Museum of Manhattan, New York, NY.
$15,000 to Columbia University, New York, NY.
$15,000 to Lenox Hill Neighborhood House, New York, NY.
$7,500 to Dalton Schools, New York, NY.
$7,500 to Union Settlement Association, New York, NY.
$5,000 to Bay Point Schools, Miami, FL.
$5,000 to High 5 Tickets to the Arts, New York, NY.
$5,000 to Orpheon, The Little Orchestra Society, New York, NY.
$5,000 to Spanish Theater Repertory Company, New York, NY.

6074
The Gordon Family Foundation ✧
c/o Goldman Sachs & Co.
85 Broad St., Tax Dept.
New York, NY   10004

Established in 1999 in CA.
Donor: Andrew M. Gordon.
Foundation type: Independent foundation.
Financial data (yr. ended 8/31/05): Assets, $996,929 (M); gifts received, $315,450; expenditures, $357,654; qualifying distributions, $355,080; giving activities include $355,080 for 24 grants (high: $115,250; low: $100).
Fields of interest: Diabetes; Pediatrics; Jewish federated giving programs; Jewish agencies & temples.
Limitations: Applications not accepted. Giving primarily in CA. No grants to individuals.
Application information: Contributes only to pre-selected organizations.
Trustees: Amy S. Gordon; Andrew M. Gordon.
EIN: 134048199
Selected grants: The following grants were reported in 2004.
$29,100 to Los Angeles Philharmonic, Los Angeles, CA.
$25,000 to Wesleyan University, Middletown, CT.

$2,500 to Alliance for Childrens Rights, Los Angeles, CA.

$2,500 to Carmelite Monastery, Beacon, NY.

$2,000 to American Diabetes Association, Emeryville, CA.

$2,000 to Neil Bogart Memorial Fund, Los Angeles, CA.

$2,000 to Project ALS, New York, NY.

$1,000 to American Ballet Theater, New York, NY.

$500 to American Heart Association, Dallas, TX.

$200 to Keep Memory Alive, Las Vegas, NV.

6075
The Michael Gordon Foundation, Inc. ✧

c/o Holtz Rubenstein Reminick
1430 Broadway, 17th Fl.
New York, NY 10018

Established in 1991 in NY.
Donor: Michael Gordon†.
Foundation type: Independent foundation.
Financial data (yr. ended 12/31/05): Assets, $14,949,142 (M); gifts received, $51,719; expenditures, $883,533; qualifying distributions, $770,009; giving activities include $661,815 for 34 grants (high: $66,250; low: $30; average: $10,000–$30,000).
Fields of interest: Secondary school/education; Education.
Limitations: Applications not accepted. Giving primarily in the metropolitan New York, NY, area.
Application information: Contributes only to pre-selected organizations.
Officers: Thomas Tillander, Pres.; Martin J. Salzman, V.P. and Treas.; William McSherry, Secy.
EIN: 133585393
Selected grants: The following grants were reported in 2005.

$30,000 to Hebrew Academy for Special Children, Brooklyn, NY.

$30,000 to Notre Dame Academy, Staten Island, NY.

$30,000 to Preston High School, Bronx, NY.

$30,000 to Staten Island Academy, Staten Island, NY.

$25,000 to Cathedral School, New York, NY.

$25,000 to Gillen Brewer School, New York, NY.

$20,000 to Nazareth Regional High School, Brooklyn, NY.

$15,000 to Cathedral Preparatory Seminary, Elmhurst, NY.

$15,000 to Lighthouse International, New York, NY.

$15,000 to Saint Saviour High School, Brooklyn, NY.

6076
The John R. and Kiendl Dauphinot Gordon Fund ✧

(formerly The John R. Gordon Fund)
c/o Sullivan & Cromwell LLP
125 Broad St.
New York, NY 10004-2498
Contact: James I. Black III

Established in 1988 in NY.
Donors: Albert H. Gordon; John R. Gordon.
Foundation type: Independent foundation.
Financial data (yr. ended 12/31/05): Assets, $285,678 (M); gifts received, $569,050; expenditures, $997,726; qualifying distributions, $985,601; giving activities include $985,401 for 42 grants (high: $250,000; low: $200).

Fields of interest: Performing arts, theater; Higher education; Business school/education; Education; Mental health, addictions; Mental health, eating disorders; Boys clubs; Human services; Children/youth, services; Foundations (private grantmaking).
Limitations: Applications not accepted. Giving primarily in New York, NY. No grants to individuals.
Application information: Contributes only to pre-selected organizations.
Trustees: John R. Gordon; Kiendl D. Gordon.
EIN: 136920431
Selected grants: The following grants were reported in 2005.

$100,000 to National Foundation for Facial Reconstruction, New York, NY.

$83,460 to Boys Club of New York, New York, NY.

$80,000 to Church of the Heavenly Rest.

$61,500 to Saint Davids School for Child Development and Family Services, Minnetonka, MN.

$25,000 to Future Generations, Franklin, WV.

$20,000 to ARC, Arlington, TX.

$5,000 to American Red Cross.

$5,000 to Salvation Army.

$500 to Duke University, Durham, NC.

6077
The Gordon Fund ✧

(formerly The Gordon/Rousmaniere/Roberts Fund)
c/o Sullivan & Cromwell
125 Broad St.
New York, NY 10004-2498
Contact: James I. Black III

Established in 1985 in NY.
Donor: Albert H. Gordon.
Foundation type: Independent foundation.
Financial data (yr. ended 12/31/03): Assets, $7,281,136 (M); expenditures, $2,677,134; qualifying distributions, $2,636,481; giving activities include $2,634,000 for 51 grants (high: $400,000; low: $5,000).
Purpose and activities: Giving primarily for higher, secondary, and elementary education; support also for health associations, cultural programs, international relations, and environmental programs.
Fields of interest: Historic preservation/historical societies; Arts; Elementary school/education; Secondary school/education; Higher education; Theological school/education; Environment; Hospitals (general); Health organizations, association; International affairs.
Limitations: Giving primarily in CA, CT, MA, and NY. No grants to individuals.
Application information:
  Initial approach: Proposal
  Deadline(s): None
Trustee: Mary Gordon Roberts.
EIN: 133257793
Selected grants: The following grants were reported in 2004.

$100,000 to Boys Club of New York, New York, NY.

$100,000 to Smith College, Northampton, MA.

$90,000 to Saint Ignatius Loyola Church, New York, NY. 2 grants: $40,000, $50,000

$80,000 to Teach for America, New York, NY.

$70,000 to Harvard University, Cambridge, MA.

$50,000 to National Judicial College, Reno, NV.

$25,000 to Achilles Track Club, New York, NY.

$25,000 to Plimoth Plantation, Plymouth, MA.

$20,000 to Metropolitan Opera, New York, NY.

6078
Owen T. Gorman & Alice M. Gorman Testamentary Charitable Trust ☆

(doing business as The Gorman Foundation)
447 Kinsley St.
Sherrill, NY 13461-1349
Contact: Amanda Larson, Pres.
FAX: (315) 366-0170; *URL:* http://www.gormanfoundation.org

Established in 2003 in NY.
Donors: Alice M. Gorman†; Owen Gorman†.
Foundation type: Independent foundation.
Financial data (yr. ended 12/31/04): Assets, $18,968,833 (M); gifts received, $460,000; expenditures, $1,700,903; qualifying distributions, $1,637,071; giving activities include $1,395,699 for 20 grants (high: $500,000; low: $20), and $11,400 for 2 employee matching gifts.
Purpose and activities: Giving primarily for human services, particularly for a housing project for elderly women, and to day care centers; funding also for the arts, higher and other education, YMCAs and a healthcare center.
Fields of interest: Historic preservation/historical societies; Arts; Higher education; Education; Health care; Human services; YM/YWCAs & YM/YWHAs; Children, day care; Aging; Women.
Limitations: Giving primarily in NY, with emphasis on Oneida. No grants to individuals, or for debt reduction drives, or lobbying activities as defined by the IRS; no organizations that do not agree with the foundation's policy on non-discrimination.
Publications: Application guidelines; Grants list; Informational brochure.
Application information: Letter of inquiry serves as a full proposal application for requests of $5,000 or less; application required for grants over $5,000. Application form required.
  Initial approach: Letter (not exceeding 2 pages)
  Deadline(s): None
  Board meeting date(s): Monthly
  Final notification: 1 month
Officers: Amanda A. Larson, Pres.; James F. Sullivan, Sr., V.P.; Joanne G. Larson, Treas.
EIN: 226927092

6079
The Gorter Family Foundation ✧

(formerly Green Bay Foundation)
c/o BCRS Group/Marcum & Kliegman, LLP
100 Wall St., 11th Fl.
New York, NY 10005 (212) 902-6897

Established in 1977 in IL.
Donor: James P. Gorter.
Foundation type: Independent foundation.
Financial data (yr. ended 12/31/05): Assets, $10,846,143 (M); gifts received, $2,162,847; expenditures, $639,456; qualifying distributions, $424,825; giving activities include $424,805 for 102 grants (high: $200,000; low: $100).
Purpose and activities: Giving primarily to education, hospitals, and human services.
Fields of interest: Higher education; Hospitals (general); Health organizations, association; Human services; Children/youth, services; Federated giving programs; Christian agencies & churches.
Type of support: General/operating support.
Limitations: Applications not accepted. Giving primarily in IL and NC. No grants to individuals.

Application information: Contributes only to pre-selected organizations.
Officer and Directors:* James P. Gorter,* Pres.; Audrey F. Gorter; David F. Gorter; James P. Gorter, Jr.; Mary Gorter Krey.
EIN: 362950350
Selected grants: The following grants were reported in 2005.
$205,000 to Lake Forest Country Day School, Lake Forest, IL. 2 grants: $200,000, $5,000
$45,000 to Duke University, Durham, NC. 2 grants: $10,000, $35,000
$11,000 to Thacher School, Ojai, CA. 2 grants: $5,500 each
$10,000 to Lake Forest Academy, Lake Forest, IL.
$10,000 to Lake Forest College, Lake Forest, IL.
$5,000 to Gilman School, Baltimore, MD.
$4,000 to Daniel Murphy Scholarship Foundation, Chicago, IL.

6080
Adolph and Esther Gottlieb Foundation, Inc. ✧

380 W. Broadway
New York, NY 10012-5115 (212) 226-0581
Contact: Sheila Ross, Grants Mgr.

Established in 1976 in NY.
Donors: Adolph Gottlieb†; Esther Gottlieb†; Alice Yamin†; Ann Cooper†.
Foundation type: Independent foundation.
Financial data (yr. ended 6/30/05): Assets, $28,778,366 (M); gifts received, $70,000; expenditures, $891,471; qualifying distributions, $829,294; giving activities include $461,505 for 38 grants to individuals (high: $25,000; low: $1,500).
Purpose and activities: The foundation maintains two separate grant programs: 1) Individual support program for painters, sculptors, and printmakers who have worked at least 20 years in a mature phase of their art, and are in current financial need; and 2) Emergency assistance program for painters, sculptors, and printmakers who have worked at least 10 years in a mature phase of their art and are in current financial need in excess of and unrelated to their normal economic situation, and which is the result of a recent emergency occurrence such as a fire, flood or medical emergency.
Type of support: Emergency funds; Grants to individuals.
Limitations: Giving on a national basis. No support for charitable organizations, educational institutions or projects, or to artists working in crafts.
Publications: Application guidelines; Informational brochure.
Application information: Emergency grant applications may be submitted and reviewed year-round. Application form required.
  Initial approach: Letter
  Copies of proposal: 1
  Deadline(s): Dec. 15 for Individual Support Program grants
  Board meeting date(s): Quarterly
  Final notification: Mar.
Officers and Directors:* Dick Netzer,* Pres.; Charlotta Kotik, V.P.; Sanford Hirsch,* Secy.-Treas.; Lynda Benglis; Robert Mangold.
Number of staff: 3 full-time professional; 1 part-time support.
EIN: 132853957

6081
Lee Gottlieb Fund, Inc. ✧ ☆

1 Liberty Plz.
New York, NY 10006

Established in 1955 in NY.
Donor: Leo Gottlieb.
Foundation type: Independent foundation.
Financial data (yr. ended 12/31/05): Assets, $8,766 (M); expenditures, $1,571,552; qualifying distributions, $1,569,122; giving activities include $1,561,932 for 34 grants (high: $948,480; low: $200).
Purpose and activities: Giving primarily for children's services, higher education, and for health and medical services; some funding also for correctional facility associations.
Fields of interest: Higher education; Health care; Health organizations, association; Crime/law enforcement, association; Human services; Children/youth, services.
Type of support: General/operating support.
Limitations: Applications not accepted. Giving primarily in NY. No grants to individuals.
Application information: Contributes only to pre-selected organizations.
Officers: Elinor Gottlieb Mannucci, Pres. and Treas.; Mark Lee Mannucci, V.P. and Secy.; Anthony James Mannucci, V.P.
EIN: 136088831
Selected grants: The following grants were reported in 2005.
$948,480 to General Electric Company, Fairfield, CT.

6082
Gould Family Foundation ✧ ☆

c/o Baker & McKenzie LLP
1114 Ave. of the Americas
New York, NY 10036
Contact: Edwin S. Matthews, Jr., Tr.

Established in 2003 in NY.
Foundation type: Independent foundation.
Financial data (yr. ended 12/31/05): Assets, $24,283,374 (M); expenditures, $1,085,147; qualifying distributions, $879,028; giving activities include $825,000 for 13 grants (high: $250,000; low: $5,000).
Fields of interest: Museums; Performing arts; Arts; Higher education; Environment.
Limitations: Giving primarily in CT, Washington, DC, and NY.
Application information:
  Initial approach: Letter
  Deadline(s): None
Trustees: Anthony Gould; Edwin S. Matthews, Jr.
EIN: 020595263

6083
Edwin Gould Foundation for Children

55 Exchange Pl.
New York, NY 10005 (646) 442-1086
Contact: Wendy Gilles, Admin. Asst.
FAX: (212) 982-6886; E-mail: wgilles@egf-ny.org

Incorporated in 1923 in NY.
Donors: Edwin Gould†; Gould 1919 Trust; Gould 1923 Trust; Gould Trust (Woodycrest Greer); Stevens Richardson Trust.
Foundation type: Independent foundation.

Financial data (yr. ended 12/31/05): Assets, $58,847,855 (M); gifts received, $73,779; expenditures, $4,137,106; qualifying distributions, $3,551,009; giving activities include $1,760,498 for 32+ grants (high: $1,598,743; average: $1,000–$25,000), and $2,092,605 for 4 foundation-administered programs.
Purpose and activities: Giving to promote the welfare of children and to improve their social and living conditions; support primarily to children's services, with priority to agencies formerly affiliated with the foundation; some scholarship support to institutions for young people who have passed through foundation-affiliated institutions and programs developed by the foundation.
Fields of interest: Education, early childhood education; Higher education; Education; Crime/violence prevention, youth; Children/youth, services; Family services; Civil rights, race/intergroup relations; Marine science; Native Americans/American Indians; Economically disadvantaged.
Type of support: General/operating support; Continuing support; Emergency funds; Program development; Conferences/seminars; Seed money; Internship funds; Scholarship funds; Technical assistance; Exchange programs.
Limitations: Giving primarily in New York, NY, and throughout the U.S. for special projects. No grants to individuals, or for building or endowment funds, or matching gifts; no loans.
Publications: Financial statement; Grants list; Multi-year report.
Application information: Applications generally not encouraged; current giving limited to previous recipients; accepts NYRAG Common Grant Application Form. Application form not required.
  Initial approach: Letter of request
  Copies of proposal: 1
  Deadline(s): None
  Board meeting date(s): Monthly except July and Aug.
  Final notification: Less than 1 month
Officers and Trustees:* Michael W. Osheowitz,* Chair. and C.E.O.; Cynthia Rivera Weissblum,* Exec. V.P.; Herschel E. Sparks, Jr.,* Secy.; Kassie Seetaram, Treas.; Mark Bieler; Steven Brown; Lofton Holder; Truda C. Jewett; Edward A. Lesser; Rosell Mack III; Josh Parker; Bruce Senzel; Alan Weinstein.
Number of staff: 5 full-time professional; 2 full-time support; 2 part-time support.
EIN: 135675642

6084
The Florence Gould Foundation ▼

c/o Cahill Gordon & Reindel LLP
80 Pine St.
New York, NY 10005 (212) 701-3400
Contact: John R. Young, Pres.

Incorporated in 1957 in NY.
Donor: Florence J. Gould†.
Foundation type: Independent foundation.
Financial data (yr. ended 12/31/04): Assets, $93,228,523 (M); expenditures, $7,357,534; qualifying distributions, $6,851,138; giving activities include $6,464,168 for 169 grants (high: $240,000; low: $300).
Purpose and activities: Essential aim is to promote French-American amity and understanding.
Fields of interest: Arts.
International interests: France.

Limitations: Giving primarily in the U.S. and France. No grants to individuals.
Application information: Application form not required.
   Initial approach: Letter or telephone inquiry
   Copies of proposal: 1
   Deadline(s): None
   Board meeting date(s): As necessary
   Final notification: Varies
Officers and Directors:* John R. Young,* Pres.; Walter C. Cliff,* V.P. and Secy.; Daniel P. Davison,* V.P. and Treas.; Ursula Cliff; Katusha Davison; Mary R. Young.
Number of staff: 1 full-time professional.
EIN: 136176855
Selected grants: The following grants were reported in 2004.
$250,000 to Metropolitan Museum of Art, New York, NY. For exhibition, Ruhlmann: The Genius of Art Deco.
$225,000 to Brooklyn Academy of Music, Brooklyn, NY. For French programming.
$200,000 to New York City Ballet, New York, NY. For season support.
$190,829 to French Heritage Society, New York, NY. For restoration of Collegiate Church of Candes Saint Martin.
$160,000 to Thomas Jefferson Memorial Foundation, Charlottesville, VA. To restore kitchen at Monticello.
$153,270 to Athenaeum of Philadelphia, Philadelphia, PA. To exhibit architectural drawings of Paul Phillippe Cret.
$150,000 to Foundation for French Museum, New York, NY. For French Regional American Museums Exchange.
$150,000 to Fund for Independent Publishing, New York, NY. For translations and for Paris office of New Press.
$114,000 to New York Public Library, New York, NY. For exhibition, Rose Adler and Pierre Legrain: Bindings for Jacques Doucet.
$20,000 to Chamber Music Society of Lincoln Center, New York, NY. For season of French programming.

6085
The Gould-Shenfeld Family Foundation ◇
(formerly The Gould Family Charitable Foundation of New York)
60 Cuttermill Rd.
Great Neck, NY   11021

Established in 1995 in NY.
Donors: Fredric H. Gould; Jeffrey Gould; Matthew Gould; Steven Shenfeld.
Foundation type: Independent foundation.
Financial data (yr. ended 12/31/05): Assets, $1,155,011 (M); gifts received, $1,571,148; expenditures, $1,089,811; qualifying distributions, $1,087,063; giving activities include $1,087,063 for 206 grants (high: $350,000; low: $75).
Purpose and activities: Giving primarily for Jewish organizations, as well as for the arts, health, and children, youth and social services.
Fields of interest: Arts; Education; Hospitals (general); Health care; Health organizations, association; Medical research, association; Youth development, services; Human services; Children/youth, services; International peace/security; International conflict resolution; Civil rights, race/intergroup relations; Jewish federated giving programs; Jewish agencies & temples.

Limitations: Applications not accepted. Giving primarily in New York, NY. No grants to individuals.
Application information: Contributes only to pre-selected organizations.
Trustees: Fredric H. Gould; Helaine Gould; Jeffrey A. Gould; Matthew J. Gould; Wendy Shenfeld.
EIN: 113262391
Selected grants: The following grants were reported in 2005.
$229,000 to United Jewish Appeal-Federation of Jewish Philanthropies. 2 grants: $500, $228,500
$10,860 to Old Westbury Hebrew Congregation, Old Westbury, NY. 2 grants: $860, $10,000
$6,200 to Chabad of Port Washington, Port Washington, NY. 2 grants: $5,000, $1,200
$5,000 to Park East Synagogue, New York, NY.
$1,800 to Hampton Synagogue, Hampton, NY.
$1,315 to Temple Judea of Manhasset, Manhasset, NY.
$1,000 to AISH International, New York, NY.

6086
The Grand Marnier Foundation ◇ ☆
717 5th Ave., 22nd Fl.
New York, NY   10022
Contact: Michel Roux, Pres.
Fellowship application address: c/o Grand Marnier Film Fellowships, 165 W. 65th St., 4th Fl., New York, NY 10023

Established in 1985 in NY.
Donor: Carillon Importers, Ltd.
Foundation type: Company-sponsored foundation.
Financial data (yr. ended 12/31/05): Assets, $5,823,573 (M); expenditures, $632,678; qualifying distributions, $510,000; giving activities include $510,000 for grants.
Purpose and activities: The foundation supports organizations involved with arts and culture, including French cultural organizations, education, health, and human services and awards fellowships.
Fields of interest: Media/communications; Arts; Higher education; Human services; International affairs, goodwill promotion.
Type of support: Fellowships.
Application information:
   Initial approach: Proposal
   Deadline(s): None
Officers and Directors:* Michel Roux,* Pres.; Joel Buchman,* Secy.; Jerry Ciraulo,* Treas.; Maxime Coury; Francois De Gasperis; Jacques Marnier-Lapostolle.
EIN: 133258414

6087
Grandison Foundation ◇
c/o Kurzman & Eisenberg
1 N. Broadway, Ste. 1004
White Plains, NY   10601-2317

Established in 1996 in NY.
Donors: Garry B. Trudeau; Jane P. Trudeau.
Foundation type: Independent foundation.
Financial data (yr. ended 12/31/04): Assets, $1,410,016 (M); gifts received, $462,714; expenditures, $369,918; qualifying distributions, $355,100; giving activities include $353,100 for 48 grants (high: $100,000; low: $100).
Purpose and activities: Support primarily to the United Way; giving also for education, health,

women's organizations, children's services, and journalism.
Fields of interest: Media, journalism/publishing; Education; Health care; Children, services; Women, centers/services; Federated giving programs.
Limitations: Giving primarily in NY. No grants to individuals.
Application information: Generally limits contributions to pre-selected organizations; the foundation occasionally makes grants to other organizations based on unsolicited requests for funds. Application form not required.
   Board meeting date(s): Annually, usually in Dec.
Officers and Directors:* Jane P. Trudeau,* Chair. and Secy.; Garry B. Trudeau,* Pres. and Treas.; Lee Harrison Corbin; Ann Pauley.
EIN: 133883296
Selected grants: The following grants were reported in 2003.
$279,700 to United Way of Tri-State, New York, NY. For general support.
$16,700 to Childrens Health Fund, New York, NY. For general support.
$13,500 to Yale University, New Haven, CT. For general support.
$5,000 to Brown University, Providence, RI. For general support.
$2,500 to Michael J. Fox Foundation for Parkinsons Research, New York, NY. For general support.
$2,100 to Baby Buggy, New York, NY. For general support.
$2,000 to Ann Schreiber Ovarian Cancer Research Fund, New York, NY. For general support.
$1,250 to New-York Historical Society, New York, NY. For general support.
$500 to Citymeals-on-Wheels, New York, NY. For general support.
$250 to Science Center of Connecticut, West Hartford, CT. For general support.

6088
Grandview-Steers Foundation ◇ ☆
15 Hilltop Pl.
Rye, NY   10580

Established in 2001 in NY.
Donors: Robert H. Steers; Lauren J. Steers.
Foundation type: Independent foundation.
Financial data (yr. ended 12/31/05): Assets, $6,067,870 (M); gifts received, $1,203,918; expenditures, $541,598; qualifying distributions, $515,500; giving activities include $515,500 for grants.
Fields of interest: Higher education, university; Education.
Limitations: Applications not accepted. No grants to individuals.
Application information: Contributes only to pre-selected organizations.
Trustees: Lauren J. Steers; Robert H. Steers.
EIN: 137297946

6089
The Perry and Martin Granoff Family Foundation, Inc. ◇
c/o Hogan & Hartson LLP, attn.: BJT
875 3rd Ave.
New York, NY   10176

Established in 1993 in NJ.
Donor: Martin J. Granoff.

Foundation type: Independent foundation.
Financial data (yr. ended 12/31/05): Assets, $3,384,752 (M); expenditures, $2,777,685; qualifying distributions, $2,777,685; giving activities include $2,683,876 for 42 grants (high: $1,040,000; low: $500).
Fields of interest: Media, film/video; Performing arts, ballet; Performing arts, theater; Higher education; Health organizations, association; Medical research, institute; Jewish federated giving programs.
Limitations: Applications not accepted. Giving primarily in Washington, DC, NJ and NY; some funding also in MA. No grants to individuals.
Application information: Contributes only to pre-selected organizations.
Officers and Trustees:* Martin J. Granoff,* Pres.; Perry Granoff,* V.P.; Michael Granoff,* Secy.-Treas.
EIN: 521647009
Selected grants: The following grants were reported in 2005.
$1,040,000 to Brown University, Providence, RI.
$200,000 to Millennium Park, Chicago, IL.
$50,000 to American Ballet Theater, New York, NY.
$50,000 to New York City Ballet, New York, NY.
$50,000 to Syracuse University, Syracuse, NY.
$44,576 to Morehouse College, Atlanta, GA.
$21,000 to National D-Day Museum, New Orleans, LA.
$10,000 to Symphony Space, New York, NY.
$5,000 to Momenta Foundation, New York, NY.
$5,000 to Special Olympics Rhode Island, Warwick, RI.

6090
Eugene and Emily Grant Family Foundation ◇
277 Park Ave., 47th Fl.
New York, NY 10172 (212) 688-4700
Contact: Eugene M. Grant, Tr.

Established in 1998 in NY.
Donors: Eugene M. Grant; Terry E. Grant.
Foundation type: Independent foundation.
Financial data (yr. ended 12/31/04): Assets, $991,851 (M); gifts received, $1,400,000; expenditures, $1,734,144; qualifying distributions, $1,728,256; giving activities include $1,728,256 for grants.
Purpose and activities: Giving primarily to Jewish agencies, the arts and health care; support also to American and Israeli universities, environmental conservation, intermarriage, and holocaust studies.
Fields of interest: Performing arts, music; Performing arts, orchestra (symphony); Performing arts, opera; History/archaeology; Arts; Higher education, university; Environment, natural resources; Health care; Health organizations, association; Jewish federated giving programs; Jewish agencies & temples.
International interests: Israel.
Type of support: Scholarships—to individuals; Scholarship funds; Grants to individuals; Fellowships; Curriculum development; Annual campaigns.
Limitations: Giving in the U.S. and Israel.
Application information:
Initial approach: Letter
Deadline(s): None
Trustees: Emily Grant; Eugene M. Grant.
EIN: 133997005

6091
Charles M. & Mary D. Grant Foundation
c/o JPMorgan Chase Bank, N.A.
345 Park Ave., 4th Fl.
New York, NY 10154
Contact: Jacqueline E. Elias, V.P.
URL: http://foundationcenter.org/grantmaker/grant/

Established in 1967 in NY.
Donor: Mary D. Grant‡.
Foundation type: Independent foundation.
Financial data (yr. ended 12/31/05): Assets, $9,333,541 (M); expenditures, $536,189; qualifying distributions, $452,336; giving activities include $440,000 for 15 grants (high: $50,000; low: $15,000).
Purpose and activities: Support for organizations involved with health and human services, economic and community development, education and literacy.
Fields of interest: Adult education—literacy, basic skills & GED; Education; Health care; Human services; Children/youth, services; Economic development; Community development.
Type of support: General/operating support; Program development; Seed money; Technical assistance.
Limitations: Giving limited to the southeastern U.S. No support for organizations lacking 501(c)(3) status. No grants to individuals, or for research, endowment funds, or matching gifts; generally no scholarships or fellowships; no loans.
Publications: Application guidelines; Grants list.
Application information: See foundation Web site for application guidelines and requirements. Application form not required.
Initial approach: E-mail or letter
Copies of proposal: 1
Deadline(s): Apr. 30
Board meeting date(s): Aug.
Final notification: Sept.
Trustee: JPMorgan Chase Bank, N.A.
EIN: 136264329
Selected grants: The following grants were reported in 2004.
$50,000 to Shepherds Hope, Orlando, FL.
$50,000 to Union Mission, Savannah, GA.
$40,000 to World Wildlife Fund, DC.
$35,000 to United Negro College Fund, New York, NY.
$30,000 to Vanderbilt University, Nashville, TN.
$25,000 to ACCION USA, Boston, MA.
$25,000 to Union College, Barbourville, KY.
$20,000 to Warren Wilson College, Asheville, NC.

6092
William T. Grant Foundation ▼ ◇
570 Lexington Ave., 18th Fl.
New York, NY 10022-6837 (212) 752-0071
Contact: Grants Coord.
FAX: (212) 752-1398; E-mail: info@wtgrantfdn.org;
URL: http://www.wtgrantfoundation.org/

Incorporated in 1936 in DE.
Donor: William T. Grant‡.
Foundation type: Independent foundation.
Financial data (yr. ended 12/31/04): Assets, $262,365,521 (M); expenditures, $12,634,629; qualifying distributions, $11,446,928; giving activities include $7,019,240 for 162 grants (high: $275,981; low: $2,500; average: $5,000–$60,000).

Purpose and activities: The mission of the foundation is to help create a society that values young people and enables them to reach their full potential. In pursuit of this goal, the foundation invests in research and in people and projects that use evidence-based approaches. Current grantmaking for research, policy analyses, and evaluations of interventions is restricted to the three interrelated topics that follow: 1) Youth Development: Understanding how youth develop strengths and assets such as the skills and relationships that contribute to their development and well-being; 2) Improving Systems, Organizations, and Programs: Understanding how to improve the quality of youth-serving systems, organizations, and programs; and 3) Adults' Use of Evidence and Their Views of Youth: Understanding how adults who are key constituents (influential policymakers, practitioners, scholars, advocates, and members of the media) view youth, and the policies and services that affect youth. The foundation also supports promising post-doctoral scholars from diverse disciplines through the William T. Grant Scholars Program, and through Youth Service Grants. Support also for local programs in the Tri-State area that actively engage young people and enable them to reach their full potential.
Fields of interest: Education, research; Youth development; Social sciences, research; Psychology/behavioral science; Social sciences, interdisciplinary studies; Social sciences; Public policy, research.
Type of support: Program development; Conferences/seminars; Publication; Fellowships; Research; Program evaluation.
Limitations: Giving on a national basis; giving limited to NY, NJ, and CT for youth service grants. No grants to individuals (except for W.T. Grant Scholars Program), or for annual fundraising campaigns, equipment and materials, land acquisition, building or renovation projects, operating budgets, endowments, or scholarships; no loans.
Publications: Application guidelines; Annual report; Financial statement; Grants list; Informational brochure; Informational brochure (including application guidelines).
Application information: Letter of inquiry may be submitted online via foundation Web site. The foundation will invite applicants to submit proposals through its Web site following review of the letter of inquiry. Application to William T. Grant Scholars Program by nomination only. Application form not required.
Initial approach: Letter of inquiry for major grants; NYRAG common application form for youth service grants
Copies of proposal: 6
Deadline(s): July 1 for William T. Grant Scholars Program nominations; Nov. 30 and Apr. 30 for Youth Service Improvement Grants
Board meeting date(s): Quarterly
Final notification: Following each quarterly board meeting
Officers and Trustees:* Gary Walker,* Chair.; Henry E. Gooss,* Vice-Chair.; Robert C. Granger, Ed.D., Pres.; Edward Seidman, Ph.D., Sr. V.P., Progs.; Larry Moreland, V.P., Finance and Admin.; J. Lawrence Aber, Ph.D.; Paula Allen-Meares, Ph.D.; Robert F. Boruch, Ph.D.; Kathleen Hall-Jamieson, Ph.D.; Lisa Hess; Christine James-Brown; Bridget MacAskill; Sara McLanahan, Ph.D.; Russell Pennoyer.

Number of staff: 5 full-time professional; 13 full-time support.
EIN: 131624021
Selected grants: The following grants were reported in 2005.

$916,026 to Developmental Studies Center, Oakland, CA. For research project entitled, A Comprehensive Evaluation of the Making Meaning, Reading Comprehension Program, which will examine if Making Meaning, elementary school reading comprehension program, is effective. Study will include 37 elementary schools in the Worchester, Massachusetts Public School District, payable over 4 years.

$605,419 to University of Michigan, Ann Arbor, MI. For research project entitled, A Multi-University Evaluation of Educational Effects of Intergroup Dialogues, which will examine if participation in race and gender Intergroup Dialogue has educational effects. Intergroup Dialogues bring students from two or more social identity groups together into a small group, co-learning environment through which students learn to recognize both intergroup differences and commonalities, and to negotiate intergroup conflicts, payable over 4 years.

$574,977 to University of Colorado Health Sciences Center, Denver, CO. For research project entitled, Trial of Intervention to Increase Participant Retention in Home Visiting, which will examine how Nurse Family Partnership (NFP), voluntary program of prenatal and infancy home visiting by nurses for low-income women bearing first babies program, can increase how long and how frequently the women participate in the program. Investigators will examine whether giving more control to families over certain aspects of the program affects retention rates. Study will focus on low-income women and children ages 8-25, payable over 3 years.

$500,000 to University of Georgia, Athens, GA. For research project entitled, Informal Mentoring: Rural African-American Emerging Adults, and Substance Use, which will examine whether trained informal mentors are more effective in reducing rates of substance use among rural, low-income African-Americans making transition from adolescence to adulthood than just training families to be supportive of these young adults (17-22). Based on their findings researchers plan to prepare and disseminate substance use prevention curriculum, payable over 3 years.

$367,207 to Georgetown University, DC. For research project entitled, Estimating Neighborhood Effects on Low-Income Youth (ages 8-25), which will examine non-experimental methods as viable alternative to randomized experiments when trying to assess effects of neighborhood on youth outcomes. Project will use data from randomized housing-voucher program in Chicago and examine congruence between experimental and non-experimental estimates of effects for variety of youth outcomes, payable over 3 years.

$317,315 to National Campaign to Prevent Teen Pregnancy, DC. For research project entitled, Adding It Up: Public and Private Costs of Teen Childbearing, which will examine economic, social, and individual costs of teen pregnancy and childbearing. Study will focus on updating national cost estimates for childbearing among teens aged 17 and younger, generating state-level cost estimates, broadly disseminating these analyses and estimates, and providing technical assistance to help state-level partners educate influential leaders about value of investing in teen pregnancy prevention, payable over 3 years.

$315,583 to Cornell University, Ithaca, NY. For research project entitled, One Hundred Families: Growing Up in Rural Poverty, Wave III, which will examine how poverty affects youth development in rural areas and which physical and psychosocial factors in children's homes and communities explain why some children do well while others do poorly. Study will focus on white, rural, low- and middle-income youth ages 16-17, payable over 4 years.

$286,738 to Yale University, New Haven, CT. For research project entitled, Addressing the Academic Performance Gap between Minority and White Students, which will examine whether academic performance of Black students can be increased using interventions designed to reduce their stress and anxiety about being negatively stereotyped. Investigators will randomly assign 6th-8th grade students from racially balanced middle school to receive either intervention or control exercises prior to academic tests. Survey will be given throughout the year to assess students' perception of school climate. Test scores, grades, attendance, and disciplinary incidents will be used to compare and measure effects of interventions.

$225,000 to Impact Strategies, Forum for Youth Investment, Tolland, CT. For research project entitled, Lessons, Links, and Levers: Bridging Research, Policy, and Practice in Allied Youth Fields. Work includes carrying out program quality improvement case studies; supporting various Foundation programs and grantees by planning and facilitating meetings and providing regular grantee updates and resource guides; providing materials for the Foundation's website; assisting in evaluation of pilot-test on Distinguished Fellows Program; and conducting other activities to improve impact of Foundation's grantmaking, especially for children and youth ages 10-21, payable over 2 years.

$175,000 to Urban Institute, DC. For research project conducted by William T. Grant Distinguished Fellow entitled, Child, Family, and Youth Policymaking for Behind the Scenes. Fellow will work with Democratic staff within Human Resources Subcommittee of House Committee on Ways and Means. Work will provide first-hand experience in how federal child welfare policy decisions are made, while at the same time giving insights into how child welfare policy fits within the larger agenda for low-income children, youth, and families, payable over 2 years.

6093
The Grateful Foundation, Inc. ✧
250 Park Ave.
New York, NY 10177

Established in 1987 in DE.
Donor: Jordan Seaman.
Foundation type: Independent foundation.
Financial data (yr. ended 10/31/05): Assets, $7,447,960 (M); expenditures, $408,819; qualifying distributions, $358,365; giving activities include $352,500 for 25 grants (high: $50,000; low: $2,000).

Purpose and activities: Giving primarily for Jewish agencies; funding also for children and youth services, and health organizations, including medical research, and social services, particularly food distribution services to the elderly, and the homeless.
Fields of interest: Arts; Animal welfare; Health organizations, association; Health organizations; Genetics/birth defects research; Food distribution, meals on wheels; Disasters, Hurricane Katrina; Human services; Children/youth, services; Family services; Jewish agencies & temples.
Type of support: Research.
Limitations: Applications not accepted. Giving primarily in CA and NY. No grants to individuals.
Application information: Contributes only to pre-selected organizations.
Officers: Jordan Seaman, Pres.; Dana Manning, V.P.; Robert Krissoff, Secy.
EIN: 112897411
Selected grants: The following grants were reported in 2003.
$25,000 to Citymeals-on-Wheels, New York, NY.
$25,000 to Friends of Animals, New York, NY.
$25,000 to North Shore Child and Family Guidance Center, Roslyn Heights, NY.
$25,000 to Pediatric Kidney Foundation, New Hyde Park, NY.
$20,000 to Aish HaTorah.
$20,000 to Sallie Foundation, New York, NY.
$15,000 to Memorial Sloan-Kettering Cancer Center, New York, NY.
$12,500 to Help USA, New York, NY.
$10,000 to American Civil Liberties Union (ACLU), New York, NY.
$10,000 to Love Heals, New York, NY.

6094
Peter T. and Laura M. Grauer Foundation ✧
c/o M. Blumenreich & Co.
295 Madison Ave., Ste. 1125
New York, NY 10017-8393
Contact: Peter T. Grauer, Pres. and Treas.

Established in 1989 in NY and DE.
Donor: Peter T. Grauer.
Foundation type: Independent foundation.
Financial data (yr. ended 12/31/04): Assets, $224,535 (M); gifts received, $618,076; expenditures, $511,266; qualifying distributions, $511,125; giving activities include $504,300 for 29 + grants (high: $75,000).
Purpose and activities: Giving primarily for education and human services.
Fields of interest: Arts; Elementary/secondary education; Higher education; Education; Health organizations, association; Human services; Family services.
Limitations: Giving on a national basis.
Application information:
Initial approach: Letter
Deadline(s): None
Officers: Peter T. Grauer, Pres. and Treas.; Laura M. Grauer, V.P. and Secy.
EIN: 521702126
Selected grants: The following grants were reported in 2004.
$75,000 to Family Centers, Greenwich, CT.
$75,000 to University of North Carolina, Chapel Hill, NC.
$50,000 to Pomfret School, Pomfret, CT.
$25,000 to Big Apple Circus, New York, NY.

$25,000 to Eisenhower Medical Center, Rancho
    Mirage, CA.
$25,000 to Hobart and William Smith Colleges,
    Geneva, NY.
$25,000 to Purnell School, Pottersville, NJ.
$15,000 to Gildas Club Worldwide, New York, NY.
$10,000 to Anchor, Inc., New York, NY.
$5,000 to Greenwich Hospital, Greenwich, CT.

6095
Green Charitable Foundation, Inc. ✧
14 E. 60th St., No. 702
New York, NY 10022

Established in 1999 in NY.
Donor: The Green Fund, Inc.
Foundation type: Independent foundation.
Financial data (yr. ended 1/31/06): Assets,
$12,668,687 (M); gifts received, $70,000;
expenditures, $570,373; qualifying distributions,
$503,952; giving activities include $440,810 for 29
grants (high: $250,000; low: $500).
Purpose and activities: Giving primarily for higher
education.
Fields of interest: Media, television; Museums (art);
Arts; Higher education; Law school/education;
Education; Botanical gardens; Legal services, public
interest law; Human services; Public affairs,
government agencies; Jewish agencies & temples.
Limitations: Applications not accepted. Giving
primarily in NY. No grants to individuals.
Application information: Contributes only to
pre-selected organizations.
Officers: Patricia Green, Pres.; Louis Green, Secy.;
Catherine Green, Treas.
EIN: 134041346

6096
The Green Fund, Inc. ✧
14 E. 60th St., Ste. 702
New York, NY 10022
Contact: Cynthia Green Colin, Pres.

Incorporated in 1947 in NY.
Donors: Evelyn Green Davis†; Louis A. Green†.
Foundation type: Independent foundation.
Financial data (yr. ended 1/31/05): Assets,
$22,462,604 (M); expenditures, $1,075,813;
qualifying distributions, $949,209; giving activities
include $824,925 for 30 grants (high: $475,675;
low: $500).
Purpose and activities: Giving primarily for Jewish
welfare funds, services to the aged and mentally
handicapped, higher and secondary education, the
performing arts, social services, and youth
agencies.
Fields of interest: Performing arts; Secondary
school/education; Higher education; Hospitals
(general); Reproductive health, family planning;
Reproductive health, fertility; Mental health/crisis
services; Human services; Youth, services; Aging,
centers/services; Community development; Jewish
federated giving programs; Jewish agencies &
temples; Aging.
Limitations: Applications not accepted. Giving
primarily in the metropolitan New York, NY, area. No
grants to individuals.
Application information: Grants initiated by the
fund's members.
    Board meeting date(s): Varies

Officers: Cynthia Green Colin, Pres.; Patricia F.
Green, Treas.
Number of staff: 1 full-time professional.
EIN: 136160950

6097
Glenn Greenberg and Linda Vester
Foundation ✧
c/o Chieftain Capital Mgmt., Inc.
12 E. 49th St.
New York, NY 10017

Established in 2003 in NY.
Donors: Glenn H. Greenberg; Linda J. Vester.
Foundation type: Independent foundation.
Financial data (yr. ended 12/31/05): Assets,
$5,456,655 (M); gifts received, $1,576,310;
expenditures, $900,853; qualifying distributions,
$874,770; giving activities include $874,520 for 21
grants (high: $405,000; low: $5,000).
Fields of interest: Higher education; Education;
Legal services.
Limitations: Applications not accepted. Giving on a
national basis. No grants to individuals.
Application information: Contributes only to
pre-selected organizations.
Officers and Directors:* Linda J. Vester,* Pres.;
Glenn H. Greenberg,* Secy.-Treas.; Thomas D.
Stern.
EIN: 200405627

6098
The Maurice R. & Corinne P. Greenberg
Foundation, Inc. ✧
c/o Marks Paneth
622 3rd Ave., 7th Fl.
New York, NY 10017

Established around 1984 in NY.
Donors: Corinne P. Greenberg; Maurice R.
Greenberg; Greenberg Charitable Trust No. 1.
Foundation type: Independent foundation.
Financial data (yr. ended 9/30/05): Assets,
$25,441,363 (M); gifts received, $6,000,000;
expenditures, $983,496; qualifying distributions,
$975,597; giving activities include $975,597 for 20
grants (high: $334,000; low: $80).
Purpose and activities: Giving primarily for health
care and medical research, as well as for higher
education, including a college for veterinary
medicine, and a Jewish temple.
Fields of interest: Museums; Higher education; Law
school/education; Hospitals (general); Medical
research, institute; Children/youth, services; Jewish
agencies & temples.
Type of support: General/operating support.
Limitations: Applications not accepted. Giving
primarily in New York, NY. No grants to individuals.
Application information: Contributes only to
pre-selected organizations.
Officers and Directors:* Maurice R. Greenberg,*
Chair.; Corinne P. Greenberg,* Pres.; Evan G.
Greenberg,* V.P.; Jeffrey W. Greenberg, V.P.;
Lawrence S. Greenberg,* V.P.
EIN: 133208725
Selected grants: The following grants were reported
in 2003.
$1,310,000 to Weill Medical College of Cornell
    University, New York, NY.
$1,023,237 to Greenberg Medical Research
    Institute, New York, NY.

$176,666 to Cornell University, College of
    Veterinary Medicine, Ithaca, NY.
$100,000 to Hebrew Home for the Aged at
    Riverdale, Riverdale, NY.
$52,500 to Rockefeller University, New York, NY.
$50,000 to American Museum of Natural History,
    New York, NY.
$35,000 to Museum of Modern Art, New York, NY.
$35,000 to Saint Lukes Chamber Ensemble, New
    York, NY.
$25,000 to Council on Foreign Relations, New York,
    NY.
$20,000 to Animal Medical Center, New York, NY.

6099
The David and Alan Greene Family
Foundation ✧
(formerly The David J. Greene Foundation, Inc.)
599 Lexington Ave.
New York, NY 10022-6303

Incorporated in 1966 in NY.
Donors: David J. Greene†; and members of the
Greene family.
Foundation type: Independent foundation.
Financial data (yr. ended 12/31/05): Assets,
$20,214,241 (M); expenditures, $927,033;
qualifying distributions, $868,298; giving activities
include $861,653 for 121 grants (high: $254,700;
low: $100).
Fields of interest: Performing arts, music;
Secondary school/education; Higher education;
Education; Environment; Hospitals (general); Eye
diseases; Eye research; Human services; Children/
youth, services; Aging, centers/services; Jewish
federated giving programs; Aging.
Type of support: General/operating support.
Limitations: Applications not accepted. Giving
primarily in the metropolitan New York, NY, area. No
grants to individuals.
Application information: Contributes only to
pre-selected organizations.
    Board meeting date(s): Mar., June, Sept., and
    Dec.
Officers: Alan I. Greene, Pres.; Michael C. Greene,
V.P.; Robert Ravitz, V.P.; James Greene, Treas.
EIN: 136209280
Selected grants: The following grants were reported
in 2004.
$121,600 to United Jewish Appeal, New York, NY.
$10,100 to Colgate University, Hamilton, NY.
$10,000 to National Center for Learning
    Disabilities, New York, NY.
$10,000 to United Cerebral Palsy, DC.
$7,000 to YMCA of Greater New York, New York, NY.
$5,000 to Jewish Federation of Palm Springs and
    Desert Area, Palm Springs, CA.
$5,000 to Soundview Preparatory School, Mount
    Kisco, NY.
$1,000 to Beginning with Children Foundation, New
    York, NY.
$500 to Cystic Fibrosis Foundation, Bethesda, MD.
$500 to Ronald McDonald House of Long Island,
    New Hyde Park, NY.

6100
Jerome L. Greene Foundation, Inc. ▼ ✧
950 Third Ave., Ste. 1900
New York, NY 10022 (212) 688-1550

Established in 1978.

Donor: Jerome L. Greene†.
Foundation type: Independent foundation.
Financial data (yr. ended 12/31/05): Assets, $72,370,197 (M); gifts received, $200,000; expenditures, $10,448,539; qualifying distributions, $10,171,492; giving activities include $10,051,300 for 33 grants (high: $4,600,000; low: $100; average: $1,000–$500,000).
Purpose and activities: Support primarily for museums, the performing arts, and higher education.
Fields of interest: Museums; Performing arts; Arts; Law school/education; Jewish federated giving programs.
Limitations: Giving primarily in NY. No grants to individuals.
Application information:
  Deadline(s): None
Officers and Directors:* Dawn M. Greene,* Pres. and Treas.; Christina McInerney,* V.P. and Secy.
EIN: 132960852
Selected grants: The following grants were reported in 2005.
$6,665,000 to Columbia University, New York, NY. 3 grants: $4,600,000 to Law School (For Jerome L. Green Hall renovations), $2,050,000 to Mailman School of Public Health (For endowed professorship), $15,000 to Law School (For David W. Leebron Human Rights Fund).
$2,400,000 to Juilliard School, New York, NY. For new fellowships in music, dance, and drama.
$500,000 to Lincoln Center for the Performing Arts, New York, NY. For general support.
$250,750 to Jewish Museum, New York, NY. For Sarah Bernhardt Exhibit.
$62,500 to Vivian Beaumont Theater, New York, NY. For general production support.
$60,000 to Young Concert Artists, New York, NY. For general support.
$45,000 to Educational Broadcasting Corporation, New York, NY. For American Masters Series on Balanchine.

6101
Greenhill Family Foundation ✧
c/o Greenhill & Co., LLC
300 Park Ave., 23rd Fl.
New York, NY 10022

Established in 1997 in CT.
Donor: Robert F. Greenhill.
Foundation type: Independent foundation.
Financial data (yr. ended 12/31/05): Assets, $1,117,502 (M); gifts received, $1,134,625; expenditures, $342,730; qualifying distributions, $330,360; giving activities include $330,360 for 33 grants (high: $145,460; low: $400).
Purpose and activities: Giving primarily to a photography center, as well as for education, hospitals, an institute for sports medicine research, human services, and federated giving programs.
Fields of interest: Visual arts, photography; Higher education; Education; Hospitals (general); Medical research, institute; Human services; Federated giving programs.
Limitations: Applications not accepted. Giving primarily in CT, MA, and NY. No grants to individuals.
Application information: Contributes only to pre-selected organizations.
Trustees: Gayle G. Greenhill; Robert F. Greenhill.
EIN: 061488779
Selected grants: The following grants were reported in 2005.

$145,460 to International Center of Photography, New York, NY.
$50,000 to Good Shepherd Services, New York, NY.
$25,000 to Metropolitan Opera Association, New York, NY.
$10,000 to American Rivers, DC.
$10,000 to Vassar College, Poughkeepsie, NY.
$5,000 to Low Country Institute, Okatie, SC.
$5,000 to Museum of Arts and Design, New York, NY.
$5,000 to Yale University, New Haven, CT.
$4,000 to Harvard-Radcliffe Parents Fund, Cambridge, MA.
$3,000 to Phillips Academy, Andover, MA.

6102
Greentree Foundation ✧
400 Madison Ave., Ste. 1001
New York, NY 10017 (212) 888-7755
Contact: George Patterson, Grants Mgr.

Established in 1982 in NY.
Donor: Betsey C. Whitney†.
Foundation type: Independent foundation.
Financial data (yr. ended 12/31/04): Assets, $305,323,296 (M); gifts received, $842,228; expenditures, $8,753,652; qualifying distributions, $21,860,153; giving activities include $1,301,320 for 35 grants (high: $175,000; low: $170), and $20,558,905 for foundation-administered programs.
Purpose and activities: Supports focused projects initiated by local community groups that provide clearly defined participatory roles for schools, parents, children and community-based organizations in order to enhance educational achievements and lessen social and cultural tensions. Giving also for the furtherance of peace, human rights, international cooperation and the preservation of the environment.
Fields of interest: Museums; Arts; Higher education; Education; Environment; Human services; Children/youth, services; International peace/security; International terrorism.
Type of support: Program development.
Limitations: Giving primarily in the metropolitan New York, NY, area. No grants to individuals.
Application information: Application form not required.
  Initial approach: Letter
  Copies of proposal: 1
  Board meeting date(s): Mar., June, Sept., and Dec.
Officers and Trustees:* Robert Schaffer,* Pres.; Kate R. Whitney,* V.P.; Sara R. Wilford,* V.P.; Robert Carswell,* Treas.; Franklin A. Thomas; Ronald A. Wilford.
Number of staff: 6 full-time professional; 24 full-time support; 2 part-time support.
EIN: 133132117
Selected grants: The following grants were reported in 2003.
$150,000 to Long Island Community Foundation, Jericho, NY. To establish Greentree Foundation Fund.
$25,000 to East Harlem Tutorial Program, New York, NY. For Parental Involvement workshops.
$25,000 to Project Reach Youth, Brooklyn, NY. For Parental Involvement Program.
$20,000 to Horticultural Society of New York, New York, NY. For Apple Seed Program.

$20,000 to Northside Center for Child Development, New York, NY. For Remedial Reading Program.
$15,000 to Girls Inc., New York, NY.
$15,000 to TEAK Fellowship, New York, NY. For academic enrichment program.
$15,000 to Washington Heights-Inwood Coalition, New York, NY. For Parents as Educational Partners programs.
$10,000 to Hamilton-Madison House, New York, NY. For after-school program.
$10,000 to New York Botanical Garden, Bronx, NY. For Bronx Green-Up.

6103
The Greenwall Foundation ▼
420 Lexington Ave., Ste. 2500
New York, NY 10170 (212) 679-7266
Contact: Fredrica Jarcho Ph.D., V.P., Progs.
FAX: (212) 679-7269; E-mail: admin@greenwall.org;
URL: http://www.greenwall.org

Incorporated in 1949 in NY.
Donors: Anna A. Greenwall†; Frank K. Greenwall†.
Foundation type: Independent foundation.
Financial data (yr. ended 12/31/05): Assets, $81,590,924 (M); expenditures, $4,464,755; qualifying distributions, $3,961,940; giving activities include $3,166,239 for 108 grants (high: $401,455; low: $1,000; average: $15,000–$100,000).
Purpose and activities: The foundation makes philanthropic grants to support work in two program areas: 1) Bioethics, and 2) Arts and Humanities.
Fields of interest: Arts; Health care, public policy; Health care, ethics; Medical research, public policy; Medical research, ethics.
Type of support: Program development; Research.
Limitations: Giving primarily in New York, NY, for arts and humanities; giving nationally for bioethics. No grants for building or endowment funds, operating budgets, annual campaigns, deficit financing, or conferences; no loans.
Publications: Application guidelines; Financial statement; Grants list; Program policy statement.
Application information: The foundation's two program areas have different application requirements. Please refer to the website. Application form not required.
  Initial approach: Proposal or telephone call
  Deadline(s): Feb. 1 and Aug. 1
  Board meeting date(s): May and Nov.
  Final notification: After next board meeting
Officers and Directors:* Harvey J. Goldschmid, J.D.*, Chair.; Joseph G. Perpich, M.D., J.D.*, Vice-Chair.; William C. Stubing,* Pres.; Fredrica Jarcho, Ph.D., V.P., Progs.; Rosmarie E. Homberger, Corp. Secy.; T. Dennis Sullivan,* Treas.; Troyen A. Brennan, M.D., J.D., MPH; George L. Bunting, Jr.; Christine K. Cassel, M.D.; John E. Craig, Jr.; Conrad K. Harper, L.L.B.; Matina S. Horner, Ph.D.; Gayle Pemberton, Ph.D.; Barbara Paul Robinson, J.D.; Roger Rosenblatt; Richard L. Salzer, Jr., M.D.; James A. Tulsky, M.D.
Number of staff: 2 full-time professional; 2 full-time support.
EIN: 136082277

6104
The William and Mary Greve Foundation, Inc. ✧

c/o Anthony C.M. Kiser
665 Broadway, Ste. 1001
New York, NY 10112

Incorporated in 1964 in NY.
Donor: Mary P. Greve†.
Foundation type: Independent foundation.
Financial data (yr. ended 12/31/05): Assets, $36,280,839 (M); expenditures, $3,591,233; qualifying distributions, $2,997,613; giving activities include $2,616,863 for 47 grants (high: $932,455; low: $5,000; average: $10,000–$100,000).
Purpose and activities: Grants largely for education and related fields, U.S.-Eastern European relations, the performing arts, and the environment.
Fields of interest: Education; Environment; International affairs, goodwill promotion.
Type of support: General/operating support; Continuing support; Endowments; Matching/challenge support.
Limitations: Applications not accepted. Giving on a national basis, with emphasis on New York, NY. No grants to individuals, or for scholarships or fellowships; no loans.
Application information: Unsolicited requests for funds not accepted.
    Board meeting date(s): Varies
Officers and Directors:* John W. Kiser III,* Chair.; Anthony C.M. Kiser,* Pres.; Victoria Bjorklund, Secy.; Robert E. Cohen; James W. Sykes, Jr.
Number of staff: 1 full-time professional; 1 part-time professional; 1 part-time support.
EIN: 136020724
Selected grants: The following grants were reported in 2004.
$952,713 to Nature Conservancy of Montana, Helena, MT.
$213,896 to Second Stage Theater, New York, NY.
$200,362 to Best Practices in Education, New York, NY.
$150,000 to Common Good Institute, New York, NY.
$110,000 to Friends of Open House, Acton, MA.
$75,000 to New York Theater Workshop, New York, NY.
$50,000 to Manhattan Institute for Policy Research, New York, NY.
$25,000 to Teach for America, New York, NY.
$15,000 to Peconic Land Trust, Southampton, NY.
$10,000 to Brooklyn Academy of Music, Brooklyn, NY.

6105
John A. Griffin Foundation, Inc. ✧

Blue Ridge Capital LLC
660 Madison Ave.
New York, NY 10021
Contact: John Griffin, Pres.

Established in 2001 in NY.
Donor: John A. Griffin.
Foundation type: Independent foundation.
Financial data (yr. ended 11/30/04): Assets, $7,279,813 (M); gifts received, $5,134,149; expenditures, $1,036,876; qualifying distributions, $996,409; giving activities include $996,409 for 19 grants (high: $348,250; low: $1,000; average: $10,000–$50,000).
Fields of interest: Education.

Limitations: Applications not accepted. Giving primarily in NY.
Application information: Contributes only to pre-selected organizations.
Officers and Director:* John A. Griffin,* Pres.; Richard Bello, Secy.-Treas.
EIN: 020562020

6106
The Griffin-Cole Fund ✧ ☆

c/o Goldman Sachs & Co.
1 New York Plz., 40th Fl.
New York, NY 10004

Established in 1996 in NJ.
Donors: Christopher A. Cole; Goldman Sachs & Co.
Foundation type: Independent foundation.
Financial data (yr. ended 7/31/05): Assets, $11,751,552 (M); expenditures, $991,835; qualifying distributions, $896,050; giving activities include $896,050 for 27 grants (high: $350,000; low: $100).
Fields of interest: Arts; Education; Human services.
Type of support: General/operating support.
Limitations: Applications not accepted. Giving primarily in Princeton, NJ. No grants to individuals.
Application information: Contributes only to pre-selected organizations.
Trustees: Christopher A. Cole; Barbara Griffin-Cole.
EIN: 137109406
Selected grants: The following grants were reported in 2003.
$150,000 to Ivy 1879 Foundation, Princeton, NJ.
$10,000 to Princeton Day School, Princeton, NJ.
$10,000 to Saint Pauls School, Concord, NH.
$3,500 to Princeton University, Princeton, NJ. 2 grants: $2,500 (For Junior Annual Fund), $1,000.
$500 to Drumthwacket Foundation, Princeton, NJ.
$500 to HomeFront, Lawrenceville, NJ.

6107
The Griffis Foundation, Inc. ✧

c/o Baker Nye
477 Madison Ave., Rm. 1600
New York, NY 10022
Application address: c/o Hughes Griffis, Waller, Smith & Palmer, 52 Eugene O'Neill Dr., New London, CT 06320, tel.: (860) 442-0367

Incorporated in 1943 in NY.
Donors: Stanton Griffis†; Nixon Griffis.
Foundation type: Independent foundation.
Financial data (yr. ended 12/31/05): Assets, $4,896,220 (M); expenditures, $579,306; qualifying distributions, $530,845; giving activities include $470,818 for 88 grants (high: $75,000; low: $100).
Purpose and activities: Giving primarily for art activities in Connecticut, primarily southeastern Connecticut and various art and education activities in Colorado.
Fields of interest: Arts, multipurpose centers/programs; Humanities; Arts; Education; Health care; Medical research, institute.
Type of support: General/operating support; Continuing support; Debt reduction; Professorships; Publication; Seed money; Fellowships; Research.
Limitations: Giving primarily in CO and southeastern CT. No grants to individuals, or for capital or endowment funds, annual campaigns, emergency funds, matching gifts, or conferences; no loans.

Publications: Application guidelines; Program policy statement.
Application information: Application form not required.
    Initial approach: Letter
    Copies of proposal: 1
    Deadline(s): None
    Board meeting date(s): 10 times per year
    Final notification: 2 months
Officers and Directors:* Hughes Griffis,* Pres.; Elizabeth Nye,* V.P.; Charles Chu; Buckly Griffis; Jennifer Griffis; Nickolas Griffis; Patricia M. Shippee.
EIN: 135678764

6108
Grigg-Lewis Foundation, Inc.

76 West Ave.
Lockport, NY 14094 (716) 478-0002
Contact: William B. May, Exec. Dir.
FAX: (716) 478-0281;
E-mail: grigglewis@grigglewis.org; URL: http://www.grigglewis.org

Established in 1968 in NY.
Donor: Henrietta G. Lewis†.
Foundation type: Independent foundation.
Financial data (yr. ended 12/31/05): Assets, $45,060,125 (M); gifts received, $524,481; expenditures, $1,844,895; qualifying distributions, $1,559,923; giving activities include $1,428,396 for 90 grants (high: $20,000; low: $14).
Fields of interest: Arts; Education; Human services; Aging, centers/services; Community development; Youth; Young adults.
Type of support: General/operating support; Continuing support; Capital campaigns; Building/renovation; Equipment; Emergency funds; Program development; Conferences/seminars; Research; Matching/challenge support.
Limitations: Giving primarily in western NY. No support for religious or political organizations. No grants to individuals.
Publications: Annual report; Program policy statement.
Application information: Application can be downloaded from foundation Web site. Application form required.
    Initial approach: Mail completed application or submit online
    Copies of proposal: 1
    Deadline(s): None
    Board meeting date(s): Quarterly
    Final notification: 1 month
Officers: Norman W. Sinclair, Pres.; William B. May, Secy. and Exec. Dir.; Dan L. Wilson, Treas.
Directors: Christa R. Caldwell; R. Thomas Weeks.
Number of staff: 1 full-time support.
EIN: 161550858

6109
Grin Family Foundation, Inc. ✧ ☆

825 3rd Ave., 14th Fl.
New York, NY 10022

Established in 2005 in NY.
Donor: Eugene Grin.
Foundation type: Operating foundation.
Financial data (yr. ended 5/31/05): Assets, $79,759 (M); gifts received, $1,600,000; expenditures, $1,521,314; qualifying distributions,

$1,520,000; giving activities include $1,520,000 for 6 grants (high: $500,000; low: $20,000).
Fields of interest: Jewish agencies & temples.
Application information:
Deadline(s): None
Officer: Eugene Grin, Pres.
EIN: 201289311

6110
Allen I. Gross Charitable Foundation ✧ ☆
50 Broadway, 3rd Fl.
New York, NY 10004

Established in 1987 in NY.
Donors: Allen I. Gross; AIG 2001 Trust.
Foundation type: Independent foundation.
Financial data (yr. ended 11/30/05): Assets, $8,609,489 (M); gifts received, $685,000; expenditures, $399,074; qualifying distributions, $373,637; giving activities include $367,698 for 17 + grants (high: $100,100).
Fields of interest: Jewish federated giving programs; Jewish agencies & temples.
Type of support: General/operating support.
Limitations: Giving primarily in NY. No grants to individuals.
Officer: Allen I. Gross, Pres.
Trustees: Brian Gross; Edie Gross; Jonathan Gross; Carolyn Weiser.
EIN: 112906887

6111
J. & H. Gross Family Foundation ✧
1224 E. 24th St.
Brooklyn, NY 11210
Contact: Jonathan Gross, Tr.

Established in 1996 in NY.
Donor: Jonathan Gross.
Foundation type: Independent foundation.
Financial data (yr. ended 6/30/05): Assets, $2,304,026 (M); gifts received, $10,000; expenditures, $560,636; qualifying distributions, $516,885; giving activities include $502,728 for 29 + grants (high: $251,936).
Purpose and activities: Giving primarily to Jewish organizations, temples, and schools.
Fields of interest: Education; Jewish agencies & temples.
Limitations: Giving primarily in NY. No grants to individuals.
Application information:
Initial approach: Proposal
Deadline(s): None
Trustees: Ben Gross; Heddy Gross; Jonathan Gross.
EIN: 113344451

6112
Gross Foundation, Inc. ✧
1660 49th St.
Brooklyn, NY 11204 (718) 851-7724
Contact: Chaim Gross, Pres.

Established in 1991 in NY.
Donors: Chaim Gross; Arie Herzog; Pinchus Gross; Esther Gross; Naftali Weiser; Esther Weiser; Shea Rosenfeld; Rachel Rosenfeld; David Spira; Daniel Gross.
Foundation type: Independent foundation.

Financial data (yr. ended 2/28/05): Assets, $45,324,714 (M); expenditures, $2,126,179; qualifying distributions, $1,977,642; giving activities include $1,977,642 for 82 grants (high: $1,566,640; low: $72).
Purpose and activities: Giving primarily for Orthodox Jewish educational and charitable organizations and temples.
Fields of interest: Education; Jewish agencies & temples.
Limitations: Giving primarily in NY. No grants to individuals.
Application information: Application form not required.
Deadline(s): None
Officer: Chaim Gross, Pres.
Directors: Daniel Gross; Faigie Gross.
EIN: 113006419
Selected grants: The following grants were reported in 2003.
$250,000 to Fidelity Investments Charitable Gift Fund, Boston, MA.
$190,000 to FJC-A Foundation of Donor-Advised Funds, New York, NY.
$160,000 to Congregation Ahavas Tzdokah V Chesed, Brooklyn, NY.
$30,000 to Mesifta Bevet Chazon Ish, Monsey, NY.
$20,000 to Tiferet Teveria. 2 grants: $10,000 each
$15,000 to Friends of Arachim, Spring Valley, NY.
$5,000 to Yeshivas Wiznitz Beth Israel V Damesek Eliezer, Brooklyn, NY.
$3,000 to Bnos Jerusalem, Brooklyn, NY.
$1,500 to Congregation Khal Toras Chaim, Brooklyn, NY.

6113
The Grubman Compton Foundation ✧
(formerly Eric P. Grubman Foundation)
c/o BCRS Assocs., LLC
100 Wall St., 11th Fl.
New York, NY 10005

Established in 1996 in NJ.
Donor: Eric P. Grubman.
Foundation type: Independent foundation.
Financial data (yr. ended 7/31/05): Assets, $1,702,996 (M); expenditures, $1,098,270; qualifying distributions, $1,094,770; giving activities include $1,093,205 for 24 grants (high: $250,000; low: $500).
Fields of interest: Museums (history); Elementary/secondary education; Higher education; Hospitals (general); Human services; Federated giving programs; Protestant agencies & churches.
Limitations: Applications not accepted. Giving primarily in MD, NJ and NY. No grants to individuals.
Application information: Contributes only to pre-selected organizations.
Trustees: Elizabeth K. Compton; Eric P. Grubman.
EIN: 133936474
Selected grants: The following grants were reported in 2005.
$750,000 to United States Naval Academy Foundation, Annapolis, MD. 3 grants: $250,000 each
$150,000 to Hippodrome Foundation, Baltimore, MD.
$110,000 to Northfield Mount Hermon School, Northfield, MA.
$5,200 to Tufts University, Medford, MA.
$5,000 to Baltimore School for the Arts Foundation, Baltimore, MD.

$2,500 to Urban Education Exchange, New York, NY.

6114
Oscar and Regina Gruss Charitable and Educational Foundation, Inc. ✧
74 Broad St.
New York, NY 10004

Incorporated in 1952 in NY.
Donors: Emanuel Gruss; Oscar Gruss†; Regina Gruss†.
Foundation type: Independent foundation.
Financial data (yr. ended 3/31/05): Assets, $41,733,492 (M); gifts received, $347,313; expenditures, $810,859; qualifying distributions, $795,325; giving activities include $712,376 for 38 grants (high: $500,000; low: $100; average: $1,000–$5,000).
Purpose and activities: Giving primarily for education and to Jewish agencies and temples.
Fields of interest: Education; Health organizations, association; Jewish federated giving programs; Jewish agencies & temples.
Limitations: Applications not accepted. Giving primarily in New York, NY. No grants to individuals.
Application information: Contributes only to pre-selected organizations.
Officers: Riane Gruss, Pres.; Elizabeth Goldberg, V.P.; Emanuel Gruss, V.P.
Directors: Brenda Gruss; Donald Hamburg.
EIN: 136061333
Selected grants: The following grants were reported in 2005.
$52,560 to Solomon Schechter High School, New York, NY.
$15,000 to Life Needs Coop, Great Barrington, MA.
$5,000 to International Center of Photography, New York, NY.
$5,000 to Ronald McDonald House.
$4,516 to Lincoln Center Theater, New York, NY.
$3,000 to Dorot, New York, NY.
$1,700 to Leo Baeck Institute, New York, NY.
$1,000 to McLean School of Maryland, Potomac, MD.
$500 to Solomon Schechter School of Manhattan, New York, NY.
$300 to Bikur Cholim of Manhattan, New York, NY.

6115
Emanuel & Riane Gruss Charitable Foundation, Inc. ✧
74 Broad St.
New York, NY 10004

Established in 1978 in NY.
Donors: Emanuel Gruss; Riane Gruss.
Foundation type: Independent foundation.
Financial data (yr. ended 3/31/05): Assets, $11,020,101 (M); expenditures, $560,322; qualifying distributions, $531,917; giving activities include $522,142 for 39 grants (high: $429,000; low: $35).
Purpose and activities: Giving primarily for education, to Jewish organizations, and minor support also for social services and the arts.
Fields of interest: Arts; Education; Hospitals (general); Human services; Jewish agencies & temples.
Limitations: Applications not accepted. Giving primarily in New York, NY. No grants to individuals.

Application information: Contributes only to pre-selected organizations.
Officers: Riane Gruss, Pres.; Emanuel Gruss, V.P.
Directors: Brenda Gruss; Leslie Gruss.
EIN: 132969811
Selected grants: The following grants were reported in 2005.
$14,250 to Abraham Joshua Heschel School, New York, NY.
$10,000 to Foundation Fighting Blindness, Owings Mills, MD.
$8,650 to Jewish Museum, New York, NY.
$5,000 to American Friends of the Israel Philharmonic Orchestra, New York, NY.
$4,275 to Fifth Avenue Synagogue, New York, NY.
$2,000 to Community Access, New York, NY.
$1,800 to Brotherhood Synagogue, New York, NY.
$1,500 to Folksbiene Yiddish Theater, New York, NY.
$1,500 to Wall Street Synagogue, New York, NY.
$1,000 to YIVO Institute for Jewish Research, New York, NY.

6116

The Gruss-Lipper Family Foundation

(formerly The Kenneth & Evelyn Lipper Foundation)
c/o Grusso & Co.
667 Madison Ave.
New York, NY 10021-8029
Contact: Evelyn Gruss Lipper, Tr.; Erika L. Aronson

Established about 1982 in NY.
Donors: Gruss Petroleum Corp.; Evmar Oil Corp.
Foundation type: Independent foundation.
Financial data (yr. ended 8/31/05): Assets, $99,314,866 (M); gifts received, $9,868,708; expenditures, $4,318,248; qualifying distributions, $3,483,125; giving activities include $3,451,991 for 15 grants (high: $1,000,000; low: $4,400; average: $25,000–$150,000).
Purpose and activities: Giving exclusively for Jewish causes.
Fields of interest: Medical research, institute; Human services; Children/youth, services; Jewish agencies & temples.
International interests: Israel.
Type of support: Annual campaigns; Program development; Curriculum development; Research.
Limitations: Applications not accepted. Giving on a national basis and in Israel.
Application information: Unsolicited requests for funds not accepted.
Trustees: Evelyn Gruss Lipper; Daniella Lipper-Coules; Joanna Lipper.
Number of staff: 1 part-time professional.
EIN: 133188873
Selected grants: The following grants were reported in 2005.
$1,000,000 to Sesame Workshop, New York, NY. For general support.
$652,622 to Center for Jewish History, New York, NY. For general support.
$500,000 to Gift of Life Bone Marrow Foundation, Boca Raton, FL. For general support.
$493,553 to Museum of Jewish Heritage, New York, NY. For general support.
$192,983 to Combined Jewish Philanthropies of Greater Boston, Boston, MA. For general support.
$150,000 to Hebrew Home for the Aged at Riverdale, Riverdale, NY. For general support.
$102,100 to American Society for Technion-Israel Institute of Technology, Newton, MA.

$48,000 to Bar-Ilan University in Israel, New York, NY.
$25,000 to New York Public Library, New York, NY. For general support.
$21,000 to Jewish Opportunities Institute, New York, NY. For general support.

6117

The Daniel and Florence Guggenheim Foundation

950 3rd Ave., 30th Fl.
New York, NY 10022 (212) 755-3199
Contact: Oscar S. Straus II, Chair.

Incorporated in 1924 in NY.
Donors: Daniel M. Guggenheim†; Florence Guggenheim†.
Foundation type: Independent foundation.
Financial data (yr. ended 12/31/05): Assets, $6,239,973 (M); expenditures, $802,907; qualifying distributions, $723,663; giving activities include $571,600 for 17 grants (high: $60,000; low: $6,600).
Purpose and activities: Giving primarily to criminal justice organizations. Support also for UJA/Federation of Jewish Philanthropies annual campaign.
Fields of interest: Crime/violence prevention.
Type of support: Seed money; Internship funds; Research.
Limitations: Giving primarily in CT, NJ, and NY. No grants to individuals, or for scholarships or fellowships.
Publications: Multi-year report.
Application information: Proposals should not exceed five pages. Application form not required.
  Initial approach: Letter
  Copies of proposal: 1
  Deadline(s): Jan. 30
  Board meeting date(s): May
  Final notification: June 1
Officers and Directors:* Oscar S. Straus II,* Chair.; Oscar S. Schafer,* Pres.; Percy Preston, Jr.,* V.P. and Treas.; Anne Lindgren,* V.P.; Charles T. Locke III, Secy.; Michael B. Davies; Dana Draper; Mrs. Max A. Hart; Mrs. Walter Metcalf III; Deborah S. Robie; Susan H. Salomon; David A. Straus; Laura Straus; Hon. Kenneth Taylor.
Number of staff: 1 part-time support.
EIN: 135562232
Selected grants: The following grants were reported in 2004.
$50,000 to Princeton University, Princeton, NJ.
$40,000 to Center for Court Innovation, New York, NY.
$40,000 to Safe Horizons, Port Huron, MI.
$35,000 to Bronx Defenders, Bronx, NY.
$35,000 to Brooklyn Law School, Brooklyn, NY.
$30,000 to Barnard College, New York, NY.
$30,000 to Sanctuary for Families, New York, NY.
$25,000 to Court Appointed Special Advocates (CASA) of New Jersey, Trenton, NJ.

6118

The Harry Frank Guggenheim Foundation

25 W. 53rd St., 16th Fl.
New York, NY 10019-5401 (646) 428-0971
Contact: Staff
FAX: (646) 428-0981; E-mail: info@hfg.org;
URL: http://www.hfg.org

Incorporated in 1929 in NY.
Donor: Harry Frank Guggenheim†.
Foundation type: Operating foundation.
Financial data (yr. ended 12/31/05): Assets, $87,741,759 (M); gifts received, $17,500; expenditures, $3,756,618; qualifying distributions, $3,141,133; giving activities include $229,624 for grants, $732,228 for grants to individuals, $107,406 for employee matching gifts, and $2,319,926 for foundation-administered programs.
Purpose and activities: Grants for research projects at the postdoctoral level (though not necessarily requiring a Ph.D.) directed toward providing a better understanding of violence, aggression, and dominance in relation to social change; Dissertation Fellowship program to support individuals only during the writing of their Ph.D. thesis; research grants can be applied for directly. Primary areas of support include anthropology, biological sciences, sociology, history, political science, and psychology.
Fields of interest: History/archaeology; Crime/law enforcement; Child development, services; International peace/security; International affairs, arms control; International affairs, foreign policy; International human rights; International affairs; Civil rights, race/intergroup relations; Biological sciences; Science; Social sciences; Anthropology/sociology; Psychology/behavioral science; Political science; Law/international law; International studies; Public policy, research; Government/public administration; Public affairs; Minorities.
Type of support: Fellowships; Research; Employee matching gifts; Grants to individuals.
Limitations: Giving on a national and international basis. No grants for capital or endowment funds, or for matching funds; no loans. No funds for overhead costs of institutions, travel to professional meetings, publications, conferences (except for those organized by the foundation), subsidiaries, self-education, elaborate fixed equipment, or pre-doctoral support (apart from that indirectly involved in research assistantships and except for a special program of support for dissertation writing).
Publications: Application guidelines; Multi-year report; Occasional report.
Application information: Application guidelines and application forms may be downloaded on foundation Web site. Application form required.
  Initial approach: Letter or telephone
  Copies of proposal: 4
  Deadline(s): Feb. 1 for Ph.D. support; Aug. 1 for research grants
  Board meeting date(s): June and Dec.
  Final notification: Within 3 days of meeting
Officers and Directors:* Peter O. Lawson-Johnston,* Chair.; Josiah Bunting III,* Pres.; Mary-Alice Yates, Secy.; Deirdre Hamill, Treas.; Tina Bennett; Dana Draper; James B. Edwards; Victor Davis Hanson; Donald C. Hood; Carol Langstaff; Lewis H. Lapham; Peter Lawson-Johnston II; Reeve Lindbergh; Gillian Lindt; Tania L.J. McCleery; J.M. Millbank III; Lois Dixon Rice; Patricia Rosenfield.
Number of staff: 4 full-time professional; 2 part-time professional.
EIN: 136043471

6119
John Simon Guggenheim Memorial Foundation ▼
90 Park Ave.
New York, NY 10016 (212) 687-4470
Contact: Edward Hirsch, Pres.
FAX: (212) 697-3248; E-mail: fellowships@gf.org;
URL: http://www.gf.org

Incorporated in 1925 in NY.
Donors: Simon Guggenheim†; Mrs. Simon Guggenheim†.
Foundation type: Independent foundation.
Financial data (yr. ended 12/31/05): Assets, $263,951,799 (M); gifts received, $1,030,838; expenditures, $14,289,744; qualifying distributions, $11,416,382; giving activities include $8,164,150 for 400 grants to individuals (high: $49,000; low: $2,000; average: $18,000–$36,000).
Purpose and activities: Fellowships offered to further the development of scholars and artists by assisting them to engage in research in any field of knowledge and creation in any of the arts, under the freest possible conditions and irrespective of race, color, or creed. Fellowships are awarded by the trustees upon nomination by a Committee of Selection. Awards are made to citizens and permanent residents of the U.S., Canada, Latin America, and the Caribbean.
Fields of interest: Visual arts; Humanities; Science; Social sciences.
International interests: Canada; Caribbean; Latin America.
Type of support: Fellowships.
Limitations: Giving to citizens and permanent residents of the U.S., Canada, Latin America, and the Caribbean. No grants for endowments, operating budgets, special projects, or any other expenses of institutions.
Publications: Application guidelines; Annual report; Financial statement; Informational brochure (including application guidelines).
Application information: Grants are awarded to individuals rather than institutions. Application guidelines available on Web site. Application form required.
   Initial approach: Letter
   Copies of proposal: 1
   Deadline(s): Oct. 1 for U.S. and Canada; Dec. 1 for Latin America and the Caribbean
   Board meeting date(s): Apr., June, and as required
   Final notification: Approximately 6 months
Officers and Trustees:* Joseph A. Rice,* Chair.; Edward Hirsch,* Pres.; G. Thomas Tanselle, Sr. V.P. and Secy.; Andre Bernard, V.P. and Secy.; Coleen P. Higgins-Jacob, V.P., C.F.O., and Treas.; Robert A. Caro; Joel Conarroe; A. Alex Porter; Richard A. Rifkind; Waddell W. Stillman; Charles Andrew Ryskamp; Ellen Taaffe Zwilich.
Number of staff: 10 full-time professional; 14 full-time support.
EIN: 135673173

6120
Aaron & Marion Gural Foundation ✧ ☆
c/o Newmark & Co.
125 Park Ave., 11th Fl.
New York, NY 10017

Established in 1986 in NY.
Donors: Aaron Gural; Jane Gural Senders.

Foundation type: Independent foundation.
Financial data (yr. ended 12/31/05): Assets, $2,578,176 (M); gifts received, $500,000; expenditures, $379,983; qualifying distributions, $379,983; giving activities include $371,354 for 22 + grants (high: $61,250).
Purpose and activities: Giving for health and Jewish organizations; funding also for art museums.
Fields of interest: Museums (art); Performing arts centers; Higher education, college; Hospitals (general); Health organizations, association; Human services; YM/YWCAs & YM/YWHAs; Civil rights; Jewish federated giving programs; Jewish agencies & temples.
Limitations: Applications not accepted. Giving primarily in New York, NY. No grants to individuals.
Application information: Contributes only to pre-selected organizations.
Officer: Aaron Gural, Pres.
Directors: Barbara Gural; Jane Gural Senders.
EIN: 133377362
Selected grants: The following grants were reported in 2005.
$21,000 to Boca Raton Community Hospital, Boca Raton, FL.
$21,000 to I Have A Dream Foundation, New York, NY.
$20,000 to Lincoln Center for the Performing Arts, New York, NY.
$10,000 to Corcoran Gallery of Art, DC.
$10,000 to Israel Special Kids Fund, New York, NY.
$7,500 to Alzheimers Association, New York, NY.
$5,283 to Young Israel of Woodmere, Woodmere, NY.
$4,000 to Georgetown Day School, DC.
$3,800 to Chemotherapy Foundation, New York, NY.
$3,000 to Metropolitan Museum of Art, New York, NY.

6121
J. Gurwin Foundation, Inc. ✧
c/o Kofler, Levenstein, Romanotto & Co.
100 Merrick Rd., Ste. 210E
Rockville Centre, NY 11570-4881

Incorporated in 1959 in NY.
Donors: Joseph Gurwin; Kings Point Industries, Inc.
Foundation type: Independent foundation.
Financial data (yr. ended 7/31/05): Assets, $24,913,479 (M); gifts received, $48; expenditures, $1,299,121; qualifying distributions, $919,474; giving activities include $919,474 for 81 grants (high: $200,000; low: $15).
Purpose and activities: Giving primarily for Jewish-affiliated organizations, including welfare funds, temples, educational institutions, geriatric centers and other health facilities, and a holocaust museum.
Fields of interest: Museums (specialized); Higher education; Hospitals (general); Health care; Health organizations, association; Human services; Jewish federated giving programs; Jewish agencies & temples.
International interests: Israel.
Limitations: Applications not accepted. Giving primarily in NY. No grants to individuals.
Application information: Contributes only to pre-selected organizations.
Officers: Joseph Gurwin, Pres.; Eric Gurwin, V.P.; Laura Flug, Secy.-Treas.
EIN: 136059258

6122
The Gutman Family Foundation ✧ ☆
c/o Ayco Co., L.P.
P.O. Box 15014
Albany, NY 12212-5014

Established in 1997 in IL.
Donor: Joseph D. Gutman.
Foundation type: Independent foundation.
Financial data (yr. ended 12/31/05): Assets, $4,023,611 (M); gifts received, $12,000; expenditures, $382,840; qualifying distributions, $373,760; giving activities include $373,760 for 42 grants (high: $60,000; low: $250).
Fields of interest: Museums (specialized); Graduate/professional education; Hospitals (general); Health organizations, association; Recreation; Human services; Federated giving programs; Jewish federated giving programs; Jewish agencies & temples.
Type of support: Scholarship funds.
Limitations: Applications not accepted. Giving primarily in Chicago, IL and New York, NY. No grants to individuals; no loans.
Application information: Contributes only to pre-selected organizations.
Trustees: Joseph D. Gutman; Sheila H. Gutman.
EIN: 133936473
Selected grants: The following grants were reported in 2004.
$54,000 to Jewish United Fund of Metropolitan Chicago, Chicago, IL.
$42,500 to University of Illinois Foundation, Urbana, IL.
$10,000 to Childrens Memorial Hospital, Chicago, IL.
$2,500 to Northwestern University, Evanston, IL.
$1,000 to Highland Park High School, Highland Park, IL.
$1,000 to Museum of Contemporary Art, Chicago, IL.
$500 to National Vietnam Veterans Art Museum, Chicago, IL.
$500 to University of Illinois at Chicago, Chicago, IL.
$250 to American Lung Association of Metropolitan Chicago, Chicago, IL.
$250 to Erikson Institute, Chicago, IL.

6123
The Leo and Karen Gutmann Foundation ✧
c/o Lawrence Putterman
470 West End Ave., Ste. 8F
New York, NY 10024

Established in 2001 in NY.
Donor: Karen Gutmann†.
Foundation type: Independent foundation.
Financial data (yr. ended 12/31/05): Assets, $90,880 (M); expenditures, $1,950,991; qualifying distributions, $1,940,147; giving activities include $1,934,567 for 7 grants (high: $386,670; low: $176,000).
Fields of interest: Higher education.
Type of support: Scholarship funds.
Limitations: Applications not accepted. Giving primarily in DE and NY. No grants to individuals.
Application information: Contributes only to pre-selected organizations.
Officers: Lawrence Putterman, Pres.; Constance Lowenthal, V.P.
EIN: 311751468

6124

Stella and Charles Guttman Foundation, Inc. ✧

122 E. 42nd St. Ste. 2010
New York, NY 10168
Contact: Elizabeth Olofson, Exec. Dir.
FAX: (212) 371-8936;
E-mail: info@guttmanfoundation.org; URL: http://www.guttmanfoundation.org/

Incorporated in 1959 in NY.
Donors: Charles Guttman†; Stella Guttman†.
Foundation type: Independent foundation.
Financial data (yr. ended 12/31/05): Assets, $49,278,064 (M); expenditures, $2,605,763; qualifying distributions, $2,174,870; giving activities include $1,647,460 for 70+ grants (high: $135,000).
Purpose and activities: Support for organizations providing health, social, and educational services for children and youth; support also for programs that promote the general welfare of the elderly and enhance their quality of life, and for a limited number of charities that conduct activities in the State of Israel, including programs that foster improved relations between Jews and Arabs.
Fields of interest: Elementary/secondary education; Education, early childhood education; Education; Human services; Children/youth, services; Aging, centers/services; Aging; Economically disadvantaged.
International interests: Israel.
Type of support: General/operating support; Continuing support; Program development; Matching/challenge support.
Limitations: Giving primarily in the metropolitan New York, NY, area. No support for religious organizations for religious purposes, or for public interest litigation or antivivisectionist causes. No grants to individuals, or for foreign travel or foreign study.
Publications: Application guidelines; Grants list; Informational brochure (including application guidelines); Multi-year report.
Application information: The foundation accepts the New York Area Common Application Form. Review funding guidelines and application procedures on foundation Web site before submitting letter of inquiry. Application form not required.
  Initial approach: Letter of inquiry (not exceeding 2 pages); submit formal funding proposal upon invitation
  Copies of proposal: 2
  Deadline(s): None
  Board meeting date(s): Quarterly
  Final notification: 30-60 days
Officers and Directors:* Robert S. Gassman,* Pres.; Peter A. Herbert,* V.P.; Ernest Rubenstein,* Secy.; Edgar H. Brenner,* Treas.; Elizabeth Olofson, Exec. Dir.; Charles S. Brenner; Paul R. Gassman; Benjamin Herbert; William S. Rubenstein.
Number of staff: 3 full-time professional.
EIN: 136103039
Selected grants: The following grants were reported in 2005.
$135,000 to New Israel Fund, Jerusalem, Israel. For Shatil, which provides technical assistance to Israeli nonprofits; for programs that promote Jewish-Arab equality and co-existence; for Hillel/Open Gates for the newly secular; and for general program support.
$50,000 to Harlem Childrens Zone, New York, NY. For after-school, weekend, and summer programs serving youth and their families at newly built community center in Central Harlem, including students attending new charter school, Promise Academy.
$45,000 to Creative Center for Women with Cancer, New York, NY. For artist-in-residence program in New York area hospitals and hospices.
$45,000 to YM-YWHA, Samuel Field, Little Neck, NY. For nursing services at new model of Naturally-Occurring Retirement Communities (NORC) supportive service program, serving seniors in community of one- and two-family homes in Northeast Queens.
$40,000 to Tel Aviv University: American Council, New York, NY. For Price Brodie Initiative, providing educational enrichment programs to disadvantaged Arab and Jewish elementary school children in Jaffa, Israel.
$30,000 to Claremont Neighborhood Centers, Bronx, NY. For capacity building project to improve leadership and management.
$30,000 to KIPP (Knowledge is Power Program) Academy, Bronx, NY. For KIPP to College, 4-year program that offers academic support, test preparation services and college placement guidance for KIPP middle school alumni.
$25,000 to Givat Haviva Educational Foundation, New York, NY. For program of Jewish-Arab Center for Peace that foster improve relations between Jewish and Arab high school students.
$10,000 to Partner for Surgery, McLean, VA. For general support.
$10,000 to Womens Project and Productions, New York, NY. For Ten Centuries of Women Playwrights, curriculum-based theater art education program sponsored by nation's oldest theater company, dedicated to development and production of new plays by women.

6125

H.R.C. Foundation, Inc. ✧

c/o John M. Emery
909 3rd Ave., 5th Fl.
New York, NY 10022

Donors: Hays Clark; H. Lawrence Clark.
Foundation type: Independent foundation.
Financial data (yr. ended 12/31/05): Assets, $888,520 (M); expenditures, $740,201; qualifying distributions, $728,726; giving activities include $706,000 for 9 grants (high: $150,000; low: $1,000).
Fields of interest: Education; Disasters, Hurricane Katrina; Human services; Community development.
Limitations: Applications not accepted. Giving on a national basis, with some emphasis on the greater metropolitan Washington, DC, area, including MD and VA. No grants to individuals.
Application information: Contributes only to pre-selected organizations.
Officers and Directors:* Rosamond S. Clark,* Chair.; H. Lawrence Clark,* Pres. and Treas.; Harris W. Clark,* V.P.; Valerie C. McNeely,* V.P.; Edward H. Hein, Secy.
EIN: 132962149

6126

The Marc Haas Foundation, Inc. ✧

c/o Blank Rome LLP
405 Lexington Ave., 14th Fl.
New York, NY 10174-0208
Contact: Robert H. Haines, Pres.

Established in 1985 in NY.
Foundation type: Independent foundation.
Financial data (yr. ended 12/31/03): Assets, $45,805,364 (M); expenditures, $2,742,331; qualifying distributions, $1,991,520; giving activities include $1,877,500 for 65 grants (high: $250,000; low: $5,000; average: $10,000–$25,000).
Purpose and activities: Giving primarily for the arts and education.
Fields of interest: Media/communications; Museums; Performing arts centers; Education; Health organizations.
Type of support: General/operating support; Fellowships.
Limitations: Giving primarily in NJ, and New York, NY. No loans or program-related investments.
Application information: Application form not required.
  Initial approach: Letter
  Deadline(s): None
Officers and Directors:* Stanley S. Shuman,* Chair.; Robert H. Haines,* Pres.
EIN: 133073137
Selected grants: The following grants were reported in 2003.
$250,000 to Columbia University, New York, NY.
$250,000 to Harvard University, Cambridge, MA.
$62,500 to American Museum of Natural History, New York, NY.
$50,000 to Metropolitan Museum of Art, New York, NY.
$50,000 to Museum of Television and Radio, New York, NY.
$50,000 to Rockefeller University, New York, NY.
$30,000 to Manhattan Theater Club, New York, NY.
$25,000 to Museum of Modern Art, New York, NY.
$25,000 to Solomon R. Guggenheim Museum, New York, NY.
$25,000 to Whitney Museum of American Art, New York, NY.

6127

The Helen Hotze Haas Foundation, Inc. ✧

c/o Blank Rome LLP
405 Lexington Ave., 14th Fl.
New York, NY 10174 (212) 885-5000
Contact: Robert H. Haines, Pres.

Established in 1995 in DE and NY.
Foundation type: Independent foundation.
Financial data (yr. ended 12/31/04): Assets, $25,785,029 (M); expenditures, $1,701,910; qualifying distributions, $1,136,787; giving activities include $1,066,000 for 48 grants (high: $150,000; low: $5,000).
Purpose and activities: Giving primarily for education, hospitals, children and social services, federated giving programs, a community fund, and a park conservancy.
Fields of interest: Performing arts, orchestra (symphony); Higher education; Education; Environment, natural resources; Hospitals (general); Human services; Children, services; Federated giving programs.

Limitations: Giving primarily in NY. No grants to individuals.
Application information:
 Initial approach: Letter
 Deadline(s): None
Officers and Directors:* Stanley S. Shuman,* Chair.; Robert H. Haines,* Pres.
EIN: 133836626
Selected grants: The following grants were reported in 2004.
$150,000 to Rockefeller University, New York, NY.
$56,000 to New York Community Trust, New York, NY.
$25,000 to Hospital for Special Surgery, New York, NY.
$25,000 to Lenox Hill Hospital, New York, NY.
$25,000 to Mount Sinai Medical Center, New York, NY.
$25,000 to Prep for Prep, New York, NY.
$25,000 to Trickle Up Program, New York, NY.
$15,000 to Caramoor Center for Music and the Arts, Katonah, NY.
$15,000 to Literacy Partners, New York, NY.
$10,000 to Childrens Museum of Manhattan, New York, NY.

6128
The Habe Foundation ✧ ☆
c/o Tanton & Co., LLP
37 W. 57th St., 5th Fl.
New York, NY   10019

Established in 2004 in NY.
Donor: John Klingenstein.
Foundation type: Independent foundation.
Financial data (yr. ended 12/31/05): Assets, $8,678,151 (M); gifts received, $3,969,368; expenditures, $858,953; qualifying distributions, $700,000; giving activities include $700,000 for grants.
Fields of interest: Museums (history).
Limitations: Applications not accepted.
Application information: Unsolicited requests for funds not accepted.
Officers: Nancy K. Simpkins, Pres.; Thomas D. Klingenstein, V.P. & Secy.; Andrew D. Klingen, Treas.
EIN: 201366114

6129
Amy and James Haber Foundation ✧
340 E. 64th St., Ste. 5K
New York, NY   10021

Established in 2000 in NY.
Donor: James Haber.
Foundation type: Independent foundation.
Financial data (yr. ended 12/31/05): Assets, $651,984 (M); gifts received, $725,550; expenditures, $542,135; qualifying distributions, $537,265; giving activities include $536,232 for 69 grants (high: $52,000; low: $70; average: $1,000–$10,000).
Purpose and activities: Giving primarily for Jewish agencies, temples and schools.
Fields of interest: Education; Human services; Jewish agencies & temples.
Limitations: Applications not accepted. No grants to individuals.
Application information: Contributes only to pre-selected organizations.

Trustee: James Haber.
EIN: 134144231

6130
Hagedorn Fund ✧
c/o JPMorgan Chase Bank, N.A., Global Foundations Group
345 Park Ave., 4th Fl.
New York, NY   10154   (212) 464-2443
Contact: Monica J. Neal, V.P., JPMorgan Chase Bank, N.A.
E-mail: neal_monica@jpmorgan.com; URL: http://foundationcenter.org/grantmaker/hagedorn/

Trust established in 1953 in NY.
Donor: William Hagedorn†.
Foundation type: Independent foundation.
Financial data (yr. ended 12/31/05): Assets, $43,597,957 (M); expenditures, $2,290,236; qualifying distributions, $2,070,543; giving activities include $1,900,000 for 90 grants (high: $50,000; low: $1,000).
Purpose and activities: Support for health (including cancer, HIV/AIDS, blindness), gardens, social services, youth, education, senior services, and housing and community development.
Fields of interest: Education; Botanical gardens; Health care; Cancer; AIDS; Housing/shelter; Youth development; Human services; Community development; Aging.
Type of support: General/operating support; Building/renovation; Program development.
Limitations: Giving primarily in New York, NY. No grants to individuals, or for continuing support, seed money, emergency funds, deficit financing, endowment funds, matching gifts, scholarships, fellowships, research, special projects, publications, or conferences; no loans.
Publications: Application guidelines; Grants list.
Application information: Almost all grants represent renewed support for previous grantees; few new grantees may be considered each year. Application form not required.
 Initial approach: Proposal
 Copies of proposal: 1
 Deadline(s): Sept. 15
 Board meeting date(s): Dec.
 Final notification: Dec. 31
Trustees: John J. Kindred III; Malcolm E. Martin; JPMorgan Chase Bank, N.A.
EIN: 136048718
Selected grants: The following grants were reported in 2004.
$65,000 to Wells College, Aurora, NY.
$35,000 to Riverdale Presbyterian Church, Bronx, NY.
$30,000 to New York Botanical Garden, Bronx, NY.
$25,000 to Brooklyn Botanic Garden, Brooklyn, NY.
$25,000 to Brooklyn Bureau of Community Service, Brooklyn, NY.
$25,000 to Cancer Research Institute, New York, NY.
$25,000 to Community Service Society of New York, New York, NY.
$25,000 to Inner-City Scholarship Fund, New York, NY.
$25,000 to New York University, School of Medicine, New York, NY.
$20,000 to Highbridge Community Life Center, Bronx, NY.

6131
Hager Family Charitable Trust ✧ ☆
2202 Ave. J
Brooklyn, NY   11210
Contact: Markus Hager, Tr.

Established in 2004 in NY.
Donor: Mala Wassner†.
Foundation type: Independent foundation.
Financial data (yr. ended 12/31/05): Assets, $530,841 (M); expenditures, $378,204; qualifying distributions, $374,077; giving activities include $373,577 for 196+ grants (high: $50,000).
Fields of interest: Jewish agencies & temples.
Limitations: Giving primarily in NY.
Application information: Application form not required.
 Deadline(s): None
Trustees: Avery Hager; Markus Hager.
EIN: 116590952

6132
Margaret Voorhies Haggin Trust in Memory of Her Late Husband, James Ben Ali Haggin ✧
c/o The Bank of New York, Tax Dept.
1 Wall St., 28th Fl.
New York, NY   10286

Established in 1938 in NY.
Donor: Margaret Voorhies Haggin†.
Foundation type: Independent foundation.
Financial data (yr. ended 12/31/05): Assets, $24,350,470 (M); expenditures, $1,151,235; qualifying distributions, $1,056,481; giving activities include $1,009,465 for 13 grants (high: $334,975; low: $3,000).
Purpose and activities: Giving primarily for higher education, health care, and to Episcopal churches.
Fields of interest: Higher education; Hospitals (general); Protestant agencies & churches.
Limitations: Applications not accepted. Giving limited to KY. No grants to individuals.
Application information: Contributes only to pre-selected organizations.
Trustee: The Bank of New York.
EIN: 136078494

6133
Peter and Helen Haje Foundation ✧
44 W. 77th St., Ste. 14W
New York, NY   10024

Established in 2000 in NY.
Donor: Peter R. Haje.
Foundation type: Independent foundation.
Financial data (yr. ended 12/31/04): Assets, $9,204,387 (M); expenditures, $754,660; qualifying distributions, $665,000; giving activities include $665,000 for 53 grants (high: $70,000; low: $2,000).
Purpose and activities: Support primarily for higher education and the performing arts; giving also for legal services.
Fields of interest: Performing arts, dance; Higher education; Law school/education; Education; Legal services; Human services; Children/youth, services; Civil rights.
Limitations: Applications not accepted. Giving on a national basis. No grants to individuals.

Application information: Contributes only to pre-selected organizations.
Officers: Peter R. Haje, Chair.; Helen Haje, Pres. and Treas.; Katie Haje, V.P. and Secy.; Michael Haje, V.P.
EIN: 134112185
Selected grants: The following grants were reported in 2003.
$85,000 to Dance Theater Workshop, New York, NY.
$60,000 to Legal Aid Society, New York, NY.
$25,000 to Harvard University, Law School, Cambridge, MA.
$20,000 to School of American Ballet, New York, NY.
$20,000 to Yale University, Law School, New Haven, CT.
$15,000 to Brearley School, New York, NY.
$15,000 to Cornell University, Ithaca, NY.
$10,000 to Human Rights First, New York, NY.
$5,000 to Legal Action Center, DC.
$5,000 to Queens College of the City University of New York Foundation, Flushing, NY.

6134
The Hajim Family Foundation ◇
c/o Mahoney, Cohen & Co.
1065 Ave. of the Americas
New York, NY 10018-2506

Established in 1987 in NY.
Donor: Edmund A. Hajim.
Foundation type: Independent foundation.
Financial data (yr. ended 12/31/05): Assets, $4,293,291 (M); gifts received, $162,950; expenditures, $492,086; qualifying distributions, $473,736; giving activities include $473,736 for 43 grants (high: $241,806; low: $100).
Purpose and activities: Giving to higher education, hospitals, health associations, and Jewish agencies; some funding also to community funds and the arts.
Fields of interest: Museums (art); Performing arts centers; Historic preservation/historical societies; Arts; Elementary/secondary education; Higher education; Education; Environment; Hospitals (general); Human services; Children/youth, services; Community development.
Limitations: Applications not accepted. Giving primarily in CT, MA, and NY. No grants to individuals.
Application information: Contributes only to pre-selected organizations.
Trustees: Barbara Hajim; Edmund A. Hajim.
EIN: 136893956
Selected grants: The following grants were reported in 2005.
$63,550 to Nantucket Historical Association, Nantucket, MA.
$25,000 to Nantucket Conservation Foundation, Nantucket, MA.
$11,350 to Ocean Reef Medical Center, Key Largo, FL.
$10,000 to Greenwich Hospital, Greenwich, CT.
$5,000 to New York Academy of Art, New York, NY.
$3,500 to Metropolitan Museum of Art, New York, NY.
$1,000 to Nantucket Cottage Hospital, Nantucket, MA.
$1,000 to Nantucket Film Festival, New York, NY.
$1,000 to Nantucket Land Council, Nantucket, MA.
$100 to Berkshire Hills Music Academy, Newton, MA.

6135
Halcyon Hill Foundation ◇
c/o JPMorgan Chase Bank, N.A.
P.O. Box 506
Webster, NY 14580   (585) 442-6560
Contact: Annette Weld Ph.D., Dir.
FAX: (315) 524-6240; E-mail: hhf@hhf.org;
URL: http://www.hhf.org

Established in 1991 in NY.
Donors: Anne G. Whitman; Anne Whitman Charitable Lead Trust.
Foundation type: Independent foundation.
Financial data (yr. ended 6/30/05): Assets, $14,028,745 (M); gifts received, $79,920; expenditures, $788,452; qualifying distributions, $654,094; giving activities include $588,570 for 60 grants (high: $169,370; low: $20).
Purpose and activities: Giving primarily for programs that benefit children ages 0-5.
Fields of interest: Arts; Education, early childhood education; Education; Health care; Children/youth, services.
Limitations: Giving primarily in Rochester, NY. No grants to individuals.
Publications: Grants list; Informational brochure.
Application information: The foundation accepts the Rochester Grantmakers Forum Common Application and Common Report forms, which may be downloaded from URL: http://www.grantmakers.org. Application form required.
Initial approach: Letter or telephone
Deadline(s): None
Board meeting date(s): May and Nov.
Directors: Rennie Chaintreuil; Bradley R. Whitman; Catherine A. Whitman; Sara G. Whitman.
Trustee: JPMorgan Chase Bank, N.A.
Number of staff: 1 part-time professional.
EIN: 161553256
Selected grants: The following grants were reported in 2004.
$169,370 to Strong Memorial Hospital of the University of Rochester, Golisano Children's Hospital, Rochester, NY.
$50,000 to Rochester Area Community Foundation, Rochester, NY.
$25,000 to Strategies for Children, Boston, MA.
$19,500 to Hearing and Speech Center of Rochester, Rochester, NY.
$15,000 to Growing Place at Corpus Christi, Rochester, NY.
$12,500 to David Hochstein Memorial Music School, Rochester, NY.
$10,000 to Rochester Institute of Technology, Rochester, NY.
$10,000 to Rochester Philharmonic Orchestra, Rochester, NY.
$10,000 to United Way of Greater Rochester, Rochester, NY.
$10,000 to Westside Health Services, Rochester, NY.

6136
Halis Family Foundation ◇ ☆
c/o Tyndall Management, LLC
559 Lexington Ave., Ste. 4100
New York, NY 10022
Contact: Jeffrey Halis, Tr.

Established in 2003 in NY.
Donors: Jeffrey Halis; Nancy Halis.
Foundation type: Independent foundation.

Financial data (yr. ended 12/31/05): Assets, $3,526,265 (M); gifts received, $2,600,137; expenditures, $477,701; qualifying distributions, $461,431; giving activities include $460,350 for 20 grants (high: $200,000; low: $250).
Fields of interest: Performing arts centers; Elementary/secondary education; Higher education; Education; Human services; Children/youth, services; Family services; Jewish federated giving programs.
Limitations: Giving primarily in New York, NY; some funding nationally.
Application information:
Initial approach: Submit resume
Deadline(s): None
Trustees: Jeffrey Halis; Nancy Halis.
EIN: 306060775

6137
The George E. Hall Childhood Diabetes Foundation ◇
c/o Clinton Group, Inc.
9 W. 57th St., 26th Fl.
New York, NY 10019

Established in 2002 in NJ.
Donor: George E. Hall.
Foundation type: Independent foundation.
Financial data (yr. ended 12/31/03): Assets, $2,064 (M); gifts received, $301,315; expenditures, $385,010; qualifying distributions, $381,342; giving activities include $376,000 for 3 grants (high: $150,000; low: $86,000).
Purpose and activities: Giving primarily for pediatric diabetes.
Fields of interest: Medical school/education; Hospitals (general); Diabetes research.
Limitations: Applications not accepted. Giving primarily in New York, NY.
Application information: Contributes only to pre-selected organizations.
Trustee: George E. Hall.
EIN: 226919353

6138
Mary P. Dolciani Halloran Foundation ◇ ☆
825 3rd Ave., 25th Fl.
New York, NY 10022-7519

Established in 1982.
Donor: Mary P. Dolciani Halloran†.
Foundation type: Independent foundation.
Financial data (yr. ended 12/31/05): Assets, $6,365,080 (M); expenditures, $542,023; qualifying distributions, $521,589; giving activities include $335,500 for 28 grants (high: $65,000; low: $5,000).
Purpose and activities: Giving primarily for Catholic organizations.
Fields of interest: Elementary/secondary education; Education; Health care; Human services; Roman Catholic agencies & churches.
Type of support: General/operating support; Equipment.
Limitations: Applications not accepted. Giving on a national basis. No grants to individuals.
Application information: Contributes only to pre-selected organizations.
Officers: Concepcion G. Halloran, V.P.; Denise Lyn Halloran, V.P.; Eugene J. Callahan, V.P.

Trustees: Thomas D. Quinn; Emilio Torres.
EIN: 133147449
Selected grants: The following grants were reported in 2004.
$35,000 to Sequim High School, Sequim, WA. For general support.
$25,000 to Mathematical Association of America, DC. For general support.
$15,000 to Port Angeles High School, Port Angeles, WA. For scholarships.
$13,000 to YWCA of Olympia, Olympia, WA. For general support.
$10,000 to Inner-City Scholarship Fund, New York, NY. For general support.
$10,000 to John F. Kennedy Catholic High School, Warren, OH. For general support.
$10,000 to Resurrection School. For general support.
$10,000 to Saint Michaels School, Olympia, WA. For general support.
$10,000 to Sequim Aquatic Recreation Center, Sequim, WA. For general support.
$10,000 to Sequim Food Bank, Sequim, WA. For general support.

6139
The Hammerman and Fisch Foundation ◇
(formerly The Stephen & Eleanor Hammerman Foundation)
1806 Bay Blvd.
Atlantic Beach, NY 11509

Established in 1993 in NY.
Donor: Stephen Hammerman.
Foundation type: Independent foundation.
Financial data (yr. ended 12/31/05): Assets, $5,118,127 (M); expenditures, $2,003,998; qualifying distributions, $1,958,921; giving activities include $1,958,742 for 169 grants (high: $500,000; low: $64).
Purpose and activities: Giving primarily to Jewish causes, including temples. Some support also for medicine and health associations, higher education, and community.
Fields of interest: Education; Health organizations, association; Human services; Federated giving programs; Jewish federated giving programs; Jewish agencies & temples.
Limitations: Applications not accepted. Giving primarily in NY. No grants to individuals.
Application information: Contributes only to pre-selected organizations.
Trustees: Caryn Fisch; Charles Hammerman; Eleanor Hammerman; Ira Hammerman; Michael Hammerman; Stephen Hammerman.
EIN: 116436649

6140
The Handler Family Foundation ◇
25 Woodway Rd.
South Salem, NY 10590

Established in 2001 in NY.
Donors: Martha Handler; Richard Handler.
Foundation type: Independent foundation.
Financial data (yr. ended 11/30/04): Assets, $1,113,506 (M); expenditures, $735,865; qualifying distributions, $735,565; giving activities include $735,470 for 42 grants (high: $149,000; low: $25).

Purpose and activities: Giving primarily for health care including cancer research, youth, community and social services; some giving also for education and the environment.
Fields of interest: Arts; Business school/education; Libraries (public); Education; Environment, water resources; Environment, land resources; Environment; Health care; Health organizations, association; Prostate cancer research; Recreation, parks/playgrounds; Athletics/sports, fishing/hunting; Big Brothers/Big Sisters; Human services.
Limitations: Applications not accepted. Giving in the U.S., primarily in NY and CA. No grants to individuals.
Application information: Contributes only to pre-selected organizations.
Officers: Richard Handler, Pres.; Martha Handler, V.P.
EIN: 137314630

6141
Milton and Miriam Handler Foundation ◇
225 Broadway, Ste. 1806
New York, NY 10007 (212) 964-5485
Contact: Albert Kalter, Secy.

Established in 1963.
Donor: Milton Handler‡.
Foundation type: Independent foundation.
Financial data (yr. ended 12/31/05): Assets, $11,462,528 (M); expenditures, $1,193,299; qualifying distributions, $910,851; giving activities include $801,580 for 28 grants (high: $100,000; low: $2,500).
Purpose and activities: Giving primarily for higher education, particularly to law schools and medical schools; funding also for Jewish organizations.
Fields of interest: Higher education, university; Law school/education; Medical school/education; Jewish agencies & temples.
Limitations: Giving on a national basis, with some emphasis on NY. No grants to individuals.
Application information:
Initial approach: Letter
Deadline(s): Oct. 31
Officers: Lawrence Newman, Pres.; Albert Kalter, Secy.
Director: Dahlia Kalter.
EIN: 136136957
Selected grants: The following grants were reported in 2003.
$50,000 to Columbia University, New York, NY. For general support.
$50,000 to New York University, School of Law, New York, NY. For general support.
$25,000 to American Friends of the Hebrew University, New York, NY. For general support.
$25,000 to Pace University, New York, NY. For general support.
$25,000 to Stanford University, Law School, Stanford, CA. For general support.
$25,000 to University of Chicago, Law School, Chicago, IL. For general support.
$25,000 to University of Pennsylvania, Law School, Philadelphia, PA. For general support.
$10,000 to NAACP Legal Defense and Educational Fund, New York, NY. For general support.
$10,000 to Touro Law Center Development Foundation, New York, NY. For general support.
$5,000 to Drexel University, Philadelphia, PA. For general support.

6142
Hansen Family Foundation, Inc. ◇ ☆
c/o Bessemer Trust
630 5th Ave.
New York, NY 10111

Established in 2000 in WI.
Donors: Donna L. Hansen; John J. Hansen.
Foundation type: Independent foundation.
Financial data (yr. ended 12/31/05): Assets, $10,553,048 (M); expenditures, $459,129; qualifying distributions, $407,662; giving activities include $404,652 for 8 grants (high: $100,000; low: $10,000).
Fields of interest: Roman Catholic federated giving programs; Roman Catholic agencies & churches.
Limitations: Applications not accepted. Giving primarily in La Crosse, WI. No grants to individuals.
Application information: Contributes only to pre-selected organizations.
Officers: Donna L. Hansen, Chair.; John J. Hansen, Pres.; Mary B. Brennan, 1st V.P.; Paul E. Hansen, 2nd V.P.; Amy L. Hansen-Strom, Secy.; Mark W. Hansen, Treas.
EIN: 392011330
Selected grants: The following grants were reported in 2005.
$100,000 to Franciscan Skemp Foundation, La Crosse, WI.
$25,000 to Viterbo University, La Crosse, WI.
$10,000 to La Crosse Symphony Orchestra, La Crosse, WI.
$10,000 to Starboard Media Foundation, Green Bay, WI.

6143
The Jerry and Janet Harary Family Foundation ◇ ☆
1942 E. 5th St.
Brooklyn, NY 11223
Contact: Jerry Harary, Pres.

Established in 2004 in NY.
Donors: Michael Harary; Jerry Harary.
Foundation type: Independent foundation.
Financial data (yr. ended 12/31/05): Assets, $5,713 (M); gifts received, $79,980; expenditures, $347,657; qualifying distributions, $343,703; giving activities include $343,701 for 43 grants (high: $116,000; low: $100).
Fields of interest: Jewish agencies & temples.
Limitations: Giving primarily in NY.
Application information: Application form not required.
Initial approach: Letter
Deadline(s): None
Officers and Directors:* Jerry Harary,* Pres.; Janet Harary, V.P.; Michael Harary,* Secy.; Leon Harary,* Treas.
EIN: 562444173

6144
Harbor Lights Foundation ◇
c/o BCRS Assocs., LLC
100 Wall St., 11th Fl.
New York, NY 10005

Established in 1980 in CT.
Donor: J. Fred Weintz, Jr.
Foundation type: Independent foundation.

Financial data (yr. ended 4/30/05): Assets, $11,245,974 (M); gifts received, $451,146; expenditures, $555,851; qualifying distributions, $510,224; giving activities include $465,500 for 41 grants (high: $150,000; low: $250).
Fields of interest: Higher education; Business school/education; Medicine/medical care, public education; Health organizations, association; Human services; Children/youth, services; Foundations (community).
Limitations: Applications not accepted. Giving on a national basis, primarily in CT, NY, and MA. No grants to individuals.
Application information: Contributes only to pre-selected organizations.
Trustees: Elizabeth Weintz Cerf; H. Frederick Krimendahl II; Polly Weintz Sanna; Elisabeth B. Weintz; Eric Cortelyou Weintz; J. Fred Weintz, Jr.; Karl Fredrick Weintz.
EIN: 133052490
Selected grants: The following grants were reported in 2005.
$125,000 to Stanford University, Stanford, CA.
$50,000 to Norwich University, Northfield, VT.
$30,000 to Pace University, New York, NY.
$15,000 to Christ Episcopal Church, Greenwich, CT.
$13,000 to AmeriCares, Stamford, CT. 2 grants: $1,000, $12,000
$2,500 to University of Denver, Denver, CO.
$2,000 to Brunswick School, Greenwich, CT.
$1,500 to Chapin School, New York, NY.
$750 to Greenwich Library, Greenwich, CT.

6145
Harkness Foundation for Dance ◇

145 E. 48th St., Ste. 26C
New York, NY 10017
Contact: Theodore S. Bartwink, Exec. Dir.

William Hale Harkness Foundation established in 1936 in NY; Harkness Ballet Foundation established in 1959 in NY; adopted current name in 1973.
Donors: William Hale Harkness†; Rebekah Harkness†.
Foundation type: Independent foundation.
Financial data (yr. ended 12/31/05): Assets, $17,167,803 (M); expenditures, $1,888,189; qualifying distributions, $1,620,614; giving activities include $1,373,900 for 199 grants (high: $119,000; low: $250; average: $1,500–$10,000).
Purpose and activities: Support primarily for arts and cultural programs.
Fields of interest: Performing arts; Performing arts, dance; Arts.
Type of support: General/operating support; Program development; Curriculum development; Scholarship funds.
Limitations: Giving primarily in NY. No support for private schools, or for religious organizations. No grants to individuals, or for endowments, capital projects, or for film and video projects.
Publications: Application guidelines.
Application information: Application form not required.
  Initial approach: Letter; no telephone calls
  Copies of proposal: 1
  Deadline(s): None
  Board meeting date(s): Quarterly
  Final notification: After meetings
Officers and Directors: * William A. Perlmuth,* Pres.; Etta Brandman, V.P.; Theodore S. Bartwink,* Secy.-Treas. and Exec. Dir.

Number of staff: 2 full-time professional.
EIN: 131926551

6146
Gladys and Roland Harriman Foundation ▼

c/o Brown Brothers Harriman Trust Co., LLC
140 Broadway, 4th Fl.
New York, NY 10005
Contact: Barbara O'Connell, Secy.

Established in 1966 in NY.
Donors: Roland Harriman†; Gladys Harriman†.
Foundation type: Independent foundation.
Financial data (yr. ended 12/31/04): Assets, $114,831,776 (M); expenditures, $6,617,568; qualifying distributions, $6,200,285; giving activities include $6,000,059 for 114 grants (high: $500,000; low: $1,000; average: $5,000–$250,000).
Purpose and activities: Giving primarily for education; support also for youth and social service agencies, arts and cultural organizations, and health agencies and hospitals.
Fields of interest: Education; Hospitals (general); Health care; Health organizations, association; Human services; Children/youth, services.
Type of support: General/operating support; Employee matching gifts; Matching/challenge support.
Limitations: Giving on a national basis. No grants to individuals.
Application information: Application form not required.
  Initial approach: Letter
  Copies of proposal: 1
  Deadline(s): None
  Board meeting date(s): May and Nov.
Officers and Directors: * Elbridge T. Gerry, Jr.,* Pres.; Thomas F. Dixon,* V.P.; Barbara O'Connell,* Secy.; Anna T. Korniczky, Treas.; Crispin H. Connery; Anthony T. Enders; Terrence M. Farley; Wilhelm E. Northrop.
Number of staff: 2 full-time professional; 2 full-time support.
EIN: 510193915
Selected grants: The following grants were reported in 2004.
$575,000 to Boys Club of New York, New York, NY. 2 grants: $175,000 (For general support), $400,000 (For general support).
$500,000 to American Red Cross in Greater New York, New York, NY. For general support.
$400,000 to American Museum of Natural History, New York, NY. For general support.
$250,000 to University of Minnesota, Medical School, Minneapolis, MN. For general support.
$125,000 to Montefiore Medical Center, Bronx, NY. For general support.
$25,000 to American Red Cross, Mid-Coast Chapter, Brunswick, ME. For general support.
$25,000 to Weill Medical College of Cornell University, New York, NY. For general support.
$20,000 to Bowdoin Summer Music Festival, Brunswick, ME. For general support.
$10,000 to Tuxedo Volunteer Ambulance Corps, Tuxedo Park, NY. For general support.

6147
Mary W. Harriman Foundation

c/o Brown Brothers Harriman Trust Co.
140 Broadway, 4th Fl.
New York, NY 10005
Contact: Barbara O'Connell, Secy.

Trust established in 1925 in NY; incorporated in 1973.
Donor: Mary W. Harriman†.
Foundation type: Independent foundation.
Financial data (yr. ended 12/31/04): Assets, $29,366,613 (M); expenditures, $1,363,524; qualifying distributions, $1,267,929; giving activities include $1,198,500 for 121 grants (high: $60,000; low: $1,000).
Fields of interest: Media, television; Media, radio; Performing arts; Arts; Elementary/secondary education; Higher education; Education; Animals/wildlife; Hospitals (general); Health organizations, association; Human services; Children/youth, services.
Type of support: General/operating support; Annual campaigns; Capital campaigns.
Limitations: Giving primarily in the metropolitan New York, NY, area, and in New York State; some funding nationally, particularly in CO, CT, MA and VT. No grants to individuals.
Application information: Application form not required.
  Initial approach: Typewritten proposal
  Copies of proposal: 1
  Deadline(s): None
  Board meeting date(s): Dec.
  Final notification: 1 month
Officers and Directors: * David H. Mortimer,* Pres.; Kathleen L.F. Ames,* V.P.; Barbara O'Connell, Secy.; Anna T. Korniczky, Treas.; Marjorie Northrop Friedman; Kathleen H. Mortimer.
Number of staff: 2 full-time professional; 2 full-time support.
EIN: 237356000
Selected grants: The following grants were reported in 2003.
$60,000 to School for Language and Communication Development, Glen Cove, NY.
$45,000 to World Wildlife Fund, DC.
$25,000 to Storm King Art Center, Mountainville, NY.
$15,000 to W G B H Educational Foundation, Boston, MA.
$15,000 to Yale University, New Haven, CT.
$10,000 to Harness Racing Museum and Hall of Fame, Goshen, NY.
$10,000 to Memorial Sloan-Kettering Cancer Center, New York, NY.
$6,000 to Grosvenor Neighborhood House, New York, NY.
$5,000 to Bates College, Lewiston, ME.
$5,000 to University of Colorado, Boulder, CO.

6148
J. Ira and Nicki Harris Foundation, Inc. ◇

c/o Rothstein Kass & Co.
1350 Ave. of the Americas, 15th fl.
New York, NY 10019

Donor: J. Ira Harris.
Foundation type: Independent foundation.
Financial data (yr. ended 3/31/05): Assets, $35,094,697 (M); expenditures, $2,411,710; qualifying distributions, $2,002,600; giving

activities include $2,002,600 for 86 grants (high: $360,000; low: $500).

Purpose and activities: Giving primarily for education, the arts, human services, health care, and Jewish giving.

Fields of interest: Museums (art); Performing arts; Higher education; Education; Health care; Youth development; Human services; Federated giving programs; Jewish federated giving programs; Jewish agencies & temples.

Type of support: General/operating support.

Limitations: Applications not accepted. Giving primarily in Washington, DC, Palm Beach and West Palm Beach, FL, Chicago, IL, and New York, NY. No grants to individuals.

Application information: Contributes only to pre-selected organizations.

Officers and Directors:* J. Ira Harris,* Pres.; Nicki Harris,* V.P.; Newton N. Minow, Secy.-Treas.; Jacqueline S. Harris; Jonathan Harris.

EIN: 650805468

Selected grants: The following grants were reported in 2003.

$300,000 to Norton Museum of Art, West Palm Beach, FL. 2 grants: $150,000 each (For general support).

$200,000 to Hostelling International-American Youth Hostels (HI-AYH), Silver Spring, MD. For general support.

$200,000 to Millennium Park, Chicago, IL. For general support.

$150,000 to John F. Kennedy Center for the Performing Arts, DC. For general support.

$50,000 to Community Chest-United Way of Palm Beach, Palm Beach, FL. For general support.

$50,000 to Jewish Federation of Palm Beach County, West Palm Beach, FL. For general support.

$50,000 to Jewish United Fund of Metropolitan Cincinnati, Cincinnati, OH. For general support.

$50,000 to Raymond F. Kravis Center for the Performing Arts, West Palm Beach, FL. For general support.

$50,000 to United Way of Metropolitan Chicago, Chicago, IL. For general support.

6149

Francena T. Harrison Foundation Trust ✧
c/o Deutsche Bank Trust Co. of NY
P.O. Box 1297, Church St. Sta.
New York, NY   10008

Established in 1986 in VA.

Donor: Francena T. Harrison†.

Foundation type: Independent foundation.

Financial data (yr. ended 4/30/05): Assets, $6,430,881 (M); expenditures, $541,943; qualifying distributions, $511,446; giving activities include $488,500 for grants.

Purpose and activities: Giving primarily to cultural institutions.

Fields of interest: Museums; Performing arts centers; Performing arts, theater; Performing arts, opera; Elementary school/education; Human services.

Type of support: General/operating support.

Limitations: Applications not accepted. Giving primarily in NY. No grants to individuals.

Application information: Contributes only to pre-selected organizations.

Trustee: Deutsche Bank Trust Co. of NY.

EIN: 136911262

Selected grants: The following grants were reported in 2004.

$95,000 to Brooklyn Academy of Music, Brooklyn, NY. For general support.

$60,000 to Metropolitan Opera, New York, NY. For general support.

$60,000 to Save Venice, New York, NY. For general support.

$25,000 to Lincoln Center Theater, New York, NY. For general support.

$25,000 to Manhattan School of Music, New York, NY. For general support.

$25,000 to New York City Opera, New York, NY. For general support.

$25,000 to Stuart Country Day School of the Sacred Heart, Princeton, NJ. For general support.

$25,000 to Trinity Counseling Service, Princeton, NJ. For general support.

$15,000 to Spoleto Festival USA, Charleston, SC. For general support.

$10,000 to Pomfret School, Pomfret, CT. For general support.

6150

The John A. Hartford Foundation, Inc. ▼ ✧
55 E. 59th St., 16th Fl.
New York, NY   10022   (212) 832-7788
Contact: Corrine H. Rieder, Exec. Dir.
FAX: (212) 593-4913; E-mail: mail@jhartfound.org;
URL: http://www.jhartfound.org

Established in 1929; incorporated in 1942 in NY.

Donors: John A. Hartford†; George L. Hartford†.

Foundation type: Independent foundation.

Financial data (yr. ended 12/31/05): Assets, $614,197,200 (M); expenditures, $35,566,319; qualifying distributions, $29,834,451; giving activities include $25,613,073 for 95 grants (high: $2,633,314; low: $500; average: $10,000–$608,230), $720,341 for employee matching gifts, and $611,225 for 3 foundation-administered programs.

Purpose and activities: The foundation addresses the unique health needs of the elderly, including long-term care, the use of medication in chronic health problems, increasing the nation's geriatric research and training capability, and improving the integration of financing and care delivery for comprehensive geriatric services.

Fields of interest: Health care; Geriatrics; Aging, centers/services; Aging.

Type of support: Continuing support; Program development; Conferences/seminars; Publication; Curriculum development; Fellowships; Research; Program evaluation; Employee matching gifts.

Limitations: Giving primarily on a national basis. No grants to individuals, or for annual or capital campaigns, building renovations, equipment, general operating support, technical assistance, seed money, emergency or endowment funds, or deficit financing.

Publications: Application guidelines; Annual report; Newsletter.

Application information: See foundation's Web site for exact guidelines. Do not send correspondence by fax or e-mail. Application form not required.

Initial approach: Letter or proposal
Copies of proposal: 1
Deadline(s): No set deadline, but initial inquiry should be made at least 6 months before funding is required

Board meeting date(s): Mar., June, Sept., and Dec.

Final notification: 6 weeks

Officers and Trustees:* Norman H. Volk,* Chair.; Kathryn D. Wriston,* Pres.; William T. Comfort, Jr.,* Secy.; Corrine H. Rieder, Treas. and Exec. Dir.; Samuel R. Gische, Cont. and Dir., Finance; James D. Farley, Chair. Emeritus; John H. Allen; Anson McCook Beard, Jr.; John J. Curley; James G. Kenan III; Christopher T.H. Pell; Barbara Paul Robinson; Margaret L. Wolff.

Number of staff: 8 full-time professional; 7 full-time support.

EIN: 131667057

Selected grants: The following grants were reported in 2005.

$10,740,685 to American Academy of Nursing, Milwaukee, WI. For Nursing Initiative Coordinating Center and Scholar Stipends renewal grant.

$2,595,890 to American Association of Colleges of Nursing, DC. For Enhancing Gerontology Content in Baccalaureate Nursing Education Programs.

$1,050,000 to Oregon Health and Science University, Portland, OR. For Center for Geriatric Nursing Excellence.

$1,050,000 to University of Arkansas for Medical Sciences, Little Rock, AR. For Center for Geriatric Nursing Excellence.

$473,742 to American Federation for Aging Research (AFAR), New York, NY. For Hartford Center of Excellence Network Resource Center.

6151

Shamai & Richu Hartman Family Foundation ✧
1639 52nd St.
Brooklyn, NY   11204

Established in 1993 in NY.

Donors: Alexander Hartman; Sima Hartman.

Foundation type: Independent foundation.

Financial data (yr. ended 11/30/04): Assets, $12,237,935 (M); expenditures, $496,630; qualifying distributions, $459,374; giving activities include $464,533 for 34+ grants (high: $31,000).

Fields of interest: Jewish federated giving programs; Jewish agencies & temples.

Limitations: Applications not accepted. No grants to individuals.

Application information: Contributes only to pre-selected organizations.

Trustees: Alexander Hartman; Sima Hartman.

EIN: 113189198

Selected grants: The following grants were reported in 2003.

$30,480 to Yeshiva Novominsk, Brooklyn, NY.

$15,950 to Congregation Sharei Tefila, Las Vegas, NV.

$10,500 to Sinai Academy, Brooklyn, NY.

$5,803 to Congregation Yismach Moshe, Brooklyn, NY.

$5,100 to Congregation Ohr Hachaim, Kew Gardens, NY.

$5,000 to Yeshiva of Spring Valley, Monsey, NY.

$4,772 to Agudath Israel of America, New York, NY.

$3,600 to Rabbinical Seminary of America, Forest Hills, NY.

$3,234 to Beth Medrash Govoha, Brooklyn, NY.

$1,550 to Kollel Shomrei Hachomos, Brooklyn, NY.

6152
William A. Haseltine Charitable Foundation ◆ ☆
c/o Starr and Co., LLC
350 Park Ave., 9th Fl.
New York, NY 10022

Established in 2001.
Donor: William A. Haseltine.
Foundation type: Independent foundation.
Financial data (yr. ended 12/31/04): Assets, $8,459,204 (M); gifts received, $130,950; expenditures, $459,493; qualifying distributions, $456,500; giving activities include $456,500 for grants.
Purpose and activities: Giving primarily to a health museum, a children's medical center, and for social services and philanthropy.
Fields of interest: Museums; Hospitals (general); Human services; Children, services; Family services; Civil rights; Philanthropy/voluntarism.
Limitations: Applications not accepted. No grants to individuals.
Application information: Contributes only to pre-selected organizations.
Officer: William A. Haseltine, Pres.
EIN: 134158761
Selected grants: The following grants were reported in 2004.
$125,000 to Brookings Institution, DC.
$25,000 to Amnesty International USA, New York, NY.
$25,000 to New York Academy of Sciences, New York, NY.
$25,000 to W N E T Channel 13, New York, NY.
$20,000 to American Academy in Berlin, New York, NY.
$5,000 to National Health Museum, DC.
$4,000 to Council on Foreign Relations, New York, NY.
$3,000 to Academy of American Poets, New York, NY.
$2,000 to Asia Society, New York, NY.
$2,000 to Meridian International Center, DC.

6153
A. & Z. Hasenfeld Foundation, Inc. ◆
580 5th Ave.
New York, NY 10036 (212) 575-0290
Contact: Alexander Hasenfeld, Pres.

Established in 1969.
Donors: Alexander Hasenfeld; Zissy Hasenfeld; Hasenfeld-Stein Inc.
Foundation type: Independent foundation.
Financial data (yr. ended 3/31/05): Assets, $95,959 (M); gifts received, $416,782; expenditures, $334,460; qualifying distributions, $334,114; giving activities include $334,114 for 478+ grants (high: $120,000).
Purpose and activities: Giving primarily to Jewish organizations.
Fields of interest: Elementary/secondary education; Human services; Jewish federated giving programs; Jewish agencies & temples.
Limitations: Giving on a national basis. No grants to individuals.
Application information: Application form not required.
Deadline(s): None

Officers and Trustees:* Alexander Hasenfeld,* Pres.; Zissy Hasenfeld,* Treas.
EIN: 237017589

6154
The Hau'Oli Mau Loa Foundation ◆
c/o Debevoise & Plimpton LLP
919 3rd Ave., 31st Fl.
New York, NY 10022-3902 (212) 909-6000

Established in 1990 in NY.
Donor: Helga Glaesel-Hollenback†.
Foundation type: Operating foundation.
Financial data (yr. ended 4/30/05): Assets, $4,737,389 (M); expenditures, $504,263; qualifying distributions, $460,462; giving activities include $370,000 for 4 grants (high: $250,000; low: $20,000).
Fields of interest: Food services; Human services.
Limitations: Applications not accepted. Giving primarily in HI; some funding nationally. No grants to individuals.
Application information: Contributes only to pre-selected organizations.
Officers and Directors:* Hans Bertram-Nothnagel,* Pres.; Wayne M. Pitluck,* V.P.; Gary M. Friedman, Secy.-Treas.
EIN: 133588071
Selected grants: The following grants were reported in 2004.
$372,500 to Aloha Harvest, Honolulu, HI.
$65,000 to Storybook Theater of Hawaii, Makaweli, HI.
$20,000 to College Connections Hawaii, Honolulu, HI.

6155
The Hauser Foundation, Inc. ◆
712 5th Ave.
New York, NY 10019-4102 (212) 956-3645
Contact: Rita E. Hauser, Pres.

Established in 1989 in NY.
Donors: Gustave M. Hauser; Rita E. Hauser.
Foundation type: Independent foundation.
Financial data (yr. ended 11/30/05): Assets, $43,134,580 (M); expenditures, $3,932,365; qualifying distributions, $3,643,989; giving activities include $3,342,141 for 38 grants (high: $1,251,000; low: $100).
Purpose and activities: Giving primarily for community funds and international affairs; some support for cultural organizations and the arts.
Fields of interest: Media/communications; Visual arts; Performing arts; Performing arts, music; Arts; International peace/security; International affairs, foreign policy; International human rights; Law/international law; Public policy, research; Government/public administration; General charitable giving; Women.
International interests: Israel; Middle East.
Type of support: Annual campaigns; Capital campaigns; Endowments; Program development; Conferences/seminars.
Limitations: Applications not accepted. No grants to individuals.
Application information: Unsolicited requests for funds not accepted.
Board meeting date(s): Fall

Officers and Directors:* Rita E. Hauser,* Pres.; Gustave M. Hauser, V.P. and Secy.-Treas.; Ronald J. Stein.
Number of staff: 1 full-time support.
EIN: 110016142
Selected grants: The following grants were reported in 2005.
$1,251,000 to Lincoln Center for the Performing Arts, New York, NY.
$500,000 to Museum of Television and Radio, New York, NY.
$100,000 to Human Rights Watch, New York, NY.
$100,000 to International Peace Academy, New York, NY.
$100,000 to International Rescue Committee, New York, NY.
$100,000 to New America Foundation, DC.
$100,000 to RAND Corporation, Santa Monica, CA.
$10,000 to Fulbright Association, DC.
$2,000 to Chamber Music Society of Lincoln Center, New York, NY.
$1,000 to American Associates of the Royal Academy Trust, New York, NY.

6156
The Havens Relief Fund Society
475 Riverside Dr., Rm. 1940
New York, NY 10115
Contact: Joyce R. Willis, Exec. Dir.

Incorporated in 1870 in NY.
Foundation type: Operating foundation.
Financial data (yr. ended 12/31/05): Assets, $24,939,450 (M); gifts received, $10,600; expenditures, $1,237,027; qualifying distributions, $1,074,339; giving activities include $708,231 for grants, and $73,871 for 57 grants to individuals (high: $2,500; low: $1,000; average: $1,000–$1,500).
Purpose and activities: A private operating foundation established for the relief of poverty and distress, and especially the affording of temporary relief to the unobtrusive suffering endured by industrious or worthy persons. Income distributed solely by almoners appointed by the Society, who are responsible for distribution of their respective grants among individual beneficiaries of their own selection in the five boroughs of New York City. All grants are strictly by invitation only.
Type of support: Grants to individuals.
Limitations: Applications not accepted. Giving limited to New York, NY. No support for institutions, organizations, or agencies.
Application information: Unsolicited requests for funds not accepted.
Board meeting date(s): Feb. and Dec.
Officers and Board Members:* Arthur V. Savage,* Pres.; Michael Loening,* V.P.; Russell G. D'Oench III,* Secy.; Paul J. Brignola,* Treas.; Joyce R. Willis, Exec. Dir.; Bayard D. Clarkson, M.D.; David C. Condliffe; JoAnn Delafield; Mildred Garcia, Ed. D.; Hon. Charles S. Haight, Jr.; Dianne Mack; Hon. Robert P. Patterson, Jr.; David L. Plimpton, Ph.D.; Hon. Charles P. Sifton; Hon. Laura Taylor Swain; Jose Tavares.
Number of staff: 2 full-time professional.
EIN: 135562382

6157
Hayden Family Foundation ✧
c/o WTAS, Inc.
452 5th Ave., 23rd Fl.
New York, NY 10018 (212) 525-4700
Contact: Marilyn Calister

Established in 1984 in NY.
Donor: Richard M. Hayden.
Foundation type: Independent foundation.
Financial data (yr. ended 2/28/05): Assets, $7,909,667 (M); expenditures, $527,533; qualifying distributions, $478,818; giving activities include $478,818 for 29 grants (high: $200,000; low: $6).
Purpose and activities: Giving primarily for education, and arts and culture, particularly theater, as well as for health and human services.
Fields of interest: Performing arts, theater; Arts; Secondary school/education; Higher education; Education; Health care; Health organizations, association; Human services.
International interests: England.
Limitations: Applications not accepted. Giving primarily in the U.S. and London, England. No grants to individuals, or for scholarships, gifts; no loans.
Publications: Financial statement; Grants list.
Application information: Contributes only to pre-selected organizations.
Trustees: Richard M. Hayden; Susan F. Hayden; Peter M. Sacerdote; Anthony Verdecchia.
EIN: 133248046

6158
Charles Hayden Foundation ▼
140 Broadway, 51st Fl.
New York, NY 10005 (212) 785-3677
Contact: Kenneth D. Merin, C.E.O. and Pres.
FAX: (212) 785-3689; E-mail: fdn@chf.org; Boston Office: c/o Grants Mgmt. Assocs., 77 Summer St., 8th Fl., Boston, MA 02110, tel.: (617) 426-7080, ext. 306; URL: http://www.charleshaydenfoundation.org

Incorporated in 1937 in NY.
Donor: Charles Hayden†.
Foundation type: Independent foundation.
Financial data (yr. ended 6/30/05): Assets, $326,305,440 (M); expenditures, $18,138,369; qualifying distributions, $16,273,382; giving activities include $15,068,395 for 185 grants (high: $599,350; low: $1,500; average: $15,000–$225,000).
Purpose and activities: To promote the mental, moral and physical development of children and youth ages five to eighteen, especially low-income youth, in the Boston, MA and New York, NY metropolitan areas. Program support grants are available for the expansion of programs with well-defined goals that are expected to be met in a specified time frame. "Bricks and mortar" capital support grants are available for renovation, expansion, construction, and acquisition of physical facilities and purchase of non-expendable equipment.
Fields of interest: Museums (children's); Elementary school/education; Secondary school/education; Education; Youth development; Children/youth, services.
Type of support: Continuing support; Capital campaigns; Building/renovation; Equipment; Land acquisition; Program development; Matching/challenge support.

Limitations: Giving limited to the metropolitan Boston, MA, and New York, NY areas (including the cities of Newark, Jersey City, and Paterson, NJ). No support for fraternal groups, religious organizations other than community youth-related projects, arts exposure programs, institutions of higher education except to support work on precollegiate programs (other than recruitment programs for a particular college), hospitals, hospices, or projects essentially medical in nature. No grants to individuals, or for endowment funds, operating budgets, fellowships, annual campaigns, emergency funds, deficit financing, publications, or conferences; no loans.
Publications: Application guidelines; Grants list.
Application information: Accepts NYRAG and AGM Common Grant Application forms; Boston area, 2 copies of proposal (one copy sent to New York City and one copy sent to Boston, MA); 1 copy for the NY/NJ area. Application form not required.
Initial approach: Proposal
Deadline(s): None
Board meeting date(s): 10 times per year
Final notification: Approximately 2 months
Officers and Trustees:* Kenneth D. Merin,* C.E.O. and Pres.; Kristen J. McCormack,* V.P.; Carol Van Atten, V.P., Progs.; Dean H. Steeger,* Secy.; Robert Howitt,* Treas.; Howard G. Wachenfeld.
Number of staff: 4 full-time professional; 1 full-time support.
EIN: 135562237
Selected grants: The following grants were reported in 2005.
$1,000,000 to Trust for Public Land, New York, NY. Toward construction of community playgrounds in New York City.
$525,000 to Good Shepherd Services, New York, NY. Toward youth programming in Red Hook, Brooklyn, payable over 3 years.
$350,000 to Brotherhood/Sister Sol, New York, NY. Toward purchase of land and support for sustaining their current programming.
$350,000 to Sports and Arts in Schools Foundation, Woodside, NY. Toward Summer School Sports and Arts Day Camps and Middle School Academics and Sports Summer Camps.
$300,000 to Goddard-Riverside Community Center, New York, NY. Toward continued support of OPTIONS replicaton project.
$275,000 to Cristo Rey High School, New York, NY. Toward renovations.
$200,000 to Building Educated Leaders for Life (BELL) Foundation, Dorchester, MA. Toward Black and Hispanic Boys Initiative.
$150,000 to Amer-I-Can Program, New York, NY. For program support in Brooklyn.
$150,000 to Center for Educational Innovation-Public Education Association (CEI-PEA), New York, NY. For program support.
$125,000 to ROCA, Chelsea, MA. Toward SOL Project (Strengthening Our Lives).
$100,000 to Bottom Line, Jamaica Plain, MA. Toward College Access and College Success Programs.
$100,000 to Boys and Girls Clubs of Boston, Boston, MA. For Youth Service Providers Network (YSPN) program.
$100,000 to Harlem RBI (Reviving Baseball in Inner-Cities), New York, NY. Toward construction of Field of Dreams.
$100,000 to Thompson Island Outward Bound Education Center, Boston, MA. Toward Choices program.

$97,500 to Wildlife Conservation Society, Bronx, NY. Toward After-School Adventures in Wildlife science program.
$75,000 to Project Hope-The New Direction, Queens Village, NY. Toward after-school program.
$75,000 to Rocking the Boat, Bronx, NY. To expand Student Advocate Program.
$75,000 to Womens Housing and Economic Development Corporation, Bronx, NY. Toward After-School Program.
$60,900 to Dorchester Youth Collaborative, Dorchester, MA. Toward Safe City Initiative.
$50,000 to StreetSquash, New York, NY. Toward After-School Program.

6159
The Lita Annenberg Hazen Foundation ✧
667 Madison Ave.
New York, NY 10021 (212) 751-4917

Established in 1996 in NY.
Foundation type: Independent foundation.
Financial data (yr. ended 12/31/04): Assets, $21,356,984 (M); expenditures, $1,313,244; qualifying distributions, $1,136,615; giving activities include $1,055,000 for 9 grants (high: $250,000; low: $5,000).
Purpose and activities: Giving primarily to an art museum, as well as for scientific and medical research.
Fields of interest: Museums (art); Organ diseases; Biomedicine; Cancer research; Biomedicine research.
Limitations: Applications not accepted. Giving primarily in NY. No grants to individuals.
Application information: Contributes only to pre-selected organizations.
Officers: Cynthia Polsky, Pres.; Adam Z. Cherry, V.P.; Alexander Polsky, V.P.; Nicholas Polsky, V.P.; Alison Cherry Zuber, V.P.; Leon Polsky, Secy. and Admin.
EIN: 137067727

6160
The Edward W. Hazen Foundation, Inc.
90 Broad St., Ste. 604
New York, NY 10004 (212) 889-3034
Contact: Lori Bezahler, Pres. and Secy.
FAX: (212) 889-3039; E-mail: hazen@hazenfoundation.org; URL: http://www.hazenfoundation.org

Incorporated in 1925 in CT.
Donors: Edward Warriner Hazen†; Helen Russell Hazen†; Lucy Abigail Hazen†; Mary Hazen Arnold†.
Foundation type: Independent foundation.
Financial data (yr. ended 12/31/05): Assets, $29,926,956 (M); expenditures, $2,033,937; qualifying distributions, $2,192,505; giving activities include $1,232,560 for grants, and $2,650 for 8 employee matching gifts.
Purpose and activities: The foundation's work is currently focused on public education and youth development. In the area of public education, interest is primarily in parent and community organizing and training around school reform issues. Similarly, in the area of youth development, proposals which focus on training young people to become community or peer organizers around concrete social issues are favored. Funding is

targeted at community-based and grassroots organizations.

Fields of interest: Education, public education; Youth development.

Type of support: Program development; Employee matching gifts.

Limitations: Applications not accepted. Giving on a national basis, with emphasis on Los Angeles, CA, Miami Dade County, FL, New York, NY, and the Mississippi Delta area. No support for service-oriented programs or projects in medicine or health sciences, engineering, law, public and business administration, juvenile justice, or schools or school districts. No grants to individuals, or for annual campaigns, deficit financing, building deficits, capital or endowment funds, scholarships, research, or fellowships; no loans.

Publications: Annual report.

Application information: Unsolicited requests for funds not accepted. Periodically, the foundation will issue requests for proposals and calls for letters of inquiry.

Board meeting date(s): Spring and fall

Officers and Trustees:* Madeline deLone,* Chair.; Marsha Bonner,* Vice-Chair.; Lori Bezahler,* Pres. and Secy.; Edward M. Sermier,* Treas.; Beverly Cross; Beverly Divers-White; Daniel HoSang; Angela Sanbrano.

Number of staff: 2 full-time professional; 2 full-time support.

EIN: 060646671

Selected grants: The following grants were reported in 2003.

$135,000 to Alliance for Quality Education, Brooklyn, NY.

$135,000 to Association of Community Organizations for Reform Now (ACORN), Chicago, IL. For Chicago Learning Campaign.

$120,000 to Cypress Hills Local Development Corporation, Brooklyn, NY.

$120,000 to Southern California Education Fund, Los Angeles, CA. For Los Angeles Metro Education Strategy.

$100,000 to Funders Collaborative on Youth Organizing, New York, NY.

$90,000 to Farmworker Association of Florida, Apopka, FL. For Family Empowerment Program.

$90,000 to Youth United for Change, Philadelphia, PA.

$80,000 to Power U Center for Social Change, Miami, FL. For Saving Our Public Schools.

$50,000 to Robert A. Taft Institute of Government, Flushing, NY. For Leadership Development for Parent Leaders.

$50,000 to Temple University, Philadelphia, PA. For Center for Public Policy.

6161
The Hearst Foundation, Inc. ▼

Hearst Twrs.
300 W. 57th St., 26th Fl.
New York, NY   10019-3741   (212) 586-5404
Contact: For east of the Mississippi River: Robert M. Frehse, Jr., V.P. and Exec. Dir.; For west of the Missipi River: Paul I. Dinovitz, V.P. and Western Dir.
FAX: (212) 586-1917; Address for applicants from west of the Mississippi River: c/o Paul I. Dinovitz, V.P. and Western Dir., 90 New Montgomery St., Ste. 1212, San Francisco, CA 94105, tel.: (415) 543-0400; URL: http://www.hearstfdn.org/

Incorporated in 1945 in NY.
Donor: William Randolph Hearst†.

Foundation type: Independent foundation.

Financial data (yr. ended 12/31/05): Assets, $258,471,887 (M); expenditures, $14,658,394; qualifying distributions, $14,693,394; giving activities include $9,450,000 for 108 grants (high: $350,000; low: $25,000).

Purpose and activities: Within a general policy of assisting institutions to provide access and opportunity to underrepresented, low-income and minority populations, the foundation's primary focus is on undergraduate education with support also for professional study at the undergraduate and graduate levels. Giving also in the areas of health, social service, and culture.

Fields of interest: Arts, cultural/ethnic awareness; Arts education; Museums; Performing arts; Performing arts, education; Arts; Higher education; Graduate/professional education; Theological school/education; Adult education—literacy, basic skills & GED; Hospitals (general); Medical care, rehabilitation; Public health; Medical research, institute; Medical research; Employment, services; Housing/shelter; Youth development, services; Children/youth, services; Family services; Human services; Homeless, human services; Rural development; Minorities.

Type of support: General/operating support; Capital campaigns; Endowments; Program development; Fellowships; Scholarship funds; Research; Technical assistance; Matching/challenge support.

Limitations: Giving limited to the U.S. and its territories. No support for public policy, or public policy research, advocacy, or foreign countries. No grants to individuals, or for media or publishing projects, conferences, workshops, seminars, seed funding, multi-year grants, special events, tables, or advertising for fundraising events; no loans or program-related investments.

Publications: Application guidelines.

Application information: Only fully documented appeals will be considered; accepts NYRAG Common Application Form. Application form not required.

Initial approach: Proposal
Copies of proposal: 1
Deadline(s): None
Board meeting date(s): Mar., June, Sept., and Dec.
Final notification: 4 - 6 weeks

Officers and Directors:* George R. Hearst, Jr.,* Pres.; Robert M. Frehse, Jr., V.P. and Exec. Dir.; Paul I. Dinovitz, V.P. and Western Dir.; Frank A. Bennack, Jr.,* V.P.; John G. Conomikes,* V.P.; Richard E. Deems,* V.P.; Victor F. Ganzi,* V.P.; John R. Hearst, Jr.,* V.P.; William R. Hearst III,* V.P.; Harvey L. Lipton,* V.P.; Gilbert C. Maurer,* V.P.; Mark F. Miller,* V.P.; Raymond J. Petersen,* V.P.; James M. Asher, Secy.; Ralph J. Cuomo, Treas.; Catherine A. Bostron, Asst. Secy.; Eve B. Burton, Asst. Secy.; Ronald J. Doerfler, Asst. Treas.; Jon D. Smith, Jr., Asst. Treas.; John P. Spisak, Asst. Treas.; Anissa B. Balson; Virginia Randt.

EIN: 136161746

6162
William Randolph Hearst Foundation ▼

Hearst Twrs.
300 W. 57th St., 26th Fl.
New York, NY   10019-3741   (212) 586-5404
Contact: For east of the Mississippi River: Robert M. Frehse, Jr., V.P. and Exec. Dir.; For west of the Mississippi River: Paul I. Dinovitz, V.P. and Western Dir.
FAX: (212) 586-1917; Address for applicants from west of the Mississippi River: c/o Paul I. Dinovitz, V.P. and Western Dir., 90 New Montgomery St., Ste. 1212, San Francisco, CA 94105, tel.: (415) 543-0400; URL: http://www.hearstfdn.org

Incorporated in 1948 in CA.
Donor: William Randolph Hearst†.
Foundation type: Independent foundation.

Financial data (yr. ended 12/31/05): Assets, $597,342,514 (M); expenditures, $39,896,539; qualifying distributions, $31,446,545; giving activities include $26,991,685 for 154 grants (high: $7,500,000; low: $25,000), and $2,674,156 for foundation-administered programs.

Purpose and activities: Assisting institutions to provide access and opportunity to underrepresented, low-income, and minority populations. The foundation's primary focus is on undergraduate education with support also for professional study at the undergraduate and graduate level. Giving also in the areas of health, social services, and culture.

Fields of interest: Arts, cultural/ethnic awareness; Arts education; Museums; Performing arts; Performing arts, education; Arts; Higher education; Graduate/professional education; Theological school/education; Adult education—literacy, basic skills & GED; Hospitals (general); Medical care, rehabilitation; Public health; Medical research, institute; Medical research; Employment, services; Housing/shelter; Youth development, services; Children/youth, services; Family services; Homeless, human services; Rural development; Minorities.

Type of support: General/operating support; Capital campaigns; Endowments; Program development; Fellowships; Scholarship funds; Research; Technical assistance; Matching/challenge support.

Limitations: Giving limited to the U.S. and its territories. No support for public policy, public schools, advocacy, or foreign countries. No grants to individuals, or for media projects, conferences, workshops, seminars, multi-year grants, publishing projects, special events, seed funding, public policy research, tables, or advertising for fundraising events; no loans or program-related investments.

Publications: Application guidelines.

Application information: Only fully documented appeals will be considered; accepts NYRAG Common Application Form. Application form not required.

Initial approach: Proposal
Copies of proposal: 1
Deadline(s): None
Board meeting date(s): Mar., June, Sept., and Dec.
Final notification: 4 to 6 weeks

Officers and Directors:* William R. Hearst III,* Pres.; Robert M. Frehse, Jr., V.P. and Exec. Dir.; Paul I. Dinovitz, V.P. and Western Dir.; Frank A. Bennack, Jr.,* V.P.; John G. Conomikes,* V.P.; Richard E. Deems,* V.P.; Victor F. Ganzi,* V.P.; George R. Hearst, Jr.,* V.P.; John R. Hearst, Jr.,* V.P.; Harvey L. Lipton,* V.P.; Gilbert C. Maurer,* V.P.; Mark F. Miller,* V.P.; Raymond J. Petersen,* V.P.; James M. Asher, Secy.; Ralph J. Cuomo, Treas.; Catherine A. Bostron, Asst. Secy.; Eve B. Burton, Asst. Secy.; Ronald J. Doerfler, Asst. Treas.; Jon D. Smith, Jr., Asst. Treas.; John P. Spisak, Asst. Treas.; Anissa B. Balson; Virginia Randt.

Number of staff: 3 full-time professional; 1 full-time support.

EIN: 136019226

6163
The Heckmann Family Foundation ✧ ☆
c/o U.S. Trust
114 W. 47th St.
New York, NY 10036

Established in 1997 in CA.
Donor: Richard J. Heckmann.
Foundation type: Independent foundation.
Financial data (yr. ended 12/31/05): Assets, $8,033 (M); expenditures, $1,776,947; qualifying distributions, $1,768,253; giving activities include $1,723,000 for 2 grants (high: $1,623,000; low: $100,000).
Fields of interest: Higher education.
Limitations: Applications not accepted. Giving primarily in CA. No grants to individuals.
Application information: Contributes only to pre-selected organizations.
Officers: Richard J. Heckmann, Pres. and Treas.; Mary M. Heckmann, Secy.
Directors: Brock P. Heckmann; Scott M. Heckmann; Thomas R. Heckmann.
EIN: 330758328

6164
The Heckscher Foundation for Children ▼
123 E. 70th St.
New York, NY 10021 (212) 744-0190
Contact: Virginia Sloane, Pres.
FAX: (212) 744-2761; URL: http://foundationcenter.org/grantmaker/heckscher/

Incorporated in 1921 in NY.
Donor: August Heckscher‡.
Foundation type: Independent foundation.
Financial data (yr. ended 12/31/04): Assets, $216,974,495 (M); expenditures, $9,513,598; qualifying distributions, $9,142,470; giving activities include $7,581,877 for 219 grants (high: $900,000; low: $130; average: $5,000–$125,000).
Purpose and activities: Giving primarily to youth-serving organizations in the greater New York, NY metropolitan area.
Fields of interest: Arts education; Performing arts, dance; Performing arts, theater; Performing arts, education; Education, early childhood education; Child development, education; Vocational education; Higher education; Teacher school/education; Student services/organizations; Scholarships/financial aid; Health organizations; Recreation, camps; Recreation, parks/playgrounds; Athletics/sports, school programs; Recreation; Youth development; Human services; Neighborhood centers; Children, foster care; Children, services; Youth, services; Family services; Minorities/immigrants, centers/services; Foundations (private grantmaking); Leadership development.
Type of support: Building/renovation; Equipment; Program development; Seed money; Curriculum development; Fellowships; Internship funds; Scholarship funds; Research; Program evaluation; Matching/challenge support.
Limitations: Giving primarily in the greater New York, NY, area. No grants to individuals, or for operating budgets, annual campaigns, deficit financing, fundraising events, political efforts, or endowment funds; no loans.
Publications: Application guidelines; Informational brochure.
Application information: Application form not required.

Initial approach: 3-page letter of inquiry, after which some applicants will then be invited to submit full proposals
Copies of proposal: 2
Deadline(s): None
Board meeting date(s): Jan., Mar., May, July, Sept., and Nov.
Final notification: Depends upon complexity
Officers and Trustees:* Howard G. Sloane,* Chair.; Virginia Sloane,* Pres.; Phyllis Fannan; Carole S. Landman; Philippe Laub; Mark Magowan; Gail Meyers; Fred Obser; Howard Rosenbaum; Marlene Shyer; Arthur J. Smadbeck; Louis Smadbeck, Jr.; Paul Smadbeck; David Tillson.
Number of staff: 2 full-time professional; 2 part-time professional; 1 full-time support.
EIN: 131820170
Selected grants: The following grants were reported in 2004.
$300,000 to Teach for America, New York, NY.
$100,000 to Take the Field, New York, NY.
$100,000 to Urban Assembly, New York, NY.
$50,000 to Big Brothers Big Sisters of New York City, New York, NY.
$50,000 to Childrens Aid Society, New York, NY.
$50,000 to De La Salle Academy, New York, NY.
$50,000 to East Side House Settlement, Chicago, IL.
$50,000 to Edwin Gould Academy, Chestnut Ridge, NY.
$25,000 to Roundabout Theater Company, New York, NY.
$25,000 to Theater for a New Audience, New York, NY.

6165
Heineman Foundation for Research, Educational, Charitable and Scientific Purposes, Inc. ✧
140 Broadway
New York, NY 10005

Incorporated in 1947 in DE.
Donor: Dannie N. Heineman‡.
Foundation type: Independent foundation.
Financial data (yr. ended 12/31/03): Assets, $15,027,891 (M); expenditures, $762,011; qualifying distributions, $664,348; giving activities include $661,000 for grants.
Purpose and activities: Primary areas of interest include the medical sciences and physics. Support for research programs in mathematical sciences and medicine; grants for higher education, specialized libraries (including the Heineman Library of Rare Books and Manuscripts given to the Pierpont Morgan Library, New York, NY), music schools, and two annual physics awards.
Fields of interest: Visual arts; Performing arts; Performing arts, dance; Performing arts, theater; Performing arts, music; Language/linguistics; Literature; Arts; Education, research; Education, early childhood education; Child development, education; Elementary school/education; Higher education; Adult/continuing education; Adult education—literacy, basic skills & GED; Libraries/library science; Education, reading; Education; Environment, natural resources; Environment, energy; Environment; Animals/wildlife, preservation/protection; Health care; Health organizations, association; Heart & circulatory diseases; Biomedicine; Medical research, institute; Heart & circulatory research; Food services; Human

services; Children/youth, services; Child development, services; Women, centers/services; Civil rights, race/intergroup relations; Civil rights; Physical/earth sciences; Chemistry; Mathematics; Physics; Engineering/technology; Biological sciences; Science; Minorities; Women; Economically disadvantaged.
Type of support: General/operating support; Endowments; Program development; Publication; Seed money; Fellowships; Research; Technical assistance.
Limitations: Giving on a national basis. No grants to individuals.
Application information: Application form not required.
Copies of proposal: 1
Board meeting date(s): Apr. and Nov.
Officers and Directors:* Ann R. Podlipny, Pres.; Maria Heineman Bergendahl, V.P.; Andrew Podlipny, Secy.; Agnes Gautier,* Treas.; Anders Bergendahl; Edith Fehr; Marilyn Heineman; June Heineman-Morris; Joan Heineman-Schur; Glen Morris; David Heineman Rose; James A. Rose; Marian Heineman Rose; Simon Rose.
EIN: 136082899
Selected grants: The following grants were reported in 2003.
$76,000 to Heineman Medical Research Center of Charlotte, Charlotte, NC.
$70,000 to American Friends of the Verbier Festival and Academy, Greenwich, CT.
$60,000 to Childrens Hospital of Philadelphia, Philadelphia, PA.
$46,000 to Kneisel Hall, Blue Hill, ME.
$20,000 to Child Health Services, Teen Health Clinic, Manchester, NH.
$20,000 to Intermountain Centers for Human Development, Tucson, AZ.
$6,000 to American Fertility Association, New York, NY.
$5,000 to Columbia University, New York, NY.
$5,000 to Cystic Fibrosis Foundation, Melbourne, FL.
$4,000 to Infertility Focus, Pittsford, NY.

6166
Solomon and Clara Heisler Family Foundation ✧
c/o Solomon Heisler
1661 53rd St.
Brooklyn, NY 11204
Contact: Solomon Heisler, Pres.

Established in 1992 in NY.
Donors: Solomon Heisler; Clara Heisler.
Foundation type: Independent foundation.
Financial data (yr. ended 12/31/04): Assets, $7,985,341 (M); gifts received, $341,276; expenditures, $464,927; qualifying distributions, $355,925; giving activities include $353,175 for 7 grants (high: $150,000; low: $500).
Purpose and activities: Giving primarily to Jewish agencies, temples, and schools.
Fields of interest: Education; Human services; Jewish agencies & temples.
Limitations: Applications not accepted. Giving primarily in Brooklyn, NY.
Application information: Unsolicited requests for funds not accepted.
Officers: Solomon Heisler, Pres.; Clara Heisler, V.P.; Rosemarie Weingarten, Secy.; Anna Schon, Treas.
Director: Harold Feinberg.
EIN: 113133210

6167
Max, Rose and Anna Heller Foundation ✧
(formerly Lawrence Klosk Foundation)
1123 Broadway, Ste. 1011
New York, NY 10010

Established in 1947 in NY.
Donors: Tobias Heller†; Lawrence Klosk.
Foundation type: Independent foundation.
Financial data (yr. ended 12/31/03): Assets,
$30,534 (M); gifts received, $291,448;
expenditures, $540,443; qualifying distributions,
$439,350; giving activities include $439,350 for 17
+ grants (high: $182,500).
Purpose and activities: Giving primarily to Jewish
agencies, temples, and federated giving programs,
and to hospitals.
Fields of interest: Hospitals (general); Jewish
federated giving programs; Jewish agencies &
temples.
International interests: Israel.
Limitations: Applications not accepted. Giving
primarily in Israel; some giving in NY. No grants to
individuals.
Application information: Contributes only to
pre-selected organizations.
Directors: Nathan Bernstein; Rachel Heller
Bernstein; Debbie Lifschitz; Moshe Lifschitz.
EIN: 136154543

6168
The Heller Foundation ✧
c/o Lazar, Levine & Felix
350 5th Ave., Ste. 6820
New York, NY 10118

Established in 2001 in NY.
Donors: Benjamin Heller; Fanny Heller; Jacqueline
Heller.
Foundation type: Independent foundation.
Financial data (yr. ended 12/31/04): Assets,
$98,904 (M); gifts received, $2,087,463;
expenditures, $2,135,489; qualifying distributions,
$2,135,437; giving activities include $2,135,437
for 186 grants (high: $250,000; low: $250;
average: $1,000–$100,000).
Fields of interest: Higher education; Education;
Jewish agencies & temples.
Limitations: Applications not accepted. No grants to
individuals.
Application information: Contributes only to
pre-selected organizations.
Officers: Fanya Heller, Chair.; Benjamin Heller,
Pres.; Jacqueline Heller, V.P.
EIN: 134150736
Selected grants: The following grants were reported
in 2004.
$210,000 to Yeshiva University Museum, New York,
NY. 3 grants: $100,000, $10,000, $100,000
$50,000 to Jewish Museum, New York, NY.
$25,000 to Aleph Society, New York, NY.
$13,575 to Fifth Avenue Synagogue, New York, NY.
2 grants: $3,575, $10,000
$10,000 to Yad Eliezer, Brooklyn, NY.
$8,500 to Wildwood School, Los Angeles, CA.
$5,000 to Hebrew Academy of Long Beach, Long
Beach, NY.

6169
The David B. Heller Foundation ✧ ☆
c/o Goldman Sachs and & Co.
1 New York Plz., 40th Fl.
New York, NY 10004

Donor: David B. Heller.
Foundation type: Independent foundation.
Financial data (yr. ended 2/28/06): Assets,
$12,484,299 (M); gifts received, $2,929,454;
expenditures, $486,222; qualifying distributions,
$392,420; giving activities include $392,420 for 23
grants (high: $80,000; low: $300).
Fields of interest: Higher education; Legal services;
Disasters, Hurricane Katrina; Children, services;
Human services; Jewish agencies & temples.
Limitations: Applications not accepted. Giving
primarily in New York, NY; some giving in MA. No
grants to individuals.
Application information: Contributes only to
pre-selected organizations.
Trustees: David B. Heller; Robert M. Heller.
EIN: 133936476

6170
The Leona M. and Harry B. Helmsley
Charitable Trust ✧
230 Park Ave., Ste. 659
New York, NY 10169

Established in 1999 in NY.
Donors: Leona M. Helmsley; Sierra Towers & Fresh
Meadows, LLP; Eastdil Realty, Inc., LLC; Helmsley
Enterprises, Inc.
Foundation type: Independent foundation.
Financial data (yr. ended 3/31/05): Assets,
$40,349,228 (L); expenditures, $3,159,676;
qualifying distributions, $3,153,845; giving
activities include $3,153,000 for 22 grants (high:
$1,000,000; low: $1,000).
Fields of interest: Philanthropy/voluntarism.
Limitations: Applications not accepted. Giving
primarily in NY. No grants to individuals.
Application information: Contributes only to
pre-selected organizations.
Trustee: Leona M. Helmsley.
EIN: 137184401
Selected grants: The following grants were reported
in 2005.
$400,000 to Greenwich Hospital, Greenwich, CT.
$25,000 to Make-A-Wish Foundation of America,
Phoenix, AZ.
$10,000 to American Cancer Society, New York, NY.
$10,000 to American Diabetes Association, New
York, NY.
$10,000 to American Heart Association, New York,
NY.
$10,000 to March of Dimes Birth Defects
Foundation, New York, NY.
$5,000 to American Parkinson Disease
Association, Staten Island, NY.
$5,000 to Greenwich Emergency Medical Service,
Riverside, CT.
$1,000 to Alzheimers Association, New York, NY.
$1,000 to Foundation for the Prevention and
Treatment of Eye Disease, New York, NY.

6171
Leona and Harry B. Helmsley Foundation,
Inc. ✧ ☆
(formerly The Harry B. Helmsley Foundation, Inc.)
230 Park Ave., Ste. 659
New York, NY 10169

Incorporated in 1954 in NY.
Donor: Harry B. Helmsley†.
Foundation type: Independent foundation.
Financial data (yr. ended 5/31/06): Assets,
$9,142,660 (M); expenditures, $519,481;
qualifying distributions, $515,500; giving activities
include $515,500 for 3 grants (high: $500,000;
low: $500).
Fields of interest: Health care, EMS; Health care.
Limitations: Applications not accepted. Giving
primarily in CT. No grants to individuals.
Application information: Contributes only to
pre-selected organizations.
Officers and Directors:* Leona M. Helmsley,* Pres.
and Treas.; John Codey,* V.P. and Secy.; Harold
Hoffman.
EIN: 136123336

6172
Stephen and Ruth Hendel Foundation ✧ ☆
10 Dundee Rd.
Larchmont, NY 10538

Established in 1989 in NY.
Donor: Stephen Hendel.
Foundation type: Independent foundation.
Financial data (yr. ended 2/28/06): Assets,
$229,406 (M); gifts received, $680,898;
expenditures, $454,446; qualifying distributions,
$454,376; giving activities include $454,376 for
grants.
Purpose and activities: Giving primarily for theater,
education, including a Jewish seminary, human
services, and Jewish organizations.
Fields of interest: Performing arts, theater; Higher
education; Health organizations, association;
Human services; Federated giving programs; Jewish
federated giving programs; Jewish agencies &
temples.
Limitations: Applications not accepted. Giving
primarily in CT and NY. No grants to individuals.
Application information: Contributes only to
pre-selected organizations.
Trustees: Myron Hendel; Ruth Hendel; Stephen
Hendel.
EIN: 133532037
Selected grants: The following grants were reported
in 2005.
$20,585 to Westchester Jewish Center,
Mamaroneck, NY. 4 grants: $225, $15,000,
$360, $5,000
$3,100 to Long Wharf Theater, New Haven, CT. 2
grants: $100, $3,000
$2,500 to Second Stage Theater, New York, NY.
$250 to Emelin Theater, Mamaroneck, NY.

6173
Herdrich 1985 Charitable Trust ✧
c/o Donald J. Herdrich
1 S. Greeley Ave., Ste. 3
Chappaqua, NY 10514

Established in 1986 in NY.
Donors: Donald J. Herdrich; Frances I. Herdrich.

Foundation type: Independent foundation.
Financial data (yr. ended 11/30/03): Assets, $6,791,534 (M); expenditures, $418,413; qualifying distributions, $358,453; giving activities include $356,700 for 14 grants (high: $50,000; low: $500).
Purpose and activities: Giving primarily for health associations, particularly for pediatric AIDS and breast cancer awareness; funding also for children and youth services, and Roman Catholic organizations.
Fields of interest: Hospitals (general); Health organizations, association; Breast cancer; AIDS; Children/youth, services; Children, day care; Roman Catholic agencies & churches.
Limitations: Applications not accepted. Giving primarily in NY; some funding nationally. No grants to individuals.
Application information: Contributes only to pre-selected organizations.
Trustee: Donald J. Herdrich.
EIN: 136855419
Selected grants: The following grants were reported in 2004.
$150,000 to Mayo Foundation, Rochester, MN.
$100,000 to Patrons Program, New York, NY.
$50,000 to Daniel Murphy Scholarship Foundation, Chicago, IL.
$50,000 to Elizabeth Glaser Pediatric AIDS Foundation, Santa Monica, CA.
$50,000 to Marquette University, Milwaukee, WI.
$50,000 to Saint Clare of Assisi, Edwards, CO.
$50,000 to Saint Raymond Parish, Bronx, NY.
$25,000 to Boys and Girls Club of Northern Westchester, Mount Kisco, NY.
$25,000 to Saint Bonaventure University, Saint Bonaventure, NY.
$500 to American Cancer Society, Bloomington, IN.

6174
The Alexander & Charlotte Herman Foundation ✧ ☆
c/o Abe I Friedman
1555 54th St., Ste. 3
Brooklyn, NY   11219
Application address: c/o Debby Rebenwurzel, 609 Ave. K, Brooklyn, NY 11230, tel.: (718) 338-2996

Established in 1995 in NY.
Donor: Charlotte Herman.
Foundation type: Independent foundation.
Financial data (yr. ended 12/31/05): Assets, $195,135 (M); gifts received, $84,270; expenditures, $366,230; qualifying distributions, $366,180; giving activities include $366,180 for grants.
Fields of interest: Human services; Jewish agencies & temples.
International interests: Israel.
Limitations: Giving primarily in Brooklyn, NY; some giving also in Israel.
Application information:
   Initial approach: Letter
   Deadline(s): None
Trustees: Charlotte Herman; Debby Rebenwurzel; Miriam Widawsky; Naomi Wiener.
EIN: 113230339

6175
Hermione Foundation ✧
c/o Laura J. Sloate
35 E. 75th St., Apt. 16C
New York, NY   10021-2762
Contact: Donna Leone, Tr.

Established in 1992 in NY.
Donor: Laura J. Sloate.
Foundation type: Independent foundation.
Financial data (yr. ended 12/31/04): Assets, $1,433,472 (M); gifts received, $1,000,000; expenditures, $687,450; qualifying distributions, $684,035; giving activities include $684,035 for 65 grants (high: $250,000; low: $36).
Fields of interest: Performing arts, opera; Arts; Higher education; Hospitals (general); Health organizations; Medical research, institute; Human services; Jewish agencies & temples.
Type of support: General/operating support; Continuing support; Endowments; Emergency funds; Program development; Conferences/seminars; Scholarship funds; Research; Program-related investments/loans.
Limitations: Applications not accepted. Giving primarily in NY. No grants to individuals.
Application information: Unsolicited requests for funds not accepted.
   Board meeting date(s): May 15
Officer: Laura J. Sloate, Pres.
Trustees: Donna Leone; Michael J. Schwartz.
EIN: 133673826

6176
The F. B. Heron Foundation ▼
100 Broadway, 17th Fl.
New York, NY   10005
Contact: Mary Jo Mullan, V.P., Progs.
URL: http://www.heronfdn.org

Established in 1992 in DE.
Foundation type: Independent foundation.
Financial data (yr. ended 12/31/05): Assets, $279,896,147 (M); expenditures, $19,043,843; qualifying distributions, $17,157,532; giving activities include $11,623,340 for 293 grants (high: $200,000; low: $25; average: $25,000–$125,000), $34,683 for 39 employee matching gifts, $78,512 for foundation-administered programs and $3,383,834 for 8 loans/program-related investments (high: $500,000; low: $250,000).
Purpose and activities: The foundation focuses its grantmaking and mission-related investing on five wealth-creation strategies for low-income families and communities. These five areas are: 1) access to capital; 2) quality and affordable child care; 3) comprehensive community development; 4) enterprise development; and 5) home ownership. The foundation concentrates its support on organizations with a national focus and in some cases, regional focus where these organizations are advancing solutions that have broad application for Heron's Wealth Creation Strategies.
Fields of interest: Housing/shelter, home owners; Children, day care; Community development, neighborhood development; Community development, citizen coalitions; Economic development.
Type of support: General/operating support; Continuing support; Program development; Technical assistance; Program evaluation;

Program-related investments/loans; Employee matching gifts; Matching/challenge support.
Limitations: Giving primarily in Appalachia; CA; Chicago, IL; MI; Kansas City, MO; Twin Cities, MN; the Mississippi Delta; NC; NJ; New York, NY; and TX. No grants to individuals, or for endowments or capital campaigns.
Publications: Application guidelines; Annual report (including application guidelines); Grants list; Occasional report.
Application information: Information is also available on the foundation's Web site. Videotapes, CDs, DVDs, etc. will not be accepted. Application form not required.
   Initial approach: Letter of inquiry (2 - 3 pages)
   Copies of proposal: 1
   Deadline(s): None
   Board meeting date(s): Quarterly
   Final notification: 1 week to initial letter of inquiry; 4 weeks max to full proposal, if requested
Officers and Directors:* William M. Dietel,* Chair.; Sharon B. King,* Pres.; Mary Jo Mullan, V.P., Progs. and Secy.-Treas.; Patricia J. Kozu, V.P., Finance and Admin.; Luther M. Ragin, Jr., V.P., Investments; John Otterlei; Buzz Schmidt; Tom Tinsley.
Number of staff: 9 full-time professional; 1 part-time professional; 4 full-time support.
EIN: 133647019
Selected grants: The following grants were reported in 2005.
$400,000 to National Community Reinvestment Coalition, DC. For general and project support, payable over 2 years.
$250,000 to Corporation for Enterprise Development (CFED), DC. For general support, payable over 2 years.
$250,000 to Family Conservancy, Kansas City, KS. For project support, payable over 2 years.
$250,000 to Neighborhood Housing Services of New York City, New York, NY. For general support, payable over 2 years.
$200,000 to Greater Minnesota Housing Fund, Saint Paul, MN. For general support, payable over 2 years.
$150,000 to Metro Industrial Areas Foundation (IAF), Rego Park, NY. payable over 2 years.
$80,000 to La Casa de Don Pedro, Newark, NJ. For general support, payable over 2 years.
$70,000 to California Reinvestment Coalition, San Francisco, CA. For general support, payable over 2 years.
$65,000 to Innovest Strategic Value Advisors, New York, NY. For project support.
$60,000 to Saint Josephs Carpenter Society, Camden, NJ. For general support.

6177
Abraham & Esther Hersh Foundation, Inc. ▼ ✧
10 W. 33rd St., No. 312
New York, NY   10001

Established in 1994 in NY.
Donors: Ahron Hersh; Toby Hersh; Chi Yueh Chen; Rosetti Handbags, Ltd.
Foundation type: Independent foundation.
Financial data (yr. ended 10/31/05): Assets, $1,084,119 (M); gifts received, $7,300,000; expenditures, $6,732,953; qualifying distributions, $6,732,905; giving activities include $6,732,905 for 106 grants (high: $100,000; low: $180; average: $1,000–$30,000).

Purpose and activities: Giving primarily to Jewish federated giving programs and Jewish agencies and temples.
Fields of interest: Jewish federated giving programs; Jewish agencies & temples.
Limitations: Applications not accepted. No grants to individuals.
Application information: Contributes only to pre-selected organizations.
Directors: Ahron Hersh; Toby Hersh.
EIN: 113188332
Selected grants: The following grants were reported in 2003.
$360,000 to Kollel Ohr Yakov Yosef, Brooklyn, NY. 2 grants: $180,000 each
$360,000 to Kollel Tiferes Yaakov Yosef, Brooklyn, NY. 2 grants: $180,000 each
$360,000 to Notzer Chesed, New York, NY. 2 grants: $180,000 each
$360,000 to Nveh Shalom, Brooklyn, NY. 2 grants: $180,000 each
$180,000 to Mosdos Spinka International, Brooklyn, NY.
$180,000 to United Spinka International, Brooklyn, NY.

6178
Hettinger Foundation
c/o Oberfest & Assocs.
P.O. Box 318
Chappaqua, NY 10514

Trust established in 1961 in NY.
Donors: Albert J. Hettinger, Jr.†; John Hettinger.
Foundation type: Independent foundation.
Financial data (yr. ended 12/31/04): Assets, $17,745,987 (M); expenditures, $736,328; qualifying distributions, $670,477; giving activities include $670,000 for 34 grants (high: $200,000; low: $1,000).
Purpose and activities: Giving primarily for education, health care, and children, youth, and social services; funding also for the welfare of thoroughbred racehorses.
Fields of interest: Education; Animal welfare; Hospitals (general); Health care; Cancer research; Athletics/sports, equestrianism; Human services; American Red Cross; Salvation Army; Children/youth, services.
Type of support: General/operating support; Scholarship funds.
Limitations: Applications not accepted. Giving primarily in NY; funding also nationally. No grants to individuals.
Application information: Contributes only to pre-selected organizations.
Trustees: Betty Hettinger; Corina Hettinger; John Hettinger; William R. Hettinger.
Number of staff: None.
EIN: 136097726
Selected grants: The following grants were reported in 2004.
$200,000 to New Milford Hospital Foundation, New Milford, CT.
$15,000 to Mount Tremper Outdoor Ministries, Patterson, NY.
$2,000 to Saratoga Care Foundation, Saratoga Springs, NY.

6179
The DuBose and Dorothy Heyward Memorial Fund ◇ ☆
c/o The Bank of New York, Tax Dept.
1 Wall St., 28th Fl.
New York, NY 10286
Contact: Peter McDermott, Asst. V.P.
Application address: c/o The Bank of New York, 1290 Ave. of the Americas, New York, NY 10104

Established in 1985 in NY.
Donor: Jenifer Heyward†.
Foundation type: Independent foundation.
Financial data (yr. ended 12/31/05): Assets, $11,629,875 (M); expenditures, $1,348,285; qualifying distributions, $983,000; giving activities include $983,000 for grants.
Purpose and activities: Giving primarily for the arts, and cancer research and treatment.
Fields of interest: Arts; Cancer; Cancer research.
Type of support: General/operating support; Research; Grants to individuals.
Limitations: Giving primarily in New York, NY.
Publications: Program policy statement.
Application information:
    Initial approach: Letter
    Copies of proposal: 2
    Deadline(s): None
Trustees: Albert J. Cardinali; The Bank of New York.
EIN: 136840999
Selected grants: The following grants were reported in 2003.
$25,000 to Metropolitan Opera, New York, NY. For operating support.
$20,000 to MacDowell Colony, New York, NY. For operating support.
$15,000 to Carnegie Hall Corporation, New York, NY. For operating support.
$15,000 to Lincoln Center for the Performing Arts, New York, NY. For operating support.
$10,000 to Charleston Ballet, Charleston, WV. For operating support.
$10,000 to Glimmerglass Opera, Cooperstown, NY. For operating support.
$7,000 to Pearl Theater Company, New York, NY. For operating support.
$5,000 to International Arts Relations (INTAR), New York, NY. For operating support.
$3,000 to Teatro Grattacielo, New York, NY. For operating support.
$2,000 to Theater by the Blind Corporation, New York, NY. For operating support.

6180
Hickrill Foundation, Inc. ◇
c/o Norman Foundation Inc.
147 E. 48th St.
New York, NY 10017
Contact: Denie S. Weil, V.P. and Secy.

Incorporated in 1946 in NY.
Donors: Frank A. Weil; The Norman Foundation; Denie S. Weil; Debbie Weil Harrington; William S. Weil; Samuel P. Harrington.
Foundation type: Independent foundation.
Financial data (yr. ended 12/31/04): Assets, $5,101,394 (M); gifts received, $180,067; expenditures, $907,569; qualifying distributions, $869,512; giving activities include $864,390 for 92 grants (high: $390,000; low: $100).
Purpose and activities: The foundation primarily supports a selected few community organizations in

the communities of the members of the foundation, and a very few special projects of particular interest to members of the foundation.
Limitations: Giving on a national basis. No grants to individuals.
Application information:
    Initial approach: Letter
    Deadline(s): None
Officers: Frank A. Weil, Pres.; Denie S. Weil, V.P. and Secy.
EIN: 136002949

6181
The Grace Hidary Foundation, Inc. ◇
c/o Jack A. Hidary
10 W. 33rd St., Ste. 900
New York, NY 10001

Established in 1994 in NY.
Donors: Abraham J. Hidary; Jack A. Hidary; Morris Hidary; M. Hidary & Co., Inc.
Foundation type: Independent foundation.
Financial data (yr. ended 12/31/05): Assets, $273,112 (M); gifts received, $223,350; expenditures, $323,269; qualifying distributions, $322,963; giving activities include $320,263 for 132 grants (high: $76,955; low: $52).
Fields of interest: Elementary/secondary education; Jewish federated giving programs; Jewish agencies & temples.
Limitations: Applications not accepted. Giving primarily in NY. No grants to individuals.
Application information: Contributes only to pre-selected organizations.
Officers: Abraham J. Hidary, Pres.; Jack A. Hidary, V.P.; Morris Hidary, Secy.-Treas.
EIN: 133785660
Selected grants: The following grants were reported in 2005.
$17,000 to Magen David Yeshiva, Brooklyn, NY.
$6,404 to Sephardic Bikur Holim, Brooklyn, NY.
$4,200 to Yeshiva of Kings Bay, Brooklyn, NY.
$4,000 to Ozar Hatorah, New York, NY.
$3,109 to Magen Israel Society, Brooklyn, NY.
$3,100 to Sephardic Community Center, Brooklyn, NY.
$3,000 to Deal Yeshiva, Deal, NJ.
$2,000 to Ahi Ezer Congregation, Brooklyn, NY.
$1,500 to ZAKA, Brooklyn, NY.
$1,153 to P.E.F. Israel Endowment Funds, New York, NY.

6182
Jacob Hidary Foundation, Inc. ◇
10 W. 33rd St.
New York, NY 10001
Contact: Isaac Hidary, Pres.; David J. Hidary, V.P.

Established in 1961.
Donors: M. Hidary Co., Inc.; and members of the Hidary family.
Foundation type: Independent foundation.
Financial data (yr. ended 12/31/05): Assets, $17,495 (M); gifts received, $429,628; expenditures, $448,809; qualifying distributions, $448,845; giving activities include $446,330 for 493 grants (high: $37,003; low: $18).
Purpose and activities: Giving primarily to Jewish agencies, temples, and schools.

Fields of interest: Elementary/secondary education; Human services; Jewish federated giving programs; Jewish agencies & temples.
Limitations: Giving primarily in NY.
Application information:
Initial approach: Letter
Deadline(s): None
Officers: Isaac Hidary, Pres.; David J. Hidary, V.P.; Jacob I. Hidary, Secy.; Abraham B. Hidary, Treas.
EIN: 136125420

6183
Tommy Hilfiger Corporate Foundation, Inc. ✧
601 W. 26th St., 6th Fl.
New York, NY 10001 (212) 548-1762
URL: http://usa.tommy.com/opencms/opencms/foundation

Established in 1995 in NY.
Donor: Tommy Hilfiger U.S.A., Inc.
Foundation type: Company-sponsored foundation.
Financial data (yr. ended 3/31/04): Assets, $2,014,060 (M); expenditures, $562,349; qualifying distributions, $561,874; giving activities include $560,943 for 67 grants (high: $55,000; low: $400).
Purpose and activities: The foundation supports organizations involved with arts and culture, education, health, youth development, minorities, and women. Special emphasis is directed toward programs designed to empower youth.
Fields of interest: Arts; Elementary/secondary education; Higher education; Education; Hospitals (general); Public health; Health care; Youth development; Youth; Minorities; Women.
Limitations: No support for political parties or discriminatory organizations. No grants to individuals, or for political campaigns or causes, endowments, or film, video, television, or radio projects.
Application information: Telephone calls during the application process are not encouraged. Proposals should be no longer than 3 to 5 pages. Application form not required.
Initial approach: Proposal
Deadline(s): Apr. 1 and Oct. 1
Officer and Directors: R. Guy Vickers,* Pres.; Steven R. Gursky; Joel H. Newman.
EIN: 133856562

6184
The Hilibrand Foundation ✧
c/o Steven M. Loeb, Cleary Gottlieb
1 Liberty Plz.
New York, NY 10006

Established in 1991 in NY.
Donors: Deborah Z. Hilibrand; Lawrence E. Hilibrand.
Foundation type: Independent foundation.
Financial data (yr. ended 12/31/05): Assets, $12,918,493 (M); gifts received, $1,082,600; expenditures, $570,918; qualifying distributions, $556,872; giving activities include $551,272 for 20 grants (high: $167,950; low: $1,000).
Purpose and activities: Giving primarily to Jewish organizations, including youth associations, education, autism research, and health associations.

Fields of interest: Higher education; Health organizations, association; Autism research; Human services; Children, services; Aging, centers/services; Jewish federated giving programs; Jewish agencies & temples.
Type of support: General/operating support.
Limitations: Applications not accepted. Giving primarily in CT and New York, NY. No grants to individuals.
Application information: Contributes only to pre-selected organizations.
Trustees: Deborah Z. Hilibrand; Lawrence E. Hilibrand.
EIN: 133632625
Selected grants: The following grants were reported in 2004.
$215,000 to National Alliance for Autism Research, Princeton, NJ.
$132,360 to ARC of Greenwich, Greenwich, CT.
$50,000 to Dorot, New York, NY.
$30,000 to Cato Institute, DC.
$30,000 to Hebrew Immigrant Aid Society (HIAS), New York, NY.
$30,000 to Institute for Justice, DC.
$25,000 to Massachusetts Institute of Technology, Cambridge, MA.
$5,000 to University of Chicago, Chicago, IL.

6185
The Margaret M. Hill Foundation ✧ ☆
c/o Lutz & Carr, LLP
300 E. 42nd St.
New York, NY 10017
Contact: Margaret M. Hill, Pres.

Established in 1997 in NY.
Donor: The Rosenkranz Foundation.
Foundation type: Independent foundation.
Financial data (yr. ended 12/31/05): Assets, $4,883,261 (M); expenditures, $646,942; qualifying distributions, $565,310; giving activities include $560,095 for 81 grants (high: $139,650; low: $75).
Purpose and activities: Giving primarily for education, human services, and for arts and culture.
Fields of interest: Arts; Higher education; Housing/shelter; Human services.
Limitations: Applications not accepted. Giving primarily in IN and NY. No grants to individuals.
Application information: Contributes only to pre-selected organizations.
Officer: Margaret M. Hill, Pres.
EIN: 137088667
Selected grants: The following grants were reported in 2005.
$139,650 to Angela House, Bronx, NY.
$125,000 to Fordham University, New York, NY.
$50,000 to Catholic Relief Services, Baltimore, MD.
$30,200 to National Theater Workshop of the Handicapped, Belfast, ME.
$7,600 to Saint Marys College, Notre Dame, IN.
$7,500 to Theater Development Fund, New York, NY.
$5,000 to Alliance for School Choice, Phoenix, AZ.
$2,500 to Historic Hudson Valley, Tarrytown, NY.
$550 to Irish Georgian Society, New York, NY.
$350 to Thorpe Family Residence, Bronx, NY.

6186
The Alex Hillman Family Foundation ✧
630 5th Ave., Rm. 2604
New York, NY 10111 (212) 265-3115
Contact: Rita K. Hillman, Pres. and Secy.-Treas.

Incorporated in 1966 in NY.
Donors: Alex L. Hillman†; Rita K. Hillman.
Foundation type: Independent foundation.
Financial data (yr. ended 12/31/05): Assets, $96,838,229 (M); expenditures, $2,193,054; qualifying distributions, $1,994,583; giving activities include $1,794,667 for 23 grants (high: $812,081; low: $100).
Purpose and activities: Giving primarily for higher education, with emphasis on schools of nursing; support also for the arts.
Fields of interest: Museums; Performing arts; Performing arts, music; Arts; Higher education; Nursing school/education; Hospitals (general); Jewish agencies & temples.
Type of support: General/operating support.
Limitations: Applications not accepted. Giving primarily in the metropolitan New York, NY, area. No grants to individuals, or for continuing support.
Application information: Contributes only to pre-selected organizations.
Board meeting date(s): Semiannually
Officer and Directors:* Rita K. Hillman,* Pres.; James Marcus,* V.P. and Secy.; Henry Christensen III,* Treas.; Polly Beere; Paul Garfinkle; William M. Griffin; Raymond J. McGuire; Ahrin Mishan; William Spiro.
EIN: 132560546
Selected grants: The following grants were reported in 2005.
$259,000 to Phillips Beth Israel School of Nursing, New York, NY.
$209,376 to Lenox Hill Hospital, New York, NY.
$79,000 to Brooklyn Academy of Music, Brooklyn, NY.
$62,000 to International Center of Photography, New York, NY.
$20,000 to Metropolitan Museum of Art, New York, NY.
$10,000 to Muse Film and Television, New York, NY.
$10,000 to University of Dallas, Irving, TX.
$500 to Freedom Institute, New York, NY.
$250 to American Red Cross.
$100 to Doe Fund, New York, NY.

6187
Douglas A. Hirsch & Holly S. Andersen Family Foundation, Inc. ✧ ☆
c/o Seneca Capital Advisors, LLC
950 3rd Ave., 29th Fl.
New York, NY 10022
Contact: Douglas A. Hirsch

Foundation type: Independent foundation.
Financial data (yr. ended 12/31/05): Assets, $184,127 (M); gifts received, $253,559; expenditures, $369,662; qualifying distributions, $369,456; giving activities include $369,456 for grants.
Fields of interest: Education; Medical research, institute; Federated giving programs; Roman Catholic federated giving programs; Jewish agencies & temples.
Application information:
Initial approach: Letter
Deadline(s): None

Officers: Douglas A. Hirsch, Pres.; Barry S. Berger, Secy.; Holly S. Andersen, Treas.
EIN: 300218948

6188
Neil S. Hirsch Foundation ◇ ☆
40 E. 52nd St., 23rd Fl.
New York, NY 10022

Established in 1986 in NY.
Donor: Neil S. Hirsch.
Foundation type: Independent foundation.
Financial data (yr. ended 12/31/05): Assets, $158,253 (M); expenditures, $321,418; qualifying distributions, $320,600; giving activities include $320,000 for 5 grants (high: $255,000; low: $5,000).
Fields of interest: Museums (art); Higher education; Medical research, institute; Boys & girls clubs; Disabilities, people with.
Limitations: Applications not accepted. Giving primarily in FL; some giving also in MO, NY, and PA. No grants to individuals.
Application information: Contributes only to pre-selected organizations.
Trustees: Neil S. Hirsch; Steven N. Rappaport.
EIN: 136881621

6189
His Will Foundation ◇
(formerly The Azariah Foundation)
c/o BCRS Group Assocs., LLC
100 Wall St., 11th Fl.
New York, NY 10005

Established in 2000 in NJ.
Donor: John E. Urban.
Foundation type: Independent foundation.
Financial data (yr. ended 8/31/05): Assets, $10,924,715 (M); gifts received, $11,098,152; expenditures, $696,800; qualifying distributions, $671,400; giving activities include $670,000 for 4 grants (high: $500,000; low: $20,000).
Fields of interest: Higher education; Christian agencies & churches.
Limitations: Applications not accepted. Giving on a national basis. No grants to individuals.
Application information: Contributes only to pre-selected organizations.
Trustees: Carolyn L. Urban; John E. Urban.
EIN: 134043877

6190
HKH Foundation ◇
521 5th Ave., Ste. 1612
New York, NY 10175-1699
Contact: Harriet Barlow
FAX: (212) 687-8877; E-mail: hkh@hkhfdn.org; URL: http://www.hkhfdn.org

Foundation established in 1980 in NY.
Foundation type: Independent foundation.
Financial data (yr. ended 12/31/05): Assets, $31,651,892 (M); expenditures, $2,578,865; qualifying distributions, $2,362,666; giving activities include $2,185,750 for 43 grants (high: $200,000; low: $750; average: $50,000–$100,000).
Purpose and activities: Funding considered only in the following areas: 1) disarmament and the

prevention of war; 2) civil liberties; and 3) environmental protection.
Fields of interest: Environment, natural resources; Environment; International peace/security; International affairs, arms control; Civil liberties, advocacy; Civil rights.
Type of support: General/operating support; Program development; Program-related investments/loans.
Limitations: Applications not accepted. Giving on a national basis. No grants to individuals.
Application information: Unsolicited requests for funds not accepted.
  Board meeting date(s): Spring and fall (actual dates vary each year)
Trustees: Hermann Hatzfeldt; Adam Hochschild; David Hochschild; Frederick A. Terry, Jr.; Robert R. Worth.
Number of staff: 2 part-time professional; 1 part-time support.
EIN: 136784950
Selected grants: The following grants were reported in 2003.
$225,000 to Tides Center, San Francisco, CA. For A Better Way program.
$100,000 to Center for Constitutional Rights, New York, NY.
$100,000 to Earth Island Institute, San Francisco, CA.
$75,000 to Adirondack Community Trust, Lake Placid, NY.
$50,000 to Earth Day Network, DC.
$50,000 to Institute for Americas Future, DC.
$25,000 to Alliance for Justice, DC.
$25,000 to Project Vote, Brooklyn, NY.
$10,000 to Center for International Policy, DC.
$10,000 to Peace Action Education Fund, Silver Spring, MD.

6191
Peter & Stacy Hochfelder Charitable Foundation, Inc. ◇
2 Lincoln Ln.
Purchase, NY 10577

Established in 1994 in NY.
Donors: Peter Hochfelder; Stacy Hochfelder.
Foundation type: Independent foundation.
Financial data (yr. ended 12/31/04): Assets, $74,051 (M); gifts received, $1,050,000; expenditures, $977,760; qualifying distributions, $977,735; giving activities include $977,640 for 52 grants (high: $378,000; low: $180).
Purpose and activities: Giving primarily to health associations and foundations, human services, and Jewish agencies and temples.
Fields of interest: Health organizations, association; Human services; Civil rights; Federated giving programs; Jewish federated giving programs; Jewish agencies & temples.
Limitations: Applications not accepted. Giving primarily in NY. No grants to individuals.
Application information: Contributes only to pre-selected organizations.
Officers: Peter Hochfelder, Pres.; Mitchell Kuflik, V.P.; Stacy Hochfelder, Secy.
EIN: 133799164

6192
Hochstein Foundation, Inc. ◇
6 E. 45th St.
New York, NY 10017

Established in 1960 in NY.
Donor: Bernard Hochstein.
Foundation type: Independent foundation.
Financial data (yr. ended 12/31/04): Assets, $18,660,490 (M); gifts received, $1,818,000; expenditures, $2,122,678; qualifying distributions, $2,103,003; giving activities include $2,103,003 for 7 grants (high: $1,490,760; low: $50,000).
Purpose and activities: Giving primarily to Jewish agencies, temples, and schools.
Fields of interest: Elementary/secondary education; Human services; Jewish federated giving programs; Jewish agencies & temples.
Type of support: General/operating support.
Limitations: Applications not accepted. Giving primarily in NJ and NY. No grants to individuals.
Application information: Contributes only to pre-selected organizations.
Officer and Board Members:* Bernard Hochstein,* Pres.; Helen Fuss; Michael Hochstein; Miriam Hochstein; Richard Hochstein; Stephen Hochstein.
EIN: 136161765
Selected grants: The following grants were reported in 2003.
$1,699,000 to P.E.F. Israel Endowment Funds, New York, NY. 2 grants: $878,000 (For general support), $821,000 (For general support).
$218,000 to American Friends of Bet El Yeshiva Center, Hempstead, NY. For general support.
$100,000 to Return-United Fund for the Education of Russian Immigrant Children in Israel, Brooklyn, NY. For general support.
$73,000 to American Friends of Yeshiva Tifereth, Monsey, NY. For general support.
$26,000 to American Friends of Chasdei Yosef, Brooklyn, NY. For general support.
$15,000 to American Friends of Ramot Torah Schools, Brooklyn, NY. For general support.
$12,000 to Neve Yerushalayim Institutions, New York, NY. For general support.
$8,000 to Otzar Haposkin, Friends of, Garden City, NY. For general support.
$3,000 to American Friends of Yeshiva Aish HaTorah, New York, NY. For general support.

6193
Hod Foundation ◇
c/o American Stock Transfer
59 Maiden Ln., Plaza Level
New York, NY 10038
Contact: Henry Reinhold, Tr.

Established in 2000 in NY.
Donors: Michael Karfunkel; Karfunkel Family Foundation.
Foundation type: Operating foundation.
Financial data (yr. ended 6/30/04): Assets, $32,166,627 (M); gifts received, $500,000; expenditures, $1,803,934; qualifying distributions, $1,678,740; giving activities include $1,678,740 for 53 grants (high: $500,000; low: $100).
Fields of interest: Jewish agencies & temples.
Application information: Application form not required.
  Initial approach: Letter
  Deadline(s): None

Trustees: Leah Karfunkel; Michael Karfunkel; Henry Reinhold.
EIN: 133922069

6194
Hoerle Foundation ◇

c/o Reich & Tang
600 5th Ave.
New York, NY 10020 (212) 830-5353
Contact: Robert F. Hoerle, Pres.
Additional tel.: (212) 830-5357

Established in 1987 in NY.
Donors: Robert F. Hoerle; Sheila A. Hoerle.
Foundation type: Independent foundation.
Financial data (yr. ended 12/31/04): Assets, $13,340,935 (M); gifts received, $418,826; expenditures, $616,567; qualifying distributions, $519,344; giving activities include $519,344 for 69 grants (high: $125,000; low: $50).
Purpose and activities: Giving primarily for education.
Fields of interest: Arts; Higher education; Education; Human services.
Type of support: General/operating support; Annual campaigns; Matching/challenge support.
Limitations: Giving primarily in NY. No grants to individuals.
Application information: Application form not required.
Initial approach: Letter
Copies of proposal: 1
Deadline(s): None
Board meeting date(s): Dec.
Officers: Robert F. Hoerle, Pres.; Sheila A. Hoerle, V.P.; Pierre J. De Vegh, Treas.
EIN: 133419592

6195
Marion O. & Maximilian Hoffman Foundation ◇

6000 Northern Blvd.
P.O. Box 130
East Norwich, NY 11732
Contact: Ursula C. Niarakis, Pres.

Established in 1984 in NY.
Donors: Marion O. Hoffman; Maximilian Hoffman†.
Foundation type: Independent foundation.
Financial data (yr. ended 6/30/05): Assets, $29,080,677 (M); expenditures, $1,603,478; qualifying distributions, $1,454,596; giving activities include $1,289,425 for 22 grants (high: $950,000; low: $200).
Purpose and activities: Giving primarily for natural resource conservation; funding also for human services.
Fields of interest: Environment, natural resources; Environment; Human services; Foundations (private grantmaking).
Limitations: Applications not accepted. Giving primarily in New York, NY. No grants to individuals.
Application information: Contributes only to pre-selected organizations.
Officers: Ursula C. Niarakis, Pres.; William Niarakis, V.P.
Director: Margareta Jackel.
EIN: 112697957
Selected grants: The following grants were reported in 2005.
$950,000 to Hoffman Center, Upper Brookville, NY.

$253,700 to Planting Fields Foundation, Oyster Bay, NY. 3 grants: $250,000, $1,200, $2,500
$15,200 to Theodore Roosevelt Sanctuary, Oyster Bay, NY. 2 grants: $200, $15,000
$4,000 to Natural Heritage Trust, Albany, NY.
$2,000 to Old Westbury Gardens, Old Westbury, NY. 2 grants: $1,000 each
$500 to Erase Racism, Syosset, NY.

6196
Helen Hoffritz Charitable Trust ◇ ☆

c/o JPMorgan Chase Bank, N.A.
345 Park Ave., 4th Fl.
New York, NY 10154
Contact: Jacqueline Elias, V.P., JPMorgan Chase Bank, N.A.

Established in 1994 in NY.
Donor: Helen Hoffritz†.
Foundation type: Independent foundation.
Financial data (yr. ended 12/31/05): Assets, $13,715,418 (M); gifts received, $40,000; expenditures, $562,155; qualifying distributions, $431,795; giving activities include $410,000 for 9 grants (high: $60,000; low: $25,000).
Purpose and activities: Financial assistance for individuals in need of medical equipment. Priority is given to hospital-based programs that target patients preparing for discharge or those in rehabilitation centers; and community-based programs that help people with disabilities or degenerative illnesses. The trust also provides annual grants to four organizations named by the donor.
Type of support: Equipment.
Limitations: Applications not accepted. Giving primarily in New York City and Long Island, NY. No grants to individuals; no loans or matching gifts.
Publications: Grants list.
Trustee: JPMorgan Chase Bank, N.A.
EIN: 136655406
Selected grants: The following grants were reported in 2004.
$62,500 to Good Samaritan Hospital, Suffern, NY. For general support.
$62,500 to Helen Keller Services for the Blind, Brooklyn, NY. For general support.
$62,500 to New York-Presbyterian Fund, New York, NY. For general support.
$62,500 to Southside Hospital, Bay Shore, NY. For general support.

6197
The Hollyhock Foundation, Inc. ◇

c/o Robert A. Karr
55 E. 59th St., 15th Fl.
New York, NY 10022

Established in 2002 in NY.
Donor: Robert A. Karr.
Foundation type: Operating foundation.
Financial data (yr. ended 12/31/03): Assets, $50,292,717 (M); expenditures, $463,661; qualifying distributions, $432,287; giving activities include $428,500 for 14 grants (high: $300,000; low: $500).
Purpose and activities: Giving primarily for human services, particularly for the fight against poverty; funding also for education.
Fields of interest: Education; Human services; Economically disadvantaged.

Limitations: Applications not accepted. Giving primarily in New York, NY; funding also in Santa Fe, NM, and MA. No grants to individuals.
Application information: Contributes only to pre-selected organizations.
Officers: Robert A. Karr, Pres.; Susanne Karr, V.P.; Timothy K. McManus, Secy.-Treas.
EIN: 542091336

6198
Jacob L. and Lillian Holtzmann Foundation ◇

c/o Howard M. Holtzmann
630 5th Ave., Ste. 2000
New York, NY 10111
FAX: (212) 332-7142; E-mail: Holtzmann@cs.com

Established in 1958 in NY.
Donors: Jacob L. Holtzmann†; Lillian Holtzmann†; Howard M. Holtzmann.
Foundation type: Independent foundation.
Financial data (yr. ended 12/31/05): Assets, $20,587,003 (M); gifts received, $100,000; expenditures, $798,168; qualifying distributions, $724,435; giving activities include $724,435 for 69 grants (high: $150,000; low: $50).
Purpose and activities: Giving primarily for Jewish organizations and temples, human services, education, and the arts.
Fields of interest: Arts; Higher education; Human services; Jewish federated giving programs; Jewish agencies & temples.
Application information: Application form not required.
Initial approach: Letter
Copies of proposal: 1
Deadline(s): None
Trustees: Howard M. Holtzmann; Susan H. Richardson.
Number of staff: 1 part-time professional; 1 part-time support.
EIN: 136174349
Selected grants: The following grants were reported in 2004.
$200,000 to Jewish Theological Seminary of America, New York, NY. For general support.
$75,000 to Ackerman Institute for the Family, New York, NY. For general support.
$50,000 to UJA-Federation of New York, New York, NY. For general support.
$40,000 to Jewish Child Care Association of New York, New York, NY. For general support.
$30,000 to Environmental Law Institute, DC. For general support.
$30,000 to Joseph Slifka Center for Jewish Life at Yale, New Haven, CT. For general support.
$25,000 to Yale University, School of Law, New Haven, CT. For general support.
$24,900 to Metropolitan Opera Association, New York, NY. For general support.
$16,000 to American Ballet Theater, New York, NY. For general support.
$15,000 to Facing History and Ourselves National Foundation, New York, NY. For general support.

6199
Homeland Foundation, Inc. ✧
c/o Montrose Acctg.
505 Park Ave., 20th Fl.
New York, NY 10022-1106
Application address: E. Lisk Wyckoff, Jr. c/o
Wethersfield, 214 Pugsley Hill Rd., Amenia, NY
12501

Incorporated in 1938 in NY.
Donor: Chauncey Stillman†.
Foundation type: Independent foundation.
Financial data (yr. ended 4/30/05): Assets,
$80,659,662 (M); gifts received, $50,470;
expenditures, $4,918,031; qualifying distributions,
$4,066,824; giving activities include $2,078,647
for 45 grants (high: $350,000; low: $250), and
$1,580,076 for foundation-administered programs.
Purpose and activities: Giving primarily for
museums, higher education, human services, and
Roman Catholic organizations and churches.
Fields of interest: Museums; Museums (art);
Museums (specialized); Performing arts, theater;
Historic preservation/historical societies; Higher
education; Law school/education; Education;
Animals/wildlife, preservation/protection; Human
services; Roman Catholic federated giving
programs; Roman Catholic agencies & churches.
International interests: Canada; Peru; Vatican City.
Type of support: General/operating support;
Curriculum development; Scholarship funds.
Limitations: Giving primarily in the U.S., with some
emphasis on Old Lyme, CT, and New York, NY;
funding also in Ontario, Canada, Vatican City, and
Huancavelica, Peru. No grants to individuals.
Application information: Application form not
required.
　Initial approach: Letter
　Deadline(s): None
Officers and Board Members:* E. Lisk Wyckoff, Jr.,*
Pres. and Treas.; Rev. Msgr. Eugene V. Clark,* V.P.
and Secy.; Robert B. MacKay,* V.P.; Rev. Ralph F.
Caamano; Lucy Flemming-McGrath; Carl Schmitt;
Charles Scribner III.
EIN: 136113816
Selected grants: The following grants were reported
in 2005.
$350,000 to Metropolitan Museum of Art, New
　York, NY.
$170,000 to Wyckoff House and Association,
　Brooklyn, NY.
$60,000 to Society for the Preservation of Long
　Island Antiquities, Cold Spring Harbor, NY.
$50,000 to Duke University, Durham, NC.
$50,000 to Florence Griswold Museum, Old Lyme,
　CT.
$50,000 to New York Genealogical and Biographical
　Society, New York, NY.
$50,000 to Pierpont Morgan Library, New York, NY.
$45,000 to Bard College, Annandale on Hudson,
　NY.
$35,000 to Musical Masterworks, Old Lyme, CT.
$25,000 to Eaglebrook School, Deerfield, MA.

6200
Horncrest Foundation, Inc. ✧
6 Sleator Dr.
Ossining, NY 10562
Contact: Lawrence Blau, Pres.

Established in 1960 in NY.
Foundation type: Independent foundation.

Financial data (yr. ended 9/30/05): Assets,
$1,536,698 (M); gifts received, $30,546;
expenditures, $463,782; qualifying distributions,
$458,187; giving activities include $452,937 for 9
grants (high: $253,737; low: $1,000).
Purpose and activities: Scholarship programs
primarily for minorities; support also for programs
for the disadvantaged, cultural programs, medical
research and education, and organizations that
focus on social change issues, especially poverty,
housing, and civil rights.
Fields of interest: Arts; Medical school/education;
Housing/shelter, development; Economic
development; Minorities; African Americans/Blacks;
Economically disadvantaged.
Type of support: General/operating support; Seed
money; Scholarship funds; Matching/challenge
support.
Limitations: Applications not accepted. Giving
primarily in the Twin Cities, MN, St. Louis, MO, and
Madison, WI. No grants to individuals.
Application information: Unsolicited requests for
funds not accepted.
Officers and Directors:* Lawrence Blau,* Pres.;
Olivia Blau,* V.P. and Secy.
EIN: 136021261
Selected grants: The following grants were reported
in 2003.
$201,209 to Sarah Lawrence College, Bronxville,
　NY. For general support.
$130,850 to National Low Income Housing
　Coalition and Low Income Housing Information
　Service, DC. For general support.
$100,000 to Washington University, School of
　Medicine, Saint Louis, MO. For general support.
$20,000 to Emmanuel Episcopal Church, Webster
　Groves, MO. For general support.
$18,013 to Missouri Association for Social Welfare,
　Jefferson City, MO. For general support.
$10,000 to Adequate Housing for Missourians,
　Hazelwood, MO. For general support.

6201
Linda Horowitz Cancer Research
Foundation ✧
445 Broadhollow Rd., Ste. 100
Melville, NY 11747

Established in 2004 in NY.
Foundation type: Independent foundation.
Financial data (yr. ended 12/31/05): Assets,
$41,128 (M); gifts received, $500,650;
expenditures, $523,332; qualifying distributions,
$523,332; giving activities include $400,000 for 1
grant.
Fields of interest: Cancer research.
Limitations: Applications not accepted. Giving
primarily in NY.
Application information: Unsolicited requests for
funds not accepted.
Officers: Richard Horowitz, Pres.; Jill Libshutz, V.P.
Director: Dennis Kalick.
EIN: 200460429

6202
The G. & B. Horowitz Family Foundation,
Inc. ✧
(formerly Gedale B. and Barbara S. Horowitz
Foundation)
c/o Cleary Gottlieb
1 Liberty Plz.
New York, NY 10006

Established in 1970 in NY.
Donors: Gedale B. Horowitz; Gedale B. Horowitz
Charitable Lead Trust.
Foundation type: Independent foundation.
Financial data (yr. ended 6/30/05): Assets,
$4,234,085 (M); gifts received, $91,200;
expenditures, $790,051; qualifying distributions,
$788,825; giving activities include $786,300 for 23
grants (high: $353,000; low: $500).
Purpose and activities: Grants primarily for Jewish
giving, including welfare and temple support;
support also for higher education and human
services.
Fields of interest: Museums; Higher education;
Health organizations; Human services; Jewish
federated giving programs; Jewish agencies &
temples.
Type of support: General/operating support.
Limitations: Applications not accepted. Giving
primarily in New York, NY. No grants to individuals.
Application information: Contributes only to
pre-selected organizations.
Officers: Gedale B. Horowitz, Pres.; Ruth Horowitz,
V.P.; Seth Horowitz, V.P.; Steven M. Loeb, Secy.;
Barbara Horowitz, Treas.
EIN: 237101730
Selected grants: The following grants were reported
in 2005.
$353,000 to Barnard College, New York, NY.
$130,000 to Jewish Museum, New York, NY.
$75,000 to Jewish Theological Seminary of
　America, New York, NY.
$50,000 to New Museum of Contemporary Art, New
　York, NY.
$5,000 to Educational Alliance, New York, NY.
$2,000 to American Friends of the Israel Museum,
　New York, NY.
$1,000 to Lehigh University, Bethlehem, PA.
$1,000 to New York Landmarks Conservancy, New
　York, NY.
$1,000 to North Shore Hebrew Academy, Great
　Neck, NY.
$500 to Fordham University, New York, NY.

6203
Stewart W. & Willma C. Hoyt Foundation,
Inc. ☆
70 Front St.
Binghamton, NY 13905 (607) 772-0780
Contact: Catherine Schwoeffermann, Exec. Dir.
FAX: (607) 722-0747;
E-mail: hoytfoundation@stny.rr.com; URL: http://
www.hoytfoundation.org

Established in 1993 in NY as successor to Stewart
W. & Willma C. Hoyt Foundation, which was
established in 1970; status changed to a private
foundation in 2006.
Donor: Willma C. Hoyt†.
Foundation type: Independent foundation.
Financial data (yr. ended 12/31/04): Assets,
$19,935,999 (M); expenditures, $1,122,114;
qualifying distributions, $970,028; giving activities

include $771,441 for 23 grants (high: $130,000; low: $1,600), and $198,587 for in-kind gifts.

Purpose and activities: The foundation aims to use its resources to enhance the quality of life of the people of Broome County, NY, primarily through judicious grantmaking. The foundation focuses broadly on the areas of the arts, humanities, education, health and human services. The foundation is particularly interested in assisting programs that meet an urgent community need, that do not unnecessarily duplicate the work of other organizations, that have explored alternative funding sources, and that have some reasonable assurance of ongoing support.

Fields of interest: Humanities; Arts; Child development, education; Higher education; Education; Health care; Substance abuse, services; Human services; Children/youth, services; Aging, centers/services; Disabilities, people with.

Type of support: Capital campaigns; Building/renovation; Equipment; Emergency funds; Program development; Seed money; Curriculum development; Technical assistance; Consulting services; Program-related investments/loans; Matching/challenge support.

Limitations: Giving limited to Broome County, NY. No support for religious purposes. No grants to individuals, or for annual campaigns of local chapters of national organizations, deficit financing, general endowments, research, or publications.

Publications: Application guidelines; Annual report; Financial statement; Grants list.

Application information: A meeting with the Exec. Dir. must precede submission of a full proposal to the foundation. Application guidelines available on foundation Web site. Application form required.

Initial approach: Telephone or letter
Copies of proposal: 1
Deadline(s): 1st of the month prior to board meeting dates
Board meeting date(s): Quarterly; grantmaking meetings in May and Oct.
Final notification: 1 to 3 days following board meetings

Officers and Directors:* Fannie R. Linder,* Chair.; Bonnie Donovan,* Vice-Chair.; William H. Rincker,* Secy.-Treas.; Catherine Schwoeffermann, Exec. Dir.; Teri Goodall-Komar; John M. Keeler; Albert Mamary; Maria Motsavage; Gary David Rein.

Number of staff: 3 full-time professional; 1 full-time support.

EIN: 223209342

6204
HSBC in the Community USA Inc. Foundation ✧

c/o Group Public Affairs
452 5th Ave.
New York, NY 10018 (212) 525-8239
Contact: Kristen Alvanson
URL: http://www.hsbcusa.com/corporateresponsibility/contributions_grants/hsbc_in_the_community_foundation.html

Established in 2000 in NY.

Donors: HSBC Bank USA, Inc.; HSBC Bank USA, N.A.

Foundation type: Company-sponsored foundation.

Financial data (yr. ended 12/31/05): Assets, $5,007,986 (M); gifts received, $1,000,000; expenditures, $959,330; qualifying distributions, $954,950; giving activities include $951,500 for 58 grants (high: $100,000; low: $4,000).

Purpose and activities: The foundation supports organizations involved with K-12, higher, and adult education, the environment, and employment.

Fields of interest: Elementary/secondary education; Higher education; Adult/continuing education; Libraries (public); Environment, research; Environment, public education; Environment, waste management; Environment, natural resources; Environment, energy; Environment, beautification programs; Environmental education; Environment; Employment; Economically disadvantaged.

Type of support: Program development; Research.

Limitations: Giving primarily in areas of company operations. No support for political organizations. No grants to individuals.

Application information: Application form not required.

Initial approach: Proposal
Deadline(s): None

Officers: Linda Stryker, Pres.; Robert H. Muth, V.P. and Treas.; Philip S. Toohey, Secy.

EIN: 161593742

Selected grants: The following grants were reported in 2004.

$100,000 to Junior Achievement of New York, New York, NY.
$50,000 to City Parks Foundation, New York, NY.
$50,000 to New York Public Library, New York, NY.
$50,000 to Queens Botanical Garden Society, Flushing, NY.
$40,000 to Rochester Institute of Technology, Rochester, NY.
$25,000 to YMCA of Albany, Albany, NY.
$15,000 to Prospect Park Alliance, Brooklyn, NY.
$15,000 to YWCA of the City of New York, New York, NY.
$14,350 to ESF College Foundation, Syracuse, NY.
$10,000 to Genesee Land Trust, Pittsford, NY.

6205
Huberfeld Family Foundation, Inc. ✧

152 W. 57th St.
New York, NY 10019
Contact: Murray Huberfeld, Pres.

Established in 1999 in NY.

Donor: Huberfeld-Bodner Family Foundation.

Foundation type: Independent foundation.

Financial data (yr. ended 12/31/04): Assets, $15,801,361 (M); gifts received, $360,000; expenditures, $1,154,454; qualifying distributions, $1,151,450; giving activities include $1,151,450 for 28 grants (high: $387,000; low: $500).

Fields of interest: Jewish agencies & temples.

Limitations: Giving primarily in New York, NY.

Application information:

Initial approach: Letter
Deadline(s): None

Officers and Directors:* Murray Huberfeld,* Pres.; Laura Huberfeld,* Secy.-Treas.; Rae Huberfeld.

EIN: 134042543

Selected grants: The following grants were reported in 2003.

$700,000 to Congregation Ahavas Tzdokah V Chesed, Brooklyn, NY.
$35,000 to Ezer Mzion, Brooklyn, NY.
$18,000 to Agudath Israel of America, New York, NY.

6206
Huberfeld-Bodner Family Foundation, Inc. ✧

152 W. 57th St.
New York, NY 10022
Contact: Murray Huberfeld, Secy.

Established in 1994 in NY.

Donors: David Bodner; Naomi Bodner; Laura Huberfeld; Murray Huberfeld.

Foundation type: Independent foundation.

Financial data (yr. ended 12/31/03): Assets, $6,321,126 (M); expenditures, $4,721,968; qualifying distributions, $1,715,070; giving activities include $1,715,070 for 64 grants (high: $1,500,000; low: $36).

Purpose and activities: Giving primarily to Jewish organizations and temples and for education.

Fields of interest: Education; Jewish agencies & temples.

Limitations: Giving primarily in the New York, NY, area.

Application information: Application form not required.

Initial approach: Letter
Deadline(s): None

Officers: Naomi Bodner, Pres.; Laura Huberfeld, V.P.; Murray Huberfeld, Secy.; David Bodner, Treas.

EIN: 133682951

Selected grants: The following grants were reported in 2004.

$360,000 to Huberfeld Family Foundation, New York, NY.
$50,000 to Yeshiva University of Los Angeles, Los Angeles, CA.
$15,500 to Rabbi Jacob Joseph School, Edison, NJ.
$15,000 to Aish HaTorah, Brooklyn, NY.
$6,000 to Yad Lachim, New York, NY.
$5,000 to Yeshiva University, New York, NY.
$2,000 to Aleph Institute, Surfside, FL.
$1,000 to Ohr Chadash, Fresh Meadows, NY.
$1,000 to Yeshiva Bais Mikroh, Brooklyn, NY.
$1,000 to Yeshiva of Spring Valley, Monsey, NY.

6207
Hudson River Bancorp, Inc. Foundation ✧

1 Hudson City Centre
P.O. Box 76
Hudson, NY 12534 (518) 828-4600, ext. 4303
Contact: Holly Rappleyea, Secy.

Established in 1998 in NY.

Donors: Hudson River Bank & Trust Co.; Carl Florio.

Foundation type: Company-sponsored foundation.

Financial data (yr. ended 3/31/05): Assets, $18,141,568 (M); gifts received, $251,475; expenditures, $849,599; qualifying distributions, $762,561; giving activities include $762,561 for 462 grants (high: $100,000; low: $25).

Purpose and activities: The foundation supports organizations involved with arts and culture, education, health, human services, and community development.

Fields of interest: Historic preservation/historical societies; Arts; Elementary/secondary education; Higher education, university; Libraries (public); Education; Hospitals (general); Health care; Children/youth, services; Human services; Community development; Federated giving programs.

Type of support: General/operating support; Building/renovation; Equipment; Program development.

Limitations: Giving primarily in upstate NY.
Application information: Application form not required.
Initial approach: Telephone foundation
Deadline(s): None
Officers: Marilyn A. Herrington, Pres.; William H. Jones, V.P.; Holly Rappleyea, Secy.; Carl Florio, Treas.
Director: Joseph Phelan.
EIN: 223595668

6208

Geoffrey C. Hughes Foundation, Inc.
c/o Cahill Gordon & Reindel LLP
80 Pine St.
New York, NY   10005   (212) 701-3400
Contact: John R. Young, Pres.

Established in 1991 in NY.
Donor: Geoffrey C. Hughes†.
Foundation type: Independent foundation.
Financial data (yr. ended 3/31/06): Assets, $32,796,311 (M); expenditures, $2,290,334; qualifying distributions, $2,218,938; giving activities include $2,201,975 for 29 grants (high: $300,000; low: $2,000).
Purpose and activities: Support primarily for environmental protection, opera, and ballet, with preference given to organizations supported by Mr. Hughes during his lifetime.
Fields of interest: Performing arts, ballet; Performing arts, opera; Environment, natural resources.
Limitations: Giving on a national basis. No grants to individuals.
Application information: Application form not required.
Initial approach: Letter of inquiry or telephone
Copies of proposal: 1
Deadline(s): None
Board meeting date(s): As necessary
Final notification: Varies
Officers and Directors:* John R. Young,* Pres.; Ursula Cliff,* V.P. and Secy.; Walter C. Cliff,* V.P. and Treas.; Mary K. Young,* V.P.; June McCandless.
EIN: 133622255
Selected grants: The following grants were reported in 2005.
$900,000 to Marine Mammal Center, Sausalito, CA. 2 grants: $300,000, $600,000
$400,000 to Nature Conservancy, Arlington, VA. 2 grants: $200,000 each
$100,000 to New York City Ballet, New York, NY.
$50,000 to Berkshire Natural Resources Council, Pittsfield, MA.
$50,000 to Literary Classics of the United States, New York, NY.
$50,000 to New York City Opera, New York, NY.
$25,000 to American Friends of the Paris Opera and Ballet, New York, NY.
$25,000 to Pascal Rioult Dance Theater, New York, NY.

6209

The Charles Evans Hughes Memorial Foundation, Inc. ◇
130 E. 59th St., 12th Fl.
New York, NY   10022-1302   (212) 836-1358
Contact: Lauren Katzowitz Shenfield, Secy.

Incorporated in 1962 in NY.

Donors: Catherine Hughes Waddell†; Chauncey L. Waddell†.
Foundation type: Independent foundation.
Financial data (yr. ended 7/31/05): Assets, $22,156,551 (M); expenditures, $1,441,957; qualifying distributions, $1,116,112; giving activities include $1,034,000 for 48 grants (high: $75,000; low: $500).
Purpose and activities: Giving primarily to organizations engaged in: 1) education, including legal education, social sciences 2) combating prejudice based on race, color, or religious belief; 3) protecting the environment, including population aspects and AIDS prevention; and 4) the arts.
Fields of interest: Arts; Law school/education; Education; Environment; Health care; Legal services; Civil rights.
Type of support: Fellowships; Continuing support; Annual campaigns; Scholarship funds.
Limitations: Applications not accepted. Giving primarily in New York, NY. No grants to individuals.
Application information: Unsolicited requests for funds not accepted.
Board meeting date(s): Oct. and June
Officers and Directors:* Theodore H. Waddell,* Pres.; Wendy J. Williamson, V.P.; Lauren Shenfield Katzowitz, Secy.; William G. Kirkland,* Treas.; Christopher Angell; Derek Kirkland; Karen A.G. Loud; Susan Johnson McLean; Brewster Waddell; Sandra Hughes Waddell.
Number of staff: None.
EIN: 136159445
Selected grants: The following grants were reported in 2003.
$75,000 to Columbia University, School of Law, New York, NY.
$75,000 to NAACP Legal Defense and Educational Fund, New York, NY.
$75,000 to Nature Conservancy, Arlington, VA.
$60,000 to National Trust for Historic Preservation, DC.
$50,000 to American Museum of Natural History, New York, NY.
$50,000 to Legal Aid Society, New York, NY.
$50,000 to New Leaders for New Schools, New York, NY.
$35,000 to Henry Street Settlement, New York, NY.
$35,000 to Waterkeeper Alliance, Tarrytown, NY.
$30,000 to Bank Street College of Education, New York, NY.

6210

Hugoton Foundation ◇
900 Park Ave., Ste. 17E
New York, NY   10021   (212) 734-5447
Contact: Joan K. Stout, Pres.

Established in 1981 in DE.
Donor: Wallace Gilroy†.
Foundation type: Independent foundation.
Financial data (yr. ended 12/31/05): Assets, $40,201,610 (M); expenditures, $2,082,872; qualifying distributions, $2,064,292; giving activities include $1,826,000 for 65 grants (high: $500,000; low: $1,000).
Purpose and activities: Giving primarily for hospitals, medical research, and equipment needs; some support for higher and pre-college education and religious welfare, and Roman Catholic churches.
Fields of interest: Higher education; Hospitals (general); Nursing care; Medical research, institute; Human services; Roman Catholic agencies & churches.

Type of support: Equipment; Program development; Research.
Limitations: Giving primarily in Miami, FL, and New York, NY. No grants to individuals.
Application information:
Initial approach: Proposal
Copies of proposal: 1
Deadline(s): None
Board meeting date(s): As necessary
Final notification: Calendar year
Officers and Directors:* Joan K. Stout, Pres.; Ray E. Stout,* V.P.; Joan M. Stout,* Secy.; Jean C. Stout,* Treas.; Frank S. Fejes; John K. Stout.
Number of staff: 1 full-time professional.
EIN: 341351062
Selected grants: The following grants were reported in 2005.
$555,000 to Lenox Hill Hospital, New York, NY. 2 grants: $500,000, $55,000
$100,000 to Archdiocese of Miami, Miami Shores, FL. 2 grants: $50,000 each
$100,000 to Columbia University, New York, NY.
$100,000 to Florida Center for Theological Studies, Miami, FL.
$50,000 to College of Mount Saint Vincent, Riverdale, NY.
$45,000 to Miami Childrens Hospital, Miami, FL.
$10,000 to Siena College, Loudonville, NY.
$5,000 to Saint Jean Baptiste Church, New York, NY.

6211

Hultquist Foundation, Inc. ◇
c/o Price, Flowers, Malin & Westerberg
P.O. Box 1219
Jamestown, NY   14701-1219   (716) 664-5210
Contact: Thomas I. Flowers, Pres.

Established in 1965 in NY.
Foundation type: Independent foundation.
Financial data (yr. ended 6/30/05): Assets, $15,026,209 (M); expenditures, $794,462; qualifying distributions, $688,710; giving activities include $680,896 for 13 grants (high: $250,000; low: $5,000).
Purpose and activities: Giving primarily for higher education.
Fields of interest: Higher education; Libraries/library science; Recreation, camps; Human services; YM/YWCAs & YM/YWHAs; Philanthropy/voluntarism.
Type of support: General/operating support; Continuing support; Annual campaigns; Capital campaigns; Building/renovation; Equipment; Land acquisition.
Limitations: Giving limited to Chautauqua County, NY, with emphasis on Jamestown, NY. No grants to individuals.
Application information: Application form required.
Initial approach: Letter
Copies of proposal: 4
Deadline(s): Generally in June and Dec.
Board meeting date(s): Quarterly
Officers: Thomas I. Flowers, Pres.; Charles H. Price, V.P.; William L. Wright, V.P.; Robert F. Rohm, Jr., Secy.-Treas.
Trustee: John K. Plumb.
EIN: 160907729
Selected grants: The following grants were reported in 2005.
$250,000 to Jamestown Community College, Jamestown, NY. For building.

$141,000 to Chautauqua Institution, Chautauqua, NY. For building.

$100,000 to Boys and Girls Club of Jamestown, Jamestown, NY. For building.

$43,246 to James Prendergast Library, Jamestown, NY. For literature program.

$30,000 to Chautauqua Striders Youth Development Coalition, Jamestown, NY.

$28,000 to United Way of Southern Chautauqua County, Jamestown, NY. For annual fund.

$25,050 to YMCA of Jamestown, Jamestown, NY. For operating support.

$25,000 to Roger Tory Peterson Institute for the Study of Natural History, Jamestown, NY.

$12,000 to YWCA of Jamestown, Jamestown, NY. For operating support.

$11,600 to Audubon Society of Jamestown, Jamestown, NY. For building.

6212
The Humanitas Foundation
(formerly Brencanda Foundation)
1114 Ave. of the Americas, 28th Fl.
New York, NY 10036 (212) 704-2300
Contact: Kathleen A. Mahoney, Pres.
E-mail: humanitas@humanitasfoundation.org;
URL: http://www.humanitasfoundation.org

Established in 1979.
Donors: American Retail Group, Inc.; American Retail Properties, Inc.; Argidius Foundation.
Foundation type: Independent foundation.
Financial data (yr. ended 12/31/05): Assets, $279,899 (M); gifts received, $3,419,493; expenditures, $3,348,888; qualifying distributions, $3,348,053; giving activities include $3,348,053 for 130 grants (high: $150,000; low: $3,500; average: $10,000–$50,000).
Purpose and activities: Grants only for Roman Catholic organizations within the U.S.
Fields of interest: Roman Catholic agencies & churches.
Type of support: General/operating support; Management development/capacity building; Equipment; Program development; Conferences/seminars; Seed money; Curriculum development; Research; Consulting services; Matching/challenge support.
Limitations: Giving on a national basis. No support for individual parishes, schools or colleges not solicited by the foundation. No grants to individuals, or for scholarships, endowments, large construction projects, or capital campaigns.
Publications: Application guidelines.
Application information: Application form required.
Initial approach: Request guidelines by telephone, e-mail, or letter
Copies of proposal: 1
Deadline(s): Feb. 1 and July 1
Board meeting date(s): Apr. and Oct.
Final notification: Following board meeting
Officer and Director:* Kathleen A. Mahoney,* Pres.
Number of staff: 2 full-time professional; 1 full-time support.
EIN: 133005012

6213
Lawrence S. Huntington Fund ◇
46 E. 70th St., 4th Fl.
New York, NY 10021 (212) 717-8633
Contact: Lawrence S. Huntington, Dir.

Established in 1997 in NY.
Donor: Lawrence S. Huntington.
Foundation type: Independent foundation.
Financial data (yr. ended 12/31/04): Assets, $71,909 (M); gifts received, $482,503; expenditures, $450,515; qualifying distributions, $440,576; giving activities include $394,975 for 34 grants.
Fields of interest: Higher education; Law school/education; Education; Animals/wildlife; Hospitals (general); Human services.
Limitations: Giving primarily in NY.
Application information: Application form not required.
Deadline(s): None
Director: Lawrence S. Huntington.
EIN: 133985928

6214
Syde Hurdus 1992 Charitable Trust ◇
2438 McCord Ave.
Merrick, NY 11566-4229

Established in 1992 in NY.
Donor: Syde Hurdus†.
Foundation type: Independent foundation.
Financial data (yr. ended 8/31/04): Assets, $13,583,238 (M); gifts received, $940,077; expenditures, $700,840; qualifying distributions, $569,000; giving activities include $569,000 for 36 grants (high: $150,000; low: $1,000).
Fields of interest: Hospitals (general); Health care; Health organizations, association; Eye diseases; Cancer research; Breast cancer research.
Limitations: Applications not accepted. No grants to individuals.
Application information: Contributes only to pre-selected organizations.
Trustees: Herbert S. Fitzgibbon; Salvatore Romanotto.
EIN: 113163290

6215
The Hurford Foundation ◇
c/o Davidson, Dawson & Clark
60 E. 42nd St.
New York, NY 10165

Established in 1986.
Donors: John B. Hurford†; BEA Assocs., Inc.
Foundation type: Independent foundation.
Financial data (yr. ended 12/31/04): Assets, $15,250,762 (M); expenditures, $1,155,729; qualifying distributions, $1,010,345; giving activities include $892,850 for 9 grants (high: $437,850; low: $3,000).
Fields of interest: Arts; Higher education; Human services; Children/youth, services; International affairs.
Type of support: General/operating support.
Limitations: Applications not accepted. Giving primarily in NY. Generally no grants to individuals.
Application information: Contributes only to pre-selected organizations.
Board meeting date(s): Quarterly
Officers and Directors:* Robert C. Miller,* Pres. and Treas.; Jayne M. Kurzman,* V.P.; William W. Priest, Jr.,* Secy.
EIN: 133394688

6216
Hurst Family Foundation ◇
(formerly The Robert J. Hurst Foundation)
c/o Crestview Partners
667 Madison Ave., 10th Fl.
New York, NY 10021

Established in 1997 in NY.
Donors: Robert J. Hurst; RJH Investment Partners, L.P.
Foundation type: Independent foundation.
Financial data (yr. ended 12/31/05): Assets, $25,021,064 (M); gifts received, $1,480,594; expenditures, $4,019,506; qualifying distributions, $3,725,355; giving activities include $2,724,604 for 102 grants (high: $1,000,000; low: $1).
Purpose and activities: Giving primarily for the arts.
Fields of interest: Arts; Education; Health care; Human services; Jewish federated giving programs; Jewish agencies & temples.
Limitations: Applications not accepted. Giving primarily in NY. No grants to individuals.
Application information: Contributes only to pre-selected organizations.
Trustees: Alexander B. Hurst; Amanda K. Hurst; Robert J. Hurst; Soledad D. Hurst.
EIN: 311568195

6217
Hutchins Family Foundation, Inc. ◇ ☆
c/o Glenn H. Hutchins, Silver Lake Partners
9 W. 57th St., 25th Fl.
New York, NY 10019

Established in 2004 in NY.
Donor: Glenn H. Hutchins.
Foundation type: Independent foundation.
Financial data (yr. ended 12/31/05): Assets, $8,375,903 (M); gifts received, $7,082,807; expenditures, $649,641; qualifying distributions, $647,831; giving activities include $646,000 for 6 grants (high: $344,000; low: $1,000).
Fields of interest: Hospitals (general); Human services.
Limitations: Applications not accepted. Giving on a national basis. No grants to individuals.
Application information: Contributes only to pre-selected organizations.
Officers: Glenn H. Hutchins, Chair. and Treas.; Deborah O. Hutchins, Pres. and Secy.
EIN: 371501785

6218
Mary J. Hutchins Foundation, Inc. ◇
50 E. 42nd St., 19th Fl.
New York, NY 10017 (212) 599-2234

Incorporated in 1935 in NY.
Donors: Mary J. Hutchins†; Caspar J. Voorhis†; Waldo H. Hutchins, Jr.†.
Foundation type: Independent foundation.
Financial data (yr. ended 12/31/05): Assets, $35,678,200 (M); expenditures, $2,439,105; qualifying distributions, $2,331,286; giving activities include $2,201,636 for grants, and $16,906 for 2 grants to individuals (high: $9,230; low: $7,676).
Purpose and activities: The foundation supports social services organizations serving low-income populations in New York City. There is some support for health services to the same populations.

Fields of interest: Hospitals (general); Health care; Human services; Federated giving programs; Economically disadvantaged.
Type of support: General/operating support; Program development; Grants to individuals.
Limitations: Applications not accepted. Giving primarily in the New York, NY, area. No support for educational purposes or national health funds. No grants for seed money, scholarships, or annual campaigns.
Application information: Unsolicited requests for proposals not accepted.
Board meeting date(s): Mar., June, Sept., and Dec.
Officers: Waldo Hutchins III, Pres.; Elizabeth E. Hutchins, V.P.; Edwin Sheffield, V.P.; Hildy Simmons, V.P.; Sidney S. Whelan, Jr., V.P.
Directors: Richard J. Mirabella; Richard G. Mulholland.
EIN: 136083578
Selected grants: The following grants were reported in 2004.
$100,000 to NYU Downtown Hospital, New York, NY.
$75,000 to Henry Street Settlement, New York, NY.
$50,000 to Planned Parenthood of Nassau County, Hempstead, NY.
$50,000 to Primary Care Development Corporation, New York, NY.
$50,000 to Visiting Nurse Service of New York, New York, NY.
$40,000 to Academy for Clinical and Applied Psychoanalysis, West Orange, NJ.
$40,000 to CityKids Foundation, New York, NY.
$30,000 to Womens Housing and Economic Development Corporation, Bronx, NY.
$25,000 to Childrens Advocacy Center of Manhattan, New York, NY.
$25,000 to Make the Road By Walking, Brooklyn, NY.

6219

I Have a Dream Foundation - New York ✧
330 7th Ave., 20th Fl.
New York, NY 10001 (212) 293-5480
Contact: Kara Forte, Exec. Dir.
FAX: (212) 293-5478; E-mail: info@ihad.org; URL: http://www.ihad.org

Established in 1986 in NY.
Donors: Eugene M. Lang; and various other donors.
Foundation type: Operating foundation.
Financial data (yr. ended 8/31/05): Assets, $141,889 (M); gifts received, $1,365,930; expenditures, $1,369,847; qualifying distributions, $1,366,039; giving activities include $1,030 for 1 grant, and $515,291 for grants to individuals.
Purpose and activities: Projects include programs to motivate disadvantaged grade school students to attend college by offering scholarships, reading materials, support groups, counseling services, tutoring, mentoring and enrichment programs.
Fields of interest: Education; Human services; Neighborhood centers; Youth, services; Minorities; Economically disadvantaged.
Type of support: Continuing support; Scholarship funds; Technical assistance.
Limitations: Applications not accepted.
Publications: Financial statement; Informational brochure.

Application information: Giving only for pre-determined educational projects organized by the foundation's sponsors.
Board meeting date(s): Annually; executive committee meets every other month
Officers: Jeff Gural, Chair.; Stanley Picheny, Vice-Chair.; Barbara Eisold, Secy.; Brian Hiedtke, Treas.
Directors: Rick Aidekman; Joseph S. Brosnan; Bill A. Duffy; Warren Eisenberg; Harold Friedman; Nathan Ganther; Sharon Kaufman; Howard Kaye; Susan Pinco; Bernie Robinson; Jefry Rosmarin.
Number of staff: 12 full-time professional; 1 part-time professional; 2 part-time support.
EIN: 133370648

6220

The IAC Foundation ✧
(formerly USA Networks Foundation, Inc.)
152 W. 57th St., 40th Fl.
New York, NY 10019
Contact: William Severance, Treas. and Cont.

Established in 1998 in NY.
Donors: USA Networks, Inc.; USA Interactive; InterActiveCorp; IAC/InterActiveCorp.
Foundation type: Company-sponsored foundation.
Financial data (yr. ended 12/31/04): Assets, $3,397,856 (M); gifts received, $21,483; expenditures, $1,308,310; qualifying distributions, $1,261,114; giving activities include $1,261,114 for 600 grants (high: $100,000; low: $40).
Purpose and activities: The foundation supports organizations involved with arts and culture, education, health, and human services.
Fields of interest: Arts; Higher education; Education; Environment, natural resources; Health organizations, association; Children/youth, services; Human services; International development; International affairs.
Limitations: Applications not accepted. Giving on a national basis.
Application information: Contributes only to pre-selected organizations.
Officers: Victor Kaufman, Pres.; Eric Degraw, V.P.; Julius Genachowski, V.P.; David Ellen, Secy.; William Severance, Treas. and Cont.
EIN: 133994361
Selected grants: The following grants were reported in 2003.
$25,000 to Educational Broadcasting Corporation, New York, NY.
$25,000 to Multiple Sclerosis Society, National, New York, NY.
$25,000 to Starbright Foundation, Los Angeles, CA.
$25,000 to UJA-Federation of New York, New York, NY.
$24,613 to Literacy Partners, New York, NY.
$23,500 to Project ALS, New York, NY.
$23,500 to Whitney Museum of American Art, New York, NY.
$19,073 to United Way of Roanoke Valley, Roanoke, VA.
$16,602 to American Red Cross, National Headquarters, DC.
$10,000 to Miami Childrens Museum, Miami, FL.

6221

IBM International Foundation ✧
(formerly IBM South Africa Projects Fund)
New Orchard Rd.
Armonk, NY 10504-1709 (914) 765-1900
E-mail: phdfellow@us.ibm.com; URL: http://www.ibm.com/ibm/ibmgives/

Established in 1985 in NY.
Donor: International Business Machines Corp.
Foundation type: Company-sponsored foundation.
Financial data (yr. ended 12/31/04): Assets, $164,195,806 (M); gifts received, $8,175,000; expenditures, $11,918,255; qualifying distributions, $11,054,279; giving activities include $1,597,710 for grants, $1,632,437 for grants to individuals, and $7,275,025 for employee matching gifts.
Purpose and activities: The foundation supports organizations involved with arts and culture, education, the environment, health, human services, civic affairs, and science and technology. Special emphasis is directed toward programs designed to promote childhood education.
Fields of interest: Arts; Education, reform; Education, early childhood education; Higher education; Education; Environment; Public health; Health care; Aging, centers/services; Human services; Science.
Type of support: General/operating support; Program development; Fellowships; Employee matching gifts.
Limitations: Giving on a national and international basis. No support for fraternal, labor, political, or religious organizations or private or parochial schools. No grants to individuals (except for fellowships), or for scholarships, capital campaigns, fundraising, construction or renovation projects, chairs, endowments, conferences, symposia, or sports competitions.
Publications: Application guidelines; Informational brochure.
Application information: Proposals should be no longer than 2 pages. Application form not required.
Initial approach: Proposal
Copies of proposal: 1
Deadline(s): None
Officers and Directors:* Samuel J. Palmisano,* Chair.; Abby F. Kohnstamm,* Vice-Chair.; Stanley S. Litow,* Pres.; Paula W. Baker, V.P.; A. Bonzani, Secy.; Richard Obetz, Treas.; Richard J. Carroll, Cont.; Mark Loughridge; Robin G. Willner.
Number of staff: 1 full-time professional.
EIN: 133267906

6222

The Icahn Charitable Foundation ✧
c/o Icahn Assoc. Corp.
767 5th Ave., Ste. 4700
New York, NY 10153
Contact: Gail Golden-Icahn, V.P.

Established in 1995 in DE.
Foundation type: Independent foundation.
Financial data (yr. ended 11/30/05): Assets, $715,144 (M); expenditures, $368,098; qualifying distributions, $367,538; giving activities include $366,400 for 25 grants (high: $192,000; low: $1,000).
Purpose and activities: Giving for health associations and human services.
Fields of interest: Education; Hospitals (general); Health organizations, association; Food distribution,

meals on wheels; Recreation; Youth development, scouting agencies (general); Human services; Children/youth, services; Foundations (private grantmaking).
Limitations: Giving primarily in NY; some giving nationally. No grants to individuals.
Application information: Application form not required.
  Initial approach: Letter
  Deadline(s): None
Officers and Directors:* Carl C. Icahn,* Pres. and Treas.; Gail Golden-Icahn,* V.P. and Secy.
EIN: 133863205

6223

The Icahn Family Foundation ▼ ✧
c/o Icahn Assocs.
767 5th Ave., Ste. 4700
New York, NY 10153
Contact: Gail Golden Icahn, V.P.

Established in 1996 in DE and NY.
Donor: Carl C. Icahn.
Foundation type: Independent foundation.
Financial data (yr. ended 8/31/05): Assets, $15,955,705 (M); expenditures, $4,573,966; qualifying distributions, $4,573,391; giving activities include $4,572,000 for 14 grants (high: $4,250,000; low: $1,000; average: $1,000–$25,000).
Purpose and activities: Giving primarily for higher education, as well as for a school of medicine.
Fields of interest: Performing arts centers; Higher education; Medical school/education; Medical research; Human services; Foundations (public).
Limitations: Giving primarily in New York, NY; some funding also in Princeton, NJ.
Application information: Application form not required.
  Initial approach: Letter
  Deadline(s): None
Officers: Carl C. Icahn, Pres. and Treas.; Gail Golden Icahn, V.P. and Secy.
EIN: 133906935
Selected grants: The following grants were reported in 2005.
$4,250,000 to Mount Sinai School of Medicine of New York University, New York, NY. For general and program support.
$250,000 to Lincoln Center for the Performing Arts, New York, NY. For general and program support.
$25,000 to Miami City Ballet, Miami Beach, FL. For general and program support.
$15,000 to Lincoln Center Hedge Fund Council, New York, NY. For general and program support.
$10,000 to Southampton Hospital Association, Southampton, NY. For general and program support.

6224

The Carl C. Icahn Foundation ✧
c/o Icahn Assoc. Corp.
767 5th Ave., Ste. 4700
New York, NY 10153-0023
Contact: Gail Golden-Icahn, V.P.

Established in 1980 in NY and DE.
Donor: Carl C. Icahn.
Foundation type: Independent foundation.
Financial data (yr. ended 11/30/05): Assets, $3,953,602 (M); expenditures, $1,537,585;

qualifying distributions, $1,536,965; giving activities include $1,536,000 for 3 grants (high: $1,500,000; low: $1,000).
Fields of interest: Arts; Higher education; Hospitals (general); Health organizations, association; Recreation; Children/youth, services; Jewish agencies & temples.
Type of support: General/operating support; Annual campaigns; Building/renovation; Matching/challenge support.
Limitations: Giving primarily in NJ and New York, NY. No grants to individuals.
Application information: Include brief description of project.
  Initial approach: Letter
  Deadline(s): None
  Board meeting date(s): As necessary
Officers: Carl C. Icahn, Pres.; Gail Golden-Icahn, V.P.
Number of staff: 1
EIN: 133091588

6225

IDF Memorial Foundation ✧
(formerly L & H Family Foundation)
1555 Rockaway Pkwy.
Brooklyn, NY 11236
Contact: Barry Friedman, Pres.

Established in 1998 in NY.
Donor: Lawrence Friedman.
Foundation type: Independent foundation.
Financial data (yr. ended 8/31/05): Assets, $2,414,518 (M); gifts received, $392,500; expenditures, $870,333; qualifying distributions, $845,442; giving activities include $820,551 for 158 grants (high: $350,000; low: $25).
Purpose and activities: Giving primarily to Jewish agencies and temples.
Fields of interest: Federated giving programs; Jewish agencies & temples.
Limitations: Applications not accepted. Giving primarily in Brooklyn, NY. No grants to individuals.
Application information: Contributes only to pre-selected organizations.
Officer: Barry Friedman, Pres.
EIN: 113455324
Selected grants: The following grants were reported in 2005.
$10,000 to Ohr Chodosh, Brooklyn, NY.
$3,600 to Yeshiva Tiferes Elimelech, Brooklyn, NY.
$720 to Yeshiva Torah Vodaath, Brooklyn, NY. 2 grants: $360 each
$700 to Congregation Yismach Moshe, Brooklyn, NY.
$600 to Sinai Academy, Brooklyn, NY. 2 grants: $240, $360
$540 to Talmudical Yeshiva of Philadelphia, Philadelphia, PA.
$225 to Agudath Israel of America, New York, NY.
$100 to Beth Medrash Govoha, Brooklyn, NY.

6226

IF Hummingbird Foundation, Inc. ✧ ☆
(formerly The Iscol Family Foundation, Inc.)
63 Lyndel Rd.
Pound Ridge, NY 10576   (914) 764-8479
Contact: Jill Iscol, Pres.

Established in 1990 in NY.
Donor: Kenneth Iscol.
Foundation type: Independent foundation.

Financial data (yr. ended 6/30/05): Assets, $1,472,200 (M); expenditures, $747,081; qualifying distributions, $481,757; giving activities include $469,494 for 40 grants (high: $60,000; low: $25).
Fields of interest: Elementary/secondary education; Higher education; Environment, natural resources; Health organizations, association; Human services; Children/youth, services; Civil liberties, advocacy; Public affairs.
Type of support: General/operating support; Continuing support; Annual campaigns; Endowments; Conferences/seminars; Curriculum development; Scholarship funds; Matching/challenge support.
Limitations: Giving primarily in CT and NY. No grants to individuals.
Application information:
  Initial approach: Letter
  Deadline(s): None
Officers and Directors:* Jill Iscol,* Pres. and Treas.; Kenneth Iscol,* V.P. and Secy.
Number of staff: 1 part-time professional; 2 part-time support.
EIN: 061314468
Selected grants: The following grants were reported in 2005.
$60,000 to Bank Street College of Education, New York, NY.
$36,375 to City Year New York, New York, NY.
$16,000 to Kayne-ERAS Center, Culver City, CA.
$15,000 to Acumen Fund, New York, NY.
$10,000 to Harvard University, Cambridge, MA.
$3,000 to Childrens Museum of Manhattan, New York, NY.
$2,750 to Jewish Museum, New York, NY.
$2,300 to Boys and Girls Club of Northern Westchester, Mount Kisco, NY.
$1,000 to PEN American Center, New York, NY.
$700 to Bank Street School for Children, New York, NY.

6227

The IFF Foundation, Inc. ✧
521 W. 57th St.
New York, NY 10019

Incorporated in 1963 in NY.
Donor: International Flavors & Fragrances, Inc.
Foundation type: Company-sponsored foundation.
Financial data (yr. ended 12/31/03): Assets, $20,416 (M); gifts received, $662,140; expenditures, $687,745; qualifying distributions, $687,068; giving activities include $626,662 for 89 grants (high: $40,000; low: $100), and $60,406 for employee matching gifts.
Purpose and activities: The foundation supports hospitals and organizations involved with arts and culture, education, health, and human services.
Fields of interest: Arts; Higher education; Education; Hospitals (general); Health organizations, association; Human services; Children/youth, services; Family services; Federated giving programs.
Type of support: Research; Employee matching gifts.
Limitations: Applications not accepted. Giving primarily in NJ and New York, NY. No grants to individuals.
Application information: Contributes only to pre-selected organizations.

Officers: R.A. Goldstein, Pres.; G. Belmuth, V.P.; D.M. Meany, Secy.; D.J. Wetmore, Treas.
EIN: 136159094
Selected grants: The following grants were reported in 2004.
$63,000 to Cosmetic Executive Women Foundation, New York, NY. 2 grants: $40,000 (For CEW Achiever Awards sponsorship), $23,000 (For Beauty Awards sponsorship).
$50,000 to Institute for the Study of Aging, New York, NY. For in memory of Mrs. Estee Lauder.
$40,000 to March of Dimes Birth Defects Foundation, New York, NY. For Million Dollar Beauty Ball.
$25,000 to Whitney Museum of American Art, New York, NY. For American Art Awards.
$20,000 to Lincoln Center Consolidated Corporate Fund, New York, NY. For annual campaign.
$15,000 to International Tennis Hall of Fame, New York, NY.
$12,500 to Fashion Group International, New York, NY. For Beauth Luncheon Symposium.
$12,500 to Saint Lukes-Roosevelt Hospital Center, New York, NY. For Seventh Annual gala.
$10,000 to Rockefeller University, New York, NY. For honoring Evelyn Lauder at annual Women and Science lecture luncheon.

6228
IIMI, Inc. ✧
c/o Hertz, Herson & Company, LLP
2 Park Ave., Ste. 1500
New York, NY 10016

Established in 1997 in DE and NY.
Donor: Susan Wexner Revocable Trust.
Foundation type: Independent foundation.
Financial data (yr. ended 6/30/05): Assets, $22,106,084 (M); expenditures, $1,194,819; qualifying distributions, $1,063,522; giving activities include $1,054,000 for 7 grants (high: $300,000; low: $1,302).
Fields of interest: Foundations (public); Jewish federated giving programs.
Limitations: Applications not accepted. Giving primarily in Washington, DC, and New York, NY. No grants to individuals.
Application information: Contributes only to pre-selected organizations.
Officer and Directors:* Susan Wexner,* Pres. and Secy.-Treas.; Bertrand Agus.
EIN: 134077817

6229
Independence Community Foundation ▼ ✧
182 Atlantic Ave.
Brooklyn, NY 11201 (718) 722-2300
Contact: Marilyn G. Gelber, Exec. Dir.
FAX: (718) 722-5757; E-mail: inquiries@icfny.org;
URL: http://www.icfny.org

Established in 1998 in NY.
Donors: Independence Community Bank Corp.; Rockefeller Brothers Fund; Penguin Putnam Inc.; St. Joseph Hill Academy.
Foundation type: Independent foundation.
Financial data (yr. ended 12/31/04): Assets, $84,643,459 (M); expenditures, $8,176,155; qualifying distributions, $7,906,462; giving activities include $7,224,764 for 897 grants (high:

$250,000; low: $10), and $300,000 for 1 loan/program-related investment.
Purpose and activities: The foundation supports organizations involved with arts and culture, education, neighborhood beautification, health, hunger, human services, and community development.
Fields of interest: Arts; Education; Environment, beautification programs; Health care; Agriculture/food; Human services; Community development.
Type of support: Sponsorships; General/operating support; Capital campaigns; Building/renovation; Equipment; Land acquisition; Endowments; Emergency funds; Program development; Publication; Seed money; Internship funds; Scholarship funds; Technical assistance; Program-related investments/loans; Employee matching gifts; Matching/challenge support.
Limitations: Giving primarily in Nassau, New York, Suffolk, and Westchester counties, NY, and Bergen, Essex, Hudson, Middlesex, Monmouth, Ocean, and Union counties, NJ. No support for political or religious organizations. No grants to individuals, or for tickets for dinners, golf outings, or fundraising events.
Publications: Application guidelines; Financial statement; Grants list; Newsletter; IRS Form 990-PF.
Application information: Letters of inquiry should be no longer than 2 to 3 pages. Application form not required.
　　Initial approach: Letter of inquiry; download application form and mail to foundation for Small Grants
　　Deadline(s): Jan. 1 through Mar. 31 and July 1 through Sept. 30; none for Small Grants
　　Board meeting date(s): Mar., June, Sept., and Dec.
　　Final notification: 1 month
Officers and Directors:* Charles J. Hamm,* Chair.; Alan H. Fishman,* Pres.; Edward F. Genter, Jr.,* Secy. and Genl. Counsel; Willard N. Archie; Robert B. Catell; Rohit M. Desai; Chaim Y. Edelstein; Donald H. Elliott; Scott M. Hand; Sr. Elizabeth A. Hill; Donald M. Karp; Malcolm MacKay; Raymond Ocasio; Maria Fiorini Ramirez; Victor M. Richel; Mikki Shepard; Lester Young, Jr.
EIN: 113422729
Selected grants: The following grants were reported in 2004.
$250,000 to YMCA of Greater New York, Bedford-Stuyvesant Branch, Brooklyn, NY.
$200,000 to Brooklyn Academy of Music, Brooklyn, NY.
$100,000 to Queens Library Foundation, Jamaica, NY.
$100,000 to Settlement Housing Fund, New York, NY.
$63,290 to Fifth Avenue Committee, Brooklyn, NY.
$25,000 to Community Resource Exchange, New York, NY.
$25,000 to Cooke Center for Learning and Development, New York, NY.
$25,000 to Fairmount Housing Corporation, Jersey City, NJ.
$20,000 to La Casa de Don Pedro, Newark, NJ.
$20,000 to Old Stone House, New York, NY.

6230
Elizabeth & Frank Ingrassia Foundation ✧ ☆
c/o Goldman Sachs & Co.
1 New York Plz., 40th Fl.
New York, NY 10004

Established in 1994 in NY.
Donor: Francis J. Ingrassia.
Foundation type: Independent foundation.
Financial data (yr. ended 9/30/05): Assets, $6,213,526 (M); gifts received, $837,960; expenditures, $789,903; qualifying distributions, $739,300; giving activities include $739,300 for grants.
Purpose and activities: Giving primarily for secondary and higher education; some giving for children and health services.
Fields of interest: Secondary school/education; Higher education; Health care; Children, services.
Limitations: Applications not accepted. Giving primarily in NY. No grants to individuals, or for scholarships; no loans.
Application information: Contributes only to pre-selected organizations.
Trustees: Francis J. Ingrassia; Elizabeth McCaul.
EIN: 133801229
Selected grants: The following grants were reported in 2004.
$25,000 to Dartmouth College, Hanover, NH.
$22,100 to Friends Academy, Locust Valley, NY. 3 grants: $10,000, $2,100, $10,000
$20,000 to Boys and Girls Club, Grenville Baker, Locust Valley, NY. 2 grants: $10,000 each
$5,000 to Lehigh University, Bethlehem, PA.
$3,300 to Long Island Childrens Museum, Garden City, NY.

6231
Initial Teaching Alphabet Foundation ✧
32 Thornwood Ln.
Roslyn Heights, NY 11577 (516) 621-6772
Contact: Betty E. Thompson, Exec. Dir.
URL: http://www.itafoundation.org

Incorporated in 1965 in NY.
Donors: Eugene Kelly†; Eugene Kelly Trust.
Foundation type: Operating foundation.
Financial data (yr. ended 12/31/05): Assets, $252,731 (M); gifts received, $742,381; expenditures, $768,306; qualifying distributions, $766,386; giving activities include $370,392 for 16 grants (high: $41,781; low: $12,600), and $359,649 for foundation-administered programs.
Purpose and activities: A private operating foundation; giving to promote, maintain, and advance education, in all its fields, and in particular, but without limiting the generality of the foregoing, by the development, standardization, propagation, dissemination, teaching, and use of the Initial Teaching Alphabet, with the aim of improving reading and writing skills.
Fields of interest: Education, research; Education, early childhood education; Elementary school/education; Secondary school/education; Higher education, university; Adult/continuing education; Education.
Type of support: Program development; Conferences/seminars; Publication; Research; Technical assistance; Consulting services.
Publications: Application guidelines; Informational brochure; Occasional report; Program policy statement.

Application information: Grant guidelines available on foundation Web site. Application form required.

Initial approach: Letter requesting guidelines

Copies of proposal: 2

Deadline(s): Pre-proposal letter by Mar. 15; detailed proposal (by invitation only) deadline Apr. 15

Board meeting date(s): May or June

Final notification: 1 month

Officers and Directors:* Frank G. Jennings,* Pres.; Maurice S. Spanbock,* Secy.-Treas.; Betty E. Thompson,* Exec. Dir.; Martha Bogart; Max Bogart; Shelly Jerviss.

Number of staff: 2 full-time professional.

EIN: 112074243

6232
Institute for the Study of Aging, Inc. ◇

1414 Ave. of the Americas, Ste. 1502
New York, NY 10019 (212) 935-2402
Contact: Monika Halarewicz, Exec. Coord.
FAX: (212) 935-2408; E-mail:
mhalarewicz@aging-institute.org; URL: http://www.aging-institute.org

Established in 1998 in NY.

Donors: Estee Lauder Charitable Trust; Pfizer Inc.; Emisphere Technologies, Inc.; Neurochem, Inc.; Elan Pharmaceuticals, Inc.; Barnhill Family Fund.

Foundation type: Independent foundation.

Financial data (yr. ended 12/31/05): Assets, $4,590,248 (M); gifts received, $3,451,286; expenditures, $4,156,351; qualifying distributions, $4,255,616; giving activities include $2,441,028 for 31+ grants (high: $359,515), and $122,350 for 1 loan/program-related investment.

Purpose and activities: The Institute is a biomedical venture philanthropy whose mission is to catalyze and fund the discovery and development of new therapies to prevent and treat Alzheimer's disease.

Fields of interest: Higher education; Medical school/education; Hospitals (general); Alzheimer's disease; Biological sciences.

Type of support: Conferences/seminars; Seed money; Research; Program-related investments/loans.

Limitations: Giving on a national and international basis. No support for political or religious organizations. No grants to individuals.

Publications: Annual report; Financial statement; Grants list; Informational brochure (including application guidelines); Occasional report.

Application information: See institute Web site for more application information. After review of the letter of intent, the institute will either send a declination e-mail explaining why it cannot invite an application at this time, or invite a full application, whereupon the applicant will be sent an e-mail with a link to the electronic application form. Applicants are required to submit a complete electronic application, including attachments and appendices. In addition, a hard copy of all materials with original signatures should be submitted. Application form required.

Initial approach: Electronic letter of intent on institute's Web site

Copies of proposal: 5

Deadline(s): None

Officers: Leonard A. Lauder, Co-Pres.; Ronald S. Lauder, Co-Pres.; Susan Reynolds Foley, C.O.O.; Howard M. Fillit, M.D., Exec. Dir.

Directors: Robert N. Butler, M.D.; Barbara J. Dalton, Ph.D.; Lanny Edelsohn, M.D.; Allan Green, M.D.,

Ph.D.; Julia P. Gregory; Elias K. Michaelis, M.D., Ph.D.

Number of staff: 5 full-time professional; 1 full-time support.

EIN: 134024149

Selected grants: The following grants were reported in 2003.

$216,527 to University of Illinois at Urbana-Champaign, Beckman Institute, Urbana, IL. For research project, Influence of Fitness on the Neurodegenerative Function of Older Adults.

$150,000 to Sun Health Research Institute, Sun City, AZ. For Phase II trial investigating Effect of the HMG-CoA Reductase Inhibitor Atorvastin Calcium, Lipitor, in the Treatment of Alzheimer's Disease.

$120,247 to Nathan S. Kline Institute for Psychiatric Research, Dementia Research Group, Orangeburg, NY. For research project, Pharmacogenetic Effects of Human ApoE on the Amyloid Reducing Activity of Cholesterol Lowering Drugs in a Transgenic Mouse Model for Alzheimer's Disease.

$100,000 to Massachusetts General Hospital, Genetics and Aging Unit, Boston, MA. For research project, Alzheimer's Disease Drug Discovery Targeted to the APP-mRNA 5'Untranslated Region.

$92,733 to Columbia University, College of Physicians and Surgeons, New York, NY. For research project, Imaging Mouse Models of Alzheimer's Disease.

$86,920 to University of North Carolina, School of Medicine, Department of Neurology, Chapel Hill, NC. For research project, Alzheimer's Therapeutics Neurotrophin Small Molecule Mimetics.

$86,714 to University of California, School of Medicine, Los Angeles, CA. For Phase II Double Blind Placebo-Controlled Study.

$80,949 to Weizmann Institute of Science, Rehovot, Israel. For research project, Structural and Functional Analysis of Beta Sciences as a Potential Target for Therapeutic Intervention in Alzheimer's Disease.

$79,380 to Northwestern University, Department of Cell and Molecular Biology, Evanston, IL. For research project, Ligands that Suppress Neuroinflammatory Responses, at Medical School in Chicago.

$77,979 to University of Illinois at Chicago, College of Pharmacy, Chicago, IL. For research project, A Combinatorial Search for Beta-Cyclodextrins to Abate the Neurotoxicity of Amyloid-Beta-Peptide in Alzheimer's.

6233
International Federation of Red Cross and Red Crescent Societies at the United Nations, Inc. ◇ ☆

800 2nd Ave., Ste. 355
New York, NY 10017

Established in 1992 in NY.

Foundation type: Independent foundation.

Financial data (yr. ended 12/31/05): Assets, $0 (L); gifts received, $15,330,337; expenditures, $15,342,561; qualifying distributions, $14,751,111; giving activities include $14,751,111 for 61 grants (high: $3,000,000; low: $90).

Fields of interest: American Red Cross; International relief.

Limitations: Giving on an international basis.

Application information:

Initial approach: Letter

Officers: Elise Baudot; Mike Davis; Andre Doren; Ibrahim Osman.

EIN: 133682664

Selected grants: The following grants were reported in 2005.

$1,860,177 to Motorola Foundation, Schaumburg, IL. 4 grants: $20,000, $550,702, $289,475, $1,000,000

$170,000 to Avon Foundation, New York, NY. 3 grants: $75,000, $75,000, $20,000

$20,000 to New York Community Trust, New York, NY.

$15,000 to Community Foundation of Collier County, Naples, FL.

6234
International Fund for Health & Family Planning ◇

c/o Alan Dolinsky
9 Spruce Pl.
Great Neck, NY 11021

Incorporated in 1979.

Donor: Philip D. Harvey.

Foundation type: Independent foundation.

Financial data (yr. ended 12/31/05): Assets, $30,656,375 (M); expenditures, $766,525; qualifying distributions, $757,040; giving activities include $750,253 for 2 grants (high: $500,253; low: $250,000).

Purpose and activities: Giving to organizations for family planning in developing countries, including those organizations providing abortion services, sterilization services, and/or the sale of contraceptives through social marketing in Asia, Africa, and Latin America.

Fields of interest: Reproductive health, family planning; AIDS.

International interests: Developing countries.

Limitations: Applications not accepted. Giving on a national and international basis. No grants to individuals.

Application information: Contributes only to pre-selected organizations.

Board meeting date(s): Varies

Officers and Directors:* Philip D. Harvey,* V.P.; Alan Dolinsky,* Treas.; Timothy Black; Robert Ciszewski.

EIN: 133000463

6235
International Shinto Foundation, Inc. ◇

300 W. 55th St., Ste. 20B
New York, NY 10019

Donor: International Shinto Foundation.

Foundation type: Independent foundation.

Financial data (yr. ended 6/30/05): Assets, $8,946 (M); gifts received, $661,057; expenditures, $671,398; qualifying distributions, $671,398; giving activities include $505,980 for 6 grants (high: $500,000; low: $100), and $500 for 1 grant to an individual.

Purpose and activities: Giving primarily to spread the knowledge and understanding of the Shinto religion and its culture.

Fields of interest: Higher education; Human services.

Limitations: Applications not accepted. Giving primarily in NY. No grants to individuals.
Application information: Contributes only to pre-selected organizations.
Officers: Toshu Fukami, Pres.; Kathy Hobbs, V.P.; Yoshimi Umeda, V.P.; Lloyd Rothenberg, Secy.
EIN: 133903933

6236
The Iovino Family Foundation ✧
26-15 Ulmer St.
College Point, NY   11356

Established in 2001 in NY.
Donors: Thomas Iovino; Judlau Contracting, Inc.; The Iovino Charitable Lead Annuity Trust.
Foundation type: Independent foundation.
Financial data (yr. ended 12/31/04): Assets, $1,316,775 (M); gifts received, $690,000; expenditures, $777,942; qualifying distributions, $756,515; giving activities include $756,515 for 18 + grants (high: $280,702).
Purpose and activities: Giving primarily for Episcopal churches, and for higher and other education; funding also for human services.
Fields of interest: Higher education; Education; Human services; Family services; Protestant agencies & churches.
Limitations: Applications not accepted. No grants to individuals.
Application information: Contributes only to pre-selected organizations.
Directors: Judith Iovino; Lauren Iovino; Michael Iovino; Thomas Iovino.
EIN: 113619538

6237
The Iris Foundation ▼ ✧
400 W. 59th St., 4th Fl.
New York, NY   10019

Established in 1991 in NY.
Donors: George Soros; Tivadar Charitable Lead Trust; George Soros 1982 Charitable Lead Trust; Soros Foundation; Open Society Institute; Murray Weber; Andrea Colombel; Eric Colombel.
Foundation type: Independent foundation.
Financial data (yr. ended 8/31/05): Assets, $109,970,359 (M); gifts received, $6,003,705; expenditures, $5,663,033; qualifying distributions, $3,742,356; giving activities include $3,740,831 for 5 grants (high: $3,629,831; low: $10,000).
Purpose and activities: Giving primarily for higher education.
Fields of interest: Museums (art); Higher education.
Type of support: General/operating support.
Limitations: Applications not accepted. Giving limited to NY. No grants to individuals.
Application information: Contributes only to pre-selected organizations.
Trustees: George Soros; Susan Weber Soros; William D. Zabel.
EIN: 136977690
Selected grants: The following grants were reported in 2004.
$5,363,871 to Bard College, Annandale on Hudson, NY. For on-going activities.

6238
The Moshe Isaac Foundation ✧
c/o Max Wasser
132 Nassau St., Ste. 300
New York, NY   10038   (212) 962-6100

Established in 1986 in NY.
Donors: Michael Konig; Esther Konig.
Foundation type: Independent foundation.
Financial data (yr. ended 9/30/03): Assets, $5,604,964 (M); gifts received, $163,529; expenditures, $625,042; qualifying distributions, $625,042; giving activities include $625,000 for 1 grant.
Fields of interest: Education.
Limitations: Applications not accepted. Giving primarily in Cherry Hill, NJ. No grants to individuals.
Application information: Contributes only to pre-selected organizations.
Directors: Esther Konig; Michael Konig.
EIN: 133385009

6239
Isdell Foundation ✧
(formerly Kevin C. Toner Foundation)
381 5th Ave., 6th Fl.
New York, NY   10016   (212) 842-8920
Contact: Yodon Thonden, Exec. Dir.

Established in 1994 in NY.
Foundation type: Independent foundation.
Financial data (yr. ended 12/31/05): Assets, $5,037,234 (M); expenditures, $370,078; qualifying distributions, $360,749; giving activities include $359,850 for 12 grants (high: $125,000; low: $250).
Purpose and activities: Giving for international affairs and public affairs.
Fields of interest: International affairs; Public affairs.
Application information: Application form required.
Initial approach: Letter of inquiry
Deadline(s): Dec. 31
Officer and Directors:* Yodon Thonden,* Exec. Dir.; Phintso Thonden; Kevin Tower.
EIN: 223341359
Selected grants: The following grants were reported in 2003.
$89,010 to Students for a Free Tibet, New York, NY. For general support.
$50,611 to Human Rights Watch, New York, NY. For general support.
$30,748 to International Campaign for Tibet, DC. For general support.
$26,890 to Tibet Justice Center, Berkeley, CA. For general support.
$25,000 to American Refugee Committee, DC. For general support.
$12,000 to Tibet Fund, New York, NY. For general support.
$8,322 to US Tibet Committee, New York, NY. For general support.
$6,500 to Tibet Information Network USA, Jackson, WY. For general support.
$5,000 to Drug Policy Alliance, DC. For general support.
$1,250 to International Tibetan Independence Movement, Fishers, IN. For general support.

6240
A. C. Israel Foundation, Inc. ✧
c/o Barry W. Gray
707 Westchester Ave., Ste. 405
White Plains, NY   10604-3102
Contact: Barry W. Gray, V.P.

Incorporated in 1967 in DE as successor to the foundation of the same name incorporated in 1946 in NY.
Donors: Adrian C. Israel†; Adrian & James, Inc.; Stanley Aberman.
Foundation type: Independent foundation.
Financial data (yr. ended 12/31/04): Assets, $29,963,173 (M); gifts received, $10,000; expenditures, $1,225,785; qualifying distributions, $1,148,247; giving activities include $1,148,247 for 76 grants (high: $250,000; low: $100).
Purpose and activities: Giving primarily for education, and to hospitals and health associations; funding also for the arts and human services.
Fields of interest: Museums; Historical activities; Arts; Secondary school/education; Higher education; Hospitals (general); Health organizations, association; Human services.
Type of support: General/operating support.
Limitations: Applications not accepted. Giving primarily in CA, CT, MA, and NY. No grants to individuals.
Application information: Contributes only to pre-selected organizations.
Officers and Directors:* Thomas C. Israel,* Pres.; Barry W. Gray,* V.P.; Jay M. Howard, Secy.; Stephen R. Finkelstein, Treas.; John P. Campbell.
EIN: 516021414
Selected grants: The following grants were reported in 2004.
$250,000 to Phillips Academy, Andover, MA. For general support.
$200,000 to Yale University, New Haven, CT. For general support.
$144,850 to Eisenhower Medical Center, Rancho Mirage, CA. For general support.
$130,000 to Middlebury College, Middlebury, VT. For general support.
$100,000 to Masters School, Dobbs Ferry, NY. For general support.
$75,000 to Montefiore Medical Center, Bronx, NY. For general support.
$25,000 to Citizens for NYC, New York, NY. For general support.
$15,175 to McCallum Theater, Palm Desert, CA. For general support.
$15,000 to Jewish Federation of Palm Springs and Desert Area, Palm Springs, CA. For general support.
$10,000 to White Plains Hospital Center, White Plains, NY. For general support.

6241
Ittleson Foundation, Inc. ✧
15 E. 67th St., 5th Fl.
New York, NY   10021   (212) 794-2008
Contact: Anthony C. Wood, Exec. Dir.
FAX: (212) 794-0351; URL: http://www.ittlesonfoundation.org

Trust established in 1932 in NY.
Donors: Henry Ittleson†; Blanche F. Ittleson†; Henry Ittleson, Jr.†; Lee F. Ittleson†; Nancy S. Ittleson†.
Foundation type: Independent foundation.

Financial data (yr. ended 12/31/03): Assets, $18,412,930 (M); expenditures, $1,384,334; qualifying distributions, $1,307,016; giving activities include $892,865 for grants.
Purpose and activities: The foundation provides seed money for start-up programs and pilot, model, and demonstration projects with a plan for dissemination, whose significance goes beyond the local area of implementation, in the fields of AIDS, mental health, and the environment, with a special interest in youth and adolescents. The foundation seeks to play a leverage role and is willing to take risks on new ideas and inspired yet untested new leaders, in addition to supporting proven professionals.
Fields of interest: Environment; Mental health/crisis services; AIDS.
Type of support: Program development; Publication; Seed money; Research; Technical assistance; Matching/challenge support.
Limitations: Giving on a national basis. No support for the humanities or cultural projects, general education, social service agencies offering direct service to people in local communities, or projects or organizations that are international in scope or purpose. No grants to individuals, or for continuing support, scholarships, fellowships, internships, annual or capital campaigns, travel, emergency or endowment funds, biomedical research, or deficit financing; no loans.
Publications: Annual report (including application guidelines).
Application information: Application form not required.
    Initial approach: Letter
    Copies of proposal: 1
    Deadline(s): Apr. 1 and Sept. 1
    Board meeting date(s): June and Dec.
    Final notification: 3 weeks to 3 months
Officers and Directors:* H. Anthony Ittleson,* Chair. and Pres.; Pamela Lee Syrmis,* V.P.; Anthony C. Wood,* Secy. and Exec. Dir.; Stephen M. Watson, Treas.; H. Philip Ittleson; Lionel I. Pincus; Christine Ittleson Smith; Victor Syrmis, M.D.
Number of staff: 1 full-time professional; 1 part-time support.
EIN: 510172757
Selected grants: The following grants were reported in 2004.
$60,000 to Marine Conservation Biology Institute, Redmond, WA. For From Sea to Shining Sea project.
$50,000 to Natural Resources Defense Council, New York, NY.
$45,000 to Family Justice, New York, NY.
$40,000 to Center for Whole Communities, Fayston, VT.
$40,000 to Education Development Center, Newton, MA.
$31,000 to New York Times Neediest Cases Fund, New York, NY.
$20,000 to AIDS Housing of Washington, Seattle, WA.
$20,000 to Medicare Rights Center, New York, NY.
$20,000 to South Carolina Aquarium, Charleston, SC.
$20,000 to Tellus Institute for Resource and Environmental Strategies, Boston, MA.

6242
Ivor Foundation ◇
667 Madison Ave., 21st Fl.
New York, NY   10021

Established in 1989 in NY.
Donor: Thomas A. Saunders III.
Foundation type: Independent foundation.
Financial data (yr. ended 12/31/05): Assets, $180,340 (M); expenditures, $1,162,278; qualifying distributions, $1,154,849; giving activities include $1,153,627 for 55 grants (high: $260,000; low: $50).
Fields of interest: Museums (art); Arts; Higher education; Education; Environment, natural resources; Hospitals (general); Health care; Health organizations, association; Human services; Children/youth, services; Federated giving programs; Protestant agencies & churches.
Limitations: Applications not accepted. Giving primarily in NY and VA. No grants to individuals.
Application information: Contributes only to pre-selected organizations.
Officers and Directors:* Thomas A. Saunders III,* Pres. and Treas.; Calvert Sanders Moore,* Secy.; George H. Roberts, Jr.; Thomas A. Saunders IV.
EIN: 133506932
Selected grants: The following grants were reported in 2003.
$895,000 to University of Virginia, Charlottesville, VA.
$315,000 to Thomas Jefferson Memorial Foundation, Charlottesville, VA.
$47,370 to School of American Ballet, New York, NY.
$30,000 to Darden School Foundation, Charlottesville, VA.
$29,110 to Boys Club of New York, New York, NY.
$9,250 to National Gallery of Art, DC.
$6,000 to Marine Corps University Foundation, Quantico, VA.
$4,000 to Old Westbury Gardens, Old Westbury, NY.
$2,350 to American Cancer Society, New York, NY.
$2,000 to Museum of the Confederacy, Richmond, VA.

6243
J & AR Foundation ◇
c/o Yohalem Gillman & Co.
477 Madison Ave.
New York, NY   10022-5802
Contact: Elizabeth Morin, Acct.

Established in 1990 in NY.
Donors: Janet C. Ross; Arthur Ross.
Foundation type: Independent foundation.
Financial data (yr. ended 12/31/05): Assets, $15,241,102 (M); gifts received, $984,775; expenditures, $824,443; qualifying distributions, $658,815; giving activities include $655,310 for 34 grants (high: $150,000; low: $300).
Purpose and activities: Giving primarily to pre-selected charitable organizations.
Limitations: Applications not accepted. Giving primarily in NY. No grants to individuals.
Application information: Contributes only to pre-selected organizations.
Trustees: George J. Gillespie III; Janet C. Ross.
EIN: 136962028
Selected grants: The following grants were reported in 2004.
$200,450 to Rockefeller University, New York, NY. 3 grants: $50,000, $150,000, $450
$25,000 to East Hampton Healthcare Foundation, East Hampton, NY.
$25,000 to International Womens Health Coalition, New York, NY.
$10,000 to Blair House Restoration Fund, DC.

$2,500 to Gracie Mansion Conservancy, New York, NY.
$1,000 to East Hampton Historical Society, East Hampton, NY.
$1,000 to Second Stage Theater, New York, NY.
$1,000 to Tryall Fund, New York, NY.

6244
The J G Foundation ◇
(formerly The Jacob Goldfield Foundation)
c/o Neufield Doudna, LLC
103 5th Ave., 5th Fl.
New York, NY   10003

Established in 1993 in NJ.
Donor: Jacob D. Goldfield.
Foundation type: Independent foundation.
Financial data (yr. ended 1/31/05): Assets, $25,094,444 (M); gifts received, $6,534,878; expenditures, $1,058,591; qualifying distributions, $944,718; giving activities include $910,000 for 1 grant.
Fields of interest: Hospitals (general); Jewish agencies & temples.
Limitations: Applications not accepted. Giving primarily in the New York, NY, area. No grants to individuals.
Application information: Contributes only to pre-selected organizations.
Trustees: Herschel Goldfield; Jacob D. Goldfield; Priscilla Goldfield.
EIN: 133748049

6245
The Jaaaa Foundation ◇ ☆
25 Rosalind Pl.
Lawrence, NY   11559-1522

Established in 2003 in NY.
Donor: S.K. Liebhard Foundation.
Foundation type: Independent foundation.
Financial data (yr. ended 12/31/05): Assets, $851,011 (M); expenditures, $1,765,325; qualifying distributions, $1,633,400; giving activities include $1,633,400 for grants.
Fields of interest: Federated giving programs; Jewish federated giving programs; Jewish agencies & temples.
Limitations: Applications not accepted. No grants to individuals.
Application information: Contributes only to pre-selected organizations.
Trustees: Ezra Birnbaum; Sandy Liedhard.
EIN: 470914136

6246
Jackson Hole Preserve, Inc. ◇
30 Rockefeller Plz., Rm. 5600
New York, NY   10112   (212) 649-5819
Contact: Carmen Reyes, Treas.

Incorporated in 1940 in NY.
Donors: John D. Rockefeller, Jr.‡; Laurance S. Rockefeller‡; Rockefeller Brothers Fund.
Foundation type: Independent foundation.
Financial data (yr. ended 12/31/04): Assets, $699,163 (M); expenditures, $718,873; qualifying distributions, $697,244; giving activities include $569,500 for 10 grants (high: $500,000; low: $1,000).

Purpose and activities: Grants to restore, protect, and preserve for the benefit of the public the primitive grandeur and natural beauties of the landscape in areas notable for picturesque scenery; and to promote, encourage, and conduct other activities germane to these purposes.
Fields of interest: Environment, natural resources; Environment.
Type of support: General/operating support; Land acquisition; Program development; Publication; Consulting services; Matching/challenge support.
Limitations: Giving primarily in the Hudson River Valley, NY, area, and WY. No grants to individuals, or for building or endowment funds, scholarships, or fellowships; no loans.
Application information: Application form not required.
  Initial approach: Letter
  Copies of proposal: 1
  Deadline(s): None
  Board meeting date(s): Oct. or Nov.; executive committee meets frequently
Officers and Trustees:* Clayton W. Frye, Jr.,* Pres.; James S. Sligar,* Secy.; Henry L. Diamond, Treas.; Ellen R.C. Pomeroy; Chet Williamson, Jr.
Number of staff: 2 part-time professional; 1 part-time support.
EIN: 131813818
Selected grants: The following grants were reported in 2003.
$500,000 to American Conservation Association, New York, NY. For general support.
$50,000 to Americans for Our Heritage and Recreation, DC. For public education programs.
$25,000 to Historic Hudson Valley, Tarrytown, NY. For general support.
$10,000 to Jackson Hole Alliance for Responsible Planning, Jackson, WY. For general support.
$10,000 to Wildlife Conservation Society, Bronx, NY. For conservation in Greater Yellowstone.
$5,000 to American Farmland Trust, Saratoga Springs, NY. For protection of farmland in Hudson Valley.
$5,000 to Greater Yellowstone Coalition, Bozeman, MT. For general support.
$5,000 to Jackson Hole Land Trust, Jackson, WY. For general support.
$5,000 to University of Wyoming Foundation, Institute for Environment and Natural Resources, Laramie, WY. For Open Space Initiative.
$1,000 to Teton Science School, Kelly, WY. For Island Outreach Education Program.

6247
The Benjamin Jacobson & Sons Foundation ◇
c/o Press Schonig & Co.
500 Bi-County Blvd., Ste. 201
Farmingdale, NY 11735

Established in 1968 in NY and DE.
Donors: Benjamin Jacobson & Sons; Robert J. Jacobson, Jr.; James A. Jacobson; Earl Ellis; Arthur Jacobson, Jr.
Foundation type: Company-sponsored foundation.
Financial data (yr. ended 6/30/05): Assets, $461,534 (M); gifts received, $379,608; expenditures, $535,846; qualifying distributions, $531,288; giving activities include $531,288 for 179 grants (high: $200,000; low: $40).
Purpose and activities: The foundation supports organizations involved with arts and culture,

education, health, children and youth, human services, and religion.
Fields of interest: Arts, multipurpose centers/programs; Arts; Education; Health care; Children/youth, services; Human services; Jewish federated giving programs; Christian agencies & churches; Jewish agencies & temples; Religion.
Limitations: Applications not accepted. Giving primarily in the metropolitan New York, NY, area. No grants to individuals.
Application information: Contributes only to pre-selected organizations.
Officers and Director: Robert J. Jacobson, Sr., Pres.; Benjamin Jacobson, Jr., V.P.; Robert J. Jacobson, Jr., Secy.; Arthur L. Jacobson, Treas.; James A. Jacobson.
EIN: 132630862
Selected grants: The following grants were reported in 2004.
$25,000 to Taft School, Watertown, CT.
$16,075 to Long Island University, Tilles Center for the Performing Arts, Brookville, NY.
$10,000 to Women in Need (WIN), New York, NY.
$1,500 to American Museum of Natural History, New York, NY.
$1,500 to Marymount School, New York, NY.
$1,000 to Juvenile Diabetes Research Foundation International, New York, NY.
$1,000 to North Shore-Long Island Jewish Health System, Westbury, NY.
$500 to Canine Companions for Independence, Farmingdale, NY.
$500 to Hackers for Hope, Danbury, CT.
$450 to Metropolitan Museum of Art, New York, NY.

6248
The Jacobson Family Foundation ◇
152 W. 57th St., 56th Fl.
New York, NY 10019

Established in 1997 in NY.
Donor: Mitchell Jacobson.
Foundation type: Independent foundation.
Financial data (yr. ended 12/31/04): Assets, $25,580,412 (M); gifts received, $3,650,000; expenditures, $777,894; qualifying distributions, $388,852; giving activities include $387,380 for 37 grants (high: $200,000; low: $100).
Purpose and activities: Giving primarily for the arts and Jewish organizations.
Fields of interest: Arts; Law school/education; Health care; Jewish agencies & temples.
Limitations: Applications not accepted. Giving primarily in New York, NY, and Southeastern, PA. No grants to individuals.
Application information: Contributes only to pre-selected organizations.
Officers and Directors:* Kathy Howard Jacobson,* Pres. and Secy.; Mitchell Jacobson,* Exec. V.P.; Erik Gershwind.
EIN: 133922461

6249
Sydney & Helen Jacoff Foundation, Inc. ◇ ☆
c/o Brown, Rudnick, Berlack, and Israels
7 Times Sq.
New York, NY 10036

Established in 1990 in NY.
Donors: Sydney Jacoff; Helen Jacoff†.

Foundation type: Independent foundation.
Financial data (yr. ended 12/31/05): Assets, $707,200 (M); gifts received, $47,720; expenditures, $1,007,769; qualifying distributions, $1,000,000; giving activities include $1,000,000 for 1 grant.
Purpose and activities: Giving primarily for health and education.
Fields of interest: Higher education.
Type of support: General/operating support.
Limitations: Applications not accepted. Giving primarily in NY. No grants to individuals.
Application information: Contributes only to pre-selected organizations.
Officers: Sydney Jacoff, Pres.; Daniel Jacoff, V.P. and Secy.; Michael Jacoff, V.P. and Treas.
EIN: 133570162

6250
The Jaffe Family Foundation ◇
c/o Elliot S. Jaffe
30 Dunnigan Dr.
Suffern, NY 10901

Established in 1986 in NY.
Donors: Elliot Jaffe; Roslyn Jaffe.
Foundation type: Independent foundation.
Financial data (yr. ended 12/31/04): Assets, $54,105,119 (M); expenditures, $2,823,143; qualifying distributions, $2,575,536; giving activities include $2,532,463 for 209+ grants (high: $500,000), and $1,473 for 1 employee matching gift.
Purpose and activities: Giving primarily for the arts, higher education, Jewish support organizations, medical research, and children, families, and social services.
Fields of interest: Media, television; Museums; Museums (art); Performing arts; Arts; Higher education; Education; Environment, natural resources; Hospitals (general); Health organizations, association; Cancer research; Allergies research; Food services; Youth development, services; Human services; Children/youth, services; Family services; Community development, neighborhood development; Jewish agencies & temples.
Limitations: Applications not accepted. Giving on a national basis. No grants to individuals.
Application information: Contributes only to pre-selected organizations.
Officer: Elliot S. Jaffe, Pres.
Directors: David R. Jaffe; Elise P. Jaffe; Richard E. Jaffe; Roslyn Jaffe.
EIN: 222827692
Selected grants: The following grants were reported in 2004.
$500,000 to New York Community Trust, New York, NY.
$200,000 to American Cancer Society, Atlanta, GA.
$168,878 to Food Allergy Initiative, New York, NY.
$100,000 to Nature Conservancy, Arlington, VA.
$65,000 to Childrens Hospital and Health System Foundation, Milwaukee, WI.
$50,000 to American Museum of Natural History, New York, NY.
$50,000 to Simmons College, Boston, MA.
$5,000 to United Way.
$3,000 to American Liver Foundation, New York, NY.
$1,000 to Norwalk Youth Symphony, Norwalk, CT.

6251
JAM Anonymous Foundation, Inc. ✧
(formerly The Dakota Foundation, Inc.)
c/o Barragato
950 3rd Ave., 8th Fl.
New York, NY 10022
Application address: c/o Nancy B. Mulheren, 17 N. Ward Ave., Rumson, NJ 07760

Established in 1984 in NJ.
Donors: John Mulheren†; Nancy Mulheren; John Mulheren, Jr.
Foundation type: Independent foundation.
Financial data (yr. ended 10/31/05): Assets, $192,697 (M); gifts received, $804,131; expenditures, $771,915; qualifying distributions, $752,950; giving activities include $752,950 for 53 grants (high: $125,000; low: $250; average: $5,000–$25,000).
Fields of interest: Performing arts, orchestra (symphony); Higher education, university; Education; Health care; Crime/law enforcement, police agencies; Christian agencies & churches.
Type of support: General/operating support.
Limitations: Giving primarily in NJ. No grants to individuals.
Application information: Application form not required.
Deadline(s): None
Trustees: Arthur Aeder; Stephen Cutler; Alexander Mulheren; Nancy Mulheren.
EIN: 222621688

6252
Robert & Ardis James Foundation ✧
80 Ludlow Dr.
Chappaqua, NY 10514
Contact: Catherine James Paglia, Tr.
Application address: 475 5th Ave., Ste. 1700, New York, NY 10017

Established in 1986 in NY.
Donor: Robert James.
Foundation type: Independent foundation.
Financial data (yr. ended 9/30/04): Assets, $57,759,286 (M); gifts received, $34,017,000; expenditures, $2,374,678; qualifying distributions, $1,801,806; giving activities include $1,774,903 for 70 grants (high: $939,885; low: $25).
Fields of interest: Higher education; International affairs, arms control; International affairs, foreign policy; International human rights; Public policy, research.
Limitations: Applications not accepted. No grants to individuals.
Application information: Unsolicited requests for funds not accepted.
Trustees: Ardis James; Ralph M. James; Robert James; Catherine James Paglia.
Number of staff: 1 part-time support.
EIN: 136880057

6253
Jandon Foundation ✧
c/o Donald Cecil, Cumberland Assocs.
3 Stratford Rd.
Harrison, NY 10528

Established in 1966 in NY.
Donor: Donald Cecil.
Foundation type: Independent foundation.

Financial data (yr. ended 12/31/05): Assets, $10,050,954 (M); gifts received, $392,010; expenditures, $548,796; qualifying distributions, $530,344; giving activities include $429,994 for 114 grants (high: $25,943; low: $25).
Fields of interest: Arts; Higher education; Education; Human services.
Limitations: Applications not accepted. Giving primarily in CT, MA, and Westchester County and New York, NY. No grants to individuals; or program-related investments; no loans.
Application information: Contributes only to pre-selected organizations.
Officers and Directors:* Donald Cecil,* Pres.; Alec Cecil,* V.P.; Leslie Cecil,* Secy.; Jane Cecil,* Treas.
EIN: 136199442

6254
Janklow Foundation ✧
445 Park Ave.
New York, NY 10022-2606
Contact: Maria Aydin

Established in 1986 in NY.
Donor: Morton L. Janklow.
Foundation type: Independent foundation.
Financial data (yr. ended 6/30/05): Assets, $4,630,405 (M); expenditures, $503,018; qualifying distributions, $465,170; giving activities include $462,975 for 108 grants (high: $100,000; low: $100).
Purpose and activities: Giving primarily for arts and cultural institutions.
Fields of interest: Museums; Performing arts, theater; Arts; Education; Hospitals (general); Human services; International affairs.
Limitations: Applications not accepted. Giving primarily in New York, NY. No grants to individuals.
Application information: Contributes only to pre-selected organizations.
Trustees: Angela Janklow Harrington; Linda LeRoy Janklow; Lucas Janklow; Morton L. Janklow.
EIN: 133357111
Selected grants: The following grants were reported in 2005.
$100,000 to Central Park Conservancy, New York, NY.
$35,000 to Lincoln Center Theater, New York, NY.
$32,500 to Greater Los Angeles Zoo Association, Los Angeles, CA.
$15,000 to Ann Schreiber Ovarian Cancer Research Fund, New York, NY.
$15,000 to Center for Early Education, West Hollywood, CA.
$15,000 to New York Landmarks Conservancy, New York, NY.
$15,000 to United Nations International School, New York, NY.
$5,500 to Doctors Without Borders USA, New York, NY.
$2,500 to New Visions for Public Schools, New York, NY.
$1,875 to American Museum of Natural History, New York, NY.

6255
The Jarx Foundation, Inc. ✧ ☆
c/o Janet Moses
P.O. Box 407
Harrison, NY 10528

Established in 1997.
Donors: Ellen M. Capra; James R. Capra.
Foundation type: Independent foundation.
Financial data (yr. ended 12/31/04): Assets, $1,502,762 (M); gifts received, $418,113; expenditures, $626,907; qualifying distributions, $626,382; giving activities include $626,382 for grants.
Fields of interest: Scholarships/financial aid; Children, services.
Limitations: Applications not accepted. Giving primarily in New York, NY. No grants to individuals.
Application information: Contributes only to pre-selected organizations.
Officers and Directors:* James R. Capra,* Pres.; Ellen M. Capra,* V.P.; Janet Moses,* Secy.
EIN: 133946523

6256
JCT Foundation ✧
c/o Jeff C. Tarr
145 Central Park West, Ste. 25C
New York, NY 10023

Established in 1984 in NY.
Donor: Jeff C. Tarr.
Foundation type: Independent foundation.
Financial data (yr. ended 12/31/04): Assets, $20,415,730 (M); expenditures, $1,058,775; qualifying distributions, $1,013,825; giving activities include $1,008,375 for 28+ grants (high: $600,000).
Purpose and activities: Giving primarily for the arts, education, nature conservancy, animal welfare, health associations, and human services.
Fields of interest: Media, television; Museums (art); Arts; Higher education; Environment; Animal welfare; Health organizations, association; Human services.
Limitations: Applications not accepted. Giving primarily in New York, NY; funding also in Cambridge, MA. No grants to individuals.
Application information: Contributes only to pre-selected organizations.
Directors: Jeff C. Tarr; Patricia G. Tarr.
Trustees: Jeff Tarr, Jr.; Jennifer Tarr.
EIN: 133237111
Selected grants: The following grants were reported in 2003.
$600,000 to Harvard University, Cambridge, MA. For general support.
$68,000 to Metropolitan Museum of Art, New York, NY. For general support.
$25,000 to Central Park Conservancy, New York, NY. For general support.
$10,000 to Boys and Girls Harbor, New York, NY. For general support.
$10,000 to Columbia University, New York, NY. For general support.
$10,000 to W N E T Channel 13, New York, NY. For general support.
$5,000 to Animal Medical Center, New York, NY. For general support.
$5,000 to Whitney Museum of American Art, New York, NY. For general support.
$2,500 to Citymeals-on-Wheels, New York, NY. For general support.
$2,500 to Joyce Theater, New York, NY. For general support.

6257
JEHT Foundation ▼
120 Wooster St., 2nd Fl.
New York, NY 10012 (212) 965-0400
FAX: (212) 966-9606;
E-mail: info@jehtfoundation.org; URL: http://
www.jehtfoundation.org

Established in 2000 in NY.
Donor: Jeanne Levy-Church.
Foundation type: Independent foundation.
Financial data (yr. ended 12/31/05): Assets,
$3,483,194 (M); gifts received, $27,235,000;
expenditures, $28,085,504; qualifying
distributions, $27,864,188; giving activities include
$24,360,503 for 165 grants (high: $734,871; low:
$5,000; average: $75,000–$500,000).
Purpose and activities: The JEHT Foundation was
established in Apr. 2000 to support its donors'
interests in human rights, social justice and
community building. The name JEHT stands for the
core values that underlie the foundation's mission:
Justice, Equality, Human dignity and Tolerance. The
foundation's programs reflect these interests and
values.
Fields of interest: International affairs; Civil rights;
Public affairs.
Type of support: General/operating support;
Continuing support; Management development/
capacity building; Capital campaigns; Program
development; Research; Program evaluation;
Matching/challenge support.
Limitations: Giving primarily in the U.S. No grants to
individuals or for direct services.
Publications: Application guidelines; Grants list.
Application information: Do not send video or audio
cassettes, press clippings, books, pamphlets, etc.
unless they are requested by the foundation.
    Initial approach: Letter of inquiry (no more than 3
    pages)
    Copies of proposal: 1
    Deadline(s): None
Officers and Trustees:* Robert Crane,* C.E.O. and
Pres.; Debra Kendall, Treas. and Admin. Dir.; Jeanne
Levy-Church; Jeffrey Levy-Hinte; William D. Zabel.
Number of staff: 15 full-time professional; 3 full-time
support.
EIN: 137232160
Selected grants: The following grants were reported
in 2005.
$810,000 to Common Cause Education Fund, DC.
    2 grants: $110,000 (For state-based reform
    program), $700,000 (For general operating
    support).
$600,000 to Annie E. Casey Foundation, Baltimore,
    MD. For Juvenile Detention Alternatives
    Initiatives.
$500,000 to Human Rights First, New York, NY. For
    U.S. Law and Security Program.
$500,000 to Innocence Project, New York, NY. For
    internal capacity building.
$350,000 to Advancement Project, DC. For
    Partnership for Fair Elections.
$350,000 to New Jersey Association on Correction,
    Trenton, NJ. For New Jersey Death Penalty
    Repeal Project.
$160,000 to New York University, Center for Human
    Rights and Global Justice, New York, NY. For
    special Rapporteur Study on U.S. Use of
    Commissions of Inquiry.
$125,000 to Juvenile Justice Project of Louisiana,
    New Orleans, LA. For general operating support.
$100,000 to Juvenile Law Center, Philadelphia, PA.
    For general operating support.

6258
Jephson Educational Trust No. 2
c/o JPMorgan Chase Bank, N.A.
345 Park Ave., 4th Fl.
New York, NY 10154 (212) 464-2441
Contact: Edward L. Jones, V.P.
FAX: (212) 464-2305;
E-mail: jones_ed_1@JPmorgan.com

Trust established in 1979 in NY.
Donor: Lucretia Davis Jephson†.
Foundation type: Independent foundation.
Financial data (yr. ended 9/30/05): Assets,
$11,342,268 (M); expenditures, $615,304;
qualifying distributions, $530,515; giving activities
include $465,000 for 36 grants (high: $100,000;
low: $2,500).
Purpose and activities: Giving primarily for the arts
and education.
Fields of interest: Arts; Secondary school/
education; Higher education.
Type of support: Scholarship funds.
Limitations: Applications not accepted. Giving on a
national basis, with emphasis on NY. No grants to
individuals, or for matching gifts; no loans.
Publications: Grants list; Informational brochure.
Application information: Contributes only to
pre-selected organizations.
Trustees: John Parkin; Robert D. Taisey; JPMorgan
Chase Bank, N.A.
Number of staff: 1
EIN: 136777236
Selected grants: The following grants were reported
in 2005.
$100,000 to Keuka College, Keuka Park, NY.
$25,000 to Metropolitan Opera Association, New
    York, NY.
$20,000 to Cornell University, Ithaca, NY.
$20,000 to Recording for the Blind and Dyslexic,
    Princeton, NJ.
$20,000 to University of Vermont, Burlington, VT.
$15,000 to American Composers Orchestra, New
    York, NY.
$15,000 to Long Trail School, Dorset, VT.
$10,000 to Harvey Mudd College, Claremont, CA.
$10,000 to Saint Lukes Chamber Ensemble, New
    York, NY.
$10,000 to Seeing Eye, Morristown, NJ.

6259
Jesselson Foundation ◇
450 Park Ave., Ste. 2603
New York, NY 10022-2605 (212) 751-3666
Contact: Michael Jesselson, 1st V.P.

Incorporated in 1955 in NY.
Donor: Ludwig Jesselson†.
Foundation type: Independent foundation.
Financial data (yr. ended 4/30/05): Assets,
$38,902,165 (M); expenditures, $2,455,972;
qualifying distributions, $2,225,023; giving
activities include $2,190,046 for 185 grants (high:
$259,250; low: $18).
Purpose and activities: Grants largely for higher and
Jewish education, welfare funds, health agencies,
and synagogues; some support for cultural
programs.
Fields of interest: Museums (ethnic/folk arts); Arts;
Secondary school/education; Higher education;
Theological school/education; Education; Health
organizations, association; Human services; Jewish
federated giving programs; Jewish agencies &
temples.

International interests: Israel.
Limitations: Giving primarily in Brooklyn and New
York, NY; some funding nationally.
Application information:
    Initial approach: Typewritten letter
    Deadline(s): None
Officers: Erica Jesselson, Pres.; Michael Jesselson,
1st V.P. and Secy.; Benjamin Jesselson, 2nd V.P.
and Treas.
EIN: 136075098
Selected grants: The following grants were reported
in 2005.
$259,250 to Yeshiva University Museum, New York,
    NY.
$250,000 to University of Pennsylvania,
    Philadelphia, PA.
$155,000 to Partnership for Excellence in Jewish
    Education, Boston, MA.
$45,123 to Riverdale Jewish Center, Bronx, NY.
$45,000 to Jewish Community Center in Manhattan,
    New York, NY.
$5,000 to American Friends of MESHI, Staten
    Island, NY.
$5,000 to FJC-A Foundation of Donor-Advised
    Funds, New York, NY.
$5,000 to Yad Eliezer, Brooklyn, NY.
$3,000 to Jewish Museum, New York, NY.
$1,000 to Ohel Childrens Home and Family
    Services, Brooklyn, NY.

6260
Jewish Foundation for Education of
Women ◇
135 E. 64 St.
New York, NY 10021 (212) 288-3931
Contact: Marge Goldwater, Exec. Dir.
FAX: (212) 288-5798; E-mail: FdnScholar@aol.com;
URL: http://www.jfew.org

Incorporated in 1884 in NY.
Foundation type: Independent foundation.
Financial data (yr. ended 6/30/05): Assets,
$57,584,279 (M); gifts received, $79,638;
expenditures, $2,679,773; qualifying distributions,
$2,512,322; giving activities include $2,233,862
for 692 grants to individuals.
Purpose and activities: The foundation's mission is
to help women of all ages attain the education and
training they need to make them productive,
economically independent members of the
community. The foundation does this by providing
scholarship assistance for higher education to
women in the New York, NY area with financial need
on a nonsectarian basis.
Fields of interest: Scholarships/financial aid;
Women.
Type of support: Fellowships; Internship funds;
Scholarships—to individuals.
Limitations: Giving limited to female students
whose permanent residence is within a 50-mile
radius of the New York NY, area. No support for law
studies, or for MBA studies. No grants for general
support, operating budgets, capital or endowment
funds, matching gifts, research, special projects,
publications, or conferences.
Publications: Application guidelines; Informational
brochure.
Application information: Applicants who are eligible
for a Biller/JFEW and a JFEW Emigres in the Health
Sciences Scholarship need to fill out only one
application and they will automatically be
considered for both. No student will receive more
than one scholarship. Telephone requests not

accepted. Direct applications accepted only for emigres in the health sciences, and emigres pursuing careers in Jewish education programs, and financially needy Jewish women. All other scholarships are offered by institutional referral. Application form required.

Initial approach: Letter, fax or e-mail
Copies of proposal: 1
Deadline(s): Varies according to program
Board meeting date(s): Oct., Jan., Apr., June and as required
Final notification: June

Officers and Directors:* Jean Bronstein,* Chair.; Marcy Russo,* Pres.; Neil Grabois,* V.P.; Sharon L. Weinberg,* V.P.; Jill W. Smith, Secy.; Alan R. Kahn,* Treas.; Marge Goldwater, Exec. Dir.; Jack R. Ackerman; Bernice Block; Alan D. Cohn; Marcia Goldsmith; Irving Kahn; Ellen B. Kallman; Michael S. Katz; Suzanne H. Keusch*; Phyllis Korff; Reeva S. Mager; Hon. Ruth Messinger; David Rosenberg; Susan Schatz; Marion Spanbock; Charles J. Tanenbaum; James Wood.
Number of staff: 1 full-time professional; 1 full-time support.
EIN: 131860415

6261
Jewish Renaissance Foundation, Inc. ◇ ☆
767 5th Ave., Ste. 4600
New York, NY 10153

Established in 1996 in NY.
Donor: Ronald S. Lauder.
Foundation type: Independent foundation.
Financial data (yr. ended 12/31/05): Assets, $9,068,322 (M); gifts received, $18,000; expenditures, $1,883,430; qualifying distributions, $2,463,764; giving activities include $1,420,000 for 2 grants (high: $1,400,000; low: $20,000), and $125,809 for foundation-administered programs.
Purpose and activities: Giving primarily for Jewish educational and cultural heritage programs.
Limitations: Applications not accepted. No grants to individuals.
Application information: Contributes only to pre-selected organizations.
Officers and Directors:* Ronald S. Lauder,* Pres.; Charles A. Goldstein, V.P.; Jacob Z. Schuster, Treas.; Rabbi Chaskel O. Besser; Malcolm Hoenlein.
EIN: 133906533

6262
The JKW Foundation ◇
c/o Jean Stein
10 Gracie Sq., PH. N
New York, NY 10028

Established in 1997 in NY.
Donor: Doris Jones Stein Charitable Lead Trust.
Foundation type: Independent foundation.
Financial data (yr. ended 12/31/04): Assets, $13,804,812 (M); gifts received, $586,411; expenditures, $1,768,179; qualifying distributions, $1,660,606; giving activities include $1,646,181 for 149 grants (high: $619,152; low: $200).
Purpose and activities: Giving for art and cultural programs, education, children, women and human services, and for a wide variety of charitable giving, including various forms of journalism.
Fields of interest: Media, journalism/publishing; Performing arts, theater; Arts; Higher education.

Limitations: Applications not accepted. No grants to individuals.
Application information: Contributes only to pre-selected organizations.
Trustees: Jean Stein; Katrina Vanden Heuvel; Wendy Vanden Heuvel.
EIN: 137127165

6263
The JM Foundation
654 Madison Ave., Ste. 1605
New York, NY 10021 (212) 687-7735
Contact: Carl Helstrom, Exec. Dir.
FAX: (212) 697-5495; *URL:* http://foundationcenter.org/grantmaker/jm

Incorporated in 1924 in NY.
Donors: Jeremiah Milbank†; Katharine S. Milbank†.
Foundation type: Independent foundation.
Financial data (yr. ended 12/31/05): Assets, $25,865,369 (M); expenditures, $2,096,033; qualifying distributions, $1,134,049; giving activities include $800,000 for 29 grants (high: $150,000; low: $5,000), and $46,873 for 49 employee matching gifts.
Purpose and activities: The foundation has a strong interest in educational activities which strengthen America's pluralistic system of free markets, entrepreneurship, and private enterprise.
Fields of interest: Children/youth, services; Public policy, research.
Type of support: Management development/capacity building; Program development; Publication; Seed money; Fellowships; Internship funds; Research; Technical assistance; Employee matching gifts; Matching/challenge support.
Limitations: Giving on a national basis. No support for the arts, government agencies, public schools, or international activities. No grants to individuals, or for operating expenses, annual fundraising campaigns, equipment, or endowment funds; no loans.
Publications: Application guidelines; Grants list.
Application information: See Web site for guidelines. Faxes, e-mails or overnight mail requests not accepted. Application form not required.
Initial approach: Summary letter accompanied by proposal
Copies of proposal: 1
Deadline(s): No firm deadlines. Proposals processed as received. Grant decisions made at board meetings in May and Oct
Board meeting date(s): May and Oct
Final notification: In writing within 30 working days
Officers and Directors:* Jeremiah Milbank III,* Pres.; Jeremiah Milbank, Jr., Pres. Emeritus; Jeremiah M. Bogert, V.P.; Peter C. Morse, Secy.; William Lee Hanley, Jr.,* Treas.; Carl Helstrom, Exec. Dir.; Chris Olander, Exec. Dir. Emeritus; Mary Caslin Ross.
Number of staff: 1 full-time professional; 1 part-time professional; 2 part-time support.
EIN: 136068340
Selected grants: The following grants were reported in 2004.
$100,000 to Boys and Girls Clubs of America, Atlanta, GA. 3 grants: $75,000 (To evaluate impact), $15,000, $10,000 (For Presidents Club Dinner).
$75,000 to State Policy Network, Richmond, CA. For SPN's Strategic Plan and Member Intern Program.

$35,000 to Atlas Economic Research Foundation, Arlington, VA. For Think Tanks for Secure Free Society.
$30,000 to Hoover Institution on War, Revolution and Peace, Stanford, CA. For research on health care and property rights.
$20,000 to Mackinac Center for Public Policy, Midland, MI. For leadership conferences and mentoring.

6264
The Jockey Club Foundation ◇
40 E. 52nd St., 15th Fl.
New York, NY 10022-5911
Contact: Nancy Kelly, Secy.

Incorporated in 1943 in NY.
Donors: New York Racing Assn.; Clark Foundation; The John C. Cavanagh Trust; Edith Allen Clark Trust; Cedar Hill Foundation; Hettinger Foundation; NYRA Charities; Thoroughbred Racing Associations of America; and others.
Foundation type: Independent foundation.
Financial data (yr. ended 12/31/05): Assets, $9,495,511 (M); gifts received, $107,122; expenditures, $704,664; qualifying distributions, $591,882; giving activities include $144,580 for 5 grants (high: $75,000; low: $5,000), and $446,693 for 77 grants to individuals (high: $25,255; low: $71).
Purpose and activities: The foundation's mission is to assist needy individuals in the Thoroughbred Racing Industry.
Fields of interest: Economically disadvantaged.
Type of support: General/operating support; Grants to individuals.
Limitations: Giving on a national basis.
Application information: Applicants must have been, at one time, associated (even via relatives) with the thoroughbred industry. Applications from individuals not associated with the industry will not be accepted.
Initial approach: Proposal outlining need for assistance
Deadline(s): None
Officers: Nancy Kelly, Secy.; Laura Barillaro, Treas.
Trustees: John Hettinger, Managing Tr.; C. Steven Duncker; Daniel G. VanClef.
EIN: 136124094

6265
The Joelson Foundation ◇
c/o Thelen, Reid & Priest, LLP, Attn.: Donald Scheier
875 3rd Ave., 12th Fl.
New York, NY 10022-6225

Established in 1966 in NY.
Donors: Julius Joelson†; Grt. Grand Charitable Remainder Unitrust.
Foundation type: Independent foundation.
Financial data (yr. ended 3/31/05): Assets, $18,308,641 (M); gifts received, $136,536; expenditures, $1,048,784; qualifying distributions, $968,735; giving activities include $815,470 for 185 grants.
Purpose and activities: Giving primarily for the arts, with emphasis on the performing arts, health, education, and social services; giving also to Jewish organizations.
Fields of interest: Museums; Performing arts; Performing arts, theater; Arts; Higher education;

Education; Environment, natural resources; Health care; Human services; Children/youth, services; Jewish federated giving programs; Jewish agencies & temples.

Limitations: Applications not accepted. Giving primarily in New York, NY; some funding also in CA and MA. No grants to individuals.

Application information: Contributes only to pre-selected organizations.

Officers: Barbara J. Fife, Pres.; Joseph C. Mitchell, Secy.-Treas.

Director: Stephen Fife.

EIN: 136220799

6266
The 1994 Christopher W. Johnson Charitable Trust No. 33 ✧
(formerly The Christopher W. Johnson Charitable Trust)
c/o The Johnson Co., Inc.
630 5th Ave., Ste. 1510
New York, NY 10111-0100

Established in 1994 in NY.
Donors: Betty W. Johnson; Christopher W. Johnson.
Foundation type: Independent foundation.
Financial data (yr. ended 12/31/05): Assets, $9,110,612 (M); expenditures, $447,090; qualifying distributions, $430,700; giving activities include $430,450 for 11 grants (high: $265,000; low: $450).
Purpose and activities: Giving primarily for education, particularly schools for girls, as well as to a school for children with learning difficulties.
Fields of interest: Elementary/secondary education; Education.
Limitations: Applications not accepted. Giving primarily in New York, NY. No grants to individuals.
Application information: Contributes only to pre-selected organizations.
Trustees: Betty W. Johnson; Christopher W. Johnson.
EIN: 137046311

6267
The 1994 Elizabeth R. Johnson Charitable Trust ✧
c/o Tag Assocs., Ltd.
75 Rockefeller Plz.
New York, NY 10019

Established in 1994 in NY.
Foundation type: Independent foundation.
Financial data (yr. ended 12/13/05): Assets, $7,313,526 (M); gifts received, $2,750; expenditures, $352,782; qualifying distributions, $350,282; giving activities include $350,000 for 9 grants (high: $165,000; low: $5,000).
Fields of interest: Education; Human services; American Red Cross; Children/youth, services; Foundations (private grantmaking).
Limitations: Applications not accepted. Giving primarily in New York, NY. No grants to individuals.
Application information: Contributes only to pre-selected organizations.
Trustees: Betty Wold Johnson; Elizabeth Ross Johnson.
EIN: 137046313
Selected grants: The following grants were reported in 2004.

$270,960 to Golden Children, New York, NY. 2 grants: $10,000, $260,960
$35,000 to Global Children, New York, NY. 2 grants: $30,000, $5,000
$24,000 to New York Jets Foundation, New York, NY.
$5,000 to Center for Khmer Studies, New York, NY.
$2,000 to Joyful Heart foundation, New York, NY.
$1,930 to School of American Ballet, New York, NY.
$1,000 to Kathmandu Valley Preservation Trust, Cambridge, MA.

6268
Christian A. Johnson Endeavor Foundation ▼
1060 Park Ave.
New York, NY 10128-1033 (212) 534-6620
Contact: Julie J. Kidd, Pres.

Incorporated in 1952 in NY.
Donors: Christian A. Johnson†; Charlotte Johnson Charitable Lead Trust.
Foundation type: Independent foundation.
Financial data (yr. ended 12/31/05): Assets, $202,052,122 (M); gifts received, $366,228; expenditures, $10,549,968; qualifying distributions, $9,914,776; giving activities include $8,659,322 for 91 grants (high: $4,181,292; low: $250; average: $1,000–$100,000).
Purpose and activities: Giving concentrated on private institutions of higher learning at the baccalaureate level and on educational outreach programs of visual and performing arts organizations in New York City; occasional support for perceived needs in other areas of education and the arts.
Fields of interest: Arts; Higher education; Education.
International interests: Europe.
Type of support: General/operating support; Program development; Seed money; Curriculum development; Scholarship funds; Matching/challenge support.
Limitations: No support for government agencies, or for community or neighborhood projects, religious institutions, or for health care. No grants to individuals, or for annual campaigns, emergency funds, deficit financing, land acquisitions, building projects, medical services, demonstration projects, publications, or conferences; no loans (except for program-related investments).
Publications: Application guidelines; Financial statement; Program policy statement.
Application information: Arts proposals by invitation only. Application form not required.
  Initial approach: Letter of inquiry
  Copies of proposal: 1
  Board meeting date(s): Spring and fall
Officers and Trustees:* Julie J. Kidd,* Pres. and Treas.; Christen L. Kidd, Secy.; Donald W. Harward; Ann B. Spence.
Number of staff: 3 full-time professional; 1 part-time professional; 1 full-time support.
EIN: 136147952
Selected grants: The following grants were reported in 2005.
$4,181,292 to European College of Liberal Arts, Berlin, Germany. For general operating support.
$500,000 to Bradford College, Bradford, MA. For endowment.
$282,473 to Artes Liberales Institute, Warsaw, Poland. For general operating support.

$250,018 to Bennington College, Bennington, VT. For Presidential Discretionary Fund. Grant made in form of stock.
$160,000 to Art Education for the Blind, New York, NY. For general operating support.
$125,022 to Bucknell University, Lewisburg, PA. For Chair in Comparative Humanities. Grant made in form of stock.
$100,023 to National Humanities Center, Research Triangle Park, NC. For education programs fund. Grant made in form of stock.
$96,000 to Orpheon, The Little Orchestra Society, New York, NY. For general operating support.
$50,000 to Learning Matters, New York, NY. For Experiencing College documentary.
$25,000 to Young Audiences-New York, New York, NY. For professional development.

6269
The Johnson Family Foundation, Inc. ✧ ☆
149 E. 73rd St.
New York, NY 10021

Established in 1997 in NY.
Donor: Thomas S. Johnson.
Foundation type: Independent foundation.
Financial data (yr. ended 12/31/05): Assets, $11,546,818 (M); gifts received, $5,965,500; expenditures, $1,851,578; qualifying distributions, $1,731,070; giving activities include $1,731,070 for grants.
Purpose and activities: Giving for higher education, art and cultural programs, and for cancer and medical research.
Fields of interest: Arts; Higher education; Cancer; Medical research, institute; Cancer research; Religion.
Limitations: Applications not accepted. Giving primarily in CT, IL, MA, NJ, and the metropolitan New York, NY, area. No grants to individuals.
Application information: Contributes only to pre-selected organizations.
Officers and Directors:* Margaret Ann Johnson,* Chair.; Thomas S. Johnson, Treas.; Thomas P. Johnson.
EIN: 137118242
Selected grants: The following grants were reported in 2004.
$50,000 to Trinity College, Hartford, CT.
$16,500 to Mountainside Hospital, Montclair, NJ.
$15,000 to Cancer Research Institute, New York, NY.
$10,000 to Boys and Girls Clubs of America, Atlanta, GA.
$10,000 to Harvard University, Business School, Cambridge, MA.
$10,000 to Inner-City Scholarship Fund, New York, NY.
$7,000 to Asia Society, New York, NY.
$5,000 to Saint Catherines High School, Racine, WI.
$2,500 to HealthCare Chaplaincy, New York, NY.
$1,400 to Futures in Education Foundation, Brooklyn, NY.

6270
Willard T. C. Johnson Foundation, Inc. ✧
c/o The Johnson Company, Inc.
630 5th Ave., Ste. 1510
New York, NY 10111
Contact: Robert W. Johnson IV, Pres.

Incorporated in 1979 in NY.

Donors: Willard T.C. Johnson†; Keith W. Johnson†.

Foundation type: Independent foundation.

Financial data (yr. ended 12/31/05): Assets, $59,964,425 (M); expenditures, $3,328,976; qualifying distributions, $2,791,235; giving activities include $2,771,000 for 8 grants (high: $1,500,000; low: $50,000).

Purpose and activities: Emphasis on health, including pediatric AIDS and juvenile diabetes; some support also for museums and performing arts groups.

Fields of interest: Museums; Performing arts; Hospitals (general); Reproductive health, family planning; Health organizations, association; AIDS; Medical research, institute; AIDS research.

Limitations: Giving primarily in CT, NJ, and NY. No grants to individuals.

Application information: Application form not required.

Deadline(s): None

Officers and Directors:* Betty W. Johnson,* Chair.; Robert W. Johnson IV,* Pres.; Christopher W. Johnson,* V.P. and Secy.-Treas.

EIN: 132993310

6271
Suzanne M. Nora Johnson and David G. Johnson Foundation ✧

c/o Goldman Sachs & Co., Family Dept.
1 New York Plz., 40th Fl.
New York, NY 10004-1950

Established in 1993 in NY and CA.

Donor: Suzanne M. Nora Johnson.

Foundation type: Independent foundation.

Financial data (yr. ended 1/31/05): Assets, $9,878,512 (M); gifts received, $1,466,264; expenditures, $583,440; qualifying distributions, $429,905; giving activities include $429,905 for 134 grants (high: $90,000; low: $25).

Purpose and activities: Giving for higher and other education including a school for people who are blind, as well as for the arts, particularly museums; funding also for health care, Christian churches, children, youth and family services, and for social services.

Fields of interest: Museums (art); Arts; Higher education; Law school/education; Medical school/education; Education; Hospitals (general); Health organizations, association; Legal services, public interest law; Human services; American Red Cross; Children/youth, services; International affairs; Science, research; Public affairs, research; Public policy, research; Christian agencies & churches; LGBTQ; Economically disadvantaged.

Limitations: Applications not accepted. Giving on a national basis, with emphasis on CA and NY. No grants to individuals; no loans.

Application information: Contributes only to pre-selected organizations.

Trustees: David G. Johnson; Suzanne M. Nora Johnson.

EIN: 133748062

6272
The Johnson Foundation ✧

17 Christopher St.
New York, NY 10014

Established in 1992 in NY and DE.

Donor: Peter James Johnson.

Foundation type: Independent foundation.

Financial data (yr. ended 6/30/05): Assets, $4,346,434 (M); expenditures, $321,069; qualifying distributions, $315,549; giving activities include $316,500 for 16 grants (high: $125,000; low: $500).

Fields of interest: Elementary/secondary education; Dental school/education; Health care, clinics/centers; Health organizations, association; Cancer research; Lung research; Skin disorders research; Human services; Roman Catholic agencies & churches.

Type of support: General/operating support; Continuing support; Research.

Limitations: Applications not accepted. Giving primarily in NY. No grants to individuals.

Application information: Contributes only to pre-selected organizations.

Officers and Directors:* Christopher Johnson,* Chair. and Pres.; Peter James Johnson, Jr.,* V.P. and Secy.; Veronica Johnson,* Treas.; Peter James Johnson.

EIN: 133696561

6273
The 1994 Robert W. Johnson IV Charitable Trust ✧

c/o The Johnson Co., Inc.
630 5th Ave., Ste. 1510
New York, NY 10111-0100

Established in 1994 in NY.

Donor: Betty W. Johnson.

Foundation type: Independent foundation.

Financial data (yr. ended 12/31/05): Assets, $7,139,344 (M); expenditures, $348,781; qualifying distributions, $334,700; giving activities include $334,450 for 58 grants (high: $101,000; low: $450).

Purpose and activities: Giving primarily for education and for medical research.

Fields of interest: Performing arts, orchestra (symphony); Arts; Higher education; Education; Health organizations; Medical research, institute; Human services; Community development; Protestant agencies & churches.

Limitations: Applications not accepted. Giving on a national basis. No grants to individuals.

Application information: Contributes only to pre-selected organizations.

Trustees: Betty W. Johnson; Robert W. Johnson IV.

EIN: 137046310

Selected grants: The following grants were reported in 2004.

$25,000 to Greater Houston Community Foundation, Houston, TX.

$20,000 to Hampton Classic Horse Show, Bridgehampton, NY.

$15,000 to Jazz at Lincoln Center, New York, NY.

$10,000 to After School Matters, Chicago, IL.

$10,000 to Dwight School Foundation, New York, NY.

$10,000 to Millbrook School, Millbrook, NY.

$10,000 to New World Symphony, Miami Beach, FL.

$10,000 to New York Shakespeare Festival, New York, NY.

$10,000 to Whitney Museum of American Art, New York, NY.

$7,500 to Safe Horizon, New York, NY.

6274
Daisy Marquis Jones Foundation ✧

1600 South Ave., Ste. 250
Rochester, NY 14620-3921 (585) 461-4950
Contact: Roger L. Gardner, Pres.
FAX: (585) 461-9752; E-mail: mail@dmjf.org;
URL: http://www.dmjf.org

Established in 1968 in NY.

Donors: Daisy Marquis Jones†; Leo M. Lyons†.

Foundation type: Independent foundation.

Financial data (yr. ended 12/31/05): Assets, $47,263,779 (M); expenditures, $2,125,298; qualifying distributions, $1,953,988; giving activities include $1,712,370 for 73 grants (high: $150,000; low: $400).

Purpose and activities: Grants primarily to stabilize and support families in the City of Rochester, NY; support also for services for senior citizens and youth, with special emphasis on the disadvantaged, special attention to preventive programs, and community development with neighborhood services for young children.

Fields of interest: Education, early childhood education; Children, services; Community development; Public affairs; Women; Economically disadvantaged.

Type of support: General/operating support; Building/renovation; Program development; Technical assistance; Matching/challenge support.

Limitations: Giving limited to Monroe and Yates counties, NY. No support for the arts, religious purposes, private schools, local chapters of national health-related organizations, or private foundations. No grants to individuals, or for endowment funds, research, scholarships, fellowships, or annual campaigns.

Publications: Application guidelines; Annual report; Annual report (including application guidelines); Grants list.

Application information: The foundation accepts the Rochester Area Common Application Form which is available on the foundation's Web site, as are the application guidelines and procedures. Application form required.

Initial approach: Letter of inquiry, or visit foundation Web site for inquiry form

Copies of proposal: 1

Deadline(s): None

Board meeting date(s): Monthly (except July and Aug.)

Final notification: 2 to 3 months

Officers and Trustees:* Donald W. Whitney,* Chair.; Roger L. Gardner,* Pres.; Pearl W. Rubin; HSBC Bank USA; M&T Bank.

Number of staff: 1 full-time professional; 1 full-time support.

EIN: 237000227

Selected grants: The following grants were reported in 2004.

$200,000 to Childrens Institute, Rochester, NY. For Rochester Early Enhancement Project.

$125,000 to Enterprise Foundation, Rochester, NY.

$110,800 to Genesee Country Museum, Mumford, NY. For Hands on History program.

$75,000 to Lifespan of Greater Rochester, Rochester, NY. For Geriatric Addictions program.

$75,000 to Planned Parenthood of the Rochester/Syracuse Region, Rochester, NY. To renovate a building to replace the current clinic and to expand services in the northwest.

$52,200 to Sojourner Hall for Women, Rochester, NY. For program support.

$50,000 to Rochester General Hospital Foundation, Rochester, NY. For Youth Apprenticeship program.

$25,000 to Children Awaiting Parents, Rochester, NY. For One Child at A Time.

$25,000 to Rochester Area Community Foundation, Rochester, NY.

$20,000 to Monroe Community College, Rochester, NY. For early childhood practitioners program.

6275
Joukowsky Family Foundation ▼

410 Park Ave., Ste. 1610
New York, NY 10022-4407
Contact: Nina J. Koprulu, Pres. and Dir.
FAX: (212) 355-3147; E-mail: info@joukowsky.org;
URL: http://www.joukowsky.org

Established in 1981 in NY as a trust; incorporated in 1983.

Foundation type: Independent foundation.

Financial data (yr. ended 10/31/05): Assets, $59,041,982 (M); expenditures, $6,669,088; qualifying distributions, $6,379,533; giving activities include $5,157,878 for 133 grants (high: $1,000,000; low: $200; average: $1,000–$50,000), and $78,492 for foundation-administered programs.

Purpose and activities: Giving primarily for higher and secondary education; support also for a wide range of cultural, social, archaeological and historical activities.

Fields of interest: Education.

Type of support: General/operating support; Continuing support; Endowments; Program-related investments/loans.

Limitations: Giving primarily in the northeastern U.S. No grants to individuals.

Publications: Grants list; IRS Form 990-PF.

Application information: Please refer to foundation Web site for future application changes.
Initial approach: Brief letter of inquiry
Final notification: None

Officers and Directors: * Nina J. Koprulu,* Pres.; Emily R. Kessler, Exec. Dir.; Randall G. Drain; Artemis A.W. Joukowsky; Martha S. Joukowsky.

Number of staff: 3 full-time professional; 1 part-time professional.

EIN: 133242753

Selected grants: The following grants were reported in 2004.

$250,000 to Brown University, Providence, RI. For general support.

$50,000 to Nightingale-Bamford School, New York, NY. For annual fund.

$25,000 to American Center of Oriental Research in Amman, Boston, MA. For ongoing restoration, Great Southern Temple at Petra.

$20,000 to No Limits Media, Brookline, MA. For general support.

$10,000 to New York University, Institute of Fine Arts, New York, NY. For Aphrodisias Excavations.

$10,000 to Robert College of Istanbul, New York, NY. For general support.

$10,000 to World Monuments Fund, New York, NY. For annual fund.

$5,000 to United Negro College Fund, Fairfax, VA. For general support.

6276
Joy Family Foundation

5436 Main St., Ste. 1
Williamsville, NY 14221 (716) 633-6600
Contact: Marsha J. Sullivan, Exec. Dir.
FAX: (716) 633-0600;
E-mail: info@joyfamilyfoundation.org; URL: http://www.joyfamilyfoundation.org

Established in 1989 in NY.

Donors: Paul W. Joy; H. Joan Joy‡.

Foundation type: Independent foundation.

Financial data (yr. ended 12/31/05): Assets, $5,742,699 (M); gifts received, $26,420; expenditures, $497,003; qualifying distributions, $393,386; giving activities include $305,881 for 68 grants (high: $25,000; low: $250), and $55,670 for 32 employee matching gifts.

Purpose and activities: To make a significant impact on the communities in which we live by assisting the economically disadvantaged through tax-exempt organizations with funding emphasis in the areas of arts and humanities, education, health care and human services.

Fields of interest: Performing arts, orchestra (symphony); Education; Hospitals (general); Substance abuse, services; Health organizations, association; Medical research, institute; Human services; Children/youth, services; Christian agencies & churches; Women.

Type of support: General/operating support; Continuing support; Annual campaigns; Capital campaigns; Building/renovation; Program development; Conferences/seminars; Curriculum development; Scholarship funds; Technical assistance; Program-related investments/loans; Matching/challenge support.

Limitations: Giving primarily in Erie and Niagara counties, NY; limited funding available to geographic regions in which trustees reside. No support for political activities. No grants to individuals.

Publications: Application guidelines; Grants list; Informational brochure (including application guidelines); Occasional report.

Application information: As a family foundation, grants are most often made to organizations where a family member is involved. Application form required.
Initial approach: Letter requesting application form
Copies of proposal: 1
Deadline(s): 3 weeks prior to quarterly board meetings
Board meeting date(s): Quarterly
Final notification: 2 weeks after review by board

Officer and Trustees: * Marsha Joy Sullivan,* Exec. Dir.; Lene Joy; Mary Alice Joy; Paul W. Joy; Stephen T. Joy; Edward C. Northwood; John Reinhold; Paula Joy Reinhold; Michael Sullivan.

Number of staff: 1 part-time support.

EIN: 166335211

Selected grants: The following grants were reported in 2003.

$100,000 to Heart, Love and Soul, Niagara Falls, NY. For renovation of new facility.

$25,000 to Business in Support of Neighborhoods (BISON) Fund, Buffalo, NY. For Children's Scholarship fund.

$19,000 to Elizabeth Pierce Olmsted, MD, Center for the Visually Impaired, Buffalo, NY. 2 grants: $10,000, $9,000

$17,500 to Burchfield-Penney Art Center, Buffalo, NY. For building campaign for new Burchfield-Penny Art Center.

$10,742 to Mount Saint Marys Hospital Foundation, Lewiston, NY. 2 grants: $5,742 (For matching fund), $5,000 (For giving campaign/emergency room project).

$10,000 to Western New York Public Broadcasting Association, Buffalo, NY. To establish Niagara Falls High School as Digital Innovation Site.

$8,500 to Nardin Academy, Buffalo, NY. To establish a named full-scholarship for elementary school division.

$5,000 to Alcohol and Drug Dependency Services Foundation, Buffalo, NY. For development of West Seneca Renaissance Campus by addition of new buildings.

6277
The JPMorgan Chase Foundation ▼ ✧

(formerly The Chase Manhattan Foundation)
270 Park Ave.
New York, NY 10017 (212) 270-6000
E-mail: jpmorgan.chase.grants@jpmchase.com;
URL: http://www.jpmorganchase.com/grants

Incorporated in 1969 in NY; name changed in 2001 as a result of the merger of Chase Manhattan Corp. with J.P. Morgan & Co. Inc.

Donors: The Chase Manhattan Bank; JPMorgan Chase Bank, N.A.; Chatham Ventures, Inc.; CMRCC, Inc.; Chemical Investments, Inc.

Foundation type: Company-sponsored foundation.

Financial data (yr. ended 12/31/04): Assets, $122,701,486 (M); gifts received, $111,606,094; expenditures, $59,158,273; qualifying distributions, $58,943,833; giving activities include $46,828,870 for 3,857 grants (high: $1,334,004; low: $100), and $9,957,213 for 42,707 employee matching gifts.

Purpose and activities: The foundation supports organizations involved with arts and culture, education, employment, housing, parks, children, financial literacy, community development, public policy, and civic affairs.

Fields of interest: Museums; Arts; Elementary/secondary education; Education; Employment, training; Employment; Housing/shelter; Recreation, parks/playgrounds; Children, services; Human services, financial counseling; Economic development; Urban/community development; Community development; Public policy, research; Public affairs.

Type of support: Employee matching gifts; General/operating support; Program development; Technical assistance; Program-related investments/loans.

Limitations: Giving on a national basis in areas of company operations; giving also to U.S.-based international organizations active in areas of company operations abroad. No support for religious, fraternal, social, or other membership organizations not of direct benefit to the entire community. No grants for capital campaigns or endowments, scholarships, fundraising, or special events or other short-term projects.

Publications: Corporate giving report.

Application information:
Initial approach: Visit Web site for application information; complete online application form for Recoverable Grant Program

EIN: 237049738

Selected grants: The following grants were reported in 2004.

$3,000,000 to United Way of Tri-State, New York, NY.

$1,334,004 to United Negro College Fund, Fairfax, VA. For employee programs.

$1,000,000 to Acorn Housing Corporation of Pennsylvania, Philadelphia, PA.

$1,000,000 to Raza Development Fund, Phoenix, AZ.

$250,000 to Urban League, National, New York, NY.

$200,000 to New Museum of Contemporary Art, New York, NY.

$25,000 to Fund for the City of New York, New York, NY.

$25,000 to San Francisco Foundation Community Initiative Funds, San Francisco, CA.

$22,000 to Delaware Housing Coalition, Dover, DE.

$20,000 to Howard University, DC.

6278
Alfred Jurzykowski Foundation, Inc. ✧
15 E. 65th St.
New York, NY 10021-6501 (212) 535-8930
Contact: Mrs. Bluma D. Cohen, Exec. Dir.

Incorporated in 1960 in NY.
Donor: Alfred Jurzykowski‡.
Foundation type: Independent foundation.
Financial data (yr. ended 12/31/05): Assets, $39,822,204 (M); expenditures, $2,993,116; qualifying distributions, $2,722,512; giving activities include $2,650,000 for 3 grants (high: $1,100,000; low: $450,000).
Purpose and activities: Giving primarily to organizations that support educational exchange, environmental projects, and entrepreneurship programs in Poland, Brazil and the United States; some funding also for health care, human services, and the arts with emphasis on children and youth.
International interests: Brazil; Poland.
Limitations: Applications not accepted. Giving primarily in the New York, NY, metropolitan area; some giving also in VA. No grants to individuals, or for endowment funds; no loans.
Application information: The foundation is undergoing major a reorganization. No new grants will be paid during this time. Only pre-existing awards will be paid. Unsolicited requests for funds will not be accepted or acknowledged.
Officers and Trustees:* Yolande L. Jurzykowski,* Exec. V.P.; Bluma D. Cohen,* V.P. and Exec. Dir.; M. Christine Jurzykowski,* Secy.-Treas.; Karin Falencki.
EIN: 136192256
Selected grants: The following grants were reported in 2004.
$390,574 to Kosciuszko Foundation, New York, NY. 2 grants: $300,574 (For fellowship program and general support), $90,000 (To establish Department of Environmental Sciences at AGH University of Science and Technology in Krakow, Poland).
$100,000 to Ashoka: Innovators for the Public, Arlington, VA. For general support.
$93,334 to Cornell University, Ithaca, NY. For polish component of their International Agriculture Programs.

6279
JW & DW Charitable Foundation, Inc. ✧
276 Riverside Dr.
New York, NY 10025

Established in 2002 in NY.

Donors: Deborah Weinreb; Jacob Weinreb; Sabina Weinreb.
Foundation type: Independent foundation.
Financial data (yr. ended 12/31/04): Assets, $4,916,144 (M); expenditures, $1,130,746; qualifying distributions, $1,130,470; giving activities include $1,129,850 for 84 grants (high: $115,000; low: $180).
Purpose and activities: Giving primarily to Jewish agencies, temples, and schools.
Fields of interest: Education; Jewish agencies & temples.
Limitations: Applications not accepted. No grants to individuals.
Application information: Contributes only to pre-selected organizations.
Officers: Jacob Weinreb, Pres.; Deborah Weinreb, V.P.; Abraham Reiss, Secy.-Treas.
EIN: 010719926

6280
The JW Foundation ✧ ☆
520 Woodmere Blvd.
Woodmere, NY 11598
Contact: Jeffrey Weinberg, Tr.

Established in 1997 in NY.
Donors: Jeffrey Weinberg; Sharona Weinberg.
Foundation type: Independent foundation.
Financial data (yr. ended 11/30/05): Assets, $57,231 (M); gifts received, $400,000; expenditures, $393,117; qualifying distributions, $393,114; giving activities include $393,114 for grants.
Fields of interest: Jewish federated giving programs; Jewish agencies & temples.
Limitations: Applications not accepted. Giving primarily in NY. No grants to individuals.
Application information: Contributes only to pre-selected organizations.
Trustees: Jeffrey Weinberg; Sharona Weinberg.
EIN: 113412512
Selected grants: The following grants were reported in 2003.
$35,000 to Shulamith School for Girls, Brooklyn, NY.
$25,000 to Torah Academy for Girls, Far Rockaway, NY.
$10,000 to Knesset Yehuda, Spring Valley, NY.
$5,000 to Chabad of the Five Towns, Cedarhurst, NY.
$1,900 to Bnei Torah Movement, New York, NY.
$500 to One Israel Fund, New York, NY.
$300 to Yeshiva Ateres Yisroel, Brooklyn, NY.
$100 to Ezras Torah Fund, New York, NY.
$36 to Mesivta of Long Beach, Long Beach, NY.
$36 to Young Israel of Woodmere, Woodmere, NY.

6281
Max Kade Foundation, Inc. ▼ ✧
6 E. 87th St., 5th Fl.
New York, NY 10128-0505 (646) 672-4354
Contact: Lya Friedrich Pfeifer, Pres. and Treas.

Incorporated in 1944 in NY.
Donor: Max Kade‡.
Foundation type: Independent foundation.
Financial data (yr. ended 12/31/05): Assets, $91,226,553 (M); expenditures, $5,145,986; qualifying distributions, $5,027,456; giving activities include $4,597,835 for 175 grants (high: $300,000; low: $1,000; average: $10,000–$100,000).
Purpose and activities: Grants primarily to higher educational institutions, with present emphasis on post-doctoral research exchange programs between the United States and Europe in medicine or in the natural and physical sciences. Foreign scholars and scientists are selected by the sponsoring universities upon nomination by the respective Academy of Sciences. Grants also for visiting faculty exchange programs and the training of language teachers.
Fields of interest: Language/linguistics; Literature; Higher education; Biomedicine; Medical research, institute; Physical/earth sciences; Chemistry; Engineering; Biological sciences.
International interests: Europe; Germany.
Type of support: Program development; Exchange programs.
Limitations: Giving primarily in the U.S. and Europe. No grants to individuals, or for operating budgets, capital funds, development campaigns, or endowment funds; no loans.
Publications: Occasional report.
Application information:
  Initial approach: Letter or proposal
  Deadline(s): None
  Board meeting date(s): As required
Officers and Directors:* Lya Friedrich Pfeifer,* Pres. and Treas.; Berteline Baier Dale,* Secy.; Guenter Blobel; Hans G. Hachmann; Fritz Kade, Jr., M.D.
Number of staff: 4 full-time professional.
EIN: 135658082
Selected grants: The following grants were reported in 2005.
$300,000 to Free University of Berlin, Friends of the, New York, NY. For renovation and refurbishment of Max Kade auditorium.
$250,000 to Allegheny College, Meadville, PA. For renovation and furnishing of Max Kade International Wing.
$200,000 to Middlebury College, Middlebury, VT. For renovation and furnishing of Max Kade House and Center for German Studies.
$100,000 to Friends of the German Historical Institute, DC. In support of German history documentation project.
$56,300 to Washington University, Department of Medicine, Saint Louis, MO. For research and training in field of medicine focusing on novel natural killer cell receptor involved in tumor cell recognition.
$48,800 to University of California, Department of Chemistry, Davis, CA. For research and training in field of inorganic chemistry.
$42,000 to University of Virginia, Cardiovascular Research Center, Charlottesville, VA. For research and training in field of innate immunity.
$33,500 to University of California, Department of Physics, Berkeley, CA. For research and training in field of physics.
$19,740 to Carnegie Mellon University, Pittsburgh, PA. In support of study program in Weimar, Germany.
$14,600 to Colgate University, Hamilton, NY. For teaching fellowship in field of foreign languages and literature.

6282
**Kadrovach/Duckworth Family
Foundation** ◇
c/o BCRS Group/Marcum & Kliegman, LLP
655 3rd Ave., 16th Fl.
New York, NY   10017-5617

Established in 1991 in IL.
Donor: Connie K. Duckworth.
Foundation type: Independent foundation.
Financial data (yr. ended 2/28/05): Assets,
$12,001,808 (M); gifts received, $2,774,914;
expenditures, $366,356; qualifying distributions,
$364,731; giving activities include $363,000 for 33
grants (high: $200,000; low: $500).
Purpose and activities: Giving primarily for the arts,
health care and research, and to Christian
organizations.
Fields of interest: Performing arts, theater;
Elementary/secondary education; Higher education;
Business school/education; Environment; Health
care; Cancer research; Children/youth, services;
Foundations (private grantmaking); Christian
agencies & churches.
Limitations: Applications not accepted. Giving
primarily in IL and New York, NY. No grants to
individuals; no loans or scholarships.
Application information: Contributes only to
pre-selected organizations.
Trustees: Connie K. Duckworth; Thomas J.
Duckworth; David B. Ford.
EIN: 133634387
Selected grants: The following grants were reported
in 2006.
$50,000 to Church of the Holy Spirit, Lake Forest,
    IL.
$50,000 to Global Heritage Fund, Palo Alto, CA.
$50,000 to University of Pennsylvania, Philadelphia,
    PA.
$36,500 to Lake Forest Open Lands Association,
    Lake Forest, IL. 2 grants: $4,000, $32,500
$25,000 to Council on Foreign Relations, New York,
    NY.
$25,000 to Gorton Community Center, Lake Forest,
    IL.
$13,250 to Asia Society, New York, NY. 2 grants:
    $8,250, $5,000
$5,000 to Washington National Cathedral, DC.

6283
**The Louise and Gerald Kaiser Family
Foundation, Inc.** ◇
44 Bacon Rd.
Old Westbury, NY   11568

Established in 2001 in NY.
Donors: Christina Kaiser; Gerald Kaiser.
Foundation type: Independent foundation.
Financial data (yr. ended 12/31/05): Assets,
$1,061,121 (M); expenditures, $542,220;
qualifying distributions, $529,250; giving activities
include $529,250 for 22 grants (high: $322,900;
low: $700).
Fields of interest: Education; Children/youth,
services; Christian agencies & churches.
Limitations: Applications not accepted. No grants to
individuals.
Application information: Contributes only to
pre-selected organizations.
Director: Christina Kaiser.
EIN: 113640058

Selected grants: The following grants were reported
in 2005.
$322,900 to Boy Scouts of America, Anchorage, AK.
$20,000 to Doctors Without Borders USA, New
    York, NY.
$20,000 to Glaucoma Foundation, New York, NY.
$20,000 to Nassau County Coalition Against
    Domestic Violence, Hempstead, NY.
$15,000 to Molloy College, Rockville Centre, NY.

6284
**The Moshe and Frady Kalter Foundation,
Inc.** ◇
c/o Moshe Kalter
1558 55th St.
Brooklyn, NY   11219

Established in 1995.
Donor: Moshe Kalter.
Foundation type: Independent foundation.
Financial data (yr. ended 12/31/03): Assets,
$1,173,470 (M); expenditures, $520,417;
qualifying distributions, $518,380; giving activities
include $518,380 for grants.
Purpose and activities: Giving primarily to Jewish
temples and for Jewish education.
Fields of interest: Elementary/secondary
education; Theological school/education; Jewish
federated giving programs; Jewish agencies &
temples.
Limitations: Giving primarily in Brooklyn, NY. No
grants to individuals.
Officers: Moshe Kalter, Pres.; Frady Kalter, Secy.;
Aryeh L. Kalter; Sheindy E. Saffer; Mindy L. Steger.
EIN: 113283510
Selected grants: The following grants were reported
in 2003.
$200,000 to Beth Jacob of Boro Park, Brooklyn, NY.
$150,000 to Bais Rivka Rochel, Lakewood, NJ.
$86,000 to Kolel Shomre Hachomos of Jerusalem,
    Brooklyn, NY.
$50,000 to Yeshivas Mir Yerushalayin, Brooklyn,
    NY.
$10,000 to Yeshiva Bais Hatalmud, Brooklyn, NY.
$7,100 to Congregation Bnei Moshe, Brooklyn, NY.
$5,000 to Baisker Yeshiva, Friends of, Brooklyn, NY.
$5,000 to Beth Aba Trust, Brooklyn, NY.
$3,600 to Torche Shabbos of Boro Park, Brooklyn,
    NY.

6285
Kaminer Foundation ◇
95 Charles St., Ste. 5
New York, NY   10014
Application address: c/o Henry Kaminer, 119
Hudson Ave., Tenafly, NJ 07670

Established in 1985 in NJ.
Donors: Henry Kaminer; Phyllis Kaminer†.
Foundation type: Independent foundation.
Financial data (yr. ended 12/31/04): Assets,
$4,053,507 (M); gifts received, $585;
expenditures, $556,035; qualifying distributions,
$539,036; giving activities include $533,147 for 19
grants (high: $423,897; low: $200).
Purpose and activities: Giving to Jewish agencies,
including Jewish education; some funding also for
health associations and human services.
Fields of interest: Health organizations,
association; Human services; Jewish federated
giving programs; Jewish agencies & temples.

Limitations: Giving primarily in MA and NY. No
grants to individuals.
Application information:
    Initial approach: Letter
    Deadline(s): None
Trustees: Ariel Kaminer; Henry Kaminer; Martin
Kaminer.
EIN: 222595518

6286
**John and Elaine Kanas Family
Foundation** ◇
c/o North Fork Bank
275 Broadhollow Rd., 4th Fl.
Melville, NY   11747
Contact: John A. Kanas, Pres.

Established in 1998 in NY.
Donors: John Kanas; Elaine Kanas.
Foundation type: Independent foundation.
Financial data (yr. ended 12/31/05): Assets,
$7,638,530 (M); gifts received, $75,000;
expenditures, $391,438; qualifying distributions,
$352,009; giving activities include $352,009 for 28
+ grants (high: $120,000).
Fields of interest: Education; Health organizations,
association; Children/youth, services; Family
services; Christian agencies & churches.
Limitations: Giving primarily in NY.
Application information: Application form not
required.
    Initial approach: Letter
    Deadline(s): None
Officers: John A. Kanas, Pres.; Elaine Kanas, V.P.
Director: Patricia Blake.
EIN: 113440709
Selected grants: The following grants were reported
in 2004.
$115,000 to Stony Brook School, Stony Brook, NY.
$2,500 to Cystic Fibrosis Foundation, Bethesda,
    MD.
$2,500 to Safe Horizon, New York, NY.
$1,500 to Adoption Alliance, Aurora, CO.

6287
The Kandell Fund ◇
59 E. 54th St.
New York, NY   10022-4211

Established in 1952 in NY.
Donors: Leslie Friedberg; Alice Joseph; Florence
Kandell†; Leonard Kandell†; Cynthia Marvell Brown;
Elinor Friedberg; Andrew Joseph†; Benjamin Joseph;
Alice Kandell.
Foundation type: Independent foundation.
Financial data (yr. ended 12/31/05): Assets,
$455,223 (M); gifts received, $595,000;
expenditures, $426,052; qualifying distributions,
$425,881; giving activities include $425,581 for
293 grants (high: $10,000; low: $200).
Fields of interest: Museums; Arts; Environment,
natural resources; Hospitals (general); Human
services; Jewish federated giving programs.
Limitations: Applications not accepted. Giving
primarily in New York, NY. No support for political
organizations. No grants to individuals.
Application information: Contributes only to
pre-selected organizations.

Officers and Directors: * Donald Gordon,* Pres. and Treas.; Debbie Fechter, Secy.; Alice Kandell; Leslie Kandell.
EIN: 136117648
Selected grants: The following grants were reported in 2005.
$11,000 to Metropolitan Museum of Art, New York, NY.
$10,000 to George Mason University Foundation, Fairfax, VA.
$10,000 to New York City Police Foundation, New York, NY.
$3,000 to Lenox Hill Hospital, New York, NY.
$2,500 to National Osteoporosis Foundation, DC.
$1,500 to American Red Cross.
$1,000 to Carnegie Hall Society, New York, NY.
$500 to Gesher Foundation, New York, NY.
$500 to Glaucoma Foundation, New York, NY.
$500 to League for the Hard of Hearing, New York, NY.

6288
Rita J. and Stanley H. Kaplan Family Foundation, Inc. ◇
866 United Nations Plz., Ste. 306
New York, NY 10017 (212) 688-1047
Contact: Rita J. Kaplan, Secy.

Incorporated in 1984 in NY.
Donors: Stanley H. Kaplan; Rita J. Kaplan; The Rita J. and Stanley H. Kaplan Charitable Lead Annuity Trust.
Foundation type: Independent foundation.
Financial data (yr. ended 12/31/05): Assets, $24,948,906 (M); gifts received, $288,407; expenditures, $2,392,858; qualifying distributions, $2,049,230; giving activities include $1,787,594 for 299 grants (high: $100,000; low: $25).
Purpose and activities: Support for cultural programs, including music, arts, theater, performing arts, and museums; libraries; medical research and education, including mental illness, AIDS and cancer research; social and family services, including programs for the homeless, children, and women; Jewish giving, including Jewish education; and organizations promoting human rights.
Fields of interest: Arts; Theological school/ education; Education; Health care; Civil rights, advocacy; Jewish federated giving programs; Jewish agencies & temples.
Type of support: General/operating support; Continuing support; Annual campaigns; Capital campaigns; Building/renovation; Endowments; Program development; Professorships; Seed money; Fellowships; Internship funds; Scholarship funds; Research; In-kind gifts.
Limitations: Applications not accepted. Giving primarily in Boston, MA, and New York, NY; giving also in Israel. No grants to individuals.
Application information: Contributes only to pre-selected organizations.
Board meeting date(s): May and Oct.
Officers and Directors: * Stanley H. Kaplan,* Pres.; Nancy Kaplan Belsky, V.P.; Susan Beth Kaplan, V.P.; Rita J. Kaplan,* Secy.; Nancy W. Greenblatt, Exec. Dir.; Scott Kaplan Belsky.
Number of staff: 1 full-time professional; 1 full-time support.
EIN: 133221298
Selected grants: The following grants were reported in 2004.
$30,000 to Brooklyn Academy of Music, Brooklyn, NY.

$26,000 to City Year New York, New York, NY. 2 grants: $25,000, $1,000
$25,000 to Jewish Womens Archive, Brookline, MA.
$25,000 to New Israel Fund, DC.
$18,000 to Sutton Place Synagogue, New York, NY.
$3,000 to Jewish Foundation for the Righteous, New York, NY.
$2,500 to Boston Symphony Orchestra, Boston, MA.
$1,700 to Rashi School, Newton, MA.
$1,500 to Reboot, New York, NY.

6289
Robert S. Kaplan Foundation ◇
c/o Goldman Sachs & Co., Family Office
1 New York Plz., 40th Fl.
New York, NY 10004

Established in 1991 in NY.
Donor: Robert S. Kaplan.
Foundation type: Independent foundation.
Financial data (yr. ended 3/31/06): Assets, $1,928,544 (M); gifts received, $2,339,900; expenditures, $1,923,150; qualifying distributions, $1,873,800; giving activities include $1,873,800 for 75 grants (high: $500,000; low: $1,000).
Purpose and activities: Giving primarily for medical research, including Amyotrophic Lateral Sclerosis (Lou Gehrig's disease), as well as social services, and Jewish and other federated giving programs.
Fields of interest: Higher education; Multiple sclerosis; Medical research, institute; Cystic fibrosis research; Cancer research; Diabetes research; Neuroscience research; Legal services; Human services; Children, services; Federated giving programs; Jewish federated giving programs.
Limitations: Applications not accepted. Giving on a national basis, with emphasis on New York, NY. No grants to individuals; no loans.
Application information: Contributes only to pre-selected organizations.
Trustee: Robert S. Kaplan.
EIN: 133637444
Selected grants: The following grants were reported in 2003.
$1,000,000 to Jewish Museum, New York, NY.
$850,000 to Project ALS, New York, NY. 3 grants: $500,000, $250,000, $100,000
$700,000 to UJA-Federation of New York, New York, NY. 2 grants: $350,000 each
$250,000 to Entertainment Industry Foundation, Los Angeles, CA.
$150,000 to Everybody Wins Foundation, New York, NY.
$150,000 to Jonsson Cancer Center Foundation, Los Angeles, CA.
$125,000 to Cystic Fibrosis Foundation, New York, NY.

6290
The J. M. Kaplan Fund, Inc. ▼ ◇
261 Madison Ave., 19th Fl.
New York, NY 10016 (212) 767-0630
Contact: William P. Falahee, Cont.
FAX: (212) 767-0639; E-mail: info@jmkfund.org;
Application address for Furthermore Grants in Publishing program:, c/o Ann Birckmayer, Prog. Assoc., P.O. Box 667, Hudson, NY 12534; tel.: (518) 828-8900; URL: http://www.jmkfund.org

Incorporated in 1948 in NY as Faigel Leah Foundation, Inc.; The J.M. Kaplan Fund, Inc., a DE corporation, merged with it in 1975 and was renamed The J.M. Kaplan Fund, Inc.
Donor: Members of the J.M. Kaplan family.
Foundation type: Independent foundation.
Financial data (yr. ended 12/31/04): Assets, $147,631,563 (M); gifts received, $1,558,706; expenditures, $10,344,823; qualifying distributions, $7,981,183; giving activities include $6,572,035 for 375 grants (high: $250,000; low: $435; average: $5,000–$150,000).
Purpose and activities: Giving primarily in three areas: environment, historic preservation, and human migrations. The fund offers program-related investments to encourage ventures of particular interest. The fund also has a trustee-initiated grants program that considers grant requests invited by the trustees.
Fields of interest: Historic preservation/historical societies; Environment, natural resources; Environment; Human services; International migration/refugee issues; Community development.
Type of support: General/operating support; Continuing support; Program development; Publication; Seed money; Research; Technical assistance; Program-related investments/loans.
Limitations: Giving primarily in New York City, NY; cross-borders of North America; and worldwide. No grants to individuals, including scholarships and fellowships, or for construction or building programs, endowment funds, operating budgets of educational or medical institutions, film or video, or sponsorship of books, dances, plays, or other works of art.
Publications: Annual report (including application guidelines).
Application information: Proposals received by fax will not be considered.
Initial approach: 2- to 3-page letter of inquiry
Copies of proposal: 1
Deadline(s): None; requests received after Oct. 1 will be carried over to next year
Board meeting date(s): Quarterly
Final notification: Applicants will be notified within 30 days of receipt of letter of inquiry if they are to submit a full proposal
Officers and Trustees: * Peter W. Davidson,* Chair.; Conn Nugent, Exec. Dir.; William P. Falahee, Cont.; Joan K. Davidson,* Pres. Emeritus; Betsy Davidson; G. Bradford Davidson; J. Matthew Davidson; Caio Fonseca; Elizabeth K. Fonseca; Isabel Fonseca; Quina Fonseca; Mary E. Kaplan; Richard D. Kaplan.
Number of staff: 4 full-time professional; 1 full-time support.
EIN: 136090286
Selected grants: The following grants were reported in 2004.
$250,000 to Malpai Borderlands Group, Douglas, AZ. For matching grant toward purchase of conservation easements on Krentz Ranch.
$250,000 to Migration Policy Institute, DC. For Migration Information Source.
$180,000 to New York Foundation for the Arts, New York, NY. For Artists' Fund.
$150,000 to Manhattan Institute for Policy Research, New York, NY. For Social Entrepreneurship Initiative and Fund.
$125,000 to Atlas Economic Research Foundation, Arlington, VA. For Fund for the Study of Spontaneous Orders.
$100,000 to City Parks Foundation, New York, NY. For Envisioning Catalyst Parks.

$70,000 to Essential Information, DC. For general support.

$40,000 to Point Community Development Corporation, Bronx, NY. For general support.

$25,000 to Sonoran Institute, Tucson, AZ. For Rio Santa Cruz Project.

$15,000 to PEN American Center, New York, NY. For Freedom to Write Program.

6291
The Karan-Weiss Foundation ◇
c/o Urban Zen, LLC
570 7th Ave.
New York, NY   10018-1603

Established in 1999.
Donors: Donna Karan; Stephan Weiss.
Foundation type: Independent foundation.
Financial data (yr. ended 12/31/03): Assets, $2,623,511 (M); expenditures, $1,046,812; qualifying distributions, $983,388; giving activities include $948,011 for 26 grants (high: $360,000; low: $1).
Fields of interest: Arts; Cancer; Breast cancer; Medical research, institute; Human services.
Limitations: Applications not accepted. No grants to individuals.
Application information: Contributes only to pre-selected organizations.
Trustee: Donna Karan.
EIN: 134084069
Selected grants: The following grants were reported in 2003.
$360,000 to Ann Schreiber Ovarian Cancer Research Fund, New York, NY.
$100,000 to Breast Cancer Research Foundation, New York, NY.
$100,000 to Byrd Hoffman Water Mill Foundation, New York, NY.
$50,000 to Elizabeth Glaser Pediatric AIDS Foundation, Santa Monica, CA.
$25,000 to Beth Israel Medical Center, New York, NY.
$25,000 to Dia Art Foundation, New York, NY.
$25,000 to Whitney Museum of American Art, New York, NY.
$10,000 to Brooklyn Academy of Music, Brooklyn, NY.
$10,000 to Healthy Foundation, Murrieta, CA.
$7,500 to Metropolitan Museum of Art, New York, NY.

6292
Karches Foundation ◇ ☆
84 Feeks Ln.
Locust Valley, NY   11560-2022

Established in 1997 in DE.
Donors: Peter Karches†; Susan Karches.
Foundation type: Independent foundation.
Financial data (yr. ended 12/31/04): Assets, $10,395,453 (M); gifts received, $411,409; expenditures, $435,377; qualifying distributions, $356,300; giving activities include $356,300 for grants.
Purpose and activities: Giving primarily for education.
Fields of interest: Education.
Limitations: Applications not accepted. Giving primarily in NY. No grants to individuals.

Application information: Contributes only to pre-selected organizations.
Trustees: Charles Harris; Susan Karches.
EIN: 137106278
Selected grants: The following grants were reported in 2004.
$75,000 to Shackleton Schools, Boston, MA.
$25,000 to Georgetown University, DC.
$20,000 to Bowdoin College, Brunswick, ME.
$10,000 to Hope House Ministries, Port Jefferson, NY.
$5,000 to Lymphoma Research Foundation, New York, NY.
$3,075 to Boys and Girls Harbor, New York, NY.

6293
Mel Karmazin Foundation ◇
1 Central Park W., Ste. 48B
New York, NY   10023

Established in DE and NY in 1998.
Donors: Melvin Karmazin; Karmazin Char. Lead Annuity Trust; Karmazin Char. Lead Annuity Trust II.
Foundation type: Independent foundation.
Financial data (yr. ended 12/31/04): Assets, $4,303,490 (M); gifts received, $1,966,175; expenditures, $1,766,079; qualifying distributions, $1,766,079; giving activities include $1,674,113 for 30 grants (high: $333,333; low: $5,000).
Purpose and activities: Giving primarily to specialized museums, particularly to a museum of television and radio, higher education, health associations, particularly for Tourette Syndrome, children and social services and public foundations.
Fields of interest: Media, television; Museums (specialized); Higher education; Health organizations; Human services; Children/youth, services; Foundations (public).
Limitations: Applications not accepted. Giving primarily in NY. No grants to individuals.
Application information: Contributes only to pre-selected organizations.
Trustees: Dina K. Elkins; Melvin Karmazin.
EIN: 311620186
Selected grants: The following grants were reported in 2003.
$350,000 to Museum of Television and Radio, New York, NY.
$250,000 to GAVI Fund, DC.
$100,000 to Tomorrows Childrens Fund, Hackensack, NJ.
$97,000 to Harlem Childrens Zone, New York, NY.
$50,000 to Intrepid Museum Foundation, New York, NY.
$25,000 to Alliance for Lupus Research, New York, NY.
$25,000 to Hollygrove Children and Family Services, Los Angeles, CA.
$10,000 to Tourette Syndrome Association, Bayside, NY.
$5,000 to Starlight Starbright Childrens Foundation, Los Angeles, CA.
$5,000 to Variety-The Childrens Charity, Los Angeles, CA.

6294
Ellen Philips Schwarzman Katz Foundation, Inc. ◇ ☆
(formerly Ellen Philips Schwarzman Foundation, Inc.)
c/o BCRS Associates, LLC
100 Wall St., 11th Fl.
New York, NY   10005

Established in 1996 in NY.
Donor: Ellen Philips Schwarzman Katz.
Foundation type: Independent foundation.
Financial data (yr. ended 4/30/05): Assets, $425,452 (M); gifts received, $1,226,499; expenditures, $896,680; qualifying distributions, $895,480; giving activities include $894,130 for 27 grants (high: $500,000; low: $50).
Purpose and activities: Giving primarily for arts and culture, particularly an art institute, higher education, hospitals, social services, and Jewish federated giving programs.
Fields of interest: Arts; Higher education; Libraries (public); Hospitals (general); Human services; Jewish federated giving programs.
Limitations: Applications not accepted. Giving primarily in New York, NY. No grants to individuals; no loans or scholarships.
Application information: Contributes only to pre-selected organizations.
Officers: Ellen Katz, Pres.; Elizabeth B. Schwarzman Right, Secy.; Howard Katz, Treas.
EIN: 133925902

6295
The Iris & Saul Katz Foundation, Inc. ◇
111 Great Neck Rd., Ste. 408
Great Neck, NY   11021
Contact: Saul B. Katz, Pres.

Established in 1982 in DE and NY.
Donor: Saul B. Katz.
Foundation type: Independent foundation.
Financial data (yr. ended 12/31/04): Assets, $5,161,427 (M); expenditures, $528,147; qualifying distributions, $490,051; giving activities include $490,051 for 57 grants (high: $220,200; low: $200).
Purpose and activities: Giving primarily for education, human services, and Jewish organizations.
Fields of interest: Performing arts centers; Secondary school/education; Higher education; Health organizations, association; Human services; Federated giving programs; Jewish federated giving programs; Jewish agencies & temples.
Limitations: Giving primarily in NY, with some emphasis on Long Island.
Application information: Application form not required.
Initial approach: Letter
Deadline(s): None
Officer and Directors:* Saul B. Katz,* Pres.; David M. Katz; Iris J. Katz.
EIN: 112626656
Selected grants: The following grants were reported in 2003.
$82,500 to National Center for Disability Services, Albertson, NY. For general support.
$36,900 to North Shore University Hospital Foundation, Manhasset, NY. For general support.
$9,800 to North Country Reform Temple, Glen Cove, NY. For general support.

$6,000 to Greenvale School, Glen Head, NY. For general support.

$5,000 to American Jewish Committee, New York, NY. For general support.

$2,500 to Brooklyn College Foundation, Brooklyn, NY. For general support.

$1,000 to North Shore Child and Family Guidance Center, Roslyn Heights, NY. For general support.

$1,000 to Starlight Starbright Childrens Foundation, New York, NY. For general support.

$500 to Boys and Girls Club at Lincoln House, Glen Cove, Glen Cove, NY. For general support.

$500 to Posse Foundation, New York, NY. For general support.

6296
The Jane and Robert Katz Foundation ◇
c/o Goldman Sachs & Co.
1 New York Plz., 40th Fl.
New York, NY 10004

Established in 1989 in NY.
Donors: Robert J. Katz; Goldman Sachs & Co.
Foundation type: Independent foundation.
Financial data (yr. ended 2/28/05): Assets, $7,935,690 (M); expenditures, $1,045,028; qualifying distributions, $995,850; giving activities include $995,850 for 90 grants (high: $300,000; low: $100).
Purpose and activities: Giving primarily to charitable gift funds, as well as for education, hospitals and health associations, human services, and Jewish organizations and temples.
Fields of interest: Elementary/secondary education; Higher education; Medical school/education; Education; Hospitals (general); Health organizations, association; Human services; Children/youth, services; Jewish federated giving programs; Philanthropy/voluntarism; Jewish agencies & temples.
Limitations: Applications not accepted. Giving primarily in New York, NY; some giving nationally. No grants to individuals, or for scholarships; no loans.
Application information: Contributes only to pre-selected organizations.
Trustees: Jane L. Katz; Robert J. Katz.
EIN: 133534735
Selected grants: The following grants were reported in 2004.
$50,000 to Cornell University, Ithaca, NY.
$50,000 to Survivors of the Shoah Visual History Foundation, Los Angeles, CA.
$25,000 to Graduate Center, City University of New York, New York, NY.
$15,000 to Central Synagogue, New York, NY.
$10,000 to Camphill Foundation, Hudson, NY.
$10,000 to Lincoln Center for the Performing Arts, New York, NY.
$5,000 to Teach for America, New York, NY.
$2,500 to Jewish Museum, New York, NY.
$1,000 to Boy Scouts of America, Greater New York Council, New York, NY.
$1,000 to Juvenile Diabetes Research Foundation International, East Brunswick, NJ.

6297
The Katz Foundation ◇
(formerly Howard & Holly Katz Foundation)
c/o BCRS Assocs., LLC
100 Wall St., 11th Fl.
New York, NY 10005

Established in 1983 in NY.
Donor: Howard C. Katz.
Foundation type: Independent foundation.
Financial data (yr. ended 8/31/05): Assets, $440,192 (M); gifts received, $459,444; expenditures, $418,936; qualifying distributions, $411,786; giving activities include $409,540 for 43 grants (high: $200,000; low: $250).
Purpose and activities: Giving for higher and other education, including medical school education, the arts, particularly art museums, Jewish organizations, and children, youth and social services.
Fields of interest: Museums (art); Arts; Elementary/secondary education; Higher education; Medical school/education; Education; Hospitals (general); Health organizations, association; Human services; Children/youth, services; Jewish agencies & temples.
Limitations: Applications not accepted. Giving primarily in New York, NY; some funding also in AZ. No grants to individuals, or for scholarships; no loans.
Application information: Contributes only to pre-selected organizations.
Trustees: Ellen Katz; Howard C. Katz; Ronald S. Tauber.
EIN: 133199938
Selected grants: The following grants were reported in 2004.
$50,000 to Mount Sinai Medical Center.
$10,000 to Choate Rosemary Hall, Wallingford, CT.
$10,000 to Lincoln Center Theater, New York, NY.
$6,100 to Philharmonic-Symphony Society of New York, New York, NY. 3 grants: $3,000, $2,500, $600
$2,500 to Rockefeller University, New York, NY.
$600 to National Foundation for Jewish Culture, New York, NY.
$500 to Guild Hall of East Hampton, East Hampton, NY.
$350 to American Friends of the Israel Museum, New York, NY.

6298
The Katzenberger Foundation, Inc. ◇
200 Park Ave. S., Ste. 1700
New York, NY 10003
Contact: Margaret G. Axelrod, Treas.

Incorporated in 1952 in NY.
Donors: Walter B. Katzenberger†; Helen Katherine Katzenberger†.
Foundation type: Independent foundation.
Financial data (yr. ended 11/30/05): Assets, $15,345,878 (M); gifts received, $5,000; expenditures, $1,369,661; qualifying distributions, $1,277,092; giving activities include $1,113,500 for 36 grants (high: $500,000; low: $1,000).
Fields of interest: Performing arts centers; Arts; Elementary/secondary education; Higher education; Human services; Children/youth, services.
Type of support: General/operating support; Continuing support; Annual campaigns; Emergency funds.
Limitations: Giving primarily in AZ, Chicago, IL, and NY. No support for religious organizations (except for Christian Science organizations), or for medical or medical research organizations. No grants to individuals, or for scholarships; no loans.
Publications: Annual report; Financial statement.
Application information: Application form not required.

Initial approach: Letter
Copies of proposal: 1
Deadline(s): Sept. 1
Board meeting date(s): Nov. and May
Final notification: Nov. 30
Officers and Directors:* Abner J. Golieb,* Pres.; Edward Davis,* Secy.; Margaret G. Axelrod,* Treas.; John A. Golieb; George Haibloom; Earl Swanson.
EIN: 136094434

6299
Marion Esser Kaufmann Foundation ◇
c/o Allen Webber
2525 Palmer Ave.
New Rochelle, NY 10801 (914) 636-8400

Established in 1986 in NY.
Donor: Marion Esser Kaufmann†.
Foundation type: Independent foundation.
Financial data (yr. ended 12/31/05): Assets, $11,107,257 (M); expenditures, $841,453; qualifying distributions, $705,000; giving activities include $705,000 for 17 grants (high: $100,000; low: $10,000).
Purpose and activities: Giving for higher education, health care, including research in cancer, the fields of sudden infant death syndrome (SIDS) and Alzheimer's disease.
Fields of interest: Child development, education; Elementary school/education; Higher education; Hospitals (general); Health care, infants; Health care; Medical research, institute; Cancer research; Alzheimer's disease research; Pediatrics research; Child development, services; Aging.
Type of support: Program development; Scholarship funds; Research.
Limitations: Giving on a national basis, with some emphasis on New York, NY, CO, and Washington, DC. No grants to individuals.
Application information:
Deadline(s): None
Final notification: Within 3 months
Trustees: Frederick L. Bissinger; Richard Esser.
EIN: 133339941
Selected grants: The following grants were reported in 2004.
$100,000 to Cancer Research Institute, New York, NY. For research for Cancer Vaccine Collaborative.
$100,000 to Columbia University, New York, NY. For scholarship fund.
$85,000 to Childrens Hospital Foundation, Denver, CO. To purchase equipment.
$75,000 to Cancer Care, New York, NY. For research.
$50,000 to Alzheimers Disease and Related Disorders Association, Champaign, IL. For research.
$50,000 to American Federation for Aging Research (AFAR), New York, NY. For research program.
$50,000 to Colorado Academy, Denver, CO. For financial aid endowment.
$50,000 to Saint Marys Home for Children, North Providence, RI. For renovations to Sophia Little Building.
$30,000 to Kingsbury Center, DC. For Upper School Transition program.
$15,000 to Colorado SIDS Program, Denver, CO.

6300
Kautz Family Foundation ◇

c/o BCRS Assocs., LLC
100 Wall St., 11th Fl.
New York, NY 10005

Established in 1981 in NY.
Donors: James C. Kautz; Peter Levy; Ron Tauber; Bob Friedman; Ann Brown Farrell; Martha Barnes Miller.
Foundation type: Independent foundation.
Financial data (yr. ended 2/28/05): Assets, $17,522,778 (M); expenditures, $692,806; qualifying distributions, $620,181; giving activities include $620,181 for 55 grants (high: $110,000; low: $230).
Purpose and activities: Giving primarily for the arts and higher and other education.
Fields of interest: Arts; Education, association; Higher education; Education; Hospitals (specialty); Health organizations, association; Children/youth, services; Human services; International affairs, foreign policy; Social sciences.
Type of support: Continuing support; Annual campaigns; Capital campaigns; Endowments; Fellowships.
Limitations: Applications not accepted. Giving primarily in Washington, DC, NY, OH, and PA. No grants to individuals; no loans.
Application information: Contributes only to pre-selected organizations.
Trustees: Caroline M. Kautz; Daniel B. Kautz; James C. Kautz; Leslie B. Kautz; Roy J. Zuckerberg.
EIN: 133103149
Selected grants: The following grants were reported in 2005.
$120,000 to Carleton College, Northfield, MN. 2 grants: $20,000, $100,000
$110,000 to Vassar College, Poughkeepsie, NY.
$60,000 to Tucson Botanical Gardens, Tucson, AZ. 2 grants: $20,000, $40,000
$25,000 to University of Cincinnati Foundation, Cincinnati, OH.
$5,000 to Baldwin School, Bryn Mawr, PA.
$5,000 to University of Wisconsin Foundation, Madison, WI.
$1,000 to Heal The Bay, Santa Monica, CA.
$1,000 to Nature Conservancy, Phoenix, AZ.

6301
The Harvey & Gloria Kaylie Foundation, Inc. ◇

238 Kings Point Rd.
Great Neck, NY 11024-1022

Established in 1999 in NY.
Donor: Scientific Components Corp.
Foundation type: Company-sponsored foundation.
Financial data (yr. ended 12/31/05): Assets, $13,457,588 (M); gifts received, $2,000,000; expenditures, $838,314; qualifying distributions, $829,379; giving activities include $829,379 for 48 grants (high: $175,000; low: $100).
Purpose and activities: The foundation supports organizations involved with arts and culture, education, health, cancer research, human services, and Judaism.
Fields of interest: Arts; Education; Health care; Cancer research; Children, services; Human services; Jewish federated giving programs; Jewish agencies & temples.
Type of support: General/operating support.

Limitations: Applications not accepted. Giving primarily in Brooklyn and New York, NY. No grants to individuals.
Application information: Contributes only to pre-selected organizations.
Officers and Directors:* Harvey Kaylie,* Pres.; Gloria Kaylie,* V.P.; Alicia Kaylie Yacoby,* Secy.-Treas.; Roberta Kaylie.
EIN: 113502781
Selected grants: The following grants were reported in 2004.
$237,000 to Aleh Foundation, Brooklyn, NY.
$152,700 to Israel Cancer Research Fund, New York, NY.
$90,000 to American Friends of the Jaffa Institute, Flushing, NY.
$33,359 to Hampton Synagogue, Hampton, NY.
$27,900 to Womens International Zionist Organization, New York, NY.
$19,024 to Medical Development for Israel, New York, NY.
$3,500 to Hineni, New York, NY.
$3,000 to Manhattan Beach Jewish Center, Brooklyn, NY.
$2,800 to American Friends of Nishmat, New York, NY.
$360 to Manhattan Sephardic Congregation, New York, NY.

6302
The Kazickas Family Foundation, Inc. ◇

120 E. 38th St.
New York, NY 10016

Established in 1998 in NY.
Donors: Victor Gruodis; John A. Kazickas; Joseph M. Kazickas; Joseph P. Kazickas; Michael Kazickas.
Foundation type: Independent foundation.
Financial data (yr. ended 12/31/03): Assets, $12,103,788 (M); expenditures, $361,660; qualifying distributions, $339,464; giving activities include $339,464 for 9+ grants.
Fields of interest: Museums (children's); Arts; Higher education; Children/youth, services.
Limitations: Applications not accepted. Giving primarily in New York, NY. No grants to individuals.
Application information: Contributes only to pre-selected organizations.
Officers and Directors:* Jurate Kazickas,* Pres.; John A. Kazickas,* Secy.-Treas.; Alexandra Kazickas; Joseph P. Kazickas; Lucy Muhlfeld.
EIN: 134011883
Selected grants: The following grants were reported in 2003.
$85,000 to Childrens Museum of the East End, Bridgehampton, NY. For general support.
$35,333 to Kaunas University of Technology, Kaunas, Lithuania. 2 grants: $22,231 (For general support), $13,102 (For scholarships).
$15,000 to U.S.-Baltic Foundation, DC. For general support.
$5,000 to Lithuanian National Foundation, New York, NY. For general support.
$5,000 to Lithuanian Research and Studies Center, Chicago, IL. For general support.
$5,000 to Weill Medical College of Cornell University, New York, NY. For general support.
$4,000 to International Council of Ophthalmology, San Francisco, CA. For general support.
$2,500 to Lithuanian American Community of the United States, Chicago, IL. For general support.
$2,500 to Naujojo Dienovidzio Fondas. For general support.

6303
Kealy Family Foundation ◇

c/o BCRS Assocs., LLC, attn.: William J. Kealy
100 Wall St., 11th Fl.
New York, NY 10005

Established in 1985.
Donors: William F. Kealy; William J. Kealy; Ellen M. Kealy.
Foundation type: Independent foundation.
Financial data (yr. ended 5/31/05): Assets, $1,905,541 (M); expenditures, $413,111; qualifying distributions, $406,413; giving activities include $397,700 for 63 grants (high: $50,000; low: $240).
Purpose and activities: Giving primarily for education; support also for the arts, conservation, mental health, and social services.
Fields of interest: Arts; Higher education; Education; Environment, natural resources; Environment, water resources; Environment, land resources; Mental health/crisis services; Human services; Children/youth, services; Family services; Civil rights, race/intergroup relations; Marine science; Christian agencies & churches; Minorities.
Type of support: General/operating support; Annual campaigns; Capital campaigns; Land acquisition.
Limitations: Applications not accepted. Giving primarily in the metropolitan New York, NY, area; some giving nationally. No grants to individuals or for scholarships; no loans.
Application information: Contributes only to pre-selected organizations.
Trustees: Leon Cooperman; Ellen M. Kealy; William J. Kealy.
Number of staff: 1 part-time support.
EIN: 133318124
Selected grants: The following grants were reported in 2005.
$35,000 to African Medical Mission, Hendersonville, NC.
$25,000 to Saint Johns University, Jamaica, NY.
$10,000 to Group Psychotherapy Foundation, New York, NY.
$7,500 to Boys and Girls Club of Morris County, Pequannock, NJ.
$5,000 to Baruch College Fund, New York, NY.
$5,000 to Thomas Jefferson Memorial Foundation, Charlottesville, VA.
$3,000 to Craig School, Boonton, NJ.
$3,000 to New York City Opera, New York, NY.
$1,250 to New York Public Library, New York, NY.
$1,000 to Museum of Arts and Design, New York, NY.

6304
William H. Kearns Foundation ◇

c/o Marks Paneth & Shron, LLP
622 3rd Ave., 7th Fl.
New York, NY 10017
Contact: Michael Bekas

Established in 1965.
Foundation type: Independent foundation.
Financial data (yr. ended 12/31/05): Assets, $8,606,925 (M); expenditures, $705,643; qualifying distributions, $434,612; giving activities include $352,250 for 32 grants (high: $85,000; low: $500).
Purpose and activities: Giving primarily for the arts and health care.
Fields of interest: Museums (art); Performing arts; Performing arts centers; Performing arts, ballet;

Performing arts, theater; Performing arts, orchestra (symphony); Arts; Education; Hospitals (general); Community development, neighborhood development.
Limitations: Applications not accepted. Giving primarily in NY. No grants to individuals.
Application information: Contributes only to pre-selected organizations.
Officers and Directors:* Milton Warshaw,* Pres. and Treas.; Maxine D. Prisyon,* V.P. and Secy.
EIN: 136199107

6305
Keefe Family Foundation ◇
375 Park Ave., Ste. 2301
New York, NY   10152

Established in 1989 in NY.
Donor: Harry V. Keefe, Jr.
Foundation type: Independent foundation.
Financial data (yr. ended 12/31/05): Assets, $7,636,214 (M); expenditures, $395,177; qualifying distributions, $380,818; giving activities include $375,000 for 13 grants (high: $100,000; low: $10,000).
Purpose and activities: Giving primarily for education, and children and family services.
Fields of interest: Secondary school/education; Higher education; Education; Aquariums; Cancer research; Human services; Children/youth, services; Family services; Disabilities, people with; Economically disadvantaged.
Type of support: General/operating support; Capital campaigns; Program development.
Limitations: Applications not accepted. Giving on a national basis, with some emphasis in New England and the East Coast. No support for private foundations. No grants to individuals.
Application information: Contributes only to pre-selected organizations. Unsolicited requests for funds not accepted.
Officers: Anita L. Keefe, Pres.; Harry V. Keefe III, V.P.; Kathleen Keefe Raffel, Secy.-Treas.
EIN: 133520397
Selected grants: The following grants were reported in 2005.
$100,000 to Boston Latin School, Boston, MA.
$60,000 to Hudson School, Hoboken, NJ.
$35,000 to Ronald McDonald House.
$15,000 to Paige Whitney Babies Center, Basking Ridge, NJ.
$10,000 to Amherst College, Amherst, MA.

6306
Ruth Keeler Charitable Trust ◇ ☆
c/o Fiduciary Trust Co. International
600 5th Ave.
New York, NY   10020   (212) 632-3000

Established in 1988 in NY.
Donor: Ruth Keeler‡.
Foundation type: Independent foundation.
Financial data (yr. ended 12/31/05): Assets, $1,492,931 (M); gifts received, $1,926,552; expenditures, $496,374; qualifying distributions, $485,135; giving activities include $480,000 for 7 grants (high: $250,000; low: $10,000).
Purpose and activities: Giving primarily to an Episcopal church, a guide dog service for people who are blind, and to a public library.

Fields of interest: Education, special; Libraries (public); Health care, home services; Youth development, centers/clubs; Human services; Protestant agencies & churches.
Limitations: Giving limited to Westchester County, NY. No grants to individuals.
Application information:
  Initial approach: Proposal
  Deadline(s): None
Trustees: Robert Scheff; Fiduciary Trust Co. International.
EIN: 136918074

6307
The Denis P. and Carol A. Kelleher Charitable Foundation ◇
17 Battery Pl., 11th Fl.
New York, NY   10004-1101

Established in 2000 in NY.
Donor: Denis P. Kelleher.
Foundation type: Independent foundation.
Financial data (yr. ended 10/31/05): Assets, $2,365,677 (M); expenditures, $485,894; qualifying distributions, $479,271; giving activities include $475,053 for 103 grants (high: $75,000; low: $100).
Purpose and activities: Giving primarily for higher education, health associations, Roman Catholic organizations and churches, and social services, including Irish organizations.
Fields of interest: Arts; Higher education; Health organizations; Human services; Roman Catholic agencies & churches.
Limitations: Applications not accepted. Giving primarily in New York, NY. No grants to individuals.
Application information: Contributes only to pre-selected organizations.
Directors: Carol A. Kelleher; Denis P. Kelleher; Denis P. Kelleher, Jr.; Sean M. Kelleher; Colleen P. Sorrentino.
EIN: 134149751
Selected grants: The following grants were reported in 2003.
$75,000 to Cardinals Appeal, New York, NY. For unrestricted support.
$27,571 to Project Hospitality, Staten Island, NY. For unrestricted support.
$26,000 to American Ireland Fund, Boston, MA. For unrestricted support.
$26,000 to Saint Johns University, Jamaica, NY. For unrestricted support.
$12,500 to UJA-Federation of New York, New York, NY. For unrestricted support.
$10,000 to Jewish Community Center in Manhattan, New York, NY. For unrestricted support.
$10,000 to Staten Island Academy, Staten Island, NY. For unrestricted support.
$7,000 to Lenox Hill Hospital, New York, NY. For unrestricted support.
$5,000 to Classroom, Inc., New York, NY. For unrestricted support.
$2,000 to Animal Medical Center, New York, NY. For unrestricted support.

6308
Anna Maria & Stephen Kellen Foundation, Inc. ▼ ◇
1345 Ave. of the Americas, 44th Fl.
New York, NY   10105

Established in 1984.
Donors: Stephen M. Kellen‡; Anna-Maria Kellen.
Foundation type: Independent foundation.
Financial data (yr. ended 4/30/06): Assets, $80,525,585 (M); gifts received, $250,000; expenditures, $8,235,568; qualifying distributions, $8,149,812; giving activities include $8,127,951 for 78 grants (high: $2,023,716; low: $250; average: $1,000–$200,000).
Purpose and activities: Giving primarily for cultural programs, including a music school, a school of design, museums, and performing arts groups; support also for higher and secondary education, Protestant churches, and media and communications.
Fields of interest: Media/communications; Museums; Performing arts, music; Arts; Secondary school/education; Higher education; Medical care, outpatient care; Protestant agencies & churches.
Limitations: Applications not accepted. Giving primarily in New York, NY. No grants to individuals.
Application information: Contributes only to pre-selected organizations.
Officers and Directors:* Anna-Maria Kellen,* Pres.; Marina K. French,* V.P.; Michael Kellen,* Secy.-Treas.
EIN: 133173593
Selected grants: The following grants were reported in 2005.
$1,686,741 to American Academy in Berlin, New York, NY.
$560,000 to Metropolitan Museum of Art, New York, NY.
$525,000 to Cancer Research Institute, New York, NY.
$350,000 to Council on Foreign Relations, New York, NY.
$250,000 to Interfaith Center of New York, New York, NY.
$200,000 to New School, Parsons School of Design, New York, NY.
$52,700 to Cathedral Church of Saint John the Divine, New York, NY.
$15,000 to French American Cultural Exchange (FACE), New York, NY.
$10,000 to Wellesley College, Wellesley, MA.
$2,500 to Corcoran Gallery of Art, DC.

6309
The Kellner Foundation ◇
c/o Kellner, Dileo, & Co.
900 3rd Ave., 10th Fl.
New York, NY   10022
URL: http://www.kellner.hu/main.html

Established in 1996 in NY.
Donors: George Kellner; Martha Kellner.
Foundation type: Independent foundation.
Financial data (yr. ended 12/31/05): Assets, $4,191,230 (M); gifts received, $294,504; expenditures, $360,503; qualifying distributions, $335,853; giving activities include $335,853 for 14 grants (high: $158,923; low: $1,000).
Fields of interest: Higher education; Education.
Limitations: Applications not accepted. Giving primarily in NY.
Application information: Unsolicited requests for funds not accepted.
Trustees: Catherine Kellner; George Kellner; Martha Kellner; Peter Kellner.
EIN: 137084979

6310
J. C. Kellogg Foundation, Inc. ▼ ✧
c/o IAT Reinsurance Co., Ltd.
48 Wall St., 30th Fl.
New York, NY 10005
Contact: Peter R. Kellogg, V.P.

Established in 1954 in NY.
Donors: Morris W. Kellogg; James C. Kellogg IV; Elizabeth I. Kellogg; Richard I. Kellogg; Peter R. Kellogg.
Foundation type: Independent foundation.
Financial data (yr. ended 8/31/05): Assets, $72,499,160 (M); gifts received, $3,588,347; expenditures, $4,388,509; qualifying distributions, $4,154,093; giving activities include $4,116,718 for 149 grants (high: $500,000; low: $500).
Purpose and activities: Giving primarily for education.
Fields of interest: Elementary/secondary education; Higher education; Education; Hospitals (general); Health organizations, association; Boys & girls clubs; Human services; Children/youth, services; Federated giving programs.
Limitations: Applications not accepted. Giving primarily in MA, NJ, and NY. No grants to individuals.
Application information: Contributes only to pre-selected organizations.
Officers: James C. Kellogg IV, Pres. and Treas.; Peter R. Kellogg, V.P.
Trustees: Nancy K. Gifford; Morris W. Kellogg; Richard I. Kellogg.
EIN: 136092448
Selected grants: The following grants were reported in 2005.
$500,000 to Trinitas Health Foundation, Elizabeth, NJ.
$400,000 to Planned Parenthood of Greater Northern New Jersey, Morristown, NJ.
$235,000 to Union County College Foundation, Cranford, NJ.
$160,000 to New Jersey Center for Visual Arts, Summit, NJ.
$100,000 to Boys and Girls Clubs of Boston, Boston, MA.
$100,000 to Grand Street Settlement, New York, NY.
$50,000 to Tomorrows Childrens Fund, Hackensack, NJ.
$20,000 to Ottawa Couple and Family Institute, Ottawa, Canada. .
$15,000 to Free Arts for Abused Children of New York City, New York, NY.
$5,000 to Morristown-Beard School, Morristown, NJ.

6311
Peter R. & Cynthia K. Kellogg Foundation ▼ ✧
c/o IAT RE, Ltd.
48 Wall St., 30th Fl.
New York, NY 10005

Established in 1983 in NJ.
Donors: Charles K. Kellogg; Lee I. Kellogg; Peter R. Kellogg; IAT Syndicate, Inc.
Foundation type: Independent foundation.
Financial data (yr. ended 6/30/05): Assets, $201,014,011 (M); gifts received, $3,435,398; expenditures, $13,216,523; qualifying distributions, $10,222,182; giving activities include $10,222,182 for 482 grants (high: $2,000,000; low: $50; average: $1,000–$100,000).

Purpose and activities: Giving primarily for education.
Fields of interest: Museums; Historic preservation/historical societies; Arts; Education; Recreation; Children/youth, services.
Limitations: Giving primarily in NJ. No grants to individuals.
Application information:
  Deadline(s): None
Officers: Peter R. Kellogg, Pres.; Cynthia K. Kellogg, Secy.; Marguerite R. Gorman, Treas.
EIN: 222472914
Selected grants: The following grants were reported in 2005.
$2,000,000 to Berkshire School, Sheffield, MA.
$600,000 to Trinitas Hospital, Elizabeth, NJ.
$275,000 to YMCA, Frost Valley, Montclair, NJ. 2 grants: $25,000, $250,000
$250,000 to Classical American Homes Preservation Trust, New York, NY.
$250,000 to United States Ski and Snowboard Association, Park City, UT.
$50,000 to College of Charleston, Charleston, SC. For Cougar Club - Cougar Classic.
$25,000 to Ocean County College, Toms River, NJ.
$25,000 to Tuckerton Seaport, Tuckerton, NJ.
$10,000 to Winthrop-University Hospital, Mineola, NY.

6312
Ellsworth Kelly Foundation, Inc. ✧
c/o Ellsworth M. Kelly
P.O. Box 220
Spencertown, NY 12165

Established in 1991 in NY.
Donor: Ellsworth Kelly.
Foundation type: Independent foundation.
Financial data (yr. ended 12/31/05): Assets, $22,858,174 (M); gifts received, $3,000,000; expenditures, $956,833; qualifying distributions, $827,731; giving activities include $825,000 for 12 grants (high: $200,000; low: $25,000).
Fields of interest: Arts; Higher education; Environment, natural resources; Animals/wildlife, bird preserves.
Limitations: Applications not accepted. Giving on a national basis, with some emphasis on the East Coast. No grants to individuals.
Application information: Contributes only to pre-selected organizations.
Officers: Ellsworth Kelly, Pres.; Jack Shear, Secy.-Treas.
Directors: Roberta Bernstein; Emily Pulitzer.
EIN: 223132379
Selected grants: The following grants were reported in 2004.
$100,000 to Columbia Land Conservancy, Chatham, NY.
$100,000 to National Gallery of Art, DC.
$50,000 to Columbia University, New York, NY.
$50,000 to Friends of Hudson, Hudson, NY.

6313
Thomas L. Kempner, Jr. Foundation ✧
885 3rd Ave., Ste. 3300
New York, NY 10022

Established in 1987 in NY.
Donor: Thomas L. Kempner, Jr.
Foundation type: Independent foundation.

Financial data (yr. ended 12/31/04): Assets, $18,225,950 (M); gifts received, $91,881; expenditures, $2,499,667; qualifying distributions, $550,219; giving activities include $548,469 for 12 grants (high: $300,000; low: $469).
Purpose and activities: Giving primarily for higher and other education; funding also for a children's hospital.
Fields of interest: Higher education; Business school/education; Education; Hospitals (specialty); Children/youth, services.
Limitations: Applications not accepted. No grants to individuals.
Application information: Contributes only to pre-selected organizations.
Officers: Thomas L. Kempner, Jr., Pres.; Dean C. Berry, V.P.; Katheryn C. Patterson, Secy.
EIN: 133407819

6314
Karen A. & Kevin W. Kennedy Foundation ✧
c/o Goldman Sachs & Co.
85 Broad St., 30th Fl.
New York, NY 10004

Established 1985 in NY.
Donor: Kevin W. Kennedy.
Foundation type: Independent foundation.
Financial data (yr. ended 4/30/06): Assets, $4,138,706 (M); gifts received, $1,022,520; expenditures, $1,191,800; qualifying distributions, $1,170,709; giving activities include $1,170,709 for 137 grants (high: $100,000; low: $475).
Purpose and activities: Giving primarily for the arts, conservation, education, health care and human services.
Fields of interest: Performing arts, opera; Arts; Higher education; Medical school/education; Nursing school/education; Environment, natural resources; Health care; Human services.
Type of support: General/operating support; Continuing support; Annual campaigns; Capital campaigns; Building/renovation; Endowments; Emergency funds; Professorships; Fellowships; Scholarship funds.
Limitations: Applications not accepted. Giving primarily in MA, NJ, and NY. No grants to individuals, or for scholarships; no loans.
Application information: Contributes only to pre-selected organizations.
Trustees: Coleman W. Kennedy; Karen A. Kennedy; Kevin W. Kennedy; William F. Kennedy.
EIN: 133318161
Selected grants: The following grants were reported in 2006.
$100,000 to Fordham University, Bronx, NY.
$100,000 to Hamilton College, Clinton, NY.
$77,000 to New York City Opera, New York, NY. 2 grants: $27,000, $50,000
$59,400 to Metropolitan Opera, New York, NY.
$50,000 to College Summit, DC.
$48,350 to New York Public Library, New York, NY.
$40,000 to Collegiate Chorale, New York, NY.
$7,500 to Metropolitan Opera Guild, New York, NY.
$2,000 to Deerfield Academy, Deerfield, MA.

6315
Marion E. Kenworthy - Sarah H. Swift Foundation, Inc.
130 E. 67th St.
New York, NY 10021-6136 (212) 988-0473
Contact: Rosalind W. Harris, Admin.
FAX: (212) 988-2483; E-mail: ksfdtn@aol.com

Established in 1962 in NY.
Donor: Marion E. Kenworthy‡.
Foundation type: Independent foundation.
Financial data (yr. ended 12/31/05): Assets, $7,877,468 (M); expenditures, $389,457; qualifying distributions, $340,000; giving activities include $340,000 for 31 grants (high: $20,000; low: $5,000; average: $10,000–$15,000).
Purpose and activities: Giving primarily to promote and advance the mental and emotional health and well being of children and young persons under 21 years of age, through the development and improvement of understanding and practice in the fields of adoption, guidance, preventive psychiatry and in other fields of child welfare.
Fields of interest: Education, early childhood education; Mental health/crisis services, research; Mental health, treatment; Mental health/crisis services; Crime/violence prevention, youth; Human services; Children/youth, services; Child development, services; Family services.
Type of support: General/operating support; Continuing support; Program development; Publication; Seed money; Research; Program evaluation.
Limitations: Giving primarily in New York City and the surrounding tri-state area. No support for political organizations, or for narcotics addiction treatment or autism. No grants to individuals, or for building or capital funds or for bricks and mortar projects.
Publications: Application guidelines; Informational brochure (including application guidelines).
Application information: Application form not required.
  Initial approach: Proposal
  Copies of proposal: 3
  Deadline(s): Mar. 31 and Oct. 30
  Board meeting date(s): May and Dec.
  Final notification: 1 month after board meeting
Officers and Directors:* Michael G. Kalogerakis, M.D.*, Pres.; Trudy Festinger,* V.P.; Alice Lin,* V.P.; Stephen Wise Tulin,* Secy.-Treas.; Rosalind W. Harris, Admin.
Number of staff: 1 part-time support.
EIN: 136140940
Selected grants: The following grants were reported in 2004.
$25,000 to Legal Aid Society of Salt Lake, Salt Lake City, UT.
$15,000 to Childrens Health Fund, New York, NY.
$15,000 to Good Shepherd Services, New York, NY.
$10,000 to Andrew Glover Youth Program, New York, NY.
$10,000 to Brooklyn Kindergarten Society, Brooklyn, NY.
$10,000 to Creative Alternatives, Houston, TX.
$10,000 to Friends of Green Chimneys, Brewster, NY.
$10,000 to Learning Leaders, New York, NY.
$10,000 to Osborne Association, Long Island City, NY.
$10,000 to Turtle Bay Music School, New York, NY.

6316
Keren Eliyahu, Inc. ✧
c/o Alexander Scharf
305 West End Ave.
New York, NY 10024

Established in NY.
Donors: Solomon T. Scharf; Senior Home Care, Inc.; Zakain Assocs., LP; White Plains Hotel Limited Partnership; The Esplanade Venture Partnership LP.
Foundation type: Independent foundation.
Financial data (yr. ended 12/31/05): Assets, $2,174,345 (M); gifts received, $55,360; expenditures, $524,854; qualifying distributions, $516,546; giving activities include $516,546 for 123 grants (high: $37,000; low: $100).
Purpose and activities: Giving primarily to Jewish agencies, temples, and schools.
Fields of interest: Elementary/secondary education; Jewish agencies & temples.
Limitations: Applications not accepted. Giving primarily in Brooklyn and New York, NY. No grants to individuals.
Application information: Contributes only to pre-selected organizations.
Officers: Alexander Scharf, Pres. and Treas.; Susan Diamond, Secy.
Director: David Scharf.
EIN: 133978200
Selected grants: The following grants were reported in 2005.
$37,000 to Yeshiva Darchei Torah, Far Rockaway, NY.
$25,000 to Yeshiva Mir Yerushalayim, Brooklyn, NY.
$16,000 to Kedushat Zion, Brooklyn, NY.
$15,400 to Yeshiva Ketana of Manhattan, New York, NY.
$14,000 to Agudath Israel of America, New York, NY.
$12,000 to Agudath Israel of Long Island, Far Rockaway, NY.
$11,000 to Congregation Zichron Shlomo, Monsey, NY.
$11,000 to Mesivta of Long Beach, Long Beach, NY.
$6,000 to Manhattan High School for Girls, New York, NY.
$5,000 to Yeshiva of the South Shore, Hewlett, NY.

6317
Keren Keshet - The Rainbow Foundation ✧
1015 Park Ave.
New York, NY 10028 (212) 396-8800
Contact: Linda Sakacs, Secy.

Established in 1999 in NY.
Donor: Zalman C. Bernstein.
Foundation type: Independent foundation.
Financial data (yr. ended 12/31/05): Assets, $270,169,082 (M); gifts received, $5,500,000; expenditures, $5,099,497; qualifying distributions, $4,699,686; giving activities include $1,922,826 for 23 grants (high: $150,000; low: $500; average: $10,000–$100,000), and $66,667 for 2 grants to individuals.
Purpose and activities: Giving for technology education.
Fields of interest: Education.
Type of support: Grants to individuals.
Limitations: Giving on a national and international basis.
Application information:
  Initial approach: Letter
  Deadline(s): None

Officers: Arthur W. Fried, Pres.; Mem Dryan Bernstein, V.P. and Treas.; Linda Sakacs, Secy.
EIN: 134069592

6318
The Keren Zichron Aron Foundation ✧ ☆
c/o Weiss & Co.
22 W. 38th St., 12th Fl.
New York, NY 10018-6269
Application address: c/o Abraham Weiss, 3442 Bedford Ave., Brooklyn, NY 11210-5235, tel.: (212) 302-3400

Established in 1996 in NY.
Donors: Abraham Weiss; Barry Weiss.
Foundation type: Independent foundation.
Financial data (yr. ended 12/31/05): Assets, $123,462 (M); gifts received, $230,046; expenditures, $355,292; qualifying distributions, $355,260; giving activities include $355,260 for grants.
Fields of interest: Education; Hospitals (general); Jewish agencies & temples.
Limitations: Giving primarily in Brooklyn, NY.
Application information: Application form not required.
  Deadline(s): None
Trustees: Jeffry Hollander; Abraham Weiss.
EIN: 137101887
Selected grants: The following grants were reported in 2003.
$14,500 to Congregation Bnai Levi, Brooklyn, NY.
$12,000 to Yeshiva Toras Chaim, New York, NY.
$10,000 to Yeshivas Boyan Tifereth Mordechai Shlomo, Brooklyn, NY.
$5,400 to Torah Academy High School of Brooklyn, Brooklyn, NY.
$5,000 to Moisdois Beer Avraham Slonim, Brooklyn, NY.
$3,650 to Gomlei Chesed of Boyan, Brooklyn, NY.
$3,150 to Masores Bais Yaakov, Brooklyn, NY.
$3,000 to Yeshiva of Flatbush, Brooklyn, NY.
$2,500 to Bnos Malka Academy, Flushing, NY.
$2,000 to Beth Jacob of Boro Park, Brooklyn, NY.

6319
Keshet Foundation ✧
c/o Abraham Family
200 W. 57th St., Ste. 1005
New York, NY 10019

Established in 1997 in NY.
Donors: Rebecca Gridish; Eli Gridish; RLTS II.
Foundation type: Independent foundation.
Financial data (yr. ended 11/30/05): Assets, $386,875 (M); gifts received, $810,000; expenditures, $845,455; qualifying distributions, $842,280; giving activities include $842,080 for 33 grants to individuals (high: $131,300; low: $500).
Fields of interest: Jewish agencies & temples.
Limitations: Applications not accepted. Giving primarily in NY.
Application information: Unsolicited requests for funds not accepted.
Trustees: Estanne Abraham; Eli Gridish; Rebecca Gridish; Richard A. Sauer.
EIN: 137132997
Selected grants: The following grants were reported in 2003.
$500,000 to Nahalat Shmuel, New York, NY. For general support.

$250,000 to Shuvu Bonim, Brooklyn, NY. For general support.
$180,000 to Yad Avraham Institute, New York, NY. For general support.
$100,000 to American Friends of Kiryat Chinuch Labomim, Kew Gardens, NY. For general support.
$70,000 to Yosef Torah Leyacov. For general support.
$20,000 to Gmach Sheta Tova. For general support.
$18,000 to Ezer Mizion, Bnei Brak, Israel. For general support.
$18,000 to Israel Special Kids Fund, New York, NY. For general support.
$5,000 to Tikva LMarpeh. For general support.
$1,500 to Ohel Avraham, Jerusalem, Israel. For general support.

6320
The KeySpan Foundation ◇
175 E. Old Country Rd.
Hicksville, NY   11801   (516) 545-5147
Contact: Robert G. Keller, Exec. Dir.
FAX: (516) 545-6094;
E-mail: foundation@keyspanenergy.com;
Application address in New England: Susan E. Carlson, Mgr., KeySpan Energy Delivery, 52 2nd Ave., Waltham, MA 02451, tel.: (781) 466-5101; URL: http://www.keyspanenergy.com/corpinfo/community/foundation_all.jsp

Established in 1998 in NY.
Donors: MarketSpan Corp.; KeySpan Corp.
Foundation type: Company-sponsored foundation.
Financial data (yr. ended 12/31/04): Assets, $23,672,557 (M); expenditures, $1,200,357; qualifying distributions, $1,118,834; giving activities include $880,400 for 49 grants (high: $175,000; low: $1,000).
Purpose and activities: The foundation supports organizations involved with education and the environment.
Fields of interest: Elementary/secondary education; Higher education; Scholarships/financial aid; Education; Environment, natural resources; Environment, beautification programs; Environment; Federated giving programs.
Limitations: Giving primarily in MA and Brooklyn, Nassau, Queens, Staten Island, and Suffolk counties, NY; some giving on an international basis. No support for religious, political, or fraternal organizations. No grants to individuals, or for capital campaigns or endowments, advertisements, or tables or tickets at dinners or other functions.
Publications: Application guidelines; Annual report.
Application information: Application form required.
  Initial approach: Complete online eligibility quiz
  Copies of proposal: 1
  Deadline(s): Oct. 31
  Board meeting date(s): Quarterly
  Final notification: 60 to 90 days
Officers and Directors:* Basil A. Paterson,* Chair.; Donald H. Elliot,* Vice-Chair.; Michael J. Taunton, Treas.; Robert G. Keller, Exec. Dir.; Pamela Adamo; Carmen Fields; Elaine Weinstein.
Number of staff: 1 full-time professional; 1 full-time support.
EIN: 113466416

6321
The Peter and Eaddo Kiernan Foundation ◇
c/o BCRS Group/Marcum & Kliegman, LLP
100 Wall St., 11th Fl.
New York, NY   10005

Established in 1991 in NY.
Donor: Peter D. Kiernan.
Foundation type: Independent foundation.
Financial data (yr. ended 5/31/05): Assets, $210,426 (M); gifts received, $115,000; expenditures, $350,853; qualifying distributions, $335,835; giving activities include $335,503 for 14 grants (high: $116,000; low: $200).
Purpose and activities: Giving primarily to a charitable investment foundation, as well as for medical research, and to hospitals.
Fields of interest: Education; Hospitals (general); Spine disorders research; Human services; Neighborhood centers; Philanthropy/voluntarism; Disabilities, people with; Economically disadvantaged.
Limitations: Applications not accepted. Giving primarily in Greenwich, CT, and New York, NY; some giving nationally. No grants to individuals; no loans or scholarships.
Application information: Contributes only to pre-selected organizations.
Trustees: Eaddo H. Kiernan; Peter D. Kiernan.
EIN: 133637705
Selected grants: The following grants were reported in 2005.
$166,000 to Robin Hood Foundation, New York, NY. 2 grants: $116,000, $50,000
$100,000 to Christopher Reeve Paralysis Foundation, Springfield, NJ.
$1,000 to NYU Downtown Hospital, New York, NY.

6322
The Kimmelman Family Foundation ◇
c/o BCRS Group/Marcum & Kliegman, LLP
655 3rd Ave., 16th Fl.
New York, NY   10017

Established in 1997 in NJ.
Donor: Douglas W. Kimmelman.
Foundation type: Independent foundation.
Financial data (yr. ended 8/31/05): Assets, $2,229,723 (M); gifts received, $939,200; expenditures, $1,301,757; qualifying distributions, $1,271,482; giving activities include $1,271,470 for 49 grants (high: $450,000; low: $45).
Purpose and activities: Giving primarily for education and human services; funding also for community foundations, a medical center, and a community theater.
Fields of interest: Performing arts, theater; Historic preservation/historical societies; Higher education; Education; Hospitals (general); Human services; Foundations (community); Philanthropy/voluntarism.
Limitations: Applications not accepted. Giving primarily in CA and NJ. No grants to individuals; no loans.
Application information: Contributes only to pre-selected organizations.
Trustees: Carol Kimmelman; Douglas W. Kimmelman.
EIN: 133933319
Selected grants: The following grants were reported in 2004.
$200,000 to Stanford University, Stanford, CA.

$30,000 to Far Hills Country Day School, Far Hills, NJ.
$10,000 to Anchor, Inc., New York, NY.
$10,000 to Morristown Memorial Health Foundation, Morristown, NJ.
$10,000 to YMCA, Somerset Hills, Basking Ridge, NJ.
$5,000 to Deirdres House, Morristown, NJ.
$2,475 to Community Theater, Morristown, NJ.
$2,000 to Several Sources Foundation, Ramsey, NJ.
$1,000 to Saint Philips Academy, Newark, NJ.
$500 to Somerset Hills Learning Institute, Gladstone, NJ.

6323
Charles & Lucille King Family Foundation, Inc. ◇
366 Madison Ave., 10th Fl.
New York, NY   10017   (212) 682-2913
Contact: Michael Donovan, Educational Dir.; Karen E. Kennedy, Asst. Educational Dir.
E-mail: info@kingfoundation.org; URL: http://www.kingfoundation.org

Established in 1988 in NJ.
Donors: Diana King; Karen Rabe.
Foundation type: Independent foundation.
Financial data (yr. ended 12/31/05): Assets, $3,099,553 (M); gifts received, $573,950; expenditures, $628,873; qualifying distributions, $624,954; giving activities include $518,295 for 113 grants (high: $200,000).
Purpose and activities: Tuition scholarships to junior and senior undergraduate college students of film and television currently attending a four year accredited university in the United States.
Type of support: Scholarships—to individuals.
Limitations: Giving on a national basis.
Publications: Application guidelines; Informational brochure (including application guidelines).
Application information: See foundation Web site for application guidelines and procedures. Scholarship application forms can be downloaded from foundation Web site between Sept. and Apr. Also, grant guidelines for various programs available on Web site.
  Initial approach: Letter, telephone, e-mail to request application
  Deadline(s): Apr. 15 for the following academic year
  Board meeting date(s): Annually
Officers and Directors:* Diana King,* Chair. and Pres.; Charles J. Brucia,* V.P. and Treas.; Eugene V. Kokot,* Secy.; M. Graham Coleman.
EIN: 133489257

6324
Gioconda & Joseph H. King Foundation ◇
15 W. 53rd St., Ste. 49F
New York, NY   10109-1910   (212) 765-5656
Contact: Diana Barrett, Exec. Dir.

Established in 1992 in NY.
Donor: Gioconda King.
Foundation type: Independent foundation.
Financial data (yr. ended 12/31/04): Assets, $10,117,752 (M); expenditures, $605,469; qualifying distributions, $456,480; giving activities include $447,720 for 19 grants (high: $105,000; low: $2,500).

Fields of interest: Higher education, college; Human services; Women's studies.
Limitations: Giving primarily in MA, NY and Washington, DC. No grants to individuals.
Application information:
   Initial approach: General letter of inquiry
   Deadline(s): Nov. 15
Trustees: Diana Barrett; Gioconda King; U.S. Trust.
EIN: 133679578

6325
The King Street Charitable Trust ◇ ☆
c/o King Street Capital Mgmt. LLC
65 E. 55th St., 30th Fl.
New York, NY 10022

Established in 2004 in NY.
Donors: Brian J. Higgins; O. Francis Biondi, Jr.
Foundation type: Independent foundation.
Financial data (yr. ended 12/31/05): Assets, $748,636 (M); expenditures, $550,977; qualifying distributions, $519,607; giving activities include $519,607 for grants.
Fields of interest: Education; Youth development; Human services; Jewish federated giving programs.
Application information:
   Deadline(s): None
Trustees: O. Francis Biondi, Jr.; Brian J. Hiiggins.
EIN: 137425331
Selected grants: The following grants were reported in 2005.
$25,000 to Saint Jude Childrens Research Hospital, New York, NY.
$10,000 to American Diabetes Association, New York, NY.
$10,000 to Inner-City Scholarship Fund, New York, NY.
$10,000 to New York University Medical Center, New York, NY.
$10,000 to Villanova University, Villanova, PA.
$5,000 to Food Allergy Initiative, New York, NY.
$5,000 to Jewish Board of Family and Childrens Services, New York, NY.
$5,000 to Tulane University, New Orleans, LA.
$2,000 to Henry Street Settlement, New York, NY.
$1,000 to Smile Train, New York, NY.

6326
Mark and Anla Cheng Kingdon Fund ◇
c/o Peter J. Cobos
152 W. 57th St., 50th Fl.
New York, NY 10019

Established in 1997 in NY.
Donor: Mark Kingdon.
Foundation type: Independent foundation.
Financial data (yr. ended 12/31/05): Assets, $53,169,804 (M); gifts received, $1,864,899; expenditures, $6,890,812; qualifying distributions, $6,862,824; giving activities include $6,861,324 for 112 grants (high: $2,000,000; low: $300; average: $2,000–$10,000).
Purpose and activities: Giving primarily for the arts, education, and human services.
Fields of interest: Arts; Higher education; Health organizations, association; Human services; Children, services; Jewish federated giving programs; Jewish agencies & temples.
Limitations: Applications not accepted. Giving primarily in NY. No grants to individuals.

Application information: Contributes only to pre-selected organizations.
Officers: Mark Kingdon, Chair.; Peter J. Cobos, Secy.
EIN: 133948023
Selected grants: The following grants were reported in 2004.
$505,000 to Harlem Childrens Zone, New York, NY.
$230,000 to Spence School, New York, NY. 3 grants: $5,000, $100,000, $125,000
$50,000 to Human Rights Watch, New York, NY.
$25,000 to American Friends of the Shanghai Museum, New York, NY.
$10,000 to American Red Cross, National Headquarters, DC.
$10,000 to China Institute, Louisville, KY.
$5,000 to American Red Cross.
$5,000 to Jewish Museum, New York, NY.

6327
Kitov Foundation ◇
c/o BCRS Assocs., LLC
100 Wall St., 11th Fl.
New York, NY 10005

Established in 1987 in NY.
Donor: Jacob Z. Schuster.
Foundation type: Independent foundation.
Financial data (yr. ended 6/30/05): Assets, $2,292,958 (M); expenditures, $404,718; qualifying distributions, $403,018; giving activities include $401,023 for 331 grants (high: $50,000; low: $10).
Purpose and activities: Giving primarily for Jewish organizations, temples, and yeshivas.
Fields of interest: Elementary/secondary education; Jewish agencies & temples.
International interests: Israel.
Limitations: Applications not accepted. Giving primarily in NY and Israel. No grants to individuals.
Application information: Contributes only to pre-selected organizations.
Trustees: Diane T. Schuster; Jacob Z. Schuster.
EIN: 133437905
Selected grants: The following grants were reported in 2004.
$25,000 to Shalom Torah Centers.
$10,000 to Ohr Somayach Institutions, Monsey, NY.
$10,000 to Young Israel of Riverdale, Bronx, NY.
$5,000 to Yeshiva Degel Hatorah, Spring Valley, NY.
$200 to Yeshiva Torah Vodaath, Brooklyn, NY.
$180 to Fifth Avenue Synagogue, New York, NY.
$180 to Yeshiva Rabbi Samson Raphael Hirsch, New York, NY.
$100 to Tzedakah Vchesed, Brooklyn, NY.
$18 to Mesivta of Long Beach, Long Beach, NY.
$18 to Yeshiva of Far Rockaway, Far Rockaway, NY.

6328
Klaus Family Foundation, Inc. ◇
c/o Mortimer Klaus
21-09 Borden Ave.
Long Island City, NY 11101

Established in 1979 in NY.
Donor: Burma Bibas, Inc.
Foundation type: Independent foundation.
Financial data (yr. ended 11/30/05): Assets, $11,478,659 (L); gifts received, $300,000; expenditures, $463,490; qualifying distributions, $426,291; giving activities include $426,291 for 49 grants (high: $150,000; low: $500).

Purpose and activities: Giving primarily to Jewish temples and yeshivas; some support also for health care.
Fields of interest: Elementary/secondary education; Hospitals (general); Human services; Jewish federated giving programs; Jewish agencies & temples.
Limitations: Applications not accepted. Giving primarily in NY. No grants to individuals.
Application information: Contributes only to pre-selected organizations.
Trustees: Arthur Klaus; Lester Klaus; Mortimer Klaus.
EIN: 133053197

6329
The Conrad and Virginia Klee Foundation, Inc.
84 Court St., Ste. 500
Binghamton, NY 13901 (607) 722-2266
Contact: Judith C. Peckham, Exec. Dir.
FAX: (607) 722-2264;
E-mail: kleefoundation@stny.rr.com

Incorporated in 1957 in NY.
Donors: Conrad C. Klee†; Virginia Klee†.
Foundation type: Independent foundation.
Financial data (yr. ended 12/31/05): Assets, $19,843,066 (M); gifts received, $1,675; expenditures, $1,036,804; qualifying distributions, $974,234; giving activities include $964,807 for grants.
Purpose and activities: Giving primarily for the arts, health care, and human services.
Fields of interest: Arts; Hospitals (general); Health care; Human services; Children/youth, services; Federated giving programs.
Type of support: Equipment; Program development; Fellowships.
Limitations: Giving limited to Broome County, NY. No support for religious or political organizations. No grants to individuals.
Application information: Application form required.
   Initial approach: Letter or telephone call
   Copies of proposal: 1
   Deadline(s): None
   Board meeting date(s): Apr., May, Oct. and Nov.
Officers: Linda Biemer, Chair.; William J. Orband, Jr., Vice-Chair.; Gary Holcomb, Secy.-Treas.; Judith C. Peckham, Exec. Dir.
Directors: Ron Akel; Larry Anderson; Armond George; Patricia Ingraham; Jeffrey Lake; Arthur Orr.
Number of staff: 1 part-time professional; 1 part-time support.
EIN: 156019821
Selected grants: The following grants were reported in 2005.
$60,000 to YMCA.
$39,022 to Roberson Museum and Science Center, Binghamton, NY.
$37,885 to Family and Childrens Society, Baltimore, MD.
$37,042 to Southern Tier Zoological Society, Binghamton, NY.
$33,865 to Southern Tier Independence Center, Binghamton, NY.
$33,333 to Family Enrichment Network, Binghamton, NY.
$33,000 to Binghamton Philharmonic, Binghamton, NY.
$30,000 to Urban League.
$26,899 to YWCA.

$4,268 to Humane Society.

6330
The Reb Ephraim Chaim & Miriam Rochel Klein Charitable Foundation ✧
614 Ave. J
Brooklyn, NY   11230

Established in 1989 in NY.
Donors: Abraham Klein; Sarah Dinah Klein; L. Rubin; Abraham Leizirowitz; Fairview Nursing Care Center, Inc.; Hyde Park Nursing Home, Inc.
Foundation type: Independent foundation.
Financial data (yr. ended 12/31/04): Assets, $41,186,029 (M); gifts received, $55,597; expenditures, $1,678,042; qualifying distributions, $1,576,659; giving activities include $1,575,909 for 280 grants (high: $92,650; low: $4).
Purpose and activities: Giving primarily to Jewish agencies and temples.
Fields of interest: Elementary/secondary education; Human services; Jewish federated giving programs; Jewish agencies & temples; Religion.
International interests: Israel.
Limitations: Applications not accepted. Giving primarily in the U.S., with emphasis on Brooklyn, NY; giving also in Jerusalem, Israel. No grants to individuals.
Application information: Contributes only to pre-selected organizations.
Directors: Abraham Klein; Sarah Dinah Klein.
EIN: 223000780
Selected grants: The following grants were reported in 2003.
$351,000 to American Friends of Tiferet Moshe Betzalel, Brooklyn, NY.
$286,537 to Mosdot Goor, Friends of, Brooklyn, NY.
$79,510 to Agudath Israel of America, New York, NY.
$77,650 to American Friends of Congregation Litzirim, Brooklyn, NY.
$28,800 to Friends of Harim, Brooklyn, NY.
$18,000 to Press Foundation of America, Brooklyn, NY.
$18,000 to Yeshiva Torah Temimah, Brooklyn, NY.
$17,050 to Mesivta Bais Yisroel, Brooklyn, NY.
$17,000 to Mesorah Heritage Foundation, Brooklyn, NY.
$10,000 to Educational Institute Oholei Torah, Brooklyn, NY.

6331
Klein Family Foundation ✧ ☆
c/o Park Terrace Care Ctr.
109-40 Saultell Ave.
Corona, NY   11368

Established in 1999 in NY.
Donors: Abraham Klein; Sarah Dinah Klein.
Foundation type: Independent foundation.
Financial data (yr. ended 12/31/04): Assets, $12,967,714 (M); gifts received, $3,969,057; expenditures, $430,089; qualifying distributions, $404,568; giving activities include $403,490 for 24 grants (high: $100,000; low: $180).
Fields of interest: Jewish agencies & temples.
Limitations: Applications not accepted. Giving primarily in NY. No grants to individuals.
Application information: Contributes only to pre-selected organizations.

Trustees: Abraham Klein; Sarah Dinah Klein.
EIN: 134092608

6332
George & Adele Klein Foundation ✧
c/o Park Tower Realty Corp.
499 Park Ave.
New York, NY   10022

Established in 1968 in NY.
Donors: Adele Klein; George Klein.
Foundation type: Independent foundation.
Financial data (yr. ended 3/31/05): Assets, $466,403 (M); gifts received, $391,000; expenditures, $393,616; qualifying distributions, $393,139; giving activities include $393,139 for 69 grants (high: $36,000; low: $180).
Purpose and activities: Giving primarily to Jewish organizations, temples, and schools.
Fields of interest: Secondary school/education; Education; Human services; Jewish federated giving programs; Jewish agencies & temples.
Limitations: Applications not accepted. No grants to individuals.
Application information: Contributes only to pre-selected organizations.
Officers: George Klein, Pres.; Adele Klein, V.P.
EIN: 136279924
Selected grants: The following grants were reported in 2005.
$36,000 to Hebrew Academy of Cleveland, Cleveland, OH.
$18,000 to Bnei Torah Movement, New York, NY.
$10,000 to Jewish Community Relations Council, Cincinnati, OH.
$10,000 to Ner Israel Rabbinical College, Baltimore, MD.
$10,000 to Telshe Yeshiva Chicago, Chicago, IL.
$6,600 to Yeshiva Chaim Berlin, Brooklyn, NY.
$5,000 to Yeshiva Mkor Chaim, Brooklyn, NY.
$5,000 to Yeshiva Torah Vodaath, Brooklyn, NY.
$3,600 to Mesorah Heritage Foundation, Brooklyn, NY.
$2,500 to Yeshiva Ketana of Manhattan, New York, NY.

6333
Ruth & Seymour Klein Foundation, Inc. ✧
16 Tallwoods Rd.
Armonk, NY   10504
Contact: Barbara G. Klein, V.P.

Established in 1947.
Donors: Seymour M. Klein†; Ruth L. Klein†.
Foundation type: Independent foundation.
Financial data (yr. ended 4/30/06): Assets, $6,551,144 (M); expenditures, $365,032; qualifying distributions, $319,100; giving activities include $319,100 for grants.
Purpose and activities: Giving primarily for health care and the arts.
Fields of interest: Museums; Arts; Education; Hospitals (general); Health care; Human services.
Type of support: General/operating support; Annual campaigns; Capital campaigns; Endowments; Scholarship funds.
Limitations: Giving primarily in NY. No grants to individuals.
Application information: Application form not required.
   Initial approach: Letter

Copies of proposal: 1
Deadline(s): Dec. 31
Officers and Directors:* Barbara G. Klein,* V.P.; Zoe S. Klein,* Secy.; Jason A. Klein,* Treas.
EIN: 136114763
Selected grants: The following grants were reported in 2005.
$37,500 to Connecticut College, New London, CT.
$25,000 to Lehigh University, Bethlehem, PA.
$10,000 to Greenwich Hospital, Greenwich, CT.
$10,000 to Metropolitan Museum of Art, New York, NY.
$5,000 to National Center for Learning Disabilities, New York, NY.
$1,000 to Musical Theater Works, New York, NY.
$100 to American Heart Association, Dallas, TX.

6334
The Kleinman Family Foundation ✧ ☆
171 Kings Hwy.
Brooklyn, NY   11223-1023

Donor: Martin Kleinman.
Foundation type: Independent foundation.
Financial data (yr. ended 12/31/05): Assets, $2,169,350 (M); gifts received, $1,237,450; expenditures, $423,321; qualifying distributions, $422,836; giving activities include $422,836 for grants.
Fields of interest: Jewish agencies & temples.
Limitations: Applications not accepted. No grants for individuals.
Application information: Contributes only to pre-selected organizations.
Officers: Martin Kleinman, Pres. and Treas.; Beth Kleinman, Secy.
Directors: Aliza Freedman; Josph S. Kleinman; Deena Schuss.
EIN: 200136129

6335
Andrew & Julie Klingenstein Family Fund, Inc. ✧ ☆
c/o Tanton and Co., LLP
37 W. 57th St., 5th Fl.
New York, NY   10019

Established in 2000 in MD.
Donors: Andrew Klingenstein; Andrew Klingenstein Charitable Lead Trust; John Klingenstein; Patricia Klingenstein.
Foundation type: Independent foundation.
Financial data (yr. ended 12/31/05): Assets, $11,064,207 (M); gifts received, $4,792,090; expenditures, $618,974; qualifying distributions, $465,730; giving activities include $465,515 for 26 grants (high: $215,000; low: $100).
Fields of interest: Higher education; Education; Health organizations, association; Jewish agencies & temples; Religion.
Limitations: Giving on a national basis. No grants to individuals.
Officers and Directors:* Julie Klingenstein,* Pres.; Thomas D. Klingenstein,* V.P.; Andrew Klingenstein,* Secy.-Treas.
EIN: 522126870
Selected grants: The following grants were reported in 2004.
$105,000 to Congregation Or Chadash, Gaithersburg, MD. For general support.

$20,000 to Hastings Center, Garrison, NY. For general support.

$17,000 to Klingenstein Third Generation Foundation, New York, NY. For general support.

$12,500 to Children and Adults with Attention-Deficit/Hyperactivity Disorder (CHADD), Landover, MD. For general support.

$10,000 to Deerfield Academy, Deerfield, MA. For general support.

$10,000 to Mental Health Association, National, Alexandria, VA. For general support.

$5,000 to Belgrade Regional Conservation Alliance, Smithfield, ME. For general support.

$5,000 to University of Maryland-College Park, College Park, MD. For general support.

$5,000 to Waynflete School, Portland, ME. For general support.

$5,000 to Yale University, New Haven, CT. For general support.

6336
Klingenstein Fund ✧

(formerly Clara Buttenwieser Unger Memorial Foundation)
31 Oxford Rd.
Scarsdale, NY   10583
Contact: Lee P. Klingenstein, Pres.

Established in 1940 in NY.

Donors: Alan Klingenstein; Lee Paul Klingenstein; Paul H. Klingenstein; Joanne K. Ziesing.

Foundation type: Independent foundation.

Financial data (yr. ended 12/31/03): Assets, $4,499,219 (M); expenditures, $357,187; qualifying distributions, $332,129; giving activities include $329,719 for 163 grants (high: $75,000; low: $25).

Purpose and activities: Support primarily for education including a wilderness education program, as well as for arts, health, and human services.

Fields of interest: Arts; Education; Environmental education; Environment; Hospitals (general); Human services; Jewish agencies & temples.

Limitations: Giving primarily in CT and NY. No grants to individuals.

Application information:
  Initial approach: Letter
  Deadline(s): None

Officers: Lee Paul Klingenstein, Pres.; Paul H. Klingenstein, V.P.; Joanne K. Ziesing, Secy.; Alan Klingenstein, Treas.

EIN: 136077894

Selected grants: The following grants were reported in 2004.

$105,000 to White Plains Hospital Center, White Plains, NY. 2 grants: $5,000, $100,000

$50,000 to Acumen Fund, New York, NY.

$25,550 to Expeditionary Learning Outward Bound, Garrison, NY.

$25,000 to Outward Bound, Garrison, NY.

$16,000 to Princeton University, Princeton, NJ. 2 grants: $15,000, $1,000

$1,500 to United Way.

$1,500 to Visiting Nurse Service of New York, New York, NY.

$1,000 to Greenbelt Alliance, San Francisco, CA.

6337
Frederick & Sharon Klingenstein Fund ✧

c/o Tanton & Co., LLP
37 W. 57th St., 5th Fl.
New York, NY   10019-3411
Application address: c/o Frederick A. Klingenstein, 787 7th Ave., 6th Fl., New York, NY 10019-6016

Established in 1997 in NY.

Donor: Frederick A. Klingenstein.

Foundation type: Independent foundation.

Financial data (yr. ended 12/31/04): Assets, $5,496,710 (M); gifts received, $1,049,370; expenditures, $961,741; qualifying distributions, $915,785; giving activities include $912,325 for 81 grants (high: $350,000; low: $50).

Purpose and activities: Giving primarily to cultural institutions, hospitals, and social services.

Fields of interest: Museums (natural history); Arts; Education; Hospitals (general); Cancer research; Breast cancer research; Recreation, parks/playgrounds; Human services; Children/youth, services; Community development.

Limitations: Giving primarily in New York, NY.

Application information: Application form not required.
  Deadline(s): None

Trustees: Frederick A. Klingenstein; Sharon Klingenstein.

EIN: 061471980

Selected grants: The following grants were reported in 2003.

$700,000 to Mount Sinai Medical Center, New York, NY.

$300,000 to American Museum of Natural History, New York, NY.

$2,789 to Metropolitan Museum of Art, New York, NY.

$2,500 to Memorial Sloan-Kettering Cancer Center, New York, NY.

$1,600 to Jazz at Lincoln Center, New York, NY.

$1,000 to Metropolitan Opera, New York, NY.

$1,000 to Museum of Modern Art, New York, NY.

$1,000 to Safe Horizon, New York, NY.

$1,000 to Women in Need (WIN), New York, NY.

$500 to W N E T Channel 13, New York, NY.

6338
The Esther A. & Joseph Klingenstein Fund, Inc. ▼ ✧

787 7th Ave., 6th Fl.
New York, NY   10019-6016   (212) 492-6181
Contact: John Klingenstein, Pres.; Kathleen Pomerantz
FAX: (212) 492-7007;
E-mail: kathleen.pomerantz@klingenstein.com;
URL: http://www.klingfund.org

Incorporated in 1945 in NY.

Donors: Esther A. Klingenstein†; Joseph Klingenstein†.

Foundation type: Independent foundation.

Financial data (yr. ended 9/30/05): Assets, $126,875,123 (M); expenditures, $6,636,002; qualifying distributions, $5,041,002; giving activities include $4,573,965 for 81 grants (high: $788,765; low: $500; average: $25,000–$50,000).

Purpose and activities: Primary interests in neuroscientific research bearing on epilepsy and in independent school education. Some support also

for the use of animals in biomedical research and church and state separation.

Fields of interest: Elementary/secondary education; Epilepsy research; Neuroscience research; Civil liberties, first amendment; Public policy, research.

Type of support: General/operating support; Continuing support; Program development; Conferences/seminars; Publication; Seed money; Fellowships; Research; Grants to individuals.

Publications: Informational brochure.

Application information: Application forms are required for the Klingenstein Fellowship Awards, and are available from department heads or from the foundation's Web site.
  Initial approach: Letter or proposal
  Copies of proposal: 1
  Deadline(s): Dec. 10 for Klingenstein Fellowship Awards applications
  Board meeting date(s): Generally 4 or 5 times a year

Officers and Directors:* John Klingenstein,* Pres. and Treas.; Frederick A. Klingenstein,* 1st V.P. and Secy.; Patricia D. Klingenstein; Sharon L. Klingenstein.

Number of staff: 2 full-time professional; 2 part-time professional; 1 full-time support.

EIN: 136028788

Selected grants: The following grants were reported in 2003.

$400,000 to Teachers College Columbia University, New York, NY. For Klingenstein Center for Independent School Education.

$50,000 to Johns Hopkins University, Baltimore, MD.

$45,000 to North Carolina Association for Biomedical Research, Raleigh, NC. For general operating support.

$45,000 to States United for Biomedical Research, Raleigh, NC. For general operating support.

$40,000 to Americans United for Separation of Church and State, DC. For general operating support.

$35,000 to Epilepsy Foundation, Landover, MD.

$20,000 to TEAK Fellowship, New York, NY. For general operating support.

6339
John & Patricia Klingenstein Fund ✧

c/o Tanton & Co., LLP
37 W. 57th St., 5th Fl.
New York, NY   10019
Contact: Janet L. Mulligan, Acct.

Established in 1999 in NY.

Donor: John Klingenstein.

Foundation type: Independent foundation.

Financial data (yr. ended 12/31/04): Assets, $13,416,017 (M); gifts received, $1,116,062; expenditures, $610,436; qualifying distributions, $544,113; giving activities include $542,010 for 28 grants (high: $200,000; low: $2,000).

Purpose and activities: Giving primarily for education and the arts.

Fields of interest: Arts; Education.

Limitations: Applications not accepted. Giving primarily in NY. No grants to individuals.

Trustees: Kenneth H. Fields; John Klingenstein; Patricia Klingenstein.

EIN: 134062589

Selected grants: The following grants were reported in 2003.

$150,000 to Rensselaerville Institute, Rensselaerville, NY.

$30,000 to Teachers College Columbia University, New York, NY.

$25,000 to Deerfield Academy, Deerfield, MA.

$24,585 to New York Public Library, New York, NY.

$16,000 to New-York Historical Society, New York, NY.

$14,500 to Metropolitan Museum of Art, New York, NY.

$10,000 to Emma Willard School, Troy, NY.

$10,000 to Yale University, New Haven, CT.

$5,000 to Smith College, Northampton, MA.

$5,000 to Waynflete School, Portland, ME.

6340
The Klingenstein Third Generation Foundation

787 7th Ave., 6th Fl.
New York, NY   10019-6016   (212) 492-6179
Contact: Sally Klingenstein Martell, Exec. Dir.
FAX: (212) 492-7007; E-mail: sally@ktgf.org;
URL: http://www.ktgf.org/

Established in 1993 in NY.

Donors: Thomas Klingenstein; Nancy Simpkins; Sarah Martell; Andrew Klingenstein; Esther A. and Joseph Klingenstein Fund; Amy Pollinger.

Foundation type: Independent foundation.

Financial data (yr. ended 9/30/05): Assets, $6,799,000 (M); gifts received, $117,000; expenditures, $515,766; qualifying distributions, $447,862; giving activities include $365,000 for 13 grants (high: $45,000; low: $5,000).

Purpose and activities: Support for programs that strive to improve the lives of families afflicted by depression, with a focus on those that address child and adolescent depression and Attention Deficit Hyperactivity Disorder (ADHD). The foundation operates three funding programs. Two are post-doctoral fellowship programs to fund clinical or basic research. One of these programs supports researchers investigating childhood and adolescent depression. The other supports researchers investigating ADHD in children. Investigators must hold a Ph.D. and/or an M.D. degree, and have completed all research training, including post-doctoral training. The foundation's third funding program supports medical student training programs at a number of institutions. These programs increase students' exposure to the field of child psychiatry. The foundation no longer funds outside the three fellowship programs.

Fields of interest: Medical school/education; Mental health, depression; Mental health/crisis services; Child development, services.

Type of support: Fellowships.

Limitations: Applications not accepted. Giving on a national basis, with emphasis on the New York, NY, Chicago, IL, and Washington, DC, areas. No support for direct service programs (unless they include a research or program evaluation component). No grants to individuals.

Application information: Send e-mail requesting addition to the mailing list for fellowship announcements. Unsolicited applications are not accepted. Fellowship nominations are solicited by invitation only. Applications for funding outside of fellowship programs not accepted.

Board meeting date(s): 3 times per year

Officers and Trustees:* Andrew Klingenstein,* Pres.; Susan Klingenstein,* V.P.; Nancy Simpkins,* Secy.; Thomas Klingenstein,* Treas.; Sally

Klingenstein Martell,* Exec. Dir.; Kathy Klingenstein; Amy Pollinger.

Number of staff: 2 part-time professional.

EIN: 133732439

6341
Knafel Family Foundation ✧

810 7th Ave., 41st Fl.
New York, NY   10019-5864

Established in 1994 in NY.

Donor: Sidney R. Knafel.

Foundation type: Independent foundation.

Financial data (yr. ended 12/31/04): Assets, $28,967,083 (M); gifts received, $252,229; expenditures, $1,218,921; qualifying distributions, $1,100,175; giving activities include $1,099,425 for 25 grants (high: $1,000,000; low: $125).

Purpose and activities: Giving primarily for higher and other education, and for human services; funding also for the arts and Jewish agencies and temples.

Fields of interest: Arts; Higher education; Education; Environment; Health organizations, association; Human services; Jewish agencies & temples.

Limitations: Applications not accepted. Giving primarily in MA and NY. No grants to individuals.

Application information: Contributes only to pre-selected organizations.

Officers: Sidney R. Knafel, Pres.; Andrew G. Knafel, Treas.

Director: Douglas R. Knafel.

EIN: 133779562

Selected grants: The following grants were reported in 2003.

$275,000 to Rogosin Institute, New York, NY. For general support.

$200,000 to Environmental Defense, New York, NY. For general support.

$100,000 to Harvard Business School Fund, Boston, MA. For general support.

$100,000 to Phillips Academy, Andover, MA. For general support.

$100,000 to Wellesley College, Wellesley, MA. For general support.

$5,000 to Heifer Project International, Little Rock, AR. For general support.

$2,500 to Regional Affordable Housing Corporation, Bennington, VT. For general support.

$1,000 to Doe Fund, New York, NY. For general support.

$1,000 to Grand Street Settlement, New York, NY. For general support.

$500 to Xerces Society, Portland, OR. For general support.

6342
Knapp-Swezey Foundation, Inc. ✧

P.O. Box 2549
Patchogue, NY   11772
Contact: Priscilla S. Knapp Teich, Pres.

Established in 1989 in NY.

Donor: Priscilla S. Knapp.

Foundation type: Independent foundation.

Financial data (yr. ended 6/30/05): Assets, $7,459,079 (M); gifts received, $45,793; expenditures, $566,041; qualifying distributions, $536,624; giving activities include $520,624 for 72 grants, and $16,000 for 8 grants to individuals.

Fields of interest: Arts; Education, fund raising/fund distribution; Education; Health organizations, association; Human services; Youth, services; Economically disadvantaged.

Type of support: Continuing support; Annual campaigns; Building/renovation; Scholarship funds.

Limitations: Giving primarily in the Suffolk County, NY, area, with emphasis on the town of Brookhaven. No support for religious organizations. No grants for individual scholarships; no loans to individuals.

Application information: The foundation no longer makes grants to individuals. Application form not required.

Initial approach: Proposal
Copies of proposal: 1
Deadline(s): None
Board meeting date(s): Quarterly
Final notification: Next board meeting

Officers and Directors:* Priscilla S. Knapp Teich,* Pres.; Carroll M. Swezey, Jr.,* V.P.; Nancy Swezey,* Secy.; William L. Knapp,* Treas.; Carol Knapp; David E. Knapp*; Jane Knapp; Carol Maust; Dori Osborne; John J. Roe III; John Swezey; Jerome Teich.

EIN: 113038738

6343
Max & Rika Knopf Foundation ✧

1362 51st St.
Brooklyn, NY   11219

Established in 1988 in NY.

Donors: Max Knopf; Rika Knopf.

Foundation type: Independent foundation.

Financial data (yr. ended 11/30/05): Assets, $1,446,423 (M); gifts received, $259,308; expenditures, $375,565; qualifying distributions, $364,678; giving activities include $362,553 for 36 grants (high: $167,241; low: $500).

Fields of interest: Elementary/secondary education; Human services; Jewish agencies & temples.

Limitations: Applications not accepted. No grants to individuals.

Application information: Contributes only to pre-selected organizations.

Managers: Max Knopf; Rika Knopf.

EIN: 133523504

Selected grants: The following grants were reported in 2004.

$114,043 to Shuvu Bonim, Brooklyn, NY.

$40,500 to Beth Medrash Govoha, Brooklyn, NY.

$18,000 to Yeshiva Torah Temimah, Brooklyn, NY.

$7,200 to Talmudical Yeshiva of Philadelphia, Philadelphia, PA.

$6,100 to Lakewood Cheder, Lakewood, NJ.

$5,800 to Tashbar of Lakewood, Lakewood, NJ.

$5,000 to Congregation Agudath Israel, Monsey, NY.

$5,000 to Pesach Relief Fund.

$2,144 to Yad Eliezer, Brooklyn, NY.

$2,000 to Congregation Zichron Yitzchok, Monsey, NY.

6344
The Knossos Foundation, Inc. ✧

c/o Rothstein, Kass & Co.
1350 Ave. of the Americas
New York, NY   10019
Contact: David Wilson, V.P.

Established in 1990 in NY.

Donors: Andrea Wilson†; Fred W. Wilson†.
Foundation type: Independent foundation.
Financial data (yr. ended 12/31/04): Assets, $9,324,167 (M); expenditures, $562,987; qualifying distributions, $481,672; giving activities include $481,672 for 42 grants (high: $48,080; low: $250).
Purpose and activities: Giving primarily for education, as well as for children, youth, and family services; some funding also for social services including services for the blind, and for summer employment search programs for older teenagers.
Fields of interest: Elementary/secondary education; Higher education; Education; Medical research, institute; Housing/shelter, development; Human services; Children/youth, services; Family services.
Limitations: Giving primarily in New York, NY and MA. No grants to individuals.
Application information: Application form not required.
  Initial approach: Letter
Officers and Directors:* David Wilson,* V.P.; Linda Wilson,* Secy.-Treas.
EIN: 133579596
Selected grants: The following grants were reported in 2004.
$40,000 to Foundation for the Mid South, Jackson, MS.
$30,000 to Homeless Prenatal Program, San Francisco, CA.
$25,017 to Laney College, Oakland, CA. For Project Bridge.
$20,000 to Mount Holyoke College, South Hadley, MA.
$20,000 to Summer Search Napa-Sonoma, Petaluma, CA.
$20,000 to Summer Search Seattle, Seattle, WA.
$15,000 to Planned Parenthood.
$15,000 to Summer Search New York City, Brooklyn, NY.
$7,500 to University of Puget Sound, Tacoma, WA.
$5,000 to Lighthouse for the Blind.

6345
The Seymour H. Knox Foundation ✧
1 HSBC Ctr., Ste. 3840
Buffalo, NY   14203

Incorporated in 1945 in NY.
Donors: Seymour H. Knox†; Marjorie K.C. Klopp†; Dorothy K.G. Rogers†.
Foundation type: Independent foundation.
Financial data (yr. ended 12/31/05): Assets, $22,524,867 (M); expenditures, $1,451,885; qualifying distributions, $1,086,986; giving activities include $951,478 for 130 grants (high: $120,000; low: $500).
Fields of interest: Arts education; Arts; Education; Zoos/zoological societies; Health care; Human services; YM/YWCAs & YM/YWHAs; Federated giving programs.
Type of support: General/operating support.
Limitations: Giving primarily in the Buffalo, NY, area; some funding nationally. No grants to individuals.
Application information:
  Initial approach: Letter
  Deadline(s): None
Officers and Directors:* Hazard K. Campbell,* Chair.; Northrup R. Knox, Jr.,* Pres.; Seymour H. Knox IV,* V.P. and Secy.; Benjamin K. Campbell,*

V.P. and Treas.; Charles W. Banta; Randolph A. Marks; Henry Z. Urban.
EIN: 160839066

6346
The Kohlberg Foundation, Inc. ▼ ✧
111 Radio Cir.
Mount Kisco, NY   10549
Contact: Nancy White McCabe, Exec. V.P. and Exec. Dir.
FAX: (914) 241-1195; E-mail: dehaan@kfound.org

Established in 1989 in NY.
Donor: The Kohlberg Foundation.
Foundation type: Independent foundation.
Financial data (yr. ended 12/31/05): Assets, $286,902,686 (M); gifts received, $12,336,705; expenditures, $15,872,361; qualifying distributions, $13,761,406; giving activities include $12,969,499 for 157 grants (high: $4,000,000; low: $250; average: $10,000–$250,000).
Purpose and activities: Support for environmental and conservation programs, integrative medicine, community, educational and cultural organizations.
Fields of interest: Environment; Health organizations, association; Medical research, institute; Children/youth, services.
International interests: Mexico.
Type of support: Annual campaigns; Land acquisition; Program development; Seed money; Program evaluation.
Limitations: Applications not accepted. Giving primarily in the U.S., with emphasis on CA and MA; giving also in Baja CA, Mexico. No grants to individuals.
Publications: Annual report.
Application information: Contributes only to pre-selected organizations.
  Board meeting date(s): Spring and Fall
Officers and Trustees:* Jerome Kohlberg,* Chair. and Pres.; Nancy White McCabe, Exec. V.P. and Exec. Dir.; Eileen M. Capone, Secy.; Walter W. Farley, Treas.; Karen K. Davis; Leslie G. Fagen; Andrew Kohlberg; Karen B. Kohlberg; Pamela Kohlberg.
Number of staff: 4 full-time professional; 1 full-time support.
EIN: 133496263
Selected grants: The following grants were reported in 2004.
$5,000,000 to Swarthmore College, Swarthmore, PA. For Parrish Hall renovation.
$2,000,000 to Jewish Communal Fund of New York, New York, NY.
$820,554 to University of Maryland-College Park, School of Medicine, College Park, MD. For integrative medicine program.
$650,000 to Proteus Fund, Amherst, MA. For Progressive projects with Bill Moyers.
$150,000 to International Community Foundation, San Diego, CA. For Baja Land acquisition fund to conserve land through easement and purchase.
$27,000 to National Center for Family Philanthropy, DC. For research on administrative costs in Family Foundations.
$25,000 to Hudson River Sloop Clearwater, Poughkeepsie, NY. For Clearwater Documentary Educational Outreach.
$15,000 to New Rochelle Fund for Educational Excellence, New Rochelle, NY. For general support.
$15,000 to Northern Westchester Hospital Center, Mount Kisco, NY. For Physician's Retreat.

$7,000 to Mount Kisco, Town of, Mount Kisco, NY. For Clock Fund for Kirby Plaza.

6347
The Komansky Foundation, Inc. ✧
c/o Morrison & Foerster
1290 6th Ave.
New York, NY   10104-0050
Contact: John D. Dadakis

Established in 1997 in NY.
Donors: David H. Komansky; Phyllis J. Komansky.
Foundation type: Independent foundation.
Financial data (yr. ended 12/31/04): Assets, $18,258,720 (M); expenditures, $4,135,935; qualifying distributions, $4,100,117; giving activities include $4,067,500 for 5 grants (high: $4,000,000; low: $2,500).
Purpose and activities: Giving primarily for a hospital's pediatrics division.
Fields of interest: Hospitals (general); Pediatrics; Children/youth.
Limitations: Giving primarily in New York, NY.
Application information:
  Initial approach: Proposal
  Deadline(s): None
Officers and Directors:* David H. Komansky,* Pres.; Phyllis J. Komansky,* Secy.; Elyssa M. Komansky,* Treas.; Evan Holod; Jennifer R. Komansky.
EIN: 133978765
Selected grants: The following grants were reported in 2005.
$4,500,000 to New York-Presbyterian Hospital, New York, NY. 2 grants: $4,000,000 (For pediatric hospital), $500,000 (For pediatric craniofacial surgery program).
$25,000 to Ronald McDonald House of New York, New York, NY. For general support.
$15,000 to Inner-City Scholarship Fund. For general support.
$10,000 to Damon Runyon Cancer Research Foundation, New York, NY. For general support.
$10,000 to Juvenile Diabetes Research Foundation International, New York, NY. For general support.

6348
Kopf Family Foundation ✧
(formerly Kopf Foundation, Inc.)
c/o Kelley, Drye & Warren, LLP
101 Park Ave.
New York, NY   10178

Incorporated in 1967 in NY.
Donor: R.C. Kopf†.
Foundation type: Independent foundation.
Financial data (yr. ended 12/31/04): Assets, $12,724,452 (L); expenditures, $726,925; qualifying distributions, $596,262; giving activities include $574,882 for 22 grants (high: $100,000; low: $882).
Purpose and activities: Giving primarily for higher and other education, including a culinary institute; funding also for health and human services.
Fields of interest: Performing arts; Elementary/secondary education; Higher education; Business school/education; Education; Hospitals (general); Health organizations, association; Eye diseases; Health organizations; Human services; Christian agencies & churches.

Type of support: General/operating support; Continuing support; Seed money; Fellowships; Scholarship funds; Matching/challenge support.
Limitations: Applications not accepted. Giving on a national basis. No grants to individuals.
Application information: Contributes only to pre-selected organizations.
Officers: Patricia Colagiuri, Pres.; Nancy Sue Mueller, V.P.; Michael S. Insel, Secy.; Brenda Helies, Treas.
EIN: 136228036
Selected grants: The following grants were reported in 2004.
$100,000 to Wellesley College, Wellesley, MA.
$75,000 to Culinary Institute of America, Hyde Park, NY.
$53,000 to University of Virginia, Charlottesville, VA.
$50,000 to Rockefeller University, New York, NY.
$45,000 to American Heart Association, Dallas, TX.
$25,000 to Boston University, Boston, MA.
$25,000 to Cornell University, Ithaca, NY.
$25,000 to Saint Christophers Inn, Garrison, NY.
$20,000 to Flint Hill School, Oakton, VA.

6349
The Koppelman Family Foundation ✧
230 Park Ave., 7th Fl.
New York, NY   10169-0005
Contact: Murray Koppelman, Tr.

Established in 1989 in NY.
Donor: Murray Koppelman.
Foundation type: Independent foundation.
Financial data (yr. ended 10/31/05): Assets, $2,009,669 (M); expenditures, $645,558; qualifying distributions, $643,556; giving activities include $641,346 for 41+ grants (high: $205,000).
Fields of interest: Arts; Higher education; Human services; Jewish federated giving programs; Jewish agencies & temples.
Limitations: Giving primarily in NY. No grants to individuals.
Application information: Application form not required.
Deadline(s): None
Trustees: Janet Koppelman; Lisa Koppelman; Murray Koppelman; Suzanne Koppelman.
EIN: 133543828
Selected grants: The following grants were reported in 2005.
$205,000 to Brooklyn College Foundation, Brooklyn, NY.
$40,850 to Washington Institute, DC.
$12,250 to Jewish Museum, New York, NY.
$5,000 to W N E T Channel 13, New York, NY.
$3,500 to Center for Jewish History, New York, NY.
$1,000 to Concord Coalition, Arlington, VA.
$1,000 to Westchester/Fairfield Hebrew Academy, Greenwich, CT.

6350
Emily Davie and Joseph S. Kornfeld Foundation
41 Schermerhorn St., Ste. 208
Brooklyn, NY   11201   (718) 624-7969
Contact: Bobye G. List, Exec. Dir.
FAX: (718) 834-1204;
E-mail: office@kornfeldfdn.org; *URL:* http://foundationcenter.org/grantmaker/kornfeld/
Additional URL: http://www.kornfeldfdn.org

Established in 1979.
Donor: Emily Davie Kornfeld†.
Foundation type: Independent foundation.
Financial data (yr. ended 12/31/04): Assets, $33,730,626 (M); expenditures, $2,136,056; qualifying distributions, $1,849,219; giving activities include $1,549,000 for 26 grants (high: $505,000; low: $2,500), and $3,647 for 1 grant to an individual.
Purpose and activities: The foundation supports literacy enrichment programs for New York City Public School children, the Robert Packard Center for ALS Research at Johns Hopkins Medical School, and grants in palliative care and bioethics, which are currently limited to a collaboration with The National Palliative Care Research and Training Center at Mount Sinai Hospital. Medical grantmaking strategies are currently under review.
Fields of interest: Education, management/technical aid; Elementary/secondary education; Medical school/education; Education, reading; Health care, ethics; Health care; Medical research, institute.
Type of support: Program development; Seed money; Curriculum development; Fellowships; Research; Program evaluation.
Limitations: Giving limited to the continental U.S., with emphasis on New York, NY, for educational grants.
Publications: Annual report (including application guidelines); Grants list.
Application information: Application information available on foundation Web site. The grants listed in current program areas include major ongoing commitments undertaken pursuant to this strategy. Accordingly, only minimal grants to other organizations will be available in the near future. Application form not required.
Initial approach: Letter
Copies of proposal: 1
Deadline(s): March 1, July 15, and Nov. 15
Board meeting date(s): 3 times per year
Final notification: Winter, spring, and fall
Officers and Directors:* Christopher C. Angell,* Pres.; Emme L. Deland, V.P.; Barry Smith,* Secy.; Morris S. Roberts,* Treas.; Bobye G. List, Exec. Dir.
Number of staff: 1 full-time professional; 1 part-time support.
EIN: 133042360
Selected grants: The following grants were reported in 2004.
$500,000 to Johns Hopkins University, Robert Packard Center for ALS Research, Baltimore, MD.
$300,000 to Open Society Institute, New York, NY. For joint palliative care fellowship program.
$176,500 to New York City Department of Education, New York, NY. For City-wide Teacher Program.
$40,000 to Claremont Neighborhood Centers, Bronx, NY. For after school and weekend literacy activities for youth and their families at on-site Education Learning Center school.
$35,000 to Henry Street Settlement, New York, NY. For enhanced and expanded literacy curriculum at Boys and Girls Republic, a co-ed educational, recreational and leadership development program.
$25,000 to Education Through Music, New York, NY. For New Partnership program at P.S. 6, integrating music instruction into school curriculum.
$25,000 to New York Academy of Medicine, New York, NY. For Office of School of Health Programs.

$20,000 to Colony-South Brooklyn Houses, Brooklyn, NY. For Literacy and arts after-school program at two child care centers, in collaboration with Marquis Studios.
$20,000 to Free Arts for Abused Children of New York City, New York, NY. For professional social service facilitators to improve training of volunteers bringing group art therapy.
$20,000 to Young Dancemakers Company, Bronx, NY. For Summer dance program connecting New York City public school students to professional dance world through instruction and performance, field trips and special sessions with guest artists.

6351
Kraft Foods Fund ✧
(formerly Nabisco Foundation Trust)
c/o Deutsche Trust Co. of NY
P.O. Box 1297
Church St. Sta.
New York, NY   10008
Application address: c/o Henry A. Sandbach, Dir., Contribs., Nabisco Plz., 7 Campus Dr., Parsippany, NJ 07054

Incorporated in 1953 in NJ.
Donor: Nabisco Holdings Corp.
Foundation type: Company-sponsored foundation.
Financial data (yr. ended 12/31/05): Assets, $10,341 (M); expenditures, $430,643; qualifying distributions, $430,421; giving activities include $430,000 for 5 grants (high: $180,000; low: $25,000).
Purpose and activities: The fund supports organizations involved with education and hunger.
Fields of interest: Higher education; Education; Food services.
Type of support: Building/renovation; Emergency funds; Scholarship funds; Employee matching gifts.
Limitations: Giving on a national basis. No grants to individuals.
Publications: Occasional report.
Application information: Application form not required.
Initial approach: Proposal
Deadline(s): None
Board meeting date(s): As needed
Final notification: Varies
Trustee: Deutsche Trust Co. of NY.
EIN: 136042595

6352
The Kraus Family Foundation ✧ ☆
c/o BCRS Group/Marcum & Kliegman LLP
10 Melville Park Rd.
Melville, NY   11747
Application address: c/o Peter S. Kraus, 1965 Broadway, Apt. 517, New York, NY 10023

Established in 1996 in NY.
Donor: Peter S. Kraus.
Foundation type: Independent foundation.
Financial data (yr. ended 8/31/05): Assets, $11,854,295 (M); gifts received, $2,799,902; expenditures, $839,775; qualifying distributions, $798,325; giving activities include $798,325 for grants.
Fields of interest: Arts; Education; Hospitals (general); Human services; Civil rights, gays/lesbians; Federated giving programs.

Type of support: General/operating support.
Limitations: Giving primarily in New York, NY. No grants to individuals.
Application information: Application form not required.
  Deadline(s): None
Trustees: Jill G. Kraus; Peter S. Kraus.
EIN: 133921376
Selected grants: The following grants were reported in 2005.
$93,000 to Carnegie Museum of Art, Pittsburgh, PA. 2 grants: $50,000, $43,000
$20,000 to Hospital for Special Surgery, New York, NY.
$20,000 to Jewish Womens Archive, Brookline, MA.
$15,000 to World Studio Foundation, New York, NY.
$5,000 to Richard J. Caron Foundation, Wernersville, PA.
$3,500 to Carnegie Mellon University, Pittsburgh, PA.
$2,500 to Abington Memorial Hospital, Abington, PA.
$2,000 to Loomis Chaffee School, Windsor, CT.
$1,000 to SculptureCenter, Long Island City, NY.

6353

The Raymond and Bessie Kravis Foundation ✧
c/o James Goldrick
9 W. 57th St.
New York, NY   10019

Established in 1992 in OK.
Donors: Bessie R. Kravis; Raymond F. Kravis.
Foundation type: Independent foundation.
Financial data (yr. ended 12/31/03): Assets, $21,151,813 (M); expenditures, $1,273,490; qualifying distributions, $1,102,154; giving activities include $934,000 for 10 grants (high: $350,000; low: $12,500).
Purpose and activities: Giving primarily for the arts and higher education.
Fields of interest: Museums; Museums (art); Performing arts; Arts; Higher education; Hospitals (general).
Limitations: Applications not accepted. Giving primarily in Tulsa, OK. No grants to individuals.
Application information: Contributes only to pre-selected organizations.
Trustees: George R. Kravis II; Henry R. Kravis; Kimberly R. Kravis; Robert S. Kravis.
EIN: 731393621
Selected grants: The following grants were reported in 2003.
$350,000 to Philbrook Museum of Art, Tulsa, OK. For general support.
$200,000 to Saint John Medical Center, Tulsa, OK. For general support.
$100,000 to Gilcrease Museum, Tulsa, OK. For general support.
$59,000 to Tulsa Library Trust, Tulsa, OK. For general support.
$50,000 to Campaign for the Center, Tulsa, OK. For general support.
$50,000 to Oklahoma Arts Institute, Oklahoma City, OK. For general support.
$50,000 to Price Tower Arts Center, Bartlesville, OK. For general support.
$50,000 to University of Tulsa, Tulsa, OK. For general support.
$12,500 to Circle Cinema Foundation, Tulsa, OK. For general support.

$12,500 to Tulsa Foundation for Architecture, Tulsa, OK. For general support.

6354

Henry R. Kravis Foundation, Inc. ▼ ✧
c/o KKR & Co.
9 W. 57th St.
New York, NY   10019   (212) 750-8300

Established in 1985 in NY.
Donor: Henry R. Kravis.
Foundation type: Independent foundation.
Financial data (yr. ended 11/30/05): Assets, $6,391,084 (M); expenditures, $5,746,094; qualifying distributions, $5,654,258; giving activities include $5,558,301 for 39 grants (high: $625,000; low: $1,000; average: $25,000–$500,000).
Purpose and activities: Support primarily for arts and culture, including a museum, and for Jewish welfare.
Fields of interest: Museums; Arts; Human services; Jewish federated giving programs.
Type of support: General/operating support.
Limitations: Applications not accepted. No grants to individuals.
Application information: Contributes only to pre-selected organizations.
Officers: Henry R. Kravis, Chair.; Leslie Harrison, Secy.; James M. Goldrick, Treas.
Director: Richard I. Beattie.
EIN: 133341521
Selected grants: The following grants were reported in 2004.
$3,300,000 to Robin Hood Foundation, New York, NY. 3 grants: $1,000,000, $1,500,000, $800,000
$3,000,000 to Mount Sinai Medical Center, New York, NY.
$2,000,000 to Columbia University, Graduate School of Business, New York, NY.
$1,260,000 to Claremont McKenna College, Claremont, CA. 2 grants: $630,000 each
$1,250,000 to Loomis Chaffee School, Windsor, CT.
$1,000,000 to Eaglebrook School, Deerfield, MA.
$1,000,000 to New York City Host Committee, New York, NY.

6355

The Robert Kravis and Kimberly Kravis Foundation ✧ ☆
c/o Kohlberg Kravis Roberts & Co.
9 W. 57th St.
New York, NY   10019

Established in 1998 in NY.
Donors: Kimberly R. Kravis; Robert S. Kravis.
Foundation type: Independent foundation.
Financial data (yr. ended 11/30/05): Assets, $47,083,316 (M); expenditures, $6,861,211; qualifying distributions, $6,332,834; giving activities include $6,300,875 for 14 grants (high: $3,000,000; low: $500).
Fields of interest: Museums (art); Higher education; Education; Heart & circulatory diseases; Human services; Philanthropy/voluntarism.
Limitations: Applications not accepted. Giving primarily in NY. No grants to individuals.
Application information: Contributes only to pre-selected organizations.

Directors: Richard I. Beattie; Kimberly R. Kravis; Robert S. Kravis.
EIN: 134000922
Selected grants: The following grants were reported in 2004.
$1,260,000 to Loomis Chaffee School, Windsor, CT. 2 grants: $1,250,000, $10,000
$10,500 to Robin Hood Foundation, New York, NY.
$6,000 to Spence School, New York, NY.
$500 to Animal Medical Center, New York, NY.

6356

The Lee S. Kreindler Foundation ✧ ☆
100 Park Ave., 18th Fl.
New York, NY   10017-5590

Established in 2004 in NY.
Donors: Kreindler & Kreindler, LLP; Speiser, Krause, Nolan & Granito; Baumeisters & Samuels; Patton Boggs, LLP; Waite, Scheinder, Bayless & Cheley Co.; James Kreidler; Steve Pounion.
Foundation type: Independent foundation.
Financial data (yr. ended 12/31/05): Assets, $1,437,029 (M); gifts received, $1,032,104; expenditures, $7,799,265; qualifying distributions, $7,799,172; giving activities include $7,780,000 for 26 grants (high: $3,000,000; low: $5,000).
Fields of interest: Arts; Higher education; Medical care, in-patient care; Community development; Philanthropy/voluntarism.
Limitations: Applications not accepted. Giving on a national basis. No grants to individuals.
Application information: Contributes only to pre-selected organizations.
Officers: Ruth Kreindler, Pres.; James Kreindler, V.P.; Steve Pounion, Secy.
EIN: 300259779

6357

Samuel H. Kress Foundation ▼
174 E. 80th St.
New York, NY   10021   (212) 861-4993
Contact: Lisa M. Ackerman, Exec. V.P.
FAX: (212) 628-3146; E-mail: lisa@shkf.org;
URL: http://www.kressfoundation.org

Incorporated in 1929 in NY.
Donors: Samuel H. Kress†; Claude W. Kress†; Rush H. Kress†.
Foundation type: Independent foundation.
Financial data (yr. ended 6/30/05): Assets, $101,594,197 (M); expenditures, $6,588,891; qualifying distributions, $5,322,060; giving activities include $4,168,461 for 350 grants (high: $289,000; low: $25; average: $5,000–$50,000), and $267,200 for 22 grants to individuals (high: $22,500; low: $1,500; average: $5,000–$22,500).
Purpose and activities: Giving through five main programs: 1) fellowships for pre-doctoral research in art history; 2) advanced training and research in conservation of works of art; 3) development of scholarly resources in the fields of art history and conservation; 4) conservation and restoration of monuments in Europe; and 5) occasional related projects.
Fields of interest: Visual arts; Museums; History/archaeology; Arts.
International interests: Europe.
Type of support: Conferences/seminars; Professorships; Publication; Fellowships; Internship funds; Research; Employee matching gifts.

Limitations: Giving primarily in the U.S. and Europe. No support for art history programs below the pre-doctoral level, or the purchase of works of art. No grants for living artists, or for operating budgets, continuing support, annual campaigns, endowments, deficit financing, capital funds exhibitions, or films; no loans.

Publications: Application guidelines; Annual report (including application guidelines).

Application information: Application forms required for fellowships in art history and art conservation. Applications sent by fax not considered. Application form not required.

 Initial approach: Proposal
 Copies of proposal: 1
 Deadline(s): Nov. 30 for research fellowships in art history
 Board meeting date(s): Usually in May and Oct.
 Final notification: 3 months

Officers and Trustees: * John C. Fontaine,* Chair.; Daniel N. Belin,* Vice-Chair.; Marilyn Perry,* Pres.; Lisa M. Ackerman, Exec. V.P.; Frederick W. Beinecke,* Secy.-Treas.; Havilah Stewart, Cont.; Cheryl Hurley; David Rumsey; Barbara A. Shailor; Inmaculada Von Habsburg-Lothringen; Walter L. Weisman.

Number of staff: 3 full-time professional; 4 full-time support.

EIN: 131624176

Selected grants: The following grants were reported in 2005.

$289,000 to World Monuments Fund, New York, NY. For collections management and preservation.

$200,000 to National Gallery of Art, DC. For fellowships.

$100,000 to Harvard University, Cambridge, MA. For building renovation.

$90,000 to New York University, New York, NY. 2 grants: $70,000 (For fellowships), $20,000 (For fellowships).

$80,000 to American Academy in Rome, New York, NY. For fellowship.

$80,000 to Cincinnati Art Museum, Cincinnati, OH. For exhibitions.

$75,000 to Rutgers, The State University of New Jersey, New Brunswick, NJ. For exhibitions.

$50,000 to Cambridge in America, New York, NY. For exhibitions.

$25,000 to High Museum of Art, Atlanta, GA. For conferences and seminars.

6358

The Jeannette & H. Peter Kriendler Charitable Trust ✧

c/o Fiduciary Trust International
600 5th Ave.
New York, NY   10020

Established in 1986 in NY.

Donor: H. Peter Kriendler†.

Foundation type: Independent foundation.

Financial data (yr. ended 12/31/05): Assets, $14,211,678 (M); gifts received, $95,112; expenditures, $946,038; qualifying distributions, $865,733; giving activities include $810,000 for 79 grants (high: $20,000; low: $2,000).

Fields of interest: Museums; Historic preservation/historical societies; Arts; Higher education; Environment, natural resources; Health organizations, association; Children/youth, services; Jewish agencies & temples.

Limitations: Applications not accepted. Giving primarily in NY. No grants to individuals.

Application information: Contributes only to pre-selected organizations.

Trustees: Blair Axel; John Kriendler.

EIN: 136880589

6359

The H. Frederick Krimendahl II Foundation ✧

c/o BCRS Group/Marcum & Kliegman, LLP
100 Wall St., 11th Fl.
New York, NY   10005

Established in 1968 in NY.

Donors: H. Frederick Krimendahl II; Elizabeth K. Krimendahl.

Foundation type: Independent foundation.

Financial data (yr. ended 5/31/05): Assets, $8,914,717 (M); expenditures, $402,027; qualifying distributions, $396,937; giving activities include $394,722 for 78 grants (high: $60,000; low: $25).

Purpose and activities: Giving primarily for education, the arts, and animal welfare.

Fields of interest: Performing arts; Performing arts, theater; Performing arts, music; Arts; Libraries/library science; Education; Animal welfare; Veterinary medicine, hospital; Hospitals (general); Health organizations, association; Children/youth, services.

Limitations: Applications not accepted. Giving primarily in New York, NY. No grants to individuals.

Application information: Contributes only to pre-selected organizations.

Trustees: Elizabeth K. Krimendahl; H.F. Krimendahl II; Nancy C. Krimendahl; James S. Marcus; Emilia A. Saint-Amand.

EIN: 237000391

Selected grants: The following grants were reported in 2004.

$60,000 to Ohio State University Foundation, Columbus, OH.

$25,900 to Animal Medical Center, New York, NY.

$25,000 to Animal Rescue Fund of the Hamptons, Wainscott, NY.

$6,446 to Metropolitan Museum of Art, New York, NY.

$3,500 to Metropolitan Opera Guild, New York, NY.

$1,600 to Jazz at Lincoln Center, New York, NY.

$1,500 to Manhattan Theater Club, New York, NY.

$1,000 to Chapin School, New York, NY.

$500 to New York Youth Symphony, New York, NY.

$108 to New York City Ballet, New York, NY.

6360

Mitchell and Karen Kuflik Charitable Foundation ✧

14 Beverly Rd.
Purchase, NY   10577

Established in 1999 in NY.

Donor: Mitchell Kuflik.

Foundation type: Independent foundation.

Financial data (yr. ended 12/31/04): Assets, $196,582 (M); gifts received, $2,355,307; expenditures, $2,430,430; qualifying distributions, $2,428,502; giving activities include $2,428,402 for 85 grants (high: $697,500; low: $36).

Fields of interest: Education; Hospitals (general); Human services; Jewish agencies & temples.

Limitations: Applications not accepted. Giving primarily in NY. No grants to individuals.

Application information: Contributes only to pre-selected organizations.

Officers: Mitchell Kuflik, Pres.; Karen Kuflik, V.P.

EIN: 137197004

Selected grants: The following grants were reported in 2004.

$697,500 to Aish HaTorah New York, New York, NY.

$153,000 to Colel Chabad, Brooklyn, NY.

$30,000 to Yeshiva Rabbi Samson Raphael Hirsch, New York, NY.

$19,800 to American Friends of Ramot Torah Schools, Brooklyn, NY.

$18,000 to Jewish Opportunities Institute, New York, NY.

$10,000 to Solomon Schechter School of Westchester, White Plains, NY.

$10,000 to Torah Academy High School of Brooklyn, Brooklyn, NY.

$3,000 to American Friends of the Hebrew University, New York, NY.

$2,233 to Aish HaTorah. 2 grants: $1,583, $650

6361

The Kumble Foundation ✧

c/o Waldman, Hirsch & Co.
855 Ave. of Americas, Rm. 623
New York, NY   10001-4115

Established in 1999 in NY.

Donor: Steven J. Kumble.

Foundation type: Independent foundation.

Financial data (yr. ended 12/31/03): Assets, $1,000 (M); gifts received, $411,250; expenditures, $411,250; qualifying distributions, $411,250; giving activities include $411,250 for 4 grants (high: $150,000; low: $5,000).

Fields of interest: Higher education; Hospitals (general); Jewish agencies & temples.

Limitations: Applications not accepted. No grants to individuals.

Application information: Contributes only to pre-selected organizations.

Directors: Peggy Kumble; Roger Kumble; Steven J. Kumble; Todd Kumble.

EIN: 134013985

6362

The Albert Kunstadter Family Foundation ✧

1035 5th Ave.
New York, NY   10028-0135   (212) 794-3951
Contact: Geraldine S. Kunstadter, Chair.
FAX: (212) 794-1273; E-mail: akff@aol.com;
Additional tel.: (212) 249-1733

Incorporated in 1952 in IL.

Donor: Members of the Kunstadter family.

Foundation type: Independent foundation.

Financial data (yr. ended 12/31/05): Assets, $1,271,324 (M); expenditures, $409,253; qualifying distributions, $391,558; giving activities include $390,000 for 78 grants (high: $13,500; low: $1,000).

Purpose and activities: Local, national, and where possible, international general grantmaking.

International interests: China; Southeast Asia.

Type of support: General/operating support; Continuing support; Management development/capacity building; Building/renovation; Program development; Conferences/seminars; Exchange programs.

Limitations: Applications not accepted. Giving in the U.S., primarily to organizations based in New York, NY, and Washington, DC; funding also in Hanoi, Vietnam, Vientiane, Laos, Phnom Penh, Cambodia, and Beijing, China. No support for religious purposes. No grants to individuals or matching gifts; no loans.

Application information: The foundation is currently, and for the foreseeable future, not able to take on any new projects.

Officers and Directors:* Geraldine S. Kunstadter,* Chair. and Pres.; Lisa Kunstadter,* V.P. and Secy.; Christopher T.W. Kunstadter,* V.P. and Treas.; Elizabeth Von Habsburg,* V.P.

EIN: 366047975

Selected grants: The following grants were reported in 2004.

$25,000 to Fund for Reconciliation and Development, New York, NY. 3 grants: $10,000, $5,000, $10,000

$10,000 to Amrita Performing Arts, Oakland, CA.

$10,000 to Spoleto Festival USA, Charleston, SC.

$9,000 to Massachusetts Institute of Technology, Cambridge, MA.

$7,000 to National Fund for Vietnamese Children, Hanoi, Vietnam. .

$4,000 to Coalition for the Homeless, New York, NY.

$4,000 to Dieu Donne Papermill, New York, NY.

$3,000 to Tsinghua University Education Foundation, Beijing, China. .

6363
The Kupferberg Foundation ✧
131-38 Sanford Ave.
Flushing, NY   11352

Established in 1961 in NY.

Donors: Jesse Kupferberg; Max Kupferberg; Kepco, Inc.

Foundation type: Company-sponsored foundation.

Financial data (yr. ended 11/30/05): Assets, $11,632,324 (M); expenditures, $683,492; qualifying distributions, $623,432; giving activities include $621,000 for 54 grants (high: $130,000; low: $500).

Purpose and activities: The foundation supports organizations involved with arts and culture, education, health, human services, and Judaism.

Fields of interest: Museums (science/technology); Arts; Education; Botanical gardens; Hospitals (general); Health care; YM/YWCAs & YM/YWHAs; Children/youth, services; Human services; Jewish federated giving programs; Jewish agencies & temples.

Limitations: Applications not accepted. Giving primarily in New York and Queens, NY. No grants to individuals.

Application information: Contributes only to pre-selected organizations.

Officers and Trustees: Max Kupferberg, Pres.; Jesse Kupferberg, V.P.; Martin Kupferberg; Saul Kupferberg.

EIN: 116008915

6364
The Kurtz Family Foundation, Inc. ✧ ☆
c/o U.S. Trust
114 W. 47th St., TAXRGR
New York, NY   10036

Established in 1996 in NJ.

Donors: Ronald Kurtz; Carol Kurtz; Steven Levitt.

Foundation type: Independent foundation.

Financial data (yr. ended 12/31/05): Assets, $2,914,548 (M); expenditures, $352,287; qualifying distributions, $341,000; giving activities include $341,000 for 27 grants (high: $100,000; low: $500).

Purpose and activities: Giving primarily for education, particularly to a business school, as well as to a program for minorities within that school; funding also for museums, health associations, human services, and Jewish federated giving programs.

Fields of interest: Museums; Higher education; Business school/education; Education; Environment; Health organizations, association; Human services; Jewish federated giving programs; Minorities.

Limitations: Applications not accepted. Giving primarily in MA. No grants to individuals.

Application information: Contributes only to pre-selected organizations.

Officers: Ronald Kurtz, Pres.; Carol Kurtz, Secy.

Trustee: Steven Levitt.

EIN: 223479749

Selected grants: The following grants were reported in 2004.

$200,000 to Massachusetts Institute of Technology, Cambridge, MA. 2 grants: $100,000 (For operating support for President's Fellowship), $100,000 (For operating support for minority program).

$5,000 to Museum of Modern Art, New York, NY. For operating support.

$2,500 to Haverford College, Haverford, PA. For operating support.

$2,000 to UJA-Federation of New York, New York, NY. For operating support.

$1,000 to Antioch College, Yellow Springs, OH. For operating support.

$1,000 to Center for Food Action in New Jersey, Englewood, NJ. For operating support.

$1,000 to Doctors Without Borders USA, New York, NY. For operating support.

$1,000 to Greater Yellowstone Coalition, Bozeman, MT. For operating support.

$1,000 to Trout Unlimited, Arlington, VA. For operating support.

6365
The Kurz Family Foundation, Ltd. ✧ ☆
69 Lydecker St.
Nyack, NY   10960-2103   (845) 358-2300
Contact: Herbert Kurz

Established in 1992 in NY.

Donor: Herbert Kurz.

Foundation type: Independent foundation.

Financial data (yr. ended 12/31/05): Assets, $14,627,719 (M); gifts received, $761,600; expenditures, $740,766; qualifying distributions, $620,328; giving activities include $620,328 for grants.

Fields of interest: Higher education; Environment, natural resources; Hospitals (general); Human services; Children/youth, services; International peace/security; Community development; Jewish agencies & temples.

Limitations: Giving primarily in NY. No grants to individuals.

Application information:

Initial approach: Letter
Deadline(s): None

Directors: Ellen Kurz; Leonard Kurz; Brenda Neal; Lewis Wechsler.

EIN: 133680855

Selected grants: The following grants were reported in 2004.

$20,000 to Arcadia Pictures, New York, NY.

$15,146 to Dakota Wesleyan University, Mitchell, SD.

$15,000 to Film Arts Foundation, San Francisco, CA. 2 grants: $5,000, $10,000

$12,730 to Nyack Hospital, Nyack, NY.

$5,000 to Shared Human Assistance Resources (SHARE), Kansas City, MO.

$5,000 to Southern Poverty Law Center, Montgomery, AL.

$2,000 to Union Child Day Care Center, White Plains, NY.

$1,000 to Friends of Young Achievers, Jamaica Plain, MA.

$1,000 to People for the American Way, DC.

6366
L and L Foundation ✧
570 Park Ave.
New York, NY   10021
Contact: Mildred C. Brinn, Pres.

Incorporated in 1963 in NY.

Foundation type: Independent foundation.

Financial data (yr. ended 12/31/05): Assets, $7,726,459 (M); expenditures, $504,124; qualifying distributions, $449,601; giving activities include $400,920 for 31 grants (high: $133,750; low: $100).

Purpose and activities: Giving primarily for the arts, health care, and human services.

Fields of interest: Arts education; Visual arts; Museums (art); Performing arts; Arts; Hospitals (general); Children/youth, services; Protestant agencies & churches.

Limitations: Giving primarily in NY. No grants to individuals.

Application information: Application form not required.

Initial approach: Letter
Deadline(s): None

Officers and Directors:* Mildred C. Brinn,* Pres. and Treas.; Peter F. De Gaetano,* Secy.

EIN: 136155758

Selected grants: The following grants were reported in 2005.

$133,750 to Ballet Theater Foundation, New York, NY.

$27,000 to Parrish Art Museum, Southampton, NY.

$21,000 to Lenox Hill Hospital, New York, NY.

$10,000 to New York Landmarks Conservancy, New York, NY.

$10,000 to Southampton Hospital Foundation, Southampton, NY.

$4,500 to American Associates of the Royal Academy Trust, New York, NY.

$500 to Municipal Art Society of New York, New York, NY.

$250 to ArtTable, New York, NY.

6367
L'Maan Ameinu Foundation, Inc. ✧
315 Westchester Ave., 2nd Fl.
Port Chester, NY   10573

Established in 2001 in NY.
Donor: Betty S. Cohen.
Foundation type: Independent foundation.
Financial data (yr. ended 12/31/05): Assets, $10,502 (M); gifts received, $549,489; expenditures, $575,775; qualifying distributions, $570,150; giving activities include $570,150 for 54 grants (high: $82,000; low: $25).
Fields of interest: Jewish federated giving programs; Jewish agencies & temples.
Limitations: Applications not accepted. No grants to individuals.
Application information: Contributes only to pre-selected organizations.
Officers: Betty S. Cohen, Pres. and Treas.; Zev Cohen, V.P.; Esther Cohen Brooks, Secy.
EIN: 311775151
Selected grants: The following grants were reported in 2005.
$60,000 to Chesed Avraham, Brooklyn, NY.
$43,500 to Wexner Heritage House, Columbus, OH.
$37,850 to Tzedakah Vchesed, Brooklyn, NY.
$9,100 to Orthodox Council of Jerusalem, Jerusalem, Israel. .
$5,000 to Bais Medrash Elyon, Monsey, NY.
$5,000 to Lev LAchim, Brooklyn, NY.

6368
L. & L. Foundation ◇
48 Lawrence Ave.
Lawrence, NY 11559 (516) 239-8884
Contact: Joshua Guttman, Mgr.

Foundation type: Independent foundation.
Financial data (yr. ended 12/31/05): Assets, $4,550,000 (M); gifts received, $5,141,125; expenditures, $2,042,768; qualifying distributions, $2,039,063; giving activities include $2,039,063 for 335 grants (high: $180,000; low: $50).
Fields of interest: Education; Human services; Jewish agencies & temples.
Limitations: Giving primarily in NY.
Application information:
  Deadline(s): None
Manager: Joshua Guttman.
EIN: 113416458

6369
Ladenburg Foundation ◇
c/o Anchin Block & Anchin, LLP
1375 Broadway
New York, NY 10018-7001

Established in 2001 in NY.
Donors: Claudia Bussmann; Martin Bussmann; Margaret Bussmann; Richard Bussmann; Courtney Bussman.
Foundation type: Operating foundation.
Financial data (yr. ended 12/31/04): Assets, $1,555 (M); gifts received, $465,000; expenditures, $474,525; qualifying distributions, $474,254; giving activities include $471,400 for 11 grants (high: $100,000; low: $1,700).
Purpose and activities: Giving primarily to human rights organizations and to the Special Olympics.
Fields of interest: Higher education; Athletics/ sports, Special Olympics; International human rights.
Limitations: Applications not accepted. No grants to individuals.

Application information: Contributes only to pre-selected organizations.
Officers and Directors:* Claudia Bussmann,* Chair.; Martin Bussmann,* Pres. and Treas.; Henry Christensen III.
EIN: 134156286

6370
Lambert Family Foundation ◇
c/o Bessemer Trust Co., N.A.
630 5th Ave.
New York, NY 10111 (212) 708-9100
Contact: Bill Lambert, Tr.; Sheila Lambert, Tr.

Established in 2001 in NY.
Donors: Bill Lambert; Sheila Lambert.
Foundation type: Independent foundation.
Financial data (yr. ended 12/31/05): Assets, $11,798,913 (M); expenditures, $554,389; qualifying distributions, $516,460; giving activities include $512,635 for 15 grants (high: $120,000; low: $1,000).
Purpose and activities: Giving primarily for education, with an emphasis on health education; support also for women's issues, civil rights and civil liberties, and organizations that provide health care, shelter, food and other services to poor and disadvantaged persons.
Fields of interest: Higher education; Human services; Jewish agencies & temples.
Limitations: Giving primarily in NY. No grants to individuals.
Application information:
  Initial approach: Letter
  Deadline(s): None
Trustees: Bill Lambert; Sheila Lambert.
EIN: 316665497

6371
The Landegger Charitable Foundation, Inc. ◇
4 International Dr., Ste. 300
Rye Brook, NY 10573
Contact: William A. Monde, Jr.

Established in 1975 DE and FL.
Foundation type: Independent foundation.
Financial data (yr. ended 10/31/05): Assets, $12,123,860 (M); expenditures, $905,765; qualifying distributions, $785,832; giving activities include $785,832 for 55 grants (high: $319,000; low: $250).
Purpose and activities: Giving primarily for higher education, health associations, and social services.
Fields of interest: Higher education; Education; Health organizations, association; Human services; Protestant agencies & churches.
Limitations: Giving on a national basis. No grants to individuals.
Application information: Application form not required.
  Deadline(s): None
Officers: George F. Landegger, Pres.; Arthur L. Schwartz, V.P.; Jewel L. Fair, Secy.; Carl Landegger, Treas.
EIN: 510180544
Selected grants: The following grants were reported in 2004.
$352,000 to Georgetown University, DC.
$50,000 to Abraham House, Bronx, NY.

$20,000 to Lenox Hill Neighborhood House, New York, NY.
$5,500 to Saint Davids School for Child Development and Family Services, Minnetonka, MN.
$5,000 to Institute for Student Achievement, Lake Success, NY.
$5,000 to Taft School, Watertown, CT.
$2,000 to Blair Academy, Blairstown, NJ.
$2,000 to Operational Emergency Center, Seattle, WA.
$1,000 to Becket Fund for Religious Liberty, DC.
$1,000 to Spring of Tampa Bay, Tampa, FL.

6372
Lane Family Foundation ◇
c/o BCRS Assocs., LLC
100 Wall St., 11th Fl.
New York, NY 10005

Established in 1987 in NY.
Donors: James N. Lane; Susan W. Lane.
Foundation type: Independent foundation.
Financial data (yr. ended 6/30/05): Assets, $1,271,292 (M); expenditures, $399,900; qualifying distributions, $394,650; giving activities include $393,150 for 37 grants (high: $100,000; low: $100).
Purpose and activities: Giving to religion and higher education.
Fields of interest: Education; Human services; Children/youth, services; International affairs; Federated giving programs; Christian agencies & churches.
Limitations: Applications not accepted. Giving on a national basis. No grants to individuals.
Application information: Contributes only to pre-selected organizations.
Trustees: James N. Lane; Susan W. Lane.
EIN: 133437903
Selected grants: The following grants were reported in 2005.
$100,000 to Chicago Hope, Chicago, IL.
$13,000 to New York Fellowship, New York, NY. 3 grants: $10,000, $2,000, $1,000
$10,000 to Brooklyn Tabernacle, Brooklyn, NY.
$4,000 to Pioneers, Inc., Orlando, FL. 2 grants: $3,000, $1,000
$1,500 to World Impact, Los Angeles, CA.
$1,000 to Saint Georges Church, New York, NY.
$500 to Salvation Army, Yonkers, NY.

6373
Jeffrey and Nancy Lane Foundation ◇
c/o The Ayco Co., LP
P.O. Box 8019
Ballston Spa, NY 12020-8019
Contact: Stephen M. Cutting

Established in 1987 in NY.
Donor: Jeffrey B. Lane.
Foundation type: Independent foundation.
Financial data (yr. ended 12/31/05): Assets, $897,096 (M); gifts received, $550,800; expenditures, $1,099,903; qualifying distributions, $1,074,225; giving activities include $1,074,225 for 77+ grants (high: $405,000).
Purpose and activities: Giving to Jewish agencies and to public schools.
Fields of interest: Higher education; Medical school/education; Education; Human services;

Jewish federated giving programs; Jewish agencies & temples.
Type of support: General/operating support.
Limitations: Applications not accepted. Giving primarily in NY. No grants to individuals.
Application information: Contributes only to pre-selected organizations.
Officers: Jeffrey B. Lane, Pres. and Treas.; Nancy Z. Lane, Secy.
EIN: 112842376
Selected grants: The following grants were reported in 2005.
$20,000 to National Academy Foundation, New York, NY.
$20,000 to Norton Museum of Art, West Palm Beach, FL.
$13,550 to Memorial Sloan-Kettering Cancer Center, New York, NY.
$10,500 to American Friends of Israel.
$10,000 to Bruce and Marsha Moskowitz Foundation, Palm Beach, FL.
$10,000 to Federation Employment and Guidance Service, New York, NY.
$4,000 to Mount Sinai Hospital, New York, NY.
$2,300 to American Friends of the Israel Museum, New York, NY.
$1,000 to American Friends of the Hebrew University, New York, NY.
$1,000 to Sanctuary for Families, New York, NY.

6374
Eugene M. Lang Foundation ◇

535 5th Ave., Ste. 906
New York, NY   10017   (212) 949-4100
Contact: Mary Sivak, Fiscal Mgr.

Established in 1968 in NY.
Donor: Eugene M. Lang.
Foundation type: Independent foundation.
Financial data (yr. ended 12/31/05): Assets, $47,334,611 (M); gifts received, $100,000; expenditures, $2,787,410; qualifying distributions, $2,490,863; giving activities include $2,371,315 for 159 grants (high: $500,000; low: $100).
Purpose and activities: Support for higher and other education, cultural programs, and health and hospitals, including medical research.
Fields of interest: Performing arts; Arts; Education, early childhood education; Higher education; Education; Hospitals (general); Health care; Health organizations, association; Medical research, institute; Minorities.
Type of support: General/operating support; Continuing support; Annual campaigns; Program development; Conferences/seminars; Professorships; Seed money; Fellowships; Internship funds; Scholarship funds.
Limitations: Giving primarily in NY and neighboring areas, including PA. No grants to individuals, or for building funds, equipment and materials, capital or endowment funds, deficit financing, publications, or matching gifts; no loans.
Publications: Annual report (including application guidelines); Grants list; Program policy statement.
Application information: Application form not required.
Initial approach: Letter
Deadline(s): None
Board meeting date(s): Apr. and Nov.
Trustees: Belinda Lang; Eugene M. Lang; Jane Lang; Kristina Lang; Stephen Lang; Theresa Lang; Paul Sprenger.

Number of staff: 2 full-time professional.
EIN: 136153412
Selected grants: The following grants were reported in 2005.
$600,000 to Atlas Performing Arts Center, DC. 3 grants: $50,000, $300,000, $250,000
$275,000 to Project Pericles, New York, NY.
$100,000 to New York-Presbyterian Hospital, New York, NY.
$52,500 to Townsend Harris Alumni Association, Flushing, NY.
$50,000 to American Museum of Natural History, New York, NY.
$5,000 to Barnard College, New York, NY.
$3,000 to Frick Collection, New York, NY.
$750 to Doctors Without Borders USA, New York, NY.

6375
The Jacob and Valeria Langeloth Foundation ▼

521 5th Ave., Ste. 1612
New York, NY   10175-1699   (212) 687-1133
Contact: Scott Moyer, Pres.
FAX: (212) 681-2628; E-mail: info@langeloth.org;
URL: http://www.langeloth.org

Incorporated in 1915 in NY as the Valeria Home; renamed in 1975.
Donor: Jacob Langeloth‡.
Foundation type: Independent foundation.
Financial data (yr. ended 11/30/05): Assets, $92,009,832 (M); expenditures, $4,652,797; qualifying distributions, $3,969,273; giving activities include $3,431,221 for 43 grants (high: $200,000; low: $5,000; average: $10,000–$100,000).
Purpose and activities: The foundation's grantmaking program is centered on the concepts of health and well-being. The foundation's purpose is to promote and support effective and creative programs, practices and policies related to healing from illness, accident, physical, social or emotional trauma and to extend the availability of programs that promote healing to underserved populations.
Fields of interest: Health care.
Type of support: Program development; Research; Program evaluation; Matching/challenge support.
Limitations: Giving primarily in NY and for projects that hold promise of national impact or extensive replication. No support for preventive medicine, direct patient care services (unless part of a research project) or religious purposes. No grants to individuals, or for capital campaigns, building or renovation projects, or loan or emergency funds.
Publications: Application guidelines; Grants list; Informational brochure.
Application information: See foundation's Web site. Application form required.
Initial approach: Online registration for letter of intent
Copies of proposal: 5
Deadline(s): Feb. 1 and Aug. 1
Board meeting date(s): Spring and Fall
Final notification: Varies
Officers and Directors:* Adam Hochschild,* Chair.; Scott W. Moyer, Pres.; Alexandra L. Driscoll, Secy.-Treas.; Aileen Adams; Dominique Boillot, M.D.; David R. Hochschild; George Labalme, Jr.*; John L. Loeb, Jr.; Deborah Prothrow-Stith, M.D.; Harvey Weinstein, M.D.

Number of staff: 3 full-time professional.
EIN: 131773646
Selected grants: The following grants were reported in 2004.
$292,806 to State University of New York at Albany, College of Optometry, Albany, NY. For investigation of tactile alphabets and clinical protocols to aid in the rehabilitation of the visually impaired. The proposed study would target severely visually impaired elders to determine the utility of tactile alphabets for use in accomplishing daily living tasks in order to achieve and/or retain independence after vision loss.
$200,000 to Paraprofessional Healthcare Institute, Bronx, NY. For Front Line Caregivers Training Institute to identify front-line caregivers home health aides and nursing home aides in communities across northern New England. The institute will provide training and a network of support to these caregivers, and in turn educate northern New England families in order to prepare for the depth and severity of the coming Care Gap in order to serve and support our elderly.
$168,774 to University of Nebraska Foundation, Lincoln, NE. For anterior dentition extraction and restoration among Nuer and Dinka refugees from the Sudan: A unique perspective on the biology and culture of healing, multidisciplinary effort to improve the readjustment and healing process for refugees from the Sudan as they transition from Africa to the US, to demonstrate the need for a shift from generic to culture specific resettlement systems, and to investigate the importance of anterior dentition to overall health.
$167,767 to Saint Charles Hospital and Rehabilitation Center, Port Jefferson, NY. For rehabilitation nursing internship program.
$165,393 to Survivors International, San Francisco, CA. For Gender Asylum and Recovery Project. The collaborative will provide assistance to women fleeing female genital cutting, women fleeing violent domestic abuse, lesbian and gay men fleeing violent persecution in their home countries, and women fleeing other human rights violations and violence commonly inflicted upon women.
$158,128 to New York University, School of Medicine, New York, NY. For an innovative intervention for adult-child caregivers. To implement and evaluate a caregiver intervention for adult children of people with Alzheimer's disease, with the goal of improving quality of life and reducing the incidence and magnitude of frequently experienced negative effects, including stress, anxiety, and depression.
$157,103 to Greater New York Hospital Foundation, New York, NY. For Health Information Tool for Empowerment. Web based tool that will provide a single portal to locally tailored information and resources for the uninsured and under-insured.
$156,432 to National Bone Marrow Transplant Link, Southfield, MI. For families and caregivers empowered (FACE) project to meet the information and support needs of prospective bone marrow/stem cell transplant (BMT) patients and their families.
$152,623 to Youth ALIVE, Oakland, CA. For Caught in the Crossfire hospital peer intervention and healing program for young adults injured by violence, implementation in Los Angeles and expansion in Oakland, CA.
$150,000 to College of Physicians of Philadelphia, Philadelphia, PA. For Regional Community Health

Information System (RCHIS). Feasibility study and pilot program to test a regional community health information system that will provide access to area consumer-oriented health information, establish local access sites, train and support intermediaries to aid the public in accessing this information.

6376
Irving Langer Charitable Trust ✧
1465A Flatbush Ave.
Brooklyn, NY   11210

Established in 1999 in NY.
Donor: Irving Langer.
Foundation type: Independent foundation.
Financial data (yr. ended 12/31/03): Assets, $44,649 (M); gifts received, $570,487; expenditures, $574,545; qualifying distributions, $574,437; giving activities include $574,437 for grants (high: $34,193).
Fields of interest: Human services; Jewish agencies & temples.
Limitations: Applications not accepted. No grants to individuals.
Application information: Contributes only to pre-selected organizations.
Director: Irving Langer.
EIN: 116449730

6377
LaSalle Adams Fund
c/o Rockefeller Philanthropy Advisors
437 Madison Ave., 37th Fl.
New York, NY   10112
Contact: Chris Page, Philanthropic Advisor

Established in 1953 in IL; incorporated in 1999 in NY.
Donor: Sydney Stein, Jr.‡.
Foundation type: Independent foundation.
Financial data (yr. ended 12/31/03): Assets, $28,676,668 (M); expenditures, $1,363,560; qualifying distributions, $1,179,685; giving activities include $1,097,275 for 12 grants (high: $250,000; low: $45,000).
Purpose and activities: Giving primarily for conservation and wildlife preservation; funding also for violence prevention.
Fields of interest: Environment, natural resources; Animals/wildlife, bird preserves.
International interests: Canada; Mexico.
Type of support: Land acquisition; Program development; Seed money; Program evaluation; Matching/challenge support.
Limitations: Applications not accepted. Giving primarily in the Rocky Mountain states and the Grand Traverse Bay region, MI. No grants to individuals.
Application information: Contributes only to pre-selected organizations.
Board meeting date(s): 3 times a year
Officer and Directors:* Carol Stein,* Pres.; Craig Kennedy.
EIN: 161562907

6378
William and Mildred Lasdon Foundation, Inc. ✧
575 Madison Ave., Ste. 1006
New York, NY   10022-2588
Contact: Nanette L. Laitman, Tr.

Established in 1947 in DE.
Donors: Jacob S. Lasdon; William S. Lasdon; Mildred D. Lasdon‡; Nanetta L. Leitman.
Foundation type: Independent foundation.
Financial data (yr. ended 12/31/04): Assets, $32,892,596 (M); gifts received, $381,118; expenditures, $2,354,755; qualifying distributions, $2,153,012; giving activities include $2,038,799 for 88 grants (high: $1,499,935; low: $100).
Purpose and activities: Giving primarily to arts and culture, particularly the American Craft Museum in NY, as well as to other museums, health associations, and human services.
Fields of interest: Museums; Arts; Hospitals (general); Jewish federated giving programs; Jewish agencies & temples.
Limitations: Giving primarily in New York, NY. No grants to individuals.
Application information:
Deadline(s): None
Trustees: Bonnie Eletz; Nanette L. Laitman; Cathy Seligman.
EIN: 237380362
Selected grants: The following grants were reported in 2004.
$133,000 to Museum of Arts and Design, New York, NY. 3 grants: $100,000, $8,000, $25,000
$30,000 to Solomon R. Guggenheim Foundation, New York, NY.
$22,500 to Central Park Conservancy, New York, NY. 3 grants: $2,500, $10,000, $10,000
$5,500 to Philharmonic-Symphony Society of New York, New York, NY.
$5,000 to National Academy of Design, New York, NY.
$1,500 to Ballet Theater Foundation, New York, NY.

6379
Mary Woodard Lasker Charitable Trust ✧
110 E. 42nd St., Ste. 1300
New York, NY   10017   (212) 286-0222
FAX: (212) 286-0924;
E-mail: info@laskerfoundation.org; Additional E-mail: nhunt@laskerfoundation.org; URL: http://www.laskerfoundation.org

Established in 1994 in NY.
Donor: Mary W. Lasker‡.
Foundation type: Independent foundation.
Financial data (yr. ended 12/31/03): Assets, $21,149,420 (M); gifts received, $451,088; expenditures, $1,583,341; qualifying distributions, $1,495,629; giving activities include $679,490 for 17 grants (high: $530,000; low: $250), and $455,500 for foundation-administered programs.
Purpose and activities: Giving primarily for medical research as well as for significant public service on behalf of medical science.
Fields of interest: Higher education; Libraries/library science; Health organizations, association; Medical research, institute.
Limitations: Applications not accepted. Giving primarily in NY; some giving in MD, VA and PA. No grants to individuals.

Application information: Contributes only to pre-selected organizations.
Board meeting date(s): Quarterly
Officers and Trustees:* James W. Fordyce,* Chair.; Neen Hunt, Pres.; Michael W. Brown,* Secy.; Christopher Brody,* Treas.; Purnell W. Choppin, M.D.; Robert Cullen; Jordan U. Gutterman; Daniel E. Koshland, Jr.; Alfred Sommer; Humphrey Taylor; Martin Tolchin.
Number of staff: 1 full-time professional; 2 full-time support.
EIN: 137049274
Selected grants: The following grants were reported in 2003.
$530,000 to Lasker Foundation, New York, NY. For general support.
$70,000 to Research America, Alexandria, VA. For general support.
$20,000 to Mount Desert Island Biological Laboratory, Salsbury Cove, ME. For general support.
$20,000 to Salute to the Seasons Fund for a More Beautiful New York, New York, NY. For general support.
$15,893 to Public Agenda Foundation, New York, NY. For general support.
$10,000 to National Health Museum, DC. For general support.
$1,000 to National Coalition for Cancer Research Public Education Campaign, DC. For general support.
$1,000 to National Organization for Hearing Research Foundation, Narberth, PA. For general support.
$500 to National Library of Medicine, Friends of the, DC. For general support.
$250 to University of California, Department of Biochemistry, San Francisco, CA. For general support.

6380
Abe and Frances Lastfogel Foundation ✧
c/o William Morris Agency, Inc.
1325 Ave. of the Americas, 15th Fl.
New York, NY   10019   (212) 586-5100
Contact: Alan Kannof, Exec. V.P.

Established in 1972 in CA.
Donors: Abe Lastfogel‡; Frances Lastfogel‡; Norman Brokaw; Walter Zifkin; William Morris Agency, Inc.
Foundation type: Independent foundation.
Financial data (yr. ended 12/31/04): Assets, $3,048,675 (M); gifts received, $250,000; expenditures, $1,378,709; qualifying distributions, $1,378,341; giving activities include $1,378,306 for 287 grants (high: $49,000; low: $40).
Purpose and activities: Giving primarily for the arts and human services.
Fields of interest: Media, film/video; Performing arts; Arts; Health organizations; Human services; Children/youth, services; Jewish federated giving programs.
Type of support: Annual campaigns; Endowments; Program development; Research.
Limitations: Giving primarily in the Los Angeles, CA, area and NY.
Application information:
Initial approach: Proposal
Deadline(s): None
Officers and Directors:* Walter Zifkin,* Pres.; Jim Wiatt, C.E.O.; Michael Dates, C.F.O.; Irving J.

Weintraub, Secy.; Norman Brokaw; Steven Kram; Louis P. Weiss.
EIN: 237146829
Selected grants: The following grants were reported in 2003.
$25,000 to American Film Institute, Los Angeles, CA.
$25,000 to United Jewish Fund of Greater Los Angeles, Los Angeles, CA.
$23,750 to Parents Action for Children, DC.
$13,500 to International Radio and Television Society Foundation (IRTSF), New York, NY.
$13,250 to American Museum of the Moving Image, Astoria, NY.
$9,400 to Los Angeles Philharmonic Association, Los Angeles, CA.
$9,300 to Public Theater, New York, NY.
$5,000 to Family Center, Los Angeles, CA.
$3,000 to Boys Hope Girls Hope of New York, Staten Island, NY.
$1,250 to Drama League, New York, NY.

6381
Lauder Foundation, Inc. ✧
767 5th Ave., 40th Fl.
New York, NY   10153
Contact: Joan Krupskas, Pres.

Incorporated in 1962 in NY.
Donors: Estee Lauder†; Joseph H. Lauder†; Leonard A. Lauder; Ronald S. Lauder; Evelyn Lauder; William Lauder; Estee Lauder, Inc.; LWG Family Partners; EL 2002 Trust.
Foundation type: Independent foundation.
Financial data (yr. ended 11/30/04): Assets, $36,963,446 (M); gifts received, $18,300,000; expenditures, $1,551,743; qualifying distributions, $1,535,281; giving activities include $1,505,482 for 21 grants (high: $800,000; low: $100; average: $500–$5,000).
Purpose and activities: Emphasis on museums and cultural programs, education, medical research, Jewish organizations, social service agencies, and conservation; some support for public affairs organizations and hospitals.
Fields of interest: Museums; Arts; Education, fund raising/fund distribution; Education; Hospitals (general); Cancer; Medical research, institute; Cancer research; Human services; Jewish agencies & temples.
Type of support: General/operating support; Continuing support; Annual campaigns; Capital campaigns.
Limitations: Giving primarily in the metropolitan New York, NY, area. No grants to individuals.
Publications: Financial statement.
Application information:
  Initial approach: Proposal letter
  Deadline(s): None
Officers and Directors:* Joan Krupskas, Pres.; Ronald S. Lauder,* V.P.; Leonard A. Lauder,* Secy.-Treas.; Aerin Lauder; William Lauder.
EIN: 136153743
Selected grants: The following grants were reported in 2003.
$250,000 to Breast Cancer Research Foundation, New York, NY.
$50,000 to Whitney Museum of American Art, New York, NY.
$40,000 to Nightingale-Bamford School, New York, NY.
$30,500 to Trinity School, New York, NY.
$27,000 to YM-YWHA, 92nd Street, New York, NY.

$12,646 to Central Synagogue, New York, NY.
$11,100 to Mount Sinai Medical Center, New York, NY.
$10,000 to Crohns and Colitis Foundation of America, New York, NY.
$10,000 to International Center of Photography, New York, NY.

6382
The Leonard and Evelyn Lauder Foundation ▼ ✧
767 5th Ave., 40th Fl.
New York, NY   10153
Contact: Joan Krupskas, Secy.-Treas.

Established in 2001 in DE.
Donors: The Lauder Foundation; Mrs. Estee Lauder†; EL 2002 Trust.
Foundation type: Independent foundation.
Financial data (yr. ended 12/31/04): Assets, $55,002,708 (M); gifts received, $61,154,580; expenditures, $7,502,066; qualifying distributions, $7,495,463; giving activities include $7,467,928 for 209 grants (high: $2,440,181; low: $250; average: $1,000–$10,000).
Purpose and activities: Giving primarily for education, health care, and human services.
Fields of interest: Arts education; Museums; Performing arts; Performing arts centers; Arts; Higher education; Environment; Health care; Health organizations, association; Breast cancer research; Recreation, parks/playgrounds; Human services; Foundations (community); Jewish agencies & temples.
Limitations: Applications not accepted. Giving primarily in New York, NY; funding also in Aspen, CO. No grants to individuals.
Application information: Contributes only to pre-selected organizations.
Officers: Leonard A. Lauder, Pres.; Evelyn H. Lauder, V.P.; Joan Krupskas, Secy.-Treas.
EIN: 134139448
Selected grants: The following grants were reported in 2004.
$2,440,181 to Whitney Museum of American Art, New York, NY.
$1,517,300 to Memorial Sloan-Kettering Cancer Center, New York, NY.
$566,368 to Breast Cancer Research Foundation, New York, NY.
$343,000 to Gideon Hausner Jewish Day School, Palo Alto, CA.
$255,000 to New York-Presbyterian Hospital, New York, NY.
$50,000 to Society of the Four Arts, Palm Beach, FL.
$10,000 to Hospital for Special Surgery Fund, New York, NY.
$5,000 to Literacy Partners, New York, NY.
$2,500 to National Marfan Foundation, Port Washington, NY.
$2,500 to World Monuments Fund, New York, NY.

6383
The Ronald S. Lauder Foundation ✧
767 5th Ave., Ste. 4200
New York, NY   10153-0185   (212) 319-6300
Contact: George Ban, C.E.O. and Exec. V.P.
FAX: (212) 319-9411; URL: http://www.rslfoundation.org

Established in 1987 in NY.
Donors: Estee Lauder†; Ronald S. Lauder; Estee Lauder, Inc.; The Estee Lauder 2002 Trust.
Foundation type: Independent foundation.
Financial data (yr. ended 12/31/04): Assets, $71,430,435 (M); gifts received, $65,681,717; expenditures, $11,202,174; qualifying distributions, $11,727,685; giving activities include $2,965,600 for 33 grants (high: $600,000; average: $10,000–$280,000), and $4,788,616 for foundation-administered programs.
Purpose and activities: Support for Central and Eastern European organizations dedicated to revitalization of Jewish life through educational and cultural programs, and the preservation of Jewish monuments and buildings; support also for a nonsectarian international student exchange program at the secondary level.
Fields of interest: Historic preservation/historical societies; Arts; Elementary/secondary education; Education; Jewish agencies & temples; Religion.
International interests: Austria; Belarus; Bulgaria; Czech Republic; Eastern Europe; Estonia; Europe; Germany; Hungary; Latvia; Lithuania; Moldova; Poland; Romania; Slovakia; Ukraine.
Type of support: General/operating support; Continuing support; Building/renovation; Program development; Grants to individuals; Exchange programs.
Limitations: Applications not accepted. Giving primarily in Central and Eastern Europe.
Publications: Financial statement; Informational brochure; Newsletter.
Application information: Unsolicited requests for funds are not considered.
  Board meeting date(s): Varies
Officers and Directors:* Ronald S. Lauder,* Chair. and Pres.; George Ban,* C.E.O. and Exec. V.P.; Rabbi Binyamin Krauss, V.P.; Rabbi Joshua Spinner, V.P.; Jacob Z. Schuster, Treas.; Rabbi Chaskel O. Besser; Rabbi Jacob I. Biderman; Micki Edelsohn; Rabbi Pinchas Goldschmidt; Malcolm Hoenlein; Jo Carole Lauder; Richard D. Parsons; Steven Schwager.
EIN: 133445910

6384
Lavelle Fund for the Blind, Inc. ▼
80 Maiden Ln., Ste. 1207
New York, NY   10038   (212) 668-9801
Contact: Andrew S. Fisher, Exec. Dir.
FAX: (212) 668-9803;
E-mail: afisher@lavellefund.org; URL: http://foundationcenter.org/grantmaker/lavellefund/

Established in 1999; Converted to an independent foundation in 2003.
Foundation type: Independent foundation.
Financial data (yr. ended 12/31/05): Assets, $95,449,372 (M); expenditures, $5,216,926; qualifying distributions, $4,461,668; giving activities include $4,199,231 for 23 grants (high: $500,000; low: $2,500; average: $100,000–$300,000).
Purpose and activities: The fund seeks to promote the spiritual, moral, intellectual, and physical development of blind and visually impaired people of all ages, and programs that help people avoid vision loss.
Fields of interest: Eye diseases; Disabilities, people with.
Type of support: Program development.

Limitations: Giving primarily in the New York City metropolitan area. No grants to individuals, or for deficit reduction, emergency funds, medical research programs, conferences or media events (unless an integral part of a broader program of direct service), or advocacy programs; no loans.
Publications: Grants list; Informational brochure (including application guidelines).
Application information: See Web site for application information. Application form not required.
  Initial approach: Letter of inquiry
  Copies of proposal: 1
  Deadline(s): None
  Board meeting date(s): Quarterly
  Final notification: 1 week
Officers and Trustees:* John J. McNally,* Pres.; John J. Caffrey,* Treas.; Andrew S. Fisher, Exec. Dir.; Nancy L. Brown; Bro. James Kearney, F.M.S.; J. Robert Lunney; Jane B. O'Connell; Victor D. Ziminsky, Jr.
Number of staff: 2 full-time professional.
EIN: 131740463
Selected grants: The following grants were reported in 2005.
$1,728,267 to Helen Keller International, New York, NY. 3 grants: $450,000 (To extend Helen Keller International's ChildSight vision care program to low-income children attending New York City pre-schools, payable over 3 years), $202,073 (To expand Helen Keller International's vision services in tsunami-affected areas in and near Aceh Province in Indonesia), $1,076,194 (For continued support for ChildSight, domestic, school-based vision screening and eyeglass distribution program for vulnerable and low-income children and youth).
$958,426 to Lavelle School for the Blind, Bronx, NY. 2 grants: $500,000 (To replenish School's fund balance), $458,426 (To launch program to provide Lavelle School alumni with ongoing peer support activities and skills training in such areas as career exploration and job readiness, social and community adjustment, and activities of daily living, payable over 2 years).
$385,000 to Jewish Guild for the Blind, New York, NY. For partnership with Columbia University Medical Center's Department of Ophthalmology to establish Center of Excellence for Vision Care that links primary vision care to low vision rehabilitation services, payable over 3 years.
$300,000 to Memorial Sloan-Kettering Cancer Center, New York, NY. To help support comprehensive training of physician-fellow and nurse in Center's new Ophthalmic Oncology Clinic, payable over 3 years.
$245,358 to International Eye Foundation, Bethesda, MD. To enable Magrabi Eye Hospital in Cairo, Egypt to train Egyptian ophthalmologists in micro-surgery techniques, establish management and sustainability program for other eye hospitals, and help two selected Cairo area eye hospitals, payable over 3 years.
$210,000 to South Street Seaport Museum, New York, NY. For project that would annually use Museum resources to build academic, social and independent travel skills of 50 visually impaired K-8 students in two Brooklyn public schools, and enable 20 visually impaired 4th-8th graders and 20 of their non-disabled siblings to attend an adapted summer sailing camp, payable over 3 years.
$200,000 to Christian Blind Mission International, Greenville, SC. For building of cataract surgery

capacity and services throughout Cuba, payable over 2 years.

6385
The Lawrence Charitable Foundation ✧ ☆
388 Kendridge Rd.
Lawrence, NY   11559   (516) 295-5350
Contact: Lynn Gettenberg, Tr.

Established in 2000 in NY.
Foundation type: Independent foundation.
Financial data (yr. ended 12/31/05): Assets, $701,077 (M); gifts received, $856,180; expenditures, $436,771; qualifying distributions, $436,771; giving activities include $435,971 for 34 + grants (high: $55,000).
Purpose and activities: Giving primarily for Jewish organizations.
Fields of interest: Scholarships/financial aid; Jewish agencies & temples; Economically disadvantaged.
Limitations: Giving primarily in NY.
Application information:
  Initial approach: Letter
  Deadline(s): None
Trustees: Gary Gettenberg; Lynn Gettenberg.
EIN: 311709120
Selected grants: The following grants were reported in 2005.
$12,368 to Torah Academy for Girls, Far Rockaway, NY.
$6,000 to Shor Yoshuv Institute, Lawrence, NY.
$4,500 to Central Fund of Israel, New York, NY.
$1,000 to Yeshiva Bnei Torah, Far Rockaway, NY.

6386
LBC Foundation ✧
c/o Lewis B. Cullman
767 3rd Ave., 36th Fl.
New York, NY   10017-2023

Established in 2001 in NY.
Donor: Lewis B. Cullman.
Foundation type: Independent foundation.
Financial data (yr. ended 6/30/06): Assets, $1,559,645 (M); expenditures, $668,999; qualifying distributions, $654,456; giving activities include $643,743 for 68 grants (high: $50,000; low: $50).
Purpose and activities: Giving primarily for the arts, education, and civil rights.
Fields of interest: Museums (art); Arts; Education; Botanical gardens; Civil rights; Jewish agencies & temples.
Limitations: Applications not accepted. Giving primarily in NY. No grants to individuals.
Application information: Contributes only to pre-selected organizations.
Trustee: Lewis B. Cullman.
EIN: 316665976
Selected grants: The following grants were reported in 2005.
$50,000 to Business Leaders for Sensible Priorities, New York, NY.
$40,000 to Aspen Institute, DC.
$25,000 to New York Botanical Garden, Bronx, NY.
$15,000 to Brooklyn Childrens Museum, Brooklyn, NY.
$10,650 to Teach for America, New York, NY.
$2,000 to Poets House, New York, NY.
$2,000 to Young Concert Artists, New York, NY.

$1,000 to Center for Khmer Studies, New York, NY.
$1,000 to Literacy Partners, New York, NY.
$1,000 to Philharmonic-Symphony Society of New York, New York, NY.

6387
LCU Foundation ✧
1123 Broadway, Ste. 1107
New York, NY   10010

Donors: Kathryn I. Fowler†; Youth Foundation, Inc.
Foundation type: Independent foundation.
Financial data (yr. ended 12/31/05): Assets, $18,953,550 (M); expenditures, $1,450,208; qualifying distributions, $1,255,386; giving activities include $1,129,200 for 26 grants (high: $100,000; low: $20,000).
Purpose and activities: Giving primarily to colleges and universities for housing stipends for female students.
Fields of interest: Higher education, college; Higher education, university; Women.
Limitations: Applications not accepted. Giving limited to New York, NY. No grants to individuals.
Application information: Contributes only to pre-selected organizations.
Directors: Vivien Clark; Janis Downey; Carol Farris; Joan Grein; and 9 additional directors.
EIN: 135562262

6388
Charles Henry Leach II Foundation ✧
c/o The Bank of New York, Tax Dept.
1 Wall St., 28th Fl.
New York, NY   10286
Application address: c/o Bank of New York, 1290 Ave. of the Americas, New York, NY 10024

Established in 1992 in NY.
Donor: Charles Henry Leach II†.
Foundation type: Independent foundation.
Financial data (yr. ended 12/31/05): Assets, $15,179,464 (M); expenditures, $986,478; qualifying distributions, $951,886; giving activities include $925,000 for 59 grants (high: $30,000; low: $2,500).
Purpose and activities: Giving primarily for care of underprivileged or emotionally damaged children, prevention of cruelty to animals, environmental protection, and promotion of science research.
Fields of interest: Child development, education; Environment, natural resources; Animal welfare; Human services; Children/youth, services; Child development, services; Economically disadvantaged.
Type of support: Research.
Limitations: Giving primarily in FL and NY.
Application information:
  Initial approach: Letter
  Deadline(s): None
Trustees: Jennifer B. Jordan; Philip E. Leone; The Bank of New York.
EIN: 133651713

6389
Lead International, Inc. ✧ ☆
(also known as Leadership for Environment &
Development International, Inc.)
c/o Simpson, Thacher, & Bartlett
425 Lexington Ave.
New York, NY 10017-3954

Established in NY and DE. Classified as a private
operating foundation in 1998.
Foundation type: Operating foundation.
Financial data (yr. ended 12/31/04): Assets,
$14,324,125 (M); gifts received, $1,204,005;
expenditures, $4,823,137; qualifying distributions,
$1,679,807; giving activities include $1,555,754
for 10 grants (high: $228,960; low: $37,319), and
$3,403,459 for foundation-administered programs.
Fields of interest: Arts.
Limitations: Applications not accepted. Giving on an
international basis. No grants to individuals.
Application information: Contributes only to
pre-selected organizations.
Officers: Jose Maria Figureres, Pres.; Teya Ryan,
V.P.; Julia Marton-Lefevre, Secy. and Exec. Dir.
Directors: Samuel Abiola Adenekan; Akin Oludele
Adesola; Julia Carabias; C.J. Chetsanga; Anjuly Chib
Duggal; Fabio Feldmann; Parvez Hassan; Song Jian;
Saburo Kawai; Geoffrey Lean; Reginald A. Mengi;
Marie Angelique Savane; Maurice Strong.
EIN: 133723995

6390
The M. J. and Caral G. Lebworth
Foundation ✧
c/o Anchin Block & Anchin LLP
1375 Broadway
New York, NY 10018

Established in 1998 in NY.
Donors: Caral G. Lebworth; Marion J. Lebworth.
Foundation type: Independent foundation.
Financial data (yr. ended 12/31/04): Assets,
$6,500,643 (M); expenditures, $546,205;
qualifying distributions, $407,562; giving activities
include $404,941 for 119 grants (high: $50,000;
low: $25).
Purpose and activities: Giving primarily for the arts,
education, and health and human services.
Fields of interest: Museums; Museums (art);
Museums (ethnic/folk arts); Historic preservation/
historical societies; Arts; Higher education,
university; Education; Human services; Jewish
agencies & temples.
Limitations: Applications not accepted. Giving
primarily in New York, NY. No grants to individuals.
Application information: Contributes only to
pre-selected organizations.
Trustees: Caral G. Lebworth; Marion J. Lebworth.
EIN: 134000723

6391
James T. Lee Foundation, Inc. ✧
FDR Station
P.O. Box 606
New York, NY 10150

Incorporated in 1958 in NY.
Donor: James T. Lee‡.
Foundation type: Independent foundation.
Financial data (yr. ended 11/30/05): Assets,
$5,006,243 (M); expenditures, $574,434;

qualifying distributions, $535,584; giving activities
include $525,000 for 49 grants (high: $25,000;
low: $2,500).
Purpose and activities: Giving primarily for higher
and other education as well as for the arts with
emphasis on the performing arts; some giving also
for health care with emphasis on specialized
hospitals, and social services including a guide dog
program for the blind.
Fields of interest: Performing arts, theater;
Performing arts, circus arts; Arts; Elementary/
secondary education; Education, early childhood
education; Education; Environment; Hospitals
(general); Hospitals (specialty); Health
organizations, association; Boy scouts; Human
services; YM/YWCAs & YM/YWHAs; Children/
youth, services; Economically disadvantaged.
Type of support: Continuing support; Annual
campaigns; Debt reduction; Emergency funds;
Program development; Scholarship funds;
Research.
Limitations: Applications not accepted. Giving
primarily in the New York, NY, metropolitan area. No
grants to individuals, or for operating budgets, seed
money, capital or endowment funds, publications, or
conferences; no loans.
Application information: Contributes only to
pre-selected organizations.
Officers: Raymond T. O'Keefe, Jr., Pres.; Delcour S.
Potter, V.P.
Directors: Thomas Appleby; Verne S. Atwater;
Leelee D'Olier Brown; Rick Curry; Paul Duffy;
Stephen B. Siegel; Richard W. Wheeless; Madelyn
Wils; Vincent Ziccolella.
EIN: 131878496
Selected grants: The following grants were reported
in 2004.
$20,000 to Big Apple Circus, New York, NY.
$20,000 to Borough of Manhattan Community
College Fund, New York, NY.
$20,000 to Boy Scouts of America, Greater New
York Councils, New York, NY.
$20,000 to Municipal Art Society of New York, New
York, NY.
$20,000 to National Council on Alcoholism and
Drug Dependence, New York, NY.
$20,000 to NYU Hospital for Joint Diseases, New
York, NY.
$20,000 to Saint Philips Academy, Newark, NJ.
$12,000 to Leake and Watts Services, Yonkers, NY.
$10,000 to Independent College Fund of New York,
Albany, NY.
$10,000 to Iona Preparatory School, New Rochelle,
NY.

6392
Andrea and Michael Leeds Family
Foundation ✧
P.O. Box 718
Syosset, NY 11791-0718

Established in 1999 in NY.
Donors: Michael S. Leeds; Liselotte J. Leeds;
Gerard G. Leeds; Andrea Leeds.
Foundation type: Independent foundation.
Financial data (yr. ended 3/31/06): Assets,
$7,409,767 (M); expenditures, $548,179;
qualifying distributions, $604,910; giving activities
include $586,887 for 18 grants (high: $222,079;
low: $2).
Purpose and activities: Giving primarily for higher
and other education, as well as for health

associations and medical research, and to Jewish
organizations.
Fields of interest: Higher education; Education;
Health organizations, association; Medical
research, institute; Human services; Jewish
federated giving programs; Jewish agencies &
temples.
Limitations: Applications not accepted. Giving
primarily in NY; some funding also in CO. No grants
to individuals.
Application information: Contributes only to
pre-selected organizations.
Trustees: Andrea R. Leeds; Michael S. Leeds.
EIN: 134055742
Selected grants: The following grants were reported
in 2005.
$200,000 to Institute for Student Achievement,
Lake Success, NY.
$50,600 to North Shore Child and Family Guidance
Center, Roslyn Heights, NY.
$5,000 to University of Colorado Foundation,
Boulder, CO.

6393
Lisa and Michael Leffell Family
Foundation ✧
c/o M.H. Davidson & Co.
65 E. 55th St., 19th Fl.
New York, NY 10022

Established in 1999 in NY.
Donor: Michael Leffell.
Foundation type: Independent foundation.
Financial data (yr. ended 12/31/05): Assets,
$2,983,769 (M); gifts received, $3,010,773;
expenditures, $679,747; qualifying distributions,
$675,297; giving activities include $675,297 for 45
grants (high: $300,600; low: $100).
Fields of interest: Education; Cancer; Human
services; Jewish federated giving programs; Jewish
agencies & temples.
Limitations: Applications not accepted. Giving
primarily in Westchester County, NY. No grants to
individuals.
Application information: Contributes only to
pre-selected organizations.
Trustees: Lisa Leffell; Michael Leffell.
EIN: 316633021

6394
Legacy Heritage Fund Limited ▼ ✧
(formerly KBRK, Inc.)
c/o Hertz, Herson & Co., LLP
2 Park Ave., Ste. 1500
New York, NY 10016

Established in 1997 in NY and DE.
Donors: VHIV, Inc.; IIMI, Inc.; JLRJ, Inc.; MRHM,
Inc.; Susan Wexner Revocable Trust; LMCL, Inc.
Foundation type: Independent foundation.
Financial data (yr. ended 6/30/05): Assets,
$23,161,175 (M); gifts received, $2,542,000;
expenditures, $4,983,697; qualifying distributions,
$5,004,549; giving activities include $2,918,099
for 30 grants (high: $515,550; low: $2,000;
average: $2,500–$200,000), $355,811 for 16
grants to individuals (high: $30,829; low: $16,666;
average: $19,000–$24,000), and $209,232 for 2
foundation-administered programs.

Purpose and activities: Giving primarily to Jewish organizations and federated giving programs; funding also for Jewish education.

Fields of interest: Education; Jewish federated giving programs; Jewish agencies & temples.

Limitations: Applications not accepted. Giving primarily in New York, NY, as well as in Tucson, AZ, MA, and Washington, DC. No grants to individuals.

Application information: Contributes only to pre-selected organizations.

Officer and Directors:* Susan Wexner,* Pres. and Secy.-Treas.; Bertrand Agus.

EIN: 134077801

Selected grants: The following grants were reported in 2004.

$1,000,000 to American Committee for the Weizmann Institute of Science, New York, NY.

$1,000,000 to American Society for Technion-Israel Institute of Technology, New York, NY.

$900,000 to American Friends of Alyn Hospital, New York, NY.

$350,000 to American Friends of the Israel Free Loan Association, Oceanside, NY. 2 grants: $100,000, $250,000

$309,400 to American Friends of Hatzalah Yehuda and Shomron, Brooklyn, NY. 2 grants: $154,700 each

$100,000 to American Israel Education Foundation (AIEF), DC.

$100,000 to American Physicians Fellowship for Medicine in Israel, Boston, MA.

$83,164 to Middle East Media Research Institute, DC.

6395
The Lehman Brothers Foundation ◇

745 7th Ave., 30th Fl.
New York, NY 10019

Established in 2000 in NY.

Donors: Lehman Brothers Holdings Inc.; Joseph M. Gregory; LB Foundation.

Foundation type: Company-sponsored foundation.

Financial data (yr. ended 11/30/04): Assets, $11,711,224 (M); gifts received, $12,570,793; expenditures, $2,463,815; qualifying distributions, $2,395,215; giving activities include $2,378,300 for 28 grants (high: $1,000,000; low: $10,000).

Purpose and activities: The foundation supports organizations involved with arts and culture, health, and youth development.

Fields of interest: Arts; Health care; Youth development.

Limitations: Applications not accepted. Giving primarily in New York, NY.

Application information: Contributes only to pre-selected organizations.

Officers and Directors:* Joseph M. Gregory,* Chair.; Francine S. Kittredge, Pres.; David Erickson; Jeremey M. Isaacs; Theodore P. Janulis; Andy A. Johnson; Akio Katsuragi; Alex Kirk; Jeffrey B. Lane; Stephen M. Lessing; Daniel Marcus; James P. Quismorio; Thomas A. Russo; Peter R. Sherratt; Laurie E. Stearn.

EIN: 311736689

Selected grants: The following grants were reported in 2003.

$1,500,000 to NYU Downtown Hospital, New York, NY. For renovation/expansion of Lehman Brothers Emergency Center.

$250,000 to New York-Presbyterian Hospital, New York, NY. To replace ambulances destroyed on September 11th.

$125,000 to Grand Street Settlement, New York, NY. For College and Career Discovery Center at Beacon.

$100,000 to University Settlement Society of New York, New York, NY. For College Prep Program/ Project Wise at the Beacon.

$30,000 to TEAK Fellowship, New York, NY. For Summer Institute.

$25,000 to Girl Scouts of the U.S.A., Greater New York Council, New York, NY. For general operating support.

$10,000 to Childrens Aid Society, New York, NY. For Dunlevy-Milbank Center.

6396
Edith and Herbert Lehman Foundation, Inc.

c/o Wendy Lehman Lash
151 E. 79th St.
New York, NY 10021-0417
FAX: (212) 744-2065; E-mail: wlash@nyc.rr.com

Incorporated in 1952 in NY.

Donors: Edith A. Lehman†; Herbert H. Lehman†.

Foundation type: Independent foundation.

Financial data (yr. ended 9/30/05): Assets, $8,453,203 (M); expenditures, $464,002; qualifying distributions, $395,170; giving activities include $392,500 for 53 grants (high: $100,000; low: $250).

Purpose and activities: Giving primarily for the arts and education.

Fields of interest: Arts; Higher education; Education; Animals/wildlife; Health care; Human services; Children, services.

International interests: United Kingdom.

Type of support: Equipment; General/operating support; Continuing support; Annual campaigns; Capital campaigns; Building/renovation; Endowments; Emergency funds; Professorships; Seed money; Curriculum development.

Limitations: Applications not accepted. Giving primarily in NY. No support for political organizations. No grants to individuals.

Publications: Annual report.

Application information: Proposals are accepted by invitation only. Preference is given to organizations which historically have been of interest to the Lehman family and to those in which the family is personally involved.

Board meeting date(s): Quarterly

Officers and Directors:* Wendy Lehman Lash,* Pres.; Robert C. Graham, Jr., V.P. and Treas.; Abigail S. Lash; Herbert Rosenfield; Deborah Sheridan; Catherine J. Wise.

EIN: 136094015

Selected grants: The following grants were reported in 2005.

$40,000 to Animal Medical Center, New York, NY.

$21,000 to Williams College, Williamstown, MA.

$12,500 to National Academy of Design, New York, NY.

$12,000 to Lab School of Washington, DC.

$10,000 to New England Wildlife Center, Hingham, MA.

$8,000 to Henry Street Settlement, New York, NY.

$6,000 to Greenwich Adult Day Care, Greenwich, CT.

$6,000 to Nightingale-Bamford School, New York, NY.

$5,000 to Museum of the City of New York, New York, NY.

$5,000 to New York Landmarks Conservancy, New York, NY.

6397
Robert Lehman Foundation, Inc. ▼ ◇

488 Madison Ave., 9th Fl.
New York, NY 10022
Contact: Francesca C. Valerio, Exec. Dir.
FAX: (212) 593-9175;
E-mail: info@robertlehmanfoundation.org;
URL: http://www.robertlehmanfoundation.org

Incorporated in 1943 in NY.

Donor: Robert Lehman†.

Foundation type: Independent foundation.

Financial data (yr. ended 9/30/05): Assets, $62,265,738 (M); expenditures, $2,783,823; qualifying distributions, $1,978,550; giving activities include $1,587,208 for 24 grants (high: $363,106; low: $400; average: $6,000–$250,000).

Purpose and activities: Support for the maintenance, conservation, and preservation of the Robert Lehman collection at the Metropolitan Museum of Art; visual arts and related teaching activities and publications.

Fields of interest: Visual arts; Arts; Higher education.

Limitations: Giving primarily in the northeastern U.S., with emphasis on New York, NY.

Application information: Application form not required.

Initial approach: Proposal (no more than three pages, two pages if applying for Art Lectureship)

Copies of proposal: 1

Deadline(s): None except for Art Lectureship, due Sept. 15

Board meeting date(s): As required

Officers and Directors:* Philip H. Isles,* Pres.; Edwin L. Weisl, Jr.,* V.P.; Michael M. Thomas,* Treas.; Francesca C. Valerio, Exec. Dir.; Robert A. Bernhard; James M. Hester; Marie Lehman; Robert Owen Lehman.

Number of staff: 2 full-time professional.

EIN: 136094018

Selected grants: The following grants were reported in 2004.

$1,647,707 to Metropolitan Museum of Art, New York, NY. To establish endowment fund, for capital projects, and to provide maintenance for Robert Lehman Wing.

$1,000,000 to Museum of Modern Art, New York, NY. For Annual Fund.

$600,000 to Harley School, Rochester, NY. For construction of Visual Arts building.

$138,370 to Institute of Fine Arts Foundation, New York, NY. To publish Lehman Collection Scholarly Catalogue.

$20,000 to Harlem School of the Arts, New York, NY. For College Prep Program.

$20,000 to National Gallery of Art, DC. For membership dues in Collectors Committee and for Teacher Institute.

$15,000 to Corning Museum of Glass, Corning, NY. For artist-in-residence program of The Studio.

$12,000 to Bowdoin College, Brunswick, ME. For Robert Lehman Lecture series.

$12,000 to Carleton College, Northfield, MN. For Robert Lehman Lecture series.

$10,000 to Alliance for the Arts, New York, NY. For NYCkidsARTS calendar.

6398
Leibowitz and Greenway Family Charitable Foundation ✧
80 Pierrepoint St., Ste. 4
Brooklyn, NY 11201

Established in 2000 in FL and NY.
Donors: Lawrence Leibowitz; Dorothy Liebowitz†.
Foundation type: Independent foundation.
Financial data (yr. ended 12/31/04): Assets, $5,481,945 (M); gifts received, $2,100,130; expenditures, $1,153,820; qualifying distributions, $1,140,000; giving activities include $1,140,000 for 61 grants (high: $40,000; low: $5,000).
Fields of interest: AIDS research; Human services; American Red Cross; Children, services; Federated giving programs.
Limitations: Applications not accepted. Giving primarily in Washington, DC, FL, GA, MA, MD, NY, and PA. No grants to individuals.
Application information: Contributes only to pre-selected organizations.
Trustees: Tara Greenway-Leibowitz; Lawrence Leibowitz.
EIN: 656358233
Selected grants: The following grants were reported in 2004.
$40,000 to American Red Cross.
$40,000 to Doctors Without Borders USA, New York, NY.
$40,000 to FINCA International, DC.
$40,000 to Habitat for Humanity International.
$40,000 to Oxfam America, Boston, MA.
$40,000 to Project Hope, Brooklyn, NY.
$30,000 to Childrens Defense Fund, DC.
$20,000 to Christopher Reeve Paralysis Foundation, Springfield, NJ.
$20,000 to Covenant House.
$20,000 to Gay Mens Health Crisis (GMHC), New York, NY.

6399
The Reuben and Jane Leibowitz Foundation, Inc. ✧
c/o Jen Partners LLC
551 Madison Ave., Rm. 300
New York, NY 10022
Contact: Reuben S. Leibowitz, Pres.

Established in 1986 in NY.
Donor: Reuben S. Leibowitz.
Foundation type: Independent foundation.
Financial data (yr. ended 11/30/05): Assets, $3,617,225 (M); gifts received, $302,197; expenditures, $459,345; qualifying distributions, $430,375; giving activities include $430,375 for 59 grants (high: $100,000; low: $100).
Purpose and activities: Giving primarily for education and Jewish organizations.
Fields of interest: Law school/education; Education; Jewish federated giving programs; Jewish agencies & temples.
Limitations: Applications not accepted. Giving primarily in NY. No grants to individuals.
Application information: Contributes only to pre-selected organizations.
Officer and Trustees:* Reuben S. Leibowitz,* Pres.; Jane Leibowitz.
EIN: 133382812

6400
The Abby and Mitch Leigh Foundation ✧
c/o Burton G. Lipsky
100 Park Ave., 33rd Fl.
New York, NY 10017-5586

Established in 1987 in NY.
Donor: Milton A. Kimmelman.
Foundation type: Independent foundation.
Financial data (yr. ended 12/31/05): Assets, $11,816,409 (M); expenditures, $889,474; qualifying distributions, $769,313; giving activities include $765,345 for 35 grants (high: $510,000; low: $200).
Fields of interest: Performing arts, ballet; Historic preservation/historical societies; Arts; Higher education; Hospitals (general); Health organizations, association; Jewish federated giving programs; Jewish agencies & temples.
Limitations: Applications not accepted. Giving primarily in New York, NY. No grants to individuals.
Application information: Contributes only to pre-selected organizations.
Trustees: Abby Leigh; Mitch Leigh.
EIN: 133398045
Selected grants: The following grants were reported in 2004.
$100,000 to Yale University, New Haven, CT.
$50,000 to Hospital for Special Surgery, New York, NY.
$50,000 to New York University, Graduate School of Arts and Science, New York, NY. For Institute of Fine Arts.
$47,570 to Dieu Donne Papermill, New York, NY.
$30,000 to Center for Reproductive Rights, New York, NY.
$30,000 to Museum of Modern Art, New York, NY.
$15,000 to American Israel Education Fund, Troy, MI.
$12,000 to Drawing Center, New York, NY.
$10,000 to Perlman Music Program, New York, NY.
$10,000 to Women Make Movies, New York, NY.

6401
Lemberg Foundation, Inc.
430 Park Ave., Ste. 505
New York, NY 10022 (212) 682-9595
Contact: John Usdan, Pres.

Incorporated in 1945 in NY.
Donor: Samuel Lemberg†.
Foundation type: Independent foundation.
Financial data (yr. ended 12/31/05): Assets, $39,096,329 (M); gifts received, $1,270,548; expenditures, $2,206,621; qualifying distributions, $1,995,127; giving activities include $1,995,127 for 66 grants (high: $1,250,000; low: $250; average: $1,000–$30,000).
Purpose and activities: Giving primarily for arts and culture, education, children and youth services, and Jewish federated giving programs and temples.
Fields of interest: Museums; Performing arts; Arts; Higher education; Human services; Children/youth, services; Jewish federated giving programs; Jewish agencies & temples.
Type of support: Building/renovation; Endowments; Program development; Fellowships; Scholarship funds; Research.
Limitations: Giving primarily in NY. No grants for matching gifts.
Application information:
  Initial approach: Letter, proposal, or telephone
  Copies of proposal: 1

Deadline(s): None
Board meeting date(s): As required
Officers: John Usdan, Pres.; Adam Usdan, V.P. and Treas.; Esme Usdan, Secy.
Number of staff: 2 part-time support.
EIN: 136082064
Selected grants: The following grants were reported in 2004.
$125,000 to Usdan Center for the Creative and Performing Arts, New York, NY.
$35,000 to W N E T Channel 13, New York, NY.
$25,000 to Carnegie Hall Society, New York, NY.
$20,000 to Bronx House, Bronx, NY.
$14,633 to Town School, New York, NY.
$6,000 to New York Shakespeare Festival, New York, NY.
$1,500 to Public Art Fund, New York, NY.
$1,000 to Metropolitan Museum of Art, New York, NY.
$1,000 to School of American Ballet, New York, NY.
$1,000 to Yale University, New Haven, CT.

6402
Reginald A. & Elizabeth S. Lenna Foundation, Inc. ✧
(doing business as The Lenna Foundation)
214 W. 5th St.
Jamestown, NY 14701
E-mail: lennafoundation@alltel.net; Application address: Elizabeth S. Lenna, Pres., 86 E. Terrace Ave., Lakewood, NY 14750

Established in 1985 in NY.
Donors: Reginald A. Lenna†; Elizabeth S. Lenna.
Foundation type: Independent foundation.
Financial data (yr. ended 12/31/05): Assets, $11,815,710 (M); expenditures, $568,566; qualifying distributions, $522,608; giving activities include $499,193 for 20 grants (high: $100,000; low: $1,000).
Fields of interest: Historic preservation/historical societies; Arts; Environment; Hospitals (general); Human services; YM/YWCAs & YM/YWHAs; Children, day care; Community development.
Type of support: Scholarship funds; Program-related investments/loans; Matching/challenge support; Capital campaigns; Building/renovation; General/operating support.
Limitations: Giving primarily in southwestern NY. No support for political or religious organizations. No grants to individuals.
Application information: Application form required.
  Initial approach: Letter of interest (2 page maximum)
  Copies of proposal: 2
  Deadline(s): Jan. 15 and July 31
  Board meeting date(s): Mar., June and Nov.
  Final notification: 90 days
Officers: Elizabeth S. Lenna, Pres.; Joseph Johnson, Exec. V.P.; Florence Cass, Secy.; Randy Ordines, Treas.
Director: Thomas Price.
Number of staff: 1 part-time professional; 1 part-time support.
EIN: 112800733

6403
The Dorothea L. Leonhardt Foundation, Inc. ✧
c/o G. Gaylord
1 Chase Manhattan Plz., 47th Fl.
New York, NY 10005 (212) 530-5016

Incorporated in 1988 in NY.
Donor: Frederick H. Leonhardt‡.
Foundation type: Independent foundation.
Financial data (yr. ended 7/31/05): Assets, $12,267,480 (M); expenditures, $946,219; qualifying distributions, $779,216; giving activities include $691,926 for 66 grants (high: $225,560; low: $250).
Fields of interest: Museums; Performing arts; Arts; Education; Health organizations, association; Legal services; Human services; Children, services.
Type of support: General/operating support; Continuing support; Building/renovation; Endowments; Professorships; Research.
Limitations: Giving primarily in NY. No grants to individuals.
Application information: Contributes mainly to pre-selected organizations. Application form not required.
  Initial approach: Letter or telephone
  Copies of proposal: 1
  Deadline(s): None
  Board meeting date(s): Varies, 2 or 3 times per year
  Final notification: Through the next board meeting
Officers and Directors:* Joanne L. Cassullo,* Pres.; Alexander D. Forger, V.P.; Richard A. Stark, V.P.; Guilford W. Gaylord,* Secy.-Treas.
Number of staff: 1 full-time professional.
EIN: 133420520
Selected grants: The following grants were reported in 2003.
$298,500 to Whitney Museum of American Art, New York, NY.
$195,666 to Roanoke College, Salem, VA.
$55,500 to Childrens Advocacy Center of Manhattan, New York, NY.
$15,600 to New Museum of Contemporary Art, New York, NY.
$15,000 to Architectural League of New York, New York, NY.
$15,000 to RX Art, New York, NY.
$7,500 to Thread Waxing Space, New York, NY.
$5,500 to Help USA, New York, NY.
$5,000 to Art 21, New York, NY.
$5,000 to Cancer Support Team, Mamaroneck, NY.

6404
The Lessing Family Foundation ✧ ☆
c/o Stephen M. Lessing
9 Snake Hill Rd.
Cold Spring Harbor, NY 11724

Established in 2003 in NY.
Donors: Stephen M. Lessing; Sandra M. Lessing; Morton S. Bouchard III.
Foundation type: Independent foundation.
Financial data (yr. ended 12/31/05): Assets, $5,003,659 (M); gifts received, $215,000; expenditures, $541,366; qualifying distributions, $438,529; giving activities include $438,529 for 3 grants (high: $338,516; low: $13).
Fields of interest: Education.
Limitations: Applications not accepted. Giving primarily in NY. No grants to individuals.

Application information: Contributes only to pre-selected organizations.
Trustees: Sandra M. Lessing; Stephen M. Lessing.
EIN: 030518473

6405
David M. Leuschen Foundation ✧
c/o BCRS Associates LLC
100 Wall St., 11th Fl.
New York, NY 10005-3720

Established in 1988 in CT.
Donor: David M. Leuschen.
Foundation type: Independent foundation.
Financial data (yr. ended 4/30/05): Assets, $2,126 (M); gifts received, $676,033; expenditures, $689,760; qualifying distributions, $689,760; giving activities include $689,760 for 13 grants (high: $223,360; low: $400).
Purpose and activities: Giving to a museum.
Fields of interest: Museums (specialized); Education; Human services; Philanthropy/voluntarism; Christian agencies & churches.
Limitations: Applications not accepted. Giving primarily in MT and WY; some funding nationally. No grants to individuals or for scholarships; no loans.
Application information: Contributes only to pre-selected organizations.
Trustees: Jonathan L. Cohen; David M. Leuschen; Patricia A. Napoli.
EIN: 133501179
Selected grants: The following grants were reported in 2005.
$423,360 to Buffalo Bill Historical Center, Cody, WY. 2 grants: $200,000 (For general support), $223,360 (For general support).
$50,000 to Eagle Mount Bozeman, Bozeman, MT. 2 grants: $25,000 each (For general support).
$40,000 to Childrens Scholarship Fund, New York, NY. For general support.
$5,000 to Houston Livestock Show and Rodeo, Houston, TX. For general support.

6406
Ira and Beth Leventhal Foundation ✧
10 Bessel Ln.
Chappaqua, NY 10514

Donors: Ira Leventhal; Beth Leventhal.
Foundation type: Operating foundation.
Financial data (yr. ended 12/31/04): Assets, $6,587,187 (M); expenditures, $2,028,714; qualifying distributions, $2,027,054; giving activities include $2,019,710 for 56 grants (high: $500,000; low: $50).
Purpose and activities: Giving primarily for the performing arts, children and social services, and for higher education.
Fields of interest: Performing arts, ballet; Arts; Boys & girls clubs; Human services; Children, services; Jewish federated giving programs.
Limitations: Applications not accepted. Giving primarily in NY. No grants to individuals.
Application information: Contributes only to pre-selected organizations.
Officers and Trustees:* Beth Leventhal, Pres.; Ira Leventhal, V.P.; Richard Cayne,* Secy.
EIN: 134092955

6407
Betty & John A. Levin Fund
(formerly Elisabeth & John Levin Fund)
c/o Levin Capital Strategies
595 Madison Ave., 17th Fl.
New York, NY 10020

Established in 1964.
Donors: Elisabeth L. Levin; John Levin.
Foundation type: Independent foundation.
Financial data (yr. ended 11/30/04): Assets, $1,324,349 (M); gifts received, $1,230; expenditures, $705,493; qualifying distributions, $704,857; giving activities include $704,560 for 36 grants (high: $150,000; low: $250).
Purpose and activities: Giving for the arts, education, hospitals, and Jewish organizations.
Fields of interest: Museums; Arts; Higher education; Medical school/education; Hospitals (general); Human services; Jewish federated giving programs; Jewish agencies & temples.
Limitations: Applications not accepted. Giving primarily in New York, NY. No grants to individuals.
Application information: Contributes only to pre-selected organizations.
Officers: Elisabeth L. Levin, Pres.; John A. Levin, Secy.-Treas.
EIN: 136168345
Selected grants: The following grants were reported in 2003.
$140,000 to Yale University, New Haven, CT. For general support.
$110,000 to Jazz at Lincoln Center, New York, NY. For general support.
$67,000 to Mount Sinai Hospital, School of Medicine, New York, NY. For general support.
$50,000 to UJA-Federation of New York, New York, NY. For general support.
$50,000 to Whitney Museum of American Art, New York, NY. For general support.
$25,000 to W N E T Channel 13, New York, NY. For general support.
$15,000 to Jewish Board of Family and Childrens Services, New York, NY. For general support.
$12,500 to Council on Foreign Relations, New York, NY. For general support.
$12,500 to Philharmonic-Symphony Society of New York, New York, NY. For general support.
$5,000 to Memorial Sloan-Kettering Cancer Center, New York, NY. For general support.

6408
Laurence W. Levine Foundation, Inc. ✧ ☆
c/o Fiduciary Trust Co. International
600 5th Ave.
New York, NY 10020

Established in 1994 in FL.
Donor: Laurence W. Levine‡.
Foundation type: Independent foundation.
Financial data (yr. ended 12/31/05): Assets, $12,452,262 (M); gifts received, $376,081; expenditures, $1,128,637; qualifying distributions, $1,079,608; giving activities include $535,000 for 51 grants (high: $30,000; low: $2,500).
Purpose and activities: Giving primarily for human services, including services for people who are deaf or blind; funding also for the arts, heath care, and Jewish organizations.
Fields of interest: Arts; Health care; Human services; Jewish agencies & temples; Blind/visually impaired; Deaf/hearing impaired.

Limitations: Applications not accepted. Giving primarily in NY. No grants to individuals.
Application information: Contributes only to pre-selected organizations.
Officers: Susan Kane, Pres. and Treas.; Jay Levine, V.P.; Eric Kane, Secy.
Directors: Beth Feldman; Russell Kane; James Levine; Michael Levine; Lesley Logue.
EIN: 650535001

6409
Levitt Foundation

c/o The Philanthropic Group
630 5th Ave., 20th Fl.
New York, NY 10111 (212) 501-7785
Contact: Barbara R. Greenberg, Fdn. Advisor
FAX: (212) 501-7788;
E-mail: BGreenberg@philanthropicgroup.com;
URL: http://foundationcenter.org/grantmaker/levitt/

Incorporated in 1949 in NY.
Donors: Levitt and Sons, Inc.; Abraham Levitt‡; Alfred Levitt‡; William Levitt.
Foundation type: Independent foundation.
Financial data (yr. ended 4/30/06): Assets, $15,905,415 (M); expenditures, $695,616; qualifying distributions, $629,885; giving activities include $553,800 for 37 grants (high: $75,000; low: $500).
Purpose and activities: To enhance the abilities of children and youth in the greater metropolitan New York, NY, areas including Nassau and Suffolk counties on Long Island, so they may understand and value their environment, and take action to improve and protect the built and natural environments in their own neighborhoods. The foundation prefers to support neighborhood-based and community-based organizations, rather than school-based programs.
Fields of interest: Environment; Children/youth, services; Community development, neighborhood development.
Type of support: Program development; Internship funds.
Limitations: Applications not accepted. Giving limited to Long Island and New York, NY. No grants to individuals.
Publications: Grants list.
Application information: Applications accepted by invitation only. However, if an organization believes their project fits the criteria of the foundation, they may telephone Barbara Greenberg, to discuss the project. See foundation Web site for details.
Board meeting date(s): 3 times per year
Officers and Trustees: May W. Newburger,* Pres.; Stephen J. Mathes,* Secy.; Robert J. Appel,* Treas.; John M. Brickman; Prudence Brown; Elaine S. Hutchinson.
EIN: 136128226
Selected grants: The following grants were reported in 2005.
$75,000 to Fund for the City of New York, New York, NY.
$65,000 to Rocking the Boat, Bronx, NY.
$50,000 to Green Guerillas, New York, NY.
$50,000 to United Neighborhood Houses of New York, New York, NY.
$35,000 to Fresh Youth Initiatives, New York, NY.
$30,000 to Prospect Park Alliance, Brooklyn, NY.
$25,000 to Cornell Cooperative Extension of Suffolk County, Riverhead, NY.
$25,000 to Trust for Public Land, New York, NY.

$20,000 to Groundswell Community Mural Project, Brooklyn, NY.
$20,000 to Sustainable Long Island, Garden City, NY.

6410
The Paul and Karen Levy Family Foundation ◇

c/o Schwartz & Co.
2580 Sunrise Hwy.
Bellmore, NY 11710-3608
Contact: Paul Levy, Tr.

Established in 1997 in NY.
Donor: Paul Levy.
Foundation type: Independent foundation.
Financial data (yr. ended 11/30/04): Assets, $1,486,149 (L); gifts received, $1,004,036; expenditures, $491,424; qualifying distributions, $473,660; giving activities include $473,660 for grants.
Purpose and activities: Giving primarily for education, the arts, and to Jewish organizations.
Fields of interest: Arts; Higher education; Law school/education; Education; Athletics/sports, golf; Jewish federated giving programs; Jewish agencies & temples.
Limitations: Giving on a national basis.
Application information: Application form not required.
Deadline(s): None
Trustee: Paul Levy.
EIN: 133982379
Selected grants: The following grants were reported in 2003.
$675,000 to University of Pennsylvania, Philadelphia, PA. 3 grants: $25,000 to School of Law, $50,000 to School of Law, $600,000 to School of Law
$200,000 to Brown University, Providence, RI.
$25,000 to Metropolitan Opera, New York, NY.
$25,000 to Ohr Somayach International, Brooklyn, NY.
$10,000 to American Jewish Committee, New York, NY.
$10,000 to Anti-Defamation League of Bnai Brith, Philadelphia, PA.
$10,000 to Scarsdale Synagogue, Scarsdale, NY.
$9,000 to Jerusalem Fellowships, New York, NY.

6411
Frances and Jack Levy Foundation ◇ ☆

820 Fifth Ave., 8th Fl.
New York, NY 10021

Established in 2001 in NY.
Donors: Jack Levy; Frances Levy.
Foundation type: Independent foundation.
Financial data (yr. ended 6/30/05): Assets, $1,124,665 (M); expenditures, $608,171; qualifying distributions, $585,040; giving activities include $585,040 for 45 grants (high: $325,000; low: $25).
Fields of interest: Arts, multipurpose centers/programs; Elementary/secondary education; Higher education, university; Education; Hospitals (general); Eye diseases; Human services; Jewish agencies & temples.
Limitations: Applications not accepted. Giving primarily in CA and NY. No grants to individuals.

Application information: Contributes only to pre-selected organizations.
Trustees: Frances Levy; Jack Levy.
EIN: 137279189

6412
The Betty & Norman F. Levy Foundation, Inc. ◇

885 3rd Ave., 31st Fl., Ste. 3180
New York, NY 10022

Established in 1965 in NY.
Donor: Norman F. Levy‡.
Foundation type: Independent foundation.
Financial data (yr. ended 9/30/05): Assets, $40,075,436 (M); expenditures, $1,429,970; qualifying distributions, $1,360,350; giving activities include $1,360,350 for 26 grants (high: $1,000,000; low: $250).
Purpose and activities: Giving primarily for the arts, health care, human services, and Jewish organizations.
Fields of interest: Performing arts centers; Arts; Higher education; Health care; Health organizations, association; Human services; Jewish federated giving programs; Jewish agencies & temples.
Type of support: General/operating support; Program development.
Limitations: Applications not accepted. Giving primarily in New York, NY. No grants to individuals.
Application information: Contributes only to pre-selected organizations.
Officers and Directors:* Norman F. Levy,* Pres.; Francis N. Levy,* V.P.
EIN: 132553674
Selected grants: The following grants were reported in 2003.
$1,000,000 to Mount Sinai Medical Center, New York, NY.
$100,000 to Lincoln Center for the Performing Arts, New York, NY.
$100,000 to UJA-Federation of New York, New York, NY.
$50,000 to Metropolitan Opera Association, New York, NY.
$25,000 to University of Miami, Department of Surgery, Coral Gables, FL.
$10,000 to Metropolitan Museum of Art, New York, NY.
$10,000 to United Cerebral Palsy of New York City, New York, NY.
$7,500 to Carnegie Hall Society, New York, NY.
$5,000 to Starlight Starbright Childrens Foundation, New York, NY.
$1,000 to Henry Street Settlement, New York, NY.

6413
Jerome Levy Foundation ◇

c/o Warshaw, Burstein, et al.
555 5th Ave.
New York, NY 10017

Trust established in 1955 in NY.
Donors: Leon Levy‡; S. Jay Levy.
Foundation type: Independent foundation.
Financial data (yr. ended 10/31/05): Assets, $18,962,700 (M); expenditures, $4,241,439; qualifying distributions, $4,201,000; giving activities include $4,201,000 for 4 grants (high: $4,170,000; low: $1,000).

Purpose and activities: Giving primarily for land conservation. Support also for the fine arts, higher education and organizations interested in freedom of expression.
Fields of interest: Visual arts; Museums; Performing arts; Higher education; Environment, land resources; Human services; Civil rights; Jewish federated giving programs.
Limitations: Applications not accepted. Giving primarily in the metropolitan New York, NY, area. No grants to individuals.
Application information: Contributes only to pre-selected organizations.
Trustees: S.J. Levy; Shelby White.
EIN: 136159573

6414
Leon Levy Foundation ✧ ☆
280 Park Ave., 21st Fl. W.
New York, NY   10017
Application address: John Bernstein, c/o Leon Levy Foundation, 280 Park Ave., 21st Fl., New York, NY 10012

Established in 2005 in NY.
Donor: Leon Levy†.
Foundation type: Independent foundation.
Financial data (yr. ended 3/31/05): Assets, $533,617,130 (M); gifts received, $535,207,333; expenditures, $2,106,002; qualifying distributions, $19,554,017; giving activities include $1,522,233 for 31 grants (high: $1,000,000; low: $250), and $17,542,857 for 1 foundation-administered program.
Purpose and activities: Giving primarily for higher education and the arts.
Fields of interest: Museums; Arts; Higher education; Environment, natural resources.
Limitations: Applications not accepted. Giving primarily in the Boston, MA, area, and New York, NY. No grants to individuals.
Application information: Contributes only to pre-selected organizations.
Officer: John Bernstein, Pres. and C.F.O.
Trustees: Elizabeth Moynihan; Shelby White.
EIN: 306085406

6415
The Martin R. Lewis Charitable
  Foundation ✧
c/o Martin R. Lewis
52 W. 11th St.
New York, NY   10011-8602

Established in 1996 in DE and NY.
Donor: Martin R. Lewis.
Foundation type: Independent foundation.
Financial data (yr. ended 12/31/05): Assets, $2,052,961 (M); expenditures, $669,343; qualifying distributions, $659,643; giving activities include $641,250 for 121 grants (high: $275,000; low: $100).
Purpose and activities: Giving primarily to services and medical research for people who are blind, including glaucoma research; funding also for higher education, human services, health associations, and Jewish organizations.
Fields of interest: Higher education; Health organizations; Medical research, institute; Eye research; Human services; Federated giving

programs; Jewish federated giving programs; Jewish agencies & temples.
Limitations: Applications not accepted. Giving on a national basis, with emphasis on the greater metropolitan areas of Washington, DC, including VA and MD, and New York, NY. No grants to individuals.
Application information: Contributes only to pre-selected organizations.
Officers and Directors:* Martin R. Lewis,* Pres.; Diane Carol Brandt, Secy.-Treas.; Lisa Lewis Cartolano; Wendy Lewis Kaye; Jeffrey S. Lewis.
EIN: 133877209
Selected grants: The following grants were reported in 2004.
$275,000 to UJA-Federation of New York, New York, NY.
$55,000 to Glaucoma Foundation, New York, NY.
$51,500 to New York University, New York, NY.
$25,000 to Colel Chabad, Brooklyn, NY.
$25,000 to Cornell Glaucoma Fund, New York, NY.
$25,000 to Dystonia Medical Research Foundation, Chicago, IL.
$3,600 to Union County Torah Center, Westfield, NJ.
$2,500 to Food Allergy Initiative, New York, NY.
$1,000 to Milton and Rose D. Friedman Foundation, Indianapolis, IN.
$250 to Cancer Care, New York, NY.

6416
Reginald F. Lewis Foundation, Inc. ✧
115 E. 57th St., Ste. 1430
New York, NY   10022
Contact: Beverly A. Cooper, Dir.

Established in 1987 in NY.
Donors: Reginald F. Lewis†; Loida N. Lewis; Leslie Lewis Sword; Christina S.N. Lewis.
Foundation type: Independent foundation.
Financial data (yr. ended 6/30/05): Assets, $23,357,909 (M); gifts received, $60,007; expenditures, $1,348,162; qualifying distributions, $1,348,162; giving activities include $1,247,500 for 10 grants (high: $1,000,000; low: $500; average: $5,000–$10,000).
Purpose and activities: Giving primarily for education and to children's programs.
Application information: Application form required.
  Initial approach: Letter
  Deadline(s): June 1 and Dec. 1
Officer and Directors:* Loida N. Lewis,* Chair.; Beverly A. Cooper; Anthony S. Fugett; Christina S.N. Lewis; Leslie Lewis Sword.
EIN: 133429965

6417
LGR Foundation ✧
c/o U.S. Trust
114 W. 47th St.
New York, NY   10036-1532

Established in 2000 in TX.
Donors: Lawrence G. Rawl; LGR Charitable Lead Annuity Trust.
Foundation type: Independent foundation.
Financial data (yr. ended 12/31/05): Assets, $10,345,548 (M); gifts received, $442,454; expenditures, $480,347; qualifying distributions, $437,013; giving activities include $418,700 for 3 grants (high: $203,700; low: $85,000).
Fields of interest: Foundations (community).

Limitations: Applications not accepted. Giving primarily in TX. No grants to individuals.
Application information: Contributes only to pre-selected organizations.
Officers: Kelly R. Guziejka, Pres. and Treas.; Lawrence V. Rawl, V.P.; Kent H. McMahan, Secy.
Director: Gail W. Rawl.
EIN: 742955428
Selected grants: The following grants were reported in 2003.
$105,000 to Community Foundation of Metropolitan Tarrant County, Fort Worth, TX.
$105,000 to Greater Houston Community Foundation, Houston, TX.
$98,350 to Austin Community Foundation for the Capital Area, Austin, TX.

6418
The Li Foundation, Inc. ✧
57 Glen St.
Glen Cove, NY   11542   (516) 676-1315
Contact: Taie Li, Pres.
FAX: (516) 676-2538;
E-mail: thelifoundation@usa.net

Established in 1944 in NY.
Foundation type: Independent foundation.
Financial data (yr. ended 12/31/05): Assets, $8,744,459 (M); expenditures, $613,261; qualifying distributions, $506,300; giving activities include $462,883 for 20 grants to individuals (high: $40,000; low: $500).
Purpose and activities: Primarily awards scholarships and fellowships by nomination only, to Chinese students for study in the U.S.
Fields of interest: Higher education; Disasters, 9/11/01.
International interests: China.
Type of support: Fellowships; Scholarships—to individuals.
Limitations: Giving on a national and international basis.
Application information: Grants are awarded to institutions for individuals. Application form required.
  Copies of proposal: 2
  Deadline(s): Feb. 1
  Board meeting date(s): May and Sept.
Officers and Directors:* Taie Li,* Pres.; Marie Chun,* V.P.; Mildred L. Distin,* Secy.; Eric Leong Way,* Treas.; Craig Mar Chun; Gail Chun-Deduonni; Minfong Ho Dennis; Carlos Chang Koo; Anna Li; Ling Li; Poco Li; Sebastian Li; Taimim Li; Eric Leong Way.
Number of staff: 3
EIN: 136098783
Selected grants: The following grants were reported in 2004.
$84,000 to American Council of Learned Societies, New York, NY.
$42,000 to Colorado School of Mines, Golden, CO.
$21,000 to East Asian History of Science Trust, Cambridge, England. .

6419
Bertha & Isaac Liberman Foundation,
  Inc. ✧
480 Park Ave.
New York, NY   10022
Contact: Jeffrey Klein, Pres.

Established in 1947 in NY.

Donor: Isaac Liberman†.
Foundation type: Independent foundation.
Financial data (yr. ended 6/30/05): Assets, $7,952,905 (M); expenditures, $386,913; qualifying distributions, $373,424; giving activities include $336,000 for 58 grants (high: $61,000; low: $250).
Fields of interest: Museums; Performing arts, music; Arts; Education.
Type of support: General/operating support; Capital campaigns; Building/renovation; Program development.
Limitations: Giving primarily in New York, NY. No grants to individuals.
Application information: Application form not required.
   Deadline(s): None
Officers: Jeffrey Klein, Pres.; Michelle Klein, V.P.; Jerome Tarnoff, Secy.; David B. Forer, Treas.
EIN: 136119056
Selected grants: The following grants were reported in 2004.
$61,000 to Museum of Modern Art, New York, NY. For operating support.
$10,000 to New York City Opera, New York, NY.
$10,000 to New York University, New York, NY. For operating support.
$7,500 to Metropolitan Museum of Art, New York, NY.
$4,000 to New Museum of Contemporary Art, New York, NY.
$3,000 to Brearley School, New York, NY.
$2,500 to Solomon R. Guggenheim Museum, New York, NY.
$1,000 to Colgate University, Hamilton, NY.
$1,000 to Columbia University, School of Business, New York, NY.
$1,000 to Lincoln Center for the Performing Arts, New York, NY.

6420
David L. Lieb Foundation, Inc. ✧
c/o Mahoney, Cohen & Co.
111 W. 40th St.
New York, NY   10018

Established in 1959.
Donor: David L. Lieb†.
Foundation type: Independent foundation.
Financial data (yr. ended 12/31/04): Assets, $9,259,934 (M); expenditures, $436,405; qualifying distributions, $369,087; giving activities include $331,765 for 81 grants (high: $100,000; low: $100).
Purpose and activities: Giving primarily for a Jewish welfare fund and other Jewish organizations; support also for higher education, hospitals, the arts, and human services.
Fields of interest: Performing arts, theater; Arts; Higher education; Hospitals (general); Human services; Jewish federated giving programs; Jewish agencies & temples.
Limitations: Applications not accepted. Giving primarily in NY. No grants to individuals.
Application information: Contributes only to pre-selected organizations.
Officers: Barbara Lieb Baumstein, V.P.; Toby Lieb, Secy.; Richard Baumstein, Treas.
EIN: 136077728
Selected grants: The following grants were reported in 2004.

$83,200 to Maharishi University of Management, Fairfield, IA. 6 grants: $1,500, $15,000, $1,000, $25,000, $15,700, $25,000
$22,500 to Maharishi Vedic Foundation, Hillsboro, NH.
$10,000 to Womens Campaign International, Bala Cynwyd, PA. 2 grants: $5,000 each
$500 to Saint Andrews Episcopal Church, Madison, WI.

6421
The Dolores Zohrab Liebmann Fund
c/o JPMorgan Chase Bank, N.A., Global Foundations Group
345 Park Ave., 4th Fl.
New York, NY   10154   (212) 464-2441
Contact: Edward L. Jones, V.P.; Alternate Contact: Sara Rosen
FAX: (212) 464-2305;
E-mail: jones_ed_l@jpmorgan.com; Additional tel.: (212) 464-2470; e-mail for Sara Rosen: sara.j.rosen@jpmchase.com; URL: http://foundationcenter.org/grantmaker/liebmann/

Established in 1995 in NY.
Foundation type: Independent foundation.
Financial data (yr. ended 12/31/05): Assets, $25,159,383 (M); expenditures, $1,824,667; qualifying distributions, $1,660,818; giving activities include $1,531,206 for 116 grants (high: $42,154; low: $1,843; average: $9,000–$26,550).
Purpose and activities: The foundation awards fellowships to United States citizens who have earned a baccalaureate degree, have an outstanding academic record, who are enrolled in an accredited university in the United States, and who plan to pursue a program of study in the humanities, social sciences, or natural sciences; the fund also makes grants to support the publication of dissertations, historical or literary works focusing on Armenian culture or history.
Fields of interest: Higher education.
Type of support: Publication; Fellowships.
Limitations: Giving on a national basis.
Publications: Application guidelines; Grants list; Informational brochure.
Application information: Application information available on foundation Web site. Fellowships are restricted to graduate students who are United States citizens attending an accredited and designated institution of higher education within the United States. Independent research and study grants are restricted to scholars who are based in and conducting research in the United States. Publication grants support the publication of dissertations or historical or literary works focusing on Armenian culture or history. Application form required.
   Copies of proposal: 6
   Deadline(s): None
Trustee: JPMorgan Chase Bank, N.A.
EIN: 137060094

6422
The Liman Foundation, Inc. ✧
c/o U.S. Trust
114 W. 47th St.
New York, NY   10036-1510
Contact: Carolyn Larke, V.P.

Established in 2000 in NY, as a result of a transfer of assets from the Joe and Emily Lowe Foundation.
Foundation type: Independent foundation.
Financial data (yr. ended 12/31/03): Assets, $8,403,652 (M); expenditures, $554,190; qualifying distributions, $501,090; giving activities include $497,050 for 93 grants (high: $15,000; low: $1,000).
Purpose and activities: Giving with an emphasis on the arts, education, legal services, medical research, the environment, and Jewish philanthropy.
Limitations: Applications not accepted. Giving primarily in the New York, NY metropolitan area. No grants to individuals.
Application information: Unsolicited requests for funds not accepted.
Officers: Ellen Liman, Pres. and Treas.; Douglas Liman, V.P.; Emily Liman, V.P.; Lewis Liman, Secy.
EIN: 134062758
Selected grants: The following grants were reported in 2004.
$40,000 to Ethical Culture Fieldston Schools, New York, NY. For operating support.
$20,000 to Barnard College, New York, NY. For operating support.
$15,000 to American Folk Art Museum, New York, NY. For operating support.
$15,000 to Brooklyn Museum, Brooklyn, NY. For operating support.
$15,000 to Norton Museum of Art, West Palm Beach, FL. For operating support.
$12,000 to Brown University, Providence, RI. For operating support.
$10,000 to Community Synagogue Museum Fund, Rye, NY. For operating support.
$10,000 to Human Rights Watch, New York, NY. For operating support.
$10,000 to National Academy of Design, New York, NY. For operating support.
$10,000 to Teachers College Columbia University, New York, NY. For operating support.

6423
The Lincoln Fund ✧
295 Madison Ave., Ste. 700
New York, NY   10017   (212) 686-4797
Contact: Duer McLanahan, Pres.

Incorporated in 1898 in NY.
Foundation type: Independent foundation.
Financial data (yr. ended 6/30/05): Assets, $9,250,574 (M); expenditures, $600,118; qualifying distributions, $526,408; giving activities include $490,000 for 24 grants (high: $30,000; low: $10,000).
Purpose and activities: Giving primarily for educational programs, scholarships, youth organizations, and human services.
Fields of interest: Medical school/education; Education; Cancer research; Crime/violence prevention, domestic violence; Employment, services; Children/youth, services; Children, services; Human services; Aging, centers/services; Women, centers/services; Homeless, human services.
Type of support: Continuing support; Program development; Seed money; Scholarship funds; Matching/challenge support.
Limitations: Giving limited to the greater metropolitan New York, NY, area. No grants to individuals, or for building or endowment funds, operating budgets, or general corporate purposes.

Application information: Application form not required.

Initial approach: Letter
Copies of proposal: 1
Deadline(s): None
Board meeting date(s): Mar., June, Sept., and Dec.

Officers and Directors:* Duer McLanahan,* Pres.; Phyllis Brown,* Secy.; Christopher Moore,* Treas.; Paule R. Alexander; Richard Brown; Monte Gray; E. Eldred Hill; John Reddick; Keith Thomas.

Number of staff: 1 part-time support.

EIN: 131740466

Selected grants: The following grants were reported in 2005.

$30,000 to East Harlem Tutorial Program, New York, NY.

$30,000 to Hope Program, Brooklyn, NY.

$25,000 to Inwood House, New York, NY.

$25,000 to Lenox Hill Neighborhood House, New York, NY.

$25,000 to National Medical Fellowships, New York, NY.

$20,000 to Getting Out and Staying Out, New York, NY.

$20,000 to Mosholu Preservation Corporation, Bronx, NY.

$20,000 to Washington Irving High School, New York, NY.

$15,000 to Project Reach Youth, Brooklyn, NY.

$15,000 to Student Sponsor Partners, New York, NY.

6424

Lawrence and Dana Linden Family Foundation ✧

c/o Marcum & Kliegman LLP
655 3rd Ave., 16th Fl.
New York, NY 10017

Established in 1993 in NY.

Donors: Lawrence H. Linden; Goldman Sachs & Co.

Foundation type: Independent foundation.

Financial data (yr. ended 2/28/05): Assets, $37,545,027 (M); expenditures, $1,608,179; qualifying distributions, $1,366,150; giving activities include $1,365,400 for 46 grants (high: $470,000; low: $100).

Purpose and activities: Giving primarily for environmental conservation and wildlife preservation, education, and to Jewish organizations.

Fields of interest: Arts; Higher education; Graduate/professional education; Environment, natural resources; Animals/wildlife, preservation/protection; Health care; Human services; Jewish federated giving programs; Jewish agencies & temples.

Limitations: Applications not accepted. Giving primarily in NY; some funding nationally with emphasis on Washington, DC, and MA. No grants, or scholarships, gifts, or for loans to individuals.

Application information: Contributes only to pre-selected organizations.

Trustees: Dana Wechsler Linden; Lawrence H. Linden.

EIN: 133748063

Selected grants: The following grants were reported in 2005.

$470,000 to Massachusetts Institute of Technology, Cambridge, MA.

$273,500 to World Wildlife Fund, DC. 2 grants: $250,000, $23,500

$150,000 to Resources for the Future, DC.

$100,000 to Columbia University, New York, NY.

$80,000 to Congregation Rodeph Sholom, New York, NY.

$50,000 to Wildlife Conservation Society, Bronx, NY.

$25,000 to World Resources Institute, DC.

$10,000 to Yale University, New Haven, CT.

$5,000 to Environmental Defense, New York, NY.

6425

The Lindmor Foundation ✧ ☆

(formerly The Reimers Family Foundation)
c/o BCRS Group/Marcum & Kliegman, LLP
100 Wall St., 11th Fl.
New York, NY 10005

Established in 1991 in NJ.

Donor: Arthur J. Reimers III.

Foundation type: Independent foundation.

Financial data (yr. ended 12/31/05): Assets, $28,779,114 (M); gifts received, $5,082,353; expenditures, $1,348,444; qualifying distributions, $893,867; giving activities include $893,867 for grants.

Purpose and activities: Giving primarily for education, health associations, and Christian churches; funding also for the arts, social services, and federated giving programs.

Fields of interest: Performing arts; Arts; Higher education; Education; Health care; Health organizations, association; Human services; Federated giving programs; Christian agencies & churches.

Type of support: General/operating support.

Limitations: Applications not accepted. Giving primarily in Greenwich, CT, and New York, NY. No grants to individuals.

Application information: Contributes only to pre-selected organizations.

Trustees: Arthur J. Reimers III; Lindsay Reimers.

EIN: 133636205

Selected grants: The following grants were reported in 2003.

$260,000 to Boys and Girls Club of Greenwich, Greenwich, CT. 2 grants: $250,000 (For general support), $10,000 (For general support).

$75,000 to YWCA of Greenwich, Greenwich, CT. For general support.

$65,000 to Audubon Society of Greenwich, Greenwich, CT. For general support.

$50,000 to Stanwich Congregational Church, Greenwich, CT. For general support.

$45,000 to Greenwich Country Day School, Greenwich, CT. For general support.

$30,000 to Trinity Church, Greenwich, CT. For general support.

$10,000 to University of Miami, Coral Gables, FL. For general support.

$5,000 to Family Centers, Greenwich, CT. For general support.

$1,000 to American Ballet Theater, New York, NY. For general support.

6426

The Fay J. Lindner Foundation ✧

1161 Meadowbrook Rd.
North Merrick, NY 11566

Established in 1966.

Donor: Fay J. Lindner‡.

Foundation type: Independent foundation.

Financial data (yr. ended 8/31/05): Assets, $26,832,707 (M); expenditures, $1,368,481; qualifying distributions, $1,310,427; giving activities include $1,259,739 for 77 grants (high: $200,000; low: $400).

Purpose and activities: Giving primarily for hospitals, child welfare, the elderly, nursing homes, and social services; grants also to a university and Jewish organizations, including a welfare fund.

Fields of interest: Performing arts; Hospitals (general); Nursing home/convalescent facility; Health care; Health organizations, association; Human services; Children/youth, services; Residential/custodial care, hospices; Aging, centers/services; Developmentally disabled, centers & services; Jewish agencies & temples; Aging; Disabilities, people with.

Type of support: Building/renovation; Program development; Seed money; Fellowships; Program-related investments/loans.

Limitations: Applications not accepted. Giving primarily on Long Island, NY. No grants to individuals.

Application information: Contributes only to pre-selected organizations.

Officers and Directors:* Robert M. Goldberg,* Pres.; Norman A. Schefer, V.P. and Secy.-Treas.; Robin Goldberg,* Secy.; David S. Goldberg.

Board Member: Norman Gross.

EIN: 116043320

Selected grants: The following grants were reported in 2005.

$200,000 to Parker Jewish Institute for Health Care and Rehabilitation Foundation, New Hyde Park, NY.

$115,000 to Gurwin Jewish Geriatric Foundation, Commack, NY.

$50,000 to Hospice Care Network, Woodbury, NY.

$50,000 to Peninsula Counseling Center, Woodmere, NY.

$43,730 to Salvation Army of Greater New York, New York, NY.

$40,100 to Hagedorn Little Village School, Seaford, NY.

$21,865 to American Cancer Society, Atlanta, GA.

$10,750 to Institute for Student Achievement, Lake Success, NY.

$5,000 to Pride of Judea Mental Health Center, Douglaston, NY.

$3,000 to Rosary Hill Home, Hawthorne, NY.

6427

Robert and Teresa Lindsay Family Foundation ✧

630 5th Ave., 30th Fl.
New York, NY 10111   (212) 708-9237

Established in 1997 in NY.

Donor: Robert D. Lindsay.

Foundation type: Independent foundation.

Financial data (yr. ended 9/30/05): Assets, $1,341,646 (M); gifts received, $2,380,566; expenditures, $2,289,383; qualifying distributions, $2,285,188; giving activities include $2,285,188 for 39 grants (high: $805,250; low: $50).

Purpose and activities: Giving primarily for education; funding also for social services.

Fields of interest: Higher education; Business school/education; Education; Health care; Human services; Community development; Federated giving programs.

Limitations: Giving on a national basis, with emphasis on CA and NY. No grants to individuals.
Application information:
  Initial approach: Letter or telephone
  Deadline(s): None
Trustees: Robert D. Lindsay; Teresa Lindsay.
EIN: 137142605
Selected grants: The following grants were reported in 2005.
$805,250 to Saint Pauls School, Concord, NH.
$360,000 to Cold Spring Harbor Laboratory Association, Cold Spring Harbor, NY.
$337,500 to East Woods School, Oyster Bay, NY.
$250,000 to Wildlife Conservation Society, Bronx, NY.
$200,000 to Harvard University, Cambridge, MA.
$5,000 to A Better Chance, New York, NY.
$5,000 to Epiphany School, Dorchester, MA.
$1,345 to Trout Unlimited, Arlington, VA.

6428
The Link Foundation ✧
c/o Binghamton University Fdn.
P.O. Box 6005
Binghamton, NY 13902-6005
Contact: Cheryl Dimick
URL: http://www.linkfoundation.org

Established in 1953 in NY.
Donors: Edwin A. Link†; Mrs. Edwin A. Link†; Lawrence Clayton; Link Div. of CAE.
Foundation type: Independent foundation.
Financial data (yr. ended 6/30/05): Assets, $10,772,261 (M); gifts received, $18,075; expenditures, $581,539; qualifying distributions, $535,886; giving activities include $497,800 for 10 grants (high: $162,300; low: $9,000), and $18,500 for 14 employee matching gifts.
Purpose and activities: The foundation supports programs to foster the theoretical basis, practical knowledge, and application of energy, simulation, and ocean engineering and instrumentation research, and to disseminate the results of that research through lectures, seminars and publications.
Fields of interest: Environment, energy; Marine science; Space/aviation; Engineering/technology.
Type of support: Continuing support; Fellowships; Research.
Limitations: Giving primarily in FL and NY. No grants to individuals (except through programs).
Application information: Unsolicited requests for funds not accepted. For specific program guidelines, see foundation Web site.
  Board meeting date(s): Feb. and June
Officers and Trustees:* David M. Gouldin,* Chair.; Thomas F. Kelly,* Secy.; Douglas R. Johnson, Treas.; Andrew Clark; Jon Forbes.
Special Advisors: Frank Cardullo; Ronald N. Hendricks; Barry Kelly; Marilyn Link; Lee Lynd; Stuart McCarty; Richard Murray; Robert Sproull; Brian J. Thompson; William D. Turner.
Number of staff: 1 part-time professional.
EIN: 536011109
Selected grants: The following grants were reported in 2004.
$169,000 to Dartmouth College, Hanover, NH.
$112,000 to University of Central Florida Foundation, Orlando, FL.
$93,000 to Florida Institute of Technology, Melbourne, FL. 2 grants: $8,000, $85,000
$15,000 to Embry-Riddle Aeronautical University, Daytona Beach, FL.

$15,000 to Indian River Community College, Fort Pierce, FL.
$9,700 to University of Rochester, Rochester, NY.
$3,000 to United Way of Volusia-Flagler Counties, Daytona Beach, FL.
$1,750 to State University of New York at Binghamton Foundation, Binghamton, NY.
$1,250 to Broome County Council of Churches, Binghamton, NY.

6429
George Link, Jr. Foundation, Inc. ✧
c/o The Bank of New York
1290 Ave. of The Americas, 5th Fl.
New York, NY 10104
Contact: Michael J. Catanzaro, V.P.

Incorporated in 1980 in NY.
Donor: George Link, Jr.†.
Foundation type: Independent foundation.
Financial data (yr. ended 12/31/05): Assets, $32,943,976 (M); expenditures, $1,578,869; qualifying distributions, $1,358,371; giving activities include $1,337,373 for 116 grants (high: $125,000; low: $1,000; average: $1,000–$25,000).
Purpose and activities: Giving primarily for hospitals and medical research, higher and secondary education, welfare, culture and fine arts, and Christian religious giving.
Fields of interest: Visual arts; Performing arts; Arts; Secondary school/education; Higher education; Hospitals (general); Medical research, institute; Human services; Christian agencies & churches.
Type of support: Building/renovation; Endowments; Fellowships; Scholarship funds.
Limitations: Giving primarily in MA, NJ, and NY. No grants to individuals, or for general support, operating budgets, continuing support, annual campaigns, seed money, emergency funds, deficit financing, equipment, land acquisition, renovation projects, or matching gifts; no loans.
Application information: Application form not required.
  Initial approach: Proposal
  Copies of proposal: 5
  Deadline(s): None
  Board meeting date(s): Monthly except July and Aug.
  Final notification: 6 weeks
Officers and Directors:* Newton P.S. Merrill,* Chair.; Robert Emmet Link,* Vice-Chair.; Michael J. Catanzaro, V.P.; Bernard F. Joyce, V.P.; Kevin J. Bannon, Secy.-Treas.
EIN: 133041396
Selected grants: The following grants were reported in 2004.
$125,000 to Museum of Modern Art, New York, NY.
$41,666 to New York City Partnership Foundation, New York, NY.
$30,000 to Gerald J. Ryan Outreach Center, Wyandanch, NY.
$30,000 to Wells College, Aurora, NY.
$25,000 to RENEW International, Plainfield, NJ.
$25,000 to Saint Vincents Medical Center, Bridgeport, CT.
$20,000 to Carmelite Monastery, Beacon, NY.
$10,000 to Cooke Center for Learning and Development, New York, NY.
$10,000 to Sanctuary for Families, New York, NY.
$8,700 to Battery Conservancy, New York, NY.

6430
Jacques and Yulla Lipchitz Foundation, Inc. ✧ ☆
369 Lexington Ave.
New York, NY 10017
Contact: Hanno D. Mott, Pres. and Treas.

Established in 1962.
Donor: Yulla Lipchitz†.
Foundation type: Independent foundation.
Financial data (yr. ended 2/28/06): Assets, $1,787,414 (M); gifts received, $125,000; expenditures, $553,827; qualifying distributions, $527,500; giving activities include $527,500 for 4 grants (high: $486,000; low: $8,500), and $26,327 for foundation-administered programs.
Purpose and activities: Giving only for the display works of art by Jacques Lipchitz to various museums.
Fields of interest: Visual arts; Museums.
Limitations: Giving on a national and international basis, particularly in New York, NY, and Valencia, Spain. No grants to individuals, or for the disposition of gifted works.
Application information:
  Initial approach: Letter on organization letterhead indicating interest in obtaining Lipchitz plaster sculptures for permanent display
  Deadline(s): None
Officers: Hanno D. Mott, Pres. and Treas.; Lolya Lipchitz, V.P.
EIN: 136151503

6431
Margaret & Richard Lipmanson Foundation, Inc. ✧
c/o Miller, Ellin & Co., LLP
750 Lexington Ave., 23rd Fl.
New York, NY 10022-1200

Established in 1986 in DE.
Donors: Gerard G. Leeds; Liselotte J. Leeds.
Foundation type: Independent foundation.
Financial data (yr. ended 6/30/05): Assets, $22,398,202 (M); expenditures, $3,792,638; qualifying distributions, $3,729,308; giving activities include $3,689,500 for 11 grants (high: $1,400,000; low: $500).
Purpose and activities: Giving primarily for educational institutions and programs.
Fields of interest: Higher education; Teacher school/education; Education; Legal services; Human services; Civil rights, advocacy; Jewish agencies & temples.
Limitations: Applications not accepted. Giving primarily in Washington, DC and NY. No grants to individuals.
Application information: Contributes only to pre-selected organizations.
Officers: Gerard G. Leeds, Chair.; Greg Jobin-Leeds, Pres. and Secy.; Liselotte J. Leeds, V.P. and Treas.
EIN: 112856656
Selected grants: The following grants were reported in 2005.
$1,600,000 to Institute for Student Achievement, Lake Success, NY.
$1,050,000 to Tides Foundation, San Francisco, CA.
$750,000 to Alliance for Excellent Education, DC.
$100,000 to Institute for Healthcare Improvement, Cambridge, MA.
$7,500 to AAUW Legal Advocacy Fund, DC.

$500 to Leo Baeck Institute, New York, NY.

6432

The Bari Lipp Foundation, Inc. ✧
P.O. Box 15014
Albany, NY 12212-5073
Contact: David Quinn

Established in 1996 in NY.
Donor: Robert I. Lipp.
Foundation type: Independent foundation.
Financial data (yr. ended 12/31/04): Assets, $38,204,849 (M); expenditures, $2,592,933; qualifying distributions, $2,321,801; giving activities include $2,321,801 for 74 grants (high: $1,200,000; low: $100).
Purpose and activities: Giving primarily for the arts, education, and health and human services.
Fields of interest: Media/communications; Performing arts centers; Performing arts, dance; Performing arts, ballet; Arts; Higher education; Health care; Human services; Children/youth, services; Federated giving programs; Jewish agencies & temples.
Limitations: Applications not accepted. Giving primarily in MA and NY, some funding nationally. No grants to individuals.
Application information: Contributes only to pre-selected organizations.
Directors: Jeffrey D. Lipp; Robert I. Lipp; Wendy A. Lipp.
EIN: 133921302

6433

The Lisabeth Foundation ✧
(formerly The Seldon Foundation)
54 Valley Rd.
Katonah, NY 10536
Contact: Lisa Joyce, Tr.

Established in 1999 in NY.
Donor: Daniel C. Benton.
Foundation type: Independent foundation.
Financial data (yr. ended 11/30/04): Assets, $19,393,756 (M); gifts received, $5,843,597; expenditures, $2,052,163; qualifying distributions, $2,026,877; giving activities include $2,024,077 for 20 grants (high: $800,000; low: $1,000).
Purpose and activities: Giving primarily for education, hospitals, and youth organizations.
Fields of interest: Higher education; Hospitals (general); Health organizations, association; Boys & girls clubs.
Limitations: Applications not accepted. Giving primarily in NY. No grants to individuals.
Application information: Contributes only to pre-selected organizations.
Trustees: Daniel C. Benton; Lisa Joyce; Kevin E. O'Brien.
EIN: 066486254
Selected grants: The following grants were reported in 2003.
$1,500,000 to Colgate University, Hamilton, NY.
$200,000 to Beginning with Children Foundation, New York, NY.
$100,000 to Kasparov Chess Foundation, Montville, NJ.
$100,000 to National Action Council for Minorities in Engineering (NACME), White Plains, NY.
$60,000 to Sadie Nash Leadership Project, Brooklyn, NY.

$25,000 to Hospital for Special Surgery, New York, NY.
$25,000 to League for the Hard of Hearing, New York, NY.
$11,000 to Make-A-Wish Foundation of the Hudson Valley, Tarrytown, NY.
$10,000 to State University of New York at Albany, Albany, NY. For Neil D. Levin Graduate Institute of International Relations and Commerce in New York City.

6434

The Lucius N. Littauer Foundation, Inc. ✧
60 E. 42nd St., Ste. 4600
New York, NY 10165
Contact: William Lee Frost, Pres.

Incorporated in 1929 in NY.
Donor: Lucius N. Littauer‡.
Foundation type: Independent foundation.
Financial data (yr. ended 12/31/05): Assets, $42,123,937 (M); gifts received, $3,038; expenditures, $2,996,197; qualifying distributions, $2,772,853; giving activities include $2,772,835 for 157 grants (high: $1,000,000; low: $100).
Purpose and activities: Grants for scholarly research on Jewish studies, for the endowment of Judaica book funds at university libraries, for medical ethics and palliative medical care, and NY public projects.
Fields of interest: Humanities; History/archaeology; Language/linguistics; Literature; Higher education; Environment; Medical care, bioethics; Social sciences; Political science; Jewish agencies & temples; Religion.
International interests: Israel.
Type of support: Endowments; Program development; Conferences/seminars; Publication; Seed money; Research; Employee matching gifts; Matching/challenge support.
Limitations: Giving primarily in NY for medical ethics, and environmental related projects. No support for synagogues. No grants to individuals, or for capital projects or operating funds.
Application information: Application form not required.
  Initial approach: Proposal
  Copies of proposal: 1
  Deadline(s): None
  Board meeting date(s): Annually and as required
  Final notification: 3 months
Officers and Directors:* William Lee Frost,* Pres. and Treas.; Henry A. Lowett,* V.P. and Secy.; Charles Berlin; Berthold Bilski; Mark A. Bilski; Robert D. Frost; George Harris; Noah Perlman; Peter J. Solomon.
Number of staff: 1 full-time professional; 1 part-time support.
EIN: 131688027

6435

The Litterman Family Foundation ✧
(formerly The Robert & Mary Litterman Foundation)
c/o Goldman Sachs & Co., Family Office
1 New York Plz., 40th Fl.
New York, NY 10004

Established in 1994 in NJ.
Donor: Robert Litterman.
Foundation type: Independent foundation.

Financial data (yr. ended 9/30/05): Assets, $11,404,009 (M); gifts received, $521,450; expenditures, $579,507; qualifying distributions, $544,500; giving activities include $544,500 for 54 grants (high: $105,000; low: $1,000).
Purpose and activities: Giving primarily to health associations, and for medical research; funding also for human services and federated giving programs.
Fields of interest: Arts; Education; Environment; Health organizations, association; Medical research, institute; Human services; Federated giving programs.
Type of support: General/operating support.
Limitations: Applications not accepted. Giving primarily in NJ and New York, NY; some funding nationally. No grants to individuals.
Application information: Contributes only to pre-selected organizations.
Trustees: Adam J. Litterman; Mary Litterman; Nadia K. Litterman; Robert Litterman.
EIN: 133805239
Selected grants: The following grants were reported in 2004.
$25,000 to Cora Hartshorn Arboretum and Bird Sanctuary, Short Hills, NJ. For general support.
$20,000 to College of New Jersey Foundation, Ewing, NJ. For general support.
$10,000 to Brain Trauma Foundation, New York, NY. For general support.
$10,000 to Healthcare Foundation for the Yampa Valley, Steamboat Springs, CO. For general support.
$10,000 to Multiple Sclerosis Society, National, Paramus, NJ. For general support.
$10,000 to Overlook Hospital Foundation, Summit, NJ. For general support.
$10,000 to United Negro College Fund, Fairfax, VA. For general support.
$10,000 to United Way of Millburn-Short Hills, Millburn, NJ. For general support.
$10,000 to University of Minnesota Foundation, Saint Paul, MN. For general support.
$5,000 to National Foundation for Facial Reconstruction, New York, NY. For general support.

6436

The Litwin Foundation, Inc. ✧
1200 Union Tpke.
New Hyde Park, NY 11040
Contact: Leonard Litwin, Pres.

Established in 1989 in NY.
Donor: Leonard Litwin.
Foundation type: Independent foundation.
Financial data (yr. ended 12/31/05): Assets, $59,819,425 (M); expenditures, $2,646,570; qualifying distributions, $2,540,200; giving activities include $2,540,200 for 125 grants (high: $1,000,000; low: $500; average: $5,000–$15,000).
Purpose and activities: Giving primarily for disease research organizations, children's services, human services, education, and the environment.
Fields of interest: Museums; Education; Environment, natural resources; Hospitals (general); Health organizations, association; Medical research, institute; Human services; Children/youth, services; Jewish agencies & temples; Aging; Disabilities, people with; Homeless.
Type of support: General/operating support; Research.

Limitations: Giving primarily in New York, NY. No grants to individuals.
Application information:
Initial approach: Letter
Deadline(s): None
Officers and Director: Leonard Litwin,* Pres.; Diane Miller, V.P.; Morton Sanders, Secy.; Carole Pittelman, Treas.
EIN: 133501980

6437
The Liu Foundation ◇
c/o Multicultural Radio Broadcasting, Inc.
449 Broadway
New York, NY 10013 (212) 966-1059
Contact: Yvonne Liu, Pres.

Established in 1997 in NY.
Donors: Arthur Liu; Yvonne Liu.
Foundation type: Independent foundation.
Financial data (yr. ended 12/31/05): Assets, $6,050,441 (M); expenditures, $410,098; qualifying distributions, $343,414; giving activities include $335,300 for 7 grants (high: $122,500; low: $6,000).
Fields of interest: Museums (science/technology); Higher education; Education; Big Brothers/Big Sisters.
Type of support: General/operating support.
Limitations: Giving primarily in New York, NY; funding also in Syracuse, NY. No grants to individuals.
Application information:
Initial approach: Letter
Deadline(s): None
Officers and Directors: Yvonne Liu,* Pres. and Treas.; Laura Parsons,* V.P.; Arthur Liu,* Secy.; Fred Teng; Whiting Wu.
EIN: 133945839

6438
Daniel S. Loeb - Third Point Foundation ◇
7 MacDougal Alley
New York, NY 10011
Contact: Daniel S. Loeb, Pres.

Established in 2000 in NY.
Donor: Daniel S. Loeb.
Foundation type: Independent foundation.
Financial data (yr. ended 12/31/05): Assets, $1,570,670 (M); gifts received, $2,566,000; expenditures, $1,943,141; qualifying distributions, $1,920,719; giving activities include $1,909,181 for 46 grants (high: $1,000,000; low: $60).
Fields of interest: Museums (art); Education; Human services; Children/youth, services.
Application information:
Initial approach: Letter
Deadline(s): None
Officers and Directors: Daniel S. Loeb,* Pres. and Treas.; John Josephson, Secy.; Ronald Loeb; Carter Pottash.
EIN: 522251371

6439
Arthur L. Loeb Foundation, Inc. ◇
c/o Loeb Partners Corp.
61 Broadway, Ste. 2400
New York, NY 10006

Established around 1977 in NY.
Donor: Arthur L. Loeb.
Foundation type: Independent foundation.
Financial data (yr. ended 11/30/04): Assets, $19,011,045 (M); expenditures, $1,810,159; qualifying distributions, $1,697,530; giving activities include $1,697,530 for 320 grants (high: $100,000; low: $150).
Purpose and activities: Giving for higher education, cultural institutes, Jewish organizations, social services, health services, and boys and girls clubs.
Fields of interest: Museums; Museums (art); Performing arts; Performing arts, theater; Performing arts, opera; Arts; Higher education; Hospitals (specialty); Reproductive health, family planning; Health organizations, association; Food distribution, meals on wheels; Boys & girls clubs; Human services; Community development, citizen coalitions; Community development, neighborhood associations.
Limitations: Applications not accepted. Giving primarily in New York, NY. No grants to individuals.
Application information: Contributes only to pre-selected organizations.
Officers: Arthur L. Loeb, Pres.; William L. Berhard, V.P.; Jerome Manning, Secy.-Treas.
EIN: 132933768

6440
John L. Loeb, Jr. Foundation ◇
c/o Barry M. Strauss Assocs., Ltd.
307 5th Ave., 8th Fl.
New York, NY 10016-6517

Established in 1964.
Donor: John L. Loeb, Jr.
Foundation type: Independent foundation.
Financial data (yr. ended 12/31/05): Assets, $17,612,852 (M); expenditures, $1,119,877; qualifying distributions, $1,060,340; giving activities include $972,453 for 81 grants (high: $160,840; low: $25).
Purpose and activities: Giving primarily for the arts, education, and Jewish organizations.
Fields of interest: Arts; Education; Environment; Health organizations, association; Human services; International affairs, U.N.; International affairs; Jewish federated giving programs; Jewish agencies & temples.
Limitations: Applications not accepted. Giving primarily in NY. No grants to individuals.
Application information: Contributes only to pre-selected organizations.
Officer: John L. Loeb, Jr., Pres.
EIN: 136142345

6441
Frederick Loewe Foundation, Inc. ◇
c/o Fitelson, Lasky, Aslan & Couture
551 5th Ave.
New York, NY 10176

Established in 1959 in NY.
Donor: Frederick Loewe†.
Foundation type: Independent foundation.
Financial data (yr. ended 11/30/04): Assets, $7,593,596 (M); expenditures, $532,503; qualifying distributions, $455,800; giving activities include $455,800 for 53 grants (high: $100,000; low: $1,000).

Purpose and activities: Giving primarily for the arts, particularly theater.
Fields of interest: Arts, association; Arts education; Performing arts; Performing arts, theater; Arts; Higher education; Jewish agencies & temples.
Limitations: Applications not accepted. Giving primarily in NY. No grants to individuals.
Application information: Contributes only to pre-selected organizations.
Officers: Floria V. Lasky, Pres.; Jerold L. Couture, V.P.; Robert A. Schlesinger, V.P.; Clifford Forster, Secy.; David S. Rhine, Treas.
EIN: 136111444

6442
Loewenberg Foundation, Inc. ◇
430 Park Ave., Ste. 1402
New York, NY 10022 (212) 753-4100
Contact: Diana Loewenberg, Pres.

Established in 1959 in NY.
Donors: Ralph E. Loewenberg; Kurt Loewenberg†.
Foundation type: Independent foundation.
Financial data (yr. ended 10/31/05): Assets, $18,100,387 (M); expenditures, $729,201; qualifying distributions, $494,250; giving activities include $493,500 for 4 grants (high: $400,000; low: $5,000).
Purpose and activities: Giving primarily for Jewish federated giving programs; funding also for an arts center.
Fields of interest: Arts; Higher education; Jewish federated giving programs.
Type of support: Research.
Limitations: Giving primarily in New York, NY, and TX. No grants to individuals.
Application information:
Initial approach: Letter
Deadline(s): None
Officers and Directors: Diana Loewenberg,* Pres. and Treas.; Jeffrey N. Grabel,* Secy.; Frederick Lubcher.
EIN: 136075586
Selected grants: The following grants were reported in 2004.
$2,000,000 to P.E.F. Israel Endowment Funds, New York, NY. For general support.
$25,000 to Storm King Art Center, Mountainville, NY. For general support.
$7,500 to Leo Baeck Institute, New York, NY. For general support.
$5,000 to Childrens Blood Foundation, New York, NY. For general support.
$1,000 to Central Park Conservancy, New York, NY. For general support.
$500 to Metropolitan Museum of Art, New York, NY. For general support.

6443
Loews Foundation ◇
c/o John J. Kenny
655 Madison Ave.
New York, NY 10021-8043 (212) 521-2650
Contact: Candace Leeds, V.P., Public Affairs

Trust established in 1957 in NY.
Donor: Loews Corp.
Foundation type: Company-sponsored foundation.
Financial data (yr. ended 12/31/03): Assets, $106,265 (M); expenditures, $842,733; qualifying distributions, $842,198; giving activities include

$786,138 for 69 grants (high: $75,000; low: $250), and $55,060 for employee matching gifts.
Purpose and activities: The foundation supports Jewish agencies and temples and organizations involved with arts and culture, higher education, youth development, and human services.
Fields of interest: Arts; Higher education; Youth development; Human services; Jewish federated giving programs; Jewish agencies & temples.
Type of support: Employee matching gifts; Employee-related scholarships.
Application information: Application form not required.
> *Initial approach:* Telephone or proposal
> *Deadline(s):* None
> *Board meeting date(s):* As required
Trustees: Peter W. Keegan; John J. Kenny; Andrew Tisch; Preston R. Tisch.
EIN: 136082817

6444
Loewy Family Foundation, Inc. ✧
80 Wall St., No. 1018
New York, NY 10005-3601
Contact: John P. Reiner, Treas.

Established in 1966 in NY.
Donors: Alfred Loewy†; Edna Loewy Butler†.
Foundation type: Independent foundation.
Financial data (yr. ended 6/30/05): Assets, $9,624,868 (M); expenditures, $522,906; qualifying distributions, $439,939; giving activities include $430,000 for 6 grants (high: $150,000; low: $15,000).
Purpose and activities: Giving primarily for education.
Fields of interest: Arts; Elementary/secondary education; Higher education.
Limitations: Giving on a national basis. No grants to individuals.
Application information: Application form not required.
> *Initial approach:* Proposal
> *Copies of proposal:* 1
> *Deadline(s):* None
Officers and Directors:* Brigitte Linz,* Chair. and Pres.; Michael Green,* V.P.; Erik A. Hanson,* V.P.; Peter Erwin Linz,* V.P.; Mischa A. Zabotin,* V.P.; John P. Reiner,* Treas.
EIN: 136225288
Selected grants: The following grants were reported in 2004.
$200,000 to Columbia University, New York, NY. For advancement of transplant medicine.
$75,000 to Trinity School, New York, NY. For Tercentennial History Project.
$50,000 to Georgetown University, DC. For lectureship program in science, technology, and international.
$50,000 to San Diego Blood Bank Foundation, San Diego, CA. For research on blood disorders.
$35,000 to Lehigh University, Bethlehem, PA. For graduate fellowship assistance.
$18,000 to Catching the Dream, Albuquerque, NM. For scholarship assistance.
$15,000 to Association for Development of Dramatic Arts, New York, NY. For student matinee series.

6445
The Lookout Fund, Inc. ✧
c/o Meyer Handelman Co.
P.O. Box 817
Purchase, NY 10577-0817

Established in 1966 in NY.
Donors: Fowler Merle-Smith; Annette C. Merle-Smith.
Foundation type: Independent foundation.
Financial data (yr. ended 12/31/05): Assets, $1,463,667 (M); expenditures, $340,343; qualifying distributions, $328,850; giving activities include $328,500 for 7 grants (high: $325,000; low: $500).
Purpose and activities: Giving primarily to a medical research institute in San Diego, CA; funding also for health care and conservation.
Fields of interest: Environment; Health care; Medical research, institute.
Limitations: Applications not accepted. Giving primarily in Elizabethtown and Keene Valley, NY; some funding also in San Diego, CA, and NJ. No grants to individuals.
Application information: Contributes only to pre-selected organizations.
Officers: Annette C. Merle-Smith, Pres.; William R. Handelman, V.P. and Treas.; Margaret F. Bergstrand, V.P.; Donald E. Handelman, V.P.; Russell J. Handelman, Secy.
EIN: 136213665

6446
The Lopatin Family Foundation ✧ ☆
c/o BCRS Assocs., LLP
100 Wall St., 11th Fl.
New York, NY 10005

Established in 1994 in NY.
Donor: Jonathan M. Lopatin.
Foundation type: Independent foundation.
Financial data (yr. ended 8/31/05): Assets, $15,048,776 (M); gifts received, $3,713,314; expenditures, $607,552; qualifying distributions, $463,975; giving activities include $460,510 for 39 grants (high: $250,000; low: $250).
Purpose and activities: Giving primarily for Jewish organizations.
Fields of interest: Theological school/education; Education; Mental health, association; Human services; Jewish federated giving programs; Jewish agencies & temples.
Limitations: Applications not accepted. Giving on a national basis, with emphasis on the greater metropolitan New York, NY, area. No grants to individuals, or for scholarships; no loans.
Application information: Contributes only to pre-selected organizations.
Trustee: Jonathan M. Lopatin.
EIN: 133797381

6447
The Lucille Lortel Foundation, Inc.
322 8th Ave., 21st Fl.
New York, NY 10001
Contact: Jeffrey Shubart, Prog. Coord.
FAX: (212) 989-0036; E-mail: jshubart@lortel.org;
URL: http://www.lortel.org

Established in 1980 in NY.
Donor: Lucille Lortel Schweitzer†.

Foundation type: Independent foundation.
Financial data (yr. ended 6/30/05): Assets, $32,504,651 (M); expenditures, $1,932,976; qualifying distributions, $1,735,206; giving activities include $1,075,900 for 64 grants (high: $399,900; low: $2,500), and $4,665 for foundation-administered programs.
Purpose and activities: Giving primarily to not-for-profit theater companies and organizations in New York, NY.
Fields of interest: Performing arts, theater; Arts.
Type of support: Fellowships; General/operating support; Continuing support.
Limitations: Giving primarily in New York, NY. No grants to individuals.
Application information: Applications sent by fax or e-mail are not accepted. Application guidelines and form are available on foundation Web site. Application form not required.
> *Initial approach:* Letter
> *Copies of proposal:* 2
> *Deadline(s):* See Web site for current deadlines
Officers and Directors:* James J. Ross,* Pres.; George Shaskan,* V.P.; Richard M. Ticktin,* Secy.; Michael Hecht,* Treas.; George Forbes, Exec. Dir.
Number of staff: 3 full-time professional; 1 part-time support.
EIN: 133036521
Selected grants: The following grants were reported in 2005.
$25,000 to Atlantic Theater Company, New York, NY.
$25,000 to Signature Theater Company, New York, NY.
$25,000 to Vera Institute of Justice, New York, NY.
$25,000 to Vineyard Theater and Workshop Center, New York, NY.
$20,000 to CSC Repertory, New York, NY.
$15,000 to New Group, New York, NY.
$12,500 to Flea Theater, New York, NY.
$12,500 to LAByrinth, Inc., New York, NY.
$12,500 to Mint Theater Company, New York, NY.
$5,000 to Epic Theater Center, New York, NY.

6448
Lostand Foundation, Inc. ✧
c/o Jonathan F.P. Rose
33 Katonah Ave.
Katonah, NY 10536

Established in 1997 in NY.
Donors: Jonathan F.P. Rose; Sandra Rose.
Foundation type: Independent foundation.
Financial data (yr. ended 10/31/05): Assets, $8,602,358 (M); gifts received, $1,355,000; expenditures, $719,394; qualifying distributions, $369,835; giving activities include $351,374 for 48 grants (high: $50,000; low: $500).
Purpose and activities: Giving primarily for the arts, education, and Jewish organizations.
Fields of interest: Performing arts; Performing arts, music; Arts; Higher education; Education; Environment, natural resources; Family services, domestic violence; Jewish federated giving programs; Jewish agencies & temples; Religion.
Limitations: Applications not accepted. Giving primarily in Brooklyn, NY. No grants to individuals.
Application information: Contributes only to pre-selected organizations.
Officers: Jonathan F.P. Rose, Pres.; Diana C. Rose, V.P.; Michael Sullivan, Treas.
Director: Charles L. Mandelstam.
EIN: 133945705

Selected grants: The following grants were reported in 2005.
$50,000 to Mind and Life Institute, Louisville, CO.
$49,440 to Jewel Heart Cho-Tsok Temple.
$30,000 to Jazz at Lincoln Center, New York, NY.
$26,000 to Brooklyn Academy of Music, Brooklyn, NY.
$24,000 to Greyston Foundation, Yonkers, NY.
$5,350 to Drawing Center, New York, NY.
$5,000 to Audubon Society, National, New York, NY.
$4,500 to Lincoln Center for the Performing Arts, New York, NY.
$2,200 to Friends of Hudson, Hudson, NY.
$2,000 to Scenic Hudson, Poughkeepsie, NY.

6449
Leon Lowenstein Foundation, Inc. ▼
126 E. 56th St., 28th Fl.
New York, NY 10022   (212) 319-0670
Contact: John Van Gorder, Exec. Dir.

Incorporated in 1941 in NY.
Donor: Leon Lowenstein†.
Foundation type: Independent foundation.
Financial data (yr. ended 12/31/05): Assets, $141,809,143 (M); expenditures, $7,359,629; qualifying distributions, $6,611,578; giving activities include $5,872,750 for 175 grants (high: $750,000; low: $100; average: $5,000–$50,000).
Purpose and activities: Support primarily for New York City public education and medical research, with emphasis on child and adolescent psychiatry, and Parkinson's Disease.
Fields of interest: Elementary school/education; Secondary school/education; Education; Medical research.
Type of support: General/operating support; Program development; Seed money; Research.
Limitations: Giving primarily in the metropolitan New York, NY, area. No support for international organizations. No grants to individuals.
Application information: Application form not required.
Initial approach: Letter
Copies of proposal: 1
Deadline(s): None
Board meeting date(s): Twice per year
Final notification: 3 months
Officers and Directors:* Robert Bendheim,* Pres.; John M. Bendheim,* V.P.; Bernard R. Rapoport, Secy.-Treas.; John Van Gorder, Exec. Dir.; Andrew Bendheim; John M. Bendheim, Jr.; Kim Bendheim; Thomas L. Bendheim; Joanna Schulman; Lynn B. Thoman; Thomas H. Wright.
Number of staff: 2 full-time professional.
EIN: 136015951
Selected grants: The following grants were reported in 2005.
$1,000,000 to University of Pennsylvania, Philadelphia, PA. 2 grants: $500,000 each (For Loan Forgiveness Fund).
$750,000 to Columbia University, New York, NY.
$700,000 to Memorial Sloan-Kettering Cancer Center, New York, NY. 2 grants: $200,000 (For Prostate Cancer Research), $500,000.
$500,000 to New York Eye and Ear Infirmary, New York, NY. For Retina Center.
$350,000 to Mount Sinai School of Medicine of New York University, New York, NY. For Robert and John M. Bendheim Parkinson's Disease Center.
$250,000 to North Shore-Long Island Jewish Health System Foundation, Great Neck, NY. For Schneider Children's Hospital.

$250,000 to Princeton University, Princeton, NJ. For Bendheim Center for Finance.
$25,000 to Classroom, Inc., New York, NY. For completion of What's Up Magazine.

6450
M. & E. Lowinger Foundation ✧
105 Madison Ave.
New York, NY 10016
Contact: Edith Lowinger, Tr.

Established in 2001 in NY.
Donors: Andrew Lowinger; Edith Lowinger; Ronald Lowinger.
Foundation type: Independent foundation.
Financial data (yr. ended 12/31/04): Assets, $86,381 (M); expenditures, $1,734,585; qualifying distributions, $1,734,164; giving activities include $1,734,164 for 38 grants (high: $900,000; low: $1,000).
Purpose and activities: Giving primarily for Jewish agencies, temples, and yeshivas.
Fields of interest: Elementary/secondary education; Family services; Jewish agencies & temples.
Limitations: Giving primarily in NY. No grants to individuals.
Application information:
Initial approach: Letter
Deadline(s): None
Trustees: Andrew Lowinger; Edith Lowinger; Ronald Lowinger.
EIN: 134043481

6451
LSR Fund ▼ ✧
c/o The Rockefeller Trust Co.
30 Rockefeller Plz., Rm. 5600
New York, NY 10112
Contact: Mary Haldi

Established in 1994 in NY.
Donor: Laurance S. Rockefeller†.
Foundation type: Independent foundation.
Financial data (yr. ended 12/31/04): Assets, $19,089,494 (M); expenditures, $4,123,199; qualifying distributions, $4,091,520; giving activities include $4,044,377 for 51 grants (high: $500,000; low: $1,000; average: $10,000–$250,000).
Purpose and activities: Giving primarily for environmental support, health care, and historic preservation.
Fields of interest: Historic preservation/historical societies; Environment; Health care.
Limitations: Applications not accepted. Giving on a national basis. No grants to individuals.
Application information: Contributes only to pre-selected organizations.
Trustees: Clayton W. Frye, Jr.; Donal C. O'Brien, Jr.; Ellen R.C. Pomeroy; James S. Sligar.
Number of staff: 1 part-time support.
EIN: 137039108
Selected grants: The following grants were reported in 2004.
$1,386,221 to Memorial Sloan-Kettering Cancer Center, New York, NY. 3 grants: $500,000, $386,221, $500,000
$500,000 to Blanchette Rockefeller Neurosciences Institute, Morgantown, WV.

$500,000 to Samueli Institute for Information Biology, Alexandria, VA. 2 grants: $250,000 each
$250,000 to Philanthropic Collaborative, New York, NY.
$250,000 to Rockefeller Philanthropy Advisors, Philanthropic Collaborative, New York, NY.
$50,000 to Americans for Our Heritage and Recreation, DC.
$15,000 to Natural Resources Council of America, DC.

6452
Theodore Luce Charitable Trust
c/o JPMorgan Chase Bank, N.A., Philanthropic Svcs.
345 Park Ave., 4th Fl.
New York, NY 10154   (212) 464-2467
Contact: Lisa Philp, V.P. & Tr. Off.. JPMorgan Chase Bank, N.A.
FAX: (212) 464-2305;
E-mail: philp_lisa@JPMorgan.com; URL: http://foundationcenter.org/grantmaker/luce/

Established in 1940's in NY.
Foundation type: Independent foundation.
Financial data (yr. ended 7/31/05): Assets, $13,070,451 (M); expenditures, $621,248; qualifying distributions, $513,174; giving activities include $500,000 for 23 grants (high: $25,000; low: $15,000).
Purpose and activities: The trust supports comprehensive youth development organizations in New York City.
Fields of interest: Youth development.
Type of support: Income development; Management development/capacity building; Program development; Program evaluation.
Limitations: Giving limited to New York, NY. No support for organizations lacking 501(c)(3) status. No grants to individuals, or for matching gifts; no loans.
Publications: Grants list.
Application information: Contributes only to pre-selected organizations. Grants made during the annual cycle in the summer. An open grant cycle will not occur until 2008.
Board meeting date(s): July
Trustee: JPMorgan Chase Bank, N.A.
EIN: 136029703
Selected grants: The following grants were reported in 2005.
$25,000 to Church Avenue Merchants Block Association (CAMBA), Brooklyn, NY. For conducting program evaluation.
$25,000 to Coalition for Hispanic Family Services, Brooklyn, NY. For expanding Arts and Literacy program.
$25,000 to DreamYard Drama Project, New York, NY.
$20,000 to StreetSquash, New York, NY. For expanding College Prep program.

6453
The Henry Luce Foundation, Inc. ▼ ✧
111 W. 50th St., Ste. 4601
New York, NY 10020   (212) 489-7700
Contact: Michael Gilligan, Pres.
FAX: (212) 581-9541; E-mail: hlf@hluce.org;
URL: http://www.hluce.org

Incorporated in 1936 in NY.
Donors: Henry R. Luce†; Clare Boothe Luce†.

Foundation type: Independent foundation.
Financial data (yr. ended 12/31/05): Assets, $792,916,471 (M); expenditures, $43,909,166; qualifying distributions, $41,362,206; giving activities include $35,235,693 for grants, $398,536 for grants to individuals, and $320,060 for employee matching gifts.
Purpose and activities: Grants for specific projects in the broad areas of Asian affairs, American art, public policy and the environment, theology, advancement of women in science and engineering, and higher education. The Luce Scholars Program gives a select group of young Americans, not Asian specialists, a year's work experience in East and Southeast Asia. Asia grants support the creation of new scholarly and public resources on East and Southeast Asia as well as innovative cultural and intellectual exchange between the Asia-Pacific and the United States. The Henry R. Luce Professorship Program, which supports innovative programs at private colleges and universities, no longer accepts proposals for new grants. The Clare Boothe Luce Program is designed to enhance the careers of women in science and engineering through scholarships, fellowships, and professorships at invited institutions. Funding in the arts focuses on research, scholarship and exhibitions in American art; direct support for specific projects at major museums and service organizations; dissertation support for topics in American art history through the American Council of Learned Societies. Theology grants are made primarily to seminaries and divinity schools for educational purposes. The Henry Luce III Theology Fellows Program is administered through the Association of Theological Schools. Public Policy and the Environment grants are made to support the study of critical issues and environmental training and research.
Fields of interest: Visual arts; Museums; Humanities; Theology; Higher education; Theological school/education; Environment; Engineering/technology; Social sciences; International studies; Public policy, research.
International interests: Asia; China; Japan; Korea; Mongolia; Southeast Asia.
Type of support: Grants to individuals; Program development; Professorships; Fellowships; Internship funds; Scholarship funds; Employee matching gifts; Matching/challenge support.
Limitations: Giving on a national and international basis; international activities limited to East and Southeast Asia. No support for journalism, medical or media projects. No grants to individuals (except for specially designated programs), or for endowments, domestic building campaigns, general operating support, annual fund drives; no loans.
Publications: Biennial report (including application guidelines); Grants list; Informational brochure; Newsletter.
Application information: Nominees for Luce Scholars Program accepted from invited institutions only; Clare Boothe Luce Program by invitation to institutions only, individual applications cannot be considered; American Art Program requires prior inquiry by Mar.1. Application form not required.
Initial approach: Letter
Copies of proposal: 1
Deadline(s): June 15, for American Art; 1st Mon. in Dec. for Luce Scholars nominations; all others, no specific deadlines
Board meeting date(s): Mar., June, Oct., and Dec.
Officers and Directors:* Margaret Boles Fitzgerald,* Chair.; Michael Gilligan,* Pres.; Terrill E. Lautz, V.P., Secy., and Prog. Dir., Asia and Higher

Ed.; John C. Evans,* V.P. and Treas.; John P. Daley, V.P., Finance and Admin.; Helene E. Redell, V.P. and Prog. Dir., Luce Scholars; Robert E. Armstrong; Anne d'Harnoncourt; Claire L. Gaudiani; Kenneth T. Jackson; James T. Laney; Thomas L. Pulling; David V. Ragone.
Number of staff: 11 full-time professional; 9 full-time support.
EIN: 136001282

6454
Lucerne Foundation ✧
(formerly SLEN Foundation)
519 8th Ave.
New York, NY 10018
Contact: Robert Rimsky, Tr.

Established in 1985 in NY.
Donors: Robert Rimsky; DLD Assocs.
Foundation type: Independent foundation.
Financial data (yr. ended 9/30/05): Assets, $5,340,939 (M); gifts received, $142,354; expenditures, $1,154,049; qualifying distributions, $1,151,127; giving activities include $1,150,818 for 26 grants (high: $1,000,000; low: $36).
Purpose and activities: Giving primarily for social services and to Jewish agencies, temples, and federated giving programs.
Fields of interest: Arts; Health care; Health organizations, association; Cancer, leukemia; Human services; Jewish federated giving programs; Jewish agencies & temples.
Limitations: Applications not accepted. Giving primarily in NY. No grants to individuals.
Application information: Contributes to pre-selected organizations.
Trustee: Robert Rimsky.
EIN: 133316334
Selected grants: The following grants were reported in 2005.
$25,000 to Lets Get Ready, New York, NY.
$25,000 to United Jewish Appeal, New York, NY.
$500 to Gesher Foundation, New York, NY.
$500 to Stony Brook Foundation, Stony Brook, NY.

6455
The Luckow Family Foundation, Inc. ✧
c/o Jeff Reynolds, IAT, RE
48 Wall St., 30th Fl.
New York, NY 10005

Established in 1996 in NJ.
Donors: Robert Luckow; The Robert W. Luckow Corp.; Education for Youth Society.
Foundation type: Independent foundation.
Financial data (yr. ended 9/30/05): Assets, $7,054,193 (M); gifts received, $2,099,000; expenditures, $1,989,558; qualifying distributions, $1,976,597; giving activities include $1,976,000 for 32 grants (high: $1,479,524; low: $100).
Purpose and activities: Giving primarily for hospitals; some giving also for health organizations and education.
Fields of interest: Education; Hospitals (general); Health organizations, association; Autism; Cancer research; Recreation, parks/playgrounds; Athletics/sports, Olympics; Christian agencies & churches.
International interests: New Zealand.
Limitations: Applications not accepted. Giving on a national basis. No grants to individuals.

Application information: Contributes only to pre-selected organizations.
Officers: Robert W. Luckow, Pres.; Audrey Luckow, Secy.-Treas.
EIN: 223479153
Selected grants: The following grants were reported in 2003.
$175,250 to Academy of Holy Angels, New Orleans, LA. 3 grants: $150,000, $250, $25,000
$26,250 to Adaptive Sports Foundation, Windham, NY. 2 grants: $25,000, $1,250
$10,000 to Monroe Education Foundation, Jamesburg, NJ.
$3,700 to Bergen Catholic High School, Oradell, NJ.
$1,000 to Clarke School for the Deaf, Northampton, MA.
$100 to University of Dayton, Dayton, OH.

6456
Lucky Star Foundation ✧
c/o Anchin Block & Anchin LLP
1375 Broadway
New York, NY 10018
Contact: Sonja Lepkowski

Established in 1993.
Donors: Judith O'Connor Gluckstern; Steven M. Gluckstern; One Heart, Inc.
Foundation type: Independent foundation.
Financial data (yr. ended 12/31/05): Assets, $799,769 (M); gifts received, $1,777,444; expenditures, $2,026,852; qualifying distributions, $2,016,852; giving activities include $2,015,852 for 40 grants (high: $552,500; low: $500).
Fields of interest: Performing arts; Education.
Limitations: Applications not accepted. Giving on a national basis. No grants to individuals.
Application information: Contributes only to pre-selected organizations.
Officers: Judith O'Connor Gluckstern, Pres.; Steven M. Gluckstern, V.P.; Steve Germaine, Secy.
EIN: 133710572

6457
Lui and Wan Foundation ✧
Murray Hill Station
P.O. Box 150
New York, NY 10156 (212) 689-4939
Contact: Francis C. Lui, Pres.

Established in 2001 in NY.
Donors: Francis C. Lui; Livia Wan Lui.
Foundation type: Independent foundation.
Financial data (yr. ended 2/28/06): Assets, $206,141 (M); gifts received, $949,222; expenditures, $1,009,409; qualifying distributions, $1,009,349; giving activities include $1,004,600 for 3 grants (high: $1,000,000; low: $1,600).
Fields of interest: Higher education.
Type of support: General/operating support.
Limitations: Giving primarily in VA.
Application information:
Initial approach: Proposal
Deadline(s): None
Officers and Directors:* Francis C. Lui,* Pres.; Lawrence Lui,* V.P.; Yvonne Lui,* Secy.; Livia Wan Lui,* Treas.; Deborah Chan.
EIN: 134161117

6458
Georges Lurcy Charitable and Educational Trust ✧
125 W. 55th St.
New York, NY 10019
Contact: Seth E. Frank, Tr.

Established in 1985 in NY.
Donor: Georges Lurcy‡.
Foundation type: Independent foundation.
Financial data (yr. ended 6/30/06): Assets, $30,189,415 (M); expenditures, $3,055,661; qualifying distributions, $2,858,403; giving activities include $2,665,500 for 75 grants (high: $600,000; low: $1,000; average: $5,000–$25,000).
Purpose and activities: Support primarily for education including fellowships for students of American colleges or universities to study in France, and students of French colleges or universities to study in the U.S.; some support for cultural organizations.
Fields of interest: Arts; Higher education.
International interests: France.
Type of support: Fellowships.
Limitations: Giving on a national basis.
Application information: Fellowship applicants from America must be recommended by their universities; applicants from France must apply to the Franco-American Commission for Educational Exchange. Applicants cannot apply directly to the foundation.
Trustees: Alan S. Bernstein; Daniel L. Bernstein; Georges Lurcy Bernstein; Seth E. Frank.
EIN: 136372044
Selected grants: The following grants were reported in 2004.
$82,000 to University of Chicago, Chicago, IL.
$58,000 to Amherst College, Amherst, MA.
$45,000 to Harvard University, Cambridge, MA.
$35,000 to Yale University, New Haven, CT.
$30,000 to New York University, New York, NY.
$26,000 to Lafayette College, Easton, PA.
$20,300 to Stanford University, Stanford, CA.
$20,000 to University of Michigan, Ann Arbor, MI.
$15,000 to Columbia University, New York, NY.
$15,000 to Georgetown University, DC.

6459
The Helen & Rita Lurie Foundation, Inc. ✧
c/o A. Lesk-Fried Frank
1 New York Plz.
New York, NY 10004

Established in NY.
Donors: Philip Morris Cos. Inc.; Helen Lurie‡.
Foundation type: Independent foundation.
Financial data (yr. ended 10/31/05): Assets, $11,729,782 (M); gifts received, $36,000; expenditures, $749,668; qualifying distributions, $617,000; giving activities include $617,000 for 12 grants (high: $120,000; low: $25,000).
Fields of interest: Medical school/education; Jewish federated giving programs; Jewish agencies & temples.
Type of support: General/operating support; Scholarship funds.
Limitations: Applications not accepted. Giving primarily in New York, NY. No grants to individuals.
Application information: Contributes only to pre-selected organizations.

Directors: Helen Armel; Ann B. Lesk; Frederick Lubcher; Joseph A. Stern.
EIN: 133316656

6460
The Lutece Foundation, Inc. ✧ ☆
c/o Kelley Drye & Warren LLP
101 Park Ave.
New York, NY 10178

Foundation type: Independent foundation.
Financial data (yr. ended 12/31/05): Assets, $7,415,895 (M); expenditures, $950,986; qualifying distributions, $860,000; giving activities include $860,000 for grants.
Fields of interest: Museums (art).
Limitations: Applications not accepted. No grants to individuals.
Application information: Contributes only to pre-selected organizations.
Officers and Directors: * Carolyn R. Caufield,* Pres.; Michael S. Insel,* Secy.-Treas.; Olivier Lefuel.
EIN: 237296158

6461
The Lyle Foundation ✧
500 Fifth Ave., Ste. 5200
New York, NY 10110

Established in 2003 in NY.
Donor: James R. Lyle.
Foundation type: Independent foundation.
Financial data (yr. ended 12/31/05): Assets, $662,710 (M); gifts received, $700,000; expenditures, $669,288; qualifying distributions, $666,700; giving activities include $666,700 for grants.
Fields of interest: Education.
Limitations: Applications not accepted. Giving primarily in New York, NY.
Application information: Unsolicited requests for funds not accepted.
Officer: James R. Lyle, Exec. Dir.
EIN: 200466096

6462
Michael R. Lynch & Susan Baker Foundation ✧
c/o BCRS Group/Marcum & Kliegman, LLP
655 3rd Ave., 16th Fl.
New York, NY 10017

Established in 1987 in NY.
Donor: Michael R. Lynch.
Foundation type: Independent foundation.
Financial data (yr. ended 7/31/05): Assets, $3,647,735 (M); gifts received, $2,200; expenditures, $2,204,144; qualifying distributions, $2,174,406; giving activities include $2,170,481 for 80 grants (high: $400,000; low: $250).
Purpose and activities: Funding primarily for human services, arts and culture, and education.
Fields of interest: Historic preservation/historical societies; Arts; Higher education; Health care; Human services; Religion.
Limitations: Applications not accepted. Giving primarily in New York, NY. No grants to individuals.
Application information: Contributes only to pre-selected organizations.

Trustees: Susan L. Baker; Michael R. Lynch.
EIN: 133438049
Selected grants: The following grants were reported in 2005.
$850,000 to New York City Opera, New York, NY. 3 grants: $50,000, $400,000, $400,000
$299,000 to Rice University, Houston, TX. 2 grants: $50,000, $249,000
$60,000 to Collegiate Chorale, New York, NY.
$50,000 to Glimmerglass Opera, Cooperstown, NY.
$14,630 to School of American Ballet, New York, NY.
$5,000 to Student Sponsor Partners, New York, NY.
$5,000 to Teach for America, New York, NY.

6463
The Lynton Foundation ✧ ☆
c/o Carol Lynton
33 W. 81st St.
New York, NY 10024

Established in 1993 in NY.
Donors: Marion Lynton; Carol Lynton; Michael Lynton.
Foundation type: Independent foundation.
Financial data (yr. ended 12/31/05): Assets, $6,099,809 (M); gifts received, $1,000,000; expenditures, $395,483; qualifying distributions, $323,119; giving activities include $323,119 for 51 grants (high: $110,000; low: $40).
Purpose and activities: Giving primarily for education and health care.
Fields of interest: Museums (children's); Arts; Higher education; Journalism school/education; Libraries/library science; Education, services; Education, reading; Mental health, association; Civil liberties, reproductive rights; Jewish agencies & temples.
Limitations: Applications not accepted. Giving primarily in NY. No grants to individuals.
Application information: Contributes only to pre-selected organizations.
Trustees: Carol Lynton; Michael Lynton.
EIN: 133743511
Selected grants: The following grants were reported in 2003.
$65,000 to Columbia University, School of Journalism, New York, NY. For general support.
$20,000 to Mental Health Association of Westchester County, Elmsford, NY. For general support.
$10,000 to Harvard College Fund, Cambridge, MA. For general support.
$5,000 to Sarah Lawrence College, Bronxville, NY. For general support.
$4,000 to Purchase College Foundation, Purchase, NY. For general support.
$1,650 to Westchester Community College Foundation, Valhalla, NY. For general support.
$1,500 to American Federation of Arts, New York, NY. For general support.
$1,000 to Planned Parenthood Federation of America, New York, NY. For general support.
$1,000 to White Plains Hospital Center, White Plains, NY. For general support.
$250 to National Student Partnerships, DC. For general support.

6464
The M & E Foundation ◇
(formerly Moric & Elsa Bistricer Foundation)
c/o Moric Bistricer
4611 12th Ave.
Brooklyn, NY 11219

Established in 1988 in NY.
Donors: Moric Bistricer; Elsa Bistricer; 1999 Bistricer Family Trust.
Foundation type: Independent foundation.
Financial data (yr. ended 4/30/05): Assets, $5,682,332 (M); expenditures, $573,725; qualifying distributions, $452,178; giving activities include $451,108 for 216 grants (high: $36,000; low: $18).
Purpose and activities: Giving primarily to Jewish organizations for the purpose of advancing education and assisting the needy.
Fields of interest: Education; Jewish federated giving programs; Jewish agencies & temples.
Limitations: Applications not accepted. No grants to individuals.
Application information: Contributes only to pre-selected organizations.
Officer: Moric Bistricer, Mgr.
EIN: 112914881
Selected grants: The following grants were reported in 2004.
$36,000 to Congregation Ohel Yehoshea, Brooklyn, NY.
$36,000 to Yeshiva Beth Hillel of Krasna, Brooklyn, NY.
$36,000 to Yeshiva Beth Yitzchok, Brooklyn, NY.
$36,000 to Yeshiva Machizikei Hadas.
$36,000 to Yeshiva Machzika Hadas.
$36,000 to Yeshiva Machzikei Torah, Monsey, NY.
$18,000 to Congregation Bais Shmuel.
$18,000 to Kollel Tiferes Yakov Yosef.
$18,000 to United Talmudical Academy of Borough Park, Brooklyn, NY.
$10,000 to Congregation Anshei Harim.

6465
The M & T Charitable Foundation ▼ ◇
1 Fountain Plz., 12th Fl.
Buffalo, NY 14203
Contact: Debbie Pringle

Established in 1993 in NY.
Donors: Manufacturers and Traders Trust Co.; M&T Bank.
Foundation type: Company-sponsored foundation.
Financial data (yr. ended 12/31/04): Assets, $29,586,319 (M); gifts received, $25,101,487; expenditures, $11,501,132; qualifying distributions, $11,496,132; giving activities include $11,496,132 for 1,787 grants (high: $475,310; low: $20).
Purpose and activities: The foundation supports organizations involved with arts and culture, education, health, and human services.
Fields of interest: Arts; Education; Health care; Human services; Children/youth, services.
Type of support: Annual campaigns; Capital campaigns; Building/renovation; Program development; Seed money; Curriculum development; Scholarship funds; Research; In-kind gifts; Matching/challenge support.
Limitations: Giving on a national basis, with emphasis on Washington, DC, DE, MD, NY, PA, and WV. No support for political, fraternal, or veterans' organizations. No grants to individuals.

Application information: Application form required.
Initial approach: Contact foundation for application form
Copies of proposal: 1
Deadline(s): 2nd Tue. of every month
Board meeting date(s): 3rd Tue. of every month
Officers and Directors:* Shelley C. Drake,* Chair. and Pres.; Michael P. Pinto,* Treas.; John A. Carmichael; Richard A. Lammert; Robert E. Sadler, Jr.; Robert G. Wilmers.
EIN: 161448017
Selected grants: The following grants were reported in 2004.
$475,310 to Westminster Community School, Buffalo, NY.
$360,500 to Banking Partnership for Community Development, New York, NY.
$275,000 to United Way of Central Maryland, Baltimore, MD.
$225,000 to Albright-Knox Art Gallery, Buffalo, NY.
$135,836 to Roswell Park Alliance Foundation, Buffalo, NY.
$81,000 to Catholic Charities of the Archdiocese of Baltimore, Baltimore, MD.
$25,000 to Baltimore Development Corporation, Baltimore, MD.
$24,000 to Baltimore School for the Arts, Baltimore, MD.
$17,000 to United Way of Schuylkill, Pottsville, PA.
$16,000 to State University of New York College at Fredonia Foundation, Fredonia, NY.

6466
The M.A.C. Global Foundation ◇
c/o The Estee Lauder Co.
767 5th Ave.
New York, NY 10153
Contact: Nancy M. Louden, Secy.

Established in 2000 in NY.
Donor: Make-Up Art Cosmetics Inc.
Foundation type: Independent foundation.
Financial data (yr. ended 12/31/03): Assets, $1,131,609 (M); gifts received, $2,610,770; expenditures, $2,507,593; qualifying distributions, $2,501,596; giving activities include $2,486,236 for 129 grants (high: $410,000; low: $282; average: $5,000–$25,000).
Purpose and activities: Giving primarily to AIDS research organizations.
Fields of interest: AIDS; International affairs.
Limitations: Applications not accepted. Giving primarily in New York, NY. No grants to individuals.
Application information: Contributes only to pre-selected organizations.
Officers and Directors:* John D. Demsey,* Chair. and Pres.; Nancy M. Louden, Secy.; Robert Charles Richards,* Treas.; Frank Doyle; Michael Laucke; Ian Ness.
EIN: 134144722

6467
M.U.S.-J. R. Hyde, Jr. Scholarship Fund ◇
c/o The Bank of New York, Tax Dept.
1 Wall St., 28th Fl.
New York, NY 10286

Established in 1991 in NY.
Donor: Joseph R. Hyde, Jr.†
Foundation type: Independent foundation.

Financial data (yr. ended 7/31/05): Assets, $12,871,778 (M); expenditures, $668,282; qualifying distributions, $619,187; giving activities include $611,360 for 1 grant.
Purpose and activities: Scholarships only for students at Memphis University School, Memphis, TN.
Fields of interest: Higher education.
Type of support: Scholarship funds.
Limitations: Applications not accepted. Giving limited to Memphis, TN.
Application information: Unsolicited requests for funds not accepted.
Trustee: The Bank of New York.
EIN: 136967610
Selected grants: The following grants were reported in 2005.
$611,360 to Memphis State University, Memphis, TN.

6468
James A. Macdonald Foundation ◇
1 N. Broadway, Ste. 1001
White Plains, NY 10601 (914) 428-9305
Contact: Walter J. Handelman, Secy.

Incorporated in 1966 in NY.
Donor: Flora Macdonald Bonney†.
Foundation type: Independent foundation.
Financial data (yr. ended 12/31/05): Assets, $8,857,133 (M); expenditures, $617,206; qualifying distributions, $562,032; giving activities include $523,080 for 246 grants (high: $24,200; low: $300).
Fields of interest: Historic preservation/historical societies; Secondary school/education; Hospitals (general); Children/youth, services; Federated giving programs; Protestant agencies & churches.
Type of support: General/operating support; Continuing support; Annual campaigns; Building/renovation; Equipment; Land acquisition; Endowments; Emergency funds; Program development; Seed money; Fellowships; Scholarship funds; Research.
Limitations: Giving primarily in NY. No grants to individuals, or for matching gifts.
Publications: Annual report.
Application information: Application form not required.
Initial approach: Letter
Copies of proposal: 1
Deadline(s): None
Board meeting date(s): Generally, on a quarterly basis
Officers and Directors:* Alice H. Model,* Pres.; Walter J. Handelman,* V.P. and Secy.; Alan L. Model,* Treas.
EIN: 136199690

6469
The Christy and John Mack Foundation ◇
(formerly The C. J. Mack Foundation)
6 Club Rd.
Rye, NY 10580

Established in 1993 in NY and DE.
Donors: Christy K. Mack; John J. Mack.
Foundation type: Independent foundation.
Financial data (yr. ended 12/31/04): Assets, $40,694,478 (M); gifts received, $919,237; expenditures, $4,872,918; qualifying distributions,

$4,718,776; giving activities include $4,718,776 for 12 grants (high: $1,500,000; low: $15,000).
Purpose and activities: Giving primarily for hospitals and education.
Fields of interest: Arts; Education; Hospitals (general); Health organizations, association; Human services.
Limitations: Applications not accepted. Giving on a national basis. No grants to individuals.
Application information: Contributes only to pre-selected organizations.
Officers: Christy K. Mack,* Pres.; John J. Mack,* V.P.; Sally Newcomb, Secy.; Jenna A. Mack.
EIN: 133746731

6470
The Paul MacKall & Evanina MacKall Trust ✧

c/o JPMorgan Chase Bank, N.A.
345 Park Ave.
New York, NY 10154-1002 (212) 464-2599
Contact: Sarah Rubin, V.P., JPMorgan Chase Bank, N.A.

Established in 1982 in NY.
Foundation type: Independent foundation.
Financial data (yr. ended 8/31/05): Assets, $16,400,436 (M); expenditures, $849,437; qualifying distributions, $819,812; giving activities include $817,100 for 1 grant.
Purpose and activities: Giving limited to ophthalmological research for the cause, prevention, alleviation and cure of blindness.
Fields of interest: Eye research.
Limitations: Giving primarily in Philadelphia, PA. No grants to individuals, or for building funds.
Application information:
  Initial approach: Letter
  Deadline(s): None
Trustee: JPMorgan Chase Bank, N.A.
EIN: 136794686
Selected grants: The following grants were reported in 2005.
$817,100 to University of Pennsylvania, Philadelphia, PA.

6471
Josiah Macy, Jr. Foundation ▼

44 E. 64th St.
New York, NY 10021 (212) 486-2424
Contact: June E. Osborn M.D., Pres.
FAX: (212) 644-0765;
E-mail: jmacyinfo@josiahmacyfoundation.org;
URL: http://www.josiahmacyfoundation.org

Incorporated in 1930 in NY.
Donor: Kate Macy Ladd‡.
Foundation type: Independent foundation.
Financial data (yr. ended 6/30/05): Assets, $149,786,079 (M); expenditures, $8,064,586; qualifying distributions, $7,081,443; giving activities include $5,098,387 for 42+ grants (high: $577,766; average: $25,000–$400,000), $354,264 for employee matching gifts, and $380,487 for foundation-administered programs.
Purpose and activities: Major interest in medicine and health. Support for enhancing and improving health professional and medical education in ways that will better the health of the public. Priorities include: medical and health professional education programs in the context of the changing healthcare

system; programs which devise or complement educational strategies likely to improve and/or increase care for the underserved populations; programs that demonstrate or encourage ways to increase teamwork between and among healthcare professionals; and projects that increase diversity in medical and health professional education and in the health professions.
Fields of interest: Medical school/education; Nursing school/education; Public health school/education; Health sciences school/education; Health care; Biomedicine; Civil liberties, reproductive rights; African Americans/Blacks; Hispanics/Latinos; Native Americans/American Indians; Women; Economically disadvantaged.
Type of support: Program development; Conferences/seminars; Publication; Curriculum development; Program evaluation.
Publications: Annual report; Grants list; Occasional report; Program policy statement.
Application information: Additional program information is available on the foundation's Web site. The foundation does not accept submission of applications via E-mail. Application form not required.
  Initial approach: Letter of inquiry
  Copies of proposal: 1
  Deadline(s): None
  Board meeting date(s): Jan., May, and Oct.
  Final notification: Within 3 months
Officers and Directors:* Lawrence S. Huntington,* Chair.; Marc A. Nivet, C.O.O. and Treas.; June E. Osborn, M.D.*, Pres.; Lawrence K. Altman, M.D.; Jordan J. Cohen, M.D.; John W. Frymoyer, M.D.; S. Parker Gilbert; Patricia Albjerg Graham, Ph.D.; Arthur H. Hayes, Jr., M.D.; John Jay Iselin, Ph.D.; Mary Patterson McPherson, Ph.D.; Herbert Pardes, M.D.; William H. Wright II.
Number of staff: 2 full-time professional; 4 full-time support.
EIN: 135596895
Selected grants: The following grants were reported in 2005.
$2,065,000 to Association of American Medical Colleges, DC. To develop models that will lead to integration of teaching of chronic diseases into both undergraduate and graduate medical education, payable over 3 years.
$948,052 to Columbia University, School of Nursing, New York, NY. For project, Establishing Standards for the Clinical Doctorate in Nursing, payable over 3 years.
$942,016 to Association of Academic Health Centers, DC. 2 grants: $421,578 (To maintain and further develop ExploreHealthCareers.org website, payable over 2 years), $520,438 (For study of health workforce shortages: causes, implications, and solutions across the health professions, payable over 3 years).
$682,884 to Stanford University, School of Medicine, Stanford, CA. For The Stanford Faculty Development Program for Professionalism in Contemporary Practice, payable over 3 years.
$500,000 to Cold Spring Harbor Laboratory, Cold Spring Harbor, NY. For project, Preserving the Past and the Present, Looking to the Future: Preserving and Digitizing the Cold Spring Harbor Laboratory Archives Collections, payable over 2 years.
$497,218 to Association of Teachers of Preventive Medicine, DC. For development of common curriculum framework for education about prevention among seven health professions and to establish web-based Prevention Education

Resource Center for faculty in health profession disciplines, payable over 3 years.
$205,858 to Adult Literacy Media Alliance, New York, NY. For Health Smarts While You Wait, project to train students to teach adult health literacy in ambulatory clinic settings.
$200,000 to Task Force for Child Survival and Development, Decatur, GA. For project documenting the history of Epidemic Intelligence Service of the Centers for Disease Control and Prevention, payable over 2 years.
$25,000 to New York University, Faculty Resource Network, New York, NY. For faculty enrichment seminar: Selected Topics in Health and Mental Health - Women, Race, and Social Class.

6472
Magen Ezra Foundation ✧

c/o Jack Cattan
37 W. 37th St., Rm. 10
New York, NY 10018

Established in 1998 in NY.
Donors: Judah Cattan; Ezra Jack Cattan; Jack Cattan; Ezrasons, Inc.; Keter Torah Synagogue Sephardic Community.
Foundation type: Independent foundation.
Financial data (yr. ended 11/30/05): Assets, $496,138 (M); gifts received, $294,099; expenditures, $349,232; qualifying distributions, $340,033; giving activities include $339,033 for 336 grants (high: $60,000; low: $18).
Purpose and activities: Giving primarily for Jewish organizations, temples and yeshivas.
Fields of interest: Children, services; Jewish agencies & temples.
Limitations: Applications not accepted. No grants to individuals.
Application information: Contributes only to pre-selected organizations.
Directors: Ezra Jack Cattan; Jack Cattan; Judah Cattan.
EIN: 133980258

6473
The Magowan Family Foundation, Inc. ✧

c/o Lebowitz & Selznick
145 Bedford Rd., Ste. 201
Armonk, NY 10504

Incorporated in 1954 in NY.
Donors: Charles E. Merrill, Sr.‡; Robert A. Magowan, Sr.‡; Doris M. Magowan; Mark Magowan; Merrill L. Magowan; Robert A. Magowan, Jr.; Merchants National Properties, Inc.
Foundation type: Independent foundation.
Financial data (yr. ended 12/31/05): Assets, $7,482,498 (M); gifts received, $68,033; expenditures, $404,290; qualifying distributions, $388,429; giving activities include $388,429 for 210 grants (high: $15,000; low: $25).
Purpose and activities: Giving primarily for arts and culture, education, health, parks and recreation, and children, youth and social services.
Fields of interest: Media, television; Performing arts, theater; Arts; Elementary/secondary education; Higher education; Libraries (academic/research); Education; Zoos/zoological societies; Hospitals (general); Health organizations, association; Recreation, parks/playgrounds;

Recreation; Human services; Children/youth, services; Christian agencies & churches.
Limitations: Applications not accepted. Giving on a national basis. No grants to individuals.
Application information: Contributes only to pre-selected organizations.
Directors: Mark E. Magowan; Merrill L. Magowan; Peter A. Magowan; Robin Magowan; Bernat Rosner.
EIN: 136085999
Selected grants: The following grants were reported in 2004.
$100,000 to American Friends of the Royal Court Theater, New York, NY.
$100,000 to Saint Andrews Dune Church, Southampton, NY.
$75,000 to Saint Bernards School, New York, NY.
$50,000 to Rogosin Institute, Polycystic Kidney Disease Center, New York, NY.
$14,500 to Calvert Social Investment Foundation, San Francisco, CA.
$12,000 to Earthwatch Institute, Maynard, MA.
$10,000 to Americans for Oxford, New York, NY.
$10,000 to Chapin School, New York, NY.
$10,000 to Harvard University, Cambridge, MA.
$10,000 to Town School, New York, NY.

6474
MAH Foundation ✧ ☆
40 Windy Hill Rd.
Millbrook, NY 12545 (845) 677-9297
Contact: Munir Abu-Haidar, Tr.

Established in 1996 in NY.
Donor: Munir Abu-Haidar.
Foundation type: Independent foundation.
Financial data (yr. ended 12/31/05): Assets, $1,832 (M); gifts received, $500,000; expenditures, $500,012; qualifying distributions, $500,000; giving activities include $500,000 for 1 grant.
Fields of interest: Higher education, university; Education.
Limitations: Giving primarily in NY.
Application information: Application form not required.
Initial approach: Letter
Deadline(s): None
Trustees: Munir Abu-Haidar; Susan Abu-Haidar.
EIN: 133895871

6475
Maheras Foundation ✧ ☆
24 Gramercy Park. S., Ste. 5
New York, NY 10003

Established in 2000 in NY.
Donor: Thomas G. Maheras.
Foundation type: Independent foundation.
Financial data (yr. ended 12/31/05): Assets, $795,185 (M); gifts received, $148,095; expenditures, $437,814; qualifying distributions, $433,208; giving activities include $431,083 for 28 grants (high: $245,000; low: $500).
Fields of interest: Museums (children's); Performing arts centers; Performing arts, dance; Education; Cancer research; Food services; Human services; American Red Cross; Children/youth, services; Religion.
Limitations: Applications not accepted. Giving primarily in New York, NY. No grants to individuals.

Application information: Contributes only to pre-selected organizations.
Trustees: Leslie L. Maheras; Thomas G. Maheras.
EIN: 134150699
Selected grants: The following grants were reported in 2004.
$32,000 to Grace Church School, New York, NY.
$20,000 to Carnegie Hall Society, New York, NY.
$10,000 to Boomer Esiason Foundation, New York, NY.
$10,000 to Cancer Research Institute, New York, NY.
$10,000 to Inner-City Scholarship Fund, New York, NY.
$5,000 to Harlem Childrens Zone, New York, NY.
$5,000 to Kids of NYU Foundation, New York, NY.
$5,000 to Marist High School, Chicago, IL.
$5,000 to Matheny School and Hospital, Peapack, NJ.
$2,000 to Henry Street Settlement, New York, NY.

6476
The Mai Family Foundation ✧
c/o Mahoney Cohen & Co.
1065 Ave. of the Americas
New York, NY 10018

Established in 1996 in NY.
Donor: Vincent A. Mai.
Foundation type: Independent foundation.
Financial data (yr. ended 12/31/05): Assets, $6,099,358 (M); gifts received, $2,310,910; expenditures, $1,829,071; qualifying distributions, $1,778,300; giving activities include $1,778,300 for 42 grants (high: $350,000; low: $2,500).
Purpose and activities: Giving primarily to a school for the arts, as well as for human services, environmental conservation, and to a U.S.-based organization for the development of South African youth and young adults.
Fields of interest: Arts education; Higher education; Environment, natural resources; Youth development; Human services; Children/youth, services; Civil rights.
Limitations: Applications not accepted. Giving primarily in New York, NY. No grants to individuals.
Application information: Contributes only to pre-selected organizations.
Officers and Directors:* Vincent A. Mai,* Pres. and Treas.; Anne Mai,* V.P.; Lisa Moore, Secy.; Sanford Krieger.
EIN: 133915987

6477
A. L. Mailman Family Foundation, Inc.
707 Westchester Ave.
White Plains, NY 10604 (914) 683-8089
Contact: Luba H. Lynch, Exec. Dir.
FAX: (914) 686-5519; E-mail: almf@mailman.org; URL: http://www.mailman.org

Established in 1976 in FL as the Dr. Marilyn M. Segal Foundation, Inc.
Donors: Abraham L. Mailman†; The Mailman Foundation, Inc.
Foundation type: Independent foundation.
Financial data (yr. ended 12/31/05): Assets, $22,163,677 (M); expenditures, $1,800,189; qualifying distributions, $1,575,462; giving activities include $1,065,011 for 70 grants (high: $290,000; low: $400; average: $10,000–

$35,000), and $57,039 for 4 foundation-administered programs.
Purpose and activities: To enhance the ability of families and communities to nurture their children by focusing on early childhood care and education, particularly for infants and toddlers.
Fields of interest: Education, early childhood education.
Type of support: Program development; Publication; Curriculum development; Research; Technical assistance.
Limitations: Giving on a national basis. No support for locally based service organizations or programs, or for religious organizations. No grants to individuals, operating budgets, or for capital expenditures endowment campaigns.
Publications: Application guidelines; Grants list; Program policy statement.
Application information: Full proposals are by invitation only upon review of letters of inquiry. The foundation encourages applicants to submit letters and solicited proposals via e-mail and to fax and/or mail attachments. Application form not required.
Initial approach: Letter (2-3 pages)
Copies of proposal: 1
Deadline(s): Jan. 15 and June 15
Board meeting date(s): Apr. and Oct.
Final notification: 5 months
Officers and Trustees:* Patricia S. Lieberman,* Chair.; Wendy S. Masi,* Vice-Chair.; Richard D. Segal,* Pres.; Betty S. Bardige,* V.P.; Luba H. Lynch, Secy. and Exec. Dir.; Donna Tookmanian, Treas.; Myla Kore Bardige; Jay B. Langner; Marilyn M. Segal.
Number of staff: 2 full-time professional; 1 full-time support.
EIN: 510203866
Selected grants: The following grants were reported in 2004.
$374,000 to Nova Southeastern University, Fort Lauderdale, FL. 3 grants: $290,000, $70,000, $14,000
$34,500 to National Association for the Education of Young Children, DC.
$33,000 to Yale University, New Haven, CT.
$25,000 to Zero to Three: National Center for Infants, Toddlers and Families, DC. 2 grants: $15,000, $10,000
$20,000 to Docs for Tots, DC.
$15,000 to United States Association for Child Care, Vienna, VA.
$15,000 to Voices for Americas Children, DC.

6478
The Mailman Foundation, Inc. ✧
111 W. 40th St., 20th Fl.
New York, NY 10018

Incorporated in 1943 in DE.
Donors: Joseph L. Mailman†; Joseph S. Mailman†; Joshua L. Mailman; Phyllis Mailman.
Foundation type: Independent foundation.
Financial data (yr. ended 12/31/04): Assets, $50,456,446 (M); expenditures, $2,323,925; qualifying distributions, $1,954,738; giving activities include $1,923,572 for 97 grants (high: $1,194,052; low: $250).
Fields of interest: Museums (art); Performing arts, theater; Arts; Higher education; Education; Health organizations, association; Human services; Jewish agencies & temples.
Limitations: Applications not accepted. Giving on a national basis. No grants to individuals.

Application information: Contributes only to pre-selected organizations.

Officers and Trustees:* Phyllis Mailman,* Pres.; Joshua L. Mailman,* V.P.; Joan M. Wolfe, V.P.; Johanna L. Wolfe,* V.P.; Judson A. Wolfe, V.P.; Joseph V. Hastings, Secy.-Treas.

EIN: 136161556

Selected grants: The following grants were reported in 2004.

$1,194,052 to Columbia University, New York, NY.

$115,320 to Lincoln Center Theater, New York, NY. 4 grants: $40,000, $5,000, $23,440, $46,880

$75,000 to Ransom Everglades School, Miami, FL. 2 grants: $25,000, $50,000

$25,000 to Lincoln Center for the Performing Arts, New York, NY.

$10,000 to American Council of Trustees and Alumni, DC.

$10,000 to Duke University, Durham, NC.

6479
Maleh-Shalom Foundation, Inc. ◇

c/o Children's Apparel Network, Ltd.
112 W. 34th St.
New York, NY 10120

Established in 1967 in NY.

Donors: Cradle Togs, Inc.; Children's Apparel Network, Ltd.

Foundation type: Independent foundation.

Financial data (yr. ended 12/31/05): Assets, $338,490 (M); gifts received, $730,000; expenditures, $786,948; qualifying distributions, $786,600; giving activities include $786,600 for 55 grants (high: $300,000; low: $50).

Purpose and activities: Giving primarily to Jewish organizations, temples and schools.

Fields of interest: Elementary/secondary education; Jewish federated giving programs; Jewish agencies & temples.

Limitations: Applications not accepted. Giving limited to NJ and NY. No grants to individuals.

Application information: Contributes only to pre-selected organizations. Unsolicited requests for funds not accepted.

Officer: Murray Maleh, Mgr.

EIN: 136265282

6480
Malkin Fund, Inc. ◇

c/o Wien & Malkin, LLP
60 E. 42nd St.
New York, NY 10165

Established in 1994 in NY.

Donor: Peter L. Malkin.

Foundation type: Independent foundation.

Financial data (yr. ended 12/31/04): Assets, $14,867,070 (M); gifts received, $2,432,212; expenditures, $1,712,197; qualifying distributions, $1,705,941; giving activities include $1,705,941 for 276 grants (high: $100,000; low: $100).

Purpose and activities: Giving primarily for education, the arts, human services and welfare. Funding also for medical associations.

Fields of interest: Arts; Education; Health organizations, association; Medical research, institute; Human services; Jewish federated giving programs.

Limitations: Giving primarily in the Northeast, with emphasis on CT, MA, and NY. No grants to individuals.

Application information:

Initial approach: Letter or proposal
Deadline(s): None

Officers and Directors:* Peter L. Malkin,* Chair. and Secy.; Isabel W. Malkin,* Pres. and Treas.; Cynthia M. Blumenthal; Anthony E. Malkin; Scott D. Malkin.

EIN: 133749046

6481
The Yvette and Joel Mallah Family Foundation ◇

P.O. Box 1297
Bridgehampton, NY 11932

Established in 1999 in NY.

Donor: Joel Mallah.

Foundation type: Independent foundation.

Financial data (yr. ended 12/31/05): Assets, $5,487,237 (M); gifts received, $3,000,000; expenditures, $382,640; qualifying distributions, $382,000; giving activities include $382,000 for 21 grants (high: $100,000; low: $500).

Purpose and activities: Giving primarily for health care with emphasis on hospitals, as well as for education including a medical college; some giving also to Jewish organizations, and social services.

Fields of interest: Medical school/education; Education; Animal welfare; Hospitals (general); Health organizations, association; Medical research, association; Children, day care; Jewish agencies & temples.

Limitations: Applications not accepted. Giving primarily in NY. No grants to individuals.

Application information: Contributes only to pre-selected organizations.

Trustees: Joel Mallah; Yvette Mallah.

EIN: 137172805

Selected grants: The following grants were reported in 2004.

$200,000 to Saint Francis Hospital Foundation, Roslyn, NY. 2 grants: $100,000 each

$50,000 to Beth Israel Medical Center, New York, NY. 2 grants: $25,000 each

$50,000 to Rabbi Arthur Schneier Park East Day School, New York, NY. 2 grants: $25,000 each

$40,000 to Jewish Center of the Hamptons, East Hampton, NY. 2 grants: $15,000, $25,000

$10,000 to FACT Foundation, Burbank, CA.

$5,000 to Maryhaven Center of Hope, Port Jefferson, NY.

6482
The Harry T. Mangurian, Jr. Foundation, Inc. ◇ ☆

(formerly The Mangurian Foundation, Inc.)
c/o Brophy, Dailey & Incardona, L.L.P.
150 Allen Creek Rd.
Rochester, NY 14618-3308

Established in 1999 in NY.

Donor: Harry T. Mangurian, Jr.

Foundation type: Independent foundation.

Financial data (yr. ended 12/31/05): Assets, $21,496,426 (M); expenditures, $709,596; qualifying distributions, $531,715; giving activities include $520,000 for 5 grants (high: $500,000; low: $5,000).

Fields of interest: Cancer research; Disasters, preparedness/services; Human services, research; YM/YWCAs & YM/YWHAs; Human services, victim aid; Human services.

Limitations: Applications not accepted. Giving primarily in Rochester, NY. No grants to individuals.

Application information: Contributes only to pre-selected organizations.

Officers and Directors:* Harry T. Mangurian, Jr.,* Chair.; Stephen G. Mehallis,* Pres.; Terry M. Skuse,* V.P.; J. Ernest Brophy,* Secy.; Gordon W. Latz,* Treas.; Beth Panesh Piana, Compt.

EIN: 161578255

6483
The Manitoba Foundation ◇

c/o First Spring Corp.
499 Park Ave., 26th Fl.
New York, NY 10022
Contact: Guido Goldman, Pres.

Established in 1996 in DE and NY.

Foundation type: Independent foundation.

Financial data (yr. ended 12/31/05): Assets, $11,523,911 (M); expenditures, $345,255; qualifying distributions, $343,107; giving activities include $341,948 for 9 grants (high: $118,948; low: $5,000).

Fields of interest: Museums (art); Cancer; Jewish federated giving programs; Jewish agencies & temples.

Limitations: Giving primarily in NY. No grants to individuals.

Application information: Application form not required.

Deadline(s): None

Officers and Directors:* Guido Goldman,* Pres.; Mark O'Donnell, V.P. and Treas.; Kenneth M. Musen, Secy.; Jean De Gunzburg; Terry De Gunzburg; Avrom Udovitch.

EIN: 133775261

6484
The James Hilton Manning and Emma Austin Manning Foundation, Inc. ◇

c/o Davidson Dawson & Clark
60 E. 42nd St., 38th Fl.
New York, NY 10165

Incorporated in 1958 in NY.

Donors: Beatrice Austin Manning†; Alfred M. Hoelzer†.

Foundation type: Independent foundation.

Financial data (yr. ended 7/31/05): Assets, $4,498,523 (M); expenditures, $721,143; qualifying distributions, $658,143; giving activities include $658,143 for 2 grants (high: $633,143; low: $25,000).

Purpose and activities: Giving primarily for higher education; some giving also for sports medicine research.

Fields of interest: Higher education, university; Medical research, institute; Medical specialty research.

Type of support: Research.

Limitations: Applications not accepted. Giving primarily in New York, NY. No grants to individuals, or for student aid, general support, capital or endowment funds, scholarships, fellowships, or matching gifts; no loans.

Publications: Annual report.

Application information: Contributes only to pre-selected organizations.
Officers and Directors:* John H. Bell, Jr.,* Pres.; Juliet Alexander,* Secy.; Ralph A. Baer, M.D.; Susan Porter; Martin R. Post, M.D.
Number of staff: 1 part-time professional.
EIN: 136123540

6485
Robert Mapplethorpe Foundation, Inc. ☆
477 Madison Ave., 15 Fl.
New York, NY   10022   (212) 755-3025
Contact: Ms. Joree Adilman, Mgr.
FAX: (212) 941-4764; URL: http://www.mapplethorpe.org/foundation.html

Established in 1988 in NY.
Donor: Robert Mapplethorpe†.
Foundation type: Independent foundation.
Financial data (yr. ended 5/31/05): Assets, $145,731,265 (M); expenditures, $4,700,300; qualifying distributions, $512,490; giving activities include $512,490 for 19+ grants (high: $250,000).
Purpose and activities: Support for medical research to advance the cure and treatment of AIDS and HIV infection; support also for photography as an art form through assisting museums, universities, and other institutions, and by publishing quality books and materials.
Fields of interest: Visual arts, photography; Museums; Arts; AIDS; Medical research, institute; AIDS research.
Type of support: Program development; Publication; Research.
Limitations: Giving on a national basis. No support for social services or for international organizations that are based outside of the U.S. No grants to individuals.
Publications: Application guidelines.
Application information: Application form not required.
  Initial approach: Letter
  Copies of proposal: 1
  Deadline(s): None
  Board meeting date(s): Approximately every 3 months
  Final notification: Approximately 1 week after board meeting
Officers: Michael Ward Stout, Pres.; Dimitri Levas, V.P.; Stewart Shining, V.P.; Burton G. Lipsky, Secy.-Treas.; Joree Adilman, Mgr.
Number of staff: 2 full-time professional; 1 full-time support; 2 part-time support.
EIN: 133480472
Selected grants: The following grants were reported in 2005.
$45,000 to Walker Art Center, Minneapolis, MN.
$31,490 to Whitney Museum of American Art, New York, NY.
$15,000 to New Museum of Contemporary Art, New York, NY. 2 grants: $1,000, $14,000
$9,400 to Dallas Museum of Art, Dallas, TX.
$5,000 to International Center of Photography, New York, NY.
$4,000 to Museum of Modern Art, New York, NY.
$2,500 to Long Beach Museum of Art, Long Beach, CA.
$2,000 to Alliance for the Arts, New York, NY.

6486
The James S. Marcus Foundation ◇
c/o The BCRS Assocs., LLC
100 Wall St., 11th Fl.
New York, NY   10005

Established in 1969 in NY.
Donor: James S. Marcus.
Foundation type: Independent foundation.
Financial data (yr. ended 5/31/05): Assets, $6,651,384 (M); expenditures, $774,253; qualifying distributions, $756,753; giving activities include $756,403 for 98 grants (high: $67,150; low: $70).
Purpose and activities: Giving primarily to the arts with emphasis on the performing arts in music, opera, and theater; some giving also for education, and health and human services.
Fields of interest: Media, television; Museums; Performing arts, ballet; Performing arts, theater; Performing arts, music; Performing arts, orchestra (symphony); Arts; Higher education; Environment, natural resources; Animal welfare; Animals/wildlife, preservation/protection; Hospitals (general); Human services; Children/youth, services.
Limitations: Applications not accepted. Giving primarily in New York, NY. No grants to individuals (including scholarships); no loans.
Application information: Contributes only to pre-selected organizations.
Trustees: H.F. Krimendahl II; Ellen F. Marcus; James S. Marcus.
EIN: 237044611
Selected grants: The following grants were reported in 2004.
$83,500 to Animal Medical Center, New York, NY. For general support.
$51,000 to Eos Orchestra, New York, NY. For general support.
$48,500 to W N E T Channel 13, New York, NY. 2 grants: $23,500 (For general support), $25,000 (For general support).
$48,025 to Lenox Hill Hospital, New York, NY. For general support.
$43,334 to Nature Conservancy, New York, NY. For general support.
$40,000 to Harvard University, Cambridge, MA. For general support.
$35,000 to Manhattan Theater Club, New York, NY. For general support.
$28,400 to Marilyn Horne Foundation, New York, NY. For general support.
$25,000 to New York City Opera, New York, NY. For general support.

6487
Mariposa Foundation, Inc. ◇
c/o Dorian A. Vergos & Co., LLP
592 5th Ave., 2nd Fl.
New York, NY   10036

Established around 1976.
Donor: Lewis W. Bernard.
Foundation type: Independent foundation.
Financial data (yr. ended 12/31/05): Assets, $67,119,753 (M); gifts received, $5,149,300; expenditures, $2,948,853; qualifying distributions, $2,500,000; giving activities include $2,500,000 for 49 grants (high: $1,001,000; low: $2,000).
Purpose and activities: Giving primarily for social services, the arts, and for education.

Fields of interest: Arts; Education; Environment; Hospitals (general); Human services; Children/youth, services.
Limitations: Applications not accepted. Giving primarily in New York, NY. No grants to individuals.
Application information: Contributes only to pre-selected organizations.
Officers: Lewis W. Bernard, Pres. and Treas.; Jill V. Bernard, V.P. and Secy.
Directors: Adam T. Bernard; Claire E. Bernard.
Number of staff: 1 full-time support.
EIN: 510170409
Selected grants: The following grants were reported in 2003.
$500,000 to American Museum of Natural History, New York, NY.
$100,000 to Good Shepherd Services, New York, NY.
$50,000 to Community Resource Exchange, New York, NY.
$15,000 to Children of Alcoholics Foundation, New York, NY.
$5,000 to Chess in the Schools, New York, NY.
$5,000 to Whitney Museum of American Art, New York, NY.
$4,000 to Beginning with Children Foundation, New York, NY.
$1,500 to Neighborhood Coalition for Shelter, New York, NY.
$1,000 to Gay Mens Health Crisis (GMHC), New York, NY.
$1,000 to New Museum of Contemporary Art, New York, NY.

6488
Mark Family Foundation ◇
c/o RSM McGladrey, Inc.
1185 Ave. of the Americas
New York, NY   10036

Established in 1994 in NY.
Donors: Morris Mark; Susan Mark.
Foundation type: Independent foundation.
Financial data (yr. ended 11/30/05): Assets, $3,704,625 (M); gifts received, $323,524; expenditures, $379,945; qualifying distributions, $379,886; giving activities include $379,620 for 45 grants (high: $10,000; low: $100).
Purpose and activities: Giving primarily for Jewish federated giving programs, the arts, health care, and medical research.
Fields of interest: Arts; Education; Health organizations, association; Human services; Jewish federated giving programs; Jewish agencies & temples.
Limitations: Applications not accepted. No grants to individuals.
Application information: Contributes only to pre-selected organizations.
Trustees: Morris Mark; Susan Mark.
EIN: 137052586
Selected grants: The following grants were reported in 2005.
$11,000 to Guild Hall, New York, NY.
$10,000 to Jewish Museum, New York, NY.
$5,000 to Brooklyn College Foundation, Brooklyn, NY.
$5,000 to National Foundation for Facial Reconstruction, New York, NY.
$2,500 to East Hampton Healthcare Foundation, East Hampton, NY.
$2,000 to Dalton Schools, New York, NY.
$1,500 to Ballet Theater Foundation, New York, NY.

$800 to Carnegie Hall Society, New York, NY.
$500 to Eldridge Street Project, New York, NY.
$250 to New Dramatists, New York, NY.

6489
Marks Family Foundation

c/o Carl Marks & Co.
900 3rd Ave., 33rd Fl.
New York, NY 10022-4775
Contact: Lisa Schantz

Established in 1986 in NY.
Donors: Edwin S. Marks†; Nancy A. Marks.
Foundation type: Independent foundation.
Financial data (yr. ended 6/30/06): Assets, $23,207,171 (M); gifts received, $3,210,349; expenditures, $3,803,692; qualifying distributions, $3,639,540; giving activities include $3,639,540 for 57 grants (high: $1,229,942; low: $500; average: $5,000–$100,000).
Purpose and activities: Giving primarily for the arts.
Fields of interest: Museums; Performing arts; Arts; Education; Human services; Jewish federated giving programs.
Type of support: General/operating support.
Limitations: Applications not accepted. Giving primarily in NY. No grants to individuals.
Application information: Contributes only to pre-selected organizations.
Officer and Directors:* Nancy A. Marks,* Pres. and Secy.; Linda Marks Katz; Carolyn Marks; Constance Marks Miller.
EIN: 133385770
Selected grants: The following grants were reported in 2005.
$47,749 to Bard College, Annandale on Hudson, NY.
$25,000 to Charter Oak Challenge Foundation, Westport, CT.
$20,000 to Mount Desert Island Biological Laboratory, Salsbury Cove, ME.
$15,000 to Friends of Hudson, Hudson, NY.
$15,000 to Scenic Hudson, Poughkeepsie, NY.
$11,700 to Rockefeller University, New York, NY.
$10,000 to Fund for Public Schools, New York, NY.
$10,000 to New Visions for Public Schools, New York, NY.
$6,920 to International Dyslexia Association, Baltimore, MD.
$6,500 to Legal Aid Society.

6490
Carl Marks Foundation, Inc.

900 3rd Ave., 33rd Fl.
New York, NY 10022-4775
Contact: Lisa Schantz

Established in 1986 in NY.
Donors: Mark Claster; Susan Claster; Andrew M. Boas; and members of the Boas family.
Foundation type: Independent foundation.
Financial data (yr. ended 6/30/05): Assets, $26,149,503 (M); expenditures, $1,129,520; qualifying distributions, $1,071,879; giving activities include $1,013,141 for 49 grants (high: $697,353; low: $180).
Fields of interest: Higher education; Jewish federated giving programs; Jewish agencies & temples.
Type of support: General/operating support.

Limitations: Applications not accepted. Giving primarily in New York, NY. No grants to individuals.
Application information: Contributes only to pre-selected organizations.
Officers: Andrew M. Boas, Pres. and Secy.; Mark Claster, V.P. and Treas.
EIN: 136169215
Selected grants: The following grants were reported in 2005.
$697,353 to FJC-A Foundation of Donor-Advised Funds, New York, NY.
$55,000 to United Jewish Appeal, New York, NY.
$50,000 to Duke University, Durham, NC.
$30,000 to University of Pennsylvania, Philadelphia, PA.
$6,500 to Jewish Federation of Palm Beach County, West Palm Beach, FL.
$5,000 to Canterbury School, New Milford, CT.
$5,000 to McLean School of Maryland, Potomac, MD.
$2,000 to Center for Jewish History, New York, NY.

6491
The Yacov and Rita Marmurstein Charitable Foundation Trust ◇ ☆

5307 17th Ave.
Brooklyn, NY 11204

Established in 1999 in NY.
Donors: Yacov Marmurstein; Rita Marmurstein; Jacob Marmurstein; Private One of NY, LLC.
Foundation type: Independent foundation.
Financial data (yr. ended 12/31/04): Assets, $702,817 (M); gifts received, $300,610; expenditures, $668,750; qualifying distributions, $667,950; giving activities include $667,500 for grants.
Fields of interest: Elementary/secondary education; Jewish agencies & temples.
Limitations: Applications not accepted. Giving primarily in Brooklyn, NY. No grants to individuals.
Application information: Contributes only to pre-selected organizations.
Trustees: Rita Marmurstein; Yacov Marmurstein.
EIN: 116532361
Selected grants: The following grants were reported in 2004.
$45,000 to Ezer Mzion, Brooklyn, NY.
$25,000 to Aleh Foundation, Brooklyn, NY.

6492
Donald B. Marron Charitable Trust ◇

c/o Starr & Co.
850 Park Ave.
New York, NY 10022
Contact: Donald B. Marron, Tr.
Application address: c/o Donald Marron, Lightyear Capital, 375 Park Ave., New York, NY 10152

Established in 2000 in NY.
Donor: Donald B. Marron.
Foundation type: Independent foundation.
Financial data (yr. ended 12/31/04): Assets, $17,785,085 (M); expenditures, $5,369,899; qualifying distributions, $5,364,591; giving activities include $5,309,591 for 16 grants (high: $4,083,984; low: $737).
Purpose and activities: Giving primarily for the arts, particularly an art museum, as well as for education and human services; funding also for a cancer center.

Fields of interest: Museums (art); Arts; Education; Cancer research; Human services.
Limitations: Giving primarily in New York, NY.
Application information:
Initial approach: Letter
Deadline(s): None
Trustee: Donald B. Marron.
EIN: 137260354
Selected grants: The following grants were reported in 2004.
$4,083,984 to Museum of Modern Art, New York, NY.
$1,001,000 to Memorial Sloan-Kettering Cancer Center, New York, NY.
$100,000 to Coalition for the Homeless, DC.
$50,000 to Green Acres School, Rockville, MD.
$20,000 to Concord Coalition, Arlington, VA.
$5,000 to City College Fund, New York, NY.
$5,000 to Fresh Air Fund, New York, NY.
$2,520 to Alumni Association of the Bronx High School of Science, Bronx, NY.
$2,000 to Concord Hill School, Chevy Chase, MD.
$1,900 to Henry Street Settlement, New York, NY.

6493
Donald B. & Catherine C. Marron Foundation ◇

c/o Starr and Co.
350 Park Ave., 9th Fl.
New York, NY 10022
Contact: Donald B. Marron, Pres.
Application address: c/o Lightyear Capital, 375 Park Ave., New York, NY 10152

Established in 1972 as the Mitchell, Hutchins, Inc. Foundation.
Donor: Donald B. Marron.
Foundation type: Independent foundation.
Financial data (yr. ended 12/31/03): Assets, $2,055,663 (M); expenditures, $625,491; qualifying distributions, $617,811; giving activities include $617,355 for 36 grants (high: $200,000; low: $100).
Fields of interest: Media, television; Museums (art); Education; Human services; Jewish agencies & temples; Economically disadvantaged; Homeless.
Limitations: Giving primarily in NY.
Application information:
Initial approach: Letter
Deadline(s): None
Officer: Donald B. Marron, Pres.
EIN: 237243134
Selected grants: The following grants were reported in 2003.
$200,000 to Spence School, New York, NY.
$163,160 to Museum of Modern Art, New York, NY.
$25,000 to Saint Bernards School, New York, NY.
$25,000 to Saint James Church, New York, NY.
$15,000 to Metropolitan Opera, New York, NY.
$10,000 to Abyssinian Development Corporation, New York, NY.
$10,000 to American Academy in Rome, New York, NY.
$10,000 to People for the American Way, DC.
$8,750 to International Womens Health Coalition, New York, NY.
$7,500 to Teaching Matters, New York, NY.

6494
Virginia Cretella Mars Foundation
c/o Brown Brothers Harriman Trust Co.
140 Broadway
New York, NY 10005 (212) 493-8594
Contact: Joseph L. Fuschetto

Established in 1994 in DE.
Foundation type: Independent foundation.
Financial data (yr. ended 12/31/05): Assets, $8,209,705 (M); gifts received, $463,162; expenditures, $390,071; qualifying distributions, $354,010; giving activities include $345,501 for 13 grants.
Purpose and activities: Giving primarily for education.
Fields of interest: Visual arts; Performing arts; Elementary school/education; Secondary school/education; Higher education; Environment.
Type of support: General/operating support; Land acquisition; Seed money; Curriculum development.
Limitations: Giving primarily in NY and WY. No grants to individuals.
Officers: Pamela M. Wright, Pres.; Marijke E. Mars, V.P.; Valerie A. Mars, Secy.; Stephanie J. Schuetz, Secy.; Victoria B. Mars, Treas.
EIN: 133798973
Selected grants: The following grants were reported in 2004.
$60,000 to Rosemount Center, DC.
$50,000 to Wildlife Trust, New York, NY.
$25,000 to Open Space Institute, New York, NY.
$25,000 to Salvation Army.
$15,000 to Charities Aid Foundation (CAF) America, Alexandria, VA.

6495
The Margot Marsh Biodiversity Foundation ◇
c/o Trainer Wortham & Co.
1230 Ave. of the Americas
New York, NY 10020

Established in 1996 in CA.
Foundation type: Independent foundation.
Financial data (yr. ended 12/31/05): Assets, $8,966,746 (M); expenditures, $643,394; qualifying distributions, $594,877; giving activities include $529,500 for 28 grants (high: $135,000; low: $4,500).
Purpose and activities: Support for organizations which operate wildlife and conservation protection programs on a worldwide basis.
Fields of interest: Environment, natural resources; Animals/wildlife, preservation/protection.
Type of support: Program development; Research.
Limitations: Applications not accepted. Giving on a national basis. No grants to individuals.
Application information: Contributes only to pre-selected organizations.
Officers: Russell Mittermeier, Pres.; Karl Zobell, V.P. and Secy.; H. Williamson Ghriskey, Jr., V.P. and C.F.O.
Director: William Konstant.
EIN: 330683174
Selected grants: The following grants were reported in 2004.
$195,500 to Conservation International, DC. 5 grants: $26,000, $75,000, $24,500, $20,000, $50,000
$25,000 to Arcadia University, Glenside, PA.
$24,000 to Houston Zoo, Houston, TX.

$20,000 to Zoological Society of San Diego, San Diego, CA.
$15,000 to African Wildlife Foundation, DC.
$8,000 to Arizona State University, Tempe, AZ.

6496
Martin Family Foundation ◇
c/o Marcum & Kliegman, LLP
655 3rd Ave., 16th Fl.
New York, NY 10017

Established in 1989 in CA.
Donors: Eff W. Martin; Goldman Sachs & Co.
Foundation type: Independent foundation.
Financial data (yr. ended 3/31/05): Assets, $10,957,030 (M); gifts received, $1,506,600; expenditures, $1,483,434; qualifying distributions, $1,365,730; giving activities include $1,363,491 for 67 grants (high: $260,000; low: $150).
Purpose and activities: Giving primarily for higher education, as well as for health associations, social services, and for Presbyterian churches.
Fields of interest: Performing arts, orchestra (symphony); Elementary/secondary education; Higher education; Business school/education; Health organizations, association; Athletics/sports, school programs; Human services; Children/youth, services; Protestant agencies & churches.
Limitations: Applications not accepted. Giving primarily in Atherton, Menlo Park, San Francisco, and Stanford, CA. No grants to individuals.
Application information: Contributes only to pre-selected organizations.
Trustees: Eff W. Martin; Patricia M. Martin.
EIN: 133532032
Selected grants: The following grants were reported in 2004.
$110,000 to Westmont College, Santa Barbara, CA. 2 grants: $100,000, $10,000
$100,000 to Church of the Pioneers Foundation, Menlo Park, CA.
$25,000 to Alzheimers Association, Mountain View, CA.
$25,000 to Hope Unlimited International, San Francisco, CA.
$25,000 to Pepperdine University, Malibu, CA.
$5,000 to Child Advocates of Santa Clara and San Mateo Counties, Milpitas, CA.
$5,000 to Malibu Presbyterian Church, Malibu, CA.
$3,800 to San Francisco Symphony, San Francisco, CA.
$2,620 to Stanford University, Stanford, CA.

6497
Virginia & Leonard Marx Foundation ◇
708 3rd Ave., 15th Fl.
New York, NY 10017 (212) 557-1400
Contact: Jennifer Gruenberg, Secy.

Established in 1959 in NY.
Donors: Leonard Marx‡; Virginia Marx; Dollar Land Syndicate; Guest Realty; Rier Realty Co., Inc.; Argin Realty; Joseph E. Marx Co., Inc.; 26 East Realty; 17 West Orange Realty Corp.; Merchants National Prop. Inc.
Foundation type: Independent foundation.
Financial data (yr. ended 12/31/04): Assets, $54,367,260 (M); gifts received, $4,771,332; expenditures, $3,083,589; qualifying distributions, $2,825,088; giving activities include $2,825,000 for 7 grants (high: $1,000,000; low: $5,000).

Fields of interest: Higher education; Libraries (public); Education; Hospitals (general); Reproductive health, family planning; Human services.
Limitations: Giving primarily in New York, NY. No grants to individuals.
Application information: Application form not required.
Initial approach: Proposal
Deadline(s): None
Officers: Edwin Solot, Jr., Pres.; Jennifer Gruenberg, Secy.
EIN: 136162557

6498
The William Marx Foundation ◇
c/o H.J. Behrman & Co., LLP
2 Penn Plz., Ste. 1970
New York, NY 10121

Donors: Helen Schulman Marx; William Marx; Cynthia Marks.
Foundation type: Independent foundation.
Financial data (yr. ended 10/31/05): Assets, $1,179,873 (M); gifts received, $800,000; expenditures, $596,191; qualifying distributions, $592,561; giving activities include $588,500 for 18 grants (high: $200,000; low: $500).
Purpose and activities: Giving primarily to services for the developmentally disabled, hospice care, and medical sciences; support also for Jewish welfare organizations.
Fields of interest: Hospitals (general); Medical research, institute; Residential/custodial care, hospices; Civil rights; Jewish federated giving programs; Jewish agencies & temples; Disabilities, people with.
Limitations: Applications not accepted. Giving primarily in NY. No grants to individuals.
Application information: Contributes only to pre-selected organizations.
Officers: Cynthia Marks, Pres.; Laurie Lederman, V.P.
EIN: 116020448

6499
The Page and Otto Marx, Jr. Foundation ◇
c/o Joseph W. Levy
3000 Marcus Ave., Ste. 3W10
New Hyde Park, NY 11042

Established in 1984 in NY.
Donors: Otto Marx, Jr.; Page M. Marx‡.
Foundation type: Independent foundation.
Financial data (yr. ended 12/31/05): Assets, $22,354,459 (M); expenditures, $1,120,661; qualifying distributions, $991,260; giving activities include $943,893 for 88 grants (high: $55,000; low: $250).
Purpose and activities: Giving primarily for education, health care and health associations.
Fields of interest: Arts; Education; Health care; Health organizations, association; Human services.
Limitations: Applications not accepted. Giving primarily in NY. No grants to individuals.
Application information: Contributes only to pre-selected organizations.
Officers and Directors:* Bruce J. Westcott,* Pres.; Joseph W. Levy,* V.P. and Treas.; Jeffrey S. Levin, Secy.; Jill S. Levy; Helen Westcott.
EIN: 133200783

Selected grants: The following grants were reported in 2005.

$55,000 to Life Needs Coop, Great Barrington, MA.

$25,000 to Alzheimers Association, Chicago, IL.

$20,000 to American Lung Association, New York, NY.

$15,000 to Camphill Foundation, Hudson, NY.

$14,000 to Deborah Hospital Foundation, Browns Mills, NJ.

$12,500 to New York Academy of Medicine, New York, NY.

$10,000 to Saint Ignatius Loyola Church, New York, NY.

$7,500 to Art Resources Transfer, New York, NY.

$7,000 to Trenton Childrens Chorus, Princeton, NJ.

$6,000 to Boston College, Chestnut Hill, MA.

6500
Masada Foundation ✦ ☆

137-05 72nd Rd.

Flushing, NY 11367

Contact: Richard Kirschner, Pres.

Established in 2002 in NY.

Donor: Richard Kirschner.

Foundation type: Independent foundation.

Financial data (yr. ended 9/30/05): Assets, $51,010 (M); gifts received, $519,530; expenditures, $659,607; qualifying distributions, $659,557; giving activities include $659,557 for grants.

Fields of interest: Jewish agencies & temples.

Limitations: Applications not accepted.

Application information: Contributes only to pre-selected organizations.

Officers and Directors:* Richard Kirschner,* Pres.; Stanley Fleishman,* Secy.; Rachelle Kirschner,* Treas.

EIN: 161622664

6501
Mashala Foundation, Inc. ✦

1957 E. 4th St.

Brooklyn, NY 11223 (212) 695-4510

Contact: Max Shalom, Dir.

Donors: Max Shalom; Allura Imports, Inc.

Foundation type: Independent foundation.

Financial data (yr. ended 12/31/05): Assets, $1,388,660 (M); gifts received, $591,911; expenditures, $582,710; qualifying distributions, $581,653; giving activities include $581,653 for 304 grants (high: $200,000; low: $10; average: $1,000–$20,000).

Purpose and activities: Support for Jewish temples and organizations.

Fields of interest: Jewish agencies & temples.

Application information:

Initial approach: Letter

Deadline(s): None

Directors: Max Shalom; Raymond Shalom.

EIN: 116100993

Selected grants: The following grants were reported in 2005.

$236,000 to Magen David Yeshiva, Brooklyn, NY. 2 grants: $36,000, $200,000

$60,050 to Yeshiva Shaare Torah, Brooklyn, NY. 2 grants: $60,000, $50

$3,600 to Ozar Hatorah, New York, NY.

$250 to Yeshiva of Greater Washington, Silver Spring, MD.

6502
Massry Charitable Foundation, Inc. ✦

c/o Norman Massry

255 Washington Ave. Ext.

Albany, NY 12205

Established in 1994.

Donor: Morris Massry.

Foundation type: Independent foundation.

Financial data (yr. ended 12/31/03): Assets, $12,199,654 (M); gifts received, $1,450,120; expenditures, $404,687; qualifying distributions, $356,932; giving activities include $356,932 for 64 grants (high: $105,000; low: $100).

Purpose and activities: Giving primarily for education, health and human services, federated giving programs, and Jewish organizations.

Fields of interest: Education; Health care; Human services; Family services; Federated giving programs; Jewish federated giving programs; Jewish agencies & temples.

Limitations: Applications not accepted. Giving primarily in NY. No grants to individuals.

Application information: Unsolicited requests for funds not accepted.

Officers: Morris Massry, Pres.; Esther Massry, V.P.; Norman Massry, Secy.-Treas.

EIN: 141777179

Selected grants: The following grants were reported in 2003.

$105,000 to Daughters of Sarah Jewish Foundation, Albany, NY. For general support.

$74,000 to United Jewish Foundation, Bloomfield Hills, MI. For general support.

$30,500 to Seton Health Foundation, Troy, NY. For general support.

$20,000 to Equinox, Albany, NY.

$14,730 to United Way. For general support.

$11,500 to Beit Edmond Safra Congregation, New York, NY. For general support.

$11,500 to Boy Scouts of America, Twin Rivers Council, Albany, NY. For general support.

$10,850 to Rensselaer County Historical Society, Troy, NY. For general support.

$10,000 to State University of New York at Albany Foundation, Albany, NY. For general support.

$5,000 to Temple Beth-El, Troy, NY. For general support.

6503
The MAT Charitable Foundation, Inc. ✦

740 Broadway, 2nd Fl.

New York, NY 10003

Established in 1992 in NY.

Donor: Ruth Uris†.

Foundation type: Independent foundation.

Financial data (yr. ended 6/30/03): Assets, $18,476,740 (M); expenditures, $1,983,446; qualifying distributions, $1,776,014; giving activities include $1,321,184 for 60 grants (high: $360,000; low: $225; average: $10,000–$25,000).

Purpose and activities: Giving primarily for the arts, especially visual and performing arts, as well as to support children's education.

Fields of interest: Visual arts; Performing arts; Elementary/secondary education; Higher education; Education; Human services; Children/youth, services.

Type of support: General/operating support.

Limitations: Giving primarily in NY. No grants to individuals.

Application information:

Initial approach: Letter

Deadline(s): None

Officers: Jane U. Bayard, Pres.; Timothy U. Nye, V.P.; Amy Nye Wolf, Secy.-Treas.

Number of staff: 1 part-time professional.

EIN: 136991067

Selected grants: The following grants were reported in 2003.

$190,000 to Foundation 20 21, New York, NY.

$125,000 to Brearley School, New York, NY.

$35,000 to Whitney Museum of American Art, New York, NY.

$20,000 to Brooklyn Museum, Brooklyn, NY.

$5,000 to Artists Space, New York, NY.

$5,000 to Studio Museum in Harlem, New York, NY.

$3,500 to Haleakala, Kitchen Center for Video, Music, and Dance, New York, NY.

$2,390 to National Arts Club, New York, NY.

$2,000 to Cunningham Dance Foundation, New York, NY.

$110 to Childrens Museum of Manhattan, New York, NY.

6504
The G. Harold & Leila Y. Mathers
Charitable Foundation ▼ ✦

118 N. Bedford Rd., Ste. 203

Mount Kisco, NY 10549-2555 (914) 242-0465

Contact: James H. Handelman, Exec. Dir.

FAX: (914) 242-0665;

E-mail: admin@mathersfoundation.org; Additional e-mail (for James H. Handelman): jh@mathersfoundation.org; URL: http://www.mathersfoundation.org

Established in 1975 in NY.

Donors: G. Harold Mathers†; Leila Y. Mathers†.

Foundation type: Independent foundation.

Financial data (yr. ended 12/31/05): Assets, $173,280,289 (M); expenditures, $13,150,754; qualifying distributions, $10,704,914; giving activities include $10,100,270 for 62 grants (high: $600,000; low: $7,500; average: $10,000–$350,000).

Purpose and activities: The foundation is primarily interested in supporting fundamental basic research in the life sciences. Support is provided for specific projects from established researchers at top universities and independent research institutions within the United States.

Fields of interest: Science, research; Biological sciences.

Type of support: General/operating support; Research.

Limitations: Giving on a national basis. No grants to individuals.

Publications: Application guidelines.

Application information: General inquiries can be made via e-mail. Specific detailed queries must be received by mail. Application form not required.

Initial approach: Letter

Copies of proposal: 1

Deadline(s): None

Board meeting date(s): 2 or 3 times per year

Final notification: Within 90 days of submission of request

Officers and Directors:* Donald E. Handelman,* Pres.; William R. Handelman,* V.P.; Don Fizer,* Secy.; Joseph W. Handelman,* Treas.; James H. Handelman, Exec. Dir.; William S. Young.

Number of staff: 1 full-time professional; 1 full-time support.
EIN: 237441901
Selected grants: The following grants were reported in 2005.
$875,000 to Columbia University, New York, NY. 2 grants: $600,000 (For research, Molecular Approach T Complex Neural Circuitry and Their Transient and Persistent Modulation by Different Forms of Attention), $275,000 (For research, Regulation of Vesicle Transport Pathway Established By Genome Scale Function of Scans).
$567,100 to University of California, San Francisco, CA. For Prion research.
$559,875 to Yale University, New Haven, CT. 2 grants: $284,845 (For research, Structural Studies in Cellular Transport), $275,030 (For research, Molecular Mechanism of Synaptic Vesicle Biogenesis).
$395,011 to Whitehead Institute for Biomedical Research, Cambridge, MA. For research in protein folding.
$350,000 to Southwest Foundation for Biomedical Research, San Antonio, TX. For research in brain function.
$333,300 to University of California, Los Angeles, CA. For research, Functional Characterization of the Vault Ribonucleoprotein Particle.
$288,000 to Salk Institute for Biological Studies, San Diego, CA. For research, An Integrated Approach to Understand Embryonic Form - The Vertebrate Heart.
$164,982 to Harvard University, Cambridge, MA. For research, Molecules and Mechanisms of Hearing, at Medical School in Boston.

6505

Pierre and Maria-Gaetana Matisse Charitable Foundation ◇

1 E. 53rd St.
New York, NY 10022-4200

Established in 1995 in DE and NY.
Donors: Maria-Gaetana Matisse; The Maria-Gaetana Matisse Revocable Trust.
Foundation type: Independent foundation.
Financial data (yr. ended 12/31/03): Assets, $104,404,581 (M); gifts received, $78,954,150; expenditures, $859,307; qualifying distributions, $707,171; giving activities include $460,000 for 6 grants (high: $200,000; low: $10,000; average: $10,000–$25,000).
Fields of interest: Museums (art).
Limitations: Applications not accepted. No grants to individuals.
Application information: Contributes only to pre-selected organizations.
Officers and Directors:* Robert H. Horowitz, Pres. and Secy.; Janos Farkas,* V.P.; Eugene V. Thaw,* V.P.
EIN: 133838457

6506

Matlin Family Foundation ◇

c/o Cleary Gottlieb
1 Liberty Plz.
New York, NY 10006

Established in 2003 in NY.
Donors: David J. Matlin; Lisa Hoffer Matlin.

Foundation type: Independent foundation.
Financial data (yr. ended 12/31/05): Assets, $43,609 (M); gifts received, $417,508; expenditures, $708,895; qualifying distributions, $708,724; giving activities include $704,862 for 12 grants (high: $384,393; low: $200; average: $5,000–$16,098).
Fields of interest: Diabetes research; Children/youth, services.
Limitations: Applications not accepted. Giving primarily in NY; with some giving in PA. No grants to individuals.
Application information: Contributes only to pre-selected organizations.
Trustees: David L. Matlin; Lisa Hoffer Matlin.
EIN: 200216086

6507

The Edward E. & Marie L. Matthews Foundation ◇

c/o Chadbourne & Parke, LLP
30 Rockeffeler Plz.
New York, NY 10112

Established in 2003 in NY and DE.
Donors: Edward E. Matthews; Marie L. Matthews.
Foundation type: Independent foundation.
Financial data (yr. ended 12/31/05): Assets, $25,378,865 (M); expenditures, $1,683,553; qualifying distributions, $1,526,344; giving activities include $1,440,000 for 59 grants (high: $252,500; low: $890).
Fields of interest: Elementary/secondary education; Higher education; Education; Health care; Human services; Family services; Protestant agencies & churches.
Type of support: General/operating support; Capital campaigns; Building/renovation; Program development; Scholarship funds; Research.
Limitations: Applications not accepted. Giving on a national basis, with some emphasis on CA, DE, IL, NJ, and NY. No grants to individuals.
Application information: Contributes only to pre-selected organizations.
Officers and Directors:* Edward E. Matthews,* Pres.; Douglas L. Matthews,* Secy.; Louise M. Flickinger; Gregory E. Matthews; Marie L. Matthews; Russell E. Matthews.
EIN: 020656117

6508

The Mayday Fund ◇

c/o SPG
136 W. 21st St., 6th Fl.
New York, NY 10011   (212) 366-6970
Contact: Christina Spellman, Exec. Dir.
FAX: (212) 366-6979;
E-mail: inquiry@maydayfund.org; URL: http://www.painandhealth.org/mayday/mayday-home.html

Established in 1992 in NY.
Donors: Shirley S. Katzenbach†; John C. Beck; Pamela M. Thye; Caroline N. Sidnam.
Foundation type: Independent foundation.
Financial data (yr. ended 12/31/03): Assets, $24,869,603 (M); expenditures, $1,188,744; qualifying distributions, $1,114,798; giving activities include $735,583 for 16 grants (high: $146,524; low: $750).

Purpose and activities: The foundation is dedicated to the reduction of the profound human problems associated with physical pain and its consequences. The fund is particularly interested in projects that result in clinical interventions to reduce the toll of physical pain, pediatric pain, pain in non-verbal populations, and pain in the context of emergency medicine. The fund also promotes networking between veterinary and human medicine.
Fields of interest: Medical research, institute.
Limitations: Giving on a national basis. No grants to individuals, or generally for endowments, capital projects, equipment, general operating expenses, ongoing activities, or annual fundraising drives.
Publications: Annual report; Financial statement; Grants list.
Application information: Mail and phone contacts only after initial E-mail communications. Application form not required.
   Initial approach: E-mail to Exec. Dir.
   Copies of proposal: 1
   Deadline(s): None
   Board meeting date(s): Quarterly
Officer: Christina Spellman, Exec. Dir.
Trustees: John C. Beck; Robert D.C. Meeker, Jr.; Caroline N. Sidnam; Pamela M. Thye.
EIN: 133645438
Selected grants: The following grants were reported in 2003.
$146,524 to American Society of Law, Medicine and Ethics, Boston, MA. For general support.
$143,750 to Emergency Medicine Foundation, Dallas, TX. For general support.
$108,136 to University of California, Berkeley, CA. For research on pain medication in emergency room treatment.
$80,418 to Massachusetts General Hospital, Boston, MA. For Cares About Pain project.
$67,365 to Newport Hospital, Newport, RI. For interventions to enhance pain management.
$62,500 to Persephone Productions, DC. For pediatric pain public education program.
$37,500 to Village Center for Care, New York, NY. For pain management initiative.
$15,134 to University of Iowa, College of Nursing, Iowa City, IA. For state of the art review of tools for pain management in nonverbal populations.
$5,000 to Caring Connections, DC. For national consensus project for quality palliative care.
$4,000 to Center for the Advancement of Health, DC. For general support.

6509

Chaim Mayer Foundation, Inc. ◇

80 Broad St., 29th Fl.
New York, NY 10004
Contact: Hirsch Wulliger, Cont.

Established in 1981 in NY.
Donor: Joseph Neumann.
Foundation type: Independent foundation.
Financial data (yr. ended 4/30/06): Assets, $13,267 (M); gifts received, $1,135,012; expenditures, $1,128,812; qualifying distributions, $2,255,960; giving activities include $1,127,980 for grants.
Purpose and activities: Giving limited to Jewish concerns, including yeshivas, synagogues, and grants to individuals for research and study of the Bible, the Talmud, and similar theological works.
Fields of interest: Theological school/education; Education; Jewish agencies & temples.

Type of support: General/operating support; Grants to individuals; Scholarships—to individuals.
Limitations: Giving on a national basis.
Application information: Application form not required.
  Initial approach: Letter
  Deadline(s): None
Officers: Joseph Neumann, Pres.; Rachel Neumann, V.P.; Donald Press, V.P.; Rabbi J.A. Luria, Cont.; Hirsch Wulliger, Cont.
EIN: 133119407

6510
The Louis B. Mayer Foundation
67A E. 77th St.
New York, NY 10021-1813
Contact: Ann Brownell Sloane, Admin.

Established in 1947 in CA.
Donor: Louis B. Mayer†.
Foundation type: Independent foundation.
Financial data (yr. ended 12/31/05): Assets, $12,035,895 (M); expenditures, $600,694; qualifying distributions, $531,696; giving activities include $505,937 for 11 grants (high: $170,000; low: $5,000).
Purpose and activities: Support for cutting edge medical research for the treatment of cancer and for film preservation.
Fields of interest: Media, film/video; Medical research.
Type of support: Continuing support; Program development; Research.
Limitations: Applications not accepted. Giving on a national basis. No support for filmmaking. No grants to individuals; no loans.
Application information: Contributes only to pre-selected organizations.
  Board meeting date(s): Quarterly
Officers and Trustees:* Robert A. Gottlieb,* Pres.; Carol Farkas,* Secy.-Treas.; Elliot R. Cattarulla.
EIN: 952232340
Selected grants: The following grants were reported in 2003.
$150,000 to Dana-Farber Cancer Institute, Boston, MA. For development of molecular-based fusion cell vaccine for treatment of human cancer.
$150,000 to Mount Sinai Medical Center, New York, NY. 2 grants: $25,000 (For matching challenge grant for MRI Technology Program), $125,000 (For The Role of Coronary CTA and Cardiac MRI in the Screening Evaluation of Coronary Artery Disease).
$52,450 to George Eastman House/International Museum of Photography and Film, Rochester, NY. 2 grants: $12,500 (For matching grant for Curatorial Assistant position), $39,950 (For further support of L. Jeffrey Selznick School of Film Preservation).
$50,000 to Miami City Ballet, Miami Beach, FL. For general support.
$10,000 to University of California, Pacific Film Archive, Berkeley, CA. For part-time support to incorporate new information into FIAF Treasures Database.

6511
Mayore Foundation, Ltd. ◇
100 Henry St.
Brooklyn, NY 11201

Established in 2000 in NY.
Donor: Sholom Drizin.
Foundation type: Independent foundation.
Financial data (yr. ended 12/31/03): Assets, $24,823 (M); gifts received, $747,000; expenditures, $720,028; qualifying distributions, $719,795; giving activities include $719,795 for 1 grant.
Fields of interest: Jewish agencies & temples.
Limitations: Applications not accepted. Giving primarily in Brooklyn, NY. No grants to individuals.
Application information: Contributes only to pre-selected organizations.
Officers: Sholom Drizin, Pres.; Shoshana Drizin, Secy.; Moshe Drizin, Treas.
EIN: 113432602

6512
MBIA Foundation, Inc. ◇
113 King St.
Armonk, NY 10504 (914) 765-3832
Contact: Nancy Paulercio

Established in 2001 in NY.
Donors: MBIA Insurance Corp.; John Caouette; Francie Heller; Kathleen Okenica; Kevin Silva; Kutak Rock LLP; Richard L. Weil; Moody's Corp.
Foundation type: Company-sponsored foundation.
Financial data (yr. ended 12/31/04): Assets, $2,278,238 (M); gifts received, $2,015,000; expenditures, $1,457,790; qualifying distributions, $1,440,971; giving activities include $1,440,971 for 477 grants (high: $105,000; low: $100).
Purpose and activities: The foundation supports organizations involved with education, health, and human services.
Fields of interest: Arts; Higher education; Education; Health care; Medical research; Disasters, 9/11/01; Human services; Community development; Jewish federated giving programs; Christian agencies & churches.
Type of support: Program development; Employee volunteer services; Employee matching gifts.
Limitations: Giving on a national basis with some emphasis on CT, NJ, NY, and PA. No support for discriminatory organizations or political or lobbying organizations, religious, fraternal, athletic, social, or veterans' organizations not of direct benefit to the entire community, or federated giving programs. No grants to individuals, or for fundraising activities related to individual sponsorship, capital campaigns, endowments, or fundraising events.
Application information: A site visit may be requested. Application form required.
  Initial approach: Contact foundation for application form
Officers and Directors: Susan A. Voltz,* Pres.; Kevin D. Silva,* V.P.; Lisa Wilson, Secy.; Neil G. Budnick,* Treas.; Jack Caouette; Gary C. Dunton; Harold Wagner; Richard I. Weill.
EIN: 134163899
Selected grants: The following grants were reported in 2005.
$100,000 to New York City 2012, New York, NY.
$33,000 to John F. Kennedy Center for the Performing Arts, DC.
$30,000 to Boston College, Chestnut Hill, MA.
$20,000 to Saint Rose of Lima Church, Short Hills, NJ.
$10,000 to Norwalk River Rowing Association, Norwalk, CT.
$10,000 to Westchester Hispanic Coalition, White Plains, NY.

$2,000 to Owls Head Transportation Museum, Owls Head, ME.
$1,500 to Saint Anthony of Padua Parish, Ambler, PA.
$1,000 to Energy Outreach Colorado, Denver, CO.
$1,000 to Princeton University, Princeton, NJ.

6513
The McCaddin-McQuirk Foundation, Inc. ◇
P.O. Box 5001
New York, NY 10185-5001 (914) 282-3714
Contact: Frank J. Hardart III, V.P.

Incorporated in 1902 in NY.
Donors: Rt. Rev. John McQuirk†; Ann Eliza McCaddin Walsh†.
Foundation type: Independent foundation.
Financial data (yr. ended 12/31/05): Assets, $5,421,571 (M); expenditures, $344,312; qualifying distributions, $334,631; giving activities include $327,900 for 100 grants (high: $39,000; low: $300).
Purpose and activities: To foster educational opportunities for poorer students to be priests, deacons, catechists, or lay teachers of the Roman Catholic Church in the U.S. or elsewhere.
Fields of interest: Theological school/education; Roman Catholic agencies & churches.
International interests: Africa; Asia; Canada; South America.
Type of support: Scholarship funds.
Limitations: Giving primarily in the U.S., Canada, South America, Africa, and Asia.
Application information: Applications must be made through a bishop, rector, or head of a seminary. Application form not required.
  Initial approach: Letter
  Deadline(s): Dec. 1
Officers: Robert G. Ix, Pres.; Frank J. Hardart III, V.P.; Thomas F. Blaney, Secy.; John J. Eager, Treas.
Trustees: John Caffrey; Francis M. Hartman; Henry J. Humphreys; Patrick Maloney; Rev. Msgr. Thomas A. Modugno; Carrol A. Muccia, Jr.; Martin W. Ronan, Jr.; Thomas A. Turley; Julien N. Vachon; William A. White.
EIN: 136134444

6514
James J. McCann Charitable Trust and McCann Foundation, Inc. ◇
(also known as McCann Foundation)
35 Market St.
Poughkeepsie, NY 12601 (845) 452-3085
Contact: Michael G. Gartland, Secy.

The foundation was established in 1967, the trust in 1969. They function as a single entity; financial data is combined.
Donor: James J. McCann†.
Foundation type: Independent foundation.
Financial data (yr. ended 12/31/04): Assets, $35,410,580 (M); expenditures, $2,020,589; qualifying distributions, $1,817,118; giving activities include $1,695,012 for 3+ grants.
Purpose and activities: Giving primarily for secondary and higher education (including scholarship funds), recreation, civic projects, social services, cultural programs, church support and religious associations, and hospitals.
Fields of interest: Arts; Secondary school/education; Higher education; Hospitals (general);

Recreation; Human services; Government/public administration; Christian agencies & churches.
Type of support: Continuing support; Annual campaigns; Building/renovation; Equipment; Land acquisition; Conferences/seminars; Publication; Seed money; Fellowships; Scholarship funds.
Limitations: Giving primarily in Poughkeepsie and Dutchess County, NY. No grants to individuals, or for operating budgets, emergency or endowment funds, deficit financing, or matching gifts; generally no loans.
Publications: Annual report.
Application information: Application form not required.
Initial approach: Letter or proposal
Copies of proposal: 1
Deadline(s): Submit proposal preferably in Feb. or Aug.; no deadline
Board meeting date(s): Jan. and July
Final notification: 60 days
Officers and Trustees:* Richard V. Corbally,* Pres.; Dennis J. Murray, V.P.; Michael G. Gartland, Secy.
Number of staff: 1 part-time professional; 1 part-time support.

6515
The McCarthy Charities, Inc. ✧
P.O. Box 1090
Troy, NY   12181-1090

Incorporated in 1917 in NY.
Donors: Robert H. McCarthy†; Lucy A. McCarthy†; Peter F. McCarthy†.
Foundation type: Independent foundation.
Financial data (yr. ended 12/31/05): Assets, $18,278,201 (M); expenditures, $773,695; qualifying distributions, $713,674; giving activities include $643,753 for 184 grants (high: $25,000; low: $18).
Purpose and activities: Giving for Roman Catholic church support and church-related education and welfare agencies; support also for community funds, social service agencies, and hospitals.
Fields of interest: Arts; Education; Hospitals (general); Human services; Roman Catholic federated giving programs; Roman Catholic agencies & churches.
Type of support: General/operating support; Continuing support; Annual campaigns; Capital campaigns; Program development; Seed money; Program evaluation; Scholarship funds; Matching/challenge support.
Limitations: Applications not accepted. Giving primarily in the Albany Capital District, NY, area. No grants to individuals.
Application information: Contributes only to pre-selected organizations.
Officers: Pamela McCarthy, Pres.; Denis McCarthy, V.P.; Lucy McCarthy, V.P.; Roseanne M. Hall, Secy.; Robert P. McCarthy, Treas.
Director: Winifred McCarthy.
EIN: 146019064

6516
The Michael W. McCarthy Foundation ✧
c/o Patrick C. McCarthy
400 Townline Rd., Ste. 155
Hauppauge, NY   11788

Trust established in 1958 in NY.

Donors: Michael W. McCarthy†; Margaret E. McCarthy.
Foundation type: Independent foundation.
Financial data (yr. ended 12/31/05): Assets, $29,841,796 (M); gifts received, $20,000; expenditures, $1,829,078; qualifying distributions, $1,695,164; giving activities include $1,587,600 for 40 grants (high: $100,000; low: $5,000).
Purpose and activities: Giving primarily for higher education, a foundation for people who are mentally handicapped, and an international piano competition; funding also for health associations, and human services.
Fields of interest: Museums; Education, special; Higher education; Health organizations, association; Recreation; Human services; Developmentally disabled, centers & services; Federated giving programs.
Type of support: General/operating support.
Limitations: Applications not accepted. Giving primarily in NY; also some giving nationwide. No grants to individuals.
Application information: Contributes only to pre-selected organizations.
Trustees: Brian A. McCarthy; Patrick C. McCarthy; Patrick M. McCarthy.
EIN: 136150919
Selected grants: The following grants were reported in 2004.
$100,000 to College of the Desert Foundation, Palm Desert, CA.
$50,000 to American Foundation for AIDS Research (AMFAR), New York, NY.
$50,000 to City Harvest, New York, NY.
$50,000 to Harlem Childrens Zone, New York, NY.
$50,000 to International Center in New York, New York, NY.
$50,000 to John F. Kennedy Memorial Foundation, Palm Desert, CA.
$50,000 to Ministry for Hope, Port Jefferson, NY.
$50,000 to Saint Francis Hospital Foundation, Roslyn, NY.
$50,000 to W G B H Educational Foundation, Boston, MA.
$25,000 to Harlem United Community AIDS Center, New York, NY.

6517
The Stephanie and Carter McClelland Foundation ✧
c/o RSM McGladrey, Inc.
1185 Ave. of the Americas
New York, NY   10036

Established in 1997 in NY.
Donor: W. Carter McClelland.
Foundation type: Independent foundation.
Financial data (yr. ended 11/30/05): Assets, $3,791,932 (M); gifts received, $2,321,350; expenditures, $1,141,010; qualifying distributions, $1,126,260; giving activities include $1,126,260 for 66 grants (high: $350,000; low: $250).
Fields of interest: Arts; Higher education; Human services.
Limitations: Applications not accepted. Giving primarily in NY. No grants to individuals.
Application information: Contributes only to pre-selected organizations.
Trustees: Stephanie P. McClelland; W. Carter McClelland.
EIN: 137154217

6518
Dextra Baldwin McGonagle Foundation, Inc.
P.O. Box 709
South Salem, NY   10590
Contact: Jonathan G. Spanier, Pres.

Incorporated in 1967 in NY.
Donor: Dextra Baldwin McGonagle†.
Foundation type: Independent foundation.
Financial data (yr. ended 12/31/05): Assets, $16,386,654 (M); expenditures, $988,414; qualifying distributions, $882,902; giving activities include $809,126 for 94 grants (high: $200,000; low: $15).
Purpose and activities: Primary areas of interest include hospitals, the medical sciences, and medical research, including cancer research; grants also for higher and medical education, social service agencies, and cultural programs.
Fields of interest: Arts; Higher education; Medical school/education; Hospitals (general); Health care; Cancer; Biomedicine; Medical research, institute; Cancer research; Human services; Biological sciences; Aging.
Type of support: Annual campaigns; Equipment; Endowments; Seed money; Research.
Limitations: Giving primarily in CA and NY. No grants to individuals, or for matching gifts.
Application information: Application form not required.
Initial approach: 1-page summary of proposal
Copies of proposal: 1
Deadline(s): None
Board meeting date(s): As required
Officers and Directors:* Maury L. Spanier,* Chair.; David B. Spanier,* Vice-Chair.; Jonathan G. Spanier, Pres. and Treas.; Helen G. Spanier,* V.P. and Secy.
Number of staff: 1 full-time professional; 3 part-time support.
EIN: 136219236

6519
The Donald C. McGraw Foundation, Inc. ✧
c/o Deutsche Trust Co. of NY
P.O. Box 1297
Church St. Sta.
New York, NY   10008
Application address: c/o Charles Fischer, Deutsche Bank, FL, 350 Royal Palm Way, Palm Beach, FL 33480

Incorporated in 1963 in NY.
Donors: Donald C. McGraw; D. McGraw Charitable Trust.
Foundation type: Independent foundation.
Financial data (yr. ended 1/31/05): Assets, $26,870,677 (M); gifts received, $91,600; expenditures, $941,549; qualifying distributions, $846,674; giving activities include $830,000 for 31 grants (high: $200,000; low: $5,000).
Purpose and activities: Giving primarily for the arts, particularly to museums, as well as for education, health care, hospices, and medical research, and children, youth, and social services, including an emergency shelter providing health care to homeless individuals and families.
Fields of interest: Museums; Museums (marine/maritime); Education; Hospitals (general); Health organizations, association; Breast cancer research; Boys & girls clubs; Human services; Residential/custodial care, hospices.

Limitations: Giving primarily to FL and MA. No grants to individuals.
Application information: Available funds for new applicants are very limited.
Initial approach: Letter
Deadline(s): Dec. 31
Officer: Donald C. McGraw, Pres.
Directors: John L. Cady; J. Patterson Cooper; David W. McGraw; Donald C. McGraw III.
EIN: 136165603
Selected grants: The following grants were reported in 2004.
$200,000 to Community Hospice of Northeast Florida, Jacksonville, FL. For general support.
$100,000 to Mystic Seaport Museum, Mystic, CT. For general support.
$50,000 to Boca Raton Community Hospital, Boca Raton, FL. For general support.
$50,000 to Mayo Clinic Jacksonville, Jacksonville, FL. For general support.
$25,000 to Baptist Medical Center, Wolfson Childrens Hospital, Jacksonville, FL. For general support.
$25,000 to National Maritime Historical Society, Peekskill, NY. For general support.
$25,000 to U.S.S. Massachusetts Memorial Committee, Fall River, MA. For general support.
$20,000 to Museum of Science and History, Jacksonville, FL. For general support.
$15,000 to Edward Waters College, Jacksonville, FL. For general support.
$15,000 to Heritage Plantation of Sandwich, Sandwich, MA. For general support.

6520
Elizabeth McGraw Foundation, Inc. ◇
c/o Deutsche Bank Trust Co. of NY
P.O. Box 1297
Church St. Sta.
New York, NY 10008
Application address: c/o John McGraw, 157 Eel River Rd., Osterville, MA 02655

Established in 1990 in NY.
Donor: Donald C. McGraw Foundation, Inc.
Foundation type: Independent foundation.
Financial data (yr. ended 9/30/05): Assets, $25,298,520 (M); expenditures, $1,095,625; qualifying distributions, $982,242; giving activities include $965,000 for 10 grants (high: $250,000; low: $5,000).
Fields of interest: Museums (art); Performing arts, ballet; Performing arts, opera; Historic preservation/historical societies; Higher education; Human services.
Limitations: Giving primarily in FL and MA. No grants to individuals.
Application information:
Initial approach: Letter
Deadline(s): None
Officers: John McGraw, Pres.; John Cady, Secy.
Directors: Charles B. Fischer, Jr.; John L. McGraw, Jr.; Ms. Lee McGraw.
EIN: 133591829
Selected grants: The following grants were reported in 2003.
$250,000 to Norton Gallery and School of Art, West Palm Beach, FL. For general support.
$200,000 to Lupus Foundation of New England, Framingham, MA. For general support.
$150,000 to Metropolitan Opera, New York, NY. For general support.

$100,000 to Winterthur Museum, Garden and Library, Winterthur, DE. For general support.
$60,000 to W G B H Educational Foundation, Boston, MA. For general support.
$50,000 to Boston Ballet, Boston, MA. For general support.
$50,000 to Stetson University, DeLand, FL. For general support.
$50,000 to University of Puget Sound, Tacoma, WA. For general support.
$30,000 to Delray Beach Historical Society, Delray Beach, FL. For general support.
$15,000 to Ellis Memorial and Eldredge House, Boston, MA. For general support.

6521
John P. & Anne Welsh McNulty Foundation ◇
c/o BCRS Group/Marcum & Kliegman, LLP
100 Wall St., 11th Fl.
New York, NY 10005

Established in 1985 in FL.
Donors: John P. McNulty; Anne Welsh McNulty.
Foundation type: Independent foundation.
Financial data (yr. ended 11/30/04): Assets, $26,229,369 (M); gifts received, $40,411; expenditures, $1,198,564; qualifying distributions, $1,160,851; giving activities include $1,132,615 for 57 grants (high: $150,000; low: $250).
Fields of interest: Arts; Education; Hospitals (general); Health organizations, association; Medical research, institute; Human services; Residential/custodial care, senior continuing care; Federated giving programs.
Limitations: Applications not accepted. Giving primarily in NY and PA. No grants to individuals.
Application information: Contributes only to pre-selected organizations.
Trustees: Anne Welsh McNulty; John P. McNulty.
EIN: 521445003

6522
The Scott & Suling Mead Foundation ◇
c/o Goldman Sachs, Family Office
1 New York Plz., 40th Fl.
New York, NY 10004

Established in 1996 in DC.
Donor: E. Scott Mead.
Foundation type: Independent foundation.
Financial data (yr. ended 4/30/05): Assets, $10,253,112 (M); gifts received, $5,456,600; expenditures, $696,427; qualifying distributions, $632,927; giving activities include $632,927 for 19 grants (high: $293,323; low: $456).
Purpose and activities: Giving primarily for education and health associations.
Fields of interest: Education; Health organizations, association; Children/youth, services.
Limitations: Applications not accepted. Giving on a national and international basis, with emphasis on London, England; funding also in MA, NY and TX. No grants to individuals.
Application information: Contributes only to pre-selected organizations.
Trustees: E. Scott Mead; James M. Mead; Suling C. Mead.
EIN: 133921104

6523
William M. & Miriam F. Meehan Foundation, Inc. ◇
1192 Park Ave., Ste. 3A
New York, NY 10128 (212) 534-8607
Contact: John D. O'Leary, Exec. Dir.

Established in 1951.
Donors: Terence S. Meehan; Miriam F. Meehan†; Maureen M. O'Leary; Joanne M. Berghold.
Foundation type: Independent foundation.
Financial data (yr. ended 12/31/03): Assets, $7,407,874 (M); gifts received, $22,556; expenditures, $690,442; qualifying distributions, $625,823; giving activities include $594,590 for 43 grants (high: $250,590; low: $500).
Purpose and activities: Giving primarily to Roman Catholic agencies, and for human services and education.
Fields of interest: Arts; Education; Environment; Children/youth, services; Roman Catholic agencies & churches.
Type of support: General/operating support; Continuing support; Annual campaigns; Capital campaigns.
Limitations: Applications not accepted. Giving primarily in New York, NY. No grants to individuals.
Application information: Contributes only to pre-selected organizations.
Board meeting date(s): May and Nov.
Officers and Directors:* Maureen Meehan O'Leary,* V.P.; Terence S. Meehan,* Treas.; John D. O'Leary,* Exec. Dir.; Amy Berghold; David Berghold; Elisabetta Berghold; Joanne M. Berghold; William D. Berghold; William Mark Berghold; Jennifer Kellogg; Emily Souvaine Meehan; William M. Meehan, Ph.D.; Laura Roebuck, M.D.; Tad Sennott.
Number of staff: 1 part-time professional; 2 part-time support.
EIN: 136062834

6524
Megrue Family Foundation ◇ ☆
445 Park Ave., 11th Fl.
New York, NY 10022

Established in 2001 in CT.
Donors: John F. Megrue, Jr.; Lizanne G. Megrue; Delaware Community Foundation.
Foundation type: Independent foundation.
Financial data (yr. ended 12/31/05): Assets, $2,526,756 (M); gifts received, $949,400; expenditures, $326,626; qualifying distributions, $328,749; giving activities include $315,700 for 19 grants (high: $250,000; low: $250; average: $2,500–$10,000).
Purpose and activities: Giving primarily for higher edcuation, including a center for real estate education and research; funding also for youth services.
Fields of interest: Performing arts; Higher education; Youth, services; Foundations (private grantmaking).
Limitations: Applications not accepted. Giving primarily in CT and Hanover, NH; some funding also in Philadelphia, PA. No grants to individuals.
Application information: Contributes only to pre-selected organizations.
Officer and Trustees:* John F. Megrue, Jr.,* Pres.; Lizanne G. Megrue.
EIN: 800004702

Selected grants: The following grants were reported in 2005.
$10,000 to Dartmouth College, Hanover, NH.
$10,000 to Noroton Presbyterian Church, Darien, CT.
$6,200 to Columbus School for Girls, Columbus, OH.
$5,000 to Fairfield County Community Foundation, Wilton, CT.
$5,000 to Shakespeare on the Sound, Norwalk, CT.
$2,500 to Greens Farms Academy, Greens Farms, CT.
$2,500 to New Canaan Country School, New Canaan, CT.
$2,500 to Saint Lukes Foundation, New Canaan, CT.

6525
The Andrew W. Mellon Foundation ▼
140 E. 62nd St.
New York, NY 10021 (212) 838-8400
Contact: Michele S. Warman, Secy. and Genl. Counsel
FAX: (212) 223-2778; URL: http://www.mellon.org

Trust established in 1940 in DE as Avalon Foundation; incorporated in 1954 in NY; merged with Old Dominion Foundation and renamed The Andrew W. Mellon Foundation in 1969.
Donors: Ailsa Mellon Bruce†; Paul Mellon†.
Foundation type: Independent foundation.
Financial data (yr. ended 12/31/05): Assets, $5,586,112,000 (M); expenditures, $253,050,000; qualifying distributions, $227,836,000; giving activities include $199,246,000 for 466 grants, $94,000 for 97 employee matching gifts, and $5,036,000 for foundation-administered programs.
Purpose and activities: Grants on a selective basis for higher education; cultural affairs, including the humanities, museums, art conservation, and performing arts; conservation and the environment; and public affairs.
Fields of interest: Museums; Performing arts; Humanities; Arts; Higher education; Environment, natural resources; Environment; Public affairs.
Type of support: Continuing support; Endowments; Program development; Fellowships; Research; Matching/challenge support.
Limitations: Giving on a national basis. No support for primarily local organizations. No grants to individuals (including scholarships); no loans.
Publications: Annual report; Grants list.
Application information: Please direct inquiries to appropriate program officers. Contact should be by writing or E-mail. Unsolicited proposals are rarely funded. Application form not required.
Initial approach: Letter
Copies of proposal: 1
Deadline(s): None
Board meeting date(s): Mar., June, Sept., and Dec.
Final notification: After board meetings
Officers and Trustees:* Anne M. Tatlock,* Chair.; Don Michael Randel, Pres.; Harriet Zuckerman, Sr. V.P.; Ira H. Fuchs, V.P., Research and Inf. Tech.; John E. Hull, V.P., Finance and C.I.O.; Patricia L. Irvin, V.P., Opers. and Planning; Mary Patterson McPherson, V.P.; Michele S. Warman, Secy. and Genl. Counsel; Thomas J. Sanders, Cont.; William G. Bowen, Ph.D.*, Pres. Emeritus; Lewis W. Bernard; Drew Gilpin Faust; Paul LeClerc; Colin Lucas; Walter

E. Massey; W. Taylor Reveley III; Lawrence R. Ricciardi.
Number of staff: 42 full-time professional; 24 full-time support.
EIN: 131879954
Selected grants: The following grants were reported in 2005.
$9,700,000 to Ithaka Harbors, New York, NY. 2 grants: $3,700,000 (For capital support, payable over 4 years), $6,000,000 (For NITLE (National Institute for Technology and Liberal Education) Funding, payable over 1.50 years).
$6,500,000 to ARTstor, New York, NY. For general support, payable over 2.75 years.
$5,000,000 to American Museum of Natural History, New York, NY. For endowment challenge grant, payable over 5 years.
$5,000,000 to Center for Advanced Study in the Behavioral Sciences, Stanford, CA. For Humanities Fellowships Endowment, payable over 10 years.
$4,622,000 to Woodrow Wilson National Fellowship Foundation, Princeton, NJ. For Mellon Fellowship Program, payable over 1.50 years.
$4,000,000 to American Philosophical Society, Philadelphia, PA. For sabbatical fellowships, payable over 5 years.
$4,000,000 to George Eastman House/International Museum of Photography and Film, Rochester, NY. For Phase III of Advanced Residency Program, payable over 4.50 years.
$225,000 to Second Stage Theater, New York, NY. For National Theater Program, payable over 3 years.
$161,000 to University of Pennsylvania, Philadelphia, PA. For New Directions Fellowships, payable over 3.50 years.

6526
The Alice Pack Melly and L. Thomas Melly Foundation ✧
(formerly L. Thomas Melly Foundation)
c/o BCRS Group/Marcum & Kliegman, LLP
100 Wall St., 11th Fl.
New York, NY 10005-3720

Established in 1969 in NY.
Donors: L. Thomas Melly; Alice Pack Melly.
Foundation type: Independent foundation.
Financial data (yr. ended 5/31/06): Assets, $7,020,312 (M); expenditures, $547,662; qualifying distributions, $525,330; giving activities include $524,585 for 44 grants (high: $328,000; low: $250).
Purpose and activities: Funding primarily for higher education; funding also for health care and social and family services.
Fields of interest: Museums (art); Arts; Elementary/secondary education; Higher education; Education; Health care; Human services; Family services.
Limitations: Applications not accepted. Giving primarily in CT and NY. No grants to individuals.
Application information: Contributes only to pre-selected organizations.
Trustees: Alice P. Melly; David Randolph Melly; L. Thomas Melly; Laura A. Melly; Lee Scott Melly; Thomas L. Melly.
EIN: 237059703
Selected grants: The following grants were reported in 2005.
$353,000 to Hobart and William Smith Colleges, Geneva, NY. 2 grants: $25,000, $328,000

$27,000 to Trinity College, Hartford, CT. 2 grants: $12,000, $15,000
$5,000 to Chatham Hall, Chatham, VA.
$5,000 to Greenwich Library, Greenwich, CT.
$5,000 to Kent School, Kent, CT.
$3,000 to Greenwich Country Day School, Greenwich, CT.
$1,000 to Hill School, Pottstown, PA.
$1,000 to United Negro College Fund, New York, NY.

6527
Johny Melohn Foundation ✧
c/o Altman & Dick
350 Broadway, Ste. 205
New York, NY 10013

Established in 1986 in NY.
Donor: Johny Melohn.
Foundation type: Independent foundation.
Financial data (yr. ended 11/30/04): Assets, $567,393 (M); gifts received, $490,552; expenditures, $577,143; qualifying distributions, $522,475; giving activities include $522,475 for 80 grants (high: $100,000; low: $18).
Purpose and activities: Giving primarily for Jewish temples, agencies, and yeshivas.
Fields of interest: Elementary/secondary education; Jewish agencies & temples.
Limitations: Applications not accepted. Giving primarily in NY. No grants to individuals.
Application information: Contributes only to pre-selected organizations.
Officer: Johny Melohn, Pres.
EIN: 133395220
Selected grants: The following grants were reported in 2003.
$100,000 to Congregation Mesifta Ohel Torah, Monsey, NY.
$25,000 to American Friends of Even Yisroel Charitable Foundation, Passaic, NJ.
$25,000 to Congregation Gvul Yavetz.
$15,000 to Congregation Nachlas Yitzchok, Brooklyn, NY.
$15,000 to Yeshiva Mishkon Yosef, Brooklyn, NY.
$10,000 to Bais Medrash L Torah, Monsey, NY.
$5,000 to Yeshiva Chofetz Chaim of Radun, Philadelphia, PA.
$3,000 to Temple Shaaray Tefila, New York, NY.
$2,600 to Yeshivah Harbotzas Torah Zichron Schneur, Brooklyn, NY.
$1,000 to Yeshiva of Far Rockaway, Far Rockaway, NY.

6528
The Melohn Foundation, Inc. ✧
c/o Melohn Properties
1995 Broadway, 14th Fl.
New York, NY 10023-5882

Established in 1965 in NY.
Donors: Alfons Melohn; Leon Melohn; and members of the Melohn family.
Foundation type: Independent foundation.
Financial data (yr. ended 7/31/05): Assets, $13,893,951 (M); expenditures, $1,324,443; qualifying distributions, $577,234; giving activities include $570,912 for 98 grants (high: $300,000; low: $25).
Purpose and activities: Giving primarily for Jewish religious organizations, including yeshivas and temples.

Fields of interest: Elementary/secondary education; Jewish federated giving programs; Jewish agencies & temples.
Limitations: Giving primarily in Brooklyn and New York, NY. No grants to individuals.
Application information:
Initial approach: Letter
Deadline(s): None
Officers: Martha Melohn, Pres.; Leon Melohn, V.P.; Alfons Melohn, Secy.
EIN: 136197827

6529
The Memton Fund, Inc. ✧
515 Madison Ave., Ste. 3702
New York, NY 10022
Contact: Lillian I. Daniels, Exec. Dir.

Incorporated in 1936 in NY.
Donors: Albert G. Milbank‡; Charles M. Cauldwell‡.
Foundation type: Independent foundation.
Financial data (yr. ended 12/31/05): Assets, $12,018,115 (M); expenditures, $649,515; qualifying distributions, $475,262; giving activities include $356,570 for 132 grants (high: $15,000; low: $500).
Fields of interest: Museums; Performing arts; Historic preservation/historical societies; Arts; Adult education—literacy, basic skills & GED; Libraries/library science; Education; Environment, natural resources; Environment; Animal welfare; Animals/wildlife; Health care; AIDS; Youth development, citizenship; Human services; Children/youth, services; Family services; Science; Public affairs, citizen participation.
Type of support: General/operating support; Continuing support; Annual campaigns; Capital campaigns; Building/renovation; Endowments; Program development; Curriculum development; Internship funds; Scholarship funds.
Limitations: Applications not accepted. Giving limited to the U.S. and U.S. Pacific Islands. No support for religious or political organizations. No grants to individuals.
Application information: Unsolicited requests for funds not accepted.
Board meeting date(s): Apr. and the fall
Officers and Directors:* Samuel L. Milbank,* Pres.; Elenita M. Drumwright,* V.P.; Lillian I. Daniels,* Secy. and Exec. Dir.; Elizabeth Shepard Farrar,* Treas.; Elizabeth R.M. Drumwright; Robert V. Edgar; Alexandra Giordano; Ellen White Levy; Michelle Milbank; Thomas L. Milbank; Debbie Piccone; Barrie M. White; Pamela White.
Number of staff: 1 full-time professional; 1 part-time support.
EIN: 136096608
Selected grants: The following grants were reported in 2004.
$15,000 to International Center of Photography, New York, NY.
$7,500 to Monadnock Music, Peterborough, NH.
$5,000 to Georgetown University, DC.
$5,000 to Natural Resources Defense Council, New York, NY.
$5,000 to Student Conservation Association, Charlestown, NH.
$3,000 to Arts Habitat, Monterey, CA.
$3,000 to Folger Shakespeare Library, DC.
$2,500 to Nature Conservancy, Arlington, VA.
$2,250 to New Victory Theater, New York, NY.
$1,500 to Bridgewater College, Bridgewater, VA.

6530
Menche Family Charitable Trust ✧
241 Viola Rd.
Monsey, NY 10952-1732

Established in 2000 in NY.
Donors: Solomon Menche; Robert Menche; Daniella Menche; Michael Menche; Lauren Menche.
Foundation type: Independent foundation.
Financial data (yr. ended 12/31/04): Assets, $225,937 (M); gifts received, $974,403; expenditures, $1,321,511; qualifying distributions, $1,296,126; giving activities include $1,271,370 for 107 grants (high: $120,000; low: $500).
Fields of interest: Jewish agencies & temples.
Limitations: Applications not accepted. Giving primarily in NY. No grants to individuals.
Application information: Contributes only to pre-selected organizations.
Trustees: Pinchus Menche; Rochelle Menche; Solomon Menche.
EIN: 137224566

6531
The Robert and Joyce Menschel Family Foundation ✧
(formerly The Robert and Joyce Menschel Foundation)
c/o Goldman Sachs & Co.
85 Broad St., Tax Dept.
New York, NY 10004

Established in 1958 in NY.
Donor: Robert B. Menschel.
Foundation type: Independent foundation.
Financial data (yr. ended 10/31/05): Assets, $13,953,577 (M); expenditures, $741,955; qualifying distributions, $725,205; giving activities include $722,605 for 53 grants (high: $190,000; low: $100).
Fields of interest: Arts; Higher education; Hospitals (general); Human services.
Limitations: Applications not accepted. Giving on a national basis. No grants to individuals.
Application information: All grants initiated by the foundation.
Officers and Directors:* Robert B. Menschel,* Pres. and Treas.; Joyce F. Menschel,* V.P. and Secy.; Henry Christensen III; David F. Menschel; Lauren E. Menschel.
EIN: 136098443
Selected grants: The following grants were reported in 2004.
$127,000 to Museum of Modern Art, New York, NY.
4 grants: $2,000, $40,000, $50,000, $35,000
$90,000 to Metropolitan Museum of Art, New York, NY.
$10,000 to Tulane University, New Orleans, LA.
$5,000 to Albert G. Oliver Program, New York, NY.
$5,000 to Rockefeller University, New York, NY.
$5,000 to Syracuse University, Syracuse, NY.
$1,200 to New York Public Library, New York, NY.

6532
The Johnny Mercer Foundation
630 9th Ave., Ste. 610
New York, NY 10036
URL: http://www.johnnymercerfoundation.org/

Established in 1982 in CA.
Donor: Elizabeth M. Mercer‡.

Foundation type: Operating foundation.
Financial data (yr. ended 7/31/05): Assets, $3,451,548 (M); gifts received, $116,760; expenditures, $1,085,277; qualifying distributions, $723,540; giving activities include $580,850 for 14 grants (high: $110,000; low: $1,350).
Purpose and activities: The mission of the foundation is to distribute funds to preserve and enhance the legacy of Johnny Mercer, to assist children with illness or disability, to provide educational programs for music appreciation, to assist in the development of songwriters, and to enhance the general appreciation of American popular music.
Fields of interest: Performing arts, music; Arts; Education; Health care; Human services.
Type of support: General/operating support; Fellowships.
Limitations: Applications not accepted. Giving on a national basis.
Application information: Unsolicited requests for funds not accepted.
Board meeting date(s): Apr., June, Sept., and Dec.
Officers and Directors:* Joseph Harris,* Chair.; Margaret Whiting,* Pres.; Jeanne Humphrey, V.P.; Charles S. Tigerman,* Secy.; John Marshall,* Treas.; Frank P. Scardino, Exec. Dir.; Alan Bergman; Alvin Deutsch; Erin Drake; Ray Evans; Neil J. Gillis; Michael A. Kerker; Al Kohn; Patrick Lattore; Amanda McBroom; Phil Ramone; Nancy Rishagen; George C. White.
Advisory Board: Tony Bennett; Leslie E. Binder; Michael Feinstein; David Friedman; Barry Manilow; Andre Previn.
Number of staff: 1 full-time professional; 1 part-time professional.
EIN: 953728115

6533
Mercury Foundation of New York, Inc. ✧
(formerly Amy and Larry Robbins Foundation, Inc.)
767 5th Ave., 44th Fl.
New York, NY 10153

Established in NY.
Donors: Amy Robbins; Larry Robbins.
Foundation type: Independent foundation.
Financial data (yr. ended 12/31/05): Assets, $12,402,485 (M); gifts received, $12,500,000; expenditures, $6,783,540; qualifying distributions, $6,782,161; giving activities include $6,782,161 for 40 grants (high: $2,155,500; low: $100).
Fields of interest: Elementary/secondary education; Health care; Human services; Children/youth, services.
Limitations: Applications not accepted. Giving primarily in NY. No grants to individuals.
Application information: Contributes only to pre-selected organizations.
Trustees: Amy Robbins; Larry Robbins.
EIN: 134201308

6534
The Sue and Eugene Mercy, Jr. Foundation, Inc. ✧
c/o BCRS Associates, LLC
100 Wall St., 11th Fl.
New York, NY 10005

Established in 1967 in NY.
Donor: Eugene Mercy, Jr.

Foundation type: Independent foundation.
Financial data (yr. ended 12/31/05): Assets, $5,292,264 (M); gifts received, $662,045; expenditures, $953,395; qualifying distributions, $901,120; giving activities include $897,575 for 184 grants (high: $135,000; low: $100).
Purpose and activities: Giving primarily for the arts, education, and health associations.
Fields of interest: Performing arts, music; Arts; Secondary school/education; Higher education; Hospitals (general); Health organizations, association; Human services; Children/youth, services; Jewish federated giving programs; Jewish agencies & temples.
Limitations: Applications not accepted. Giving primarily in New York, NY. No grants to individuals.
Application information: Contributes only to pre-selected organizations.
Officers: Eugene Mercy, Jr., Pres.; Sue Mercy, V.P.; Robert E. Mnuchin, Secy.
Directors: Andrew Seth Mercy; Eugene Mercy III.
EIN: 136217050
Selected grants: The following grants were reported in 2004.
$135,000 to Philharmonic-Symphony Society of New York, New York, NY.
$75,000 to Lehigh University, Bethlehem, PA.
$50,000 to Beth Israel Medical Center, New York, NY.
$50,000 to Museum of Modern Art, New York, NY.
$26,000 to Connecticut College, New London, CT. 2 grants: $25,000, $1,000
$25,000 to Humanity in Action, New York, NY.
$2,500 to Seeds of Peace, New York, NY.
$1,500 to American Federation of Arts, New York, NY.
$1,000 to Hospital for Special Surgery, New York, NY.

6535
The Meriwether Foundation ◇ ☆
c/o Steven Loeb, Cleary Gottlieb, et al.
1 Liberty Plz.
New York, NY 10006

Established in 1991 in NY.
Donors: John W. Meriwether; Mimi Murray Meriwether.
Foundation type: Independent foundation.
Financial data (yr. ended 12/31/05): Assets, $355,020 (M); expenditures, $323,200; qualifying distributions, $316,600; giving activities include $316,600 for grants.
Purpose and activities: Giving primarily for education and to Roman Catholic organizations and churches.
Fields of interest: Higher education; Human services; Roman Catholic agencies & churches.
Limitations: Applications not accepted. Giving on a national basis. No grants to individuals.
Application information: Contributes only to pre-selected organizations.
Trustees: John W. Meriwether; Mimi Murray Meriwether.
EIN: 133620935

6536
Merlin Foundation ◇
c/o Schulte, Roth & Zabel
919 3rd Ave.
New York, NY 10022

Established in 1978 in NY.
Donor: Audrey Sheldon Poon†.
Foundation type: Independent foundation.
Financial data (yr. ended 12/31/05): Assets, $2,681,768 (M); expenditures, $603,073; qualifying distributions, $524,607; giving activities include $498,745 for 77 grants (high: $125,000; low: $95).
Purpose and activities: Emphasis on human rights, higher education, and cultural programs, including music and the arts; some support also for health and hospitals.
Fields of interest: Performing arts, music; Arts; Elementary/secondary education; Higher education; Health care; Health organizations, association; Recreation; International human rights; Roman Catholic agencies & churches; Jewish agencies & temples.
Limitations: Applications not accepted. Giving on a national basis. No grants to individuals.
Application information: Contributes only to pre-selected organizations. Unsolicited requests for funds not considered.
Board meeting date(s): Nov.
Officers: William D. Zabel, Pres. and Treas.; Roger C. Altman, V.P.; Thomas H. Baer, V.P.; John J. McLaughlin, Secy.
EIN: 237418853

6537
Merrill Lynch & Co. Foundation, Inc. ▼ ◇
c/o Merrill Lynch & Co., Inc.
Global Philanthropy and Community Relations
2 World Financial Center, 5th Fl
New York, NY 10281 (212) 236-4319
Contact: Eddy Bayardelle, Pres.
FAX: (212) 236-3821;
E-mail: philant7@exchange.ml.com; URL: http://community.ml.com/index.asp?id=66319_67036

Incorporated in 1950 in DE.
Donors: Merrill Lynch & Co., Inc.; Pierce, Fenner & Smith, Inc.
Foundation type: Company-sponsored foundation.
Financial data (yr. ended 12/31/05): Assets, $19,643,940 (M); gifts received, $19,322,009; expenditures, $21,979,671; qualifying distributions, $21,769,818; giving activities include $15,967,510 for 126 grants (high: $1,576,417; low: $30), and $5,257,733 for 4,686 employee matching gifts.
Purpose and activities: The foundation supports organizations involved with education, career planning, youth development, financial literacy, business, and entrepreneurship. Special emphasis is directed toward programs designed to educate underserved children and youth.
Fields of interest: Education; Employment, job counseling; Youth development, business; Youth development; Children/youth, services; Human services, financial counseling; Business/industry; Community development, small businesses.
Type of support: Continuing support; Capital campaigns; Program development; Fellowships; Scholarship funds; Employee matching gifts; Employee-related scholarships.
Limitations: Giving to national and international organizations. No support for private foundations, political candidates or lobbying organizations, religious, fraternal, social, or other membership organizations not of direct benefit to the entire community, or United Way-supported organizations (except for emergency needs). No grants to

individuals (except for employee-related scholarships) or for fundraising activities related to individual sponsorships, seed money, political causes or campaigns, athletic events or sports tournaments (except for the Special Olympics), fundraising events, endowments, construction or renovation, special purpose campaigns, chairs, or equipment, conferences, workshops, or seminars, research, or video or film production; no loans.
Publications: Application guidelines; Corporate giving report; Grants list; Program policy statement.
Application information: Support is limited to 1 contribution per organization during any given year. Telephone calls are not encouraged. Application form not required.
Initial approach: Complete online application
Deadline(s): None
Board meeting date(s): Mar., June, Sept., and Dec.
Final notification: 30 days
Officers and Trustees:* Claudia J. Kahn,* Chair.; Eddy Bayardelle, Pres.; Paul W. Critchlow, V.P.; E. Stanley O'Neal, V.P.; Westina L. Matthews Shatteen, V.P.; Larry Sharpe, Secy.; Kevin McGovern, Treas.
Number of staff: 3 full-time professional; 1 part-time professional; 3 full-time support; 2 part-time support.
EIN: 136139556
Selected grants: The following grants were reported in 2004.
$1,545,138 to Scholarship America, Saint Peter, MN. 2 grants: $483,000 (For McCarthy Scholarship Program), $1,062,138 (For September 11th Disaster Relief scholarships).
$1,250,000 to Bronx Preparatory Charter School, Friends of, Bronx, NY. 2 grants: $1,000,000 (For general support), $250,000 (For general support).
$200,000 to Baruch College of the City University of New York, New York, NY. For general support.
$150,000 to Tower Hamlets Education Business Partnership, London, England. For general support.
$127,500 to Sheltering Arms Childrens Service, New York, NY. For general support.
$100,000 to Academy of Business Leadership, Rosemead, CA. For general support for Investing Pays Off (IPO) program.
$100,000 to Tsinghua University, Friends of, New York, NY. For general support for School of Economics and Management.
$90,000 to Pennsylvania Council on Economic Education, Selinsgrove, PA. For general support.

6538
Mertz Gilmore Foundation ▼ ◇
(formerly Joyce Mertz-Gilmore Foundation)
218 E. 18th St.
New York, NY 10003-3694 (212) 475-1137
Contact: Jay Beckner, Exec. Dir.
FAX: (212) 777-5226;
E-mail: info@mertzgilmore.org; URL: http://www.mertzgilmore.org

Incorporated in 1959 in NY.
Donors: Robert Gilmore†; Joyce Mertz†.
Foundation type: Independent foundation.
Financial data (yr. ended 12/31/04): Assets, $103,436,389 (M); expenditures, $7,913,868; qualifying distributions, $7,040,403; giving activities include $5,626,085 for 147 grants (high:

$1,700,000; low: $500; average: $1,000–$125,000).

Purpose and activities: Current concerns include human rights, the environment, and New York City cultural, social, and civic concerns.

Fields of interest: Performing arts, dance; Environment, energy; Community development, equal rights; Community development, citizen coalitions; Community development.

Type of support: Program-related investments/loans; General/operating support; Continuing support; Program development; Seed money; Technical assistance; Matching/challenge support.

Limitations: Giving on a national basis with some emphasis on the New York City Program. No support for sectarian religious concerns. No grants to individuals, or for endowments, annual fund appeals, fundraising events, conferences, workshops, publications, film or media projects, scholarships, research, fellowships, or travel.

Publications: Application guidelines; Biennial report (including application guidelines); Grants list; Informational brochure.

Application information: The foundation will send an application form to those it feels fall within its guidelines based on the initial inquiry letter. The foundation prefers to receive all inquiries by regular mail. Do not submit videos, CDs, audiocassettes, press clippings, books, or other materials unless they are requested. Application form required.

> *Initial approach:* Letter of inquiry (1-3 pages)
> *Copies of proposal:* 1
> *Deadline(s):* None
> *Board meeting date(s):* May and Nov. for grant decisions
> *Final notification:* Within 3 weeks

Officers and Directors:* Larry E. Condon,* Chair.; Elizabeth Burke Gilmore,* Vice-Chair. and Secy.; Lukas Haynes, V.P.; Denise Nix Thompson,* Treas.; Jay Beckner, Exec. Dir.; Franklin W. Wallin, Dir. Emeritus; Harlan Cleveland; Robert Crane; Patricia Ramsay; Peggy Saika; Mikki Shepard.

Number of staff: 5 full-time professional; 1 part-time professional; 5 full-time support; 2 part-time support.

EIN: 132872722

Selected grants: The following grants were reported in 2003.

$1,700,000 to Energy Foundation, San Francisco, CA.

$175,000 to Danspace Project, New York, NY.

$165,000 to Green Guerillas, New York, NY.

$125,000 to People of Faith Network, Brooklyn, NY.

$100,000 to New York City Environmental Justice Alliance, New York, NY.

$75,000 to Field, The, Performance Zone, New York, NY.

$75,000 to Historic Districts Council, New York, NY.

$75,000 to Trisha Brown Dance Company, New York, NY.

$70,000 to Centro de Derechos Economicos y Sociales, Quito, Ecuador. .

$65,000 to Arts Resources in Collaboration, New York, NY.

6539
The Mesdag Family Foundation ◇
c/o BCRS Group/Marcum & Kliegman, LLP
100 Wall St., 11th Fl.
New York, NY   10005

Established in 1991 in NY.

Donors: T. Willem Mesdag; Goldman Sachs & Co.

Foundation type: Independent foundation.

Financial data (yr. ended 3/31/05): Assets, $12,917,628 (M); gifts received, $2,568,300; expenditures, $1,079,338; qualifying distributions, $961,439; giving activities include $956,994 for 34 grants (high: $265,000; low: $100).

Purpose and activities: Giving primarily for higher education and the arts.

Fields of interest: Museums (art); Performing arts, music; Performing arts, opera; Higher education; Medical school/education; Athletics/sports, water sports.

Type of support: General/operating support; Scholarship funds.

Limitations: Applications not accepted. Giving primarily in CA; funding also in CO, Cambridge, MA, and Princeton, NJ. No grants to individuals.

Application information: Contributes only to pre-selected organizations.

Trustees: Lisa Ann Mesdag; T. Willem Mesdag.

EIN: 133651269

6540
The Messer Foundation ◇ ☆
120 W. Tupper St.
Buffalo, NY   14201   (716) 853-8671
Contact: Thomas R. Beecher, Jr., Tr.

Donor: Thomas R. Beecher, Jr.

Foundation type: Independent foundation.

Financial data (yr. ended 12/31/05): Assets, $230,513 (M); expenditures, $376,683; qualifying distributions, $375,000; giving activities include $375,000 for 8 grants (high: $105,000; low: $1,000).

Fields of interest: Arts; Education; Human services.

Limitations: Giving primarily in Buffalo, NY. No grants to individuals.

Application information: Application form not required.

> *Initial approach:* Letter
> *Deadline(s):* None

Trustees: Judy C. Beecher; Thomas R. Beecher, Jr.; Kathleen Beecher Moore.

EIN: 166025317

Selected grants: The following grants were reported in 2005.

$105,000 to Buffalo Inner-City Scholarship Opportunity Network (BISON), Buffalo, NY.

$50,000 to Buffalo Academy of the Sacred Heart, Buffalo, NY.

$50,000 to Canisius High School, Buffalo, NY.

$50,000 to College of the Holy Cross, Worcester, MA.

$40,000 to DYouville College, Buffalo, NY.

$29,000 to Nardin Academy, Buffalo, NY.

$1,000 to United Way, NY.

6541
The Stanley W. Metcalf Foundation, Inc. ☆
120 Genesee St., Rm. 503
Auburn, NY   13021
Contact: Walter M. Lowe, Exec. Dir.

Established in 1962.

Donor: Stanley W. Metcalf‡.

Foundation type: Independent foundation.

Financial data (yr. ended 12/31/05): Assets, $9,243,588 (M); expenditures, $491,140; qualifying distributions, $428,251; giving activities

include $391,000 for 41 grants (high: $90,000; low: $500).

Purpose and activities: Emphasis on youth organizations and church support; grants also for hospitals, welfare, and education.

Fields of interest: Arts; Education; Hospitals (general); Human services; Youth, services; Federated giving programs; Protestant agencies & churches; Roman Catholic agencies & churches; Aging; Disabilities, people with.

Type of support: General/operating support; Continuing support; Annual campaigns; Capital campaigns; Building/renovation; Endowments; Emergency funds; Scholarship funds; Matching/challenge support.

Limitations: Giving primarily in Cayuga County, NY. No support for political organizations. No grants to individuals.

Application information: Application form not required.

> *Initial approach:* Letter
> *Copies of proposal:* 1
> *Deadline(s):* None
> *Board meeting date(s):* Jan., Apr., July, and Oct.

Officers and Directors:* Ronald D. West, Pres.; Caryl W. Adams, Secy.; Walter M. Lowe,* Exec. Dir.; James P. Costello; John P. McLane.

EIN: 156017859

6542
MetLife Foundation ▼ ◇
(formerly Metropolitan Life Foundation)
27-01 Queens Plz. N.
Long Island City, NY   11101   (212) 578-6272
Contact: Sibyl C. Jacobson, C.E.O. and Pres.
URL: http://www.metlife.org

Incorporated in 1976 in NY.

Donor: Metropolitan Life Insurance Co.

Foundation type: Company-sponsored foundation.

Financial data (yr. ended 12/31/05): Assets, $148,885,452 (M); gifts received, $1,239,220; expenditures, $30,087,479; qualifying distributions, $33,292,834; giving activities include $28,833,924 for 621 grants (high: $1,125,000; low: $82), and $1,065,666 for employee matching gifts.

Purpose and activities: The foundation supports organizations involved with arts and culture, education, health, substance abuse, HIV/AIDS, Alzheimer's disease, geriatrics, employment, nutrition, housing, parks and playgrounds, youth development, human services, diversity, economic development, civic affairs, minorities, and economically disadvantaged people. Special emphasis is directed toward programs designed to strengthen communities; promote good health; and improve education.

Fields of interest: Arts, cultural/ethnic awareness; Arts education; Media/communications; Arts; Education, reform; Elementary/secondary education; Higher education; Education; Public health; Health care; Substance abuse, services; AIDS; Alzheimer's disease; Geriatrics; Alzheimer's disease research; Employment, services; Nutrition; Housing/shelter; Recreation, parks/playgrounds; Youth development; Children, services; Family services, parent education; Human services; Economic development; Public affairs; Aging; Minorities; Economically disadvantaged.

Type of support: General/operating support; Continuing support; Program development; Publication; Seed money; Research;

Program-related investments/loans; Employee matching gifts; Employee-related scholarships; Grants to individuals; In-kind gifts.

Limitations: Giving on a national basis. No support for private foundations, religious, fraternal, athletic, political, social, or veterans' organizations, hospitals, United Way-supported organizations, local chapters of national organizations, disease-specific organizations, labor groups, international organizations, organizations primarily engaged in patient care or direct treatment, drug treatment centers or community health clinics, or elementary or secondary schools. No grants to individuals (except for Medical Research Awards and employee-related scholarships), or for endowments, courtesy advertising, or festival participation.

Publications: Application guidelines; Corporate giving report.

Application information: Additional information may be requested at a later date. Multi-year funding is not automatic. Application form not required.

Initial approach: Proposal
Copies of proposal: 1

Officers and Directors:* Catherine A. Rein,* Chair.; Sibyl C. Jacobson,* C.E.O. and Pres.; Jonathan Rosenthal,* Treas.; C. Robert Henrikson; James Lipscomb; William J. Toppeta; Lisa M. Weber.

EIN: 132878224

Selected grants: The following grants were reported in 2005.

$1,125,000 to United Way of America, Alexandria, VA. To disperse to various chapters around the U.S. through annual United Way Campaign.

$400,000 to Enterprise Community Partners, Columbia, MD. For Community Recovery Fund, Louisiana and Mississippi activities.

$350,000 to Education Trust, DC. For MetLife Equity Audit.

$300,000 to Big Brothers Big Sisters of America, Philadelphia, PA. For school-based mentoring growth initiative, with boomer focus.

$300,000 to University of Pennsylvania, Philadelphia, PA. For Alzheimer's Disease/Healthy Brain Outreach.

$275,000 to Philharmonic-Symphony Society of New York, New York, NY. For education and national radio program.

$150,000 to Alliance for Aging Research, DC. For Alzheimer's Caregiver Initiative.

$70,000 to National Medical Fellowships, New York, NY. For Awards for Program for Academic Excellence in Medicine.

$39,000 to Discovery Place, Charlotte, NC. For Partnership for Lifelong Learning.

$10,000 to United Way of the Greater Dayton Area, Dayton, OH. For Community Ventures Grant.

6543
Metropolitan Philanthropic Fund, Inc. ◇

(formerly Jane P. & Charles D. Klein Foundation)
666 3rd Ave., 29th Fl.
New York, NY 10017-4011 (212) 476-8062
Contact: Charles D. Klein, V.P.

Established in 1982 in NY.

Donors: Charles D. Klein; Laila Hafner; Jane P. Klein.

Foundation type: Independent foundation.

Financial data (yr. ended 6/30/05): Assets, $8,865,305 (M); gifts received, $343,575; expenditures, $684,447; qualifying distributions, $612,390; giving activities include $612,045 for 91 grants (high: $200,000; low: $35).

Purpose and activities: Giving primarily for the arts, higher and other education, human services, and to Jewish organizations.

Fields of interest: Museums; Performing arts, theater; Elementary/secondary education; Higher education; Environment, natural resources; Health organizations, association; Human services; Jewish agencies & temples.

Type of support: General/operating support.

Limitations: Giving primarily in New York, NY. No grants to individuals.

Application information: Application form not required.

Initial approach: Proposal
Deadline(s): None

Officers and Directors:* Jane P. Klein,* Pres.; Charles D. Klein,* V.P.; David P. Steinmann,* Secy.-Treas.; Alex Anagnos.

EIN: 133128811

Selected grants: The following grants were reported in 2004.

$210,000 to New York University, New York, NY. 2 grants: $100,000 (For unrestricted support), $110,000 to School of Law (For unrestricted support).

$107,500 to Columbia University, New York, NY. For unrestricted support.

$50,200 to Bard College, Annandale on Hudson, NY. For unrestricted support.

$40,000 to Population Council, New York, NY. For unrestricted support.

$37,016 to Initiative for a Competitive Inner-City (ICIC), Boston, MA. For unrestricted support.

$36,000 to Amherst College, Amherst, MA. For unrestricted support.

$25,000 to Ciesla Foundation, DC. For unrestricted support.

$8,000 to United States Ski Team Foundation, Park City, UT.

$7,250 to Metropolitan Opera, New York, NY. For unrestricted support.

6544
Edward & Sandra Meyer Foundation, Inc. ◇

c/o Philip I. Pollack
21 E. 40th St., Ste. 400
New York, NY 10016-0501

Established in 1966.

Donor: Edward H. Meyer.

Foundation type: Independent foundation.

Financial data (yr. ended 12/31/04): Assets, $20,949,487 (M); gifts received, $15,448,160; expenditures, $748,666; qualifying distributions, $742,141; giving activities include $741,841 for 34 grants (high: $500,000; low: $100).

Purpose and activities: Giving primarily for Jewish agencies and federated giving programs, as well as for the arts, and education; funding also for a medical center.

Fields of interest: Museums; Arts; Education; Hospitals (general); Health care; Jewish federated giving programs; Jewish agencies & temples.

Limitations: Applications not accepted. Giving primarily in the New York, NY, area. No grants to individuals.

Application information: Contributes only to pre-selected organizations.

Officers: Edward H. Meyer, Pres. and Treas.; Sandra Meyer, Secy.

Directors: Anthony Meyer; Margaret Meyer.

EIN: 136204325

Selected grants: The following grants were reported in 2004.

$500,000 to New York University Medical Center, New York, NY.

$18,300 to Film Society of Lincoln Center, New York, NY.

$10,000 to Jewish Museum, New York, NY.

$4,400 to Jazz at Lincoln Center, New York, NY.

$1,000 to East Hampton Healthcare Foundation, East Hampton, NY.

$1,000 to Hamptons International Film Festival, East Hampton, NY.

$100 to New Dramatists, New York, NY.

6545
Roslyn Milstein Meyer and Jerome Meyer Foundation ◇

(formerly Roslyn Milstein Meyer Foundation)
335 Madison Ave., 15th Fl.
New York, NY 10017
Contact: Eric Kaplan

Established in 1996 in NY.

Donors: Irma Milstein; Paul Milstein; Roslyn Meyer; Jerome Meyer; Milstein Family Foundation.

Foundation type: Independent foundation.

Financial data (yr. ended 12/31/05): Assets, $2,220,872 (M); gifts received, $2,300,000; expenditures, $1,622,837; qualifying distributions, $1,622,590; giving activities include $1,622,553 for 29 grants (high: $959,053; low: $500).

Purpose and activities: Giving primarily for the arts, particularly theater, and for Jewish organizations, particularly a Jewish theological seminary; funding also for social services.

Fields of interest: Museums; Performing arts, theater; Arts; Theological school/education; Education; Human services; Federated giving programs; Jewish agencies & temples.

Limitations: Applications not accepted. Giving primarily in CT. No grants to individuals.

Application information: Contributes only to pre-selected organizations.

Trustees: Jerome Meyer; Roslyn Meyer; Irma Milstein; Paul Milstein.

EIN: 133921828

Selected grants: The following grants were reported in 2003.

$200,000 to Learning Through an Expanded Arts Program (LEAP), New York, NY.

$150,000 to Jewish Theological Seminary of America, New York, NY.

$100,000 to Long Wharf Theater, New Haven, CT.

$75,000 to New Haven International Festival of Arts and Ideas, New Haven, CT.

$70,000 to Amistad Academy, New Haven, CT.

$20,000 to Arts Council of Greater New Haven, New Haven, CT.

$20,000 to Greater New Haven Arts Stabilization Project, New Haven, CT.

$20,000 to Landmark College, Putney, VT.

$20,000 to Read to Grow, Branford, CT.

$12,000 to United Way of Greater New Haven, New Haven, CT.

6546
The Meyer Foundation ◇

c/o Lazard Freres & Co., LLC
30 Rockefeller Plz.
New York, NY 10020

Established in 1985 in NY.
Donor: George J. Ames†.
Foundation type: Independent foundation.
Financial data (yr. ended 12/31/05): Assets, $11,958,206 (M); expenditures, $675,486; qualifying distributions, $583,350; giving activities include $575,000 for 6 grants (high: $200,000; low: $25,000).
Fields of interest: Performing arts, theater; Performing arts, orchestra (symphony); Performing arts, education; Higher education.
Type of support: General/operating support; Research.
Limitations: Applications not accepted. Giving primarily in New York, NY; some funding also in Washington, DC, and Philadelphia, PA. No grants to individuals.
Application information: Contributes only to pre-selected organizations.
Officers: Phillipe Meyer, Pres.; Vincent Meyer, V.P.; Charles M. Stieglitz, Secy.; Paul Cohen, Treas.
EIN: 133317912

6547
Milbank Foundation for Rehabilitation
654 Madison Ave., Ste. 1605
New York, NY 10021   (212) 687-7735
Contact: Carl Helstrom, Exec. Dir.
FAX: (212) 697-5495; URL: http://foundationcenter.org/grantmaker/milbank/

Established in 1995 in NY; converted through an affiliation between the ICD International Center for the Disabled and the New York Hospital-Cornell Medical Center Network.
Foundation type: Independent foundation.
Financial data (yr. ended 12/31/04): Assets, $32,164,699 (M); expenditures, $1,429,593; qualifying distributions, $1,100,045; giving activities include $760,000 for 25 grants, and $25,500 for 4 employee matching gifts.
Purpose and activities: The foundation's mission is to integrate people with disabilities into all aspects of American life. Current priorities include, but are not limited to: consumer-focused initiatives that enable people with disabilities to lead fulfilling, independent lives; innovative policy research and education on market-based approaches to health care and rehabilitation; improving and expanding quality health services, especially palliative care, and education and training of allied health and rehabilitation professionals.
Fields of interest: Health care, public policy; Medical care, rehabilitation; Health care; Disabilities, people with.
Type of support: Research; Publication; Program development; Conferences/seminars; Fellowships; Employee matching gifts.
Limitations: Giving limited to the U.S., with some emphasis on New York, NY. No support for government agencies. No grants to individuals, or for general operating funds, annual appeals, dinners or events, capital campaigns, building funds, direct mailings, solicitations, equipment, music, theater, multi-year grants, or campaigns.
Publications: Annual report (including application guidelines).
Application information: See Web site for guidelines and limitations. Inquiries and proposals are to be sent by regular mail only. Unless requested, please do not send by fax, E-mail, or overnight mail. Application form not required.
 Initial approach: Letter or proposal

Copies of proposal: 1
Deadline(s): None
Board meeting date(s): May and Oct.
Final notification: Within 1 month of application
Officers and Directors: * Jeremiah M. Bogert,* Chair. and Secy.; Jeremiah Milbank III,* Pres. and Treas.; Carl Helstrom,* Exec. Dir.; Chris Olander, Exec. Dir. Emeritus; Jeremiah M. Bogert, Jr.; Jeremiah Milbank, Jr.; Michael Sanger; Ezra K. Zilkha.
Number of staff: 1 full-time professional; 1 part-time professional; 2 part-time support.
EIN: 115125050
Selected grants: The following grants were reported in 2004.
$100,000 to International Center for the Disabled (ICD), New York, NY. For Margaret Milbank Bogert Chair of Rehabilitation.
$60,000 to Rehabilitation Institute of Chicago, Chicago, IL. To establish Margaret Milbank Bogert Pediatric fellowship.
$50,000 to American Red Cross, Falls Church, VA. To enhance disaster preparedness for people with disabilities.
$50,000 to Memorial Sloan-Kettering Cancer Center, New York, NY. For Pain and Palliative Care fellowship Program.
$50,000 to National Foundation for Facial Reconstruction, New York, NY. For Margaret Milbank Bogert Orthodontic Research Fellowship.
$25,000 to Boy Scouts of America, Greater New York Council, New York, NY. Toward scouting programs for children with disabilities.
$25,000 to National Organization on Disability, DC. Toward Harris Survey of Americans with Disabilities.
$20,000 to Big Brothers Big Sisters of New York City, New York, NY. For mentoring relationships for children with disabilities.
$15,000 to Foundation Center, New York, NY. Toward services for people with disabilities.
$5,000 to TIRR Rehabilitation Centers, Houston, TX. For educational forum by National Council on Disability.

6548
Robert & Bethany Millard Charitable Foundation ◇
(formerly Robert B. Millard Charitable Foundation)
c/o Mahoney Cohen & Co.
111 W. 40th St.
New York, NY   10018

Established in 1989 in NY.
Donor: Robert B. Millard.
Foundation type: Independent foundation.
Financial data (yr. ended 12/31/05): Assets, $10,716,807 (M); expenditures, $2,013,679; qualifying distributions, $1,970,391; giving activities include $1,969,641 for 78 grants (high: $975,796; low: $20).
Purpose and activities: Giving primarily for the arts and higher education; funding also for Jewish organizations.
Fields of interest: Museums (specialized); Performing arts, dance; Performing arts, theater; Arts; Higher education; Education; Jewish federated giving programs.
Limitations: Applications not accepted. Giving primarily in New York, NY. No grants to individuals.
Application information: Contributes only to pre-selected organizations.

Trustee: Robert B. Millard.
EIN: 133566723
Selected grants: The following grants were reported in 2004.
$110,000 to Manhattan Theater Club, New York, NY. 3 grants: $15,000, $70,000, $25,000
$100,000 to Bard College, Annandale on Hudson, NY.
$50,000 to Elaine Kaufman Cultural Center, New York, NY.
$50,000 to Island Institute, Rockland, ME.
$25,000 to American Museum of Natural History, New York, NY.
$25,000 to Conservation International, DC.
$15,000 to National Parks Conservation Association, DC.
$10,000 to Carnegie Institution of Washington, DC.

6549
Millbrook Tribute Garden, Inc. ◇
c/o D'Arcangelo & Co., LLP
P.O. Box D, Franklin Ave.
Millbrook, NY   12545   (845) 677-6823

Incorporated in 1943 in NY.
Foundation type: Independent foundation.
Financial data (yr. ended 9/30/05): Assets, $41,260,577 (M); expenditures, $2,155,439; qualifying distributions, $1,871,263; giving activities include $1,712,500 for 66 grants (high: $202,000; low: $500), and $41,048 for 1 loan/program-related investment.
Purpose and activities: Emphasis on secondary education, church support, child welfare, hospitals, and civic projects; operates and maintains a playground and memorial park in honor of war veterans.
Fields of interest: Elementary/secondary education; Hospitals (general); Children/youth, services; Government/public administration; Christian agencies & churches; Protestant agencies & churches.
Type of support: General/operating support; Capital campaigns; Scholarship funds.
Limitations: Giving primarily in Millbrook, Poughkeepsie, and New York, NY and in Chicago, IL. No grants to individuals.
Application information:
 Initial approach: Proposal
 Deadline(s): None
Officers: Oakleigh B. Thorne, Pres.; Felicitas S. Thorne, V.P.; Vincent N. Turletes, Secy.; George T. Whalen, Jr., Treas.
Trustees: Oakleigh Thorne; Robert W. Whalen.
EIN: 141340079
Selected grants: The following grants were reported in 2005.
$202,500 to Dutchess Day School, Millbrook, NY.
$138,000 to Saint Francis Hospital, Poughkeepsie, NY.
$133,500 to Washington, Town of, Millbrook, NY.
$115,000 to Millbrook School, Millbrook, NY.
$105,000 to Millbrook Central School, Millbrook, NY.
$67,500 to Saint Josephs Church, Millbrook, NY.
$55,500 to Millbrook, Village of, Millbrook, NY.
$50,000 to Bard College, Annandale on Hudson, NY.
$30,000 to Maplebrook School, Amenia, NY.
$17,500 to Grace Episcopal Church, Millbrook, NY.

6550
The Miller Family Foundation, Inc. ✧
(formerly The William R. & Irene D. Miller Foundation)
c/o Bessemer Trust Co.
630 5th Ave.
New York, NY 10111
Contact: Judith R. Miller, Pres.
Application address: 9462 Brownsboro Rd., No.
131, Louisville, KY 40241, tel.: (502) 243-1252;
FAX: (502) 243-0951

Established in 1991 in NY; reorganized in 1995 as
The Miller Family Foundation.
Donors: William R. Miller; Irene D. Miller.
Foundation type: Independent foundation.
Financial data (yr. ended 12/31/05): Assets,
$281,566 (M); expenditures, $740,777; qualifying
distributions, $722,778; giving activities include
$628,726 for grants.
Purpose and activities: Giving primarily for
education, the arts, and children, youth, and social
services.
Fields of interest: Performing arts; Performing arts,
opera; Arts; Higher education; Education; Health
organizations; Human services; Children/youth,
services; Biological sciences; Christian agencies &
churches.
International interests: Asia; United Kingdom.
Type of support: Program development.
Limitations: Giving primarily in Louisville, KY, and
the metropolitan New York, NY, area. No grants to
individuals.
Publications: Application guidelines; Program policy
statement.
Application information: Application form required.
   Initial approach: Letter requesting update form
   Copies of proposal: 1
   Deadline(s): Feb. 1 and Aug. 1
   Board meeting date(s): Sept. and Mar.
   Final notification: Letter
Officers and Directors:* William R. Miller,* Chair.
and C.E.O.; Irene D. Miller,* Vice-Chair.; Judith R.
Miller,* Pres. and Exec. Dir.; Jane S. Tierney,*
Secy.; Ian W. Miller,* Treas.
Number of staff: 1 part-time professional.
EIN: 133826612
Selected grants: The following grants were reported
in 2005.
$250,000 to Metropolitan Opera Association, New
   York, NY.
$50,000 to Michael J. Fox Foundation for
   Parkinsons Research, New York, NY.
$34,500 to Kentucky Country Day School,
   Louisville, KY. 5 grants: $1,000, $25,000,
   $1,000, $5,000, $2,500
$12,000 to Opera Orchestra of New York, New York,
   NY.
$12,000 to Saint Andrew Nativity School, Portland,
   OR.
$5,000 to American Trust for the British Library, New
   York, NY.

6551
Charles Lawrence Keith and Clara Miller
Foundation ✧ ☆
217 Thompson St., No. 7
New York, NY 10012

Established in 1976 as Clara Miller Foundation.
Donor: Charles L. Keith†.
Foundation type: Independent foundation.

Financial data (yr. ended 1/31/05): Assets,
$8,255,474 (M); expenditures, $477,530;
qualifying distributions, $386,916; giving activities
include $336,250 for 30 grants (high: $45,000;
low: $2,000).
Purpose and activities: Support for institutions
involved in the preservation of human rights and the
elimination of human suffering, and for cultural,
scientific, and literary pursuits.
Fields of interest: Arts; Legal services; Food
services; International human rights; Civil rights.
Type of support: Continuing support; Annual
campaigns; Conferences/seminars; Curriculum
development.
Limitations: Giving limited to the greater
metropolitan New York, NY, area. No grants for
scholarships, fellowships, or prizes; no loans.
Application information: Application form not
required.
   Initial approach: Letter
   Deadline(s): None
Directors: Linda Fisher; Brian O'Dwyer; Susan Ould;
Honie Ann Peacock.
EIN: 132918230
Selected grants: The following grants were reported
in 2006.
$10,000 to College of Saint Rose, Albany, NY.
$10,000 to Tzu Chi Foundation, Columbus, OH.
$5,000 to Friends of Inside Albany, Albany, NY.
$5,000 to In the Spirit of the Children, New York,
   NY.
$5,000 to New York City Mission Society, New York,
   NY.
$5,000 to People for the American Way, DC.
$2,500 to American Place Theater, New York, NY.

6552
Milliken Foundation ✧
c/o Citibank, N.A.
153 E. 53rd St.
New York, NY 10043

Trust established in 1945 in NY.
Donor: Milliken and Co.
Foundation type: Company-sponsored foundation.
Financial data (yr. ended 12/31/05): Assets,
$10,805,164 (M); gifts received, $1,000,000;
expenditures, $1,515,433; qualifying distributions,
$1,512,578; giving activities include $1,509,914
for 84+ grants (high: $275,000).
Purpose and activities: The foundation supports
organizations involved with arts and culture,
education, health, human services, and
Protestantism.
Fields of interest: Arts; Higher education;
Education; Health care; Salvation Army; Children/
youth, services; Human services; Federated giving
programs; Protestant agencies & churches.
Limitations: Applications not accepted. Giving on a
national basis, with some emphasis on SC. No
grants to individuals.
Application information: Contributes only to
pre-selected organizations.
Trustee: Citibank, N.A.
Advisory Committee: G. Ashley Allen; J.L. Hamrick;
Thomas J. Malone; Gerrish H. Milliken; Roger
Milliken.
EIN: 136055062
Selected grants: The following grants were reported
in 2005.
$275,000 to Salvation Army, Greenwood, SC.
$133,333 to Georgia Tech Foundation, Atlanta, GA.

$100,000 to Arts Partnership of Greater
   Spartanburg, Spartanburg, SC.
$53,400 to Hospital for Special Surgery, New York,
   NY.
$52,500 to Charles Lea Center for Rehabilitation
   and Special Education, Spartanburg, SC.
$50,000 to National Right to Work Legal Defense
   and Education Foundation, Springfield, VA.
$33,000 to Miracle Hill Ministries, Greenville, SC.
$10,000 to Independent College Fund of North
   Carolina, Raleigh, NC.
$10,000 to Total Ministries of Spartanburg County,
   Spartanburg, SC.
$5,000 to LaFayette Society for Performing Arts, La
   Grange, GA.

6553
Ira M. and Diane G. Millstein Family
Foundation ✧
1240 Flagler Dr.
Mamaroneck, NY 10543-4601

Established in 1997 in NY.
Donors: Diane G. Millstein; Ira Millstein.
Foundation type: Independent foundation.
Financial data (yr. ended 11/30/05): Assets,
$1,298,219 (M); expenditures, $531,751;
qualifying distributions, $526,159; giving activities
include $526,159 for 61 grants (high: $150,000;
low: $100).
Purpose and activities: Giving primarily for medical
school education, and medical research; funding
also for human services.
Fields of interest: Medical school/education;
Health organizations, association; Medical
research, institute; Human services.
Limitations: Applications not accepted. Giving
primarily in New York, NY. No grants to individuals.
Application information: Contributes only to
pre-selected organizations.
Trustees: Diane G. Millstein; Ira M. Millstein.
EIN: 137131232
Selected grants: The following grants were reported
in 2005.
$15,000 to American Museum of Natural History,
   New York, NY. 2 grants: $5,000, $10,000
$12,500 to Manhattan Theater Club, New York, NY.
   2 grants: $5,500, $7,000
$10,000 to United Way. 2 grants: $5,000 each
$10,000 to White Plains Hospital Center, White
   Plains, NY.
$5,000 to American Red Cross.
$3,000 to Cystic Fibrosis Foundation, Bethesda,
   MD.
$1,000 to March of Dimes Birth Defects Foundation,
   White Plains, NY.

6554
Edward L. Milstein Foundation ✧
c/o Paul Milstein
335 Madison Ave., Ste. 1500
New York, NY 10017

Established in 1996 in NY.
Donors: Irma Milstein; Paul Milstein; Edward L.
Milstein; Milstein Family Foundation.
Foundation type: Independent foundation.
Financial data (yr. ended 12/31/05): Assets,
$1,001,997 (M); gifts received, $300,000;
expenditures, $965,572; qualifying distributions,

$954,108; giving activities include $954,108 for 50 grants (high: $100,000; low: $275).
Purpose and activities: Giving for youth services, and for Jewish organizations.
Fields of interest: Arts, cultural/ethnic awareness; Arts; Crime/violence prevention; Jewish agencies & temples.
Limitations: Applications not accepted. No grants to individuals.
Application information: Contributes only to pre-selected organizations.
Trustees: Edward L. Milstein; Irma Milstein; Paul Milstein.
EIN: 133921821
Selected grants: The following grants were reported in 2005.
$135,000 to Chesed Avraham, Brooklyn, NY.
$125,000 to Yeshiva University, New York, NY.
$50,000 to American Skin Association, New York, NY.
$10,000 to Dysautonomia Foundation, New York, NY.
$7,000 to Congregation Agudath Sholom, Stamford, CT.
$6,000 to Westchester Hebrew High School, Mamaroneck, NY.
$1,800 to American Cancer Society, Atlanta, GA.

6555
Howard P. Milstein Foundation ✦
c/o Paul Milstein
335 Madison Ave., Ste. 1500
New York, NY   10017

Established in 1998 in NY.
Donors: Irma Milstein; Howard P. Milstein; Paul Milstein; Milstein Family Foundation.
Foundation type: Independent foundation.
Financial data (yr. ended 12/31/05): Assets, $77,543 (M); gifts received, $300,000; expenditures, $349,208; qualifying distributions, $349,184; giving activities include $348,884 for 33 grants (high: $50,000; low: $200).
Fields of interest: Museums; Museums (ethnic/folk arts); Arts; Higher education; Medical school/education; Health organizations, association; Human services; Children/youth, services; Aging, centers/services; Community development; Foundations (private operating); Federated giving programs; Jewish agencies & temples.
Limitations: Applications not accepted. No grants to individuals.
Application information: Contributes only to pre-selected organizations.
Trustees: Howard P. Milstein; Irma Milstein; Paul Milstein.
EIN: 133921824
Selected grants: The following grants were reported in 2003.
$130,250 to Cornell University, Ithaca, NY. 2 grants: $67,750, $62,500
$100,000 to Riverdale Country School, Bronx, NY.
$100,000 to Weill Medical College of Cornell University, New York, NY.
$55,000 to New York City Public/Private Initiatives, New York, NY.
$50,000 to American Skin Association, New York, NY.
$50,000 to Corcoran Gallery of Art, DC.
$25,000 to Jewish Museum, New York, NY.
$25,000 to New York Legal Assistance Group, New York, NY.
$25,000 to New York Public Library, New York, NY.

6556
Paul and Irma Milstein Foundation ▼ ✦
335 Madison Ave., Ste. 1500
New York, NY   10017   (212) 708-0280
Contact: Paul Milstein, Pres.

Established in 1995.
Donors: Paul Milstein; Irma Milstein; PIM Holding Co.
Foundation type: Independent foundation.
Financial data (yr. ended 12/31/04): Assets, $10,672,071 (M); gifts received, $8,505,485; expenditures, $4,115,757; qualifying distributions, $4,110,312; giving activities include $4,105,844 for 30 grants (high: $1,175,979; low: $1,000; average: $5,000–$100,000).
Purpose and activities: Giving to a public library and for education, the arts and Jewish causes.
Fields of interest: Museums; Secondary school/education; Higher education; Theological school/education; Libraries (public); Cancer; Jewish federated giving programs; Jewish agencies & temples.
Limitations: Applications not accepted. Giving primarily in New York, NY. No grants to individuals.
Application information: Contributes only to pre-selected organizations.
Officer: Paul Milstein, Pres.
Directors: Roslyn M. Meyer; Edward Milstein; Howard Milstein; Irma Milstein; Barbara M. Zalaznick.
EIN: 133771891
Selected grants: The following grants were reported in 2004.
$1,175,979 to American Museum of Natural History, New York, NY. Grant made in form of stock.
$1,010,513 to Columbia University, New York, NY. Grant made in form of stock.
$1,010,513 to UJA-Federation of New York, New York, NY. Grant made in form of stock.
$202,312 to American Jewish Committee, New York, NY. Grant made in form of stock.
$115,000 to W N E T Channel 13, New York, NY.
$100,000 to Anti-Defamation League of Bnai Brith, New York, NY.
$93,847 to Bank Street College of Education, New York, NY. Grant made in form of stock.
$50,000 to Long Wharf Theater, New Haven, CT.
$50,000 to New York Public Library, New York, NY.
$30,000 to Jewish Museum, New York, NY.

6557
The Mindel Foundation ✦
c/o Morris Tuchman
134 Lexington Ave.
New York, NY   10016-8107

Established in 1998 in NY.
Donors: Morris Tuchman; Nelson Tuchman; Mitchell Adler.
Foundation type: Independent foundation.
Financial data (yr. ended 12/31/05): Assets, $973,393 (M); gifts received, $1,007,062; expenditures, $962,500; qualifying distributions, $962,073; giving activities include $961,973 for 171+ grants (high: $200,000).
Purpose and activities: Giving primarily for Jewish organizations, temples, and schools.
Fields of interest: Education; Jewish federated giving programs; Jewish agencies & temples.
Limitations: Applications not accepted. Giving primarily in NY. No grants to individuals.

Application information: Contributes only to pre-selected organizations.
Trustees: Mitchell Adler; Morris Tuchman; Nelson Tuchman.
EIN: 066462625
Selected grants: The following grants were reported in 2005.
$146,700 to Aleh Foundation, Brooklyn, NY.
$75,000 to Notzer Chesed, New York, NY.
$68,000 to Keren Shlomo Memorial, Brooklyn, NY.
$7,634 to Hampton Synagogue, Hampton, NY.
$2,100 to Yad Eliezer, Brooklyn, NY.
$1,668 to Young Israel of Scarsdale, Scarsdale, NY.
$540 to Hineni, New York, NY.
$360 to Friends of Hatzolah Israel, Monsey, NY.
$360 to Young Israel of Queens Valley, Queens, NY.
$100 to Scarsdale Volunteer Ambulance Corps, Scarsdale, NY.

6558
The Mindich Family Foundation ✦
c/o Neufield Doudna, LLC
103 5th Ave., 5th Fl.
New York, NY   10004

Established in 1996 in NY.
Donor: Eric M. Mindich.
Foundation type: Independent foundation.
Financial data (yr. ended 7/31/05): Assets, $8,351,694 (M); expenditures, $800,971; qualifying distributions, $796,245; giving activities include $793,650 for 76 grants (high: $200,000; low: $200).
Fields of interest: Museums (art); Performing arts, theater; Hospitals (general); Jewish federated giving programs; Jewish agencies & temples.
Limitations: Applications not accepted. Giving primarily in New York, NY. No grants to individuals.
Application information: Contributes only to pre-selected organizations.
Trustees: Eric M. Mindich; Stacey B. Mindich.
EIN: 137085272
Selected grants: The following grants were reported in 2005.
$200,000 to Mount Sinai Medical Center, New York, NY.
$35,000 to Lincoln Center Theater, New York, NY.
$25,000 to Burden Center for the Aging, New York, NY.
$15,000 to Horace Mann School, Riverdale, NY.
$10,000 to ArtsConnection, New York, NY.
$10,000 to Prep for Prep, New York, NY.
$5,000 to Whitney Museum of American Art, New York, NY.
$1,000 to American Friends of the Hebrew University, New York, NY.
$1,000 to Harlem Childrens Zone, New York, NY.
$1,000 to Kids of NYU Foundation, New York, NY.

6559
The Joan Mitchell Foundation, Inc. ✦ ☆
c/o Carolyn Somers
155 Avenue of the Americas, 14th Fl.
New York, NY   10013   (212) 524-0100
FAX: (212) 524-0101;
E-mail: joanmitchellfdn@mindspring.com;
URL: http://foundationcenter.org/grantmaker/joanmitchellfdn/

Donor: Joan Mitchell†.
Foundation type: Independent foundation.

Financial data (yr. ended 12/31/05): Assets, $61,362,765 (M); gifts received, $398,727; expenditures, $1,950,246; qualifying distributions, $1,398,396; giving activities include $122,000 for 5 grants (high: $42,000; low: $5,000), $622,500 for 56 grants to individuals (high: $12,000; low: $10,000), and $135,506 for 3 foundation-administered programs.

Purpose and activities: The Joan Mitchell Foundation seeks to demonstrate that painting and sculpture are significant cultural necessities. To further this mandate, the Foundation provides grants, stipends and scholarships for painters and sculptors. The Foundation also seeks out avenues to meet the needs of artists such as colloquiums and workshops, classes and other resource facilities. These educational activities are to further the development of painters and sculptors. Applications are accepted only in the field of art.

Fields of interest: Arts; Scholarships/financial aid; Disasters, 9/11/01.

Type of support: Scholarships—to individuals; Grants to individuals.

Limitations: Giving on a national basis.

Application information: Application form required.
  Initial approach: Letter
  Deadline(s): See application form for deadlines

Officers: Adrian Gaines, Pres.; Carolyn Somers, Secy. and Prog. Dir.; Yolanda Shashaty, Treas.; Dan Bergman, Exec. Dir.

Directors: Alejandro Anreus; Grace Hartigan; John Koos.

EIN: 113161054

6560
Mitsubishi International Corporation Foundation ◇ ☆

(also known as MIC Foundation)
c/o Mitsubishi International Corp.
655 3rd Ave.
New York, NY 10017 (212) 605-2000
Contact: Mark Keegan, Prog. Off.
E-mail: mic.foundation@org.mitsubishicorp.com;
URL: http://www.micfoundation.org

Established in 1992 in NY.

Donors: Mitsubishi Corp.; Mitsubishi International Corp.

Foundation type: Company-sponsored foundation.

Financial data (yr. ended 12/31/05): Assets, $5,198,077 (M); gifts received, $450,000; expenditures, $482,688; qualifying distributions, $404,716; giving activities include $404,716 for grants.

Purpose and activities: The foundation supports programs designed to help educate the public in ecology and the importance of the environment; support the development of civil society through coalition-building, human rights programs, and poverty alleviation; and help alleviate poverty through educational programs for economically disadvantaged people in the areas of arts education, economic education, and basic education and literacy. Special emphasis is directed toward programs with an environmental component.

Fields of interest: Education, reading; Education; Environmental education; Human services, financial counseling; Civil rights; Economically disadvantaged.

International interests: Canada; Latin America.

Type of support: Continuing support; Land acquisition; Program development; Curriculum development; Scholarship funds; Research.

Limitations: Giving primarily in the Americas, with emphasis on areas of company operations. No support for religious, political, or lobbying organizations or discriminatory organizations. No grants to individuals.

Publications: Application guidelines; Annual report; Grants list.

Application information: Proposals should be brief. Application form not required.
  Initial approach: Proposal
  Copies of proposal: 3
  Deadline(s): None; June is preferred
  Board meeting date(s): Fall
  Final notification: Summer

Officers and Directors:* Ryoichi Ueda,* Chair.; James E. Brumm,* Pres.; Shunichiro Kimpara, Treas.; Tracy L. Austin, Exec. Dir.; Tsutomu Awaya; Tsunao Kijima; Akira Kudo; Yasuyuki Sugiura; Hiroyuki Tarumi.

Number of staff: 3 full-time professional; 3 full-time support.

EIN: 133676166

Selected grants: The following grants were reported in 2004.
$125,000 to Wildlife Conservation Society, Bronx, NY.
$53,900 to American Bird Conservancy, The Plains, VA.
$15,000 to New York Botanical Garden, Bronx, NY.
$11,000 to Earthwatch Institute, Maynard, MA.
$10,000 to Japanese American National Museum, Los Angeles, CA.
$5,000 to Katalysis Partnership, Stockton, CA.

6561
The Mitsui U.S.A. Foundation ◇

200 Park Ave.
New York, NY 10166
URL: http://www.mitsui.com/about_mitUSAfound.shtml

Established in 1987 in NY.

Donor: Mitsui & Co. (U.S.A.), Inc.

Foundation type: Company-sponsored foundation.

Financial data (yr. ended 3/31/04): Assets, $775,981 (M); gifts received, $662,750; expenditures, $548,680; qualifying distributions, $548,599; giving activities include $532,337 for 48 grants (high: $64,333; low: $1,000), and $6,807 for employee matching gifts.

Purpose and activities: The foundation supports organizations involved with arts and culture, education, and human services.

Fields of interest: Arts; Higher education; Education; Human services; International affairs; Federated giving programs.

Type of support: Conferences/seminars; Fellowships; Employee matching gifts; Exchange programs.

Limitations: Applications not accepted. Giving primarily in Los Angeles, CA, Atlanta, GA, Chicago, IL, New York, NY, Houston, TX, and Seattle, WA. No support for religious, fraternal, or athletic organizations or political or lobbying organizations. No grants to individuals, or for endowments, capital campaigns, or television productions.

Publications: Informational brochure.

Application information: Contributes only to pre-selected organizations.
  Board meeting date(s): Quarterly

Officers and Directors:* Hiroshi Tada, Chair.; Shinichi Hirabayashi,* C.E.O. and Pres.; Alan Getz,* Secy.-Treas.; Lawrence Bruser; Glenn Clarke; Hiroyuki Kato; Yoshiyuki Kawashima; Merlin Nelson.

EIN: 133415220

6562
Mizuho USA Foundation, Inc.

(formerly The IBJ Foundation, Inc.)
1251 Ave. of the Americas, 31st Fl.
New York, NY 10020-1104 (212) 282-4192
Contact: Lesley Palmer, Exec. Dir.
FAX: (212) 282-4250;
E-mail: mizuho.usa.foundation@mizuhocbus.com

Established in 1989 in NY.

Donors: The Industrial Bank of Japan Trust Co.; Mizuho Corporate Bank (USA); The Industrial Bank of Japan, Ltd.; Mizuho Securities USA Inc.

Foundation type: Company-sponsored foundation.

Financial data (yr. ended 12/31/04): Assets, $13,551,149 (M); gifts received, $12,465; expenditures, $705,341; qualifying distributions, $643,653; giving activities include $452,330 for 24 grants (high: $40,000; low: $5,000), and $41,030 for employee matching gifts.

Purpose and activities: The foundation supports organizations involved with workforce development, affordable housing, economic development, and community development.

Fields of interest: Employment; Housing/shelter; Economic development; Community development.

Type of support: Continuing support; Program development; Seed money; Employee matching gifts.

Limitations: Giving primarily in Los Angeles, CA, Chicago, IL, and New York, NY. No support for religious or sectarian, fraternal, veterans', labor, or political organizations. No grants to individuals, or for building or construction, capital campaigns, general operating support, fundraising, dinners, benefits, sporting events, journal advertising, or tickets.

Publications: Grants list; Informational brochure (including application guidelines).

Application information: Proposals may be submitted using the NY/NJ Common Area Application Form. Application form not required.
  Initial approach: Telephone or proposal
  Copies of proposal: 2
  Deadline(s): 1st Fri. in July
  Board meeting date(s): Spring and fall
  Final notification: Dec.

Officers and Directors:* Merlin E. Nelson,* Chair.; Michisuke Araki,* Pres.; Yukio Yasuda, Secy.; Paul Dankers, Treas.; Lesley Palmer, Exec. Dir.; John H. Higgs; Mitsuhiro Nagahama; Akio Nekoshima.

EIN: 133550008

Selected grants: The following grants were reported in 2004.
$25,000 to Neighborhood Housing Services of New York City, New York, NY. For general operating support.
$25,000 to United Way of New York City, New York, NY. For Neighborhood Opportunities Fund.
$15,000 to Enterprise Foundation, New York, NY. For capacity building.
$12,500 to National Federation of Community Development Credit Unions, New York, NY. To expand the Each One, Teach Many financial literacy training program at community development credit unions as across the country.

6563
MJPM Foundation
c/o McLaughlin & Stern, LLP
260 Madison Ave.
New York, NY 10016
Contact: Huyler C. Held
E-mail: hheld@Mclaughlinstern.com

Established in 1999 in NY.
Donor: Mary J.P. Moore.
Foundation type: Independent foundation.
Financial data (yr. ended 12/31/04): Assets, $12,685,373 (M); expenditures, $587,398; qualifying distributions, $542,298; giving activities include $518,069 for 8 grants (high: $255,000; low: $8,069).
Purpose and activities: Giving primarily to a community foundation, and for land and other natural resource conservation; funding also for human services.
Fields of interest: Historic preservation/historical societies; Environment, natural resources; Environment, land resources; Food services; Human services; Foundations (community).
Limitations: Applications not accepted. Giving primarily in the northwest corner of CT. No grants to individuals.
Application information: Contributes only to pre-selected organizations. Unsolicited applications strongly discouraged.
Officers: Mary J.P. Moore, Pres.; Samuel F. Posey, Jr., V.P.; Nicholas J. Moore, Secy.; David W. Moore, Treas.
Number of staff: 1 part-time support.
EIN: 134043598
Selected grants: The following grants were reported in 2003.
$248,500 to Berkshire Taconic Community Foundation, Great Barrington, MA.
$100,000 to Trust for Public Land, Boston, MA. For Skiff Mountain N. Parcel Acquisition.
$25,000 to Connecticut Farmland Trust, Hartford, CT. For general support.
$25,000 to Sharon Land Trust, Sharon, CT. For general support.
$20,000 to Hotchkiss School, Lakeville, CT. For scholarships.
$10,000 to Kent Land Trust, Kent, CT. For Southern Gateway Barns.
$285 to Hotchkiss Library of Sharon, Sharon, CT. For children's library renovation.

6564
The Steven and Heather Mnuchin Foundation ◇ ☆
(formerly The Steven T. Mnuchin Foundation)
c/o BCRS Associates, LLC
100 Wall St., 11th Fl.
New York, NY 10005

Established in 1996 in NY.
Donor: Steven T. Mnuchin.
Foundation type: Independent foundation.
Financial data (yr. ended 11/30/05): Assets, $9,114,364 (M); expenditures, $691,643; qualifying distributions, $682,066; giving activities include $682,066 for grants.
Fields of interest: Museums (history); Performing arts, theater; Arts; Higher education, university; Education; Foundations (public); Federated giving programs.
Limitations: Applications not accepted. No grants to individuals; no loans or scholarships.

Application information: Contributes only to pre-selected organizations.
Trustees: Heather Crosby Mnuchin; Robert E. Mnuchin; Steven T. Mnuchin.
EIN: 133990500
Selected grants: The following grants were reported in 2004.
$50,000 to Smithsonian Institution, DC.
$50,000 to Whitney Museum of American Art, New York, NY.
$25,000 to Ackerman Institute for the Family, New York, NY.
$10,000 to Riverdale Country School, Bronx, NY.
$8,600 to City Harvest, New York, NY.
$5,000 to UJA-Federation of New York, New York, NY.
$3,900 to Henry Street Settlement, New York, NY.
$3,500 to Metropolitan Opera, New York, NY.
$1,000 to Columbia University, New York, NY.
$1,000 to Yale University, New Haven, CT.

6565
Leo Model Foundation, Inc. ◇
c/o Peter Model
500 E. 63rd St., No. 24K
New York, NY 10021
Additional address: c/o Model Entities, 1500 Walnut St., Ste. 1300, Philadelphia, PA 19103

Established in 1970 in NY.
Donors: Model Charitable Lead Trust; Jane and Leo Model Foundation; Leo Model†.
Foundation type: Independent foundation.
Financial data (yr. ended 12/31/05): Assets, $40,251,043 (M); expenditures, $1,269,650; qualifying distributions, $1,198,968; giving activities include $1,179,907 for 36 grants (high: $139,750; low: $100).
Purpose and activities: Support for museums and the arts, secondary and higher education (including colleges and universities), and public interest organizations.
Fields of interest: Museums; Arts; Higher education; Education; Environment; Human services; International peace/security; International migration/refugee issues; Public affairs.
International interests: Israel.
Limitations: Applications not accepted. Giving primarily in New York, NY, and Philadelphia, PA. No grants to individuals.
Application information: Contributes only to pre-selected organizations.
Board meeting date(s): Mar.
Officers and Directors:* Allen Model,* Chair.; Peter H. Model,* Pres.; Pamela Model,* V.P.; Marjorie Russel,* Secy.-Treas.; Roberta Gausas; Paul Model.
EIN: 237084119
Selected grants: The following grants were reported in 2004.
$145,000 to Jerusalem Foundation, New York, NY.
$94,730 to Wildlife Trust, Prospect Park, PA.
$55,000 to Planned Parenthood Southeastern Pennsylvania, Philadelphia, PA.
$54,000 to American Bird Conservancy, The Plains, VA.
$35,000 to Nature Conservancy, Arlington, VA.
$25,900 to Pennsylvania Academy of the Fine Arts, Philadelphia, PA.
$21,500 to Middlesex School, Concord, MA.
$3,000 to Bat Conservation International, Austin, TX.
$2,000 to Berea College, Berea, KY.

$2,000 to Metropolitan Museum of Art, New York, NY.

6566
The Ambrose Monell Foundation ▼ ◇
c/o Fulton, Rowe, & Hart
1 Rockefeller Plz., Ste. 301
New York, NY 10020-2002
Contact: George Rowe, Jr., Pres.
FAX: (212) 245-1863;
E-mail: info@monellvetlesen.org; URL: http://www.monellvetlesen.org/

Incorporated in 1952 in NY.
Donor: Maude Monell Vetlesen†.
Foundation type: Independent foundation.
Financial data (yr. ended 12/31/05): Assets, $223,002,711 (M); expenditures, $11,978,145; qualifying distributions, $10,868,950; giving activities include $10,628,333 for 169 grants (high: $500,000; low: $2,500; average: $10,000–$100,000).
Purpose and activities: Giving for the improvement of the physical, mental, and moral condition of humanity throughout the world. Giving largely for hospitals and health services, scientific research, museums, performing arts, and other cultural activities, and higher and secondary education; support also for social services, research in political science, mental health, and aid to the handicapped.
Fields of interest: Education; Animal welfare; Hospitals (general); Health care; Mental health/crisis services; Health organizations, association; Alcoholism; Medical research, institute; AIDS research; Human services; Physical/earth sciences; Political science; Public policy, research; Aging; Disabilities, people with.
Type of support: General/operating support; Continuing support; Annual campaigns; Capital campaigns; Building/renovation; Equipment; Curriculum development; Scholarship funds; Research; Matching/challenge support.
Publications: Application guidelines; Annual report; Financial statement; Grants list.
Application information: After receiving and reviewing letters of inquiry, the foundation may wish to meet with prospective grantees if it feels a meeting will be helpful to the prospective grantee and the foundation. The foundation may then request a detailed proposal. Application form not required.
Initial approach: Letter of inquiry
Copies of proposal: 1
Deadline(s): Apr. 30 and Oct. 31
Board meeting date(s): June and Dec.
Final notification: 4-6 weeks for letter of inquiry
Officers and Directors:* George Rowe, Jr.,* Pres. and Treas.; Eugene P. Grisanti,* V.P.; Ambrose K. Monell,* V.P.; Maurizio J. Morello, Secy.; Gary K. Beauchamp.
EIN: 131982683
Selected grants: The following grants were reported in 2005.
$500,000 to Harvard University, Cambridge, MA. For general operating support for School of Public Health in Boston.
$333,333 to Monell Chemical Senses Center, Philadelphia, PA. For renovations.
$300,000 to American Museum of Natural History, New York, NY. For general operating support.
$300,000 to Educational Broadcasting Corporation, New York, NY. For general operating support.

$200,000 to Brookdale University Hospital and Medical Center, Brooklyn, NY. For Emergency Department.

$200,000 to Lenox Hill Hospital, New York, NY. To install computer information system in Emergency Department.

$50,000 to Breast Cancer Research Foundation, New York, NY. For general operating support.

$50,000 to Saint Lukes-Roosevelt Hospital Center, New York, NY. For general operating support.

$25,000 to Admiral Nimitz Foundation, Fredericksburg, TX. For expansion of National Museum of the Pacific War.

$25,000 to Teaching Matters, New York, NY. For general operating support.

6567
The Monteforte Foundation, Inc. ✧ ☆
61 E. 80th St.
New York, NY 10021

Established in 1992 in NJ.
Donors: Willem Kooyker; Judith-Ann Corrente.
Foundation type: Independent foundation.
Financial data (yr. ended 8/31/05): Assets, $11,824 (M); gifts received, $508,483; expenditures, $464,965; qualifying distributions, $437,965; giving activities include $436,850 for 7 + grants (high: $163,750).
Fields of interest: Arts; Education; Human services.
Type of support: Annual campaigns.
Limitations: Applications not accepted. Giving primarily in NJ and NY. No grants to individuals.
Application information: Contributes only to pre-selected organizations.
Officers: Judith-Ann Corrente, Pres.; Willem Kooyker, V.P.; Carmela June Bruno, Secy.
EIN: 223198329

6568
Monterey Fund, Inc. ▼ ✧
c/o Bear Stearns & Co.
1 Metrotech Ctr. N., 9th Fl.
Brooklyn, NY 11201
Contact: Gilbert Sherman

Incorporated in 1967 in NY.
Donor: Employees of Bear Stearns & Co.
Foundation type: Independent foundation.
Financial data (yr. ended 11/30/05): Assets, $18,477,256 (M); gifts received, $13,173,145; expenditures, $11,305,848; qualifying distributions, $11,217,635; giving activities include $11,111,008 for 1,632 grants (high: $381,100; low: $25; average: $1,000–$25,000).
Purpose and activities: Contributions for hospitals, health services, higher and other education, social services, and youth and child welfare.
Fields of interest: Higher education; Education; Hospitals (general); Health care; Human services; Children/youth, services; Federated giving programs; Jewish federated giving programs; Jewish agencies & temples.
Type of support: General/operating support.
Limitations: Applications not accepted. No grants to individuals.
Publications: Annual report.
Application information: Contributes only to pre-selected organizations.
Board meeting date(s): As required

Officers and Directors: Kenneth Edlow,* Pres.; Robert Janukowicz, Exec. V.P.; Lawrence E. Royes, Exec. V.P.; Robert Steinberg, Exec. V.P.; Jeffrey M. Lipman, Secy.; David Margulies, Treas.; Ray Aronson.
EIN: 136255661
Selected grants: The following grants were reported in 2005.
$381,100 to Greater Houston Community Foundation, Houston, TX.
$257,500 to New-York Historical Society, New York, NY.
$210,750 to Samuel Waxman Cancer Research Foundation, New York, NY.
$210,000 to Darcy School, Chatham, NJ.
$122,175 to American Red Cross, National Headquarters, DC.
$100,000 to Saint Josephs Health Fund, Yonkers, NY.
$74,250 to National Foundation for Ectodermal Dysplasias, Mascoutah, IL.
$50,000 to Follow Your Dream, New York, NY.
$25,000 to Jewish Federation of Lee and Charlotte Counties, Fort Myers, FL.
$17,725 to People About Changing Education (PACE), New York, NY.

6569
The Moody's Foundation ✧
c/o Mgr., Community Progs.
99 Church St.
New York, NY 10007 (212) 553-3667
Contact: Jennifer Dwyer, Philanthropy Coord.
E-mail: philanthropy@moodys.com; URL: http://philanthropy.moodys.com/page.asp?template=tmf&context=tmf&section=hglts

Established in 2002 in NY.
Donor: Moody's Investors Service, Inc.
Foundation type: Company-sponsored foundation.
Financial data (yr. ended 12/31/05): Assets, $19,788,893 (M); gifts received, $6,000,000; expenditures, $3,101,833; qualifying distributions, $3,092,333; giving activities include $2,213,001 for 67 grants (high: $200,142; low: $573), and $757,338 for employee matching gifts.
Purpose and activities: The foundation supports organizations involved with arts and culture, education, health, mental health, human services, civic affairs, minorities, and women.
Fields of interest: Arts; Elementary/secondary education; Secondary school/education; Higher education; Business school/education; Education; Health care; Mental health/crisis services; Human services; Mathematics; Public affairs; Minorities; Women.
International interests: United Kingdom.
Type of support: General/operating support; Continuing support; Management development/capacity building; Equipment; Program development; Fellowships; Scholarship funds; Research; Employee volunteer services; Employee matching gifts.
Limitations: Giving primarily in areas of company operations in New York, NY, San Francisco, CA, and London, England. No support for religious organizations not of direct benefit to the entire community, political candidates or lobbying organizations, fraternal, labor, or similar organizations not of direct benefit to the entire community, or anti-business groups. No grants to individuals, or for travel, national conferences, sponsorships or advertising, or team sponsorships

or athletic scholarships; generally, no general operating support or capital campaigns.
Publications: Application guidelines; Grants list; Informational brochure (including application guidelines); Newsletter; Program policy statement.
Application information: Letters of inquiry should be no longer than 1 page. Telephone calls during the application process are not encouraged. Application form not required.
Initial approach: Mail or E-mail letter of inquiry
Deadline(s): None
Board meeting date(s): Quarterly
Final notification: Within 8 weeks
Officers and Directors:* Fran Laserson,* Pres.; Michelle Berninger, V.P.; Jane Clark, Secy.; Brian Clarkson; Jeanne Dering; Jennifer Elliot; John Goggins; Linda Huber; Chris Mahoney; Chester Murray.
EIN: 134200757
Selected grants: The following grants were reported in 2005.
$712,648 to JK Group, Plainsboro, NJ. 4 grants: $150,482, $280,423, $110,158, $171,585
$147,250 to Mathematical Association of America, DC.
$100,000 to American Red Cross.
$86,650 to Working in Support of Education, New York, NY.
$50,000 to Rockefeller University, New York, NY.
$35,000 to Metropolitan Museum of Art, New York, NY.
$10,000 to American Museum of the Moving Image, Astoria, NY.

6570
The Moore Charitable Foundation, Inc. ✧
c/o Moore Capital Mgmt., LLC
1251 Ave. of the Americas, 17th Fl.
New York, NY 10020
Contact: Ann Colley

Established in 1992 in NY; funded in 1993.
Donors: One to One Charitable Foundation; Carl Palash; David Waddill; Moore Capital Mgmt., LLC.
Foundation type: Independent foundation.
Financial data (yr. ended 12/31/05): Assets, $30,875,934 (M); gifts received, $10,028,760; expenditures, $3,829,595; qualifying distributions, $3,829,595; giving activities include $3,486,150 for 126 grants (high: $2,040,000; low: $500).
Purpose and activities: The mission of the foundation is land and water conservation.
Fields of interest: Environment, natural resources; Environment.
Limitations: Applications not accepted. Giving on a national basis. No grants to individuals.
Application information: Contributes only to pre-selected organizations. Unsolicited requests for funds not considered.
Officers: Louis M. Bacon, Pres.; Ann Stevenson-Colley, Exec. V.P.; Lawrence M. Noe, V.P.; Paula Stzurma, Secy.-Treas.
EIN: 133741954
Selected grants: The following grants were reported in 2005.
$2,040,000 to Middlebury College, Middlebury, VT.
$117,000 to Peconic Land Trust, Southampton, NY.
$100,000 to Land Trust Alliance, DC.
$67,000 to Riverkeeper, Tarrytown, NY.
$58,450 to Group for the South Fork, Bridgehampton, NY.
$18,000 to Communities in Schools, Alexandria, VA.

$15,000 to Episcopal High School, Alexandria, VA.

$12,000 to Colorado Conservation Trust, Boulder, CO.

$10,000 to University of Virginia, Charlottesville, VA.

$5,000 to Saint Michaels College, Colchester, VT.

6571
David and Katherine Moore Family Foundation ◇

c/o D'Arcangelo Co.
3000 Westchester Ave., Ste. 100
Purchase, NY 10577 (914) 694-4600
Contact: David E. Moore, Tr.
E-mail: pwarner@darcangelo.com

Established in 1997 in NY.
Donor: David E. Moore, Sr.
Foundation type: Independent foundation.
Financial data (yr. ended 12/31/05): Assets, $20,894,644 (M); gifts received, $111,055; expenditures, $1,000,304; qualifying distributions, $869,459; giving activities include $860,500 for 4 grants.
Purpose and activities: Giving primarily to art museums, as well as to arts and culture, education, family planning, and human services.
Fields of interest: Museums (art); Arts; Education; Reproductive health, family planning; Human services.
Type of support: General/operating support; Continuing support; Annual campaigns; Capital campaigns; Endowments; Scholarship funds.
Limitations: Giving primarily in the northeastern U.S.
Application information: Application form not required.
   Deadline(s): None
Trustees: David E. Moore; Katherine C. Moore.
EIN: 137103979

6572
Edward S. Moore Family Foundation, Inc. ◇ ☆

248 Creamer St., No. 9
Brooklyn, NY 11231

Established in 2005 in NY.
Foundation type: Independent foundation.
Financial data (yr. ended 3/31/05): Assets, $22,776,816 (M); expenditures, $933,949; qualifying distributions, $933,849; giving activities include $765,100 for 62 grants (high: $50,000; low: $1,000).
Fields of interest: Arts, formal/general education; Higher education; Education; Hospitals (general); Human services; Children/youth, services; Family services.
Limitations: Giving primarily in CT and NY; some funding nationally.
Officers and Directors:* Marion M. Gilbert,* Pres.; Roger Gilbert,* V.P.; Katrina Gilbert Millard,* Secy.; Jeffrey Z. Gilbert,* Treas.; Jane Gilbert; Louisa Gilbert.
EIN: 200249777

6573
James A. Moore Foundation for Otologic Research ◇

c/o Eleanor M. Sterne
117 E. 72nd St.
New York, NY 10021

Established in NY.
Foundation type: Independent foundation.
Financial data (yr. ended 12/31/04): Assets, $4,467 (M); expenditures, $410,086; qualifying distributions, $400,000; giving activities include $400,000 for 2 grants (high: $375,000; low: $25,000).
Fields of interest: Medical school/education.
Type of support: Scholarship funds.
Limitations: Applications not accepted. Giving primarily in NY. No grants to individuals.
Application information: Contributes only to pre-selected organizations.
Officers: Eleanor M. Sterne, Pres. and Treas.; Douglas Moore, V.P. and Secy.
EIN: 136153634

6574
The Tom and Judy Moore Foundation ◇ ☆

1133 5th Ave.
New York, NY 10128

Donor: Thomas A. Moore.
Foundation type: Independent foundation.
Financial data (yr. ended 12/31/05): Assets, $4,921,475 (M); expenditures, $829,636; qualifying distributions, $820,000; giving activities include $820,000 for 10 grants (high: $50,000; low: $3,000).
Fields of interest: Elementary/secondary education; Human services; Community development.
Limitations: Applications not accepted. Giving primarily in NY. No grants to individuals.
Application information: Unsolicited requests for funds not accepted.
Officers: Thomas A. Moore, Pres.; Judith A. Livingston, V.P. and Secy.-Treas.
Director: Mary Rose Smith.
EIN: 201258563

6575
Daniel and Janet Mordecai Foundation ◇ ☆

c/o U.S. Trust Company of New York
114 W. 47th St., TAXRGR
New York, NY 10036

Established in 2003 in CO.
Donor: Janet Mordecai.
Foundation type: Independent foundation.
Financial data (yr. ended 12/31/05): Assets, $12,873,702 (M); gifts received, $600,000; expenditures, $777,962; qualifying distributions, $669,783; giving activities include $665,500 for 28 grants (high: $385,500; low: $1,000).
Fields of interest: Arts; Higher education; Education; Boys & girls clubs; Human services.
Limitations: Applications not accepted. Giving primarily in CO. No grants to individuals.
Application information: Contributes only to pre-selected organizations.
Officer: Janet Mordecai, Pres. and Treas.
EIN: 200185059

6576
John E. Morgan Roundation, Inc. ◇ ☆

c/o Bessemer Trust
630 5th Ave.
New York, NY 10111

Foundation type: Independent foundation.
Financial data (yr. ended 12/31/04): Assets, $64,607,244 (M); expenditures, $2,153,927; qualifying distributions, $1,765,489; giving activities include $1,493,971 for 12 grants (high: $1,000,650; low: $1,000), and $30,000 for 12 grants to individuals (high: $2,500; low: $2,500).
Purpose and activities: Giving primarily for higher education.
Fields of interest: Higher education; Human services.
Limitations: Applications not accepted. Giving primarily in PA.
Application information: Unsolicited requests for funds not accepted.
Officers and Directors:* Harry Loder,* Pres.; James Zigmant,* V.P.; Jay Wagner,* Secy.; John Eddy,* Treas.
EIN: 562290010

6577
Morgan Stanley Foundation ▼

(formerly Morgan Stanley Dean Witter Foundation)
c/o Community Affairs
1633 Broadway, 20th Fl.
New York, NY 10019 (212) 537-1400
FAX: (646) 519-5460;
E-mail: whatadifference@morganstanley.com;
URL: http://www.morganstanley.com/about/community/index.html

Trust established in 1961 in NY.
Donors: Morgan Stanley Group Inc.; Morgan Stanley & Co. Inc.; Morgan Stanley, Dean Witter, Discover & Co.; Morgan Stanley Dean Witter & Co.; Morgan Stanley.
Foundation type: Company-sponsored foundation.
Financial data (yr. ended 12/31/04): Assets, $47,240,957 (M); gifts received, $6,950,973; expenditures, $4,662,236; qualifying distributions, $4,661,953; giving activities include $4,661,953 for 829 grants (high: $168,366; low: $72).
Purpose and activities: The foundation supports organizations involved with arts and culture, K-12 education, minority education, children's health, human services, and diversity.
Fields of interest: Arts; Elementary/secondary education; Secondary school/education; Higher education; Medical care, in-patient care; Health care; Human services; Civil rights, equal rights; Children; Minorities.
Type of support: General/operating support; Program development; Fellowships; Scholarship funds; Employee volunteer services; Scholarships—to individuals.
Limitations: Giving primarily in areas of company operations, with emphasis on the Phoenix, AZ, Los Angeles and San Francisco, CA, Wilmington, DE, Chicago, IL, Baltimore, MD, New York, NY, Columbus, OH, Philadelphia, PA, Dallas and Houston, TX, and Salt Lake City, UT, metropolitan areas; giving also to national organizations. No support for local organizations with which Morgan Stanley employees are not involved, political candidates or lobbying organizations, religious, fraternal, or professional sports organizations, or individual performing arts organizations. No grants

to individuals (except for the Morgan Stanley Scholars Program), or for capital campaigns or endowments, construction or renovation (except for self-identified children's health improvement projects), political causes or campaigns, or documentaries or productions.

Publications: Application guidelines; Corporate giving report; Informational brochure; Program policy statement.

Application information: Letters of inquiry should be no longer than 1 to 2 pages. Unsolicited requests from local organizations are accepted from Morgan Stanley employees on behalf of nonprofit organizations only. Application form not required.

Initial approach: Letter of inquiry
Board meeting date(s): Mar., June, Sept., and Dec.

Officers and Trustees:* Carla Harris,* Chair.; Joan E. Steinberg,* Exec. Dir.; Marianne Bachynski; Kathy Beiser; Marilyn Booker; Charlie Chasin; Frank English; Bill McMahon; Kelly McNamara-Corley; Eileen Murray; Tom Nides; Jose Rivera; Bill Wright.
EIN: 136155650

Selected grants: The following grants were reported in 2004.

$168,366 to Columbia University, Business School, New York, NY.
$150,000 to American Association of School Administrators, Arlington, VA.
$150,000 to College Summit, DC.
$150,000 to United Way of New York City, New York, NY.
$123,987 to United Way of Metropolitan Chicago, Chicago, IL.
$32,500 to Childrens Aid Society, New York, NY.
$25,000 to Covenant House, New York, NY.
$25,000 to New York Cares, New York, NY.
$12,500 to Midtown West Parents Association, New York, NY.
$10,000 to Drueding Center, Project Rainbow, Philadelphia, PA.

6578
Norman M. Morris Foundation, Inc. ✦
c/o Wendy Aglietti
9 Rustling Ln.
Bedford, NY 10506 (914) 694-2000

Incorporated in 1947 in NY.
Donor: Norman M. Morris†.
Foundation type: Independent foundation.
Financial data (yr. ended 12/31/04): Assets, $11,858,056 (M); gifts received, $1,174,599; expenditures, $466,210; qualifying distributions, $404,761; giving activities include $404,761 for 76 grants (high: $50,000; low: $50).
Purpose and activities: Giving primarily for health care.
Fields of interest: Elementary/secondary education; Higher education; Hospitals (general); Human services.
Limitations: Giving on a national basis, with emphasis on NY and CT. No grants to individuals.
Application information: Application form not required.
Initial approach: Letter
Deadline(s): None
Officers and Trustees:* Arline J. Lubin, Pres.; Marvin Lubin,* V.P.; Robert E. Morris,* Secy.-Treas.; Kenneth A. Lubin; Leland M. Morris.
EIN: 136119134
Selected grants: The following grants were reported in 2005.

$50,000 to Hebrew Home for the Aged at Riverdale, Riverdale, NY.
$50,000 to White Plains Hospital Center, White Plains, NY.
$30,000 to Guiding Eyes for the Blind, Yorktown Heights, NY. 2 grants: $15,000 each
$10,000 to Boca Raton Community Hospital Foundation, Boca Raton, FL.
$10,000 to Israel at Heart, New York, NY.
$10,000 to Saint Andrews School, Boca Raton, FL.
$6,000 to Bridges to Community, Ossining, NY.
$6,000 to Puppies Behind Bars, New York, NY.
$4,000 to Oakwood School, North Hollywood, CA.

6579
The William T. Morris Foundation, Inc.
230 Park Ave., Ste. 622
New York, NY 10169-0622
Contact: Bruce A. August, Pres.

Trust established in 1937; incorporated in 1941 in DE.
Donor: William T. Morris†.
Foundation type: Independent foundation.
Financial data (yr. ended 6/30/05): Assets, $48,864,480 (M); expenditures, $3,176,877; qualifying distributions, $2,532,847; giving activities include $1,915,000 for 30 grants (high: $125,000; low: $10,000).
Purpose and activities: Giving primarily to charitable, scientific, and/or educational institutions.
Fields of interest: Arts; Higher education; Hospitals (general); Health care; Children/youth, services.
Type of support: Scholarship funds.
Limitations: Applications not accepted. Giving primarily in the northeastern states, especially NY, CT, and RI.
Application information:
Board meeting date(s): As required
Officers and Directors:* Bruce A. August,* Pres.; Arthur C. Laske, Jr.,* Treas.; E.W. Burns.
Number of staff: 2 full-time professional.
EIN: 131600908
Selected grants: The following grants were reported in 2005.

$125,000 to Assumption College, Worcester, MA.
$125,000 to Dartmouth College, Hanover, NH.
$125,000 to Fairfield University, Fairfield, CT.
$125,000 to Roger Williams University, Bristol, RI.
$110,000 to Arthritis Foundation, Atlanta, GA.
$100,000 to Bowdoin College, Brunswick, ME.
$100,000 to Hospital for Special Surgery, New York, NY.
$100,000 to Metropolitan Opera Association, New York, NY.
$100,000 to Saint Vincents Medical Center Foundation, Bridgeport, CT.
$25,000 to Mystic Seaport Museum, Mystic, CT.

6580
The William C. and Susan F. Morris Foundation ✦
c/o J & W Seligman & Co.
100 Park Ave., 8th Fl.
New York, NY 10017

Established in 2000 in DE.
Donor: William Morris.
Foundation type: Independent foundation.

Financial data (yr. ended 12/31/05): Assets, $2,257,978 (M); expenditures, $2,727,896; qualifying distributions, $2,724,315; giving activities include $2,721,500 for 7 grants (high: $2,013,390; low: $10,000).
Purpose and activities: Giving primarily to the opera.
Fields of interest: Performing arts, opera; Elementary/secondary education; Higher education.
Limitations: Applications not accepted. Giving primarily in Santa Fe, NM, and NY. No grants to individuals.
Application information: Contributes only to pre-selected organizations.
Officers: William Morris, Chair., Pres. and Treas.; Susan Morris, V.P. and Secy.
EIN: 134128044

6581
The Allan Morrow Foundation, Inc.
c/o Imowitz Koenig & Co., LLP
622 3rd Ave., 33rd Fl.
New York, NY 10017

Established in 1989 in NY.
Donor: Allan Morrow†.
Foundation type: Independent foundation.
Financial data (yr. ended 12/31/05): Assets, $1,886,127 (M); gifts received, $14,742; expenditures, $380,399; qualifying distributions, $380,274; giving activities include $370,500 for 8 grants (high: $100,000; low: $10,000).
Fields of interest: Jewish agencies & temples; LGBTQ.
Limitations: Giving primarily in New York, NY.
Publications: Annual report.
Application information: Application form not required.
Initial approach: Letter
Copies of proposal: 1
Deadline(s): None
Board meeting date(s): Oct.
Officers: James Pepper, Pres.; Vivian Shapiro, V.P.; Arline West, Secy.; Mark R. Imowitz, Treas.
Directors: Bernice Manocherian; Lawrence Newman; Jeffrey Soref.
Number of staff: None.
EIN: 133566764
Selected grants: The following grants were reported in 2004.

$100,000 to Lincoln Center for the Performing Arts, New York, NY. For general support.
$100,000 to Museum of Jewish Heritage, New York, NY. For general support.
$50,500 to Jewish Association for Services for the Aged, New York, NY. For general support.
$35,000 to Stonewall Community Foundation, New York, NY. For general support.
$12,500 to Jewish Museum, New York, NY. For general support.

6582
Morse Family Foundation, Inc. ✦
(formerly Enid & Lester S. Morse, Jr. Foundation, Inc.)
c/o Lester Morse Co.
60 E. 42nd St., Ste. 1807
New York, NY 10165

Established in 1967 in NY.
Donor: Lester S. Morse, Jr.

Foundation type: Independent foundation.
Financial data (yr. ended 3/31/05): Assets, $14,023,327 (M); expenditures, $515,492; qualifying distributions, $496,375; giving activities include $493,875 for 161 grants (high: $70,000; low: $25).
Purpose and activities: Giving primarily for education and the arts, including music and the performing arts.
Fields of interest: Museums; Performing arts; Performing arts, dance; Performing arts, music; Arts; Higher education; Libraries/library science; Education; Health care; Human services; Jewish federated giving programs.
Limitations: Applications not accepted. Giving primarily in New York, NY. No grants to individuals.
Application information: Contributes only to pre-selected organizations.
  Board meeting date(s): Apr.
Officers: Lester S. Morse, Jr., Pres.; Enid W. Morse, V.P.; Douglas A. Morse, Treas.
EIN: 136220174

6583
The Morse Foundation ✧
c/o Phillip H. Morse
P.O. Box 723
Glens Falls, NY 12801

Established in 1998 in MA.
Donors: Phillip H. Morse; The Waterhouse Family Foundation.
Foundation type: Independent foundation.
Financial data (yr. ended 12/31/05): Assets, $1,436,681 (M); gifts received, $2,200; expenditures, $1,207,580; qualifying distributions, $1,205,080; giving activities include $1,191,918 for 33 grants (high: $500,000; low: $30).
Purpose and activities: Giving primarily for education, as well as for hospitals and health associations, and human services.
Fields of interest: Museums; Historical activities; Secondary school/education; Higher education; Hospitals (general); Health organizations; Cancer research; Human services; Family services; Federated giving programs.
Limitations: Applications not accepted. Giving primarily in NY. No grants to individuals.
Application information: Contributes only to pre-selected organizations.
Trustees: Michael L. Brown; Katherine S. Morse; Lindsey A. Morse; Phillip H. Morse; Shelley H. Morse; Susan K. Morse.
EIN: 046868099
Selected grants: The following grants were reported in 2004.
$500,000 to Albany Medical Center Foundation, Albany, NY.
$250,000 to YMCA, Glens Falls Area Family, Glens Falls, NY.
$25,000 to American Cancer Society, North Brunswick, NJ.
$10,000 to Jupiter Medical Center Foundation, Jupiter, FL.
$10,000 to National Baseball Hall of Fame and Museum, Cooperstown, NY.
$500 to Maine Handicapped Skiing, Bethel, ME.
$250 to Cystic Fibrosis Foundation, New York, NY.
$250 to Junior Achievement of Northeastern New York, Latham, NY.

6584
Morse Hill Foundation, Inc. ✧ ☆
20 Corporate Woods Blvd.
Albany, NY 12211

Established in 1990 in NY.
Donors: Kathleen M. Picotte†; Michael B. Picotte; KMP Charitable Trust II; KMP Charitable Trust VI.
Foundation type: Independent foundation.
Financial data (yr. ended 12/31/05): Assets, $9,958,885 (M); gifts received, $447,764; expenditures, $507,453; qualifying distributions, $463,385; giving activities include $429,200 for 5 grants (high: $150,000; low: $10,000).
Purpose and activities: Giving for higher education, performing arts centers, hospital funding, and Christian organizations.
Fields of interest: Performing arts centers; Higher education; Education; Hospitals (general); Christian agencies & churches.
Limitations: Applications not accepted. Giving primarily in FL, NY, and PA. No grants to individuals.
Application information: Contributes only to pre-selected organizations.
Officers: Michael B. Picotte, Pres.; Margaret L. Picotte, V.P.; Margaret Ryhanych, Secy.-Treas.
EIN: 223083890
Selected grants: The following grants were reported in 2004.
$160,000 to Rosarian Academy, West Palm Beach, FL. 2 grants: $10,000 (For annual fund), $150,000.
$50,000 to South Florida Science Museum, West Palm Beach, FL.
$50,000 to Villanova University, Villanova, PA.
$25,000 to Saint Peters Hospital Foundation, Albany, NY.
$24,400 to Raymond F. Kravis Center for the Performing Arts, West Palm Beach, FL.
$20,000 to Dreher Park Zoo, West Palm Beach, FL.
$10,000 to American Red Cross, West Palm Beach, FL.
$10,000 to Diocese of Albany, Albany, NY.
$5,000 to Hospice of Palm Beach County, West Palm Beach, FL.

6585
The Morton Foundation, Inc. ✧
c/o Rosalind Davidowitz
44 Wall St., 2nd Fl.
New York, NY 10005

Established in 1961.
Donor: J. Morton Davis.
Foundation type: Independent foundation.
Financial data (yr. ended 12/31/04): Assets, $3,565,815 (M); expenditures, $347,758; qualifying distributions, $327,824; giving activities include $323,924 for 33+ grants (high: $125,000).
Purpose and activities: Emphasis on Jewish organizations, including educational institutions and temple support; support also for higher education.
Fields of interest: Arts; Higher education; Jewish agencies & temples.
Limitations: Applications not accepted. Giving primarily in NY. No grants to individuals, or for scholarships.
Application information: Contributes only to pre-selected organizations.
Officers and Directors:* Rosalind Davidowitz,* Pres.; Ruki Renov,* Secy.; Esther Stahler,* Treas.
EIN: 136107817

6586
The Mosaic Fund ▼ ✧
c/o Howard G. Seitz
230 Park Ave., Ste. 1130
New York, NY 10169-0079

Established in 1994 in NY.
Donors: Clattesad Trust; Clapttrap Trust; Clatpag Trust; Clatscatt Trust; Clattaur Trust; Clattecam Trust.
Foundation type: Independent foundation.
Financial data (yr. ended 12/31/05): Assets, $350,311 (M); gifts received, $8,373,031; expenditures, $8,468,951; qualifying distributions, $8,468,951; giving activities include $8,462,290 for 43 grants (high: $3,700,000; low: $500; average: $1,000–$10,000).
Purpose and activities: Giving primarily for environmental conservation and protection, including urban parks and gardens; some support also for secondary education and the arts.
Fields of interest: Arts; Elementary/secondary education; Environment, natural resources; Environment.
Limitations: Applications not accepted. Giving primarily in NY. No grants to individuals.
Application information: Contributes only to pre-selected organizations.
Trustees: Howard G. Seitz; Richard T. Watson.
EIN: 137045257
Selected grants: The following grants were reported in 2005.
$3,700,000 to Los Luceros Foundation, Alcalde, NM. For general operating support.
$3,600,000 to Stonecrop Gardens, Cold Spring, NY. For general operating support.
$200,000 to Palisades Interstate Park Commission, Bear Mountain, NY. For general operating support for Sterling Forest program.
$130,000 to Garden Conservancy, Cold Spring, NY. For general operating support and endowment.
$70,000 to Heritage Charlevoix, Canada. For general operating support.
$20,000 to Wave Hill, Bronx, NY. For general operating support.
$10,000 to Maud Morgan Visual Arts Center, Cambridge, MA. For general support.
$7,500 to Trust for Public Land, San Francisco, CA.
$5,000 to W N E T Channel 13, New York, NY.
$2,500 to American Museum of Natural History, New York, NY.

6587
Henry and Lucy Moses Fund, Inc.
c/o Moses and Singer
405 Lexington Ave.
New York, NY 10174
Contact: Irving Sitnick, Pres.

Incorporated in 1942 in NY.
Donors: Henry L. Moses†; Lucy G. Moses†.
Foundation type: Independent foundation.
Financial data (yr. ended 12/31/04): Assets, $1,026,855 (M); gifts received, $1,565,000; expenditures, $1,750,752; qualifying distributions, $1,730,768; giving activities include $1,721,840 for 92 grants (high: $100,000; low: $2,500).
Purpose and activities: Support for hospitals; Jewish and other welfare funds; higher and legal education and educational programs for minorities; social service agencies, including those for youth, child welfare, minorities, the aged, and the handicapped; arts and cultural programs, including

dance; and environmental concerns, including Central Park in New York, NY.
Fields of interest: Performing arts; Performing arts, dance; Performing arts, music; Arts; Higher education; Environment; Hospitals (general); Human services; Children/youth, services; Aging, centers/services; Jewish federated giving programs; Disabilities, people with.
Type of support: General/operating support; Continuing support; Annual campaigns; Endowments; Professorships; Scholarship funds; Research; Matching/challenge support.
Limitations: Giving primarily in the New York, NY, area. No grants to individuals; no loans.
Application information: Support generally limited to previous grant recipients. Application form not required.
> *Initial approach:* Letter
> *Copies of proposal:* 1
> *Deadline(s):* None
> *Board meeting date(s):* Usually in Feb., May, Aug., and Oct.
Officers and Directors: * Irving Sitnick,* Pres.; Joseph Fishman,* V.P. and Secy.; Jacqueline Schneider, V.P.
EIN: 136092967
Selected grants: The following grants were reported in 2003.
$100,000 to Montefiore Medical Center, Bronx, NY.
$100,000 to UJA-Federation of New York, New York, NY.
$25,000 to Jewish Association for Services for the Aged, New York, NY.
$25,000 to New York City Ballet, New York, NY.
$15,000 to Childrens Aid Society, New York, NY.
$15,000 to Wildlife Conservation Society, Bronx, NY.
$10,000 to Alvin Ailey Dance Foundation, New York, NY.
$10,000 to Dance Theater of Harlem, New York, NY.
$10,000 to Visiting Nurse Service of New York, New York, NY.
$10,000 to Young Peoples Chorus of New York City, New York, NY.

6588
The Henry & Rose Moskowitz 1999 Family Foundation ✧
50 W. 17th St.
New York, NY   10011

Established in 2000 in NY.
Donor: Henry Moskowitz.
Foundation type: Independent foundation.
Financial data (yr. ended 12/31/03): Assets, $1,757,309 (M); expenditures, $499,208; qualifying distributions, $496,418; giving activities include $493,902 for 259 grants (high: $68,000).
Fields of interest: Jewish agencies & temples.
Limitations: Applications not accepted. No grants to individuals.
Application information: Contributes only to pre-selected organizations.
Officers: Henry Moskowitz, Pres.; Rose Moskowitz, V.P.; Mark Moskowitz, Secy.
EIN: 116537576

6589
Stephen Moss Foundation, Inc. ✧ ☆
c/o JAD Consulting, LLC
61 Broadway, Ste. 1710
New York, NY   10006

Established in 1994 in NY.
Donors: Stephen Moss; Education for Youth Society.
Foundation type: Independent foundation.
Financial data (yr. ended 10/31/05): Assets, $313,633 (M); gifts received, $418,782; expenditures, $326,500; qualifying distributions, $325,875; giving activities include $325,099 for 57 grants (high: $100,000; low: $65).
Fields of interest: Hospitals (general); Art & music therapy; Health organizations, association; Human services; Jewish agencies & temples.
Type of support: Research.
Limitations: Applications not accepted. Giving primarily in NY. No grants to individuals.
Application information: Contributes only to pre-selected organizations.
Officers: Stephen Moss, Pres. and Treas.; Robert Moss, Sr. V.P.; Linda Burns, V.P.; Nicole Moss, V.P.; Steven Moss, V.P.
EIN: 133799260
Selected grants: The following grants were reported in 2005.
$120,000 to New York University Medical Center, New York, NY. 2 grants: $20,000 (For Haddenfeld Children's Center), $100,000 to Child Life and Creative Arts Therapies (For Child Life and Creative Arts Therapies).
$80,000 to Be-A-Friend Program, Buffalo, NY.
$10,000 to New York University, Institute for Surgical Research, New York, NY.
$5,150 to Leukemia & Lymphoma Society, White Plains, NY.
$5,000 to UJA-Federation of New York, New York, NY. For Tsunami relief.
$3,000 to American Red Cross, National Headquarters, DC. For Hurrican 2005.
$2,000 to New York Public Library, New York, NY.
$1,000 to Learning Leaders, New York, NY.
$500 to Sanctuary for Families, New York, NY.

6590
The Mosse Foundation for Education and the Arts ✧
(formerly The Hilde L. Mosse Foundation)
217 Broadway, Ste. 600A
New York, NY   10007-2941
Contact: Henry H. Muller, Secy.

Established in 1985 in NY.
Foundation type: Independent foundation.
Financial data (yr. ended 9/30/05): Assets, $18,361,015 (M); expenditures, $825,272; qualifying distributions, $715,000; giving activities include $715,000 for 11 grants (high: $200,000; low: $10,000).
Purpose and activities: Giving for reading disorders and related problems in children, the effects of violence in mass media on children, and to promote the works of Frederic Wertham.
Fields of interest: Performing arts, theater; Child development, education; Higher education; Child development, services; Federated giving programs; Jewish agencies & temples.
Limitations: Giving primarily in CA, MA, and NY. No grants to individuals.
Application information:

Initial approach: Letter
Deadline(s): None
Officers: Roger Strauch, Co-Pres. and Treas.; Hans Strauch, Co-Pres.; Henry H. Muller, Secy.
EIN: 133284797
Selected grants: The following grants were reported in 2004.
$250,000 to Mathematical Sciences Research Institute, Berkeley, CA. 2 grants: $100,000 (For after-school math), $150,000 (For science programs).
$150,000 to Berkeley Repertory Theater, Berkeley, CA. For Touring productions and Matinee programs.
$100,000 to Northside Center for Child Development, New York, NY. For after-school Reading and Math.
$95,000 to Lesley University, Cambridge, MA. For reading recovery and early literacy.
$50,000 to Temple Beth-El of Great Neck, Great Neck, NY. For after-school program for children with Learning Disabilities.
$45,000 to Brandeis University, Waltham, MA. For lecture programs.
$25,000 to Combined Jewish Philanthropies of Greater Boston, Boston, MA. To promote literacy and reading skills in young children.
$12,500 to Humboldt-Universitat zu Berlin, Berlin, Germany. For lecture programs.
$10,000 to Institute of Contemporary Art, Boston, MA. For Art and Reading program.

6591
Mostyn Foundation, Inc.
c/o Silvercrest Asset Mgmt. Group
1330 Ave. of the Americas
New York, NY   10019
Contact: Jeremiah M. Bogert

Trust established in 1949 in NY; incorporated in 1965.
Donors: Harvey D. Gibson†; Mrs. Harvey D. Gibson†; Whitney Bourne Atwood.
Foundation type: Independent foundation.
Financial data (yr. ended 12/31/05): Assets, $5,037,397 (M); expenditures, $373,411; qualifying distributions, $323,000; giving activities include $323,000 for 37 grants (high: $60,000; low: $1,000).
Fields of interest: Higher education; Environment, natural resources; Health care; Human services; Protestant agencies & churches.
Type of support: General/operating support; Endowments.
Limitations: Applications not accepted. Giving in the U.S., with emphasis on FL and NY. No grants to individuals.
Application information: Contributes only to pre-selected organizations.
Officers: Arthur B. Choate, Pres.; Timothy Choate, V.P.; Nicholas E. Christin, Secy.-Treas.
EIN: 136171217
Selected grants: The following grants were reported in 2004.
$50,000 to University of Miami, Coral Gables, FL. For capital fund for Education Center.
$35,000 to Episcopal Diocese of Maine, Portland, ME.
$25,000 to National Coalition for Marine Conservation, Leesburg, VA.
$20,000 to Washburn-Norlands Living History Center, Livermore, ME. For Unique Programs for the Public.

$15,000 to Diabetes Research Institute, Miami, FL.

$15,000 to Parish Resource Center, Valley Stream, NY. For general support.

$15,000 to Scarborough Land Conservation Trust, Scarborough, ME. For general support.

$10,000 to Bermuda Institute of Ocean Sciences, Saint George, Bermuda. For research fund.

$10,000 to International Game Fish Association, Dania, FL. For Marine Conservation.

$8,000 to Pine Tree Legal Assistance, Bangor, ME.

6592
MRM Foundation, Inc. ✧
100 Jericho Quadrangle, Ste. 212
Jericho, NY 11753 (516) 935-4200
Contact: Julia Greenblatt, Dir.
Application address: 245 Middle Neck Rd., Sands Point, NY 11050

Established in 1994 in NY.
Donor: Joel N. Greenblatt.
Foundation type: Independent foundation.
Financial data (yr. ended 11/30/05): Assets, $638,197 (M); gifts received, $1,946,888; expenditures, $2,459,768; qualifying distributions, $2,445,000; giving activities include $2,443,950 for 54 grants (high: $600,000; low: $1,000).
Purpose and activities: Giving primarily for education.
Fields of interest: Higher education; Theological school/education; Cancer research; Medical research; Jewish agencies & temples.
Type of support: General/operating support.
Limitations: Giving primarily in NY.
Application information: Application form not required.
Initial approach: Letter
Deadline(s): Nov. 30
Directors: Joel N. Greenblatt; Julia Greenblatt; Richard Greenblatt.
EIN: 113243133
Selected grants: The following grants were reported in 2004.
$850,000 to Success for All Foundation, Baltimore, MD. 3 grants: $300,000, $350,000, $200,000
$250,000 to Institute for Student Achievement, Lake Success, NY.
$140,000 to Jewish Opportunities Institute, New York, NY.
$115,000 to Temple Beth Israel, Port Washington, NY. 2 grants: $100,000, $15,000
$10,000 to Solomon Schechter School of Manhattan, New York, NY.
$2,500 to Chabad of Port Washington, Port Washington, NY.
$1,800 to Temple Israel of Great Neck, Great Neck, NY.

6593
Mulago Foundation ✧
c/o Joel E. Sammet & Co.
20 Exchange Pl.
New York, NY 10005

Established around 1968 in CA.
Donors: Rainer Arnhold Trust; Ruth Steiner†.
Foundation type: Independent foundation.
Financial data (yr. ended 12/31/03): Assets, $83,181,069 (M); gifts received, $17,829,418; expenditures, $4,539,421; qualifying distributions,

$4,227,023; giving activities include $4,226,683 for 51 grants (high: $1,251,603; low: $250).
Purpose and activities: Giving primarily for education, conservation, and health.
Fields of interest: Education; Environment; Health care; Human services; Children/youth, services; Family services; International relief.
Limitations: Applications not accepted. Giving on a national basis, with some emphasis on New York, NY. No grants to individuals.
Application information: Contributes only to pre-selected organizations.
Officers: Henry H. Arnhold, Pres.; Patricia Finnen, Secy.; John P. Arnhold, Treas.
EIN: 946182697

6594
Mary Muldoon Fund ✧ ☆
800 Troy-Schenectady Rd.
Latham, NY 12110-2455
Contact: Board of Trustees

Established in 1927.
Foundation type: Independent foundation.
Financial data (yr. ended 8/31/05): Assets, $2,052,929 (M); gifts received, $10,600; expenditures, $409,886; qualifying distributions, $382,849; giving activities include $382,849 for grants.
Purpose and activities: Giving for disaster relief and aid to the elderly who are retired teachers in NY.
Fields of interest: Human services.
Type of support: Consulting services; Grants to individuals.
Limitations: Giving limited to NY.
Application information: Application form not required.
Deadline(s): None
Officer: Richard Iannuzzi, Chair.
Trustees: Tom Pappas; Dennis Tracey.
EIN: 146030191
Selected grants: The following grants were reported in 2004.
$138,690 to New York State United Teachers, Latham, NY.

6595
Donald R. Mullen Family Foundation, Inc. ✧ ☆
516 5th Ave., 11th Fl.
New York, NY 10036

Established in 2004 in NY.
Donor: Donald R. Mullen.
Foundation type: Independent foundation.
Financial data (yr. ended 12/31/05): Assets, $25,798 (M); gifts received, $200,000; expenditures, $535,897; qualifying distributions, $488,312; giving activities include $488,312 for grants.
Fields of interest: Arts; Education; Digestive diseases; Digestive disorders research; Medical research; Human services; Christian agencies & churches.
Limitations: Applications not accepted. Giving on a national basis, with some emphasis on NY. No grants to individuals.
Application information: Contributes only to pre-selected organizations.
Director: Donald R. Mullen.
EIN: 200786906

6596
The Hilda Mullen Foundation ✧
c/o Simpson Thacher & Bartlett
425 Lexington Ave.
New York, NY 10017

Established in 1997 in NY.
Donors: Lois Q. Whitman; Martin J. Whitman.
Foundation type: Independent foundation.
Financial data (yr. ended 12/31/03): Assets, $7,526,646 (M); expenditures, $1,117,294; qualifying distributions, $1,111,422; giving activities include $1,105,252 for 12 grants (high: $354,000; average: $5,000–$10,000).
Purpose and activities: Giving primarily for human rights, education, health services, and Jewish agencies.
Fields of interest: Education; Environment; Health care; Human services; Civil rights; Jewish agencies & temples.
Limitations: Applications not accepted. No grants to individuals.
Application information: Contributes only to pre-selected organizations.
Trustees: Lois Q. Whitman; Martin J. Whitman.
EIN: 137120449
Selected grants: The following grants were reported in 2003.
$354,000 to New York Community Trust, New York, NY. For Dora Fund.
$150,000 to Foundation of Cognitive Therapy and Research, Bala Cynwyd, PA.
$50,000 to Rutgers, The State University of New Jersey, New Brunswick, NJ.
$10,000 to American Jewish World Service, New York, NY.
$5,100 to Smith College, Northampton, MA.
$5,000 to Human Rights Watch, New York, NY.
$3,000 to Amnesty International USA, New York, NY.
$2,500 to Wall Street Synagogue, New York, NY.
$2,000 to Central Park Conservancy, New York, NY.
$1,000 to Doctors Without Borders USA, New York, NY.

6597
The Philip D. & Tammy S. Murphy Foundation ✧
1 New York Plz., 40th Fl.
New York, NY 10004

Established in 1993 in NY.
Donors: Philip D. Murphy; Goldman Sachs.
Foundation type: Independent foundation.
Financial data (yr. ended 7/31/05): Assets, $15,103,783 (M); gifts received, $2,085,900; expenditures, $621,867; qualifying distributions, $517,881; giving activities include $517,881 for 48 grants (high: $200,000; low: $50).
Fields of interest: Higher education; Education; Health organizations, association; Human services; Roman Catholic agencies & churches.
Limitations: Applications not accepted. Giving primarily in NJ, NY, and PA. No grants to individuals.
Application information: Contributes only to pre-selected organizations.
Trustees: Philip D. Murphy; Tammy S. Murphy.
EIN: 133742910
Selected grants: The following grants were reported in 2004.
$100,000 to Center for American Progress, DC. For general support.

$100,000 to NAACP Special Contribution Fund, Baltimore, MD. For general support.

$100,000 to William J. Clinton Presidential Foundation, Little Rock, AR. For general support.

$55,000 to Count Basie Theater, Red Bank, NJ. For general support.

$54,000 to 180, Turning Lives Around, Hazlet, NJ. For general support.

$50,000 to American Majority Institute, DC. For general support.

$25,000 to Phillips Academy, Andover, MA. For general support.

$25,000 to Services for Children with Hidden Intelligence (SCHI), Lakewood, NJ. For general support.

$20,000 to Monmouth Medical Center Foundation, Long Branch, NJ. For general support.

$17,000 to Acumen Fund, New York, NY. For general support.

6598
Naddisy Foundation, Inc. ✧ ☆
c/o Invus Group Ltd.
126 E. 56th St., 16th Fl.
New York, NY 10022

Established in 2002 in NY.
Donor: Sacha Lainovic.
Foundation type: Independent foundation.
Financial data (yr. ended 12/31/05): Assets, $24,820,756 (M); expenditures, $1,171,464; qualifying distributions, $1,141,250; giving activities include $1,140,500 for 10 grants (high: $200,000; low: $2,500).
Fields of interest: Education; Medical research.
Limitations: Applications not accepted. Giving primarily in New York, NY. No grants to individuals.
Application information: Contributes only to pre-selected organizations.
Officers and Director:* Sacha Lainovic,* Pres.; Rebecca Lainovic, Secy.-Treas.
EIN: 050544092
Selected grants: The following grants were reported in 2004.
$200,000 to Robin Hood Foundation, New York, NY.
$188,000 to Memorial Sloan-Kettering Cancer Center, New York, NY.
$25,000 to Buckley School, Sherman Oaks, CA.
$2,500 to Food Allergy and Anaphylaxis Network, Fairfax, VA.
$2,000 to Hole in the Wall, New Britain, CT.
$1,000 to African Medical and Research Foundation, New York, NY.
$1,000 to Gods Love We Deliver, New York, NY.
$1,000 to Prep for Prep, New York, NY.

6599
The Nagle Family Foundation ✧ ☆
19 Garden Ave.
Bronxville, NY 10708-3007
Contact: Arthur J. Nagle, Chair.

Established in 1987 in NY.
Donor: Arthur J. Nagle.
Foundation type: Independent foundation.
Financial data (yr. ended 12/31/05): Assets, $926,622 (M); gifts received, $575,126; expenditures, $433,134; qualifying distributions, $433,134; giving activities include $430,810 for 135 grants (high: $200,000; low: $25).

Fields of interest: Higher education; Education; Hospitals (general); Protestant agencies & churches; Religion.
Limitations: Giving primarily in NY. No grants to individuals.
Application information:
Initial approach: Letter
Deadline(s): None
Officer: Arthur J. Nagle, Chair.
Director: Paige L. Nagle.
EIN: 133453422
Selected grants: The following grants were reported in 2004.
$7,130 to Lawrence Hospital, Bronxville, NY.
$5,600 to Telluride Film Festival, Telluride, CO.
$5,200 to University of Vermont, Burlington, VT.
$1,200 to Bay Street Theater Festival, Sag Harbor, NY.
$1,000 to Cystic Fibrosis Foundation, Bethesda, MD.
$1,000 to March of Dimes Birth Defects Foundation, White Plains, NY.
$450 to Metropolitan Museum of Art, New York, NY.
$200 to Bridgehampton Historical Society, Bridgehampton, NY.
$200 to Crohns and Colitis Foundation of America, New York, NY.
$150 to K E E T-TV Redwood Empire Public Television, Eureka, CA.

6600
Nakash Family Foundation ✧
c/o Jordache Enterprises, Inc.
1400 Broadway, 14th Fl.
New York, NY 10018-5300
Contact: Joseph Nakash, Pres.; Ralph Nakash, Secy.-Treas.

Established in 1984 in NY.
Donors: Jordache Ltd.; Jordache Enterprises, Inc.
Foundation type: Company-sponsored foundation.
Financial data (yr. ended 12/31/05): Assets, $2,170,264 (M); gifts received, $1,376,630; expenditures, $1,416,947; qualifying distributions, $1,375,970; giving activities include $1,375,970 for grants.
Purpose and activities: The foundation supports organizations involved theological education, youth development, and Judaism.
Fields of interest: Theological school/education; Youth development, centers/clubs; Jewish agencies & temples.
Type of support: General/operating support.
Application information: Application form not required.
Initial approach: Proposal
Deadline(s): None
Officers: Joseph Nakash, Pres.; Avi Nakash, V.P.; Ralph Nakash, Secy.-Treas.
EIN: 133030267

6601
NAON, Inc. ✧
c/o Hertz, Herson & Co., LLP
2 Park Ave., Rm. 1500
New York, NY 10016

Established in 2000 in NY and DE.
Donor: Susan R. Wexner.
Foundation type: Independent foundation.

Financial data (yr. ended 12/31/05): Assets, $22,109,469 (M); expenditures, $1,183,980; qualifying distributions, $978,106; giving activities include $962,000 for 10 grants (high: $800,000; low: $5,000).
Purpose and activities: Giving primarily for Jewish education, temples, and organizations.
Fields of interest: Education; Jewish agencies & temples.
Limitations: Applications not accepted. Giving primarily in NY. No grants to individuals.
Application information: Contributes only to pre-selected organizations.
Officer and Director:* Susan R. Wexner,* Pres. and Secy.-Treas.
EIN: 134099539
Selected grants: The following grants were reported in 2003.
$1,075,000 to Vanguard Charitable Endowment Program, Southeastern, PA. For donor advised endowment fund.

6602
The Nash Family Foundation, Inc. ▼
25 W. 45th St., Ste. 1400
New York, NY 10036 (212) 221-9491
Contact: Judith Ginsberg, Exec. Dir.
FAX: (212) 221-9487; E-mail: info@nashff.org;
Additional E-mail: judith@nashff.org; URL: http://www.nashff.org

Established in 1964 in NY.
Donors: Jack Nash; Leo Levy; Helen Nash.
Foundation type: Independent foundation.
Financial data (yr. ended 6/30/04): Assets, $103,563,011 (M); gifts received, $10,095,273; expenditures, $6,226,190; qualifying distributions, $6,075,808; giving activities include $5,754,060 for 356 grants (high: $600,000; low: $18; average: $1,000–$100,000).
Purpose and activities: Support primarily for arts and culture, health care organizations, and Jewish giving.
Fields of interest: Arts; Elementary/secondary education; Theological school/education; Human services; Jewish agencies & temples.
International interests: Israel.
Limitations: Giving primarily in New York, NY and Israel. No support for political organizations. No grants to individuals or for conferences.
Application information: Application for Israeli doctors seeking to apply for the foundation's Medical Training Fellowship may be downloaded from the foundation Web site. Application form not required.
Initial approach: Telephone, letter or E-mail
Copies of proposal: 2
Deadline(s): None
Board meeting date(s): Throughout the year
Final notification: 6 months
Officers and Directors:* Jack Nash,* Pres.; Joshua Nash, V.P.; Pamela Rohr, V.P.; Morris H. Rosenthal, Secy.; Helen Nash,* Treas.; Judith Ginsberg, Exec. Dir.; Beth Goldberg Nash; George Rohr.
Number of staff: 1 full-time professional; 1 full-time support.
EIN: 136168559
Selected grants: The following grants were reported in 2005.
$2,000,000 to Birthright Israel Foundation, New York, NY.
$600,000 to Mount Sinai Hospital, New York, NY.
$275,000 to W N E T Channel 13, New York, NY.

$222,223 to UJA-Federation of New York, New York, NY.

$205,000 to New York Public Library, New York, NY.

$200,000 to Jewish Television Network, Beverly Hills, CA.

$69,500 to Metropolitan Council on Jewish Poverty, New York, NY.

$37,500 to P.E.F. Israel Endowment Funds, New York, NY.

$25,000 to Hebrew Academy for Special Children, Brooklyn, NY.

$20,000 to Mount Sinai Medical Center, New York, NY.

6603
National Hockey League Foundation ◇
c/o National Hockey League
1251 Ave. of the Americas, 47th Fl.
New York, NY 10020-1104

Established in 1991 in NY.
Donor: National Hockey League.
Foundation type: Independent foundation.
Financial data (yr. ended 6/30/05): Assets, $2,910,355 (M); gifts received, $38,777; expenditures, $466,718; qualifying distributions, $451,830; giving activities include $436,806 for grants.
Purpose and activities: Giving for programs promoting the development of youth hockey and for charities supported by players and member clubs affiliated with this foundation.
Fields of interest: Education; Health organizations, association; Genetics/birth defects; Recreation; Youth development; American Red Cross; Disabilities, people with.
International interests: Canada; China.
Type of support: Equipment; Emergency funds; Program development; Internship funds; In-kind gifts.
Limitations: Applications not accepted. Giving primarily in the U.S., Canada, and Europe; with some support in South Africa. No grants to individuals.
Application information: Contributes only to pre-selected organizations.
Officers: William Daly, Pres.; Bernadette Mansur, V.P. and Secy.; Craig C. Harnett, Treas.
Directors: Joseph DeSousa; David Zimmerman.
EIN: 133498589

6604
National Video Resources, Inc. ◇
73 Spring St., Ste. 403
New York, NY 10012 (212) 274-8080
FAX: (212) 274-8081; E-mail: info@nvr.org;
URL: http://www.nvr.org

Incorporated in 1990 in NY and DE.
Donors: John D. and Catherine T. MacArthur Foundation; National Endowment for the Humanities; National Science Foundation; The Rockefeller Foundation.
Foundation type: Operating foundation.
Financial data (yr. ended 12/31/04): Assets, $1,189,585 (M); gifts received, $1,615,020; expenditures, $2,024,084; qualifying distributions, $2,071,031; giving activities include $865,850 for 61 grants to individuals (high: $35,000; low: $1,000), and $1,039,865 for foundation-administered programs.

Purpose and activities: The organization seeks to increase the public's awareness of and access to independently produced media and film and video as well as motion media delivered through the new digital technologies by awarding fellowships and technical assistance grants to individuals.
Fields of interest: Media, film/video.
Type of support: Fellowships; Research; Technical assistance.
Limitations: Giving in the U.S. and Mexico.
Officers and Directors:* Alberta B. Arthurs,* Chair.; Steve Savage,* Treas.; Brian Newman, Exec. Dir.; Peggy Charren; Eli Evans; Sam Pollard; John Roche; N. Bird Runningwater; Suzanne M. Sato; Rea Tajiri; Diana E. Williams.
EIN: 133572353

6605
NEC Foundation of America ◇
2950 Expressway Dr. S., Ste. 102
Islandia, NY 11749-1412 (631) 753-7021
Contact: Sylvia Clark, Exec. Dir.
FAX: (631) 232-2212;
E-mail: foundation@necusa.com; URL: http://necfoundation.org

Established in 1991 in NY.
Donors: NEC Corp.; NEC USA, Inc.
Foundation type: Company-sponsored foundation.
Financial data (yr. ended 3/31/04): Assets, $12,406,776 (M); expenditures, $804,730; qualifying distributions, $740,295; giving activities include $394,000 for 11 grants (high: $50,000; low: $9,000).
Purpose and activities: The foundation supports programs designed to have national reach and impact in the areas of science and technology education, principally at the secondary level; and apply technology to assist people with disabilities.
Fields of interest: Secondary school/education; Science; Disabilities, people with.
Type of support: General/operating support; Program development; Conferences/seminars; Publication; Seed money; Research.
Limitations: Giving to national organizations. No support for sectarian or religious organizations, political organizations, sports teams, individual elementary or secondary schools or school districts, local chapters of national organizations, or organizations located outside of the U.S. No grants to individuals, or for equipment or devices for individuals, endowments, capital campaigns, fundraising, advertising, or athletic competitions.
Publications: Grants list; Informational brochure (including application guidelines).
Application information: Proposals should be no longer than 100 words or 1 page. Proposals may be submitted using the NYRAG Common Application Form. Support is limited to 1 contribution per organization during any given year. Application form not required.
Initial approach: E-mail proposal to headquarters
Copies of proposal: 1
Deadline(s): Mar. 1 and Sept. 1
Board meeting date(s): Quarterly
Final notification: Within 4 to 6 weeks following receipt of proposal
Officers and Board Members:* Hisashi Kaneko,* Pres.; Hirofumi Okuyama,* Sr. Exec. V.P.; Deon Retemeyer, Secy.; Jun Tada, Treas.; Sylvia Clark, Exec. Dir.; Toshimitsu Iwanami; Hisashi Kaneko; Kunitomo Matsuoka; Toshio Nakajima; Hirofumi Okuyama; Nobuhito Yagi.

Number of staff: 1 full-time professional; 1 full-time support.
EIN: 113059554
Selected grants: The following grants were reported in 2004.
$50,000 to Albert Einstein Healthcare Network, Philadelphia, PA. To disseminate user-friendly computer assisted program, MossTalkWords, to national network of researchers and clinicians who will select and train appropriate patients with aphasia to use software, then evaluate effectiveness.
$50,000 to Carnegie Mellon University, Pittsburgh, PA. For deployment of handhelds as assistive technologies for people with muscular disabilities.
$45,000 to National Organization on Disability, DC. For section on assistive technology (AT) to 2004 National Organization on Disability/Harris Survey of Americans with Disabilities, highly regarded and frequently referenced source of information for policymakers, media, business leaders, and academia.
$40,000 to Adaptive Environments Center, Boston, MA. Toward Designing for the 21st Century III: An International Conference on Universal design, to take place in Rio de Janeiro, Brazil.
$40,000 to Deaf Counseling, Advocacy and Referral Agency, San Leandro, CA. Toward equipment and software associated with start up of CaptionsOnline, new remote real-time captioning service (RTCC) for deaf people.
$40,000 to Music Intelligence Neural Development (MIND) Institute, Costa Mesa, CA. For national expansion of technology-based Math Plus Music (M Plus M) program for grades 2 through 4, toward goal of reaching students within 3-5 years.
$40,000 to World Institute on Disability, Oakland, CA. For business plan and prototype of website to provide information to people with disabilities about accessibility features embedded in mainstream electronic and information technology.
$35,000 to Center for Applied Special Technology (CAST), Wakefield, MA. Toward creation of new version of CAST eReader.
$20,000 to American Association of Homes and Services for the Aging, DC. For planning related to creation of framework for CAST Online Clearinghouse, comprehensive database and virtual center that will provide up-to-date information in technical developments in field of aging.
$20,000 to Recording for the Blind and Dyslexic, Princeton, NJ. For implementation of new Operations Management System, to increase efficiency in recording, translating, and disseminating production information at headquarters and through network of volunteer-manned recording studios across country.

6606
Daniel M. Neidich & Brooke Garber Foundation ◇
c/o BCRS Group/Marcum & Kliegman, LLP
100 Wall St., 11th Fl.
New York, NY 10005

Established in 1985 in NY.
Donor: Daniel M. Neidich.
Foundation type: Independent foundation.

Financial data (yr. ended 1/31/05): Assets, $11,588,025 (M); expenditures, $2,819,613; qualifying distributions, $2,794,865; giving activities include $2,790,128 for 351 grants (high: $200,000; low: $50).
Purpose and activities: Funding primarily for education; some funding also for arts and culture, human services, and Jewish agencies.
Fields of interest: Museums; Performing arts; Arts; Elementary/secondary education; Higher education; Education; Environment, natural resources; Hospitals (general); Children/youth, services; Jewish federated giving programs; Protestant agencies & churches; Jewish agencies & temples.
Limitations: Applications not accepted. Giving primarily in New York, NY. No grants to individuals.
Application information: Contributes only to pre-selected organizations.
Trustees: Brooke Garber Neidich; Daniel M. Neidich.
EIN: 133318126
Selected grants: The following grants were reported in 2005.
$200,000 to Brown University, Providence, RI.
$100,000 to Museum of Modern Art, New York, NY.
$100,000 to NYU Hospitals Center, New York, NY.
$99,220 to Lincoln Center Theater, New York, NY. 2 grants: $49,220, $50,000
$33,000 to Prep for Prep, New York, NY.
$15,000 to Peer Health Exchange, New York, NY.
$10,000 to Collegiate School, New York, NY.
$4,700 to International Womens Health Coalition, New York, NY.
$2,500 to Lar Lubovitch Dance Company, New York, NY.

6607
Leroy Neiman Foundation, Inc. ✧
1 W. 67th St.
New York, NY 10023-6223

Established in 1987 in NY.
Donors: Leroy Neiman; Janet Neiman.
Foundation type: Independent foundation.
Financial data (yr. ended 12/31/05): Assets, $7,135,579 (M); gifts received, $500,000; expenditures, $395,399; qualifying distributions, $390,000; giving activities include $390,000 for 6 grants (high: $200,000; low: $5,000).
Fields of interest: Higher education; Human services; Federated giving programs.
Limitations: Applications not accepted. Giving limited to NY. No grants to individuals.
Application information: Contributes only to pre-selected organizations.
Officers: Leroy Neiman, Pres.; Janet Neiman, V.P.; Jason Jacobs, Secy.; Steven Bond, Treas.
EIN: 133385053

6608
The Nelkin Foundation ✧
111 Great Neck Rd., Ste. 304
Great Neck, NY 11021

Established in 1968 in NY.
Donors: Harold Nelkin; Leslie Andrew Nelkin.
Foundation type: Independent foundation.
Financial data (yr. ended 4/30/05): Assets, $138,119 (M); gifts received, $2,015,000; expenditures, $2,016,671; qualifying distributions, $2,014,093; giving activities include $2,014,093 for 12+ grants (high: $2,000,000).

Purpose and activities: Giving to Jewish agencies, and to higher education.
Fields of interest: Human services; Jewish federated giving programs; Jewish agencies & temples.
Limitations: Applications not accepted. Giving primarily in the greater metropolitan New York, NY, area, including Long Island. No grants to individuals.
Application information: Contributes only to pre-selected organizations.
Officers: Harold Nelkin, Pres.; Amy Nelkin, V.P. and Secy.-Treas.; Ruth Nelkin, V.P. and Secy.
EIN: 136261501

6609
Netzach Foundation ✧
200 W. 57th St., Ste. 1005
New York, NY 10019

Established in 1992 in NY.
Donors: Laurie Pinck; Menachem Pinck; Jerry Solomon; Esther Solomon; Estanne Abraham; Bron Industries; Reliable Health Systems; Laurie Abraham; William Bron Family Fund.
Foundation type: Independent foundation.
Financial data (yr. ended 3/31/05): Assets, $7,288,427 (M); gifts received, $103,949; expenditures, $1,190,397; qualifying distributions, $1,159,773; giving activities include $1,159,428 for 47 grants (high: $262,545; low: $800).
Fields of interest: Jewish agencies & temples.
Type of support: Grants to individuals; Scholarships —to individuals.
Limitations: Applications not accepted. Giving primarily in NY.
Application information: Contributes only to pre-selected organizations. Unsolicited requests for funds not accepted.
Trustees: Hirschell E. Levine; Laurie Pinck; Menachem Pinck; Richard A. Sauer.
EIN: 136967224
Selected grants: The following grants were reported in 2003.
$318,000 to Toras Simcha, Israel. .
$250,000 to Kiryat Chinuch Abonim Ashdod.
$100,000 to Toras Simcha, Friends of, New York, NY.
$50,000 to Rabbi Jacob Joseph School, Staten Island, NY.
$50,000 to Ramot Torah Schools, Brooklyn, NY.
$43,000 to P.E.F. Israel Endowment Funds, New York, NY.
$12,000 to Bayis Leshem Uletiferes.
$11,700 to Kollel Ohr Hanev, Brooklyn, NY.
$8,000 to Kupat Matan Beseter, Israel. .
$3,000 to Heritage House, Jerusalem, Israel. .

6610
The John L. Neu Family Foundation, Inc. ✧
110 5th Ave., Ste. 70
New York, NY 10011

Established in 1990 in NY.
Donor: Hugo Neu Corp.
Foundation type: Independent foundation.
Financial data (yr. ended 12/31/05): Assets, $8,524,729 (M); gifts received, $5,000,000; expenditures, $1,271,983; qualifying distributions, $1,266,067; giving activities include $1,264,400 for 48 grants (high: $400,000; low: $200).

Purpose and activities: Giving primarily for animal welfare; support also for hospitals and rehabilitation centers. Some giving for environmental conservation.
Fields of interest: Museums; Education; Environment; Animal welfare; Hospitals (general); Youth development.
Limitations: Applications not accepted. Giving primarily in NJ and NY. No grants to individuals.
Application information: Contributes only to pre-selected organizations.
Officers and Directors: * John L. Neu,* Pres.; Donald Hamaker, Secy.-Treas.; Robert T. Neu; Wendy K. Neu.
EIN: 133731089
Selected grants: The following grants were reported in 2003.
$255,000 to Companion Animal Placement, Weehawken, NJ. For general support.
$200,000 to Natural Resources Defense Council, New York, NY. For general support.
$30,500 to Cornell University, Ithaca, NY. For general support.
$30,000 to Spence School, New York, NY.
$20,500 to Humane Society, Liberty, Jersey City, NJ. For general support.
$20,000 to Last Chance for Animals, West Hollywood, CA. For general support.
$17,000 to Edison Wetlands Association, Edison, NJ. For general support.
$15,000 to Riverdale Country School, Bronx, NY. For general support.
$12,000 to YM-YWHA, 92nd Street, New York, NY. For general support.
$10,000 to Mount Sinai Childrens Center Foundation, New York, NY. For general support.

6611
Roy R. and Marie S. Neuberger Foundation, Inc. ✧
605 3rd Ave., 41st Fl.
New York, NY 10158-0180
Contact: Gloria Silverman

Incorporated in 1954 in NY.
Donors: Roy R. Neuberger; Marie S. Neuberger†.
Foundation type: Independent foundation.
Financial data (yr. ended 12/31/04): Assets, $15,989,380 (M); expenditures, $738,026; qualifying distributions, $613,748; giving activities include $572,055 for 148 grants (high: $100,000; low: $212).
Purpose and activities: Giving primarily for education and arts and culture organizations.
Fields of interest: Visual arts; Performing arts; Arts; Higher education.
Type of support: General/operating support; Continuing support; Annual campaigns.
Limitations: Giving primarily in NY. No grants to individuals.
Application information: Application form not required.
  Initial approach: Letter
  Copies of proposal: 1
  Deadline(s): None
  Board meeting date(s): Apr.
Officers and Directors: * Roy R. Neuberger,* Pres.; Roy S. Neuberger,* V.P. and Treas.; Ann N. Aceves,* V.P.; James A. Neuberger,* V.P.
EIN: 136066102

6612
Neuwirth Foundation, Inc. ✧
539 Split Rock Rd.
Syosset, NY   11791

Established in 1991 in NY.
Donor: Marvin R. Neuwirth.
Foundation type: Independent foundation.
Financial data (yr. ended 8/31/05): Assets, $7,377,637 (L); expenditures, $710,168; qualifying distributions, $690,450; giving activities include $690,450 for 32 grants (high: $216,000; low: $100).
Purpose and activities: Giving primarily to health associations, and to a hospital; funding also for museums as well as for a horse show, natural resource conservation, children services, and Jewish and other federated giving programs.
Fields of interest: Museums (art); Environment, natural resources; Hospitals (general); Cancer; Alzheimer's disease research; Athletics/sports, equestrianism; Children, services; Federated giving programs; Jewish federated giving programs.
Limitations: Applications not accepted. Giving primarily in NY. No grants to individuals.
Application information: Contributes only to pre-selected organizations.
Officers and Directors:* Marvin R. Neuwirth,* Pres.; Richard J. Birnbach,* V.P.; Barbara Braun,* V.P.; Felice Neuwirth,* Secy.-Treas.
EIN: 113048776
Selected grants: The following grants were reported in 2005.
$216,000 to Nature Conservancy, Arlington, VA.
$150,000 to North Shore University Hospital, Manhasset, NY.
$10,000 to United Way.
$5,000 to Saint John Lutheran School, Random Lake, WI.
$3,500 to Metropolitan Museum.
$2,500 to Boca Raton Community Hospital, Boca Raton, FL.
$1,000 to Chemotherapy Foundation, New York, NY.
$1,000 to Wadsworth Atheneum, Hartford, CT.
$650 to American Cancer Society, Atlanta, GA.
$500 to East End Hospice, Westhampton Beach, NY.

6613
The New York Community Trust ▼ ✧
909 Third Ave., 22nd Fl.
New York, NY   10022   (212) 686-0010
Contact: Lorie A. Slutsky, Pres.; For grant inquiries: Judith Lopez, Exec. Asst., Grants and Special Projects
FAX: (212) 532-8528;
E-mail: info@nycommunitytrust.org; Additional E-mail: las@nyct-cfi.org; Grant application E-mail: grants@nycommunitytrust.org; URL: http://www.nycommunitytrust.org

Established in 1924 in NY by resolution and declaration of trust.
Foundation type: Community foundation.
Financial data (yr. ended 12/31/05): Assets, $1,897,604,374 (M); gifts received, $126,518,677; expenditures, $146,649,839; giving activities include $136,970,963 for 1,135+ grants (high: $3,053,080).
Purpose and activities: Priority given to applications for projects having particular significance for the New York City area. Program areas of major interest are: 1) Children, Youth, and Families - includes issues of hunger and homelessness, social services, substance abuse, youth development, girls and young women; 2) Community Development and the Environment - includes civic affairs, community development, conservation, environment, and technical assistance; 3) Education, Arts, and the Humanities - includes arts and culture, education, historic preservation, and human justice; and 4) Health and People With Special Needs - includes health services and policy, biomedical research, AIDS, visual handicaps, children and youth with disabilities, the elderly, and mental health and retardation. In addition, the trust has established divisions that reach out to the greater New York metropolitan area: the Westchester Community Foundation and the Long Island Community Foundation.
Fields of interest: Historic preservation/historical societies; Arts; Education, public education; Child development, education; Education; Environment; Health care; Substance abuse, services; Mental health/crisis services; Health organizations, association; Cancer; AIDS; Biomedicine research; Crime/violence prevention, domestic violence; Legal services; Employment; Food services; Housing/shelter, development; Youth development; Children/youth, services; Family services; Aging, centers/services; Women, centers/services; Homeless, human services; Human services; Civil rights, immigrants; Civil rights, minorities; Civil rights, disabled; Civil rights, women; Civil rights, aging; Civil rights, gays/lesbians; Civil liberties, reproductive rights; Community development; Government/public administration; Girls; Young adults, female.
Type of support: Income development; Management development/capacity building; Program development; Publication; Seed money; Fellowships; Scholarship funds; Research; Technical assistance; Consulting services; Program evaluation; Employee matching gifts.
Limitations: Giving limited to the metropolitan New York, NY, area. No support for religious purposes. No grants to individuals (except for scholarships), or for deficit financing, emergency funds, building campaigns, films, endowment funds, capital projects or general operating support.
Publications: Application guidelines; Annual report; Financial statement; Grants list; Informational brochure (including application guidelines); Newsletter; Occasional report; Program policy statement (including application guidelines).
Application information: Visit foundation Web site for application cover sheet and guidelines. Please submit all written materials before calling the foundation to discuss ideas. Faxed or e-mailed proposals are not accepted. Application form required.
   Initial approach: Submit proposal with cover letter
   Copies of proposal: 1
   Deadline(s): None
   Board meeting date(s): Feb., Apr., June, July, Oct., and Dec.
   Final notification: Within 2 weeks for initial response; up to 25 weeks for grant determination
Officers and Distribution Committee:* Samuel S. Polk,* Chair.; Robert M. Kaufman,* Vice-Chair.; Lorie A. Slutsky,* Pres.; Joyce M. Bove, Sr. V.P., Grants and Special Projects; Robert V. Edgar, V.P., Donor Rels.; Mercedes M. Leon, V.P., Admin.; Kathryn "Kit" Conroy, C.F.O.; Mary Greenebaum, C.I.O.; Heidi Hotzler, Cont.; Jane L. Wilton, Genl. Counsel; Bruce W. Calvert; Anla Cheng-Kingdon; Ernest J. Collazo; Charlynn Goins; Roger Juan Maldonado; Anne Moore, M.D.; Donaldson C. Pillsbury; Anne P. Sidamon-Eristoff; Estelle "Nicki" Newman Tanner.
Trustee Banks: Bank of America, N.A.; The Bank of New York; Bessemer Trust Co., N.A.; Brown Brothers Harriman Trust Co.; Citibank, N.A.; Deutsche Bank Americas; Fiduciary Trust Co. International; HSBC Bank USA; JPMorgan Chase Bank, N.A.; Lehman Brothers Trust Co., N.A.; Merrill Lynch Trust Co.; Rockefeller Trust Co.; U.S. Trust.
Number of staff: 23 full-time professional; 2 part-time professional; 18 full-time support; 1 part-time support.
EIN: 133062214
Selected grants: The following grants were reported in 2005.
$1,000,000 to Adelphi University, Garden City, NY. For Hagedorn Child Activity Center.
$1,000,000 to Winthrop-University Hospital, Mineola, NY. For Hagedorn Pediatric Center.
$900,000 to Harvard University, Cambridge, MA.
$833,000 to Grameen Foundation USA, DC. For multi-year McKinley/Grameen Foundation USA memorandum of understanding for strategic growth.
$717,000 to Charles B. Wang Community Health Center, New York, NY.
$600,000 to Cancer Care, New York, NY. For financial assistance to needy cancer patients.
$600,000 to London School of Hygiene and Tropical Medicine, London, England. For Initiative for Diagnostic and Epidemiological Assays for Leprosy (IDEAL) consortium to develop diagnostic test for leprosy.
$575,000 to International AIDS Vaccine Initiative, New York, NY. For research in New York City to develop AIDS vaccine.
$550,000 to Hofstra University, Hempstead, NY. For general support.
$500,000 to Princeton University, Princeton, NJ. For general support of Council of Humanities.

6614
New York Crohns Foundation ✧
1200 Union Tpke.
New Hyde Park, NY   11040
Contact: Leonard Litwin, Pres.

Established in 1998 in NY.
Donors: Leonard Litwin; Litwin Foundation; M&R Management.
Foundation type: Independent foundation.
Financial data (yr. ended 12/31/05): Assets, $57,993 (M); gifts received, $540,000; expenditures, $560,150; qualifying distributions, $560,000; giving activities include $560,000 for 3 grants (high: $335,000; low: $60,000).
Purpose and activities: Giving primarily for health care and medical research for the cure of Crohn's disease.
Fields of interest: Hospitals (general); Health care; Digestive diseases; Medical research.
Limitations: Giving primarily in New York, NY.
Application information: Application form required.
   Initial approach: Letter
   Copies of proposal: 1
   Deadline(s): None
Officers and Directors:* Leonard Litwin,* Pres.; Michael Kerr,* V.P.; Carole Pittelman,* V.P.; Howard Swarzman,* Secy.-Treas.
EIN: 113437172

Selected grants: The following grants were reported in 2004.

$165,000 to Mount Sinai School of Medicine of New York University, New York, NY. For Crohn's Disease research.

$75,000 to North Shore-Long Island Jewish Health System, Westbury, NY. For Crohn's Disease research.

$75,000 to Weill Medical College of Cornell University, New York, NY. For Crohn's Disease research.

$50,000 to Lenox Hill Hospital, New York, NY. For Crohn's Disease research.

$25,000 to Association of Prevention and Treatment for Gastrointestinal Disorders. For Crohn's Disease research.

6615

New York Foundation ▼

350 5th Ave., No. 2901
New York, NY 10118-2996
Contact: Maria Mottola, Exec. Dir.
URL: http://www.nyf.org/

Incorporated in 1909 in NY.

Donors: Louis A. Heinsheimer‡; Alfred M. Heinsheimer‡; Lionel J. Salomon‡.

Foundation type: Independent foundation.

Financial data (yr. ended 12/31/05): Assets, $75,291,000 (M); gifts received, $100,000; expenditures, $5,736,000; qualifying distributions, $4,569,000; giving activities include $4,569,000 for 96 grants (high: $50,000; low: $6,500; average: $40,000–$42,500).

Purpose and activities: The foundation supports groups in New York City that are working on problems of urgent concern to residents of disadvantaged communities and neighborhoods. The foundation is particularly interested in start-up grants to new, untested programs that have few other sources of support. Grants are not limited to specified issue areas, although under the terms of a restricted endowment, half the foundation's grants are reserved for projects involving the elderly. Instead, the foundation looks at the characteristics of the organization or project applying. Because the foundation believes in a pluralist, inclusive democracy, it seeks to support programs emerging from communities where existing services and institutions do not reach, neighborhoods taking action for their own betterment, and population groups organizing to create a collective voice where they have not been heard.

Fields of interest: Housing/shelter, development; Disasters, 9/11/01; Youth development, services; Human services; Children/youth, services; Aging, centers/services; Minorities/immigrants, centers/services; Homeless, human services; Civil rights, alliance; Civil rights, immigrants; Civil rights, minorities; Civil rights, disabled; Civil rights, women; Civil rights, aging; Civil rights, gays/lesbians; Civil rights, race/intergroup relations; Civil liberties, reproductive rights; Community development; Aging; Disabilities, people with; Minorities; African Americans/Blacks; Hispanics/Latinos; AIDS, people with; Immigrants/refugees; Economically disadvantaged; Homeless.

Type of support: General/operating support; Continuing support; Program development; Seed money; Technical assistance.

Limitations: Giving limited to local programs in the New York, NY, metropolitan area. No grants to individuals, or for capital campaigns, research

studies, films, conferences, or publications (except for those initiated by the foundation).

Publications: Annual report (including application guidelines); Grants list.

Application information: Accepts New York-New Jersey Common Application Form. This form is available on the foundation Web site. Proposals not accepted via fax or e-mail. Application form not required.

Initial approach: Letter outlining project and budget needs
Copies of proposal: 1
Deadline(s): Mar. 1, July 1, and Nov. 1
Board meeting date(s): Feb., June, and Oct.
Final notification: 3 to 6 months

Officers and Trustees:* Gladys Carrion,* Chair.; Thomas I. Acosta,* Vice-Chair.; Margaret Booth,* Secy.; Madeline Glick,* Treas.; Maria Mottola, Exec. Dir.; Rose Dobrof, DSW, Tr. Emeritus; Sayu V. Bhojwani; Seth Borgos; John P. Daley; Dana Michelle Davis; A. Carleton Dukess; Stephen Heyman; Chung Wha Hong; William Kelly; Peter Kwong; Thomas J. Mackell, Jr.; Ana Oliveira; Mike Pratt; Paul Spivey; Jason Warwin.

Number of staff: 4 full-time professional; 3 full-time support; 1 part-time support.

EIN: 135626345

Selected grants: The following grants were reported in 2005.

$79,500 to Community Resource Exchange, New York, NY. To provide individual technical assistance to New York Foundation grantees.

$50,000 to El Puente de Williamsburg, Brooklyn, NY. For campaign to close only radioactive nuclear and toxic chemical storage facility in New York City.

$50,000 to Nah We Yone, Staten Island, NY. To provide assistance for displaced Sierra Leonean war victims in New York area and facilitate their adjustment within United States.

$47,500 to Ali Forney Center, New York, NY. For start-up support for shelter serving homeless lesbian, gay, bisexual, and transgendered youth and for organizing and advocacy work.

$47,500 to Ansob Center for Refugees, Astoria, NY. For general support for community-based center providing services to refugees from former Yugoslavia.

$47,500 to Dwa Fanm, Brooklyn, NY. For general support for community-based organization addressing womens rights in Haitian immigrant communities.

$47,500 to Girls for Gender Equity, Brooklyn, NY. To promote physical, psychological, social, and economic development of girls and women through education, organizing, and physical fitness.

$47,500 to New York City Tibetan Outreach Center, New York, NY. For general support to link Tibetan refugees and immigrants residing in New York City with information and services they need.

$47,500 to Picture the Homeless, New York, NY. For general support for organization led by homeless people working to end criminalization of homelessness and build movement that demands housing as human right.

$47,500 to Sista II Sista, Brooklyn, NY. For general support for organization that addresses challenges of teenaged women in Brooklyn.

6616

New York Jets Foundation, Inc. ◇ ☆

c/o New York Jets Football Club, Inc.
1000 Fulton Ave.
Hempstead, NY 11550 (516) 560-8100
Contact: Michael Gerstle, Treas.
URL: http://www.newyorkjets.com/community/index.php?
sect=programs&content_id=2031#2031

Established in 1969.

Donors: New York Jets Football Club, Inc.; NFL Charities.

Foundation type: Company-sponsored foundation.

Financial data (yr. ended 12/31/05): Assets, $1,120,435 (M); gifts received, $564,571; expenditures, $685,547; qualifying distributions, $358,000; giving activities include $358,000 for grants.

Purpose and activities: The foundation supports organizations involved with education, health, and recreation.

Fields of interest: Secondary school/education; Education; Health care; Cancer research; Recreation, parks/playgrounds; Recreation; Human services; Community development.

Limitations: Giving primarily in NY.

Application information: Application form not required.

Initial approach: Proposal
Deadline(s): None

Officers and Trustees:* Robert Wood Johnson IV,* Chair.; Loren J. Cross,* Pres. and Secy.; Neil Burmeister,* V.P.; Michael Gerstle,* Treas.

EIN: 237108291

Selected grants: The following grants were reported in 2004.

$11,000 to New York Cares, New York, NY.
$5,000 to Youth Foundation, Edwards, CO.
$1,000 to American Cancer Society, Atlanta, GA.
$1,000 to Big Brothers/Big Sisters.
$1,000 to Boomer Esiason Foundation, New York, NY.
$1,000 to Connecticut Renaissance, Norwalk, CT.
$1,000 to Hale House Center, New York, NY.
$1,000 to Holy Cross High School.
$1,000 to Moore Catholic High School, Staten Island, NY.
$1,000 to Sledge Group, Bronx, NY.

6617

New York Life Foundation ▼ ◇

51 Madison Ave., Ste. 604
New York, NY 10010-1655 (212) 576-7341
Contact: Peter J. Bushyeager, Pres.
URL: http://www.newyorklifefoundation.org

Established in 1979 in NY.

Donor: New York Life Insurance Co.

Foundation type: Company-sponsored foundation.

Financial data (yr. ended 12/31/05): Assets, $97,380,953 (M); gifts received, $278,636; expenditures, $9,199,806; qualifying distributions, $9,170,925; giving activities include $8,419,160 for 411 grants (high: $1,000,000; low: $500), and $746,485 for 860 employee matching gifts.

Purpose and activities: The foundation supports organizations involved with K-12 education and youth development.

Fields of interest: Arts, cultural/ethnic awareness; Elementary/secondary education; Child development, education; Education, reading; Youth development, adult & child programs; Youth development, citizenship; Youth development; Science, formal/general education; Mathematics; Science.

Type of support: General/operating support; Continuing support; Program development; Employee volunteer services; Employee matching gifts; Employee-related scholarships.

Limitations: Giving primarily in New York and Westchester County, NY; giving also to national organizations serving two or more of the following cities and regions: Tampa, FL, Atlanta, GA, Minneapolis, MN, Clinton/Hunterdon counties and Morris/Parsippany counties, NJ, Cleveland, OH, Dallas, TX, and the Gulf Coast region. No support for religious or sectarian organizations not of direct benefit to the entire community, fraternal, social, professional, veterans', or athletic organizations, or discriminatory organizations. No grants for seminars, conferences, or trips, endowments, memorials, or capital campaigns, fundraising events, telethons, races, or other benefits, goodwill advertising, or basic or applied research.

Publications: Application guidelines; Annual report; Grants list; Informational brochure (including application guidelines).

Application information: Interviews and site visits may be requested. Multi-year funding is not automatic. Application form required.

Initial approach: Complete online application form
Board meeting date(s): Apr. and Dec.

Officers and Directors: * Sy Sternberg,* Chair.; Peter Bushyeager,* Pres.; Richard W. Zuccaro, V.P.; Charles F. Holek, Treas.; Carolyn M. Buscarino; Sheila K. Davidson; Thomas Smoot.

EIN: 132989476

Selected grants: The following grants were reported in 2005.

$1,000,000 to American Red Cross, National Headquarters, DC. For relief effort for Hurricane Katrina.
$650,000 to United Way of Tri-State, New York, NY.
$400,000 to City University of New York, New York, NY.
$400,000 to Foundation for the National Archives, DC.
$400,000 to New York-Presbyterian Hospital, New York, NY.
$333,334 to New York City Partnership Foundation, New York, NY.
$312,500 to Camp Fire USA, Kansas City, MO.
$199,200 to Child Welfare League of America, DC.
$101,400 to Harlem Educational Activities Fund, New York, NY.
$21,000 to Girl Scouts of the U.S.A., Westchester-Putnam Council, Pleasantville, NY.

6618
New York Mercantile Exchange Charitable Foundation
(also known as NYMEX Charitable Foundation)
c/o Grant Prog.
1 North End Ave., Ste. 1437
New York, NY 10282-1101 (212) 299-2427
Contact: Laura Cavallaro, Mgr., Philanthropic Affairs
FAX: (212) 301-4700;
E-mail: lcavallaro@nymex.com; URL: http://www.nymex.com/cs_main.aspx

Established in 1989 in NY.
Donors: New York Mercantile Exchange, Inc.; Steven Berkson.
Foundation type: Company-sponsored foundation.

Financial data (yr. ended 12/31/04): Assets, $2,701,270 (M); gifts received, $3,661,526; expenditures, $1,885,363; qualifying distributions, $1,831,409; giving activities include $1,805,580 for 275 grants (high: $100,000; low: $500).

Purpose and activities: The foundation supports summer camps and organizations involved with arts and culture, education, health, medical research, youth development, human services, senior citizens, and disabled people.

Fields of interest: Museums; Arts; Medical school/education; Education; Health care; Medical research; Recreation, camps; Youth development; Children/youth, services; Children, day care; Human services; General charitable giving; Aging; Disabilities, people with.

Type of support: General/operating support; Annual campaigns; Building/renovation; Equipment; Emergency funds; Program development; Seed money; Scholarship funds; Research; Sponsorships.

Limitations: Giving primarily in NJ and New York, NY. No grants to individuals.

Publications: Application guidelines; Annual report; Newsletter.

Application information: Unsolicited requests are accepted from New York Mercantile Exchange members and employees on behalf of nonprofit organizations only. Application form required.

Initial approach: Contact foundation for application form
Copies of proposal: 1
Deadline(s): None
Board meeting date(s): 2nd Wed. of every month
Final notification: Approximately 1 month

Officers and Directors: * Mitchell Steinhause,* Chair.; Richard Schaeffer,* Vice-Chair.; Gary Rizzi,* Secy.; Kenneth Shifran, C.F.O.

EIN: 133586378

Selected grants: The following grants were reported in 2003.

$100,000 to American Camping Association, New York, NY. For camperships for inner-city children.
$10,000 to New York Cares, New York, NY.
$10,000 to NYU Downtown Hospital, New York, NY. For general operating support.
$10,000 to Safe Space, New York, NY.
$7,500 to Association for Children with Down Syndrome, Plainview, NY. For general operating support.
$7,500 to On Your Mark, Staten Island, NY.
$5,000 to Bronx Arts Ensemble, Bronx, NY. For arts education in schools in the Bronx.
$5,000 to Youth Service League, Brooklyn, NY. For scholarship program.
$2,500 to Children for Children Foundation, New York, NY. For youth community outreach programs.
$1,000 to New York Public Library, New York, NY. For general support.

6619
New York Stock Exchange Foundation, Inc.
11 Wall St.
New York, NY 10005
Contact: David L. Shuler, Secy.
FAX: (212) 656-5629;
E-mail: foundation@nyse.com; URL: http://www.nysefoundation.org

Incorporated in 1983 in NY.

Donors: New York Stock Exchange, Inc.; New York Stock Exchange LLC.
Foundation type: Company-sponsored foundation.

Financial data (yr. ended 12/31/04): Assets, $22,754,835 (M); gifts received, $695,471; expenditures, $1,886,433; qualifying distributions, $1,877,153; giving activities include $1,760,253 for 56 grants (high: $150,000; low: $100), and $116,900 for 121 employee matching gifts.

Purpose and activities: The foundation supports organizations involved with arts and culture, education, environmental beautification, crime prevention, disaster relief, youth development, financial counseling, civil rights, senior citizens, minorities, economically disadvantaged people, and homeless people.

Fields of interest: Visual arts; Performing arts; History/archaeology; Literature; Arts; Elementary/secondary education; Business school/education; Education; Environment, beautification programs; Crime/violence prevention; Safety/disasters; Youth development; Human services, financial counseling; Civil rights, equal rights; Civil rights; Science; Aging; Minorities; Economically disadvantaged; Homeless.

Type of support: General/operating support; Annual campaigns; Capital campaigns; Program development; Scholarship funds; Employee matching gifts.

Limitations: Giving primarily in New York, NY.

Publications: Annual report; IRS Form 990-PF.

Application information: Application form not required.

Initial approach: Proposal
Copies of proposal: 1
Deadline(s): None
Board meeting date(s): Rolling
Final notification: Varies

Officers and Directors: * John A. Thain,* Chair.; David L. Shuler, Secy.; Amy S. Butte, Treas.; Anne Giviskos, Cont.; Arthur D. Cashin, Jr.; John F. X. Dolan; Karen Nelson Hackett; Catherine R. Kinney; George M.L. LaBranche IV; Robert H. McCooey, Jr.; Daniel W. Tandy; Margaret DeB. Tutwiler.

EIN: 133203195

Selected grants: The following grants were reported in 2004.

$100,550 to Metropolitan Museum of Art, New York, NY.
$100,000 to Floor Members Outreach Program, New York, NY.
$100,000 to YMCA of Greater New York, New York, NY.
$72,993 to United Way of New York City, New York, NY.
$50,000 to Lincoln Center for the Performing Arts, New York, NY.
$50,000 to Quinnipiac University, Hamden, CT.
$50,000 to Seton Hall University, South Orange, NJ.
$25,000 to Salvation Army of Greater New York, New York, NY.
$10,000 to Lower East Side Tenement Museum, New York, NY.
$500 to University of Dayton, Dayton, OH.

6620
The New York Times Company Foundation, Inc. ▼
229 W. 43rd St., 10 Fl.
New York, NY 10036-3959 (212) 556-1091
Contact: Jack Rosenthal, Pres.
FAX: (212) 556-4450; URL: http://www.nytimes.com/scholarship

http://www.nytco.com/foundation
Tel. for scholarships: (212) 556-1923

Incorporated in 1955 in NY.
Donor: The New York Times Co.
Foundation type: Company-sponsored foundation.
Financial data (yr. ended 12/31/05): Assets, $2,421,566 (M); gifts received, $7,399,000; expenditures, $7,937,301; qualifying distributions, $8,030,081; giving activities include $6,521,160 for grants.
Purpose and activities: The foundation supports organizations involved with arts and culture, secondary and higher education, the environment, human services, community development, and minorities.
Fields of interest: Media, journalism/publishing; Museums; Performing arts; Arts; Education, association; Secondary school/education; Higher education; Environment; Human services; Community development; Minorities.
Type of support: General/operating support; Continuing support; Annual campaigns; Program development; Seed money; Fellowships; Internship funds; Scholarship funds; Research; Employee matching gifts; Scholarships—to individuals; Matching/challenge support.
Limitations: Giving primarily in areas of company operations, with emphasis on the New York, NY, metropolitan area. No support for religious organizations not of direct benefit to the entire community. No grants to individuals (except for scholarships), or for capital campaigns or health, drug, or alcohol therapy purposes; no loans.
Publications: Annual report (including application guidelines).
Application information: Application form required.
  Initial approach: Download application form
  Copies of proposal: 1
  Deadline(s): Sept. 1
  Board meeting date(s): Apr.
  Final notification: Varies
Officers and Directors:* Cathy J. Sulzberger,* Chair.; Jack Rosenthal,* Pres.; Janet L. Robinson,* Exec. V.P.; Leonard P. Forman, Sr. V.P.; Michael Golden,* Sr. V.P.; Solomon B. Watson IV, Sr. V.P.; James C. Lessersohn, V.P.; Rhonda L. Brauer, Secy.; R. Anthony Benten, Treas.; Doreen A. Toben.
Number of staff: 2 full-time professional; 5 full-time support.
EIN: 136066955
Selected grants: The following grants were reported in 2005.
$100,000 to Alliance of Resident Theaters/New York (ART/NY), New York, NY. For regranting program for small and mid-size theaters.
$80,000 to American Museum of Natural History, New York, NY. For Electronic Newspaper exhibit for fossil-dinosaur hall.
$75,000 to Lincoln Center Consolidated Corporate Fund, New York, NY. For general operating support.
$65,000 to New York Public Library, New York, NY. For operations of research libraries.
$50,000 to CARE, Atlanta, GA. For disaster relief, including Hurricane Katrina and Asian tsunami relief.
$50,000 to Oxfam America, Boston, MA. For disaster relief, including Hurricane Katrina and Asian tsunami relief.
$50,000 to Save the Children Federation, New York, NY. For disaster relief, including Hurricane Katrina and Asian tsunami relief.

$26,870 to National Merit Scholarship Corporation, Evanston, IL. For four-year college Merit Scholarships for employee children.
$10,000 to Asian American Journalists Association, San Francisco, CA. For general operating support.
$10,000 to Graham-Windham Services to Families and Children, New York, NY. For early childhood literacy programs.

6621
The New-Land Foundation, Inc. ◇
1114 Ave. of the Americas, 46th Fl.
New York, NY   10036-7798   (212) 479-6162

Incorporated in 1941 in NY.
Donor: Muriel M. Buttinger†.
Foundation type: Independent foundation.
Financial data (yr. ended 12/31/04): Assets, $38,255,188 (M); expenditures, $2,196,586; qualifying distributions, $1,948,427; giving activities include $1,861,132 for 123 grants (high: $75,000; low: $792).
Purpose and activities: Grants for child development, civil rights and justice, family planning, environmental preservation, peace, and arms control and disarmament.
Fields of interest: Museums (specialized); Child development, education; Environment; International peace/security; International affairs, arms control; Civil rights; Population studies.
International interests: England.
Type of support: General/operating support; Continuing support; Annual campaigns; Program development; Seed money; Research; Matching/challenge support.
Limitations: Giving on a national basis with emphasis on CA, CO, Washington, DC, and New York, NY; some funding also in London, England. No support for educational institutions, medicine, religion and general social programs. No grants to individuals or for capital campaigns, publications, films, endowment campaigns, building campaigns, or conferences; no loans.
Publications: Application guidelines.
Application information: Application form required.
  Initial approach: Proposal
  Copies of proposal: 1
  Deadline(s): Feb. 1 and Aug. 1
  Board meeting date(s): Spring and fall
  Final notification: Positive responses only; June 1 (spring cycle) and Dec. 31 (fall cycle)
Officers and Directors:* Hal Harvey,* Pres.; Constance Harvey,* V.P.; Renee G. Schwartz,* Secy.-Treas.; Anne Ehrlich; Ann Harvey; Joan Harvey; George Perkovich, Ph.D.
EIN: 136086562

6622
Newcastle Foundation ◇ ☆
c/o Brown Brothers Harriman Trust Co.
140 Broadway
New York, NY   10005   (212) 493-8594

Established in 2000 in MA.
Foundation type: Independent foundation.
Financial data (yr. ended 12/31/05): Assets, $2,694,056 (M); gifts received, $150; expenditures, $412,975; qualifying distributions, $339,000; giving activities include $339,000 for grants.

Fields of interest: Historical activities; Education; Hospitals (general); Health organizations, association; Human services.
Type of support: General/operating support.
Limitations: Applications not accepted. Giving primarily in MA. No grants to individuals.
Application information: Contributes only to pre-selected organizations.
Trustees: Timothy J. Barberich; Eileen P. Gebrian; Brown Brothers Harriman Trust Co.
EIN: 522283813
Selected grants: The following grants were reported in 2005.
$100,000 to Concord Land Conservation Trust, Concord, MA.
$15,000 to Catholic Schools Foundation, Boston, MA.
$10,000 to Kings College, Wilkes Barre, PA.
$10,000 to Northfield Mount Hermon School, Northfield, MA.
$7,500 to Berklee College of Music, Boston, MA.

6623
Samuel I. Newhouse Foundation, Inc. ▼ ◇
c/o Paul Scherer & Co. LLP
335 Madison Ave., 9th Fl.
New York, NY   10017

Incorporated in 1945 in NY.
Donors: Samuel I. Newhouse†; Mitzi E. Newhouse†; The Conde Nast Publications, Inc.; Advance Publications, Inc.
Foundation type: Independent foundation.
Financial data (yr. ended 10/31/05): Assets, $90,611,305 (M); gifts received, $6,117,169; expenditures, $13,239,424; qualifying distributions, $12,684,713; giving activities include $12,684,713 for 397 grants (high: $1,000,000; low: $100).
Purpose and activities: Establishment of Newhouse Communications Center at Syracuse University for education and research in mass communications; giving for community funds, hospitals, Jewish welfare funds, higher and secondary education, music and the arts, and youth agencies; support also for journalism associations.
Fields of interest: Media/communications; Media, journalism/publishing; Performing arts, music; Arts; Secondary school/education; Higher education; Hospitals (general); Human services; Children/youth, services; Federated giving programs; Jewish federated giving programs.
Application information:
  Deadline(s): None
Officers and Directors:* Samuel I. Newhouse, Jr.,* Pres. and Treas.; Donald E. Newhouse,* V.P. and Secy.
EIN: 116006296
Selected grants: The following grants were reported in 2005.
$1,000,000 to American Red Cross of the National Capital Area, Fairfax, VA.
$1,000,000 to American Red Cross, National Headquarters, DC. For relief effort for Hurricane Katrina.
$500,000 to New York-Presbyterian Fund, New York, NY.
$500,000 to United Negro College Fund, New York, NY.
$487,500 to UJA-Federation of New York, New York, NY.
$450,000 to New York City Opera, New York, NY.
$25,000 to Jerusalem Foundation, New York, NY.

$10,000 to Oregon Museum of Science and Industry, Portland, OR.
$9,000 to Loyola University, New Orleans, LA.
$5,000 to Staten Island Childrens Campaign Charitable Trust, Staten Island, NY.

6624
Jerome A. and Estelle R. Newman Assistance Fund, Inc. ✧
925 Westchester Ave., Ste. 308
White Plains, NY   10604-3564   (914) 993-0777
Contact: Michael Greenberg, Treas.

Incorporated in 1954 in NY.
Donors: Howard A. Newman†; Jerome A. Newman†.
Foundation type: Independent foundation.
Financial data (yr. ended 6/30/05): Assets, $8,570,032 (M); expenditures, $463,319; qualifying distributions, $444,500; giving activities include $444,500 for 18 grants (high: $150,000; low: $1,000).
Purpose and activities: Giving primarily to Jewish education and welfare organizations, including a guild for the blind; support also for higher and other education.
Fields of interest: Media/communications; Performing arts, theater; Arts; Higher education; Human services; Jewish federated giving programs.
Limitations: Giving primarily in NY. No loans or grants to individuals.
Application information:
   Initial approach: Letter
   Deadline(s): None
   Board meeting date(s): Sept.
   Final notification: Varies
Officers and Directors:* William C. Newman,* Pres.; Patricia Nanon,* V.P.; Robert H. Haines,* Secy.; Michael Greenberg,* Treas.; Andrew H. Levy; Victoria Woolner Samuels; William C. Scott; Jerry I. Speyer.
EIN: 136096241
Selected grants: The following grants were reported in 2005.
$150,000 to JustWorld International, White Plains, NY.
$40,000 to Bennington College, Bennington, VT.
$25,000 to Joyce Theater, New York, NY.
$25,000 to Juilliard School, New York, NY.
$20,000 to American Jewish Committee, New York, NY.
$2,500 to JBI International, New York, NY.
$2,500 to Puppies Behind Bars, New York, NY.

6625
The Lizbeth & Frank Newman Charitable Foundation
767 3rd Ave., 27th Fl.
New York, NY   10017-2023
Contact: Mary Reen, Treas.

Established in 1999 in NY.
Donors: Frank N. Newman; Lizbeth Newman.
Foundation type: Independent foundation.
Financial data (yr. ended 12/31/05): Assets, $163,275 (M); gifts received, $440,000; expenditures, $452,069; qualifying distributions, $393,530; giving activities include $393,530 for 18 grants (high: $81,000; low: $500).
Purpose and activities: Giving primarily to performing arts and cultural institutions.

Fields of interest: Museums; Performing arts centers; Arts; Higher education; Education.
Limitations: Applications not accepted. Giving primarily in NY. No grants to individuals.
Application information: Contributes only to pre-selected organizations.
Officers: Frank Newman, Pres.; Lizabeth Newman, V.P. and Secy.; Mary Reen, Treas.
EIN: 134067790

6626
Newman-Tanner Foundation ✧
c/o Harold Tanner
950 3rd Ave.
New York, NY   10022

Established in 1990 in NY.
Donors: Estelle Tanner; Harold Tanner.
Foundation type: Independent foundation.
Financial data (yr. ended 12/31/05): Assets, $500,733 (M); gifts received, $365,315; expenditures, $385,812; qualifying distributions, $384,000; giving activities include $383,900 for 70 grants (high: $101,800; low: $200).
Fields of interest: Higher education; Human services; Jewish agencies & temples.
Limitations: Applications not accepted. Giving primarily in NY. No grants to individuals.
Application information: Contributes only to pre-selected organizations.
Trustees: Karen Tanner Allen; David A. Tanner; Estelle Newman Tanner; Harold Tanner; James M. Tanner.
EIN: 136942897

6627
Nicholas Family Charitable Trust ✧ ☆
c/o Nicholas J. Nicholas, Jr.
45 W. 67th St., NM 19F
New York, NY   10023

Established in 1992 in NY.
Donors: Nicholas J. Nicholas, Jr.; Llewellyn J. Nicholas.
Foundation type: Independent foundation.
Financial data (yr. ended 12/31/05): Assets, $2,743,561 (M); gifts received, $233,547; expenditures, $430,450; qualifying distributions, $421,905; giving activities include $419,548 for 61 grants (high: $170,000; low: $1).
Purpose and activities: Giving for higher and other education, cultural programs, and for health and human services.
Fields of interest: Arts; Higher education; Education; Environment, natural resources; Environment; Mental health, treatment; Human services.
Type of support: General/operating support; Capital campaigns.
Limitations: Applications not accepted. Giving primarily in NY. No grants to individuals.
Application information: Contributes only to pre-selected organizations.
Trustees: Llewellyn J. Nicholas; Nicholas J. Nicholas, Jr.
EIN: 136990536
Selected grants: The following grants were reported in 2005.
$40,000 to Fountain House, New York, NY. 2 grants: $25,000, $15,000

$35,000 to Princeton Prospect Foundation, Princeton, NJ.
$25,000 to Phillips Academy, Andover, MA.
$20,000 to Princeton University, Princeton, NJ. 2 grants: $10,000 each
$9,515 to Whitney Museum of American Art, New York, NY.
$5,000 to Nantucket Conservation Foundation, Nantucket, MA.
$2,000 to Nantucket Land Council, Nantucket, MA.
$1,000 to Artists Association of Nantucket, Nantucket, MA.

6628
Nichols Foundation, Inc.
c/o Fiduciary Trust Co. International
600 5th Ave.
New York, NY   10020   (212) 632-3000
Contact: David H. Nichols, Pres.
FAX: (212) 632-3198; E-mail: jwetmo@ftci.com

Incorporated in 1923 in NY.
Donor: Members of the Nichols family.
Foundation type: Independent foundation.
Financial data (yr. ended 12/31/03): Assets, $17,073,772 (M); gifts received, $270,000; expenditures, $1,225,983; qualifying distributions, $1,134,961; giving activities include $1,003,913 for 130 grants (high: $76,200; low: $75).
Purpose and activities: Giving primarily for education, health care, and human services.
Fields of interest: Secondary school/education; Higher education; Education, reading; Education; Environment, natural resources; Environment; Animals/wildlife, preservation/protection; Hospitals (general); Reproductive health, family planning; Cancer; Biomedicine; Cancer research; Human services; Children/youth, services; Family services; Disabilities, people with; Economically disadvantaged.
Type of support: Continuing support; Annual campaigns; Capital campaigns; Building/renovation; Equipment; Land acquisition; Program development; Scholarship funds; Research; Matching/challenge support.
Limitations: Applications not accepted. Giving primarily in Santa Barbara, CA, Hinsdale County, CO, FL, and the metropolitan New York, NY area. No support for religious institutions. No grants to individuals, or for individual scholarships or general support; no loans.
Application information: Contributes only to pre-selected organizations. Unsolicited requests for funds not considered.
   Board meeting date(s): Jan. and June
Officers and Directors:* David H. Nichols,* Pres.; Peter Coxhead,* V.P.; Jessica Wetmore, Secy.; C. Walter Nichols III, Treas.; Marguerite D.R. Buttrick; Ralph N. Coxhead; Kathleen C. Moseley.
EIN: 136400615

6629
Nicholson Foundation ✧
419 E. 50th St.
New York, NY   10022
Contact: Jan Nicholson, V.P.

Established in 1980 in NJ.
Donor: Marion G. Nicholson.
Foundation type: Independent foundation.

Financial data (yr. ended 6/30/05): Assets, $11,359,066 (M); expenditures, $1,231,907; qualifying distributions, $1,238,482; giving activities include $733,127 for 19 grants.
Purpose and activities: Giving primarily for the development of the state of NJ.
Fields of interest: Community development.
Limitations: Applications not accepted. Giving primarily in NJ and NY. No grants to individuals.
Application information: Contributes only to pre-selected organizations.
Officers: William B. Nicholson, Pres.; Jan Nicholson, V.P. and Treas.; Barbara McFadyen, V.P.; Marion G. Nicholson, Secy.
EIN: 222344110
Selected grants: The following grants were reported in 2004.
$100,000 to National Alliance for Research on Schizophrenia and Depression (NARSAD), Great Neck, NY. To support scientists in schizophrenia research.
$75,000 to Integrity, Newark, NJ. For position of Program Coordinator.
$62,500 to Prevent Child Abuse New Jersey, New Brunswick, NJ. 2 grants: $25,000 (To aid volunteers in improving parenting skills), $37,500.
$60,000 to Essex, County of, Newark, NJ. For Human Resource Development Consultant.
$54,000 to Kids Corporation, Newark, NJ. For cost of full-time employee.
$40,000 to Jersey Urban Debate League (JUDL), Newark, NJ. For program support.
$35,000 to Child Advocacy Resource and Education, Greeley, CO. For start up activities for Hispanic foster parents.
$25,000 to Leadership Newark, Newark, NJ. For training program.
$25,000 to Regional Plan Association, New York, NY.

6630
The Dragomir Nicolitch Charitable Trust ✧
c/o Kranz & Co.
145 E. 57th St.
New York, NY 10022
Application addresses: c/o Silas Mountsier, 205 Rutgers Pl., Nutley, NJ 07110, and The Most Rev. Metropolitan Christopher Serbian Orthodox Church, 32377 N. Milwaukee Ave., Libertyville, IL 60048

Established in 1996 in NY.
Donor: Dragomir Nicolitch†.
Foundation type: Independent foundation.
Financial data (yr. ended 12/31/05): Assets, $5,108,372 (M); expenditures, $655,537; qualifying distributions, $594,541; giving activities include $585,500 for 5 grants (high: $290,500; low: $1,500).
Purpose and activities: Scholarships given to recent university graduates of Serbian parentage from any state that made up the former Yugoslav nation for graduate courses at an institution of higher learning in the U.S. Also, awards scholarships to students of the Serbian Orthodox Community who desire to become priests of the Serbian Orthodox Church, and to ordained priests of the Serbian Orthodox Church who desire higher educational opportunities.
Fields of interest: Religion.
Limitations: Giving on a national basis.
Application information:
Initial approach: Letter
Deadline(s): None

Trustees: Silas R. Mountsier III; The Most Reverend Metropolitan Christopher Serbian Orthodox Church.
EIN: 137082276

6631
The Robert and Kate Niehaus Foundation ✧
105 Evergreen Ave.
Rye, NY 10580
Contact: Robert H. Neihaus, Pres.

Established in 1998 in NY.
Donor: Robert H. Niehaus.
Foundation type: Independent foundation.
Financial data (yr. ended 12/31/05): Assets, $12,836,937 (M); gifts received, $800; expenditures, $2,865,040; qualifying distributions, $2,315,860; giving activities include $2,300,023 for 6 grants (high: $2,000,000; low: $40,000).
Fields of interest: Education; Cystic fibrosis; Cancer; YM/YWCAs & YM/YWHAs; Children, services.
Limitations: Giving primarily in New York, NY; some funding also in MA, MD, and KY.
Application information:
Initial approach: Letter
Deadline(s): None
Officers: Robert H. Niehaus, Pres.; Kate Niehaus, V.P.
Director: Jerome L. Levine.
EIN: 134007527
Selected grants: The following grants were reported in 2003.
$100,000 to Cystic Fibrosis Foundation, Bethesda, MD.
$60,000 to Sitesalive Foundation, Boston, MA.
$50,000 to Bronx Preparatory Charter School, Friends of, Bronx, NY.
$50,000 to Good Shepherd Church, Owensboro, KY.
$40,000 to Student Sponsor Partners, New York, NY.
$10,000 to Port Chester Carver Center, Port Chester, NY.
$10,000 to YMCA of Rye, Rye, NY.
$31 to Through Greenhill.

6632
John H. and Ethel G. Noble Charitable Trust ✧
c/o Deutsche Trust Co. of NY
P.O. Box 1297, Church St. Sta.
New York, NY 10008
Contact: Paul J. Bisset, V.P., Deutsche Bank

Established in 1969 in CT.
Donors: Ethel G. Noble†; John H. Noble†.
Foundation type: Independent foundation.
Financial data (yr. ended 5/31/05): Assets, $19,508,673 (M); expenditures, $1,062,821; qualifying distributions, $921,368; giving activities include $850,000 for 43 grants (high: $35,000; low: $2,500).
Purpose and activities: Grants for organizations that provide shelter or support to the low-income aged and places for the care and treatment of crippled or handicapped children.
Fields of interest: Hospitals (general); Medical care, rehabilitation; Health care; Aging, centers/services; Aging; Disabilities, people with.
Limitations: Applications not accepted. Giving limited to CT, FL, and NY. No grants to individuals.

Application information: Contributes only to pre-selected organizations.
Trustee: Deutsche Trust Co. of NY.
EIN: 136307313
Selected grants: The following grants were reported in 2004.
$25,000 to Rebuilding Together, Stamford, CT. For general support.
$20,000 to American School for the Deaf, West Hartford, CT.
$20,000 to ARC of Greenwich, Greenwich, CT. For general support.
$20,000 to Camp Horizons, South Windham, CT. For general support.
$20,000 to Easter Seal Rehabilitation Center of Southwestern Connecticut, Stamford, CT. For general support.
$20,000 to Family Centers, Greenwich, CT. For general support.
$20,000 to Heartsong, Bronxville, NY. For general support.
$20,000 to Marvelwood Preparatory School, Kent, CT. For general support.
$20,000 to Northern Westchester Center for the Arts, Mount Kisco, NY. For general support.
$20,000 to Saint Anthonys Health Care Foundation, Saint Petersburg, FL. For general support.

6633
Edward John Noble Foundation, Inc. ▼ ✧
32 E. 57th St.
New York, NY 10022 (212) 759-4212
Contact: E.J. Noble Smith, Chair.

Trust established in 1940 in CT; incorporated in 1982.
Donors: Edward John Noble†; St. Catherine's Island Foundation, Inc.
Foundation type: Independent foundation.
Financial data (yr. ended 12/31/05): Assets, $134,248,527 (M); expenditures, $10,281,589; qualifying distributions, $9,243,776; giving activities include $8,083,030 for 67 grants (high: $2,000,000; low: $5,000; average: $10,000–$50,000).
Purpose and activities: Grants to major cultural organizations in New York City, especially for educational programs and management training internships. Selected projects concerned with conservation and ecology primarily related to activities on an island off the coast of GA. Supports programs to improve educational opportunities for gifted and talented disadvantaged children in NY. Programs in health education efforts related to family planning and population education.
Fields of interest: Performing arts, music; Arts; Education; Environment, natural resources; Environment; Reproductive health, family planning.
Type of support: General/operating support; Continuing support; Endowments; Program development; Internship funds; Matching/challenge support.
Limitations: Giving primarily in the metropolitan New York, NY, area for arts organizations; St. Catherine's Island, GA, and the eastern states for conservation projects and family planning; and the Northeast for private colleges and universities. No grants to individuals, or for publications, building funds, equipment, television, films, or performances; no loans.
Publications: Biennial report (including application guidelines).

Application information: Application form not required.

> *Initial approach:* Brief letter
> *Copies of proposal:* 1
> *Deadline(s):* None
> *Board meeting date(s):* Dec.
> *Final notification:* 3 months

Officers and Directors: * E.J. Noble Smith,* Chair. and Pres.; Jeremy T. Smith,* Vice-Chair. and V.P.; Deborah Menton-Nightlinger, Secy. and Exec. Dir; E. Mary Heffernan, Treas.; June Noble Larkin, Chair. Emeritus; Dr. William G. Conway; Harold B. Johnson; Mrs. June Noble Larkin; Daniel L. Mosley; Howard Phipps, Jr.; Ms. Marnie Pillsbury; Joseph W. Polisi; Bradford D. Smith; David S. Smith; Mr. E. J. Noble Smith; Mr. Jeremy T. Smith; Maribeth Smith; Carroll L. Wainwright, Jr.

Number of staff: 3 full-time professional; 1 full-time support; 1 part-time support.

EIN: 061055586

Selected grants: The following grants were reported in 2004.

$2,882,000 to Fernbank Museum of Natural History, Atlanta, GA. For grant in the form of archaeological items from Saint Catherine's Island.

$2,000,000 to Juilliard School, New York, NY. For June Nobel Larkin Humanities Program.

$2,000,000 to Museum of Modern Art, New York, NY. For endowment, renovation and expansion activities.

$941,169 to Wildlife Conservation Society, Bronx, NY. For Wildlife Survival Center on Saint Catherine's Island.

$800,000 to Saint Catherines Island Foundation, Midway, GA. For general support.

$400,362 to American Museum of Natural History, New York, NY. For collection management and transfer.

$150,000 to Jazz at Lincoln Center, New York, NY. For general support.

$37,500 to Chamber Music Society of Lincoln Center, New York, NY. For program support.

$35,000 to LightHawk, Lander, WY. For general support.

$12,500 to Florida Keys Wild Bird Rehabilitation Center, Tavernier, FL. For internship program.

6634
Norcross Wildlife Foundation, Inc.

250 W. 88th St., Ste. 806
Caller Box No. 611
New York, NY 10024 (212) 362-4831
Contact: Richard S. Reagan, Pres.; John McMurray, Prog. Off.
Application address: Grants Admin., P.O. Box 269, Wales, MA 01081; Additional tel.: (718) 791-2094; E-mail for John Murray, Prog. Off.: johnmcmurray@ez2net; URL: http://www.norcrossws.org

Established in 1964 in NY.

Donors: Arthur D. Norcross†; June Norcross Webster†.

Foundation type: Independent foundation.

Financial data (yr. ended 12/31/05): Assets, $70,000,095 (M); expenditures, $3,583,635; qualifying distributions, $4,405,544; giving activities include $1,086,584 for 304+ grants (high: $55,000), and $1,164,000 for 9 loans/program-related investments.

Purpose and activities: The foundation gives to: 1) protect, enhance and expand habitat for wildlife,

primarily at The Norcross Wildlife Sanctuary (known as Tupper Hill), in the form of holdings in the surrounding towns of Monson, Wales, Holland, Brimfield and Hardwick, MA, and Stafford, CT; 2) to protect wild land wherever it is threatened; 3) to propagate, establish, restore and maintain populations of threatened and endangered plants native to New England; 4) to provide the public with educational programs in natural and environmental science; and 5) to support, through grants, gifts, easements and loans-for-land, the activities of a national and international constituency of not-for-profit wildlife conservation organizations. Funding also for historical preservation, and extremely limited support also for health organizations, assistance for the handicapped, drug abuse programs, and education.

Fields of interest: Environment, natural resources; Environment; Animals/wildlife, preservation/protection.

Type of support: Building/renovation; Equipment; Land acquisition; Publication.

Limitations: Giving primarily in North America. No support for animal welfare or wildlife rehabilitation. No grants to individuals, or for operating support, fundraising, overhead expenses, research endowments, conferences, matching gifts, or multi-year grants.

Publications: Application guidelines; Annual report (including application guidelines); Grants list; Multi-year report.

Application information: The foundation will accept grant requests only for amounts under $10,000. Grants average less than $5,000. Fax, express mail applications or proposals without an attached application form not accepted; no 990-PF forms or annual reports required; only 1 copy of IRS letter is required. Application form required.

> *Initial approach:* 1-page letter on organization letterhead requesting guidelines and application form; guidelines and application form also available on foundation Web site
> *Copies of proposal:* 1
> *Deadline(s):* None
> *Board meeting date(s):* Quarterly

Officers and Directors: * Richard S. Reagan,* Pres.; Joseph A. Catalano,* V.P.; Karen Outlaw, Treas.; Warren Balgooyen; Angelica Braestrup; Albia Dugger; Arthur D. Norcross, Jr.; Michael D. Patrick; Denise Schlener; Christof von Strasser; Ted Williams.

Number of staff: 3 full-time professional; 1 full-time support.

EIN: 132041622

Selected grants: The following grants were reported in 2004.

$7,000 to Tar River Land Conservancy, Louisburg, NC.

$6,800 to Ecologic Development Fund, Cambridge, MA.

$6,500 to Georgia Forestwatch, Ellijay, GA.

$6,300 to Trout Unlimited, Arlington, VA.

$6,000 to Wyoming Wildlife Federation, Cheyenne, WY.

$5,400 to Southern Utah Wilderness Alliance, Salt Lake City, UT.

$5,100 to National Wildlife Refuge Association, DC.

$5,000 to Caribbean Conservation Corporation, Gainesville, FL.

$4,000 to Xerces Society, Portland, OR.

$3,300 to Rivers Council of Minnesota, Sauk Rapids, MN.

6635
Norman Foundation, Inc. ✧

147 E. 48th St.
New York, NY 10017 (212) 230-9830
Contact: June Makela, Prog. Dir.
FAX: (212) 230-9849; E-mail: info@normanfdn.org; URL: http://www.normanfdn.org/

Incorporated in 1935 in NY.

Donors: Aaron E. Norman†; and directors of the foundation.

Foundation type: Independent foundation.

Financial data (yr. ended 12/31/03): Assets, $23,157,196 (M); expenditures, $1,494,078; qualifying distributions, $1,358,340; giving activities include $1,105,500 for 99 grants (high: $21,000; low: $1,000).

Purpose and activities: The foundation funds in three broad areas: economic justice, environmental justice and civil rights. The current priorities for the civil rights program are education equity and criminal justice reform. The foundation is interested in community-based organizing projects that could have a potentially national impact as well as provide potential models for social change. Collaborative projects welcome.

Fields of interest: Environment; legal rights; Employment; Civil rights; Economic development; Community development; Public affairs; Minorities; Economically disadvantaged.

Type of support: General/operating support; Continuing support; Program development; Seed money; Matching/challenge support.

Limitations: Giving limited to the U.S. No support for universities or direct social service agencies. No grants to individuals, or for building or endowment funds, publications, conferences, capital funding projects, fundraising, research, scholarships, films, and arts projects or fellowships.

Publications: Application guidelines; Financial statement; Grants list.

Application information: Accepts NYRAG & NNG Common Application Forms. The foundation does not accept applications by E-mail and does not open attached files. Updated guidelines available on Web site. The foundation only accepts full proposals upon positive response to the letter of inquiry. Application form not required.

> *Initial approach:* A short 2- to 3- page letter of inquiry
> *Copies of proposal:* 1
> *Deadline(s):* See foundation Web site for current deadlines
> *Board meeting date(s):* 3 times per year
> *Final notification:* 1 month to 1 year

Officers and Directors: * Honor Lassalle,* Pres.; Alice Franklin,* V.P.; Amanda Weil,* V.P.; Margaret Norman,* Secy.; Melissa Bunnen,* Treas.; Robert L. Bunnen, Jr.; Andrew D. Franklin; Deborah Weil Harrington; Philip E. Lassalle; Abigail Norman; Rebecca Norman; Sarah Norman; Belinda Bunnen Reusch; Diana Lassalle Turner; Sandison E. Weil; William S. Weil.

Number of staff: 1 part-time professional; 1 part-time support.

EIN: 131862694

Selected grants: The following grants were reported in 2003.

$25,000 to Carolina Alliance for Fair Employment (CAFE), Greenville, SC. For educational activities.

$20,000 to Alternatives for Community and Environment (ACE), Roxbury, MA. For community education work.

$20,000 to Chicago Coalition for the Homeless, Chicago, IL.

$20,000 to Indigenous Environmental Network, Bemidji, MN. For youth training program.

$20,000 to Kentucky Environmental Foundation, Berea, KY. For public education work.

$20,000 to People Acting for Community Together (PACT), Miami, FL. For public education work.

$20,000 to Sentencing Project, DC. For criminal justice education.

$20,000 to Western Prison Project, Portland, OR. For criminal justice education.

$15,000 to Center for Economic Justice, DC. For educational activities.

$15,000 to Community Environmental Legal Defense Fund, Chambersburg, PA. For community education.

6636
Normandie Foundation, Inc.
147 E. 48th St.
New York, NY 10017

Incorporated in 1966 in NY.
Donors: Andrew E. Norman†; The Aaron E. Norman Fund, Inc.
Foundation type: Independent foundation.
Financial data (yr. ended 12/31/04): Assets, $7,927,947 (M); gifts received, $1,025,963; expenditures, $371,193; qualifying distributions, $326,688; giving activities include $323,506 for 50 grants (high: $75,000; low: $100).
Purpose and activities: Grants primarily for civil liberties and the environment.; support also for civic, charitable, educational, and cultural institutions.
Fields of interest: Environment; Civil liberties, advocacy.
Type of support: General/operating support; Continuing support; Annual campaigns; Seed money.
Limitations: No support for religious organizations. No grants to individuals, or for conferences, building or endowment funds, scholarships, fellowships, or matching gifts; generally no loans.
Application information: Generally, grants are only to organizations with which the officers are personally familiar. Application form not required.
  Initial approach: Letter
  Copies of proposal: 1
  Deadline(s): None
  Board meeting date(s): Aug.
  Final notification: 1 month after board meeting
Directors: Abigail Norman; Margaret Norman; Rebecca D. Norman; Sarah Norman.
Number of staff: None.
EIN: 136213564
Selected grants: The following grants were reported in 2003.
$100,000 to International Rescue Committee, New York, NY.
$25,000 to American Civil Liberties Union (ACLU), New York, NY.
$15,000 to JusticeWorks Community, Brooklyn, NY.
$10,000 to Center for Constitutional Rights, New York, NY.
$10,000 to Government Accountability Project (GAP), DC.
$1,250 to New York Public Library, New York, NY.
$700 to Food First, Brooklyn, NY.
$500 to Amnesty International USA, New York, NY.
$300 to Brooklyn Academy of Music, Brooklyn, NY.
$250 to Gay Mens Health Crisis (GMHC), New York, NY.

6637
North Fork Foundation ▼ ✧
(formerly The GreenPoint Foundation, Inc.)
275 Broadhollow Rd.
Melville, NY 11747
E-mail: scooper@nfb.com
Scholarship application address: c/o North Fork Foundation Scholarship Prog., Scholarship America, Inc., 1 Scholarship Way, P.O. Box 297, St. Peter, MN 56082, tel.: (507) 931-1682, FAX: (507) 931-9278, E-mail: gmiller@csfa.org

Established in 1994 in NY.
Donor: GreenPoint Bank.
Foundation type: Company-sponsored foundation.
Financial data (yr. ended 9/30/05): Assets, $46,331,081 (M); expenditures, $6,274,309; qualifying distributions, $6,023,086; giving activities include $5,802,039 for 741 grants (high: $494,779; low: $30), and $101,361 for 170 employee matching gifts.
Purpose and activities: The foundation supports organizations involved with health, cancer research, housing, human services, and community development and awards college scholarships to high school seniors located in New Haven County, Connecticut, Bergen, Essex, Hudson, Mercer, Middlesex, Monmouth, Morris, Passaic, Somerset, and Union counties, New Jersey, and Bronx, Brooklyn, Manhattan, Nassau, Queens, Rockland, Staten Island, Suffolk, and Westchester counties, New York.
Fields of interest: Health care; Cancer research; Housing/shelter; Children/youth, services; Human services; Community development; Federated giving programs.
Type of support: General/operating support; Employee matching gifts; Scholarships—to individuals.
Limitations: Giving primarily in areas of company operations in New Haven County, Connecticut, Bergen, Essex, Hudson, Mercer, Middlesex, Monmouth, Morris, Passaic, Somerset, and Union counties, New Jersey, and Bronx, Brooklyn, Manhattan, Nassau, Queens, Rockland, Staten Island, Suffolk, and Westchester counties, New York.
Application information: An application form is required for scholarships.
  Initial approach: Contact foundation for application information; contact foundation for application form for scholarships
  Deadline(s): Mar. 1 for scholarships
Officers and Directors: John Adam Kanas, Pres.; Carolyn Drexel, Exec. V.P.; Stacey Cooper, V.P.; Linda Mangan, V.P.; Aurelie S. Campbell, Secy.; John N. DiGiacomo, Treas.; Rev. Calvin O. Butts; Regina S. Peruggi; Bishop Joseph M. Sullivan.
EIN: 113276603
Selected grants: The following grants were reported in 2004.
$956,250 to Scholarship America, Saint Peter, MN. 2 grants: $868,750, $87,500
$500,000 to Fund for Public Schools, New York, NY.
$258,250 to Jeffersons Ferry, South Setauket, NY.
$72,000 to Neighborhood Housing Services of New York City, New York, NY.
$39,240 to United Way of New York City, New York, NY.
$32,850 to United Way of the Bay Area, San Francisco, CA.
$25,000 to Institute of International Education, New York, NY. For benefit.

$25,000 to National American Indian Housing Council, DC.
$25,000 to Scripps Ranch Civic Association, San Diego, CA.

6638
Northern Chautauqua Community Foundation, Inc.
212 Lake Shore Dr. W.
Dunkirk, NY 14048 (716) 366-4892
Contact: Diane Hannum, Exec. Dir.
FAX: (716) 366-3905;
E-mail: nccf@nccfoundation.org; Grant application E-mails: grants@nccfoundation.org; URL: http://www.nccfoundation.org

Incorporated in 1986 in NY.
Foundation type: Community foundation.
Financial data (yr. ended 12/31/05): Assets, $12,845,825 (M); gifts received, $1,675,787; expenditures, $532,349; giving activities include $172,151 for 80 grants (high: $27,000; low: $76), and $172,010 for 212 grants to individuals (high: $7,000; low: $25).
Purpose and activities: The mission of the foundation is to enrich the area in which the community lives and works. Primary areas of interest include education, libraries, family services, community funds, cultural programs, and other general charitable activities.
Fields of interest: Arts; Higher education; Adult education—literacy, basic skills & GED; Libraries/library science; Education, reading; Education; Environment, public education; Environment, water resources; Environment; Animal welfare; Hospitals (general); Substance abuse, services; Recreation, parks/playgrounds; Recreation; Family services; Residential/custodial care, hospices; Aging, centers/services; Community development; Voluntarism promotion; Aging.
Type of support: Building/renovation; Equipment; Endowments; Program development; Seed money; Scholarship funds; Scholarships—to individuals; Matching/challenge support.
Limitations: Giving limited to northern Chautauqua County, NY. No support for religious organizations. No grants to individuals (except for designated scholarship funds), or for capital campaigns, general operating budgets, publication of books, conferences, or annual fundraising campaigns.
Publications: Application guidelines; Annual report (including application guidelines); Financial statement; Newsletter.
Application information: Visit foundation Web site for application form and guidelines. Application form required.
  Initial approach: Letter or telephone
  Copies of proposal: 1
  Deadline(s): Mar. 1 and Sept. 1
  Board meeting date(s): Quarterly
  Final notification: 10 days following board meeting
Officers and Directors:* Susan Marsh,* Pres.; Kurt Maytum,* V.P.; George "Pete" Holt,* Secy.; Richard Ketcham,* Treas.; Diane Hannum, Exec. Dir.; Rosemary Banach; Michael Brunecz; Jon Cooke; Patti Daughrity; Rose Ann Falcone; James S. Koch; David Larson, Ph.D.; Jean Malinoski; Robert Miller, Jr.; Jeffrey G. Passafaro; Daniel Reininga; Gerard Rocque; R. Bard Schaack.
Number of staff: 1 full-time professional; 2 part-time professional; 1 full-time support.
EIN: 161271663

6639
Northern New York Community Foundation, Inc. ◇

(formerly Watertown Foundation, Inc.)
120 Washington St., Ste. 400
Watertown, NY 13601 (315) 782-7110
Contact: Alex C. Velto, Exec. Dir.
FAX: (315) 782-0047; E-mail: info@nnycf.org;
URL: http://www.nnycf.org

Incorporated in 1929 in NY.
Foundation type: Community foundation.
Financial data (yr. ended 12/31/04): Assets,
$26,666,244 (M); gifts received, $1,124,994;
expenditures, $2,120,469; giving activities include
$1,612,129 for 35 grants (high: $116,666; low:
$1,000).
Purpose and activities: The foundation raises,
manages and administers an endowment and
collection of funds for the benefit of the community,
built and added to by gifts from individuals and
organizations committed to meeting the changing
needs of Northern New York.
Fields of interest: Historic preservation/historical
societies; Arts; Education, fund raising/fund
distribution; Child development, education; Adult/
continuing education; Libraries/library science;
Education; Environment; Hospitals (general);
Nursing care; Health care; Substance abuse,
services; Health organizations, association; AIDS;
Food services; Housing/shelter, development;
Recreation; Children/youth, services; Child
development, services; Family services;
Residential/custodial care, hospices; Aging,
centers/services; Homeless, human services;
Human services; Community development;
Federated giving programs; Government/public
administration; Aging; Disabilities, people with;
Economically disadvantaged; Homeless.
Type of support: Annual campaigns; Capital
campaigns; Building/renovation; Equipment; Land
acquisition; Program development; Conferences/
seminars; Publication; Seed money; Scholarship
funds; Technical assistance; Scholarships—to
individuals; Matching/challenge support.
Limitations: Giving limited to organizations and
individuals in Jefferson and Lewis counties, NY. No
support for churches or religious organizations
(except where projects clearly benefit the entire
community). No grants to individuals (except for
scholarships), or for endowment funds or deficit
financing.
Publications: Annual report; Grants list; Newsletter.
Application information: Visit foundation Web site
to request grant application guidelines or download
scholarship application forms.
  Initial approach: Letter, telephone, or E-mail
  Copies of proposal: 1
  Deadline(s): Jan. 31, May 2, Sept. 6, and Oct. 31;
    Apr. 1 for scholarships
  Board meeting date(s): Mar., June, Sept., and
    Dec.
  Final notification: 1 to 2 months for grants; June
    1 for scholarships
Officers and Directors:* Philip J. Sprague,* Pres.;
Lee Clary,* V.P.; James R. Kanik,* Secy.-Treas.;
Alex C. Velto, Exec. Dir.; Terry Ierlan, Cont.; Donald
C. Alexander; Douglas Brodie; Bernard H. Brown, Jr.;
John W. Deans; Judith J. Foster; Susan B. Horr; Mary
McDonald Mascott; Kenneth J. McAuliffe; Catherine
B. Quencer; D. Peter Van Eenenaam; Anderson
Wise.

Number of staff: 1 full-time professional; 1 full-time
support; 1 part-time support.
EIN: 156020989

6640
Novartis US Foundation

(formerly Sandoz Foundation of America)
608 5th Ave.
New York, NY 10020
Contact: Brandi Robinson, Exec. Dir.
FAX: (212) 830-2424;
E-mail: brandi.robinson@novartis.com; Additional
E-mail: us.foundation@novartis.com; URL: http://
www.novartis.com/about_novartis/en/
foundations.shtml

Incorporated in 1965 in DE; adopted current name
in 1997 following a merger with the Ciba Educational
Foundation, Inc.
Donors: Sandoz Corp.; Novartis Inc.
Foundation type: Company-sponsored foundation.
Financial data (yr. ended 12/31/05): Assets,
$17,774,046 (M); gifts received, $795,728;
expenditures, $1,292,882; qualifying distributions,
$1,182,858; giving activities include $616,131 for
2 grants (high: $416,000; low: $200,131), and
$566,727 for employee matching gifts.
Purpose and activities: The foundation supports
organizations involved with education, health, and
human services.
Fields of interest: Education; Health care; Human
services.
Type of support: Employee matching gifts; Program
development; Scholarship funds; Employee-related
scholarships.
Limitations: Giving on a national basis, with
emphasis on areas of company operations. No
support for religious organizations or social, labor,
veterans', fraternal, athletic, or alumni
organizations. No grants to individuals (except for
employee-related scholarships).
Publications: Application guidelines.
Application information: Application form not
required.
  Initial approach: Proposal
  Deadline(s): None
  Board meeting date(s): As required
Officers and Trustees:* Terry Barnett,* Pres.;
Brandi Robinson, Exec. Dir.; Brenda Blanchard;
Martin Henrich; Urs Naegelin; Burt Rosen; Erwin
Schillinger.
EIN: 136193034

6641
NoVo Foundation ▼

(formerly The Spirit Foundation)
11 E. 44th St., Ste. 1600
New York, NY 10017 (212) 808-5400
Contact: Bob Dandrew, Exec. Dir.
FAX: (212) 252-0927;
E-mail: info@novofoundation.org; URL: http://
www.novofoundation.org

Established in 1999 in NE; classified as a private
operating foundation in 2000; reclassified as an
independent foundation in 2001.
Donor: Warren E. Buffett.
Foundation type: Independent foundation.
Financial data (yr. ended 12/31/04): Assets,
$129,863,364 (M); gifts received, $20,812;
expenditures, $11,088,752; qualifying

distributions, $11,061,355; giving activities include
$10,780,254 for 104 grants (high: $2,940,004;
low: $100; average: $10,000–$500,000).
Purpose and activities: Giving primarily for
exemplary organizations that advance sustainable
change in community building, women's
empowerment and early childhood development.
Fields of interest: Child development, services;
Women, centers/services; Community
development; Women; Adults, women.
Limitations: Applications not accepted. Giving
primarily in Portland, OR and WI, as well as some
international giving. No grants to individuals.
Application information: Does not accept
unsolicited applications.
Officer and Directors:* Peter A. Buffett,* Chair.;
Jennifer Buffett,* Pres. and Treas.; Shawn Perrin,*
Secy.; Bob Dandrew, Exec. Dir.
Number of staff: 4 full-time professional; 1 part-time
professional; 1 part-time support.
EIN: 470824753
Selected grants: The following grants were reported
in 2004.
$2,940,004 to Tides Center, San Francisco, CA. For
  general support.
$1,000,000 to Next Door Foundation, Milwaukee,
  WI. For EduCare of Milwaukee.
$970,000 to New World Foundation, New York, NY.
  2 grants: $250,000 (For general support),
  $720,000 (For general support).
$500,000 to Human Rights Watch, New York, NY.
  For general support.
$350,000 to Rainforest Action Network, San
  Francisco, CA. For general support.
$250,000 to First Nations Development Institute,
  Fredericksburg, VA. For general support.
$250,000 to Friends of the International Freedom
  Center, New York, NY. For general support.
$250,000 to Gynuity Health Projects, New York, NY.
  For program support.
$15,000 to HeartLove Place, Milwaukee, WI. For
  capital support.

6642
The Novogratz-Caceres Family Foundation ◇

(formerly The Novogratz Family Foundation)
c/o BCRS Assocs., LLC
100 Wall St., 11th Fl.
New York, NY 10005

Established in 1999 in NY.
Donor: Michael Novogratz.
Foundation type: Independent foundation.
Financial data (yr. ended 12/31/05): Assets,
$1,460,509 (M); expenditures, $359,358;
qualifying distributions, $359,275; giving activities
include $359,075 for 27 grants (high: $100,000;
low: $900).
Fields of interest: Performing arts, orchestra
(symphony); Performing arts, education; Education;
Animals/wildlife, association; Health organizations,
association; Human services.
Limitations: Applications not accepted. Giving
primarily in New York, NY. No grants to individuals;
no loans.
Application information: Contributes only to
pre-selected organizations.
Trustees: Dora Caceres; Jacqueline Novogratz;
Michael Novogratz.
EIN: 134083989
Selected grants: The following grants were reported
in 2005.

$100,000 to Tsunami Relief, New York, NY.

$25,000 to School for Strings, New York, NY.

$12,500 to National Fish and Wildlife Foundation, DC.

$10,000 to Creative Alternatives of New York, New York, NY.

$10,000 to Windward School, Los Angeles, CA.

$5,000 to Princeton University, Princeton, NJ.

6643
Jessie Smith Noyes Foundation, Inc. ▼

6 E. 39th St., 12th Fl.
New York, NY   10016-0112   (212) 684-6577
Contact: Victor De Luca, Pres.
FAX: (212) 689-6549; E-mail: noyes@noyes.org;
URL: http://www.noyes.org

Incorporated in 1947 in NY.
Donor: Charles F. Noyes†.
Foundation type: Independent foundation.
Financial data (yr. ended 12/31/04): Assets, $61,345,357 (M); gifts received, $200; expenditures, $4,614,765; qualifying distributions, $4,208,132; giving activities include $3,102,780 for 186 grants, and $18,315 for foundation-administered programs.
Purpose and activities: The foundation seeks to protect and restore the planet's capacity for renewal by supporting grassroots organizations and movements whose work promotes healthy, just and sustainable social and natural systems. The foundation views the Earth as one community, an indivisible web of life with human society an integral part. The foundation's grantmaking addresses two general themes: 1) healthy, just and sustainable environments and communities; and 2) reproductive rights. Grants are designed to help organizations increase and sustain their effectiveness. With first time grants, the foundation tries to bring diverse voices and approaches into the movements it supports.
Fields of interest: Environment, toxics; Environment; Agriculture; Civil liberties, reproductive rights.
Type of support: General/operating support; Continuing support; Program development; Seed money.
Limitations: Giving limited to the U.S. No grants to individuals, or for scholarships, fellowships, endowment funds, deficit financing, capital construction funds, or general fundraising drives; generally no support for conferences, research, college and university based programs, or media; no loans.
Publications: Annual report; Financial statement.
Application information: Applications not accepted for discretionary or founder-designated funds. Accepts National Network of Grantmakers Common Application Form, which can be downloaded from the foundation website. Full proposal will be requested after review of letter of intent, background of organization, summary of activities for funding and expected outcome. The foundation encourages requests that address multiple priorities, as well as those that bring together organizations and activists from diverse movements. The foundation prefers to make general support grants and does not limit the number of renewal grants. Application form not required.
Initial approach: 1- or 2-page letter of inquiry, including budget estimate
Copies of proposal: 1
Deadline(s): None

Board meeting date(s): Spring, summer, and fall
Final notification: Within 6 weeks of receipt of letters; within 2 weeks of board meetings for final proposals
Officers and Directors:* Heather Findlay,* Chair.; Victor De Luca, Pres.; Leslie Lowe,* Secy.; Nicholas Jacangelo,* Treas.; Dorothy Anderson; George Beardsley; Jerry Beardsley; Peter Bedell, Jr.; Steven M. Carbo; Stephen Falci; Betty Hung; Laurel Kearns; Pamela Kingfisher; Carol Kuhre; LaDonna Redmond; Chitra Staley; Ann Wiener.
Number of staff: 2 full-time professional; 2 part-time professional; 2 part-time support.
EIN: 135600408
Selected grants: The following grants were reported in 2005.

$60,000 to Comite de Apoyo a los Trabajadores Agricolas, Glassboro, NJ. For general support for grassroots organizing work on environmental, economic justice and sustainable agriculture issues with farmworkers in Northeast and Mid-Atlantic States, payable over 2 years.

$50,000 to Farmworker Association of Florida, Apopka, FL. For general support for statewide farmworker organization organizing primarily Latino and immigrant farmworkers to address workplace, health, environment and political issues, payable over 2 years.

$50,000 to Farmworker Health and Safety Institute, Glassboro, NJ. For general support to work with Latino and immigrant farmworker organizations to address environmental and health issues, and to impact public policy, payable over 2 years.

$50,000 to Healthy Environment Alliance of Utah, Salt Lake City, UT. For general support to protect health and environment of Utah from industrial pollution, and toxic and nuclear waste disposal, payable over 2 years.

$50,000 to Religious Coalition for Reproductive Choice, Missouri, Saint Louis, MO. For general support to protect and expand reproductive choice for all people in Missouri, with emphasis on African-American community, payable over 2 years.

$50,000 to SouthWest Organizing Project, Albuquerque, NM. For general support for grassroots organizing work on environmental and economic justice issues in New Mexico, payable over 2 years.

$50,000 to Utah Progressive Network Education Fund, Salt Lake City, UT. For program support for Gender Justice initiative, collaborative effort to integrate reproductive health and rights issues into broader social justice movement, payable over 2 years.

$45,000 to West Virginia FREE, Charleston, WV. For general support for statewide coalition working for reproductive freedom for all West Virginia women, payable over 2 years.

$45,000 to Western States Center, Portland, OR. For program support to broaden reproductive rights debate among Western social justice organizations through sharing of strategies and models that prevent use of wedge tactics around gender issues, payable over 2 years.

$40,000 to California Coalition for Food and Farming, Santa Cruz, CA. For general support to promote sustainable agriculture in California and nationally through policy advocacy, networking and education, payable over 2 years.

6644
Jane W. Nuhn Charitable Trust ◇

c/o Van DeWater & Van DeWater
P.O. Box 112
Poughkeepsie, NY   12602
Contact: Michael De Cordova, Tr.

Established in 1988 in NY.
Foundation type: Independent foundation.
Financial data (yr. ended 12/31/04): Assets, $11,741,090 (M); expenditures, $531,833; qualifying distributions, $467,846; giving activities include $414,250 for 13 grants (high: $100,000; low: $2,250).
Purpose and activities: Areas of support include the arts, music, and prevention of cruelty to animals.
Fields of interest: Arts; Animal welfare; Community development; Federated giving programs.
Type of support: General/operating support; Building/renovation; Equipment; Endowments; Matching/challenge support.
Limitations: Giving primarily in Dutchess County, NY. No grants to individuals.
Publications: Annual report.
Application information: Unsolicited requests for funds not accepted.
Deadline(s): None
Board meeting date(s): Monthly
Trustees: Edward V.K. Cunningham, Jr.; Michael De Cordova; Noel De Cordova, Jr.
EIN: 146134057

6645
A. Lindsay and Olive B. O'Connor Foundation ◇

c/o Partners Trust Bank, Trust Dept.
P.O. Box 1056
Binghamton, NY   13902-1056   (607) 538-9248
Contact: Donald F. Bishop II, Exec. Dir.
FAX: (607) 538-9136; Application address: P.O. Box D, Hobart, NY 13788

Trust established in 1965 in NY.
Donor: Olive B. O'Connor†.
Foundation type: Independent foundation.
Financial data (yr. ended 12/31/05): Assets, $65,422,482 (M); expenditures, $3,339,614; qualifying distributions, $2,949,146; giving activities include $2,696,484 for 209 grants (high: $500,000; low: $325; average: $1,000–$25,000).
Purpose and activities: Emphasis on quality of life, including hospitals, libraries, community centers, higher education, nursing and other vocational education, child development and youth agencies, religious organizations, museums, and historic restoration; support also for civic affairs and town, village, and environmental conservation and improvement.
Fields of interest: Visual arts, architecture; Museums; Performing arts; History/archaeology; Historic preservation/historical societies; Arts; Education, early childhood education; Child development, education; Vocational education; Higher education; Business school/education; Libraries/library science; Environment, natural resources; Environment; Animal welfare; Animals/ wildlife, preservation/protection; Hospitals (general); Nursing care; Substance abuse, services; Alcoholism; Crime/violence prevention, youth; Employment; Agriculture; Housing/shelter, development; Human services; Children/youth, services; Child development, services; Women,

centers/services; Rural development; Community development; Federated giving programs; Religious federated giving programs; Biological sciences; Economics; Government/public administration; Christian agencies & churches; Protestant agencies & churches; Religion; Women; Economically disadvantaged.

Type of support: Continuing support; Annual campaigns; Capital campaigns; Building/renovation; Equipment; Land acquisition; Endowments; Emergency funds; Program development; Conferences/seminars; Publication; Seed money; Scholarship funds; Research; Technical assistance; Program-related investments/loans; Matching/challenge support.

Limitations: Giving primarily in Delaware County, NY, and 7 contiguous rural counties in upstate NY (Broome, Chenango, Greene, Otsego, Schoharie, Sullivan, and Ulster). No grants to individuals, or for operating budgets, or deficit financing.

Publications: Application guidelines; Multi-year report; Program policy statement.

Application information: Complete application guidelines and form are available by contacting the foundation. Application form required.

> Initial approach: Letter or telephone
> Copies of proposal: 1
> Deadline(s): Apr. 1 and Sept. 1; 1st of each month for grants under $5,000
> Board meeting date(s): May or June and Sept. or Oct.; committee meets monthly to consider grants under $5,000
> Final notification: 7 to 10 days after semiannual meeting

Officers and Directors:* Robert L. Bishop II,* Chair.; Charlotte Bishop Hill,* Vice-Chair.; Donald F. Bishop II, Pres. and Exec. Dir.; Pamela Hill, Secy.-Treas.; Amy Bishop; Suzanne Hill; Eugene Peckham.

Trustee: Partners Trust Bank.

Number of staff: 2 full-time professional.

EIN: 166063485

Selected grants: The following grants were reported in 2004.

$521,986 to Catskill Revitalization Corporation, Stamford, NY. 3 grants: $124,656, $388,200, $9,130

$165,000 to Catskill Forest Association, Arkville, NY. 2 grants: $35,000, $130,000

$64,000 to Hanford Mills Museum, East Meredith, NY. 2 grants: $40,000, $24,000

$62,000 to College Foundation at Delhi, Delhi, NY.

$10,000 to Broome Community College Foundation, Binghamton, NY.

$10,000 to West Kortright Center, East Meredith, NY.

6646

The O'Herron Family Foundation ◇

(formerly Jonathan & Shirley O'Herron Foundation)
c/o Lazard, LLC
30 Rockefeller Plz.
New York, NY 10020-2102
Contact: Jonathan O'Herron, Pres.

Established in 1984 in NY.

Donors: Jonathan O'Herron; Shirley O'Herron‡.

Foundation type: Independent foundation.

Financial data (yr. ended 6/30/05): Assets, $125,027 (M); gifts received, $516,320; expenditures, $414,070; qualifying distributions, $411,866; giving activities include $410,950 for 42 grants (high: $60,000; low: $500).

Purpose and activities: Giving primarily for higher and other education; funding also for health associations, human services, and Roman Catholic churches.

Fields of interest: Higher education; Business school/education; Medical school/education; Education; Health organizations, association; Human services; American Red Cross; Roman Catholic agencies & churches.

Type of support: General/operating support; Scholarship funds.

Limitations: Giving primarily in CT, MA, NY, and VT. No grants to individuals.

Application information: Application form not required.

> Initial approach: Letter
> Deadline(s): None

Officers and Directors:* Jonathan O'Herron,* Pres.; Charles M. Stieglitz,* V.P.; Paul Cohen,* Secy.-Treas.

EIN: 133244207

Selected grants: The following grants were reported in 2005.

$77,500 to Saint Pauls School, Concord, NH. 2 grants: $60,000, $17,500

$49,000 to New Canaan Country School, New Canaan, CT. 2 grants: $25,000, $24,000

$35,000 to Quissett Harbor Preservation Trust, Falmouth, MA.

$25,000 to Fordham University, New York, NY.

$21,700 to Horizons Student Enrichment Program, New Canaan, CT.

$10,000 to Diocese of Bridgeport, Bridgeport, CT.

$10,000 to Saint Johns Church, Salisbury, CT.

$7,500 to Greenwich Academy, Greenwich, CT.

6647

The T. D. & M. A. O'Malley Foundation, Inc. ◇

c/o Berdon, LLP
360 Madison Ave.
New York, NY 10017-1111

Established in 1985 in CT.

Donor: Thomas D. O'Malley.

Foundation type: Independent foundation.

Financial data (yr. ended 9/30/05): Assets, $18,294,447 (M); gifts received, $11,231,500; expenditures, $2,414,570; qualifying distributions, $2,406,270; giving activities include $2,397,922 for 22 grants (high: $1,000,000; low: $500).

Purpose and activities: Giving primarily for health care and medical research, particularly children's health; funding also for education, and children and youth services.

Fields of interest: Higher education; Education; Hospitals (general); Medical research, institute; Children/youth, services.

Limitations: Applications not accepted. Giving primarily in CT and New York, NY; some funding nationally. No grants to individuals.

Application information: Contributes only to pre-selected organizations.

Officers: Thomas D. O'Malley, Pres. and Treas.; Mary Alice O'Malley, V.P. and Secy.; Timothy O'Malley, Treas.

EIN: 061157580

Selected grants: The following grants were reported in 2004.

$500,000 to Childrens National Medical Center, DC.

$100,000 to Greenwich Hospital, Greenwich, CT.

$60,000 to American Red Cross, Greenwich, CT.

$60,000 to Brunswick School, Greenwich, CT.

$25,000 to Boston College, Chestnut Hill, MA.

$25,000 to Manhattan College, Riverdale, NY.

$20,000 to Stamford Hospital, Stamford, CT.

$5,000 to Xavier High School, New York, NY.

$1,450 to Kids in Crisis, Cos Cob, CT.

$500 to Greenwich Land Trust, Greenwich, CT.

6648

The O'Malley Foundation, Inc. ◇

3 Old Farm Rd.
Amawalk, NY 10501

Established in 1987 in NY.

Donors: James J. O'Malley; Contractors Register, Inc.

Foundation type: Independent foundation.

Financial data (yr. ended 12/31/05): Assets, $519,357 (M); gifts received, $597,840; expenditures, $554,200; qualifying distributions, $554,200; giving activities include $554,100 for grants.

Fields of interest: Performing arts, music; Elementary/secondary education; Christian agencies & churches; Religion.

Type of support: General/operating support.

Limitations: Applications not accepted. Giving primarily in Westchester County and New York, NY. No grants to individuals.

Application information: Unsolicited requests for funds not accepted.

Officers: James J. O'Malley, Pres.; Mary O'Malley, Treas.

Director: Sheila O'Malley.

EIN: 133447954

6649

Cyril F. and Marie E. O'Neil Foundation ◇

c/o Sacks Press & Lacher
600 3rd Ave.
New York, NY 10016
Contact: Ralph M. O'Neil, Pres.

Incorporated in 1957 in OH.

Donor: Members of the O'Neil family.

Foundation type: Independent foundation.

Financial data (yr. ended 12/31/05): Assets, $6,405,757 (M); expenditures, $380,671; qualifying distributions, $330,000; giving activities include $330,000 for grants.

Purpose and activities: Giving primarily for education, health care, and for religious purposes.

Fields of interest: Secondary school/education; Higher education; Health care; Roman Catholic agencies & churches.

Limitations: Applications not accepted. Giving primarily in NY. No grants to individuals.

Application information: Contributes only to pre-selected organizations.

Officers: Ralph M. O'Neil, Pres.; Priscilla O'Neil, V.P.

EIN: 346523819

Selected grants: The following grants were reported in 2004.

$300,000 to Maryknoll Fathers and Brothers.

$205,000 to Maryknoll Sisters of Saint Dominic, New York, NY.

$65,000 to Cleveland Clinic, Cleveland, OH.

$45,000 to Saint Timothys School, Stevenson, MD.

$36,000 to Saint Michaels Church.

$15,500 to Colorado Academy, Denver, CO.

$12,500 to Maryknoll Cloister.

$12,000 to University School.
$11,750 to Vail Valley Foundation, Vail, CO.
$6,500 to Freedom Institute, New York, NY.

6650
The Timothy J. and Linda D. O'Neill Foundation ✧
c/o Goldman Sachs & Co., Family Office
1 New York Plz., 40th Fl.
New York, NY   10004

Established in 1991 in NY.
Donor: Timothy J. O'Neill.
Foundation type: Independent foundation.
Financial data (yr. ended 4/30/06): Assets, $13,338,135 (M); gifts received, $954,038; expenditures, $1,390,017; qualifying distributions, $1,234,722; giving activities include $1,234,722 for 34 grants (high: $400,000; low: $20).
Fields of interest: Elementary/secondary education; Higher education; Health organizations; Human services.
Limitations: Applications not accepted. Giving primarily in CT, Washington DC, and NY. No grants to individuals.
Application information: Contributes only to pre-selected organizations.
Trustees: Linda D. O'Neill; Timothy J. O'Neill.
EIN: 133642501
Selected grants: The following grants were reported in 2004.
$600,000 to Georgetown University, DC. 4 grants: $200,000 (For general support), $100,000 (For general support), $100,000 (For general support), $200,000 (For general support).
$75,000 to Brunswick School, Greenwich, CT. 2 grants: $25,000 (For general support), $50,000 (For general support).
$10,000 to Cystic Fibrosis Association of Greater New York, New York, NY. For general support.
$10,000 to Cystic Fibrosis Foundation, New York, NY.
$10,000 to Greenwich Academy, Greenwich, CT. For capital campaign.
$10,000 to New York Foundling Hospital, New York, NY. For general support.

6651
The O'Shea Family Foundation ✧
(formerly The Robert J. and Michele K. O'Shea Foundation)
c/o BCRS Assocs., LLC
100 Wall St., 11th Fl.
New York, NY   10005

Established in 1996 in NJ.
Donor: Robert J. O'Shea.
Foundation type: Independent foundation.
Financial data (yr. ended 10/31/05): Assets, $10,368,002 (M); gifts received, $500; expenditures, $429,155; qualifying distributions, $417,133; giving activities include $415,351 for 63 grants (high: $50,000; low: $100).
Fields of interest: Hospitals (general); Health organizations, association; Human services; Roman Catholic agencies & churches.
Limitations: Applications not accepted. Giving primarily in NJ, with some emphasis on Wyckoff. No grants to individuals or for scholarships; no loans.
Application information: Contributes only to pre-selected organizations.

Trustees: Michele K. O'Shea; Robert J. O'Shea.
EIN: 133926380
Selected grants: The following grants were reported in 2005.
$35,000 to Covenant House, New York, NY.
$25,000 to New York-Presbyterian Hospital, New York, NY.
$15,000 to World Emergency Relief, Carlsbad, CA.
$10,000 to Childrens Hunger Fund, Mission Hills, CA.
$10,000 to Oasis Haven for Women and Children, Paterson, NJ.
$10,000 to Valley Hospital Foundation, Ridgewood, NJ.
$7,500 to Catholic Charities of the Archdiocese of Newark, Newark, NJ. 2 grants: $2,500, $5,000
$5,000 to UNICEF, DC.

6652
The O'Sullivan Children Foundation, Inc. ✧
4 Bridle Path Dr.
Old Westbury, NY   11568   (516) 334-3209

Established in 1981 in NY.
Donors: Kevin P. O'Sullivan†; Carole O'Sullivan.
Foundation type: Independent foundation.
Financial data (yr. ended 9/30/05): Assets, $3,692,711 (M); gifts received, $43,840; expenditures, $706,253; qualifying distributions, $566,420; giving activities include $450,005 for 69 grants (high: $50,000; low: $45).
Purpose and activities: Giving primarily for education, health associations and hospitals, children, youth, family and social services, and Roman Catholic schools and organizations; funding also for a public television station.
Fields of interest: Media, television; Education; Hospitals (general); Health organizations; Human services; Children/youth, services; Family services; International human rights; Roman Catholic federated giving programs.
Type of support: Capital campaigns; Endowments; Scholarships—to individuals.
Limitations: Applications not accepted. Giving primarily in the greater metropolitan New York, NY, area, with some emphasis on Long Island.
Application information: Unsolicited requests for funds not accepted.
Officers and Director: * Carole O'Sullivan,* Exec. V.P.; Joseph W. Muldoon, Sr. V.P. and Secy.
Number of staff: 1 full-time professional.
EIN: 133126389
Selected grants: The following grants were reported in 2005.
$50,000 to Robert F. Kennedy Memorial, DC.
$45,000 to Catholic Home Bureau, New York, NY.
$10,000 to American Red Cross, Princeton, NJ.
$6,500 to National Ethnic Coalition of Organizations, New York, NY.
$6,000 to LIFT, Trenton, NJ.
$5,000 to Parkinsons Disease Foundation, New York, NY.
$4,750 to National Alliance for Autism Research, Princeton, NJ.
$2,005 to Mustard Seed Communities, Tucker, GA.
$250 to Girls and Boys Town, Boys Town, NE.

6653
The O'Toole Family Foundation ✧ ☆
c/o Ayco Company
P.O. Box 15014
Albany, NY   12212-5014

Established in 1993 in NJ.
Donor: Terence M. O'Toole.
Foundation type: Independent foundation.
Financial data (yr. ended 3/31/06): Assets, $9,995,592 (M); gifts received, $1,301,800; expenditures, $627,033; qualifying distributions, $584,015; giving activities include $584,015 for 22 grants (high: $500,000; low: $50).
Fields of interest: Arts; Higher education; Education; Health organizations, association; Medical research, institute; Human services; Children/youth, services.
Limitations: Applications not accepted. Giving primarily in CA, NJ, and NY. No grants to individuals; no loans.
Application information: Contributes only to pre-selected organizations.
Trustees: Paula M. O'Toole; Terence M. O'Toole.
EIN: 133748068
Selected grants: The following grants were reported in 2005.
$500,000 to Villanova University, Villanova, PA.
$5,000 to Rosemont College, Rosemont, PA.
$1,000 to Literacy Partners, New York, NY.
$500 to University of Pennsylvania, Philadelphia, PA.
$250 to Summit Speech School, New Providence, NJ.

6654
Theresa and Edward O'Toole Foundation ▼ ✧
c/o The Bank of New York, Tax Dept.
1 Wall St., 28th Fl.
New York, NY   10286   (212) 635-1622

Established in 1971.
Donor: Theresa O'Toole†.
Foundation type: Independent foundation.
Financial data (yr. ended 6/30/05): Assets, $63,826,906 (M); expenditures, $451,236; qualifying distributions, $4,207,821; giving activities include $3,965,000 for 27 grants (high: $1,000,000; low: $10,000; average: $25,000–$500,000).
Purpose and activities: Giving primarily for religious and educational purposes, as well as for the performing arts, medical purposes, public health, population research, and certain environmental and public affairs areas.
Fields of interest: Performing arts; Education; Hospitals (general); Medical research, institute; Human services; Roman Catholic federated giving programs; Roman Catholic agencies & churches.
Type of support: General/operating support; Continuing support; Annual campaigns; Capital campaigns; Building/renovation; Emergency funds; Program development; Seed money; Research; Matching/challenge support.
Limitations: Applications not accepted. Giving primarily in FL, NJ, and NY. No grants to individuals, or for endowment funds, scholarships, or fellowships; no loans.
Application information: Contributes only to pre-selected organizations.
Board meeting date(s): Apr. and Oct.

Trustees: Bert Degheri; The Bank of New York.
EIN: 136350175
Selected grants: The following grants were reported in 2005.
$1,500,000 to University of San Diego, San Diego, CA. 2 grants: $1,000,000 (For operating support), $500,000 (For operating support).
$785,000 to Saint Catherines Church. 3 grants: $275,000 (For operating support), $235,000 (For operating support), $275,000 (For operating support).
$500,000 to University of Southern California, Los Angeles, CA. For operating support for Our Savior Parish and Catholic Center.
$175,000 to Servants of Relief for Incurable Cancer, Hawthorne, NY. 2 grants: $75,000 (For operating support), $100,000 (For operating support).
$100,000 to Xavier Society for the Blind, New York, NY. For operating support.
$50,000 to Saint Gabriels Church. For operating support.

6655
OCLO, Inc. ✧
c/o Hertz, Herson & Co., LLP
2 Park Ave., Ste. 1500
New York, NY 10016

Established in 1999 in DE and NY.
Donors: Susan R. Wexner; Naon, Inc.
Foundation type: Independent foundation.
Financial data (yr. ended 12/31/05): Assets, $37,691,834 (M); expenditures, $1,899,812; qualifying distributions, $956,106; giving activities include $945,000 for 1 grant.
Fields of interest: Federated giving programs.
Limitations: Applications not accepted. Giving primarily in NY, NY. No grants to individuals.
Application information: Contributes only to pre-selected organizations.
Officer and Director:* Susan R. Wexner,* Pres. and Secy.-Treas.
EIN: 522171831
Selected grants: The following grants were reported in 2003.
$1,625,000 to Vanguard Charitable Endowment Program, Southeastern, PA.

6656
Sylvan and Ann Oestreicher Foundation, Inc. ✧
c/o Marks Paneth & Shron, LLP
622 3rd Ave.
New York, NY 10017

Incorporated in 1948 in NY.
Donor: Sylvan Oestreicher†.
Foundation type: Independent foundation.
Financial data (yr. ended 4/30/05): Assets, $11,729,716 (M); expenditures, $486,770; qualifying distributions, $459,406; giving activities include $448,690 for 119 grants (high: $50,000; low: $200).
Purpose and activities: Giving primarily for health associations, particularly for cancer research, as well as for the arts, education, children, youth and social services, Roman Catholic organizations, and to organizations for people who are blind.
Fields of interest: Arts; Higher education; Education; Animal welfare; Hospitals (general);

Health organizations, association; Cancer research; Human services; Children/youth, services; Roman Catholic federated giving programs; Roman Catholic agencies & churches; Blind/visually impaired; Native Americans/American Indians.
Limitations: Applications not accepted. Giving primarily in Chicago, IL and NY.
Application information: Contributes only to pre-selected organizations.
Officer: Ann Oestreicher, Pres.
EIN: 136085974
Selected grants: The following grants were reported in 2005.
$25,000 to Richard Nixon Library and Birthplace Foundation, Yorba Linda, CA.
$25,000 to W N E T Channel 13, New York, NY.
$10,200 to Calvary Fund, Bronx, NY.
$10,000 to Carter Center, Atlanta, GA.
$8,000 to Alfred E. Smith Memorial Foundation, New York, NY.
$8,000 to Hospital for Special Surgery, New York, NY.
$5,000 to Catholic Charities.
$5,000 to United Cerebral Palsy Association, Kansas City, MO.
$4,000 to Manhattan School of Music, New York, NY.
$1,700 to Bar Harbor Music Festival, Bar Harbor, ME.

6657
Ralph E. Ogden Foundation, Inc. ✧
Pleasant Hill Rd.
P.O. Box 290
Mountainville, NY 10953

Incorporated in 1947 in DE.
Donors: Ralph E. Ogden†; H. Peter Stern; Margaret H. Ogden†.
Foundation type: Independent foundation.
Financial data (yr. ended 12/31/03): Assets, $34,463,593 (M); expenditures, $2,175,036; qualifying distributions, $1,767,963; giving activities include $1,727,300 for 42 grants (high: $1,410,000; low: $500; average: $1,000–$25,000).
Purpose and activities: Support primarily for the arts, especially for a local art center; minor support for international understanding, higher education, and community welfare.
Fields of interest: Museums (art).
Limitations: Applications not accepted. Giving primarily in Mountainville and New York, NY. No grants to individuals.
Application information: Contributes only to pre-selected organizations.
Officers and Trustees:* H. Peter Stern,* Pres.; Leslie A. Jacobson,* V.P.; Georgene Zlock, Secy.; Eugene L. Cohan,* Treas.; Frederick Lubcher; Beatrice Stern; Elisabeth Ellen Stern; John Peter Stern.
EIN: 141455902

6658
The Norio Ohga Foundation ✧
550 Madison Ave., 35th Fl.
New York, NY 10022
Application address: c/o Sony Electronics, Inc., attn.: Kenneth Nees, 12451 Gateway Blvd., Fort Myers, FL 33913

Established in 1991 in NY.
Donor: Sony Corp. of America.
Foundation type: Independent foundation.
Financial data (yr. ended 12/31/05): Assets, $6,476,559 (M); expenditures, $563,391; qualifying distributions, $560,000; giving activities include $560,000 for 3 grants (high: $500,000; low: $10,000).
Purpose and activities: Support for the arts, with giving primarily for the benefit of the Tokyo Philharmonic Orchestra.
Fields of interest: Arts, association; Performing arts, orchestra (symphony).
Type of support: General/operating support; Capital campaigns; Scholarship funds.
Limitations: Giving primarily in the U.S. and in Tokyo, Japan. No grants to individuals.
Application information:
Initial approach: Letter
Deadline(s): None
Officers and Directors:* Norio Ohga,* Pres.; Kenneth L. Nees,* V.P. and Secy.; H. Paul Burak,* V.P.; Midori Ohga,* V.P.
EIN: 133617866
Selected grants: The following grants were reported in 2003.
$500,000 to Tokyo Philharmonic Orchestra, Tokyo, Japan. For operating support.

6659
The Ohrstrom Foundation, Inc. ✧
c/o TCC Group
50 E. 42nd St., 19th Fl.
New York, NY 10017 (212) 949-0990, ext. 225
Contact: Carol Gallo

Incorporated in 1953 in DE.
Donor: Members of the Ohrstrom family.
Foundation type: Independent foundation.
Financial data (yr. ended 5/31/05): Assets, $70,916,745 (M); expenditures, $3,361,809; qualifying distributions, $3,232,867; giving activities include $3,051,074 for 25 grants (high: $732,905; low: $5,000).
Purpose and activities: Emphasis on elementary, secondary, and higher education; support also for civic affairs, conservation, hospitals and medical research, and museums.
Fields of interest: Museums; Education, fund raising/fund distribution; Elementary/secondary education; Elementary school/education; Secondary school/education; Higher education; Libraries/library science; Environment, natural resources; Environment; Animal welfare; Hospitals (general); Alcoholism; Medical research, institute; Government/public administration; Religion.
Type of support: General/operating support; Continuing support; Annual campaigns; Building/renovation; Equipment; Land acquisition; Endowments; Emergency funds; Program development; Seed money; Matching/challenge support.
Limitations: Applications not accepted. Giving primarily in VA. No grants to individuals, or for deficit financing, scholarships, fellowships, research, special projects, publications, or conferences; no loans.
Application information: Contributes only to pre-selected organizations.
Officers and Directors:* George F. Ohrstrom,* Pres.; George L. Ohrstrom, Jr.,* Pres. Emeritus; Magalen O. Bryant,* V.P.; Peter A. Kalat,* Secy.; Dorothy Barry, Treas.; W. Carey Crane II; Winifred O.

Nichols; Kristiane C. Graham; Clarke Ohrstrom; George L. Ohrstrom II; Richard R. Ohrstrom.
EIN: 546039966
Selected grants: The following grants were reported in 2005.
$732,905 to Vanguard Charitable Endowment Program, Southeastern, PA.
$125,000 to Shenandoah Valley Discovery Museum, Winchester, VA. For capacity building.
$100,000 to Wakefield School, The Plains, VA. For capital campaign.
$60,000 to EARTH University Foundation, Atlanta, GA. For endowed scholarship.
$50,000 to Environmental Defense, DC. For project to transition U.S. fisheries to a market-based system.
$50,000 to Falmouth Heritage Renewal, The Plains, VA. For position of development and communication director.
$50,000 to Kent School, Kent, CT. For construction of new faculty housing.
$50,000 to Lord Fairfax Community College Educational Foundation, Middletown, VA. For building endowment to fund student scholarships.
$25,000 to Committee to Reduce Infection Deaths, New York, NY. For forums for hospital executives on prevention of infection.
$20,000 to Fauquier Hospital Foundation, Warrenton, VA. For capital campaign for renovation of emergency department.

6660
The John R. Oishei Foundation ▼
1 HSBC Ctr., Ste. 3650
Buffalo, NY 14203 (716) 856-9490
Contact: Thomas E. Baker, Pres.
FAX: (716) 856-9493; E-mail: info@oisheifdt.org; URL: http://www.oisheifdt.org

Incorporated in 1941 in NY.
Donors: Peter C. Cornell Trust; John R. Oishei; R. John Oishei†; Jean R. Oshei; Oishei Consolidated Trust No. 1; Oishei Consolidated Trust No. 2.
Foundation type: Independent foundation.
Financial data (yr. ended 12/31/05): Assets, $287,522,534 (M); gifts received, $485,896; expenditures, $18,285,222; qualifying distributions, $15,336,112; giving activities include $13,589,957 for 95 grants (high: $1,500,000; low: $1,000; average: $10,000–$200,000); and $700,000 for 2 loans/program-related investments (high: $500,000; low: $200,000).
Purpose and activities: Emphasis on medical research, health care, higher and secondary education, cultural, social, civic and other charitable needs of the community. Grants are restricted to qualified nonprofit organizations in the Buffalo, NY area.
Fields of interest: Arts; Secondary school/education; Higher education; Health care; Medical research, institute; Human services; Community development; Science, research.
Type of support: Program-related investments/loans; Program evaluation; Program development; Professorships; Seed money; Curriculum development; Scholarship funds; Research; Matching/challenge support.
Limitations: Giving limited to the Buffalo, NY, area. No support for religious organizations for sectarian or propagation of faith purposes. Generally, no grants to individuals, including scholarships and fellowships (except within specific foundation

programs), or for deficit financing, endowment, ongoing program expenses, general operating expenses, travel, conferences, capital expenditures, seminars, workshops or fundraising.
Publications: Annual report; Grants list; Informational brochure (including application guidelines).
Application information: Application form not required.
Initial approach: Letter of inquiry; Telephone or submission of brief proposal summary
Copies of proposal: 1
Deadline(s): None
Board meeting date(s): Bimonthly
Final notification: Within 3 to 6 months
Officers and Directors:* James M. Wadsworth,* Chair.; Mary S. Martino,* Vice-Chair.; Thomas E. Baker,* Pres.; Gayle L. Houck, Secy.; Allan R. Wiegley,* Treas.; Robert M. Bennett; Ruth D. Bryant; Clotilde Perez-Bode Dedecker; Christopher T. Dunstan; Erland E. Kailbourne.
Number of staff: 3 full-time professional; 1 full-time support.
EIN: 160874319
Selected grants: The following grants were reported in 2004.
$1,032,000 to University of Buffalo Foundation, Buffalo, NY. 4 grants: $250,000 (To establish interdisciplinary Center for Research in Cardiovascular Medicine), $341,000 (For recruitment of leading scientist and development of program in Nanomedicine), $141,000 (For Center of Excellence in Augmentative Communication), $300,000 (To establish Ira G. Ross Eye Institute in cooperation with Olmsted Center for the Visually Impaired and School of Medicine).
$500,000 to Sheas Performing Arts Center, Buffalo, NY. For major funding initiative to address both fiscal and physical restoration.
$480,000 to Roswell Park Alliance Foundation, Buffalo, NY. For Center for Cancer Genetics and Pharmacology at Buffalo Niagara Life Sciences Complex.
$250,000 to Buffalo State College Foundation, Buffalo, NY. For Center of Excellence in Urban and Rural Education.
$107,000 to State University of New York Empire State College, Saratoga Springs, NY. For Fast-Track-to-the-Classroom Master of Arts in Teaching Program.
$75,000 to Buffalo Philharmonic Orchestra, Buffalo, NY. For reestablishment of summer concert series at Artpark.
$25,000 to Saint Vincent de Paul Society, Buffalo, NY. For basic human needs.

6661
Olayan Charitable Trust ✧
c/o Olayan America Corp.
505 Park Ave., 11th Fl.
New York, NY 10022-9319

Established in 1993 in NY.
Foundation type: Independent foundation.
Financial data (yr. ended 12/31/04): Assets, $532,623 (M); expenditures, $1,232,390; qualifying distributions, $1,222,790; giving activities include $1,222,790 for 11 grants (high: $1,000,000; low: $3,500).
Purpose and activities: Giving primarily for health and medical care in the Middle East.

Fields of interest: Higher education; Health care; Medical research, institute; Human services.
International interests: Middle East.
Limitations: Applications not accepted. Giving on an international basis. No grants to individuals.
Application information: Contributes only to pre-selected organizations.
Trustees: Nazeeh S. Habachy; Hutham S. Olayan.
EIN: 137031747
Selected grants: The following grants were reported in 2003.
$100,000 to Columbia University, New York, NY.
$50,000 to Institute for International Economics, DC.
$50,000 to Rockefeller University, New York, NY.
$25,000 to Memorial Sloan-Kettering Cancer Center, New York, NY.
$21,600 to International Management Education Foundation (INSEAD), Fontainebleau, France. .
$15,000 to Middle East Policy Council, DC.
$10,000 to American Near East Refugee Aid, DC.
$10,000 to Americans for Middle East Understanding, New York, NY.
$5,850 to Southern Illinois University, Edwardsville, IL.
$5,000 to International Documentary Foundation, Los Angeles, CA.

6662
Olive Bridge Fund, Inc. ✧
c/o Ralph E. Hansmann
500 5th Ave., 50th Fl.
New York, NY 10110 (212) 391-8960

Incorporated in 1952 in NY.
Donors: Harold F. Linder†; Joshua Steiner; Susan E. Linder; Elizabeth Steiner; Daniel L. Steiner; Prudence L. Steiner.
Foundation type: Independent foundation.
Financial data (yr. ended 12/31/04): Assets, $35,363,260 (M); gifts received, $157,750; expenditures, $2,739,114; qualifying distributions, $2,463,535; giving activities include $2,305,804 for 175 grants (high: $1,000,000; low: $25).
Purpose and activities: Giving primarily for higher education.
Fields of interest: Performing arts, music; Performing arts, education; Higher education; Education; Health care; Health organizations, association; Human services; Jewish federated giving programs.
Type of support: General/operating support.
Limitations: Applications not accepted. Giving primarily in MA and NY. No grants to individuals.
Application information: Contributes only to pre-selected organizations.
Officers and Directors:* Daniel L. Steiner,* Pres.; Susan E. Linder,* V.P. and Secy.; William T. Golden,* V.P. and Treas.; Prudence L. Steiner,* V.P.; Anna Lou Dehavenon; Ralph E. Hansmann; William M. Kelly.
EIN: 136161669
Selected grants: The following grants were reported in 2003.
$750,000 to Harvard University, Cambridge, MA.
$547,000 to New England Conservatory of Music, Boston, MA.
$70,000 to Combined Jewish Philanthropies of Greater Boston, Boston, MA.
$7,500 to P.E.F. Israel Endowment Funds, New York, NY.
$2,000 to Boston Arts Academy, Boston, MA.
$1,000 to Lenox Hill Hospital, New York, NY.

$1,000 to Memorial Sloan-Kettering Cancer Center, New York, NY.
$1,000 to Project Step, Boston, MA.
$500 to Hamilton College, Clinton, NY.
$100 to Fordham University, Bronx, NY.

6663
Morton & Carole Olshan Foundation ◇
c/o Morton Olshan, Mall Properties, Inc.
654 Madison Ave.
New York, NY 10021

Established in 1991 in NY.
Donor: Morton Olshan.
Foundation type: Independent foundation.
Financial data (yr. ended 12/31/05): Assets, $20,911 (M); gifts received, $550,000; expenditures, $548,198; qualifying distributions, $548,172; giving activities include $548,172 for 31 grants (high: $165,000; low: $40).
Fields of interest: Education; Human services; Jewish federated giving programs; Jewish agencies & temples.
Limitations: Applications not accepted. Giving primarily in NY. No grants to individuals.
Application information: Contributes only to pre-selected organizations.
Officers and Directors:* Morton Olshan,* Pres.; Carole Olshan,* V.P.; Robert Steinberg.
EIN: 133601794
Selected grants: The following grants were reported in 2004.
$115,480 to Jewish Center of the Hamptons, East Hampton, NY.
$115,000 to Horace Mann School, Riverdale, NY.
$15,000 to Columbus Coalition Against Family Violence, Columbus, OH.
$15,000 to Graduate Center, City University of New York, New York, NY.

6664
The Opatrny Family Foundation ◇
(formerly Donald C. and Judith T. Opatrny, Jr. Charitable Foundation)
c/o BCRS Group/Marcum & Kliegman, LLP
100 Wall St., 11th Fl.
New York, NY 10005

Established in 1988 in NY.
Donor: Donald C. Opatrny, Jr.
Foundation type: Independent foundation.
Financial data (yr. ended 5/31/05): Assets, $8,317,882 (M); gifts received, $2,983,750; expenditures, $338,995; qualifying distributions, $335,895; giving activities include $335,550 for 34 grants (high: $100,000; low: $100).
Purpose and activities: Giving primarily for education.
Fields of interest: Arts; Education; Health organizations, association; Human services.
Limitations: Applications not accepted. Giving primarily in Greenwich, CT. No grants to individuals.
Application information: Contributes only to pre-selected organizations.
Trustees: Donald C. Opatrny, Jr.; Judith T. Opatrny.
EIN: 133502411
Selected grants: The following grants were reported in 2004.
$115,000 to Cornell University, Ithaca, NY. 2 grants: $100,000 (For general support),

$15,000 to College of Arts and Sciences (For general support).
$100,000 to Greenwich Hospital, Greenwich, CT. For general support.
$100,000 to Lawrenceville School, Lawrenceville, NJ. For general support.
$50,000 to Nantucket Cottage Hospital, Nantucket, MA. For general support.
$50,000 to Oxford Academy, Westbrook, CT. For general support.
$20,000 to Aldrich Contemporary Art Museum, Ridgefield, CT. For general support.
$10,000 to Round Hill Community Church, Greenwich, CT. For general support.
$10,000 to Suffield Academy, Suffield, CT. For general support.
$10,000 to YWCA of Greenwich, Greenwich, CT. For general support.

6665
Open Society Institute ▼
400 W. 59th St.
New York, NY 10019 (212) 548-0600
Contact: Inquiry Mgr.
FAX: (212) 548-4600; *URL:* http://www.soros.org

Established in 1993 in NY.
Donor: George Soros.
Foundation type: Operating foundation.
Financial data (yr. ended 12/31/05): Assets, $858,935,162 (M); expenditures, $113,704,430; qualifying distributions, $45,565,966; giving activities include $45,565,966 for grants.
Purpose and activities: The Open Society Institute (OSI), a private operating and grantmaking foundation, aims to shape public policy to promote democratic governance, human rights, and economic, legal, and social reform. On a local level, OSI implements a range of initiatives to support the rule of law, education, public health, and independent media. At the same time, OSI works to build alliances across borders and continents on issues such as combating corruption and rights abuses. OSI was created in 1993 by investor and philanthropist George Soros to support his foundations in Central and Eastern Europe and the former Soviet Union. Those foundations were established, starting in 1984, to help countries make the transition from communism. OSI has expanded the activities of the Soros foundations network to other areas of the world where the transition to democracy is of particular concern. The Soros foundations network encompasses more than 60 countries, including the United States.
Fields of interest: Media/communications; Arts; Education; Public health; International economic development; International human rights; Law/international law.
Type of support: General/operating support; Equipment; Program development; Professorships; Fellowships; Internship funds; Scholarship funds; Research; Program-related investments/loans; Employee matching gifts; Grants to individuals; Scholarships—to individuals; In-kind gifts.
Limitations: Giving on a national and international basis.
Publications: Annual report; Newsletter; Program policy statement.
Application information: For program application guidelines and deadlines see foundation Web site.

The site includes a wizard to help determine eligibility and submit an inquiry electronically.
Initial approach: Letter of inquiry, only if grantseeker does not have internet access
Officers and Trustees:* George Soros,* Chair.; Aryeh Neier, C.E.O. and Pres.; Stewart J. Paperin, Exec. V.P. and Treas.; Gara LaMarche, V.P. and Dir., U.S. Progs.; Stephen Gutmann, Secy. and Audit. Dir.; Maija Arbolino, C.F.O.; Ricardo A. Castro, Genl. Counsel and Legal Off.; Morton Halperin, Dir., OSI Washington; Leon Botstein; Geoffrey Canada; Joan B. Dunlop; Lani Guinier; David Rothman; Thomas M. Scanlon, Jr.; John G. Simon; Jonathan Soros; Herbert Sturz.
EIN: 137029285
Selected grants: The following grants were reported in 2004.
$4,425,000 to Media Development Loan Fund, New York, NY. 2 grants: $2,500,000 (For PRI pool), $1,925,000 (For operating and program support).
$4,000,000 to Trust for Civil Society in Central and Eastern Europe, DC. To establish Trust, including program support in New York City.
$2,000,000 to New Visions for Public Schools, New York, NY. To implement New Century High Schools for New York City program.
$808,248 to Baltic-American Partnership Fund, New York, NY. For general support.
$800,000 to Sundance Institute, Beverly Hills, CA. To operate Sundance Documentary Fund.
$750,000 to Parrish Art Museum, Southampton, NY. For general support.
$667,000 to Calvert Social Investment Foundation, Bethesda, MD. For credit enhancements supporting Foundation loan to Media Development Loan Fund.
$600,000 to Microfinance Management Institute, DC.
$500,000 to Brooklyn Institute of Arts and Sciences, Brooklyn, NY. For general support.

6666
Leo Oppenheimer & Flora Oppenheimer Haas Foundation ◇
c/o JPMorgan Chase Bank, N.A.
345 Park Ave., 4th Fl.
New York, NY 10154
Contact: Jacqueline Elias, V.P., JPMorgan Chase Bank, N.A.

Trust established in 1950 in NY.
Donor: Flora Oppenheimer Haas†.
Foundation type: Independent foundation.
Financial data (yr. ended 12/31/04): Assets, $18,754,615 (M); expenditures, $861,698; qualifying distributions, $766,727; giving activities include $705,000 for 20 grants (high: $100,000; low: $15,000).
Purpose and activities: Giving to programs and agencies that provide care, aid and comfort to needy Jewish children; particular interest in helping Jewish children recovering from illness; funding also for other Jewish organizations.
Fields of interest: Health organizations, association; Children/youth, services; Jewish federated giving programs; Jewish agencies & temples.
Type of support: General/operating support.
Limitations: Applications not accepted. Giving primarily in the New York, NY, metropolitan area. No support for hospitals. No grants to individuals, or for matching gifts; no loans.

Publications: Grants list.
Application information: Unsolicited requests for funds not accepted.
   Board meeting date(s): June and Dec.
Trustee: JPMorgan Chase Bank, N.A.
EIN: 136013101

6667

The Orentreich Family Foundation ◇

909 5th Ave.
New York, NY   10021-1415

Established in 1986 in NY.
Donors: David Orentreich; Norman Orentreich; Orentreich Medical Group.
Foundation type: Independent foundation.
Financial data (yr. ended 9/30/05): Assets, $26,580,157 (M); expenditures, $1,612,951; qualifying distributions, $1,535,750; giving activities include $1,528,677 for 92+ grants.
Purpose and activities: Support primarily for an affiliated medical research facility. Funding also for the arts and city parks.
Fields of interest: Arts; Education; Environment, natural resources; Botanical gardens; Hospitals (general); Health organizations, association; Biomedicine research; Recreation, parks/playgrounds; Jewish federated giving programs; Jewish agencies & temples.
Limitations: Applications not accepted. Giving primarily in New York, NY. No grants to individuals.
Application information: Contributes only to pre-selected organizations.
Trustees: David Orentreich; Norman Orentreich.
EIN: 136879797

6668

The Arthur and Mae Orvis Foundation, Inc. ◇

(formerly The Arthur Emerton Orvis Foundation)
c/o Alston & Bird, LLP
60 E. 42nd St., 45th Fl.
New York, NY   10165
Application address: c/o Grover O'Neill, Jr., Pres., 30 Rockefeller Plz., New York, NY 10112

Established in 1967 in NY.
Donor: Mae Zenke Orvis‡.
Foundation type: Independent foundation.
Financial data (yr. ended 9/30/05): Assets, $11,462,465 (M); expenditures, $546,693; qualifying distributions, $490,998; giving activities include $435,500 for 25 grants (high: $50,000; low: $5,000).
Purpose and activities: Giving primarily for cultural institutions, and for nursing.
Fields of interest: Performing arts, music; Performing arts, orchestra (symphony); Performing arts, opera; Higher education; Nursing school/education.
Limitations: Giving limited to Honolulu, HI, Reno, NV, and New York, NY. No grants to individuals.
Application information: Application form not required.
   Initial approach: Letter
   Deadline(s): None
Officers and Directors:* Grover O'Neill, Jr.,* Pres.; Roger M. Gerber,* V.P. and Treas.; Wallace L. Cook,* V.P.; Paul M. Frank,* Secy.; Robert S. Hines; T.A. Nigro.
EIN: 136217675

Selected grants: The following grants were reported in 2005.
$90,000 to Hawaii Opera Theater, Honolulu, HI. 2 grants: $40,000, $50,000
$50,000 to Honolulu Symphony, Honolulu, HI. 2 grants: $25,000 each
$40,000 to Manhattan School of Music, New York, NY. 2 grants: $25,000, $15,000
$35,000 to Sierra Arts Foundation, Reno, NV.
$26,500 to University of Hawaii Foundation, Honolulu, HI.
$15,000 to Reno Philharmonic, Reno, NV. 2 grants: $10,000, $5,000

6669

Edward B. Osborn Charitable Trust ◇

c/o U.S. Trust Co.
114 W. 47th St., 7th Fl., Tax Div.
New York, NY   10036

Trust established in 1961 in NY.
Donor: Edward B. Osborn.
Foundation type: Independent foundation.
Financial data (yr. ended 12/31/05): Assets, $7,453,873 (M); expenditures, $387,306; qualifying distributions, $354,682; giving activities include $343,129 for grants.
Fields of interest: Museums; Arts; Higher education; Environment; Cancer; Boys clubs; Children/youth, services; Federated giving programs.
Limitations: Giving primarily in MN and NY. No grants to individuals.
Application information: Application form not required.
   Initial approach: Letter
   Deadline(s): None
Trustee: U.S. Trust.
EIN: 136071296

6670

OSI Pharmaceuticals Foundation, Inc. ☆

41 Pinelawn Rd.
Melville, NY   11747   (631) 962-2031
Contact: Ann McDermott-Kave, Dir.
FAX: (631) 962-2022;
E-mail: amcdermott@osip.com; URL: http://www.osip.com/OSI/about.asp?id=177

Established in 2005 in NY.
Donor: OSI Pharmaceuticals, Inc.
Foundation type: Company-sponsored foundation.
Financial data (yr. ended 12/31/05): Assets, $99,881 (M); gifts received, $600,000; expenditures, $500,119; qualifying distributions, $500,000; giving activities include $500,000 for 1 grant.
Purpose and activities: The foundation supports organizations involved with patient supportive care, scientific and medical research, and science education. Special emphasis is directed toward programs designed to address cancer, eye diseases, and diabetes.
Fields of interest: Health care, patient services; Cancer; Eye diseases; Diabetes; Medical research; Science, research; Science, formal/general education.
International interests: United Kingdom.
Limitations: Giving on a national basis, with emphasis on CO and NY, and in Oxford, United Kingdom. No support for political organizations. No

grants to individuals, or for religious events or capital campaigns.
Application information: Support is limited to 1 contribution per organization during any given year. Proposals should be no longer than 5 pages. Application form not required.
   Initial approach: Proposal
   Copies of proposal: 1
   Final notification: 6 to 8 weeks
Officers and Trustees:* G. Morgan Browne,* Chair.; Stephan Grillo, Treas.; Linda E. Amper, Ph.D.; Colin Goddard, Ph.D.; John P. White.
EIN: 202373033

6671

Harry & Helen Ostreicher Family Foundation ◇ ☆

c/o Wasser Brettler, CPA
132 Nassau St., Ste. 300
New York, NY   10038

Established in 1996 in DE.
Donor: Harry Ostreicher.
Foundation type: Independent foundation.
Financial data (yr. ended 7/31/05): Assets, $3,557,006 (M); gifts received, $117,550; expenditures, $706,223; qualifying distributions, $704,844; giving activities include $700,315 for 13 grants (high: $125,000; low: $13,050).
Purpose and activities: Giving primarily for Jewish education.
Fields of interest: Education; Jewish agencies & temples.
Type of support: General/operating support.
Limitations: Applications not accepted. Giving primarily in NY. No grants to individuals.
Application information: Contributes only to pre-selected organizations.
Officers: Harry Ostreicher, Pres.; Helen Ostreicher, V.P.
EIN: 113241598
Selected grants: The following grants were reported in 2005.
$125,000 to Aleh Foundation, Brooklyn, NY.
$75,000 to Notzer Chesed, New York, NY.

6672

Marvin & Susan Ostreicher Family Foundation ◇ ☆

184 Wildacre Ave.
Lawrence, NY   11559-1413
Application address: c/o Zell & Ettinger, C.P.A., 3001 Ave. M, Brooklyn, NY 11210

Established in 1994 in NY.
Donors: Marvin Ostreicher; Susan Ostreicher.
Foundation type: Independent foundation.
Financial data (yr. ended 11/30/04): Assets, $161,474 (M); gifts received, $45,000; expenditures, $425,785; qualifying distributions, $413,490; giving activities include $411,220 for 9 + grants (high: $75,000).
Fields of interest: Jewish federated giving programs; Jewish agencies & temples.
Limitations: Applications not accepted.
Application information: Contributes only to pre-selected organizations.
Officers: Marvin Ostreicher, Pres.; Susan Ostreicher, Secy.
EIN: 113241597

6673

Ostrovsky Family Fund, Inc. ✧

c/o Horowitz and Ullmann
275 Madison Ave., Ste. 902
New York, NY 10016
Contact: Michael Winicki

Established in 1987.
Donors: Vivian S. Ostrovsky; LKC Foundation.
Foundation type: Independent foundation.
Financial data (yr. ended 11/30/04): Assets,
$734,905 (M); gifts received, $605,000;
expenditures, $614,158; qualifying distributions,
$542,500; giving activities include $542,000 for 3
grants (high: $347,500; low: $10,000).
Purpose and activities: Giving primarily to Jewish
organizations and agencies, including a Jewish
cinema in Jerusalem, Israel, and to a nonprofit
cinema in New York, NY.
Fields of interest: Media, film/video; Jewish
federated giving programs.
International interests: Israel.
Type of support: Continuing support.
Limitations: Applications not accepted. Giving
primarily in New York, NY, and Jerusalem, Israel. No
grants to individuals.
Application information: Contributes only to
pre-selected organizations.
Officers and Directors:* Vivian S. Ostrovsky,*
Pres.; Jacob Friedman,* Secy.; Rose Ostrovsky.
EIN: 133389580

6674

The Ottinger Foundation ✧

80 Broad St., Ste. 1600
New York, NY 10004 (212) 764-1508
FAX: (917) 438-4639;
E-mail: info@ottingerfoundation.org; URL: http://
www.ottingerfoundation.org

Incorporated in 1945 in NY.
Donor: Lawrence Ottinger‡.
Foundation type: Independent foundation.
Financial data (yr. ended 12/31/04): Assets,
$6,283,951 (M); gifts received, $19,766;
expenditures, $549,471; qualifying distributions,
$416,394; giving activities include $348,797 for 14
grants (high: $50,000; low: $10,000).
Purpose and activities: Supports selected projects
designed to advance democracy, social and
economic justice, citizen activism, and
environmental protection. The foundation is
implementing a program area focusing on economic
security issues.
Fields of interest: Environment; Social sciences;
Public policy, research.
Type of support: General/operating support;
Program development; Seed money; Matching/
challenge support.
Limitations: Applications not accepted. Giving on a
national basis. No support for local organizations,
human services, or for organizations which typically
receive popular support like universities, museums,
hospitals, or schools. No grants to individuals, or for
capital or annual campaigns, deficit financing,
building or endowment funds, equipment and
materials, land acquisition, construction or
renovation of buildings, publications, conferences,
books, film or video projects or academic research.
Publications: Grants list.
Application information: Unsolicited requests for
funds not accepted. Proposals are reviewed by

invitation only. See foundation Web site for
complete details.
Board meeting date(s): Biannually
Directors: Michael Goldberg; Karen Heath; Jennifer
Ottinger; June Godfrey Ottinger; Lawrence Ottinger;
Lea Anne Ottinger; Randy Ottinger; Richard L.
Ottinger; Ronald Ottinger; Cinthia Schumann; Peter
Smith; Betsy Taylor; Bill Zabel.
EIN: 136118423
Selected grants: The following grants were reported
in 2003.
$50,000 to Center for Community Change, DC.
$35,000 to Front Range Economic Strategy Center,
Denver, CO.
$30,000 to Institute on Taxation and Economic
Policy, DC.
$30,000 to Strategic Actions for a Just Economy
(SAJE), Los Angeles, CA.
$25,000 to National Womens Law Center, DC.
$25,000 to Project Vote, Brooklyn, NY.
$20,000 to Economic Opportunity Institute, Seattle,
WA.
$10,000 to Environmental and Energy Study
Institute, DC.
$10,000 to Legal Environmental Assistance
Foundation, Tallahassee, FL.
$10,000 to South Carolina Fair Share Education
Fund, Columbia, SC.

6675

The Overbrook Foundation ▼

122 E. 42nd St., Ste. 2500
New York, NY 10168-2500 (212) 661-8710
Contact: M. Sheila McGoldrick, Grants Mgr.
FAX: (212) 661-8664;
E-mail: contact@overbrookfoundation.org;
URL: http://www.overbrook.org

Incorporated in 1948 in NY.
Donors: Frank Altschul‡; Helen G. Altschul‡; Arthur
G. Altschul‡; Margaret A. Lang‡.
Foundation type: Independent foundation.
Financial data (yr. ended 12/31/05): Assets,
$170,072,025 (M); expenditures, $11,406,297;
qualifying distributions, $9,290,684; giving
activities include $4,855 for 1 employee matching
gift.
Purpose and activities: The foundation strives to
improve the lives of people by supporting projects
that protect human and civil rights, advance the
self-sufficiency and well being of individuals and
their communities, and conserve the natural
environment. The foundation recognizes the
importance of a strong community that promotes
health, education and opportunity for all of its
members. The foundation values the individual
rights of all people and encourages the discussion
and analysis of public issues. It is deeply committed
to protecting our natural resources.
Fields of interest: Environment, natural resources;
AIDS; International human rights; Civil rights,
advocacy; Civil liberties, advocacy; Civil liberties,
reproductive rights; Civil rights.
International interests: Latin America; South Africa.
Type of support: General/operating support;
Program development; Fellowships.
Limitations: Giving primarily in the United States,
South Africa, and Latin America— especially Brazil,
Mexico and Ecuador. No grants to individuals.
Publications: Application guidelines; Financial
statement; Grants list; Newsletter; Program policy
statement.

Application information: Detailed proposal
requirements are found on website. Application form
required.
Initial approach: Letter of inquiry
Deadline(s): None
Board meeting date(s): Varies
Final notification: 3 to 6 months
Officers and Directors:* Stephen F. Altschul,*
Chair.; Frances Labaree,* Vice-Chair. and Secy.;
Robert C. Graham, Jr.,* Vice-Chair. and Treas.;
Stephen A. Foster, C.E.O. and Pres.; Arthur G.
Altschul, Jr.; Charles Altschul; Serena Altschul; Julie
Graham; Kathryn C. Graham; Kathryn G. Graham;
Aaron Labaree; Helen Lang; Vincent McGee; Isaiah
Orozco.
Number of staff: 4 full-time professional.
EIN: 136088860
Selected grants: The following grants were reported
in 2004.
$208,334 to People for the American Way
Foundation, DC. For Election Protection,
Sanctified Seven and Mi Familia Vota programs.
$135,000 to Columbia University, New York, NY. 2
grants: $100,000 to Center for Environmental
Research and Conservation (For classes of
Overbrook Conservation Fellows Program),
$35,000 to School of Law (For project,
Reconsidering the Guilt of Executed Defendants
and the Reliability of the Death Penalty in the
U.S).
$100,000 to Human Rights Watch, New York, NY.
For general operating support.
$100,000 to National Public Radio, DC. For
Endowment Fund for Excellence.
$100,000 to Saint Bernards School, New York, NY.
For school's 100th anniversary.
$75,000 to American Civil Liberties Union
Foundation, New York, NY. For general operating
support for litigation.
$50,600 to Gay Mens Health Crisis (GMHC), New
York, NY. For New York City Youth to Youth
Project.
$25,000 to Fundacion Futuro Latinoamericano,
Quito, Ecuador. For strengthening natural
resources management in Galapagos Marine
Reserve.
$6,000 to Byrd Hoffman Water Mill Foundation, New
York, NY. For general operating support.

6676

Overhills Foundation ✧

c/o MGF Mgmt., Inc.
P.O. Box 5315, FDR Station
New York, NY 10150-5315

Established in 2000 in DE.
Donors: Omnibus Charitable Trust; Underhill
Foundation; Wild Wings Foundation.
Foundation type: Independent foundation.
Financial data (yr. ended 11/30/04): Assets,
$13,554,848 (M); gifts received, $477,675;
expenditures, $837,916; qualifying distributions,
$705,377; giving activities include $680,000 for 51
grants (high: $35,000; low: $1,000).
Purpose and activities: Giving primarily for nature
conservancies and the environment.
Fields of interest: Museums (specialized); Law
school/education; Environment, land resources;
Environment, forests; Environment; Employment,
services; Human services; Children/youth, services.
Limitations: Applications not accepted. Giving
primarily in NY; some funding also in CT and VA. No
grants to individuals.

Application information: Contributes only to pre-selected organizations.
Officers and Directors:* Ann R. Elliman,* Pres.; Lucia R. Brown,* V.P.; Edward H. Elliman,* V.P.; Christopher J. Elliman,* Secy.-Treas.
EIN: 133922745
Selected grants: The following grants were reported in 2004.
$25,500 to Open Space Institute, New York, NY.
$25,000 to Adirondack Council, Elizabethtown, NY.
$25,000 to We Can, New York, NY.
$25,000 to Wilderness Society, DC.
$20,000 to Appalachian Mountain Club, Boston, MA.
$20,000 to Georgetown University, DC.
$20,000 to Nature Conservancy, Brunswick, ME.
$10,000 to Adirondack Museum, Blue Mountain Lake, NY.
$7,000 to Natural History Museum of the Adirondacks, Tupper Lake, NY.
$5,000 to Yale University, New Haven, CT.

6677
Daniel P. and Nancy C. Paduano Family Foundation ◇
c/o Daniel Paduano
19 E. 72nd St.
New York, NY 10021

Established in 1994 in NY.
Donors: Daniel P. Paduano; Nancy C. Paduano.
Foundation type: Independent foundation.
Financial data (yr. ended 11/30/05): Assets, $448,601 (M); gifts received, $809,220; expenditures, $945,975; qualifying distributions, $933,093; giving activities include $933,093 for 70 grants (high: $300,000; low: $500).
Purpose and activities: Giving primarily for health associations and hospitals, as well as to medical colleges; funding also for the arts, education, and family and social services.
Fields of interest: Arts; Higher education; Medical school/education; Education; Hospitals (general); Health organizations, association; Cancer research; Human services; Family services.
Limitations: Applications not accepted. Giving primarily in New York, NY. No grants to individuals.
Application information: Contributes only to pre-selected organizations.
Directors: Daniel P. Paduano; James A. Paduano; Nancy C. Paduano.
EIN: 133796430

6678
The Paestum Foundation, Inc. ◇
c/o Hecht & Co., PC
111 W. 40th St.
New York, NY 10018

Established in 2000 in DE and NY.
Foundation type: Independent foundation.
Financial data (yr. ended 9/30/05): Assets, $18,599,826 (M); expenditures, $1,187,062; qualifying distributions, $942,862; giving activities include $909,500 for 12 grants (high: $225,000; low: $10,000).
Purpose and activities: Giving primarily to a medical college, as well as to a committee for human rights; funding also for the arts.

Fields of interest: Arts; Medical school/education; International human rights; Community development, neighborhood development.
Limitations: Applications not accepted. Giving primarily in New York, NY. No grants to individuals.
Application information: Contributes only to pre-selected organizations.
Director: Michael Rudell.
EIN: 134082016
Selected grants: The following grants were reported in 2004.
$300,000 to Yale University, New Haven, CT.
$125,000 to Friendly Planet, Cambridge, MA.
$100,000 to Studio in a School Association, New York, NY.

6679
William S. Paley Foundation, Inc. ▼ ◇
c/o Bencivenga Ward & Company CPAS, PC
420 Columbus Ave.
Valhalla, NY 10595-1382 (914) 739-5005
Contact: Patrick S. Gallagher, Exec. Dir.

Incorporated in 1936 in NY.
Donor: William S. Paley‡.
Foundation type: Independent foundation.
Financial data (yr. ended 12/31/05): Assets, $122,914,074 (M); expenditures, $6,593,085; qualifying distributions, $3,961,846; giving activities include $3,762,227 for 40 grants (high: $2,110,000; low: $500; average: $2,500–$100,000).
Purpose and activities: Endowment funds held for and emphasis on the Museum of Television and Radio and the Greenpark Foundation (Paley Park). Support for other museums, health services, education, and cultural programs.
Fields of interest: Museums; Arts; Education; Health care.
Type of support: General/operating support; Continuing support; Annual campaigns.
Limitations: Giving on a national basis. No grants to individuals.
Application information: Application form not required.
 Initial approach: Proposal
 Copies of proposal: 1
 Deadline(s): None
 Board meeting date(s): Nov.
Officers and Directors:* Henry A. Kissinger,* Chair.; William C. Paley,* V.P.; Daniel L. Mosley,* Secy.-Treas.; Patrick S. Gallagher,* Exec. Dir.; George J. Gillespie III.
Number of staff: 1 full-time professional; 1 part-time professional.
EIN: 136085929
Selected grants: The following grants were reported in 2004.
$3,776,035 to Museum of Television and Radio, New York, NY. 3 grants: $2,852,045 (For general program), $423,990 (For capital campaign), $500,000 (For Paley TV Festival).
$100,000 to Museum of Modern Art, New York, NY. For general program.
$75,000 to Jerusalem Foundation, New York, NY. For Paley Art Center.
$50,000 to Auburn Theological Seminary, New York, NY. For Auburn Media Program.
$25,000 to Saint Vincents Hospital and Medical Center of New York, Westchester Branch, Harrison, NY. For general program.
$20,000 to University of Alabama, School of Law, Tuscaloosa, AL. For general program.

$14,500 to Tulane University, New Orleans, LA. For Classical and Byzantine Program.
$13,000 to Metropolitan Museum of Art, New York, NY. For general program.

6680
The Vincent and Harriet Palisano Foundation
P.O. Box 1133
Buffalo, NY 14205-1133
Contact: James M. Beardsley, Tr.

Established in 1962 in NY.
Donors: Vincent H. Palisano‡; Harriet A. Palisano‡.
Foundation type: Independent foundation.
Financial data (yr. ended 5/31/05): Assets, $4,616,894 (M); expenditures, $416,826; qualifying distributions, $382,223; giving activities include $371,500 for 33 grants (high: $100,000; low: $1,000).
Purpose and activities: Emphasis on higher and secondary education, including scholarship funds for selected colleges and high schools in western NY; also giving for cancer research.
Fields of interest: Secondary school/education; Higher education; Cancer research.
Type of support: General/operating support; Equipment; Scholarship funds; Research.
Limitations: Applications not accepted. Giving primarily in the Buffalo, NY, area. No grants to individuals.
Application information: Unsolicited requests for funds not considered.
Trustees: James M. Beardsley; Beverly A. Leek; Angeline D. Smith.
EIN: 166052186
Selected grants: The following grants were reported in 2004.
$160,000 to Roswell Park Alliance Foundation, Buffalo, NY. For research.
$25,000 to DYouville College, Buffalo, NY. For nursing program.
$25,000 to Niagara University, Niagara Falls, NY. For equipment and travel for language department.
$25,000 to Trocaire College, Buffalo, NY. For computers.
$20,000 to Buffalo Philharmonic Orchestra, Buffalo, NY. For concert.
$20,000 to Medaille College, Buffalo, NY. For capital campaign.
$10,000 to Annunciation Roman Catholic Church, New York, NY.
$10,000 to Business in Support of Neighborhoods (BISON) Fund, Buffalo, NY. For scholarship.
$3,500 to Hilbert College, Hamburg, NY. For scholarship.
$1,500 to Villa Maria College of Buffalo, Buffalo, NY. For scholarship.

6681
Michael Palm Foundation ◇
c/o Yohalem Gillman & Co., LLP
477 Madison Ave.
New York, NY 10022-5802

Established in 1993 in NY.
Donor: Michael Palm‡.
Foundation type: Independent foundation.
Financial data (yr. ended 12/31/05): Assets, $3,293,521 (M); gifts received, $600;

expenditures, $1,350,553; qualifying distributions, $1,341,259; giving activities include $1,334,940 for 12 grants (high: $1,000,000; low: $2,500; average: $5,000–$40,000).

Purpose and activities: Funding is primarily focused on national or NY community-based organizations working in AIDS services, prevention, gay and lesbian civil rights, community-based interests; and cultural and arts-related interests.

Fields of interest: Arts, multipurpose centers/programs; Performing arts; Arts; AIDS; Civil rights, gays/lesbians.

Type of support: General/operating support; Program development.

Limitations: Applications not accepted. Giving on a national basis, with emphasis on New York City. No grants to individuals.

Application information: Unsolicited requests for funds not accepted.

Board meeting date(s): Quarterly

Officers and Directors:* M. Melissa Jamula,* Chair.; David W. Prager, Treas.; Craig Anderson; Eugene D. Falk; Judith O'Connor Gluckstern; Steven M. Gluckstern.

EIN: 133745516

Selected grants: The following grants were reported in 2004.

$500,000 to Gay and Lesbian Alliance Against Defamation (GLAAD), New York, NY. 2 grants: $250,000 each

$125,000 to Lincoln Center for the Performing Arts, New York, NY.

$80,000 to Telluride School District R-1, Telluride, CO.

$50,000 to Friends of the Mothers Programmes, New York, NY.

$40,000 to Classical Action, New York, NY.

$25,000 to Eos Orchestra, New York, NY.

$15,000 to Hetrick-Martin Institute, New York, NY.

$15,000 to North Bennet Street School, Boston, MA.

$2,500 to Reading School District, Reading, PA.

6682

The Francis Asbury Palmer Foundation ◇

c/o The Solaris Group, LLC
598 Madison Ave.
New York, NY 10022

Incorporated in 1897 in NY.

Donor: Francis Asbury Palmer†.

Foundation type: Independent foundation.

Financial data (yr. ended 4/30/06): Assets, $7,481,775 (M); expenditures, $520,210; qualifying distributions, $375,411; giving activities include $359,583 for 17 grants (high: $47,500; low: $2,500).

Purpose and activities: Support for Christian theological seminaries and other higher education organizations.

Fields of interest: Higher education; Theological school/education; Christian agencies & churches.

Limitations: Applications not accepted. Giving on a national basis. No grants to individuals.

Application information: Contributes only to pre-selected organizations. Unsolicited requests for funds not accepted.

Officer: Diana L. Reed, Pres.

Directors: Allison C. Hansen; Page Hughes; E. Gayle McGuigan, Jr.; Phillip P. McGuigan; Susan K. Reed.

EIN: 136400635

Selected grants: The following grants were reported in 2006.

$45,000 to Hartford Seminary, Hartford, CT.

$40,000 to New York Theological Seminary, New York, NY.

$40,000 to Night Ministry, Chicago, IL.

$15,000 to Community Ministries of Rockville, Rockville, MD.

$5,000 to Worcester County Food Bank, Shrewsbury, MA.

6683

The Palmer Foundation, Inc. ◇

40 W. 57th St., 20th Fl.
New York, NY 10019
Contact: Barbara R. Palmer, Pres.

Established in 1988 in PA.

Donor: James R. Palmer.

Foundation type: Independent foundation.

Financial data (yr. ended 12/31/05): Assets, $1,767,868 (M); expenditures, $875,865; qualifying distributions, $860,889; giving activities include $860,889 for 25 grants (high: $286,351; low: $100).

Purpose and activities: Giving primarily to universities. Some funding also for research purposes and the arts.

Fields of interest: Museums; Higher education; Environment, natural resources; Reproductive health, family planning; Heart & circulatory diseases; Cancer research; YM/YWCAs & YM/YWHAs.

Type of support: General/operating support; Grants to individuals.

Limitations: Giving primarily in NY and PA.

Application information: Application form not required.

Deadline(s): None

Officers: Barbara R. Palmer, Pres.; Wayne Reisner, Secy.-Treas.

Directors: Janet Lipcon; Charles Palmer; David Palmer.

EIN: 251568606

Selected grants: The following grants were reported in 2005.

$286,351 to Iowa State University Foundation, Ames, IA.

$25,000 to Centre County Community Foundation, State College, PA.

$20,100 to Centre Peace, Bellefonte, PA.

$15,000 to United Way.

$12,500 to Smithsonian American Art Museum, DC.

$10,000 to Pennsylvania Academy of the Fine Arts, Philadelphia, PA.

$1,500 to Nittany Valley Symphony, State College, PA.

6684

The Panaphil Foundation ◇

c/o U.S. Trust Company of New York, N.A.
114 W. 47th St.
New York, NY 10036
Contact: Jean Crawford

Established in 1990 in PA and NY.

Donor: Frances A. Velay.

Foundation type: Independent foundation.

Financial data (yr. ended 12/31/05): Assets, $35,424,902 (M); expenditures, $3,471,834; qualifying distributions, $3,275,906; giving activities include $3,273,156 for 59 grants (high:

$850,000; low: $5,000; average: $10,000–$100,000).

Purpose and activities: Giving primarily for environmental concerns, preservation of animal and plant species threatened with extinction, and prevention of cruelty to animals.

Fields of interest: Environment, natural resources; Animal welfare; Reproductive health, family planning; Human services.

Limitations: Giving primarily on the East Coast. No grants to individuals.

Application information:
Initial approach: Proposal
Deadline(s): None

Trustees: Barbara Paul Robinson; Christopher J. Velay; Frances A. Velay.

EIN: 136959472

6685

The Paneth Family Charitable Trust ◇ ☆

3900 Shore Pkwy.
Brooklyn, NY 11235

Established in 1992 in NY.

Donors: Morton Paneth; Samuel Paneth; Leah Werner; Thomas Paneth.

Foundation type: Independent foundation.

Financial data (yr. ended 12/31/05): Assets, $6,072,015 (M); gifts received, $1,185,360; expenditures, $552,224; qualifying distributions, $453,880; giving activities include $453,880 for grants.

Fields of interest: Jewish agencies & temples.

Limitations: Applications not accepted. Giving primarily in Brooklyn, NY. No grants to individuals.

Application information: Contributes only to pre-selected organizations.

Trustees: Morton Paneth; Samuel Paneth; Thomas Paneth; Leah Werner.

EIN: 116415770

Selected grants: The following grants were reported in 2003.

$50,000 to Congregation Maatei Ephraim, Brooklyn, NY.

$3,600 to Yad Eliezer, Brooklyn, NY.

$2,000 to Congregation Ahavas Tzdokah V Chesed, Brooklyn, NY.

$1,000 to Chabad Lubavitch of Rockland, New City, NY.

$1,000 to Chesed Avraham, Brooklyn, NY.

$1,000 to Congregation Chakal Yitzchok, Brooklyn, NY.

$1,000 to Congregation Sheves Achim, Brooklyn, NY.

$1,000 to Mesivta Tifereth Zvi Spinka, Brooklyn, NY.

$1,000 to Yeshiva Nachlas Yaakov, Brooklyn, NY.

$1,000 to Yeshivas Novominsk-Kol Yehuda, Brooklyn, NY.

6686

Pannonia Foundation ◇ ☆

c/o Marks Paneth, et al.
622 3rd Ave., 7th Fl.
New York, NY 10017

Established in 2003 in NY.

Foundation type: Independent foundation.

Financial data (yr. ended 12/31/05): Assets, $110,075 (M); expenditures, $433,899; qualifying distributions, $430,600; giving activities include $430,600 for grants.

Fields of interest: Museums; Arts; Libraries/library science; Education; Hospitals (general).
Limitations: Applications not accepted. No grants to individuals.
Application information: Contributes only to pre-selected organizations.
Directors: Adam Bartos; Steve C. Baum; Mahnaz Ispahani.
EIN: 134112882
Selected grants: The following grants were reported in 2005.
$50,000 to American Museum of the Moving Image, Astoria, NY.
$48,350 to Schomburg Center for Research in Black Culture, New York, NY.
$30,000 to Zest for Life Foundation, New York, NY.
$15,000 to Wellesley College, Wellesley, MA.
$10,000 to Drawing Center, New York, NY.
$10,000 to El Museo Francisco Oller y Diego Rivera, Buffalo, NY.
$5,000 to FINCA International, DC.
$5,000 to International Center for Global Communications, New York, NY.
$5,000 to Oxfam America, Boston, MA.
$3,500 to New Art Publications, New York, NY.

6687
Park Charitable Trust ◇
(formerly Park Foundation)
5223 15th Ave.
Brooklyn, NY   11219   (718) 851-4811
Contact: Efraim Landau, Dir.

Donors: Efraim Landau; A. Landau Trust; Triangle Trust.
Foundation type: Operating foundation.
Financial data (yr. ended 12/31/05): Assets, $8,511,588 (M); gifts received, $150,000; expenditures, $413,024; qualifying distributions, $379,500; giving activities include $379,500 for 15 grants (high: $128,600; low: $500).
Fields of interest: Jewish agencies & temples.
Type of support: General/operating support.
Limitations: Giving primarily in NY. No grants to individuals.
Application information:
Initial approach: Letter
Deadline(s): None
Directors: Chaim Landau; David Landau; Efraim Landau.
EIN: 116450788

6688
Park Foundation, Inc. ▼ ◇
P.O. Box 550
Ithaca, NY   14851
Contact: Linda W. Madeo, Exec. Dir.

Established in 1966.
Donors: RHP, Inc.; Roy H. Park†.
Foundation type: Independent foundation.
Financial data (yr. ended 12/31/04): Assets, $387,531,644 (M); expenditures, $17,963,411; qualifying distributions, $15,745,457; giving activities include $15,007,929 for 315 grants (high: $600,000; low: $10; average: $5,000–$100,000).
Purpose and activities: Giving primarily for scholarships in higher education, quality public affairs media that heightens public awareness of critical issues, and protection of the environment. In addition to these core program areas, interests

include a broad range of charitable giving in communities where the trustees reside.
Fields of interest: Media/communications; Media, film/video; Media, television; Higher education; Education; Environment, water resources; Animal welfare.
Type of support: Employee matching gifts; General/operating support; Program development; Seed money; Scholarship funds; Matching/challenge support.
Limitations: Giving limited to the eastern U.S., primarily in central NY, Washington, DC, and North Carolina. No grants to individuals.
Publications: Informational brochure (including application guidelines).
Application information: After receipt of the letter of inquiry, the foundation may request a full proposal, along with a completed application form provided by the foundation. Proposal may be submitted in hard copy or electronically. Application form required.
Initial approach: Letter of inquiry
Copies of proposal: 2
Deadline(s): None
Board meeting date(s): Mar., June, Sept., and Dec.
Final notification: Varies
Officers and Directors:* Dorothy D. Park,* Pres.; Adelaide P. Gomer,* V.P.; Alicia P. Wittink,* Secy.; Richard G. Robb,* Treas.; Linda W. Madeo, Exec. Dir.; William L. Bondurant; Jerome B. Libin; John F. McNair III.
Number of staff: 6 full-time professional.
EIN: 166071043
Selected grants: The following grants were reported in 2004.
$3,937,453 to North Carolina State University, Raleigh, NC. 8 grants: $484,638 (For Park Scholarships), $484,638 (For Park Scholarships), $504,357 (For Park Scholarships), $504,357 (For Park Scholarships), $507,223 (For Park Scholarships), $507,223 (For Park Scholarships), $531,258 (For Park Scholarships), $413,759 (For Park Scholarships).
$824,941 to Ithaca College, Ithaca, NY. 2 grants: $387,761 to Roy H. Park School of Communications (For scholarships for students in Class of 2006), $437,180 to Roy H. Park School of Communications (For Park Scholars Program).

6689
The Park Foundation ◇
500 5th Ave., Ste. 1710
New York, NY   10110

Incorporated in 1949 in DC.
Donors: Eunice K. Shriver; Joseph P. Kennedy, Jr. Foundation.
Foundation type: Independent foundation.
Financial data (yr. ended 12/31/04): Assets, $139,872 (M); gifts received, $190,000; expenditures, $1,052,259; qualifying distributions, $1,050,064; giving activities include $1,050,064 for 45+ grants (high: $756,090).
Fields of interest: Performing arts, theater; Arts; Libraries/library science; Children/youth, services; International human rights; Federated giving programs; Disabilities, people with.
Type of support: General/operating support; Annual campaigns; Research.

Limitations: Applications not accepted. Giving primarily in Washington, DC, MA, and NY. No grants to individuals; no loans or program-related investments.
Application information: Contributes only to pre-selected organizations.
Officers and Trustees:* Eunice K. Shriver,* V.P.; Robert W. Corcoran, Treas.; Patricia K. Lawford; Jean K. Smith.
EIN: 136163065

6690
The Jack Parker Foundation, Inc. ◇
1700 Broadway, 34th Fl.
New York, NY   10019

Established in 1998 in NY.
Foundation type: Independent foundation.
Financial data (yr. ended 12/31/05): Assets, $1,951,937 (M); expenditures, $455,003; qualifying distributions, $451,878; giving activities include $451,878 for 41 grants (high: $100,000; low: $15).
Purpose and activities: Giving primarily for arts and culture, as well as for education, human services, and Jewish organizations.
Fields of interest: Museums (art); Arts; Education; Health organizations; Human services; Aging, centers/services; Jewish federated giving programs; Jewish agencies & temples.
Limitations: Applications not accepted. Giving primarily in NY. No grants to individuals.
Application information: Contributes only to pre-selected organizations.
Officers: Jack Parker, Pres.; Adam P. Glick, V.P.
EIN: 116101542

6691
Parkview Foundation ◇
2600 Nostrand Ave.
Brooklyn, NY   11210

Established in 2000 in NY.
Donor: Parkview Realty Co.
Foundation type: Independent foundation.
Financial data (yr. ended 6/30/05): Assets, $7,140,190 (M); expenditures, $622,821; qualifying distributions, $376,000; giving activities include $376,000 for 8 grants (high: $104,000; low: $10,000).
Purpose and activities: Giving primarily to Jewish agencies, temples, and schools.
Fields of interest: Education; Jewish federated giving programs; Jewish agencies & temples.
Limitations: Applications not accepted. Giving primarily in Brooklyn, NY. No grants to individuals.
Application information: Contributes only to pre-selected organizations.
Trustees: Issack Bernstein; Emil Fischman.
EIN: 113544307
Selected grants: The following grants were reported in 2004.
$222,000 to Chevra Zichron Yisroel Dovid, Brooklyn, NY. For unrestricted support.
$174,000 to Kahal Adath Krasna, Brooklyn, NY. For unrestricted support.
$91,000 to Yeshiva Beth Hillel of Krasna, Brooklyn, NY. For unrestricted support.
$30,000 to Yeshiva Minchas Eluzar, Brooklyn, NY. For unrestricted support.

$29,000 to Congregation Ohel Baruch, Brooklyn, NY. For unrestricted support.

$20,000 to United Munkacser Yeshivos, Brooklyn, NY. For unrestricted support.

$16,000 to Cong Ohel Moshe, Brooklyn, NY. For unrestricted support.

$10,000 to United Krasna, Brooklyn, NY. For unrestricted support.

6692
The Gary W. Parr Family Foundation, Inc. ✧ ☆
174 E. Lake Rd.
Tuxedo Park, NY 10987-4243
Contact: Gary W. Parr, Chair.

Established in 1996 in NC.
Donor: Gary W. Parr.
Foundation type: Independent foundation.
Financial data (yr. ended 12/31/05): Assets, $1,234,280 (M); gifts received, $219; expenditures, $1,055,719; qualifying distributions, $1,055,000; giving activities include $1,055,000 for 2 grants (high: $1,050,000; low: $5,000).
Fields of interest: Higher education; Education.
Limitations: Giving primarily in NC. No grants to individuals.
Application information:
  Initial approach: Letter
  Deadline(s): None
Officers: Gary W. Parr, Chair.; Cheri S. Parr, V.P.
EIN: 562003520

6693
Moses L. Parshelsky Foundation ✧
26 Court St., Rm. 904
Brooklyn, NY 11242 (718) 875-8883
Contact: Tony B. Berk, Tr.

Established in 1949 in NY.
Donor: Moses L. Parshelsky†.
Foundation type: Independent foundation.
Financial data (yr. ended 12/31/04): Assets, $7,661,723 (M); expenditures, $435,989; qualifying distributions, $353,952; giving activities include $316,600 for 43 grants (high: $39,000; low: $250).
Purpose and activities: Emphasis on the aged, the handicapped, and hospitals; support also for higher and secondary education, temple support and religious activities, youth agencies, mental health, and Jewish welfare funds.
Fields of interest: Performing arts, dance; Arts; Secondary school/education; Higher education; Hospitals (general); Mental health/crisis services; Cancer; Cancer research; Human services; Children/youth, services; Aging, centers/services; Jewish federated giving programs; Jewish agencies & temples; Aging; Disabilities, people with.
Limitations: Giving primarily in Brooklyn and Queens County, NY. No grants to individuals, or for building or endowment funds, or operating budgets.
Application information: Application form not required.
  Initial approach: Letter
  Copies of proposal: 1
  Deadline(s): May 31
  Board meeting date(s): Monthly
Trustees: Tony B. Berk; Robert D. Krinsky.
Number of staff: 1 part-time professional.
EIN: 111848260

Selected grants: The following grants were reported in 2004.

$44,000 to Brookdale University Hospital and Medical Center, Brooklyn, NY. 2 grants: $34,000, $10,000

$30,000 to Vacamas Programs for Youth, New York, NY. 2 grants: $20,000, $10,000

$25,000 to Jewish Guild for the Blind, New York, NY. 2 grants: $17,500, $7,500

$24,000 to National Jewish Medical and Research Center, New York, NY. 2 grants: $16,500, $7,500

$2,500 to Brooklyn Bureau of Community Service, Brooklyn, NY.

$2,000 to Hebrew Free Loan Society, New York, NY.

6694
Ann Parsons Memorial Foundation ✧
c/o C.F. Burger, Troutman Sanders LLP
405 Lexington Ave., 8th Fl
New York, NY 10174
Contact: Carol F. Burger

Established in 1994 in TX.
Foundation type: Independent foundation.
Financial data (yr. ended 12/31/05): Assets, $5,615,765 (M); expenditures, $419,017; qualifying distributions, $418,185; giving activities include $418,185 for 12 grants (high: $100,118; low: $2,122).
Fields of interest: AIDS; Diabetes; Cancer research; Orthodox Catholic agencies & churches.
Limitations: Applications not accepted. Giving on a national basis. No grants to individuals.
Application information: Contributes only to pre-selected organizations.
Officers and Directors:* Roger Parsons,* Pres. and Treas.; Sofia Kartsotis,* Secy.; Mary Beth Cook; Kathy Elliot; Cheri Friedman; Bill Kartsotis.
EIN: 752550555

6695
The Partridge Foundation ✧
c/o Rockefeller & Co., Inc.
30 Rockefeller Plz., Rm. 5600
New York, NY 10112

Established in 1992 in NY.
Donors: Polly Guth; P.W. Guth Charitable Lead Unitrust.
Foundation type: Independent foundation.
Financial data (yr. ended 11/30/05): Assets, $50,396,775 (M); gifts received, $7,700,832; expenditures, $4,247,395; qualifying distributions, $3,606,666; giving activities include $3,606,666 for 17 grants (high: $1,433,333; low: $30,000).
Fields of interest: Arts, cultural/ethnic awareness; Performing arts; Environment, land resources; Reproductive health, family planning; Cancer research; Public affairs; Women.
Limitations: Applications not accepted. Giving primarily in NY. No grants to individuals.
Application information: Unsolicited requests for funds not accepted.
Trustees: Virginia Montgomery; Richard T. Watson.
EIN: 341742512
Selected grants: The following grants were reported in 2004.

$333,333 to Island Institute, Rockland, ME. For general support.

$200,000 to Asia Society, New York, NY. For general support.

$100,000 to Cancer Research Institute, New York, NY. For general support.

$100,000 to Chatham Hall, Chatham, VA. For general support.

$100,000 to Glimmerglass Opera, Cooperstown, NY. For general support.

$100,000 to Institute for Democracy Studies, New York, NY. For general support.

$100,000 to Maine Coast Heritage Trust, Topsham, ME. For general support.

$100,000 to New York Womens Foundation, New York, NY. For general support.

$100,000 to Planned Parenthood of New York City, New York, NY. For general support.

6696
Pascucci Family Foundation ✧
270 S. Service Rd., Ste. 45
Melville, NY 11747-2339

Established in 1996 in NY.
Donors: Christopher S. Pascucci; Ralph P. Pascucci.
Foundation type: Independent foundation.
Financial data (yr. ended 9/30/04): Assets, $12,047,682 (M); gifts received, $4,000; expenditures, $1,448,203; qualifying distributions, $1,401,973; giving activities include $1,387,613 for 72 grants (high: $200,000; low: $500).
Purpose and activities: Giving primarily to health and human services, and to Roman Catholic churches and organizations.
Fields of interest: Higher education; Education; Health organizations, association; Medical research, institute; Food services; Human services; Children/youth, services; Roman Catholic agencies & churches.
Limitations: Applications not accepted. No grants to individuals.
Application information: Contributes only to pre-selected organizations.
Officers and Directors:* Michael C. Pascucci,* Pres.; Peter I. Cavallaro, V.P. and Counsel; Christopher S. Pascucci,* V.P.; Ralph P. Pascucci,* Secy.-Treas.
EIN: 113346466
Selected grants: The following grants were reported in 2005.

$245,000 to Evergreen Association, New York, NY.

$25,000 to Priestly Fraternity of Saint Peter, Elmhurst, PA.

$25,000 to Youth With A Mission, Kealakekua, HI.

$22,500 to Nicklaus Childrens Health Care Foundation, West Palm Beach, FL.

$22,000 to Hope House Ministries, Port Jefferson, NY.

$10,000 to Archdiocese for the Military Services, Silver Spring, MD.

$10,000 to Bridge to Life, Bayside, NY.

$5,000 to Vitae Caring Foundation, Jefferson City, MO.

$3,000 to Catholic Charities.

$1,000 to Gift of Life Bone Marrow Foundation, Boca Raton, FL.

6697
Andrew M. Paul Family Foundation ✧ ☆
283 Pondfield Rd.
Bronxville, NY 10708
Contact: Andrew M. Paul, Tr.

Established in 1997 in NY.
Donor: Andrew M. Paul.
Foundation type: Independent foundation.
Financial data (yr. ended 8/31/05): Assets, $928,339 (M); gifts received, $101,201; expenditures, $350,218; qualifying distributions, $339,813; giving activities include $339,813 for 36 grants (high: $100,000; low: $100).
Fields of interest: Arts; Higher education; Business school/education; Hospitals (general); Cancer research; Foundations (public); Christian agencies & churches.
Limitations: Giving on a national basis, with emphasis on NY.
Application information:
   Initial approach: Letter
   Deadline(s): None
Trustees: Andrew M. Paul; Margaret B. Paul.
EIN: 137143442

6698
PBHP, Inc. ✧
c/o Hertz, Herson & Co., LLP
2 Park Ave.
New York, NY   10016

Established in 1999 in DE and NY.
Donors: Susan R. Wexner; Naon, Inc.
Foundation type: Independent foundation.
Financial data (yr. ended 12/31/04): Assets, $37,960,472 (M); gifts received, $45,889; expenditures, $1,659,254; qualifying distributions, $1,547,413; giving activities include $1,450,000 for 1 grant.
Fields of interest: Philanthropy/voluntarism.
Limitations: Applications not accepted. Giving primarily in PA. No grants to individuals.
Application information: Contributes only to pre-selected organizations.
Officer and Director:* Susan R. Wexner,* Pres. and Treas.
EIN: 522171835
Selected grants: The following grants were reported in 2003.
$1,630,000 to Vanguard Charitable Endowment Program, Southeastern, PA.

6699
PBO Fund, Inc. ✧
c/o American Express Tax & Business Svcs.
1185 Ave. of the Americas
New York, NY   10036

Established in 1961.
Donors: William J. Oppenheim; Paula K. Oppenheim.
Foundation type: Independent foundation.
Financial data (yr. ended 8/31/04): Assets, $11,570,292 (M); expenditures, $509,945; qualifying distributions, $456,731; giving activities include $449,014 for 118 grants (high: $75,000; low: $25).
Purpose and activities: Giving primarily for health organizations, with emphasis on hospitals and a medical center; funding also for education, libraries, and social services, especially children and family services.
Fields of interest: Museums; Arts; Higher education; Education; Environment; Hospitals (general); Health organizations, association; Human

services; Family services; Jewish federated giving programs; Jewish agencies & temples.
Limitations: Applications not accepted. Giving primarily in Greenwich, CT, and New York, NY. No grants to individuals.
Application information: Contributes only to pre-selected organizations.
Officers: William J. Oppenheim, Pres. and Treas.; Paula K. Oppenheim, V.P. and Secy.
EIN: 136158857
Selected grants: The following grants were reported in 2004.
$75,000 to Greenwich Hospital, Greenwich, CT.
$40,000 to Taft School, Watertown, CT.
$10,000 to Fresh Air Fund, New York, NY.
$5,000 to Montefiore Medical Center, Bronx, NY.
$5,000 to New York Times Neediest Cases Fund, New York, NY.
$3,000 to Greenwich Academy, Greenwich, CT.
$3,000 to United Way of Greenwich, Greenwich, CT.
$1,000 to Rockefeller University, New York, NY.
$750 to Lenox Hill Hospital, New York, NY.
$500 to City Harvest, New York, NY.

6700
Peale Foundation, Inc.
665 Old Quaker Hill Rd.
Pawling, NY   12564
Contact: Elizabeth P. Allen, Secy.-Treas.

Established in 1991 in NY and DE.
Donors: JME II Charitable Lead Trust; JME Charitable Lead Trust; Ruth S. Peale Trust; Schiff, Hardin & Waite; Pawling Charitable Lead Annuit.
Foundation type: Independent foundation.
Financial data (yr. ended 9/30/05): Assets, $6,754,843 (M); gifts received, $151,078; expenditures, $479,309; qualifying distributions, $402,374; giving activities include $366,000 for 27 grants (high: $40,000; low: $500).
Purpose and activities: Giving primarily for religion, community and educational programs.
Fields of interest: Education; Community development; Protestant agencies & churches.
Limitations: Applications not accepted. Giving primarily in NY.
Application information: Unsolicited requests for funds not accepted.
   Board meeting date(s): June
Officers and Directors:* Margaret P. Everett,* Pres.; John Peale,* V.P.; Elizabeth P. Allen,* Secy.-Treas.
EIN: 141746478

6701
Pearson-Rappaport Foundation ✧ ☆
c/o The Ayco Co., LP
P.O. Box 15014
Albany, NY   12212-5014

Established in 1997 in CT.
Donors: Andrall E. Pearson; Jill P. Rappaport; Joanne P. Pearson.
Foundation type: Independent foundation.
Financial data (yr. ended 12/31/05): Assets, $3,836,346 (M); gifts received, $2,061,820; expenditures, $409,370; qualifying distributions, $403,250; giving activities include $403,250 for 46 grants (high: $50,000; low: $250).
Fields of interest: Museums (art); Education; Veterinary medicine, hospital; Hospitals (general);

Health organizations, association; Cancer; Human services; Christian agencies & churches; Women.
Limitations: Applications not accepted. Giving on a national basis. No grants to individuals.
Application information: Contributes only to pre-selected organizations.
Trustees: Andrall E. Pearson; Joanne P. Pearson; Alan H. Rappaport; Jill P. Rappaport.
EIN: 061484929

6702
Peckham Family Foundation ✧
29 Old Aspetong Rd.
Katonah, NY   10536
Contact: John R. Peckham, Tr.

Established in 1999 in NY.
Foundation type: Independent foundation.
Financial data (yr. ended 12/31/05): Assets, $1,012,868 (M); gifts received, $487,475; expenditures, $582,775; qualifying distributions, $569,700; giving activities include $569,700 for 142 grants (high: $100,000; low: $50).
Fields of interest: Arts; Health care; Human services.
Limitations: Applications not accepted. Giving primarily in NY. No grants to individuals.
Application information: Unsolicited requests for funds not accepted.
Trustees: Amy Peckham; John R. Peckham.
EIN: 141814765

6703
Peco Foundation ✧
c/o Jeffrey S. Feinman
1 Penn Plz, 54th Fl.
New York, NY   10119

Established in 1969 in NY.
Donor: Catherine G. Curran.
Foundation type: Independent foundation.
Financial data (yr. ended 12/31/04): Assets, $10,070,039 (M); expenditures, $406,659; qualifying distributions, $391,762; giving activities include $390,354 for 151 grants (high: $50,065; low: $100).
Purpose and activities: Giving for arts and culture, education, health associations and human services.
Fields of interest: Arts; Education; Botanical/horticulture/landscape services; Health organizations, association; Human services; Children, services; Women.
Type of support: General/operating support.
Limitations: Applications not accepted. Giving primarily in New York, NY. No grants to individuals.
Application information: Contributes only to pre-selected organizations.
   Board meeting date(s): Dec.
Trustee: Catherine G. Curran.
EIN: 237031675
Selected grants: The following grants were reported in 2005.
$40,000 to Middlebury College, Middlebury, VT.
$20,000 to Saint Hildas and Saint Hughs School, New York, NY.
$15,000 to YMCA.
$8,300 to Brooklyn Botanic Garden, Brooklyn, NY.
$7,500 to Metropolitan Museum of Art, New York, NY.
$5,000 to Brooklyn Museum, Brooklyn, NY.
$1,000 to Nature Conservancy, Arlington, VA.

$650 to Shakespeare Society, New York, NY.
$500 to Library of Congress, DC.
$450 to Doe Fund, New York, NY.

6704
Peer & Mary Pedersen Charitable Trust ◇
c/o Montrose Acctg. Co., LLC
505 Park Ave., 20th Fl.
New York, NY 10022

Established in 1994 in NY.
Donors: Peer Pedersen; Mary Pedersen.
Foundation type: Independent foundation.
Financial data (yr. ended 11/30/04): Assets,
$528,282 (M); gifts received, $504,828;
expenditures, $430,095; qualifying distributions,
$432,236; giving activities include $429,750 for 15
grants (high: $173,000; low: $500).
Purpose and activities: Giving primarily for
education, medical research, and human services.
Fields of interest: Elementary/secondary
education; Education; Health organizations; Medical
research; Human services; Children/youth,
services; Community development; Foundations
(private grantmaking); Economically disadvantaged.
Limitations: Applications not accepted. Giving
primarily in CT, with some emphasis on Greenwich;
giving also in NY. No grants to individuals.
Application information: Contributes only to
pre-selected organizations.
Officers: Peer Pedersen, Pres.; Mary Pedersen,
Treas.
EIN: 133762413
Selected grants: The following grants were reported
in 2004.
$173,000 to Eagle Hill School, Greenwich, CT.
$132,000 to Greenwich Academy, Greenwich, CT.
$50,000 to Robin Hood Foundation, New York, NY.
$25,000 to De La Salle Academy, New York, NY.
$1,000 to Fairfield County Community Foundation,
Wilton, CT.

6705
Peierls Foundation ▼ ◇
c/o U.S. Trust
114 W. 47th St.
New York, NY 10036
Contact: E. Jeffrey Peierls, Pres.
Application address: 73 S. Holman Way, Golden, CO
80401

Incorporated in 1956 in NY.
Donors: Brian E. Peierls; Edgar S. Peierls†; Ethel F.
Peierls; E. Jeffrey Peierls; and sons.
Foundation type: Independent foundation.
Financial data (yr. ended 10/31/04): Assets,
$93,626,367 (M); gifts received, $1,733,853;
expenditures, $3,887,069; qualifying distributions,
$3,723,045; giving activities include $3,713,950
for 52 grants (high: $412,500; low: $5,500;
average: $10,000–$70,000).
Purpose and activities: Primary areas of interest
include higher education, international relief, and
programs benefiting minorities.
Fields of interest: Higher education; Reproductive
health, family planning; Health organizations,
association; Medical research, institute; Children/
youth, services; Minorities/immigrants, centers/
services; International relief; Civil rights, race/
intergroup relations; Minorities.

Type of support: Annual campaigns; Endowments;
Scholarship funds.
Limitations: Giving on a national basis. No grants to
individuals.
Application information: Application form not
required.
Deadline(s): None
Final notification: Only positive responses will be
sent
Officers: E. Jeffrey Peierls, Pres.; Brian Eliot Peierls,
V.P.; Malcolm A. Moore, Secy.
EIN: 136082503
Selected grants: The following grants were reported
in 2003.
$455,400 to American Red Cross, National
Headquarters, DC. For unrestricted support.
$375,000 to Hispanic Scholarship Fund, San
Francisco, CA. For unrestricted support.
$315,000 to International Rescue Committee, New
York, NY. For unrestricted support.
$213,000 to United Negro College Fund, Fairfax, VA.
For unrestricted support.
$162,800 to Planned Parenthood Federation of
America, New York, NY. For unrestricted support.
$78,000 to American Indian College Fund, Denver,
CO. For unrestricted support.
$73,800 to I Have A Dream Foundation, Denver, CO.
For unrestricted support.
$71,500 to Metropolitan State College of Denver
Foundation, Denver, CO. For unrestricted
support.
$69,100 to Planned Parenthood Association of
Hidalgo County, McAllen, TX. For unrestricted
support.
$63,600 to Francis I. Proctor Foundation for
Research in Ophthalmology, San Francisco, CA.
For unrestricted support.

6706
Donald A. Pels Charitable Trust ◇
63 E. 79th St., Apt. 4B
New York, NY 10021

Established in 1992 in NY.
Donor: Donald A. Pels.
Foundation type: Independent foundation.
Financial data (yr. ended 12/31/05): Assets,
$37,504,999 (M); gifts received, $739,598;
expenditures, $965,349; qualifying distributions,
$946,145; giving activities include $934,200 for 59
grants (high: $151,000; low: $100).
Purpose and activities: Giving primarily to cultural
institutions and for education.
Fields of interest: Media/communications;
Performing arts; Arts; Higher education;
Environment, natural resources; Hospitals (general);
Human services.
Type of support: General/operating support.
Limitations: Applications not accepted. Giving
primarily in NY. No grants to individuals.
Application information: Contributes only to
pre-selected organizations.
Trustee: Donald A. Pels.
EIN: 136998091
Selected grants: The following grants were reported
in 2004.
$75,000 to Barnard College, New York, NY.
$50,000 to Philharmonic-Symphony Society of New
York, New York, NY.
$50,000 to Rockefeller University, New York, NY.
$25,000 to Asphalt Green, New York, NY.
$25,000 to Central Park Conservancy, New York,
NY.

$25,000 to Chess in the Schools, New York, NY.
$25,000 to Cold Spring Harbor Laboratory, Cold
Spring Harbor, NY.
$25,000 to Museum of Natural History, Denver, CO.
$10,000 to Friends of the High Line, New York, NY.
$10,000 to Solomon R. Guggenheim Museum, New
York, NY.

6707
The Laura Pels Foundation ◇
200 W. 57th St., Ste. 803
New York, NY 10019 (212) 382-1404
Contact: Diane Morrison, Exec. Dir.
E-mail: dmorrison@LauraPels.com

Established in 1985 in NY; became The Laura Pels
Foundation in 1992.
Donor: Laura J. Pels.
Foundation type: Independent foundation.
Financial data (yr. ended 12/31/04): Assets,
$10,443,292 (M); gifts received, $5,000;
expenditures, $569,678; qualifying distributions,
$497,022; giving activities include $363,000 for 23
grants (high: $60,000; low: $1,000).
Purpose and activities: The foundation is
committed to the support of theatrical productions
and theater organizations that make a significant
contribution to the vitality of the field. Its primary
mission is to encourage the production of classic
plays, including great works of the 20th century;
foster the creation, growth, and production of new
work by recognized contemporary playwrights; and
develop an arena for theater to flourish so that it is
accessible to the general public.
Fields of interest: Performing arts, theater.
Limitations: Applications not accepted. Giving
primarily in New York, NY. No grants to individuals.
Application information: Unsolicited requests for
funds not accepted. Grants are by invitation only.
Board meeting date(s): First week of June and
Dec.
Officers: Laura J. Pels, Pres.; Laurence Y. Pels,
Secy.; Jeffrey S. Feinman, Treas.; Diane Morrison,
Exec. Dir.
Number of staff: 1 full-time professional; 1 full-time
support.
EIN: 136865620
Selected grants: The following grants were reported
in 2003.
$500,000 to Roundabout Theater Company, New
York, NY. For general support.
$25,000 to American Friends of the Royal Court
Theater, New York, NY. For general support.
$16,000 to National Corporate Theater Fund, New
York, NY. For general support.
$7,500 to CSC Repertory, Classic Stage Company,
New York, NY. For general support.
$5,000 to New Victory Theater, New York, NY. For
general support.
$5,000 to Signature Theater Company, New York,
NY. For general support.
$2,500 to Second Stage Theater, New York, NY. For
general support.
$1,000 to Mint Theater Company, New York, NY. For
general support.
$1,000 to Play Company, New York, NY. For general
support.
$500 to Playwrights Horizons, New York, NY. For
general support.

6708
Laura Pels International Foundation ✧ ☆
200 W. 57th St., Ste. 803
New York, NY 10019

Established in 1997 in NY.
Donor: Laura Pels.
Foundation type: Independent foundation.
Financial data (yr. ended 12/31/05): Assets, $3,056 (M); expenditures, $795,876; qualifying distributions, $367,500; giving activities include $367,500 for grants.
Purpose and activities: Giving for theater productions.
Fields of interest: Performing arts, theater.
Limitations: Applications not accepted. No grants to individuals.
Application information: Contributes only to pre-selected organizations. Grants are by invitation only.
Officers: Laura J. Pels, Pres.; Jeffrey S. Feinman, Treas.
Directors: Michael Colgan; Wilma Jordan; Juliette Meeus; Francis X. Morrissey.
EIN: 133926887

6709
Albert Penick Fund ✧
c/o JPMorgan Chase Bank, N.A.
1211 6th Ave., 34th Fl.
New York, NY 10036
Application address: c/o K. Philip Dresdner, 65 S. Main St., Pennington, NJ 08534

Trust established in 1951 in NY.
Donors: A.D. Penick†; Mrs. Albert D. Penick†.
Foundation type: Independent foundation.
Financial data (yr. ended 12/31/04): Assets, $3,456,708 (M); expenditures, $436,521; qualifying distributions, $386,406; giving activities include $376,100 for 43 grants (high: $100,000; low: $250).
Purpose and activities: Giving primarily for higher education, including pharmacy and nursing schools.
Fields of interest: Higher education; Education; Environment, natural resources; Animal welfare; Health care.
Type of support: Continuing support; Annual campaigns; Capital campaigns; Building/renovation; Equipment; Professorships; Scholarship funds.
Limitations: Giving primarily in CT, MA, NJ, and NY.
Application information: Application form not required.
   Initial approach: Letter
   Deadline(s): None
   Board meeting date(s): Spring and fall
Trustees: K. Philip Dresdner; V. Susan Penick.
EIN: 136161137
Selected grants: The following grants were reported in 2003.
$110,000 to Mills College, Oakland, CA. 2 grants: $100,000 (For general support), $10,000 (For annual support).
$50,000 to Pitzer College, Claremont, CA. For general support.
$50,000 to Yale University, Saybrook College, New Haven, CT. For renovation.
$26,000 to Lawrenceville School, Lawrenceville, NJ. For general support.
$25,000 to New Jersey SEEDS (Scholars, Educators, Excellence, Dedication, Success), Newark, NJ. For general support.

$16,500 to Planned Parenthood of the Mid-Hudson Valley, Poughkeepsie, NY. For general support.
$10,000 to Nature Conservancy, Arlington, VA. For general support.
$5,000 to North Star Fund, New York, NY. For general support.
$5,000 to Thoroughbred Retirement Foundation, Shrewsbury, NJ. For general support.

6710
Arnold S. Penner Foundation, Inc. ✧ ☆
249 E. 71st St.
New York, NY 10021
Contact: Arnold S. Penner, Dir.

Donor: Arnold S. Penner.
Foundation type: Independent foundation.
Financial data (yr. ended 2/28/06): Assets, $522,198 (M); gifts received, $1,185,148; expenditures, $1,188,098; qualifying distributions, $1,185,148; giving activities include $1,185,148 for grants.
Fields of interest: Museums (children's); Higher education, university; Medical school/education; Human services; Jewish agencies & temples.
Application information:
   Initial approach: Letter
   Deadline(s): None
Directors: Amy Berley; Jennifer Berley; Madaleine Berley; Mark Berley; Nancy Berley; Arnold S. Penner.
EIN: 133935352
Selected grants: The following grants were reported in 2005.
$22,000 to Yeshiva University, New York, NY.
$10,000 to Rabbi Arthur Schneier Park East Day School, New York, NY.
$3,000 to Carnegie Hall Society, New York, NY.
$2,800 to Jewish Museum, New York, NY.
$2,480 to Richmond Childrens Foundation, Yonkers, NY.
$500 to National Center for Victims of Crime, DC.
$250 to Community Access, New York, NY.

6711
Shannon and Andrew S. Penson Foundation ✧
551 5th Ave., 34th Fl.
New York, NY 10176

Established in 2002 in NY.
Donors: Andrew S. Penson; Shannon S. Penson.
Foundation type: Independent foundation.
Financial data (yr. ended 12/31/05): Assets, $2,896,804 (M); gifts received, $1,299,000; expenditures, $1,263,032; qualifying distributions, $1,246,368; giving activities include $1,233,165 for 52 grants (high: $258,500; low: $360).
Fields of interest: Law school/education; Hospitals (general); Big Brothers/Big Sisters; Jewish agencies & temples.
Limitations: Applications not accepted. No grants to individuals.
Application information: Contributes only to pre-selected organizations.
Trustees: Andrew S. Penson; Shannon S. Penson; Citibank, N.A.
EIN: 134226290

6712
Penzance Foundation ✧
909 Third Ave., 5th Fl.
New York, NY 10022

Established in 1981 in DE.
Donor: Edna McConnell Clark†.
Foundation type: Independent foundation.
Financial data (yr. ended 4/30/05): Assets, $52,334,182 (M); expenditures, $3,234,886; qualifying distributions, $2,992,889; giving activities include $2,933,900 for 18 grants (high: $1,000,000; low: $1,500; average: $5,000–$25,000).
Purpose and activities: The foundation's grantmaking reflects personal preferences of donor.
Fields of interest: Elementary/secondary education; Higher education; Environment, land resources; Environmental education; Hospitals (general); Marine science.
Type of support: General/operating support.
Limitations: Applications not accepted. Giving on a national basis. No grants to individuals.
Application information: Contributes only to pre-selected organizations.
Officers and Trustees:* Hays Clark,* Pres.; John M. Emery,* V.P. and Secy.; James McConnell Clark,* V.P. and Treas.
Number of staff: 1
EIN: 133081557
Selected grants: The following grants were reported in 2003.
$540,000 to Simons Rock College of Bard, Great Barrington, MA.
$512,000 to Loomis Chaffee School, Windsor, CT.
$194,250 to Thompson Island Outward Bound Education Center, Boston, MA.
$30,000 to Landing School of Boatbuilding and Design, Kennebunkport, ME.
$20,000 to Gordon School, East Providence, RI.
$17,000 to Childrens Medical Center of Dallas, Dallas, TX.
$11,000 to Save the Bay, Providence, RI.
$10,000 to Audubon Society, National, New York, NY.
$10,000 to Sippican Lands Trust, Marion, MA.

6713
The Pepsi Bottling Group Foundation, Inc. ✧
c/o The Pepsi Bottling Group, Inc.
1 Pepsi Way
Somers, NY 10589-2201 (914) 767-6000
Contact: Angela Buonocore, Asst. Secy.

Established in 1999 in NY.
Donors: The Pepsi Bottling Group, Inc.; Bottling Group, LLC.
Foundation type: Company-sponsored foundation.
Financial data (yr. ended 12/31/05): Assets, $7,645,403 (M); gifts received, $4,035,206; expenditures, $2,614,460; qualifying distributions, $2,614,460; giving activities include $2,468,520 for 1,990+ grants (high: $200,163).
Purpose and activities: The foundation supports organizations involved with higher education, disaster relief, human services, philanthropy, and the disabled people.
Fields of interest: Higher education; Disasters, preparedness/services; American Red Cross; Human services; Federated giving programs; Philanthropy/voluntarism; Disabilities, people with.

Type of support: General/operating support; Scholarship funds; Employee volunteer services; Employee matching gifts.

Limitations: Applications not accepted. Giving on a national basis in areas of company operations. No grants to individuals.

Application information: Contributes only to pre-selected organizations.

Officers and Directors:* John T. Cahill,* Chair.; Eric J. Foss,* Vice-Chair.; Steven M. Rapp, Secy.; Alfred H. Drewes,* Treas.; John L. Bensford.

EIN: 134090130

6714
The PepsiCo Foundation, Inc. ▼ ✧

c/o Dir., Corp. Contribs.
700 Anderson Hill Rd.
Purchase, NY   10577   (914) 253-3153
Contact: Jacqueline R. Millan, V.P.
URL: http://www.pepsico.com/PEP_Citizenship/ Contributions/index.cfm

Incorporated in 1962 in NY.

Donor: PepsiCo, Inc.

Foundation type: Company-sponsored foundation.

Financial data (yr. ended 12/31/05): Assets, $106,561,857 (M); gifts received, $21,000,000; expenditures, $22,014,844; qualifying distributions, $22,014,844; giving activities include $17,730,902 for 195 grants (high: $3,560,630; low: $16), and $4,125,626 for employee matching gifts.

Purpose and activities: The foundation supports organizations involved with education, water resources management, health, employment, small business, youth, minorities, women, and economically disadvantaged people.

Fields of interest: Education; Environment, water resources; Public health; Health care; Employment; Community development, small businesses; Youth; Minorities; Adults, women; Economically disadvantaged.

Type of support: General/operating support; Employee volunteer services; Employee matching gifts; Employee-related scholarships; Scholarships —to individuals.

Limitations: Giving on a national basis. No support for religious, fraternal, or political organizations. No grants to individuals (except for employee-related and Diamond scholarships), or for fundraising or sponsorship events.

Publications: Grants list; Informational brochure (including application guidelines).

Application information: Application form not required.

Initial approach: Mail proposal to foundation for requests of up less than $100,000; mail concept paper to foundation for requests of over $100,000

Deadline(s): None for requests of less than $100,000; Mar. 1 and Sept. 1 for requests of over $100,000

Board meeting date(s): May and Nov.

Final notification: Within 1 month for requests of over $100,000

Officers and Directors:* Steven S. Reinemund,* Chair.; Larry D. Thompson,* Pres.; Jacqueline R. Millan, V.P.; Christine Griff, Secy.; Lionel L. Nowell III, Treas.; David L. Gonzales; Donald M. Kendall; Brock Leach; Tod J. MacKenzie; Margaret D. Moore; Indra K. Nooyi; Ron Parker; Michael D. White.

Number of staff: 2 full-time professional; 2 full-time support.

EIN: 136163174

Selected grants: The following grants were reported in 2005.

$3,560,630 to Scholarship America, Saint Peter, MN.

$1,000,000 to American Red Cross, National Headquarters, DC. For relief effort for Hurricane Katrina.

$1,000,000 to National Council of La Raza, DC.

$1,000,000 to Salvation Army National Headquarters, Alexandria, VA. For relief effort for Hurricane Katrina.

$864,200 to Give2Asia, San Francisco, CA.

$600,000 to Girl Scouts of the U.S.A..

$500,000 to Community Foundation for the National Capital Region, DC.

$250,000 to Mercy Corps, Portland, OR.

$37,151 to United Way of Greater Topeka, Topeka, KS.

$25,000 to William Carey College, School of Business, Hattiesburg, MS.

6715
The A. J. Perella Foundation ✧ ☆

998 5th Ave., Apt. 11E
New York, NY   10028
Contact: Joseph R. Perella, Tr.

Established in 2001 in NY.

Donors: Mrs. Joseph Perella; Joseph Perella.

Foundation type: Independent foundation.

Financial data (yr. ended 12/31/05): Assets, $336,844 (M); gifts received, $916,662; expenditures, $760,535; qualifying distributions, $752,160; giving activities include $752,160 for grants.

Fields of interest: Arts; Elementary/secondary education; Business school/education; Libraries/ library science; Education; Cancer; Boys & girls clubs; Human services.

Limitations: Applications not accepted. Giving primarily in NY. No grants to individuals.

Application information: Contributes only to pre-selected organizations.

Trustees: Amy M. Perella; Joseph R. Perella.

EIN: 134200954

Selected grants: The following grants were reported in 2004.

$50,000 to Metropolitan Opera, New York, NY. For general support.

$25,000 to Boys and Girls Harbor, New York, NY. For general support.

$15,000 to Graduate Center Foundation, New York, NY. For general support.

$10,000 to Atlantic Salmon Federation, New York, NY. For general support.

$10,000 to Council on Foreign Relations, New York, NY. For general support.

$10,000 to De La Salle Academy, New York, NY. For general support.

$10,000 to Lehigh University, Bethlehem, PA. For general support.

$10,000 to New York Eye and Ear Infirmary, New York, NY. For general support.

$10,000 to Studio Museum in Harlem, New York, NY. For general support.

$2,500 to New York Public Library, New York, NY. For general support.

6716
Perelman Family Foundation ▼ ✧

c/o Mafco Holdings
35 E. 62nd St.
New York, NY   10021

Established in 1999 in NY.

Donor: R G I Group Incorporated.

Foundation type: Independent foundation.

Financial data (yr. ended 12/31/04): Assets, $0 (M); gifts received, $7,378,400; expenditures, $7,279,098; qualifying distributions, $7,275,148; giving activities include $7,275,148 for 129 grants (high: $1,000,000; low: $45; average: $500– $100,000).

Purpose and activities: Giving primarily for arts and culture, hospitals, human services, and Jewish agencies.

Fields of interest: Arts; Hospitals (general); Health organizations, association; Human services; Federated giving programs; Jewish agencies & temples.

Limitations: Applications not accepted. Giving on a national basis. No grants to individuals.

Application information: Contributes only to pre-selected organizations.

Officers and Directors:* Ronald O. Perelman,* Chair. and C.E.O.; Donald G. Drapkin, Vice-Chair.; Howard Gittis,* Vice-Chair.; Todd J. Slotkin, Exec. V.P. and C.F.O.; Barry F. Schwartz, Exec. V.P. and Gen. Counsel; Laurence Winoker, Sr. V.P., Treas. and Cont.; Christine Taylor, Sr. V.P.; Michael C. Borofsky, V.P. and Secy.; Gerry R. Kessel, V.P.; Debra G. Perelman, V.P.; Hope G. Perelman, V.P.; Joshua G. Perelman, V.P.; Steven G. Perelman, V.P.; Marvin Schaffer, V.P.

EIN: 134008528

Selected grants: The following grants were reported in 2004.

$1,000,000 to New York University Medical Center, New York, NY.

$750,000 to Memorial Sloan-Kettering Cancer Center, New York, NY. For campaign.

$453,310 to Machne Israel, Brooklyn, NY. 2 grants: $203,310, $250,000

$211,355 to Dana-Farber Cancer Institute, Boston, MA.

$200,000 to Rainforest Foundation US, New York, NY.

$131,300 to East 62nd Street Association, New York, NY.

$100,000 to Lubavitch of the East End, Patchogue, NY.

$100,000 to Ohr Torah Stone Colleges and Graduate Programs, New York, NY.

$50,000 to Brearley School, New York, NY.

6717
The Perkin Fund ✧

c/o Morris & McVeigh
767 3rd Ave.
New York, NY   10017
Contact: Mrs. Winifred P. Gray, Tr.

Established in 1967 in NY.

Donor: Richard S. Perkin‡.

Foundation type: Independent foundation.

Financial data (yr. ended 12/31/05): Assets, $30,063,775 (M); expenditures, $904,814; qualifying distributions, $558,928; giving activities include $514,000 for 14 grants (high: $100,000; low: $5,000).

Purpose and activities: Support for advanced scientific education, especially for astronomy, optics and bio-medicine, medical research, especially in bio-medicine, and giving for the performing arts.

Fields of interest: Performing arts; Performing arts, music; Arts; Higher education; Animal welfare; Hospitals (general); Biomedicine; Medical research, institute.

Type of support: General/operating support; Continuing support; Annual campaigns; Capital campaigns; Building/renovation; Equipment; Emergency funds; Program development; Conferences/seminars; Fellowships; Matching/challenge support.

Limitations: Giving primarily in CT, MA, and NY. No grants to individuals, or for scholarships; no loans.

Publications: Annual report; Financial statement; Informational brochure (including application guidelines).

Application information: Application form not required.

   Initial approach: Letter
   Copies of proposal: 2
   Deadline(s): Mar. 15 or Sept. 15
   Board meeting date(s): May and Nov.

Trustees: Kristina P. Davison; Alexandra T. Gray; John M. Gray; Matthew E.P. Gray; Winifred P. Gray; Peter W. Oldershaw; Christopher T. Perkin; Nicolas R. Perkin; Richard S. Perkin II; Robert S. Perkin; Thorne L. Perkin.

Number of staff: 1 part-time professional.

EIN: 136222498

Selected grants: The following grants were reported in 2004.

$600,000 to Rockefeller University, New York, NY.
$100,000 to TASIS Foundation, DC.
$83,000 to Wildlife Conservation Society, Bronx, NY.
$60,000 to Boston Ballet, Boston, MA.
$60,000 to Boston University, Boston, MA.
$50,000 to Lynchburg College, Lynchburg, VA.
$25,000 to Harvard University, Cambridge, MA.
$11,652 to Citizens for NYC, New York, NY.
$10,000 to Boston Modern Orchestra Project, Roslindale, MA.

6718

The Persepolis Foundation ✧ ☆

c/o Goldman Sachs & Co.
1 New York Plz., 40th Fl.
New York, NY   10004

Established in 1999 in NY.

Donor: Sharmin Mossavar-Rahmani.

Foundation type: Independent foundation.

Financial data (yr. ended 12/31/05): Assets, $10,297,838 (M); gifts received, $2,250,859; expenditures, $2,088,118; qualifying distributions, $2,060,381; giving activities include $2,031,647 for 12 grants (high: $1,961,876; low: $1,000).

Fields of interest: Museums; Higher education; Hospitals (general).

Limitations: Applications not accepted. Giving primarily in MA and NY. No grants to individuals.

Application information: Contributes only to pre-selected organizations.

Trustees: Bijan Mossavar-Rahmani; Sharmin Mossavar-Rahmani.

EIN: 134093707

Selected grants: The following grants were reported in 2005.

$1,961,876 to Harvard University, Cambridge, MA.

$10,000 to American Friends of the British Museum, New York, NY.
$6,100 to School of American Ballet, New York, NY.
$4,469 to Metropolitan Museum of Art, New York, NY.
$2,578 to Princeton University, Princeton, NJ.
$2,250 to Rockefeller University, New York, NY.
$1,500 to United Way, NY.
$1,000 to Friends School, Boulder, CO.

6719

The Pevaroff Cohn Family Foundation ✧

c/o Goldman Sachs-Family Office
1 New York Plz., 40th Fl.
New York, NY   10004

Donor: Gary D. Cohn.

Foundation type: Independent foundation.

Financial data (yr. ended 8/31/05): Assets, $10,338,101 (M); gifts received, $5,846,817; expenditures, $1,467,480; qualifying distributions, $1,402,270; giving activities include $1,402,270 for 67 grants (high: $300,000; low: $100).

Purpose and activities: Giving primarily for higher and other education, including a child study center; funding also for the arts, particularly museums.

Fields of interest: Museums (art); Museums (natural history); Arts; Elementary/secondary education; Education; Environment, natural resources; Reproductive health, family planning; Health care; Health organizations; Human services; Children/youth, services; Foundations (public); Jewish federated giving programs; Jewish agencies & temples.

Limitations: Applications not accepted. Giving primarily in NY. No grants to individuals; no loans or scholarships.

Application information: Contributes only to pre-selected organizations.

Trustees: Gary D. Cohn; Lisa Pevaroff-Cohn; James Riley, Jr.

EIN: 133797393

Selected grants: The following grants were reported in 2004.

$234,850 to New York University, New York, NY. For Child Study Center.
$150,000 to Ethical Culture Fieldston Schools, New York, NY. For general support.
$67,962 to Congregation Rodeph Sholom, New York, NY. 2 grants: $17,962 (For general support), $50,000 (For general support).
$34,000 to Johns Hopkins University, Baltimore, MD. For Next Generation Venture Fund.
$29,520 to Planned Parenthood of New York City, New York, NY. 2 grants: $15,220 (For general support), $14,300 (For general support).
$25,000 to Chai Lifeline, New York, NY. For general support.
$25,000 to Ronald McDonald House of New York, New York, NY. For general support.
$23,000 to Robin Hood Foundation, New York, NY. For general support.

6720

The Pfizer Foundation, Inc. ▼

235 E. 42nd St.
New York, NY   10017   (212) 733-4250
URL: http://www.pfizer.com/pfizer/subsites/philanthropy/index.jsp

Incorporated in 1953 in NY.

Donor: Pfizer Inc.

Foundation type: Company-sponsored foundation.

Financial data (yr. ended 12/31/05): Assets, $357,567,030 (M); expenditures, $24,876,968; qualifying distributions, $24,428,726; giving activities include $22,874,796 for grants.

Purpose and activities: The foundation supports organizations involved with K-12 science education, health, and HIV/AIDS.

Fields of interest: Elementary/secondary education; Education; Health care, equal rights; Medicine/medical care, public education; Health care; AIDS; Science.

Type of support: Program development; Curriculum development; Technical assistance; Employee volunteer services; Program evaluation; Employee matching gifts.

Limitations: Applications not accepted. No support for political organizations. No grants to individuals, or for capital campaigns or scholarships; no loans to individuals.

Publications: Financial statement.

Application information: Contributes only to pre-selected organizations.

   Board meeting date(s): As required

Officers and Directors:* C.L. Clemente,* V.P. and Genl. Counsel; Henry A. McKinnell, Jr., Ph.D.*, V.P.; Robert Norton,* V.P.; William C. Steere, Jr.,* V.P.; Caroline Roan, Secy.; R. Luftglass, Exec. Dir.; Jeffrey Kindler; Alan Levin; Robert Mallett.

EIN: 136083839

Selected grants: The following grants were reported in 2004.

$500,000 to C-Change, DC.
$500,000 to Project HOPE - People-to-People Health Foundation, Millwood, VA. For grant made through Global Community Matching Fund.
$500,000 to University of Virginia, Charlottesville, VA.
$380,298 to Morehouse School of Medicine, Atlanta, GA. 2 grants: $150,000 (For grant made through Healthcare Program), $230,298 (For grant made through Healthcare Program).
$300,000 to Asia Foundation, San Francisco, CA. For grant made through Healthcare Program.
$204,956 to CDC Foundation, Atlanta, GA. For grant made through Global Community Matching Fund.
$200,000 to Trust for Civil Society in Central and Eastern Europe, Warsaw, Poland. For grant made through Healthcare Program.
$150,000 to Irish American Endowment for Education, New York, NY. For grant made through Education Program.
$150,000 to San Diego Foundation, San Diego, CA. For grant made through Education Program.

6721

The Carl and Lily Pforzheimer Foundation, Inc. ▼

950 Third Ave., 30th Fl.
New York, NY   10022
Contact: Carl H. Pforzheimer III, Pres.

Incorporated in 1942 in NY.

Donor: Members of the Pforzheimer family.

Foundation type: Independent foundation.

Financial data (yr. ended 12/31/05): Assets, $23,184,132 (M); expenditures, $5,378,708; qualifying distributions, $5,158,538; giving activities include $4,838,225 for 49 grants (high: $1,000,000; low: $5,000; average: $10,000–$200,000), and $262,207 for 1 foundation-administered program.

Purpose and activities: The foundation maintains publishing and research activities in connection with the Carl H. Pforzheimer Library collection at the New York Public Library in the general field of American and English literature; giving primarily for higher and secondary education; support also for libraries, and cultural programs, public administration, a national municipal organization, and health care.

Fields of interest: Performing arts; Performing arts, theater; Language/linguistics; Literature; Arts; Secondary school/education; Higher education; Adult education—literacy, basic skills & GED; Libraries/library science; Education, reading; Education; Hospitals (general); Nursing care; Health care; Health organizations, association; Youth development, citizenship; Government/public administration; Public affairs, citizen participation.

Type of support: Endowments; Program development; Professorships; Publication; Seed money; Fellowships; Internship funds; Scholarship funds; Matching/challenge support.

Limitations: No support for religious or political organizations. No grants to individuals, or for building funds; no loans.

Application information: Application form not required.

   Initial approach: Letter or proposal
   Copies of proposal: 1
   Deadline(s): None
   Board meeting date(s): Apr., Oct., and Dec.
   Final notification: Generally, following board meeting

Officers and Directors:* Carl H. Pforzheimer III,* Pres. and Treas.; Nancy P. Aronson,* V.P.; Martin F. Richman, Secy.; Anthony L. Ferranti, Compt.; Edgar D. Aronson; George L.K. Frelinghuysen; Carl A. Pforzheimer; Carol K. Pforzheimer; Elizabeth S. Pforzheimer; Richard M. Sullick; Alison A. Sherman.

Number of staff: 3 full-time professional; 1 part-time professional; 2 full-time support.

EIN: 135624374

Selected grants: The following grants were reported in 2005.

$1,000,000 to Wellesley College, Wellesley, MA. To endow staff and program of the Learning and Teaching Center, as part of a capital campaign.

$400,000 to Harvard University, Radcliffe Institute for Advanced Study, Cambridge, MA. For fellowships program and Schlesinger Library endowment fund.

$400,000 to Pace University, New York, NY. For Pforzheimer Honors College endowment.

$250,000 to Americans for Oxford, New York, NY. For purchase of manuscript of Mary Shelley's Frankenstein for the Bodleian Library.

$250,000 to Horace Mann School, Riverdale, NY. For financial aid endowment fund.

$207,500 to Mount Sinai Medical Center, New York, NY. For Employee Assistance Program and SAVI program.

$150,000 to Dance Theater of Harlem, New York, NY. For educational programs in public schools.

$127,525 to Visiting Nurse Service of New York, New York, NY. For fundraising campaign for the Research Institute.

$100,000 to White Plains Hospital Center, White Plains, NY. For nursing student scholarships.

$50,000 to Lincoln Center Institute, New York, NY. For Mark Schubart Endowment.

6722
Phaedrus Foundation ✧

c/o Peyser & Alexander Mgmt.
500 5th Ave., Ste. 2700
New York, NY 10110
Contact: Thomas W. Buckner, Pres.

Established in 1991 in NY.

Donor: Foundation for the Needs of Others, Inc.

Foundation type: Independent foundation.

Financial data (yr. ended 12/31/05): Assets, $2,827,654 (M); expenditures, $387,289; qualifying distributions, $352,738; giving activities include $352,738 for 28 grants (high: $74,500; low: $900).

Purpose and activities: Giving primarily for the arts; funding also for education, and children and youth services.

Fields of interest: Performing arts; Performing arts, music; Performing arts, education; Arts; Higher education; Human services; Children/youth, services.

Limitations: Giving primarily in New York, NY. No grants to individuals.

Application information: Generally unsolicited requests for funds are not accepted. Application form not required.

   Deadline(s): None

Officers and Director:* Thomas W. Buckner,* Pres.; Kamala Buckner, Secy.

Number of staff: 1 full-time support; 2 part-time support.

EIN: 223120375

6723
The Phelan Foundation ✧ ☆

c/o Frank Phelan
7 Split Rock Ct.
Melville, NY 11747

Established in 2000 in NY.

Donor: Frank Phelan.

Foundation type: Independent foundation.

Financial data (yr. ended 12/31/05): Assets, $94,138 (M); gifts received, $1,475,000; expenditures, $1,470,912; qualifying distributions, $1,470,598; giving activities include $1,468,125 for 36 grants (high: $1,201,000; low: $25).

Fields of interest: Higher education; Roman Catholic federated giving programs; Roman Catholic agencies & churches.

Type of support: General/operating support.

Limitations: Applications not accepted. Giving primarily in NY. No grants to individuals.

Application information: Contributes only to pre-selected organizations.

Officers: Frank Phelan, Pres.; Mary Phelan, V.P. and Secy.

Director: Charles Feuerstein.

EIN: 113531781

6724
The Charles G. Phillips Family Foundation ✧

775 Park Ave.
New York, NY 10021

Established in 1997 in NY.

Donors: Charles G. Phillips; Candace Phillips.

Foundation type: Independent foundation.

Financial data (yr. ended 10/31/05): Assets, $1,002,148 (M); expenditures, $627,797; qualifying distributions, $591,950; giving activities include $591,950 for 20 grants (high: $500,000; low: $100).

Purpose and activities: Giving primarily for education.

Fields of interest: Education; Children/youth, services.

Limitations: Applications not accepted. Giving primarily in New York, NY. No grants to individuals.

Application information: Contributes only to pre-selected organizations.

Trustees: Candace Phillips; Charles G. Phillips.

EIN: 133981242

6725
Phillips-Van Heusen Foundation, Inc. ✧ ☆

200 Madison Ave., 10th Fl.
New York, NY 10016 (212) 381-3500
Contact: Tiffany Vargas
FAX: (212) 381-3960

Incorporated in 1969 in NY.

Donor: Phillips-Van Heusen Corp.

Foundation type: Company-sponsored foundation.

Financial data (yr. ended 12/31/05): Assets, $2,383,073 (M); gifts received, $3,993,738; expenditures, $1,676,828; qualifying distributions, $1,676,828; giving activities include $1,676,828 for grants.

Purpose and activities: The foundation supports organizations involved with health, human services, international affairs, and Judaism.

Fields of interest: Health care; Children/youth, services; Human services; International affairs; Federated giving programs; Jewish agencies & temples.

International interests: Israel.

Type of support: General/operating support; Continuing support; Annual campaigns; Emergency funds; Program development; Research.

Application information: Application form not required.

   Initial approach: Proposal
   Copies of proposal: 1
   Deadline(s): None
   Board meeting date(s): Sept.

Officers: Bruce J. Klatsky, Chair.; Pamela N. Hootkin, V.P. and Secy.; Emanuel Chirico, V.P. and Treas.

EIN: 237104639

Selected grants: The following grants were reported in 2005.

$101,200 to Metropolitan Museum of Art, New York, NY. 2 grants: $100,000, $1,200

$79,843 to United Way. 2 grants: $78,806, $1,037

$50,000 to Human Rights Watch, New York, NY.

$50,000 to Muscular Dystrophy Association, Tucson, AZ.

$50,000 to Safe Horizon, New York, NY.

$2,000 to Volunteers of America.

$1,000 to Brazil Foundation, New York, NY.

$500 to March of Dimes Birth Defects Foundation, White Plains, NY.

6726
The Pincus Family Fund ▼ ✧

466 Lexington Ave.
New York, NY 10017 (212) 878-9291
Contact: Evelyn Lipori, Fund Admin.

Established in 1961 in NY.
Donors: Lionel I. Pincus; Suzanne Pincus†.
Foundation type: Independent foundation.
Financial data (yr. ended 12/31/05): Assets, $27,182,495 (M); expenditures, $4,940,983; qualifying distributions, $4,893,483; giving activities include $4,845,030 for 60 grants (high: $1,000,000; low: $2,000; average: $10,000–$100,000).
Purpose and activities: The program fund focuses primarily on disadvantaged and at-risk youth in New York City from early childhood to adolescence. The fund seeks to support programs leveraging change, having an impact beyond their immediate location, and at a critical phase in their evolution. Of special interest are programs working with the public schools. The institutional giving fund is only open to pre-selected organizations.
Fields of interest: Education; Youth development, community service clubs; Youth development; Children, services; Child development, services; Family services; Community development.
Type of support: Program development.
Limitations: Applications not accepted. Giving primarily in NY. No loans or grants to individuals, or for capital funds, construction and equipment, scholarships, or fellowships.
Application information: Grants from the Institutional Fund are made only to pre-selected organizations; unsolicited applications not accepted.
Officers and Directors:* Lionel I. Pincus,* Pres.; Edwin Gustafson, Jr.,* Secy.-Treas.; Henry Pincus; Matthew Pincus.
EIN: 136089184
Selected grants: The following grants were reported in 2004.
$1,412,500 to Columbia University, New York, NY. 4 grants: $1,000,000 to School of Business, $50,000 to School of Buisness, $312,500, $50,000
$1,100,000 to New York Public Library, New York, NY. 2 grants: $1,000,000, $100,000
$200,000 to Peace Games, Boston, MA. 2 grants: $100,000 each
$75,000 to Community Impact, New York, NY.
$50,000 to Women in Need (WIN), New York, NY.

6727
The Pines Bridge Foundation ◇
1114 Ave. of the Americas, Ste. 3400
New York, NY   10036

Established in 1986 in NY.
Donors: Alan G. Weiler; Elaine Weiler; The Weiler-Arnow Investment Co.
Foundation type: Independent foundation.
Financial data (yr. ended 12/31/05): Assets, $2,206 (M); gifts received, $50,000; expenditures, $323,832; qualifying distributions, $323,450; giving activities include $323,250 for 39 grants (high: $55,000; low: $250).
Purpose and activities: Giving primarily for the arts; funding also for education, and for medical research, particularly a glaucoma foundation.
Fields of interest: Media/communications; Museums; Performing arts; Arts; Higher education; Education; Health organizations, research.
Limitations: Applications not accepted. Giving primarily in NY. No grants to individuals.
Application information: Contributes only to pre-selected organizations.

Trustees: Alan G. Weiler; Elaine Weiler.
EIN: 136872045

6728
The Pinkerton Foundation ▼ ◇
610 5th Ave., Ste. 316
New York, NY   10020   (212) 332-3385
Contact: Joan Colello, Exec. Dir.
FAX: (212) 332-3399;
E-mail: pinkfdn@pinkertonfdn.org; *URL:* http://www.thepinkertonfoundation.org

Incorporated in 1966 in DE.
Donor: Robert A. Pinkerton†.
Foundation type: Independent foundation.
Financial data (yr. ended 12/31/05): Assets, $138,602,820 (M); expenditures, $8,627,017; qualifying distributions, $8,183,039; giving activities include $7,023,563 for 128 grants (high: $281,789; low: $1,000; average: $10,000–$100,000), and $2,586 for employee matching gifts.
Purpose and activities: Giving to economically disadvantaged children, youth, and families; support also for severely learning-disabled children and adults of borderline intelligence. The foundation is also interested in endeavors that strengthen youth programming in poor communities; and programs that develop an individual's competencies, instill values, and increase opportunities to participate in society.
Fields of interest: Children/youth, services; Economically disadvantaged.
Type of support: General/operating support; Program development; Seed money; Research; Technical assistance; Employee matching gifts; Matching/challenge support.
Limitations: Giving primarily in New York, NY. No support for medical research, the media, the direct provision of health care, or religious education. Generally no grants to individuals, or for emergency assistance, conferences, publications, media, building renovations, or other capital projects, unless they are integrally related to foundation's program objectives or an outgrowth of grantee's programs; no loans.
Publications: Grants list.
Application information: Accepts NYRAG Common Application Form. Application form required.
   Initial approach: Letter (no more than 2 pages)
   Copies of proposal: 1
   Deadline(s): Submit proposal by Feb. 1 for May meeting and Sept. 1 for Dec. meeting
   Board meeting date(s): May and Dec.
Officers and Trustees:* George J. Gillespie III,* Pres.; Joan Colello,* Secy. and Exec. Dir.; Daniel L. Mosley,* Treas.; Christopher H. Browne; Richard M. Smith; Thomas J. Sweeney.
Number of staff: 2 full-time professional; 1 part-time professional; 1 part-time support.
EIN: 136206624
Selected grants: The following grants were reported in 2005.
$1,000,000 to Fund for the City of New York, New York, NY. For operating support for Young Adult Capacity Building Initiative.
$426,808 to Fund for Public Health in New York, New York, NY. For operating support.
$281,789 to Good Shepherd Services, New York, NY. For operating support.
$175,000 to Cristo Rey High School, New York, NY. For operating support.

$100,000 to Center for Arts Education, New York, NY. For operating support.
$51,000 to Jewish Home and Hospital for the Aged, New York, NY. For operating support.
$49,941 to Bank Street College of Education, New York, NY. For operating support.
$40,000 to Lenox Hill Neighborhood House, New York, NY. For operating support.
$40,000 to Summer Search New York City, Brooklyn, NY. For operating support.
$25,000 to Museum of Jewish Heritage, New York, NY. For operating support.

6729
The Pioneer Fund, Inc. ◇ ☆
954 Lexington Ave., Ste. 211
New York, NY   10021   (212) 459-4084
Contact: J. Philippe Rushton, Pres.
E-mail: info@pioneerfund.org; *URL:* http://www.pioneerfund.org

Incorporated in 1937 in NY.
Donor: Kistler Instruments Inc.
Foundation type: Independent foundation.
Financial data (yr. ended 12/31/05): Assets, $3,038,186 (M); gifts received, $50,000; expenditures, $404,175; qualifying distributions, $369,316; giving activities include $369,316 for grants.
Fields of interest: Media, journalism/publishing; Higher education; Social sciences, research; Psychology/behavioral science.
Type of support: Research.
Application information: Submit letter on institutional stationery (typically a university). Application form not required.
   Initial approach: Brief letter (no more than 500 words)
   Copies of proposal: 1
   Deadline(s): None
   Board meeting date(s): Annually
Officer and Directors:* J. Philippe Rushton, B.Sc., Ph.D.*, Pres.; Richard Lynn; T. Travis Osborne; Stephen Rushton; Michelle Weyher.
EIN: 510181036
Selected grants: The following grants were reported in 2004.
$55,175 to University of Western Ontario, London, Canada. .
$45,000 to Ulster Institute for Social Research, Bristol, United Kingdom. .
$25,000 to University of Arizona, Tucson, AZ.
$20,000 to New Century Fund, DC.
$12,000 to Arizona State University, Tempe, AZ.
$11,000 to Western Carolina University, Cullowhee, NC.
$5,125 to University of Texas, Austin, TX.
$5,000 to Forest Institute of Professional Psychology, Springfield, MO.

6730
The Pittman Family Foundation ◇
c/o TAG Assocs.
75 Rockefeller Plz.
New York, NY   10019

Established in 1997.
Donor: Robert W. Pittman.
Foundation type: Independent foundation.
Financial data (yr. ended 4/30/05): Assets, $6,901,050 (M); gifts received, $3,161,494;

expenditures, $2,430,363; qualifying distributions, $2,387,013; giving activities include $2,387,013 for 104 grants (high: $500,000; low: $100).
Purpose and activities: Giving primarily for arts and culture, as well as for education; funding also for health associations, human services, and federated giving programs.
Fields of interest: Performing arts, ballet; Performing arts, theater; Arts; Education; Health organizations, association; Human services; Federated giving programs.
Limitations: Applications not accepted. Giving on a national basis, with emphasis on New York, NY. No grants to individuals.
Application information: Contributes only to pre-selected organizations.
Trustees: Robert W. Pittman; Veronique Choa Pittman.
EIN: 541876548
Selected grants: The following grants were reported in 2005.
$400,000 to Robin Hood Foundation, New York, NY.
$333,333 to University of Pennsylvania, Philadelphia, PA.
$91,140 to New York City Ballet, New York, NY. 3 grants: $28,070, $13,070, $50,000
$50,000 to Whitney Museum of American Art, New York, NY.
$15,000 to Christ Church Day School, New York, NY.
$10,000 to Bank Street College of Education, New York, NY.
$1,000 to International Center for Journalists, DC.
$1,000 to New York Cares, New York, NY.

6731
Henry B. Plant Memorial Fund, Inc. ✧
c/o U.S. Trust
114 W. 47th St., 8th Fl.
New York, NY 10036-1532
Contact: Andrew D. Lane, Secy.-Treas.

Incorporated in 1947 in NY.
Donor: Amy P. Statter.
Foundation type: Independent foundation.
Financial data (yr. ended 12/31/04): Assets, $12,175,652 (M); expenditures, $566,528; qualifying distributions, $523,545; giving activities include $520,000 for grants.
Purpose and activities: Giving primarily for arts and culture, education, health, and human services.
Fields of interest: Museums; Performing arts; Performing arts, music; Arts; Higher education; Law school/education; Education; Environment; Health organizations, association; Human services; Children/youth, services; Family services; Federated giving programs.
Limitations: Applications not accepted. No grants to individuals.
Application information: Contributes only to pre-selected organizations.
Officers and Directors:* Amy Roberts Lee,* Pres.; Phyllis S. Oxman,* V.P.; Andrew D. Lane, Secy.-Treas.
Advisor: U.S. Trust.
Number of staff: 1 part-time professional.
EIN: 136077327
Selected grants: The following grants were reported in 2004.
$51,000 to Saint Georges School, Newport, RI. For annual fund.
$28,600 to Caramoor Center for Music and the Arts, Katonah, NY.

$23,000 to World Learning, Brattleboro, VT. For EIL Scholarship Fund.
$21,000 to Tabor Academy, Marion, MA. For Schooner Tabor Boy endowment.
$20,000 to Dana-Farber Cancer Institute, Boston, MA. For Women's Cancer Program.
$15,000 to Chewonki Foundation, Wiscasset, ME.
$15,000 to Marlboro College, Marlboro, VT. For endowment fund.
$15,000 to Williams College, Williamstown, MA. For Parents Fund.
$12,000 to Ashoka: Innovators for the Public, Arlington, VA. For unrestricted support.
$10,000 to Yale University, New Haven, CT. For unrestricted support.

6732
PLM Foundation ✧
390 Park Ave., Ste. 600
New York, NY 10022

Established in 1996 in NY.
Donor: Philip L. Milstein.
Foundation type: Independent foundation.
Financial data (yr. ended 12/31/04): Assets, $9,249,681 (M); gifts received, $3,186,707; expenditures, $2,776,491; qualifying distributions, $2,774,837; giving activities include $2,774,192 for 89 grants (high: $1,000,619; low: $500).
Fields of interest: Arts; Higher education; Education; Health care; Human services; YM/YWCAs & YM/YWHAs.
Limitations: Applications not accepted. Giving primarily in NY. No grants to individuals.
Application information: Contributes only to pre-selected organizations.
Trustees: Cheryl Milstein; Philip L. Milstein.
EIN: 137105558
Selected grants: The following grants were reported in 2004.
$1,002,619 to Columbia University, New York, NY.
$511,250 to Barnard College, New York, NY.
$400,000 to New York University, New York, NY.
$5,000 to Yale University, New Haven, CT.
$1,000 to Scranton Hebrew Day School, Scranton, PA.

6733
The Polisseni Foundation, Inc. ✧ ☆
c/o G.P. Associates
375 Woodcliff Dr.
Fairport, NY 14450

Established in 2001 in NY.
Donor: Wanda Polisseni.
Foundation type: Independent foundation.
Financial data (yr. ended 8/31/05): Assets, $5,285,199 (M); gifts received, $3,470,484; expenditures, $1,384,132; qualifying distributions, $1,265,500; giving activities include $1,265,500 for 9 grants (high: $1,000,000; low: $500).
Fields of interest: Higher education; Hospitals (general).
Limitations: Applications not accepted. Giving primarily in NY. No grants to individuals.
Application information: Contributes only to pre-selected organizations.
Officer: Wanda Polisseni, Pres.
Directors: Gary Polisseni; Gregory Polisseni; Valerie Polisseni Wilcox.
EIN: 161611263

6734
Yvonne & Leslie Pollack Family Foundation, Inc. ✧
8 Long Meadow Rd.
Bedford, NY 10506 (212) 476-5888
Contact: Leslie Pollack, Pres; Yvonne Pollack, Secy.

Established in 1998 in NY.
Donors: Leslie Pollack; Rae Pollack†.
Foundation type: Independent foundation.
Financial data (yr. ended 12/31/03): Assets, $3,689,469 (M); expenditures, $336,188; qualifying distributions, $336,188; giving activities include $317,367 for 81 grants (high: $113,739; low: $100).
Purpose and activities: Giving primarily for the arts, health, human services, and to Jewish organizations.
Fields of interest: Arts; Education; Hospitals (general); Health care; Health organizations, association; Human services; Jewish federated giving programs; Jewish agencies & temples.
Limitations: Giving primarily in New York, NY. No grants to individuals.
Application information: Application form not required.
  Deadline(s): None
Officers and Directors:* Leslie Pollack,* Pres.; Yvonne Pollack,* Secy.; Fredrica Pollack; Jonathan Pollack; Jennifer Pollack Reiner.
EIN: 133985619
Selected grants: The following grants were reported in 2004.
$100,000 to UJA-Federation of New York, New York, NY. For unrestricted support.
$32,600 to Katonah Museum of Art, Katonah, NY. 3 grants: $3,600 (For unrestricted support), $4,000 (For unrestricted support), $25,000 (For unrestricted support).
$25,000 to Anti-Defamation League of Bnai Brith, New York, NY. For unrestricted support.
$25,000 to Yale University, New Haven, CT. For unrestricted support.
$20,000 to American Jewish Historical Society, New York, NY. 2 grants: $5,000 (For unrestricted support), $15,000 (For unrestricted support).
$10,000 to Jewish Museum, New York, NY. For unrestricted support.
$5,000 to Northern Westchester Hospital Center, Mount Kisco, NY. For unrestricted support.

6735
The Geri & Lester Pollack Family Foundation, Inc. ✧ ☆
(formerly The Pollack Family Foundation, Inc.)
c/o Lazard
30 Rockefeller Plz.
New York, NY 10020
Contact: Lester Pollack, Pres.

Established in 1986 in NY.
Donor: Lester Pollack.
Foundation type: Independent foundation.
Financial data (yr. ended 9/30/05): Assets, $1,387,902 (M); gifts received, $317,294; expenditures, $486,681; qualifying distributions, $486,331; giving activities include $486,331 for grants.
Purpose and activities: Giving primarily for social services and to Jewish agencies and temples.
Fields of interest: Museums (specialized); Arts; Education; Health organizations, association;

Human services; Children/youth, services; Federated giving programs; Jewish federated giving programs; Jewish agencies & temples.
Type of support: General/operating support; Capital campaigns; Scholarship funds.
Limitations: Giving primarily in New York, NY. No grants to individuals.
Application information:
   Initial approach: Letter
   Deadline(s): None
Officers and Directors: * Lester Pollock,* Pres.; Geri Pollack,* V.P.; Howard Sontag,* Secy.-Treas.
EIN: 133384943
Selected grants: The following grants were reported in 2005.
$83,000 to American Friends of the Israel Museum, New York, NY.
$50,000 to American Friends of Shalom Hartman Institute, New York, NY.
$20,000 to Tel Aviv University: American Council, New York, NY.
$14,500 to Jewish Museum, New York, NY.
$4,200 to Abraham Joshua Heschel School, New York, NY.
$3,000 to New York Landmarks Conservancy, New York, NY.
$2,500 to Beacon Cultural Foundation, Beacon, NY.
$2,000 to Katonah Museum of Art, Katonah, NY.
$2,000 to Public Theater, New York, NY.
$1,000 to Kolbe Cathedral High School, Bridgeport, CT.

6736
The Pollock-Krasner Foundation, Inc. ◇
863 Park Ave.
New York, NY 10021 (212) 517-5400
Contact: Caroline Black, Prog. Off.
FAX: (212) 288-2836; E-mail: grants@pkf.org;
URL: http://www.pkf.org

Established in 1984 in DE.
Donor: Lee Krasner‡.
Foundation type: Independent foundation.
Financial data (yr. ended 6/30/05): Assets, $60,720,134 (M); gifts received, $20,000; expenditures, $4,562,184; qualifying distributions, $3,769,810; giving activities include $2,690,200 for grants to individuals.
Purpose and activities: Giving exclusively to needy and worthy individual working artists (painters, sculptors, artists who work on paper, including printmakers) who have embarked on professional careers; grants may be used for professional or personal requirements.
Fields of interest: Visual arts.
Type of support: Grants to individuals.
Limitations: Giving on a national and international basis. No support for organizations or institutions. No grants for past debt, legal fees, purchase of real estate, tuition reimbursement, moving expenses, costs of installations, commissions or projects ordered by others, or individual grants to students, photographers, commercial, performance, or video artists, filmmakers or craftsmen.
Publications: Application guidelines; Annual report; Informational brochure (including application guidelines).
Application information: Application forms and information on the application procedure can be obtained from the foundation Web site. The foundation cannot respond to application requests by telephone or in person; therefore, write, fax or E-mail. Application form required.

Initial approach: Letter, fax or E-mail, requesting application
Deadline(s): None
Board meeting date(s): Regularly throughout the year
Final notification: As soon as possible
Officers and Directors: * Charles C. Bergman,* Chair.; Samuel Sachs II,* Pres.; Kerrie Buitrago, Exec. V.P.
Number of staff: 5 full-time professional; 2 full-time support.
EIN: 133255693

6737
The Polo Ralph Lauren Foundation ◇
c/o Mahoney Cohen, C.P.A.
1065 Ave. of the Americas
New York, NY 10018
URL: http://about.polo.com/philanthropy/default.asp

Established in 2001 in NY.
Donor: Polo Ralph Lauren Corp.
Foundation type: Company-sponsored foundation.
Financial data (yr. ended 4/3/05): Assets, $12,398,205 (M); gifts received, $1,455,672; expenditures, $982,416; qualifying distributions, $844,558; giving activities include $844,557 for 68 grants (high: $150,000; low: $500).
Purpose and activities: The foundation supports programs designed to benefit medically underserved persons in cancer care and prevention; and enhance artistic expression and cultural development for underserved groups, with an emphasis on American heritage and values.
Fields of interest: Arts; Cancer; Economically disadvantaged.
Limitations: Applications not accepted. Giving on a national basis. No grants to individuals.
Application information: Contributes only to pre-selected organizations.
Officers and Directors: * Ralph Lauren,* Chair.; David Lauren, Pres.; Paul Campbell, V.P.; Bette-Ann Gwathmey, V.P.; Edward Scheuermann, Secy.; Tracy Travis, Treas.; Oscar Cohen, Exec. Dir.; Roger Farah; Mitch Kosh.
EIN: 522316766

6738
The Hazen Polsky Foundation, Inc. ◇
(formerly The Polsky Foundation, Inc.)
667 Madison Ave.
New York, NY 10021

Established in NY.
Donors: Alexander Polsky; Cynthia Polsky.
Foundation type: Independent foundation.
Financial data (yr. ended 12/31/04): Assets, $2,245,665 (M); gifts received, $161,003; expenditures, $846,830; qualifying distributions, $828,702; giving activities include $762,326 for 45 + grants (high: $220,000).
Purpose and activities: Giving for cultural activities.
Fields of interest: Arts; Higher education; Education.
Limitations: Applications not accepted. Giving primarily in NY. No grants to individuals.
Application information: Contributes only to pre-selected organizations.

Officers: Cynthia H. Polsky, Chair.; Leon Polsky, Pres.; N. Polsky, V.P. and Secy.; A. Polsky, V.P. and Treas.
EIN: 510245812

6739
Sam Pomeranz Trust ◇
c/o Sheldon G. Kall
3522 James St., Ste. 101
Syracuse, NY 13206 (315) 437-3321

Established in 2001.
Foundation type: Independent foundation.
Financial data (yr. ended 12/31/04): Assets, $6,752,460 (M); expenditures, $498,642; qualifying distributions, $341,393; giving activities include $341,393 for 15 grants (high: $204,970; low: $1,000).
Purpose and activities: Giving primarily to Jewish charities in central NY.
Fields of interest: Jewish federated giving programs; Jewish agencies & temples.
Limitations: Giving primarily in NY.
Application information:
   Initial approach: Letter
   Deadline(s): 90 days prior to year end
Trustees: Sheldon G. Kall; Abraham Shankman.
EIN: 166514459

6740
The Generoso Pope Foundation ◇
(formerly The Pope Foundation)
24 Depot Sq.
Tuckahoe, NY 10707
Contact: David Pope, C.E.O.

Incorporated in 1947 in NY.
Donor: Generoso Pope‡.
Foundation type: Independent foundation.
Financial data (yr. ended 12/31/04): Assets, $33,196,456 (M); expenditures, $1,583,628; qualifying distributions, $3,727,777; giving activities include $794,234 for 78 grants (high: $115,500; low: $450).
Purpose and activities: Emphasis on Roman Catholic church support, including religious associations and welfare funds, and higher and secondary education; funding also for medical research and hospitals, and community funds, and education.
Fields of interest: Performing arts, music; Secondary school/education; Higher education; Education; Hospitals (general); Medical research, institute; Human services; Roman Catholic agencies & churches.
Type of support: General/operating support.
Limitations: Giving primarily in the metropolitan New York, NY, area, including Westchester County. No grants to individuals.
Application information: Application form required for the foundation's Awards for the Arts program.
   Initial approach: Letter
   Deadline(s): Dec. 31 for Awards for the Arts program; no set deadlines for other grants
Officer: David Pope, C.E.O.
EIN: 136096193
Selected grants: The following grants were reported in 2003.
$113,600 to Lawrence Hospital, Bronxville, NY.
$100,000 to Blythedale Childrens Hospital, Valhalla, NY. For medical research.

$36,500 to Amherst College, Amherst, MA.

$32,248 to Northfield Mount Hermon School, Northfield, MA.

$30,000 to Fairfield University, Fairfield, CT.

$28,200 to Diabetes Institutes Foundation, Norfolk, VA.

$25,000 to Yonkers Fire Department, Yonkers, NY.

$20,500 to Fairfield College Preparatory School, Fairfield, CT.

$15,000 to Catholic University of America, DC.

$12,220 to Greenwich Adult Day Care, Greenwich, CT.

6741

The Popplestone Foundation ◇

c/o JPMorgan Chase Bank, N.A.
345 Park Ave., 4th Fl.
New York, NY 10154
Contact: Lisa Philp, V.P., JPMorgan Chase Bank, N.A.
FAX: (212) 464-2305;
E-mail: philp_lisa@JPMorgan.com

Established in 2000 in MA.
Donors: Alan J. Dworsky; Suzanne E. Werber.
Foundation type: Independent foundation.
Financial data (yr. ended 12/31/04): Assets, $56,882,019 (M); expenditures, $2,632,746; qualifying distributions, $2,367,863; giving activities include $2,359,065 for 15 grants (high: $365,000; low: $31,000).
Fields of interest: Media/communications; Performing arts, opera; Performing arts, music (choral); Education.
Type of support: General/operating support.
Limitations: Applications not accepted. Giving on a national basis. No grants to individuals, or for matching gifts; no loans.
Application information: Contributes only to pre-selected organizations.
Trustees: Alan J. Dworsky; Suzanne E. Werber.
EIN: 043528004
Selected grants: The following grants were reported in 2004.
$300,000 to Center for American Progress, DC.
$250,000 to Center on Budget and Policy Priorities, DC.
$200,000 to Center for Public Integrity, DC.
$175,000 to Communications Consortium Media Center, DC.
$150,000 to Chorus America, DC.
$150,000 to Institute on Taxation and Economic Policy, DC.
$150,000 to Metropolitan Opera Guild, New York, NY.
$62,000 to Cambridge Public Schools, Cambridge, MA.
$50,000 to Boston Childrens Chorus, Boston, MA.
$31,000 to Brown University, Providence, RI.

6742

The Philip E. Potter Foundation ◇

6 Ford Ave.
Oneonta, NY 13820 (607) 432-6720
Contact: Henry L. Hulbert, Mgr.

Established in 1973.
Donors: Philip E. Potter; Mrs. Philip E. Potter; Lillian W. Potter†.
Foundation type: Independent foundation.

Financial data (yr. ended 10/31/05): Assets, $10,625,596 (M); expenditures, $663,279; qualifying distributions, $645,986; giving activities include $530,000 for grants to individuals.
Purpose and activities: Awards scholarships mostly to Oneonta High School graduates.
Type of support: Scholarships—to individuals.
Limitations: Giving limited to residents of Otsego and Delaware counties, NY, with emphasis on residents of Oneonta.
Application information: Application forms available at local high schools or from foundation office. Application form required.
 Deadline(s): May 15
Officer and Trustees:* Henry L. Hulbert,* Mgr.; SueAnne T. DeBergh; Maureen P. Hulbert; Robert W. Moyer; Anne T. Wolek.
EIN: 166169167

6743

The Potter's Wheel Foundation, Inc. ◇

c/o Anchin, Block & Anchin LLP
1375 Broadway
New York, NY 10018-7001

Established in 1997 in NY.
Donor: Alice Jacobs.
Foundation type: Independent foundation.
Financial data (yr. ended 3/31/05): Assets, $6,547,710 (M); expenditures, $454,128; qualifying distributions, $333,649; giving activities include $321,035 for 1 grant.
Fields of interest: Disasters, 9/11.01.
Limitations: Applications not accepted. Giving primarily in New York, NY. No grants to individuals.
Application information: Contributes only to pre-selected organizations.
Officers: Alice Jacobs, Pres.; Brian D. Altman, V.P.; Barbara Bruno, V.P.; Donald B. Altman, Secy.-Treas.
Director: Diego Hidalgo.
EIN: 133949433
Selected grants: The following grants were reported in 2004.
$295,144 to Park Avenue Charitable Fund, New York, NY. For general support.
$400 to Temple Beth Judah, Wildwood, NJ. For general support.

6744

The Powers Family Foundation ◇

c/o Goldman Sachs & Co.
1 New York Plz., 40th Fl.
New York, NY 10004

Established in 1991 in NY.
Donor: John J. Powers.
Foundation type: Independent foundation.
Financial data (yr. ended 6/30/05): Assets, $11,744,067 (M); expenditures, $345,547; qualifying distributions, $336,750; giving activities include $336,750 for 18 grants (high: $200,000; low: $750).
Fields of interest: Education, early childhood education; Higher education, college; Education; Hospitals (general).
Limitations: Applications not accepted. Giving primarily in Boston, MA, and New York, NY. No grants to individuals.
Application information: Contributes only to pre-selected organizations.

Trustees: Charles A. Davis; John J. Powers; Linda E. Powers.
EIN: 133637704
Selected grants: The following grants were reported in 2006.
$230,000 to Boston College, Chestnut Hill, MA. 3 grants: $25,000, $200,000, $5,000
$10,000 to Boys and Girls Club of Martin County, Hobe Sound, FL.
$10,000 to Buckley Country Day School, Roslyn, NY.
$10,000 to College of Charleston, Charleston, SC.
$10,000 to Fairfield University, Fairfield, CT.
$10,000 to One to One New York, New York, NY.
$5,000 to Mountain Mission School, Grundy, VA.
$750 to Boys Club of New York, New York, NY.

6745

Tina & Steven Price Charitable Foundation ◇ ☆

c/o Tag Assoc., LLC
75 Rockefeller Plz., Ste. 900
New York, NY 10019

Established in 2003 in NY.
Donors: Steven Price; Tina Price.
Foundation type: Independent foundation.
Financial data (yr. ended 12/31/05): Assets, $1,469,432 (M); gifts received, $975,000; expenditures, $345,209; qualifying distributions, $344,900; giving activities include $344,900 for 25 grants (high: $180,000; low: $100).
Officers and Trustees:* Steven Price,* Mgr.; Tina Price,* Mgr.
EIN: 206019600

6746

Price Chopper's Golub Foundation ◇

(formerly Golub Foundation)
501 Duanesburg Rd.
Schenectady, NY 12306 (518) 356-9450
FAX: (518) 374-4259; Application address: P.O. Box 1074, Schenectady, NY 12301; Additional tel.: (877) 877-0870; URL: http://www.pricechopper.com/GolubFoundation/GolubFoundation_S.las?-token.S=0C2T9R7F6221 1b8P73922412RLWN6L5J64CA5D|24634| 0507251403||||
Scholarship application address: c/o Price Chopper Scholarship Office, P.O. Box 1074, Schenectady, NY 12301

Established in 1981 in NY.
Donors: Jane Golub; Neil M. Golub; Golub Corp.
Foundation type: Company-sponsored foundation.
Financial data (yr. ended 3/31/05): Assets, $70,608 (M); gifts received, $450,000; expenditures, $776,824; qualifying distributions, $776,807; giving activities include $680,225 for 529 grants (high: $50,000; low: $30), $59,000 for 54 grants to individuals (high: $3,000; low: $500), and $120 for 5 employee matching gifts.
Purpose and activities: The foundation supports organizations involved with arts and culture, education, health, youth development, and human services and awards college scholarships to students located in areas of company operations.
Fields of interest: Arts; Higher education; Education; Health care; Youth development; Human services; Federated giving programs; Jewish agencies & temples; Minorities.

Type of support: General/operating support; Continuing support; Annual campaigns; Program development; Sponsorships; Employee matching gifts; Scholarships—to individuals.
Limitations: Giving limited to areas of company operations in CT, MA, NH, NY, PA, and VT. No grants to individuals (except for scholarships), or for annual meetings, endowments, film or video projects, advertising, travel, conferences, conventions, or symposiums, publishing, or capital campaigns of national, religious, or political organizations.
Publications: Informational brochure (including application guidelines).
Application information: Proposals should be submitted using organization letterhead. An application form is required for scholarships.
  Initial approach: Proposal; download application form and mail to foundation for scholarships
  Deadline(s): 6 weeks prior to need; Mar. 15 for scholarships
  Final notification: 3 to 4 months; Apr. 15 for scholarships
Trustees: Cindy Breslin; Pamela Cerrone; George Coleman; David Golub.
EIN: 222341421
Selected grants: The following grants were reported in 2003.
$43,125 to United Jewish Federation of Northeastern New York, Latham, NY.
$20,000 to Ellis Hospital Foundation, Schenectady, NY.
$10,000 to Albany College of Pharmacy, Albany, NY. For capital campaign.
$10,000 to Albany Symphony Orchestra, Albany, NY.
$10,000 to Empire State College Foundation, Saratoga Springs, NY.
$10,000 to Jewish Community Center of Albany, Albany, NY.
$10,000 to Regional Food Bank of Northeastern New York, Latham, NY. For capital campaign.
$10,000 to Saratoga Springs Performing Arts Center, Saratoga Springs, NY.
$5,000 to Albany Medical Center, Albany, NY.
$2,500 to Siena College, Loudonville, NY. For scholarships.

6747

The Price Family Foundation, Inc. ✧
25 E. 86th St.
New York, NY 10028
Contact: Robert Price, Dir.

Established in 1998 in NY.
Donor: Robert Price.
Foundation type: Independent foundation.
Financial data (yr. ended 12/31/05): Assets, $337,209 (M); gifts received, $1,670,250; expenditures, $2,030,737; qualifying distributions, $2,020,665; giving activities include $2,020,465 for 50 grants (high: $975,000; low: $85).
Purpose and activities: Giving primarily to health organizations.
Fields of interest: Health organizations, association.
Limitations: Giving primarily in NY.
Application information:
  Initial approach: Letter
  Deadline(s): None
Directors: Catherine Dana; Robert Price.
EIN: 134003955
Selected grants: The following grants were reported in 2003.

$179,000 to Mount Sinai School of Medicine of New York University, New York, NY. For Gastrointestinal Research Lab.
$50,000 to Hospital for Special Surgery, New York, NY. For Chair in Pediatrics.
$45,000 to My Sisters Place, White Plains, NY. For unrestricted support.
$35,000 to Council on Foreign Relations, New York, NY. For unrestricted support.
$35,000 to Montefiore Medical Center, Bronx, NY. For unrestricted support.
$26,000 to Park Avenue Synagogue, New York, NY. For unrestricted support.
$25,000 to Hudson Institute, Indianapolis, IN. For unrestricted support.
$25,000 to Middle East Forum, Philadelphia, PA. For unrestricted support.
$20,500 to American Committee for Shaare Zedek Hospital in Jerusalem, New York, NY. For unrestricted support.
$20,000 to Baruch College Fund, New York, NY. For unrestricted support.

6748

William E. and Maude S. Pritchard Charitable Trust
(formerly Maude Pritchard Charitable Trust)
c/o JPMorgan Chase Bank, N.A.
345 Park Ave., 4th Fl.
New York, NY 10154
Contact: Lisa L. Philp, V.P
FAX: (212) 464-2305;
E-mail: philip_lisa@jpmorgan.com

Established in 1983 in NY.
Foundation type: Independent foundation.
Financial data (yr. ended 12/31/05): Assets, $17,515,952 (M); expenditures, $957,250; qualifying distributions, $794,347; giving activities include $755,000 for 15 grants (high: $295,000; low: $5,000).
Purpose and activities: Giving primarily for education, health care, and human services.
Fields of interest: Elementary/secondary education; Health care; Human services; Biological sciences; Christian agencies & churches.
Type of support: General/operating support.
Limitations: Applications not accepted. Giving primarily in Suffolk County, NY. No grants to individuals or for matching gifts or loans.
Application information: Unsolicited requests for funds not accepted.
  Board meeting date(s): December
Trustees: Herbert J. Wellington, Jr.; JPMorgan Chase Bank, N.A.
EIN: 136824965
Selected grants: The following grants were reported in 2004.
$295,000 to Stony Brook Foundation, Stony Brook, NY.
$286,000 to Portledge School, Locust Valley, NY.
$15,000 to Hazelden Foundation, Center City, MN.
$8,000 to Humane Society of New York, New York, NY.
$7,500 to Society of Saint Johnland, Kings Park, NY.
$7,000 to Ministry for Hope, Port Jefferson, NY.
$5,000 to North Shore Wildlife Sanctuary, Mill Neck, NY.
$5,000 to Visiting Nurse Association of Oyster Bay and Glen Cove, Oyster Bay, NY.

6749

Morris and Anna Propp Sons Fund, Inc. ✧ ☆
405 Park Ave., Ste. 1103
New York, NY 10022

Incorporated in 1944 in NY.
Donor: Members of the Propp family.
Foundation type: Independent foundation.
Financial data (yr. ended 12/31/05): Assets, $8,891,739 (M); gifts received, $73,986; expenditures, $386,462; qualifying distributions, $358,270; giving activities include $358,270 for grants.
Purpose and activities: Giving primarily for Jewish welfare funds, temple support, and religious education; some support for higher education.
Fields of interest: Museums; Higher education; Theological school/education; Health care; Human services; Jewish federated giving programs; Jewish agencies & temples.
Limitations: Applications not accepted. Giving primarily in NY. No grants to individuals.
Application information: Contributes only to pre-selected organizations.
Directors: Ephraim Propp; M.J. Propp; Morris S. Propp.
EIN: 136099110
Selected grants: The following grants were reported in 2003.
$35,750 to UJA-Federation of New York, New York, NY.
$7,500 to Yeshiva University, New York, NY.
$7,200 to Westchester Day School, Mamaroneck, NY.
$2,000 to Lakewood Chedar School, Lakewood, NJ.
$1,800 to Gesher Foundation, New York, NY.
$1,000 to Chai Lifeline, New York, NY.
$750 to National Jewish Outreach Program, New York, NY.
$750 to New York University, School of Medicine, New York, NY.
$500 to Jewish National Fund, New York, NY.
$500 to PTACH, Brooklyn, NY.

6750

The Prospect Hill Foundation, Inc. ✧
99 Park Ave., Ste. 2220
New York, NY 10016-1601 (212) 370-1165
FAX: (212) 599-6282; URL: http://foundationcenter.org/grantmaker/prospecthill/

Incorporated in 1960 in NY; absorbed The Frederick W. Beinecke Fund in 1983.
Donor: William S. Beinecke.
Foundation type: Independent foundation.
Financial data (yr. ended 6/30/05): Assets, $63,716,311 (M); expenditures, $4,043,644; qualifying distributions, $3,763,149; giving activities include $2,910,250 for 103 grants (high: $100,000; low: $5,000; average: $10,000–$25,000), and $242,482 for 203 employee matching gifts.
Purpose and activities: The foundation's mission is to advance the human experience while ensuring the well being of the earth. The foundation pursues this mission by making grants in four main program areas: 1) environmental conservation - to support conservation strategies that protect natural systems and to improve air quality for the benefit of human and ecological health; 2) nuclear nonproliferation - to limit the spread of nuclear weapons by providing reliable information to U.S. policy makers, the

media, and the public; 3) reproductive health and rights - to support the right of women and men to be informed of and have access to safe, effective, affordable and acceptable methods of fertility regulation of their choice; and 4) criminal justice - to promote a fair and humane criminal justice system. In addition, the foundation makes a number of core grants that support the general philanthropic interests and goals of the foundation's directors and their family.

Fields of interest: Arts; Education; Environment, natural resources; Reproductive health, family planning; Courts/judicial administration; International affairs, arms control.

International interests: Latin America.

Type of support: General/operating support; Capital campaigns; Land acquisition; Employee matching gifts; Matching/challenge support.

Limitations: Giving primarily on a national basis with emphasis on MA, NJ, NY, and RI; limited support is directed towards environmental conservation and reproductive health projects in the Mayan Region of Latin America. No support for sectarian religious activities, political organizations or non-tax exempted organizations. No grants to individuals, or for basic scientific research.

Publications: Grants list; Informational brochure.

Application information: Unsolicited proposals are not normally considered. Invited applicants should see the foundation Web site for specific guidelines.

Board meeting date(s): 3 times annually

Officers and Directors:* William S. Beinecke,* Chair.; John B. Beinecke,* Pres.; Elizabeth G. Beinecke,* V.P.; Frederick W. Beinecke, V.P. and Secy.; Robert J. Barletta, Treas.; Frances Beinecke Elston; Sarah Beinecke Richardson.

Number of staff: 1 full-time professional; 1 part-time support.

EIN: 136075567

Selected grants: The following grants were reported in 2003.

$200,000 to Yale University, School of Forestry and Environmental Studies, New Haven, CT. For New Century Fund.

$75,000 to Nature Conservancy, Arlington, VA. Toward purchase of acres in Connecticut owned by Kelda Group water utility.

$50,000 to Adirondack Council, Elizabethtown, NY. Toward Forever Wild Capital Campaign.

$50,000 to New York Botanical Garden, Bronx, NY. For capital campaign to partially endow Chair of the Director of the Graduate Studies Program.

$50,000 to New York City Ballet, New York, NY. For capital campaign for education programs for students.

$50,000 to Planned Parenthood of New York City, New York, NY. For general support.

$50,000 to Saint Lukes-Roosevelt Hospital Center, New York, NY. Toward Richard G. Eaton, MD Hand Surgery Fellowship.

$35,000 to Centro para los Adolescentes de San Miguel de Allende (CASA), San Miguel de Allende, Mexico. Toward Professional Midwifery School.

$35,000 to Guttmacher Institute, New York, NY. To improve access to family planning, abortion, and emergency contraception in the U.S.

$35,000 to Natural Resources Defense Council, New York, NY. Toward Oceans Protection Initiative.

6751
Providence Foundation, Inc. ✧
1637 50th St.
Brooklyn, NY 11204

Established in 1997 in NY.

Donors: Michael Melnicke; Samuel Chmelnicki; Jack Rosen; Mr. Weingarten.

Foundation type: Independent foundation.

Financial data (yr. ended 6/30/05): Assets, $8,021,977 (M); gifts received, $315,000; expenditures, $1,094,649; qualifying distributions, $1,081,110; giving activities include $1,067,570 for 44 grants (high: $565,000; low: $360).

Fields of interest: Education; Human services; Jewish agencies & temples.

Limitations: Applications not accepted. Giving primarily in Brooklyn, NY; some funding also in Los Angeles, CA. No grants to individuals.

Application information: Contributes only to pre-selected organizations.

Officer and Directors:* Michael Melnicke,* Pres.; Cila Chmelnicki; Samuel Chmelnicki; Briendy Melnicke.

EIN: 113350828

Selected grants: The following grants were reported in 2003.

$456,100 to Friends of Mosdos Gur, Brooklyn, NY.

$160,000 to American Friends of Rabbinical College, New York, NY.

$125,000 to Echud Mosdos gur, Brooklyn, NY.

$58,500 to Mesivta Bais Yisroel, Brooklyn, NY.

$31,500 to Kollel Chasidei Gur, Brooklyn, NY.

$25,000 to Long Island University, C.W. Post Center, Brookville, NY.

$25,000 to Mosdos Spinka International, Brooklyn, NY.

$25,000 to Rabbinical College Academy, Brooklyn, NY.

$25,000 to Yeshiva Imrei Yosef, Brooklyn, NY.

$20,000 to Congregation Yetev Lev D Jerusalem, Brooklyn, NY.

6752
The PTM Charitable Foundation ✧ ☆
c/o R. Bradford Evans
791 Park Ave., Ste. 7B
New York, NY 10021

Donor: R. Bradford Evans.

Foundation type: Independent foundation.

Financial data (yr. ended 12/31/05): Assets, $1,980,544 (M); expenditures, $391,830; qualifying distributions, $363,972; giving activities include $358,383 for 106 grants (high: $100,000; low: $100).

Fields of interest: Elementary/secondary education; Higher education; Business school/education; Human services.

Limitations: Applications not accepted. Giving primarily in CA, CT, and NY. No grants to individuals.

Application information: Contributes only to pre-selected organizations.

Officers and Directors:* R. Bradford Evans,* Pres. and Treas.; Barbara Reed Evans,* V.P. and Secy.; Robert H. Arnold.

EIN: 133800384

Selected grants: The following grants were reported in 2004.

$85,000 to Columbia University, Business School, New York, NY.

$6,000 to A Better Chance, New York, NY.

$5,000 to Robin Hood Foundation, New York, NY.

$5,000 to Teach for America, New York, NY.

$1,000 to De La Salle Academy, New York, NY.

$1,000 to Prep for Prep, New York, NY.

$500 to City Harvest, New York, NY.

$500 to Yale University, New Haven, CT.

$250 to Citymeals-on-Wheels, New York, NY.

$250 to Covenant House, New York, NY.

6753
Benjamin & Seema Pulier Charitable Foundation, Inc. ✧ ☆
7 Cayuga Trail
Harrison, NY 10528

Established in 1993 in NY.

Foundation type: Independent foundation.

Financial data (yr. ended 12/31/05): Assets, $7,915,278 (M); expenditures, $805,231; qualifying distributions, $718,950; giving activities include $718,950 for grants.

Purpose and activities: Giving primarily for education and health care, particularly for an institute for research and treatment of kidney disease.

Fields of interest: Museums (specialized); Arts; Higher education; Hospitals (general); Health organizations, association; Medical research, institute; Kidney research; Human services; Jewish agencies & temples.

Limitations: Applications not accepted. Giving primarily in FL, MA, and NY. No grants to individuals.

Application information: Contributes only to pre-selected organizations.

Officers and Directors:* Edith Freedman,* Pres.; Sol Karsch,* V.P.; Bruce A. Rosen,* Secy.-Treas.

EIN: 133683886

Selected grants: The following grants were reported in 2003.

$129,600 to P.E.F. Israel Endowment Funds, New York, NY.

$110,000 to Rogosin Institute, New York, NY.

$35,000 to United States Holocaust Memorial Museum Campaign, New York, NY.

$25,000 to American Committee for the Weizmann Institute of Science, New York, NY.

$20,000 to Beer Sheva Foundation, Beer Sheva, Israel. .

$10,000 to Gildas Club Westchester, White Plains, NY.

$7,500 to New York University Medical Center, Tisch Hospital, New York, NY.

$7,500 to Ronald McDonald House of New York, New York, NY.

$2,500 to Bnai Brith Hillel-Jewish Association for College Youth, New York, NY.

$2,500 to Mothers Against Drunk Driving (MADD), Irving, TX.

6754
The Pumpkin Foundation ✧
575 Lexington Ave., 33rd Fl.
New York, NY 10022

Established in 1969.

Donors: Joseph H. Reich; Carol F. Reich; Janet Reich Elsbach; Deborah Reich.

Foundation type: Independent foundation.

Financial data (yr. ended 6/30/05): Assets, $22,247,188 (M); gifts received, $899,104; expenditures, $2,772,140; qualifying distributions,

$2,605,214; giving activities include $2,593,294 for 89 grants (high: $1,150,000; low: $250).

Purpose and activities: Giving primarily for education and the arts, particularly programs for children; funding also for other children services, as well as for legal services, family and social services, and federated giving programs.

Fields of interest: Arts education; Museums (natural history); Performing arts; Performing arts, ballet; Performing arts, theater; Performing arts, orchestra (symphony); Arts; Education, association; Elementary/secondary education; Higher education; Education; Botanical gardens; Health care; Legal services; Housing/shelter, development; Human services; Children/youth, services; Family services; Federated giving programs.

Limitations: Applications not accepted. Giving primarily in New York, NY; some funding nationally. No grants to individuals.

Application information: Contributes only to pre-selected organizations.

Trustees: Janet Reich Elsbach; Tracy S. Nagler; Carol F. Reich; Joseph H. Reich.

Number of staff: 1 full-time professional.

EIN: 136279814

Selected grants: The following grants were reported in 2004.

$500,000 to New York City Center for Charter Excellence, New York, NY. For general support.

$25,000 to Brooklyn Childrens Museum, Brooklyn, NY. For general support.

$15,000 to American Ballet Theater, New York, NY. For general support.

$12,000 to Children for Children Foundation, New York, NY. For general support.

$10,000 to City Lights Youth Theater, New York, NY. For general support.

$10,000 to Lawyers for Children, New York, NY. For general support.

$10,000 to Prep for Prep, New York, NY. For general support.

$10,000 to Yale University, New Haven, CT.

$9,352 to I Have A Dream Foundation, New York, NY. For general support.

$5,000 to Cornell University, Ithaca, NY. For general support.

6755
The Purchase Fund ✧
c/o Barry M. Strauss Assocs., Ltd.
307 5th Ave., 8th Fl.
New York, NY 10016-6517

Established in 1992 in NY.
Donor: Peter M. Flanigan.
Foundation type: Independent foundation.
Financial data (yr. ended 9/30/05): Assets, $405,944 (M); gifts received, $568,992; expenditures, $703,926; qualifying distributions, $694,825; giving activities include $693,250 for 112 grants (high: $180,000; low: $100).
Fields of interest: Arts; Education; Health organizations, association; Human services; Roman Catholic agencies & churches.
Limitations: Applications not accepted. Giving on a national basis, with emphasis on NY. No grants to individuals.
Application information: Contributes only to pre-selected organizations.
Trustees: Brigid S. Flanigan; Peter M. Flanigan; Robert W. Flanigan; Timothy P. Flanigan; Brigid S. Flanigan Lezak; Megan F. Skakel.
EIN: 137005756

6756
Pyewacket Foundation ✧
c/o Reminick, Aarons & Co., LLP
1430 Broadway, 17th Fl.
New York, NY 10018

Established in 1997 in NY.
Donor: William H. Janeway.
Foundation type: Independent foundation.
Financial data (yr. ended 12/31/03): Assets, $6,748,738 (M); expenditures, $449,667; qualifying distributions, $335,732; giving activities include $330,050 for 6 grants (high: $211,550; low: $500).
Fields of interest: Performing arts, orchestra (symphony); Higher education, college; Aging, centers/services; Social sciences.
Limitations: Applications not accepted. Giving primarily in Cambridge, MA. No grants to individuals.
Application information: Contributes only to pre-selected organizations.
Officer: William H. Janeway, Pres.
EIN: 137051522
Selected grants: The following grants were reported in 2003.
$211,550 to Social Science Research Council, New York, NY.
$80,000 to Cambridge in America, New York, NY.
$21,000 to Hunter College of the City University of New York, New York, NY.
$10,000 to Deerfield Academy, Deerfield, MA.
$7,000 to Jackson Laboratory, Bar Harbor, ME.
$500 to New York Society Library, New York, NY.

6757
QIBQ Foundation ✧
(also known as Susan Wexner Charitable Foundation)
c/o Hertz, Herson & Co., LLP
Two Park Ave., Rm. 1500
New York, NY 10016

Established in 1986 in NY.
Donor: Susan R. Wexner.
Foundation type: Independent foundation.
Financial data (yr. ended 12/31/04): Assets, $7,624,927 (M); gifts received, $45,986; expenditures, $430,779; qualifying distributions, $406,896; giving activities include $333,500 for 2 grants (high: $325,000; low: $8,500).
Fields of interest: Philanthropy/voluntarism.
Limitations: Applications not accepted. Giving primarily in PA. No grants to individuals.
Application information: Contributes only to pre-selected organizations.
Trustees: Eliot D. Hawkins; Solomon M. Kamm; Susan R. Wexner.
EIN: 133424462

6758
Quadrangle Group Foundation, Inc. ✧
375 Park Ave.
New York, NY 10152

Established in 2001 in NY and DE.
Donors: Peter Ezersky; Steven Rattner; Joshua Steiner; David Tanner.
Foundation type: Independent foundation.
Financial data (yr. ended 12/31/05): Assets, $0 (M); gifts received, $345,139; expenditures, $547,310; qualifying distributions, $538,345;

---

giving activities include $534,845 for 91 grants (high: $60,000; low: $75).
Fields of interest: Museums (art); Higher education; Libraries (public); Environment; Recreation, camps; Human services; Jewish agencies & temples.
Limitations: Applications not accepted. Giving primarily in NY. No grants to individuals.
Application information: Contributes only to pre-selected organizations.
Directors: Peter Ezersky; Steven Rattner; Joshua Steiner; David Tanner.
EIN: 134193512

6759
Quarry Hill Foundation ✧
c/o U.S. Trust Co. of NY
114 W. 47th St., TAXVAS
New York, NY 10036

Established in 2000 in NY.
Donor: H. Marshall Schwarz.
Foundation type: Independent foundation.
Financial data (yr. ended 12/31/04): Assets, $3,719,628 (M); gifts received, $500,000; expenditures, $582,325; qualifying distributions, $552,105; giving activities include $550,000 for 2 grants (high: $500,000; low: $50,000).
Fields of interest: Higher education; Education; Human services.
Limitations: Applications not accepted. Giving primarily in NY. No grants to individuals.
Application information: Contributes only to pre-selected organizations.
Trustees: H. Marshall Schwarz; Rae Paige Schwarz.
EIN: 134129864
Selected grants: The following grants were reported in 2003.
$1,000,236 to Milton Academy, Milton, MA. For operating support.
$50,000 to Oberlin College, Oberlin, OH. For operating support.
$10,195 to Family Care International, New York, NY. For operating support.
$9,000 to Central Park Conservancy, New York, NY. For operating support.

6760
Queensgate Foundation ✧
c/o TAG Assocs., Ltd.
75 Rockefeller Plz., Ste. 900
New York, NY 10019
Contact: Mark Friedman

Established in 1985 in NY.
Donors: Peter A. Joseph; Elizabeth H. Scheuer.
Foundation type: Independent foundation.
Financial data (yr. ended 11/30/05): Assets, $3,154,959 (M); gifts received, $1,034,892; expenditures, $1,171,714; qualifying distributions, $1,149,125; giving activities include $1,146,375 for 95 grants (high: $250,000; low: $180).
Purpose and activities: Giving primarily for Jewish agencies and temples; funding also for education, human services, and the arts.
Fields of interest: Arts; Higher education; Education; Health care; Human services; Jewish agencies & temples.
Limitations: Applications not accepted. Giving primarily in NY. No grants to individuals.
Application information: Contributes only to pre-selected organizations.

Officers and Directors:* Peter A. Joseph,* Pres.; Elizabeth H. Scheuer,* V.P.; Carol Joseph.
EIN: 133336710

6761
Patricia Quick Charitable Trust ◇
c/o AMCO
505 Park Ave., 20th Fl.
New York, NY   10022-1106

Established in 1996 in FL.
Donor: Patricia Quick.
Foundation type: Independent foundation.
Financial data (yr. ended 12/31/04): Assets, $15,335 (M); gifts received, $323,031; expenditures, $579,684; qualifying distributions, $575,073; giving activities include $575,073 for grants.
Purpose and activities: Giving primarily for medical research.
Fields of interest: Breast cancer research; Developmentally disabled, centers & services.
Limitations: Applications not accepted. Giving on a national basis. No grants to individuals.
Application information: Contributes only to pre-selected organizations.
Officer: Patricia Quick, Pres.
EIN: 656228829

6762
Leslie C. Quick, Jr. & Regina A. Quick Charitable Trust Foundation ◇
c/o Montrose Acctg.
505 Park Ave., 20th Fl.
New York, NY   10022-9306

Established in 1988 in FL.
Donors: Leslie C. Quick, Jr.; Regina A. Quick.
Foundation type: Independent foundation.
Financial data (yr. ended 10/31/05): Assets, $5,361,100 (M); expenditures, $3,779,860; qualifying distributions, $3,731,706; giving activities include $3,728,750 for 26 grants (high: $2,000,000; low: $500).
Purpose and activities: Support primarily for higher education, Roman Catholic churches, a mission, and a diocese; grants also for hospitals and medical research.
Fields of interest: Elementary/secondary education; Higher education; Health organizations, association; Medical research, institute; Roman Catholic agencies & churches.
Limitations: Applications not accepted. Giving primarily in FL and NY. No grants to individuals.
Application information: Contributes only to pre-selected organizations.
Trustee: Regina A. Quick.
EIN: 650083436
Selected grants: The following grants were reported in 2005.
$312,500 to Fairfield University, Fairfield, CT.
$250,000 to Breast Cancer Research Foundation, New York, NY.
$100,000 to Arthritis Foundation, Melville, NY.
$100,000 to Widener University, Chester, PA.
$50,000 to Eagle Hill School, Greenwich, CT.
$45,000 to Sisters of Mercy, Orchard Park, NY.
$25,250 to American Cancer Society, Oklahoma City, OK.
$2,500 to Saint Thomas Church, New York, NY.

6763
The Stephen D. Quinn Foundation ◇
c/o Behan, Ling & Ruta
475 Park Ave. S., 31st Fl.
New York, NY   10016

Established in 1993 in CT.
Donor: Stephen D. Quinn.
Foundation type: Independent foundation.
Financial data (yr. ended 7/31/05): Assets, $3,299,661 (M); expenditures, $417,585; qualifying distributions, $409,691; giving activities include $410,575 for 2 grants (high: $270,575; low: $140,000).
Purpose and activities: Giving primarily to a federated giving program of the Church of Jesus Christ of Latter-day Saints.
Limitations: Applications not accepted. Giving primarily in UT. No grants to individuals.
Application information: Contributes only to pre-selected organizations.
Trustees: Cydney P. Quinn; Stephen D. Quinn.
EIN: 133789066
Selected grants: The following grants were reported in 2003.
$250,000 to Church of Jesus Christ of Latter Day Saints, Salt Lake City, UT.
$1,500 to New Canaan Basketball Association, New Canaan, CT.
$100 to Boy Scouts of America, Connecticut Yankee Council, Milford, CT.

6764
R & TP Family Foundation, Inc. ◇
c/o Bessemer Trust Co.
630 5th Ave., 34th Fl.
New York, NY   10111
Contact: Era Yoo

Established in 2001 in NY.
Donors: Robert A. Pruzan; Tracey Pruzan.
Foundation type: Independent foundation.
Financial data (yr. ended 4/30/05): Assets, $1,230,057 (M); expenditures, $446,987; qualifying distributions, $436,712; giving activities include $434,747 for 27 grants (high: $230,000; low: $1,000).
Purpose and activities: Giving primarily for elementary/secondary education, the arts, and children, youth, family, and social services.
Fields of interest: Museums (art); Museums (children's); Arts; Higher education; Business school/education; Education; Environment; Human services; Children/youth, services; Family services; Human services, emergency aid; Jewish agencies & temples.
Limitations: Giving primarily in New York, NY.
Application information:
    Initial approach: Letter
    Deadline(s): None
Officers and Directors:* Robert A. Pruzan,* Pres.; Tracey Pruzan,* Secy.-Treas.; Jeffrey Silverman.
EIN: 134175476

6765
Radio Drama Network, Inc. ◇
285 Central Park W., No. 8N
New York, NY   10024
Contact: Himan Brown Ph.D., Pres.

Established in 1990.

Donor: Himan Brown.
Foundation type: Independent foundation.
Financial data (yr. ended 6/30/05): Assets, $17,445,708 (M); gifts received, $4,000,000; expenditures, $563,077; qualifying distributions, $512,338; giving activities include $486,526 for 5 grants (high: $200,000).
Purpose and activities: The foundation is devoted to the spoken word and audiodramas, so as to discover the joy of listening.
Fields of interest: Media, radio.
Limitations: Applications not accepted. Giving primarily in New York, NY. No grants to individuals.
Application information: Unsolicited requests for funds not accepted.
    Board meeting date(s): June and Dec.
Officers and Directors:* Himan Brown,* Pres.; Arnold Sheiffer,* V.P.; Richard Kay,* Secy.
Number of staff: 2 part-time support.
EIN: 133253712
Selected grants: The following grants were reported in 2005.
$200,000 to Brooklyn College of the City University of New York, School of Law, Brooklyn, NY.
$150,000 to Brooklyn College Foundation, Brooklyn, NY.
$100,000 to Visiting Nurse Association of Brooklyn, Brooklyn, NY.
$25,000 to School of Visual Arts, New York, NY.
$800 to Learning Leaders, New York, NY.

6766
Raether 1985 Charitable Trust ◇
c/o Kohlberg, Kravis, Roberts & Co.
9 W. 57th St.
New York, NY   10019

Established in 1985 in NY.
Donors: Paul E. Raether; Wendy S. Raether.
Foundation type: Independent foundation.
Financial data (yr. ended 11/30/05): Assets, $26,461,866 (M); gifts received, $6,209,865; expenditures, $1,124,488; qualifying distributions, $999,364; giving activities include $828,754 for 47 grants (high: $410,479; low: $500; average: $1,000–$30,000).
Purpose and activities: Funding primarily for education and for a boys and girls club. Funding also for human services and health care.
Fields of interest: Arts; Elementary/secondary education; Higher education, college; Health organizations; Medical research, institute; Boys & girls clubs; Human services.
Type of support: General/operating support.
Limitations: Applications not accepted. Giving primarily in CT and NY. No grants to individuals.
Application information: Contributes only to pre-selected organizations.
Trustees: Paul E. Raether; Wendy S. Raether.
EIN: 136855420
Selected grants: The following grants were reported in 2004.
$2,032,265 to Trinity College, Hartford, CT. 3 grants: $100,000 (For general support), $1,519,901 (For general support), $412,364 (For general support).
$1,960,000 to Dartmouth College, Hanover, NH. 3 grants: $30,000 to Amos Tuck School of Business (For general support), $250,000 to Amos Tuck School of Business (For general support), $1,680,000 to Amos Tuck School of Business (For general support).

$115,000 to Greenwich Academy, Greenwich, CT. 2
grants: $15,000 (For general support),
$100,000 (For general support).
$48,000 to Robin Hood Foundation, New York, NY.
For general support.
$25,000 to Boys and Girls Club of Greenwich,
Greenwich, CT. For general support.

6767
Raffiani Family Foundation, Inc. ✧ ☆
24 Claudet Way
Eastchester, NY 10709
Contact: Laura Raffiani, V.P.
E-mail: phil@raffiani.com

Established in 1999 in CT and NY.
Donors: Philip Raffiani; Laura Raffiani.
Foundation type: Independent foundation.
Financial data (yr. ended 12/31/05): Assets,
$2,112,590 (M); expenditures, $2,144,931;
qualifying distributions, $2,132,001; giving
activities include $2,132,001 for grants.
Fields of interest: Education; Health care; Health
organizations, association; Housing/shelter,
development; Human services; Youth, services;
Community development.
Type of support: General/operating support;
Continuing support; Annual campaigns; Capital
campaigns; Building/renovation; Equipment;
Emergency funds; Program development;
Curriculum development; Scholarship funds;
Research; Program-related investments/loans.
Limitations: Giving primarily in the New York
Tri-State area.
Application information:
Initial approach: E-mails only
Deadline(s): None
Officers and Board Members:* Philip Raffiani,*
Pres.; Laura Raffiani,* V.P.
EIN: 061566990
Selected grants: The following grants were reported
in 2004.
$20,000 to Hope Community Services, New
Rochelle, NY. For general support.
$14,000 to Parents of Autistic Children of Ocean
County (POAC), Hazlet, NJ. 2 grants: $5,000 (For
general support), $9,000 (For general support).
$10,000 to Habitat for Humanity of Westchester,
New Rochelle, NY. For general support.
$5,002 to Family and Community Services,
Eastchester, NY. For general support.
$5,000 to Blythedale Childrens Hospital, Valhalla,
NY. For general support.
$3,000 to Sudden Infant Death Syndrome (SIDS)
Center of New Jersey, New Brunswick, NJ. For
general support.
$2,500 to Kids Alive International, Valparaiso, IN.
For general support.
$2,000 to Heartsong, Bronxville, NY. For general
support.
$1,000 to TechnoServe, Norwalk, CT. For general
support.

6768
The Raiff Foundation ✧
Carnegie Hall Twr.
152 W. 57th St., 29th Fl.
New York, NY 10019

Established in 1995 in NY.
Donor: Robert M. Raiff.

Foundation type: Independent foundation.
Financial data (yr. ended 12/31/05): Assets,
$16,117,158 (M); expenditures, $641,982;
qualifying distributions, $548,500; giving activities
include $548,500 for 26 grants (high: $100,000;
low: $1,000).
Fields of interest: Higher education; Hospitals
(general); Jewish agencies & temples.
Type of support: Annual campaigns; Emergency
funds.
Limitations: Applications not accepted. Giving
primarily in New York, NY, and Providence, RI.
Application information: Contributes only to
pre-selected organizations.
Trustee: Robert M. Raiff.
EIN: 137070078
Selected grants: The following grants were reported
in 2005.
$100,000 to Brown University, Providence, RI.
$35,000 to Roundabout Theater Company, New
York, NY.
$25,000 to Brown Hillel Foundation, Providence, RI.
$25,000 to Columbia Grammar and Preparatory
School, New York, NY.
$25,000 to Museum of Jewish Heritage, New York,
NY.
$25,000 to New York Public Library, New York, NY.
$5,000 to American Friends of the Israel Museum,
New York, NY.
$5,000 to Center for Arts Education, New York, NY.
$5,000 to New York City Opera, New York, NY.

6769
Ramapo Trust
950 3rd Ave., 19th Fl.
New York, NY 10022
Contact: For inquiry by mail:: Stephen L. Schwartz,
Tr.; For telephone inquiries: Nora O'Brien
URL: http://www.BrookdaleFoundation.org

Trust established in 1973 in NY.
Donors: Henry L. Schwartz†; Montebello Trust.
Foundation type: Independent foundation.
Financial data (yr. ended 6/30/04): Assets,
$83,457,883 (M); expenditures, $4,577,848;
qualifying distributions, $3,624,281; giving
activities include $2,505,886 for 117 grants (high:
$1,000,000; low: $343).
Purpose and activities: Giving for gerontological and
geriatric research and innovative services; support
also for health, higher and other education.
Fields of interest: Higher education; Health care;
Health organizations, association; Medical
research, institute; Human services; Aging, centers/
services; Jewish agencies & temples; Aging.
Type of support: Program development;
Conferences/seminars; Seed money; Research;
Matching/challenge support.
Limitations: Applications not accepted. No grants to
individuals, or for capital or building campaigns,
operating budgets, continuing support, annual
campaigns, media or the arts, or deficit financing;
no loans.
Application information: Contributes only to
pre-selected organizations.
Board meeting date(s): Quarterly
Trustees: Arthur Norman Field; Karen Schwartz Hart;
Stephen L. Schwartz; Rebecca Shaffer; Mary Ann
Van Clief.
Number of staff: 3 full-time professional; 2 part-time
support.
EIN: 136594279

Selected grants: The following grants were reported
in 2004.
$1,000,000 to Mount Sinai Hospital, New York, NY.
$125,000 to Mount Sinai School of Medicine of New
York University, New York, NY. 2 grants:
$100,000, $25,000
$100,000 to New York Studio School of Drawing,
Painting and Sculpture, New York, NY.
$85,000 to Research Foundation of the City
University of New York, New York, NY.
$60,000 to University of Colorado, Boulder, CO.
$60,000 to University of North Carolina, Chapel Hill,
NC.
$60,000 to Yale University, New Haven, CT.
$50,000 to Philharmonic Center for the Arts,
Naples, FL.
$25,000 to Eckerd College, Saint Petersburg, FL.

6770
The Ranger Family Charitable Trust ✧ ☆
c/o The Bank of New York
One Wall St., Tax Dept., 28th Flr.
New York, NY 10286

Established in 1999 in NJ.
Foundation type: Independent foundation.
Financial data (yr. ended 12/31/05): Assets,
$3,255,364 (M); expenditures, $890,169;
qualifying distributions, $877,989; giving activities
include $870,000 for 9 grants (high: $300,000;
low: $5,000).
Fields of interest: Museums (marine/maritime);
Performing arts, theater; Elementary/secondary
education; Higher education, university; Libraries
(public); Eye diseases; Christian agencies &
churches.
Limitations: Applications not accepted. No grants to
individuals.
Application information: Contributes only to
pre-selected organizations.
Distribution Committee: Michael W. Ranger;
Virginia Ray Ranger.
Trustee: Winthrop Trust Co.
EIN: 137213551
Selected grants: The following grants were reported
in 2004.
$260,000 to Darcy School, Chatham, NJ.
$200,000 to Family Service.
$60,000 to Morristown-Beard School, Morristown,
NJ.
$25,000 to First Presbyterian Church of New
Vernon, New Vernon, NJ.
$10,000 to Seeing Eye, Morristown, NJ.
$5,000 to Shakespeare Theater of New Jersey,
Madison, NJ.

6771
Rapaport Shallat Foundation ✧ ☆
Bay Pl. and Forest Ct.
Huntington, NY 11743

Foundation type: Independent foundation.
Financial data (yr. ended 12/31/05): Assets,
$5,408,950 (M); expenditures, $367,587;
qualifying distributions, $343,900; giving activities
include $340,400 for 63 grants (high: $60,000;
low: $250).
Purpose and activities: Giving primarily for Jewish
organizations, schools, and federated giving
programs, and for the arts.

Fields of interest: Arts; Education; Jewish federated giving programs; Jewish agencies & temples.
Limitations: Applications not accepted. Giving primarily in New York, NY. No grants to individuals.
Application information: Contributes only to pre-selected organizations.
Manager: Rabbi Barton A. Shallat.
EIN: 137027583
Selected grants: The following grants were reported in 2004.
$35,750 to Mount Sinai Hospital, New York, NY.
$29,000 to Jewish Museum, New York, NY.
$25,000 to Temple Beth-El, Cedarhurst, NY.
$10,000 to Huntington Hospital, Huntington, NY.
$6,000 to Lincoln Center Theater, New York, NY.
$5,000 to Metropolitan Opera, New York, NY.
$1,500 to Music Festival of the Hamptons, Amagansett, NY.
$700 to Bay Street Theater Festival, Sag Harbor, NY.

6772
The Paul Rapoport Foundation, Inc.
220 E. 60th St., Ste. 3H
New York, NY 10022 (212) 888-6578
Contact: Jane D. Schwartz, Exec. Dir.
FAX: (212) 980-0867; Tel. for application information: (212) 888-6577; URL: http://foundationcenter.org/grantmaker/rapoport/

Established in 1987 in NY.
Donor: Paul Rapoport†.
Foundation type: Independent foundation.
Financial data (yr. ended 6/30/06): Assets, $11,721,294 (M); expenditures, $999,894; qualifying distributions, $813,085; giving activities include $587,100 for 47 grants.
Purpose and activities: The foundation's primary focus is the support of organizations that provide social services, advocacy, and community empowerment to and for the LGBT community. HIV/AIDS remains a strong area of interest, but only as it specifically intersects with the LGBT community. The foundation is particularly interested in supporting: 1) the most underserved segments of the LGBT community; 2) new and emerging needs and unique work; and 3) organizational development. It will give priority to organizations, strategies, and types of grants that may not be easily funded elsewhere. It will also give consideration to organizations in transition, faced with changes in leadership, major funding reductions, etc. The foundation will also consider funding programs of organizations not focused exclusively on the LGBT community if at least 50 percent of the clients served are LGBT. If these organizations wish to request general operating support, at least 50 percent of the clients they serve agency-wide must be LGBT.
Fields of interest: AIDS; Civil rights, gays/lesbians; LGBTQ.
Type of support: General/operating support; Continuing support; Building/renovation; Program development; Conferences/seminars; Publication; Seed money; Technical assistance; Matching/challenge support.
Limitations: Giving primarily in the metropolitan New York, NY, area. No support for medical research, cultural or artistic activities, or other foundations. No grants to individuals, or for endowment funds or building campaigns, deficits, operating support (to organizations whose budgets exceed $5 million) scholarships or building campaigns.

Publications: Application guidelines; Grants list; Program policy statement.
Application information: Proposals submitted without application coversheet will not be accepted. See foundation Web site for new application guidelines. Application form required.
Initial approach: Telephone for application information
Copies of proposal: 3
Deadline(s): Feb. 1, June 1, and Oct. 1 (or previous Friday if the 1st falls on a weekend)
Board meeting date(s): June, Oct., and Feb.
Final notification: 5 months
Officers and Directors:* Andrew D. Lane,* Pres.; Soraya Elcock,* V.P.; Paul D.C. Huang,* Secy.; B. Kevin Sterns,* Treas.; Jane D. Schwartz, Exec. Dir.; Ryan Chavez; Laurie Goldberger; Bea Hanson; Tyra Liebmann; Kimberleigh Smith.
Number of staff: 2 full-time professional.
EIN: 136892333
Selected grants: The following grants were reported in 2005.
$22,500 to Ali Forney Center, New York, NY. For general support.
$20,000 to Gay Men of African Descent, New York, NY. For general support.
$20,000 to Heights Hill Mental Health Service, Brooklyn, NY. For Rainbow Heights Club.
$20,000 to Hispanic AIDS Forum, New York, NY. For transgender Latina services.
$15,000 to Forest Hills Community House, Forest Hills, NY. For services for lesbian, gay, bisexual, and transexual seniors in Queens.
$15,000 to Immigration Equality, New York, NY. For general support.
$15,000 to Queers for Economic Justice, New York, NY. For Shelter Organizing Project.
$10,000 to Bronx Lesbian and Gay Health Care Consortium, Bronx, NY. For general support.
$10,000 to Urban Justice Center, New York, NY. For Sylvia Rivera Law Project.

6773
Steven L. Rattner and P. Maureen White Foundation, Inc. ◈
c/o Quadrangle Group LLC
375 Park Ave., 14th Fl.
New York, NY 10152

Established in 1989 in NY.
Donors: Steven L. Rattner; The Steven Rattner 2000 LT Trust.
Foundation type: Independent foundation.
Financial data (yr. ended 12/31/04): Assets, $3,778,483 (M); gifts received, $551,915; expenditures, $1,096,860; qualifying distributions, $1,081,250; giving activities include $1,080,731 for 89 grants (high: $500,000; low: $40).
Purpose and activities: Giving primarily for an institution of higher education; support also for outdoor education, cultural institutions, including museums and the media, Jewish organizations and public policy institutes.
Fields of interest: Media/communications; Museums; Arts; Higher education; Education; Public policy, research; Jewish agencies & temples.
Limitations: Applications not accepted. Giving primarily in New York, NY. No grants to individuals.
Application information: Contributes only to pre-selected organizations.

Officers and Directors:* Steven L. Rattner, Pres.; P. Maureen White,* V.P.; Howard Sontag, Secy.-Treas.; Joy Conlon, C.F.O.
EIN: 133519099
Selected grants: The following grants were reported in 2003.
$83,290 to Brown University, Providence, RI. For general support.
$75,000 to W N E T Channel 13, New York, NY. For general support.
$40,000 to Metropolitan Museum of Art, New York, NY. For general support.
$15,000 to Collegiate School, New York, NY. For general support.
$10,000 to Council on Foreign Relations, New York, NY. For general support.
$10,000 to New York City Outward Bound Center, Long Island City, NY. For general support.
$5,000 to International Womens Media Foundation, DC. For general support.
$2,500 to New York Pops, New York, NY. For general support.
$2,000 to Lincoln Center Theater, New York, NY. For general support.
$1,000 to American Museum of Natural History, New York, NY. For general support.

6774
Rauch Foundation ◈
229 7th St., Ste. 306
Garden City, NY 11530-5766 (516) 873-9808
Contact: John McNally
FAX: (516) 873-0708;
E-mail: info@rauchfoundation.org; URL: http://www.rauchfoundation.org

Incorporated in 1960 in NY.
Donors: Philip Rauch; Louis J. Rauch†; Ruth T. Rauch; Philip J. Rauch; Nancy R. Douzinas.
Foundation type: Independent foundation.
Financial data (yr. ended 11/30/04): Assets, $40,278,608 (M); expenditures, $2,688,963; qualifying distributions, $2,214,480; giving activities include $1,819,288 for 125 grants (high: $91,840; low: $210).
Purpose and activities: The foundation's mission is to: 1) promote positive outcomes for young children, ages newborn to 6, with particular focus on those with a disadvantaged socio-economic start. The foundation's first priority is to support programs that facilitate systemic change for those children and their families; 2) to protect the environment and improve the quality of life on Long Island, NY, and in MD; and 3) to strengthen the organizational effectiveness of nonprofit institutions that work on these issues through capactiy building and leadership development. The foundation focuses its work in the places where Rauch family members have lived and worked- Long Island, NY, and MD. The foundation concentrates the majority of its grantmaking on prevention programs that benefit young children (ages birth to 6) and their families in Nassau County, NY. The foundation has small programs on Long Island, NY, concerning the environment and community development. The foundation also has an environmental program in MD.
Fields of interest: Education, early childhood education; Environment; Family services; Community development.
Type of support: Program development; Conferences/seminars; Seed money; Technical

assistance; Consulting services; Program evaluation; Matching/challenge support.

Limitations: Giving primarily in Nassau and Suffolk counties, NY; some giving also in MD. Generally, no grants to individuals, capital expenditures, or emergency funding.

Publications: Annual report (including application guidelines); Grants list.

Application information: If a full proposal is requested, applicants may follow the New York/New Jersey Common Application Form. The foundation requests that organizations not send videotapes. Application guidelines available on foundation Web site. Application form not required.

Initial approach: Concept paper (no more than 3 pages)

Copies of proposal: 1

Deadline(s): None

Board meeting date(s): Feb., June, and Oct.

Final notification: Within 3 months

Officers and Trustees:* Nancy R. Douzinas,* Pres.; Philip J. Rauch,* V.P.; George W. Frank; Lance E. Lindblom; Gerald I. Lustig; Brooke W. Mahoney; Lisa Mars; Philip Rauch; Ruth T. Rauch; John Wenzel.

Number of staff: 1 full-time professional; 1 part-time professional; 2 full-time support.

EIN: 112001717

Selected grants: The following grants were reported in 2004.

$91,840 to New School, New York, NY.

$55,000 to Neighborhood Network Research Center, East Farmingdale, NY. 2 grants: $25,000, $30,000

$50,000 to Project GRAD Roosevelt, Roosevelt, NY.

$40,000 to Boys and Girls Club, Hempstead, Hempstead, NY.

$30,000 to Citizens Planning and Housing Association, Baltimore, MD.

$30,000 to Conservation Fund, New York, NY.

$30,000 to Eastern Shore Land Conservancy, Queenstown, MD.

$28,240 to State University of New York Health Sciences Center of Stony Brook, Stony Brook, NY.

$23,200 to Regional Plan Association, New York, NY.

6775
N. & D. Rausman Foundation ✧
20 Herschel Terr.
Monsey, NY   10952

Established in 1999 in NY.
Donor: Norman Rausman.
Foundation type: Independent foundation.
Financial data (yr. ended 11/30/03): Assets, $1,726,703 (M); gifts received, $145,800; expenditures, $319,254; qualifying distributions, $318,960; giving activities include $318,960 for 17 grants (high: $116,000; low: $360).
Fields of interest: Theological school/education; Jewish federated giving programs; Jewish agencies & temples.
Limitations: Giving primarily in NY. No grants to individuals.
Application information: Application form not required.
Initial approach: Letter
Deadline(s): None
Trustee: Norman Rausman.
EIN: 134036959
Selected grants: The following grants were reported in 2003.

$27,000 to Stam Gemilas Chesed Fund, Lakewood, NJ.

6776
Richard Ravitch Foundation, Inc. ✧ ☆
c/o Richard Ravitch
31 E. 79th St., Apt. 9E
New York, NY   10021

Established in 1949 in NY.
Donor: Richard Ravitch.
Foundation type: Independent foundation.
Financial data (yr. ended 11/30/05): Assets, $1,883,618 (M); expenditures, $379,329; qualifying distributions, $365,830; giving activities include $365,830 for grants.
Purpose and activities: Giving primarily for education, hospitals, and public affairs.
Fields of interest: Education; Hospitals (general); Jewish federated giving programs; Public affairs.
Limitations: Applications not accepted. Giving primarily in NY. No grants to individuals.
Application information: Contributes only to pre-selected organizations.
Officers and Directors:* Richard Ravitch,* Pres. and Principal Mgr.; Judah Gribetz,* V.P.; Joseph Ravitch,* V.P.; Michael Ravitch,* Treas.
EIN: 136093139

6777
Reader's Digest Foundation ✧
Reader's Digest Rd.
Pleasantville, NY   10570-7000   (914) 244-5370
Contact: Janis L. Braun, Secy.
FAX: (914) 238-7642;
E-mail: carolyn.malile@readersdigest.com;
URL: http://www.readersdigest.com/corporate/rd_foundation.html

Incorporated in 1938 in NY.
Donor: The Reader's Digest Association, Inc.
Foundation type: Company-sponsored foundation.
Financial data (yr. ended 6/30/04): Assets, $14,237,259 (M); gifts received, $94,422; expenditures, $1,701,182; qualifying distributions, $1,628,079; giving activities include $983,061 for 45 grants (high: $402,200; low: $200), $162,600 for 53 grants to individuals (high: $10,000; low: $1,000), and $319,458 for 664 employee matching gifts.
Purpose and activities: The foundation supports libraries and organizations involved with K-12 and higher education, literacy, and human services.
Fields of interest: Elementary/secondary education; Higher education; Libraries/library science; Education, reading; Human services.
Type of support: Scholarship funds; Employee volunteer services; Employee matching gifts; Employee-related scholarships.
Limitations: Giving primarily in Westchester County, NY. No support for religious organizations, veterans' or fraternal organizations, private foundations, cultural organizations, environmental organizations, or local chapters of national organizations. No grants to individuals (except for employee-related scholarships), or for capital campaigns, endowments, general operating support, annual campaigns, start-up needs, emergency needs, debt reduction, special projects, charitable dinners or fundraising events, television, film, or video productions, publications, workshops, conferences,

---

seminars, religious endeavors, medical research, or health-related activities; no loans.
Publications: Annual report (including application guidelines).
Application information: Application form not required.
Initial approach: Proposal
Copies of proposal: 1
Deadline(s): Apr. 1, Aug. 1, and Dec. 1
Board meeting date(s): June, Nov., and Feb.
Final notification: Within 2 weeks
Officers and Directors:* Thomas O. Ryder,* Chair.; Janis L. Braun, Secy.; William H. Magill, Treas.; Susan F. Russ,* Exec. Dir.; William Adler; Bonnie Bachar; Richard Clark; Paul Gillow; Jeffrey Spar.
Number of staff: 3
EIN: 136120380
Selected grants: The following grants were reported in 2003.

$417,906 to Richard Nixon Library and Birthplace Foundation, Yorba Linda, CA. For program support.

$301,000 to Boys and Girls Clubs of America, Atlanta, GA. For Youth of the Year Program.

$250,000 to United Way of Westchester and Putnam, White Plains, NY. For general support.

$150,000 to Girl Scouts of the U.S.A., Northwest Georgia Council, Atlanta, GA. For general support.

$111,111 to Marshfield Clinic, Marshfield, WI. For general support.

$110,000 to United Way of the National Capital Area, Vienna, VA. For European flood relief.

$100,000 to Eisenhower Foundation, Abilene, KS. For Eisenhower Library.

$100,000 to Northern Westchester Hospital Center Foundation, Mount Kisco, NY. For general support.

$75,000 to Educators for Social Responsibility, Cambridge, MA. For general support.

$35,000 to United Negro College Fund, Excellence in Journalism, Fairfax, VA. For scholarships for students in journalism at historically black colleges and universities.

6778
Reader's Digest Partners for Sight Foundation ✧
Reader's Digest Rd.
Pleasantville, NY   10570-7000   (914) 244-5349
Contact: Susan Olivo, V.P.
FAX: (914) 244-7481; E-mail: rdpfs@rd.com;
Additional E-mail: partnersforsight@rd.com;
URL: http://www.rdpfs.org

Established in 1955.
Donors: Elise M. Schlicker; George Cornell.
Foundation type: Company-sponsored foundation.
Financial data (yr. ended 6/30/05): Assets, $11,134,466 (M); gifts received, $37,771; expenditures, $775,789; qualifying distributions, $735,410; giving activities include $521,450 for 17 grants (high: $150,000; low: $5,000).
Purpose and activities: The foundation supports programs designed to increase the self-reliance and dignity of blind and visually impaired people.
Fields of interest: Human services; Blind/visually impaired.
Type of support: Program development; Seed money; Matching/challenge support; General/operating support; Continuing support.

Limitations: Giving on a national basis. No support for lobbying organizations. No grants to individuals, or for medical research.
Publications: Application guidelines; Informational brochure (including application guidelines); Newsletter; IRS Form 990-PF.
Application information: Proposals should be no longer than 2 pages. Application form not required.
  Initial approach: Mail or E-mail proposal
  Copies of proposal: 1
  Deadline(s): None; contact foundation for deadlines for multi-year support of over $1,000,000
  Board meeting date(s): Mar., June, Sept., and Dec.
  Final notification: 1 month
Officers and Directors:* Barry Liebman,* Pres.; Susan Olivo,* V.P.; Andrea Newborn,* Secy.; Caroline Dale,* Treas.
Number of staff: 1 full-time professional; 1 part-time professional.
EIN: 136120440
Selected grants: The following grants were reported in 2005.
$38,450 to Association for the Visually Impaired, Spring Valley, NY. For Employment Placement Services Program.
$35,000 to American Foundation for the Blind, New York, NY. For program that trains Braille transcribers.
$35,000 to Hudson Valley Lighthouse, Ghent, NY. For Career Services Program.
$30,250 to Visions Services for the Blind and Visually Impaired, New York, NY. To restore and sustain rehab services to children who are blind and multi-handicapped.
$25,000 to Guide Dog Foundation for the Blind, Smithtown, NY. For general support.
$25,000 to National Association for Visually Handicapped, New York, NY. For Homebound Seniors Program.
$15,000 to Enrichment Audio Resource Services (EARS), New York, NY. For Community Outreach Program.
$14,700 to Saint Coletta and Cardinal Cushing Schools of Massachusetts, Hanover, MA. To create low vision clinic for students with very special needs.
$10,000 to BlindSkills, Salem, OR. For general support.
$10,000 to Chicago Lighthouse for People Who Are Blind or Visually Impaired, Chicago, IL.

6779
Realty Foundation of New York ✧ ☆
551 5th Ave., Ste. 415
New York, NY 10176 (212) 697-3943
Contact: Scholarship and Aid Comm.

Established in 1956 in NY.
Foundation type: Independent foundation.
Financial data (yr. ended 6/30/06): Assets, $1,760,540 (M); gifts received, $239,500; expenditures, $506,877; qualifying distributions, $320,782; giving activities include $320,782 for grants.
Purpose and activities: Provides assistance to financially needy employees, and awards scholarships to employees and children of employees of the real estate industry in New York City.
Type of support: Grants to individuals; Scholarships—to individuals.

Limitations: Giving limited to the five boroughs of New York City.
Publications: Informational brochure.
Application information: Application form required.
  Deadline(s): None
Officers: Larry Silverstein, Chair.; Jerry Cohen, Pres.; Charles Borrok, Exec. V.P.; H. Dale Hemmerdinger, Exec. V.P.; John Avlon, V.P.; David Baldwin, V.P.; Charles Benenson, V.P.; Maureen K. Clancy, V.P.; Douglas Durst, V.P.; Harold A. Fetner, V.P.; Richard Fisher, V.P.; Joseph Grotto, V.P.; Aaron Gural, V.P.; Jeffrey R. Gural, V.P.; Peter Kalikow, V.P.; Peter Malkin, V.P.; Raymond T. O'Keere, Jr., V.P.; Burton Resnick, V.P.; Stephen Ross, V.P.; Irving Schneider, V.P.; Robert Shapiro, V.P.; Stephen Siegel, V.P.; Sheldon Solow, V.P.; Jerry Speyer, V.P.; Kent Swig, V.P.; Alan Weiler, V.P.; Fred Wilpon, V.P.; William Zeckendorf, V.P.; Daniel Rose, Secy.; Eugene Grant, Treas.; Patricia Frank, Exec. Dir.
Directors: Lawrence Ackman; and 41 additional directors.
EIN: 136016622

6780
REBNY Foundation, Inc. ✧ ☆
570 Lexington Ave.
New York, NY 10022 (212) 532-3100
Contact: Marolyn Davenport

Incorporated in 1985 in NY.
Donors: The Real Estate Board of New York, Inc.; Morgan Guaranty Trust Co. of New York.
Foundation type: Independent foundation.
Financial data (yr. ended 6/30/05): Assets, $285,402 (M); gifts received, $634,655; expenditures, $623,618; qualifying distributions, $614,498; giving activities include $369,154 for grants.
Purpose and activities: Giving primarily for projects concerning housing and the homeless.
Fields of interest: Education; Housing/shelter, development; Homeless, human services; Homeless.
Limitations: Giving limited to New York, NY.
Application information:
  Initial approach: Letter
  Deadline(s): None
Officers and Trustees:* J. Zuccoti, Pres.; Daniel Brodsky,* V.P.; Samuel Lindenbaum,* V.P.; B. Resnick, V.P.; Edward Riguardi,* V.P.; William Rudin,* V.P.; Steven Spinola,* V.P.; Elizabeth Stribling,* V.P.; M. Tighe, V.P.; K. Witkin, V.P.; D. Zucker, V.P.; Leonard Litwin,* Secy.; A. Wiener, Treas.
EIN: 133317104
Selected grants: The following grants were reported in 2003.
$22,818 to Big Apple Circus, New York, NY. For educational and school programs.
$21,830 to Broadway Housing Communities, New York, NY.
$21,830 to Common Ground Community Housing Development Fund Corporation, New York, NY.
$8,500 to Metropolitan Museum of Art, New York, NY.
$5,000 to Alliance for the Arts, New York, NY.
$5,000 to Learning Leaders, New York, NY. For parent education.
$4,350 to New York Housing Conference, New York, NY.
$4,250 to Inner Circle, New York, NY.
$4,000 to World Hunger Year, New York, NY.
$2,500 to Skyscraper Museum, New York, NY.

6781
The Rechler Family Foundation, Inc. ✧
(formerly Morton & Beverley Rechler Foundation, Inc.)
c/o Katzman, Weinstein & Co., LLP
131 Jericho Tpke., Ste. 400
Jericho, NY 11753 (516) 333-6881
Contact: Morton Rechler, Pres.

Established in 1986 in FL.
Donors: Morton Rechler; Beverley Rechler; Yvetta Rechler-Newman; Bennett Rechler; Hannah Rabinowitz.
Foundation type: Independent foundation.
Financial data (yr. ended 12/31/05): Assets, $11,566,527 (M); gifts received, $1,324,657; expenditures, $951,856; qualifying distributions, $951,650; giving activities include $951,650 for 46 grants (high: $600,000; low: $500).
Purpose and activities: Giving to Jewish agencies, education, and community services.
Fields of interest: Arts; Higher education; Education; Human services; Jewish federated giving programs; Jewish agencies & temples.
Limitations: Applications not accepted. Giving primarily in New York, NY. No grants to individuals.
Application information: Contributes only to pre-selected organizations.
Officers: Morton Rechler, Pres.; Beverley Rechler, Secy.; Bennett Rechler, Treas.
Directors: Hannah Rabinowitz; Yvetta Rechler-Newman.
EIN: 592828631

6782
The Reed Foundation, Inc. ✧
444 Madison Ave., Ste. 2901
New York, NY 10022 (212) 223-1330
FAX: (212) 754-0078;
E-mail: trf@reedfoundation.org

Incorporated in 1949 in NY.
Donor: Samuel Rubin†.
Foundation type: Independent foundation.
Financial data (yr. ended 12/31/05): Assets, $15,754,800 (M); expenditures, $1,874,304; qualifying distributions, $1,859,439; giving activities include $1,601,132 for 98 grants (high: $210,000; low: $230).
Purpose and activities: The foundation's focus is on the support of programs in the arts, related libraries, social services, and both domestic and international civil rights. The arts and literature of the Caribbean Basin, through programs at a university and a research institute, are of major interest at present.
Fields of interest: Visual arts; Performing arts; Performing arts, theater; Arts; Higher education; Libraries/library science; Education; Minorities/immigrants, centers/services; International human rights; Civil rights.
International interests: Caribbean.
Type of support: General/operating support; Continuing support; Endowments; Program development; Fellowships; Scholarship funds; Research; Exchange programs; Matching/challenge support.
Limitations: Giving primarily in the metropolitan New York, NY, area; some funding also in the Caribbean Basin. No grants to individuals.
Publications: Program policy statement.
Application information: Applications generally considered only from organizations that have been

pre-selected or those with which the foundation has a funding history. Application form not required.

Initial approach: Letter
Copies of proposal: 1
Deadline(s): None
Board meeting date(s): Varies
Final notification: Immediately following board meetings

Officers and Directors:* Reed Rubin,* Pres.; Jane Gregory Rubin,* Secy.; Maia A. Rubin, Treas.; Lara R. Rubin; Peter L. Rubin.
Number of staff: 1 part-time professional.
EIN: 131990017

6783
John & Cynthia Reed Foundation ▼ ◇
c/o U.S. Trust
114 W. 47th St.
New York, NY 10036
Contact: Andrew Lane, V.P., U.S. Trust

Established in 2000 in NY.
Donor: John S. Reed.
Foundation type: Independent foundation.
Financial data (yr. ended 12/31/04): Assets, $64,089,793 (M); gifts received, $5,038,972; expenditures, $5,004,708; qualifying distributions, $4,827,385; giving activities include $4,821,290 for 35 grants (high: $1,740,000; low: $5,000; average: $10,000–$200,000).
Purpose and activities: Giving primarily for education and arts and culture.
Fields of interest: Museums (art); Performing arts, theater; Higher education; Higher education, university; Animals/wildlife, preservation/ protection; Recreation, parks/playgrounds; Big Brothers/Big Sisters.
Type of support: General/operating support; Continuing support; Annual campaigns; Capital campaigns; Building/renovation; Land acquisition; Program development.
Limitations: Applications not accepted. Giving on a national basis, with some emphasis on Princeton, NJ, and the greater metropolitan New York, NY, area.
Application information: Unsolicited requests for funds not accepted.
Trustees: Cynthia Reed; John S. Reed.
Number of staff: 1 part-time professional; 1 part-time support.
EIN: 137219392
Selected grants: The following grants were reported in 2004.
$1,740,000 to Massachusetts Institute of Technology, Cambridge, MA. For annual unrestricted support.
$500,000 to Institut des Hautes Etudes Scientifiques (IHES), Friends of the, New York, NY. For unrestricted support.
$279,648 to Union Square Partnership, New York, NY. 2 grants: $100,000 (For annual unrestricted support for Union Square Park projects), $179,648 (For unrestricted support for capital campaign).
$200,000 to CERGE-EI Foundation, Teaneck, NJ. For annual unrestricted support.
$200,000 to MDRC, New York, NY. For unrestricted support.
$175,000 to National Academies, DC. For unrestricted support.
$102,790 to University of Michigan, Ann Arbor, MI. For unrestricted support.

$75,000 to Philharmonic-Symphony Society of New York, New York, NY. For annual unrestricted support.
$50,000 to Metropolitan Museum of Art, New York, NY. For annual unrestricted support.

6784
The Reich Family Charitable Trust ◇ ☆
131 Dover St.
Brooklyn, NY 11235

Established in 1993 in NY.
Donors: Raymond Reich; Sue Reich.
Foundation type: Independent foundation.
Financial data (yr. ended 12/31/05): Assets, $288,721 (M); gifts received, $426,751; expenditures, $385,161; qualifying distributions, $378,135; giving activities include $378,135 for grants.
Purpose and activities: Giving to Jewish organizations, including temples, yeshivas, and funds.
Fields of interest: Elementary/secondary education; Health care; Human services; Jewish federated giving programs; Jewish agencies & temples.
Limitations: Applications not accepted. Giving primarily in Brooklyn, NY. No grants to individuals.
Application information: Contributes only to pre-selected organizations.
Trustees: Raymond Reich; Sue Reich.
EIN: 137029481
Selected grants: The following grants were reported in 2003.
$48,500 to Yeshiva of Manhattan Beach, Brooklyn, NY.
$20,060 to Yeshiva DZikuv Ateres Yehoshua, Brooklyn, NY.
$2,180 to Child Life Society, Brooklyn, NY.
$2,061 to Yeshivath Beth Moshe, Scranton, PA.
$2,030 to Aleh Foundation, Brooklyn, NY.
$1,800 to Prospect Park Yeshiva, Brooklyn, NY.
$1,000 to Beer Hagolah Institutes, Brooklyn, NY.
$1,000 to Israel Cancer Research Fund, New York, NY.
$1,000 to Yeshiva of Brooklyn, Brooklyn, NY.
$1,000 to Yeshiva Torah Temimah, Brooklyn, NY.

6785
Mahir A. & Helene Reiss Foundation, Inc. ◇
444 Madison Ave., Ste. 1800
New York, NY 10022
Contact: Helene Reiss, Dir.

Established in 1981 in NY.
Donors: Mahir A. Reiss; Helene Reiss.
Foundation type: Independent foundation.
Financial data (yr. ended 12/31/05): Assets, $57,412 (M); gifts received, $1,750,000; expenditures, $1,627,937; qualifying distributions, $1,627,937; giving activities include $1,626,078 for 247 grants (high: $130,000; low: $10).
Purpose and activities: Giving primarily for Jewish agencies, temples, and schools.
Fields of interest: Elementary/secondary education; Jewish federated giving programs; Jewish agencies & temples.
Limitations: Giving primarily in NY.
Application information:

Initial approach: Letter
Deadline(s): None
Directors: Helene Reiss; Mahir A. Reiss.
EIN: 133050322
Selected grants: The following grants were reported in 2005.
$130,000 to Mesivta Chaim Berlin, Brooklyn, NY.
$5,000 to Monsey Academy for Girls, Monsey, NY.
$4,500 to Mosdos Viznitz, New York, NY.
$2,800 to Bais Rivka Rochel, Lakewood, NJ.
$1,800 to Bais Medrash Taharos, Monsey, NY.
$1,200 to Yeshiva Ketana of Manhattan, New York, NY.
$750 to Bais Yakov Dchasidei Gur, Brooklyn, NY.
$680 to Yeshiva Ohr Yisroel, Forest Hills, NY.
$620 to Sinai Academy, Brooklyn, NY.
$360 to Yeshiva Mkor Chaim, Brooklyn, NY.

6786
Harold and Beatrice Renfield Foundation, Inc. ◇
888 Park Ave.
New York, NY 10021
Contact: Jean Renfield-Miller, Pres.

Established in 1974 in NY.
Donor: Beatrice Renfield‡.
Foundation type: Independent foundation.
Financial data (yr. ended 12/31/05): Assets, $15,235,167 (M); expenditures, $873,388; qualifying distributions, $699,257; giving activities include $669,414 for 18 grants (high: $250,000; low: $2,500; average: $5,000–$10,000).
Purpose and activities: Giving for education, nursing homes, and arts and culture.
Fields of interest: Arts; Higher education; Education; Health care, patient services; Nursing care; Health organizations, association; Human services.
Limitations: Giving primarily in New York, NY. No support for private foundations. No grants to individuals.
Application information:
Initial approach: Letter
Deadline(s): None
Officers: Jean Renfield-Miller, Pres.; Martin J. Milston, Treas.
Director: Joseph W. Renfield.
EIN: 510156925

6787
The Ira M. Resnick Foundation, Inc. ◇
133 E. 58th St.
New York, NY 10022 (212) 223-1009
Contact: Ira M. Resnick, Pres.

Established in 1994 in NY.
Donor: Ira M. Resnick.
Foundation type: Independent foundation.
Financial data (yr. ended 5/31/05): Assets, $977,647 (M); gifts received, $1,592,039; expenditures, $623,540; qualifying distributions, $575,115; giving activities include $575,115 for 174 grants (high: $140,000; low: $100).
Purpose and activities: Giving primarily for the arts, health associations, children, youth and social services, and to Jewish organizations.
Fields of interest: Media, film/video; Museums; Museums (specialized); Performing arts; Performing arts centers; Performing arts, theater; Arts; Health organizations, association; Human services;

Children/youth, services; Jewish agencies & temples.
Limitations: Giving primarily in NY.
Application information: Application form not required.
  Deadline(s): None
Officers: Ira M. Resnick, Pres.; Gilbert A. Wang, Secy.-Treas.
Director: Charles F. Crames.
EIN: 133775995
Selected grants: The following grants were reported in 2005.
$140,000 to Film Society of Lincoln Center, New York, NY.
$62,000 to Ethical Culture Fieldston Schools, New York, NY.
$6,000 to Lincoln Center Theater, New York, NY.
$6,000 to Roundabout Theater Company, New York, NY.
$5,000 to Jacobs Pillow, New York, NY.
$5,000 to Joyce Theater, New York, NY.
$2,500 to Jewish Womens Archive, Brookline, MA.
$1,500 to Childrens Storefront, New York, NY.
$1,000 to Museum of Jewish Heritage, New York, NY.
$500 to United Negro College Fund, Fairfax, VA.

6788
Allene Reuss Memorial Trust ✧
c/o The Bank of New York, Tax Dept.
1 Wall St., 28th Fl.
New York, NY 10286
Contact: Richard Pershan, Tr.
Application address: c/o Leboeuf, Lamb, Greene and McRae, 125 W. 55th St., New York, NY 10019

Established in 1996 in France.
Donor: Henry Reuss†.
Foundation type: Independent foundation.
Financial data (yr. ended 12/31/04): Assets, $13,276,810 (M); gifts received, $3,035,503; expenditures, $5,343,834; qualifying distributions, $597,385; giving activities include $557,246 for 18 grants (high: $83,333; low: $5,000).
Purpose and activities: Giving primarily for the aiding, prevention, and cure of vision problems.
Fields of interest: Higher education; Eye diseases.
Limitations: Giving primarily in NY.
Application information: Application form not required.
  Initial approach: Letter
  Deadline(s): None
Trustees: Richard Pershan; The Bank of New York.
EIN: 137086745
Selected grants: The following grants were reported in 2004.
$83,333 to American Foundation for the Blind, New York, NY.
$25,043 to State University of New York College of Optometry, New York, NY.
$25,000 to Freedom Guide Dogs for the Blind, Cassville, NY.
$20,000 to Catholic Charities.

6789
Charles H. Revson Foundation, Inc. ▼ ✧
55 E. 59th St., 23rd Fl.
New York, NY 10022-1112   (212) 935-3340
FAX: (212) 688-0633;
E-mail: info@revsonfoundation.org; URL: http://www.revsonfoundation.org

Incorporated in 1956 in NY.
Donor: Charles H. Revson†.
Foundation type: Independent foundation.
Financial data (yr. ended 12/31/04): Assets, $167,488,377 (M); expenditures, $7,812,582; qualifying distributions, $6,694,046; giving activities include $5,653,442 for 48 grants (high: $850,000; low: $2,500; average: $5,000–$150,000).
Purpose and activities: Grants for urban affairs and public policy, with a special emphasis on New York, NY, problems, as well as national policy issues; education, including higher education; biomedical research policy; and Jewish philanthropy and education. Particular emphasis within these program areas are: the future of New York, accountability of government, the changing role of women (especially leadership development for public life), minority groups, and the role of modern communications in education and other aspects of society.
Fields of interest: Media/communications; Higher education; Education; Civil rights, minorities; Civil rights, women; Civil rights; Community development, public education; Biological sciences; Public policy, research; Government/public administration; Public affairs; Minorities; African Americans/Blacks; Women; Homeless.
International interests: Israel.
Type of support: Continuing support; Program development; Fellowships; Internship funds; Research; Program-related investments/loans.
Limitations: Giving primarily in New York, NY. No support for local or national health appeals or direct service programs. No grants to individuals, or for endowment funds, building, renovation, or construction funds, book projects, charity events, travel expenses, or budgetary support.
Publications: Application guidelines; Biennial report (including application guidelines); Occasional report.
Application information: Application form not required.
  Initial approach: Letter or full proposal
  Copies of proposal: 1
  Deadline(s): None
  Board meeting date(s): Apr., June, Oct., and Dec.
  Final notification: 6 months
Officers and Directors:* Phillip Leder,* Chair.; Charles H. Revson, Jr.,* Secy.-Treas.; Red Burns; Henry Louis Gates, Jr.; Suzanne Gluck; Jerome Groopman; Ruth Mandel; Martha Minow; Louis Perlmutter; Robert S. Rifkind; Harold Tanner.
Number of staff: 2 full-time professional; 1 part-time professional; 3 full-time support.
EIN: 136126105
Selected grants: The following grants were reported in 2004.
$1,545,429 to New York University, School of Law, New York, NY. For Charles H. Revson Law Students' Public Interest Fellowship Program (LSPIN), which enables New York-area law students to work in public interest law organizations during upcoming summers.
$900,000 to Center on Budget and Policy Priorities, DC. For continued support of Center's monitoring and public education activities related to federal budget.
$550,000 to Citizens Union Foundation of the City of New York, New York, NY. To strengthen and expand gothamgazette.corn, web site launched by Citizens Union Foundation providing one-stop-shopping in public policy and NYC affairs.

$494,964 to Columbia University, New York, NY. For continued support of Charles H. Revson Fellows Program on the Future of the City of New York.
$450,000 to United States Holocaust Memorial Museum, DC. For continued support of Charles H. Revson Fellowships for Archival Research at Museum's Center for Advanced Holocaust Studies.
$300,000 to Fiscal Policy Institute, New York, NY. For support of research, public education and advocacy work on budget, economic, and related policy issues that affect low-and moderate-income New Yorkers.
$250,000 to Tides Center, San Francisco, CA. For Media Voting Project to join with other foundations to support national nonpartisan media campaign for television, radio, print and Internet outlets, urging Americans to register and vote.
$100,000 to Center for National Independence in Politics (CNIP), Project Vote Smart, Philipsburg, MT. For database, web site, and national 800 number.
$30,000 to Documentary Preservation Project, New York, NY. Toward collection and preservation of award-winning films of Marcus Ophusl, The Sorrow and Pity, Memory of Justice, and Hotel Terminus, in particular.
$25,000 to New York Law School, New York, NY. To provide final year of support to Center for New York City Law, to continue to develop and expand web site while Center seeks support from other funders.

6790
The Christopher Reynolds Foundation, Inc. ✧
267 5th Ave., Ste. 1001
New York, NY 10016   (212) 532-1606
Contact: Andrea Panaritis, Exec. Dir.
FAX: (212) 532-1403;
E-mail: inquiries@creynolds.org; URL: http://www.creynolds.org

Incorporated in 1952 in NY.
Donor: Libby Holman Reynolds†.
Foundation type: Independent foundation.
Financial data (yr. ended 1/31/05): Assets, $30,198,696 (M); expenditures, $1,824,548; qualifying distributions, $1,563,801; giving activities include $1,085,643 for 54 grants (high: $67,000; low: $500).
Purpose and activities: The foundation is now concentrating its resources on U.S. relations with Cuba.
Fields of interest: Human services; International affairs.
International interests: Cuba.
Type of support: General/operating support; Continuing support; Conferences/seminars; Technical assistance; Exchange programs.
Limitations: Giving on a national and international basis. No grants to individuals, or for capital or endowment funds, annual campaigns, emergency funds, deficit financing, scholarships, or matching gifts; no loans.
Publications: Financial statement; Grants list; Multi-year report (including application guidelines).
Application information: Application form available on foundation Web site. Application form required.
  Initial approach: Telephone, or fax or E-mail letter of inquiry, no more than 3 typewritten pages. Formal proposal upon request

Copies of proposal: 6
Deadline(s): Submit proposal preferably 30 days prior to board meeting
Board meeting date(s): Quarterly
Final notification: 1 week
Officers and Directors:* Michael Kahn,* Pres.; Suzanne Derrer, V.P.; Andrea Panaritis,* Secy. and Exec. Dir.; John R. Boettiger, Ph.D., Treas.; Virginia Kahn.
Number of staff: 1 full-time professional; 1 part-time professional; 1 full-time support.
EIN: 136129401
Selected grants: The following grants were reported in 2004.
$60,000 to Center for International Policy, DC.
$55,000 to World Policy Institute at the New School, New York, NY.
$43,000 to Social Science Research Council, New York, NY. For Cuba Project.
$24,000 to Fund for Reconciliation and Development, New York, NY. For general support.
$24,000 to Puentes Cubanos, Miami, FL.
$22,500 to Global Exchange, San Francisco, CA.
$22,000 to Center for Constitutional Rights, New York, NY.
$16,500 to International Crane Foundation, Baraboo, WI.
$12,793 to Interreligious Foundation for Community Organization, New York, NY.
$10,000 to Center for National Policy, DC.

6791
Rhodebeck Charitable Trust
c/o McLaughin & Stern LLP
260 Madison Ave.
New York, NY 10016
Contact: Huyler C. Held, Tr.

Established in 1987 in AZ.
Donor: Mildred T. Rhodebeck‡.
Foundation type: Independent foundation.
Financial data (yr. ended 4/30/05): Assets, $25,703,865 (M); expenditures, $2,683,978; qualifying distributions, $2,447,842; giving activities include $1,937,500 for 54 grants (high: $125,000; low: $3,000), and $487,500 for 7 employee matching gifts.
Purpose and activities: To alleviate the plight of disadvantaged people in the New York, NY, metropolitan area, including people who are homeless, hungry, elderly, or sick, and children by making grants to publicly supported tax-exempt organizations concerned with one or more of these objectives.
Fields of interest: Mental health/crisis services; Legal services; Food services; Human services; Children/youth, services; Family services; Aging, centers/services; Homeless, human services; Federated giving programs; Aging; Economically disadvantaged; Homeless.
Type of support: General/operating support; Capital campaigns; Building/renovation; Endowments; Program development; Seed money; Matching/challenge support.
Limitations: Giving limited to the metropolitan New York, NY, area. No grants to individuals.
Application information: Unsolicited applications are strongly discouraged.
Trustee: Huyler C. Held.
Number of staff: 1 part-time support.
EIN: 133413293
Selected grants: The following grants were reported in 2004.

$455,000 to Community Funds, New York, NY. For Rhodebeck Charitable Fund.
$50,000 to Brooklyn Legal Services Corporation A, Brooklyn, NY. For capital campaign.
$50,000 to West Side Center for Community Life, New York, NY. For renovation project.
$50,000 to Womens Housing and Economic Development Corporation, Bronx, NY. For general support.
$35,000 to Jericho Project, New York, NY. For general support.
$25,000 to Friends of Island Academy, New York, NY. For Mental Health Program.
$25,000 to Montefiore Medical Center, Bronx, NY. For general support.
$25,000 to Project Hospitality, Staten Island, NY. For general support.
$25,000 to Volunteers of Legal Service, New York, NY. For general support.
$10,000 to Peter Westbrook Foundation, New York, NY. For general support.

6792
The Rhodes Foundation ✧
1120 5th Ave., Ste. 8B
New York, NY 10128
Contact: William R. Rhodes, Pres.

Established in 2002 in DE.
Donor: William R. Rhodes.
Foundation type: Independent foundation.
Financial data (yr. ended 12/31/05): Assets, $943,950 (M); gifts received, $9,378; expenditures, $1,444,684; qualifying distributions, $1,435,000; giving activities include $1,435,000 for 2 grants (high: $1,035,000; low: $400,000).
Purpose and activities: Giving primarily for education.
Fields of interest: Secondary school/education; Higher education.
Limitations: Applications not accepted. Giving primarily in Northfield, MA, and Providence, RI. No grants to individuals.
Application information: Contributes only to pre-selected organizations.
Officers: William R. Rhodes, Pres. and Treas.; Robert E. Dineen, Jr., V.P.; Jeanne C. Olivier, Secy.
EIN: 800003840

6793
The Rice Family Foundation ✧
P.O. Box 319
Bedford, NY 10506
Contact: Eve H. Rice, V.P. and Treas.

Established in 1989 in NY.
Donor: Henry Hart Rice‡.
Foundation type: Independent foundation.
Financial data (yr. ended 12/31/05): Assets, $41,778,237 (M); expenditures, $3,030,501; qualifying distributions, $1,058,874; giving activities include $1,058,519 for 47 grants (high: $200,000; low: $19; average: $25,000–$50,000).
Purpose and activities: Support for higher educational institutions, cultural programs, and health and human service agencies.
Fields of interest: Arts; Higher education; Health care; Human services.
Limitations: Applications not accepted. Giving primarily in NY. No grants to individuals.

Application information: Contributes only to pre-selected organizations.
Board meeting date(s): Annually
Officers: Margaret S. Rice, Pres.; Edward H. Rice, V.P. and Secy.; Eve H. Rice, V.P. and Treas.
EIN: 133542090
Selected grants: The following grants were reported in 2004.
$350,000 to George Mason University Foundation, Fairfax, VA.
$200,000 to Yale University, New Haven, CT.
$45,000 to Westchester Community College, Valhalla, NY.
$25,000 to Metropolitan Museum of Art, New York, NY.
$25,000 to Music Conservatory of Westchester, White Plains, NY.
$10,000 to New York University, New York, NY.
$10,000 to Northern Westchester Center for the Arts, Mount Kisco, NY.

6794
The Rice Family Foundation ✧ ☆
c/o Clayton, Dubilier & Rice, Inc.
375 Park Ave.
New York, NY 10152

Established in 1998 in NY.
Donor: Joseph L. Rice III.
Foundation type: Independent foundation.
Financial data (yr. ended 12/31/05): Assets, $5,110,857 (M); expenditures, $464,076; qualifying distributions, $430,250; giving activities include $430,000 for 6 grants (high: $250,000; low: $10,000).
Fields of interest: Human services.
Limitations: Applications not accepted. Giving primarily in NY. No grants to individuals.
Application information: Contributes only to pre-selected organizations.
Trustees: Franci J. Blassberg; Joseph L. Rice.
EIN: 137152866
Selected grants: The following grants were reported in 2005.
$250,000 to New York City Ballet, New York, NY.
$110,000 to Cornell University, Ithaca, NY.
$25,000 to Memorial Sloan-Kettering Cancer Center, New York, NY.
$25,000 to New School, New York, NY.
$10,000 to Guild Hall of East Hampton, East Hampton, NY.
$10,000 to Historic Deerfield, Deerfield, MA.

6795
Rich Family Foundation ✧
(formerly Rich Foundation)
1150 Niagara St.
P.O. Box 245
Buffalo, NY 14240-0245
Contact: David A. Rich, Exec. Dir.

Established in 1961.
Donors: Robert E. Rich; Rich Products Corp.
Foundation type: Company-sponsored foundation.
Financial data (yr. ended 12/31/03): Assets, $4,646,824 (M); gifts received, $720,000; expenditures, $499,645; qualifying distributions, $476,470; giving activities include $463,753 for 158 grants (high: $75,000; low: $25).
Purpose and activities: The foundation supports Christian agencies and churches and organizations

involved with arts and culture, higher education, health, human services, and children and youth services.

Fields of interest: Historic preservation/historical societies; Arts; Higher education; Health care; Health organizations, association; Human services; Children/youth, services; Federated giving programs; Christian agencies & churches.

Limitations: Giving primarily in Buffalo and western NY.

Application information:
Initial approach: Proposal
Deadline(s): None

Officers: Robert E. Rich, Pres. and Treas.; Robert E. Rich, Jr., Secy.; David A. Rich, Exec. Dir.

EIN: 166026199

Selected grants: The following grants were reported in 2004.

$75,000 to Students in Free Enterprise, Springfield, MO.

$25,000 to Buffalo Fine Arts Academy, Buffalo, NY. For annual fund.

$19,600 to Hunters Hope Foundation, Orchard Park, NY. 2 grants: $10,000, $9,600

$15,500 to United Way of Buffalo and Erie County, Buffalo, NY. 2 grants: $7,750 each

$10,000 to Baptist Health Systems of South Florida Foundation, Miami, FL. For annual fund.

$10,000 to International Game Fish Association, Dania, FL. For general support.

$10,000 to Jackson Memorial Foundation, Miami, FL.

$10,000 to Roswell Park Cancer Institute, Buffalo, NY.

6796
The Richardson Foundation ✧
(formerly Frank E. and Nancy M. Richardson Foundation)
245 Park Ave., 41st Fl.
New York, NY 10167

Established in 1987 in NY.
Donor: Frank E. Richardson III.
Foundation type: Independent foundation.
Financial data (yr. ended 12/31/05): Assets, $1,630,673 (M); expenditures, $882,257; qualifying distributions, $880,379; giving activities include $879,379 for 58 grants (high: $236,327; low: $30).

Purpose and activities: Giving to a museum of art; support also for other cultural programs and education.

Fields of interest: Museums (art); Performing arts; Performing arts, ballet; Performing arts, opera; Higher education; Law school/education; Medical school/education; Education; Breast cancer research; Human services.

Type of support: General/operating support.

Limitations: Applications not accepted. Giving primarily in NY; some giving also in MA and NJ. No grants to individuals.

Application information: Contributes only to pre-selected organizations.

Trustee: Frank E. Richardson.

EIN: 133440317

6797
Anne S. Richardson Fund
(formerly Anne S. Richardson Charitable Trust)
c/o JPMorgan Chase Bank, N.A.
345 Park Ave., 4th Fl.
New York, NY 10154 (212) 464-2443
Contact: Rohit Burman
FAX: (212) 464-2305; URL: http://foundationcenter.org/grantmaker/richardson/

Trust established in 1965 in CT.
Donor: Anne S. Richardson†.
Foundation type: Independent foundation.
Financial data (yr. ended 7/31/05): Assets, $13,135,657 (M); expenditures, $704,487; qualifying distributions, $586,856; giving activities include $575,000 for 23 grants (high: $70,000; low: $2,500).

Purpose and activities: Funding interests include: 1) eight organizations recommended by the donor; 2) programs in Ridgefield, CT, that assist lower-income people or are of broad interest to the community; and 3) programs in Fairfield County, CT, that promote the independence of women, support the lesbian and gay community, foster youth development, or enhance the natural beautification of communities through parks or gardens.

Fields of interest: Botanical/horticulture/landscape services; Recreation, parks/playgrounds; Youth development; Women; LGBTQ.

Type of support: General/operating support; Capital campaigns; Program development.

Limitations: Giving primarily in western CT. No support for private foundations or organizations lacking 501(c)(3) status. No grants to individuals; no loans.

Publications: Application guidelines; Grants list.

Application information: See foundation Web site for application guidelines and requirements. Application form not required.
Initial approach: Proposal
Copies of proposal: 1
Deadline(s): Mar. 1
Board meeting date(s): July
Final notification: July 31

Trustee: JPMorgan Chase Bank, N.A.

Number of staff: None.

EIN: 136192516

Selected grants: The following grants were reported in 2004.

$50,000 to Saint Stephens Church, Ridgefield, CT. For organ renovation and church restoration.

$50,000 to YMCA of Western Connecticut, Regional, Danbury, CT. For Escape to the Arts.

$42,500 to Pro Bono Partnership, White Plains, NY. For pilot project addressing special legal needs of organizations in Fairfield County that address domestic violence of other issues affecting independence of women.

$40,000 to Norwalk Hospital Foundation, Norwalk, CT. For digital mammography unit and computer aided detection units.

$40,000 to Yale University, New Haven, CT. For scholarships or fellowships in the area of Women's and Gender Studies.

$35,000 to Connecticut Womens Educational and Legal Fund, Hartford, CT.

$25,000 to Aldrich Contemporary Art Museum, Ridgefield, CT. For capital campaign.

$25,000 to True Colors, Manchester, CT. For capacity building.

$20,000 to Ridgefield Symphony Orchestra, Ridgefield, CT. For youth program.

$15,000 to Ridgefield Historical Society, Ridgefield, CT. For education project.

6798
Richenthal Foundation ✧
122 E. 42nd St., Ste. 4400
New York, NY 10168-0002 (212) 687-8360
Contact: Arthur Richenthal, Dir.

Established in 1964 in NY.
Foundation type: Independent foundation.
Financial data (yr. ended 12/31/05): Assets, $6,552,344 (M); expenditures, $1,059,341; qualifying distributions, $1,050,310; giving activities include $1,050,310 for 22 grants.

Purpose and activities: Giving primarily for the arts and education.

Fields of interest: Arts, multipurpose centers/programs; Performing arts; Education; Hospitals (general).

Limitations: Giving primarily in NY. No grants to individuals.

Application information:
Initial approach: Proposal
Deadline(s): None

Directors: Arthur Richenthal; Donald Richenthal.

EIN: 136113616

6799
The Richman Family Foundation ✧
(formerly The Fred & Rita Richman Foundation)
261 5th Ave.
New York, NY 10016

Established in 1985 in NY.
Donors: Fred Richman; Richloom Sales Corp.; Richloom Fabrics Group, Inc.
Foundation type: Independent foundation.
Financial data (yr. ended 11/30/05): Assets, $34,751,708 (M); gifts received, $1,337,355; expenditures, $2,202,710; qualifying distributions, $1,877,105; giving activities include $1,539,000 for 10 grants (high: $600,000; low: $5,000).

Fields of interest: Museums (art); International development; Jewish federated giving programs; Jewish agencies & temples.

Limitations: Applications not accepted. Giving on a national basis. No grants to individuals.

Application information: Contributes only to pre-selected organizations.

Directors: Fred Richman; James Richman; Rita Richman.

EIN: 133332711

6800
Richmond County Savings Foundation ▼
900 South Ave., Exec. Ste. 17
Staten Island, NY 10314 (718) 568-3516
Contact: Cesar Claro, Exec. Dir.
FAX: (718) 568-3551; E-mail: Staff@rcsf.org;
Additional tels.: (718) 568-3517 and (718) 568-3631; URL: http://www.rcsf.org

Established in 1998 in DE.
Donor: Richmond County Financial Corp.
Foundation type: Independent foundation.
Financial data (yr. ended 12/31/05): Assets, $73,386,990 (M); expenditures, $3,766,067; qualifying distributions, $4,022,528; giving activities include $3,509,422 for 309 grants (high:

$200,000; low: $100; average: $5,000–$100,000).

Purpose and activities: The foundation supports 501(c)(3) organizations involved with the arts, education, health and human services, housing/shelter, and community development in their service areas. The foundation also supports religious institutions. Support also given in the following four areas of eligibility: 1) Capital Initiative - Construction, renovations and enhancements are included in this category; 2) Programmatic Funding - Priority is given to organizations providing programs and services in the areas of human services, public benefit, health, education, environment, arts and culture; 3) Organizational Effectiveness and Advancement - Funding is considered for initiatives that strengthen the performance of community organizations. Areas for consideration include governance, leadership, strategy, program implementation, financial management, and fund development; and 4) Partnerships for Community Enhancement - The foundation encourages nonprofit organizations to establish programmatic partnerships in order to provide new vital services to the community. Funding consideration in this category is for new-shared initiatives only.

Fields of interest: Arts, multipurpose centers/programs; Arts; Education; Environment; Hospitals (general); Health organizations, association; Housing/shelter; Youth development, services; Human services; Community development, neighborhood development; Economic development; Community development; Religion.

Type of support: General/operating support; Management development/capacity building; Annual campaigns; Capital campaigns; Building/renovation; Equipment; Emergency funds; Program development; Conferences/seminars; Publication; Research; Technical assistance; Program evaluation; Program-related investments/loans; Matching/challenge support.

Limitations: Giving primarily in Staten Island, NY. No support for political organizations. No grants to individuals.

Publications: Application guidelines; Annual report; Program policy statement (including application guidelines).

Application information: An application form is available online. Only one grant larger than $5,000 shall be awarded to any organization in a given year. Organizations receiving grants of more than $10,000 will be required to file a final report with the foundation. See foundation Web site for more application information. Application form required.

    Initial approach: Complete online application form or download application form and mail it to foundation. Organizations submitting online are required to confirm, by phone, the receipt of the submission with foundation staff
    Copies of proposal: 1
    Deadline(s): None
    Board meeting date(s): Quarterly
Officers and Directors:* Michael F. Manzulli,* C.E.O. and Pres.; Kim Seggio, Secy. and Sr. Prog. Off.; Anthony E. Burke,* Treas.; Cesar J. Claro, Exec. Dir.; Godfrey H. Carstens, Jr.; Edward Cruz; Alfred B. Curtis, Jr.; Robert S. Farrell; Joseph R. Ficalora; James L. Kelley; Patrick F.X. Nilan; Maurice K. Shaw.
Number of staff: 4 full-time support.
EIN: 061503051
Selected grants: The following grants were reported in 2004.

$267,000 to Saint Peters Church, Staten Island, NY. For capital campaign.
$200,000 to Our Lady of Mount Carmel-Saint Benedicta, Staten Island, NY. For school roof replacement project.
$150,000 to Art Lab, Staten Island, NY. For Dolphin Sightings Temporary Public Art Display.
$150,000 to New York Blood Center, New York, NY. For Blood Donor Coach Sponsorship.
$150,000 to Ronald McDonald House of Long Island, New Hyde Park, NY. For Extensions of Love Expansion Project.
$130,000 to Eden II School for Autistic Children, Staten Island, NY. For capital campaign.
$100,000 to New York Hall of Science, Corona, NY. For teacher professional development.
$100,000 to Noble Maritime Collection, Staten Island, NY. For exhibitions, technology upgrades and art collection restoration.
$100,000 to Olympia Activity Center, Staten Island, NY. For Community Center: Interior Construction.
$100,000 to Queens Library Foundation, Jamaica, NY. For Programmatic Matching Challenge.

6801

The Anita B. and Howard S. Richmond Foundation, Inc. ✧

(formerly Kings Piont Richmond Foundation, Inc.)
266 W. 37th St., 17th Fl.
New York, NY 10018-6609
Contact: Howard S. Richmond, Pres.

Established in 1965 in NY.
Donors: Howard S. Richmond; Lawrence Richmond; Phillip Richmond; Robert Richmond; Elizabeth Richmond-Schulman.
Foundation type: Independent foundation.
Financial data (yr. ended 12/31/05): Assets, $5,390,387 (M); gifts received, $375,730; expenditures, $522,114; qualifying distributions, $478,920; giving activities include $478,920 for 167 grants (high: $100,000; low: $50).
Purpose and activities: Giving primarily to health associations, including a children's hospital, education, and social services including a free cancer support community group.
Fields of interest: Museums (children's); Arts; Higher education; Education; Hospitals (general); Health organizations, association; Human services; Children, services; Federated giving programs; Jewish agencies & temples.
Limitations: Giving on a national basis. No grants to individuals.
Application information: Application form not required.
    Initial approach: Letter
    Deadline(s): None
Officers and Directors:* Howard S. Richmond, Pres.; Lawrence Richmond,* V.P.; Phillip Richmond,* V.P.; Robert Richmond,* V.P.; Elizabeth Richmond-Schulman,* V.P.; Bernard D. Gartlir, Secy.; Frank Richmond,* Treas.
EIN: 136180873

6802

The Ridgefield Foundation ✧

c/o American Express Tax & Business Svc. of New York
1185 6th Ave.
New York, NY 10036-2602

Incorporated in 1956 in NY.
Donors: Henry J. Leir‡; Erna D. Leir‡; Continental Ore Corp.; International Ore and Fertilizer Corp.
Foundation type: Independent foundation.
Financial data (yr. ended 12/31/03): Assets, $43,188,434 (M); expenditures, $3,051,955; qualifying distributions, $2,540,381; giving activities include $2,212,750 for 113 grants (high: $300,000; low: $250; average: $5,000–$50,000).
Purpose and activities: Support for education in the U.S. and Israel, Jewish welfare funds, social service agencies, and cultural programs; most support is for past donees or for organizations recommended by board members.
Fields of interest: Arts; Education; Human services; Jewish federated giving programs; Jewish agencies & temples.
International interests: Israel.
Limitations: Applications not accepted. Giving primarily in NY for local services; giving in the U.S. and Israel for education. No grants to individuals, or for scholarships, fellowships, or matching gifts; no loans.
Application information: Contributes only to pre-selected organizations.
    Board meeting date(s): Oct.
Officers and Directors:* Arthur S. Hoffman, Pres. and Treas.; Margot Gibis,* V.P.; Fred M. Lowenfels, Secy.; Mary-Ann Fribourg.
Number of staff: 1 part-time professional.
EIN: 136093563
Selected grants: The following grants were reported in 2004.
$300,000 to Montclair Art Museum, Montclair, NJ.
$100,000 to American Friends of the Hebrew University, New York, NY.
$52,500 to Stanley M. Isaacs Neighborhood Center, New York, NY. 2 grants: $2,500, $50,000
$50,000 to American Friends of the Alliance Israelite Universelle, New York, NY.
$50,000 to Rogosin Institute, New York, NY.
$30,000 to Beth Israel Medical Center, New York, NY.
$10,000 to America-Israel Cultural Foundation, New York, NY.
$5,000 to Lincoln Center Consolidated Corporate Fund, New York, NY.
$5,000 to University of Denver, Denver, CO.

6803

The A. & M. Rieder Family Foundation ✧ ☆

1673 51st St.
Brooklyn, NY 11204 (732) 821-1500
Contact: Leslie Rieder, Tr.

Established in 1999 in NY.
Donor: Leslie Rieder.
Foundation type: Operating foundation.
Financial data (yr. ended 12/31/05): Assets, $0 (M); gifts received, $490,000; expenditures, $458,182; qualifying distributions, $458,182; giving activities include $456,379 for 645 grants (high: $150,000; low: $18).
Purpose and activities: Giving primarily to Jewish organizations.
Fields of interest: Education; Jewish agencies & temples.
Application information:
    Initial approach: Letter
    Deadline(s): None

Trustees: Leslie Rieder; Miriam Rieder.
EIN: 113471866
Selected grants: The following grants were reported in 2003.
$10,000 to Sinai Academy, Brooklyn, NY.
$5,000 to Beth Medrash Govoha, Brooklyn, NY.
$5,000 to Lev Aryeh, Baltimore, MD.
$4,000 to Nechomas Yisroel, Brooklyn, NY.
$3,000 to Congregation of New Square, Spring Valley, NY.
$3,000 to Lev LAchim, Brooklyn, NY.
$3,000 to Rofeh Cholim Cancer Society, Brooklyn, NY.
$1,500 to Congregation Divrei Yecheskel of Shinive, Monsey, NY.
$1,000 to Child Life Society, Brooklyn, NY.
$1,000 to Shekel Hakodesh, Brooklyn, NY.

6804
The Riedman Foundation ✧
45 East Ave.
Rochester, NY 14604 (585) 232-4424
Contact: John R. Riedman, Mgr.

Established in 1980 in NY.
Donors: John R. Riedman; Susan Holliday; Riedman Corp.
Foundation type: Independent foundation.
Financial data (yr. ended 12/31/04): Assets, $12,453,940 (M); gifts received, $141,620; expenditures, $531,497; qualifying distributions, $519,300; giving activities include $503,996 for 29 grants (high: $200,000; low: $100).
Fields of interest: Museums; Arts; Education; Hospitals (general); Health organizations, association; Human services; Community development.
Type of support: General/operating support.
Limitations: Giving primarily in NY, with emphasis on Rochester.
Application information: Application form not required.
Deadline(s): None
Manager: John R. Riedman.
EIN: 222279168

6805
The Rieger Charitable Foundation Trust ✧
c/o Noam Mgmt.
1646 49th St.
Brooklyn, NY 11204 (718) 436-2326
Contact: Abraham Rieger, Dir.

Established in 1998 in NY.
Donors: Abraham Jacob Rieger; A & E Trust; Triangle Trust.
Foundation type: Independent foundation.
Financial data (yr. ended 12/31/04): Assets, $5,404,216 (M); gifts received, $1,260,000; expenditures, $320,446; qualifying distributions, $318,183; giving activities include $319,400 for 24 grants (high: $150,000; low: $500).
Fields of interest: Jewish agencies & temples.
Limitations: Giving primarily in Brooklyn, NY.
Application information: Application form not required.
Deadline(s): None
Directors: Abraham Rieger; Rachel Rieger.
EIN: 116508164
Selected grants: The following grants were reported in 2003.

$73,000 to Mosdos Skolya, Brooklyn, NY.
$50,000 to Bobover Yeshiva Bnei Zion, Brooklyn, NY.
$50,000 to Ichus Mosdei Bobov.
$25,000 to Mesivta Eitz Chaim, Brooklyn, NY.
$25,000 to Rabbinical College Academy, Brooklyn, NY.
$23,200 to Congregation Shaare Zion, Brooklyn, NY.
$18,000 to Bnos Zion of Bobov, Brooklyn, NY.
$5,000 to Congregation Khal Yereim, Woodridge, NY.
$2,000 to Kedushat Zion, Brooklyn, NY.
$1,000 to Kollel Medrash Shmuel, Brooklyn, NY.

6806
The Robert S. Rifkind Charitable Foundation ✧
c/o Cravath, Swaine & Moore
825 8th Ave.
New York, NY 10019

Established in 1986 in NY.
Donors: Robert S. Rifkind; Arleen Rifkind.
Foundation type: Independent foundation.
Financial data (yr. ended 12/31/05): Assets, $1,749,926 (M); gifts received, $87,808; expenditures, $406,870; qualifying distributions, $393,000; giving activities include $393,000 for 11 grants (high: $200,000; low: $5,000).
Purpose and activities: Giving primarily for higher education and to Jewish organizations, including Jewish education.
Fields of interest: Higher education; Theological school/education; Jewish agencies & temples.
Limitations: Applications not accepted. Giving primarily in MA and NY. No grants to individuals.
Application information: Contributes only to pre-selected organizations.
Trustee: Robert S. Rifkind.
EIN: 133374924
Selected grants: The following grants were reported in 2005.
$45,000 to Brandeis University, Waltham, MA. 2 grants: $20,000, $25,000
$31,000 to American Jewish Committee, New York, NY.
$15,000 to Yale Alumni Fund, New Haven, CT.
$5,000 to Center for Jewish History, New York, NY.
$5,000 to New York Public Library, New York, NY.

6807
The Riggio Foundation ▼ ✧
c/o Bryan Cave Robinson Silverman
1290 Ave. of the Americas
New York, NY 10104-3300

Established in 1994 in NY.
Donor: Leonard Riggio.
Foundation type: Independent foundation.
Financial data (yr. ended 8/31/05): Assets, $78,541,708 (M); expenditures, $1,730,065; qualifying distributions, $1,355,950; giving activities include $1,355,950 for 146 grants (high: $275,000; low: $100; average: $1,000–$50,000).
Purpose and activities: Giving primarily for the arts; funding also for human services, higher education, hospitals and health associations, and children's services.
Fields of interest: Arts, multipurpose centers/programs; Museums; Museums (art); Performing

arts; Arts; Higher education; Hospitals (general); Health organizations, association; Disasters, 9/11/01; Human services; Children, services.
Type of support: General/operating support; Capital campaigns.
Limitations: Applications not accepted. Giving primarily in NY, with emphasis on the greater metropolitan New York City area; some funding on a national basis also. No grants to individuals.
Application information: Contributes only to pre-selected organizations.
Trustees: Leonard Riggio; Louise Riggio.
EIN: 137039631
Selected grants: The following grants were reported in 2004.
$3,150,000 to Dia Art Foundation, New York, NY.
$500,000 to Childrens Defense Fund, DC.
$85,000 to Orpheon, The Little Orchestra Society, New York, NY. 2 grants: $75,000, $10,000
$50,000 to Hemophilia Association of New York, New York, NY.
$25,000 to Columbus Citizens Foundation, New York, NY.
$25,000 to Materials for the Arts, Long Island City, NY.
$25,000 to Preservation League of New York State, Albany, NY.
$20,000 to Metropolitan Opera, New York, NY. 2 grants: $10,000 each

6808
The Riklis Family Foundation, Inc. ✧
c/o Starr & Co., LLC
850 3rd Ave.
New York, NY 10022 (212) 861-1595
Application address: c/o Simona R. Ackerman, Pres., 1020 5th Ave., New York, NY 10028

Incorporated in 1960 in NY.
Foundation type: Independent foundation.
Financial data (yr. ended 6/30/05): Assets, $1,084,250 (M); expenditures, $392,820; qualifying distributions, $388,489; giving activities include $387,085 for 23 grants (high: $100,000; low: $500).
Purpose and activities: Giving primarily for Jewish agencies and temples; funding also for education, health care, and the arts.
Fields of interest: Arts; Education; Health care; Cancer; Jewish agencies & temples.
Limitations: Giving on a national basis, with emphasis on New York, NY. No grants to individuals.
Application information: Application form not required.
Initial approach: Letter
Deadline(s): None
Officers: Simona R. Ackerman, Pres.; Meeshulam Riklis, V.P.
EIN: 136163061
Selected grants: The following grants were reported in 2005.
$30,000 to Metropolitan Opera, New York, NY.
$25,000 to Congregation Kehilath Jeshurun, New York, NY.
$10,000 to New Yorkers for Children, New York, NY.
$10,000 to Partnership for Public Service, DC.
$8,000 to American Friends of Keshet Eilon, New York, NY.
$6,940 to Israel Heart Fund, New York, NY.
$5,000 to Hampton Synagogue, Hampton, NY.
$3,000 to Public Theater, New York, NY.
$1,000 to Concord Coalition, Arlington, VA.

6809

Riley Family Foundation ✧
c/o Behan, Ling & Ruta
475 Park Ave. S., 31st Fl.
New York, NY 10016

Established in 1991 in NY.
Donor: James P. Riley, Jr.
Foundation type: Independent foundation.
Financial data (yr. ended 2/28/05): Assets, $14,159,488 (M); expenditures, $445,864; qualifying distributions, $379,450; giving activities include $378,700 for 38 grants (high: $150,000; low: $100).
Purpose and activities: Giving primarily to Roman Catholic organizations, schools, and churches, as well as for higher education, and children, families, and social services.
Fields of interest: Secondary school/education; Higher education; Nursing school/education; Hospitals (general); Hospitals (specialty); Health care; Health organizations, association; Human services; Children/youth, services; Family services; Foundations (private grantmaking); Roman Catholic agencies & churches.
Type of support: General/operating support.
Limitations: Applications not accepted. Giving primarily in New York, NY. No grants to individuals; no loans.
Application information: Contributes only to pre-selected organizations.
Officers: James P. Riley, Jr., Pres.; Brigid A. Riley, V.P.; Shannon C. Riley, V.P.; Ellen C. Riley, Secy.-Treas.
Director: Kerrylyn Riley.
EIN: 133638509
Selected grants: The following grants were reported in 2005.
$150,000 to Saint Johns University, Jamaica, NY.
$51,000 to Robin Hood Foundation, New York, NY.
$30,000 to Childrens Aid Society, New York, NY.
$30,000 to Family and Childrens Association, Mineola, NY.
$23,500 to Winthrop-University Hospital, Mineola, NY.
$20,000 to New York Foundling Hospital, New York, NY.
$11,000 to Little Sisters of the Assumption Family Health Services, Dorchester, MA.
$10,500 to Villanova University, Villanova, PA.
$5,000 to NYU Downtown Hospital, New York, NY.
$3,500 to Swim Across America, Boston, MA.

6810

The Riordan Fund ✧
767 5th Ave., Ste. 4701
New York, NY 10153-4798

Established in 2001 in NY.
Donor: William J. Ruane.
Foundation type: Independent foundation.
Financial data (yr. ended 12/31/05): Assets, $1,341,176 (M); expenditures, $1,008,239; qualifying distributions, $1,001,250; giving activities include $1,001,250 for grants.
Fields of interest: Performing arts, orchestra (symphony); Arts; Education; Cancer research.
Limitations: Applications not accepted. Giving primarily in NY. No grants to individuals.
Application information: Contributes only to pre-selected organizations.
Trustee: Joy M. Ruane; William J. Ruane.
EIN: 137298631

Selected grants: The following grants were reported in 2003.
$100,000 to Mannes College of Music, New York, NY.
$25,000 to United Hospital Fund of New York, New York, NY.
$1,000 to American Cancer Society, Atlanta, GA.
$1,000 to Catholic Big Sisters of the Archdiocese of New York, New York, NY.
$1,000 to Friends of Winterthur, Winterthur, DE.
$1,000 to Gateway School of New York, New York, NY.
$1,000 to Lenox Hill Hospital, New York, NY.
$1,000 to Philharmonic-Symphony Society of New York, New York Philharmonic, New York, NY.
$1,000 to Republican Majority for Choice, DC.
$1,000 to Saint Vincent Catholic Medical Centers of New York, New York, NY.

6811

The Ripple Foundation ✧ ☆
c/o Wien & Malkin, LLP
60 E. 42nd St.
New York, NY 10165
Contact: Richard Shapiro

Established in 1999 in DE.
Donors: Anthony E. Malkin; Rachelle B. Malkin.
Foundation type: Independent foundation.
Financial data (yr. ended 12/31/04): Assets, $5,238,570 (L); gifts received, $3,662,054; expenditures, $392,800; qualifying distributions, $390,950; giving activities include $390,950 for 32 grants (high: $100,000; low: $150).
Fields of interest: Arts; Elementary/secondary education; Higher education; Education; Environment, natural resources; Children/youth, services; Federated giving programs.
Application information:
Initial approach: Letter
Deadline(s): None
Officer: Anthony E. Malkin, Pres.
Director: Rachelle B. Malkin.
EIN: 134081347
Selected grants: The following grants were reported in 2003.
$82,000 to Greenwich Country Day School, Greenwich, CT.
$25,000 to Greenwich Reform Synagogue, Greenwich, CT.
$20,000 to Choate Rosemary Hall, Wallingford, CT.
$16,200 to Natural Resources Defense Council, New York, NY.
$15,000 to Yeshiva University, New York, NY.
$7,500 to Boys Club of New York, New York, NY.
$7,000 to Metropolitan Museum of Art, New York, NY.
$5,000 to Fresh Air Fund, New York, NY.
$3,000 to New York Landmarks Preservation Foundation, New York, NY.
$2,500 to United Way of Greenwich, Greenwich, CT.

6812

Ripplewood Foundation, Inc. ✧ ☆
1 Rockefeller Plz., 32nd Fl.
New York, NY 10020

Established in 1997 in DE and NY.
Donors: Ripplewood Holdings LLC; Timothy C. Collins.
Foundation type: Company-sponsored foundation.

Financial data (yr. ended 12/31/05): Assets, $5,331,470 (M); gifts received, $24,414; expenditures, $5,326,555; qualifying distributions, $5,233,000; giving activities include $5,233,000 for 36 grants (high: $1,000,000; low: $1,000).
Purpose and activities: The foundation supports organizations involved with arts and culture, education, animal welfare, human services, and civic affairs.
Fields of interest: Arts; Higher education; Business school/education; Theological school/education; Education; Animals/wildlife, preservation/protection; Animals/wildlife, fisheries; Children, services; Human services; Public policy, research; Public affairs, finance; Public affairs.
Type of support: Scholarship funds; Program development; General/operating support.
Limitations: Applications not accepted. Giving on a national basis, with some emphasis on NY. No grants to individuals.
Application information: Contributes only to pre-selected organizations.
Officer: Timothy C. Collins, Pres.
EIN: 522036080
Selected grants: The following grants were reported in 2004.
$50,000 to Syracuse University, Syracuse, NY.
$25,000 to Global Business Coalition on HIV/AIDS, New York, NY.
$15,000 to La Leche League International, Schaumburg, IL.
$12,500 to Columbia University, New York, NY.
$10,000 to American Society for the Prevention of Cruelty to Animals, New York, NY.
$10,000 to Asia Society, New York, NY.
$10,000 to Boy Scouts of America, New York, NY.
$10,000 to Music Center of Los Angeles County, Los Angeles, CA.
$10,000 to Phoenix House, New York, NY.
$10,000 to Student Sponsor Partners, New York, NY.

6813

May Ellen and Gerald Ritter Foundation ✧
9411 Shore Rd.
Brooklyn, NY 11209-6755
Contact: Emma Daniels, Pres.

Established in 1980 in NY.
Donors: Gerald Ritter†; May Ellen Ritter†.
Foundation type: Independent foundation.
Financial data (yr. ended 12/31/03): Assets, $12,743,384 (M); expenditures, $903,477; qualifying distributions, $752,406; giving activities include $679,565 for 27 grants (high: $210,000; low: $1,000).
Purpose and activities: Giving primarily for Roman Catholic causes, including a cultural center and welfare funds.
Fields of interest: Arts; Education; Health care; Human services; Roman Catholic federated giving programs; Roman Catholic agencies & churches; Economically disadvantaged.
Limitations: Giving primarily in NY. No grants to individuals.
Application information: Application form not required.
Initial approach: Letter
Deadline(s): None
Board meeting date(s): Quarterly
Officers: Emma Daniels, Pres.; Vincent Rohan, V.P.; Helen Rohan, Secy.; Sophie Stanovich, Treas.
EIN: 136114269

6814
The Ritter Foundation, Inc. ✧
1450 Flagler Dr.
Mamaroneck, NY 10543
Contact: David Ritter, V.P. and Secy.

Incorporated in 1947 in NY.
Donors: Gladys Ritter Livingston†; Irene Ritter†; Lena Ritter†; Louis Ritter†; Sidney Ritter†.
Foundation type: Independent foundation.
Financial data (yr. ended 11/30/05): Assets, $30,123,083 (M); expenditures, $1,687,736; qualifying distributions, $1,534,923; giving activities include $1,503,740 for 197 grants (high: $123,000; low: $100).
Purpose and activities: Grants for higher education, including medical education; giving also to Israel, mental health, and local Jewish welfare funds.
Fields of interest: Higher education; Medical school/education; Mental health/crisis services; Human services; Jewish federated giving programs.
International interests: Israel.
Type of support: General/operating support; Capital campaigns; Building/renovation; Endowments; Emergency funds; Scholarship funds; Research.
Limitations: Applications not accepted. Giving on a national basis. No grants to individuals.
Publications: Annual report.
Application information: Contributes only to pre-selected organizations.
Board meeting date(s): May and Nov.
Officers and Trustees:* Toby G. Ritter,* V.P. and Secy.; David Ritter,* V.P.; Alan I. Ritter,* Treas.
Number of staff: 1 part-time support.
EIN: 136082276
Selected grants: The following grants were reported in 2004.
$105,000 to Vanderbilt University Medical Center, Nashville, TN.
$75,000 to National Alliance for Research on Schizophrenia and Depression (NARSAD), Great Neck, NY.
$62,500 to Alliance for Cancer Gene Therapy, Stamford, CT.
$50,500 to Central Park Conservancy, New York, NY.
$49,000 to Center for Childrens Advocacy, Hartford, CT.
$35,000 to Connecticut Civil Liberties Union Foundation, Hartford, CT.
$24,675 to I Have A Dream Foundation, New York, NY.
$12,500 to Wadsworth Atheneum, Hartford, CT.
$1,000 to Beth Israel Hospital.
$1,000 to Miracle House, Ventura, CA.

6815
The Riversville Foundation ✧
600 5th Ave., 26th Fl.
New York, NY 10020 (212) 332-5182
Contact: Barton M. Biggs, Tr.

Established in 2000 in NY.
Donors: Barton M. Biggs; Richard Fisher.
Foundation type: Independent foundation.
Financial data (yr. ended 12/31/05): Assets, $15,522,770 (M); gifts received, $3,844,332; expenditures, $757,643; qualifying distributions, $597,900; giving activities include $597,900 for 19 grants (high: $124,000; low: $500).
Fields of interest: Arts; Higher education; Education; Medical care, in-patient care; Human services.

Limitations: Giving in the U.S., with emphasis on NY.
Application information:
Initial approach: Letter
Deadline(s): None
Trustees: Barton M. Biggs; Ann D. Thivierge; Arthur Thivierge.
EIN: 066504128
Selected grants: The following grants were reported in 2003.
$1,000,000 to Bard College, Annandale on Hudson, NY.
$50,000 to Elihu Club, Purchase, NY.
$20,000 to Highbridge Voices, Bronx, NY.
$20,000 to Nightingale-Bamford School, New York, NY. For minority scholarship.
$10,000 to Boys Club of Greenwich, Greenwich, CT.
$3,000 to Lighthouse International, New York, NY.
$1,000 to New York City Opera, New York, NY.

6816
The RJM Foundation ✧
c/o Brown Brothers Harriman Trust. Co., LLC
140 Broadway, 4th Fl.
New York, NY 10005-1108

Donor: R. James MacAleer.
Foundation type: Independent foundation.
Financial data (yr. ended 7/31/05): Assets, $14,153,243 (M); expenditures, $747,408; qualifying distributions, $679,932; giving activities include $670,000 for 3 grants (high: $400,000; low: $60,000).
Fields of interest: Higher education.
Limitations: Applications not accepted. Giving primarily in Princeton, NJ. No grants to individuals.
Application information: Contributes only to pre-selected organizations.
Trustee: R. James MacAleer.
EIN: 236953316

6817
Jerome Robbins Foundation ✧
18 W. 21st St., 6th Fl.
New York, NY 10010
Contact: Christopher Pennington, Admin. Dir.
FAX: (212) 367-8966;
E-mail: pennington@jeromerobbins.org;
URL: http://www.jeromerobbins.org

Established about 1970 in NY.
Donor: Jerome Robbins†.
Foundation type: Independent foundation.
Financial data (yr. ended 9/30/05): Assets, $18,911,163 (M); expenditures, $2,125,299; qualifying distributions, $1,575,179; giving activities include $1,381,163 for 66 grants (high: $500,000; low: $1,000), and $33,687 for foundation-administered programs.
Purpose and activities: Financial support for dance, theater and organizations dedicated to serving those with HIV and AIDS.
Fields of interest: Performing arts, dance; Performing arts, theater; AIDS.
Limitations: Giving primarily in New York, NY.
Publications: Application guidelines; Grants list.
Application information: Application information and application guidelines available on foundation Web site. Videotape required for performance-related applications. AIDS-related grants only to organizations addressing the basic

adult necessities of life including medication and direct care, shelter, food and employment training. Additionally, issues of HIV or AIDS must be the primary focus of an organization and at least two-thirds of the organization's client base must be effected by such issues. Application form not required.
Initial approach: Proposal not exceeding 3 pages (excluding financials)
Copies of proposal: 4
Deadline(s): None
Board meeting date(s): Quarterly
Final notification: 4 to 6 months
Trustees: Allen Greenberg; Floria V. Lasky; Daniel Stern.
Number of staff: 1 full-time professional.
EIN: 136021425
Selected grants: The following grants were reported in 2005.
$100,000 to Brooklyn Academy of Music, Brooklyn, NY.

6818
Robertson Foundation ▼ ✧
c/o Dorian A. Vergos & Co., LLC
592 5th Ave., 2nd Fl.
New York, NY 10036-2602 (212) 307-7180

Established in 1996 in NY.
Donor: Julian H. Robertson, Jr.
Foundation type: Independent foundation.
Financial data (yr. ended 11/30/04): Assets, $546,995,309 (M); gifts received, $19,900,300; expenditures, $27,872,133; qualifying distributions, $27,360,805; giving activities include $26,708,917 for 88 grants (high: $8,500,000; low: $1,000; average: $1,000–$200,000).
Purpose and activities: Support for education, general and rehabilitative medicine, medical research and philanthropy and voluntarism.
Fields of interest: Arts; Education; Hospitals (general); Youth development, centers/clubs; Protestant agencies & churches.
Limitations: Applications not accepted. No grants to individuals.
Application information: Contributes only to pre-selected organizations.
Trustees: William R. Goodell; Josephine T. Robertson; Julian H. Robertson, Jr.
EIN: 137068398
Selected grants: The following grants were reported in 2004.
$8,500,000 to Wildlife Conservation Society, Bronx, NY.
$1,500,000 to Harlem Childrens Zone, New York, NY.
$1,500,000 to University of North Carolina at Chapel Hill Foundation, Chapel Hill, NC.
$1,107,917 to National Parks Conservation Association, DC.
$1,000,000 to Communities in Schools, Alexandria, VA.
$1,000,000 to New-York Historical Society, New York, NY.
$750,000 to Saint Bartholomews Episcopal Church, New York, NY.
$500,000 to Environmental Defense, New York, NY.
$100,000 to Duke University, Durham, NC.
$55,000 to Saint Johns of Lattingtown, Locust Valley, NY.

6819
The Jim and Linda Robinson Foundation, Inc. ✧ ☆
c/o Daniel J. Curran, The Ayco Co., LLP
P.O. Box 860
Saratoga Springs, NY 12866-0860

Established in NY.
Donors: Linda Gosden Robinson; James D. Robinson III.
Foundation type: Independent foundation.
Financial data (yr. ended 12/31/05): Assets, $787,077 (M); gifts received, $78,042; expenditures, $602,197; qualifying distributions, $587,000; giving activities include $581,750 for 46 grants (high: $250,000; low: $250).
Purpose and activities: Giving for art and cultural institutes, education, law enforcement, and for human services.
Fields of interest: Arts; Higher education; Medical school/education; Education; Hospitals (specialty); Crime/law enforcement; Human services; American Red Cross; Children/youth, services; Military/veterans' organizations.
Limitations: Applications not accepted. Giving on a national basis. No grants to individuals.
Application information: Contributes only to pre-selected organizations.
Officers: James D. Robinson III, Pres.; Linda G. Robinson, V.P. and Treas.; Karen Marshon, Secy.
EIN: 133981478
Selected grants: The following grants were reported in 2004.
$11,000 to Memorial Sloan-Kettering Cancer Center, New York, NY.
$10,000 to Brookings Institution, DC.
$10,000 to Carnegie Hall Society, New York, NY.
$10,000 to Federal Law Enforcement Foundation, New York, NY.
$10,000 to Harvard Business School Fund, Boston, MA.
$10,000 to Sarah Lawrence College, Bronxville, NY.
$10,000 to Woodberry Forest School, Woodberry Forest, VA.
$5,000 to Council on Foreign Relations, New York, NY.
$5,000 to Marlborough School, Los Angeles, CA.
$1,560 to Museum of Television and Radio, Beverly Hills, CA.

6820
Robinson-Broadhurst Foundation, Inc.
c/o Charles K. McKenzie
101 Main St.
P.O. Box 160
Stamford, NY 12167
FAX: (607) 652-2453; E-mail: rbfi@stny.rr.com

Established in 1984 in NY.
Donors: Anna Broadhurst†; R. Avery Robinson†; Winnie M. Robinson†.
Foundation type: Independent foundation.
Financial data (yr. ended 4/30/06): Assets, $48,160,800 (M); expenditures, $3,017,909; qualifying distributions, $2,719,789; giving activities include $2,548,025 for 97 grants (high: $300,000; low: $467).
Purpose and activities: Support for local community services.
Fields of interest: Arts; Health care; Community development; Government/public administration.
Type of support: Building/renovation; Equipment; Scholarship funds; Matching/challenge support.

Limitations: Applications not accepted. Giving limited to Winchendon, MA; and Stamford and Worcester, NY. No grants to individuals, or for annual operating expenditures or debt reduction.
Application information: Unsolicited requests for funds not accepted.
Board meeting date(s): May
Officers and Trustees:* Charles K. McKenzie,* Pres. and Exec. Dir.; Martin A. Parks,* V.P.; Ralph Beisler,* Secy.; Ernest P. Fletcher, Jr.,* Treas.; William H. Lister.
Number of staff: 1 full-time professional; 1 full-time support.
EIN: 222558699
Selected grants: The following grants were reported in 2004.
$342,860 to Winchendon, Town of, Winchendon, MA. 3 grants: $174,000 (For educational program support), $80,000 (For highway repairs), $88,860 (For facility improvements, HVAC system).
$305,471 to Wendell P. Clark Memorial Association, Winchendon, MA. 2 grants: $155,471 (For capital improvement), $150,000 (For program support).
$125,000 to Stamford, Village of, Stamford, NY. 2 grants: $50,000 (For Fire Department equipment acquisition), $75,000 (For road equipment).
$35,985 to Stamford Central School, Stamford, NY. For Camp H.E.R.E. summer program.
$35,000 to Girl Scouts of the U.S.A., Indian Hills Council, Binghamton, NY. For facility improvement.
$35,000 to Winchendon Historical Society, Winchendon, MA. For facility improvement.

6821
Robison Family Foundation ✧
(formerly The Ellis H. and Doris B. Robison Foundation)
51 Collins Ave.
Troy, NY 12180

Established in 1980 in NY.
Donor: Ellis Robison†.
Foundation type: Independent foundation.
Financial data (yr. ended 12/31/05): Assets, $9,573,593 (M); expenditures, $600,105; qualifying distributions, $584,634; giving activities include $583,000 for 70 grants (high: $110,000; low: $250).
Purpose and activities: Grants for educational, religious, social services, and medical purposes initiated solely by the president.
Fields of interest: Arts; Education; Hospitals (general); Health care; Health organizations, association; Human services; Christian agencies & churches; Protestant agencies & churches.
Type of support: General/operating support; Continuing support; Building/renovation.
Limitations: Applications not accepted. Giving primarily in the Troy and Albany, NY, area, and in Cincinnati, OH. No grants to individuals, or for endowment funds, scholarships, fellowships, or matching gifts; no loans.
Application information: Contributes only to pre-selected organizations.
Officers: James A. Robison, Pres.; Richard G. Robison, V.P.; Elissa R. Prout, Secy.-Treas.
Director: Barbara R. Sporck.
EIN: 222470695
Selected grants: The following grants were reported in 2004.

$120,000 to Albany Academy, Albany, NY.
$117,000 to Emma Willard School, Troy, NY.
$30,000 to American Music Scholarship Association, Cincinnati, OH.
$15,000 to YMCA of Troy, Troy, NY.
$13,000 to Church of the Redeemer, Cincinnati, OH.
$10,000 to Cincinnati Childrens Hospital Medical Center, Cincinnati, OH.
$10,000 to Saint Johns Episcopal Church.
$5,000 to Albany College of Pharmacy, Albany, NY.
$5,000 to Troy Savings Bank Music Hall Corporation, Troy, NY.
$5,000 to Unity House, Troy, NY.

6822
Roche Foundation, Inc. ✧
c/o Robert G. Wilmers
350 Park Ave., 6th Fl.
New York, NY 10022 (212) 350-2497

Established in 1997 in NY.
Donor: Robert G. Wilmers.
Foundation type: Independent foundation.
Financial data (yr. ended 11/30/04): Assets, $10,200,311 (M); expenditures, $422,907; qualifying distributions, $420,011; giving activities include $420,011 for 5 grants (high: $313,511; low: $500).
Fields of interest: Historic preservation/historical societies; Arts; Higher education.
Limitations: Applications not accepted. Giving primarily in Buffalo, NY; funding also in Lenox, MA. No grants to individuals.
Application information: Contributes only to pre-selected organizations.
Officers: Robert G. Wilmers, Pres.; Elisabeth Roche Wilmers, Treas.
EIN: 161543635
Selected grants: The following grants were reported in 2003.
$133,654 to Williams College, Williamstown, MA. 2 grants: $72,000, $61,654 (For grant made in form of stock).
$100,000 to Discalced Carmelite Friars, Hartford, WI.
$50,000 to Berkshire Theater Festival, Stockbridge, MA.
$30,000 to Council on Foreign Relations, New York, NY. 2 grants: $25,000, $5,000 to Center on Preventive Action.
$17,000 to French Institute Alliance Francaise, New York, NY.
$5,000 to Hospice Foundation of Western New York, Cheektowaga, NY.
$5,000 to Oxfam America, Boston, MA.
$1,000 to Benedict House of Western New York, Buffalo, NY.

6823
Rochester Area Community Foundation ▼
(formerly Rochester Area Foundation)
500 East Ave.
Rochester, NY 14607-1912 (585) 271-4100
Contact: Edward Doherty, V.P., Community Progs.; For grants: Mairead Hartmann, Prog. Admin.
FAX: (585) 271-4292; E-mail: edoherty@racf.org; Grant application E-mail: mhartmann@racf.org; URL: http://www.racf.org

Incorporated in 1972 in NY.

Foundation type: Community foundation.
Financial data (yr. ended 3/31/06): Assets, $203,121,585 (M); gifts received, $28,151,502; expenditures, $18,256,110; giving activities include $21,433,391 for 6,272 grants.
Purpose and activities: Giving for broad purposes related to community betterment, including education, the environment, arts and cultural programs, historic preservation, health services, especially for youth, community development and responsibility, and social services, including family and legal services, minorities, women, and youth. Scholarship recipients are chosen by institutions. Primary interests include early childhood education, community development, including leadership programs for young people, and strengthening families and children through expansion of housing counseling and resource management counseling to low-income families. The foundation also provides management guidance to area nonprofit organizations for capacity building.
Fields of interest: Historic preservation/historical societies; Arts; Education, early childhood education; Child development, education; Adult education—literacy, basic skills & GED; Education, services; Education; Environment, natural resources; Environment; Health care; Legal services; Housing/shelter, development; Recreation; Youth development, services; Children/youth, services; Child development, services; Family services; Women, centers/services; Minorities/immigrants, centers/services; Human services; Community development; Voluntarism promotion; Leadership development; Children; Aging; Minorities; Women.
Type of support: General/operating support; Management development/capacity building; Building/renovation; Equipment; Program development; Conferences/seminars; Publication; Seed money; Scholarship funds; Technical assistance; Consulting services; Program evaluation; Program-related investments/loans.
Limitations: Giving limited to Genesee, Livingston, Monroe, Ontario, Orleans, and Wayne counties, NY, except for donor-designated funds. No support for religious projects. No grants to individuals (except from restricted funds), or for capital or annual campaigns, debt reduction, special events, land acquisition, or endowment or emergency funds.
Publications: Annual report (including application guidelines); Financial statement; Grants list; Informational brochure; Newsletter; Program policy statement.
Application information: Visit foundation Web site for application forms and specific guidelines per grant type. Scholarship recipients chosen by institutions. Application form required.
   Initial approach: Submit application form and attachments
   Copies of proposal: 1
   Deadline(s): Varies
   Board meeting date(s): Jan., Feb., Mar., May, June, July, Oct., and Nov.
   Final notification: Ongoing
Officers and Board Members:* Margaret A. Sanchez,* Chair.; Linda W. Davey,* Vice-Chair.; Mimi Hwang,* Vice-Chair.; Michael B. Millard,* Vice-Chair.; Sarah H. Trafton,* Vice-Chair.; Philip H. E. Yawman,* Vice-Chair.; Jennifer Leonard, Pres. and Exec. Dir.; Jeffrie B. Leahy, V.P. and C.O.O.; Edward Doherty, V.P., Community Progs.; Jeffrey Hough, V.P., Devel. and Comms.; Bonita Wallace, V.P., Donor Svcs.; Michael F. Buckley,* Secy.; Edward Adams, Treas.; Ted A. Boucher,*

Chair.-Elect; Hanif Abdul-Wahid; Edward D. Bloom; Philip L. Burke; Jill M. Cicero; Ellen H. Croog; Barbara Williams de Leeuw; Malik Evans; Joan L. Feinbloom; Carlos A. Garcia; Suzanne Gouvernet; Margaret "Peggy" Hubbard; Barbara J. Jones; Hoffman Moka Lantum, M.D.; Laura Loomis; Richard J. Mengel; Michael P. Morley; Kamesh Nagarajan; Nannette Nocon; Alan H. Resnick; Terry M. Richman; Gregory W. Smith; Judy von Bucher; Heidi N. Zimmer-Meyer.
Number of staff: 10 full-time professional; 1 part-time professional; 6 full-time support; 1 part-time support.
EIN: 237250641
Selected grants: The following grants were reported in 2005.
$61,000 to Rural Housing Opportunities Corporation, Rochester, NY. For grant made through Muriel H. Marshall Fund for the Aging in Genesee County.
$50,000 to Common Good Planning Center, Rochester, NY.
$50,000 to Odyssey of Humanity, Rochester, NY. To implement next phase of Biracial Partnership Program, which aims to build trust and tolerance among people of different races and ethnicities.
$40,000 to Rochester Museum and Science Center, Rochester, NY. For Science Linkages in Community's Science Co-Explorers Program, which offers workshops, in-home demonstrations, and reference material on science education projects appropriate for in-home child care providers.
$36,624 to Rochester Childfirst Network, Rochester, NY. For professional development workshops for Family Child Care Satellite Network at Toy Resource Center.
$33,000 to Orleans Community Action Committee, Albion, NY. For Quality of Care Initiative, which will provide training and accreditation to increase professionalism of family child care providers in Orleans County.
$20,000 to Candy Apple Preschool Center, Newark, NY. To hire health coordinator to assist with telemedicine project and coordinate health and early intervention resources at child care center.
$20,000 to Center for Youth Services, Rochester, NY.
$20,000 to Interfaith Action, Rochester, NY. To engage broad range of residents, community institutions and City agencies in redeveloping neighborhoods on west side.
$20,000 to LeRoy Christian Community Project, LeRoy, NY. To enhance quality of after-school programs.

6824
Rock River Foundation, Inc. ✧
230 W. 41st St., Ste. 1500
New York, NY 10036
Contact: Stuart J. Hammer, Treas.
FAX: (212) 382-2686;
E-mail: sjhammer@akmcpa.com

Established in 1994 in MS.
Donor: Morgan Freeman.
Foundation type: Independent foundation.
Financial data (yr. ended 12/31/05): Assets, $2,801,076 (M); gifts received, $805,000; expenditures, $486,399; qualifying distributions, $386,628; giving activities include $386,628 for 23 grants.
Fields of interest: Elementary/secondary education; Youth development.

Type of support: Continuing support; Scholarship funds.
Limitations: Applications not accepted. Giving primarily in MS. No grants to individuals.
Application information: Unsolicited requests for funds not accepted.
Officers and Trustees:* Morgan Freeman,* Pres.; Otey Sherman,* V.P.; Myrna Colley-Lee,* Secy.; Stuart J. Hammer,* Treas.
EIN: 640838346
Selected grants: The following grants were reported in 2005.
$26,000 to Delta State University Foundation, Cleveland, MS.
$12,500 to Delta Blues Museum, Clarksdale, MS.
$10,000 to Mississippi Museum of Art, Jackson, MS.
$10,000 to Sunflower County Freedom Project, Sunflower, MS.
$8,557 to Delta State University, Cleveland, MS.
$7,500 to Z Space Studio, San Francisco, CA.
$7,000 to Piney Woods School, Piney Woods, MS.

6825
Rockefeller Brothers Fund, Inc. ▼ ✧
437 Madison Ave., 37th Fl.
New York, NY 10022-7001 (212) 812-4200
Contact: Benjamin R. Shute, Jr., Secy.
FAX: (212) 812-4299; E-mail: info@rbf.org; E-mail for annual report: anreport@rbf.org; URL: http://www.rbf.org

Incorporated in 1940 in NY.
Donors: John D. Rockefeller, Jr.†; Martha Baird Rockefeller†; Abby Rockefeller Mauze†; David Rockefeller; John D. Rockefeller III†; Laurance S. Rockefeller†; Nelson A. Rockefeller†; Winthrop Rockefeller†.
Foundation type: Independent foundation.
Financial data (yr. ended 12/31/05): Assets, $815,561,407 (M); gifts received, $113,500; expenditures, $41,584,516; qualifying distributions, $33,914,557; giving activities include $22,591,496 for 392 grants (high: $500,000; low: $900; average: $5,000–$200,000), $1,147,500 for 101 grants to individuals (high: $108,000; low: $1,200; average: $2,500–$8,000), $30,844 for 155 employee matching gifts, and $4,747,536 for 4 foundation-administered programs.
Purpose and activities: The Rockefeller Brothers Fund promotes social change that contributes to a more just, sustainable, and peaceful world. Through its grantmaking, the Fund supports efforts to expand knowledge, clarify values and critical choices, nurture creative expression, and shape public policy. The Fund's programs are intended to develop leaders, strengthen institutions, engage citizens, build community, and foster partnerships that include government, business, and civil society. Respect for cultural diversity and ecological integrity pervades the Fund's activities.
Fields of interest: Arts, cultural/ethnic awareness; Arts; Environment, global warming; Environment, natural resources; Environment; Health care; International peace/security; Leadership development.
International interests: Serbia; South Africa.
Type of support: General/operating support; Continuing support; Program development; Conferences/seminars; Seed money; Fellowships; Technical assistance; Consulting services; Program evaluation; Program-related investments/loans;

Employee matching gifts; Grants to individuals; Matching/challenge support.

Limitations: Giving on a national basis, and in Central and Eastern Europe, East and Southeast Asia, and South Africa. No grants to individuals (including research, graduate study, or the writing of books or dissertations by individuals, with 3 exceptions: the RBF Fellowships under the education program, which are limited to those students nominated by the colleges that have been selected to participate in this program, the Ramon Magsaysay Awards through the Program for Asian Projects, and the Culpeper Medical Scholarships), or land acquisitions or building funds.

Publications: Annual report (including application guidelines); Grants list; Informational brochure; Occasional report; IRS Form 990-PF.

Application information: Application form not required.

  Initial approach: Letter (not exceeding 2 to 3 pages) except for Arts and Culture
  Copies of proposal: 1
  Deadline(s): From Jan. 15 to Mar. 15 for Arts and Culture; all others, none
  Board meeting date(s): Mar., June, Oct., and Dec.
  Final notification: 3 months

Officers and Trustees:* Steven C. Rockefeller,* Chair.; Neva R. Goodwin,* Vice-Chair.; Stephen B. Heintz,* Pres.; William F. McCalpin, C.O.O. and Exec. V.P.; Geraldine F. Watson, V.P., Opers. and Finance; Benjamin R. Shute, Jr., Secy. and Prog. Off., Democratic Practice Prog.; Boris A. Wessely, Treas.; Jonathan F. Fanton, Advisory Tr.; William H. Luers, Advisory Tr.; Abby M. O'Neill, Advisory Tr.; Richard D. Parsons, Advisory Tr.; David Rockefeller, Advisory Tr.; Richard Chasin; Jessica P. Einhorn; James E. Moltz; John Morning; Robert B. Oxnam; David Rockefeller, Jr.; Richard G. Rockefeller; Edmond D. Villani; Valerie Rockefeller Wayne; Frank G. Wisner; Tadataka Yamada, M.D.

Number of staff: 20 full-time professional; 2 part-time professional; 22 full-time support.
EIN: 131760106

6826

The Rockefeller Foundation ▼

420 5th Ave.
New York, NY 10018-2702 (212) 869-8500
Contact: Richard Tofel, V.P., Secy. and Genl. Counsel
URL: http://www.rockfound.org

Incorporated in 1913 in NY.
Donor: John D. Rockefeller, Sr.†.
Foundation type: Independent foundation.
Financial data (yr. ended 12/31/05): Assets, $3,417,557,613 (M); expenditures, $175,812,481; qualifying distributions, $148,240,608; giving activities include $111,083,354 for grants, $6,788,968 for foundation-administered programs and $650,000 for 2 loans/program-related investments.
Purpose and activities: The foundation was established by John D. Rockefeller, Sr. to "promote the well being" of humanity by addressing the root causes of serious problems. With assets of more than $3 billion, it is one of the nation's largest private foundations. The foundation works internationally to expand opportunities for poor and vulnerable people and to help ensure that the benefits of globalization are shared more equitably.
Fields of interest: Humanities; Arts; Education; Health care; Employment; Agriculture/food, public

education; Housing/shelter; International development; International affairs; Community development.
International interests: Africa; Southeast Asia.
Type of support: General/operating support; Continuing support; Program development; Conferences/seminars; Publication; Seed money; Curriculum development; Fellowships; Research; Technical assistance; Program-related investments/loans; Employee matching gifts; Scholarships—to individuals.
Limitations: Giving primarily in Africa, North America, and Southeast Asia. No grants to individuals for personal aid, or except in rare cases, for endowment funds or building or operating funds.
Publications: Application guidelines; Annual report (including application guidelines); Financial statement; Grants list; Informational brochure; Program policy statement.
Application information: The foundation seeks opportunities that will advance its long-term goals of improving the lives of poor and excluded people and the communities in which they live. To determine if your organization's project aligns with the foundation's goals, please visit the foundation Web site. Applicants may then want to send a brief letter of inquiry addressed to the director of the subject area of interest, at the foundation's address. Inquiries can also be sent electronically to the e-mail addresses on each program description page on the foundation Web site. Organizations submitting inquiries that foundation staff thinks might contribute to a defined area of work will be asked to submit a full proposal. Application form not required.

  Initial approach: Letter of inquiry addressed to director of subject area of interest
  Copies of proposal: 1
  Deadline(s): Letters of inquiry will be considered as they are received throughout the year
  Board meeting date(s): Apr., Aug., and Dec.
  Final notification: 6 to 8 weeks

Officers and Trustees:* James F. Orr III,* Chair.; Peter Madonia, C.O.O.; Dr. Judith Rodin,* Pres.; Richard Tofel, V.P., Secy. and Genl. Counsel; Nadya K. Shmavonian, V.P., Fdn. Initiatives; Darren Walker, V.P., Fdn. Initiatives; Lynda Mullen, Corp. Secy.; Lawrence Mangan, C.F.O.; Donna Dean, Treas. and C.I.O.; William H. Foege; Ann M. Fudge; Rajat Gupta; Margaret Hambug; Thomas J. Healey; Antonia Hernandez; Alice Huang; Strive Masiyiwa; Jessica T. Mathews; Diana Natalicio; Sandra Day O'Connor; Mamphela Ramphele; David Rockefeller, Jr.; Raymond Smith; Vo-Tong Xuan.
Number of staff: 82 full-time professional; 28 full-time support.
EIN: 131659629
Selected grants: The following grants were reported in 2004.
$7,000,000 to Global Alliance for TB Drug Development, New York, NY. For general support for efforts to develop new, more effective medicines to treat tuberculosis that will be affordable and available in developing countries.
$3,550,000 to Regional Universities Forum for Capacity Building in Agriculture Limited, Kampala, Uganda. For general support.
$2,225,000 to Harvard University, Cambridge, MA. Toward Global Equity Initiative, to promote global equity through expanding ideas, mobilizing diverse actors and setting policy agenda.
$2,166,000 to Living Cities: The National Community Development Initiative, New York, NY. For continued support of second ten-year

phase of National Community Development Initiative.
$2,000,000 to California Endowment, Los Angeles, CA. For second phase of California Works for Better Health project, which is designed to improve health and economic opportunity of residents of Fresno, Los Angeles, Sacramento and San Diego regions.
$1,300,010 to Creative Capital Foundation, New York, NY. Toward Multi-Arts Production Fund, program that supports creation of new work in performing arts.
$1,092,733 to National Video Resources, New York, NY. Toward Program for Media Artists, program that supports film, video and multimedia artists.
$1,000,000 to Columbia University, New York, NY. Toward Security Council Report, designed to provide information on current and prospective work of United Nations Security Council.
$1,000,000 to World Conference of Religions for Peace, New York, NY. For continued support of efforts to build and expand sustainable multi-religious networks collaborating for common good.
$885,597 to Africa Rice Center (WARDA), Cotonou, Benin. Toward field and laboratory research aimed at developing more drought-tolerant varieties of rice for farmers in drought-prone areas of sub-Saharan Africa.

6827

The David Rockefeller Fund, Inc.

30 Rockefeller Plz., Rm. 5600
New York, NY 10112
Contact: Marnie Pillsbury, Exec. Dir.

Established in 1989 in NY.
Donor: David Rockefeller.
Foundation type: Independent foundation.
Financial data (yr. ended 12/31/04): Assets, $4,432,907 (M); gifts received, $537,147; expenditures, $797,344; qualifying distributions, $747,424; giving activities include $652,000 for 128 grants (high: $30,000; low: $500; average: $1,000–$25,000), and $30,500 for employee matching gifts.
Purpose and activities: Giving primarily for conservation and historic preservation, community services, and health services; minor support also for the arts, local fire departments, and recreation.
Fields of interest: Historic preservation/historical societies; Arts; Education; Environment; Health care; Recreation; Community development.
Type of support: Continuing support; Annual campaigns.
Limitations: Giving limited to Mount Desert Island, ME, the Tarrytown area in Westchester County, NY, and the Livingston Communities of Columbia County, NY, for the Citizenship Program. No grants to individuals, or for film/video projects.
Publications: Annual report.
Application information: Unsolicited applications and subsequent guideline attachments are accepted for the Citizenship Program only. Unsolicited applications are not accepted for the Family Interest grants program. Application form not required.

  Initial approach: Letter of inquiry to Exec. Dir. for the Citizenship Program only
  Copies of proposal: 1
  Deadline(s): None

Board meeting date(s): May and Nov.
Final notification: Positive responses only
Officers and Directors: * David Rockefeller,* Pres.;
Richard E. Salomon,* Secy.-Treas.; Marnie S.
Pillsbury, Exec. Dir.; Colin G. Campbell; Adam
Growald; Daniel Growald; Eileen Growald; Lee
Halprin; Miranda Kaiser; Abby Rockefeller; Camilla
Rockefeller; James Sligar.
Number of staff: 1 part-time professional; 1
part-time support.
EIN: 133533359

6828
The Rodgers Family Foundation, Inc. ✧
(formerly Richard and Dorothy Rodgers Foundation)
c/o J. Rubenstein
575 Madison Ave.
New York, NY   10022

Established in 1952 in NY.
Donors: Richard Rodgers†; Dorothy F. Rodgers†.
Foundation type: Independent foundation.
Financial data (yr. ended 12/31/05): Assets,
$12,674,734 (M); gifts received, $200,000;
expenditures, $878,947; qualifying distributions,
$720,780; giving activities include $700,000 for
103 grants (high: $200,000; low: $100).
Purpose and activities: Giving primarily to arts
organizations; some support also for education,
hospitals and Jewish organizations.
Fields of interest: Museums; Performing arts;
Performing arts, education; Arts; Higher education;
Education; Health care; Human services.
Limitations: Applications not accepted. Giving
primarily in New York, NY. No grants to individuals.
Application information: Contributes only to
pre-selected organizations.
Officers: Linda Rodgers Emory, Pres.; Mary Rogers
Guettel, V.P.; Jasmine M. Hanif, Secy.; Joshua S.
Rubenstein, Treas.
EIN: 136062852

6829
The David & Tricia Rogers Foundation ✧
c/o BCRS Assocs. LLC
100 Wall St., 11th Fl.
New York, NY   10005

Established in 1994 in CT.
Donors: J. David Rogers; Patricia Rogers.
Foundation type: Independent foundation.
Financial data (yr. ended 2/28/05): Assets,
$7,037,615 (M); gifts received, $1,686,480;
expenditures, $1,389,764; qualifying distributions,
$1,312,085; giving activities include $1,309,600
for 22 grants (high: $1,140,000; low: $200).
Purpose and activities: Giving primarily for higher
education; funding also for human services, and to
a Presbyterian church.
Fields of interest: Arts; Higher education, college;
Recreation; Human services; Philanthropy/
voluntarism; Protestant agencies & churches.
Limitations: Applications not accepted. Giving
primarily in Darien, CT, and New York, NY; some
giving in University Park, PA. No grants to
individuals, or for scholarships; no loans.
Application information: Contributes only to
pre-selected organizations.
Trustees: J. David Rogers; Tricia Rogers.
EIN: 133789004

Selected grants: The following grants were reported
in 2005.
$1,160,200 to Pennsylvania State University,
   University Park, PA. 3 grants: $1,140,000,
   $20,000, $200

6830
The Felix and Elizabeth Rohatyn Foundation, Inc.
(formerly Felix G. Rohatyn Foundation)
114 W. 47th St., 3rd Fl.
New York, NY   10036
Contact: Andrew Lane

Established in 1968.
Donors: Felix G. Rohatyn; Elizabeth F. Rohatyn.
Foundation type: Independent foundation.
Financial data (yr. ended 12/31/04): Assets,
$8,735,150 (M); gifts received, $2,500,000;
expenditures, $2,610,468; qualifying distributions,
$2,570,304; giving activities include $2,527,667
for 131 grants (high: $453,500; low: $50; average:
$1,000–$25,000).
Purpose and activities: Giving primarily for
elementary schools, secondary schools, and
education.
Fields of interest: Elementary school/education;
Secondary school/education; Education.
Type of support: General/operating support;
Program development.
Limitations: Applications not accepted. Giving
primarily in the New York, NY, area. No grants to
individuals.
Application information:
   Board meeting date(s): Quarterly
Officers and Directors: * Felix G. Rohatyn,* Pres.;
Elizabeth F. Rohatyn,* V.P.; Nicolas Rohatyn,*
Secy.-Treas.; Vivien Stiles Duffy, Exec. Dir.
Number of staff: 1 part-time professional.
EIN: 237015644
Selected grants: The following grants were reported
in 2004.
$700,000 to Carnegie Hall Society, New York, NY.
   3 grants: $200,000 (For unrestricted support),
   $400,000 (For expansion campaign), $100,000
   (For Isaac Stern Endowment Fund).
$453,500 to Teaching Matters, New York, NY. For
   unrestricted support.
$333,333 to Middlebury College, Middlebury, VT.
   For unrestricted support.
$100,000 to New York Public Library, New York, NY.
   For Literary Lions.
$50,000 to Center for Strategic and International
   Studies, DC. For unrestricted support.
$33,333 to Columbia University, New York, NY. For
   Professorship in Hypertension.
$30,000 to International Rescue Committee, New
   York, NY. For unrestricted support.
$29,000 to Bank Street College of Education, New
   York, NY. For unrestricted support.

6831
The George Rohr Foundation, Inc. ✧
c/o Ulysses Partners, LLC
280 Park Ave., 21st Fl.
New York, NY   10017

Established in 1986 in NY.
Donor: George Rohr.
Foundation type: Independent foundation.

Financial data (yr. ended 12/31/03): Assets,
$7,519,066 (M); gifts received, $13,500;
expenditures, $882,923; qualifying distributions,
$807,855; giving activities include $807,510 for 32
grants (high: $328,010; low: $300).
Purpose and activities: Giving primarily to Jewish
organizations.
Fields of interest: Hospitals (general); Jewish
federated giving programs; Jewish agencies &
temples.
Limitations: Applications not accepted. Giving
primarily in NY. No grants to individuals.
Application information: Contributes only to
pre-selected organizations.
Officers and Directors: * George Rohr,* Pres.;
Pamela Rohr,* V.P.; Scott Korman,* Treas.
EIN: 133267203

6832
The Aaron, Martha, Isidore & Blanche Rosansky Foundation ✧
c/o Aronauer, Goldfarb, et al.
444 Madison Ave., 17th Fl.
New York, NY   10022
Contact: Alan Sills, Dir.

Donor: B. Rosanksy Trust.
Foundation type: Independent foundation.
Financial data (yr. ended 12/31/05): Assets,
$1,269,274 (M); expenditures, $488,738;
qualifying distributions, $456,244; giving activities
include $440,000 for 5 grants (high: $130,000;
low: $10,000).
Purpose and activities: Giving primarily to Jewish
temples and for Jewish education.
Fields of interest: Higher education, college; Higher
education, university; Diabetes; Human services;
Jewish agencies & temples.
Limitations: Giving primarily in NY.
Application information:
   Initial approach: Letter or proposal
   Deadline(s): None
Directors: Zevulun Charlop; Jonathan I. Ginsberg;
Betty Rifkin; Alan Sills; Leo N. Sokol.
EIN: 112594677
Selected grants: The following grants were reported
in 2004.
$130,000 to Yeshiva University, New York, NY.
$100,000 to Beth Medrash Govoha, Brooklyn, NY.
$100,000 to Columbia University, New York, NY.
$100,000 to Joslin Diabetes Center, Boston, MA.
$10,000 to Queens Jewish Center and Talmud
   Torah, Forest Hills, NY.

6833
Marshall Rose Family Foundation, Inc. ✧
(formerly Jill & Marshall Rose Foundation, Inc.)
c/o Georgetown Mgmt. Assn.
667 Madison Ave.
New York, NY   10021
Contact: Marshall Rose, Dir.

Established around 1980.
Donors: Marshall Rose; Alan R. Grossman.
Foundation type: Independent foundation.
Financial data (yr. ended 11/30/05): Assets,
$3,290,403 (M); gifts received, $101,281;
expenditures, $557,697; qualifying distributions,
$552,891; giving activities include $552,891 for 72
grants (high: $125,000; low: $75).

Fields of interest: Arts; Higher education; Theological school/education; Education; Human services; Jewish federated giving programs; Jewish agencies & temples.
Type of support: General/operating support; Annual campaigns; Endowments; Curriculum development.
Limitations: Applications not accepted. Giving primarily in New York, NY. No grants to individuals.
Application information: Contributes only to pre-selected organizations.
Directors: Simeon Brinberg; Marshall Rose.
EIN: 133036439
Selected grants: The following grants were reported in 2005.
$125,000 to Brown University, Providence, RI.
$31,600 to Breast Cancer Research Foundation, New York, NY.
$25,750 to New York Public Library, New York, NY.
$25,000 to Hackley School, Tarrytown, NY.
$10,500 to Doctors Without Borders USA, New York, NY.
$5,000 to Literacy Partners, New York, NY.
$2,500 to Montefiore Medical Center, Bronx, NY.
$2,000 to City College Fund, New York, NY.
$1,000 to Free Library of Philadelphia, Philadelphia, PA.
$1,000 to Montessori School.

6834
Adam R. Rose Foundation ✧
200 Madison Ave., 5th Fl.
New York, NY 10016

Established in 1996 in DE.
Donor: Adam Rose.
Foundation type: Independent foundation.
Financial data (yr. ended 12/31/03): Assets, $62,588 (M); gifts received, $705,000; expenditures, $650,805; qualifying distributions, $650,575; giving activities include $650,575 for grants.
Purpose and activities: Giving for education, music, human rights, lesbian and gay services, and public gardens.
Fields of interest: Performing arts, music; Education; Botanical gardens; International human rights; LGBTQ.
Limitations: Applications not accepted. Giving primarily in NY. No grants to individuals.
Application information: Contributes only to pre-selected organizations.
Officers: Adam M. Rose, Pres.; Michael D. Sullivan, Secy.
EIN: 137095495
Selected grants: The following grants were reported in 2003.
$200,000 to New York Botanical Garden, Bronx, NY.
$75,000 to Human Rights Campaign Foundation, DC.
$25,000 to Battery Conservancy, New York, NY.
$25,000 to Broadway Cares/Equity Fights AIDS, New York, NY.
$25,000 to Gay, Lesbian and Straight Education Network (GLSEN), New York, NY.
$20,000 to Yale University, New Haven, CT.
$15,000 to Senior Action in a Gay Environment (SAGE), New York, NY.
$3,000 to Caramoor Garden Club, Katonah, NY.
$1,000 to Melrose School, Brewster, NY.
$1,000 to Richard Tucker Music Foundation, New York, NY.

6835
The Deborah Rose Foundation ✧ ☆
200 Madison Ave., 5th Fl.
New York, NY 10016

Established in 1999 in DE.
Foundation type: Independent foundation.
Financial data (yr. ended 12/31/05): Assets, $31,733 (M); gifts received, $1,450,000; expenditures, $1,842,453; qualifying distributions, $1,829,920; giving activities include $1,829,920 for grants.
Fields of interest: Higher education.
Limitations: Applications not accepted. No grants to individuals.
Application information: Contributes only to pre-selected organizations.
Director: Deborah Rose.
EIN: 134088811

6836
Susan and Elihu Rose Foundation, Inc. ✧
200 Madison Ave., 5th Fl.
New York, NY 10016

Established in 1988 in DE.
Donors: Elihu Rose; Samuel and David Rose Charitable Foundation.
Foundation type: Independent foundation.
Financial data (yr. ended 12/31/03): Assets, $24,632,003 (M); expenditures, $1,833,878; qualifying distributions, $1,724,559; giving activities include $1,724,559 for 138 grants (high: $200,000; low: $250).
Purpose and activities: Support primarily for the arts, education, and Jewish giving.
Fields of interest: Performing arts; Historic preservation/historical societies; Arts; Higher education; Health organizations, association; Human services; Jewish federated giving programs; Jewish agencies & temples.
Type of support: Annual campaigns; Capital campaigns; Building/renovation; Endowments.
Limitations: Applications not accepted. Giving primarily in New York, NY. No grants to individuals.
Application information: Contributes only to pre-selected organizations.
Officer and Directors:* Elihu Rose,* Pres. and Secy.; Susan Rose.
EIN: 133484181
Selected grants: The following grants were reported in 2003.
$200,000 to Carnegie Hall Society, New York, NY.
$200,000 to Central Synagogue, New York, NY.
$115,000 to International Center of Photography, New York, NY.
$67,500 to UJA-Federation of New York, New York, NY.
$50,000 to Juilliard School, New York, NY.
$32,500 to Teachers College Columbia University, New York, NY.
$5,000 to New York Public Library, New York, NY.
$1,500 to New York City Opera, New York, NY.
$1,000 to Orpheus Chamber Orchestra, New York, NY.
$1,000 to Rockefeller University, New York, NY.

6837
Frederick P. & Sandra P. Rose Foundation ▼ ✧
200 Madison Ave., 5th Fl.
New York, NY 10016

Established in 1982 in DE.
Donors: Frederick P. Rose†; Samuel and David Rose Charitable Foundation; Sandra Priest Rose.
Foundation type: Independent foundation.
Financial data (yr. ended 11/30/04): Assets, $4,073,547 (M); gifts received, $1,500,000; expenditures, $7,404,246; qualifying distributions, $7,314,150; giving activities include $7,263,454 for 119+ grants (high: $833,333; average: $100–$100,000).
Purpose and activities: Giving primarily for performing arts and other cultural organizations; support also for higher education.
Fields of interest: Performing arts; Arts; Higher education.
Limitations: Applications not accepted. Giving primarily in New York, NY. No grants to individuals.
Application information: Contributes only to pre-selected organizations.
Officers and Directors:* Sandra Priest Rose,* Pres.; Jonathan F.P. Rose,* V.P.; Adam R. Rose,* Secy.-Treas.; Deborah Rose.
EIN: 133136740
Selected grants: The following grants were reported in 2004.
$863,333 to Metropolitan Museum of Art, New York, NY. 2 grants: $833,333, $30,000
$500,000 to Yale University, New Haven, CT.
$250,000 to Lincoln Center for the Performing Arts, New York, NY. For Live From Lincoln Center.
$113,333 to Selfhelp Community Services, New York, NY. 2 grants: $30,000, $83,333
$100,000 to American Museum of Natural History, New York, NY.
$100,000 to New York Public Library, New York, NY.
$50,000 to College of New Rochelle, New Rochelle, NY.
$50,000 to Reading Reform Foundation of New York, New York, NY.

6838
Billy Rose Foundation, Inc. ✧
805 3rd Ave., 23rd Fl.
New York, NY 10022 (212) 407-7745
Contact: Terri C. Mangino, Asst. Secy.

Incorporated in 1958 in NY.
Donor: Billy Rose†.
Foundation type: Independent foundation.
Financial data (yr. ended 12/31/05): Assets, $13,367,759 (M); expenditures, $735,343; qualifying distributions, $576,392; giving activities include $537,000 for grants.
Purpose and activities: Support for museums, particularly a museum in Israel, and the performing and fine arts; some giving also for higher education.
Fields of interest: Arts, research; Visual arts; Museums; Performing arts; Performing arts, theater (playwriting); Performing arts, orchestra (symphony); Arts; Higher education; Libraries (public).
Type of support: Program development; Research.
Limitations: Giving primarily in New York, NY. No grants to individuals.
Application information: Application form not required.
Initial approach: Letter

Deadline(s): None
Board meeting date(s): Usually in June
Final notification: Varies
Officers: Paul Silberberg, Pres.; Edward J. Walsh, Jr., Secy.; John Wohlstetter, Treas.
Number of staff: 1 full-time professional.
EIN: 136165466

6839
Daniel and Joanna S. Rose Fund, Inc. ◇
200 Madison Ave., 5th Fl.
New York, NY 10016

Established in 1988 in DE.
Donors: Daniel Rose; Samuel and David Rose Charitable Foundation.
Foundation type: Independent foundation.
Financial data (yr. ended 12/31/03): Assets, $730,182 (M); gifts received, $600,000; expenditures, $1,554,208; qualifying distributions, $1,543,874; giving activities include $1,543,874 for 164 grants (high: $200,000; low: $100; average: $500–$50,000).
Purpose and activities: Giving exclusively for the grantees' general charitable, educational, scientific, religious, or literary purposes.
Fields of interest: Museums; Performing arts; Historic preservation/historical societies; Arts; Higher education; International affairs, foreign policy; Public policy, research; Jewish agencies & temples.
Limitations: Applications not accepted. Giving primarily in NY. No grants to individuals.
Application information: Contributes only to pre-selected organizations.
Officer and Director:* Daniel Rose,* Pres.
EIN: 133484179

6840
Rosedorf Foundation ◇
1139 57th St.
Brooklyn, NY 11219
Contact: David Weisz, Pres.

Established in 1999 in NY.
Donor: David Weisz.
Foundation type: Independent foundation.
Financial data (yr. ended 12/31/03): Assets, $216,250 (M); expenditures, $351,392; qualifying distributions, $351,118; giving activities include $351,118 for 21 grants (high: $190,000; low: $18).
Fields of interest: Jewish agencies & temples.
Application information:
 Initial approach: Letter
 Deadline(s): None
Officers: David Weisz, Pres.; Rachelle Weisz, V.P.
EIN: 113523188

6841
The Benjamin M. Rosen Family Foundation ▼ ◇
1 Central Park W.
New York, NY 10023
Contact: Benjamin M. Rosen, Tr.

Established in 1998 in NY.
Donor: Benjamin M. Rosen.
Foundation type: Independent foundation.
Financial data (yr. ended 12/31/04): Assets, $23,953,212 (M); expenditures, $3,657,462;

qualifying distributions, $3,460,482; giving activities include $3,445,033 for 24 grants (high: $1,060,000; low: $4,460; average: $5,000–$175,000).
Purpose and activities: Giving primarily for the arts including museums, education, specialty hospitals, health organizations and associations, and cancer.
Fields of interest: Museums; Education; Hospitals (specialty); Health organizations, association; Cancer.
Limitations: Applications not accepted. Giving primarily in NY. No grants to individuals.
Application information: Contributes only to pre-selected organizations.
Trustees: Benjamin M. Rosen; Donna Rosen; Frederic A. Rubinstein; Jean Wenzel.
EIN: 134034465
Selected grants: The following grants were reported in 2004.
$1,060,000 to California Institute of Technology, Pasadena, CA. For unrestricted support.
$1,050,000 to Memorial Sloan-Kettering Cancer Center, New York, NY. For unrestricted support.
$345,880 to Metropolitan Opera, New York, NY. For unrestricted support.
$238,700 to Dia Art Foundation, New York, NY. For unrestricted support.
$188,783 to Philharmonic-Symphony Society of New York, New York, NY. For unrestricted support.
$175,000 to Columbia University, Business School, New York, NY. For unrestricted support.
$74,550 to Museum of Modern Art, New York, NY. For unrestricted support.
$43,550 to Second Stage Theater, New York, NY. For unrestricted support.
$23,050 to Hospital for Special Surgery, New York, NY. For unrestricted support.
$15,000 to Tulane University, New Orleans, LA. For unrestricted support.

6842
The Abner Rosen Foundation, Inc. ☆
40 E. 69th St.
New York, NY 10021
Contact: Jonathan P. Rosen, Pres.
FAX: (212) 249-5451; *E-mail:* jon@urmci.com

Donor: Miriam N. Rosen†.
Foundation type: Independent foundation.
Financial data (yr. ended 6/30/06): Assets, $3,625,643 (M); gifts received, $4,204,763; expenditures, $641,429; qualifying distributions, $640,553; giving activities include $640,553 for grants.
Limitations: Applications not accepted. No grants to individuals.
Application information: Contributes only to pre-selected organizations.
Officers and Directors:* Jonathan P. Rosen,* Pres.; Irving S. Bobrow,* Secy.; Jeanette D. Rosen,* Treas.
EIN: 133841307

6843
Joseph Rosen Foundation, Inc. ◇
P.O. Box 334
Lenox Hill Sta.
New York, NY 10021

Incorporated in 1948 in NY.

Donor: Tranel, Inc.
Foundation type: Independent foundation.
Financial data (yr. ended 6/30/05): Assets, $24,295,750 (M); gifts received, $4,700; expenditures, $2,464,383; qualifying distributions, $1,484,102; giving activities include $1,484,102 for 348 grants (high: $126,000; low: $25).
Purpose and activities: Giving primarily for higher education, the arts, with emphasis on museums, as well as for Jewish organizations and temples, medical research, and for children, youth, families, and social services.
Fields of interest: Museums; Museums (art); Museums (children's); Performing arts; Arts; Higher education; Law school/education; Environment, natural resources; Environment; Animals/wildlife, preservation/protection; Animals/wildlife; Hospitals (specialty); Health care; Health organizations, association; Cancer research; Human services; International affairs; Civil rights; Jewish federated giving programs; Public affairs; Christian agencies & churches; Jewish agencies & temples.
Limitations: Applications not accepted. Giving on a national basis. No grants to individuals.
Application information: Contributes only to pre-selected organizations.
Officers: Jonathan P. Rosen, Pres. and Secy.; Irving S. Bobrow, V.P. and Secy.; Jeannette Rosen, V.P. and Treas.
EIN: 136158412
Selected grants: The following grants were reported in 2004.
$100,000 to Amherst College, Amherst, MA.
$65,500 to UJA-Federation of New York, New York, NY.
$40,000 to Dalton Schools, New York, NY.
$32,725 to Metropolitan Museum of Art, New York, NY.
$25,000 to American ORT Federation, New York, NY.
$25,000 to Metropolitan Opera Association, New York, NY.
$23,000 to Brooklyn Museum, Brooklyn, NY.
$18,000 to Cornell University, Ithaca, NY.
$14,500 to Roundabout Theater Company, New York, NY.
$10,000 to Jewish National Fund, New York, NY.

6844
Reb Moishe Rosen Fund, Inc. ◇
271 Madison Ave., 22nd Fl.
New York, NY 10016-1001

Donors: Charles Alpert; Joseph Alpert.
Foundation type: Independent foundation.
Financial data (yr. ended 6/30/05): Assets, $303,856 (M); gifts received, $1,002,104; expenditures, $978,848; qualifying distributions, $978,838; giving activities include $978,643 for 220+ grants (high: $30,000).
Fields of interest: Jewish agencies & temples.
Limitations: Applications not accepted. Giving primarily in NY. No support for private foundations. No grants to individuals, or for scholarships.
Application information: Contributes only to pre-selected organizations.
Officers: Joseph Alpert, Secy.; Charles Alpert, Treas.
EIN: 116036649

6845
Sunny and Abe Rosenberg Foundation, Inc. ✧
888 7th Ave., 24th Fl.
New York, NY 10019
Contact: Karen McQuade, Exec. Asst.
FAX: (212) 660-1218;
E-mail: info@rosenbergfoundation.org; URL: http://www.rosenbergfoundation.org

Incorporated in 1966 in NY.
Donors: Abraham Rosenberg‡; Sonia Rosenberg‡.
Foundation type: Independent foundation.
Financial data (yr. ended 12/31/03): Assets, $13,123,590 (M); gifts received, $1,450; expenditures, $1,047,423; qualifying distributions, $675,401; giving activities include $520,636 for 56 grants (high: $44,500; low: $400).
Purpose and activities: The foundation focuses its giving directly towards foster care and education.
Fields of interest: Education; Children, foster care.
Type of support: General/operating support; Continuing support; Program development; Seed money; Curriculum development; Research; Program evaluation.
Limitations: Applications not accepted. Giving primarily in New York, NY. No support for private foundations. No grants to individuals, or for capital campaigns.
Application information: Unsolicited requests for funds not accepted.
Board meeting date(s): Spring and fall
Officers and Directors:* Susan R. Goldstein,* Pres.; Michael L. Rosenberg,* Sr. V.P.; Stuart D. Goldstein,* V.P. and Secy.-Treas.; Danielle Goldstein; Darin Goldstein.
Number of staff: 2 full-time professional; 1 part-time professional; 1 part-time support.
EIN: 136210591
Selected grants: The following grants were reported in 2004.
$60,000 to Professional Childrens School, New York, NY. 3 grants: $5,000, $50,000, $5,000
$20,000 to Planned Parenthood Federation of America, New York, NY.
$15,000 to Citymeals-on-Wheels, New York, NY.
$10,000 to Friends of Island Academy, New York, NY.
$10,000 to Harlem Childrens Zone, New York, NY.
$10,000 to Israel Youth Training Fund, Wayland, MA.
$10,000 to Metropolitan Museum of Art, New York, NY.
$5,000 to Educational Alliance, New York, NY.

6846
Thomas Jefferson Rosenberg Foundation, Inc. ✧
5 Hanover Sq., Ste. 200
New York, NY 10004-2614 (212) 869-1490
Contact: Henry Rosenberg, Pres.

Established around 1989 in NY.
Donor: Henry Rosenberg.
Foundation type: Independent foundation.
Financial data (yr. ended 12/31/05): Assets, $685,770 (M); gifts received, $470,420; expenditures, $451,503; qualifying distributions, $445,125; giving activities include $439,295 for 23 grants (high: $247,300; low: $25).
Purpose and activities: Giving for higher education, Jewish agencies, and human service organizations.

Fields of interest: Arts; Education; Health organizations, association; Human services; Jewish agencies & temples.
Limitations: Giving primarily in NY.
Application information: Application form not required.
Deadline(s): None
Officers: Henry Rosenberg, Pres. and Treas.; Gail Rosenberg, V.P.; Carol Rosner, V.P.; Eitan Eadan, Secy.
EIN: 133436858

6847
Murray & Sydell Rosenberg Foundation ▼ ✧
(formerly Murray M. Rosenberg Foundation)
75 Montebello Rd.
Suffern, NY 10901

Established in 1991 in GA.
Donor: Greystone Funding Corp.
Foundation type: Company-sponsored foundation.
Financial data (yr. ended 6/30/05): Assets, $5,831,176 (M); gifts received, $11,767,643; expenditures, $7,082,065; qualifying distributions, $7,114,715; giving activities include $6,776,567 for 87 grants (high: $2,313,983; low: $200), and $63,407 for 7 grants to individuals.
Purpose and activities: The foundation supports programs designed to help impoverished Jewish families.
Fields of interest: Education; Jewish agencies & temples; Economically disadvantaged.
International interests: Argentina; Israel; Soviet Union (Former).
Type of support: Grants to individuals.
Limitations: Giving primarily in NY, NJ, and Israel.
Application information: Application form required.
Initial approach: Contact foundation for application form
Copies of proposal: 1
Directors: Lisa Lifshitz; Cheryl Rosenberg; Stephen Rosenburg.
Number of staff: 3 full-time professional.
EIN: 581947342
Selected grants: The following grants were reported in 2005.
$2,313,983 to Ahavas Chesed Israel Relief, Monsey, NY.
$1,566,968 to Keren Ahavas Chesed and Torah, Jerusalem, Israel. .
$734,376 to American Friends of Yad Yemin, Brooklyn, NY.
$220,000 to Mirrer Yerushalayim, Brooklyn, NY.
$150,000 to Shuvu/Return: The United Fund for the Education of Russian Immigrant Children in Israel, New York, NY.
$107,748 to Yeshiva Bais Binyomin, Stamford, CT.
$57,552 to Congregation Ohel Yitzchok Chesed Foundation, Monsey, NY.
$47,070 to Union of Councils for Soviet Jews, DC.
$32,000 to Keren Chaim Shlomo, Brooklyn, NY.
$17,500 to American Foundation for Yeshivath Rashbi, Brooklyn, NY.

6848
Rosenblatt Family Foundation, Inc. ✧
155 Riverside Dr.
New York, NY 10024-2207

Incorporated in 1956 in NY.

Donors: Marcus Retter; Betty Retter‡; C. Rosenblatt.
Foundation type: Independent foundation.
Financial data (yr. ended 11/30/05): Assets, $40,524,242 (M); expenditures, $323,770; qualifying distributions, $320,770; giving activities include $320,770 for 214 grants (high: $49,900; low: $18).
Purpose and activities: Giving primarily to Jewish temples and yeshivas.
Fields of interest: Education; Human services; Jewish agencies & temples.
International interests: Israel.
Limitations: Giving primarily in NY.
Application information: Application form not required.
Deadline(s): None
Officers: Marcus Retter, Pres.; Lea Eisenberg, V.P.; Margot Pollak, V.P.; Mary Schreiber, Secy.-Treas.
EIN: 136145385

6849
Louis & Emanuel G. Rosenblatt Foundation, Inc. ✧
360 Central Ave., Ste. 106
Lawrence, NY 11559
Application address: c/o Linda R. Kaminow, 2003 N. Ocean Blvd., Boca Raton, FL 33431

Established around 1966 in NY.
Donors: Master Equities Corp.; E.G. Rosenblatt Trust.
Foundation type: Independent foundation.
Financial data (yr. ended 6/30/05): Assets, $2,356,608 (M); expenditures, $559,924; qualifying distributions, $555,000; giving activities include $555,000 for 8 grants (high: $275,000; low: $5,000).
Purpose and activities: Giving primarily for health and health associations, as well as for Jewish agencies, temples, and education.
Fields of interest: Hospitals (specialty); Health care; Cancer; Medical research, institute; Human services; Jewish federated giving programs; Jewish agencies & temples.
Limitations: Giving primarily in FL and NY. No grants to individuals.
Application information:
Initial approach: Letter
Deadline(s): None
Officers: Linda R. Kaminow, Pres.; Lois Lustig, V.P.; Ira Panzier, Secy.-Treas.
EIN: 136189436

6850
Daniel Rosenblum Family Foundation, Inc. ✧
257 Park Ave. S.
New York, NY 10010

Established in 1989 in NY.
Donor: Daniel Rosenblum.
Foundation type: Independent foundation.
Financial data (yr. ended 12/31/05): Assets, $5,495,648 (M); gifts received, $4,755; expenditures, $841,835; qualifying distributions, $805,459; giving activities include $798,009 for 42 grants (high: $261,800; low: $200).
Purpose and activities: Giving primarily for arts and culture, including an institute for classical architecture and a ballet school, education,

particularly a girls' school, health associations, children and youth services, including a foundation for special children, and for Jewish organizations and temples.

Fields of interest: Arts education; Visual arts, architecture; Performing arts, ballet; Arts; Elementary/secondary education; Hospitals (general); Health organizations, association; Genetics/birth defects; American Red Cross; Children/youth, services; Residential/custodial care, half-way house; Jewish agencies & temples.

Limitations: Applications not accepted. Giving primarily in NY. No grants to individuals.

Application information: Contributes only to pre-selected organizations.

Officers and Directors: * Daniel Rosenblum,* Pres.; Leonard Rosenblum,* Secy.; N. Barry Ross,* Treas.

EIN: 133520602

Selected grants: The following grants were reported in 2005.

$261,800 to March of Dimes Birth Defects Foundation, New York, NY.

$180,000 to Charities Aid Foundation (CAF) America, Alexandria, VA.

$84,720 to Allen-Stevenson School, New York, NY.

$74,700 to Hewitt School, New York, NY.

$28,000 to New Yorks Finest Foundation, Cedarhurst, NY.

$2,000 to Dysautonomia Foundation, New York, NY.

$1,000 to East Harlem School at Exodus House, New York, NY.

$1,000 to Learning Leaders, New York, NY.

6851
The Rosenkranz Foundation, Inc.
590 Madison Ave., 30th Fl.
New York, NY 10022

Established in 1997 in DE and NY.

Donor: Robert Rosenkranz.

Foundation type: Independent foundation.

Financial data (yr. ended 10/31/05): Assets, $17,010,157 (M); expenditures, $1,683,544; qualifying distributions, $1,619,599; giving activities include $1,609,545 for 92 grants (high: $383,000; low: $75).

Purpose and activities: Giving primarily for arts and culture, as well as for higher education.

Fields of interest: Museums (art); Performing arts; Performing arts, orchestra (symphony); Arts; Higher education; Law school/education; Education.

Limitations: Applications not accepted. Giving primarily in New York, NY. No grants to individuals.

Application information: Contributes only to pre-selected organizations.

Officers and Directors: * Robert Rosenkranz,* Pres.; Stephanie Rosenkranz, V.P.; Jean De LaPoer, Secy.; S. Dana Wolfe, Treas.; Nicholas Rosenkranz.

Number of staff: 1 full-time professional; 1 part-time professional.

EIN: 133940017

Selected grants: The following grants were reported in 2003.

$194,700 to New York University, School of Law, New York, NY. For Dean's Merit Scholarship Program.

$100,000 to Community Funds, New York, NY.

$50,000 to New York-Presbyterian Hospital, New York, NY.

$48,670 to Metropolitan Museum of Art, New York, NY.

$25,000 to Harvard University, Art Museum, Cambridge, MA.

$20,000 to Princeton University, Princeton, NJ.

$14,000 to Film Society of Lincoln Center, New York, NY.

$10,000 to American Enterprise Institute for Public Policy Research, DC.

$10,000 to Center for Individual Rights, DC.

$10,000 to Council on Foreign Relations, New York, NY.

6852
The Rosenstiel Foundation ✧
575 Madison Ave., 11th Fl.
New York, NY 10022-2511
Contact: Maurice C. Greenbaum, Secy.-Treas.

Incorporated in 1950 in OH.

Donor: Lewis S. Rosenstiel†.

Foundation type: Independent foundation.

Financial data (yr. ended 12/31/05): Assets, $22,887,638 (M); expenditures, $1,087,995; qualifying distributions, $861,039; giving activities include $840,200 for 127 grants (high: $195,000; low: $500).

Purpose and activities: Grants largely for Polish cultural programs, the performing arts, health organizations, hospitals, and higher education.

Fields of interest: Performing arts; Arts; Higher education; Education; Medical care, rehabilitation; Health care; Health organizations, association.

International interests: Poland.

Type of support: General/operating support; Continuing support; Seed money.

Limitations: Applications not accepted. Giving primarily in FL and NY. No grants to individuals.

Application information: Contributes only to pre-selected organizations.

Officers and Trustees: * Elizabeth R. Kabler,* Pres.; Robert I. Fisher,* V.P.; Blanka A. Rosenstiel,* V.P.; Maurice C. Greenbaum,* Secy.-Treas. and Admin.

EIN: 066034536

6853
Juliet Rosenthal Foundation, Inc. ✧
1370 Broadway
New York, NY 10018

Established in 1958.

Donor: Rosenthal & Rosenthal, Inc.

Foundation type: Independent foundation.

Financial data (yr. ended 12/31/03): Assets, $8,448,527 (M); expenditures, $355,057; qualifying distributions, $350,842; giving activities include $353,254 for grants (high: $51,000).

Purpose and activities: Giving primarily for health care and human services.

Fields of interest: Arts; Education; Hospitals (general); Health organizations, association; Medical research, institute; Human services; Jewish federated giving programs.

Limitations: Applications not accepted. Giving primarily in New York, NY. No grants to individuals or for program-related investments.

Application information: Contributes only to pre-selected organizations.

Officers: Stephen Rosenthal, Pres.; Julie Sanjenis, V.P.; Eric Rosenthal, Treas.

EIN: 136161085

6854
The Rosenthal Fund ✧
784 Park Ave., Apt. 19B
New York, NY 10021

Established in 1996 in NY.

Donor: Charles Rosenthal.

Foundation type: Independent foundation.

Financial data (yr. ended 9/30/05): Assets, $5,407,616 (M); gifts received, $1,410,320; expenditures, $587,708; qualifying distributions, $577,595; giving activities include $575,500 for 75 grants (high: $425,000; low: $50).

Purpose and activities: Giving primarily for higher education; funding also for animal welfare, and human services.

Fields of interest: Arts; Higher education; Animal welfare; Animals/wildlife; Human services; Jewish agencies & temples.

Type of support: General/operating support.

Limitations: Applications not accepted. Giving primarily in NY and Providence, RI. No grants to individuals.

Application information: Contributes only to pre-selected organizations.

Officers: Charles Rosenthal, Pres.; Phyllis Rosenthal, V.P.

EIN: 133919545

6855
The William Rosenwald Family Fund, Inc. ✧
666 3rd Ave., 29th Fl.
New York, NY 10017
Contact: David P. Steinmann, Pres.

Incorporated in 1938 in CT.

Donors: William Rosenwald†; and family.

Foundation type: Independent foundation.

Financial data (yr. ended 12/31/04): Assets, $24,035,765 (M); gifts received, $1,652,725; expenditures, $1,929,029; qualifying distributions, $1,605,300; giving activities include $1,604,550 for 85 grants (high: $360,000; low: $200), and $50,000 for 1 loan/program-related investment.

Purpose and activities: Support for higher education, the arts, hospitals, and Jewish organizations.

Fields of interest: Arts; Education; Hospitals (general); Medical research, institute; Human services; Jewish federated giving programs; Orthodox Catholic agencies & churches; Jewish agencies & temples.

Type of support: General/operating support.

Limitations: Applications not accepted. Giving primarily in NY. No grants to individuals.

Application information: Contributes only to pre-selected organizations.

Officers: David P. Steinmann, Pres. and Treas.; Elizabeth R. Varet, V.P. and Secy.; Nina Rosenwald, V.P.; Alice R. Sigelman, V.P.

EIN: 131635289

Selected grants: The following grants were reported in 2003.

$360,000 to UJA-Federation of New York, New York, NY. For general support.

$250,000 to Bard College, Annandale on Hudson, NY. For general support.

$50,000 to Central Park Conservancy, New York, NY. For general support.

$25,000 to School of American Ballet, New York, NY. For general support.

$24,975 to National Tuberous Sclerosis Association, New York, NY. For general support.

$24,500 to Jewish Institute for National Security Affairs, DC. For general support.

$18,000 to Jewish Foundation for the Righteous, New York, NY. For general support.

$11,000 to Greek Orthodox Archdiocese of North and South America, New York, NY. For general support.

$10,000 to Center for Reproductive Rights, New York, NY. For general support.

$10,000 to Freedom House, DC. For general support.

6856

The Edward John & Patricia Rosenwald Foundation ✧ ☆

c/o Anchin, Block & Anchin LLP
1375 Broadway
New York, NY 10018

Established in 2004 in NY.
Donor: Edward John Rosenwald, Jr.
Foundation type: Independent foundation.
Financial data (yr. ended 12/31/05): Assets, $10,372,581 (M); gifts received, $12,152,539; expenditures, $2,123,979; qualifying distributions, $1,999,873; giving activities include $1,995,000 for 19 grants (high: $300,000; low: $10,000).
Fields of interest: Museums (art); Higher education; Environment.
Limitations: Applications not accepted. Giving primarily in New York, NY. No grants to individuals.
Application information: Contributes only to pre-selected organizations.
Officers: Edward John Rosenwald, Jr., Pres.; Patricia Rosenwald, V.P.
Director: Lawrence B. Buttenwieser.
EIN: 743107995

6857

Rosenwald Foundation, Inc. ✧

6 Forest Ln.
Lawrence, NY 11559

Established in 1993 in NY.
Donor: Lindsay Rosenwald.
Foundation type: Independent foundation.
Financial data (yr. ended 11/30/05): Assets, $1,955,354 (M); expenditures, $2,211,999; qualifying distributions, $2,202,490; giving activities include $2,139,838 for 86+ grants (high: $69,000).
Purpose and activities: Giving primarily for Jewish organizations, temples, and schools.
Fields of interest: Jewish federated giving programs; Jewish agencies & temples.
Limitations: Applications not accepted. Giving on a national basis.
Application information: Unsolicited requests for funds not accepted.
Officers and Directors:* Bernard Gross,* Pres.; Bernard Suss,* Treas.; Jay Lobell*.
EIN: 133746216

6858

Rosh Foundation ✧

c/o Neufield Doudna, LLC
103 5th Ave., 5th Fl.
New York, NY 10003-1009

Established in 1991 in NY.
Donor: Robin Neustein.
Foundation type: Independent foundation.
Financial data (yr. ended 3/31/05): Assets, $6,092,710 (M); gifts received, $748,680; expenditures, $1,530,384; qualifying distributions, $1,519,540; giving activities include $1,499,736 for 25 grants (high: $500,000; low: $250).
Purpose and activities: Giving primarily to universities, Jewish temples, and the arts, with emphasis on the ballet.
Fields of interest: Performing arts, ballet; Higher education; Medical school/education; Jewish agencies & temples.
Type of support: Scholarship funds.
Limitations: Applications not accepted. Giving primarily in the metropolitan New York, NY, area; funding also in Providence, RI and in South Hadley, MA. No grants to individuals, or for scholarships; no loans.
Application information: Contributes only to pre-selected organizations.
Trustees: Robin Neustein; Shimon Neustein.
EIN: 133637441
Selected grants: The following grants were reported in 2005.

$500,000 to Rockefeller University, New York, NY.

$271,885 to Brown University, Providence, RI. 2 grants: $71,885, $200,000

$126,916 to Ballet Theater Foundation, New York, NY. 3 grants: $100,000, $13,958, $12,958

$112,610 to Mount Holyoke College, South Hadley, MA. 2 grants: $57,610, $55,000

$80,350 to Congregation Shearith Israel, New York, NY. 2 grants: $30,175, $50,175

6859

The Roslyn Savings Foundation ✧

1400 Old Northern Blvd.
Roslyn, NY 11576-2127 (516) 484-1344
Contact: Sharon G. Grosser, Exec. Dir.
FAX: (516) 484-1599;
E-mail: info@roslynsavingsfoundation.org;
URL: http://www.roslynsavingsfoundation.org

Established in 1997 in NY.
Donor: Roslyn Bancorp, Inc.
Foundation type: Company-sponsored foundation.
Financial data (yr. ended 12/31/05): Assets, $24,692,783 (M); expenditures, $1,948,108; qualifying distributions, $1,970,035; giving activities include $1,706,899 for 143 grants (high: $100,000; low: $1,000).
Purpose and activities: The foundation supports organizations involved with arts and culture, education, health, employment, housing, child care, and community development.
Fields of interest: Arts; Education; Health care; Employment; Housing/shelter; Children, day care; Economic development; Community development.
Type of support: Continuing support; General/operating support.
Limitations: Giving primarily in Long Island and Queens, NY. No support for religious, political, or fraternal organizations. No grants to individuals.
Publications: Application guidelines; Grants list; Program policy statement.
Application information: Multi-year funding is not automatic. Organizations receiving support are asked to submit periodic progress reports. A site visit may be requested. Application form not required.
Initial approach: Proposal

Deadline(s): None
Final notification: Within 3 months
Officers and Directors: Joseph L. Mancino, Pres.; John R. Bransfield, Jr., V.P.; R. Patrick Quinn, Secy.; Michael P. Puorro, Treas.; Sharon G. Grosser, Exec. Dir.; Dominick Ciampa; Joseph Ficalora; Victor C. McCuaig; Walter Mullins; Daniel L. Murphy; James E. Swiggett; John M. Tsimbinos; Richard C. Webel.
EIN: 113354472
Selected grants: The following grants were reported in 2004.

$80,000 to Boy Scouts of America, Massapequa, NY. 2 grants: $40,000 each to Theodore Roosevelt Council (For capital campaign).

$50,000 to Columbus Citizens Foundation, New York, NY. For scholarships.

$46,500 to Long Island University, C.W. Post Center, Tilles Center for the Performing Arts, Brookville, NY. To sponsor Swing for Kids, annual gala, and performance.

$43,000 to Community Development Corporation of Long Island, Centereach, NY. For Home Maintenance Training in Nassau and Suffolk.

$35,000 to Saint Johns Episcopal Hospital-South Shore, Far Rockaway, NY. To purchase Endoscopy equipment.

$30,000 to North Shore-Long Island Jewish Health System Foundation, Great Neck, NY. For capital campaign.

$30,000 to Ronald McDonald House of Long Island, New Hyde Park, NY.

$25,000 to Asian Americans for Equality, New York, NY. For Working Immigrants Saving for a Home Program.

$15,000 to Friends of the Arts, Locust Valley, NY. For Arts in Education Program.

6860

Leo Rosner Foundation, Inc.

6 Westway
White Plains, NY 10605
Contact: William D. Robbins, Pres.

Established in 1960 in NY.
Foundation type: Independent foundation.
Financial data (yr. ended 10/31/05): Assets, $10,915,131 (M); expenditures, $608,807; qualifying distributions, $567,126; giving activities include $491,000 for 36 grants (high: $30,000; low: $2,000).
Purpose and activities: Giving for Jewish organizations and human services; funding also for museums, education and hospitals.
Fields of interest: Museums (specialized); Arts; Higher education; Education; Hospitals (general); Housing/shelter; Human services; Community development; Jewish federated giving programs; Jewish agencies & temples.
Type of support: Scholarship funds; Program development; Conferences/seminars.
Limitations: Giving primarily in New York, NY.
Application information: Application form not required.
Initial approach: Sept. 30
Deadline(s): None
Board meeting date(s): Mid-Oct.
Officers and Directors:* William D. Robbins,* Pres.; Mildred R. Caplow,* V.P.; June Rosner,* V.P.; Marcy Wachtel,* V.P.; Amy H. Caplow Chan,* Secy.-Treas.
Number of staff: 1 part-time professional.
EIN: 136161637

6861

Ross Family Charitable Foundation ✧
c/o Starr & Co., LLC
350 Park Ave., Ste. 9
New York, NY 10022-6022 (212) 759-6556
Application address: 15 Railroad Ave., Ste.1, East
Hampton, NY 11937, tel.: (631) 324-0790

Established in 1989 in NY.
Donor: Steven J. Ross†.
Foundation type: Independent foundation.
Financial data (yr. ended 11/30/04): Assets,
$2,373,999 (M); expenditures, $1,402,637;
qualifying distributions, $1,222,776; giving
activities include $1,222,681 for 8 grants (high:
$832,000; low: $10,000).
Purpose and activities: Giving primarily to
education, the arts, and health and human services.
Fields of interest: Arts; Education; Health care;
Human services.
Limitations: Applications not accepted. Giving
primarily in the greater metropolitan New York, NY,
area, including Long Island. No grants to individuals.
Application information: Contributes only to
pre-selected organizations.
Trustees: Bertram Fields; Elizabeth McCormack;
Courtney S. Ross; Kenneth I. Starr.
EIN: 133552082

6862

Ross Family Fund ✧
(formerly Lynn & George M. Ross Foundation)
c/o BCRS Assocs., LLC
100 Wall St., 11th Fl.
New York, NY 10005

Established in 1977.
Donors: George M. Ross; Merry Ross; Patrick
Zimski.
Foundation type: Independent foundation.
Financial data (yr. ended 2/28/05): Assets,
$12,204,104 (M); gifts received, $10,000;
expenditures, $1,077,099; qualifying distributions,
$981,828; giving activities include $981,758 for
187 grants (high: $250,000; low: $25).
Purpose and activities: Giving primarily for arts and
culture, education, and to Jewish organizations;
funding also for health associations, federated
giving programs, and children, youth, and social
services.
Fields of interest: Museums (art); Performing arts;
Arts; Vocational education; Higher education;
Education; Health organizations, association;
Human services; Children/youth, services;
Federated giving programs; Jewish federated giving
programs; Jewish agencies & temples.
Limitations: Applications not accepted. Giving
primarily in Philadelphia, PA; some funding
nationally, particularly in Oakland and San
Francisco, CA, Palm Beach and West Palm Beach,
FL, and New York, NY. No grants to individuals.
Application information: Contributes only to
pre-selected organizations.
Officers: George M. Ross, Pres. and Treas.; Lyn M.
Ross, Secy.
EIN: 232049592
Selected grants: The following grants were reported
in 2005.
$278,960 to National Museum of American Jewish
History, Philadelphia, PA. 3 grants: $250,000,
$25,000, $3,960
$150,200 to Drexel University, Philadelphia, PA. 3
grants: $10,000, $130,200, $10,000

$50,000 to Philadelphia Orchestra Association,
Philadelphia, PA.
$25,000 to Norton Museum of Art, West Palm
Beach, FL.
$5,000 to Park Day School, Oakland, CA.
$950 to Gesu School, Philadelphia, PA.

6863

The Dorothea Haus Ross Foundation
1036 Monroe Ave.
Rochester, NY 14620 (585) 473-6006
Contact: Wayne S. Cook, Fdn. Exec.
FAX: (585) 473-6007;
E-mail: rossfoundation@frontiernet.net;
URL: http://www.dhrossfoundation.org

Established in 1979 in NY.
Donor: Dorothea Haus Ross†.
Foundation type: Independent foundation.
Financial data (yr. ended 12/31/05): Assets,
$17,144,427 (M); expenditures, $936,758;
qualifying distributions, $734,338; giving activities
include $499,056 for 32 grants (high: $62,500;
low: $2,429).
Purpose and activities: To advance the moral,
mental, and physical well-being of children of all
races and creeds in all parts of the world; to aid and
assist in providing for the basic needs of food,
shelter, and education of such children by whatever
means and methods necessary or advisable; to
prevent by medical research or otherwise the mental
and physical handicaps of children. Funding also for
the research of pediatric diseases.
Fields of interest: Child development, education;
Medical care, rehabilitation; Health care; Health
organizations, association; Pediatrics; Medical
research, institute; Pediatrics research; Children/
youth, services; Child development, services; Native
Americans/American Indians; Economically
disadvantaged.
Type of support: Income development; Building/
renovation; Equipment; Land acquisition;
Emergency funds; Program development;
Publication; Seed money; Scholarship funds;
Research; Technical assistance; Matching/
challenge support.
Limitations: Giving on a national and international
basis. No support for day care or public education in
America. No grants to individuals, or for operating
budgets, continuing support, annual campaigns,
deficit financing, conferences, or fellowships; no
loans.
Publications: Application guidelines; Grants list.
Application information: 1 copy only of appendix
material. Application guidelines available on
foundation Web site. Application form not required.
Initial approach: Telephone call prior to sending
proposal strongly encouraged
Copies of proposal: 5
Deadline(s): None
Board meeting date(s): May, Aug., Nov., and Feb.
Final notification: 2 to 6 months
Officer and Trustees: Wayne S. Cook, Ph.D.*, Fdn.
Exec.; Charles C. Chamberlain; Kathryn C.
Chamberlain; Edward C. Radin; Bank of America,
N.A.
Number of staff: 1 full-time professional; 1 part-time
support.
EIN: 161080458

6864

Arthur Ross Foundation, Inc. ✧
c/o Anchin Block & Anchin, LLP
1375 Broadway
New York, NY 10018 (212) 737-7311
Contact: Arthur Ross, Pres.

Incorporated in 1955 in NY.
Donor: Arthur Ross.
Foundation type: Independent foundation.
Financial data (yr. ended 12/31/04): Assets,
$14,651,839 (M); gifts received, $4,812,436;
expenditures, $4,249,303; qualifying distributions,
$4,059,145; giving activities include $3,988,307
for 74+ grants (high: $1,000,000).
Purpose and activities: Giving for higher education
and cultural institutions, especially museums and
parks; support also for environmental organizations
and historic preservation.
Fields of interest: Museums; Historic preservation/
historical societies; Arts; Higher education; Medical
school/education; Environment; International
affairs; Aging; Disabilities, people with; Homeless.
Type of support: Continuing support; Capital
campaigns; Endowments; Conferences/seminars;
Scholarship funds; Matching/challenge support.
Limitations: Applications not accepted. Giving
primarily in NY.
Application information: Unsolicited requests for
funds not accepted.
Officers and Directors: Arthur Ross,* Pres. and
Treas.; Janet C. Ross,* Exec. V.P.; George J.
Gillespie III,* Secy.; Gail Lloyd, Exec. Dir.; William T.
Golden; Hon. William J. vanden Heuvel; Edgar
Wachenheim III.
Number of staff: 2
EIN: 136121436
Selected grants: The following grants were reported
in 2005.
$1,700,000 to Mount Sinai Medical Center, New
York, NY.
$1,202,210 to Asia Society, New York, NY.
$1,130,000 to American Academy in Rome, New
York, NY.
$1,000,915 to University of Pennsylvania,
Philadelphia, PA.
$1,000,500 to New York Botanical Garden, Bronx,
NY.
$100,000 to Horace Mann School, Riverdale, NY.
$75,000 to Mount Sinai Hospital, New York, NY.
$50,000 to Lincoln Center Theater, New York, NY.
$30,000 to Peconic Land Trust, Southampton, NY.
$25,000 to World Federation of United Nations
Associations, Friends of, New York, NY.

6865

**The Jon & Susan Rotenstreich Foundation,
Inc.** ✧
770 Park Ave.
New York, NY 10021

Established in 1975.
Donors: Jon W. Rotenstreich; Glenda Susan
Rotenstreich.
Foundation type: Independent foundation.
Financial data (yr. ended 6/30/05): Assets,
$590,250 (M); gifts received, $500,000;
expenditures, $548,146; qualifying distributions,
$544,210; giving activities include $544,110 for
120 grants (high: $20,000; low: $100).
Purpose and activities: Giving primarily for the arts
and education.

Fields of interest: Museums; Performing arts, opera; Arts; Education; Human services.
Limitations: Applications not accepted. Giving primarily in NY. No grants to individuals.
Application information: Contributes only to pre-selected organizations.
Officers and Directors:* Jon W. Rotenstreich,* Pres.; Glenda Susan Rotenstreich,* Treas.; James I. Rotenstreich.
EIN: 510180076

6866
The Judith Rothschild Foundation ✧
1110 Park Ave.
New York, NY 10128 (212) 831-4114
Contact: Elizabeth Slater, V.P., Grant Prog.
FAX: (212) 831-6222; E-mail: slatereliz@aol.com;
URL: http://www.judithrothschildfdn.org

Established in 1993 in NY.
Donor: Judith Rothschild‡.
Foundation type: Operating foundation.
Financial data (yr. ended 12/31/05): Assets, $27,524,343 (M); gifts received, $74,283; expenditures, $63,235,967; qualifying distributions, $63,082,297; giving activities include $60,855,837 for grants, and $8,108,000 for foundation-administered programs.
Purpose and activities: The unique mission of the grant program focuses on encouraging interest in recently deceased American painters, sculptors, and photographers whose work is of the highest quality but lacks adequate recognition. The grant program is dedicated to ensuring that the work of under-recognized, deceased artists has meaningful opportunities for public viewing and critical reassessment. The foundation also has responsibility for the stewardship of Judith Rothschild's own work and a collection of European masterworks.
Fields of interest: Visual arts, photography; Visual arts, sculpture; Visual arts, painting; Museums (art).
Type of support: Research; Grants to individuals.
Limitations: Giving on a national and international basis. No support for multi-media, performance, or conceptual art. No grants for general operating support, capital projects, endowment funds, scholarships, or travel unrelated to art activities under juried grant program.
Publications: Application guidelines; Grants list.
Application information: Request grant program guidelines. Application form required.
  Initial approach: 2- to 3-page letter; do not fax
  Copies of proposal: 1
  Deadline(s): Applications accepted between Apr. 15 and Sept. 15
  Final notification: Apr. 1
Officer: Elizabeth Simonson Slater, V.P., Grant Prog.
Trustee: Harvey S. Shipley Miller.
Number of staff: 1 full-time professional; 2 part-time professional; 2 part-time support.
EIN: 133736320

6867
The Roxe Foundation ✧ ☆
c/o Bessemer Trust
630 5th Ave.
New York, NY 10111

Established in 1997 in CT.
Donors: Joseph D. Roxe; Maureen L. Roxe.

Foundation type: Independent foundation.
Financial data (yr. ended 12/31/05): Assets, $5,323,340 (M); expenditures, $573,865; qualifying distributions, $548,441; giving activities include $437,235 for 75 grants (high: $100,000; low: $500).
Purpose and activities: Giving to support education, the performing arts, health care, and medical research.
Fields of interest: Performing arts, orchestra (symphony); Arts; Secondary school/education; Higher education; Medical school/education; Education; Cancer; Medical research, institute; Christian agencies & churches; Religion.
Limitations: Giving primarily in CT and NY. No grants to individuals.
Application information: Contributes only to pre-selected organizations.
Officers and Trustees:* Joseph D. Roxe,* Chair.; Maryann B. Tolan,* V.P.
Number of staff: 1 part-time support.
EIN: 061480884
Selected grants: The following grants were reported in 2004.
  $25,000 to New York Medical College, Valhalla, NY. For general support.
  $10,000 to Harvard University, John F. Kennedy School of Government, Cambridge, MA. For general support.
  $10,000 to Washington Opera, DC. For general support.
  $10,000 to Woods Hole Oceanographic Institution, Woods Hole, MA. For general support.
  $5,000 to Museum of Fine Arts, Boston, MA. For general support.
  $3,000 to Saint Jude Childrens Research Hospital, Memphis, TN. For general support.
  $2,500 to Princeton University, Princeton, NJ. For general support.
  $1,500 to Cardinal Shehan Center, Bridgeport, CT. For general support.
  $1,500 to Colgate University, Hamilton, NY. For general support.
  $1,070 to Metropolitan Museum of Art, New York, NY. For general support.

6868
Lawrence Ruben Foundation ✧
(formerly The Selma and Lawrence Ruben Foundation)
c/o Lawrence Ruben Co.
600 Madison Ave., 21st Fl.
New York, NY 10022

Established in 1982 in NY.
Donors: Lawrence Ruben; Selma Ruben.
Foundation type: Independent foundation.
Financial data (yr. ended 12/31/05): Assets, $6,100,226 (M); gifts received, $100,000; expenditures, $652,754; qualifying distributions, $595,900; giving activities include $595,900 for grants.
Fields of interest: Higher education; Hospitals (general); Cancer research; Jewish federated giving programs; Jewish agencies & temples.
Limitations: Applications not accepted. Giving primarily in New York, NY. No grants to individuals.
Application information: Contributes only to pre-selected organizations.
Directors: Rochelle Kivell; Lawrence Ruben; Lenore Ruben; Richard Ruben.
EIN: 133124700

Selected grants: The following grants were reported in 2003.
  $225,000 to Jewish Communal Fund of New York, New York, NY. For general support.
  $7,500 to American Friends of the Israel Museum, New York, NY. For general support.
  $7,000 to Parkinsons Disease Foundation, New York, NY. For general support.
  $5,000 to Breast Cancer Research Foundation, New York, NY. For general support.
  $1,500 to America-Israel Cultural Foundation, New York, NY. For general support.
  $1,000 to Alzheimers Association, New York, NY. For general support.
  $1,000 to Foundation for the Prevention and Treatment of Eye Disease, New York, NY. For general support.

6869
The Selma Ruben Foundation ✧
c/o Lawrence Ruben Co.
600 Madison Ave., 21st Fl.
New York, NY 10022-1615

Established in 1997 in NY.
Donor: Selma Ruben.
Foundation type: Independent foundation.
Financial data (yr. ended 12/31/05): Assets, $6,976,124 (M); expenditures, $485,328; qualifying distributions, $383,333; giving activities include $383,333 for grants.
Fields of interest: Higher education; Jewish federated giving programs.
Limitations: Applications not accepted. Giving primarily in NY. No grants to individuals.
Application information: Contributes only to pre-selected organizations.
Trustees: Rochelle Kivell; Lenore Ruben; Richard Ruben.
EIN: 137113807

6870
The Marilyn and Barry Rubenstein Family Foundation ✧
68 Wheatley Rd.
Glen Head, NY 11545

Established in 1992 in NY.
Donors: Barry Rubenstein; Marilyn Rubenstein.
Foundation type: Independent foundation.
Financial data (yr. ended 6/30/05): Assets, $2,014,139 (M); expenditures, $624,874; qualifying distributions, $617,318; giving activities include $617,318 for 78 grants (high: $500,000; low: $18; average: $10–$50,000).
Purpose and activities: Giving primarily to Jewish affiliated institutions and for health care.
Fields of interest: Museums (ethnic/folk arts); Elementary/secondary education; Hospitals (general); Health organizations, association; Medical research, institute; Children/youth, services; Jewish federated giving programs; Jewish agencies & temples.
Type of support: Continuing support; Annual campaigns; Capital campaigns; Building/renovation.
Limitations: Applications not accepted. Giving primarily in NY. No grants to individuals.
Application information: Contributes only to pre-selected organizations.

Trustees: Barry Rubenstein; Brian Rubenstein; Marilyn Rubenstein; Rebecca Rubenstein.
EIN: 116417671
Selected grants: The following grants were reported in 2004.
$500,000 to American Society for Yad Vashem, New York, NY.
$78,500 to Sid Jacobson Jewish Community Center, East Hills, NY. 2 grants: $72,000, $6,500
$5,600 to Folksbiene Yiddish Theater, New York, NY.
$2,500 to North Shore-Long Island Jewish Health System, Westbury, NY. 2 grants: $1,000, $1,500
$2,000 to Jewish Womens Foundation of New York, New York, NY.
$1,800 to UJA-Federation of New York, New York, NY.
$1,000 to Jewish Museum, New York, NY.
$1,000 to Queens College of the City University of New York Foundation, Flushing, NY.

6871
The Rubin Family Foundation, Inc. ✧
1441 59th St.
Brooklyn, NY   11219

Established in 1991 in NY.
Donors: Liebul Rubin; Abraham Klein; Solomon Rubin; Long Beach Grandell Co., Inc.; Oceanside Care Center Inc., Inc.; Park Terrace Care Center; Beach Terrace Care Center; Queens Nassau Nursing Home.
Foundation type: Independent foundation.
Financial data (yr. ended 12/31/04): Assets, $22,172,926 (M); gifts received, $1,516,500; expenditures, $879,574; qualifying distributions, $865,007; giving activities include $856,933 for 48 + grants (high: $172,000).
Fields of interest: Jewish agencies & temples.
Limitations: Applications not accepted. Giving primarily in Brooklyn, NY.
Application information: Contributes only to pre-selected organizations.
Officers: Liebel Rubin, Pres.; Dorothy Rubin, V.P.; Eugene Rubin, Secy.; Dina Rubin, Treas.
EIN: 113047773
Selected grants: The following grants were reported in 2003.
$125,000 to Kollel Zichron Mordechai.
$102,000 to Bobover Yeshiva Bnei Zion, Brooklyn, NY.
$18,000 to Yeshiva Beis Meir, Brooklyn, NY.
$13,000 to Od Yosef Chai, Brooklyn, NY.
$12,533 to Yeshiva Kedushat Zion, Brooklyn, NY.
$2,700 to Talmud Torah Imrei Chaim Dvishnitz, Brooklyn, NY.
$1,800 to Tzedakah Vchesed, Brooklyn, NY.
$500 to Congregation Ohr Hachaim, Kew Gardens, NY.
$500 to Tomchei Shabbos of Boro Park and Flatbush, Brooklyn, NY.
$360 to Chai Lifeline, New York, NY.

6872
Samuel Rubin Foundation, Inc.
777 United Nations Plz.
New York, NY   10017-3521   (212) 697-8945
Contact: Lauranne Jones, Grants Admin.

FAX: (212) 682-0886;
E-mail: info@samuelrubinfoundation.org;
URL: http://www.samuelrubinfoundation.org

Established in 1958 in NY.
Donor: Samuel Rubin Foundation, Inc.
Foundation type: Independent foundation.
Financial data (yr. ended 6/30/05): Assets, $12,685,283 (M); expenditures, $1,116,339; qualifying distributions, $965,465; giving activities include $780,695 for 73+ grants (high: $150,000).
Purpose and activities: Grants for the pursuit of peace and justice; for an equitable reallocation of the world's resources; and to promote social, economic, political, civil, and cultural rights.
Fields of interest: Higher education; International peace/security; International affairs, arms control; International affairs, foreign policy; International human rights; Civil rights; Women.
Type of support: Film/video/radio; General/operating support; Seed money.
Limitations: Giving on a national and international basis. No grants to individuals, or for endowments, scholarships, or building funds.
Publications: Grants list; Program policy statement.
Application information: The foundation accepts the National Network of Grantmakers Common Grant Application Form. Applications sent by e-mail or fax will not be accepted, nor will telephone solicitations. Application form not required.
  Initial approach: Proposal (not to exceed 5 pages)
  Copies of proposal: 1
  Deadline(s): First Fri. in Jan., May, and Sept.
  Board meeting date(s): 3 times per year; generally at the end of Feb., June, and Oct.
  Final notification: 2 weeks following board meetings
Officers: Cora Weiss, Pres.; Daniel Weiss, V.P.; Judy Weiss, V.P.; Tamara Weiss, V.P.; Charles L. Mandelstam, Secy.; Peter Weiss, Treas.
Number of staff: 2 full-time professional.
EIN: 136164671
Selected grants: The following grants were reported in 2005.
$150,000 to Transnational Institute, Amsterdam, Netherlands. .
$100,000 to Hague Appeal for Peace, New York, NY.
$35,000 to Center for Constitutional Rights, New York, NY.
$35,000 to Downtown Community Television Center, New York, NY.
$5,000 to Abortion Access Project, Cambridge, MA.
$5,000 to Jane Addams Peace Association, New York, NY.
$5,000 to Promises Film Company, Berkeley, CA.

6873
The Shelley & Donald Rubin Foundation, Inc. ✧
115 5th Ave., 7th Fl.
New York, NY   10003   (212) 780-2035
Contact: Evelyn Jones Rich, Exec. Dir.
FAX: (212) 780-0410;
E-mail: eejrich54@sdrubin.org; *URL:* http://www.sdrubin.org

Established in 1991 in NY.
Donors: Donald Rubin; Shelley Rubin.
Foundation type: Independent foundation.
Financial data (yr. ended 6/30/05): Assets, $9,518,684 (M); gifts received, $6,000,000; expenditures, $769,762; qualifying distributions,

$747,661; giving activities include $628,167 for 77 grants (high: $50,000; low: $250).
Purpose and activities: Major interest is Himalayan art; funding also for health care, AIDS and its effects on society's institutions, at-risk children and families, and the celebration of ethnic and cultural diversity. Please refer to foundation Web site for further information.
Fields of interest: Arts, cultural/ethnic awareness.
Limitations: Giving limited to the U.S. and PR, with emphasis on New York, NY. No grants to individuals, or for fundraising activities, capital funds, direct services, operating support, scholarships, fellowships, building funds, endowment funds, or for the delivery of direct services.
Publications: Application guidelines; Grants list.
Application information: The range of funding is between $5,000-$10,000 maximum. Application form not required.
  Initial approach: Letter of intent (letters sent via e-mail will not be accepted)
  Copies of proposal: 1
  Deadline(s): None
  Board meeting date(s): As needed
  Final notification: Within 90 days
Officers and Directors:* Donald Rubin,* Pres.; Shelley Rubin,* Secy.; Evelyn Jones Rich, Exec. Dir.; Harvey Sigelbaum.
Number of staff: 1 part-time professional.
EIN: 133639542

6874
The Nancy & Miles Rubin Foundation ✧
(formerly The Jacob & Mae D. Rubin Foundation)
c/o Graf Repetti & Co. LLP
1114 6th Ave
New York, NY   10036

Established in 1961 in CT.
Donors: Miles Rubin; Andrew Rosen.
Foundation type: Independent foundation.
Financial data (yr. ended 10/31/05): Assets, $304,285 (M); expenditures, $488,046; qualifying distributions, $486,120; giving activities include $482,370 for 78+ grants (high: $62,800).
Fields of interest: Performing arts centers; Arts; Higher education; Health care; Human services; International affairs; Civil rights; Jewish agencies & temples.
Limitations: Applications not accepted. Giving on a national basis. No grants to individuals.
Application information: Contributes only to pre-selected organizations.
Trustees: Miles Rubin; Nancy Rubin.
EIN: 136092976
Selected grants: The following grants were reported in 2003.
$70,500 to John F. Kennedy Center for the Performing Arts, DC.
$30,000 to Dakota Wesleyan University, Mitchell, SD.
$25,250 to Didi Hirsch Community Mental Health Center, Culver City, CA.
$17,500 to Temple Sinai.
$15,000 to Adopt-a-Minefield, New York, NY.
$15,000 to Harvard University, Cambridge, MA.
$12,500 to National Mental Health Awareness Campaign, DC.
$12,500 to Salzburg Seminar, Middlebury, VT.
$10,275 to Aspen Institute, DC.
$10,000 to Brady Center to Prevent Gun Violence, DC.

6875
The Rubin-Henry Family Foundation ✧
c/o Howard Rubin
120 East End Ave., Apt. 2
New York, NY 10028-7552

Established in 2000 in NY.
Donors: Mary Henry; Howard Rubin.
Foundation type: Independent foundation.
Financial data (yr. ended 8/31/05): Assets, $903,362 (M); expenditures, $634,200; qualifying distributions, $631,088; giving activities include $631,088 for 87 grants (high: $100,000; low: $25).
Fields of interest: Human services; Children/youth, services.
Limitations: Applications not accepted. No grants to individuals.
Application information: Contributes only to pre-selected organizations.
Trustees: Mary Henry; Howard Rubin.
EIN: 137255537

6876
Helena Rubinstein Foundation, Inc.
477 Madison Ave., 7th Fl.
New York, NY 10022-5802 (212) 750-7310
Contact: Diane Moss, C.E.O. and Pres.
URL: http://www.helenarubinsteinfdn.org

Incorporated in 1953 in NY.
Donor: Helena Rubinstein Gourielli‡.
Foundation type: Independent foundation.
Financial data (yr. ended 5/31/05): Assets, $32,352,176 (M); expenditures, $3,106,436; qualifying distributions, $2,640,280; giving activities include $2,107,374 for 143 grants (high: $150,000; low: $190).
Purpose and activities: Focus on projects that benefit women and children. Funding primarily for education, community services, health, the arts and arts in education.
Fields of interest: Arts education; Arts; Vocational education; Higher education; Education; Health care; Human services; Children/youth, services; Women; Economically disadvantaged.
Type of support: General/operating support; Continuing support; Endowments; Program development; Seed money; Fellowships; Internship funds; Scholarship funds.
Limitations: Giving primarily in New York, NY. No grants to individuals, or for emergency funds or film or video projects; no loans.
Publications: Application guidelines; Grants list.
Application information: Accepts NYRAG Common Grant Application Form. Application form not required.
Initial approach: Letter
Copies of proposal: 1
Deadline(s): None
Board meeting date(s): May and Nov.
Final notification: 1 to 6 months
Officers and Directors:* Gertrude G. Michelson,* Chair.; Diane Moss,* C.E.O. and Pres.; Robert Moss,* V.P.; Louis E. Slesin,* Secy.-Treas.; Laurie Shapley, Exec. Dir.; Robin F. Grossman; Suzanne Slesin; Deborah A. Zoullas.
Number of staff: 4 full-time professional; 1 full-time support.
EIN: 136102666
Selected grants: The following grants were reported in 2005.

$150,000 to W N E T Channel 13, New York, NY. To sponsor children's educational television programming.
$35,000 to Goddard-Riverside Community Center, New York, NY. For college-counseling program to help low-income minority youth gain access to college and professional development workshops to help staff at other agencies replicate programs.
$35,000 to Womens Housing and Economic Development Corporation, Urban Horizons Economic Development Center, Bronx, NY. For job training and support services for family day care providers.
$25,000 to Careers Through Culinary Arts Program, New York, NY. For general support of organization that prepares New York City public high school students for careers in food service industry, and scholarships for program graduates.
$25,000 to Lincoln Center Institute, New York, NY. For aesthetic literacy programs for students and teachers.
$25,000 to Montefiore Medical Center, Childrens Hospital, Bronx, NY. For after-school program that trains high school and college students to provide technical assistance to patients using bedside computer workstations.
$18,000 to Hunter College of the City University of New York, New York, NY. For stipend support for internships at government agencies and nonprofit organizations that introduce undergraduate women to careers in public service.
$15,000 to Cooper Union for the Advancement of Science and Art, New York, NY. For studio art instruction for disadvantaged high school students.
$15,000 to Figure Skating in Harlem, New York, NY. For general support of organization that provides after-school sports and tutoring program for girls.
$15,000 to Groundwork, Brooklyn, NY. For general support of orgagnization that provides educational enrichment, community service, and recreational activities for children in East New York section of Brooklyn.

6877
May and Samuel Rudin Family Foundation, Inc. ▼ ✧
c/o Rudin
345 Park Ave.
New York, NY 10154 (212) 407-2400
Contact: Mark L. Bodden, Admin. and Prog. Dir.

Established in 1996 in NY.
Foundation type: Independent foundation.
Financial data (yr. ended 12/31/05): Assets, $470,603 (M); gifts received, $5,200,000; expenditures, $5,158,394; qualifying distributions, $5,158,394; giving activities include $4,698,732 for 215 grants (high: $650,000; low: $550; average: $5,000–$100,000).
Purpose and activities: Grants are mainly to charitable organizations, museums, and educational institutions in New York City.
Fields of interest: Museums; Education.
Type of support: General/operating support.
Limitations: Giving primarily in New York City.
Application information: Application form not required.
Initial approach: Letter
Deadline(s): None

Officers and Directors:* Jack Rudin,* Chair.; Beth Rudin DeWoody,* Pres.; Eric C. Rudin,* V.P. and Secy.-Treas.; James Carlton DeWoody III,* V.P.; Kyle Hardin DeWoody,* V.P.; Madeleine Rudin Johnson,* V.P.; David B. Levy,* V.P.; Katherine L. Rudin,* V.P.; Samantha Mia Rudin,* V.P.; William C. Rudin,* V.P.; Mark P.H. Rudin.
EIN: 133875171
Selected grants: The following grants were reported in 2004.
$207,000 to City University of New York, New York, NY. For general support.
$155,410 to Whitney Museum of American Art, New York, NY. For general support.
$104,650 to New York University, New York, NY. For general support.
$100,000 to Columbia University, College of Physicians and Surgeons, New York, NY. For general support.
$94,200 to Metropolitan Museum of Art, New York, NY. For general support.
$78,520 to New York City Police Museum, New York, NY. For general support.
$73,750 to George C. Marshall Research Foundation, Lexington, VA. For general support.
$65,000 to Iona College, New Rochelle, NY. For general support.
$54,950 to Brooklyn Academy of Music, Brooklyn, NY. For general support.
$53,750 to Drawing Center, New York, NY. For general support.

6878
The Louis and Rachel Rudin Foundation, Inc. ✧
c/o Rudin
345 Park Ave.
New York, NY 10154 (212) 407-2400
Contact: Mark L. Bodden, Admin. & Program Dir.

Incorporated in 1968 in NY.
Foundation type: Independent foundation.
Financial data (yr. ended 12/31/05): Assets, $65,359,764 (M); expenditures, $3,303,813; qualifying distributions, $2,388,619; giving activities include $2,245,000 for 52 grants (high: $210,000; low: $10,000).
Purpose and activities: Grants to medical and nursing schools only for educational training programs.
Fields of interest: Medical school/education; Nursing school/education.
Type of support: Scholarship funds.
Limitations: Giving primarily in New York, NY. No grants to individuals, or for building funds.
Application information:
Initial approach: Letter
Officers and Directors:* Jack Rudin,* Chair.; Beth Rudin DeWoody,* Pres.; Stephen Lewin,* Exec. V.P.; Madeleine Rubin Johnson,* V.P.; John Lewin,* V.P.; Katherine L. Rudin,* V.P.; William C. Rudin,* V.P.; Peter D. Steinman,* V.P.; Eric C. Rudin,* Secy.; Jeffrey Steinman,* Treas.
EIN: 237039549
Selected grants: The following grants were reported in 2004.
$50,000 to Phillips Beth Israel School of Nursing, New York, NY.
$40,000 to New York Medical College, Valhalla, NY. 2 grants: $10,000, $30,000
$25,000 to Rockefeller University, New York, NY.
$20,000 to Rogosin Institute, New York, NY.

6879
The Rudin Foundation, Inc. ✧
c/o Rudin
345 Park Ave.
New York, NY 10154 (212) 407-2400
Contact: Mark L. Bodden, Admin. & Prog. Dir.

Incorporated in 1960 in NY.
Donors: Clarkton Estates, Inc.; Corliss Estates, Inc.; Graceton Estates, Inc.; Marshall Estates, Inc.; Rudin Estates Co., LP; Taylor Estates, Inc.; 136 East 55th Street, Inc.; 144 West Corp.; 415 Madison, Inc.
Foundation type: Independent foundation.
Financial data (yr. ended 12/31/05): Assets, $126,455 (M); gifts received, $1,055,600; expenditures, $963,900; qualifying distributions, $963,900; giving activities include $848,035 for 104 grants (high: $100,000; low: $400).
Purpose and activities: Giving to the arts, education, health and human services, and to Jewish and Roman Catholic organizations.
Fields of interest: Arts, alliance; Arts; Higher education; Hospitals (general); Human services; Community development; Jewish federated giving programs; Roman Catholic agencies & churches.
Limitations: Giving primarily in New York, NY. No grants to individuals.
Application information:
Initial approach: Letter
Deadline(s): None
Officers and Directors:* Jack Rudin,* Chair.; Beth Rudin DeWoody,* Pres.; Jeffrey Steinman,* Exec. V.P.; Madeleine Rudin Johnson,* V.P.; John Lewin,* V.P.; Stephen Lewin,* V.P.; Eric C. Rudin,* V.P.; William C. Rudin,* V.P.; Gregory Sills,* V.P.; John L. Sills,* V.P.; Robert Steinman,* V.P.; Richard C. Snider,* Secy.; David B. Levy,* Treas.
EIN: 136113064

6880
Peter B. & Adeline W. Ruffin Foundation, Inc.
240 Madison Ave., Ste. 704
New York, NY 10016
Contact: Edward G. McAnaney, Pres.

Established in 1964 in NY.
Foundation type: Independent foundation.
Financial data (yr. ended 11/30/05): Assets, $30,723,545 (M); gifts received, $874,948; expenditures, $1,955,742; qualifying distributions, $1,749,750; giving activities include $1,740,000 for 48 grants (high: $700,000; low: $1,000).
Purpose and activities: Support for minority scholarship funds.
Fields of interest: Secondary school/education; Higher education; Education; Human services; Minorities.
Type of support: General/operating support; Capital campaigns; Endowments; Professorships; Scholarship funds.
Limitations: Applications not accepted. Giving primarily in CT, Washington, DC, NJ, NY, PA, and VA. No grants to individuals.
Application information: Contributes only to pre-selected organizations.
Officers and Trustees:* Edward G. McAnaney,* Pres., Treas., and Mgr.; Brian T. McAnaney, Secy.; Sheila K. Kostanecki; Kevin G. McAnaney.
Number of staff: 1 part-time professional.
EIN: 136170484

Selected grants: The following grants were reported in 2005.
$700,000 to University of Virginia, Charlottesville, VA.
$100,000 to Fordham Preparatory School, Bronx, NY.
$100,000 to University of North Carolina, Chapel Hill, NC.
$100,000 to University of Notre Dame, Notre Dame, IN.
$80,000 to Inner-City Scholarship Fund, New York, NY.
$75,000 to Salvation Army, Yonkers, NY. 2 grants: $50,000, $25,000
$25,000 to Catching the Dream, Albuquerque, NM.
$25,000 to New York Times Neediest Cases Fund, New York, NY.
$10,000 to Covenant House, New York, NY.

6881
Rukal Foundation, Inc. ✧
c/o Renov
9 Beachwood Dr.
Lawrence, NY 11559

Established in 1993 in NY.
Donors: Kalman M. Renov; Joseph Davdowitz; Rosalind Davdowitz.
Foundation type: Independent foundation.
Financial data (yr. ended 11/30/04): Assets, $703,601 (M); gifts received, $202,745; expenditures, $365,213; qualifying distributions, $362,185; giving activities include $363,615 for 76 + grants (high: $55,300).
Purpose and activities: Giving primarily for Jewish agencies, temples, and federated giving programs.
Fields of interest: Education; Human services; Jewish federated giving programs; Jewish agencies & temples.
Limitations: Applications not accepted. Giving on a national basis.
Application information: Unsolicited requests for funds not accepted.
Officers and Directors:* Tova Katz,* Pres.; Nathan Renov,* Secy.
EIN: 113189193
Selected grants: The following grants were reported in 2004.
$14,350 to Congregation Shaaray Tefila, Lawrence, NY.
$12,000 to Knesseth Israel Congregation, Birmingham, AL.
$10,600 to Aish HaTorah.
$5,400 to Hebron Fund, Brooklyn, NY.
$5,000 to Congregation Bnei Moshe, Brooklyn, NY.
$1,800 to American Friends of Yad Aharon, New York, NY.
$1,500 to Jerusalem Fund, DC.
$1,000 to Hebrew Academy of West Queens, Richmond Hill, NY.
$1,000 to Yeshiva University, New York, NY.

6882
Mary A. H. Rumsey Foundation
c/o Brown Brothers Harriman Trust Co.
140 Broadway, 4th Fl.
New York, NY 10005
Contact: William F. Hibbard, Secy.

Established in 1984 in NY.
Donor: Mary A.H. Rumsey†.

Foundation type: Independent foundation.
Financial data (yr. ended 9/30/04): Assets, $8,324,359 (M); expenditures, $712,318; qualifying distributions, $633,736; giving activities include $621,700 for 15 grants (high: $60,000; low: $500).
Purpose and activities: Giving primarily for education, wildlife, and nature preservation, and the arts.
Fields of interest: Arts; Secondary school/ education; Higher education; Environment, natural resources; Animals/wildlife, preservation/ protection; Medical care, in-patient care; Health organizations, association; Human services; Children/youth, services; Christian agencies & churches.
Limitations: Applications not accepted. Giving primarily in the greater metropolitan New York, NY, area. No grants to individuals.
Application information: Contributes only to pre-selected organizations.
Officers and Directors:* Charles Cary Rumsey,* Pres.; Mary M. Rumsey,* V.P.; William F. Hibberd, Secy.; Anna T. Korniczky, Treas.; Edwin R. Ward; Douglas F. Williamson, Jr.
EIN: 133244314

6883
The Richard W. Rupp Foundation ✧
1806 Liberty Bldg.
Buffalo, NY 14202
Contact: William R. Rupp, Treas.

Established in 1998 in NY.
Donor: Richard W. Rupp.
Foundation type: Independent foundation.
Financial data (yr. ended 12/31/04): Assets, $11,980,332 (M); expenditures, $741,665; qualifying distributions, $573,043; giving activities include $536,399 for 70 grants (high: $50,000; low: $100).
Fields of interest: Human services.
Type of support: General/operating support.
Limitations: Applications not accepted. Giving primarily in Buffalo, NY. No grants to individuals.
Application information: Contributes only to pre-selected organizations.
Officers: Frances O. Rupp, Pres.; Christina D. Rupp, V.P.; Susan S. Rupp, Secy.; William R. Rupp, Treas.
Director: Chester E. Borczynski.
EIN: 161551594

6884
The Nina M. Ryan Foundation, Inc. ✧
Box 321
Cold Spring, NY 10516

Incorporated in 1947 in NY.
Foundation type: Independent foundation.
Financial data (yr. ended 12/31/05): Assets, $16,005,597 (M); expenditures, $713,945; qualifying distributions, $709,393; giving activities include $707,500 for 2 grants (high: $705,000; low: $2,500).
Purpose and activities: Giving primarily to a community trust.
Fields of interest: Health organizations, association; Foundations (community).
Limitations: Applications not accepted. Giving primarily in NY. No grants to individuals, or for scholarships; no loans.

Application information: Contributes only to pre-selected organizations.
Officers: Leroy M. Parker, Pres; Rosalie L. Parker, V.P. and Treas.; Katherine Parker, Secy.
EIN: 136111038
Selected grants: The following grants were reported in 2004.
$593,594 to New York Community Trust, New York, NY. For general support.

6885
RZH Foundation ◇

c/o Meridian Capital Group LLC
1 Battery Park Plz.
New York, NY   10004

Established in 1994 in NY.
Donor: Ralph Herzka.
Foundation type: Independent foundation.
Financial data (yr. ended 12/31/04): Assets, $6,240,791 (M); gifts received, $245,800; expenditures, $547,733; qualifying distributions, $510,678; giving activities include $508,634 for 31 + grants.
Fields of interest: Theological school/education; Jewish agencies & temples.
Limitations: Applications not accepted. Giving primarily in NY. No grants to individuals.
Application information: Contributes only to pre-selected organizations.
Trustees: Judy Herzka; Ralph Herzka.
EIN: 113242489

6886
S.O. Charitable Trust ◇

135 Ocean Pkwy., No. 1N
Brooklyn, NY   11218

Established in 2002 in NY.
Donor: Emunah Trust.
Foundation type: Independent foundation.
Financial data (yr. ended 5/31/05): Assets, $228,678 (M); expenditures, $493,001; qualifying distributions, $402,608; giving activities include $402,000 for 12 grants (high: $100,000; low: $10,000).
Fields of interest: Jewish federated giving programs; Jewish agencies & temples.
Limitations: Applications not accepted. No grants to individuals.
Application information: Contributes only to pre-selected organizations.
Trustee: Rebecca Offen.
EIN: 010617948

6887
The Peter M. Sacerdote Foundation ◇

c/o BCRS Group/Marcum & Kliegman, LLP
655 3rd. Ave., 16th Fl.
New York, NY   10017

Established in 1981 in NY.
Donors: Peter M. Sacerdote; P.M. Sacerdote Charitable Lead Trust.
Foundation type: Independent foundation.
Financial data (yr. ended 2/28/05): Assets, $23,323,561 (M); gifts received, $1,730,600; expenditures, $1,881,050; qualifying distributions, $1,868,125; giving activities include $1,867,375 for 31 grants (high: $905,540; low: $1,000).

Purpose and activities: Giving primarily for higher and other education, particularly medical schools as well as for cancer research, the arts, youth development, and environmental protection and conservation.
Fields of interest: Museums (art); Arts; Elementary/secondary education; Higher education; Medical school/education; Education; Environment; Hospitals (general); Cancer research; Youth development; Human services.
Limitations: Applications not accepted. Giving primarily in New York, NY; some funding also in Nantucket, MA. No grants to individuals.
Application information: Contributes only to pre-selected organizations.
Trustee: Peter M. Sacerdote.
EIN: 133102940
Selected grants: The following grants were reported in 2006.
$252,500 to Metropolitan Museum of Art, New York, NY. 2 grants: $2,500, $250,000
$241,000 to Nantucket Conservation Foundation, Nantucket, MA.
$15,000 to Greenwich Land Trust, Greenwich, CT.
$5,000 to Nantucket Land Council, Nantucket, MA.
$1,000 to Museum of the City of New York, New York, NY.
$1,000 to Nantucket Historical Association, Nantucket, MA.
$1,000 to Sconset Trust, Siasconset, MA.

6888
Sachs Family Foundation ◇ ☆

c/o Allison Sachs
454 Succabone Rd.
Bedford Corners, NY   10549

Established in 2004 in NY.
Donors: David Sachs; Allison Sachs.
Foundation type: Independent foundation.
Financial data (yr. ended 12/31/05): Assets, $264,621 (M); gifts received, $447,180; expenditures, $332,131; qualifying distributions, $331,920; giving activities include $331,920 for 29 grants (high: $225,000; low: $500).
Fields of interest: Education; Human services; Children/youth, services; Jewish federated giving programs.
Limitations: Applications not accepted.
Application information: Contributes only to pre-selected organizations.
Director: Allison Sachs; David Sachs.
EIN: 201966808

6889
The Else Sackler Charitable Foundation ◇

c/o Pillsbury Winthrop
1540 Broadway
New York, NY   10036

Established in 2000 in NY.
Donor: The Else Sackler Charitable Remainder Trust.
Foundation type: Independent foundation.
Financial data (yr. ended 12/31/05): Assets, $15,713,900 (M); expenditures, $6,145,640; qualifying distributions, $6,084,398; giving activities include $6,060,000 for 4 grants (high: $2,770,000; low: $40,000).
Purpose and activities: Giving primarily to Jewish federated giving programs.

Fields of interest: Foundations (private independent); Jewish federated giving programs.
Limitations: Applications not accepted. Giving primarily in New York, NY. No grants to individuals.
Application information: Contributes only to pre-selected organizations.
Officers: Elizabeth A. Sackler, Pres.; Carol Master, V.P. and Treas.; Susan P. Serota, Secy.
EIN: 133933972
Selected grants: The following grants were reported in 2003.
$1,485,800 to Elizabeth A. Sackler Foundation, New York, NY. For public charities and program support.
$550,000 to Arthur M.Sackler Foundation, New York, NY. For program support.
$70,000 to Else Sackler Foundation, New York, NY. For public charities.

6890
Mortimer D. Sackler Foundation, Inc. ◇

17 E. 62nd St.
New York, NY   10021-7204

Established in 1967 in NY.
Donor: Varns Investments, Ltd.
Foundation type: Independent foundation.
Financial data (yr. ended 12/31/04): Assets, $16,847,378 (M); expenditures, $1,374,950; qualifying distributions, $1,370,800; giving activities include $1,370,800 for 19 grants (high: $400,000; low: $300).
Fields of interest: Economics; Political science.
Type of support: General/operating support.
Limitations: Applications not accepted. Giving primarily in New York, NY. No grants to individuals.
Application information: Contributes only to pre-selected organizations.
Officers and Directors:* Mortimer D. Sackler,* Pres.; K.A. Sackler,* V.P. and Secy.; M.D.A. Sackler,* V.P. and Treas.; I. Lefcourt,* V.P.; S.S. Sackler,* V.P.; T.E. Sackler,* V.P.
EIN: 237022461
Selected grants: The following grants were reported in 2004.
$500,000 to Solomon R. Guggenheim Foundation, New York, NY. For general support.
$400,000 to American Fund for the Tate Gallery, New York, NY. For general support.
$130,000 to Georgetown University, DC. For general support.
$30,000 to Asia Society, New York, NY. For general support.
$25,000 to Tel Aviv University, Tel Aviv, Israel. For general support.
$10,000 to Greens Farms Academy, Greens Farms, CT. For general support.
$4,000 to Westport Country Playhouse, Westport, CT. For general support.
$1,500 to Save the Children Federation, Westport, CT. For general support.
$1,000 to Near and Far Aid Association, Southport, CT. For general support.
$1,000 to Temple Israel Westport, Westport, CT. For general support.

6891
The Elizabeth A. Sackler Foundation, Inc. ◇

461 E. 57th St.
New York, NY   10022

Established in 2001 in NY.
Donor: Elizabeth A. Sackler.
Foundation type: Independent foundation.
Financial data (yr. ended 12/31/05): Assets, $3,056 (M); gifts received, $2,816,433; expenditures, $2,827,285; qualifying distributions, $2,825,785; giving activities include $2,791,600 for 2 grants (high: $2,788,100; low: $3,500), and $34,185 for foundation-administered programs.
Fields of interest: Museums; Arts.
Type of support: General/operating support.
Limitations: Applications not accepted. Giving primarily in NY. No grants to individuals.
Application information: Contributes only to pre-selected organizations.
Directors: Janet Bajan; Janet McKay; Elizabeth A. Sackler.
EIN: 134180717

6892
Raymond & Beverly Sackler Fund for the Arts & Sciences ◇

c/o Chadbourne & Parke
30 Rockefeller Plz., Ste. 3218
New York, NY 10112-0129

Established in 2001 in DE.
Donors: Raymond R. Sackler, M.D.; Beverly Sackler; Richard S. Sackler, M.D.; Jonathan D. Sackler.
Foundation type: Independent foundation.
Financial data (yr. ended 12/31/04): Assets, $4,293,402 (M); expenditures, $709,922; qualifying distributions, $672,590; giving activities include $672,590 for 15 grants (high: $301,590; low: $1,500).
Purpose and activities: Giving primarily for the arts and for higher education.
Fields of interest: Museums (art); Performing arts, ballet; Performing arts, opera; Arts; Higher education; Education; Hospitals (general); Medical research, institute.
Limitations: Applications not accepted. Giving primarily in CT, MA, and NY. No grants to individuals.
Application information: Contributes only to pre-selected organizations.
Officers and Directors:* Beverly Sackler,* Chair. and Secy.-Treas.; Jonathan D. Sackler,* C.E.O. and Pres.; Raymond R. Sackler, M.D.*, V.P.; Richard S. Sackler, M.D.*, V.P.
EIN: 134085037
Selected grants: The following grants were reported in 2004.
$316,590 to Yale University, New Haven, CT. 2 grants: $15,000, $301,590
$50,000 to Harvard University, Cambridge, MA.
$26,500 to Research America, Alexandria, VA. 2 grants: $25,000, $1,500
$25,000 to New York City Ballet, New York, NY.

6893
Safra Foundation, Inc. ◇

546 5th Ave.
New York, NY 10036

Established in 2002 in NY.
Donor: Safra National Bank of New York.
Foundation type: Independent foundation.
Financial data (yr. ended 12/31/04): Assets, $16,076,190 (M); gifts received, $4,800,000; expenditures, $554,759; qualifying distributions,

$530,800; giving activities include $530,800 for 8 grants (high: $428,000; low: $1,800).
Purpose and activities: Giving primarily to Jewish organizations, federated giving programs and yeshivas.
Fields of interest: Education; Hospitals (general); Jewish federated giving programs; Jewish agencies & temples.
Limitations: Applications not accepted. Giving primarily in New York, NY. No grants to individuals.
Application information: Contributes only to pre-selected organizations.
Directors: Carlos Bertaco Bomfim; Luiz Antonio Bull; Jacob Safra; Joseph Yacoub Safra.
EIN: 061640434

6894
Russell Sage Foundation ◇

112 E. 64th St.
New York, NY 10021
Contact: Christopher Brogna, C.F.O.
FAX: (212) 371-4761; E-mail: info@rsage.org;
URL: http://www.russellsage.org

Incorporated in 1907 in NY.
Donor: Mrs. Russell Sage†.
Foundation type: Operating foundation.
Financial data (yr. ended 8/31/05): Assets, $262,786,860 (M); gifts received, $1,000; expenditures, $13,632,830; qualifying distributions, $12,032,132; giving activities include $4,872,502 for 75 grants (high: $434,845; low: $229; average: $1,700–$99,101), and $11,543,192 for 3 foundation-administered programs.
Purpose and activities: The foundation is a private operating foundation devoted exclusively to the conduct and dissemination of research in the social sciences. Its current programs include research on the causes and consequences of the decline in demand for low-skilled workers in advanced economies; the adaptation of U.S. immigrants and their children to American society; efforts by American institutions to accommodate greater racial and ethnic diversity; and a variety of smaller special projects and research initiatives. The foundation sponsors a Visiting Scholar Program in which individual scholars and collaborative groups pursue research and writing projects related to the foundation's interests at its headquarters in New York City for periods of up to one year. The foundation also provides support for scholars at other institutions to pursue research projects that advance the foundation's research interests. The foundation disseminates the resulting research findings through its own book publishing program.
Fields of interest: Social sciences.
Type of support: Program development; Conferences/seminars; Publication; Research; Employee matching gifts.
Limitations: Giving on a national basis. No grants for capital or endowment funds, independent ongoing activities of other institutions, scholarships, annual campaigns, emergency funds, deficit financing, operating budgets, or continuing support; no loans.
Publications: Application guidelines; Biennial report; Financial statement; Informational brochure (including application guidelines); Newsletter.
Application information: Awards are given to post-Ph.D.s only. Application form not required.
Initial approach: Letter
Copies of proposal: 2

Deadline(s): All major proposals must be submitted 8 weeks prior to board meetings
Board meeting date(s): Feb., June, and Nov.
Final notification: 3 months
Officers and Trustees:* Robert E. Denham, Chair.; Eric Wanner,* Pres.; Madeline Spitaleri, V.P. and Secy.; Christopher Brogna, C.F.O.; Alan S. Blinder; Christine K. Cassel; Thomas D. Cook; Christopher Edley; John A. Ferejohn; Larry V. Hedges; Jennifer L. Hochschild; Timothy A. Hultquist; Kathleen Hall Jamieson; Melvin Konner; Alan B. Krueger; Cora B. Marrett; Mary C. Waters.
Number of staff: 11 full-time professional; 19 full-time support; 6 part-time support.
EIN: 131635303

6895
Robert Saligman Charitable Trust ◇

c/o Alice Saligman
830 Park Ave., Ste. 7B
New York, NY 10021-2757

Established in 1987 in PA.
Donor: Robert Saligman†.
Foundation type: Independent foundation.
Financial data (yr. ended 12/31/05): Assets, $14,764,646 (M); expenditures, $634,103; qualifying distributions, $552,952; giving activities include $550,475 for 29 grants (high: $150,000; low: $200).
Purpose and activities: Giving primarily for Jewish agencies, temples and education; funding also for the arts health and human services.
Fields of interest: Museums (art); Museums (ethnic/folk arts); Arts; Higher education; Nursing school/education; Education; Health organizations; Disasters, 9/11/01; Human services; Children, services; Family services; Jewish federated giving programs; Jewish agencies & temples.
Limitations: Giving primarily in Philadelphia, PA. No grants to individuals.
Application information: Application form not required.
Initial approach: Letter
Copies of proposal: 1
Deadline(s): None
Board meeting date(s): Several times a year
Final notification: Within 90 days
Trustees: Herschel Cravitz; Alice Saligman; Carolyn Saligman; Ira Saligman.
EIN: 236875203
Selected grants: The following grants were reported in 2004.
$119,500 to National Museum of American Jewish History, Philadelphia, PA.
$3,020 to Metropolitan Museum of Art, New York, NY.
$2,000 to Carnegie Hall Society, New York, NY.
$1,500 to Israel Guide Dog Center for the Blind, Warrington, PA.
$1,500 to Philadelphia Museum of Art, Philadelphia, PA.
$1,450 to Jewish Museum, New York, NY.
$350 to A Better Chance, Philadelphia, PA.

6896
The Salmon Foundation, Inc.

67A E. 77th St.
New York, NY 10021
Contact: Ann Brownell Sloane, Admin.

Established in 1991 in NY.
Donor: Lois S. Duffey.
Foundation type: Independent foundation.
Financial data (yr. ended 12/31/05): Assets, $15,088,375 (M); gifts received, $1,000,000; expenditures, $825,492; qualifying distributions, $762,991; giving activities include $720,600 for 35 grants (high: $40,000; low: $2,500; average: $15,000–$30,000).
Purpose and activities: Giving primarily for children and family services, and education.
Fields of interest: Education; Children/youth, services.
Limitations: Giving primarily in CO, CT, MD, NH, and VT. No grants to individuals.
Publications: Application guidelines.
Application information: Application form required.
  Initial approach: Letter
  Copies of proposal: 1
  Deadline(s): Feb. 15 and Aug. 15
  Board meeting date(s): May and Nov.
Officers and Directors:* Amanda D. Rutledge,* Pres.; Peter L. Rutledge,* Secy.; Harry J. Duffey III,* Treas.; Sarah J. R. Krimmel; Catherine D. MacGlashan; Patricia D. Parkhurst; Diana D. Pedinielli.
EIN: 133637630

6897
The Richard Salomon Family Foundation, Inc. ✧

(formerly Richard & Edna Salomon Foundation, Inc.)
c/o Richard E. Salomon
610 5th Ave., 7th Fl.
New York, NY   10020

Established in 1964 in NY.
Donors: Richard B. Salomon†; Richard E. Salomon.
Foundation type: Independent foundation.
Financial data (yr. ended 12/31/04): Assets, $14,100,025 (M); expenditures, $750,034; qualifying distributions, $545,312; giving activities include $545,312 for 46 grants (high: $100,000; low: $500).
Purpose and activities: Giving for the arts, including public television and the performing arts.
Fields of interest: Media/communications; Arts.
Type of support: General/operating support.
Limitations: Applications not accepted. Giving primarily in New York, NY. No grants to individuals.
Application information: Contributes only to pre-selected organizations.
Officers and Directors:* Richard E. Salomon,* Pres.; Jennifer Salomon,* Secy.; Robyn S. Transport, Treas.; Evanne S. Gargiulo; Laura A. Landro; Frederick Lubcher; Christina Salomon; David Salomon.
EIN: 136163521

6898
William R. Salomon Scholarship Fund ✧ ☆
c/o Patricia David, Smith Barney
388 Greenwich St., 7th Fl.
New York, NY   10013

Donor: Salomon Brothers Inc.
Foundation type: Company-sponsored foundation.
Financial data (yr. ended 6/30/05): Assets, $620,335 (M); expenditures, $338,504; qualifying distributions, $338,504; giving activities include $338,400 for 192 grants (high: $8,000; low: $500).

Purpose and activities: The foundation supports organizations involved with higher education.
Fields of interest: Higher education.
Type of support: General/operating support; Employee-related scholarships.
Limitations: Applications not accepted. Giving limited to areas of company operations.
Application information: Contributes only through employee-related scholarships and to pre-selected organizations.
Officers: John L. Donnelly, Pres.; Patricia David, Secy.; Gedale B. Horowitz, Treas.
EIN: 132986194
Selected grants: The following grants were reported in 2005.
$16,000 to New York University, New York, NY. 2 grants: $8,000 each
$16,000 to University of Pennsylvania, Philadelphia, PA. 2 grants: $8,000 each
$8,000 to Boston College, Chestnut Hill, MA.
$8,000 to Cornell University, Ithaca, NY.
$8,000 to Duke University, Durham, NC.
$8,000 to Massachusetts College of Art, Boston, MA.
$8,000 to Skidmore College, Saratoga Springs, NY.
$500 to Oregon State University, Corvallis, OR.

6899
The Gary Saltz Foundation, Inc. ✧
c/o High Pro 2 Assocs., LLC
600 Madison Ave., 11th Fl.
New York, NY   10022

Incorporated in 1985 in NY.
Donors: Jack Saltz; Anita Saltz‡; Leonard Saltz Charitable Lead Annuity Trust; Ronald Saltz Charitable Lead Annuity Trust; Susan Saltz Charitable Lead Annuity Trust.
Foundation type: Independent foundation.
Financial data (yr. ended 4/30/05): Assets, $18,677,990 (M); gifts received, $2,739,900; expenditures, $809,536; qualifying distributions, $747,000; giving activities include $747,000 for 24 grants (high: $152,000; low: $1,500).
Purpose and activities: Grants primarily for education, health associations, and to museums.
Fields of interest: Museums; Elementary/ secondary education; Higher education; Education; Health organizations, association; Medical research, institute; Human services; Children/youth, services; Jewish agencies & temples.
Type of support: Research.
Limitations: Applications not accepted. Giving primarily in New York, NY; some giving in Los Angeles and Santa Barbara, CA. No grants to individuals.
Application information: Contributes only to pre-selected organizations.
Officers: Jack Saltz, Pres.; Ronald Saltz, V.P.; Susan Saltz, Secy.; Leonard Saltz, Treas.
EIN: 133267114

6900
Saltzman Foundation, Inc. ✧
c/o Arnold A. Saltzman
350 5th Ave., Ste. 8008
New York, NY   10118-0001

Established in 1950 in NY.
Donors: Eric Saltman Charitable Lead Trust; Arnold Saltzman.

Foundation type: Independent foundation.
Financial data (yr. ended 3/31/04): Assets, $6,195,792 (M); gifts received, $99,039; expenditures, $583,653; qualifying distributions, $572,612; giving activities include $569,788 for 63 grants (high: $400,000; low: $100).
Purpose and activities: Giving primarily to museums and for education.
Fields of interest: Museums; Education; Hospitals (general); Children/youth, services; International development; Community development, neighborhood development; Jewish agencies & temples.
International interests: Africa; Central America; Eastern Europe; South America.
Limitations: Applications not accepted. Giving on a national basis.
Application information: Contributes only to pre-selected organizations.
Officers: Arnold A. Saltzman, Pres. and Treas.; Joan R. Saltzman, Secy.
Director: Ruth S. Taishoff.
EIN: 136142471

6901
The Fan Fox and Leslie R. Samuels Foundation, Inc. ▼ ✧
350 5th Ave., Ste. 4301
New York, NY   10118   (212) 239-3030
Contact: Joseph C. Mitchell, Pres.
FAX: (212) 239-3039; E-mail: info@samuels.org; URL: http://www.samuels.org

Incorporated in 1959 in UT; reincorporated in 1981 in NY.
Donors: Leslie R. Samuels†; Fan Fox Samuels†.
Foundation type: Independent foundation.
Financial data (yr. ended 7/31/05): Assets, $201,463,938 (M); expenditures, $11,422,935; qualifying distributions, $9,982,471; giving activities include $8,551,088 for 310 grants (high: $350,000; low: $50; average: $5,000–$100,000).
Purpose and activities: Grants for the performing arts, and health care and social services for the elderly, including palliative and end-of-life care, health systems, and quality measurement.
Fields of interest: Performing arts; Performing arts, dance; Performing arts, theater; Performing arts, music; Performing arts, opera; Medical care, outpatient care; Health care, support services; Housing/shelter, aging; Human services; Aging.
Type of support: Program evaluation; Program development; Seed money; Program-related investments/loans.
Limitations: Giving limited to New York, NY. No support for education. No grants to individuals, or for scholarships, fellowships, or film or video projects.
Application information: Do not submit musical scores. Application form not required.
  Initial approach: Letter of inquiry not exceeding 3 typed pages
  Copies of proposal: 1
  Deadline(s): Mar. 1, June 1, Sept. 1, and Dec.1
  Board meeting date(s): Jan., Apr., July, Oct., and as necessary
  Final notification: 3 months
Officers and Directors:* Marvin A. Kaufman,* Chair.; Joseph C. Mitchell,* Pres. and Treas.; Robert Marx,* V.P. and Secy.; Carlos D. Moseley, Dir. Emeritus; Morton J. Bernstein; Joseph W. Polisi; Jacqueline M. Taylor; Michael L. Ziegler.

Number of staff: 4 full-time professional; 2 full-time support.
EIN: 133124818
Selected grants: The following grants were reported in 2005.
$350,000 to New York City Opera, New York, NY. For season support.
$300,000 to Philharmonic-Symphony Society of New York, New York, NY. For Saturday Matinee Concerts and Rush Hour Concerts.
$250,000 to Brooklyn Academy of Music, Brooklyn, NY. For season support.
$200,000 to Bronx-Lebanon Hospital Center, Bronx, NY. 2 grants: $100,000 each (For implementation of culturally competent, elder-focused, in-patient palliative care consultation service).
$147,250 to YM-YWHA, Samuel Field, Little Neck, NY. 2 grants: $63,250 (To implement NORC supportive services to community of free-standing one- and two-family homes), $84,000 (To implement NORC supportive services to community of free-standing one- and two-family homes).
$45,000 to North General Hospital, New York, NY. For initiative to develop teams comprised of physicians, nurse practitioners, and social workers that would visit frail elderly in their homes, become their primary care providers, and coordinate all aspects of care.
$34,000 to New York Citizens Committee on Health Care Decisions, New York, NY. For development of pilot program to educate the deaf elderly about advanced care planning.
$15,000 to Symphony Space, New York, NY. For Wall to Wall Stephen Sondheim.

6902
The Mara & Ricky Sandler Foundation ✧ ☆
c/o Ricky Sandler
65 E. 55th St., 25th Fl.
New York, NY 10022

Donors: Mara Sandler; Ricky Sandler.
Foundation type: Independent foundation.
Financial data (yr. ended 12/31/04): Assets, $2,008,628 (M); gifts received, $2,675,000; expenditures, $732,878; qualifying distributions, $732,825; giving activities include $732,680 for 58 grants (high: $140,000; low: $100).
Fields of interest: Health organizations, association; Children/youth, services; Jewish federated giving programs; Jewish agencies & temples.
Limitations: Applications not accepted. Giving primarily in New York, NY. No grants to individuals.
Application information: Contributes only to pre-selected organizations.
Trustees: Mara Sandler; Ricky Sandler.
EIN: 412091688

6903
Sandy Hill Foundation ✧ ☆
P.O. Box 30
Hudson Falls, NY 12839 (518) 747-5805
Contact: Floyd H. Rourke, Tr.

Established in 1953.
Donor: J. Walter Juckett.
Foundation type: Independent foundation.

Financial data (yr. ended 8/31/05): Assets, $8,724,601 (M); expenditures, $553,210; qualifying distributions, $529,137; giving activities include $426,553 for 108 grants (high: $200,000; low: $200), and $69,500 for 46 grants to individuals (high: $1,500; low: $100).
Purpose and activities: Giving primarily for a camp for critically ill children, the arts and culture, higher education, hospitals, health associations, children's and social services, and federated giving programs. Also offers scholarship grants for college education to assist young men and women graduating from designated local area schools.
Fields of interest: Arts; Higher education; Hospitals (general); Health organizations, association; Recreation, camps; Human services; Children/youth, services; Community development; Federated giving programs; Protestant agencies & churches.
Type of support: General/operating support.
Limitations: Giving primarily in the greater Hudson Falls, NY, area. No grants to individuals directly.
Application information: Scholarships paid directly to educational institutions on behalf of named recipients; application form must be typed or printed in black ink. Application form required.
Deadline(s): Apr. 1 for scholarship program only
Final notification: May 15
Trustees: Nancy Juckett Brown; Floyd H. Rourke.
EIN: 146018954

6904
Sani Family Foundation, Inc. ✧ ☆
c/o RSM McGladrey, Inc.
750 3rd Ave., 9th Fl.
New York, NY 10017

Established in 1965 in NY.
Donors: Lal C. Sani; Ashok Sani; CGS Industries, Inc.
Foundation type: Independent foundation.
Financial data (yr. ended 1/31/06): Assets, $3,470,305 (M); gifts received, $200,000; expenditures, $348,171; qualifying distributions, $343,732; giving activities include $343,732 for grants.
Fields of interest: Higher education; Education; Hospitals (general); Health organizations, association; Human services; Hinduism; Religion.
Limitations: Applications not accepted. Giving primarily in NY. No grants to individuals.
Application information: Contributes only to pre-selected organizations.
Officers and Directors:* Sham G. Sani, Pres.; Lal C. Sani,* V.P. and Secy.
Trustees: Sunil Sani; Suresh Sani.
EIN: 136201183

6905
Santa Maria Foundation, Inc. ✧
c/o M. Mastrogiorgio
35 Underhill St.
Tuckahoe, NY 10707
Contact: Margaret Devine, Admin. Asst.

Established in 1978 in NY.
Donors: J. Peter Grace†; Margaret F. Grace.
Foundation type: Independent foundation.
Financial data (yr. ended 12/31/03): Assets, $8,695,654 (M); expenditures, $420,518;

qualifying distributions, $364,801; giving activities include $362,500 for grants.
Purpose and activities: Giving primarily for Catholic organizations, focusing on spiritual and religious renewal, and shelters for the homeless and unwed mothers.
Fields of interest: Housing/shelter, homeless; Human services; Roman Catholic agencies & churches.
Type of support: General/operating support; Continuing support; Seed money.
Limitations: Applications not accepted. Giving primarily in NY. No grants to individuals.
Application information: Contributes only to pre-selected organizations.
Board meeting date(s): As necessary
Officers and Directors:* Margaret F. Grace,* Pres.; Patrick P. Grace,* V.P. and Treas.; Theresa G. Sears,* Secy.; Mary Grace Benson.
EIN: 132938749
Selected grants: The following grants were reported in 2003.
$142,500 to John Carroll University, University Heights, OH. For general operating support.
$30,000 to Thorpe Family Residence, Bronx, NY. For general operating support.
$20,000 to Tuesdays Children, Manhasset, NY. For general operating support.
$10,000 to Christophers, New York, NY. For general operating support.
$10,000 to Gregorian University Foundation, New York, NY. For general operating support.
$10,000 to Mercy Center, Bronx, NY. For general operating support.
$5,000 to Abraham House, Bronx, NY. For general operating support.
$5,000 to Broward Coalition for the Homeless, Fort Lauderdale, FL. For general operating support.
$5,000 to Russell Byers Charter School, Philadelphia, PA. For general operating support.
$5,000 to Sisters of Life, New York, NY. For general operating support.

6906
The Sapp Family Foundation ✧
c/o Goldman Sachs & Co.
1 New York Plz., 40th Fl.
New York, NY 10004

Established in 1991 in NY.
Donor: Richard A. Sapp.
Foundation type: Independent foundation.
Financial data (yr. ended 4/30/04): Assets, $8,674,851 (M); expenditures, $1,163,533; qualifying distributions, $1,155,000; giving activities include $1,155,000 for 3 grants (high: $1,000,000; low: $5,000).
Fields of interest: Higher education; Diabetes.
Limitations: Applications not accepted. Giving on a national basis. No grants to individuals.
Application information: Contributes only to pre-selected organizations.
Trustees: Richard A. Sapp; Shari M. Sapp.
EIN: 133632757
Selected grants: The following grants were reported in 2005.
$10,000 to BRIDGE, Inc., Baltimore, MD.
$10,000 to Rancho Santa Fe Community School Endowment Fund, Rancho Santa Fe, CA.

6907
Sasco Foundation ◇
c/o JPMorgan Chase Bank, N.A.
345 Park Ave., 6th Fl.
New York, NY 10154
Contact: Mr. Uwe Lindner

Trust established in 1951 in NY.
Donors: Leila E. Riegel†; Katherine R. Emory†.
Foundation type: Independent foundation.
Financial data (yr. ended 12/31/05): Assets, $6,561,874 (M); expenditures, $378,421; qualifying distributions, $335,979; giving activities include $331,500 for 48 grants (high: $110,000; low: $1,000).
Purpose and activities: Giving for the arts, education, the environment, health, and human services.
Fields of interest: Arts; Environment, natural resources; Health care; Human services; Family services; Women.
Type of support: Continuing support.
Limitations: Giving primarily in CT, ME, and NY. No grants to individuals.
Application information: Currently supporting trustee-sponsored projects only. Application form not required.
  Copies of proposal: 1
  Deadline(s): Sept. 1
  Board meeting date(s): Fall
Trustees: Lucy E. Ambach; Benjamin Riegel Emory; Katherine Emory Stookey.
EIN: 136046567

6908
The Sato Family Foundation, Inc ◇
c/o Diamond Assocs.
415 Madison Ave., 16th Fl.
New York, NY 10017 (212) 308-2441
Contact: Yeshai Teichman

Established in 2001 in NY.
Donors: Joseph Wechsler; Samuel Wechsler; MTS Assocs. LLC.
Foundation type: Independent foundation.
Financial data (yr. ended 12/31/05): Assets, $4,468,970 (M); gifts received, $350,000; expenditures, $361,050; qualifying distributions, $360,550; giving activities include $360,550 for 15 grants (high: $100,000; low: $300).
Fields of interest: Education; Human services; Jewish agencies & temples.
Limitations: Giving on a national and international basis, with emphasis on New York, NY, and the Kyrghz Republic.
Application information: Application form not required.
  Deadline(s): None
Directors: Joseph Wechsler; Samuel Wechsler.
EIN: 134140924

6909
Saunders Foundation ◇
760 Brooks Ave.
Rochester, NY 14619-2259

Incorporated in 1986 in NY.
Foundation type: Independent foundation.
Financial data (yr. ended 12/31/05): Assets, $1,927,456 (L); gifts received, $15,845; expenditures, $826,949; qualifying distributions,

$814,165; giving activities include $814,165 for 56 grants (high: $600,000; low: $100).
Fields of interest: Higher education, college; Medical school/education; Hospitals (general); Human services; Federated giving programs; Protestant agencies & churches.
Limitations: Applications not accepted. Giving primarily in upstate NY. No grants to individuals.
Application information: Contributes only to pre-selected organizations.
Officers: Carole M. Saunders, Pres.; William Burslem III, Treas.
Director: Max Stoner.
EIN: 161289330

6910
Schafer Family Foundation ◇ ☆
c/o Executive Monetary Mgmt.
220 E. 42nd St., 32nd Fl.
New York, NY 10017 (212) 536-9700

Established in 1986 in NY.
Donor: Oscar S. Schafer.
Foundation type: Independent foundation.
Financial data (yr. ended 12/31/05): Assets, $1,563,885 (M); expenditures, $453,966; qualifying distributions, $448,460; giving activities include $448,460 for grants.
Purpose and activities: Giving primarily for social services.
Fields of interest: Media, television; Performing arts; Historic preservation/historical societies; Education; Animal welfare; Health care; Children/youth, services; Christian agencies & churches; Jewish agencies & temples.
Limitations: Applications not accepted. Giving primarily in the metropolitan New York, NY, area. No grants to individuals.
Application information: Contributes only to pre-selected organizations.
Officer: Oscar S. Schafer, Pres.
Directors: Myer Berlow; Sigrid U. Schafer; Michael Stein.
EIN: 133382931
Selected grants: The following grants were reported in 2005.
$30,000 to Tulane University, New Orleans, LA. 2 grants: $25,000, $5,000
$10,000 to Long Wharf Theater, New Haven, CT.
$10,000 to New York University, New York, NY.
$10,000 to Yorkville Common Pantry, New York, NY.
$750 to American Cancer Society, Atlanta, GA.

6911
The H. Schaffer Foundation, Inc.
809 State St.
Schenectady, NY 12307
Contact: Sonya A. Stall, Pres.

Established in 1982 in NY, by Henry Schaffer, the owner of Empire Supermarkets.
Donor: Henry Schaffer†.
Foundation type: Independent foundation.
Financial data (yr. ended 10/31/05): Assets, $5,157,807 (M); expenditures, $449,140; qualifying distributions, $409,762; giving activities include $328,600 for 10 grants (high: $250,000; low: $1,000).
Purpose and activities: Giving primarily for higher education, libraries, cultural/arts support, and

community support services in Quad City area of NY State.
Fields of interest: Performing arts, theater; Higher education; Hospitals (general); Reproductive health, family planning; Health care; Human services; Children, foster care; Aging, centers/services.
Type of support: General/operating support; Continuing support; Annual campaigns; Capital campaigns; Building/renovation; Endowments; Program development; Conferences/seminars; Professorships; Seed money; Curriculum development; Research; In-kind gifts.
Limitations: Giving primarily in NY, with emphasis on the Capital District Region: Schenectady, Albany, Troy, and Saratoga Springs. No grants to individuals (usually).
Application information: Application form not required.
  Initial approach: Letter of request
  Copies of proposal: 1
  Deadline(s): None
  Board meeting date(s): Annually
  Final notification: 3-12 months
Officers: Sonya A. Stall, Pres.; Andrea B. Shay, V.P.; Jeffrey R. Stall, M.D., Secy.-Treas.; Lorna H. Stall, Treas.
Number of staff: 3 part-time support.
EIN: 222325485
Selected grants: The following grants were reported in 2004.
$255,000 to Albany Medical College, Albany, NY. 2 grants: $250,000, $5,000
$12,000 to Planned Parenthood Mohawk Hudson, Utica, NY.
$5,000 to Girls Inc..
$5,000 to Proctors Theater, Schenectady, NY.
$5,000 to Siena College, Loudonville, NY.

6912
The Morris and Alma Schapiro Fund ◇
(formerly M. A. Schapiro Fund)
c/o Kronish, Lieb, Weiner and Hellman, LLP
1114 Ave. of the Americas, 46th Fl.
New York, NY 10036-7798 (212) 479-6040

Established in 1955 in NY.
Donor: Morris A. Schapiro†.
Foundation type: Independent foundation.
Financial data (yr. ended 12/31/03): Assets, $41,282,035 (M); gifts received, $6,019,276; expenditures, $2,448,643; qualifying distributions, $2,225,423; giving activities include $2,123,333 for 24 grants (high: $500,000; low: $10,000).
Purpose and activities: Giving primarily for medical research; funding also for the arts and education.
Fields of interest: Museums (art); Arts; Higher education; Education; Hospitals (general); Neuroscience; Jewish agencies & temples.
Limitations: Giving primarily in New York, NY. No grants to individuals.
Application information:
  Deadline(s): None
Officers and Directors:* Linda S. Collins,* Pres.; Stephen J. Paluszek,* V.P.; Daniel E. Schapiro, Secy.-Treas.
EIN: 136089254
Selected grants: The following grants were reported in 2003.
$500,000 to Lenox Hill Hospital, New York, NY.
$400,000 to Columbia University, New York, NY.
$120,000 to New York University, School of Medicine, New York, NY.
$100,000 to Yaddo, Saratoga Springs, NY.

$60,000 to School of American Ballet, New York, NY.

$50,000 to Brooklyn Public Library Foundation, Brooklyn, NY.

$50,000 to Poets House, New York, NY.

$20,000 to Westhampton Beach Performing Arts Center, Westhampton Beach, NY.

$15,000 to Lark Quartet, Minneapolis, MN.

$10,000 to New York New Music Ensemble, New York, NY.

6913
Morris & Dvora Scharf Foundation, Inc. ◇
1659 58th St.
Brooklyn, NY 11204

Established in 2000 in NY.
Donors: Morris Scharf; Dvora Scharf.
Foundation type: Independent foundation.
Financial data (yr. ended 12/31/03): Assets, $2,639,825 (M); gifts received, $80,087; expenditures, $342,520; qualifying distributions, $332,192; giving activities include $335,118 for 15 grants (high: $80,000; low: $1,000).
Fields of interest: Jewish agencies & temples.
Limitations: Applications not accepted. No grants to individuals.
Application information: Contributes only to pre-selected organizations.
Directors: Dvora Scharf; Lipa Scharf; Morris Scharf.
EIN: 134115138

6914
The Harold & Blanche Schechter Foundation, Inc. ◇
2600 Nostrand Ave.
Brooklyn, NY 11210

Established in 1999 in NY.
Donors: Saul Schechter; Dov Schechter; Benjamin Brecher; Richard Schechter; Shelly Schechter; Mordechai Schechter.
Foundation type: Independent foundation.
Financial data (yr. ended 6/30/05): Assets, $980,104 (M); gifts received, $207,318; expenditures, $338,309; qualifying distributions, $337,688; giving activities include $336,467 for 308 grants (high: $36,000; low: $36).
Fields of interest: Jewish federated giving programs; Jewish agencies & temples.
Limitations: Applications not accepted. Giving primarily in Brooklyn and Far Rockaway, NY. No grants to individuals.
Application information: Contributes only to pre-selected organizations.
Officers: Saul Schechter, Pres.; Benjamin Brecher, V.P.; Richard Schechter, V.P.; Dov Schechter, Treas.
EIN: 113494145
Selected grants: The following grants were reported in 2005.

$10,000 to Yeshiva Darchei Torah, Far Rockaway, NY.

$4,480 to Chesed Avraham, Brooklyn, NY. 2 grants: $1,980, $2,500

$4,180 to Beth Oloth, Monsey, NY.

$1,500 to Sinai Academy, Brooklyn, NY.

$1,500 to Zichron Menachem, Monsey, NY.

$1,200 to Yeshiva of Spring Valley, Monsey, NY.

$720 to Chai Lifeline, New York, NY.

$500 to National Society for Hebrew Day Schools - Torah Umesorah, New York, NY.

$250 to Arachim, Brooklyn, NY.

6915
The Schenectady Foundation ◇
c/o United Way of Schenectady County
P.O. Box 916
Schenectady, NY 12301 (518) 272-6402
Contact: Robert A. Carreau, Secy.
E-mail: racarreau@outcomeswork.com; *URL:* http://www.schenectadyfoundation.org

Established in 1963 in NY.
Donors: Eleanor F. Green†; Mabel Birdsall†; Agnes Macdonald†; Laura Ayer†; S. Wells Corbin†; John N. Erbacher†; Kathryn Rice†; Martin Rice†; Willis R. Whitney†; Herman Blumer†; Patrick Garey†; Irving Handelman†; Sara Handelman†; Adelaide Parker†; Alice Stackpole†; Charles W. Carl, Jr.†; Edna Wood†; General Electric Foundation.
Foundation type: Community foundation.
Financial data (yr. ended 12/31/05): Assets, $11,235,470 (M); gifts received, $335,065; expenditures, $846,233; giving activities include $758,785 for grants.
Purpose and activities: The foundation seeks to assist and promote the welfare of Schenectady County, New York and the people who live and/or work there. Support for general charitable purposes; awards scholarships to graduating seniors of Schenectady County, NY, high schools planning to enter the teaching profession.
Fields of interest: Education; Animals/wildlife, preservation/protection; Health care; Youth development; Child development, services; Community development; Engineering/technology; Children.
Type of support: Scholarship funds; Capital campaigns; Building/renovation; Equipment; Land acquisition; Seed money; Research; Matching/challenge support.
Limitations: Giving limited to Schenectady County, NY. No grants for operating budgets, continuing support, annual campaigns, emergency or deficit financing, general or special endowments, demonstration projects, publications, or conferences or seminars; no loans.
Publications: Application guidelines; Annual report; Grants list; Informational brochure.
Application information: Visit foundation Web site for application form and guidelines. Interested organizations first submit a Concept Paper; upon approval of the concept paper, a grant proposal is requested. Application form required.
  Initial approach: Telephone
  Copies of proposal: 1
  Deadline(s): Sept.
  Board meeting date(s): Mar., June, Sept., Dec.
Officers and Distribution Committee:* Mark Handelman,* Chair.; Robert A. Carreau,* Secy. and Grant Prog. Mgr.; Robert T. Cushing, Treas. and Chair., Trustee's Comm.; Cornelia Hume; Grace Jorgensen; Thomas O. Maggs; Dr. Walter L. Robb; Sarah J. Schermerhorn; Herbert L. Shultz.
EIN: 146019650

6916
The Schenker Family Foundation ◇
c/o Curtis Schenker
1175 Park Ave., Apt. 8A
New York, NY 10128

Established in 1998 in NY.
Donors: Curtis Schenker; Leo Schenker; CJS Partnership.
Foundation type: Independent foundation.
Financial data (yr. ended 12/31/04): Assets, $809,344 (M); gifts received, $971,646; expenditures, $823,935; qualifying distributions, $810,666; giving activities include $810,666 for 71 grants (high: $105,120; low: $30).
Purpose and activities: Giving primarily for education, health, children and youth services, human services, and Jewish organizations.
Fields of interest: Arts; Education; Animals/wildlife; Hospitals (general); Health organizations, association; Human services; Children/youth, services; Jewish federated giving programs; Jewish agencies & temples.
Type of support: General/operating support.
Limitations: Applications not accepted. Giving primarily in the greater metropolitan New York, NY, area. No grants to individuals.
Application information: Contributes only to pre-selected organizations.
Officer: Livia Schenker, Secy.
Directors: Curtis Schenker; Leo Schenker; Jeffrey Schwarz.
EIN: 133992998

6917
Leopold Schepp Foundation ◇
551 5th Ave., Ste. 3000
New York, NY 10176 (212) 692-0191
Contact: SuzanneClair Guard, Exec. Dir.
URL: http://www.scheppfoundation.org

Incorporated in 1925 in NY.
Donors: Leopold Schepp†; Florence L. Schepp†.
Foundation type: Independent foundation.
Financial data (yr. ended 2/28/06): Assets, $15,598,017 (M); gifts received, $98,363; expenditures, $1,279,259; qualifying distributions, $1,106,147; giving activities include $810,200 for 145 grants to individuals (high: $8,000; low: $1,000; average: $3,000–$5,000).
Purpose and activities: Giving primarily to assist young men and women of character and ability who have insufficient means to complete their vocational or professional education. Undergraduate scholarships to individuals under 30 years of age; graduate scholarships to individuals under 40 years of age; a small number of fellowships for independent study and research to individuals in the arts and literature, medicine, and oceanography.
Fields of interest: Human services.
Type of support: Fellowships; Grants to individuals; Scholarships—to individuals.
Limitations: Giving to students on a national basis.
Publications: Application guidelines; Informational brochure; Informational brochure (including application guidelines); Newsletter.
Application information: Application form required.
  Initial approach: Letter responding to questions on Web site
  Copies of proposal: 1
  Deadline(s): When a sufficient number of requests has been received
  Board meeting date(s): May and Oct.
  Final notification: 3 weeks
Officers and Trustees:* Barbara McLendon,* Pres.; William L.D. Barrett,* V.P.; Kathryn Batchelder Cashman,* V.P.; Sue Ann Dawson,* V.P.; James G. Turino, Treas.; SuzanneClair Guard, Exec. Dir.; Edythe Bobrow; Louise M. Bozorth; Susan Brenner;

Andrew Butterfield; Carvel H. Cartmell; Anne Coffin; Emily Crawford; Betty David; William G. Gridley, Jr.; Diana P. Hermann; Michele A. Paige; Elizabeth Stone Potter; Bruno A. Quinson; Robert F. Reder; Banning Repplier; George R. Walker.
Number of staff: 1 full-time professional; 1 full-time support; 2 part-time support.
EIN: 135562353

6918
The Scherman Foundation, Inc. ▼
16 E. 52nd St., Ste. 601
New York, NY   10022-5306   (212) 832-3086
Contact: Sandra Silverman, Pres. and Exec. Dir.
FAX: (212) 838-0154; E-mail: info@scherman.org;
URL: http://www.scherman.org

Incorporated in 1941 in NY.
Donor: Members of the Scherman family.
Foundation type: Independent foundation.
Financial data (yr. ended 12/31/05): Assets, $77,673,022 (M); expenditures, $5,513,509; qualifying distributions, $4,922,175; giving activities include $4,242,200 for 138 grants (high: $135,000; low: $500; average: $5,000–$40,000).
Purpose and activities: Grants largely for environment, peace and security, reproductive rights and services, and human rights and liberties, the arts and social welfare. In the social welfare field, grants are made to New York City organizations concerned with social justice, community organizing, and community self-help. Arts grants are generally limited to New York City.
Fields of interest: Performing arts; Performing arts, theater; Performing arts, music; Environment, natural resources; Environment; Reproductive health, family planning; Legal services; Human services; International peace/security; International affairs, arms control; International human rights; Civil rights, minorities; Civil liberties, reproductive rights; Civil rights; Community development; Economically disadvantaged.
Type of support: General/operating support; Continuing support; Annual campaigns; Technical assistance; Matching/challenge support.
Limitations: Giving in NY and nationally in all areas, except for the arts and social welfare, which are primarily in New York City. No support for colleges, universities, or other higher educational institutions. No grants to individuals, or for building or endowment funds, capital campaigns scholarships, fellowships, conferences or symposia, specific media or arts production, medical, science or engineering research.
Publications: Annual report (including application guidelines); Grants list.
Application information: The foundation does not accept proposals via fax or the Internet. Do not submit video or audio cassettes or CDs, unless requested to do so. Application form not required.
   Initial approach: Letter
   Copies of proposal: 1
   Deadline(s): None
   Board meeting date(s): Quarterly
   Final notification: 8 to 10 weeks
Officers and Directors:* Karen R. Sollins,* Chair.; Sandra Silverman, Pres. and Exec. Dir.; Susanna Bergtold,* Secy.; Mitchell C. Pratt, Treas. and Prog. Off.; Axel G. Rosin,* Chair. Emeritus; Katharine S. Rosin, Dir. Emeritus; Hillary Brown; David R. Jones; Gordon N. Litwin; John J. O'Neil; Anthony M. Schulte; Marcia Thompson; John Wroclawski.

Number of staff: 2 full-time professional; 1 full-time support; 1 part-time support.
EIN: 136098464
Selected grants: The following grants were reported in 2005.
$70,000 to NAACP Legal Defense and Educational Fund, New York, NY. For general support.
$65,000 to Conservation Law Foundation, Boston, MA. For general support.
$60,000 to Planned Parenthood of New York City, New York, NY. For general support.
$55,000 to New York Lawyers for the Public Interest, New York, NY. For Environmental Justice and Community Development Project.
$45,000 to American Civil Liberties Union Foundation, New York, NY. For Reproductive Freedom Project.
$40,000 to Make the Road By Walking, Brooklyn, NY. For general support.
$40,000 to New York City Opera, New York, NY. For general support.
$35,000 to Population Action International, DC. For general support.
$30,000 to New Yorkers for Parks, New York, NY. For general support.
$20,000 to New York Youth Symphony, New York, NY. For general support.

6919
Richard J. & Joan G. Scheuer Family Foundation, Inc. ◇
c/o TAG Assocs., Ltd.
75 Rockefeller Plz., Ste. 900
New York, NY   10019

Established in 1966 in NY.
Donors: Joan G. Scheuer; Richard J. Scheuer.
Foundation type: Independent foundation.
Financial data (yr. ended 10/31/05): Assets, $44,406 (M); gifts received, $404,144; expenditures, $377,776; qualifying distributions, $361,369; giving activities include $359,344 for 124 grants (high: $31,000; low: $50).
Purpose and activities: Giving primarily for the arts, and for archaeological research; funding also for social services and Jewish organizations and temples.
Fields of interest: Museums (ethnic/folk arts); Performing arts, theater; History/archaeology; Arts; Education, association; Higher education; Environment, land resources; Human services; Jewish agencies & temples.
Limitations: Applications not accepted. Giving on a national basis, with emphasis on MA, NY, and OH. No grants to individuals.
Application information: Contributes only to pre-selected organizations.
Officers and Directors:* Richard J. Scheuer,* Pres. and Treas.; Joan G. Scheuer,* V.P. and Secy.
EIN: 136197447

6920
S. H. and Helen R. Scheuer Family Foundation, Inc. ◇
c/o 61 Assocs.
350 5th Ave., Ste. 1413
New York, NY   10118   (212) 947-9009
Contact: Linda Ehrlich, Admin. Dir.

Incorporated in 1943 in NY.
Donor: Members of the Scheuer family.

Foundation type: Independent foundation.
Financial data (yr. ended 11/30/05): Assets, $9,670,334 (M); expenditures, $2,082,869; qualifying distributions, $1,932,172; giving activities include $1,932,172 for 118 grants (high: $166,000; low: $1,000).
Purpose and activities: Emphasis on local Jewish welfare funds, higher education, and cultural programs.
Fields of interest: Arts; Higher education; Health organizations, association; Human services; Children, services; Jewish federated giving programs; Jewish agencies & temples.
Limitations: Giving primarily in NY, with emphasis on the metropolitan New York, NY, area; some funding also nationally.
Application information: The foundation only makes contributions to pre-selected charitable organizations; however the foundation does review unsolicited applications for funds.
   Board meeting date(s): As necessary
Officers: Richard J. Scheuer, Pres.; Laura L. Scheuer, V.P.; Elizabeth H. Scheuer, Secy.; David Zahner, Treas.
Number of staff: 1 full-time professional.
EIN: 136062661
Selected grants: The following grants were reported in 2005.
$60,000 to Cambridge College, Cambridge, MA.
$55,000 to Jewish Museum, New York, NY.
$52,000 to Jewish Community Council of Greater Coney Island, Brooklyn, NY.
$31,000 to American Jewish World Service, New York, NY.
$30,000 to American Supporters of YEDID, New York, NY.
$22,500 to American Society for the Protection of Nature in Israel, Great Neck, NY.
$10,000 to Jubilee Community Center, Montgomery, AL.
$10,000 to Sandy Spring Friends School, Sandy Spring, MD.
$7,000 to AmeriCares, Stamford, CT.
$5,000 to Chamber Music Society of Lincoln Center, New York, NY.

6921
The Steven H. and Alida Brill Scheuer Foundation, Inc. ◇
320 E. 54th St.
New York, NY   10022

Established around 1993 in NY.
Donor: The S.H. and Helen R. Scheuer Family Foundation.
Foundation type: Independent foundation.
Financial data (yr. ended 12/31/03): Assets, $1,195,700 (M); expenditures, $648,073; qualifying distributions, $426,795; giving activities include $421,547 for 44 grants (high: $73,725; low: $50).
Purpose and activities: Giving primarily to Jewish programs including education, the arts and human services; funding also for other arts and culture, and human services.
Fields of interest: Performing arts, theater; Arts; Health organizations, association; Disasters, 9/11/01; Human services; Jewish agencies & temples.
Limitations: Applications not accepted. Giving on a national basis. No grants to individuals.

Application information: Contributes only to pre-selected organizations.

Board meeting date(s): 3 times a year

Officers: Alida Brill Scheuer, Pres. and Treas.; Steven H. Scheuer, V.P. and Secy.

Trustee: Daniel Kurtz.

Number of staff: 1 part-time professional.

EIN: 133725704

6922

Sarah I. Schieffelin Residuary Trust ◇

c/o The Bank of New York
1 Wall St., 28th Fl.
New York, NY 10286 (212) 635-1520
Contact: Grace Allen
Application address: c/o The Bank of New York, 1290 6th Ave., New York, NY 10104

Established in 1976.

Donor: Sarah I. Schieffelin†.

Foundation type: Independent foundation.

Financial data (yr. ended 3/31/05): Assets, $13,716,296 (M); expenditures, $712,947; qualifying distributions, $653,728; giving activities include $613,934 for 44 grants (high: $61,393; low: $1,000).

Purpose and activities: Giving primarily to the American Red Cross, and for a historical society, human services, and animals and wildlife.

Fields of interest: Historic preservation/historical societies; Arts; Libraries (public); Education; Environment, natural resources; Animals/wildlife, preservation/protection; Health care; Health organizations, association; Human services; American Red Cross; Children/youth, services; Christian agencies & churches; Roman Catholic agencies & churches.

Type of support: Continuing support.

Limitations: Giving primarily in New York, NY. No grants to individuals.

Application information: Application form not required.

Initial approach: Letter
Copies of proposal: 1
Deadline(s): Mar. 31
Board meeting date(s): May 31
Final notification: June 30

Trustees: David M. Daly; The Bank of New York.

EIN: 136724459

6923

The Schiff Foundation

50 Rockefeller Plz., 15th Fl.
New York, NY 10020-1605
Contact: David T. Schiff, Pres.

Incorporated in 1946 in NY.

Donors: John M. Schiff†; Edith B. Schiff†; David T. Schiff; Peter G. Schiff.

Foundation type: Independent foundation.

Financial data (yr. ended 12/31/05): Assets, $11,232,582 (M); expenditures, $579,814; qualifying distributions, $501,190; giving activities include $501,190 for 86 grants (high: $150,000; low: $100; average: $150,000).

Purpose and activities: Giving for special medical programs, certain youth and social service agencies, museums, animal welfare, and education; funds substantially committed to organizations of interest to the donors.

Fields of interest: Museums; Arts; Education; Animal welfare; Health care; Human services; Children/youth, services.

Type of support: General/operating support; Annual campaigns; Capital campaigns; Program development.

Limitations: Applications not accepted. Giving primarily in NY. No grants to individuals.

Application information: Contributes only to pre-selected organizations.

Officers and Directors:* David T. Schiff,* Pres.; Peter G. Schiff,* V.P.; Sandra Frey Davies, Secy.; Andrew N. Schiff,* Treas.

EIN: 136088221

Selected grants: The following grants were reported in 2003.

$173,500 to Wildlife Conservation Society, Bronx, NY. 3 grants: $125,000 (For general support), $23,500 (For general support), $25,000 (For general support).

$50,000 to Brooks School, New York, NY. For general support.

$50,000 to Jazz at Lincoln Center, New York, NY. For general support.

$50,000 to Lake Forest College, Lake Forest, IL. For general support.

$15,000 to Metropolitan Museum of Art, New York, NY. For general support.

$15,000 to North Shore-Long Island Jewish Health System Foundation, Great Neck, NY. For general support q.

$10,000 to Lincoln Center for the Performing Arts, New York, NY. For general support.

$9,000 to Save Venice, New York, NY. For general support.

6924

Jeannette F. Schlobach Article 4 Trust ◇

c/o Mark Dennis, C.P.A.
504 Haight Ave.
Poughkeepsie, NY 12603

Established in 2001 in NY.

Foundation type: Independent foundation.

Financial data (yr. ended 12/31/05): Assets, $12,050,251 (M); expenditures, $645,522; qualifying distributions, $567,500; giving activities include $567,500 for 28 grants (high: $110,000; low: $2,500).

Purpose and activities: Giving primarily for education, including education in the culinary arts, as well as for medical research, and children, youth and social services.

Fields of interest: Performing arts; Higher education, college; Medical research, institute; Human services; YM/YWCAs & YM/YWHAs; Children/youth, services.

Limitations: Applications not accepted. Giving primarily in NY, with emphasis on Poughkeepsie. No grants to individuals.

Application information: Contributes only to pre-selected organizations.

Trustee: Mark V. Dennis.

EIN: 226863221

6925

Schlosstein Hartley Foundation ◇

c/o Barry M. Strauss Assocs., Ltd.
307 5th Ave., Ste. 8th Fl.
New York, NY 10016-6517

Established in 2000 in NY.

Donor: Ralph L. Schlosstein.

Foundation type: Independent foundation.

Financial data (yr. ended 9/30/05): Assets, $2,393,746 (M); gifts received, $137,586; expenditures, $653,949; qualifying distributions, $610,700; giving activities include $610,450 for 77 grants (high: $100,000; low: $250).

Fields of interest: Education; Hospitals (general); Religion.

Limitations: Applications not accepted. No grants to individuals.

Application information: Contributes only to pre-selected organizations.

Trustees: Jane Hartley; Ralph L. Schlosstein.

EIN: 137268307

Selected grants: The following grants were reported in 2005.

$100,000 to Dartmouth College, Hanover, NH.

$50,000 to Museum of Natural History, Denver, CO.

$35,000 to American Museum of Natural History, New York, NY.

$25,000 to Conservation International, DC.

$25,000 to New York Shakespeare Festival, New York, NY.

$15,000 to International Womens Health Coalition, New York, NY.

$10,000 to Denison University, Granville, OH.

$6,000 to Bank Street College of Education, New York, NY.

$1,500 to Lower East Side Tenement Museum, New York, NY.

$1,000 to New York University Medical Center, New York, NY.

6926

Schlumberger Foundation, Inc. ◇

153 E. 53rd St., 57th Fl.
New York, NY 10022 (212) 350-9400
URL: http://www.slb.com/content/about/foundation/index.asp

Established as a company-sponsored trust in 1954 in TX; terminated in 1982 and transferred its assets to the new Schlumberger Foundation, established as a company-sponsored foundation in DE by a company incorporated in the Netherlands Antilles.

Donor: Schlumberger N.V.

Foundation type: Independent foundation.

Financial data (yr. ended 12/31/04): Assets, $27,406,918 (M); expenditures, $752,605; qualifying distributions, $544,313; giving activities include $459,927 for grants.

Purpose and activities: The foundation supports organizations involved with arts and culture, education, and medicine. The foundation also supports colleges and universities with scholarships and fellowships in engineering and other natural sciences.

Fields of interest: Arts; Higher education; Engineering school/education; Education; Engineering.

Type of support: General/operating support; Program development; Fellowships; Scholarship funds; Research; Program-related investments/loans.

Limitations: Giving on a national and international basis. No grants to individuals, or for building funds or operating budgets.

Application information: Application form not required.

Deadline(s): None

Board meeting date(s): Feb. or Mar.
Final notification: Within 3 weeks
Officers: Maarten Scholten, Chair. and Pres.;
Stephanie Cox, V.P. and Secy.; Jamal Ainul, V.P. and
Treas.; Michael Benjamin, V.P. and Cont.; Thierry
Pilenko, V.P.; Arthur W. Alexander, Exec. Secy.
EIN: 237033142

6927
Priscilla & Richard J. Schmeelk Foundation, Inc. ✧ ☆
c/o J. Anderson
1003 Park Blvd.
Massapequa Park, NY   11762
Contact: Richard J. Schmeelk, Pres. and Treas.

Established in 1983 in NY.
Donor: Richard J. Schmeelk.
Foundation type: Independent foundation.
Financial data (yr. ended 12/31/05): Assets,
$1,914,121 (M); expenditures, $595,554;
qualifying distributions, $572,810; giving activities
include $572,810 for grants.
Fields of interest: Education; Hospitals (general);
Health care; Children/youth, services; Roman
Catholic agencies & churches; Jewish agencies &
temples.
Type of support: Continuing support; Annual
campaigns; Endowments; Scholarship funds.
Limitations: Applications not accepted. Giving
primarily in New York, NY. No grants to individuals.
Application information: Contributes only to
pre-selected organizations.
Officers and Directors:* Richard J. Schmeelk,*
Pres. and Treas.; Priscilla M. Schmeelk,* V.P. and
Secy.
EIN: 133126387

6928
The Kilian J. and Caroline F. Schmitt Foundation, Inc. ✧
c/o Gary J. Lindsay, Secy.-Treas.
349 W. Commercial St., Ste. 2360
East Rochester, NY   14445   (585) 238-7721

Established in 1991 in NY as successor to Kilian J.
and Caroline F. Schmitt Foundation.
Donors: Kilian J. Schmitt†; Caroline F. Schmitt†.
Foundation type: Independent foundation.
Financial data (yr. ended 2/28/05): Assets,
$10,285,702 (M); expenditures, $453,791;
qualifying distributions, $508,395; giving activities
include $357,500 for 27 grants (high: $125,000;
low: $1,000).
Purpose and activities: Giving primarily for
education, human services, aging centers and
services, and Christian agencies and churches.
Fields of interest: Media, television; Media, radio;
Arts; Education, special; Higher education;
Hospitals (general); Human services; Children/
youth, services; Aging, centers/services; Christian
agencies & churches.
Type of support: General/operating support; Annual
campaigns; Capital campaigns; Equipment;
Endowments.
Limitations: Giving primarily in the metropolitan
Rochester, NY, area. No grants to individuals.
Application information: Application form required.
Deadline(s): None
Officers: Robert H. Fella, Pres.; Michael Walker,
V.P.; Gary J. Lindsay, Secy.-Treas.

Directors: James R. Dray; Leon Fella; Alfred
Hallenbeck; James D. Ryan.
EIN: 223087449
Selected grants: The following grants were reported
in 2005.
$125,000 to University of Rochester, Rochester,
NY.
$109,000 to Rochester Institute of Technology,
Rochester, NY. 2 grants: $4,000, $105,000
$50,000 to Nazareth College of Rochester,
Rochester, NY.
$10,000 to Hope Hall, Rochester, NY.
$5,000 to Wilson Commencement Park, Rochester,
NY.
$2,000 to Womens Foundation of Genesee Valley,
Rochester, NY.
$1,500 to Food Bank of Western New York, Buffalo,
NY.
$1,500 to Rochester Museum and Science Center,
Rochester, NY.

6929
Helen & Irving Schneider Foundation, Inc. ✧
880 5th Ave., Ste. 17F
New York, NY   10021

Donors: Irving Schneider; Helen Schneider.
Foundation type: Independent foundation.
Financial data (yr. ended 12/31/05): Assets,
$4,735,668 (M); expenditures, $600,976;
qualifying distributions, $600,976; giving activities
include $551,200 for 4 grants (high: $500,000;
low: $1,000).
Fields of interest: Museums; Performing arts;
Recreation, community facilities; Recreation, social
clubs; Children/youth, services; Jewish agencies &
temples.
Limitations: Applications not accepted. Giving
primarily in New York, NY. No grants to individuals.
Application information: Contributes only to
pre-selected organizations.
Officers: Irving Schneider, Pres.; Lynn C. Schneider,
V.P. and Secy.; Mindy Schneider, V.P. and Treas.
EIN: 136165503
Selected grants: The following grants were reported
in 2003.
$50,000 to Metropolitan Opera Association, New
York, NY.
$25,000 to American Friends of the Open University
of Israel, New York, NY.
$25,000 to Fresh Air Fund, New York, NY.
$25,000 to Magic Circle Opera Repertory Ensemble,
New York, NY.
$25,000 to New York University, Child Study Center,
New York, NY.
$10,000 to Big Apple Circus, New York, NY.
$10,000 to National Association on Drug Abuse
Problems, New York, NY.
$7,500 to Bailey House, New York, NY.

6930
Adolph & Ruth Schnurmacher Foundation, Inc.
551 5th Ave., Ste. 1210
New York, NY   10176   (212) 986-1533
Contact: Janet Plotkin, Pres.
FAX: (212) 972-2303;
E-mail: info@arsfoundation.com; URL: http://
www.arsfoundation.com

Established in 1977 in NY.
Donors: Adolph Schnurmacher†; Ruth
Schnurmacher†.
Foundation type: Independent foundation.
Financial data (yr. ended 12/31/05): Assets,
$27,138,973 (M); expenditures, $2,055,813;
qualifying distributions, $1,870,136; giving
activities include $1,669,617 for 144 grants (high:
$52,500; low: $500; average: $7,500–$15,000).
Purpose and activities: Giving for the arts,
education, social services, health-related programs,
and other charitable purposes.
Fields of interest: Arts; Education; Health
organizations, association; Human services; Public
affairs.
Type of support: General/operating support;
Continuing support; Equipment; Emergency funds;
Conferences/seminars; Curriculum development;
Scholarship funds; Research; Matching/challenge
support.
Limitations: Giving in the metropolitan New York,
NY, area; funding also in Fairfield County, CT. No
support for projects and organizations outside of the
U.S., or for political organizations. No grants to
individuals.
Publications: IRS Form 990-PF.
Application information: Application form not
required.
Initial approach: Letter
Copies of proposal: 5
Deadline(s): None
Board meeting date(s): 6 to 8 times a year
Officers and Trustees:* Janet Plotkin,* Pres.;
Amanda Plotkin,* V.P.; Carolyn Plotkin,* V.P.;
Jonathan Plotkin,* V.P.; Fred Plotkin,* Secy.-Treas.
Number of staff: 1 full-time support; 4 part-time
support.
EIN: 132938935
Selected grants: The following grants were reported
in 2005.
$50,000 to Fairfield University, Fairfield, CT.
$50,000 to Lenox Hill Hospital, New York, NY.
$40,000 to Anti-Defamation League of Bnai Brith,
New York, NY.
$27,500 to Salvation Army of Greater New York,
New York, NY.
$25,000 to Bronx Museum of the Arts, Bronx, NY.
$25,000 to Childrens Health Fund, New York, NY.
$25,000 to G and P Foundation for Cancer
Research, New York, NY.
$15,000 to Westport Public Library, Westport, CT.
$10,000 to Jazz at Lincoln Center, New York, NY.
$10,000 to Mid-Fairfield Hospice, Norwalk, CT.

6931
Charles & Mildred Schnurmacher Foundation, Inc.
155 E. 55th St., Ste. 6J
New York, NY   10022   (212) 838-7766
Contact: Ira J. Weinstein, Pres.

Established in 1977 in NY.
Donor: Charles M. Schnurmacher†.
Foundation type: Independent foundation.
Financial data (yr. ended 12/31/05): Assets,
$25,253,937 (M); expenditures, $2,145,209;
qualifying distributions, $1,919,072; giving
activities include $1,625,677 for grants.
Purpose and activities: Support primarily for music
organizations, art therapy, social services, health
care, Jewish agencies and temples, food banks,
animal spay-neuter programs, and botanical

gardens and garden restoration. Limited funding for mental health treatment.

Fields of interest: Arts; Education; Botanical gardens; Animal population control; Hospitals (general); Mental health, treatment; Medical research, institute; Food banks; Human services, victim aid; Jewish federated giving programs; Jewish agencies & temples; Homeless.

Type of support: Internship funds; General/ operating support; Continuing support; Management development/capacity building; Capital campaigns; Equipment; Endowments; Emergency funds; Program development; Conferences/seminars; Publication; Seed money; Curriculum development; Scholarship funds; Research; Technical assistance; Program-related investments/loans; Matching/challenge support.

Limitations: Giving limited to the metropolitan New York, NY area, but all requests will be considered. No grants to individuals or charities without an IRS determination letter.

Publications: Annual report.

Application information: Application form not required.

> *Initial approach:* Letter (preferred)
> *Copies of proposal:* 4
> *Deadline(s):* None
> *Board meeting date(s):* 6 times per year, and special meetings as needed
> *Final notification:* Up to 2 months

Officers and Directors: Ira J. Weinstein,* Pres.; Barbara Packer,* V.P. and Secy.; Peter Weinstein, DVM*, V.P.

Number of staff: 1 part-time support.

EIN: 132937218

Selected grants: The following grants were reported in 2004.

$200,000 to Neurosciences Research Foundation, San Diego, CA.

$65,000 to Lenox Hill Hospital, New York, NY.

$50,000 to Temple Beth-El of Great Neck, Great Neck, NY.

$40,000 to Fountain House, New York, NY.

$35,000 to Varicella Zoster Virus (VZV) Research Foundation, New York, NY.

$30,000 to Metropolitan Opera Association, New York, NY.

$25,000 to Catching the Dream, Albuquerque, NM.

$25,000 to New York Blood Center, New York, NY.

$25,000 to Safe Horizon, New York, NY.

$12,500 to Holocaust Documentation and Education Center, North Miami, FL.

6932

The Scholarships Foundation, Inc. ✧ ☆

P.O. Box 6020
New York, NY   10128

Established in 1921.

Donor: Audrey Dexter Hedge Trust.

Foundation type: Independent foundation.

Financial data (yr. ended 6/30/05): Assets, $81,523 (M); expenditures, $409,176; qualifying distributions, $383,700; giving activities include $383,700 for grants to individuals.

Purpose and activities: Awards grants to undergraduate and graduate students enrolled in academic or vocational programs either full or part-time. Priority is given to students who do not fit into defined scholarship categories. Preference is also given to students for study in New York State or residents of New York State who plan to study elsewhere.

Type of support: Scholarships—to individuals.

Limitations: Giving primarily in NY. No support for study abroad.

Application information: Application form required.

> *Initial approach:* Typewritten letter, no more than 1 page, with SASE; form letters not accepted
> *Deadline(s):* None
> *Board meeting date(s):* Monthly

Officers: Mrs. Charles L. Fleming, Pres.; Mrs. Warren Gunderson, V.P.; Mrs. Gerald R. Philips, Recording Secy.; Mrs. Rodman Benedict, Corresponding Secy.; Phoebe R. Stanton, Treas.

Directors: Ann Spindler; Mrs. Philip D. Wiedel.

Number of staff: 1 part-time professional.

EIN: 066043809

6933

Schon Family Foundation ✧

1534 53rd St.
Brooklyn, NY   11219
Contact: Henry A. Schon, Pres.

Established in 1992 in NY.

Donors: Henry A. Schon; Baron Schon; Heidi Gelley; Abraham Shaulson; Mesivta Torah Institute.

Foundation type: Independent foundation.

Financial data (yr. ended 12/31/05): Assets, $11,232,237 (M); gifts received, $618,000; expenditures, $542,151; qualifying distributions, $505,525; giving activities include $502,250 for 25 grants (high: $151,000; low: $1,000).

Purpose and activities: Giving primarily to Jewish temples and schools.

Fields of interest: Education; Jewish agencies & temples.

Limitations: Applications not accepted. Giving primarily in Brooklyn, NY. No grants to individuals.

Application information: Contributes only to pre-selected organizations.

Officers: Henry A. Schon, Pres.; Anna Schon, V.P.; Heidi Gelley, Secy.; Baron Schon, Treas.

EIN: 113133066

6934

Lewis Schott Foundation ✧

c/o A. Kozak and Co., LLP
192 Lexington Ave., Ste. 1100
New York, NY   10016-6823

Established in 1992 in DE and FL.

Donor: Lewis M. Schott.

Foundation type: Independent foundation.

Financial data (yr. ended 12/31/05): Assets, $3,001,118 (M); expenditures, $757,745; qualifying distributions, $732,305; giving activities include $730,926 for 45 grants (high: $243,001; low: $500).

Purpose and activities: Giving primarily for education, health and social services.

Fields of interest: Performing arts, orchestra (symphony); Arts; Higher education; Education; Health care; Health organizations; Athletics/sports, racquet sports; Human services; Federated giving programs; Jewish federated giving programs.

Limitations: Applications not accepted. Giving primarily in FL. No grants to individuals.

Application information: Contributes only to pre-selected organizations.

Officers: Lewis M. Schott, Pres.; Nash W. Schott, Secy.

Directors: Victoria de Rothschild; Steven G. Schott.

EIN: 581969908

6935

Schulhof Family Foundation ✧

c/o Michael Schulhof
375 Park Ave., Ste. 1506
New York, NY   10152

Established in 2000 in NY.

Donor: Michael P. Schulhof.

Foundation type: Independent foundation.

Financial data (yr. ended 11/30/05): Assets, $2,752,243 (M); gifts received, $525,000; expenditures, $523,667; qualifying distributions, $523,667; giving activities include $473,667 for 102 grants.

Fields of interest: Arts; Education; Health organizations, association; Human services; Children/youth, services; Jewish federated giving programs.

Limitations: Giving primarily in NY. No support for foreign students to attend colleges outside of the U.S.

Application information: Application form required.

> *Deadline(s):* None

Trustees: Michael P. Schulhof; Paola Schulhof.

EIN: 134150938

6936

The Schulweis Family Foundation ✧

c/o H. Schulweis, Schulweis Realty
9 W. 57th St., 50th Fl.
New York, NY   10019

Established in 1989 in NY.

Donors: Harvey Schulweis; Carol Schulweis.

Foundation type: Independent foundation.

Financial data (yr. ended 12/31/05): Assets, $1,588,755 (M); gifts received, $884,282; expenditures, $620,399; qualifying distributions, $620,149; giving activities include $620,149 for 63 grants (high: $165,500; low: $28).

Purpose and activities: Giving primarily to Jewish organizations and temples, as well as for the arts, particularly museums, hospitals and health organizations, social services and federated giving programs.

Fields of interest: Museums; Arts; Higher education; Education; Hospitals (general); Health organizations, association; Human services; Federated giving programs; Jewish federated giving programs; Jewish agencies & temples.

International interests: Israel.

Limitations: Applications not accepted. Giving primarily in New York, NY. No grants to individuals.

Application information: Contributes only to pre-selected organizations.

Trustee: Harvey Schulweis.

EIN: 136930204

6937

The Paul D. Schurgot Foundation, Inc. ✧

280 Madison Ave., Ste. 1102
New York, NY   10016   (212) 725-5505
Contact: William J. Butler, Pres.

Foundation type: Independent foundation.

Financial data (yr. ended 12/31/05): Assets, $10,156,614 (M); expenditures, $505,523;

qualifying distributions, $470,208; giving activities include $437,370 for 48 grants (high: $120,000; low: $100).

Fields of interest: Health care; Health organizations, association; Human services; Children/youth, services.

Limitations: Giving primarily in New York, NY. No grants to individuals.

Application information:
Initial approach: Letter
Deadline(s): None
Officers: William Butler, Pres.; Jane Butler, Secy.
Board Member: Tom Sweeney.
EIN: 237137799

Selected grants: The following grants were reported in 2004.
$50,000 to Metropolitan Museum of Art, New York, NY.
$50,000 to Washington and Jefferson College, Washington, PA.
$10,000 to Center for International Policy, DC.
$5,000 to NPR Foundation, DC.
$4,000 to American Diabetes Association, Alexandria, VA.
$2,500 to American Cancer Society, Atlanta, GA.
$2,500 to British Institute of Human Rights, London, England. .
$2,500 to Canadian Human Rights Foundation, Montreal, Canada. .
$2,500 to City and Country School, New York, NY.
$2,000 to Meretz USA, New York, NY.

6938
Schwartz Family Foundation ✧
c/o BCRS Associates, LLP
100 Wall St., 11th Fl.
New York, NY 10005

Established in 1991 in NY.
Donor: Mark Schwartz.
Foundation type: Independent foundation.
Financial data (yr. ended 4/30/05): Assets, $653,476 (M); gifts received, $933,400; expenditures, $613,401; qualifying distributions, $593,484; giving activities include $591,498 for 36 grants (high: $200,000; low: $100; average: $500–$25,000).

Purpose and activities: Giving primarily for higher education, health associations, particularly to a children's hospital, Jewish organizations and temples, social services, and the arts, particularly to a cultural foundation.
Fields of interest: Arts; Higher education; Business school/education; Education; Hospitals (specialty); Health organizations, association; Human services; Children, services; Community development, neighborhood development; Jewish federated giving programs; Jewish agencies & temples.
Limitations: Applications not accepted. Giving primarily in NY, with emphasis on New York City; funding also in MA. No grants to individuals, or for scholarships; no loans.
Application information: Contributes only to pre-selected organizations.
Trustees: Lisa H. Schwartz; Mark Schwartz.
EIN: 133632755
Selected grants: The following grants were reported in 2004.
$2,750,000 to Harvard University, Business School, Cambridge, MA. For general support.
$2,000,000 to Childrens Hospital Building Fund, New York, NY. For general support.

$1,438,280 to Northern Westchester Hospital Center Foundation, Mount Kisco, NY. 3 grants: $250,000 (For general support), $973,404 (For general support. Grant made in form of stock), $214,876 (For general support. Grant made in form of stock).
$1,000,000 to Bard College, Annandale on Hudson, NY. For general support.
$1,000,000 to Bet Torah Synagogue, Mount Kisco, NY. For general support.
$100,000 to Beacon Cultural Foundation, Beacon, NY. 2 grants: $50,000 each (For general support).
$100,000 to Massachusetts General Hospital, Boston, MA. For general support for Partners AIDS Research Center.

6939
Schwartz Family Foundation ✧
c/o Bear Stearns
383 Madison Ave., 42nd Fl.
New York, NY 10179
Contact: Alan Schwartz, Tr.

Established in 1997 in NY.
Donor: Alan Schwartz.
Foundation type: Independent foundation.
Financial data (yr. ended 12/31/05): Assets, $11,190,120 (M); gifts received, $4,749,130; expenditures, $1,017,183; qualifying distributions, $1,009,000; giving activities include $1,009,000 for 50 grants (high: $300,000; low: $500).
Purpose and activities: Giving primarily for higher education.
Fields of interest: Higher education.
Limitations: Applications not accepted. Giving primarily in NC. No grants to individuals.
Application information: Contributes only to pre-selected organizations.
Trustees: Alan Schwartz; Nancy M. Seaman.
EIN: 137138217
Selected grants: The following grants were reported in 2004.
$196,848 to National Mentoring Partnership, Alexandria, VA. 2 grants: $25,000, $171,848
$25,000 to Apollo Theater Foundation, New York, NY.
$25,000 to Brookings Institution, DC.
$25,000 to Duke University, Durham, NC.
$25,000 to Saint Vincents Services, Brooklyn, NY.
$15,000 to Eagle Hill School, Greenwich, CT.
$12,000 to Masters School, Dobbs Ferry, NY.
$10,000 to Brunswick School, Greenwich, CT.
$10,000 to Covenant House, New York, NY.

6940
Barry K. Schwartz Family Foundation, Inc. ✧ ☆
159 Mahopac Ave.
Granite Springs, NY 10527

Established in 1987 in DE.
Donor: Barry K. Schwartz.
Foundation type: Independent foundation.
Financial data (yr. ended 10/31/05): Assets, $25,978 (M); gifts received, $248,570; expenditures, $366,023; qualifying distributions, $363,125; giving activities include $363,125 for grants.

Fields of interest: Arts; Higher education, university; Health organizations, research; Family services; Religion.
Limitations: Applications not accepted. Giving primarily in NY and Providence, RI. No grants to individuals.
Application information: Contributes only to pre-selected organizations.
Officers: Barry K. Schwartz, Pres.; Sheryl R. Schwartz, V.P.
EIN: 133472786
Selected grants: The following grants were reported in 2005.
$100,000 to Sanctuary for Families, New York, NY.
$29,850 to Double H Hole in the Woods Ranch, Lake Luzerne, NY.
$25,125 to Ronald McDonald House.
$10,000 to Auburn Theological Seminary, New York, NY.
$2,250 to New York Service for the Handicapped, New York, NY.
$2,000 to Belmont Child Care Association, Elmont, NY.
$500 to Special Olympics, DC.

6941
Peter A. and Marion W. Schwartz Family Foundation Trust ✧
5337 Black Point Rd.
Canandaigua, NY 14424

Established in 1997 in CT.
Donor: Peter A. Schwartz.
Foundation type: Independent foundation.
Financial data (yr. ended 12/31/05): Assets, $26,370,727 (M); expenditures, $1,430,290; qualifying distributions, $1,349,000; giving activities include $1,349,000 for 58 grants (high: $185,000; low: $1,000).
Purpose and activities: Giving primarily for the arts, education, and human services.
Fields of interest: Museums (natural history); Higher education; Reproductive health, family planning; Cancer; Medical research; Human services.
Limitations: Applications not accepted. Giving primarily in CT and NY. No grants to individuals.
Application information: Contributes only to pre-selected organizations.
Trustees: Marion W. Schwartz; Peter A. Schwartz.
EIN: 066447457
Selected grants: The following grants were reported in 2005.
$100,000 to American Red Cross.
$100,000 to Brothers Brother Foundation, Pittsburgh, PA.
$75,000 to American Museum of Natural History, New York, NY.
$75,000 to Finger Lakes Land Trust, Ithaca, NY.
$60,000 to Yale University, New Haven, CT.
$40,000 to Project Hope, Brooklyn, NY. 2 grants: $20,000 each
$40,000 to SEE International, Santa Barbara, CA.
$30,000 to Endangered Language Fund, New Haven, CT.
$20,000 to Mercy Flight Central, Canandaigua, NY.

6942
Schwartz Foundation ✧
c/o Goldman Sachs
1 New York Plz., 40th Fl.
New York, NY 10004

Established in 1996 in NY.
Donor: Eric S. Schwartz.
Foundation type: Independent foundation.
Financial data (yr. ended 8/31/05): Assets, $5,204,900 (M); gifts received, $312,150; expenditures, $530,956; qualifying distributions, $522,218; giving activities include $522,218 for 42 grants (high: $162,645; low: $100).
Fields of interest: Elementary/secondary education; Higher education; Health organizations, association; Human services; Jewish federated giving programs; Jewish agencies & temples.
Limitations: Applications not accepted. Giving primarily in NY. No grants to individuals, or for scholarships; no loans.
Application information: Contributes only to pre-selected organizations.
Trustees: Eric S. Schwartz; Erica Schwartz.
EIN: 133957291

6943
The Donna and Marvin Schwartz Foundation ✧
c/o Neuberger & Berman
605 3rd Ave.
New York, NY 10158-3698

Established in 1997 in NY.
Donors: Donna Schwartz; Marvin C. Schwartz.
Foundation type: Independent foundation.
Financial data (yr. ended 4/30/05): Assets, $97,241,568 (M); gifts received, $1,951,725; expenditures, $2,358,461; qualifying distributions, $2,283,760; giving activities include $2,283,760 for grants.
Purpose and activities: Giving primarily to a university; some funding also for the arts, health, and medical research.
Fields of interest: Arts; Higher education; Environment, natural resources; Health organizations, association; Medical research, institute; Human services; Community development; Religion.
Limitations: Applications not accepted. No grants to individuals.
Application information: Contributes only to pre-selected organizations.
Trustees: Donna Schwartz; Marvin C. Schwartz.
EIN: 137114848
Selected grants: The following grants were reported in 2004.
$1,600,000 to Emory University, Atlanta, GA.
$273,500 to Baruch College Fund, New York, NY. 2 grants: $250,000, $23,500
$150,000 to Metropolitan Opera, New York, NY.
$48,600 to Neuberger Museum, Friends of the, Purchase, NY. 2 grants: $25,000, $23,600
$33,000 to Philharmonic-Symphony Society of New York, New York Philharmonic, New York, NY.
$25,000 to Columbia University, Mailman School of Public Health, New York, NY.
$25,000 to Westhampton Beach Performing Arts Center, Westhampton Beach, NY.
$15,000 to Glaucoma Foundation, New York, NY.

6944
Bernard & Irene Schwartz Foundation, Inc. ▼ ✧
c/o Loral Corp.
944 5th Ave.
New York, NY 10021

Established in 1981 in NY.
Donors: Bernard L. Schwartz; Irene Schwartz.
Foundation type: Independent foundation.
Financial data (yr. ended 11/30/05): Assets, $5,196,990 (M); gifts received, $5,582,600; expenditures, $8,957,704; qualifying distributions, $8,937,602; giving activities include $8,866,173 for 65 grants (high: $2,979,000; low: $600; average: $5,000–$500,000).
Purpose and activities: Giving primarily for health care, education, and the arts.
Fields of interest: Arts; Higher education; Education; Hospitals (general); Jewish federated giving programs.
Limitations: Applications not accepted. Giving primarily in New York, NY. No grants to individuals.
Application information: Contributes only to pre-selected organizations.
Officers and Directors:* Irene Schwartz,* Pres.; Karen Schwartz Paddock,* V.P.; Francesca Schwartz,* V.P.; Judith Linksman, Secy.-Treas.; Robert B. Hodes; Ronald Kissner; Bernard L. Schwartz.
EIN: 133099518
Selected grants: The following grants were reported in 2005.
$2,979,000 to New School, New York, NY. For general support.
$1,250,000 to New America Foundation, DC. For general support.
$672,531 to Johns Hopkins University, Baltimore, MD. For general support.
$548,791 to Baruch College of the City University of New York, New York, NY. For general support.
$500,000 to New River Education Fund, DC. For general support.
$350,000 to W N E T Channel 13, New York, NY. For general support.
$150,000 to Brookings Institution, DC. For general support.
$50,000 to Franklin and Eleanor Roosevelt Institute (FERI), Hyde Park, NY. For general support.
$25,000 to American ORT Federation, New York, NY. For general support.
$25,000 to Institute for Americas Future, DC. For general support.

6945
David Schwartz Foundation, Inc. ✧
c/o Siegel, Sacks Press & Lacher PC
600 3rd Ave., 18th Fl.
New York, NY 10016-1901

Incorporated in 1945 in NY.
Donors: David Schwartz; Jonathan Logan, Inc.; and others.
Foundation type: Independent foundation.
Financial data (yr. ended 5/31/05): Assets, $10,714,582 (M); expenditures, $1,162,942; qualifying distributions, $909,960; giving activities include $832,375 for grants.
Purpose and activities: Giving primarily for arts and culture; funding also for higher education, and Jewish organizations.
Fields of interest: Arts, alliance; Museums; Performing arts, theater; Historic preservation/historical societies; Arts; Higher education; Medical school/education; Jewish federated giving programs; Jewish agencies & temples.
Type of support: General/operating support.
Limitations: Applications not accepted. Giving primarily in NY, with emphasis on New York City. No grants to individuals.

Application information: Contributes only to pre-selected organizations.
Board meeting date(s): Annually, usually in May or June
Officers and Directors:* Richard J. Schwartz,* Pres.; Sheila Schwartz,* V.P.; Stephen D. Gardner,* Secy.; Irene Schwartz.
EIN: 226075974
Selected grants: The following grants were reported in 2004.
$396,600 to Cornell University, Ithaca, NY.
$60,000 to Queens Theater in the Park, Flushing, NY.
$50,000 to Brandeis University, Waltham, MA.
$50,000 to Juilliard School, New York, NY.
$50,000 to UJA-Federation of New York, New York, NY.
$20,000 to Frederick Douglass Creative Arts Center, New York, NY.
$20,000 to Working Playground, New York, NY.
$12,500 to New York Foundation for the Arts, New York, NY.
$10,000 to Albert Einstein College of Medicine of Yeshiva University, Bronx, NY.
$10,000 to Fresh Air Fund, New York, NY.

6946
The Jack and Billie Schwartz Foundation ✧
39 Kenilworth Rd.
Rye, NY 10580

Established in 1997 in DE.
Donor: Pearl T. Schwartz.
Foundation type: Independent foundation.
Financial data (yr. ended 12/31/05): Assets, $272,608 (M); gifts received, $778,469; expenditures, $682,490; qualifying distributions, $682,350; giving activities include $682,350 for 10 grants (high: $215,000; low: $100).
Purpose and activities: Giving primarily for higher education and human services; funding also for an art museum, and a camp.
Fields of interest: Museums (art); Higher education; Hospitals (general); Human services; Jewish agencies & temples.
Limitations: Applications not accepted. Giving primarily in NY. No grants to individuals.
Application information: Contributes only to pre-selected organizations.
Officers: Harriet Johnson, Secy.; Deborah Raizes, Treas.
Director: Pearl T. Schwartz.
EIN: 133920688
Selected grants: The following grants were reported in 2005.
$215,000 to Lesley University, Cambridge, MA.
$110,150 to Surprise Lake Camp, New York, NY.
$100,000 to Saint Marys Foundation for Children, Bayside, NY.
$45,000 to Westchester Community College Foundation, Valhalla, NY.
$10,000 to New York University Medical Center, New York, NY.

6947
Schwarz Family Foundation ✧ ☆
c/o 3
211 E. 70th St., Ste. 23A
New York, NY 10021

Established in 1998 in NY.
Donor: Jeffrey E. Schwarz.
Foundation type: Independent foundation.
Financial data (yr. ended 12/31/05): Assets, $463,869 (M); gifts received, $430,875; expenditures, $407,708; qualifying distributions, $397,410; giving activities include $397,410 for 49 grants (high: $100,000; low: $180).
Purpose and activities: Giving primarily for Jewish organizations and education.
Fields of interest: Education; Jewish agencies & temples.
Limitations: Applications not accepted. Giving primarily in New York, NY. No grants to individuals.
Application information: Contributes only to pre-selected organizations.
Trustees: Joel Greenblatt; Rabbi Irwin Kula; Jeffrey E. Schwarz; Sherwood Schwarz.
EIN: 226743828
Selected grants: The following grants were reported in 2005.
$100,000 to University of Pennsylvania, Philadelphia, PA.
$25,900 to Limmud, London, England. .
$23,630 to Abraham Joshua Heschel School, New York, NY.
$10,000 to Abrahams Vision Of Peace, New York, NY.
$10,000 to American Friends of Shalom Hartman Institute, New York, NY.
$1,800 to Solomon Schechter School of Manhattan, New York, NY.

6948
Irene & Mac Schwebel Foundation, Inc. ✧
2 Leith Pl.
White Plains, NY   10605-3316

Established in 1959.
Donor: M. Mac Schwebel.
Foundation type: Independent foundation.
Financial data (yr. ended 12/31/03): Assets, $5,243,245 (M); expenditures, $1,008,145; qualifying distributions, $1,000,000; giving activities include $1,000,000 for 1 grant.
Purpose and activities: Giving primarily to the opera, and for Jewish education.
Fields of interest: Performing arts, opera; Education.
Limitations: Applications not accepted. Giving primarily in Palm Beach, FL, and NY. No grants to individuals.
Application information: Contributes only to pre-selected organizations.
Officer: M. Mac Schwebel, Pres.
EIN: 136161504

6949
The Thomas P. & Cynthia D. Sculco Foundation ✧
c/o Cynthia D. Sculco
132 E. 95th St.
New York, NY   10128
Contact: Thomas P. Sculco M.D., Pres.

Established in 1997 in NY.
Donors: Thomas P. Sculco, M.D.; Cynthia D. Sculco.
Foundation type: Independent foundation.
Financial data (yr. ended 2/28/05): Assets, $6,920,896 (M); gifts received, $1,492,780; expenditures, $503,939; qualifying distributions,

$460,045; giving activities include $459,700 for 51 grants (high: $240,000; low: $250).
Purpose and activities: Giving primarily for education.
Fields of interest: Performing arts, theater; Performing arts, opera; Higher education; Hospitals (general); Arthritis.
Limitations: Giving primarily in NY. No grants to individuals.
Application information: Application form not required.
Initial approach: Letter
Deadline(s): None
Officers: Thomas P. Sculco, M.D., Pres.; Cynthia D. Sculco, Secy.
EIN: 133952927
Selected grants: The following grants were reported in 2005.
$240,000 to Hospital for Special Surgery, New York, NY.
$1,000 to Westerly Hospital, Westerly, RI.

6950
The SDA Foundation ✧
c/o Lindsay Goldberg & Bessemer, LLC
630 5th Ave.
New York, NY   10111

Established in 2000 in NY.
Donor: Alan E. Goldberg.
Foundation type: Independent foundation.
Financial data (yr. ended 12/31/03): Assets, $7,543,504 (M); gifts received, $750,000; expenditures, $1,389,712; qualifying distributions, $1,387,000; giving activities include $1,387,000 for 18 grants (high: $250,000; low: $1,000).
Purpose and activities: Giving primarily for medical research and education, as well as for Jewish education and to Jewish organizations.
Fields of interest: Medical school/education; Education; Medical research, institute; Jewish federated giving programs; Jewish agencies & temples.
Limitations: Applications not accepted. Giving primarily in New York, NY. No grants to individuals.
Application information: Contributes only to pre-selected organizations.
Trustees: Alan E. Goldberg; Miriam P. Goldberg.
EIN: 137235530
Selected grants: The following grants were reported in 2003.
$250,000 to Cold Spring Harbor Laboratory, Cold Spring Harbor, NY.
$200,000 to Ohr Torah Stone Colleges and Graduate Programs, New York, NY.
$100,000 to Destiny Foundation, Monsey, NY.
$100,000 to EDAH, New York, NY.
$50,000 to Brandeis-Bardin Institute, Brandeis, CA.
$50,000 to Etzion Foundation, New York, NY.
$50,000 to Hebrew Institute of Riverdale, Bronx, NY.
$25,000 to P.E.F. Israel Endowment Funds, New York, NY.
$25,000 to Yeshiva University, New York, NY.
$1,000 to Mount Sinai School of Medicine of New York University, New York, NY.

6951
The Sealark Foundation, Inc. ✧
c/o Bessemer Trust Co., N.A.
630 5th Ave.
New York, NY   10111

Established in 1997 in DE.
Donor: James M. Clark.
Foundation type: Independent foundation.
Financial data (yr. ended 12/31/05): Assets, $8,996,736 (M); expenditures, $515,262; qualifying distributions, $493,070; giving activities include $470,000 for 9 grants (high: $100,000; low: $25,000).
Purpose and activities: Giving primarily for oceanographic research. Some funding for hospitals and education.
Fields of interest: Historic preservation/historical societies; Higher education, university; Hospitals (general); Health care; Marine science.
Limitations: Applications not accepted. Giving primarily in Woods Hole and Falmouth, MA; with some giving in NY. No grants to individuals.
Application information: Contributes only to pre-selected organizations.
Officers: James M. Clark, Pres.; James M. Clark, Jr., V.P. and Secy.; Mrs. James M. Clark, Treas.
EIN: 133747240

6952
Beatrice & Samuel A. Seaver Foundation ✧
c/o Eisner & Lubin
444 Madison Ave.
New York, NY   10022

Established in 1986 in NY.
Donor: Beatrice Seaver†.
Foundation type: Independent foundation.
Financial data (yr. ended 11/30/05): Assets, $74,014,692 (M); gifts received, $166,900; expenditures, $6,096,555; qualifying distributions, $5,869,579; giving activities include $5,342,795 for 47 grants (high: $3,900,078; low: $500).
Purpose and activities: Giving primarily for medical education and research, hospitals, cancer care, human services, and Jewish organizations.
Fields of interest: Higher education; Medical school/education; Hospitals (general); Cancer; Medical research, institute; Human services; Jewish federated giving programs; Jewish agencies & temples.
Type of support: Research.
Limitations: Applications not accepted. Giving primarily in New York, NY. No grants to individuals.
Application information: Contributes only to pre-selected organizations.
Trustees: John Cohen; Hirschell E. Levine.
EIN: 133251432
Selected grants: The following grants were reported in 2005.
$180,000 to New York University, New York, NY. 4 grants: $45,000 each
$31,200 to National Alliance for Research on Schizophrenia and Depression (NARSAD), Great Neck, NY. 2 grants: $1,200, $30,000
$25,000 to Beginning with Children Foundation, New York, NY.

6953
Seevers Family Foundation ✧ ☆
c/o BCRS Assocs., LLP
100 Wall St., 11th Fl.
New York, NY 10005

Established in 1987 in NY.
Donor: Gary L. Seevers.
Foundation type: Independent foundation.
Financial data (yr. ended 7/31/05): Assets,
$3,309,872 (M); gifts received, $104,300;
expenditures, $600,509; qualifying distributions,
$545,948; giving activities include $542,507 for 22
grants (high: $250,000; low: $250).
Purpose and activities: Giving primarily for the arts,
education, environmental conservation, and human
service organizations.
Fields of interest: Museums; Performing arts,
opera; Higher education; Libraries (public);
Education; Environment, natural resources;
Hospitals (general); Human services.
Limitations: Applications not accepted. Giving on a
national basis, with emphasis on MI and NY. No
grants to individuals.
Application information: Contributes only to
pre-selected organizations.
Trustees: Gary L. Seevers; Gary L. Seevers, Jr.;
Sharon Seevers.
EIN: 133437890

6954
**Nathan & Lena Seiler Family Foundation,
Inc.** ✧
c/o Lenat Co.
315 Westchester Ave.
Port Chester, NY 10573

Established in 1981 in NY.
Donors: Lena Seiler†; Nathan Seiler.
Foundation type: Independent foundation.
Financial data (yr. ended 12/31/05): Assets,
$9,084,376 (M); gifts received, $500,000;
expenditures, $471,253; qualifying distributions,
$384,700; giving activities include $384,700 for 33
grants (high: $50,000; low: $500).
Purpose and activities: Giving primarily to Jewish
agencies and temples, and for social services.
Fields of interest: Education; Animal welfare; Health
organizations, association; Human services;
International affairs; Jewish federated giving
programs; Jewish agencies & temples.
Limitations: Applications not accepted. Giving
primarily in the greater New York, NY, area. No
grants to individuals.
Application information: Contributes only to
pre-selected organizations.
Officers: Gloria S. Deitsch, Pres.; Irving Kaplan, V.P.
and Secy.; Betty S. Cohen, Treas.
EIN: 133106906
Selected grants: The following grants were reported
in 2005.
$30,000 to Chofetz Chaim Heritage Foundation,
 Monsey, NY.
$29,900 to Lev LAchim, Brooklyn, NY.
$25,000 to Center for Constitutional Rights, New
 York, NY.
$19,500 to Yeshiva Zichron Yaakov, Spring Valley,
 NY.
$18,000 to Wexner Heritage House, Columbus, OH.
$10,000 to Innocence Project, New York, NY.
$10,000 to New York Cares, New York, NY.
$5,000 to Chesed Avraham, Brooklyn, NY.

$500 to Delaware Valley Torah Institute, Cherry Hill,
NJ.

6955
Irving and Sara Selis Foundation, Inc. ✧ ☆
c/o Michael D. Robbins
40 E. 88th St., Ste. 3A
New York, NY 10128-1176

Established in NY.
Donors: Sara Selis†; Sara Selis Article Fourth Trust.
Foundation type: Independent foundation.
Financial data (yr. ended 12/31/05): Assets,
$2,861,412 (M); gifts received, $101,765;
expenditures, $418,251; qualifying distributions,
$411,078; giving activities include $406,000 for 3
grants (high: $400,000; low: $3,000).
Fields of interest: Libraries (public).
Limitations: Applications not accepted. Giving
primarily in New York, NY. No grants to individuals.
Application information: Contributes only to
pre-selected organizations.
Officers: Michael D. Robbins, Pres.; Lois O.
Robbins, V.P.; Carol Joy Heller, Secy.-Treas.
EIN: 270066678

6956
The SES Foundation, Inc. ✧ ☆
c/o Gericare
1650 63rd St.
Brooklyn, NY 11204-2713

Established in 2000 in NY.
Donors: Gericare Pharmaceuticals; Eli Shindler.
Foundation type: Independent foundation.
Financial data (yr. ended 11/30/05): Assets, $0
(M); gifts received, $320,000; expenditures,
$343,635; qualifying distributions, $343,520;
giving activities include $343,520 for 85 grants
(high: $45,000; low: $100).
Fields of interest: Jewish agencies & temples.
Application information:
 Initial approach: Letter
Officer: Eli Shindler, Pres.
EIN: 113579451

6957
The Setton Foundation ✧
85 Austin Blvd.
Commack, NY 11725

Established in 2000 in NY.
Donor: Setton International Foods of Brooklyn.
Foundation type: Independent foundation.
Financial data (yr. ended 12/31/05): Assets,
$916,738 (M); gifts received, $500,000;
expenditures, $421,823; qualifying distributions,
$422,821; giving activities include $422,821 for
228 grants (high: $54,677; low: $50).
Fields of interest: Jewish agencies & temples.
Limitations: Applications not accepted. No grants to
individuals.
Application information: Contributes only to
pre-selected organizations.
Officers and Directors:* Joshua Setton,* Pres. and
Secy.; Morris Setton,* V.P.; Rachel Souede.
EIN: 113577481

6958
Seventeen Torah Foundation, Inc. ✧
c/o Glass & Shiechel, LLP
110 Stewart Ave.
Hicksville, NY 11801

Established in 2000 in NY.
Donor: Chaim Wachsman.
Foundation type: Independent foundation.
Financial data (yr. ended 12/31/03): Assets,
$1,932,983 (M); expenditures, $335,050;
qualifying distributions, $334,750; giving activities
include $334,750 for grants.
Fields of interest: Jewish agencies & temples;
Religion.
Limitations: Applications not accepted. No grants to
individuals.
Directors: Yitty Eichenstein; Chaya Shaindy Tauber;
Benzion A. Wachsman; Boruch J. Wachsman; Chaim
Wachsman; Naftali Wachsman.
EIN: 113529422

6959
**Joseph and Libby Shapiro Family
Foundation** ✧
5 Fairchild Ct.
Plainview, NY 11803

Established in 2002 in NY.
Foundation type: Independent foundation.
Financial data (yr. ended 12/31/04): Assets,
$40,243 (M); gifts received, $206,584;
expenditures, $564,030; qualifying distributions,
$562,625; giving activities include $562,625 for 23
grants (high: $500,000; low: $25).
Purpose and activities: Giving primarily for health,
especially pediatrics and hematology research.
Fields of interest: Education; Health organizations;
Pediatrics research; Medical research; Hematology
research; Jewish agencies & temples.
Limitations: Applications not accepted. Giving
primarily in NY.
Application information: Contributes only to
pre-selected organizations.
Directors: Joseph Shapiro; Leonard Shapiro; Libby
Shapiro.
EIN: 010728257

6960
Shapiro-Silverberg Foundation ✧
c/o Yohalem, Gillman & Co.
477 Madison Ave.
New York, NY 10022

Established in 2000 in NY.
Donor: John M. Shapiro.
Foundation type: Independent foundation.
Financial data (yr. ended 12/31/05): Assets,
$25,974,477 (M); gifts received, $4,912,145;
expenditures, $1,870,799; qualifying distributions,
$1,809,950; giving activities include $1,809,200
for 27 grants (high: $450,000; low: $1,000).
Fields of interest: Children/youth, services.
Limitations: Applications not accepted. Giving
primarily in NY. No grants to individuals.
Application information: Contributes only to
pre-selected organizations.
Officers: John M. Shapiro, Pres.; Shonni J.
Silverberg, V.P.
EIN: 134151366

Selected grants: The following grants were reported in 2004.

$450,000 to Wesleyan University, Middletown, CT.

$330,000 to Dalton Schools, New York, NY.

$250,000 to American Jewish Committee, New York, NY.

$200,000 to Lawyers for Children, New York, NY.

$25,000 to New Israel Fund, DC.

$10,000 to Dorot, New York, NY.

$10,000 to Washington Institute, DC.

$5,000 to Institute of International Education, New York, NY.

$5,000 to Montefiore Medical Center, Bronx, NY.

6961
The Evelyn Sharp Foundation ✧

c/o Peter Sharp & Co.
545 Madison Ave.
New York, NY 10022 (212) 977-1300

Incorporated in 1952 in NY.

Donor: Evelyn Sharp†.

Foundation type: Independent foundation.

Financial data (yr. ended 12/31/05): Assets, $10,071,593 (M); expenditures, $558,102; qualifying distributions, $530,276; giving activities include $493,906 for 73 grants (high: $75,000; low: $250).

Fields of interest: Arts education; Museums; Performing arts; Performing arts, theater; Arts; Higher education; Hospitals (general).

Limitations: Giving primarily in New York, NY. No grants to individuals.

Application information: Generally contributes to pre-selected organizations. Application form not required.

Initial approach: Letter
Deadline(s): None

Officers and Trustees:* Mary Cronson,* Pres.; Paul Cronson,* Secy.; Barry Tobias,* Treas.; Claus Virch.

EIN: 136119532

6962
The Peter Jay Sharp Foundation ▼ ✧

(formerly Sharp Foundation)
545 Madison Ave., 11th Fl.
New York, NY 10022 (212) 397-6060

Established in 1984 in NY.

Donor: Peter J. Sharp†.

Foundation type: Independent foundation.

Financial data (yr. ended 12/31/04): Assets, $218,988,742 (M); gifts received, $1,200,000; expenditures, $31,025,347; qualifying distributions, $29,830,994; giving activities include $28,228,210 for 124+ grants (high: $2,600,000; average: $25,000–$250,000), and $799,278 for 2 foundation-administered programs.

Purpose and activities: Support primarily for museums; giving also for the performing arts, with emphasis on music.

Fields of interest: Museums; Performing arts; Performing arts, music; Education; Health organizations.

Limitations: Applications not accepted. Giving primarily in New York, NY. No grants to individuals.

Application information: Contributes only to pre-selected organizations.

Officers: Norman Peck, Pres.; Barry Tobias, Treas.

Directors: Edmund Duffy; Dan Lufkin; Jack Nash.

EIN: 133253731

Selected grants: The following grants were reported in 2004.

$2,600,000 to Mount Sinai School of Medicine of New York University, New York, NY. For Melanoma Initiative.

$1,025,000 to National Center for Disability Services, Albertson, NY. For Integrative Technology Programs.

$1,000,000 to Johns Hopkins University, Brady Urological Institute, Baltimore, MD. For Molecular Gene Array Laboratory.

$825,000 to Metropolitan Museum of Art, New York, NY. For Fund for Ruth and Harold D. Uris Center for Education.

$750,000 to Rockefeller University, New York, NY. For Attention Deficit Hyperactivity research project.

$700,000 to Harlem Day Charter School, New York, NY. To establish Charter School.

$375,000 to Beth Israel Deaconess Medical Center, Boston, MA. For Peter Jay Sharp Program in Reconstructive Breast Surgery.

$116,000 to Young Concert Artists, New York, NY. For advertising for Playing for Real.

$100,000 to Clearpool, Carmel, NY. To establish scholarships for Programs.

$80,000 to Bailey House, New York, NY. For renovations.

6963
Eric P. Sheinberg Foundation ✧

c/o Goldman Sachs & Co.
85 Broad St., Tax Dept.
New York, NY 10004

Established in 1971.

Donor: Eric P. Sheinberg.

Foundation type: Independent foundation.

Financial data (yr. ended 6/30/05): Assets, $10,007,955 (M); expenditures, $482,673; qualifying distributions, $473,150; giving activities include $469,275 for 53 grants (high: $75,000; low: $250).

Fields of interest: Museums; Libraries (public); Education; Environment; Hospitals (general); Health organizations; Crime/law enforcement, police agencies; Human services; Community development; Federated giving programs.

Type of support: General/operating support.

Limitations: Applications not accepted. Giving primarily in CT and New York, NY. No grants to individuals.

Application information: Contributes only to pre-selected organizations.

Trustees: Eric P. Sheinberg; Michael Steinhardt.

EIN: 137004291

Selected grants: The following grants were reported in 2004.

$116,500 to Mount Sinai Medical Center, New York, NY.

$25,000 to New York Public Library, New York, NY.

$14,000 to Central Park Conservancy, New York, NY.

$10,000 to American Red Cross, New Canaan, CT.

$10,000 to New Canaan Library, New Canaan, CT.

$10,000 to United Way of New Canaan, New Canaan, CT.

$6,000 to Human Rights Watch, New York, NY.

$5,000 to Memorial Sloan-Kettering Cancer Center, New York, NY.

$3,750 to Safe Horizon, New York, NY.

$300 to East Side Settlement House, New York, NY.

6964
Ralph C. Sheldon Foundation, Inc. ✧

P.O. Box 417
Jamestown, NY 14702-0417 (716) 664-9890
Contact: Miles L. Lasser, Exec. Dir.
FAX: (716) 483-6116; Application address: 7 E. 3rd St., Jamestown, NY 14701; FAX: (716) 483-6116

Incorporated in 1948 in NY.

Donors: Julia S. Livengood†; Isabell M. Sheldon†; Ralph C. Sheldon Trust.

Foundation type: Independent foundation.

Financial data (yr. ended 12/31/05): Assets, $11,201,070 (M); gifts received, $1,854,717; expenditures, $1,928,863; qualifying distributions, $1,893,465; giving activities include $1,868,480 for 86 grants (high: $400,150; low: $100).

Purpose and activities: Support for youth development organizations, community improvement, cultural organizations, hospitals, social service organizations, and education.

Fields of interest: Visual arts; Performing arts; Performing arts, theater; Arts; Libraries/library science; Education; Environment; Hospitals (general); Human services; Youth, services; Community development.

Type of support: General/operating support; Annual campaigns; Capital campaigns; Building/renovation; Equipment; Emergency funds.

Limitations: Giving limited to southern Chautauqua County, NY. No support for religious organizations. No grants to individuals.

Publications: Application guidelines.

Application information: Contact foundation for deadlines. Application form required.

Initial approach: Letter or telephone for application
Copies of proposal: 8
Deadline(s): Varies with meeting dates
Board meeting date(s): Varies, approx. 5 times a year
Final notification: Immediately after determination

Officers and Directors:* Jane E. Sheldon,* Pres.; Mark Hampton,* V.P.; Peter B. Sullivan,* V.P.; Miles L. Lasser,* Secy. and Exec. Dir.; Barclay O. Wellman,* Treas.; Betsy Shults; Alexis Theofilactidis.

Number of staff: 1 part-time professional; 1 part-time support.

EIN: 166030502

Selected grants: The following grants were reported in 2004.

$500,000 to Womans Christian Association Hospital, Jamestown, NY. For capital campaign.

$300,000 to Boys and Girls Club of Jamestown, Jamestown, NY. For swimming pool project.

$50,000 to Audubon Society of Jamestown, Jamestown, NY. For Natural Center renovations.

$50,000 to YMCA of Jamestown, Jamestown, NY. For Joint Outreach Program.

$45,000 to Chautauqua Institution, Chautauqua, NY. For annual fund drive.

$25,000 to Lucille Ball Little Theater of Jamestown, Jamestown, NY. For new sound system.

$15,000 to American Red Cross, Jamestown, NY. For delivery vehicle.

$15,000 to Meals on Wheels of the Jamestown Area, Jamestown, NY. For vehicle replacement project.

$15,000 to Nature Conservancy, Rochester, NY. For French Creek Watershed Project.

$11,650 to Chautauqua Adult Day Care Centers, Jamestown, NY. For Family Transportation Program.

6965
The Hope Sheridan Foundation ✧

c/o Schulte Roth & Zabel
919 3rd Ave., 24th Fl.
New York, NY 10022

Established in 2001 in NY.
Donor: Hope Sheridan†.
Foundation type: Independent foundation.
Financial data (yr. ended 12/31/04): Assets, $262,218 (M); gifts received, $1,200,000; expenditures, $1,295,279; qualifying distributions, $1,285,666; giving activities include $1,285,666 for 3 grants (high: $1,000,000; low: $119,000).
Fields of interest: Cancer research.
Limitations: Applications not accepted. Giving primarily in New York, NY. No grants to individuals.
Application information: Contributes only to pre-selected organizations.
Trustees: Linda Dawson; Howard F. Scharfstein.
EIN: 137257964

6966
Susan Stein Shiva Foundation ✧

c/o Starr & Co., LLC
350 Park Ave., 9th Fl.
New York, NY 10022

Established in 1997 in CA.
Foundation type: Independent foundation.
Financial data (yr. ended 12/31/03): Assets, $19,548,357 (M); gifts received, $856,417; expenditures, $1,001,547; qualifying distributions, $910,098; giving activities include $850,210 for 79 grants (high: $178,800; low: $500).
Purpose and activities: Giving primarily to health care, education and the arts.
Fields of interest: Arts; Higher education; Hospitals (general).
Limitations: Giving primarily in NY. No grants to individuals.
Application information:
   Initial approach: Letter
   Deadline(s): None
Officers: Alexandra Shiva, Pres.; Andrew Shiva, V.P. and Treas.
EIN: 954620752
Selected grants: The following grants were reported in 2003.
$178,800 to Public Theater, New York, NY. For general operating support.
$100,000 to John Jay College of Criminal Justice of the City University of New York, New York, NY. For general operating support.
$50,000 to Bellevue Hospital Center, New York, NY. For general operating support.
$16,452 to New York City Ballet, New York, NY. For general operating support.
$12,500 to Hewitt School, New York, NY. For general operating support.
$5,000 to International Center of Photography, New York, NY. For general operating support.
$5,000 to Juilliard School, New York, NY. For general operating support.
$1,070 to Metropolitan Museum of Art, New York, NY. For general operating support.
$1,000 to Chamber Music Society of Lincoln Center, New York, NY. For general operating support.
$500 to Ballet Theater Foundation, New York, NY. For general operating support.

6967
The Edith Glick Shoolman Children's Foundation ✧ ☆

c/o O'Connor Davies Munns & Dobbins, LLP
60 E. 42nd St.
New York, NY 10165
URL: http://www.shoolman.org

Donor: Edith Glick Shoolman†.
Foundation type: Independent foundation.
Financial data (yr. ended 12/31/05): Assets, $25,458,342 (M); gifts received, $1,066,000; expenditures, $651,163; qualifying distributions, $454,675; giving activities include $454,675 for grants.
Fields of interest: Child development, education; Child development, services; Children.
Type of support: General/operating support.
Limitations: Giving primarily in the metropolitan New York, NY and Boston, MA, areas. No support for organizations lacking 501(c)(3) status. No grants to individuals.
Application information: Application form required.
   Initial approach: See foundation Web site for guidelines and deadlines
Trustees: Henry L. Berman; Deborah B. Breznay.
EIN: 043414101

6968
The Shoreland Foundation ✧

c/o Carol Ann Mealy
1 Comac Loop
Ronkonkoma, NY 11779

Established in 1994 in NY.
Donor: Anthony W. Wang.
Foundation type: Independent foundation.
Financial data (yr. ended 12/31/04): Assets, $38,848,130 (M); expenditures, $3,368,923; qualifying distributions, $3,367,389; giving activities include $3,360,855 for 75 grants (high: $2,300,000; low: $100).
Purpose and activities: Giving primarily to education; also to human services, horticulture and garden clubs, education and museums.
Fields of interest: Museums; Higher education, university; Horticulture/garden clubs; Children/youth, services; Philanthropy/voluntarism.
Type of support: General/operating support; Endowments.
Limitations: Applications not accepted. Giving primarily in NY. No grants to individuals.
Application information: Contributes only to pre-selected organizations.
Officers: Anthony W. Wang, Pres.; Lulu C. Wang, V.P.; Gary E. Martinelli, Secy.-Treas.
EIN: 113241828

6969
The SHS Foundation ✧

c/o Richard Feldman
888 7th Ave., Ste. 501
New York, NY 10106

Established in 2002 in NY.
Donor: Samuel H. Scripps.
Foundation type: Independent foundation.
Financial data (yr. ended 12/31/05): Assets, $2,067,523 (M); gifts received, $3,151,227; expenditures, $1,846,540; qualifying distributions,

$1,835,080; giving activities include $1,835,080 for 11 grants (high: $585,000; low: $10,000).
Purpose and activities: Giving primarily for the arts.
Fields of interest: Performing arts, theater; Arts; Education.
Limitations: Applications not accepted. Giving primarily in NY.
Application information: Contributes only to pre-selected organizations.
Officers and Directors:* Richard E. Feldman,* Pres.; Sara Throne,* Secy.; Joyce Bove.
EIN: 256819008

6970
The Shubert Foundation, Inc. ▼

234 W. 44th St.
New York, NY 10036 (212) 944-3777
Contact: Vicki Reiss, Exec. Dir.
FAX: (212) 944-3767; *URL:* http://www.shubertfoundation.org

Incorporated in 1945 in DE.
Donors: Lee Shubert†; J.J. Shubert†.
Foundation type: Independent foundation.
Financial data (yr. ended 5/31/05): Assets, $258,743,621 (M); gifts received, $136,401; expenditures, $18,656,477; qualifying distributions, $15,313,510; giving activities include $14,598,500 for 386 grants (high: $275,000; low: $3,000; average: $5,000–$75,000), and $374,198 for 1 foundation-administered program.
Purpose and activities: To build and perpetuate the live performing arts, particularly the professional theater, in the United States. Emphasis is on theater and a secondary focus on dance. Support for theatrical organizations with demonstrated artistic and administrative track records, and arts-related institutions necessary to maintain and support the theater. The foundation also operates a theatrical archive. Grants almost always made exclusively for general operating funds.
Fields of interest: Performing arts; Performing arts, dance; Performing arts, theater.
Type of support: General/operating support.
Limitations: Giving limited to the U.S. No grants to individuals, or for capital or endowment funds, conduit organizations, renovation projects, audience development, direct subsidy of reduced-price admissions, no loans.
Publications: Annual report (including application guidelines).
Application information: The foundation does not acknowledge receipt of proposals. Interviews with applicants are granted by appointment. Unaudited financial statements are not accepted. Grant requests must be submitted on the foundation's current application form. Application form is available on foundation Web site. E-mailed applications will not be accepted. Application form required.
   Initial approach: Letter or telephone
   Copies of proposal: 2
   Deadline(s): Non-Theater: Oct. 15; Theater: Dec. 1
   Final notification: Late May
Officers and Directors:* Gerald Schoenfeld,* Chair.; Michael I. Sovern,* Pres.; John W. Kluge,* V.P.; Philip J. Smith,* V.P.; Stuart Subotnick,* Secy.; Lee J. Seidler,* Treas.; Vicki Reiss, Exec. Dir.
Number of staff: 2 full-time professional; 1 full-time support.
EIN: 136106961

Selected grants: The following grants were reported in 2005.

$275,000 to Lincoln Center Theater, New York, NY. For general support.

$240,000 to Goodman Theater, Chicago, IL. For general support.

$240,000 to South Coast Repertory Theater, Costa Mesa, CA. For general support.

$220,000 to Public Theater, New York, NY. For general support.

$220,000 to Washington Drama Society, Arena Stage, DC. For general support.

$210,000 to Manhattan Theater Club, New York, NY. For general support.

$210,000 to Roundabout Theater Company, New York, NY. For general support.

$185,000 to Center Theater Group of Los Angeles, Los Angeles, CA. For general support for Mark Taper Forum.

$175,000 to Long Wharf Theater, New Haven, CT. For general support.

$175,000 to Playwrights Horizons, New York, NY. For general support.

6971

Rachel Bat Shulamit Foundation, Inc. ✧

c/o Fleet Street, Ltd.
512 7th Ave.
New York, NY 10018

Established in 2000 in NY.

Foundation type: Independent foundation.

Financial data (yr. ended 4/30/05): Assets, $522,140 (M); expenditures, $426,626; qualifying distributions, $426,525; giving activities include $426,425 for 12 grants (high: $112,500; low: $5,000).

Fields of interest: Jewish agencies & temples.

Limitations: Applications not accepted. Giving primarily in Brooklyn and New York, NY and NJ, especially Lakewood; giving also in Israel. No grants to individuals.

Application information: Contributes only to pre-selected organizations.

Officers: Manny Haber, Pres.; Shari Haber, V.P.; Stephen Haber, Secy.; Raymond Haber, Treas.

EIN: 134122676

6972

SI Bank & Trust Foundation ▼

(formerly SISB Community Foundation)
260 Christopher Ln., Ste. 3B
Staten Island, NY 10314 (718) 697-2831
FAX: (718) 697-3180; *URL:* http://www.sibtf.org

Established in 1998 in DE and NY.

Donors: Staten Island Savings Bank; SI Bank & Trust.

Foundation type: Independent foundation.

Financial data (yr. ended 6/30/05): Assets, $81,788,807 (M); expenditures, $5,531,645; qualifying distributions, $4,877,203; giving activities include $4,720,424 for 284 grants (high: $500,000; low: $75; average: $1,000–$100,000), $22,350 for 12 employee matching gifts, and $100,000 for foundation-administered programs.

Purpose and activities: The foundation supports organizations involved with arts and culture, education, health, housing, human services, and community development in the borough Staten Island.

Fields of interest: Arts; Education; Health care; Housing/shelter; Human services; Community development.

Type of support: Matching/challenge support; General/operating support; Capital campaigns; Building/renovation; Technical assistance; Sponsorships.

Limitations: Giving only in Staten Island, NY. No support for political causes, candidates, or lobbying efforts, fraternal or veterans organizations, business, professional, or civic associations or clubs, animal welfare groups, cemetery associations, or private foundations. No grants to individuals, or for renovations/repairs to places of worship, yearbook advertisements, research including medical research, memorial fundraising events, or tickets to fundraising events.

Publications: Application guidelines; Biennial report.

Application information: An application form is available online. Application form required.

Initial approach: Download application form, call to discuss application, mail proposal and application form to foundation if advised to do so

Copies of proposal: 1

Deadline(s): 2 months prior to board meeting

Board meeting date(s): Mar., June, Sept., and Dec.

Final notification: 2 months

Officers and Directors:* Harry P. Doherty,* Chair. and Pres.; Allan Weissglass,* V.P.; John R. Morris,* Treas.; Elizabeth Dubovsky, Exec. Dir.; Arthur W. Decker; Alice B. Diamond; John G. Hall; Dennis P. Kelleher.

Number of staff: 3 full-time professional.

EIN: 133993115

Selected grants: The following grants were reported in 2005.

$500,000 to Jewish Community Center of Staten Island, Staten Island, NY. For capital campaign to build a flagship facility.

$200,000 to Saint Peters Church, Staten Island, NY. For capital campaign for renovation of Farrell Hall.

$192,796 to Staten Island University Hospital, Staten Island, NY. For matching grant for Emergency Department expansion and modernization.

$150,000 to Seton Foundation for Learning, Staten Island, NY. For Bishop Patrick V. Ahern High School.

$70,000 to College of Staten Island Foundation, Staten Island, NY. For renewed funding for Strategies for Success at IS 49 and PS 57.

$60,000 to Council on the Arts and Humanities for Staten Island, Staten Island, NY. For Arts-in-Education Re-grant Program and related technical assistance for Staten Island public and private schools (K-12).

$40,000 to Project Hospitality, Staten Island, NY. For general operating support.

$20,000 to Oakwood Heights Community Church, Staten Island, NY. For new boiler system for church hall building.

$20,000 to Poets House, New York, NY. For Poetry in the Branches, initiative at Staten Island branches of New York Public Library.

$20,000 to Saint Vincent Catholic Medical Centers of New York, New York, NY. For fundraising events.

6973

The Sicherman Family Foundation, Inc. ✧

1451 52nd St.
Brooklyn, NY 11219
Contact: Wolf Sicherman, Pres.

Established in 1995 in NY.

Foundation type: Independent foundation.

Financial data (yr. ended 2/28/05): Assets, $140,873 (L); gifts received, $642,028; expenditures, $891,989; qualifying distributions, $891,941; giving activities include $891,000 for 28 grants (high: $50,000; low: $2,000).

Fields of interest: Elementary/secondary education; Jewish agencies & temples.

Limitations: Giving on a national basis.

Application information:

Initial approach: Letter

Deadline(s): None

Officer: Wolf Sicherman, Pres.

EIN: 510365530

Selected grants: The following grants were reported in 2003.

$100,000 to Yeshiva Minchas Eluzar, Brooklyn, NY.

$25,000 to Congregation Ohel Yehoshua, Brooklyn, NY.

6974

Harold W. Siebens Charitable Foundation, Inc. ✧

c/o Sullivan & Cromwell LLP
125 Broad St.
New York, NY 10004-2498

Established in 2001 in NY, IA, and MO.

Donors: Famsea Corporation; Seafam Corporation; Seacay Corporation.

Foundation type: Independent foundation.

Financial data (yr. ended 12/31/05): Assets, $1,423,343 (M); gifts received, $4,248,516; expenditures, $3,118,221; qualifying distributions, $3,114,602; giving activities include $2,866,359 for 40 grants (high: $500,000; low: $10,000).

Purpose and activities: Giving primarily for education, including a school for the deaf, as well as for community programs, health care, and children, youth, and social services.

Fields of interest: Elementary/secondary education; Higher education; Health care; Human services; Children/youth, services; Family services; Roman Catholic agencies & churches.

Type of support: General/operating support; Building/renovation; Endowments; Emergency funds; Program development; Scholarship funds.

Limitations: Applications not accepted. Giving primarily in IA and MO. No grants to individuals.

Application information: Contributes only to pre-selected organizations.

Officers and Directors:* Clifford A. Rae,* Pres. and Treas.; Henry Christensen III,* Secy.; Heather Rae Johnson,* Exec. Dir.; Charles T. Dowling; Stewart D. Siebens; William W. Siebens.

EIN: 133666768

Selected grants: The following grants were reported in 2003.

$500,000 to Central Institute for the Deaf, Saint Louis, MO. For scholarships.

$160,000 to Whitfield School, Saint Louis, MO. For endowment support.

$150,000 to Sierra Nevada College, Incline Village, NV. For scholarships for low-income students.

$145,000 to Salvation Army of Dallas, Dallas, TX. For program support.

$125,000 to Mentor Saint Louis, Saint Louis, MO. For program expansion and mentor recruitment.

$110,000 to New City School, Saint Louis, MO. For scholarship endowment fund support.

$80,000 to Anawim Housing, Des Moines, IA. For salary support for Shelter Care Program.

$75,000 to Salvation Army of Houston, Houston, TX. For program operating support.

$75,000 to Salvation Army of San Antonio, San Antonio, TX. For program operating support.

$50,000 to Family Gateway, Dallas, TX. For general operating support.

6975
Muriel F. Siebert Foundation, Inc. ◆
435 E. 52nd St.
New York, NY 10022

Donor: Muriel F. Siebert.
Foundation type: Independent foundation.
Financial data (yr. ended 12/31/04): Assets, $10,198,207 (M); gifts received, $250; expenditures, $441,547; qualifying distributions, $380,131; giving activities include $343,127 for 111 grants (high: $32,437; low: $35).
Purpose and activities: Giving primarily for arts and culture, and human services.
Fields of interest: Arts; Education; Medical care, rehabilitation; Health care; Cancer; Human services; Women, centers/services; Jewish agencies & temples; Women.
Limitations: Applications not accepted. Giving primarily in NY. No grants to individuals.
Application information: Contributes only to pre-selected organizations.
Officers: Muriel F. Siebert, Pres.; Patricia L. Francy, V.P.; Jane H. Macon, V.P.; June Jaffee, Secy.
EIN: 136266367
Selected grants: The following grants were reported in 2004.
$32,437 to Varicella Zoster Virus (VZV) Research Foundation, New York, NY.
$22,000 to Animal Rescue Fund of the Hamptons, Wainscott, NY.
$21,000 to Breast Cancer Research Foundation, New York, NY.
$15,000 to Animal Medical Center, New York, NY.
$15,000 to Coudert Institute Villa Dei Fiori, Palm Beach, FL.
$15,000 to Jazz at Lincoln Center, New York, NY.
$5,600 to Working in Support of Education, New York, NY.
$2,500 to Parrish Art Museum, Southampton, NY.
$2,000 to Aspen Institute, Queenstown, MD.
$1,200 to New York Public Library, New York, NY.

6976
Ruth and Jerome A. Siegel Foundation ◆ ☆
1175 Old White Plains Rd.
Mamaroneck, NY 10543-1018

Incorporated in 1951 in NY.
Donors: Titan Industrial Corp.; Jerome Siegel; Ruth Siegel.
Foundation type: Company-sponsored foundation.
Financial data (yr. ended 11/30/05): Assets, $1,312,339 (M); gifts received, $419,247; expenditures, $647,148; qualifying distributions, $637,704; giving activities include $637,704 for grants.

Purpose and activities: The foundation supports hospitals and organizations involved with arts and culture, education, human services, and religion.
Fields of interest: Museums; Performing arts; Arts; Higher education; Education; Hospitals (general); Cancer research; Big Brothers/Big Sisters; Human services; Federated giving programs; Jewish federated giving programs; Jewish agencies & temples; Religion.
Limitations: Applications not accepted. Giving primarily in NY. No grants to individuals.
Application information: Contributes only to pre-selected organizations.
Officer: Jerome A. Siegel, Pres. and Treas.
EIN: 136066216
Selected grants: The following grants were reported in 2005.
$200,000 to Sarah Lawrence College, Bronxville, NY.
$125,000 to White Plains Hospital Center, White Plains, NY.
$10,030 to Congregation Rodeph Sholom, New York, NY.
$6,020 to Westchester Reform Temple, Scarsdale, NY.
$5,000 to HealthCare Chaplaincy, New York, NY.
$5,000 to Union for Reform Judaism, New York, NY.
$2,500 to Magen David Adom USA, Skokie, IL.
$2,400 to Learning Leaders, New York, NY.
$2,000 to Central Reform Congregation, Saint Louis, MO.
$1,000 to Harvard Business School Fund, Boston, MA.

6977
Sigma Chi Greystone Foundation, Inc. ◆ ☆
c/o Sciarabba Walker & Co. LLP
P.O. Box 788
Ithaca, NY 14851 (607) 272-5550
Contact: Barbara Verna

Donor: William G. Geiger.
Foundation type: Independent foundation.
Financial data (yr. ended 12/31/04): Assets, $203,856 (M); gifts received, $505,098; expenditures, $768,829; qualifying distributions, $768,829; giving activities include $735,405 for 1 grant.
Fields of interest: Students, sororities/fraternities; Education.
Limitations: Giving primarily in Ithaca, NY. No grants for For educational scholarships.
Application information:
  Initial approach: Letter
  Deadline(s): None
Directors: George Agle; Mark Deangelis; John Foote; Jeff Gibb; Steve Gregg; John Way; Peter Wilhelm; Bob Williams; Gordon J. Whiting.
EIN: 161529623

6978
The William & Sylvia Silberstein Foundation, Inc. ◆
c/o Silberstein Holdings LLC
1600 Harrison Ave.
Mamaroneck, NY 10543 (914) 698-6636

Established in 1969 in NY.
Donors: William Silberstein†; Sylvia Silberstein.
Foundation type: Independent foundation.

Financial data (yr. ended 11/30/05): Assets, $8,232,157 (M); expenditures, $362,793; qualifying distributions, $332,600; giving activities include $332,600 for 13 grants (high: $100,000; low: $3,000).
Purpose and activities: Support primarily for Jewish welfare and health associations.
Fields of interest: Hospitals (general); Human services; Jewish agencies & temples.
Limitations: Applications not accepted. Giving primarily in the New York, NY, area. No grants to individuals.
Application information: Contributes only to pre-selected organizations.
Officers: Bruce Silberstein, Co-Pres.; Richard J. Stricof, Co-Pres.; Martin Rome, V.P.; Mary Farren, Secy.; Richard J. Stricof, Treas.
EIN: 237108375
Selected grants: The following grants were reported in 2004.
$695,457 to White Plains Hospital Center, White Plains, NY. 3 grants: $10,000, $100,000, $585,457
$37,000 to Cystic Fibrosis Foundation, Mineola, NY. 2 grants: $12,000, $25,000
$20,000 to CF Foundation, Atlanta, GA.
$1,000 to Jewish Guild for the Blind, New York, NY.
$600 to Congregation Emanu-El of Westchester, Rye, NY. 2 grants: $500, $100
$500 to Emelin Theater, Mamaroneck, NY.

6979
Silberstein-Boesky Family Foundation, Inc. ◆ ☆
340 Sarles St.
Mount Kisco, NY 10549

Established in 1997 in NY.
Foundation type: Independent foundation.
Financial data (yr. ended 12/31/05): Assets, $2,700,307 (M); expenditures, $361,065; qualifying distributions, $354,262; giving activities include $353,650 for 26 grants (high: $157,400; low: $250).
Purpose and activities: Giving primarily to youth programs, a hospital, and for the environment.
Fields of interest: Arts; Environment, natural resources; Health care; Health organizations, association; Disasters, 9/11/01; Boys & girls clubs.
Limitations: Applications not accepted. Giving primarily in NY. No grants to individuals.
Application information: Contributes only to pre-selected organizations.
Officers: Seema S. Boesky, Pres.; William T. Ward, Secy.
Directors: Leslie Steinau; William T. Ward, Jr.
EIN: 061498058
Selected grants: The following grants were reported in 2003.
$120,000 to Boys and Girls Club of Northern Westchester, Mount Kisco, NY.
$50,000 to Waterkeeper Alliance, Tarrytown, NY.
$25,000 to Childrens Hospital Foundation at Westchester Medical Center, Valhalla, NY.
$20,000 to Westchester Land Trust, Bedford Hills, NY.
$10,750 to Caramoor Center for Music and the Arts, Katonah, NY.
$6,000 to Northern Westchester Hospital Center, Mount Kisco, NY.
$1,000 to National Center for Learning Disabilities, New York, NY.

$625 to Audubon New York, Albany, NY.
$500 to Visiting Nurse Association of Hudson Valley, Mount Kisco, NY.
$300 to Westchester Community College Foundation, Valhalla, NY.

6980

The David and Lyn Silfen Foundation ✧

c/o BCRS Group/Marcum & Kliegman, LLP
100 Wall St., 11th Fl.
New York, NY 10005
Contact: David M. Silfen, Tr.

Established in 1981 in NY.
Donor: David M. Silfen.
Foundation type: Independent foundation.
Financial data (yr. ended 3/31/05): Assets, $2,345,667 (M); gifts received, $550,250; expenditures, $767,276; qualifying distributions, $754,739; giving activities include $754,370 for 67 grants (high: $150,000; low: $100).
Purpose and activities: Giving primarily for higher education and Jewish organizations; funding also for museums, health associations, particularly for cancer research, and to golf-related organizations.
Fields of interest: Museums; Museums (art); Elementary/secondary education; Higher education; Veterinary medicine, hospital; Hospitals (general); Health organizations; Cancer research; Athletics/sports, equestrianism; Athletics/sports, golf; Children/youth, services; Jewish federated giving programs; Jewish agencies & temples.
Limitations: Applications not accepted. Giving on a national basis, with emphasis on Bridgehampton, and New York, NY; some giving also in CA, CT, and PA. No grants to individuals.
Application information: Contributes only to pre-selected organizations.
Trustees: Adam Gordon Silfen; David M. Silfen; Lyn Silfen.
EIN: 133103011
Selected grants: The following grants were reported in 2005.
$155,000 to Temple Israel, Lawrence, NY. 2 grants: $5,000, $150,000
$100,000 to University of Pennsylvania, Philadelphia, PA.
$25,000 to Smithsonian Institution, DC.
$22,000 to Animal Medical Center, New York, NY. 2 grants: $12,000, $10,000
$20,500 to Connecticut College, New London, CT.
$20,000 to Riverdale Country School, Bronx, NY.
$5,000 to New-York Historical Society, New York, NY.
$5,000 to Prep for Prep, New York, NY.

6981

The Jack S. & Shirley M. Silver Foundation ✧ ☆

920 5th Ave.
New York, NY 10021

Established in 1985 in NY.
Donors: Jack S. Silver; Shirley M. Silver.
Foundation type: Independent foundation.
Financial data (yr. ended 5/31/05): Assets, $648,995 (M); expenditures, $375,902; qualifying distributions, $375,830; giving activities include $375,830 for grants.
Fields of interest: Performing arts, theater; Arts; Education; Children, services; Jewish federated giving programs; Jewish agencies & temples; Women.
Type of support: General/operating support.
Limitations: Applications not accepted. Giving primarily in New York, NY. No grants to individuals.
Application information: Contributes only to pre-selected organizations.
Trustees: Jack S. Silver; Shirley M. Silver.
EIN: 133343294

6982

The Harvey Silverman Foundation, Inc. ✧

c/o Kellogg Grp. LLC, attn.: Jeffrey Reynolds
48 Wall St., 30th Fl.
New York, NY 10005

Established in 1985 in DE and NY.
Donor: Harvey Silverman.
Foundation type: Independent foundation.
Financial data (yr. ended 11/30/05): Assets, $4,899,639 (M); expenditures, $861,367; qualifying distributions, $826,579; giving activities include $777,135 for 73 grants (high: $225,000; low: $25).
Purpose and activities: Giving primarily for health care, medical research, and to Jewish agencies and temples.
Fields of interest: Secondary school/education; Higher education; Education; Health care; Health organizations, association; Medical research, institute; Recreation; Human services; Jewish federated giving programs; Jewish agencies & temples.
Limitations: Applications not accepted. Giving primarily in NJ and New York, NY. No grants to individuals.
Application information: Contributes only to pre-selected organizations.
Officers: Harvey Silverman, Pres.; Jeffrey Reynolds, Secy.-Treas.
EIN: 133343289
Selected grants: The following grants were reported in 2003.
$200,000 to UJA-Federation of New York, New York, NY.
$100,000 to Adaptive Sports Foundation, Windham, NY.
$100,000 to Aish HaTorah, Brooklyn, NY.
$50,000 to Variety-The Childrens Charity, Los Angeles, CA.
$40,000 to Maryhaven Center of Hope, Port Jefferson, NY.
$10,000 to Berkshire School, Sheffield, MA.
$10,000 to Catskill Mountain Foundation, Hunter, NY.
$10,000 to Make-A-Wish Foundation of New Jersey, Union, NJ.
$10,000 to North Shore-Long Island Jewish Health System Foundation, Great Neck, NY.
$10,000 to Windham Foundation, Windham, NY.

6983

Marty and Dorothy Silverman Foundation ▼ ✧

830 3rd Ave., 6th Fl.
New York, NY 10022 (212) 832-9170
Contact: Lorin Silverman, Secy.-Treas.

Established in 1986.
Donor: Marty Silverman†.
Foundation type: Independent foundation.
Financial data (yr. ended 7/31/05): Assets, $351,241,274 (M); gifts received, $17,971; expenditures, $7,211,112; qualifying distributions, $17,200,624; giving activities include $6,876,470 for 145 grants (high: $1,000,000; low: $6,000; average: $15,000–$100,000), and $10,324,154 for 14 loans/program-related investments (high: $2,500,000; low: $153,654; average: $100,000–$1,000,000).
Purpose and activities: Support for programs that address the special needs of indigent senior citizens, including nursing homes and hospitals. Grants may also be made to educational and cultural organizations, and health and welfare agencies.
Fields of interest: Arts; Education, association; Hospitals (general); Health organizations, association; Human services; Aging, centers/services; Aging.
Type of support: Program-related investments/loans.
Limitations: Applications not accepted. Giving primarily in NY. No grants to individuals.
Application information: Contributes only to pre-selected organizations.
Officers and Directors: Patty Lipshutz,* V.P.; Lorin Silverman,* Secy.-Treas.
EIN: 222777449
Selected grants: The following grants were reported in 2005.
$1,000,000 to Rensselaer Polytechnic Institute, Troy, NY. For Noble Enterprise Constellation's biotechnology research.
$500,000 to Albany Medical Center, Albany, NY.
$300,000 to West Point Jewish Chapel Fund, New York, NY.
$253,000 to YM-YWHA of Riverdale, Bronx, NY.
$180,000 to Dorot, New York, NY.
$150,000 to American ORT Federation, New York, NY.
$137,900 to New York Legal Assistance Group, New York, NY.
$125,000 to Fund for the City of New York, New York, NY.
$50,000 to Fund for Public Health in New York, New York, NY.
$30,000 to Edith and Carl Marks Jewish Community House of Bensonhurst, Brooklyn, NY.

6984

The Raine & Stanley Silverstein Family Foundation, Inc. ✧

c/o Krusch & Modell
10 Rockefeller Plz., Ste. 710
New York, NY 10020-1966

Established in 1996 in NY.
Donors: Raine Silverstein; Stanley Silverstein.
Foundation type: Independent foundation.
Financial data (yr. ended 11/30/05): Assets, $472,611 (M); gifts received, $677,550; expenditures, $932,125; qualifying distributions, $896,114; giving activities include $896,114 for 58 grants (high: $130,000; low: $500).
Purpose and activities: Giving primarily for human services and Jewish agencies and temples.
Fields of interest: Education; Human services; Jewish agencies & temples.
Limitations: Applications not accepted. Giving primarily in NY. No grants to individuals.
Application information: Contributes only to pre-selected organizations.

Officers: Stanley Silverstein, Pres.; Raine Silverstein, V.P. and Treas.; Nina Miner, V.P.; Flori Silverstein, V.P.
EIN: 113353084

6985
Silverweed Foundation, Inc. ✧
c/o Anchin Block & Anchin, LLP
1375 Broadway
New York, NY 10018
Contact: Elizabeth Morin, Acct.

Established in 1989.
Foundation type: Independent foundation.
Financial data (yr. ended 12/31/05): Assets, $18,288,588 (M); expenditures, $2,835,763; qualifying distributions, $2,376,067; giving activities include $2,267,200 for 68 grants (high: $230,000; low: $1,000).
Purpose and activities: Giving primarily for education, the arts and to Jewish agencies and temples.
Fields of interest: Arts; Elementary/secondary education; Legal services; Human services; Children/youth, services; Family services; Federated giving programs; Jewish agencies & temples.
Limitations: Applications not accepted. Giving primarily in New York, NY. No grants to individuals.
Application information: Contributes only to pre-selected organizations.
Officers: Karen Freedman, Pres.; Susan K. Freedman, V.P. and Secy.; Nina P. Freedman, V.P. and Treas.
Number of staff: 1 full-time professional.
EIN: 133496446
Selected grants: The following grants were reported in 2004.
$250,000 to Wesleyan University, Middletown, CT.
$210,000 to Brown University, Providence, RI.
$200,000 to Lawyers for Children, New York, NY. 2 grants: $100,000 each
$200,000 to Public Art Fund, New York, NY. 2 grants: $80,000, $120,000
$100,000 to Educational Broadcasting Corporation, New York, NY.
$100,000 to Manhattan Theater Club, New York, NY.
$34,000 to Big Apple Circus, New York, NY.
$25,000 to Albright College, Reading, PA.

6986
The Arnold Simon Family Foundation, Inc. ✧
c/o Schneider, Schecter and Yoss, LLP
7 Penn Plz., Ste. 830
New York, NY 10001

Established in 1996 in NJ.
Donor: Arnold Simon.
Foundation type: Operating foundation.
Financial data (yr. ended 12/31/05): Assets, $5,264,237 (M); expenditures, $780,050; qualifying distributions, $706,079; giving activities include $706,079 for 12 grants (high: $400,000; low: $142).
Purpose and activities: Giving primarily for hospitals, and children and youth services, particularly to a center for research into child and adolescent mental health problems.

Fields of interest: Hospitals (general); Health organizations, association; Children/youth, services.
Limitations: Applications not accepted. Giving primarily in NY. No grants to individuals.
Application information: Contributes only to pre-selected organizations.
Trustee: Arnold Simon.
EIN: 223480373

6987
William E. Simon Foundation, Inc. ▼ ✧
(formerly William E. & Carol G. Simon Foundation, Inc.)
140 E. 45th St., Ste. 14D
New York, NY 10017 (212) 661-8366
FAX: (212) 661-9450; URL: http://www.wesimonfoundation.org

Established in 1967 in NJ.
Donor: William E. Simon†.
Foundation type: Independent foundation.
Financial data (yr. ended 12/31/04): Assets, $154,734,151 (M); gifts received, $5,983,725; expenditures, $8,557,664; qualifying distributions, $8,347,795; giving activities include $7,330,100 for 344 grants (high: $500,000; low: $25; average: $5,000–$100,000).
Purpose and activities: The main purpose of the foundation is to assist those in need by providing the means through which they may help themselves. The foundation seeks to fund programs that are effective in promoting independence and responsibility.
Fields of interest: Education; Human services; Children/youth, services; Religion; General charitable giving; Economically disadvantaged.
Type of support: General/operating support; Scholarship funds; Employee matching gifts; Matching/challenge support.
Limitations: Giving on a national basis, with emphasis on New York, NY, and Los Angeles and the San Francisco Bay Area, CA. No support for foreign charities. No grants to individuals.
Publications: Application guidelines; Grants list; Informational brochure.
Application information: Application form required.
  Initial approach: Telephone, write, or download for application guidelines
  Copies of proposal: 1
  Deadline(s): None
  Board meeting date(s): Varies
Officers and Directors:* J. Peter Simon,* Co-Chair.; William E. Simon, Jr.,* Co-Chair.; Leigh Simon Porges,* V.P. and Secy.; Aimee Simon Bloom,* V.P. and Treas.; Johanna K. Simon Morris; Daniel L. Mosley; Julie Simon Munro; James Piereson; Mary B. Simon Streep; William T. Wachenfeld.
Number of staff: 1 full-time professional; 1 full-time support; 1 part-time support.
EIN: 136217788
Selected grants: The following grants were reported in 2004.
$800,000 to Morristown Memorial Health Foundation, Morristown, NJ.
$500,000 to University of Rochester, Rochester, NY.
$250,000 to David Robinson Foundation, San Antonio, TX.
$150,000 to Archdiocese of Newark, Newark, NJ.
$100,000 to Missionaries of Charity, Bronx, NY.
$60,000 to California Community Foundation, Los Angeles, CA.

$60,000 to Hoover Institution on War, Revolution and Peace, Stanford, CA.
$25,000 to First Presbyterian Church of New Vernon, New Vernon, NJ.
$25,000 to Newark Academy, Livingston, NJ.
$20,000 to Union Hospital Foundation, Union, NJ.

6988
Carl and Fay Simons Family Charitable Trust No. 2
900 Park Ave., Rm. 27E
New York, NY 10021
Contact: Carl Simons, Tr.

Established in 1987 in MO.
Foundation type: Independent foundation.
Financial data (yr. ended 12/31/05): Assets, $2,385,400 (M); expenditures, $447,808; qualifying distributions, $414,757; giving activities include $413,030 for 31 grants (high: $150,000; low: $100).
Purpose and activities: Giving primarily for human services and health care, including deafness research; giving also for disadvantaged inner city youth.
Fields of interest: Hospitals (general); Health organizations, association; Human services; Jewish agencies & temples.
Type of support: General/operating support; Annual campaigns; Capital campaigns; Building/renovation; Endowments; Emergency funds; Program development; Research.
Limitations: Applications not accepted. Giving primarily in NY. No grants to individuals.
Application information: Contributes only to pre-selected organizations.
Trustees: Carl Simons; Fay Simons.
Number of staff: None.
EIN: 436335969

6989
The Simons Foundation ▼ ✧
101 Fifth Ave., 5th Fl.
New York, NY 10003
Contact: Marilyn Simons, Pres.
E-mail: admin@simonsfoundation.org; URL: http://www.simonsfoundation.org

Established in 1994 in NY.
Foundation type: Independent foundation.
Financial data (yr. ended 6/30/05): Assets, $324,809,625 (M); gifts received, $56,800,935; expenditures, $17,945,805; qualifying distributions, $17,185,475; giving activities include $17,185,475 for grants.
Purpose and activities: The primary mission of the foundation is to advance the frontiers of research in the basic sciences and mathematics.
Fields of interest: Autism research; Science, research; Mathematics.
Type of support: General/operating support; Capital campaigns; Endowments; Professorships; Research.
Limitations: Applications not accepted. No grants to individuals.
Publications: Annual report; Financial statement.
Application information: Contributes only to pre-selected organizations.
  Board meeting date(s): Throughout the year

Officers and Directors:* Marilyn Simons,* Pres.; James H. Simons, Ph.D.*, V.P. and Treas.; Mark Silber.
Number of staff: 2 part-time professional; 1 full-time support.
EIN: 133794889
Selected grants: The following grants were reported in 2005.
$1,450,741 to Cold Spring Harbor Laboratory, Cold Spring Harbor, NY. 2 grants: $225,000, $1,225,741
$1,144,425 to Stony Brook Foundation, Stony Brook, NY.
$1,061,500 to Rockefeller University, New York, NY. 2 grants: $61,500, $1,000,000
$1,000,000 to Mathematical Sciences Research Institute, Berkeley, CA.
$800,000 to Institute for Advanced Study, Princeton, NJ. 2 grants: $500,000, $300,000
$667,000 to Institut des Hautes Etudes Scientifiques (IHES), Friends of the, New York, NY.
$500,000 to Learning Spring Elementary School, New York, NY.

6990
Herbert & Nell Singer Foundation, Inc. ◇
c/o Singer, Netter, Dowd & Berman
460 Park Ave., 12th Fl.
New York, NY 10022

Donors: Herbert M. Singer†; The Peter Singer Trust; The Steven Singer Trust.
Foundation type: Independent foundation.
Financial data (yr. ended 12/31/05): Assets, $24,397,004 (M); expenditures, $419,459; qualifying distributions, $340,750; giving activities include $334,500 for 11 grants (high: $100,000; low: $2,000).
Purpose and activities: Giving primarily for human services, Jewish federated giving programs, and Jewish agencies and temples.
Fields of interest: Arts; Human services; Jewish federated giving programs; Jewish agencies & temples.
Limitations: Applications not accepted. Giving primarily in New York, NY. No grants to individuals.
Application information: Contributes only to pre-selected organizations.
Officers: Nell Singer, Pres.; Richard Netter, V.P.; Hector Dowd, Treas.
Director: Jay Sandak.
EIN: 133151548
Selected grants: The following grants were reported in 2004.
$400,000 to American Jewish Joint Distribution Committee, New York, NY.
$100,000 to Rockefeller University, New York, NY.
$50,000 to Thanks to Scandinavia, New York, NY.
$10,000 to Lincoln Center Theater, New York, NY.
$3,500 to Philharmonic-Symphony Society of New York, New York, NY.

6991
Singh Family Foundation ◇ ☆
c/o Goldman Sachs- Family Office
1 New York Plz., 40th Fl.
New York, NY 10004

Established in 1999 in NY.
Donor: Dinakar Singh.

Foundation type: Independent foundation.
Financial data (yr. ended 10/31/05): Assets, $28 (M); gifts received, $1,000; expenditures, $483,302; qualifying distributions, $482,102; giving activities include $482,102 for 2 grants (high: $367,802; low: $114,300).
Purpose and activities: Giving primarily for Spinal Muscular Atrophy medical research to develop a treatment or cure for SMA, a leading genetic disease of infants and toddlers.
Fields of interest: Genetics/birth defects research; Infants/toddlers.
Limitations: Applications not accepted. Giving primarily in New York, NY. No grants to individuals.
Application information: Contributes only to pre-selected organizations.
Trustees: Dinakar Singh; Florence Ann Singh; Ravi Mo Singh.
EIN: 134115900

6992
The Sirus Fund
750 3rd Ave.
New York, NY 10017-2703
Contact: Yancy R. Garrido, Grants Admin.

Established in 1996 in NY.
Donor: Susan U. Halpern.
Foundation type: Independent foundation.
Financial data (yr. ended 6/30/05): Assets, $20,222,959 (M); expenditures, $1,057,483; qualifying distributions, $897,672; giving activities include $787,068 for 51 grants (high: $112,968; low: $100).
Purpose and activities: Giving primarily for services to young children in the metropolitan New York, NY, area.
Fields of interest: Education, early childhood education; Child development, services; Family services.
Type of support: General/operating support; Continuing support; Program development.
Limitations: Giving primarily in the metropolitan New York, NY, area. No support for religious organizations. No grants to individuals.
Application information: NYRAG Common Application Form preferred. Application form not required.
  Initial approach: Proposal
  Copies of proposal: 1
  Deadline(s): Varies
  Board meeting date(s): June and Sept.
  Final notification: 1-2 months
Officer and Directors:* Susan U. Halpern,* Pres.; Robert Abrams; Robert Bachner; Bernard Fisher.
Number of staff: None.
EIN: 137100236
Selected grants: The following grants were reported in 2005.
$105,000 to Good Shepherd Services, New York, NY.
$50,000 to Appleseed Foundation, DC.
$45,000 to Save the Children Federation, Westport, CT.
$35,000 to Broadway Housing Communities, New York, NY.
$30,000 to Association to Benefit Children, New York, NY.
$30,000 to Edwin Gould Academy, Chestnut Ridge, NY.
$25,000 to Adaptive Design Association, New York, NY.

$25,000 to Friends of Island Academy, New York, NY.
$15,000 to New York Public Library, New York, NY.
$10,000 to Childrens Aid Society, New York, NY.

6993
Branna and Irv Sisenwein Fund, Inc. ◇
(formerly Eliscu and Sisenwein Fund, Inc.)
c/o Buck Sturmer & Co.
521 5th Ave.
New York, NY 10175

Established in NY.
Donor: Branna Sisenwein.
Foundation type: Independent foundation.
Financial data (yr. ended 12/31/05): Assets, $737,262 (M); gifts received, $147,506; expenditures, $345,587; qualifying distributions, $338,468; giving activities include $338,468 for 15 grants (high: $333,500; low: $18).
Purpose and activities: Giving primarily for medical education; funding also for human services.
Fields of interest: Arts; Medical school/education; Health organizations, association; Human services; Jewish agencies & temples.
Limitations: Applications not accepted. Giving in the U.S., primarily in New York, NY. No grants to individuals.
Application information: Contributes only to pre-selected organizations.
Officers: Irving Sisenwein, Pres.; Branna Sisenwein, Treas.
EIN: 136141483

6994
The Sister Fund
(formerly The Hunt Alternatives Fund)
79 5th Ave., 4th Fl.
New York, NY 10003 (212) 260-4446
Contact: Kanyere Eaton, Exec. Dir.
FAX: (212) 260-4633; E-mail: info@sisterfund.org;
URL: http://www.sisterfund.org/

Established in 1981 in NY; in Dec. 1992, the New York, NY, office officially became a private women's fund with the current name; the Denver, CO, office has become a separate entity called the Hunt Alternatives Fund.
Donors: Helen Lakelly Hunt; Helen Hunt Alternative Fund.
Foundation type: Independent foundation.
Financial data (yr. ended 11/30/04): Assets, $22,284 (M); gifts received, $960,965; expenditures, $1,036,922; qualifying distributions, $959,738; giving activities include $510,500 for 78 grants (high: $30,000; low: $75).
Purpose and activities: The Sister Fund is a private women's foundation that works at a nexus of faith and social justice. The fund envisions universal equity in our society that includes women's full development through spiritual, social, economic and political empowerment. In supporting faith-based feminism, the fund hopes to encourage the transformation that faith can bring to the women's movement, religious institutions and our culture at large. The fund dedicates most of its resources to defining and supporting faith and feminism.
Fields of interest: Women, centers/services; Minorities/immigrants, centers/services; International human rights; Leadership

development; Religion; Women; Economically disadvantaged.

Type of support: General/operating support; Income development; Management development/capacity building; Program development; Seed money; Technical assistance; Matching/challenge support.

Limitations: Applications not accepted. Giving primarily in the metropolitan New York, NY, area for local programs. No support for federal, state, or municipal agencies or cultural, educational, or religious projects except those concerned with the disabilities stated in the fund's purpose. No grants to individuals, or for institutional or general program needs, capital/building acquisition or improvements, research, scholarship funds or student aid, or deficit financing.

Publications: Newsletter; Occasional report.

Application information: Unsolicited requests for funds not accepted.

Board meeting date(s): Apr. and Nov.

Officers and Trustees:* Helen LaKelly Hunt,* Pres.; Harville Hendrix,* V.P.; Vincent McGee,* Secy.; Hildy Simmons,* Treas.; Kanyere Eaton, Exec. Dir.

Number of staff: 3 full-time professional; 1 part-time support.

EIN: 751763787

Selected grants: The following grants were reported in 2003.

$190,000 to Womens Funding Network, San Francisco, CA. For general support, payable over 3 years.

$25,000 to Center for Anti-Violence Education/ Brooklyn Womens Martial Arts, Brooklyn, NY. For general support.

$25,000 to Women for Afghan Women, New York, NY. For general support.

$15,000 to Amethyst Womens Project, Brooklyn, NY. For general support.

$15,000 to Maura Clarke-Ita Ford Center, Brooklyn, NY. For general support.

$12,000 to Jewish Womens Archive, Brookline, MA. For general support.

$10,000 to Albanian American Womens Organization, Motrat Qiriaz, New York, NY. For general support.

$10,000 to Womens eNews, New York, NY. For general support.

$5,000 to Womens Learning Partnership for Rights, Development, and Peace, Bethesda, MD.

$3,000 to Women and Philanthropy, DC.

6995
David and Marjorie Sitt Chesed Fund ◇ ☆
2043 E. 4th St.
Brooklyn, NY 11223

Established in 2004 in NY.

Donor: David Sitt.

Foundation type: Independent foundation.

Financial data (yr. ended 12/31/05): Assets, $405 (M); gifts received, $866,750; expenditures, $866,410; qualifying distributions, $866,344; giving activities include $866,344 for 47 grants (high: $25,000; low: $100).

Fields of interest: Jewish agencies & temples.

Type of support: General/operating support.

Limitations: Applications not accepted. Giving primarily in New York City. No grants to individuals.

Application information: Contributes only to pre-selected organizations.

Officers: David Sitt, Pres.; Marjorie Sitt, V.P.

EIN: 341994530

6996
The Sitt Family Foundation ◇ ☆
(formerly Morris & Eddie Sitt Family Foundation)
1127 E. 7th St.
Brooklyn, NY 11230
Application address: c/o Blusand USA, Attn.: Morris Sitt, 37 Bridge St., Brooklyn, NY 11201, tel.: (718) 858-5530

Established in 1977 in NY.

Donors: Morris Sitt; and members of the Sitt family.

Foundation type: Independent foundation.

Financial data (yr. ended 6/30/05): Assets, $2,909 (M); gifts received, $3,236,982; expenditures, $3,247,421; qualifying distributions, $3,247,378; giving activities include $3,241,200 for 15 grants (high: $801,600; low: $50).

Purpose and activities: Giving primarily for Jewish organizations; funding also for health associations.

Fields of interest: Health organizations, association; Human services; Children, services; Jewish agencies & temples.

Limitations: Giving primarily in NY. No grants to individuals.

Application information:

Initial approach: Letter

Deadline(s): None

Directors: David Sitt; Jeffrey Sitt; Morris Sitt.

EIN: 132886778

6997
The Isaac Sitt Foundation ◇
501 Ave. S
Brooklyn, NY 11223-3048

Established in 1999 in NY.

Foundation type: Independent foundation.

Financial data (yr. ended 9/30/05): Assets, $577,324 (M); expenditures, $359,080; qualifying distributions, $350,931; giving activities include $350,931 for 53 grants (high: $100,000; low: $3).

Fields of interest: Jewish agencies & temples.

Limitations: Applications not accepted. Giving primarily in NY. No grants to individuals.

Application information: Contributes only to pre-selected organizations.

Officer: Isaac J. Sitt, Pres.

EIN: 137200888

6998
The Skadden Fellowship Foundation, Inc. ◇
(formerly Skadden, Arps, Slate, Meagher & Flom Fellowship Foundation)
4 Times Sq., Rm. 40-228
New York, NY 10036 (212) 735-2956
Contact: Susan Butler Plum, Dir.
FAX: (917) 777-2956; URL: http:// www.skaddenfellowships.org/

Established in 1988 in NY.

Donor: Skadden, Arps, Slate, Meagher & Flom.

Foundation type: Company-sponsored foundation.

Financial data (yr. ended 12/31/04): Assets, $3,958,670 (M); gifts received, $2,656,661; expenditures, $2,903,344; qualifying distributions, $2,897,439; giving activities include $2,573,040 for 83 grants to individuals (high: $58,607; low: $5,000).

Purpose and activities: The foundation awards fellowships to graduating law students and outgoing

judicial clerks who create projects at public interest organizations designed to provide legal services to the poor, the elderly, the disabled, and those deprived of their civil rights or human rights.

Type of support: Fellowships.

Limitations: Giving on a national basis. No grants to individuals not securing a potential position with a sponsoring public interest organization.

Publications: Application guidelines; Informational brochure; Multi-year report.

Application information: Application form required.

Initial approach: Download application form and mail application form and supporting materials to foundation

Copies of proposal: 1

Deadline(s): Oct. 4

Board meeting date(s): Dec. 7

Final notification: Dec. 8

Trustees: Judith Areen; Joseph H. Flom; Barry H. Garfinkel; Elena Kagan; Jose Lozano; Suzanne Mckechnie Klahr; Peter P. Mullen; Kurt Schmoke; Robert C. Sheehan; Solomon Watson IV; Gregory H. Williams.

Advisory Committee: Lauren E. Aguiar; Jose R. Allen; Thomas J. Allingham II; Margaret A. Brown; C. Benjamin Crisman, Jr.; N. Lynn Hiestand; Frances Kao; Alan C. Myers; Peter Simshauser; Ronald J. Tabak; Harold M. Williams; Vaughn C. Williams.

Number of staff: 1 full-time professional; 1 part-time support.

EIN: 133455231

6999
Skirball Foundation ▼ ◇
767 5th Ave., 50th Fl.
New York, NY 10153 (212) 832-8500
Contact: Martin Blackman, Pres.

Established in 1950 in OH.

Donors: Members of the Skirball family; Skirball Investment Co.

Foundation type: Independent foundation.

Financial data (yr. ended 12/31/05): Assets, $230,578,263 (M); gifts received, $8,817,787; expenditures, $46,966,290; qualifying distributions, $44,764,037; giving activities include $43,269,726 for 107 grants (high: $14,858,334; low: $1,000; average: $10,000–$500,000).

Purpose and activities: Giving primarily for Jewish welfare and temple support; support also for education, the arts, and medicine.

Fields of interest: Media/communications; Arts; Education; Human services; Jewish federated giving programs; Jewish agencies & temples.

Limitations: Giving primarily in CA. No grants to individuals.

Application information: Contributes primarily to pre-selected organizations and accepts limited applications for funds.

Officers and Trustees:* Martin Blackman,* C.E.O. and Pres.; Robert D. Goldfarb,* V.P. and Treas.; Marvin Goldstein, Secy. and C.F.O.; Nympha H. Cody, Cont.; Uri D. Herscher.

EIN: 346517957

Selected grants: The following grants were reported in 2004.

$7,200,000 to Hebrew Union College-Jewish Institute of Religion, Skirball Cultural Center, Los Angeles, CA. For operating support.

$2,025,000 to New York University, Jack H. Skirball Center for New Media and Film, New York, NY. For operating support.

$1,833,333 to Geffen Playhouse, Los Angeles, CA. For operating support.

$1,550,000 to University of Southern California, Los Angeles, CA. For operating support.

$1,500,000 to Stephen S. Wise Temple, Los Angeles, CA. For operating support.

$1,000,000 to Motion Picture and Television Fund Foundation, Woodland Hills, CA. For operating support.

$750,000 to Los Angeles Opera Company, Los Angeles, CA. For operating support.

$650,000 to Jewish Museum, New York, NY. For operating support.

$635,000 to Oxford Centre for Hebrew and Jewish Studies, Oxford, England. For operating support.

$625,000 to Roman Catholic Archbishop of Los Angeles, Los Angeles, CA. For operating support.

7000

The Slant/Fin Foundation, Inc. ✧

100 Forest Dr.
Greenvale, NY   11548-1205   (516) 484-2600
Contact: Melvin Dubin, Pres.

Established in 1985 in NY.
Donors: Melvin Dubin; Slant/Fin Corp.
Foundation type: Company-sponsored foundation.
Financial data (yr. ended 6/30/05): Assets, $159,220 (M); gifts received, $533,000; expenditures, $533,046; qualifying distributions, $533,046; giving activities include $532,765 for 67 grants (high: $100,000; low: $100).
Purpose and activities: The foundation supports Jewish agencies and temples and organizations involved with education, health, and human services.
Fields of interest: Education; Health care; Human services; Jewish federated giving programs; Jewish agencies & temples.
Limitations: Giving primarily in NY. No grants to individuals.
Application information: Application form not required.
Initial approach: Proposal
Deadline(s): None
Officers: Melvin Dubin, Pres.; Adam Dubin, V.P.; Donald Brown, Secy.-Treas.
EIN: 112752009
Selected grants: The following grants were reported in 2005.
$100,000 to North Shore-Long Island Jewish Health System, Westbury, NY.
$70,000 to American Society for Technion-Israel Institute of Technology, New York, NY.
$10,000 to Jewish Institute for National Security Affairs, DC.
$10,000 to National Liberty Museum, Philadelphia, PA.
$10,000 to Zionist Organization of America, New York, NY.
$5,000 to Livnot ULehibanot, Safed, Israel. .
$5,000 to Reconstructionist Rabbinical College, Wyncote, PA.
$2,500 to Roundabout Theater Company, New York, NY.
$2,000 to Maimonides Medical Center, Brooklyn, NY.
$1,500 to Friends of the Israel Defense Forces, New York, NY.

7001

Alan B. Slifka Foundation, Inc. ▼

477 Madison Ave., 8th Fl.
New York, NY   10022-5802   (212) 303-9408
Contact: Adina H. Dubin, Prog. Off.
E-mail: programofficer@halcyonllc.com

Established in 1963 in NY.
Donors: Alan B. Slifka; Sylvia Slifka†.
Foundation type: Independent foundation.
Financial data (yr. ended 11/30/04): Assets, $7,744,490 (M); gifts received, $8,370,000; expenditures, $4,698,454; qualifying distributions, $4,695,724; giving activities include $4,411,023 for 410 grants (high: $300,000; low: $50; average: $1,000–$25,000).
Purpose and activities: Support primarily for Jewish interest projects and cultural activities and for endeavors that promote coexistence and a world safe for difference.
Fields of interest: Elementary/secondary education; International peace/security; International affairs; Jewish federated giving programs; Jewish agencies & temples; Religion, interfaith issues; Religion.
International interests: Israel; Middle East.
Type of support: General/operating support; Continuing support; Annual campaigns; Emergency funds; Program development; Conferences/seminars; Seed money; Curriculum development; Program evaluation; Matching/challenge support.
Limitations: Giving primarily in NY. No support for political organizations, environmental, medical, or health-related fields. No grants to individuals, or for endowments, for-profit organizations or acquisitions of land. Generally no grants for major equipment purchases, individual research or media projects.
Application information: Contact the foundation for a copy of the current guidelines which has all the necessary information for applying.
Initial approach: Letter
Copies of proposal: 1
Board meeting date(s): Varies
Officers and Board Members:* Alan B. Slifka,* Pres. and Treas.; Shira Levin,* Secy.; Sarah Silver, Exec. Dir.; Rachelle Markowitz.
Number of staff: 2 full-time professional; 1 part-time professional.
EIN: 136192257
Selected grants: The following grants were reported in 2004.
$300,000 to Abraham Fund Initiatives, New York, NY. For unrestricted support.
$300,000 to Brandeis University, Waltham, MA. For unrestricted support.
$100,000 to Coexistence Initiative, New York, NY. For unrestricted support.
$100,000 to Interfaith Center of New York, New York, NY. For unrestricted support.
$100,000 to Jewish Community Center in Manhattan, New York, NY. For unrestricted support.
$10,000 to Jerusalem Foundation, New York, NY. For unrestricted support.
$10,000 to Reboot, New York, NY. For unrestricted support.
$5,000 to P.E.F. Israel Endowment Funds, New York, NY.
$2,500 to William J. Clinton Presidential Foundation, New York, NY.
$1,350 to Walter Kaner Childrens Foundation, Great Neck, NY.

7002

Joseph & Sylvia Slifka Foundation, Inc.

c/o Hecht & Co. PC
111 W. 40th St.
New York, NY   10018

Established in 1944 in NY.
Donors: Joseph Slifka†; Sylvia Slifka†; Barbara Slifka.
Foundation type: Independent foundation.
Financial data (yr. ended 10/31/05): Assets, $37,378,936 (M); gifts received, $20,000,000; expenditures, $1,284,791; qualifying distributions, $1,140,354; giving activities include $1,100,000 for grants.
Fields of interest: Education; Jewish federated giving programs.
Limitations: Applications not accepted. Giving primarily in the metropolitan New York, NY, area. No grants to individuals.
Application information: Contributes only to pre-selected organizations.
Officers and Trustees:* Barbara S. Slifka,* Pres.; Michael Hecht,* V.P. and Treas.; John J. O'Neil,* Secy.
EIN: 136106433
Selected grants: The following grants were reported in 2004.
$450,000 to Abraham Joshua Heschel School, New York, NY.

7003

Alfred P. Sloan Foundation ▼ ✧

630 5th Ave., Ste. 2550
New York, NY   10111-0242   (212) 649-1649
Contact: Ralph E. Gomory, Pres.
FAX: (212) 757-5117; URL: http://www.sloan.org

Incorporated in 1934 in DE.
Donors: Alfred P. Sloan, Jr.†; Irene Jackson Sloan†; New Castle Corp.
Foundation type: Independent foundation.
Financial data (yr. ended 12/31/05): Assets, $1,581,350,875 (M); expenditures, $67,237,794; qualifying distributions, $61,165,933; giving activities include $61,165,933 for grants.
Purpose and activities: The foundation is interested in: 1) Science and Technology: direct support of research; 2) Standard of Living, and Economic Performance: industries, dual-career middle-class working families, the role of corporations and nonprofit sectors; and 3) Education and Careers in Science and Technology: anywhere, anytime learning, minorities and women in science and technology, the university as a system, and public understanding of science and technology.
Fields of interest: Higher education; Employment; Family services; Science, research; Engineering/technology; Minorities.
Type of support: Program development; Research.
Limitations: No support for the creative or performing arts, humanities, religion, or primary or secondary education. No grants to individuals (except for research and publication), or for endowment or building funds, medical research, or equipment not related directly to foundation-supported projects; no loans.
Publications: Annual report; Grants list; Informational brochure (including application guidelines).
Application information: Nomination forms available on foundation Web site for fellowship

candidates; direct applications not accepted. Application form not required.

Initial approach: Letter of inquiry
Copies of proposal: 1
Deadline(s): Sept. 15 for Sloan Research Fellowship program; no deadline for others
Board meeting date(s): Throughout the year (grants of $45,000 or less); 4 times a year (grants over $45,000)
Final notification: Early in year for research fellowships; within 3 months for others

Officers and Trustees:* Harold T. Shapiro,* Chair.; Ralph E. Gomory,* Pres.; June M. Yearwood, V.P. and Secy.; William B. Petersen, V.P. and C.I.O.; Christopher T. Sia, Treas. and Chief Tech. Off.; Stephen L. Brown; S. Parker Gilbert; William E. Hoglund; Sandra O. Moose; Richard E. Salomon; Roger M. Solow; Marta Tienda; Dennis Weatherstone; Sheila E. Widnall.
Number of staff: 12 full-time professional; 1 part-time professional; 11 full-time support.
EIN: 131623877
Selected grants: The following grants were reported in 2005.

$4,701,642 to National Action Council for Minorities in Engineering (NACME), White Plains, NY. For Minority Ph.D. Program and American Indian Program, payable over 5 years.

$2,990,474 to Boston College, Chestnut Hill, MA. For Sloan Center on Flexible Work Options and Older Workers, payable over 3 years.

$2,401,316 to Families and Work Institute, New York, NY. For When Work Works, public engagement campaign to promote and facilitate more flexible workplace, payable over 1.50 years.

$2,343,264 to Georgetown University, DC. For Workplace Flexibility 2010, whose goal is to find consensus in Washington, D.C. by 2010 for national policy on workplace flexibility.

$2,000,000 to Internet Archive, San Francisco, CA. To launch building of open access archive of millions of books, payable over 2 years.

$1,665,422 to ICPO-Interpol, Lyon, France. To provide renewed support for development of capacity to counter bioterrorism by raising awareness, developing police training programs and strengthening law enforcement, payable over 2 years.

$120,000 to University of the Pacific, Stockton, CA. To advance global strategy to prevent bioterrorism through rule of law.

$45,000 to Iowa State University, Ames, IA. For project to develop and implement citizen-based performance measures for e-government in small rural communities, payable over 2 years.

$45,000 to Princeton University, Princeton, NJ. For Alfred P. Sloan Fellowship to Dr. Markus K. Brunnermierer in Economics, payable over 2 years.

$45,000 to University of California at San Diego, La Jolla, CA. For Alfred P. Sloan Fellowship to Dr. Serge Belongie for Computer Science, payable over 2 years.

7004
Slovin Foundation ✧
c/o Bruce Slovin
111 E. 61st St.
New York, NY 10021

Established in 1988 in NY.
Donor: Bruce Slovin.

Foundation type: Independent foundation.
Financial data (yr. ended 2/28/05): Assets, $223,420 (M); gifts received, $900,875; expenditures, $753,945; qualifying distributions, $635,386; giving activities include $635,386 for 117 grants (high: $55,000; low: $50).
Purpose and activities: Giving primarily to Jewish organizations as well as to organizations for Jewish history, funding also for the arts, education, and social services.
Fields of interest: Arts; Education; Human services; Jewish federated giving programs; Jewish agencies & temples.
Limitations: Applications not accepted. Giving primarily in NY. No grants to individuals.
Application information: Contributes only to pre-selected organizations.
Officer: Bruce Slovin, Pres.
EIN: 236912396
Selected grants: The following grants were reported in 2005.

$157,000 to Center for Jewish History, New York, NY. 4 grants: $50,000, $55,000, $2,000, $50,000

$31,125 to Park East Synagogue, New York, NY. 2 grants: $11,125, $20,000

$10,000 to American Friends of the Tel Aviv Museum, New York, NY.

$5,000 to Gomez Foundation for Mill House, New York, NY.

$3,318 to Rodeph Shalom Congregation, Philadelphia, PA.

$2,000 to Perlman Music Program, New York, NY.

7005
SMBC Global Foundation, Inc.
(formerly Sumitomo Bank Global Foundation)
277 Park Ave.
New York, NY 10172
Contact: Elizabeth Usui, Asst. Secy.
E-mail: globalfoundation@smbcgroup.com

Established in 1994 in DE and NY.
Donors: Sumitomo Bank Capital Markets, Inc.; SMBC Capital Markets, Inc.
Foundation type: Company-sponsored foundation.
Financial data (yr. ended 12/31/04): Assets, $13,494,936 (M); expenditures, $718,993; qualifying distributions, $700,830; giving activities include $454,690 for 51 grants (high: $238,000; low: $50), and $50,000 for 280 grants to individuals (high: $275; low: $150).
Purpose and activities: The foundation supports organizations involved with arts and culture, education, and human services and awards college scholarships to Asian citizens or residents in financial need. The scholarship program is administered by the Institute of International Education.
Fields of interest: Arts; Education; Human services; Asians/Pacific Islanders.
International interests: China; Indonesia; Malaysia; Singapore; Thailand; Vietnam.
Type of support: General/operating support; Annual campaigns; Program development; Scholarship funds; Scholarships—to individuals.
Limitations: Giving on a national and international basis, including in China, Indonesia, Malaysia, Singapore, Thailand, and Vietnam. No grants to individuals (except for scholarships).
Application information: Application form required.

Initial approach: Contact foundation for application form; contact foundation for application information for scholarships
Copies of proposal: 1
Deadline(s): Contact foundation for deadlines for scholarships
Officers and Directors:* Tetsufumi Fujisawa,* Pres.; Jane Hutta, Secy.; Naoki Okubo, Treas.; William Haney; Yoshinori Kawamura; D. Scarborough Smith III; Elizabeth Usui; David A. Ward.
EIN: 133766226

7006
The Park B. Smith and Carol Smith Family Foundation ✧ ☆
270 Madison Ave., 16th Fl.
New York, NY 10016

Established in 1994 in NY.
Donors: Park B. Smith; Carol Smith†.
Foundation type: Independent foundation.
Financial data (yr. ended 12/31/03): Assets, $687,710 (M); gifts received, $495,000; expenditures, $410,012; qualifying distributions, $409,729; giving activities include $409,729 for 9 grants (high: $200,000; low: $500).
Fields of interest: Higher education; Education; Human services.
Limitations: Applications not accepted. No grants to individuals.
Application information: Contributes only to pre-selected organizations.
Trustees: Carol Smith; Park B. Smith.
EIN: 237050320

7007
George Graham and Elizabeth Galloway Smith Foundation, Inc. ✧ ☆
84 S. Davis St., Ste. A
Orchard Park, NY 14127-2651 (716) 662-9749
Contact: Mary Jane C. Smith, Pres.

Established in 1960.
Donors: Elizabeth G. Smith; Beatrice Erlin†; George G. Smith†.
Foundation type: Independent foundation.
Financial data (yr. ended 5/31/06): Assets, $6,684,811 (M); gifts received, $296,941; expenditures, $403,534; qualifying distributions, $373,675; giving activities include $373,675 for grants.
Purpose and activities: Funding primarily for an arts center and other music and arts organizations; funding also for education and human services.
Fields of interest: Museums (science/technology); Performing arts centers; Performing arts, orchestra (symphony); Higher education; Education; Human services; Federated giving programs.
Type of support: Building/renovation; Equipment; Program development.
Limitations: Giving primarily in western NY, with emphasis on Buffalo and Orchard Park. No grants to individuals.
Application information:
Initial approach: Letter
Deadline(s): June 15 for requests above $1,000
Board meeting date(s): July
Officers and Directors:* Mary Jane C. Smith,* Pres.; George G. Smith III,* V.P.; Elizabeth S.

Morehouse,* Secy.-Treas.; C. Schuyler Morehouse; Janet Smith.

EIN: 166031530

Selected grants: The following grants were reported in 2003.

$106,250 to Orchard Park Symphony Orchestra, Orchard Park, NY. For endowment fund and provision for artists.

$100,000 to Sheas Performing Arts Center, Buffalo, NY. For development and renovation of arts center.

$15,000 to Buffalo Museum of Science, Buffalo, NY. For Byron Dig.

$8,000 to Durham Memorial A.M.E. Zion Church, Buffalo, NY. For construction of new building.

$6,000 to Mendelssohn Club, Philadelphia, PA. For obtaining artist for concert.

$5,000 to Niagara Frontier Radio Reading Service, Buffalo, NY. For moving to new headquarters.

$2,500 to University of Rochester, Rochester, NY. For annual campaign.

$1,000 to Mercy Hospital Foundation, Buffalo, NY. For annual campaign.

$1,000 to Sisters Hospital Foundation, Buffalo, NY. For annual fund.

$1,000 to United Way of Buffalo and Erie County, Buffalo, NY. For annual fund drive.

7008
The Randall & Kathryn Smith Foundation ◇ ☆
c/o Smith Mgmt., LLC
885 3rd Ave., 34th Fl.
New York, NY 10022
Contact: John W. Adams

Established in 1982 in NJ.

Donors: John W. Adams; Randall Smith.

Foundation type: Independent foundation.

Financial data (yr. ended 12/31/05): Assets, $3,943,950 (M); gifts received, $91,278; expenditures, $337,234; qualifying distributions, $322,370; giving activities include $322,370 for grants.

Purpose and activities: Giving primarily for higher education, as well as for the environment, health associations and hospitals, and the arts.

Fields of interest: Museums (art); Higher education; Environment, air pollution; Hospitals (general); Health organizations, association; Human services.

Type of support: General/operating support; Annual campaigns; Research.

Limitations: Giving primarily in NC and NY.

Application information:
 Initial approach: Letter
 Deadline(s): None

Officers: Randall D. Smith, Pres.; Jeffrey A. Smith, Secy.

Trustee: Robert Haribson.

EIN: 222422965

7009
George D. Smith Fund, Inc. ▼ ◇
900 3rd Ave.
New York, NY 10022 (212) 895-2000
Contact: Lawrence W. Milas, V.P.

Incorporated in 1956 in DE.

Donor: George D. Smith, Sr.‡.

Foundation type: Independent foundation.

Financial data (yr. ended 12/31/05): Assets, $155,017,174 (M); expenditures, $8,643,400; qualifying distributions, $8,580,100; giving activities include $8,580,100 for 12 grants (high: $2,000,000; low: $100; average: $400,000–$800,000).

Purpose and activities: The fund primarily supports basic cell research at the molecular level at university medical centers.

Fields of interest: Media, television; Higher education; Biomedicine; Medical research, institute.

Type of support: Research.

Limitations: Applications not accepted. Giving primarily in CA and UT.

Application information: Unsolicited requests for funds not considered.

Officers: George D. Smith, Jr., Pres. and Secy.-Treas.; Lawrence W. Milas, V.P.; Camilla M. Smith, V.P.

Director: Sarah A. Smith.

EIN: 136138728

Selected grants: The following grants were reported in 2005.

$2,000,000 to Stanford University Hospital, Stanford, CA.

$1,500,000 to University of California at San Francisco Foundation, San Francisco, CA. For cardiovascular research.

$1,200,000 to University of California, Berkeley, CA.

$950,000 to University of Utah, Salt Lake City, UT. 2 grants: $350,000, $600,000 (For special collections).

$800,000 to Carter Center, Atlanta, GA.

$800,000 to Council for Secular Humanism, Amherst, NY.

$500,000 to Planned Parenthood Federation of America, New York, NY.

$400,000 to National Public Radio, DC.

$400,000 to W G B H Educational Foundation, Boston, MA.

7010
The Christopher D. Smithers Foundation, Inc. ◇
P.O. Box 67
Mill Neck, NY 11765 (516) 676-0067
Contact: Adele C. Smithers-Fornaci, Pres.
FAX: (516) 676-0323;
E-mail: info@smithersfoundation.org; URL: http://www.smithersfoundation.org

Incorporated in 1952 in NY.

Donors: Christopher D. Smithers‡; Mabel B. Smithers‡; R. Brinkley Smithers‡; Adele C. Smithers-Fornaci.

Foundation type: Independent foundation.

Financial data (yr. ended 12/31/05): Assets, $12,193,336 (M); gifts received, $87,485; expenditures, $2,033,476; qualifying distributions, $1,967,669; giving activities include $1,366,500 for 80 grants (high: $161,028; low: $100).

Purpose and activities: Supports prevention, educational service, treatment, and research programs in the field of alcoholism; initiates its own projects in this field primarily by writing and publishing specialized booklets for industry, educational organizations, and the general public.

Fields of interest: Higher education; Medical school/education; Hospitals (general); Alcoholism; Human services.

Type of support: General/operating support; Capital campaigns; Program development; Conferences/seminars; Seed money; Research; Matching/challenge support.

Limitations: Giving on a national basis, with some emphasis on New York, particularly Long Island. No grants to individuals, or for building or endowment funds or matching gifts; no loans.

Publications: Annual report.

Application information: Application form not required.
 Initial approach: Proposal
 Copies of proposal: 2
 Deadline(s): None
 Board meeting date(s): May

Officers and Directors: Adele C. Smithers-Fornaci,* Pres.; Christopher B. Smithers,* V.P. and Secy.; Thomas D. Croci,* V.P. and Treas.; M. Elizabeth Brothers,* V.P.; Joseph J. Calandra, M.D.; Lt. Thomas D.A. Croci.

Number of staff: 1 full-time support; 1 part-time support.

EIN: 131861928

Selected grants: The following grants were reported in 2004.

$195,009 to National Council on Alcoholism and Drug Dependence, New York, NY.

$79,000 to Boys and Girls Clubs of Tampa Bay, Tampa, FL.

$64,000 to Boys and Girls Club.

$60,000 to Turn 2 Foundation, Kalamazoo, MI.

$50,000 to North Shore-Long Island Jewish Health System Foundation, Great Neck, NY.

$45,000 to Freedom Institute, New York, NY.

$33,000 to New York Medical College, Valhalla, NY.

$25,500 to American Society of Addiction Medicine, Chevy Chase, MD.

$10,000 to Advocates for Children of New York, New York, NY.

$5,000 to North Shore Child and Family Guidance Center, Roslyn Heights, NY.

7011
John Ben Snow Memorial Trust ◇
50 Presidential Plz., Ste. 106
Syracuse, NY 13202
Contact: (For NY): Jonathan L. Snow, Tr.; (For NV): Emelie M. Williams, Tr.; (For MD): Allen R. Malcom, Tr.

Regional offices: c/o Allen R. Malcom, 104 Church Alley, Chestertown, MD 21620; c/o Emelie M. Williams, 2975 Knight Rd., Reno, NV 89509; URL: http://www.johnbensnow.com/jbsmt

Established in 1975 in NY.

Donor: John Ben Snow‡.

Foundation type: Independent foundation.

Financial data (yr. ended 12/31/05): Assets, $25,060,521 (M); expenditures, $1,247,037; qualifying distributions, $1,107,165; giving activities include $970,962 for 69 grants (high: $50,000; low: $2,000).

Purpose and activities: Support primarily for higher education, scholarship funds, the humanities and cultural institutions, especially libraries, the performing arts, theater, and historical preservation; environmental groups; media and communications; and community development. Support also for organizations for people who are handicapped.

Fields of interest: Media, journalism/publishing; Performing arts; Performing arts, theater; Historic preservation/historical societies; Arts; Higher education; Libraries/library science; Education; Environment; Health organizations, association;

Children/youth, services; Youth, services; Community development; Disabilities, people with.

Type of support: Building/renovation; Equipment; Program development; Publication; Seed money; Curriculum development; Fellowships; Scholarship funds; Matching/challenge support.

Limitations: Giving primarily in MD, NV, and central NY. No support for unspecified projects, religious organizations, or for-profit groups. No grants to individuals, or for operating budgets, endowment funds, or contingency financing; no loans.

Publications: Annual report (including application guidelines).

Application information: Contact closest regional office. Application form required.

Initial approach: Letter of inquiry by Jan. 1 of the year for which funding is requested

Copies of proposal: 1

Deadline(s): Submit proposal preferably from July through Feb.; deadline Apr. 1

Board meeting date(s): June

Final notification: July 1

Trustees: Allen R. Malcolm; Jonathan L. Snow; Emelie Melton Williams; The Bank of New York.

EIN: 136633814

Selected grants: The following grants were reported in 2003.

$135,000 to National Judicial College, Reno, NV. 2 grants: $100,000 (For operating support), $35,000 (For operating support).

$50,000 to Wesleyan University, Middletown, CT. For operating support.

$30,000 to Nevada Museum of Art, Reno, NV. For operating support.

$25,000 to Munson-Williams-Proctor Institute, Utica, NY. For operating support.

$20,000 to New York State Historical Association, Cooperstown, NY. For operating support.

$15,000 to Delaware Valley College, Doylestown, PA. For operating support.

$15,000 to Desert Research Institute, Reno, NV. For operating support.

$10,000 to Recording for the Blind and Dyslexic, Princeton, NJ. For operating support.

$10,000 to VSA Arts of Nevada, Reno, NV. For operating support.

7012

The Ted Snowdon Foundation ✧

(formerly The Snowdon Foundation)
50 Riverside Dr., No. 15-C
New York, NY 10024-6508
Contact: Edward W. Snowdon, Jr., Pres.
E-mail: snowdonfound@aol.com; Tel./FAX: (212) 787-2413

Established in 1997 in DE and NY.

Donor: Edward W. Snowdon, Jr.

Foundation type: Independent foundation.

Financial data (yr. ended 4/30/05): Assets, $6,507,237 (M); gifts received, $1,830,900; expenditures, $656,405; qualifying distributions, $656,405; giving activities include $583,550 for 37 grants (high: $50,000; low: $5,000).

Purpose and activities: Giving to promote research and study, production and dissemination of the performing arts, and to encourage interest in many forms of artistic endeavor; provide financial aid and assistance to organizations attending principally to the concerns and needs of the lesbian and gay community.

Fields of interest: Performing arts, theater; Performing arts, theater (musical); Performing arts,

opera; Arts; Health care; AIDS; Human services; Civil rights, gays/lesbians; LGBTQ.

Limitations: Giving primarily in New York, NY. No grants to individuals.

Publications: Application guidelines.

Application information:

Initial approach: Letter of introduction requesting the grant application procedure

Deadline(s): Feb. 1 and Aug. 1

Board meeting date(s): Apr. and Oct.

Final notification: Apr. 30 and Oct. 31

Officers and Directors:* Edward W. Snowdon, Jr., Pres.; Richard W. Snowdon,* V.P.; Robert S. Blaustein, Secy.; Deborah Ensign.

Number of staff: 1 part-time support.

EIN: 133948662

Selected grants: The following grants were reported in 2005.

$50,000 to In the Life Media, New York, NY.

$25,000 to Lambda Legal Defense and Education Fund, New York, NY.

$25,000 to YMCA of Greater New York, New York, NY.

$20,000 to Freedom to Marry, New York, NY.

$15,000 to Doe Fund, New York, NY.

$15,000 to Foundation for National Progress, San Francisco, CA.

$15,000 to Lincoln Center Theater, New York, NY.

$15,000 to Point Foundation, Chicago, IL.

$12,250 to Riverside Park Fund, New York, NY.

$10,000 to New York Youth Symphony, New York, NY.

7013

Beatrice Snyder Foundation ✧

c/o Arthur J. Fox
126 E. 56th St., 12th Fl.
New York, NY 10022

Established in 1998 in NJ.

Donors: Harold Snyder; Beryl L. Snyder; Jay Snyder.

Foundation type: Independent foundation.

Financial data (yr. ended 5/31/05): Assets, $3,018,011 (M); gifts received, $126,399; expenditures, $793,576; qualifying distributions, $720,060; giving activities include $720,000 for 25 grants (high: $150,000; low: $2,500).

Purpose and activities: Giving for art and cultural programs, health care, including a medical center, and human services.

Fields of interest: Performing arts centers; Performing arts, music; Performing arts, orchestra (symphony); Arts; Higher education; Education; Hospitals (general); Hospitals (specialty); Human services.

Limitations: Applications not accepted. Giving primarily in NY. No grants to individuals.

Application information: Contributes only to pre-selected organizations.

Trustees: Beryl L. Snyder; Brian S. Snyder; Harold Snyder; Jay T. Snyder.

EIN: 223595071

Selected grants: The following grants were reported in 2005.

$102,000 to Philharmonic-Symphony Society of New York, New York, NY.

$50,000 to Jazz at Lincoln Center, New York, NY. 2 grants: $25,000 each

$37,500 to Lenox Hill Neighborhood House, New York, NY.

$6,000 to Musicians on Call, New York, NY.

$5,000 to Doctors Without Borders USA, New York, NY.

$5,000 to McCarton School, New York, NY.

$5,000 to Moberly Area Community College, Moberly, MO.

$2,500 to Intrepid Fallen Heroes Fund, New York, NY.

7014

Valentine Perry Snyder Fund ✧

c/o JPMorgan Chase Bank, N.A., Global Foundations Group
345 Park Ave., 4th Fl.
New York, NY 10154
Contact: Lisa L. Philp, V.P.
E-mail: philp_lisa@jpmorgan.com; URL: http://foundationcenter.org/grantmaker/snyder/

Trust established in 1942 in NY.

Donor: Sheba Torbert Snyder†.

Foundation type: Independent foundation.

Financial data (yr. ended 12/31/05): Assets, $9,634,560 (M); expenditures, $515,065; qualifying distributions, $425,920; giving activities include $418,000 for 17 grants (high: $25,000; low: $20,000).

Purpose and activities: Giving primarily for youth and other human services, community workforce development programs, and public affairs.

Fields of interest: Employment, training; Human services; Children/youth, services; Public affairs.

Type of support: General/operating support; Building/renovation; Equipment; Program development; Seed money.

Limitations: Giving limited to New York, NY. No support for organizations lacking 501(c)(3) status. No grants to individuals, or for research-related programs, scholarships, fellowships, or matching gifts; no loans.

Publications: Application guidelines; Grants list.

Application information: See foundation Web site for application guidelines and requirements. Application form not required.

Initial approach: Proposal

Copies of proposal: 2

Deadline(s): Sept. 1

Board meeting date(s): Dec.

Final notification: Dec. 30

Officer: Lisa L. Philp, V.P.

Trustee: JPMorgan Chase Bank, N.A.

EIN: 136036765

Selected grants: The following grants were reported in 2004.

$30,000 to Child Care, Inc., New York, NY. For the Talk Reach Read program.

$30,000 to Community Voices Heard, New York, NY. For general support.

$30,000 to Women for Afghan Women, New York, NY. For general support.

$25,000 to Battered Womens Resource Center, Brooklyn, NY. For general support.

$25,000 to Fund for New Citizens, New York, NY. For Community Legal Services project.

$25,000 to Harlem Congregations for Community Improvement, New York, NY. For construction of Trades Academy.

$25,000 to In the Spirit of the Children, New York, NY. For general support.

$25,000 to Neighborhood Family Services Coalition, New York, NY. For activities related to the Out-of-School-Time initiative.

$20,000 to Center for Anti-Violence Education/ Brooklyn Womens Martial Arts, Brooklyn, NY. For Teen Program.

$20,000 to Institute for Labor and the Community, Brooklyn, NY. For Boys Project.

7015
The SO Charitable Trust ✧
c/o Oded Aboodi
1700 Broadway, 17th Fl.
New York, NY   10019

Established in 1980 in NJ.
Donors: Oded Aboodi; Moses Marx; Kenneth Wang; Vera Wang-Becker; Victor Yen; Vincent Yen; Summer Assocs.
Foundation type: Independent foundation.
Financial data (yr. ended 11/30/04): Assets, $1,866,915 (M); expenditures, $467,740; qualifying distributions, $466,893; giving activities include $466,893 for 221 grants (high: $101,510; low: $108).
Purpose and activities: Giving primarily for Jewish education, agencies and temples; funding also for the arts, children and social services, education and health care.
Fields of interest: Museums; Arts; Higher education; Theological school/education; Education; Health organizations, association; Human services; Children, services; Jewish federated giving programs; Jewish agencies & temples.
Limitations: Applications not accepted. Giving primarily in NY. No grants to individuals.
Application information: Contributes only to pre-selected organizations.
Trustees: Oded Aboodi; Solomon M. Weiss.
EIN: 133050892
Selected grants: The following grants were reported in 2003.
$100,193 to Jewish Theological Seminary of America, New York, NY.
$72,000 to New York-Presbyterian Hospital, New York, NY.
$30,000 to Montefiore Medical Center, Bronx, NY.
$28,000 to Philharmonic-Symphony Society of New York, New York, NY.
$25,230 to American Committee for the Weizmann Institute of Science, New York, NY.
$24,180 to Congregation Shearith Israel, New York, NY.
$12,600 to Rutgers, The State University of New Jersey Foundation, New Brunswick, NJ.
$12,500 to Queens College of the City University of New York Foundation, Flushing, NY.
$10,000 to Aspen Center for New Medicine, Aspen, CO.
$10,000 to Prep for Prep, New York, NY.

7016
The Jonathan Sobel and Marcia Dunn Foundation ✧
c/o Goldman Sachs- Family Office
1 New York Plz., 40th Fl.
New York, NY   10004-2456

Established in 1999 in NY.
Donor: Jonathan Sobel.
Foundation type: Independent foundation.
Financial data (yr. ended 11/30/05): Assets, $2,181,449 (M); gifts received, $290,462; expenditures, $370,772; qualifying distributions, $360,473; giving activities include $360,473 for 66 grants (high: $81,850; low: $28).

Fields of interest: Museums; Arts; Higher education, university; Federated giving programs; Jewish agencies & temples.
Limitations: Applications not accepted. Giving primarily in New York, NY. No grants to individuals.
Application information: Contributes only to pre-selected organizations.
Trustees: Marcia Dunn; Jonathan Sobel.
EIN: 134050663

7017
Peter J. Solomon Foundation ✧
(formerly Peter J. & Linda N. Solomon Foundation)
c/o Barry M. Strauss Assocs., Ltd.
307 5th Ave., 8th Fl.
New York, NY   10016-6517

Established in 1986 in NY.
Donor: Peter J. Solomon.
Foundation type: Independent foundation.
Financial data (yr. ended 3/31/05): Assets, $11,603,911 (M); gifts received, $676,167; expenditures, $1,165,919; qualifying distributions, $1,011,690; giving activities include $1,011,440 for 90 grants (high: $453,573; low: $2).
Purpose and activities: Giving primarily for the arts and to cultural organizations; support also for human services.
Fields of interest: Museums; Museums (natural history); Performing arts, theater; Arts; Higher education; Education; Environment; Human services; Federated giving programs; Jewish agencies & temples.
Type of support: Annual campaigns; Capital campaigns; Building/renovation; Endowments; Scholarship funds.
Limitations: Applications not accepted. Giving on a national basis, with some emphasis on New York, NY. No grants to individuals.
Application information: Contributes only to pre-selected organizations.
Trustee: Peter J. Solomon.
EIN: 133384028

7018
Alfred Z. Solomon Testamentary Trust ✧ ☆
160 West Ave.
P.O. Box 4367
Saratoga Springs, NY   12866
Application address: c/o Harry D. Snyder, P.O. Box 108 Saratoga Springs, NY 12866

Established in 2005 in NY.
Donor: Alfred L. Solomon†.
Foundation type: Independent foundation.
Financial data (yr. ended 12/31/05): Assets, $6,591,462 (M); gifts received, $7,051,470; expenditures, $532,138; qualifying distributions, $523,335; giving activities include $517,992 for 10 grants (high: $150,000; low: $6,692).
Fields of interest: Museums (specialized); Education; Health care; Jewish agencies & temples.
Limitations: Giving primarily in NY.
Trustees: Robert E. Ingmire; Harry D. Snyder.
EIN: 137430894

7019
Solow Foundation ✧
9 W. 57th St., Ste. 4500
New York, NY   10019-2601
Contact: Sheldon H. Solow, Pres.

Established in 1978 in DE.
Donor: Sheldon H. Solow.
Foundation type: Independent foundation.
Financial data (yr. ended 10/31/05): Assets, $7,237,919 (M); expenditures, $1,505,856; qualifying distributions, $1,496,272; giving activities include $1,495,000 for 11 grants (high: $1,200,000; low: $2,000).
Fields of interest: Visual arts, architecture; Museums (art); Arts; Higher education; Education; Jewish agencies & temples.
Type of support: General/operating support; Continuing support; Professorships; Fellowships.
Limitations: Giving primarily in New York, NY. No grants to individuals.
Application information: Application form not required.
Initial approach: Letter
Copies of proposal: 1
Deadline(s): None
Officers: Sheldon H. Solow, Pres.; Rosalie S. Wolff, V.P.; Leonard Lazarus, Secy.; Steven M. Cherniak, Treas.
EIN: 132950685
Selected grants: The following grants were reported in 2004.
$300,000 to American Society for Technion-Israel Institute of Technology, New York, NY.
$50,000 to Metropolitan Museum of Art, New York, NY.
$25,000 to Partnership for Public Service, DC.
$19,500 to Solow Art and Architecture Foundation, New York, NY. 2 grants: $9,500, $10,000
$10,000 to American Spectator Foundation, Arlington, VA.
$9,500 to Lincoln Center for the Performing Arts, Real Estate and Construction Council, New York, NY.
$6,000 to New York University, New York, NY. For Leadership Award.
$5,000 to American Jewish Committee, New York, NY.
$5,000 to Covenant House, New York, NY.

7020
Sheldon H. Solow Foundation, Inc. ✧
9 W. 57th St., Ste. 4500
New York, NY   10019-2601   (212) 754-0284
Contact: Rosalie S. Wolff, Secy.

Incorporated in 1986 in DE.
Donor: Sheldon H. Solow.
Foundation type: Independent foundation.
Financial data (yr. ended 11/30/04): Assets, $3,054,376 (M); gifts received, $15,000; expenditures, $1,270,586; qualifying distributions, $1,260,615; giving activities include $1,260,250 for 14 grants (high: $1,000,000; low: $250).
Purpose and activities: Giving primarily for the arts, including visual arts organizations and programs.
Fields of interest: Visual arts; History/archaeology; Arts; Animals/wildlife, preservation/protection; Human services; Jewish federated giving programs.
Type of support: General/operating support; Continuing support; Endowments; Professorships; Fellowships.

Limitations: Giving on a national basis. No grants to individuals.
Application information: Application form not required.
  Initial approach: Letter
  Copies of proposal: 1
  Deadline(s): None
Officers: Sheldon H. Solow, Pres.; Steven Cherniak, V.P.; Rosalie Wolff, Secy.
EIN: 133386646
Selected grants: The following grants were reported in 2004.
$1,000,000 to UJA-Federation of New York, New York, NY. For general support.
$100,000 to Museum of Jewish Heritage, New York, NY. For general support.
$50,000 to Anti-Defamation League of Bnai Brith, New York, NY. For general support.
$30,000 to Federal Law Enforcement Foundation, New York, NY. For general support.
$15,000 to Museum of Modern Art, New York, NY. For general support.
$15,000 to Riverdale Country School, Bronx, NY. For general support.
$15,000 to Stonington Historical Society, Stonington, CT.
$13,000 to Solow Art and Architecture Foundation, New York, NY. For general support.
$10,000 to City Center of Music and Drama, New York, NY. For general support.
$5,000 to Teach for America, New York, NY. For general support.

7021
Soros Charitable Foundation ✧ ☆
400 W. 59th St.
New York, NY 10019
Contact: Steve Gutmann

Established in 1992 in NY.
Donor: George Soros.
Foundation type: Independent foundation.
Financial data (yr. ended 11/30/05): Assets, $90,731,433 (M); expenditures, $20,024,975; qualifying distributions, $4,132,707; giving activities include $4,100,000 for 1 grant.
Fields of interest: International affairs.
Type of support: Program-related investments/loans.
Limitations: Applications not accepted. Giving primarily in New York, NY. No grants to individuals.
Application information: Contributes only to pre-selected organizations.
Trustees: Armando Belly; Daniel R. Eule; George Soros; Jonathan Allan Soros; Susan Weber Soros; William D. Zabel.
EIN: 137003532

7022
Paul & Daisy Soros Foundation
400 W. 59th St.
New York, NY 10019 (212) 547-6926
FAX: (212) 548-4623;
E-mail: pdsoros_fellows@sorosny.org; URL: http://www.pdsoros.org

Established in 1994 in NY.
Donor: Paul Soros.
Foundation type: Independent foundation.
Financial data (yr. ended 12/31/04): Assets, $3,193,880 (M); gifts received, $2,933,000;

expenditures, $2,457,388; qualifying distributions, $1,790,628; giving activities include $165,675 for 15+ grants, and $1,624,953 for 70 grants to individuals (high: $55,935; low: $2,000).
Purpose and activities: Grants to new Americans for graduate study.
Fields of interest: Education.
Type of support: Grants to individuals.
Limitations: Giving on a national basis.
Publications: Application guidelines.
Application information: Application forms are available on foundation Web site. Application form required.
  Initial approach: See Web site for details
  Deadline(s): Nov. 1 (it is encouraged that materials be submitted prior to this date)
Director: Warren F. Ilchman.
Trustee: Daisy Soros.
EIN: 137057096
Selected grants: The following grants were reported in 2003.
$40,000 to Center for Early Education, West Hollywood, CA. For general support.
$20,000 to Creative Capital Foundation, New York, NY. For general support.
$17,500 to Santa Monica Museum of Art, Santa Monica, CA. For general support.
$16,300 to Lincoln Center for the Performing Arts, New York, NY. For general support.
$12,000 to Animal Medical Center, New York, NY. For general support.
$11,700 to Philharmonic-Symphony Society of New York, New York Philharmonic, New York, NY. For general support.
$10,000 to Collegiate Chorale, New York, NY. For general support.
$8,000 to New York City Opera, New York, NY. For general support.
$7,000 to Young Concert Artists, New York, NY. For general support.
$5,100 to Waveny Care Center, New Canaan, CT. For general support.

7023
The Soros Foundation-Hungary, Inc. ☆
400 W. 59th St.
New York, NY 10019 (212) 548-0630

Established in 1983 in NY.
Donors: George Soros; George Soros Charitable Lead Trust; Tivadar Charitable Lead Trust.
Foundation type: Independent foundation.
Financial data (yr. ended 12/31/04): Assets, $47,363,669 (M); expenditures, $22,126,109; qualifying distributions, $20,999,243; giving activities include $20,991,148 for 2 grants (high: $10,991,148; low: $10,000,000).
Fields of interest: Youth development, services.
Limitations: Applications not accepted. Giving limited to New York, NY. No grants to individuals.
Publications: Annual report.
Application information: Contributes only to pre-selected organizations.
Officers and Directors:* George Soros,* Chair.; Aryeh Neier,* Pres.; Stewart J. Paperin, Secy.-Treas.; Armando Belly; Daniel R. Eule; Jonathan Soros; William D. Zabel.
EIN: 133210361

7024
Soros Fund Charitable Foundation
(formerly SGM Scholarship Foundation)
888 7th Ave., 33rd Fl.
New York, NY 10106-0011

Established in 1986 in NY.
Donors: George Soros; Soros Charitable Foundation; Soros Foundation-Hungary; Centennial Foundation.
Foundation type: Independent foundation.
Financial data (yr. ended 12/31/05): Assets, $100,522,221 (M); expenditures, $3,874,185; qualifying distributions, $3,829,237; giving activities include $3,811,179 for 252 grants (high: $417,900; low: $75).
Purpose and activities: Awards scholarships to students who have demonstrated an ability for contributing to the scientific, cultural, or economic development of China, and fellowships to individuals involved in the fields of culture, economics, and science. The scholarships and fellowships may be used for trips to the U.S. and other countries by Chinese nationals and trips to China by non-Chinese nationals. Support also for international organizations and U.S. philanthropic organizations supporting international issues.
Fields of interest: Education; Health care; Health organizations, association; Human services; Children/youth, services; International affairs, goodwill promotion; Civil rights, race/intergroup relations; Christian agencies & churches; Jewish agencies & temples.
International interests: China & Mongolia.
Type of support: General/operating support; Fellowships; Scholarship funds.
Limitations: Applications not accepted. Giving primarily in CT, NJ, and NY. No grants to individuals.
Application information: Contributes only to pre-selected organizations.
Officers and Directors:* Gary Gladstein,* Pres.; Daniel R. Eule,* V.P. and Secy.; Jennifer Glassman, Treas.; Armando Belly; George Soros; Jonathan Allan Soros; Susan Weber Soros; William D. Zabel.
EIN: 133388177
Selected grants: The following grants were reported in 2005.
$294,675 to San Francisco Foundation, San Francisco, CA.
$223,350 to Harvard University, Cambridge, MA.
$200,000 to Village Community School, New York, NY.
$171,000 to Wesleyan University, Middletown, CT.
$150,567 to Girls Preparatory School, Chattanooga, TN.
$100,000 to Foundation for the Protection of Children, New York, NY.
$45,000 to Westchester Land Trust, Bedford Hills, NY.
$30,000 to Robin Hood Foundation, New York, NY.
$8,000 to North Carolina Outward Bound School, Asheville, NC.
$1,500 to Yeshiva Rabbi Samson Raphael Hirsch, New York, NY.

7025
Martin and Toni Sosnoff Foundation ✧
(formerly Martin T. Sosnoff Foundation)
P.O. Box 135
Rhinebeck, NY 12572

Established in 1978 in NY.
Donor: Martin T. Sosnoff.

Foundation type: Independent foundation.
Financial data (yr. ended 11/30/05): Assets, $8,812,167 (M); gifts received, $2,896,454; expenditures, $675,212; qualifying distributions, $638,228; giving activities include $625,871 for 57 grants (high: $250,000; low: $15).
Purpose and activities: Giving primarily for higher education, animal welfare, health associations, the arts, and children and social services.
Fields of interest: Museums (art); Performing arts; Performing arts, theater; Performing arts, opera; Higher education; Animal welfare; Health organizations, association; Human services; Children/youth, services.
Type of support: General/operating support; Building/renovation.
Limitations: Applications not accepted. Giving primarily in NY. No support for private foundations. No grants to individuals.
Application information: Contributes only to pre-selected organizations.
Trustees: Martin T. Sosnoff; Toni Sosnoff.
EIN: 222231640

7026
The Sperry Fund
99 Park Ave., Ste. 2220
New York, NY   10016-1601
Contact: Thomas L. Parkinson Ph.D., Prog. Dir.
FAX: (610) 625-7919;
E-mail: BeineckeScholarship@earthlink.net
Application address: c/o Beinecke Scholarship Prog., Box 125, Fogelsville, PA 18051-0125, tel.: (610) 395-5560

Established in 1962 in NY.
Foundation type: Independent foundation.
Financial data (yr. ended 6/30/05): Assets, $16,582,685 (M); expenditures, $1,055,513; qualifying distributions, $983,197; giving activities include $232,000 for 6 grants (high: $125,000; low: $10,000), and $650,168 for 92 grants to individuals (high: $20,000; low: $2,000).
Purpose and activities: Giving primarily to college juniors for support during two years of graduate education.
Fields of interest: Education.
Type of support: Program development; Scholarships—to individuals.
Limitations: Applications not accepted. Giving primarily in NY.
Publications: Informational brochure.
Application information: College or university must be invited to nominate juniors for scholarship program; completion of application form required for nominees. Applications outside the nomination process not considered.
Board meeting date(s): Annually
Officers and Directors:* Frederick W. Beinecke,* Pres.; John B. Beinecke,* V.P.; R. Scott Greathead,* Secy.; Robert J. Barletta, Treas.; William S. Beinecke; Frances Beinecke Elston; Sarah Beinecke Richardson; Melvyn L. Shaffir.
Number of staff: 1 part-time support.
EIN: 136114308

7027
The Speyer Family Foundation, Inc. ▼ ✧
(formerly Tishman Speyer Properties Foundation, Inc.)
45 Rockefeller Plz., 7th Fl.
New York, NY   10022

Established in NY.
Donor: Jerry I. Speyer.
Foundation type: Independent foundation.
Financial data (yr. ended 9/30/04): Assets, $5,913,417 (M); gifts received, $3,483,370; expenditures, $4,796,241; qualifying distributions, $4,770,491; giving activities include $4,770,491 for 109 grants (high: $714,300; low: $500; average: $1,000–$100,000).
Purpose and activities: Giving primarily for museums, education, health care, and the arts.
Fields of interest: Museums (art); Museums (natural history); Performing arts; Arts; Higher education; Education; Hospitals (general); Health organizations; Human services; International human rights; Civil rights, immigrants; Jewish agencies & temples.
Limitations: Applications not accepted. Giving primarily in New York, NY. No grants to individuals.
Application information: Contributes only to pre-selected organizations.
Officers: Jerry I. Speyer, Pres.; Katherine G. Farley, V.P.; Paul A. Galiano, Secy.; Daniel Shapiro, Treas.
EIN: 136158848
Selected grants: The following grants were reported in 2004.
$900,000 to Columbia University, New York, NY. 4 grants: $25,000 (For College Fund), $312,500, $250,000 to School of Business, $312,500.
$724,300 to New York-Presbyterian Hospital, New York, NY. 2 grants: $10,000 to Iris Cantor Womens Health Center, $714,300
$182,500 to Alvin Ailey American Dance Theater, New York, NY. 2 grants: $175,000, $7,500
$150,000 to Lincoln Center for the Performing Arts, New York, NY.
$100,000 to International Rescue Committee, New York, NY.

7028
The SPIA Foundation
(formerly Dorinda Pell and Mark Winkelman Foundation)
c/o Michele McIntyre
717 5th Ave., 26th Fl.
New York, NY   10022
FAX: (646) 219-2257; *E-mail:* mmcintyre@jfco.com

Established in 1985 in NY.
Donors: Mark O. Winkelman; Dorinda Pell; Marius O. Winkelman.
Foundation type: Independent foundation.
Financial data (yr. ended 2/28/06): Assets, $3,255,531 (M); expenditures, $502,704; qualifying distributions, $494,270; giving activities include $492,450 for 19 grants (high: $200,000; low: $200).
Purpose and activities: Giving primarily for higher education, environmental conservation, and for health and social services.
Fields of interest: Arts; Elementary/secondary education; Higher education; Education; Environment, natural resources; Hospitals (general); Physical therapy; Health organizations, association; Food distribution, meals on wheels; Human services; Children/youth, services.

Limitations: Applications not accepted. Giving primarily in New York, NY, and CT. No grants to individuals.
Application information: Contributes only to pre-selected organizations.
Trustees: Dorinda P. Winkelman; Marius O. Winkelman.
EIN: 133318172

7029
Jerry and Emily Spiegel Family Foundation, Inc. ✧
(formerly Jerry Spiegel Foundation, Inc.)
2 E. 88th St.
New York, NY   10128-0555

Established in 1958 in NY.
Donors: Jerry Spiegel; Emily Spiegel.
Foundation type: Independent foundation.
Financial data (yr. ended 3/31/05): Assets, $16,223,396 (M); gifts received, $875,000; expenditures, $5,076,758; qualifying distributions, $5,076,758; giving activities include $5,033,074 for 126 grants (high: $3,877,300; low: $500).
Purpose and activities: Giving primarily for the arts, health associations, and to Jewish organizations and temples.
Fields of interest: Museums (art); Performing arts, orchestra (symphony); Performing arts, opera; Arts; Hospitals (general); Health organizations; Parkinson's disease research; Jewish federated giving programs; Jewish agencies & temples.
Type of support: General/operating support; Scholarship funds.
Limitations: Applications not accepted. Giving primarily in NY. No grants to individuals.
Application information: Contributes only to pre-selected organizations. Unsolicited requests for funds not accepted.
Officers: Jerry Spiegel, Pres.; Arthur D. Sanders, V.P.; Emily Spiegel, V.P.; Lise Spiegel, Secy.
EIN: 116006020

7030
Sam Spiegel Foundation ✧
30 Wall St.
New York, NY   10005   (212) 269-6720
Contact: David N. Bottoms, Jr., Dir.

Established in 1958 in NY.
Donors: Sam Spiegel; Albatros Enterprises Trust.
Foundation type: Independent foundation.
Financial data (yr. ended 12/31/05): Assets, $12,433,182 (M); expenditures, $518,184; qualifying distributions, $452,026; giving activities include $430,000 for 26 grants (high: $125,000; low: $1,000).
Purpose and activities: Giving primarily for the arts, human services, and Jewish organizations, education, and temples.
Fields of interest: Museums (art); Performing arts, theater; Performing arts, music; Performing arts, opera; Arts; Education; Health care; Legal services; Human services; Children/youth, services; Federated giving programs; Jewish federated giving programs; Jewish agencies & temples.
International interests: England.
Limitations: Giving on a national and international basis, with some emphasis on NY. No grants to individuals.
Application information:

Initial approach: Letter
Deadline(s): None
Directors: David N. Bottoms, Jr.; Raya Dreben; Alisa S. Freedman; Adam Spiegel.
EIN: 136163123
Selected grants: The following grants were reported in 2004.
$75,000 to Givat Haviva Educational Foundation, New York, NY.
$25,000 to American Fund for Charities, DC.
$25,000 to British American Arts Association, London, England. .
$25,000 to Charities Aid Foundation (CAF) America, Alexandria, VA.
$25,000 to Friends of the Princes Trust, New York, NY.
$25,000 to Israel Guide Dog Center for the Blind, Warrington, PA.
$20,000 to Center for Jewish History, New York, NY.
$20,000 to Harvard Hillel, Cambridge, MA.
$20,000 to Hebrew College, Newton Centre, MA.
$2,000 to Adelphi University, Garden City, NY.

7031
Spinal Muscular Atrophy Foundation ✧
(also known as SMA Foundation)
119 W. 72nd St., Ste. 187
New York, NY 10023 (646) 253-7100
Contact: Cynthia Joyce, Exec. Dir.
FAX: (212) 247-3079;
E-mail: info@smafoundation.org; Additional tel.:
(877) FUND-SMA (toll-free); URL: http://
www.smafoundation.org/

Established in 2003 in NY.
Donors: Loren Eng; Dinakar Singh; Muneer Satter; Jason Amiss; John Zacamy; Richard Perry; Phillip D. Murphy; Timothy Dattels; Eric Mandelblatt; Deborah Heine.
Foundation type: Independent foundation.
Financial data (yr. ended 12/31/04): Assets, $6,041,009 (M); gifts received, $936,070; expenditures, $3,749,896; qualifying distributions, $3,749,060; giving activities include $3,016,771 for 17 grants (high: $801,818; low: $3,800).
Purpose and activities: The mission of the foundation is to accelerate the development of a treatment or a cure for SMA, the number one genetic killer of infants and toddlers.
Fields of interest: Spine disorders.
Type of support: Research.
Limitations: Giving on a national basis. No grants for salaries, construction, computer equipment, memberships (in scientific societies), office supplies, tuitions, or for publication costs.
Application information: See foundation Web site for grant application requirements. Application form required.
Officers and Directors:* Dinakar Singh,* Chair.; Loren Eng,* Pres.; Cynthia Joyce, Exec. Dir.; Wendy Belzberg; Matthew T. Browne; William T. Coleman, Jr.; Darryl C. DeVivo, M.D.; Gerald Fischbach, M.D.; Alan F. Holmer; Susan S. Lin; Vishwa Singh, Ph.D.; David M. Weil.
EIN: 010759380

7032
The Spingold Foundation, Inc.
(formerly Nate B. and Frances Spingold Foundation, Inc.)
c/o Holland & Knight, LLP
195 Broadway, 23rd Fl.
New York, NY 10007
Contact: Sergio Stifelman, Legal Asst.

Incorporated in 1955 in NY.
Donors: Frances Spingold†; Nathan Breither Spingold†.
Foundation type: Independent foundation.
Financial data (yr. ended 11/30/05): Assets, $11,112,478 (M); expenditures, $688,926; qualifying distributions, $561,500; giving activities include $523,500 for 44 grants (high: $35,000; low: $1,000).
Fields of interest: Arts; Education; Mental health/crisis services; Human services; Aging, centers/services; Civil rights; Community development.
Type of support: General/operating support; Continuing support; Annual campaigns; Program development; Seed money.
Limitations: Applications not accepted. Giving primarily in the metropolitan New York, NY, area. No grants to individuals.
Application information: Contributes only to pre-selected organizations. Unsolicited requests for funds not considered or acknowledged.
Board meeting date(s): 2-3 times annually
Officers and Directors:* Daniel L. Kurtz,* Pres.; Lorance Hockert,* Secy.-Treas.; Elizabeth Olofson; Ruth Rosenblatt, M.D.
EIN: 136107659

7033
Spirit Foundation, Inc. ✧ ☆
c/o Sexter & Warmflash
115 Broadway
New York, NY 10006

Established in 1978 in NY.
Donors: John Lennon†; Yoko Ono Lennon; Bag One Arts, Inc.; Fuji Films, Japan; Nike, Inc.; Together Magazine.
Foundation type: Independent foundation.
Financial data (yr. ended 11/30/05): Assets, $915,921 (M); gifts received, $521,901; expenditures, $368,477; qualifying distributions, $368,352; giving activities include $368,352 for 9 grants (high: $210,000; low: $3,352).
Purpose and activities: Giving primarily for human services, international affairs, and women's causes.
Fields of interest: Education, early childhood education; Medical research; Human services; Children/youth, services; Community development, association; Women.
International interests: England; Hungary.
Type of support: General/operating support.
Limitations: Applications not accepted. Giving primarily in New York, NY, England and Hungary.
Application information: Unsolicited requests for funds not accepted.
Officers: Yoko Ono, Pres.; David Warmflash, Secy.-Treas.
Director: Allan S. Sexter.
EIN: 132971714
Selected grants: The following grants were reported in 2005.
$100,000 to Americas Second Harvest, Chicago, IL.
$10,000 to Bailey House, New York, NY.
$5,000 to Citizens Advice Bureau, Bronx, NY.

7034
The Bernard & Anne Spitzer Charitable Trust, Inc. ✧
(formerly The Bernard & Anne Spitzer Foundation, Inc.)
730 5th Ave., Ste. 2202
New York, NY 10019-4105 (212) 765-5170
Contact: Bernard Spitzer, Pres.; Anne Spitzer, Tr.

Established around 1982 in NY.
Donor: Bernard Spitzer.
Foundation type: Independent foundation.
Financial data (yr. ended 12/31/05): Assets, $35,115,418 (M); gifts received, $5,000,000; expenditures, $1,276,157; qualifying distributions, $579,413; giving activities include $578,663 for 33 + grants (high: $100,000).
Purpose and activities: Support primarily for health associations, education, and Jewish organizations; funding also for cultural programs.
Fields of interest: Arts; Higher education; Education; Hospitals (general); Reproductive health, family planning; Diabetes research; Jewish federated giving programs.
Type of support: General/operating support.
Limitations: Giving primarily in NY. No grants to individuals.
Application information:
Initial approach: Proposal
Deadline(s): None
Trustees: Anne Spitzer; Bernard Spitzer; Daniel Evan Spitzer; Eliot Laurence Spitzer.
EIN: 137298842
Selected grants: The following grants were reported in 2004.
$1,553,000 to American Museum of Natural History, New York, NY.
$100,000 to Horace Mann School, Riverdale, NY.
$50,000 to Jewish Museum, New York, NY.
$30,000 to Museum of Jewish Heritage, New York, NY.
$25,000 to New York Public Library, New York, NY.
$10,000 to Israel Arts and Science Academy, Jerusalem, Israel. .
$7,500 to Carnegie Hall Society, New York, NY.
$6,000 to Metropolitan Museum of Art, New York, NY.
$5,000 to Columbia University, New York, NY.

7035
The Seth Sprague Educational and Charitable Foundation ✧
c/o U.S. Trust
114 W. 47th St.
New York, NY 10036-1532
Contact: Linda R. Franciscovich, Managing Dir., U.S. Trust

Trust established in 1939 in NY.
Donor: Seth Sprague†.
Foundation type: Independent foundation.
Financial data (yr. ended 12/31/05): Assets, $60,355,919 (M); expenditures, $3,173,837; qualifying distributions, $2,881,647; giving activities include $2,604,525 for grants.
Purpose and activities: Giving primarily for health, human services, education, the arts, civic affairs, and community development.
Fields of interest: Performing arts; Arts; Secondary school/education; Higher education; Education; Hospitals (general); Health care; Human services;

Children/youth, services; Community development; Government/public administration.
Type of support: General/operating support; Program development; Matching/challenge support.
Limitations: Giving primarily in MA and NY. No grants to individuals, or for building funds; no loans.
Publications: Application guidelines.
Application information: Application form not required.
  Initial approach: 3-5 page narrative proposal
  Copies of proposal: 1
  Deadline(s): Apr. 15 and Oct. 1
  Board meeting date(s): Mar., June, Sept., and Dec. (grants awarded at June and Dec. meetings)
  Final notification: Letter
Trustees: Patricia Dunnington; Arline Ripley Greenleaf; Jacqueline D. Simpkins; U.S. Trust.
EIN: 136071886
Selected grants: The following grants were reported in 2003.
$75,000 to New York-Presbyterian Hospital, New York, NY.
$50,000 to Memorial Sloan-Kettering Cancer Center, New York, NY.
$25,000 to Philharmonic-Symphony Society of New York, New York, NY.
$25,000 to Woodberry Forest School, Woodberry Forest, VA.
$20,000 to Sturgis Library, Barnstable, MA.
$15,000 to Big Brothers Big Sisters of New York City, New York, NY.
$10,000 to Boston Ballet, Boston, MA.
$10,000 to Cape Cod Maritime Museum at Hyannis Harbor, Hyannis, MA.
$10,000 to Lesley University, Cambridge, MA.
$10,000 to Westport Country Playhouse, Westport, CT.

7036
The Spunk Fund, Inc.
780 3rd Ave., 24th Fl.
New York, NY 10017 (212) 980-8880
Contact: Marianne Gerschel, Pres.
FAX: (212) 980-8976; E-mail: mg@spunkfund.com

Incorporated in 1981 in NY.
Donor: Marianne Gerschel.
Foundation type: Independent foundation.
Financial data (yr. ended 12/31/05): Assets, $18,759,678 (M); gifts received, $1,039,956; expenditures, $2,205,654; qualifying distributions, $1,907,424; giving activities include $1,122,479 for 24 grants (high: $150,000; low: $1,790).
Purpose and activities: Supports initiatives that contribute to the enrichment and well-being of children and adolescents, including medical and psychological research, education, cultural programs, and programs for the prevention and treatment of child abuse and neglect. Giving also for international programs that enhance the quality of life and create opportunities for less-advantaged children.
Fields of interest: Arts; Child development, education; Elementary school/education; Education; Crime/violence prevention, child abuse; Children/youth, services; Child development, services; Family services; Economically disadvantaged.
Type of support: General/operating support; Seed money; Research.

Limitations: Giving primarily in NY, with growing support for international grants. No grants to individuals, or for capital programs.
Publications: Informational brochure (including application guidelines).
Application information: The fund will request proposals from organizations in which it is interested; unsolicited proposals not considered. Application form not required.
  Initial approach: Letter of inquiry
  Copies of proposal: 1
  Deadline(s): Letters of inquiry accepted year round; requested proposals due Apr. 1
  Board meeting date(s): June
  Final notification: July 1
Officer: Marianne Gerschel, Pres.
Number of staff: 2 full-time professional; 1 part-time professional; 4 full-time support.
EIN: 133116094

7037
Toufic Srour Foundation, Inc. ✧
c/o Parigi Group Ltd.
112 W. 34th St., Ste. 836
New York, NY 10120-0800

Established in 1999 in NY.
Donors: Esther Jamal; Marco Srour; Morris Srour; Parigi Group, Ltd.
Foundation type: Independent foundation.
Financial data (yr. ended 11/30/05): Assets, $639,086 (M); gifts received, $863,520; expenditures, $958,266; qualifying distributions, $957,263; giving activities include $957,163 for 25 + grants (high: $250,000).
Fields of interest: Jewish federated giving programs; Jewish agencies & temples.
Limitations: Applications not accepted. Giving primarily in NJ and NY. No grants to individuals.
Application information: Contributes only to pre-selected organizations.
Officers: Marco Srour, Pres.; Morris Srour, Secy.; Esther Jamal, Treas.
EIN: 134088570

7038
SSM Foundation, Inc. ✧ ☆
c/o Miller, Ellin & Co.
750 Lexington Ave.
New York, NY 10022

Foundation type: Independent foundation.
Financial data (yr. ended 10/31/05): Assets, $0 (M); gifts received, $1,270,000; expenditures, $1,374,822; qualifying distributions, $1,374,822; giving activities include $1,371,060 for grants.
Fields of interest: Jewish agencies & temples.
Limitations: Applications not accepted. Giving primarily in NY. No grants to individuals.
Application information: Contributes only to pre-selected organizations.
Officers: Edward Lawner, Pres.; Hilton Sokol, V.P.; Mark Peltz, Secy.-Treas.
EIN: 061691147

7039
St. Faith's House Foundation
P.O. Box 308
Ardsley-on-Hudson, NY 10503 (914) 631-6065
Contact: Ann D. Phillips, Dir.

Additional address: 16 Crest Dr., Tarrytown, NY 10591

Incorporated in 1901 in NY as St. Faith's House; reorganized in 1973 as a private foundation.
Foundation type: Independent foundation.
Financial data (yr. ended 6/30/05): Assets, $9,117,327 (M); expenditures, $672,385; qualifying distributions, $561,182; giving activities include $529,000 for 53 grants (high: $25,000; low: $4,000; average: $5,000–$10,000).
Purpose and activities: Giving for homeless children, pregnancy prevention programs for at-risk teens, and tuition assistance for day care. Grants limited to organizations that provide services to children and young people of Westchester County, NY.
Fields of interest: Children/youth, services; Children, day care; Family services; Homeless, human services.
Type of support: Continuing support; Program development; Seed money; Matching/challenge support.
Limitations: Giving restricted to Westchester County, NY. No support for public or private institutions. No grants to individuals, or for building, capital campaigns or endowment funds.
Publications: Application guidelines.
Application information: Distributions awarded twice annually. A copy of the application must be sent to each Grants Committee Member on the list provided with application. Application form required.
  Initial approach: Letter
  Copies of proposal: 12
  Deadline(s): Submit proposal preferably in Aug. or Jan.; deadlines Sept. 15 and Feb. 15
  Board meeting date(s): May and Nov.
  Final notification: June and Nov.
Officers and Directors:* Mrs. William Bush, Pres.; Mrs. C. Edward Midgley,* V.P.; Robert C. Myers,* Secy.; Daniel H. Childs,* Treas.; Bruce E. Clark; Mrs. John Diao; Mrs. John A. Dimling; Mrs. Emmet Ellis; Mrs. Brian Gardner; Mrs. Robert L. Huston; Mrs. John C. Keenan; Michael H. Lowry; Mrs. Robert W. Lyman; Ann D. Phillips; Mrs. William Shore; Harvey J. Struthers, Jr.; Mrs. Maarten Van Hengel.
EIN: 131740123

7040
St. George's Society of New York
216 E. 45th St., Ste. 901
New York, NY 10017-3304 (212) 682-6110
Contact: John Shannon, Exec. Dir.
FAX: (212) 682-3465;
E-mail: info@stgeorgessociety.org; URL: http://www.stgeorgessociety.org

Established in 1770 in NY.
Donors: Charlotte M. F. Bentley†; British Embassy; DeCoizart Charitable Trust; Andrew MacKenzie Hay†; Florence Davis; Francis Finlay; Richard Grasso; Sir Deryck C. Maughan; Sir Edwin Manton†; William R. Miller; Martin Sullivan; Aetna; Citigroup UK; D'Amato & Lynch; HSBC Bank USA; McGraw Hill Companies; Sherman & Sterling; Skaden Arps; Starr Foundation; JPMorgan Chase Bank, N.A.; Revolution Studios; CSFB; Bloomberg; AIG; Sony Corp.; WWP/Young & Rubicam; Heast Corp.; Sir Howard Stringer.
Foundation type: Operating foundation.
Financial data (yr. ended 12/31/04): Assets, $9,195,881 (M); gifts received, $60,160; expenditures, $913,762; qualifying distributions, $543,917; giving activities include $365,840 for 61

grants to individuals, and $144,575 for foundation-administered programs.

Purpose and activities: A private operating foundation dedicated to helping men and women from the United Kingdom and the British Commonwealth and their children who find themselves in need, trouble, sickness or other adversity in the New York, NY, area.

Fields of interest: Health care; Aging; Disabilities, people with; Economically disadvantaged.

International interests: United Kingdom.

Type of support: Emergency funds; Grants to individuals.

Limitations: Giving limited to the metropolitan New York, NY, area. No grants for financial aid.

Publications: Application guidelines; Annual report; Informational brochure; Newsletter.

Application information: Applicant must be a native of the United Kingdom or the British Commonwealth, residing in the New York, NY, metropolitan region, with a legal status. Personal interviews and visits from the Society's social worker. Application form not required.

Initial approach: Letter or telephone
Copies of proposal: 1
Deadline(s): None
Board meeting date(s): Quarterly
Final notification: 4-6 weeks

Officers: Natalie Thomas Pray, Pres.; Peter M Felix, 1st V.P.; Victor E. Stewart, 2nd V.P.; John C. Harvey, Secy.; Peter Buffington, Treas.

Directors: June C. Briggs; Michael H. Charles; Anita P. Cotter; Andrew Curtis; Stephen P. Foley; Kazie M. Harvey; Robin N. Hayes; Arnold Hayward Neis; Ellsworth G. Stanton III; Robert J.K. Titley; Hugh Williamson-Noble; Jonathan B. Wimpenny.

Number of staff: 1 full-time professional; 1 part-time professional; 1 full-time support.

EIN: 237426425

7041
St. Giles Foundation ✧
(formerly The House of St. Giles the Cripple)
420 Lexington Ave., Ste. 2329
New York, NY 10170 (212) 338-9001
Contact: Richard T. Arkwright, Pres.

Established around 1979.

Foundation type: Independent foundation.

Financial data (yr. ended 3/31/06): Assets, $21,037,926 (M); gifts received, $250; expenditures, $1,438,863; qualifying distributions, $1,194,526; giving activities include $1,021,513 for 8 grants (high: $350,000; low: $25,000).

Purpose and activities: Giving primarily for hospitals, particularly children's hospitals, and to organizations that help people who are handicapped, particularly youth; special interest in medical sciences, and children's orthopedics.

Fields of interest: Hospitals (general); Hospitals (specialty); Children/youth, services; Disabilities, people with.

Type of support: General/operating support; Equipment; Research.

Limitations: Giving on a national basis.

Application information:
Initial approach: Proposal
Deadline(s): None

Officers: Richard T. Arkwright, Pres.; Edward Ridley Finch, Jr., V.P.; Henry A. Braun, Secy.; Robert B. MacKay, Treas.

EIN: 111630806

Selected grants: The following grants were reported in 2004.

$500,000 to Cold Spring Harbor Laboratory, Cold Spring Harbor, NY. For Saint Giles Chair in Neurosurgery.

$187,500 to Harvard University, School of Medicine, Cambridge, MA. For Osteoprogenirtor Cells and Bone Repair.

$85,000 to New York-Presbyterian Hospital, New York, NY. For one year fellowship in subspecialty of vitreo-retinal surgery and assist the continuation of research and clinical treatment to benefit many children.

$75,000 to Manhattan Institute for Cancer Research, New York, NY. For program support.

$50,000 to Medical Benevolence Foundation, Woodville, TX. To build and equip four operating rooms in a hospital in India which will assist in many of the children of that region receive benefits of a local institution which would otherwise not be available to them.

$35,000 to Pediatric Orthopaedic Society of North America (POSNA), Rosemont, IL. For Arthur H. Huene Memorial Award to support research.

$25,000 to Saint Hildas and Saint Hughs School, New York, NY. For scholarship assistance program.

$25,000 to University of the Cumberlands, Williamsburg, KY. For Scholarship Assistance Program for disabled students.

7042
Thomas F. Staley Foundation ✧
4 Chatsworth Ave., No. 3
Larchmont, NY 10538-2932

Trust established in 1943 in MI.

Donors: Thomas F. Staley†; Shirley H. Hunter†.

Foundation type: Independent foundation.

Financial data (yr. ended 12/31/05): Assets, $6,503,389 (M); expenditures, $603,042; qualifying distributions, $529,767; giving activities include $400,000 for 48 grants (high: $72,000; low: $1,000).

Purpose and activities: Support only for Christian scholar lectureship programs on college campuses.

Fields of interest: Education; Christian agencies & churches; Protestant agencies & churches.

Type of support: Curriculum development.

Limitations: Applications not accepted. Giving on a national basis. No grants to individuals.

Publications: Informational brochure; Program policy statement.

Application information: Contributes only to pre-selected organizations.
Board meeting date(s): June

Officers: Thomas F. Staley, Jr., Pres.; Robert G. Howard, Treas.

Trustees: Diane Staley Bernard; Susan H. Canada; Janet Howard; Catherine Staley; Stuart Staley; Sarah H. Wichert.

Number of staff: 1 full-time professional.

EIN: 136071888

Selected grants: The following grants were reported in 2003.

$55,500 to Northshire Day School, Manchester Center, VT. For general support.

$55,000 to Fund for American Studies, DC. For general support.

$50,000 to Trinity Episcopal School for Ministry, Ambridge, PA. For general support.

$28,750 to Burr and Burton Seminary, Manchester, VT. For general support.

$25,000 to Migrant Association of South Florida, Boynton Beach, FL. For general support.

$18,000 to First Presbyterian Church, Harrison, OH. For general support.

$16,500 to Project of Easton, Center Valley, PA. For general support.

$15,000 to Camp Sunshine. For general support.

$11,000 to Man in the Mirror, Casselberry, FL. For general support.

$5,000 to Safe Harbour, Carlisle, PA. For general support.

7043
The Ruth Stanton Family Foundation ✧ ☆
(formerly The Ruth & Oliver Stanton Foundation)
c/o Anchin, Block & Anchin, LLP
1375 Broadway, 18th Fl.
New York, NY 10018

Established in 1994 in NY.

Donor: Ruth S. Stanton.

Foundation type: Independent foundation.

Financial data (yr. ended 12/31/05): Assets, $5,221,654 (M); expenditures, $562,490; qualifying distributions, $514,628; giving activities include $508,803 for 24+ grants (high: $380,000).

Purpose and activities: Giving primarily to arts and culture; funding also for health associations, medical research, human services, and Jewish agencies and temples.

Fields of interest: Museums; Museums (art); Performing arts, ballet; Performing arts, theater; Arts; Higher education; Health organizations, association; Medical research; Human services; Jewish agencies & temples.

Limitations: Applications not accepted. Giving primarily in New York, NY. No grants to individuals.

Application information: Contributes only to pre-selected organizations.

Trustees: Frank Giraud; Oliver K. Stanton; Ruth S. Stanton.

EIN: 137031172

Selected grants: The following grants were reported in 2004.

$81,000 to Metropolitan Museum of Art, New York, NY. For general support.

$37,450 to New York City Ballet, New York, NY. For general support.

$26,590 to Lincoln Center for the Performing Arts, New York, NY. For general support.

$8,500 to Dia Art Foundation, New York, NY. For general support.

$5,500 to American Friends of the Israel Museum, New York, NY. For general support.

$5,500 to Chinati Foundation, Marfa, TX. For general support.

$5,000 to New York-Presbyterian Hospital, New York, NY. For general support.

$4,250 to Museum of Modern Art, New York, NY. For general support.

$2,500 to Film Society of Lincoln Center, New York, NY. For general support.

$1,250 to Partnership for Public Service, DC. For general support.

7044
The Stanton Family Foundation ✧
c/o BCRS Assocs., LLC
100 Wall St., 11th Fl.
New York, NY 10005

Established in 1996 in NJ.
Donor: Daniel W. Stanton.
Foundation type: Independent foundation.
Financial data (yr. ended 9/30/05): Assets, $5,732,334 (M); expenditures, $442,532; qualifying distributions, $403,957; giving activities include $402,250 for 37 grants (high: $200,000; low: $500).
Fields of interest: Higher education, college; Higher education, university; Business school/education; Education; Health care; Medical research, institute.
Limitations: Applications not accepted. Giving primarily in NJ and NY. No grants to individuals; no loans.
Application information: Contributes only to pre-selected organizations.
Trustees: Daniel W. Stanton; Mary B. Stanton.
EIN: 137103245

7045
The Oliver & Elizabeth Stanton Foundation ✧ ☆
c/o Transommonia, Inc.
320 Park Ave.
New York, NY 10022-6815

Established in 2000 in NY.
Donors: Transammonia, Inc.; Oliver K. Stanton.
Foundation type: Independent foundation.
Financial data (yr. ended 12/31/05): Assets, $5,241,460 (M); gifts received, $3,500; expenditures, $547,657; qualifying distributions, $502,183; giving activities include $502,183 for 27 grants (high: $51,800; low: $860).
Fields of interest: Higher education; Jewish agencies & temples.
Limitations: Applications not accepted. Giving primarily in New York, NY. No grants to individuals.
Application information: Contributes only to pre-selected organizations.
Officers: Elizabeth Stanton, Pres.; Oliver K. Stanton, V.P.; Fred M. Lowenfels, Secy.; Edward G. Weiner, Treas.
EIN: 134138465

7046
The Starfish Group ✧ ☆
c/o Anchin Block & Anchin
1375 Broadway
New York, NY 10018

Established in 2000 in NY.
Foundation type: Independent foundation.
Financial data (yr. ended 12/31/05): Assets, $694,527 (M); gifts received, $498,927; expenditures, $445,167; qualifying distributions, $445,167; giving activities include $438,820 for 43 grants (high: $50,000; low: $1,000).
Fields of interest: Arts; Education; Environment; Legal services; International relief.
Limitations: Applications not accepted. No grants to individuals.
Application information: Contributes only to pre-selected organizations.
Officers: Virginia Anne Gilder, Co-Pres.; Britt-Louise Gilder, Co-Pres.; Margaret Mathews, Secy.; Lynn Slaughter, Treas.
Director: Ericka Alford.
EIN: 134128526
Selected grants: The following grants were reported in 2005.

$50,000 to International Rescue Committee, New York, NY.
$12,500 to Environmental Defense, New York, NY.
$12,500 to Natural Resources Defense Council, New York, NY.
$10,000 to New York Foundation for the Arts, New York, NY.
$7,000 to La Escuelita, Minneapolis, MN.
$7,000 to Planned Parenthood, Oak Harbor, WA.
$5,000 to De La Salle Academy, New York, NY.
$2,500 to Brooklyn Jesuit Prep, Brooklyn, NY.
$2,000 to Bovina Public Library, Bovina Center, NY.
$1,500 to Summer Search Foundation, San Francisco, CA.

7047
The Starker Family Foundation, Inc. ✧
c/o JAD Consulting, LLC
61 Broadway, Rm. 1710
New York, NY 10006
Contact: Joseph DeMaio

Established in NY.
Donor: Steven Starker.
Foundation type: Independent foundation.
Financial data (yr. ended 9/30/05): Assets, $2,564,709 (M); gifts received, $225,000; expenditures, $737,300; qualifying distributions, $734,875; giving activities include $731,917 for grants.
Fields of interest: Education; Health care; Health organizations, association; Medical research, institute; Children/youth, services.
Limitations: Applications not accepted. No grants to individuals.
Application information: Contributes only to pre-selected organizations.
Officers: Steven Starker, Pres. and Treas.; Farrel Starker, V.P. and Secy.; Stuart Dix, V.P.; Ray Starker, V.P.
EIN: 133986718
Selected grants: The following grants were reported in 2005.

$50,000 to Rye Country Day School, Rye, NY.
$25,000 to Jewish Enrichment Center, New York, NY.
$22,500 to Tsunami Relief, New York, NY.
$10,000 to A Little Hope, New York, NY.
$10,000 to City Harvest, New York, NY.
$10,000 to Help USA, New York, NY.
$10,000 to Ushers New Look, Lawrenceville, GA.
$7,500 to American Cancer Society, Atlanta, GA.
$7,500 to Cancer Research Institute, New York, NY.
$1,000 to P.S. 166, New York, NY.

7048
The Starr Foundation ▼
399 Park Ave., 17th Fl.
New York, NY 10022 (212) 909-3600
Contact: Florence A. Davis, Pres.
FAX: (212) 750-3536; Additional tel.: (212) 909-3615; URL: http://www.starrfoundation.org/

Incorporated in 1955 in NY.
Donor: Cornelius V. Starr‡.
Foundation type: Independent foundation.
Financial data (yr. ended 12/31/05): Assets, $3,344,801,753 (M); gifts received, $188,319; expenditures, $164,496,989; qualifying distributions, $163,278,823; giving activities

include $147,566,930 for 591 grants, and $11,564,022 for 1,280 grants to individuals.
Purpose and activities: The foundation makes grants in a number of areas, including education, medicine and health care, human needs, public policy, culture and the environment.
Fields of interest: Arts; Higher education; Education; Environment; Health care; Health organizations, association; Medical research; Human services; Social sciences.
Type of support: General/operating support; Program development; Professorships; Fellowships; Scholarship funds.
Limitations: Giving primarily on a national and international basis, with emphasis on New York, NY and emphasis on Asia internationally. No grants to.
Application information: Please consult foundation Web site for further application details before submitting letter. The foundation prefers not to receive videotapes. The foundation is no longer accepting applications for scholarships. Application form not required.
Initial approach: Letter
Copies of proposal: 1
Deadline(s): None
Board meeting date(s): Six times per year
Final notification: Varies
Officers and Directors:* Maurice R. Greenberg,* Chair.; Florence A. Davis,* Pres.; Gladys R. Thomas, V.P. and Secy.; Paula S. Lawrence, V.P.; Courtney O'Malley, V.P.; H.I. Smith,* Treas.; T.C. Hsu; E.E. Matthews; John J. Roberts; Ernest E. Stempel.
Number of staff: 5 full-time professional; 8 full-time support.
EIN: 136151545
Selected grants: The following grants were reported in 2005.

$25,000,000 to World Trade Center Memorial Foundation, New York, NY. For construction, operation and maintenance of World Trade Center Site Memorial Complex, payable over 5 years.
$10,800,000 to Greenberg Medical Research Institute, New York, NY. 2 grants: $5,300,000 (For Center for the Study of Hepatitus C, payable over 5 years), $5,500,000 to Center for the Study of Hepatitus C (For capital and program support, payable over 5 years).
$10,000,000 to Weill Medical College of Cornell University, New York, NY. For tri-institutional stem cell initiative, involving collaboration of Weill Cornell, Rockefeller University and Memorial-Sloan Kettering.
$6,000,000 to Hospital for Special Surgery, New York, NY. For Research Campaign, Discovery to Recovery and Capital Campaign, payable over 2 years.
$3,600,000 to Smile Train, New York, NY. For cleft care training and treatment programs in India and China, payable over 2 years.
$3,000,000 to New York Blood Center, New York, NY. For National Cord Blood Program, payable over 2 years.
$3,000,000 to Teach for America, New York, NY. For general support, payable over 3 years.
$2,500,000 to Metropolitan Museum of Art, New York, NY. For challenge grant to build educational facilities, payable over 2 years.
$2,500,000 to Young Audiences (YA), New York, NY. For Arts for Learning, payable over 2 years.

7049
The Starwood Foundation, Inc. ◇
(formerly The Sheraton Foundation, Inc.)
1111 Westchester Ave.
White Plains, NY 10604 (877) 443-4585
Contact: Beth Shanholtz
Application address: 777 Westchester Ave., White
Plains, NY 10604

Incorporated in 1950 in MA.
Donors: ITT Sheraton Corp.; The Sheraton Corp.
Foundation type: Company-sponsored foundation.
Financial data (yr. ended 12/31/04): Assets,
$2,185,096 (M); expenditures, $1,099,640;
qualifying distributions, $1,059,650.
Purpose and activities: The foundation supports
organizations involved with arts and culture,
education, health, medical research, human
services, and children and youth services.
Fields of interest: Arts; Education; Cancer;
Diabetes; Health organizations; Medical research;
Children/youth, services; Human services;
Federated giving programs.
Type of support: General/operating support;
Scholarship funds.
Limitations: Giving limited to the greater Boston,
MA, area. No grants to individuals, or for
endowments, capital campaigns, or research; no
matching gifts; no loans.
Application information: Application form not
required.
 Initial approach: Proposal
 Deadline(s): None
Officers: Barry F. Sternlicht, Pres.; Kenneth Siegal,
Clerk; Robyn Arnell, Treas.
Directors: Daniel Gibson; David Norton.
Number of staff: 2
EIN: 046039510

7050
The Statler Foundation ◇
107 Delaware Ave., Ste. 680
Buffalo, NY 14202 (716) 852-1104
Contact: Herb M. Siegel, Chair.

Trust established in 1934 in NY.
Donor: Ellsworth Milton Statler†.
Foundation type: Independent foundation.
Financial data (yr. ended 12/31/05): Assets,
$33,455,490 (M); expenditures, $1,917,878;
qualifying distributions, $1,548,659; giving
activities include $795,409 for 6 grants (high:
$254,170; low: $12,074), and $666,101 for grants
to individuals.
Purpose and activities: Education and research for
the benefit of the hotel industry in the U.S. Income
used for awards to colleges and schools teaching
hotel techniques and for grants to schools and
others for research projects and for programs to
train and increase the proficiency of hotel workers.
The foundation also supports culinary arts and hotel
management programs.
Fields of interest: Vocational education; Business
school/education.
Type of support: Building/renovation; Equipment;
Professorships; Research.
Limitations: Giving primarily in western NY. No
grants for scholarships.
Application information: The scholarship program is
offered only to students in Western New York.
Application form not required.
 Initial approach: Letter

Copies of proposal: 13
Board meeting date(s): Every 2 months
Officer and Trustees:* Herb M. Siegel,* Chair.;
Robert Bennett; Marguerite Collesano; William J.
Cunningham, Jr.; Peter J. Fiorella, Jr.; Edward M.
Flynn; Ernestine R. Green; Arthur F. DuCouet
Mussarra; Carlo M. Perfetto; Arthur V. Sabia;
Bernard A. Tolbert; Peter A. Vinolus.
Number of staff: 1 full-time professional.
EIN: 131889077
Selected grants: The following grants were reported
in 2004.
$254,166 to Niagara University, Niagara Falls, NY.
$200,000 to Culinary Institute of America, Hyde
 Park, NY.
$100,000 to Florida International University, Miami,
 FL.

7051
The Esta and Jamie Stecher Foundation ◇
c/o Goldman Sachs Family Office
1 New York Plz., 40th Fl.
New York, NY 10004

Established in NY.
Donors: Esta Eiger Stecher; Goldman Sachs Family
Office.
Foundation type: Independent foundation.
Financial data (yr. ended 7/31/05): Assets,
$1,889,677 (M); gifts received, $500,720;
expenditures, $939,895; qualifying distributions,
$939,550; giving activities include $939,550 for 40
grants (high: $300,000; low: $100).
Purpose and activities: Giving primarily for Jewish
organizations.
Fields of interest: Higher education; Law school/
education; Human services; Jewish federated giving
programs; Jewish agencies & temples.
Limitations: Applications not accepted. Giving
primarily in Minneapolis, MN and New York, NY. No
grants to individuals, or for scholarships; no loans.
Application information: Contributes only to
pre-selected organizations.
Trustees: Esta Eiger Stecher; Jamie B.W. Stecher.
EIN: 133918278

7052
The Robert K. Steel Family Foundation ◇
c/o BCRS Group/Marcum and Kliegman, LLP
655 Third Ave.
New York, NY 10017

Established in 1989 in NY.
Donors: Robert K. Steel Family; Goldman Sachs, &
Co.
Foundation type: Independent foundation.
Financial data (yr. ended 4/30/04): Assets,
$4,970,048 (M); gifts received, $3,024,090;
expenditures, $2,208,913; qualifying distributions,
$2,190,270; giving activities include $2,187,185
for 141 grants (high: $500,000; low: $100;
average: $1,000–$10,000).
Purpose and activities: Giving primarily for higher
education, and to health associations and
hospitals.
Fields of interest: Arts; Higher education; Health
care; Health organizations, association;
International studies; Protestant agencies &
churches.
Type of support: General/operating support; Annual
campaigns; Capital campaigns; Endowments.

Limitations: Applications not accepted. Giving on a
national basis, with some emphasis on CT and NY.
No grants to individuals.
Application information: Contributes only to
pre-selected organizations.
Trustees: Gillian V. Steel; Robert K. Steel.
EIN: 133531990
Selected grants: The following grants were reported
in 2003.
$3,998,450 to Duke University, Durham, NC. For
 general support. Grant made in form of stock.
$499,825 to Windward School, White Plains, NY.
 For general support. Grant made in form of stock.
$399,890 to Greenwich Academy, Greenwich, CT.
 For general support. Grant made in form of stock.
$299,880 to Brown University, Providence, RI. For
 general support. Grant made in form of stock.
$250,000 to Brunswick School, Greenwich, CT. For
 general support.
$250,000 to Reach, Derby, CT. For general support.
$249,950 to University of Chicago, Chicago, IL. For
 general support. Grant made in form of stock.
$200,000 to PAX, New York, NY. 2 grants:
 $100,000 each (For general support).
$100,000 to Global Fund for Children, DC. For
 general support.

7053
The Steele-Reese Foundation ◇
32 Washington Sq. W.
New York, NY 10011 (212) 505-2696
Contact: For general matters in NY: William T. Buice
III, Tr.; Charles U. Buice, Tr.; For the Southern
Appalachians: Jane B. Stephenson, Prog. Dir.; For
Idaho and Montana: Jeanne E. Wolverton, Prog. Dir.
Application addresses: (For Appalachia) Jane B.
Stephenson, Appalachian Prog. Dir., 3121
Grantham Way, Lexington, KY 40509, tel.: (859)
263-5313; e-mail: jane1938@alltel.net, (For Idaho
and Montana); Jeanne E. Wolverton, Western Prog.
Dir., P.O. Box 249, Alberton, MT 59820, tel.: (406)
722-4564; e-mail: jeannew@blackfoot.net;
Additional address: c/o Charles U. Buice, 1 Main
St., Apt. 6-F, Brooklyn, NY 11201,
e-mail: charles@steele-reese.org; URL: http://
www.Steele-Reese.org

Trust established in 1955 in NY.
Donors: Eleanor Steele Reese†; Emmet P. Reese†.
Foundation type: Independent foundation.
Financial data (yr. ended 8/31/05): Assets,
$42,086,800 (M); expenditures, $2,689,661;
qualifying distributions, $2,458,066; giving
activities include $2,232,170 for 69 grants (high:
$125,000; low: $5,000).
Purpose and activities: Principally to aid organized
charities in southern Appalachia, Idaho and
Montana. Support for education (primarily
elementary and secondary), health and hospices,
welfare, including programs for drug abuse and
youth, conservation, and the humanities, with a
strong preference for rural projects; student aid only
to students of Lemhi and Custer counties, Idaho,
administered autonomously by institutions.
Fields of interest: Humanities; Elementary/
secondary education; Education; Environment,
natural resources; Environment; Health care;
Substance abuse, services; Health organizations,
association; Human services; Children/youth,
services; Family services; Residential/custodial
care, hospices; Rural development.
Type of support: Management development/
capacity building; Land acquisition; General/

operating support; Equipment; Endowments; Professorships; Scholarship funds; Matching/ challenge support.

Limitations: Giving primarily in ID, MT, and the Appalachian Mountain region of KY, NC, and TN; scholarship program limited to students from Lemhi and Custer counties, ID. No support for community chests, efforts to influence school board and other elections, recreational facilities, athletic or academic competitions, or efforts to promulgate religious or political beliefs. No grants for continuing support, annual campaigns, conferences or workshops, seed money, emergency or building funds, deficit financing, research, endowments for small organizations, computers or other technology used for instruction in schools; no loans; grants to individuals confined to scholarships and paid through institutions.

Publications: Annual report (including application guidelines); Grants list.

Application Information: High school seniors in Lemhi and Custer counties, ID, should apply for scholarships through their schools. Application form not required.

Initial approach: Proposal, letter, or e-mail to regional rep.

Copies of proposal: 2

Deadline(s): Mar. 1 for payment during current fiscal year; payments are generally made in Aug. and Sept.

Board meeting date(s): Monthly

Final notification: 4 months

Trustees: Charles U. Buice; William T. Buice III; JPMorgan Chase Bank, N.A.

Number of staff: 2 part-time professional.

EIN: 136034763

Selected grants: The following grants were reported in 2005.

$125,000 to Steele Memorial Benefit Association, Salmon, ID.

$50,000 to Daly Mansion Preservation Trust, Hamilton, MT.

$50,000 to Idaho Community Foundation, Boise, ID.

$50,000 to Leadore Emergency Medical Technicians, Leadore, ID.

$50,000 to Montana Natural History Center, Missoula, MT.

$50,000 to Pierpont Morgan Library, New York, NY.

$50,000 to Ronald McDonald House Charities, Missoula, MT.

$41,000 to Renaissance Arts Center, Rupert, ID.

$37,500 to Idaho Nonprofit Development Center, Boise, ID.

$26,000 to University of Kentucky, Lexington, KY.

7054

Steffens 21st Century Foundation II ✧ ☆

c/o Spring Mountain Capital
65 E. 55th St., 32nd Fl.
New York, NY 10022-3356

Established in 2001 in NY.

Donor: John L. Steffens.

Foundation type: Independent foundation.

Financial data (yr. ended 12/31/05): Assets, $8,290,349 (M); gifts received, $100,000; expenditures, $475,323; qualifying distributions, $475,250; giving activities include $475,250 for grants.

Fields of interest: Education; Human services; Aging.

Limitations: Applications not accepted. No grants to individuals.

Application Information: Contributes only to pre-selected organizations.

Trustee: John L. Steffens.

EIN: 137284293

7055

Allen A. Stein Family Foundation, Inc. ☆

c/o DLA Piper Rudnick Gray Cary
1251 Ave. of the Americas, 38th Fl.
New York, NY 10020-1104
Contact: Christine A. Kehoe, Admin. Dir.
E-mail: aasff@piperrudnick.com

Established in 2002 in NY.

Donor: Allen A. Stein†.

Foundation type: Independent foundation.

Financial data (yr. ended 12/31/05): Assets, $9,052,104 (M); expenditures, $462,167; qualifying distributions, $368,842; giving activities include $368,842 for 67 grants (high: $50,000; low: $200).

Purpose and activities: Giving primarily for Jewish education, organizations and temples.

Fields of interest: Theological school/education; Jewish federated giving programs; Jewish agencies & temples.

International interests: Israel.

Type of support: General/operating support; Continuing support; Annual campaigns; Capital campaigns; Building/renovation; Equipment; Program development; Research.

Limitations: Applications not accepted.

Application Information: Unsolicited requests for funds not accepted.

Board meeting date(s): Quarterly

Officers and Directors:* Elaine Stein Roberts,* Pres.; Eric Stein,* V.P.; Sharon Stein,* V.P.; Margot Stein,* Secy.; Bernard Roberts,* Treas.

Number of staff: 1 part-time professional.

EIN: 134153383

Selected grants: The following grants were reported in 2005.

$50,000 to Jewish Federation of South Palm Beach County, Boca Raton, FL. 5 grants: $5,000, $5,000, $20,000, $10,000, $10,000

$20,000 to Sinai Academy of the Berkshires, Pittsfield, MA. 2 grants: $10,000 each

$12,000 to Boca Raton Kollel, Boca Raton, FL.

$3,600 to Boca Raton Synagogue, Boca Raton, FL.

$2,500 to Elat Chayyim, Accord, NY.

7056

Joseph F. Stein Family Foundation, Inc. ✧

(formerly The Steiro Foundation, Inc.)
30 Glenn St.
White Plains, NY 10603

Established in 2002 in NY.

Donors: Stuart M. Stein; Anne S. Squadron; Brian T. Kloza; David Plotkin; Edward H. Cohen; Elaine S. Stein; Jerold Goldberg; Martin Barbar; Nancy Rozen Feibus; Roger Stein; Susan Melchner; Toby Stein Rozen; Norton Spiel; Robert Spielman; Charles Selig, Jr.; Mrs. Charles Selig, Jr.; Robert Grossman; Wiss & Co; Elaine S. Stein Revocable Trust.

Foundation type: Independent foundation.

Financial data (yr. ended 12/31/05): Assets, $17,087,651 (M); gifts received, $264,715; expenditures, $893,790; qualifying distributions, $748,338; giving activities include $699,650 for 149 grants (high: $67,500; low: $150).

Fields of interest: Performing arts, theater; Arts; Higher education; Business school/education; Education; Hospitals (general); Health organizations, association; Cancer research; Human services; Children/youth, services; Jewish federated giving programs; Jewish agencies & temples.

Type of support: General/operating support.

Limitations: Applications not accepted. No grants to individuals.

Application Information: Contributes only to pre-selected organizations.

Officers: Stuart M. Stein, Pres.; Arthur J. Feibus, Treas.

EIN: 134144648

7057

The Fred & Sharon Stein Foundation, Inc. ✧

c/o Charles A. Barragato & Co., LLP
950 3rd Ave., 17th Fl.
New York, NY 10022
Contact: Fred Stein, Dir.

Established in 1985 in NY.

Donors: Fred Stein; Susan Haugh Stein.

Foundation type: Independent foundation.

Financial data (yr. ended 11/30/05): Assets, $1,226,064 (M); expenditures, $458,975; qualifying distributions, $451,097; giving activities include $451,097 for 71 grants (high: $50,000; low: $75).

Purpose and activities: Giving primarily for performing arts, with emphasis on ballet; support also for Jewish giving programs and secondary education.

Fields of interest: Performing arts; Arts; Jewish federated giving programs.

Limitations: Giving primarily in NY. No grants to individuals.

Application Information:

Initial approach: Letter

Deadline(s): None

Directors: James Kaufman; Fred Stein; Sharon Haugh Stein.

EIN: 133389107

Selected grants: The following grants were reported in 2005.

$50,000 to Bush-Clinton Katrina Fund, New York, NY.

$50,000 to Manhattan Institute for Policy Research, New York, NY.

$23,237 to Ann Schreiber Ovarian Cancer Research Fund, New York, NY.

$10,000 to Hewitt School, New York, NY.

$10,000 to Interplast, Mountain View, CA.

$10,000 to Metropolitan Opera Guild, New York, NY.

$10,000 to New-York Historical Society, New York, NY.

$10,000 to Robert Toigo Foundation, Oakland, CA.

$7,500 to Shipley School, Bryn Mawr, PA.

$2,500 to American Poetry Review, Philadelphia, PA.

7058

The Lazar Stein Memorial Foundation ✧

469 7th Ave., Ste. 1300
New York, NY 10018

Established in 1999 in NY.

Donor: Martin Stein.

Foundation type: Independent foundation.
Financial data (yr. ended 8/31/05): Assets, $76,730 (M); gifts received, $500,000; expenditures, $511,782; qualifying distributions, $500,732; giving activities include $500,732 for grants.
Fields of interest: Jewish agencies & temples.
Limitations: Applications not accepted. Giving primarily in NY. No grants to individuals.
Application information: Contributes only to pre-selected organizations.
Officers: Martin Stein, Pres. and Treas.; Arlyne Stein, Secy.
Director: Steven N. Stein.
EIN: 134119091

7059
Ruth & Milton Steinbach Fund, Inc. ✧
c/o Tanton & Co.
37 W. 57th St., 5th Fl.
New York, NY 10019

Incorporated in 1950 in NY.
Donor: Milton Steinbach†.
Foundation type: Independent foundation.
Financial data (yr. ended 10/31/05): Assets, $23,805,946 (M); expenditures, $1,290,718; qualifying distributions, $1,044,612; giving activities include $1,000,000 for 10 grants (high: $100,000; low: $100,000).
Purpose and activities: Giving primarily for higher education, and for basic biomedical research in loss of vision, specifically macular degeneration.
Fields of interest: Higher education; Eye research.
Type of support: Research.
Limitations: Applications not accepted. Giving on a national basis. No grants to individuals, or for building and endowment funds.
Application information: Contributes only to pre-selected organizations.
Officers and Directors:* John Klingenstein,* Pres.; Frederick A. Klingenstein,* V.P.; Patricia D. Klingenstein; Sharon L. Klingenstein.
EIN: 136028785
Selected grants: The following grants were reported in 2003.
$100,000 to Harvard University, Cambridge, MA. For general support.
$100,000 to Massachusetts Eye and Ear Infirmary, Boston, MA. For general support.
$100,000 to University of Basel, Basel, Switzerland. For general support.
$100,000 to University of Florida, Gainesville, FL. For general support.
$100,000 to University of Pennsylvania, Philadelphia, PA. For general support.
$100,000 to University of Rochester, Rochester, NY. For general support.
$100,000 to University of Toronto, Toronto, Canada. For general support.
$100,000 to University of Wisconsin, Madison, WI. For general support.
$100,000 to Weill Medical College of Cornell University, New York, NY. For general support.
$80,000 to Rensselaerville Institute, Rensselaerville, NY. For general support.

7060
Joseph S. & Diane H. Steinberg 1992 Charitable Trust ✧
c/o Leucadia National Corp.
315 Park Ave. S., 20th Fl.
New York, NY 10010-3607
Contact: Joseph S. Steinberg, Tr.

Established in 1992 in NY.
Donors: Joseph S. Steinberg; Diane H. Steinberg.
Foundation type: Independent foundation.
Financial data (yr. ended 6/30/05): Assets, $38,731,902 (M); gifts received, $8,713,660; expenditures, $2,632,428; qualifying distributions, $2,346,493; giving activities include $2,346,493 for 80 grants (high: $395,409; low: $100).
Purpose and activities: Giving primarily to Jewish organizations and for the arts and children's services.
Fields of interest: Arts, cultural/ethnic awareness; Performing arts, education; Arts; Higher education; Health care; Health organizations, association; Youth development; Jewish federated giving programs; Jewish agencies & temples.
Limitations: Giving primarily in NY; some giving nationally. No grants to individuals.
Application information:
Initial approach: Letter
Deadline(s): None
Trustees: Diane H. Steinberg; Joseph S. Steinberg.
EIN: 137002791
Selected grants: The following grants were reported in 2004.
$1,000,000 to Juilliard School, New York, NY.
$141,902 to Brooklyn Academy of Music, Brooklyn, NY.
$125,000 to New Israel Fund, DC.
$125,000 to Take the Field, New York, NY.
$104,360 to Playwrights Horizons, New York, NY.
$50,000 to Center for Jewish History, New York, NY.
$45,000 to New York University, New York, NY.
$10,000 to American Jewish Historical Society, New York, NY.
$2,500 to Prospect Park Alliance, Brooklyn, NY.
$2,500 to Rockefeller University, New York, NY.

7061
The Harold & Mimi Steinberg Charitable Trust ▼ ✧
c/o Schulte Roth & Zabel, LLP
919 3rd Ave.
New York, NY 10022

Established in 1986 in NY.
Donor: Harold Steinberg†.
Foundation type: Independent foundation.
Financial data (yr. ended 12/31/04): Assets, $35,687,046 (M); gifts received, $15,346,007; expenditures, $4,842,952; qualifying distributions, $4,486,648; giving activities include $4,382,900 for 177 grants (high: $1,000,000; low: $500; average: $2,000–$100,000).
Purpose and activities: Giving primarily for arts and cultural organizations, higher education, and the environment.
Fields of interest: Visual arts; Performing arts; Performing arts, theater; Higher education; Libraries/library science; Hospitals (general); Human services; Jewish federated giving programs.
Limitations: Applications not accepted. Giving primarily in New York, NY. No grants to individuals.

Application information: Contributes only to pre-selected organizations.
Trustees: Carole A. Krumland; James D. Steinberg; Michael A. Steinberg; Seth Weingarten; William D. Zabel.
EIN: 133383348
Selected grants: The following grants were reported in 2004.
$1,250,000 to Roundabout Theater Company, New York, NY. 2 grants: $250,000 (For unrestricted support), $1,000,000 (For unrestricted support).
$225,000 to Juilliard School, New York, NY. 2 grants: $25,000 (For unrestricted support), $200,000 (For unrestricted support).
$200,000 to Lincoln Center Theater, New York, NY. For unrestricted support.
$200,000 to Manhattan Theater Club, New York, NY. For unrestricted support.
$35,000 to California Institute of the Arts, Valencia, CA. For unrestricted support.
$20,000 to University of Pennsylvania, Philadelphia, PA. For unrestricted support.
$13,000 to San Francisco Shakespeare Festival, San Francisco, CA. For unrestricted support.
$5,000 to University of Judaism, Los Angeles, CA. For unrestricted support.

7062
Meyer & Jean Steinberg Family Foundation, Inc. ✧
(formerly Meyer Steinberg Foundation, Inc.)
c/o Meyer Steinberg
475 5th Ave., 12th Fl.
New York, NY 10017
Contact: Jean Steinberg, V.P.

Established in 1965 in NY.
Donors: Bonnie Englebardt; Susan Zizesgreen; Jean Steinberg; Meyer Steinberg†; Carol Weisman; Lois Zaro.
Foundation type: Independent foundation.
Financial data (yr. ended 12/31/04): Assets, $6,054,766 (L); gifts received, $81,631; expenditures, $477,514; qualifying distributions, $429,584; giving activities include $429,334 for 23 + grants (high: $110,125).
Purpose and activities: Giving to all worthy causes.
Fields of interest: Education; Health care; Human services.
Limitations: Giving primarily in NY.
Application information:
Initial approach: Letter
Deadline(s): None
Officers: Jean Steinberg, V.P. and Secy.; Bonnie Englebardt, Exec. Dir.
EIN: 136199973

7063
The Steinberg Family Fund, Inc. ✧
c/o Bear Stearns & Co., Inc.
383 Madison Ave.
New York, NY 10179-0001

Established in 1984 in NY.
Donor: Robert Steinberg.
Foundation type: Independent foundation.
Financial data (yr. ended 11/30/05): Assets, $10,967,743 (M); expenditures, $572,250; qualifying distributions, $570,825; giving activities include $568,650 for 32 grants (high: $100,000; low: $250).

Purpose and activities: Giving primarily for Jewish schools and organizations; funding also for health associations.
Fields of interest: Elementary/secondary education; Pediatrics research; Jewish federated giving programs; Jewish agencies & temples.
Limitations: Applications not accepted. Giving primarily in CT and NY. No grants to individuals.
Application information: Contributes only to pre-selected organizations.
Officers: Robert Steinberg, Pres.; Suzanne Steinberg, V.P. and Treas.
EIN: 133254493
Selected grants: The following grants were reported in 2003.
$75,000 to Yeshivat Chovevei Torah Rabbinical School, New York, NY.
$50,000 to UJA-Federation of New York, New York, NY.
$25,000 to Greenwich Emergency Medical Service, Riverside, CT.
$15,000 to Chai Lifeline, New York, NY.
$11,658 to Temple Israel Westport, Westport, CT.
$11,500 to Cystic Fibrosis Foundation, New York, NY.
$10,000 to Rutgers, The State University of New Jersey, New Brunswick, NJ.
$10,000 to UJA-Federation of Greenwich, Greenwich, CT.
$8,500 to Temple Sholom, Greenwich, CT.
$5,000 to Police Athletic League, New York, NY.

7064
The Judy and Michael Steinhardt Foundation ▼ ◇

650 Madison Ave., 17th Fl
New York, NY 10022
Contact: Michael Steinhardt, Tr.

Established in 1986 in NY.
Donor: Michael Steinhardt.
Foundation type: Independent foundation.
Financial data (yr. ended 9/30/05): Assets, $14,930,648 (M); gifts received, $12,000,000; expenditures, $14,645,077; qualifying distributions, $14,643,690; giving activities include $14,581,681 for 159 grants (high: $1,400,000; low: $50; average: $10,000–$500,000).
Purpose and activities: Support for Jewish giving and Jewish welfare, including organizations supporting Israel; support also for higher and other education and a botanical garden.
Fields of interest: Higher education; Education; Environment, natural resources; Human services; Jewish federated giving programs; Jewish agencies & temples.
International interests: Israel.
Limitations: Applications not accepted. Giving on a national basis. No grants to individuals.
Application information: Contributes only to pre-selected organizations.
Trustees: Judith Steinhardt; Michael Steinhardt.
EIN: 133357500
Selected grants: The following grants were reported in 2005.
$2,400,000 to New York University, New York, NY. 2 grants: $1,000,000 to Institute of Fine Arts, $1,400,000
$1,000,000 to Birthright Israel Foundation, New York, NY.
$664,949 to Chaverim Kol Yisrael Jewish Life Network, New York, NY. 2 grants: $115,000, $549,949

$500,000 to Hillel of Greater Philadelphia, Philadelphia, PA.
$25,000 to Brookings Institution, Saban Center for Middle East Policy, DC.
$25,000 to University of Pennsylvania, Center for Jewish Engagement, Philadelphia, PA.
$10,000 to Abraham Joshua Heschel School, New York, NY.
$10,000 to Lincoln Center for the Performing Arts, New York, NY.

7065
Edward & Joan B. Steiniger Charitable Foundation ◇

c/o Citibank, N.A.
153 E. 53rd St., 23rd St.
New York, NY 10022

Established in 1990 in NY.
Donor: Pamela S. Saelzler Unitrust.
Foundation type: Independent foundation.
Financial data (yr. ended 12/31/05): Assets, $25,654,842 (M); expenditures, $1,322,222; qualifying distributions, $1,215,418; giving activities include $1,171,473 for 4 grants (high: $450,473; low: $95,000).
Purpose and activities: Giving primarily for Roman Catholic education, as well as to a Roman Catholic archdiocese.
Fields of interest: Education, administration/regulation; Education; Roman Catholic agencies & churches.
Limitations: Applications not accepted. Giving primarily in the metropolitan New York, NY, area. No grants to individuals.
Application information: Contributes only to pre-selected organizations.
Trustee: Citibank, N.A.
EIN: 133585674

7066
B.& M. Steinmetz Foundation ◇

c/o David Soifer
24 Jackson Ave.
Spring Valley, NY 10977
Application address: c/o Mr. Bernat Steinmetz, 18 W. 33rd St., New York, NY 10001, tel.: (212) 563-5733

Established in 1969 in NY.
Donors: Bernat Steinmetz; Michael Steinmetz; Shraga Brecher; LSM Management Co.; Town Management; Shoretown Management Co.; Fort Management.
Foundation type: Independent foundation.
Financial data (yr. ended 5/31/05): Assets, $18,494,697 (M); gifts received, $358,499; expenditures, $763,374; qualifying distributions, $752,975; giving activities include $752,975 for 242 grants (high: $200,000; low: $18).
Purpose and activities: Support limited to religious organizations, with an emphasis on Jewish organizations, temples, and schools.
Fields of interest: Elementary/secondary education; Jewish agencies & temples; Religion.
Limitations: Giving primarily in New York, NY.
Application information: The foundation gives grants to religious organizations or to those with a letter of recommendation from a religious organization. Application form not required.
Deadline(s): None

Officer: Bernat Steinmetz, Pres.
EIN: 237048163

7067
D. & E. Steinmetz Foundation ◇

202 Keap St.
Brooklyn, NY 11211
Contact: David Steinmetz, Tr.

Established in 1999 in NY.
Donors: Fort Management; Sherman Management; Town Management; Emanuel & Clara Steinmetz Trust.
Foundation type: Independent foundation.
Financial data (yr. ended 6/30/05): Assets, $1,811,282 (M); gifts received, $136,000; expenditures, $422,270; qualifying distributions, $419,980; giving activities include $419,980 for 99 grants (high: $25,000; low: $50).
Fields of interest: Jewish agencies & temples.
Application information: Application form not required.
Deadline(s): None

Trustees: David Steinmetz; Esther Steinmetz.
EIN: 113522236
Selected grants: The following grants were reported in 2003.
$25,000 to Heichel Hatorah.
$10,000 to Congregation Kehilath Yosef Incorporated, Brooklyn, NY.
$5,000 to Congregation Beth Joseph, Far Rockaway, NY.
$5,000 to Congregation Toras Chaim, Brooklyn, NY.
$3,000 to Mosdos Chernobel, Brooklyn, NY.
$3,000 to Oseh Chesed.
$1,000 to Chesed Avraham, Brooklyn, NY.
$250 to Derech Chaim Academy, Baltimore, MD.
$100 to Congregation Yetev Lev D Jerusalem, Brooklyn, NY.
$50 to Tomchei Shabbos of Boro Park and Flatbush, Brooklyn, NY.

7068
S. & E. Steinmetz Foundation ◇ ☆

352 Marcy Ave.
Brooklyn, NY 11206
Contact: Solomon Steinmetz, Tr.

Established in 1999 in NY.
Donors: Chaim Babab; Joseph Babab; Riviera Mgmt.; Ridge Mgmt.; Bay Mgmt.; E & C Trust; Park Mgmt.; Solomon Steinmetz.
Foundation type: Independent foundation.
Financial data (yr. ended 6/30/06): Assets, $2,981,240 (M); gifts received, $116,878; expenditures, $338,041; qualifying distributions, $335,713; giving activities include $335,713 for grants.
Fields of interest: Jewish agencies & temples.
Limitations: Giving primarily in NY.
Application information: Application form not required.
Deadline(s): None

Trustees: Esther Steinmetz; Solomon Steinmetz.
EIN: 113481171
Selected grants: The following grants were reported in 2005.
$4,000 to Chesed Avraham, Brooklyn, NY.
$375 to Kollel Shomrei Hachomos, Brooklyn, NY.

7069
Ernest E. Stempel Foundation ◇
c/o Eisenberg
150 Broadway, Ste. 1102
New York, NY 10038-4367

Established in 1994 in DE.
Donor: Ernest E. Stempel.
Foundation type: Independent foundation.
Financial data (yr. ended 12/31/05): Assets, $26,335,544 (M); gifts received, $6,800; expenditures, $1,422,558; qualifying distributions, $1,310,751; giving activities include $1,185,626 for 46 grants (high: $250,529; low: $1,000).
Purpose and activities: Giving primarily for education, health associations, children, youth and social services, and to an organization which studies the ocean.
Fields of interest: Elementary/secondary education; Higher education; Law school/education; Education; Zoos/zoological societies; Hospitals (general); Health organizations, association; Cancer; Human services; Children/youth, services; Marine science.
International interests: Bermuda.
Limitations: Applications not accepted. Giving on a national basis, as well as in Bermuda. No grants to individuals.
Application information: Contributes only to pre-selected organizations.
Trustees: Diana S. Bergquist; Calvin P. Stempel; Ernest E. Stempel; Neil F. Stempel.
EIN: 510363381
Selected grants: The following grants were reported in 2005.
$60,631 to Florida International University, Miami, FL.
$25,237 to Asia Society, New York, NY.
$25,237 to Manhattan College, Riverdale, NY.
$25,237 to Salvation Army.
$20,313 to Nature Conservancy, Arlington, VA.
$20,313 to Saint Andrews School of Delaware, Middletown, DE.
$10,156 to Breast Cancer Resource Center, Princeton, NJ.
$10,156 to Campaign for Our Children, Baltimore, MD.
$10,156 to City Harvest, New York, NY.
$10,156 to Young Life.

7070
Jerome L. Stern Family Foundation, Inc. ◇
(formerly Jerome L. and Jane Stern Foundation, Inc.)
270 Madison Ave., 16 Fl.
New York, NY 10016-0601

Incorporated in 1944 in NY.
Donors: Jerome L. Stern; Ronald A. Stern; members of the Stern family.
Foundation type: Independent foundation.
Financial data (yr. ended 2/28/06): Assets, $7,262,770 (M); expenditures, $531,761; qualifying distributions, $458,195; giving activities include $456,815 for 75 grants (high: $68,525; low: $50).
Purpose and activities: Giving primarily for Jewish higher education, temples and agencies.
Fields of interest: Museums; Arts; Elementary/secondary education; Higher education; Human services; Jewish federated giving programs; Jewish agencies & temples; Religion.
Limitations: Applications not accepted. Giving primarily in New York, NY. No grants to individuals.

Application information: Contributes only to pre-selected organizations.
Officers and Directors:* Jerome L. Stern, Pres. and Secy.; Geoffrey S. Stern,* Treas.; Ellen L. Stern; Ronald A. Stern.
EIN: 136127063
Selected grants: The following grants were reported in 2006.
$68,525 to New Museum of Contemporary Art, New York, NY.
$31,720 to Hampton Synagogue, Hampton, NY.
$31,000 to Abraham Joshua Heschel School, New York, NY.
$29,300 to American Friends of the Israel Museum, New York, NY.
$10,000 to American Forum for New Immigrants in Israel, DC.
$7,200 to Jewish Renaissance Center, New York, NY.
$7,100 to Ramaz School, New York, NY.
$6,000 to Congregation Kehilath Jeshurun, New York, NY.
$2,000 to Friends of the Israel Defense Forces, New York, NY.
$1,000 to Parrish Art Museum, Southampton, NY.

7071
Thomas D. & Denise R. Stern Family Foundation ◇
c/o Anchin, Block & Anchin, LLP
1375 Broadway
New York, NY 10018

Established in 2001 in NY.
Donor: Thomas D. Stern.
Foundation type: Independent foundation.
Financial data (yr. ended 12/31/05): Assets, $5,089,931 (M); gifts received, $1,011,791; expenditures, $461,743; qualifying distributions, $449,403; giving activities include $449,153 for 24 grants (high: $205,000; low: $500).
Purpose and activities: Giving primarily for education.
Fields of interest: Secondary school/education; Education; Hospitals (specialty); Medical research.
Limitations: Applications not accepted. No grants to individuals.
Application information: Contributes only to pre-selected organizations.
Trustees: Denise R. Stern; Thomas D. Stern.
EIN: 134195656

7072
Bernice and Milton Stern Foundation ◇
c/o Phillips Gold & Co.
1430 Broadway, 6th Fl.
New York, NY 10018
Application address: c/o Bernice Stern, Pres., 59 E. 54th St., New York, NY 10036

Established in 1982 in DE.
Donor: Bernice Stern.
Foundation type: Independent foundation.
Financial data (yr. ended 4/30/05): Assets, $15,670,082 (M); expenditures, $1,468,782; qualifying distributions, $1,201,518; giving activities include $1,101,500 for 13 grants (high: $270,000; low: $2,000).
Purpose and activities: Grants for Jewish welfare, social services, child welfare, and health services. The foundation funds study and program

development on issues affecting the lives of needy children and families through the Stern Institute for Family Life Education of the Children's Aid Society.
Fields of interest: Hospitals (general); Health care; Human services; Children/youth, services; Jewish federated giving programs.
Type of support: Continuing support.
Limitations: Giving primarily in NY. No grants to individuals.
Application information:
Initial approach: Letter
Deadline(s): None
Officers: Bernice Stern, Pres.; Wendy S. Pesky, V.P.
EIN: 510264122

7073
Gustav and Irene Stern Foundation, Inc. ◇
(formerly Gustav Stern Foundation, Inc.)
c/o Braver, Stern Securities Corp.
641 Lexington Ave.
New York, NY 10022

Established in 1980.
Donors: Roy Stern; Steven Stern.
Foundation type: Independent foundation.
Financial data (yr. ended 3/31/05): Assets, $15,172,149 (M); gifts received, $100,000; expenditures, $1,216,180; qualifying distributions, $1,216,180; giving activities include $1,131,590 for grants.
Purpose and activities: Giving primarily to Jewish agencies and temples, and for education and the arts.
Fields of interest: Performing arts; Performing arts, opera; Higher education; Education; Human services; Jewish federated giving programs; Jewish agencies & temples.
Limitations: Giving primarily in New York, NY. No grants to individuals.
Application information: Application form not required.
Initial approach: Letter
Deadline(s): None
Officers: Steven Stern, Pres.; Joyce Herland, Secy.; Roy Stern, Treas.
Director: Irene Stern.
EIN: 136121155
Selected grants: The following grants were reported in 2004.
$110,000 to Montefiore Medical Center, Bronx, NY.
$4,500 to Metropolitan Opera, New York, NY.
$2,500 to Solomon R. Guggenheim Museum, New York, NY.
$1,350 to Metropolitan Museum of Art, New York, NY.
$1,250 to New York University, New York, NY.
$1,000 to Manhattan Day School, New York, NY.
$750 to Jewish Museum, New York, NY.
$600 to American Jewish Committee, New York, NY.
$400 to Museum of Modern Art, New York, NY.
$375 to American Museum of Natural History, New York, NY.

7074
Jean L. and Robert A. Stern Foundation, Inc. ◇
(formerly PRR Foundation, Inc.)
12 Brooks Hills Cir.
White Plains, NY 10605 (914) 686-3201
Contact: Jean L. Stern, Pres.

Established in 1992 in NY.
Donors: Joseph H. Bruening†; Jean L. Stern; Robert A. Stern.
Foundation type: Independent foundation.
Financial data (yr. ended 12/31/05): Assets, $5,353,076 (M); expenditures, $366,021; qualifying distributions, $362,125; giving activities include $360,900 for 48 grants (high: $25,350; low: $100).
Fields of interest: Arts; Health care; Human services.
Limitations: Giving primarily in the metropolitan New York, NY, area. No grants to individuals.
Application information: Application form required.
　Initial approach: Letter
　Deadline(s): None
Officers: Jean L. Stern, Pres.; Robert A. Stern, V.P. and Secy.-Treas.
Director: Robert J. Stern.
EIN: 133682636

7075
Sternberg Charitable Trust ✧ ☆
85 Bellevue Ave.
Rye, NY　10580

Established in 1994 in NY.
Donor: Stuart L. Sternberg.
Foundation type: Independent foundation.
Financial data (yr. ended 12/31/05): Assets, $7,864,688 (M); expenditures, $458,286; qualifying distributions, $442,063; giving activities include $437,660 for 42+ grants (high: $300,000).
Fields of interest: Performing arts centers; Arts; Elementary/secondary education; Health organizations, association; Human services; YM/YWCAs & YM/YWHAs; Federated giving programs; Religion.
Limitations: Applications not accepted. No grants to individuals.
Application information: Contributes only to pre-selected organizations.
Trustees: Lisa Kampfmann Sternberg; Stuart L. Sternberg.
EIN: 137046097
Selected grants: The following grants were reported in 2005.
$300,000 to Vanguard Charitable Endowment Program, Southeastern, PA.
$72,300 to Rye Country Day School, Rye, NY.
$2,500 to Cornell University, Ithaca, NY.
$1,000 to Brother Martin High School, New Orleans, LA.

7076
The Stevens Kingsley Foundation, Inc. ✧ ☆
c/o Sullivan & Cromwell
125 Broad St.
New York, NY　10004-2498　(212) 558-3845
Contact: Charles T. Dowling, Dir.

Established in 1960 in NY.
Foundation type: Independent foundation.
Financial data (yr. ended 12/31/05): Assets, $0 (M); expenditures, $2,511,989; qualifying distributions, $2,500,195; giving activities include $2,491,376 for 1 grant.
Purpose and activities: Giving primarily for community development, art and culture, and education.

Fields of interest: Historic preservation/historical societies; Arts; Libraries (public); Education; Salvation Army; YM/YWCAs & YM/YWHAs; Community development.
Type of support: Building/renovation; Equipment; Seed money.
Limitations: Giving limited to the Rome, NY, area. No grants to individuals, or for operating expenses.
Application information: Application form not required.
　Initial approach: Letter
　Copies of proposal: 1
　Deadline(s): None
　Board meeting date(s): Fall
Officers and Directors:* Donald R. Osborn,* Pres.; Henry Christensen III,* Secy.-Treas.; Charles T. Dowling; David C. Grow; Mark F. Hinman; Stephen B. Walters.
EIN: 136150722

7077
Stanley Steyer Family Foundation, Inc. ✧ ☆
c/o Harold Orlin
60 E. 42nd St., Ste. 1163
New York, NY　10165

Established in 1983 in DE.
Donors: Helen Steyer; Thomas M. Steyer.
Foundation type: Independent foundation.
Financial data (yr. ended 5/31/05): Assets, $21,962 (M); gifts received, $2,000; expenditures, $642,232; qualifying distributions, $641,590; giving activities include $640,690 for 3 grants (high: $500,000; low: $44,190).
Purpose and activities: Giving for Jewish educational and welfare organizations.
Fields of interest: Higher education; Cancer research; Jewish agencies & temples.
International interests: Israel.
Type of support: General/operating support; Research.
Limitations: Applications not accepted. Giving primarily in NY. No grants to individuals.
Application information: Contributes only to pre-selected organizations.
Officers: Stanley Steyer, Pres.; Thomas M. Steyer, V.P. and Treas.; Helen Steyer, Secy.
EIN: 133207413

7078
Stiefel Foundation for Dermatological Research, Inc. ✧
P.O. Box 97
East Durham, NY　12423
Application address: c/o Teresita L. Brunken, Secy., 255 Alhambra Cir., No. 1000, Coral Gables, FL 33134, tel.: (305) 443-3800

Established around 1968 in NY.
Donors: Werner K. Stiefel; Stiefel Laboratories.
Foundation type: Independent foundation.
Financial data (yr. ended 12/31/05): Assets, $486,521 (M); gifts received, $928,930; expenditures, $1,085,469; qualifying distributions, $1,085,469; giving activities include $1,085,465 for 104 grants (high: $150,000; low: $400).
Purpose and activities: Giving primarily for dermatological research and training.
Fields of interest: Medical school/education; Skin disorders; Skin disorders research.

Type of support: General/operating support.
Limitations: Giving on a national basis.
Application information: Application form not required.
　Initial approach: Letter
　Deadline(s): None
Officers: Charles W. Stiefel, Pres.; Teresita L. Brunken, Secy.; Matt S. Pattullo, Treas.
EIN: 237002608
Selected grants: The following grants were reported in 2003.
$267,500 to American Academy of Dermatology, Evanston, IL. 5 grants: $50,000, $50,000, $67,500, $50,000, $50,000 (For Founder's Fund).
$100,000 to Wake Forest University, School of Medicine, Winston-Salem, NC.
$85,000 to University of Miami, Miami, FL. 2 grants: $45,000 to School of Medicine, $40,000 to School of Medicine (For Cosmetic Center).
$20,000 to Skin Disease Education Foundation, Chicago, IL.
$10,000 to Dermatology Foundation, Evanston, IL.

7079
The Ernst C. Stiefel Foundation ✧
c/o Coudert Bros.
1114 Ave. of the Americas, 4th Fl.
New York, NY　10036-7703
Contact: Kenneth R. Page, Tr.

Established in 1997 in NY.
Donor: Ernst C. Stiefel†.
Foundation type: Independent foundation.
Financial data (yr. ended 12/31/05): Assets, $9,227,553 (M); expenditures, $815,000; qualifying distributions, $777,000; giving activities include $777,000 for 30 grants (high: $100,000; low: $5,000).
Fields of interest: Performing arts, music; Food services, agency eatery; Human services.
Type of support: General/operating support; Continuing support; Research; Matching/challenge support.
Limitations: Giving primarily in New York, NY. No grants to individuals.
Application information: Application form not required.
　Initial approach: Letter
　Copies of proposal: 1
　Deadline(s): None
　Final notification: Upon review and decision by Trustees
Trustees: Robert J. Gellert; Kenneth R. Page.
EIN: 137117155

7080
H. L. Stokes Charitable Trust ✧ ☆
c/o U.S. Trust Co.
114 W. 47th St.. 7th Fl.
New York, NY　10036
Contact: Andrew Lane, Trust Off., U.S. Trust Co.

Donor: Hannah L. Stokes†.
Foundation type: Independent foundation.
Financial data (yr. ended 12/31/05): Assets, $1,960,189 (M); expenditures, $535,087; qualifying distributions, $500,000; giving activities include $500,000 for 1 grant.
Fields of interest: Protestant agencies & churches.
Limitations: Giving primarily in NY.

Application information:
Initial approach: Letter
Deadline(s): None
Trustees: Susan F. Weil; U.S. Trust.
EIN: 476250147

7081
The Stone Foundation, Inc. ✧
c/o Charles A. Barragato
950 3rd Ave., 17th Fl.
New York, NY 10022-2705
Contact: Donald Stone, Dir.

Incorporated in 1985 in NY.
Donor: Donald Stone.
Foundation type: Independent foundation.
Financial data (yr. ended 11/30/05): Assets,
$1,888,024 (M); expenditures, $502,179;
qualifying distributions, $474,350; giving activities
include $474,350 for 33 grants (high: $280,000;
low: $1,000).
Fields of interest: Health care; Mental health,
association; Human services; Jewish federated
giving programs; Jewish agencies & temples.
Type of support: Scholarship funds.
Limitations: Giving primarily in New York, NY. No
grants to individuals.
Application information: Application form not
required.
Directors: Donald Stone; James Stone; Jean Stone.
EIN: 136066290
Selected grants: The following grants were reported
in 2005.
$280,000 to White Plains Hospital Center, White
Plains, NY.
$32,500 to National Alliance for Research on
Schizophrenia and Depression (NARSAD), Great
Neck, NY.
$10,000 to Hospital for Special Surgery, New York,
NY.
$1,000 to Burke Rehabilitation Hospital, White
Plains, NY.
$1,000 to Mental Health Association of
Westchester County, Elmsford, NY.

7082
The Stony Point Foundation ✧
c/o BCRS Group/Marcum & Kliegman, LLP
100 Wall St., 11th Fl.
New York, NY 10005

Established in 1993 in NY.
Donor: John O. Downing.
Foundation type: Independent foundation.
Financial data (yr. ended 1/31/05): Assets,
$13,298,366 (M); gifts received, $471,463;
expenditures, $584,543; qualifying distributions,
$486,610; giving activities include $483,340 for 65
grants (high: $100,000; low: $50).
Purpose and activities: Giving primarily for
education, the environment, and health and human
services.
Fields of interest: Museums; Elementary/
secondary education; Higher education;
Environment, natural resources; Environment, land
resources; Hospitals (general); Health care; Human
services.
Limitations: Applications not accepted. Giving on a
national basis. No grants to individuals or for
scholarships; no loans.

Application information: Contributes only to
pre-selected organizations.
Trustees: Frances V.S. Downing; John O. Downing.
EIN: 133766973

7083
Jonathan Strasser Foundation ✧
c/o Jonathan Strasser
61-35 Dry Harbor Rd.
Middle Village, NY 11379-1528

Established in 1989 in NY.
Donor: Jonathan Strasser.
Foundation type: Independent foundation.
Financial data (yr. ended 10/31/04): Assets,
$50,803,757 (M); gifts received, $3,000,000;
expenditures, $1,159,886; qualifying distributions,
$868,700; giving activities include $868,700 for 35
grants (high: $100,000; low: $500).
Fields of interest: Jewish agencies & temples.
Limitations: Applications not accepted. Giving
primarily in NY. No grants to individuals.
Application information: Contributes only to
pre-selected organizations.
Trustee: Jonathan Strasser.
EIN: 112993178

7084
The Melville Straus Charitable Trust ✧
c/o Barry M. Strauss Assocs., Ltd.
307 5th Ave., 8th Fl.
New York, NY 10016-6517

Established in 1986 in NY.
Donor: Melville Straus.
Foundation type: Independent foundation.
Financial data (yr. ended 2/28/05): Assets,
$208,960 (M); gifts received, $529,260;
expenditures, $375,143; qualifying distributions,
$368,626; giving activities include $369,507 for 54
grants (high: $165,000; low: $50).
Purpose and activities: Giving primarily for arts and
culture and educational purposes; some support
also for health and human services.
Fields of interest: Museums; Museums (art);
Performing arts; Arts; Higher education;
Environment; Health care; Women, centers/
services.
Limitations: Applications not accepted. Giving
primarily in New York, NY. No grants to individuals.
Application information: Contributes only to
pre-selected organizations.
Trustees: Richard Reiss; Melville Straus; Eugene
Zuriff.
EIN: 136881724
Selected grants: The following grants were reported
in 2006.
$104,000 to Dartmouth College, Hanover, NH.
$74,700 to Guild Hall, New York, NY.
$12,250 to Allen-Stevenson School, New York, NY.
$9,590 to Ballet Theater Foundation, New York, NY.
$4,000 to New York University, New York, NY.
$2,750 to Independent Curators International, New
York, NY.
$2,683 to Lincoln Center Theater, New York, NY.
$2,500 to Juilliard School, New York, NY.
$1,000 to Big Apple Circus, New York, NY.
$1,000 to Urban Stages, New York, NY.

7085
Martha Washington Straus & Harry H. Straus Foundation, Inc. ✧
8 Sky Meadow Farm
Lincoln Ave.
Port Chester, NY 10573
Contact: Roger J. King, Treas.

Incorporated in 1949 in NC.
Donors: Harry H. Straus, Sr.†; Louise Straus King.
Foundation type: Independent foundation.
Financial data (yr. ended 12/31/05): Assets,
$8,028,962 (M); expenditures, $455,050;
qualifying distributions, $438,900; giving activities
include $438,900 for 99 grants (high: $50,000;
low: $100).
Purpose and activities: Giving primarily for health,
including medical research and education,
hospitals, and health associations; some support
also for Roman Catholic and Jewish religious
institutions and federated giving programs, persons
with disabilities, and social services.
Fields of interest: Arts; Higher education; Hospitals
(general); Health care; Health organizations,
association; Medical research, institute; Human
services; Roman Catholic federated giving
programs; Jewish federated giving programs; Roman
Catholic agencies & churches; Jewish agencies &
temples.
Limitations: Applications not accepted. Giving
primarily in the metropolitan Washington, DC, area,
including MD, and New York, NY. No grants to
individuals.
Application information: Contributes only to
pre-selected organizations.
Board meeting date(s): As required
Officers: Louise Straus King, Pres.; David Straus,
V.P.; Thomas King, Treas. and Mgr.
EIN: 560645526

7086
The Philip A. and Lynn Straus Foundation, Inc. ✧
1037 Constable Dr. S.
Mamaroneck, NY 10543
Contact: Lynn G. Straus, Pres.
E-mail: lynnstr@earthlink.net

Incorporated about 1957 in NY.
Donors: Lynn G. Straus; Philip A. Straus†.
Foundation type: Independent foundation.
Financial data (yr. ended 3/31/06): Assets,
$20,949,436 (M); expenditures, $1,108,822;
qualifying distributions, $857,329; giving activities
include $851,835 for 85 grants (high: $275,000;
low: $100; average: $1,000–$10,000).
Purpose and activities: Giving primarily for
education from birth to age 21, the arts, libraries,
civil rights and human services. Giving also to
support the impartation of information about the
U.S. to Arabic and Farsi speaking areas (i.e. World
Security Institution).
Fields of interest: Museums; Arts; Libraries/library
science; Education; Human services; Civil rights.
Type of support: Continuing support; Annual
campaigns; Capital campaigns; Building/
renovation; Endowments; Emergency funds;
Curriculum development; Scholarship funds.
Limitations: Applications not accepted. Giving
primarily in NY. No grants to individuals.
Application information: Contributes only to
pre-selected organizations.

Officer: Lynn G. Straus, Pres.
Trustees: Donald Roy Straus; Katherine Bea Straus; Philip A. Straus, Jr.
Number of staff: None.
EIN: 136161223
Selected grants: The following grants were reported in 2004.
$2,049,594 to Jewish Board of Family and Childrens Services, New York, NY.
$275,000 to Bank Street College of Education, New York, NY. 2 grants: $250,000, $25,000
$200,000 to Zero to Three: National Center for Infants, Toddlers and Families, DC.
$50,000 to Museum of Arts and Design, New York, NY.
$50,000 to Neuberger Museum, Friends of the, Purchase, NY.
$50,000 to Vassar College, Poughkeepsie, NY.
$40,000 to Museum of Modern Art, New York, NY.
$12,500 to Metropolitan Opera, New York, NY.
$12,500 to Philharmonic-Symphony Society of New York, New York, NY.

7087
The Strauss Foundation, Inc. ✦ ☆
c/o Sacks Press & Lacher
600 3rd Ave.
New York, NY 10016

Established in 2005 in NY.
Foundation type: Independent foundation.
Financial data (yr. ended 12/31/05): Assets, $272,988 (M); gifts received, $600,000; expenditures, $335,635; qualifying distributions, $335,000; giving activities include $335,000 for 4 grants (high: $200,000; low: $25,000).
Fields of interest: Jewish agencies & temples.
Limitations: Applications not accepted. No grants to individuals.
Application information: Contributes only to pre-selected organizations.
Directors: Warren Gleicher; Ernst Strauss; Renato Strauss.
EIN: 202357393

7088
The Dorothy Strelsin Foundation, Inc. ✦
c/o The Bank of New York, Tax Dept.
1 Wall St., 28th Fl.
New York, NY 10286

Established in 1990 in NY.
Donor: Dorothy Strelsin†.
Foundation type: Independent foundation.
Financial data (yr. ended 7/31/04): Assets, $12,641,588 (M); gifts received, $892,153; expenditures, $436,440; qualifying distributions, $391,962; giving activities include $316,250 for 56 grants (high: $35,000; low: $500).
Fields of interest: Performing arts, theater; Arts; Human services.
Limitations: Applications not accepted. Giving primarily in NY. No grants to individuals.
Application information: Contributes only to pre-selected organizations.
Trustee: Enid Nemy.
EIN: 133961352
Selected grants: The following grants were reported in 2004.
$35,000 to Central Park Conservancy, New York, NY.

$25,000 to Royal Ontario Museum, Toronto, Canada. .
$25,000 to Theater Hall of Fame, New York, NY.
$15,000 to Metropolitan Museum.
$12,500 to Manhattan Theater Club, New York, NY.
$10,000 to Spanish Theater Repertory Company, New York, NY.
$8,000 to New York Shakespeare Festival, New York, NY.
$5,000 to New Group, New York, NY.
$5,000 to Talking Band, New York, NY.
$3,000 to Drama Department, New York, NY.

7089
Strypemonde Foundation
1890 Palmer Ave., Rm. 203
Larchmont, NY 10538

Established in 1999 in NY.
Donor: Paul Francis.
Foundation type: Independent foundation.
Financial data (yr. ended 6/30/05): Assets, $15,909,403 (M); gifts received, $47,212; expenditures, $2,292,303; qualifying distributions, $2,083,725; giving activities include $2,079,975 for 53 grants (high: $1,257,500; low: $100).
Fields of interest: Arts; Secondary school/ education; Higher education, university; Human services; Children/youth, services.
Type of support: General/operating support; Continuing support; Annual campaigns; Equipment; Program development; Research.
Limitations: Applications not accepted. No grants to individuals.
Application information: Contributes only to pre-selected organizations.
Officers: Paul Francis, Pres.; Titia Hulst, V.P. and Secy.
Number of staff: None.
EIN: 137204588
Selected grants: The following grants were reported in 2004.
$1,250,000 to New York University, New York, NY.
$100,000 to Purchase College Foundation, Purchase, NY.
$50,000 to Robin Hood Foundation, New York, NY.
$10,000 to Phillips Academy, Andover, MA.
$2,500 to Bronx Charter School for Excellence, Bronx, NY.
$1,000 to Children for Children Foundation, New York, NY.
$1,000 to Foster Pride, New York, NY.
$1,000 to Saint Johns University, Jamaica, NY.
$1,000 to Westchester Childrens Association, White Plains, NY.
$600 to Everybody Wins Foundation, New York, NY.

7090
The Stuart Family Foundation, Inc. ✦
c/o Kohlberg, Kravis, Roberts & Co.
9 W. 57th St.
New York, NY 10019-2600

Established in 1995 in NY.
Donor: Scott M. Stuart.
Foundation type: Independent foundation.
Financial data (yr. ended 11/30/05): Assets, $2,374,673 (M); gifts received, $1,519,750; expenditures, $609,251; qualifying distributions, $609,251; giving activities include $569,721 for 64 grants (high: $75,000; low: $500).

Fields of interest: Media, television; Education; Human services; Children/youth, services; Christian agencies & churches.
Limitations: Applications not accepted. Giving primarily in CT and NY. No grants to individuals.
Application information: Contributes only to pre-selected organizations.
Officers: Scott M. Stuart, Pres.; Lisa G. Stuart, V.P.; James M. Goldrick, Secy.-Treas.
EIN: 133861861
Selected grants: The following grants were reported in 2005.
$75,000 to Texas Childrens Hospital, Houston, TX.
$53,000 to Robin Hood Foundation, New York, NY. 2 grants: $5,000, $48,000
$25,000 to Big Apple Circus, New York, NY.
$25,000 to Equal Justice Works, DC.
$25,000 to Greenwich Country Day School, Greenwich, CT.
$23,280 to National Parks Conservation Association, DC.
$23,000 to Michael J. Fox Foundation for Parkinsons Research, New York, NY.
$10,000 to Global Kids, New York, NY.
$5,000 to Conservation International, DC.

7091
The Julien J. Studley Foundation ✦
c/o Studley New Vista Assocs.
505 Park Ave.
New York, NY 10022

Established in 1992 in NY.
Donor: Julien J. Studley.
Foundation type: Independent foundation.
Financial data (yr. ended 12/31/05): Assets, $1,438,120 (M); gifts received, $750,000; expenditures, $656,784; qualifying distributions, $636,900; giving activities include $636,900 for 26 grants (high: $100,000; low: $100).
Fields of interest: Arts; Higher education.
Limitations: Applications not accepted. Giving primarily in NY. No grants to individuals.
Application information: Contributes only to pre-selected organizations.
Trustee: Julien J. Studley.
EIN: 133703530

7092
Jay and Kelly Sugarman Foundation ✦ ☆
c/o US Trust Co.
114 W. 47th St.
New York, NY 10036

Established in 2004 in NY.
Donor: Jay Sugarman.
Foundation type: Independent foundation.
Financial data (yr. ended 12/31/05): Assets, $10,009,088 (M); expenditures, $652,325; qualifying distributions, $508,350; giving activities include $508,350 for 18 grants (high: $100,000; low: $250).
Fields of interest: Education; Youth, services; Human services; International human rights; Protestant agencies & churches.
Limitations: Applications not accepted. No grants to individuals.
Application information: Contributes only to pre-selected organizations.

Officers: Jay Sugarman, Pres.; Kelly Sugarman, V.P.; Belinda Chan, Secy.
EIN: 200911399

7093
The Sullivan & Cromwell Foundation ◇
125 Broad St., Ste. 2533
New York, NY 10004-2498

Established in 2001 in NY.
Donors: Sullivan & Cromwell LLP; Banco Popular.
Foundation type: Company-sponsored foundation.
Financial data (yr. ended 12/31/03): Assets, $207,431 (M); gifts received, $100,000; expenditures, $500,273; qualifying distributions, $500,162; giving activities include $500,000 for 5 grants (high: $125,000; low: $25,000).
Purpose and activities: The foundation supports organizations involved with arts and culture, education, human services, and community development.
Fields of interest: Arts; Education; Hospitals (general); Disasters, 9/11/01; Human services; Community development.
Limitations: Applications not accepted. Giving primarily in NY. No grants to individuals.
Application information: Contributes only to pre-selected organizations.
Officers and Directors:* H. Rodgin Cohen,* Chair. and Pres.; Ricardo A. Mestres, Jr.,* Secy.; John E. Merow,* Treas.
EIN: 311809780

7094
The Sullivan Family Foundation ◇ ☆
c/o BCRS Associates, LLC
100 Wall St., 11th Fl.
New York, NY 10005

Established in 1989 in MA.
Donors: Daniel J. Sullivan, Jr.; Marjorie O. Sullivan.
Foundation type: Independent foundation.
Financial data (yr. ended 5/31/05): Assets, $170,962 (M); gifts received, $150,000; expenditures, $332,300; qualifying distributions, $327,000; giving activities include $326,000 for 7 grants (high: $200,000; low: $1,000).
Purpose and activities: Giving primarily for education.
Fields of interest: Elementary/secondary education; Higher education; Employment, job counseling.
Limitations: Applications not accepted. Giving primarily in Washington, DC and Boston, MA. No grants to individuals.
Application information: Contributes only to pre-selected organizations.
Trustees: Daniel J. Sullivan, Jr.; Marjorie O. Sullivan.
EIN: 133531989
Selected grants: The following grants were reported in 2003.
$100,000 to Winsor School, Boston, MA. For general support.
$20,000 to Georgetown University, Office of Alumni & University Relations, DC. For general support.
$10,000 to Boston College High School, Dorchester, MA. For general support.
$10,000 to Inner-City Scholarship Fund, Boston, MA. For general support.
$10,000 to JFYNetworks, Boston, MA. For general support.

$5,000 to Saint Johns Church, Wellesley, MA. For general support.

7095
The Sulzberger Foundation, Inc.
229 W. 43rd St., Ste. 1031
New York, NY 10036
Contact: Andrea S. Markezin, Asst. Treas.

Incorporated in 1956 in NY.
Donors: Arthur Hays Sulzberger†; Iphigene Ochs Sulzberger†; Marian S. Heiskell; Ruth S. Holmberg; Judith P. Sulzberger; Arthur Ochs Sulzberger.
Foundation type: Independent foundation.
Financial data (yr. ended 12/31/04): Assets, $49,877,269 (M); gifts received, $500; expenditures, $2,924,476; qualifying distributions, $2,424,671; giving activities include $2,262,590 for 179 grants (high: $251,000; low: $100).
Purpose and activities: Giving primarily to arts and cultural programs, and to hospitals; funding also for education, including a public library, as well as for natural resource conservation and protection, and children, youth and social services.
Fields of interest: Museums (art); Museums (natural history); Arts; Education, administration/regulation; Elementary/secondary education; Higher education; Education; Environment, natural resources; Animals/wildlife; Hospitals (general); Reproductive health, family planning; Health organizations, association; Human services; Children/youth, services; Jewish agencies & temples.
Type of support: Internship funds; General/operating support; Continuing support; Annual campaigns; Building/renovation; Endowments; Emergency funds; Program development; Scholarship funds.
Limitations: Giving on a national basis, with emphasis on NY, Chattanooga, TN, CA, and Washington, DC. No grants to individuals, or for matching gifts; no loans.
Application information: Application form not required.
Initial approach: Letter
Copies of proposal: 1
Deadline(s): None
Board meeting date(s): Jan. and as required
Officers and Directors:* Marian S. Heiskell,* Pres.; Ruth S. Holmberg,* V.P.; Arthur Ochs Sulzberger,* V.P.; Judith P. Sulzberger,* V.P.
Number of staff: 1 part-time professional; 2 part-time support.
EIN: 136083166
Selected grants: The following grants were reported in 2003.
$255,000 to New York Times Neediest Cases Fund, New York, NY.
$155,500 to Council on the Environment, New York, NY.
$25,000 to Browning School, New York, NY.
$20,000 to Southampton Hospital Association, Southampton, NY.
$12,500 to Museum of Modern Art, New York, NY.
$10,000 to Dartmouth College, Hanover, NH.
$10,000 to Southern Environmental Law Center, Charlottesville, VA.
$5,000 to Wilderness Society, DC.
$1,000 to Ballet Hispanico of New York, New York, NY.
$1,000 to New York Cares, New York, NY.

7096
Sumitomo Corporation of America Foundation ◇ ☆
c/o Elizabeth Peters
600 3rd Ave.
New York, NY 10016-2001
URL: http://www.sumitomocorp.com/about/community.html

Established in 2004 in NY.
Donor: Sumitomo Corporation of America "SCOA".
Foundation type: Independent foundation.
Financial data (yr. ended 3/31/06): Assets, $9,775,819 (M); expenditures, $470,223; qualifying distributions, $470,223; giving activities include $446,760 for grants.
Purpose and activities: Giving to organizations that improve the understanding of Japan-American culture; some giving for the arts in form of play presentations and community improvement in the local Sumitomo Corporation of America areas.
Fields of interest: Arts; International relief, 2004 tsunami.
Type of support: General/operating support.
Limitations: Applications not accepted. Giving primarily in areas of company operations. No grants to individuals.
Application information: Contributes only to pre-selected organizations.
Officers and Directors:* Kunio Fujimoto,* Pres.; Elizabeth Peters, Secy.; Reiji Morooka, Treas.; Takaya Endo; Jose Tavares.
EIN: 202103634

7097
Solon E. Summerfield Foundation, Inc.
1270 Ave. of the Americas, Ste. 2114
New York, NY 10020
Contact: William W. Prager, Jr., Pres.
E-mail: sesfdn@aol.com

Incorporated in 1939 in NY.
Donor: Solon E. Summerfield†.
Foundation type: Independent foundation.
Financial data (yr. ended 12/31/05): Assets, $62,029,489 (M); expenditures, $2,556,563; qualifying distributions, $2,309,535; giving activities include $1,987,345 for 110 grants (high: $500,000; low: $500).
Purpose and activities: Giving primarily for education (including the arts), medical research and social needs.
Fields of interest: Arts education; Higher education; Hospitals (general); Health care; Health organizations; Medical research, institute; Human services; Children/youth, services.
Type of support: General/operating support; Capital campaigns; Endowments; Scholarship funds; Matching/challenge support.
Limitations: Giving on a national basis, with emphasis on the East Coast. No grants to individuals, or for fund raising events or benefits.
Application information: Eligible foundations will be invited to submit a full proposal. Attachments to the LOI are not accepted. Application form not required.
Initial approach: Letter of inquiry only (no more than 1 page)
Deadline(s): Aug. and Mar.
Board meeting date(s): Biannually
Final notification: Nov. and June

Officers and Trustees:* William W. Prager, Jr.,* Pres.; Thomas C. Treeger,* V.P. and Treas.; Ruth P. Cogen,* Secy.
Number of staff: 1 full-time support; 3 part-time support.
EIN: 131797260
Selected grants: The following grants were reported in 2004.
$457,239 to Kansas University Endowment Association, Lawrence, KS.
$50,000 to American Foundation for the Blind, New York, NY.
$50,000 to Hebrew Free Loan Society, New York, NY.
$50,000 to One Hundred Neediest Cases, Saint Louis, MO.
$45,723 to Visiting Nurse Service of New York, New York, NY.
$25,000 to Duke University Medical Center, Durham, NC.
$5,000 to American Indian College Fund, Denver, CO.
$5,000 to Berea College, Berea, KY.
$2,500 to New Alternatives for Children, New York, NY.
$2,500 to New York Public Library, New York, NY.

7098
The Summerhill Foundation ✧ ☆
c/o BCRS Assocs., LLC
100 Wall St., 11th Fl.
New York, NY 10005

Established in 1954.
Donors: Peter G. Sachs; Eleanor B. Sachs†; Howard J. Sachs†.
Foundation type: Independent foundation.
Financial data (yr. ended 11/30/05): Assets, $3,791,133 (M); gifts received, $323,959; expenditures, $354,596; qualifying distributions, $347,637; giving activities include $345,627 for 34 grants (high: $150,000; low: $250).
Purpose and activities: Giving primarily for education.
Fields of interest: Elementary/secondary education; Higher education; Health care; Health organizations, association; Cancer research; Human services; Federated giving programs.
Limitations: Applications not accepted. Giving primarily in CT, MA, and New York, NY. No grants to individuals; no loans.
Application information: Contributes only to pre-selected organizations.
Trustees: Katharine C. Sachs; Michael T. Sachs; Peter G. Sachs.
EIN: 136028811

7099
The John and Jayne Summers Foundation, Inc. ✧
P.O. Box 60620
Rochester, NY 14606-0620

Established in 2000 in NY.
Donors: John M. Summers; Jayne C. Summers.
Foundation type: Independent foundation.
Financial data (yr. ended 12/31/05): Assets, $4,729,652 (M); gifts received, $1,503,000; expenditures, $619,811; qualifying distributions, $497,459; giving activities include $476,279 for 22 grants (high: $255,720; low: $500).

Fields of interest: Higher education; Health organizations, association; Children/youth, services.
Limitations: Applications not accepted. Giving primarily in Rochester, NY. No grants to individuals.
Application information: Contributes only to pre-selected organizations.
Officers: Douglas J. Summers, Pres.; Kenneth A. Marvald, V.P. and Secy.; John M. Summers, Treas.
Directors: Susan Conrado; Jayne C. Summers.
EIN: 161596923

7100
Summit Foundation ✧ ☆
c/o BCRS Group, Marcum & Kliegman, LLP
655 3rd Ave., 16th Fl.
New York, NY 10017

Established in 1994 in NY.
Donor: Cody J. Smith.
Foundation type: Independent foundation.
Financial data (yr. ended 9/30/05): Assets, $1,924,911 (M); expenditures, $624,961; qualifying distributions, $585,275; giving activities include $584,100 for 34 grants (high: $100,000; low: $500).
Fields of interest: Higher education; Higher education, college; Youth, services; Philanthropy/voluntarism.
Limitations: Applications not accepted. Giving primarily in CA, MA, MN and NY. No grants to individuals; no loans or scholarships.
Application information: Contributes only to pre-selected organizations.
Trustee: Cody J. Smith.
EIN: 133805672
Selected grants: The following grants were reported in 2004.
$100,000 to Claremont McKenna College, Claremont, CA.
$50,000 to Stanford University, Stanford, CA.
$25,000 to Chess in the Schools, New York, NY.
$25,000 to Student Sponsor Partners, New York, NY.
$10,000 to Colorado Conservation Trust, Boulder, CO.
$5,000 to Urban Education Exchange, New York, NY.
$1,000 to Project ALS, New York, NY.
$1,000 to TEAK Fellowship, New York, NY.
$100 to Houston Food Bank, Houston, TX.

7101
The Sunrise Foundation Trust ✧
641 Lexington Ave., 25th Fl.
New York, NY 10022
Contact: Nathan Low, Tr.

Established in 1997 in NJ.
Donor: Nathan Low.
Foundation type: Independent foundation.
Financial data (yr. ended 12/31/05): Assets, $7,485,085 (M); gifts received, $2,936,362; expenditures, $3,369,349; qualifying distributions, $3,313,883; giving activities include $3,257,073 for 90 grants (high: $524,000; low: $15).
Purpose and activities: Giving to Jewish organizations.
Fields of interest: Jewish federated giving programs; Jewish agencies & temples.

Limitations: Applications not accepted. Giving primarily in New York, NY. No grants to individuals.
Application information: Contributes only to pre-selected organizations.
Trustees: Lisa Low; Nathan Low.
EIN: 226709496
Selected grants: The following grants were reported in 2003.
$34,000 to North American Conference on Ethiopian Jewry, New York, NY. For general support.
$25,000 to American Friends of Yad Ezrah, New York, NY. For general support.
$21,120 to Yad Avraham Institute, New York, NY. For general support.
$14,000 to Chabad House of Greater Boston, Boston, MA. For general support.
$7,500 to Manhattan Jewish Experience Synagogue, New York, NY. For general support.
$6,240 to American Friends of Shalva, New York, NY. For general support.
$5,000 to American Friends of Tiferet Tiberias Institutions, New York, NY. For general support.
$5,000 to National Society for Hebrew Day Schools - Torah Umesorah, New York, NY. For general support.
$5,000 to Yeshiva of Spring Valley, Monsey, NY. For general support.
$3,600 to Aleph Institute, New York, NY. For general support.

7102
The Sunrise Klein Foundation, Inc. ✧ ☆
8 Sunrise Dr.
Monsey, NY 10952-3305
Contact: Abraham Klein, Tr.

Established in 2000.
Donors: Julius Klein Diamonds Inc.; Abraham Klein; Sunrise Venture LLC.
Foundation type: Company-sponsored foundation.
Financial data (yr. ended 1/31/05): Assets, $2,576,951 (M); gifts received, $470,594; expenditures, $454,481; qualifying distributions, $388,459; giving activities include $388,459 for 46 grants (high: $61,000; low: $200).
Purpose and activities: The foundation supports Jewish agencies and temples.
Fields of interest: Jewish agencies & temples.
Type of support: General/operating support.
Application information: Application form not required.
Initial approach: Proposal
Trustee: Abraham Klein.
EIN: 134097745

7103
Surdna Foundation, Inc. ▼ ✧
330 Madison Ave., 30th Fl.
New York, NY 10017-5001 (212) 557-0010
Contact: Edward Skloot, Exec. Dir.
FAX: (212) 557-0003; E-mail: request@surdna.org;
URL: http://www.surdna.org

Incorporated in 1917 in NY.
Donor: John E. Andrus†.
Foundation type: Independent foundation.
Financial data (yr. ended 6/30/05): Assets, $769,100,511 (M); gifts received, $1,426,141; expenditures, $38,878,663; qualifying distributions, $35,814,521; giving activities include

$30,608,760 for 517 grants (high: $350,000; low: $50; average: $5,000–$100,000).

Purpose and activities: The foundation's guidelines focus on five areas: 1) The Environment, specifically transportation and energy, urban and suburban issues, and biological and cultural diversity; 2) Community Revitalization, which takes a comprehensive and holistic approach to restoring communities in America; 3) Building an Effective Citizenry, to advance social and emotional learning, enhance conflict resolution theory, practice and expand opportunities for service and citizenship, and support character development and ethical behavior; 4) The Arts; and 5) The Nonprofit Sector. The foundation is particularly interested in fostering catalytic, entrepreneurial programs that offer solutions to difficult systemic problems.

Fields of interest: Arts education; Environment, natural resources; Environment, energy; Environment; Dispute resolution; Housing/shelter, development; Disasters, 9/11/01; Economic development; Urban/community development; Community development; Philanthropy/voluntarism, association; Public affairs, citizen participation.

Type of support: General/operating support; Continuing support; Program development; Technical assistance.

Limitations: Giving on a national basis. No support for international projects, or programs addressing toxics, hazardous waste, environmental education, sustainable agriculture, food production and distribution. No grants for endowments or land acquisition. Generally, no grants to individuals, or for capital campaigns or building construction.

Publications: Annual report (including application guidelines); Grants list.

Application information: Application form not required.

> *Initial approach:* Letter by mail or online at foundation Web site
> *Copies of proposal:* 1
> *Deadline(s):* None
> *Board meeting date(s):* Feb., May, and Sept.
> *Final notification:* 90 days

Officers and Directors:* John F. Hawkins,* Chair.; Michael S. Spensley,* Vice-Chair.; Edward Skloot, Pres.; Phillip Henderson, Pres.-Elect; John J. Lynagh,* Secy.; Marc de Venoge, C.F.O. and C.A.O.; Frederick F. Moon III,* Treas.; John E. Andrus III, Chair. Emeritus; Elizabeth H. Andrus; Pamela Brill, Ed.D.; David Grant; Lawrence S.C. Griffith, M.D.; Sandra T. Kaupe; Josephine B. Lowman; Nadya K. Shmavonian; Edith D. Thorpe; Samuel S. Thorpe III.

Number of staff: 11 full-time professional; 5 full-time support.

EIN: 136108163

Selected grants: The following grants were reported in 2005.

$500,000 to John E. Andrus Memorial, Hastings on Hudson, NY. For renovations and repairs.

$450,000 to Bridgespan Group, Boston, MA. To generate and share knowledge with, and to provide consulting to high-potential nonprofits at discount, payable over 3 years.

$450,000 to Labor Community Strategy Center, Los Angeles, CA. To expand regional and national influence on transportation issues by creating new Center for Transportation Strategies, increasing work in Consent Decree Enforcement Team, and launching Clean Air, Clean Lungs, Clean Buses Campaign, payable over 3 years.

$400,000 to Funders Collaborative on Youth Organizing, New York, NY. For efforts to increase philanthropic investment in and strengthen organizational capacities of youth organizing efforts across country, payable over 2 years.

$400,000 to Sustainable Northwest, Portland, OR. For Rural Voices for Conservation Initiative, project to build ability of rural conservation leaders to engage in policy process and to promote community-based solutions to natural resource management problems in Northwest, payable over 2 years.

$375,000 to Southern Environmental Law Center, Charlottesville, VA. For project which promotes smart growth and sustainable transportation in Southeast, payable over 3 years.

$300,000 to Brookings Institution, DC. To develop and advance action agenda for U.S. cities facing significant economic, fiscal, and social challenges as part of broader, two-year project called Campaign for America's Core Cities, payable over 2 years.

$300,000 to Natural Resources Defense Council, New York, NY. To develop national standard for neighborhood design that integrates green building and smart growth, and to work with Enterprise Foundation on major initiative to build affordable housing according to these green principles, payable over 2 years.

$300,000 to Network for Good, Vienna, VA. To use Internet to increase flow of resources from citizens to nonprofits and to increase ability of nonprofits to get resources for themselves, payable over 3 years.

$255,000 to Maryland Institute College of Art, Baltimore, MD. To enable high school visual artists to attend pre-college studio residency program, hire coordinator to advise students, and recruit master faculty, and to provide financial aid to visual artists in low-residency studio master's program, payable over 3 years.

7104

The Laurie Tisch Sussman Foundation, Inc. ✧

c/o M.J. Krinsky
655 Madison Ave., 19th Fl.
New York, NY 10021-8043

Established in 1992 in NY and DE.

Donors: Preston Robert Tisch; S. Donald Sussman; Joan H. Tisch; The Sussman Family Foundation.

Foundation type: Independent foundation.

Financial data (yr. ended 12/31/05): Assets, $25,302,941 (M); gifts received, $3,724,200; expenditures, $2,468,931; qualifying distributions, $2,310,145; giving activities include $2,178,181 for 73 grants (high: $1,163,505; low: $100).

Purpose and activities: Giving primarily for the arts; funding also for education, health associations, social services and Jewish organizations.

Fields of interest: Arts, alliance; Arts, administration/regulation; Arts education; Performing arts; Performing arts, theater; Arts; Education; Health organizations, association; Human services; Jewish agencies & temples.

Limitations: Applications not accepted. Giving primarily in New York, NY. No grants to individuals.

Application information: Contributes only to pre-selected organizations.

Officers: Laurie M. Tisch, Pres.; Jonathan M. Tisch, Sr. V.P.; Mark J. Krinsky, V.P.; Thomas M. Steinberg, V.P.; Barry L. Bloom, Secy.-Treas.

EIN: 133693585

7105

Edna Bailey Sussman Fund ✧

c/o Boyce, Hughes & Farrell, LLP
1025 Northern Blvd., Ste. 300
Roslyn, NY 11576-1506
Contact: Dorothy Bertine, Admin.

Established in 1984 in NY.

Donors: Arthur H. Dean†; Edward S. Miller.

Foundation type: Independent foundation.

Financial data (yr. ended 4/30/06): Assets, $5,935,108 (M); expenditures, $384,057; qualifying distributions, $332,351; giving activities include $332,351 for grants.

Purpose and activities: To further the preservation of wildlife, the control of pollution, and the preservation of natural land and resources by funding internships for individuals in a field of study at an institution of higher learning in an area that significantly impacts the environment.

Fields of interest: Higher education; Environment.

Type of support: Internship funds.

Limitations: Giving on a national basis. No grants to individuals directly.

Application information: The fund only accepts applications from colleges and universities with whom it has established relationships. It does not accept applications from individuals. Stipends are disbursed to institution on behalf of intern selected by fund trustees.

> *Initial approach:* Application process must conform with host institution's general procedures

Trustees: Robert H. Frey; Edward S. Miller.

EIN: 133187064

7106

Norma Sutton Charitable Foundation ✧

c/o Middlegate Securities Ltd.
8 W. 40th St.
New York, NY 10018

Established in 1993 in NY.

Donors: Albert Sutton; Elliot Sutton; Isaac Sutton; Abraham Zami; Rochelle Zami; Charles Mamiye; Morris Sutton; Steve Ostrofsky; Neil Barrish; Gloria Barrish; Adam Ash; Sara Ash; Middlegate Securities, Ltd.; Herbert and Yvonne Missry Foundation; Middlegate Insurance Agency, Ltd.; Nissam Investment Group LLC; XES NY.

Foundation type: Independent foundation.

Financial data (yr. ended 3/31/05): Assets, $279,636 (M); gifts received, $754,977; expenditures, $777,578; qualifying distributions, $777,496; giving activities include $777,301 for 66 grants (high: $114,600; low: $101).

Purpose and activities: Giving primarily to Jewish agencies, temples, and schools.

Fields of interest: Education; Jewish federated giving programs; Jewish agencies & temples.

Limitations: Applications not accepted. Giving primarily in NY. No grants to individuals.

Application information: Contributes only to pre-selected organizations.

Officers: Albert Sutton, Pres.; Isaac Sutton, Secy.; Elliot Sutton, Treas.

EIN: 133747098

Selected grants: The following grants were reported in 2003.

$240,000 to Magen David Yeshiva, Brooklyn, NY. For general operating support.

$127,500 to Magen Israel Society, Brooklyn, NY. For general operating support.

$80,000 to Shaare Torah. For general operating support.

$59,500 to Nefesh Academy, Brooklyn, NY. For general operating support.

$30,000 to Torah Academy High School of Brooklyn, Brooklyn, NY. For general operating support.

$30,000 to Yeshiva Shaare Torah, Brooklyn, NY. For general operating support.

$26,800 to Yad Yosef, Brooklyn, NY. For general operating support.

$20,000 to Meorot, Brooklyn, NY. For general operating support.

$16,000 to Mattan Basseter, New York, NY. For general operating support.

$15,000 to Bnei Yitzhak Foundation. For general operating support.

7107
Joe & Eileen Sutton Family Foundation ✧ ☆
1411 Broadway, 19th Fl.
New York, NY 10018

Established in 2004 in NY.
Donor: Joseph and Eileen Sutton Fund, Inc.
Foundation type: Independent foundation.
Financial data (yr. ended 12/31/05): Assets, $5,550,916 (M); gifts received, $1,348,201; expenditures, $779,398; qualifying distributions, $776,961; giving activities include $775,036 for 110 grants (high: $65,000; low: $2).
Fields of interest: Jewish agencies & temples.
Limitations: Applications not accepted. No grants to individuals.
Application information: Contributes only to pre-selected organizations.
Officer: Joseph Sutton, Chair.
Directors: Albert J. Sutton; Eileen Sutton.
EIN: 743136392

7108
The Celia and Isaac Sutton Foundation ✧ ☆
c/o Celia and Isaac Sutton
463 Ave. S
Brooklyn, NY 11223-3024

Established in 2000 in NY.
Donors: Isaac Sutton; The Jack Sitt 1992 Charitable Trust.
Foundation type: Independent foundation.
Financial data (yr. ended 10/31/05): Assets, $2,683,485 (M); expenditures, $514,211; qualifying distributions, $424,362; giving activities include $424,362 for 16 grants (high: $338,000; low: $18).
Purpose and activities: Giving primarily to Jewish agencies, temples, and schools.
Fields of interest: Elementary/secondary education; Jewish federated giving programs; Jewish agencies & temples.
Limitations: Applications not accepted. No grants to individuals.
Application information: Contributes only to pre-selected organizations.
Trustees: Celia Sutton; Isaac Sutton.
EIN: 137200889

7109
The Sam and Jack Sutton, Abe Dweck, and Isaac Saff Family Foundation ✧
1 E. 33rd St., 6th Fl.
New York, NY 10016

Established in 2002 in NY.
Donors: Jack Sutton; Accessory Exchange LLC.
Foundation type: Independent foundation.
Financial data (yr. ended 11/30/05): Assets, $5,312 (M); gifts received, $1,000,000; expenditures, $1,007,170; qualifying distributions, $1,006,909; giving activities include $1,006,909 for 265 grants (high: $80,000; low: $18).
Fields of interest: Education; Human services; Jewish federated giving programs; Jewish agencies & temples.
Limitations: Applications not accepted. Giving primarily in NY. No grants to individuals.
Application information: Contributes only to pre-selected organizations.
Officers and Directors:* Solomon A. Sutton,* Pres.; Abe Dweck,* V.P.; Jack A. Sutton,* Secy.
EIN: 510437421

7110
SVM Foundation ✧
390 Park Ave., 6th Fl., Ste. 600
New York, NY 10022-4608
Contact: Philip L. Milstein, Tr.

Established in 1996 in NY.
Donors: Seymour Milstein†; Vivian Milstein.
Foundation type: Independent foundation.
Financial data (yr. ended 12/31/05): Assets, $14,560,193 (M); expenditures, $3,362,574; qualifying distributions, $3,357,394; giving activities include $3,351,983 for 40 grants (high: $2,000,000; low: $250).
Purpose and activities: Giving primarily for Jewish federated giving and to family-affiliated private foundations.
Fields of interest: Higher education; Jewish federated giving programs; Jewish agencies & temples.
Type of support: Grants to individuals.
Limitations: Applications not accepted. Giving on a national basis.
Application information: Unsolicited requests for funds not accepted.
Trustees: Constance J. Milstein; Philip L. Milstein; Vivian Milstein.
EIN: 137105557
Selected grants: The following grants were reported in 2004.
$225,000 to American Jewish Committee, New York, NY.
$130,000 to Metropolitan Museum of Art, New York, NY.
$55,000 to Philharmonic-Symphony Society of New York, New York, NY.
$32,500 to Neighborhood Coalition for Shelter, New York, NY.
$25,000 to Womens American ORT, New York, NY.
$12,500 to Westchester Philharmonic, White Plains, NY.
$11,500 to Jewish Museum, New York, NY.
$10,000 to Lincoln Center Theater, New York, NY.
$5,000 to Reece School, New York, NY.
$3,000 to Foundation for Excellent Schools, Cornwall, VT.

7111
The Swartz Foundation Trust ✧
c/o Brandywine Mgmt. Svcs.
880 3rd Ave., 3rd Fl.
New York, NY 10022 (212) 319-2700
Contact: James R. Swartz, Pres.
Application address: c/o Brandywine Trust Co., 7234 Lancaster Pike, Hockessin, DE 19707, tel.: (302) 234-5750

Donor: James R. Swartz.
Foundation type: Independent foundation.
Financial data (yr. ended 12/31/04): Assets, $21,195,464 (M); expenditures, $1,994,280; qualifying distributions, $1,905,389; giving activities include $1,903,932 for 54 grants (high: $400,000; low: $500).
Purpose and activities: Giving primarily to evangelical Christian organizations and to Christian churches.
Fields of interest: Arts; Higher education; Human services; Christian agencies & churches.
Limitations: Giving primarily in NJ and UT.
Application information: Application form not required.
  Deadline(s): None
Officer: James R. Swartz, Pres.
EIN: 226554026

7112
The Swartz Foundation ✧
199 Old Field Rd.
Setauket, NY 11733
URL: http://www.theswartzfoundation.org

Established in 1995 in NY.
Donor: Jerome Swartz.
Foundation type: Independent foundation.
Financial data (yr. ended 10/31/04): Assets, $14,192,409 (M); gifts received, $4,844,645; expenditures, $2,407,656; qualifying distributions, $2,300,773; giving activities include $2,300,773 for 13 grants.
Purpose and activities: The mission of the Swartz foundation is to explore the application of physics, mathematics, and computer engineering principles to neuroscience, as a path to better understanding the brain-mind relationship. Giving primarily to establish research centers devoted to advancing computational neuroscience.
Fields of interest: Higher education; Science, research.
Limitations: Applications not accepted. Giving primarily in CA and NY. No grants to individuals.
Application information: Contributes only to pre-selected organizations.
Officer: Paul Kelly, C.F.O.
Trustees: James P. King; Andrew Schenker; Jerome Swartz.
EIN: 116447242
Selected grants: The following grants were reported in 2003.
$707,000 to University of California at San Diego, La Jolla, CA. For research.
$240,039 to California Institute of Technology, Pasadena, CA. For research.
$205,000 to Brandeis University, Waltham, MA. For research.
$194,300 to New York University, New York, NY. For research.
$180,000 to Salk Institute for Biological Studies, San Diego, CA. For research.

$180,000 to University of San Francisco, San Francisco, CA. For research.

$4,500 to Stony Brook Foundation, Stony Brook, NY. For research.

7113
Sweetgrass Foundation ✧
170 Newell Rd.
Hammond, NY 13646
Contact: Allan P. Newell, Pres.

Established in 1992 in NY.
Donors: Allan P. Newell; Jean Newell†.
Foundation type: Independent foundation.
Financial data (yr. ended 12/31/05): Assets, $6,013,804 (M); expenditures, $467,316; qualifying distributions, $460,333; giving activities include $460,333 for 21 grants (high: $100,000; low: $5,000).
Fields of interest: Arts; Education; Environment, water resources; Environment; Youth development, services; Human services; Government/public administration.
Type of support: Research; General/operating support; Capital campaigns; Building/renovation; Endowments; Program development; Conferences/seminars; Publication; Seed money; Matching/challenge support.
Limitations: Applications not accepted. Giving limited to St. Lawrence County and the St. Lawrence River Valley, NY, areas. No grants to individuals.
Application information: Contributes only to pre-selected organizations. Unsolicited requests for grants not accepted.
  Board meeting date(s): 1st Wed. in Mar., June, Sept., and Dec.
Officers and Directors:* Allan P. Newell,* Pres. and Treas.; Catherine B. Newell,* V.P. and Secy.; MaryAnn Narenkivicius; Mark Scarlett.
EIN: 161414871
Selected grants: The following grants were reported in 2005.
$100,000 to Antique Boat Museum, Clayton, NY.
$25,000 to North Country Childrens Clinic, Watertown, NY.
$25,000 to Thousand Islands Performing Arts Fund, Clayton, NY.
$10,000 to Ogdensburg Command Performances, Ogdensburg, NY.
$10,000 to Potsdam College Foundation, Potsdam, NY.
$6,000 to Norwood Village Green Concert Series, Norwood, NY.

7114
Syde Hurdus Foundation, Inc. ✧ ☆
(formerly Syde Hurdus 1992 Charitable Trust)
2438 McCord Ave.
Merrick, NY 11566-4229

Donor: Syde Hurdus†.
Foundation type: Independent foundation.
Financial data (yr. ended 8/31/05): Assets, $15,448,298 (M); gifts received, $299,206; expenditures, $895,064; qualifying distributions, $667,000; giving activities include $667,000 for 37 grants (high: $200,000; low: $1,000).
Purpose and activities: Giving primarily for health care and human services, including to hospitals and to an organization that provides reconstructive surgery to people in developing countries.

Fields of interest: Hospitals (general); Hospitals (specialty); Health organizations, association; Human services; Blind/visually impaired.
Limitations: Applications not accepted. Giving nationally with some emphasis on the New York, NY, metropolitan area.
Application information: Contributes only to pre-selected organizations.
Trustees: Herbert S. Fitzgibbon; Salvatore Romanotto.
EIN: 201903001

7115
Sykes Family Foundation ✧ ☆
c/o Goldman Sachs & Co., Tax Dept.
85 Broad St.
New York, NY 10004

Established in 1993 in CA.
Donor: Gene T. Sykes.
Foundation type: Independent foundation.
Financial data (yr. ended 6/30/05): Assets, $8,715,990 (M); gifts received, $2,087,000; expenditures, $683,183; qualifying distributions, $561,300; giving activities include $561,300 for 39 grants (high: $250,000; low: $250).
Purpose and activities: Giving for higher education, and human services.
Fields of interest: Elementary/secondary education; Higher education; Scholarships/financial aid; Environment, natural resources; Environment; Human services.
Type of support: General/operating support.
Limitations: Giving on a national basis. No grants to individuals; no loans.
Trustee: Gene T. Sykes.
EIN: 133748075
Selected grants: The following grants were reported in 2004.
$25,000 to Harvard College Fund, Cambridge, MA. For general operating support.
$25,000 to Robert Packard Foundation for ALS Research, San Francisco, CA. For general operating support.
$23,900 to National Parks Conservation Association, DC. For general operating support.
$3,750 to Dolores Mission Elementary School Parochial, Los Angeles, CA. For general operating support.
$2,000 to Saint Annes Maternity Home, Los Angeles, CA. For general operating support.
$1,500 to Multiple Sclerosis Society, National, New York, NY. For general operating support.
$1,500 to Prep for Prep, New York, NY. For general operating support.
$1,000 to Homeboy Industries, Los Angeles, CA. For general operating support.
$1,000 to Project ALS, New York, NY. For general operating support.
$1,000 to Student Sponsor Partners, New York, NY. For general operating support.

7116
T-4 Foundation ✧
c/o BCRS Group, LLP
100 Wall St., 11th Fl.
New York, NY 10005

Established in 1999 in NY.
Donor: John A. Thain.
Foundation type: Independent foundation.

Financial data (yr. ended 9/30/05): Assets, $2,684,760 (M); expenditures, $663,348; qualifying distributions, $629,795; giving activities include $628,350 for 11 grants (high: $500,000; low: $1,000).
Fields of interest: Business school/education; Hospitals (general); Human services; Community development.
Limitations: Applications not accepted. Giving primarily in MA and NY. No grants to individuals.
Application information: Contributes only to pre-selected organizations.
Trustees: David W. Blood; Richard W. Sabo; Barry L. Zubrow.
EIN: 134085189
Selected grants: The following grants were reported in 2004.
$50,000 to New York Restoration Project, New York, NY.
$1,800 to Habitat for Humanity New York City, Brooklyn, NY.

7117
Taconic Foundation, Inc.
c/o JPMorgan Private Bank, N.A., Philanthropic Svcs., NY1-N040
345 Park Ave., 4th Fl.
New York, NY 10154
FAX: (212) 464-2305; Contact for Affordable Housing and Community Development: Megan Watkins, tel.: (212) 464-2440, e-mail: megan.l.watkins@jpmorgan.com; Contact for Youth Development: Lisa Philp, tel.: (212) 464-2467, e-mail: philp_lisa@jpmorgan.com; URL: http://foundationcenter.org/grantmaker/taconic/

Incorporated in 1958 in DE.
Donors: Stephen R. Currier†; Mrs. Stephen R. Currier†.
Foundation type: Independent foundation.
Financial data (yr. ended 12/31/04): Assets, $12,423,065 (M); expenditures, $1,114,027; qualifying distributions, $1,020,579; giving activities include $790,000 for 43 grants (high: $50,000; low: $2,500).
Purpose and activities: The foundation supports organizations working in the areas of housing and community development, equality of opportunity, and youth development.
Fields of interest: Housing/shelter, development; Children/youth, services; Children, foster care; Civil rights, equal rights; Community development.
Type of support: General/operating support; Continuing support; Program development.
Limitations: Giving primarily in the New York, NY, area. No support for higher education, arts and cultural programs, elderly or international programs, crime and justice, health, medicine, mental health, ecology and the environment, individual economic development projects, or local community programs outside New York City. No grants to individuals, or for building or endowment funds, mass media, scholarships, or fellowships; grants rarely made for research; no loans.
Publications: Application guidelines; Grants list.
Application information: Accepts New York/New Jersey area Common Application Form. See foundation Web site for application guidelines. Application form not required.
  Initial approach: Letter or telephone to request complete guidelines
  Copies of proposal: 1
  Deadline(s): Feb. 1, June 1, and Sept. 1

Board meeting date(s): 3 times per year
Final notification: 3 to 4 months
Trustees: L.F. Boker Doyle; Alan J. Dworsky; Jane Lee Eddy; Melvin A. Mister; John G. Simon; Hildy J. Simmons; Oliver Wesson; Veronica White.
EIN: 131873668
Selected grants: The following grants were reported in 2005.
$30,000 to Partnership for After School Education, New York, NY. For mentoring component of Summer Learning initiative.
$25,000 to ACCION New York, New York, NY. For general operating support.
$25,000 to Lawyers Alliance for New York, New York, NY. For business law services to organizations involved in community development.
$20,000 to Low Income Investment Fund, New York, NY.
$20,000 to Neighborhood Economic Development Advocacy Project, New York, NY. For general operating support.
$20,000 to Neighborhood Family Services Coalition, New York, NY. For advocacy efforts for youth employment and needs of older youth.
$20,000 to Southern Center for Human Rights, Atlanta, GA. For general operating support.
$20,000 to Urban Homesteading Assistance Board (UHAB), New York, NY. To plan to deliver and sustain tenant capacity-building services.
$15,000 to Brotherhood/Sister Sol, New York, NY. For general operating support.
$15,000 to Legal Outreach, New York, NY. For College Bound program.

7118
J. T. Tai & Company Foundation, Inc. ✧
18 E. 67th St.
New York, NY   10021

Incorporated in 1983 in DE.
Donors: Jun Tsei Tai, Inc.; J.T. Tai & Co.
Foundation type: Independent foundation.
Financial data (yr. ended 12/31/03): Assets, $29,978,192 (M); expenditures, $1,629,490; qualifying distributions, $1,358,079; giving activities include $1,309,574 for 60 grants (high: $100,000; low: $2,260).
Purpose and activities: Giving primarily for higher education and health care.
Fields of interest: Higher education; Medical school/education; Health care.
Type of support: General/operating support.
Limitations: Applications not accepted. Giving on a national basis. No grants to individuals.
Application information: Contributes only to pre-selected organizations.
Officers and Directors:* F. Richard Hsu,* Pres.; Y.C. Chen,* Secy.; Lita W. Chang; Ming Chen Hsu.
EIN: 133157279
Selected grants: The following grants were reported in 2003.
$100,000 to Childrens Hospital Foundation.
$37,597 to Columbia University, New York, NY.
$36,000 to Johns Hopkins University, Baltimore, MD.
$35,000 to Cornell University, Ithaca, NY.
$35,000 to Harvard University, Cambridge, MA.
$30,000 to Boston University, Boston, MA.
$30,000 to Brown University, Providence, RI.
$30,000 to Dartmouth College, Hanover, NH.
$25,000 to Georgetown University, DC.

$20,000 to Memorial Sloan-Kettering Cancer Center, New York, NY.

7119
Tamarind Foundation, Inc. ▼ ✧
(formerly Helaine Heilbrunn Lerner Fund, Inc.)
c/o O'Connor Davies Munns & Dobbins, LLP
60 E. 42nd St.
New York, NY   10165

Established in 1999 in DE and NY.
Donors: Robert Heilbrunn†; Helaine Lerner.
Foundation type: Independent foundation.
Financial data (yr. ended 12/31/04): Assets, $61,434,352 (M); expenditures, $6,721,756; qualifying distributions, $6,704,915; giving activities include $6,691,462 for 40 grants (high: $1,905,945; low: $120; average: $1,000–$600,000).
Purpose and activities: Giving primarily for the environment.
Fields of interest: Environment.
Limitations: Applications not accepted. No grants to individuals.
Application information: Contributes only to pre-selected organizations.
Officer: Helaine Lerner, Pres.
EIN: 134082873
Selected grants: The following grants were reported in 2004.
$2,626,807 to Global Resource Action Center for the Environment (GRACE), New York, NY. 2 grants: $1,905,945 (For general support), $720,862 (For general support. Grant made in form of stock).
$1,153,500 to Johns Hopkins University, Baltimore, MD. 2 grants: $600,000, $553,500 (For general support. Grant made in form of stock).
$944,845 to Rockefeller University, New York, NY. For general support. Grant made in form of stock.
$789,429 to Jewish Communal Fund of New York, New York, NY. 2 grants: $254,604 (For general support), $534,825 (For general support. Grant made in form of stock).
$211,782 to Long Island University, C. W. Post Center, Brookville, NY. For general support.
$15,165 to Sustainable Harvest International, Surry, ME. For general support.
$1,000 to Environmental Working Group, DC. For general support.

7120
Tanaka Memorial Foundation, Inc. ✧
230 Park Ave., 110th Fl.
New York, NY   10017   (212) 551-1778
Contact: Kenji Tanaka, Chair.

Established in 1991 in NY.
Donor: Tanaka Ikubikai Educational Corp.
Foundation type: Independent foundation.
Financial data (yr. ended 6/30/05): Assets, $17,849,959 (M); expenditures, $1,033,954; qualifying distributions, $1,033,954; giving activities include $684,000 for 26 grants (high: $108,000; low: $3,000).
Purpose and activities: Giving primarily for higher education, including support for Asian studies through programs and scholarship funds, arts, and human services.

Fields of interest: Performing arts; Higher education; Human services; Children/youth, services; International affairs, goodwill promotion.
International interests: United Kingdom.
Type of support: General/operating support; Capital campaigns; Endowments; Scholarship funds.
Limitations: Giving on a national and international basis, with emphasis on New York, NY and England. No grants to individuals.
Application information: Application form not required.
Initial approach: Proposal
Deadline(s): None
Officers and Directors:* Kenji Tanaka,* Chair.; Taeko Tanaka,* Vice-Chair.; Makiko Tanaka,* Pres.; Kimiko Tanaka,* V.P.; Takeshi Hashimoto, Secy.; Tokiwa Morimoto, Treas.; Kiyoshi Okada; Yoshihiro Tajima; Takeshi Ueshima.
EIN: 110235010

7121
Tandon Family Foundation, Inc. ✧ ☆
c/o Brucia & Co
366 Madison Ave.
New York, NY   10017

Donor: Chandrika Tandon.
Foundation type: Independent foundation.
Financial data (yr. ended 12/31/05): Assets, $384,250 (M); gifts received, $251,480; expenditures, $620,057; qualifying distributions, $615,005; giving activities include $615,005 for 5 grants (high: $255,000; low: $10,001).
Fields of interest: Arts; Education.
Directors: Martin Baharestani; Chandrika Tandon; Ranjan Tandon.
EIN: 043744965

7122
The Tang Fund ✧
600 5th Ave., 8th Fl.
New York, NY   10020
Contact: Oscar L. Tang, Pres.

Established in 1984 in NY.
Donors: Oscar L. Tang; Reich & Tang; Robert F. Hoerle; and members of the Tang family.
Foundation type: Independent foundation.
Financial data (yr. ended 11/30/04): Assets, $43,661,843 (M); gifts received, $523,977; expenditures, $3,431,464; qualifying distributions, $3,280,416; giving activities include $3,280,416 for 58 grants (high: $1,000,000; low: $100).
Purpose and activities: Giving primarily for higher and secondary education; support also for cultural programs and community development.
Fields of interest: Arts; Secondary school/education; Higher education; International affairs, goodwill promotion; Community development.
International interests: China.
Limitations: Applications not accepted. Giving on a national basis. No grants to individuals.
Application information: Contributes only to pre-selected organizations.
Officers and Directors:* Oscar L. Tang,* Pres. and Treas.; Gwenn S. Winkhaus, Secy.; Tracy L. Tang.
EIN: 133256295

7123
Tarnopol Family Foundation, Inc. ✧
(formerly Michael & Lynne Tarnopol Foundation, Inc.)
c/o Bear Stearns & Co.
383 Madison Ave.
New York, NY   10179

Established in 1969 in NY.
Donors: Michael Tarnopol†; Lynne Tarnopol; The Monterey Fund, Inc.
Foundation type: Independent foundation.
Financial data (yr. ended 12/31/04): Assets, $662,972 (M); gifts received, $441,725; expenditures, $413,318; qualifying distributions, $405,188; giving activities include $405,188 for 112 grants (high: $100,000; low: $42).
Purpose and activities: Giving primarily for education, Jewish organizations, and health care.
Fields of interest: Museums (ethnic/folk arts); Performing arts centers; Higher education; Medical school/education; Hospitals (general); Health organizations, association; Disasters, fire prevention/control; Human services; Jewish federated giving programs; Jewish agencies & temples.
Limitations: Applications not accepted. Giving primarily in New York, NY, and Philadelphia, PA. No grants to individuals.
Application information: Contributes only to pre-selected organizations. Unsolicited requests for funds not accepted.
Officers and Directors:* Lynne Tarnopol,* V.P.; Joel S. Ehrenkranz,* Secy.
EIN: 132626280

7124
Task Foundation, Inc. ✧
(formerly Consumer Action Council on Collective Purchasing, Inc.)
c/o Phil Weinper
20 S. Bayles Ave.
Port Washington, NY   11050   (516) 883-7711
Contact: Theodore W. Kheel, Pres.

Established around 1992.
Donors: Ann S. Kheel†; Theodore W. Kheel.
Foundation type: Independent foundation.
Financial data (yr. ended 12/31/03): Assets, $7,663,386 (M); gifts received, $90,000; expenditures, $1,547,347; qualifying distributions, $1,031,597; giving activities include $815,940 for 29 grants (high: $426,000; low: $50).
Purpose and activities: Giving primarily for higher education.
Fields of interest: Higher education; Environment, natural resources; Environment; Health care; Health organizations, association; Youth, services; Community development; Public affairs.
Limitations: Giving primarily in NY. No grants to individuals.
Application information: Application form not required.
Officers: Theodore W. Kheel, Pres.; Robert Kheel, Secy.
EIN: 131968353
Selected grants: The following grants were reported in 2003.
$426,000 to Persistence Foundation, Eagle Bridge, NY.
$270,000 to Carriage House Center on Global Issues, New York, NY.
$10,000 to Earth Pledge Foundation, New York, NY.
$4,000 to Americas Society, New York, NY.

$2,000 to Central Park Conservancy, New York, NY.
$2,000 to Rainforest Alliance, New York, NY.
$1,000 to Columbia University, New York, NY.
$500 to Riverdale Neighborhood House, Bronx, NY.
$400 to Cornell University, Ithaca, NY.
$100 to Literacy Partners, New York, NY.

7125
TBF Charitable Trust ✧
(formerly The Berkowitz Family Charitable Trust)
1665 47th St.
Brooklyn, NY   11204-1142

Established in 1992 in NY and NJ.
Donors: Israel Berkowitz; Leopold Berkowitz; Morris Berkowitz; Frady Zyskind; Khal Binyomin Dovid; Brooklyn Queens Nursing Home; Yeshiva Novominsk.
Foundation type: Independent foundation.
Financial data (yr. ended 12/31/05): Assets, $11,047,904 (M); gifts received, $1,242,700; expenditures, $677,073; qualifying distributions, $638,479; giving activities include $638,479 for 150 grants (high: $96,850; low: $36).
Purpose and activities: Giving primarily to Jewish agencies, temples, and schools.
Fields of interest: Education; Jewish agencies & temples.
Limitations: Applications not accepted. Giving primarily in Brooklyn, NY. No grants to individuals.
Application information: Contributes only to pre-selected organizations.
Trustees: Israel Berkowitz; Leopold Berkowitz; Morris Berkowitz; Frady Zyskind.
EIN: 226585269

7126
The Teagle Foundation ▼ ✧
10 Rockefeller Plz., Rm. 920
New York, NY   10020-1903   (212) 373-1970
Contact: Megan Bray, Office Asst.
E-mail: mbray@teaglefoundation.org; URL: http://www.teaglefoundation.org/intro.htm

Incorporated in 1944 in CT.
Donors: Walter C. Teagle†; Rowena Lee Teagle†; Walter C. Teagle, Jr.†.
Foundation type: Independent foundation.
Financial data (yr. ended 6/30/04): Assets, $141,768,589 (M); expenditures, $10,835,774; qualifying distributions, $9,330,336; giving activities include $7,871,624 for 78 grants, and $86,115 for employee matching gifts.
Purpose and activities: The goal of the Teagle Foundation is to mobilize resources, financial and intellectual, to help students "catch fire" intellectually through a challenging, wide-ranging and enriching college education. At this time, the foundation is only focusing on higher education.
Fields of interest: Arts education; Higher education; Children/youth, services.
Type of support: Continuing support; Program development; Curriculum development; Consulting services; Employee matching gifts; Matching/challenge support.
Limitations: Applications not accepted. Giving limited to the U.S. No grants to community organizations outside New York City. No grants to U.S. organizations for foreign programmatic activities. No grants to individuals; no loans.
Publications: Annual report.

Application information: Unsolicited proposals are no longer accepted. Please check the foundation's program development and implementation page on its Web site for more information.
Board meeting date(s): Feb., May, and Nov.
Officers and Directors:* John S. Chalsty,* Chair.; W. Robert Connor, Ph.D.*, C.E.O. and Pres.; Donna Heiland, V.P. and Secy.; Eli Weinberg, Treas.; Diana Kandasamy, Cont.; Kenneth P. Cohen; Sol Gittleman; William Chester Jordan; Jayne Keith; Roland M. Machold; Mary Patterson McPherson; Richard L. Morrill; Philip B. Pool, Jr.; Barbara Paul Robinson; Anne M. Tatlock; Walter C. Teagle III; Stephen H. Weiss; Pauline Yu.
Number of staff: 3 full-time professional; 1 full-time support.
EIN: 131773645

7127
The Teddy Foundation ✧
(formerly Evelyn Donaldson Charitable Foundation)
c/o Brown Brothers Harriman Trust Co., LLP
140 Broadway, 4th Fl.
New York, NY   10005

Established in 1999 in DE.
Donor: Evelyn Donaldson†.
Foundation type: Independent foundation.
Financial data (yr. ended 12/31/04): Assets, $19,083,114 (M); expenditures, $1,010,375; qualifying distributions, $925,762; giving activities include $925,762 for 34 grants (high: $207,754; low: $5,000).
Purpose and activities: Giving primarily for education, health associations, particularly a lyme disease association, and for human services.
Fields of interest: Museums; Education; Hospitals (general); Health organizations, association; Human services.
Limitations: Applications not accepted. Giving on a national basis. No grants to individuals.
Application information: Contributes only to pre-selected organizations.
Trustees: Elise Donaldson Bulger; Charlotte Donaldson D'Arcy; Judith Donaldson Jefferis.
EIN: 516511786

7128
Richard and Mary Templeton
Foundation ✧ ☆
c/o Ayco Co.
P.O. Box 15014
Albany, NY   12212-5014

Established in 2003 in TX.
Donors: Mary Templeton; Richard Templeton.
Foundation type: Independent foundation.
Financial data (yr. ended 12/31/05): Assets, $6,362,642 (M); expenditures, $366,840; qualifying distributions, $366,250; giving activities include $366,250 for 29 grants (high: $100,000; low: $300).
Fields of interest: Education; Human services; Federated giving programs.
Limitations: Applications not accepted. Giving primarily in TX. No grants to individuals.
Application information: Contributes only to pre-selected organizations.
Trustees: Mary Templeton; Richard Templeton.
EIN: 200321164

7129
Tennenbaum Family Foundation Trust ✧
c/o Breindy Melnicke
1637 50th St.
Brooklyn, NY 11204

Established in 1994 in NY.
Donor: Michael and Pola Tenenbaum Trust.
Foundation type: Independent foundation.
Financial data (yr. ended 12/31/03): Assets,
$516,044 (M); gifts received, $850,000;
expenditures, $402,056; qualifying distributions,
$402,047; giving activities include $390,156 for 25
+ grants (high: $227,000).
Purpose and activities: Giving primarily for Jewish
agencies, temples, and yeshivas.
Fields of interest: Elementary/secondary
education; Jewish agencies & temples.
Type of support: General/operating support.
Limitations: Applications not accepted. Giving
primarily in Brooklyn, NY. No grants to individuals.
Application information: Contributes only to
pre-selected organizations.
Trustees: Briendy Melnicke; Morris Tennenbaum.
EIN: 116431567

7130
Terumah Foundation, Inc. ✧
c/o Phillipe Katz, Secy.
160 Broadway, 1st Fl.
New York, NY 10038 (212) 349-2875

Established in 1993 in NY.
Donors: Moses Marx; Max Czapski†; Daniel Stein.
Foundation type: Independent foundation.
Financial data (yr. ended 12/31/05): Assets,
$18,028,987 (M); gifts received, $4,507,500;
expenditures, $3,027,363; qualifying distributions,
$2,889,886; giving activities include $2,886,630
for 115 grants (high: $500,000; low: $100).
Purpose and activities: Giving primarily to Jewish
organizations and temples.
Fields of interest: Elementary/secondary
education; Jewish agencies & temples.
Limitations: Applications not accepted. Giving
primarily in NY. No grants to individuals.
Application information: Contributes only to
pre-selected organizations.
Officers and Directors: * Moses Marx,* Pres.;
Joseph Fink,* V.P.; Phillipe Katz,* Secy.; Magda
Marx,* Treas.; Eva Fink; Esther Katz.
EIN: 133694180
Selected grants: The following grants were reported
in 2005.
$525,000 to Yeshiva University, New York, NY. 2
  grants: $500,000, $25,000
$100,000 to Mesorah Heritage Foundation,
  Brooklyn, NY.
$50,000 to Bonei Olam, Brooklyn, NY.
$47,500 to Young Israel of Riverdale, Bronx, NY. 3
  grants: $2,500, $20,000, $25,000
$25,000 to Agudath Israel of America, New York,
  NY.
$10,000 to Ozar Hatorah, New York, NY.
$2,000 to Yeshiva of Brooklyn, Brooklyn, NY.

7131
The Textor Family Foundation ✧
c/o BCRS Associates, LLP
100 Wall St., 11th Fl.
New York, NY 10005

Established in 1991 in NY.
Donors: Donald F. Textor; Elaine R. Textor.
Foundation type: Independent foundation.
Financial data (yr. ended 5/31/05): Assets,
$11,401,648 (M); gifts received, $524,325;
expenditures, $444,186; qualifying distributions,
$441,347; giving activities include $439,477 for 33
grants (high: $100,000; low: $500).
Purpose and activities: Giving primarily for higher
and other education, and to Roman Catholic
churches and dioceses.
Fields of interest: Arts; Elementary/secondary
education; Higher education; Education; Human
services; Children, services; Community
development; Roman Catholic agencies & churches.
Limitations: Applications not accepted. Giving
primarily in NY; funding also in Bethlehem, PA. No
contributions, grants, gifts, loans or scholarships to
individuals.
Application information: Contributes only to
pre-selected organizations.
Trustees: Donald F. Textor; Elaine R. Textor.
EIN: 133637703
Selected grants: The following grants were reported
in 2005.
$100,000 to Lehigh University, Bethlehem, PA.
$45,000 to Ithaca College, Ithaca, NY. 2 grants:
  $20,000, $25,000
$25,000 to Chapin School, New York, NY.
$25,000 to Futures in Education Foundation,
  Brooklyn, NY.
$22,000 to Friends Academy, Locust Valley, NY.
$20,000 to Church of the Resurrection, Rye, NY.
$10,000 to Boys and Girls Harbor, Houston, TX.
$10,000 to Fund for Teachers, Houston, TX.
$10,000 to Salvation Army, Yonkers, NY.

7132
**Third Millennium Charitable and Cultural
  Foundation** ✧
340 W. 12th St.
New York, NY 10014
Contact: Marco Stoffel, Pres.
FAX: (212) 421-5243; E-mail: tmf.usa@verizon.net;
URL: http://www.seedsoftolerance.org

Established in 1999 in NY.
Donors: Rainer Blickle; Colleen Investments, LLC.
Foundation type: Independent foundation.
Financial data (yr. ended 12/31/03): Assets,
$1,909,843 (M); gifts received, $4,724,220;
expenditures, $1,296,511; qualifying distributions,
$1,286,513; giving activities include $1,171,838
for 32 grants (high: $150,000; low: $1,800).
Purpose and activities: The foundation's principal
goal is to support initiatives designed to promote
tolerance, particularly among the young. Its four
main areas of giving are: human rights protection,
arts education, school curricula, and anti-bias
programs.
Fields of interest: International human rights.
Limitations: Giving on a national and an
international basis. No grants to individuals.
Application information: Letter of inquiry should
include focus of request (either education or human
rights). Application guidelines available on
foundation Web site.
  Initial approach: Letter of inquiry (not exceeding 3
  pages) sent by regular mail or E-mail
Officers and Directors: * Marco Stoffel,* Pres.;
Raymond Merritt,* Secy.-Treas.
EIN: 134072609

Selected grants: The following grants were reported
in 2003.
$122,188 to Harvard University, Cambridge, MA.
  For Understanding the Roots of Tolerance and
  Prejudice program.
$50,000 to Museum of Modern Art, New York, NY.
  For educational programs.
$50,000 to Studio in a School Association, New
  York, NY. For general support.
$25,000 to Brooklyn Institute of Arts and Sciences,
  Brooklyn, NY. For annual support.
$25,000 to Educators for Social Responsibility,
  Cambridge, MA. For general support.
$25,000 to Facing History and Ourselves National
  Foundation, New York, NY. For general support.
$12,500 to Winston Churchill Foundation of the
  United States, New York, NY. For scholarships.
$10,000 to Creative Time, New York, NY. For arts
  education for the public.
$10,000 to Humanity in Action, New York, NY. For
  student fellows program.
$5,000 to International Center of Photography, New
  York, NY. For Only Skin Deep education
  programs.

7133
The Daniel K. Thorne Foundation, Inc. ✧
c/o Stroock & Stroock
142 W. 57th St., 16th Fl.
New York, NY 10019

Established in 1996 in NY.
Donor: Daniel K. Thorne.
Foundation type: Independent foundation.
Financial data (yr. ended 12/31/03): Assets,
$8,970,870 (M); expenditures, $851,674;
qualifying distributions, $839,993; giving activities
include $822,200 for 36 grants (high: $250,000;
low: $500).
Purpose and activities: Giving for natural resource
conservation.
Fields of interest: Environment, natural resources.
Type of support: Continuing support; Emergency
funds; Matching/challenge support.
Limitations: Applications not accepted. Giving on a
national basis.
Application information: Unsolicited requests for
funds not accepted.
  Board meeting date(s): Mar., June, Oct. and Dec.
  15
Officers and Directors: * Daniel K. Thorne,* Pres.
and Treas.; Theodore S. Lynn,* Secy.; Alexandra T.
Thorne.
Number of staff: 1 part-time support.
EIN: 133857951
Selected grants: The following grants were reported
in 2003.
$318,000 to National Trust for Historic
  Preservation, DC. 2 grants: $68,000 (For general
  support of national trust program), $250,000
  (For National Intervention Fund).
$200,000 to South Street Seaport Museum, New
  York, NY. For Schermerhorn Row New Museum
  project.
$50,000 to South Carolina Coastal Conservation
  League, Charleston, SC. For capital support.
$50,000 to Wildlife Conservation Society, Bronx,
  NY. For Albertine Rift Program.
$40,000 to Dian Fossey Gorilla Fund International,
  Atlanta, GA. For conservation action program and
  golden monkey.
$22,000 to Fundacion Amistad, East Hampton, NY.
  For Palacio Iznaga.

$20,000 to Galveston Historical Foundation, Galveston, TX. For annual fund.
$20,000 to Mystic Seaport Museum, Mystic, CT. For annual fund and Williams and/Mystic campaign.
$15,000 to Island Institute, Rockland, ME. For island fellows program.

7134
The Thornton Foundation ✧

c/o Goldman Sachs - Family Office
1 New York Plz., 40th Fl.
New York, NY 10004

Established in 1989 in NY.
Donor: John L. Thornton.
Foundation type: Independent foundation.
Financial data (yr. ended 6/30/05): Assets, $8,091,481 (M); expenditures, $1,709,780; qualifying distributions, $1,706,888; giving activities include $1,706,888 for 14 grants (high: $980,937; low: $10,000).
Fields of interest: Arts; Education; Human services.
Type of support: General/operating support.
Limitations: Applications not accepted. Giving primarily in CT and NY. No grants to individuals.
Application information: Contributes only to pre-selected organizations.
Trustees: Robert S. Harrison; John L. Thornton.
EIN: 133543268
Selected grants: The following grants were reported in 2005.
$130,000 to Asia Society, New York, NY. 3 grants: $50,000, $50,000, $30,000
$100,000 to Acumen Fund, New York, NY.
$60,000 to Hotchkiss School, Lakeville, CT.
$25,000 to American Friends of Bilderberg, New York, NY.
$25,000 to Aspen Institute, Queenstown, MD.
$25,000 to Atlantic Salmon Federation, Calais, ME.

7135
Three Little Pigs Foundation ✧

c/o William E. Ford
1060 5th Ave., Apt. 8B
New York, NY 10128

Established in 2003 in NY.
Donor: William E. Ford.
Foundation type: Independent foundation.
Financial data (yr. ended 12/31/05): Assets, $153,888 (M); gifts received, $298,923; expenditures, $441,143; qualifying distributions, $435,000; giving activities include $435,000 for 25 grants (high: $115,000; low: $1,000).
Purpose and activities: Giving primarily for education; funding also for cancer research, natural resource conservation, and museums.
Fields of interest: Museums; Higher education; Education; Environment, natural resources; Cancer research.
Limitations: Applications not accepted. Giving primarily in New York, NY; funding also in CA, with emphasis on Stanford, and MA. No grants to individuals.
Application information: Contributes only to pre-selected organizations.
Officers: William E. Ford, Pres.; Richard Gold, Secy.
EIN: 200512645

7136
The Tianaderrah Foundation ✧

Butternut Rd.
P.O. Box 139
Unadilla, NY 13849 (607) 369-9401
Contact: Robert L. Gipson, Tr.

Established in 1996 in NY.
Donor: Robert L. Gipson.
Foundation type: Independent foundation.
Financial data (yr. ended 12/31/05): Assets, $22,557,704 (M); gifts received, $1,129,800; expenditures, $845,981; qualifying distributions, $821,163; giving activities include $819,050 for 55 grants (high: $100,000; low: $250).
Fields of interest: Historic preservation/historical societies; Education; Health organizations, association; Community development.
Limitations: Giving primarily in NY state; some funding nationally. No grants to individuals.
Application information:
Initial approach: Letter
Deadline(s): None
Trustees: Robert L. Gipson; Thomas L. Gipson; Sally Gipson Tully.
EIN: 166445118
Selected grants: The following grants were reported in 2004.
$100,000 to Bulgarian American Society, Bulgaria.
$68,000 to Princeton University, Princeton, NJ.
$35,000 to Massachusetts Institute of Technology, Cambridge, MA.
$15,000 to Sweet Briar College, Sweet Briar, VA.
$12,000 to Cornell University, Ithaca, NY.
$10,000 to Farmers Museum, Cooperstown, NY.
$10,000 to Metropolitan Museum of Art, New York, NY.
$10,000 to Williamstown Art Conservation Center, Williamstown, MA.
$5,000 to American University in Bulgaria, DC.
$5,000 to Anne Frank Center USA, New York, NY.

7137
The Tiffany & Co. Foundation ✧

600 Madison Ave.
New York, NY 10022 (212) 230-6591
Contact: Fernanda M. Kellogg, Pres.
URL: http://www.tiffanyandcofoundation.org

Established in 2000 in NY.
Donor: Tiffany & Co.
Foundation type: Company-sponsored foundation.
Financial data (yr. ended 1/31/06): Assets, $28,690,856 (M); expenditures, $4,881,502; qualifying distributions, $4,719,250; giving activities include $4,718,500 for 31 grants (high: $1,100,000; low: $10,000).
Purpose and activities: The foundation supports organizations involved with arts and culture and the environment.
Fields of interest: Arts, public education; Visual arts, art conservation; Arts, artist's services; Arts; Environment, research; Environment, natural resources; Environment, water resources; Environment, land resources; Environment.
Type of support: Management development/capacity building; Program development; Research.
Limitations: Giving on a national basis. No support for religious, political, social, or fraternal organizations or athletic teams. No grants to individuals, or for capital campaigns, fundraising benefits or events, or athletic events.

Application information: Letters of inquiry should be no longer than 2 to 3 pages. Application form not required.
Initial approach: Letter of inquiry
Copies of proposal: 1
Deadline(s): Rolling
Board meeting date(s): Jan. and July
Officers and Directors:* Fernanda M. Kellogg,* Pres.; James N. Fernandez,* Exec. V.P.; James E. Quinn, Exec. V.P.; Patrick B. Dorsey,* Secy.; Michael W. Connolly, Treas.; Michael J. Kowalski.
EIN: 134096178

7138
The Louis Comfort Tiffany Foundation ✧ ☆

c/o Artists Space
38 Greene St., 3rd Fl.
New York, NY 10013
Contact: Angela Westwater, Pres.

Association established in 1918 in NY.
Donor: Louis Comfort Tiffany†.
Foundation type: Independent foundation.
Financial data (yr. ended 12/31/05): Assets, $7,757,797 (M); expenditures, $699,684; qualifying distributions, $600,000; giving activities include $600,000 for grants.
Purpose and activities: To encourage talented and advanced artists of the fine arts (painting, sculpture, and the graphic arts) and the industrial crafts (ceramics, textile design, glass design, metal work) by awarding a limited number of grants biannually.
Fields of interest: Visual arts; Performing arts; Arts.
Type of support: Grants to individuals.
Limitations: Applications not accepted. Giving on a national basis. No grants for general support or capital or endowment funds.
Application information: Awards are by nomination only.
Officers: Angela Westwater, Pres.; Gerard Jones, Secy.; Robert Shapiro, Treas.
EIN: 131689389

7139
Tiger Foundation ▼

101 Park Ave., 48th Fl.
New York, NY 10178 (212) 984-2565
Contact: Phoebe Boyer, Exec. Dir.
FAX: (212) 949-9778;
E-mail: info@tigerfoundation.org; *URL:* http://www.tigerfoundation.org

Established in 1989 in NY.
Donors: Julian H. Robertson, Jr.; Tiger Management LLC employees.
Foundation type: Independent foundation.
Financial data (yr. ended 6/30/05): Assets, $23,374,538 (M); gifts received, $11,243,849; expenditures, $8,105,269; qualifying distributions, $7,957,774; giving activities include $7,244,150 for 77 grants (high: $225,000; low: $3,150; average: $50,000–$100,000), and $70,351 for 2 foundation-administered programs.
Purpose and activities: Giving provided to organizations working to break the cycle of poverty in New York City, rather than those which merely alleviate its symptoms. Seeking to provide families with the tools necessary to attain self-sufficiency and build productive lives. To this end, support is to a variety of educational, vocational, and social service and youth development programs designed

to catch children and families before they slip into a cycle of poverty and despair, as well as those programs designed to enable individuals to end their dependence on public assistance.

Fields of interest: Education; Employment, services; Youth development, services; Children/youth, services; Family services; Human services; Economically disadvantaged.

Type of support: Program-related investments/ loans; General/operating support; Continuing support; Management development/capacity building; Program development; Technical assistance; Program evaluation.

Limitations: Giving primarily in New York, NY. No support for political organizations or public policy. No grants to individuals, or for endowments, annual or capital campaigns, benefits, legal aid, obligations or debt.

Publications: Application guidelines; Grants list.

Application information: Foundation accepts New York/New Jersey Common application form with supplements. Application form required.

   Initial approach: 3-page letter
   Copies of proposal: 1
   Deadline(s): None
   Board meeting date(s): Quarterly

Officer: Phoebe Boyer, Exec. Dir.

Trustees: Charlie Anderson; Edna Beaudelte; Rob Butler; Gil Caffray; Trent Carmichael; Scott Chace; Chase Coleman; Quincy Fennebresque; Laurel FitzPatrick; William R. Goodwell; John A. Griffin; Mike Hodge; Bill Hwang; Kevin Hipp; Tim Jenkins; Ted Kang; Michael Kelly; Kevin Kenny; James Lee; Jon Locker; John Lykouretzos; James Lyle; Pat McCormack; Roberto Mignone; Matt Ngai; Jerry Norris; Brian Olson; Jill Olson; Steven C. Olson; Hence Orme; David Ott; Stephen Prince; Alex Rafal; Steven Rodgers; Shiva Sarram; Dave Saunders; Tim Schilt; Chris Schumway; Scott Shleifer; Carter Simonds; Scott Sinclair; Marco Tablada; Bill Welsh; Tiger Williams; Robert Williamson; Teddy Wong; Hope Woodhouse.

Number of staff: 4 full-time professional.

EIN: 133555671

Selected grants: The following grants were reported in 2005.

$300,000 to Door - A Center of Alternatives, New York, NY. For Career Pathways Program.

$225,000 to Teach for America, New York, NY. For general support.

$200,000 to Boys Club of New York, New York, NY. For After School Academy.

$200,000 to Good Shepherd Services, New York, NY. For Chelsea Foyer and South Brooklyn Community High School.

$200,000 to Opportunities for a Better Tomorrow, Brooklyn, NY. For general support.

$175,000 to Classroom, Inc., New York, NY. For general support.

$150,000 to Child Care, Inc., New York, NY. For Quality of Care Initiative.

$100,000 to Pius XII Youth and Family Services, Bronx, NY. For Now What Community Employment Program, which provides training in Microsoft Office, GED preparation, internships, and job development to young adults.

$100,000 to Turnaround for Children, New York, NY. For general support.

$80,000 to Inwood House, New York, NY. For Teen Choice Program.

7140
The Tikvah Fund ▼ ✧
1345 Ave. of the Americas
New York, NY   10105-0096   (212) 756-4385
Contact: Roger Hertog, Chair.

Established in 1992 in NY.

Donor: Zalman C. Bernstein†.

Foundation type: Independent foundation.

Financial data (yr. ended 12/31/04): Assets, $146,328,817 (M); gifts received, $21,500,000; expenditures, $7,252,687; qualifying distributions, $8,316,135; giving activities include $7,011,396 for 2 grants (high: $5,500,000; low: $1,511,396).

Purpose and activities: Giving primarily for Jewish affairs. Makes grants and program-related investments to companies located in areas of high unemployment or development in Israel, and to companies that are owned by or employ new immigrants or veteran soldiers.

Fields of interest: Religion, public policy; Jewish agencies & temples.

International interests: Israel.

Type of support: Program-related investments/ loans.

Limitations: Applications not accepted. Giving primarily in Israel.

Application information: Contributes only to pre-selected organizations.

Officers and Directors: * Roger Hertog,* Chair.; Christina Restivo, Secy.; Arthur W. Fried,* C.F.O.; Kenneth A. Abramowitz; Mem Dryan Bernstein; Morris Smith; David Stone.

Trustee: Alliance Capital Management Corp.

EIN: 133676152

Selected grants: The following grants were reported in 2004.

$5,500,000 to Shalem Center, Jerusalem, Israel. For general support.

$1,511,396 to Shalem Foundation, New York, NY. For general support.

7141
The Tilles Family Foundation ✧
7600 Jericho Tpke., Ste. LL4
Woodbury, NY   11797

Established in 1997 in NY.

Donors: Rose Tilles; Rose Tilles Revocable Trust.

Foundation type: Independent foundation.

Financial data (yr. ended 12/31/05): Assets, $171,774 (M); gifts received, $920,124; expenditures, $817,730; qualifying distributions, $817,630; giving activities include $817,630 for 50 grants (high: $253,333; low: $25).

Purpose and activities: Giving for education, youth services, health and medical services, and to Jewish organizations.

Fields of interest: Arts; Higher education; Health organizations, association; Human services; Children/youth, services; Jewish agencies & temples.

Limitations: Applications not accepted. Giving primarily in NY. No grants to individuals.

Application information: Contributes only to pre-selected organizations.

Officers and Directors: * Roger Tilles,* Pres.; Peter Tilles,* V.P.; Sol Wachtler,* Secy.-Treas.

EIN: 113372816

Selected grants: The following grants were reported in 2004.

$25,250 to Temple Beth-El, Cedarhurst, NY.

$7,500 to Telecare, Uniondale, NY.

$5,500 to Family and Childrens Association, Mineola, NY.

$3,500 to American Jewish Committee, New York, NY.

$3,000 to Cancer Care of Long Island, Woodbury, NY.

$2,500 to Center for Discovery, Harris, NY.

$2,000 to Barrington Stage Company, Sheffield, MA.

$1,000 to YMCA of Long Island, Huntington, NY.

$950 to Chamber Players International, Woodbury, NY.

$925 to American Cancer Society, Atlanta, GA.

7142
Time Warner Foundation ▼ ✧
(formerly AOL Time Warner Foundation)
1 Time Warner Ctr.
New York, NY   10019
URL: http://www.timewarner.com/corp/ citizenship/index.html

Established in 1997 in VA.

Donors: America Online, Inc.; AOL Time Warner Inc.; Time Warner Inc.

Foundation type: Company-sponsored foundation.

Financial data (yr. ended 12/31/03): Assets, $3,165,152 (M); gifts received, $9,294,892; expenditures, $7,498,391; qualifying distributions, $7,498,227; giving activities include $7,241,900 for 2,449 grants (high: $300,000; low: $10).

Purpose and activities: The foundation supports organizations involved with education, youth development, and computer science.

Fields of interest: Media/communications; Elementary school/education; Secondary school/ education; Education; Youth development; Children/youth, services; Computer science.

Type of support: Equipment; Seed money; Curriculum development; Technical assistance.

Limitations: Applications not accepted. Giving on a national basis. No support for political, labor, religious, or fraternal organizations or amateur or professional sports groups. No grants to individuals, or for book publication, film or music production, or capital campaigns.

Application information: Contributes only to pre-selected organizations.

Officers and Directors: * Richard D. Parsons,* Chair. and Pres.; Kathryn Bushkin, Pres.; Michael M. Cavataio, Exec. Dir.; Brian S. Keys, Secy.; Michael C. Sacconaghi, Treas.; Stephen Case; Ken Lerer; Henry McGee; Ken Novack; Lisa Quiroz; Sylvia Rhone; Tom Rutledge; George Vradenburg III; Audrey Weil.

EIN: 541886827

Selected grants: The following grants were reported in 2003.

$1,173,342 to Network for Good, Vienna, VA. 4 grants: $303,596 (For nonprofit effectiveness), $317,407 (For nonprofit effectiveness), $317,407 (For nonprofit effectiveness), $234,932 (For nonprofit effectiveness).

$461,000 to New York University, New York, NY. 2 grants: $230,500 each to Steinhardt School of Education (For education and literacy).

$300,000 to Girls Inc., New York, NY. For education and literacy.

$300,000 to YMCA of the U.S.A., National Council, Chicago, IL. For education and literacy.

$200,000 to National Academy of Television Arts and Sciences, New York, NY. For arts and culture.

$125,000 to Fund for Public Schools, New York, NY. For education and literacy.

7143
The Tinker Foundation Inc. ✧
55 E. 59th St., 21st Fl.
New York, NY 10022 (212) 421-6858
Contact: Renate Rennie, Pres.
FAX: (212) 223-3326; E-mail: tinker@tinker.org†.
for Margaret J Cushing: (212) 421-6858;
URL: http://foundationcenter.org/grantmaker/tinker

Trust established in 1959 in NY; incorporated in 1975 in NY.
Donor: Edward Larocque Tinker†.
Foundation type: Independent foundation.
Financial data (yr. ended 12/31/04): Assets, $78,473,670 (M); expenditures, $3,863,087; qualifying distributions, $3,334,598; giving activities include $2,359,150 for 56 grants (high: $80,000; low: $3,150).
Purpose and activities: Broadly, the purpose of the foundation is to promote better understanding among the peoples of the U.S., Latin America, Portugal and Spain. More specifically, grants are awarded in the areas of: 1) environmental issues, particularly incentive-based environmental activities, and those projects supporting the collaboration of NGOs (Nongovernmental Organizations) corporate interests; 2) projects on governance including the reform of the judicial sector, decentralization, anti-violence and anti-corruption programs, and, in general, assistance to groups promoting transparency and accountability; and 3) economic policy programs concerned with modernization, liberalization and privatization issues.
Fields of interest: Environment, natural resources; Environment; International affairs, foreign policy; International affairs; Marine science; Economics; Political science; Public policy, research; Government/public administration.
International interests: Antarctica; Latin America; Mexico; Portugal; Spain.
Type of support: Program development; Conferences/seminars; Seed money; Research; Matching/challenge support.
Limitations: Giving limited to projects related to Latin America, Spain, Portugal, and Antarctica. No support for projects concerned with health or medical issues or the arts and humanities. No grants to individuals, or for building or endowment funds, equipment, annual campaigns, operating budgets, annual appeals of community funds, or production costs for film, television, and radio projects.
Publications: Application guidelines; Annual report.
Application information: Application form for Institutional grants available on foundation Web site. Application form required.
Initial approach: Letter requesting application procedures
Copies of proposal: 2
Deadline(s): Institutional grants: Mar. 1 for summer meeting and Sept. 1 for winter meeting; Oct. 1 for Field Research Grants
Board meeting date(s): Institutional grants: June and Dec.; Field Research Grants: Dec.
Final notification: Institutional and Field Research grants: 2 weeks after board meetings
Officers and Directors:* Martha T. Muse,* Chair.; Renate Rennie,* Pres.; Richard de J. Osborne,*

Secy.; William R. Chaney; Sally Grooms Cowal; Kenneth R. Maxwell; Susan L. Segal; Alan Stoga.
Number of staff: 4 full-time professional; 1 part-time professional; 1 full-time support.
EIN: 510175449
Selected grants: The following grants were reported in 2004.
$80,000 to Universidad de la Republica de Uruguay, Montevideo, Uruguay. .
$75,000 to Rainforest Alliance, New York, NY.
$70,000 to National Wildlife Federation, Reston, VA.
$69,000 to Columbia University, New York, NY.
$65,000 to Woodrow Wilson International Center for Scholars, DC.
$63,000 to Environmental Law Institute, DC.
$60,000 to Center for Global Development, DC.
$42,000 to Transfair USA, Oakland, CA.
$30,000 to Latin American Studies Association, Pittsburgh, PA.
$15,000 to Cornell University, Ithaca, NY.

7144
The James S. & Merryl H. Tisch Foundation, Inc. ✧ ☆
c/o Mark J. Krinsky, Acct.
655 Madison Ave., 19th Fl.
New York, NY 10021-8043

Established in 1992 in DE and NY.
Donors: Laurence A. Tisch†; James S. Tisch.
Foundation type: Independent foundation.
Financial data (yr. ended 12/31/05): Assets, $13,093,668 (M); gifts received, $1,342,275; expenditures, $1,066,967; qualifying distributions, $1,026,527; giving activities include $1,026,527 for grants.
Purpose and activities: Giving primarily for education, and children and youth services; funding also for the arts, health associations, social services, and Jewish organizations.
Fields of interest: Arts; Education, association; Higher education; Education; Health organizations, association; Human services; Children/youth, services; Jewish federated giving programs; Social sciences, public policy; Jewish agencies & temples.
Limitations: Applications not accepted. Giving primarily in New York, NY. No grants to individuals.
Application information: Contributes only to pre-selected organizations.
Officers: James S. Tisch, Pres.; Merryl H. Tisch, Sr. V.P.; Mark J. Krinsky, V.P.; Thomas M. Steinberg, V.P.; Barry L. Bloom, Secy.-Treas.
EIN: 133693587

7145
Tisch Foundation, Inc. ▼ ✧
655 Madison Ave.
New York, NY 10021-8087 (212) 521-2930
Contact: Mark J. Krinsky, V.P.

Incorporated in 1957 in FL.
Donors: Hotel Americana; Tisch Hotels, Inc.; members of the Tisch family; and closely held corporations.
Foundation type: Independent foundation.
Financial data (yr. ended 12/31/05): Assets, $123,515,492 (M); expenditures, $17,197,078; qualifying distributions, $17,059,298; giving activities include $17,054,837 for 135 grants (high:

$3,000,200; low: $10; average: $1,000–$500,000).
Purpose and activities: Emphasis on higher education, including institutions in Israel, and research-related programs; support also for Jewish organizations and welfare funds, museums, and secondary education.
Fields of interest: Museums; Secondary school/education; Higher education; AIDS; Medical research, institute; Human services; Jewish federated giving programs; Jewish agencies & temples.
International interests: Israel.
Type of support: Continuing support; Building/renovation; Equipment; Research.
Limitations: Applications not accepted. Giving primarily in NY. No grants to individuals, or for endowment funds, scholarships, fellowships, or matching gifts; no loans.
Application information: Contributes only to pre-selected organizations.
Board meeting date(s): Mar., June, Sept., Dec., and as required
Officers and Directors:* Preston R. Tisch,* Pres.; Wilma S. Tisch,* Sr. V.P.; Mark J. Krinsky, V.P.; Thomas M. Steinberg, V.P.; Laurie Tisch Sussman, V.P.; Andrew H. Tisch, V.P.; Daniel R. Tisch, V.P.; James S. Tisch, V.P.; Jonathan M. Tisch, V.P.; Steven E. Tisch, V.P.; Thomas J. Tisch, V.P.; Barry L. Bloom, Secy.-Treas.; Joan H. Tisch.
EIN: 591002844
Selected grants: The following grants were reported in 2005.
$3,000,200 to New York University, New York, NY.
$2,504,260 to UJA-Federation of New York, New York, NY.
$2,198,644 to Museum of Modern Art, New York, NY.
$1,500,671 to Skidmore College, Saratoga Springs, NY.
$1,000,000 to Brown University, Providence, RI.
$600,000 to Dana-Farber Cancer Institute, Boston, MA.
$457,487 to W N Y C Foundation, New York, NY.
$102,000 to Jewish Museum, New York, NY.
$95,000 to New York-Presbyterian Hospital, New York, NY.
$50,000 to Nightingale-Bamford School, New York, NY.

7146
The Alice M. & Thomas J. Tisch Foundation, Inc. ✧
c/o Mark J. Krinsky
655 Madison Ave., 8th Fl.
New York, NY 10021-8043

Established in 1992 in NY and DE.
Donors: Laurence A. Tisch†; Thomas J. Tisch; Wilma S. Tisch.
Foundation type: Independent foundation.
Financial data (yr. ended 12/31/05): Assets, $65,371,361 (M); gifts received, $1,342,275; expenditures, $3,636,231; qualifying distributions, $3,610,544; giving activities include $3,603,672 for 120 grants (high: $765,000; low: $125).
Purpose and activities: Giving primarily for education, arts, health services, youth services, and Jewish agencies and temples.
Fields of interest: Museums (art); Performing arts; Arts; Higher education; Education; Hospitals (general); Health organizations, association; Human services; Children, services; Jewish federated giving

programs; Public policy, research; Jewish agencies & temples.
Limitations: Applications not accepted. Giving primarily in New York, NY. No grants to individuals.
Application information: Contributes only to pre-selected organizations.
Officers: Thomas J. Tisch, Pres.; Alice M. Tisch, Sr. V.P.; Mark J. Krinsky, V.P.; Barry L. Bloom, Secy.-Treas.
EIN: 133693582
Selected grants: The following grants were reported in 2005.
$233,200 to Manhattan Institute for Policy Research, New York, NY.
$204,000 to Wellesley College, Wellesley, MA.
$100,000 to New-York Historical Society, New York, NY.
$100,000 to Ohel Childrens Home and Family Services, Brooklyn, NY.
$87,500 to Suffield Academy, Suffield, CT.
$70,000 to Museum of Modern Art, New York, NY.
$64,700 to Brearley School, New York, NY.
$10,000 to Savannah College of Art and Design, Savannah, GA.
$8,475 to Historic Savannah Foundation, Savannah, GA.
$5,000 to League for the Hard of Hearing, New York, NY.

7147
The Andrew & Ann Tisch Foundation, Inc. ✧
c/o Mark J. Krinsky
655 Madison Ave., 19th Fl.
New York, NY   10021-8043

Established in 1992 in NY.
Donors: Laurence A. Tisch†; Wilma S. Tisch.
Foundation type: Independent foundation.
Financial data (yr. ended 12/31/05): Assets, $8,739,985 (M); gifts received, $1,342,275; expenditures, $1,674,265; qualifying distributions, $1,630,678; giving activities include $1,624,337 for 53 grants (high: $424,000; low: $300).
Purpose and activities: Giving primarily for education and Jewish agencies. Some funding also for human services, and medical research.
Fields of interest: Higher education; Medical school/education; Medical research, institute; Human services; Children/youth, services; Jewish federated giving programs; Jewish agencies & temples; Women.
Limitations: Applications not accepted. Giving primarily in New York, NY. No grants to individuals.
Application information: Contributes only to pre-selected organizations.
Officers: Andrew H. Tisch, Pres.; Ann R. Tisch, Sr. V.P.; Mark J. Krinsky, V.P.; Thomas M. Steinberg, V.P.; Barry L. Bloom, Secy.-Treas.
EIN: 133693583
Selected grants: The following grants were reported in 2005.
$424,000 to Young Womens Leadership Foundation, New York, NY.
$120,000 to American Jewish Joint Distribution Committee, New York, NY.
$87,500 to Suffield Academy, Suffield, CT.
$85,000 to Washington University, Saint Louis, MO.
$20,000 to United States Naval Academy Foundation, Annapolis, MD.
$12,000 to Auschwitz Jewish Center Foundation, New York, NY.

$12,000 to Theater Development Fund, New York, NY.
$10,000 to Council on Foreign Relations, New York, NY.
$10,000 to Independent Feature Project, New York, NY.
$10,000 to Washington Institute for Near East Policy, DC.

7148
The Jamie and Steve Tisch Foundation, Inc. ✧
(formerly The Steve Tisch Foundation, Inc.)
c/o Mark J. Krinsky, C.P.A.
655 Madison Ave., 19th Fl.
New York, NY   10021

Established in 1992 in NY.
Donors: Preston Robert Tisch; Joan H. Tisch.
Foundation type: Independent foundation.
Financial data (yr. ended 12/31/05): Assets, $25,561,659 (M); gifts received, $3,724,200; expenditures, $1,923,423; qualifying distributions, $1,760,796; giving activities include $1,745,771 for 82 grants (high: $273,150; low: $200).
Purpose and activities: Giving primarily to the arts, health care, medical research, and for education.
Fields of interest: Museums (children's); Performing arts; Arts; Education; Hospitals (general); Health care; Health organizations; Medical research, institute; Cancer research; Human services; Children/youth, services; Jewish federated giving programs.
Limitations: Applications not accepted. Giving primarily in CA. No grants to individuals.
Application information: Contributes only to pre-selected organizations.
Officers: Steven E. Tisch, Pres.; Jamie L. Tisch, Sr. V.P.; Mark J. Krinsky, V.P.; Thomas M. Steinberg, V.P.; Barry L. Bloom, Secy.-Treas.
EIN: 133693586

7149
Jonathan M. Tisch Foundation, Inc. ✧
c/o Mark J. Krinsky, C.P.A.
655 Madison Ave., 19th Fl.
New York, NY   10021

Established in 1995 in NY.
Donors: Joan H. Tisch; Greater Talent Network, Inc.
Foundation type: Independent foundation.
Financial data (yr. ended 12/31/05): Assets, $21,448,246 (M); gifts received, $3,724,200; expenditures, $935,238; qualifying distributions, $786,347; giving activities include $775,337 for 113 grants (high: $64,000; low: $250).
Purpose and activities: Giving primarily for education, including organizations for the culinary arts; funding also for health care and medical research, the arts, and children, youth and social services.
Fields of interest: Arts; Higher education; Education; Hospitals (general); Health organizations, association; Cancer research; Human services; Children/youth, services.
Limitations: Applications not accepted. Giving primarily in New York, NY; some funding nationally. No grants to individuals.
Application information: Contributes only to pre-selected organizations.

Officers: Jonathan M. Tisch, Pres.; Mark J. Krinsky, V.P.; Thomas M. Steinberg, V.P.; Barry L. Bloom, Secy.-Treas.
EIN: 311641042

7150
John & Daniel Tishman Family Fund, Inc. ✧
(formerly John & Daniel Tishman Fund, Inc.)
666 5th Ave.
New York, NY   10103-0001
Contact: John L. Tishman, Pres.

Established in 1957 in NY.
Donors: Rose F. Tishman; John Tishman; Daniel Tishman.
Foundation type: Independent foundation.
Financial data (yr. ended 12/31/05): Assets, $2,862,558 (M); gifts received, $1,493,343; expenditures, $2,288,046; qualifying distributions, $2,259,542; giving activities include $2,248,950 for 35 grants (high: $500,000; low: $100).
Purpose and activities: Giving primarily for higher education, and the arts.
Fields of interest: Arts; Higher education; Education; Environment; Health care; Human services; Jewish federated giving programs.
Limitations: Giving primarily in NY.
Application information:
Initial approach: Proposal
Deadline(s): None
Officers: John L. Tishman, Pres.; Daniel Tishman, V.P. and Treas.; Katherine Blacklock, V.P.; Kathleen E. Kotoun, Secy.
EIN: 136151766
Selected grants: The following grants were reported in 2005.
$45,000 to Museum for African Art, Long Island City, NY. 2 grants: $25,000, $20,000
$25,000 to National Dance Institute, New York, NY.
$10,000 to Friends of Hudson, Hudson, NY.
$250 to Grand Street Settlement, New York, NY.

7151
TNG Charitable Trust ✧ ☆
378 Crown St.
Brooklyn, NY   11225

Established in 1997 in NY.
Donors: Eli Itzinger Irrevocable Trust; Chmvel Labkowski Irrevocable Trust.
Foundation type: Independent foundation.
Financial data (yr. ended 12/31/05): Assets, $248,741 (M); gifts received, $274,307; expenditures, $350,106; qualifying distributions, $349,886; giving activities include $349,886 for 19 grants (high: $155,156; low: $630).
Purpose and activities: Giving primarily for Jewish organizations.
Fields of interest: Jewish agencies & temples.
Limitations: Applications not accepted. No grants to individuals.
Application information: Contributes only to pre-selected organizations.
Director: Tema Gurary.
EIN: 116482383
Selected grants: The following grants were reported in 2005.
$59,572 to Bnos Menachem, Brooklyn, NY.
$19,818 to United Lubavitcher Yeshiva, Brooklyn, NY.

$1,000 to Lubavitch Youth Organization, Brooklyn, NY.

$1,000 to Rabbinical College of America, Morristown, NJ.

$970 to Tzedakah Vchesed, Brooklyn, NY.

7152
Barbara and Donald Tober Foundation ✧

c/o Jack Vivinetto, Sugar Foods Corp.
950 3rd Ave.
New York, NY 10022

Established in 1999 in NY.
Donors: Barbara Tober; Donald G. Tober.
Foundation type: Independent foundation.
Financial data (yr. ended 12/31/05): Assets, $240,629 (M); expenditures, $1,253,897; qualifying distributions, $1,231,841; giving activities include $1,224,741 for 146 grants (high: $88,830; low: $100).
Fields of interest: Museums; Arts; Environment; Health care.
Limitations: Applications not accepted. No grants to individuals.
Application Information: Contributes only to pre-selected organizations.
Trustees: Myron Stein; Barbara Tober; Donald G. Tober; Jack Vivinetto.
EIN: 137192894
Selected grants: The following grants were reported in 2005.
$43,000 to Museum of Arts and Design, New York, NY.
$26,000 to Manhattan Institute for Policy Research, New York, NY.
$25,000 to Lincoln Center for the Performing Arts, New York, NY.
$25,000 to National Dance Institute, New York, NY.
$12,500 to American Jewish Committee, New York, NY.
$9,000 to Metropolitan Museum of Art, New York, NY.
$5,000 to New York City Opera, New York, NY.
$2,500 to American Museum of Natural History, New York, NY.
$2,000 to Partnership for Public Service, DC.
$1,500 to Philharmonic-Symphony Society of New York, New York, NY.

7153
Tomorrow Foundation ✧

650 Madison Ave., 16th Fl.
New York, NY 10022

Established in 1997 in NY.
Donors: Robert F.X. Sillerman; Laura Baudo Sillerman.
Foundation type: Independent foundation.
Financial data (yr. ended 12/31/05): Assets, $16,572,651 (M); gifts received, $1,500,000; expenditures, $4,375,526; qualifying distributions, $4,278,387; giving activities include $4,278,387 for 266 grants (high: $1,000,000; low: $25; average: $1,000–$100,000).
Purpose and activities: Giving primarily for higher education.
Fields of interest: Arts; Higher education; Human services; Children/youth, services.
Limitations: Applications not accepted. Giving primarily in NY. No grants to individuals.

Application information: Contributes only to pre-selected organizations.
Officers and Directors: Laura Baudo Sillerman,* Pres.; Robert F.X. Sillerman,* V.P. and Treas.; John Coughlan, Secy.; Kraig Fox, Secy.; Mitchell Nelson.
EIN: 133930172
Selected grants: The following grants were reported in 2005.
$2,000,000 to Marietta College, Marietta, OH. 2 grants: $1,000,000 each
$600,000 to Childrens Health Fund, New York, NY. 2 grants: $300,000 each
$400,000 to American Museum of Natural History, New York, NY. 2 grants: $200,000 each
$400,000 to Boston University, Boston, MA.
$200,000 to Memorial Sloan-Kettering Cancer Center, New York, NY.
$100,000 to American Red Cross.
$50,000 to Southampton Hospital Foundation, Southampton, NY. 2 grants: $25,000 each
$50,000 to Variety-The Childrens Charity, Los Angeles, CA.
$5,075 to Forward Face, New York, NY.
$5,000 to American Poetry Review, Philadelphia, PA.
$5,000 to Fidelco Guide Dog Foundation, Bloomfield, CT.
$5,000 to North Star Academy Charter School, Springfield, MA.
$5,000 to Opus 118 Harlem School of Music, New York, NY.
$5,000 to Rockefeller University, New York, NY.

7154
The John R. and Barbara A. Tormondsen Foundation ✧

c/o BCRS Group/Marcum & Kliegman, LLP
10 Melville Park Rd.
Melville, NY 11747-3146

Established in 1996 in CT.
Donor: John R. Tormondsen.
Foundation type: Independent foundation.
Financial data (yr. ended 4/30/05): Assets, $1,760,884 (M); gifts received, $312,900; expenditures, $428,175; qualifying distributions, $415,620; giving activities include $412,945 for 37 grants (high: $136,775; low: $50).
Purpose and activities: Giving primarily for higher education; funding also for human services.
Fields of interest: Higher education; Business school/education; Health organizations, association; Human services; Children/youth, services; Federated giving programs.
Limitations: Applications not accepted. Giving primarily in CT, with emphasis on Greenwich, funding also in MA, New York, NY, and Middlebury, VT. No grants to individuals, no loans.
Application information: Contributes only to pre-selected organizations.
Trustees: Roger Harper; Barbara A. Tormondsen; John R. Tormondsen.
EIN: 133921373
Selected grants: The following grants were reported in 2005.
$136,775 to Middlebury College, Middlebury, VT.
$20,000 to Dartmouth College, Hanover, NH.
$15,100 to School of the Holy Child, Rye, NY.
$500 to Stratton Foundation, Stratton Mountain, VT.
$100 to Tufts University, Medford, MA.

7155
Tortuga Foundation ✧

c/o Siegel, Sacks, Press & Lacher, PC
600 3rd Ave., 18th Fl.
New York, NY 10016-1901

Established in 1979 in NY.
Donors: William C. Breed III; J.L. Tweedy.
Foundation type: Independent foundation.
Financial data (yr. ended 9/30/05): Assets, $23,439,388 (M); gifts received, $400,000; expenditures, $1,024,198; qualifying distributions, $830,000; giving activities include $830,000 for 26 grants (high: $100,000; low: $5,000).
Purpose and activities: Support primarily for land preservation, the environment, and women's and family planning groups; support also for health organizations and education.
Fields of interest: Education; Environment, natural resources; Environment; Health organizations, association; Human services; Women, centers/services; Women.
Limitations: Applications not accepted. Giving on a national basis. No grants to individuals.
Application information: Contributes only to pre-selected organizations.
Officers: Mildred Siceloff, Pres.; Patricia Livingston, Secy.
EIN: 510245279
Selected grants: The following grants were reported in 2004.
$190,000 to League of Conservation Voters Education Fund, DC.
$115,000 to Wilderness Society, DC.
$50,000 to Population Action International, DC.
$35,000 to Connecticut Fund for the Environment, New Haven, CT.
$30,000 to National Wildlife Refuge Association, DC.
$25,000 to Alaska Conservation Foundation, Anchorage, AK.
$25,000 to Healthy Schools Network, Albany, NY.
$25,000 to Open Space Institute, New York, NY.
$18,000 to Memorial Sloan-Kettering Cancer Center, New York, NY.
$5,000 to Carrying Capacity Network (CCN), DC.

7156
Toshiba America Foundation

c/o Prog. Office
1251 Ave. of the Americas, 41st Fl.
New York, NY 10020 (212) 596-0620
Contact: Laura Cronin, Mgr.
E-mail: foundation@tai.toshiba.com; URL: http://www.taf.toshiba.com

Established in 1990 in NY.
Donor: Toshiba America, Inc.
Foundation type: Company-sponsored foundation.
Financial data (yr. ended 3/31/04): Assets, $11,387,486 (M); expenditures, $606,584; qualifying distributions, $583,861; giving activities include $506,490 for 144 grants (high: $50,000; low: $220).
Purpose and activities: The foundation supports organizations involved with K-12 science and mathematics education.
Fields of interest: Elementary/secondary education; Science, formal/general education; Mathematics.
Type of support: Equipment; Program development.
Limitations: Giving on a national basis, with some emphasis on areas of company operations in CA, NJ,

NY, SD, TN, and TX. No support for religious or political organizations or teacher training institutes. No grants to individuals, or for professional development, capital campaigns, endowments, start-up needs, general operating support, conferences, building, computer hardware or materials, audio-visual equipment, videos, textbooks, independent study, fundraising, dinners, special events, educational research, after-school programs, or educational summer programs.

Publications: Application guidelines; Corporate giving report; Grants list; Informational brochure (including application guidelines); Occasional report.

Application information: Application form required.
Initial approach: Download application form and mail to foundation
Copies of proposal: 2
Deadline(s): Varies; Feb. 1 and Aug. 1 for requests of over $5,000
Board meeting date(s): Mar. and Sept.
Final notification: 3 months

Officer and Board Member:* John Anderson,* Pres.

Number of staff: 2 full-time professional.

EIN: 133596612

Selected grants: The following grants were reported in 2005.

$50,000 to National Science Teachers Association, Arlington, VA.

$13,800 to Vestavia Hills High School, Birmingham, AL.

$13,700 to Oregon State University, Corvallis, OR.

$11,500 to Immaculate Conception Academy, San Francisco, CA.

$10,000 to Best Practices in Education, New York, NY.

$10,000 to Pingry School, Martinsville, NJ.

$5,000 to Our Lady of Mercy High School, Rochester, NY.

$4,810 to North Central Charter Essential School, Fitchburg, MA.

$4,340 to East High School, Denver, CO.

$1,565 to Colorado Springs School, Colorado Springs, CO.

7157

Touch 'n Tutor Research & Development Foundation, Inc. ◇ ☆

361 W. 125th St., Ste. 212
New York, NY 10027

Donor: Percy Sutton.

Foundation type: Independent foundation.

Financial data (yr. ended 12/31/04): Assets, $1,791,044 (M); gifts received, $810,945; expenditures, $412,265; qualifying distributions, $412,000; giving activities include $412,000 for 1 grant.

Purpose and activities: Giving primarily to a Christian educational association.

Fields of interest: Christian agencies & churches.

Limitations: Applications not accepted. Giving primarily in San Antonio, TX. No grants to individuals.

Application information: Contributes only to pre-selected organizations.

Officers: Roscoe Brown, Pres.; Charles Andrews, Secy.; Percy Sutton, Treas.

EIN: 133980657

7158

The Peter and Elizabeth C. Tower Foundation

90B John Muir Dr., Ste. 100
Amherst, NY 14228-1148 (716) 689-0370
Contact: Glenda M. Cadwallader, Exec. Dir.
FAX: (716) 689-3716;
E-mail: info@thetowerfoundation.org; tel. for Michael Kustreba: (716) 689-0370, ext. 12;
URL: http://www.thetowerfoundation.org

Established in 1990 in NY.

Donors: Elizabeth C. Tower; Peter Tower; Peter Tower, Inc.; Peter Tower Living Trust.

Foundation type: Independent foundation.

Financial data (yr. ended 12/31/05): Assets, $57,075,493 (M); gifts received, $300,000; expenditures, $2,799,459; qualifying distributions, $2,571,227; giving activities include $2,216,876 for 100 grants.

Purpose and activities: Support for organizations providing services to children, youth and their families, in the areas of mental health, substance abuse, development disabilities and education.

Fields of interest: Elementary/secondary education; Education, early childhood education; Education; Substance abuse, services; Mental health, treatment; Mental health/crisis services.

Type of support: Management development/capacity building; Program development; Seed money; Technical assistance; Program evaluation; Matching/challenge support.

Limitations: Applications not accepted. Giving primarily in Essex County, MA, east of I-95, Martha's Vineyard; and in Erie and Niagara counties in NY. No grants to individuals.

Publications: Grants list; Program policy statement.

Application information: Unsolicited requests for funds not accepted.
Board meeting date(s): Quarterly

Officer: Glenda M. Cadwallader, Exec. Dir.

Trustees: John H. Byrnes; Mollie Tower Byrnes; Dorcas L. Colvin; Cynthia Tower Doyle; Robert M. Doyle; Todd M. Joseph; Richard A. Steinberg; Elizabeth C. Tower; Peter Tower.

Number of staff: 3 full-time professional; 1 part-time support.

EIN: 166350753

Selected grants: The following grants were reported in 2004.

$117,028 to Childrens Friend, Worcester, MA.

$33,000 to Bob Lanier Center for Educational, Physical and Cultural Development, Buffalo, NY.

$27,289 to Camp Fire USA, Buffalo, NY.

$25,000 to Buffalo Philharmonic Orchestra Society, Buffalo, NY.

$25,000 to Providence Center for Counseling and Psychiatric Services, Providence, RI.

$25,000 to United Way of Buffalo and Erie County, Buffalo, NY.

$25,000 to Vista Vocational and Life Skills Center, Westbrook, CT.

$5,000 to Community Foundation for Greater Buffalo, Buffalo, NY.

$5,000 to YMCA, Danvers Community, Danvers, MA.

$1,500 to Buffalo Society of Natural Sciences, Buffalo, NY.

7159

The Townsend Family Foundation ◇

c/o Goldman Sachs- Family Office
1 New York Plz., 40th Fl.
New York, NY 10004

Established in 1993 in NY.

Donor: John L. Townsend III.

Foundation type: Independent foundation.

Financial data (yr. ended 6/30/05): Assets, $6,994,030 (M); gifts received, $137,157; expenditures, $412,201; qualifying distributions, $389,815; giving activities include $389,815 for 55 grants (high: $259,814; low: $50).

Purpose and activities: Giving primarily for education, the arts, human services, and for Episcopal education and churches.

Fields of interest: Museums (art); Secondary school/education; Higher education; Education; Health organizations, association; Human services; Children/youth, services; Protestant agencies & churches.

Limitations: Applications not accepted. Giving primarily in CT, NC, NY, and VA. No grants to individuals.

Application information: Contributes only to pre-selected organizations.

Trustees: John L. Townsend III; Marree S. Townsend.

EIN: 133748079

Selected grants: The following grants were reported in 2005.

$15,000 to Greenwich Hospital, Greenwich, CT.

$3,000 to Boys and Girls Club of Greenwich, Greenwich, CT.

$3,000 to United Way of Greenwich, Greenwich, CT.

$3,000 to University of North Carolina, Chapel Hill, NC.

$2,500 to Frick Collection, New York, NY.

$2,500 to Museum of Modern Art, New York, NY.

$2,500 to Reach, Derby, CT.

$1,500 to Greenwich Academy, Greenwich, CT.

$1,500 to Whitney Museum of American Art, New York, NY.

$500 to Port Chester Carver Center, Port Chester, NY.

7160

Toyota USA Foundation ◇

c/o Fdn. Admin.
9 W. 57th St., Ste. 4900
New York, NY 10019 (212) 715-7486
URL: http://www.toyota.com/foundation

Established in 1987 in CA.

Donors: Toyota Motor Sales, U.S.A., Inc.; Toyota Motor Manufacturing North America, Inc.

Foundation type: Company-sponsored foundation.

Financial data (yr. ended 6/30/05): Assets, $42,269,133 (M); gifts received, $2,000,000; expenditures, $2,249,240; qualifying distributions, $2,221,470; giving activities include $2,221,470 for 18 grants (high: $300,000; low: $29,365).

Purpose and activities: The foundation supports organizations involved with K-12 math and science education and higher education. Special emphasis is directed toward programs designed to be broad in scope and incorporate interdisciplinary curriculum, "real world" classroom applications, and high student expectations; develop the potential of students and/or teachers; and possess a high potential for success with relatively low duplication of effort.

Fields of interest: Elementary/secondary education; Higher education; Science, formal/general education; Mathematics.

Type of support: Program development; Seed money; Curriculum development; Program evaluation.

Limitations: Giving on a national basis. No support for government agencies, private or public K-12 schools, or religious, fraternal, or lobbying organizations. No grants to individuals, or for general operating support, annual campaigns, or debt reduction, endowments, capital campaigns, fundraising events, or construction or equipment, conferences, meals, or travel, or publication subsidies, advertising, or mass mailings.

Publications: Application guidelines; Grants list; Informational brochure (including application guidelines).

Application information: A site visit may be requested. Additional information may be requested at a later date. Application form required.

Initial approach: Download application form and mail to foundation
Copies of proposal: 1
Deadline(s): None
Board meeting date(s): Twice per year
Final notification: Approximately 6 months

Officers and Directors:* Yoshumi Inaba,* Pres.; James Press,* Exec. V.P.; Douglas M. West, Sr. V.P.; Michael Deaderick, V.P.; James Olson,* V.P.; Yuzo Ushiyama, V.P.; Dian Ogilvie,* Secy.; Akimasa Yamamoto, Treas.; Chuck Brown; Dennis Cuneo; Dave Illingworth; Irv Miller; Atsushi Nimi; Toshiaki Taguchi; Jim Weisman.

Number of staff: 2 full-time professional; 1 full-time support.

EIN: 953255038

Selected grants: The following grants were reported in 2005.

$250,000 to College Board, New York, NY.
$186,469 to Wayne State University, Detroit, MI.
$150,000 to Challenger Center for Space Science Education, Alexandria, VA.
$150,000 to National Park Foundation, DC.
$150,000 to University of California, Irvine, CA.
$150,000 to University of Michigan, Ann Arbor, MI.
$145,836 to University of Southern California, Los Angeles, CA.
$127,500 to Earths Birthday Project, Santa Fe, NM.
$112,000 to Fairleigh Dickinson University, Madison, NJ.
$100,000 to Keep America Beautiful, Stamford, CT.

7161
Traditional Foundation ✧ ☆
1688 54th St.
Brooklyn, NY 11204

Established in 2005 in NY.
Foundation type: Independent foundation.
Financial data (yr. ended 10/31/05): Assets, $324 (M); gifts received, $1,050,401; expenditures, $1,050,830; qualifying distributions, $1,050,830; giving activities include $1,050,830 for grants.
Fields of interest: Jewish agencies & temples.
Limitations: Applications not accepted. Giving primarily in NY. No grants to individuals.
Application information: Contributes only to pre-selected organziations.
Directors: Fay Fink; Ann Friedman; Rebecca Hacoen.
EIN: 201891793

7162
Triad Foundation, Inc. ▼ ✧
P.O. Box 4440
Ithaca, NY 14852 (607) 257-1133
Contact: Joanne V. Florino, Exec. Dir.

Established in 2002; funded by transfer of assets from Park Foundation, Inc. in Feb., 2003.
Donors: Roy Hampton Park, Jr.; Park Foundation, Inc.
Foundation type: Independent foundation.
Financial data (yr. ended 12/31/05): Assets, $219,414,443 (M); expenditures, $12,221,544; qualifying distributions, $9,921,254; giving activities include $9,088,756 for 251 grants (high: $461,600; low: $130; average: $5,000–$50,000), $5,801 for 22 employee matching gifts, $410 for 1 in-kind gift, and $25,000 for 1 loan/program-related investment.
Purpose and activities: Giving primarily for graduate fellowships, educational programs serving children and youth, marine and tropical ecology, scientific research, and human services.
Fields of interest: Education; Environment, water resources; Human services; Children/youth, services.
Type of support: Technical assistance; Research; Seed money; Matching/challenge support; Program-related investments/loans; Internship funds; Fellowships; Conferences/seminars; Program development; Management development/capacity building; General/operating support; Employee matching gifts.
Limitations: Giving primarily in Tampa, FL., Charlotte, NC., and Central NY. No grants to individuals, or for endowments or capital campaigns.
Publications: Application guidelines.
Application information: Application form required.
Initial approach: Letter or telephone
Copies of proposal: 1
Deadline(s): Rolling basis
Board meeting date(s): Quarterly
Final notification: 2 months
Officers and Directors:* Roy Hampton Park, Jr.,* Chair. and Pres.; Roy H. Park III,* V.P. and Secy.; Elizabeth P. Fowler,* V.P. and Treas.; Joanne V. Florino, Exec. Dir.
Number of staff: 2 full-time professional; 2 full-time support.
EIN: 300108102

7163
Tribune New York Foundation ✧
220 E. 42nd St., 10th Fl.
New York, NY 10017 (212) 210-2604

Incorporated in 1958 in NY.
Donors: Daily News, LP; WPIX, Inc.
Foundation type: Independent foundation.
Financial data (yr. ended 12/31/05): Assets, $6,318,362 (M); expenditures, $475,996; qualifying distributions, $434,702; giving activities include $434,702 for grants.
Purpose and activities: Giving to improve the vitality of cultural offerings in the community and to enhance broadcasting and journalism throughout the CT, NJ, and NY tri-state area.
Fields of interest: Media/communications; Media, journalism/publishing; Arts; Education; Health care; Human services.
Type of support: General/operating support; Employee matching gifts.

Limitations: Giving limited to the tri-state CT, NJ, and NY area, with emphasis on the five boroughs of New York. No support for religious organizations. No grants to individuals, or for fundraising dinners.
Publications: Application guidelines.
Application information: Application form required.
Initial approach: Letter or telephone requesting application guidelines
Board meeting date(s): June and Dec.
Officers and Directors:* Betty Ellen Berlamino,* Pres.; Carlos Austin,* Secy.; Catherine Davis,* Treas.; Timothy Knight; Steve Mulderrig; Bill Shaw.
EIN: 136161525

7164
Barbara Davies Troisi Foundation ✧ ☆
230 Park Ave.
New York, NY 10169
Contact: Frank X. Troisi, Tr.

Established in 1989 in NY.
Donor: Frank X. Troisi.
Foundation type: Independent foundation.
Financial data (yr. ended 12/31/05): Assets, $11,255 (M); gifts received, $21,128; expenditures, $483,085; qualifying distributions, $477,105; giving activities include $468,605 for 5 grants (high: $418,754; low: $4,000), and $8,500 for 5 grants to individuals (high: $2,000; low: $1,500).
Purpose and activities: Giving limited to research and training of the learned disabled.
Fields of interest: Disabilities, people with.
Limitations: Giving primarily in NJ and NY.
Application information:
Initial approach: Letter on individual or organization letterhead
Deadline(s): None
Trustees: Costa L. Papson; James F. Sassano; Frank X. Troisi.
EIN: 133534989

7165
The Trott Family Foundation ✧
c/o BCRS Assocs., LLC
100 Wall St., 11th Fl.
New York, NY 10005

Established in 1996 in IL.
Donor: Byron D. Trott.
Foundation type: Independent foundation.
Financial data (yr. ended 8/31/05): Assets, $11,175,346 (M); gifts received, $2,782,200; expenditures, $465,588; qualifying distributions, $461,573; giving activities include $461,533 for 32 grants (high: $250,000; low: $250).
Fields of interest: Museums (art); Performing arts; ballet; Education; Hospitals (general); Human services; Children/youth, services; Federated giving programs.
Limitations: Applications not accepted. Giving primarily in IL, with emphasis on Chicago; some funding nationally. No grants or scholarships to individuals; no loans.
Application information: Contributes only to pre-selected organizations.
Trustees: Byron D. Trott; Tina L. Trott.
EIN: 133919816
Selected grants: The following grants were reported in 2004.

$75,000 to University of Chicago, Chicago, IL. 2 grants: $50,000, $25,000

$50,000 to United Way of Metropolitan Chicago, Chicago, IL. 2 grants: $25,000 each

$25,000 to Art Institute of Chicago, Chicago, IL.

$20,000 to Althoff Catholic High School, Belleville, IL.

$20,000 to Ohio State University, Columbus, OH.

$20,000 to Rush University Medical Center, Chicago, IL.

$15,000 to Writers Theater, Glencoe, IL.

$1,000 to Winnetka Historical Society, Winnetka, IL.

7166
The Troy Savings Bank Charitable Foundation, Inc. ☆
32 2nd St.
P.O. Box 598
Troy, NY 12181-0598
Contact: Leslie A. Cheu, Exec. Dir.

Established in 1998 in NY as a company-sponsored foundation; status changed to independent foundation in 2004.
Donors: The Troy Savings Bank; Troy Financial Corp.
Foundation type: Independent foundation.
Financial data (yr. ended 12/31/05): Assets, $16,197,786 (M); expenditures, $1,059,152; qualifying distributions, $977,669; giving activities include $821,792 for 108 grants (high: $210,177; low: $100).
Purpose and activities: The foundation supports organizations involved with arts and culture, education, housing, and human services.
Fields of interest: Arts; Elementary/secondary education; Education; Housing/shelter; Human services.
Type of support: Continuing support; Capital campaigns; Equipment; Program development; Curriculum development; Matching/challenge support.
Limitations: Giving primarily in NY, with emphasis on Albany, Greene, Rensselaer, Saratoga, Schenectady, Schoharie, Warren, and Washington counties. No grants to individuals.
Publications: Application guidelines; Informational brochure.
Application information: Application form required.
Initial approach: Contact foundation for application form
Copies of proposal: 11
Deadline(s): None
Final notification: 8 to 10 weeks
Officers and Directors:* Daniel J. Hogarty, Jr.,* Pres.; Richard DeVane,* Secy.; Leslie A. Cheu, Exec. Dir.
Number of staff: 2 full-time professional.
EIN: 141813865

7167
The Donald J. Trump Foundation ◇
c/o Weiser, LLP
3000 Marcus Ave., Ste. 2W1
Lake Success, NY 11042
Application address: c/o Donald J. Trump, Pres., The Trump Organization, 725 5th Ave., New York, NY 10022

Established in 1987 in NY.

Donors: Donald J. Trump; Alfons J. Schmitt; Maurice R. Povich; Beth Schwartz; Jayson Schwartz; Kinray, Inc.; Trump Park Ave., LLC; Mr. White LLC.
Foundation type: Independent foundation.
Financial data (yr. ended 12/31/04): Assets, $2,857 (M); gifts received, $725,525; expenditures, $738,225; qualifying distributions, $738,225; giving activities include $736,200 for 47 grants (high: $250,000; low: $500).
Purpose and activities: Giving primarily for health associations, youth development, and social services; funding also for the arts and Jewish organizations.
Fields of interest: Arts; Education; Health organizations, association; Cancer research; Crime/law enforcement, police agencies; Athletics/sports, golf; Youth development; Human services; Federated giving programs; Jewish federated giving programs; Jewish agencies & temples.
Limitations: Giving primarily in New York, NY.
Application information: Application form not required.
Initial approach: Letter
Deadline(s): None
Officers: Donald J. Trump, Pres.; Norma Foerderer, Secy.; Allen Weisselberg, Treas.
EIN: 133404773

7168
The Trust for Mutual Understanding ▼ ◇
30 Rockefeller Plz., Rm. 5600
New York, NY 10112 (212) 632-3405
Contact: Richard S. Lanier, Dir.
FAX: (212) 632-3409; E-mail: tmu@tmuny.org;
URL: http://www.tmuny.org

Established in 1984 in NY.
Foundation type: Independent foundation.
Financial data (yr. ended 12/31/04): Assets, $55,317,379 (M); expenditures, $5,108,497; qualifying distributions, $4,669,151; giving activities include $3,540,457 for 142 grants (high: $100,000; low: $1,500; average: $5,000–$60,000).
Purpose and activities: Support to American nonprofit organizations for professional exchanges in the arts and in environmental conservation between the United States, Russia, and Eastern and Central Europe. Approximately 75 percent of grant funds are allocated for cultural projects and approximately 25 percent for environmental projects. Support is provided primarily for travel and related expenses for exchange projects in which professional interaction plays a major role and in which there is a significant degree of collaborative effort.
Fields of interest: Visual arts; Museums; Performing arts; Performing arts, dance; Performing arts, theater; Performing arts, music; Historic preservation/historical societies; Arts; Environment, natural resources; Environment; Animals/wildlife, preservation/protection; International exchange.
International interests: Albania; Belarus; Bosnia-Herzegovina; Bulgaria; Croatia; Czech Republic; Georgia (Republic of); Hungary; Macedonia; Moldova; Mongolia; Poland; Romania; Russia; Slovakia; Slovenia; Ukraine.
Type of support: Exchange programs.
Limitations: Giving for exchanges between the U.S. and the countries of Central and Eastern Europe, primarily the Czech Republic, Hungary, Poland, Russia, and Slovakia. Support is also provided, to a lesser extent, for exchanges involving Albania, Belarus, Bosnia and Herzegovina, Bulgaria, Croatia, Georgia, Macedonia, Moldova, Mongolia, Romania, Serbia and Montenegro, Slovenia, and Ukraine. No support for large-scale institutional programs lacking an individual exchange component, youth or undergraduate exchanges, economic development, medicine, public health, agricultural issues, or activities pertaining to nuclear weapons and arms control. No grants to individuals, or for fellowships, capital campaigns, deficit financing, endowments, general program and operating costs, salaries, honoraria, publications, library and equipment purchases, film, media, or one-person exhibitions or performance tours.
Publications: Annual report (including application guidelines); Grants list.
Application information: Grants are made only to tax-exempt organizations in the United States for exchange projects involving Eastern and Central Europe. Application form required.
Initial approach: Letter; initial contact should be established at least 3 months prior to anticipated date of project implementation
Copies of proposal: 1
Deadline(s): Feb. 1 and Aug. 1
Board meeting date(s): Spring and fall
Final notification: Directly following board meeting
Director and Trustees:* Richard S. Lanier,* Dir.; Elizabeth J. McCormack; Donal C. O'Brien, Jr.
Board of Advisors: Wade Greene; William H. Luers; Joseph Polisi; Blair Ruble; Isaac Shapiro.
Number of staff: 3 full-time professional; 1 full-time support; 1 part-time support.
EIN: 133212724
Selected grants: The following grants were reported in 2005.
$53,000 to Art in General, New York, NY. For international travel and related expenses of artists and arts managers from Croatia, Czech Republic, Hungary, Poland and Unites States participating in reciprocal residency exchange program.
$50,000 to American Dance Festival, New York, NY. To enable choreographer Tatiana Baganova and members of Provincial Dances Theatre from Yekaterinburg to participate in residency programs.

7169
Tsadra Foundation ◇ ☆
P.O. Box 20192
New York, NY 10014

Established in 2000 in NY.
Donor: Eric Colombel.
Foundation type: Independent foundation.
Financial data (yr. ended 12/31/05): Assets, $16,141 (M); gifts received, $205,000; expenditures, $1,165,186; qualifying distributions, $909,357; giving activities include $909,357 for 76 grants to individuals (high: $156,000; low: $3,326).
Fields of interest: Education; International development; Buddhism.
Type of support: General/operating support; Program development; Fellowships.
Limitations: Applications not accepted. Giving on a national and international basis.
Application information: Unsolicited requests for funds not accepted.
Trustee: Eric Colombel.
EIN: 137224970

7170
Michael Tuch Foundation, Inc.
122 E. 42nd St., Ste. 1622
New York, NY 10168
Contact: Martha Tuck Rozett, Pres.

Incorporated in 1946 in NY.
Donor: Michael Tuch†.
Foundation type: Independent foundation.
Financial data (yr. ended 12/31/05): Assets, $6,645,789 (M); gifts received, $46,915; expenditures, $453,088; qualifying distributions, $408,730; giving activities include $370,250 for 78 grants (high: $16,000; low: $750).
Purpose and activities: Giving primarily for the arts, including museums, and for educational institutions and programs.
Fields of interest: Museums; Performing arts; Performing arts, theater; Performing arts, music; Arts; Libraries/library science; Education; Employment; Food services; Recreation, parks/ playgrounds; Human services; Children/youth, services; Aging, centers/services; Community development; Economically disadvantaged.
Type of support: General/operating support; Continuing support; Program development; Curriculum development; Internship funds.
Limitations: Giving primarily in New York, NY. No support for religion or health organizations. No grants to individuals.
Application information: Application form not required.
   Initial approach: Proposal
   Copies of proposal: 1
   Deadline(s): None
   Board meeting date(s): May
   Final notification: 3 months
Officers and Trustees:* Martha Tuck Rozett,* Pres. and Exec. Dir.; Jonathan S. Tuck, V.P. and Secy.-Treas.; Daniel H. Tuck; David A. Tuck.
Number of staff: 2 part-time professional; 1 part-time support.
EIN: 136002848

7171
The Tufenkian Foundation, Inc. ◇
919 3rd Ave.
New York, NY 10022 (212) 603-2560

Donors: James Tufenkian; Adrienne V. Tashjian; Alber K. Karamanoukian.
Foundation type: Operating foundation.
Financial data (yr. ended 11/30/05): Assets, $12,273,328 (M); gifts received, $38,924; expenditures, $1,074,708; qualifying distributions, $1,074,487; giving activities include $1,054,637 for 29 grants.
Purpose and activities: Giving primarily for the benefit of Armenian society.
Fields of interest: Education; Human services; Children/youth, services.
Limitations: Applications not accepted. Giving primarily in NY. No grants to individuals.
Application information: Contributes only to pre-selected organizations.
Officer and Directors:* James Tufenkian,* Pres.; Diane L. Hodges; David F. Tufenkian.
EIN: 133976159

7172
Tuft Family Foundation ◇
c/o Goldman Sachs- Family Office
1 New York Plz., 40th Fl.
New York, NY 10004

Established in 1987 in NY.
Donor: Thomas E. Tuft.
Foundation type: Independent foundation.
Financial data (yr. ended 8/31/05): Assets, $11,765,252 (M); expenditures, $1,210,653; qualifying distributions, $1,158,000; giving activities include $1,158,000 for 74 grants (high: $275,000; low: $200).
Fields of interest: Arts; Health organizations, association; Human services; Children/youth, services; Christian agencies & churches.
Limitations: Applications not accepted. Giving primarily in New York, NY. No grants to individuals.
Application information: Contributes only to pre-selected organizations.
Trustees: Lewis M. Eisenberg; Diane H. Tuft; Thomas E. Tuft.
EIN: 133437888
Selected grants: The following grants were reported in 2003.
$90,000 to Rusty Staub Foundation, Peabody, MA. For general support.
$10,000 to Ballet Theater Foundation, New York, NY. For general support.
$10,000 to Film Society of Lincoln Center, New York, NY. For general support.
$10,000 to Prep for Prep, New York, NY. For general support.
$10,000 to Robin Hood Foundation, New York, NY. For general support.
$9,300 to James Beard Foundation, New York, NY. For general support.
$7,500 to Metropolitan Museum of Art, New York, NY. For general support.
$6,000 to Lincoln Center for the Performing Arts, New York, NY. For general support.
$5,000 to Boys and Girls Harbor, New York, NY. For general support.
$5,000 to New York City Opera, New York, NY. For general support.

7173
The Alice Tully Foundation ◇
(formerly Maya Corporation)
317 Madison Ave., Rm. 1511
New York, NY 10017
Contact: James McGarry, Pres.

Established in 1953 in NY.
Donor: Alice Tully†.
Foundation type: Independent foundation.
Financial data (yr. ended 12/31/05): Assets, $40,203,050 (M); expenditures, $5,942,349; qualifying distributions, $5,674,033; giving activities include $5,605,516 for 78 grants (high: $3,200,000; low: $1,000).
Purpose and activities: Giving primarily for the arts, education, and human services.
Fields of interest: Arts education; Museums (art); Performing arts, music; Performing arts, opera; Education; Hospitals (general); Human services; Federated giving programs; Roman Catholic agencies & churches.
Limitations: Giving primarily in New York, NY. No grants to individuals.
Application information:
   Deadline(s): None

Officers and Directors:* James McGarry,* Pres.; Ettie Butler, Secy.; William A. Simon,* Treas.; Robert N. Davies; Maisie Houghton; William T. Powers.
EIN: 136135056
Selected grants: The following grants were reported in 2005.
$3,460,000 to Lincoln Center for the Performing Arts, New York, NY. 2 grants: $3,200,000, $260,000
$400,000 to Juilliard School, New York, NY.
$400,000 to Metropolitan Museum of Art, New York, NY.
$375,000 to Pierpont Morgan Library, New York, NY.
$335,000 to New York City Opera, New York, NY.
$150,000 to Philharmonic-Symphony Society of New York, New York, NY.
$5,000 to Regis High School, New York, NY.
$5,000 to Rockefeller University, New York, NY.
$3,750 to Vermont Mozart Festival, Burlington, VT.

7174
Turn 2 Foundation, Inc.
215 Park Ave. S., Ste. 1905
New York, NY 10003 (212) 475-2339
FAX: (212) 475-3378;
E-mail: mail@turn2foundation.org; URL: http:// derekjeter.mlb.com/NASApp/mlb/players/ jeter_derek/turn2/overview.jsp
Alternate URL: http://www.turn2foundation.org

Established in 1996 MI.
Donors: Derek S. Jeter; Daniel Keith; Thomas Terrill; Philip Rogers; Raniero Cortina, Jr.; Drew Doscher; Adele Smithers-Fornaci; Chris Sullivan; Jason Giambi; Matt Lalin; Dan Lavecchia; Howard Lutnick; Thomas Geller; James Krivacs; Victoria Krivacs; Jack Critchfield; Richard C. Dresdale; Bestfoods; Pharmacia & Upjohn, Inc.; Kellogg Co.; Christopher D. Smithers Foundation; FleetBoston Financial Corp.; Steiner Sports Memorabilia; Collins Building Services; AXA Foundation Charitable Gift Fund; Turn 2, Inc.; Rockmont Mgmt. Partners; All American Collectibles; Dittman Incentive Marketing; Fleer Trading Cards; 78/79 York Assocs., LLC; Forbes Foundation; Interviewing Services of America; Omdusa, Inc.; Disney Worldwide Services, Inc.; PricewaterhouseCoopers, LLC; IMG; Quaker Oates Co.; Nike, Inc.; Partnership for a Drug-Free America; Time, Inc.; Sport Fun, Inc.; Turn 2 Enterprises, Inc.; Visual Architectural Designs; BBDO; Acclaim Entertainment; ConAgra Foods, Inc.; Credit Suisse First Boston LLC; Ernest & Young, LLP; Fenway Partners; Pfizer Inc.; Millsport; Marquis Jet; Del Frisco's New York; Goldman Sachs; Pepsi Cola Company; The Packer Family Foundation; The Promotions Network; The Upper Deck Co.; Twenty Ones Inc.; Christopher D. Smithers Foundation; Danker-Basham Foundation; Bank of America; NetJets Aviation, Inc.; Prudential Financial; Seminole Hard Rock Hotel & Casino; Tri State Quality Ford Dealers; JPMorgan Private Client Svcs.; Nature's Therapy, Inc.; NFL Ventures LP; New York Merchantile Exchange; Bloomberg; Cantor Fitzgerald Securities; Pro Performance Sports, LLC; Schenker Family Foundation; Straub Lincoln Mercury; Take 2 Interactive.
Foundation type: Independent foundation.
Financial data (yr. ended 12/31/05): Assets, $2,868,860 (M); gifts received, $1,850,758; expenditures, $1,540,334; qualifying distributions, $1,528,736; giving activities include $1,004,930 for 30 grants (high: $175,000; low: $600).

Purpose and activities: Giving primarily to organizations which focus on substance abuse prevention and treatment for youth, and programs that promote healthy lifestyles, academics and leadership development among youth in the Tampa, FL, Kalamazoo, MI, and New York, NY, areas.
Fields of interest: Secondary school/education; Substance abuse, prevention; Substance abuse, treatment; Recreation, parks/playgrounds; Boys & girls clubs; Human services; Children/youth, services; Foundations (community).
Limitations: Giving primarily in and around the Tampa, FL, Kalamazoo, MI, and New York, NY, areas. No support for organizations lacking 501(c) (3) status. No grants to individuals, or for endowment funds, building or renovation projects, or conferences or travel expenses.
Application information: See foundation Web site for application guidelines and requirements.
 Initial approach: Letter or telephone requesting guidelines
 Board meeting date(s): Jan. and July
Officers: Derek S. Jeter, Pres.; Sanderson Charles Jeter, V.P.; Dorothy Jeter, Exec. Dir.
EIN: 341847687
Selected grants: The following grants were reported in 2004.
$175,000 to Camp Sussex, Forest Hills, NY.
$154,053 to Abyssinian Development Corporation, New York, NY.
$40,000 to Hillsborough Educational Partnership Foundation, Tampa, FL.
$20,000 to Kalamazoo Public Schools, Kalamazoo, MI.
$10,000 to Daytop Village Foundation, New York, NY.
$10,000 to Outreach Project, Richmond Hill, NY.
$10,000 to Phoenix House, New York, NY.

7175
Ruth Turner Fund, Inc. ✧
c/o Davidson, Dawson & Clark
60 E. 42nd St., 38 Fl.
New York, NY 10165

Established in 1973 in NY.
Donor: Ruth Turner†.
Foundation type: Independent foundation.
Financial data (yr. ended 12/31/05): Assets, $5,589,695 (M); expenditures, $461,605; qualifying distributions, $423,658; giving activities include $402,500 for 19 grants (high: $55,000; low: $5,000).
Purpose and activities: Support for medical research and programs for the visually impaired; grants also for youth and social services, and primary and secondary education.
Fields of interest: Education, early childhood education; Secondary school/education; Medical research, institute; Human services; Children/youth, services; Homeless, human services; Civil rights; Disabilities, people with; Homeless.
Type of support: General/operating support; Continuing support; Program development; Seed money; Research.
Limitations: Applications not accepted. Giving primarily in New York, NY. No grants to individuals.
Application information: Contributes only to pre-selected organizations.
Officers and Directors:* Gloria S. Neuwirth,* Pres.; Jessica Neuwirth,* Secy.; Stephanie P. Mermin,

Treas.; Suzanne Black; Joyce Hartman; Veronica Jordan*; Chris Sorensen.
EIN: 237240889
Selected grants: The following grants were reported in 2004.
$50,000 to Equality Now, New York, NY.
$40,000 to Fountain House, New York, NY.
$30,000 to Educational Alliance, New York, NY.
$25,000 to City Harvest, New York, NY.
$25,000 to Coalition for the Homeless, New York, NY.
$25,000 to Friends of Green Chimneys, Brewster, NY.
$10,000 to Associated Blind, New York, NY.
$8,000 to Childrens Hospital.
$5,000 to Bide-A-Wee Home Association, New York, NY.

7176
Isaac H. Tuttle Fund
1155 Park Ave.
New York, NY 10128-1209 (212) 831-0429
Contact: Stephanie A. Raneri, Exec. Dir.
FAX: (212) 426-5684; E-mail: info@tuttlefund.org;
URL: http://www.tuttlefund.org

Incorporated in 1872 as a public charity; status changed to a private foundation in 2001.
Donors: Martin S. Paine Foundation; Mary Phelps Foundation.
Foundation type: Independent foundation.
Financial data (yr. ended 12/31/05): Assets, $52,130,849 (M); gifts received, $1,111,346; expenditures, $2,571,604; qualifying distributions, $2,392,701; giving activities include $1,135,000 for 45 grants, and $563,664 for 129 grants to individuals.
Purpose and activities: The fund gives direct financial support to elderly individuals and not-for-profit community-based organizations that provide services to seniors in the borough of Manhattan in New York City, with the goal of enabling older persons to continue living in their own homes so long as they are physically and mentally able to do so.
Fields of interest: Aging, centers/services.
Type of support: General/operating support; Continuing support; Building/renovation; Equipment; Program development; Technical assistance; Grants to individuals.
Limitations: Giving limited to New York, NY.
Publications: Application guidelines; Financial statement.
Application information: Contact Exec. Dir. for grants, or Stipend Prog. Dir. for stipends. Application form required for stipends. Application form required.
 Initial approach: Telephone, E-mail or letter of inquiry
 Copies of proposal: 1
 Deadline(s): 3 months prior to board meetings for grants and stipends
 Board meeting date(s): 5 times per year
 Final notification: Following board meetings
Officers and Trustees:* Molly O. Parkinson,* Pres.; Kenneth R. Page,* V.P.; Christine Valentine,* Secy.; Anne H. Lindgren,* Treas.; Stephanie A. Raneri, Exec. Dir.; Sia Arnason; Shirley B. Bresler; Susan P. Cole; William H. Forsyth, Jr.; John C. Harpole; Martha V. Johns; Ann R. Loeb; Edward D. Pardoe III; Oscar S. Straus III.

Number of staff: 5 full-time professional; 1 full-time support; 1 part-time support.
EIN: 135628325

7177
Solomon and Machla Tzedaka Fund Trust ✧ ☆
1830 59th St.
Brooklyn, NY 11204

Established in 1998 in NY.
Donors: Solomon Abramczyk; Machla Abramczyk.
Foundation type: Independent foundation.
Financial data (yr. ended 11/30/05): Assets, $963,723 (M); gifts received, $390,000; expenditures, $418,993; qualifying distributions, $416,384; giving activities include $416,384 for 16 + grants (high: $54,000).
Fields of interest: Jewish agencies & temples.
Limitations: Applications not accepted. Giving primarily in Brooklyn, NY. No grants to individuals.
Application information: Contributes only to pre-selected organizations.
Trustees: Machla Abramczyk; Solomon Abramczyk.
EIN: 116516261
Selected grants: The following grants were reported in 2003.
$50,000 to Gemach Chemed Shlomo, Brooklyn, NY.
$35,000 to Congregation Oholey Shem, Brooklyn, NY.
$11,000 to Congregation Boruch Yisroel, Brooklyn, NY.
$10,000 to Beth Feiga, Brooklyn, NY.
$10,000 to Emergency Aid Fund, Brooklyn, NY.
$7,500 to Beth Jacob Parent Teacher Association, Brooklyn, NY.
$6,400 to Congregation Zvi Lzadik, Brooklyn, NY.
$2,600 to Gmach Moshe Aron, Brooklyn, NY.
$2,500 to Khal Zichron Avraham Yaakov, Brooklyn, NY.
$1,000 to Tzedaka Vachesed, Brooklyn, NY.

7178
Tziterman Memorial Trust ✧ ☆
195 Wildacre Ave.
Lawrence, NY 11559

Established in 2000 in NY.
Donor: IDT Corp.
Foundation type: Company-sponsored foundation.
Financial data (yr. ended 6/30/03): Assets, $0 (M); gifts received, $125,000; expenditures, $485,284; qualifying distributions, $485,218; giving activities include $483,101 for grants.
Purpose and activities: The foundation supports organizations involved with Judaism.
Fields of interest: Jewish agencies & temples.
Limitations: Applications not accepted. No grants to individuals.
Application information: Contributes only to pre-selected organizations.
Trustee: Devora May Smith.
EIN: 137257263
Selected grants: The following grants were reported in 2003.
$100,500 to Yeshiva Darchei Torah, Far Rockaway, NY. 3 grants: $500, $50,000, $50,000
$10,000 to Hebrew Academy of Long Beach, Long Beach, NY.
$10,000 to SAR Scholarship Fund.

$225 to Yeshiva of Far Rockaway, Far Rockaway, NY.

$200 to Torah Academy for Girls, Far Rockaway, NY.

$100 to National Society for Hebrew Day Schools - Torah Umesorah, New York, NY.

$50 to Machon Academy, New York, NY.

$36 to Diaspora Yeshiva, Brooklyn, NY.

7179
Maoz Tzur Foundation, Inc. ◇
1860 Flatbush Ave.
Brooklyn, NY 11210
Contact: Charles Neiss, Pres.

Donors: Charles Neiss; Fay Neiss; Berger Boiler Corp.
Foundation type: Operating foundation.
Financial data (yr. ended 12/31/04): Assets, $17,301 (M); gifts received, $1,059,567; expenditures, $1,160,812; qualifying distributions, $1,158,739; giving activities include $671,429 for 92 grants (high: $207,883; low: $50), and $487,310 for grants to individuals (high: $94,000; low: $50).
Purpose and activities: Giving for Jewish organizations.
Fields of interest: Jewish agencies & temples.
International interests: Israel.
Limitations: Giving on an international and national basis, with emphasis on Israel.
Application information:
  Initial approach: Letter
  Deadline(s): None
Officers: Charles Neiss, Pres.; Jacob Neiss, V.P.
EIN: 113423569
Selected grants: The following grants were reported in 2004.
$5,000 to Camp United Methodist Church, Shallotte, NC.
$2,000 to Keren Chaim Shlomo, Brooklyn, NY.

7180
U.S. Trust Corporation Foundation ◇
(formerly United States Trust Company of New York Foundation)
c/o United States Trust Co. of New York
114 W. 47th St.
New York, NY 10036
Contact: Carol A. Strickland, Corp. Contrib. Comm. Chair.
FAX: (212) 852-1341;
E-mail: foundation@ustrust.com; *URL:* http://www.ustrust.com/public/ustrust/our_firm/community_contributions

Trust established in 1955 in NY.
Donors: United States Trust Co. of New York; U.S. Trust Corp.
Foundation type: Company-sponsored foundation.
Financial data (yr. ended 12/31/03): Assets, $2,645 (M); gifts received, $491,446; expenditures, $500,115; qualifying distributions, $500,113; giving activities include $500,000 for 34 grants (high: $75,000; low: $5,000).
Purpose and activities: The foundation supports organizations involved with arts and culture, employment, housing, community economic development, and economically disadvantaged people.
Fields of interest: Museums; Performing arts; Performing arts, dance; Performing arts, theater;

Performing arts, music; Arts; Employment; Housing/shelter; Urban/community development; Economically disadvantaged.
Type of support: General/operating support; Continuing support; Annual campaigns; Capital campaigns; Building/renovation; Program development; Program evaluation; Matching/challenge support.
Limitations: Giving on a national basis in areas of company operations, with emphasis on Costa Mesa, Los Angeles, Palo Alto, and San Francisco, CA, Essex, Greenwich, Hartford, Stamford, and West Hartford, CT, Washington, DC, Wilmington, DE, Boca Raton, Naples, Palm Beach, Sarasota, and Vero Beach, FL, Boston and Oesterville, MA, the Twin Cities, MN, Manchester, NH, Morristown and Princeton, NJ, Garden City and New York, NY, Charlotte, Greensboro, and Raleigh, NC, Portland, OR, Philadelphia, PA, Dallas and Houston, TX, McLean, VA, and Seattle, WA. No support for religious or political organizations. No grants to individuals, or for emergency needs, debt reduction, scholarships, or fellowships; no loans.
Application information: Proposals may be submitted using the NYRAG Common Application Form. Application form not required.
  Initial approach: Letter of inquiry or proposal to nearest company facility; letter of inquiry or proposal to foundation for organizations located in New York, NY
  Copies of proposal: 1
  Deadline(s): Mar. 1 for arts and culture; Sept. 1 for community services
  Board meeting date(s): Spring for arts and culture; fall for community services
  Final notification: June 31 or Dec. 31
Corporate Contributions Committee: Carol A. Strickland, Chair.
Number of staff: 1
EIN: 136072081

7181
Albert L. Ueltschi Foundation ◇
c/o Flightsafety International
Marine Air Terminal, LaGuardia Airport
Flushing, NY 11371

Established in 2003 in FL as a successor to the original Albert L. Ueltschi Foundation (Irvine, CA).
Donor: Albert L. Ueltschi.
Foundation type: Independent foundation.
Financial data (yr. ended 12/31/05): Assets, $9,217,518 (M); gifts received, $780,000; expenditures, $448,186; qualifying distributions, $448,177; giving activities include $439,363 for grants.
Purpose and activities: Giving primarily to organizations involved with aeronautics.
Fields of interest: Health organizations, association; Space/aviation.
Limitations: Applications not accepted. Giving primarily in NY. No grants to individuals.
Application information: Contributes only to pre-selected organizations.
Trustees: Albert L. Ueltschi; James T. Ueltschi.
EIN: 550838858

7182
The C. & J. Unanue Foundation, Inc. ◇
c/o Bessemer Trust Co., N.A.
630 5th Ave.
New York, NY 10111

Established in 1995 in NJ.
Donors: Joseph A. Unanue; Carmen Unanue; Joseph A. Unanue Charitable Lead Trust.
Foundation type: Independent foundation.
Financial data (yr. ended 6/30/05): Assets, $9,969,231 (M); gifts received, $1,100,000; expenditures, $422,313; qualifying distributions, $372,992; giving activities include $372,000 for 6 grants (high: $300,000; low: $3,000).
Fields of interest: Museums (art); Higher education, university.
Limitations: Applications not accepted. Giving primarily in NJ and NY. No grants to individuals.
Application information: Contributes only to pre-selected organizations.
Officers and Trustees:* Carmen Unanue,* Pres.; Andrew Unanue,* V.P.; Joseph A. Unanue,* Secy.-Treas.
EIN: 223382542
Selected grants: The following grants were reported in 2003.
$70,000 to El Museo del Barrio, New York, NY. 2 grants: $50,000, $20,000
$50,000 to Academy of the Holy Angels, Demarest, NJ.
$50,000 to Holy Name Hospital, Teaneck, NJ.
$25,000 to Bergen Catholic High School, Oradell, NJ.
$25,000 to Casa Corazon de la Misericordia, San Pedro Sula, Honduras. .
$25,000 to Fred Hutchinson Cancer Research Center Foundation, Seattle, WA.
$15,000 to Mercy Center Corporation, Asbury Park, NJ. For Sisters Academy scholarships.
$8,000 to Georgian Court University, Lakewood, NJ. 2 grants: $3,000, $5,000 (For scholarships).

7183
The Ungar Foundation ◇
P.O. Box 752
Copake, NY 12516
Contact: Mrs. Aine Ungar, Tr.

Established in NY.
Foundation type: Independent foundation.
Financial data (yr. ended 11/30/04): Assets, $1,521,232 (M); expenditures, $407,017; qualifying distributions, $400,108; giving activities include $352,001 for 11 grants (high: $162,100; low: $3,000).
Purpose and activities: Giving to education, Native American organizations, and human services, including a residence for families and caregivers of people living with AIDS.
Fields of interest: Museums; Performing arts, dance; Education; Health organizations, association; Human services; Foundations (community); Native Americans/American Indians.
Type of support: Continuing support; Annual campaigns; Building/renovation; Program development; Professorships; Internship funds; Scholarship funds; Research.
Limitations: Giving primarily in New York, NY. No grants to individuals.
Application information:
  Initial approach: Letter
  Deadline(s): None

Trustee: Mrs. Aine D. Ungar.
Number of staff: 1 part-time support.
EIN: 136937282
Selected grants: The following grants were reported in 2004.
$162,100 to Miracle House of New York, New York, NY.
$40,000 to Native American Rights Fund, Boulder, CO.
$38,000 to TREATY Total Immersion School, Porcupine, SD. 2 grants: $23,000 (For endowment), $15,000.
$37,301 to Berkshire Taconic Community Foundation, Great Barrington, MA.
$25,000 to Yukon-Kuskokwim Health Corporation, Bethel, AK.
$23,500 to Olga Dunn Dance Company, Great Barrington, MA.
$10,000 to Taconic Hills Central School District, Craryville, NY.
$5,000 to Brain Tumor Society, Watertown, MA.
$3,000 to Copake Commission Revitalization.

7184
Union Square Awards
(formerly The Union Square Fund, Inc.)
281 Park Ave. S., 2nd Fl.
New York, NY 10010 (212) 213-6140
FAX: (212) 213-6372;
E-mail: info@unionsquareawards.org; URL: http://www.unionsquareawards.org

Established in 1997 in NY.
Foundation type: Independent foundation.
Financial data (yr. ended 12/31/05): Assets, $52,435,237 (M); expenditures, $2,936,141; qualifying distributions, $2,274,757; giving activities include $2,224,631 for 3 grants (high: $2,109,631; low: $15,000).
Purpose and activities: Giving primarily for homelessness and hunger, HIV/AIDS prevention, education and treatment, youth leadership and organizing, family and community development, economic self-sufficiency, and conflict resolution.
Fields of interest: AIDS research; Youth, services; Family services; Community development; Homeless.
Limitations: Applications not accepted. Giving limited to New York, NY. No grants to individuals.
Publications: Informational brochure.
Application information: Contributes only to pre-selected organizations.
Officers: Jeane Ungerleider, Pres.; Steven Baum, Secy.-Treas.
Number of staff: 3 full-time professional; 1 part-time professional.
EIN: 311574700

7185
United States-Japan Foundation
145 E. 32nd St., 12th Fl.
New York, NY 10016 (212) 481-8753
FAX: (212) 481-8762; E-mail: info@us-jf.org; Tokyo, Japan office address: Reinanzaka Bldg. 1F, 1-14-2 Akasaka, Minato-ku, Tokyo 107-0052, Japan, tel.: (03) 3586-0541; FAX: (03) 3586-1128; E-mail: infotokyo-usjf@nifty.com; URL: http://www.us-jf.org

Foundation incorporated in 1980 in NY.
Donor: The Nippon Foundation.
Foundation type: Independent foundation.

Financial data (yr. ended 12/31/05): Assets, $85,975,684 (M); gifts received, $20,372; expenditures, $3,843,660; qualifying distributions, $3,486,918; giving activities include $1,484,729 for grants.
Purpose and activities: The United States-Japan Foundation is committed to promoting stronger ties between Americans and Japanese by supporting projects that foster mutual knowledge and education, deepen understanding, create effective channels of communication, and address common concerns in an increasingly interdependent world. The current focus of grantmaking activities is in the areas of communication/public opinion, precollege education and policy studies.
Fields of interest: Elementary school/education; Secondary school/education; Education; Environment, energy; Environment; International economic development; International affairs, foreign policy; International affairs; Economics; Public policy, research; Government/public administration.
International interests: Asia; Japan.
Type of support: Program development; Publication; Curriculum development; Research; Matching/challenge support.
Limitations: Giving primarily in the U.S. and Japan. No support for projects in the arts involving performances, exhibitions, or productions, or for sports exchanges or student exchanges. No grants to individuals, or for building or endowment funds, capital campaigns, deficit operations.
Publications: Application guidelines; Financial statement; Grants list.
Application information: The foundation only accepts unsolicited letters of inquiry, not proposals. Application form not required.
  Initial approach: Letter (no longer than 4 pages)
  Copies of proposal: 2
  Deadline(s): July 15 and Dec. 15
  Board meeting date(s): Apr. and Oct.
  Final notification: 1 to 3 months
Officers and Trustees:* Thomas S. Johnson, Chair.; Shinji Fukukawa,* Vice-Chair.; George R. Packard,* Pres.; Takeo Takuma,* V.P. and Dir., Tokyo office; Yusuke Saraya,* Board Secy.; Christine Manapat-Sims, Treas.; John Brademas; Gerald L. Curtis; Robin Chandler Duke; Thomas S. Foley; Yotaro Kobayashi; Ahira Kojima; T. Timothy Ryan, Jr.; Yohei Sasakawa; Thomas W. Strauss.
Number of staff: 5 full-time professional; 1 part-time support.
EIN: 133054425
Selected grants: The following grants were reported in 2004.
$220,000 to Japan Society, New York, NY. 2 grants: $165,000, $55,000
$101,145 to Stanford University, Stanford, CA. 2 grants: $40,260, $60,885
$27,500 to Projectile Arts, Brooklyn, NY.
$26,766 to Yamaguchi University, Yamaguchi, Japan. .
$25,000 to Japan Society of Boston, Boston, MA.
$25,000 to Midori Foundation, New York, NY.
$25,000 to University of Vermont, Burlington, VT.
$25,000 to W G B H Educational Foundation, Boston, MA.

7186
Marjorie & Clarence E. Unterberg Foundation, Inc. ✧
c/o C.E. Unterberg Towbin
350 Madison Ave., 9th Fl.
New York, NY 10017

Established in 1994 in NY.
Donors: Mary A. Debare; Thomas I. Unterberg.
Foundation type: Independent foundation.
Financial data (yr. ended 12/31/04): Assets, $9,181,970 (M); gifts received, $1,609,250; expenditures, $2,004,639; qualifying distributions, $1,987,100; giving activities include $1,987,100 for 91 grants (high: $250,000; low: $100).
Purpose and activities: Giving primarily to a neighborhood center, as well as for human services; funding also for the arts, higher education, health care, children and youth services, and Jewish federated giving programs.
Fields of interest: Museums (art); Museums (children's); Performing arts, theater; Historic preservation/historical societies; Arts; Higher education; Health care; Health organizations, association; Human services; Neighborhood centers; Children/youth, services; Jewish federated giving programs.
Limitations: Applications not accepted. Giving primarily in NJ and NY. No grants to individuals.
Application information: Contributes only to pre-selected organizations.
Officers: Thomas I. Unterberg, Pres.; Mary A. Debare, V.P. and Secy.; Andrew Arno, Treas.
EIN: 133792809
Selected grants: The following grants were reported in 2003.
$125,000 to UJA-Federation of New York, New York, NY.
$62,000 to Grand Street Settlement, New York, NY.
$50,000 to Deerfield Academy, Deerfield, MA.
$30,000 to American Jewish Committee, New York, NY.
$30,000 to International Womens Health Coalition, New York, NY.
$25,000 to Princeton University, Princeton, NJ.
$10,000 to Monmouth Medical Center Foundation, Long Branch, NJ.
$5,000 to Jewish Museum, New York, NY.
$5,000 to Monmouth University, West Long Branch, NJ.
$250 to Oceanic Free Library, Rumson, NJ.

7187
Uphill Foundation ✧
c/o U.S. Trust
114 W. 47th St., TAXRGR
New York, NY 10036
Contact: Barry Waldorf

Established in 2000 in PA.
Donor: Frances A. Velay.
Foundation type: Independent foundation.
Financial data (yr. ended 12/31/05): Assets, $7,787,920 (M); expenditures, $384,054; qualifying distributions, $334,900; giving activities include $332,500 for 10 grants (high: $75,000; low: $5,000).
Purpose and activities: Giving primarily for the preservation of animal and vegetal species threatened with extinction, and for the prevention of cruelty to animals.
Fields of interest: Libraries (public); Human services.

Application information:
Initial approach: Letter
Trustees: Dan McCarthy; Barbara Paul Robinson; Frances A. Velay.
EIN: 137196672
Selected grants: The following grants were reported in 2003.
$50,000 to Heifer Project International, Little Rock, AR. For general support.
$50,000 to Project Hope, Brooklyn, NY. For general support.
$50,000 to ProLiteracy Worldwide, Syracuse, NY. For general support.
$50,000 to Wave Hill, Bronx, NY. For general support.
$15,000 to Arnold P. Gold Foundation, Englewood Cliffs, NJ. For general support.
$15,000 to TechnoServe, Norwalk, CT. For general support.
$10,000 to Asheville Art Museum Association, Asheville, NC. For general support.
$10,000 to CARE, San Francisco, CA. For general support.
$10,000 to FINCA International, DC. For general support.
$10,000 to Trickle Up Program, New York, NY. For general support.

7188
Ushkow Foundation, Inc. ✧ ☆
c/o Bama Equities, Inc.
200 E. 61st St., Ste. 15E
New York, NY   10021

Incorporated in 1956 in NY.
Donor: Joseph Ushkow.
Foundation type: Independent foundation.
Financial data (yr. ended 12/31/05): Assets, $1,774,460 (M); expenditures, $459,100; qualifying distributions, $444,548; giving activities include $430,950 for 72 grants (high: $145,000; low: $50).
Purpose and activities: Giving primarily to Jewish agencies and temples and for education.
Fields of interest: Museums; Higher education; Education; Health care; Human services; Jewish federated giving programs; Public affairs; Jewish agencies & temples.
Limitations: Applications not accepted. Giving primarily in NY, with some emphasis on Nassau County. No grants to individuals.
Application information: Contributes only to pre-selected organizations.
Officers: Barbara Deane, Pres.; Maurice A. Deane, Secy.-Treas.
EIN: 116006274
Selected grants: The following grants were reported in 2004.
$45,000 to Hofstra University, Hempstead, NY.
$26,700 to Temple Beth-El, Cedarhurst, NY. 4 grants: $600, $1,000, $25,000, $100
$10,000 to Bennington College, Bennington, VT.
$10,000 to Jewish Museum, New York, NY.
$10,000 to Raymond F. Kravis Center for the Performing Arts, West Palm Beach, FL.
$1,250 to Dalton Schools, New York, NY.
$500 to Metropolitan Museum of Art, New York, NY.

7189
The Valentine Charitable Foundation, Inc. ✧
61 Broadway, 18th Fl.
New York, NY   10006-2794

Established in 1998 in FL.
Donors: Audrey I. Clark Charitable Lead Trust; Reed Clark Dynasty Charitable Lead Unitrust.
Foundation type: Independent foundation.
Financial data (yr. ended 12/31/04): Assets, $703,935 (M); gifts received, $463,661; expenditures, $365,895; qualifying distributions, $354,067; giving activities include $353,620 for 29 grants (high: $50,000; low: $300).
Fields of interest: Education, services; Christian agencies & churches.
Type of support: General/operating support.
Limitations: Applications not accepted. Giving primarily in NY. No grants to individuals.
Application information: Contributes only to pre-selected organizations.
Officers and Directors:* Audrey I. Clark,* Pres.; Peter R. Clark,* V.P. and Treas.; Sandra C. Moore,* Secy.
EIN: 223603584

7190
H. van Ameringen Foundation ✧
509 Madison Ave.
New York, NY   10022-5501   (212) 758-6221
Contact: Henry P. van Ameringen, Tr.

Established in 1967 in NY.
Donor: Henry P. van Ameringen.
Foundation type: Independent foundation.
Financial data (yr. ended 12/31/04): Assets, $30,399,724 (M); gifts received, $1,015,000; expenditures, $3,200,462; qualifying distributions, $3,185,990; giving activities include $3,183,150 for 117 grants (high: $130,000; low: $1,000; average: $1,000–$50,000).
Purpose and activities: Giving primarily for human service agencies, AIDS programs, health organizations, and civil rights agencies.
Fields of interest: Health care; AIDS; Human services; Civil rights, advocacy; LGBTQ.
Type of support: General/operating support; Program development; Seed money; Matching/challenge support.
Limitations: Applications not accepted. Giving primarily in NY. No grants to individuals.
Application information: Contributes only to pre-selected organizations.
Trustee: Henry P. van Ameringen.
EIN: 136215329

7191
van Ameringen Foundation, Inc. ▼
509 Madison Ave.
New York, NY   10022-5501   (212) 758-6221
Contact: Henry P. van Ameringen, Pres.
URL: http://www.vanamfound.org/

Incorporated in 1950 in NY.
Donor: Arnold Louis van Ameringen†.
Foundation type: Independent foundation.
Financial data (yr. ended 12/31/05): Assets, $78,705,804 (M); expenditures, $4,800,510; qualifying distributions, $3,928,556; giving activities include $3,928,556 for 82 grants (high:

$150,000; low: $3,500; average: $5,000–$50,000).
Purpose and activities: Grants primarily to promote mental health and social welfare through preventive measures, treatment, and rehabilitation. Support also for the field of psychiatry. Within its broad focus on mental health, the foundation is interested in encouraging and attracting innovative and practical programs in areas which: 1) increase the accessibility of the poor and needy to mental health services; and 2) offer preventative and early intervention strategies.
Fields of interest: Mental health, treatment; Mental health/crisis services.
Type of support: General/operating support; Program development; Seed money; Matching/challenge support.
Limitations: Giving primarily in metropolitan New York, NY, and Philadelphia, PA. No support for international activities and institutions, or for programs for the mentally retarded, the physically handicapped, drug abuse, or alcoholism. No grants to individuals, or for endowments, annual campaigns, deficit financing, emergency funds, capital campaigns, scholarships, or fellowships; no loans.
Publications: Application guidelines; Annual report; Financial statement; Grants list.
Application information: NYRAG Common Application Form required. Proposals received after a deadline will not be considered for the upcoming meeting. Application form required.
Initial approach: Letter of inquiry
Copies of proposal: 1
Deadline(s): Apr. 1 (for June meeting), July 1 (for Nov. meeting), and Dec. 1 (for Mar. meeting)
Board meeting date(s): Mar., June, and Nov.
Final notification: Within 60 days
Officers and Directors:* Henry P. van Ameringen,* Pres. and Treas.; George Rowe, Jr.,* V.P. and Secy.; Eleanor K. Sypher, Exec. Dir.; Christina K. Baiocchi; Judith Beck; Alexandra Herzan; Kenneth A. Kind; Patricia Kind; Valerie Kind-Rubin; Andrew Kindfuller; Laura K. McKenna; Clarence J. Sundram.
Number of staff: 1 full-time professional; 1 full-time support.
EIN: 136125699
Selected grants: The following grants were reported in 2005.
$225,000 to Disability Advocates, Albany, NY. For ongoing advocacy and litigation for mentally ill inmates in New York State, payable over 2 years.
$200,000 to MFY Legal Services, New York, NY. For ongoing support of advocacy and litigation for mentally ill in adult homes.
$200,000 to Urban Justice Center, New York, NY. For social security benefits restoration project, which would initiate a class action suit and media and policy campaign to restore benefits to mentally ill, elderly, and disabled who are wrongly accused of felonies in NYC, payable over 2 years.
$199,356 to Schuyler Center for Analysis and Advocacy, Albany, NY. For continued support of mental health advocates for adult home reform, payable over 2 years.
$132,490 to New York City Health and Hospitals Corporation, New York, NY. For psychologist and related expenses to deliver short-term, solution-based therapy to low-income Black and Hispanic patients with HIV at Jacobi Hospital, payable over 2 years.
$102,119 to North Shore-Long Island Jewish Health System Foundation, Great Neck, NY. For start-up of Intensive Outpatient Program for treatment of

children and adolescents with eating disorders, payable over 2 years.

$100,000 to Breakthrough Club of Sedgwick County, Wichita, KS. For training, education, communication hub, developed to allow clubhouses for mentally ill around the world to communicate and to take website courses, payable over 2 years.

$50,000 to Hudson Guild, New York, NY. For anger management program for low-income emotionally disturbed young people.

$50,000 to Montgomery County Emergency Service, Norristown, PA. For training small municipal police force in mental health treatment and crisis intervention.

$50,000 to Saint Lukes-Roosevelt Hospital Center, New York, NY. For developing mindfulness-based stress reduction meditation and yoga program as specialty care for individuals with HIV/AIDS.

7192
Van Pelt Foundation ✧

c/o Konigsberg, Wolf & Co.
440 Park Ave. S.
New York, NY 10016

Established in 1977 in NJ.
Donors: Edwin Van Pelt†; Henry Bass†.
Foundation type: Independent foundation.
Financial data (yr. ended 9/30/05): Assets, $6,105,508 (M); expenditures, $353,604; qualifying distributions, $319,595; giving activities include $319,570 for 68 grants (high: $53,000; low: $250).
Purpose and activities: Support for smaller organizations that have been hurt by cutbacks in federal monies or individual contributions.
Fields of interest: Performing arts; Education; Hospitals (general); Human services; Children/youth, services; Family services; Homeless, human services; Homeless.
Type of support: General/operating support; Continuing support; Building/renovation; Equipment; Program development; Seed money; Research; Matching/challenge support.
Limitations: Giving primarily in FL, NJ, and NY. No grants to individuals, or for building renovations, or for capital campaigns.
Publications: Application guidelines.
Application information: Telephone requests not accepted. Application form not required.
  Initial approach: Proposal
  Copies of proposal: 5
  Deadline(s): Apr. 10 and Oct. 10
  Board meeting date(s): May 1 and Nov. 1
  Final notification: Within 2 weeks of meetings on or about May 1 and Nov. 1
Officers and Trustees:* Lawrence D. Bass,* Pres.; Stanley Cooper, V.P.; Robert DuBois,* Secy.; Henry Gerke,* Treas.; John Schmidt.
Number of staff: 1 part-time support.
EIN: 222188141
Selected grants: The following grants were reported in 2005.
$53,000 to Pascack Valley Hospital Foundation, Westwood, NJ.
$20,500 to University of Pennsylvania, Philadelphia, PA.
$20,000 to Valley Hospital Foundation, Ridgewood, NJ.
$10,000 to Kennedy Krieger Institute, Baltimore, MD.

$6,000 to National Center for Learning Disabilities, New York, NY.
$4,000 to Deborah Hospital Foundation, Browns Mills, NJ.
$3,500 to New Jersey Theater Alliance, Morristown, NJ.
$2,500 to New York University, New York, NY.
$2,000 to Bucknell University, Lewisburg, PA.
$2,000 to Signature Theater Company, New York, NY.

7193
Lee and Cynthia Vance Foundation ✧ ☆

c/o BCRS Associates, LLC
100 Wall St., 11th Fl.
New York, NY 10005

Established in 1993 in NY.
Donor: Lee G. Vance.
Foundation type: Independent foundation.
Financial data (yr. ended 6/30/05): Assets, $9,907,381 (M); expenditures, $488,981; qualifying distributions, $356,367; giving activities include $345,466 for 124 grants (high: $100,000; low: $35).
Fields of interest: Media, radio; Museums; Performing arts, theater; Performing arts, music; Arts; Higher education; Education; Recreation, parks/playgrounds; Human services; Civil rights, women.
Limitations: Applications not accepted. Giving primarily in New York, NY; some funding also in CT. No grants to individuals.
Application information: Contributes only to pre-selected organizations.
Trustees: Cynthia King Vance; Lee G. Vance.
EIN: 133789060

7194
The Gopal Varadhan Memorial Foundation ✧ ☆

c/o Goldman Sachs- Family Office
1 New York Plz., 40th Fl.
New York, NY 10004

Established in 2003 in NY.
Foundation type: Independent foundation.
Financial data (yr. ended 12/31/05): Assets, $2,188,415 (M); expenditures, $357,872; qualifying distributions, $351,000; giving activities include $351,000 for 3 grants (high: $250,000; low: $1,000).
Fields of interest: Higher education; Children/youth, services.
Limitations: Applications not accepted. Giving primarily in NY. No grants to individuals.
Application information: Contributes only to pre-selected organizations.
Trustees: Ashok Varadhan; Srinivasa Varadhan.
EIN: 476262237

7195
Miles Hodsdon Vernon Foundation, Inc. ✧

c/o Chadbourne, et al.
P.O. Box 701
Sleepy Hollow, NY 10591-0701 (914) 923-8499
Contact: Robert C. Thomson, Jr., Pres.

Incorporated in 1953 in NY.

Donors: Miles Hodsdon Vernon†; Martha Hodsdon Kinney†; Louise Hodsdon†.
Foundation type: Independent foundation.
Financial data (yr. ended 12/31/04): Assets, $9,015,985 (M); expenditures, $589,485; qualifying distributions, $372,776; giving activities include $343,500 for 33 grants (high: $55,000; low: $1,000).
Purpose and activities: Giving primarily for education, YMCAs, children and youth services, federated giving programs, and to a Presbyterian church.
Fields of interest: Secondary school/education; Higher education; Scholarships/financial aid; Education; Agriculture/food; Human services; YM/YWCAs & YM/YWHAs; Children/youth, services; Homeless, human services; Federated giving programs; Christian agencies & churches; Economically disadvantaged.
Type of support: Scholarship funds; Research.
Limitations: Giving primarily in NY. No grants to individuals directly.
Application information:
  Initial approach: Proposal
  Deadline(s): None
  Final notification: Positive responses only
Officers and Directors:* Robert C. Thomson, Jr.,* Pres. and Treas.; Dennis M. Fitzgerald,* V.P. and Secy.; Michele C. Fitzgerald; Linda T. Murray; Eloise T. Schundler.
EIN: 136076836
Selected grants: The following grants were reported in 2004.
$68,500 to YMCA. 4 grants: $10,000, $13,500, $25,000, $20,000
$55,000 to Wolfeboro Area Childrens Center, Wolfeboro, NH.
$10,000 to Independent College Fund.
$10,000 to Lake Wentworth Foundation, Wolfeboro, NH.
$5,500 to Cardinal Hayes High School, Bronx, NY.
$5,000 to Brewster Academy, Wolfeboro, NH.
$5,000 to Westfield Day Care Center, Westfield, NJ.

7196
The G. Unger Vetlesen Foundation ▼ ✧

c/o Fulton, Rowe, & Hart
1 Rockefeller Plz., Ste. 301
New York, NY 10020-2002 (212) 586-0700
Contact: George Rowe, Jr., Pres.
FAX: (212) 245-1863;
E-mail: info@monellvetlesen.org; URL: http://www.monellvetlesen.org/

Incorporated in 1955 in NY.
Donor: George Unger Vetlesen†.
Foundation type: Independent foundation.
Financial data (yr. ended 12/31/05): Assets, $96,313,287 (M); expenditures, $4,844,384; qualifying distributions, $4,140,055; giving activities include $4,010,809 for 31 grants (high: $700,000; low: $2,500; average: $25,000–$100,000).
Purpose and activities: Established a biennial international science award for discoveries in the earth sciences; grants for biological, geophysical, and environmental research, including scholarships, and cultural organizations, including those emphasizing Norwegian-American relations and maritime interests. Support also for public policy research and libraries.
Fields of interest: Arts; Libraries/library science; Environment; Marine science; Physical/earth

sciences; Engineering/technology; Biological sciences; Science; Public policy, research.
Type of support: General/operating support; Continuing support; Annual campaigns; Capital campaigns; Building/renovation; Equipment; Endowments; Program development; Professorships; Scholarship funds; Research.
Limitations: Giving on a national basis. No grants to individuals.
Publications: Application guidelines; Annual report; Financial statement; Grants list.
Application information: Application form not required.
  Initial approach: Letter
  Copies of proposal: 1
  Deadline(s): Apr. 30 and Oct. 31
  Board meeting date(s): June and Dec.
Officers and Directors:* George Rowe, Jr.,* Pres. and Treas.; Maurizio J. Morello, Secy.; Gary K. Beauchamp; Eugene P. Grisanti; Ambrose K. Monell.
EIN: 131982695
Selected grants: The following grants were reported in 2004.
$940,139 to Columbia University, New York, NY. 3 grants: $500,000 to Lamont-Doherty Earth Observatory (For general operating support), $200,000 to Lamont-Doherty Earth Observatory (For Climate Center programs), $240,139 to Lamont-Doherty Earth Observatory (For Vetlesen Award).
$700,000 to Scripps Institution of Oceanography, La Jolla, CA. For global change program.
$700,000 to Woods Hole Oceanographic Institution, Woods Hole, MA. For general operating support.
$350,000 to Marine Biological Laboratory, Josephine Bay Paul Center in Comparative Molecular Biology and Evolution, Woods Hole, MA. For veterinary services at Marine Resources Center.
$125,000 to Oregon State University, College of Oceanic and Atmospheric Sciences, Corvallis, OR. For general operating support.
$125,000 to University of Miami, Rosenstiel School of Marine and Atmospheric Science, Coral Gables, FL. For climate studies.
$100,000 to Massachusetts Institute of Technology, Cambridge, MA. For MIT Joint Program on Science and Policy of Global Change.
$25,000 to Wildlife Conservation Society, Bronx, NY. For Marine Program.

7197
VHIV, Inc. ✧
(formerly The Bella Wexner Charitable Foundation)
c/o Hertz, Herson, & Co., LLP
Two Park Ave., Ste. 1500
New York, NY 10016

Established in 1990 in OH.
Donor: Bella Wexner.
Foundation type: Independent foundation.
Financial data (yr. ended 12/31/03): Assets, $36,166,304 (M); gifts received, $15,365; expenditures, $2,637,081; qualifying distributions, $2,294,572; giving activities include $2,239,000 for 22 grants (high: $154,700; low: $2,000).
Fields of interest: Philanthropy/voluntarism.
Limitations: Applications not accepted. No grants to individuals.
Application information: Contributes only to a pre-selected organization.

Officers and Directors:* Susan R. Wexner,* Pres. and Secy.-Treas.; Bertrand Agus.
EIN: 311324522

7198
The Vidda Foundation
250 W. 57th St., Ste. 916
New York, NY 10107
Contact: John B. Roberts, Admin.
URL: http://www.vidda.org

Established in 1979 in NY.
Donor: Ursula Corning†.
Foundation type: Independent foundation.
Financial data (yr. ended 5/31/06): Assets, $8,079,034 (M); gifts received, $600,000; expenditures, $1,416,677; qualifying distributions, $1,351,326; giving activities include $1,285,990 for 30 grants (high: $300,000; low: $2,000).
Purpose and activities: Giving primarily to higher education and educational projects, cultural programs, including fine arts and museums, church music funds, animal welfare, the environment and conservation, hospitals, and social services, including child welfare and the elderly.
Fields of interest: Humanities; Arts; Education; Environment, beautification programs; Environment; Animal welfare; Animals/wildlife, preservation/protection; Medical care, in-patient care; Human services; Children/youth, services; Aging, centers/services; Economic development; Community development; Protestant agencies & churches.
Type of support: General/operating support; Continuing support; Annual campaigns; Building/renovation; Endowments; Program development; Seed money; Research.
Limitations: Giving primarily in NY. No grants to individuals.
Publications: Application guidelines; Financial statement.
Application information: New York/New Jersey Area Common Grant Application Form is required from proposed grantees that receive a positive response to their letter of intent. Please refer to application guidelines on foundation Web site. Application form required.
  Initial approach: Letter of interest
  Copies of proposal: 1
  Deadline(s): None
  Board meeting date(s): Dec. and May
  Final notification: Approximately 2 months
Officer and Trustees:* Gerald E. Rupp,* Chair.; John A. Downey, M.D.; Helen C. Evarts; Ian Fraser; John B. Roberts.
EIN: 132981105
Selected grants: The following grants were reported in 2005.
$330,000 to Columbia University, New York, NY. 3 grants: $250,000, $65,000, $15,000
$300,000 to World Wildlife Fund, DC.
$100,000 to American Museum of Natural History, New York, NY.
$50,000 to Trust for Public Land, New York, NY.
$25,000 to Nature Conservancy, East Hampton, NY.
$25,000 to Waverly Consort, Patterson, NY.
$10,000 to Nature Conservancy, Arlington, TX.
$5,000 to High School for Environmental Studies, New York, NY.

7199
The Vilcek Foundation, Inc.
(formerly The Friderika Fischer Foundation)
c/o Jan Vilcek, M.D.
920 5th Ave., No. 2A
New York, NY 10021
Contact: Rick A. Kinsel, Exec. Dir.
FAX: (212) 794-9652; E-mail: rick.kinsel@vilcek.org;
URL: http://www.vilcek.org

Established in 2000 in NY. Classified as a private operating foundation in 2001.
Donor: Jan Vilcek.
Foundation type: Operating foundation.
Financial data (yr. ended 11/30/05): Assets, $15,842,156 (M); gifts received, $51,980; expenditures, $747,311; qualifying distributions, $557,348; giving activities include $445,500 for 7 grants (high: $340,000; low: $5,000).
Purpose and activities: The foundation honors foreign-born scientists and artists living in the U.S. who have made outstanding contributions to U.S. society that benefit mankind. Each year the foundation bestows upon certain individuals the Vilcek Prize to honor such achievement in biomedical research and in arts or humanities. Giving primarily for higher education and to fund a research project to develop treatments for chronic inflammatory auto-immune diseases.
Fields of interest: Performing arts, opera; Higher education; Arthritis research; Medical research; Immunology research.
Type of support: Conferences/seminars; Research.
Limitations: Applications not accepted. Giving primarily in NY and NM. No grants to individuals.
Application information: Contributes only to pre-selected organizations.
Officers and Directors:* Jan Vilcek,* Pres. and Treas.; Marica Vilcek,* V.P. and Secy.; Rick A. Kinsel,* Exec. Dir.; Bruce Cronstein, M.D.; Jennifer Olshin.
Number of staff: 1 full-time professional.
EIN: 510404790
Selected grants: The following grants were reported in 2003.
$224,584 to New York University, New York, NY. For medical research.
$25,000 to Santa Fe Opera, Santa Fe, NM.
$10,000 to Saint Anns School, Brooklyn, NY.
$7,000 to Ballet Folklorico Mexicano De Nueva York, Sunnyside, NY.
$7,000 to International Cytokine Society, Augusta, GA.

7200
Ellen M. Violett and Mary P. R. Thomas Foundation ✧
(formerly Ellen M. Violett Foundation, Inc.)
230 E. 50th St.
New York, NY 10022

Established in 1994 in NY.
Donor: Ellen M. Violett.
Foundation type: Independent foundation.
Financial data (yr. ended 12/31/05): Assets, $2,900 (M); gifts received, $345,000; expenditures, $349,609; qualifying distributions, $346,933; giving activities include $344,290 for 48 grants (high: $200,000; low: $100).
Purpose and activities: Giving primarily for the arts, gays and lesbians, and medical research, human services, and civil rights.

Fields of interest: Media, film/video; Performing arts; Literature; Arts, artist's services; Adult education—literacy, basic skills & GED; Cancer; AIDS; Cancer research; Medical research; Human services; Civil rights, advocacy; Minorities; LGBTQ.
Limitations: Applications not accepted. Giving primarily in New York, NY. No grants to individuals.
Application information: Contributes only to pre-selected organizations.
Officers: Ellen M. Violett, Pres.; Mary P.R. Thomas, V.P.; Herbert Bard, Secy.
EIN: 133767145
Selected grants: The following grants were reported in 2003.
$37,000 to Stella Adler Studio of Acting, New York, NY.
$27,852 to Manhattan Theater Club, New York, NY.
$10,000 to Hetrick-Martin Institute, New York, NY.
$10,000 to New York City Public/Private Initiatives, New York, NY.
$10,000 to New York Times Neediest Cases Fund, New York, NY.
$8,500 to Municipal Art Society of New York, New York, NY.
$5,000 to Carter Center, Atlanta, GA.
$5,000 to Writers Guild Foundation, Los Angeles, CA.
$5,000 to Writers Guild of America East Foundation, New York, NY.
$4,500 to Bay Street Theater Festival, Sag Harbor, NY.

7201
John L. Vogelstein Charitable Trust ✧
c/o Warburg Pincus
466 Lexington Ave., 10th Fl.
New York, NY   10017-3147

Established in 1999 in NY.
Donor: John L. Vogelstein.
Foundation type: Independent foundation.
Financial data (yr. ended 11/30/04): Assets, $2,600,673 (M); gifts received, $2,275,394; expenditures, $3,789,661; qualifying distributions, $3,726,500; giving activities include $3,726,500 for 84 grants (high: $320,000; low: $500).
Purpose and activities: Giving primarily for education, and the arts, particularly the performing arts as well as for health and human services.
Fields of interest: Museums (art); Performing arts, ballet; Performing arts, opera; Arts; Elementary/secondary education; Higher education; Education; Hospitals (general); Reproductive health, family planning; Health organizations, association; Medical research, association; Human services; Children/youth, services; Jewish agencies & temples.
Limitations: Applications not accepted. Giving primarily in the metropolitan New York, NY area; some giving nationally. No grants to individuals.
Application information: Contributes only to pre-selected organizations.
Trustees: Andrew A. Vogelstein; Barbara Manfrey Vogelstein; Hans A. Vogelstein; John L. Vogelstein.
EIN: 137177278
Selected grants: The following grants were reported in 2003.
$360,000 to Taft School, Watertown, CT. 2 grants: $80,000, $280,000
$250,000 to New York City Ballet, New York, NY. 2 grants: $50,000, $200,000
$250,000 to Pomona College, Claremont, CA.

$230,000 to Jewish Museum, New York, NY. 2 grants: $30,000, $200,000
$200,000 to Vassar College, Poughkeepsie, NY.
$175,000 to RAND Corporation, Santa Monica, CA. 2 grants: $75,000, $100,000

7202
Barry & Teri Volpert Foundation ✧
c/o BCRS Assocs., LLC
100 Wall St., 11th Fl.
New York, NY   10005

Established in 1995 in NY.
Donor: Barry S. Volpert.
Foundation type: Independent foundation.
Financial data (yr. ended 8/31/05): Assets, $3,668,434 (M); expenditures, $395,648; qualifying distributions, $367,060; giving activities include $364,166 for 83 grants (high: $75,000; low: $75).
Fields of interest: Museums (art); Performing arts, orchestra (symphony); Higher education; Higher education, university; Hospitals (general); Youth development, centers/clubs; Federated giving programs; Jewish agencies & temples.
Limitations: Applications not accepted. Giving on a national basis; some funding also in London, England. No grants to individuals.
Application information: Contributes only to pre-selected organizations.
Trustees: Joel Beckman; Barry S. Volpert; Teri C. Volpert.
EIN: 133802670
Selected grants: The following grants were reported in 2004.
$179,120 to Amherst College, Amherst, MA. For grant made in form of stock.
$25,000 to Tufts University, Medford, MA. For general support.
$10,000 to Jewish Museum, New York, NY. For general support.
$10,000 to Rye Country Day School, Rye, NY. For general support.
$10,000 to UJA-Federation of New York, New York, NY. For general support.
$9,178 to American School in London Foundation, London, England. For general support.
$5,016 to Temple Sholom, Greenwich, CT. For general support.
$5,000 to University of Oregon, Institute for the Development of Educational Achievement, Eugene, OR. For general support.
$3,000 to Los Angeles Clippers Foundation, Los Angeles, CA. For general support.
$2,850 to Common Ground Community Housing Development Fund Corporation, New York, NY. For general support.

7203
The von der Heyden Foundation ✧
c/o Karl M. von der Heyden
25 Central Park W., No. 24K
New York, NY   10023

Established in 1994 in CT.
Donors: Ingolf M. von der Heyden; Karl von der Heyden.
Foundation type: Independent foundation.
Financial data (yr. ended 12/31/05): Assets, $2,386,542 (M); gifts received, $879,527; expenditures, $947,499; qualifying distributions,

$943,665; giving activities include $936,849 for 14 grants (high: $677,600; low: $150).
Purpose and activities: Giving primarily for higher education.
Fields of interest: Museums; Arts; Higher education; Education; Human services; YM/YWCAs & YM/YWHAs; Federated giving programs.
Limitations: Applications not accepted. Giving primarily in NC and NY. No grants to individuals.
Application information: Contributes only to pre-selected organizations.
Trustees: Karl von der Heyden; Mary Ellen von der Heyden.
EIN: 061410915

7204
Sue and Edgar Wachenheim Foundation ▼
3 Manhattanville Rd.
Purchase, NY   10577-2116
Contact: Edgar Wachenheim III, Pres.

Established in 1969 in NY.
Donors: Sue W. Wachenheim; Edgar Wachenheim III; Greenhaven Assocs.
Foundation type: Independent foundation.
Financial data (yr. ended 10/31/05): Assets, $102,994,264 (M); expenditures, $5,353,006; qualifying distributions, $4,982,650; giving activities include $4,981,150 for 54 grants (high: $1,400,000; low: $500; average: $2,500–$250,000).
Purpose and activities: Giving primarily for higher education and for health and human services.
Fields of interest: Arts; Higher education; Libraries/library science; Education; Health care; Human services.
Type of support: Annual campaigns; Capital campaigns; Building/renovation; Scholarship funds.
Limitations: Applications not accepted. Giving primarily in NY. No grants to individuals.
Application information: Contributes only to pre-selected organizations.
Officers and Directors:* Edgar Wachenheim III,* Pres.; Sue W. Wachenheim,* Exec. V.P.; Kenneth L. Wallach, Secy.; Kim Wachenheim Wagman; Ira D. Wallach.
Number of staff: None.
EIN: 237011002
Selected grants: The following grants were reported in 2005.
$2,300,000 to New York Public Library, New York, NY. 3 grants: $1,400,000 (For general support), $50,000 (For general support), $850,000 (For general support).
$1,115,000 to Museum of Modern Art, New York, NY. 3 grants: $1,000,000 (For general support), $90,000 (For general support), $25,000 (For general support).
$500,000 to Williams College, Williamstown, MA. For general support.
$300,000 to Rye Country Day School, Rye, NY. For general support.
$250,000 to Memorial Sloan-Kettering Cancer Center, New York, NY. For general support.
$12,500 to HealthCare Chaplaincy, New York, NY. For general support.

7205
The Wachtell, Lipton, Rosen & Katz Foundation ▼ ◇
51 W. 52nd St.
New York, NY 10019

Established in 1981 in NY.
Donor: Wachtell, Lipton, Rosen & Katz.
Foundation type: Company-sponsored foundation.
Financial data (yr. ended 9/30/05): Assets, $10,501,230 (M); gifts received, $4,000,000; expenditures, $3,259,896; qualifying distributions, $3,259,350; giving activities include $3,259,000 for 19 grants (high: $1,000,000; low: $5,000).
Purpose and activities: The foundation supports organizations involved with higher and legal education.
Fields of interest: Higher education; Law school/education; Jewish federated giving programs.
Type of support: Scholarship funds; Annual campaigns; Endowments; General/operating support.
Limitations: Applications not accepted. Giving limited to New York, NY. No grants to individuals.
Application information: Contributes only to pre-selected organizations.
  Board meeting date(s): As necessary
Officers and Directors: Martin Lipton, Pres.; Herbert M. Wachtell, V.P. and Secy.; Richard D. Katcher, V.P.; Constance Monte, Treas.; Edward D. Herlihy; Daniel A. Neff.
EIN: 133099901
Selected grants: The following grants were reported in 2004.
$2,000,000 to New York University, New York, NY. 2 grants: $1,000,000 (For Neuroscience Program), $1,000,000 (For President's Endowment Fund).
$750,000 to UJA-Federation of New York, New York, NY. For general support.
$400,000 to Prep for Prep, New York, NY. For general support.
$200,000 to New York City Leadership Academy, New York, NY. For general support.
$200,000 to University of Pennsylvania, Philadelphia, PA.
$100,000 to University of Chicago, School of Law, Chicago, IL.
$97,000 to Harvard University, Cambridge, MA. For Law School Fund.
$50,000 to Jewish Theological Seminary of America, New York, NY. For general support.
$50,000 to Mount Sinai School of Medicine of New York University, New York, NY.

7206
Leonard Wagner Trust ◇
c/o Paul Eichler
1375 Broadway, 16th Fl.
New York, NY 10018

Established in 1994.
Donor: Leonard Wagner†.
Foundation type: Independent foundation.
Financial data (yr. ended 12/31/03): Assets, $22,394,586 (M); expenditures, $1,794,480; qualifying distributions, $1,500,000; giving activities include $1,500,000 for grants.
Purpose and activities: Giving primarily for higher education, and to support hospitals and medical research.
Fields of interest: Higher education; Hospitals (general); Medical research, institute.

Limitations: Applications not accepted. Giving primarily in NY. No grants to individuals.
Application information: Contributes only to pre-selected organizations.
Trustees: Paul Eichler; Alexander Forger.
EIN: 137012051

7207
The Walbridge Fund ◇
c/o William S. Phillips, C.P.A.
26 Firemans Memorial Dr., Ste. 110
Pomona, NY 10970-3569

Established in 1997 in NY.
Foundation type: Independent foundation.
Financial data (yr. ended 12/31/05): Assets, $15,187,327 (M); expenditures, $1,119,570; qualifying distributions, $1,017,000; giving activities include $1,017,000 for 60 grants (high: $100,000; low: $2,500).
Purpose and activities: Giving primarily for environmental programs.
Fields of interest: Museums; Elementary/secondary education; Higher education; Environment, natural resources; Environment; Human services.
Limitations: Applications not accepted. Giving primarily in NY and UT. No grants to individuals.
Application information: Contributes only to pre-selected organizations.
Officers: George W. Perkins, Jr., Pres.; Jennifer P. Speers, V.P.; Arthur V. Savage, Secy.; William S. Phillips, Treas.
Trustees: Arthur Yorke Allen; Nancy F. Perkins; Randon W. Wilson.
EIN: 133936131

7208
Thomas B. Walker III Foundation ◇
c/o Goldman Sachs & Co.
1 New York Plz., 40th Fl.
New York, NY 10004

Established in 1991 in NY.
Donor: Thomas B. Walker III.
Foundation type: Independent foundation.
Financial data (yr. ended 4/30/05): Assets, $1,093,259 (M); gifts received, $1,311,000; expenditures, $369,947; qualifying distributions, $366,800; giving activities include $366,800 for 30 grants (high: $50,000; low: $1,000).
Purpose and activities: Giving primarily for education and Protestant agencies and churches.
Fields of interest: Arts; Education; Health organizations, association; Human services; Protestant agencies & churches.
Limitations: Applications not accepted. Giving primarily in New York, NY. No grants to individuals.
Application information: Contributes only to pre-selected organizations.
Trustee: Thomas B. Walker III.
EIN: 133632752
Selected grants: The following grants were reported in 2004.
$50,000 to Brearley School, New York, NY.
$25,000 to New York University, Child Study Center, New York, NY.
$25,000 to Saint Bernards School, New York, NY.
$10,000 to Brick Presbyterian Church, New York, NY.
$10,000 to Enterprise Foundation, New York, NY.

$10,000 to Juvenile Law Center, Philadelphia, PA.
$10,000 to New York City Opera, New York, NY.
$10,000 to Princeton University, Princeton, NJ.
$10,000 to Project ALS, New York, NY.
$10,000 to Saint Marks School of Texas, Dallas, TX.

7209
The Wallace Foundation ▼
(formerly Wallace-Reader's Digest Funds)
5 Penn Plz., 7th Fl.
New York, NY 10001 (212) 251-9700
Contact: Genl. Mgmt.
FAX: (212) 679-6990;
E-mail: info@wallacefoundation.org; URL: http://www.wallacefoundation.org

Lila Wallace-Reader's Digest Fund and DeWitt Wallace-Reader's Digest Fund Inc., incorporated in NY in 1956 and 1965 respectively; in 2003, the foundations merged and adopted the current name.
Donors: DeWitt Wallace†; Lila Acheson Wallace†.
Foundation type: Independent foundation.
Financial data (yr. ended 12/31/05): Assets, $1,447,299,661 (M); gifts received, $148,759; expenditures, $86,861,389; qualifying distributions, $65,000,000; giving activities include $56,649,828 for 113 grants (high: $5,000,000; low: $10,000; average: $100,000–$500,000), and $15,454 for 38 employee matching gifts.
Purpose and activities: The foundation's mission is to enable institutions to expand learning and enrichment opportunities for all people. The foundation does this by supporting and sharing effective ideas and practices. To achieve their mission, they have three objectives: strengthen education leadership to improve student achievement; improve after-school learning opportunities; and expand participation in arts and culture.
Fields of interest: Arts; Education, services; Education, community/cooperative; Education; Leadership development.
Type of support: General/operating support; Management development/capacity building; Endowments; Program development; Conferences/seminars; Publication; Research; Technical assistance; Program evaluation; Employee matching gifts.
Limitations: Giving on a national basis. No support for religious or fraternal organizations; environmental or conservation programs, health, medical or social service programs, international programs, or for private foundations. No grants to individuals, or for annual campaigns, emergency funds, conferences, historical restoration, capital campaigns, or for deficit financing.
Publications: Annual report (including application guidelines); Financial statement; Grants list; Newsletter; Occasional report.
Application information: Unsolicited proposals are rarely funded. Additional knowledge products are available on foundation Web site. Application form not required.
  Initial approach: Letter of inquiry; no proposals for initial approach
  Deadline(s): None
  Board meeting date(s): 4 times per year
  Final notification: Usually within 4 weeks from receipt of letter of inquiry
Officers and Directors:* Walter V. Shipley,* Chair.; M. Christine DeVita,* Pres.; Holly Dodge, Corp. Secy. and Exec. Assoc.; Rob D. Nagel, Treas. and Dir., Investments; Gordon M. Ambach; Lawrence T.

Babbio, Jr.; W. Don Cornwell; Augusta Souza Kappner; Kevin W. Kennedy; Susan J. Kropf; Peter C. Marzio; Ann S. Moore; Joseph Shenker.
Number of staff: 30 full-time professional; 20 full-time support.
EIN: 136183757
Selected grants: The following grants were reported in 2005.
$5,000,000 to Harvard University, Cambridge, MA. For implementation support to establish Executive Leadership Programs for Educators.
$5,000,000 to New York City Leadership Academy, New York, NY. For Innovation Sites, effort to determine kinds of legislative and regulatory changes needed to ensure that school districts can develop, prepare and train leaders capable of improving student performance, and to support high-need districts within those states.
$5,000,000 to University of Virginia, Charlottesville, VA. For implementation support to establish Executive Leadership Programs for Educators.
$2,000,000 to Brooklyn Museum, Brooklyn, NY. For matching grant to expand endowment or establish cash reserves to support continuing participation-building as part of Wallace Excellence Awards, initiative for arts organizations to attract broad attention to effective practices in building appreciation and demand for the arts, encourage continued commitment to maintaining those practices, and keep the issue of participation-building high among practitioners and thought leaders.
$2,000,000 to Chicago Symphony Orchestra, Chicago, IL. For matching grant to expand endowment or establish cash reserves to support continuing participation-building as part of Wallace Excellence Awards, initiative for arts organizations to attract broad attention to effective practices in building appreciation and demand for the arts, encourage continued commitment to maintaining those practices, and keep the issue of participation-building high among practitioners and thought leaders.
$2,000,000 to Jazz at Lincoln Center, New York, NY. For matching grant to expand endowment or establish cash reserves to support continuing participation-building as part of Wallace Excellence Awards, initiative for arts organizations to attract broad attention to effective practices in building appreciation and demand for the arts, encourage continued commitment to maintaining those practices, and keep the issue of participation-building high among practitioners and thought leaders.
$2,000,000 to San Francisco Symphony, San Francisco, CA. For matching grant to expand endowment or establish cash reserves to support continuing participation-building as part of Wallace Excellence Awards, initiative for arts organizations to attract broad attention to effective practices in building appreciation and demand for the arts, encourage continued commitment to maintaining those practices, and keep the issue of participation-building high among practitioners and thought leaders.
$1,750,000 to Southern Regional Education Board, Atlanta, GA. To revise leadership training modules and add new ones as needed to better focus on how leadership improves school and classroom practice; and to strengthen work of states in that region and promote development and spread of effective leadership ideas within membership and beyond.

$1,060,000 to Big Thought, Dallas, TX. To bring together education, civic and cultural leaders in Dallas to develop plan that will aim at improvements in quality, access and sustainability of high-quality arts education services as part of Arts for Young People Initiative.
$300,000 to New York State Department of Education, Albany, NY. For Innovation Sites, effort to determine kinds of legislative and regulatory changes needed to ensure that school districts can develop, prepare and train leaders capable of improving student performance, and to support high-need districts within those states.

7210
Miriam G. and Ira D. Wallach Foundation ✧
3 Manhattanville Rd.
Purchase, NY   10577-2110

Incorporated in 1956 in NY.
Foundation type: Independent foundation.
Financial data (yr. ended 10/31/04): Assets, $27,587,764 (M); expenditures, $3,742,541; qualifying distributions, $3,097,507; giving activities include $3,016,439 for 92 grants (high: $1,000,000; low: $100).
Purpose and activities: Support primarily for higher education, and international relations, including peace; support also for social services, Jewish organizations, and cultural programs.
Fields of interest: Media, television; Museums; Performing arts; Historical activities; Higher education; Libraries/library science; Environment; Hospitals (general); AIDS; Medical research, institute; Human services; International peace/security; International affairs; Community development, neighborhood development; Jewish federated giving programs; Jewish agencies & temples.
Limitations: Applications not accepted. Giving primarily in NY. No grants to individuals.
Application information: Contributes only to pre-selected organizations.
Officers and Directors:* Ira D. Wallach,* Chair.; Miriam G. Wallach,* Vice-Chair.; Kenneth L. Wallach,* Pres.; Edgar Wachenheim III,* V.P.; Peter C. Siegfried, Secy.; Reginald Reinhardt, Treas.; Kate W. Cassidy; Martin W. Cassidy; Sue W. Wachenheim; Mary K. Wallach; Susan S. Wallach.
EIN: 136101702
Selected grants: The following grants were reported in 2005.
$300,000 to People for the American Way Foundation, DC.
$135,000 to United Nations Association of the United States of America, New York, NY.
$125,000 to Metropolitan Museum of Art, New York, NY.
$50,000 to New York Public Library, New York, NY.
$30,000 to South Kent School, South Kent, CT.
$15,000 to Ploughshares Fund, San Francisco, CA.
$6,600 to Philharmonic-Symphony Society of New York, New York, NY.
$5,000 to Synergos Institute, New York, NY.
$5,000 to Wellesley College, Wellesley, MA.
$2,500 to Museum of Modern Art, New York, NY.

7211
Otto and Fran Walter Foundation, Inc.
(formerly Walter & Lorenz Foundation, Inc.)
90 Park Ave., Ste. 1600
New York, NY   10017-1822   (212) 786-7448
Contact: Martha H. Peak, V.P. and Grants Dir.
E-mail: grants@walterfoundation.org

Established in 1952 in NY.
Donors: Anton Lorenz†; Otto L. Walter†; Fran D. Walter†.
Foundation type: Independent foundation.
Financial data (yr. ended 12/31/05): Assets, $14,671,473 (M); gifts received, $7,991; expenditures, $1,258,930; qualifying distributions, $977,368; giving activities include $529,300 for 8 grants (high: $205,000; low: $5,000), and $235,000 for 1 loan/program-related investment.
Purpose and activities: Primary areas of interest include education and legal education, hunger, the disadvantaged, and international projects, especially in Germany.
Fields of interest: Museums; Arts; Secondary school/education; Higher education; Law school/education; Adult/continuing education; Education; Food services; Human services; Aging, centers/services; International affairs, goodwill promotion; International affairs, foreign policy; Civil rights, race/intergroup relations; Public policy, research; Aging; Economically disadvantaged.
International interests: Germany.
Type of support: Seed money; Professorships; Matching/challenge support.
Limitations: Giving primarily on a national and international basis. No support for purely religious or ethnic programs, or for programs with political agendas or programs that discriminate. No grants to individuals.
Publications: Application guidelines; Annual report.
Application information: Application form not required.
    Initial approach: E-mail
    Copies of proposal: 1
    Deadline(s): Ongoing
    Board meeting date(s): As necessary
    Final notification: Up to 6 weeks
Officers and Directors:* Frank G. Helman,* Pres.; Martha H. Peak,* V.P.; Susanne Nadel, Secy.; Fritz Weinschenk,* Treas.
Number of staff: 1 part-time support.
EIN: 131625529

7212
The Rosalind P. Walter Foundation ✧
509 Madison Ave., Ste. 1216
New York, NY   10022

Established in 1951 as the Walter Foundation.
Donors: Henry G. Walter, Jr.†; Rosalind P. Walter.
Foundation type: Independent foundation.
Financial data (yr. ended 12/31/05): Assets, $658,307 (M); expenditures, $565,498; qualifying distributions, $556,650; giving activities include $555,150 for 31 grants (high: $100,000; low: $150).
Fields of interest: Media/communications; Media, television; Museums (natural history); Animals/wildlife; Athletics/sports, racquet sports; Boys & girls clubs; Human services; Federated giving programs.
Limitations: Applications not accepted. Giving primarily in NY. No grants to individuals.

Application information: Contributes only to pre-selected organizations.
Trustee: Rosalind P. Walter.
EIN: 136177284

7213
The William G. Walters Foundation ◇ ☆
c/o Laidlaw & Co.
90 Park Ave.
New York, NY   10016

Established in 1986.
Donor: William G. Walters.
Foundation type: Independent foundation.
Financial data (yr. ended 11/30/05): Assets, $428,642 (M); expenditures, $357,482; qualifying distributions, $354,000; giving activities include $354,000 for grants.
Purpose and activities: Giving for higher education and Jewish organizations.
Fields of interest: Higher education; Jewish agencies & temples.
Limitations: Applications not accepted. Giving primarily in New York, NY. No grants to individuals.
Application information: Contributes only to pre-selected organizations.
Officers: William G. Walters, Pres.; Elliot J. Smith, V.P. and Treas.
EIN: 133387377

7214
The Warburg Pincus Foundation ◇ ☆
466 Lexington Ave., 10th Fl.
New York, NY   10017

Established in 2000 in NY.
Donor: Warburg Pincus Partners LLC.
Foundation type: Company-sponsored foundation.
Financial data (yr. ended 11/30/05): Assets, $284,928 (M); gifts received, $1,050,000; expenditures, $875,591; qualifying distributions, $875,384; giving activities include $875,384 for grants.
Purpose and activities: The foundation supports organizations involved with higher education.
Fields of interest: Higher education.
Limitations: Applications not accepted. Giving on a national basis, with some emphasis on New York, NY, PA, and the East Coast. No grants to individuals.
Application information: Contributes only to pre-selected organizations.
Officers: Steven G. Schneider, Pres.; Scott A. Arenare, Secy.; Timothy J. Curt, Treas.
EIN: 134148834
Selected grants: The following grants were reported in 2005.
$25,000 to Damon Runyon Cancer Research Foundation, New York, NY.
$10,000 to Building With Books, Stamford, CT.
$10,000 to United Neighborhood Houses of New York, New York, NY.
$10,000 to University of Virginia Alumni Association, Charlottesville, VA. 2 grants: $5,000 each
$4,500 to Harvard University, Cambridge, MA. 2 grants: $1,500, $3,000
$3,000 to Oxford University, Balliol College, Oxford, England. .
$2,514 to Yale University, New Haven, CT.
$2,500 to Abraham Joshua Heschel School, New York, NY.

7215
The Andy Warhol Foundation for the Visual Arts ▼
65 Bleecker St., 7th Fl.
New York, NY   10012   (212) 387-7555
Contact: Pamela Clapp, Prog. Dir.
FAX: (212) 387-7560; *URL:* http://www.warholfoundation.org

Established in 1987 in NY.
Donor: Andy Warhol‡.
Foundation type: Independent foundation.
Financial data (yr. ended 4/30/05): Assets, $230,461,192 (M); expenditures, $11,806,489; qualifying distributions, $7,421,852; giving activities include $6,010,471 for 112 grants (high: $1,000,000; low: $1,000; average: $5,000–$75,000).
Purpose and activities: The foundation's purpose is the advancement of the visual arts. The foundation's principal activities are twofold: it awards grants to not-for-profit cultural organizations working in the visual arts; and it has responsibility for all aspects of its collection of Andy Warhol's art.
Fields of interest: Visual arts; Museums; Arts, artist's services; Arts.
Type of support: Program development; Conferences/seminars; Publication; Seed money; Research.
Publications: Application guidelines; Biennial report; Financial statement; Grants list; Multi-year report.
Application information: Application form not required.
Initial approach: Letter
Copies of proposal: 1
Deadline(s): Mar. 1 and Sept. 1
Board meeting date(s): Apr., June, Oct., and Dec.
Final notification: Jan.1 and July 1
Officers and Directors:* Sherri Geldin,* Chair.; Joel Wachs,* Pres.; John Warhola,* V.P.; M. Antoinette Thomas, Secy.; K.C. Maurer, C.F.O. and Treas.; James Keith Brown; Patricia Cruz; David Dechmon; Jane Hammoud; Ann R. Leven; Rick Lowe; Ann Philbin; Lisa Phillips; Jock Reynolds; Cindy Sherman; Michael Straus; John Waters; Patricia Williams; Robert G. Wilmers.
Number of staff: 22 full-time professional; 2 part-time professional.
EIN: 133410749

7216
The Joseph Leroy and Ann C. Warner Fund, Inc. ◇
233 Broadway, 38th Fl.
New York, NY   10279
E-mail: warnerfund@aol.com

Established in 1998 in NY.
Foundation type: Independent foundation.
Financial data (yr. ended 12/31/05): Assets, $27,398,912 (M); expenditures, $1,687,851; qualifying distributions, $1,401,551; giving activities include $1,234,515 for grants.
Purpose and activities: Grants are made for the benefit of orphans and children with disabilities.
Fields of interest: Elementary school/education; Education, special; Children, foster care; Children, services.
Type of support: General/operating support; Continuing support; Building/renovation; Equipment; Emergency funds.

Limitations: Giving primarily in the metropolitan New York, NY, area.
Application information: NYRAG Common Application Form is preferred. Application form required.
Initial approach: Proposal
Deadline(s): None
Trustees: Barbara Fei; Jo Ann Ferdinand; Peter Sherman.
Number of staff: 1
EIN: 113426508
Selected grants: The following grants were reported in 2003.
$170,000 to Columbia University, New York, NY.
$80,000 to YMCA of Greater New York, West Side, New York, NY.
$50,000 to Advocates for Children of New York, New York, NY.
$50,000 to Berkeley-Carroll Street School, Brooklyn, NY.
$50,000 to Brooklyn Public Library Foundation, Brooklyn, NY.
$50,000 to Childrens Village, Dobbs Ferry, NY.
$50,000 to Montefiore Medical Center, Bronx, NY.
$50,000 to Saint Marys Foundation for Children, Bayside, NY.
$35,000 to Resources for Children with Special Needs, New York, NY.
$20,000 to Achilles Track Club, New York, NY.

7217
Riley J. and Lillian N. Warren and Beatrice W. Blanding Foundation ◇
6 Ford Ave.
Oneonta, NY   13820   (607) 432-6720
Contact: Henry L. Hulbert, Mgr.

Trust established in 1972 in NY.
Donor: Beatrice W. Blanding.
Foundation type: Independent foundation.
Financial data (yr. ended 12/31/05): Assets, $20,819,886 (M); expenditures, $1,095,155; qualifying distributions, $1,072,449; giving activities include $952,000 for 37 grants (high: $200,000; low: $3,000).
Fields of interest: Arts; Elementary/secondary education; Higher education; Hospitals (general); Human services; Children/youth, services; Protestant agencies & churches; Jewish agencies & temples.
Limitations: Giving primarily in the Oneonta, NY, area.
Application information:
Initial approach: Letter
Deadline(s): Nov. 1
Officer and Trustees:* Henry L. Hulbert,* Mgr.; Robert A. Harlem; Maureen P. Hulbert.
EIN: 237203341

7218
The Bert & Sandra Wasserman Foundation ◇
126 E. 56th St., Ste. 12N
New York, NY   10022-3613

Established in 1997 in NY.
Donor: Bert W. Wasserman.
Foundation type: Independent foundation.
Financial data (yr. ended 12/31/05): Assets, $8,539,030 (M); gifts received, $140,124; expenditures, $375,049; qualifying distributions,

$363,609; giving activities include $363,359 for 42 grants (high: $114,360; low: $180).

Purpose and activities: Giving for higher education, Jewish organizations, and art and cultural programs.

Fields of interest: Arts; Higher education; Jewish federated giving programs; Jewish agencies & temples.

Limitations: Applications not accepted. Giving primarily in New York. No grants to individuals.

Application information: Contributes only to pre-selected organizations.

Officers and Directors:* Sandra Wasserman,* Pres. and Treas.; Debra Wasserman,* V.P. and Secy.

EIN: 133961422

Selected grants: The following grants were reported in 2003.

$61,000 to Baruch College of the City University of New York, New York, NY.

$54,000 to UJA-Federation of New York, New York, NY.

$25,000 to Hewitt School, New York, NY.

$18,000 to Gurwin Jewish Geriatric Foundation, Commack, NY.

$16,000 to Israel Policy Forum, New York, NY.

$11,250 to Metropolitan Opera, New York, NY.

$10,300 to Jewish Federation of South Palm Beach County, Boca Raton, FL.

$5,000 to Jewish Museum, New York, NY.

$3,600 to Prep for Prep, New York, NY.

$1,800 to American Jewish Committee, New York, NY.

7219

Waterfowl Research Foundation, Inc.

57 Dunemere Ln.
East Hampton, NY 11937
Contact: Carroll L. Wainwright, Jr., Pres.

Established in 1955 in NY.

Donor: M.E. Davis†.

Foundation type: Independent foundation.

Financial data (yr. ended 12/31/05): Assets, $9,387,643 (M); expenditures, $616,088; qualifying distributions, $500,000; giving activities include $500,000 for 6 grants (high: $225,000; low: $30,000).

Purpose and activities: To support waterfowl preservation programs.

Fields of interest: Animals/wildlife, research; Animals/wildlife, preservation/protection.

Type of support: Land acquisition; Research.

Limitations: Giving primarily in the U.S. and Canada. No grants to individuals.

Application information: Application form not required.

Board meeting date(s): Apr. and Dec.

Officers: Carroll L. Wainwright, Jr., Pres.; Lincoln P. Lyman, Secy.

Number of staff: 1 part-time support.

EIN: 136122167

Selected grants: The following grants were reported in 2004.

$220,000 to Delta Waterfowl Foundation, Bismarck, ND.

7220

The Thomas J. Watson Fellowship Program

(formerly The Thomas J. Watson Foundation)
810 7th Ave.
New York, NY 10019
FAX: (212) 245-8860;
E-mail: TJW@WatsonFellowship.org; URL: http://www.watsonfellowship.org

Trust established in 1961 in NY.

Donors: Jeannette K. Watson†; Arthur K. Watson†; Thomas J. Watson, Jr.†; Mrs. John N. Irwin II†; Helen W. Buckner†.

Foundation type: Independent foundation.

Financial data (yr. ended 5/31/05): Assets, $70,642,877 (M); expenditures, $3,700,152; qualifying distributions, $2,950,276; giving activities include $1,799,615 for 126 grants (high: $37,000; low: $500; average: $500–$237,000).

Purpose and activities: Sponsors fellowship program for independent study and travel abroad for graduating seniors at up to 50 private colleges and universities.

Fields of interest: Higher education; Education.

Type of support: General/operating support; Continuing support; Fellowships.

Limitations: Giving on a national basis. No grants to individuals (except for seniors attending the 50 member colleges of The Watson Fellowship Program).

Publications: Informational brochure.

Application information: Applicants for fellowships must be nominated by a participating private college or university and must be a graduating senior; independent applications not accepted. For information about the Watson Fellowship Program and a list of the participating colleges, see Web site. Application form required.

Copies of proposal: 1

Deadline(s): 1st Tues. in Nov.

Board meeting date(s): As required

Final notification: Approximately Mar. 15

Officer: Rosemary Macedo, Exec. Dir.

Advisory Committee: Liz Buckner; Walker Buckner; John Irwin, III; David McKinney; Daniel L. Mosley; Jeanne Olivier; Stuart Watson; Thomas J. Watson III.

Director: Alice Ilchman, Dir.

Trustee: JPMorgan Chase Bank, N.A.

Number of staff: 4 full-time professional.

EIN: 136038151

Selected grants: The following grants were reported in 2004.

$81,000 to Middlebury College, Middlebury, VT. For general operating support.

$60,000 to Saint Lukes School, New Canaan, CT.

$57,700 to Pomona College, Claremont, CA. For Watson fellowship program.

$50,402 to University of Puget Sound, Tacoma, WA. For Watson fellowship program.

$48,936 to Hamilton College, Clinton, NY. For Watson fellowship program.

$47,870 to Colby College, Waterville, ME. For Watson fellowship program.

$47,860 to Wellesley College, Wellesley, MA. For Watson fellowship program.

$45,052 to Amherst College, Amherst, MA. For Watson fellowship program.

$44,975 to Davidson College, Davidson, NC. For Watson fellowship program.

$44,650 to Whitman College, Walla Walla, WA. For Watson fellowship program.

7221

The Watts Family Foundation ◇

c/o Bessemer Trust Co., N.A.
630 5th Ave.
New York, NY 10111

Established in 1997 in MA.

Donors: Beverly Watts; David B. Watts; Scudder Charitable Foundation.

Foundation type: Operating foundation.

Financial data (yr. ended 6/30/05): Assets, $6,617,298 (M); gifts received, $12,859; expenditures, $381,673; qualifying distributions, $327,139; giving activities include $324,711 for 14 grants (high: $271,711; low: $1,000).

Purpose and activities: Giving primarily for higher and other education; funding also for human services.

Fields of interest: Elementary/secondary education; Higher education; Human services; Foundations (private grantmaking); Federated giving programs.

Limitations: Applications not accepted. Giving primarily in MA; funding also in VI. No grants to individuals.

Application information: Contributes only to pre-selected organizations.

Trustees: Beverly Watts; David B. Watts.

EIN: 043402936

Selected grants: The following grants were reported in 2005.

$271,711 to Harvard University, Cambridge, MA.

$10,000 to Connecticut College, New London, CT.

$10,000 to Thayer Academy, Braintree, MA.

$1,000 to Carroll School, Lincoln, MA.

7222

The Weatherup Family Foundation ◇ ☆

c/o AYCO Co., Tax Dept.
P.O. Box 15014
Albany, NY 12212-5014

Established in 1998 in CT.

Donors: Craig E. Weatherup; Constance K. Weatherup.

Foundation type: Independent foundation.

Financial data (yr. ended 12/31/05): Assets, $13,808,631 (M); gifts received, $2,687,250; expenditures, $1,102,048; qualifying distributions, $991,500; giving activities include $991,500 for 20 grants (high: $250,000; low: $1,000).

Fields of interest: Environment, natural resources; Animals/wildlife; Roman Catholic agencies & churches.

Limitations: Applications not accepted. Giving primarily in Tucson, AZ, Charlotte, NC, and NY. No grants to individuals.

Application information: Contributes only to pre-selected organizations.

Trustees: Constance K. Weatherup; Craig E. Weatherup.

EIN: 066469433

7223

Weeden Foundation

(formerly Frank Weeden Foundation)
747 3rd Ave., 34th Fl.
New York, NY 10017 (212) 888-1672
Contact: Donald A. Weeden, Exec. Dir.

FAX: (212) 888-1354;
E-mail: weedenfdn@weedenfdn.org; URL: http://
www.weedenfdn.org

Established 1963 in CA.
Donors: Frank Weeden†; Alan N. Weeden; Donald
E. Weeden; John D. Weeden; William F. Weeden,
M.D.; Frank Weeden Fund.
Foundation type: Independent foundation.
Financial data (yr. ended 6/30/05): Assets,
$31,956,785 (M); expenditures, $2,462,440;
qualifying distributions, $1,991,808; giving
activities include $1,798,200 for grants.
Purpose and activities: Giving primarily to
environmental organizations working to preserve
biological diversity. Program interests also include
organizations working to stabilize human population
and organizations working to address the over
consumption of the earth's resources.
Fields of interest: Environment, natural resources;
Environment; Population studies.
International interests: Chile; Russia.
Type of support: General/operating support;
Continuing support; Land acquisition; Program
development; Seed money.
Limitations: Giving on a national and international
basis, primarily in northern CA, the Pacific
Northwest, Latin America (Chile), Central Siberia
and the Altai Republic in Russia. No grants to
individuals; generally no funding for films,
conferences, or scientific research.
Publications: Application guidelines; Annual report;
Financial statement; Grants list; Program policy
statement.
Application information: E-mail copy of proposal
and executive summary. Annual Report, Grants List,
Application Guidelines, and Program Policy
Statement are available on foundation Web site.
Application form not required.
 Initial approach: Letter of inquiry 1 month before
  proposal deadline
 Copies of proposal: 2
 Deadline(s): 6 weeks prior to each board meeting;
  check Web site for dates
 Board meeting date(s): 3 times a year
 Final notification: 8-10 weeks
Officers and Directors:* Norman Weeden, Ph.D.*,
Pres.; William F. Weeden, M.D.*, V.P.; John D.
Weeden,* Secy.-Treas.; Donald A. Weeden, Exec.
Dir.; Barbara Daugherty; David Davies; Christina
Roux; Alan N. Weeden; Donald E. Weeden; Leslie
Weeden; Robert Weeden.
Number of staff: 2 full-time professional.
EIN: 946109313
Selected grants: The following grants were reported
in 2004.
$50,000 to American Folk Art Museum, New York,
 NY.
$50,000 to National Tropical Botanical Garden,
 Kalaheo, HI.
$20,000 to California Wilderness Coalition, Davis,
 CA.
$20,000 to ForestEthics, San Francisco, CA.
$20,000 to Island Conservation, Santa Cruz, CA.
$20,000 to Pacific Environment, San Francisco, CA.
$20,000 to Wilderness Watch, Missoula, MT.
$15,000 to Montana Wilderness Association,
 Helena, MT.
$10,000 to Alaska Conservation Foundation,
 Anchorage, AK.
$2,500 to Consultative Group on Biological
 Diversity, San Francisco, CA.

7224
The Weezie Foundation ◇
c/o JPMorgan Chase Bank, N.A.
345 Park Ave, 7th Fl.
New York, NY 10154
Contact: Shannon Hennessey, V.P., JPMorgan
Chase Bank, N.A.

Trust established in 1961 in NY.
Donor: Adelaide T. Corbett†.
Foundation type: Independent foundation.
Financial data (yr. ended 12/31/04): Assets,
$27,053,498 (M); expenditures, $1,573,255;
qualifying distributions, $1,383,399; giving
activities include $1,374,500 for 20 grants (high:
$200,000; low: $10,000).
Purpose and activities: Giving primarily for
education and human services.
Fields of interest: Secondary school/education;
Education; Hospitals (general); Housing/shelter,
development; Human services; Youth, services;
Community development.
Limitations: Giving primarily in MA and New York,
NY.
Application information: Application form not
required.
 Initial approach: Letter
 Deadline(s): None
 Board meeting date(s): Nov.
Advisory Committee: D. Nelson Adams; Mrs.
Thomas W. Carroll; Mrs. George F. Fiske, Jr.; Mrs.
William H. Hays III; Kirke T. Hall; Tyler P. Hoffman;
Mrs. H.S. Graham McBride; William Parsons, Jr.
Trustee: JPMorgan Chase Bank, N.A.
EIN: 136090903
Selected grants: The following grants were reported
in 2004.
$200,000 to Massachusetts Horticultural Society,
 Wellesley, MA.
$125,000 to Nantucket Atheneum, Nantucket, MA.
$100,000 to Grymes Memorial School, Orange, VA.
$100,000 to National Hypertension Association,
 New York, NY.
$100,000 to New England Wildlife Center, Hingham,
 MA.
$90,000 to Miss Porters School, Farmington, CT.
$75,000 to Brantwood Camp, Peterborough, NH.
$75,000 to W G B H Educational Foundation,
 Boston, MA.
$75,000 to Youth Counseling League, New York,
 NY.
$50,000 to Reach Out and Read, Somerville, MA.

7225
Weil, Gotshal & Manges Foundation ◇
767 5th Ave.
New York, NY 10153 (212) 310-8000
Contact: Jesse D. Wolff, Dir.

Established in 1983 in NY.
Donors: Weil, Gotshal & Manges LLP; Robert Todd
Lang; Ira M. Millstein; Harvey R. Miller.
Foundation type: Company-sponsored foundation.
Financial data (yr. ended 12/31/04): Assets,
$1,920,748 (M); gifts received, $3,519,003;
expenditures, $2,883,213; qualifying distributions,
$2,882,918; giving activities include $2,882,868
for 215 grants (high: $500,000; low: $75).
Purpose and activities: The foundation supports law
schools and organizations involved with legal
services, human services, and civic affairs.
Fields of interest: Law school/education; Legal
services; Boy scouts; Human services; Federated

giving programs; Jewish federated giving programs;
Public affairs.
Limitations: Giving primarily in NY. No grants to
individuals.
Application information: Application form not
required.
 Initial approach: Proposal
 Deadline(s): Nov. 1
Directors: Robert Todd Lang; Ira M. Millstein; Jesse
D. Wolff.
EIN: 133158325
Selected grants: The following grants were reported
in 2003.
$400,000 to UJA-Federation of New York, New York,
 NY.
$250,000 to Legal Aid Society, New York, NY.
$25,000 to Human Rights First, New York, NY.
$20,000 to New York Lawyers for the Public
 Interest, New York, NY.
$11,000 to Lawyers for Children, New York, NY.
$10,000 to Coalition for the Homeless, New York,
 NY.
$10,000 to Solomon Schechter School of
 Manhattan, New York, NY.
$6,500 to Steppingstone Foundation, Boston, MA.
$5,000 to Covenant House, New York, NY.
$5,000 to Henry Street Settlement, New York, NY.

7226
**Theodore & Renee Weiler Foundation,
 Inc.** ◇
24 Rock St.
Brooklyn, NY 11206

Established in 1965 in NY.
Donor: Theodore R. Weiler†.
Foundation type: Independent foundation.
Financial data (yr. ended 12/31/05): Assets,
$11,014,036 (M); expenditures, $827,169;
qualifying distributions, $775,255; giving activities
include $738,900 for 17 grants (high: $30,000;
low: $500).
Purpose and activities: Giving primarily for arts and
culture, hospitals and health associations,
children's and human services, and Jewish agencies
and temples.
Fields of interest: Museums; Museums (art);
Museums (ethnic/folk arts); Performing arts;
Performing arts, theater; Arts; Hospitals (general);
Health organizations, association; Human services;
Children, services; Jewish federated giving
programs; Jewish agencies & temples.
Limitations: Applications not accepted. Giving
primarily in Palm Beach, FL, and New York, NY. No
grants to individuals.
Application information: Contributes only to
pre-selected organizations.
Officers and Directors:* Alan Safir,* Pres.; Richard
Kandel,* Treas. and Mgr.
EIN: 136181441
Selected grants: The following grants were reported
in 2005.
$30,000 to Blythedale Childrens Hospital, Valhalla,
 NY.
$25,000 to Center for Jewish History, New York, NY.
$25,000 to Film Society of Lincoln Center, New
 York, NY.
$25,000 to Katonah Museum of Art, Katonah, NY.
$10,000 to American Jewish Joint Distribution
 Committee, New York, NY.
$10,000 to Greenwich House, New York, NY.
$5,000 to New York Foundation for the Arts, New
 York, NY.

$5,000 to White Plains Hospital Center, White Plains, NY.

$2,500 to Lee David Pesky Center for Learning Enrichment, Boise, ID.

$1,500 to Marty Lyons Foundation, New York, NY.

7227

The Weill Family Foundation ◇

(formerly Sanford I. Weill Charitable Foundation, Inc.)

c/o Independent Family Office, LLC
123 Great Oaks Blvd.
P.O. Box 3977
Albany, NY   12203
Contact: Sanford I. Weill, Chair.

Established around 1967.
Donor: Sanford I. Weill.
Foundation type: Independent foundation.
Financial data (yr. ended 12/31/05): Assets, $212,871,739 (M); gifts received, $1,147,207; expenditures, $26,901,135; qualifying distributions, $26,443,175; giving activities include $26,443,175 for 11 grants (high: $14,825,000; low: $200).
Purpose and activities: Support primarily for higher education and the arts; support also for human services, hospitals, and Jewish agencies.
Fields of interest: Arts; Education; Hospitals (general); Human services; Aging, centers/services; Jewish agencies & temples.
Type of support: Program development.
Limitations: Applications not accepted. Giving primarily in the metropolitan New York, NY, area. No grants to individuals.
Application information: Contributes only to pre-selected organizations.
Officers and Directors:* Sanford I. Weill,* Chair and Treas.; Joan H. Weill,* Pres.; Jessica Bibliowicz,* V.P.; Michael T. Masin,* Secy.; Ken Bialkin; Arthur Mahon.
EIN: 136223609
Selected grants: The following grants were reported in 2003.
$25,000 to Catholic Foreign Mission Society of America, Maryknoll, NY. For general support.

7228

Peter A. and Deborah L. Weinberg Family Foundation ◇

c/o Goldman Sachs- Family Office
1 New York Plz., 40th Fl.
New York, NY   10004

Established in 1996 in CT.
Donor: Peter A. Weinberg.
Foundation type: Independent foundation.
Financial data (yr. ended 7/31/05): Assets, $12,481,980 (M); expenditures, $873,010; qualifying distributions, $817,510; giving activities include $817,510 for 26 grants (high: $500,000; low: $250).
Purpose and activities: Giving for education and health.
Fields of interest: Higher education; Higher education, university; Education; Hospitals (general); Cystic fibrosis research; Human services; Children, services; Federated giving programs; Jewish agencies & temples.
International interests: England.

Limitations: Applications not accepted. Giving in the U.S., with emphasis on New York, NY, and London, England. No grants to individuals.
Application information: Contributes only to pre-selected organizations.
Trustees: Deborah L. Weinberg; Peter A. Weinberg.
EIN: 133920469
Selected grants: The following grants were reported in 2004.
$500,000 to Deerfield Academy, Deerfield, MA.
$112,000 to University of Michigan, Ann Arbor, MI.
$15,000 to Brunswick School, Greenwich, CT.
$10,000 to American School.
$10,000 to Educational Opportunity Fund, New York, NY.
$5,000 to Prep for Prep, New York, NY.
$1,000 to TEAK Fellowship, New York, NY.

7229

The John S. & Amy S. Weinberg Foundation ◇

c/o Goldman Sachs- Family Office
1 New York Plz., 40th Fl.
New York, NY   10004

Established in 1993 in NY.
Donor: John S. Weinberg.
Foundation type: Independent foundation.
Financial data (yr. ended 7/31/05): Assets, $15,236,107 (M); gifts received, $1,898,169; expenditures, $626,745; qualifying distributions, $568,895; giving activities include $568,895 for 70 grants (high: $250,000; low: $20).
Fields of interest: Arts; Education; Health organizations, association; Big Brothers/Big Sisters; Youth development; Human services.
Limitations: Applications not accepted. Giving primarily in the metropolitan New York, NY, area. No grants to individuals; no loans or scholarships.
Application information: Contributes only to pre-selected organizations.
Trustees: Robert S. Kaplan; Amy S. Weinberg; John S. Weinberg.
EIN: 133749671

7230

The Sue Ann and John L. Weinberg Foundation ◇

(formerly The Sue and John L. Weinberg Foundation)
c/o BCRS Group/Marcum & Kliegman, LLP
100 Wall St., 11th Fl.
New York, NY   10005

Established in 1959 in NY.
Donor: John L. Weinberg‡.
Foundation type: Independent foundation.
Financial data (yr. ended 4/30/05): Assets, $42,887,589 (M); gifts received, $359,695; expenditures, $2,611,304; qualifying distributions, $2,407,851; giving activities include $2,363,157 for 344 grants (high: $100,000; low: $35).
Purpose and activities: Giving primarily for education, health care, and human services.
Fields of interest: Secondary school/education; Higher education; Hospitals (general); Medical research, institute; Human services; International relief; Jewish federated giving programs.
Type of support: General/operating support; Annual campaigns; Capital campaigns; Building/renovation; Endowments; Professorships; Research; Program-related investments/loans.

Limitations: Applications not accepted. Giving primarily in Greenwich, CT, and New York, NY. No grants to individuals, or for scholarships.
Application information: Contributes only to pre-selected organizations.
Trustees: Jean Weinberg Rose; Elizabeth Weinberg Smith; Sue Ann Weinberg.
Number of staff: 2 part-time support.
EIN: 136028813
Selected grants: The following grants were reported in 2004.
$999,215 to University of Delaware, Newark, DE.
$102,675 to New York Public Library, New York, NY. 2 grants: $100,000, $2,675
$50,000 to Mayo Foundation, Jacksonville, FL.
$45,000 to Greenwich Hospital, Greenwich, CT. 2 grants: $20,000, $25,000
$39,610 to Hospital for Special Surgery Fund, New York, NY. 2 grants: $30,000, $9,610
$10,000 to Columbia University, New York, NY.
$3,000 to New York-Presbyterian Hospital, New York, NY.

7231

Sidney J. Weinberg, Jr. Foundation ◇

c/o BCRS Assocs., LLC
100 Wall St., 11th Fl.
New York, NY   10005

Established in 1979 in NY.
Donor: Sidney J. Weinberg, Jr.
Foundation type: Independent foundation.
Financial data (yr. ended 5/31/05): Assets, $38,663,428 (M); gifts received, $502,925; expenditures, $3,440,013; qualifying distributions, $3,039,754; giving activities include $2,951,850 for 80 grants (high: $1,000,000; low: $100).
Purpose and activities: Giving primarily for education and health and human services.
Fields of interest: Museums (marine/maritime); Historic preservation/historical societies; Arts; Higher education; Education; Environment; Hospitals (general); Health organizations, association; Human services; Children/youth, services; Community development; Federated giving programs; Christian agencies & churches.
Type of support: General/operating support.
Limitations: Applications not accepted. Giving primarily in MA and New York, NY; some funding also in CA. No grants to individuals or for scholarships; no loans.
Application information: Contributes only to pre-selected organizations.
Trustees: Elizabeth W. Smith; Peter A. Weinberg; Sidney J. Weinberg, Jr.; Sydney H. Weinberg.
EIN: 132998603
Selected grants: The following grants were reported in 2005.
$1,000,000 to Carnegie Institution of Washington, DC.
$125,000 to New Bedford Whaling Museum, New Bedford, MA. 2 grants: $100,000, $25,000
$50,000 to Claremont University Consortium, Claremont, CA.
$50,000 to Deerfield Academy, Deerfield, MA.
$50,000 to Pomfret School, Pomfret, CT.
$50,000 to Scripps College, Claremont, CA.
$25,000 to Woods Hole Oceanographic Institution, Woods Hole, MA.
$10,000 to Anchor, Inc., New York, NY.
$10,000 to Metropolitan Opera Guild, New York, NY.

7232
Isak and Rose Weinman Foundation, Inc. ✧
c/o BDO Seidman, LLP
330 Madison Ave.
New York, NY 10017

Established in 1956.
Donor: Lilliana Teruzzi†.
Foundation type: Independent foundation.
Financial data (yr. ended 12/31/04): Assets, $13,169,771 (M); expenditures, $1,043,470; qualifying distributions, $975,010; giving activities include $932,000 for 56 grants (high: $100,000; low: $1,000).
Purpose and activities: Giving primarily for the arts, hospitals and health associations, education, Jewish organizations, and social services.
Fields of interest: Museums; Museums (art); Performing arts; Performing arts centers; Performing arts, theater; Performing arts, orchestra (symphony); Performing arts, opera; Arts; Education, alliance; Higher education; Education; Hospitals (general); Health organizations, association; Human services; Children, services; Jewish agencies & temples.
Limitations: Applications not accepted. Giving primarily in New York, NY. No grants to individuals.
Application information: Contributes only to pre-selected organizations.
Officers and Directors:* W. Loeber Landau, Chair. and Secy.; Alexander E. Slater,* Pres. and Treas.; Donna Landau Hardiman; Barbara Landau; Frederick A. Terry; Blair Landau Trippe.
EIN: 136110132
Selected grants: The following grants were reported in 2004.
$100,000 to New York City Opera, New York, NY.
$70,000 to Metropolitan Museum of Art, New York, NY.
$65,000 to Brooklyn Academy of Music, Brooklyn, NY.
$35,000 to Chapel Haven, Westville, CT.
$25,000 to Rockefeller University, New York, NY.
$10,000 to Glimmerglass Opera, Cooperstown, NY.
$10,000 to Legal Aid Society of Salt Lake, Salt Lake City, UT.
$10,000 to Prep for Prep, New York, NY.
$10,000 to Reece School, New York, NY.
$5,000 to Jewish Association for Services for the Aged, New York, NY.

7233
The Irving Weinstein Foundation, Inc. ✧
c/o Thelen Reid & Priest, LLP
875 3rd Ave.
New York, NY 10022-6225
Contact: Douglas F. Allen

Established in 1961.
Donors: Irving Weinstein†; Steven Lipkin; Millbrook Partners LLC.
Foundation type: Independent foundation.
Financial data (yr. ended 3/31/05): Assets, $9,621,899 (M); gifts received, $500; expenditures, $483,464; qualifying distributions, $465,793; giving activities include $340,000 for 5 grants (high: $170,000; low: $20,000).
Fields of interest: Higher education; Medical school/education; Hospitals (general); Cancer research.
Limitations: Applications not accepted. Giving on a national basis. No grants to individuals.

Application information: Contributes only to pre-selected organizations.
Directors: Joan Lipkin; Martin Lipkin; Richard Lipkin; Steven M. Lipkin.
EIN: 136093068
Selected grants: The following grants were reported in 2003.
$173,525 to Preventive Medicine Institute, Strang Cancer Prevention Center, New York, NY. For research.
$90,000 to University of California, Irvine, CA. For research.
$50,000 to Montefiore Medical Center, Bronx, NY. For research.
$25,000 to American Association for Cancer Research Foundation for the Prevention and Cure of Cancer, Philadelphia, PA. For general support.
$10,000 to Marine Biological Laboratory, Woods Hole, MA. For program support.

7234
Candace King Weir Foundation ✧
c/o C.L. King & Assocs., Inc.
9 Elk St.
Albany, NY 12207
Contact: Candace K. Weir, Tr.

Established in 1994 in NY.
Donor: Candace K. Weir.
Foundation type: Operating foundation.
Financial data (yr. ended 12/31/05): Assets, $10,265,448 (M); gifts received, $365,000; expenditures, $1,226,188; qualifying distributions, $1,226,188; giving activities include $1,212,350 for 85 grants (high: $180,000; low: $100).
Purpose and activities: Giving primarily for Roman Catholic churches and agencies, and to an institute of history and art. Support also for higher education, human services, and health care.
Fields of interest: Historical activities; Arts; Higher education; Hospitals (general); Human services; Roman Catholic agencies & churches.
Limitations: Giving primarily in New York, NY. No grants to individuals.
Application information:
Initial approach: Letter
Deadline(s): None
Trustees: Meredith Prime; Amelia F. Weir; Candace K. Weir.
EIN: 133797919
Selected grants: The following grants were reported in 2005.
$751,000 to Albany Institute of History and Art, Albany, NY.
$180,000 to Albany Academy for Girls, Albany, NY.
$100,300 to Albany Medical Center, Albany, NY.
$11,000 to Yaddo, Saratoga Springs, NY.
$10,000 to National Trust for Historic Preservation, DC.
$2,500 to Brighter Choice Foundation, Clifton Park, NY.
$2,000 to Wildwood Programs, Schenectady, NY.
$1,500 to Literacy Volunteers of America, Syracuse, NY.
$1,000 to Elizabethtown Community Hospital, Elizabethtown, NY.
$1,000 to Saint Peters Hospital Foundation, Albany, NY.

7235
The Joseph H. & Miriam F. Weiss Foundation, Inc. ✧ ☆
551 5th Ave., Ste. 1600
New York, NY 10176

Established in 1995 in NY.
Donors: Joseph H. Weiss; Miriam F. Weiss.
Foundation type: Independent foundation.
Financial data (yr. ended 12/31/05): Assets, $616,658 (M); gifts received, $914,239; expenditures, $577,880; qualifying distributions, $577,880; giving activities include $577,680 for grants.
Purpose and activities: Giving primarily to Jewish temples, organizations, and schools.
Fields of interest: Education; Jewish federated giving programs; Jewish agencies & temples.
Limitations: Applications not accepted. Giving primarily in Brooklyn, NY. No grants to individuals.
Application information: Contributes only to pre-selected organizations.
Officers: Joseph H. Weiss, Pres.; Miriam F. Weiss, V.P.; Howard Weiser, Secy.
EIN: 133800609
Selected grants: The following grants were reported in 2003.
$40,000 to Maimonides Academy of Western Connecticut, Danbury, CT.
$10,000 to Torah Academy High School of Brooklyn, Brooklyn, NY.
$5,000 to Chai Lifeline, New York, NY.
$2,000 to Yad Eliezer, Brooklyn, NY.
$1,000 to National Jewish Outreach Program, New York, NY.
$780 to Tzedakah Vchesed, Brooklyn, NY.
$750 to Westchester Day School, Mamaroneck, NY.
$650 to Tomchei Shabbos of Boro Park and Flatbush, Brooklyn, NY.
$500 to Young Israel of Staten Island, Staten Island, NY.
$100 to Nefesh Academy, Brooklyn, NY.

7236
The Stephen and Suzanne Weiss Foundation, Inc. ✧ ☆
c/o Neuberger Berman
605 3rd Ave., 41st Fl.
New York, NY 10158

Established in 1986 in NY.
Donors: Stephen Weiss; Suzanne Weiss.
Foundation type: Independent foundation.
Financial data (yr. ended 12/31/05): Assets, $5,101,080 (M); gifts received, $12,707; expenditures, $373,923; qualifying distributions, $355,883; giving activities include $351,883 for 42 grants (high: $125,000; low: $300).
Purpose and activities: Giving primarily to a university; support also for secondary education, civic affairs, culture, and Jewish organizations.
Fields of interest: Secondary school/education; Higher education; Hospitals (general); Government/public administration; Jewish agencies & temples.
Limitations: Applications not accepted. Giving primarily in New York, NY. No grants to individuals.
Application information: Contributes only to pre-selected organizations.
Officers: Stephen Weiss, Pres.; Suzanne Weiss, V.P.; Roger J. Weiss, Secy.-Treas.
EIN: 133384021

Selected grants: The following grants were reported in 2005.

$101,000 to Cornell University, Ithaca, NY.

$33,333 to National Humanities Center, Research Triangle Park, NC.

$20,000 to Centurion Foundation, Valley Stream, NY.

$10,000 to American Cancer Society, White Plains, NY.

$7,500 to Carnegie Hall Society, New York, NY.

$2,500 to Cystic Fibrosis Foundation, New York, NY.

$2,000 to American Cancer Society, New York, NY.

$1,000 to American Friends of the Israel Museum, New York, NY.

$1,000 to American Theater Wing, New York, NY.

$1,000 to Greenwich Country Day School, Greenwich, CT.

7237
Weissman Family Foundation, Inc. ✧

81 Manursing Way

Rye, NY   10580

Contact: George Weissman, Chair.

Established in 1992 in NY.

Donor: George Weissman.

Foundation type: Independent foundation.

Financial data (yr. ended 12/31/05): Assets, $11,610,340 (M); expenditures, $868,029; qualifying distributions, $830,035; giving activities include $830,035 for grants.

Purpose and activities: Giving primarily for education and for human services.

Fields of interest: Arts; Education; Environment; Human services; Jewish agencies & temples.

Type of support: General/operating support; Continuing support; Annual campaigns; Capital campaigns; Endowments; Emergency funds; Publication; Seed money.

Limitations: Applications not accepted. Giving primarily in New York, NY. No grants to individuals.

Application information: Contributes only to pre-selected organizations.

Board meeting date(s): Annually

Officers: George Weissman, Chair.; Mildred Weissman, Pres.; Daniel Weissman, V.P.; Ellen Weissman, Secy.; Paul Weissman, Treas.

Number of staff: 1 part-time support.

EIN: 133688122

Selected grants: The following grants were reported in 2004.

$200,000 to Jewish Museum, New York, NY.

$25,000 to Lincoln Center for the Performing Arts, New York, NY.

$17,500 to Gomez Foundation for Mill House, New York, NY. 2 grants: $10,000, $7,500

$10,000 to Israel Policy Forum, New York, NY.

$10,000 to US Israel Women to Women, New York, NY.

$7,000 to Childrens Museum of Manhattan, New York, NY.

$5,000 to Freedom from Hunger, Davis, CA.

$1,000 to Metropolitan Museum of Art, New York, NY.

$100 to AFS-USA, New York, NY.

7238
The Paul and Harriet Weissman Family Foundation, Inc. ✧

(formerly The Paul M. Weissman Family Foundation)

2 Oxford Rd.

White Plains, NY   10605

Established in 1969 in NY.

Donor: Paul M. Weissman.

Foundation type: Independent foundation.

Financial data (yr. ended 2/28/05): Assets, $12,849,059 (M); expenditures, $488,241; qualifying distributions, $481,803; giving activities include $479,560 for 103 grants (high: $290,000; low: $25).

Purpose and activities: Support primarily to private schools and universities, the arts, health and social services, and child welfare associations.

Fields of interest: Arts; Higher education; Health care; Human services; Children/youth, services; Jewish agencies & temples.

Limitations: Applications not accepted. Giving primarily in MA and NY. No grants to individuals.

Application information: Contributes only to pre-selected organizations.

Officers and Directors: * Paul M. Weissman,* Pres. and Treas.; Harriet L. Weissman,* V.P. and Secy.; Michael A. Weissman,* V.P.; Peter A. Weissman,* V.P.; Stephanie T. Weissman,* V.P.

EIN: 237049744

Selected grants: The following grants were reported in 2005.

$340,000 to Mount Holyoke College, South Hadley, MA. 2 grants: $50,000, $290,000

$50,000 to White Plains Public Library, White Plains, NY.

$1,000 to Connecticut College, New London, CT.

$1,000 to Mercy College, Dobbs Ferry, NY.

$1,000 to University of Pennsylvania, Philadelphia, PA.

$250 to American Trust for the British Library, New York, NY.

$250 to Harvard University, Cambridge, MA.

$100 to Student Advocacy, Elmsford, NY.

7239
The George W. & Patricia A. Wellde Foundation ✧

c/o Goldman Sachs & Co., Family Office

1 New York Plz., 40th Fl.

New York, NY   10004

Established in 1993 in NY.

Donor: George W. Wellde, Jr.

Foundation type: Independent foundation.

Financial data (yr. ended 7/31/05): Assets, $6,755,087 (M); expenditures, $2,057,750; qualifying distributions, $1,996,572; giving activities include $1,996,572 for 57 grants (high: $99,999; low: $50).

Purpose and activities: Giving primarily for higher and other education.

Fields of interest: Higher education; Education; Hospitals (general); Children/youth, services; Federated giving programs.

Limitations: Applications not accepted. Giving primarily in New York, NY; funding also in CT, Washington, DC, and VA. No grants to individuals, or for scholarships; no loans.

Application information: Contributes only to pre-selected organizations.

Trustees: George W. Wellde, Jr.; Patricia A. Wellde.

EIN: 133749673

7240
Wellin Family Foundation, Inc. ✧

c/o Weiser, LLP

50 Charles Lindbergh Blvd., Ste. 400

Uniondale, NY   11553

Established in 2002 in FL.

Donor: Keith S. Wellin.

Foundation type: Operating foundation.

Financial data (yr. ended 12/31/05): Assets, $663,585 (M); gifts received, $603,860; expenditures, $905,364; qualifying distributions, $875,000; giving activities include $875,000 for 11 grants (high: $710,000; low: $1,000).

Purpose and activities: Giving primarily for higher and other education, and to a Christian organization; funding also for human services.

Fields of interest: Performing arts, dance; Higher education; Education; Human services; Christian agencies & churches.

Limitations: Applications not accepted. No grants to individuals.

Application information: Contributes only to pre-selected organizations.

Officers: Keith S. Wellin, Pres.; Peter J. Wellin, V.P.; Marjorie W. King, Secy.; Cynthia W. Plum, Treas.

EIN: 753087525

7241
The Joseph H. Wender Foundation ✧ ☆

c/o BCRS Associates, LLC

100 Wall St., 11th Fl.

New York, NY   10005

Established in 1985 in NY.

Donor: Joseph H. Wender.

Foundation type: Independent foundation.

Financial data (yr. ended 4/30/05): Assets, $2,970,900 (M); expenditures, $378,961; qualifying distributions, $366,590; giving activities include $364,410 for 35 grants (high: $100,000; low: $250).

Purpose and activities: Giving primarily to arts organizations and federated giving programs; funding also for a center for wine, food and the arts.

Fields of interest: Arts, multipurpose centers/programs; Museums (art); Arts; Higher education; Hospitals (general); Children, services; Federated giving programs.

Limitations: Applications not accepted. Giving primarily in CA, and New York, NY; some funding nationally. No grants to individuals; no loans.

Application information: Contributes only to pre-selected organizations.

Trustees: Jonathan L. Cohen; Ann Colgin Wender; Joseph H. Wender.

EIN: 133318170

Selected grants: The following grants were reported in 2005.

$101,000 to Northwestern University, Evanston, IL. 2 grants: $1,000, $100,000

$35,000 to Naples Children and Education Foundation, Naples, FL.

$21,204 to High Museum of Art, Atlanta, GA. 2 grants: $9,675, $11,529

$16,930 to Saint Helena Hospital Foundation, Deer Park, CA. 2 grants: $10,330, $6,600

$15,150 to Napa Valley Museum, Yountville, CA.

$15,000 to Performing Arts Center of Los Angeles County, Los Angeles, CA. 2 grants: $5,000, $10,000

7242
The Wendling Foundation ◇
80 Broad St., 17th Fl.
New York, NY 10004
Contact: Michelle Lord
FAX: (212) 764-4298

Established in 1984 in FL.
Donor: Helen C. Vanderbilt†.
Foundation type: Independent foundation.
Financial data (yr. ended 12/31/04): Assets, $10,853,985 (M); gifts received, $53,537; expenditures, $531,325; qualifying distributions, $493,760; giving activities include $405,000 for 32 grants (high: $50,000; low: $1,000; average: $1,000–$50,000).
Purpose and activities: Giving primarily for educational reform, the environment, organizational and leadership development, including job development, and international rights and women's rights.
Fields of interest: Education, reform; Environment; Employment; International human rights; Civil rights, women; Community development; Leadership development.
Type of support: General/operating support; Continuing support; Program development; Conferences/seminars; Seed money; Research; Technical assistance.
Limitations: Applications not accepted. Giving on a national basis, with emphasis on Washington, DC, and the New England states, especially ME. No grants to individuals.
Publications: Grants list.
Application information: Application process, initiated by the board of directors, includes completion of application in Apr. and Nov. (1 month prior to board meeting). Grantees must be invited to submit proposals; unsolicited requests not accepted.
  Board meeting date(s): 2 weeks following board meetings for board-initiated application process
Officers and Directors:* Averill Cook,* Co-Chair.; John Cook, Jr.,* Co-Chair.; Heleny Cook,* Pres.; Rebecca Cook,* Secy.; Willard Cook,* Treas.; Warren C. Cook.
EIN: 133249448

7243
The Margaret L. Wendt Foundation ▼ ◇
40 Fountain Plz., Ste. 277
Buffalo, NY 14202-2220 (716) 855-2146
Contact: Robert J. Kresse

Trust established in 1956 in NY.
Donor: Margaret L. Wendt†.
Foundation type: Independent foundation.
Financial data (yr. ended 1/31/05): Assets, $118,571,051 (M); expenditures, $7,725,463; qualifying distributions, $6,159,733; giving activities include $5,871,065 for 155 grants (high: $500,000; low: $224; average: $5,000–$50,000).
Purpose and activities: Emphasis on education, the arts, and social services; support also for churches and religious organizations, health associations, public interest organizations, and youth agencies.

Fields of interest: Visual arts; Museums; Performing arts; Performing arts, theater; History/archaeology; Historic preservation/historical societies; Arts; Education, fund raising/fund distribution; Education, early childhood education; Higher education; Libraries/library science; Education; Environment, natural resources; Hospitals (general); Substance abuse, services; Mental health/crisis services; Health organizations, association; Cancer; AIDS; Alcoholism; Biomedicine; Medical research, institute; Cancer research; AIDS research; Legal services; Crime/law enforcement; Human services; Children/youth, services; Residential/custodial care, hospices; Aging, centers/services; Minorities/immigrants, centers/services; International human rights; Community development; Federated giving programs; Political science; Government/public administration; Public affairs; Religion; Aging; Disabilities, people with; Minorities; Economically disadvantaged.
Type of support: Program-related investments/loans.
Limitations: Giving primarily in Buffalo and western NY. No grants to individuals, or for scholarships.
Publications: Application guidelines.
Application information: Application form not required.
  Initial approach: Letter or application form
  Copies of proposal: 4
  Deadline(s): 1 month prior to board meeting
  Board meeting date(s): Quarterly; no fixed dates
  Final notification: Usually 4 to 6 months
Trustees: Janet L. Day; Thomas D. Lunt; Robert J. Kresse.
Number of staff: 1 part-time support.
EIN: 166030037
Selected grants: The following grants were reported in 2005.
$500,000 to Hauptman-Woodward Medical Research Institute, Buffalo, NY. To construct and equip large open laboratory study center within new facility.
$500,000 to Roswell Park Cancer Institute, Buffalo, NY. For construction of new science research building.
$500,000 to University of Buffalo Foundation, Buffalo, NY. For Buffalo Center of Excellence in Bioinformatics.
$300,000 to Buffalo Fine Arts Academy, Buffalo, NY. For anticipated loss for Masterworks from The Philips Collection exhibition.
$250,000 to Summit Educational Resources, Tonawanda, NY. To construct new facility.
$155,296 to Buffalo, City of, Buffalo, NY. For renovation of wading pool and basketball courts in Martin Luther King, Jr. Park.
$87,500 to Buffalo Zoological Gardens, Buffalo, NY. For state-of-the art exhibit, Otter Creek.
$20,000 to Northwest Buffalo Community Health Care Center, Buffalo, NY. For salary of executive director and office assistant and to hire consultants.
$18,750 to New York Charter School Resource Center, New York, NY. To serve increased needs of Buffalo Charter Schools.
$18,486 to Niagara Aerospace Museum, Niagara Falls, NY. For general support.

7244
Wenner-Gren Foundation for Anthropological Research, Inc. ◇
470 Park Ave. S., 8th Fl.
New York, NY 10016 (212) 683-5000
FAX: (212) 683-9151;
E-mail: inquiries@wennergren.org; URL: http://www.wennergren.org

Incorporated in 1941 in DE.
Donor: Axel L. Wenner-Gren†.
Foundation type: Operating foundation.
Financial data (yr. ended 12/31/04): Assets, $138,297,947 (M); expenditures, $7,171,680; qualifying distributions, $6,299,663; giving activities include $3,305,328 for grants to individuals, and $1,334,588 for 5 foundation-administered programs.
Purpose and activities: A private operating foundation; international support of research in all branches of anthropology including cultural/social anthropology, ethnology, biological/physical anthropology, archaeology, and anthropological linguistics, and in closely related disciplines so far as they pertain to human origins, development, and variation; grants-in-aid for programs of research; subsidies for conferences for anthropologists to promote reporting on results of research; publishes a journal and provides clearinghouse services for anthropological information.
Fields of interest: History/archaeology; Language/linguistics; Anthropology/sociology.
Type of support: Conferences/seminars; Publication; Seed money; Fellowships; Research; Grants to individuals.
Limitations: Giving on a national and international basis. Individuals from all countries are invited to apply for individual research grants. No support for intermediary funding agencies, nonproject personnel, or institutional overhead or support. No grants for salaries or fringe benefits, tuition or travel to meetings; low priority given to dissertation write-up or revision, publication subvention, or filmmaking.
Publications: Application guidelines; Annual report; Annual report (including application guidelines); Grants list; Informational brochure.
Application information: Application form required.
  Initial approach: Web site
  Copies of proposal: 5
  Deadline(s): Contact foundation for program deadlines
  Board meeting date(s): Apr. and Oct.
  Final notification: Approximately 6 months after deadline
Officers and Trustees:* Richard C. Hackney, Jr.,* Chair.; Seth J. Masters,* Vice-Chair. and Treas.; Leslie C. Aiello,* Pres. and Secy.; David Alexander; Beverly F. Chase; William L. Cobb, Jr.; Joan S. Girgus; John Immerwahr; Darcy Kelley; Ruth Kennedy; Ellen Mickiewicz; David Patterson; William B. Peterson; Lorraine Sciarra; Frank W. Wadsworth.
Number of staff: 9 full-time professional; 2 full-time support; 1 part-time support.
EIN: 131813827

7245
Nina W. Werblow Charitable Trust ◇
c/o Ehrenkranz and Ehrenkranz, LLP
375 Park Ave., Ste. 2800
New York, NY 10152-0067 (212) 751-5959
Contact: Roger A. Goldman, Tr.

Established in 1977 in NY.
Donor: Nina W. Werblow†.
Foundation type: Independent foundation.
Financial data (yr. ended 2/28/05): Assets, $12,880,679 (M); expenditures, $882,813; qualifying distributions, $827,251; giving activities include $815,400 for 64 grants (high: $110,000; low: $1,000).
Purpose and activities: Giving primarily to the arts with emphasis on museums of art; some giving also for education, health care, and social services.
Fields of interest: Visual arts, photography; Museums; Museums (art); Arts; Higher education; Dental school/education; Law school/education; Education; Hospitals (general); Hospitals (specialty); Health organizations, association; Cancer research; Human services; Children/youth, services; Family services; Federated giving programs; Jewish agencies & temples.
Limitations: Giving limited to New York, NY.
Application information:
 Initial approach: Letter
 Deadline(s): Sept. 30
Trustees: Joel S. Ehrenkranz; Roger A. Goldman.
EIN: 136742999

7246
West Ferry Foundation ✧
c/o Robert G. Wilmers
350 Park Ave., 6th Fl.
New York, NY 10022 (212) 350-2497

Established in 1992 in NY.
Donor: Robert G. Wilmers.
Foundation type: Independent foundation.
Financial data (yr. ended 11/30/04): Assets, $19,883,507 (M); expenditures, $798,506; qualifying distributions, $793,125; giving activities include $793,125 for 15 grants (high: $250,000; low: $1,000).
Fields of interest: Arts; Higher education; Education; Environment, natural resources.
Limitations: Applications not accepted. Giving primarily in Buffalo, NY and MA. No grants to individuals.
Application information: Contributes only to pre-selected organizations.
Trustee: Robert G. Wilmers.
EIN: 133715532
Selected grants: The following grants were reported in 2003.
$802,890 to Martin House Restoration Corporation, Buffalo, NY.
$30,000 to Buffalo Museum of Science, Buffalo, NY.
$25,000 to United Way of Buffalo and Erie County, Buffalo, NY.
$15,000 to Natural Resources Defense Council, New York, NY.
$10,000 to Harvard University, Cambridge, MA.
$10,000 to Studio Arena Theater and School, Buffalo, NY.
$5,000 to Buffalo Prep, Buffalo, NY.
$4,340 to Williams College, Williamstown, MA.
$2,000 to Buffalo Niagara Partnership Foundation, Buffalo, NY.
$1,000 to Central Park Conservancy, New York, NY.

7247
Westchester Artificial Kidney Foundation, Inc. ✧
234 Tarrytown Rd.
Elmsford, NY 10523 (914) 592-5858
Contact: Ronnie Greenberg, Admin.

Foundation type: Operating foundation.
Financial data (yr. ended 12/31/05): Assets, $4,339,919 (L); gifts received, $1,485; expenditures, $515,036; qualifying distributions, $393,571; giving activities include $288,639 for 3 + grants (high: $220,605), and $104,932 for 4 grants to individuals (high: $50,000; low: $2,466).
Purpose and activities: The purpose of the foundation is to support renal research and education.
Fields of interest: Kidney diseases; Kidney research.
Application information:
 Initial approach: Letter with supporting information
 Deadline(s): None
Officers and Directors:* M. Charles Ross,* Pres.; Richard Marasco,* Treas.; Stephen Adler, M.D.; Khalid M.H. Butt, M.D.; Veronica Delaney, M.D.; Robert P. Dohn; Anjani K. Dubey, M.D.; Renee E. Garrick, M.D.; Michael Golgorsky, M.D.; Alvin I. Goodman; Richard Rosenberg; Karim B. Solangi, M.D.; Peter P. Zeltner.
EIN: 132761067

7248
The Western New York Foundation ✧
11 Summer St.
Buffalo, NY 14209 (716) 839-4225
Contact: Richard E. Moot, Pres.
FAX: (716) 839-3152;
E-mail: info@wnyfoundation.org; URL: http://www.wnyfoundation.org

Incorporated in 1951 in NY as the Wildroot Foundation; present name adopted in 1958.
Donor: Welles V. Moot†.
Foundation type: Independent foundation.
Financial data (yr. ended 7/31/05): Assets, $13,364,281 (M); expenditures, $642,919; qualifying distributions, $553,699; giving activities include $436,869 for 41 grants (high: $50,000; low: $750).
Purpose and activities: Grants to nonprofit institutions, with emphasis on capital needs, seed funds for new projects, or expanding services. Support primarily for the fine and performing arts, youth agencies, the natural sciences, and social service agencies; some support also for health services and libraries and other educational institutions.
Fields of interest: Visual arts; Museums; Performing arts; Performing arts, dance; Performing arts, theater; Performing arts, music; Arts; Child development, education; Secondary school/education; Libraries (public); Medical care, rehabilitation; Substance abuse, services; Mental health/crisis services; Alcoholism; Legal services; Crime/law enforcement; Housing/shelter, development; Human services; Children/youth, services; Family services; Residential/custodial care, hospices; Aging, centers/services; Women, centers/services; Community development; Aging; Disabilities, people with; Minorities.

Type of support: Capital campaigns; Building/renovation; Equipment; Land acquisition; Emergency funds; Program development; Conferences/seminars; Publication; Seed money; Technical assistance; Program-related investments/loans; Matching/challenge support.
Limitations: Giving limited to the 8th Judicial District of NY (Erie, Niagara, Genesee, Wyoming, Allegany, Cattaraugus, and Chautauqua counties). No support for hospitals or religious organizations. No grants to individuals, or for scholarships, fellowships, or generally for operating budgets or deficit financing.
Publications: Annual report (including application guidelines); Informational brochure.
Application information: Application form available on foundation Web Site. Application form required.
 Initial approach: One-and-a-half-page letter
 Copies of proposal: 2
 Deadline(s): None
 Board meeting date(s): 3 or 4 times a year
 Final notification: Usually within 3 months
Officers and Trustees:* Richard E. Moot,* Pres.; John N. Walsh III, V.P.; John R. Moot,* Secy.; Welles V. Moot, Jr., Treas.; Anthony Johnson; Jennifer Johnson; Ann F. McCarthy; James A.W. McLeod; Trudy A. Mollenberg.
Number of staff: 1 full-time professional; 1 part-time support.
EIN: 160845962
Selected grants: The following grants were reported in 2005.
$27,787 to Irish Classical Theater, Buffalo, NY. For Tessitura Software Program.
$25,000 to Food Bank of Western New York, Buffalo, NY. For freezer.
$25,000 to Zoological Society of Buffalo, Buffalo, NY.
$20,000 to Child and Family Services of Erie County, Buffalo, NY. For capital campaign.
$15,223 to Legal Services for the Elderly, New York, NY. For Emergency Gap Funding.
$10,000 to Benedict House of Western New York, Buffalo, NY. For new van.
$10,000 to People Inc., Buffalo, NY. For Family Respite Center.
$10,000 to Ronald McDonald House, Buffalo, NY. For renovation.
$5,420 to Botanical Gardens of Buffalo and Erie County, Buffalo, NY. For Portable Cart Design.
$4,500 to Tremendous Teens of WNY, West Seneca, NY. For computers.

7249
Leslie H. Wexner Charitable Fund ▼ ✧
c/o George V. Delson Assocs.
110 E. 59th St.
New York, NY 10022

Established in 1990 in OH.
Donor: Leslie H. Wexner.
Foundation type: Independent foundation.
Financial data (yr. ended 12/31/04): Assets, $107,346,462 (M); expenditures, $19,861,518; qualifying distributions, $19,172,935; giving activities include $19,172,500 for 33 grants (high: $5,000,000; low: $5,000; average: $100,000–$500,000).
Purpose and activities: Giving primarily to Jewish organizations, with an emphasis on Jewish education.
Fields of interest: Education; Reproductive health, family planning; Federated giving programs; Jewish agencies & temples.

Limitations: Applications not accepted. Giving on a national basis. No grants to individuals.
Application information: Contributes only to pre-selected organizations.
Officers: Leslie H. Wexner, Pres.; Jeffrey E. Epstein, V.P.; Abigail S. Wexner, Treas.
EIN: 311318013
Selected grants: The following grants were reported in 2004.
$8,000,000 to Wexner Foundation, New Albany, OH. 2 grants: $5,000,000 (For unrestricted support), $3,000,000 (For unrestricted support).
$2,400,000 to Jewish Federation, Columbus, Columbus, OH. 3 grants: $1,200,000 (For unrestricted support), $600,000 (For unrestricted support), $600,000 (For unrestricted support).
$2,000,000 to Columbus Foundation, Columbus, OH. For unrestricted support.
$550,000 to UJA-Federation of New York, New York, NY. For unrestricted support.
$500,000 to Birthright Israel North America, New York, NY. For unrestricted support.
$300,000 to Partnership for Excellence in Jewish Education, Boston, MA. For unrestricted support.
$300,000 to United Way of Central Ohio, Columbus, OH. For unrestricted support.

7250
Whispering Bells Foundation ✧
c/o McLaughlin & Stern, LLP
260 Madison Ave., 18th Fl.
New York, NY 10016
Contact: Edward Klagsbrun, Tr.

Established in 1990 in NY.
Donors: Peter Workman; Carolan Workman; Workman Publishing Co.
Foundation type: Independent foundation.
Financial data (yr. ended 12/31/05): Assets, $1,404,228 (M); gifts received, $600,000; expenditures, $580,902; qualifying distributions, $576,300; giving activities include $575,950 for 113 grants (high: $105,000; low: $50).
Fields of interest: Education; Human services; Neighborhood centers; International human rights; Jewish federated giving programs.
Limitations: Applications not accepted. Giving primarily in NY. No grants to individuals.
Application information: Contributes only to pre-selected organizations.
Officer and Trustees:* Peter Workman,* Pres.; Edward Klagsbrun; Carolan Workman.
EIN: 136962126

7251
White Flowers Foundation ✧
c/o Neufield Doudna LLC
103 5th Ave., 5th Fl.
New York, NY 10003

Established in 1989 in NY.
Donor: J. Christopher Flowers.
Foundation type: Independent foundation.
Financial data (yr. ended 5/31/04): Assets, $1,027,320 (M); gifts received, $10,301,817; expenditures, $9,970,608; qualifying distributions, $9,963,718; giving activities include $9,962,773 for 71 grants (high: $8,933,500; low: $25; average: $1,000–$100,000).

Purpose and activities: Giving primarily for higher education and Christian churches.
Fields of interest: Performing arts, orchestra (symphony); Higher education; Education; Human services; Christian agencies & churches.
Type of support: General/operating support; Continuing support; Annual campaigns; Capital campaigns; Endowments; Emergency funds; Research.
Limitations: Applications not accepted. Giving primarily in New York, NY. No grants to individuals, or for scholarships; no loans.
Application information: Contributes only to pre-selected organizations.
Trustees: J. Christopher Flowers; Mary H. White.
EIN: 133532030
Selected grants: The following grants were reported in 2004.
$8,933,500 to Harvard University, Cambridge, MA.
$99,340 to Rockefeller University, New York, NY.
$27,340 to Brearley School, New York, NY. 2 grants: $25,000, $2,340
$5,000 to North Haven Foundation, North Haven, ME.
$5,000 to Wellesley College, Wellesley, MA.
$2,000 to Cooke Center for Learning and Development, New York, NY. 2 grants: $1,000 each
$1,000 to Classroom, Inc., New York, NY.
$1,000 to Early Steps, New York, NY.

7252
The Whitehead Foundation ✧
c/o Denise Emmett
65 E. 55th St.
New York, NY 10022

Established in 1982 in NY.
Donor: John C. Whitehead.
Foundation type: Independent foundation.
Financial data (yr. ended 6/30/05): Assets, $5,387,755 (M); gifts received, $2,200,000; expenditures, $2,072,425; qualifying distributions, $2,072,425; giving activities include $2,070,771 for 344 grants (high: $38,000; low: $100).
Purpose and activities: Primary categories of interest are international affairs, higher education, and youth; support also for the arts, civic affairs, and public policy.
Fields of interest: Arts; Higher education; Environment, natural resources; Children/youth, services; International affairs; Public policy, research.
International interests: Eastern Europe.
Type of support: Annual campaigns; Capital campaigns; Program-related investments/loans.
Limitations: Applications not accepted. Giving primarily in NY. No grants to individuals.
Application information: Unsolicited proposals are rarely approved.
Board meeting date(s): Quarterly
Trustees: Wade Greene; Anne Whitehead; John C. Whitehead; John Gregory Whitehead.
EIN: 133119344
Selected grants: The following grants were reported in 2005.
$40,000 to Pierpont Morgan Library, New York, NY.
$34,800 to Museum of Modern Art, New York, NY.
$33,000 to Sabre Foundation, Cambridge, MA.
$25,000 to Common Good Institute, New York, NY.
$20,000 to Nantucket Sustainable Development Corporation, Nantucket, MA.

$7,500 to Council for Excellence in Government, DC.
$5,000 to Mountain Institute, DC.
$5,000 to Rockefeller University, New York, NY.
$5,000 to TechnoServe, Norwalk, CT.
$3,510 to Lincoln Center for the Performing Arts, New York, NY.

7253
Mrs. Giles Whiting Foundation ✧
1133 Ave. of the Americas, 22nd Fl.
New York, NY 10036-6710 (212) 336-2000
Contact: Kellye M. Rosenheim, Dir. of Opers.
URL: http://www.whitingfoundation.org

Incorporated in 1963 in NY.
Donor: Mrs. Giles Whiting†.
Foundation type: Independent foundation.
Financial data (yr. ended 11/30/04): Assets, $63,904,638 (M); expenditures, $4,079,954; qualifying distributions, $3,214,431; giving activities include $2,368,851 for 43 grants (high: $460,000; low: $1,500), and $350,000 for 20 grants to individuals (high: $17,500; low: $17,500).
Purpose and activities: The foundation is dedicated to the support of the humanities and of creative writing. Seven universities with distinguished graduate programs in the humanities receive yearly grants from the foundation to support their best scholars as they complete their dissertations. Doctoral students at Bryn Mawr, University of Chicago, Columbia, Harvard, Princeton, Stanford, and Yale are eligible. Each university sets up its own procedures to select its Fellows; most use a jury of faculty members from various disciplines within the graduate school of the Arts and Sciences. Applicants to this program apply to the committee within their school. The foundation has no other program to assist students.
Fields of interest: Humanities; Literature; Higher education.
Type of support: Fellowships; Grants to individuals.
Limitations: Applications not accepted. Giving on a national basis. No grants to individuals (except for Whiting Writers' Award program for which applications are not invited), or for general support, capital funds, matching gifts, research, special projects, publications, or conferences; no loans.
Publications: Multi-year report.
Application information: See Web site for application information.
Board meeting date(s): May and Oct.
Officers: Robert L. Belknap, Pres.; John N. Irwin III,* V.P. and Treas.; Antonia M. Grumbach,* V.P.; Peter Pennoyer, V.P.; Kate Douglas Torrey,* V.P.; Robin Krause, Secy.
Number of staff: 1 full-time professional; 2 part-time professional.
EIN: 136154484
Selected grants: The following grants were reported in 2004.
$460,000 to Yale University, New Haven, CT.
$290,000 to Stanford University, Stanford, CA.
$245,000 to University of Chicago, Chicago, IL. 2 grants: $145,000, $100,000
$230,000 to Columbia University, New York, NY.
$230,000 to Harvard University, Cambridge, MA.
$150,000 to Brooklyn College Foundation, Brooklyn, NY.
$100,000 to Kenyon College, Gambier, OH.
$65,000 to Bryn Mawr College, Bryn Mawr, PA.
$32,000 to Princeton University, Princeton, NJ.

7254
The Helen Hay Whitney Foundation
20 Squadron Blvd., Ste. 630
New City, NY   10956   (845) 639-6799
Contact: Robert Weinberger, Admin. Dir.
FAX: (845) 639-6798; E-mail: hhwf@earthlink.net;
URL: http://www.hhwf.org/

Charitable trust established in 1943; established as a private foundation in 1947; incorporated in 1951 in NY.
Donor: Mrs. Charles S. Payson†.
Foundation type: Independent foundation.
Financial data (yr. ended 6/30/05): Assets, $46,149,070 (M); gifts received, $592,844; expenditures, $3,239,449; qualifying distributions, $2,890,566; giving activities include $2,486,105 for 58 grants (high: $48,000; low: $23,500), and $2,890,566 for 1 foundation-administered program.
Purpose and activities: To support beginning postdoctoral training in basic biomedical research through research fellowships for residents of the United States, Canada, or Mexico. Fellowships are awarded to individuals but funds are administered largely by research institutions. American citizenship is not required, but foreign nationals are expected to pursue their research in the U.S.
Fields of interest: Medical research, institute.
Type of support: Fellowships.
Limitations: Giving limited to North America, including Canada and Mexico.
Publications: Application guidelines; Annual report; Financial statement; Informational brochure (including application guidelines).
Application information: Application forms available Apr. 15 on foundation Web site. For application guidelines and procedures, and any inquiries, please E-mail or see foundation Web site. Application form required.
  Initial approach: Complete application form on-line
  Deadline(s): Submit proposal in July; deadline July 15
  Final notification: 3 months
Officers and Trustees:* Averil Payson Meyer,* Pres.; Stephen C. Harrison, Ph.D.*, V.P. and Chair., Scientific Advisory Comm.; Lisa A. Steiner, M.D.*, V.P.; W. Perry Welch, Treas.; Milton N. Allen; Jerome Gross, M.D.; Payne Middleton; Thomas Sakmar, M.D.; Stephen C. Sherrill; Christopher Walsh, Ph.D.
Scientific Advisory Committee: Thomas M. Jessell, Ph.D.; Daniel Kahne, Ph.D.; Barbara J. Meyer, Ph.D.; Erin K. O'Shea, Ph.D.; Matthew D. Scharff, M.D.; Julie Theriot, Ph.D.; S. Lawrence Ziporsky, Ph.D.
Number of staff: 1 full-time professional.
EIN: 131677403
Selected grants: The following grants were reported in 2005.
$93,000 to Harvard University, Cambridge, MA. 2 grants: $46,500 each
$90,750 to Childrens Hospital. 2 grants: $45,750, $45,000
$90,000 to Cold Spring Harbor Laboratory, Cold Spring Harbor, NY. 2 grants: $45,000 each
$48,000 to Columbia University, New York, NY.
$46,500 to New York University, New York, NY.
$46,500 to Stanford University, Stanford, CA.
$45,000 to Ludwig Institute for Cancer Research, La Jolla, CA.

7255
The Widgeon Point Charitable Foundation ✧
(formerly The Beinecke Foundation, Inc.)
c/o Weiser LLP
3000 Marcus Ave.
Lake Success, NY   11042-1066

Incorporated in 1966 in NY as The Kerry Foundation, Inc. and absorbed the Edwin J. Beinecke Trust, NY, in April 1985. The new name for the combined foundations was adopted in Dec. 1985.
Donor: Sylvia B. Robinson†.
Foundation type: Independent foundation.
Financial data (yr. ended 12/31/04): Assets, $67,588,559 (M); expenditures, $3,458,374; qualifying distributions, $2,481,977; giving activities include $1,871,270 for 144 grants (high: $150,000; low: $100; average: $1,000–$125,000), and $13,380 for 1 in-kind gift.
Purpose and activities: Giving primarily for secondary, higher, and medical education, conservation, and Protestant church support.
Fields of interest: Secondary school/education; Higher education; Medical school/education; Environment, natural resources; Protestant agencies & churches.
Type of support: General/operating support; Capital campaigns; Building/renovation; Equipment; Endowments; Conferences/seminars; Publication.
Limitations: Applications not accepted. Giving primarily in CT and NY. No grants to individuals; no loans.
Publications: Annual report.
Application information: Contributes only to pre-selected organizations.
  Board meeting date(s): Spring and fall
Officers and Directors:* John R. Robinson,* Pres.; Abigail Phipps Bowers,* V.P.; Jean W. Painter, Secy.; Rowland P. Robinson, Treas.
Number of staff: 2 full-time professional; 1 full-time support.
EIN: 136201175
Selected grants: The following grants were reported in 2003.
$850,000 to Harvard University, Cambridge, MA. For endowment.
$25,000 to Columbia University, New York, NY. For general support.
$15,000 to University of Southern Maine, Portland, ME. For general support.
$5,000 to American Farmland Trust, DC. For general support.
$5,000 to Breakwater School, Portland, ME. For general support.
$5,000 to City Parks Foundation, New York, NY. For general support.
$5,000 to Rye Country Day School, Rye, NY. For general support.
$5,000 to Yale University, New Haven, CT. For general support.
$2,000 to Natural Resources Defense Council, New York, NY. For general support.
$1,000 to New York Landmarks Preservation Foundation, New York, NY. For general support.

7256
The Wiegers Family Foundation ✧ ☆
c/o Barry M. Strauss Assocs., Ltd.
307 5th Ave., 8th Fl.
New York, NY   10016-6517

Established in 1992 in CO.

Donor: George A. Wiegers.
Foundation type: Independent foundation.
Financial data (yr. ended 2/28/05): Assets, $4,526,206 (M); expenditures, $442,367; qualifying distributions, $409,033; giving activities include $402,888 for 23 grants (high: $97,592; low: $100).
Fields of interest: Arts; Higher education; Business school/education; Environment; Animals/wildlife, preservation/protection.
Limitations: Applications not accepted. Giving primarily in CO and NY. No grants to individuals.
Application information: Contributes only to pre-selected organizations.
Trustees: Hans P. Utsch; E. Alexander Wiegers; Elizabeth C. Wiegers; George A. Wiegers.
EIN: 841214070

7257
Zena & Michael A. Wiener Foundation ✧
c/o Lewis Braff & Co.
60 E. 42nd St., Ste. 850
New York, NY   10165

Established in 1993 in NH.
Donors: Michael A. Wiener; Zena Wiener.
Foundation type: Independent foundation.
Financial data (yr. ended 12/31/05): Assets, $3,590,382 (M); expenditures, $357,914; qualifying distributions, $339,932; giving activities include $339,932 for 28 grants (high: $45,000; low: $500).
Purpose and activities: Giving primarily for the arts and health care.
Fields of interest: Performing arts, music; Arts; Elementary/secondary education; Health care; Human services; Children/youth, services; Jewish agencies & temples.
Limitations: Applications not accepted. Giving primarily in NY. No grants to individuals.
Application information: Contributes only to pre-selected organizations.
Officers and Directors:* Michael A. Wiener,* Pres.; Jennifer Wiener,* V.P.; Zena Wiener,* Secy.
EIN: 020468920
Selected grants: The following grants were reported in 2003.
$50,000 to CASA-Voices for Children, Buffalo, NY.
$50,000 to Mount Sinai Hospital, New York, NY. For Crystal Ball.
$15,000 to Katonah Museum of Art, Katonah, NY.
$10,000 to Orpheus Chamber Orchestra, New York, NY.
$5,000 to Atlantic Theater Company, New York, NY.
$5,000 to New York Stage and Film, New York, NY.
$2,500 to Center for Independence of the Disabled in New York, New York, NY.
$2,500 to National Center for Learning Disabilities, New York, NY.
$2,500 to Weill Medical College of Cornell University, New York, NY.
$1,500 to Playwrights Horizons, New York, NY.

7258
Barrie A. & Dee Dee Wigmore Foundation ✧
c/o BCRS Assocs., LLP
100 Wall St., 11th Fl.
New York, NY   10005

Established in 1978 in NY.

Donor: Barrie A. Wigmore.
Foundation type: Independent foundation.
Financial data (yr. ended 3/31/05): Assets, $10,762,312 (M); gifts received, $951; expenditures, $1,067,301; qualifying distributions, $1,019,658; giving activities include $1,017,505 for 53 grants (high: $200,000; low: $500).
Purpose and activities: Giving primarily for arts and culture, particularly art museums; support also for human services and education.
Fields of interest: Museums (art); Arts; Higher education; Human services; Federated giving programs.
International interests: Canada.
Limitations: Applications not accepted. Giving on a national basis, with emphasis on NY, especially the New York, NY metropolitan area; giving also internationally, primarily in Canada. No grants to individuals; no loans.
Application information: Contributes only to pre-selected organizations.
Trustees: Donald Lenz; Barrie A. Wigmore; DeeDee Wigmore.
EIN: 132967487
Selected grants: The following grants were reported in 2004.
$114,575 to Metropolitan Museum of Art, New York, NY. 3 grants: $49,125 (For general support), $13,500 (For general support), $51,950 (For general support).
$30,000 to Cooper-Hewitt Museum, The Smithsonians National Museum of Design, New York, NY. For general support.
$10,000 to American Friends of Oxford Centre for Hebrew and Jewish Studies, New York, NY. For general support.
$10,000 to Munson-Williams-Proctor Institute, Utica, NY. For general support.
$10,000 to New Jersey Historical Society, Newark, NJ. For general support.
$10,000 to Salvation Army of Greater New York, New York, NY. For general support.
$10,000 to Visiting Nurse Service of New York, New York, NY. For general support.
$5,000 to Bide-A-Wee Home Association, New York, NY. For general support.

7259
The Wildwood Foundation ✧
(formerly The Morgens East Foundation)
c/o Morgen, Waterfall, Vintiadis
600 5th Ave., 27th Fl.
New York, NY   10020

Established in 1968 in CT.
Donors: Edwin H. Morgens; Howard J. Morgens; Wildwood Trust.
Foundation type: Independent foundation.
Financial data (yr. ended 12/31/05): Assets, $14,070,728 (M); gifts received, $3,006,062; expenditures, $1,411,505; qualifying distributions, $1,409,125; giving activities include $1,408,000 for 9 grants (high: $1,000,000; low: $1,000).
Purpose and activities: Giving primarily to a museum of natural history, and a lab of ornithology.
Fields of interest: Museums (natural history); Business school/education; Medical school/education; Animals/wildlife, formal/general education; Hospitals (general); Anatomy (animal).
Limitations: Applications not accepted. Giving primarily in NY; funding also nationally. No grants to individuals.

Application information: Contributes only to pre-selected organizations.
Trustees: Edwin H. Morgens; Linda M. Morgens; Lauren Morgens.
EIN: 316090956

7260
Dave H. & Reba W. Williams
Foundation ✧ ☆
c/o White, William, Holding
41 W. 57th St., 4th Fl.
New York, NY   10019

Established in 1986 in NY.
Donors: Dave H. Williams; Reba W. Williams.
Foundation type: Independent foundation.
Financial data (yr. ended 6/30/05): Assets, $30,007 (M); expenditures, $827,901; qualifying distributions, $827,222; giving activities include $826,887 for 21 grants (high: $300,000; low: $120).
Purpose and activities: Funding primarily for museums and arts and cultural programs.
Fields of interest: Museums; Arts; Education; Animals/wildlife, clubs; Government/public administration.
Limitations: Applications not accepted. Giving primarily in New York, NY and Fairfield County, CT. No grants to individuals.
Application information: Contributes only to pre-selected organizations.
Trustees: Dave H. Williams; Reba W. Williams.
EIN: 133381821
Selected grants: The following grants were reported in 2003.
$50,000 to Skyscraper Museum, New York, NY.
$25,000 to Foreign Policy Association, New York, NY.
$25,000 to Intrepid Museum Foundation, New York, NY.
$2,500 to Lady Bird Johnson Wildflower Center, Austin, TX.
$1,000 to Episcopal Charities of the Diocese of New York, New York, NY.
$1,000 to Franklin and Eleanor Roosevelt Institute (FERI), Hyde Park, NY.
$1,000 to Institute for Advanced Study, Princeton, NJ.
$1,000 to PEN American Center, New York, NY.
$1,000 to United Service Organization of Metropolitan New York, New York, NY.
$1,000 to University of Michigan, Ann Arbor, MI.

7261
Judy and Fred Wilpon Family Foundation, Inc. ✧
111 Great Neck Rd., Ste. 408
Great Neck, NY   11021-5476   (516) 773-3800
Contact: Fred Wilpon, Pres.

Established in 1982.
Donor: Fred Wilpon.
Foundation type: Independent foundation.
Financial data (yr. ended 12/31/05): Assets, $555,344 (M); expenditures, $1,071,073; qualifying distributions, $1,070,695; giving activities include $1,070,695 for 62 grants (high: $625,000; low: $100).
Purpose and activities: Giving for animal welfare, and for medical and health purposes.

Fields of interest: Health care; Recreation; Youth development, centers/clubs.
Type of support: General/operating support.
Limitations: Giving primarily in the greater metropolitan New York, NY, area, including Long Island. No grants to individuals.
Application information: Application form not required.
Initial approach: Letter
Deadline(s): None
Officer and Directors:* Fred Wilpon,* Pres.; Robin Wilpon Wachtler; Jeffrey Wilpon; Judith Wilpon.
EIN: 112626618
Selected grants: The following grants were reported in 2003.
$62,066 to City Center Fifty-Fifth Street Theater, New York, NY. For general support.
$15,000 to Alliance for Lupus Research, New York, NY. For general support.
$10,000 to Project ALS, New York, NY. For general support.
$10,000 to Saint Barnabas Medical Center, Livingston, NJ. For general support.
$5,000 to National Center for Disability Services, Albertson, NY. For general support.
$4,000 to Golden Retriever Foundation, Elkhorn, NE. For general support.
$1,000 to American Cancer Society, New York, NY. For general support.
$1,000 to Elizabeth Glaser Pediatric AIDS Foundation, New York, NY. For general support.
$1,000 to Multiple Sclerosis Society, National, New York, NY. For general support.
$250 to Equine Advocates, Chatham, NY. For general support.

7262
The Robert W. Wilson Charitable
Trust ▼ ✧
c/o Robert W. Wilson
520 83rd St., Ste. 1R
Brooklyn, NY   11209

Established in 2003 in NY.
Donors: Robert W. Wilson; Bowman Family Foundation.
Foundation type: Independent foundation.
Financial data (yr. ended 12/31/05): Assets, $166,865,173 (M); gifts received, $54,910,484; expenditures, $54,004,274; qualifying distributions, $52,824,088; giving activities include $52,452,518 for 52 grants (high: $21,984,923; low: $50; average: $20,000–$3,000,000), and $318,437 for 1 loan/program-related investment.
Purpose and activities: Giving primarily for art museums, civil rights associations, historic preservation/historical societies, and environmental conservation and protection.
Fields of interest: Museums (art); Historic preservation/historical societies; Environment, natural resources; Environment; Civil rights, association.
Type of support: Program-related investments/loans.
Limitations: Applications not accepted. Giving primarily in NY. No grants to individuals.
Application information: Contributes only to pre-selected organizations.
Trustee: Robert W. Wilson.
EIN: 516536168

7263
The H. W. Wilson Foundation, Inc. ✧
950 University Ave.
Bronx, NY 10452
Contact: William E. Stanton, Pres.

Incorporated in 1952 in NY.
Donors: H.W. Wilson†; Mrs. H.W. Wilson†; The H.W. Wilson Co., Inc.
Foundation type: Independent foundation.
Financial data (yr. ended 11/30/05): Assets, $16,970,226 (M); gifts received, $50,000; expenditures, $866,139; qualifying distributions, $811,714; giving activities include $800,300 for grants.
Purpose and activities: Grants largely to accredited library schools for scholarships; support also for cultural programs, including historical societies, and library associations.
Fields of interest: Higher education; Libraries/library science.
Type of support: Scholarship funds; Research.
Limitations: Giving on a national basis. No grants for building or endowment funds or operating budgets.
Application information: Application form not required.
Initial approach: Proposal
Copies of proposal: 1
Deadline(s): None
Board meeting date(s): Jan., Mar., May, Aug., and Oct.
Final notification: 3 months
Officers and Directors:* William E. Stanton,* Pres. and Treas.; William T. Hayden,* V.P.; James M. Matarazzo,* V.P.
EIN: 237418062

7264
Marie C. and Joseph C. Wilson Foundation
160 Allens Creek Rd.
Rochester, NY 14618-3309 (585) 461-4699
Contact: Ruth H. Fleischmann-Colgan, Exec. Dir.
FAX: (585) 473-5206;
E-mail: mcjcwilsonfdn@frontiernet.net; Additional tel.: (585) 461-4696; URL: http://www.mcjcwilsonfoundation.org

Trust established in 1963 in NY.
Donors: Katherine M. Wilson†; Joseph C. Wilson†; Marie C. Wilson†.
Foundation type: Independent foundation.
Financial data (yr. ended 12/31/05): Assets, $18,833,275 (M); expenditures, $1,006,510; qualifying distributions, $882,933; giving activities include $648,782 for 85 grants (high: $171,245; low: $500).
Purpose and activities: Our mission is to improve the quality of life through initiating and supporting projects that measurably demonstrate a means of creating a sense of belonging within the family and the community. Currently focusing on a strategic initiative to promote transformational housing (see foundation Web site).
Fields of interest: Housing/shelter; Community development.
Type of support: General/operating support; Continuing support; Equipment; Emergency funds; Program development; Conferences/seminars; Seed money; Fellowships; Scholarship funds; Technical assistance; Program evaluation.
Limitations: Giving primarily in Rochester, NY. No grants to individuals or for capital campaigns.

Publications: Application guidelines; Financial statement; Grants list; Program policy statement.
Application information: Application form required.
Initial approach: Proposal via e-mail as a Word document
Copies of proposal: 1
Deadline(s): Apr. 20
Board meeting date(s): Fall
Final notification: Usually 2-3 months
Officers and Board of Managers:* Deirdre Wilson Garton, Chair.; Marie D. Tabah,* Chair., Nominating Comm.; Katherine Dalbey Ensign, Secy.; Joseph R. Wilson,* Treas.; Ruth H. Fleischmann-Colgan,* Exec. Dir.; Caitlin Garton; Elenore Garton; Josie Garton; Breckenridge Kling; Christian G. Kling; Josh Kling; Jessa Martin; Judith W. Martin; Katherine W. Roby; J. Christine Wilson; J. Richard Wilson.
Trustee: JPMorgan Chase Bank, N.A.
Number of staff: 1 part-time professional; 1 part-time support.
EIN: 166042022

7265
Jon and Abby Winkelried Foundation ✧ ☆
(formerly The Winkelried Family Foundation)
c/o Goldman Sachs & Co.
1 New York Plz., 40th Fl.
New York, NY 10004

Established in 1991 in NJ.
Donor: Jon Winkelried.
Foundation type: Independent foundation.
Financial data (yr. ended 5/31/05): Assets, $5,708,190 (M); gifts received, $2,085,900; expenditures, $1,502,144; qualifying distributions, $1,501,684; giving activities include $1,501,684 for 56 grants (high: $998,880; low: $100).
Purpose and activities: Giving for Jewish organizations and education.
Fields of interest: Elementary/secondary education; Higher education; Business school/education; Hospitals (general); Jewish federated giving programs; Jewish agencies & temples.
International interests: England.
Limitations: Applications not accepted. Giving primarily in NJ and NY; some giving also in London, England. No grants to individuals; no loans or scholarships.
Application information: Contributes only to pre-selected organizations.
Trustees: Mark Schwartz; Abby Winkelried; Jon Winkelried.
EIN: 133634388
Selected grants: The following grants were reported in 2005.
$998,880 to University of Chicago, Chicago, IL.
$100,000 to Rocky Mountain Elk Foundation, Missoula, MT.
$51,000 to Winston School, Short Hills, NJ. 2 grants: $1,000, $50,000
$600 to Summit Speech School, New Providence, NJ.
$250 to ECLC Foundation, Chatham, NJ.

7266
Winley Foundation ✧
2303 Salt Point Tpke.
Clinton Corners, NY 12514 (845) 266-3065
Contact: Anna M. Barone, Treas.

Established in NY.

Foundation type: Independent foundation.
Financial data (yr. ended 12/31/05): Assets, $21,699,123 (M); gifts received, $50; expenditures, $2,105,992; qualifying distributions, $1,990,000; giving activities include $1,990,000 for 8 grants (high: $975,000; low: $5,000).
Purpose and activities: Giving is limited to the benefit of animals.
Fields of interest: Animal welfare.
Limitations: Giving primarily in Washington, DC and New York, NY. No grants to individuals.
Application information:
Initial approach: Letter
Deadline(s): None
Officers: Heidi Prescott, Pres.; Marian Probst, V.P.; Edward J. Walsh, Jr., Secy.; Anna M. Barone, Treas.
EIN: 521230146

7267
The Norman and Rosita Winston Foundation, Inc. ▼ ✧
c/o John O'Neil, Paul Weiss et. al.
1285 Ave. of the Americas
New York, NY 10019-6064 (212) 373-3000
Contact: John J. O'Neil

Incorporated in 1954 in NY.
Donors: Norman K. Winston†; The N.K. Winston Foundation, Inc.
Foundation type: Independent foundation.
Financial data (yr. ended 6/30/05): Assets, $92,997,572 (M); expenditures, $5,690,182; qualifying distributions, $5,168,753; giving activities include $5,040,000 for 138 grants (high: $273,000; low: $2,000; average: $5,000–$100,000).
Purpose and activities: Emphasis on higher education, including medical and theological education, hospitals, and cultural programs.
Fields of interest: Arts; Secondary school/education; Higher education; Medical school/education; Theological school/education; Hospitals (general).
Type of support: General/operating support.
Limitations: Giving in the U.S., with emphasis on national and local organizations in NY. No grants to individuals.
Application information: Application form not required.
Deadline(s): None
Board meeting date(s): 2 to 4 times per year
Officers and Directors:* Richard A. Rifkind,* Pres.; Lauri Levitt Friedland,* Secy.; Jan Krukowski,* Treas.
EIN: 136161672
Selected grants: The following grants were reported in 2005.
$273,000 to Hospital for Special Surgery, New York, NY. For general support.
$250,000 to Westport Country Playhouse, Westport, CT. For general support.
$210,000 to Artists House Foundation, Norwalk, CT. For Jazz Masters Series.
$195,000 to Hamilton College, Clinton, NY. For general support.
$150,000 to International Rescue Committee, New York, NY. For general support.
$110,000 to Teachers College Columbia University, New York, NY. For Symposium of Education Equity.
$30,000 to Barnard College, New York, NY. For faculty fellowship.

$25,000 to Human Rights Watch, New York, NY. For Video Project.

$25,000 to Martin Memorial Foundation, Stuart, FL. For general support.

$20,000 to Whitney Museum of American Art, New York, NY. For general support.

7268
The Meryl & Charles Witmer Charitable Foundation ✧ ☆

237 Park Ave., Ste. 800
New York, NY   10017

Established in 2000 in NY.
Donors: Charles H. Witmer; Meryl B. Witmer.
Foundation type: Independent foundation.
Financial data (yr. ended 12/31/05): Assets, $3,043,558 (M); gifts received, $1,482,742; expenditures, $854,132; qualifying distributions, $833,490; giving activities include $833,490 for grants.
Fields of interest: Higher education; Education; Hospitals (general); Children/youth, services.
Limitations: Applications not accepted. Giving primarily in New York, NY. No grants to individuals.
Application information: Contributes only to pre-selected organizations.
Trustees: Charles H. Witmer; Meryl B. Witmer.
EIN: 134129627
Selected grants: The following grants were reported in 2004.
$50,000 to Robin Hood Foundation, New York, NY.
$40,000 to Parrish Art Museum, Southampton, NY.
$30,000 to Student Sponsor Partners, New York, NY.
$25,000 to Ronald McDonald House.
$20,000 to Saint Pius V High School, Bronx, NY.
$20,000 to Tulane University, New Orleans, LA.
$15,000 to Harlem Childrens Zone, New York, NY.
$7,500 to Rice High School, New York, NY.
$5,000 to Prep for Prep, New York, NY.
$3,500 to Metropolitan Museum of Art, New York, NY.

7269
WJS Foundation, Inc. ✧

c/o TAG Associates, LLC
75 Rockefeller Plz., 9th Fl.
New York, NY   10019

Established in 1997 in NJ.
Donor: Walter V. Shipley.
Foundation type: Independent foundation.
Financial data (yr. ended 12/31/05): Assets, $5,206,077 (M); expenditures, $548,911; qualifying distributions, $498,530; giving activities include $498,500 for 23 grants (high: $200,000; low: $1,000).
Purpose and activities: Funding primarily for arts and culture, the environment, and historical preservation; funding also for human services.
Fields of interest: Media, television; Arts; Education; Environment, natural resources; Hospitals (general).
Limitations: Applications not accepted. Giving primarily in NJ and NY. No grants to individuals.
Application information: Contributes only to pre-selected organizations.
Officers and Directors:* Walter V. Shipley,* Pres.; Judith L. Shipley,* V.P. and Secy.; Allison P. Shipley,

Treas.; Barbara S. Pandoli; Dorothy B. Shipley; John P. Shipley; Pamela J. Shipley.
EIN: 223514762

7270
Wolfensohn Family Foundation

1350 Ave. of the Americas, Ste. 2900
New York, NY   10019
Contact: Bridget Batson, Asst. Dir.
FAX: (212) 974-1437; *E-mail:* info@wolfensohn.org
URL: http://www.wolfensohn.org

Established in 1995 in NY.
Foundation type: Independent foundation.
Financial data (yr. ended 12/31/04): Assets, $16,954,491 (M); expenditures, $3,195,924; qualifying distributions, $1,981,136; giving activities include $1,860,270 for 253 grants (high: $168,000; low: $20).
Purpose and activities: Giving primarily to arts and cultural programs, environment and community.
Fields of interest: Arts; Education; Environment; Cancer research; Community development, neighborhood development; Jewish agencies & temples.
Type of support: General/operating support; Continuing support; Annual campaigns; Capital campaigns; Program development; Seed money; Research; Technical assistance.
Limitations: Applications not accepted. Giving primarily on the East Coast, with emphasis on NY and Washington, DC. Giving for environmental programs in AK and WY. Giving for religious pluralism and Jewish-Arab coexistence in Israel; giving also in Australia and England. No grants to individuals.
Application information: Contributes only to pre-selected organizations.
Director: Sara R. Wolfensohn.
Trustees: Adam R. Wolfensohn; Elaine R. Wolfensohn; James D. Wolfensohn; Naomi R. Wolfensohn.
Number of staff: 2 full-time professional.
EIN: 133781581
Selected grants: The following grants were reported in 2003.
$200,000 to Institute for Advanced Study, Princeton, NJ. For general support.
$20,000 to National Symphony Orchestra, DC. For endowment.
$15,000 to Trustees for Alaska, Anchorage, AK. For general operating support.
$5,000 to Bang On A Can, New York, NY. For general operating support.
$2,500 to Jackson Hole Conservation Alliance, Jackson, WY. For general support.
$1,500 to American Symphony Orchestra League, New York, NY. For annual fund.
$1,500 to Studio in a School, New York, NY. For general support.
$1,000 to Dance Theater of Harlem, New York, NY. For general support.
$1,000 to Fund for Arts And Culture in Central and Eastern Europe, McLean, VA. For general support.
$1,000 to People and Stories-Gente y Cuentos, Trenton, NJ. For general support.

7271
Louis S. & Molly B. Wolk Foundation ✧

1600 East Ave., Ste. 701
Rochester, NY   14610   (585) 442-6900
Contact: Grants Committee

Established in 1982 in NY.
Donor: Louis S. Wolk.
Foundation type: Independent foundation.
Financial data (yr. ended 12/31/05): Assets, $28,113,666 (M); expenditures, $1,575,773; qualifying distributions, $1,435,664; giving activities include $1,340,500 for 8 grants (high: $407,000; low: $7,500).
Purpose and activities: Giving primarily to organizations in the greater Rochester area whose goals are focused on health related, educational, geriatric and social issues.
Fields of interest: Zoos/zoological societies; Health care; Health organizations; Youth development, scouting agencies (general); Human services; Family services, domestic violence; Jewish agencies & temples.
Limitations: Giving primarily in Rochester, NY. No grants to individuals.
Application information: Application form required.
  Copies of proposal: 2
  Deadline(s): None
  Board meeting date(s): May and Oct.
  Final notification: June 1
Officer and Trustees:* Alvin L. Ureles, M.D.*, Chair.; Michael B. Berger; Audrey P. Cooke; Leon Germanow; Harold Samloff; David M. Wolk; Marvin L. Wolk.
EIN: 222405596
Selected grants: The following grants were reported in 2005.
$400,000 to Monroe Community College, Rochester, NY.
$26,000 to Garth Fagan Dance, Rochester, NY. 2 grants: $25,000, $1,000
$25,000 to Bnai Brith Hillel Foundation.
$25,000 to Rochester Institute of Technology, Rochester, NY.
$10,000 to Temple Brith Kodesh, Rochester, NY. 2 grants: $5,000 each
$5,000 to Strong Museum, Rochester, NY.
$1,000 to Writers and Books, Rochester, NY.

7272
Charles R. Wood Foundation ✧

499 Glen St.
Glens Falls, NY   12801-2205
Contact: Georgia Beckos-Wood, Chair.; Shirley Myott, Treas.

Established in 1978.
Donor: Charles R. Wood†.
Foundation type: Independent foundation.
Financial data (yr. ended 12/31/05): Assets, $36,798,114 (M); gifts received, $20,911,781; expenditures, $692,753; qualifying distributions, $475,218; giving activities include $451,400 for grants.
Purpose and activities: Giving primarily to medical centers; support also for arts and culture. The foundation supports a ranch for children with cancer and other blood-related diseases.
Fields of interest: Arts; Hospitals (general).
Type of support: General/operating support.
Limitations: Applications not accepted. Giving primarily in NY. No grants to individuals.

Publications: Financial statement; Informational brochure.
Application information: Contributes only to pre-selected organizations.
Officers and Trustees:* Georgia Beckos-Wood,* Chair.; Barbara Wages,* Pres.; Dean Beckos,* V.P.; Charlene Courtney,* Secy.; Shirley Myott,* Treas.
Number of staff: None.
EIN: 222237193
Selected grants: The following grants were reported in 2005.
$100,000 to Glens Falls Hospital, Glens Falls, NY.
$28,000 to Alzheimers Association, Chicago, IL.
$10,000 to Habitat for Humanity International.
$7,250 to Big Brothers/Big Sisters.
$5,000 to Childrens Hospital.

7273
The Woodcock Foundation ✧
437 Madison Ave., 37th Fl.
New York, NY 10022
Contact: Alexandra Christy, Exec. Dir.

Established in 1988 in NY.
Donors: Polly Guth; John H.J. Guth.
Foundation type: Independent foundation.
Financial data (yr. ended 11/30/04): Assets, $37,490,820 (M); expenditures, $2,349,149; qualifying distributions, $1,859,976; giving activities include $1,519,000 for 17 grants (high: $165,000; low: $10,000).
Fields of interest: Education; Environment, natural resources; Health care; Youth, services; Women.
Type of support: General/operating support; Continuing support; Income development; Program development.
Limitations: Applications not accepted. No grants to individuals.
Application information: Contributes only to pre-selected organizations.
Trustees: Stuart Davidson; Jeremy Guth; John H.J. Guth; Polly Guth; Virginia Montgomery; Holly Davidson Nagy; Herschel Post; Lindsay Davidson Shea; Richard T. Watson.
Number of staff: 1 full-time professional.
EIN: 341606285

7274
The Woodheath Foundation, Inc. ✧
c/o Barry M. Strauss Assocs., Ltd.
307 5th Ave., 8th Fl.
New York, NY 10016-6517

Incorporated in 1956 in NY.
Donors: Frederick L. Ehrman†; Edith K. Ehrman†; F. Warren Hellman.
Foundation type: Independent foundation.
Financial data (yr. ended 6/30/05): Assets, $3,719,992 (M); expenditures, $734,145; qualifying distributions, $733,500; giving activities include $732,000 for 10 grants (high: $225,000; low: $10,000).
Purpose and activities: Giving primarily for the arts and education; some giving also for medical research for scleroderma.
Fields of interest: Museums (art); Performing arts; Arts; Elementary/secondary education; Higher education; Environment, natural resources; Medical research, institute.

Limitations: Applications not accepted. Giving primarily in San Francisco, CA. No grants to individuals.
Application information: Contributes only to pre-selected organizations.
Officers: F. Warren Hellman, Pres.; Nancy Bechtle, V.P.; Patricia C. Hellman, Secy.
Director: Joachim Bechtle.
EIN: 136094025
Selected grants: The following grants were reported in 2003.
$2,500,000 to Music Concourse Community Partnership, San Francisco, CA. For general support.
$1,050,000 to San Francisco Symphony, San Francisco, CA. For general support.
$125,000 to Johns Hopkins Medical Institutions, Baltimore, MD. For general support.
$35,000 to San Francisco Opera, San Francisco, CA. For general support.
$30,000 to National Park Foundation, DC. For general support.
$30,000 to Scleroderma Research Foundation, San Francisco, CA. For general support.
$25,000 to Katherine Delmar Burke School, San Francisco, CA. For general support.
$25,000 to New World Symphony, Miami Beach, FL. For general support.
$25,000 to San Francisco Conservatory of Music, San Francisco, CA. For general support.

7275
Woodland Foundation ✧
c/o White & Case, LLP
1155 6th Ave.
New York, NY 10036

Incorporated in 1950 in DE.
Donor: William Durant Campbell‡.
Foundation type: Independent foundation.
Financial data (yr. ended 12/31/05): Assets, $2,602,108 (M); expenditures, $401,645; qualifying distributions, $355,500; giving activities include $355,500 for 26 grants (high: $200,000; low: $500).
Purpose and activities: Giving primarily for the arts, education, and Christian and Episcopal organizations and churches.
Fields of interest: Performing arts; Arts; Higher education; Education; Hospitals (general); Youth development, scouting agencies (general); Christian agencies & churches; Protestant agencies & churches.
Type of support: Annual campaigns; Capital campaigns; Building/renovation; Endowments.
Limitations: Applications not accepted. Giving on a national basis, with emphasis on New York and Westchester County, NY. No grants to individuals.
Application information: Contributes only to pre-selected organizations.
Board meeting date(s): Dec.
Officers and Trustees:* Margot C. Bogert,* Pres.; Jeremiah M. Bogert,* V.P. and Treas.; Winthrop Rutherfurd, Jr.,* Secy.; Jeremiah M. Bogert, Jr.; Milicient D. Bogert; Rev. Terence L. Elsberry.
EIN: 136018244

7276
Woodmere Foundation ✧
c/o Ayco Co.
P.O. Box 860
Saratoga Springs, NY 12866

Established in 1993 in PA.
Donor: Robert B. Knutson.
Foundation type: Independent foundation.
Financial data (yr. ended 12/31/05): Assets, $5,187,000 (M); expenditures, $702,497; qualifying distributions, $634,770; giving activities include $634,770 for 29 grants (high: $100,000; low: $500).
Purpose and activities: Giving for the arts, human services, conservation, education, and medical services and research.
Fields of interest: Museums; Arts; Education; Environment, natural resources; Mental health/crisis services, research; Human services.
Limitations: Applications not accepted. Giving nationwide, with emphasis on PA. No grants to individuals.
Application information: Contributes only to pre-selected organizations.
Officer: Robert B. Knutson, Pres.
EIN: 251705913
Selected grants: The following grants were reported in 2004.
$105,000 to Phi Gamma Delta Educational Foundation, Lexington, KY.
$50,000 to Extra Mile Education Foundation, Pittsburgh, PA.
$50,000 to University of Michigan, Ann Arbor, MI.
$30,300 to Historical Society of Western Pennsylvania, Pittsburgh, PA.
$25,000 to Western Pennsylvania Conservancy, Pittsburgh, PA.
$24,100 to Pittsburgh Parks Conservancy, Pittsburgh, PA.
$20,000 to Frick Art and Historical Center, Pittsburgh, PA.
$15,000 to Solomon R. Guggenheim Foundation, New York, NY.
$10,000 to Career College Foundation, DC.
$5,000 to DePaul Institute, Pittsburgh, PA.

7277
The A. Woodner Fund, Inc. ✧
c/o Andrea Woodner
35 W. 9th St., Ste. 8A
New York, NY 10011

Established in 2000 in NY.
Donor: Ian Woodner Family Collection, Inc.
Foundation type: Independent foundation.
Financial data (yr. ended 12/31/05): Assets, $279,847 (M); expenditures, $420,099; qualifying distributions, $419,000; giving activities include $419,000 for 24 grants (high: $90,000; low: $1,000).
Fields of interest: Visual arts, drawing; Arts; Education.
Limitations: Applications not accepted. Giving primarily in NY. No grants to individuals.
Application information: Contributes only to pre-selected organizations.
Board meeting date(s): Annually
Officer and Director:* Andrea Woodner,* Pres.
EIN: 134092338
Selected grants: The following grants were reported in 2005.
$90,000 to Drawing Center, New York, NY.

$35,000 to Servicemembers Legal Defense Network, DC.

$10,000 to Ethels Foundation for the Arts, New York, NY.

$7,000 to National Coalition Against Censorship, New York, NY.

$5,000 to Cygnet Foundation, New York, NY.

$3,500 to North Shore Animal League, Port Washington, NY.

$2,500 to Lauderdale Outreach and Volunteer Effort (LOVE), Meridian, MS.

7278

The Woods Foundation ✧

(formerly The Ward W. Woods Foundation)
c/o Bessemer Trust Co., N.A.
630 5th Ave.
New York, NY 10111
Contact: Ward W. Woods, Jr., Pres.

Established in 1985 in NY.
Donors: Ward W. Woods, Jr.; Priscilla B. Woods; Katherine Weld Bacon.
Foundation type: Independent foundation.
Financial data (yr. ended 9/30/05): Assets, $1,663 (M); gifts received, $356,400; expenditures, $436,318; qualifying distributions, $436,259; giving activities include $426,834 for 34 grants (high: $75,000; low: $500).
Purpose and activities: Giving primarily for wildlife conservation and the environment; funding also for the arts, education, recreation, and international affairs.
Fields of interest: Arts; Environment, natural resources; Animals/wildlife, preservation/protection; Athletics/sports, amateur leagues; International affairs, U.N..
Limitations: Giving on a national basis, with some emphasis on national organizations headquartered in New York, NY, and Washington, DC. No grants to individuals.
Application information:
  Initial approach: Letter
  Deadline(s): None
Officers and Directors:* Ward W. Woods, Jr.,* Pres.; Priscilla B. Woods,* V.P.; Robert Roriston,* Secy.-Treas.; Katherine Woods Emerick; Alexandra Woods.
EIN: 133314966

7279

Ann Eden Woodward Foundation ✧ ☆

c/o J. Lapatin
977 6th Ave., No. 810
New York, NY 10018

Established in 1963 in NY.
Donor: Ann Eden Woodward†.
Foundation type: Independent foundation.
Financial data (yr. ended 5/31/05): Assets, $5,085,083 (M); gifts received, $2,549,015; expenditures, $342,230; qualifying distributions, $333,500; giving activities include $333,500 for 34 grants (high: $50,000; low: $1,000).
Purpose and activities: Giving for the arts, including museums, and for hospitals, environmental and wildlife preservation, and public libraries.
Fields of interest: Museums; Arts; Libraries/library science; Environment, natural resources; Animals/wildlife, preservation/protection; Hospitals (general).

Limitations: Applications not accepted. Giving primarily in New York, NY. No grants to individuals.
Trustees: J. Lapatin; J.A. Wood.
EIN: 136126021
Selected grants: The following grants were reported in 2005.

$50,000 to Metropolitan Museum of Art, New York, NY.

$25,000 to Society of Saint Johnland, Kings Park, NY.

$10,000 to Metropolitan Opera Association, New York, NY.

$10,000 to Nature Conservancy, Arlington, VA.

$5,000 to Salvation Army.

$2,500 to Calvary Hospital, Bronx, NY.

$2,500 to Visions Services for the Blind and Visually Impaired, New York, NY.

$1,500 to American Cancer Society, Atlanta, GA.

$1,500 to Circle in the Square, New York, NY.

$1,000 to Audubon New York, Albany, NY.

7280

The Wright Family Foundation, Inc. ✧

P.O. Box 1046
Schenectady, NY 12301 (518) 347-4530
Contact: Adeline W. Graham, Chair.
FAX: (518) 347-6201;
E-mail: info@wrightfamilyfoundation.org;
URL: http://www.wrightfamilyfoundation.org

Established in 1997 in Schenectady, NY.
Donor: Schenectady International, Inc.
Foundation type: Independent foundation.
Financial data (yr. ended 9/30/05): Assets, $23,443,438 (M); expenditures, $1,315,639; qualifying distributions, $1,315,639; giving activities include $1,315,639 for 32 grants (high: $100,000; low: $2,000).
Purpose and activities: Funding for community, education, health, social needs, and the arts.
Fields of interest: Museums; Arts; Higher education; Environment; Health care; Human services; Community development.
Type of support: Capital campaigns; Building/renovation; Equipment; Matching/challenge support.
Limitations: Giving limited to Schenectady County, NY, and surrounding counties, Cocke County, TN, and Brazoria County, TX. No support for religious or political organizations. No grants to individuals, or for annual campaigns, athletic events, social functions, advertising, underwriting or administrative support.
Publications: Application guidelines; Annual report.
Application information: Application form available on foundation Web site. Funding requests under $1,000 will not be considered. Application form required.
  Initial approach: Applications must be submitted through foundation Web site
  Copies of proposal: 1
  Deadline(s): Jan. 20, May 20, Aug. 20, and Nov. 20
  Board meeting date(s): Quarterly
Officers: Adeline W. Graham, Chair.; A. Malcolm MacCormick, Vice-Chair.; Heather M. Ward, Secy.; Robert D. McQueen, Treas.
Trustees: Gregg W. Brown; Ashley G. Palm.
EIN: 141798255
Selected grants: The following grants were reported in 2005.

$100,000 to Ellis Hospital Foundation, Schenectady, NY.

$100,000 to Glens Falls Hospital Foundation, Glens Falls, NY.

$100,000 to Proctors Theater, Schenectady, NY.

$100,000 to Schenectady Museum Association, Schenectady, NY.

$98,736 to Union College, Schenectady, NY.

$25,000 to Brazosport College, Lake Jackson, TX. 2 grants: $5,000, $20,000

$25,000 to City Mission of Schenectady, Schenectady, NY.

$25,000 to United Way of Schenectady County, Schenectady, NY.

$3,000 to United Way of Brazoria County, Angleton, TX.

7281

Wunsch Foundation, Inc. ✧ ☆

902 Broadway, Ste. 1603
New York, NY 10010
Contact: Eric M. Wunsch, Pres.

Incorporated in 1943 in NY.
Donors: Joseph W. Wunsch; Eric M. Wunsch; Samuel Wunsch; WEA Enterprises Co., Inc.; 9th Avenue Equities; 63rd Street Equities.
Foundation type: Independent foundation.
Financial data (yr. ended 12/31/05): Assets, $7,690,523 (M); gifts received, $81,560; expenditures, $367,137; qualifying distributions, $357,633; giving activities include $357,633 for grants.
Purpose and activities: Funding primarily for higher education and for museums.
Fields of interest: Visual arts; Museums; Museums (art); Education; Jewish federated giving programs.
Limitations: Applications not accepted. Giving primarily in NY. No grants to individuals.
Application information: Contributes only to pre-selected organizations.
Officers: Eric M. Wunsch, Pres.; Ethel Wunsch, Secy.; Peter Wunsch, Treas.
EIN: 116006013
Selected grants: The following grants were reported in 2004.

$60,000 to United Jewish Appeal, New York, NY.

$41,500 to Saint Louis Art Museum, Saint Louis, MO.

$25,000 to Massachusetts Institute of Technology, Cambridge, MA.

$18,000 to Corning Museum of Glass, Corning, NY.

$9,900 to New York State Museum, Albany, NY.

$6,000 to Cornell University, Ithaca, NY.

$3,000 to Xavier High School, New York, NY.

$2,500 to Metropolitan Museum of Art, New York, NY.

$1,000 to Grace Church School, New York, NY.

$100 to American Heart Association, New York, NY.

7282

Yellow Chair Foundation ✧ ☆

c/o Nancy Funari, The Ayco Company, L.P.
321 Broadway
P.O. Box 860
Saratoga Springs, NY 12866-0860

Established in 2000 in CA.
Donor: David Filo.
Foundation type: Independent foundation.
Financial data (yr. ended 12/31/04): Assets, $102,222,389 (M); gifts received, $57,070,000; expenditures, $5,010,800; qualifying distributions,

$3,256,860; giving activities include $3,225,000 for 8 grants (high: $2,700,000; low: $5,000).

Purpose and activities: Giving primarily for higher education.

Fields of interest: Higher education; Human services; Children/youth, services.

Limitations: Applications not accepted. Giving primarily in CA. No grants to individuals.

Application information: Contributes only to pre-selected organizations.

Officers and Director:* David Filo,* Pres.; Diana Hastings Temple, Secy. and C.F.O.

EIN: 943380194

7283
Divrei Yitzchok Foundation ✧ ☆
1165 E. 24th St.
Brooklyn, NY 11210 (718) 871-1039
Contact: Marvin Beinhorn, Tr.

Established in 2001 in NY.

Donor: Marvin Beinhorn.

Foundation type: Independent foundation.

Financial data (yr. ended 12/31/05): Assets, $611,260 (M); gifts received, $180,000; expenditures, $366,610; qualifying distributions, $366,040; giving activities include $366,040 for 15 grants (high: $53,500; low: $650).

Fields of interest: Education; Human services; Jewish agencies & temples.

Type of support: General/operating support.

Limitations: Giving primarily in Brooklyn, NY.

Application information:
Initial approach: Letter
Deadline(s): None

Trustees: Esther Beinhorn; Marvin Beinhorn.

EIN: 113603802

Selected grants: The following grants were reported in 2005.
$8,500 to Monsey Academy for Girls, Monsey, NY.
$5,000 to Masores Bais Yaakov, Brooklyn, NY.

7284
YLRY, Inc. ✧
c/o Hertz, Herson & Co., LLP
2 Park Ave., Ste. 1500
New York, NY 10016

Established in 1992 in NY.

Donor: Legacy Heritage Fund Limited.

Foundation type: Independent foundation.

Financial data (yr. ended 12/31/05): Assets, $36,690,034 (M); expenditures, $1,319,279; qualifying distributions, $1,138,041; giving activities include $1,120,000 for 7 grants (high: $600,000; low: $6,698).

Purpose and activities: Giving primarily to Jewish federated giving programs, as well as to Jewish medical relief organizations.

Fields of interest: Health organizations, association; Jewish federated giving programs.

Limitations: Applications not accepted. Giving on a national and international basis, primarily in New York, NY, and in Jerusalem, Israel. No grants to individuals.

Application information: Contributes only to pre-selected organizations.

Officer and Directors:* Susan R. Wexner,* Pres. and Secy.-Treas.; Bertrand Agus.

EIN: 133722745

Selected grants: The following grants were reported in 2003.
$1,660,000 to Vanguard Charitable Endowment Program, Southeastern, PA.

7285
The Young Family Charitable Foundation ✧ ☆
c/o EOS Partners, LP
320 Park Ave., 22nd Fl.
New York, NY 10022

Established in 1991 in NY.

Donors: Brian D. Young; Anne Young.

Foundation type: Independent foundation.

Financial data (yr. ended 6/30/05): Assets, $1,674,131 (M); gifts received, $1,462,008; expenditures, $448,045; qualifying distributions, $445,663; giving activities include $445,000 for 7 grants (high: $400,000; low: $2,500).

Fields of interest: Elementary/secondary education; Higher education; Human services; Roman Catholic agencies & churches.

Limitations: Applications not accepted. Giving primarily in Bridgeport, CT and Cambridge, MA. No grants to individuals.

Application information: Contributes only to pre-selected organizations.

Trustee: Brian D. Young.

EIN: 136976453

Selected grants: The following grants were reported in 2003.
$100,000 to Diocese of Bridgeport, Bridgeport, CT. 2 grants: $60,000 (For general support), $40,000 (For Annual Bishop's Appeal).
$12,500 to Horizons Student Enrichment Program, New Canaan, CT. For general support.
$10,000 to Wheaton College, Norton, MA. For general support.
$2,825 to Johns Hopkins University, Baltimore, MD. For Charter Oak Scholarships.
$2,500 to Small Steps Nurturing Center, Houston, TX. For general support.
$500 to Nursing and Home Care, Wilton, CT. For general support.

7286
The Bracebridge H. Young, Jr. Foundation ✧
c/o BCRS Assocs., LLP
100 Wall St., 11th Fl.
New York, NY 10005

Established in 1989 in NY.

Donor: Bracebridge H. Young, Jr.

Foundation type: Independent foundation.

Financial data (yr. ended 5/31/05): Assets, $2,141,854 (M); expenditures, $621,310; qualifying distributions, $591,570; giving activities include $587,875 for 25 grants (high: $180,000; low: $500).

Purpose and activities: Giving primarily for education, with some giving for historical preservation and children's services.

Fields of interest: History/archaeology; Elementary/secondary education; Higher education; Hospitals (general); Human services.

Limitations: Applications not accepted. Giving primarily in MA. No grants to individuals; no loans or scholarships.

Application information: Contributes only to pre-selected organizations.

Trustees: Bracebridge H. Young, Jr.; Mary-Elizabeth Young; Yuriko Jane Young.

EIN: 133531986

Selected grants: The following grants were reported in 2005.
$170,000 to Buckingham Browne and Nichols School, Cambridge, MA. 2 grants: $20,000, $150,000
$100,000 to Nantucket Cottage Hospital, Nantucket, MA.
$55,000 to New England Aquarium, Boston, MA. 2 grants: $25,000, $30,000
$25,000 to Alliance to Protect Nantucket Sound, Hyannis, MA.
$1,000 to Nantucket Conservation Foundation, Nantucket, MA.
$1,000 to Nantucket Land Council, Nantucket, MA.
$1,000 to Sconset Trust, Siasconset, MA.
$500 to Dana-Farber Cancer Institute, Boston, MA.

7287
Youth Foundation, Inc.
36 W. 44th St., Ste. 716
New York, NY 10036-8144 (212) 840-6291
Contact: Johanna M. Lee
FAX: (212) 840-6747; E-mail: youthfdn@aol.com;
URL: http://foundationcenter.org/grantmaker/youthfdn

Incorporated in 1940 in NY.

Donors: Alexander M. Hadden†; Mrs. Alexander M. Hadden†.

Foundation type: Independent foundation.

Financial data (yr. ended 12/31/05): Assets, $10,299,180 (M); gifts received, $20,150; expenditures, $588,436; qualifying distributions, $483,338; giving activities include $17,500 for 7 grants (high: $2,500; low: $2,500), and $331,000 for grants to individuals.

Purpose and activities: Youth Foundation's basic objective is the awarding of Hadden Scholarships to exceptionally worthy, financially needy, secondary school seniors for their undergraduate college education.

Fields of interest: Scholarships/financial aid; Education.

Type of support: General/operating support; Scholarships—to individuals.

Limitations: Giving on a national basis.

Publications: Application guidelines; Informational brochure; Program policy statement.

Application information: Applications limited to U.S. citizens. Application form required.
Initial approach: Letter requesting application (include SASE)
Copies of proposal: 1
Deadline(s): Sept. 1 to Dec. 1 or earlier for application request; Feb. 28 for application
Board meeting date(s): 3rd or 4th Wed. of every month except Apr., July, Aug., Oct., and Dec.
Final notification: May

Officers and Directors:* Robert W. Radsch,* Pres.; Pamela S. Fulweiler,* V.P.; Guy N. Robinson,* Secy.; S. Scott Nicholls, Jr.,* Treas.; and 9 additional directors.

Number of staff: 1 full-time professional.

EIN: 136093036

7288
Barbara M. Zalaznick Foundation ✧
c/o Eric Kaplan
335 Madison Ave., Ste. 1500
New York, NY 10017

Established in 1996 in NY.
Donors: Irma Milstein; Paul Milstein; Barbara Zalaznick; David Zalaznick; Milstein Family Foundation.
Foundation type: Independent foundation.
Financial data (yr. ended 12/31/05): Assets, $14,870,618 (M); gifts received, $300,000; expenditures, $907,828; qualifying distributions, $875,190; giving activities include $874,265 for 61 grants (high: $735,000; low: $95).
Fields of interest: Performing arts; Arts; Higher education, university; Medical school/education; Children/youth, services; Jewish federated giving programs; Jewish agencies & temples.
Limitations: Applications not accepted. Giving primarily in New York, NY. No grants to individuals.
Application information: Contributes only to pre-selected organizations.
Trustees: Irma Milstein; Paul Milstein; Barbara Zalaznick; David Zalaznick.
EIN: 133921831

7289
The Zankel Fund ✧
(formerly The Arthur & Nancy Zankel Foundation)
16 Bayberry Rd.
Armonk, NY 10504
Application address: c/o Arthur Zankel, 535 Madison Ave., New York, NY 10022, tel.: (212) 421-7548

Established in 1969 in NY.
Donor: Arthur Zankel.
Foundation type: Independent foundation.
Financial data (yr. ended 12/31/04): Assets, $27,036,601 (M); gifts received, $5,952,025; expenditures, $895,024; qualifying distributions, $804,459; giving activities include $803,614 for 96 grants (high: $200,000; low: $200).
Fields of interest: Arts; Higher education; Hospitals (general); Human services; Business/industry; Jewish federated giving programs; Jewish agencies & temples.
Limitations: Giving primarily in NY. No grants to individuals.
Application information:
Initial approach: Letter
Deadline(s): None
Trustees: Arthur Zankel; Judy E. Zankel.
EIN: 136284496

7290
Zarin/Rosenfeld Family Foundation ✧
110 Riverside Dr., Ste. 13AC
New York, NY 10024

Established in 2000 in NY.
Donors: Gerald Rosenfeld; Judith Zarin.
Foundation type: Independent foundation.
Financial data (yr. ended 12/31/03): Assets, $367,206 (M); gifts received, $250,200; expenditures, $493,888; qualifying distributions, $487,070; giving activities include $487,000 for 11 grants (high: $350,000; low: $1,000).

Fields of interest: Education; Jewish agencies & temples.
Limitations: Applications not accepted. No grants to individuals.
Application information: Contributes only to pre-selected organizations.
Trustees: Gerald Rosenfeld; Judith Zarin.
EIN: 134116103
Selected grants: The following grants were reported in 2004.
$506,296 to New York University, New York, NY. 2 grants: $12,200 to Stern School of Business (For general support), $494,096 (For general support).
$276,000 to Jewish Theological Seminary of America, New York, NY. For general support.
$30,000 to Horace Mann School, Riverdale, NY. For general support.
$15,000 to Congregation Bnai Jeshurun, New York, NY. For general support.
$10,000 to City College 21st Century Foundation, New York, NY. For general support.
$6,000 to NARAL Foundation, Nashville, TN. For general support.
$5,000 to Barrel of Monkeys Productions, Chicago, IL. For general support.
$5,000 to UJA-Federation of New York, New York, NY. For general support.
$2,500 to Young Audiences (YA), New York, NY. For general support.

7291
S. Z. & P. R. Zedakah Fund ✧
c/o Pauline Gutfreund
P.O. Box 16
Far Rockaway, NY 11691

Established in 1995 in NY.
Donor: S. Gutfruend.
Foundation type: Independent foundation.
Financial data (yr. ended 11/30/03): Assets, $13,478 (M); gifts received, $497,488; expenditures, $506,730; qualifying distributions, $506,028; giving activities include $506,028 for 74 + grants (high: $278,960).
Fields of interest: Jewish agencies & temples.
Limitations: Applications not accepted. No grants to individuals.
Application information: Contributes only to pre-selected organizations.
Trustees: Pauline Gutfreund; S. Gutfruend.
EIN: 113335250

7292
Zedukah Vechesed Foundation, Inc. ✧ ☆
c/o David Soifer
24 Jackson Ave.
Spring Valley, NY 10977-1908
Contact: Clara Steinmetz, Tr.
Application address: 465 Bedford Ave., Brooklyn, NY 11211, tel.: (718) 387-7171

Established in 1967.
Donors: Emanuel Steinmetz; Yitzchak Steinmetz; Rita Wagshall; Solomon Steinmetz; Steinmetz Bros., Inc.; Jrr Mgmt.; Shoretown Mgmt.; Sherman Mgmt.
Foundation type: Independent foundation.
Financial data (yr. ended 5/31/06): Assets, $8,014,997 (M); gifts received, $32,016; expenditures, $362,766; qualifying distributions,

$345,599; giving activities include $345,599 for grants.
Fields of interest: Jewish agencies & temples.
Limitations: Giving primarily in NY. No grants to individuals.
Application information: Application form not required.
Deadline(s): None
Trustee: Clara Steinmetz.
EIN: 237057565

7293
The Jacquelyn & Gregory Zehner Foundation ✧
c/o BCRS Assocs., LLC
100 Wall St.
New York, NY 10005

Established in 1996 in NY.
Donors: Gregory Zehner; Jacquelyn Zehner.
Foundation type: Independent foundation.
Financial data (yr. ended 7/31/05): Assets, $9,613,750 (M); gifts received, $2,946,223; expenditures, $456,809; qualifying distributions, $362,245; giving activities include $360,500 for grants.
Fields of interest: Arts; Higher education, university; Boy scouts; Philanthropy/voluntarism; Christian agencies & churches.
Type of support: General/operating support.
Limitations: Applications not accepted. Giving primarily in CT and the New York, NY, area. No grants to individuals.
Application information: Contributes only to pre-selected organizations.
Trustees: Jacquelyn M. Hoffman-Zehner; Gregory Zehner.
EIN: 133971019
Selected grants: The following grants were reported in 2005.
$50,000 to Give Me an Answer, New Canaan, CT.
$50,000 to University of British Columbia, Vancouver, Canada. .
$10,000 to Girls Inc., New York, NY.
$10,000 to International Dyslexia Association, New York, NY.
$5,000 to Center for Reproductive Rights, New York, NY.
$5,000 to National Partnership for Women and Families, DC.
$3,000 to Biblical Ministries Worldwide, Lawrenceville, GA.
$2,500 to Jewish Womens Archive, Brookline, MA.
$2,000 to Young Life, Norwalk, CT.
$1,000 to New Canaan Library, New Canaan, CT.

7294
Zemsky Family Foundation ✧
(formerly Russer Foods/Zemsky Family Trust)
c/o Taurus Partners
70 W. Chippewa St., Rm. 500
Buffalo, NY 14202

Established in 1987 in NY.
Donors: Zemco Industries, Inc.; Sam Zemsky; Mrs. Sam Zemsky.
Foundation type: Independent foundation.
Financial data (yr. ended 12/31/04): Assets, $3,856,923 (M); gifts received, $400,000; expenditures, $725,512; qualifying distributions,

$712,143; giving activities include $712,143 for 56 grants (high: $75,000; low: $360).

Purpose and activities: Giving primarily for religion, health research, human services, art and culture and education.

Fields of interest: Performing arts; Arts; Education; Medical research, institute; Human services; Children/youth, services; Jewish federated giving programs; Jewish agencies & temples.

Type of support: Scholarships—to individuals.

Limitations: Applications not accepted. Giving primarily in FL, western MA, and NY, with emphasis on Buffalo.

Application information: Unsolicited requests for funds not accepted.

Trustees: Howard Zemsky; Sam Zemsky; Shirley Zemsky.

EIN: 112867625

7295
Zenkel Foundation ✧

15 W. 53rd St.
New York, NY   10019-5410
Contact: Lois Zenkel, Pres.

Established in 1987 in NY.

Foundation type: Independent foundation.

Financial data (yr. ended 12/31/05): Assets, $3,063,775 (M); expenditures, $371,161; qualifying distributions, $353,203; giving activities include $343,432 for grants.

Purpose and activities: Giving primarily for Jewish welfare, the arts, higher education, the environment, and human rights.

Fields of interest: Visual arts, photography; Museums (art); Arts; Higher education; Environment; Hospitals (general); Health organizations, association; Medical research, institute; Human services; International human rights; Civil rights, race/intergroup relations; Community development; Jewish federated giving programs; Jewish agencies & temples.

Type of support: General/operating support; Annual campaigns; Capital campaigns; Building/renovation; Professorships; Scholarship funds.

Limitations: Applications not accepted. No grants to individuals.

Application information: Contributes only to pre-selected organizations.

Board meeting date(s): Apr.

Officers and Directors:* Lois S. Zenkel,* Pres.; Daniel R. Zenkel,* Secy.-Treas.; Gary B. Zenkel; Bruce L. Zenkel; Lisa R. Zenkel.

EIN: 133380631

Selected grants: The following grants were reported in 2004.

$100,000 to International Center of Photography, New York, NY.

$30,000 to Greenwich Hospital, Greenwich, CT.

$7,500 to Dartmouth College, Hanover, NH.

$2,500 to Amherst College, Amherst, MA.

$2,500 to Film Society of Lincoln Center, New York, NY.

$2,500 to Stanwich School, Greenwich, CT.

$2,000 to Lincoln Center Theater, New York, NY.

$1,000 to Center for Jewish History, New York, NY.

$1,000 to Greenwich Library, Greenwich, CT.

$1,000 to New Museum of Contemporary Art, New York, NY.

7296
Zichron Alter Meir Wilamowsky Foundation ✧ ☆

49 Sealy Dr.
Lawrence, NY   11559

Established in 2001 in NY.

Donors: David Rybak; Eli Wilamowsky.

Foundation type: Independent foundation.

Financial data (yr. ended 12/31/05): Assets, $8,971,338 (M); expenditures, $674,306; qualifying distributions, $336,729; giving activities include $336,729 for grants.

Fields of interest: Education; Health care; Human services; Jewish agencies & temples.

Limitations: Applications not accepted. Giving primarily in NY. No grants to individuals.

Application information: Contributes only to pre-selected organizations.

Directors: Eli Wilamowsky; Rhone Wilamowsky; Steven Wilamowsky.

EIN: 311795391

Selected grants: The following grants were reported in 2004.

$15,000 to Refuah Helpline, Brooklyn, NY.

$12,000 to UJA-Federation of New York, New York, NY.

$4,000 to Shor Yoshuv Institute, Lawrence, NY.

$2,000 to Yeshiva Rtzahd Hebrew Academy of Brooklyn, Brooklyn, NY.

$1,800 to Keren Hachesed, Monsey, NY.

$1,800 to Yeshiva Toras Yisrael, Brooklyn, NY.

$1,000 to American Friends of Yad Eliezer, Brooklyn, NY.

$1,000 to Bnos Bais Yaakov of Far Rockaway, Far Rockaway, NY.

$1,000 to Etzion Foundation, New York, NY.

$1,000 to One Israel Fund, New York, NY.

7297
Zichron Avraham Abba Foundation ✧

1360 E. 14th St., Ste. 101
Brooklyn, NY   11230

Established in 1998 in NY.

Donors: Leon Goldenberg; Chaim Goldenberg.

Foundation type: Independent foundation.

Financial data (yr. ended 12/31/05): Assets, $1,492,981 (M); gifts received, $365,000; expenditures, $453,236; qualifying distributions, $448,798; giving activities include $448,798 for 69 + grants.

Purpose and activities: Giving primarily for Jewish education, temples, and organizations.

Fields of interest: Education; Jewish agencies & temples.

Type of support: General/operating support.

Limitations: Applications not accepted. Giving primarily in NY. No grants to individuals.

Application information: Contributes only to pre-selected organizations.

Officers: Leon Goldenberg, Pres.; Agnes Goldenberg, V.P.

Trustee: Chaim Goldenberg.

EIN: 113412101

Selected grants: The following grants were reported in 2004.

$30,050 to Agudath Israel of America, New York, NY.

$10,190 to Yeshiva Tiferes Yisroel, Brooklyn, NY.

$8,840 to Yad Eliezer, Brooklyn, NY.

$6,300 to Yeshiva Darchei Torah, Far Rockaway, NY.

$5,000 to Yeshiva Torah Temimah, Brooklyn, NY.

$1,800 to National Society for Hebrew Day Schools - Torah Umesorah, New York, NY.

$1,000 to Project Chazon, Brooklyn, NY.

$1,000 to Tomchei Shabbos, Monsey, NY.

7298
Zichron Yisroel Vesther Foundation ✧ ☆

5401 15th Ave.
Brooklyn, NY   11219   (718) 894-2000
Contact: Albert Weinstock, Tr.

Established in 1999 in NY.

Foundation type: Independent foundation.

Financial data (yr. ended 9/30/05): Assets, $881,344 (M); gifts received, $774,185; expenditures, $417,936; qualifying distributions, $417,936; giving activities include $416,680 for 15 grants (high: $208,600; low: $5,000), and $1,256 for foundation-administered programs.

Fields of interest: Theological school/education; Jewish agencies & temples.

Type of support: Building/renovation; Scholarship funds.

Limitations: Giving primarily in NJ and Brooklyn, NY.

Application information:

Initial approach: Letter with recommendation on organization letterhead

Deadline(s): None

Trustees: Albert Weinstock; Mendel Weinstock.

EIN: 113519911

7299
ZIIZ, Inc. ✧

c/o Hertz, Herson & Co., LLP
2 Park Ave., Ste. 1500
New York, NY   10016

Established in 2000 in DE and NY.

Donor: Susan Wexner Revocable Trust.

Foundation type: Independent foundation.

Financial data (yr. ended 3/31/05): Assets, $39,206,154 (M); expenditures, $1,860,452; qualifying distributions, $1,677,970; giving activities include $1,645,000 for 1 grant.

Fields of interest: Foundations (public); Jewish agencies & temples.

Limitations: Applications not accepted. Giving primarily in PA. No grants to individuals.

Application information: Contributes only to pre-selected organizations.

Officer and Directors:* Susan Wexner,* Pres. and Secy.-Treas.; Bernard Agus.

EIN: 134031038

Selected grants: The following grants were reported in 2004.

$1,675,000 to Vanguard Charitable Endowment Program, Southeastern, PA.

$14,500 to Center for Jewish Community Studies, Philadelphia, PA.

7300
The Zilkha Foundation, Inc.

450 Park Ave., Ste. 2102
New York, NY   10022
Contact: Ezra K. Zilkha, Pres. and Treas.

Incorporated in 1948 in NY.

Donors: Zilkha & Sons, Inc.; Ezra K. Zilkha; Cecile E. Zilkha.

Foundation type: Company-sponsored foundation.
Financial data (yr. ended 8/31/05): Assets, $5,038,790 (M); gifts received, $2,009,000; expenditures, $846,272; qualifying distributions, $807,125; giving activities include $803,775 for 75 grants (high: $230,000; low: $50).
Purpose and activities: The foundation supports organizations involved with performing arts, higher education, human services, international affairs, race relations, and Judaism.
Fields of interest: Performing arts; Higher education; Human services; International affairs; Civil rights, race/intergroup relations; Jewish federated giving programs; Jewish agencies & temples.
Limitations: Applications not accepted. Giving on a national basis. No grants to individuals.
Application information: Contributions only to pre-selected organizations.
  Board meeting date(s): Dec.
Officers: Ezra K. Zilkha, Pres. and Treas.; Cecile E. Zilkha, V.P. and Secy.
EIN: 136090739
Selected grants: The following grants were reported in 2005.
$120,000 to Wesleyan University, Middletown, CT. 2 grants: $40,000, $80,000
$20,000 to Hospital for Special Surgery Fund, New York, NY. 2 grants: $10,000 each
$20,000 to Lycee Francais de New York, New York, NY.
$10,000 to Pierpont Morgan Library, New York, NY.
$10,000 to Spence School, New York, NY.
$5,000 to Museum of the City of New York, New York, NY.
$2,000 to Frick Collection, New York, NY.
$2,000 to Layalina Productions, DC.

7301
Marie and John Zimmermann Fund, Inc. ✧
114 W. 47th St.
New York, NY 10036-1532
Contact: Linda Franciscovich, Sr. V.P.; Carolyn L. Larke, Asst. V.P.

Incorporated in 1942 in NY.
Donor: Marie Zimmermann†.
Foundation type: Independent foundation.
Financial data (yr. ended 12/31/04): Assets, $8,079,428 (M); expenditures, $381,678; qualifying distributions, $353,658; giving activities include $323,682 for grants.
Fields of interest: Higher education; Medical school/education.
Limitations: Applications not accepted. Giving primarily in the Northeast. No grants to individuals.
Application information: Contributes only to pre-selected organizations.
  Board meeting date(s): June
Officers and Directors:* John C. Zimmermann III,* Pres.; Robert Perret, Jr.,* Secy.; J. Robert Buchanan, M.D.; Anne C. Heller; Edward C. Kline.
EIN: 136158767

7302
Charlotte & Arthur Zitrin Foundation ✧
56 Ruxton Rd.
Great Neck, NY 11023
Application address: 32 Lockerman Sq., Ste. L-100, Dover, DE 19901

Established in 1991 in DE.
Donors: Arthur Zitrin; Charlotte Zitrin.
Foundation type: Independent foundation.
Financial data (yr. ended 10/31/05): Assets, $8,251,347 (M); expenditures, $404,560; qualifying distributions, $391,683; giving activities include $388,650 for grants.
Purpose and activities: Giving for the arts, education, the environment, housing, and human services.
Fields of interest: Arts; Higher education; Education; Environment; Legal services; Housing/shelter; Human services; Jewish federated giving programs.
Type of support: Scholarship funds.
Limitations: Giving primarily in New York, NY. No grants to individuals.
Application information: Application form not required.
  Initial approach: Letter or proposal
  Deadline(s): None
Officers: Arthur Zitrin, Pres.; Charlotte Zitrin, V.P.
EIN: 510337212
Selected grants: The following grants were reported in 2005.
$35,000 to Southern Center for Human Rights, Atlanta, GA.
$26,000 to Oberlin College, Oberlin, OH.
$25,000 to City College 21st Century Foundation, New York, NY.
$10,000 to Natural Resources Defense Council, New York, NY.
$5,000 to City Arts and Lectures, San Francisco, CA.
$5,000 to Nature Conservancy, Arlington, VA.
$5,000 to People for the American Way Foundation, DC.
$5,000 to Sunburst Projects, Rohnert Park, CA.
$3,000 to Luther Burbank Center for the Arts, Santa Rosa, CA.
$2,500 to Arriba Juntos, San Francisco, CA.

7303
The Donald & Barbara Zucker Foundation, Inc. ✧
103 W. 55th St.
New York, NY 10019

Established in 1998.
Donors: Donald Zucker; Barbara Hrbek Zucker.
Foundation type: Independent foundation.
Financial data (yr. ended 9/30/05): Assets, $7,575 (M); gifts received, $973,176; expenditures, $964,883; qualifying distributions, $964,883; giving activities include $964,335 for 165 grants (high: $150,000; low: $15).
Purpose and activities: Giving primarily to Jewish organizations, and to hospitals; funding also for arts and culture, education, wildlife preservation, and youth and social services.
Fields of interest: Arts; Higher education; Education; Animals/wildlife, preservation/protection; Hospitals (general); Human services; Youth, services; Jewish federated giving programs; Jewish agencies & temples.
Limitations: Applications not accepted. Giving primarily in NY. No grants to individuals.
Application information: Contributes only to pre-selected organizations.

Officers: Donald Zucker, Pres.; Barbara Zucker Albinder, V.P.; Laurie Zucker, V.P.; Barbara Hrbek Zucker, Secy.-Treas.
EIN: 134032142
Selected grants: The following grants were reported in 2004.
$150,000 to United Jewish Communities, New York, NY.
$125,000 to Sisters of Saint Dominic, Brooklyn, NY. 2 grants: $100,000, $25,000
$100,000 to Anti-Defamation League of Bnai Brith, New York, NY.
$75,000 to North Shore-Long Island Jewish Health System, Westbury, NY.
$50,000 to Jewish Museum, New York, NY. 2 grants: $25,000 each
$50,000 to Wildlife Conservation Society, Bronx, NY.
$39,067 to Jewish Center of the Hamptons, East Hampton, NY.
$20,000 to Hebrew Union College-Jewish Institute of Religion, New York, NY.

7304
Roy J. Zuckerberg Family Foundation ✧
(also known as Roy J. Zuckerberg Foundation)
c/o BCRS Assocs., LLC
100 Wall St.
New York, NY 10005

Established in 1980 in NY.
Donor: Roy J. Zuckerberg.
Foundation type: Independent foundation.
Financial data (yr. ended 9/30/05): Assets, $11,339,032 (M); gifts received, $1,044,350; expenditures, $1,355,411; qualifying distributions, $1,142,059; giving activities include $1,141,698 for 188 grants (high: $72,455; low: $115).
Purpose and activities: Giving primarily to museums, hospitals, health associations, human services and Jewish federated giving programs.
Fields of interest: Museums; Hospitals (general); Health organizations, association; Human services; Jewish federated giving programs.
Limitations: Applications not accepted. Giving primarily in the greater metropolitan New York, NY, area. No grants to individuals, or for scholarships; no loans.
Application information: Contributes only to pre-selected organizations.
Trustees: James C. Kautz; Barbara Zuckerberg; Dina R. Zuckerberg; Lloyd P. Zuckerberg; Roy J. Zuckerberg.
EIN: 133052489

NORTH CAROLINA

7305
Arthur F. and Alice E. Adams Charitable Foundation ◇
c/o Wachovia Bank, N.A.
100 N. Main St., 13th Fl.
Winston-Salem, NC 27150
Application address: c/o Wachovia Bank, N.A.,
Attn.: Susan Best, 200 S. Biscayne Blvd., 14th Fl.,
Miami, FL 33131

Established in 1987 in FL.
Donor: Alice E. Adams†.
Foundation type: Independent foundation.
Financial data (yr. ended 9/30/05): Assets,
$20,549,336 (M); expenditures, $2,024,120;
qualifying distributions, $1,698,342; giving
activities include $1,668,800 for 49 grants (high:
$700,000; low: $1,000).
Fields of interest: Performing arts; Performing arts
centers; Performing arts, opera; Arts; Higher
education; Libraries/library science; Botanical
gardens.
Limitations: Giving primarily in FL and TN. No grants
to individuals.
Application information:
  Initial approach: Letter
  Deadline(s): None
  Board meeting date(s): May and Nov.
Governors: Virginia Clark; Renee Clark Guibao.
Trustees: William B. Warren; Wachovia Bank, N.A.
EIN: 656003785

7306
The Anonymous Fund
P.O. Box 9908
Greensboro, NC 27429

Established in 1995 in NC.
Foundation type: Independent foundation.
Financial data (yr. ended 12/31/05): Assets,
$17,129,467 (M); expenditures, $1,567,005;
qualifying distributions, $1,445,624; giving
activities include $1,360,000 for 27 grants (high:
$250,000; low: $10,000).
Fields of interest: Historic preservation/historical
societies; Arts; Higher education; Environment,
natural resources; Human services; Children,
services; Federated giving programs.
Limitations: Applications not accepted. Giving on a
national basis, with emphasis on NC. No grants to
individuals.
Application information: Contributes only to
pre-selected organizations.
Officers: Joseph M. Bryan, Jr., Pres.; Ronald P.
Johnson, Secy.
Trustee: William P. Massey.
EIN: 562152734

7307
The Edward M. Armfield, Sr. Foundation, Inc. ◇
P.O. Box 9436
Greensboro, NC 27429

Established in 2000 in NC.
Donor: Edward M. Armfield, Sr.†.

Foundation type: Independent foundation.
Financial data (yr. ended 12/31/04): Assets,
$53,240,402 (M); gifts received, $7,947,684;
expenditures, $1,449,674; qualifying distributions,
$1,010,038; giving activities include $386,985 for
4 grants (high: $100,000; low: $5,000), and
$423,927 for grants to individuals.
Fields of interest: Elementary/secondary
education; Higher education; Education.
Limitations: Applications not accepted. Giving
primarily in NC.
Application information: Unsolicited requests for
funds not accepted.
Directors: Adair P. Armfield; W.J. Armfield; Bedford
Cannon; Steve Joyce.
EIN: 562156876

7308
Mary Reynolds Babcock Foundation, Inc. ▼ ◇
2920 Reynolda Rd.
Winston-Salem, NC 27106 (336) 748-9222
Contact: Gayle Williams, Exec. Dir.
FAX: (336) 777-0095; E-mail: info@mrbf.org;
URL: http://www.mrbf.org

Incorporated in 1953 in NC.
Donors: Mary Reynolds Babcock†; Charles H.
Babcock†.
Foundation type: Independent foundation.
Financial data (yr. ended 12/31/05): Assets,
$173,290,609 (M); gifts received, $23,325,303;
expenditures, $7,867,402; qualifying distributions,
$7,509,093; giving activities include $5,219,335
for 153 grants (high: $300,000; low: $2,500;
average: $10,000–$75,000), $236,609 for 3
foundation-administered programs and $1,000,000
for 7 loans/program-related investments.
Purpose and activities: The foundation supports
people in the southeast to build just and caring
communities that nurture people, spur enterprise,
bridge differences, and foster fairness. Its mission
is to help people and places to move out of poverty
and achieve greater social and economic justice.
The foundation carries out this commitment through
three funding areas: enterprise and asset
development, community problem solving, and
grassroots leadership development.
Fields of interest: Human services; Civil rights,
race/intergroup relations; Community development;
Leadership development; Economically
disadvantaged.
Type of support: Program development; Seed
money; Technical assistance; Program-related
investments/loans.
Limitations: Giving in the southeastern U.S., with
emphasis on eastern AL, AR, GA, LA, MS, NC, SC,
TN, north and central FL, and the Appalachian
regions of KY and WV. No grants to individuals,
capital improvements, direct services (such as food
or medical assistance), or for satellite operations of
organizations outside the southeast.
Publications: Annual report (including application
guidelines); Grants list.
Application information: Organization summary may
be submitted via mail, fax, or e-mail. An online
organization summary may also be completed on the
foundation's Web site. Applications should wait for
a response to the summary before submitting a
proposal. Application form required.
  Initial approach: Organizational summary (no
    longer than 2 pages)

Copies of proposal: 2
Deadline(s): Feb. 1 and July 1
Board meeting date(s): Feb., June, and Oct.
Final notification: Mid-June
Officers and Directors:* Carol P. Zippert,* Pres.;
Kenneth F. Mountcastle III,* V.P.; Victoria Creed,*
Secy.; Laura L. Mountcastle,* Treas.; Gayle
Williams, Exec. Dir.; Bruce M. Babcock; Wayne Flynt;
Otis Johnson; Wendy S. Johnson; Barbara B.
Millhouse; Katharine B. Mountcastle; Katherine R.
Mountcastle; Mary Mountcastle.
Number of staff: 5 full-time professional; 3 full-time
support; 1 part-time support.
EIN: 560690140
Selected grants: The following grants were reported
in 2005.
$300,000 to Enterprise Corporation of the Delta,
  Jackson, MS. For program support.
$225,000 to Mountain Microenterprise Fund,
  Asheville, NC. For program support.
$200,000 to Southeastern Organizational
  Development Initiative, Raleigh, NC. For program
  support.
$200,000 to Southern Rural Development Initiative,
  Raleigh, NC. For regional capacity building work.
$160,000 to Center for Participatory Change,
  Asheville, NC. For program support.
$150,000 to Southern Mutual Help Association,
  New Iberia, LA. For Hurricane Katrina relief.
$108,000 to Appalachian Community Enterprises,
  Cleveland, GA. For program support.
$100,000 to Alabama Association of Community
  Development Corporations Education Fund,
  Gadsden, AL. For regional capacity building work.
$100,000 to Alabama Organizing Project,
  Montgomery, AL. For Grassroots Leadership
  Development Program.
$40,000 to East Baker Historical and Twenty-First
  Community Corporation, Newton, GA. For
  Grassroots Organizations Program.

7309
Bobbie Bailey Foundation, Inc. ◇ ☆
c/o Bank of America, N.A.
101 S. Tryon St., NC1-002-11-18
Charlotte, NC 28255-0001
Contact: Ms. Bobbie Bailey, Tr.
Application address: c/o Bank of America, N.A., 600
Peachtree St. N.E., Atlanta, GA 30308

Established in 1994 in GA.
Donor: Bobbie Bailey.
Foundation type: Independent foundation.
Financial data (yr. ended 12/31/05): Assets,
$2,652,619 (M); expenditures, $420,095;
qualifying distributions, $397,979; giving activities
include $392,000 for 4 grants (high: $375,000;
low: $2,500).
Purpose and activities: Giving primarily for a
medical center; some funding for education.
Fields of interest: Higher education; Education;
Human services.
Limitations: Giving primarily in GA.
Application information:
  Initial approach: Letter
  Deadline(s): None
Trustee: Ms. Bobbie Bailey.
EIN: 582085849
Selected grants: The following grants were reported
in 2003.
$75,000 to Georgia State University Foundation,
  Atlanta, GA.
$20,000 to Musicares Foundation, Atlanta, GA.

$11,500 to Friends of Georgia Music Scholarship Fund, Atlanta, GA.

$10,000 to United Jewish Appeal of the Southeast Region, Atlanta, GA. For general support.

$6,000 to Latin Academy, Atlanta, GA. For general support.

$5,000 to Georgia Music Industry Association, Atlanta, GA. For general support.

$5,000 to LARAS, Atlanta, GA. For general support.

$550 to Our House, Decatur, GA.

7310
The Bank of America Charitable Foundation, Inc. ▼ ✧
101 S. Tryon St., NC1-002-33-77
Charlotte, NC   28255-0001
URL: http://www.bankofamerica.com/foundation/index.cfm?template=fd_funding

Established in 1958; current name adopted in 1998 following the merger of NationsBank Corporation and BankAmerica Corporation; reincorporated in 2004.

Donors: Bank of America Corp.; Bank of America, N.A.; FleetBoston Financial Foundation.

Foundation type: Company-sponsored foundation.

Financial data (yr. ended 12/31/05): Assets, $41,742,644 (M); gifts received, $80,041,243; expenditures, $123,360,380; qualifying distributions, $123,291,488; giving activities include $123,287,819 for grants.

Purpose and activities: The foundation supports organizations involved with arts and culture, education, health, human services, community development, and religion. Special emphasis is directed toward programs designed to address critical issues in local communities.

Fields of interest: Arts; Education; Health care; Human services; Community development; Religion.

Type of support: General/operating support; Continuing support; Annual campaigns; Building/renovation; Equipment; Emergency funds; Program development; Internship funds; Scholarship funds; Employee volunteer services; Employee matching gifts; Employee-related scholarships; Matching/challenge support.

Limitations: Giving limited to areas of major company operations. No support for political, labor, or fraternal organizations, civic clubs, religious organizations not of direct benefit to the entire community, public or private pre-K-12 schools, United Way- or arts council-supported organizations, or disease advocacy organizations. No grants to individuals (except for Joe Martin Scholarships), or for fellowships, advertising, sports, athletic events, or athletic programs, travel-related events, student trips, or tours, development or production of books, films, videos, or television programs, endowments, or memorial campaigns.

Publications: Application guidelines; Grants list.

Application information: Application form required.

  Initial approach: Complete online eligibility quiz

Officers and Trustees:* Charles K. Gifford,* Chair.; Catherine P. Bessant,* Vice-Chair.; Andrew D. Plepler, Pres.; Thomas M. Brantley, Sr. V.P.; Mary A. Brown, Sr. V.P.; Stephen B. Fitzgerald, Sr. V.P.; Michelle C. Hartzell, Sr. V.P.; Gregory S. Mroz, Sr. V.P.; David R. Smith, Sr. V.P.; Duane L. Smith, Sr. V.P.; Brenda L. Suits, Sr. V.P.; Deidre W. Martin, V.P.; Phyllis B. Woollen, V.P.; Merrily S. Gerrish, Secy.; Christopher C. Deville, Treas.

EIN: 200721133

Selected grants: The following grants were reported in 2004.

$1,000,000 to National Council on Economic Education, New York, NY.

$1,000,000 to University of California, San Francisco, CA.

$700,000 to Enterprise Community Partners, Columbia, MD.

$700,000 to Local Initiatives Support Corporation (LISC), New York, NY.

$600,000 to National Council of La Raza, DC.

$500,000 to Orange County Performing Arts Center, Costa Mesa, CA.

$440,000 to Arts and Science Council of Charlotte-Mecklenburg, Charlotte, NC.

$300,000 to National Baseball Hall of Fame and Museum, Cooperstown, NY.

$279,500 to Scholarship America, Saint Peter, MN.

$258,333 to Action Greensboro, Greensboro, NC.

7311
The Baruch Fund ✧
c/o Richard U. Puryear
82 Old Pasture Way
Hendersonville, NC   28739-3133
Application address: c/o Jordan J. Baruch, 5630 Wisconsin Ave., Ste. 905, Chevy Chase, MD 20815

Established about 1964 in MA as the Jordan J. Baruch Foundation.

Donors: Jordan J. Baruch; Rhoda W. Baruch.

Foundation type: Independent foundation.

Financial data (yr. ended 12/31/04): Assets, $5,241,115 (M); gifts received, $531,988; expenditures, $1,322,652; qualifying distributions, $1,267,523; giving activities include $1,267,523 for 168 grants (high: $325,650; low: $50).

Purpose and activities: Giving primarily for education, particularly engineering schools, and to Jewish organizations and temples; funding also for the arts, health and human services.

Fields of interest: Arts; Engineering school/education; Education; Hospitals (general); Health organizations, association; Human services; Jewish federated giving programs; Jewish agencies & temples.

Limitations: Giving primarily in Washington, DC, MA, MD, NJ, and NY. No grants to individuals.

Application information: Application form not required.

  Initial approach: Letter
  Deadline(s): None

Trustees: Jordan J. Baruch; Lawrence K. Baruch; Rhoda W. Baruch.

EIN: 046112483

Selected grants: The following grants were reported in 2004.

$325,650 to American Jewish Committee, New York, NY.

$200,000 to Massachusetts Institute of Technology, Cambridge, MA.

$200,000 to National Academy of Engineering, DC.

$55,300 to Jewish Federation of Greater Washington, Rockville, MD.

$6,000 to Jewish Womens Archive, Brookline, MA.

$1,300 to University of Chicago, Chicago, IL.

$1,000 to Boston University, Boston, MA.

$1,000 to Brooklyn College Foundation, Brooklyn, NY.

$1,000 to Carnegie Institution of Washington, DC.

$500 to National Partnership for Women and Families, DC.

7312
BB&T Charitable Foundation ▼
P.O. Box 1547, M.C. 001-05-04-30
Winston-Salem, NC   27102-1547
Contact: Rodney Hughes, Exec. Dir.
FAX: (336) 733-0118;
E-mail: rodney.hughes@bbandt.com

Established in 1998 in NC.

Donors: BB&T Corp.; First Virginia Bank.

Foundation type: Company-sponsored foundation.

Financial data (yr. ended 12/31/05): Assets, $34,640,801 (M); expenditures, $6,153,731; qualifying distributions, $6,037,625; giving activities include $6,037,275 for grants.

Purpose and activities: The foundation supports organizations involved with arts and culture, education, the environment, health, human services, and community development.

Fields of interest: Arts; Education; Environment; Health care; Human services; Economic development; Community development.

Type of support: General/operating support; Annual campaigns; Capital campaigns; Building/renovation; Endowments; Emergency funds; Program development; Professorships; Curriculum development; Matching/challenge support.

Limitations: Applications not accepted. Giving primarily in areas of company operations. No grants to individuals.

Application information: Contributes only to pre-selected organizations.

  Board meeting date(s): Bi-monthly

Trustee: BB&T Corp.

Officer: Rodney Hughes, Exec. Dir.

EIN: 562093089

Selected grants: The following grants were reported in 2004.

$400,003 to Ayn Rand Institute, Irvine, CA.

$300,000 to Winston-Salem Foundation, Winston-Salem, NC.

$250,000 to University of Kentucky, Lexington, KY.

$202,500 to Duke University, Durham, NC.

$200,000 to Clemson University Foundation, Clemson, SC.

$200,000 to Riverpark Center, Owensboro, KY.

$120,840 to United Way of Wilson County, Wilson, NC.

$20,000 to Virginia Polytechnic Institute and State University, Blacksburg, VA.

$15,000 to Cultural Events for Educating Frederick, Frederick, MD.

$15,000 to United Way of Gaston County, Gastonia, NC.

7313
Beaver Family Foundation, Inc. ✧
(formerly Donald C. Beaver Family Foundation, Inc.)
2425 N. Center St., No. 227
Hickory, NC   28601
E-mail: margaretglaze@charter.net

Established in 1997 in NC.

Donors: Donald C. Beaver; Patricia Anderson; Rob Simons; Angela Simons.

Foundation type: Independent foundation.

Financial data (yr. ended 4/30/06): Assets, $11,034,216 (M); gifts received, $53,074; expenditures, $975,682; qualifying distributions, $854,571; giving activities include $854,571 for 82 grants (high: $289,507; low: $25).

Purpose and activities: Funding for Christian agencies, human services, and arts and culture.

Fields of interest: Arts; Human services; Christian agencies & churches.

Limitations: Applications not accepted. No grants to individuals.

Application information: Contributes only to pre-selected organizations.

Officers: Donald C. Beaver, Pres.; Patricia A. Anderson, V.P.; Angela B. Simmons, Secy.; Donna Fleming, Treas.

Director: Deborah E. Beaver.

Number of staff: 1 part-time professional; 1 part-time support.

EIN: 562028723

Selected grants: The following grants were reported in 2005.

$100,000 to Sipes Orchard Home, Conover, NC.

$51,000 to Lenoir-Rhyne College, Hickory, NC. 2 grants: $50,000, $1,000

$30,000 to YMCA.

$20,000 to Habitat for Humanity of Catawba Valley, Hickory, NC.

$20,000 to Patrick Beaver Learning Resource Center, Hickory, NC.

$15,000 to Boys and Girls Club.

$15,000 to Catawba County Council for the Arts, Hickory, NC.

$5,000 to Girl Scouts of the U.S.A..

$5,000 to South Caldwell Christian Ministries, Granite Falls, NC.

7314
Irwin Belk Educational Foundation ◇

6100 Fairview Rd., Ste. 640
Charlotte, NC   28210-3277   (704) 553-8296
Contact: Carl G. Belk, Dir.

Established in 1992.

Donors: Carl G. Belk; Irwin Belk; Irwin Belk Charitable Lead Trusts.

Foundation type: Independent foundation.

Financial data (yr. ended 12/31/05): Assets, $652,391 (M); gifts received, $390,171; expenditures, $369,160; qualifying distributions, $364,000; giving activities include $364,000 for grants.

Purpose and activities: Giving primarily for arts and culture, libraries, and to religious organizations.

Fields of interest: Museums (science/technology); Arts; Libraries (public); Protestant agencies & churches.

Type of support: General/operating support.

Limitations: Giving primarily in NC. No grants to individuals.

Application information: Application form required.

  Initial approach: Letter

  Deadline(s): None

Directors: Bill Belk; Carl G. Belk; Irene Belk Miltimore; Marilyn Belk Wallis.

EIN: 561783301

7315
The Belk Foundation

2801 W. Tyvola Rd.
Charlotte, NC   28217-4500   (704) 426-8396
Contact: Susan Blount, Admin.
E-mail: susan_blount@belk.com; URL: http://www.belk.com/main/belk_foundation.jsp

Trust established in 1928 in NC.

Donors: The Belk Department Stores; Matthews Belk; Belk Enterprises; Belk, Inc.

Foundation type: Company-sponsored foundation.

Financial data (yr. ended 5/31/05): Assets, $56,678,286 (M); gifts received, $1,000,000; expenditures, $2,607,661; qualifying distributions, $2,334,018; giving activities include $2,334,018 for 99 grants (high: $110,322; low: $1,000).

Purpose and activities: The foundation supports organizations involved with arts and culture, education, health, human services, and Christianity.

Fields of interest: Arts; Higher education; Education; Hospitals (general); Health care; Children/youth, services; Human services; Federated giving programs; Christian agencies & churches.

Type of support: General/operating support; Continuing support; Annual campaigns; Capital campaigns; Building/renovation; Endowments; Emergency funds; Program development; Professorships; Sponsorships; Matching/challenge support.

Limitations: Applications not accepted. Giving primarily in NC and in areas of company operations. No support for government or quasi-governmental organizations. No grants to individuals.

Publications: Financial statement; Informational brochure.

Application information: Contributes only to pre-selected organizations.

Officer and Trustees:* John M. Belk,* Chair.; Paul B. Wyche, Jr.; Wachovia Bank, N.A.

Advisors: Claudia W. Belk; Katherine McKay Belk-Cook; James Kirk Glenn, Jr.; B. Frank Matthews II; Katherine Belk Morris; Mary Claudia Belk Pilon; Leroy Robinson.

EIN: 566046450

Selected grants: The following grants were reported in 2005.

$203,593 to Charlotte Country Day School, Charlotte, NC. 2 grants: $103,593, $100,000

$166,667 to Converse College, Spartanburg, SC.

$83,000 to United Way, NC. 2 grants: $50,000, $33,000

$75,947 to High Point University, High Point, NC.

$49,603 to YMCA, Rocky Mount Family, Rocky Mount, NC.

$49,344 to Crossnore School, Crossnore, NC.

$25,000 to United Family Services, Charlotte, NC.

$5,000 to United Way, GA.

7316
Frank and Lydia Bergen Foundation ◇

c/o Wachovia Bank, N.A.
100 N. Main St., 13th Fl.
Winston-Salem, NC   27150
Contact: Gale Y. Sykes
E-mail: grantinquiriesnj@wachovia.com; Application address: c/o Wachovia Bank, N.A., 190 River Rd., Summit, NJ 07901

Incorporated in 1983 in NJ.

Donor: Charlotte V. Bergen†.

Foundation type: Independent foundation.

Financial data (yr. ended 12/31/05): Assets, $10,346,493 (M); expenditures, $651,394; qualifying distributions, $602,940; giving activities include $600,940 for grants.

Purpose and activities: The foundation supports the musical arts with emphasis on orchestral presentations and education. Specific areas of interest include the educational outreach activities of performing arts organizations. Grants are provided to institutions to assist students from NJ who are studying orchestral instruments.

Fields of interest: Performing arts, music; Arts; Education.

Type of support: Program development; Scholarship funds.

Limitations: Giving limited to NJ. No grants to individuals, or for endowments or general operating support; fundraising events including dinners, benefits and athletic events; no loans.

Publications: Application guidelines.

Application information: Applicants must submit a Common Grant Application Form along with proposal. Application form required.

  Initial approach: Proposal

  Copies of proposal: 2

  Deadline(s): Mar. 15 - Sept. 15

  Board meeting date(s): June and Dec.

  Final notification: 1 month after board meets

Trustee: Wachovia Bank, N.A.

EIN: 226359304

7317
The Mary Duke Biddle Foundation ◇

1044 W. Forest Hills Blvd.
Durham, NC   27707   (919) 493-5591
Contact: Douglas C. Zinn, Exec. Dir.
URL: http://mdbf.org

Trust established in 1956 in NY.

Donors: Mary Duke Biddle†; Nicholas Duke Biddle 1960 Trust; Nicholas D. Biddle Trust #2.

Foundation type: Independent foundation.

Financial data (yr. ended 12/31/05): Assets, $26,527,949 (M); gifts received, $3,281,200; expenditures, $2,652,735; qualifying distributions, $2,421,529; giving activities include $2,107,178 for 214 grants (high: $1,000,000; low: $480).

Purpose and activities: Support for private higher and secondary education, specified churches, cultural programs, particularly music, dance and theater, projects in the arts, and aid to the community and to the handicapped; half of the income is committed to Duke University.

Fields of interest: Performing arts, dance; Performing arts, theater; Performing arts, music; Arts; Secondary school/education; Higher education; Education; Community development; Disabilities, people with.

Type of support: Program development; Conferences/seminars; Seed money; Fellowships; Scholarship funds; Matching/challenge support.

Limitations: Giving limited to NC and New York, NY. No support for public education. No grants to individuals, or for building or endowment funds; generally no operating budgets; no loans.

Publications: Annual report.

Application information: Application form not required.

  Initial approach: Telephone

  Copies of proposal: 1

  Deadline(s): Call for deadlines

  Board meeting date(s): Mar., June, Sept., and Dec.

  Final notification: Approximately 90 days for negative responses

Officers and Trustees:* Mary T. Jones,* Chair.; Thomas S. Kenan III,* Vice-Chair. and Secy.; John G. Mebane,* Treas.; C. Russell Bryan; James D.B.T. Semans; Jon Zeljo.

Number of staff: 1 part-time professional; 2 part-time support.

EIN: 136068883

7318
BIN Charitable Foundation ✧
P.O. Box 3127
Durham, NC 27715

Established in 1999 in NC.
Donor: Barbara Newborg.
Foundation type: Independent foundation.
Financial data (yr. ended 12/31/05): Assets, $10,436,264 (M); gifts received, $4,300; expenditures, $537,055; qualifying distributions, $403,505; giving activities include $403,505 for 37 grants (high: $75,000; low: $814).
Purpose and activities: Giving to enhance the Durham, NC and surrounding community by making grants to support environmental concerns, affordable housing, unity of diverse citizens, the arts, and children.
Fields of interest: Housing/shelter, development; Human services; Children/youth, services.
Type of support: Matching/challenge support; Curriculum development; Equipment; Building/renovation; Annual campaigns.
Limitations: Applications not accepted. Giving primarily in NC. No grants to individuals.
Application information: Unsolicited requests for funds not accepted.
Officers: Barbara Newborg, Pres.; Bond Anderson III, Secy.; Sarah F. Preyer, Treas.
EIN: 562111550
Selected grants: The following grants were reported in 2005.
$30,000 to Durham Nativity School, Durham, NC.
$15,000 to Habitat for Humanity International.
$12,000 to Carnivore Preservation Trust, Pittsboro, NC.
$11,675 to Ronald McDonald House.
$9,160 to South Eastern Efforts Developing Sustainable Spaces (SEEDS), Durham, NC.
$9,000 to Southern Documentary Fund, Durham, NC.
$7,500 to All Kinds of Minds, Chapel Hill, NC.
$5,000 to Durham Symphony, Durham, NC.
$4,000 to Durham Technical Community College, Durham, NC.
$3,000 to Eno River Association, Durham, NC.

7319
Blue Cross and Blue Shield of North Carolina Foundation ✧
c/o Grant Review Comm.
P.O. Box 2291
Durham, NC 27702 (919) 765-4114
FAX: (919) 765-2433;
E-mail: foundation@bcbsnc.com; URL: http://www.bcbsnc.com/foundation

Established in 2000 in NC.
Donors: Blue Cross and Blue Shield of North Carolina, Inc.; Golden Leaf Foundation.
Foundation type: Company-sponsored foundation.
Financial data (yr. ended 6/30/04): Assets, $44,642,303 (M); gifts received, $10,000,000; expenditures, $3,334,018; qualifying distributions, $3,190,540; giving activities include $3,106,121 for 46 grants (high: $2,000,000; low: $2,100), and $84,419 for 4 foundation-administered programs.
Purpose and activities: The foundation supports organizations involved with health and human services.
Fields of interest: Health care; Children/youth, services; Family services; Human services.

Type of support: General/operating support; Program development; Curriculum development; Technical assistance; Program evaluation; Matching/challenge support.
Limitations: Giving primarily in NC. No support for religious organizations, individual sports teams, or organizations with the sole purpose of receiving goods and entitlements from other charitable organizations. No grants for annual campaigns, political campaigns, endowments, or advertising.
Publications: Application guidelines; Financial statement; Grants list.
Application information: Application form required.
Initial approach: Download application form and mail to foundation
Copies of proposal: 6
Deadline(s): Visit Web site for deadlines
Final notification: Visit Web site for dates
Officers: Robert J. Greczyn, Jr., Pres.; Kathy Higgins, V.P.; Maureen O'Connor, Secy.; Steve Cherrier, Treas.
Trustees: Roberta B. Bowman; Lynne Garrison; Daniel E. Glaser; John T. Roos; Rhone Sasser; J. Bradley Wilson.
EIN: 562226009

7320
The Blumenthal Foundation
P.O. Box 34689
Charlotte, NC 28234-4689 (704) 688-2305
Contact: Philip Blumenthal, Tr.
FAX: (704) 688-2401;
E-mail: foundation@gunk.com; URL: http://www.blumenthalfoundation.org/index.htm

Trust established in 1953 in NC.
Donors: I.D. Blumenthal†; Herman Blumenthal†; Radiator Specialty Co.
Foundation type: Independent foundation.
Financial data (yr. ended 12/31/04): Assets, $0 (M); gifts received, $4,250,000; expenditures, $6,203,221; qualifying distributions, $5,930,008; giving activities include $5,828,716 for 135 grants (high: $2,000,000; low: $500).
Purpose and activities: Giving for higher education, Jewish welfare organizations, and programs in the arts and humanities; also supports Wildacres Leadership Initiative, a conference center in NC, which invites nonprofit groups with planned educational programs in a variety of disciplines to use its facilities, as well as WA Retreat.
Fields of interest: Humanities; Arts; Higher education; Education; Environment; Health care; Human services; Jewish federated giving programs; Jewish agencies & temples.
Type of support: General/operating support; Annual campaigns; Capital campaigns; Building/renovation; Endowments; Emergency funds; Program development; Conferences/seminars; Professorships; Publication; Seed money; Research; Matching/challenge support.
Limitations: Giving primarily in NC, with emphasis on Charlotte and Mecklenburg County. No grants to individuals, or for scholarships or fellowships; no loans.
Publications: Application guidelines; Annual report; Grants list; Multi-year report.
Application information: Application form not required.
Initial approach: Letter or telephone
Copies of proposal: 1
Deadline(s): None

Board meeting date(s): Mar., June, Sept., and Dec.
Final notification: 1-2 months
Trustees: Philip Blumenthal, Dir.; Alan Blumenthal; Samuel Blumenthal, Ph.D.
Number of staff: 2 full-time professional; 1 part-time professional.
EIN: 560793667
Selected grants: The following grants were reported in 2004.
$2,163,763 to Wildacres Retreat, Little Switzerland, NC. 6 grants: $20,000, $2,000,000, $20,000, $88,763, $20,000, $15,000
$350,000 to Foundation of Shalom Park, Charlotte, NC.
$15,000 to Foundation for the Carolinas, Charlotte, NC.
$7,500 to United Way of Central Carolinas, Charlotte, NC. 2 grants: $3,750 each

7321
The Bolick Foundation ✧
P.O. Box 307
Conover, NC 28613

Established in 1967 in NC.
Donor: Southern Furniture Co. of Conover, Inc.
Foundation type: Company-sponsored foundation.
Financial data (yr. ended 6/30/05): Assets, $10,143,584 (M); expenditures, $539,738; qualifying distributions, $435,650; giving activities include $435,650 for 74 grants (high: $111,250; low: $100).
Purpose and activities: The foundation supports organizations involved with higher education, health, human services, and Christianity.
Fields of interest: Higher education; Health care; Children/youth, services; Residential/custodial care, hospices; Human services; Christian agencies & churches.
Limitations: Applications not accepted. Giving primarily in NC. No grants to individuals.
Application information: Contributes only to pre-selected organizations.
Trustee: Jerome W. Bolick.
EIN: 566086348
Selected grants: The following grants were reported in 2005.
$25,000 to Lenoir-Rhyne College, Hickory, NC.
$20,000 to Concordia Theological Seminary, Fort Wayne, IN.
$20,000 to Tri-City Christian School, Independence, MO.
$14,000 to Boy Scouts of America.
$10,000 to Lutheran Theological Southern Seminary, Columbia, SC.
$5,000 to Independent College Fund of North Carolina, Raleigh, NC.
$5,000 to Lutheran Services for the Aging, Salisbury, NC.
$2,500 to Catawba Medical Foundation, Hickory, NC.
$2,500 to Dallas Baptist University, Dallas, TX.
$2,000 to Young Life.

7322
Charles I. Branan Trust ✧
c/o Wachovia Bank, N.A.
100 N. Main St., 13th Fl.
Winston-Salem, NC 27150

Established in 2003 in GA.
Foundation type: Independent foundation.
Financial data (yr. ended 12/31/05): Assets, $28,952,271 (M); expenditures, $1,260,603; qualifying distributions, $1,112,280; giving activities include $1,112,280 for 51 grants (high: $68,500; low: $500).
Fields of interest: Historic preservation/historical societies; Education; Food banks; Human services; Children/youth, services; Residential/custodial care; Community development; Federated giving programs; Protestant agencies & churches.
Limitations: Applications not accepted. Giving primarily in Atlanta, GA.
Application information: Contributes only to pre-selected organizations.
Trustee: Wachovia Bank, N.A.
EIN: 586026401

7323
James R. and Bronnie L. Braswell Trust ◇

c/o George L. Bower, Jr., Poisson, Poisson, Bower & Clodfelter
300 E. Wade St.
Wadesboro, NC   28170

Established in 2001 in NC.
Donor: James R. Braswell†.
Foundation type: Independent foundation.
Financial data (yr. ended 12/31/05): Assets, $10,505,441 (M); expenditures, $585,479; qualifying distributions, $502,500; giving activities include $502,500 for 16 grants (high: $75,000; low: $2,500).
Fields of interest: Education; Housing/shelter; Human services; Christian agencies & churches; Protestant agencies & churches.
Limitations: Applications not accepted. Giving primarily in NC. No grants to individuals.
Application information: Contributes only to pre-selected organizations.
Trustee: George L. Bower, Jr.
EIN: 736339730

7324
The Breeden Family Foundation ◇ ☆

100 Europa Dr., Ste. 200
Chapel Hill, NC   27514   (919) 967-7221
Contact: Douglas T. Breeden, Pres.

Donor: Douglas T. Breeden.
Foundation type: Independent foundation.
Financial data (yr. ended 12/31/05): Assets, $1,143 (M); gifts received, $154,000; expenditures, $377,263; qualifying distributions, $377,263; giving activities include $377,177 for 3 grants (high: $306,177; low: $14,000).
Fields of interest: Secondary school/education; Libraries (school).
Limitations: Giving primarily in IN. No grants to individuals.
Application information:
   Initial approach: Letter
   Deadline(s): None
Officers: Douglas T. Breeden, Pres.; Josie C. Breeden, V.P.; Russell Breeden III, V.P.; Annabelle T. Breeden, Secy.-Treas.
EIN: 562006787

7325
Brody Brothers Foundation, Inc.

P.O. Box 1046
Kinston, NC   28503

Established in 1966.
Donors: David S. Brody; J.S. Brody; Leo Brody; J. & S. Investment Co.
Foundation type: Independent foundation.
Financial data (yr. ended 7/31/05): Assets, $5,514,767 (M); expenditures, $583,453; qualifying distributions, $534,100; giving activities include $534,100 for 29 grants (high: $250,000; low: $100).
Fields of interest: Higher education; Medical school/education; Education; Human services.
Limitations: Applications not accepted. Giving primarily in NC. No grants to individuals.
Application information: Contributes only to pre-selected organizations.
Officers: David S. Brody, Pres.; Hyman J. Brody, V.P.; Laura C. Brody, Secy.; Stacy C. Brody, Treas.
EIN: 560858144
Selected grants: The following grants were reported in 2005.
$2,500 to Duke University, Durham, NC.
$2,200 to Lenoir Committee of 100, Kinston, NC. 2 grants: $200, $2,000
$2,200 to Lenoir Community College, Kinston, NC. 2 grants: $1,000, $1,200
$1,500 to United Way, Lenoir/Greene, Kinston, NC.
$1,000 to Nature Conservancy, Durham, NC.
$500 to North Carolina Museum of Art Foundation, Raleigh, NC.
$250 to Alzheimers Association, Raleigh, NC.
$100 to Salvation Army, NC.

7326
The A. Pat and Kathryne L. Brown Foundation, Inc. ☆

c/o Thomas F. Foster
P.O. Box 1550
High Point, NC   27261-1550

Established in 1991 in NC.
Donor: Kathryne L. Brown†.
Foundation type: Independent foundation.
Financial data (yr. ended 12/31/05): Assets, $5,048,199 (M); expenditures, $382,996; qualifying distributions, $343,000; giving activities include $343,000 for grants.
Purpose and activities: Giving for education, hospitals, and human services.
Fields of interest: Higher education; Education; Hospitals (general); Human services; Christian agencies & churches.
Limitations: Applications not accepted. Giving primarily in NC. No grants to individuals.
Application information: Contributes only to pre-selected organizations.
   Board meeting date(s): May and Nov.
Officers and Directors:* David L. Maynard,* Pres.; W. Calvin Reynolds,* V.P.; Norma Smith,* Secy.; Thomas F. Foster,* Treas.; Tom Blount; Ann Busby; Jeff Horney.
EIN: 561761750
Selected grants: The following grants were reported in 2005.
$50,200 to YMCA. 2 grants: $25,000, $25,200
$25,200 to Baptist Retirement Homes of North Carolina, Winston-Salem, NC.
$25,200 to High Point Regional Hospital, High Point, NC.

$25,000 to Community Clinic of High Point, High Point, NC.
$25,000 to North Carolina Shakespeare Festival, High Point, NC.
$14,000 to Presbyterian Home, Quitman, GA.
$10,000 to Westchester Academy, High Point, NC.
$5,000 to Communities in Schools, Alexandria, VA.
$5,000 to United Way.

7327
Frank E. Brown Trust 1 ◇ ☆

c/o Wachovia Bank, N.A.
100 N. Main St.
Winston-Salem, NC   27150-6732

Established in 2005 in NC.
Foundation type: Independent foundation.
Financial data (yr. ended 12/31/05): Assets, $254,509 (M); gifts received, $1,261,585; expenditures, $1,027,910; qualifying distributions, $1,021,796; giving activities include $1,021,796 for 1 grant (high: $1,021,796).
Fields of interest: Higher education.
Limitations: Applications not accepted. Giving primarily in NC. No grants to individuals.
Application information: Contributes only to pre-selected organizations.
Trustee: Wachovia Bank, N.A.
EIN: 546161145

7328
Broyhill Family Foundation, Inc. ◇

P.O. Box 500, Golfview Park
Lenoir, NC   28645-0472
Contact: Sheila Triplett-Brady, Exec. Dir.

Incorporated in 1945 in NC.
Donors: Broyhill Furniture Industries, Inc.; James E. Broyhill; Paul H. Broyhill.
Foundation type: Independent foundation.
Financial data (yr. ended 12/31/05): Assets, $45,630,976 (M); expenditures, $2,344,318; qualifying distributions, $2,144,699; giving activities include $1,717,498 for grants.
Purpose and activities: Support for education, health, youth development and welfare, civic and community services, and the free enterprise system.
Fields of interest: Museums; Arts; Child development, education; Higher education; Health care; Health organizations, association; Recreation, parks/playgrounds; Human services; Children/youth, services; Child development, services; Federated giving programs; Public policy, research; Government/public administration.
Type of support: Program development; Scholarship funds.
Limitations: Giving primarily in NC, with emphasis on Caldwell County. No grants to individuals.
Application information: Brief initial inquiry with SASE.
   Initial approach: Letter
   Copies of proposal: 1
   Deadline(s): None
   Board meeting date(s): Quarterly
   Final notification: Within calendar year
Officers and Directors:* Paul H. Broyhill,* Chair.; M. Hunt Broyhill,* Pres.; Sheila Triplett-Brady, Exec. Dir.
Number of staff: 2 full-time professional.
EIN: 566054119
Selected grants: The following grants were reported in 2004.

$200,000 to Caldwell Community College and
Technical Institute, Lenoir, NC.

$109,000 to Caldwell Arts Council, Lenoir, NC. For
donation of building.

$66,668 to Converse College, Spartanburg, SC.

$60,000 to Medical Foundation of North Carolina,
Chapel Hill, NC.

$58,000 to Lenoir-Rhyne College, Hickory, NC. For
Broyhill Leadership.

$50,000 to First Baptist Church, NC.

$50,000 to Tomorrows America Foundation,
Charlotte, NC.

$50,000 to Wake Forest University, Winston-Salem,
NC. For Baptist Medical Center.

$34,000 to Lees-McRae College, Banner Elk, NC.

$25,000 to Hickory Day School, Hickory, NC.

7329
The Joseph M. Bryan Foundation of Greater Greensboro, Inc. ✧
P.O. Box 14829
Greensboro, NC 27415
Contact: Carole W. Bruce, Secy.-Treas.

Established in 1986 in NC.
Donor: Joseph M. Bryan.
Foundation type: Independent foundation.
Financial data (yr. ended 12/31/03): Assets,
$111,769,286 (M); expenditures, $3,963,127;
qualifying distributions, $8,921,976; giving
activities include $1,866,688 for 42 grants (high:
$450,750; low: $25; average: $1,000–$75,000),
$1,017,738 for 2 foundation-administered
programs and $5,571,536 for loans/
program-related investments.
Purpose and activities: Support for the economic,
cultural and recreational enrichment of the lives of
the citizens of the greater Greensboro, NC, area; a
primary purpose of the foundation is the making of
improvements to and enhancements of the Joseph
M. and Kathleen Bryan Park.
Fields of interest: Arts; Higher education;
Recreation.
Type of support: Program-related investments/
loans.
Limitations: Applications not accepted. Giving
limited to NC. No grants to individuals.
Application information: Contributes only to
pre-selected organizations.
Officers and Directors:* David DeVries, Chair.; E.S.
Melvin,* Pres.; Carole W. Bruce,* Secy.-Treas.;
Shirley Frye; Michael W. Haley; H. Michael Weaver.
EIN: 561548051
Selected grants: The following grants were reported
in 2004.
$300,000 to United Way.
$200,000 to Guilford College, Greensboro, NC.
$200,000 to YMCA.
$60,000 to United Arts Council, Saint Paul, MN.
$50,000 to Girl Scouts of the U.S.A..
$37,500 to Action Greensboro, Greensboro, NC.
$20,000 to Room at the Inn, Charlotte, NC.
$15,000 to Eastern Music Festival, Greensboro,
NC.
$10,000 to Greensboro College, Greensboro, NC.
$10,000 to Guilford Battleground Company,
Greensboro, NC.

7330
R. A. Bryan Foundation, Inc. ✧
400 Patetown Rd.
P.O. Drawer 919
Goldsboro, NC 27533-0919 (919) 734-8400
Contact: R.A. Bryan, Jr., Pres.

Established in 1956 in NC.
Donors: R.A. Bryan, Jr.; Ruby M. Bryan†; Aviation
Fuel Terminals, Inc.; Ridgewood, Inc.; T.A. Loving
Co.
Foundation type: Independent foundation.
Financial data (yr. ended 12/31/05): Assets,
$17,429,454 (M); expenditures, $978,596;
qualifying distributions, $806,349; giving activities
include $797,099 for 59 grants (high: $431,650;
low: $200).
Purpose and activities: Giving to public day schools,
higher education, youth services, and health and
medical organizations.
Fields of interest: Arts; Higher education; Animals/
wildlife, preservation/protection; Health care;
Health organizations, association; Cancer; Medical
research, institute; Cancer research; Human
services; Christian agencies & churches.
Type of support: General/operating support;
Continuing support; Annual campaigns; Capital
campaigns; Building/renovation; Endowments;
Program development; Scholarship funds;
Research.
Limitations: Applications not accepted. Giving
primarily in NC. No grants to individuals.
Publications: Annual report.
Application information: Contributes only to
pre-selected organizations.
Officers and Trustees:* R.A. Bryan, Jr.,* Pres.;
Stephen C. Bryan,* V.P.; Thomas R. Howell,*
Treas.; Ann M. Bryan; R.A. Bryan III.
EIN: 566044320

7331
J. W. Burress Foundation ✧
380 Knollwood St., Ste. 610
Winston-Salem, NC 27103
Contact: John W. Burress III, Pres.

Established in 1986 in NC.
Donors: J.W. Burress, Inc.; John W. Burress III; Mary
Louise Walker Burress.
Foundation type: Company-sponsored foundation.
Financial data (yr. ended 12/31/04): Assets, $0
(M); expenditures, $417,179; qualifying
distributions, $405,957; giving activities include
$405,957 for grants.
Purpose and activities: The foundation supports
organizations involved with arts and culture,
education, human services, and Christianity.
Fields of interest: Arts; Education; Human services;
Federated giving programs; Christian agencies &
churches.
Limitations: Giving primarily in NC. No grants to
individuals.
Application information: Application form not
required.
Initial approach: Proposal
Deadline(s): None
Officers: John W. Burress III, Pres. and Treas.; Sue
Burress Wall, Secy.
EIN: 561554131

7332
N. R. Burroughs Educational Fund ✧
c/o BB&T
P.O. Box 2907
Wilson, NC 27894-2907
Application address: c/o Lynanne Newman, P.O. Box
5228, Martinsville, VA 24115; tel.: (276) 666-3198

Established in 1983 in VA.
Donor: Burroughs Scholarship Trust.
Foundation type: Independent foundation.
Financial data (yr. ended 6/30/05): Assets,
$5,684,325 (M); gifts received, $113,191;
expenditures, $758,643; qualifying distributions,
$700,500; giving activities include $697,933 for
244 grants to individuals (high: $3,000; low:
$1,350).
Purpose and activities: Students loans to qualified,
deserving, and credit-worthy residents of the
Martinsville, VA, area.
Type of support: Student loans—to individuals.
Limitations: Giving limited to residents who live
within a 200-mile radius of Martinsville, VA.
Application information: Application form required.
Initial approach: Letter or telephone
Deadline(s): None
Trustees: Opal Gilbert; Ron Holt; Lynanne H.
Newman; Ricky L. Scott; BB&T.
EIN: 521303602

7333
Burroughs Wellcome Fund ▼ ✧
21 T. W. Alexander Dr.
P.O. Box 13901
Research Triangle Park, NC 27709-3901
(919) 991-5100
Contact: Russ Campbell III, Comms. Off.
FAX: (919) 991-5160; E-mail: info@bwfund.org;
Contact info. for Russ Campbell III tel.: (919)
991-5119; Fax: (919) 991-5179, E-mail:
rcampbell@bwfund.org; URL: http://
www.bwfund.org

Incorporated in 1955 in NY.
Donors: Burroughs Wellcome Co.; The Wellcome
Trust.
Foundation type: Independent foundation.
Financial data (yr. ended 8/31/05): Assets,
$702,980,765 (M); expenditures, $36,040,587;
qualifying distributions, $28,181,718; giving
activities include $24,350,797 for 491 grants (high:
$500,000; low: $800; average: $20,000–
$125,000).
Purpose and activities: The fund is an independent
private foundation dedicated to advancing the
medical sciences by supporting research and other
scientific and educational activities. Major program
areas include: basic biomedical sciences, infectious
diseases, interfaces between physical and
biological sciences, translational research, and
science education.
Fields of interest: Medical research, institute;
Biological sciences.
International interests: Canada.
Type of support: Program development; Research.
Limitations: Giving limited to the U.S. and Canada.
No grants to individuals, or for building or
endowment funds, equipment, operating budgets,
continuing support, annual campaigns, deficit
financing, publications, conferences, or matching
gifts; no loans.
Publications: Annual report (including application
guidelines); Informational brochure (including

application guidelines); Newsletter; Occasional report.

Application information: See fund Web site for application information. Application form required.

Deadline(s): Varies depending on the program

Board meeting date(s): Feb., Apr., July, and Oct.

Final notification: Varies

Officers and Directors: * Enriqueta C. Bond, Ph.D.*, Pres.; Scott G. Schoedler, V.P., Finance; Carlos J. Bustamante, Ph.D.; Gail H. Cassell, Ph.D.; Stephen D. Corman; Marye Anne Fox, Ph.D.; Phil Gold, M.D., Ph.D.; Albert James Hudspeth, M.D., Ph.D.; I. George Miller, M.D.; Mary Lou Pardue, Ph.D.; Jerome F. Strauss III, M.D., Ph.D.; Judith L. Swain, M.D.; Philip R. Tracy, J.D.; Jean D. Wilson, M.D.

Number of staff: 17 full-time professional; 4 full-time support; 2 part-time support.

EIN: 237225395

Selected grants: The following grants were reported in 2005.

$2,500,000 to North Carolina Science, Mathematics and Technology Education Center, Research Triangle Park, NC. For general support.

$750,000 to Mayo Clinic, Rochester, MN. For Clinical Scientist Award in Translational Research for Novel antiapoptotic therapies for sepsis.

$750,000 to University of Michigan, Medical School, Ann Arbor, MI. For Clinical Scientist Award in Translational Research for Acute lung injury after SCT: from laboratory insights to novel strategies for diagnosis and treatment.

$750,000 to Vanderbilt University, School of Medicine, Nashville, TN. For Clinical Scientist Award in Translational Research for Immunology and cell biology of human metapneumovirus infections.

$466,473 to Public School Forum of North Carolina, Raleigh, NC. For International Studies Program and the North Carolina Institute for Educational Policymakers.

$400,000 to Northwestern University, Feinberg School of Medicine, Evanston, IL. For Investigators in Pathogenesis of Infectious Disease grant for research, Coordination of herpes virus assembly and transport in axons of sensory neurons.

$240,000 to Marine Biological Laboratory, Woods Hole, MA. For interdisciplinary physiology course.

$180,000 to Duke University, Durham, NC. For Student Science Enrichment Program grant for Techtronics: Hands-on exploration of technology in everyday life.

$10,000 to Society of Toxicology, Reston, VA. For graduate students to attend society's annual meeting.

$5,000 to North Carolina Central University, Durham, NC.

7334

Alice Butler Foundation ✧

(formerly J. D. and Alice Butler Memorial Scholarship Foundation)

c/o Wachovia Bank, N.A.

100 N. Main St., 13th Fl.

Winston-Salem, NC 27150

Application address: c/o Principal, Deerfield Beach Senior High School, 910 S.W. 15th St., Deerfield Beach, FL 33461

Established in 1987 in FL.

Foundation type: Independent foundation.

Financial data (yr. ended 8/31/05): Assets, $9,810,146 (M); expenditures, $559,881; qualifying distributions, $467,677; giving activities include $467,677 for 820 grants to individuals (high: $34,357; low: $49).

Purpose and activities: Scholarships only to graduates of Deerfield Beach Senior High School, FL.

Type of support: Scholarships—to individuals.

Limitations: Giving limited to residents of Deerfield Beach, FL.

Application information: Application form required.

Initial approach: Letter requesting application form

Trustee: Wachovia Bank, N.A.

EIN: 596878169

7335

The Cannon Foundation, Inc. ▼ ✧

P.O. Box 548

Concord, NC 28026-0548 (704) 786-8216

Contact: Frank Davis, Exec. Dir.

URL: http://www.thecannonfoundationinc.org

Incorporated in 1943 in NC.

Donors: Charles A. Cannon†; Cannon Mills Co.

Foundation type: Independent foundation.

Financial data (yr. ended 9/30/05): Assets, $181,705,242 (M); expenditures, $10,343,848; qualifying distributions, $9,427,475; giving activities include $9,100,000 for 123 grants (high: $2,127,778; low: $250; average: $10,000–$100,000).

Purpose and activities: Support for hospitals, secondary and higher education, and cultural programs; grants also for Protestant church support, and social service and youth agencies.

Fields of interest: Arts; Secondary school/education; Higher education; Hospitals (general); Human services; Children/youth, services; Protestant agencies & churches.

Type of support: Capital campaigns; Building/renovation; Equipment; Debt reduction; Matching/challenge support.

Limitations: Giving primarily in NC, with emphasis on the Cabarrus County area. No grants to individuals, or for operating budgets, seed money, emergency funds, deficit financing, land acquisition, endowment funds, demonstration projects, research, publications, conferences, seminars, scholarships, or fellowships; no loans.

Publications: Application guidelines; Informational brochure (including application guidelines).

Application information: Initial contacts by E-mail are not accepted. Application form required.

Initial approach: Letter or telephone

Copies of proposal: 1

Deadline(s): Jan. 5, Apr. 5, July 5, and Oct. 5

Board meeting date(s): Mar., June, Sept., and Dec.

Final notification: Within 10-12 weeks following each deadline date

Officers and Directors: * W.C. Cannon, Jr.,* Pres.; W.S. Fisher,* V.P.; Dan L. Gray,* Secy.-Treas.; Frank Davis, Exec. Dir.; William M. Connolly; T.M. Grady; Mariam C. Hayes; R.C. Hayes; George W. Liles, Jr.; Elizabeth L. Quick.

Number of staff: 2 full-time professional; 2 full-time support.

EIN: 566042532

Selected grants: The following grants were reported in 2005.

$2,127,778 to NorthEast Medical Center, Concord, NC. For medical technology upgrades.

$500,000 to American Red Cross, Concord, NC. For Hurricane Katrina emergency relief.

$500,000 to Charles A. Cannon, Jr. Memorial Hospital, Linville, NC. For debt restructuring.

$300,000 to YMCA, Stanly County Family, Albemarle, NC. For facility renovation.

$250,000 to Campbell University, Buies Creek, NC. For Convocation Center construction.

$250,000 to Tryon Palace Council of Friends, New Bern, NC. For North Carolina History Education Center site preparation.

$50,000 to North Carolina Center for Public Policy Research, Raleigh, NC. For North Carolina Community College System evaluation.

$35,000 to Davidson Medical Ministries Clinic, Lexington, NC. For durable medical equipment.

$35,000 to Granville County Historical Society, Oxford, NC. For exhibit construction.

$25,000 to REACH of Jackson County, Sylva, NC. For facility expansion.

7336

Cape Fear Memorial Foundation

2508 Independence Blvd., Ste. 200

Wilmington, NC 28412

Contact: Garry A. Garris, Pres.

FAX: (910) 452-5879; *E-mail:* beth@cfmfdn.org

Established in 1996 in NC; converted from the sale of Cape Fear Memorial Hospital to Columbia/HCA.

Donor: Cape Fear Memorial Health Care Corp.

Foundation type: Independent foundation.

Financial data (yr. ended 6/30/05): Assets, $57,344,160 (M); expenditures, $2,774,632; qualifying distributions, $2,588,195; giving activities include $2,259,300 for 47+ grants (high: $100,000).

Purpose and activities: Giving for health and medical needs.

Fields of interest: Education; Health care; Human services.

Type of support: General/operating support; Continuing support; Income development; Management development/capacity building; Capital campaigns; Building/renovation; Equipment; Land acquisition; Debt reduction; Program development; Publication; Seed money; Curriculum development; Technical assistance; Matching/challenge support.

Limitations: Giving limited to southeastern NC, generally within a 50-mile radius of Wilmington, NC. No grants to individuals.

Publications: Application guidelines; Informational brochure (including application guidelines).

Application information: 1 original and 1 electronic copy of proposal must be submitted. Application form required.

Initial approach: Letter

Copies of proposal: 2

Deadline(s): Jan. 15 and July 15

Board meeting date(s): Varies

Final notification: Approx. 90 days

Officers and Board Members: * R.T. Sinclair, Jr., M.D.*, Chair.; W. Carter Mebane III,* Vice-Chair.; Garry A. Garris,* Pres. and Treas.; Agnes R. Beane,* Secy.; William H. Cameron; J. Richard Corbett, M.D., F.A.C.R.; James D. Hundley, M.D., F.A.C.O.S; Ronald Sinclair; Robert F. Warwick; Richard L. Woodbury.

Number of staff: 1 full-time professional; 2 part-time support.

EIN: 561974747

Selected grants: The following grants were reported in 2003.

$256,000 to New Hanover County Partnership for Children, Wilmington, NC.

$100,000 to Wilmington Health Access for Teens, Wilmington, NC.

$95,000 to Domestic Violence Shelter and Services, Wilmington, NC.

$95,000 to Elderhaus, Wilmington, NC.

$90,000 to American Red Cross, Cape Fear Chapter, Wilmington, NC.

$90,000 to Black River Health Services, Burgaw, NC.

$90,000 to University of North Carolina, Chapel Hill, NC.

$85,000 to Coastal Horizons Center, Wilmington, NC.

$70,000 to Pender County Schools, Burgaw, NC.

$65,000 to Yahweh Center, Wilmington, NC.

7337

The Cemala Foundation, Inc.
330 S. Greene St., Ste. 101
Greensboro, NC 27401
Contact: Susan Schwartz, Exec. Dir.
FAX: (336) 272-8153; E-mail: cemala@cemala.org;
Additional e-mail address: sschwartz@cemala.org;
URL: http://www.cemala.org

Established in 1986 in NC.
Donors: Martha A. Cone†; Ceasar Cone II†.
Foundation type: Independent foundation.
Financial data (yr. ended 12/31/04): Assets, $43,375,531 (M); expenditures, $2,865,498; qualifying distributions, $2,742,661; giving activities include $2,448,262 for 53+ grants (high: $52,700).
Purpose and activities: The foundation's primary purpose is to continue a family tradition of commitment to enhancing the quality of life of the community through grants to qualified charitable organizations.
Fields of interest: Performing arts; Arts; Education, association; Child development, education; Higher education; Adult education—literacy, basic skills & GED; Education, reading; Health care; Health organizations, association; Housing/shelter, development; Human services; Children/youth, services; Residential/custodial care, hospices; Minorities/immigrants, centers/services; Minorities.
Type of support: Emergency funds; General/operating support; Capital campaigns; Building/renovation; Equipment; Land acquisition; Program development; Conferences/seminars; Seed money; Fellowships; Internship funds; Matching/challenge support.
Limitations: Giving limited to Guilford County, NC, and projects with statewide benefit. No support for sectarian religious activities. No grants to individuals or for annual campaigns, endowments or requests under $1,000.
Publications: Application guidelines.
Application information: The fall 2006 grant cycle is suspended. Please visit the foundation Web site for information regarding grant guidelines. Application available on the foundation Web site. The foundation does not accept online submissions of applications. Application form required.
 Initial approach: Letter or telephone
 Copies of proposal: 1
 Deadline(s): Mar. 1 and Sept. 1

Board meeting date(s): May and Nov.
Final notification: Within 3 months
Officers and Directors:* Martha C. Wright,* Chair.; Ceasar Cone III,* Vice-Chair.; Merritt Richmond,* Secy.; Walter "Butch" Cone, Treas.; Susan Schwartz, Exec. Dir.; John L. Bakane; Carole W. Bruce; Janet G. Cone; Katherine K. Richmond; Matthew D. Richmond.
Number of staff: 2 full-time professional; 1 full-time support.
EIN: 561528982
Selected grants: The following grants were reported in 2004.

$1,436,896 to Action Greensboro, Greensboro, NC.

$50,000 to North Carolina Museum of Art, Raleigh, NC.

$41,000 to United Arts Council of Greensboro, Greensboro, NC. 2 grants: $26,000, $15,000

$25,000 to Eastern Music Festival, Greensboro, NC.

$20,000 to Triad Stage, Greensboro, NC.

$10,000 to Greensboro Childrens Museum, Greensboro, NC.

7338

Charlotte Merchants Foundation ◇ ☆
c/o Wachovia Bank, N.A.
100 N. Main St., 13th Fl.
Winston-Salem, NC 27150
Contact: Palmer Wilson

Established in 1994 in NC.
Foundation type: Independent foundation.
Financial data (yr. ended 12/31/05): Assets, $17,231,950 (M); expenditures, $1,011,899; qualifying distributions, $956,472; giving activities include $858,000 for grants.
Fields of interest: Education; Human services; YM/YWCAs & YM/YWHAs; Children/youth, services.
Limitations: Giving primarily in Mecklenburg County and Charlotte, NC. No grants to individuals.
Application information: Application form required.
 Initial approach: Letter
 Copies of proposal: 1
 Board meeting date(s): June and Dec.
Trustee: Wachovia Bank, N.A.
EIN: 561853632

7339

The Coffey Foundation, Inc. ◇
P.O. Box 1170
Lenoir, NC 28645
Contact: Harriet Hailey
Application address: 406 Norwood St. S.W., Lenoir, NC 28645

Established about 1979 in NC.
Donor: Harold F. Coffey Trust.
Foundation type: Independent foundation.
Financial data (yr. ended 11/30/05): Assets, $9,265,636 (M); expenditures, $594,611; qualifying distributions, $411,704; giving activities include $153,500 for 27 grants (high: $31,665; low: $1,000), and $252,000 for 37 grants to individuals (high: $10,500; low: $3,500).
Purpose and activities: Giving for higher education, youth, and social services; support also for student loans and individual scholarships.
Fields of interest: Higher education; Education; Hospitals (general); Food services; Human services; Children/youth, services; Residential/custodial

care, hospices; Aging, centers/services; Women, centers/services; Federated giving programs.
Type of support: General/operating support; Scholarships—to individuals.
Limitations: Giving primarily in Caldwell County, NC; scholarships limited to residents of Caldwell County.
Application information: Application forms for student grants available at high schools in Caldwell County, NC. Application form required. Application form required.
 Deadline(s): Apr. 15 for scholarships
Trustees: Gary W. Bradford; Charles E. Dobbin; Leslie D. Hines, Jr.; Betty Lou Miller; Wayne J. Miller, Jr.
EIN: 566047501
Selected grants: The following grants were reported in 2005.

$15,000 to Caldwell County Yokefellow, Lenoir, NC.

$10,000 to Shelter Home of Caldwell County, Lenoir, NC.

$10,000 to United Way of Caldwell County, Lenoir, NC.

$5,500 to Caldwell County Hospice, Lenoir, NC.

$5,000 to Caldwell County Schools, Lenoir, NC.

$5,000 to Grandfather Home for Children, Banner Elk, NC.

$5,000 to Riddle Institute, Morganton, NC.

$4,000 to Helping Hands Clinic of Caldwell County, Lenoir, NC.

$3,000 to Crossnore School, Crossnore, NC.

$3,000 to South Caldwell Christian Ministries, Granite Falls, NC.

7340

The Thomas B. and Robertha K. Coleman Foundation, Inc. ◇ ☆
P.O. Box 1169
New Bern, NC 28563

Established in 1998 in NC.
Donor: Robertha K. Coleman.
Foundation type: Independent foundation.
Financial data (yr. ended 12/31/05): Assets, $2,714,012 (M); expenditures, $394,855; qualifying distributions, $360,632; giving activities include $359,950 for 24 grants (high: $250,000; low: $30).
Fields of interest: Historic preservation/historical societies; Arts; Education; Environment; Health care; Human services; Christian agencies & churches.
Type of support: Building/renovation.
Limitations: Applications not accepted. Giving primarily in New Bern, NC. No grants to individuals.
Application information: Contributes only to pre-selected organizations.
Officers: Katherine C. Haroldson, Pres. and Secy.; Thomas Brooks Coleman III, V.P.; John O. Haroldson, Treas.
EIN: 562086113
Selected grants: The following grants were reported in 2004.

$27,150 to Tryon Palace Council of Friends, New Bern, NC.

$5,000 to North Carolina Symphony, Raleigh, NC.

$4,500 to East Carolina University, Greenville, NC.

$1,700 to Merci Clinic, New Bern, NC.

$1,000 to American Red Cross, New Bern, NC.

$500 to Coastal Womens Shelter, New Bern, NC.

$500 to North Carolina Museum of Art, Raleigh, NC.

$250 to Craven Community College, New Bern, NC.

$250 to North Carolina Shakespeare Festival, High Point, NC.

$100 to Craven Arts Council and Gallery, New Bern, NC.

7341

Robert & Sara S. Comloquoy Charitable Foundation ✧

c/o Wachovia Bank, N.A.
100 N. Main St., 13th Fl.
Winston Salem, NC 27150

Established in PA.
Foundation type: Independent foundation.
Financial data (yr. ended 12/31/05): Assets, $10,096,199 (M); expenditures, $415,414; qualifying distributions, $376,313; giving activities include $376,313 for 56 grants (high: $29,164; low: $2,601).
Purpose and activities: Support primarily for education, hospitals, human services, and Protestant churches.
Fields of interest: Elementary/secondary education; Higher education; Hospitals (general); Health organizations; Youth development; Human services; Protestant agencies & churches.
Type of support: General/operating support.
Limitations: Applications not accepted. Giving primarily in PA, with emphasis on Reading, Philadelphia, Pottsville, and St. Davids; some giving also in Boyne City, MI. No grants to individuals.
Application information: Contributes only to pre-selected organizations.
Trustees: Philip C. Herr II; Wachovia Bank, N.A.
EIN: 236604053

7342

Community Foundation of Gaston County, Inc.

P.O. Box 123
Gastonia, NC 28053 (704) 864-0927
Contact: John A. Edgerton, Exec. Dir.
FAX: (704) 869-0222; E-mail: info@cfgaston.org;
Additional E-mail: jedgerton@cfgaston.org;
URL: http://www.cfgaston.org

Incorporated in 1978 in NC.
Foundation type: Community foundation.
Financial data (yr. ended 12/31/05): Assets, $55,561,824 (M); gifts received, $5,704,046; expenditures, $7,793,692; giving activities include $7,067,421 for 267 grants (high: $3,175,312; low: $59).
Purpose and activities: The foundation is the primary steward of philanthropic giving by connecting donors with community needs to enhance the lives of present and future generations.
Fields of interest: Community development.
Type of support: Curriculum development; Capital campaigns; Building/renovation; Equipment; Program development; Seed money.
Limitations: Giving primarily in Gaston County, NC. No support for private schools or religious organizations for religious purposes. No grants to individuals (except for scholarship funds), or for operating costs of established programs, exchange programs, fellowships, annual campaigns, deficit financing, continuing support, technical assistance, professorships, or internships.
Publications: Annual report; Informational brochure; Newsletter.
Application information: Visit foundation Web site for application guidelines. Full proposal by invitation

only, after consideration of letter of inquiry. Application form required.
Initial approach: Letter of inquiry
Copies of proposal: 1
Deadline(s): Jan. 1 and July 1 for letter of inquiry; Jan. 31 and July 31 for formal proposal
Board meeting date(s): Quarterly
Final notification: Sept. 30
Officers and Directors:* Henry H. Massey, Jr.,* Pres.; Natalie M. Tindol,* V.P.; May C. Barger,* Secy.; Ernest W. Sumner,* Treas.; John A. Edgerton, Exec. Dir.; Susanne D. Albright; William P. Carstarphen; John L. Fraley, Jr.; Hon. Ralph C. Gingles, Jr.; George F. Henry III; W. Duke Kimbrell; John K. Long; Gene R. Matthews II; Dr. Charles J. Meakin III; Johan T. Newcombe; H. William Palmer; Charles W. Pearson, Jr.; Kim S. Price; Ralph S. Robinson, Jr.; Ben R. Rudisill; Wayne F. Shovelin; T.J. Solomon II; Fred P. Spach, Jr.; Elizabeth N. Sumner; Elizabeth G. Wren.
Number of staff: 3 full-time professional; 1 full-time support.
EIN: 581340834

7343

Community Foundation of Greater Greensboro, Inc. ✧

(formerly The Foundation of Greater Greensboro, Inc.)
Foundation Place
330 S. Greene St., Ste. 100
Greensboro, NC 27401 (336) 379-9100
Contact: H. Walker Sanders, Pres.; For grant applications: Tara Sandercock, V.P., Progs.; For scholarship applications: Michiko Stavert, Dir., Scholarships
FAX: (336) 378-0725; E-mail: info@cfgg.org; Application address: P.O. Box 20444, Greensboro, NC 27420; Grant application E-mail: grants@cfgg.org; URL: http://www.cfgg.org
Scholarship application E-mail: mstavert@cfgg.org

Established in 1983 in NC.
Foundation type: Community foundation.
Financial data (yr. ended 12/31/04): Assets, $83,379,047 (M); gifts received, $22,971,457; expenditures, $15,969,741; giving activities include $13,390,745 for grants.
Purpose and activities: The foundation is dedicated to strengthening the community for both present and future generations by promoting philanthropy, building a collection of endowment funds, and serving as a leader in shaping effective responses to community issues and opportunities in the greater Greensboro, NC, area.
Fields of interest: Humanities; Arts; Education; Environment; Health care; Health organizations, association; AIDS; Housing/shelter, development; Children/youth, services; Human services; Community development, neighborhood development; Community development; Government/public administration.
Type of support: Equipment; Land acquisition; Emergency funds; Program development; Conferences/seminars; Seed money; Technical assistance; Consulting services; Program evaluation; Program-related investments/loans; Employee-related scholarships; Matching/challenge support.
Limitations: Giving primarily in the greater Greensboro, NC, area. No support for partisan purposes, or for programs in which religious teachings are an integral part. No grants to

individuals (except for scholarships), or for capital campaigns, multi-year commitments, debt retirement, building funds, operating budgets or endowments.
Publications: Application guidelines; Annual report; Financial statement; Grants list; Informational brochure; Newsletter; Program policy statement.
Application information: Visit foundation Web site for application Cover Sheet and guidelines. Faxed or e-mailed applications are not accepted. The foundation strongly encourages attending a Grantseeker Orientation Workshop held approximately one month prior to each proposal deadline; registration is required. Application form required.
Initial approach: Mail Cover Sheet with proposal, and attachments
Copies of proposal: 1
Deadline(s): Feb. 15, June 15, and Oct. 13
Board meeting date(s): Monthly
Final notification: Late Apr., late Aug., and mid-Dec.
Officers and Directors:* R. David Sprinkle,* Chair.; Henry E. Frye,* Chair.-Elect; H. Walker Sanders, Pres.; Lisa Martin, V.P., Finance and Admin.; Tara McKenzie Sandercock, V.P., Progs.; Patrick A. Weiner, V.P., Donor Svcs. and Devel.; Nettie L. Coad,* Secy.; Craven Williams,* Treas.; John L. Bakane; David Ball; Louise F. Brady; Chester H. "Trip" Brown, Jr.; Lisa Bullock; Molly Carrison; Elizabeth W. "Betty" Cone; Luck Davidson; Eunice Dudley; Jed Dunn; William F. Geter; Patrice A. Hinnant; Tomasita Jacubowitz; Ron Johnson; Randall Kaplan; Carter Leinster; Paul H. Livingston, Jr.; Lee Lloyd; Robert E. "Bobby" Long; Michael T. Marshall; Robert L. Powell; Norman Samet; Mac Sims; Linda E. Sloan; Melvin C. Swann, Jr.; Stuart A. Taylor; Jerry R. Tolley; James T. "Butch" Williams, Jr.; Otis Wilson; David Worth; Ann Zuraw.
Number of staff: 8 full-time professional; 3 part-time professional.
EIN: 561380249

7344

Community Foundation of Henderson County, Inc.

401 N. Main St., 3rd Fl.
P.O. Box 1108
Hendersonville, NC 28793 (828) 697-6224
Contact: McCray V. Benson, C.E.O. and Pres.
FAX: (828) 696-4026;
E-mail: info@cfhendersoncounty.org; Grant application E-mail: kmcconnell@cfhendersoncounty.org; URL: http://www.cfhendersoncounty.org
Scholarship E-mail: arobinson@cfhendersoncounty.org

Incorporated in 1982 in NC.
Foundation type: Community foundation.
Financial data (yr. ended 6/30/05): Assets, $55,532,411 (M); gifts received, $7,739,602; expenditures, $3,136,131; giving activities include $2,038,029 for 206 grants (high: $227,000; low: $50), $218,843 for 136 grants to individuals (high: $5,000; low: $500), and $354,176 for 1 foundation-administered program.
Purpose and activities: The foundation exists to enrich the quality of life in the greater Henderson County, NC, area, through building and increasing endowments in perpetuity.
Fields of interest: Arts; Child development, education; Higher education; Education;

Environment; Health care; Disasters, Hurricane Katrina; Child development, services; Aging, centers/services; Homeless, human services; Human services; Community development; Public affairs; Aging; Homeless.
Type of support: Equipment; Emergency funds; Program development; Publication; Seed money; Curriculum development; Scholarship funds; Technical assistance; Scholarships—to individuals; Matching/challenge support.
Limitations: Giving limited to the Henderson County, NC, area. No support for religious purposes. No grants to individuals (except for scholarships), or for capital campaigns, annual campaigns, fundraising events, or augmenting endowments; no loans.
Publications: Application guidelines; Annual report; Informational brochure; Newsletter.
Application information: Visit foundation Web site for application guidelines. Scholarship availability is announced in Nov. Application form required.
  Initial approach: Letter or telephone
  Copies of proposal: 2
  Deadline(s): Mar. 1, June 1, Sept. 1, and Dec. 1; Mar. 1 for scholarships
  Board meeting date(s): Monthly
  Final notification: 3 months
Officers and Directors:* Jan Shefter,* Chair.; Rick Austin,* Vice-Chair.; McCray V. Benson, C.E.O. and Pres.; Kathryn McConnell, V.P., Community Philanthropy; Crystal Reese, V.P., Finance and Admin.; Stan Duncan,* Secy.; F. Lee Thomas,* Treas.; Becky Banadyga; Susie Bender; Gus Campano; Ed Cushing; Madeline Daubert; Jim Hendrix; Jana Johnson Humleker; Pat Jones; Sharon Koffman; Sherri Metzger; Theron "Tim" Mullinax; Cheryl S. Smith; Art Stuenkel; Dirk Wilms.
Number of staff: 4 full-time professional; 2 full-time support.
EIN: 561330792
Selected grants: The following grants were reported in 2005.
$54,500 to Children and Family Resource Center of Henderson County, Hendersonville, NC.
$37,000 to Boys and Girls Club of Henderson County, Hendersonville, NC.
$25,000 to First United Methodist Church.
$20,000 to Blue Ridge Community Health Services, Hendersonville, NC.
$20,000 to First Congregational Church.
$20,000 to Henderson County Council on Aging, Hendersonville, NC. For capital project.
$18,700 to Brevard Music Center, Brevard, NC.
$15,300 to Blue Ridge Community College Education Foundation, Flat Rock, NC.
$15,000 to Emory University, School of Medicine, Atlanta, GA.
$12,899 to Arts Council of Henderson County, Hendersonville, NC. For matching funds for projects, merger consultant services and for marketing of unified arts organization.

7345
Community Foundation of Southeastern North Carolina
(formerly Cape Fear Community Foundation, Inc.)
P.O. Box 119
Wilmington, NC 28402-0119 (910) 251-3911
Contact: Stephen J. Dillon, Exec. Dir.
FAX: (910) 251-3911;
E-mail: info@communityfoundationsenc.org;
Additional E-mail:

sjdillon@communityfoundationsenc.org;
URL: http://www.communityfoundationsenc.org

Incorporated in 1987 in NC.
Foundation type: Community foundation.
Financial data (yr. ended 9/30/05): Assets, $2,435,221 (M); gifts received, $950,306; expenditures, $860,373; giving activities include $709,594 for 517 grants.
Purpose and activities: The foundation seeks to encourage and facilitate charitable giving, serve the needs of donors and client organizations, and help donors realize their charitable objectives.
Type of support: Scholarship funds; General/operating support; Continuing support; Annual campaigns; Capital campaigns; Building/renovation; Equipment; Endowments; Emergency funds; Program development; Conferences/seminars; Publication; Seed money; Curriculum development; Research; Technical assistance; Consulting services; Program-related investments/loans; In-kind gifts; Matching/challenge support.
Limitations: Applications not accepted. Giving limited to the Cape Fear, NC, area, including Bladen, Brunswick, Columbus, New Hanover, and Pender counties for discretionary giving. No grants to individuals (except for scholarships); no loans.
Publications: Annual report; Informational brochure; Newsletter.
Application information: The foundation has suspended discretionary grant applications and inquiries. Please visit foundation Web site for updates.
  Board meeting date(s): 6 times per year
Officers and Directors:* Frank B. Gibson, Jr.,* Pres.; Laurie H. Taylor,* Secy.; Anna G. Toconis,* Treas.; Stephen J. Dillon, Exec. Dir.; Jonathan Alper; Zeb E. Barnhardt; Stephen Gaskins; John A. Moore; William A. Raney, Jr.; Jasper P. Reed; Jane C. Sullivan; George Taylor; R. Bertram Williams III; Frederick Willetts III.
Number of staff: 2 full-time professional.
EIN: 561560364

7346
The Community Foundation of Western North Carolina, Inc. ▼
The BB&T Bldg., Ste. 1600
1 W. Pack Sq., P.O. Box 1888
Asheville, NC 28802 (828) 254-4960
Contact: Pat Smith, Pres.
FAX: (828) 251-2258; E-mail: dollar@cfwnc.org;
Additional E-mail: sandlin@cfwnc.org; URL: http://www.cfwnc.org
Scholarship E-mail: juarez@cfwnc.org

Incorporated in 1978 in NC.
Foundation type: Community foundation.
Financial data (yr. ended 6/30/06): Assets, $144,084,286 (M); gifts received, $14,210,160; expenditures, $8,519,687; giving activities include $6,304,636 for grants, and $516,708 for grants to individuals.
Purpose and activities: The foundation promotes and expands regional philanthropy and develops local funds that address changing needs and opportunities in the 18 counties of Western North Carolina.
Fields of interest: Arts; Education, public education; Education; Environment; Health care; Children/youth, services; Human services; Nonprofit management; Community development; Economically disadvantaged.

Type of support: General/operating support; Income development; Management development/capacity building; Equipment; Emergency funds; Program development; Curriculum development; Scholarship funds; Technical assistance; Consulting services; Program evaluation; Scholarships—to individuals; Matching/challenge support.
Limitations: Giving limited to Avery, Buncombe, Burke, Cherokee, Clay, Graham, Haywood, Henderson, Jackson, Macon, Madison, McDowell, Mitchell, Polk, Rutherford, Swain, Transylvania, and Yancey counties, NC. No support for religious organizations or sectarian purposes (except from designated funds). No grants to individuals (except for undergraduate student scholarships), or for capital campaigns, endowment funds, start-up funds, or debt retirement.
Publications: Application guidelines; Annual report; Informational brochure (including application guidelines); Newsletter.
Application information: Visit foundation Web site for application forms, guidelines, and specific deadlines. Application form required.
  Initial approach: Telephone or letter
  Copies of proposal: 1
  Deadline(s): Varies
  Board meeting date(s): Quarterly, 2nd Wed. in Feb., May, Aug., and Nov.
  Final notification: Varies
Officers and Directors:* Eleanor M. Owen,* Chair.; John G. Winkenwerder,* Vice-Chair.; Pat Smith,* Pres.; Sheryl Aikman, V.P., Devel.; Graham Keever, V.P., Finance and Admin.; Bob Wagner, V.P., Progs.; Isabel H. Nichols,* Secy.; William N. Lewin,* Treas.; Marla Adams; Louise W. Baker; William Michael Begley; E. Mitchell Betty; Janice W. Brumit; Sandra P. Byrd; Vincent D. Childress, Jr.; Donald R. Cooper; S. Jerome Crow; Paul "Bubba" Crutchfield; Barbara W. Dark; Carol Deutsch; John N. Fleming; Kerry A. Friedman; Fred F. Groce, Jr.; Kenneth M. Hughes; Lewis J. Isaac; John G. Kelso; Adelaide Daniels Key; William W. Mance, Jr.; James H. Miller; James B. Powell II; Arthea "Charlie" Reed; George D. Renfro; Robby Russell; A. Clay Smith; Michael S. Tanner; Pamela M. Turner; Kate Vogel; Laura A. Webb; Glenn W. Wilcox, Sr.; Willis H. Willey.
Number of staff: 14 full-time professional; 2 part-time professional; 2 full-time support.
EIN: 561223384
Selected grants: The following grants were reported in 2005.
$75,000 to United Methodist Church, Western North Carolina Conference, Charlotte, NC. For Disaster Response Western North Carolina Conference.
$50,000 to Caring for Children, Asheville, NC. To strengthen financial sustainability, increase volunteer support, and expand partnerships, ensuring access to programs for abused, neglected, and troubled children and their families.
$50,000 to Center for Participatory Change, Asheville, NC. To expand partnerships, build sustainable funding base, and strengthen board of directors to improve capacity building services to Latino-led grassroots organizations.
$32,000 to Haywood Waterways Association, Waynesville, NC. To provide water quality educational and monitoring programs, and to implement Haywood Watershed Action Plan.
$25,000 to Mitchell-Yancey County Partnership for Children, Burnsville, NC. To expand program providing families with tools to develop strong parenting practices and improve family relations.

$25,000 to Mountain Microenterprise Fund, Asheville, NC. For services to entrepreneurs during critical first years of opening small businesses.

$25,000 to Pisgah Legal Services, Asheville, NC. To improve affordable housing in Bucombe, Madison, Henderson, Rutherford, Polk, and Transylvania counties.

$24,000 to Mountain Housing Opportunities, Asheville, NC. For major expansion of affordable housing production and services for people in Asheville and Buncombe County.

$23,400 to Hearts With Hands, Asheville, NC. For flood relief.

$20,000 to Southeastern Jurisdictional of the United Methodist Church, Lake Junaluska, NC. To improve lake nutrient management cycle and habitat for fish and birds by creating lake edge wetland and littoral shelf.

7347
Maxwell M. Corpening, Jr. Memorial Foundation

P.O. Box 2400
Marion, NC   28752
Contact: Terri Laws
Additional address: c/o YMCA, 1388 Sugar Hill Rd., Marion, NC 28752

Established in 1972 in NC.

Donors: M.M. Corpening Foundation; Duke Power Co.; Mrs. M.M. Corpening†.

Foundation type: Operating foundation.

Financial data (yr. ended 12/31/05): Assets, $145,882 (M); gifts received, $675,237; expenditures, $668,824; qualifying distributions, $664,954; giving activities include $544,949 for 5 grants (high: $538,949; low: $500), and $111,954 for 465 grants to individuals (high: $500; low: $25; average: $100–$250).

Purpose and activities: Grants to needy individuals only in McDowell County, NC.

Fields of interest: Economically disadvantaged.

Type of support: Grants to individuals; In-kind gifts.

Limitations: Giving limited to residents of McDowell County, NC.

Application information: Mailed applications not accepted. Unsolicited requests for funds accepted from McDowell County, NC residents only. All other unsolicited requests not accepted. Application form required.

Initial approach: Personal interview with completed application
Copies of proposal: 1
Deadline(s): None
Board meeting date(s): Weekly, on Wed.
Final notification: Within 24 hours

Officers and Trustee:* Jackie Turner,* Chair.; James Wiken,* Vice-Chair.; David Wooten,* Treas.

Number of staff: 1 part-time support.

EIN: 237201488

7348
Edward E. Crutchfield Family Foundation ◇

401 S. Tryon St., Ste. 2880
Charlotte, NC   28288-0001

Established in 2000 in NC.

Donor: Edward E. Crutchfield.

Foundation type: Independent foundation.

Financial data (yr. ended 12/31/05): Assets, $2,723,609 (M); gifts received, $160; expenditures, $1,150,236; qualifying distributions, $1,146,830; giving activities include $1,141,230 for 44 grants (high: $500,000; low: $1,000; average: $10,000–$25,000).

Purpose and activities: Giving primarily for education, cancer research, children, youth, and social services, as well as for Christian organizations and Presbyterian churches.

Fields of interest: Higher education; Cancer research; Human services; Children/youth, services; Christian agencies & churches; Protestant agencies & churches.

Limitations: Applications not accepted. Giving primarily in NC. No grants to individuals.

Application information: Contributes only to pre-selected organizations.

Officers: Edward E. Crutchfield, Chair. and Pres.; Sarah Crutchfield Davis, V.P.; Edward E. Crutchfield, Jr., Secy.-Treas.

EIN: 562220389

Selected grants: The following grants were reported in 2004.

$250,000 to Asheville School, Asheville, NC.

$76,000 to Nature Conservancy, Arlington, VA. 3 grants: $1,000, $25,000, $50,000

$25,000 to United Way.

$25,000 to YMCA.

$17,500 to Linville Foundation, Linville, NC. 2 grants: $7,500, $10,000

$1,000 to Salvation Army.

7349
Cumberland Community Foundation, Inc.

308 Green St.
P.O. Box 2345
Fayetteville, NC   28302   (910) 483-4449
Contact: Mary M. Holmes, Exec. Dir.
FAX: (910) 483-2905;
E-mail: mary@cumberlandcf.org; URL: http://www.cumberlandcf.org

Established in 1980 in NC by Dr. Lucile Hutaff.

Donor: Lucile Hutaff†.

Foundation type: Community foundation.

Financial data (yr. ended 6/30/05): Assets, $28,074,571 (M); gifts received, $1,047,052; expenditures, $2,234,640; giving activities include $1,676,594 for 790 grants (high: $70,000; low: $50), and $1,350 for 1 grant to an individual.

Purpose and activities: The foundation exists to foster creative change, to encourage and test new ideas, and to work for the common good of all citizens of Cumberland County and the surrounding area by: 1) promoting local philanthropy and its rewards; 2) building and maintaining a permanent endowment for the benefit of the community; 3) providing a flexible vehicle for prospective donors with varied charitable interests and abilities to give; and 4) developing solutions to changing community needs through effective grantmaking.

Fields of interest: Museums; Performing arts; Performing arts, dance; Humanities; History/archaeology; Language/linguistics; Literature; Arts; Education, early childhood education; Child development, education; Vocational education; Higher education; Adult/continuing education; Libraries/library science; Education; Environment, natural resources; Environment; Animals/wildlife, preservation/protection; Reproductive health, family planning; Medical care, rehabilitation; Health care; Substance abuse, services; Mental health/

crisis services; AIDS; Crime/violence prevention, youth; Crime/law enforcement; Employment; Nutrition; Housing/shelter, development; Recreation; Youth development, services; Children/youth, services; Child development, services; Family services; Residential/custodial care, hospices; Aging, centers/services; Women, centers/services; Minorities/immigrants, centers/services; Homeless, human services; Human services; Civil rights, race/intergroup relations; Civil rights; Economic development; Urban/community development; Rural development; Community development; Voluntarism promotion; Population studies; Military/veterans' organizations; Leadership development; Youth; Disabilities, people with; Minorities; Native Americans/American Indians; Women; Economically disadvantaged; Homeless.

Type of support: General/operating support; Income development; Management development/capacity building; Program development; Conferences/seminars; Publication; Seed money; Scholarship funds; Technical assistance; Scholarships—to individuals; In-kind gifts; Matching/challenge support.

Limitations: Giving limited to Cumberland County, NC. No support for religious purposes. No grants to individuals (except for scholarships), or for annual campaigns, special event fundraisers or sponsorships, capital campaigns, endowment, trips for schools or clubs, or deficit funding or debt retirement.

Publications: Application guidelines; Annual report; Financial statement; Grants list; Informational brochure; Newsletter; Occasional report; Program policy statement.

Application information: Visit foundation Web site for application forms and guidelines. The foundation reviews letters of intent and the organizations that are most likely to be funded are invited to submit a detailed grant application. First time applicants are required to attend a Grant Overview Session, held the first Monday of every month; call to register. Application form required.

Initial approach: Attend a Grant Overview Session for grants
Copies of proposal: 1
Deadline(s): Mar. 31 for scholarships; Aug. 1 for letters of intent; Oct. 1 for full grant applications
Board meeting date(s): 2nd Thurs. of every other month
Final notification: May 11 for scholarships; Nov. 15 for grants

Officers and Directors:* Robert W. Drake,* Pres.; Samuel E. Short,* V.P.; Eleanor W. Fleishman,* Secy.; Samuel H. Meares,* Treas.; Mary M. Holmes, Exec. Dir.; John S. Ayers; Kamal M. Bakri; Mildred M. Braxton; Mary Lynn M. Bryan; Elaine M. Bryant; Loleta Wood Foster; Aston L. Fox; Leslie A. Griffin; John "Mac" Healy; Lucy H. Jones; S. Lynn Legatski; O. Raymond Manning, Jr.; Ellen K. Parker; Donald L. Porter; Barbara B. Richardson; Eugene E. Wright, Jr.; Dot Wyatt.

Number of staff: 4 full-time professional.

EIN: 581406831

7350
The Michael G. Curran Family Foundation ◇ ☆

301 Champions Point Way
Cary, NC   27513

Established in 2003 in NC.
Donor: Michael Curran.
Foundation type: Independent foundation.
Financial data (yr. ended 12/31/05): Assets, $13,996,425 (M); gifts received, $646,845; expenditures, $538,198; qualifying distributions, $510,111; giving activities include $510,111 for 11 grants (high: $484,400; low: $100).
Fields of interest: Health organizations; Recreation; Human services; Christian agencies & churches.
Limitations: Giving primarily in NC. No grants to individuals.
Director: Michael Curran.
EIN: 061691227

7351

The Katherine H. Daveler and David R. Hayworth Foundation ◇

c/o Wachovia Bank, N.A.
100 N. Main St., 13th Fl.
Winston-Salem, NC 27150
Application address: c/o David Hayworth, 800 Rockford Rd., High Point, NC 27262-4653, tel.: (336) 889-4439

Established in 1986 in NC.
Foundation type: Independent foundation.
Financial data (yr. ended 12/31/05): Assets, $6,644,971 (M); expenditures, $340,589; qualifying distributions, $329,551; giving activities include $322,250 for grants.
Fields of interest: Arts; Higher education; Nursing home/convalescent facility; Protestant federated giving programs.
Limitations: Giving limited to NC, with emphasis on High Point. No grants to individuals.
Application information: Application form not required.
Deadline(s): None
Directors: David R. Hayworth; John C. Slane; Marsha B. Slane.
Custodian: Wachovia Bank, N.A.
EIN: 581705607
Selected grants: The following grants were reported in 2003.
$100,000 to High Point University, High Point, NC.
$100,000 to Wesley Memorial United Methodist Church, High Point, NC.
$81,000 to Maryfield Nursing Home, High Point, NC.

7352

Champion McDowell Davis Charitable Foundation ◇

P.O. Drawer 2178
Wilmington, NC 28402 (910) 763-4565
Contact: Carter Mebane, Treas.

Established in 1963 in NC.
Donor: Champion McDowell Davis†.
Foundation type: Independent foundation.
Financial data (yr. ended 12/31/05): Assets, $17,501,011 (M); expenditures, $739,894; qualifying distributions, $711,168; giving activities include $669,000 for 8 grants (high: $625,000; low: $1,000).
Purpose and activities: Giving primarily for a health center; support for other health services and care for the elderly; limited to capital projects.
Fields of interest: Health care; YM/YWCAs & YM/YWHAs; Aging, centers/services; Aging.

Type of support: Capital campaigns; Building/renovation.
Limitations: Giving primarily in Wilmington, NC. No grants to individuals.
Application information: Application form not required.
Initial approach: Letter
Copies of proposal: 1
Deadline(s): 2 weeks before meetings
Board meeting date(s): Bimonthly meetings on 2nd Wed. commencing in Feb.
Officers and Trustees:* R.T. Sinclair, Jr., M.D.*, Chair.; William O.J. Lynch,* Secy.; W. Carter Mebane III, Treas.; William H. Cameron; Thomas L. Dodson; Dan Gottovi; John R. Murchinson III; Cyrus D. Hogue, Jr.
Number of staff: 1 part-time support.
EIN: 566055716

7353

Tom Davis Fund ◇

P.O. Box 25864
Winston-Salem, NC 27114-5864
(336) 765-4363
Contact: Cherryl Hartman, Exec. Dir.
FAX: (336) 765-1248;
E-mail: cherrylhartman@triad.rr.com

Established in 1988 in NC.
Donor: Thomas H. Davis†.
Foundation type: Independent foundation.
Financial data (yr. ended 12/31/04): Assets, $7,403,060 (M); expenditures, $622,542; qualifying distributions, $492,611; giving activities include $472,475 for 32 grants (high: $320,000; low: $100).
Purpose and activities: Giving primarily to medical education and research, youth development and aviation-related programs and safety.
Fields of interest: Museums (specialized); Medical school/education; Lung research; Asthma research; Medical research; Youth development, services; Space/aviation.
Limitations: Giving primarily in NC; also giving in FL. No grants to individuals.
Application information:
Initial approach: Letter
Deadline(s): None
Officers and Directors:* Winifred Davis Pierce,* Pres.; G. Franklin T. Davis,* V.P.; Thomas H. Davis, Jr.,* V.P.; Cherryl L. Hartman, Exec. Dir.; Nancy D. McGlothlin; Juliana D. West.
EIN: 581813100

7354

Davis Hospital Foundation, Inc. ◇

P.O. Box 7109
Statesville, NC 28687-0908

Established in 1983 in NC; converted from the sale of Davis Hospital.
Foundation type: Independent foundation.
Financial data (yr. ended 6/30/05): Assets, $6,921,761 (M); expenditures, $374,053; qualifying distributions, $327,781; giving activities include $314,611 for 6 grants (high: $152,640; low: $8,513), and $9,749 for grants to individuals.
Purpose and activities: Giving primarily for nursing education; limited support also for health care for individuals.

Fields of interest: Nursing school/education; Health care.
Type of support: Grants to individuals.
Limitations: Applications not accepted. Giving primarily in Boiling Springs and Statesville, NC.
Application information: Unsolicited requests for funds not accepted.
Officers and Board Members:* John N. Gilbert, Jr.,* Chair.; John S. Steele,* Vice-Chair.; Sammy Black,* Secy. and Chair., Nominating Comm.; F. Anderson Sherrill, Jr.,* Treas. and Chair., Investment Mgmt. Comm.; Ralph Bentley,* Chair., Prog. Review Comm.; Doug Hendrix,* Chair., Financial Assistance Comm.; H. Brown Kimball,* Chair., Bylaws Comm.; William A. Long,* Mgr.; Marie Brendle; Maxine Middlesworth; John L. West; Hoyle L. Whiteside; Margaret Wilhide.
EIN: 581528127
Selected grants: The following grants were reported in 2003.
$184,720 to Gardner-Webb University, Boiling Springs, NC.
$110,958 to Mitchell Community College, Statesville, NC.
$20,000 to Hospice of Iredell County, Statesville, NC.

7355

The Dickson Foundation, Inc. ◇

301 S. Tryon St., Ste. 1800
Charlotte, NC 28202 (704) 372-5404
Contact: Alan T. Dickson, Pres.; Susan W. Patterson, Secy.-Treas.

Incorporated in 1944 in NC.
Donor: American and Efird Mills, Inc.
Foundation type: Independent foundation.
Financial data (yr. ended 12/31/04): Assets, $55,899,552 (M); expenditures, $2,354,552; qualifying distributions, $2,238,241; giving activities include $2,128,000 for 180 grants (high: $10,000; low: $100).
Purpose and activities: Giving primarily to local charities including health, human services and education.
Fields of interest: Education, association; Secondary school/education; Higher education; Hospitals (general); Human services; Youth, services; Federated giving programs.
Type of support: General/operating support; Scholarship funds.
Limitations: Giving primarily in NC. No grants to individuals, or for building or endowment funds.
Application information:
Initial approach: Letter
Deadline(s): None
Board meeting date(s): Annually and as required
Officers and Directors:* R. Stuart Dickson,* Chair.; Alan T. Dickson,* Pres.; Rush S. Dickson III,* V.P.; Thomas W. Dickson,* V.P.; Susan W. Patterson, Secy.-Treas.
EIN: 566022339

7356

The Dover Foundation, Inc. ◇

P.O. Box 208
Shelby, NC 28151 (704) 487-8888
Contact: Hoyt Q. Bailey, Pres.
FAX: (704) 482-6818; E-mail: doverfnd@shelby.net

Incorporated in 1944 in NC.

Foundation type: Independent foundation.
Financial data (yr. ended 8/31/05): Assets, $23,054,423 (M); expenditures, $1,124,744; qualifying distributions, $954,695; giving activities include $830,225 for 137 grants (high: $100,000; low: $100).
Purpose and activities: Giving for museums, education, environment, health care, youth development, religion, particularly Baptist churches, and human services.
Fields of interest: Museums; Arts; Secondary school/education; Higher education; Education; Environment; Health care; Youth development, services; Human services; Public affairs; Protestant agencies & churches.
Type of support: General/operating support; Continuing support; Annual campaigns; Capital campaigns; Building/renovation; Endowments; Emergency funds; Professorships; Fellowships; Scholarship funds; Research; Matching/challenge support.
Limitations: Giving primarily in Cleveland County, NC.
Publications: Informational brochure (including application guidelines).
Application information: Application form not required.
Initial approach: Letter
Copies of proposal: 9
Board meeting date(s): Jan., April, July, and Oct.
Officers and Directors:* Hoyt Q. Bailey,* Pres.; Kathleen H. Wilson,* V.P.; Harvey B. Hamrick,* Secy.; Jay Linton Suttle,* Treas.; Cynthia B. Buckingham; Harvey B. Hamrick, Jr.; Melanie Ann Knight.
Number of staff: 1 full-time professional.
EIN: 560769897
Selected grants: The following grants were reported in 2005.
$50,000 to Cleveland Community College, Shelby, NC.
$50,000 to Gardner-Webb University, Boiling Springs, NC.
$50,000 to Life Enrichment Center of Cleveland County, Shelby, NC.
$25,000 to Hospice of Cleveland County, Shelby, NC.
$10,500 to Boys and Girls Club.
$10,000 to American Heart Association, Dallas, TX.
$10,000 to American Red Cross.
$10,000 to Young Life.
$5,000 to Cleveland-Rutherford Kidney Association, Shelby, NC.
$5,000 to Johnson C. Smith University, Charlotte, NC.

7357
Dowd Foundation, Inc. ✧
P.O. Box 35430
Charlotte, NC   28235

Established in 1951.
Donor: Charlotte Pipe and Foundry Co.
Foundation type: Independent foundation.
Financial data (yr. ended 12/31/05): Assets, $20,906,855 (M); gifts received, $6,000,000; expenditures, $1,342,359; qualifying distributions, $1,230,455; giving activities include $1,230,455 for grants.
Purpose and activities: Support is directed to a few educational, religious, and civic institutions and organizations in NC and VA.

Fields of interest: Arts; Secondary school/education; Higher education; Education; Health organizations, association; Human services; Protestant agencies & churches.
Limitations: Applications not accepted. Giving limited to NC and VA. No grants to individuals.
Application information: Contributes only to pre-selected organizations.
Officers: Edward H. Hardison, Pres.; W. Frank Dowd IV, V.P.; E. Hooper Hardison, Jr., Secy.; William R. Hutaff III, Treas.
EIN: 566061389

7358
S. May Drue Trust ✧ ☆
c/o Wachovia Bank, N.A.
100 N. Main St., 13th Fl.
Winston-Salem, NC   27150

Established in CT.
Foundation type: Independent foundation.
Financial data (yr. ended 12/31/05): Assets, $24,140 (M); expenditures, $334,763; qualifying distributions, $330,272; giving activities include $324,073 for 9 grants (high: $115,372; low: $5,503).
Fields of interest: Higher education; Education.
Limitations: Applications not accepted.
Application information: Contributes only to pre-selected organizations.
Trustee: Wachovia Bank, N.A.
EIN: 066269650

7359
The Duke Endowment ▼
100 N. Tryon St., Ste. 3500
Charlotte, NC   28202-4012   (704) 376-0291
Contact: Eugene W. Cochrane, Jr., Pres.
FAX: (704) 376-9336; E-mail: cperleins@tde.org;
URL: http://www.dukeendowment.org

Trust established in 1924 in NJ.
Donor: James Buchanan Duke†.
Foundation type: Independent foundation.
Financial data (yr. ended 12/31/05): Assets, $2,708,834,085 (M); expenditures, $141,122,291; qualifying distributions, $129,700,000; giving activities include $125,629,926 for 796 grants (high: $25,000,000), and $329,600 for 4 foundation-administered programs.
Purpose and activities: Grants to nonprofit health care and child care institutions in NC and SC; rural United Methodist churches and its pastors in NC; and Duke, Furman, and Johnson C. Smith Universities, and Davidson College.
Fields of interest: Higher education; Hospitals (general); Health care; Children/youth, services; Protestant agencies & churches.
Type of support: General/operating support; Continuing support; Capital campaigns; Building/renovation; Equipment; Endowments; Emergency funds; Program development; Conferences/seminars; Professorships; Publication; Seed money; Curriculum development; Fellowships; Internship funds; Scholarship funds; Research; Technical assistance; Consulting services; Matching/challenge support.
Limitations: Giving limited to NC and SC. No grants to individuals or for deficit financing; no loans.

Publications: Annual report (including application guidelines); Grants list; Informational brochure (including application guidelines); Occasional report.
Application information: Application form required.
Initial approach: Letter
Copies of proposal: 1
Deadline(s): Jan. 15 and June 15
Board meeting date(s): 10 months of the year
Final notification: 2 to 6 months
Officers and Trustees:* Russell M. Robinson II,* Chair.; William G. Anlyan, M.D.*, Vice-Chair.; Hugh M. Chapman,* Vice-Chair.; Eugene W. Cochrane, Jr., Pres.; Terri W. Honeycutt, Secy.; Janice C. Walker, C.F.O. and Treas.; Karen H. Rogers, Cont.; Stephanie S. Lynch, C.I.O.; William Barnet III; Dennis M. Campbell, Ph.D.; Constance F. Gray; Richard H. Jenrette; Mary D.T. Jones; Thomas S. Kenan III; Charles C. Lucas III; John G. Medlin, Jr.; Mary D.B.T. Semans; Minor M. Shaw; Lanty L. Smith; Jean G. Spaulding, M.D.; Neil Williams.
Number of staff: 22 full-time professional; 18 full-time support.
EIN: 560529965
Selected grants: The following grants were reported in 2005.
$38,384,000 to Duke University, Durham, NC. 2 grants: $13,384,000 (For general operating support), $25,000,000 (For Financial Aid Endowment).
$2,000,000 to Duke University Health System, Durham, NC. Toward Leadership Development Fund.
$1,000,000 to North Carolina Hospital Foundation, Cary, NC. Toward establishing North Carolina Hospital Association Center for Hospital Quality and Patient Safety.
$989,263 to United Methodist Church, Western North Carolina Conference, Charlotte, NC. For assistance to retired ministers and widows and dependent children of deceased ministers from list provided by Duke Endowment based on qualified service years according to policy.
$613,245 to South Carolina Association of Childrens Homes and Family Services, Columbia, SC. To make significant upgrades and enhancements to KIDS operating system.
$170,000 to Elon Homes for Children, Elon, NC. For second year of two-year period to construct multi-purpose educational center and to accomplish other capital and programmatic improvements for enhancing educational services.
$66,750 to Pender Memorial Hospital, Burgaw, NC. To assist in expanding capacity of Pender County Emergency Medical Services.
$50,000 to Epworth Childrens Home, Columbia, SC. For unrestricted operating support.
$32,000 to Mount Zion United Methodist Church, Pinnacle, NC. To assist in second year of two-year period for renovations to fellowship hall.

7360
Duke Energy Foundation ▼ ✧
(formerly Duke Power Company Foundation)
526 S. Church St., M.C. EC03ZJ
P.O. Box 1006
Charlotte, NC   28201-1006   (704) 382-7200
Contact: Kay Saville, Exec. Dir.
FAX: (704) 382-7600; URL: http://www.duke-energy.com/community/foundations/duke_foundation

Established in 1984 in NC.

Donors: Duke Power Co.; Duke Energy Corp.; Duke Energy Field Services, LP.

Foundation type: Company-sponsored foundation.

Financial data (yr. ended 12/31/05): Assets, $30,569,139 (M); gifts received, $15,917,442; expenditures, $15,489,582; qualifying distributions, $15,481,582; giving activities include $15,481,432 for grants.

Purpose and activities: The foundation supports organizations involved with arts and culture, education, the environment, health, employment, human services, community development, civic affairs, and economically disadvantaged people.

Fields of interest: Media/communications; Arts; Elementary/secondary education; Vocational education; Higher education; Education; Environment; Health care; Employment; Human services; Community development; Voluntarism promotion; Philanthropy/voluntarism; Mathematics; Science; Economically disadvantaged.

Type of support: General/operating support; Professorships; Scholarship funds; Employee matching gifts; Employee-related scholarships; In-kind gifts; Matching/challenge support.

Limitations: Giving primarily in areas of company operations in NC and SC; giving also in Canada. No support for discriminatory or political organizations, individual agencies of the United Way or the Charlotte Arts and Science Council, religious organizations, fraternal, veterans', or labor organizations, or family foundations. No grants to individuals (except for employee-related scholarships), or for new ticket sales, memberships, banquets, sponsorships, advertising, or special event fundraisers, capital campaigns or endowments, athletics, films, video or television productions, utility service reductions, conferences, trips or tours, advertising, membership fees or association fees, or dinners or tables.

Application information: Application form required.
Initial approach: Complete online application form
Board meeting date(s): Quarterly

Officers and Directors: Roberta B. Bowman,* Pres.; Hilary Davidson, V.P.; Erika Young, Secy.; Dale Carpenter, Treas.; Fred J. Fowler; Richard J. Osborne; Ruth G. Shaw.

Number of staff: 2 full-time professional.

EIN: 581586283

Selected grants: The following grants were reported in 2004.

$3,000,000 to University of North Carolina at Charlotte Foundation, Charlotte, NC. For capital support.

$2,196,321 to Vancouver Foundation, Vancouver, Canada. For operating support.

$1,667,853 to Foundation for the Carolinas, Charlotte, NC. For operating support.

$781,528 to United Way of America, Alexandria, VA. For operating support for various United Ways.

$291,657 to Arts and Science Council of Charlotte-Mecklenburg, Charlotte, NC. For operating support.

$288,500 to University of North Carolina, Charlotte, NC. For operating support.

$75,000 to Friends of the Hunley, Summerville, SC. For operating support.

$29,169 to United Way of Rockingham County, Wentworth, NC. For operating support.

$20,000 to Project Yes, Houston, TX. For operating support.

$15,000 to Theater Under the Stars, Houston, TX. For operating support.

7361
Andrew H. & Anne O. Easley Trust ✧
(also known as The Easley Foundation)
c/o Wachovia Bank, N.A. Charitable Funds Dept.
401 S. Tryon St., 4th Fl.
Charlotte, NC 28288-5709
Contact: Secy., The Easley Foundation
Application address: c/o Wachovia Bank, 1021 E. Cary St., VA9610, Richmond, VA 23219

Established in 1968 in VA.

Donor: Andrew H. Easley†.

Foundation type: Independent foundation.

Financial data (yr. ended 6/30/06): Assets, $10,183,258 (M); expenditures, $578,111; qualifying distributions, $470,727; giving activities include $470,727 for 24 grants (high: $50,000; low: $2,611).

Purpose and activities: Giving primarily for the arts, education and human services.

Fields of interest: Arts; Higher education; Environment; Recreation; Family services; Native Americans/American Indians.

Type of support: General/operating support; Continuing support; Capital campaigns; Building/renovation; Equipment; Land acquisition; Endowments; Emergency funds; Program development; Curriculum development; Scholarship funds; Technical assistance; Matching/challenge support.

Limitations: Giving limited to the central VA, area, within a 30-mile radius of Lynchburg. No support for religious organizations. No grants to individuals, or for research, deficit financing, seed money, annual campaigns, or conferences and seminars; no loans.

Publications: Application guidelines.

Application information: Application form not required.
Initial approach: Proposal (not exceeding 2 pages)
Copies of proposal: 6
Deadline(s): Apr. 1 and Oct. 1
Board meeting date(s): June and Dec.

Trustee: Wachovia Bank, N.A.

EIN: 546074720

Selected grants: The following grants were reported in 2005.

$43,975 to Lynchburg Covenant Fellowship, Lynchburg, VA.

$30,000 to Ferrum College, Ferrum, VA.

$30,000 to Hampden-Sydney College, Hampden Sydney, VA.

$30,000 to Lynchburg College, Lynchburg, VA.

$30,000 to Randolph-Macon Womans College, Lynchburg, VA.

$30,000 to Sweet Briar College, Sweet Briar, VA.

$25,000 to Historic Sandusky Foundation, Lynchburg, VA.

$25,000 to YMCA, Altavista Area, Altavista, VA.

$20,000 to National D-Day Memorial Foundation, Bedford, VA.

$16,270 to Virginia University of Lynchburg, Lynchburg, VA.

7362
Horatio B. Ebert Charitable Foundation
c/o Mark B. Edwards
P.O. Box 830
Mooresville, NC 28115-0830

Established in 1985.

Donors: Lyda G. Ebert†; Robert O. Ebert.

Foundation type: Independent foundation.

Financial data (yr. ended 12/31/05): Assets, $10,318,545 (M); expenditures, $559,958; qualifying distributions, $460,000; giving activities include $460,000 for grants.

Purpose and activities: Giving primarily for higher education.

Fields of interest: Museums (sports/hobby); Higher education; Human services; Children/youth, services; Christian agencies & churches.

Type of support: General/operating support; Building/renovation.

Limitations: Applications not accepted. Giving primarily in FL, KY, MD, NC, OH, and TN. No grants to individuals.

Application information: Unsolicited requests for funds not accepted.
Board meeting date(s): Aug. 1

Trustees: Catherine G. Ebert; Cecile G. Ebert; Michael L. Ebert; Robert O. Ebert; Mark B. Edwards; Adrienne E. Miller.

Number of staff: 1 part-time support.

EIN: 592602801

Selected grants: The following grants were reported in 2004.

$210,000 to College of Wooster, Wooster, OH. 2 grants: $10,000, $200,000

$90,000 to Berea College, Berea, KY.

$40,000 to Youth Villages, Arlington, TN.

$10,000 to Hospice of Iredell County, Statesville, NC.

$10,000 to Johns Hopkins Hospital, Baltimore, MD.

$7,500 to Childrens Home Society Foundation, Greensboro, NC.

$5,000 to Helping Up Mission, Baltimore, MD.

$5,000 to Johns Hopkins Childrens Center, Baltimore, MD.

$5,000 to Teen Health, Statesville, NC.

7363
Harold T. Edgar Charitable Trust ✧
c/o Wachovia Bank, N.A.
100 N. Main St., 13th Fl.
Winston-Salem, NC 27150

Established in NJ.

Foundation type: Independent foundation.

Financial data (yr. ended 12/31/05): Assets, $7,292,026 (M); expenditures, $434,548; qualifying distributions, $410,829; giving activities include $405,692 for 6 grants (high: $108,184; low: $47,331).

Fields of interest: Human services.

Limitations: Applications not accepted. No grants to individuals.

Application information: Contributes only to pre-selected organizations.

Trustee: Wachovia Bank, N.A.

EIN: 226023917

Selected grants: The following grants were reported in 2003.

$54,482 to Reformed Church of Metuchen, Metuchen, NJ.

$54,482 to YMCA of Metuchen-Edison-Woodbridge, Metuchen, NJ.

$23,849 to Boy Scouts of America, Central New Jersey Council, Monmouth Junction, NJ.

$23,849 to Boys and Girls Clubs of America, Atlanta, GA.

$23,849 to New Brunswick Theological Seminary, New Brunswick, NJ.

$23,849 to Northwood School, Lake Placid, NY.

7364

The Herschel H. & Cornelia N. Everett Foundation ☆

c/o Wachovia Bank, N.A.
401 S. Tryon St., TH-2
Charlotte, NC 28288-1159
Contact: Rachel Reilly
E-mail: rachel.reilly@wachovia.com

Established in 2001 in NC.
Foundation type: Independent foundation.
Financial data (yr. ended 6/30/04): Assets,
$5,036,540 (M); expenditures, $381,045;
qualifying distributions, $338,000; giving activities
include $338,000 for grants (high: $50,000; low:
$1,000).
Fields of interest: Education; Health care; Cancer;
Christian agencies & churches.
Limitations: Applications not accepted. Giving
primarily in NC. No grants to individuals.
Application information: Contributes only to
pre-selected organizations.
Trustee: Wachovia Bank, N.A.
EIN: 566093697

7365

The Family Foundation ✧

(formerly The Cash Family Foundation)
c/o F.A. Cash, Jr.
1601 Queens Rd. W.
Charlotte, NC 28207

Established in 1991 in NC.
Donors: F.A. Cash; Scott Cash; United Way.
Foundation type: Independent foundation.
Financial data (yr. ended 12/31/04): Assets,
$1,849,529 (M); gifts received, $1,563,029;
expenditures, $598,553; qualifying distributions,
$598,400; giving activities include $598,400 for
grants (high: $269,600).
Purpose and activities: Giving primarily for youth
services.
Fields of interest: Children/youth, services;
Protestant agencies & churches.
Limitations: Applications not accepted. Giving
primarily in Charlotte, NC. Generally no grants to
individuals.
Application information: Contributes only to
pre-selected organizations.
Officers: F.A. Cash, Jr., Pres.; Barbara Cash, Secy.
EIN: 566382881

7366

Thomas Austin Finch Foundation ✧

c/o Wachovia Bank, N.A.
100 N. Main St., 13th Fl.
Winston-Salem, NC 27150 (336) 732-6488
Contact: Ed Loflin, Admin., Wachovia Bank, N.A.

Trust established in 1944 in NC.
Donors: Ernestine L. Finch Mobley†; Thomas Austin
Finch, Jr.†.
Foundation type: Independent foundation.
Financial data (yr. ended 12/31/05): Assets,
$10,094,292 (M); expenditures, $560,452;
qualifying distributions, $471,399; giving activities
include $470,899 for 20 grants (high: $100,000;
low: $3,000).
Fields of interest: Elementary/secondary
education; Secondary school/education; Libraries/
library science; Hospitals (general); Federated giving

programs; Government/public administration;
Protestant agencies & churches; Religion.
Type of support: General/operating support;
Continuing support; Annual campaigns; Building/
renovation; Equipment; Program development;
Scholarship funds.
Limitations: Giving limited to Thomasville, NC. No
grants to individuals, or for emergency funds, deficit
financing, endowment funds, or fellowships; no
loans.
Publications: Informational brochure (including
application guidelines).
Application information: Application form required.
Initial approach: Letter
Copies of proposal: 1
Deadline(s): None
Board meeting date(s): Mar. and Nov.
Final notification: 2 weeks
Foundation Committee: David Finch, Chair.; Kermit
Cloninger; John L. Finch; Sumner Finch; Meredith
Slane Person.
Trustee: Wachovia Bank, N.A.
EIN: 566037907

7367

A. E. Finley Foundation, Inc. ✧

P.O. Box 98266
Raleigh, NC 27624 (919) 782-0565
Contact: Robert C. Brown, Pres.
E-mail: lesaaeff@nc.rr.com; Additional tel.: (919)
782-0529; FAX: (919) 235-3348; URL: http://
www.aefinleyfoundationinc.org

Incorporated in 1957 in NC.
Donor: A.E. Finley†.
Foundation type: Independent foundation.
Financial data (yr. ended 11/30/05): Assets,
$31,537,870 (M); expenditures, $2,683,198;
qualifying distributions, $1,699,875; giving
activities include $1,699,875 for grants.
Purpose and activities: Support primarily for
religion, health care, human services, arts and
culture, youth development, and education.
Fields of interest: Higher education; Education;
Human services; Youth, services; Community
development; Christian agencies & churches.
Type of support: General/operating support;
Continuing support; Annual campaigns; Building/
renovation; Equipment; Endowments; Program
development; Seed money; Curriculum
development; Fellowships; Scholarship funds;
Research; Matching/challenge support.
Limitations: Giving primarily in NC. No grants to
individuals.
Publications: Informational brochure.
Application information: Application form not
required.
Initial approach: Letter
Copies of proposal: 1
Deadline(s): None
Board meeting date(s): Monthly
Directors: Robert C. Brown; A. Earle Finley II; David
A. Goodwin; A.E. Howard; Ben G. Nottingham; C.D.
Nottingham II.
Number of staff: 1 full-time professional; 2 part-time
professional; 1 full-time support.
EIN: 566057379
Selected grants: The following grants were reported
in 2005.
$190,000 to Exploris, Raleigh, NC.
$176,357 to Peace College, Raleigh, NC.
$151,000 to Duke University, Durham, NC.

$140,000 to Ravenscroft School, Raleigh, NC.
$85,000 to YMCA.
$38,000 to Broadwater Academy, Exmore, VA.
$14,000 to Tammy Lynn Memorial Foundation,
Raleigh, NC.
$10,500 to North Carolina Theater, Raleigh, NC.
$2,000 to Hampden-Sydney College, Hampden
Sydney, VA.
$2,000 to Ronald McDonald House.

7368

Flow Foundation, Inc. ✧ ☆

1425 Plaza Dr.
Winston-Salem, NC 27103

Established in 2004 in NC.
Donor: Donald E. Flow.
Foundation type: Independent foundation.
Financial data (yr. ended 12/31/05): Assets,
$145,633 (M); gifts received, $612,726;
expenditures, $477,468; qualifying distributions,
$470,784; giving activities include $470,784 for 14
grants (high: $200,000; low: $1,000).
Fields of interest: Higher education; Human
services; Federated giving programs.
Limitations: Applications not accepted. Giving
primarily in NC and VA. No grants to individuals.
Application information: Contributes only to
pre-selected organizations.
Officers: Donald E. Flow, Pres.; Robbin B. Flow,
Secy.-Treas.
EIN: 201983806

7369

Food Lion Charitable Foundation, Inc. ✧

P.O. Box 1330
Salisbury, NC 28145-1330 (704) 633-8250
Contact: John Mercer, Chair.
FAX: (704) 633-9724; E-mail: flcf@foodlion.com;
URL: http://charitablefoundation.foodlion.org

Established as a company-sponsored operating
foundation in 2001 in NC.
Foundation type: Operating foundation.
Financial data (yr. ended 12/31/05): Assets,
$1,500,231 (M); gifts received, $715,000;
expenditures, $435,789; qualifying distributions,
$435,789; giving activities include $435,789 for
108 grants (high: $25,000; low: $495).
Purpose and activities: The foundation supports
organizations involved with K-12 education and
hunger.
Fields of interest: Elementary/secondary
education; Food services; Food banks; Food
distribution, meals on wheels.
Limitations: Giving primarily in areas of company
operations in the mid-Atlantic and Southeast. No
grants to individuals.
Application information: Application form required.
Initial approach: Download application form and
mail to foundation
Deadline(s): Apr. 30
Officers and Directors:* John Mercer,* Chair.;
Cathy Cherry,* Vice-Chair.; James Mack, Secy.
EIN: 562279572

7370
Foundation for the Carolinas ▼ ✧
217 S. Tryon St.
Charlotte, NC 28202 (704) 973-4500
Contact: Donald K. Jonas Ph.D., Sr. V.P., Community
Philanthropy
FAX: (704) 973-4599; E-mail: infor@fftc.org;
Additional tel.: (800) 973-7244; Additional E-mail:
djonas@fftc.org; URL: http://www.fftc.org

Incorporated in 1958 in NC.
Foundation type: Community foundation.
Financial data (yr. ended 12/31/05): Assets,
$424,272,918; gifts received, $64,829,466;
expenditures $70,248,252; giving activities
include $59,551,103 for 608+ grants.
Purpose and activities: The foundation exists to
advance philanthropy by serving donors, increasing
charitable giving, and improving communities.
Fields of interest: Arts, cultural/ethnic awareness;
Historic preservation/historical societies; Arts;
Education; Environment; Health care; Health
organizations, association; Medical research,
institute; Disasters, Hurricane Katrina; Children/
youth, services; Aging, centers/services; Human
services; Civil rights, equal rights; Civil rights,
minorities; Economic development; Leadership
development; Public affairs; Religion; African
Americans/Blacks; Economically disadvantaged.
Type of support: Seed money; Scholarship funds;
Grants to individuals; Matching/challenge support.
Limitations: Giving primarily to organizations serving
the citizens of NC and SC, with emphasis on the
greater Charlotte, NC, region. No grants to
individuals (except for scholarships), or for deficit
financing, capital campaigns, ongoing operating
budgets, publications, conferences, videos, travel,
equipment, small businesses, business start-up, or
advertising.
Publications: Application guidelines; Annual report
(including application guidelines); Newsletter.
Application information: Visit foundation Web site
for application guidelines per grant type and specific
deadlines. Faxed or e-mail applications are not
accepted. Application form required.
 Initial approach: Varies
 Deadline(s): Varies
 Board meeting date(s): Distribution Committee
 meets 3 times per year
 Final notification: 2 months
Officers and Directors:* Harvey B. Gantt,* Chair.;
Michael Marsicano, C.E.O. and Pres.; Laura L.
Meyer, Exec. V.P.; Donald K. Jonas, Ph.D., Sr. V.P.,
Community Philanthropy; Judy L. Kerns, Sr. V.P.,
Finance and Admin.; C. Barton Landess, Sr. V.P.,
Devel. and Planned Giving; Jenene H. Seymour, Sr.
V.P., Scholarships; Debra S. Watt, Sr. V.P., Opers.;
Charity L. Perkins, V.P., Comms.; Holly K. Welch
Stubbing, V.P., Client Svcs.; Elaine Rhodes, Assoc.
V.P., Community Philanthropy; Mark R. Bernstein;
Catherine P. Bessant; Howard C. Bissell; H.W.
Close; Michael R. Coltrane; Alvaro de Molina; Alan
T. Dickson; Polly C. Jackson; C. Ray Kennedy;
Margaret Kluttz; Thomas C. Nelson; Martha
"Brownie" Plaster; Sally Robinson; Lynne Scott
Safrit; Ruth G. Shaw; Geraldine Sumter; G. Kennedy
Thompson.
Number of staff: 17 full-time professional; 10
full-time support; 1 part-time support.
EIN: 566047886
Selected grants: The following grants were reported
in 2004.
$200,000 to Community Building Initiative,
 Charlotte, NC. For Crossroads Charlotte program,

which engages community through storytelling
and focuses on productive approach to
community's future in terms of access, equity,
inclusion and trust for citizens. Grant made
through Charlotte Mecklenburg Community
Foundation.
$150,000 to Richmond County Arts Council,
 Rockingham, NC. For renovation of existing Arts
 Richmond Center. Grant made through the Cole
 Foundation.
$141,343 to Partners in Out-of-School Time (POST),
 Charlotte, NC. For collaborative effort to increase
 quantity and quality of out-of-school time
 programming, to provide technical assistance
 and training for providers and to increase public
 awareness of out-of-school time issues. Grant
 made through Charlotte Mecklenburg Community
 Foundation.
$125,000 to Richmond Community College
 Foundation, Hamlet, NC. To build Grimsley Health
 Sciences Building. Grant made through the Cole
 Foundation.
$117,257 to Voices and Choices of the Central
 Carolinas, Charlotte, NC. For State of the Region
 Report and Catawha Regional Trail project. Grant
 made through Charlotte Mecklenburg Community
 Foundation.
$100,000 to Lynwood Foundation, Charlotte, NC. 2
 grants: $50,000 to Lee Institute (For United
 Agenda for Children initiative, with goal of
 ensuring that all children in Mecklenburg County
 are healthy, safe and well-educated. Grant made
 through Charlotte Mecklenburg Community
 Foundation), $50,000 to Lee Institute (For United
 Agenda for Children initiative, with goal of
 ensuring that all children in Mecklenburg County
 are healthy, safe and well educated. Grant made
 through Charlotte Mecklenburg Community
 Foundation).
$65,000 to Mecklenburg Medical Alliance
 Endowment, Charlotte, NC. For Reach Out and
 Read literacy program, to provide books and
 educational materials for children and their
 parents.
$54,000 to Womenfolk Unlimited, Hamlet, NC. To
 provide shelter and services for victims who are
 escaping domestic violence. Grant made through
 the Cole Foundation.
$50,100 to Mineral Springs Middle School,
 Winston-Salem, NC. To complete Barry Ridley
 Memorial Learning Garden. Grant made through
 the Cole Foundation.

7371
Fox Family Foundation, Inc. ✧
2726 Croasdaile Dr., Ste. 102
Durham, NC 27705-2500 (919) 383-5575
Contact: David D. Beischer, Exec. Dir.
FAX: (919) 383-5577;
E-mail: dbeischer@foxfoundation.org

Established in 1991 in NC.
Donor: Frances Hill Fox‡.
Foundation type: Independent foundation.
Financial data (yr. ended 12/31/05): Assets,
$6,550,308 (M); gifts received, $469,911;
expenditures, $461,216; qualifying distributions,
$352,133; giving activities include $346,000 for
grants.
Purpose and activities: Giving for health care, family
and youth services, and the arts, and human
services.

Fields of interest: Arts; Education; Pharmacy/
prescriptions; Health organizations, association;
Youth development; Human services.
Type of support: General/operating support;
Continuing support; Annual campaigns; Capital
campaigns; Building/renovation; Endowments;
Curriculum development; Internship funds.
Limitations: Giving to organizations that are
headquartered in Durham, Orange, and Wake
counties, NC. No support for religious or political
organizations. No grants to individuals.
Publications: Application guidelines; Grants list.
Application information: Application form required.
 Initial approach: Letter of inquiry or telephone
 Copies of proposal: 1
 Deadline(s): Sept. 1
 Board meeting date(s): 2nd Wed. in May and Nov.
 Final notification: Dec. 1
Officers and Directors:* Randolph Dudley Fox,*
Pres.; Susan Fox Beischer,* V.P.; A. William
Kennon,* Secy.; J. David Ross,* Treas.; David D.
Beischer,* Exec. Dir.; John W. Mallard.
Number of staff: 1 full-time professional; 1 part-time
support.
EIN: 561756144
Selected grants: The following grants were reported
in 2003.
$20,000 to Planned Parenthood of Central North
 Carolina, Chapel Hill, NC. For operating support.
$17,000 to Literacy Council of Durham County,
 Durham, NC. To underwrite volunteer
 coordinator.
$15,000 to Dispute Settlement Center, Carrboro,
 NC. For operating support.
$15,000 to Senior PharmAssist, Durham, NC. For
 operating support.
$12,500 to Durham Arts Council, Durham, NC. For
 art school financial aid.
$10,000 to North Carolina Museum of Life and
 Science, Durham, NC. For operating support.
$8,000 to Carolina Theater of Durham, Durham, NC.
 For ticket subsidies.
$7,500 to Alliance of AIDS Services-Carolina,
 Raleigh, NC. For operating support.
$5,000 to Adolescent Pregnancy Prevention
 Coalition of North Carolina, Chapel Hill, NC. For
 operating support.
$5,000 to Threshold, Durham, NC. For program
 support.

7372
George Foundation, Inc.
P.O. Box 800
Hickory, NC 28603
Contact: Boyd George, Pres.

Established in 1980 in NC.
Donors: Boyd George; G. Lee George‡; Merchants
Distributors, Inc.; Lowe's Food Stores, Inc.;
Institution Food House, Inc.
Foundation type: Independent foundation.
Financial data (yr. ended 11/30/05): Assets,
$6,032,829 (M); gifts received, $980,000;
expenditures, $909,451; qualifying distributions,
$880,400; giving activities include $880,400 for 95
grants (high: $130,000; low: $150).
Purpose and activities: Giving primarily for a
college; support also for community development
and a program fighting hunger.
Fields of interest: Higher education; Food services;
Community development.
Limitations: Giving primarily in Hickory, NC. No
grants to individuals.

Officers and Trustees:* Boyd George,* Pres.; John B. Orgain, Secy.; Ron Knedlik,* Treas.; Joyce George Corbett; William R. Waddell.
EIN: 561282417

7373
Price Gilbert, Jr. Charitable Fund ◇
c/o Wachovia Bank, N.A.
100 N. Main St., 13th Fl.
Winston-Salem, NC   27150
Contact: Alice Sheets; Lydia Whitman
E-mail: grantinquiriesga@wachovia.com; Application address: c/o Wachovia Bank, N.A, 3414 Peachtree Rd, 5th Fl., MC-GA8023, Atlanta, GA 30326;
URL: http://www.wachovia.com/corp_inst/charitable_services/0,,3298,00.html

Established in 1973 in GA.
Foundation type: Independent foundation.
Financial data (yr. ended 5/31/05): Assets, $9,004,457 (M); expenditures, $629,871; qualifying distributions, $557,013; giving activities include $557,013 for 30 grants (high: $100,000; low: $3,000).
Purpose and activities: Giving primarily for arts and culture, education, human services, and federated giving programs.
Fields of interest: Arts; Education; Human services; Federated giving programs.
Limitations: Giving limited to the Atlanta, GA, area. No grants to individuals.
Application information: Application form required.
  Initial approach: 1-page letter
  Deadline(s): Feb. 1 and Aug. 1
  Board meeting date(s): Mar. and Sept.
Officers and Distribution Committee Members:*
Isaiah Tidwell,* Chair.; Beverly Blake,* Secy.; Bennie Boswell, Jr.; D. Gary Thompson.
Trustee: Wachovia Bank, N.A.
Number of staff: 4
EIN: 582064640

7374
The Lucille P. and Edward C. Giles Foundation
(formerly The Edward C. Giles Foundation)
P.O. Box 830
Mooresville, NC   28115
Contact: Bernard R. Fitzgerald, Pres.

Established in 1981 in NC.
Donor: Lucille P. Giles†.
Foundation type: Independent foundation.
Financial data (yr. ended 12/31/05): Assets, $15,908,366 (M); expenditures, $577,794; qualifying distributions, $373,324; giving activities include $113,500 for 18 grants (high: $20,000; low: $1,000), and $259,824 for grants to individuals.
Purpose and activities: Scholarships to descendants of employees of Caraustar Industries, Inc. and subsidiaries.
Fields of interest: Education, association; Higher education; Education; Human services.
Type of support: Employee-related scholarships.
Limitations: Applications not accepted. Giving primarily in the Charlotte, NC, area.
Application information: Unsolicited requests for funds not accepted.
  Board meeting date(s): Spring and late fall

Officers: Bernard Fitzgerald, Pres.; Van L. Weatherspoon, V.P.; Mark B. Edwards, Secy.-Treas.
EIN: 581450874

7375
Gipson Family Foundation ◇ ☆
7340 Six Forks Rd.
Raleigh, NC   27615
Application address: c/o Thomas L. Gipson, 609 Brookfield Rd., Raleigh, NC 27615

Established in 1996.
Foundation type: Independent foundation.
Financial data (yr. ended 12/31/05): Assets, $17,391,356 (M); expenditures, $394,859; qualifying distributions, $370,355; giving activities include $370,355 for grants.
Fields of interest: Higher education, college; Education; Muscular dystrophy; Food banks; Housing/shelter; Human services; Children, services; Foundations (community); Christian agencies & churches.
Limitations: Giving primarily in NC.
Application information: Application form required.
  Initial approach: Letter
  Deadline(s): None
Trustees: Elizabeth Cheatham; Cary Gipson; Clay Gipson; Donald Gipson; Patricia Gipson; Thomas L. Gipson.
EIN: 562001414
Selected grants: The following grants were reported in 2003.
$75,000 to Triangle Community Foundation, Research Triangle Park, NC. For general support.
$50,000 to Habitat for Humanity of Wake County, Raleigh, NC. For general support.
$5,000 to Food Bank of Central and Eastern North Carolina, Raleigh, NC. For general support.
$5,000 to Listening Hearts Ministries, Baltimore, MD. For general support.
$5,000 to North Carolina Symphony, Raleigh, NC. For general support.
$5,000 to Pan Lutheran Ministries of Wake County, Raleigh, NC. For general support.
$3,500 to Assistance League of the Triangle Area, Raleigh, NC. For general support.
$3,200 to Muscular Dystrophy Association, Raleigh, NC. For general support.
$2,500 to Franklin and Marshall College, Lancaster, PA. For general support.
$2,500 to University of Pennsylvania, Philadelphia, PA. For general support for Wharton Annual Fund.

7376
Glenn Family Foundation ◇
P.O. Box 2736
Winston-Salem, NC   27102-2736

Established in 1987 in NC.
Donors: James K. Glenn; James K. Glenn, Jr.
Foundation type: Independent foundation.
Financial data (yr. ended 12/31/05): Assets, $8,251,402 (M); gifts received, $5,100; expenditures, $477,311; qualifying distributions, $422,200; giving activities include $422,200 for 37 grants (high: $150,000; low: $200).
Fields of interest: Elementary/secondary education; Higher education; Human services; Federated giving programs; Protestant agencies & churches.

Type of support: General/operating support; Building/renovation; Professorships.
Limitations: Applications not accepted. Giving primarily in Winston-Salem, NC. No grants to individuals.
Application information: Contributes only to pre-selected organizations.
Officer and Directors:* J. Kirk Glenn, Jr.,* Pres. and Treas.; Frances G. Porter; Sally G. Williams.
EIN: 581748268
Selected grants: The following grants were reported in 2005.
$226,000 to First Presbyterian Church, Charlotte, NC. 3 grants: $16,000, $60,000, $150,000
$70,000 to United Way, NC.
$20,000 to Crisis Control Ministry, Winston-Salem, NC.
$8,500 to Senior Services, Winston-Salem, NC.
$1,000 to North Carolina Victim Assistance Network, Raleigh, NC.
$1,000 to Ronald McDonald House, Chapel Hill, NC.
$1,000 to Trinity Center, Winston-Salem, NC.
$1,000 to Winston-Salem Foundation, Winston-Salem, NC.

7377
Goodnight Educational Foundation ◇
100 SAS Campus Dr.
Cary, NC   27513

Established in 1998 in NC.
Foundation type: Independent foundation.
Financial data (yr. ended 12/31/05): Assets, $8,237,713 (M); expenditures, $426,128; qualifying distributions, $410,008; giving activities include $410,008 for 10 grants (high: $205,008; low: $5,000; average: $10,000–$20,000).
Purpose and activities: Giving primarily for higher education, and the arts.
Fields of interest: Museums (art); Performing arts; Arts; Elementary/secondary education; Higher education; Libraries (school); Education; Human services; Salvation Army; Children/youth, services.
Limitations: Applications not accepted. Giving primarily in NC, with emphasis on Raleigh. No support for political campaigns. No grants to individuals.
Application information: Contributes only to pre-selected organizations.
Directors: Susan G. Ellis; Ann Baggett Goodnight; James H. Goodnight; Leah A. Goodnight.
EIN: 566533546

7378
The Goodrich Foundation, Inc. ◇
(formerly The B.F.Goodrich Foundation, Inc.)
4 Coliseum Center
2730 W. Tyvola Rd.
Charlotte, NC   28217-4578   (704) 423-7000
Contact: Natalie English, Secy.

Established in 1989 in OH.
Donors: The B.F.Goodrich Co.; Goodrich Corp.
Foundation type: Company-sponsored foundation.
Financial data (yr. ended 12/31/04): Assets, $15,376,122 (M); expenditures, $1,579,629; qualifying distributions, $1,567,313; giving activities include $1,566,413 for 629+ grants (high: $174,653).
Purpose and activities: The foundation supports organizations involved with arts and culture,

education, health, employment training, human services, community development, and civic affairs.

Fields of interest: Arts; Elementary/secondary education; Higher education; Engineering school/education; Adult/continuing education; Education; Medical care, in-patient care; Health care; Employment, training; Human services; Economic development; Community development; Federated giving programs; Mathematics; Science; Public affairs.

Type of support: General/operating support; Continuing support; Annual campaigns; Capital campaigns; Building/renovation; Equipment; Emergency funds; Scholarship funds; Research; Employee matching gifts.

Limitations: Giving primarily in areas of company operations. No support for private foundations, religious organizations, political, international, fraternal, social, labor, or veterans' organizations, or churches. No grants to individuals, or for endowments, lobbying, travel, tours, exhibitions, local athletics, equipment, advertising, benefits, tables, or tickets.

Publications: Application guidelines; Informational brochure.

Application information: Application form required.
  Initial approach: Download application form and mail to foundation
  Deadline(s): None
  Board meeting date(s): 3 to 4 times per year
  Final notification: Within 2 weeks

Officers: Terrence G. Linnert, Pres.; Jack Carmola, V.P.; Rick Schmidt, V.P.; Natalie English, Secy.; Scott Kuechle, Treas.

Number of staff: 1 full-time professional; 1 full-time support.

EIN: 341601879

Selected grants: The following grants were reported in 2004.

$174,653 to United Way of Central Carolinas, Charlotte, NC.

$50,500 to Purdue Foundation, West Lafayette, IN.

$50,000 to Childrens Learning Center, Charlotte, NC.

$50,000 to Mint Museum of Art, Charlotte, NC.

$27,453 to Discovery Place, Charlotte, NC.

$25,000 to Foundation of Shalom Park, Charlotte, NC.

$21,600 to Council for Children, Charlotte, NC.

$250 to Arts in Stark, Canton, OH.

$200 to San Diego State University, San Diego, CA.

$100 to Covenant House, New York, NY.

7379
The Jeff Gordon Foundation ◆

P.O. Box 880
Harrisburg, NC 28075
Contact: Amanda L. Hollingsworth, Dir., Progs.
FAX: (704) 455-0623;
E-mail: foundation@jgracing.com; URL: http://www.jeffgordonfoundation.org

Established in 1999 in NC.

Donor: Jeffrey M. Gordon.

Foundation type: Independent foundation.

Financial data (yr. ended 12/31/05): Assets, $411,768 (M); gifts received, $737,549; expenditures, $1,367,671; qualifying distributions, $1,281,690; giving activities include $1,099,734 for 14+ grants (high: $335,834; average: $10,000–$100,000).

Purpose and activities: The foundation is dedicated to helping support the physical, social, and

intellectual needs of children and their families in the U.S.

Fields of interest: Arts; Education; Hospitals (specialty); Health care; Human services; Children/youth, services; Family services; Religion.

Limitations: Giving primarily in NC; some giving nationally. No grants to individuals.

Publications: Informational brochure.

Application information: Must submit proposal with the Jeff Gordon Foundation grant application form. Application form required.
  Initial approach: Letter
  Copies of proposal: 1
  Deadline(s): Aug. 16
  Final notification: Dec. 31

Officer: Jeffrey M. Gordon, Pres. and Treas.

Number of staff: 1 full-time professional.

EIN: 562174163

7380
Shelton Gorelick Family Foundation ◆ ☆

c/o Shelton Gorelick
6000 Fairview Rd., Ste. 1415
Charlotte, NC 28210

Established in 1990; funded in 1991.

Donor: Shelton Gorelick.

Foundation type: Independent foundation.

Financial data (yr. ended 6/30/05): Assets, $4,605,529 (M); gifts received, $90,000; expenditures, $363,393; qualifying distributions, $349,724; giving activities include $349,724 for 7 grants (high: $296,774; low: $1,000).

Purpose and activities: Giving primarily for arts and culture, Jewish agencies and temples.

Fields of interest: Arts; Recreation; Human services; Jewish federated giving programs; Jewish agencies & temples.

Type of support: Annual campaigns; Capital campaigns; Building/renovation; Endowments; Matching/challenge support.

Limitations: Applications not accepted. Giving limited to Charlotte, NC. No grants to individuals.

Application information: Contributes only to pre-selected organizations.

Officers: Shelton Gorelick, Pres. and Treas.; Scott Gorelick, V.P. and Secy.; Jeff Gorelick, V.P.; Pamela Gorelick, V.P.

EIN: 561743194

7381
William and Patricia Gorelick Family Foundation ◆

4064 Colony Rd., Ste. 340
Charlotte, NC 28211-5117
Contact: William Gorelick, Pres.

Established in 1990 in NC.

Donor: William Gorelick.

Foundation type: Independent foundation.

Financial data (yr. ended 6/30/05): Assets, $4,657,479 (M); gifts received, $389,012; expenditures, $718,192; qualifying distributions, $687,275; giving activities include $686,400 for 31 + grants (high: $222,500).

Purpose and activities: Giving primarily to Jewish organizations.

Fields of interest: Museums; Arts; Education; Jewish agencies & temples.

Type of support: Annual campaigns; Capital campaigns; Building/renovation; Endowments.

Limitations: Applications not accepted. Giving primarily in NC. No grants to individuals.

Application information: Contributes only to pre-selected organizations.

Officers and Trustee:* William Gorelick,* Pres. and Treas.; Patricia Gorelick, V.P.; Todd A. Gorelick, Secy.

EIN: 561743190

Selected grants: The following grants were reported in 2005.

$222,500 to Foundation of Shalom Park, Charlotte, NC.

$42,500 to Charlotte Country Day School, Charlotte, NC.

$21,400 to Penland School of Crafts, Penland, NC.

$20,000 to Childrens Theater of Charlotte, Charlotte, NC.

$10,000 to United Way.

$7,500 to Charlotte Jewish Day School, Charlotte, NC.

$2,500 to Charlotte Symphony Orchestra, Charlotte, NC.

$2,500 to Duke University, Durham, NC.

$2,500 to Opera Carolina, Charlotte, NC.

$1,000 to Foundation for the Carolinas, Charlotte, NC.

7382
The Graham Foundation ◆

c/o Bank of America, N.A.
101 S. Tryon St., NC1-002-11-18
Charlotte, NC 28280-0002
FAX: (864) 233-3667; Application address: c/o William A. Bridges, 2 Liberty Sq., 75 Beattie Pl., Ste. 610, Greenville, SC 29601, tel.: (864) 233-3666; e-mail: bill@thegrahamfoundation.org; URL: http://www.thegrahamfoundation.org

Established in 1985 in SC.

Donors: Allen J. Graham†; Frances G. MacIlwinen; Allen J. Graham Marital Trust.

Foundation type: Independent foundation.

Financial data (yr. ended 8/31/05): Assets, $49,467,785 (M); gifts received, $33,547,813; expenditures, $2,069,264; qualifying distributions, $1,844,950; giving activities include $1,512,715 for 32 grants (high: $200,000; low: $2,000).

Purpose and activities: Giving to organizations that make a significant difference for the betterment of residents of Greenville, SC, and upstate SC, and focused on needs that are specific and contained. The primary areas of focus are the arts, children, community welfare, education, the environment, and religion.

Fields of interest: Performing arts; Historic preservation/historical societies; Arts; Elementary/secondary education; Education; Health care, clinics/centers; Food distribution, groceries on wheels; Human services; Protestant agencies & churches.

Type of support: Endowments; Capital campaigns; General/operating support.

Limitations: Giving primarily in Greenville, SC. No support for political purposes. No grants to individuals or for scholarships.

Application information: See foundation Web site for application guidelines, procedures, and downloading of application form. Application form required.
  Initial approach: Letter or telephone, or e-mail
  Copies of proposal: 5
  Deadline(s): None

Trustees: Wilbur Y. Bridges; William A. Bridges; Stephen J. Lambert; Susan R. Lambert; Frances G. MacIlwinen.
Agent: Bank of America, N.A.
EIN: 570805774
Selected grants: The following grants were reported in 2005.
$200,000 to Hospice House of Greenville, Greenville, SC.
$100,000 to Historic Greenville Foundation, Greenville, SC.
$75,515 to Christ Church Episcopal School, Greenville, SC.
$50,000 to American Red Cross, Greenville, SC.
$50,000 to Davidson College, Davidson, NC.
$28,000 to Furman University, Greenville, SC.
$25,000 to Pendleton Place, Greenville, SC.
$25,000 to Walker Foundation, Spartanburg, SC.
$15,000 to Center for Developmental Services, Greenville, SC.
$10,000 to Peace Center for the Performing Arts, Greenville, SC.

7383
Greensboro Jaycees Charitable Foundation, Inc. ✧ ☆
401 N. Greene St.
Greensboro, NC 27401

Established in 1967 in NC.
Foundation type: Independent foundation.
Financial data (yr. ended 12/31/05): Assets, $1,992,753 (M); gifts received, $1,064,772; expenditures, $9,361,145; qualifying distributions, $862,679; giving activities include $862,679 for grants.
Purpose and activities: Giving primarily for health and human services.
Fields of interest: Hospitals (general); Health organizations, association; Human services; Children/youth, services; Protestant agencies & churches.
Limitations: Applications not accepted. No grants to individuals.
Application information: Contributes only to pre-selected organizations.
Officers: Barbara Esquibel, Chair.; Randy Harris, Pres.; James Latta, V.P.; Gregory Fons, Secy.; Michael Fogarty, Treas.
EIN: 566085407
Selected grants: The following grants were reported in 2003.
$25,000 to Tanglewood Park Foundation, Clemmons, NC.
$15,000 to Childrens Home Society.
$10,000 to American Junior Golf Association, Braselton, GA.
$10,000 to Music Academy of North Carolina, Greensboro, NC.
$5,000 to After Gateway, Greensboro, NC. 2 grants: $1,000, $4,000
$5,000 to Womens Resource Center.
$3,700 to YMCA. 2 grants: $2,500, $1,200
$800 to Urban Ministry, Birmingham, AL.

7384
Gunzenhauser-Chapin Fund ✧
c/o Piedmont Financial Trust Co., Inc.
P.O. Box 20124
Greensboro, NC 27420

Established in 1998 in NC.
Donor: Lynne R. and Karl E. Prickett Fund.
Foundation type: Independent foundation.
Financial data (yr. ended 12/31/04): Assets, $14,129,277 (M); gifts received, $1,670,000; expenditures, $542,780; qualifying distributions, $487,572; giving activities include $470,000 for 29 grants (high: $94,000; low: $1,000).
Purpose and activities: Giving for health, including children's health, and family planning services; funding also for higher education, children and youth services, and animal welfare.
Fields of interest: Higher education; Animal welfare; Hospitals (specialty); Reproductive health, family planning; Health care; Health organizations, association; Human services; Children/youth, services.
Limitations: Applications not accepted. Giving primarily in CA.
Application information: Unsolicited requests for funds not accepted.
Officers and Directors:* Charles S. Chapin,* Chair. and Pres.; Chester F. Chapin,* V.P.; Lynn C. Gunzenhauser,* V.P.; Lisa Prochnow,* Secy.; Samuel C. Chapin,* Treas.
EIN: 562089195
Selected grants: The following grants were reported in 2004.
$94,000 to Community Foundation of Greater Greensboro, Greensboro, NC.
$27,000 to Candlelighters Childhood Cancer Foundation, Kensington, MD.
$22,000 to Population Connection, DC.
$17,000 to Center for Public Integrity, DC.
$17,000 to National Center for Youth Law, Oakland, CA.
$15,000 to San Jose State University Foundation, San Jose, CA.
$10,000 to Arthritis Foundation, Concord, NH.

7385
Michael W. Haley Foundation, Inc. ✧
c/o Mike Winnig
228 W. Market St.
Greensboro, NC 27401

Established in 1990 in NC.
Donor: Michael W. Haley.
Foundation type: Independent foundation.
Financial data (yr. ended 10/31/04): Assets, $12,891,848 (M); expenditures, $640,753; qualifying distributions, $631,710; giving activities include $631,710 for 38 grants (high: $230,000; low: $400).
Purpose and activities: Giving primarily for higher education; funding also for the arts, health, children and youth services, and federated giving programs.
Fields of interest: Performing arts, orchestra (symphony); Arts; Higher education; Health organizations, association; Children/youth, services; Federated giving programs.
Limitations: Applications not accepted. Giving primarily in Greensboro, NC. No grants to individuals.
Application information: Contributes only to pre-selected organizations.
Officers and Directors:* Michael W. Haley,* Pres. and Treas.; Lynn C. Haley,* Secy.; Leigh H. Jones; Elizabeth L. Stanley.
EIN: 561720197
Selected grants: The following grants were reported in 2003.
$213,000 to Greensboro College, Greensboro, NC.

$12,000 to Carolina Pediatric-Family Center, Chapel Hill, NC.
$6,000 to Childrens Home Society of North Carolina, Greensboro, NC.
$5,000 to Duke University, Durham, NC.
$5,000 to United Way of Greater Greensboro, Greensboro, NC.
$1,000 to Boy Scouts of America, Old North State Council, Greensboro, NC.
$1,000 to Eastern Music Festival, Greensboro, NC.
$1,000 to Greensboro Independent School Corporation, Greensboro, NC.
$1,000 to United Arts Council of Greensboro, Greensboro, NC.
$1,000 to University of North Carolina, Greensboro, NC.

7386
D. F. Halton Foundation, Inc. ✧
(formerly Pepsi-Cola of Charlotte Foundation, Inc.)
P.O. Box 241167
Charlotte, NC 28224-1167   (704) 523-6761

Established in 1987 in NC.
Donor: Pepsi-Cola Bottling Co. of Charlotte.
Foundation type: Company-sponsored foundation.
Financial data (yr. ended 12/31/03): Assets, $24,592 (M); gifts received, $200,000; expenditures, $415,179; qualifying distributions, $415,173; giving activities include $415,175 for 73 grants (high: $250,000; low: $25).
Purpose and activities: The foundation supports organizations involved with arts and culture, education, health, medical research, social services, human services, and community development.
Fields of interest: Museums; Performing arts; Performing arts, dance; Performing arts, music; Historic preservation/historical societies; Arts; Education, association; Vocational education; Business school/education; Education; Substance abuse, services; Cancer; Heart & circulatory diseases; Cancer research; Heart & circulatory research; Housing/shelter, development; Children/youth, services; Family services; Residential/custodial care, hospices; Homeless, human services; Human services; Community development; Homeless.
Type of support: General/operating support; Annual campaigns; Capital campaigns; Scholarship funds.
Limitations: Giving limited to Cabarrus, Cleveland, Gaston, Lincoln, Mecklenburg, Stanly, and Union counties, NC. No grants to individuals.
Application information: Application form not required.
  Initial approach: Proposal
  Copies of proposal: 1
  Deadline(s): None
  Board meeting date(s): Quarterly
Officers: Dale F. Halton, Pres.; Darrell Holland, Secy.
EIN: 561591985

7387
The John W. and Anna H. Hanes Foundation
c/o Wachovia Bank N.A.
P.O. Box 3099, MC-NC6732
Winston-Salem, NC 27150   (336) 732-5991
Contact: Christopher W. Spaugh, V.P., Wachovia Bank, N.A.

Trust established in 1947 in NC.
Foundation type: Independent foundation.
Financial data (yr. ended 12/31/05): Assets, $26,497,990 (M); expenditures, $1,490,782; qualifying distributions, $1,382,391; giving activities include $1,366,233 for 32 grants (high: $400,000; low: $1,500).
Purpose and activities: Giving primarily for the arts.
Fields of interest: Historic preservation/historical societies; Arts; Education; Environment, natural resources; Environment; Health care; Human services; Children/youth, services.
Type of support: Annual campaigns; Capital campaigns; Building/renovation; Equipment; Land acquisition; Endowments; Emergency funds; Program development; Seed money; Matching/challenge support.
Limitations: Giving limited to NC, with emphasis on Forsyth County. No grants to individuals, or for operating expenses.
Publications: Application guidelines; Program policy statement.
Application information: Application form required.
  Initial approach: Telephone or letter
  Copies of proposal: 1
  Deadline(s): 15th day of month preceding board meeting
  Board meeting date(s): Jan., Apr., July, and Oct.
  Final notification: 10 days following board meeting
Trustees: Frank B. Hanes, Sr.; F. Borden Hanes, Jr.; R. Philip Hanes, Jr.; Drewry H. Nostitz; Ralph H. Womble; Wachovia Bank, N.A.
EIN: 566037589

7388
James G. Hanes Memorial Fund

(formerly James G. Hanes Memorial Fund/Foundation)
P.O. Box 26134
Winston-Salem, NC   27114   (336) 794-7832
Contact: George Burns
FAX: (336) 794-9944; Application address: c/o Southern Community Bank and Trust 4505 Country Club Rd., Ste. 200 Winston-Salem, NC 27104

Established in 1957 in NC. The James G. Hanes Memorial Fund reincorporated under its current name following the formal merger and transfer of all foundation assets to the fund in Dec. 1991. The foundation terminated in 1992.
Foundation type: Independent foundation.
Financial data (yr. ended 10/31/05): Assets, $20,312,703 (M); expenditures, $1,054,998; qualifying distributions, $892,492; giving activities include $767,492 for 12 grants (high: $349,992; low: $5,000), and $125,000 for 3 employee matching gifts.
Purpose and activities: Giving primarily for arts and culture, with emphasis on a contemporary art center.
Fields of interest: Museums (art); Arts; Environment, natural resources; Health care; Health organizations; Community development.
Type of support: General/operating support; Annual campaigns; Capital campaigns; Building/renovation; Equipment; Land acquisition; Endowments; Emergency funds; Program development; Conferences/seminars; Publication; Seed money; Research; Matching/challenge support.
Limitations: Giving primarily in NC, with emphasis on Winston-Salem. No grants to individuals, or for

maintenance purposes, or salary requests or funding on a recurring basis.
Publications: Application guidelines; Informational brochure.
Application information: Application form required.
  Initial approach: Proposal
  Copies of proposal: 1
  Deadline(s): Jan. 1, Apr. 1, July 1, and Oct. 1
  Board meeting date(s): Jan., Apr., Aug., and Oct.
  Final notification: 10 business days
Trustee: Southern Community Bank and Trust.
EIN: 566036987

7389
Haney Memorial Fund ◇

c/o Wachovia Bank, N.A.
100 N. Main St., 13th Fl.
Winston-Salem, NC   27150

Established in 1999 in PA.
Foundation type: Independent foundation.
Financial data (yr. ended 12/31/05): Assets, $8,531,126 (M); expenditures, $408,932; qualifying distributions, $321,194; giving activities include $320,794 for 9 grants (high: $318,794; low: $250).
Fields of interest: Higher education.
Limitations: Applications not accepted. Giving primarily in Philadelphia, PA. No grants to individuals.
Application information: Contributes only to pre-selected organizations.
Trustee: Wachovia Bank, N.A.
EIN: 236220412
Selected grants: The following grants were reported in 2004.
$319,839 to University of Pennsylvania, Philadelphia, PA.
$250 to American Academy of Political and Social Science, Philadelphia, PA.
$250 to Historical Society of Pennsylvania, Philadelphia, PA.

7390
James J. and Angelia M. Harris Foundation ◇

P.O. Box 220427
Charlotte, NC   28222   (704) 364-6046
Contact: Sherri McDaniel Harrell

Established in 1984 in NC.
Donor: James J. Harris†.
Foundation type: Independent foundation.
Financial data (yr. ended 11/30/05): Assets, $13,885,011 (M); expenditures, $1,826,050; qualifying distributions, $1,696,300; giving activities include $1,696,300 for 51 grants (high: $250,000; low: $1,000).
Purpose and activities: Primary areas of interest include higher and other education, health services and hospitals, social services, and youth.
Fields of interest: Arts; Elementary/secondary education; Education, early childhood education; Higher education; Theological school/education; Adult/continuing education; Education; Hospitals (general); Health care; Human services; YM/YWCAs & YM/YWHAs; Children/youth, services; Family services; Community development.
Type of support: Annual campaigns; Capital campaigns; Building/renovation; Program

development; Seed money; Scholarship funds; Matching/challenge support.
Limitations: Giving limited to Clarke County, GA, and Mecklenburg County, NC (except where otherwise provided in trust agreement). No grants to individuals.
Publications: Application guidelines; Informational brochure.
Application information: Application form not required.
  Initial approach: Letter (no more than 3 pages)
  Copies of proposal: 1
  Deadline(s): None
  Board meeting date(s): May and Nov.
Officers and Managers:* Cameron M. Harris,* Chair.; Sara H. Bissell; John W. Harris; James E.S. Hynes; James E. Johnson, Jr.
EIN: 561465696
Selected grants: The following grants were reported in 2005.
$250,000 to YMCA of Greater Charlotte, Charlotte, NC.
$100,000 to Billy Graham Evangelistic Association, Charlotte, NC.
$75,000 to Sharon Towers, Charlotte, NC.
$60,000 to University of Georgia, Athens, GA.
$50,000 to Charlotte Symphony Orchestra, Charlotte, NC.
$50,000 to Childrens Learning Center, Charlotte, NC.
$50,000 to Union Theological Seminary, Winston-Salem, NC.
$35,000 to Charlotte-Mecklenburg Schools, Charlotte, NC.
$30,000 to Fletcher School, Charlotte, NC.
$10,000 to Family Center, Charlotte, NC.

7391
The Hartquist Foundation

c/o Wachovia Bank, N.A.
401 S. Tryon St., TH-2
Charlotte, NC   28288-1159
Contact: Palmer Wilson

Established in 1998 in NC.
Donor: Mildred Hartquist Trust.
Foundation type: Independent foundation.
Financial data (yr. ended 12/31/05): Assets, $10,349,631 (M); gifts received, $89,941; expenditures, $691,110; qualifying distributions, $682,595; giving activities include $675,000 for 9 grants (high: $100,000; low: $25,000).
Purpose and activities: Giving primarily for higher education.
Fields of interest: Higher education; Hospitals (general).
Limitations: Applications not accepted. Giving primarily in NC. No grants to individuals.
Application information: Contributes only to pre-selected organizations.
Directors: Anne Marie Kean; Janet H. Kean; Teresa Anne Kean; Thomas J. Kean, Jr.
EIN: 911912805

7392
Harvest Charities ◇ ☆

(formerly Belk-Simpson Foundation)
c/o Wachovia Bank, N.A.
100 N. Main St., 13th Fl.
Winston-Salem, NC   27150
Contact: Todd Ripley

Application address: c/o Wachovia Bank, N.A., 15 S. Main St., Greenville, SC 29601, tel.: (864) 467-2802

Trust established in 1944 in SC.
Donors: Belk-Simpson Co.; J.A. Kuhn.
Foundation type: Company-sponsored foundation.
Financial data (yr. ended 12/31/05): Assets, $10,845,835 (M); expenditures, $571,282; qualifying distributions, $493,065; giving activities include $488,565 for 72 grants (high: $60,000; low: $100).
Purpose and activities: The foundation supports hospitals and organizations involved with arts and culture, education, cancer, human services, and Protestantism.
Fields of interest: Historic preservation/historical societies; Arts; Higher education; Education; Hospitals (general); Cancer; Cancer research; Children/youth, services; Residential/custodial care, hospices; Human services; Federated giving programs; Protestant agencies & churches.
Type of support: General/operating support; Capital campaigns; Matching/challenge support.
Limitations: Giving primarily in SC. No grants to individuals.
Application information: Letters of inquiry should be submitted using organization letterhead.
Initial approach: Letter of inquiry
Copies of proposal: 5
Deadline(s): Apr. 30 and Oct. 31
Board meeting date(s): May 1 and Nov. 1
Trustee: Wachovia Bank, N.A.
Board of Advisors: Claire Efird; John A. Kuhn; Lucy S. Kuhn; Nell M. Rice; Caroline Schmitt; Kate M. Simpson.
EIN: 576020261

7393
The C. Felix Harvey Foundation, Inc. ✧
P.O. Box 189
Kinston, NC   28502

Established around 1970 in NC.
Donors: Felix Harvey; Margaret B. Harvey; Dixie Denning Supply Co.
Foundation type: Independent foundation.
Financial data (yr. ended 8/31/05): Assets, $14,089,953 (M); gifts received, $395,000; expenditures, $496,914; giving activities include $465,701 for 63 grants (high: $80,000; low: $1).
Purpose and activities: Giving for education, health, religion, social services, and the arts and humanities.
Fields of interest: Humanities; Secondary school/education; Higher education; Health care; Human services; Christian agencies & churches.
Limitations: Giving primarily in NC. No grants to individuals.
Officers: Margaret B. Harvey, Pres.; C. Felix Harvey, V.P.; Leigh H. McNairy, V.P.; Ruth Heath, Secy.-Treas.
EIN: 237038942
Selected grants: The following grants were reported in 2005.
$60,000 to Westminister School. 2 grants: $50,000, $10,000
$25,000 to Mount Olive College, Mount Olive, NC.
$11,000 to Salvation Army. 2 grants: $1,000, $10,000
$10,000 to Woodberry Forest School, Woodberry Forest, VA. 2 grants: $5,000 each
$7,000 to Lenoir Memorial Hospital, Kinston, NC.

$5,000 to Hood Theological Seminary, Salisbury, NC.
$2,500 to Independent College Fund.

7394
Hayden-Harman Foundation ✧
c/o J. Patrick Harman
P.O. Box 1762
Burlington, NC   27216-1762

Established in 2000 in NC.
Foundation type: Independent foundation.
Financial data (yr. ended 12/31/05): Assets, $11,674,122 (M); expenditures, $584,669; qualifying distributions, $479,171; giving activities include $420,567 for 33 grants (high: $62,000; low: $1,000; average: $5,000–$25,000).
Fields of interest: Museums (history); Arts; Education; Youth development.
Limitations: Applications not accepted. Giving primarily in NC. No grants to individuals.
Application information: Contributes only to pre-selected organizations.
Officers: J. Patrick Harman, Pres.; David L. Harman, V.P.; Patrick H. Harman, V.P.; Phoebe Harman, Secy.-Treas.
EIN: 562180022

7395
Hendrick Foundation for Children ✧ ☆
6000 Monroe Rd.
Charlotte, NC   28212   (704) 568-5550
Application address: c/o Grant Request, P.O. Box 240070, Charlotte, NC 28224-0070; URL: http://www.thehendrickfoundation.org

Established in 2004 in NC.
Donors: Hendrick Automotive Group; Marrow Foundation; Hendrick Motorsports, Inc.
Foundation type: Company-sponsored foundation.
Financial data (yr. ended 12/31/05): Assets, $696,568 (M); gifts received, $277,072; expenditures, $480,772; qualifying distributions, $480,735; giving activities include $480,735 for 7 grants (high: $100,000; low: $15,000).
Purpose and activities: The foundation supports programs designed to provide health, medical, social welfare, and educational services to benefit children with illness, disease, injury, pain, disability, incapacity, or other disadvantages; and improve quality of life for children with life-threatening or chronic injuries, illness, and disabilities.
Fields of interest: Elementary/secondary education; Health care; Children, services; Physically disabled.
Type of support: General/operating support; Building/renovation; Scholarship funds.
Limitations: Giving primarily in Charlotte, NC.
Application information: Proposals should be submitted using organization letterhead. Application form not required.
Initial approach: Proposal
Deadline(s): None
Officers and Directors:* Charles V. Ricks,* Pres. and Treas.; Brad McClough,* V.P.; Gregory H. Gach,* Secy.
EIN: 201786855

7396
The Leonard G. Herring Family Foundation, Inc.
310 Coffey St.
North Wilkesboro, NC   28659

Established in 1994 in NC.
Donor: Leonard G. Herring.
Foundation type: Independent foundation.
Financial data (yr. ended 12/31/05): Assets, $16,518,900 (M); gifts received, $6,911,813; expenditures, $442,173; qualifying distributions, $438,392; giving activities include $438,392 for 63 grants (high: $40,000; low: $500).
Fields of interest: Higher education; Environment, natural resources; Health organizations, association; YM/YWCAs & YM/YWHAs; Children/youth, services; Federated giving programs; Protestant agencies & churches.
Limitations: Applications not accepted. No grants to individuals.
Application information: Contributes only to pre-selected organizations.
Officers: Leonard G. Herring, Pres.; Rozelia S. Herring, V.P.; Sandra Herring Gaddy, Secy.; Albert Lee Herring, Treas.
EIN: 561881015

7397
High Point Community Foundation ✧
101 S. Main St., Ste. 815
P.O. Box 1371
High Point, NC   27261-1371   (336) 882-3298
Contact: Paul Lessard, Exec. Dir.; For grants: Sarah O'Hearn, Office Mgr.
FAX: (336) 882-3293;
E-mail: paul@hpcommunityfoundation.org; Grant application tel.: (336) 882-3297 and E-mail: sarah@hpcommunityfoundation.org; URL: http://www.hpcommunityfoundation.org

Established in 1990 in NC.
Foundation type: Community foundation.
Financial data (yr. ended 6/30/05): Assets, $37,358,101 (M); gifts received, $12,989,879; expenditures, $2,544,744; giving activities include $2,138,559 for grants.
Purpose and activities: The mission of the foundation is to contribute toward meeting the changing needs of the High Point Community and its residents.
Fields of interest: Arts; Elementary/secondary education; Education; Boys & girls clubs; Children/youth, services; Human services; Jewish agencies & temples.
Limitations: Giving limited to the High Point, NC, area. No grants to individuals.
Publications: Application guidelines; Annual report; Grants list; Informational brochure; Newsletter.
Application information: Visit foundation Web site for application form and information. "Guidelines for Grantseekers" and "Grants Policies and Procedures" must be reviewed before submitting complete application; materials may be requested from foundation office. Faxed applications are not accepted. Application form required.
Initial approach: Letter
Copies of proposal: 15
Deadline(s): Sept. 1
Final notification: Late Dec.
Officers and Trustees:* Nido Qubein,* Chair.; Bill McGuinn,* 1st Vice-Chair.; A.B. Henley,*

Vice-Chair.; Bill Horney,* Vice-Chair.; Judy Mendenhall,* Vice-Chair.; Marsha Slane,* Vice-Chair.; Charles A. Green,* Secy.; Dan Odom,* Treas.; Paul Lessard, Exec. Dir.; Elizabeth Aldridge; Tom Blount; Robert J. Brown; Ray Burrow; Susan Culp; P. Hunter Dalton, Jr.; Danny Davis; Meredith Eanes; Tom Haggai; David Hayworth; Milton Kirkland; Ray McAllister, Sr.; Wade McInnis; George Marsh; Kay Maynard; Max Meeks; David S. Miller; James F. Morgan; Jim Morgan; Charles L. Odom; Ed Price; Joe Rawley; Jan Samet; Otis Tillman; Yogi Yarborough; W. Vann York.
Number of staff: 2 full-time professional.
EIN: 561695787

7398

Hillsdale Fund, Inc. ✧
c/o Piedmont Financial Co.
P.O. Box 20124
Greensboro, NC 27420-0124 (336) 274-5471
Contact: Edward E. Doolan, Fdn. Mgr.

Incorporated in 1963 in NC.
Donor: The L. Richardson family.
Foundation type: Independent foundation.
Financial data (yr. ended 12/31/04): Assets, $33,430,019 (M); gifts received, $24,239; expenditures, $1,701,802; qualifying distributions, $1,574,005; giving activities include $1,422,628 for 84 grants (high: $100,000; low: $1,000).
Purpose and activities: Giving primarily to education, natural resource conservation and protection, and arts and culture.
Fields of interest: Arts councils; Arts; Elementary/secondary education; Higher education; Environment; Hospitals (specialty); Food banks; Human services; Children/youth, services; Christian agencies & churches.
Limitations: Giving primarily in NC and the Eastern Seaboard. No grants to individuals, or for operating budgets.
Application information: Application form required.
  Initial approach: Completed application form
  Copies of proposal: 1
  Deadline(s): Spring and fall (contact foundation for exact dates)
  Board meeting date(s): Usually in Apr. or June and Nov.
Officers and Trustees:* Lunsford Richardson, Jr.,* Chair.; Sion A. Boney,* Fdn. Mgr.; Edward E. Doolan, Fdn. Mgr.; Sion A. Boney III; Laurinda Lowenstein Douglas; Barbara R. Evans; J. Peter Gallagher; Margaret W. Gallagher; Louise Boney McCoy; Beatrix W. Richardson; Eudora L. Richardson; James Lunsford Richardson; L.R. Smith; Molly R. Smith; Richard G. Smith III; Margaret R. White.
Number of staff: 1 part-time professional; 1 part-time support.
EIN: 566057433

7399

The R. P. Holding Foundation, Inc. ✧
(formerly The Robert P. Holding Foundation)
P.O. Box 1377
Smithfield, NC 27577-1377

Incorporated in 1955 in NC.
Donors: Robert Holding†; Maggie B. Holding.
Foundation type: Independent foundation.
Financial data (yr. ended 12/31/05): Assets, $26,358,444 (M); expenditures, $1,195,086;

qualifying distributions, $1,188,180; giving activities include $1,188,180 for 22 grants (high: $810,152; low: $500).
Purpose and activities: Giving primarily for a community foundation, as well as to museums, education, children and social services, federated giving programs, and a cancer center. Grants also for education-specified scholarships to select individuals in financial distress.
Fields of interest: Museums (art); Higher education; Education; Cancer research; Human services; Children, services; Foundations (community); Federated giving programs.
Type of support: General/operating support; Scholarship funds.
Limitations: Applications not accepted. Giving primarily in NC.
Application information: Contributes only to pre-selected organizations and individuals.
Officers: Frank B. Holding, Pres.; Lewis R. Holding, V.P.; Virginia Hopkins, Secy.; Doris T. Allen, Treas.
EIN: 566044205
Selected grants: The following grants were reported in 2004.
$589,959 to North Carolina Community Foundation, Raleigh, NC. 2 grants: $10,000, $579,959
$200,440 to Campbell University, Buies Creek, NC. 2 grants: $500, $199,940
$100,000 to Louisburg College, Louisburg, NC.
$25,000 to Duke University Medical Center, Durham, NC.
$10,000 to Healing Place of Wake County, Raleigh, NC.
$5,000 to Ravenscroft School, Raleigh, NC.
$2,500 to Lee University, Cleveland, TN.
$2,500 to Salvation Army.

7400

The Julius and Katheryn Hommer Foundation ✧
c/o Wachovia Bank, N.A.
100 N. Main St., 13th Fl.
Winston-Salem, NC 27150
Application address: c/o Peter L. Kern or Carol H. Kern, P.O. Box 8, Brodheadsville, PA 18322

Established in 1996 in PA.
Donor: Katheryn M. Hommer.
Foundation type: Independent foundation.
Financial data (yr. ended 12/31/05): Assets, $14,319,041 (M); expenditures, $638,291; qualifying distributions, $570,000; giving activities include $570,000 for 27 grants (high: $115,000; low: $2,000).
Fields of interest: Secondary school/education; Libraries/library science; Libraries (public); Education; Hospitals (general); Christian agencies & churches.
Application information:
  Initial approach: Letter
  Deadline(s): None
Trustees: Carol H. Kern; Peter L. Kern; Wachovia Bank, N.A.
EIN: 232847257

7401

O. C. Hubert Charitable Trust ✧
c/o Bank of America, N.A.
101 S. Tryon St.
Charlotte, NC 28255

Established in 1997 in GA.
Foundation type: Independent foundation.
Financial data (yr. ended 5/31/05): Assets, $15,681,291 (M); expenditures, $1,123,750; qualifying distributions, $995,875; giving activities include $942,667 for 5 grants (high: $466,667; low: $1,000).
Purpose and activities: Giving primarily for public health education.
Fields of interest: Public health school/education; Scholarships/financial aid.
Limitations: Applications not accepted. Giving primarily in NC. No grants to individuals.
Application information: Contributes only to pre-selected organizations.
Trustees: William Foege, M.D.; Richard N. Hubert; Bank of America, N.A.
EIN: 586316941
Selected grants: The following grants were reported in 2004.
$466,666 to Rollins College, School of Public Health, Winter Park, FL. For Foege chair.
$250,000 to Global Health Action, Atlanta, GA.
$200,000 to Duke University, Durham, NC. For resident program.
$100,000 to Emory University, Nell Hodgson Woodruff School of Nursing, Atlanta, GA. For Lillian Carter Center for International Nursing.
$100,000 to Medshare International, Lithonia, GA. For global medical resources and supplies.
$100,000 to Wellstar Foundation, Marietta, GA. For Center for Nursing Excellence.
$25,000 to Baptist Medical Dental Fellowship, Memphis, TN. For student practicum.

7402

J. F. Hurley Foundation
P.O. Box 4354
Salisbury, NC 28145-4354
Contact: Gordon P. Hurley, Pres.

Established in 1982 in NC.
Donors: Gordon P. Hurley; J.F. Hurley III.
Foundation type: Independent foundation.
Financial data (yr. ended 12/31/05): Assets, $3,201,811 (M); expenditures, $536,127; qualifying distributions, $508,960; giving activities include $508,960 for 23 grants (high: $400,000; low: $100).
Purpose and activities: Giving primarily for general and higher education institutions, health, and medical associations; support also for child welfare organizations and children's homes.
Fields of interest: Higher education; Education; Health organizations, association; Children/youth, services.
Type of support: General/operating support; Continuing support; Building/renovation; Program development.
Limitations: Applications not accepted. Giving primarily in Rowan County, NC, with emphasis on Salisbury.
Application information: Unsolicited requests for funds not accepted.
  Board meeting date(s): 1st Tues. in Feb.
Officers and Directors:* J.F. Hurley III,* Chair. and Secy.-Treas.; Gordon P. Hurley,* Pres.; Elizabeth V. Rankin, Exec. V.P.
Number of staff: None.
EIN: 561318937
Selected grants: The following grants were reported in 2004.
$415,000 to YMCA.

$10,000 to Rufty-Holmes Senior Center, Salisbury, NC.

$5,000 to First Presbyterian Church, Salisbury, NC.

$5,000 to Livingstone College, Salisbury, NC.

$1,000 to Davidson College, Davidson, NC.

$1,000 to Rowan Helping Ministries, Salisbury, NC.

$500 to Crossnore School, Crossnore, NC.

$500 to Nazareth Childrens Home, Rockwell, NC.

7403
The Hurley-Trammell Foundation ☆
c/o Elizabeth V. Rankin
126 W. Innes St.
P.O. Box 4354
Salisbury, NC 28145-4354

Established in 1987 in NC.
Donors: James F. Hurley; Geraldine T. Hurley.
Foundation type: Independent foundation.
Financial data (yr. ended 12/31/05): Assets, $78,652 (M); expenditures, $367,023; qualifying distributions, $354,000; giving activities include $354,000 for 32 grants (high: $100,000; low: $500).
Purpose and activities: Giving to children and family services, higher education, religion, public services, and aid to the aged.
Fields of interest: Arts; Higher education, college; Family services; Christian agencies & churches.
Type of support: General/operating support; Continuing support; Building/renovation.
Limitations: Applications not accepted. Giving primarily in Salisbury, NC. No grants to individuals.
Application information: Unsolicited requests for funds not accepted.
Board meeting date(s): 1st Tues. in Feb.
Officers and Directors:* Geraldine T. Hurley,* Pres.; Elizabeth V. Rankin,* Exec. V.P.; James F. Hurley,* Secy.-Treas.; Gordon P. Hurley; Linda Alexander Weaver; Mark Wineka.
Number of staff: 1 full-time support.
EIN: 561576470
Selected grants: The following grants were reported in 2004.
$50,000 to Rape, Child and Family Abuse Crisis Council, Salisbury, NC.

$40,000 to First Presbyterian Church, Salisbury, NC.

$28,000 to Salisbury High School, Salisbury, NC.

$15,000 to Winthrop University, Rock Hill, SC.

$10,000 to Catawba College, Salisbury, NC.

$10,000 to Livingstone College, Salisbury, NC. For scholarships.

$10,000 to United Way of Rowan County, Salisbury, NC.

$5,000 to Rufty-Holmes Senior Center, Salisbury, NC.

$5,000 to Woodberry Forest School, Woodberry Forest, VA.

$1,000 to Rowan Helping Ministries, Salisbury, NC.

7404
Janirve Foundation ▼ ◇
1 N. Pack Sq., Ste. 416
Asheville, NC 28801   (828) 258-1877
Contact: E. Charles Dyson, Chair.
FAX: (828) 258-1837;
E-mail: janirve@charterinternet.com

Established in 1954 in FL.
Donors: Irving J. Reuter†; Jeannett M. Reuter†.

Foundation type: Independent foundation.
Financial data (yr. ended 12/31/05): Assets, $42,723,799 (M); expenditures, $8,535,887; qualifying distributions, $8,260,433; giving activities include $7,903,300 for 91 grants (high: $500,000; low: $1,000; average: $10,000–$125,000).
Purpose and activities: Giving primarily for colleges and universities and human services, including child welfare, family services, and housing programs; some support also for hospitals and health associations and community development projects.
Fields of interest: Higher education; Environment, natural resources; Environment, plant conservation; Environment; Hospitals (general); Health organizations, association; Housing/shelter, development; Human services; Children/youth, services; Family services; Community development; Aging; Disabilities, people with; Minorities; Economically disadvantaged.
Type of support: Capital campaigns; Building/renovation; Equipment.
Limitations: Giving primarily in western NC. No support for public and private elementary schools, or churches and religious programs. No grants to individuals (except for scholarships), or generally for operating budgets, endowments or for research programs, publication of books or printed material, theatrical productions, videos, radio or television programs; no loans.
Publications: Application guidelines; Annual report; Grants list.
Application information: Applicants should contact Asheville, NC, office for application procedures. A grantee must wait at least two years from the date of approval of a grant before applying for another grant. Proposals from colleges and universities are considered only in the front quarter. Application form required.
Initial approach: Telephone or letter
Copies of proposal: 5
Deadline(s): Mar. 1, June 1, Sept. 1, and Dec. 1
Board meeting date(s): At least monthly
Final notification: Within 4 months
Officers and Advisory Committee Members:* E. Charles Dyson,* Chair.; Richard B. Wynne,* Vice-Chair.; John W. Erichson,* Secy.; Met R. Poston; James W.G. Woollcott.
Trustee: First National in Palm Beach.
Number of staff: 1 full-time professional; 1 part-time professional.
EIN: 596147678
Selected grants: The following grants were reported in 2005.
$500,000 to Habitat for Humanity, Asheville Area, Asheville, NC. To develop land on which Habitat will build affordable homes.

$500,000 to Pack Square Conservancy, Asheville, NC.

$400,000 to Mission Saint Josephs Healthcare Foundation, Asheville, NC.

$300,000 to Asheville City and Buncombe County Education Coalition, Asheville, NC. For tutoring and mentoring program for under-performing students in Asheville City and Buncombe County schools.

$250,000 to Crossnore School, Crossnore, NC. To renovate old Sloop Hospital to use as guesthouse during family reunification and adoption placement.

$145,000 to Asheville Symphony, Asheville, NC. To update acoustics in Thomas Wolfe Auditorium, purchase electronic keyboard, update rehearsal space and provide office for music director.

$100,000 to Colburn Earth Science Museum, Asheville, NC. To expand and upgrade permanent exhibits.

$100,000 to Macon County Public Library, Friends of, Franklin, NC. To purchase furnishings, fixtures and equipment for new facility.

$75,000 to Partnership for Health, Hendersonville, NC.

$45,000 to Kids Inter-Disciplinary Services, Franklin, NC. Toward mortgage reduction on facility used in child abuse prevention program.

7405
Jefferson-Pilot Foundation ◇
P.O. Box 21008, Dept. 3602
Greensboro, NC 27420-1008   (336) 691-3000
Contact: May Whitaker

Established in 1951 in NC.
Donor: Jefferson-Pilot Corp.
Foundation type: Company-sponsored foundation.
Financial data (yr. ended 11/30/05): Assets, $13,023 (M); gifts received, $1,375,000; expenditures, $2,866,489; qualifying distributions, $2,874,270; giving activities include $2,874,270 for 1,066 grants (high: $255,000; low: $25).
Purpose and activities: The foundation supports organizations involved with arts and culture, education, health, and human services.
Fields of interest: Arts; Higher education; Education; Hospitals (general); Health organizations, association; Residential/custodial care, hospices; Human services; Federated giving programs.
Limitations: Giving primarily in the Southeast.
Application information: Application form not required.
Initial approach: Proposal
Deadline(s): None
Trustees: Dennis Glass; John C. Ingram; Hoyt Phillips; Russell Simpson.
EIN: 566040780
Selected grants: The following grants were reported in 2004.
$250,000 to United Way of Greater Greensboro, Greensboro, NC.

$166,667 to Community Foundation of Greater Greensboro, Greensboro, NC.

$60,000 to United Arts Council, Saint Paul, MN.

$50,000 to Bennett College, Greensboro, NC.

$50,000 to Greensboro College, Greensboro, NC.

$50,000 to YMCA of Greensboro, Greensboro, NC.

$4,675 to United Way of Gaston County, Gastonia, NC.

$500 to Brookwood Community, Brookshire, TX.

$500 to Nebraska Shakespeare Festival, Omaha, NE.

$350 to Cannon School, Concord, NC.

7406
Victoria Jenkins Charitable Foundation ◇
c/o Bank of America, N.A.
101 S. Tryon St., NC1-002-08-12
Charlotte, NC 28255-0001

Established in 1993 in GA.
Donor: Victoria Jenkins†.
Foundation type: Independent foundation.
Financial data (yr. ended 12/31/05): Assets, $20,898,362 (M); expenditures, $881,910; qualifying distributions, $780,658; giving activities

include $750,000 for 7 grants (high: $225,000; low: $75,000).

Purpose and activities: Giving primarily to a Presbyterian church, as well as for education.

Fields of interest: Elementary/secondary education; Boys clubs; Protestant agencies & churches.

Limitations: Applications not accepted. Giving primarily in Savannah, GA. No grants to individuals.

Application information: Contributes only to pre-selected organizations.

Trustee: Bank of America, N.A.

EIN: 586281550

7407

The Jolley Foundation ✧

c/o Wachovia Bank N.A.
100 N. Main St., 13th Fl.
Winston-Salem, NC 27150
Application address: c/o Wachovia Bank, N.A., Attn.: Todd Ripley, P.O. Box 969, 15 S. Main St., Greenville, SC 29601, tel.: (864) 467-2836; fax number to request application form: (864) 467-2846

Established in 1947 in SC.

Donors: R.A. Jolley, Jr.; James E. Jolley; Mamie J. Bruce.

Foundation type: Independent foundation.

Financial data (yr. ended 12/31/05): Assets, $29,123,573 (M); expenditures, $793,099; qualifying distributions, $672,000; giving activities include $670,000 for 15 grants (high: $150,000; low: $15,000).

Purpose and activities: The foundation awards grants to local charities in the Greenville County, SC, area for higher education, human services, and scouting programs.

Fields of interest: Higher education; Boys & girls clubs; Boy scouts; Girl scouts; Human services.

Type of support: Capital campaigns.

Limitations: Giving primarily in the Greenville, SC, area. No grants to individuals, or for annual campaigns, operating budgets or endowment funds.

Application information: E-mailed or faxed applications will not be accepted. Application form required.

Initial approach: Request application guidelines
Copies of proposal: 4
Deadline(s): Apr. 1 and Sept. 1
Board meeting date(s): May and Oct.

Trustees: James McDuffie Bruce III; Jolley Bruce Christman; James E. Jolley.

EIN: 576024996

Selected grants: The following grants were reported in 2003.

$8,000,000 to Citadel, The, Charleston, SC. For general support.

7408

The Seby B. Jones Family Foundation, Inc. ✧

P.O. Box 19067
Raleigh, NC 27619-9067
Contact: Seby Russell Jones, Secy.

Established in 1983 in NC.

Donors: Seby B. Jones; Christina B. Jones†; Seby B. Jones Charitable Lead Trust.

Foundation type: Independent foundation.

Financial data (yr. ended 6/30/06): Assets, $12,666,397 (M); gifts received, $380,000; expenditures, $889,588; qualifying distributions, $846,160; giving activities include $846,160 for 53 grants (high: $200,000; low: $500).

Fields of interest: Museums (history); Arts; Elementary/secondary education; Higher education; Medical research, institute; Youth development; Human services; Christian agencies & churches.

Type of support: General/operating support; Building/renovation; Research.

Limitations: Giving primarily in NC; no giving outside the U.S.

Application information: Application form not required.

Initial approach: Letter
Copies of proposal: 1
Deadline(s): None
Board meeting date(s): Usually quarterly

Officers: Robert L. Jones, Chair.; James R. Jones, Pres.; Seby B. Jones, Jr., V.P.; Seby Russell Jones, Secy.; Alice J. Harrod, Treas.

EIN: 311578859

Selected grants: The following grants were reported in 2005.

$123,000 to Ravenscroft School, Raleigh, NC.

$50,000 to New Directions International, Burlington, NC.

$30,000 to North Carolina Community Foundation, Raleigh, NC.

$26,750 to YWCA of the Greater Triangle, Raleigh, NC.

$25,000 to Samaritans Purse, Boone, NC.

$10,000 to Passage Home, Raleigh, NC.

$10,000 to Raleigh Rescue Mission, Raleigh, NC.

$10,000 to Voorhees College, Denmark, SC.

$5,000 to Peace College, Raleigh, NC.

7409

H. G. and A. G. Keasbey Memorial Fund ✧

c/o Wachovia Bank, N.A.
100 N. Main St., 13th Fl.
Winston-Salem, NC 27150
Application address: c/o Angus Russell, Morgan, Lewis & Backus, 1 Logan Sq., Ste. 2000, Philadelphia, PA 19103-6993

Foundation type: Independent foundation.

Financial data (yr. ended 12/31/05): Assets, $7,401,496 (M); expenditures, $460,197; qualifying distributions, $423,311; giving activities include $375,642 for 36 grants to individuals (high: $65,298; low: $864).

Purpose and activities: Giving primarily for scholarships for higher education.

Type of support: Scholarships—to individuals.

Application information: Application form required.

Initial approach: Request application
Deadline(s): Contact foundation for deadlines

Trustees: Philip J. Greven, Jr.; Angus M. Russell; Wachovia Bank, N.A.

Number of staff: 1 part-time support.

EIN: 236447014

7410

The Greg and India Keith Foundation ✧ ☆

5201 Gorham Dr.
Charlotte, NC 28226
Contact: India Keith, Secy.

Established in 2004 in NC.

Donors: Greg Keith; India E. Keith.

Foundation type: Independent foundation.

Financial data (yr. ended 12/31/05): Assets, $290,020 (M); gifts received, $433,917; expenditures, $416,453; qualifying distributions, $402,148; giving activities include $402,148 for 17 grants (high: $125,000; low: $500).

Fields of interest: Arts; Education; YM/YWCAs & YM/YWHAs; Christian agencies & churches.

Limitations: Giving primarily in GA and NC.

Application information: Application form not required.

Officers: Graeme M. Keith, Jr., Pres.; India E. Keith, Secy.

EIN: 202016795

7411

The William R. Kenan, Jr. Fund for Engineering, Technology and Science

c/o Richard M. Krasno
P.O. Box 4150
Chapel Hill, NC 27515-4150

Established in 1991 in NC.

Foundation type: Independent foundation.

Financial data (yr. ended 6/30/05): Assets, $28,826,733 (M); expenditures, $1,638,889; qualifying distributions, $1,475,559; giving activities include $1,375,000 for 2 grants (high: $1,275,000; low: $100,000).

Fields of interest: Higher education; Engineering school/education; Science.

Type of support: General/operating support; Continuing support.

Limitations: Applications not accepted. Giving primarily in Raleigh, NC. No grants to individuals.

Application information: Contributes only to pre-selected organizations.

Officers and Directors:* Daniel W. Drake,* Chair.; Richard M. Krasno,* Pres.; Thomas S. Kenan III,* V.P.; Braxton Schell,* Secy.-Treas.; Christopher H. Cecil; J. Haywood Davis; Elizabeth Price Kenan; Thomas J. Sweeney.

EIN: 561761145

Selected grants: The following grants were reported in 2004.

$1,250,600 to North Carolina State University, Raleigh, NC. 3 grants: $1,090,600 to Institute of Engineering, $100,000 (For National Science Foundation project), $60,000 (For teaching fellows program).

7412

William R. Kenan, Jr. Fund for the Arts ✧

P.O. Box 4150
Chapel Hill, NC 27515-4150

Established in 1991 in NC.

Donor: William R. Kenan, Jr. Charitable Trust.

Foundation type: Independent foundation.

Financial data (yr. ended 6/30/05): Assets, $29,291,296 (M); expenditures, $1,497,910; qualifying distributions, $1,347,934; giving activities include $1,225,000 for 2 grants (high: $1,025,000; low: $200,000).

Fields of interest: Arts education; Higher education.

Type of support: General/operating support; Continuing support.

Limitations: Applications not accepted. Giving primarily in NC. No grants to individuals.

Application information: Contributes only to pre-selected organizations.
Officers and Directors:* Thomas S. Kenan III,* Chair.; Richard M. Krasno,* Pres.; Braxton Schell,* Secy.-Treas.; Christopher H. Cecil;* J. Haywood Davis; Daniel W. Drake; Elizabeth Price Kenan; Thomas J. Sweeney.
EIN: 581976597
Selected grants: The following grants were reported in 2004.
$615,940 to Kenan Institute for the Arts Foundation, Winston-Salem, NC. For general support.
$350,000 to University of North Carolina, Greensboro, NC. For A+ program.
$90,000 to Spoleto Festival USA, Charleston, SC. For program support.
$75,000 to New World Symphony, Miami Beach, FL. For Internet 2 program.
$25,000 to North Carolina School of the Arts, Winston-Salem, NC. For program support.

7413
The William R. Kenan, Jr. Fund
c/o Richard M. Krasno
P.O. Box 3808
Chapel Hill, NC 27515-3808

Established in 1983 in NC.
Donors: Frank H. Kenan†; William R. Kenan, Jr. Charitable Trust; Thomas S. Kenan III.
Foundation type: Independent foundation.
Financial data (yr. ended 6/30/05): Assets, $56,691,533 (M); expenditures, $3,432,865; qualifying distributions, $2,462,191; giving activities include $2,200,000 for 1 grant.
Purpose and activities: Grants awarded to an institute for the study of private enterprise and to the University of North Carolina for the support of the Kenan Center.
Fields of interest: Business school/education.
Type of support: Continuing support; Seed money.
Limitations: Applications not accepted. Giving primarily in NC. No grants to individuals.
Application information: Contributes only to pre-selected organizations.
Officers and Directors:* Richard M. Krasno,* Pres.; Thomas S. Kenan III,* V.P.; Braxton Schell,* Secy.; Robert P. Baynard; J. Haywood Davis; Daniel W. Drake; Elizabeth Kenan Howell; Elizabeth Kenan; Thomas J. Sweeney.
Number of staff: 2 full-time professional; 1 full-time support; 2 part-time support.
EIN: 570757568
Selected grants: The following grants were reported in 2004.
$2,250,000 to University of North Carolina, Chapel Hill, NC. 2 grants: $2,200,000 to Kenan Flagler Business School (For Frank H. Kenan Institute), $50,000 to Kenan Flagler Business School (For operating support).
$10,000 to Union Baptist Church, Durham, NC. For education fund.

7414
KPB Corporation ✦ ☆
P.O. Box 11902
Charlotte, NC 28220

Donor: Julian Price Family Foundation.
Foundation type: Independent foundation.

Financial data (yr. ended 12/31/04): Assets, $6,634,251 (M); gifts received, $120,000; expenditures, $1,074,666; qualifying distributions, $991,413; giving activities include $975,127 for 54 grants (high: $500,000; low: $50).
Fields of interest: Arts; Higher education; Health care; Community development.
Limitations: Applications not accepted. No grants to individuals.
Application information: Contributes only to pre-selected organizations.
Trustees: J.M. Bryan Taylor; John Taylor; Shawn Taylor.
EIN: 943418538

7415
Kulynych Family Foundation I, Inc. ✦
(formerly Petro Kulynych Foundation, Inc.)
1727 Spring Valley Rd.
Wilkesboro, NC 28697

Established in 1992 in NC.
Donor: Petro Kulynych.
Foundation type: Independent foundation.
Financial data (yr. ended 6/30/05): Assets, $10,291,687 (M); gifts received, $501,532; expenditures, $503,841; qualifying distributions, $483,750; giving activities include $483,750 for 155 grants (high: $10,000; low: $500).
Purpose and activities: Giving primarily for arts and culture, education, health, human services, children's services, and Baptist and Lutheran churches and organizations.
Fields of interest: Arts; Education; Health care; Health organizations, association; Cancer; Human services; Children/youth, services; Protestant agencies & churches.
Limitations: Applications not accepted. Giving primarily in NC. No grants to individuals.
Application information: Contributes only to pre-selected organizations.
Officers: Petro Kulynych, Chair. and Treas.; Brenda Cline, Pres.; Dale Cline, V.P.; Sydney Warren, Secy.
EIN: 237335353
Selected grants: The following grants were reported in 2004.
$10,000 to Brenner Childrens Hospital, Winston-Salem, NC.
$10,000 to Girl Scouts of the U.S.A., Tarheel Triad Council, Colfax, NC.
$10,000 to Holy Trinity Lutheran Church, Hickory, NC.
$10,000 to Providence Day School, Charlotte, NC.
$3,000 to Independent College Fund of North Carolina, Raleigh, NC.
$3,000 to Salem Academy and College, Winston-Salem, NC.
$3,000 to Wilkes Art Gallery, North Wilkesboro, NC.
$3,000 to Winston-Salem Foundation, Winston-Salem, NC.
$2,500 to Wilkes Central Senior High School, Wilkesboro, NC.
$1,000 to Special Olympics of North Carolina, Raleigh, NC.

7416
Kulynych Family Foundation II, Inc. ✦
1727 Spring Valley Rd.
Wilkesboro, NC 28697

Established in 1996 in NC.

Donor: Petro Kulynych.
Foundation type: Independent foundation.
Financial data (yr. ended 6/30/05): Assets, $10,288,603 (M); gifts received, $423,724; expenditures, $430,370; qualifying distributions, $421,000; giving activities include $421,000 for 92 grants (high: $20,000; low: $500).
Purpose and activities: Giving primarily for youth services, Christian organizations, education, and hospitals.
Fields of interest: Education; Health care; Athletics/sports, soccer; Children/youth, services; Christian agencies & churches.
Limitations: Applications not accepted. No grants to individuals.
Application information: Contributes only to pre-selected organizations.
Officers: Petro Kulynych, Chair. and Treas.; Janice Story, Pres.; Thomas E. Story, V.P.; Sydney Warren, Secy.
EIN: 561982360

7417
The Ladane Foundation, Ltd. ✦
c/o Ladane Williamson
P.O. Box 2588
Shallotte, NC 28459-2588

Established in 2000 in NC.
Donor: Ladane Williamson.
Foundation type: Independent foundation.
Financial data (yr. ended 12/31/05): Assets, $10,901,602 (M); gifts received, $11,145,000; expenditures, $542,791; qualifying distributions, $541,237; giving activities include $539,053 for 6 grants (high: $400,000; low: $100; average: $500–$100,000).
Purpose and activities: Giving primarily to a Presbyterian church; funding also for higher education.
Fields of interest: Higher education; Protestant agencies & churches.
Limitations: Applications not accepted. Giving primarily in NC, and New York, NY. No grants to individuals.
Application information: Contributes only to pre-selected organizations.
Officer: Ladane Williamson, Pres.
EIN: 134105176
Selected grants: The following grants were reported in 2003.
$990,000 to Fifth Avenue Presbyterian Church, New York, NY. For improvements to the church.
$400,000 to Duke University, Durham, NC. For scholarships.
$47,613 to Brunswick Community College Foundation, Supply, NC. For scholarships.
$588 to Blue Ridge Community College, Flat Rock, NC. For scholarships.
$100 to American Cancer Society, Charlotte, NC. For general support.

7418
Lance Foundation ✦
c/o Bank of America, N.A.
101 S. Tryon St., NC1-002-11-18
Charlotte, NC 28255-0001 (704) 554-1421
Contact: Zean Jamison, Dir.
Application address: P.O. Box 32368, Charlotte, NC 28232

Trust established in 1956 in NC.
Donor: Lance, Inc.
Foundation type: Company-sponsored foundation.
Financial data (yr. ended 6/30/05): Assets, $3,317,702 (M); expenditures, $513,390; qualifying distributions, $494,496; giving activities include $485,500 for 51 grants (high: $145,000; low: $1,000).
Purpose and activities: The foundation supports organizations involved with arts and culture, education, health, medical research, children and youth, and human services.
Fields of interest: Arts; Higher education; Education; Health care; Medical research; Children/youth, services; Human services; Federated giving programs.
Type of support: General/operating support; Scholarship funds.
Limitations: Giving primarily in NC. No grants to individuals, or for scholarships or fellowships; no loans.
Application information: Application form not required.
   Initial approach: Proposal
   Copies of proposal: 1
   Deadline(s): None
   Board meeting date(s): As required
   Final notification: 2 to 3 months
Directors: Zean Jamison, Jr.; Earl D. Leake; Clyde Preslar; Paul A. Stroup III; Richard G. Tucker.
Trustee: Bank of America, N.A.
Number of staff: 1
EIN: 566039487
Selected grants: The following grants were reported in 2004.
$140,000 to United Way of Central Carolinas, Charlotte, NC. For general support.
$15,000 to Fletcher School, Charlotte, NC. For general support.
$10,000 to Discovery Place, Charlotte, NC. For general support.
$10,000 to Junior Achievement of the Central Carolinas, Charlotte, NC. For general support.
$6,860 to Boy Scouts of America, Charlotte, NC. For general support.
$5,000 to American Red Cross, Charlotte, NC. For general support.
$5,000 to Carolina Youth Commission, Charlotte, NC. For general support.
$5,000 to Medical University of South Carolina (MUSC), Charleston, SC. For general support.
$4,000 to Young Life, Charlotte, NC. For general support.
$2,500 to United Way of Gaston County, Gastonia, NC. For general support.

7419
The Layden Family Foundation ✧
c/o Wachovia Bank, N.A.
100 N. Main St., 13th Fl.
Winston-Salem, NC 27150

Established in 2000 in PA.
Foundation type: Independent foundation.
Financial data (yr. ended 12/31/05): Assets, $1,193,259 (M); expenditures, $363,719; qualifying distributions, $337,504; giving activities include $334,200 for 26 grants (high: $50,000; low: $1,000).
Fields of interest: Museums; Elementary/secondary education; Food services; Human services; Federated giving programs.

Limitations: Applications not accepted. No grants to individuals.
Application information: Unsolicited requests for funds not accepted.
Trustees: Barbara Layden; Donald W. Layden.
EIN: 233039715
Selected grants: The following grants were reported in 2005.
$35,000 to National Center for Disability Services, Albertson, NY.
$25,000 to Chief Executive Leadership Institute, Atlanta, GA.
$10,000 to Childrens Hospital.
$10,000 to Roanoke College, Salem, VA.
$5,000 to Child and Parent Resources, Tacoma, WA.
$5,000 to Christophers, New York, NY. 2 grants: $2,500 each

7420
Legatus Foundation ✧ ☆
1 W. 4th St.
Winston-Salem, NC 27101-3806

Established in 2000 in NC.
Donors: Virginia Durand Shelden†; William Warren Shelden†.
Foundation type: Independent foundation.
Financial data (yr. ended 12/31/05): Assets, $13,237,994 (M); gifts received, $280,316; expenditures, $484,067; qualifying distributions, $484,067; giving activities include $407,347 for 41 grants (high: $228,532; low: $200).
Fields of interest: Higher education; Environment; Health organizations, association; Residential/custodial care, hospices; Foundations (community); Protestant agencies & churches.
Limitations: Applications not accepted. Giving on a national basis, with emphasis on Winston-Salem, NC. No grants to individuals.
Application information: Contributes only to pre-selected organizations.
Officers and Director:* Ranlet S. Bell,* Pres.; Frank M. Bell, Jr., Secy.-Treas.
EIN: 311737683
Selected grants: The following grants were reported in 2005.
$57,100 to Winston-Salem Foundation, Winston-Salem, NC.
$11,600 to Southeastern Center for Contemporary Art, Winston-Salem, NC.
$10,250 to Hospice and Palliative Care Center, Winston-Salem, NC.
$6,000 to Forsyth Medical Center Foundation, Winston-Salem, NC.
$6,000 to Vassar College, Poughkeepsie, NY.
$4,000 to Miss Porters School, Farmington, CT.
$4,000 to Nature Conservancy, Durham, NC.
$3,000 to Duke University, Durham, NC.
$1,250 to Penland School of Crafts, Penland, NC.
$1,000 to Reynolda House, Winston-Salem, NC.

7421
The Leon Levine Foundation ▼ ✧
P.O. Box 1017
Charlotte, NC 28201-1017
Contact: Leon Levine, Pres. and Treas.

Established in 1981 in NC.
Donors: Leon Levine; Howard Levine.
Foundation type: Independent foundation.

Financial data (yr. ended 6/30/05): Assets, $178,358,472 (M); gifts received, $1,514,750; expenditures, $9,427,053; qualifying distributions, $7,614,025; giving activities include $7,614,025 for 117 grants (high: $3,275,000; low: $50; average: $2,000–$10,000).
Purpose and activities: Giving primarily to arts and culture, human services, medical associations and Jewish agencies and temples.
Fields of interest: Arts; Health care; Human services; Foundations (community); Jewish agencies & temples.
Limitations: Applications not accepted. Giving primarily in Charlotte, NC. No grants to individuals.
Application information: Contributes only to pre-selected organizations.
Officers: Leon Levine, Pres. and Treas.; Sandra Levine, V.P. and Secy.; Lori Levine Sklut, V.P.
EIN: 581427515
Selected grants: The following grants were reported in 2005.
$3,275,000 to Carolinas Medical Center, Levine Children's Hospital, Charlotte, NC.
$1,800,000 to Foundation of Shalom Park, Charlotte, NC. 2 grants: $1,500,000, $300,000
$420,000 to Central Piedmont Community College Foundation, Charlotte, NC.
$400,000 to Levine Museum of the New South, Charlotte, NC. For endowment fund.
$250,000 to Levine Senior Center, Matthews, NC.
$10,000 to Crisis Assistance Ministry, Charlotte, NC.
$10,000 to Jewish Preschool on Sardis, Charlotte, NC.
$5,000 to Teen Health Connection, Charlotte, NC.
$1,000 to Carolinas Concert Association, Charlotte, NC.

7422
The Betty J. and J. Stanley Livingstone Charitable Foundation, Inc. ✧
119 Chestnut Tree Rd.
Mooresville, NC 28117

Established in 1986 in NC.
Donor: Betty J. Livingstone†.
Foundation type: Independent foundation.
Financial data (yr. ended 5/31/06): Assets, $390,181 (M); expenditures, $487,811; qualifying distributions, $473,005; giving activities include $459,500 for 11 grants (high: $250,000; low: $1,500).
Purpose and activities: Giving primarily for the arts, particularly a symphony orchestra, as well as for children and social services.
Fields of interest: Museums (art); Performing arts, orchestra (symphony); Human services; YM/YWCAs & YM/YWHAs; Children, services.
Limitations: Applications not accepted. Giving primarily in Charlotte, NC. No grants to individuals.
Application information: Contributes only to pre-selected organizations.
Officers: Margaret D. Callen, Pres.; David M. Bishop, Secy.; Mary S. Stokes, Treas.
EIN: 566233211

7423
Lowe's Charitable and Educational Foundation ◇

c/o Community Rels.
1000 Lowe's Blvd.
Mooresville, NC   28117   (704) 758-2831
Contact: Cindy Williams
FAX: (704) 757-4766;
E-mail: cindy.l.williams@lowes.com; Additional address: P.O. Box 1000, Mooresville, NC 28115; Application address for Outdoor Classroom Grant Prog.: Outdoor Classroom Grant Prog., P.O. Box 3292, Memphis, TN 38173-0292; Tel. for Lowe's Toolbox for Education: (800) 644-3561, ext. 208; E-mail for Lowe's Toolbox for Education: info@toolboxforeducation.com; URL: http://www.lowes.com/community

Established in 1957.
Donor: Lowe's Cos., Inc.
Foundation type: Company-sponsored foundation.
Financial data (yr. ended 1/31/06): Assets, $4,465,002 (M); gifts received, $16,961,336; expenditures, $14,098,581; qualifying distributions, $14,039,851; giving activities include $13,982,051 for 562 grants (high: $5,000,000; low: $500).
Purpose and activities: The foundation supports parks and playgrounds and organizations involved with K-12 education, environmental beautification, environmental education, home safety, and community development.
Fields of interest: Elementary/secondary education; Vocational education; Education, PTA groups; Environment, beautification programs; Environmental education; Safety, education; Recreation, parks/playgrounds; Community development; Science.
Type of support: General/operating support; Employee volunteer services.
Limitations: Giving on a national basis in areas of company operations; giving on a national basis for the Outdoor Classroom Grant Program and Lowe's Toolbox for Education. No support for national health organizations or their local affiliates, religious organizations, political, labor, veterans', or fraternal organizations, civic clubs, or candidates, sports teams, animal rescue and support organizations, organizations not of direct benefit to the entire community, private schools, or local affiliates or chapters of Habitat for Humanity, the American Red Cross, the United Way, or the Home Safety Council; no support for schools established less than two years ago for Lowe's Toolbox for Education. No grants to individuals or families, or for academic or medical research, religious programs or events, special events, sponsorship of fundraising events, advertising or marketing, athletic events or athletic programs, arts-based programs, travel-related events, book, film, video, or television program development or production, capital campaigns, endowments, or endowed chairs, continuing education for teachers and staff, institutional overhead and/or indirect costs, memorial campaigns, continuing support, international programs, or tickets to events; no grants for stipends, salaries, scholarships, or third party funding for Lowe's Toolbox for Education.
Publications: Application guidelines; Grants list.
Application information: Support is limited to 1 contribution per organization during any given year. The foundation reviews the first 1,500 applications only for Lowe's Toolbox for Education. Application form required.

Initial approach: Complete online application form; download application form and mail proposal and application form to application address for Outdoor Classroom Grant Program; complete online application form for Lowe's Toolbox for Education
Copies of proposal: 1
Deadline(s): None; postmarked by Dec. 31, Apr. 30, and Aug. 31 for the Outdoor Classroom Grant Program; Oct. 15 and Feb. 15 for Lowe's Toolbox for Education
Final notification: Mid-Jan., mid-May, and mid-Sept. for the Outdoor Classroom Grant Program; Dec. 15 and Apr. 15 for Lowe's Toolbox for Education
Officers: Larry D. Stone, Chair.; N. Brian Peace, Secy.; Larry W. Stanley, Treas.
Trustees: Darryl K. Henderson; Perry G. Jennings; Dale C. Pond.
EIN: 566061689

7424
Margaret Lee Martin Charitable Trust ◇

c/o Bank of America, N.A.
101 S. Tryon St., NC1-002-11-18
Charlotte, NC   28255
Application address: The Martin Scholarship Committee, c/o James M. Floyd, Sr., The Heritage Bank, P.O. Box 1009, Hinesville, GA 31310-8009

Established in 1995 in GA.
Foundation type: Independent foundation.
Financial data (yr. ended 12/31/05): Assets, $9,626,506 (M); expenditures, $510,197; qualifying distributions, $470,394; giving activities include $441,987 for 11 grants (high: $252,500; low: $3,790).
Purpose and activities: Giving primarily for the arts, and education; funding also for a Presbyterian church.
Fields of interest: Museums; Arts; Education; Federated giving programs; Protestant agencies & churches.
Type of support: Scholarship funds; Scholarships—to individuals.
Limitations: Giving limited to Liberty County, GA.
Application information: Applicant must be a legal resident of Liberty County, GA, or the child of a legal resident of Liberty County, GA; be in the top 10 percent of their high school class, score a minimum of 1,000 on the SAT or the equivalent on the ACT, and must be accepted by and/or attending a regionally accredited college, university, or nursing school.
Deadline(s): May 1
Final notification: Varies
Trustees: James M. Floyd, Sr.; Bank of America, N.A.
Number of staff: 1 part-time professional.
EIN: 586305150

7425
Thomas R. & Elizabeth E. McLean Foundation, Inc.

P.O. Box 58329
Fayetteville, NC   28305
Contact: Alfred Cleveland, Tr.
Application address: P.O. Box 58329, Fayetteville, NC 28305, tel.: (910) 483-8104

Established in 1998 in NC.

Donor: Tom McLean.
Foundation type: Independent foundation.
Financial data (yr. ended 12/31/05): Assets, $16,865,078 (M); gifts received, $250,000; expenditures, $904,369; qualifying distributions, $700,466; giving activities include $700,466 for 16 grants (high: $166,666; low: $6,000).
Purpose and activities: Giving to improve the quality of life in Cumberland County, NC.
Fields of interest: Museums (science/technology); Performing arts, theater; Higher education; YM/YWCAs & YM/YWHAs; Foundations (community).
Limitations: Applications not accepted. Giving limited to Cumberland County, NC. No support for religious or political organizations.
Application information: Unsolicited requests for funds not accepted.
Board meeting date(s): Monthly
Trustees: Alfred Cleveland; Harry Shaw.
EIN: 311470721
Selected grants: The following grants were reported in 2003.
$255,000 to Methodist College, Fayetteville, NC. For unrestricted support.
$83,333 to Airborne and Special Operations Museum Foundation, Fayetteville, NC. For unrestricted support.
$75,000 to Fayetteville Technical Community College, Fayetteville, NC. For unrestricted support.
$75,000 to Nature Conservancy, Arlington, VA. For unrestricted support.
$50,000 to Cumberland Community Foundation, Fayetteville, NC. For unrestricted support.
$50,000 to Fayetteville, City of, Fayetteville, AR. For unrestricted support.
$26,000 to Cape Fear Regional Theater at Fayetteville, Fayetteville, NC. For unrestricted support.
$25,000 to Festival of Flight 2003, Fayetteville, NC. For unrestricted support.
$20,000 to Fayetteville Symphony Orchestra, Fayetteville, NC. For unrestricted support.
$1,500 to Garden Club of North Carolina, Raleigh, NC. For unrestricted support.

7426
The McMichael Family Foundation ◇

P.O. Box 507
Madison, NC   27025

Established in 1992 in NC.
Donor: Dalton L. McMichael, Sr.‡.
Foundation type: Independent foundation.
Financial data (yr. ended 9/30/05): Assets, $57,466,331 (M); gifts received, $219,429; expenditures, $2,814,301; qualifying distributions, $2,717,325; giving activities include $2,717,325 for 71 grants (high: $250,000; low: $500).
Purpose and activities: Giving primarily for education and recreation.
Fields of interest: Higher education; Education; Recreation, government agencies; Protestant agencies & churches.
Limitations: Applications not accepted. Giving primarily in NC. No grants to individuals.
Application information: Contributes only to pre-selected organizations.
Officers and Directors:* Dalton L. McMichael, Jr.,* Pres.; Gail McMichael Drew,* V.P.; Flavel McMichael Godfrey,* V.P.; Louise McMichael Miracle, Secy.-Treas.
EIN: 561774976

7427

Mebane Charitable Foundation, Inc. ◇
232 S. Main St.
P.O. Box 339
Mocksville, NC 27028 (336) 936-0041
Contact: Misty Green, Admin. Asst.
FAX: (336) 936-0038;
E-mail: mgreen@mebanefoundation.com;
URL: http://www.mebanefoundation.com

Established in 1992 in NC.
Donor: G. Allen Mebane IV.
Foundation type: Independent foundation.
Financial data (yr. ended 12/31/05): Assets, $21,742,966 (M); expenditures, $1,239,378; qualifying distributions, $1,158,537; giving activities include $886,196 for 40 grants (high: $152,909; low: $200).
Purpose and activities: The foundation promotes and supports the highest quality early childhood education initiatives for children in NC. The foundation also supports nonprofit initiatives in Davie and Yadkin counties, NC, that can improve the lifestyle of its citizens.
Fields of interest: Education, early childhood education; Children/youth, services.
Type of support: General/operating support; Continuing support; Annual campaigns; Capital campaigns; Building/renovation; Endowments; Debt reduction; Program development; Seed money; Curriculum development; Scholarship funds; Research; Program evaluation; In-kind gifts; Matching/challenge support.
Limitations: Giving limited to NC. No grants to individuals; no loans.
Publications: Application guidelines; Annual report; Financial statement; Grants list; Multi-year report; Program policy statement.
Application information: Letter of intent form available on foundation Web site. Questions regarding letter of intent maybe made by telephone, Mon.-Fri., between 9:00am-4:00pm. Application form required.
Initial approach: Letter of intent
Copies of proposal: 1
Deadline(s): July 1 for consideration at fall board meeting and Jan. 1 for consideration at spring board meeting
Board meeting date(s): 3rd Tues. in Mar. and Sept.
Final notification: 90 days
Officers and Directors:* Michelle C. Speas, C.E.O.; G. Allen Mebane IV,* Pres.; Marianne Mebane,* V.P.; Clifford Frazier, Jr.,* Secy.; John H. Minehan,* Treas.; Carl N. Boon; John C. Lathrop; Donald C. McMillion; G. Allen Mebane V; Edward C. Smith, Jr.
Number of staff: 1 full-time professional; 2 full-time support.
EIN: 561853390
Selected grants: The following grants were reported in 2004.
$230,000 to Berea College, Berea, KY.
$147,200 to Hill Center, Durham, NC.
$45,800 to Christ School, Arden, NC.
$20,000 to Communities in Schools of Wilkes County, North Wilkesboro, NC.
$2,500 to Kanuga Conferences, Hendersonville, NC.
$600 to North Carolina Network of Grantmakers, Chapel Hill, NC.

7428

Merancas Foundation, Inc. ◇
(formerly Mermans Foundation, Inc.)
14051 Island Dr.
Huntersville, NC 28078 (704) 992-0705
Contact: Cornelis A.M. Mermans, Pres.

Established in 1989 in NC.
Donors: Cornelis A.M. Mermans; Johanna K. Mermans.
Foundation type: Independent foundation.
Financial data (yr. ended 12/31/05): Assets, $43,405,954 (M); gifts received, $98,698; expenditures, $2,551,118; qualifying distributions, $2,486,575; giving activities include $2,486,575 for 54 grants (high: $310,800; low: $400).
Fields of interest: Employment, training; Employment, vocational rehabilitation; Disasters, preparedness/services; Human services; Children/youth, services.
Type of support: Annual campaigns; Capital campaigns.
Limitations: Giving primarily in the Charlotte, NC, area. No support for arts organizations, or for political or religious organizations. No grants to individuals.
Application information: Application form not required.
Initial approach: Proposal
Copies of proposal: 1
Deadline(s): None
Board meeting date(s): Dec.
Officers: Cornelis A.M. Mermans, Pres.; Johanna K. Mermans, Secy.
Directors: Barry A. Bruno; Jennifer E. Bruno; Andy Mermans; Bryan K. Mermans; Nicole A. Mermans; Robin B. Mermans; Tasha B. Mermans.
EIN: 561677733
Selected grants: The following grants were reported in 2003.
$170,000 to Central Piedmont Community College, Charlotte, NC. For general support.
$150,000 to American Red Cross, Charlotte, NC. For general support.
$75,000 to Community Link Programs of Travelers Aid Society, Charlotte, NC. For general support.
$50,000 to Community Food Rescue, Charlotte, NC. For general support.
$50,000 to Crisis Assistance Ministry, Charlotte, NC. For general support.
$50,000 to Friendship Trays, Charlotte, NC. For general support.
$50,000 to Habitat for Humanity, Our Towns, Cornelius, NC. For general support.
$50,000 to Thompson Child and Family Focus, Matthews, NC. For general support.
$25,000 to Hospice and Palliative Care Charlotte Region, Charlotte, NC. For general support.
$25,000 to Salvation Army of Charlotte, Charlotte, NC. For general support.

7429

Mills Family Foundation, Inc. ◇ ☆
P.O. Box 8100
Asheville, NC 28814-8100
Contact: Pamela M. Turner, Pres.

Established around 1963.
Foundation type: Independent foundation.
Financial data (yr. ended 5/31/06): Assets, $1,007,577 (M); gifts received, $300,000; expenditures, $362,285; qualifying distributions, $355,042; giving activities include $355,042 for grants.
Purpose and activities: Giving primarily for arts and culture, education, and health and human services.
Fields of interest: Arts; Education; Environment, natural resources; Health care; Health organizations, association; Human services; YM/YWCAs & YM/YWHAs; Federated giving programs.
Type of support: General/operating support; Continuing support; Annual campaigns; Capital campaigns; Building/renovation; Equipment; Endowments; Emergency funds; Seed money; Scholarship funds; Matching/challenge support.
Limitations: Applications not accepted. Giving primarily in Asheville, Buncombe, and Madison counties, NC. No grants to individuals.
Application information: Unsolicited requests for funds not accepted.
Officers and Directors:* Pamela M. Turner,* Pres.; James W. Turner,* V.P.; Robin Turner Oswald; Brian Mills Turner.
EIN: 566060644
Selected grants: The following grants were reported in 2005.
$226,170 to Health Adventure, Asheville, NC.
$275 to Lewis Rathbun Wellness Center, Asheville, NC.

7430

The John Motley Morehead Foundation ▼ ◇
P.O. Box 690
Chapel Hill, NC 27514-0690
Contact: Charles E. Lovelace, Jr., Exec. Dir.
FAX: (919) 962-1615; E-mail: morehead@unc.edu;
URL: http://www.moreheadfoundation.org

Trust established in 1945 in NY.
Donor: John Motley Morehead III‡.
Foundation type: Independent foundation.
Financial data (yr. ended 6/30/05): Assets, $112,295,627 (M); expenditures, $6,485,665; qualifying distributions, $5,694,418; giving activities include $1,176,851 for 3+ grants (high: $708,455; low: $119,156), and $3,323,781 for 175 grants to individuals (high: $41,209; low: $6,900; average: $13,800–$28,672).
Purpose and activities: To attract outstanding, well-rounded students to study at the University of North Carolina at Chapel Hill. Currently makes awards for undergraduate study only at the University of North Carolina at Chapel Hill to graduates of NC high schools and preparatory and public schools, of selected preparatory schools outside the state and in Canada, and of 32 selected public schools in the United Kingdom; candidates for undergraduate scholarships must be nominated by their secondary schools.
Fields of interest: Higher education.
Type of support: Internship funds; Scholarships—to individuals.
Limitations: Giving primarily in NC and selected secondary schools. No support for secondary schools outside NC except by invitation from the foundation.
Publications: Annual report; Informational brochure.
Application information: Nomination form required.
Initial approach: By nomination only; no one may apply directly for Morehead Award
Deadline(s): Oct. 1 for nominations
Board meeting date(s): Mar., Apr., Aug., and Nov.
Final notification: Mar. 1

Officers and Trustees:* Lucy Hanes Chatham,* Chair.; Timothy Brooks Burnett,* Vice-Chair.; Steven R. Michalak, Treas.; Charles E. Lovelace, Jr., Exec. Dir.; Russell M. Robinson II,* Genl. Counsel; Holly Cluett Gwynne-Timothy; John A. Laskin, III; George Kennedy Thompson.

Number of staff: 5 full-time professional; 3 full-time support.

EIN: 560599225

Selected grants: The following grants were reported in 2004.

$1,092,648 to University of North Carolina, Chapel Hill, NC. 3 grants: $104,040 (To maintain Morehead House for Distinguished Guests), $293,481 (For support and promotion of Morehead Scholarship Program), $695,127 (For summer enrichment programs).

7431
The Morgan Foundation, Inc.
P.O. Box 1167
Laurel Hill, NC 28351
Contact: James L. Morgan Sr., Chair.

Established in 1992 in NC as successor to Morgan Trust for Charity, Religion, and Education which was established in 1949.

Donors: Edwin Morgan†; Elise Morgan†; Morgan Mills, Inc.; The Morgan Co. of Laurel Hill, Inc.; Morgan Farms, Inc.; Walden Court, Inc.

Foundation type: Independent foundation.

Financial data (yr. ended 4/30/06): Assets, $8,499,800 (M); expenditures, $744,850; qualifying distributions, $741,403; giving activities include $695,090 for 23 grants (high: $200,000; low: $100).

Purpose and activities: Support for higher education, Protestant churches, and community charities.

Fields of interest: Higher education; Community development; Protestant agencies & churches.

Type of support: Continuing support; Annual campaigns; Capital campaigns; Building/renovation; Endowments; Debt reduction; Seed money; Matching/challenge support.

Limitations: Giving primarily in the Laurel Hill, NC, area. No grants to individuals, or for scholarships or fellowships; no loans. Generally no grants for operating budgets.

Publications: Financial statement.

Application information: Application form not required.

Initial approach: Letter
Copies of proposal: 1
Deadline(s): None
Board meeting date(s): As required

Officers and Trustees:* James L. Morgan, Sr.,* Chair. and Pres.; James L. Morgan, Jr.,* Vice-Chair.; Elizabeth E. Morgan,* V.P.; Mary C. Oxendine,* Secy.-Treas.; Susan Farrell.

EIN: 561790979

Selected grants: The following grants were reported in 2004.

$200,000 to Saint Andrews Presbyterian College, Laurinburg, NC.
$100,000 to Montreat College, Montreat, NC.
$100,000 to Montreat Conference Center, Montreat, NC.
$100,000 to Scotia Village Foundation, Jamestown, NC.
$25,000 to Scotland County Band Boosters, Laurinburg, NC.
$12,500 to Saint James Church.

$10,000 to Domestic Violence and Rape Crisis Center of Scotland County, Laurinburg, NC.
$7,000 to Childrens Harbor, Alexander City, AL. For Church in the Pines.
$1,000 to Child Care Directions, Laurinburg, NC.
$1,000 to Hospice of Scotland County, Laurinburg, NC.

7432
E. A. Morris Charitable Foundation ◇
3802 Swarthmore Rd.
Durham, NC 27707-5438
Contact: John S. Thomas, Pres.

Established in 1980 in NC.

Donors: E.A. Morris; Mrs. E.A. Morris.

Foundation type: Independent foundation.

Financial data (yr. ended 12/31/04): Assets, $16,403,174 (M); expenditures, $1,087,407; qualifying distributions, $731,500; giving activities include $731,500 for 43 grants (high: $200,000; low: $1,000).

Fields of interest: Higher education; Boy scouts; Human services; Public affairs; Christian agencies & churches.

Limitations: Giving on a national basis, with some emphasis on NC.

Application information:
Initial approach: Letter
Deadline(s): None

Officers and Directors:* John S. Thomas,* Pres.; K. Barry Morgan,* V.P. and Treas.; E. Jack Walker,* Secy.; James Lofton; Dorothy S. Shaw; Katharine Thomas.

EIN: 581413060

Selected grants: The following grants were reported in 2003.

$193,000 to Duke University, Durham, NC. For cancer research.
$50,000 to John Locke Foundation, Raleigh, NC. For general support.
$35,000 to National Taxpayers Union Foundation, Alexandria, VA. For general support.
$30,000 to Outreach, Greensboro, NC. For general support.
$26,000 to Boy Scouts of America, Old North State Council, Greensboro, NC. For addition to headquarters building.
$20,000 to National Right to Work Legal Defense and Education Foundation, Springfield, VA. For general support.
$10,000 to Columbia International University, Columbia, SC. For general support.
$10,000 to Global Action, Colorado Springs, CO. For general support.
$10,000 to North Carolina Council on Economic Education, Raleigh, NC. For general support.
$3,000 to Junior Achievement of Central North Carolina, Greensboro, NC. For general support.

7433
The Neal Family Foundation ◇
P.O. Box 561109
Charlotte, NC 28256-1109

Established in 1994 in NC.

Donors: Tobianne M. Neal; Thomas C. Neal.

Foundation type: Independent foundation.

Financial data (yr. ended 12/31/05): Assets, $5,573,800 (M); expenditures, $1,873,932; qualifying distributions, $1,821,558; giving

activities include $1,821,558 for 67 grants (high: $373,334; low: $1,000; average: $4,000–$100,000).

Purpose and activities: Giving mostly for evangelical Christian activities.

Fields of interest: Christian agencies & churches.

Limitations: Applications not accepted. Giving on a national basis. No grants to individuals.

Application information: Contributes only to pre-selected organizations.

Officers: Tobianne M. Neal, Pres.; Melinda Neal Bastedo, V.P.; Peter C. Neal, V.P.; William T. Barnes, Secy.-Treas.

EIN: 582081294

7434
NFM Charitable Trust ◇ ☆
Bank of America Plz., NC1-002-11-18
Charlotte, NC 28255

Established in GA.

Foundation type: Independent foundation.

Financial data (yr. ended 12/31/05): Assets, $2,568,211 (M); gifts received, $1,194,737; expenditures, $360,404; qualifying distributions, $354,771; giving activities include $354,123 for 20 grants (high: $100,000; low: $300).

Fields of interest: Family services; Christian agencies & churches.

Limitations: Applications not accepted. Giving primarily in GA. No grants to individuals.

Application information: Contributes only to pre-selected organizations.

Trustee: Norman F. Miller.

EIN: 586456369

7435
Henry Nias Foundation, Inc. ◇
277 Glendale Dr.
Carthage, NC 28327 (910) 824-4413
Contact: Richard Edelman, Treas.

Incorporated in 1955 in NY.

Donor: Henry Nias†.

Foundation type: Independent foundation.

Financial data (yr. ended 11/30/03): Assets, $23,531,945 (M); expenditures, $1,442,591; qualifying distributions, $1,259,013; giving activities include $1,213,000 for 22 grants.

Purpose and activities: Emphasis on medical sciences, including hospitals, aid to the handicapped, and medical school student loan funds; support also for education, cultural programs, child welfare and youth, the aged, and Jewish organizations, including welfare funds.

Fields of interest: Arts; Medical school/education; Education; Hospitals (general); Human services; Children/youth, services; Aging, centers/services; Jewish federated giving programs; Jewish agencies & temples; Aging; Disabilities, people with.

Type of support: Continuing support.

Limitations: Giving limited to the metropolitan New York, NY, area.

Application information: Applications by invitation only. Unsolicited requests for funds not accepted.

Deadline(s): Aug.
Board meeting date(s): Sept. and Oct.
Final notification: Grants paid in Nov.

Officers and Directors:* Stanley Edelman, M.D.*, Chair.; Charles D. Fleischman,* Pres.; William F. Rosenberg,* Secy.; Richard J. Fleischman,* Treas.
EIN: 136075785

7436
Nickel Producers Environmental Research Association, Inc. ✧ ☆

2605 Meridian Pkwy., Ste. 200
Durham, NC 27713-2203 (919) 544-8500
Contact: Hudson K. Bates, Exec. Dir.
FAX: (919) 544-7724; E-mail: nipera@nipera.org;
Additional tel.: (919) 544-7722; URL: http://www.nipera.org

Established in 1980.
Donors: Anglo Platinum; Billiton; Empress Nickel Refinery, Ltd.; Eramet; Inco, Ltd.; International Cobalt; Nippon Yakin; Noranda; Sumitomo; Pharma; Unicore.
Foundation type: Independent foundation.
Financial data (yr. ended 12/31/05): Assets, $1,808,155 (M); gifts received, $2,076,610; expenditures, $3,048,473; qualifying distributions, $838,528; giving activities include $838,528 for grants.
Purpose and activities: Giving primarily for research investigations, studies, and surveys relating to occupational health and safety aspects of the nickel producing industries and related environmental matters.
Fields of interest: Higher education; Environment; Health care; Health organizations, association; Safety/disasters; Engineering/technology; Science.
International interests: Canada; Europe; Japan.
Type of support: Fellowships; Research.
Limitations: Giving primarily in the U.S., Europe, Canada, and Japan.
Application information:
Initial approach: Proposal
Board meeting date(s): Sept.
Officers: Toshiharu Kanai, Chair.; Tim E. Aiken, Vice-Chair.; Bert Swennen, Secy.; Bruce R. Conrad, Treas.; Hudson K. Bates, Exec. Dir.
Board Members: Michael Chalkley; Gordon Hall; Tetsuya Kubota; L.J.G. Nacken; Jacques-Antoine Rondeau; Catherine Tissot-Colle.
EIN: 133070077

7437
Mark A. and Rena R. Norcross Family Foundation ✧ ☆

1049 Rockford Rd.
High Point, NC 27262

Established in 2000 in NC.
Donor: Mark David, Inc.
Foundation type: Independent foundation.
Financial data (yr. ended 12/31/05): Assets, $403,084 (M); gifts received, $454,000; expenditures, $379,522; qualifying distributions, $377,913; giving activities include $377,913 for 25 grants (high: $250,000; low: $50).
Fields of interest: Arts; Elementary/secondary education; Higher education; Human services.
Limitations: Applications not accepted. No grants to individuals.
Application information: Contributes only to pre-selected organizations.

Officers: Mark A. Norcross, Chair., Pres. and Treas.; Rena R. Norcross, V.P. and Secy.
EIN: 562191282
Selected grants: The following grants were reported in 2005.
$250,000 to High Point University, High Point, NC.
$16,667 to Vineyard, The, Westfield, NC.
$15,000 to United Way.
$2,000 to Community Clinic of High Point, High Point, NC.
$1,000 to Family Service of the Piedmont, High Point, NC.
$1,000 to High Point Regional Health System, High Point, NC.
$500 to American Red Cross.
$500 to Peace College, Raleigh, NC.
$500 to Salvation Army.

7438
North Carolina Community Foundation ✧

4601 Six Forks Rd., Ste. 524
Raleigh, NC 27609 (919) 828-4387
Contact: Elizabeth C. Fentress, Pres.
FAX: (919) 828-5495;
E-mail: general@nccommf.org; Additional tel.: (800) 201-9533; Western Regional Office: P.O. Box 2148, Sylva, NC 28779, tel.: (828) 586-4616, FAX: (828) 631-3951, E-mail: slelievre@nccomf.org; Northeastern Regional Office: Harbinger Ctr., Ste. 4, Point Harbor, NC 27964, tel.: (252) 491-8166, FAX: (252) 491-5714, E-mail: pbirk@nccommf.org; Central and Western Piedmont Regional Office: P.O. Box 2851, Hickory, NC 28603, tel.: (828) 328-1237, FAX: (828) 328-3948, E-mail: jcorrell@nccommf.org; New Bern Office: P.O. Box 13276, New Bern, NC 28651, tel.: (252) 635-1001; FAX: (252) 635-3265; E-mail: jalcock@nccommf.org; URL: http://www.nccommunityfoundation.org

Established in 1988 in NC.
Foundation type: Community foundation.
Financial data (yr. ended 3/31/05): Assets, $85,307,887 (M); gifts received, $9,508,941; expenditures, $4,499,029; giving activities include $2,179,761 for 863 grants (high: $227,400; low: $42).
Purpose and activities: Primary areas of interest include higher and other education, conservation, community funds, and other general charitable activities.
Fields of interest: Museums; Performing arts; Historic preservation/historical societies; Arts; Higher education; Adult education—literacy, basic skills & GED; Education, reading; Education; Environment, natural resources; Environment; Health care; Substance abuse, services; Health organizations, association; Children/youth, services; Residential/custodial care, hospices; Aging, centers/services; Women, centers/services; Homeless, human services; Human services; Community development; Federated giving programs; Science; Christian agencies & churches; Religion; Aging; Women; Homeless.
Type of support: Endowments; Program development; Conferences/seminars; Scholarship funds; Technical assistance; Consulting services.
Limitations: Giving primarily in NC.
Publications: Annual report; Informational brochure; Newsletter.
Application information: Visit foundation Web site for application information.

Initial approach: E-mail foundation
Board meeting date(s): June and Nov.
Officers and Directors:* C. Ronald Scheeler, Chair.; Robert L. Jones, Vice-Chair.; Sherwood H. Smith, Vice-Chair.; Elizabeth C. Fentress,* Pres.; Cherry Ballard, V.P., Donor Rels. and Grants; Esther S. Hall, V.P., Opers.; Billy T. Woodard, Secy.; John Berngartt, C.F.O.; Dean E. Painter, Jr., Treas.; Martha Guy, Dir. Emeritus; Lewis R. Holding, Dir. Emeritus; Gov. James E. Holshouser, Jr., Dir. Emeritus; Karl G. Hudson, Dir. Emeritus; W. Trent Ragland, Jr., Emeritus; Robert W. Scott, Emeritus; Robert E. Barnhill, Jr.; James B. Black III; George H. Broadrick; David S. Brody; Felton J. Capel, Sr.; J. Keith Crisco; Brian C. Crutchfield; Hugh Cullman; Donald W. Curtis; Stuart B. Dorsett; Charles D. Evans; Annabelle L. Fetterman; Henry E. Frye; Charles W. Gaddy; Sarah Belk Gambrell; Margaret J. Gates; Clyde P. Harris, Jr.; Jeannette Hyde; D. Kim Johnson; John R. Jordan, Jr.; William J. Kealy; H. Martin Lancaster; Rodney E. Martin; James W. Narron; Joy E. Paige; W. Trent Ragland III; Ken G. Reece; Clyde J. Rhyne; Harley F. Shuford; Linda J. Staunch; Laurie Trexler; James A. Weathers; Elmer J. Wellons, Jr.; Dr. Norman A. Wiggins.
Number of staff: 10 full-time professional; 1 part-time professional; 5 full-time support; 1 part-time support.
EIN: 581661700

7439
The North Carolina GlaxoSmithKline Foundation ✧

(formerly The Glaxo Wellcome Foundation)
5 Moore Dr.
P.O. Box 13398
Research Triangle Park, NC 27709
(919) 483-2140
Contact: Marilyn E. Foote-Hudson, Exec. Dir.
FAX: (919) 315-3015; URL: http://us.gsk.com/community/ncfound.htm

Established in 1986 in NC.
Donors: Glaxo Wellcome Americas Inc.; GlaxoSmithKline Holdings (Americas) Inc.
Foundation type: Company-sponsored foundation.
Financial data (yr. ended 12/31/05): Assets, $63,807,914 (M); expenditures, $4,037,518; qualifying distributions, $3,819,871; giving activities include $3,479,486 for 11 grants (high: $825,000; low: $25,000).
Purpose and activities: The foundation supports organizations involved with education, health, and science. Special emphasis is directed toward programs designed to advance education.
Fields of interest: Education; Health care; Science.
Type of support: Program development; Seed money; Fellowships; Scholarship funds.
Limitations: Giving primarily in NC. No support for international organizations. No grants to individuals, or for construction or restoration projects.
Publications: Annual report (including application guidelines); Financial statement; Grants list; Informational brochure (including application guidelines).
Application information: Application form not required.
Initial approach: Proposal
Copies of proposal: 1
Deadline(s): Jan. 1, Apr. 1, July 1, and Oct. 1

Board meeting date(s): Mar., June, Sept., and Dec.

Final notification: Within 15 days following board meetings

Officers and Directors:* Robert A. Ingram,* Chair.; Margaret B. Dardess,* Pres.; Paul S. Holcombe, Jr.,* Secy.; Marilyn E. Foote-Hudson, Exec. Dir.; Julius L. Chambers; W. Robert Connor; Shirley T. Frye; Thomas R. Haber; Charles A. Sanders, M.D.; Joseph Spagnardi; David M. Stout; Christopher A. Viehbacher; Janice M. Whitaker.

Number of staff: 2 full-time professional; 1 part-time professional.

EIN: 581698610

Selected grants: The following grants were reported in 2003.

$669,000 to North Carolina State University, Friday Institute, Raleigh, NC.

$668,000 to Duke University, Durham, NC. For a new Sanford Institute Program for Cross-Sectoral Public Policy.

$250,000 to Carolina Ballet, Raleigh, NC.

$195,000 to Research Triangle Institute, Research Triangle Park, NC. For North Carolina Science, Mathematics, and Technology Center, to champion efforts to improve science, mathematics, and technology education in the state's K-12 public schools.

$123,135 to Hill Center, Durham, NC. For Reading Achievement Program.

$83,334 to North Carolina State University Foundation, Raleigh, NC. For fellowship program.

$45,000 to Recording for the Blind and Dyslexic, Princeton, NJ.

$35,363 to Family Resources of Rutherford County, Spindale, NC. For Dental Learning Libraries program in a rural area of the state.

$33,050 to Task Force for Child Survival and Development, Decatur, GA. For awards for public health departments to encourage and recognize the development of creative and successful approaches toward improving the health status and quality life of children in North Carolina.

7440
Nucor Foundation ✧

2100 Rexford Rd.
Charlotte, NC 28211-3418
Contact: James M. Coblin, Dir.

Established in 1973 in NC.

Donor: Nucor Corp.

Foundation type: Company-sponsored foundation.

Financial data (yr. ended 12/31/04): Assets, $18,760 (M); gifts received, $900,000; expenditures, $992,277; qualifying distributions, $992,270; giving activities include $991,609 for 444 grants to individuals (high: $5,250; low: $120).

Purpose and activities: The foundation awards college scholarships to students pursuing an undergraduate degree in engineering or metallurgy.

Type of support: Employee-related scholarships; Scholarships—to individuals.

Limitations: Giving primarily in areas of company operations.

Publications: Application guidelines.

Application information: Application form required.

Initial approach: Contact foundation for application form

Deadline(s): Mar. 1

Final notification: mid-Apr.

Directors: James M. Coblin; Daniel R. Dimicco; Terry S. Lisenby.

EIN: 237318064

7441
O'Herron Foundation, Inc. ✧

6827-C Fairview Rd.
Charlotte, NC 28210 (704) 364-6531
Contact: Edward M. O'Herron, Jr., Pres. and Treas.

Established in 1962 in NC.

Donor: Edward M. O'Herron, Jr.

Foundation type: Independent foundation.

Financial data (yr. ended 12/31/04): Assets, $8,886,066 (M); expenditures, $669,184; qualifying distributions, $555,700; giving activities include $555,700 for 39 grants (high: $120,000; low: $250).

Purpose and activities: Giving for education, the arts, and children, youth, and social services.

Fields of interest: Museums; Arts; Elementary/secondary education; Higher education; Education; Health organizations, association; Human services; YM/YWCAs & YM/YWHAs; Children/youth, services; Federated giving programs; Christian agencies & churches.

Limitations: Giving primarily in Palm Beach County, FL, Mecklenburg and Wake counties, NC, and Horry County, SC. No grants to individuals.

Application information:

Initial approach: Proposal

Deadline(s): None

Officers and Directors:* Edward M. O'Herron, Jr., Pres. and Treas.; Patricia Norman,* Secy.; Kenneth Coe; Kennedy O'Herron; William O'Herron.

EIN: 566061256

7442
P & B Foundation ✧

2004 Valencia Terr.
Charlotte, NC 28226 (704) 365-9757
Contact: C. Wilbur Peters, Pres.

Established in 1970.

Donors: Kurt Cunningham; Pam Cunningham; C. Wilbur Peters; Eli Scholarship Fund; Grace Baptist Church; International Bible College; Providence Development Partners, LLC.

Foundation type: Independent foundation.

Financial data (yr. ended 8/31/05): Assets, $15,494,211 (M); gifts received, $300,558; expenditures, $1,024,811; qualifying distributions, $779,793; giving activities include $623,963 for 34 grants (high: $258,964; low: $50).

Purpose and activities: Giving primarily for Baptist church-related educational and religious institutions.

Fields of interest: Protestant agencies & churches.

Limitations: Giving on a national basis. No grants to individuals.

Application information:

Initial approach: Letter

Deadline(s): None

Officers: C. Wilbur Peters, Pres.; Bessie Peters, V.P.

Director: Larry C. Pratt.

EIN: 237083912

Selected grants: The following grants were reported in 2003.

$360,000 to International Baptist Church, Brooklyn, NY.

$182,650 to Northside Baptist Church, Charlotte, NC.

$35,000 to Fourth Baptist Church, Plymouth, MN.

$32,640 to Sweet Briar College, Sweet Briar, VA.

$12,000 to Baptist Mid-Mission, Cleveland, OH.

$3,650 to Lutheran Academy, Rockford, IL.

$2,000 to Baptist World Mission, Decatur, AL.

$1,000 to Baptist International Mission, Chattanooga, TN.

$1,000 to Hearts for Heaven, Charlotte, NC.

7443
The Palin Foundation ✧

P.O. Box 97365
Raleigh, NC 27624-7365
Contact: Clifton L. Benson III

Established in 1985 in NC.

Donor: Clifton L. Benson, Jr.

Foundation type: Independent foundation.

Financial data (yr. ended 12/31/05): Assets, $8,415,798 (M); gifts received, $702,000; expenditures, $766,041; qualifying distributions, $629,750; giving activities include $629,750 for 20 grants (high: $525,000; low: $100).

Purpose and activities: Giving primarily to churches and religious organizations.

Fields of interest: Higher education; Human services; Christian agencies & churches.

Type of support: General/operating support; Building/renovation.

Limitations: Giving primarily in NC. No grants to individuals.

Application information: Application form not required.

Initial approach: Proposal

Copies of proposal: 1

Deadline(s): None

Directors: Clifton L. Benson, Jr.; Margaret P. Benson; John F. Philips.

EIN: 561490228

Selected grants: The following grants were reported in 2004.

$75,000 to Alliance Defense Fund, Scottsdale, AZ.

$50,000 to Boy Scouts of America, Atlanta, GA.

$40,000 to Fore the Lord, Raleigh, NC.

$35,000 to Raleigh Rescue Mission, Raleigh, NC.

$20,000 to North Carolina Family Policy Council, Raleigh, NC.

$18,000 to Samaritans Purse, Boone, NC.

$5,000 to Boys and Girls Club, Warren Memorial, Atlanta, GA.

$3,000 to House of Hope, Raleigh, NC.

$2,000 to Turning Point, Santa Monica, CA.

$500 to International Foundation, DC.

7444
Annie Penn Community Trust ✧

P.O. Box 1169
Reidsville, NC 27323 (336) 951-4552
Contact: Susan J. Richardson

Established in 2001 in NC.

Foundation type: Independent foundation.

Financial data (yr. ended 9/30/05): Assets, $32,161,247 (L); gifts received, $152,714; expenditures, $1,680,294; qualifying distributions, $1,358,582; giving activities include $1,358,582 for 68 grants (high: $100,000; low: $600).

Fields of interest: Health care; Human services.

Limitations: Giving primarily in the Reidsville, NC, area. No grants to individuals.
Application information:
  Initial approach: Letter or telephone
  Deadline(s): Jan. 17 and June 30
Officers: Jacob B. Balsley III, Chair.; Robert L. Watt, Vice-Chair.; Larry K. Johnson, Secy.; Barry Z. Dodson, Treas.
Directors: James Burston; R. Craig Caldwell; Susan H. Fitzgibbon; Edward L. Hawkins; Gerald K. Hill; Barbara L. Johnson; J. Wayne Keeling; Glenn Martin; Barbara L. McMichael; Lee Niegelsky.
EIN: 562255809
Selected grants: The following grants were reported in 2004.
$165,000 to Rockingham County Schools, Reidsville Elementary School, Eden, NC. For obesity initiative.
$20,000 to Rockingham Community College, Wentworth, NC. For literacy project.
$10,000 to Annie Penn Hospital, Reidsville, NC. For fund for needy patients.
$4,800 to REMMSCO, Reidsville, NC. For general operating support.
$3,300 to Reidsville Soup Kitchen, Reidsville, NC. For general operating support.
$1,800 to Salvation Army of Reidsville, Reidsville, NC. For general operating support.
$1,400 to Reidsville Senior High School, Reidsville, NC. For general operating support.
$1,200 to HELP, Wentworth, NC. For general operating support.
$1,200 to Hospice of Rockingham County, Wentworth, NC. For general operating support.
$900 to Free Clinic of Reidsville and Vicinity, Reidsville, NC. For general operating support.

7445
James J. and Mamie R. Perkins Memorial Fund ✧

c/o Bank of America, N.A., Private Client Group
1 Hanover Sq., Ste. 306
Raleigh, NC 27601-1754
Application address: c/o James G. Sullivan, P.O. Box 20067, Greenville, NC 27858, tel.: (252) 756-8888

Established in 1989 in NC.
Foundation type: Independent foundation.
Financial data (yr. ended 9/30/05): Assets, $13,393,301 (M); expenditures, $657,322; qualifying distributions, $600,211; giving activities include $544,677 for 21 grants (high: $122,943; low: $1,138).
Purpose and activities: Giving primarily for the arts, education, hospitals, social services, community development, federated giving programs, and Christian churches and agencies.
Fields of interest: Arts education; Performing arts, music; Arts; Elementary/secondary education; Education; Hospitals (general); Disasters, fire prevention/control; Human services; Community development; Federated giving programs; Christian agencies & churches.
Limitations: Giving limited to Pitt County, NC. No grants to individuals.
Application information: Application form required.
  Copies of proposal: 4
  Deadline(s): Jan. 15, Apr. 15, July 15, and Oct. 15
  Board meeting date(s): 1st Tues. of Feb., May, Aug., and Nov.
Officer and Director:* James Sullivan,* Chair.
Members: Danny McNally; Thomas Midyette.

Trustee: Bank of America, N.A.
EIN: 566325764
Selected grants: The following grants were reported in 2003.
$128,779 to Pitt County Memorial Hospital Foundation, Greenville, NC.
$70,000 to Pitt-Greenville Soccer Association, Greenville, NC.
$56,779 to Saint Pauls Episcopal Church, Greenville, NC.
$51,250 to Music Academy of Eastern Carolina, Greenville, NC.
$35,000 to Historical Society of Pitt County, Greenville, NC.
$28,779 to Salvation Army, Greenville, NC.
$15,340 to Little Willie Center, Greenville, NC.
$15,000 to North Pitt High School, Bethel, NC.
$10,542 to Pitt County Educational Foundation, Greenville, NC.
$10,000 to South Greenville School, Greenville, NC.

7446
The Pharmacy Network Foundation, Inc. ✧

4020 Old Wake Forest Rd., Ste. 102
Raleigh, NC 27609 (919) 772-4371
Contact: J. Andrew Barrett, Exec. V.P.
Application address: Jimmy S. Jackson, V.P. and Secy., 2015 Navan Ln., Garner, NC 27529

Donors: Pharmacy Network National Corp.; United Pharmacy Cooperative Inc.; Pharmacy Network National Corporation Trust.
Foundation type: Company-sponsored foundation.
Financial data (yr. ended 12/31/05): Assets, $22,373,471 (M); expenditures, $1,505,979; qualifying distributions, $1,129,329; giving activities include $1,073,000 for 11 grants (high: $400,000; low: $8,000).
Purpose and activities: The foundation supports organizations involved with education and health and awards college scholarships to pharmacy students enrolled at the University of North Carolina at Chapel Hill and Campbell University.
Fields of interest: Education; Pharmacy/prescriptions; Health care.
Type of support: Building/renovation; Scholarships—to individuals.
Limitations: Giving limited to NC.
Application information: Application form required.
  Initial approach: Contact foundation for application form
  Copies of proposal: 1
  Deadline(s): May 15
  Board meeting date(s): 4th Tue. of each month
  Final notification: 2 months
Officers: Mitchell W. Watts, Pres.; J. Andrew Barrett, Exec. V.P.; Jimmy S. Jackson, V.P. and Secy.; Julian E. Upchurch, V.P.; Jonathan A. Hill, Sr., Treas.
EIN: 561690027

7447
Piedmont Natural Gas Foundation ✧ ☆

c/o Wachovia Bank, N.A.
100 N. Main St., NC-6732
Winston-Salem, NC 27150-6732
URL: http://www.piedmontng.com/itc/pngFoundation/organization

Established in 2004 in NC.
Donor: Piedmont Natural Gas Co., Inc.
Foundation type: Company-sponsored foundation.

Financial data (yr. ended 12/31/05): Assets, $8,152,731 (M); gifts received, $1,108,333; expenditures, $451,120; qualifying distributions, $414,933; giving activities include $414,933 for 8 grants (high: $180,300; low: $10,000).
Purpose and activities: The foundation supports organizations involved with arts and culture, K-12 public education, literacy, the environment, low-income energy assistance, health, human services, and community development.
Fields of interest: Arts; Elementary/secondary education; Education, reading; Environment, research; Environment, public policy; Environment, natural resources; Environment, energy; Environmental education; Environment; Health care; Human services; Economic development; Community development; Federated giving programs; Economically disadvantaged.
Limitations: Giving primarily in NC, SC, and TN. No support for religious organizations not of direct benefit to the entire community, fraternal or political organizations, athletic organizations, private foundations, social or veterans' organizations, K-12 private schools, third-party professional fundraising organizations, or private clubs. No grants to individuals, or for scholarships, travel or conferences, controversial social causes, athletic events or programs, or causes from which Piedmont Natural Gas will receive any benefit.
Publications: Application guidelines.
Application information: The foundation may request additional information at a later date. An interview or site visit may be requested. Application form required.
  Initial approach: Complete online application form
  Deadline(s): 6 weeks prior to board meetings
  Board meeting date(s): Quarterly, including June 28 and Dec. 6
Officers and Directors:* Kevin O'Hara, Chair.; George Baldwin, Pres.; Ranelle Q. Warfield, V.P.; Jane Lewis-Raymond, Secy.; Robert O. Pritchard, Treas.; David Trusty; Theresa VonCannon.
Trustee: Wachovia Bank, N.A.
EIN: 201786431

7448
Louis Planseon Foundation ✧

c/o Wachovia Bank, N.A.
100 N. Main St., 13th Fl.
Winston-Salem, NC 27150

Established in 2002 in NJ.
Foundation type: Operating foundation.
Financial data (yr. ended 12/31/05): Assets, $7,179,978 (M); expenditures, $426,175; qualifying distributions, $361,960; giving activities include $361,436 for 34 grants (high: $25,000; low: $3,000).
Fields of interest: Arts; Hospitals (general); Human services; Federated giving programs; Christian agencies & churches.
Limitations: Applications not accepted. Giving on a national basis. No grants to individuals.
Application information: Contributes only to pre-selected organizations.
Trustees: Hector L. Planseon; John L. Planseon; Richard G. Post; Wachovia Bank, N.A.
EIN: 016182253
Selected grants: The following grants were reported in 2004.
$40,000 to Chilton Memorial Hospital Foundation, Pompton Plains, NJ.

$15,000 to Indian River Memorial Hospital, Vero Beach, FL.

$15,000 to Salem Hospital, Salem, OR.

$15,000 to Visiting Nurse Association and Hospice Foundation, Vero Beach, FL.

$14,500 to Presbyterian Church, Westfield, NJ.

$10,000 to Christ Church of Lake Forest, Lake Forest, IL.

$9,000 to Humane Society of the Willamette Valley, Salem, OR.

$8,000 to Voice of the Martyrs, Bartlesville, OK.

$8,000 to Word of Life Fellowship, Schroon Lake, NY.

$5,000 to Radio Bible Class, Grand Rapids, MI.

7449
The Polk County Community Foundation, Inc.
255 S. Trade St.
Tryon, NC   28782-3707   (828) 859-5314
Contact: Elizabeth Nager, Exec. Dir.
FAX: (828) 859-6122;
E-mail: foundation@polkccf.org; URL: http://www.polkccf.org

Incorporated in 1975 in NC.
Foundation type: Community foundation.
Financial data (yr. ended 12/31/05): Assets, $16,416,759 (M); gifts received, $763,985; expenditures, $1,512,740; giving activities include $1,143,848 for 21+ grants.
Purpose and activities: The foundation seeks to improve the quality of life in Polk County, NC, and surrounding areas.
Fields of interest: Humanities; Arts; Education; Environment, natural resources; Health care; Human services; Community development.
Type of support: General/operating support; Continuing support; Capital campaigns; Building/renovation; Equipment; Program development; Conferences/seminars; Publication; Seed money; Curriculum development; Internship funds; Scholarship funds; Scholarships—to individuals; Matching/challenge support.
Limitations: Giving limited to Polk County, NC, and Landrum, SC. No grants to individuals (except for scholarships), or for debt reduction, medical research, courtesy advertising, or benefit tickets.
Publications: Application guidelines; Annual report; Financial statement; Informational brochure (including application guidelines); Occasional report.
Application information: Visit foundation Web site for application form, guidelines, and specific deadlines. Faxed or incomplete applications are not accepted. Application form required.
   Initial approach: Submit application form and attachments
   Copies of proposal: 1
   Deadline(s): Varies
   Board meeting date(s): 3rd Thurs. in Feb., June, and Sept.; 2nd Thurs. in Apr., Nov., and Dec.
   Final notification: Approx. 3 months
Officers and Directors:* Larry Wassong,* Pres.; Donald Lessig,* V.P.; Melanie Talbot,* Secy.; David Slater,* Treas.; Elizabeth Nager, Exec. Dir.; Arthur Brown; Jeanne Byrd; Laura Fields; Wayne Inks; Grant Libramento; Nancy Mahler; Donna S. Martin; Renee McDermott; Alberta Phayer.
Number of staff: 1 full-time professional; 2 part-time professional; 1 full-time support.
EIN: 510168751

7450
John William Pope Foundation ▼ ✧ ☆
3401 Greshams Lake Rd.
Raleigh, NC   27615   (919) 876-6000
Contact: James Arthur Pope, Pres.

Established in 1986 in NC.
Donor: Members of the Pope family.
Foundation type: Independent foundation.
Financial data (yr. ended 6/30/05): Assets, $53,579,851 (M); gifts received, $3,862,402; expenditures, $7,775,937; qualifying distributions, $7,407,728; giving activities include $7,406,097 for 186 grants (high: $500,000; low: $40).
Fields of interest: Education; Public policy, research.
Application information: Application form not required.
   Initial approach: Letter
   Deadline(s): Jan. 1
Officers and Directors:* Joyce W. Pope,* Chair.; James Arthur Pope,* Pres.; Amanda Joyce Pope.
EIN: 581691765
Selected grants: The following grants were reported in 2004.
$236,112 to John Locke Foundation, Raleigh, NC. 2 grants: $118,056 each
$228,000 to North Carolina State University, Raleigh, NC.
$100,000 to Carolina Ballet, Raleigh, NC.
$100,000 to Institute for Humane Studies, Arlington, VA.
$100,000 to Pennsylvania Institute of Technology, Media, PA.
$25,000 to Mercatus Center, Arlington, VA.
$20,000 to Fund for American Studies, DC.
$20,000 to Opera Company of North Carolina, Raleigh, NC.
$10,000 to Center for Education Reform, DC.

7451
The Julian Price Family Foundation
c/o Wachovia Bank, N.A.
100 N. Main St.
Winston-Salem, NC   27150
Application address: c/o Wachovia Bank, N.A., Attn: Jim Gallaher, NC 6732, 100 N. Main St., Winston-Salem, NC 27150, tel.: (800) 576-5135, Ext. 26478, E-mail: Jim.gallaher@wachovia.com

Established in 1996 in NC.
Foundation type: Independent foundation.
Financial data (yr. ended 12/31/05): Assets, $0 (M); expenditures, $1,286,853; qualifying distributions, $1,260,277; giving activities include $1,133,709 for 92 grants (high: $125,000; low: $100).
Purpose and activities: Giving primarily for environmental conservation programs, as well as for education, the arts, community development, and health and human services.
Fields of interest: Media, television; Arts; Education; Environment, natural resources; Environment; Hospitals (general); Human services; Community development; Christian agencies & churches.
Limitations: Giving primarily in NC. No grants to individuals.
Application information: Application form not required.
   Initial approach: Letter
   Copies of proposal: 5
   Deadline(s): None

Trustees: Laura Deboisfeuillet Edwards; Susan Jarrell Edwards; Melaine Taylor Farland; Mary P.T. Harrison.
EIN: 311665269

7452
Lynn R. and Karl E. Prickett Fund ✧
P.O. Box 20124
Greensboro, NC   27420

Established in 1964 in NC.
Donor: Lynn R. Prickett†.
Foundation type: Independent foundation.
Financial data (yr. ended 6/30/05): Assets, $19,672,044 (M); expenditures, $1,105,440; qualifying distributions, $1,003,152; giving activities include $975,000 for 40 grants (high: $325,000; low: $2,000).
Purpose and activities: Giving for education, health and social services.
Fields of interest: Education; Health care; Human services.
Type of support: General/operating support.
Limitations: Applications not accepted. Giving on a national basis.
Application information: Unsolicited requests for funds not accepted.
Trustees: Chester F. Chapin; Samuel C. Chapin; Lynn C. Gunzenhauser; Katherine Kentfield; Lisa V. Prochnow.
EIN: 566064788
Selected grants: The following grants were reported in 2005.
$367,500 to Community Foundation of Greater Greensboro, Greensboro, NC. 2 grants: $42,500, $325,000
$45,000 to Doctors Without Borders USA, New York, NY. 2 grants: $20,000, $25,000
$25,000 to International Rescue Committee, New York, NY.
$20,000 to Human Rights Watch, New York, NY.
$20,000 to Ocean Conservancy, DC.
$20,000 to Planned Parenthood Federation of America, New York, NY.
$15,000 to Center for International Policy, DC.
$15,000 to North Carolina Outward Bound School, Asheville, NC.

7453
Progress Energy Foundation, Inc. ▼
(formerly CP&L Foundation, Inc.)
P.O. Box 2591
Raleigh, NC   27602-2591
Contact: Kellan Moore Chapin, Contribs. Specialist
FAX: (919) 546-4338;
E-mail: kellan.chapin@pgnmail.com; URL: http://www.progress-energy.com/community/foundation/grantguidelines.asp

Established in 1990 in NC.
Donors: Carolina Power & Light Co.; Progress Energy, Inc.; Florida Progress Corp.
Foundation type: Company-sponsored foundation.
Financial data (yr. ended 12/31/05): Assets, $102,333 (M); gifts received, $7,503,000; expenditures, $7,479,227; qualifying distributions, $7,475,797; giving activities include $7,473,797 for 205 grants (high: $500,000; low: $165; average: $10,000–$110,000).

Purpose and activities: The foundation supports organizations involved with education, the environment, and economic development.
Fields of interest: Elementary/secondary education; Higher education; Teacher school/education; Engineering school/education; Education; Environment, association; Environment, water pollution; Environmental education; Environment; Economic development; Mathematics; Science.
Type of support: General/operating support; Continuing support; Annual campaigns; Program development; Conferences/seminars; Curriculum development; Scholarship funds; Research.
Limitations: Giving primarily in areas of company operations in FL, NC, and SC. No support for fraternal, veterans', or labor organizations, athletic teams, religious organizations not of direct benefit to the entire community, or individual K-12 schools. No grants to individuals, or for memberships or courtesy advertising.
Publications: Application guidelines; Annual report; Grants list.
Application information: Application form required.
 Initial approach: Complete online application form
 Deadline(s): Feb. 1, May 1, Aug. 1, and Nov. 1
 Board meeting date(s): Quarterly
 Final notification: Within 2 weeks following board meetings
Officers and Directors: * Robert B. McGehee,* Pres.; Mary Woodley Dicus, Secy.; Fred Day; William Johnson; Jeff Lyash; John McArthur; Peter Scott.
Trustee: Wachovia Bank, N.A.
EIN: 561720636
Selected grants: The following grants were reported in 2005.
$500,000 to Wake Forest University, Winston-Salem, NC. For general support.
$393,146 to United Way, Triangle, Research Triangle Park, NC. For general support.
$351,000 to North Carolina State University, Raleigh, NC. For general support.
$300,000 to North Carolina Symphony Society, Raleigh, NC. For general support.
$286,000 to American Red Cross, Triangle Area Chapter, Raleigh, NC. For general support.
$200,000 to Carolina Ballet, Raleigh, NC. For general support.
$100,000 to Performing Arts Center Foundation, Clearwater, FL. For general support.
$30,000 to Foundation for Osceola Education, Kissimmee, FL. For general support.
$21,986 to United Way of Tampa Bay, Tampa, FL. For general support.
$20,589 to Boys and Girls Homes of North Carolina, Lake Waccamaw, NC. For general support.

7454
Provident Benevolent Foundation
(formerly Providence Charitable Foundation)
c/o Wachovia Bank, N.A.
100 N. Main St., 13th Fl.
Winston-Salem, NC 27150
Contact: Rachel Reilly, Trust Off., Wachovia Bank, N.A.
E-mail: rachel.reilly@wachovia.com

Established in 1989 in NC.
Donor: Jesse J. Thompson†.
Foundation type: Independent foundation.
Financial data (yr. ended 6/30/05): Assets, $17,389,017 (M); expenditures, $1,191,742;

qualifying distributions, $1,074,414; giving activities include $1,054,385 for grants.
Purpose and activities: Giving primarily for education, health, and human services.
Fields of interest: Arts; Education; Environment, natural resources; Hospitals (general); Human services; Children/youth, services.
Type of support: General/operating support.
Limitations: Giving limited to NC and TN. No grants for endowments or deficit financing.
Application information: Application form required.
 Initial approach: Letter (not to exceed 2 pages)
 Copies of proposal: 1
 Deadline(s): Aug. 15
 Board meeting date(s): Oct. (annually)
Director: Jesse J. Thompson.
Trustee: Wachovia Bank, N.A.
EIN: 581881092
Selected grants: The following grants were reported in 2004.
$500,000 to Boys and Girls Club of Sarasota County, Sarasota, FL.
$30,000 to Medassist of Mecklenburg, Charlotte, NC.
$20,000 to Charlotte Emergency Housing, Charlotte, NC.
$20,000 to Clemson University, Clemson, SC.
$20,000 to Hospitality House of Charlotte, Charlotte, NC.
$10,000 to Mountain Area Child and Family Center, Montreat, NC.
$10,000 to Steps to Hope, Columbus, NC.
$10,000 to Summit House, Charlotte, NC.
$9,806 to Charlotte Rescue Mission, Charlotte, NC.
$1,250 to North Carolina School of the Arts Foundation, Winston-Salem, NC.

7455
Carolyn King Ragan Charitable Foundation ✧ ☆
(formerly Ragan and King Charitable Foundation)
c/o Wachovia Bank, N.A.
100 N. Main St., 13th Fl.
Winston-Salem, NC 27150
Contact: Susanna Adams

Established in 1972 in GA.
Donor: Carolyn King Ragan†.
Foundation type: Independent foundation.
Financial data (yr. ended 9/30/05): Assets, $5,048,905 (M); expenditures, $505,705; qualifying distributions, $464,849; giving activities include $464,849 for 13 grants (high: $68,849; low: $1,000).
Purpose and activities: Giving primarily for Baptist organizations and churches; funding also for higher education and human services.
Fields of interest: Higher education; Human services; Protestant agencies & churches.
Limitations: Giving limited to GA (except for two specific out-of-state beneficiaries). No grants to individuals.
Application information: Application form not required.
 Initial approach: Letter
 Copies of proposal: 1
 Deadline(s): None
 Board meeting date(s): Fall
Trustee: Wachovia Bank, N.A.
EIN: 586138950

7456
Randleigh Foundation Trust
c/o Thomas S. Kenan III
P.O. Box 4150
Chapel Hill, NC 27515

Established in 1965 in NY.
Donor: William R. Kenan, Jr.†.
Foundation type: Independent foundation.
Financial data (yr. ended 3/31/06): Assets, $21,306,580 (M); expenditures, $979,421; qualifying distributions, $942,507; giving activities include $918,500 for 23 grants (high: $147,000; low: $7,500).
Purpose and activities: Giving primarily for education and the arts.
Fields of interest: Arts; Education; Christian agencies & churches.
Type of support: General/operating support; Continuing support.
Limitations: Applications not accepted. Giving primarily in KY and NC. No grants to individuals.
Application information: Contributes only to pre-selected organizations.
 Board meeting date(s): Annually
Trustees: Annice H. Kenan; James G. Kenan III; Thomas S. Kenan III; Garrett Kirk, Jr.
Number of staff: None.
EIN: 136207897
Selected grants: The following grants were reported in 2005.
$60,000 to Colorado College, Colorado Springs, CO.
$40,000 to Phillips Academy, Andover, MA.
$40,000 to Williams College, Williamstown, MA.
$35,000 to Duplin County Board of Education, Kenansville, NC.
$25,000 to Ackland Art Museum, Chapel Hill, NC.
$25,000 to North Carolina School of the Arts Foundation, Winston-Salem, NC.
$25,000 to North Carolina Veterinary Medical Foundation, Raleigh, NC.
$25,000 to Woodberry Forest School, Woodberry Forest, VA.
$15,000 to Henry Morrison Flagler Museum, Palm Beach, FL.
$10,000 to Lexington School, Lexington, KY.

7457
Kate B. Reynolds Charitable Trust ▼
128 Reynolda Village
Winston-Salem, NC 27106-5123
(336) 723-1456
Contact: Karen McNeil-Miller, Pres.; John H. Frank, Dir., Health Care Div.; Joyce T. Adger, Dir., Poor and Needy Div.
FAX: (336) 723-7765; *E-mail:* Karen@kbr.org; Additional tel. (for Karen Yoak Lewis, Dir., Admin.): (336) 721-2273; *URL:* http://www.kbr.org

Established in 1947 in NC.
Donor: Kate B. Reynolds†.
Foundation type: Independent foundation.
Financial data (yr. ended 8/31/06): Assets, $569,540,075 (M); expenditures, $21,466,911; qualifying distributions, $19,327,315; giving activities include $19,327,315 for 339 grants (high: $750,000; low: $9,212; average: $20,000–$200,000).
Purpose and activities: To improve the quality of life and quality of health for the financially needy of North Carolina. The trust accomplishes its work through its

two divisions. The Health Care Division and The Poor and Needy Division.

Fields of interest: Education, early childhood education; Child development, education; Nursing school/education; Education; Hospitals (general); Dental care; Medical care, rehabilitation; Nursing care; Health care; Substance abuse, services; Mental health/crisis services; Health organizations, association; Cancer; AIDS; Alcoholism; Diabetes; Crime/violence prevention, domestic violence; Food services; Nutrition; Housing/shelter, development; Human services; Children/youth, services; Child development, services; Family services; Residential/custodial care, hospices; Aging, centers/services; Homeless, human services; Aging; Disabilities, people with; Economically disadvantaged; Homeless.

Type of support: General/operating support; Continuing support; Annual campaigns; Capital campaigns; Building/renovation; Equipment; Program development; Seed money; Matching/challenge support.

Limitations: Giving limited to NC; social welfare grants limited to Winston-Salem and Forsyth County; health care giving, statewide. No support for political organizations. No grants to individuals, or for endowment funds or medical research; grants on a highly selective basis for construction of facilities or purchase of equipment.

Publications: Application guidelines; Annual report (including application guidelines); Financial statement; Newsletter.

Application information: Applicant should contact the trust staff to discuss the proposal prior to submitting a written application. Advance consultation is required before an application can be accepted for consideration. Applications will not be accepted electronically. Application form required.

Initial approach: Telephone to inquire about guidelines and to request an application or access Web site

Copies of proposal: 1

Deadline(s): Jan. 15 and July 15 for Poor and Needy Division; Mar. 15 and Sept. 15 for Health Care Division; or the 1st business day thereafter if any deadline falls on a weekend or holiday

Board meeting date(s): Poor and Needy Division Advisory Board - Mar. and Sept.; Health Care Division Advisory Board - May and Nov.

Final notification: Within 2 weeks after advisory board meeting

Officer: Karen McNeil-Miller, Pres.

Trustee: Wachovia Bank, N.A.

Number of staff: 9 full-time professional; 2 full-time support.

EIN: 566036515

Selected grants: The following grants were reported in 2006.

$850,000 to Mission Hospitals, Asheville, NC. 2 grants: $350,000 (For construction of new children's outpatient center, featuring advanced specialty care, to serve as referral center for 21 western North Carolina counties with high percentage of children from low-income families), $500,000 (For operating and capital support to begin dental residency program in collaboration with Mountain Air Health Education Center, including dental clinic to primarily serve children from low-income families from western North Carolina, payable over 3 years).

$500,000 to Bethesda Center for the Homeless, Winston-Salem, NC. For capital support to renovate and expand facilities providing services to homeless individuals in Forsyth County.

$500,000 to Senior Services, Winston-Salem, NC. For capital support for new Senior Services Center to expand and increase services provided to low-income, elderly residents of Forsyth County.

$500,000 to United Way of Forsyth County, Winston-Salem, NC. For relief efforts for the victims of Hurricane Katrina who relocated to Forsyth County to rebuild their lives.

$456,203 to Wake Forest University Health Sciences, Winston-Salem, NC. For operating support to begin diabetic retinopathy screening program, I See in NC, in two community care network regions covering eleven counties, payable over 3 years.

$395,314 to PORT Human Services, Greenville, NC. For operating support to develop, implement, and monitor Rural Adolescent Access Program (RAAP), community-based substance abuse treatment program targeting adolescents in rural eastern Non Carolina counties, payable over 3 years.

$196,580 to Mountain Area Health Education Center, Asheville, NC. For expansion of Primary Care Integration Initiative to improve children's access to mental health services in nonprofit primary care practices in Mitchell, Henderson, Rutherford, Transylvania, Yancey, and Buncombe counties.

$150,000 to Alleghany Memorial Hospital, Sparta, NC. For capital support to replace, upgrade, or add medical equipment at Tier One rural hospital.

$136,445 to East Carolina Health, Greenville, NC. For operating support to expand diabetes education to financially needy sixth grade students in Perquimans, Tyrrell, Chowan, and Washington counties. Program administered through Chowan Hospital Division, payable over 3 years.

$125,000 to Koala, Inc., Brevard, NC. For construction of adult day care/day health center for elderly and disabled adults of Transylvania County.

7458
Z. Smith Reynolds Foundation, Inc. ▼
147 S. Cherry St., Ste. 200
Winston-Salem, NC 27101-5287
(336) 725-7541
Contact: Thomas W. Ross, Secy.
FAX: (336) 725-6069; E-mail: info@zsr.org;
Additional tel.: (800) 443-8319; URL: http://
www.zsr.org

Incorporated in 1936 in NC.

Donors: Nancy S. Reynolds†; Mary Reynolds Babcock†; Richard J. Reynolds, Jr.†; William N. Reynolds†.

Foundation type: Independent foundation.

Financial data (yr. ended 12/31/05): Assets, $18,877,765 (M); gifts received, $19,466,328; expenditures, $16,725,877; qualifying distributions, $16,727,957; giving activities include $14,077,512 for 288 grants (high: $1,200,000; low: $3,000), $1,750 for 5 employee matching gifts, and $733,594 for 3 foundation-administered programs.

Purpose and activities: The goals of the foundation are: 1) to promote social, economic and environmental justice; 2) to strengthen democracy, through an educated and informed populace; 3) to encourage innovation and excellence in a dynamic nonprofit sector; 4) to support progressive public policy and social change; 5) to foster cooperation and respect among all racial, ethnic, and socio-economic groups; and 6) to build strong, vibrant, economically sound, and peaceful communities. To accomplish its purpose, the foundation currently gives special attention to certain focus areas: community and economic development; environment; democracy and civic engagement; pre-collegiate education; and social justice and equity.

Fields of interest: Education, early childhood education; Child development, education; Elementary school/education; Secondary school/education; Education; Environment, natural resources; Environment; Crime/violence prevention, youth; Crime/violence prevention, domestic violence; Legal services; Housing/shelter, public housing; Women, centers/services; Minorities/immigrants, centers/services; Civil rights, formal/general education; Civil rights, minorities; Civil rights, women; Civil rights, race/intergroup relations; Civil liberties, reproductive rights; Civil rights; Rural development; Community development; Voluntarism promotion; Public policy, research; Public affairs, citizen participation; Leadership development; Public affairs; Minorities; African Americans/Blacks; Hispanics/Latinos; Native Americans/American Indians; Women.

Type of support: General/operating support; Continuing support; Program development; Publication; Seed money; Technical assistance; Employee matching gifts; Matching/challenge support.

Limitations: Giving limited to NC. No support for athletic teams, civic clubs, day care centers, fraternal groups, parent/teachers associations, private K-12 schools, single site public schools, volunteer fire departments, or emergency medical service organizations, art organizations, historic preservation organizations, homeless shelters, or health care (physical and mental health). No grants to individuals (except for Nancy Susan Reynolds Awards and Sabbatical Program), or for endowment funds, equipment purchases, research, athletic events, building projects or renovations (including construction materials and labor costs), capital campaigns, computer hardware or software purchases (where it is the principal purpose of the grant), conferences, seminars, symposiums, fundraising events, initiatives promoting religious education or doctrine, land purchases, payment of debts, salaries for personnel or other general operating expenses in public schools, or after-school programs. Additionally, no grants for adoption and foster care, annual species preservation or rehabilitation, crisis intervention, greenways, senior citizen services, social/human direct services, substance abuse treatment, transitional housing, or treatment or rehabilitation.

Publications: Annual report (including application guidelines); Informational brochure; Informational brochure (including application guidelines); Occasional report.

Application information: The foundation will not accept applications via mail, fax, or e-mail. Application forms and guidelines available on foundation Web site. Application form required.

Initial approach: Letter or telephone for specifics. Review the foundation's Web site and then telephone for questions not answered by online resources. All applications must be submitted using the foundation's online application system

Copies of proposal: 1

Deadline(s): For grants, Feb. 1 and Aug. 1; for Sabbatical Program, Dec. 1; for Nancy Susan Reynolds Awards, June 1

Board meeting date(s): 3rd Fri. in May and Nov.

Final notification: 4 months after deadline

Officers and Trustees: * Mary Mountcastle,* Pres.; Lloyd P. Tate, Jr.,* V.P.; Thomas W. Ross, Secy. and Exec. Dir.; Jane S. Patterson,* Treas.; Katharine B. Mountcastle, Life Tr.; Zachary T. Smith, Life Tr.; Nancy R. Bagley; Smith W. Bagley; Daniel G. Clodfelter; Anita Brown Graham; John O. McNairy; David L. Neal; Stephen L. Neal; Virgil L. Smith.

Number of staff: 7 full-time professional; 1 part-time professional; 6 full-time support.

EIN: 586038145

Selected grants: The following grants were reported in 2005.

$1,250,000 to North Carolina Community Development Initiative, Raleigh, NC. For general operating support to increase community-based economic development.

$1,200,000 to Wake Forest University, Winston-Salem, NC. For general support, faculty development, and scholarships.

$750,000 to North Carolina Justice Center, Raleigh, NC. For general operating support to continue its antipoverty efforts on behalf of North Carolina's poor.

$400,000 to Conservation Fund, Chapel Hill, NC. For general operating support to enhance Resourceful Communities Program, which helps grassroots organizations to promote environmental, economic and social justice in their communities.

$350,000 to Democracy North Carolina, Carrboro, NC. For general operating support.

$300,000 to North Carolina Center for Voter Education, Raleigh, NC. For general operating support.

$75,000 to North Carolina Coalition Against Domestic Violence, Durham, NC. For general operating support to coordinate public policy and public awareness efforts on behalf of battered women.

$40,000 to Corporation for Enterprise Development (CFED), Durham, NC. For New Directions in Economic Development and Adjustment, advocacy and education project focused on economic incentives and other reform policies that will produce jobs and address needs of displaced workers.

$40,000 to University of North Carolina, Chapel Hill, NC. To facilitate collaboration among stakeholders affected by school site selection in rapidly-growing counties in NC.

$25,000 to WildLaw, Asheville, NC. For its work in sustainable forestry.

7459
R. J. Reynolds Foundation ◇

(formerly RJR Nabisco Foundation)
P.O. Box 2959
Winston-Salem, NC   27102-2959
(336) 741-5315
Contact: Stephen R. Strawsburg, Pres.
URL: http://www.brownandwilliamson.com/values/communityLegacy.asp

Established in 1986 in NC.

Donors: RJR Nabisco Holdings Corp.; R.J. Reynolds Tobacco Co.; Nabisco Brands, Inc.; Planters LifeSavers Co.; RJR Tobacco Intl.; RJR Acquisition Corp.

Foundation type: Company-sponsored foundation.

Financial data (yr. ended 12/31/04): Assets, $51,951,267 (M); gifts received, $5,000,000; expenditures, $1,997,548; qualifying distributions, $1,923,434; giving activities include $1,923,434 for 72+ grants (high: $550,000).

Purpose and activities: The foundation supports organizations involved with arts and culture, education, and human services.

Fields of interest: Arts, association; Arts; Child development, education; Elementary school/education; Higher education; Education; Human services; Federated giving programs; Economically disadvantaged.

Type of support: Continuing support; Program development; Scholarship funds; Employee matching gifts; Employee-related scholarships.

Limitations: Giving primarily in areas of company operations in NC; giving also in PR. No support for religious organizations not of direct benefit to the entire community, political organizations, or discriminatory organizations. No grants to individuals (except for employee-related scholarships), or for endowments, general operating support, or travel expenses; generally, no sponsorships.

Publications: Application guidelines.

Application information: Proposals should be no longer than 5 pages. Support is limited to 3 years. Application form not required.

Initial approach: Proposal

Deadline(s): Feb. 1, May 1, Aug. 1, and Nov. 1

Board meeting date(s): Quarterly

Final notification: 2 months

Officers: Stephen R. Strawsburg, Pres.; Tommy J. Payne, V.P.; Frank H. Skinner, V.P.; Jackson W. Henson, Secy.

Number of staff: 1 full-time professional; 1 full-time support.

EIN: 581681920

7460
Richard J. Reynolds III and Marie Mallouk Reynolds Foundation ◇

c/o Norwood Robinson
370 Knollwood St., Ste. 600
Winston-Salem, NC   27103-1886

Established in 1995 in NC.

Donor: Richard J. Reynolds III†.

Foundation type: Independent foundation.

Financial data (yr. ended 6/30/05): Assets, $17,833,644 (M); expenditures, $944,383; qualifying distributions, $826,078; giving activities include $808,000 for 21 grants (high: $235,000; low: $7,000).

Purpose and activities: Giving primarily for education, health care including medical research, and children, youth, families, and social services.

Fields of interest: Museums; Arts; Elementary/secondary education; Higher education; Education; Health care; Brain research; Housing/shelter, development; Safety/disasters; Human services; Salvation Army; Children/youth, services; Family services; Residential/custodial care; Community development; Foundations (community); Aging; Disabilities, people with; Mentally disabled; Economically disadvantaged.

Type of support: Building/renovation.

Limitations: Applications not accepted. Giving primarily in NC. No grants to individuals.

Application information: Contributes only to pre-selected organizations.

Committee Members: Hon. Robert Collier; Robinson & Lawing, LLP.

Trustee: Mercantile-Safe Deposit & Trust Co.

EIN: 561925457

7461
H. Smith Richardson Charitable Trust ◇

(formerly Randolph Foundation)
701 Green Valley Rd., Ste. 300
Greensboro, NC   27408-7096
Contact: Heather R. Higgins, Dir.

Trust established in 1976 in NC.

Donor: H. Smith Richardson†.

Foundation type: Independent foundation.

Financial data (yr. ended 12/31/05): Assets, $61,029,218 (M); gifts received, $55,178; expenditures, $3,196,921; qualifying distributions, $2,750,106; giving activities include $2,333,044 for 14 grants (high: $274,868; low: $85,343).

Purpose and activities: Primary areas of interest include the study and research of cultural values and civic virtues.

Fields of interest: Social sciences; Public affairs.

Type of support: Publication; Research.

Limitations: Applications not accepted. Giving limited to the U.S. No grants to individuals.

Application information: Contributes only to pre-selected organizations.

Trustees: Winburne King; Peter L. Richardson; Stuart S. Richardson; E. William Stetson III.

Number of staff: 1 full-time professional; 2 full-time support.

EIN: 237245123

7462
Grace Jones Richardson Trust ◇

c/o Piedmont Financial Co.
P.O. Box 20124
Greensboro, NC   27420-0124
Contact: P.L. Richardson, Tr.

Trust established in 1962 in CT.

Donor: Grace Jones Richardson†.

Foundation type: Independent foundation.

Financial data (yr. ended 12/31/04): Assets, $70,304,963 (M); gifts received, $930,000; expenditures, $1,912,464; qualifying distributions, $1,831,394; giving activities include $1,667,000 for 376 grants (high: $55,000; low: $500).

Purpose and activities: Giving primarily for the arts, education, and human services.

Fields of interest: Arts; Higher education; Environment, natural resources; Health care; Human services; Federated giving programs; Christian agencies & churches.

Type of support: General/operating support.

Limitations: Giving on a national basis. No grants to individuals.

Application information:

Initial approach: Proposal

Deadline(s): None

Board meeting date(s): As required

Trustees: P.L. Richardson; S.S. Richardson.

EIN: 066023003

Selected grants: The following grants were reported in 2003.

$60,000 to Montshire Museum of Science, Norwich, VT.

$37,000 to Childrens Hospital Foundation, Denver, CO. 2 grants: $17,000, $20,000

$35,000 to Santa Barbara Museum of Art, Santa Barbara, CA.

$30,000 to Downtown Community Television Center, New York, NY.

$25,000 to Victory Programs, Boston, MA.

$20,000 to Connecticut Audubon Society, Fairfield, CT.

$18,000 to Stuart Country Day School of the Sacred Heart, Princeton, NJ.

$16,000 to UrbanGlass, Brooklyn, NY.

$10,000 to Davidson College, Davidson, NC.

7463
Richmond Community Foundation, Inc. ◇
217 S. Tryon St.
Charlotte, NC 28202   (704) 973-4500

Established in 2001 in NC.
Donors: Richmond Memorial Hospital Foundation; First Union National Bank.
Foundation type: Independent foundation.
Financial data (yr. ended 12/31/05): Assets, $26,624,985 (M); expenditures, $2,132,912; qualifying distributions, $2,134,094; giving activities include $1,488,745 for 5 grants (high: $1,000,000; low: $3,500).
Purpose and activities: Giving primarily for hospitals, education, and to a United Methodist church.
Fields of interest: Higher education, college; Education; Hospitals (general); Health care; Protestant agencies & churches.
Limitations: Giving primarily in the Richmond County, NC, area. No grants to individuals.
Application information: Application form required.
  Deadline(s): Oct. 15
Directors: Russell E. Bennett, Jr.; Raymond E. "Gene" Burrell; R. Larry Campbell; Betty Dorsett; Robert E. Hutchinson; John J. Jackson; Franklin Clay Jenkins; John D. Price; Paul R. Smart; Roger Staley; Bruce Stanback; Bill M. Thompson.
EIN: 562168849

7464
Roanoke-Chowan Foundation, Inc.
500 S. Academy St.
Ahoskie, NC 27910
Contact: Peter N. Geilich, Pres.

Established in 1997 in NC.
Foundation type: Independent foundation.
Financial data (yr. ended 9/30/05): Assets, $0 (M); expenditures, $687,530; qualifying distributions, $516,808; giving activities include $516,808 for 4 grants (high: $424,508; low: $4,300).
Purpose and activities: Grants are made only to promote the health and wellness of persons living in Bertie, Gates, Hertford, or Northampton, counties in NC.
Fields of interest: Hospitals (general); Health care.
Type of support: General/operating support; Program development.
Limitations: Giving limited to Bertie, Gates, Hertford, and Northampton counties, NC.
Publications: Application guidelines; Grants list; Informational brochure; Informational brochure

(including application guidelines); Occasional report; Program policy statement.
Application information: Application form required.
  Initial approach: Contact foundation
  Copies of proposal: 2
  Deadline(s): Jan. 1, Apr. 1, July 1, and Oct. 1
  Board meeting date(s): Quarterly
  Final notification: 3-6 months
Officers: Ernest L. Evans, Chair.; James W. Mason, Vice-Chair.; Peter N. Geilich, Pres.; J.S. Almario, M.D., Secy.-Treas.
Directors: Ernest Carter; Gif Daughtridge; Hon. Cy Grant; Reba Green-Holley; Charles Hughes; Robert C. Kahn, M.D.; Carl D. Taylor; Charles L. Revelle III.
Number of staff: 1 part-time professional; 1 part-time support.
EIN: 561535057
Selected grants: The following grants were reported in 2004.
$644,286 to Roanoke-Chowan Hospital, Ahoskie, NC. 4 grants: $398,672 (For operating support), $51,605 (For equipment), $81,009 (For program support), $113,000.
$24,171 to University Health System, Ahoskie, NC.

7465
Percival Roberts, Jr. Trust ◇ ☆
c/o Wachovia Bank, N.A.
100 N. Main St.
Winston-Salem, NC 27150

Foundation type: Independent foundation.
Financial data (yr. ended 12/31/05): Assets, $15,156,484 (M); expenditures, $1,091,814; qualifying distributions, $1,088,000; giving activities include $1,088,000 for 5 grants (high: $250,000; low: $164,000).
Purpose and activities: Giving primarily to children's hospitals. Support also for a school of nursing and for a rehabilitation hospital.
Fields of interest: Nursing school/education; Hospitals (specialty); Medical care, rehabilitation.
Limitations: Giving primarily in Philadelphia, PA.
Trustee: Wachovia Bank, N.A.
EIN: 236219291

7466
The Blanche and Julian Robertson Family Foundation, Inc. ◇
P.O. Box 4242
Salisbury, NC 28145-4242   (704) 637-0511
Contact: David E. Setzer, Exec. Dir.
FAX: (704) 637-0177;
E-mail: bjrfoundation@aol.com; Additional address: 141 E. Council St., Salisbury, NC 28144

Established in 1997 in NC.
Donors: Julian H. Robertson, Jr.; Wyndham Robertson.
Foundation type: Independent foundation.
Financial data (yr. ended 12/31/05): Assets, $18,730,595 (M); expenditures, $1,748,018; qualifying distributions, $1,728,467; giving activities include $1,682,691 for 57 grants (high: $250,000; low: $1,000).
Purpose and activities: The foundation, committed to improving the quality of life in Salisbury, NC, and its surrounding area, is interested in funding programs that address social, family, educational, health, and neighborhood issues, and those which enrich lives through cultural, artistic and

recreational opportunities. Preference is given to projects that encourage constructive change, strive toward achieving excellence, and have a significant component of public service.
Fields of interest: Historic preservation/historical societies; Arts; Education; Environment; Health care; Recreation; Youth, services; Family services; Community development.
Type of support: General/operating support; Continuing support; Capital campaigns; Building/renovation; Equipment; Land acquisition; Emergency funds; Program development; Conferences/seminars; Curriculum development; Technical assistance; Program evaluation; Matching/challenge support.
Limitations: Giving limited to Salisbury, NC, and its surrounding area.
Publications: Application guidelines; Annual report; Grants list; Informational brochure (including application guidelines); Occasional report.
Application information: Application form required.
  Initial approach: Telephone, personal visit, or letter
  Copies of proposal: 1
  Deadline(s): Mar. 31
  Board meeting date(s): Twice a year, as determined by board
  Final notification: Upon board's decision and action, usually in mid-May
Officers and Directors:* James F. Hurley,* Chair.; James G. Whitton,* Vice-Chair.; Margaret H. Kluttz,* Secy.; Catrelia Hunter; B. Clay Lindsay, Jr.; R. Scott Maddox; Lillian A. Morgan; Alex T. Robertson; Spencer R. Robertson; Wyndham Robertson; Fred J. Stanback, Jr.
Number of staff: 1 part-time professional.
EIN: 562027907
Selected grants: The following grants were reported in 2005.
$200,000 to Rowan Regional Medical Center, Salisbury, NC.
$100,000 to Hood Theological Seminary, Salisbury, NC.
$100,000 to Salisbury, City of, Salisbury, NC.
$75,000 to Rowan Helping Ministries, Salisbury, NC. 2 grants: $25,000, $50,000
$70,000 to Catawba College, Salisbury, NC.
$50,000 to Livingstone College, Salisbury, NC.
$50,000 to Nazareth Childrens Home, Rockwell, NC.
$25,000 to Community Care Clinic, Albemarle, NC.
$15,000 to Rowan Partnership for Children, Salisbury, NC.

7467
Rostan Family Foundation
P.O. Box 970
Valdese, NC 28690-0970

Established in 1995 in NC.
Donors: John P. Rostan, Jr.†; Naomi B. Rostan.
Foundation type: Independent foundation.
Financial data (yr. ended 12/31/05): Assets, $7,320,074 (M); expenditures, $374,869; qualifying distributions, $335,500; giving activities include $335,500 for 22 grants (high: $57,000; low: $2,500).
Purpose and activities: Giving primarily for education and for human services.
Fields of interest: Higher education, university; Libraries (public); Boy scouts; Girl scouts; Salvation Army; Residential/custodial care, hospices; Christian agencies & churches.

Limitations: Applications not accepted. Giving limited to NC, with emphasis on Burke County. No grants to individuals.
Application information: Contributes only to pre-selected organizations. Unsolicited requests for funds not accepted.
Officers and Trustees:* Mrs. John P. Rostan, Jr.,* C.E.O. and Pres.; John P. Rostan III,* V.P. and Secy.; James H. Rostan,* V.P. and Treas.
Number of staff: None.
EIN: 561901626

7468
J. H. & R. H. Rumbaugh Foundation ◇
c/o Wachovia Bank, N.A.
100 N. Main St., 13th Fl.
Winston-Salem, NC 27150

Established in 1986 in FL.
Foundation type: Independent foundation.
Financial data (yr. ended 3/31/05): Assets, $7,326,512 (M); expenditures, $392,466; qualifying distributions, $336,421; giving activities include $338,610 for 3 grants (high: $112,870; low: $112,870).
Fields of interest: Higher education.
Type of support: General/operating support.
Limitations: Applications not accepted. Giving primarily in PA. No grants to individuals.
Application information: Contributes only to pre-selected organizations.
Trustee: Wachovia Bank, N.A.
EIN: 596851866

7469
Ida Alice Ryan Trust ◇
c/o Wachovia Bank, N.A.
100 N. Main St., 13th Fl.
Winston-Salem, NC 27150

Established in GA.
Foundation type: Independent foundation.
Financial data (yr. ended 12/31/05): Assets, $37,903,207 (M); expenditures, $1,213,660; qualifying distributions, $956,732; giving activities include $956,732 for 46 grants (high: $134,316; low: $3,000).
Fields of interest: Arts; Elementary/secondary education; Higher education; Education; Animal welfare; Mental health/crisis services; Biomedicine; Human services; YM/YWCAs & YM/YWHAs; Children/youth, services; Federated giving programs.
Limitations: Applications not accepted. Giving primarily in the Atlanta, GA, area. No grants to individuals.
Application information: Contributes only to pre-selected organizations.
Trustee: Wachovia Bank, N.A.
EIN: 586026603

7470
S.R.C. Education Alliance ◇ ☆
P.O. Box 12053
Research Triangle Park, NC 27709
URL: http://srcea.src.org

Donors: Microelectronics Advanced Research Corp.; Semiconductor Research Corp.; Intel Foundation; IBM.

Foundation type: Independent foundation.
Financial data (yr. ended 12/31/04): Assets, $1,457,620 (M); gifts received, $796,116; expenditures, $882,947; qualifying distributions, $837,975; giving activities include $815,487 for 27 grants (high: $300,000; low: $6,000), and $2,000 for 2 grants to individuals (high: $1,000; low: $1,000).
Purpose and activities: Giving primarily for higher education.
Limitations: Giving on a national basis.
Directors: Ralph K. Cavin III; Dinesh Mehta; Larry W. Sumney.
EIN: 581807204

7471
Sall Family Foundation, Inc. ◇
201 Vineyard Ln.
Cary, NC 27513-3067 (919) 677-8000
Contact: John Phillip Sall, Pres.

Established in 1993 in NC.
Donors: John Phillip Sall; Virginia B. Sall.
Foundation type: Independent foundation.
Financial data (yr. ended 12/31/04): Assets, $8,299,433 (M); expenditures, $2,205,266; qualifying distributions, $2,172,184; giving activities include $2,151,648 for 2 grants (high: $1,800,000; low: $351,648).
Purpose and activities: Giving primarily for health, education, environmental protection, and community development.
Fields of interest: Education; Environment, natural resources; Health care; Community development.
Limitations: Giving on a national basis. No grants to individuals.
Application information:
  Initial approach: Letter
  Deadline(s): Sept. 30
Officers: John Phillip Sall, Pres.; Virginia B. Sall, Treas.
Agent: Citibank, N.A.
EIN: 582016050

7472
The Simpson Foundation ◇
c/o Wachovia Bank, N.A.
P.O. Box 3099
Winston-Salem, NC 27102-3099
Contact: C. Gerald Lane, V.P. and Trust Off., Wachovia Bank, N.A.
Application address: 1401 Main St., Columbia, SC 29226, tel.: (803) 765-3671

Trust established in 1956 in SC.
Donors: W.H.B. Simpson†; Mrs. W.H.B. Simpson.
Foundation type: Independent foundation.
Financial data (yr. ended 12/31/05): Assets, $10,184,090 (M); expenditures, $541,133; qualifying distributions, $466,863; giving activities include $462,113 for 58 grants (high: $60,000; low: $500).
Purpose and activities: Giving primarily for human services, the arts, and cancer research.
Fields of interest: Historic preservation/historical societies; Arts; Education; Hospitals (general); Cancer research; Human services; Federated giving programs; Protestant agencies & churches.
Type of support: Capital campaigns; Matching/challenge support.

Limitations: Giving primarily in SC. No support for educational purposes. No grants to individuals, or for scholarships; no loans.
Application information: Application form not required.
  Initial approach: Letter or proposal
  Copies of proposal: 5
  Deadline(s): Apr. 1 and Oct. 1
  Board meeting date(s): Middle of May and Nov.
Directors: Claire Efrid; Wilma Johnson; J.A. Kuhne; Lucy Kuhne; Nell M. Rice; Kate Simpson.
Trustee: Wachovia Bank, N.A.
EIN: 576017451

7473
Lori L. Sklut Foundation ◇
c/o Eric Ridenour and Ama Charlotte
4064 Colony Rd., Ste. 195
Charlotte, NC 28211

Established in 1995 in NC.
Donor: Lori L. Sklut.
Foundation type: Independent foundation.
Financial data (yr. ended 12/31/04): Assets, $11,097,536 (M); expenditures, $357,122; qualifying distributions, $342,598; giving activities include $340,484 for 21 grants (high: $155,000; low: $1,321).
Purpose and activities: Giving generally for health, Jewish organizations, community arts and sciences, and education.
Fields of interest: Museums (history); Education; Human services; Children/youth, services; Family services; Residential/custodial care, hospices; Jewish federated giving programs.
Limitations: Applications not accepted. Giving primarily in Charlotte, NC. No grants to individuals.
Application information: Contributes only to pre-selected organizations.
Directors: Eric R. Sklut; Lori Levine Sklut.
Trustee: Bank of America, N.A.
EIN: 561904190

7474
Slick Family Foundation ◇
P.O. Box 5958
Winston-Salem, NC 27113

Established in 1997 in NC.
Donor: Earl F. Slick.
Foundation type: Independent foundation.
Financial data (yr. ended 12/31/05): Assets, $6,369,221 (M); expenditures, $785,077; qualifying distributions, $726,659; giving activities include $634,166 for 20 grants (high: $200,000; low: $5,000).
Purpose and activities: Giving for the arts, the environment, human services, and education.
Fields of interest: Arts; Education; Environment; Human services.
Limitations: Applications not accepted. Giving primarily in NC. No grants to individuals.
Application information: Contributes only to pre-selected organizations.
Officers and Directors:* Earl F. Slick,* Pres.; Phyllis S. Cowell,* V.P.; Jane P. Slick,* V.P.; Mary Caroline Gamble,* Secy.-Treas.; R. Elaine Addison; John Cowell; John L.W. Garrou; Lynn C. Ives.
EIN: 311500854

7475
O. Temple Sloan, Jr. Foundation ✧ ☆
P.O. Box 26006
Raleigh, NC   27611   (919) 573-3211
Contact: Carol Sloan, Tr.
Additional tel.: (919) 573-3000

Established in 1994 in NC.
Donors: O. Temple Sloan, Jr.; O. Temple Sloan, Jr. Charitable Lead Trust.
Foundation type: Independent foundation.
Financial data (yr. ended 12/31/05): Assets, $8,877,405 (M); gifts received, $1,278,915; expenditures, $1,597,262; qualifying distributions, $1,566,609; giving activities include $1,566,609 for grants.
Purpose and activities: Giving primarily for education, hospitals, and religious organizations.
Fields of interest: Higher education; Hospitals (general); Federated giving programs; Christian agencies & churches; Protestant agencies & churches.
Type of support: Capital campaigns; Scholarships—to individuals.
Limitations: Giving primarily in NC; some funding also in MT.
Application information: Application form required.
  Deadline(s): None
Trustees: Malcolm C. Graham; Carson S. Henline; Carol C. Sloan; W. Gerald Thornton; George C. Turner.
EIN: 561870844
Selected grants: The following grants were reported in 2004.
$98,298 to First Presbyterian Church, Raleigh, NC.
$30,000 to Duke University, Durham, NC.
$13,910 to Saint Andrews Presbyterian College, Laurinburg, NC.
$10,000 to American Humanics, Kansas City, MO.
$5,000 to Meredith College, Raleigh, NC.
$5,000 to Peace College, Raleigh, NC.
$2,000 to Hospice of Wake County, Raleigh, NC.
$1,000 to American Red Cross, Raleigh, NC.
$1,000 to United Way of Beaverhead County, Dillon, MT.

7476
John I. Smith Charities, Inc. ✧
c/o Bank of America, N.A.
101 S. Tryon St., NC1-002-11-18
Charlotte, NC   28255-0001
Application address: c/o Cindy L. Wilson, Bank of America, N.A., P.O. Box 608, Greenville, SC 29608, tel.: (864) 271-5930

Established in 1985 in SC.
Donor: John I. Smith†.
Foundation type: Independent foundation.
Financial data (yr. ended 7/31/05): Assets, $26,860,952 (M); expenditures, $1,310,430; qualifying distributions, $1,180,466; giving activities include $1,135,500 for 43 grants (high: $200,000; low: $1,500).
Purpose and activities: Giving primarily for higher education, human services, and the arts.
Fields of interest: Museums; Arts; Higher education; Medical school/education; Theological school/education; Education; YM/YWCAs & YM/YWHAs; Children/youth, services; Federated giving programs; Christian agencies & churches.
Type of support: General/operating support; Capital campaigns; Endowments; Emergency funds; Scholarship funds.

Limitations: Giving primarily in SC. No grants to individuals.
Application information: Application form not required.
  Initial approach: Form provided by foundation directors
  Board meeting date(s): Quarterly
Officer: Wilbur Y. Bridges, Pres. and Secy.
Directors: Elizabeth Clayton; Jefferson V. Smith III.
Trustee: Bank of America, N.A.
EIN: 570806327

7477
G. Gregory Smith Family Foundation, Inc. ✧ ☆
5201 Hedrick Dr.
Greensboro, NC   27410
Contact: John R. Perkinson, Jr., Asst. Secy.

Established in 1994 in NC.
Donor: George Gregory Smith.
Foundation type: Independent foundation.
Financial data (yr. ended 9/30/05): Assets, $1,720,418 (M); gifts received, $503,500; expenditures, $507,599; qualifying distributions, $501,000; giving activities include $501,000 for 2 grants (high: $500,000; low: $1,000).
Fields of interest: Education; Human services; Christian agencies & churches.
Limitations: Giving primarily in Greensboro, NC. No grants to individuals.
Application information:
  Initial approach: Letter
  Deadline(s): None
Officers: George Gregory Smith, Pres.; George Gregory Smith, Jr., V.P.; Carol Belk Smith, Secy.-Treas.
EIN: 561902026

7478
Edward C. Smith, Jr. & Christopher B. Smith Foundation, Inc. ✧
(also known as Eddie and Jo Allison Smith Family Foundation, Inc.)
P.O. Box 1527
Greenville, NC   27835

Established in 1993 in NC.
Donors: Edward C. Smith, Jr.; Christopher B. Smith; C & E Enterprises; Grady-White Boats, Inc.
Foundation type: Independent foundation.
Financial data (yr. ended 6/30/05): Assets, $30,996,952 (M); gifts received, $4,001,100; expenditures, $1,256,778; qualifying distributions, $964,530; giving activities include $964,530 for 88 grants (high: $333,000; low: $200).
Purpose and activities: Giving primarily for the arts, education, natural resource conservation, health, children, youth and social services, federated giving programs, and Baptist and Episcopal churches.
Fields of interest: Museums; Museums (science/technology); Performing arts, opera; Arts; Higher education; Education; Environment, natural resources; Animals/wildlife, fisheries; Hospitals (general); Health organizations, association; Human services; Children/youth, services; Family services; Foundations (community); Federated giving programs; Protestant agencies & churches.
Limitations: Applications not accepted. Giving primarily in NC; some funding nationally. No grants to individuals.

Application information: Contributes only to pre-selected organizations.
Directors: Christopher B. Smith; Edward C. Smith, Jr.; Jo A. Smith.
EIN: 561844198
Selected grants: The following grants were reported in 2005.
$50,000 to Lexington Memorial Hospital Foundation, Lexington, NC.
$35,000 to Family Services of Davidson County, Lexington, NC.
$16,000 to United Way of Pitt County, Greenville, NC. 2 grants: $3,000, $13,000
$8,500 to Graveyard of the Atlantic Museum, Hatteras, NC.
$8,500 to Turnage Theaters Foundation, Washington, NC.
$6,000 to Appalachian Voices, Boone, NC.
$6,000 to Oak Ridge Military Academy, Oak Ridge, NC.
$2,500 to Ronald McDonald House, Chapel Hill, NC.
$1,000 to William Byrd Community House, Richmond, VA.

7479
The General William A. Smith Trust ✧
c/o BB&T, Trust Dept.
P.O. Box 2907
Wilson, NC   27894-2907
Contact: Judy Micha
Application address: 200 S. College St., Charlotte, NC 28202-2005, tel.: (704) 954-1125

Trust established in 1940 in NC.
Donor: Genl. William A. Smith.
Foundation type: Independent foundation.
Financial data (yr. ended 12/31/05): Assets, $5,541,266 (M); expenditures, $433,725; qualifying distributions, $380,952; giving activities include $380,952 for grants.
Fields of interest: Higher education; Education; Children/youth, services; Government/public administration; Protestant agencies & churches.
Type of support: General/operating support; Continuing support; Annual campaigns; Capital campaigns; Building/renovation; Equipment; Endowments; Emergency funds; Program development; Professorships; Scholarship funds.
Limitations: Giving primarily in Anson County, NC. No grants to individuals.
Application information: Application form not required.
  Deadline(s): Dec. 31
Trustees: Joe E. Gaddy; James A. Hardison, Jr.; Joanne Huntley; Frank F. Mills; BB&T.
EIN: 566042630
Selected grants: The following grants were reported in 2005.
$91,752 to Anson County Schools, Wadesboro, NC.
$6,000 to Anson County Arts Council, Wadesboro, NC.
$5,500 to Historical Society Anson County, Wadesboro, NC.
$2,500 to Girl Scouts of the U.S.A..
$2,500 to United Way.
$1,000 to Humane Society.

7480
SOL Foundation Agency ✧ ☆
(formerly Ken A. & Gail B. Miller Family Foundation)
c/o U.S. Trust
P.O. Box 26262
Greensboro, NC   27420

Established in 1998 in NC.
Donor: Kenneth D. Miller.
Foundation type: Independent foundation.
Financial data (yr. ended 12/31/05): Assets, $476,645 (M); expenditures, $458,725; qualifying distributions, $455,915; giving activities include $455,000 for 5 grants (high: $420,000; low: $5,000).
Fields of interest: Elementary/secondary education; Higher education; Community development.
Type of support: General/operating support.
Limitations: Applications not accepted. Giving primarily in NC. No grants to individuals.
Application information: Contributes only to pre-selected organizations.
Officer: Kenneth D. Miller, Pres.
EIN: 562113226

7481
Southern Bank Foundation ✧
P.O. Box 729
Mount Olive, NC   28365-0729
Contact: David A. Bean, Treas.

Established in 1996 in NC.
Donors: Southern Bank and Trust Co.; Southern Bancshares, Inc.
Foundation type: Company-sponsored foundation.
Financial data (yr. ended 12/31/05): Assets, $9,805,307 (M); gifts received, $172,215; expenditures, $528,187; qualifying distributions, $415,964; giving activities include $415,964 for 98 grants (high: $150,000; low: $100).
Purpose and activities: The foundation supports organizations involved with education and human services.
Fields of interest: Education; Human services, emergency aid; Human services.
Type of support: General/operating support; Annual campaigns; Capital campaigns; Building/renovation; Equipment; Debt reduction; Program development; Scholarship funds.
Limitations: Giving primarily in eastern NC. No grants to individuals.
Application information: Application form required.
Initial approach: Contact foundation for application form
Deadline(s): None
Board meeting date(s): Varies
Officers: Frank B. Holding,* Pres.; John N. Walker,* V.P.; John E. Pegram, Jr., Secy.; David A. Bean, Treas.
Directors: Hope Holding Connell; Charles L. Revelle, Jr.
EIN: 562002871
Selected grants: The following grants were reported in 2004.
$70,000 to Mount Olive College, Mount Olive, NC.
$42,652 to Pungo District Hospital Corporation, Belhaven, NC.
$20,000 to Chowan College, Murfreesboro, NC.
$20,000 to North Carolina Community Foundation, Raleigh, NC.
$20,000 to YMCA. 2 grants: $10,000 each
$15,000 to Campbell University, Buies Creek, NC.

$10,000 to Boy Scouts of America.
$8,500 to North Carolina Community College Foundation, Raleigh, NC.
$5,000 to Historic Hope Foundation, Windsor, NC.

7482
C. D. Spangler Foundation, Inc. ▼ ✧
P.O. Box 36007
Charlotte, NC   28236-6007
Contact: W.D. Cornwell, Jr., V.P. and Secy.-Treas.

Established in 1956 in NC.
Donors: C.D. Spangler‡; PTI Investments Inc.; Delcap, Inc.; C.D. Spangler Construction Co.; Delcor, Inc.
Foundation type: Independent foundation.
Financial data (yr. ended 12/31/05): Assets, $348,251,347 (M); gifts received, $35,542,000; expenditures, $12,697,264; qualifying distributions, $12,440,051; giving activities include $12,433,955 for 43 grants (high: $7,500,000; low: $1,000; average: $5,000–$125,000).
Purpose and activities: Emphasis on higher education.
Fields of interest: Museums; Arts; Higher education; Human services.
Type of support: Employee matching gifts.
Limitations: Applications not accepted. Giving primarily in NC. No grants to individuals.
Application information: Unsolicited requests for funds not considered.
Officers and Directors:* Meredith R. Spangler,* Chair.; Abigail R. Spangler,* Pres.; W.D. Cornwell, Jr.,* V.P. and Secy.-Treas.; Denise E. Gardner, V.P.; Anna Spangler Nelson,* V.P.; C.D. Spangler, Jr.
EIN: 566061548
Selected grants: The following grants were reported in 2005.
$7,500,000 to Harvard University, Cambridge, MA. For program support for Business School in Boston.
$2,416,350 to Myers Park Baptist Church, Charlotte, NC. 2 grants: $166,350 (For Cornwell Center operating support), $2,250,000 (For Cornwell Center endowment).
$1,000,000 to Wellesley College, Wellesley, MA.
$200,000 to YMCA of Greater Charlotte, Charlotte, NC.
$125,000 to American Red Cross, National Headquarters, DC. For program support.
$125,000 to Salvation Army of Charlotte, Charlotte, NC. For program support.
$25,680 to National Merit Scholarship Corporation, Evanston, IL.
$25,000 to Public Library of Charlotte and Mecklenburg County, Charlotte, NC. For program support.
$10,000 to College Foundation of the University of Virginia, Charlottesville, VA.

7483
Spring Charitable Trust ✧
c/o Wachovia Bank, N.A.
100 N. Main St., 13th Fl.
Winston-Salem, NC   27150

Established in 1998 in PA.
Foundation type: Independent foundation.
Financial data (yr. ended 1/31/05): Assets, $11,805,981 (M); expenditures, $652,101; qualifying distributions, $567,644; giving activities

include $567,244 for 5 grants (high: $226,898; low: $28,362).
Fields of interest: Hospitals (general); Hospitals (specialty); Human services; Salvation Army; Residential/custodial care, senior continuing care.
Limitations: Applications not accepted. Giving primarily in Tampa, FL and PA. No grants to individuals.
Application information: Contributes only to pre-selected organizations.
Trustee: Wachovia Bank, N.A.
EIN: 236290545
Selected grants: The following grants were reported in 2003.
$280,000 to Shriners Hospitals for Children, Tampa, FL.
$175,000 to Temple Lower Bucks Hospital, Bristol, PA.
$140,000 to Methodist Home for the Aged, Philadelphia, PA.
$70,000 to Bucks County Association for the Blind, Newtown, PA.
$35,000 to Salvation Army Divisional Headquarters, Philadelphia, PA.

7484
SPX Foundation
(formerly Sealed Power Foundation)
13515 Ballantyne Corporate Pl.
Charlotte, NC   28277   (704) 752-4400
Contact: Tina L. Betlejewski, Pres.
E-mail: spx@spx.com

Established in 1982 in MI.
Donors: SPX Corp.; EGS Electrical Group LLC; O-Z Gedney Co., LLC.
Foundation type: Company-sponsored foundation.
Financial data (yr. ended 12/31/04): Assets, $1,249,910 (M); expenditures, $860,001; qualifying distributions, $833,051; giving activities include $451,459 for 21 grants (high: $100,000; low: $1,000), and $381,592 for 362 employee matching gifts.
Purpose and activities: The foundation supports organizations involved with arts and culture, education, health, human services, and civic affairs.
Fields of interest: Arts; Education; Health care; Human services; Public affairs.
Type of support: General/operating support; Capital campaigns; Employee matching gifts.
Publications: Informational brochure (including application guidelines).
Application information: Application form not required.
Initial approach: Proposal
Copies of proposal: 1
Deadline(s): None
Board meeting date(s): Quarterly
Officers and Trustees:* Tina L. Betlejewski,* Pres.; Robert B. Foreman,* V.P.; Patrick J. O'Leary,* Secy.-Treas.; Christopher J. Kearney.
EIN: 386058308

7485
The Stewards Fund ✧
P.O. Box 6575
Raleigh, NC   27628
Contact: Joyce Adler, Asst. Secy.

Established in 1986 in NC.
Foundation type: Independent foundation.

Financial data (yr. ended 12/31/04): Assets, $34,920,647 (M); expenditures, $2,819,093; qualifying distributions, $2,773,746; giving activities include $2,734,620 for 53 grants (high: $300,000; low: $5,000).

Purpose and activities: Support for organizations meeting basic needs including food, clothing, and shelter in the triangle area of NC only.

Fields of interest: Health care; Housing/shelter, development; Children/youth, services; Family services; Residential/custodial care, hospices; Homeless, human services; Religious federated giving programs; Homeless.

Limitations: Applications not accepted. Giving limited to Wake, Durham, and Orange counties, NC. No grants to individuals.

Application information: Contributes only to pre-selected organizations. Unsolicited requests for funds not accepted.

Officers and Trustees:* Anne B. Faircloth,* Pres. and Treas.; Thomas H. McGuire,* V.P. and Secy.; Anna Neal Blanchard, Genl. Mgr.; Marian Bergdolt; David Dodson; Martin Eakes; Haywood Holderness; Wyndham Robertson.

Number of staff: 1 part-time support.

EIN: 561482138

Selected grants: The following grants were reported in 2004.

$160,000 to Raleigh Rescue Mission, Raleigh, NC. 2 grants: $100,000, $60,000

$105,000 to Inter-Faith Council for Social Service, Carrboro, NC. 2 grants: $70,000, $35,000

$100,000 to Inter-Faith Food Shuttle, Raleigh, NC.

$100,000 to SAFEchild, Raleigh, NC. 2 grants: $50,000 each

$100,000 to Salvation Army, NC.

$50,000 to Hospice of Wake County, Raleigh, NC.

$50,000 to Loaves and Fishes, Charlotte, NC.

7486
Stonecutter Foundation, Inc. ✧ ☆

400 Spindale St.
Spindale, NC   28160
Contact: Terri Barringer
Application address: P.O. Box 157, Spindale, NC 28160

Incorporated in 1944 in NC.

Donors: Stonecutter Mills Corp.; Ivy Cowan.

Foundation type: Company-sponsored foundation.

Financial data (yr. ended 3/31/05): Assets, $9,187,108 (M); gifts received, $600; expenditures, $485,982; qualifying distributions, $487,187; giving activities include $400,356 for 51 grants (high: $45,000; low: $256), and $46,000 for loans to individuals.

Purpose and activities: The foundation supports organizations involved with secondary and higher education, human services, and Protestantism and awards student loans.

Fields of interest: Secondary school/education; Higher education; Children/youth, services; Human services; Philanthropy/voluntarism; Protestant agencies & churches.

Type of support: General/operating support; Student loans—to individuals.

Limitations: Giving primarily in NC; giving in Rutherford and Polk County, NC, for student loans.

Application information: Application form required.

Initial approach: Contact foundation for application form for student loans

Deadline(s): None

Officers and Directors: Z.E. Dobbins, Jr., Pres.; James R. Cowan, V.P.; James M. Perry, V.P.; Thomas P. Walker, Secy.; D. Daniel Briscoe; Dillard Morrow; James T. Strickland; M.L. Summey; K.S. Tanner, Jr.

EIN: 566044820

7487
Robert Lee Stowe, Jr. Foundation, Inc. ✧ ☆

P.O. Box 351
Belmont, NC   28012   (704) 825-1340
Contact: Robert L. Stowe III, Pres.; Daniel Harding Stowe, V.P.

Incorporated in 1945 in NC.

Donors: Robert Lee Stowe, Jr.‡; Robert Lee Stowe III; R.L. Stowe Mills, Inc.

Foundation type: Independent foundation.

Financial data (yr. ended 12/31/05): Assets, $3,165,962 (M); expenditures, $537,329; qualifying distributions, $507,603; giving activities include $507,603 for grants.

Purpose and activities: Giving primarily for human services and to Protestant agencies and churches.

Fields of interest: Elementary/secondary education; Higher education; Botanical gardens; Human services; Protestant agencies & churches.

Limitations: Giving primarily in NC, with emphasis on the Charlotte area. No grants to individuals.

Application information:

Initial approach: Letter

Deadline(s): None

Officers: Robert Lee Stowe III, Pres.; Daniel Harding Stowe, V.P.; Richmond H. Stowe, V.P.; Jean H. Gibson, Secy.-Treas.

EIN: 566034773

Selected grants: The following grants were reported in 2003.

$110,000 to YMCA of Gaston County, Gastonia, NC.

$10,000 to Carolina Educational Opportunity Fund, Winston-Salem, NC.

$10,000 to Charlotte Country Day School, Charlotte, NC.

$4,500 to Belmont Abbey College, Belmont, NC.

$4,350 to United Way of Gaston County, Gastonia, NC.

$4,000 to Community Foundation of Gaston County, Gastonia, NC.

$2,100 to Presbyterian Hospital Foundation, Charlotte, NC.

$2,000 to Gaston Together, Dallas, NC.

$1,000 to Daniel Stowe Botanical Garden, Belmont, NC.

$1,000 to Hinds Feet Farm, Huntersville, NC.

7488
Strowd Roses, Inc. ✧

1526 E. Franklin St., Ste. 5-202
P.O. Box 3558
Chapel Hill, NC   27515-3558
Contact: Jennifer B. Boger, Pres.
E-mail: jboger@strowdroses.org; *Application address:* P.O. Box 3558, Chapel Hill, NC 27515-3558, tel.: (919) 929-1984; URL: http://www.strowdroses.org

Established in 2001 in NC.

Donors: Irene H. Strowd‡; Gladis H. Adams Charitable Trust.

Foundation type: Independent foundation.

Financial data (yr. ended 12/31/05): Assets, $7,948,820 (M); expenditures, $416,862; qualifying distributions, $413,862; giving activities include $376,345 for 60 grants (high: $23,560; low: $1,000).

Purpose and activities: To support programs and projects which improve the quality of life for citizens of Chapel Hill and Carrboro.

Fields of interest: Arts; Elementary/secondary education; Environment; Health care; Recreation; Children/youth, services; Aging; Hispanics/Latinos.

Type of support: General/operating support; Continuing support; Capital campaigns; Debt reduction; Program development; Conferences/seminars; Seed money; Internship funds; Program evaluation; Grants to individuals; Matching/challenge support.

Limitations: Giving primarily in Chapel Hill, Carrboro, and Orange County, NC.

Publications: Application guidelines; Annual report; Grants list.

Application information: Application guidelines and form available on foundation Web site. Application form required.

Initial approach: Letter requesting application

Deadline(s): Jan. 31, Apr. 30, July 31, and Oct. 31

Board meeting date(s): Quarterly (Feb., May., Aug., Nov.)

Final notification: Two weeks following board meeting

Officers and Directors:* Jennifer B. Boger,* Pres.; Sydenham B. Alexander,* V.P.; Stephen B. Miller,* Secy.; Donald A. Williams,* Treas.

Board Members: Doris L. Hicks; Edward A. Norfleet.

Number of staff: None.

EIN: 562241874

7489
Summer Rest Foundation ✧ ☆

P.O. Box 18953
Raleigh, NC   27619

Established in 1998 in NC.

Donors: George C. Turner; Sue M. Turner.

Foundation type: Independent foundation.

Financial data (yr. ended 12/31/05): Assets, $6,239,325 (M); gifts received, $85,775; expenditures, $342,219; qualifying distributions, $323,491; giving activities include $323,491 for 27 grants (high: $85,000; low: $300).

Fields of interest: Education; Human services; Youth, services; Protestant agencies & churches.

Type of support: General/operating support.

Limitations: Giving primarily in NC.

Application information: Contributes to pre-selected organizations, and grants education-specific scholarships to limited individuals in financial need.

Directors: Jay G. Loftin, Jr.; Sue M. Turner.

EIN: 566534008

7490
The Sunshine Lady Foundation, Inc. ▼ ✧

P.O. Box 1074
Morehead City, NC   28557-1074
(252) 240-2788
Contact: Doris B. Buffett, Pres.
Application address: 4900 Raudall PKWY, STE H, Willington, NC 28403; Tel: (910) 397-7742; URL: http://www.sunshineladyfdn.org

Established in 1996 in NC.
Donor: Doris B. Bryant.
Foundation type: Independent foundation.
Financial data (yr. ended 12/31/05): Assets, $2,389,690 (M); gifts received, $8,896,600; expenditures, $7,129,068; qualifying distributions, $6,970,644; giving activities include $6,438,859 for 1,803 grants (high: $348,283; low: $50; average: $1,000–$10,000).
Purpose and activities: The mission of the Sunshine Lady Foundation is to invest in organizations and programs dedicated to providing opportunities for the advancement of education, well being and new life choices for disadvantaged people with special empathy for the working poor and families in crisis. Furthermore, the foundation believes in spreading responsibility in philanthropy through encouraging its growth in our educational system.
Fields of interest: Higher education; Education; Health care; Youth development; Human services; Family services, domestic violence.
Type of support: Program-related investments/loans; Scholarships—to individuals; Matching/challenge support.
Limitations: Giving on a national basis. No grants for endowments or deficit funding.
Application information: Unsolicited requests for grants are not accepted. See foundation Web site for program application information.
Officers and Directors:* Doris B. Buffett,* Pres.; Diane Grimsley,* V.P.; Robin Haymes,* Secy.; Barbara Kriegsman,* Treas.; Mitty Beal.
Number of staff: 3 full-time professional; 2 part-time professional; 2 part-time support.
EIN: 561977987
Selected grants: The following grants were reported in 2004.
$260,000 to Center for Child and Family Health - North Carolina, Durham, NC. 2 grants: $250,000, $10,000 (For Sunbeam Fund).
$212,170 to Mercy College, Dobbs Ferry, NY. 2 grants: $106,170, $106,000
$100,000 to George Washingtons Fredericksburg Foundation, Fredericksburg, VA.
$50,000 to Berks County Women in Crisis, Reading, PA. For domestic violence programs.
$42,000 to Head Start, Stafford County, Stafford, VA. For preschool mental health programs.
$25,000 to Clemson University Foundation, Clemson, SC.
$19,470 to Central Virginia Battlefields Trust, Fredericksburg, VA. For history publication and sites.
$10,000 to 1736 Family Crisis Center, Los Angeles, CA. For operating support.

7491
SunTrust Carolinas Group Foundation, Inc. ◇
(formerly CCB Foundation, Inc.)
1414 Raleigh Rd., Ste. 150
Chapel Hill, NC   27517   (919) 918-2449
Contact: David Kimball
Application address: P.O. Box 931, Durham, NC 27702

Established in 1985 in NC.
Donors: CCB Financial Corp.; Central Carolina Bank and Trust Co.; SunTrust Bank.
Foundation type: Company-sponsored foundation.
Financial data (yr. ended 12/31/04): Assets, $2,942,950 (M); gifts received, $1,516,704; expenditures, $1,653,915; qualifying distributions,

$1,640,586; giving activities include $1,537,032 for 254 grants (high: $128,000; low: $20), and $91,441 for 118 employee matching gifts.
Purpose and activities: The foundation supports organizations involved with arts and culture, education, the environment, health, human services, community development, and religion.
Fields of interest: Arts; Higher education; Education; Environment; Health care; Human services; Community development; Federated giving programs; Religion.
Type of support: General/operating support; Employee matching gifts.
Limitations: Giving primarily in NC. No grants to individuals.
Application information: Application form not required.
  Initial approach: Proposal
  Deadline(s): None
  Board meeting date(s): Monthly
Officers: Eileen Sarro, Pres.; J. Scott Edwards, Secy.
Board Members: William L. Burns, Jr.; Mariela Cabaleiro; Richard L. Furr; David Kimball; John Stallings.
EIN: 581611223

7492
F. W. Symmes Foundation ◇
c/o Wachovia Bank, N.A.
100 N. Main St., 13th Fl.
Winston-Salem, NC   27150
Application address: c/o Wachovia Bank, Char. Svcs., SC5455, P.O. Box 969, Greenville, SC 29602

Established in 1954 in SC.
Donor: F.W. Symmes†.
Foundation type: Independent foundation.
Financial data (yr. ended 3/31/05): Assets, $14,165,739 (M); expenditures, $724,130; qualifying distributions, $634,587; giving activities include $631,000 for grants.
Purpose and activities: Giving primarily for the performing arts, theater, human services, and higher education.
Fields of interest: Performing arts; Performing arts, theater; Arts; Higher education; Human services.
Limitations: Giving primarily in the Greenville, SC, area. No grants to individuals.
Publications: Application guidelines; Informational brochure.
Application information: Application form not required.
  Initial approach: Letter
  Copies of proposal: 10
  Deadline(s): None
  Board meeting date(s): Semiannually
  Final notification: 2 weeks following meeting
Trustees: O. Perry Earle III; Eleanor Welling; F. McKinnon Wilkinson; Wachovia Bank, N.A.
EIN: 576017472

7493
Tannenbaum-Sternberger Foundation, Inc.
(formerly Sigmund Sternberger Foundation, Inc.)
600 Bank of America Bldg.
P.O. Box 3112
Greensboro, NC   27402   (336) 373-1500
Contact: Sally B. Cone, Exec. Dir.
FAX: (336) 272-8258;
E-mail: scone@sternlawnc.com; URL: http://www.TSFoundation.com

Incorporated in 1957 in NC.
Donors: Sigmund Sternberger†; Leah Louise B. Tannenbaum†; Rosa Sternberger Williams†.
Foundation type: Independent foundation.
Financial data (yr. ended 3/31/05): Assets, $16,656,769 (M); expenditures, $777,794; qualifying distributions, $707,694; giving activities include $638,958 for 50 grants (high: $92,250; low: $1,000), and $26,100 for 15 grants to individuals (high: $3,000; low: $1,000).
Purpose and activities: Support for higher education, including scholarship funds, and individual scholarships for children and grandchildren of members of the Revolution Masonic Lodge in Greensboro, NC; grants also for the arts and human service agencies serving Guilford County, NC. Emphasis on special one-time projects, seed money and emergency needs.
Fields of interest: Arts; Higher education; Human services.
Type of support: Matching/challenge support; Building/renovation; General/operating support; Capital campaigns; Emergency funds; Program development; Seed money; Scholarship funds; Scholarships—to individuals.
Limitations: Giving primarily in Guilford County, NC. No grants for endowments.
Publications: Application guidelines.
Application information: Application form required.
  Initial approach: Letter
  Copies of proposal: 1
  Deadline(s): 1 month prior to board meeting
  Board meeting date(s): Usually in Mar., June, Dec., and as required
  Final notification: 3 months
Officers and Directors:* Susan M. Tannenbaum,* Chair.; Jeanne L. Tannenbaum, Vice-Chair.; Nancy B. Tannenbaum, Vice-Chair.; Sigmund I. Tannenbaum,* Chair., Scholarship, and V.P.; John T. Warmath, Jr., Chair., Invest.; Charles M. Reid,* Secy.-Treas.; Sally B. Cone, Exec. Dir.; Sue W. Cole; Edward F. Cone.
Number of staff: 1 part-time professional; 1 part-time support.
EIN: 566045483
Selected grants: The following grants were reported in 2004.
$116,000 to Eastern Music Festival, Greensboro, NC.
$80,000 to Duke University, Durham, NC.
$50,000 to Greensboro Public Library Foundation, Greensboro, NC.
$20,000 to Childrens Home Society of North Carolina, Greensboro, NC.
$10,000 to Marys House, Greensboro, NC.
$8,000 to Greensboro College, Greensboro, NC.
$8,000 to University of North Carolina, Greensboro, NC.
$8,000 to Wake Forest University, Winston-Salem, NC.
$7,500 to Greensboro Opera Company, Greensboro, NC.
$7,500 to Womens Resource Center of Greensboro, Greensboro, NC.

7494
R. B. Terry Charitable Foundation, Inc. ◇
P.O. Box 2003
High Point, NC   27261-2003
Contact: Charles L. Odom, Treas.

Established in 1998 in NC.
Foundation type: Independent foundation.

Financial data (yr. ended 12/31/04): Assets, $50,454,525 (M); gifts received, $2,771,719; expenditures, $2,244,498; qualifying distributions, $2,010,000; giving activities include $2,010,000 for 4 grants (high: $995,000; low: $10,000).
Fields of interest: Higher education, university; Education.
Type of support: General/operating support.
Limitations: Giving primarily in Raleigh, NC and Woodberry Forest, VA. No grants to individuals.
Publications: Annual report.
Application information:
   Initial approach: In writing
Officers and Directors:* Arch K. Schoch IV,* Pres.; Walter Craigie, Secy.; Charles L. Odom,* Treas.; Oscar Fletcher.
EIN: 562066238
Selected grants: The following grants were reported in 2003.
$956,569 to North Carolina State University, College of Veterinary Medicine, Raleigh, NC.
$956,569 to Woodberry Forest School, Woodberry Forest, VA.
$10,000 to United Animal Coalition, Greensboro, NC.
$5,000 to Montpelier Foundation, Montpelier Station, VA.

7495
The Toleo Foundation ◇ ☆
(formerly The Kaplan Family Foundation)
c/o Cathy K. Levinson
445 Dolley Madison Rd., Ste. 208
Greensboro, NC 27410
FAX: (336) 851-0410; E-mail: Toleo@toleo.net

Established in 1982 in NC.
Donors: Leonard J. Kaplan; Tobee W. Kaplan.
Foundation type: Independent foundation.
Financial data (yr. ended 12/31/05): Assets, $4,106,453 (M); gifts received, $100,000; expenditures, $729,784; qualifying distributions, $689,723; giving activities include $487,257 for 81 grants (high: $200,000; low: $100).
Fields of interest: Education; Human services; Jewish federated giving programs; Jewish agencies & temples.
Limitations: Applications not accepted. Giving primarily in NC. No grants to individuals.
Application information: Contributes only to pre-selected organizations.
Officers: Leonard J. Kaplan, Pres. and Treas.; Tobee W. Kaplan, V.P. and Secy.
Number of staff: 1 full-time professional; 1 part-time support.
EIN: 581496345
Selected grants: The following grants were reported in 2005.
$204,300 to Bnai Shalom Day School, Greensboro, NC. 2 grants: $4,300, $200,000
$8,500 to Eastern Music Festival, Greensboro, NC.
$5,000 to Greensboro Childrens Museum, Greensboro, NC.
$5,000 to United Arts Council, Saint Paul, MN.
$1,500 to Roanoke College, Salem, VA.
$1,000 to Bullis School, Potomac, MD.
$1,000 to Greensboro Opera Company, Greensboro, NC.
$1,000 to High Point University, High Point, NC.
$1,000 to North Carolina Museum of Art, Raleigh, NC.

7496
Triangle Community Foundation ▼
4813 Emperor Blvd., Ste. 130
P.O. Box 12834
Research Triangle Park, NC 27709
(919) 474-8370
Contact: Krystin Jorgenson, Cont.
FAX: (919) 941-9208; E-mail: info@trianglecf.org
Additional E-mails: krystin@trianglecf.org and cathy@trianglecf.org; URL: http://www.trianglecf.org

Incorporated in 1983 in NC.
Foundation type: Community foundation.
Financial data (yr. ended 6/30/05): Assets, $100,752,459 (M); gifts received, $6,862,970; expenditures, $10,417,732; giving activities include $9,115,831 for grants.
Purpose and activities: The mission of the foundation is to expand private philanthropy in the communities of Chatham, Durham, Orange, and Wake counties.
Fields of interest: Visual arts; Museums; Performing arts; Performing arts, dance; Performing arts, theater; Performing arts, music; Humanities; Historic preservation/historical societies; Arts; Education, early childhood education; Child development, education; Elementary school/education; Vocational education; Higher education; Adult/continuing education; Adult education—literacy, basic skills & GED; Libraries/library science; Education, reading; Education; Environment, natural resources; Environment, energy; Environment; Animal welfare; Animals/wildlife, preservation/protection; Reproductive health, family planning; Medical care, rehabilitation; Health care; Substance abuse, services; Mental health/crisis services; Health organizations, association; AIDS; Alcoholism; Crime/violence prevention, youth; Legal services; Crime/law enforcement; Food services; Housing/shelter, development; Recreation; Youth development, services; Children/youth, services; Child development, services; Family services; Residential/custodial care, hospices; Aging, centers/services; Women, centers/services; Minorities/immigrants, centers/services; Homeless, human services; Human services; International peace/security; Civil rights, race/intergroup relations; Urban/community development; Rural development; Community development; Voluntarism promotion; Government/public administration; Leadership development; Public affairs; Aging; Disabilities, people with; Minorities; Native Americans/American Indians; Women; LGBTQ; Economically disadvantaged; Homeless.
Type of support: Capital campaigns; Continuing support; Annual campaigns; Emergency funds; Program development; Seed money; Scholarship funds; Technical assistance; Program-related investments/loans; Employee matching gifts; Employee-related scholarships; Scholarships—to individuals; In-kind gifts.
Limitations: Giving limited to Chatham, Durham, Orange, and Wake counties, NC. No grants for operating budgets.
Publications: Annual report; Newsletter.
Application information: The foundation does not accept unsolicited proposals; information on completing an Impact Profile for grant funding is available on the foundation's Web site, or by telephone or e-mail. Visit Web site for scholarship

application guidelines, deadlines, and forms. Application form required.
   Initial approach: Contact foundation
   Deadline(s): None
   Board meeting date(s): Feb., May, Aug., and Nov.
   Final notification: Ongoing
Officers and Directors:* Peter J. Meehan,* Chair.; Jean Gordon Carter,* Vice-Chair. and Chair.-Elect; Andrea Bazan-Manson, Pres.; Mary B. Mountcastle, Secy.; Ronald A. Strom,* Treas. and Chair., Finance Comm.; Carol Bilbro, Chair., Foundation Leadership Council; Elizabeth B. Craven,* Chair., Philanthropic Svcs. Comm.; Krystin Jorgenson, Cont.; Carrie Bolton; David R. Carr; Bill Cavanaugh; Kip Frey; Alice K. Horton; Fred D. Hutchinson; James H. Johnson; James A. Joseph; Frank Phoenix; Joel M. Sheer; Dr. Phail Wynn, Jr.
Number of staff: 12 full-time professional.
EIN: 561380796
Selected grants: The following grants were reported in 2005.
$471,000 to Massachusetts General Hospital, Boston, MA.
$425,000 to United States Naval Academy Foundation, Annapolis, MD.
$100,000 to Eno River Unitarian Universalist Fellowship, Durham, NC.
$100,000 to North Carolina Museum of Art Foundation, Raleigh, NC.
$47,784 to Wake, County of, Human Services Department, Raleigh, NC.
$5,400 to Temple Beth Or, Raleigh, NC.
$5,000 to National Foundation for Transplants, Memphis, TN.
$3,450 to Playmakers Repertory Company, Chapel Hill, NC.
$2,500 to Christian Life Home, Raleigh, NC.
$2,500 to University of North Carolina, Chapel Hill, NC. For Arts and Sciences Foundation.

7497
Tzedakah Foundation ◇ ☆
c/o Wachovia Bank, N.A.
401 S. Tryon St., 4th Fl.
Charlotte, NC 28288-5709

Established in 2002 in PA.
Donors: Erlbaum Foundation; Wellington Management.
Foundation type: Independent foundation.
Financial data (yr. ended 12/31/04): Assets, $2,605,988 (M); gifts received, $1,277,740; expenditures, $427,500; qualifying distributions, $385,755; giving activities include $385,755 for 46 grants (high: $60,000; low: $200).
Purpose and activities: Giving primarily for Jewish organizations.
Fields of interest: Museums; Education; Hospitals (general); Health organizations, association; Federated giving programs; Jewish federated giving programs; Jewish agencies & temples.
Limitations: Applications not accepted. No grants to individuals.
Application information: Contributes only to pre-selected organizations.
Trustees: Steven Erlbaum; Amy Kurtzman; Wachovia Bank, N.A.
EIN: 233090755

7498
V.F. Foundation ✧
105 Corporate Center Blvd.
Greensboro, NC 27408

Established in 2002 in NC.
Donor: V.F. Corp.
Foundation type: Company-sponsored foundation.
Financial data (yr. ended 12/31/05): Assets, $2,362,328 (L); expenditures, $1,464,931; qualifying distributions, $1,458,786; giving activities include $1,458,786 for 138 grants (high: $260,000; low: $50).
Purpose and activities: The foundation supports organizations involved with arts and culture, education, and human services.
Fields of interest: Arts; Higher education; Business school/education; Education; Human services.
Type of support: General/operating support; Capital campaigns.
Limitations: Applications not accepted. Giving primarily in WA. No grants to individuals.
Application information: Contributes only to pre-selected organizations.
Officers and Directors:* Mackey J. McDonald,* Pres.; Candace Cummings,* Secy.; Frank C. Pickard, Treas.; Susan L. Williams.
EIN: 562322084

7499
Philip L. Van Every Foundation ✧
c/o Bank of America, N.A.
101 S. Tryon St, NC1-002-11-18
Charlotte, NC 28255-0001

Established in 1961 in NC.
Donor: Philip Van Every.
Foundation type: Independent foundation.
Financial data (yr. ended 12/31/05): Assets, $29,483,537 (M); expenditures, $1,135,918; qualifying distributions, $1,098,315; giving activities include $1,077,500 for grants.
Purpose and activities: Giving for arts and culture, social services, health care and medical research, higher education, and federated giving programs.
Fields of interest: Arts; Higher education; Education; Health care; Health organizations, association; Medical research, institute; Human services; Federated giving programs.
Limitations: Applications not accepted. Giving primarily in NC and SC. No grants to individuals.
Application information: Contributes only to pre-selected organizations.
Officer: Zean Jamison, Jr., Secy.-Treas.
Directors: J.W. Disher; James S. Howell; Willie Royal; Albert F. Sloan; Paul A. Stroup.
Trustee: Bank of America, N.A.
Number of staff: 1
EIN: 566039337

7500
The Edward W. and Stella C. Van Houten Memorial Fund ✧
c/o Wachovia Bank, N.A.
100 N. Main St., 13th Fl.
Winston-Salem, NC 27150
Contact: Susan Head
E-mail: grantinquiriesnj@wachovia.com; Application address: 190 River Rd., Summit, NJ 07901

Established in 1979 in NJ.

Donor: Stella C. Van Houten†.
Foundation type: Independent foundation.
Financial data (yr. ended 11/30/05): Assets, $20,922,405 (M); expenditures, $1,036,984; qualifying distributions, $954,634; giving activities include $952,634 for 42 grants.
Purpose and activities: Interests include: 1) human service activities in Bergen and Passaic counties in NJ; specific areas of interest include orphaned children, the disabled, and the elderly; 2) hospitals and health organizations in Bergen and Passaic counties, NJ, to improve or expand healthcare services; 3) higher education, primarily medical and nursing training; and 4) education and care of children.
Fields of interest: Education, early childhood education; Child development, education; Medical school/education; Education; Hospitals (general); Nursing care; Health care; Health organizations, association; Biomedicine; Medical research, institute; Human services; Children/youth, services; Child development, services; Aging, centers/services; Aging.
Type of support: Capital campaigns; Building/renovation; Equipment; Program development; Seed money; Scholarship funds.
Limitations: Giving primarily in Bergen and Passaic counties, NJ. No grants to individuals, or for general operating support or endowments; no loans.
Publications: Application guidelines.
Application information: Application form not required.
 Initial approach: Proposal
 Copies of proposal: 1
 Deadline(s): Apr. 15
 Board meeting date(s): Mar., June, Sept., and Dec.
 Final notification: 1 month after board meets
Trustee: Wachovia Bank, N.A.
EIN: 226311438

7501
R. T. Vanderbilt Trust ✧
c/o Wachovia Bank, N.A.
100 North Main St.
Winston-Salem, NC 27150-6732

Established in 1951 in CT.
Foundation type: Independent foundation.
Financial data (yr. ended 12/31/05): Assets, $8,500,007 (M); expenditures, $514,790; qualifying distributions, $459,449; giving activities include $425,544 for 65 grants (high: $100,000; low: $200).
Purpose and activities: Emphasis on education and conservation; support also for hospitals, cultural programs, and historic preservation.
Fields of interest: Historic preservation/historical societies; Arts; Education; Environment, natural resources; Hospitals (general); Reproductive health, family planning.
Type of support: General/operating support; Building/renovation; Endowments; Program development.
Limitations: Applications not accepted. Giving primarily in CT and NY. No grants to individuals.
Application information: Contributes only to pre-selected organizations.
 Board meeting date(s): Apr., June, Sept., and Dec.
Officer and Trustees:* Hugh B. Vanderbilt, Jr.,* Chair.; P. Vanderbilt; R.T. Vanderbilt; Wachovia Bank, N.A.

Number of staff: 2 part-time support.
EIN: 066040981
Selected grants: The following grants were reported in 2004.
$95,485 to Connecticut Audubon Society, Fairfield, CT. 2 grants: $45,485, $50,000
$30,000 to Historical Society of the Town of Greenwich, Cos Cob, CT. 2 grants: $12,000, $18,000
$20,000 to Greenwich Hospital, Greenwich, CT.
$10,000 to Historic Deerfield, Deerfield, MA.
$10,000 to Mayo Foundation, Rochester, MN.
$10,000 to Mount Sinai Hospital, New York, NY.
$5,000 to Berkshire School, Sheffield, MA.
$5,000 to Choate Rosemary Hall, Wallingford, CT.

7502
The Wachovia Foundation, Inc. ▼ ✧
100 N. Main St., NC 6755
Winston-Salem, NC 27150-6755
(336) 732-6138
E-mail: communityaffairs@wachovia.com; Additional address: 301 S. College St., NC 0143, Charlotte, NC 28288-0143. tel.: (704) 715-8579; E-mail for Teachers and Teaching Initiative: tti@wachovia.com; URL: http://www.wachovia.com/inside/page/0,,139_414_430,00.html

Incorporated in 1982 in NC.
Donors: Wachovia Corp.; Wachovia Bank, N.A.
Foundation type: Company-sponsored foundation.
Financial data (yr. ended 12/31/05): Assets, $70,227,017 (M); gifts received, $44,900,000; expenditures, $59,143,473; qualifying distributions, $58,994,452; giving activities include $48,130,787 for 2,707 grants (high: $700,000; low: $100), and $9,232,841 for employee matching gifts.
Purpose and activities: The foundation supports organizations involved with arts and culture, education, health, human services, and community development.
Fields of interest: Arts, equal rights; Arts; Education, equal rights; Elementary/secondary education; Education, early childhood education; Education; Health care, equal rights; Public health; Health care; Employment; Housing/shelter; Human services, financial counseling; Human services; Economic development; Community development; Minorities; Economically disadvantaged.
Type of support: General/operating support; Employee volunteer services; Employee matching gifts.
Limitations: Giving primarily in CT, DE, Washington, DC, FL, GA, MD, NC, NJ, NY, PA, SC, and VA; giving also to national organizations active in areas of company operations. No support for international organizations, political organizations, veterans', fraternal, or alumni organizations, religious organizations not of direct benefit to the entire community, private foundations, individual pre-college, private, parochial, charter, or home schools, or individual public schools (except to benefit system-wide programs and initiatives or as a part of a Wachovia-sponsored partnership program). No grants to individuals, or for travel or conferences, books, research papers, or articles in professional journals, general operating support for United Way-supported organizations or organizations supported by united arts drives in which Wachovia participates, or sponsorships, events, or projects for which Wachovia and/or its employees receive tangible benefits or privileges.

Publications: Application guidelines; Annual report; Corporate giving report.
Application information:
Initial approach: Complete online application form
Deadline(s): None
Board meeting date(s): Semi-annually
Officer and Directors:* G. Kennedy Thompson,* Chair.; David M. Carroll; Stephen E. Cummings; Gerald A. Enos, Jr.; Benjamin P. Jenkins III; Stanhope A. Kelly; Shannon W. McFayden; Michael P. Rizer; Thomas J. Wurtz.
Trustee: Wachovia Bank, N.A.
EIN: 581485946
Selected grants: The following grants were reported in 2004.
$400,000 to University of North Carolina, Chapel Hill, NC.
$400,000 to YMCA of Greater Charlotte, Charlotte, NC.
$380,000 to Arts and Science Council of Charlotte-Mecklenburg, Charlotte, NC.
$300,000 to North Carolina Dance Theater, Charlotte, NC.
$300,000 to North Carolina State University Foundation, Raleigh, NC.
$300,000 to Philadelphia Museum of Art, Philadelphia, PA.
$240,000 to Art Museum of Western Virginia, Roanoke, VA.
$200,000 to Davidson College, Davidson, NC.
$200,000 to North Carolina Partnership for Children, Raleigh, NC.
$200,000 to University of North Carolina at Charlotte Foundation, Charlotte, NC.

7503
Warner Foundation ◆ ☆
(formerly The D. Michael Warner Foundation, Inc.)
c/o Tony Pipa
501 Washington St., Ste. D
Durham, NC   27701   (919) 530-8842
FAX: (919) 530-8852;
E-mail: info@thewarnerfoundation.org; URL: http://www.thewarnerfoundation.org

Established in 1996 in NC.
Donor: D. Michael Warner.
Foundation type: Independent foundation.
Financial data (yr. ended 12/31/05): Assets, $8,584,523 (M); expenditures, $908,822; qualifying distributions, $813,936; giving activities include $725,000 for 3 grants (high: $500,000; low: $100,000).
Purpose and activities: Giving to NC organizations working to foster long-term improvements in economic opportunities for low-wealth African-Americans.
Fields of interest: Education; Minorities; Economically disadvantaged.
Type of support: General/operating support; Continuing support; Income development; Management development/capacity building; Program development; Seed money; Technical assistance; Matching/challenge support.
Limitations: Applications not accepted. Giving limited to NC. No grants to individuals.
Application information: Contributes only to pre-selected organizations.
Officers and Directors:* D. Michael Warner,* Pres.; Elizabeth Craven,* V.P.; Mimi Gredy; Daryl Lester; Carla Smith.
Number of staff: 5 full-time professional.
EIN: 561969171

7504
Weaver Foundation, Inc.
324 W. Wendover Ave., Ste. 300
Greensboro, NC   27408   (336) 378-7910
Contact: Richard L. Moore, Pres.
FAX: (336) 275-9602;
E-mail: RLM@weaverfoundation.com; Application address: P.O. Box 26040, Greensboro, NC 27420-6040; URL: http://www.weaverfoundation.com

Incorporated in 1967 in NC.
Donors: W.H. Weaver‡; E.H. Weaver; H. Michael Weaver.
Foundation type: Independent foundation.
Financial data (yr. ended 12/31/05): Assets, $26,895,346 (M); gifts received, $172,000; expenditures, $2,023,107; qualifying distributions, $1,815,564; giving activities include $1,527,385 for 78 grants (high: $250,000; low: $200), and $39,136 for 62 employee matching gifts.
Purpose and activities: The purpose of the foundation is to help the greater Greensboro, NC, community, enhance and improve the quality of life and the economic environment for its citizens while developing a sense of philanthropy, civic education, and commitment in current and future generations of the founders' families. Focus areas include education, children and youth, environment, reducing poverty, advancement of civil rights, and economic development.
Fields of interest: Arts; Education, early childhood education; Higher education; Education; Environment, natural resources; Environment; Housing/shelter, development; Human services; Children/youth, services; Homeless, human services; Community development; Leadership development; Economically disadvantaged.
Type of support: General/operating support; Continuing support; Management development/capacity building; Annual campaigns; Capital campaigns; Building/renovation; Equipment; Land acquisition; Endowments; Debt reduction; Emergency funds; Program development; Professorships; Seed money; Scholarship funds; Technical assistance; Consulting services; Program evaluation; Employee matching gifts; Matching/challenge support.
Limitations: Applications not accepted. Giving limited to the greater Greensboro, NC, area. No support for fraternal or religious organizations. No grants to individuals, or for conferences, travel or group trips, or video productions.
Publications: Annual report; Grants list.
Application information: Unsolicited requests for funds not accepted.
Board meeting date(s): Quarterly
Officers and Trustees:* Ashley W. Hodges,* Chair.; Richard L. Moore, Pres.; Katherine Weaver,* Secy.; Mark Wilson, Treas.; Greg Shutter.
Number of staff: 1 full-time professional; 1 part-time professional.
EIN: 566093527
Selected grants: The following grants were reported in 2003.
$300,000 to Community Foundation of Greater Greensboro, Greensboro, NC. 2 grants: $50,000, $250,000 (For Action Greensboro program support).
$115,865 to University of North Carolina, School of Education, Chapel Hill, NC. For Bridges to Success Program.
$100,000 to YMCA of Greensboro, Greensboro, NC. For Weaver Outdoor Center campaign.

$50,000 to Guilford Technical Community College Foundation, Jamestown, NC. For Adult High School Workforce Preparedness Project.
$50,000 to United Way of Greater Greensboro, Greensboro, NC.
$46,150 to Childrens Home Society of North Carolina, Greensboro, NC. For Adoption Alliance Program.
$45,805 to Family Service of the Piedmont, High Point, NC. For Children Advocacy Center program.
$35,000 to Welfare Reform Liaison Project, Greensboro, NC. For warehouse rental and operation.
$30,000 to Greensboro College, Greensboro, NC. For capital campaign.

7505
The Richard and Carol Weingarten Foundation ◆ ☆
P.O. Box 370
Tryon, NC   28782

Established in 1997 in DE.
Donors: Richard Weingarten; Carol Weingarten.
Foundation type: Independent foundation.
Financial data (yr. ended 12/31/05): Assets, $1,794 (M); expenditures, $328,817; qualifying distributions, $328,300; giving activities include $328,300 for grants.
Limitations: Applications not accepted. Giving primarily in CA, IL, and NY. No grants to individuals.
Application information: Contributes only to pre-selected organizations.
Officers: Richard Weingarten, Chair.; Carol Weingarten, Pres. and Secy.
EIN: 582267858

7506
The Wilson Family Foundation ◆
(formerly Janet H. and T. Henry Wilson, Jr. Foundation)
c/o Janet H. Wilson
411 Tremont Cir.
Lenoir, NC   28645

Established in 1997 in NC.
Donors: Janet Wilson; Henry Wilson.
Foundation type: Independent foundation.
Financial data (yr. ended 12/31/05): Assets, $33,004,518 (M); expenditures, $1,381,831; qualifying distributions, $1,259,100; giving activities include $1,259,100 for 68 grants (high: $346,000; low: $100).
Fields of interest: Education; Human services; Christian agencies & churches.
Limitations: Applications not accepted. Giving primarily in NC. No grants to individuals.
Application information: Contributes only to pre-selected organizations.
Officers: Janet Wilson, Pres; Amy Wilson Scott, V.P.
Trustees: David Wilson; Henry Wilson III.
EIN: 562042058
Selected grants: The following grants were reported in 2005.
$115,000 to American Red Cross.
$100,000 to North Carolina Wildlife Habitat Foundation, Greensboro, NC.
$50,000 to Aldersgate Homes, Atlanta, GA.
$50,000 to Carter Center, Atlanta, GA.
$40,000 to Simonian Little League, Anchorage, AK.

$30,500 to Caldwell Memorial Hospital Foundation, Lenoir, NC.

$25,000 to Army Emergency Relief, Alexandria, VA.

$25,000 to North Carolina Stroke Association, Winston-Salem, NC.

$20,000 to Shelter Home of Caldwell County, Lenoir, NC.

$10,000 to Global Health Action, Atlanta, GA.

7507
The Winston Family Foundation, Inc. ✧
2626 Glenwood Ave., Ste. 200
Raleigh, NC 27608 (919) 510-6018
Contact: Thomas M. Herbert

Established in 1997 in NC.
Donors: Charles M. Winston; Florence B. Winston.
Foundation type: Independent foundation.
Financial data (yr. ended 12/31/05): Assets, $332,081 (M); gifts received, $294,986; expenditures, $580,333; qualifying distributions, $575,074; giving activities include $575,074 for grants.
Purpose and activities: Giving for the arts, education, and to an Episcopal church and high school.
Fields of interest: Museums; Historic preservation/historical societies; Arts; Secondary school/education; Higher education; Education; Health care; Human services; Federated giving programs; Protestant agencies & churches.
Application information:
Initial approach: Letter or telephone
Deadline(s): Usually Nov. 15
Officers: Charles M. Winston, Co-Chair. and V.P.; Florence B. Winston, Co-Chair. and V.P.; Charles M. Winston, Jr., V.P.; Marion T. Winston, Secy.; Robert W. Winston III, Treas.
EIN: 562058027

7508
The Winston-Salem Foundation ▼
860 W. 5th St.
Winston-Salem, NC 27101-2506
Contact: Scott F. Wierman, Pres.
FAX: (336) 727-0581;
E-mail: info@wsfoundation.org; Toll free tel.: (866) 227-1209; Additional E-mail: swierman@wsfoundation.org; URL: http://www.wsfoundation.org

Established in 1919 in NC by declaration of trust.
Foundation type: Community foundation.
Financial data (yr. ended 12/31/05): Assets, $241,479,110 (M); gifts received, $59,589,458; expenditures, $27,458,532; giving activities include $21,480,659 for grants.
Purpose and activities: The foundation invests in the community by making philanthropy and its benefits available to all. Student aid primarily to bona fide residents of Forsyth County, NC; support also for nonprofit organizations of all types, especially educational, social service and health programs, the arts, and civic affairs.
Fields of interest: Arts; Education; Health organizations, association; Recreation; Youth, services; Human services; Public affairs, government agencies; Government/public administration.
Type of support: Capital campaigns; Building/renovation; Endowments; Emergency funds; Program development; Seed money; Scholarship funds; Technical assistance; Consulting services; Program-related investments/loans; Employee matching gifts; Grants to individuals; Scholarships—to individuals; Matching/challenge support; Student loans—to individuals.
Limitations: Giving primarily in the greater Forsyth County, NC, area. No support for religious organizations for religious purposes. No grants to individuals (except for scholarships), or for long-term operating support, annual campaigns, land acquisition, publications, equipment or conferences.
Publications: Application guidelines; Annual report (including application guidelines); Grants list; Newsletter; Occasional report.
Application information: Visit foundation Web site for grant proposal cover sheet and application guidelines. Application form required for student aid or student loans only and requires a $20 application fee. Application form required.
Initial approach: Telephone
Copies of proposal: 1
Deadline(s): July 17 and Nov. 15
Board meeting date(s): Mar., June, and Oct.
Final notification: Within 4 months
Officers and Foundation Committee:* James T. Lambie,* Chair.; Dr. Harold L. Martin,* Vice-Chair.; Scott F. Wierman, Pres.; Annette Lynch, V.P., Donor Svcs.; Donna Rader, V.P., Grants and Progs.; Todd Slate, V.P., Finance and Admin.; Simpson "Skip" O. Brown, Jr.; John W. Burress III; Rence Callahan; Peggy Carter; Gregory A. Cox; Lynn Brenner Eisenberg; Robert E. Greene; Drew Hancock; Kay Lord; Paul Wiles; Ralph Hanes Womble.
Trustees: Bank of America, N.A.; BB&T; First Citizens Bank; SunTrust Bank; Wachovia Bank, N.A.
Number of staff: 13 full-time professional; 8 full-time support.
EIN: 566037615
Selected grants: The following grants were reported in 2005.

$200,000 to Childrens Center for the Physically Handicapped, Winston-Salem, NC. Toward Children's Center Fund endowment.

$99,443 to Senior Services, Winston-Salem, NC. To provide nutritious food to homebound older adults.

$84,615 to Winston-Salem/Forsyth County School System, Winston-Salem, NC. 2 grants: $39,615 (To acquire inventory of assistive technology devices for new Assistive Technology Center), $45,000 (For development of Career Start curriculum for Middle Schools).

$75,000 to Bethesda Center for the Homeless, Winston-Salem, NC. For renovation and expansion through capital campaign.

$57,500 to Neighbors for Better Neighborhoods, Winston-Salem, NC. For general operating support.

$50,000 to Winston-Salem Industries for the Blind, Winston-Salem, NC. Toward multipurpose meeting area and transportation for the blind and visually impaired.

$40,000 to Catholic Social Services, Winston-Salem, NC. Toward salary and benefits of full-time Spanish-speaking counselor.

$40,000 to Liberty Community Development Corporation, Winston-Salem, NC. For operational expenses, capacity building and program development.

$35,000 to Sawtooth Center for Visual Art, Winston-Salem, NC. For position of Development Director.

7509
Margaret C. Woodson Foundation, Inc. ✧
225 N. Main St.
Salisbury, NC 28144-0829 (704) 633-5000
Contact: Beulah H. Hillard, Dir.
Application address: P.O. Box 829, Salisbury, NC 28145-0829

Incorporated in 1954 in NC.
Donor: Margaret C. Woodson†.
Foundation type: Independent foundation.
Financial data (yr. ended 12/31/05): Assets, $897,231 (M); gifts received, $928,093; expenditures, $847,387; qualifying distributions, $795,600; giving activities include $795,600 for grants.
Purpose and activities: Giving primarily for education and human services, with designated funds for Davidson College, Mary Baldwin College and Barium Springs Childrens Home.
Fields of interest: Arts, association; Museums; Performing arts; Historic preservation/historical societies; Arts; Secondary school/education; Higher education; Theological school/education; Libraries (public); Animal welfare; Hospitals (general); Food distribution, meals on wheels; Recreation, parks/playgrounds; Youth development, services; Human services; YM/YWCAs & YM/YWHAs; Children/youth, services; Family services; Family services, counseling; Residential/custodial care.
Type of support: General/operating support.
Limitations: Giving primarily in Davie and Rowan counties, NC. No grants for research.
Application information: Application form not required.
Initial approach: Letter with 2 years' accounting statements
Deadline(s): Mar. 1
Officers and Directors:* Mary H. Woodson,* Pres.; Mary Anne Woodson,* V.P.; Paul B. Woodson, Jr.,* Secy.; Donald D. Sayers,* Treas.; Paul Leake Bernhardt; John B.E. Cunningham; Beulah H. Hillard; William G. Johnson; Robert P. Shay, Jr.
EIN: 566064938

7510
George & Harriet Woodward Trust
c/o Wachovia Bank, N.A.
100 N. Main St., 13th Fl.
Winston-Salem, NC 27150

Foundation type: Independent foundation.
Financial data (yr. ended 11/30/05): Assets, $29,292,569 (M); expenditures, $1,854,607; qualifying distributions, $1,540,400; giving activities include $1,540,000 for 7 grants (high: $220,000; low: $220,000).
Purpose and activities: Giving primarily for the arts and culture.
Fields of interest: Arts education; Museums (art); Performing arts, orchestra (symphony); Higher education; Hospitals (general); Physical/earth sciences; Religion.
Type of support: General/operating support.
Limitations: Applications not accepted. No grants to individuals.
Application information: Contributes only to pre-selected organizations.
Trustees: James Stevens; Richard Stevens; Wachovia Bank, N.A.
EIN: 237750367

7511

The Yeargan Foundation Charitable Trust ✧ ☆

7777 White Oak Rd.
Garner, NC 27529-8808

Established in 1998.

Foundation type: Independent foundation.

Financial data (yr. ended 12/31/05): Assets, $5,624,934 (M); gifts received, $342,358; expenditures, $362,588; qualifying distributions, $353,200; giving activities include $353,200 for 3 grants (high: $200,000; low: $20,000).

Purpose and activities: Giving primarily for higher education and religion.

Fields of interest: Higher education; Higher education, university; Christian agencies & churches; Religion.

Limitations: Applications not accepted. Giving primarily in NC. No grants to individuals.

Application information: Contributes only to pre-selected organizations.

Trustees: Rowann Yeargan; Sherman Yeargan.

EIN: 581846281

Selected grants: The following grants were reported in 2004.

$135,200 to University of North Carolina, Chapel Hill, NC. 2 grants: $5,000, $130,200

$75,000 to Duke University, Durham, NC. 2 grants: $25,000 (For endowment), $50,000 (For endowment).

7512

J. Smith & Helen W. Young Family Foundation ✧

P.O. Box 867
Lexington, NC 27292

Established in 1996 in NC.

Donor: J. Smith & Helen W. Young Irrevocable Living Unitrust.

Foundation type: Independent foundation.

Financial data (yr. ended 12/31/05): Assets, $120,468 (M); gifts received, $400,000; expenditures, $431,326; qualifying distributions, $431,302; giving activities include $430,000 for 5 grants (high: $200,000; low: $10,000).

Fields of interest: Higher education; Hospitals (general).

Limitations: Applications not accepted. Giving primarily in Lexington, NC. No grants to individuals.

Application information: Contributes only to pre-selected organizations.

Officers: J. Smith Young, Jr., Pres.; Charles Jeffery Young, V.P.; Sydney Y. Beck, Secy.

EIN: 561977282

7513

The Zelnak Private Foundation ✧ ☆

c/o U.S. Trust
P.O. Box 26262
Greensboro, NC 27420

Contact: Stephen P. Zelnak, Jr., Tr.

Established in 1998 in NC.

Donor: Stephen P. Zelnak, Jr.

Foundation type: Independent foundation.

Financial data (yr. ended 12/31/05): Assets, $3,133,737 (M); gifts received, $1,727,132; expenditures, $389,267; qualifying distributions, $359,354; giving activities include $355,500 for 20 grants (high: $100,000; low: $5,000).

Purpose and activities: Giving primarily for education and religious organizations.

Fields of interest: Education, reform; Protestant agencies & churches; Religion.

Type of support: General/operating support.

Limitations: Applications not accepted. Giving primarily in NC. No grants to individuals.

Application information: Contributes only to pre-selected organizations.

Trustees: Judy D. Zelnak; Stephen P. Zelnak, Jr.

EIN: 562115096

Selected grants: The following grants were reported in 2004.

$60,000 to Alexander-Tharpe Fund, Atlanta, GA.

$25,000 to White Memorial Presbyterian Church, Raleigh, NC.

$20,000 to Angel Ministries, Raleigh, NC.

$20,000 to Campus Crusade for Christ International, Orlando, FL.

$15,000 to Capital Ministries, Santa Clarita, CA.

$7,500 to Liberty University, Lynchburg, VA.

$5,000 to Fellowship of Christian Athletes, Kansas City, MO.

$5,000 to Georgia Tech Foundation, Atlanta, GA.

$1,000 to North Carolina State University, Raleigh, NC.

NORTH DAKOTA

7514

Fargo-Moorhead Area Foundation

502 1st Ave. N., Ste. 202
Fargo, ND 58102-4804   (701) 234-0756
Contact: Karla Aaland, Exec. Dir.
FAX: (701) 234-9724;
E-mail: nyla@areafoundation.org; Additional E-mail: Karla@areafoundation.org; Grant application E-mail: Wendy@areafoundation.org; URL: http://www.areafoundation.org

Established in 1960 in ND.
Foundation type: Community foundation.
Financial data (yr. ended 12/31/05): Assets, $41,619,487 (M); gifts received, $1,171,002; expenditures, $2,048,960; giving activities include $1,367,722 for 343+ grants, $85,486 for 69 grants to individuals (high: $4,000; low: $100), and $5,829 for foundation-administered programs.
Purpose and activities: The foundation seeks to enrich the quality of life of the people in the Clay County, MN, and Cass County, ND, area by encouraging philanthropy and developing permanent endowment, assessing and responding to emerging and changing community needs, providing flexibility for donors with varied interests and levels of giving capabilities, and serving as a resource and catalyst for other organizations.
Fields of interest: Arts; Education; Health organizations, association; Children/youth, services; Human services; Community development; Government/public administration; Youth.
Type of support: Capital campaigns; Building/renovation; Equipment; Emergency funds; Program development; Conferences/seminars; Publication; Seed money; Scholarship funds; Technical assistance; In-kind gifts; Matching/challenge support.
Limitations: Giving limited to Clay County, MN, and Cass County, ND. No support for religious purposes. No grants to individuals, or for operating expenses (except for limited experimental or start-up periods), annual appeals or membership drives, or organizations which have outstanding reports from previous Fargo-Moorhead Foundation grants.
Publications: Application guidelines; Annual report; Informational brochure; Newsletter; Program policy statement.
Application information: Visit foundation Web site for application form and guidelines. Application form required.
Initial approach: Submit application form and attachments
Copies of proposal: 1
Deadline(s): Feb. 16
Board meeting date(s): Every other month
Final notification: July 15
Officers and Governors:* Tracy Hartman,* Chair.; Tracy Moorhead,* Vice-Chair.; James Stenerson,* Secy.; Karla Aaland, Exec. Dir.; Susan Andrews; Kelley P. Boyum; Matt Butler; Roland Dille; William Guy III; Neil Jordheim; Sandy Korbel; Mary Locken; Phyllis May-Machunda; Beth Renner; Paul T. Sather; Thomas Schaffer; John Stibbe; Joyce Wallman.
Trustee Banks: Alerus Financial; Bank of the West; Bremer Bank, N.A.; Heartland Trust Co.; State Bank and Trust; U.S. Bank, N.A.; Wells Fargo Bank, N.A.

Number of staff: 3 full-time professional; 1 part-time professional; 1 full-time support.
EIN: 456010377

7515

L. W. Huncke Foundation ◈

P.O. Box 5008
Bismarck, ND   58502-5008

Established in 1980 in KS.
Donor: L.W. Huncke.
Foundation type: Independent foundation.
Financial data (yr. ended 9/30/04): Assets, $9,407,471 (M); gifts received, $250,000; expenditures, $587,155; qualifying distributions, $338,391; giving activities include $340,000 for 4 grants (high: $300,000; low: $5,000).
Fields of interest: Higher education; Human services.
Limitations: Applications not accepted. Giving primarily in IA and ND. No grants to individuals.
Application information: Contributes only to pre-selected organizations.
Trustee: Otto W. Dohn.
EIN: 480912892
Selected grants: The following grants were reported in 2004.
$300,000 to Iowa State University, Ames, IA. For endowment fund.
$25,000 to Gods Child Project, Bismarck, ND. For general support.
$10,000 to Cathedral of the Holy Spirit School, Bismarck, ND. For general support.

7516

Tom and Frances Leach Foundation, Inc.

(also known as Leach Foundation)
1720 Burnt Boat Dr.
P.O. Box 1136
Bismarck, ND   58502-1136   (701) 255-0479
Contact: Delanis M. Eckroth, Grants Coord. and Admin. Secy.
URL: http://www.leachfoundation.org

Established in 1955 in ND.
Donors: Thomas W. Leach†; Frances V. Leach†.
Foundation type: Independent foundation.
Financial data (yr. ended 12/31/05): Assets, $11,949,286 (M); expenditures, $942,597; qualifying distributions, $715,546; giving activities include $650,000 for 61 grants (high: $95,000; low: $1,000).
Purpose and activities: Primary areas of interest include the arts, higher and other education, social services, youth, and health-related programs.
Fields of interest: Visual arts; Performing arts; Arts; Education, early childhood education; Child development, education; Higher education; Public health school/education; Medicine/medical care, public education; Hospitals (general); Health care; Human services; Children/youth, services; Child development, services; Disabilities, people with.
Type of support: Curriculum development; General/operating support; Continuing support; Capital campaigns; Building/renovation; Equipment; Emergency funds; Program development; Scholarship funds; Technical assistance; Matching/challenge support.
Limitations: Giving primarily in ND, particularly in Bismarck and Mandan, and the upper Midwest. No grants for travel, or for fellowships or conferences;

generally, limited grants for capital expenditures or endowments.
Publications: Application guidelines; Annual report; Informational brochure.
Application information: Application guidelines and form available on foundation Web site. Application form required.
Initial approach: Letter
Copies of proposal: 1
Deadline(s): June 30
Board meeting date(s): May and Nov.
Final notification: Dec.
Officers and Directors:* Gilbert N. Olson,* Chair.; Frank J. Bavendick,* Pres.; Brian R. Bjella,* V.P.; William L. "Bill" Daniel,* Secy.-Treas.; John T. Roswick; Paul D. Schliesman; Todd Steinward.
Number of staff: 1 full-time support; 1 part-time support.
EIN: 456012703
Selected grants: The following grants were reported in 2005.
$95,000 to Williston State College Foundation, Williston, ND. For new health science and sports facilities.
$70,000 to Bismarck Recreation Council, Bismarck, ND. For High Prairie Arts and Science Leach Complex.
$68,750 to Medcenter One, Bismarck, ND. For Tom and Frances Leach Kidney Dialysis Center.
$50,000 to North Dakota Cowboy Hall of Fame, Medora, ND. For Tom Leach tribute.
$43,750 to International Music Camp, Minot, ND. For International Arts Music Center and for Frances Leach library.
$20,000 to Jamestown College, Jamestown, ND. For start-up support for Character in Leadership Program.
$15,000 to Bismarck-Mandan Orchestral Association, Bismarck, ND. For concert season and educational school programs.
$15,000 to Charles Hall Youth Services, Bismarck, ND. For Impact Creative Arts Program for at-risk children.
$15,000 to Fort Abraham Lincoln Foundation, Mandan, ND. For Native American Interpretive Program.
$12,500 to Salvation Army of Bismarck, Bismarck, ND. For operating support for emergency help, transitional housing for homeless women and children, after-school and daycare services.

7517

MDU Resources Foundation ◈

P.O. Box 5650
Bismarck, ND   58506-5650   (701) 530-1085
Contact: Dennis W. Boyd, Pres.
FAX: (701) 222-7607; URL: http://www.mdu.com/the_vision/vision_foundation.htm

Established in 1983 in ND.
Donors: MDU Resources Group, Inc.; WBI Holdings, Inc.; Knife River Corp.; Montana Dakota Utilities Co.; Williston Basin Interstate Pipeline Co.
Foundation type: Company-sponsored foundation.
Financial data (yr. ended 12/31/05): Assets, $3,163,300 (M); gifts received, $1,300,084; expenditures, $1,248,578; qualifying distributions, $1,247,293; giving activities include $1,211,789 for 512 grants (high: $25,000; low: $50), and $30,000 for 25 grants to individuals (high: $1,200; low: $1,200).
Purpose and activities: The foundation supports organizations involved with arts and culture,

education, the environment, health, human services, community development, and civic affairs.

Fields of interest: Arts councils; Media, television; Media, radio; Performing arts, theater; Arts; Secondary school/education; Higher education; Business school/education; Libraries (public); Education; Environment, natural resources; Environment; Hospitals (general); Health care; Youth, services; Aging, centers/services; Human services; Community development; Federated giving programs; Public affairs.

Type of support: General/operating support; Continuing support; Annual campaigns; Capital campaigns; Building/renovation; Scholarship funds; Employee-related scholarships.

Limitations: Giving primarily in areas of company operations. No support for athletic, labor, fraternal, veterans', political, lobbying, social, or religious organizations or regional or national organizations without local affiliation. No grants to individuals (except for employee-related scholarships); generally, no endowments.

Publications: Application guidelines; Annual report; Program policy statement.

Application information: Application form required.

Initial approach: Contact foundation for application form

Deadline(s): None

Officers and Directors:* Dennis W. Boyd,* Pres.; Warren L. Robinson,* Secy.-Treas.; John K. Castleberry; Paul Gatzemeier; John Harp; Terry D. Hildestad; Bruce T. Imsdahl; Paul K. Sandness; William Schneider; Robert E. Wood.

EIN: 450378937

Selected grants: The following grants were reported in 2005.

$30,000 to Scholarship America, Saint Peter, MN. For scholarships.

$25,000 to Northern Plains Ballet, Bismarck, ND. For general support.

$20,000 to CentraCare Foundation, Saint Cloud, MN. For capital construction.

$20,000 to Dickinson Building Authority, Dickinson, ND. For capital construction.

$20,000 to Saint Cloud Technical College (SCTC) Foundation, Saint Cloud, MN. For endowment.

$17,500 to North Dakota Lewis and Clark Bicentennial Foundation, Washburn, ND. For general support.

$15,000 to American Red Cross, National Headquarters, DC. For general support.

$15,000 to United Way, Missouri Slope Areawide, Bismarck, ND. For general support.

$10,000 to Beavers Charitable Trust, Los Altos, CA. For scholarship.

$10,000 to La Clinica del Valle Family Health Care Center, Medford, OR. For capital construction.

7518
The R. B. Nordick Foundation ✧

675 12th Ave. N.
West Fargo, ND 58078-3500

Established in 1995 in ND.
Donor: Ralph B. Nordick.
Foundation type: Independent foundation.
Financial data (yr. ended 12/31/04): Assets, $21,018,700 (M); gifts received, $4,030,000; expenditures, $863,923; qualifying distributions, $851,233; giving activities include $840,000 for 16 grants (high: $200,000; low: $2,400).
Fields of interest: Christian agencies & churches.

Limitations: Applications not accepted. Giving limited to ND. No grants to individuals.
Application information: Contributes only to pre-selected organizations.
Officers: Ralph B. Nordick, Pres.; Brett A. Nordick, V.P.; Douglas R. Geeslin, Secy.-Treas.
Director: Yvonne Nordak.
EIN: 450442920
Selected grants: The following grants were reported in 2004.

$200,000 to Operation Mobilization, Tyrone, GA.

$130,000 to Emmanuel Ministries International, Brainerd, MN.

$129,782 to Reaching Indians Ministries International, Round Lake Beach, IL.

$78,000 to China Harvest, Wichita, KS.

$75,750 to Trans World Radio, Cary, NC.

$52,000 to Christar, Reading, PA.

$50,068 to Cornerstone Ministries International, Tustin, CA.

$35,000 to Systematic Asian Leadership Training (SALT), Belmont, NC.

$15,000 to Dunwoody College of Technology, Minneapolis, MN.

$15,000 to Masters Theater, Fargo, ND.

7519
North Dakota Community Foundation

P.O. Box 387
Bismarck, ND 58502-0387 (701) 222-8349
Contact: Kevin J. Dvorak, C.E.O.
E-mail: kdvorak@ndcf.net; Additional E-mail: valerie@ndcf.net; URL: http://www.ndcf.net

Established in 1977 in ND.
Foundation type: Community foundation.
Financial data (yr. ended 12/31/05): Assets, $27,291,653 (L); gifts received, $3,594,861; expenditures, $1,559,483; giving activities include $875,674 for 310 grants (high: $75,000; low: $70), and $116,748 for 161 grants to individuals.
Purpose and activities: The foundation seeks to improve the quality of life for North Dakota's citizens through charitable giving and promoting philanthropy. Unrestricted funds largely for aid to the elderly and disadvantaged; support also for health services, including mental health, youth agencies, parks and recreation, and arts and cultural programs in ND.
Fields of interest: Arts; Higher education; Education; Environment; Health care; Mental health/crisis services; Recreation; Children/youth, services; Aging, centers/services; Human services; Community development; Aging; Economically disadvantaged.
Type of support: Scholarships—to individuals; General/operating support; Annual campaigns; Building/renovation; Equipment; Program development; Conferences/seminars; Publication; Seed money; Scholarship funds; Research; Matching/challenge support.
Limitations: Giving primarily in ND. No support for sectarian projects or national organizations (generally). No grants to individuals (except for scholarships), or for multi-year commitments.
Publications: Application guidelines; Annual report; Informational brochure; Newsletter.
Application information: Visit foundation Web site for application guidelines. Foundation will contact applicant by Oct. 1 for additional materials; grants normally do not exceed $2,000; faxed or e-mailed letters are not accepted. Application form not required.

Initial approach: Letter (not exceeding 2 pages)
Copies of proposal: 1
Deadline(s): Aug. 15
Board meeting date(s): 3rd quarter of year, annually
Final notification: Late Nov. or Dec.
Officers and Directors:* Chad Peterson,* Chair.; Joanne H. Ottmar,* Vice-Chair.; Kevin J. Dvorak,* C.E.O. and Pres.; Dennis Johnson, Secy.-Treas.; Neil Fedje; Rod Gayton; H. Michael Hardy; Joe Hauer; Dan Liberda; Barbara Mayer; Rosemarie Myrdahl; Lynn Nelson; Patsy Thompson; Jim Weisser.
Number of staff: 2 full-time professional; 1 full-time support.
EIN: 450336015
Selected grants: The following grants were reported in 2004.

$75,000 to Arthur Good Samaritan Center, Arthur, ND.

$71,929 to Bismarck Public Schools, Bismarck, ND. For planning and implementation.

$50,000 to Arthur, City of, Arthur, ND.

$50,000 to Casselton Park District, Casselton, ND.

$50,000 to North Dakota State University Development Foundation, Fargo, ND.

$25,000 to Dollars for Scholars, Casselton, ND.

$15,000 to American Red Cross, Minn-Kota Chapter, Fargo, ND.

$13,500 to Wayzata Sailing Foundation, Wayzata, MN.

$11,000 to Saint Martins Lutheran Church, Casselton, ND. For endowment fund.

$10,000 to Central Cass Public School District, Casselton, ND.

7520
North Dakota Natural Resources Trust, Inc.

(formerly North Dakota Wetlands Trust, Inc.)
1605 E. Capitol Ave., Ste. 101
Bismarck, ND 58501-2102
Contact: Keith Trego
FAX: (701) 223-6937; *E-mail:* nrtlinda@btinet.net; URL: http://www.ndnrt.com

Established in 1986 in ND.
Foundation type: Independent foundation.
Financial data (yr. ended 12/31/05): Assets, $16,947,251 (M); gifts received, $1,472,329; expenditures, $2,007,457; giving activities include $245,158 for 11 grants (high: $125,000; low: $2,000; average: $5,000–$20,000), and $1,411,801 for 4 foundation-administered programs.
Purpose and activities: Giving to preserve, enhance, restore, and manage wetlands and associated habitat, grasslands, and riparian areas.
Fields of interest: Environment, natural resources.
Type of support: Equipment; Land acquisition; Program development; Matching/challenge support.
Limitations: Giving limited to ND. No grants to individuals.
Publications: Annual report; Informational brochure; Newsletter.
Application information: Application form available on foundation Web site. Application form required.

Initial approach: Telephone
Copies of proposal: 1
Deadline(s): Oct. 15th
Board meeting date(s): Spring, summer, and winter
Final notification: By Dec. 31

Officers: Dick Kroger, V.P.; Scott Peterson, Secy.-Treas.
Directors: Bruce Adams; Dean Hildebrand; Duane Liffrig; Jack Olin; Genevieve Thompson.
Number of staff: 3 full-time professional; 1 part-time professional.
EIN: 363512179
Selected grants: The following grants were reported in 2004.
$22,400 to North Dakota Game and Fish Department, Bismarck, ND. For public hunting access.
$20,000 to Ducks Unlimited, Bismarck, ND. To promote crop production in Drift Praine region of North Dakota.
$20,000 to U.S. Fish and Wildlife Service, Woodworth, ND. For Chase Lake area habitat creation program.
$14,949 to North Dakota State University, Fargo, ND. To improve wetlands in Sheridian and McIntosh counties.
$10,000 to Sheyenne River Valley, Valley City, ND. For placement of interpretive wetland habitat signs along scenic byway.

7521
Alex Stern Family Foundation
4152 30th Ave. S., No. 102
Fargo, ND 58104
Contact: Donald L. Scott, Exec. Dir.

Established in 1964 in ND.
Donors: William Stern†; Sam Stern†; Edward A. Stern†.
Foundation type: Independent foundation.
Financial data (yr. ended 12/31/05): Assets, $9,496,191 (M); expenditures, $637,608;

qualifying distributions, $575,217; giving activities include $553,230 for 47 grants (high: $100,000; low: $1,000).
Purpose and activities: Primary areas of interest include the arts, child welfare, the elderly, alcohol abuse programs, and community funds. Support also for family and social services, including legal services, and welfare for the homeless and disabled; community organizations; higher, business, minority, and other education; and hospices and cancer research.
Fields of interest: Museums; Performing arts; Performing arts, dance; Performing arts, theater; Historic preservation/historical societies; Arts; Child development, education; Higher education; Substance abuse, services; Alcoholism; Legal services; Housing/shelter, development; Human services; Children/youth, services; Child development, services; Family services; Residential/custodial care, hospices; Aging, centers/services; Homeless, human services; Aging; Disabilities, people with; Minorities; Native Americans/American Indians; Economically disadvantaged; Homeless.
Type of support: General/operating support; Continuing support; Annual campaigns; Capital campaigns; Building/renovation; Equipment; Emergency funds; Program development; Scholarship funds; Research; Technical assistance; Matching/challenge support.
Limitations: Giving limited to the Moorhead, MN, and Fargo, ND areas. No grants to individuals, or for endowment funds; no loans.
Publications: Application guidelines; Annual report.
Application information: Application form required.
Initial approach: Letter requesting application and guidelines
Copies of proposal: 3

Deadline(s): Mar. 31 for spring consideration and Aug. 31 for fall consideration
Board meeting date(s): Varies
Final notification: Within a few months
Officer and Trustees:* Donald L. Scott,* Exec. Dir.; Dan Carey; H. Michael Hardy.
Number of staff: 1 part-time professional.
EIN: 456013981
Selected grants: The following grants were reported in 2005.
$100,000 to Impact Foundation, Fargo, ND. For general operating support and for grantwriting support.
$100,000 to Trollwood Performing Arts School, Fargo, ND. For general operating support.
$20,000 to Prairie Public Broadcasting, Fargo, ND. For general operating support.
$15,000 to Blessing Way Family Services, Cushing, WI. For Partners in Housing.
$15,000 to FutureBuilders in Support of the Trollwood Performing Arts School, Fargo, ND. For Star Program.
$15,000 to YWCA, Cass Clay, Fargo, ND. For general operating support.
$12,000 to Fargo-Moorhead Opera, Fargo, ND. For general operating support.
$12,000 to Fraser, Limited, Fargo, ND. For social skills program.
$10,000 to Fargo-Moorhead Dorothy Day House of Hospitality, Moorhead, MN. For general operating support.
$10,000 to Nokomis Child Care Center, Fargo, ND. For general operating support.

OHIO

7522
A Good Day Foundation ✧
414 Walnut St., Ste. 1014
Cincinnati, OH   45202-3913
Contact: Michelle Kelley, Secy.-Treas.

Established in 2002 in OH.
Donor: Gloria J. Fehr.
Foundation type: Operating foundation.
Financial data (yr. ended 6/30/05): Assets, $443,143 (M); gifts received, $400,000; expenditures, $676,125; qualifying distributions, $657,925; giving activities include $619,153 for 94 grants to individuals (high: $26,000; low: $55).
Fields of interest: Cancer; Children, services; Human services, emergency aid; Children.
Type of support: General/operating support; Grants to individuals.
Limitations: Giving primarily in KY and OH.
Application information:
  Initial approach: Letter
  Deadline(s): None
Officers and Directors: A.V. Katz, Jr.,* Pres.; Betty Bassett,* V.P.; Gloria J. Fehr,* V.P.; Donald Feldman,* V.P.; Michelle Kelley,* Secy.-Treas.
EIN: 223885978

7523
A Good Neighbor Foundation ✧
414 Walnut St., Ste. 1014
Cincinnati, OH   45202-3913   (513) 651-9333
Contact: M. Kelley

Established in 2002 in OH.
Donor: Gloria J. Fehr.
Foundation type: Independent foundation.
Financial data (yr. ended 6/30/05): Assets, $35,628,584 (M); expenditures, $5,619,585; qualifying distributions, $5,324,402; giving activities include $5,147,162 for 134 grants (high: $1,000,000; low: $100).
Purpose and activities: Giving primarily for children and social services.
Fields of interest: Education; Health care; Human services; Children/youth, services.
Type of support: General/operating support; Grants to individuals.
Limitations: Giving primarily in OH, with emphasis on the Cincinnati area; giving also in KY.
Application information:
  Deadline(s): None
Officers and Directors: A.V. Katz, Jr.,* Pres.; Betty Bassett,* V.P.; Gloria J. Fehr,* V.P.; Donald Feldman,* V.P.; Michelle Kelley,* Secy.-Treas.
EIN: 223885976
Selected grants: The following grants were reported in 2003.
$30,000 to CareNet Pregnancy Services of Northern Kentucky, Florence, KY. For renovations and ultrasound equipment.
$25,000 to Prospect House, Cincinnati, OH. For new heating and air conditioning.
$25,000 to Saint Ursula Academy, Cincinnati, OH. For program support.
$20,000 to Saint Joseph Infant and Maternity Home, Cincinnati, OH. For feasibility study.

$16,500 to Easter Seal Society of Southwestern Ohio, Reading, OH. For summer speech program.
$13,500 to AAA Cincinnati Orphans Outing, Cincinnati, OH.
$13,500 to Shepherds Crook Ministries, West Chester, OH. For the adoption of a blind infant.
$10,000 to Animal Rescue Fund, Amelia, OH. For driveway renovation.
$5,000 to Ault Park Advisory Council, Cincinnati, OH.
$5,000 to W G U C-FM, Cincinnati, OH. For spring fund raiser.

7524
The Abington Foundation
c/o Foundation Mgmt. Svcs., Inc.
1422 Euclid Ave., Ste. 627
Cleveland, OH   44115-1952   (216) 621-2901
Contact: Janet E. Narten, Consultant
FAX: (216) 621-8198;
E-mail: abington@fmscleveland.com; *URL:* http://www.fmscleveland.com/abington

Established in 1983 in OH.
Donors: David Knight Ford‡; Elizabeth Brooks Ford‡.
Foundation type: Independent foundation.
Financial data (yr. ended 12/31/05): Assets, $35,569,087 (M); expenditures, $2,204,819; qualifying distributions, $1,937,268; giving activities include $1,789,323 for 92 grants (high: $100,000; low: $775; average: $5,000–$10,000).
Purpose and activities: Giving primarily for educational programs, geriatrics, health care, social services, and the arts and cultural programs in Cuyahoga County, OH.
Fields of interest: Arts; Education; Health care; Human services; Aging.
Type of support: Capital campaigns; Equipment; Emergency funds; Program development; Seed money; Matching/challenge support.
Limitations: Giving primarily in Cleveland, OH. No grants to individuals; no support for endowments, sponsorships, seminars, or general operating support.
Publications: Application guidelines; Annual report (including application guidelines); Grants list.
Application information: Application guidelines and procedures available on foundation Web site. Mass mailings not accepted. Application form not required.
  Initial approach: Proposal (no more than 2 pages)
  Copies of proposal: 2
  Deadline(s): May 1, Sept. 1, and Dec. 1
  Board meeting date(s): Jan., June, and Oct.
  Final notification: 2 weeks after board meeting
Trustees: Allen H. Ford; Charles K. Ford; David Kingsley Ford; Edward C. Ford; John Ford; Oliver M. Ford; Hope Ford Murphy; Tomas Revesz.
EIN: 341404854
Selected grants: The following grants were reported in 2004.
$66,666 to Cleveland Foundation, Cleveland, OH.
$50,000 to Cleveland Foodbank, Cleveland, OH.
$50,000 to Laurel School, Shaker Heights, OH.
$40,000 to Eliza Bryant Center, Cleveland, OH.
$30,000 to Great Lakes Theater Festival, Cleveland, OH.
$28,000 to Recovery Resources, Cleveland, OH.
$18,000 to Positive Education Program, Cleveland, OH.
$14,400 to John Carroll University, University Heights, OH.

$10,300 to Far West Center, Westlake, OH.
$10,000 to Western Reserve Historical Society, Cleveland, OH.

7525
AK Steel Foundation ✧
703 Curtis St.
Middletown, OH   45043   (513) 425-5038
Contact: Alan H. McCoy, Exec. Dir.
URL: http://www.aksteel.com/events/event_detail.asp?e=69

Established in 1989 in OH.
Donors: AK Steel Corp.; Kawasaki Steel Investments, Inc.
Foundation type: Company-sponsored foundation.
Financial data (yr. ended 12/31/04): Assets, $16,148,187 (M); expenditures, $935,139; qualifying distributions, $915,645; giving activities include $841,438 for 75 grants (high: $312,000; low: $250), and $52,807 for 178 employee matching gifts.
Purpose and activities: The foundation supports organizations involved with arts and culture, higher education, health, youth development, and human services and awards college scholarships to the children of employees of AK Steel and to African-American high school seniors attending high schools in Butler and Warren counties, Ohio.
Fields of interest: Arts; Higher education; Health care; Youth development; Human services; Federated giving programs; African Americans/Blacks.
Type of support: General/operating support; Employee matching gifts; Employee-related scholarships; Scholarships—to individuals.
Limitations: Giving primarily in OH.
Application information: An application form is required for scholarships. Application form required.
  Initial approach: Contact foundation for application information; download application form and mail to foundation for scholarships
  Deadline(s): Dec. 30 for scholarships
Officers and Trustees: James L. Wainscott,* Chair.; Joe Plye, Secy.; Roger K. Newport, Treas.; Alan H. McCoy,* Exec. Dir.; Al Ferrara; David Horn; Lawrence F. Zizzo.
Number of staff: 1 part-time professional.
EIN: 311284344

7526
Akron Community Foundation ▼ ✧
345 W. Cedar St.
Akron, OH   44307-2407   (330) 376-8522
Contact: Jody Bacon, Pres.
FAX: (330) 376-0202;
E-mail: acfmail@akroncommunityfdn.org;
URL: http://www.akroncommunityfdn.org

Incorporated in 1955 in OH.
Foundation type: Community foundation.
Financial data (yr. ended 3/31/05): Assets, $116,597,576 (M); gifts received, $7,298,000; expenditures, $7,117,815; giving activities include $6,133,815 for 835 grants (high: $572,333; low: $100).
Purpose and activities: The foundation seeks to promote charitable, benevolent, educational, recreational, health, esthetic, cultural, and public welfare activities; to support a program of research leading to the improvement of the health, education,

and general well-being of all citizens of the Akron, OH, area; to give toward the support of experimental and demonstration programs, through established or new agencies; to test the validity of research findings in various fields of community planning directed toward the efficient and adequate coordination of public and private services organized to meet human needs.

Fields of interest: Media, film/video; Museums; Performing arts; Historic preservation/historical societies; Arts; Education; Environment; Health care; Mental health/crisis services; Health organizations, association; Medical research, institute; Medical research; Employment; Disasters, fire prevention/control; Disasters, Hurricane Katrina; Recreation; Children/youth, services; Children, day care; Family services; Aging, centers/ services; Human services; Civil rights, advocacy; Community development; Consumer protection; Public affairs; Aging; Disabilities, people with; African Americans/Blacks; Women; AIDS, people with; LGBTQ; Immigrants/refugees; Economically disadvantaged; Homeless.

Type of support: Program development; Seed money; Scholarship funds; Research; Matching/ challenge support.

Limitations: Giving primarily in Summit County, OH. No support for religious organizations for religious purposes. No grants to individuals, or for endowment funds, capital campaigns, or fellowships; no loans.

Publications: Application guidelines; Annual report (including application guidelines); Newsletter.

Application information: Visit foundation Web site for online pre-application form and application guidelines. The foundation accepts full proposals based on pre-application form. No more than 1 grant to an organization in a 12-month period. Application form required.

Initial approach: Complete online pre-application form

Deadline(s): Jan. 2 for Education, Apr. 1 for Arts and Culture, July 1 for Civic Affairs, and Oct. 1 for Health and Human Services (full proposals)

Board meeting date(s): Generally Feb., May, Aug., and Nov.

Final notification: 8 weeks

Officers and Trustees:* Kathryn Dindo,* Chair.; Gregory McDermott,* Vice-Chair.; Jody Bacon, Pres.; Sandy Auburn, V.P., Devel.; Tina Boyes, V.P., Comms.; Donae Eckert, V.P., Progs.; Steven Schloenbach, V.P., Finance; Patricia Pacenta,* Secy.; Steve Marks,* Treas.; F. Steven Albrecht; Rennick Andreoli; Mark Bober; Ellen Burg; Cynthia Capers; James Crutchfield; George Daverio, Jr.; Timothy Fitzwater; Dorothy Gaffney; Terry Haines; Susan Kinnamon; Dale Koblenzer; Richard Kramer; Mike Lewis; Scott A. Lyons, Jr.; Hon. Carla Moore; Robert Reffner; George Sarkis; Rev. Sandra F. Selby; Bill Sharp.

Trustee Banks: Brandes Investment Partners; Clover Capital Mgmt.; FirstMerit Bank, N.A.; Frontier Capital Mgmt.; JPMorgan Chase Bank, N.A.; National City Bank; Oak Assocs.; Osprey Investment Partners.

Number of staff: 4 full-time professional; 1 part-time professional; 3 full-time support.

EIN: 341087615

Selected grants: The following grants were reported in 2005.

$300,000 to Akron Art Museum, Akron, OH. For Inaugural Celebration for re-opening.

$75,000 to Akron Community Service Center and Urban League, Akron, OH. For capital campaign.

$50,000 to Akron, City of, Akron, OH. For Neighborhood Partnership Program.

$35,000 to Greater Akron Musical Association, Akron, OH. For Concert for Kids series.

$33,402 to Battered Womens Shelter, Akron, OH. For community outreach program.

$30,000 to Ohio and Erie Canal Corridor Coalition, Akron, OH. For restoration of 1836 Richard Howe House to serve as Towpath Trail visitors' information center.

$25,000 to Boys and Girls Clubs of Summit County, Akron, OH. For after-school program at Eller Unit.

$25,000 to Community Hall Foundation Program, Akron, OH. For in-house programming.

$25,000 to Good Neighbors, Akron, OH. For Food Center project, which supplies emergency food assistance to those facing immediate hunger in community.

$25,000 to Musical Arts Association, Blossom Music Center, Cleveland, OH. For sponsorship of Blossom Festival's Bravo Broadway's Music of the Night.

7527

The Alpaugh Foundation ◇

525 Vine St., 21st Fl.
Cincinnati, OH 45202-3121

Established in 1986 in OH.

Donor: Peter A. Alpaugh.

Foundation type: Independent foundation.

Financial data (yr. ended 6/30/05): Assets, $2,861,807 (M); gifts received, $36,692; expenditures, $806,241; qualifying distributions, $797,923; giving activities include $793,160 for 100 grants (high: $434,700; low: $50).

Purpose and activities: Giving for arts and culture, education, and human services and community development.

Fields of interest: Arts; Education; Environment; Health organizations, association; Medical research; Disasters, fire prevention/control; Recreation; Human services; Community development; Federated giving programs; Religion.

Limitations: Applications not accepted. Giving on a national basis.

Application information: Unsolicited requests for funds not accepted.

Officer: Peter A. Alpaugh, Mgr.

EIN: 316314074

7528

The American Foundation Corporation ◇

629 Euclid Ave., Ste. 720
Cleveland, OH 44114

Incorporated in 1974 as successor to trust established in 1944 in OH.

Donors: Members of the Corning family; and members of the Murfey family.

Foundation type: Independent foundation.

Financial data (yr. ended 12/31/05): Assets, $34,748,181 (M); expenditures, $2,391,399; qualifying distributions, $2,313,766; giving activities include $2,243,507 for 96 grants (high: $510,814; low: $28).

Purpose and activities: Giving primarily to an arboretum, as well as for education, health associations, animal welfare, and youth, family, and social services.

Fields of interest: Museums (natural history); Education; Environment; Animals/wildlife; Health organizations, association; Human services; Children/youth, services; Family services.

Type of support: General/operating support; Continuing support; Annual campaigns.

Limitations: Applications not accepted. Giving primarily in the Cleveland, OH, area. No grants to individuals, or for capital or endowment funds, special projects, research, scholarships, fellowships, or matching gifts; no loans.

Publications: Annual report.

Application information: Contributes only to pre-selected organizations. Funds presently committed.

Board meeting date(s): As necessary

Officers and Trustees:* William W. Murfey,* Pres.; Maria G. Muth, Secy.-Treas.; Dwight B. Corning.

EIN: 237348126

Selected grants: The following grants were reported in 2005.

$510,814 to Holden Arboretum, Kirtland, OH.

$123,860 to Cleveland Museum of Natural History, Cleveland, OH.

$100,000 to Carrabassett Valley Academy, Kingfield, ME.

$80,000 to Best Friends Animal Society, Kanab, UT.

$75,000 to Huntington Memorial Hospital, Huntington, IN.

$40,000 to American Red Cross.

$35,000 to Defenders of Wildlife, DC.

$30,000 to Winchester Medical Center, Winchester, VA.

$13,343 to Cleveland Botanical Garden, Cleveland, OH.

$5,000 to New York University, New York, NY.

7529

Anderson Foundation

480 W. Dussel Dr.
P.O. Box 119
Maumee, OH 43537-0119
Application address: c/o Ms. Fredi Heywood, 608 Madison Ave., Ste. 1540, Toledo, OH 43604, tel.: (419) 243-1706

Trust established in 1949 in OH.

Donor: Partners in The Andersons, Inc.

Foundation type: Independent foundation.

Financial data (yr. ended 12/31/04): Assets, $4,633,464 (M); gifts received, $455,500; expenditures, $484,450; qualifying distributions, $460,365; giving activities include $450,858 for 122 grants (high: $83,333; low: $50).

Purpose and activities: Grants primarily for community funds, higher and secondary education, and cultural programs; support also for social service and youth agencies, civic and community efforts, educational and research associations, and religion.

Fields of interest: Arts; Education, association; Secondary school/education; Higher education; Education; Agriculture; Human services; Children/ youth, services; Community development; Federated giving programs; Government/public administration; Religion.

Type of support: General/operating support; Annual campaigns; Capital campaigns; Building/ renovation; Emergency funds; Program development; Conferences/seminars; Publication; Seed money; Scholarship funds; Research; Matching/challenge support.

Limitations: Giving primarily in the greater Toledo, OH, area, including Maumee and Columbus. Giving also to organizations located within the areas of the Anderson plants in the following cities: Champaign, IL, Delphi and Dunkirk, IN, and Albion, Potterville, Webberville, and White Pigeon, MI. No support for private foundations, public high schools or elementary schools. No grants to individuals, or for endowment funds, travel, or building or operating funds for churches or elementary schools.
Publications: Application guidelines.
Application information: Application form not required.
  Initial approach: Proposal not exceeding 5 pages
  Copies of proposal: 1
  Deadline(s): 3 weeks before board meetings
  Board meeting date(s): Mar., June, Sept., and Dec., usually the 3rd Mon. of the month
  Final notification: Generally 3 months; depends on completeness of proposal
Officer and Trustees:* Thomas H. Anderson,* Chair.; Charles W. Anderson; Jeffrey W. Anderson; Matthew C. Anderson; Richard M. Anderson; Richard P. Anderson; Dale W. Fallat; John P. Kraus.
EIN: 346528868
Selected grants: The following grants were reported in 2004.
$83,333 to Catholic Diocese of Toledo, Toledo, OH.
$75,000 to United Way of Greater Toledo, Toledo, OH. 2 grants: $37,500 each
$25,000 to Notre Dame Academy, Toledo, OH.
$16,666 to Central Catholic High School, Toledo, OH.
$16,666 to COSI Toledo, Toledo, OH.
$5,000 to Cardinal Stritch High School, Oregon, OH.
$5,000 to Toledo Opera Association, Toledo, OH.
$1,000 to Ohio Grantmakers Forum, Columbus, OH.
$1,000 to Ursuline Sisters of Toledo, Toledo, OH.

7530
The Andrews Foundation
13111 Shaker Sq., Ste. 208
Cleveland, OH 44120-2345 (216) 751-2115
Contact: Laura Baxter-Heuer, Pres.
FAX: (216) 751-2105;
E-mail: andrewsfoundation@sbcglobal.net

Incorporated in 1951 in OH.
Donor: Mrs. Matthew Andrews†.
Foundation type: Independent foundation.
Financial data (yr. ended 12/31/04): Assets, $9,124,092 (M); expenditures, $540,130; qualifying distributions, $477,672; giving activities include $443,300 for 18 grants (high: $50,000; low: $500).
Purpose and activities: Giving primarily for education.
Fields of interest: Performing arts; Secondary school/education; Higher education; Alcoholism.
Type of support: General/operating support; Annual campaigns; Capital campaigns; Endowments.
Limitations: Giving limited to OH. No grants to individuals.
Application information: Application form not required.
  Initial approach: E-mail is preferred method for initial contact
  Copies of proposal: 1
  Deadline(s): None
  Board meeting date(s): Spring and Fall
Officers and Trustees:* Laura Baxter-Heuer,* Pres.; Michael A. Heuer,* V.P.; Ann Garson,* Secy.-Treas.

Number of staff: 1 full-time professional.
EIN: 346515110

7531
Arab Student Aid International Corp. ◇
P.O. Box 3546
Dublin, OH 43016 (614) 889-9420
FAX: (614) 889-9430; E-mail: info@asai2000.org;
URL: http://www.asai2000.org

Established in 1998 in NJ.
Donor: HRH Prince Turkin bin Abdul Aziz.
Foundation type: Operating foundation.
Financial data (yr. ended 6/30/05): Assets, $5,087,512 (M); gifts received, $10,070; expenditures, $637,364; qualifying distributions, $468,614; giving activities include $233,723 for 6 grants (high: $98,723; low: $15,000), and $117,500 for 42 loans to individuals (high: $5,000; low: $1,500).
Purpose and activities: Support primarily for loans to full-time students of Arab descent who will be studying in the U.S. on a student visa, are pursuing a Ph.D., and who plan to return to the Arab world after graduation. Funding also for scholarship grants to Palestinian universities.
Fields of interest: Graduate/professional education; Scholarships/financial aid.
International interests: Middle East.
Type of support: Scholarship funds; Student loans—to individuals.
Limitations: Giving primarily in the U.S. and the Middle East. No support for the study of languages before enrolling at a university, or for more than one student per family. No grants for trips or travel expenses.
Publications: Application guidelines; Newsletter.
Application information: Institutions must be accredited and students must maintain a "B" average. See foundation Web site for complete application guidelines. Application form required.
  Initial approach: Letter
  Deadline(s): Aug. 1
Officers: Ishaq Y. Al-Qutub, Pres.; Mustafa D. Shamy, V.P. and Treas.; Robert W. Thabit, Secy.
EIN: 223519297

7532
The Evenor Armington Fund ◇
c/o The Huntington National Bank
917 Euclid Ave., CM24
Cleveland, OH 44115

Established in 1954 in OH.
Donors: Everett Armington; and members of the Armington family.
Foundation type: Independent foundation.
Financial data (yr. ended 6/30/05): Assets, $4,629,921 (M); expenditures, $618,852; qualifying distributions, $588,477; giving activities include $581,500 for 30 grants (high: $100,000; low: $2,000).
Purpose and activities: Grants primarily for special projects, usually short-term, in education, child welfare, medical research, health, the arts, the environment, and public policy organizations, including human rights, peace and justice, and the struggle against poverty.
Fields of interest: Arts; Education; Environment; natural resources; Environment; Health care; Medical research, institute; Human services;

Children/youth, services; International peace/security; International human rights; Civil rights; Public policy, research.
Type of support: General/operating support; Continuing support; Annual campaigns; Emergency funds; Program development; Publication; Research; Consulting services.
Limitations: Applications not accepted. Giving on a national basis. No grants to individuals, or for deficit financing or general purposes.
Application information: Contributes only to pre-selected organizations. Unsolicited requests for funds not considered or acknowledged.
  Board meeting date(s): Summer
Advisors: David E. Armington; Paul Armington; Peter Armington.
Trustee: The Huntington National Bank.
EIN: 346525508
Selected grants: The following grants were reported in 2005.
$30,000 to Nature Conservancy, Arlington, VA.
$25,000 to Trust for Public Land, San Francisco, CA.
$25,000 to University Hospital, Zagreb, Croatia. .
$15,000 to Mountain Top Music Center, North Conway, NH. 2 grants: $7,500 each
$15,000 to New England Medical Center, Boston, MA.
$15,000 to Peace Development Fund, Amherst, MA.
$10,000 to Catalytic Diplomacy, Chevy Chase, MD.
$10,000 to Humane Society.
$10,000 to NARAL Foundation, Nashville, TN.

7533
Ashland County Community Foundation ☆
300 College Ave.
Ashland, OH 44805 (419) 281-4733
Contact: Lucille G. Ford Ph.D., Pres.
FAX: (419) 289-5540; E-mail: accf@hmcltd.net;
URL: http://www.ashlandcountycommunityfoundation.org

Established in 1995 in OH.
Foundation type: Community foundation.
Financial data (yr. ended 6/30/05): Assets, $7,870,462 (M); gifts received, $1,145,543; expenditures, $423,223; giving activities include $275,503 for grants, $69,839 for 77 grants to individuals (high: $5,000; low: $100), and $37,200 for 31 loans to individuals (high: $1,200; low: $1,200).
Purpose and activities: The mission of the foundation is to advance philanthropy and improve the quality of life in Ashland County by supporting charitable activities in the community, providing and administering a variety of planned giving programs, and serving as responsible stewards of scholarship, as well as individual and organizational funds for specific charities.
Fields of interest: Arts; Education; Environment; Health care; Human services; Community development.
Type of support: Seed money; Capital campaigns; Building/renovation; Equipment; Program development; Scholarship funds; Scholarships—to individuals; Matching/challenge support; Student loans—to individuals.
Limitations: Giving limited to Ashland County, OH. No support for religious organizations for religious purposes. No grants to individuals (except for designated scholarship funds and educational loans), or for ongoing operating expenses, annual campaigns, endowment funds, cash reserves, or debt reduction.

Publications: Application guidelines; Annual report; Informational brochure; Newsletter.

Application information: An interview to discuss a grant proposal is required. Visit foundation Web site for application form and guidelines. Call or e-mail foundation for an ACCF Scholarship Guide. Application form required.

Initial approach: Letter, telephone, or e-mail
Copies of proposal: 1
Deadline(s): Feb. 15 and Sept. 15; Sept. 8 for Teacher Mini-Grants
Board meeting date(s): Last Mon. of Jan., Apr., July, and Oct.
Final notification: May 1 and Nov. 1

Officers and Trustees:* James Hess,* Chair.; Anne Beer,* Vice-Chair.; Lucille G. Ford, Ph.D.,* Pres.; Sue E. Banks,* Secy.; Irene Moore, Recording Secy.; David Steury,* Treas.; Janet L. Archer; Michael Bandy; Stan Brechbuhler; William Buckingham; Suzanne Carruthers; Robert C. Ingmand; Susanne Reineke; Loreen Simonson; Charles Taylor; Robert Ward II.

Number of staff: 1 full-time professional; 1 part-time support.

EIN: 341812908

7534
The Ashtabula Foundation, Inc. ◇

4510 Collins Blvd., Ste. 6
Ashtabula, OH 44004 (440) 992-6818
Contact: Roberta Martin, Admin.
FAX: (440) 992-0724;
E-mail: ashtabulafdn@suite224.net; URL: http://www.ashtabulafoundation.org

Incorporated in 1922 in OH.

Foundation type: Independent foundation.

Financial data (yr. ended 12/31/05): Assets, $17,132,960 (M); expenditures, $1,117,019; qualifying distributions, $955,855; giving activities include $893,817 for 43 grants (high: $130,000; low: $300).

Purpose and activities: The mission of the foundation is the betterment of Ashtabula County, OH, through the administration of funds consistent with the intent of donors to address the significant needs of Ashtabula County.

Fields of interest: Arts; Education; Recreation; Human services; Religion.

Type of support: Annual campaigns; Building/renovation; Equipment; Land acquisition; Debt reduction; Emergency funds; Program development; Curriculum development; Scholarships—to individuals; Matching/challenge support.

Limitations: Giving limited to Ashtabula County, OH.

Publications: Application guidelines; Informational brochure.

Application information: Application forms and guidelines for scholarship funds available on foundation Web site. Application form required.

Initial approach: Proposal
Copies of proposal: 12
Deadline(s): The 1st Tues. in the following months: Feb. (Education), Apr. (Human Services), June (Arts/Culture/History), Aug. (Religion), Oct. (Community Development and Other), and Dec. (Recreation and Conservation) grants
Board meeting date(s): 2nd Tues. of each month
Final notification: 2 weeks following review

Officers and Trustees:* Thomas D. Anderson,* Pres.; Jerry Brockway,* V.P.; Liz Campbell,* Secy.-Treas.; W.L. Anderson; Roy H. Bean; Cheryle

Chiaramonte; Rick Coblitz; Roger Corlett; William W. Hill; Eleanor A. Jammal; Glen W. Warner; Barbara P. Wiese.

Number of staff: 1 part-time support.

EIN: 346538130

7535
The Austin Memorial Foundation ◇

251 W. Garfield Rd., Ste. 230
Aurora, OH 44202-8856
Contact: Donald G. Austin, Jr., Pres.

Incorporated in 1961 in OH.

Donor: Members of the Austin family.

Foundation type: Independent foundation.

Financial data (yr. ended 12/31/05): Assets, $12,567,010 (M); expenditures, $667,431; qualifying distributions, $603,852; giving activities include $514,249 for 41 grants (high: $76,000; low: $500).

Fields of interest: Education, fund raising/fund distribution; Environment; Human services; Religion.

Type of support: Seed money; Matching/challenge support; General/operating support; Continuing support; Capital campaigns; Building/renovation.

Limitations: Applications not accepted. Giving limited to the U.S. No support for political organizations. No grants to individuals.

Application information: Contributes only to pre-selected organizations. Unsolicited requests for funds not accepted.

Board meeting date(s): Semiannually

Officers and Trustees:* Donald G. Austin, Jr.,* Pres.; Paul W. Austin, Secy.; David A. Rodgers,* Treas.; James W. Austin; Samuel H. Austin; Stewart G. Austin, Sr.; Stewart G. Austin, Jr.; Thomas G. Austin; Winifred N. Austin; Sarah R. Cole; Gretchen Cole-Corona; Ann R. Loeffler; Ellen Austin Smith.

Number of staff: 1 part-time professional.

EIN: 346528879

7536
Austin-Bailey Health and Wellness Foundation

2719 Fulton Dr. N.W., Ste. D
Canton, OH 44718 (330) 580-2380
Contact: Don A. Sultzbach, Exec. Dir.
FAX: (330) 580-2381; E-mail: abfdn@sbcglobal.net;
URL: http://foundationcenter.org/grantmaker/austinbailey/

Established in 1996 in OH.

Foundation type: Independent foundation.

Financial data (yr. ended 6/30/06): Assets, $9,137,554 (M); expenditures, $579,800; qualifying distributions, $416,502; giving activities include $415,702 for 31 grants (high: $80,000; low: $5,000), and $800 for 4 employee matching gifts.

Purpose and activities: The purpose of the foundation is to support programs that promote the physical and mental well-being of citizens of Holmes, Stark, Tuscarawas and Wayne counties, OH. The foundation emphasizes healthcare affordability concerns of people who are uninsured and underinsured, economically disadvantaged, children, single parents and the aging. The foundation also advocates programs that speak to the mental health needs of individuals and families.

Fields of interest: Dental care; Public health; Health care, insurance; Health care; Mental health/crisis services; Human services; Family services.

Type of support: General/operating support; Continuing support; Equipment; Emergency funds; Program development; Conferences/seminars; Seed money; Curriculum development; Scholarship funds; Employee matching gifts; Matching/challenge support.

Limitations: Giving primarily in Holmes, Stark, Tuscarawas, and Wayne counties, OH. No support for religious organizations for overtly religious purposes. No grants to annual and capital campaigns, membership drives, fundraising, advertising, or endowment funds.

Publications: Application guidelines; Financial statement; Grants list; Informational brochure; Informational brochure (including application guidelines).

Application information: Call foundation to request grant guidelines. Application form required.

Initial approach: Telephone or letter
Copies of proposal: 6
Deadline(s): June 30 and Dec. 30
Board meeting date(s): 2nd Thurs. in Mar., June, Sept., and Dec.
Final notification: 14 days after board meeting in Mar. and Sept.

Officers and Trustees:* John L. Muhlbach, Jr.,* Chair.; Charles R. Conklin, D.O.*, Vice-Chair.; Virginia Neutzling,* Secy.; Peter Kopko,* Treas.; Don A. Sultzbach, Exec. Dir.; William G. Bittle, Ph.D.; Hon. James S. Gwin; Stephen S. Higley; Candace Lautenschleger; Elton D. Lehman, D.O.; Daniel N. Moretta, D.O.; Frederick W. Rohrig.

Number of staff: 2 part-time professional; 1 part-time support.

EIN: 341845584

Selected grants: The following grants were reported in 2005.

$80,000 to Mercy Medical Center, Canton, OH. To assist with start-up of dental residency program for two dental examination/treatment rooms.

$75,000 to Stark Prescription Assistance Network, Canton, OH. For program support.

$30,000 to Wayne, County of, Department of Health, Wooster, OH. For operating support.

$12,000 to Doughty View Midwifery Center, Millersburg, OH. To purchase a GSI Audio Screener for hearing screening for newborns.

7537
The Mary E. Babcock Foundation ◇ ☆

c/o Jean Wright
9889 Hollow Rd.
Pataskala, OH 43062
Application address: c/o Thomas E. Gibson, 1650 Lake Shore Dr., Ste. 285, Columbus, OH 43204

Established in OH.

Donor: Mary Babcock†.

Foundation type: Independent foundation.

Financial data (yr. ended 3/31/06): Assets, $1,715,702 (M); expenditures, $1,017,579; qualifying distributions, $1,006,188; giving activities include $1,006,188 for grants.

Fields of interest: Libraries (public); Education; Community development; Government/public administration.

Type of support: Building/renovation.

Limitations: Giving primarily in the Johnstown, OH, area.

Application information: Application form not required.
Initial approach: Letter
Deadline(s): None
Officers: Jean Wright, Pres.; Stuart Parsons, V.P.; Mary C. Thomas, Secy.; Thomas E. Gibson, Treas.
Directors: Richard T. Clark; Sharon Johnson; Allen Reeves; Richard Scovell; Steven H. Williams.
EIN: 311170451

7538
Bachman Foundation ✧
7824 Laurel Ave.
Cincinnati, OH 45253
Contact: Nathan D. Bachman, Pres.

Established in 2002 in OH.
Donor: Nathan D. Bachman.
Foundation type: Independent foundation.
Financial data (yr. ended 12/31/05): Assets, $2,381,147 (M); gifts received, $1,000,000; expenditures, $331,242; qualifying distributions, $331,242; giving activities include $330,985 for 78 grants (high: $42,000; low: $100).
Purpose and activities: Scholarship awards paid directly to the college or university of graduating high school students with a GPA of 3.0 or better, attending a four-year college; must choose a college major approved by Bachman Foundation.
Fields of interest: Higher education.
Type of support: Scholarship funds.
Limitations: Giving primarily in OH.
Application information: Application form required.
Initial approach: Letter
Deadline(s): None
Officers and Directors:* Nathan D. Bachman,* Pres.; Lynda A. Bachman,* V.P.; Edward A. Bachman, Secy.-Treas.
EIN: 010712009
Selected grants: The following grants were reported in 2005.
$40,000 to Saint Xavier High School, Cincinnati, OH.
$18,000 to Sun Valley Adaptive Sports, Ketchum, ID.
$10,000 to George Mason University Foundation, Fairfax, VA.
$10,000 to Heritage Foundation, DC.
$10,000 to Indian Hill Church, Cincinnati, OH.
$6,000 to Saint Thomas Episcopal Church, Ketchum, ID.
$5,000 to Sun Valley Summer Symphony, Sun Valley, ID.
$1,000 to Friends of Idaho Public Television, Pocatello, ID.
$1,000 to Tax Foundation, DC.
$500 to Princeton University, Princeton, NJ.

7539
Barberton Community Foundation
460 W. Paige Ave.
Barberton, OH 44203 (330) 745-5995
Contact: Thomas L. Harnden, Exec. Dir.; Carl D. Bako, Dir., Comms.
FAX: (330) 745-3990; E-mail: cbako@bcfcharity.org;
Additional E-mail: tharden@bcfcharity.org;
URL: http://www.bcfcharity.org

Established in 1996 in OH; converted from the sale of Barberton Citizens Hospital to Quorum Health Group, Inc.

Foundation type: Community foundation.
Financial data (yr. ended 12/31/05): Assets, $100,944,021 (M); gifts received, $287,476; expenditures, $3,578,404; giving activities include $2,799,557 for 63 grants (high: $1,698,587; low: $309).
Purpose and activities: The foundation supports projects that benefit the citizens of Barberton, OH.
Fields of interest: Education; Health organizations, association; Recreation; Urban/community development.
Type of support: Capital campaigns; Building/renovation; Equipment; Land acquisition; Program development; Conferences/seminars; Curriculum development; Scholarship funds; Technical assistance; Program-related investments/loans; Matching/challenge support.
Limitations: Giving limited to Barberton, OH. No support for religious organizations for religious purposes. No grants to individuals (except for scholarships), or for debt reduction, deficits or previous obligations, annual fundraising drives, ongoing operational expenses, sabbatical leaves or scholarly research, or for endowments housed at institutions other than the foundation.
Publications: Application guidelines; Annual report; Informational brochure (including application guidelines); Newsletter; Quarterly report.
Application information: Visit foundation Web site for application forms and additional guidelines per grant type; number of copies vary per grant type. The Small Grants program accepts applications for grants of up to $1,000. Application form required.
Initial approach: Letter or telephone
Copies of proposal: 10
Deadline(s): Jan. 3, Apr. 3, July 3, and Oct. 2 for quarterly program; last Fri. of each month for Small Grants program
Board meeting date(s): 3rd Thurs. of each month
Final notification: Within 3 to 4 weeks for Small Grants program; within 7 to 8 weeks for quarterly grants
Officers and Trustees:* Thomas D. Doak,* Chair.; Diane E. McConnell,* Vice-Chair.; Phillip H. Canfora,* Secy.; Dennis Liddle, Jr.,* Treas.; Thomas L. Harnden, Exec. Dir.; Ronald J. Burkhard, Cont.; Thomas Anders; Larry Bidlingmeyer; Beth Gagnon; Robert J. Genet; Thomas Gough; Randy Hart; Lois Matney; Bruce May; Scott McQuaide; Jerome Pecko; Richard R. Wiley.
Number of staff: 4 full-time professional; 1 part-time support.
EIN: 341846432
Selected grants: The following grants were reported in 2004.
$2,341,082 to Barberton City Schools, Barberton, OH. 2 grants: $27,000 (For Decker Grant Development Program), $2,314,082.
$333,083 to Barberton, City of, Barberton, OH. 5 grants: $20,000 (For sidewalk replacement program), $60,000 (For Barberton Comprehensive Plan), $75,000 (For Project Impact), $128,083 (For Senior Center Interest payment), $50,000 (For military honor roll renovation).
$100,000 to Barberton Community Health Clinic, Barberton, OH.
$75,000 to Barberton Community Development Corporation, Barberton, OH. For program support.
$20,000 to United Way of Summit County, Akron, OH. For direct assistance in barberton.

7540
The John C. Bates Foundation ✧
2401 Front St.
Toledo, OH 43605

Established in 1993 in OH.
Donors: Heidtman Steel Products, Inc.; Centaur, Inc.; HS Processing, LP.
Foundation type: Company-sponsored foundation.
Financial data (yr. ended 3/31/06): Assets, $3,662 (M); gifts received, $400,000; expenditures, $397,620; qualifying distributions, $390,882; giving activities include $390,882 for 18 grants (high: $251,500; low: $200).
Purpose and activities: The foundation supports zoological societies, community foundations, and organizations involved with education, health, human services, and Christianity.
Fields of interest: Elementary/secondary education; Higher education; Education; Zoos/zoological societies; Health care; Cancer; Family services; Human services; Foundations (community); Christian agencies & churches.
Type of support: Capital campaigns; Program development; Scholarship funds.
Limitations: Applications not accepted. Giving primarily in IN, MI, and OH. No grants to individuals.
Application information: Contributes only to pre-selected organizations.
Officers and Trustees:* Darlene B. Dotson,* Pres.; John M. Carey,* Secy.; Mark E. Ridenour,* Treas.; Sarah J. Bates; Debra A. Shinkle.
EIN: 341749094

7541
The Beaverson Foundation ✧
1474 Ramblewood Dr.
Wooster, OH 44691-3038

Established in 1992 in OH.
Donor: Audrey L. Beaverson.
Foundation type: Independent foundation.
Financial data (yr. ended 9/30/05): Assets, $403,397 (M); gifts received, $70,000; expenditures, $346,034; qualifying distributions, $339,345; giving activities include $339,345 for 15 grants (high: $100,000; low: $1,150).
Fields of interest: Arts; Elementary school/education; Higher education; Hospitals (general); Disasters, fire prevention/control; Recreation, parks/playgrounds; Human services; Children/youth, services; Residential/custodial care, hospices; Protestant agencies & churches.
Type of support: Capital campaigns.
Limitations: Applications not accepted. Giving primarily in Wayne County, OH. No grants to individuals.
Application information: Contributes only to pre-selected organizations.
Officers: Audrey L. Beaverson, Chair.; Robert E. Mapes, V.P.; John C. Johnston III, Secy.
EIN: 341722868

7542
The Molly Bee Fund ✧
c/o Thomas F. Allen
20325 Center Ridge Rd., Ste. 629
Rocky River, OH 44116-3554

Established in 1995 in OH.
Donor: Elizabeth B. Blossom.

Foundation type: Independent foundation.
Financial data (yr. ended 12/31/05): Assets, $4,893,546 (M); expenditures, $468,135; qualifying distributions, $439,168; giving activities include $430,000 for 11 grants (high: $100,000; low: $10,000).
Purpose and activities: Giving primarily for the arts as well as for education, human services, a nature center, and a wheelchair sports fund.
Fields of interest: Arts, association; Performing arts; Performing arts, ballet; Performing arts, music; Environment, natural resources; Recreation; Human services.
Type of support: General/operating support; Capital campaigns; Building/renovation; Equipment; Endowments; Program-related investments/loans.
Limitations: Applications not accepted. Giving primarily in Palm Beach and West Palm Beach, FL, Cleveland, OH, and Charleston, SC. No grants to individuals.
Application information: Contributes only to pre-selected organizations. Unsolicited requests for funds not accepted.
Officers and Trustees: Mary E. Gale,* Pres.; Benjamin Gale,* V.P.; Thomas F. Allen, Secy.-Treas.; Thomas H. Gale; Kevin R. Kneisly.
EIN: 341812998

7543
The Beerman Foundation, Inc. ◇

11 W. Monument Bldg., 8th Fl.
Dayton, OH 45402
Contact: William S. Weprin, Pres.

Incorporated in 1945 in OH.
Donors: Arthur Beerman†; Jessie Beerman.
Foundation type: Independent foundation.
Financial data (yr. ended 12/31/04): Assets, $4,918,029 (M); gifts received, $455; expenditures, $1,205,569; qualifying distributions, $963,989; giving activities include $867,375 for 52 grants (high: $166,666; low: $40), and $26,440 for foundation-administered programs.
Purpose and activities: Giving primarily for Jewish organizations, education, and the economically disadvantaged.
Fields of interest: Elementary/secondary education; Higher education; Health organizations; Human services; Jewish federated giving programs; Jewish agencies & temples; Economically disadvantaged.
Type of support: General/operating support; Building/renovation.
Limitations: Giving primarily in the Dayton, OH, area. No grants to individuals.
Publications: Annual report.
Application information:
Initial approach: Letter
Deadline(s): None
Officers: William S. Weprin, Pres.; Barbara B. Weprin, V.P.; Eric S. Hungerford, Secy.; Larry McCord, Treas.
EIN: 316024369

7544
The Bonne Bell Foundation ◇

(formerly The J. G. Bell Foundation)
18519 Detroit Ave.
Lakewood, OH 44107 (216) 221-0800

Established in 1969 in OH.

Donors: Jess A. Bell†; Bonne Bell, Inc.
Foundation type: Independent foundation.
Financial data (yr. ended 6/30/05): Assets, $1,477,827 (M); gifts received, $352,490; expenditures, $336,747; qualifying distributions, $327,762; giving activities include $326,985 for 81 grants (high: $52,150; low: $175).
Fields of interest: Education; Health organizations, association; Medical research, institute; Recreation; Salvation Army; Children/youth, services; Roman Catholic agencies & churches.
Limitations: Giving primarily in OH. No grants to individuals.
Application information:
Initial approach: Letter
Deadline(s): None
Trustees: Jess A. Bell; Julianna Bell.
EIN: 341018779

7545
The Louis and Sandra Berkman Foundation ◇

330 N. 7th St.
P.O. Box 576
Steubenville, OH 43952-5576
Application address: c/o John R. Koren, P.O. Box 820, Steubenville, OH 43952, tel.: (740) 283-3722

Incorporated in 1952 in OH.
Donors: Louis Berkman†; Mrs. Louis Berkman; The Louis Berkman Co.; Follansbee Steel Corp.
Foundation type: Independent foundation.
Financial data (yr. ended 12/31/05): Assets, $13,232,504 (M); expenditures, $680,165; qualifying distributions, $680,165; giving activities include $679,575 for 60 grants (high: $122,200; low: $50).
Purpose and activities: Giving primarily for higher education and health care.
Fields of interest: Higher education; Hospitals (general); Health organizations, association; Cancer; Medical research, institute; Human services; Jewish federated giving programs; Christian agencies & churches; Jewish agencies & temples.
Limitations: Giving primarily in OH and PA. No grants to individuals.
Application information:
Initial approach: Proposal
Deadline(s): July 1 of year prior to year of grant
Officers and Trustees: Louis Berkman,* Pres. and Treas.; Robert A. Paul,* V.P.; Linda L. Pirkle,* Secy.; Donna Berkman Paul.
EIN: 346526694

7546
Berlin Family Foundation, Inc. ◇

(formerly Berlin Family Charitable Corporation)
c/o Judi Roman
1795 Brookwood Dr.
Akron, OH 44313

Established in 1990 in FL and OH.
Foundation type: Independent foundation.
Financial data (yr. ended 10/31/05): Assets, $5,449,337 (M); gifts received, $1,074,543; expenditures, $378,047; qualifying distributions, $371,450; giving activities include $370,700 for 36 grants (high: $160,000; low: $50).
Purpose and activities: Giving for Jewish organizations and health associations.

Fields of interest: Health organizations, association; Medical research, institute; Jewish agencies & temples.
Limitations: Applications not accepted. Giving primarily in Miami, FL, and Akron and Cleveland, OH. No grants to individuals.
Application information: Unsolicited requests for funds not accepted.
Officers: Madeline Berlin, Pres.; Robin Berlin Kane, V.P.
EIN: 650230453

7547
Berry Family Foundation ◇

(formerly Loren M. Berry Foundation)
3055 Kettering Blvd., Ste. 418
Dayton, OH 45439
Contact: William T. Lincoln, Treas.

Incorporated in 1960 in OH.
Donors: Loren M. Berry†; George W. Berry.
Foundation type: Independent foundation.
Financial data (yr. ended 12/31/05): Assets, $19,959,737 (M); gifts received, $2,000,000; expenditures, $1,008,090; qualifying distributions, $883,500; giving activities include $845,500 for 71 grants (high: $50,000; low: $150).
Purpose and activities: Giving primarily for education.
Fields of interest: Arts; Higher education; Education; Hospitals (general); Health organizations, association; Human services; Public policy, research.
Limitations: Applications not accepted. Giving primarily in Dayton, OH; giving on a national basis for education. No grants to individuals, or for operating budgets.
Application information: Unsolicited requests for funds not accepted.
Board meeting date(s): June and Dec.
Officers and Trustees: John W. Berry, Jr.,* Pres.; William T. Lincoln,* Treas.; Charles D. Berry; David L. Berry; George W. Berry; Martha B. Fraim; William L. Fraim; Elizabeth B. Gray; Leland W. Henry; James O. Payne.
EIN: 316026144

7548
Bicknell Fund

c/o Advisory Svcs., Inc.
1422 Euclid Ave., Ste. 1010
Cleveland, OH 44115-2078 (216) 363-6482
Contact: Robert G. Acklin, Secy.-Treas.
FAX: (216) 363-6488; URL: http://foundationcenter.org/grantmaker/bicknellfund

Incorporated in 1949 in OH.
Donors: Kate H. Bicknell†; Warren Bicknell, Jr.†; Warren Bicknell III; Kate B. Kirkham.
Foundation type: Independent foundation.
Financial data (yr. ended 12/31/05): Assets, $8,275,745 (M); expenditures, $495,873; qualifying distributions, $387,495; giving activities include $374,149 for 53 grants (high: $50,000; low: $148).
Purpose and activities: The Bicknell Fund was formed for the purpose of promoting the well-being of mankind, and to that end to engage in such forms of charitable, benevolent, educational, scientific and research work as from time to time shall seem expedient to the trustees. Main areas of focus

include social and human services to help the needy and homeless in the Cleveland, OH, area, and education.

Fields of interest: Elementary/secondary education; Secondary school/education; Education, special; Higher education; Health care; Mental health/crisis services; Youth development, adult & child programs; Human services; Children/youth, services; Child development, services; Family services.

Type of support: Annual campaigns; Capital campaigns; Building/renovation; Program development; Scholarship funds.

Limitations: Giving primarily in the greater Cleveland, OH, area. No grants to individuals; or for endowments, or multi-year pledges; no loans.

Publications: Application guidelines.

Application information: Multi-year grants not awarded. Application guidelines are available on foundation Web site. Application form not required.

> *Initial approach:* Proposal; questionnaire available on foundation Web site. Proposals sent by fax or E-mail will not be accepted
> *Copies of proposal:* 1
> *Deadline(s):* Submit proposal prior to Apr. 1 or Sept. 1
> *Board meeting date(s):* June and Nov.
> *Final notification:* 4 weeks following board meeting

Officers and Trustees:* Kate B. Luzius,* Pres.; Warren Bicknell III,* V.P.; Robert G. Acklin, Secy.-Treas.; Wendy H. Bicknell; Samantha K. Crowley; W. Gates Kirkham; Henry L. Meyer III; Henry E. Seibert; Alexander S. Taylor II.

EIN: 346513799

7549

The William Bingham Foundation

20325 Center Ridge Rd., Ste. 629
Rocky River, OH   44116-3554   (440) 331-6350
Contact: Laura H. Gilbertson, Dir.
E-mail: info@WBinghamFoundation.org; URL: http://foundationcenter.org/grantmaker/bingham/

Incorporated in 1955 in OH.

Donor: Elizabeth B. Blossom†.

Foundation type: Independent foundation.

Financial data (yr. ended 12/31/05): Assets, $19,687,775 (M); gifts received, $696,223; expenditures, $890,160; qualifying distributions, $696,223; giving activities include $561,500 for 10 grants (high: $400,000; low: $1,000).

Purpose and activities: The foundation furthers the philanthropic intent of its founder, Elizabeth Bingham Blossom. It supports organizations in the fields of education, science, health and human services, and the arts. It works for a world that is environmentally self-sustaining; seeks to strengthen civil society and its institutions; educates family members and others in the values and practice of philanthropy, community service, and stewardship; and it seeks to build a sense of community. In 2007 the foundation will be considering only those grant proposals from organizations providing Adult Day Care services to Seniors in Southern New England.

Fields of interest: Education; Environment; Aging.

Type of support: General/operating support; Continuing support; Management development/capacity building; Capital campaigns; Building/renovation; Equipment; Endowments; Program development; Conferences/seminars; Curriculum development; Technical assistance; Matching/challenge support.

Limitations: Giving primarily to organizations in communities in which the foundation trustees reside. No support for foreign organizations. No grants to individuals; no loans.

Publications: Application guidelines; Financial statement; Grants list.

Application information: Application form available on foundation Web site. Use is strongly encouraged by the foundation. Application form required.

> *Initial approach:* On-line application form or letter of inquiry (2 pages or less). Complete proposals will not be accepted
> *Copies of proposal:* 1
> *Deadline(s):* May 31 (for adult daycare programs in Southern New England)
> *Board meeting date(s):* Usually Feb. and Aug.

Officers and Trustees:* C. Bingham Blossom,* Pres.; Virginia O. Blossom,* V.P.; Thomas F. Allen, Secy.; C. Perry Blossom,* Treas.; David B. Blossom; Jonathan B. Blossom; Laurel Blossom; Robin Dunn Blossom; Rebecca B. Kovacik; Elizabeth B. Meers.

Director: Laura H. Gilbertson.

Number of staff: 1 full-time professional.

EIN: 346513791

Selected grants: The following grants were reported in 2006.

$75,000 to Pawtucket Armory Association, Pawtucket, RI. Toward renovation of regional arts center.

$25,000 to Cleveland Sight Center, Cleveland, OH. For Bright Futures program.

$25,000 to Cleveland Zoological Society, Cleveland, OH. For African Elephant Crossing capital campaign.

$25,000 to Hawken School, Cleveland, OH. Toward construction of new middle school.

$25,000 to McKee Botanical Garden, Vero Beach, FL. For general operating support.

$25,000 to National Association of College and University Attorneys, DC. For study of preventive law training programs at colleges and universities.

$25,000 to Rhode Islanders Sponsoring Education (RISE), Providence, RI. For mentoring program.

$25,000 to Spoleto Festival USA, Charleston, SC. For education and outreach during 2006 Festival.

$25,000 to Western Reserve Land Conservancy, Novelty, OH. For capacity building activities.

$15,000 to Sustainability Institute, North Charleston, SC. For general operating support.

7550

Isadore Binzer Fund ✧

c/o KeyBank N.A.
P.O. Box 10099
Toledo, OH   43699-0099

Established in 2002 in OH.

Foundation type: Independent foundation.

Financial data (yr. ended 12/31/05): Assets, $8,855,057 (M); expenditures, $504,838; qualifying distributions, $462,175; giving activities include $444,694 for 10 grants (high: $88,939; low: $22,235).

Fields of interest: Human services; Jewish federated giving programs; Jewish agencies & temples.

Limitations: Applications not accepted. Giving primarily in Toledo, OH; some funding also in New York, NY. No grants to individuals.

Application information: Contributes only to pre-selected organizations.

Trustee: KeyBank N.A.

EIN: 020534833

Selected grants: The following grants were reported in 2003.

$82,445 to United Jewish Council of Greater Toledo, Sylvania, OH. For general support.

$82,444 to Anti-Defamation League of Bnai Brith, New York, NY. For general support.

$41,222 to Bellefaire Jewish Childrens Bureau, Shaker Heights, OH. For general support.

$41,222 to Hadassah, The Womens Zionist Organization of America, New York, NY. For general support.

$41,222 to Jewish Family Service of Toledo, Sylvania, OH. For general support.

$41,222 to Jewish Senior Services of Toledo, Toledo, OH. For general support.

$20,611 to Toledo Board of Jewish Education, Sylvania, OH. For general support.

$20,611 to Toledo Community Foundation, Toledo, OH. For general support.

$20,611 to Toledo Orchestra Association, Toledo, OH. For general support.

$20,611 to Toledo Zoological Society, Toledo, OH. For general support.

7551

Elizabeth S. Black Charitable Trust ✧ ☆

c/o National City Bank
P.O. Box 94651
Cleveland, OH   44101-4651
Application address: c/o Steven P. Kosak, P.O. Box 374, Oil City, PA 16301, tel.: (814) 677-5085

Foundation type: Independent foundation.

Financial data (yr. ended 10/31/04): Assets, $9,021,064 (M); expenditures, $603,734; qualifying distributions, $575,941; giving activities include $530,156 for 86 grants (high: $85,264; low: $400).

Fields of interest: Education, services; Human services.

Type of support: General/operating support.

Limitations: Giving limited in and around Oil City, PA. No grants to individuals.

Application information:

> *Initial approach:* Letter
> *Deadline(s):* None

Trustee: National City Bank.

EIN: 043731472

7552

Walter W. Born Foundation ✧ ☆

c/o FirstMerit Bank, N.A.
106 S. Main St., Ste. 1600
Akron, OH   44308
Application address: c/o Mark Mosley, V.P. and Client Advisor, FirstMerit Bank, N.A., 121 S. Main St, Akron, Oh 44308, tel.: (330) 384-7314

Established in 2005 in OH.

Donor: Walter W. Born Trust.

Foundation type: Independent foundation.

Financial data (yr. ended 4/30/06): Assets, $6,170,095 (M); expenditures, $387,951; qualifying distributions, $317,000; giving activities include $317,000 for grants.

Purpose and activities: Giving primarily to hospitals that demonstrate financial need.

Fields of interest: Hospitals (specialty); Human services; Children/youth, services.

Limitations: Giving primarily in Akron, Canton, and Cleveland, OH.
Application information:
  Initial approach: Letter
  Deadline(s): None
Trustee: FirstMerit Bank, N.A.
EIN: 550869606

7553
The Sam and Rachel Boymel
Foundation ◇
P.O. Box 477, Mail Location: 4928
Hamilton, OH 45012-0477
Application address: c/o Nancy Wenning, High St. and Journal Sq., Hamilton, OH 45011, tel.: (513) 867-5133

Established in 1997 in OH.
Donors: Rachel Boymel; Samuel Boymel.
Foundation type: Independent foundation.
Financial data (yr. ended 12/31/05): Assets, $2,840,095 (M); gifts received, $300,000; expenditures, $356,271; qualifying distributions, $335,500; giving activities include $335,500 for 11 grants (high: $100,000; low: $5,000).
Purpose and activities: Giving primarily to Jewish agencies, temples, and schools.
Fields of interest: Education; Human services; Jewish federated giving programs; Jewish agencies & temples.
Limitations: Giving primarily in Cincinnati, OH.
Application information:
  Initial approach: Proposal
  Deadline(s): None
Trustees: Rachel Boymel; Samuel Boymel; Steven Boymel; Gidon Eldad; Fay Sosna.
EIN: 311578615

7554
Brennan Family Foundation
1200 Sunset View Dr.
Akron, OH 44313 (330) 864-5528
Contact: Ann Brennan, Pres.
E-mail: annamer@aol.com

Established in 1995 in OH.
Donors: David L. Brennan; Mrs. David L. Brennan; Hayes Industrial Brake, Inc.; White Hat Management.
Foundation type: Independent foundation.
Financial data (yr. ended 12/31/04): Assets, $3,625,456 (M); gifts received, $500,000; expenditures, $1,458,204; qualifying distributions, $1,419,250; giving activities include $1,419,250 for 82 grants (high: $350,000; low: $500).
Purpose and activities: Giving primarily for the arts, education, and health and human services.
Fields of interest: Arts; Elementary/secondary education; Higher education; Health care; Diabetes; Children/youth, services; Women, centers/services; Community development; Religion.
Type of support: General/operating support; Continuing support; Annual campaigns; Capital campaigns; Building/renovation; Endowments; Scholarship funds.
Limitations: Giving primarily in northeastern OH, with emphasis on Summit County. No grants to individuals.
Application information: Application form not required.
  Initial approach: Letter outlining project

Copies of proposal: 1
Deadline(s): None
Board meeting date(s): No formal meetings
Officers: Ann Brennan, Pres.; David L. Brennan, V.P.; Nancy Brennan, Secy.; Joseph R. Weber, Treas.
EIN: 341812978
Selected grants: The following grants were reported in 2004.
$350,000 to Summa Health System Foundation, Akron, OH.
$55,000 to United Way.
$50,000 to Akron Civic Theater, Akron, OH.
$30,000 to Catholic Charities.
$25,000 to Hiram College, Hiram, OH.
$20,000 to United Way Endowment Fund, AL.
$12,500 to Stillman College, Tuscaloosa, AL.
$5,000 to American Red Cross.
$5,000 to Case Western Reserve University, Cleveland, OH.
$2,000 to Ohio Arts Foundation, Columbus, OH.

7555
Brentwood Foundation
c/o Anthea R. Daniels
1400 McDonald Investment Ctr.
800 Superior Ave.
Cleveland, OH 44114-2688 (330) 334-9294
Contact: Terri Kovach, Dir.
FAX: (330) 334-9219; *E-mail:* terriK@apk.net; Application address: 3593 Medina Rd., PMB 303, Medina, OH 44256; URL: http:// www.brentwood-foundation.org/

Established in 1994 in OH; converted following the merger of Brentwood Hospital, which was an osteopathic hospital, with Meridia Suburban Hospital.
Foundation type: Independent foundation.
Financial data (yr. ended 12/31/05): Assets, $23,486,318 (M); gifts received, $11,970; expenditures, $827,761; qualifying distributions, $620,546; giving activities include $497,500 for 6 grants (high: $360,000; low: $2,500).
Purpose and activities: Giving to enhance osteopathic medicine, research and patient care by: 1) providing educational opportunities designed to strengthen the capabilities of students and practitioners, (including interns and residents), 2) supporting research efforts which focus upon the acquisition, advancement, and dissemination of knowledge in this field, 3) educating the public about osteopathic services and trends, and 4) initiating activities designed to advance and improve patient care in osteopathic hospitals and in the community.
Fields of interest: Medical school/education; Hospitals (general).
Type of support: General/operating support; Continuing support; Equipment; Program development; Conferences/seminars; Curriculum development; Research; Consulting services; Matching/challenge support.
Limitations: Giving primarily to northeastern OH, but the foundation does some collaborations statewide, in OH as well as on a national basis. No support for activities which are in direct competition with the osteopathic education and medical activities being conducted within the Cleveland Clinic Health System. No grants to individuals.
Publications: Application guidelines; Annual report; Annual report (including application guidelines); Financial statement; Grants list; Informational brochure (including application guidelines).

Application information: Grant requests submitted from South Pointe Hospital and other hospitals or programs within the Cleveland Clinic Health System must follow South Pointe Hospital's grant application procedures. See Web site for application guidelines. Application form required.
  Initial approach: Letter requesting guidelines
  Copies of proposal: 2
  Deadline(s): Apr. 1 or Sept. 1 (If a deadline date falls on a weekend, the following Mon. will be considered the deadline date)
  Board meeting date(s): June and Nov.
Officers and Trustees:* Roger F. Classen, D.O.*, Chair.; Anthea R. Daniels,* Secy.; Parry Keller,* Treas.; Richard Barone; Robert M. Biggar; Dennis J. Bodziony; Vincent F. DeCrane; Thomas J. Ebner, D.O.; Raymond J. Grabow; George Kappos, Jr.*; Michael F. Killeen; David Krahe, D.O.; Gregory P. Kurtz; Michael McClain; Michael Merriman; Lucille Reed Narducci; Wayne Sevier, D.O.; Jeffrey A. Stanley, D.O.
Number of staff: 1 full-time professional.
EIN: 341783117
Selected grants: The following grants were reported in 2004.
$810,530 to South Pointe Hospital, Warrensville Heights, OH. 4 grants: $10,000, $52,250, $30,280, $718,000
$100,000 to Osteopathic Heritage Foundation, Columbus, OH. For OMT Pneumonia research project.
$25,000 to Cleveland Academy of Osteopathic Medicine, Beachwood, OH.
$10,000 to Cleveland Foundation, Cleveland, OH.
$6,000 to Ohio University, College of Osteopathic Medicine, Athens, OH.

7556
Britton Fund ◇
1422 Euclid Ave., Ste. 1010
Cleveland, OH 44115-2078 (216) 363-6489
Contact: Nick Valentino, Treas.

Incorporated in 1952 in OH.
Donors: Gertrude H. Britton†; Charles S. Britton II†; Brigham Britton†.
Foundation type: Independent foundation.
Financial data (yr. ended 12/31/05): Assets, $22,674,943 (M); expenditures, $1,420,708; qualifying distributions, $1,284,159; giving activities include $1,258,640 for 37 grants (high: $265,200; low: $2,000).
Purpose and activities: Giving primarily for health and human services; support also for the arts and education.
Fields of interest: Museums (art); Museums (natural history); Arts; Education, research; Secondary school/education; Higher education; Hospitals (general); Reproductive health, family planning; Health care; Medical research, institute; Alzheimer's disease research; Food services; Human services; Children/youth, services; Women, centers/services; Disabilities, people with; Women.
Type of support: General/operating support; Continuing support; Annual campaigns; Endowments; Emergency funds; Scholarship funds; Research.
Limitations: Giving primarily in the greater Cleveland, OH area, including Cuyahoga, Geauga and Lake counties. No grants to individuals.
Publications: Annual report.
Application information: Funds substantially committed. Application form not required.

Initial approach: Letter
Copies of proposal: 1
Deadline(s): May 1 and Nov. 1
Board meeting date(s): May and Nov.
Officers and Trustees:* Lynda R. Britton,* Pres.;
Terence B. Britton,* V.P.; Timothy C. Britton,* V.P.;
Jennifer Davis, Secy.; Nick Valentino, Treas.
EIN: 346513616
Selected grants: The following grants were reported
in 2005.
$200,000 to Planned Parenthood of Greater
   Cleveland, Cleveland, OH.
$50,000 to American Red Cross.
$30,000 to Ohio Foundation of Independent
   Colleges, Columbus, OH.
$27,000 to Salvation Army.
$25,000 to Cleveland Orchestra, Cleveland, OH.
$20,000 to CityMusic Cleveland, Cleveland Heights,
   OH.
$11,000 to Playhouse Square Center, Cleveland,
   OH.
$10,000 to Cleveland Hearing and Speech Center,
   Cleveland, OH.
$10,000 to Cleveland Scholarship Programs,
   Cleveland, OH.
$10,000 to Harbor Heritage Society, Cleveland, OH.

7557
Broussard Charitable Foundation Trust ✧
c/o Fifth Third Bank, Trust Tax Dept.
38 Fountain Sq. Plz., MD 1COM31
Cincinnati, OH   45263

Established in 1996 in IN.
Donor: Jerome T. Broussard.
Foundation type: Independent foundation.
Financial data (yr. ended 12/31/04): Assets,
$7,527,236 (M); gifts received, $32,078;
expenditures, $352,607; qualifying distributions,
$332,300; giving activities include $332,300 for 13
grants (high: $60,000; low: $2,000).
Fields of interest: Business school/education;
Athletics/sports, equestrianism; Human services;
Federated giving programs.
Limitations: Giving primarily in IN.
Trustee: Fifth Third Bank.
EIN: 356634227

7558
Eva L. and Joseph M. Bruening
Foundation ▼
1422 Euclid Ave., Ste. 627
Cleveland, OH   44115-1952   (216) 621-2632
Contact: Janet E. Narten, Exec. Dir.
FAX: (216) 621-8198; URL: http://
www.fmscleveland.com/bruening

Established in 1987 in OH.
Donors: Joseph M. Bruening‡; Eva L. Bruening‡.
Foundation type: Independent foundation.
Financial data (yr. ended 12/31/05): Assets,
$63,690,061 (M); expenditures, $5,495,401;
qualifying distributions, $5,072,204; giving
activities include $4,731,284 for 141 grants (high:
$375,000; low: $400; average: $5,000–$50,000).
Purpose and activities: The foundation's current
focus areas are education and social services with
an emphasis on educating youth, care for the
elderly, disabled, and disadvantaged.
Fields of interest: Education, early childhood
education; Higher education; Education; Crime/

violence prevention, domestic violence; Human
services; Children/youth, services; Aging, centers/
services; Roman Catholic agencies & churches;
Aging; Disabilities, people with; Minorities; Women;
AIDS, people with; Economically disadvantaged;
Homeless.
Type of support: Capital campaigns; Building/
renovation; Equipment; Emergency funds; Program
development; Seed money; Matching/challenge
support.
Limitations: Giving limited to the Cuyahoga, OH. No
support for international funding. No grants to
individuals, or for endowment funds, general
operating budgets, research, symposia or seminars,
mass mailings, or annual campaigns.
Publications: Annual report (including application
guidelines); Financial statement; Grants list.
Application information: The foundation does not
respond to mass mailings or annual campaign
appeals. Application form not required.
   Initial approach: Proposal
   Copies of proposal: 2
   Deadline(s): Mar. 1, July 1, and Oct. 1
   Board meeting date(s): May, Aug., and Dec.
   Final notification: Within several weeks of board
      meeting
Officer: Janet E. Narten, Exec. Dir.
Distribution Committee: Marilyn A. Cunin, Chair.;
Douglas Bannerman; Robert J. Kane; Karen R.
Nestor; Anne B. Springer.
Trustee: KeyBank N.A.
EIN: 341584378
Selected grants: The following grants were reported
in 2005.
$500,000 to Mental Health Services for Homeless
   Persons, Cleveland, OH. To acquire and renovate
   building to serve as headquarters, payable over
   2 years.
$375,000 to Cleveland Central Catholic High
   School, Cleveland, OH. For program and facility
   expansion.
$200,000 to West Side Community House,
   Cleveland, OH. To build new facility, payable over
   2 years.
$100,000 to Care Alliance, Cleveland, OH. For
   renovation of Health Center on St. Clair
   Boulevard.
$50,000 to Cleveland Restoration Society,
   Cleveland, OH. For Sacred Landmarks
   Assistance program, payable over 2 years.
$38,800 to Recovery Resources, Cleveland, OH. For
   start-up support for substance abuse and alcohol
   treatment program for older adult men.
$35,000 to Free Medical Clinic of Greater
   Cleveland, Cleveland, OH. To expand dental
   clinic.
$25,000 to New Avenues to Independence,
   Cleveland, OH. For renovations to create staff
   training room.
$20,000 to Positive Education Program, Cleveland,
   OH. For training and certification of staff for
   Wilson Reading System.
$15,000 to Beck Center for the Cultural Arts,
   Lakewood, OH. For education outreach
   programs.

7559
Bryan Area Foundation, Inc.
102 N. Main St.
P.O. Box 651
Bryan, OH   43506   (419) 633-1156
Contact: Mitchell S. Owens, Exec. Dir.

E-mail: foundation@bryanareafoundation.org;
URL: http://www.bryanareafoundation.org

Established in 1969 in OH.
Foundation type: Community foundation.
Financial data (yr. ended 6/30/06): Assets,
$15,641,589 (M); gifts received, $1,060,021;
expenditures, $1,232,744; giving activities include
$649,014 for grants, and $84,355 for grants to
individuals.
Purpose and activities: The foundation seeks to
enhance the quality of life for all citizens of the
Bryan, OH area, now and for generations to come by
building community endowment, addressing needs
through grantmaking, and serving as a leader,
catalyst and resource for charitable giving. Focus
areas include historic preservation, higher
education, health care, agriculture, recreation,
children and youth services, community
development and religion.
Fields of interest: Historic preservation/historical
societies; Arts; Higher education; Education; Health
care; Agriculture; Recreation, parks/playgrounds;
Recreation; Youth development, adult & child
programs; Aging, centers/services; Community
development; Religion.
Type of support: Capital campaigns; Building/
renovation; Equipment; Program development;
Conferences/seminars; Curriculum development;
Research; Technical assistance; Grants to
individuals; Scholarships—to individuals;
Matching/challenge support.
Limitations: Giving limited to the Bryan, OH, area.
Publications: Application guidelines; Occasional
report.
Application information: Bryan Area Foundation
grant application is required for consideration.
Scholarships are paid directly to universities on
behalf of recipient. Application form required.
   Initial approach: Telephone
   Copies of proposal: 13
   Deadline(s): Call for grant guidelines and
      deadlines
   Board meeting date(s): Quarterly
   Final notification: Jan., May, Aug., and Oct.
Officers and Trustees:* James R. Bard,* Pres.; Julie
A. Brown, V.P.; Michael Shaffer, Secy.; George
Gardner, Treas.; Mitchell S. Owens, Exec. Dir.; Dean
B. Blaser; Jack E. Brace; Philip L. Ennen; Beth
Hollabaugh; Bill Pepple; Carol Rogers; C. Gregory
Spangler; Dean Spangler.
Number of staff: 1 full-time professional; 2 part-time
professional.
EIN: 237041310

7560
Clement and Ann Buenger Foundation ✧
P.O. Box 630858
Cincinnati, OH   45263-0858
Application address: c/o Fifth Third Bank, 38
Fountain Sq. Plz., Cincinnati, OH 45263, tel.: (513)
534-5472

Established in 1988 in OH.
Donors: Clement L. Buenger; Ann M. Buenger.
Foundation type: Independent foundation.
Financial data (yr. ended 9/30/05): Assets,
$18,440,870 (M); expenditures, $1,047,989;
qualifying distributions, $982,718; giving activities
include $981,970 for 9 grants (high: $606,970;
low: $5,000).

Purpose and activities: Giving primarily for secondary and higher education; funding also for human services.

Fields of interest: Performing arts, orchestra (symphony); Secondary school/education; Higher education; Education; Human services.

Limitations: Giving primarily in the greater Cincinnati, OH, area. No support for religious or political purposes. No grants to individuals.

Application information: Application form required.
  Initial approach: Write for application form
  Deadline(s): None

Directors: Ann M. Buenger; Michael K. Keating; William J. Keating; Charles S. Mechem, Jr.

EIN: 311259480

Selected grants: The following grants were reported in 2005.

$606,970 to Xavier University, Cincinnati, OH.

$200,000 to Saint Xavier High School, Cincinnati, OH.

$60,000 to University of Cincinnati, Cincinnati, OH.

$50,000 to Milford Spiritual Center, Milford, OH.

$25,000 to Lighthouse Youth Services, Cincinnati, OH.

$20,000 to Boys Hope Girls Hope, Cincinnati, OH.

$10,000 to Cincinnati Symphony Orchestra, Cincinnati, OH.

$5,000 to American Red Cross, Cincinnati Area Chapter, Cincinnati, OH.

$5,000 to Bethany House Services, Cincinnati, OH.

7561
Burleigh Family Foundation ◈
125 E. Court St., Ste. 950
Cincinnati, OH 45202-1241

Established in 1996 in OH.

Donors: William R. Burleigh; Catherine Anne Husted Burleigh.

Foundation type: Independent foundation.

Financial data (yr. ended 12/31/05): Assets, $4,076,031 (M); gifts received, $1,193,099; expenditures, $1,291,432; qualifying distributions, $1,224,694; giving activities include $1,222,944 for 40 grants (high: $700,000; low: $250).

Purpose and activities: Giving primarily to Roman Catholic organizations, churches, and schools.

Fields of interest: Arts; Education; Human services; Roman Catholic agencies & churches.

Type of support: General/operating support.

Limitations: Applications not accepted. Giving on a national basis, with some emphasis on KY. No grants to individuals.

Application information: Contributes only to pre-selected organizations.

Trustees: Margaret W. Brecount; Anne Catherine Burleigh; Catherine Anne Husted Burleigh; David W. Burleigh; William R. Burleigh.

EIN: 316543121

7562
Robert M. Butler Memorial Foundation ☆
P.O. Box 75020
Cincinnati, OH 45275-0020 (859) 292-5534
Contact: Barbara Baumann Schaefer
FAX: (859) 292-5599;
E-mail: bschaefer@corporex.com

Established in 1979 in OH.

Donor: Corporex Cos., Inc.

Foundation type: Independent foundation.

Financial data (yr. ended 9/30/05): Assets, $3,257,192 (M); gifts received, $243,500; expenditures, $350,775; qualifying distributions, $320,490; giving activities include $320,490 for 53 grants (high: $82,500; low: $50).

Purpose and activities: Giving primarily for the basic needs of the poor in northern KY and in Cincinnati, OH.

Fields of interest: Education; Health organizations, association; Human services; Youth, services; Roman Catholic agencies & churches.

Type of support: General/operating support; Emergency funds; Scholarship funds; Matching/challenge support.

Limitations: Giving limited to northern KY and Cincinnati, OH. No support for private foundations or for veterans', fraternal or labor organizations. No grants for event sponsorships, capital campaigns or endowment funds.

Application information:
  Initial approach: Letter
  Copies of proposal: 7
  Deadline(s): None
  Board meeting date(s): Semiannually
  Final notification: 6 to 9 months

Trustees: Tom Banta; Christa Butler; Kevin Butler; Marty Butler; Mary Sue Butler; William P. Butler; Barbara Schaefer.

EIN: 310981683

Selected grants: The following grants were reported in 2005.

$15,000 to New Perceptions, Edgewood, KY.

$10,000 to Be Concerned, Covington, KY.

$10,000 to Childrens Law Center of Connecticut, Hartford, CT.

$10,000 to Saint Camillus Academy, Corbin, KY.

$5,200 to Diocesan Catholic Childrens Home, Fort Mitchell, KY.

$5,000 to Kids Helping Kids, Cincinnati, OH.

$3,500 to Campbell Lodge Boys Home, Cold Spring, KY.

$3,000 to Family Nurturing Center of Massachusetts, Boston, MA.

$3,000 to Hosea House, Saint Louis, MO.

$1,000 to Literacy Network of Greater Cincinnati, Cincinnati, OH.

7563
The William M. & A. Cafaro Family Foundation ◈
c/o The Cataro Co.
2445 Belmont Ave.
P.O. Box 2186
Youngstown, OH 44504-0186
Contact: Joseph S. Nohra, Tr.

Established in 1998 in OH.

Donors: Anthony M. Cafaro; Alyce Cafaro Charitable Lead Trust; William M. Cafaro Charitable Lead Trust.

Foundation type: Independent foundation.

Financial data (yr. ended 3/31/06): Assets, $17,730,089 (M); gifts received, $1,870,063; expenditures, $734,844; qualifying distributions, $663,218; giving activities include $616,718 for 228 grants (high: $150,000; low: $25; average: $1,000–$5,000), and $46,000 for 13 grants to individuals (high: $5,000; low: $2,000).

Purpose and activities: Giving primarily for education, including college and university scholarships; funding also for health associations, children, youth and social services, and Roman Catholic organizations and churches.

Fields of interest: Elementary/secondary education; Higher education; Health organizations, association; Cancer; Human services; Children/youth, services; Roman Catholic agencies & churches.

Type of support: General/operating support; Scholarships—to individuals.

Limitations: Giving primarily in OH.

Application information:
  Initial approach: Proposal
  Deadline(s): None

Trustees: Anthony M. Cafaro; Flora M. Cafaro; Joseph S. Nohra.

EIN: 311550874

7564
M. E. & F. J. Callahan Foundation ◈
4760 Richmond Rd., Ste. 400
Warrensville Heights, OH 44128-5656

Established in 1975 in OH.

Donor: F.J. Callahan.

Foundation type: Independent foundation.

Financial data (yr. ended 12/31/04): Assets, $1,293,747 (M); expenditures, $859,257; qualifying distributions, $838,750; giving activities include $838,750 for 14 grants (high: $546,000; low: $1,000).

Purpose and activities: Giving primarily for the fine and musical arts; support also for education.

Fields of interest: Arts education; Museums (art); Performing arts; Performing arts, music; Arts; Elementary/secondary education; Higher education.

Type of support: General/operating support.

Limitations: Applications not accepted. Giving primarily in Cleveland, OH. No grants to individuals.

Application information: Contributes only to pre-selected organizations.

Officers: F.J. Callahan, Pres.; T.J. Callahan, V.P.; Ernest P. Mansour, Secy.

EIN: 510164320

Selected grants: The following grants were reported in 2004.

$546,000 to Cleveland Institute of Music, Cleveland, OH.

$20,000 to Lima Central Catholic High School, Lima, OH.

$10,000 to Case Western Reserve University, Cleveland, OH.

$6,000 to Cleveland School of the Arts, Cleveland, OH.

$3,750 to Rochester Institute of Technology, Rochester, NY.

$2,500 to Cleveland Institute of Art, Cleveland, OH.

7565
Estelle S. Campbell Charitable Foundation ◈
c/o National City Bank
P.O. Box 94651
Cleveland, OH 44101-4651
Application address: c/o William M. Schmidt, National City Bank, 20 Stanwix St., Pittsburgh, PA 15222, tel.: (412) 644-8332

Established in 1998 in PA.

Foundation type: Independent foundation.

Financial data (yr. ended 12/31/05): Assets, $16,722,716 (M); gifts received, $1,017; expenditures, $995,183; qualifying distributions,

$923,867; giving activities include $874,250 for 22 grants (high: $250,000; low: $10,000).
Fields of interest: Historic preservation/historical societies; Education; Boys & girls clubs; Big Brothers/Big Sisters; Youth, services; Aging, centers/services.
Limitations: Giving primarily in Pittsburgh, PA.
Application information: Application form required.
Initial approach: Letter
Copies of proposal: 3
Deadline(s): None
Trustee: National City Bank.
EIN: 251809360

7566
The Cardinal Foundation ✧ ☆
3055 Kettering Blvd., Ste. 310
Dayton, OH 45439

Established in 1998 in OH.
Donor: Thomas D. MacLeod.
Foundation type: Independent foundation.
Financial data (yr. ended 11/30/05): Assets, $1,153,854 (M); expenditures, $649,568; qualifying distributions, $629,000; giving activities include $629,000 for grants.
Fields of interest: Education; Health organizations, association; Roman Catholic agencies & churches.
Limitations: Applications not accepted. Giving in the U.S., with emphasis on NY and OH. No grants to individuals.
Application information: Contributes only to pre-selected organizations.
Officer: Thomas D. MacLeod, Pres.
Trustees: William J. Leibold; Barbara B. MacLeod.
EIN: 311681353
Selected grants: The following grants were reported in 2003.
$93,560 to Cornell University, Ithaca, NY. For general support.
$65,400 to Butte Central High School, Butte, MT. For general support.
$55,000 to Dayton Foundation, Dayton, OH. For scholarships.
$40,000 to Delta Gamma Center for Children with Visual Impairments, Saint Louis, MO. For general support.
$32,000 to Chaminade Julienne High School, Dayton, OH. For general support.
$3,000 to University of Dayton, Dayton, OH. For general support.
$1,000 to Ronald McDonald House Charities, Oak Brook, IL. For general support.
$500 to Hospice of Dayton, Dayton, OH. For general support.

7567
Cardinal Health Foundation ✧
7000 Cardinal Pl.
Dublin, OH 43017 (614) 757-7450
Contact: Debra Hadley, Exec. Dir.
E-mail: cardinalfoundation@cardinal.com;
URL: http://www.cardinal.com/aboutus/what/community/foundation/index.asp

Established in 2000 in OH.
Donors: The Baxter Allegiance Foundation; Cardinal Health, Inc.
Foundation type: Company-sponsored foundation.
Financial data (yr. ended 6/30/05): Assets, $51,948,740 (M); gifts received, $7,684;

expenditures, $4,541,742; qualifying distributions, $4,443,183; giving activities include $3,665,898 for 197 grants (high: $300,000; low: $210), and $627,456 for employee matching gifts.
Purpose and activities: The foundation supports organizations involved with arts and culture, education, health, and youth development.
Fields of interest: Arts; Education; Health care; Youth development.
Type of support: General/operating support; Equipment; Program development; Scholarship funds; Employee volunteer services; Employee matching gifts; Matching/challenge support.
Limitations: Giving on a national basis; giving also to national and international organizations. No support for local chapters of organizations already receiving national support from Cardinal Health, hospitals or hospital foundations, disease-specific organizations, sports teams, religious organizations not of direct benefit to the entire community, veterans', labor, or political organizations, fraternal, athletic, or social clubs, or discriminatory organizations. No grants to individuals, or for capital campaigns, endowments, debt reduction, advertising, sponsorships, or athletic competitions; no loans.
Application information: Project summaries should be no longer than 2 to 3 pages. A proposal will be requested following receipt of an eligible project summary. Application form not required.
Initial approach: Project summary
Deadline(s): None
Officers and Directors:* Sandy Rigopoulos,* Chair.; Aneezal Mohamed, Secy.; Debra Hadley, Exec. Dir.; Michael Bender; Tony Caprio; Cathy Cooney; Geoffrey Fenton; Ivan Fong; Linda Harty; John Lowry; Don Moseley; Mark Stauffer; Carol Watkins; Connie Woodburn.
EIN: 311746458
Selected grants: The following grants were reported in 2005.
$300,000 to AmeriCares, Stamford, CT.
$300,000 to CARE, Chicago, IL.
$250,000 to American Red Cross, National Headquarters, DC. For relief effort for Hurricane Katrina.
$200,000 to Oxfam America, Boston, MA.
$125,000 to World of Children, Columbus, OH.
$100,000 to Burn Institute, San Diego, CA.
$100,000 to United Negro College Fund, Fairfax, VA.
$10,000 to American Society of Consultant Pharmacists Research and Education Foundation, Alexandria, VA.
$5,000 to Mount Carmel College of Nursing, Columbus, OH.
$3,000 to American Red Cross of Greater Columbus, Columbus, OH.

7568
Castellini Foundation ✧
312 Elm St., Ste. 2600
Cincinnati, OH 45202 (513) 651-9400
Contact: Christopher L. Fister, Secy.-Treas.

Established in 1991 in OH.
Donors: Robert H. Castellini; Susan F. Castellini.
Foundation type: Independent foundation.
Financial data (yr. ended 3/31/06): Assets, $10,752,155 (M); gifts received, $50,000; expenditures, $1,412,346; qualifying distributions, $1,361,570; giving activities include $1,339,811 for 145 grants (high: $106,000; low: $50).

Purpose and activities: Giving primarily for education, health care, and the arts.
Fields of interest: Museums (art); Arts; Higher education; Education; Environment; Animal welfare; Hospitals (general); Health organizations, association; Human services; Children/youth, services; Federated giving programs; Roman Catholic agencies & churches.
Limitations: Giving limited to the greater Cincinnati, OH, area; some funding nationally. No grants to individuals.
Application information: Application form not required.
Initial approach: Letter
Deadline(s): None
Officers and Trustees:* Robert H. Castellini,* Chair. and Pres.; Christopher L. Fister,* Secy.-Treas.; Susan F. Castellini.
Agent: Fifth Third Bank.
EIN: 316429763
Selected grants: The following grants were reported in 2003.
$250,000 to Archdiocese of Cincinnati, Cincinnati, OH.
$126,000 to Good Samaritan Hospital Foundation, Cincinnati, OH. For da Vinci Robotic System Program.
$100,000 to National Underground Railroad Freedom Center, Cincinnati, OH. For capital campaign.
$100,000 to University of Pennsylvania, Wharton School of Business, Philadelphia, PA. For student center.
$90,000 to Canterbury School, New Milford, CT. For Squash Pavilion.
$65,500 to Catholic Inner-City Schools Educational Fund (CISE), Cincinnati, OH. For challenge grant.
$56,500 to Saint Margaret Hall, Cincinnati, OH.
$50,000 to United Way of Greater Cincinnati, Cincinnati, OH.
$21,000 to Taft Museum, Cincinnati, OH.
$20,000 to Sisters of Notre Dame de Namur, Cincinnati, OH. For Growing God's Goodness campaign.

7569
Charities Foundation ✧
1 Seagate, 5-OSG
Toledo, OH 43666 (419) 247-2929
Contact: Cher Johnson, Contribs. Admin.
Additional tel.: (419) 247-1386

Established in 1937 in OH.
Donors: Owens-Illinois, Inc.; William E. Levis†; Harold Boeschenstein†.
Foundation type: Company-sponsored foundation.
Financial data (yr. ended 12/31/05): Assets, $369,172 (M); gifts received, $1,570,757; expenditures, $1,622,944; qualifying distributions, $1,613,040; giving activities include $1,268,586 for 3,444,560 grants (high: $200,000; low: $25), and $344,454 for 169 employee matching gifts.
Purpose and activities: The foundation supports organizations involved with arts and culture, education, natural resources, health, human services, and civic affairs.
Fields of interest: Visual arts; Museums; Performing arts; Arts; Education, fund raising/fund distribution; Higher education; Business school/education; Education, natural resources; Environment; Hospitals (general); Health care; Children/youth, services; Human services; Federated giving

programs; Government/public administration; Public affairs.

Type of support: General/operating support; Employee matching gifts.

Limitations: Applications not accepted. Giving primarily in OH, with emphasis on Toledo. No grants to individuals, or for scholarships.

Publications: Annual report.

Application information: Contributes only to pre-selected organizations.

> Board meeting date(s): Jan. 26, Apr. 27, Aug. 3, and Oct. 26

Trustees: Jim Baehren; Jeffrey Denker; Henry Page; Carter Smith.

Number of staff: 1 part-time support.

EIN: 346554560

Selected grants: The following grants were reported in 2004.

$283,172 to United Way of Greater Toledo, Toledo, OH.

$225,000 to Toledo Museum of Art, Toledo, OH.

$112,775 to University of Toledo Foundation, Toledo, OH.

$54,536 to Toledo Orchestra Association, Toledo, OH.

$30,800 to Saint Johns High School, Delphos, OH. 2 grants: $10,800, $20,000

$30,000 to Bowling Green State University, Bowling Green, OH.

$28,000 to Saint Johns Jesuit High School, Toledo, OH.

$10,000 to Notre Dame Academy, Toledo, OH.

$10,000 to Toledo Opera Association, Toledo, OH.

7570
Children's Family Care, Inc. ◇ ☆

245 Locust St.
Akron, OH 44302

Application address: c/o Donald D. Shook, 4019 Highpoint Dr., Uniontown, OH 44685-7947

Established in 1999 in OH.

Donor: Maxene D. Darrah Revocable Trust.

Foundation type: Independent foundation.

Financial data (yr. ended 12/31/04): Assets, $5,551,282 (M); expenditures, $438,637; qualifying distributions, $360,942; giving activities include $362,008 for 15 grants (high: $241,000; low: $821).

Fields of interest: Hospitals (general); Human services; Children/youth, services; Family services; Christian agencies & churches.

Limitations: Giving primarily in OH. No grants to individuals.

Application information:

> Initial approach: Letter (no more than 2 pages)
> Deadline(s): Sept. 15
> Final notification: Dec. 31

Officers: Keith Kilgore, Pres.; Jim Stroble, Secy.; Michael G. Soful, Treas.

Trustees: Sheldon W. Barlette, Jr.; John Blickle; Robert Bobbitt; Steve Cox; Dale G. Freygang; Richard Heidman; Emily B. Petrarca; John Shaffer; Steve Shriber; John P. Stoner; Dana Zahuranec.

EIN: 341405958

7571
Chiquita Brands International Foundation ◇ ☆

(formerly United Brands Foundation)
250 E. 5th St.
Cincinnati, OH 45202

Contact: Cynthia Godby

Incorporated in 1954 in IL.

Donor: Chiquita Brands International, Inc.

Foundation type: Company-sponsored foundation.

Financial data (yr. ended 12/31/05): Assets, $901 (M); gifts received, $557,675; expenditures, $558,363; qualifying distributions, $558,363; giving activities include $558,335 for 51 grants (high: $300,000; low: $5).

Purpose and activities: The foundation supports organizations involved with natural resources, agriculture, and nutrition.

Fields of interest: Environment, natural resources; Agriculture; Nutrition.

Type of support: Program development; In-kind gifts.

Limitations: Giving on a national basis, with emphasis on areas of company operations. No support for individual sports teams or religious or political organizations. No grants to individuals, or for scholarships, research or travel, or stipends.

Publications: Application guidelines; Annual report.

Application information: Telephone calls are not encouraged. Letters of inquiry should be submitted using organization letterhead. Application form not required.

> Initial approach: Letter of inquiry
> Copies of proposal: 1
> Deadline(s): None
> Final notification: 6 to 12 weeks

EIN: 366051081

Selected grants: The following grants were reported in 2004.

$50,000 to United Way.

$35,000 to Rainforest Alliance, New York, NY.

$15,000 to Freedom Center, Lakeland, FL.

$15,000 to Social Accountability International, New York, NY.

$2,500 to Otto Armleder Memorial Education Center, Cincinnati, OH.

$2,000 to Hispanic Scholarship Fund, San Francisco, CA.

$1,000 to College of Mount Saint Joseph, Cincinnati, OH.

$1,000 to Fabretto Childrens Foundation, Evanston, IL.

$1,000 to University of Cincinnati, Cincinnati, OH.

$1,000 to Urban League.

7572
Anne Kilcawley Christman Foundation ◇

City Centre 1
100 Federal Plz. E.
Youngstown, OH 44503

Established in 2002 in OH.

Donor: Anne Christman Irrevocable Trust.

Foundation type: Independent foundation.

Financial data (yr. ended 12/31/05): Assets, $26,545,780 (M); gifts received, $7; expenditures, $1,104,987; qualifying distributions, $995,927; giving activities include $947,200 for 8 grants (high: $118,400; low: $118,400).

Fields of interest: Arts; Education; Health care; Human services; Christian agencies & churches.

Limitations: Applications not accepted. Giving primarily in OH, with emphasis on Youngstown. No grants to individuals.

Application information: Contributes only to pre-selected organizations.

Trustees: Herbert H. Pridham; Butler Wick Trust Co.

EIN: 356735706

7573
The Cincinnati Foundation for the Aged ◇

2100 4th and Vine Twr.
5 W. 4th St.
Cincinnati, OH 45202   (513) 381-6859

Established in 1891 in OH.

Donors: Oscar Cohrs†; Otto Luedeking†; William Meyer†.

Foundation type: Independent foundation.

Financial data (yr. ended 3/31/06): Assets, $21,966,080 (M); gifts received, $155,065; expenditures, $1,089,700; qualifying distributions, $1,041,177; giving activities include $1,026,489 for 13 grants (high: $388,200; low: $12,000).

Purpose and activities: The sole purpose of the foundation is to assist indigent persons in the greater Cincinnati, OH, area, to gain admission to nonprofit nursing homes.

Fields of interest: Aging, centers/services; Aging.

Limitations: Giving primarily in the greater Cincinnati, OH, area; some funding also in KY. No grants to individuals.

Application information: Disbursements limited to the foundation's single mission described in Purpose & Activities; funding requests for studies or any other activity not eligible for consideration. Application form required.

> Deadline(s): None
> Board meeting date(s): Mar., June, Sept., and Dec.

Officers: Robert C. Porter, Jr., Pres.; Jon Hoffheimer, 1st V.P.; Gene Weber, 2nd V.P. and Treas.; Ruth Avram, Secy.

Trustees: Jon Blohm; Boyd Colglazier; Leigh Deaton; Bernice Gartrell; Jack Greer; Richard Hoefinghoff; Sr. Jean Marie Hoffman; Vince Hopkins; Heather Jansen; Robert Porter III; William H. Strietmann.

Number of staff: 1 full-time support.

EIN: 310536971

Selected grants: The following grants were reported in 2006.

$388,200 to Cedar Village, Cincinnati, OH.

$113,333 to Bayley Place, Cincinnati, OH.

$82,625 to Saint Margaret Hall, Cincinnati, OH.

$66,680 to Madonna Manor, Villa Hills, KY.

$45,200 to Carmel Manor, Fort Thomas, KY.

7574
The Greater Cincinnati Foundation ▼

200 W. 4th St.
Cincinnati, OH 45202-2602   (513) 241-2880

Contact: Ellen M. Gilligan, V.P., Community Investment; For grants: Kay Pennington, Community Investment Coord.

FAX: (513) 852-6886;
E-mail: info@greatercincinnatifdn.org; Grant application E-mail: penningtonk@greatercincinnatifdn.org; URL: http://www.greatercincinnatifdn.org

Established in 1963 in OH by bank resolution and declaration of trust.

Foundation type: Community foundation.
Financial data (yr. ended 12/31/05): Assets, $453,932,746 (M); gifts received, $51,684,097; expenditures, $37,362,109; giving activities include $32,130,666 for grants.
Purpose and activities: Grants for a broad range of both new and existing activities in general categories of arts and culture, community progress, environmental needs, education, health, and social and human services, including youth agencies. The foundation actively seeks to promote access, equity and diversity, and to end discrimination based on race, ethnicity, gender, disability and age.
Fields of interest: Arts; Education, early childhood education; Education; Environment; Health care; Housing/shelter, home owners; Disasters, Hurricane Katrina; Children/youth, services; Human services; Community development; Voluntarism promotion; Aging; Disabilities, people with; African Americans/Blacks; Economically disadvantaged; Homeless.
Type of support: Capital campaigns; Building/renovation; Equipment; Emergency funds; Program development; Seed money; Technical assistance; Matching/challenge support.
Limitations: Giving limited to southeastern IN, northern KY, and the greater Cincinnati, OH area. No support for private or parochial religious purposes, units of government or government agencies, schools, hospitals, nursing homes, or retirement centers. No grants to individuals (except for scholarships), or for operating budgets, fundraising drives, event sponsorship or underwriting, equipment, stand-alone publications or videos, annual campaigns, deficit financing, endowments, travel, fellowships, internships, exchange programs, or scholarly or medical research; no loans.
Publications: Application guidelines; Annual report (including application guidelines); Informational brochure (including application guidelines); Newsletter.
Application information: Visit foundation Web site for application form and guidelines. Common Grant Application form used after invitation; proposals must be invited for submission. Application form required.
  Initial approach: Telephone, followed by interview
  Copies of proposal: 2
  Deadline(s): Pre-application due Jan. 2, Apr. 1, July 1, and Oct. 1; full proposal due Feb. 15, May 15, Aug. 15, and Nov. 15
  Board meeting date(s): Mar., June, Sept., and Dec.
  Final notification: Mar., June, Sept., and Dec.
Officers and Governing Board:* William C. Portman III,* Chair.; Nancy K. Swanson,* Vice-Chair.; Kathryn E. Merchant, C.E.O. and Pres.; Amy L. Cheney, V.P., Giving Strategies; Ellen M. Gilligan, V.P., Community Investment; J. Scott McReynolds, V.P., Finance and Admin.; Elizabeth Bower Reiter, V.P., Comms. and Mktg.; Liane M. Szucs, Cont.; Richard J. Ruebel,* Legal Counsel; Thomas A. Brennan; Paul W. Chellgren; Thomas G. Cody; Cathy T. Crain; Alva Jean Crawford; Jane V. Domaschko; David Ellis III; Linda C. Fath; Barbara G. Lewis; Myrtis H. Powell, Ph.D.; Marvin H. Rorick, M.D.; Peter S. Strange; Joseph P. Tomain; Ron D. Wright, Ph.D.
Trustee Banks: Fifth Third Bank; The Huntington National Bank; JPMorgan Chase Bank, N.A.; KeyBank N.A.; The Lebanon Citizens National Bank; North Side Bank & Trust Co.; PNC Bank, N.A.; The Provident Bank; U.S. Bank, N.A.

Number of staff: 17 full-time professional; 10 full-time support; 1 part-time support.
EIN: 310669700
Selected grants: The following grants were reported in 2005.
$100,000 to Crossroad Health Center, Cincinnati, OH. For capital campaign.
$100,000 to Saint Vincent de Paul Society, Cincinnati, OH. For capital campaign.
$75,000 to Cincinnati Early Learning Centers, Cincinnati, OH. For Riverview East Academy Early Learning Center.
$75,000 to Cincinnati-Hamilton County Community Mental Health and Retardation Board, Cincinnati, OH. For construction of Facility at Jordan Crossing.
$75,000 to Covington Community Center, Covington, KY. For capital campaign.
$75,000 to Forward Quest, Covington, KY. For strategic planning.
$75,000 to University of Cincinnati Foundation, Cincinnati, OH. For University of Cincinnati Diabetes Center.
$75,000 to Xavier University, Cincinnati, OH. For Community Engagement Process.
$70,000 to Booker T. Washington Community Center, Hamilton, OH. For Executive Director.
$68,200 to Cincinnati Youth Collaborative, Cincinnati, OH. For continued support of COACH program.

7575
The M. Roger and Anne Melby Clapp Foundation ✧
9100 Billings Rd.
Kirtland, OH 44094
Contact: Anne Melby Clapp, Secy.

Established in 1988 in OH.
Donors: Anne Melby Clapp; M. Roger Clapp.
Foundation type: Independent foundation.
Financial data (yr. ended 12/31/04): Assets, $1,781,506 (M); gifts received, $800,000; expenditures, $723,755; qualifying distributions, $710,612; giving activities include $700,000 for 1 grant.
Fields of interest: Protestant agencies & churches; Aging.
Limitations: Giving primarily in OH.
Application information:
  Initial approach: Proposal
  Deadline(s): None
Officers and Trustees:* Anne Melby Clapp,* Pres. and Secy.; Jane Sedgwick, Treas.; Suzanne Munn; Martha Roediger.
EIN: 341543994

7576
The Cleveland Foundation ▼
1422 Euclid Ave., Ste. 1300
Cleveland, OH 44115-2001 (216) 861-3810
Contact: Ronald B. Richard, C.E.O.
FAX: (216) 861-1729;
E-mail: grantsmgmt@clevefdn.org; *TTY:* (216) 861-3806; *URL:* http://www.clevelandfoundation.org

Established in 1914 in OH by bank resolution and declaration of trust.
Foundation type: Community foundation.

Financial data (yr. ended 12/31/05): Assets, $1,716,136,165 (M); gifts received, $29,029,674; expenditures, $82,274,592; giving activities include $66,364,087 for grants, $57,768 for grants to individuals, and $1,310,000 for 4 loans/program-related investments.
Purpose and activities: The Cleveland Foundation is the nation's first community foundation and model for community foundations nationwide and around the world. Its purpose is to enhance the quality of life for all the citizens of greater Cleveland by building community endowment, addressing needs through grantmaking, and providing leadership on key community issues. The foundation awards grants in seven program areas: arts and culture, civic affairs, economic development, education, the environment, health, and social services. Special cross-functional grantmaking initiatives include neighborhoods and housing, strengthening mid-size arts organizations, public school improvement, early childhood, successful aging, and economic transformation.
Fields of interest: Arts education; Visual arts; Performing arts; Arts; Elementary school/education; Secondary school/education; Higher education; Medical school/education; Education; Environment; Health care; Health organizations, association; AIDS; Medical research, institute; AIDS research; Housing/shelter, development; Disasters, Hurricane Katrina; Youth, services; Family services; Aging, centers/services; Human services; Economic development; Urban/community development; Community development; Economics; Government/public administration; Aging.
Type of support: Capital campaigns; Program development; Seed money; Scholarship funds; Research; Technical assistance; Consulting services; Program-related investments/loans; Matching/challenge support.
Limitations: Giving limited to the greater Cleveland, OH, area, with primary emphasis on Cleveland, Cuyahoga, Lake, and Geauga counties, unless specified by donor. No support for sectarian or religious activities, community services such as fire and police protection, government staff positions, or library and welfare services. No grants to individuals (except for scholarships), or for endowment funds, operating costs, debt reduction, fundraising campaigns, publications, films and audiovisual materials (unless they are an integral part of a program already being supported), memberships, travel for bands, sports teams, classes and similar groups; no capital support for planning, construction, renovation, or purchase of buildings, equipment and materials, land acquisition, or renovation of public space unless there is strong evidence that the program is of priority to the foundation.
Publications: Application guidelines; Annual report (including application guidelines); Financial statement; Grants list; Informational brochure; Newsletter; Occasional report.
Application information: Visit foundation Web site for Grant Inquiry Form and application guidelines. Applicants will be notified as to whether to submit a full proposal based on Grant Inquiry Form. Application form required.
  Initial approach: Submit Grant Inquiry Form
  Copies of proposal: 1
  Deadline(s): None

Board meeting date(s): Distribution committee meets in Mar., June, Sept., and Dec.

Final notification: Within a few weeks for Grant Inquiry Form determination; varies for full proposals

Officers and Directors:* Jacqueline F. Woods,* Chair.; Rev. Otis Moss, Jr.,* Vice-Chair.; Ronald B. Richard, C.E.O. and Pres.; J.T. Mullen, Sr. V.P., C.F.O. and Treas.; Caprice H. Bragg, V.P., Gift Planning and Donor Rels.; Leslie A. Dunford, V.P., Corp. Gov. and Admin.; Robert E. Eckardt, V.P., Progs. and Evaluation; Kathy S. Parker, Cont.; Charles P. Bolton; Terri Hamilton Brown; Tana N. Carney; David Goldberg; Joseph P. Keithley; Benson P. Lee; Frederick R. Nance; Sandra Pianalto; Maria Jose Pujana, M.D.; James A. Ratner; Alayne L. Reitman; Rev. Hilton O. Smith; Frank C. Sullivan.

Trustees: FirstMerit Bank, N.A.; The Huntington National Bank; JPMorgan Chase Bank, N.A.; KeyBank N.A.; National City Bank.

Number of staff: 41 full-time professional; 1 part-time professional; 15 full-time support; 3 part-time support.

EIN: 340714588

Selected grants: The following grants were reported in 2005.

$6,850,000 to Cleveland Foundation Inc., Cleveland, OH. 4 grants: $2,550,000 (For continuation of Neighborhood Connections program, payable over 3 years), $3,000,000 (For Fund for Our Economic Future for continuation of regional economic transformation program), $650,000 (For Arts Advancement Project management), $650,000 (For planning and development-related efforts in Greater University Circle area).

$5,762,101 to Case Western Reserve University, Cleveland, OH. 2 grants: $762,101 to Mandel Center for Nonprofit Organizations (For Treu-Mart Youth Initiative Project, payable over 2 years), $5,000,000 to School of Medicine (To establish Case Proteomics Center and Department of Immunology, payable over 3 years).

$3,000,000 to Cleveland Orchestra, Cleveland, OH. For transformational business model and educational and outreach programs, payable over 2 years.

$1,600,000 to Cuyahoga County Board of Commissioners, Cleveland, OH. For Invest in Children, Cuyahoga County's early childhood development program, payable over 2 years.

$1,250,000 to Cleveland Scholarship Programs, Cleveland, OH. For post-secondary advisory services and scholarships associated with Six to Success Program, Adult Learner Program and operation of Resource Center, payable over 2 years.

$1,000,000 to Westminster School, Simsbury, CT. For new academic center and library, payable over 2 years.

7577

Cleveland Indians Charities, Inc. ✧

c/o Jacobs Field
2401 Ontario St.
Cleveland, OH 44115 (216) 420-4400
Contact: Melissa Zapanta, Dir.
E-mail: cic@indians.com; Additional tel.: (216) 420-HITS; URL: http://cleveland.indians.mlb.com/NASApp/mlb/cle/community/cic.jsp

Established in 1989 in OH.

Donors: Huntington Bancshares Inc.; McDonald Investments, Inc.; Cleveland Indians Baseball Co., Inc.; Jim Thome; Ellis Burks.

Foundation type: Company-sponsored foundation.

Financial data (yr. ended 12/31/03): Assets, $573,254 (M); gifts received, $406,164; expenditures, $731,267; qualifying distributions, $356,000; giving activities include $356,000 for 8 grants (high: $100,000; low: $1,000), and $248,016 for 4 foundation-administered programs.

Purpose and activities: The foundation primarily supports the youth of northeast Ohio by providing educational and recreational opportunities.

Fields of interest: Education; Recreation; Youth development, centers/clubs; Children/youth, services.

Type of support: General/operating support; Continuing support; Annual campaigns; Program development; Scholarship funds; In-kind gifts.

Limitations: Applications not accepted. Giving limited to Cleveland, OH. No grants to individuals.

Application information: Contributes only to pre-selected organizations.

Officers and Trustees:* Robert A. DiBiasio,* Pres.; Kenneth E. Stefanov,* Treas.; E. Dennis Lehman; Mark Shapiro; Jon Starrett.

Number of staff: 2 full-time professional; 12 part-time support.

EIN: 341618536

Selected grants: The following grants were reported in 2004.

$82,400 to Boys and Girls Club. 2 grants: $80,000, $2,400

$60,000 to Cleveland Baseball Federation, Cleveland, OH.

$50,000 to United Black Fund, DC.

$6,900 to Center for Families and Children, Cleveland, OH.

$6,000 to North American Indian Cultural Center, Tallmadge, OH.

$4,346 to Providence House, Cleveland, OH.

$4,346 to Womens Center of Greater Cleveland, Cleveland, OH.

7578

The George W. Codrington Charitable Foundation

c/o KeyBank N.A.
800 Superior Ave., 4th Fl.
Cleveland, OH 44114
Contact: Craig Martahus, Chair.
Application address: 127 Public Sq., 39th Fl., Cleveland, OH 44114

Trust established in 1955 in OH.

Donor: George W. Codrington†.

Foundation type: Independent foundation.

Financial data (yr. ended 12/31/05): Assets, $19,123,146 (M); expenditures, $1,210,579; qualifying distributions, $1,029,452; giving activities include $1,011,000 for 101 grants (high: $50,000; low: $1,000).

Purpose and activities: Giving primarily for higher education, hospitals, arts groups, and youth.

Fields of interest: Museums; Performing arts; Arts; Higher education; Education; Hospitals (general); Children/youth, services.

Type of support: General/operating support; Continuing support; Annual campaigns; Capital campaigns; Equipment; Program development; Research.

Limitations: Giving limited to Cuyahoga County, OH, and the surrounding area. No grants to individuals, or for endowment funds; no loans.

Publications: Annual report (including application guidelines).

Application information: Application form not required.

Initial approach: Full proposal
Copies of proposal: 4
Deadline(s): Submit proposal preferably the month before board meetings
Board meeting date(s): Apr., June, Sept., Nov., and Dec.
Final notification: Promptly after board meeting

Officers: Craig R. Martahus, Chair.; William R. Seelbach, Vice-Chair; Raymond T. Sawyer, Secy.

Supervisory Board: Curtis E. Moll; William R. Seelbach; Craig T. Martahus.

Trustee: KeyBank N.A.

EIN: 346507457

7579

Lester E. & Kathleen A. Coleman Foundation ✧

14849 Trappers Trail
Novelty, OH 44072-9543 (216) 861-1148
Contact: Kathleen A. Coleman, Pres.

Established in 1994 in OH.

Donor: Lester E. Coleman.

Foundation type: Independent foundation.

Financial data (yr. ended 12/31/05): Assets, $167,622 (M); expenditures, $415,742; qualifying distributions, $412,500; giving activities include $412,500 for grants.

Purpose and activities: Giving primarily for education and health care.

Fields of interest: Higher education; Medical school/education; Hospitals (general); Health care; Boy scouts.

Limitations: Giving primarily in OH. No grants to individuals.

Application information: Application form not required.

Initial approach: Letter
Deadline(s): None

Officer: Kathleen A. Coleman, Pres.

Trustees: Kenneth J. Coleman; Mark W. Meister.

EIN: 341788395

7580

The Columbus Foundation and Affiliated Organizations ▼ ✧

(formerly The Columbus Foundation)
1234 E. Broad St.
Columbus, OH 43205-1453 (614) 251-4000
Contact: Raymond J. Biddiscombe, V.P., Finance
FAX: (614) 251-4009;
E-mail: tcfinfo@columbusfoundation.org; Additional E-mail: rbiddisc@columbusfoundation.org;
URL: http://www.columbusfoundation.org

Established in 1943 in OH by resolution and declaration of trust.

Foundation type: Community foundation.

Financial data (yr. ended 12/31/05): Assets, $850,089,853 (M); gifts received, $67,974,224; expenditures, $72,617,157; giving activities include $65,626,215 for 4,720 grants.

Purpose and activities: The foundation seeks to assist donors and others in strengthening and improving the community for the benefits of all its citizens. Grants are made to strengthen existing agencies or to initiate new programs in the following categories: arts and humanities, urban affairs, conservation and environmental protection, education, health, mental health and the developmentally disabled, and social service agencies.

Fields of interest: Performing arts; Humanities; Historic preservation/historical societies; Arts; Education, association; Child development, education; Adult education—literacy, basic skills & GED; Education, reading; Education; Environment, natural resources; Environment, energy; Environment; Animal welfare; Reproductive health, family planning; Health care; Mental health/crisis services; Health organizations, association; AIDS; AIDS research; Employment, training; Housing/ shelter; Disasters, Hurricane Katrina; Youth, services; Child development, services; Women, centers/services; Homeless, human services; Human services; Civil rights, race/intergroup relations; Economic development; Community development; Voluntarism promotion; Philanthropy/ voluntarism; Government/public administration; Public affairs; Disabilities, people with; Women; Economically disadvantaged; Homeless.

Type of support: Continuing support; Capital campaigns; Building/renovation; Land acquisition; Program development; Publication; Seed money; Scholarship funds; Technical assistance; Matching/ challenge support.

Limitations: Giving limited to central OH. No support for religious purposes, or for projects normally the responsibility of a public agency. No grants to individuals, or generally for budget deficits, conferences, scholarly research, or endowment funds.

Publications: Application guidelines; Annual report; Informational brochure (including application guidelines); Newsletter.

Application information: Visit foundation Web site for online application, guidelines, and specific deadlines. Application form required.
 Initial approach: Submit proposal coversheet and attachments
 Copies of proposal: 4
 Deadline(s): Varies
 Board meeting date(s): Feb., Apr., May, July, Sept., Oct., and Dec.
 Final notification: Approximately 3 months after the given deadline

Officers and Governing Committee: Ann Isaly Wolfe,* Chair.; David R. Meuse,* Vice-Chair.; Ann Pizzuti,* Vice-Chair.; Douglas F. Kridler,* C.E.O. and Pres.; Raymond J. Biddiscombe, V.P., Finance and Admin.; Lisa S. Courtice, Ph.D., V.P., Community Research and Grants Mgmt.; Philip T. "Terry" Schavone, V.P., Donor Svcs. and Devel.; Renilda Marshall, Exec. Secy.; Tanny Crane; John B. Gerlach, Jr.; Archie M. Griffin; Leonard A. Schlesinger; Barbara Trueman; Frank Wobst.

Trustee Banks: The Huntington National Bank; JPMorgan Chase Bank, N.A.; KeyBank N.A.; National City Bank, Columbus.

Number of staff: 23 full-time professional; 14 full-time support; 3 part-time support.

EIN: 316044264

Selected grants: The following grants were reported in 2005.
$1,000,000 to COSI Columbus, Columbus, OH. For operating support.
$1,000,000 to Williams College, Williamstown, MA.

$500,000 to OhioHealth Foundation, Columbus, OH.
$225,000 to United Way of Central Ohio, Columbus, OH.
$150,000 to KidsOhio.org, Columbus, OH. For operations.
$22,000 to Allen Eiry Senior Center, Tiffin, OH. To provide facility for Senior Community Services activities.
$20,000 to Community Foundation of Delaware County, Delaware, OH.
$20,000 to Edison State Community College, Piqua, OH. For general operating support.
$17,000 to Columbus Public Schools, Columbus, OH. To provide support on WCBE-FM.
$15,000 to Greenewood Manor Nursing Home, Xenia, OH.

7581
Community Foundation of Delaware County

P.O. Box 261
40 N. Sandusky St., Ste. 202
Delaware, OH 43015 (740) 369-0095
FAX: (740) 369-1140; E-mail: cfdc@midohio.net;
URL: http://www.delawarecf.org

Established in 1995 in OH.
Foundation type: Community foundation.
Financial data (yr. ended 12/31/04): Assets, $6,235,910 (M); gifts received, $4,745,856; expenditures, $456,560; giving activities include $221,686 for 13+ grants, and $142,826 for 27 grants to individuals.
Purpose and activities: The foundation seeks to provide for various charitable, cultural, educational and community purposes in Delaware County, OH. Also provides scholarships to local graduating seniors.
Fields of interest: Arts; Scholarships/financial aid; Education; Environment; Health care; Human services; Community development; Public affairs.
Type of support: Seed money; Equipment; Program development; Scholarships—to individuals.
Limitations: Giving limited to Delaware County, OH. No support for religious purposes. No grants to individuals (except for scholarships), or for deficit reduction, operating expenses, or special fundraising events.
Publications: Application guidelines; Financial statement; Grants list; Informational brochure; Newsletter.
Application information: Visit foundation Web site for grant application Coversheet and guidelines. Application form required.
 Initial approach: Letter and proposal
 Copies of proposal: 2
 Deadline(s): Oct. 1 for grants; June 15 for the Gooding Memorial Scholarship
 Board meeting date(s): 2nd Wed. of every other month
 Final notification: 45 days
Officers and Trustees: Richard Lombardi,* Chair.; D.G. Edgerton,* Vice-Chair.; Teri Meider,* Vice-Chair.; Jeffrey T. Benton,* Secy.; E. Jane Van Fossen,* Treas.; Sherry Barbosky; Susan Beavers; Mark W. Huddleston, Ph.D.; William Lane; Thomas Louden; Gary Madich; Stephen D. Martin; Rozella Miller; William D. Rogers.
Number of staff: 1 full-time professional; 2 part-time support.
EIN: 311450786

7582
The Community Foundation of Greater Lorain County ▼

1865 N. Ridge Rd. E., Ste. A
Lorain, OH 44055 (440) 277-0142
Contact: Brian R. Frederick, C.E.O.
FAX: (440) 277-6955;
E-mail: foundation@peoplewhocare.org; Additional tel.: (440) 323-4445; Additional E-mail: info@peoplewhocare.org; URL: http://www.peoplewhocare.org

Incorporated in 1980 in OH.
Foundation type: Community foundation.
Financial data (yr. ended 12/31/05): Assets, $73,103,012 (M); gifts received, $3,190,165; expenditures, $4,403,760; giving activities include $3,139,695 for 481 grants (high: $459,020; low: $50), and $353,320 for 302 grants to individuals (high: $4,000; low: $250).
Purpose and activities: The foundation seeks to improve the quality of life and to instill a greater sense of unity in the Greater Lorain County community by mobilizing individuals to become active partners in building a better community; providing a permanent instrument for receiving and managing charitable gifts and bequests; supporting innovative programs and acting as a catalyst in identifying problems and sharing information with individuals, other foundations, corporations, and organizations; and exercising and promoting leadership in meeting the changing needs and opportunities of the entire community.
Fields of interest: Arts; Education; Environment; Health care; Health organizations, association; Human services; Community development, neighborhood development; Economic development; Asians/Pacific Islanders; African Americans/Blacks; Hispanics/Latinos; Women.
Type of support: General/operating support; Endowments; Program development; Seed money; Scholarship funds; Technical assistance; Scholarships—to individuals; Matching/challenge support.
Limitations: Giving primarily in Lorain County, OH. No support for religious purposes, street repair, government services, public or non-public school services required by law, or self-help clubs that meet the needs of a small population. No grants to individuals (except for scholarships), or for annual campaigns, medical research, deficit financing, membership fees, tickets for benefits, tours, equipment, group travel, or capital campaigns; no loans.
Publications: Application guidelines; Annual report (including application guidelines); Financial statement; Informational brochure (including application guidelines); Newsletter; Program policy statement.
Application information: Grantseekers should contact the Sr. Prog. Off. to discuss the proposal before submitting an application. Visit foundation Web site for application form and guidelines. Application form required.
 Initial approach: Letter or telephone
 Copies of proposal: 1
 Deadline(s): Feb. 1 and Aug. 1 for grants; Feb. 10 for scholarships
 Board meeting date(s): Bimonthly
 Final notification: July and Dec. for grants; June for scholarships
Officers and Directors: James Park,* Chair.; Jane Norton,* Vice-Chair. and Chair., Grants; Brian R. Frederick, C.E.O. and Pres.; John Keyse-Walker,*

Secy.; Cheryl McKenna, C.F.O.; Don Arnold,* Treas.; Andrew Culberson, Chair., Devel.; Michael I. Goodman, Chair., Governance; Joel Arredondo; Robert T. Bowman; James Bucci; Judith Crocker; Maria Escuro; Donald Illig; Derrick Johnson; Claudia Jones; Pat Lindley; Russell McLaughlin; Gayle Reeves; Helen Woodward.

Number of staff: 6 full-time professional; 1 part-time professional; 2 full-time support; 1 part-time support.

EIN: 341322781

Selected grants: The following grants were reported in 2005.

$250,000 to Common Ground, Oberlin, OH. For general support, payable over 2 years.

$55,000 to Neighborhood House Association of Lorain County, Lorain, OH. For Haven Center Emergency Shelter general operating support.

$50,000 to Oberlin Historical and Improvement Organization, Oberlin, OH. For Oberlin Heritage Center Museum Fellow Program, payable over 2 years.

$45,000 to Catholic Charities Services of Lorain County, Elyria, OH. For Community Connections and Family Night.

$42,000 to Community Health Partners Foundation, Lorain, OH. For Rural Parish Nurse Program.

$35,000 to Boys and Girls Club of Lorain County, Oberlin, OH. For general operating support.

$25,000 to Community Impact Organization, Elyria, OH. For program support.

$25,000 to Firelands Symphony Orchestra, Milan, OH. For season in Lorain County.

$15,000 to Horizon Activities Center, North Olmsted, OH. For Greater Lorain County Early Learning Consortium.

$15,000 to MAD Factory, Oberlin, OH. For Theater-based Arts Programming.

7583
Community Foundation of Mount Vernon & Knox County ✧

(formerly The Mount Vernon/Knox County Community Trust)
c/o The First-Knox National Bank
1 S. Main St.
P.O. Box 1270
Mount Vernon, OH 43050 (740) 392-3270
Contact: Sam Barone, Exec. Dir.
FAX: (740) 399-5296;
E-mail: sbarone@mvkcfoundation.org; URL: http://www.mvkcfoundation.org

Established in 1944 in OH by declaration of trust.
Foundation type: Community foundation.
Financial data (yr. ended 12/31/04): Assets, $27,797,399 (M); gifts received, $1,455,295; expenditures, $896,552; giving activities include $450,358 for 92 grants (high: $82,544; low: $8), and $195,289 for 154 grants to individuals (high: $10,000; low: $400).
Purpose and activities: The foundation seeks to assist public, educational, charitable or benevolent enterprises. Grants, in accordance with the donors' wishes, for student loan and scholarship funds, community funds, youth agencies, nursing and the health profession, and museums.
Fields of interest: Museums; Humanities; Arts; Education; Environment, natural resources; Nursing care; Health care; Health organizations, association; Recreation, parks/playgrounds; Children/youth, services; Human services;

Community development; Federated giving programs.
Type of support: Capital campaigns; Building/renovation; Equipment; Program development; Conferences/seminars; Seed money; Scholarship funds; Program evaluation; Scholarships—to individuals; Matching/challenge support.
Limitations: Giving primarily in Mount Vernon and Knox County, OH. No support for religious purposes, or police and fire protection. No grants to individuals (except for scholarships), or for ongoing operating expenses, equipment, existing obligations, liabilities, debt reduction, endowment funds, staff positions for government agencies, or research; no loans.
Publications: Application guidelines; Annual report; Informational brochure; Occasional report.
Application information: Visit foundation Web site for application form, deadlines, and additional guidelines per grant type. Application form required.
Initial approach: Submit application form and attachments
Copies of proposal: 1
Deadline(s): Varies
Board meeting date(s): Feb., Apr., June, Aug., Oct., and Dec.
Final notification: Following next board meeting
Officers and Board Members:* Mark R. Ramser,* Chair.; Douglas O. Brenneman, Sr.,* Vice-Chair.; Robert L. Rauzi,* Secy.; Sally A. Nelson,* Treas.; Samuel Barone, Exec. Dir.; E. LeBron Fairbanks; Thomas R. Fosnaught; Ronald G. Godfrey; Bruce E. Hawkins; L. Bruce Levering; Deborah J. Reeder; Dennis L. Snyder.
Investment Manager: The First-Knox National Bank.
Number of staff: 1 part-time professional; 1 part-time support.
EIN: 311768219

7584
The Community Foundation of Shelby County

(formerly The Community Foundation of Sidney and Shelby County)
100 S. Main Ave., Ste. 202
Sidney, OH 45365-2771 (937) 497-7800
Contact: Marian Spicer, Exec. Dir.
FAX: (937) 497-7799; E-mail: info@commfoun.com;
Additional E-mail: mspicer@commfoun.com;
URL: http://www.commfoun.com

Incorporated in 1952 in OH.
Foundation type: Community foundation.
Financial data (yr. ended 12/31/06): Assets, $8,732,885 (M); gifts received, $760,832; expenditures, $743,104; giving activities include $562,570 for grants.
Purpose and activities: The foundation seeks to cultivate, administer, and distribute legacy gifts for the benefit of the community. Primary areas of giving include: Arts and Culture, Family and Community, Education, Environment, and Health.
Fields of interest: Arts; Education; Environment, natural resources; Environment, beautification programs; Environment; Health care; Health organizations, association; Recreation; Family services; Human services; Community development.
Type of support: Capital campaigns; Equipment; Program development; Seed money; Scholarship funds; Scholarships—to individuals.

Limitations: Giving limited to Shelby County, OH, and surrounding areas. No support for religious organizations. No grants to individuals (except for scholarships), or for endowments, fundraising campaigns from existing organizations, specific scientific, medical, or academic research, or general operating expenses.
Publications: Annual report; Informational brochure; Newsletter.
Application information: Visit foundation Web site for preliminary grant proposal form and guidelines. Preliminary grant proposal form and proposals will not be accepted if applicant has not discussed grant request with foundation staff. Application form required.
Initial approach: Telephone
Copies of proposal: 4
Deadline(s): Mar. 15 and Aug. 15 for preliminary grant proposal; May 1 and Oct. 1 for full proposal; Mar. 31 for scholarships
Board meeting date(s): Bimonthly
Final notification: June and Dec.
Officers and Trustees:* Edward Borchers,* Chair.; Patrick Milligan,* Vice-Chair.; Linda Scott,* Secy.; Bruce Boyd,* Treas.; Marian Spicer, Exec. Dir.; Daniel Bensman; Kenneth Monnier; Kenneth Schlater; Sandra Shoemaker; Judy Westerheide.
Number of staff: 1 part-time professional; 1 part-time support.
EIN: 346565194

7585
Community Foundation of the Mahoning Valley

Metropolitan Twr.
11 Federal Plaza Central, Ste. 1600
Youngstown, OH 44503-1592 (330) 743-5555
Contact: Patricia Brozik, Exec. Dir.
FAX: (330) 746-0330; E-mail: info@cfmv.org;
URL: http://www.cfmv.org

Established in 1999 in OH.
Foundation type: Community foundation.
Financial data (yr. ended 6/30/05): Assets, $9,505,821 (M); gifts received, $102,699; expenditures, $2,332,675; giving activities include $2,212,464 for 76 grants (high: $760,150; low: $100).
Purpose and activities: The mission of the foundation is to attract and invest permanent resources, with the purpose of enhancing the quality of life for the residents of the Mahoning Valley and future generations, in accordance with the charitable intentions of its donors.
Fields of interest: Historic preservation/historical societies; Arts; Education; Environment; Health care; Recreation; Children/youth, services; Aging, centers/services; Human services; Economic development; Science, research.
Type of support: Continuing support; Capital campaigns; Building/renovation; Equipment; Endowments; Technical assistance; Matching/challenge support.
Limitations: Giving limited to Mahoning County and Trumbull County, OH.
Publications: Application guidelines; Financial statement; Informational brochure.
Application information: Visit foundation Web site for application form and guidelines. Application form required.
Initial approach: Submit application form and attachments

Copies of proposal: 5
Deadline(s): Feb. 1, May 1, Aug. 1, and Nov. 1
Board meeting date(s): Mar., June, Sept., and Dec.
Final notification: 45 days
Officers and Directors:* Janice E. Strasfeld,* Chair.; William J. Bresnahan,* Vice-Chair.; Gerald Walsh,* Secy.; Frank J. Dixon,* Treas.; Patricia Brozik, Exec. Dir.; Bruce R. Beeghly; Thomas Fleming; Earnest Perry, M.D.; E. Jeffrey Rossi; Molly S. Seals.
Number of staff: 1 part-time professional; 1 full-time support.
EIN: 341904353

7586
Community Foundation of Union County, Inc.

(doing business as Union County Foundation)
126 N. Main St.
P.O. Box 608
Marysville, OH 43040-0608 (937) 642-9618
Contact: David A. Vollrath, Exec. Dir.
FAX: (937) 642-7376;
E-mail: info@unioncountyfoundation.org;
URL: http://www.unioncountyfoundation.org

Established in 1962 in OH.
Foundation type: Community foundation.
Financial data (yr. ended 12/31/05): Assets, $3,279,915 (M); gifts received, $700,679; expenditures, $515,525; giving activities include $365,046 for 61 grants (high: $24,000; low: $50), and $37,815 for 20 grants to individuals (high: $4,500; low: $500).
Purpose and activities: The foundation seeks to enhance the quality of life for all the citizens of Union County, and to provide a vehicle whereby gifts of any size might be invested and used in perpetuity to that end.
Fields of interest: Arts; Higher education; Education; Environment; Health care; Recreation; Religion; Youth; Aging.
Type of support: Capital campaigns; General/operating support; Endowments; Scholarships—to individuals; In-kind gifts.
Limitations: Giving limited to Union County, OH. No support for sectarian religious programs. No grants to individuals (except from designated funds), or for buildings or equipment, unrestricted operating support, endowments, fundraising campaigns, conferences, or annual meetings.
Publications: Application guidelines; Annual report; Informational brochure.
Application information: Visit foundation Web site for application form and guidelines. Application form required.
Initial approach: Phone or personal contact with Director
Copies of proposal: 1
Deadline(s): Jan., Apr., July, and Oct.
Board meeting date(s): 3rd Thurs. of Feb., May, Aug., and Nov.
Final notification: Quarterly
Officers and Trustees:* J. Daniel Fitzgerald,* Chair.; Thomas A. McCarthy,* Vice-Chair.; Phillip Connolly,* Secy.-Treas.; David Vollrath, Exec. Dir.; David F. Allen, Counsel; Robert Buckley, Fdn., C.P.A.; Robin Craft; Barbara Holcomb; Thomas C. Kruse; Robert Lewis; John Linscott; Frank Miller; Carolyn Mitchell; Dorothy Mudgett; Pat Nuckles; Frank Raymond; Greg Sehnert; Barbara Timmons.

Number of staff: 1 part-time professional; 1 part-time support.
EIN: 310628641

7587
The Convergys Foundation, Inc. ✧

201 E. 4th St., Ste. 102-1400
Cincinnati, OH 45202

Established in 1999 in OH.
Donor: Convergys Corp.
Foundation type: Company-sponsored foundation.
Financial data (yr. ended 12/31/04): Assets, $185,324 (M); gifts received, $660,000; expenditures, $955,870; qualifying distributions, $955,862; giving activities include $919,036 for 35 grants (high: $270,000; low: $100), and $36,645 for 72 employee matching gifts.
Purpose and activities: The foundation supports organizations involved with arts and culture, education, youth development, and human services.
Fields of interest: Museums; Performing arts; Arts; Higher education; Education; Youth development; Children/youth, services; Human services; Federated giving programs.
International interests: Asia; Canada; Europe; India; Latin America; Oceania.
Type of support: Capital campaigns; Building/renovation; Endowments; Seed money; Internship funds; Research; Sponsorships; Employee matching gifts.
Limitations: Giving primarily in Jacksonville and Orlando, FL, Cincinnati, OH, TX, Salt Lake City, UT, and on an international basis in Asia, Canada, Europe, India, Latin America, and Oceania. No support for political or religious organizations. No grants to individuals.
Publications: Application guidelines; Corporate giving report; Informational brochure.
Application information: Application form not required.
Initial approach: Proposal
Copies of proposal: 1
Deadline(s): None
Board meeting date(s): Spring and fall
Final notification: Varies
Officer: James F. Orr, Pres.
Trustees: Cheryl N. Campbell; David F. Dougherty; William H. Hawkins II; Steven G. Rolls; Earl Shanks.
EIN: 311619871

7588
Ruth J. & Robert A. Conway Foundation, Inc. ✧

5799 Mariemont Ave.
Cincinnati, OH 45227
Contact: Robert A. Conway Sr., Treas.

Established in 1998 in OH.
Donors: Robert A. Conway, Sr.; Ruth J. Conway.
Foundation type: Independent foundation.
Financial data (yr. ended 12/31/04): Assets, $18,106,527 (M); expenditures, $869,284; qualifying distributions, $801,533; giving activities include $765,488 for 82 grants (high: $100,000; low: $200).
Fields of interest: Human services; Federated giving programs; Roman Catholic agencies & churches.
Type of support: Program development; Matching/challenge support.

Limitations: Giving primarily in OH, with emphasis on the metropolitan Cincinnati area, Pittsburgh, PA, and Louisville and northern KY. No grants to individuals.
Application information: Proposals will not be accepted in person. Application form required.
Initial approach: Letter
Copies of proposal: 1
Deadline(s): 10 days before board meeting
Board meeting date(s): Mar., June, Sept., Dec.
Final notification: 1 week after board meeting
Officers and Trustees:* Ruth J. Conway,* Chair. and Pres.; Thomas H. Clark, Secy.; Robert A. Conway, Sr.,* Treas.; Sean P. Conway; Sr. Jean Patrice Harrington; William J. Keating; Mary Ruth Smyjunas.
EIN: 311575184

7589
Cooper Tire & Rubber Foundation ✧

701 Lima Ave.
Findlay, OH 45840
Contact: Philip G. Weaver, V.P. and C.F.O., Cooper Tire & Rubber Co.
Application address: c/o Cooper Tire & Rubber Co., Lima & Western Aves., Findlay, OH 45840, tel.: (419) 423-1321

Established in 1953 in OH.
Donor: Cooper Tire & Rubber Co.
Foundation type: Company-sponsored foundation.
Financial data (yr. ended 12/31/04): Assets, $20,188 (M); gifts received, $675,803; expenditures, $683,998; qualifying distributions, $683,998; giving activities include $683,364 for 233 grants (high: $109,116; low: $50).
Purpose and activities: The foundation supports organizations involved with arts and culture, education, health, and youth development.
Fields of interest: Museums; Museums (art); Arts; Elementary/secondary education; Higher education; Education; Health care; Boy scouts; Youth development; YM/YWCAs & YM/YWHAs; Federated giving programs.
Type of support: General/operating support; Capital campaigns; Employee matching gifts.
Limitations: Giving on a national basis.
Application information: Application form not required.
Initial approach: Proposal
Deadline(s): None
Trustees: Philip G. Weaver; E.B. White.
EIN: 237025013
Selected grants: The following grants were reported in 2004.
$109,116 to United Way of Hancock County, Findlay, OH.
$41,000 to United Way. 3 grants: $15,000, $11,000, $15,000
$25,000 to Ohio Foundation of Independent Colleges, Columbus, OH.
$22,450 to University of Findlay, Findlay, OH.
$20,000 to Kettering University, Flint, MI.
$20,000 to Owens Community College Foundation, Toledo, OH.
$19,000 to United Way of Greater Texarkana, Texarkana, TX.
$400 to Tiffin University, Tiffin, OH.

7590
The Corbett Foundation ✧
127 W. 9th St., Ste. 3
Cincinnati, OH 45202 (513) 241-3320
Contact: Karen P. McKim, Exec. Dir.

Incorporated in 1958 in OH.
Donors: J. Ralph Corbett†; Patricia A. Corbett.
Foundation type: Independent foundation.
Financial data (yr. ended 4/30/05): Assets, $14,955,022 (M); expenditures, $2,442,738; qualifying distributions, $2,368,903; giving activities include $2,252,241 for 23 grants (high: $1,000,000; low: $1,000).
Purpose and activities: Giving primarily for arts and cultural organizations, and education.
Fields of interest: Arts, association; Arts education; Media/communications; Arts; Libraries (public); Education; Community development.
Type of support: General/operating support; Capital campaigns; Equipment; Program development; Matching/challenge support.
Limitations: Giving primarily in the greater Cincinnati, OH, area. No grants to individuals.
Application information:
Initial approach: Proposal
Deadline(s): None
Final notification: Within 2 months
Officers: Patricia A. Corbett, Pres.; James A. Markley, Jr., V.P.; Karen P. McKim, Exec. Dir.
Trustees: Thomas R. Corbett; Joyce J. Salinger; Nancy F. Walker.
EIN: 316050360
Selected grants: The following grants were reported in 2005.
$1,000,000 to Cincinnati Symphony Orchestra, Cincinnati, OH.
$13,000 to Eccentric Theater Company, Anchorage, AK.
$5,000 to Boys and Girls Club.
$2,500 to Behringer-Crawford Museum, Covington, KY.
$2,000 to Visionaries and Voices, Cincinnati, OH.
$1,000 to Special Olympics-Egypt, Egypt. .

7591
Mary S. & David C. Corbin Foundation
910 Key Bldg.
159 S. Main St.
Akron, OH 44308 (330) 762-6427
Contact: Erika J. May, Office Mgr. and Grants Admin.
FAX: (330) 762-6428; E-mail: corbin@nls.net;
URL: http://foundationcenter.org/grantmaker/corbin/

Established about 1968.
Donor: David C. Corbin†.
Foundation type: Independent foundation.
Financial data (yr. ended 12/31/05): Assets, $21,289,168 (M); expenditures, $1,013,077; qualifying distributions, $805,524; giving activities include $761,340 for 70 grants (high: $60,000; low: $500).
Purpose and activities: Giving primarily for arts and culture, civic and community issues, education, environment, health care, housing, human and social services, medical research, and youth issues.
Fields of interest: Arts; Hospitals (general); Health care, home services; Housing/shelter; Recreation; Human services; Children/youth, services.
Type of support: General/operating support; Building/renovation; Equipment; Seed money; Research; Matching/challenge support.

Limitations: Giving primarily in Akron and Summit County, OH. No support for organizations which in turn make grants to others. No grants to individuals, or for annual fundraising campaigns, ongoing requests for general operating support, or operating deficits.
Publications: Application guidelines.
Application information: Guidelines and coversheet available on foundation Web site. Application form required.
Copies of proposal: 2
Deadline(s): Mar. 1 for consideration in May; Sept. 1 for consideration in Nov.
Board meeting date(s): Quarterly, beginning early Feb.
Officers and Trustees:* Joseph M. Holden,* Pres. and Secy.; James S. Hartenstein,* V.P. and Treas.; Sophie E. Albrecht; Robert M. Bonchack; Louis A. Maglione; Roger T. Read; Raymond R. Wernig.
Number of staff: 1 part-time support.
EIN: 237052280
Selected grants: The following grants were reported in 2004.
$150,000 to Akron Art Museum, Akron, OH. 2 grants: $50,000 (For capital and endowment campaign), $100,000 (For capital and endowment campaign).
$100,000 to Stan Hywet Hall Foundation, Akron, OH. 2 grants: $50,000 each (For Gothic Style Conservatory).
$73,140 to Childrens Hospital Foundation, Akron, OH. For renovation of Corbin Outpatient Burn Center.
$60,000 to United Way of Summit County, Akron, OH.
$50,000 to Akron City Hospital, Akron, OH. For Critical Care Pavilion.
$25,000 to Interval Brotherhood Homes Corporation, Akron, OH. For upgrade Education Center Auditorium Ceiling and Walls.
$20,000 to East Akron Community House (EACH), Akron, OH. For equipment and furnishings for Excel Classroom in New Addition.
$19,000 to Visiting Nurse Service and Hospice Development Foundation, Akron, OH. For Volunteer Room Renovation.

7592
Cornerstone Foundation ✧ ☆
765 Hedgerow Ln.
Cincinnati, OH 45246
Contact: Ronald H. McSwain, Pres.

Established in 1987 in OH.
Donor: Ronald H. McSwain.
Foundation type: Independent foundation.
Financial data (yr. ended 12/31/04): Assets, $3,233,495 (M); gifts received, $207,454; expenditures, $544,004; qualifying distributions, $527,545; giving activities include $526,965 for 19 grants (high: $420,000; low: $500).
Fields of interest: Education; Urban/community development; Protestant agencies & churches; Economically disadvantaged.
Limitations: Giving primarily in Cincinnati, OH.
Application information: Giving restricted to inner-city projects among the poor in which board members take an active role.
Initial approach: Letter
Deadline(s): None
Officers: Ronald H. McSwain, Pres. and Treas.; Phyllis McSwain, V.P.; Jason McSwain, Secy.
EIN: 311220787

7593
Coshocton Foundation
220 S. 4th St.
P.O. Box 55
Coshocton, OH 43812 (740) 622-0010
Contact: James Gauerke, Treas.
FAX: (740) 622-1660;
E-mail: jamesg@coshoctonfoundation.org;
URL: http://www.coshoctonfoundation.org

Established in 1966 in OH.
Donors: Adolph Golden†; Fred Johnston; Edward E. Montgomery†; Edith Schooler†; Seward Schooler†; Mary F. Taylor; Robert M. Thomas; Willard Baughman†; Willard S. Breon; James E. Wilson†; Herbert E. Carlson†; Ralph Wisenburg; Richard Barthebaug; Mrs. Richard Barthebaug; Ed Mulligan; Marion Mulligan Sutton.
Foundation type: Community foundation.
Financial data (yr. ended 9/30/05): Assets, $18,734,261 (M); gifts received, $223,469; expenditures, $800,325; giving activities include $347,641 for grants, and $204,108 for grants to individuals.
Purpose and activities: The mission of the foundation is to provide a community controlled organization dedicated to the betterment and long term development of Coshocton County's natural, community, and human resources.
Fields of interest: Museums; Performing arts, dance; Arts; Child development, education; Secondary school/education; Higher education; Education; Hospitals (general); Health care; Substance abuse, services; Mental health/crisis services; Alcoholism; Crime/law enforcement; Safety/disasters; Athletics/sports, water sports; Youth development, services; Youth development, citizenship; Children/youth, services; Child development, services; Community development; Government/public administration; Public affairs, citizen participation; Leadership development.
Type of support: Continuing support; Capital campaigns; Building/renovation; Equipment; Program development; Conferences/seminars; Seed money; Curriculum development; Scholarship funds; Employee matching gifts; Scholarships—to individuals; Matching/challenge support.
Limitations: Giving limited to Coshocton County, OH.
Publications: Application guidelines; Annual report; Financial statement; Informational brochure (including application guidelines); Newsletter; Occasional report.
Application information: Visit foundation Web site for application form, guidelines, and specific deadlines. Scholarships granted directly to college or university. Application form required.
Initial approach: Submit application form and attachments
Copies of proposal: 6
Deadline(s): One week before quarterly meeting
Board meeting date(s): Quarterly
Final notification: 45 days after receipt
Officers and Trustees:* Sheila Parkhill,* Pres.; John Snyder,* V.P.; Geneva Martin,* Secy.; James Gauerke,* Treas. and Exec. Dir.; Sally Bullens; Don Parkhill; Bruce Wallace.
Distribution Committee: Tom Thompson, Chair., Distrib. Comm.; Bill Brown; Rick Davis; Tom Edwards; Barbara Warren.
Investment Committee: Richard Corbett, Chair., Investment Comm.; Dick Baker; Fred E. Johnston; Steve Nelson; Marion Sutter.

Number of staff: 1 full-time professional; 1 full-time support.
EIN: 316064567

7594

The Cotswold Foundation ✦ ☆

c/o Fifth Third Bank
38 Fountain Sq. Plz., Trust Tax Dept., MD1COM31
Cincinnati, OH 45263 (513) 579-6034
Contact: Stephanie A. Smith, Fdn. Dir.
Application address: Fifth Third Bank, MD 1090CA, Cincinnati, OH, 45263

Established in 1998 in OH.
Donor: Beth B. Jones.
Foundation type: Independent foundation.
Financial data (yr. ended 12/31/05): Assets, $4,372,314 (M); expenditures, $374,057; qualifying distributions, $349,432; giving activities include $348,982 for 29 grants (high: $100,000; low: $5,000).
Purpose and activities: Giving primarily for the preservation of wilderness areas, the prevention of cruelty to animals and to promote the welfare of children.
Fields of interest: Education; Environment, natural resources; Animals/wildlife, preservation/protection; Aquariums; Children, services.
Type of support: General/operating support.
Limitations: Giving primarily in FL, MT and OH. No grants to individuals.
Application information:
  Initial approach: Letter
  Deadline(s): None
Trustees: Catherine J. Bournstein; Martha L. Burchenal; Beth B. Jones; Fifth Third Bank.
EIN: 316611702
Selected grants: The following grants were reported in 2003.
$60,000 to Nature Conservancy of Montana, Helena, MT. 2 grants: $25,000, $35,000
$25,000 to Seven Hills School, Cincinnati, OH.
$15,000 to Five Valleys Land Trust, Missoula, MT.
$15,000 to University of Central Florida, Orlando, FL.
$10,000 to Brown Bear Resources, Missoula, MT.
$10,000 to Cincinnati Parks Foundation, Cincinnati, OH.
$10,000 to Civic Garden Center of Greater Cincinnati, Cincinnati, OH.
$7,000 to IMAGO, Cincinnati, OH.
$6,000 to Cheetah Conservation Fund, Cincinnati, OH.

7595

Covenant Foundation, Inc. ✦

c/o Timothy E. Johnson
5807 McCray Ct.
Cincinnati, OH 45224

Established in 1987 in OH.
Foundation type: Independent foundation.
Financial data (yr. ended 12/31/05): Assets, $17,170,643 (M); gifts received, $1,816,441; expenditures, $845,226; qualifying distributions, $833,202; giving activities include $828,504 for 24 grants (high: $581,304; low: $1,000).
Purpose and activities: Giving to organizations that further Christian missions with a meaningful evangelical component.
Fields of interest: Christian agencies & churches.

Type of support: General/operating support; Continuing support; Capital campaigns; Building/renovation; Equipment; Land acquisition; Debt reduction; Emergency funds; Program development; Research; Program-related investments/loans; Matching/challenge support.
Limitations: Applications not accepted. Giving on a national basis. No grants to individuals.
Application information: Unsolicited requests for grants not accepted. Grants only to organizations known to trustees.
  Board meeting date(s): Mar.
Trustees: Timothy C. Gehner; Janet L. Johnson; Paul T. Johnson; Timothy E. Johnson.
Number of staff: None.
EIN: 311225037
Selected grants: The following grants were reported in 2004.
$257,554 to North Park University, Chicago, IL.
$20,000 to Victory Videos, Cincinnati, OH.
$4,500 to Frontiers, Mesa, AZ.
$4,000 to Reformed Theological Seminary, Charlotte, NC.
$3,000 to Coalition for Christian Outreach, Pittsburgh, PA.
$3,000 to InterVarsity Christian Fellowship/USA, Madison, WI.
$2,000 to Asbury Theological Seminary, Wilmore, KY.
$1,000 to Gathering, The, Tyler, TX.
$840 to McCormick Theological Seminary, Chicago, IL.

7596

James M. Cox, Jr. Foundation, Inc. ✦

4th and Ludlow Sts.
Dayton, OH 45402
Contact: Leigh Ann Launius, Tr.
Application address: c/o Cox Enterprises, Inc., P.O. Box 105720, Atlanta, GA 30348, tel.: (678) 645-0000

Established in 1969 in GA.
Donor: James M. Cox, Jr.†
Foundation type: Independent foundation.
Financial data (yr. ended 12/31/04): Assets, $45,304,856 (M); expenditures, $2,354,699; qualifying distributions, $2,200,000; giving activities include $2,200,000 for 35 grants (high: $500,000; low: $500).
Purpose and activities: Support for environmental conservation, higher education (through scholarship program), including schools of journalism and media communications, and social services.
Fields of interest: Media, journalism/publishing; Higher education; Environment, natural resources; Environment; Human services.
Type of support: Capital campaigns; Building/renovation.
Limitations: Giving limited to cities where Cox Enterprises does business.
Publications: Application guidelines.
Application information: Application form not required.
  Initial approach: Letter
  Copies of proposal: 3
  Deadline(s): One month before meeting
  Board meeting date(s): Quarterly
Officers and Trustees:* Barbara Cox Anthony,* Chair.; Timothy W. Hughes,* V.P.; Andrew A. Merdek, Secy.; John G. Bayette, Treas.; Richard Braunstein; James Cox Kennedy; Leigh Ann Launius.
EIN: 237256190

Selected grants: The following grants were reported in 2003.
$1,000,000 to Little Star, Aspen, CO. For general operating support.
$750,000 to Colorado State University, Fort Collins, CO. For capital campaign.
$135,000 to PATH Foundation, Atlanta, GA. For capital campaign.
$50,000 to University of Georgia Athletic Association, Athens, GA. For scholarships.
$45,000 to Wilderness Society, DC. For general operating support.
$40,000 to Wittenberg University, Springfield, OH. For Science Center capital campaign.
$25,000 to Air Force Museum Foundation, Wright Patterson AFB, OH. For capital campaign.
$25,000 to James M. Cox, Jr. Arboretum Foundation, Dayton, OH. For capital campaign.
$10,000 to Florida Atlantic University Foundation, Boca Raton, FL. For scholarships.
$5,000 to East Central University Foundation, Ada, OK. For scholarships.
$2,500 to Ohio University, Athens, OH. For scholarships.

7597

The Creech Family Charitable Trust ▼ ✦

(formerly The Akey Charitable Trust)
c/o Frederick J. Caspar
10 Courthouse Plz. S.W., Ste. 1100
Dayton, OH 45402 (937) 449-2800
Contact: David R. Wickham

Established in 1997 in OH.
Donors: Kay Akey Creech; Randolph S. Creech.
Foundation type: Independent foundation.
Financial data (yr. ended 12/31/05): Assets, $2,536,206 (M); expenditures, $6,830,977; qualifying distributions, $6,770,595; giving activities include $6,706,500 for 11 grants (high: $5,866,900; low: $1,200; average: $6,000–$60,000), and $64,095 for 10 grants to individuals (high: $16,964; low: $682; average: $1,020–$7,888).
Purpose and activities: Support primarily for Christian-based organizations and activities.
Fields of interest: Higher education; Education; Athletics/sports, training; Christian agencies & churches.
Type of support: Grants to individuals.
Limitations: Giving primarily in OH.
Application information:
  Initial approach: Contact foundation
  Deadline(s): None
Trustees: Kay Akey Creech; Randolph S. Creech.
EIN: 311574878
Selected grants: The following grants were reported in 2005.
$5,866,900 to Campus Crusade for Christ International, Orlando, FL.
$680,000 to Legacy Ministries International, Xenia, OH.
$60,000 to Miami Valley Womens Center, Dayton, OH.
$30,000 to American Values, Arlington, VA.
$30,000 to In Word Ministry, Middletown, OH.
$21,000 to Word of Life Institute, Pottersville, NY.
$7,800 to Navigators, The, Colorado Springs, CO.
$1,800 to Son Reign Ministries, Beavercreek, OH.

7598
CRN Foundation ◇
1900 E. 9th St., Rm. 3200
Cleveland, OH 44114-3485

Established in 2004 in OH.
Foundation type: Independent foundation.
Financial data (yr. ended 12/31/05): Assets, $895,523 (M); gifts received, $1,500; expenditures, $327,627; qualifying distributions, $323,050; giving activities include $321,550 for 15 grants (high: $250,000; low: $50; average: $1,000–$10,000).
Fields of interest: Higher education; Human services; Family services; Foundations (private grantmaking).
Limitations: Applications not accepted. Giving primarily in OH and TX; some funding nationally. No grants to individuals.
Application information: Contributes only to pre-selected organizations.
Officers and Trustees: Richard Neu,* Pres.; Cheryl Neu,* Secy.; Troy Decello,* Treas.
EIN: 201413635

7599
Dana Corporation Foundation ◇
P.O. Box 1000
Toledo, OH 43697 (419) 535-4500
Contact: Ed McNeal

Incorporated in 1956 in OH.
Donor: Dana Corp.
Foundation type: Company-sponsored foundation.
Financial data (yr. ended 3/31/05): Assets, $3,498,249 (L); gifts received, $500,000; expenditures, $1,811,961; qualifying distributions, $1,782,571; giving activities include $1,401,701 for 172 grants (high: $264,916; low: $200), $14,000 for 7 grants to individuals (high: $2,000; low: $2,000), and $364,370 for employee matching gifts.
Purpose and activities: The foundation supports organizations involved with arts and culture, education, health, human services, community development, international law, and government and public administration.
Fields of interest: Arts; Higher education; Education; Health care; American Red Cross; Children/youth, services; Human services; Community development; Federated giving programs; Law/international law; Government/public administration.
Type of support: General/operating support; Continuing support; Annual campaigns; Capital campaigns; Building/renovation; Equipment; Land acquisition; Emergency funds; Employee matching gifts; Scholarships—to individuals.
Limitations: Giving primarily in areas of company operations. No grants to individuals (except for the Driveshaft Scholarship Fund), or for fellowships; no loans.
Publications: Informational brochure (including application guidelines).
Application information: Application form not required.
> *Initial approach:* Proposal
> *Copies of proposal:* 1
> *Deadline(s):* None
> *Board meeting date(s):* Apr., Aug., and Dec. or May, Sept., and Jan.
> *Final notification:* 60 to 90 days

Officers and Directors: Mike Burns,* Pres.; Anne Marie Riley,* V.P.; Joe Stancati,* Secy.; Kathy Chang,* Treas.; Bob Fesenmyer; Cheryl Kline.
Number of staff: 1 part-time professional.
EIN: 346544909
Selected grants: The following grants were reported in 2003.
$291,000 to United Way of Greater Toledo, Toledo, OH.
$65,000 to United Way of Allen County, Fort Wayne, IN.
$50,000 to Central City Ministries of Toledo, Toledo, OH.
$50,000 to Toledo Museum of Art, Toledo, OH.
$25,000 to Crawford County Foundation, Cuba, MO.
$10,000 to Big Brothers/Big Sisters of Iredell County, Statesville, NC.
$10,000 to Intersection, Columbia, MO.
$7,550 to Union University, Jackson, TN.
$5,000 to Junior Achievement of San Joaquin County, Stockton, CA.
$2,893 to North Panola Vocational Complex, Como, MS.

7600
Charles H. Dater Foundation, Inc. ◇
302 Gwynne Bldg.
602 Main St., Ste. 302
Cincinnati, OH 45202 (513) 241-2658
Contact: Bruce A. Krone, Secy.
FAX: (513) 241-2731;
E-mail: info@DaterFoundation.org; *URL:* http://www.daterfoundation.org

Established in 1985 in OH.
Donor: Charles H. Dater†.
Foundation type: Independent foundation.
Financial data (yr. ended 8/31/05): Assets, $46,848,560 (M); expenditures, $2,404,543; qualifying distributions, $1,741,722; giving activities include $1,281,468 for 71 grants (high: $100,000; low: $100).
Purpose and activities: The foundation makes grants to private, nonprofit organizations and public agencies in Greater Cincinnati for programs that benefit children in the region in the areas of arts/culture, education, health care, social services and other community needs.
Fields of interest: Historic preservation/historical societies; Arts; Child development, education; Higher education; Libraries/library science; Education; Hospitals (general); Medical care, rehabilitation; Crime/violence prevention, youth; Recreation; Human services; Children/youth, services; Child development, services; Family services; Christian agencies & churches; Disabilities, people with; Economically disadvantaged.
Type of support: General/operating support; Continuing support; Annual campaigns; Building/renovation; Equipment; Program development; Seed money; Scholarship funds; Consulting services; Program-related investments/loans.
Limitations: Giving primarily in the greater Cincinnati, OH, area. No grants to individuals, or for scholarships, debt reduction, or for capital projects.
Publications: Application guidelines; Annual report; Multi-year report.
Application information: Application guidelines and form available on foundation Web site. Application form required.
> *Initial approach:* Letter requesting application form

Copies of proposal: 6
Deadline(s): None
Board meeting date(s): Monthly
Final notification: Within 2 months
Officers and Directors: John D. Silvati,* V.P.; Bruce A. Krone,* Secy.; Stanley J. Frank, Jr.,* Treas.
EIN: 311150951

7601
The Paul & Carol David Foundation ◇
(formerly The David Family Foundation)
4840 Dressler Rd., No. 200
Canton, OH 44718 (330) 590-0200
Contact: Jeffrey David, Pres.

Established in 1980 in OH.
Donor: Paul David.
Foundation type: Independent foundation.
Financial data (yr. ended 12/31/05): Assets, $54,378,769 (M); gifts received, $1,470,833; expenditures, $3,187,089; qualifying distributions, $2,850,194; giving activities include $2,143,680 for 65 grants (high: $500,000; low: $30), and $522,792 for grants to individuals.
Purpose and activities: Giving primarily for children's issues in Stark County, OH; also awards college scholarships to high school students in Stark County, OH.
Fields of interest: Children/youth, services.
Type of support: Capital campaigns; Building/renovation; Equipment; Scholarships—to individuals.
Limitations: Giving limited to Stark County, OH.
Application information: Application form required.
> *Initial approach:* Proposal or application form
> *Copies of proposal:* 5
> *Deadline(s):* None
> *Board meeting date(s):* As needed

Officers and Trustees: Carol David,* Chair.; Jeffrey David,* Pres.; Tom Knoll; Walt Stanislawski.
EIN: 341319236
Selected grants: The following grants were reported in 2003.
$250,000 to YMCA of Central Stark County, Canton, OH.
$70,800 to Domestic Violence Project, Canton, OH. For capital campaign.
$50,000 to United Way of Greater Stark County, Canton, OH. For annual campaign.
$25,000 to Community Services of Stark County, Canton, OH. For program support.
$20,000 to Pegasus Farm, Hartville, OH. For arena roof and siding repair.
$7,500 to Big Brothers/Big Sisters of Massillon, Massillon, OH. For annual campaign.
$3,750 to Stark Community Foundation, Canton, OH. For traumatized child workshop.
$3,000 to Wilderness Center, Wilmot, OH. For general support.
$2,000 to Saint Johns Villa, Childrens Home, Carrollton, OH. For benefit dinner.
$250 to Siffrin Residential Association, Canton, OH. For general support.

7602
Carleton F. & Ruth T. Davidson Trust ◇
285 Ridge Mall
Springfield, OH 45504
Contact: Norma Dillon, Tr.

Established in 1987 in OH.

Donor: Carleton F. Davidson.
Foundation type: Independent foundation.
Financial data (yr. ended 12/31/05): Assets, $8,734,408 (M); expenditures, $488,462; qualifying distributions, $432,978; giving activities include $432,978 for 13 grants (high: $280,400; low: $1,000).
Fields of interest: Museums (art); Higher education; Housing/shelter, services; Recreation, parks/playgrounds; Recreation; Christian agencies & churches.
Limitations: Giving primarily in Springfield, and Clark County, OH. No grants to individuals.
Application information:
  Initial approach: Letter
  Deadline(s): None
Trustees: Norma Dillon; Ed Rice.
EIN: 316328010

7603
The Dayton Foundation ▼
2300 Kettering Twr.
Dayton, OH 45423-1395 (937) 222-0410
Contact: Michael M. Parks, Pres.
FAX: (937) 222-0636;
E-mail: info@daytonfoundation.org; Additional tel.: (877) 222-0410; Additional E-mail: Dtimmons@daytonfoundation.org and Bstonerock@daytonfoundation.org; URL: http://www.daytonfoundation.org

Established in 1921 in OH by resolution and declaration of trust.
Foundation type: Community foundation.
Financial data (yr. ended 6/30/06): Assets, $298,963,813 (M); gifts received, $61,275,205; expenditures, $43,886,391; giving activities include $32,628,442 for 14,354 grants (high: $500,000; low: $10), and $1,230,120 for 928 grants to individuals (high: $5,000; low: $100).
Purpose and activities: The mission of the foundation is to advance charitable giving and provide leadership to meet changing needs in the local community.
Fields of interest: Humanities; Arts; Education; Environment; Animal welfare; Health care; Youth development; Children/youth, services; Human services; Public affairs.
Type of support: Capital campaigns; Building/renovation; Equipment; Land acquisition; Program development; Publication; Seed money; Technical assistance; Consulting services.
Limitations: Giving limited to the greater Dayton and Miami Valley, OH, area. No support for religious organizations for religious purposes, or public or private schools. No grants to individuals (except for specific scholarships and award programs), or for operating budgets, exchange programs, professorships, continuing support, travel, fundraising drives, special events, annual campaigns, deficit financing, endowments, or scientific, medical, or academic research; no loans or program-related investments.
Publications: Application guidelines; Annual report; Financial statement; Informational brochure; Newsletter; Program policy statement.
Application information: Visit foundation Web site for application guidelines. The foundation highly recommends attending a free discretionary grants program orientation before applying for funding; online registration is required. Application form required.
  Initial approach: Submit Letter of Intent

Copies of proposal: 1
Deadline(s): Jan. 15 and July 13 for Letter of Intent; Mar. 30 and Sept. 28 for full application
Board meeting date(s): Mar., June, Sept., and Dec.
Final notification: 4 to 6 weeks
Officers and Governing Board:* Fred C. Setzer, Jr.,* Chair.; Michael M. Parks, Pres.; Joseph B. Baldasare, V.P., Devel.; Stephen D. Darnell, V.P., Finance; Carol Siyahi Hicks, V.P., Mktg. and Public Rels.; Pamela S. Sunderland, V.P., Admin.; Diane K. Timmons, V.P., Grants and Progs.; Thomas G. Breitenbach,* Treas.; Franz J. Hoge; Ellen Ireland; Charles A. Jones; Helen Jones-Kelley; Jamie King; Leo E. Knight, Jr.; Gary L. LeRoy; Judy D. McCormick; Vicki Pegg; Douglas C. Scholz; Richard W. Schwartz; Jerome F. Tatar; Fred E. Weber.
Trustees: Fifth Third Bank; JPMorgan Chase Bank, N.A.; KeyBank N.A.; Merrill Lynch Pierce Fenner & Smith; National City Bank; PNC Bank, N.A.
Number of staff: 13 full-time professional; 3 part-time professional; 9 full-time support; 5 part-time support.
EIN: 316027287
Selected grants: The following grants were reported in 2005.
$50,000 to Aullwood Audubon Center and Farm, Dayton, OH. For capital campaign.
$25,000 to Dayton Theater Guild, Dayton, OH. For New Theatre Project.
$25,000 to Dayton Visual Arts Center, Dayton, OH. For capital campaign.
$15,200 to Technology Resource Center, Dayton, OH. For Committee to Aid Blind.
$15,000 to Masonic Learning Centers for Children. For Tutoring Project.
$12,000 to Aviation Heritage Foundation, Dayton, OH.
$10,900 to YMCA of Metropolitan Dayton, Dayton, OH. For Camp Kern.
$10,000 to Clothes That Work, Dayton, OH. For Clothing Resale Boutique.
$10,000 to Dayton Society of Natural History, Dayton, OH. For SunWatch Indian Village Renovation.
$10,000 to Human Race Theater Company, Dayton, OH. For Educational Programming.

7604
The Dayton Power and Light Company Foundation ◇
1065 Woodman Dr.
Dayton, OH 45432 (937) 259-7924
Contact: Ginny Strausburg, Exec. Dir.

Established in 1985 in OH.
Donor: The Dayton Power and Light Co.
Foundation type: Company-sponsored foundation.
Financial data (yr. ended 12/31/04): Assets, $30,045,533 (M); gifts received, $500,000; expenditures, $1,746,403; qualifying distributions, $1,506,984; giving activities include $1,472,889 for 71 grants (high: $170,000; low: $500).
Purpose and activities: The foundation supports organizations involved with arts and culture, education, health, human services, and community development.
Fields of interest: Museums; Arts; Engineering school/education; Adult education—literacy, basic skills & GED; Education, reading; Education; Environment, energy; Environment; Health care; Human services; Civil rights, race/intergroup relations; Community development; Federated

giving programs; Engineering; Government/public administration; General charitable giving.
Type of support: General/operating support.
Limitations: Giving primarily in west central OH. No support for fraternal, religious, labor, conduit, or veterans' organizations, college fundraising associations, or sports leagues. No grants to individuals, or for endowments, development campaigns, capital campaigns, or general operating support for hospitals, or telephone or mass mail solicitations.
Publications: Informational brochure (including application guidelines).
Application information: Application form not required.
  Initial approach: Proposal
  Copies of proposal: 1
  Deadline(s): None
  Board meeting date(s): Quarterly
Officers and Trustees:* James F. Dicke II,* Pres.; Jane Haley, Secy.; W. August Hillenbrand, Treas.; Ginny Strausburg, Exec. Dir.; Paul R. Bishop; Ernie Green; Allen M. Hill.
Number of staff: 1 full-time professional.
EIN: 311138883

7605
The DBJ Foundation ◇
(formerly The David H. and Barbara M. Jacobs Foundation)
127 Public Sq., Ste. 3300
Cleveland, OH 44114-1303 (216) 589-1300
Contact: Patrick S. Mullin, Tr.

Established in 1990 in OH.
Donors: David H. Jacobs; Barbara M. Jacobs.
Foundation type: Independent foundation.
Financial data (yr. ended 12/31/04): Assets, $14,535,878 (M); gifts received, $1,253,047; expenditures, $732,325; qualifying distributions, $692,000; giving activities include $686,000 for 52 grants (high: $50,000; low: $2,500).
Purpose and activities: Giving primarily for medical research, the arts, and human services.
Fields of interest: Museums (art); Museums (natural history); Museums (specialized); Performing arts; Arts; Higher education; Education; Botanical gardens; Zoos/zoological societies; Hospitals (general); Health care; Health organizations, association; Human services; YM/YWCAs & YM/YWHAs; Neighborhood centers; Developmentally disabled, centers & services; Protestant agencies & churches.
Type of support: General/operating support.
Limitations: Giving primarily in Cleveland, OH. No grants to individuals.
Application information:
  Initial approach: Letter
  Deadline(s): None
Trustees: Barbara M. Jacobs; Patrick S. Mullin.
EIN: 341661482
Selected grants: The following grants were reported in 2004.
$50,000 to Cleveland Play House, Cleveland, OH. For general support.
$35,000 to Bay United Methodist Church, Bay Village, OH. For general support.
$25,000 to American Cancer Society, Cuyahoga County Unit, Cleveland, OH. For general support.
$20,000 to American Heart Association, N.E. Ohio Affiliate, Cleveland, OH. For general support.
$20,000 to YMCA of Lakewood, Lakewood, OH. For general support.

$15,000 to AIDS Task Force of Greater Cleveland, Cleveland, OH. For general support.

$15,000 to Ocean Reef Community Foundation, Key Largo, FL. For general support.

$15,000 to Ocean Reef Medical Center Foundation, Key Largo, FL. For general support.

$15,000 to Our Lady of the Wayside, Avon, OH. For general support.

$10,000 to Providence House, Cleveland, OH. For general support.

7606

Ann and Ari Deshe Foundation ◇

1800 Moler Rd.
Columbus, OH 43207

Established in 1997 in OH.
Donors: Ann Deshe; Ari Deshe.
Foundation type: Independent foundation.
Financial data (yr. ended 12/31/04): Assets, $1,783,782 (M); expenditures, $351,567; qualifying distributions, $351,567; giving activities include $351,367 for 9 grants (high: $350,000; low: $45).
Fields of interest: Health organizations, association; Jewish federated giving programs; Jewish agencies & temples.
Limitations: Applications not accepted. Giving primarily in Columbus, OH. No grants to individuals.
Application information: Contributes only to pre-selected organizations.
Officers: Ann Deshe, Pres.; Ari Deshe, V.P.
EIN: 311499050
Selected grants: The following grants were reported in 2004.

$350,000 to Columbus Jewish Foundation, Columbus, OH.

$500 to Kidney F oundation, New York, NY.

$250 to Henry Hacker Memorial Scholarship Fund, Columbus, OH.

$250 to Leukemia & Lymphoma Society, White Plains, NY.

$100 to Bexley City Schools, Columbus, OH. For Lions Pride.

$100 to Columbus Community Kollel, Columbus, OH.

$72 to Ahavas Sholom Sisterhood, Columbus, OH.

$50 to American Heart Association, Dallas, TX.

$45 to Agudas Achim Synagogue, Columbus, OH.

7607

The George H. Deuble Foundation ◇

5757 Mayfair Rd.
P.O. Box 2288
North Canton, OH 44720
Contact: Andrew H. Deuble, Secy.

Established in 1995 in OH.
Foundation type: Independent foundation.
Financial data (yr. ended 12/31/05): Assets, $28,032,976 (M); expenditures, $1,723,249; qualifying distributions, $1,534,633; giving activities include $1,370,000 for 166 grants (high: $77,700; low: $75; average: $1,000–$10,000).
Purpose and activities: Giving primarily for arts, education, health care, and human services.
Fields of interest: Humanities; Arts; Education; Hospitals (general); Boys & girls clubs; Big Brothers/Big Sisters; Human services; Federated giving programs.

Application information: Only accepts unsolicited applications from the North Canton, OH, area. Application form not required.
   Initial approach: Letter
   Copies of proposal: 1
   Deadline(s): None
   Board meeting date(s): Quarterly
   Final notification: 6 weeks
Officers and Trustees:* Steven G. Deuble,* Pres.; Andrew H. Deuble,* Secy.; Walter C. Deuble; Walter J. Deuble; Charles A. Morgan, Jr.
Number of staff: 3 part-time professional.
EIN: 341806245

7608

The Dewald Family Charitable Foundation, Inc. ◇ ☆

c/o S.R. Susskind
600 Vine St., Ste. 2800
Cincinnati, OH 45202-2409
Application address: c/o Margery Dewald Glaser, 10124 Stephens Young Rd., Camden, OH 43111, tel.: (937) 452-3082

Established in 2003 in OH.
Foundation type: Independent foundation.
Financial data (yr. ended 12/31/05): Assets, $1,442,850 (M); gifts received, $101,250; expenditures, $342,861; qualifying distributions, $342,861; giving activities include $318,799 for 15 grants (high: $126,000; low: $2,000).
Purpose and activities: Giving primarily for healthcare education.
Fields of interest: Arts, alliance; Historic preservation/historical societies; Medical school/ education; Health care; Medical research; Human services, mind/body enrichment.
Limitations: Giving on an national basis.
Application information: Application form not required.
   Deadline(s): None
Officers: Margery E. Glaser, Pres.; Gary Glaser, V.P.; Reuben Glaser, Secy.-Treas.
EIN: 311772229

7609

The Christine and Guido Di Geronimo Foundation ◇ ☆

c/o Lee Di Geronimo
33325 Chagrin Blvd.
Moreland Hills, OH 44022

Established in 1994 in OH.
Donor: Guido E. Di Geronimo.
Foundation type: Independent foundation.
Financial data (yr. ended 11/30/05): Assets, $1,276,945 (M); expenditures, $342,348; qualifying distributions, $333,775; giving activities include $333,775 for 18 grants (high: $214,500; low: $900).
Fields of interest: Higher education; Scholarships/ financial aid; Health organizations, association; Human services.
Limitations: Applications not accepted. Giving primarily in OH. No grants to individuals.
Application information: Contributes only to pre-selected organizations.
Trustees: Lee Di Geronimo; Lynn Di Geronimo House.
EIN: 341788087

7610

The Jon & Susan Diamond Family Foundation ◇ ☆

1800 Moler Rd.
Columbus, OH 43207
Contact: Susan Diamond, Pres.
E-mail: Jond@safeauto.com; Additional E-mail: SSDiamond2@aol.com

Established in 1997 in OH.
Donors: Susan Diamond; Jon Diamond; Schottenstein Stores Corp.
Foundation type: Independent foundation.
Financial data (yr. ended 12/31/04): Assets, $6,529,793 (M); gifts received, $1,724,824; expenditures, $351,410; qualifying distributions, $351,410; giving activities include $344,000 for 1 grant.
Purpose and activities: Giving primarily to Jewish agencies and temples.
Fields of interest: Jewish agencies & temples.
Type of support: General/operating support; Continuing support; Annual campaigns; Capital campaigns; Building/renovation; Endowments; Emergency funds; Curriculum development; Scholarship funds; Research; Program-related investments/loans; Grants to individuals; Scholarships—to individuals; Matching/challenge support.
Limitations: Applications not accepted. Giving primarily in NY and OH.
Application information: Contributes only to pre-selected organizations.
Officers: Susan Diamond, Pres.; Jon Diamond, V.P.; Ann Deshe, Secy.; Geraldine Schottenstein, Treas.
EIN: 311523574
Selected grants: The following grants were reported in 2003.

$200,356 to Columbus Jewish Foundation, Columbus, OH.

7611

Diebold Foundation ◇

c/o Tax Dept.
P.O. Box 3077
North Canton, OH 44720-8077

Established in 1993 in OH.
Donor: Diebold, Inc.
Foundation type: Company-sponsored foundation.
Financial data (yr. ended 12/31/05): Assets, $8,486,520 (M); expenditures, $636,328; qualifying distributions, $612,324; giving activities include $573,017 for 60 grants (high: $252,333; low: $30).
Purpose and activities: The foundation supports organizations involved with arts and culture, education, health, and human services.
Fields of interest: Museums; Arts; Higher education; Education; Hospitals (general); Health care; Children/youth, services; Human services; Federated giving programs.
Type of support: General/operating support; Annual campaigns; Capital campaigns; Equipment; Emergency funds; Employee matching gifts.
Limitations: Applications not accepted. Giving primarily in OH. No grants to individuals.
Application information: Contributes only to pre-selected organizations.
Officers: Kevin Krakora, Pres.; Sheila Rutt, V.P. and Treas.; Paul Feaser, Secy.
EIN: 341757351

Selected grants: The following grants were reported in 2004.

$40,225 to Walsh University, North Canton, OH.

$30,000 to Ohio Foundation of Independent Colleges, Columbus, OH.

$18,334 to Stark Development Board, Canton, OH.

$14,000 to Stark State College of Technology, Canton, OH.

$10,000 to Stark Education Partnership, Canton, OH.

$5,000 to United Negro College Fund, Fairfax, VA.

$1,000 to Canton Student Loan Foundation, Canton, OH.

$1,000 to Lake Superior State University, Sault Sainte Marie, MI.

$600 to Bowling Green State University, Bowling Green, OH.

$200 to Columbia University, New York, NY.

7612
Randolph J. & Estelle M. Dorn Foundation ◇

165 E. Washington Row
Sandusky, OH   44870-2610   (419) 625-8324
Contact: M.J. Stauffer, Pres.

Established around 1971.
Donor: Estelle M. Dorn.
Foundation type: Independent foundation.
Financial data (yr. ended 4/30/05): Assets, $24,529,418 (M); expenditures, $1,501,193; qualifying distributions, $1,312,374; giving activities include $1,236,019 for 123 grants (high: $200,000; low: $450).
Purpose and activities: Giving primarily for the arts, education, health associations, youth development, social services, YMCAs, and community development.
Fields of interest: Arts, multipurpose centers/programs; Arts education; Museums; Performing arts, orchestra (symphony); Arts; Elementary/secondary education; Higher education; Libraries/library science; Education; Health organizations, association; Cancer; Boys & girls clubs; Big Brothers/Big Sisters; Human services; Community development, neighborhood development; Community development; Christian agencies & churches.
Type of support: General/operating support; Equipment; Endowments; Program development; Employee matching gifts.
Limitations: Giving limited to northern OH, with strong emphasis on Sandusky. No grants to individuals.
Application information: Application form not required.
Deadline(s): None
Officers and Trustees:* M.J. Stauffer,* Pres.; Mary Jane Hill,* V.P. and Secy.; David F. Reid,* V.P.; Bobbie J. Hummel,* Treas.; John O. Bacon.
EIN: 237099592

7613
Helen G., Henry F. & Louise T. Dornette Foundation ◇ ☆

c/o Fifth Third Bank
P.O. Box 630858
Cincinnati, OH   45263

Established in 1991 in OH.
Donor: Helen G. Dornette†.

Foundation type: Independent foundation.
Financial data (yr. ended 3/31/06): Assets, $13,628,284 (M); expenditures, $968,161; qualifying distributions, $893,852; giving activities include $852,500 for 28 grants (high: $200,000; low: $5,000).
Fields of interest: Media/communications; Museums; Arts; Botanical gardens; Zoos/zoological societies; Health organizations, association; Human services; American Red Cross; Salvation Army.
Limitations: Applications not accepted. Giving primarily in OH. No grants to individuals.
Application information: Contributes only to pre-selected organizations.
Trustees: Stanley Koller; Fifth Third Bank.
EIN: 316425317
Selected grants: The following grants were reported in 2006.

$200,000 to Cincinnati Zoo and Botanical Garden, Cincinnati, OH.

$50,000 to CET, Cincinnati, OH.

$50,000 to Cincinnati Nature Center, Milford, OH.

$50,000 to Cincinnati Parks Foundation, Cincinnati, OH.

$30,000 to American Lung Association of Ohio, Cincinnati, OH.

$25,000 to American Heart Association, Cincinnati, OH.

$25,000 to Boys and Girls Clubs of Greater Cincinnati, Cincinnati, OH.

$25,000 to Disabled Veterans LIFE Memorial Foundation, Arlington, VA.

$25,000 to Mariemont Preservation Foundation, Cincinnati, OH.

$25,000 to WAVE Foundation, Newport, KY.

7614
Downing Foundation ◇

7 Grandin Ln.
Cincinnati, OH   45208-3363   (513) 321-2230
Contact: W. Charles Blum, Secy.

Established in 1994 in OH.
Donor: Jack G. Downing.
Foundation type: Independent foundation.
Financial data (yr. ended 5/31/05): Assets, $6,995,511 (M); expenditures, $423,639; qualifying distributions, $367,013; giving activities include $368,752 for 25 grants (high: $100,000; low: $200).
Purpose and activities: Giving primarily for Roman Catholic agencies, churches, and schools.
Fields of interest: Education; Human services; Roman Catholic agencies & churches.
Type of support: General/operating support.
Limitations: Giving primarily in Cincinnati, OH; some giving also in Helena, MT. No grants to individuals.
Application information:
Initial approach: Proposal
Deadline(s): None
Officers: Mary J. Blum, Chair.; W. Charles Blum, Secy.
Directors: Christine L. Blum; Tracy A. Blum.
EIN: 311416687

7615
Lola G. Duff & William H. Duff II Scholarship ◇ ☆

P.O. Box 94651
Cleveland, OH   44101

Foundation type: Independent foundation.
Financial data (yr. ended 3/31/05): Assets, $79,954,778 (M); expenditures, $2,498,759; qualifying distributions, $2,298,067; giving activities include $2,047,000 for 209 grants to individuals (high: $26,500; low: $5,000).
Fields of interest: Scholarships/financial aid.
Type of support: Scholarships—to individuals.
Limitations: Applications not accepted.
Application information: Unsolicited requests for funds not accepted.
Trustee: National City Bank of Pennsylvania.
EIN: 256020949

7616
George Edward Durell Foundation ◇

623-J Park Meadow Rd.
Westerville, OH   43081-2873

Established in 1985 in VA.
Donor: George Edward Durell†.
Foundation type: Independent foundation.
Financial data (yr. ended 12/31/05): Assets, $34,652,357 (M); expenditures, $1,601,018; qualifying distributions, $1,381,911; giving activities include $1,131,000 for 24 grants (high: $560,000; low: $1,500; average: $10,000–$125,000).
Purpose and activities: Giving primarily for youth services, as well as for education, including a center of science and industry, and for Christian education, organizations and churches.
Fields of interest: Higher education; Education; Human services; Youth, services; Science; Christian agencies & churches; Protestant agencies & churches; Religion.
Type of support: General/operating support; Program development; Conferences/seminars.
Limitations: Applications not accepted. Giving on a national basis, with some emphasis on Columbus, OH, and VA. No grants to individuals.
Application information: Contributes only to pre-selected organizations. Unsolicited requests for funds not considered.
Board meeting date(s): Jan., Apr., July, and Oct.
Officer and Trustees:* David A. Durell,* Chair.; James Landaker; Paul A. Schoonover; Alson H. Smith; William S. Weiant.
EIN: 311111800
Selected grants: The following grants were reported in 2003.

$312,000 to Shenandoah University, Winchester, VA.

$200,000 to COSI Columbus, Columbus, OH.

$20,000 to El Centro de los Ninos, Tierra Amarilla, NM.

$15,000 to Advancing Churches in Missions Commitment, Atlanta, GA.

$10,000 to Fellowship of Christian Athletes, Columbus, OH.

$5,000 to Boy Scouts of America, Shenandoah Area Council, Winchester, VA.

$5,000 to Josephine School Community Museum, Berryville, VA.

$5,000 to Man in the Mirror, Casselberry, FL.

$3,500 to National Association of Street Schools, Denver, CO.

$2,500 to Indiana Wesleyan University, Marion, IN.

7617
The Eaton Charitable Fund ▼
c/o Eaton Corp.
1111 Superior Ave.
Cleveland, OH 44114-2584   (216) 523-4944
Contact: William B. Doggett, Chair.
FAX: (216) 479-7013;
E-mail: barrydoggett@eaton.com; URL: http://
www.eaton.com/NASApp/cs/ContentServer?
pagename=EatonCom%2FPage%
2FEC_T_ArticleFull&c=Page&cid=1007421140590

Trust established in 1953 in OH.
Donor: Eaton Corp.
Foundation type: Company-sponsored foundation.
Financial data (yr. ended 12/31/05): Assets,
$11,839,937 (M); expenditures, $5,328,752;
qualifying distributions, $5,285,508; giving
activities include $5,280,308 for 1,659 grants
(high: $350,000).
Purpose and activities: The fund supports
organizations involved with arts and culture,
education, children and youth, families, and
community development. Special emphasis is
directed toward organizations with which employees
of Eaton are involved.
Fields of interest: Arts; Higher education;
Education; Children/youth, services; Family
services; Community development.
Type of support: General/operating support; Capital
campaigns; Building/renovation; Program
development; Employee volunteer services;
Employee matching gifts; In-kind gifts.
Limitations: Giving on a national and international
basis in areas of company operations. No support
for religious organizations, fraternal or labor
organizations, or organizations that could be
members of a United Fund or federated community
fund but choose not to participate. No grants to
individuals, or for endowments, medical research,
general operating support for United Way agencies
or hospitals, or debt reduction; no loans.
Publications: Application guidelines; Annual report;
Corporate giving report.
Application information: Application form not
required.
  Initial approach: Proposal to nearest company
    facility
  Copies of proposal: 1
  Deadline(s): None
  Board meeting date(s): Bimonthly
  Final notification: 2 to 3 months
Corporate Contributions Committee: William B.
Doggett, Chair.; Craig Arnold; William W. Blausey,
Jr.; Susan J. Cook; Ken D. Semelsberger; James E.
Sweetnam.
Trustee: KeyBank N.A.
EIN: 346501856
Selected grants: The following grants were reported
in 2005.
$350,000 to Cleveland Clinic Foundation,
  Cleveland, OH. For capital campaign for new
  heart center.
$200,000 to Cleveland Museum of Art, Cleveland,
  OH. For capital campaign for expansion.
$150,000 to Cleveland Scholarship Programs,
  Cleveland, OH. For scholarships.
$126,577 to United Way Services of Greater
  Cleveland, Cleveland, OH.
$25,000 to Center for Families and Children,
  Cleveland, OH. For renovations and construction.
$19,770 to United Way of Asheville and Buncombe
  County, Asheville, NC.

$15,000 to Great Lakes Theater Festival, Cleveland,
  OH. For arts education.
$15,000 to Vocational Guidance Services,
  Cleveland, OH. For basic life skills program for
  individuals with disabilities.
$10,000 to American Cancer Society, Jackson, MI.
  For Relay for Life.
$10,000 to Ohio State University, College of
  Engineering, Columbus, OH.

7618
The Edwards Foundation, Inc. ✧ ☆
(formerly J. T. Edwards Company Foundation)
495 S. High St., Ste. 150
Columbus, OH 43215

Established in 1964 in OH.
Donors: Edwards Industries, Inc.; Ross Willoughby
Co.; Edwards Insulation; Duffy Homes; Swan
Manufacturing Co.; Mooney and Moses of Ohio, Inc.;
Jeffrey W. Edwards; Multicon Builders, Inc.
Foundation type: Company-sponsored foundation.
Financial data (yr. ended 6/30/05): Assets,
$871,914 (M); gifts received, $1,396,203;
expenditures, $801,018; qualifying distributions,
$801,018; giving activities include $800,935 for 24
grants (high: $341,635; low: $250).
Purpose and activities: The foundation supports
organizations involved with arts and culture,
education, health, and human services.
Fields of interest: Museums; Arts; Higher
education; Education; Hospitals (general);
Reproductive health, family planning; Health care;
Salvation Army; Human services; Federated giving
programs.
Type of support: Capital campaigns; Annual
campaigns; General/operating support; Building/
renovation.
Limitations: Applications not accepted. Giving
primarily in OH, with emphasis on Columbus. No
grants to individuals; no loans or program-related
investments.
Application information: Contributes only to
pre-selected organizations.
Officer and Trustees: John A. Leibold, Treas.; Paula
Cochran; Jeffrey W. Edwards; Peter H. Edwards, Sr.;
Judith Sandbo.
EIN: 237447588
Selected grants: The following grants were reported
in 2003.
$100,000 to Ohio State University Foundation,
  Columbus, OH. 2 grants: $50,000 each
$40,000 to Columbus Museum of Art, Columbus,
  OH.
$30,000 to Salvation Army, Columbus, OH.
$25,000 to United Way of Central Ohio, Columbus,
  OH.
$20,000 to Ohio State University, Columbus, OH.
$10,000 to Wellington School, Columbus, OH.
$3,600 to Columbus Foundation, Columbus, OH.
$2,000 to Boca Raton Historical Society, Boca
  Raton, FL.
$1,000 to Boca Raton Community Hospital, Boca
  Raton, FL.

7619
The Thomas J. Emery Memorial
c/o The Greater Cincinnati Foundation
200 W. 4th St.
Cincinnati, OH 45202   (513) 241-2880
Contact: Mary LeRoy, Prog. Off.

Incorporated in 1925 in OH.
Donor: Mary Muhlenberg Emery†.
Foundation type: Independent foundation.
Financial data (yr. ended 12/30/04): Assets,
$27,750,135 (M); expenditures, $1,484,409;
qualifying distributions, $1,319,903; giving
activities include $1,249,750 for 62 grants (high:
$120,000; low: $500).
Purpose and activities: The purpose of the
foundation is to secure a citizenry which shall be
more sane, sound and effective because of more
satisfactory initial conditions of environment and
education. The foundation is used for the physical,
social, civic and educational betterment of
individuals.
Fields of interest: Performing arts; Arts;
Elementary/secondary education; Higher education;
Health care; Human services.
Type of support: Capital campaigns; Building/
renovation; Program development.
Limitations: Giving primarily in the greater Cincinnati
area, including Hamilton, Butler, Clermont and
Warren counties in OH, and Boone, Campbell and
Kenton counties in KY. No support for non 501(c)(3)
organizations. No grants to individuals, or for
continuing support or conferences; no loans.
Publications: Application guidelines.
Application information: Letter of inquiry available
at http://www.greatercincinnatifdn.org, under
Grants/Private Foundations/The Thomas J. Emery
Memorial. Application form required.
  Copies of proposal: 2
  Deadline(s): Feb. 1, July 1 and Oct. 1
  Board meeting date(s): Apr., Sept., and Dec.
  Final notification: 30 days after meeting
Officers and Trustees:* Lee A. Carter,* Pres.; John
T. Lawrence, Jr.,* V.P.; James S. Wachs,* Secy.;
John F. Barrett,* Treas.; Thomas L. Williams.
EIN: 310536711
Selected grants: The following grants were reported
in 2004.
$120,000 to Cincinnati Institute of Fine Arts,
  Cincinnati, OH.
$97,500 to United Way of Greater Cincinnati,
  Cincinnati, OH.
$62,500 to Greater Cincinnati Foundation,
  Cincinnati, OH.
$54,000 to Cincinnati Opera Association,
  Cincinnati, OH.
$50,000 to Miami Valley Christian Academy,
  Newtown, OH.
$50,000 to Taft Museum, Cincinnati, OH.
$40,000 to Cincinnati Arts School, Cincinnati, OH.
$25,000 to American Classical Music Hall of Fame
  and Museum, Cincinnati, OH.
$25,000 to Cincinnati Nature Center, Milford, OH.
$25,000 to Crayons to Computers, Cincinnati, OH.

7620
The Thomas J. Evans Foundation ✧
36 N. 2nd St.
Newark, OH 43055
Contact: J. Gilbert Reese, Chair. and C.E.O.

Established in 1965 in OH.
Donors: Thomas J. Evans†; Dan Evans; Peggy
Evans.
Foundation type: Independent foundation.
Financial data (yr. ended 10/31/05): Assets,
$23,049,156 (M); expenditures, $944,559;
qualifying distributions, $807,938; giving activities
include $701,443 for 11 grants (high: $350,000;
low: $44).

Purpose and activities: Grants primarily for community development.
Fields of interest: Human services; Community development; Foundations (community).
Type of support: General/operating support; Building/renovation; Seed money; Scholarship funds.
Limitations: Giving primarily in the Licking County, OH, area. No grants to individuals.
Application information: Application form not required.

Initial approach: Letter
Deadline(s): None
Board meeting date(s): Quarterly

Officers: J. Gilbert Reese, Chair. and C.E.O.; Sarah Wallace, Pres. and Secy.; Louella H. Reese, V.P. and Treas.
EIN: 316055767
Selected grants: The following grants were reported in 2005.
$400,000 to Licking County Foundation, Newark, OH. 2 grants: $350,000, $50,000
$25,000 to A Call to College, Newark, OH.

7621
The Fairfax Foundation ✧
29425 Chagrin Blvd., Ste. 203
Pepper Pike, OH 44122
Contact: Gerald A. Conway, Tr.; Kevin C. Conway, Tr.
Application address: 30195 Chagrin Blvd., Ste. 350W, Cleveland, OH 44124

Established in 1986 in OH.
Donors: Gerald A. Conway; Martine V. Conway.
Foundation type: Independent foundation.
Financial data (yr. ended 12/31/05): Assets, $2,346,365 (M); expenditures, $487,642; qualifying distributions, $422,287; giving activities include $422,287 for 18 grants (high: $250,000; low: $287; average: $2,500–$10,000).
Purpose and activities: Giving primarily for environmental protection, religion and education.
Fields of interest: Education; Environment, forests; Brain research; Human services; International affairs; Religion.
International interests: Central America.
Type of support: Annual campaigns; Capital campaigns; Research; Matching/challenge support.
Limitations: Giving primarily in OH. No grants to individuals.
Application information: Contributes primarily to pre-selected organizations. Application form required.

Initial approach: Letter
Copies of proposal: 1
Deadline(s): None
Board meeting date(s): Varies
Final notification: 2 months

Officer and Trustees:* Gerald A. Conway,* Chair.; Gerald A. Conway, Jr.; Kevin C. Conway; Martine V. Conway.
Number of staff: 1 part-time professional.
EIN: 341553708
Selected grants: The following grants were reported in 2003.
$75,000 to Trees, Water and People, Fort Collins, CO.
$40,000 to NARSAD Research Institute, Great Neck, NY.
$40,000 to Stella Maris, Inc., Cleveland, OH.
$2,000 to Cleveland Music School Settlement, Cleveland, OH.
$1,000 to Benjamin Rose Institute, Cleveland, OH.

$1,000 to Gilmour Academy, Gates Mills, OH.
$1,000 to NAMI-Metro Cleveland, Shaker Heights, OH.
$500 to Neighbor to Neighbor, Dayton, OH.
$500 to Providence House, Cleveland, OH.
$500 to Spectrum of Supportive Services, Cleveland, OH.

7622
Fairfield County Foundation
162 E. Main St.
P.O. Box 159
Lancaster, OH 43130 (740) 654-8451
Contact: Amy Eyman, Exec. Dir.
FAX: (740) 654-3971;
E-mail: info@fairfieldcountyfoundation.org;
Additional E-mail: aeyman@fairfieldcountyfoundation.org; URL: http://www.fairfieldcountyfoundation.org

Established in 1989 in OH.
Foundation type: Community foundation.
Financial data (yr. ended 12/31/05): Assets, $24,007,925 (M); gifts received, $2,278,397; expenditures, $1,110,530; giving activities include $465,427 for 162 grants (high: $35,000; low: $25), and $337,060 for 195 grants to individuals (high: $5,500; low: $500).
Purpose and activities: The foundation was created to receive and administer charitable gifts that will provide long-term, continuing benefits to Fairfield County and its residents by supporting educational, scientific, cultural, social, environmental, medical and other charitable purposes.
Fields of interest: Arts; Education, early childhood education; Elementary/secondary school reform; Education, continuing education; Education; Environment, beautification programs; Environment; Hospitals (general); Health care; Mental health/crisis services; Health organizations, association; Employment; Housing/shelter; Recreation; Children/youth, services; Aging, centers/services; Human services; Community development; Aging; Disabilities, people with; Economically disadvantaged; Homeless.
Type of support: Technical assistance; Publication; Continuing support; Capital campaigns; Building/renovation; Equipment; Program development; Seed money; Curriculum development; Scholarship funds; Scholarships—to individuals; Matching/challenge support.
Limitations: Giving limited to Fairfield County, OH. No grants for operating expenses, annual drives, or debt retirement.
Publications: Application guidelines; Annual report; Financial statement; Grants list; Informational brochure (including application guidelines); Newsletter.
Application information: Visit foundation Web site for preliminary grant proposal form and guidelines. Based on the preliminary application, the foundation's Grants Committee will confirm if project fits within the foundation's guidelines and invite the applicant to submit a full proposal. Applications submitted by e-mail or fax not accepted. Application form required.

Initial approach: Telephone or letter confirming request falls within foundation guidelines
Copies of proposal: 3
Deadline(s): Mar. 15 and Aug. 15 for preliminary application; May 2 and Oct. 3 for full proposal

Board meeting date(s): 3rd Thurs. in Jan., Mar., May, July, Sept., and Nov.
Final notification: 2 weeks for preliminary application response

Officers and Trustees:* Milt Taylor, Jr.,* Chair.; Rick Snider,* Vice-Chair.; Barbara Kumler,* Secy.; Mark Bibler,* Treas.; Amy Eyman, Exec. Dir.; Marilyn Clark; John Furlow, Jr.; Sky Gettys; June Harcum; David Jones; Sue Sidwell; Gordon Snider; Dwayne Spence; Dane Swinehart; Barry Walker; Steve Wells.
Number of staff: 1 full-time professional; 2 part-time professional.
EIN: 341623983
Selected grants: The following grants were reported in 2005.
$35,000 to Lancaster Festival, Lancaster, OH. For Lancaster Festival Orchestra.
$20,000 to Maywood Mission, Lancaster, OH. For Thrift Store Pantry.
$15,000 to Decorative Arts Center of Ohio, Lancaster, OH. For art exhibition.
$15,000 to New Horizons Youth and Family Center, Lancaster, OH. For Columbia TeenScreen project.
$7,000 to Fairfield County Parks, Lancaster, OH. For phase one of Rock Mill Restoration roof project.
$7,000 to Sanderson Parent-Teacher Organization, Lancaster, OH. For walking trail paving.
$6,580 to Fairfield Industries, Lancaster, OH. For expansion of Blue Shoe Arts experience.
$5,700 to Fairfield County Health Department, Lancaster, OH. For purchase of three automatic external defibrillators.
$4,705 to Ohio University, Lancaster, OH. For Childcare Center Playground.
$2,800 to Recovery Center, Lancaster, OH. For Fairfield County Family Festival.

7623
Farmer Family Foundation
P.O. Box 625737
Cincinnati, OH 45262-5737 (513) 573-3996

Established in 1988 in OH.
Donors: Brynne F. Coletti; Richard T. Farmer; Amy F. Joseph; Scott D. Farmer.
Foundation type: Independent foundation.
Financial data (yr. ended 12/31/04): Assets, $127,151,110 (M); gifts received, $57,121,215; expenditures, $3,479,902; qualifying distributions, $2,554,040; giving activities include $2,449,059 for 72 grants (high: $800,000; low: $500).
Purpose and activities: To provide funding for charities that will assist and protect primarily children through education, health care, and assistance to the handicapped; giving also to fund programs to assist individuals to enter the work force.
Fields of interest: Education; Medical research; Human services.
Type of support: General/operating support; Capital campaigns; Building/renovation; Program development; Scholarship funds; Research; Matching/challenge support.
Limitations: Giving primarily in Cincinnati, OH. No grants to individuals.
Application information:

Initial approach: Letter
Deadline(s): None
Board meeting date(s): As needed

Officer and Trustees:* Richard T. Farmer,* Chair. and Pres.; Brynne F. Coletti; Robert E. Coletti; Joyce E. Farmer; Mary J. Farmer; Scott D. Farmer; Amy F. Joseph; George R. Joseph.

Number of staff: 1 part-time professional.
EIN: 311256614
Selected grants: The following grants were reported in 2004.
$800,000 to M. D. Anderson Cancer Center Outreach Corporation, Houston, TX.
$373,333 to Summit Country Day School, Cincinnati, OH.
$125,000 to Citizens for Community Values, Cincinnati, OH.
$100,000 to Crayons to Computers, Cincinnati, OH.
$100,000 to Marine Corps Heritage Foundation, Quantico, VA.
$77,500 to Xavier University, Cincinnati, OH.
$50,000 to Cincinnati Nature Center, Milford, OH.
$44,791 to Archbishop Moeller High School, Cincinnati, OH.
$40,202 to Intrepid Fallen Heroes Fund, New York, NY.
$40,000 to Free Store, Cincinnati, OH.

7624
Federated Department Stores Foundation ▼
7 W. 7th St.
Cincinnati, OH 45202 (513) 579-7000
Contact: Dixie Barker, Mgr., Corp. Contribs.
FAX: (513) 579-7185;
E-mail: foundationapps@fds.com; *URL:* http://www.federated-fds.com/community/foundation

Established in 1995 in OH.
Donor: Federated Department Stores, Inc.
Foundation type: Company-sponsored foundation.
Financial data (yr. ended 1/29/05): Assets, $17,628,585 (M); gifts received, $12,300,000; expenditures, $12,240,429; qualifying distributions, $12,249,026; giving activities include $10,191,677 for 1,104 grants (high: $331,522; low: $250), and $1,911,221 for 1,245 employee matching gifts.
Purpose and activities: The foundation supports organizations involved with arts and culture, education, HIV/AIDS, minorities, and women.
Fields of interest: Arts; Education; AIDS; Minorities; Women.
Type of support: General/operating support; Continuing support; Annual campaigns; Capital campaigns; Program development; Seed money; Employee volunteer services; Employee matching gifts; Matching/challenge support.
Limitations: Giving on a national basis in areas of company operations. No support for private foundations, fraternal organizations, political or advocacy organizations, religious organizations not of direct benefit to the entire community, or fiscal agents or other umbrella organizations providing funding to nonprofit organizations. No grants to individuals, or for event or program sponsorships or salaries.
Publications: Application guidelines; Annual report; Corporate giving report; Informational brochure (including application guidelines).
Application information: Letters of inquiry are forwarded by the foundation to the nearest company division. Application form not required.
Initial approach: Contact nearest company division for invitation to apply or E-mail letter of inquiry to foundation
Copies of proposal: 1
Board meeting date(s): Quarterly

Officers and Trustees:* Thomas G. Cody,* Pres.; Klaus M. Ziermaier, Secy.; Susan R. Robinson, Treas.; David W. Clark; Karen Hoguet.
EIN: 311427325
Selected grants: The following grants were reported in 2004.
$257,693 to Cincinnati Institute of Fine Arts, Cincinnati, OH.
$200,000 to National Underground Railroad Freedom Center, Cincinnati, OH.
$103,000 to Florida Education Foundation, Tallahassee, FL.
$80,000 to Elizabeth Glaser Pediatric AIDS Foundation, Santa Monica, CA.
$75,000 to Robert W. Woodruff Arts Center, Atlanta, GA.
$75,000 to San Francisco Symphony, San Francisco, CA.
$70,000 to University of Arizona, Tucson, AZ.
$61,000 to New York Police and Fire Widows and Childrens Benefit Fund, New York, NY.
$61,000 to Scholarship America, Saint Peter, MN.
$60,000 to Cincinnati Museum Center for Natural and Cultural History and Science, Cincinnati, OH.

7625
Leonard C. & Mildred F. Ferguson Foundation ✧
c/o Sky Bank
39 E. Market St., Ste. 402
Akron, OH 44308 (330) 258-2362
Contact: Irene Gray

Established in 1998 in FL.
Donor: Mildred F. Ferguson Irrevocable Trust.
Foundation type: Independent foundation.
Financial data (yr. ended 1/31/05): Assets, $11,763,398 (M); expenditures, $533,020; qualifying distributions, $499,731; giving activities include $488,091 for 40 grants (high: $40,000; low: $480).
Purpose and activities: Giving primarily for education, medicine, social welfare, historic preservation, religion, the environment, and the arts.
Fields of interest: Museums (specialized); Historic preservation/historical societies; Arts; Theological school/education; Education; Environment, natural resources; Hospitals (general); Human services; Youth, services; Community development; Science, single organization support; Christian agencies & churches.
Type of support: Annual campaigns; Capital campaigns; Building/renovation; Land acquisition; Program development; Seed money; Scholarship funds; Matching/challenge support.
Limitations: Giving primarily in CA, FL, IL, ME and VT. No grants to individuals or for endowments.
Application information: Application form not required.
Initial approach: Letter
Deadline(s): None
Board meeting date(s): Last week of July
Final notification: 1 - 3 months from receipt
Officers and Directors:* Nancy Seeley,* Pres.; Lynne Seeley,* V.P.
Trustee: Sky Bank.
EIN: 656245247
Selected grants: The following grants were reported in 2003.
$75,000 to First Congregational Church of Hudson, Hudson, OH. For capital campaign.

$60,000 to Freeport Regional Health Care Foundation, Freeport, IL. For scholarships.
$50,000 to Conservancy of Southwest Florida, Naples, FL. For Naples Nature Center Jason Project.
$40,000 to Committee on Temporary Shelter, Burlington, VT. To purchase building.
$40,000 to Peninsula Open Space Trust, Menlo Park, CA.
$40,000 to University of Dubuque, Theological Seminary, Dubuque, IA. For seminary housing.
$30,000 to Eastside College Preparatory School, East Palo Alto, CA. For scholarships.
$18,840 to Maine State Museum, Friends of the, Augusta, ME. For Website education programs.
$15,000 to Moorings Presbyterian Church, Naples, FL. For general support.
$10,000 to Vermont Forum on Sprawl, Burlington, VT. For general support.

7626
The Fifth Third Foundation ▼
c/o Fifth Third Bank
38 Fountain Square Plz., M.D. 1090CA
Cincinnati, OH 45263 (513) 534-7001
Contact: Heidi B. Jark, Mgr.

Trust established in 1948 in OH.
Donor: Fifth Third Bank.
Foundation type: Company-sponsored foundation.
Financial data (yr. ended 9/30/05): Assets, $10,768,834 (M); gifts received, $4,000,000; expenditures, $6,363,148; qualifying distributions, $6,286,845; giving activities include $6,254,022 for 579 grants (high: $800,000).
Purpose and activities: The foundation supports organizations involved with arts and culture, higher education, adult education, reading, health, human services, community development, and minorities.
Fields of interest: Performing arts; Arts; Higher education; Adult education—literacy, basic skills & GED; Education, reading; Hospitals (general); Health care; Children/youth, services; Human services; Community development; Minorities.
Type of support: Continuing support; Annual campaigns; Capital campaigns; Building/renovation; Equipment; Program development; Publication; Seed money; Scholarship funds; Employee matching gifts.
Limitations: Giving primarily in areas of company operations, with emphasis on the Cincinnati, OH, area. No support for public schools or elementary schools. No grants to individuals, or for capital campaigns for individual churches, endowments, or fellowships; no loans.
Publications: Application guidelines; Annual report.
Application information: Visit Web site for nearest company facility. A site visit may be requested. Application form not required.
Initial approach: Letter of inquiry to nearest company facility
Copies of proposal: 1
Deadline(s): None
Board meeting date(s): Jan., Mar., June, and Sept.
Final notification: Following board meetings
Trustee: Fifth Third Bank.
EIN: 316024135
Selected grants: The following grants were reported in 2005.
$800,000 to Lucas, County of, Toledo, OH. For capital support.
$375,000 to University of Cincinnati Foundation, Cincinnati, OH. For capital support.

$330,000 to United Way of Greater Cincinnati, Cincinnati, OH. For annual fund.
$200,000 to Cincinnati, City of, Cincinnati, OH. For capital support.
$200,000 to Greater Cincinnati Arts and Education Center, Cincinnati, OH. For capital support.
$150,000 to Grand Action Foundation, Grand Rapids, MI. For capital support.
$50,000 to Muhammad Ali Museum and Education Center, Louisville, KY. For capital support.
$25,000 to Queen City Foundation, Cincinnati, OH. For program support.
$20,000 to Lagrange Development Corporation, Toledo, OH. For capital support.
$20,000 to United Way of Hancock County, Findlay, OH. For annual fund.

7627
The Findlay Hancock County Community Foundation

101 W. Sandusky St., Ste. 207
Findlay, OH 45840 (419) 425-1100
Contact: Pat Margraf, C.F.O.; Barbara Deerhake, Exec. Dir.
FAX: (419) 425-9339; E-mail: commfdn@bright.net;
URL: http://www.community-foundation.com
For scholarships:
mswaisgood@community-foundation.com

Established in 1992 in OH as a supporting organization of the Cleveland Foundation; became a community foundation independent of the Cleveland Foundation in Feb. 1999.
Foundation type: Community foundation.
Financial data (yr. ended 12/31/05): Assets, $59,665,653 (M); gifts received, $25,868,302; expenditures, $1,863,869; giving activities include $988,262 for 114 grants, and $219,050 for grants to individuals.
Purpose and activities: The foundation is dedicated to improving the quality of life in the Hancock County area through responsible grantmaking. The foundation seeks to facilitate philanthropic efforts through the development and stewardship of donor funds. The foundation builds permanent endowed funds contributed by individuals, corporations and institutions, provides grants and assistance to develop and strengthen organizations located in our community, encourages partnerships with other foundations, businesses and government entities to increase funds distributed to the community, and inspires philanthropic and community involvement.
Fields of interest: Arts; Adult education—literacy, basic skills & GED; Education; Health care; Youth development; Human services; Economic development; Public affairs.
Type of support: Management development/ capacity building; Capital campaigns; Building/ renovation; Program development; Seed money; Scholarship funds; Technical assistance; Consulting services; Program evaluation; Program-related investments/loans; Student loans —to individuals.
Limitations: Giving limited to the greater Hancock County, OH, area. No support for religious organizations for religious purposes, community services such as the police and fire protection, or for staff positions for government agencies. No grants to individuals (except for scholarships), or for endowment campaigns. Generally no grants for ongoing operating expenses, annual appeals or membership drives, fundraising projects or advertisements, travel, existing obligations, debts

or liabilities, or for the printing of publications, audiovisual projects or video productions. Support for capital requests are seldom considered.
Publications: Application guidelines; Annual report; Financial statement; Informational brochure; Informational brochure (including application guidelines).
Application information: Visit foundation Web site for application forms and requirements. Proposals submitted by fax or e-mail are not accepted. Application form required.
Initial approach: Submit cover sheet, budget forms, and proposal
Copies of proposal: 2
Deadline(s): 1st Fri. of Mar., June, Sept. and Dec.
Board meeting date(s): Feb., Apr., May, July, Sept., and Nov.
Final notification: Within 3 weeks of board meeting
Officers and Trustees:* Charles J. Younger,* Chair.; David S. Healy,* Vice-Chair.; Barbara M. Deerhake,* Pres. and Exec. Dir.; Pat Margraf, C.F.O.; Charles F. Stumpp, Jr.,* Treas.; Karl L. Heminger; Michael S. Needler; G. Norman Nicholson; Jennifer Payne-White; J. Alec Reinhardt; Judy M. Rower; Ralph D. Russo.
Number of staff: 5 full-time professional; 1 full-time support.
EIN: 341713261
Selected grants: The following grants were reported in 2005.
$87,000 to Hancock County Agency on Aging, Findlay, OH. For coordinator to recruit, train, monitor, and evaluate volunteers to provide legal guardianship for Hancock County adult wards.
$47,116 to Century Health, Findlay, OH. For consultants to attain national accreditation to provide services to Hancock County residents.
$37,500 to Findlay, City of, Findlay, OH. For consultant fees.
$30,000 to Findlay-Hancock County Community Foundation, Findlay, OH. For The Family Center start-up costs.
$27,875 to Findlay Hope House for the Homeless, Findlay, OH. For revolving loan fund to assist low-income residents with security deposits and financial literacy.
$25,000 to Arts Partnership of Greater Hancock County, Findlay, OH. For afterschool arts-based intervention for at-risk youth.
$12,800 to Hancock Parks Foundation, Findlay, OH. For consultant fees to create a Hancock County parks, recreation, and open space plan and map.
$8,000 to Wilson Vance Intermediate School, Findlay, OH. For staff training and utilization of the Classroom Performance System (CPS) to increase students' academic achievement.
$1,551 to Howard United Methodist Church. For afterschool tutoring and enrichment activities for elementary students.
$300 to Fort Findlay Kiwanis, Findlay, OH. For age-appropriate books during the summer months for elementary students.

7628
Firman Fund ◇

c/o H & I Advisors
1422 Euclid Ave., 1030 Hanna Bldg.
Cleveland, OH 44115-2078 (216) 363-1030
Contact: Royal Firman, III, Pres.

Incorporated in 1951 in OH.
Donor: Pamela H. Firman†.

Foundation type: Independent foundation.
Financial data (yr. ended 12/31/05): Assets, $10,998,122 (M); expenditures, $642,001; qualifying distributions, $586,080; giving activities include $572,100 for 26 grants (high: $200,000; low: $500).
Purpose and activities: Giving primarily for the arts, education, health care, the environment, and human services.
Fields of interest: Performing arts; Arts; Secondary school/education; Higher education; Environment, natural resources; Health care; Human services; Government/public administration.
Type of support: General/operating support; Annual campaigns; Capital campaigns; Building/ renovation; Scholarship funds.
Limitations: Applications not accepted. Giving primarily in Denver, CO, Tallahassee, FL, Thomasville, GA, and Cleveland, OH. No grants to individuals, or for research; no loans.
Application information: Unsolicited requests for funds not accepted.
Board meeting date(s): Apr. and Nov.
Officers and Trustees:* Royal Firman III, Pres.; Cynthia F. Webster,* V.P.; Neil A. Brown, Secy.; Carole M. Nowak, Treas.; Stephanie Firman; Robert Webster, Jr.
EIN: 346513655

7629
First Place Bank Community Foundation
(formerly First Federal of Warren Community Foundation)

P.O. Box 551
Warren, OH 44482-0551
Contact: David J. Jenkins, Secy. and Exec. Dir.

Established in 1998 in DE.
Donors: First Place Financial Corp.; The Cleveland Clinic Foundation.
Foundation type: Company-sponsored foundation.
Financial data (yr. ended 6/30/05): Assets, $14,325,960 (M); expenditures, $641,955; qualifying distributions, $580,386; giving activities include $580,386 for grants.
Purpose and activities: The foundation supports organizations involved with arts and culture, education, health, human services, and urban affairs and economic development.
Fields of interest: Humanities; Arts; Education; Health care; Human services; Urban/community development.
Type of support: General/operating support; Continuing support; Annual campaigns; Capital campaigns; Building/renovation; Equipment; Land acquisition; Program development; Curriculum development; Scholarship funds; Consulting services; Employee matching gifts; Matching/ challenge support.
Limitations: Giving primarily in areas of company operations. No support for political organizations or religious organizations.
Application information: Telephone calls are not encouraged. Application form required.
Initial approach: Write to foundation for application form
Copies of proposal: 1
Deadline(s): Jan. 5, Apr. 5, July 5, and Oct. 5
Board meeting date(s): 4th Thurs. of Jan., Apr., July, and Oct.
Final notification: End of month following board meetings

Officers and Directors: * Richard P. Cowin,* Chair.; Steven R. Lewis,* Pres.; David J. Jenkins, Secy. and Exec. Dir.; Robert S. McGeough; E.J. Rossi.
Number of staff: 1 part-time professional.
EIN: 341879025

7630
FirstEnergy Foundation ▼ ◇
(formerly Centerior Energy Foundation)
76 S. Main St.
Akron, OH   44308   (330) 761-4246
Contact: Mary Beth Carroll, Pres.
URL: http://www.firstenergycorp.com/community

Incorporated in 1961 in OH.
Donors: The Cleveland Electric Illuminating Co.; Centerior Energy Corp.; FirstEnergy Corp.; The Toledo Edison Co.; GPU Service, Inc.; Metropolitan Edison Co.; Jersey Central Power & Light Co.; Ohio Edison Co.; Pennsylvania Electric Co.
Foundation type: Company-sponsored foundation.
Financial data (yr. ended 12/31/05): Assets, $57,851,681 (M); expenditures, $5,106,336; qualifying distributions, $5,106,336; giving activities include $4,918,900 for 949 grants (high: $241,500).
Purpose and activities: The foundation supports organizations involved with education, public and personal safety, human services, and economic development.
Fields of interest: Education; Crime/law enforcement; Human services; Economic development; Federated giving programs.
Type of support: Annual campaigns; Capital campaigns; Building/renovation; Program development; Curriculum development; Employee matching gifts; Matching/challenge support.
Limitations: Giving primarily in areas of company operations in NJ, OH, and PA. No support for largely tax-supported organizations, fraternal, religious, labor, athletic, social, or veterans' organizations not of direct benefit to the entire community, national or international organizations, United Way-supported organizations, public or private schools, or foundations. No grants to individuals, or for political or legislative activities, research, equipment, endowments, or debt reduction; no loans.
Publications: Application guidelines; Informational brochure; Program policy statement.
Application information: Proposals should be no longer than 2 pages. Application form not required.
   Initial approach: Mail proposal to foundation
   Board meeting date(s): As needed
   Final notification: 12 to 16 weeks
Officer and Trustees: * Mary Beth Carroll,* Pres.; Charles E. Jones; Richard Marsh; Leila Vespoli.
EIN: 346514181
Selected grants: The following grants were reported in 2005.
$241,500 to United Way Services of Greater Cleveland, Cleveland, OH.
$150,000 to Musical Arts Association, Cleveland, OH.
$110,400 to Kent State University Foundation, Kent, OH. 2 grants: $10,400, $100,000
$52,500 to Economic Growth Foundation, Cleveland, OH.
$50,000 to Akron Community Service Center and Urban League, Akron, OH.
$20,000 to United Way of Lebanon County, Lebanon, PA.

$10,000 to Chamber of Commerce of New Jersey, Chamber of Commerce Education Foundation, Trenton, NJ.
$10,000 to COSI Toledo, Toledo, OH.
$10,000 to Family Service of Morris County, Morristown, NJ.

7631
Samuel H. Fleming Charitable Trust ◇
c/o National City Bank
P.O. Box 94651
Cleveland, OH   44101

Established in OH.
Foundation type: Independent foundation.
Financial data (yr. ended 12/31/05): Assets, $10,836,204 (M); expenditures, $546,552; qualifying distributions, $528,177; giving activities include $521,768 for 8 grants (high: $65,221; low: $65,221).
Purpose and activities: Giving for health and medical care as well as for children, youth, and family services, and social services.
Fields of interest: Medical care, rehabilitation; Speech/hearing centers; Nursing care; Goodwill Industries; Human services; Children/youth, services; Family services; Blind/visually impaired.
Limitations: Applications not accepted. Giving primarily in Cleveland, OH. No grants to individuals.
Application information: Contributes only to pre-selected organizations.
Trustee: National City Bank.
EIN: 346511196

7632
Focus Foundation ◇ ☆
29550 Detroit Rd., Ste. 102
Westlake, OH   44145-1994   (440) 892-5022
Contact: Keith A. Brown, Pres.

Established in 1997 in OH.
Donor: Keith A. Brown.
Foundation type: Independent foundation.
Financial data (yr. ended 12/31/05): Assets, $2,637,259 (M); expenditures, $685,833; qualifying distributions, $658,220; giving activities include $650,000 for 2 grants (high: $325,000; low: $325,000).
Purpose and activities: Giving primarily for education.
Fields of interest: Higher education, university; Education.
Limitations: Giving primarily in OH.
Application information:
   Initial approach: Letter
   Deadline(s): None
Officer: Keith A. Brown, Pres.
Trustee: Dale Kucaj.
EIN: 311526199
Selected grants: The following grants were reported in 2004.
$100,000 to Lawrence School, Broadview Heights, OH.
$14,000 to Juvenile Diabetes Research Foundation International, Cleveland, OH.
$9,920 to National Foundation for Philanthropy, Chicago, IL.
$6,000 to University School of Nova University, Fort Lauderdale, FL.
$5,000 to Big Brothers and Sisters of Gallatin County, Bozeman, MT.

$5,000 to Doctors Without Borders USA, New York, NY.
$2,000 to Lake Ridge Academy, North Ridgeville, OH.
$1,000 to Phi Gamma Delta Educational Foundation, Lexington, KY.
$500 to Boys and Girls Clubs of Broward County, Fort Lauderdale, FL.
$500 to Girl Scouts of the U.S.A., Lorain, OH.

7633
The S. N. Ford and Ada Ford Fund ◇
c/o KeyBank N.A
P.O. Box 10099
Toledo, OH   43699-0099
Contact: Nick Gesouras, Trust Off., KeyBank N.A
Application address: c/o KeyBank N.A., 42 N. Main St., Mansfield, OH 44902, tel.: (419) 525-7665

Established in 1947 in OH.
Donors: Ada Ford, M.D.†; James F. Jolley†.
Foundation type: Independent foundation.
Financial data (yr. ended 12/31/05): Assets, $11,884,944 (M); expenditures, $559,385; qualifying distributions, $541,700; giving activities include $536,500 for 7 grants (high: $385,000; low: $3,000).
Purpose and activities: Assistance to the aged and the sick, and scholarships for the youth of Richland County, OH.
Fields of interest: Education; Roman Catholic federated giving programs; Aging; Economically disadvantaged.
Type of support: Building/renovation; Grants to individuals; Scholarships—to individuals.
Limitations: Giving primarily in Richland County, OH. No grants for endowment funds, or for operating budgets, special projects, general support, research, or matching gifts; no loans.
Publications: Annual report.
Application information: Application form required.
   Initial approach: Telephone
   Deadline(s): None
   Board meeting date(s): Monthly
   Final notification: 2 months
Officers: W. Thomas Ross, Pres.; Stephen B. Bogner, V.P.; John W. Welsh, Secy.
Distribution Committee: Edwin M. Cook; Deborah M. Schenk.
Trustee: KeyBank N.A.
EIN: 340842282
Selected grants: The following grants were reported in 2004.
$385,000 to Catholic Charities.
$90,000 to Richland County Foundation, Mansfield, OH.
$40,000 to MedCentral College of Nursing, Mansfield, OH.
$10,000 to Salvation Army, Cambridge, OH.

7634
Forest City Enterprises Charitable Foundation, Inc. ▼ ◇
1100 Terminal Tower
50 Public Sq., Ste. 1100
Cleveland, OH   44113   (216) 621-6060
Contact: Allan Krulak, Dir., Community Affairs

Trust established in 1976 in OH.
Donor: Forest City Enterprises, Inc.
Foundation type: Company-sponsored foundation.

Financial data (yr. ended 1/31/06): Assets, $222,000 (M); gifts received, $4,996,537; expenditures, $5,174,173; qualifying distributions, $5,173,770; giving activities include $5,173,770 for 303 grants (high: $862,500; low: $100).

Purpose and activities: The foundation supports organizations involved with arts and culture, education, health, human services, community development, and religion.

Fields of interest: Arts; Elementary school/education; Higher education; Education; Health care; Health organizations, association; Food services; Youth development, services; Human services; Community development; Federated giving programs; Jewish federated giving programs; Leadership development; Christian agencies & churches; Jewish agencies & temples; Religion.

Type of support: Annual campaigns.

Limitations: Giving primarily in OH. No grants to individuals.

Application information: Application form not required.

Initial approach: Proposal
Copies of proposal: 1
Deadline(s): None

Officers and Trustees:* Charles Ratner,* Pres.; Samuel H. Miller, V.P. and Treas.; Thomas G. Smith, Secy.

Number of staff: 3

EIN: 341218895

Selected grants: The following grants were reported in 2006.

$862,500 to Jewish Community Federation of Cleveland, Cleveland, OH.

$500,000 to Tulane University, New Orleans, LA. For Rebuilding Tulane University.

$323,300 to United Way Services of Greater Cleveland, Cleveland, OH.

$250,000 to Case Western Reserve University, School of Medicine, Cleveland, OH.

$178,792 to American Red Cross, Greater Cleveland Chapter, Greater Cleveland Chapter, Cleveland, OH.

$76,000 to National Building Museum, DC.

$25,000 to Maltz Museum of Jewish Heritage, Beachwood, OH.

$25,000 to United Way of Lake County, Mentor, OH.

$22,500 to Cleveland State University, Cleveland, OH.

$12,636 to Salvation Army of Greater Cleveland, Cleveland, OH.

7635
Donald J. Foss Memorial Employees Trust ✧
604 Madison Ave.
Wooster, OH 44691-4764
Contact: Woodrow J. Zook, Tr.

Established in 1956 in OH.

Donors: Donald J. Foss†; Mrs. Donald J. Foss†; Walter R. Foss†.

Foundation type: Independent foundation.

Financial data (yr. ended 4/30/06): Assets, $8,837,636 (M); expenditures, $470,943; qualifying distributions, $463,743; giving activities include $215,000 for 4 grants (high: $75,000; low: $15,000), and $248,743 for 149 grants to individuals (high: $12,800; low: $190).

Purpose and activities: Grants to individual employees of the Wooster Brush Co. or members of their immediate families in time of sickness, death,

or other unfortunate circumstances; support also for human services and federated giving programs.

Fields of interest: Education; Human services; Federated giving programs.

Type of support: General/operating support; Grants to individuals.

Limitations: Giving primarily in Wooster, OH.

Application information: Application form required.

Deadline(s): None

Trustees: Robert L. Weiss; Thomas W. Zook; Woodrow J. Zook.

EIN: 346517801

7636
The Foundation for the Continuity of Mankind ✧
71963 Lodge Rd.
Freeport, OH 43973-8908
Application address: c/o Doris Kimble, Tr., 3596 State Rte. 39, Dover, OH 44622, tel.: (330) 343-1226

Established in 1989 in OH.

Donors: Floyd E. Kimble†; Doris Kimble.

Foundation type: Independent foundation.

Financial data (yr. ended 12/31/05): Assets, $53,417,936 (M); expenditures, $2,130,511; qualifying distributions, $1,838,263; giving activities include $1,640,300 for 39 grants (high: $200,000; low: $2,000), and $195,825 for foundation-administered programs.

Purpose and activities: Giving primarily for higher and other education, hospitals and hospices, and youth and social services; funding also for research, collection, storage and preservation of germ plasma essential to the preservation of endangered species.

Fields of interest: Historical activities; Arts; Higher education; Education; Hospitals (general); Human services; American Red Cross; Salvation Army; Youth, services; Residential/custodial care, hospices; Federated giving programs.

Type of support: General/operating support; Building/renovation.

Limitations: Giving primarily in OH. No grants to individuals.

Application information:

Initial approach: Letter
Deadline(s): None

Trustees: Doris Kimble; Greg Kimble; Phillip Raber.

EIN: 341622273

7637
The Harry K. Fox and Emma R. Fox Charitable Foundation
c/o National City Bank—Allegiant Institutional Svcs. 200 Public Sq., 5th Fl.
Cleveland, OH 44114 (216) 583-7130
FAX: (216) 583-7131;
E-mail: hfriedman@ulmer.com; *Application address:* c/o Harold E. Friedman, Secy., Skylight Office Twr., 1660 W. 2nd St., Ste. 1100, Cleveland, OH 44113-1448, tel.: (216) 583-7000 or (212) 583-7130; Addresses to send copies of grant applications: c/o Nancy S. Friedman, 23149 Laureldale Rd., Shaker Heights, OH 44122 and Stephen L. Strayer, National City Bank, c/o Linda Capezzuto, Allegiant Institutional Svcs., 200 Public Sq., 5th Fl., Cleveland, OH 44114

Established in 1959 in OH.

Donor: Emma R. Fox†.

Foundation type: Independent foundation.

Financial data (yr. ended 12/31/05): Assets, $9,107,167 (M); expenditures, $381,420; qualifying distributions, $351,393; giving activities include $324,135 for 83 grants (high: $25,000; low: $1,000).

Fields of interest: Arts; Education; Hospitals (general); Human services; Children/youth, services.

Type of support: General/operating support; Continuing support; Annual campaigns; Capital campaigns; Building/renovation; Equipment; Program development; Seed money; Scholarship funds.

Limitations: Giving primarily in northeastern OH, with emphasis on the greater Cleveland area. No grants to individuals; no loans.

Publications: Application guidelines.

Application information: 1 copy of each proposal must be sent to each of the trustees. Application form not required.

Initial approach: Letter of formal statement
Copies of proposal: 3
Deadline(s): May 15 for June meeting and Nov. 15 for Dec. meeting
Board meeting date(s): June and Dec.
Final notification: Following board meetings

Officers and Trustees:* Nancy S. Friedman,* Chair.; Stephen Strayer, Vice-Chair.; Harold E. Friedman, Secy.; National City Bank.

Number of staff: 1 part-time professional.

EIN: 346511198

Selected grants: The following grants were reported in 2005.

$25,000 to Jewish Community Federation of Cleveland, Cleveland, OH.

$10,000 to Case Western Reserve University, Cleveland, OH.

$10,000 to Council Gardens, Cleveland Heights, OH.

$10,000 to United Way Services of Greater Cleveland, Cleveland, OH.

$6,000 to Musical Arts Association, Cleveland, OH.

$5,000 to HELP Foundation, Cleveland, OH.

$5,000 to Menorah Park Foundation, Beachwood, OH.

$3,500 to YWCA of Greater Cleveland, Cleveland, OH.

$3,000 to Eleanor B. Rainey Memorial Institute, Cleveland, OH.

$2,500 to Cleveland Museum of Natural History, Cleveland, OH.

7638
Fox Foundation, Inc. ✧
284 S. Harding Rd.
Columbus, OH 43209
Contact: Robert L Fox, Dir.

Established in 1953 in OH.

Donor: Robert K. Fox.

Foundation type: Independent foundation.

Financial data (yr. ended 11/30/04): Assets, $9,790,004 (M); expenditures, $569,844; qualifying distributions, $561,084; giving activities include $560,619 for 30 grants (high: $321,059; low: $100).

Fields of interest: Arts; Education; Health organizations, association; Recreation, parks/playgrounds; Human services.

Type of support: Annual campaigns; Capital campaigns; Professorships; Exchange programs.

Limitations: Giving primarily in OH. No grants to individuals.
Application information: Application form not required.
   Initial approach: Letter
   Deadline(s): None
   Board meeting date(s): Feb.
Directors: Elizabeth O. Fox; Robert L. Fox; Donald R. Sutton.
EIN: 316023906

7639
France Stone Foundation ◇
608 Madison Ave., Ste. 1000
Toledo, OH   43604   (419) 241-2201
Contact: Joseph S. Heyman, Pres.

Established in 1952 in OH.
Donors: George A. France†; The France Stone Co.; and subsidiaries.
Foundation type: Independent foundation.
Financial data (yr. ended 12/31/05): Assets, $11,881,630 (M); expenditures, $626,049; qualifying distributions, $508,000; giving activities include $508,000 for 29 grants (high: $60,000; low: $1,000; average: $5,000–$20,000).
Purpose and activities: Giving primarily to medical, educational, and religious organizations.
Fields of interest: Arts; Higher education; Education; Health organizations, association; Human services; Children/youth, services; Community development; Federated giving programs.
Type of support: General/operating support; Continuing support; Annual campaigns; Scholarship funds; Research.
Limitations: Giving primarily in Toledo, OH. No grants to individuals, or for operating budgets or special projects.
Application information: Application form not required.
   Initial approach: Proposal
   Copies of proposal: 1
   Deadline(s): None
   Board meeting date(s): June
   Final notification: 6 months
Officers and Trustees:* Joseph S. Heyman,* Pres.; Ollie J. Risner,* V.P.; Andrew E. Anderson,* Secy.-Treas.
Number of staff: 1 part-time support.
EIN: 346523033
Selected grants: The following grants were reported in 2004.
$70,000 to Salvation Army, Cambridge, OH.
$60,000 to Sunshine Childrens Home, Maumee, OH.
$30,000 to Toledo Society for the Blind, Toledo, OH.
$25,000 to Boy Scouts of America, Toledo, OH.
$25,000 to Humane Society of Toledo, Toledo, OH.
$20,000 to Read for Literacy, Toledo, OH.
$20,000 to Saint Pauls Community Center, Toledo, OH.
$15,000 to Boys and Girls Clubs of Toledo, Toledo, OH.
$15,000 to Friendly Center, Toledo, OH.
$10,000 to University of Toledo Foundation, Toledo, OH.

7640
Walter Henry Freygang Foundation ◇
2794 Forestview Dr.
Akron, OH   44333

Incorporated in 1949 in NJ.
Donors: Walter Henry Freygang†; Marie A. Freygang†.
Foundation type: Independent foundation.
Financial data (yr. ended 8/31/05): Assets, $8,117,091 (M); expenditures, $468,654; qualifying distributions, $414,099; giving activities include $414,099 for 59 grants (high: $32,949; low: $1,390).
Purpose and activities: Grants primarily for higher education, medical research, and hospitals; support also for social services, children's services and services for the blind.
Fields of interest: Media/communications; Higher education; Engineering school/education; Hospitals (general); Health care; Medical research, institute; Human services; Children/youth, services; Disabilities, people with; Blind/visually impaired.
Limitations: Applications not accepted. Giving on a national basis, with emphasis on the East Coast. No grants to individuals.
Application information: Contributes only to pre-selected organizations.
   Board meeting date(s): Oct.
Officers: Dale G. Freygang, Pres. and Treas.; Dorothea F. Drennan, V.P.; Katherine A. Freygang, Secy.
Trustees: James Drennan; Antje Freygang; David B. Freygang; W. Nicholas F. Freygang.
EIN: 226027952
Selected grants: The following grants were reported in 2005.
$13,360 to Mobile Meals, Akron, OH.
$10,390 to Connecticut College, New London, CT.
$10,000 to McDonogh School, Owings Mills, MD.
$9,930 to Mount Holyoke College, South Hadley, MA.
$9,630 to W N E T Channel 13, New York, NY.
$7,530 to Institute for Cancer Research, Philadelphia, PA.
$7,140 to Manzano Day School, Albuquerque, NM.
$6,860 to W G B H Educational Foundation, Boston, MA.
$5,910 to National Public Radio, DC.
$5,340 to Johns Hopkins University, Baltimore, MD.

7641
The Sidney Frohman Foundation ◇
c/o Flynn, Py, and Kruse
165 E. Washington Row
Sandusky, OH   44870

Trust established in 1952 in OH.
Donors: Sidney Frohman†; Blanche P. Frohman†.
Foundation type: Independent foundation.
Financial data (yr. ended 12/31/05): Assets, $11,320,150 (M); expenditures, $564,683; qualifying distributions, $511,175; giving activities include $497,341 for 50 grants (high: $30,000; low: $500).
Purpose and activities: Giving primarily for higher and other education, as well as to educational programs, social services, community development, federated giving programs, the arts, health associations, a YMCA, and to services for people who are blind.
Fields of interest: Arts; Elementary/secondary education; Higher education; Education; Health

organizations, association; Human services; American Red Cross; Salvation Army; YM/YWCAs & YM/YWHAs; Community development; Foundations (community); Federated giving programs; Blind/visually impaired.
Type of support: General/operating support; Capital campaigns; Equipment.
Limitations: Applications not accepted. Giving primarily in OH, with emphasis on Erie County. No grants to individuals.
Application information: Contributes only to pre-selected organizations.
Trustees: Daniel C. Frohman; Donald G. Koch.
EIN: 346517809

7642
The Frost-Parker Foundation ◇
165 E. Washington Row
Sandusky, OH   44870   (419) 625-8324
Contact: Melvyn .J. Stauffer, Secy.

Established in 1986 in OH.
Donors: Ruth F. Parker; Ruth F. Parker Trust.
Foundation type: Independent foundation.
Financial data (yr. ended 4/30/05): Assets, $1,358,735 (M); gifts received, $1,329,517; expenditures, $982,800; qualifying distributions, $940,272; giving activities include $924,384 for 59 grants (high: $128,750; low: $450).
Fields of interest: Museums; Museums (marine/maritime); Performing arts, orchestra (symphony); Education, administration/regulation; Secondary school/education; Higher education; Education; Health organizations, association; Housing/shelter; Boy scouts; Human services; Community development; Foundations (community); Christian agencies & churches.
Limitations: Giving limited to northern OH, with emphasis on Sandusky. No grants to individuals.
Application information: Application form not required.
   Deadline(s): None
Officers and Trustees:* Ruth F. Parker,* Pres. and Treas.; Melvyn J. Stauffer,* Secy.; Richard B. Fuller.
EIN: 341515319
Selected grants: The following grants were reported in 2005.
$165,750 to Sandusky, City of, Sandusky, OH. 2 grants: $128,750, $37,000
$50,000 to Sandusky State Theater, Sandusky, OH. 2 grants: $25,000 each
$30,000 to YMCA.
$15,000 to Boys and Girls Club of Sandusky, Sandusky, OH.
$12,500 to Girl Scouts of the U.S.A..
$5,000 to Safe Harbour Domestic Violence Shelter, Sandusky, OH.
$3,000 to Sandusky Concert Association, Sandusky, OH.

7643
The GAR Foundation ▼
3875 Embassy Parkway, Ste. 250
Akron, OH   44309-1500   (330) 576-2926
Contact: Robert W. Briggs, Exec. Dir.
FAX: (330) 252-5584; E-mail: GAR@bdblaw.com; Temporary relocation address: 3875 Embassy Pkwy., Ste. 250 Akron OH 44333; Additional E-mail: RBriggs@BDBlaw.com; URL: http://www.garfdn.org

Trust established in 1967 in OH.

Donors: Ruth C. Roush†; Galen Roush†.
Foundation type: Independent foundation.
Financial data (yr. ended 12/31/04): Assets, $169,578,363 (M); expenditures, $9,109,884; qualifying distributions, $7,594,310; giving activities include $6,877,352 for 100 grants (high: $1,013,134; low: $2,500; average: $10,000–$100,000), and $231,501 for 3 foundation-administered programs.
Purpose and activities: Grants for education, the arts, and civic and social service agencies, including youth activities.
Fields of interest: Arts; Secondary school/education; Higher education; Human services; Youth, services; Economics; Minorities; Economically disadvantaged; Homeless.
Type of support: General/operating support; Continuing support; Annual campaigns; Capital campaigns; Building/renovation; Equipment; Land acquisition; Endowments; Debt reduction; Program development; Seed money; Curriculum development; Scholarship funds; Matching/challenge support.
Limitations: Giving primarily in the Akron-Summit County area and secondarily in Cuyahoga, Stark, Medina, Portage and Wayne counties, OH. No support for private non-operating foundations, health care institutions, or national organizations. No grants to individuals, or for medical research, capital funding for churches or synagogues, or computers for schools.
Publications: Application guidelines.
Application information: If recipient has received a grant from the foundation within the past five years, please access the online grant application form on the foundation's Web site. Proposals are not accepted by fax or e-mail. Application form required.
   Initial approach: 1-2 page letter of inquiry
   Copies of proposal: 1
   Deadline(s): Feb. 1, May 1, Aug. 1, and Nov. 1
   Board meeting date(s): Feb., May, Aug., and Nov.
   Final notification: 2 to 3 weeks after meeting
Officer and Trustees:* Robert W. Briggs,* Pres.; Christine Amer Mayer, V.P. for Grantee and Community Relations, Sr. Prog. Off.; National City Bank.
Distribution Committee: Richard A. Chenoweth; Joseph M. Clapp; Kathryn W. Dindo; James Staley; S.R. Werner; Douglas A. Wilson.
Number of staff: 2 full-time professional; 4 part-time professional; 2 full-time support; 1 part-time support.
EIN: 346577710
Selected grants: The following grants were reported in 2004.
$1,013,134 to Akron Art Museum, Akron, OH. For endowment, general operating support and general endowment in memory of Charles E. Pierson.
$300,000 to University of Akron Foundation, Akron, OH. For tuition assistance for Summit College.
$250,000 to Akron Community Service Center and Urban League, Akron, OH. For endowment.
$200,000 to Access, Akron, OH. For capital campaign to raise funds to expand emergency shelter for women and children.
$196,330 to Summit Education Initiative, Akron, OH. For development of PD3 Program and to subsidize compensation package of new executive director.
$162,743 to Kent State University Foundation, Kent, OH. For challenge grant for WKSU endowment and to fund a Research Professor

within the Research Center for Educational Techology.
$150,000 to Cleveland Institute of Music, Cleveland, OH. For challenge for endowment for building.
$150,000 to Hiram College, Hiram, OH. For challenge grant issued by National Endowment for the Humanities for the endowment of The Center for Literature, Medicine and Health Care Professions and the Biomedical Humanities Program.
$140,000 to Ohio Foundation of Independent Colleges, Columbus, OH. For Annual Campaign.
$130,000 to Info Line, Akron, OH. For general operating support of Project Connect and for business plan development.

7644
The James J. and Joan A. Gardner Family Foundation ◇
(formerly Gardner Family Foundation)
c/o Summer Hill, Inc.
P.O. Box 625737
Cincinnati, OH   45262   (513) 459-1085
Contact: James J. Gardner, Pres.

Established in 1994 in OH.
Donors: Joan A. Gardner; Margaret M. Johns; Linda G. Mueller; Lorraine G. Sommer; Spencer J. Gardner; Patricia F. Gardner; James J. Gardner; Gardner Family 2000 Charitable Trust.
Foundation type: Independent foundation.
Financial data (yr. ended 12/31/04): Assets, $37,569,435 (M); gifts received, $13,106,000; expenditures, $1,005,697; qualifying distributions, $991,137; giving activities include $963,665 for 17 grants (high: $259,665; low: $1,000).
Purpose and activities: Giving primarily for education, Christian churches and organizations, social services, and children and youth services, including a children's diabetes foundation.
Fields of interest: Museums (art); Arts; Elementary/secondary education; Human services; Children/youth, services; Christian agencies & churches.
Limitations: Giving primarily in Cincinnati, OH; some funding also in Denver, CO, and Orlando, FL. No grants to individuals.
Application information:
   Initial approach: Letter
   Deadline(s): None
Officers and Trustees:* James J. Gardner,* Pres.; Joan A. Gardner,* V.P.; Margaret M. Johns,* Secy.; Linda G. Mueller,* Treas.; Patricia F. Gardner; Spencer J. Gardner; Gary D. Johns; Thomas J. Mueller; Lorraine G. Sommer.
EIN: 311397164
Selected grants: The following grants were reported in 2004.
$259,665 to Cincinnati Institute of Fine Arts, Cincinnati, OH.
$250,000 to Summit Country Day School, Cincinnati, OH.
$150,000 to Saint Gertrude Church, Cincinnati, OH.
$125,000 to Matthew Kelly Foundation, Cincinnati, OH.
$50,000 to Purcell Marian High School, Cincinnati, OH.
$35,000 to Orlando Regional Healthcare Foundation, Orlando, FL.
$20,000 to Mercy Health Partners of Southwest Ohio Foundation, Cincinnati, OH.
$15,000 to Cincinnati Works, Cincinnati, OH.

$10,000 to Catholic Inner-City Schools Educational Fund (CISE), Cincinnati, OH.
$10,000 to Saint Xavier High School, Cincinnati, OH.

7645
Henry H. Geary, Jr. Memorial Foundation ◇
c/o KeyBank N.A.
800 Superior Ave.
Cleveland, OH   44114

Established in 1995 in OH.
Donor: H.H. Geary, Jr. Irrevocable Trust.
Foundation type: Independent foundation.
Financial data (yr. ended 12/31/05): Assets, $7,195,096 (M); expenditures, $362,606; qualifying distributions, $322,400; giving activities include $320,450 for 11 grants (high: $124,800; low: $650).
Purpose and activities: Giving primarily for social services, including YMCAs; funding also for education, and to a Presbyterian church.
Fields of interest: Education; Human services; YM/YWCAs & YM/YWHAs; Federated giving programs; Protestant agencies & churches.
Limitations: Applications not accepted. Giving primarily in Fostoria, OH. No grants to individuals.
Application information: Contributes only to pre-selected organizations.
Trustee: KeyBank N.A.
EIN: 341594662

7646
John F. and Mary A. Geisse Foundation
(formerly The Geisse Foundation)
100 N. Main St., Ste. 350
Chagrin Falls, OH   44022   (440) 247-0003
Contact: Tim Geisse, Tr.
FAX: (440) 247-8903;
E-mail: tgeisse@turnergeisse.com; Additional E-mail: timgeisse@aol.com

Established in 1969 in MO.
Donors: John F. Geisse†; Mary A. Geisse†.
Foundation type: Independent foundation.
Financial data (yr. ended 12/31/05): Assets, $12,339,950 (M); expenditures, $1,191,703; qualifying distributions, $1,046,236; giving activities include $976,862 for 49 grants (high: $250,000; low: $50), and $18,725 for 24 employee matching gifts.
Purpose and activities: Support for programs that help the very poor of the developing world reach a higher standard of living.
Fields of interest: International development.
International interests: Central America; Developing countries.
Type of support: General/operating support; Continuing support; Annual campaigns; Equipment; Scholarship funds; Program-related investments/loans; Matching/challenge support.
Limitations: Applications not accepted. Giving primarily on an international basis, with emphasis on Central America. No support for purely religious or environmental protection purposes, or for arts and culture. No grants to individuals, or for research.
Application information: Unsolicited requests for funds not accepted.
   Board meeting date(s): As needed

Trustees: Lawrence J. Geisse, M.D.; Timothy F. Geisse.
Number of staff: 1 full-time professional.
EIN: 237049780
Selected grants: The following grants were reported in 2004.
$100,000 to ACCION International, Boston, MA. For Microfinance.
$50,000 to Adelante Foundation, Miami, FL. For microfinance program in Honduras.

7647

The Generation Trust ✧
c/o Fifth Third Bank
P.O. Box 1868
Toledo, OH 43603 (419) 259-6806
Contact: J. Philip Ruyle, V.P., Fifth Third Bank

Established in 1985 in OH.
Donors: John D. Beckett; The R.W. Beckett Corp.; and members of the Beckett family.
Foundation type: Independent foundation.
Financial data (yr. ended 12/31/05): Assets, $26,203,530 (M); gifts received, $2,618,550; expenditures, $2,888,811; qualifying distributions, $2,795,800; giving activities include $2,790,000 for 71 grants (high: $250,000; low: $3,000; average: $10,000–$50,000).
Purpose and activities: Support limited to organizations with a Christian purpose, including churches and ministries.
Fields of interest: Christian agencies & churches.
Type of support: Emergency funds; Program development; Seed money; Technical assistance.
Limitations: Giving on a national and international basis. No grants to individuals.
Application information: Application form not required.
Initial approach: Letter
Copies of proposal: 1
Deadline(s): None
Advisor: John D. Beckett.
Trustee: Fifth Third Bank.
EIN: 346850815

7648

Gerlach Foundation, Inc. ✧
37 W. Broad St., 5th Fl.
Columbus, OH 43215 (614) 224-7141

Incorporated in 1953 in OH.
Donors: Pauline Gerlach†; John J. Gerlach; John B. Gerlach.
Foundation type: Independent foundation.
Financial data (yr. ended 11/30/05): Assets, $30,386,808 (M); expenditures, $1,587,494; qualifying distributions, $1,554,876; giving activities include $1,551,100 for 20 grants (high: $755,350; low: $500).
Purpose and activities: Giving primarily to a hospital foundation; giving also for higher education, the arts, and human services.
Fields of interest: Performing arts, theater; Higher education; Education; Hospitals (general); Human services; YM/YWCAs & YM/YWHAs; Children/youth, services; Foundations (community).
Type of support: General/operating support.
Limitations: Applications not accepted. Giving primarily in OH, with emphasis on Columbus. No grants to individuals.

Application information: Contributes only to pre-selected organizations.
Officers: Susan Douglass, V.P.; David P. Gerlach, V.P.; John B. Gerlach, Jr., Treas.
EIN: 316023912
Selected grants: The following grants were reported in 2005.
$755,350 to Ballet Metropolitan, Columbus, OH.
$500,000 to Upper Arlington Library Foundation, Upper Arlington, OH.
$150,000 to Recreation Unlimited Farm and Fun, Ashley, OH.
$25,900 to Ohio State University Foundation, Columbus, OH.
$11,400 to Buckeye Diamond Club, Hilliard, OH.
$10,000 to Columbus College of Art and Design, Columbus, OH.
$10,000 to Franklin University, Columbus, OH.
$10,000 to Ohio Foundation of Independent Colleges, Columbus, OH.

7649

The Gettler Family Foundation ✧
30 Garfield Pl., Ste. 1000
Cincinnati, OH 45202 (513) 621-2850
Contact: Benjamin Gettler, Chair.

Established in 1993 in OH.
Donor: Benjamin Gettler.
Foundation type: Independent foundation.
Financial data (yr. ended 2/28/05): Assets, $1,468,218 (M); gifts received, $288,820; expenditures, $338,627; qualifying distributions, $322,017; giving activities include $322,230 for 93 grants (high: $210,900; low: $11).
Purpose and activities: Giving primarily for education, conservation, and to Jewish organizations.
Fields of interest: Education; Environment, natural resources; Human services; Jewish federated giving programs; Public affairs; Jewish agencies & temples.
Type of support: General/operating support.
Application information:
Initial approach: Proposal
Deadline(s): None
Officers: Benjamin Gettler, Chair. and Treas.; Delian A. Gettler, Pres. and Secy.; Benjamin R. Gettler, V.P.
Trustee: Thomas D. Gettler.
EIN: 311374350
Selected grants: The following grants were reported in 2006.
$31,000 to Jewish Federation of Cincinnati, Cincinnati, OH.
$5,200 to Isaac M. Wise Temple, Cincinnati, OH.
$4,480 to Ohio Cancer Research Associates, Columbus, OH.
$3,800 to Cystic Fibrosis Foundation, Bethesda, MD.
$2,500 to American Jewish Committee, New York, NY.
$2,000 to Committee for Accuracy in Middle East Reporting in America (CAMERA), Boston, MA.
$300 to Israel Cancer Research Fund, New York, NY.
$250 to Capital Research Center, DC.
$40 to American Heart Association, Dallas, TX.

7650

Paul R. Gingher State Auto Insurance Companies Foundation ✧
518 E. Broad St.
Columbus, OH 43215

Established in 1989 in OH.
Donor: State Automobile Mutual Insurance Co.
Foundation type: Company-sponsored foundation.
Financial data (yr. ended 12/31/04): Assets, $3,105,719 (M); gifts received, $200,000; expenditures, $433,127; qualifying distributions, $432,618; giving activities include $429,829 for 187 grants (high: $91,211; low: $200).
Purpose and activities: The foundation supports organizations involved with arts and culture, education, health, youth development, and religion.
Fields of interest: Arts; Higher education; Education; Health care; Youth development; Federated giving programs; Religion.
Limitations: Applications not accepted. Giving primarily in Columbus, OH. No grants to individuals.
Application information: Contributes only to pre-selected organizations.
Trustees: Mark Blackburn; Noreen Johnson; Steven J. Johnston; John R. Lowther; Robert H. Moone.
EIN: 311257265

7651

The Goatie Foundation ✧
c/o KeyBank N.A.
800 Superior Ave, 4th Fl.
Cleveland, OH 44114
Application address: c/o Karen Potopsky, 127 Public Sq., Cleveland, OH 44113

Established in 2001 in OH.
Donor: Women's Project Foundation.
Foundation type: Independent foundation.
Financial data (yr. ended 12/31/04): Assets, $0 (M); gifts received, $2,994,669; expenditures, $3,268,796; qualifying distributions, $3,268,796; giving activities include $3,268,796 for 28 grants (high: $783,390; low: $3,000; average: $25,000–$150,000).
Fields of interest: Environment; Animals/wildlife; Reproductive health, family planning; Human services; Women.
Limitations: Giving on a national basis.
Application information: Application form not required.
Deadline(s): None
Trustee: KeyBank N.A.
EIN: 347158309

7652

The Roe Green Foundation ✧
925 Euclid Ave., Ste. 2000
Cleveland, OH 44115

Established in 1999 in OH.
Foundation type: Independent foundation.
Financial data (yr. ended 12/31/05): Assets, $9,822,415 (M); expenditures, $1,570,897; qualifying distributions, $1,552,992; giving activities include $1,506,736 for 21 grants (high: $982,900; low: $500).
Purpose and activities: Primarily giving to the arts, and for the restoration of a legal library.
Fields of interest: Arts; Libraries (law); Health organizations, association.

Limitations: Applications not accepted. Giving primarily in OH. No grants to individuals.
Application information: Contributes only to pre-selected organizations.
Trustees: Roe Green; Eugene A. Kratus.
EIN: 341886405

7653
Greene County Community Foundation
(doing business as Greene Giving)
25 Greene St.
Xenia, OH 45385-3101 (937) 562-5550
Contact: Edward Marrinan, Exec. Dir.
FAX: (937) 562-5556;
E-mail: emarrinan@co.greene.oh.us; URL: http://www.greenegiving.org

Established in 2001 in OH.
Foundation type: Community foundation.
Financial data (yr. ended 12/31/04): Assets, $1,574,818 (M); gifts received, $693,797; expenditures, $474,516; giving activities include $334,940 for grants.
Purpose and activities: The foundation seeks to promote philanthropy and provide stewardship and leadership to enhance the use of regional resources to meet charitable needs.
Fields of interest: Arts; Education, public education; Health care; Agriculture; Recreation; Family services; Aging, centers/services; Community development, neighborhood development; Economic development; Women.
Type of support: Building/renovation; Equipment; Scholarship funds.
Limitations: Giving limited to Greene County, OH.
Publications: Informational brochure.
Application information: Application form required.
   Initial approach: Letter, telephone, or e-mail
   Copies of proposal: 1
   Deadline(s): Prior to the first Wed. of each month
   Board meeting date(s): Monthly
Officers and Trustees:* Dennis Phillips,* Pres.; Mary Nutter,* V.P.; Edward Marrinan, Exec. Dir.; Don Anderson; "Buck" Bibb; Bob Buerger; Paul Dillaplain; Michael Foy; Jack Gayheart; Anne Gerard; Fred Gibson; Mark Guess; Joe Harkleroad; Don Hollister; "Chuck" Kanoy; Jim Kennedy; Donald Knoth; Donna Luttrell; Shannon Martin; Herman Menapace; Joe Mullins; Jane Newton; Jerry Pfeifer; Ed Phillips; Lucy Roberts; Ron Russell; John Saraga; Stephanie Stephan; Patricia Swanke; Julie Vann; Dan Young.
EIN: 311751001

7654
Gordon & Llura Gund 1993 Charitable
   Foundation ✧
925 Euclid Ave., Ste. 2000
Cleveland, OH 44115

Established in 1993 in OH.
Donor: Gordon and Llura Liggett Gund Trust.
Foundation type: Independent foundation.
Financial data (yr. ended 12/31/05): Assets, $212,005 (M); gifts received, $1,721,195; expenditures, $2,309,123; qualifying distributions, $2,239,000; giving activities include $2,239,000 for 4 grants (high: $1,234,000; low: $171,000).
Purpose and activities: Giving primarily to fight blindness.
Fields of interest: Eye diseases.

Limitations: Applications not accepted. Giving on a national basis. No grants to individuals.
Application information: Contributes only to pre-selected organizations.
Trustee: Richard T. Watson.
EIN: 341730494

7655
The Agnes Gund Foundation ✧
c/o Agnes Gund
517 Broadway, 3rd Fl.
East Liverpool, OH 43920 (330) 385-3400

Established in 1988 in OH.
Donors: Agnes Gund; The Domani Trust.
Foundation type: Independent foundation.
Financial data (yr. ended 12/31/05): Assets, $28,929,644 (M); gifts received, $40,255,620; expenditures, $11,392,497; qualifying distributions, $11,389,022; giving activities include $11,271,209 for 317 grants (high: $3,977,557; low: $250; average: $5,000–$250,000).
Purpose and activities: Support primarily for the arts and higher education.
Fields of interest: Museums; Performing arts, dance; Performing arts, music; Arts; Higher education; Health care; Health organizations, association.
Type of support: General/operating support.
Limitations: Applications not accepted. Giving primarily in New York, NY. No grants to individuals.
Application information: Contributes only to pre-selected organizations.
Trustees: Agnes Gund; Daniel Shapiro.
EIN: 341606084
Selected grants: The following grants were reported in 2003.
$2,451,581 to Museum of Modern Art, New York, NY. For general support.
$302,337 to Jazz at Lincoln Center, New York, NY. For general support.
$298,490 to Lincoln Center for the Performing Arts, New York, NY. For general support.
$293,105 to American Fund for the Tate Gallery, New York, NY. For general support.
$285,000 to Studio in a School Association, New York, NY. For general support.
$100,000 to Art 21, New York, NY. For general support.
$100,000 to Business Committee for the Arts, Long Island City, NY.
$85,000 to Brown University, Providence, RI. For general support.
$75,000 to Cleveland Museum of Art, Cleveland, OH. For general support.
$55,000 to Metropolitan Museum of Art, New York, NY.

7656
Geoffrey Gund Foundation ✧
c/o KeyBank N.A.
800 Superior Ave., 4th Fl.
Cleveland, OH 44114
Contact: Geoffrey Gund, Tr.
Application address: 40 E. 94th St., Apt. 28-E, New York, NY 10128

Established in 1987 in DC.
Donor: Geoffrey Gund.
Foundation type: Independent foundation.

Financial data (yr. ended 6/30/05): Assets, $24,041,436 (M); gifts received, $2,000,000; expenditures, $1,194,279; qualifying distributions, $1,152,625; giving activities include $1,152,425 for 55 grants (high: $1,000,000; low: $100; average: $1,000–$10,000).
Fields of interest: Arts, association; Museums (art); Performing arts, music; Arts; Education; Human services; Protestant agencies & churches.
Type of support: General/operating support; Annual campaigns; Endowments; Scholarship funds.
Limitations: Giving primarily in MA and the greater metropolitan New York, NY, area. No grants to individuals.
Application information: Application form not required.
   Initial approach: Letter
   Deadline(s): None
Trustees: Geoffrey Gund; Donald Kozuskp; James O'Hara; KeyBank N.A.
EIN: 521509128

7657
The George Gund Foundation ▼ ✧
1845 Guildhall Bldg.
45 Prospect Ave. W.
Cleveland, OH 44115-1018 (216) 241-3114
Contact: David T. Abbott, Exec. Dir.
FAX: (216) 241-6560; E-mail: info@gundfdn.org;
URL: http://www.gundfdn.org
Fellowship application address: c/o Robert Jaquay, Assoc. Dir., George Gund Foundation, 1845 Guildhall Bldg., 45 Prospect Ave., West Cleveland, Ohio 44115

Incorporated in 1952 in OH.
Donor: George Gund†.
Foundation type: Independent foundation.
Financial data (yr. ended 12/31/05): Assets, $474,375,488 (M); expenditures, $27,853,977; qualifying distributions, $23,385,277; giving activities include $21,243,043 for 414 grants (high: $2,000,000; low: $982; average: $5,000–$100,000).
Purpose and activities: Priority to education projects, with emphasis on new concepts and methods of teaching and learning, and on increasing educational opportunities for the disadvantaged; programs advancing economic revitalization and job creation; projects promoting neighborhood development; projects for improving human services, employment opportunities, housing for minority and low-income groups; support also for ecology, civic affairs, and the arts. Preference is given to pilot projects and innovative programs which present prospects for broad replication.
Fields of interest: Arts; Education, research; Education, early childhood education; Elementary school/education; Secondary school/education; Higher education; Education; Environment, natural resources; Environment; AIDS; AIDS research; Crime/law enforcement; Employment; Housing/shelter, development; Human services; Children/youth, services; Women, centers/services; Minorities/immigrants, centers/services; Civil rights, race/intergroup relations; Urban/community development; Community development; Government/public administration; Public affairs; Minorities; Women; Economically disadvantaged.
Type of support: General/operating support; Continuing support; Land acquisition; Emergency funds; Program development; Conferences/seminars; Publication; Seed money; Internship

funds; Scholarship funds; Research; Technical assistance; Program-related investments/loans; Matching/challenge support.

Limitations: Giving primarily in northeastern OH and the greater Cleveland, OH, area. No support for political groups, services for the physically, mentally or developmentally disabled, or the elderly. Generally, no grants to individuals, or for building or endowment funds, political campaigns, debt reduction, equipment, renovation projects, or to fund benefit events.

Publications: Application guidelines; Annual report (including application guidelines); Grants list; Informational brochure (including application guidelines).

Application information: Proposals sent by fax not considered. Please do not submit proposals in notebooks, binders, or plastic folders. Proposals are due the next business day if a deadline falls on a weekend. Application form not required.

Initial approach: Proposal (including 1-page cover letter)

Copies of proposal: 1

Deadline(s): Mar. 30, June 30, Sept. 30, and Dec. 30

Board meeting date(s): Mar., June, Sept., and Dec.

Final notification: 8 weeks

Officers and Trustees:* Geoffrey Gund,* Pres. and Treas.; Llura A. Gund,* V.P.; Ann L. Gund,* Secy.; David T. Abbott, Exec. Dir.; David Goodman; Catherine Gund; George Gund III; Zachary Gund; Cathy M. Lewis.

Number of staff: 8 full-time professional; 5 full-time support.

EIN: 346519769

Selected grants: The following grants were reported in 2005.

$2,100,000 to Museum of Contemporary Art Cleveland, Cleveland, OH. For capital campaign to build new facility in University Circle, payable over 5 years.

$2,000,000 to Foundation Fighting Blindness, Owings Mills, MD. For retinal degenerative disease research.

$1,000,000 to Musical Arts Association, Cleveland, OH. For support during time of transition, payable over 4 years.

$500,000 to Cuyahoga County Planning Commission, Cleveland, OH. For Cuyahoga Valley Initiative organizational planning and start-up, payable over 2 years.

$500,000 to Ideastream, Cleveland, OH. For news and public affairs programming, payable over 2 years.

$320,000 to Community Renewal Society, Chicago, IL. For CATALYST: Cleveland newsmagazine, payable over 2 years.

$230,000 to Center for Community Solutions, Cleveland, OH. For comprehensive health plan in Cleveland Municipal School District, payable over 2 years.

$210,000 to EcoCity Cleveland, Cleveland, OH. For Greater Ohio operating support, payable over 2 years.

$35,000 to Cleveland Municipal School District, Cleveland, OH. For CEO search.

$22,000 to Cleveland Contemporary Dance Theater, Cleveland, OH. For operating and planning support.

7658
H.C.S. Foundation ▼ ✧
1801 E. 9th St., Ste. 1105
Cleveland, OH 44114-3103 (216) 781-3502
Contact: Trustees

Trust established in 1959 in OH.
Donor: Harold C. Schott†.
Foundation type: Independent foundation.
Financial data (yr. ended 12/31/05): Assets, $111,539,839 (M); expenditures, $5,719,157; qualifying distributions, $4,644,085; giving activities include $4,250,500 for 46 grants (high: $500,000; low: $5,000; average: $25,000–$250,000).
Purpose and activities: Grants primarily for health care, education, the arts, and the United Way.
Fields of interest: Arts; Education; Health care; Human services; Federated giving programs; Roman Catholic agencies & churches.
Type of support: General/operating support; Capital campaigns; Building/renovation; Endowments; Program development; Scholarship funds.
Limitations: Giving limited to OH. No grants to individuals.
Application information: Application form not required.
Initial approach: Letter
Copies of proposal: 1
Deadline(s): None
Trustees: Francie S. Hiltz; L. Thomas Hiltz; Betty Jane Mulcahy; William D. Saal; Milton B. Schott, Jr.
Number of staff: 1 full-time professional.
EIN: 346514235
Selected grants: The following grants were reported in 2004.

$1,000,000 to Summit Country Day School, Cincinnati, OH. Toward Capital Campaign Fund for endowment for middle school maintenance.

$250,000 to Starfire Council of Greater Cincinnati, Cincinnati, OH. For operating support and building expansion.

$100,000 to Dominican Sisters of Saint Cecilia, Nashville, TN. For repair and restoration of Cincinnati facility.

$100,000 to University of Cincinnati, College of Medicine, Department of Ophthamology, Cincinnati, OH. Toward establishment of chair in Ophthalmology.

$70,000 to Cincinnati Association for the Blind, Cincinnati, OH. For general support.

$50,000 to Redwood Rehabilitiation Center, Fort Mitchell, KY. For operating support.

$50,000 to University of Chicago, Department of Surgery Section of Transplantation, Chicago, IL. For organ transplant research.

$50,000 to Xavier College Preparatory School, Phoenix, AZ. Toward Fine Arts programs and reducing indebtedness.

$35,000 to Community of Holy Rosary and Saint John, Columbus, OH. For support of learning center programs for adult education, workforce development and after-school tutoring.

$25,000 to Notre Dame College of Ohio, South Euclid, OH. Toward Smart Classroom multimedia instruction project.

7659
Carol & Ralph Haile, Jr. Foundation ✧
c/o U.S. Bank, N.A.
P.O. Box 1118, ML CN-OH-W10X
Cincinnati, OH 45201

Established in 2003 in OH.
Donor: Ralph V. Haile.
Foundation type: Independent foundation.
Financial data (yr. ended 12/31/05): Assets, $610,579 (M); gifts received, $1,256,000; expenditures, $1,257,092; qualifying distributions, $1,256,200; giving activities include $1,256,000 for 22 grants (high: $335,000; low: $3,000; average: $10,000–$100,000).
Purpose and activities: Giving primarily for higher education as well as for the arts, including a visual and performing arts center; funding also for hospitals and cancer research.
Fields of interest: Arts, multipurpose centers/programs; Museums; Arts; Elementary/secondary education; Higher education; Education; Hospitals (general); Cancer research; Human services; Children/youth, services; Developmentally disabled, centers & services; Economic development; Foundations (community); Federated giving programs.
Limitations: Applications not accepted. Giving primarily in KY and OH. No grants to individuals.
Application information: Contributes only to pre-selected organizations.
Advisory Committee: Jennie P. Carlson; Jerry A. Grundhofer; Carol Ann Haile; Ralph V. Haile, Jr.; Timothy J. Maloney.
Trustee: U.S. Bank, N.A.
EIN: 542135984

7660
The Hamilton Community Foundation, Inc. ▼
319 N. 3rd St.
Hamilton, OH 45011-1624 (513) 863-1717
Contact: John J. Guidugli, C.E.O.
FAX: (513) 863-2868;
E-mail: info@hamiltonfoundation.org; Additional E-mail: hcf@one.net; URL: http://www.hamiltonfoundation.org

Incorporated in 1951 in OH.
Foundation type: Community foundation.
Financial data (yr. ended 12/31/05): Assets, $68,777,525 (M); gifts received, $4,624,979; expenditures, $5,757,992; giving activities include $4,132,259 for 1,232 grants (high: $337,000; low: $10).
Purpose and activities: The foundation is dedicated to improving the quality of life in its community by supporting a wide variety of both new and old organizations committed to projects in the areas of arts & culture, civic beautification & development, education, health care, housing, recreation, and social services.
Fields of interest: Arts; Elementary school/education; Education; Environment, beautification programs; Health care; Substance abuse, services; Health organizations, association; Alcoholism; Housing/shelter, development; Recreation; Children/youth, services; Human services; Community development.
Type of support: Emergency funds; Program development; Conferences/seminars; Seed money; Scholarship funds; Program-related investments/loans.
Limitations: Giving limited to Butler County, OH. No support for individual religious organizations, including churches and parochial schools. No grants to individuals (except for scholarships), or for operating budgets, continuing support, annual campaigns, deficit financing, capital or endowment

funds, matching gifts, research, demonstration projects, equipment, or publications; no loans (except for program related-investments).
Publications: Application guidelines; Annual report; Newsletter.
Application information: Visit foundation Web site for application guidelines. Application form not required.
  Initial approach: Telephone
  Copies of proposal: 12
  Deadline(s): Jan. 15, Mar. 15, May 15, Sept. 15, and Nov. 15
  Board meeting date(s): Feb., Apr., June, Oct., and Dec.
  Final notification: Immediately following Board meetings
Officers and Trustees: * Mary Reimer,* Chair.; Craig Wilks,* Vice-Chair.; John J. Guidugli, C.E.O. and Pres.; Kelli Kurtz, V.P., Devel.; Rebecca P. Fitton,* Secy.; William A. Groth,* Treas.; Cynthia V. Parrish, Exec. Dir.; Lee H. Parrish, Legal Counsel; David L. Belew, Tr. Emeritus; Donald M. Cisle; John R. Moser; Frank Pfirrman; Emily B. Reed; George Schmidt; Karen Underwood-Kramer.
Trustee Banks: First Financial Bank; U.S. Bank, N.A.
Number of staff: 1 full-time professional; 2 part-time professional; 2 full-time support; 1 part-time support.
EIN: 316038277
Selected grants: The following grants were reported in 2005.
$717,647 to Fort Hamilton-Hughes Healthcare Corporation, Hamilton, OH. 3 grants: $117,647, $300,000, $300,000
$429,462 to Fitton Center for Creative Arts, Hamilton, OH. 2 grants: $92,462, $337,000
$200,000 to Fort Hamilton Healthcare Foundation, Hamilton, OH. 2 grants: $100,000 each
$100,000 to Stephen T. Badin High School, Hamilton, OH.
$93,333 to YMCA, Great Miami Valley, Hamilton, OH.
$50,000 to Pyramid Hill Sculpture Park and Museum, Hamilton, OH.

7661
Richard M. & Yvonne Hamlin Foundation ◇
3560 W. Market St., Ste. 300
Akron, OH 44333
Contact: Rosemary Lombardi

Donor: McDowell Manufacturing.
Foundation type: Independent foundation.
Financial data (yr. ended 12/31/05): Assets, $3,137,728 (M); gifts received, $86,582; expenditures, $608,046; qualifying distributions, $567,900; giving activities include $567,900 for 19 grants (high: $500,000; low: $200; average: $1,000–$10,000).
Purpose and activities: Giving primarily for education.
Fields of interest: Elementary/secondary education; Higher education; Hospitals (general); Health care; Federated giving programs; Roman Catholic agencies & churches.
Type of support: General/operating support.
Limitations: Giving primarily in OH.
Application information: Application form required.
  Deadline(s): None

Trustees: R. Mark Hamlin; Richard M. Hamlin; Yvonne F. Hamlin.
EIN: 341812974

7662
The Hankins Foundation ◇
c/o R.A. Bumblis, C.P.A.
1900 E. 9th St., Ste. 3200
Cleveland, OH 44114   (216) 861-7623
Contact: Richard R. Hollington, Jr., Tr.

Established in 1952 in OH.
Donors: Edward R. Hankins†; Ann H. Long†; Jane H. Lockwood†; Ruth Leale Hankins.
Foundation type: Independent foundation.
Financial data (yr. ended 12/31/04): Assets, $6,302,540 (M); expenditures, $362,686; qualifying distributions, $341,079; giving activities include $332,200 for 62 grants (high: $25,000; low: $500).
Fields of interest: Arts; Education; Health care; Health organizations, association; Human services; Children/youth, services; Federated giving programs.
Type of support: General/operating support.
Limitations: Giving primarily in AZ and OH. No grants to individuals; no loans.
Application information: Application form not required.
  Copies of proposal: 1
  Deadline(s): None
  Board meeting date(s): As required
Trustees: Richard R. Hollington, Jr.; Gordon Long; Janet L. Tarwater.
Number of staff: 1 full-time professional; 4 part-time support.
EIN: 346565426
Selected grants: The following grants were reported in 2004.
$25,000 to American Red Cross, Akron, OH.
$15,000 to Connecticut College, New London, CT.
$13,000 to Ohio Foundation of Independent Colleges, Columbus, OH.
$10,000 to Benjamin Rose Institute, Cleveland, OH.
$10,000 to Hathaway Brown School, Shaker Heights, OH.
$10,000 to Playhouse Square Foundation, Cleveland, OH.
$10,000 to United Way Services of Greater Cleveland, Cleveland, OH.
$5,000 to Salvation Army, Cambridge, OH.
$5,000 to Summit Education Initiative, Akron, OH.
$2,000 to Great Lakes Science Center, Cleveland, OH.

7663
Harding Family Charitable Trust ◇ ☆
c/o National City Bank
P.O. Box 94651
Cleveland, OH 44101
Application address: c/o Susan C. Murphy, National City Bank, P.O. Box 5756, LOC 2030, Cleveland, OH 44101, tel.: (216) 222-2747

Donors: Clara E. Harding; R. Amelia Harding.
Foundation type: Independent foundation.
Financial data (yr. ended 12/31/05): Assets, $595,259 (M); gifts received, $602,770; expenditures, $726,133; qualifying distributions, $724,451; giving activities include $719,664 for grants.

Fields of interest: Health care, clinics/centers.
Limitations: Giving primarily in Cleveland, OH.
Application information: Application form not required.
  Deadline(s): None
Trustees: Clara E. Harding; R. Amelia Harding; National City Bank.
EIN: 300021471

7664
Sandra L. and Dennis B. Haslinger Family Foundation, Inc. ◇
2524 Ira Rd.
Akron, OH 44333
Application address: Sandra L. Haslinger, c/o Seikel & Co., Inc., 686 W. Market St., Akron, OH 44303, tel.: (330) 761-1040

Established in 1997 in OH.
Donor: Sandra L. Haslinger.
Foundation type: Independent foundation.
Financial data (yr. ended 12/31/04): Assets, $3,300,241 (M); expenditures, $2,755,835; qualifying distributions, $2,559,003; giving activities include $2,559,003 for 15 grants (high: $1,600,000; low: $3).
Purpose and activities: Giving for human services and education; funding also for a children's hospital.
Fields of interest: Education; Hospitals (specialty); Human services; Community development.
Type of support: General/operating support; Building/renovation; Equipment; Endowments; Program development; Scholarship funds.
Limitations: Giving primarily in OH.
Application information:
  Initial approach: Letter
  Deadline(s): None
Officers and Trustees: * Sandra L. Haslinger,* Pres.; Douglas S. Haslinger,* Secy.; Jennifer S. Haslinger,* Treas.; Benjamin G. Haslinger; Kimberly M. Haslinger; Melissa A. Haslinger; Myriam Eve Haslinger.
EIN: 341848698

7665
E. Kenneth & Esther Marie Hatton Foundation ◇
2486 Charwood Ct.
Cincinnati, OH 45211   (513) 762-5150
Contact: Linda Ranz

Established in 1997 in OH.
Donors: Esther Marie Hatton; Kenneth Hatton.
Foundation type: Independent foundation.
Financial data (yr. ended 12/31/05): Assets, $27,215,652 (M); expenditures, $1,529,200; qualifying distributions, $1,302,893; giving activities include $1,248,123 for 10 grants (high: $1,042,208; low: $190; average: $2,400–$50,000).
Purpose and activities: The focus of the foundation is on medical organizations and mentoring programs.
Fields of interest: Hospitals (general); Human services; Roman Catholic agencies & churches.
Limitations: Giving primarily in OH; some giving in KY. No grants to individuals.
Application information:
  Initial approach: Letter or telephone
  Deadline(s): None

Officers: Steve Scherzinger, Pres.; Jeffrey Holtmeier, V.P.; Robert Robinson, Secy.; Margaret Lunsford, Treas.; Walter Lunsford, Exec. Dir.
EIN: 311533046

7666
John Hauck Foundation ✧

c/o Fifth Third Bank
P.O. Box 630858
Cincinnati, OH 45263

Established in 1989 in OH.
Donor: Frederick Hauck.
Foundation type: Independent foundation.
Financial data (yr. ended 9/30/05): Assets, $12,938,942 (M); expenditures, $537,658; qualifying distributions, $435,700; giving activities include $432,500 for 3+ grants.
Purpose and activities: Giving primarily for education, museums and historical societies, and children and youth services, including a children's hospital.
Fields of interest: Museums; Historic preservation/historical societies; Higher education; Education; Hospitals (specialty); Human services; Children/youth, services.
Type of support: Capital campaigns; Building/renovation; Program development; Research.
Limitations: Applications not accepted. Giving primarily in Cincinnati, OH. No grants to individuals.
Application information: Contributes only to pre-selected organizations.
Trustees: E. Allen Elliott; Narley L. Haley; John W. Hauck; Fifth Third Bank.
EIN: 316366846

7667
HCR Manor Care Foundation

(formerly Manor Care Foundation, Inc.)
333 N. Summit St.
P.O. Box 10086
Toledo, OH 43699-0086 (419) 252-5989
Contact: Jennifer Steiner, Exec. Dir.
FAX: (419) 252-5521;
E-mail: foundation@hcr-manorcare.com;
URL: http://www.hcr-manorcare.org/

Established in 1997 in MD.
Donors: Manor Care, Inc.; HCR Manor Care, Inc.; Virginia Hill Trust; Anna Mae Lee; Mary Louise and Marjori Lord Trust Fund.
Foundation type: Company-sponsored foundation.
Financial data (yr. ended 5/31/05): Assets, $3,148,001 (M); gifts received, $821,417; expenditures, $1,379,072; qualifying distributions, $1,345,963; giving activities include $436,251 for 74 grants (high: $75,000; low: $500), and $638,074 for 4 foundation-administered programs.
Purpose and activities: The foundation supports organizations involved with Alzheimer's disease, geriatrics, hospice and palliative care, post-acute services, and senior citizens.
Fields of interest: Alzheimer's disease; Geriatrics; Geriatrics research; Residential/custodial care, hospices; Residential/custodial care, senior continuing care; Aging, centers/services; Aging.
Type of support: General/operating support; Continuing support; Program development; Seed money; Curriculum development; Research; Employee matching gifts; Matching/challenge support.

Limitations: Giving on a national basis in areas of company operations. No grants to individuals, or for building or capital campaigns, endowments, fundraising events, overhead fees, advertising, or political purposes; no multi-year awards.
Publications: Application guidelines; Annual report (including application guidelines); Grants list.
Application information: Additional information may be requested at a later date. A site visit may be requested. Application form required.
  Initial approach: Complete online application form
  Deadline(s): Apr. 1 and Oct. 1
  Board meeting date(s): June and Dec.
  Final notification: Within 1 month following board meetings
Officers and Directors:* Rick Rump,* Pres.; Matt Kang,* Treas.; Jennifer Steiner, Exec. Dir.; Kim Byk; Dan Kight; Jim Pagoaga; David Parker; Clif Porter.
Number of staff: 3 full-time professional; 2 full-time support.
EIN: 522031975
Selected grants: The following grants were reported in 2006.
$50,000 to American Medical Student Association Foundation, Chicago, IL. For End-of-Life Initiative.
$29,167 to University of Colorado Health Sciences Center, Denver, CO. For clinical implementation and testing of Alzheimer's-Hospice Placement Evaluation Scale (AHOPE).
$24,000 to Menorah Park Center for Senior Living, Beachwood, OH. For Better Visits: Improving Family Visits for Persons with Dementia and Their Families.
$15,000 to Bernal Heights Neighborhood Center, San Francisco, CA. For Neighborhood Elder Support Team (NEST) program.
$14,000 to Community Hospice of Northeast Florida, Jacksonville, FL. For Camp healing Powers.
$10,304 to Family Service of South Lake County, Highland Park, IL. For Elder Mental health Serviecs program.
$10,000 to East Liberty Family Health Care Center, Pittsburgh, PA. For Homebound Elderly Outreach Program.
$5,000 to ARK, Adult Respite Care, Summerville, SC. For A Friend Project.
$5,000 to Family Eldercare, Austin, TX. For In-Home Care and Respite Services.
$5,000 to Jewish Vocational Service and Community Workshop, Southfield, MI. For Caring Partners Project (CPP).

7668
Heavenly Hands Foundation ✧ ☆

925 Euclid Ave., Ste. 2000
Cleveland, OH 44115

Established in 2004 in OH.
Donor: Rebecca Jones-Jemison.
Foundation type: Independent foundation.
Financial data (yr. ended 12/31/05): Assets, $409,185 (M); expenditures, $503,012; qualifying distributions, $503,012; giving activities include $500,000 for 1 grant.
Purpose and activities: Giving to Baptist faith ministries.
Fields of interest: Protestant agencies & churches.
Type of support: General/operating support.
Limitations: Applications not accepted. Giving primarily in OH. No grants to individuals.
Application information: Contributes only to pre-selected organizations.

Trustees: Samuel R. Jemison; Rebecca Jones-Jemison; Eugene Kratus.
EIN: 202033858

7669
The Kim and Gary Heiman Family Foundation ✧

c/o Edward M. Frankel
P.O. Box 371805
Cincinnati, OH 45222-1805

Established in 1998 in OH.
Donors: Gary Heiman; Kim Heiman; Standard Textile Co., Inc.
Foundation type: Independent foundation.
Financial data (yr. ended 12/31/05): Assets, $870,140 (M); expenditures, $491,483; qualifying distributions, $491,483; giving activities include $488,200 for 57 grants (high: $151,440; low: $100; average: $1,000–$10,000).
Purpose and activities: Giving primarily for Jewish federated giving programs, and to Jewish organizations and temples.
Fields of interest: Education; Jewish federated giving programs; Jewish agencies & temples.
Limitations: Applications not accepted. Giving primarily in OH. No grants to individuals.
Application information: Contributes only to pre-selected organizations.
Officers: Gary Heiman, Pres.; Kim Heiman, V.P.; Edward M. Frankel, Secy.-Treas.
EIN: 316605176

7670
Heimbinder Family Foundation ✧ ☆

c/o William E. Reichard
25109 Detroit Rd., Ste. 300
Westlake, OH 44145

Established in 1989 in OH.
Donors: Isaac Heimbinder; Sheila Heimbinder.
Foundation type: Independent foundation.
Financial data (yr. ended 12/31/05): Assets, $45,658,489 (M); expenditures, $431,474; qualifying distributions, $409,101; giving activities include $409,101 for grants.
Fields of interest: Performing arts, theater; Residential/custodial care, hospices; Roman Catholic agencies & churches.
Type of support: Program-related investments/loans.
Limitations: Applications not accepted. Giving primarily in TX. No grants to individuals.
Application information: Contributes only to pre-selected organizations.
Trustees: Isaac Heimbinder; Sheila Heimbinder; William E. Reichard.
EIN: 346921501
Selected grants: The following grants were reported in 2004.
$30,000 to National Housing Endowment, DC.
$15,000 to Sanctuary for Families, New York, NY.
$5,000 to Americas Second Harvest, Chicago, IL.
$5,000 to Casa Juan Diego, Houston, TX.
$5,000 to Catholic Charities, El Paso, TX.
$5,000 to Catholic Charities of the Archdiocese of Galveston-Houston, Houston, TX.
$1,350 to Houston Symphony Orchestra, Houston, TX.
$1,000 to Menil Collection, Houston, TX.

$1,000 to Museum of Fine Arts, Houston, Houston, TX.

$500 to Fresh Arts Coalition, Houston, TX.

7671
The Hershey Foundation
10229 Prouty Rd.
Concord Township, OH 44024 (440) 256-6003
Contact: Debra Hershey Guren, Pres.
FAX: (440) 256-0233; URL: http://
foundationcenter.org/grantmaker/hershey/

Established in 1986 in OH.
Donors: Jo Hershey Selden†; Loren W. Hershey;
Debra Hershey Guren; Carole Hershey Walters.
Foundation type: Independent foundation.
Financial data (yr. ended 12/31/04): Assets,
$18,081,970 (M); expenditures, $901,678;
qualifying distributions, $890,206; giving activities
include $888,150 for 38 grants (high: $450,000;
low: $1,500; average: $10,000–$25,000).
Purpose and activities: The foundation is dedicated
to providing children in northeastern OH, from all
socio-economic and cultural backgrounds, with
special opportunities for personal growth and
development. Support from the foundation helps
schools, museums, cultural institutions, and other
non-profit organizations develop and implement
innovative programs that make the future brighter
for children by improving quality of life, building
self-esteem, enhancing learning, increasing
exposure to other cultures and ideas, and
encouraging the development of independent
thinking and problem-solving skills.
Fields of interest: Arts education; Education, early
childhood education; Child development, education;
Elementary school/education; Education; Children/
youth, services; Child development, services.
Type of support: Capital campaigns; Building/
renovation; Equipment; Endowments; Program
development; Seed money; Curriculum
development.
Limitations: Giving primarily in northeastern OH. No
grants to individuals, or for annual campaigns,
endowment funds, operating budgets, computer
systems, or research.
Publications: Application guidelines; Annual report;
Grants list; Informational brochure (including
application guidelines); Multi-year report.
Application information: See foundation Web site
for application guidelines and procedures.
Application form not required.
   Initial approach: 1-page letter or telephone
   Copies of proposal: 1
   Deadline(s): Dec. 1 and June 1
   Board meeting date(s): Feb. and Aug.
   Final notification: Mar. and Sept.
Officers and Trustees:* Debra Hershey Guren,*
C.E.O. and Pres.; Carole Hershey Walters,* V.P. and
Secy.; Loren W. Hershey,* Treas.; Georgia A.
Froelich.
Number of staff: 1 part-time support.
EIN: 341525626
Selected grants: The following grants were reported
in 2005.
$65,000 to Hershey Montessori School, Concord,
   OH. For capital support and strategic projects.
$50,000 to Goodrich-Gannett Neighborhood Center,
   Cleveland, OH. For childcare capital campaign.
$30,000 to Achievement Centers for Children,
   Highland Hills, OH. For Champ Camp playground.
$25,000 to Cleveland Play House, Cleveland, OH.
   For community education programs.

$25,000 to Das Deutsch Center for Special Needs
   Children, Middlefield, OH. For Genetic Disease
   Intervention through Education.
$25,000 to Fieldstone Farm Therapeutic Riding
   Center, Chagrin Falls, OH. For endowment.
$11,500 to Holden Arboretum, Kirtland, OH. For Big
   Bugs Exhibit.
$11,400 to Cleveland Museum of Natural History,
   Cleveland, OH. For teacher/astronomer
   partnerships.
$10,000 to Leadership Lake County, Painesville,
   OH. For youth leadership program.
$4,000 to New Life Community, Cleveland, OH. For
   equipment for campers.

7672
Home Savings Charitable Foundation ◈
c/o Home Savings and Loan Co.
P.O. Box 1111
Youngstown, OH 44501-1111 (330) 742-0500
Contact: Darlene Pavlock, Exec. Dir.
Additional tel.: (330) 742-0571

Established in 1991 in OH.
Donor: Home Savings and Loan Co.
Foundation type: Company-sponsored foundation.
Financial data (yr. ended 12/31/03): Assets,
$24,333,565 (M); expenditures, $800,545;
qualifying distributions, $718,229; giving activities
include $680,423 for 167 grants (high: $66,000;
low: $50).
Purpose and activities: The foundation supports
organizations involved with arts and culture,
education, health, and human services.
Fields of interest: Arts; Higher education;
Education; Health organizations, association;
Human services; YM/YWCAs & YM/YWHAs;
Federated giving programs.
Type of support: Annual campaigns; Capital
campaigns.
Limitations: Giving primarily in northeastern, north
central, and northwestern OH, with emphasis on
Columbiana, Mahoning, and Trumbull counties. No
grants to individuals.
Application information: An application form is
available but not required. Application form not
required.
   Initial approach: Proposal
   Copies of proposal: 15
   Deadline(s): 1 month prior to board meetings
   Board meeting date(s): Last Tues. of each month
Trustee: Butler Wick Trust Co.
Number of staff: 1 full-time professional.
EIN: 341695319

7673
Honda of America Foundation
c/o Corp. Affairs, Marysville Motorcycle Plant
24000 Honda Pkwy.
Marysville, OH 43040-9251 (937) 645-8785
Contact: Lourene Hoy, Asst. Mgr., Community Rels.
and Comms.
FAX: (937) 645-8787;
E-mail: rene_hoy@ham.honda.com; URL: http://
www.ohio.honda.com/Neighbor/dedication.cfm

Established in 1981 in OH.
Donor: Honda of America Mfg., Inc.
Foundation type: Company-sponsored foundation.
Financial data (yr. ended 12/31/05): Assets,
$9,202,716 (M); expenditures, $655,930;

qualifying distributions, $547,384; giving activities
include $547,384 for 20 grants (high: $79,434;
low: $10,000).
Purpose and activities: The foundation supports
organizations involved with arts and culture,
education, the environment, health, human
services, and community development.
Fields of interest: Arts; Education; Environment;
Health care; Human services; Community
development.
Limitations: Giving primarily in areas of company
operations in OH. No support for religious
organizations, national health, fraternal, lobbying,
political, or veterans' organizations, or sports
teams. No grants to individuals, or for courtesy
advertisements, legal advocacy, memberships,
conferences, workshops, seminars, pageants, or
extracurricular school activities.
Publications: Application guidelines.
Application information: Application form required.
   Initial approach: Complete online application form
   Deadline(s): None
   Board meeting date(s): Quarterly
   Final notification: 1 month
Officers and Trustees:* Lynn Dennison,* Pres.;
Shaun McCloskey,* Treas.; John Adams; Sue
Boggs; Steve Francis; Larry Jutte.
Number of staff: 1 full-time professional.
EIN: 311006130

7674
The Herbert W. Hoover Foundation
c/o Key Bank, N.A.
800 Superior Ave., 4th Fl., OH-01-02-0421
Cleveland, OH 44114
Contact: Ellen Beidler, Exec. Dir.
c/o: Ellen Beidler, Exec. Dir., 220 Market Ave. S.,
Ste. 40, Canton, OH 44702-2180

Established in 1990 in OH.
Donor: The Hoover Foundation.
Foundation type: Independent foundation.
Financial data (yr. ended 12/31/05): Assets,
$23,540,367 (M); expenditures, $1,198,459;
qualifying distributions, $1,144,244; giving
activities include $942,380 for 40 grants (high:
$75,000; low: $3,000; average: $10,000–
$25,000).
Purpose and activities: The focus of the Herbert W.
Hoover Foundation is on children, education, the
environment, and health and social services. The
foundation only contributes to 501c(3)
organizations.
Fields of interest: Education; Environment; Health
care; Human services; Children.
Type of support: General/operating support;
Continuing support; Capital campaigns; Equipment;
Program development; Scholarship funds;
Research; Matching/challenge support.
Limitations: Giving primarily in Stark County, OH. No
support for political organizations. No grants to
individuals, or for annual campaigns, endowments,
start-up funds, or for grassroots.
Publications: Application guidelines.
Application information: Applications not meeting
guidelines will not be accepted. Application form
required.
   Initial approach: Letter
   Deadline(s): None
   Board meeting date(s): 3 times per year
Trust Committee: Elizabeth Lacey Hoover, Chair.;
Colton Hoover Chase; Eugene A. DeChellis; Nancy
McPeek; Robert S. O'Brien.

Trustee: KeyBank N.A.
Number of staff: 1 full-time professional; 1 full-time support.
EIN: 346905388

7675
The Hoover Foundation
400 Market Ave. N., Ste. 210
Canton, OH   44702
Contact: Lawrence R. Hoover, Chair.

Trust established in 1945 in OH.
Donor: Members of the Hoover family.
Foundation type: Independent foundation.
Financial data (yr. ended 12/31/05): Assets, $50,536,533 (M); expenditures, $3,063,247; qualifying distributions, $2,854,804; giving activities include $2,801,422 for 69 grants (high: $352,000; low: $200).
Purpose and activities: Grants for youth agencies, hospital building funds, community funds, and elementary, secondary, and higher education.
Fields of interest: Education, early childhood education; Elementary school/education; Secondary school/education; Higher education; Libraries (public); Hospitals (general); Food services; Youth development, services; YM/YWCAs & YM/YWHAs; Children/youth, services; Federated giving programs.
Type of support: General/operating support; Annual campaigns; Capital campaigns; Equipment; Seed money; Curriculum development; Scholarship funds; Employee matching gifts; Matching/challenge support.
Limitations: Giving primarily in Stark County, OH. No grants to individuals.
Application information: Application form not required.
  Initial approach: Letter
  Copies of proposal: 1
  Deadline(s): None
  Board meeting date(s): As required
  Final notification: 1 to 4 months
Trust Committee: Lawrence R. Hoover, Chair.; Ronald K. Bennington; Charles H. Hoover; Thomas H. Hoover, M.D.; Timothy D. Schlitz.
Trustee: Huntington National Bank.
EIN: 346510994
Selected grants: The following grants were reported in 2004.
$340,000 to Walsh University, North Canton, OH.
$323,000 to Malone College, Canton, OH.
$120,000 to Arts in Stark, Canton, OH.
$100,000 to North Canton Medical Foundation, North Canton, OH.
$83,500 to Stark Education Partnership, Canton, OH.
$50,000 to Stark Social Workers Network, Canton, OH.
$35,000 to Pathway Caring for Children, Canton, OH.
$25,000 to Canton Museum of Art, Canton, OH.
$25,000 to YMCA, Canton Area - North Canton Center Branch, North Canton, OH.
$15,000 to Student Loan Foundation of North Canton, North Canton, OH.

7676
The Leonard and Joan Horvitz Foundation ◇
6095 Parkland Blvd., Ste. 300
Mayfield Heights, OH   44124

Established in 2000 in OH.
Donors: Leonard C. Horvitz; Joan L. Horvitz.
Foundation type: Independent foundation.
Financial data (yr. ended 12/31/05): Assets, $415,027 (M); gifts received, $834,550; expenditures, $426,991; qualifying distributions, $415,718; giving activities include $415,000 for 4 grants (high: $200,000; low: $25,000).
Fields of interest: Cancer research; Arthritis research; Jewish federated giving programs; Jewish agencies & temples.
Limitations: Applications not accepted. Giving limited to OH. No grants to individuals.
Application information: Contributes only to pre-selected organizations.
Officers: Leonard C. Horvitz, Pres.; Joan L. Horvitz, V.P.; Mark F. Polzin, Secy.-Treas.
EIN: 341894055

7677
Lois U. Horvitz Foundation ◇
(formerly HRH Family Foundation)
c/o Parkland Mgmt. Co.
1001 Lakeside Ave., Ste. 900
Cleveland, OH   44114-1151   (216) 479-2200
Contact: Thomas H. Oden, Treas.
Scholarship application address: c/o Nyles C. Ayers, Scholarship Prog. Admin., 3314 W. End Ave., Nashville, TN 37203-1022, tel.: (615) 292-4379

Established in 1988 in OH.
Foundation type: Independent foundation.
Financial data (yr. ended 12/31/05): Assets, $3,318,619 (M); expenditures, $559,360; qualifying distributions, $552,538; giving activities include $475,000 for 4 grants (high: $250,000; low: $75,000), and $66,763 for grants to individuals.
Purpose and activities: Support for hospitals, human services, and education, including scholarship awards for higher education to high school seniors attending public, private or parochial high schools in Lake, Lorain, Richland, and Tuscarawas counties, OH and Rensselaer County, NY, or children (natural or adopted) of full-time employees who were employed by Aug. 1, 1987 for at least 2 years.
Fields of interest: Museums (art); Arts; Education; Hospitals (general); Substance abuse, treatment; Human services; Civil rights, advocacy; Jewish agencies & temples.
Type of support: General/operating support; Scholarships—to individuals.
Limitations: Giving limited to residents of Lake, Lorain, Richland and Tuscarawas counties, OH and Rensselaer County, NY; some giving also in Rancho Mirage, CA.
Application information: Application form required for scholarships. Application form required.
  Initial approach: Application form for scholarships; letter of inquiry for grants
  Copies of proposal: 1
  Deadline(s): Apr. 1 for scholarships; for other grants, none
  Board meeting date(s): 3 to 4 times a year
  Final notification: July 1 for scholarships

Officers and Trustees: * Lois U. Horvitz,* Pres.; Peter A. Kuhn,* Secy. and Exec. Dir.; Thomas H. Oden,* Treas.
EIN: 341594655
Selected grants: The following grants were reported in 2003.
$358,000 to Eisenhower Medical Center, Rancho Mirage, CA. For support of hospital staff training.
$300,000 to Cleveland Museum of Art, Cleveland, OH. For restoration project.
$200,000 to Laurel School, Shaker Heights, OH. For Laurel School Centennial Campaign.
$133,333 to Temple Tifereth Israel, Beachwood, OH. For general support and renovation.
$64,713 to HRH Scholarship Fund, Cleveland, OH. For scholarships.
$50,000 to Betty Ford Center at Eisenhower Medical Center, Rancho Mirage, CA. For support of the Betty Ford Children's Program.
$38,750 to Horvitz Newspapers Charity Fund, Cleveland, OH.

7678
The Richard and Marcy Horvitz Foundation ◇
6095 Parkland Blvd., Ste. 300
Mayfield Heights, OH   44124-6140

Established in 1997 in OH.
Donors: Marcy R. Horvitz; Richard A. Horvitz.
Foundation type: Independent foundation.
Financial data (yr. ended 12/31/05): Assets, $4,212,693 (M); gifts received, $441,774; expenditures, $971,164; qualifying distributions, $573,099; giving activities include $568,268 for 167 grants (high: $120,000; low: $25).
Fields of interest: Elementary/secondary education; Higher education; Graduate/professional education; Education; Medical research, institute; Human services; Federated giving programs; Jewish agencies & temples.
Limitations: Applications not accepted. Giving primarily in OH, with emphasis on Cleveland; some giving on a national basis. No grants to individuals.
Application information: Contributes only to pre-selected organizations.
Officers and Trustee: * Richard A. Horvitz,* Pres.; Mark F. Polzin,* Secy.-Treas.
EIN: 311533634
Selected grants: The following grants were reported in 2005.
$284,708 to Childrens Tumor Foundation, New York, NY. 4 grants: $35,472, $120,000, $29,236, $100,000
$90,000 to Aish HaTorah, Cleveland, OH. 3 grants: $18,000, $18,000, $54,000
$20,000 to Claremont McKenna College, Claremont, CA.
$10,000 to University School, Hunting Valley, OH.
$4,200 to Mosdos Ohr Hatorah, Cleveland Heights, OH.

7679
George M. and Pamela S. Humphrey Fund
c/o Advisory Svcs., Inc.
1422 Euclid Ave., Ste. 1010
Cleveland, OH   44115-2078
Contact: Christopher J. Lindley, Treas.

Incorporated in 1951 in OH.

Donors: George M. Humphrey†; Pamela S. Humphrey†.

Foundation type: Independent foundation.

Financial data (yr. ended 12/31/05): Assets, $22,017,626 (M); expenditures, $746,381; qualifying distributions, $675,391; giving activities include $659,000 for 24 grants (high: $400,000; low: $500).

Purpose and activities: Support for hospitals, higher and secondary education, and community funds; support also for cultural programs and health agencies.

Fields of interest: Arts; Secondary school/education; Higher education; Hospitals (general); Health care; Federated giving programs.

Type of support: General/operating support; Continuing support; Annual campaigns; Building/renovation; Equipment; Endowments; Emergency funds; Professorships; Internship funds; Research; Technical assistance; Matching/challenge support.

Limitations: Giving primarily in OH, with emphasis on Cleveland. No grants to individuals; no loans.

Publications: Annual report.

Application information: Application form not required.

  Initial approach: Letter or proposal
  Copies of proposal: 1
  Deadline(s): Prior to board meeting
  Board meeting date(s): Nov.
  Final notification: 1 month

Officers and Trustees:* Pamela B. Keefe,* Pres.; Stephen T. Keefe,* V.P.; Priscilla Perrotti, Secy.; Christopher J. Lindley, Treas.; Peter W. Adams; Alice B. Burnham.

EIN: 346513798

Selected grants: The following grants were reported in 2004.

$775,000 to Hathaway Brown School, Shaker Heights, OH.

$100,000 to Rainbow Babies and Childrens Hospital, Cleveland, OH.

$80,000 to Cleveland Botanical Garden, Cleveland, OH.

$26,352 to Saint Martin de Porres High School, Cleveland, OH.

$25,000 to Cleveland Institute of Music, Cleveland, OH.

$25,000 to Miss Halls School, Pittsfield, MA.

$5,000 to Cleveland Scholarship Programs, Cleveland, OH.

$2,000 to Holden Arboretum, Kirtland, OH.

7680

The John Huntington Fund for Education

20620 N. Park Blvd., Ste. 215
Cleveland, OH 44118 (216) 321-7185
Contact: Ann P. Ranney, Treas.

Incorporated in 1954 in OH.

Donor: John Huntington†.

Foundation type: Independent foundation.

Financial data (yr. ended 12/31/05): Assets, $40,259,423 (M); expenditures, $2,579,767; qualifying distributions, $2,431,596; giving activities include $2,395,000 for 10 grants (high: $800,000; low: $50,000).

Purpose and activities: To provide grants to Cuyahoga County institutions to be administered for scientific and technological scholarships to Cuyahoga students.

Fields of interest: Higher education; Engineering/technology; Science.

Type of support: Scholarship funds.

Limitations: Giving limited to Cuyahoga County, OH. No grants to individuals.

Application information: Application form not required.

  Initial approach: Letter
  Copies of proposal: 1
  Deadline(s): Apr. 15
  Board meeting date(s): Usually in May

Officers and Trustees:* Peter W. Adams,* Pres.; Oakley Andrews,* Secy.; Ann P. Ranney,* Treas.; Chandler Everett; Robert M. Ginn; Robert G. McCreary III; Karen R. Nestor; Leigh H. Perkins.

Number of staff: 1 part-time professional.

EIN: 340714434

Selected grants: The following grants were reported in 2003.

$739,000 to Case Western Reserve University, Cleveland, OH. For scholarships.

$480,000 to Cleveland Scholarship Programs, Cleveland, OH. For scholarships.

$304,000 to John Carroll University, University Heights, OH. For scholarships.

$180,000 to Ursuline College, Pepper Pike, OH. For scholarships.

$96,000 to Baldwin-Wallace College, Berea, OH. For scholarships.

$96,000 to Cleveland Institute of Art, Cleveland, OH. For scholarships.

$88,000 to Central School of Practical Nursing, Cleveland, OH. For scholarships.

$80,000 to Notre Dame College of Ohio, South Euclid, OH. For scholarships.

$64,000 to Myers University, Cleveland, OH. For scholarships.

$50,000 to University Hospitals of Cleveland, Cleveland, OH. For Leaders in Nursing Careers pilot program.

7681

Edward L. Hutton Foundation ☆

2600 Chemed Ctr.
255 E. 5th St.
Cincinnati, OH 45202-4726
Contact: Sandra E. Laney, V.P.
FAX: (513) 762-6919;
E-mail: sandra.laney@chemed.com

Established in 1991 in OH.

Donors: Edward L. Hutton; Kathryn Jane Hutton.

Foundation type: Independent foundation.

Financial data (yr. ended 12/31/05): Assets, $5,554,025 (M); gifts received, $69,545; expenditures, $357,286; qualifying distributions, $336,972; giving activities include $302,694 for 78 grants (high: $90,000; low: $18); and $15,500 for 12 grants to individuals (high: $2,500; low: $500).

Purpose and activities: Giving for health associations, the arts, and education.

Fields of interest: Arts; Higher education; Education; Health organizations, association; Human services.

Type of support: Scholarships—to individuals; Scholarship funds.

Limitations: Applications not accepted. Giving on a national basis, with emphasis on IN and OH. No support for political organizations.

Publications: Annual report.

Application information: Contributes only to pre-selected organizations.

  Board meeting date(s): Mar., June, Sept., and Dec.

Officers: Edward L. Hutton, Pres.; Edward A. Hutton, V.P.; Kathryn Jane Hutton, V.P.; Thomas C. Hutton,

V.P.; Jennie Hutton Jacoby, V.P.; Sandra E. Laney, V.P.

Number of staff: 6 part-time support.

EIN: 311334189

Selected grants: The following grants were reported in 2005.

$25,000 to Lower Price Hill Community School, Cincinnati, OH.

$5,000 to Kenyon College, Gambier, OH.

$3,300 to United Way.

$3,000 to Millikin University, Decatur, IL.

$1,000 to Catching the Dream, Albuquerque, NM.

$500 to Association of Small Foundations, DC.

$300 to Wellesley Education Foundation, Wellesley, MA.

7682

Iddings Benevolent Trust ◇

(also known as Iddings Foundation)
c/o JPMorgan Chase Bank, N.A.
Kettering Twr.
40 N. Main St., Ste. 1620
Dayton, OH 45423-2490 (937) 224-1773
Contact: Maribeth A. Graham, Admin.
FAX: (937) 224-1871

Established in 1973 in OH.

Donors: Roscoe C. Iddings†; Andrew S. Iddings†.

Foundation type: Independent foundation.

Financial data (yr. ended 12/31/05): Assets, $13,296,624 (M); expenditures, $626,731; qualifying distributions, $612,905; giving activities include $534,959 for 49 grants (high: $50,000; low: $600; average: $5,000–$10,000).

Purpose and activities: Grants for improvement of the greater Dayton, OH, area, through capital and small grants; and through innovative projects which benefit at-risk youth and change the system, education, health, justice, economics, for example.

Fields of interest: Arts; Education; Reproductive health, family planning; Human services; Children/youth, services.

Type of support: Capital campaigns; Building/renovation; Equipment; Land acquisition; Program development; Seed money; Matching/challenge support.

Limitations: Giving limited to OH, with emphasis on the Dayton metropolitan area. No grants to individuals, or for endowment funds or deficit financing; no loans.

Publications: Informational brochure (including application guidelines).

Application information: Application form required.

  Initial approach: Letter (synopsis form, 3-page narrative) or telephone
  Copies of proposal: 7
  Deadline(s): Mar. 1, June 1, Sept. 1 and Nov. 1
  Board meeting date(s): Apr. July, Oct. and Dec.
  Final notification: 10 days after committee meeting

Trustee: JPMorgan Chase Bank, N.A.

Number of staff: 1 part-time professional.

EIN: 316135058

7683

IHS Foundation ◇ ☆

(formerly Skestos Family Foundation)
2700 E. Dublin Granville Rd., Ste. 01
Columbus, OH 43231
Contact: Terrie L. Rice, Secy.- Treas.

Established in 2000 in OH.
Donors: George A. Skestos; Jason Skestos; Alexandra Skestos Block; Stephanie K. Skestos Gabriele; Justine Skestos; Alexandra Skestos Holmes.
Foundation type: Independent foundation.
Financial data (yr. ended 12/31/05): Assets, $18,614,969 (M); gifts received, $2,000,000; expenditures, $544,692; qualifying distributions, $395,286; giving activities include $394,046 for 48 grants (high: $27,000; low: $200; average: $2,500–$15,000).
Purpose and activities: Giving primarily for human services, particularly food services for people who are economically disadvantaged; funding also for education, health, including a cancer hospital, children and youth services, and Christian and Lutheran churches and organizations.
Fields of interest: Museums (art); Performing arts; Education; Animal welfare; Hospitals (specialty); Reproductive health; Health organizations, association; Cancer; Food services; Human services; Children/youth, services; Pregnancy centers; Christian agencies & churches; Protestant agencies & churches; Economically disadvantaged.
Limitations: Giving primarily in Columbus, OH.
Application information: Application form required.
  Initial approach: Letter
  Deadline(s): None
Officers and Trustees: * George Arthur Skestos,* Pres.; Terrie L. Rice, Secy.-Treas.; Alexandra Skestos Holmes; George Anthony Skestos; Jason J. Skestos; Justine A. Skestos; Stephanie K. Skestos.
EIN: 311721314

7684
The Louise H. and David S. Ingalls Foundation, Inc. ✧
301 Tower E.
20600 Chagrin Blvd.
Shaker Heights, OH 44122 (216) 921-6000
Contact: Gary Lombardo

Incorporated in 1953 in OH.
Donors: Louise H. Ingalls†; Edith Ingalls Vignos; Louise Ingalls Brown†; David S. Ingalls†; David S. Ingalls, Jr.†; Jane I. Davison; Anne I. Lawrence.
Foundation type: Independent foundation.
Financial data (yr. ended 12/31/05): Assets, $30,987,554 (M); expenditures, $1,948,765; qualifying distributions, $1,692,939; giving activities include $1,653,500 for 53 grants (high: $150,000; low: $2,500).
Purpose and activities: Support mainly to organizations known to the trustees for the improvement of the physical, educational, mental, and moral condition of humanity primarily in the Cleveland OH area; grants largely for education, fine arts and culture, music, historical preservation, archaeology and anthropology, the environment and conservation, health programs, and hospital building funds, rehabilitation programs, the disadvantaged, and child development.
Fields of interest: Museums; Performing arts; Historic preservation/historical societies; Arts; Higher education; Environment, natural resources; Hospitals (general); Medical care, rehabilitation; Medical research, institute.
Type of support: Capital campaigns; Building/renovation; Program development; Research.
Limitations: Giving on a national basis, primarily in Cleveland, OH. No grants to individuals; or for annual giving.

Application information: Application form not required.
  Initial approach: Proposal
  Copies of proposal: 1
  Deadline(s): None
  Board meeting date(s): As required
Officers and Trustees: * Barbara Brown,* Pres.; Nina S. Ingalls,* V.P.; Willard W. Brown, Jr., Recording Secy.; John T. Lawrence III, Treas.; E.P. Davison, Jr.; Caren V. Sturges.
Number of staff: 2 part-time support.
EIN: 346516550
Selected grants: The following grants were reported in 2005.
$166,000 to Nature Conservancy, Brunswick, ME. 2 grants: $83,000 each
$150,000 to Vail Mountain School, Vail, CO. 2 grants: $50,000, $100,000
$130,000 to Taft Museum, Cincinnati, OH.
$102,500 to Hawken School, Lyndhurst, OH.
$50,000 to Lawrence School, Broadview Heights, OH.
$50,000 to ORBIS International, New York, NY.
$50,000 to Springer School, Cincinnati, OH.
$50,000 to Winners Walk Tall, Cincinnati, OH.

7685
John E. & Sue M. Jackson Charitable Trust ✧
c/o National City Bank
P.O. Box 94651
Cleveland, OH 44101-4651
Application address: National City Bank, Attn: John Dodson, 20 Stanwix St., Pittsburgh, PA 15222, tel.: (412) 644-6005; FAX: (412) 644-6176

Established in 1950.
Foundation type: Independent foundation.
Financial data (yr. ended 12/31/05): Assets, $10,063,985 (M); expenditures, $687,328; qualifying distributions, $632,278; giving activities include $567,500 for 62 grants (high: $40,000; low: $500).
Fields of interest: Museums; Historic preservation/historical societies; Higher education; Theological school/education; Hospitals (general); Legal services, public interest law; Employment, research; Human services; American Red Cross; Children/youth, services; Family services; Foundations (private grantmaking); Social sciences, research; Social sciences, public policy; Christian agencies & churches.
Limitations: Giving primarily to national organizations in Washington, DC, FL, MD, Pittsburgh, PA, and VA. No grants to individuals.
Application information:
  Initial approach: Letter
  Deadline(s): None
Trustee: National City Bank.
EIN: 256019484
Selected grants: The following grants were reported in 2004.
$40,000 to Heritage Foundation, DC.
$30,000 to Leadership Institute, Arlington, VA.
$27,000 to American Red Cross, National Headquarters, DC.
$18,000 to American Center for Law and Justice, DC.
$18,000 to Hollins University, Roanoke, VA.
$12,000 to Media Research Center, Alexandria, VA.
$10,000 to American Family Association, Tupelo, MS.
$10,000 to Hillsdale College, Hillsdale, MI.

$7,000 to Coalition for Christian Outreach, Pittsburgh, PA.
$3,000 to Covenant House, Charleston, WV.

7686
Isaac & Esther Jarson - Stanley & Mickey Kaplan Foundation ✧ ☆
(formerly Isaac N. and Esther M. Jarson Charitable Trust)
9435 Waterstone Blvd., Ste. 390
Cincinnati, OH 45249
Contact: Stanley M. Kaplan, Tr.; Myron J. Kaplan, Tr.

Trust established in 1955 in OH.
Foundation type: Independent foundation.
Financial data (yr. ended 12/31/05): Assets, $0 (M); expenditures, $2,079,764; qualifying distributions, $2,073,514; giving activities include $2,073,314 for 1 grant.
Fields of interest: Education; Medical research; Human services; Jewish federated giving programs; Jewish agencies & temples.
Limitations: Giving primarily in the greater Cincinnati, OH, area. No grants to individuals.
Application information:
  Initial approach: Letter
  Deadline(s): None
Trustees: Myron J. Kaplan; Stanley M. Kaplan.
EIN: 316033453

7687
The Jegs Foundation ✧ ☆
(formerly Jeg's Quarter Mile Charities)
101 Jegs Pl.
Delaware, OH 43015

Established in 2000 in OH.
Donor: Jeg's Automotive, Inc.
Foundation type: Company-sponsored foundation.
Financial data (yr. ended 12/31/04): Assets, $2,092,382 (M); gifts received, $3,551,156; expenditures, $1,625,174; qualifying distributions, $1,625,000; giving activities include $1,625,000 for 3 grants (high: $1,500,000; low: $25,000).
Purpose and activities: The foundation supports children's hospitals and organizations involved with higher education and cancer research.
Fields of interest: Higher education, university; Hospitals (specialty); Cancer research.
Type of support: General/operating support; Management development/capacity building; Research.
Limitations: Applications not accepted. Giving primarily in OH, with emphasis on Columbus. No grants to individuals.
Application information: Contributes only to pre-selected organizations.
Officers and Trustees: * Phillip Troy Coughlin,* Pres.; Edward John Coughlin,* Secy.-Treas.; Jeg Anthony Coughlin; Michael Allen Coughlin.
EIN: 311731261

7688
The Martha Holden Jennings Foundation ▼
The Halle Bldg.
1228 Euclid Ave., Ste. 710
Cleveland, OH 44115 (216) 589-5700
Contact: William T. Hiller, Exec. Dir.

FAX: (216) 589-5730; Business office: 20620 N. Park Blvd., No. 215, Cleveland, OH 44118, tel.: (216) 932-7337; URL: http://www.mhjf.org

Incorporated in 1959 in OH.

Donor: Martha Holden Jennings‡.

Foundation type: Independent foundation.

Financial data (yr. ended 12/31/05): Assets, $84,985,650 (M); gifts received, $500; expenditures, $4,922,547; qualifying distributions, $4,460,553; giving activities include $3,354,133 for 149 grants (high: $100,649; low: $75; average: $12,500–$30,000), and $380,244 for 7 foundation-administered programs.

Purpose and activities: Giving to foster development of the capabilities of young people through improving the quality of teaching in secular elementary and secondary schools; program includes awards in recognition of outstanding teaching; special educational programs for teachers in the fields of the humanities, the arts, and the sciences; curriculum development projects; school evaluation studies; and educational television programs. Preference is given to programs that target underserved student populations and districts with fewer available resources.

Fields of interest: Education, association; Elementary school/education; Secondary school/ education; Mathematics; Science.

Type of support: Program evaluation; Continuing support; Program development; Seed money; Curriculum development; Matching/challenge support.

Limitations: Giving limited to OH. No grants to individuals or operating budgets, annual campaigns, travel, emergency funds, deficit financing, capital or endowment funds, research, or publications; no loans; teacher stipends; school supplies; substitute coverage; school bus transportation or graduate study.

Publications: Application guidelines; Annual report; Newsletter; Program policy statement.

Application information: Application form required for Grants-to-Educators Program, and is available on Web site. Applicants must submit an original form, signed by the superintendent. Follow criteria on foundation Web site for Open Grants. Open Grant requests must not exceed ten pages. Application form not required.

Initial approach: 1-page project summary with cover letter and proposal
Copies of proposal: 1
Deadline(s): 20th of each month preceding month in which application is to be considered
Board meeting date(s): Distrib. Comm. meets monthly, except July and Dec.; Trustees meet monthly, except Feb., July, Oct., and Dec.
Final notification: 6 to 8 weeks

Officers and Trustees:* George B. Milbourn,* Chair. and Pres.; Arthur S. Holden, Jr.,* Chair. Emeritus; Karen R. Nestor,* V.P.; Deborah Z. Read,* Secy.; William T. Hiller, Exec. Dir.; George B. Chapman, Jr.,* Sr. Advisor; Jeanette Grasselli Brown; Julian M. Earls; Jon H. Outcalt; John F. Sideras.

Distribution Committee: Yvonne L. Allen; Lorenzo T. Carlisle; Leigh H. Carter; James V. Connell; John P. Davis III; Doreen E. Osmun; Joanne Rand Schwartz; John H. Wilharm, Jr.

Number of staff: 2 full-time professional; 1 part-time professional; 1 full-time support; 1 part-time support.

EIN: 340934478

Selected grants: The following grants were reported in 2004.

$202,000 to Kent State University Foundation, Kent, OH. For Ohio Literacy Alliance.

$79,150 to Cleveland Municipal School District, Cleveland, OH. 2 grants: $39,150 (For academic standards strategic support), $40,000 (For mathematics and science partnership).

$54,000 to Harvard University, Cambridge, MA. For Tripod Project.

$50,000 to Cleveland Foundation, Cleveland, OH. For literacy coalition.

$50,000 to Great Lakes Museum of Science, Environment and Technology, Cleveland, OH. For school tours program.

$50,000 to KnowledgeWorks Foundation, Cincinnati, OH. For Ohio 8 Coalition.

$45,000 to Cleveland Scholarship Programs, Cleveland, OH. For advisory services.

$37,000 to Cleveland State University Foundation, Cleveland, OH. For First Ring Leadership Academy.

$37,000 to Ideastream, Cleveland, OH. For NewsDepth.

7689

The Andrew Jergens Foundation

c/o The Greater Cincinnati Foundation
200 W. 4th St.
Cincinnati, OH   45202   (513) 241-2880
Contact: Mary D. LeRoy, Prog. Off.

Incorporated in 1962 in OH.

Donor: Andrew N. Jergens‡.

Foundation type: Independent foundation.

Financial data (yr. ended 8/31/05): Assets, $11,371,135 (M); expenditures, $609,644; qualifying distributions, $560,452; giving activities include $532,617 for 47 grants (high: $50,000; low: $300; average: $5,000–$20,000).

Purpose and activities: Giving to programs directly serving children in the greater Cincinnati, OH, area, with emphasis on organizations serving minority, low-income, and/or disadvantaged children.

Fields of interest: Child development, education; Children/youth, services.

Type of support: Capital campaigns; Building/ renovation; Equipment; Program development.

Limitations: Giving limited to the greater Cincinnati, OH, area. No grants to individuals, or for continuing support, annual campaigns, endowment funds, deficit financing, scholarships, fellowships, or research; no loans.

Publications: Application guidelines.

Application information: Proposal must meet requirements outlined in proposal guidelines. See http://www.greatercincinnatifdn.org under Grants/ Private Foundations/Jergens Foundation for submission information. Application form required.

Copies of proposal: 11
Deadline(s): Jan. 1, May 1, and Aug. 1
Board meeting date(s): Mar., July, and Oct.
Final notification: 1 month after meetings

Officers and Trustees:* Michael B. Hays,* Chair.; Peter H. Dine-Jergens,* Pres.; Eric H. Kearney,* V.P.; Consuelo W. Harris,* Secy.; Thomas C. Hays,* Treas.; Mary Ann Hays; Rev. Andrew M. Jergens; Linda Busken Jergens; Joyce J. Keeshin.

EIN: 316038702

Selected grants: The following grants were reported in 2005.

$50,000 to Greater Cincinnati Arts and Education Center, Cincinnati, OH.

$25,000 to Cincinnati Nature Center, Milford, OH.

$25,000 to University of Cincinnati Foundation, Cincinnati, OH.

$20,000 to College of Mount Saint Joseph, Cincinnati, OH.

$20,000 to Greater Cincinnati Foundation, Cincinnati, OH.

$15,000 to Cincinnati Opera Association, Cincinnati, OH.

$15,000 to Talbert House, Cincinnati, OH.

$10,000 to Family Service of the Cincinnati Area, Cincinnati, OH.

$10,000 to Ohio Valley Oral School, Cincinnati, OH.

$10,000 to United Way of Greater Cincinnati, Cincinnati, OH.

7690

The Jewish Foundation of Cincinnati

8044 Montgomery Rd., Ste. 700
Cincinnati, OH   45236-2926   (513) 792-2715
Contact: Connie M. Hinitz, Admin.
FAX: (513) 792-2716; E-mail: jfdncin@supern.com

Established in 1995 in OH; created when the Jewish Hospital of Cincinnati's capital assets were sold to the Health Alliance of Cincinnati.

Foundation type: Independent foundation.

Financial data (yr. ended 10/31/05): Assets, $85,130,183 (M); gifts received, $30; expenditures, $1,784,610; qualifying distributions, $4,849,700; giving activities include $1,368,865 for 13 grants (high: $340,074; low: $500).

Purpose and activities: Giving limited to health care, Jewish agencies and temples, Jewish education, and Israel experience grants.

Fields of interest: Hospitals (general); Jewish agencies & temples.

International interests: Israel.

Type of support: Capital campaigns; Building/ renovation; Equipment; Emergency funds; Scholarship funds; Matching/challenge support.

Limitations: Giving primarily in Cincinnati, OH, and to organizations benefiting Israel. No grants to individuals, or for general operating support, or for debt reduction or for endowments.

Publications: Application guidelines; Annual report.

Application information: Application form required.

Initial approach: Two-page letter of inquiry with attachments
Copies of proposal: 14
Deadline(s): None
Board meeting date(s): Varies
Final notification: 3-9 months

Officers and Trustees:* Gloria S. Haffer, Chair.; Phyllis S. Sewell,* Pres.; Gary Heiman,* V.P.; Philip T. Cohen, Secy.; Warren C. Falberg,* Treas.; Connie M. Hinitz, Admin.; Bernard L. Dave; Michael A. Fisher*; Benjamin Gettler; Robert Kanter; Sidney A. Peerless, M.D.; Jeffrey Zipkin, M.D.

Number of staff: 1 part-time professional.

EIN: 311451489

Selected grants: The following grants were reported in 2004.

$26,613 to Hillel Jewish Student Center of Cincinnati, Cincinnati, OH. For unrestricted support.

7691
Conrad & Caroline Jobst Foundation ◇
c/o KeyBank N.A.
P.O. Box 10099
Toledo, OH   43699-0099   (419) 259-8655
Contact: Diane Ohns, V.P., KeyBank N.A.

Established in 1986 in OH.
Foundation type: Independent foundation.
Financial data (yr. ended 12/31/05): Assets,
$12,812,033 (M); expenditures, $623,038;
qualifying distributions, $586,705; giving activities
include $540,000 for 4 grants (high: $210,000;
low: $60,000).
Purpose and activities: Giving primarily for health
associations and medical education; funding also
for an Episcopal church, and the symphony.
Fields of interest: Performing arts, orchestra
(symphony); Higher education; Medical research,
institute; Protestant agencies & churches.
Limitations: Giving primarily in Toledo, OH; funding
also in Ann Arbor, MI. No grants to individuals.
Application information:
  Initial approach: Letter
  Deadline(s): July 31
Trustees: John M. Curphey; Douglas Metz; Orval
Seydlitz; KeyBank N.A.
EIN: 346872214

7692
The Jochum-Moll Foundation ◇
P.O. Box 368022
Cleveland, OH   44136-9722

Incorporated in 1961 in OH.
Donors: MTD Products, Inc.; A.F. Holding Co.
Foundation type: Company-sponsored foundation.
Financial data (yr. ended 7/31/05): Assets,
$27,662,833; gifts received, $500,000;
expenditures, $1,743,526; qualifying distributions,
$1,612,694; giving activities include $1,602,000
for 65 grants (high: $345,000; low: $1,000).
Purpose and activities: The foundation supports art
museums and organizations involved with
secondary education and Christianity.
Fields of interest: Museums (art); Secondary
school/education; Federated giving programs;
Christian agencies & churches.
Type of support: Program development; Capital
campaigns; General/operating support.
Limitations: Applications not accepted. Giving
primarily in Cleveland, OH. No grants to individuals.
Application information: Contributes only to
pre-selected organizations.
Officers and Trustees:* Carol B. Manning,* Pres.;
Theodore S. Moll,* V.P.; David J. Hessler,* Secy.;
Curtis E. Moll,* Treas.; Emil Jochum; Emma
Jochum; Darrell Moll.
EIN: 346538304
Selected grants: The following grants were reported
in 2004.
$200,000 to Cleveland Museum of Art, Cleveland,
  OH.
$50,000 to City Mission, Cleveland, OH.
$34,000 to Achievement Centers for Children,
  Highland Hills, OH.
$25,000 to Kettering University, Flint, MI.
$20,000 to Inventure Place, Akron, OH.
$20,000 to Lutheran Chaplaincy Service, Cleveland,
  OH.
$20,000 to Salvation Army, Cambridge, OH.
$15,000 to Fairview General Hospital, Cleveland,
  OH.

$15,000 to Valparaiso University, Valparaiso, IN.
$10,000 to Cleveland Orchestra, Cleveland, OH.

7693
The Krishan and Vicky Joshi Foundation ◇
c/o Krishan Joshi
4401 Dayton-Xenia Rd.
Dayton, OH   45432

Established in 2002 in OH.
Donors: Krishan K. Joshi; Vicky M. Joshi.
Foundation type: Independent foundation.
Financial data (yr. ended 12/31/04): Assets,
$1,062,733 (M); gifts received, $12,700;
expenditures, $376,356; qualifying distributions,
$364,692; giving activities include $365,355 for 12
grants (high: $313,340; low: $200).
Fields of interest: Elementary/secondary
education; Higher education.
Limitations: Applications not accepted. Giving
primarily in OH. No grants to individuals.
Application information: Contributes only to
pre-selected organizations.
Officers: Krishan K. Joshi, Pres. and Treas.; Vicky
M. Joshi, V.P. and Secy.
Directors: Nina Joshi; Shashi S. Joshi.
EIN: 611432907

7694
The Jubilee Foundation ◇
(formerly Herman Miller Design Foundation)
P.O. Box 94651
Cleveland, OH   44101

Established in 1994 in MI.
Donor: Herman Miller, Inc.
Foundation type: Company-sponsored foundation.
Financial data (yr. ended 5/31/05): Assets,
$1,930,380 (M); gifts received, $2,063,721;
expenditures, $2,861,142; qualifying distributions,
$2,860,728; giving activities include $2,859,393
for grants.
Purpose and activities: The foundation supports
organizations involved with arts and culture,
education, health, human services, community
development, and minorities.
Fields of interest: Performing arts, orchestra
(symphony); Arts; Higher education; Education;
Health care; Children/youth, services; Human
services; Community development; Minorities.
Type of support: General/operating support;
Scholarship funds.
Limitations: Applications not accepted. Giving
primarily in IL, MD, and MI. No grants to individuals.
Application information: Contributes only to
pre-selected organizations.
Officers and Directors: Michael A. Volkema, Pres.;
James E. Christenson, Secy.; Elizabeth A. Nickels,
Treas.; May Vermeer Andringa; Douglas D. French;
Brian Griffiths; C. William Pollard.
EIN: 383003821
Selected grants: The following grants were reported
in 2004.
$85,484 to Goshen College, Goshen, IN. For
  general support.
$65,000 to Fuller Theological Seminary, Pasadena,
  CA. For general support.
$65,000 to Western Theological Seminary, Holland,
  MI. For general support.
$62,400 to Scholarship America, Saint Peter, MN.
  For general support.

$50,000 to Cornerstone Schools, Detroit, MI. For
  general support.
$45,000 to Calvary Christian School of Byesville,
  Byesville, OH. For general support.
$45,000 to Wycliffe Bible Translators, Orlando, FL.
  For general support.
$40,000 to World Radio Missionary Fellowship,
  Colorado Springs, CO. For general support.
$37,500 to Reformed Bible College, Grand Rapids,
  MI. For general support.
$30,000 to Potters House, Grand Rapids, MI. For
  general support.

7695
The Walter and Jean Kalberer
Foundation ◇
1259 W. Hill Dr.
Gates Mills, OH   44040-9636
Contact: Walter E. Kalberer, Tr.

Established in 1995 in OH.
Donors: Walter E. Kalberer; Jean C. Kalberer; Peter
Scheid.
Foundation type: Independent foundation.
Financial data (yr. ended 12/31/04): Assets,
$6,098,976 (M); gifts received, $3,000;
expenditures, $428,875; qualifying distributions,
$428,575; giving activities include $228,575 for 15
grants (high: $100,000; low: $500), and $200,000
for 1 employee matching gift.
Purpose and activities: Giving primarily for the
performing arts, particularly to a theater; funding
also for human services, as well as to a Presbyterian
church.
Fields of interest: Performing arts, theater;
Performing arts, orchestra (symphony); Performing
arts, opera; Human services; Youth, services;
Protestant agencies & churches.
Limitations: Applications not accepted. Giving
primarily in Cleveland, OH. No grants to individuals.
Application information: Contributes only to
pre-selected organizations.
Trustees: Jean C. Kalberer; Lori Kalberer; Walter E.
Kalberer; Gwenn S. Winkhaus.
EIN: 341817179

7696
The Kaplan Foundation ◇
9435 Waterstone Blvd., Ste. 390
Cincinnati, OH   45249-8227
Contact: Stanley M. Kaplan M.D., Pres.; Myran J.
Kaplan, Secy.

Established in 1994 in OH.
Foundation type: Independent foundation.
Financial data (yr. ended 12/31/05): Assets,
$8,084,736 (M); gifts received, $4,074,159;
expenditures, $1,053,887; qualifying distributions,
$1,019,697; giving activities include $1,019,497
for 115 grants (high: $124,669; low: $25).
Purpose and activities: Giving primarily for religion,
education, and medical and community projects.
Fields of interest: Museums; Performing arts;
Education; Health care, patient services; Human
services; Jewish agencies & temples; Religion.
Type of support: General/operating support.
Limitations: Giving primarily in the greater
Cincinnati, OH, area. No grants to individuals.
Application information:
  Initial approach: Letter
  Deadline(s): None

Officers: Stanley M. Kaplan, M.D., Pres. and Treas.; Myran Kaplan, Secy.

Trustees: Barbara S. Kaplan, M.D.; Richard M. Kaplan; Steven J. Kaplan.

EIN: 311423392

Selected grants: The following grants were reported in 2004.

$100,000 to Greater Cincinnati Arts and Education Center, Cincinnati, OH.

$60,000 to Jewish Federation of Cincinnati, Cincinnati, OH.

$33,333 to National Underground Railroad Freedom Center, Cincinnati, OH.

$25,000 to Ronald McDonald House.

$25,000 to United Way.

$20,000 to Enjoy the Arts, Cincinnati, OH.

$20,000 to Ensemble Theater of Cincinnati, Cincinnati, OH.

$15,000 to YMCA.

$2,100 to Cincinnati Arts Association, Cincinnati, OH.

$1,000 to Starfire Council of Greater Cincinnati, Cincinnati, OH.

7697
Robert T. Keeler Foundation

425 Walnut St., Ste. 1800
Cincinnati, OH 45202-3957
Contact: Mary L. Rust, Treas.

Established in 2001 in OH.

Donor: Robert T. Keeler†.

Foundation type: Independent foundation.

Financial data (yr. ended 12/31/05): Assets, $7,379,366 (M); expenditures, $678,445; qualifying distributions, $642,837; giving activities include $635,295 for 5 grants (high: $282,800; low: $25,000).

Fields of interest: Arts; Education; Health care.

Limitations: Applications not accepted. Giving primarily in OH. No grants to individuals.

Application information: Contributes only to pre-selected organizations.

Officers and Trustees:* Margaret P. Keeler,* Pres.; Peter P. Mithoefer,* Secy.; Mary L. Rust,* Treas.

Number of staff: None.

EIN: 311420552

Selected grants: The following grants were reported in 2003.

$257,100 to University of Cincinnati, Cincinnati, OH. For general support.

$100,000 to Cincinnati Childrens Hospital Medical Center, Cincinnati, OH. For general support.

$5,000 to Long Trail School, Dorset, VT. For general support.

$1,000 to Beechwood Home for Incurables, Cincinnati, OH. For general support.

$1,000 to Cincinnati Association for the Blind, Cincinnati, OH. For general support.

7698
The Kettering Family Foundation

1480 Kettering Twr.
Dayton, OH 45423
Contact: Charles F. Kettering III, Pres.
E-mail: GRANTS@Ketteringfamilyfoundation.org;
Application address: 2833 S. Colorado Blvd., Ste. 2415, Denver, CO 80222; Additional e-mail: Ketteringfamilyf@aol.com; URL: http://www.ketteringfamilyfoundation.org/

Incorporated in 1956 in IL; reincorporated in 1966 in OH.

Donors: E.W. Kettering†; Virginia W. Kettering†; Jane K. Lombard; S.K. Williamson; P.D. Williamson, M.D.; Richard D. Lombard†; B. Weiffenbach†; Charles F. Kettering III; Lisa S. Kettering, M.D.; Leslie G. Williamson; Douglas E. Williamson, M.D.; Susan S. Kettering; Kyle W. Cox; Mark A. Cox; Douglas J. Cushnie; Karen W. Cushnie; Linda K. Danneberg; William H. Danneberg; Jean S. Kettering; Richard J. Lombard; Debra L. Williamson; Nathalie R. Lombard.

Foundation type: Independent foundation.

Financial data (yr. ended 12/31/05): Assets, $20,815,675 (M); gifts received, $2,000; expenditures, $1,251,784; qualifying distributions, $1,199,081; giving activities include $1,186,369 for 54 grants (high: $100,000; low: $1,000).

Purpose and activities: Giving primarily for arts and culture, education, the environment, health care and human services.

Fields of interest: Visual arts; Performing arts; Arts; Higher education; Education; Environment, natural resources; Environment; Health care; Medical research, institute; Human services.

Type of support: General/operating support; Annual campaigns; Capital campaigns; Equipment; Endowments; Program development; Conferences/seminars; Publication; Curriculum development; Research; Technical assistance; Matching/challenge support.

Limitations: Giving on a national basis. No support for foreign purposes, religious organizations for religious purposes, public elementary or secondary schools, or local chapters of national organizations, or conduit organizations. No grants to individuals, or for scholarships, fellowships, memberships, multi-year grants, capital construction, travel expenses, or community drives; no loans.

Publications: Application guidelines; Financial statement; Grants list; Informational brochure (including application guidelines).

Application information: Unsolicited proposals considered after trustee-endorsed requests. Trustee-endorsed requests get priority. Trustees may endorse requests from generally excluded areas. Only trustee-endorsed requests will be considered for international giving. Grants list available on the foundation's Web site. E-mail communication is preferred, including proposals. Application form not required.

Initial approach: 1-page letter of inquiry, preferably via e-mail

Copies of proposal: 3

Deadline(s): Feb. 1 and Aug. 1, for letter of inquiry; Mar. 1 and Sept. 1, for proposals

Board meeting date(s): Mid-May and mid-Nov.

Final notification: 2 weeks after board meetings

Officers and Trustees:* Charles F. Kettering III, Pres.; Susan S. Kettering,* V.P.; Debra L. Williamson,* V.P.; Richard J. Lombard,* Secy.-Treas.; Kyle W. Cox; Karen W. Cushnie; Lisa S. Kettering, M.D.; Jane K. Lombard; Douglas E. Williamson, M.D.; P.D. Williamson, M.D.; Susan K. Williamson.

EIN: 310727384

Selected grants: The following grants were reported in 2005.

$130,000 to Center for School Success, West Lebanon, NH. For general operating support.

$100,000 to Childrens National Medical Center, DC. For gene therapy research.

$100,000 to Dartmouth-Hitchcock Medical Center, Lebanon, NH. For Alex Garden Reeves Professorship.

$70,000 to CEC ArtsLink, New York, NY. For Jubilee Fellowship and Art Programs.

$61,655 to American Red Cross, National Headquarters, DC. For Disaster Relief Fund.

$50,000 to Andover-Phillips Academy, Andover, MA. For Math and Science for Minority Students Program.

$50,000 to Colorado Conservation Trust, Boulder, CO. For Yampa Valley land purcahse.

$30,000 to Brooklyn Botanic Garden, Brooklyn, NY. For Childrens Education Programs.

$29,113 to Kettering University, Flint, MI. For scholarships.

$26,613 to Memorial Sloan-Kettering Cancer Center, New York, NY. For research.

7699
The Kettering Fund ▼

1480 Kettering Twr.
Dayton, OH 45423-1020 (937) 228-1021
Contact: Judith Thompson, Exec. Dir.
FAX: (937) 228-2399;
E-mail: info@ketteringfund.org; URL: http://www.ketteringfund.org

Established in 1958 in OH.

Donor: Charles F. Kettering†.

Foundation type: Independent foundation.

Financial data (yr. ended 6/30/05): Assets, $86,432,548 (M); expenditures, $5,657,795; qualifying distributions, $5,177,205; giving activities include $5,074,878 for 34 grants (high: $500,000; low: $2,000; average: $15,000–$200,000).

Purpose and activities: Grants for scientific, medical, social, and educational studies and research.

Fields of interest: Performing arts; Arts; Higher education; Education; Human services.

Type of support: Capital campaigns; Building/renovation; Equipment; Endowments; Program development; Seed money; Scholarship funds; Research; Technical assistance; Program evaluation.

Limitations: Giving limited to OH. No support for religious purposes, public elementary or secondary schools, or for efforts to carry on propaganda or otherwise attempt to influence legislation. No grants to individuals, or for travel, deficit reduction, or benefit events; no loans.

Publications: Application guidelines; Financial statement; Grants list.

Application information: Only after favorable review of initial letter of intent will application information be provided. Application form required.

Initial approach: Telephone call, or e-mail with Exec. Dir.

Copies of proposal: 7

Deadline(s): Varies

Board meeting date(s): Usually in mid-May and Nov.

Final notification: 10 days to 2 weeks after meeting date

Officer: Judith Thompson, Exec. Dir.

Distribution Committee: Susan S. Kettering; Jane K. Lombard; Debra Williamson; Susan K. Williamson.

Trustee: JPMorgan Chase Bank, N.A.

Number of staff: 1 part-time professional.

EIN: 316027115

Selected grants: The following grants were reported in 2005.

$1,000,000 to Hathaway Brown School, Shaker Heights, OH. For Student Research Program.

$1,000,000 to Kettering Medical Center Foundation, Kettering, OH. For Kettering College of Arts.

$750,000 to Dayton Philharmonic Orchestra, Dayton, OH. For Olive Kettering Endowment.

$500,000 to Wright State University Foundation, Dayton, OH. For School of Medicine Research Center.

$300,000 to Aullwood Audubon Center and Farm, Dayton, OH. For renovation and expansion of facilities.

$250,000 to Ashland University, Ashland, OH. For Science Center Renovation.

$250,000 to Sinclair Community College, Dayton, OH. For Fast Forward Program.

$100,000 to Dayton Society of Natural History, Dayton, OH. For SunWatch Indian Village/ Archaeological Park Renovation.

$100,000 to Girl Scouts of the U.S.A., Buckeye Trails Council, Dayton, OH. For facility improvements.

$36,500 to Ohio Arts Council, Columbus, OH. For ArtLinks program.

7700
Key Foundation ▼
(formerly Society Foundation)
127 Public Sq., 7th Fl.
M.C. OH-01-27-0705
Cleveland, OH   44114-1306   (216) 689-5458
Contact: Bobby Shepherd, Prog. Assoc.
FAX: (216) 689-3865;
E-mail: key_foundation@keybank.com; Additional tel.: (216) 689-4465, (216) 828-7394; Additional FAX: (216) 689-5444, (216) 828-7845;
URL: http://www.key.com/html/A-12.html

Established about 1969 in OH.
Donors: Society Corp.; Society Capital Corp.; KeyBank N.A.; KeyCorp.
Foundation type: Company-sponsored foundation.
Financial data (yr. ended 12/31/04): Assets, $17,569,860 (M); gifts received, $382,205; expenditures, $7,287,878; qualifying distributions, $7,262,400; giving activities include $6,289,072 for 1,368 grants (high: $250,000; low: $500), and $973,328 for 1,445 employee matching gifts.
Purpose and activities: The foundation supports organizations involved with arts and culture, health, employment, financial education, and human services. Special emphasis is directed toward programs designed to promote economic self sufficiency.
Fields of interest: Arts; Health care; Employment, training; Employment; Human services, financial counseling; Human services; Economically disadvantaged.
Type of support: Employee volunteer services; General/operating support; Annual campaigns; Program development; Employee matching gifts.
Limitations: Giving primarily in areas of company operations in AK, CO, ID, IN, ME, MA, MI, NY, OH, OR, UT, VT, and WA, with emphasis on the greater Cleveland, OH, area; giving also to national organizations. No support for lobbying or political organizations, veterans' or fraternal organizations, or discriminatory organizations. No grants to individuals, or for advertisements or memberships or political acitivities.

Publications: Application guidelines; Corporate giving report.
Application information: Proposals should be concise. Visit Web site for nearest company district office. Organizations receiving support are asked to provide a final report. Application form not required.
Initial approach: Mail proposal to nearest company district office
Copies of proposal: 1
Deadline(s): Feb. 7, June 20, Sept. 15, and Nov. 3
Board meeting date(s): Mar. 7, July 18, Oct. 17, and Nov. 3
Final notification: Within 2 weeks following board meetings
Officers and Trustees:* Margot J. Copeland,* Chair.; Robert B. Heisler, Jr.,* Pres.; George Emmons, V.P.; Paul Harris, Secy.; James Hoffman, Treas.; Christopher Gorman; Karen R. Haefling; Thomas E. Helfrich; Carol Klimis; Bruce D. Murphy.
Number of staff: 5 full-time professional.
EIN: 237036607
Selected grants: The following grants were reported in 2004.

$250,000 to Cuyahoga Community College Foundation, Cleveland, OH. For capital campaign.

$100,500 to Cleveland Clinic Foundation, Cleveland, OH. For program support.

$100,000 to Local Initiatives Support Corporation (LISC), Toledo, OH. For operating support.

$98,000 to United Way of Greater Portland, Portland, ME. For general operating support.

$83,333 to Urban League of Greater Cleveland, Cleveland, OH. For program support.

$66,000 to Arts Center Foundation, Dayton, OH. For capital campaign.

$20,500 to United Way of Central Indiana, Indianapolis, IN. For capital campaign.

$15,000 to COSI Toledo, Toledo, OH. For program support.

$15,000 to Roswell P. Flower Memorial Library, Watertown, NY. For capital campaign.

$15,000 to YWCA of Greater Portland, Portland, OR. For program support.

7701
Leonora H. Knowles Trust B ✦
c/o KeyBank N.A., Trust Div.
800 Superior Ave., 4th Fl.
Cleveland, OH   44114-2601

Established in 1987 in ME.
Foundation type: Independent foundation.
Financial data (yr. ended 12/31/05): Assets, $6,475,503 (M); expenditures, $480,166; qualifying distributions, $422,203; giving activities include $317,177 for 15 grants (high: $76,700; low: $5,400), and $85,000 for 65 grants to individuals (high: $2,500; low: $500; average: $750–$1,000).
Purpose and activities: Giving primarily for higher education, as well as to a school for people who are deaf; funding also for health associations, particularly an eye and ear infirmary.
Fields of interest: Education, special; Higher education; Health organizations, association; Human services.
Type of support: Scholarships—to individuals; General/operating support; Scholarship funds.
Limitations: Applications not accepted. Giving on a national basis.
Application information: Unsolicited requests for funds not accepted.

Trustee: KeyBank N.A.
EIN: 222789214

7702
Earl Knudsen Charitable Foundation ✦
c/o National City Bank of Pennsylvania
P.O. Box 94651
Cleveland, OH   44101-4651
Contact: Judith Morrison
Application address: 104 Broadway Ave., Carnegie, PA 15106, tel.: (412) 278-4118

Established about 1975.
Donor: Earl Knudsen†.
Foundation type: Independent foundation.
Financial data (yr. ended 12/31/05): Assets, $4,062,998 (M); gifts received, $1,095; expenditures, $490,101; qualifying distributions, $470,692; giving activities include $451,000 for 52 grants (high: $50,000; low: $1,000; average: $5,000–$10,000).
Fields of interest: Performing arts; Arts; Human services; Children/youth, services; Family services; Christian agencies & churches.
Type of support: General/operating support; Annual campaigns; Capital campaigns.
Limitations: Giving primarily in western PA. No grants to individuals, or for scholarships, or fellowships; no loans.
Application information: Application form available at Grantmakers of Western Pennsylvania Web site. Application form required.
Initial approach: Grantmakers of Western Pennsylvania Common Grant Application Form required
Copies of proposal: 3
Deadline(s): None
Board meeting date(s): Quarterly and as required
Final notification: Affirmative replies only
Director: National City Bank of Pennsylvania.
EIN: 256062530
Selected grants: The following grants were reported in 2004.

$30,000 to Pittsburgh Leadership Foundation, Pittsburgh, PA.

$25,000 to Wells College, Aurora, NY.

$20,000 to American Red Cross, Pittsburgh, PA.

$20,000 to Extra Mile Education Foundation, Pittsburgh, PA.

$20,000 to Family House, Pittsburgh, PA.

$15,000 to Trinity Episcopal School for Ministry, Ambridge, PA.

$10,000 to Mattress Factory, Pittsburgh, PA.

$10,000 to National Center for Civil War Photography, Tampa, FL.

$10,000 to United Methodist Church, Valley Forge, PA.

$5,000 to Family Guidance, Sewickley, PA.

7703
Bernie J. Kosar Charitable Trust ✦
c/o Chess Financial Corp.
30050 Chagrin Blvd., Ste. 100
Pepper Pike, OH   44124
Contact: Bernie J. Kosar Sr., Mgr.
Application address: 7301 West Blvd., Ste. C-5, Boardman, OH 44512, tel.: (216) 831-2400

Established in 1991 in OH.
Donor: Bernie J. Kosar, Jr.
Foundation type: Independent foundation.

Financial data (yr. ended 12/31/04): Assets, $59,631 (M); gifts received, $13,901; expenditures, $336,490; qualifying distributions, $334,519; giving activities include $334,650 for 19 grants (high: $142,600; low: $750).

Purpose and activities: Giving for recreation, youth services, and education, including Catholic education.

Fields of interest: Secondary school/education; Theological school/education; Education; Health organizations, association; Athletics/sports, training; Recreation; Human services; Children/ youth, services; Roman Catholic agencies & churches.

Type of support: General/operating support; Building/renovation; Scholarship funds; Research.

Limitations: Giving on a national basis, with some emphasis on OH, FL, and MN. No grants to individuals.

Officer and Trustees:* Bernie J. Kosar, Sr.,* Mgr.; Bernie J. Kosar, Jr.

EIN: 341673013

Selected grants: The following grants were reported in 2004.

$20,000 to Archdiocese of Miami, Miami Shores, FL.

$20,000 to Byzantine Catholic Central School, Youngstown, OH.

$20,000 to Cleveland State University, Cleveland, OH.

$12,000 to Childrens Hospital.

$10,000 to Helping Abused, Neglected, Dependent Youth (HANDY), Fort Lauderdale, FL.

$6,800 to Nova Southeastern University, Fort Lauderdale, FL.

$750 to Saint David Church, Willow Grove, PA.

7704
Milton A. and Charlotte R. Kramer Charitable Foundation ✧

Halle Bldg.
1228 Euclid Ave., Ste. 310
Cleveland, OH 44115
Contact: Charlotte R. Kramer, Tr.

Established in 1984 in OH.

Donor: Charlotte R. Kramer.

Foundation type: Independent foundation.

Financial data (yr. ended 11/30/05): Assets, $6,240,325 (M); expenditures, $362,441; qualifying distributions, $344,013; giving activities include $337,661 for 135+ grants (high: $163,500).

Purpose and activities: Giving for the arts, education, human services and Jewish agencies.

Fields of interest: Arts; Higher education; Education; Nursing care; Multiple sclerosis research; Food services; Nutrition; Children/youth, services; Disabilities, people with.

Type of support: General/operating support; Annual campaigns; Endowments; Program development; Scholarship funds; Program evaluation; Matching/ challenge support.

Limitations: Giving primarily in the Cleveland, OH, area. No grants to individuals.

Application information: Application form not required.

Initial approach: Letter
Copies of proposal: 1
Deadline(s): None
Board meeting date(s): Vary
Final notification: Varies

Trustees: Michael J. Horvitz; Charlotte R. Kramer; Mark R. Kramer; David G. Stiller.

EIN: 341467089

Selected grants: The following grants were reported in 2005.

$29,000 to Musical Arts Association, Cleveland, OH.

$25,000 to Case Western Reserve University, Cleveland, OH.

$17,522 to Park Synagogue, Cleveland Heights, OH.

$12,500 to Childrens Hospital Corporation, Boston, MA.

$12,500 to University of California, San Francisco, CA.

$5,000 to Cleveland Clinic Foundation, Cleveland, OH.

$5,000 to Cleveland Play House, Cleveland, OH.

$1,000 to Great Lakes Theater Festival, Cleveland, OH.

$900 to Temple Emanu-El, Miami Beach, FL.

$700 to Cleveland Institute of Music, Cleveland, OH.

7705
The Kroger Co. Foundation ✧

1014 Vine St.
Cincinnati, OH 45202 (513) 762-4449, ext. 3
Contact: Lynn Marmer, Pres.
FAX: (513) 762-1295; URL: http:// www.thekrogerco.com/corpnews/ corpnewsinfo_charitablegiving_foundation.htm

Established in 1987 in OH.

Donor: The Kroger Co.

Foundation type: Company-sponsored foundation.

Financial data (yr. ended 1/28/06): Assets, $3,461,275 (M); gifts received, $92,006; expenditures, $2,765,031; qualifying distributions, $2,753,996; giving activities include $2,753,996 for 710 grants (high: $364,769; low: $50).

Purpose and activities: The foundation supports organizations involved with education, women's health, breast cancer, hunger, minorities, and women.

Fields of interest: Elementary/secondary education; Education; Health care; Breast cancer; Food services; Federated giving programs; Minorities; Women.

Type of support: Capital campaigns; Seed money.

Limitations: Giving primarily in areas of company operations. No support for national or international organizations, non-educational foundations, medical research organizations, or religious organizations or institutions not of direct benefit to the entire community. No grants to individuals, or for conventions or conferences, dinners or luncheons, endowments, general operating support, sports event sponsorships, program advertisements, or membership dues.

Publications: Application guidelines.

Application information: Visit Web site for company division addresses. Application form not required.

Initial approach: Proposal to nearest company division
Deadline(s): None

Officers and Trustees: Lynn Marmer, Pres.; David Dillon, V.P.; Paul Heldman, Secy.; Scott Henderson, Treas.; John Burgon; Jon Flora; Dennis Hackett; Marnette Perry.

Number of staff: 1 part-time professional.

EIN: 311192929

Selected grants: The following grants were reported in 2004.

$60,000 to Habitat for Humanity of Greater Indianapolis, Indianapolis, IN.

$35,821 to United Way, Mile High, Denver, CO.

$25,000 to Columbus Downtown Development Corporation, Columbus, OH.

$20,000 to Salvation Army, Columbus, OH.

$20,000 to Susan G. Komen Breast Cancer Foundation, Little Rock, AR.

$20,000 to University of Cincinnati Foundation, Cincinnati, OH.

$10,000 to Omaha Childrens Museum, Omaha, NE.

$1,000 to Peoria Educational Enrichment Foundation, Peoria, AZ.

$1,000 to Salvation Army, NC.

$875 to United Way of South Central Kentucky, Somerset, KY.

7706
Kulas Foundation ✧

50 Public Sq., Ste. 924
Cleveland, OH 44113-2203 (216) 623-4770
Contact: Allan J. Zambie, V.P. and Secy.
FAX: (216) 623-4773; URL: http:// foundationcenter.org/grantmaker/kulas/

Incorporated in 1937 in OH.

Donors: Fynette H. Kulas†; E.J. Kulas†.

Foundation type: Independent foundation.

Financial data (yr. ended 12/31/05): Assets, $47,328,008 (M); gifts received, $715,924; expenditures, $3,733,554; qualifying distributions, $3,484,002; giving activities include $3,164,561 for 125 grants (high: $200,000; low: $1,000).

Purpose and activities: Grants largely to music institutions and for higher education; some support also for local performing arts and social services.

Fields of interest: Museums; Performing arts; Performing arts, music; Arts; Education, association; Education, fund raising/fund distribution; Higher education; Libraries/library science; Education; Human services.

Type of support: General/operating support; Continuing support; Annual campaigns; Capital campaigns; Building/renovation; Equipment; Land acquisition; Program development; Conferences/ seminars; Professorships; Research; Consulting services; Matching/challenge support.

Limitations: Giving limited to Cuyahoga County, OH, and its contiguous counties. No support for mental health organizations. No grants to individuals, or for endowment funds; no loans or scholarships.

Publications: Application guidelines; Financial statement; Informational brochure (including application guidelines).

Application information: There are 3 different application forms: Student Ticket Plan Requests; Music Therapy Requests; and a General Application for Grants form for requests that do not fall into the other two categories. Each form explains the information needed as well as designates the number of copies required. Applications should not include notebooks, binders or plastic folders. Application form required.

Initial approach: Letter or telephone
Copies of proposal: 5
Deadline(s): Submit proposal 6 weeks before a meeting
Board meeting date(s): 4 times per year
Final notification: Within 2-3 weeks after board meeting

Officers and Trustees:* Richard W. Pogue,* Chair. and V.P.; Nancy W. McCann,* Pres. and Treas.;

Allan J. Zambie, V.P. and Secy.; Patrick F. McCartan,* V.P.; Ellen E. Halfon.
Number of staff: 1 full-time professional; 2 full-time support.
EIN: 340770687
Selected grants: The following grants were reported in 2004.
$313,500 to Cleveland Institute of Music, Cleveland, OH. 3 grants: $200,000, $10,000, $103,500
$250,000 to Musical Arts Association, Cleveland, OH.
$80,000 to University Circle, Cleveland, OH. 2 grants: $5,000, $75,000
$50,000 to Cleveland Music School Settlement, Cleveland, OH.
$50,000 to University Hospitals Health System, Cleveland, OH.
$25,000 to Lake Hospital Foundation, Painesville, OH.
$10,000 to Akron Civic Theater, Akron, OH.

7707
Lancaster Lens, Inc. ✧
c/o Clarence Clapham
37 W. Broad St., Rm. 530
Columbus, OH 43215

Established in 1953.
Foundation type: Independent foundation.
Financial data (yr. ended 7/31/05): Assets, $7,680,546 (M); expenditures, $407,851; qualifying distributions, $390,116; giving activities include $388,480 for 13 grants (high: $133,230; low: $2,000).
Purpose and activities: Giving primarily for youth and family services, including an organization for recreational programs for disabled youth; funding also for community organizations.
Fields of interest: Higher education, university; Children/youth, services; Family services; Community development; Foundations (private grantmaking).
Limitations: Applications not accepted. Giving primarily in Columbus, OH. No grants to individuals.
Application information: Contributes only to pre-selected organizations.
Officers: Bruce L. Rosa, Pres.; Clarence Clapham, Secy.
EIN: 316023927
Selected grants: The following grants were reported in 2005.
$133,230 to Recreation Unlimited Foundation, Ashley, OH.
$105,000 to Ohio State University Foundation, Columbus, OH. 2 grants: $100,000, $5,000
$70,000 to Columbus Partnership, Columbus, OH. 2 grants: $20,000, $50,000
$15,000 to Columbus Coalition Against Family Violence, Columbus, OH.
$10,000 to Law Enforcement Foundation, Dublin, OH.
$5,000 to Columbus Museum of Art, Columbus, OH.

7708
The LaValley Foundation ✧
5800 Monroe St., Bldg. F
Sylvania, OH 43560

Established in 1992 in OH.
Donor: Richard G. LaValley.

Foundation type: Independent foundation.
Financial data (yr. ended 12/31/05): Assets, $18,445,611 (M); expenditures, $828,519; qualifying distributions, $715,500; giving activities include $715,500 for grants.
Purpose and activities: Giving primarily to Roman Catholic churches and organizations; funding also for higher education, children, youth and social services.
Fields of interest: Arts; Elementary/secondary education; Secondary school/education; Higher education; Human services; Children/youth, services; Federated giving programs; Roman Catholic agencies & churches.
Type of support: General/operating support; Scholarship funds.
Limitations: Applications not accepted. Giving primarily in Toledo, OH. No grants to individuals.
Application information: Contributes only to pre-selected organizations.
Officers and Trustees:* Richard G. LaValley,* Pres.; Daniel J. LaValley,* V.P.; Richard G. LaValley, Jr.,* V.P.
EIN: 341722402

7709
Lehner Family Foundation Trust ✧
c/o Merrill Lynch Trust Co.
50 S. Main St.
Akron, OH 44308
Contact: Gordon Ewers, Mgr.

Established in 1989 in OH.
Donors: Marie Lehner; Jane Lehner; Charles Lehner.
Foundation type: Operating foundation.
Financial data (yr. ended 12/31/04): Assets, $11,380,849 (M); expenditures, $683,937; qualifying distributions, $597,500; giving activities include $597,500 for 29 grants (high: $200,000; low: $500).
Purpose and activities: Giving primarily for the arts, and Roman Catholic agencies and churches.
Fields of interest: Museums (art); Historic preservation/historical societies; Human services; Roman Catholic agencies & churches.
Type of support: Capital campaigns; Building/renovation; Equipment; Matching/challenge support.
Limitations: Giving limited to Akron, OH. No grants to individuals.
Application information: Application form not required.
Copies of proposal: 1
Deadline(s): May 1 and Nov. 1
Board meeting date(s): May 15 and Nov. 15
Officers and Board Members:* Rick Burke, Mgr.; Gordon Ewers,* Mgr.; David M. Koly, Mgr.; Jane Lehner,* Mgr.; Michael R. Stark,* Mgr.
EIN: 346927210
Selected grants: The following grants were reported in 2003.
$125,000 to Akron Zoological Park, Akron, OH. For botanical gardens project.
$60,000 to Stan Hywet Hall and Gardens, Akron, OH. For restoration of terraces.
$27,500 to Hospice of Visiting Nurse Services, Akron, OH. For renovation of nurses station.
$25,000 to Akron Art Museum, Akron, OH. For capital campaign.
$15,775 to Mobile Meals, Akron, OH. For HVAC unit.
$15,000 to Childrens Hospital Medical Center of Akron, Akron, OH. For pet therapy program.

$15,000 to Loyola of the Lakes Jesuit Retreat House, Clinton, OH. For retreat contracts.
$10,000 to Summit County Historical Society of Akron, Akron, OH. For restoration.
$5,000 to Cleveland Orchestra, Cleveland, OH. For improvements to buildings and grounds.
$2,000 to Keep Akron Beautiful, Akron, OH. For flowerscape campaign.

7710
The Fred A. Lennon Charitable Trust ▼
29425 Chagrin Blvd., Ste. 201
Cleveland, OH 44122-4602

Established in 1993 in OH.
Donor: Fred A. Lennon†.
Foundation type: Independent foundation.
Financial data (yr. ended 12/31/05): Assets, $71,952,230 (M); expenditures, $7,530,868; qualifying distributions, $6,923,393; giving activities include $6,896,000 for 108 grants (high: $2,000,000; low: $500; average: $1,000–$400,000).
Purpose and activities: Giving primarily for health and human services, and economic development.
Fields of interest: Higher education; Hospitals (general); Health care; Health organizations, association; Alzheimer's disease research; Diabetes research; Human services; Children, services.
Type of support: Seed money; Matching/challenge support.
Limitations: Giving primarily in OH, with emphasis on Cleveland. No grants to individuals; no loans.
Publications: Informational brochure (including application guidelines).
Application information: Application form not required.
Initial approach: Letter
Copies of proposal: 1
Deadline(s): Apr. 15 and Sept. 15
Board meeting date(s): May and Oct.
Final notification: 6 months
Trustees: A. Anton; F.J. Callahan; T. Janoch; E.A. Lozick; N. Tobbe.
Number of staff: 1 part-time professional.
EIN: 341761181
Selected grants: The following grants were reported in 2005.
$2,000,000 to Cleveland Institute of Music, Cleveland, OH.
$1,225,000 to Cleveland Clinic Foundation, Cleveland, OH.
$1,000,000 to Case Western Reserve University, Cleveland, OH.
$400,000 to Achievement Centers for Children, Highland Hills, OH.
$250,000 to Ronald McDonald House Charities of Cleveland, Cleveland, OH.
$100,000 to Benedictine High School, Cleveland, OH.
$30,000 to Center for Health Affairs, Cleveland, OH.
$25,000 to MetroHealth Medical Center, Cleveland, OH.
$25,000 to Saint Edward High School, Lakewood, OH.
$11,000 to Little Sisters of the Poor, Cleveland, OH.

7711
The Lerner Foundation ▼ ✧
26500 Curtiss Wright Pkwy.
Highland Heights, OH   44143   (440) 891-5000
Contact: Douglas Jacobs

Established in 1993 in OH.
Donors: Alfred Lerner‡; Norma Lerner.
Foundation type: Independent foundation.
Financial data (yr. ended 12/31/05): Assets,
$106,167,509 (M); expenditures, $21,188,249;
qualifying distributions, $21,123,773; giving
activities include $21,123,773 for 56+ grants (high:
$12,200,800; average: $5,000–$500,000).
Purpose and activities: Support primarily for
medical care, Jewish agencies and temples and
Jewish federated giving programs.
Fields of interest: Higher education; Health care,
single organization support; Hospitals (general);
Jewish federated giving programs; Jewish agencies
& temples.
Application information:
  Initial approach: Letter
  Deadline(s): None
Officers and Trustees:* Norma Lerner,* Pres. and
Treas.; Nancy Fisher,* V.P.; Randolph Lerner,* V.P.;
James H. Berick,* Secy.
EIN: 341744726
Selected grants: The following grants were reported
in 2005.
$12,200,800 to Cleveland Clinic Foundation,
  Cleveland, OH. For general operating support.
$3,100,000 to Cleveland Orchestra, Cleveland, OH.
  For general operating support.
$2,010,000 to Columbia University Foundation,
  New York, NY. For general operating support.
$2,005,300 to Marine Corps Heritage Foundation,
  Quantico, VA. For general operating support.
$100,000 to Columbia University, New York, NY. For
  general operating support for Columbia College
  Fund.
$60,000 to Fieldstone Farm Therapeutic Riding
  Center, Chagrin Falls, OH. For general operating
  support.
$50,000 to Lawrence School, Broadview Heights,
  OH. For general operating support.
$50,000 to Wigs for Kids, Rocky River, OH. For
  general operating support.
$12,500 to Leonard and Susan Fuchs Mizrachi
  School, University Heights, OH. For general
  operating support.
$1,500 to Cleveland Play House, Cleveland, OH.

7712
Levin Family Foundation
111 W. 1st St., Ste. 849
Dayton, OH   45402   (937) 223-1669
Contact: Karen Levin, Exec. Dir.
E-mail: levinfamilyfound@ameritech.net;
URL: http://www.levinfamilyfoundation.org

Established in 1990 in OH.
Donors: Allen Levin; Louis Levin; Barbara Levin‡;
Karen Levin; Ryan Levin; Darrell Murphy; Howard
Michaels.
Foundation type: Independent foundation.
Financial data (yr. ended 12/31/04): Assets,
$23,850,970 (M); expenditures, $1,482,416;
qualifying distributions, $1,249,908; giving
activities include $1,067,448 for 172 grants (high:
$50,000; low: $50).

Fields of interest: Arts; Education; Human services;
Children, services; Jewish agencies & temples;
Women; Economically disadvantaged.
Type of support: Emergency funds; Capital
campaigns; Building/renovation; Equipment;
Program development; Conferences/seminars;
Publication; Seed money; Internship funds;
Research; Program evaluation; Matching/challenge
support.
Limitations: Giving primarily in the Dayton, OH, area.
No grants to individuals, or for endowment funds.
Publications: Application guidelines.
Application information: In addition to the 1 copy of
the letter, include 6 copies of the 1st and 2nd page
of the application; application guidelines and
application form available on foundation Web site.
Application form required.
  Initial approach: Letter of intent
  Copies of proposal: 1
  Deadline(s): May 1 and Nov. 1
  Board meeting date(s): 2nd Fri. in June and 2nd
    Fri. in Dec.
  Final notification: June and Dec.
Officer and Trustees:* Karen Levin,* Exec. Dir.;
Allen Levin; Louis Levin; Ryan Levin; Howard
Michaels; Darrell Murphy.
Number of staff: 1 full-time professional; 1 part-time
support.
EIN: 311327847
Selected grants: The following grants were reported
in 2004.
$82,500 to Jewish Federation of Greater Dayton,
  Dayton, OH. 5 grants: $5,000, $10,000,
  $12,500, $50,000, $5,000
$25,000 to Kids Helping Kids, Cincinnati, OH.
$15,000 to Wellness Connection of the Miami
  Valley, Dayton, OH. 2 grants: $5,000, $10,000
$10,000 to Jewish Agency for Israel, New York, NY.
$2,500 to Jewish Childrens Adoption Network,
  Denver, CO.

7713
The Lewis Foundation ✧
c/o The Lipson Group
1422 Euclid Ave., Ste. 1500
Cleveland, OH   44115-2001   (216) 861-1100

Established in 2002 in CO.
Donors: Adam J. Lewis; Peter B. Lewis.
Foundation type: Independent foundation.
Financial data (yr. ended 12/31/04): Assets,
$10,296,794 (M); gifts received, $6,205,251;
expenditures, $466,169; qualifying distributions,
$454,509; giving activities include $355,700 for 21
grants (high: $100,000; low: $100), and $93,469
for 1 grant to an individual.
Fields of interest: Museums; Arts; Higher
education; Recreation, community facilities;
Community development; Foundations (community).
Type of support: Grants to individuals.
Application information: Application form not
required.
  Deadline(s): None
Officer: Adam J. Lewis, Pres. and Secy.-Treas.
EIN: 412063101
Selected grants: The following grants were reported
in 2003.
$75,000 to Aspen Valley Community Foundation,
  Aspen, CO. For general operating support.
$50,000 to Aspen Sports and Recreation Complex,
  Friends of the, Aspen, CO. For general operating
  support.

$35,200 to Sustainable Settings, Carbondale, CO.
  For general operating support.
$30,000 to Work Foundation, Manhattan Beach,
  CA. For general operating support.
$10,000 to Blue Sky Associates, Honolulu, HI. For
  general operating support.
$5,000 to Heifer Project International, Merrifield,
  VA. For general operating support.

7714
Licking County Foundation
P.O. Box 4212
Newark, OH   43058   (740) 349-3863
Contact: Michael Wolfe, Exec. Dir.
FAX: (740) 322-6260;
E-mail: lcf@thelcfoundation.org; URL: http://
www.thelcfoundation.org

Established in 1956 in OH.
Foundation type: Community foundation.
Financial data (yr. ended 10/31/05): Assets,
$34,513,630 (M); gifts received, $3,776,437;
expenditures, $2,993,585; giving activities include
$2,567,167 for 158 grants (high: $275,000; low:
$100), and $72,846 for 1 foundation-administered
program.
Purpose and activities: The foundation seeks to
improve the quality of life for the citizens of Licking
County, OH. Giving primarily for arts, education,
health care, recreation, human services, and
children and youth services.
Fields of interest: Arts; Education; Health care;
Recreation; Children/youth, services; Human
services.
Type of support: Capital campaigns; Building/
renovation; Equipment; Seed money; Scholarship
funds; Matching/challenge support.
Limitations: Giving limited to Licking County, OH. No
support for religious or sectarian purposes. No
grants to individuals (except for scholarships), or for
make-up of operating deficits, post-event or
after-the-fact situations, or endowments.
Publications: Annual report (including application
guidelines); Informational brochure; Newsletter.
Application information: Grant follow-up due in 90
days from check issue. Application form required.
  Initial approach: Telephone or letter inquiry
  Copies of proposal: 5
  Deadline(s): May 15 and Nov. 15
  Board meeting date(s): Mar., June, Sept., and
    Dec.
  Final notification: By mail with grant terms within
    2 weeks after board meeting
Officers and Governing Committee:* William S.
Moore,* Chair.; Nancy Dix,* Vice-Chair.; Ronald B.
Alford,* Secy.-Treas.; Michael Wolfe, Exec. Dir.;
Howard E. LeFevre,* Chair. Emeritus; J. Gilbert
Reese,* Chair. Emeritus; Robert A. Barnes; Barbara
M. Hammond; Frank B. Murphy; David Trautman;
Sarah Wallace; Christine Warner-Powell; James T.
Young.
Trustee Banks: JPMorgan Chase Bank, N.A.; Merrill
Lynch Trust Co.; National City Bank; The Park
National Bank.
Number of staff: 1 full-time professional; 1 part-time
professional; 1 part-time support.
EIN: 316018618

7715
The Lincoln Electric Foundation ✧
c/o KeyBank N.A., Tony Blossom
127 Public Sq.
Cleveland, OH 44114 (216) 689-0959
Contact: H. Jay Elliot

Trust established in 1952 in OH.
Donor: The Lincoln Electric Co.
Foundation type: Company-sponsored foundation.
Financial data (yr. ended 12/31/05): Assets, $1,566,393 (M); gifts received, $900,000; expenditures, $476,960; qualifying distributions, $474,327; giving activities include $472,000 for 35 grants (high: $197,500; low: $1,000).
Purpose and activities: The foundation supports organizations involved with arts and culture, education, health, lung disease, and human services.
Fields of interest: Museums (history); Performing arts centers; Arts; Elementary/secondary education; Education; Hospitals (general); Health care; Lung diseases; Residential/custodial care, senior continuing care; Human services; Federated giving programs.
Type of support: General/operating support.
Limitations: Giving primarily in OH, with emphasis on Cleveland. No loans or program-related investments.
Application information: Application form not required.
Initial approach: Proposal
Deadline(s): Sept. 20
Board meeting date(s): Nov.
Trustee: KeyBank N.A.
Number of staff: 1
EIN: 346518355

7716
The Carl H. and Edyth B. Lindner Foundation ▼ ✧
(formerly Carl H. Lindner Foundation)
49 E. 4th St., Ste. 521
Cincinnati, OH 45202-3803

Established in 1993 in OH.
Donor: Carl H. Lindner, Jr.
Foundation type: Independent foundation.
Financial data (yr. ended 12/31/04): Assets, $24,619,495 (M); gifts received, $6,145; expenditures, $7,569,128; qualifying distributions, $7,562,556; giving activities include $7,559,383 for 12 grants (high: $4,999,964; low: $5,000; average: $50,000–$499,977).
Purpose and activities: Giving primarily for museums and education.
Fields of interest: Museums; Higher education; Theological school/education; Education; Cancer; Christian agencies & churches; Protestant agencies & churches.
Limitations: Applications not accepted. Giving primarily in Cincinnati, OH. No grants to individuals.
Application information: Contributes only to pre-selected organizations.
Officers and Trustees:* Carl H. Lindner, Jr.,* Pres.; Edyth B. Lindner,* V.P.; Joseph A. Pedoto,* Secy.-Treas.
EIN: 310738034
Selected grants: The following grants were reported in 2004.
$5,499,941 to University of Cincinnati Foundation, Cincinnati, OH. 2 grants: $4,999,964 (For

general support), $499,977 (For general support).
$742,475 to McLean Hospital, Belmont, MA. For general support.
$578,259 to Cincinnati Hills Christian Academy, Cincinnati, OH. 2 grants: $100,000 (For general support), $478,259 (For general support).
$499,708 to Cincinnati Pops Orchestra, Cincinnati, OH. For general support.
$14,000 to Childrens Theater of Cincinnati, Cincinnati, OH. For general support.

7717
Robert D. Lindner Foundation ✧ ☆
3955 Montgomery Rd.
Cincinnati, OH 45212-3733

Established in 1967 in OH.
Donors: Robert D. Lindner, Sr.; Provident Financial Group, Inc.
Foundation type: Independent foundation.
Financial data (yr. ended 12/31/05): Assets, $2,521,044 (M); gifts received, $2,807; expenditures, $413,957; qualifying distributions, $408,960; giving activities include $408,960 for grants.
Purpose and activities: Giving for Christian organizations.
Fields of interest: Christian agencies & churches.
Type of support: General/operating support.
Limitations: Applications not accepted. Giving primarily in Cincinnati, OH. No grants to individuals.
Application information: Contributes only to pre-selected organizations.
Officers and Trustees:* Robert D. Lindner, Sr.,* Pres.; Betty R. Lindner,* V.P. and Treas.; Joseph A. Pedoto,* Secy.
EIN: 310738035

7718
The Katherine Kenyon Lippitt Foundation ✧
c/o National City Bank
P.O. Box 94651
Cleveland, OH 44101-4651
Application address: c/o Tom Gilchrist, National City Bank, P.O. Box 5756, LOC 2020, Cleveland, OH 44101, tel.: (216) 222-9272

Established in 1987 in OH.
Donor: Esther McEwan Black‡.
Foundation type: Independent foundation.
Financial data (yr. ended 12/31/05): Assets, $4,876,519 (M); expenditures, $411,652; qualifying distributions, $388,298; giving activities include $368,500 for 28 grants (high: $105,000; low: $500).
Fields of interest: Performing arts; Arts; Education; Health organizations, association; Human services; Federated giving programs.
Type of support: General/operating support; Continuing support; Annual campaigns; Capital campaigns; Building/renovation; Land acquisition.
Limitations: Giving primarily in Mansfield and Richland County, OH. No grants to individuals.
Application information: Application form not required.
Initial approach: Letter
Copies of proposal: 1
Deadline(s): None
Board meeting date(s): July and Dec.

Officers: John B. Black, Pres.; Peter M. Black, V.P.; Kenneth G. Hochman, Secy.
EIN: 341571383

7719
Lippman Kanfer Family Foundation ✧
(formerly Jerome Lippman Family Foundation)
P.O. Box 991
Akron, OH 44309-0991
Contact: Sharon Guten, Secy.

Established in 1991 in OH.
Donor: Gojo Industries, Inc.
Foundation type: Independent foundation.
Financial data (yr. ended 12/31/05): Assets, $16,938,235 (M); expenditures, $1,030,920; qualifying distributions, $964,331; giving activities include $959,219 for 21 grants (high: $355,000; low: $250).
Purpose and activities: Giving primarily for Jewish organizations, education and the Jewish community.
Fields of interest: Education; Human services; Jewish federated giving programs; Jewish agencies & temples.
Type of support: General/operating support; Continuing support.
Limitations: Giving primarily in OH; some funding also in New York, NY. No grants to individuals.
Publications: Informational brochure.
Application information: Application form not required.
Initial approach: Narrative
Copies of proposal: 1
Deadline(s): None
Board meeting date(s): Annually, (Q3)
Final notification: 3 months
Officers and Directors:* Marcella Kanfer Rolnick,* Chair. and Pres.; Sharon Guten,* Secy.; Allan Markey,* Treas.; Stan Bober; Joseph Kanfer; Mamie Kanfer; Phillip Nabors; Joshua Rolnick.
EIN: 340974875
Selected grants: The following grants were reported in 2005.
$355,000 to Jewish Community Board of Akron, Akron, OH.
$100,000 to United Jewish Communities, New York, NY.
$25,000 to American Jewish World Service, New York, NY.
$25,000 to Jewish Family and Life, Newton, MA.
$10,000 to Partnership for Excellence in Jewish Education, Boston, MA.
$5,000 to Beth El Congregation, Akron, OH.
$900 to National Center for Family Philanthropy, DC.
$500 to KESHET, Northbrook, IL.
$500 to Sharsheret, Teaneck, NJ.

7720
LKC Foundation ✧
2737 Walsh Rd.
Cincinnati, OH 45208

Established in 1996 in DE.
Foundation type: Independent foundation.
Financial data (yr. ended 12/31/04): Assets, $10,575,625 (M); expenditures, $580,964; qualifying distributions, $458,680; giving activities include $458,680 for 132 grants (high: $50,000; low: $15).

Purpose and activities: Giving primarily for the arts, education, health and human services, and Jewish charities.

Fields of interest: Museums (art); Performing arts, theater; Performing arts, orchestra (symphony); Arts; Elementary/secondary education; Higher education; Zoos/zoological societies; Hospitals (general); Health care; Food services; Recreation; Youth development; Human services; YM/YWCAs & YM/YWHAs; Children/youth, services; Federated giving programs; Jewish federated giving programs; Jewish agencies & temples.

Type of support: General/operating support; Annual campaigns; Capital campaigns; Building/renovation.

Limitations: Applications not accepted. Giving primarily in OH, with emphasis on Cincinnati; some funding nationally. No grants to individuals.

Application information: Contributes only to pre-selected organizations.

Officers and Directors:* Lucille K. Carothers,* Pres. and Treas.; Paula K. Oppenheim,* V.P. and Secy.; Ellen Stern Kerr, V.P.

EIN: 311490185

7721
Loeb Foundation

c/o Lebanon Citizens National Bank
P.O. Box 59
Lebanon, OH 45036-0059 (513) 932-1414
Contact: B.H. Wright, Jr., Tr.
FAX: (513) 932-1492; *E-mail:* bwright@lcnb.com

Established in 1992 in OH.
Donor: Justus H. Loeb‡.
Foundation type: Independent foundation.
Financial data (yr. ended 9/30/05): Assets, $7,810,884 (M); expenditures, $478,141; qualifying distributions, $398,174; giving activities include $266,587 for 2 grants (high: $176,093; low: $90,494), and $92,592 for 30 grants to individuals (high: $3,000; low: $450).
Purpose and activities: Giving primarily for fire and police protection.
Fields of interest: Crime/law enforcement, police agencies; Disasters, fire prevention/control; Aging.
Type of support: Equipment; Grants to individuals.
Limitations: Giving limited to Warren County, OH.
Publications: Annual report.
Application information: Application form not required.
Initial approach: Letter
Copies of proposal: 3
Deadline(s): Aug. 15
Board meeting date(s): Early Sept.
Final notification: Late Sept.
Trustees: Michael E. Foley; Bernard H. Wright, Jr.; The Lebanon Citizens National Bank.
Number of staff: None.
EIN: 316225986
Selected grants: The following grants were reported in 2003.
$183,601 to Warren, City of, Warren, OH. 2 grants: $138,546 (For Loeb Fire Protection Grants), $45,055 (For Loeb Police Protection Grants).

7722
The Longaberger Foundation ✧

1500 E. Main St.
Newark, OH 43055-8847 (740) 322-5039
Contact: Matthew Elli, Dir.

Established in 1997 in OH.
Donor: The Longaberger Co.
Foundation type: Independent foundation.
Financial data (yr. ended 12/31/04): Assets, $9,393,751 (M); gifts received, $5,231; expenditures, $1,323,215; qualifying distributions, $1,294,179; giving activities include $947,050 for 32 grants (high: $220,000; low: $100).
Purpose and activities: The purpose of the foundation is to stimulate a better quality of life through philanthropy. Priority is given to organizations located in communities where employees of The Longaberger Company reside. Primary focus is on children and families, American history, entrepreneurism, and regional quality of life issues.
Fields of interest: Children/youth, services; Family services; Business/industry; American studies.
Limitations: Giving on a national basis. No grants to individuals.
Application information:
Initial approach: Brief letter of inquiry
Deadline(s): None
Officers: Rachel L. Stukey, Pres. and Treas.; Tamala Longaberger, V.P.; Richard Longaberger, Secy.
EIN: 311575931

7723
Love Family Foundation, Inc. ✧

615 Windings Ln.
Cincinnati, OH 45220 (513) 977-8236
Contact: L. Ross Love, Jr., V.P.

Established in 2001 in OH.
Donors: Cheryl Love; L. Ross Love, Jr.; Ayanna Love; LRC Love LP; LRL Investments.
Foundation type: Independent foundation.
Financial data (yr. ended 12/31/04): Assets, $257,345 (M); gifts received, $65,698; expenditures, $553,435; qualifying distributions, $548,942; giving activities include $548,742 for 18 grants (high: $200,000; low: $100).
Fields of interest: Human services; Federated giving programs.
Limitations: Giving primarily in the greater Cincinnati, OH, area. No grants to individuals.
Application information:
Initial approach: Letter
Deadline(s): None
Officers: Cheryl Love, Pres. and Secy.; L. Ross Love, Jr., V.P. and Treas.
EIN: 311809156
Selected grants: The following grants were reported in 2004.
$200,000 to United Way of Greater Cincinnati, Cincinnati, OH.
$100,000 to Greater Cincinnati Foundation, Cincinnati, OH.
$45,000 to Citizens Committee on Youth, Cincinnati, OH.
$30,625 to Cincinnati Playhouse in the Park, Cincinnati, OH.
$25,000 to Jewish Federation of Cincinnati, Cincinnati, OH.
$15,000 to Learning Through Art, Cincinnati, OH.
$3,000 to Fine Arts Fund, Cincinnati, OH.
$642 to Evanston Youth Association, Evanston, OH.
$250 to Cincinnati Black Theater Company, Cincinnati, OH.
$250 to Talbert House, Cincinnati, OH.

7724
Edward A. and Catherine L. Lozick Foundation ☆

(formerly Edward A. Lozick Foundation)
29425 Chagrin Blvd., Ste. 201
Beachwood, OH 44122-4602
Contact: Christopher P. Hitchcock

Established in 1983 in OH.
Donors: Edward Lozick; Catherine Lozick.
Foundation type: Independent foundation.
Financial data (yr. ended 12/31/05): Assets, $2,679,444 (M); gifts received, $500,000; expenditures, $523,331; qualifying distributions, $519,283; giving activities include $519,283 for 230 grants (high: $196,250; low: $50).
Purpose and activities: Giving primarily for education and human services.
Fields of interest: Education; Crime/law enforcement; Human services.
Type of support: Research.
Limitations: Giving primarily in Cleveland, OH. No grants to individuals.
Application information: Application form not required.
Initial approach: Letter
Copies of proposal: 1
Final notification: 6 months from receipt
Trustees: Thomas J. Janoch; Catherine L. Lozick; Edward A. Lozick.
Number of staff: None.
EIN: 341386776
Selected grants: The following grants were reported in 2004.
$25,800 to Crime Stoppers of Cuyahoga County, Highland Heights, OH.
$25,000 to National Psoriasis Foundation, Portland, OR.
$15,000 to Ohio Roundtable, Strongsville, OH.
$15,000 to United Way, OH.
$5,000 to Heritage Foundation, DC.
$2,500 to Cleveland Museum of Art, Cleveland, OH.
$1,000 to Capital Research Center, DC.
$250 to Aperture Foundation, New York, NY.
$250 to Eagle Forum Education and Legal Defense Fund, Alton, IL.
$250 to Washington Legal Foundation, DC.

7725
The Lubrizol Foundation

29400 Lakeland Blvd., No. 053A
Wickliffe, OH 44092-2298 (440) 347-1797
Contact: Karen Lerchbacher, Admin.
FAX: (440) 347-1858; *E-mail:* kal@lubrizol.com;
URL: http://corporate.lubrizol.com/Foundation

Incorporated in 1952 in OH.
Donor: The Lubrizol Corp.
Foundation type: Company-sponsored foundation.
Financial data (yr. ended 12/31/05): Assets, $14,535,389 (M); expenditures, $2,598,278; qualifying distributions, $2,457,765; giving activities include $1,725,700 for 264+ grants (high: $163,000), and $732,065 for 859 employee matching gifts.
Purpose and activities: The foundation supports organizations involved with arts and culture, education, the environment, health, youth development, and human services.
Fields of interest: Arts; Higher education; Education; Environmental education; Environment;

Hospitals (general); Health care; Youth development; Human services.

Type of support: General/operating support; Continuing support; Annual campaigns; Capital campaigns; Building/renovation; Equipment; Fellowships; Scholarship funds; Employee matching gifts.

Limitations: Giving primarily in areas of major company operations, with emphasis on the greater Cleveland, OH, and Houston, TX, areas. No support for religious or political organizations. No grants to individuals, or for start-up needs, debt reduction, demonstration projects, publications, or conferences; generally, no grants for endowments; no loans.

Publications: Annual report (including application guidelines).

Application information: Application form not required.

  Initial approach: Proposal
  Copies of proposal: 1
  Deadline(s): None
  Board meeting date(s): As required, usually 4
    times per year
  Final notification: 2 weeks following board
    meetings

Officers and Trustees:* George R. Hill,* Chair. and C.E.O.; Kenneth M. Iwashita,* C.O.O., Pres., and Secy.; Kenneth J. Marr,* Treas.; David J. Enzerra; Robert T. Graf; James L. Hambrick; Charles W. Jones; Fred Kidder; Fred Law; Mark W. Meister; John L. Petric; Mary F. Salomon; Julian M. Steinberg; J. Mark Sutherland; Tanya M. Travis.

Number of staff: 1 part-time professional; 1 full-time support.

EIN: 346500595

Selected grants: The following grants were reported in 2005.

$218,000 to United Way Services of Greater Cleveland, Cleveland, OH. For general operating support.

$100,000 to Lakeland Community College, Kirtland, OH. For Campaign for the Future of Lakeland.

$98,000 to United Way of Lake County, Mentor, OH. For operating support.

$75,200 to United Way of the Texas Gulf Coast, Houston, TX. For general operating support.

$30,000 to Musical Arts Association, Cleveland, OH. For general operating support.

$25,000 to American Red Cross, Central Bay Area, Pasadena, TX. For Hurricane Katrina disaster relief fund.

$25,000 to Euclid Hospital, Cleveland Clinic Health System, Euclid, OH. For renovation of emergency care facility.

$25,000 to Salvation Army, Pasadena, TX. For Hurricane Katrina disaster relief fund.

7726
The Frances R. Luther Charitable Trust ✧
c/o Fifth Third Bank
P.O. Box 630858
Cincinnati, OH 45263-0858
Application address: c/o Fifth Third Bank, Attn.: Paula Wharton, 38 Fountain Square Plz., Cincinnati, OH 45202, tel.: (513) 579-5498

Established in 2000 in OH.
Donor: Frances R. Luther Trust.
Foundation type: Independent foundation.
Financial data (yr. ended 12/31/05): Assets, $41,142,701 (M); expenditures, $2,107,555; qualifying distributions, $1,920,060; giving

activities include $1,803,000 for 42 grants (high: $250,000; low: $5,000), and $25,000 for 1 employee matching gift.

Fields of interest: Media/communications; Arts; Zoos/zoological societies; Hospitals (general); Food banks; Human services; YM/YWCAs & YM/YWHAs; Children/youth, services.

Type of support: Annual campaigns; Program development; Matching/challenge support.

Limitations: Giving primarily in Cincinnati, OH.

Application information: Application form required.

  Initial approach: Letter
  Deadline(s): Feb. 1, May 1, Aug. 1, and Nov. 1

Trustees: Narley L. Haley; Fifth Third Bank.

EIN: 316646985

Selected grants: The following grants were reported in 2005.

$250,000 to Cincinnati Arts School, Cincinnati, OH.

$200,000 to Fine Arts Fund, Cincinnati, OH. 3 grants: $100,000, $50,000, $50,000

$50,000 to Cincinnati Symphony Orchestra, Cincinnati, OH.

$50,000 to Lighthouse Youth Services, Cincinnati, OH.

$50,000 to Starfire Council of Greater Cincinnati, Cincinnati, OH.

$50,000 to Tower School, Marblehead, MA.

$25,000 to Springer School, Cincinnati, OH.

$25,000 to Xavier University, Cincinnati, OH.

7727
LZ Francis Foundation ✧
c/o Mark Mihalik
3550 Lander Rd., Ste. 200
Pepper Pike, OH 44124

Established in 1992 in OH as partial successor to the Nason Foundation.
Donors: The Nason Foundation; Katharine Nason Tipper.
Foundation type: Independent foundation.
Financial data (yr. ended 12/31/05): Assets, $11,991,456 (M); gifts received, $200; expenditures, $618,250; qualifying distributions, $540,290; giving activities include $477,000 for 26 grants (high: $100,000; low: $1,000; average: $5,000–$25,000).
Purpose and activities: Giving primarily for education and conservation.
Fields of interest: Arts; Higher education, college; Education; Environment, natural resources; Food services; Human services; Federated giving programs.
Limitations: Applications not accepted. Giving primarily in FL and VT. No grants to individuals.
Application information: Contributes only to pre-selected organizations.
Officers: Katharine Nason Tipper, Pres. and Treas.; Charles F. Tipper, V.P. and Secy.; Jessica A. Oski, V.P.
EIN: 341721860
Selected grants: The following grants were reported in 2005.
$75,000 to Intervale Foundation, Burlington, VT.
$50,000 to Nature Conservancy, Arlington, VA.
$25,000 to Living Classrooms Foundation, Baltimore, MD.
$25,000 to Oxfam America, Boston, MA.
$25,000 to Preservation Trust of Vermont, Burlington, VT.
$15,000 to Local Motion, Burlington, VT.
$10,000 to Vermont Forum on Sprawl, Burlington, VT.

$5,000 to Chittenden Emergency Food Shelf, Burlington, VT.

$4,000 to Birds of Vermont Museum, Huntington, VT.

$2,500 to Vermont Stage Company, Burlington, VT.

7728
M/B Foundation ✧
1011 Sandusky St., Ste. L
Perrysburg, OH 43551

Established in 1986 in OH.
Donors: William W. Boeschenstein; Elizabeth M. Boeschenstein.
Foundation type: Independent foundation.
Financial data (yr. ended 12/31/05): Assets, $843,693 (M); gifts received, $28,586; expenditures, $412,994; qualifying distributions, $405,777; giving activities include $402,777 for grants.
Purpose and activities: Giving primarily for education, including to a Roman Catholic high school, for arts and culture, including to an art museum, and for health care, human services, and to the United Way.
Fields of interest: Museums (art); Performing arts, orchestra (symphony); Historic preservation/ historical societies; Secondary school/education; Education; Health care; Human services; Residential/custodial care, hospices; Federated giving programs; Roman Catholic agencies & churches.
Limitations: Applications not accepted. Giving primarily in Toledo, OH; some funding nationally, especially in FL and MA. No grants to individuals.
Application information: Contributes only to pre-selected organizations.
Trustees: Josephine M. Boeschenstein; William W. Boeschenstein.
EIN: 311195114

7729
M/I Homes Foundation ✧
(formerly M/I Schottenstein Homes Foundation)
3 Easton Oval, Ste. 500
Columbus, OH 43219 (614) 418-8041
Contact: Robert H. Schottenstein, Pres.

Established in 1989 in OH.
Donor: M/I Schottenstein Homes, Inc.
Foundation type: Company-sponsored foundation.
Financial data (yr. ended 12/31/05): Assets, $6,609,887 (M); gifts received, $2,000,000; expenditures, $2,303,471; qualifying distributions, $2,292,020; giving activities include $2,292,020 for 74 grants (high: $345,500; low: $250).
Purpose and activities: The foundation supports community foundations and organizations involved with arts and culture, education, health, housing, human services, community development, and Judaism.
Fields of interest: Arts; Higher education; Law school/education; Education; Health care; Housing/shelter; Children/youth, services; Human services; Community development; Foundations (community); Federated giving programs; Jewish federated giving programs; Jewish agencies & temples.
Type of support: General/operating support; Annual campaigns; Capital campaigns; Building/ renovation; Endowments; Scholarship funds.

Limitations: Giving primarily in Columbus, OH.
Application information: Application form not required.
Initial approach: Proposal
Deadline(s): None
Officers and Trustees:* Robert H. Schottenstein,* Pres.; Steven Schottenstein,* V.P.; J. Thomas Mason, Secy.; Charlotte Stout, Treas.; Phillip G. Creek; Linda Fisher; Gary Schottenstein.
EIN: 311254013

7730
The Morton and Barbara Mandel Family Foundation ▼ ✧
(formerly Morton and Barbara Mandel Foundation)
2829 Euclid Ave.
Cleveland, OH 44115 (216) 875-6500
Contact: Morton L. Mandel, Tr.

Established in 1963 in OH.
Donors: Morton L. Mandel; Barbara A. Mandel.
Foundation type: Independent foundation.
Financial data (yr. ended 12/31/04): Assets, $90,389,439 (M); gifts received, $9,554,341; expenditures, $5,837,422; qualifying distributions, $4,089,647; giving activities include $4,028,144 for 116+ grants (high: $2,250,000; average: $333–$25,000).
Purpose and activities: Support primarily for Jewish welfare funds and organizations, including community development and the arts; support also for hospitals.
Fields of interest: Arts; Human services; Community development; Jewish federated giving programs; Government/public administration; Jewish agencies & temples.
International interests: Israel.
Type of support: General/operating support.
Limitations: Giving primarily in Cleveland, OH; giving also in MA and NY. No grants to individuals.
Application information: Application form not required.
Initial approach: Proposal
Deadline(s): None
Officers and Trustees:* Morton L. Mandel,* Pres.; Barbara A. Mandel,* V.P.; Karen A. Vereb, Secy.; Anthony J. Pishkula, Treas.; Amy C. Mandel; Jack N. Mandel; Joseph C. Mandel; Stacy L. Mandel; Thomas A. Mandel.
Number of staff: 1 full-time professional; 1 part-time professional; 2 full-time support.
EIN: 346546420
Selected grants: The following grants were reported in 2004.
$2,250,000 to Mandel Supporting Foundations, Cleveland, OH. For general support.
$345,000 to Cooper-Hewitt Museum, The Smithsonians National Museum of Design, New York, NY. For general support.
$341,667 to Jewish Community Federation of Cleveland, Cleveland, OH. For general support.
$155,000 to Jewish Community Board of Akron, Akron, OH. For general support.
$100,000 to Leader to Leader Institute, New York, NY. For general support.
$55,293 to United Way Services of Greater Cleveland, Cleveland, OH. For general support.
$33,334 to Bezalel Academy of Arts and Design, Jerusalem, Israel. For general support.
$26,000 to Temple Israel, West Palm Beach, FL. For general support.

$25,000 to Combined Jewish Philanthropies of Greater Boston, Boston, MA. For general support.
$25,000 to Jewish Fund for Justice, New York, NY. For general support.

7731
Jack N. and Lilyan Mandel Foundation ▼ ✧
2829 Euclid Ave.
Cleveland, OH 44115 (216) 875-6500
Contact: Jack N. Mandel, Pres.

Established in 1963 in OH.
Donors: Jack N. Mandel; Lilyan Mandel†.
Foundation type: Independent foundation.
Financial data (yr. ended 12/31/04): Assets, $222,839,698 (M); gifts received, $2,598,695; expenditures, $14,648,710; qualifying distributions, $10,499,435; giving activities include $10,439,133 for 73+ grants (high: $9,300,000; low: $250; average: $1,000–$25,000).
Purpose and activities: Giving primarily to Jewish agencies, temples and schools.
Fields of interest: Elementary/secondary education; Jewish federated giving programs; Jewish agencies & temples.
Limitations: Giving primarily in Cleveland, OH. No grants to individuals.
Application information: Application form not required.
Initial approach: Proposal
Deadline(s): None
Officers and Trustees:* Jack N. Mandel,* Pres.; Karen A. Vereb, Secy.; Anthony J. Pishkula, Treas.; Joseph C. Mandel; Morton L. Mandel; Bradley Smith.
EIN: 346546418
Selected grants: The following grants were reported in 2004.
$9,300,000 to Mandel Supporting Foundations, Cleveland, OH. For general support.
$341,667 to Jewish Community Federation of Cleveland, Cleveland, OH. For general support.
$90,000 to Broward CHAI Center, Hallandale, FL. For general support.
$45,000 to Catholic Diocese of Cleveland Foundation, Cleveland, OH. For general support.
$40,000 to Temple Tifereth Israel, Beachwood, OH. For general support.
$25,000 to United Way Services of Greater Cleveland, Cleveland, OH. For general support.
$17,500 to Chabad House of Cleveland, Cleveland, OH. For general support for Chabad Chai Center.
$15,000 to Nova Southeastern University, Fort Lauderdale, FL. For general support.
$10,000 to Rose and Jack Orloff Central Agency for Jewish Education of Broward County, Davie, FL. For general support.

7732
The Joseph and Florence Mandel Foundation ✧
2829 Euclid Ave.
Cleveland, OH 44115 (216) 875-6500
Contact: Joseph C. Mandel, Tr.

Established in 1963 in OH.
Donors: Florence Mandel†; Joseph C. Mandel.
Foundation type: Independent foundation.
Financial data (yr. ended 12/31/04): Assets, $68,714,353 (M); gifts received, $2,217,805; expenditures, $4,610,498; qualifying distributions,

$3,191,959; giving activities include $3,129,700 for grants.
Purpose and activities: Giving primarily to a Jewish community fund and family-affiliated foundations.
Fields of interest: Higher education; Federated giving programs; Jewish federated giving programs; Jewish agencies & temples.
Type of support: General/operating support.
Limitations: Giving primarily in OH; giving also in FL, MA, and NY. No grants to individuals.
Application information: Application form not required.
Initial approach: Proposal
Deadline(s): None
Officers and Trustees:* Joseph C. Mandel,* Pres.; Karen A. Vereb, Secy.; Anthony J. Pishkula, Treas.; Michele Beyer; Jack N. Mandel; Morton L. Mandel; Bradley S. Smith; Penni Weinberg.
EIN: 346546419

7733
Frank Mangano Foundation ✧
119 E. State St.
Alliance, OH 44601-4933

Established in 1988 in OH.
Donor: Frank J. Mangano†.
Foundation type: Independent foundation.
Financial data (yr. ended 12/31/05): Assets, $12,960,632 (M); expenditures, $518,573; qualifying distributions, $491,011; giving activities include $469,224 for 106 grants (high: $200,000; low: $100).
Purpose and activities: Giving primarily to a YMCA, and for education, youth and social services, community development, local fire departments, and to an Episcopal church.
Fields of interest: Elementary/secondary education; Education; Health care; Disasters, fire prevention/control; Human services; YM/YWCAs & YM/YWHAs; Children/youth, services; Residential/custodial care, hospices; Community development; Protestant agencies & churches.
Type of support: General/operating support; Capital campaigns; Building/renovation.
Limitations: Applications not accepted. Giving primarily in OH, VA, and WV. No grants to individuals.
Application information: Contributes only to pre-selected organizations.
Trustees: M.S. Hoover; Margaret E. Mangano.
EIN: 341600651
Selected grants: The following grants were reported in 2005.
$200,000 to YMCA, Steubenville, OH.
$78,099 to Notre Dame Academy, Middleburg, VA.
$29,000 to Tri-State Promoters, East Liverpool, OH.
$16,000 to Emmanuel Episcopal Church, Alexandria, VA.
$10,000 to Elon University, Elon College, NC.
$7,000 to Hill School of Middleburg, Middleburg, VA.
$2,500 to Middleburg Community Center, Middleburg, VA.
$1,000 to Keyes Group Home, East Liverpool, OH.
$1,000 to Sacred Heart Church, Chester, WV.
$1,000 to Trinity Episcopal Church, East Liverpool, OH.

7734
Joseph L. & Sarah S. Marcum
Foundation ◇
300 High St.
Hamilton, OH 45011

Established in 1987 in OH.
Donors: Joseph L. Marcum; Sarah Marcum.
Foundation type: Independent foundation.
Financial data (yr. ended 12/31/05): Assets, $6,474,210 (M); gifts received, $50,000; expenditures, $371,128; qualifying distributions, $341,411; giving activities include $327,020 for 35 grants (high: $136,000; low: $225).
Fields of interest: Arts; Higher education; Human services; Community development; Foundations (community); Federated giving programs; Christian agencies & churches.
Limitations: Applications not accepted. Giving primarily in OH. No grants to individuals.
Application information: Contributes only to pre-selected organizations.
Officer: Joseph L. Marcum, Chair.
Trustees: Catherine M. Lowe; M. Christina Manchester; Sarah S. Marcum; Stephen S. Marcum; Sarah S. Shuffield.
Agent: First Financial Bank.
EIN: 311190243
Selected grants: The following grants were reported in 2005.
$136,000 to Hamilton Community Foundation, Hamilton, OH.
$101,000 to Miami University, Oxford, OH.
$30,000 to Dayton Foundation, Dayton, OH.
$10,000 to United Way of Indian River County, Vero Beach, FL.
$5,000 to Antioch College, Yellow Springs, OH.
$2,500 to Ethel Walker School, Simsbury, CT.
$2,500 to Hillsdale College, Hillsdale, MI.
$2,500 to Sarah Lawrence College, Bronxville, NY.
$1,000 to East End Adult Education Center, Cincinnati, OH.
$500 to Alice Lloyd College, Pippa Passes, KY.

7735
Marietta Community Foundation ◇
121 Putman St.
P.O. Box 77
Marietta, OH 45750-0070 (740) 373-3286
Contact: Jack Moberg, C.E.O., Pres., and Exec. Dir.; For grant information: Carol Wharff, Prog. and Donor Svcs. Off.
FAX: (740) 373-3937;
E-mail: info@mariettacommunityfoundation.org;
Additional E-mail:
jack@mariettacommunityfoundation.org;
URL: http://www.mariettacommunityfoundation.org

Established in 1974 in OH.
Donors: Lillian Strecker Smith†; Mrs. William Mildren, Sr.†; Carl L. Broughton†; William Mildren, Sr.†; Jane McCoy Peterson†; Susan Marsch.
Foundation type: Community foundation.
Financial data (yr. ended 12/31/04): Assets, $1,039,063 (M); gifts received, $1,049,743; expenditures, $512,354; giving activities include $338,242 for grants.
Purpose and activities: The foundation is committed to building a strong foundation for the community and making life better for all citizens of Washington County, OH and the surrounding

communities. The foundation seeks to respond to a wide variety of needs in the community.
Fields of interest: Arts; Education; Health care; Children/youth, services; Aging, centers/services; Community development.
Type of support: General/operating support; Building/renovation; Equipment; Endowments; Program development; Conferences/seminars; Seed money; Scholarship funds; Research; Technical assistance; Program-related investments/loans; Grants to individuals; Scholarships—to individuals; Matching/challenge support.
Limitations: Giving limited to the Marietta, OH, area, including Washington County, OH, and Wood County, WV. No grants for annual funds or continuing support.
Publications: Application guidelines; Annual report; Informational brochure (including application guidelines).
Application information: Visit foundation Web site for application form and guidelines. Application form required.
  Initial approach: Telephone
  Copies of proposal: 1
  Deadline(s): Feb. 7, June 7, and Oct. 7
  Board meeting date(s): 3rd Tues. of each month
  Final notification: 45 to 65 days following deadlines
Officers and Directors:* Teri Ann Zide Pfeffer,* Chair.; Michael Iaderosa,* Vice-Chair.; John A. "Jack" Moberg, C.E.O., Pres., and Exec. Dir.; William A. Fields,* Secy.; Mark B. Schwendeman,* Treas.; David C. Barrett; Eric Erb; Louise Holmes; Joan Hushion; Karen Osborne; Mary Vituccio; Bonnie Witten.
Number of staff: 2 full-time professional.
EIN: 743054287

7736
Elizabeth Ring Mather and William Gwinn
Mather Fund ◇
1111 Superior Ave., Ste. 1000
Cleveland, OH 44114
Contact: James D. Ireland III, Pres.

Incorporated in 1954 in OH.
Donor: Elizabeth Ring Mather†.
Foundation type: Independent foundation.
Financial data (yr. ended 12/31/05): Assets, $7,840,130 (M); gifts received, $536,958; expenditures, $1,150,977; qualifying distributions, $1,089,025; giving activities include $985,367 for 50 grants (high: $479,150; low: $400; average: $5,000–$10,000).
Fields of interest: Museums (art); Historic preservation/historical societies; Secondary school/education; Higher education; Medical school/education; Education; Federated giving programs; Roman Catholic agencies & churches.
Type of support: General/operating support; Annual campaigns; Building/renovation; Endowments; Publication.
Limitations: Giving primarily in OH, with emphasis on the greater Cleveland area. No grants to individuals, or for scholarships or fellowships; no loans.
Application information: The foundation does not encourage new requests for grants. Application form not required.
  Initial approach: Letter
  Copies of proposal: 1

Deadline(s): None
  Board meeting date(s): June and Dec.
Officers and Trustees:* James D. Ireland III,* Pres.; Lucy I. Weller,* V.P.; Cornelia I. Hallinan,* Secy.; George R. Ireland,* Treas.
Number of staff: 1 part-time professional.
EIN: 346519863
Selected grants: The following grants were reported in 2004.
$400,931 to University Circle, Cleveland, OH. 3 grants: $13,431, $380,000, $7,500
$50,000 to Hawken School, Gates Mills, OH.
$33,334 to Team NEO, Cleveland, OH.
$16,000 to Fessenden School, West Newton, MA.
$16,000 to Park School, Brookline, MA.
$15,000 to Smith College, Northampton, MA.
$10,000 to Generation Foundation, Cleveland, OH.
$5,000 to Kent State University, Kent, OH.

7737
Mathile Family Foundation ▼ ◇
6450 Sand Lake Rd., Ste. 100
Dayton, OH 45414 (937) 264-4607
Contact: Angela Hayes, Grant Assoc.
FAX: (937) 264-4805;
E-mail: angela.hayes@mathilefamilyfoundation.org;
Application address: P.O. Box 13615, Dayton, OH 45413-0615

Established in 1989 in OH.
Donors: Clayton Lee Mathile; MaryAnn Mathile.
Foundation type: Independent foundation.
Financial data (yr. ended 11/30/05): Assets, $297,721,975 (M); gifts received, $40,000; expenditures, $21,605,571; qualifying distributions, $18,897,155; giving activities include $17,234,977 for 176 grants (high: $2,500,000; low: $400; average: $1,000–$1,000,000).
Purpose and activities: To create opportunities for children in need by focusing support on children and their families who have already demonstrated the motivation to succeed. The focus is on three areas: family, education and health.
Fields of interest: Education; Food services; Children/youth, services; Homeless, human services.
Type of support: General/operating support; Capital campaigns; Building/renovation; Equipment; Program development; Program-related investments/loans; Matching/challenge support.
Limitations: Giving primarily in the Dayton and Montgomery County, OH, areas. No support for political organizations. No grants to individuals, or for sponsorships, endowment funds, or mass appeals for funding.
Publications: Application guidelines; Annual report (including application guidelines).
Application information: Mass mailings not accepted. Application form not required.
  Initial approach: Letter, proposal, or telephone
  Copies of proposal: 1
  Deadline(s): Feb. 1, May 1, Aug. 1, and Nov. 1
  Board meeting date(s): Jan. 10, Apr. 10, July 10, and Oct. 10
  Final notification: 70 days after the deadline
Officers and Trustees:* MaryAnn Mathile,* Chair and C.E.O.; Clayton Lee Mathile,* Pres.; Richard J. Chernesky,* Secy.; Gregory Scott Edwards, Exec. Dir.
Number of staff: 9 full-time professional.
EIN: 311257219
Selected grants: The following grants were reported in 2005.

$2,500,000 to Sinclair Community College Foundation, Dayton, OH. For capital support.

$1,000,000 to Boy Scouts of America, Miami Valley Council, Dayton, OH. For capital support.

$1,000,000 to Glen, The, Dayton, OH. For operating support.

$1,000,000 to Saint James Catholic Church, Dayton, OH. For capital support.

$1,000,000 to Urban League of Dayton, Dayton, OH. For capital support.

$100,000 to Holy Family Church, Dayton, OH. For operating support.

$50,000 to Artemis Center for Alternatives to Domestic Violence, Dayton, OH. For operating support.

$50,000 to Dakota Center, Dayton, OH. For operating support.

$45,000 to Ohio Association of Nonprofit Organizations, Columbus, OH. For operating support.

$41,000 to University of Dayton, Dayton, OH. For operating support.

7738
David May Employees Trust Fund ✧ ☆
c/o Federated Corporate Svcs.
7 W. 7th St.
Cincinnati, OH 45202

Established in 1928.
Donors: The May Department Stores Co.; The May Department Stores Foundation.
Foundation type: Company-sponsored foundation.
Financial data (yr. ended 12/31/05): Assets, $539,719 (M); gifts received, $702,528; expenditures, $360,536; qualifying distributions, $353,825; giving activities include $353,825 for grants to individuals.
Purpose and activities: The foundation awards college scholarships to former employees of the May Department Stores Company.
Type of support: Employee-related scholarships.
Limitations: Applications not accepted. Giving limited to areas of company operations.
Application information: Contributes only through employee-related scholarships.
Trustees: Richard A. Brickson; John L. Dunham; Brian L. Keck; Jan R. Kniffen; John A. Sztukowski.
EIN: 436027540

7739
Manuel D. & Rhoda Mayerson Foundation
312 Walnut St., Ste. 3600
Cincinnati, OH 45202 (513) 621-7500
Contact: Neal H. Mayerson Ph.D., Pres.
FAX: (513) 621-2864;
E-mail: applications@mayersonfoundation.org;
URL: http://www.mayersonfoundation.org

Established in 1986 in FL.
Donors: Manuel D. Mayerson; Rhoda Mayerson.
Foundation type: Independent foundation.
Financial data (yr. ended 10/31/05): Assets, $35,077,416 (M); gifts received, $1,055,340; expenditures, $2,552,343; qualifying distributions, $1,911,753; giving activities include $1,652,373 for grants.
Purpose and activities: Primary areas of interest include youth, people with disabilities, and education. Some giving for the performing and fine arts, including museums, theater, and music

groups; funding also for Jewish welfare funds and other organizations; family and social services, and for civic engagement.
Fields of interest: Arts; Education, early childhood education; Education; Human services; Children/youth, services; Family services; Voluntarism promotion; Jewish federated giving programs; Jewish agencies & temples; Disabilities, people with.
Type of support: General/operating support; Management development/capacity building; Annual campaigns; Capital campaigns; Building/renovation; Emergency funds; Program development; Seed money; Technical assistance; Matching/challenge support.
Limitations: Giving primarily in Berkeley, CA, Boca Raton, FL, Cincinnati, OH, and Park City, UT. No support for political organizations. No grants to individuals, or for travel or study.
Publications: Grants list; Informational brochure (including application guidelines); Multi-year report.
Application information: Foundation recommends the use of The Greater Cincinnati Grant Application form for full proposals requesting more than $10,000. Initial contact regarding new initiatives in the area of Judaism should be directed to the Program Director for Jewish Giving. Application form required.
> *Initial approach:* Letter of inquiry
> *Copies of proposal:* 1
> *Deadline(s):* Ongoing
> *Board meeting date(s):* Quarterly
> *Final notification:* One quarter after full proposal is received

Officers and Trustees:* Neal H. Mayerson, Ph.D.*, Pres.; Breta C. Cooper, Exec. V.P.; Arlene B. Mayerson; Donna Mayerson, Ph.D.; Frederic H. Mayerson, J.D.; Manuel D. Mayerson; Rhoda Mayerson.
Number of staff: 3 full-time professional; 1 full-time support.
EIN: 311310431
Selected grants: The following grants were reported in 2003.
$25,387 to Cincinnati Art Museum, Cincinnati, OH. For insurance policies.

$16,500 to Hadassah, The Womens Zionist Organization of America, Hadassah Medical Center, New York, NY. For X-Ray Room at the New Center for Emergency Medicine in Jerusalem, Israel.

$11,000 to United Way of Greater Cincinnati, Cincinnati, OH.

$5,000 to Chabad House of Cincinnati, Cincinnati, OH. For hiring staff for the Inclusion Program.

$3,000 to YWCA of Cincinnati, Cincinnati, OH. For Career Women of Achievement Awards Luncheon.

$1,500 to Comprehensive Community Child Care Organization, Cincinnati, OH. For Champions for Children lecture.

$1,000 to Tender Mercies, Cincinnati, OH. In memory of Frank Harkavy.

$1,000 to Ursuline Academy of Cincinnati, Cincinnati, OH. For transportation and ticket subsidy.

$850 to Robert A. Taft Information Technology High School, Cincinnati, OH. For Taft VIP Club.

$100 to Society for the Preservation of Music Hall, Cincinnati, OH. In honor of the 50th wedding anniversary of Melvin and Zell Schulman.

7740
The Arthur B. McBride, Sr. Family Foundation ✧
2069 W. 3rd St.
Cleveland, OH 44113

Established in 1989 in OH.
Donor: Arthur B. McBride, Jr.
Foundation type: Independent foundation.
Financial data (yr. ended 12/31/05): Assets, $8,130,059 (M); expenditures, $490,881; qualifying distributions, $488,007; giving activities include $488,007 for 98 grants (high: $50,000; low: $7; average: $5,000–$20,000).
Purpose and activities: Giving primarily to Roman Catholic agencies and churches, and for health care, education, and social services.
Fields of interest: Higher education; Education; Hospitals (general); Medical research, institute; Human services; YM/YWCAs & YM/YWHAs; Roman Catholic agencies & churches.
Type of support: General/operating support.
Limitations: Applications not accepted. Giving primarily in the Cleveland, OH, area. No grants to individuals.
Application information: Contributes only to pre-selected organizations.
Trustees: Brian A. McBride; Maureen McBride; Rita McBride; Kathleen McBride Plum.
EIN: 341612197
Selected grants: The following grants were reported in 2004.
$1,020,000 to P.M. Foundation, Cleveland, OH.

$25,000 to Middleburg Early Education Center, Middleburg Heights, OH.

$17,500 to Montessori School. 3 grants: $2,000, $4,500, $11,000

$10,000 to Eden Institute Foundation, Princeton, NJ.

$3,000 to John Carroll University, University Heights, OH.

$3,000 to Magnificat High School, Rocky River, OH.

$3,000 to Seeds of Literacy, Cleveland, OH.

$2,000 to Julie Billiart School, Lyndhurst, OH.

7741
The Bill and Mae McCorkle Foundation, Inc. ✧
755 Bluffview Dr.
Columbus, OH 43235

Established in 2002 in OH.
Donors: Mae L. McCorkle; William R. McCorkle, Jr.
Foundation type: Independent foundation.
Financial data (yr. ended 12/31/05): Assets, $169,539 (M); gifts received, $400,027; expenditures, $835,512; qualifying distributions, $834,700; giving activities include $834,700 for 16 grants (high: $600,000; low: $100).
Fields of interest: Children/youth, services.
Limitations: Applications not accepted. Giving primarily in Columbus, OH. No grants to individuals.
Application information: Contributes only to pre-selected organizations.
Officers and Directors:* Mae L. McCorkle,* Pres. and Treas.; Nanci L. McCorkle, V.P.; William R. McCorkle III,* V.P.; Mark Vanatta, Secy.
EIN: 421562321

7742
The McGregor Foundation ◇
14900 Private Dr.
East Cleveland, OH 44112
Contact: Susan O. Althans
E-mail: salthans@fmscleveland.com; Application address: c/o Foundation Management Svcs., 1422 Euclid Ave., Ste. 627, Cleveland, OH 44115-1952, tel: (216) 621-2901; URL: http://www.mcgregorfoundation.org

Established in 2003 in OH from an initial endowment from The A.M. McGregor Home.
Donors: Robert Rhodes†; Mary B. Donahue†.
Foundation type: Independent foundation.
Financial data (yr. ended 4/30/05): Assets, $22,380,472 (M); expenditures, $1,169,184; qualifying distributions, $1,045,573; giving activities include $908,372 for 29 grants (high: $115,000; low: $250).
Purpose and activities: The foundation provides support for organizations that address the following priority areas for elders in need: 1) recruitment, education, training and retention of healthcare professionals in geriatrics; 2) access to care for underserved populations; 3) promotion of health and wellness; and 4) total quality of life for seniors. The Board of Directors particularly encourages requests for programs that increase the pool of workers trained in geriatrics, expand access to care for elders in need or demonstrate effective new methods and approaches.
Fields of interest: Geriatrics; Human services; Residential/custodial care, hospices; Aging, centers/services; Aging.
Limitations: Giving limited to Cuyahoga County, OH, with emphasis on the areas served by the A.M. McGregor Home. No support for long-term residential care facilities (for capital projects). No grants to individuals, or for debt reduction, annual funds, research, symposia or for endowments.
Publications: Grants list.
Application information: Application form not required.
Initial approach: See foundation Web site for application guidelines
Copies of proposal: 2
Deadline(s): Mar. 1 and Sept. 1
Board meeting date(s): Apr. and Nov.
Officers and Directors:* David P. Handke, Jr.,* Chair.; Jane K. Meyer, Vice-Chair; R. Robertson Hilton,* C.E.O. and Pres.; Sue W. Neff, Secy. and Exec. Dir.; William D. Buss II; Peter A. DeGolia; Rev. Henry C. Doll; Andrew L. Fabens III; Mary E. Mann; Bruce D. Murphy; Barbara S. Oldenburg.
EIN: 352166848

7743
John McIntire Educational Fund ◇
c/o Unizan Fin. Svcs. Group
422 Main St.
P.O. Box 2307
Zanesville, OH 43702-2307 (740) 455-7060
Contact: Neana Butler, Admin. Asst.

Established about 1937.
Donor: John McIntire†.
Foundation type: Independent foundation.
Financial data (yr. ended 6/30/05): Assets, $11,314,887 (M); expenditures, $558,688; qualifying distributions, $520,719; giving activities include $1,000 for 1 grant, and $501,783 for 139 grants to individuals (high: $8,000; low: $1,000).

Purpose and activities: Awards college scholarships to residents of Zanesville, OH, who are single and under 21 years of age.
Type of support: Scholarships—to individuals.
Limitations: Giving limited to residents of Zanesville, OH.
Publications: Annual report.
Application information: Application form required.
Deadline(s): May 1
Officers and Directors:* Milman H. Linn III,* Pres.; Charles A. Gorsuch,* V.P.; Frederic Grant,* Secy.; Nelson McCoy, Jr.,* Treas.; William Brown; Michael Leplante; Timothy H. Linn; William Stewart; Brent A Stubbins.
EIN: 316021239

7744
The Harold and Helen McMaster Foundation, Inc. ◇
c/o SJS Investment Consulting
6711 Monroe St., Bldg. 4, Ste. A
Sylvania, OH 43560 (419) 885-2626
Contact: Scott Savage

Established in 1988 in OH.
Donors: Harold A. McMaster; Helen E. McMaster.
Foundation type: Independent foundation.
Financial data (yr. ended 11/30/04): Assets, $10,513,077 (M); expenditures, $1,416,952; qualifying distributions, $1,224,505; giving activities include $1,224,505 for grants.
Purpose and activities: Giving primarily for the arts and education.
Fields of interest: Media/communications; Museums; Performing arts; Higher education; Education; Health organizations, association; Human services.
Type of support: General/operating support; Continuing support; Annual campaigns; Capital campaigns; Building/renovation; Endowments; Debt reduction; Program development; Curriculum development; Research; Technical assistance.
Limitations: Giving primarily in OH.
Publications: Application guidelines.
Application information: Application form required.
Initial approach: Letter
Copies of proposal: 1
Deadline(s): Apr. 1 and Oct. 1
Board meeting date(s): May and Nov.
Officers: Harold A. McMaster, Pres. and Treas.; Helen E. McMaster, V.P. and Secy.
Trustee: Nancy Cobie; Jeanine Dunn; Frank Jacobs; Alan McMaster; Ronald A. McMaster.
Number of staff: 1 full-time professional; 1 part-time professional.
EIN: 341576110
Selected grants: The following grants were reported in 2003.
$300,000 to Defiance College, Defiance, OH. For McMaster Institute.
$100,000 to Toledo Museum of Art, Toledo, OH. For capital campaign.
$50,000 to Bowling Green State University, College of Musical Arts, Bowling Green, OH.
$50,000 to Flower Hospital Foundation, Sylvania, OH. For pulmonary rehab facility.
$10,000 to Ohio Foundation of Independent Colleges, Columbus, OH. For annual campaign.
$10,000 to United Way of Greater Toledo, Toledo, OH. For general support.
$5,000 to Ann Arbor Symphony Orchestra, Ann Arbor, MI. For general support.

$5,000 to Owens Community College, Toledo, OH. For Brown Scholarship Endowment.
$4,000 to Adopt America Network, Toledo, OH. For general support.
$1,000 to Assistance Dogs of America, Swanton, OH. For general support.

7745
The MeadWestvaco Foundation ▼ ◇
Courthouse Plz. N.E.
Dayton, OH 45463 (937) 495-3428
Contact: Kathryn A. Strawn, V.P. and Exec. Dir.
E-mail: foundation@meadwestvaco.com;
URL: http://www.mwvfoundation.org

Established in 2003 in DE.
Foundation type: Company-sponsored foundation.
Financial data (yr. ended 12/31/05): Assets, $26,910,363 (M); expenditures, $4,595,060; qualifying distributions, $4,467,939; giving activities include $4,453,929 for 1,235 grants (high: $276,000).
Purpose and activities: The foundation supports organizations involved with arts and culture, education, the environment, health, human services, community development, and civic affairs.
Fields of interest: Arts; Education; Environment; Health care; Human services; Economic development; Community development; Public affairs.
Type of support: General/operating support; Employee volunteer services; Employee matching gifts.
Limitations: Giving primarily in areas of company operations. No support for lobbying or political organizations, religious organizations not of direct benefit to the entire community, fraternal organizations, sports teams, or student teams. No grants to individuals, or for academic fellowships or research, advertising, concert, dance, or theatrical tours, conferences, endowments, film, radio, or video productions, fundraising events, scholarships, sports events, or student trips or competitions.
Publications: Application guidelines; Program policy statement.
Application information: Application form not required.
Initial approach: Proposal to foundation or nearest company division
Deadline(s): None
Board meeting date(s): 4 times per year
Officers and Directors:* Wendell L. Willkie II,* Chair.; Cynthia A. Niekamp,* Vice-Chair.; Kathryn A. Strawn, V.P. and Exec. Dir.; P.C. Norris, Secy.; Linda C. Scheffield,* Treas.; James A. Buzzard; Jack C. Goldfrank; Neil A. McLachlan; Linda V. Schreiner; Benjamin F. Ward, Jr.
EIN: 061652243
Selected grants: The following grants were reported in 2004.
$296,000 to United Way, Trident, North Charleston, SC.
$128,035 to United Way of Tri-State, New York, NY.
$112,000 to Nature Conservancy, Arlington, VA.
$100,000 to Clark Atlanta University, Atlanta, GA.
$90,500 to Culture Works: The Arts and Cultural Alliance of the Miami Valley, Dayton, OH.
$75,000 to Sinclair Community College Foundation, Dayton, OH.
$25,000 to United Way, Berkshire, Pittsfield, MA.
$17,500 to Virginia Forestry Educational Foundation, Richmond, VA.

$16,500 to Pulp and Paper Foundation of North Carolina State University, Raleigh, NC.

$15,500 to Victoria Theater Association, Dayton, OH.

7746
George and Deborah Mehl Family Foundation, Inc. ✧

c/o W. Stuart Dornette
425 Walnut St., Ste. 1800
Cincinnati, OH 45202

Established in 1999 in OH.

Donor: George and Deborah Mehl Family Trust.
Foundation type: Independent foundation.
Financial data (yr. ended 12/31/05): Assets, $9,975,078 (M); expenditures, $527,894; qualifying distributions, $487,093; giving activities include $450,000 for 18 grants (high: $100,000; low: $1,500; average: $10,000–$25,000).
Purpose and activities: Giving primarily for Christian organizations.
Fields of interest: Education; Reproductive health, prenatal care; Offenders/ex-offenders, services; Children/youth, services; Family services; Christian agencies & churches.
Limitations: Applications not accepted. Giving on a national basis, with emphasis on AZ, CO, and OH. No grants to individuals.
Application information: Contributes only to pre-selected organizations.
Officers and Trustees:* W. Stuart Dornette,* Pres.; Bonnie Mehl,* V.P.; Martha Dornette,* Secy.; David Mehl,* Treas.
EIN: 311679603
Selected grants: The following grants were reported in 2004.

$50,000 to Focus on the Family, Colorado Springs, CO.

$30,000 to Kids Across America Foundation, Branson, MO.

$25,000 to Miami Valley Christian Academy, Newtown, OH.

$25,000 to Teen Challenge of Arizona, Tucson, AZ.

$21,500 to Young Life, Colorado Springs, CO.

$18,200 to City CURE, Cincinnati, OH.

$17,750 to City Gospel Mission, Cincinnati, OH.

$15,000 to Precept Ministries International, Chattanooga, TN.

$5,000 to AMONG Foundation, Sioux Falls, SD.

$5,000 to Fellowship of Christian Athletes, Kansas City, MO.

7747
The Mellen Foundation ✧

c/o John D. Drinko
3200 National City Ctr., 1900 E. 9th St.
Cleveland, OH 44114-3485

Established in 1963 in OH.

Donor: Edward J. Mellen.
Foundation type: Independent foundation.
Financial data (yr. ended 12/31/05): Assets, $1,303,340 (M); expenditures, $492,973; qualifying distributions, $483,625; giving activities include $475,400 for 24 grants (high: $100,000; low: $1,000).
Purpose and activities: Grants primarily for higher education; some support also for medical organizations.

Fields of interest: Performing arts, orchestra (symphony); Higher education; Law school/education; Hospitals (general); Human services.
Type of support: General/operating support; Building/renovation.
Limitations: Applications not accepted. Giving primarily in OH, with some emphasis on Cleveland; some giving nationally. No grants to individuals.
Application information: Contributes only to pre-selected organizations.
Officers and Trustees:* John D. Drinko,* Chair. and Pres.; Elizabeth G. Drinko,* V.P.; Lloyd F. Loux, Jr.,* Secy.; J. Richard Hamilton,* Treas.; J. Randall Drinko.
EIN: 346560874

7748
Miami County Foundation ✧

(formerly Piqua-Miami County Foundation)
317 N. Wayne St.
P.O. Box 1526
Piqua, OH 45356-1526 (937) 773-9012
Contact: Cheryl Stiefel-Francis, Exec. Dir.
FAX: (937) 773-9012;
E-mail: mcfoundation@peoplepc.com; Additional E-mail: director@miamicountyfoundation.org; URL: http://www.miamicountyfoundation.org

Established in 1985 in OH.

Donor: Richard E. Hunt†.
Foundation type: Independent foundation.
Financial data (yr. ended 12/31/04): Assets, $10,783,132 (M); gifts received, $5,102,340; expenditures, $511,346; qualifying distributions, $442,882; giving activities include $360,534 for 64 grants (high: $20,000; low: $220), and $65,850 for 23 grants to individuals (high: $25,000; low: $850).
Purpose and activities: The mission of the foundation is to effectively assist, encourage and promote the health, education and welfare of the citizens of Miami County, OH, by soliciting, receiving and administering assets exclusively for the charitable needs of the community. The Miami County Foundation endeavors to focus on "People Helping People" within the community.
Fields of interest: Education; Hospitals (general); Human services.
Type of support: Management development/capacity building; Capital campaigns; Building/renovation; Equipment; Program development; Conferences/seminars; Publication; Seed money; Curriculum development; Scholarship funds; Program evaluation.
Limitations: Giving limited to Miami County, OH. No support for organizations that limit their services to members of any one religious group, political organizations or those whose primary purpose is to influence legislation, political viewpoint or promotion of a particular candidate.
Publications: Application guidelines; Informational brochure; Newsletter.
Application information: Application guidelines and forms available on foundation Web site. Application form required.

Copies of proposal: 5
Deadline(s): Feb. 28 and Aug. 31
Board meeting date(s): Apr. and Oct.
Final notification: 7 weeks

Officers and Trustees:* Richard N. Adams, Ph.D., Pres.; Leesa Baker,* V.P.; Joe Duncan, Secy.; Douglas R. Murray,* Treas.; Cheryl Stiefel-Francis, Exec. Dir.; George A. Ashton; Carol Coate; Dan Dickerson; Paul Gearhardt; Candace Goodall;

Joanna Hill Heitzman; Jim Oda; Larry Polhamus; Bill Posey; Andy Pratt; Lolita Schultz.
Number of staff: 1 part-time professional.
EIN: 311142558
Selected grants: The following grants were reported in 2004.

$24,000 to Health Partners of Miami County, Troy, OH.

$20,000 to Girl Scouts of the U.S.A..

$20,000 to Rehabilitation Center for Neurological Development, Piqua, OH.

$9,000 to Miami County Agricultural Society, Troy, OH.

$8,000 to American Red Cross.

$5,010 to Upper Valley Medical Center, Troy, OH.

$5,000 to Lehman High School, Sidney, OH.

$5,000 to Salvation Army.

$3,000 to Partners in Hope, Troy, OH.

$2,795 to Piqua High School, Piqua, OH.

7749
Middletown Community Foundation ✧

36 Donham Plz.
Middletown, OH 45042 (513) 424-7369
Contact: Kay Wright, Exec. Dir.
FAX: (513) 424-7555;
E-mail: info@mcfoundation.org; URL: http://www.mcfoundation.org/

Incorporated in 1976 in OH.

Foundation type: Community foundation.
Financial data (yr. ended 12/31/03): Assets, $20,862,088 (M); gifts received, $2,054,523; expenditures, $1,926,024; giving activities include $991,091 for 388 grants (high: $37,500; low: $12); and $633,936 for 351 grants to individuals (high: $4,000; low: $40).
Purpose and activities: The mission of the foundation is to: 1) serve as a leader, catalyst and resource for philanthropy; 2) to serve as a permanent and growing endowment for the community's changing needs and opportunities; 3) to strive for excellence through strategic grantmaking in the areas of the arts, education, health, social services, recreation and community development; 4) to provide a flexible and cost-effective way for donors to improve their community.
Fields of interest: Performing arts; Arts; Elementary/secondary education; Education, early childhood education; Elementary school/education; Higher education; Libraries/library science; Education; Health care; Recreation; Youth development, services; Youth development, citizenship; Youth, services; Family services; Human services; Community development; Public affairs, citizen participation; Leadership development; Aging.
Type of support: Capital campaigns; Building/renovation; Equipment; Emergency funds; Program development; Seed money; Curriculum development; Scholarship funds; Employee matching gifts; Scholarships—to individuals; Matching/challenge support.
Limitations: Giving limited to the greater Middletown, OH, area. No support for religious organizations other than religious schools, medical or other research organizations, or national or regional organizations (unless program addresses local needs). No grants to individuals (except for scholarships), or for endowments or general operating budgets of established organizations.

Publications: Application guidelines; Annual report; Financial statement; Informational brochure (including application guidelines); Newsletter.

Application information: Visit foundation Web site for application guidelines and scholarship deadlines. Common Grant Application may be submitted for grant requests. Application form not required.

　Initial approach: Submit proposal

　Copies of proposal: 1

　Deadline(s): Mar. 1 and Sept. 1 for Recreation, Arts, Festivals, and Community Devel. grants and June 1 and Dec. 1 for Education and Human Needs grants; varies for scholarships

　Board meeting date(s): Quarterly

　Final notification: 60 to 90 days

Officers and Trustees:* Sarah Kaup,* Pres.; Doug Casper,* V.P.; Sue Butcher,* Secy.; Larry Powell,* Treas.; Kay Wright, Exec. Dir.; Ron Ely, Tr. Emeritus; C.William Verity, Tr. Emeritus; John Burley; Eugenie Campbell; Edwina Blackwell Clark; Brian Coughlin; Candice De Clark; Karl Gaston; Michael Governanti; Kathleen Gramke; Gregg Grimes; Seth Johnston; Marla Marsh; Jack O'Neill; Mary Novak; Mary Jane Palmer; Noah Powers; Michael J. Sanders; William Schaefer; Mike Scorti; Andrew Singer; Gene Snow; Bill Trick.

Number of staff: 1 full-time professional; 1 full-time support.

EIN: 310898380

7750
Midland Company Foundation ◇

c/o John I. Von Lehman

7000 Midland Blvd.

Amelia, OH 45102

Established in 1998 in OH.

Donor: The Midland Co.

Foundation type: Company-sponsored foundation.

Financial data (yr. ended 12/31/03): Assets, $764,662 (M); gifts received, $602,075; expenditures, $609,273; qualifying distributions, $604,996; giving activities include $604,996 for 118 grants (high: $200,000; low: $50).

Purpose and activities: The foundation supports organizations involved with education, health, medical research, and community development.

Fields of interest: Education; Hospitals (general); Health organizations, association; Medical research; Human services; Community development; Federated giving programs.

Limitations: Applications not accepted. Giving primarily in Cincinnati, OH. No grants to individuals.

Application information: Contributes only to pre-selected organizations.

Officers: Joseph P. Hayden III, Chair.; John W. Hayden, Pres.; John I. Von Lehman, V.P. and Secy.; W. Todd Gray, Treas.

EIN: 311580326

7751
Milacron Foundation ◇

(formerly Cincinnati Milacron Foundation)

2090 Florence Ave.

Cincinnati, OH 45206 (513) 487-5912

Contact: John C. Francy, Secy.

Incorporated in 1951 in OH.

Donors: Cincinnati Milacron Inc.; Milacron Inc.

Foundation type: Company-sponsored foundation.

Financial data (yr. ended 12/31/04): Assets, $158,431 (M); gifts received, $300,000; expenditures, $351,164; qualifying distributions, $340,763; giving activities include $341,000 for 3 grants (high: $290,000; low: $5,000).

Purpose and activities: The foundation supports organizations involved with arts and culture, education, human services, children and youth services, and community development.

Fields of interest: Arts; Higher education; Education; Children/youth, services; Human services; Community development; Federated giving programs.

Type of support: Continuing support; Annual campaigns; Capital campaigns; Building/renovation; Program development; Seed money; Scholarship funds; Research.

Limitations: Giving primarily in Cincinnati, OH; some giving also in MI. No support for United Way-supported agencies. No grants to individuals, or for endowments.

Publications: Application guidelines.

Application information: Application form not required.

　Initial approach: Proposal

　Copies of proposal: 1

　Deadline(s): None

　Board meeting date(s): Quarterly

Officer and Trustees:* R.D. Brown, Pres.; J.C. Francy, Secy.; R.A. Anderson, Treas.; R.D. Brown; J.A. Steger; C.F.C. Turner.

EIN: 316030682

Selected grants: The following grants were reported in 2004.

$290,000 to United Way of Greater Cincinnati, Cincinnati, OH.

$46,000 to Cincinnati Scholarship Foundation, Cincinnati, OH.

7752
Miller Family Foundation ◇

(formerly Arnold M. & Sydell L. Miller Foundation)

30575 Bainbridge Rd., Ste. 130

Solon, OH 44139-2275

Contact: Diane Gregerson

Application address: c/o Matrix Essentials, Inc., 30601 Carter St., Solon, OH 44139

Established in 1997 in OH.

Donor: Sydell L. Miller Charitable Lead Annuity Trust.

Foundation type: Independent foundation.

Financial data (yr. ended 12/31/05): Assets, $7,768,616 (M); gifts received, $702,320; expenditures, $493,975; qualifying distributions, $449,038; giving activities include $449,038 for 44 grants (high: $110,000; low: $18).

Fields of interest: Arts; Higher education; Health organizations; Foundations (community); Jewish agencies & temples.

Type of support: General/operating support.

Limitations: Applications not accepted. Giving primarily in FL and OH.

Publications: Financial statement.

Application information: Contributes only to pre-selected organizations.

Trustees: Stacie L. Halpern; Dennis E. Lubin; Lauren B. Spilman.

EIN: 341460324

Selected grants: The following grants were reported in 2003.

$55,000 to Jewish Community Federation of Cleveland, Cleveland, OH.

$13,400 to Musical Arts Association, Cleveland, OH.

$12,500 to Gathering Place, Cleveland, OH.

$10,000 to Cleveland Museum of Art, Cleveland, OH.

$10,000 to Hawken School, Gates Mills, OH.

$10,000 to Laurel School, Shaker Heights, OH.

$6,050 to Cleveland Zoological Society, Cleveland, OH.

$5,193 to Menorah Park Foundation, Beachwood, OH.

$5,000 to Hole in the Wall Gang Fund, New Haven, CT.

$2,500 to Childrens Museum of Cleveland, Cleveland, OH.

7753
The Miller Family Foundation ◇

32333 Aurora Rd., Ste. 300

Solon, OH 44139

Established in 1999 in OH.

Donor: Sydell L. Miller Charitable Lead Annuity Trust.

Foundation type: Independent foundation.

Financial data (yr. ended 12/31/05): Assets, $3,008,970 (M); gifts received, $500,000; expenditures, $321,241; qualifying distributions, $315,602; giving activities include $315,602 for 79 grants (high: $132,500; low: $5; average: $500–$10,000).

Purpose and activities: Giving primarily for the arts, education, Jewish giving, health, and human services, especially for children and youth.

Fields of interest: Museums; Museums (art); Performing arts centers; Arts; Elementary/secondary education; Education; Environment; Animals/wildlife; Health care, patient services; Health organizations; Human services; Children/youth, services; Family services; Community development; Jewish federated giving programs; Jewish agencies & temples.

Type of support: General/operating support; Annual campaigns; Program development.

Limitations: Applications not accepted. Giving primarily in OH, with emphasis on Cleveland. No grants to individuals.

Application information: Contributes only to pre-selected organizations.

Trustees: Stacie L. Halpern; Dennis E. Lubin; Lauren B. Spilman.

EIN: 341855841

Selected grants: The following grants were reported in 2004.

$130,400 to Jewish Community Federation of Cleveland, Cleveland, OH.

$31,000 to Playhouse Square Foundation, Cleveland, OH. 2 grants: $26,000, $5,000

$27,100 to Cleveland Zoological Society, Cleveland, OH.

$1,570 to Museum of Arts and Design, New York, NY.

$1,067 to Great Lakes Museum of Science, Environment and Technology, Cleveland, OH.

$1,000 to Maltz Museum of Jewish Heritage, Beachwood, OH.

$1,000 to Ocean Alliance, Lincoln, MA.

$500 to Childrens Museum of Cleveland, Cleveland, OH.

$500 to Pilchuck Glass School, Seattle, WA.

7754
Samuel H. Miller Family Fund, Inc. ✧
c/o Samuel H. Miller, Forest City Enterprises
1170 Terminal Twr.
50 Public Sq.
Cleveland, OH 44113

Established in 1989 in OH.
Donor: Samuel H. Miller.
Foundation type: Independent foundation.
Financial data (yr. ended 12/31/05): Assets,
$20,341,783 (M); gifts received, $149,381;
expenditures, $2,284,866; qualifying distributions,
$1,978,401; giving activities include $1,978,401
for 118 grants (high: $243,981; low: $100).
Purpose and activities: Giving primarily for
education, the arts, health care, and children, and
social services.
Fields of interest: Arts; Elementary/secondary
education; Higher education; Education; Health
care, clinics/centers; Health organizations,
association; Human services; Jewish federated
giving programs; Christian agencies & churches;
Jewish agencies & temples.
Type of support: General/operating support.
Limitations: Applications not accepted. Giving
primarily in Cleveland, OH. No grants to individuals.
Application information: Contributes only to
pre-selected organizations.
Officers and Trustees:* Samuel H. Miller,* Pres.;
Abraham Miller,* V.P.; Eleanor Fanslau,*
Secy.-Treas.; Bruce W. Lang; Maria Miller.
EIN: 341482231
Selected grants: The following grants were reported
in 2004.
$860,600 to Cleveland Clinic, Cleveland, OH.
$316,650 to Cleveland State University, Cleveland,
OH.
$76,000 to Salvation Army.
$25,000 to American Red Cross.
$25,000 to Childrens Hospital.
$25,000 to John Carroll University, University
Heights, OH.
$25,000 to Youngstown State University,
Youngstown, OH.
$24,552 to Purdue University, West Lafayette, IN.
$12,900 to Ratner School, Lyndhurst, OH.
$10,000 to Our Lady of the Wayside, Avon, OH.

7755
Mindala Family Foundation ✧
9640 Weathervane Dr.
Chagrin Falls, OH 44023

Donor: James Mindala.
Foundation type: Independent foundation.
Financial data (yr. ended 12/31/05): Assets,
$2,174,778 (M); expenditures, $622,982;
qualifying distributions, $516,515; giving activities
include $516,515 for 23 grants (high: $158,929;
low: $500).
Purpose and activities: Giving primarily to churches,
education, and children, youth, and health services.
Fields of interest: Higher education; Education;
Health care; Human services; Children/youth,
services; Christian agencies & churches; Orthodox
Catholic agencies & churches.
Limitations: Applications not accepted. Giving
primarily in OH; some giving nationally. No grants to
individuals.
Application information: Contributes only to
pre-selected organizations.

Trustees: James J. Mindala; Joanne N. Mindala;
Kelly L. Kapadia.
EIN: 341939326
Selected grants: The following grants were reported
in 2003.
$150,000 to Orthodox Church in America, Syosset,
NY.
$106,280 to Cleveland Browns Foundation, Berea,
OH.
$97,500 to George Gund Foundation, Cleveland,
OH.
$12,000 to Valley Presbyterian Church, Chagrin
Falls, OH.
$9,800 to Ohio University Foundation, Athens, OH.
$1,000 to Lauri Strauss Leukemia Foundation, New
York, NY.
$500 to Green Mountain College, Poultney, VT.
$500 to Humane Society of Broward County, Fort
Lauderdale, FL.
$500 to Juvenile Diabetes Research Foundation
International, Cleveland, OH.
$250 to Bowling Green State University Foundation,
Bowling Green, OH.

7756
Clement O. Miniger Memorial Foundation ✧
709 Madison Ave., Rm. 205
P.O. Box 1985
Toledo, OH 43603-1985

Incorporated in 1952 in OH.
Donors: George M. Jones, Jr.†; Eleanor Miniger
Jones†.
Foundation type: Independent foundation.
Financial data (yr. ended 12/31/05): Assets,
$12,906,746 (M); expenditures, $605,612;
qualifying distributions, $566,176; giving activities
include $547,983 for 27 grants (high: $75,000;
low: $5,000).
Purpose and activities: Giving primarily for
education, the arts, and children, youth, and health
care services.
Fields of interest: Media, radio; Museums (art);
Museums (science/technology); Performing arts,
orchestra (symphony); Performing arts, opera;
Historic preservation/historical societies; Arts;
Education, early childhood education; Higher
education; Education; Environment, natural
resources; Zoos/zoological societies; Boys & girls
clubs; Human services; Children/youth, services;
Residential/custodial care, hospices.
Type of support: Capital campaigns; Equipment;
Emergency funds; Matching/challenge support.
Limitations: Giving primarily in OH, with emphasis
on Toledo. No grants to individuals.
Officer and Trustees:* George M. Jones III,* Pres.;
William F. Buckley; Justice Johnson; Severn Joyce;
Marna Ramnath; Mark Schaffer; Steve Staelin;
Edward Weber.
EIN: 346523024

7757
A. Malachi Mixon III & Barbara W. Mixon Foundation ✧
Republic Bldg.
25 W. Prospect Ave., Ste.1400
Cleveland, OH 44115-1048

Established in 1991 in OH.
Donors: A. Malachi Mixon III; Barbara W. Mixon.

Foundation type: Independent foundation.
Financial data (yr. ended 11/30/04): Assets,
$290,922 (M); expenditures, $567,900; qualifying
distributions, $567,700; giving activities include
$567,700 for 55 grants (high: $100,000; low:
$100).
Purpose and activities: Giving primarily for the arts,
education, health care, and children, youth, and
social services.
Fields of interest: Museums; Performing arts;
Performing arts, music; Performing arts, orchestra
(symphony); Arts; Elementary/secondary education;
Higher education; Education; Environment, natural
resources; Botanical gardens; Health care, clinics/
centers; Health care; Human services; American
Red Cross; Federated giving programs; Christian
agencies & churches.
Limitations: Applications not accepted. Giving
primarily in Cleveland, OH. No grants to individuals.
Application information: Contributes only to
pre-selected organizations.
Officer: A. Malachi Mixon III, Pres.
Trustees: Robert N. Gudbranson; Barbara W. Mixon.
EIN: 341692992
Selected grants: The following grants were reported
in 2003.
$67,000 to Cleveland Foodbank, Cleveland, OH.
$55,000 to Hathaway Brown School, Shaker
Heights, OH.
$25,000 to Cleveland Orchestra, Cleveland, OH.
$25,000 to Mount Vernon Ladies Association,
Mount Vernon, VA.
$13,000 to Cleveland Botanical Garden, Cleveland,
OH.
$11,200 to Playhouse Square Foundation,
Cleveland, OH.
$10,000 to Elyria Memorial Hospital and Medical
Center, Elyria, OH.
$5,345 to Musical Arts Association, Cleveland, OH.
$1,500 to Cleveland Museum of Natural History,
Cleveland, OH.
$1,000 to Cleveland Museum of Art, Cleveland, OH.

7758
Montgomery Foundation
Roscoe Village
Coshocton, OH 43812
Contact: Linda M. Scott
FAX: (740) 622-4838; Application address: 365 N.
Whitewoman St., Coshocton, OH 43812

Established in 1972 in OH.
Donors: Edward E. Montgomery†; Frances B.
Montgomery†.
Foundation type: Independent foundation.
Financial data (yr. ended 12/31/05): Assets,
$22,735,027 (M); expenditures, $1,753,473;
qualifying distributions, $1,653,619; giving
activities include $1,562,677 for 16 grants (high:
$1,446,519; low: $100).
Purpose and activities: Grants primarily for local
charities in Coshocton County, OH.
Fields of interest: Historic preservation/historical
societies; Education; Community development.
Type of support: Annual campaigns; Building/
renovation; Seed money; Matching/challenge
support.
Limitations: Giving primarily in Coshocton, OH. No
grants to individuals.
Publications: Application guidelines.
Application information: Application form not
required.
   Initial approach: Letter or proposal

Copies of proposal: 4
Deadline(s): None
Board meeting date(s): Executive committee meets monthly to review requests
Final notification: 90 days
Officers and Trustees: * Richard E. Corbett,* Pres.; William Dutton,* V.P.; Randy Kreuter,* Secy.; Robert Simpson,* Treas.; Joseph S. Montgomery; Scott Montgomery.
Number of staff: 1 full-time professional; 1 part-time professional.
EIN: 237165768
Selected grants: The following grants were reported in 2006.
$1,000,000 to Roscoe Village Foundation, Coshocton, OH. To supplement operating deficit of site.
$80,000 to Central Ohio Technical College, The Coshocton Campus, Coshocton, OH. For construction.
$50,000 to Coshocton County Memorial Hospital, Coshocton, OH. To renovate Elder Care Facility.
$30,000 to Missionary Maintenance Services, Coshocton, OH. For construction of aviation repair hangar.
$25,000 to Hospice of Coshocton County, Coshocton, OH. For palliative care unit.

7759
Harry C. Moores Foundation ◇
100 S. 3rd St.
Columbus, OH 43215-4236
Contact: Mary B. Cummins

Trust established in 1961 in OH.
Donor: Harry C. Moores†.
Foundation type: Independent foundation.
Financial data (yr. ended 9/30/05): Assets, $32,444,754 (M); expenditures, $1,955,890; qualifying distributions, $1,803,465; giving activities include $1,793,662 for 89 grants (high: $50,000; low: $5,000).
Purpose and activities: Grants largely for rehabilitation of the handicapped, as well as for hospitals, higher education, cultural programs, and social service agencies concerned with the aged, child welfare, and the developmentally disabled.
Fields of interest: Arts; Higher education; Education; Hospitals (general); Health organizations, association; Food banks; Human services; YM/YWCAs & YM/YWHAs; Children/youth, services.
Type of support: General/operating support; Annual campaigns; Capital campaigns; Seed money; Scholarship funds.
Limitations: Giving primarily in the Columbus, OH, area. No support for private foundations. No grants to individuals, or for endowment funds or matching gifts; no loans.
Publications: Application guidelines.
Application information: The foundation will not review or return video tapes. Application form required.
Initial approach: Letter
Copies of proposal: 1
Deadline(s): June 1
Board meeting date(s): Aug.
Final notification: Sept. 15
Trustees: John P. Beavers; Neil B. Distelhorst; Cris J. Gillespie; Ronald D. Rardon; Kristen J. Sydney.
EIN: 316035344
Selected grants: The following grants were reported in 2005.

$50,000 to Goodwill Industries of Central Ohio, Columbus, OH.
$50,000 to Maryhaven, Columbus, OH.
$43,096 to Creative Living, Columbus, OH.
$40,000 to OhioHealth Foundation, Columbus, OH.
$30,000 to Arthritis Foundation, Columbus, OH.
$29,054 to Childhood League Center, Columbus, OH.
$27,500 to Community Shelter Board, Columbus, OH.
$25,000 to Central Ohio Diabetes Association, Columbus, OH.
$20,000 to On My Own, Columbus, OH.
$15,000 to I Know I Can, Columbus, OH.

7760
Morgan Family Foundation ☆
130 Glen St., Unit 6
P.O. Box 561
Yellow Springs, OH 45387 (937) 767-9208
Contact: Lori Kuhn, Exec. Dir.
FAX: (937) 767-9308;
E-mail: info@morganfamilyfdn.org; URL: http://www.morganfamilyfdn.org

Established in 2003 in OH.
Donors: Lee M. Morgan; Victoria A. Morgan.
Foundation type: Independent foundation.
Financial data (yr. ended 11/30/05): Assets, $47,455,286 (M); expenditures, $2,552,290; qualifying distributions, $2,083,400; giving activities include $2,083,400 for 77 grants (high: $200,000).
Purpose and activities: The foundation will be a vehicle of change and instill hope for a bright future by fostering individual human potential and the desire of communities to seek out and optimize that potential, and a movement toward a healthier, more just, more caring and sustainable society.
Fields of interest: Media, radio; Performing arts; Elementary/secondary education; Higher education; Environment; Reproductive health, family planning; Housing/shelter, development; Youth development; Human services; Foundations (community); Children/youth; Women.
Type of support: General/operating support; Capital campaigns; Building/renovation; Equipment; Endowments; Program development; Matching/challenge support.
Limitations: Giving primarily in the Yellow Springs and southwest OH, and St. Cloud and central MN, areas. No grants to individuals.
Publications: Application guidelines; Grants list.
Application information: Application form required.
Initial approach: Preliminary e-mail or telephone to determine eligibility to submit full proposal
Copies of proposal: 3
Deadline(s): Jan. and Aug.
Board meeting date(s): Mar. & Oct.
Final notification: Within three weeks of board meeting
Officers and Directors: * Lee M. Morgan,* Pres.; Victoria A. Morgan,* Treas.; Lori Kuhn, Exec. Dir.; Asha Morgan Moran; Marty Moran; Matthew Morgan.
Number of staff: 1 full-time professional; 1 full-time support.
EIN: 300205024

7761
The Burton D. Morgan Foundation ▼
22 Aurora St.
Hudson, OH 44236 (330) 655-1660
Contact: Deborah D. Hoover, Pres.
FAX: (330) 655-1673;
E-mail: admin@bdmorganfdn.org; Contact for application guidelines: Marie Erb, tel.: (330) 655-1369, e-mail: merb@bdmorganfdn.org;
URL: http://www.bdmorganfdn.org

Established in 1967 in OH.
Donor: Burton D. Morgan†.
Foundation type: Independent foundation.
Financial data (yr. ended 12/31/05): Assets, $131,570,936 (M); gifts received, $3,000,000; expenditures, $5,987,239; qualifying distributions, $4,873,307; giving activities include $4,687,250 for 54 grants (high: $1,012,000; low: $500; average: $5,000–$250,000).
Purpose and activities: The purpose of the foundation is to strengthen the free enterprise system by investing in organizations and institutions that foster the entrepreneurial spirit. The foundation is interested in supporting projects that nurture creativity, invention, entrepreneurship, and innovation. To that end, it will invest in projects that fall into three life phases (starting with and continuing through college and then into business activity): Education, on the primary and secondary levels, that instills an appreciation for free enterprise and that cultivates creativity and invention. Entrepreneurial education on the collegiate and on the adult levels that deepens free enterprise values and develops critical skills and competencies. Entrepreneurial support for organizations that provide the incubation, business planning and/or capitalization assistance critical to success.
Fields of interest: Higher education; Business school/education; Education; Economics.
Type of support: General/operating support; Capital campaigns; Building/renovation; Endowments; Program development; Seed money; Curriculum development; Scholarship funds.
Limitations: Giving primarily in northeastern OH. No support for private foundations, governmental or tax-supported organizations, or to the arts, or social service organizations and programs (including mental health), or support for lobbying or political organizations. No grants to individuals, or for annual fund drives.
Publications: Application guidelines; Annual report (including application guidelines); Financial statement; Grants list.
Application information: Please visit the foundation Web site for additional information. Before submitting a full proposal, organizations should submit a letter of inquiry to the foundation regarding a request. The Exec V.P. will then determine if the organization should proceed with a formal grant application. Organizations may only submit one grant proposal within a 12-month period. Application form not required.
Initial approach: Letter of inquiry (1 page)
Copies of proposal: 1
Deadline(s): Sept. 1, Feb. 1 and Apr. 1 for Letter of Inquiry; Oct. 1, Mar. 1 and May 1 for grant requests
Board meeting date(s): Jan., June, and Sept.
Officers and Trustees: * Deborah D. Hoover, Pres.; J. Martin Erbaugh, V.P.; Richard N. Seaman, Secy.-Treas.; Keith A. Brown; Richard A. Chenoweth; John V. Frank; Stanley C. Gault; Mark D. Robeson.

Number of staff: 2 full-time professional; 3 part-time professional; 1 full-time support; 1 part-time support.

EIN: 346598971

Selected grants: The following grants were reported in 2005.

$1,012,000 to Western Reserve Academy, Hudson, OH. For completion of Burton D. Morgan Hall.

$750,000 to Baldwin-Wallace College, Berea, OH. For Burton D. Morgan Endowed Chair in Entrepreneurship.

$400,000 to Kent State University Foundation, School of Fashion Design and Merchandising, Kent, OH. For Burton D. Morgan Foundation Technology Endowment.

$275,000 to Methodist Theological School in Ohio, Delaware, OH. 2 grants: $250,000 (To establish Burton D. Morgan Foundation Endowed Scholarship Fund in Youth Ministry), $25,000 (For Youth Ministry Institute).

$250,000 to Denison University, Granville, OH. To establish Burton D. Morgan Entrepreneurial Internship and Venture Fund.

$200,000 to Lawrence School, Broadview Heights, OH. For capital campaign.

$102,000 to Purdue University, Burton D. Morgan Center for Entrepreneurship, West Lafayette, IN. To provide programming for Center.

$50,000 to Middlesex School, Concord, MA. For Class of 1942 Memorial Scholarship Fund.

$45,000 to Norman Rockwell Museum at Stockbridge, Stockbridge, MA. For strategic planning for capital campaign.

7762
The Margaret Clark Morgan Foundation ✧
1521 Georgetown Rd., Ste. 205
Hudson, OH 44236 (330) 655-1366
Contact: Rick Kellar, Interim Exec. Dir.
FAX: (330) 655-1696;
E-mail: rkellar@mcmorganfoundation.org;
URL: http://www.mcmorganfoundation.org

Established in 2001 in OH.

Donors: Margaret Clark Morgan; Burton D. Morgan†.

Foundation type: Independent foundation.

Financial data (yr. ended 12/31/05): Assets, $71,910,702 (M); gifts received, $3,000,000; expenditures, $2,966,281; qualifying distributions, $2,393,790; giving activities include $2,263,387 for 53 grants (high: $120,000; low: $500).

Purpose and activities: Giving primarily to assist the mentally ill in leading independent lives through meaningful work and life skills training, to provide mental health public education and awareness programs, develop housing and support facilities for persons with mental illness. Giving also to strengthen visual and performing arts organizations, and to encourage collaborative and innovative educational endeavors.

Fields of interest: Visual arts; Performing arts, theater; Education; Mental health/crisis services.

Type of support: General/operating support; Continuing support; Capital campaigns; Building/renovation; Equipment; Endowments; Program development; Scholarship funds.

Limitations: Giving primarily in northeastern OH. No grants to individuals, or for lobbying or legislative activities.

Publications: Application guidelines; Grants list; Informational brochure (including application guidelines).

Application information: Only 1 application per organization in a 12-month period. See foundation Web site for application guidelines and procedures. Application form required.

Initial approach: 1-page letter
Copies of proposal: 1
Deadline(s): Mar. 1, June 1., Sept. 1, and Dec. 1
Board meeting date(s): Feb., May, Aug., and Nov.
Final notification: 3 months

Officers and Trustees:* Suzanne Morgan,* Chair.; Mary Ann Winders,* Secy.; William H. Fellows,* Treas.; Rick Kellar, Interim Exec. Dir.; Richard A. Chenoweth; Penelope Frese; A. William McGraw.

Number of staff: 2 part-time professional; 1 part-time support.

EIN: 341948246

Selected grants: The following grants were reported in 2003.

$100,000 to Hopewell Inn, Mesopotamia, OH. For endowment.

$50,000 to Kevin Coleman Foundation, Ravenna, OH. For community room.

$30,000 to Planned Life Assistance Network of Northeast Ohio, Cleveland Heights, OH. For cognitive enhancement therapy.

$17,000 to University of Akron Foundation, Archives of the History of American Psychology, Akron, OH. For graduate assistant and website consultant.

$15,000 to Actors Summit, Hudson, OH. For operating support.

$10,000 to Berea College, Berea, KY. For annual fund.

$5,000 to Cuyahoga Valley Preservation and Scenic Railway Association, Peninsula, OH. For school field trips.

$5,000 to Kent State University Foundation, The Fashion School, Kent, OH. For scholarships.

$5,000 to Ohio Chamber Ballet, Akron, OH. For Hudson performances.

$1,500 to Mental Health Association of Summit County, Cuyahoga Falls, OH. For Hudson Mental Health Week.

7763
John C. and Sally S. Morley Family Foundation
c/o Richard T. Watson
925 Euclid Ave., Ste. 2000
Cleveland, OH 44115
Contact: Elizabeth A. Shaw, Admin. Asst.

Established in OH in 1998.

Donors: John C. Morley; Sally S. Morley.

Foundation type: Independent foundation.

Financial data (yr. ended 12/31/05): Assets, $384,413 (M); gifts received, $326,448; expenditures, $352,508; qualifying distributions, $352,422; giving activities include $340,000 for 7 grants (high: $80,000; low: $20,000).

Purpose and activities: Support primarily for the arts and education.

Fields of interest: Museums (art); Performing arts, music; Higher education; Education.

Type of support: General/operating support; Annual campaigns; Building/renovation; Endowments; Professorships; Scholarship funds; Matching/challenge support.

Limitations: Applications not accepted. Giving primarily in OH. No grants to individuals.

Application information: Contributes only to pre-selected organizations.

Trustee: Richard T. Watson.

EIN: 347065759

7764
Robert S. Morrison Foundation ✧ ☆
355 Prospect Rd., Ste. 110
P.O. Box 580
Ashtabula, OH 44005 (440) 992-7674
Contact: Louise Raffa, Exec. Dir.
FAX: (440) 992-5412; URL: http://www.robertsmorrisonfoundation.org

Established in OH.

Donor: Robert S. Morrison.

Foundation type: Independent foundation.

Financial data (yr. ended 12/31/05): Assets, $12,379,942 (M); expenditures, $571,184; qualifying distributions, $547,909; giving activities include $328,116 for 17 grants (high: $112,500; low: $1,000).

Purpose and activities: The mission of the foundation is to improve the lives of people in the Ashtabula, OH area.

Fields of interest: Education; Animal welfare; Human services; Community development.

Type of support: General/operating support.

Limitations: Giving limited to within 100 miles of Ashtabula, OH.

Application information: Application form available on foundation Web site. Application form required.

Initial approach: Submit application form
Deadline(s): None

Officer: Louise Raffa, Exec. Dir.

Trustees: Gary Coblitz; Stuart W. Cordell; John Palo; Richard Rowley.

EIN: 237246162

Selected grants: The following grants were reported in 2005.

$112,500 to Oberlin College, Oberlin, OH.

$49,800 to Ashtabula County Animal Protective League, Ashtabula, OH.

$30,000 to Ashtabula County Airport Authority, Ashtabula, OH.

$10,000 to Ashtabula Arts Center, Ashtabula, OH.

$8,040 to United Way of Ashtabula County, Ashtabula, OH.

$6,000 to Partnership for Education in Ashtabula County, Jefferson, OH.

$5,000 to Fund for Our Economic Future, Cleveland, OH.

7765
The Motorists Insurance Group Foundation ✧
471 E. Broad St.
Columbus, OH 43215-3861 (614) 255-3861
Contact: John J. Bishop, Tr.

Established in 2000 in OH.

Donor: Motorists Mutual Insurance Co.

Foundation type: Company-sponsored foundation.

Financial data (yr. ended 12/31/04): Assets, $104,454 (M); gifts received, $114,917; expenditures, $364,121; qualifying distributions, $359,634; giving activities include $359,722 for 39 grants (high: $200,000; low: $50).

Purpose and activities: The foundation supports organizations involved with arts and culture, higher education, health, and youth development.

Fields of interest: Arts; Higher education; Health care; Youth development; Federated giving programs.

Type of support: General/operating support; Annual campaigns; Building/renovation.

Limitations: Giving primarily in OH, with emphasis on Columbus. No grants to individuals.
Application information: Application form not required.
 Initial approach: Proposal
 Deadline(s): None
Trustees: John J. Bishop; Thomas C. Ogg; Michael L. Wiseman.
EIN: 311712343
Selected grants: The following grants were reported in 2004.
$200,000 to Ohio State University Foundation, Columbus, OH.
$100,000 to United Way of Central Ohio, Columbus, OH.
$10,568 to United Way.
$6,000 to Insurance Education Foundation, Indianapolis, IN.
$5,000 to Franklin University, Columbus, OH.
$5,000 to Griffith Foundation for Insurance Education, Columbus, OH.
$3,500 to Ohio Foundation of Independent Colleges, Columbus, OH.
$1,949 to United Way of Greater Cincinnati, Cincinnati, OH.
$1,820 to United Way of Central Indiana, Indianapolis, IN.
$1,752 to United Way of Allegheny County, Pittsburgh, PA.

7766
The Murch Foundation ◇
830 Hanna Bldg.
Cleveland, OH 44115

Incorporated in 1956 in OH.
Donor: Maynard H. Murch‡.
Foundation type: Independent foundation.
Financial data (yr. ended 12/31/05): Assets, $17,905,121 (M); expenditures, $863,704; qualifying distributions, $838,500; giving activities include $838,500 for 77 grants (high: $212,500; low: $2,000; average: $5,000–$10,000).
Fields of interest: Museums (natural history); Arts; Higher education; Education; Health organizations, association; Human services.
Type of support: General/operating support; Annual campaigns; Capital campaigns; Building/renovation; Endowments; Scholarship funds.
Limitations: Applications not accepted. Giving primarily in OH. No grants to individuals.
Application information: Contributes only to pre-selected organizations.
 Board meeting date(s): Sept.-Dec.
Officers: Creighton B. Murch, V.P.; Robert B. Murch, V.P.
Trustee: Maynard H. Murch V.
Number of staff: 1 part-time support.
EIN: 346520188
Selected grants: The following grants were reported in 2004.
$160,000 to Cleveland Museum of Natural History, Cleveland, OH.
$19,000 to Arthritis Foundation, Atlanta, GA.
$17,000 to Cleveland Institute of Art, Cleveland, OH.
$15,000 to American Red Cross.
$13,000 to American Cancer Society, Atlanta, GA.
$13,000 to Kiskiminetas Springs School, Saltsburg, PA.
$12,000 to Western Reserve Historical Society, Cleveland, OH.
$9,000 to Playhouse Square Center, Cleveland, OH.

$6,000 to John Carroll University, University Heights, OH.
$5,000 to YMCA.

7767
The Murdough Foundation ◇
(formerly Thomas G. & Joy P. Murdough Foundation)
P.O. Box 2134
Hudson, OH 44236-0134
Contact: William M. Oldham, Exec. Dir.

Established in 1986 in OH.
Donor: Thomas G. Murdough, Jr.
Foundation type: Independent foundation.
Financial data (yr. ended 12/31/05): Assets, $7,934,180 (M); expenditures, $1,221,345; qualifying distributions, $1,152,380; giving activities include $1,149,500 for 14 grants (high: $1,000,000; low: $500).
Purpose and activities: Support for organizations whose core values include belief in God, family, and community and country.
Fields of interest: Religion.
Type of support: General/operating support; Annual campaigns; Building/renovation.
Limitations: Giving primarily in OH, with emphasis on northeastern OH. No grants to individuals.
Application information: Due to major gift commitments, the foundation is currently only accepting grant requests from organizations that it has supported in prior years. Application form not required.
 Initial approach: Letter
 Copies of proposal: 1
 Deadline(s): None
 Board meeting date(s): May and Nov.
Officers and Trustees:* Thomas G. Murdough, Jr.,* Pres. and Treas.; Joy P. Murdough,* Secy.; William M. Oldham, Exec. Dir.; Jody P. Murdough; Marshall C. Murdough; Peter R. Murdough; Thomas G. Murdough, III.
Number of staff: 1 part-time professional.
EIN: 341454379
Selected grants: The following grants were reported in 2005.
$1,000,000 to Western Reserve Academy, Hudson, OH.
$50,000 to Marine Corps Heritage Foundation, Quantico, VA.
$5,000 to Musical Arts Association, Cleveland, OH.
$1,000 to Rhode Island School of Design, Providence, RI.
$500 to Hudson Community Chorus, Hudson, OH.

7768
The Murphy Family Foundation
25800 Science Park Dr., Ste. 200
P.O. Box 22747
Beachwood, OH 44122 (216) 831-7320
Contact: Rita M. Carfagna, Pres.
FAX: (216) 831-2296; *E-mail:* mff@apk.net;
URL: http://www.fsrequests.com/murphyfamily

Established in 1986 in OH.
Donor: Members of the Murphy family.
Foundation type: Independent foundation.
Financial data (yr. ended 12/31/05): Assets, $3,721,141 (M); gifts received, $221,416; expenditures, $560,844; qualifying distributions, $516,650; giving activities include $516,650 for 77 grants (high: $50,000; low: $500).

Purpose and activities: The foundation considers its primary mission to be the support of viable programs addressing the problems of poverty in the greater Cleveland, OH, area. Grantmaking is primarily to those organizations providing food for the hungry, shelter for the homeless and educational opportunities for the disadvantaged.
Fields of interest: Education; Food services; Housing/shelter, development; Human services; Children/youth, services; Homeless, human services; Economically disadvantaged; Homeless.
Type of support: General/operating support; Continuing support; Annual campaigns; Capital campaigns; Building/renovation; Equipment; Endowments; Emergency funds; Program development; Scholarship funds; Matching/challenge support.
Limitations: Giving primarily in the greater Cleveland, OH, area. Generally no support for health or disability-related programs, or the arts. No grants to individuals.
Publications: Application guidelines; Financial statement; Informational brochure (including application guidelines).
Application information: Application information and application form available on foundation Web site. Application form not required.
 Copies of proposal: 1
 Deadline(s): Jan. 15, Apr. 15, Aug. 15, and Nov. 15
 Board meeting date(s): Feb., May, Sept., and Dec.
 Final notification: Feb. 28, May 31, Sept. 30, and Dec. 31
Officers and Trustees:* Rita Murphy Carfagna,* Pres.; Paul J. Murphy,* V.P. and Secy.-Treas.; Brian F. Murphy; Margaret S. Murphy; Murlan J. Murphy, Sr.; Murlan J. Murphy, Jr.; Raymond M. Murphy.
EIN: 341526161
Selected grants: The following grants were reported in 2005.
$55,000 to Catholic Relief Services, Baltimore, MD.
$50,000 to CARE, Atlanta, GA.
$50,000 to Cleveland Central Catholic High School, Cleveland, OH.
$26,000 to Salvation Army, Cambridge, OH.
$10,000 to New Life Community, Cleveland, OH.
$10,000 to Saint Martin de Porres High School, Cleveland, OH.
$10,000 to Saint Vincent de Paul Society, Cleveland, OH.
$10,000 to Volunteers of America, Cincinnati, OH.
$7,500 to Gilmour Academy, Gates Mills, OH.
$5,000 to Ruffing Montessori Rocky River, Rocky River, OH.

7769
John P. Murphy Foundation
Terminal Twr.
50 Public Sq., Ste. 924
Cleveland, OH 44113-2203 (216) 623-4770
Contact: Allan J. Zambie, Exec. V.P. and Secy.
FAX: (216) 623-4773;
E-mail: azambie@murphykulas.org; *Additional tel.:*
(216) 623-4771; *URL:* http://foundationcenter.org/grantmaker/jpmurphy/

Incorporated in 1960 in OH.
Donor: John P. Murphy‡.
Foundation type: Independent foundation.
Financial data (yr. ended 12/31/05): Assets, $54,789,723 (M); expenditures, $3,847,812; qualifying distributions, $3,476,576; giving

activities include $3,053,076 for 160 grants (high: $1,500,000; low: $1,000).

Purpose and activities: Giving primarily for higher education, civic affairs, the performing arts, community development and health; support also for social services and youth. The foundation's board identified the subject of economic development in Northeastern Ohio as a special interest.

Fields of interest: Visual arts; Museums; Performing arts; Performing arts, dance; Performing arts, theater; History/archaeology; Historic preservation/historical societies; Arts; Vocational education; Higher education; Libraries/library science; Education; Hospitals (general); Medical care, rehabilitation; Nursing care; Health care; Health organizations, association; Alcoholism; Youth development, services; Human services; Children/youth, services; Women, centers/services; Urban/community development; Community development; Federated giving programs; Economics; Government/public administration; Leadership development; Public affairs; Disabilities, people with; Women.

Type of support: General/operating support; Continuing support; Annual campaigns; Capital campaigns; Building/renovation; Equipment; Program development; Publication; Curriculum development; Research; Consulting services; Program-related investments/loans; Exchange programs; Matching/challenge support.

Limitations: Giving primarily in Cuyahoga County, OH, and the surrounding counties. No support for K-12 education or mental health. No grants to individuals, scholarships, or for endowment funds; no loans (except for program-related investments).

Publications: Application guidelines; Financial statement; Informational brochure.

Application information: Application should not include notebooks, binders, or plastic folders. Application can be submitted in person, by mail or messenger. Application form required.

Initial approach: Letter or telephone
Copies of proposal: 6
Deadline(s): 6 weeks before meeting
Board meeting date(s): 4 times a year
Final notification: Within 2 weeks of meeting

Officers and Trustees:* Nancy W. McCann,* Pres. and Treas.; Allan J. Zambie,* Exec. V.P. and Secy.; Robert R. Broadbent,* V.P.; R. Bruce Campbell,* V.P.; Marie S. Strawbridge,* V.P.

Number of staff: 1 full-time professional; 2 full-time support.

EIN: 346528308

Selected grants: The following grants were reported in 2004.

$200,000 to Cleveland Museum of Art, Cleveland, OH. 2 grants: $100,000 each

$100,000 to BioEnterprise Corporation, Cleveland, OH. 2 grants: $50,000 each

$100,000 to Cleveland Clinic Foundation, Cleveland, OH.

$30,000 to Cleveland Institute of Music, Cleveland, OH.

$10,000 to Cleveland Institute of Art, Cleveland, OH.

$10,000 to Cleveland Signstage Theater, Cleveland, OH.

$10,000 to Shaker Square Area Development Corporation, Cleveland, OH.

$7,500 to Planned Parenthood of Greater Cleveland, Cleveland, OH.

7770

Muskingum County Community Foundation

534 Putnam Ave.
Zanesville, OH   43701   (740) 453-5192
Contact: David P. Mitzel, Exec. Dir.; For scholarships: Heather Sands, Prog. Coord.
FAX: (740) 453-5734; E-mail: giving@mccf.org;
URL: http://www.mccf.org
Scholarship Central tel.: (740) 453-5192

Established in 1985 in OH.
Foundation type: Community foundation.
Financial data (yr. ended 12/31/05): Assets, $16,362,002 (M); gifts received, $1,702,148; expenditures, $972,957; giving activities include $331,912 for 283 grants (high: $27,225; low: $16), $39,815 for 76 grants to individuals (high: $1,000; low: $100), and $139,220 for foundation-administered programs.

Purpose and activities: The foundation seeks to support worthwhile organizations and programs that enhance the quality of life in Muskingum County, OH.

Fields of interest: Performing arts; Performing arts, music; Arts; Elementary/secondary education; Libraries/library science; Education; Animal welfare; Animals/wildlife, preservation/protection; Hospitals (general); Health care; Recreation; Youth development, services; Children/youth, services; Residential/custodial care, hospices; Community development; Leadership development; Aging.

Type of support: In-kind gifts; Program-related investments/loans; Consulting services; Technical assistance; Research; Internship funds; General/operating support; Capital campaigns; Building/renovation; Equipment; Land acquisition; Endowments; Program development; Conferences/seminars; Publication; Seed money; Fellowships; Scholarship funds; Scholarships—to individuals; Matching/challenge support.

Limitations: Giving limited to Muskingum County, OH.

Publications: Application guidelines; Annual report; Grants list; Informational brochure.

Application information: Visit foundation Web site for online application and guidelines. Application form required.

Initial approach: Complete online application and submit attachments
Deadline(s): Mar. 1 and Nov. 1 (for proposals); scholarship application deadlines vary, telephone Scholarship Central for information
Board meeting date(s): 4th Wed. of Jan., Apr., July, and Oct.

Officers and Trustees: M. Dean Young,* Pres.; Thomas M. Lyall,* V.P.; Jack Russett,* Secy.; Tim McLain,* Treas.; David P. Mitzel, Exec. Dir.; Jeff Beam; Mary V. "Vicci" Biles; Michael Bullock; Steve Carter; Andrea Walters Dowding; Richard Duncan; Robert F. Glass, Jr.; Thomas Holdren; D. Scott Moyer; J. Scott Peterson; Carl Raines; Steven G. Randles; Thomas Selock; Michael Steen; Dan Sylvester; Kristy Szemetylo; Beth Upton; Brian Wagner.

Number of staff: 2 full-time professional; 1 full-time support; 1 part-time support.

EIN: 311147022

7771

Nationwide Foundation ▼ ✧

(formerly Nationwide Insurance Enterprise Foundation)

1 Nationwide Plz., 1-22-05
Columbus, OH   43215-2220   (614) 249-4310
Additional tel.: (614) 249-0039; URL: http://www.nationwide.com/nw/about-us/community-involvement/investing-in-people/index.htm?WT.svl=3#Nationwide%20Foundation

Incorporated in 1959 in OH.
Donors: Nationwide Mutual Insurance Co.; Nationwide Corp.; Nationwide Life Insurance Co. of America.
Foundation type: Company-sponsored foundation.
Financial data (yr. ended 12/31/05): Assets, $60,770,247 (M); gifts received, $24,004,452; expenditures, $15,138,057; qualifying distributions, $14,970,050; giving activities include $13,770,449 for 636 grants (high: $6,913,298; low: $100), and $1,093,008 for 2,052 employee matching gifts.

Purpose and activities: The foundation supports organizations involved with arts and culture, higher education, the environment, health, human services, community development, government and public administration, senior citizens, disabled people, and economically disadvantaged people.

Fields of interest: Arts; Higher education; Business school/education; Environment; Health care; Human services; Community development, business promotion; Community development; Government/public administration; Aging; Disabilities, people with; Economically disadvantaged.

Type of support: General/operating support; Continuing support; Annual campaigns; Capital campaigns; Emergency funds; Program development; Seed money; Employee volunteer services; Employee matching gifts; Matching/challenge support.

Limitations: Giving primarily in areas of company operations, with emphasis on OH, including Columbus. No support for athletic teams, public or private primary or secondary schools, pass-through organizations (except the United Way), veterans', labor, religious, or fraternal organizations not of direct benefit to the entire community, or lobbying or political organizations; generally, no support for hospitals or hospital foundations or national organizations (except local branches or chapters). No grants to individuals, or for fundraising events, sponsorships, athletic events, debt reduction, research, travel, endowments, or bands or choirs.

Publications: Informational brochure (including application guidelines).

Application information: Proposals should be no longer than 3 pages. Videos, photo albums, and binders are not encouraged. Application form required.

Initial approach: Download application form and mail proposal and application form to foundation
Deadline(s): Sept. 1; Aug. 17 for Cooperative Leadership Awards
Board meeting date(s): Feb., May, and Nov.
Final notification: Mar. 31; Dec. 31 for Cooperative Leadership Awards

Officers and Trustees:* W.G. Jurgensen,* Chair. and C.E.O.; Chad A. Jester, Pres.; Robert A. Rosholt, Exec. V.P. and C.F.O.; Thomas E. Barnes, V.P. and Secy.; Alan A. Todryk, V.P., Taxation; Glenn W. Soden, V.P.; Carol L. Dove, Assoc. V.P. and Treas.;

James B. Bachman; Keith W. Eckel; Fred C. Finney; Lydia M. Marshall; David O. Miller; James F. Patterson; Arden L. Shisler.
Number of staff: 1 part-time professional; 1 full-time support.
EIN: 316022301
Selected grants: The following grants were reported in 2005.
$6,913,298 to United Way of America, Alexandria, VA.
$833,333 to Ohio State University Foundation, Columbus, OH.
$500,000 to American Red Cross, National Headquarters, DC.
$500,000 to COSI Columbus, Columbus, OH.
$150,000 to Ohio Foundation of Independent Colleges, Columbus, OH.
$125,000 to Columbus Symphony Orchestra, Columbus, OH.
$85,000 to Cooperative Development Foundation, DC.
$25,000 to Communities in Schools of Columbus, Columbus, OH.
$25,000 to Contemporary American Theater Company, Columbus, OH.
$15,000 to Council for Retarded Citizens of Franklin County, Columbus, OH.

7772
NCC Charitable Foundation ▼ ✧
(formerly NCC Charitable Foundation II)
c/o National City Bank
1900 E. 9th St., LOC 2157
Cleveland, OH 44114 (216) 222-2994
Contact: Joanne Clark, V.P.
E-mail: joanne.clark@nationalcity.com; Additional E-mail: bruce.mccrodden@nationalcity.com;
URL: http://www.nationalcity.com/about/commurelations/default.asp

Established in 1993.
Donors: National City Bank of Kentucky; National City Corp.
Foundation type: Company-sponsored foundation.
Financial data (yr. ended 6/30/05): Assets, $64,643,246 (M); expenditures, $22,748,790; qualifying distributions, $22,728,915; giving activities include $22,728,115 for 2,817 grants (high: $440,000).
Purpose and activities: The foundation supports organizations involved with arts and culture, education, health, human services, and community development.
Fields of interest: Arts; Education; Health care; Human services; Community development; Federated giving programs.
Type of support: Continuing support; Annual campaigns; Capital campaigns; Program development; Employee matching gifts.
Limitations: Giving primarily in IL, IN, KY, MI, OH, and PA, with emphasis on OH. No grants to individuals.
Publications: Corporate giving report.
Application information: Application form not required.
Initial approach: Proposal
Deadline(s): None
Board meeting date(s): Quarterly
Officers: Joanne Clark, V.P.; David A. Daberko, Off.; Bruce McCrodden, Off.; William E. McDonald, Off.
Trustee: National City Bank.
EIN: 347050989

Selected grants: The following grants were reported in 2005.
$440,000 to Western Michigan University, Kalamazoo, MI. For general support.
$392,700 to United Way, Greater Kalamazoo, Kalamazoo, MI. For general support.
$366,648 to American Red Cross, Greater Cleveland Chapter, Cleveland, OH. For general support.
$250,000 to Cleveland Museum of Art, Cleveland, OH. For general support.
$150,000 to Southwest Michigan First Corporation, Kalamazoo, MI. For general support.
$142,857 to Cleveland Clinic Foundation, Cleveland, OH. For general support.
$26,045 to United Way of the Lakeshore, Muskegon, MI. For general support.
$20,000 to Columbus Partnership, Columbus, OH. For general support.
$20,000 to Southern Illinois University, School of Medicine, Carbondale, IL. For general support.
$20,000 to Taft Museum, Cincinnati, OH. For general support.

7773
The NCR Foundation
(formerly AT&T Global Information Solutions Foundation)
1700 S. Patterson Blvd.
Dayton, OH 45479
Contact: Janet J. Brewer, V.P.

Incorporated in 1953 in OH.
Donor: NCR Corp.
Foundation type: Company-sponsored foundation.
Financial data (yr. ended 12/31/04): Assets, $2,348,026 (M); gifts received, $1,000,000; expenditures, $1,085,379; qualifying distributions, $1,075,791; giving activities include $873,334 for 7 grants (high: $300,000; low: $5,000), and $202,457 for 882 employee matching gifts.
Purpose and activities: The foundation supports organizations involved with arts and culture, education, human services, and community development.
Fields of interest: Arts; Higher education; Education; Human services; Community development; Federated giving programs.
Type of support: General/operating support; Employee matching gifts.
Limitations: Giving primarily in areas of company operations, with emphasis on San Diego, CA, Atlanta, GA, and Dayton, OH. No support for religious or political organizations. No grants to individuals; no loans.
Application information: Application form not required.
Initial approach: Proposal
Copies of proposal: 1
Deadline(s): Jan. 15 and July 15
Board meeting date(s): July and Dec.
Final notification: 3 to 4 months
Officers and Trustees:* Janet J. Brewer,* V.P.; Laura K. Nyquist,* Secy.; Bo Sawyer,* Treas.; Pete Bocian; Alan Chow; Christine Wallace.
Number of staff: 1 part-time professional; 1 part-time support.
EIN: 316030860
Selected grants: The following grants were reported in 2004.
$300,000 to United Way of America, Alexandria, VA. For general support.

$202,000 to American Red Cross, Dayton, OH. For tsunami efforts.
$200,000 to Dayton Art Institute, Dayton, OH. For traveling Egyptian exhibit sponsorship.
$25,000 to Carillon Historical Park, Dayton, OH. For historical support.
$13,000 to K12 Gallery, Dayton, OH. For traveling exhibit.

7774
The Needmor Fund
42 S. St. Clair St.
Toledo, OH 43604 (419) 255-5560
Contact: Mary Sobecki, Grants Mgr.
FAX: (419) 255-5561;
E-mail: moreinfo@needmorfund.org; URL: http://foundationcenter.org/grantmaker/needmor/

Trust established in 1956 in OH.
Donor: Members of the Stranahan family.
Foundation type: Independent foundation.
Financial data (yr. ended 12/31/05): Assets, $27,432,457 (M); expenditures, $2,555,623; qualifying distributions, $2,221,226.
Purpose and activities: The mission of The Needmor Fund is to work with others to bring about social justice. We support groups that work together to change the social, economic, or political conditions that bar access to participation in a democratic society. Needmor has identified grassroots community organizing as the most effective process by which low- and moderate-income people can build power, address the systemic barriers to the practice of democracy, hold public and corporate officials accountable for their actions, and begin to participate in shaping public policy. Our grantmaking is focused exclusively on providing support for multi-issue, democratically controlled, membership-based community organizations.
Fields of interest: Community development, citizen coalitions.
Type of support: General/operating support.
Limitations: Giving limited to the U.S. No support for public or private schools. No grants to individuals, or for capital or endowment funds, scholarships, fellowships, matching gifts, deficit financing, operating support for traditional community services, replacement of lost government funding, land acquisition, purchase of buildings or equipment, or publications, media, computer projects or research; no loans.
Publications: Application guidelines; Biennial report (including application guidelines); Grants list.
Application information: Accepts NNG Common Application Form; Do not use staples to hold proposals together; paper/binder clips are acceptable. Application form required.
Initial approach: Letter or telephone. Faxes or electronic submissions are not accepted
Copies of proposal: 4
Deadline(s): Jan. 10, 2006 for applicants in AL, AZ, LA, MS, NM, southern CA and southern TX; May 1- June 30, 2006 for the rest of the United States
Board meeting date(s): May and Nov.
Final notification: 2 weeks after board meeting
Officers and Directors:* Mary C. Stranahan,* Chair.; Dave Beckwith, Exec. Dir.; Scott Douglas; Ken Rolling; Abbot Stranahan; Daniel Stranahan; George S. Stranahan; Molly Stranahan; Sarah S. Stranahan; Steve Viederman.

Number of staff: 3 full-time professional; 1 full-time support.
EIN: 346504812
Selected grants: The following grants were reported in 2004.
$100,000 to Northern Louisiana Interfaith Sponsoring Committee, Monroe, LA. For collaboration with Pacific Institute for Community Organization.
$80,000 to American Institute for Social Justice, New Orleans, LA. 3 grants: $30,000 (For ACORN program in Florida), $30,000, $20,000 (For ACORN program in San Jose).
$40,000 to American Institute for Social Justice, Jersey City, NJ.
$30,000 to Front Range Economic Strategy Center, Denver, CO.
$30,000 to San Diego Organizing Project, San Diego, CA.
$30,000 to Virginia Organizing Project, Charlottesville, VA.
$25,000 to La Union del Pueblo Entero (LUPE), Sacramento, CA.
$25,000 to Logan Square Neighborhood Association, Chicago, IL.
$25,000 to Wisconsin Citizen Action, Milwaukee, WI.

7775
New Albany Community Foundation ◇
220 Market St., Ste. 205
New Albany, OH 43054 (614) 939-8150
Contact: J. Craig Mohre, Pres.
FAX: (614) 939-8025;
E-mail: craigmohre@newalbanyfoundation.org;
URL: http://www.newalbanyfoundation.org

Established in OH.
Foundation type: Community foundation.
Financial data (yr. ended 6/30/05): Assets, $3,765,482 (M); gifts received, $2,453,474; expenditures, $685,757; giving activities include $427,383 for 16 grants (high: $152,000; low: $50).
Purpose and activities: The foundation's mission is to assist donors and others in strengthening and improving New Albany, OH, for the benefit of all of its residents. The scope of the foundation's charitable grantmaking includes both capital and program grants. Typically, grants are awarded under the following categories: Arts, Culture, & Humanities, Civic/Community Development, Conservation & Environment, Education, Health & Wellness, and Human Services.
Fields of interest: Humanities; Arts; Education; Environment; Health care; Human services; Community development.
Limitations: Giving limited to New Albany, OH. No support for religious organizations or religious purposes. No grants to individuals (except for scholarships), or for operating expenses, deficit financing for programs or capital expenditures, endowment funds, annual appeals, membership contributions, conferences, or recognition events.
Application information: Visit foundation Web site for application form and guidelines. Application form required.
Initial approach: Contact foundation
Officers and Trustees:* David J. Ryan,* Chair.; Barbara J. Siemer,* Vice-Chair.; J. Craig Mohre,* Pres. and Exec. Dir.; Marci Ingram,* Secy.; James Gilmour,* Treas.; Michael DeAscentis, Jr.; William G. Ebbing; Carl V. English; Cindy Hilsheimer; Jonathan Kass; Michael W. Kramer; Tiney McComb;

Cherie Nelson; Rich Ramsey; Yaromir Steiner; Ron Sykes.
EIN: 311409264

7776
NFG Foundation ◇ ☆
c/o Mark Senff
65 E. State St., Ste. 2100
Columbus, OH 43215-4213
Contact: Chris Fidler, Baker & Hostetler LLP

Established around 1993.
Donors: Mildred George; Noel George Trust.
Foundation type: Independent foundation.
Financial data (yr. ended 12/31/05): Assets, $1,925,968 (M); gifts received, $65,685; expenditures, $481,935; qualifying distributions, $478,025; giving activities include $478,025 for 9 grants (high: $255,250; low: $25).
Purpose and activities: Giving primarily for higher education.
Fields of interest: Higher education, university; Health care; Eye research; Human services; Science.
Limitations: Giving primarily in Oklahoma City, OK.
Application information: Application form not required.
Initial approach: Letter
Deadline(s): None
Officers: James N. George, Pres.; Rebecca Morgan, Secy.-Treas.
Trustee: Christopher D. Fidler.
EIN: 311387062
Selected grants: The following grants were reported in 2004.
$185,625 to University of Oklahoma, Oklahoma City, OK. 2 grants: $180,375, $5,250 to Dean McGee Eye Institute
$16,000 to Gorgas Science Foundation, Brownsville, TX.
$1,000 to Paramount Baptist Church, Amarillo, TX.
$1,000 to United Way of Central Oklahoma, Oklahoma City, OK.
$500 to Nichols Hills Parks, Nichols Hills, OK.
$100 to Cornell University, Lab of Ornithology, Ithaca, NY.
$75 to National Cowboy and Western Heritage Museum, Oklahoma City, OK.
$25 to Oklahoma County Historical Society, Oklahoma City, OK.

7777
L. and L. Nippert Charitable Foundation, Inc. ◇
c/o The Randolph Co.
8255 Spooky Hollow Rd.
Cincinnati, OH 45242-6518 (513) 891-7144
Contact: Carter Randolph, V.P.
E-mail: crandolph@green-acres.org

Established in 1992 in OH as successor to L. and L. Nippert Charitable Foundation.
Donors: Louis Nippert†; Louise D. Nippert; Louise Dieterle Nippert Trust.
Foundation type: Independent foundation.
Financial data (yr. ended 12/31/05): Assets, $14,372,947 (M); expenditures, $741,423; qualifying distributions, $635,000; giving activities include $635,000 for 4 grants (high: $400,000; low: $30,000).

Purpose and activities: Support for the arts, music (especially vocal, symphonic, and chamber music), historic preservation, conservation, environmental education, and parks; funding also for visiting nurse services.
Fields of interest: Performing arts, music; Historic preservation/historical societies; Arts; Environment, natural resources; Environment; Health care, home services; Health care; Medical research, institute; Human services; Religion.
Type of support: General/operating support; Continuing support; Annual campaigns; Capital campaigns; Building/renovation; Program development; Curriculum development; Internship funds; Scholarship funds; Research.
Limitations: Giving primarily in Hamilton County, OH. No grants to individuals.
Application information: Application form not required.
Initial approach: Letter requesting guidelines
Copies of proposal: 2
Deadline(s): Sept. 15
Board meeting date(s): Annual
Final notification: Jan. of the following year
Officers and Directors:* Louise D. Nippert,* Pres.; Carter Randolph,* V.P. and Treas.; Lawrence Kyte, Secy.
EIN: 311351011

7778
Donald and Alice Noble Foundation, Inc. ◇
(formerly Donald E. and Alice M. Noble Charitable Foundation, Inc.)
2345 Gateway Dr.
Wooster, OH 44691
Contact: David D. Noble, Pres.

Established in 1990 in OH.
Donors: Donald E. Noble†; Alice M. Noble.
Foundation type: Independent foundation.
Financial data (yr. ended 12/31/04): Assets, $17,793,868 (M); gifts received, $98,000; expenditures, $2,074,620; qualifying distributions, $1,262,424; giving activities include $983,942 for 63 grants (high: $182,500; low: $100).
Purpose and activities: Giving for education and human services.
Fields of interest: Education, public education; Secondary school/education; Human services; Foundations (community).
Type of support: General/operating support; Capital campaigns; Program development.
Limitations: Applications not accepted. Giving primarily in Wooster, OH. No grants to individuals.
Application information: Contributes only to pre-selected organizations.
Officers: David D. Noble, Pres. and Treas.; Carroll Meyer, V.P.; Ron Holtman, Secy.
Trustees: Nancy L. Holland; Donald Noble II; Matthew Noble; Chris Schmid.
Number of staff: 1 full-time professional; 1 full-time support.
EIN: 341665641

7779
The Nord Family Foundation
747 Milan Ave.
Amherst, OH 44001 (440) 984-3939
Contact: John Mullaney, Exec. Dir.
FAX: (440) 984-3934; E-mail: johnm@nordft.org;
Additional tel.: (800) 745-8946; FAX: (440)

984-3934; E-mail: info@nordff.org or execdir@nordff.org; URL: http://www.nordff.org

Trust established in 1952 in OH; reorganized in 1988 under current name.
Donors: Walter G. Nord†; Mrs. Walter G. Nord†; Nordson Corp.
Foundation type: Independent foundation.
Financial data (yr. ended 12/31/05): Assets, $85,506,619 (M); gifts received, $60,000; expenditures, $4,920,578; qualifying distributions, $4,313,483; giving activities include $3,632,496 for 338 grants (high: $100,000; low: $25; average: $1,000–$25,000), and $190,970 for 1 foundation-administered program.
Purpose and activities: Emphasis on projects to assist the disadvantaged and minorities, including giving for early childhood, secondary, and higher education, social services, health, cultural affairs, and civic activities. Initiatives included a project to establish a common agenda to address factors which inhibit social and economic progress within the county and a program to strengthen nonprofit organizations which address family issues.
Fields of interest: Arts; Education, early childhood education; Child development, education; Secondary school/education; Higher education; Education; Environment; Health care; Health organizations, association; Human services; Children/youth, services; Child development, services; Minorities/immigrants, centers/services; Urban/community development; Minorities; Economically disadvantaged.
Type of support: Capital campaigns; General/operating support; Continuing support; Building/renovation; Program development; Conferences/seminars; Publication; Seed money; Technical assistance; Program-related investments/loans; Employee matching gifts; Matching/challenge support.
Limitations: Giving primarily in the Lorain and Cuyahoga County, OH, areas; also gives secondarily in Denver, CO, Boston, MA, and Columbia, SC. No support for religious or political organizations. No grants for deficit financing, research, capital campaigns, tickets, or advertising for fundraising activities.
Publications: Application guidelines; Annual report (including application guidelines); Grants list; Informational brochure (including application guidelines); Occasional report.
Application information: Only accept proposals online. Application form required.
   Initial approach: Online grant application
   Copies of proposal: 1
   Deadline(s): Apr. 1, Aug. 1, and Dec. 1
   Board meeting date(s): Feb., June, and Oct.
   Final notification: 1 to 3 months
Officers and Trustees:* Emily McClintock, Pres.; Virginia Barbato, V.P.; Cindy Nord, Secy.; Ray Cushing,* Treas.; Sharon White, Cont.; John J. Mullaney, Exec. Dir.; Sam Berk; Camille Hamlin-Allen; Eleanor Ignat; Erin Ignat; Pam Ignat; Katie Nord Peterson; Ethan Nord; Luis Villarreal.
Number of staff: 3 full-time professional; 1 part-time professional; 1 full-time support; 1 part-time support.
EIN: 341595929
Selected grants: The following grants were reported in 2004.
$100,000 to Allen Medical Center Foundation, Oberlin, OH.
$100,000 to Girl Scouts of the U.S.A..

$63,200 to Oberlin Early Childhood Center, Oberlin, OH.
$50,000 to Community Foundation of Greater Lorain County, Lorain, OH.
$50,000 to Firelands Association for the Visual Arts, Oberlin, OH.
$50,000 to Local Initiatives Support Corporation (LISC), New York, NY.
$35,000 to Oberlin Community Services Council, Oberlin, OH.
$20,000 to Community Health Partners Foundation, Lorain, OH.
$10,000 to Massachusetts Coalition for the Homeless, Boston, MA.
$5,000 to National Inventors Hall of Fame, Akron, OH.

7780
The Eric and Jane Nord Foundation
P.O. Box 457
Oberlin, OH 44074 (440) 774-3812
Contact: Eric T. Nord, Pres.
FAX: (440) 774-8607; E-mail: enord@oberlin.net

Established in 1984 in OH.
Donors: Eric T. Nord; Jane B. Nord.
Foundation type: Independent foundation.
Financial data (yr. ended 6/30/05): Assets, $12,317,234 (M); gifts received, $260,000; expenditures, $551,710; qualifying distributions, $547,001; giving activities include $541,999 for 53 grants (high: $150,000; low: $250).
Purpose and activities: Giving primarily for the arts, particularly an inter-museum association; funding also for education, and human services.
Fields of interest: Arts, association; Museums; Performing arts, opera; Arts; Education, information services; Higher education; Botanical gardens; Health care, clinics/centers; Human services; Community development; Federated giving programs.
Type of support: General/operating support.
Limitations: Giving primarily in north central OH. No support for religious organizations. No grants to individuals.
Publications: Annual report (including application guidelines).
Application information: Application form not required.
   Initial approach: Letter
Officers: Eric T. Nord, Pres. and Treas.; Jane B. Nord, V.P.; William D. Ginn, Secy.
EIN: 341465569
Selected grants: The following grants were reported in 2005.
$98,799 to Urban League, Lorain County, Elyria, OH.
$50,000 to Central Carolina Community Foundation, Columbia, SC.
$26,000 to Oberlin Early Childhood Center, Oberlin, OH.
$25,000 to Our Lady of the Wayside, Avon, OH.
$20,000 to Cleveland Opera, Cleveland, OH.
$10,000 to Buckingham Browne and Nichols School, Cambridge, MA.
$10,000 to Cleveland Museum of Art, Cleveland, OH.
$8,000 to United Way of Greater Lorain County, Lorain, OH.
$5,000 to Firelands Association for the Visual Arts, Oberlin, OH.
$4,000 to Amherst Schools Educational Foundation, Amherst, OH.

7781
The Nordson Corporation Foundation
28601 Clemens Rd.
Westlake, OH 44145-1119 (440) 892-1580, ext. 5172
Contact: Cecilia H. Render, Mgr.
E-mail: crender@nordson.com; Additional application addresses: Talladega, AL, and GA: Assoc. Prog. Off., Nordson Corp., 11475 Lakefield Dr., Duluth, GA 30097, tel.: (770) 497-3672, San Diego County, CA: Ray McHenry, Mgr., Human Resource, Asymtek, 2762 Loker Ave. W., Carlsbad, CA 92008-6603, tel.: (760) 930-7258, E-mail: rmchenry@asymtek.com, southeastern MA and RI: Janet Moy, Dir., Human Resources, EFD, Inc., 977 Waterman Ave., East Providence, RI 02914-1378, tel.: (401) 434-1680, E-mail: jmoy@efd-inc.com; URL: http://www.nordson.com/Corporate/Community/Foundation

Established in 1988 in OH as successor to the Nordson Foundation, established in 1952.
Donor: Nordson Corp.
Foundation type: Company-sponsored foundation.
Financial data (yr. ended 10/31/04): Assets, $1,372,709 (M); gifts received, $1,236,700; expenditures, $739,429; qualifying distributions, $727,305; giving activities include $727,305 for 110 grants (high: $75,000; low: $1,000).
Purpose and activities: The foundation has changed its strategic focus to education. Organizations and programs that assist individuals to become self-sufficient members of society are our main focus.
Fields of interest: Performing arts; Performing arts, education; Education, public education; Education, formal/general education; Elementary/secondary education; Education, early childhood education; Elementary school/education; Higher education; Scholarships/financial aid; Employment, formal/general education; Employment, job counseling; Housing/shelter, homeless; Housing/shelter; Youth development, centers/clubs; Neighborhood centers; Children/youth, services; Family services; Family services, parent education; Homeless, human services; Human services; Nonprofit management; Science, formal/general education; Science; Leadership development; Economically disadvantaged; Homeless.
Type of support: General/operating support; Continuing support; Annual campaigns; Capital campaigns; Building/renovation; Equipment; Emergency funds; Seed money; Scholarship funds; Technical assistance.
Limitations: Giving primarily in Talladega, AL, San Diego County, CA, GA, with emphasis on greater Atlanta, Dawsonville, and Swainsboro, southeastern MA, Cuyahoga and Lorain counties, OH, and RI, with emphasis on East Providence. No support for political organizations or candidates or discriminatory organizations. No grants to individuals, or for political causes or campaigns; generally, no grants for fundraising.
Publications: Application guidelines; Annual report; Grants list.
Application information: Organizations receiving support are asked to provide a final report. Human welfare, civic, and arts and culture applications will be reviewed for their alignment with the foundation's strategic focus on education. Application form required.
   Initial approach: Download application form and mail to foundation for organizations located in Cuyahoga and Lorain counties, OH; download

application form and mail to nearest application address for organizations located in AL, CA, GA, MA, and RI
Copies of proposal: 1
Deadline(s): May 15 and Nov. 15 for organizations located in AL and GA; May 15 for organizations located in CA; Aug. 15 for organizations located in MA and RI; and Feb. 15, May 15, Aug. 15, and Nov. 15 for organizations located in OH
Board meeting date(s): Feb., Apr., July, and Oct.
Final notification: Within 1 month following board meetings
Officer and Directors: * Edward P. Campbell,* Pres.; Doug Bloomfield; Beverly J. Coen; Peter S. Hellman; John J. Keane.
Number of staff: 3 full-time professional; 1 full-time support.
EIN: 341596194

7782
The O'Neill Brothers Foundation ✧
30000 Aurora Rd., Ste. 250
Solon, OH 44139
Contact: Robert K. Healey, Pres.

Incorporated in 1953 in MI.
Donors: William J. O'Neill†; P.J. O'Neill†; H.M. O'Neill†; Francis J. O'Neill†; George C. Fortner†; Robert K. Healey; Mrs. Robert K. Healey.
Foundation type: Independent foundation.
Financial data (yr. ended 12/31/04): Assets, $6,515,188 (M); gifts received, $136,462; expenditures, $588,546; qualifying distributions, $489,759; giving activities include $432,825 for 72 grants (high: $30,000; low: $100).
Purpose and activities: Giving primarily to Roman Catholic agencies, churches, schools, and hospitals.
Fields of interest: Secondary school/education; Higher education; Environment, natural resources; Animal welfare; Health care; Health organizations, association; Children/youth, services; Community development; Roman Catholic agencies & churches.
Type of support: General/operating support.
Limitations: Giving primarily in Cleveland, OH; giving also in FL. No grants to individuals.
Application information: Application form required.
Initial approach: Letter
Deadline(s): None
Board meeting date(s): 4 times a year
Officers and Trustees: * Robert K. Healey,* Pres.; F.J. O'Neill III,* V.P.; Hugh O'Neill,* Secy.; Robert K. Healey, Jr.
EIN: 346545084
Selected grants: The following grants were reported in 2004.
$39,000 to Gilmour Academy, Gates Mills, OH. 2 grants: $25,000, $14,000
$30,000 to Hathaway Brown School, Shaker Heights, OH.
$25,000 to Jennings Center for Older Adults, Garfield Heights, OH.
$21,500 to Catholic Charities, Youngstown, OH. 2 grants: $20,000, $1,500
$20,000 to Cleveland Mounted Police Charitable Trust, Cleveland, OH.
$15,000 to Habitat for Humanity, Geauga County, Newbury, OH.
$15,000 to Josephs Home, Cleveland, OH.
$11,875 to Little Sisters of the Poor, Cleveland, OH.

7783
The William J. and Dorothy K. O'Neill Foundation, Inc.
30195 Chagrin Blvd., Ste. 106
Cleveland, OH 44124 (216) 831-4134
Contact: Catherine T. Abbott, Dir.
FAX: (216) 378-0594; *E-mail:* oneillfdn@aol.com;
URL: http://www.oneillfdn.org

Established in 1987 in OH.
Donor: Dorothy K. O'Neill†.
Foundation type: Independent foundation.
Financial data (yr. ended 12/31/05): Assets, $83,563,282 (M); gifts received, $133,388; expenditures, $5,190,798; qualifying distributions, $4,070,770; giving activities include $3,751,212 for 248 grants (high: $494,382; low: $250; average: $1,000–$25,000).
Purpose and activities: Giving in three categories: 1) family-related programs, 2) program areas of interest to grantmaking committee, and 3) selected charitable organizations. A primary focus is capacity building for nonprofits, specifically board development, staff development, program effectiveness and strategic planning.
Fields of interest: Family services.
Type of support: Curriculum development; Income development; Management development/capacity building; Program development; Conferences/seminars; Technical assistance; Consulting services; Program evaluation; Matching/challenge support.
Limitations: Giving primarily in the Cleveland, OH, area, and in cities where family members reside, including Sonoma County, CA, Washington DC, Naples and Bonita Springs, FL, Big Island, HI, the Baltimore/Annapolis, MD, area, the New York/Long Island, NY, area, Cincinnati, Columbus, and Licking County, OH, area, Houston, TX, and Richmond, VA. No support for organizations operating outside the U.S. No grants to individuals, or for annual campaigns or scholarships.
Publications: Application guidelines; Annual report (including application guidelines); Financial statement; Grants list; Occasional report.
Application information: Will review no more than 1 proposal from the same organization in the same year, unless the request is declined. Application guidelines are available on foundation Web site. If no past funding has been received, applicant must first apply for eligibility to submit a grant request. Application form required.
Initial approach: Letter
Copies of proposal: 1
Deadline(s): 2007: Jan 2, March 26, July 2, Sept. 17
Board meeting date(s): Feb., May, Aug. and Nov.
Final notification: Upon receipt
Officers and Trustees: * Timothy M. O'Neill,* Chair, Grantmaking Comm.; William J. O'Neill, Jr.,* Pres.; Kristine I. Sadlo, Secy.; Douglas J. Smorag, Treas.; Dorothy O'Neill Donahey; Robert W. Donahey; William M. France, Jr.; John E. Kohl.
Director: Catherine T. Abbott.
Number of staff: 1 full-time professional; 0.5 part-time professional; 1 part-time support.
EIN: 341560893
Selected grants: The following grants were reported in 2005.
$494,382 to Center for Families and Children, Cleveland, OH. For Fathers and Families Together program.
$100,000 to Cleveland Foundation, Cleveland, OH.

$100,000 to Cleveland Zoological Society, Cleveland, OH.
$100,000 to Therapeutic Riding Center Foundation, Chagrin Falls, OH.
$100,000 to Western Reserve Land Conservancy, Novelty, OH.
$50,000 to Willwoods Community, Metairie, LA.
$40,000 to Boys and Girls Clubs of Cleveland, Cleveland, OH.
$40,000 to Cleveland Institute of Art, Cleveland, OH.
$31,240 to Playhouse Square Center, Cleveland, OH.

7784
Ohio Casualty Foundation, Inc. ☆
9450 Seward Rd.
Fairfield, OH 45014
Contact: Stacey Andrews, Admin. Asst.
FAX: (513) 881-1327;
E-mail: stacey.andrews@ocas.com

Established in 1992 in OH.
Donor: Ohio Casualty Corp.
Foundation type: Company-sponsored foundation.
Financial data (yr. ended 9/30/06): Assets, $4,625,686 (M); gifts received, $1,550,025; expenditures, $498,191; qualifying distributions, $494,129; giving activities include $494,129 for 22 grants (high: $219,000; low: $1,700).
Purpose and activities: The foundation supports organizations involved with arts and culture, education, health, and human services.
Fields of interest: Arts; Education; Health care; Human services.
Type of support: Continuing support; Annual campaigns; Building/renovation; Equipment; Program development; Curriculum development.
Limitations: Giving limited to areas of company operations, with emphasis on Fairfield, OH. No support for religious, political, or international organizations. No grants to individuals.
Publications: Application guidelines.
Application information: Application form required.
Initial approach: Contact foundation for application form
Copies of proposal: 1
Deadline(s): Aug. 1
Board meeting date(s): Sept.
Final notification: End of Nov.
Officers and Trustees: * Dan R. Carmichael,* Chair. and Pres.; Debra K. Crane,* V.P.; Lynn C. Schoel, Secy.; Michael A. Winner, Treas.; Paul J. Gerard; Stanley N. Pontius.
EIN: 311357883
Selected grants: The following grants were reported in 2005.
$228,245 to United Way, Butler County, Hamilton, OH.
$50,000 to Shepherd Productions, Columbia, TN.
$15,000 to YMCA, Great Miami Valley, Hamilton, OH.
$8,333 to Fitton Center for Creative Arts, Hamilton, OH.
$5,000 to Greater Cincinnati Arts and Education Center, Cincinnati, OH.
$5,000 to Huntington House Museum, Windsor, CT.
$5,000 to Public Radio International, Minneapolis, MN.
$5,000 to Womens Crisis Center of Northern Kentucky, Covington, KY.
$3,000 to Lexington Shakespeare Festival, Lexington, KY.

7785
The Ohio National Foundation ◇
1 Financial Way
Cincinnati, OH 45242 (513) 794-6493
Contact: Anthony G. Esposito, Secy.

Established in 1987 in OH.
Donors: The Ohio National Life Insurance Co.; Ohio National Financial Svcs.
Foundation type: Company-sponsored foundation.
Financial data (yr. ended 12/31/05): Assets, $514,441 (L); gifts received, $445,643; expenditures, $726,355; qualifying distributions, $725,097; giving activities include $709,609 for 90 grants (high: $116,229; low: $25), and $15,488 for 44 employee matching gifts.
Purpose and activities: The foundation supports organizations involved with arts and culture, education, health, medical research, and human services.
Fields of interest: Museums; Arts; Higher education; Education; Hospitals (general); Health care; Cancer; Heart & circulatory diseases; AIDS; Cancer research; Heart & circulatory research; AIDS research; Medical research; Children/youth, services; Human services; Federated giving programs.
Type of support: Annual campaigns; Capital campaigns; Building/renovation; Employee matching gifts.
Limitations: Giving primarily in Cincinnati, OH. No grants to individuals.
Application information: Application form not required.
Initial approach: Proposal
Copies of proposal: 1
Deadline(s): None
Trustees: Howard C. Becker; Christopher A. Carlson; Ronald J. Dolan; Anthony G. Esposito; Diane Hagenbuch; David B. O'Maley; D. Gates Smith.
EIN: 311230164
Selected grants: The following grants were reported in 2003.
$115,687 to United Way of Greater Cincinnati, Cincinnati, OH. For annual support.
$49,500 to University of Cincinnati Foundation, Cincinnati, OH. For operating support.
$33,919 to National Underground Railroad Freedom Center, Cincinnati, OH. For capital support.
$30,000 to Boy Scouts of America, Dan Beard Council, Cincinnati, OH. For operating support.
$25,500 to Greater Cincinnati Foundation, Cincinnati, OH. For operating support.
$24,258 to Fine Arts Fund, Cincinnati, OH. For annual support.
$22,500 to Childrens Hospital Medical Center of Akron, Akron, OH. For capital support.
$20,000 to Cincinnati Institute of Fine Arts, Cincinnati, OH. For operating support.
$20,000 to Cincinnati Parks Foundation, Cincinnati, OH. For capital support.
$7,100 to National Conference for Community and Justice, Cincinnati, OH. For operating support.

7786
Ohio Savings Association Charitable Foundation ◇
1801 E. 9th St., Ste. 200
Cleveland, OH 44114

Established around 1970.
Donor: Ohio Savings Bank.
Foundation type: Company-sponsored foundation.

Financial data (yr. ended 11/30/05): Assets, $7,866,474 (M); gifts received, $2,000,000; expenditures, $787,467; qualifying distributions, $726,376; giving activities include $726,376 for 101 grants (high: $170,000; low: $30).
Purpose and activities: The foundation supports Jewish agencies and temples and organizations involved with arts and culture, education, health, and human services.
Fields of interest: Arts; Education; Health care; Youth, services; Minorities/immigrants, centers/services; Human services; Federated giving programs; Jewish agencies & temples; Religion.
Type of support: General/operating support; Scholarship funds.
Limitations: Applications not accepted. Giving on a national basis, with emphasis on Cleveland, OH. No grants to individuals.
Application information: Contributes only to pre-selected organizations.
Officer and Trustees:* Robert Goldberg,* Chair.; David Goldberg.
EIN: 237055858
Selected grants: The following grants were reported in 2003.
$5,751,000 to Jewish Community Federation of Cleveland, Cleveland, OH. For unrestricted support.
$41,298 to Ishmael and Isaac, Cleveland, OH. For unrestricted support.
$40,000 to Zionism 2000, Shefayim, Israel. For unrestricted support.
$26,000 to United Jewish Communities, New York, NY. For unrestricted support.
$25,000 to MedWish International, Cleveland Heights, OH. For unrestricted support.

7787
The Olive Branch Foundation, Inc. ◇
P.O. Box 20881
Canton, OH 44701
Contact: Marshall B. Belden, Jr., Tr.
Application address: 612 Market Ave. S., Canton, OH 44702, tel.: (330) 456-7900

Established in 1998 in OH.
Donors: Marshall B. Belden, Jr.; Fay Martin Chandler.
Foundation type: Independent foundation.
Financial data (yr. ended 12/31/05): Assets, $5,186,980 (M); gifts received, $100,000; expenditures, $899,419; qualifying distributions, $874,730; giving activities include $874,730 for 17 grants (high: $300,000; low: $500).
Purpose and activities: Giving for the purpose of improving the quality of life and scope of human knowledge in the areas of science, medicine, literature, philosophy, environmental science, or sociology; some funding also for a global development fund that inspires the creation of healthy housing and world peace, and the establishment of Vedic centers throughout the world.
Fields of interest: Arts; Higher education; Education; Environment; Health organizations, association; Human services; Children/youth, services; Family services; International peace/security; Philanthropy/voluntarism.
Limitations: Giving primarily in IA, with emphasis on Fairfield, Boone, NC, and Canton, OH. No grants to individuals.
Application information:

Initial approach: Letter
Deadline(s): None
Trustees: James Bagnola; Diana Davis Belden; Marshall B. Belden, Jr.
EIN: 341862239

7788
The Oliver Family Foundation ◇
c/o U.S. Bank, N.A.
P.O. Box 1118
Cincinnati, OH 45201-1118

Established in 1992 in OH.
Donors: Gertrude M. Oliver; Richard D. Oliver.
Foundation type: Independent foundation.
Financial data (yr. ended 12/31/05): Assets, $7,528,992 (M); expenditures, $485,958; qualifying distributions, $463,000; giving activities include $463,000 for 29 grants (high: $165,000; low: $1,000).
Purpose and activities: Giving to youth services, civic organizations, the arts and federated giving programs.
Fields of interest: Arts; fund raising/fund distribution; Museums; Residential/custodial care, hospices; Federated giving programs.
Limitations: Giving primarily in Cincinnati, OH.
Trustees: Vere W. Gaynor; John J. Kropp; Gertrude M. Oliver; John C. Oliver; Richard D. Oliver.
Agent: U.S. Bank, N.A.
EIN: 311365209
Selected grants: The following grants were reported in 2004.
$220,000 to Cincinnati Nature Center, Milford, OH.
$65,000 to Cincinnati Art Museum, Cincinnati, OH.
$50,000 to Taft Museum, Cincinnati, OH.
$20,000 to Cincinnati Symphony Orchestra, Cincinnati, OH.
$10,000 to Fine Arts Fund, Cincinnati, OH.
$3,000 to Cincinnati Playhouse in the Park, Cincinnati, OH.

7789
OMNOVA Solutions Foundation Inc.
175 Ghent Rd.
Fairlawn, OH 44333-3300 (330) 869-4289
Contact: Theresa Carter, Exec. Dir.
FAX: (330) 869-4345;
E-mail: theresa.carter@omnova.com; URL: http://www.omnova.com/about/community/community.aspx

Established in 1999 in OH.
Donor: GenCorp Foundation Inc.
Foundation type: Company-sponsored foundation.
Financial data (yr. ended 11/30/05): Assets, $30,614,960 (M); expenditures, $2,081,476; qualifying distributions, $1,902,633; giving activities include $1,568,519 for 463 grants (high: $115,000; low: $25), $144,312 for 105 grants to individuals, and $41,502 for employee matching gifts.
Purpose and activities: The foundation supports organizations involved with arts and culture, education, health, drug prevention, crime prevention, disaster relief, safety, human services, urban renewal, and civic affairs. Special emphasis is directed toward programs designed to help motivate our future leaders and workers to gain the desire, knowledge, and work readiness skills

required for companies to succeed and maintain a competitive edge.

Fields of interest: Arts, public education; Arts; Elementary/secondary education; Adult education —literacy, basic skills & GED; Education, reading; Education; Medical care, in-patient care; Health care; Substance abuse, prevention; Crime/violence prevention; Disasters, preparedness/services; Safety, education; Human services; Urban/ community development; Science, formal/general education; Mathematics; Public affairs, public education; Public affairs.

International interests: Canada; China; Finland; India; Italy; Sweden; United Kingdom.

Type of support: General/operating support; Continuing support; Annual campaigns; Capital campaigns; Building/renovation; Endowments; Program development; Scholarship funds; Employee volunteer services; Employee matching gifts; Employee-related scholarships; In-kind gifts.

Limitations: Giving primarily in areas of company operations in GA, MA, MS, NC, OH, PA, SC, WI, and in Canada, China, Finland, India, Italy, Sweden, and the United Kingdom; giving also to national organizations. No support for private foundations, fraternal, social, labor, or veterans' organizations, discriminatory organizations, organizations not of direct benefit to the entire community, political parties or candidates, organizations posing a conflict of interest with OMNOVA, or churches or religious organizations. No grants to individuals (except for employee-related scholarships), or for lobbying activities, local athletic or sports programs or sports equipment, travel, advertising, benefits, raffles, or similar fundraising events, or research or conferences.

Publications: Application guidelines; Annual report.

Application information: Organizations receiving support are asked to provide periodic progress reports. Multi-year funding is not automatic. Proposals should be brief. Application form not required.

Initial approach: Mail proposal to foundation
Copies of proposal: 1
Deadline(s): None
Board meeting date(s): As required
Final notification: 4 to 6 weeks

Officers and Trustees:* Michael E. Hicks,* Pres.; Kristine C. Syrvalin,* Secy.; Frank Robers,* Treas.; Theresa Carter, Exec. Dir.; Sandra Klaasse; Nick Triantafillopoulos.

Number of staff: 1 full-time professional; 1 part-time support.

EIN: 341909350

Selected grants: The following grants were reported in 2005.

$300,000 to Akron Community Service Center and Urban League, Akron, OH.
$115,000 to United Way.
$50,000 to University of Akron, Akron, OH.
$30,000 to Western Michigan University, Kalamazoo, MI.
$25,000 to Akron Art Museum, Akron, OH.
$25,000 to YWCA.
$5,000 to United Way International, Alexandria, VA.
$2,500 to Copley Historical Society, Copley, OH.
$2,000 to Catholic Charities.
$1,308 to Mississippi State University Foundation, Mississippi State, MS.

7790
Robert O. and AnnaMae Orr Family Foundation ✧ ☆

625 Ridgecrest Rd.
Akron, OH 44303
Contact: Bruce H. Buchholzer, Tr.
Application address: c/o Philip W. Murray, 137 S. Main St., Ste. 206, Akron, OH 44308, tel.: (330) 384-7306

Established in 1998 in OH.
Donor: Robert Orr.
Foundation type: Independent foundation.
Financial data (yr. ended 12/31/05): Assets, $11,049,314 (M); gifts received, $5,940,000; expenditures, $675,622; qualifying distributions, $473,010; giving activities include $473,010 for grants.
Fields of interest: Arts; Human services; Christian agencies & churches.
Type of support: General/operating support.
Limitations: Giving primarily in OH. No grants to individuals.
Application information:
Initial approach: Letter
Deadline(s): None
Board Members: Bruce H. Buchholzer; Philip W. Murray; Michael Stark.
EIN: 341867983

7791
Osteopathic Heritage Foundations ▼

1500 Lake Shore Dr., Ste. 230
Columbus, OH 43204-3800 (614) 737-4370
Contact: Richard Vincent, Pres.
FAX: (614) 737-4371; E-mail: heritage@ohf-ohio.org; Toll-free tel.: (866) 737-4370; URL: http://www.osteopathicheritage.org/

Redesigned in 1998 in OH.
Donors: Doctors Hospital; The Columbus Foundation.
Foundation type: Independent foundation.
Financial data (yr. ended 12/31/04): Assets, $270,192,156 (M); gifts received, $1,813,735; expenditures, $11,813,878; qualifying distributions, $9,704,719; giving activities include $8,609,782 for 75+ grants (high: $1,500,000; average: $20,000–$125,000).
Purpose and activities: Comprised of two private foundations that share a common mission and vision, while maintaining separate boards and funding concentration: 1) the Osteopathic Heritage Foundation supports community health and quality of life - primarily in central Ohio - as well as osteopathic medical education and research throughout the nation, and 2) the Osteopathic Heritage Foundation of Nelsonville directs its funding support primarily to improving community health and quality of life in southeastern Ohio. The foundations' focus on health and quality of life is broad and concentrated primarily on mission-related, target priorities, including the following: improving access to oral health care; reducing the prevalence of overweight/obesity in central Ohio; resolving healthcare workforce shortages; enhancing access to healthcare services; enhancing osteopathic medical education; and medical research. In addition, the foundations have made reducing homelessness a recent funding priority.

Fields of interest: Health care, information services; Health care, formal/general education; Medical care, community health systems; Public health; Health care; Housing/shelter, homeless; Homeless, human services; Homeless.

Type of support: General/operating support; Capital campaigns; Building/renovation; Equipment; Endowments; Program development; Conferences/seminars; Professorships; Curriculum development; Research; Program evaluation; Matching/challenge support.

Limitations: Giving primarily in the following OH counties: Athens, Delaware, Fairfield, Fayette, Franklin, Hocking, Jackson, Knox, Licking, Madison, Meigs, Morgan, Perry, Pickaway, Ross, Union, Vinton, and Washington.

Publications: Grants list; Multi-year report; Newsletter.

Application information: Unsolicited requests for funds generally not accepted. Grant requests are considered through a Request for Proposals (RFP) process. See foundation Web site for RFP summary and application forms.

Officers and Directors:* J. Richard Costin, D.O.*, Chair., Osteopathic Heritage Foundation; Frederick L. Oremus,* Chair., Osteopathic Heritage Fdn. of Nelsonville; I. Robert Amerine,* Vice-Chair., Osteopathic Heritage Foundation; Joseph A. Holtel, D.O.*, Vice-Chair., Osteopathic Heritage Fdn. of Nelsonville; Richard A. Vincent,* Pres.; Van Cardaras,* Secy., Osteopathic Heritage Fdn. of Nelsonville; George O. Faerber, D.O.*, Secy., Osteopathic Heritage Foundation; Richard A. Mitchell,* Treas.; Theodore M. Ofat, Cont.; Peter E. Johnston, D.O.*; Sherry A. Lahr, Ed.D.*; and 10 additional directors.

Selected grants: The following grants were reported in 2005.

$2,000,000 to University of Medicine and Dentistry of New Jersey, Newark, NJ. To establish Endowed Chair in Primary Care Research that would develop leaders in clinical research in primary care among osteopathic physicians throughout the profession based upon mentorship model.
$1,628,668 to OhioHealth, Columbus, OH. To enhance postgraduate osteopathic medical education at Doctors OhioHealth and other central Ohio facilities owned and operated by OhioHealth.
$1,505,912 to Ohio University, Athens, OH. 3 grants: $750,000 (To construct state-of-the-art integrated research facility for the development of new diagnostics, therapeutics, treatment and education), $463,654 (To develop haptic/graphical model of human back that can be used for palpatory diagnostics and medical training), $292,258 (To build infrastructure for three programs: diabetes education and research, physician training; neuromusculoskeletal research and CORE Research Program).
$500,000 to University of North Texas Health Science Center, Fort Worth, TX. To fund Osteopathic Heritage Foundation Research Chairs and Teams at national Osteopathic Research Center to achieve research objectives of osteopathic profession.
$433,568 to Ohio State University, College of Dentistry, Columbus, OH. To support acquisition of mobile van to provide dental services to low-income children in Columbus Public Schools.
$220,048 to Columbus Neighborhood Health Center, Dental Safety Net Clinics, Columbus, OH. To increase capacity and efficiencies of existing

safety net dental clinics in Franklin County through enhanced staffing patterns.

$147,338 to Otterbein College, Westerville, OH. To increase nursing student enrollment by recruiting adult students to accelerated program leading to BSN.

$52,000 to Licking County Health Department, Newark, OH. For Funding for Oral Health Referral and Education Program.

7792
Jane and Jon Outcalt Foundation ◇ ☆
(formerly Outcalt Charitable Fund)
3201 Enterprise Pkwy., Ste. 240
Beachwood, OH   44122

Donors: Jon H. Outcalt; Jane Q. Outcalt.
Foundation type: Independent foundation.
Financial data (yr. ended 12/31/05): Assets, $7,014,682 (M); expenditures, $563,743; qualifying distributions, $562,250; giving activities include $562,050 for 36+ grants (high: $192,000).
Purpose and activities: Giving primarily for the arts, with an emphasis on museums and the performing arts; some funding also for health care and for healthcare facilities.
Fields of interest: Performing arts, theater; Higher education, university; Botanical gardens; Hospitals (general); Federated giving programs.
Limitations: Applications not accepted. Giving primarily in Cleveland, OH. No grants to individuals.
Application information: Contributes only to pre-selected organizations.
Officers: Jane Q. Outcalt, Pres.; Jon H. Outcalt, Jr., V.P.; David B. Outcalt, Secy.; Robin M. Outcalt, Treas.
EIN: 311194069
Selected grants: The following grants were reported in 2004.

$50,000 to United Way, OH.

$37,000 to Hathaway Brown School, Shaker Heights, OH.

$37,000 to University School, Shaker Heights, OH.

$25,000 to Cleveland Foundation, Cleveland, OH.

$25,000 to Cleveland Institute of Music, Cleveland, OH.

$25,000 to Golden Age Centers of Greater Cleveland, Cleveland, OH.

$500 to Intergenerational School, Cleveland, OH.

$500 to Smith College, Northampton, MA.

$250 to Boys Hope Girls Hope, Cleveland, OH.

$250 to Salvation Army of Greater Cleveland, Cleveland, OH.

7793
Owens Corning Foundation ◇ ☆
c/o Owens Corning World Headquarters
1 Owens Corning Pkwy.
Toledo, OH   43659   (419) 248-6719
Contact: George Kiemle, Chair.

Established around 1960.
Donor: Owens Corning.
Foundation type: Company-sponsored foundation.
Financial data (yr. ended 12/31/05): Assets, $6,723,242 (M); gifts received, $80,255; expenditures, $562,757; qualifying distributions, $554,765; giving activities include $554,765 for grants.
Purpose and activities: The foundation supports organizations involved with arts and culture, K-12

education, health, human services, community development, and civic affairs.
Fields of interest: Arts; Elementary/secondary education; Health care; Human services; Community development; Federated giving programs; Public affairs.
Type of support: General/operating support; Capital campaigns; Program development; Scholarship funds; In-kind gifts.
Limitations: Giving primarily in areas of company operations. No support for athletic organizations, religious organizations, or political parties, offices, or candidates. No grants to individuals, or for endowments, advertising, travel, sporting events, or debt reduction.
Publications: Annual report (including application guidelines); Program policy statement.
Application information: Application form not required.
   Initial approach: Proposal
   Copies of proposal: 1
   Deadline(s): None
   Board meeting date(s): Mar., June, Oct., and Dec.
Officers: George Kiemle, Chair.; Joseph Mikelonis, V.P.; Rod Nowland, Secy.
Directors: Terry L. Priestap; Bill Rossiter; Jeremiah M. Sullivan; Karil Vose.
Trustee: Mellon Financial Corp.
Number of staff: 1 part-time professional; 1 part-time support.
EIN: 341270856
Selected grants: The following grants were reported in 2004.

$48,000 to United Way of Greater Toledo, Toledo, OH.

$25,000 to Toledo Symphony Orchestra, Toledo, OH.

$24,650 to United Way of Licking County, Newark, OH. 2 grants: $10,250, $14,400

$15,633 to National Merit Scholarship Corporation, Evanston, IL. For program in Chicago.

$14,600 to United Way of Amarillo and Canyon, Amarillo, TX.

$10,000 to Junior Achievement of Northwestern Ohio, Toledo, OH.

$10,000 to Sunshine Childrens Home, Maumee, OH.

$9,765 to Association of Universities and Colleges of Canada, Canada. .

$7,500 to Local Initiatives Support Corporation (LISC), Toledo, OH.

7794
The Park Foundation ◇ ☆
6200 Riverside Dr.
Cleveland, OH   44135

Established in 2004 in OH.
Donors: Georgia Financial, LLC; Park Corp.
Foundation type: Company-sponsored foundation.
Financial data (yr. ended 12/31/05): Assets, $20,795,152 (M); gifts received, $102,785; expenditures, $668,805; qualifying distributions, $573,800; giving activities include $573,800 for grants.
Limitations: Applications not accepted. No grants to individuals.
Application information: Contributes only to pre-selected organizations.
Officers: Raymond P. Park, Pres.; Kelly C. Park, V.P. and Treas.; Dan K. Park, V.P.; Patrick M. Park, V.P.; Piper A. Park, V.P.; Ricky L. Bertram, Secy.
EIN: 200791170

7795
The Park National Corporation Foundation ◇
(formerly The Park National Bank Foundation)
P.O. Box 3500
Newark, OH   43058-3500

Established in 1983 in OH.
Donors: The Park National Bank; Fairfield National Bank; The Richland Trust Co.; Park National Corp.
Foundation type: Company-sponsored foundation.
Financial data (yr. ended 12/31/05): Assets, $13,055,934 (L); gifts received, $2,433,795; expenditures, $1,030,453; qualifying distributions, $1,013,508; giving activities include $1,013,508 for 132 grants (high: $112,500; low: $250).
Purpose and activities: The foundation supports organizations involved with arts and culture, education, health, youth development, and community development.
Fields of interest: Arts; Elementary/secondary education; Higher education; Education; Health care; Youth development; Family services; Community development; Federated giving programs.
Type of support: General/operating support; Scholarship funds.
Limitations: Applications not accepted. Giving primarily in OH, with emphasis on Newark. No grants to individuals.
Application information: Contributes only to pre-selected organizations.
Officers: C. Daniel DeLawder, Pres.; Cheryl L. Snyder, Secy.-Treas.
Trustees: John W. Kozak; Stuart N. Parsons; David L. Trautman.
EIN: 316249406
Selected grants: The following grants were reported in 2004.

$93,000 to United Way of Licking County, Newark, OH.

$70,000 to YMCA, Licking County Family, Newark, OH.

$30,000 to MedCentral Health System Foundation, Mansfield, OH.

$25,000 to Babe Ruth League, Trenton, NJ.

$23,950 to Ohio University Foundation, Athens, OH.

$20,000 to Lancaster Festival, Lancaster, OH.

$10,000 to Salvation Army, Cambridge, OH.

$8,000 to Genesis Healthcare Foundation, Zanesville, OH.

$7,000 to United Way, Piqua Area, Piqua, OH.

$5,000 to A Call to College, Newark, OH.

7796
The Parker-Hannifin Foundation ◇
6035 Parkland Blvd.
Cleveland, OH   44124   (216) 896-3000

Incorporated in 1953 in OH.
Donor: Parker-Hannifin Corp.
Foundation type: Company-sponsored foundation.
Financial data (yr. ended 6/30/05): Assets, $20,494,689 (M); gifts received, $2,370,365; expenditures, $2,981,669; qualifying distributions, $2,981,669; giving activities include $2,168,305 for 773 grants (high: $326,500; low: $50), and $386,560 for 507 employee matching gifts.
Purpose and activities: The foundation supports organizations involved with arts and culture, education, health, human services, and government and public administration.

Fields of interest: Arts; Secondary school/ education; Higher education; Theological school/ education; Education; Hospitals (general); Health care; Children/youth, services; Human services; Federated giving programs; Government/public administration.

Type of support: General/operating support; Employee matching gifts.

Limitations: Applications not accepted. Giving primarily in areas of company operations. No support for fraternal or labor organizations.

Application information: Contributes only to pre-selected organizations.

Board meeting date(s): Jan. and July

Officers and Trustees: D.E. Washkewicz, Pres.; Duane E. Collins, V.P.; Thomas A. Piraino, Secy.

EIN: 346555686

Selected grants: The following grants were reported in 2005.

$60,000 to Cleveland Orchestra, Cleveland, OH.

$30,000 to American Red Cross.

$20,000 to Ohio Foundation of Independent Colleges, Columbus, OH.

$10,000 to Doctors Without Borders USA, New York, NY.

$5,000 to United Way of North Central Massachusetts, Fitchburg, MA.

$2,000 to Cleveland Museum of Natural History, Cleveland, OH.

$1,000 to Childrens Hospital of Orange County, Orange, CA.

$1,000 to Hicksville High School, Hicksville, NY.

$1,000 to United Way.

$500 to Assistance League of Irvine, Irvine, CA.

7797

Proctor Patterson Foundation ✧ ☆

c/o National City Bank
P.O. Box 94651
Cleveland, OH 44101
Application address: c/o Nicole Bornhorst, National City Bank, 1900 E. 9th St., LOC 3030, Cleveland, OH 44114, tel.: (216) 222-9038

Established in 2004 in OH.

Donor: Proctor Patterson Trust.

Foundation type: Independent foundation.

Financial data (yr. ended 12/31/05): Assets, $15,852,723 (M); expenditures, $721,181; qualifying distributions, $662,384; giving activities include $559,117 for grants to individuals.

Purpose and activities: Giving grants to needy individuals and for medicare reimbursement; funding also for student scholarships for higher education.

Fields of interest: Education; Human services; Economically disadvantaged.

Type of support: Grants to individuals; Scholarships —to individuals.

Application information: Application form required.

Initial approach: Letter or telephone requesting application form

Deadline(s): None

Trustee: National City Bank.

EIN: 306081504

7798

The Payne Fund ✧

2950 Terminal Twr.
50 Public Sq.
Cleveland, OH 44113

Incorporated in 1929 in OH.

Donors: Frances P. Bolton†; UD F.P. Bolton for Payne Fund Inc.

Foundation type: Independent foundation.

Financial data (yr. ended 12/31/04): Assets, $3,973,953 (M); gifts received, $540,630; expenditures, $928,854; qualifying distributions, $864,778; giving activities include $758,872 for 34 + grants (high: $16,500).

Purpose and activities: Giving primarily for higher education and cultural programs.

Fields of interest: Arts, association; Museums; Performing arts, theater; Performing arts, music; Arts; Education, research; Higher education; Education; Environment, natural resources; Nursing care.

Type of support: General/operating support; Capital campaigns; Building/renovation.

Limitations: Applications not accepted. Giving primarily in San Francisco, CA, Atlanta, GA, Boston, Cambridge, and Milton, MA, and Cleveland and Gambier, OH. No grants to individuals.

Application information: Contributes only to pre-selected organizations.

Board meeting date(s): Nov.

Officers: Barbara Bolton Gratry, Pres.; Kenyon C. Bolton III, V.P.; Thomas C. Bolton, V.P.; William B. Bolton, V.P.; Mary Bolton Hooper, V.P.; Charles P. Bolton, Secy.-Treas.

Directors: John B. Bolton; Philip P. Bolton; Frederick B. Taylor.

Number of staff: 1 full-time professional.

EIN: 135563006

Selected grants: The following grants were reported in 2004.

$161,500 to Musical Arts Association, Cleveland, OH.

$100,000 to Case Western Reserve University, Cleveland, OH.

$75,000 to Decorative Arts Center of Ohio, Lancaster, OH.

$50,000 to HealthSpace Cleveland, Cleveland, OH.

$38,448 to Cleveland Institute of Music, Cleveland, OH.

$22,500 to Asheville Symphony, Asheville, NC.

$22,500 to Georgia State University Foundation, Atlanta, GA.

$12,500 to Society of the Four Arts, Palm Beach, FL.

$12,000 to Cleveland Opera, Cleveland, OH.

$1,500 to Palm Beach County Literacy Coalition, Delray Beach, FL.

7799

The Peninsula Foundation ✧

517 Broadway, 3rd Fl.
East Liverpool, OH 43920-3167

Established in 1997 in OH.

Donors: Agnes Gund; The Domani Trust.

Foundation type: Independent foundation.

Financial data (yr. ended 12/31/05): Assets, $9,119,193 (M); expenditures, $1,120,360; qualifying distributions, $899,242; giving activities include $886,467 for 133 grants (high: $140,000; low: $40; average: $2,000–$10,000).

Purpose and activities: Giving primarily for the arts, with emphasis on art museums; the foundation also provides consulting services to museums; funding also for colleges and universities.

Fields of interest: Museums; Museums (art); Performing arts, ballet; Performing arts, theater;

Performing arts, opera; Elementary/secondary education; Higher education.

Type of support: General/operating support.

Limitations: Applications not accepted. Giving primarily in NY. No grants to individuals.

Application information: Contributes only to pre-selected organizations.

Trustees: Agnes Gund; Daniel Shapiro.

EIN: 347070871

Selected grants: The following grants were reported in 2003.

$250,000 to Center for American Progress, DC. For general support.

$25,000 to Storm King Art Center, Mountainville, NY. For general support.

$25,000 to University of Houston-University Park, Office of University Advancement, Houston, TX. For general support.

$22,500 to Studio in a School Association, New York, NY. For general support.

$10,500 to American Museum of the Moving Image, Astoria, NY. For general support.

$10,000 to Phillips Collection, DC. For general support.

$5,000 to RX Art, New York, NY. For general support.

$3,500 to P.S. 1 Charter School, Long Island City, NY. For general support.

$3,000 to Alvin Ailey Dance Foundation, New York, NY. For general support.

$3,000 to Ricardo OGorman Garden and Center for Resources in the Humanities, New York, NY. For general support.

7800

The Perkins Charitable Foundation ✧

1030 Hanna Bldg.
1422 Euclid Ave.
Cleveland, OH 44115 (216) 621-0465
Contact: Marilyn Best, Secy.-Treas.

Trust established in 1950 in OH.

Donors: Leigh H. Perkins; Sallie Sullivan; Members of the Perkins family.

Foundation type: Independent foundation.

Financial data (yr. ended 12/31/05): Assets, $24,375,342 (M); expenditures, $1,277,505; qualifying distributions, $1,188,996; giving activities include $1,172,700 for 177 grants (high: $68,300; low: $250).

Purpose and activities: Giving primarily for education, the arts, environmental conservation, animals, wildlife, health and medical care, and children, youth and social services.

Fields of interest: Museums; Arts; Elementary/ secondary education; Higher education; Education; Environment, natural resources; Animals/wildlife, preservation/protection; Reproductive health, family planning; Health care; Human services; Children/youth, services; Federated giving programs; Christian agencies & churches.

Limitations: Giving on a national basis, with some emphasis on OH and VT. No grants to individuals.

Application information: Application form not required.

Initial approach: Letter or telephone

Deadline(s): None

Officer: Marilyn Best, Secy.-Treas.

Trustees: George Oliva III; Leigh H. Perkins; Sallie P. Sullivan.

EIN: 346549753

Selected grants: The following grants were reported in 2005.

$61,000 to Cleveland Scholarship Programs, Cleveland, OH.

$31,175 to Nature Conservancy, Arlington, VA.

$29,500 to American Museum of Fly Fishing, Manchester, VT.

$28,000 to Planned Parenthood of North Central Florida, Gainesville, FL.

$17,875 to National Philanthropic Trust, Jenkintown, PA.

$16,000 to Planned Parenthood of Greater Cleveland, Cleveland, OH.

$12,925 to United Way.

$4,000 to George Mason University, Fairfax, VA.

$2,500 to First Stage Childrens Theater, Milwaukee, WI.

$1,050 to Vermont Land Trust, Montpelier, VT.

7801

Ruth and Lovett Peters Foundation ◇

(formerly Lovett Peters Foundation)
c/o Daniel S. Peters
1500 Chiquita Ctr.
250 E. 5th St.
Cincinnati, OH 45202

Established in 1992 in MA.
Donor: Lovett C. Peters.
Foundation type: Independent foundation.
Financial data (yr. ended 12/31/05): Assets, $2,589,658 (M); expenditures, $1,617,507; qualifying distributions, $1,540,813; giving activities include $1,329,750 for 29 grants (high: $225,000; low: $5,000; average: $25,000–$100,000).
Purpose and activities: Giving primarily for public policy organizations and research; funding also for education.
Fields of interest: Education, alliance; Education, reform; Higher education; Education; Human services; Public policy, research; Public affairs.
Limitations: Applications not accepted. Giving primarily to national organizations, with emphasis on AZ, Washington, DC, and MI; some funding nationally.
Application information: Unsolicited requests for funds not accepted.
Officer and Trustees:* Daniel S. Peters,* Pres.; Lovett C. Peters; Ruth Stott Peters.
EIN: 046748820

7802

The Thomas F. Peterson Foundation ◇ ☆

c/o James D. Roseman
25 W. Prospect Ave., Ste. 1400
Cleveland, OH 44115

Established in 1953 in OH.
Donor: Ethel B. Peterson†.
Foundation type: Independent foundation.
Financial data (yr. ended 10/31/05): Assets, $4,143,571 (M); expenditures, $649,186; qualifying distributions, $627,963; giving activities include $615,413 for 17 grants (high: $102,925; low: $2,000).
Purpose and activities: Giving primarily for the arts and education.
Fields of interest: Performing arts centers; Performing arts, orchestra (symphony); Elementary/secondary education; Higher education; Human services; Federated giving programs.

Type of support: General/operating support; Scholarship funds.
Limitations: Applications not accepted. Giving primarily in OH. No support for private foundations. No grants to individuals.
Application information: Contributes only to pre-selected organizations.
Officers and Trustees:* Barbara P. Ruhlman,* Pres.; John D. Drinko,* V.P.; Randall M. Ruhlman.
EIN: 346524958
Selected grants: The following grants were reported in 2005.
$105,925 to Laurel School, Shaker Heights, OH. 2 grants: $3,000, $102,925
$104,994 to Wellesley College, Wellesley, MA. 2 grants: $3,000, $101,994
$53,462 to Lawrence School, Broadview Heights, OH. 2 grants: $2,000, $51,462
$10,000 to Musical Arts Association, Cleveland, OH.
$10,000 to United Way Services of Greater Cleveland, Cleveland, OH.
$5,000 to Vocational Guidance Services, Cleveland, OH.
$3,500 to Ohio Foundation of Independent Colleges, Columbus, OH.

7803

The Daniel and Susan Pfau Foundation ◇

c/o The Greater Cincinnati Foundation
200 W. 4th St.
Cincinnati, OH 45202 (513) 241-2880
Contact: Mary D. LeRoy

Established in 1994 in OH.
Donors: Daniel A. Pfau; Susan L. Pfau.
Foundation type: Independent foundation.
Financial data (yr. ended 12/31/04): Assets, $10,130,862 (M); gifts received, $323,112; expenditures, $507,184; qualifying distributions, $464,065; giving activities include $460,000 for 37 grants (high: $40,000; low: $3,000).
Purpose and activities: Support primarily for programs that benefit disabled children, adolescents, and young adults (to age 30). There is also a secondary focus on funding for disadvantaged children, and adolescents and young adults (to age 30).
Fields of interest: Children/youth, services.
Type of support: Program development.
Limitations: Giving primarily in the greater Cincinnati area including Hamilton, Butler, Clermont and Warren counties, OH and Boone, Campbell, and Kenton counties, KY. No grants to individuals.
Publications: Application guidelines.
Application information: Application form required.
Initial approach: Telephone to request guidelines
Copies of proposal: 9
Deadline(s): Mar. 1 and Aug. 1
Board meeting date(s): May and Oct.
Final notification: June and Nov.
Advisory Board: David Brill; Steve Brill; Lee D. Crooks; Daniel A. Pfau; Susan L. Pfau.
Trustee: PNC Bank, N.A.
EIN: 311411794

7804

The Jesse and Caryl Philips Foundation ◇

3870 Honey Hill Ln.
Dayton, OH 45405
Contact: Christine Pack, Admin. Asst.

Established in 1990 in OH.
Donor: Jesse Philips†.
Foundation type: Independent foundation.
Financial data (yr. ended 6/30/04): Assets, $24,753,189 (M); expenditures, $757,496; qualifying distributions, $613,775; giving activities include $491,755 for 51 grants (high: $100,000; low: $55).
Fields of interest: Museums; Animals/wildlife, bird preserves; Jewish federated giving programs.
Limitations: Applications not accepted. Giving primarily in Dayton, OH. No grants to individuals.
Application information: Contributes only to pre-selected organizations.
Officer and Trustees:* Caryl Philips,* Pres.; Benjamin M. Beatty; Mary Dombrowsky Beatty.
EIN: 341656718
Selected grants: The following grants were reported in 2004.
$100,000 to Jewish Federation of Greater Dayton, Dayton, OH.
$40,000 to Susquehanna Art Museum, Harrisburg, PA.
$35,000 to Northwestern University, Evanston, IL. 2 grants: $10,000, $25,000
$25,000 to Phoenix Art Museum, Phoenix, AZ.
$20,000 to Dayton Society of Natural History, Dayton, OH.
$15,000 to Dayton Contemporary Dance Company, Dayton, OH.
$10,000 to Rockefeller University, New York, NY.
$10,000 to United Way.
$7,500 to Human Race Theater Company, Dayton, OH.

7805

PLACE Fund ▼ ◇

6300 Wilson Mills Rd.
Mayfield Village, OH 44143-2182
Contact: Betty J. Powers; Peter B. Lewis, Pres.

Established in 1986 in OH.
Donor: Peter B. Lewis.
Foundation type: Independent foundation.
Financial data (yr. ended 12/31/04): Assets, $5,989,146 (M); gifts received, $4,661,010; expenditures, $3,498,576; qualifying distributions, $3,496,875; giving activities include $3,458,552 for 10 grants (high: $1,000,000; low: $250; average: $20,000–$528,512), and $1,528,302 for 2 in-kind gifts.
Purpose and activities: Giving primarily for higher education and museums.
Fields of interest: Museums (art); Arts; Higher education; Education; Civil rights; Federated giving programs; Jewish agencies & temples.
Type of support: In-kind gifts; Program development; Seed money.
Limitations: Giving on a national basis, with some emphasis on OH.
Publications: Occasional report.
Application information: Application form not required.
Initial approach: Letter
Deadline(s): None
Board meeting date(s): As necessary
Officers and Trustees:* Peter B. Lewis,* Pres.; Adam L. Lewis,* V.P.; John D. Garson,* Secy.
Number of staff: 1 part-time professional; 1 part-time support.
EIN: 341532635
Selected grants: The following grants were reported in 2004.

$999,790 to Tides Foundation, New York, NY. For general support.

$528,512 to New School, New York, NY. For general support.

$125,000 to Hermitage-Guggenheim Foundation, New York, NY. For general support.

$37,500 to Nation Institute, New York, NY. For general support.

$12,500 to Cleveland Museum of Art, Cleveland, OH. For general support.

7806

The Elisabeth Severance Prentiss Foundation ▼ ◇

c/o National City Bank, Charitable and Endowment Svcs.
1900 E. 9th St., LOC 01-2030
Cleveland, OH 44114 (216) 222-2760
Contact: Richard Mack, Secy.
FAX: (216) 222-2410;
E-mail: john.baco@nationalcity.com; URL: http://www.esprentissfoundation.org/

Trust established in 1944 in OH.
Donors: Elisabeth Severance Prentiss†; Luther L. Miller†; Kate W. Miller†.
Foundation type: Independent foundation.
Financial data (yr. ended 12/31/04): Assets, $90,537,361 (M); expenditures, $4,120,458; qualifying distributions, $3,935,339; giving activities include $3,840,534 for 42 grants (high: $460,000; low: $7,500; average: $10,000–$100,000).
Purpose and activities: Support primarily for the following five objectives: 1) to promote medical and surgical research and to assist in the acquisition, advancement and dissemination of knowledge of medicine and surgery, and of means to maintain health; 2) to promote public health; 3) to aid hospitals and health institutions in Cuyahoga County, OH, that are organized and operated exclusively for public charitable purposes by contributions for capital improvements or equipment, purchase of rare and expensive drugs, and expenses of operation or maintenance; 4) to improve methods of hospital management and administration; and 5) to aid in establishment and support of plans and programs designed to make hospital and medical care available to all, especially those of low-income.
Fields of interest: Hospitals (general); Health care; Health organizations, association; Medical research, institute.
Type of support: General/operating support; Continuing support; Building/renovation; Equipment; Program development; Seed money; Research; Matching/challenge support.
Limitations: Giving primarily in the greater Cleveland, OH, area. No support for national fundraising campaigns. No grants to individuals, or for scholarships, or generally for surveys, assessments, studies, planning activities, or endowment funds; no loans.
Publications: Annual report (including application guidelines).
Application information: Each grant application must include a cover letter. Please see foundation Web site for further details application. Application form not required.
  Initial approach: Proposal or letter
  Copies of proposal: 6
  Deadline(s): Apr. 15 (for May meeting) and Oct. 15 (for Nov. meeting)

Board meeting date(s): May and Nov.
Final notification: Shortly after board meeting
Officers and Managers:* Quentin Alexander,* Pres.; Richard Mack, Secy.; Elisabeth H. Alexander; Pamela A. Alexander; Harry J. Bolwell; William R. Robertson.
Trustee: National City Bank.
EIN: 346512433
Selected grants: The following grants were reported in 2004.
$460,000 to Achievement Centers for Children, Highland Hills, OH. For salaries of direct service staff and operating support.
$347,335 to University Hospitals Health System, Cleveland, OH. For clinical capacity building project.
$250,000 to Case Western Reserve University, Frances Payne Bolton School of Nursing, Cleveland, OH. For Center on Aging and Health Care.
$250,000 to Free Medical Clinic of Greater Cleveland, Cleveland, OH. For general operating support.
$100,000 to Lakewood Hospital, Lakewood, OH. For teen health center.
$100,000 to University Hospitals of Cleveland, Cleveland, OH. For osteoarthritis and osteoporosis programs.
$75,000 to Vanderbilt University, School of Medicine, Nashville, TN. For schizophrenia research.
$66,667 to Eliza Bryant Center, Cleveland, OH. For program support and to hire coordinator.
$50,000 to Santas Hide-A-Way Hollow, Middlefield, OH. For expansion and relocation of Santa's Headquarters.
$30,000 to Hopewell Inn, Mesopotamia, OH. For funding for residents.

7807

The Procter & Gamble Fund ▼ ◇

2 Procter & Gamble Pl.
Cincinnati, OH 45202 (513) 983-2173
Contact: Paula Long
FAX: (513) 983-2147; E-mail: pgfund.im@pg.com; URL: http://www.pg.com/company/our_commitment/community.jhtml

Incorporated in 1952 in OH.
Donor: The Procter & Gamble Co.
Foundation type: Company-sponsored foundation.
Financial data (yr. ended 6/30/05): Assets, $53,186,228 (M); expenditures, $25,554,918; qualifying distributions, $25,513,460; giving activities include $25,389,729 for 1,358 grants (high: $1,225,519; low: $22).
Purpose and activities: The fund supports organizations involved with education, youth development, human services, community development, and public policy research.
Fields of interest: Higher education; Education; Youth development; Human services; Community development; Public policy, research.
Type of support: Employee matching gifts; Employee-related scholarships; Grants to individuals.
Limitations: Giving on a national basis, with emphasis on areas of company operations.
Application information:
  Initial approach: Contact foundation for application information

Officers and Trustees:* C.R. Otto, Pres.; C.G. Talbot,* V.P.; Clayton C. Daley, Jr., Treas.; R.L. Antoine; A.R. Sempowski-Ward.
EIN: 316019594
Selected grants: The following grants were reported in 2005.
$2,451,038 to Greater Cincinnati Foundation, Cincinnati, OH. 2 grants: $1,225,519 each
$600,000 to Cincinnati Convention Center, Cincinnati, OH.
$450,000 to Scholarship Program Administrators, Nashville, TN.
$365,000 to Economics Center for Education and Research, Cincinnati, OH.
$200,000 to Cincinnati Opera Association, Cincinnati, OH.
$45,000 to United Way of Androscoggin County, Lewiston, ME.
$40,000 to Chamber of Commerce, Albany Area, Albany, GA.
$20,000 to Foundation for the National Archives, DC.
$20,000 to W G U C-FM, Cincinnati, OH.

7808

The Progressive Insurance Foundation ◇ ☆

6300 Wilson Mills Rd.
Mayfield Village, OH 44143
URL: http://www.progressive.com/progressive/foundation.asp

Established in 2001 in OH.
Donor: Progressive Casualty Insurance Co.
Foundation type: Company-sponsored foundation.
Financial data (yr. ended 12/31/04): Assets, $1,944,894 (M); gifts received, $3,605,770; expenditures, $2,053,623; qualifying distributions, $2,012,491; giving activities include $1,974,005 for 996 employee matching gifts.
Purpose and activities: The foundation supports the Institute for Highway Safety and organizations involved with other areas.
Fields of interest: Consumer protection; General charitable giving.
Type of support: Employee matching gifts; General/operating support.
Limitations: Applications not accepted.
Application information: Contributes only to pre-selected organizations.
Officers and Trustees:* Glenn M. Renwick, Pres.; Kim Price, V.P.; Charles E. Jarrett, Secy.; James Kusmer, Treas.; W. Thomas Forrester; Jeffrey D. Kelly; R. Steven Kestner.
EIN: 300013138

7809

The Pruina Corporation ◇ ☆

1801 E. 9th St., Ste. 1300
Cleveland, OH 44114-3103
Contact: Thomas F. Allen

Established in 1963 in OH.
Donors: Andrew H. Kalnow; Loretta K. Kalnow; Gertrude K. Chisholm; Carl F. Kalnow.
Foundation type: Independent foundation.
Financial data (yr. ended 12/31/05): Assets, $3,965,343 (M); expenditures, $333,583; qualifying distributions, $328,863; giving activities include $327,000 for 4 grants (high: $200,000; low: $2,000).

Fields of interest: Performing arts, theater; Education, public education.
Type of support: Endowments.
Limitations: Applications not accepted. Giving on a national basis, primarily in the Midwest. No grants to individuals.
Application information: Contributes only to pre-selected organizations.
Officers and Trustees:* Loretta K. Kalnow,* Pres. and Treas.; Gertrude K. Chisholm,* V.P.; Andrew H. Kalnow,* Secy.; Carl F. Kalnow.
EIN: 346596908

7810
Charles M. & Thelma M. Pugliese Charitable Foundation ◇
P.O. Box 141
Steubenville, OH 43952
Application address: c/o Sky Bank, 23 Federal Plz., 2nd Fl., Youngstown, OH 44501

Established in 1998 in OH.
Donors: Charles M. Pugliese; Thelma M. Pugliese.
Foundation type: Independent foundation.
Financial data (yr. ended 12/31/04): Assets, $9,523,249 (M); gifts received, $56; expenditures, $464,760; qualifying distributions, $397,458; giving activities include $379,910 for 27 grants (high: $75,000; low: $1,000).
Fields of interest: Education; Animal welfare; Disasters, fire prevention/control; Human services; Aging, centers/services; Foundations (community).
Limitations: Giving limited to within a 30-mile radius of Steubenville, OH. No grants to individuals.
Application information:
Initial approach: Letter
Deadline(s): None
Officers: William W. McElwain, Chair.; Douglas C. Naylor, Sr., Secy.
Trustee: H. Lee Kinney.
Agent: Sky Bank.
EIN: 341784660
Selected grants: The following grants were reported in 2003.
$118,766 to Unionport Volunteer Fire and Rescue, Bloomingdale, OH.
$60,972 to Harrison Hills City School District, Hopewell, OH.
$55,000 to Edison Local School District, Edison High School, Hammondsville, OH. For bleacher replacement.
$25,000 to YWCA of Steubenville Ohio, Steubenville, OH.
$10,000 to Carrollton Exempted Village Schools, Harlem Springs Elementary School, Carrollton, OH. For playground improvement.
$5,000 to Steubenville City School District, Steubenville, OH.
$2,000 to Hounds Haven, Dillonvale, OH. For contribution to build shelter.
$1,500 to Brooke County Animal Welfare League, Wellsburg, WV. For spay/neuter program.
$1,500 to Community Foundation of Jefferson County, Steubenville, OH. For civic choral society musical event.
$1,500 to Ohio Department of Rehabilitation and Correction, Marysville, OH. For holiday celebration at Eastern Ohio Correction Center in Wintersville, OH.

7811
Pulley Foundation ◇
(formerly L. L. Browning Memorial Fund)
c/o U.S. Bank, N.A.
P.O. Box 1118, ML CN-OH-W10X
Cincinnati, OH 45201-1118

Established in 1969 in OH.
Donor: L.L. Browning, Jr. Charitable Lead Unitrust.
Foundation type: Independent foundation.
Financial data (yr. ended 12/31/05): Assets, $12,605,114 (M); gifts received, $690,213; expenditures, $956,858; qualifying distributions, $945,200; giving activities include $945,000 for 26 grants (high: $210,000; low: $500).
Purpose and activities: Giving primarily for the arts, particularly the symphony, higher and other education, health associations, human services, particularly an institute for people who are deaf, children and youth services, Christian churches, and to a science center.
Fields of interest: Performing arts, orchestra (symphony); Performing arts, opera; Arts; Elementary/secondary education; Higher education; Health organizations, association; Human services; Children/youth, services; Christian agencies & churches.
Type of support: Annual campaigns.
Limitations: Applications not accepted. Giving primarily in Maysville, KY, and St. Louis, MO. No grants to individuals.
Application information: Contributes only to pre-selected organizations. Unsolicited requests for funds not accepted.
Officers and Trustees:* Janet L. Houston, Pres.; Dorothy W. Browning,* Secy.; Kathryn B. Hendrickson; Virginia B. Illick.
Agent: U.S. Bank, N.A.
EIN: 237009545
Selected grants: The following grants were reported in 2004.
$200,000 to Saint Louis Symphony Orchestra, Saint Louis, MO.
$125,000 to Central Institute for the Deaf, Saint Louis, MO.
$110,000 to Saint Louis Science Center, Saint Louis, MO.
$60,000 to Repertory Theater of Saint Louis, Saint Louis, MO.
$50,000 to Christ Church of the Ascension, Scottsdale, AZ.
$40,000 to YMCA, Limestone Family, Maysville, KY.
$30,000 to Opera Theater of Saint Louis, Saint Louis, MO.
$15,000 to Grand Center, Saint Louis, MO.
$15,000 to Sheldon Arts Foundation, Saint Louis, MO.
$5,000 to Character Education Partnership, DC.

7812
R.T. Foundation ◇
(formerly Tomsich Foundation)
6140 Parkland Blvd.
Mayfield Heights, OH 44124-4187

Donor: Robert J. Tomsich.
Foundation type: Independent foundation.
Financial data (yr. ended 12/31/04): Assets, $668,250 (M); gifts received, $150,000; expenditures, $644,369; qualifying distributions, $643,000; giving activities include $643,000 for 22 grants (high: $200,000; low: $600).

Fields of interest: Arts; Higher education; Health care, clinics/centers; Health organizations, association; Boys & girls clubs; Human services.
Limitations: Applications not accepted. Giving primarily in Cleveland, OH. No grants to individuals.
Application information: Contributes only to pre-selected organizations.
Officer: Robert J. Tomsich, Pres.
EIN: 341537777

7813
P. K. Ranney Foundation ◇ ☆
c/o Paul Feinberg
13881 Lake Ave.
Lakewood, OH 44107

Incorporated in 1973 in OH.
Foundation type: Independent foundation.
Financial data (yr. ended 12/31/05): Assets, $8,394,613 (M); expenditures, $432,320; qualifying distributions, $391,613; giving activities include $330,000 for 28 grants (high: $75,000; low: $1,000).
Purpose and activities: Funding for the interests of the founding trustees and local community foundations.
Limitations: Applications not accepted. Giving primarily in the greater Cleveland, OH, area. No grants to individuals.
Application information: Unsolicited requests for funds not accepted.
Board meeting date(s): As required
Officers: Peter K. Ranney, Pres. and Treas.; Robert K. Bissell, V.P.; Paul Feinberg, Secy.
Director: Cynthia Bassett.
Number of staff: 1 part-time professional.
EIN: 237343201
Selected grants: The following grants were reported in 2003.
$25,000 to Cleveland Clinic Foundation, Cleveland, OH. For Medical Innovations Summit.
$20,000 to Eliza Jennings Group, Eliza Jennings Home, Lakewood, OH.
$15,000 to Free Medical Clinic of Greater Cleveland, Cleveland, OH.
$12,000 to Ideastream, W V I Z, Cleveland, OH.
$10,000 to Dolphin Institute, Honolulu, HI.
$10,000 to Generation Foundation, Cleveland, OH.
$10,000 to HealthSpace Cleveland, Cleveland, OH.
$10,000 to Providence House, Cleveland, OH.
$2,000 to Cleveland Animal Protective League, Cleveland, OH.
$2,000 to Cleveland Botanical Garden, Cleveland, OH.

7814
Reeves Foundation
232-4 W. 3rd St.
P.O. Box 441
Dover, OH 44622-0441 (330) 364-4660
Contact: H. Donald Patterson, Exec. Dir.

Trust established in 1966 in OH.
Donors: Margaret J. Reeves†; Helen F. Reeves†; Samuel J. Reeves†.
Foundation type: Independent foundation.
Financial data (yr. ended 12/31/05): Assets, $23,558,503 (M); expenditures, $1,213,166; qualifying distributions, $1,146,973; giving activities include $949,652 for 38 grants (high: $250,000; low: $500; average: $5,000–$50,000).

Purpose and activities: Emphasis on health agencies, including hospitals; grants also for youth agencies, education, and public administration. Priority given to capital improvement projects.
Fields of interest: Education; Hospitals (general); Health care; Health organizations, association; Human services; Children/youth, services; Government/public administration.
Type of support: Continuing support; Building/renovation; Equipment; Program development; Matching/challenge support.
Limitations: Giving primarily in OH, with emphasis on the Dover area. No grants to individuals, or for annual campaigns, seed money, emergency funds, deficit financing, land acquisition, endowment funds, fellowships, special projects, publications, or conferences; no loans.
Application information: Application form not required.
Initial approach: Proposal
Copies of proposal: 1
Deadline(s): 21 days prior to those months when board meets
Board meeting date(s): Bimonthly starting in Feb.
Final notification: 1 month
Officers and Trustees:* W.E. Lieser,* Pres.; Thomas J. Patton,* V.P.; Jeffry Wagner,* Secy.-Treas.; H. Donald Patterson,* Exec. Dir.; Ronald L. Pissocra; Don A. Ulrich; Peter F. Wagner.
Number of staff: 1 part-time professional; 1 part-time support.
EIN: 346575477
Selected grants: The following grants were reported in 2003.
$127,050 to Buckeye Career Center, New Philadelphia, OH. For equipment for L.P.N. program.
$125,000 to Tuscarawas County University Foundation, New Philadelphia, OH. For science and technology building.
$125,000 to Union Hospital Association, Dover, OH. For Boulevard South addition.
$96,369 to Twin City Hospital, Dennison, OH. For new patient hospital beds.
$45,000 to Tuscarawas County Council Church and Community, New Philadelphia, OH. For general fund and emergency assistance fund.
$32,000 to Stone Creek Volunteer Fire Department, Stone Creek, OH. For purchase of multipurpose vehicle.
$25,000 to New Philadelphia, City of, New Philadelphia, OH. For installation of lighting at Waterworks Field.
$20,000 to Journeys End Ministries, Newcomerstown, OH. For purchase of building.
$18,154 to Moravian College, Reeves Library, Bethlehem, PA. For carillon replacement.
$13,900 to Saint Joseph Elementary School, Dover, OH. For computer lab renovation project.
$7,200 to American Red Cross, Muskingum Lakes, New Philadelphia, OH. For Save The Day Program.

7815
The Reinberger Foundation ▼
27600 Chagrin Blvd., No. 355
Cleveland, OH 44122 (216) 292-2790
FAX: (216) 292-4466;
E-mail: reinbergerfound@aol.com; URL: http://foundationcenter.org/grantmaker/reinberger/

Established in 1968 in OH.
Donors: Clarence T. Reinberger†; Louise F. Reinberger†.

Foundation type: Independent foundation.
Financial data (yr. ended 12/31/05): Assets, $77,840,616 (M); expenditures, $5,035,856; qualifying distributions, $4,467,808; giving activities include $4,188,121 for 85 grants (high: $285,714; low: $3,500; average: $10,000–$100,000).
Purpose and activities: Support for the arts, social welfare, higher education, and medical research.
Fields of interest: Media/communications; Visual arts; Museums; Performing arts; Humanities; Arts; Elementary/secondary education; Education, early childhood education; Higher education; Adult education—literacy, basic skills & GED; Libraries/library science; Education; Zoos/zoological societies; Hospitals (general); Health care, home services; Health care; Substance abuse, prevention; Substance abuse, treatment; Mental health, treatment; Medical research; Offenders/ex-offenders, rehabilitation; Employment, vocational rehabilitation; Food banks; Housing/shelter, temporary shelter; Recreation; Youth development; Children/youth, services; Family services, domestic violence.
Type of support: General/operating support; Annual campaigns; Capital campaigns; Building/renovation; Equipment; Research.
Limitations: Giving primarily in Columbus and in northeastern OH. No grants to individuals, or for seed money, emergency funds, land acquisition, demonstration projects, or conferences; no loans.
Publications: Informational brochure (including application guidelines).
Application information: The foundation does not accept unsolicited full proposals, after review of the letter of inquiry the foundation will request a proposal if desired. Application form not required.
Initial approach: Letter of inquiry
Copies of proposal: 1
Deadline(s): For letter of inquiry: Mar. 1 for Education, June 1 for Health, Sept. 1 for Social Service and Dec. 1 for Arts, Culture and Humanities
Board meeting date(s): Feb., May, Aug., and Nov.
Final notification: Request for proposal or letter of inquiry declined within 2 weeks of deadline
Trustees: Sara R. Dyer; Karen R. Hooser; Richard H. Oman; Robert N. Reinberger; William C. Reinberger.
Number of staff: 5 full-time professional.
EIN: 346574879
Selected grants: The following grants were reported in 2005.
$304,166 to Case Western Reserve University, Cleveland, OH. 2 grants: $137,500 (For Product and Process Development Lab), $166,666 to School of Medicine (For Reinberger Research Fund).
$285,714 to Cleveland Clinic Foundation, Cleveland, OH. For Heart Center.
$208,333 to Great Lakes Museum of Science, Environment and Technology, Great Lakes Science Center, Cleveland, OH. For Reinberger Special Exhibition Area.
$150,000 to Cleveland Zoological Society, Cleveland, OH. For Education Pavilion at Center For Zoological Medicine.
$100,000 to Boy Scouts of America, Greater Cleveland Council, Cleveland, OH. For interior renovation.
$80,000 to West Side Ecumenical Ministry, Cleveland, OH. For Reinberger Auditorium in new facility.
$50,000 to North Coast Community Homes, Cleveland, OH. For general support.

$42,303 to Columbus College of Art and Design, Columbus, OH. To update electronic door access system.
$25,000 to Singing Angels, Cleveland, OH. For capacity building.

7816
Marion G. Resch Foundation ☆
c/o Butler Wick Trust Co.
P.O. Box 149
Youngstown, OH 44501
Contact: James H. Sisek, Butler Wick Trust Co.

Established in 1997 in OH.
Donor: Marion G. Resch.
Foundation type: Independent foundation.
Financial data (yr. ended 12/31/05): Assets, $19,463,049 (M); gifts received, $17,431,067; expenditures, $676,492; qualifying distributions, $595,611; giving activities include $576,500 for 4 grants (high: $232,500; low: $110,000).
Fields of interest: Higher education.
Type of support: Scholarship funds; Program development.
Limitations: Applications not accepted. Giving limited within 100 miles of Youngstown, OH.
Application information: Unsolicited requests for funds not accepted.
Officers and Trustees:* George B. Pugh,* Pres.; George R. Berlin, V.P.; Neil H. Maxwell,* Secy.; James H. Sisek,* Treas.; Brian J. Wolf, Exec. Dir.; Ingrid Lundquist; George B. Woodman; Eldon S. Wright.
Agent: Butler Wick Trust Co.
Number of staff: 1
EIN: 341853367

7817
Reuter Foundation
7700 Clinton Rd.
Cleveland, OH 44144 (216) 961-1141
Contact: Bob Reuter, Pres.
FAX: (216) 651-1777; *E-mail:* mail@ReuterFdn.org;
Additional E-mail: Proposals@ReuterFdn.org (proposals) or Reports@ReuterFdn.org (reports);
URL: http://www.reuterfdn.org/

Established in 1987 in OH.
Donor: Robert Reuter.
Foundation type: Independent foundation.
Financial data (yr. ended 11/30/05): Assets, $7,480,631 (M); gifts received, $730; expenditures, $352,005; qualifying distributions, $341,972; giving activities include $336,787 for 89 grants (high: $25,609; low: $50).
Purpose and activities: Giving primarily for social services to help the needy, disadvantaged, and mentally and physically challenged.
Fields of interest: Substance abuse, services; Medical research; Crime/violence prevention, abuse prevention; Human services; Economically disadvantaged.
Type of support: General/operating support; Continuing support; Emergency funds; Program development; Research; Consulting services.
Limitations: Giving limited to Cleveland, OH, and Collin County, TX. No support for endowment programs, construction or renovation of buildings, artistic or civic projects, scholarships, tuition, conferences, or travel costs. Program limitations available on foundation Web site. No grants to

individuals directly or for endowment or educational programs.
Publications: Application guidelines; Financial statement; Grants list.
Application information: Application guidelines available on foundation Web site. Application should consist of 2 parts: the cover letter and the proposal, no more than 5 pages total. Application form not required.
Initial approach: E-mail letter of intent before sending proposal
Copies of proposal: 1
Deadline(s): None
Board meeting date(s): Monthly, except for Dec.
Final notification: 4-6 weeks after receipt of e-mail proposal
Officers: Robert A. Reuter, Pres.; Gretchen Reuter Bowen, V.P.; Heidi Reuter Paul, Secy.; Christopher R. Reuter, Treas.
Trustees: Matthew J. Bowen; Holly K. Gigante; Dana F. Paul; Richard F. Sofka.
Number of staff: 1 part-time support.
EIN: 341766081
Selected grants: The following grants were reported in 2005.
$111,733 to American Red Cross.
$29,151 to Catholic Relief Services, Baltimore, MD. 3 grants: $15,036, $2,103, $12,012
$18,431 to North Coast Community Homes, Cleveland, OH.
$16,200 to Emerald Development and Economic Network, Cleveland, OH.
$13,000 to Ed Keating Center, Cleveland, OH.
$12,730 to Cleveland Tenants Organization, Cleveland, OH.
$11,000 to Hopes Door, Plano, TX. 2 grants: $1,000, $10,000

7818
The Reynolds and Reynolds Company Foundation ◇
P.O. Box 2608
Dayton, OH 45402-2608 (937) 485-8138
Contact: Alice Davisson, Admin.
E-mail: alice_davisson@reyrey.com; URL: http://www.reyrey.com/our_company/profile/in_the_community/company_foundation.asp

Established in 1986 in OH.
Donor: The Reynolds and Reynolds Co.
Foundation type: Company-sponsored foundation.
Financial data (yr. ended 9/30/05): Assets, $4,395,593 (M); gifts received, $4,500,000; expenditures, $370,920; qualifying distributions, $370,920; giving activities include $190,820 for 23 grants (high: $27,070; low: $2,000), and $180,000 for 1 employee matching gift.
Purpose and activities: The foundation supports organizations involved with arts and culture, K-12 education, and community development.
Fields of interest: Arts; Secondary school/education; Community development.
Type of support: General/operating support; Continuing support; Annual campaigns; Program development.
Limitations: Giving limited to the Celina and Dayton, OH, areas. No support for primary or secondary schools, sectarian organizations not of direct benefit to the entire community, political organizations, or fraternal or veterans' organizations. No grants to individuals, or for general operating support for universities or

colleges, debt reduction, endowments, courtesy advertising, fundraising events, or capital campaigns.
Publications: Application guidelines.
Application information: Multi-year funding is not automatic. Application form not required.
Initial approach: E-mail proposal
Copies of proposal: 1
Deadline(s): Feb. 15, May 17, Aug. 16, and Nov. 14
Board meeting date(s): Quarterly
Final notification: 3 months
Trustees: Jeff Almoney; Greg Geswein; Jon Strawsburg; Carolyn Wall.
EIN: 311168299
Selected grants: The following grants were reported in 2005.
$180,000 to United Way of Dayton, Dayton, WA.
$7,500 to Dayton Contemporary Dance Company, Dayton, OH.
$7,500 to Dayton Opera, Dayton, OH.
$7,500 to Dayton Philharmonic Orchestra, Dayton, OH.
$7,500 to Victoria Theater, Dayton, OH.
$6,500 to Boonshoft Museum of Discovery, Dayton, OH.
$6,250 to New City School, Saint Louis, MO.
$5,000 to Muse Machine, Dayton, OH.
$2,000 to Dayton Playhouse, Dayton, OH.
$2,000 to Dayton Theater Guild, Dayton, OH.

7819
Richland County Foundation
(formerly The Richland County Foundation of Mansfield, Ohio)
24 W. 3rd St., Ste. 100
Mansfield, OH 44902-1209 (419) 525-3020
Contact: Pamela H. Siegenthaler, C.E.O.
FAX: (419) 525-1590;
E-mail: info@rcfoundation.org; URL: http://www.rcfoundation.org

Incorporated in 1945 in OH.
Foundation type: Community foundation.
Financial data (yr. ended 12/31/05): Assets, $64,016,814 (M); gifts received, $3,281,430; expenditures, $3,028,239; giving activities include $2,204,278 for 664 grants (high: $150,000; low: $50), and $246,966 for 321 grants to individuals (high: $1,000; low: $15).
Purpose and activities: The foundation seeks to improve the quality of life in Richland County, OH, through organized philanthropy. The foundation also seeks to provide leadership and act as a catalyst in identifying and addressing evolving community needs, and to distribute grants for charitable purposes in the areas of health, economic development, basic human needs, education, cultural activities, environment, and community services. Also provides grants, through other local nonprofits, to aged and incurably ill Richland County residents.
Fields of interest: Historic preservation/historical societies; Arts; Education, early childhood education; Child development, education; Elementary school/education; Secondary school/education; Vocational education; Higher education; Adult/continuing education; Adult education—literacy, basic skills & GED; Libraries/library science; Education, reading; Education; Environment; Hospitals (general); Health care; Substance abuse, services; Mental health/crisis services; Health organizations, association;

Children/youth, services; Child development, services; Aging, centers/services; Women, centers/services; Human services; Civil rights, race/intergroup relations; Economic development; Community development; Government/public administration; Aging; Disabilities, people with; Minorities; Women; Economically disadvantaged.
Type of support: General/operating support; Capital campaigns; Building/renovation; Equipment; Endowments; Emergency funds; Program development; Seed money; Scholarship funds; Technical assistance; Program-related investments/loans; Scholarships—to individuals; Matching/challenge support.
Limitations: Giving primarily in Richland County, OH. No support for sectarian religious purposes. No grants to individuals (except for scholarships), or annual campaigns, operating expenses, computer systems, fellowships, highly technical or specialized research, maintenance funds, travel, debt, or medical, scientific or academic research.
Publications: Application guidelines; Annual report (including application guidelines); Informational brochure; Newsletter.
Application information: Visit foundation Web site for grant guidelines; scholarship applications available on Web site also. Application form required.
Initial approach: Telephone for appointment
Copies of proposal: 1
Deadline(s): 1st Fri. of Jan., Mar., May, July, Sept., and Nov.; May 1 for scholarships
Board meeting date(s): 2nd Mon. of Feb., Apr., June, Aug., Oct., and Dec.; annual meeting in May
Final notification: 6 to 8 weeks
Officers and Trustees:* Linda H. Smith,* Chair.; Thomas A. Depler,* Chair.-Elect; Pamela H. Siegenthaler, C.E.O. and Pres.; Douglas C. Freer, V.P., Finance and Opers.; Deborah M. Schenk,* Secy.; Sidney A. Foltz III,* Treas.; Charma Bhenke; Dr. Tom Croghan, M.D.; Don Edwards; Gayle Gorman Freeman; Lawrence L. Gibson, M.D.; John Kastelic; Robert L. Konstam; Don Mitchell; Jason Murray; Sharlene Neumann; Cynthia O'Neal; Carol E. Payton; Jack Pollock; Rick B. Taylor; Rev. Clifford Schutjer; Richard Walters; Betty Wells.
Trustee Banks: JPMorgan Chase Bank, N.A.; KeyBank N.A.; National City Bank, Columbus; Richland Bank, Mansfield.
Number of staff: 4 full-time professional; 1 full-time support; 1 part-time support.
EIN: 340872883
Selected grants: The following grants were reported in 2003.
$200,000 to Third Street Community Clinic, Mansfield, OH. For capital campaign.
$110,000 to Braintree, Inc., Mansfield, OH. For building renovation and relaunching.
$100,000 to YMCA of Mansfield, Mansfield, OH. For capital campaign support.
$81,250 to MedCentral Health System, Mansfield, OH. For capital campaign.
$10,000 to Planned Parenthood of North Central Ohio, Mansfield, OH. For cancer prevention medical services.
$1,875 to Richland Academy of the Arts, Mansfield, OH. For Hearing the Dance.
$1,500 to Center for Individual and Family Services, Mansfield, OH. For Raemelton Day Services Program.
$1,500 to Foundation Center, Cleveland, OH. For general support.

$1,000 to Malabar Middle School, Mansfield, OH. For Teacher Assistance Program for Math Is Fun project.

$300 to Mansfield, City of, Mansfield, OH. For Hooked on Fishing-Not on Drugs program.

7820
The Rieveschl Foundation ◇

c/o Fifth Third Bank
P.O. Box 630858, MD 1090C8
Cincinnati, OH 45263
Application address: c/o Fifth Third Bank, 38 Fountain Sq. Plz., Cincinnati, OH 45202

Established in 1997 in OH.
Foundation type: Independent foundation.
Financial data (yr. ended 12/31/05): Assets, $1,629,202 (M); expenditures, $729,460; qualifying distributions, $706,939; giving activities include $704,689 for 197 grants (high: $100,000; low: $50).
Purpose and activities: Giving primarily for arts and culture, higher education, and human services.
Fields of interest: Museums (art); Performing arts; Performing arts, music; Arts; Higher education; Health care; Human services; YM/YWCAs & YM/YWHAs; Children/youth, services.
Limitations: Giving primarily in the greater Cincinnati, OH, area; some funding nationally.
Application information:
  Initial approach: Letter
  Deadline(s): None
Trustees: Ellen Rieveschl; Gary T. Rieveschl; George Rieveschl, Jr.; Jan L. Rieveschl.
Agent: Fifth Third Bank.
EIN: 311515801
Selected grants: The following grants were reported in 2004.
$550,000 to Northern Kentucky University, Highland Heights, KY. 2 grants: $300,000, $250,000
$301,000 to University of Cincinnati Foundation, Cincinnati, OH. 2 grants: $300,000, $1,000
$250,000 to Art Academy of Cincinnati, Cincinnati, OH.
$200,000 to Greater Cincinnati Arts and Education Center, Cincinnati, OH.
$68,000 to Cincinnati Art Museum, Cincinnati, OH.
$25,000 to Carnegie Visual and Performing Arts Center, Covington, KY.
$25,000 to Thomas D. Clark Foundation, Lexington, KY.
$500 to Art Links, Cincinnati, OH.

7821
The Charles E. and Mabel M. Ritchie Memorial Foundation ◇ ☆

c/o FirstMerit Bank, N.A.
106 S. Main St., 16th Fl.
Akron, OH 44308 (330) 384-7330
Contact: Ronald B. Tynan, V.P., FirstMerit Bank, N.A.

Trust established in 1954 in OH.
Donor: Mabel M. Ritchie‡.
Foundation type: Independent foundation.
Financial data (yr. ended 12/31/05): Assets, $7,524,957 (M); expenditures, $418,672; qualifying distributions, $346,300; giving activities include $346,300 for grants.

Purpose and activities: Giving primarily for social services, education, the arts, children and health care services.
Fields of interest: Arts; Higher education; Education; Hospitals (general); Children/youth, services; Community development; Government/public administration.
Type of support: General/operating support; Continuing support; Annual campaigns; Capital campaigns; Building/renovation; Equipment; Endowments; Program development; Scholarship funds; Research; Matching/challenge support.
Limitations: Giving limited to Summit County, OH. No grants to individuals.
Application information: Application form not required.
  Initial approach: Proposal
  Copies of proposal: 4
  Deadline(s): None
  Board meeting date(s): 3 or 4 times per year
Advisory Committee: Edward F. Carter; Jon Heider; Kathryn M. Hunter.
Trustee: FirstMerit Bank, N.A.
EIN: 346500802
Selected grants: The following grants were reported in 2004.
$15,000 to United Way of Summit County, Akron, OH.
$10,000 to Akron Art Museum, Akron, OH.
$8,000 to National Inventors Hall of Fame, Akron, OH.
$5,000 to Childrens Hospital Medical Center of Akron, Akron, OH.
$5,000 to Hattie Larlham Foundation, Mantua, OH.
$5,000 to Ohio Chamber Ballet, Akron, OH.
$5,000 to Regina Health Center, Richfield, OH.
$5,000 to Weaver Industries, Akron, OH.
$5,000 to YWCA of Summit County, Akron, OH.
$3,000 to Project LEARN of Summit County, Akron, OH.

7822
George W. & Mary F. Ritter Charitable Trust ◇

c/o KeyBank N.A.
P.O. Box 10099
Toledo, OH 43699-0099 (419) 259-8655
Contact: Diane Ohns, V.P., KeyBank N.A.

Established in 1982 in OH.
Donor: George W. Ritter‡.
Foundation type: Independent foundation.
Financial data (yr. ended 11/30/05): Assets, $10,944,614 (M); expenditures, $528,951; qualifying distributions, $488,853; giving activities include $478,586 for 25 grants (high: $93,550; low: $123).
Purpose and activities: Giving primarily for hospitals, higher education, and Protestant churches. Student aid limited to male graduates of Ottawa Hills High School and Vermillion High School attending Baldwin-Wallace College.
Fields of interest: Museums (art); Higher education; Hospitals (general); Youth development, scouting agencies (general); Human services; YM/YWCAs & YM/YWHAs; Protestant agencies & churches.
Type of support: General/operating support; Scholarships—to individuals.
Limitations: Giving primarily in the Toledo, OH, area.
Application information: Application form required for scholarships.
  Deadline(s): None

Trustee: KeyBank N.A.
Advisors: Larry Firestone; Edgar A. Gibson; James D. Harvey.
EIN: 346781636
Selected grants: The following grants were reported in 2005.
$41,095 to Shriners Hospitals for Children, Tampa, FL.
$21,006 to YMCA, Steubenville, OH.
$21,005 to YWCA of Greater Cleveland, Cleveland, OH.
$15,755 to Boy Scouts of America, Toledo, OH.
$13,229 to First Congregational Church, Columbus, OH. 2 grants: $2,725, $10,504
$11,161 to Saint Lukes Hospital, Cleveland, OH.
$10,901 to Riverside Hospital, Toledo, OH.
$10,511 to Toledo Bar Association, Toledo, OH.
$10,503 to Salvation Army, Cambridge, OH.

7823
Robbins & Myers Foundation ◇

1400 Kettering Tower
Dayton, OH 45423
Contact: Peter C. Wallace, Chair. and Pres.

Incorporated in 1966 in OH.
Donor: Robbins & Myers, Inc.
Foundation type: Company-sponsored foundation.
Financial data (yr. ended 8/31/04): Assets, $138,182 (L); gifts received, $341,271; expenditures, $316,738; qualifying distributions, $316,738; giving activities include $304,363 for 44 grants (high: $50,000; low: $500), and $12,275 for employee matching gifts.
Purpose and activities: The foundation supports organizations involved with arts and culture, education, human services, and community development.
Fields of interest: Performing arts, music; Arts; Secondary school/education; Higher education; Education; Human services; Community development; Federated giving programs.
Type of support: Endowments; Scholarship funds; Annual campaigns; Employee matching gifts.
Limitations: Giving primarily in areas of company operations, with emphasis on OH. No grants to individuals.
Application information: Application form not required.
  Initial approach: Proposal
  Deadline(s): None
Officers: Peter C. Wallace,* Chair. and Pres.; Kevin J. Brown, V.P. and Treas.; B.W. Walther, Secy.
EIN: 316064597

7824
The Rockwern Charitable Foundation ◇

30 Garfield Pl., Ste. 1030
Cincinnati, OH 45202-4357 (513) 621-2850
Contact: Benjamin Gettler, Exec. Dir.

Established in 1998 in OH.
Donor: S. Sumner Rockwern‡.
Foundation type: Independent foundation.
Financial data (yr. ended 5/31/06): Assets, $11,822,073 (M); expenditures, $612,381; qualifying distributions, $537,958; giving activities include $533,038 for 8 grants (high: $200,000; low: $7,500).

Purpose and activities: Giving primarily to a university, as well as to Jewish agencies and temples.

Fields of interest: Higher education, university; Jewish federated giving programs; Jewish agencies & temples.

Limitations: Giving primarily in Cincinnati, OH.

Application information:

Initial approach: Proposal

Deadline(s): None

Officer: Benjamin Gettler, Exec. Dir.

Trustees: Stephanie R. Amlung; Delian A. Gettler; Gloria S. Haffer.

EIN: 311590504

7825

Stuart Rose Family Foundation ◇

2875 Needmore Rd.
Dayton, OH   45414

Established in 1988 in OH.

Donors: Stuart A. Rose; Christy Rose.

Foundation type: Independent foundation.

Financial data (yr. ended 11/30/04): Assets, $10,137,959 (M); gifts received, $1,973,700; expenditures, $396,105; qualifying distributions, $355,604; giving activities include $355,604 for 10 grants (high: $200,000; low: $1,000).

Purpose and activities: Giving primarily for Jewish federated giving programs and temples; funding also for the arts and education.

Fields of interest: Arts; Education; Human services; Foundations (private grantmaking); Jewish federated giving programs; Jewish agencies & temples.

Limitations: Applications not accepted. Giving primarily in Dayton, OH. No grants to individuals.

Application information: Contributes only to pre-selected organizations.

Officers and Director: Stuart A. Rose, Pres.; Jaqueline T. Rose, Secy.; Eugene S. Rose, Treas.

EIN: 311274967

Selected grants: The following grants were reported in 2004.

$250,007 to Jewish Federation of Greater Dayton, Dayton, OH. 2 grants: $200,005, $50,002

$25,001 to Chabad of Greater Dayton, Dayton, OH.

$25,001 to Temple Beth Or, Dayton, OH.

$25,000 to Maimonides Academy, Los Angeles, CA.

$15,000 to Dayton Foundation, Dayton, OH.

$5,000 to Dayton Art Institute, Dayton, OH.

$5,000 to Dayton Playhouse, Dayton, OH.

$4,595 to Miami Valley School, Dayton, OH.

$1,000 to Charles F. Kettering Foundation, Dayton, OH.

7826

Lois and Richard Rosenthal Foundation ◇

123 E. Liberty St.
Cincinnati, OH   45202
Contact: Richard H. Rosenthal, Tr.

Established in 1986 in OH.

Donors: Richard Rosenthal; Lois Rosenthal.

Foundation type: Independent foundation.

Financial data (yr. ended 12/31/04): Assets, $6,223,552 (M); gifts received, $2,700; expenditures, $389,551; qualifying distributions, $355,000; giving activities include $355,000 for 1 grant.

Purpose and activities: Giving primarily for the arts; some funding also for education and human services.

Fields of interest: Museums; Performing arts, theater; Arts; Elementary/secondary education; Human services.

Type of support: General/operating support; Annual campaigns; Capital campaigns; Endowments.

Limitations: Giving primarily in the Cincinnati, OH, area. No grants to individuals.

Application information:

Initial approach: Proposal

Deadline(s): None

Trustees: Jennie Rosenthal Berliant; Lois R. Rosenthal; Richard H. Rosenthal.

EIN: 311203666

7827

The Josephine Schell Russell Charitable Trust

c/o PNC Advisors
P.O. Box 1198
Cincinnati, OH   45201   (513) 651-8463
Contact: Mary Alice Koch
Additional address: c/o PNC Advisors Charitable Trust Committee, 201 E. 5th St., M.D. B1-BM01-02-5, Cincinnati, OH 45202

Trust established in 1976 in OH.

Donor: Josephine Schell Russell†.

Foundation type: Independent foundation.

Financial data (yr. ended 6/30/05): Assets, $11,690,262 (M); expenditures, $611,431; qualifying distributions, $500,632; giving activities include $465,500 for 25 grants (high: $50,000; low: $5,000).

Purpose and activities: Giving primarily for the arts, health care and human services.

Fields of interest: Arts; Health care; Human services; Children/youth, services; Economically disadvantaged.

Type of support: Capital campaigns; Building/renovation; Equipment; Program development; Seed money.

Limitations: Giving limited to the greater Cincinnati, OH, area. No support for private foundations, or for political, fraternal, labor or advocacy groups. No grants to individuals, or for endowment funds, operating budgets, continuing support, annual campaigns, deficit financing, scholarships, or conferences; no loans.

Application information: Full proposals will not be accepted. Proposals will be invited upon review of inquiry. Application form not required.

Initial approach: Telephone or letter of inquiry

Copies of proposal: 1

Deadline(s): Feb.1, May 1, Aug. 1, and Oct. 1

Trustee: PNC Bank, N.A.

EIN: 316195446

Selected grants: The following grants were reported in 2004.

$50,000 to Zoological Society of Cincinnati, Cincinnati, OH. For animal hospital.

$30,000 to Cincinnati Art Museum, Cincinnati, OH. For Cincinnati Wing capital campaign.

$30,000 to Lincoln Heights Health Center, Cincinnati, OH. For capital campaign.

$30,000 to Mercy Health System of Southwest Ohio, Cincinnati, OH. For emergency department redesign and renovation.

$25,000 to Art Academy of Cincinnati, Cincinnati, OH. For capital campaign.

$25,000 to Bayley Place, Cincinnati, OH. To build new wellness center.

$20,000 to Stepping Stones Center for Handicapped, Cincinnati, OH. For preschool services.

$20,000 to United Way of Greater Cincinnati, Cincinnati, OH. For program support.

$10,000 to Boys and Girls Clubs of Greater Cincinnati, Cincinnati, OH. For teen education and center.

$10,000 to Goodwill Industries of the Ohio Valley, Cincinnati, OH. For assistive rehabilitation technology.

7828

The Russell Family Foundation ◇

3711 Starr Centre Rd.
Canfield, OH   44406-8004

Established in 1998 in OH.

Donor: Wayland J. Russell.

Foundation type: Independent foundation.

Financial data (yr. ended 12/31/04): Assets, $1,452,866 (M); gifts received, $2,863,320; expenditures, $3,313,591; qualifying distributions, $3,309,733; giving activities include $3,309,533 for 13 grants (high: $3,274,183; low: $200).

Purpose and activities: Giving primarily for Christian associations.

Fields of interest: Christian agencies & churches.

Limitations: Applications not accepted. Giving primarily in Youngstown, OH. No grants to individuals.

Application information: Contributes only to pre-selected organizations.

Officers and Trustees: Wayland J. Russell, Pres.; Michael Pecchia, Secy.; Donna Russell, Treas.

EIN: 341885760

7829

The Sage Cleveland Foundation ◇

(formerly The Standard Products Foundation)
c/o John D. Drinko
3200 National City Ctr.
Cleveland, OH   44114

Incorporated in 1953 in OH.

Donor: The Standard Products Co.

Foundation type: Company-sponsored foundation.

Financial data (yr. ended 6/30/05): Assets, $6,990,710 (M); expenditures, $434,837; qualifying distributions, $400,988; giving activities include $387,300 for 14 grants (high: $200,000; low: $1,000).

Purpose and activities: The foundation supports organizations involved with arts and culture, education, and human services.

Fields of interest: Museums (art); Performing arts centers; Performing arts, music; Arts; Higher education; Law school/education; Education; Human services; Federated giving programs.

Type of support: General/operating support; Capital campaigns; Professorships.

Limitations: Applications not accepted. Giving primarily in Cleveland, OH, and Cambridge, MA. No grants to individuals.

Application information: Contributes only to pre-selected organizations.

Officers and Trustees:* J.S. Reid, Jr.,* Pres.; J. Richard Hamilton,* Secy.; John D. Drinko,* Treas.; Edward B. Brandon; John D. Sigel.

EIN: 346525047

Selected grants: The following grants were reported in 2005.

$235,000 to Cleveland Museum of Art, Cleveland, OH. 2 grants: $200,000 (For capital campaign), $35,000 (For general support).

$50,000 to Musical Arts Association, Cleveland, OH. For Severence Hall Fund.

$25,000 to City Mission, Cleveland, OH. For Laura's Home project.

$20,000 to Stella Maris, Inc., Cleveland, OH. For general support.

$20,000 to United Way Services of Greater Cleveland, Cleveland, OH. For general support.

$10,000 to John Carroll University, University Heights, OH. For general support.

$10,000 to Playhouse Square Foundation, Cleveland, OH. For general support.

$4,000 to Laurel School, Shaker Heights, OH. For general support.

$3,300 to Ohio Foundation of Independent Colleges, Columbus, OH. For general support.

7830
Saint Luke's Foundation of Cleveland, Ohio ▼

4208 Prospect Ave.
Cleveland, OH 44103 (216) 431-8010
Contact: Denise S. Zeman, Pres.
FAX: (216) 431-8015;
E-mail: dzeman@saintlukesfoundation.org;
URL: http://www.saintlukesfoundation.org/

Established in 1997 in OH; converted from the Saint Luke's Medical Center.

Foundation type: Independent foundation.

Financial data (yr. ended 12/31/05): Assets, $202,578,069 (M); gifts received, $149,474; expenditures, $9,627,444; qualifying distributions, $8,238,036; giving activities include $8,238,036 for 118 grants (high: $1,212,907; low: $250).

Purpose and activities: The foundation reinvests its resources to provide leadership and support for the improvement and transformation of the health and well-being of individuals, families and communities of Greater Cleveland.

Fields of interest: Health care; Human services; Community development, neighborhood development.

Type of support: Scholarship funds; General/operating support; Equipment; Emergency funds; Conferences/seminars; Publication; Seed money; Curriculum development; Research; Technical assistance; Consulting services; Program evaluation.

Limitations: Giving primarily in Cleveland and Cuyahoga counties, OH. No support for for-profit organizations or for religious purposes. No grants to individuals or fundraising events, endowments, or debt retirement.

Publications: Application guidelines; Annual report; Grants list.

Application information: See Web site for additional application information. Application form required.
Initial approach: Letter of inquiry online through Web site
Copies of proposal: 3
Deadline(s): Nov. 1, Feb. 1, May 1, and Aug. 1

Board meeting date(s): Mar., June, Sept., and Dec.
Final notification: 4 to 5 months after receipt of application

Officers and Trustees:* Sandra Kiely Kolb,* Chair.; J. Christopher Manners,* Vice-Chair.; Denise S. Zeman,* Pres.; Leah S. Gary, V.P., Prog. and Eval.; Janet E. Burney,* Secy.; Ken Okeson,* Treas.; and 13 additional trustees.

Number of staff: 3 full-time professional; 1 part-time professional; 2 full-time support.

EIN: 340714513

Selected grants: The following grants were reported in 2004.

$892,365 to Collaborative for Organizing Mount Pleasant, Cleveland, OH. For operating budget.

$794,722 to Kidshealth 2020, Cleveland, OH. For operating support.

$352,360 to Case Western Reserve University, School of Dental Medicine, Cleveland, OH. For operating budget for Healthy Smiles Sealant Program.

$75,000 to Center for Families and Children, Cleveland, OH. For mental health advocacy coalition.

$75,000 to Cuyahoga County Planning Commission, Cleveland, OH. For Senior Transportation Initiative.

$40,000 to Covenant Adolescent Chemical Dependency Treatment and Prevention, Cleveland, OH. For Day Treatment Expansion Project.

$35,200 to Cleveland Hearing and Speech Center, Cleveland, OH. For collaborative approach to developing language, literacy, and learning skills.

$25,000 to Welcome House, Rocky River, OH. For needs assessment for aging individuals with mental retardation and developmental disabilities.

$24,731 to Retired and Senior Volunteer Program (RSVP) of Greater Cleveland, Cleveland, OH. For Medicare Outreach Complimentary Program.

$19,620 to Hanna Perkins School, Hanna Perkins Center for Child Development, Cleveland, OH. For National Day Care Consultation Alliance Cleveland Consultation Program.

7831
Salem Community Foundation, Inc.

713 E. State St.
Salem, OH 44460-2911 (330) 332-4021
Contact: John E. Tonti, Pres.
FAX: (330) 337-3474;
E-mail: scf@salemohiochamber.org; URL: http://www.salemohio.com/scf

Established in 1966 in OH.

Foundation type: Community foundation.

Financial data (yr. ended 12/31/05): Assets, $13,514,024 (M); gifts received, $1,137,281; expenditures, $1,155,321; giving activities include $1,002,409 for 42 grants (high: $761,827; low: $316), and $88,000 for grants to individuals.

Purpose and activities: Helping the Salem, OH community improve the quality of life is the foundation's primary mission. The foundation, through special grants, supports charitable, educational, scientific, literary, artistic, and civic efforts, as well as public safety, welfare, and recreational programs in Salem.

Fields of interest: Arts; Education; Children/youth, services; Government/public administration.

Type of support: Annual campaigns; Continuing support; Building/renovation; Equipment; Land acquisition; Scholarship funds.

Limitations: Giving primarily in Salem and Perry Township, OH. No support for religious purposes or federal agencies. No grants to individuals (except for scholarships), or for operating budgets of established organizations or programs, budget deficits, endowments, conferences, or scholarly research.

Publications: Annual report; Newsletter.

Application information: Visit foundation Web site for application guidelines. Application form required.
Initial approach: Contact foundation for application form
Copies of proposal: 2
Deadline(s): 2 weeks prior to quarterly board meeting
Board meeting date(s): Quarterly
Final notification: Immediately following quarterly board meetings

Officers and Trustees:* John E. Tonti,* Pres.; Bruce P. Gordon,* V.P.; Salvatore C. Apicella, M.D.*, Secy.; Gary E. Moffett,* Treas.; David Brobeck; Larry G. Cecil; Harry R. Conn; George Hays; Joseph Julian; Deb McCulloch; Rob McCulloch III; Wilma Navyosky; Larry Paxson; Joe Sedzmak; Michael J. Sevilla; Nancy Willeman.

Number of staff: 1 part-time support.

EIN: 341001130

7832
Samaritan Foundation ◇ ☆

P.O. Box 97
Haviland, OH 45851-0097 (419) 622-4611
Contact: Trent A. Stoller

Established in 2002 in OH.

Donor: Haviland Plastic Products Co.

Foundation type: Company-sponsored foundation.

Financial data (yr. ended 12/31/05): Assets, $2,412,687 (M); gifts received, $718,057; expenditures, $352,458; qualifying distributions, $350,700; giving activities include $350,700 for grants.

Purpose and activities: The foundation supports Christian agencies and churches and organizations involved with human services and awards college scholarships to students located in Paulding County, Ohio.

Fields of interest: Human services; Christian agencies & churches.

Type of support: Scholarships—to individuals.

Application information: An application form is required for scholarships.
Initial approach: Proposal; contact foundation for application form for scholarships
Deadline(s): None

Officers: Russell Stoller, Pres.; Craig Stoller, V.P.; Todd Stoller, Secy.-Treas.

EIN: 341957355

7833
Sankey Family Foundation ◇

c/o Alan J. Tobin
4040 Embassy Pkwy., Ste. 100
Akron, OH 44333-8354

Established in 1999 in OH.

Donor: James K. Sankey.

Foundation type: Independent foundation.

Financial data (yr. ended 12/31/03): Assets, $6,898,761 (M); gifts received, $6,200; expenditures, $653,405; qualifying distributions, $649,960; giving activities include $646,423 for 6 grants (high: $262,923; low: $500).
Purpose and activities: Giving primarily for children and social services, particularly international relief organizations.
Fields of interest: Human services; Children, services; International relief; Federated giving programs; Christian agencies & churches.
Type of support: General/operating support; Program development.
Limitations: Applications not accepted. Giving on a national basis, with some emphasis on OH. No grants to individuals.
Application information: Unsolicited requests for funds not accepted.
Officers: James K. Sankey, Pres.; Beth H. Sankey, V.P and Treas.; Alan J. Tobin, Secy.
Trustee: Richard W. Sankey.
EIN: 341909797

7834
The Sapirstein-Stone-Weiss Foundation ✧ ✧
(formerly The Jacob Sapirstein Foundation of Cleveland)
10500 American Rd.
Cleveland, OH 44144
Application address: c/o Gary Weiss, V.P., 1 American Rd., Cleveland, OH 44144

Incorporated in 1952 in OH.
Donor: Jacob Sapirstein†.
Foundation type: Independent foundation.
Financial data (yr. ended 5/31/05): Assets, $19,132,822 (M); expenditures, $1,686,229; qualifying distributions, $1,686,229; giving activities include $1,561,433 for 65 grants (high: $582,500; low: $100).
Purpose and activities: Giving locally, nationally, and internationally for Jewish welfare funds and secondary and higher religious education.
Fields of interest: Elementary/secondary education; Theological school/education; Human services; Jewish federated giving programs; Jewish agencies & temples.
Type of support: General/operating support.
Limitations: Giving primarily on a national basis; some giving in Jerusalem, Israel. No grants to individuals, or for scholarships or fellowships; no loans.
Application information:
  Initial approach: Letter
  Copies of proposal: 1
  Deadline(s): Jan. 15
  Board meeting date(s): Quarterly
Officers and Trustees:* Morry Weiss,* Pres.; Gary Weiss,* V.P. and Secy.; Zev Weiss,* Treas.; Steven Tatar; Elie Weiss; Jeffrey Weiss; Judith Weiss.
EIN: 346548007
Selected grants: The following grants were reported in 2005.
$511,582 to Leonard and Susan Fuchs Mizrachi School, University Heights, OH.
$50,000 to American Jewish Joint Distribution Committee, New York, NY.
$40,000 to AMIT Women, New York, NY.
$27,000 to Hebrew Academy of Cleveland, Cleveland, OH.
$25,000 to Solomon Schechter Day School, Shaker Heights, OH.

$5,000 to Bureau of Jewish Education, San Francisco, CA.
$5,000 to Mesivta Yeshiva Rabbi Chaim Berlin, Brooklyn, NY.
$3,000 to Yeshivat Chovevei Torah Rabbinical School, New York, NY.
$2,000 to Chai Lifeline, New York, NY.
$1,500 to Jewish National Fund, New York, NY.

7835
The Schiewetz Foundation, Inc. ✧
3110 Kettering Blvd.
Dayton, OH 45439

Established in 2001 in OH.
Donor: Richard F. Schiewetz.
Foundation type: Independent foundation.
Financial data (yr. ended 12/31/05): Assets, $22,631,506 (M); gifts received, $7,523,400; expenditures, $812,498; qualifying distributions, $709,949; giving activities include $639,002 for 6 grants (high: $300,000; low: $5,000).
Purpose and activities: Giving primarily to the Boy Scouts of America, as well as to a YMCA; funding also for human services.
Fields of interest: Boy scouts; Human services; YM/YWCAs & YM/YWHAs.
Limitations: Applications not accepted. Giving primarily in Dayton, OH. No grants to individuals.
Application information: Contributes only to pre-selected organizations.
Officers: Richard W. Schwartz, Pres. and Treas.; Jennifer L. Schmidt, V.P.; Amy Kress, Secy. and Exec. Dir.
Director: Jane R. Schwartz.
EIN: 311812245

7836
Robert C. & Adele R. Schiff Family Foundation ✧ ☆
c/o U.S. Bank, N.A.
P.O. Box 1118, CH-OH-W10X
Cincinnati, OH 45201

Established in 2002 in OH.
Donor: Robert C. Schiff.
Foundation type: Independent foundation.
Financial data (yr. ended 11/30/05): Assets, $42,626,113 (M); gifts received, $31,324,713; expenditures, $429,636; qualifying distributions, $410,568; giving activities include $400,000 for 6 grants (high: $190,000; low: $10,000).
Fields of interest: Media, television; Higher education; Libraries/library science; Disabilities, people with.
Limitations: Applications not accepted. No grants to individuals.
Application information: Contributes only to pre-selected organizations.
Directors: James A. Schiff; Robert C. Schiff, Jr.
EIN: 300206688

7837
John J. and Mary R. Schiff Foundation ▼ ✧
P.O. Box 145496
Cincinnati, OH 45250-5496

Established in 1983 in OH.
Donors: John J. Schiff; Mary R. Schiff.

Foundation type: Independent foundation.
Financial data (yr. ended 6/30/05): Assets, $131,637,730 (M); gifts received, $12,817,644; expenditures, $6,894,671; qualifying distributions, $6,831,129; giving activities include $6,808,000 for 25 grants (high: $2,900,000; low: $5,000; average: $10,000–$250,000).
Purpose and activities: Support primarily for a historical society; support also for higher education and hospitals.
Fields of interest: Museums (art); Historic preservation/historical societies; Higher education; Animal welfare; Hospitals (general).
Limitations: Applications not accepted. Giving primarily in Cincinnati, OH. No grants to individuals.
Application information: Contributes only to pre-selected organizations.
Officer: John J. Schiff, Jr., Chair.
Trustees: Suzanne Reid; Thomas R. Schiff.
EIN: 311077222
Selected grants: The following grants were reported in 2006.
$1,100,000 to Deaconess Hospital of Cincinnati, Cincinnati, OH. For unrestricted support.
$1,000,000 to Cincinnati Parks Foundation, Cincinnati, OH. For unrestricted support.
$1,000,000 to Xavier University, Cincinnati, OH. For unrestricted support.
$400,000 to Cincinnati Art Museum, Cincinnati, OH. For unrestricted support.
$310,000 to Society for the Prevention of Cruelty to Animals, Friends of the, Cincinnati, OH. For unrestricted support.
$300,000 to U.S.S. Constitution Museum, Boston, MA. For unrestricted support.
$225,000 to Childrens Hospital Medical Center. For unrestricted support.
$200,000 to United States Naval Institute Foundation, Annapolis, MD. For unrestricted support.
$75,000 to Northern Kentucky University, Highland Heights, KY. For unrestricted support.
$40,000 to Cape Cod Writers Center, Osterville, MA. For unrestricted support.

7838
Robert C. & Adele R. Schiff Foundation ✧
c/o U.S. Bank, N.A.
P.O. Box 1118, CN-OH-W10X
Cincinnati, OH 45201

Established in 1983 in OH.
Donors: Adele R. Schiff; Robert C. Schiff.
Foundation type: Independent foundation.
Financial data (yr. ended 11/30/05): Assets, $42,418,430 (M); expenditures, $1,985,094; qualifying distributions, $2,018,257; giving activities include $1,958,000 for 131 grants (high: $350,000; low: $1,000).
Purpose and activities: Giving primarily for education, the arts, health care, and children and social services.
Fields of interest: Museums; Performing arts; Arts; Higher education; Education; Zoos/zoological societies; Hospitals (specialty); Health organizations, association; Youth development, centers/clubs; Human services; YM/YWCAs & YM/YWHAs; Children/youth, services.
Limitations: Applications not accepted. Giving primarily in OH. No grants to individuals.
Application information: Contributes only to pre-selected organizations.

Trustees: Adele R. Schiff; Robert C. Schiff.
EIN: 311080947
Selected grants: The following grants were reported in 2005.
$275,000 to YMCA.
$100,000 to Childrens Hospital.
$60,000 to Kids Helping Kids, Cincinnati, OH.
$35,000 to Friends of Drake Foundation, Cincinnati, OH.
$25,000 to Beech Acres, Cincinnati, OH.
$25,000 to Cincinnati Playhouse in the Park, Cincinnati, OH.
$20,000 to Lighthouse Youth Services, Cincinnati, OH.
$10,000 to Cincinnati Symphony Orchestra, Cincinnati, OH.
$7,000 to Hospice of Cincinnati, Cincinnati, OH.
$5,000 to National Underground Railroad Freedom Center, Cincinnati, OH.

7839
Albert G. and Olive H. Schlink Foundation ✧
49 Benedict Ave., Ste. C
Norwalk, OH 44857 (419) 668-8211
Contact: Robert A. Wiedemann, Pres.

Established in 1966 in OH.
Donors: Albert G. Schlink‡; Olive H. Schlink‡.
Foundation type: Independent foundation.
Financial data (yr. ended 12/31/05): Assets, $14,330,663 (M); expenditures, $756,218; qualifying distributions, $706,177; giving activities include $610,267 for 26 grants (high: $154,987; low: $500).
Purpose and activities: Grants to organizations providing aid to the indigent, aged, including religious, educational, and health agencies and hospitals; support also for the blind and for hospice and other national agencies and charities.
Fields of interest: Museums; Education, fund raising/fund distribution; Medical school/education; Education; Nursing care; Health care; Medical research, institute; Human services; Residential/custodial care, hospices; Aging, centers/services; Biological sciences; Science; Aging; Disabilities, people with; Economically disadvantaged.
Type of support: Capital campaigns; Building/renovation; Equipment; Endowments; Program development; Scholarship funds; Research.
Limitations: Giving primarily in OH. No grants to individuals or for operating expenses.
Publications: Application guidelines.
Application information: Application form not required.
Initial approach: Letter
Copies of proposal: 1
Deadline(s): Oct. 1
Board meeting date(s): Monthly
Final notification: Dec.
Officers and Trustees:* Robert A. Wiedemann,* Pres. and Secy.; Curtis J. Koch,* V.P.; John D. Allton,* Treas.; James O. Miller; Dorothy E. Wiedemann.
EIN: 346574722

7840
Charlotte R. Schmidlapp Fund
(formerly C. Schmidlapp Fund)
c/o Fifth Third Bank
38 Fountain Sq. Plz., MD 1090CA
Cincinnati, OH 45263 (513) 534-7001
Contact: Heidi B. Jark, V.P. and Mgr., Fdn Office

Trust established in 1908 in OH.
Donor: Jacob G. Schmidlapp‡.
Foundation type: Independent foundation.
Financial data (yr. ended 9/30/05): Assets, $29,487,738 (M); expenditures, $1,990,149; qualifying distributions, $1,830,587; giving activities include $1,772,498 for 40 grants (high: $300,000; low: $5,905).
Purpose and activities: Giving primarily to young girls in preparation of womanhood; funding also for higher education and human services.
Fields of interest: Higher education; Human services; Women, centers/services.
Type of support: Program development; Seed money.
Limitations: Giving primarily in Cincinnati, OH.
Publications: Application guidelines; Annual report.
Application information: Application form not required.
Initial approach: Request application
Copies of proposal: 1
Deadline(s): Quarterly
Board meeting date(s): Mar., June, Sept., Dec.
Final notification: Immediately following board meetings
Trustee: Fifth Third Bank.
EIN: 310532641
Selected grants: The following grants were reported in 2003.
$125,000 to Clinton Memorial Hospital Foundation, Wilmington, OH. For capital fund support.
$100,000 to Porter County Community Foundation, Valparaiso, IN. For scholarships.
$75,000 to Bethesda Foundation of Cincinnati, Cincinnati, OH. For capital fund support.
$50,000 to Michigan Womens Foundation, Livonia, MI. For project support.
$50,000 to Sayre School, Lexington, KY. For project support.
$30,000 to Girl Scouts of the U.S.A., Fair Winds Council, Swartz Creek, MI. For project support.
$25,000 to Applewood Centers, Cleveland, OH. For capital fund support.
$25,000 to Mercy Memorial Hospital Foundation, Monroe, MI. For capital fund support.
$25,000 to West Side Catholic Center, Cleveland, OH. For project support.
$25,000 to YMCA of Greater Cincinnati, Cincinnati, OH. For general operating support.

7841
Jacob G. Schmidlapp Trust No. 1 and No. 2 ✧
(formerly Jacob G. Schmidlapp Trust No. 1)
c/o Fifth Third Bank
38 Fountain Sq. Plz., 1090CA
Cincinnati, OH 45263 (513) 534-4397
Contact: Heidi B. Jark, Mgr., Charitable and Planned Giving Svcs.

Trust established in 1927 in OH.
Donor: Jacob G. Schmidlapp‡.
Foundation type: Independent foundation.

Financial data (yr. ended 9/30/05): Assets, $62,001,361 (M); expenditures, $2,642,862; qualifying distributions, $2,388,686; giving activities include $2,296,499 for 60 grants (high: $100,000; low: $5,000; average: $10,000–$50,000).
Purpose and activities: Grants for the relief of sickness, suffering, and distress, and for care of young children or the helpless and afflicted; support also for education, including child care training.
Fields of interest: Child development, education; Education; Hospitals (general); Health care; Health organizations, association; Food services; Housing/shelter, development; Human services; Children/youth, services; Child development, services; Aging, centers/services; Homeless, human services; Aging; Minorities; Homeless.
Type of support: Equipment; Land acquisition; Endowments; Program development; Seed money; Technical assistance.
Limitations: Giving primarily in the greater Cincinnati, OH, area. No support for religious or political purposes. No grants to individuals, or for annual campaigns, deficit financing, general support, fellowships, operating budgets, or continuing support; no loans.
Publications: Application guidelines; Annual report.
Application information: Application form required.
Initial approach: Letter
Copies of proposal: 1
Deadline(s): Feb., May, Aug., and Nov.
Board meeting date(s): Mar., June, Sept., Dec.
Final notification: Immediately following meetings
Trustee: Fifth Third Bank.
Selected grants: The following grants were reported in 2004.
$500,000 to Shriners Hospitals for Children, Cincinnati, OH. For program support.
$250,000 to Bayley Place, Cincinnati, OH. 2 grants: $125,000 each (For capital support).
$100,000 to Cleveland Clinic Foundation, Cleveland, OH. For program support.
$75,000 to Trinity High School Foundation, Louisville, KY. For program support.
$66,667 to Saint Xavier High School, Cincinnati, OH. For scholarships.
$62,500 to Frazier Rehabilitation Center, Louisville, KY. For program support.
$50,000 to Catholic Inner-City Schools Educational Fund (CISE), Cincinnati, OH. For scholarships.
$50,000 to Maumee Schools Foundation, Maumee, OH. For capital support.
$10,000 to Saint Marys Medical Center of Evansville, Evansville, IN. For program support.

7842
Joseph J. Schott Foundation ✧
1801 E. 9th St., Ste. 1105
Cleveland, OH 44114-3103
Contact: L. Thomas Hiltz, Tr.
KY application tel.: (859) 431-5544

Established in 1960 in OH.
Donor: Joseph J. Schott‡.
Foundation type: Independent foundation.
Financial data (yr. ended 12/31/05): Assets, $14,716,035 (M); expenditures, $923,717; qualifying distributions, $737,183; giving activities include $692,000 for 17 grants (high: $150,000; low: $2,000; average: $10,000–$50,000).
Purpose and activities: Giving primarily for medical research for children with facial disabilities; some

giving also for youth, and social services including a program for homelessness.

Fields of interest: Museums (art); Education; Botanical gardens; Zoos/zoological societies; Reproductive health; Health care; Genetics/birth defects; Medical research, association; Human services; Children/youth, services; Disabilities, people with.

Type of support: General/operating support; Equipment; Program development; Scholarship funds; Research.

Limitations: Giving primarily in Cincinnati, OH. No grants to individuals.

Application information:

Initial approach: Letter

Deadline(s): None

Trustees: Francie S. Hiltz; L. Thomas Hiltz; Betsy Saal; William D. Saal.

EIN: 346513748

Selected grants: The following grants were reported in 2005.

$150,000 to Xavier University, Cincinnati, OH.

$50,000 to Inner-City Youth Opportunities, Cincinnati, OH.

$32,500 to Harbor Hall Foundation, Harbor Springs, MI.

$25,000 to Cincinnati Works, Cincinnati, OH.

$10,000 to Families Forward, Irvine, CA.

$7,500 to Youth Opportunities United, Cincinnati, OH.

7843
Marge & Charles J. Schott Foundation ✧ ☆

531 Murray Rd.

Cincinnati, OH 45217-2014 (513) 721-8400

Contact: Phyllis J. Cartwright, Secy.-Treas.

Established around 1980.

Donor: Margaret U. Schott†.

Foundation type: Independent foundation.

Financial data (yr. ended 6/30/05): Assets, $59,065,286 (M); gifts received, $48,820,820; expenditures, $1,553,819; qualifying distributions, $1,353,909; giving activities include $1,147,500 for 37 grants (high: $500,000; low: $1,000).

Fields of interest: Performing arts; Secondary school/education; Human services; Children/youth, services; Roman Catholic agencies & churches.

Limitations: Giving primarily in Cincinnati, OH; some funding nationally. No grants to individuals.

Application information:

Initial approach: Letter

Deadline(s): None

Officers: Frank Crane, Jr., Pres.; Carlotta Crane, V.P.; Phyllis J. Cartwright, Secy.-Treas.

Trustee: Robert Martin.

EIN: 316063407

Selected grants: The following grants were reported in 2005.

$500,000 to Society of the Sacred Heart, Saint Louis, MO.

$120,000 to Saint Mary Church, Columbus, OH.

$20,000 to Hospice of Cincinnati, Cincinnati, OH.

$20,000 to Lighthouse Youth Services, Cincinnati, OH.

$20,000 to Little Sisters of the Poor, Cincinnati, OH.

$20,000 to Milford Spiritual Center, Milford, OH.

$20,000 to Tender Mercies, Cincinnati, OH.

$10,000 to Athletes in Action, Xenia, OH.

$10,000 to Boys Hope Girls Hope, Cincinnati, OH.

$2,500 to Welcome House of Northern Kentucky, Covington, KY.

7844
The Jay and Jean Schottenstein Foundation ▼ ✧

(formerly Jay L. Schottenstein Foundation)

1800 Moler Rd.

Columbus, OH 43207-1698

Established in OH.

Donors: Jay Schottenstein; Jeffrey Schottenstein; Jonathan Schottenstein; Joseph Schottenstein.

Foundation type: Independent foundation.

Financial data (yr. ended 12/31/04): Assets, $23,147,567 (M); gifts received, $8,720,000; expenditures, $7,200,268; qualifying distributions, $7,200,268; giving activities include $7,199,874 for 50 grants (high: $2,025,000; low: $100; average: $5,000–$100,000).

Purpose and activities: Support only for Jewish agencies, temples, and schools.

Fields of interest: Elementary/secondary education; Theological school/education; Jewish federated giving programs; Jewish agencies & temples.

Type of support: General/operating support.

Limitations: Applications not accepted. Giving limited to NY and OH. No grants to individuals.

Application information: Contributes only to pre-selected organizations.

Officers: Jay Schottenstein, Pres.; Geraldine Schottenstein Hoffman, V.P.; Saul Schottenstein, Secy.

EIN: 311111955

Selected grants: The following grants were reported in 2004.

$2,025,000 to Yeshiva University, New York, NY.

$1,140,000 to Mesorah Heritage Foundation, Brooklyn, NY.

$824,400 to Chabad of Key Biscayne, Surfside, FL.

$600,000 to Congregation Mosdosh Tash, Brooklyn, NY.

$330,000 to Yad Avraham Institute, New York, NY.

$270,000 to Jewish Federation, Columbus, OH.

$200,000 to American Friends of Reshet Chabad, New York, NY.

$133,334 to Western Wall Heritage Foundation, New York, NY.

$110,156 to Columbus Torah Academy, Columbus, OH.

$101,000 to American Friends of Chasdei Yosef, Brooklyn, NY.

7845
The Scioto Foundation

(formerly The Scioto County Area Foundation)

P.O. Box 911

Portsmouth, OH 45662 (740) 354-4612

Contact: Kimberly E. Cutlip, Exec. Dir.

FAX: (740) 354-4612;

E-mail: kim.sciotofoundation@verizon.net

Established in 1974 in OH.

Foundation type: Community foundation.

Financial data (yr. ended 12/31/05): Assets, $17,598,881 (M); gifts received, $622,473; expenditures, $733,873; giving activities include $523,384 for 44 grants (high: $45,000; low: $450).

Purpose and activities: Giving for charitable purposes to benefit the citizens of Scioto County; primary areas of interest include education, health care, community development, economic development, arts and culture, social services, and civic benefit.

Fields of interest: Arts; Education; Environment, natural resources; Health care; Human services; Economic development; Community development.

Type of support: Management development/capacity building; Equipment; Program development; Conferences/seminars; Publication; Seed money; Curriculum development; Scholarship funds; Research; Technical assistance; Consulting services; Program evaluation; Matching/challenge support.

Limitations: Giving primarily in Scioto County, OH; distributions are regional depending on donor preference. No support for religious organizations for religious programs. No grants to individuals, or for continuing support, annual campaigns, emergency funds, deficit financing, building funds, land acquisition, endowments, foundation-managed projects, exchange programs, or program support; no loans.

Publications: Application guidelines; Annual report; Financial statement; Informational brochure (including application guidelines); Newsletter.

Application information: Grants accepted on a quarterly basis. Application form required.

Initial approach: Telephone

Copies of proposal: 6

Deadline(s): Quarterly: Mar. 31, June 30, Sept. 30, and Dec. 31

Board meeting date(s): 2nd Wed. of each month

Final notification: 1 month

Officers: Wayne Wheeler, M.D.*, Chair.; Kimberly E. Cutlip, Exec. Dir.

Number of staff: 1 full-time professional; 2 part-time professional.

EIN: 510157026

7846
Scotford Foundation ✧ ☆

211 S. Main St.

Poland, OH 44514 (330) 757-3761

Contact: John P. Scotford, Jr., Tr.

Established in 1978 in OH.

Donors: John Scotford; Judy Scotford; John Scotford, Jr.; Laura Scotford; Stephen L. Scotford.

Foundation type: Independent foundation.

Financial data (yr. ended 12/31/05): Assets, $4,582,212 (M); gifts received, $530,637; expenditures, $368,003; qualifying distributions, $355,385; giving activities include $354,497 for 34 grants (high: $67,600; low: $500; average: $1,000–$25,000).

Purpose and activities: Giving primarily to Protestant agencies and churches and for education.

Fields of interest: Elementary/secondary education; Higher education; Youth development; Protestant agencies & churches.

Type of support: General/operating support; Annual campaigns; Capital campaigns; Building/renovation; Land acquisition; Endowments; Matching/challenge support.

Limitations: Giving primarily in OH and FL; some funding nationally. No grants to individuals.

Application information: Application form not required.

Initial approach: Letter

Deadline(s): None

Board meeting date(s): Varies

Trustees: E. Judith Scotford; John P. Scotford; John P. Scotford, Jr.; Laura L. Scotford; Stephen L. Scotford.

EIN: 341278622

Selected grants: The following grants were reported in 2004.

$95,000 to Whitworth College, Spokane, WA.

$12,000 to Ohio Roundtable, Strongsville, OH.

$11,100 to Youngstown Foundation, Youngstown, OH.

$5,000 to Knox Theological Seminary, Fort Lauderdale, FL.

$5,000 to Westminster College, New Wilmington, PA.

$1,825 to Youngstown State University, Youngstown, OH.

7847
Kenneth A. Scott Charitable Trust ◇

c/o KeyBank N.A.

127 Public Sq., 16th Fl.

Cleveland, OH 44114-1306 (216) 556-4062

Contact: H. Richard Obermanns, Exec. Dir.

Established in 1995 in OH.

Donor: Kenneth A. Scott†.

Foundation type: Independent foundation.

Financial data (yr. ended 12/31/05): Assets, $20,268,551 (M); expenditures, $1,075,823; qualifying distributions, $934,393; giving activities include $850,539 for 56 grants (high: $83,160; low: $1,500; average: $5,000–$25,000).

Purpose and activities: Support only for organizations whose purpose is the prevention of cruelty to animals.

Fields of interest: Animal welfare.

Limitations: Giving primarily in OH for local organizations; giving outside OH only for national organizations. No grants to individuals, or for endowments, general support, capital expenditures, or deficit reduction.

Publications: Annual report.

Application information: Application form required for OH residents.

Initial approach: Letter

Deadline(s): May 1 for Ohio; Jan. 1 and Sept. 1 nationally

Officer: H. Richard Obermanns, Exec. Dir.

Trustee: KeyBank N.A.

Number of staff: 1 part-time professional.

EIN: 347034544

7848
Scripps Howard Foundation ▼ ◇

P.O. Box 5380

312 Walnut St., 28th Fl.

Cincinnati, OH 45201 (513) 977-3035

Contact: Judith G. Clabes, C.E.O. and Pres.; Patty Cottingham, V.P., Admin.

FAX: (513) 977-3800; E-mail: clabes@scripps.com; Contact for Roy W. Howard National Reporting Competition, Internships, and Top 10 Scholarships: Susan J. Porter, V.P., Progs., tel.: (800) 888-3000, E-mail: porters@scripps.com; Contact for Jack R. Howard Fellowships in International Journalism: Josh Friedman, Dir., Intl. Prog., Columbia Graduate School of Journalism, E-mail: jf125@columbia.edu; Additional tel.: (513) 997-3048, (800) 888-3847; URL: http://foundation.scripps.com/foundation/

Incorporated in 1962 in OH.

Donors: The E.W. Scripps Co.; Jack R. Howard Trust; Robert P. Scripps.

Foundation type: Company-sponsored foundation.

Financial data (yr. ended 12/31/05): Assets, $75,261,121 (M); gifts received, $3,788,991; expenditures, $7,367,536; qualifying distributions, $6,937,879; giving activities include $5,721,275 for grants.

Purpose and activities: The foundation supports organizations involved with journalism and free press issues, arts and culture, literacy, education, families, human services, and civic affairs and awards grants, scholarships, fellowships, and internship grants to journalists and journalism students.

Fields of interest: Media, journalism/publishing; Arts; Education, reading; Education; Family services; Human services; Civil liberties, first amendment; Public affairs; General charitable giving.

Type of support: General/operating support; Capital campaigns; Equipment; Endowments; Program development; Conferences/seminars; Professorships; Seed money; Fellowships; Internship funds; Research; Technical assistance; Employee volunteer services; Employee matching gifts; Employee-related scholarships; Grants to individuals; Scholarships—to individuals; Matching/challenge support.

Limitations: Giving on a national basis, with emphasis on areas of company operations. No support for religious organizations not of direct benefit to the entire community, political candidates, anti-business organizations, discriminatory organizations, private foundations, or veterans', fraternal, or labor organizations. No grants to individuals (except for fellowships, scholarships, internship grants, and National Journalism Awards), or for tables, walks, runs, golf outings, or neighborhood special events (except for employee team sponsorships), disease-related events, research-related events, political causes, advertising, or continuing support.

Publications: Application guidelines; Annual report (including application guidelines).

Application information: Proposals should be brief. An application form is required for National Reporting Competition and National Journalism Awards.

Initial approach: Proposal to nearest company facility for Community Fund and Literacy Grants; proposal to foundation for Greater Cincinnati Fund and Journalism Grants; download application form and mail to foundation for Reporting Competition and Journalism Awards

Deadline(s): Postmarked by Mar. 31 for National Reporting Competition; postmarked by Jan. 31 for National Journalism Awards; Mar. 1 for Ted Scripps Environmental Fellowships

Board meeting date(s): Semiannually

Final notification: 3 months for Community Fund and Greater Cincinnati Fund

Officers and Trustees:* Alan M. Horton,* Chair.; Judith G. Clabes,* C.E.O. and Pres.; Patty Cottingham, V.P., Admin.; Susan J. Porter, V.P., Progs.; Robert J. Benz; Rebecca Scripps Brickner; Mark Contreras; Peter Copeland; Tim Gallagher; Julia Scripps Heidt; Pamela Howard; Cindy McConkey; Crystal B. Price; William A. Scripps, Sr.; Donna Stephens; Adam Symson; E. John Wolfzorn.

Members: William R. Burleigh; John H. Burlingame; David A. Galloway; Kenneth W. Lowe; Jarl Mohn; Nicholas B. Paumgarten; Jeff Sagansky; Nackey E. Scagliotti; Edward W. Scripps, Jr.; Paul K. Scripps; Ronald W. Tysoe; Julie A. Wrigley.

Number of staff: 5 full-time professional.

EIN: 316025114

Selected grants: The following grants were reported in 2004.

$283,795 to University of Colorado Foundation, School of Journalism and Mass Communication, Boulder, CO. For Ted Scripps Fellowships.

$250,000 to Marquette University, College of Communication, Milwaukee, WI. For Professorship Endowment.

$250,000 to Ohio University Foundation, Athens, OH. For Visiting Professional Chair Endowment.

$150,000 to Columbia University, New York, NY. For Jack R. Howard International Fellowships.

$140,360 to United Way of Greater Cincinnati, Cincinnati, OH. 2 grants: $25,000 (For de Tocqueville Society Challenge Grant), $115,360 (For annual fund drive).

$100,000 to Northern Kentucky University Foundation, Highland Heights, KY. For Civic Engagement Endowment.

$40,000 to American Institute for Public Service, Wilmington, DE. For Jefferson Awards.

$25,000 to Cincinnati Institute of Fine Arts, Cincinnati, OH. For capital campaign.

$15,000 to University of California, Davis, CA. For literacy grant.

7849
Sedgwick Family Charitable Trust ◇ ☆

c/o KeyBank N.A.

800 Superior Ave., 4th Fl.

Cleveland, OH 44114

Established in 1991 in OH.

Donor: Ellery Sedgwick, Jr.†.

Foundation type: Independent foundation.

Financial data (yr. ended 12/31/05): Assets, $2,851,834 (M); expenditures, $717,307; qualifying distributions, $695,110; giving activities include $695,110 for grants.

Purpose and activities: Giving primarily for education, wildlife protection, and human services.

Fields of interest: Education; Animals/wildlife, preservation/protection; Reproductive health, family planning; Human services; Federated giving programs.

Type of support: Annual campaigns; Capital campaigns; Building/renovation; Scholarship funds; Research.

Limitations: Applications not accepted. Giving primarily in south GA. No grants to individuals.

Application information: Contributes only to pre-selected organizations the family has involvement with. Unsolicited requests for funds not accepted.

Trustees: Irene Sedgwick Briedis; Elizabeth W. Sedgwick; Ellery Sedgwick III; Theodore Sedgwick; Walter Cabot Sedgwick; KeyBank N.A.

EIN: 346958569

Selected grants: The following grants were reported in 2005.

$10,000 to Folger Shakespeare Library, DC.

$10,000 to Thomasville Community Resource Center, Thomasville, GA. 2 grants: $5,000 each

$9,500 to Winous Point Marsh Conservancy, Willoughby Hills, OH.

$5,000 to Land Trust Alliance, DC.

$4,000 to Oxfam America, Boston, MA.

$2,000 to International Rescue Committee, New York, NY.

$1,000 to Hawken School, Gates Mills, OH.

$900 to El Hogar Ministries, Winchester, MA.

$400 to Harvard University, Cambridge, MA.

7850
Dorothy T. & Myron Seifert Charitable Trust ✧ ☆

c/o National City Bank
P.O. Box 94651
Cleveland, OH 44101-4651

Established in 1996 in OH.
Foundation type: Independent foundation.
Financial data (yr. ended 12/31/05): Assets, $5,718,303 (M); expenditures, $406,000; qualifying distributions, $397,050; giving activities include $395,000 for 26 grants (high: $57,922; low: $518; average: $3,869–$19,161).
Fields of interest: Museums; Historic preservation/historical societies; Higher education; Libraries/library science; Hospitals (general); Health organizations, association; Protestant agencies & churches.
Type of support: General/operating support.
Limitations: Applications not accepted. Giving limited to OH. No grants to individuals.
Application information: Contributes only to pre-selected organizations.
Trustee: National City Bank.
EIN: 316535424
Selected grants: The following grants were reported in 2005.
$16,766 to American Cancer Society, Columbus, OH.
$6,375 to First United Methodist Church, Hamilton, OH.
$6,118 to Columbus Foundation, Columbus, OH.
$3,869 to American Heart Association, Columbus, OH.
$3,869 to Central Ohio Lung Association, Columbus, OH.

7851
The Louise Taft Semple Foundation ✧

312 Walnut St., Ste. 3560
Cincinnati, OH 45202
Contact: Penny Friedman
FAX: (513) 421-7107; *E-mail:* benefactors@fuse.net

Incorporated in 1941 in OH.
Donor: Louise Taft Semple†.
Foundation type: Independent foundation.
Financial data (yr. ended 12/31/05): Assets, $21,498,558 (M); expenditures, $1,205,349; qualifying distributions, $1,023,559; giving activities include $976,823 for 39 grants (high: $100,000; low: $2,000).
Purpose and activities: Giving primarily for the arts, private elementary and secondary education, and for civic and social purposes.
Fields of interest: Museums; Performing arts; Historical activities; Arts; Education.
Type of support: Capital campaigns; Building/renovation; Equipment; Land acquisition; Endowments; Program development; Matching/challenge support.
Limitations: Giving primarily in the Cincinnati and Hamilton County, OH, area. No grants to individuals, or for general purposes or research; no loans.
Publications: Application guidelines.
Application information: Application form required.
  Initial approach: Letter
  Copies of proposal: 2
  Deadline(s): Feb. 15, May 15, Aug. 15, and Oct. 15

Board meeting date(s): 3rd Mon. in Apr., July, Oct., and Dec.
Final notification: 3 months
Officers and Trustees:* Dudley S. Taft,* Chair.; James R. Bridgeland, Jr.,* Secy.; John T. Lawrence III,* Treas.; William O. DeWitt; Mrs. John T. Lawrence, Jr.; Mrs. Robert A. Taft II; John B. Tytus.
Number of staff: 2 part-time professional.
EIN: 310653526
Selected grants: The following grants were reported in 2005.
$100,000 to Taft Museum, Cincinnati, OH.
$72,000 to United Way, OH.
$71,428 to Cincinnati Country Day School, Cincinnati, OH.
$71,428 to Seven Hills School, Cincinnati, OH.
$30,000 to Summit Country Day School, Cincinnati, OH.
$25,800 to Governors Residence Foundation Corporation, Columbus, OH.
$25,000 to Cincinnati Hills Christian Academy, Cincinnati, OH.
$25,000 to Cincinnati Nature Center, Milford, OH.
$25,000 to Saint Xavier High School, Cincinnati, OH.
$15,000 to Northern Kentucky Symphony, Newport, KY.

7852
Shaw Family Foundation, Inc. ✧ ☆

750 White Pond Dr.
Akron, OH 44320

Established in 1999 in FL.
Donor: Gerald Shaw.
Foundation type: Independent foundation.
Financial data (yr. ended 12/31/04): Assets, $2,902,482 (M); expenditures, $552,636; qualifying distributions, $433,030; giving activities include $433,030 for 26 grants (high: $225,050; low: $20).
Fields of interest: Arts; Education; Jewish agencies & temples.
Limitations: Applications not accepted. Giving primarily in FL. No grants to individuals.
Application information: Contributes only to pre-selected organizations.
Officers: Gerald Shaw, Pres.; Deborah Lynn Shaw, V.P.; Patsy L. Shaw, V.P.; Greta Foster, Secy.; Michael Wise, Treas.
EIN: 650968251
Selected grants: The following grants were reported in 2004.
$225,050 to Jewish Community Board of Akron, Akron, OH.
$40,000 to Akron Art Museum, Akron, OH.
$10,000 to Summa Health System Foundation, Akron, OH.
$5,000 to Jewish Federation of Greater Washington, Rockville, MD.
$1,000 to American Cancer Society, Atlanta, GA.
$1,000 to American Friends of Shalva, New York, NY.
$1,000 to Radiology Mammography International, Akron, OH.
$200 to Marcus Jewish Community Center of Atlanta, Dunwoody, GA.
$200 to Muscular Dystrophy Association, Tucson, AZ.
$20 to Humane Society.

7853
The Harold W. & Mary Louise Shaw Foundation ✧

1700 Courthouse Plz. N.E.
Dayton, OH 45402

Established in 1997 in OH.
Donors: Harold Shaw; Louise Shaw.
Foundation type: Independent foundation.
Financial data (yr. ended 11/30/04): Assets, $9,002,683 (M); gifts received, $3,029,104; expenditures, $380,821; qualifying distributions, $330,000; giving activities include $330,000 for 11 grants (high: $100,000; low: $5,000).
Fields of interest: Arts; Higher education; Zoos/zoological societies; Recreation; Children/youth, services.
Limitations: Applications not accepted. Giving primarily in OH. No grants to individuals.
Application information: Contributes only to pre-selected organizations.
Officers: Mary Louise Shaw, Pres. and Treas.; Sally Louise Veitch, V.P.; Ames Gardner, Jr., Secy.
Trustee: Robert D. Veitch.
EIN: 311577890
Selected grants: The following grants were reported in 2004.
$100,000 to Cheyenne Mountain Zoological Society, Colorado Springs, CO.
$45,000 to Dayton Art Institute, Dayton, OH.
$35,000 to Wediko Childrens Services, Boston, MA.
$30,000 to Project Aware, Prescott, AZ.
$30,000 to University of Colorado Foundation, Boulder, CO.
$5,000 to Boy Scouts of America, Springfield, OH.

7854
Rhonda & Larry A. Sheakley Family Foundation ✧

c/o Larry Sheakley
100 Merchant St.
Cincinnati, OH 45246-3751

Established in 2000.
Donor: The Sheakley Group, Inc.
Foundation type: Independent foundation.
Financial data (yr. ended 12/31/05): Assets, $1,096,728 (M); gifts received, $340,000; expenditures, $451,715; qualifying distributions, $443,567; giving activities include $443,567 for grants.
Fields of interest: Arts; Health organizations, association; Cancer; Human services; Federated giving programs.
Limitations: Applications not accepted. Giving primarily in Cincinnati, OH. No grants to individuals.
Application information: Contributes only to pre-selected organizations.
Trustees: Thomas E. Pappas, Jr.; Larry A. Sheakley; Rhonda L. Sheakley.
EIN: 311679150

7855
The Sherwin-Williams Foundation ✧

101 Prospect Ave., N.W., 12th Fl.
Cleveland, OH 44115 (216) 566-2000
Contact: Barbara Gadosik, Dir., Corp. Contribs.

Incorporated in 1964 in OH.
Donor: The Sherwin-Williams Co.
Foundation type: Company-sponsored foundation.

Financial data (yr. ended 12/31/04): Assets, $14,668,714 (M); expenditures, $889,247; qualifying distributions, $874,261; giving activities include $698,221 for 92+ grants (high: $185,000), and $175,840 for employee matching gifts.
Purpose and activities: The foundation supports organizations involved with arts and culture, education, health, human services, and community development.
Fields of interest: Arts; Higher education; Education; Human services; Community development; Federated giving programs.
Type of support: General/operating support; Capital campaigns; Building/renovation; Employee matching gifts.
Limitations: Giving primarily in areas of company operations, with emphasis on Cleveland, OH. No support for sectarian, labor, veterans', or fraternal organizations, or tax-supported organizations. No grants to individuals, or for endowments, start-up needs, emergency needs, debt reduction, land acquisition, special projects, research, scholarships, fellowships, publications, advertising, or conferences; no loans.
Application information: Application form not required.
   Initial approach: Proposal
   Copies of proposal: 1
   Deadline(s): Jan., Apr., July, or Oct. is preferred
   Board meeting date(s): Mar., June, Sept., and Dec.
   Final notification: 1 month
Trustees: C.M. Connor, Chair.; S.P. Hennessy, Secy.-Treas.; T.E. Hopkins; J.M. Scaminace.
EIN: 346555476

7856
The Alvin and Laura Siegal Foundation ◇ ☆
28790 Chagrin Blvd.
Woodmere, OH   44122

Established in 1998 in OH.
Donors: Alvin Siegal; Laura Siegal.
Foundation type: Independent foundation.
Financial data (yr. ended 12/31/05): Assets, $1,655,749 (M); expenditures, $461,870; qualifying distributions, $455,729; giving activities include $455,729 for 107 grants (high: $200,000; low: $9; average: $50–$5,000).
Purpose and activities: Giving primarily to Jewish organizations.
Fields of interest: Museums (art); Performing arts, orchestra (symphony); Jewish federated giving programs; Jewish agencies & temples.
Type of support: General/operating support.
Limitations: Applications not accepted. Giving primarily in Cleveland, OH. No grants to individuals.
Application information: Contributes only to pre-selected organizations.
Officers and Trustees:* Alvin Siegal,* Pres.; Kirk Schneider,* V.P.; Michael Siegal,* V.P.; Laura Siegal,* Secy.; Raj Patel,* Treas.
EIN: 341885840

7857
Fred F. Silk Charitable Foundation ◇
1731 Edmar St.
Louisville, OH   44641-2749

Established in 1990 in OH.

Donor: Fred F. Silk†.
Foundation type: Independent foundation.
Financial data (yr. ended 9/30/05): Assets, $12,617,322 (M); expenditures, $705,251; qualifying distributions, $686,993; giving activities include $594,108 for 24 grants (high: $220,000; low: $300).
Purpose and activities: Giving primarily for higher education and community improvement.
Fields of interest: Arts; Higher education; Human services; Children, services; Community development; Foundations (private grantmaking).
Type of support: General/operating support; Capital campaigns; Building/renovation; Endowments; Scholarship funds.
Limitations: Applications not accepted. Giving primarily in Canton, OH. No grants to individuals.
Application information: Contributes only to pre-selected organizations.
Trustees: Dennis J. Fox; Paul J. Helmuth.
EIN: 341651258
Selected grants: The following grants were reported in 2005.
$220,000 to Stark State College Foundation, Canton, OH.
$17,500 to Goshen College, Goshen, IN.
$17,160 to Saint Johns Villa, Carrollton, OH.
$15,000 to Massillon Museum, Massillon, OH.
$15,000 to Stark County District Library, Canton, OH.
$9,665 to Pathway Caring for Children, Canton, OH.
$7,750 to YMCA of Central Stark County, Canton, OH.
$7,500 to Second Chance Chaplaincy, Hartville, OH.
$300 to Coalition for Christian Outreach, Pittsburgh, PA.

7858
The Sisler McFawn Foundation
P.O. Box 149
Akron, OH   44309-0149   (330) 849-8887
Contact: Charlotte M. Stanley, Grants Mgr.
FAX: (330) 996-6215;
E-mail: sisler_McFawn@yahoo.com

Trust established in 1959 in OH.
Donor: Lois Sisler McFawn†.
Foundation type: Independent foundation.
Financial data (yr. ended 12/31/05): Assets, $20,597,747 (M); expenditures, $1,165,800; qualifying distributions, $1,068,016; giving activities include $1,012,172 for 85 grants (high: $65,000; low: $200).
Purpose and activities: Giving primarily for education, social services, and for special needs populations such as the elderly, children from disadvantaged families, and the disabled.
Fields of interest: Education; Health care; Human services; Children/youth, services; Aging; Disabilities, people with; Economically disadvantaged.
Type of support: General/operating support; Continuing support; Capital campaigns; Building/renovation; Equipment; Endowments; Program development; Seed money; Curriculum development; Scholarship funds; Matching/challenge support.
Limitations: Giving primarily in Summit County, OH. No support for churches, or general units of government. No grants to individuals, or for computer equipment, annual support, or special events; no loans.
Publications: Application guidelines; Grants list.

Application information: Application form not required.
   Initial approach: Telephone call prior to submission
   Copies of proposal: 1
   Deadline(s): 45 days prior to board meeting; Mar. 15, July 15, and Oct. 15
   Board meeting date(s): May, Sept., and Dec.
   Final notification: Within 3 weeks of board meeting
Distribution Committee: Richard H. Marsh, Chair.; Nicholas V. Browning; Michael J. Connor; Patricia A. Kemph; Justin T. Rogers, Jr.
Trustee: KeyBank N.A.
Number of staff: 1 part-time professional.
EIN: 346508111

7859
Sky Foundation
221 S. Church St.
Bowling Green, OH   43402-0428
(419) 327-6300
Contact: Angie Hill, Asst. Secy. and Admin.

Established in 1998 in OH.
Donors: Sky Financial Group, Inc.; Sky Holdings, Inc.
Foundation type: Company-sponsored foundation.
Financial data (yr. ended 12/31/04): Assets, $2,557,964 (M); gifts received, $425,125; expenditures, $502,832; qualifying distributions, $481,787; giving activities include $481,787 for 56 grants (high: $50,000; low: $2,000).
Purpose and activities: The foundation supports organizations involved with arts and culture, education, health, human services, and community development.
Fields of interest: Performing arts, orchestra (symphony); Arts; Elementary/secondary education; Higher education; Libraries (public); Education; Health care; YM/YWCAs & YM/YWHAs; Human services; Community development.
Limitations: Giving limited to northeast IN, southern MI, OH, western PA, and northern WV. No support for private foundations. No grants to individuals.
Application information: Application form required.
   Initial approach: Contact foundation for application form
   Deadline(s): None
Trustees: Marty E. Adams; Jennifer L. Iliff; Darlene Minnick; Rockette "Rocky" Richardson; Curtis E. Shepherd; C.J. Keller Smith; Eric C. Stachler; Kevin T. Thompson; Paul Tomko; D.J. Valentine.
EIN: 341886344
Selected grants: The following grants were reported in 2004.
$50,000 to Bowling Green State University, Bowling Green, OH.
$25,000 to Lucas County Educational Service Center, Toledo, OH.
$20,000 to Library Legacy Foundation, Toledo, OH.
$20,000 to YMCA of Youngstown, Youngstown, OH.
$20,000 to Youngstown Symphony Society, Youngstown, OH.
$15,000 to National Aviary in Pittsburgh, Pittsburgh, PA.
$15,000 to Toledo Museum of Art, Toledo, OH.
$12,500 to Mon Valley Education Consortium, McKeesport, PA.
$12,500 to West Liberty State College, West Liberty, WV.
$10,000 to Logan County Landmark Preservation, Bellefontaine, OH.

7860
The Slemp Foundation ✧
c/o U.S. Bank, N.A., Trust Tax Dept.
P.O. Box 1118, ML CN-OH-W10X
Cincinnati, OH 45201-1118
Grant and scholarship application address: c/o
Patricia L. Durbin, Tr. Off., U.S. Bank, N.A., P.O. Box
5208, ML CN-OH-W7PT, Cincinnati, OH
45201-5208; URL: http://
www.slempfoundation.org

Trust established in 1943 in VA.
Donor: C. Bascom Slemp‡.
Foundation type: Independent foundation.
Financial data (yr. ended 6/30/05): Assets,
$20,159,044 (M); expenditures, $1,125,021;
qualifying distributions, $1,039,886; giving
activities include $732,382 for 26 grants (high:
$500,000; low: $600), and $244,000 for 244
grants to individuals (high: $1,000; low: $1,000).
Purpose and activities: Giving primarily for
education and the arts for the benefit of residents
of Lee and Wise counties, VA. Giving also for
scholarships to residents of Lee and Wise counties,
VA, or a descendant of a resident thereof.
Fields of interest: Arts; Libraries/library science;
Education; Recreation, parks/playgrounds; Youth
development, centers/clubs.
Type of support: Building/renovation; Equipment;
Endowments; Emergency funds; Seed money;
Curriculum development; Scholarship funds;
Scholarships—to individuals.
Limitations: Giving primarily in Lee and Wise
counties, VA.
Publications: Application guidelines.
Application information: See foundation Web site
for application guidelines and procedures, and
downloading of scholarship application form.
Application form required.
  Initial approach: Letter
  Copies of proposal: 1
  Deadline(s): Oct. 15 for scholarships; no
    deadlines for grants
  Board meeting date(s): Apr., July, and Nov.
Trustees: Melissa S. Smith Jensen; Pamela S.
Orcutt; James C. Smith; Nancey E. Smith.
Agent: U.S. Bank, N.A.
EIN: 316025080
Selected grants: The following grants were reported
in 2003.
$525,000 to University of Virginias College at Wise,
  Wise, VA. 3 grants: $25,000 (For construction of
  C Bascom Slemp Student Center), $299,716
  (For construction of C Bascom Slemp Student
  Center), $200,284 (For construction of C
  Bascom Slemp Student Center).
$25,000 to University of Virginias College at Wise
  Foundation, Wise, VA. For radio station operating
  support.
$20,000 to Virginia State Parks Foundation, Wise,
  VA. 2 grants: $10,000 each (For annual
  support).
$10,000 to Hospice Support Services of the
  Lenowisco Area, Duffield, VA. For operating
  support.
$7,000 to Boy Scouts of America, Johnson City, TN.
  2 grants: $5,000 to Sequoyah Council (For
  books, literature, uniform parts, and program
  material), $2,000 to Sequoyah Council (For
  summer camp scholarships).
$2,000 to J. I. Burton High School, Norton, VA. For
  tutoring program.

7861
Edward and Betty Sloat Foundation
3065 Fairfax Rd.
Cleveland Heights, OH 44118 (216) 321-7159
Contact: Anne Unverzagt, Pres.
E-mail: mektra@aol.com

Established in 1990 in OH.
Donor: Edward Sloat‡.
Foundation type: Independent foundation.
Financial data (yr. ended 12/31/05): Assets,
$3,522,089 (M); expenditures, $432,745;
qualifying distributions, $420,280; giving activities
include $420,280 for 27 grants (high: $95,000;
low: $1,000).
Purpose and activities: Helping disadvantaged
youth through Catholic, Lutheran, and Jewish
institutions and organizations.
Fields of interest: Education; Youth development;
Children/youth, services; Protestant agencies &
churches; Roman Catholic agencies & churches;
Jewish agencies & temples; Religion.
Type of support: Building/renovation; Program
development; Curriculum development; Scholarship
funds; Technical assistance.
Limitations: Giving primarily in Cleveland, OH. No
grants to individuals.
Publications: Application guidelines; Financial
statement; Grants list; Multi-year report.
Application information: Application form not
required.
  Initial approach: Letter or telephone
  Copies of proposal: 1
  Deadline(s): Sept. 1
  Board meeting date(s): 1st Tues. in June and Dec.
  Final notification: Dec.
Officers and Directors:* Anne Unverzagt,* Pres.;
Richard P. Goddard,* Secy.; Joseph F. Ciulla,*
Treas.; Patricia Ciulla.
EIN: 341657230
Selected grants: The following grants were reported
in 2004.
$10,000 to Benedictine High School, Cleveland,
  OH.
$10,000 to City Year Cleveland, Cleveland, OH.
$10,000 to Magnificat High School, Rocky River,
  OH.
$10,000 to Regina High School, South Euclid, OH.
$10,000 to Saint Edward High School, Lakewood,
  OH.
$8,000 to Cleveland Music School Settlement,
  Cleveland, OH.
$8,000 to Young Audiences of Greater Cleveland,
  Cleveland, OH.
$5,000 to International Partners in Mission,
  Cleveland Heights, OH.
$1,000 to Foundation Center, New York, NY.

7862
The Kelvin and Eleanor Smith
  Foundation ▼ ✧
30195 Chagrin Blvd., Ste. 275
Cleveland, OH 44124 (216) 591-9111
Contact: Carol W. Zett, Grants Mgr.

Incorporated in 1955 in OH.
Donor: Kelvin Smith‡.
Foundation type: Independent foundation.
Financial data (yr. ended 10/31/04): Assets,
$147,612,165 (M); expenditures, $7,602,870;
qualifying distributions, $6,332,038; giving
activities include $6,280,653 for 65 grants (high:

$1,000,000; low: $1,000; average: $3,000–
$150,000).
Purpose and activities: The foundation's principal
interests are in the fields of nonsectarian education,
the performing and visual arts, and the environment.
Fields of interest: Arts; Education; Environment;
Health care; Human services.
Type of support: General/operating support;
Continuing support; Annual campaigns; Capital
campaigns; Building/renovation.
Limitations: Giving primarily in the greater
Cleveland, OH, area. No grants to individuals, or for
endowment funds, scholarships, or fellowships; no
loans.
Publications: Application guidelines.
Application information: Application form not
required.
  Initial approach: Letter of inquiry
  Copies of proposal: 1
  Deadline(s): None
  Board meeting date(s): No set time
  Final notification: By mail
Officers and Trustees:* Lucia S. Nash,* Co-Chair.;
Cara S. Stirn,* Co-Chair.; Ellen S. Mavec,* Pres.;
Andrew L. Fabens III, Secy.; William B. LaPlace,*
Treas.; Charles L. Bolton; Michael D. Eppig, M.D.
Number of staff: 1 full-time professional.
EIN: 346555349
Selected grants: The following grants were reported
in 2004.
$950,000 to Cleveland Museum of Art, Cleveland,
  OH. 2 grants: $150,000 (For annual fund),
  $800,000 (For capital campaign).
$500,000 to Laurel School, Shaker Heights, OH. For
  capital support.
$400,000 to Hathaway Brown School, Shaker
  Heights, OH. For capital campaign.
$250,000 to Cleveland Clinic Foundation,
  Cleveland, OH. For capital campaign.
$150,000 to PM Foundation, Urban Community
  School, Cleveland, OH. For capital campaign.
$150,000 to Trinity Commons Foundation,
  Cleveland, OH. For capital campaign.
$123,419 to Hawken School, Gates Mills, OH. For
  capital campaign.
$50,000 to Cleveland Institute of Art, Cleveland,
  OH. For annual fund.
$50,000 to Great Lakes Theater Festival, Cleveland,
  OH. For general operating support.

7863
The Jack J. Smith, Jr. Charitable Trust
c/o PNC Advisors Charitable Trust Committee
P.O. Box 1198
Cincinnati, OH 45201-1198 (513) 651-8463
Contact: Mary Alice Koch

Established in 1972 in OH.
Donor: Jack J. Smith, Jr.‡.
Foundation type: Independent foundation.
Financial data (yr. ended 9/30/05): Assets,
$8,998,470 (M); expenditures, $462,686;
qualifying distributions, $394,438; giving activities
include $384,300 for 31 grants (high: $44,000;
low: $3,000).
Purpose and activities: Giving primarily for health
and social services that benefit needy or
handicapped children in greater Cincinnati, OH.
Fields of interest: Children/youth, services.
Type of support: Capital campaigns; Building/
renovation; Equipment; Program development; Seed
money.

Limitations: Giving limited to organizations serving the greater Cincinnati, OH, area, including those in Hamilton, Butler, Clermont and Warren counties in OH, and Boone, Campbell and Kenton counties in KY. No grants to individuals, or for operating budgets, continuing support, annual campaigns, emergency funds, deficit financing, endowment funds, scholarships, research, or conferences; no loans.

Publications: Application guidelines.

Application information: Application form required.

Initial approach: Greater Cincinnati Common Grant Application Form required

Copies of proposal: 3

Deadline(s): Feb. 1, Aug. 1

Board meeting date(s): Mar. and Sept.

Final notification: 1 month after meetings

Trustees: James S. Wachs; PNC Bank, N.A.

EIN: 310912146

7864

Willard E. Smucker Foundation ◇

Strawberry Ln.
Orrville, OH 44667

Established in 1968 in OH.

Donor: The J.M. Smucker Co.

Foundation type: Company-sponsored foundation.

Financial data (yr. ended 12/31/05): Assets, $9,904,727 (M); expenditures, $873,779; qualifying distributions, $866,007; giving activities include $864,687 for 43 grants (high: $350,000; low: $1,000).

Purpose and activities: The foundation supports organizations involved with arts and culture, education, health, human services, and Christianity.

Fields of interest: Arts; Higher education; Education; Health care; Children/youth, services; Human services; Christian agencies & churches.

Type of support: General/operating support.

Limitations: Applications not accepted. Giving primarily in OH. No grants to individuals.

Application information: Contributes only to pre-selected organizations.

Officers and Trustees:* Timothy P. Smucker,* Pres.; Marcella S. Clark,* Exec. V.P.; Richard K. Smucker, Treas.; Adam Ekonomon, Secy.; Carole L. Randall; Susan S. Wagstaff.

EIN: 346610889

7865

The Spaulding Foundation ◇

(formerly Joseph H. Spaulding Foundation)
8260 N. Creek Dr., Ste. 340
Cincinnati, OH 45236-6114 (513) 936-0101
Contact: Linda K. Marlow, V.P., Progs.

Established in 1997 in OH.

Donor: Ruth E. Spaulding Trust.

Foundation type: Independent foundation.

Financial data (yr. ended 2/28/06): Assets, $30,107,985 (M); expenditures, $1,602,132; qualifying distributions, $1,383,287; giving activities include $1,183,849 for 59 grants (high: $350,000; low: $2,000; average: $10,000–$25,000).

Purpose and activities: Giving to organizations that improve the quality of life in the Hamilton County, OH, community, in the areas of education, health, and human services.

Fields of interest: Education, special; Education; Zoos/zoological societies; Health care; Mental health/crisis services; Youth development; Human services; Children/youth, services.

Type of support: General/operating support; Continuing support; Capital campaigns; Building/renovation; Equipment; Program development.

Limitations: Giving limited to Hamilton County, OH, and the surrounding counties. No support for religious purposes. No grants to individuals.

Publications: Application guidelines.

Application information: Application form required.

Initial approach: Letter requesting application

Copies of proposal: 1

Deadline(s): Mar. 1, June 1, Sept. 1, and Dec. 1

Board meeting date(s): Quarterly

Officers: John E. Prather, Pres. and Treas.; Linda K. Marlow, V.P., Progs.; Lisa L. Prather, V.P.; James R. Marlow, Secy.

Number of staff: 3 full-time professional.

EIN: 311096254

7866

The Springfield Foundation

4 W. Main St., Ste. 825
Springfield, OH 45502-1323 (937) 324-8773
Contact: Robin Atwood Pfeil, C.E.O.; For grant application: Ed Baker, Prog. Off.
FAX: (937) 324-1836;
E-mail: robin@springfieldfoundation.org; E-mail for grant application: ed@springfieldfoundation.org;
URL: http://www.springfieldfoundation.org

Incorporated in 1948 in OH.

Foundation type: Community foundation.

Financial data (yr. ended 3/31/05): Assets, $31,150,487 (M); gifts received, $1,883,818; expenditures, $1,989,717; giving activities include $1,237,536 for 737 grants (high: $28,000; low: $25).

Purpose and activities: The foundation devotes emphasis to programs that enrich the life of the community in the following areas: the arts, civic affairs, education, the environment, health and social services.

Fields of interest: Arts; Education; Environment; Health care; Human services; Public affairs.

Type of support: General/operating support; Equipment; Program development; Publication; Seed money; Curriculum development; Research; Technical assistance; Program evaluation; Scholarships—to individuals.

Limitations: Giving limited to Clark County, OH. No support for private or religious schools, or religious programs. No grants to individuals (except for designated scholarships), or for debt reduction or to establish endowment funds.

Publications: Application guidelines; Annual report; Financial statement; Grants list; Informational brochure (including application guidelines); Newsletter; Program policy statement.

Application information: Visit foundation Web site for letter of inquiry form and guidelines. Faxed or e-mailed applications are not accepted. If letter of inquiry rests favorably with the foundation's committee, it shall be considered for funding during the second phase of the deliberation process. Application form required.

Initial approach: Letters of inquiry are required

Copies of proposal: 10

Deadline(s): Aug. 1 for discretionary grants; Mar. 1 for scholarship applications

Board meeting date(s): Mar., June, and Nov.

Final notification: Approx. 6 weeks for initial response; Dec. 30 for grant determination

Officers and Trustees:* Robin Atwood Pfeil, C.E.O.; Peter Gus Geil,* Pres.; David Sanders,* V.P.; Chuck Swaney,* Secy.; Robyn Koch-Schumaker,* Treas.; Jean Acton; Cindy Barnett; Andy Bell; Charley Brougher; Robert Burton; Pauline Chakere; Glenn Collier; Lula Cosby; Harry Egger; Kim Nedelman Fish; Gordon Flax; Art Gianakopoulos; Sallie Ingle; Sally Lupfer; Mel Marsh; Vurn Mullins; Phyllis Nedelman; Peter Noonan; O. Lester Smithers; Bill Stapleton; Michelle Sweeney.

Staff: Edward J. Baker, Prog. Off.; Joan Elder, Office Mgr.-Donor Svcs. Coord.; Horton Hobbs, Devel. Dir.; Ted Vander Roest, Financial Off.

Number of staff: 5 full-time professional.

EIN: 316030764

7867

Stark Community Foundation ▼

(formerly The Stark County Foundation, Inc.)
400 Market Ave., N. Ste. 200
Canton, OH 44702-2107 (330) 454-3426
Contact: James A. Bower, Pres.; For grants: Cynthia M. Lazor, V.P., Progs.
FAX: (330) 454-5855; E-mail: jbower@starkcf.org;
Additional E-mail: cmlazer@starkcf.org; URL: http://www.starkcommunityfoundation.org

Established in 1963 in OH by resolution and declaration of trust.

Foundation type: Community foundation.

Financial data (yr. ended 12/31/04): Assets, $137,086,201 (M); gifts received, $8,856,342; expenditures, $6,778,515; giving activities include $5,682,172 for grants.

Purpose and activities: The foundation seeks to enhance the sound health and general welfare of Stark County, OH, citizens through support for civic improvement programs and educational institutions. Primary areas of interest include the arts, education, community development, health and wellness, youth, and social services.

Fields of interest: Visual arts; Performing arts; Historic preservation/historical societies; Arts; Education, early childhood education; Child development, education; Elementary school/education; Higher education; Business school/education; Law school/education; Education; Environment, natural resources; Environment; Health care; Substance abuse, services; AIDS; AIDS research; Crime/law enforcement; Food services; Housing/shelter, development; Recreation; Youth development, services; Children/youth, services; Child development, services; Family services; Aging, centers/services; Minorities/immigrants, centers/services; Homeless, human services; Human services; Urban/community development; Community development; Government/public administration; Leadership development; Youth; Aging; Disabilities, people with; Minorities; Homeless.

Type of support: General/operating support; Capital campaigns; Building/renovation; Equipment; Land acquisition; Emergency funds; Program development; Seed money; Scholarship funds; Research; Technical assistance; Consulting services; Scholarships—to individuals; Matching/challenge support; Student loans—to individuals.

Limitations: Giving limited to Stark County, OH. No support for religious organizations for religious purposes. No grants for endowment funds, operating budgets, continuing support, annual campaigns, publications, conferences or deficit financing; no grants or loans to individuals (except to college students who are permanent residents of Stark County, OH).

Publications: Application guidelines; Annual report (including application guidelines); Financial statement; Grants list; Informational brochure; Newsletter; Program policy statement.

Application information: Visit foundation Web site for application cover sheet and guidelines. Upon receipt of applicant's letter of intent, the foundation will determine if project merits further consideration and contact organization by letter to either decline further review or to ask for a full proposal. Application form required.

Initial approach: Mail, fax, or e-mail letter of intent (no more than 2 pages)
Copies of proposal: 16
Deadline(s): Mar. 1, July 1, and Nov. 1 for letter of intent; Apr. 1, Aug. 1, and Dec. 1 for full grant proposals
Board meeting date(s): 8 to 10 times per year
Final notification: Feb., June, and Oct.

Officers and Board of Trustees:* Candy Wallace,* Chair.; James A. Bower, Pres.; Cynthia M. Lazor, V.P., Progs.; Patricia C. Quick, V.P., Finance; Howard S. Rubin, Jr., V.P., Devel.; Rhoda M. Blough, Corp. Secy.; Sheila Markley Black, Genl. Counsel; Nazamovia "Naz" Adams-Phillips; Robert DeHoff; Thomas V. Ferrero; Jeffrey A. Fisher; David L. Kuntzman; Patricia A. Miller; Thomas W. Schervish; John R. Werren.

Trustee Banks: CHASE; FirstMerit Bank, N.A.; The Huntington Bank; KeyBank N.A.; National City Bank; Sky Bank.

Number of staff: 4 full-time professional; 3 part-time professional; 2 full-time support; 3 part-time support.

EIN: 340943665

Selected grants: The following grants were reported in 2004.

$365,373 to Lake Local School District, Millbury, OH. For Lake Community Center YMCA project.

$257,800 to Mount Union College, Alliance, OH.

$184,038 to United Way of Greater Stark County, Canton, OH.

$100,000 to Ohio and Erie Canal Corridor Coalition, Akron, OH.

$65,000 to Stark Development Board, Canton, OH. For general operating support.

$51,891 to Multi-Development Services of Stark County, Canton, OH. To initiate Summit Neighborhood Housing Program.

$45,000 to Goodwill Industries and Rehabilitation Center of Canton, Canton, OH. For United Way Capital campaign.

$34,770 to Arts in Stark, Canton, OH. For Arts in Stark.

$29,510 to Lake Township Rotary, Hartville, OH. For Book Sculpture. Grant made through Lake Local School District.

$15,000 to Faces of Stark County, Canton, OH. To provide additional support sources to Kinship Caregivers in Stark County.

7868
Ben S. & Gerome R. Stefanski Charitable Foundation ◇
7007 Broadway Ave.
Cleveland, OH 44105-1490
Contact: Marc A. Stefanski, Pres.; Bernard S. Kobak, Secy.-Treas.

Established in 1991 in OH.
Donors: Monica Martines; Paul Stefanik; Third Federal Savings and Loan Assn.; TFS Key Trust Donations.
Foundation type: Independent foundation.
Financial data (yr. ended 12/31/04): Assets, $9,150,577 (M); gifts received, $10,139,368; expenditures, $1,144,346; qualifying distributions, $1,141,750; giving activities include $1,141,750 for 14 grants (high: $600,000; low: $1,000).
Purpose and activities: Giving primarily to a Roman Catholic school, as well as for other education, and for senior citizens services.
Fields of interest: Elementary/secondary education; Education; Human services; Aging, centers/services; Roman Catholic agencies & churches.
Limitations: Giving primarily in to the greater Cleveland, OH, area.
Application information: Application form not required.
Deadline(s): Sept. 30
Officers and Trustees:* Marc A. Stefanski,* Pres.; Rhonda Stefanski,* V.P.; Bernard S. Kobak,* Secy.-Treas.
EIN: 341691023
Selected grants: The following grants were reported in 2004.
$250,000 to Catholic Diocese of Cleveland Foundation, Cleveland, OH.
$100,000 to Jennings Center for Older Adults, Garfield Heights, OH.
$40,250 to Gilmour Academy, Gates Mills, OH.
$30,000 to Heidelberg College, Tiffin, OH.
$5,000 to Cleveland Rape Crisis Center, Cleveland, OH.
$5,000 to New Directions, Pepper Pike, OH.
$2,000 to Hathaway Brown School, Shaker Heights, OH.
$2,000 to Saint Philomena Church, Cleveland, OH.
$2,000 to University School, Shaker Heights, OH.
$1,000 to Julie Billiart School, Lyndhurst, OH.

7869
Stillson Foundation ◇
c/o Fifth Third Bank, Trust Dept.
38 Fountain Square Plz., MD 1COM31
Cincinnati, OH 45263
Application address: Fifth Third Bank Foundation Office, c/o Heidi Jark 38 Fountain Square Plz., MD1090CA, Cincinnati, OH 45263, tel.: (513) 534-4397

Foundation type: Independent foundation.
Financial data (yr. ended 12/31/05): Assets, $8,270,529 (M); expenditures, $696,993; qualifying distributions, $639,092; giving activities include $618,000 for 22 grants (high: $125,000; low: $3,000).
Fields of interest: Museums; Museums (science/technology); Performing arts; Elementary/secondary education; Higher education; Zoos/zoological societies; Physical therapy; Athletics/sports; equestrianism; Jewish agencies & temples.

Type of support: General/operating support; Capital campaigns; Program development.
Limitations: Giving primarily in the greater Cincinnati, OH area.
Application information: Application form required.
Initial approach: Request application form
Deadline(s): Quarterly
Trustee: Fifth Third Bank.
EIN: 311327107

7870
The Stocker Foundation ◇
401 Broadway Ave., Ste. 101
Lorain, OH 44052 (440) 246-5719
Contact: Patricia O'Brien, Exec. Dir.
FAX: (440) 246-5720;
E-mail: contact@stockerfoundation.org; Additional e-mails: pobrien@stockerfoundation.org (Patricia O'Brien); mwilson@stockerfoundation.org (Melanie R. Wilson); dgolba@stockerfoundation.org (Dawn Golba); URL: http://www.stockerfoundation.org

Incorporated in 1979 in OH.
Donor: Beth K. Stocker‡.
Foundation type: Independent foundation.
Financial data (yr. ended 12/31/05): Assets, $47,118,348 (M); expenditures, $3,318,963; qualifying distributions, $2,734,924; giving activities include $2,734,924 for 306 grants (high: $54,700; low: $50).
Purpose and activities: Emphasis on short-term youth development programs; social service agencies offering solutions to specific problems, such as literacy, hunger, and homelessness; education (including early childhood, elementary, secondary, and higher education); aid to the disabled; self-help programs; theater and the performing arts, and other cultural programs; women's issues and the strengthening of families.
Fields of interest: Arts education; Arts; Education, early childhood education; Elementary school/education; Secondary school/education; Adult education—literacy, basic skills & GED; Reproductive health, family planning; Mental health/crisis services; Crime/violence prevention, domestic violence; Housing/shelter; Youth development, services; Human services; Children/youth, services; Family services; Residential/custodial care, hospices; Aging, centers/services; Women, centers/services; Homeless, human services; Civil liberties, reproductive rights; Voluntarism promotion; Public affairs, citizen participation; Leadership development; Disabilities, people with; Economically disadvantaged.
Type of support: General/operating support; Building/renovation; Equipment; Endowments; Emergency funds; Program development; Seed money; Curriculum development; Technical assistance; Matching/challenge support.
Limitations: Giving primarily in Pina County, AZ, San Francisco County, CA, Dona Ana and Bernalillo counties, NM, Lorain and Cuyahoga counties, OH, and King County, WA. No support for religious organizations for religious purposes, governmental services, or public school services required by law. No grants to individuals, or for annual campaigns, conferences, deficit financing/debt reduction, mass mailings, research projects and tickets or advertising for fundraising activities; no loans. Generally no grants for capital requests except when specific criteria is met.
Publications: Annual report (including application guidelines); Grants list; Informational brochure.

Application information: Proposals received by fax not considered; proposals exceeding 10 pages will not be reviewed. Cover sheet required. See foundation Web site for application guidelines and downloading of cover sheet.

Initial approach: Telephone or letter of inquiry to discuss proposal ideas
Copies of proposal: 3
Deadline(s): May 15, Aug. 15, and Dec. 15
Board meeting date(s): Spring, summer, and fall
Final notification: 10 to 12 weeks after deadline

Officers and Trustees:* Benjamin P. Norton,* Pres.; Nancy Elizabeth Woodling,* Secy.; Patricia O'Brien, Exec. Dir.; Amy Dobras; Dawn Dobras; Mary Ann Dobras; Brent Norton; Jane Norton; Anne Woodling; Sue Woodling.
Corporate Trustee: KeyBank N.A.
Number of staff: 2 full-time professional; 1 full-time support.
EIN: 341293603

7871
Irving I. Stone Foundation ✧ ☆
1 American Rd.
Cleveland, OH   44144

Established in 1999 in OH.
Donor: Irving I. Stone.
Foundation type: Independent foundation.
Financial data (yr. ended 12/31/04): Assets, $9,605,290 (M); gifts received, $250,000; expenditures, $582,884; qualifying distributions, $530,186; giving activities include $520,000 for 3 grants (high: $310,000; low: $50,000).
Fields of interest: Higher education, university; Jewish agencies & temples.
Limitations: Applications not accepted. Giving primarily in New York, NY. No grants to individuals.
Application information: Contributes only to pre-selected organizations.
Officers and Trustees:* Gary Weiss, Pres.; Judith Stone Weiss,* Secy.; Hensha Gansbourg; Helen Stone; Myrna Tatar; Elie Weiss; Jeffrey Weiss; Morry Weiss; Zev Weiss.
EIN: 341892327
Selected grants: The following grants were reported in 2003.
$200,000 to Yeshiva University, New York, NY. For general support.

7872
Stranahan Foundation
4169 Holland-Sylvania Rd., Ste. 201
Toledo, OH   43623-2590   (419) 882-5575
Contact: Pamela G. Roberts, Grants Mgr.
FAX: (419) 882-2072;
E-mail: proberts@stranahanfoundation.org;
Additional E-mail: mail@stranahanfoundation.org;
URL: http://www.stranahanfoundation.org

Trust established in 1944 in OH.
Donors: Robert A. Stranahan†; Frank D. Stranahan†; and others.
Foundation type: Independent foundation.
Financial data (yr. ended 12/31/04): Assets, $91,904,076 (M); gifts received, $2,000; expenditures, $4,282,923; qualifying distributions, $3,903,935; giving activities include $3,395,131 for 70 grants (high: $1,250,000; low: $350; average: $10,000–$50,000), and $185,000 for 2 loans/program-related investments.

Purpose and activities: Giving largely for higher education; support also for a community foundation and a community fund, youth, social services, health agencies, and cultural organizations, including a fine arts museum and performing arts groups.
Fields of interest: Museums; Performing arts, ballet; Performing arts, orchestra (symphony); Performing arts, opera; Performing arts, music (choral); Arts; Higher education; Education; Health organizations, association; Human services; Youth, services; Business/industry; Community development; Federated giving programs.
Type of support: General/operating support; Continuing support; Annual campaigns; Capital campaigns; Building/renovation; Equipment; Program development; Program evaluation; Program-related investments/loans; Matching/challenge support.
Limitations: Giving primarily in Toledo and northwest, OH. No support for religious organizations or religious purposes, projects located outside the U.S., or government sponsored or controlled projects. No grants to individuals, or for deficit reduction, computer projects, film, television, or radio productions, or endowment funds.
Publications: Annual report; Grants list; Informational brochure (including application guidelines).
Application information: Application form available on foundation Web site. Application form required.
Initial approach: Letter (no more than 2 pages)
Copies of proposal: 1
Deadline(s): Mar. 1, July 1, and Nov. 1
Board meeting date(s): Feb., June, and Oct.
Final notification: 3 weeks after board meetings

Officers: Pat Stranahan, Pres.; Kathy Knight, Secy.; William Foster, Treas.; Pam Howell-Beach, Exec. Dir.
Trustees: Diana Foster; Paget Ferrell; Trevor Foster; Michael Foster; Julie Higgins; Marcia Piper; Bob Stranahan IV; Stephen Stranahan; Charles G. Yeager.
Number of staff: 1 full-time professional; 1 full-time support; 3 part-time support.
EIN: 346514375

7873
Robert A. Stranahan, Jr. Charitable Trust ✧
c/o KeyBank N.A.
800 Superior Ave., 4th Fl.
Cleveland, OH   44114
Contact: Diane Ohns, V.P., KeyBank N.A.

Established in 1959.
Donors: Robert A. Stranahan, Jr.; Nancy S. Jones; Lynn S. Butler.
Foundation type: Independent foundation.
Financial data (yr. ended 12/31/05): Assets, $7,862,987 (M); expenditures, $415,899; qualifying distributions, $387,415; giving activities include $380,180 for 37 grants (high: $30,000; low: $4,000; average: $5,000–$25,000).
Purpose and activities: Giving primarily for education, health associations, including children's hospitals, as well as for children, youth and social services, Christian organizations, and to federated giving programs, including the United Way; funding also for theater.
Fields of interest: Performing arts, theater; Education; Hospitals (specialty); Health organizations, association; Human services; Children/youth, services; Federated giving programs; Christian agencies & churches.

Type of support: General/operating support; Equipment; Emergency funds; Program development.
Limitations: Applications not accepted. Giving primarily in Toledo, OH. No grants to individuals; no loans or program-related investments.
Application information: Contributes only to pre-selected organizations.
Advisors: William R. Foster; Gerald W. Miller; Roberta M. Pawlak.
Trustee: KeyBank N.A.
EIN: 346504818
Selected grants: The following grants were reported in 2004.
$25,000 to Hospice of Northwest Ohio, Perrysburg, OH.
$25,000 to Mill Youth Stop, Toledo, OH.
$20,000 to Sunshine Foundation, Maumee, OH.
$20,000 to United Way of Greater Toledo, Toledo, OH.
$15,000 to Campus Crusade for Christ, San Clemente, CA.
$15,000 to Stranahan Theater Trust, Toledo, OH.
$10,000 to Adopt America Network, Toledo, OH.
$10,000 to Boys and Girls Clubs of Toledo, Toledo, OH.
$10,000 to Cherry Street Mission Ministries, Toledo, OH.
$5,000 to American Red Cross, Toledo, OH.

7874
The Summer Family Foundation ✧ ☆
20749 Beachcliff Blvd.
Rocky River, OH   44116

Foundation type: Independent foundation.
Financial data (yr. ended 12/31/05): Assets, $465,474 (M); gifts received, $652,564; expenditures, $505,651; qualifying distributions, $500,500; giving activities include $500,500 for 51 grants (high: $250,000; low: $500).
Fields of interest: Higher education; Health care; Human services.
Limitations: Applications not accepted. No grants to individuals.
Application information: Contributes only to pre-selected organizations.
Directors: Kelly B. Summers; Mark H. Summers; Pamela A. Summers; William B. Summers.
EIN: 341973147

7875
The Frank M. Tait Foundation ✧
40 N. Main St., Ste. 1530
Dayton, OH   45423   (937) 222-2401
Contact: Doris J. Adler, Exec. Dir.

Incorporated in 1955 in OH.
Donors: Frank M. Tait†; Mrs. Frank M. Tait†.
Foundation type: Independent foundation.
Financial data (yr. ended 12/31/05): Assets, $7,499,027 (M); expenditures, $369,296; qualifying distributions, $358,870; giving activities include $319,750 for 32 grants (high: $50,000; low: $1,000).
Purpose and activities: Giving primarily for youth development.
Fields of interest: Arts; Youth development.
Type of support: Annual campaigns; Building/renovation; Equipment; Program development; Seed money; Matching/challenge support.

Limitations: Giving limited to Montgomery County, OH. No support for religious purposes. No grants to individuals, or for endowment funds, operating budgets, continuing support, emergency funds, deficit financing, research, publications, conferences, scholarships, fellowships or selective capital campaigns; no loans.
Publications: Grants list; Informational brochure (including application guidelines).
Application information: Application form not required.
Initial approach: 1- to 2-page letter or telephone
Copies of proposal: 1
Deadline(s): Varies
Board meeting date(s): Quarterly
Final notification: 2 months
Officer and Trustees:* Doris J. Adler,* Secy.-Treas. and Exec. Dir.; Irven J. Bieser, Jr.; Thomas G. Breitenbach; Robert J. Kegerreis; James M. Woodhull II.
Number of staff: 1 part-time professional.
EIN: 316037499

7876
Paul P. Tell Foundation, Inc. ✧
195 S. Main St., Ste. 200
Akron, OH   44308   (330) 434-8355
Contact: David J. Schipper, Pres.

Incorporated in 1952 in OH.
Donors: Anne P. Tell; David J. Schipper; Michael Tell; members of the Tell family, and their business interests.
Foundation type: Independent foundation.
Financial data (yr. ended 12/31/05): Assets, $15,916,715 (L); gifts received, $300,000; expenditures, $1,834,727; qualifying distributions, $1,744,900; giving activities include $1,744,900 for 72 grants (high: $1,139,000; low: $1,000).
Purpose and activities: For the furtherance of Evangelical Christianity; on-going grants primarily for foreign missions.
Fields of interest: Christian agencies & churches.
Type of support: Continuing support.
Limitations: Giving on a national basis. No support for educational institutions. No grants to individuals, or for building, start-up, or endowment funds, scholarships, fellowships, or matching gifts; no loans.
Application information: Application form not required.
Deadline(s): None
Board meeting date(s): June
Officers: David J. Schipper, Pres.; Peter Keslar, V.P.; Jean Anne Schipper, Secy.-Treas.
Trustees: David Fair; Terry Hollister; Brenda Unruh.
EIN: 346537201
Selected grants: The following grants were reported in 2004.
$1,149,500 to Chapel, The, Akron, OH.
$13,000 to Greater Europe Mission, Monument, CO.
$5,000 to Bibles for the World, Colorado Springs, CO.
$5,000 to Christian World Publishers, Pleasant Hill, CA.
$5,000 to Haggai Institute for Advanced Leadership Training, Atlanta, GA.
$5,000 to International Bible Society, Colorado Springs, CO.
$5,000 to Operation Mobilization, Tyrone, GA.
$4,000 to Avant Ministries, Kansas City, MO.
$4,000 to Trans World Radio, Cary, NC.

$3,400 to Wycliffe Bible Translators, Orlando, FL.

7877
The Tetlak Foundation ✧
c/o C.J. D'Ambrosia, C.P.A.
1900 E. 9th St., Ste. 3200
Cleveland, OH   44114-3485

Established in 1998 in OH.
Donor: Joseph F. Tetlak.
Foundation type: Independent foundation.
Financial data (yr. ended 12/31/05): Assets, $2,591,911 (M); expenditures, $403,255; qualifying distributions, $403,050; giving activities include $51,750 for 12 grants (high: $14,750; low: $1,000), and $350,000 for 1 grant to an individual (high: $350,000).
Purpose and activities: Giving primarily for Roman Catholic charities and schools, the arts, veterans' health care and higher education.
Fields of interest: Arts; Higher education, university; Education; Military/veterans' organizations; Roman Catholic agencies & churches.
Limitations: Applications not accepted. Giving primarily in OH; some funding also in IN.
Application information: Unsolicited requests for funds not accepted.
Officers and Trustees:* Joseph F. Tetlak,* Pres.; Jane T. Haylor,* Secy.; Edward G. Ptaszek, Jr.,* Treas.
EIN: 341880531

7878
The Thendara Foundation, Inc. ✧
c/o James M. Anderson
3333 Burnett Ave.
Cincinnati, OH   45229

Established in 1984 in OH.
Donors: C. Lawson Reed†; Dorothy W. Reed.
Foundation type: Independent foundation.
Financial data (yr. ended 12/31/05): Assets, $9,059,558 (M); expenditures, $501,215; qualifying distributions, $383,590; giving activities include $359,250 for 107 grants (high: $40,000; low: $500; average: $1,000–$2,500).
Purpose and activities: Giving primarily for the arts, particularly museums, and for social services.
Fields of interest: Museums; Performing arts (multimedia); Arts; Education; Health care; Human services; Children, services; Social sciences, public policy.
Limitations: Applications not accepted. Giving primarily in CA and CO; some giving also in NY and OH. No grants to individuals.
Application information: Contributes only to pre-selected organizations.
Trustees: James M. Anderson; Janet Reed Goss; C.L. Reed III; Dorothy Foster Reed; Foster A. Reed.
EIN: 311126072
Selected grants: The following grants were reported in 2004.
$40,000 to Applied Information Resources, Cincinnati, OH.
$10,000 to Boulder County Arts Alliance, Boulder, CO.
$10,000 to Compass for Lifelong Discovery, Woody Creek, CO.
$10,000 to Friendship Bridge, Evergreen, CO.
$10,000 to Joy Outdoor Education Center, Clarksville, OH.

$8,000 to Hudson Valley Writers Center, Sleepy Hollow, NY.
$5,000 to Doe Fund, New York, NY.
$4,000 to Chesapeake Bay Foundation, Annapolis, MD.
$2,000 to National AIDS Memorial Grove, San Francisco, CA.
$1,000 to Mills College, Oakland, CA.

7879
The Timken Company Educational Fund, Inc. ✧
1835 Dueber Ave. S.W.
Canton, OH   44706
E-mail: palomba@timken.com

Established in 1957.
Donor: The Timken Co.
Foundation type: Company-sponsored foundation.
Financial data (yr. ended 12/31/03): Assets, $931,914 (M); expenditures, $665,733; qualifying distributions, $663,961; giving activities include $634,050 for 46 grants to individuals (low: $135).
Purpose and activities: The foundation awards college scholarships to children of associates and retirees of the Timken Company, Timken Latrobe Steel Company, Timken Aerospace & Super Precision Bearings, RBS Corporation, and Canadian Timken.
International interests: Poland; Romania.
Type of support: Employee-related scholarships.
Limitations: Applications not accepted. Giving primarily in OH and PA; some giving also in Poland and Romania.
Application information: Contributes only through employee-related scholarships.
Board meeting date(s): Quarterly
Officers and Trustees:* Ward J. Timken,* Pres.; R.W. Lindsay, Sr. V.P.; D.L. Miller, Sr. V.P.; J.W. Begg, V.P.; S.B. Bailey, Secy.-Treas.
EIN: 346520257

7880
Timken Foundation of Canton ▼
200 Market Ave. N., Ste. 210
Canton, OH   44702   (330) 452-1144
Contact: Nancy Knudsen, Secy.-Treas.

Incorporated in 1934 in OH.
Donor: Members of the Timken family.
Foundation type: Independent foundation.
Financial data (yr. ended 9/30/05): Assets, $228,313,362 (M); expenditures, $8,032,907; qualifying distributions, $7,757,332; giving activities include $7,460,995 for 96 grants (high: $350,000; low: $8,064; average: $20,000–$2,000,000).
Purpose and activities: To promote broad civic betterment by capital fund grants; support largely for colleges, schools, hospitals, cultural centers, social services and recreation, and other charitable institutions.
Fields of interest: Historic preservation/historical societies; Arts; Education, early childhood education; Child development, education; Elementary school/education; Secondary school/education; Higher education; Adult education—literacy, basic skills & GED; Libraries/library science; Education, reading; Education; Hospitals (general); Health care; Health organizations, association; Crime/violence prevention, abuse

prevention; Recreation; Youth development, services; Child development, services; Community development; Computer science; Leadership development; Economically disadvantaged.

International interests: Brazil; Canada; China; Czech Republic; France; Germany; India; Italy; Poland; Romania; South Africa; United Kingdom.

Type of support: Capital campaigns; Building/renovation; Equipment; Land acquisition; Research; Matching/challenge support.

Limitations: Giving primarily in local areas of Timken Co. domestic operations in Torrington, and Watertown, CT; Cairo, Dahlonega, and Sylvania, GA; Bucyrus, Canton, Eaton, New Philadelphia, and Wooster, OH; Ashboro, Columbus, and Lincolnton, NC; Keene, and Lebanon, NH; Latrobe, PA; Honea Path, Walhalla, Clinton, Union, and Gaffney, SC; Altavista, VA; and Mascot and Pulaski, TN. Giving also in local areas in Brazil, Canada, China, Czech Republic, France, Germany, Great Britain, India, Italy, Poland, Romania, and South Africa where Timken Co. has manufacturing facilities. No support for projects for religious or political purposes. No grants to individuals. Generally, no grants for operating budgets, endowments, or program development.

Application information: Application form not required.

   Deadline(s): None
   Board meeting date(s): As required

Officers and Trustees:* Ward J. Timken,* Pres.; W.J. Timken, Jr.,* V.P.; Nancy Knudsen,* Secy.-Treas.; Joy A. Timken.

Number of staff: 1 full-time professional; 1 part-time professional; 1 full-time support.

EIN: 346520254

Selected grants: The following grants were reported in 2005.

$333,333 to Manufacturing Institute, DC. For operating endowment fund.

$300,000 to Arts in Stark, Arts in Stark, Canton, OH. For the Funds for the Arts Campaign.

$300,000 to Sosnowiec, Town of, Sosnowiec, Poland. To purchase premature birth equipment.

$222,333 to Wilberforce University, Wilberforce, OH. For capital campaign.

$215,000 to Partners for a Healthier Honea Path, Honea Path, SC. To install sprinkler in Watkins Community Center.

$100,000 to YMCA, Altavista Area, Altavista, VA. For expansion and renovation of athletic center.

$83,090 to Gauteng Department of Education, Johannesburg, South Africa. For computer lab in Hulwazi Secondary School.

$75,000 to Home Health Care and Community Services, Keene, NH. For new homecare technologies and disease management.

$50,000 to American Red Cross, Central Stark County Chapter, Canton, OH. For furniture and equipment.

$25,000 to Montshire Museum of Science, Norwich, VT. To build sidewalk for access to museum.

7881
The C. Carlisle and Margaret M. Tippit Charitable Trust ◇
925 Euclid Ave., Ste. 2000
Cleveland, OH 44115-1496

Established in 1989 in OH.
Donor: Tippit 1992 Charitable Lead Trust.
Foundation type: Independent foundation.

Financial data (yr. ended 8/31/05): Assets, $6,868,956 (M); expenditures, $453,014; qualifying distributions, $395,000; giving activities include $350,000 for 24 grants (high: $60,000; low: $5,000).

Purpose and activities: Giving primarily for education, health and human services.

Fields of interest: Higher education; Environment; Hospitals (general); Health care; Human services.

Limitations: Applications not accepted. Giving primarily in OH, with emphasis on Cleveland. No grants to individuals.

Application information: Contributes only to pre-selected organizations.

Trustees: James R. Bright; Carl J. Tippit.
EIN: 341627297

Selected grants: The following grants were reported in 2005.

$25,000 to Orlando Regional Medical Center Foundation, Orlando, FL.

$25,000 to Planned Parenthood of Greater Cleveland, Cleveland, OH.

$25,000 to Winnie Palmer Nature Reserve, Latrobe, PA.

$12,500 to United Way.

$10,000 to Beech Brook, Cleveland, OH.

$10,000 to Fairmount Presbyterian Church, Cleveland Heights, OH.

$7,500 to Benjamin Rose Institute, Cleveland, OH.

$7,500 to Breckenridge Village, Willoughby, OH.

$7,500 to Hattie Larlham Foundation, Mantua, OH.

7882
Toledo Community Foundation Donor Directed Pooled Fund ◇ ☆
c/o KeyBank N.A.
P.O. Box 10099
Toledo, OH 43699-0099 (419) 259-8655
Application address: c/o Toledo Community Foundation, 608 Madison Ave., Ste. 1540, Toledo, OH 43604

Established in OH.
Donors: Robert Wingerter; Dorothy Wingerter; David K. Welles, Jr.; Hope J. Welles; David K. Welles, Sr.; Georgia Welles; Mary Celeste Stranahan; Duane Stranahan, Jr.; George Stranahan; Kate T. Foster; Michael Stranahan; Paul Richard Day; Mrs. Paul Richard Day; Stephen Stranahan; Ann Stranahan; Tom Anderson; Mary Pat Anderson.
Foundation type: Independent foundation.

Financial data (yr. ended 12/31/04): Assets, $5,320,420 (M); gifts received, $2,151,093; expenditures, $2,311,742; qualifying distributions, $2,300,416; giving activities include $2,272,563 for 124 grants (high: $265,000; low: $40).

Fields of interest: Arts; Education; Health care; Human services; Residential/custodial care, hospices; Foundations (community); Federated giving programs; Protestant agencies & churches; Roman Catholic agencies & churches; Jewish agencies & temples.

Limitations: Giving primarily in Toledo, OH; some funding nationally.

Application information:
   Initial approach: Letter
   Deadline(s): None

Officers: Frank D. Jacobs, Chair.; Susan Morgan, Vice-Chair.; Keith Burwell, Pres.; William Rose, Treas.

Trustees: Sara Jane Dehoff; Hon. Charles J. Doneghy; William R. Foster; Dennis Johnson; Richard G. Lavalley, Jr.; Elizabeth Ruppert; Charles

Stocking; David K. Welles, Jr.; Patricia Wise; KeyBank N.A.
EIN: 341243271

7883
Toledo Community Foundation, Inc.
608 Madison Ave., Ste. 1540
Toledo, OH 43604-1151 (419) 241-5049
Contact: For grants: Kaarina Ornelas, Sr. Prog. Off.
FAX: (419) 242-5549; E-mail: toledocf@toledocf.org; Grant inquiry E-mail: kaarina@toledocf.org; URL: http://www.toledocf.org/

Established in 1924 in OH by trust agreement; reactivated in 1973.
Foundation type: Community foundation.

Financial data (yr. ended 12/31/05): Assets, $88,990,412 (M); gifts received, $7,343,297; expenditures, $8,831,899; giving activities include $7,177,862 for 373+ grants.

Purpose and activities: The foundation provides support for projects which promise to affect a broad segment of the citizens of northwestern OH or which tend to help those living in an area not being adequately served by local community resources. Areas of interest include social services and youth programs, arts and culture, education, natural resources, government and urban affairs, and physical and mental health.

Fields of interest: Arts; Child development, education; Education; Environment, natural resources; Health care; Mental health/crisis services; Health organizations, association; Children/youth, services; Child development, services; Aging, centers/services; Homeless, human services; Human services; Community development; Public affairs; Aging; Homeless.

Type of support: Program development; Seed money; Matching/challenge support.

Limitations: Giving primarily in northwestern OH, with emphasis on the greater Toledo area. No support for sectarian activities of religious organizations. No grants to individuals (except for scholarships), or for annual campaigns, capital campaigns, operating budgets, film, video, or TV productions, equipment purchase, or endowment funds.

Publications: Annual report (including application guidelines); Newsletter.

Application information: Visit foundation Web site for online grant application and guidelines. Application form required.

   Initial approach: Telephone
   Copies of proposal: 1
   Deadline(s): Jan. 15, May 15, and Sept. 1 for community grants; varies for others
   Board meeting date(s): Apr., Sept., and Dec.
   Final notification: Approx. 3 and a half months

Officers and Trustees:* Susan E. Morgan,* Chair.; Charles Stocking,* Vice-Chair.; Keith Burwell,* Pres.; William R. Foster,* Secy.; Kim Cryan, C.F.O.; William E. Rose,* Treas.; Richard P. Anderson; Sara Jane DeHoff; Charles J. Doneghy; Frank D. Jacobs; Dennis G. Johnson; Richard G. LaValley, Jr.; Beverly J. McBride; Edward McNeal; Geoffrey G. Meyers; Elizabeth S. Ruppert, M.D.; Mark Zyndorf.

Number of staff: 6 full-time professional; 1 part-time professional; 1 full-time support.
EIN: 237284004

7884
Tomkins Corporation Foundation ◇
(formerly Philips Industries Foundation)
6450 Poe Ave., Ste. 109
Dayton, OH 45414

Established in 1986 in OH.
Donor: Tomkins Industries, Inc.
Foundation type: Company-sponsored foundation.
Financial data (yr. ended 4/30/05): Assets, $6,300,267 (M); expenditures, $371,927; qualifying distributions, $364,145; giving activities include $159,199 for 14 grants (high: $70,984; low: $260), and $204,946 for 158 employee matching gifts.
Purpose and activities: The foundation supports organizations involved with arts and culture, education, health, children and youth, and human services.
Fields of interest: Arts; Higher education; Education; Health care; YM/YWCAs & YM/YWHAs; Children/youth, services; Human services; Federated giving programs.
Type of support: General/operating support; Scholarship funds; Employee matching gifts.
Limitations: Applications not accepted. Giving on a national basis, with some emphasis on OH. No grants to individuals.
Application information: Contributes only to pre-selected organizations.
Officers and Trustees:* Daniel J. Disser,* V.P.; Teresa A. Simmons,* V.P.; Malcolm T. Swain,* V.P.
EIN: 311207183

7885
V.B. Toulmin Charitable Foundation III ◇
34 N. Main St., 4th Fl.
Dayton, OH 45401

Established in 2003 in OH.
Donor: Virginia Toulmin.
Foundation type: Independent foundation.
Financial data (yr. ended 10/31/05): Assets, $290,142 (M); gifts received, $1,001,062; expenditures, $1,241,877; qualifying distributions, $1,241,015; giving activities include $1,240,800 for 18 grants (high: $516,000; low: $100).
Fields of interest: Performing arts, opera; Health care; Human services; Children/youth, services; Religion.
Limitations: Applications not accepted. Giving primarily in FL. No grants to individuals.
Application information: Unsolicited requests for funds not accepted.
Trustee: KeyBank N.A.
EIN: 137385769

7886
The Troy Foundation ◇
U.S. Bank Bldg.
910 W. Main St.
Troy, OH 45373 (937) 339-8935
Contact: Melissa A. Kleptz, Exec. Dir.
FAX: (937) 332-8305;
E-mail: info@thetroyfoundation.org; URL: http://thetroyfoundation.org/

Established in 1924 in OH by bank resolution and declaration of trust.
Donors: Nannie Kendall†; A.G. Stouder†; J.M. Spencer†.
Foundation type: Community foundation.
Financial data (yr. ended 12/31/04): Assets, $48,465,867 (M); gifts received, $731,081; expenditures, $2,160,494; giving activities include $1,743,537 for 297 grants (high: $427,634; low: $25).
Purpose and activities: The foundation seeks to improve the quality of life for the community served by promoting philanthropy and stewardship for a better tomorrow.
Fields of interest: Museums; Historic preservation/historical societies; Arts; Elementary/secondary education; Child development, education; Elementary school/education; Vocational education; Business school/education; Libraries/library science; Education; Environment, natural resources; Environment; Hospitals (general); Health care; Substance abuse, services; Recreation; Children/youth, services; Child development, services; Residential/custodial care, hospices; Human services; Community development; Youth.
Type of support: Capital campaigns; Building/renovation; Equipment; Emergency funds; Program development; Seed money; Curriculum development; Scholarship funds; Matching/challenge support.
Limitations: Giving limited to the Troy City, OH, School District. No support for religious organizations. No grants to individuals (except for scholarships), or for endowment funds, operating budgets, continuing support, deficit financing, research, demonstration projects, publications, conferences, or fellowships; no loans.
Publications: Application guidelines; Annual report; Informational brochure; Informational brochure (including application guidelines); Newsletter.
Application information: Visit foundation Web site for application form and guidelines. Application form required.
 Initial approach: Submit grant application and attachments
 Copies of proposal: 7
 Deadline(s): 15th of the month preceding board meeting
 Board meeting date(s): 3rd Fri. of Mar., June, Sept., and Dec.
 Final notification: 1-3 business days
Officer and Trustees:* Ronald B. Scott,* Chair.; Robert M. Schlemmer, Secy.; Melissa A. Kleptz, Exec. Dir.; Paul A. Hendrick; R. Daniel Sadlier.
Distribution Committee: Elizabeth A. Earhart, Chair.; Steve M. Baker; Arthur D. Haddad; Joan C. Heidelburg; Cindy Meeker.
Number of staff: 2 full-time professional.
EIN: 316018703

7887
The Trzcinski Foundation
8050 Corporate Cir., No.2
North Royalton, OH 44133
Contact: Ronald Trzcinski, Pres.

Established in 1997 in OH.
Donors: Ronald Trzcinski; Cheryl Trzcinski.
Foundation type: Independent foundation.
Financial data (yr. ended 6/30/05): Assets, $16,074,277 (M); gifts received, $2,250,133; expenditures, $626,575; qualifying distributions, $567,710; giving activities include $567,710 for 3 grants (high: $369,475; low: $20,000).
Fields of interest: Roman Catholic agencies & churches.
Type of support: General/operating support.

Limitations: Applications not accepted. Giving primarily in Cleveland, OH. No grants to individuals.
Application information: Unsolicited requests for funds not accepted.
Officer: Ronald Trzcinski, Pres.
EIN: 341852993

7888
Susan and John Turben Foundation ◇
3201 Enterprise Pkwy., Ste. 200
Beachwood, OH 44122

Established in 1992 in OH.
Donors: John F. Turben; Susan H. Turben.
Foundation type: Independent foundation.
Financial data (yr. ended 12/31/04): Assets, $2,464,298 (M); gifts received, $967,632; expenditures, $1,031,540; qualifying distributions, $995,546; giving activities include $988,566 for 72 grants (high: $217,000; low: $50).
Purpose and activities: Giving primarily for education, as well as for the arts, health associations, social services, children and youth services, and Christian churches.
Fields of interest: Media, radio; Museums (art); Arts; Higher education; Education; Health organizations; Medical research; Human services; Children/youth, services; Christian agencies & churches.
Type of support: General/operating support.
Limitations: Applications not accepted. Giving primarily in OH; some funding nationally. No grants to individuals.
Application information: Contributes only to pre-selected organizations.
Officers and Trustees:* Susan H. Turben,* Pres.; John F. Turben,* V.P.; Sandra L. Keily; James H. Kimberly; Newton S. Kimberly, Jr.; Mary S. Prien; William R. Robertson; David C. Turben; Nicholas A. Turben.
EIN: 341725277
Selected grants: The following grants were reported in 2004.
$210,625 to University School, Hunting Valley, OH.
$48,333 to Lake Erie College, Painesville, OH.
$45,000 to National Public Radio, DC.
$43,000 to Cleveland Museum of Art, Cleveland, OH.
$37,400 to First Presbyterian Church, Willoughby, OH.
$33,333 to Fund for Our Economic Future, Cleveland, OH.
$22,167 to Chautauqua Institution, Chautauqua, NY.
$11,000 to Yale University, New Haven, CT.
$5,300 to Fine Arts Council of Trumbull County, Warren, OH.
$2,500 to Ohio Foundation of Independent Colleges, Columbus, OH.

7889
The Turner Foundation ▼
(formerly Harry and Violet Turner 95 Charitable Trust)
4 W. Main St., Ste. 800
Springfield, OH 45502 (937) 325-1300
Contact: John Landess, Exec. Dir.
FAX: (937) 325-0100;
E-mail: questions@hmturnerfoundation.org;
URL: http://www.hmturnerfoundation.org

Established in 2001 in OH.
Donors: Harry M. Turner 97 Trust; Sara Landess.
Foundation type: Independent foundation.
Financial data (yr. ended 12/31/04): Assets, $110,990,950 (M); gifts received, $202,679; expenditures, $15,082,967; qualifying distributions, $12,493,413; giving activities include $10,344,200 for 141 grants (high: $2,492,005; low: $30; average: $10,000–$100,000), and $10,601,338 for 3 loans/program-related investments (high: $5,190,823; low: $2,098,707).
Purpose and activities: The foundation's mission is to enhance the quality of life in the greater Springfield/Clark County community through artistic, educational, environmental, recreational, family, healthcare, historic preservation, community beautification and revitalization initiatives.
Fields of interest: Elementary/secondary education; Higher education; Children/youth, services; Protestant agencies & churches.
Type of support: Matching/challenge support; General/operating support; Building/renovation.
Limitations: Giving primarily in Springfield and Clark County, Ohio. No support for religious or political organizations. No grants to individuals.
Publications: Application guidelines.
Application information: Application form required.
  Initial approach: Online application
  Deadline(s): Sept. 15
  Final notification: Dec.
Officers: John Landess, Exec. Dir.; Charlie McFarland, Cont.
Trustee: Security National Bank.
Number of staff: 14 full-time professional.
EIN: 311711190
Selected grants: The following grants were reported in 2004.
$750,000 to Emmanuel Christian Academy, Springfield, OH.
$352,500 to Catholic Central High School, Springfield, OH.
$167,500 to Wittenberg University, Springfield, OH.
$150,000 to Springfield City Schools, Springfield, OH.
$128,273 to Nehemiah Foundation of Springfield-Clark County, Springfield, OH.
$120,000 to Childrens Rescue Center, Springfield, OH.
$102,500 to Catholic Social Services, Springfield, OH.
$100,000 to Cedarville University, Cedarville, OH.
$85,000 to Saint Gregory the Great School, South Euclid, OH.
$84,000 to Tri-County Womens Network, New CArlisle, OH.

7890
Tuscarawas County Community Foundation

P.O. Box 523
New Philadelphia, OH   44663-0523
(330) 602-6264
Contact: David L. Engibous, Exec. Dir.
E-mail: execdir@tuscfoundation.com; Additional E-mail: grants@tuscfoundation.org; URL: http://www.tuscfoundation.com

Established in 2001 in OH.
Foundation type: Community foundation.
Financial data (yr. ended 12/31/05): Assets, $8,956,520 (M); gifts received, $381,381; expenditures, $497,561; giving activities include

$453,229 for 36 grants (high: $25,000; low: $2,740).
Purpose and activities: The foundation's mission is to enhance the quality of life in the Tuscarawas County community through the strengthening of its educational, economic, social, and cultural fabrics by making charitable grants of investment income.
Fields of interest: Humanities; Arts; Education; Environment; Health care; Human services; Community development.
Type of support: Continuing support; Management development/capacity building; Annual campaigns; Capital campaigns; Building/renovation; Equipment; Scholarship funds; Grants to individuals; Scholarships—to individuals.
Limitations: Giving primarily limited to Tuscarawas County, OH, area. No support for religious organizations. No grants to individuals (except through scholarship funds), operating expenses of well-established organizations, deficit financing, endowment funds, annual appeals, or conference or recognition events.
Publications: Application guidelines; Financial statement; Grants list; Informational brochure; Occasional report.
Application information: Visit foundation Web site for application form, guidelines, and specific deadlines. Application form required.
  Initial approach: Personal contact by letter or telephone
  Copies of proposal: 6
  Deadline(s): Varies, usually mid-year
  Board meeting date(s): Every 3 months
  Final notification: 30 days
Officers and Directors:* Hon. Roger G. Lile,* Pres.; George Brode,* V.P.; Elizabeth W. Stephenson,* Secy.; Sally O'Donnell,* Treas.; David L. Engibous, Exec. Dir.; Vic Marsh, Counsel; David Hanhart; Blair A. Hillyer; Michael Noretto; John J. Page; Jack D. Shores.
Number of staff: 1 part-time support.
EIN: 341930804

7891
The Van Wert County Foundation

138 E. Main St.
Van Wert, OH   45891   (419) 238-1743
Contact: Larry L. Wendel, Exec. Secy.
FAX: (419) 238-3374; E-mail: wwcf@bright.net; URL: http://www.vanwert.com/foundation

Incorporated in 1925 in OH.
Donors: Charles F. Wassenberg†; Gaylord Saltzgaber†; John D. Ault†; Kernan Wright†; Richard L. Klein†; Hazel Gleason†; Constance Eirich†; James Johnson†; Bert Strote†; Vernon Poling†.
Foundation type: Community foundation.
Financial data (yr. ended 12/31/05): Assets, $37,847,562 (M); gifts received, $1,533,445; expenditures, $3,872,136; giving activities include $2,852,072 for 145+ grants (high: $2,077,222), $336,042 for 325 grants to individuals (high: $3,300; low: $250), and $115,219 for 1 foundation-administered program.
Purpose and activities: Emphasis on scholarships in art, music, agriculture, and home economics; support also for elementary, secondary and higher education, youth agencies, an art center, recreational facilities, and programs dealing with alcoholism and drug abuse.
Fields of interest: Performing arts, music; Historic preservation/historical societies; Arts; Elementary school/education; Secondary school/education;

Higher education; Libraries/library science; Substance abuse, services; Alcoholism; Agriculture; Recreation; Children/youth, services; Human services.
Type of support: General/operating support; Capital campaigns; Building/renovation; Equipment; Scholarship funds; Research; Scholarships—to individuals.
Limitations: Giving limited to Paulding and Van Wert counties, OH. No support for religious purposes. No grants to individuals (except for designated scholarship funds), or for endowment funds or matching gifts.
Publications: Application guidelines; Informational brochure; Informational brochure (including application guidelines); Newsletter.
Application information: Visit foundation Web site for application guidelines. The foundation has discontinued its loans to individuals program. Previous commitments will be honored. Application form required.
  Initial approach: Letter
  Copies of proposal: 1
  Deadline(s): May 15 and Nov. 15 for grants; June 1 for scholarships
  Board meeting date(s): June and Dec.
  Final notification: 1 week
Officers and Trustees:* Michael T. Cross,* Pres.; Clair Dudgeon,* V.P.; Gerald Thatcher,* Secy.; Larry L. Wendel, Exec. Secy.; D.L. Brumback III; William S. Derry; Larry Greve; Bruce C. Kennedy; Watson Ley; F.W. Purmort III; Paul W. Purmort, Jr.; C. Allan Runser; Donald C. Sutton; Roger K. Thompson; Robert C. Young; Michael R. Zedaker.
Number of staff: 3 full-time professional; 2 full-time support.
EIN: 340907558

7892
Vesper Foundation ✧ ☆

6950 S. Edgerton Rd.
Brecksville, OH   44141-3184

Established in 1961 in OH.
Donor: Vesper Corp.
Foundation type: Company-sponsored foundation.
Financial data (yr. ended 12/31/05): Assets, $6,499,652 (M); expenditures, $880,797; qualifying distributions, $877,097; giving activities include $877,097 for grants.
Purpose and activities: The foundation supports hospitals and organizations involved with arts and culture, education, the environment, water sports, human services, and Christianity.
Fields of interest: Museums; Arts; Elementary/secondary education; Higher education; Education; Environment, natural resources; Botanical gardens; Horticulture/garden clubs; Environment; Hospitals (general); Athletics/sports, water sports; Human services; Christian agencies & churches.
Type of support: General/operating support; Scholarship funds.
Limitations: Applications not accepted. Giving on a national basis, with emphasis on the Northeast. No grants to individuals.
Application information: Contributes only to pre-selected organizations.
Trustees: James Benenson, Jr.; James Benenson III; John V. Curci.
EIN: 236251198
Selected grants: The following grants were reported in 2004.
$300,000 to Tabor Academy, Marion, MA.

$300,000 to Tulane University, New Orleans, LA.

$146,500 to New York Botanical Garden, Bronx, NY.

$75,000 to Horticultural Society of New York, New York, NY.

$30,000 to Smith Cove Preservation Trust, Ellsworth, ME.

$15,000 to Orange County Performing Arts Center, Costa Mesa, CA.

$10,000 to Melvin Van Peebles Foundation, New York, NY.

$7,500 to Hotchkiss School, Lakeville, CT.

$6,300 to Metropolitan Opera Association, New York, NY.

$1,450 to Metropolitan Museum of Art, New York, NY.

7893
The Phil Wagler Charitable Foundation ◇
3656 Massillon Rd.
Uniontown, OH 44685

Established in 1988 in OH.
Donors: Phil Wagler; Wagler Homes of Akron, Inc.; Wagler Homes of Cleveland, Inc.
Foundation type: Independent foundation.
Financial data (yr. ended 12/31/05): Assets, $10,176,053 (M); gifts received, $295,501; expenditures, $633,718; qualifying distributions, $557,750; giving activities include $557,750 for 29 grants (high: $100,000; low: $250).
Purpose and activities: Giving primarily for human services.
Fields of interest: Food services; Housing/shelter, homeless; Human services; Salvation Army; Christian agencies & churches.
Type of support: General/operating support.
Limitations: Applications not accepted. Giving primarily in OH. No grants to individuals.
Application information: Contributes only to pre-selected organizations.
Trustee: Phil Wagler.
EIN: 346886145

7894
Fred & Alice Wallace Charitable Memorial Foundation, Inc.
32 N. Main St.
Dayton, OH 45402 (937) 609-9048
Contact: Dennis Hanaghan, Exec. Dir.

Established in 1978 in OH.
Foundation type: Independent foundation.
Financial data (yr. ended 12/31/05): Assets, $9,906,248 (M); expenditures, $1,243,910; qualifying distributions, $1,086,932; giving activities include $895,729 for 68 grants (high: $100,000; low: $85).
Fields of interest: Education; Health organizations, association; Human services.
Type of support: Continuing support; Capital campaigns; Building/renovation; Equipment; Emergency funds; Program development; Conferences/seminars; Seed money; Curriculum development; Internship funds; Matching/challenge support.
Limitations: Giving limited to OH, with emphasis on the Miami Valley area. No grants to individuals.
Publications: Financial statement; Informational brochure (including application guidelines); Program policy statement.
Application information: Application form required.

Initial approach: Letter of intent
Copies of proposal: 4
Deadline(s): None
Board meeting date(s): July and Dec.
Final notification: As appropriate
Officers: Dennis Hanaghan, Pres. and Exec. Dir.; Jacob Worner, V.P.; J.R. Hochwalt, Secy.-Treas.
Number of staff: 1 full-time professional; 3 part-time professional.
EIN: 310944135

7895
The Warrington Foundation ◇
c/o Fifth Third Bank, Trust Tax Dept.
38 Fountain Sq. Plz., MD 1090FA
Cincinnati, OH 45263
Contact: Julie Herbert, Sr. Trust Off., Fifth Third Bank

Established in 1997 in OH.
Donor: Elsie H. Warrington.
Foundation type: Independent foundation.
Financial data (yr. ended 12/31/04): Assets, $9,782,218 (M); expenditures, $665,916; qualifying distributions, $605,120; giving activities include $587,258 for 88 grants (high: $50,000; low: $500), and $13,152 for 1 grant to an individual.
Purpose and activities: Giving primarily for the arts, education, the environment, medical research, including juvenile diabetes, and to Christian churches, as well as for children, youth and family services.
Fields of interest: Museums (art); Performing arts, orchestra (symphony); Arts; Higher education; Education; Environment, natural resources; Environment; Medical research, institute; Diabetes research; Human services; YM/YWCAs & YM/YWHAs; Children/youth, services; Protestant agencies & churches.
Limitations: Giving on a national basis, with some emphasis on OH.
Application information:

Initial approach: Letter
Deadline(s): None
Trustees: Dan Bailey; John Bailey; Lesley Bailey; Sam Bailey.
Agent: Fifth Third Bank.
EIN: 311582067
Selected grants: The following grants were reported in 2004.

$50,000 to Grand Traverse Regional Land Conservancy, Traverse City, MI. For general support.

$50,000 to New Britain Museum of American Art, New Britain, CT. For general support.

$30,000 to Ducks Unlimited, Vancouver, WA. For ecosystem project.

$20,000 to YMCA, Wood River Community, Ketchum, ID. For general support.

$19,700 to Indian Hill Church, Cincinnati, OH. For general support.

$19,000 to Trinity College, Hartford, CT. For general support.

$17,300 to Salisbury School, Salisbury, CT. For general support.

$16,000 to Alliance Institute for Integrative Medicine, Cincinnati, OH. For general support.

$15,000 to Cincinnati Nature Center, Milford, OH. For general support.

$15,000 to Federated Church, West Winfield, NY. For general support.

7896
Walter E. and Caroline H. Watson Foundation ◇
c/o National City Bank
P.O. Box 94651
Cleveland, OH 44101
Contact: Myra L. Vitto, Trust Off.
Application address: P.O. Box 450, Youngstown, OH 44501, tel.: (330) 742-4159

Established in 1964 in OH.
Donor: Walter E. Watson†.
Foundation type: Independent foundation.
Financial data (yr. ended 12/31/04): Assets, $7,932,552 (M); expenditures, $441,751; qualifying distributions, $430,188; giving activities include $429,990 for 55 grants (high: $125,000; low: $1,000).
Purpose and activities: To support public institutions of learning in OH and public and charitable institutions in the Youngstown and Mahoning Valley, OH, area; emphasis on health and hospitals, child development and youth agencies, community development, health and family services, housing and other programs for the disadvantaged, Jewish welfare funds, and arts and cultural programs, including the fine and performing arts.
Fields of interest: Visual arts; Museums; Performing arts; Performing arts, theater; Historic preservation/historical societies; Arts; Child development, education; Education; Hospitals (general); Health care; Health organizations, association; Cancer; Alcoholism; Cancer research; Housing/shelter, development; Human services; Children/youth, services; Child development, services; Family services; Residential/custodial care, hospices; Community development; Jewish federated giving programs; Economically disadvantaged.
Type of support: General/operating support; Continuing support; Annual campaigns; Capital campaigns; Building/renovation; Equipment; Program development.
Limitations: Giving primarily in OH, including the Youngstown and Mahoning Valley areas. No grants to individuals, or for endowment funds.
Application information: Application form not required.

Initial approach: Letter and proposal
Copies of proposal: 4
Deadline(s): None
Board meeting date(s): 3 or 4 times per year
Trustee: Eugenia Atkinson; Thomas R. Hollern; National City Bank.
EIN: 346547726

7897
Wayne County Community Foundation ◇
(formerly Greater Wayne County Foundation, Inc.)
517 N. Market St.
P.O. Box 201
Wooster, OH 44691 (330) 262-3877
Contact: B. Diane Gordon, Exec. Dir.
FAX: (330) 262-8057; E-mail: info@gwcf.net; Additional E-mail: gwcf@gwcf.net; URL: http://www.gwcf.net

Established in 1978 in OH.
Foundation type: Community foundation.
Financial data (yr. ended 6/30/05): Assets, $27,132,212 (M); gifts received, $2,307,230; expenditures, $1,467,019; giving activities include

$1,003,873 for 338 grants (high: $130,000; low: $25), and $266,390 for 128 grants to individuals (high: $5,000; low: $100).

Purpose and activities: The foundation seeks to: 1) encourage individuals who have prospered in Wayne County to leave part of their estates for the good of the community in which they lived; 2) assist community nonprofit organizations in the creation and management of endowments to meet future financial needs; and 3) assure responsible management and expenditure of funds devoted to charitable purposes.

Fields of interest: Humanities; Arts; Education; Environment; Health care; Human services; Community development; Religion.

Type of support: General/operating support; Continuing support; Capital campaigns; Building/ renovation; Equipment; Endowments; Emergency funds; Program development; Seed money; Scholarship funds; Matching/challenge support.

Limitations: Giving limited to Wayne County, OH. No support for religious organizations for religious purposes. No grants for deficit financing, endowment funds, annual appeals or membership contributions, conferences, field trips, travel, recognition events, or general operating expenses of well-established organizations including computers and office equipment.

Publications: Application guidelines; Annual report; Financial statement; Informational brochure (including application guidelines).

Application information: Visit foundation Web site for application form and guidelines. Faxed or E-mailed proposals are not accepted. Application form required.

Initial approach: Submit application form and attachments
Copies of proposal: 3
Deadline(s): Mar. 1 and Sept. 1
Board meeting date(s): Quarterly
Final notification: June 1 and Dec. 1

Officers and Trustees:* J.C. Johnston III,* Pres.; James L. Gerber,* V.P.; Jack K. Miller,* Secy.; Mary Alice Streeter,* Treas.; B. Diane Gordon, Exec. Dir.; David M. Briggs; Don Buren; Ronald E. Holtman; Don Houglan; William D. Landers; Fred Maibach; Robert C. Seiwert; Jenny Smucker; James C. Stebbins; Philip S. Swope; Richard S. Wagner; Mickey Workman; Mildred C. Workman.

Number of staff: 1 part-time professional; 1 part-time support.

EIN: 341281026

7898
The Raymond John Wean Foundation ▼
P.O. Box 760
Warren, OH   44482-0760   (330) 394-5600
Contact: Gordon B. Wean, Chair.
FAX: (330) 394-5601; E-mail: info@rjweanfdn.org; Additional address: 108 Main Ave. S.W., Ste. 1005, Warren, OH, 44481-1058; URL: http://www.rjweanfdn.org

Established in 1949 in OH.
Donor: Raymond John Wean, Sr.†.
Foundation type: Independent foundation.
Financial data (yr. ended 12/31/05): Assets, $90,092,904 (M); expenditures, $5,560,198; qualifying distributions, $4,722,029; giving activities include $4,489,176 for 281 grants (high: $500,000; low: $1,000; average: $1,000–$50,000).

Purpose and activities: To enhance the community well-being and vitality, particularly through strategic and responsive grants which help people in need.

Fields of interest: Education, early childhood education; Child development, services; Community development.

Type of support: Capital campaigns; Program development; Curriculum development; Program evaluation.

Limitations: Giving primarily in the Mahoning Valley, OH, area. No support for sectarian religious activities, veterans' or fraternal organizations, or local or national offices of organizations combating a particular disease or family of diseases. No grants to individuals; or for endowment funds, debt reduction, foreign operations, national fundraising campaigns or film or video production.

Publications: Application guidelines; Financial statement.

Application information: Applications accepted only after pre-application review. Pre-application form is available on the foundation's Web site. Application form required.

Initial approach: Complete pre-application form
Copies of proposal: 2
Deadline(s): Mar. 1, June 1, Sept. 1, and Dec. 1
Board meeting date(s): Jan., Apr., July, and Oct.
Final notification: Following board meeting

Officer and Administrators: Gordon B. Wean, Chair.; Jennie Dennison-Budak; John L. Pogue; Patricia Sweet.

Trustee: Sky Bank.
Number of staff: 2 full-time support.
EIN: 346505038
Selected grants: The following grants were reported in 2004.

$108,733 to Info Line, Akron, OH. For Child Care Connections: The Quality Enhancement Project: Phase 2.

$100,000 to Cuyahoga County District Board of Health, Cleveland, OH. For Early Childhood Intiative.

$60,622 to Tru-Mah-Col Association for the Education of Young Children, Girard, OH. For Quality Enrichment Project.

$50,000 to Pennsylvania Partnerships for Children, Harrisburg, PA. For improving early childhood education in Pennsylvania.

$50,000 to Western Reserve Health Foundation, Warren, OH. For Asthma Prevention in Childcare Setting.

$45,000 to RAND Corporation, Santa Monica, CA. For building model maternal and child health care system in Allegheny County through policy and practice improvements.

$30,000 to Mahoning County District Board of Health, Youngstown, OH. For Mahoning County Child Immunization Coalition.

$25,000 to Child Care Resource Center of Cuyahoga County, Cleveland, OH. For Teacher Education and Compensation Helps Ohio Program.

$20,000 to YWCA of Youngstown, Youngstown, OH. For Discovery Place Childcare Accreditation Project.

$4,000 to Family and Children First Council of Mahoning County, Youngstown, OH. For Building a Community Consensus to Child Lead Poisoning.

7899
The Weatherhead Foundation ▼ ✧
20600 Chagrin Blvd., No. 701
Shaker Heights, OH   44122-5341
(216) 771-4000

Incorporated in 1953 in OH; foundation is income beneficiary of a perpetual trust; assets reflect assets of both feeder trust and foundation.

Donors: Albert J. Weatherhead, Jr.†; Weathead Charitable Trust.
Foundation type: Independent foundation.
Financial data (yr. ended 12/31/05): Assets, $7,921,955 (M); gifts received, $4,720,074; expenditures, $5,172,867; qualifying distributions, $5,134,470; giving activities include $4,976,038 for 8 grants (high: $1,846,258; low: $7,500; average: $252,500–$645,000).

Purpose and activities: Grants for endowments or programs, principally to universities and research organizations.

Fields of interest: Higher education.

Type of support: General/operating support; Endowments; Program development; Research.

Limitations: Applications not accepted. Giving on a national basis. No support for religious purposes or for general support of church or denominational institutions. No grants to individuals.

Publications: Informational brochure.

Application information: Contributes only to pre-selected organizations. Grants are initiated by the trustees.

Board meeting date(s): Spring, fall, and as required

Officers and Trustees:* Albert J. Weatherhead III,* Pres.; Eamon M. Kelly,* V.P.; Terri Lacy,* V.P.; Henry Rosovsky,* V.P.; Celia J. Weatherhead,* V.P.; Jorge I. Dominguez.

Number of staff: 1 full-time professional.
EIN: 132711998
Selected grants: The following grants were reported in 2005.

$2,491,258 to Tulane University, New Orleans, LA. 2 grants: $1,846,258 (For grant made in form of stock), $645,000.

$1,494,487 to Harvard University, Cambridge, MA. 2 grants: $1,116,987 (For grant made in form of stock), $377,500.

$975,293 to Columbia University, New York, NY. 2 grants: $722,793 (For grant made in form of stock), $252,500 (For grant made in form of stock).

$7,500 to Kinkaid School, Houston, TX.

$7,500 to University of Texas, Austin, TX.

7900
Robert and Mary Weisbrod Foundation ✧
c/o National City Bank
P.O. Box 94651
Cleveland, OH   44101-4651
Application address: c/o National City Bank, R & M Weisbrod Distribution Comm., P.O. Box 837, Pittsburgh, PA 15230, tel.: (412) 644-8114

Established in 1968 in PA.
Donors: Mary E. Weisbrod†; Mary Weisbrod Unitrust.
Foundation type: Independent foundation.
Financial data (yr. ended 12/31/05): Assets, $14,382,770 (M); expenditures, $668,895; qualifying distributions, $599,516; giving activities include $558,000 for 52 grants (high: $30,000; low: $2,500).

Purpose and activities: Giving primarily for education including a school for the deaf, the arts, health care, and children, youth, and social services.

Fields of interest: Arts; Education; Hospitals (general); Health organizations, association; Human services; Children/youth, services; Family services; Federated giving programs; Christian agencies & churches; Deaf/hearing impaired.

Type of support: General/operating support; Continuing support.

Limitations: Giving primarily in the Pittsburgh, PA, area. No grants to individuals.

Application information: Application form not required.

Initial approach: Letter
Copies of proposal: 1
Deadline(s): None
Board meeting date(s): As required

Trustee: National City Bank.

EIN: 256105924

Selected grants: The following grants were reported in 2004.

$28,000 to Western Pennsylvania School for the Deaf, Pittsburgh, PA.

$25,000 to Little Sisters of the Poor, Pittsburgh, PA.

$20,000 to Pittsburgh Mercy Foundation, Pittsburgh, PA.

$16,000 to Western Pennsylvania Hospital Foundation, Pittsburgh, PA.

$15,000 to Greater Pittsburgh Community Food Bank, Duquesne, PA.

$15,000 to Multiple Sclerosis Service Society, Pittsburgh, PA.

$15,000 to United Way of Allegheny County, Pittsburgh, PA.

$10,000 to Boy Scouts of America, Pittsburgh, PA.

$10,000 to Jane Holmes Residence, Pittsburgh, PA.

$10,000 to Make-A-Wish Foundation of Western Pennsylvania, Pittsburgh, PA.

7901
The S. K. Wellman Foundation ✧

P.O. Box 32554
Euclid, OH 44132-0554
Contact: Ethel Pearson, Secy.
URL: http://www.csuohio.edu/uored/FUNDING/Wellman.html

Incorporated in 1951 in OH.

Donor: S.K. Wellman†.

Foundation type: Independent foundation.

Financial data (yr. ended 12/31/05): Assets, $7,219,160 (M); expenditures, $643,743; qualifying distributions, $578,972; giving activities include $550,000 for 76 grants (high: $25,000; low: $1,000).

Purpose and activities: The foundation's areas of funding are the following: animals/wildlife, preservation/protection (only in Cleveland, OH); the arts; children, youth, and human services; elementary/secondary/higher education; the environment/natural resources; government/public administration and health care.

Fields of interest: Arts; Elementary/secondary education; Higher education; Nursing school/education; Environment, natural resources; Environment; Animals/wildlife; Hospitals (general); Health care; Human services; Children/youth, services; Government/public administration.

Limitations: Giving primarily in OH. No grants to individuals.

Publications: Application guidelines; Grants list.

Application information: Any requests or proposals for grants must follow the foundation's guidelines. Application guidelines are available on foundation Web site. Application form not required.

Initial approach: Written proposal, following foundation's guidelines
Copies of proposal: 1
Deadline(s): June 1
Board meeting date(s): July
Final notification: 1 week

Officers and Trustees:* John M. Wilson, Jr.,* Pres.; Ethel Pearson, Secy.; Franklin B. Floyd; Susanne Wellman O'Gara.

Number of staff: 1 part-time professional.

EIN: 346520032

Selected grants: The following grants were reported in 2004.

$25,000 to Rainbow Babies and Childrens Hospital, Cleveland, OH.

$15,000 to Salvation Army, Cambridge, OH.

$10,000 to Cleveland Museum of Art, Cleveland, OH.

$10,000 to Cleveland Museum of Natural History, Cleveland, OH.

$10,000 to Grand River Partners, Painesville, OH.

$8,000 to Central School of Practical Nursing, Cleveland, OH.

$7,500 to Fieldstone Farm Therapeutic Riding Center, Chagrin Falls, OH.

$5,000 to Cleveland Opera, Cleveland, OH.

$5,000 to Cleveland State University, Cleveland, OH.

$5,000 to Salvation Army, Redding, CA.

7902
Wendy's International Foundation ✧

4288 W. Dublin-Granville Rd.
Dublin, OH 43017
Contact: Dennis L. Lynch

Established in 2002.

Donor: Wendy's International, Inc.

Foundation type: Company-sponsored foundation.

Financial data (yr. ended 12/31/05): Assets, $3,040,502 (M); gifts received, $1,808,433; expenditures, $1,043,708; qualifying distributions, $1,043,708; giving activities include $734,776 for 66 grants (high: $100,000; low: $500), and $306,900 for grants to individuals.

Purpose and activities: The foundation supports hospitals and organizations involved with education and human services and awards disaster relief grants to employees of Wendy's International.

Fields of interest: Higher education; Education; Hospitals (general); Children/youth, services; Human services; Federated giving programs.

Type of support: General/operating support; Grants to individuals.

Limitations: Giving primarily in OH.

Application information: Application form not required.

Initial approach: Proposal
Deadline(s): None

Officers and Directors:* John T. Schuessler,* Pres.; Dennis L. Lynch,* V.P.; Leon McCorkle,* Secy.; Kerri B. Anderson,* Treas.

EIN: 311807834

7903
Western-Southern Foundation, Inc. ✧

(formerly Western-Southern Enterprise Fund, Inc.)
400 Broadway
Cincinnati, OH 45202   (513) 629-1464
Contact: Edward J. Babbit
URL: http://www.westernsouthernlife.com/aboutUs/wsfg/communityinvolvement.asp

Established in 1988 in OH.

Donors: The Western & Southern Life Insurance Co.; Columbus Life Insurance Co.

Foundation type: Company-sponsored foundation.

Financial data (yr. ended 12/31/04): Assets, $32,168,469 (M); gifts received, $4,589; expenditures, $3,291,425; qualifying distributions, $3,279,624; giving activities include $3,193,325 for 89 grants (high: $264,433; low: $200).

Purpose and activities: The foundation supports organizations involved with arts and culture, education, medical research, children and youth, human services, religion, and civic affairs.

Fields of interest: Arts; Higher education; Education; Medical research; Children/youth, services; Human services; Federated giving programs; Government/public administration; Christian agencies & churches; Jewish agencies & temples; Religion.

Limitations: Giving in the U.S., with emphasis on Cincinnati, OH.

Application information: Application form not required.

Initial approach: Proposal
Deadline(s): None

Trustees: John F. Barrett; Thomas L. Williams; William J. Williams.

EIN: 311259670

Selected grants: The following grants were reported in 2004.

$264,433 to United Way.

$247,865 to Greater Cincinnati Arts and Education Center, Cincinnati, OH.

$50,000 to Community Quarterback Foundation, Cincinnati, OH.

$46,281 to College of Mount Saint Joseph, Cincinnati, OH.

$33,850 to Salvation Army.

$30,000 to Art Academy of Cincinnati, Cincinnati, OH.

$25,000 to Cincinnati Art Museum, Cincinnati, OH.

$15,000 to Greater Cincinnati Foundation, Cincinnati, OH.

$7,500 to Economics Center for Education and Research, Cincinnati, OH.

$5,440 to Neediest Kids of All, Cincinnati, OH.

7904
Wexner Foundation ▼ ✧

8000 Walton Pkwy., Ste. 100
New Albany, OH 43054   (614) 939-6060
Contact: Larry Moses, Pres.
FAX: (614) 939-6066;
E-mail: info@wexnerfoundation.org; URL: http://www.wexnerfoundation.org

Established in 1973.

Donors: Abigail Wexner; Leslie H. Wexner; The Leslie H. Wexner Charitable Fund.

Foundation type: Independent foundation.

Financial data (yr. ended 12/31/04): Assets, $1,955,993 (M); gifts received, $8,000,000; expenditures, $9,621,276; qualifying distributions, $9,593,304; giving activities include $4,355,599 for 40 grants (high: $840,644; low: $1,200; average: $20,000–$250,000), and $822,417 for 133 grants to individuals (high: $8,333; low: $1,083; average: $6,667–$7,750).

Purpose and activities: The foundation focuses its giving on the arena of Jewish leadership. The fellowship programs address constituencies that the foundation believes are essential to the revitalization of Jewish life: North American Jewish professional leaders and Israeli public sector leaders.

Fields of interest: Youth development, services; Human services; Jewish federated giving programs; Leadership development; Jewish agencies & temples.

Type of support: Fellowships; Grants to individuals; Scholarships—to individuals.

Limitations: Giving primarily in North America.

Publications: Informational brochure; Program policy statement.

Application information: Contributes only to pre-selected organizations; applications accepted for fellowship programs. Contact the foundation for complete application information. Application form required.

   Initial approach: Letter
   Deadline(s): Feb. 1 for Wexner Graduate
      Fellowships; Nov. 30 for Wexner-Israel
      Fellowships

Officers and Trustees:* Leslie H. Wexner,* Chair.; Larry S. Moses, Pres.; Darren Indyke, Secy.; Rabbi Maurice Corson, Pres. Emeritus; Jeffrey E. Epstein.

Number of staff: 5 full-time professional; 6 full-time support.

EIN: 237320631

Selected grants: The following grants were reported in 2005.

$1,250,000 to Wexner Heritage Foundation, New Albany, OH. 5 grants: $250,000 each (For educational seminars).

$830,647 to Harvard University, Cambridge, MA. For educational fellowships.

$323,353 to Hebrew Union College-Jewish Institute of Religion, Cincinnati, OH. For educational fellowships.

$283,208 to New York University, New York, NY. For educational fellowships.

$239,197 to Jewish Theological Seminary of America, New York, NY. For educational fellowships.

$21,369 to City University of New York, CUNY Graduate School, New York, NY. For educational fellowships.

7905

The Thomas H. White No. 1 Trust

(also known as Thomas H. White Foundation)
c/o Foundation Mgmt. Svcs., Inc.
1422 Euclid Ave., Ste. 627
Cleveland, OH   44115-1952   (216) 696-7273
Contact: Susan Althans, Consultant
FAX: (216) 621-8198;
E-mail: salthans@fmscleveland.com; URL: http://www.fmscleveland.com/thomaswhite/

Trust established in 1913 in OH; became active in 1939.

Donor: Thomas H. White†.

Foundation type: Independent foundation.

Financial data (yr. ended 12/31/05): Assets, $23,315,134 (M); expenditures, $1,333,983; qualifying distributions, $1,282,798; giving activities include $1,288,697 for 88 grants (high:

$150,000; low: $1,000; average: $5,000–$10,000).

Purpose and activities: Giving to support education and charitable purposes in the city of Cleveland, OH, to promote family preservation and self-sufficiency, to provide for care of the sick, aged, or helpless, to improve living conditions and to provide recreation for all classes.

Fields of interest: Education, early childhood education; Elementary school/education; Secondary school/education; Education; Crime/violence prevention, domestic violence; Employment; Human services; Children/youth, services; Family services; Homeless, human services; Disabilities, people with; Minorities; Women; AIDS, people with; Economically disadvantaged; Homeless.

Type of support: Capital campaigns; Building/renovation; Equipment; Emergency funds; Program development; Seed money.

Limitations: Giving limited to nonprofit charitable organizations located within Cuyahoga County, OH, if such organizations, and their services and facilities, primarily serve residents of the City of Cleveland. No grants to individuals, or for annual campaigns, general operating support, scholarships, endowments, research, symposia, seminars, deficit financing, or land acquisition; no loans.

Publications: Application guidelines; Annual report (including application guidelines).

Application information: Mass mailings not accepted. Application guidelines available for download on trust's Web site. Application form not required.

   Initial approach: Proposal
   Copies of proposal: 2
   Deadline(s): Apr. 1, Aug. 1, and Dec. 1
   Board meeting date(s): Distribution Committee
      meets in Jan., May, and Sept.
   Final notification: Within several weeks

Distribution Committee: Robin Cottingham; Michael S. Galland; Cynthia Koury; Susan Locke; Charyl A. Parcych.

Trustee: KeyBank N.A.

EIN: 346505722

Selected grants: The following grants were reported in 2005.

$50,000 to Playhouse Square Foundation, Cleveland, OH. For collaboration with ideastream to build Idea Center.

$30,000 to Cleveland Scholarship Programs, Cleveland, OH. For Six to Success, a college access service program for students in grades 6-12.

$20,000 to Westside Industrial Retention and Expansion Network (WIRE-Net), Cleveland, OH. For School-to-Career Program at Max S. Hayes Vocational High School.

$15,200 to Great Lakes Theater Festival, Cleveland, OH. For Cleveland Municipal School District students to participate in School Residence Program.

$15,000 to Dress for Success Cleveland, Cleveland, OH. For workplace clothing.

$15,000 to West Side Ecumenical Ministry, Cleveland, OH. For El Barrio's Workforce Development program.

7906

The E. F. Wildermuth Foundation ✧

1014 Dublin Rd.
Columbus, OH   43215-1116   (614) 487-0040
Contact: Robert W. Lee, Treas.

Established in 1962.

Foundation type: Independent foundation.

Financial data (yr. ended 12/31/05): Assets, $4,613,728 (M); expenditures, $616,385; qualifying distributions, $562,314; giving activities include $532,333 for 18 grants (high: $383,333; low: $1,500).

Purpose and activities: Giving primarily for higher education, including to optometry programs at colleges and universities; funding also for human services, as well as to a children's hospital.

Fields of interest: Performing arts, ballet; Higher education; Hospitals (specialty); Eye research; Human services; Protestant agencies & churches.

Limitations: Giving primarily in OH and contiguous states. No grants to individuals.

Application information: Application form not required.

   Initial approach: Letter
   Deadline(s): July 31

Officers: Patrick Campbell, Chair. and Pres.; David T. Patterson, V.P. and Secy.; Karl Borton, V.P.; Robert W. Lee, Treas.

Trustees: Thomas Borton; Chris Campbell; Harriet Slaughter; Jonathon Slaughter.

EIN: 316050202

7907

The Williams Foundation ✧

c/o National City Bank
P.O. Box 94651
Cleveland, OH   44101

Established in 1938 in OH.

Donors: Harriette R. Downey; William J. Williams; Helen D. Williams; Mary Frances W. Clauder.

Foundation type: Independent foundation.

Financial data (yr. ended 12/31/04): Assets, $7,987,406 (M); gifts received, $1,482,802; expenditures, $377,236; qualifying distributions, $355,875; giving activities include $352,556 for 29 grants (high: $50,094; low: $100).

Purpose and activities: Giving primarily for health care, Roman Catholic organizations, churches, and education, including a seminary; funding also for children, youth, and social services.

Fields of interest: Museums (art); Arts; Higher education; Education; Health care; Boys & girls clubs; Human services; Children/youth, services; Roman Catholic agencies & churches.

Limitations: Applications not accepted. Giving primarily in Cincinnati, OH. Generally no grants to individuals.

Application information: Contributes only to pre-selected organizations.

Trustees: Mary Frances W. Clauder; Sharon W. Frisbie; Carol W. Jodar; Lawrence H. Kyte, Jr.; Helen D. Williams; Thomas L. Williams; William J. Williams; W. Joseph Williams, Jr.

EIN: 316032504

Selected grants: The following grants were reported in 2004.

$49,770 to Immaculate Heart of Mary Church, Cincinnati, OH.

$20,000 to Summit Country Day School, Cincinnati, OH.

$12,441 to National Underground Railroad Freedom Center, Cincinnati, OH.

$6,000 to Fine Arts Fund, Cincinnati, OH.

$5,000 to Joy Outdoor Education Center, Clarksville, OH.

$500 to Xavier University, Cincinnati, OH.

7908
Williamson Family Foundation ◇ ☆

8399 Tippecanoe Rd.
Canfield, OH 44406

Donors: WKBN Broadcasting Corp.; Warren P. Williamson III.
Foundation type: Company-sponsored foundation.
Financial data (yr. ended 12/31/05): Assets, $3,936,622 (M); expenditures, $565,999; qualifying distributions, $524,201; giving activities include $524,201 for grants.
Purpose and activities: The foundation supports historical societies and organizations involved with education.
Fields of interest: Historic preservation/historical societies; Higher education; Business school/education; Education; Speech/hearing centers; Federated giving programs.
Type of support: General/operating support.
Limitations: Applications not accepted. Giving primarily in OH. No grants to individuals.
Application information: Contributes only to pre-selected organizations.
Officers: Warren P. Williamson III, Pres.; John D. Williamson II, V.P.; Doris J. Saloom, Secy.-Treas.
EIN: 346568495

7909
J. B. Wilson & Garnet A. Wilson Charitable Trust ◇

P.O. Box 686
Waverly, OH 45690-0686 (740) 947-2727
Contact: Billy S. Moore, Tr.

Established in 1980.
Donor: Garnet A. Wilson†.
Foundation type: Independent foundation.
Financial data (yr. ended 12/31/05): Assets, $5,674,339 (M); expenditures, $597,244; qualifying distributions, $578,338; giving activities include $568,100 for grants to individuals.
Purpose and activities: Scholarships only to Pike County students attending a state-supported college or university in OH.
Type of support: Scholarships—to individuals.
Limitations: Giving limited to residents and graduates of Pike County, OH, schools.
Application information: Application form required.
   Deadline(s): Prior to 1st year of college
Trustees: William Foster; Billy S. Moore; Glenda Williams.
EIN: 310983188

7910
Edward M. Wilson Family Foundation ◇

c/o National City Bank of Indiana
P.O. Box 94651
Cleveland, OH 44101-4651
Application address: c/o Denise Andorfer, National City Bank of Indiana, P.O. Box 110, Fort Wayne, IN 46801, tel.: (260) 461-6218

Established around 1980 in IN.
Donor: William Telfer.
Foundation type: Independent foundation.
Financial data (yr. ended 9/30/05): Assets, $31,386,610 (M); expenditures, $1,568,871; qualifying distributions, $1,447,289; giving activities include $1,357,500 for 81 grants (high: $100,000; low: $1,500).
Purpose and activities: Giving primarily for arts and culture, education, parks and recreation, social services, and children and youth services.
Fields of interest: Arts; Higher education; Education; Recreation, parks/playgrounds; Human services; YM/YWCAs & YM/YWHAs; Children/youth, services.
Type of support: General/operating support.
Limitations: Giving primarily in Fort Wayne, IN. No grants to individuals.
Application information:
   Initial approach: Proposal
   Deadline(s): None
Distribution Committee: Hon. William Lee; Amy Morrill; Tom Quirk; Thomas Shoaff; Don Wolf.
Trustee: National City Bank of Indiana.
EIN: 310976337
Selected grants: The following grants were reported in 2005.
$100,000 to Fort Wayne Park Foundation, Fort Wayne, IN.
$90,000 to Indiana University-Purdue University, Fort Wayne, IN.
$75,000 to Indiana Institute of Technology, Fort Wayne, IN.
$75,000 to United Way of Allen County, Fort Wayne, IN.
$65,000 to Girl Scouts of the U.S.A., Fort Wayne, IN.
$40,000 to Arts United of Greater Fort Wayne, Fort Wayne, IN.
$30,000 to Taylor University, Upland, IN.
$20,000 to Boy Scouts of America, Fort Wayne, IN.
$10,000 to Allen County Fort Wayne Historical Society, Fort Wayne, IN.
$10,000 to Early Childhood Alliance, Fort Wayne, IN.

7911
Thomas A. Wilson Foundation ◇ ☆

c/o National City Bank
P.O. Box 94651
Cleveland, OH 44101-4651
Application address: c/o JoAnna Mayo, Trust Off., National City Bank, E. 20 Stanwix St., Pittsburgh, PA 15222, tel.: (412) 644-8002

Established in 1971 in PA.
Foundation type: Independent foundation.
Financial data (yr. ended 12/31/05): Assets, $6,974,976 (M); expenditures, $434,200; qualifying distributions, $360,000; giving activities include $360,000 for grants.
Purpose and activities: Giving primarily to the Wilson Christian Academy, McKeesport; some giving to Christian education and for health care programs.
Fields of interest: Christian agencies & churches.
Limitations: Giving limited to McKeesport, PA. No grants to individuals.
Application information: Application form not required.
   Deadline(s): None
Trustee: National City Bank.
EIN: 237358862
Selected grants: The following grants were reported in 2003.

$220,000 to Wilson Christian Academy, West Mifflin, PA. For general support.

7912
Wodecroft Foundation ◇

225 E. 5th St., Rm. 1900
Cincinnati, OH 45202 (513) 977-8236
Contact: J. Michael Cooney Esq., Chair.

Established in 1958 in OH.
Donor: Roger Drackett†.
Foundation type: Independent foundation.
Financial data (yr. ended 12/31/05): Assets, $15,826,420 (M); expenditures, $830,514; qualifying distributions, $731,500; giving activities include $731,500 for 34 grants (high: $275,000; low: $1,000).
Purpose and activities: Giving primarily for the arts, particularly a performing arts center; funding also for higher education, conservation, health and hospitals, including a children's hospital, children, youth and social services, federated giving programs, and Christian churches.
Fields of interest: Museums; Performing arts centers; Performing arts, orchestra (symphony); Arts; Higher education; Environment, natural resources; Hospitals (general); Mental health/crisis services; Health organizations, association; Human services; Children/youth, services; Federated giving programs; Christian agencies & churches.
Type of support: Annual campaigns; Capital campaigns; Building/renovation; Equipment.
Limitations: Giving primarily in southwestern FL and southwestern OH. No grants to individuals.
Application information: Few unsolicited applications granted. Application form not required.
   Initial approach: Letter
   Deadline(s): June 30
   Board meeting date(s): As required
   Final notification: Prior to Dec. 31
Officer and Trustees:* J. Michael Cooney,* Chair.; William Bahl; Jeanne Drackett.
EIN: 316047601
Selected grants: The following grants were reported in 2005.
$275,000 to Philharmonic Center for the Arts, Naples, FL.
$150,000 to National Alliance for Research on Schizophrenia and Depression (NARSAD), Great Neck, NY.
$45,000 to Sun Valley Summer Symphony, Sun Valley, ID.
$5,000 to Orcas Island Chamber Music Festival, Eastsound, WA.
$5,000 to Taft Museum, Cincinnati, OH.
$3,000 to Cincinnati Symphony Orchestra, Cincinnati, OH.

7913
The Wohlgemuth-Herschede Foundation ◇

c/o Fifth Third Bank
PO Box 630858
Cincinnati, OH 45263-0858
Contact: Elizabeth D. Wohlgemuth, Tr.
Application address: c/o Fifth Third Bank, 38 Fountain Sq. Plz., Cincinnati, OH 45263. tel: (513) 534-5472

Established in 1994 in OH.
Foundation type: Independent foundation.

Financial data (yr. ended 12/31/05): Assets, $9,329,487 (M); expenditures, $526,148; qualifying distributions, $437,319; giving activities include $406,050 for 48 grants (high: $35,000; low: $1,500; average: $5,000–$10,000).
Fields of interest: Media/communications; Performing arts; Performing arts, music; Arts; Education; Reproductive health, family planning; Human services; Developmentally disabled, centers & services; Women, centers/services.
Limitations: Giving primarily in the greater Cincinnati, OH, area.
Application information: Application form not required.
   Initial approach: Letter or telephone
   Deadline(s): None
Officers and Trustees:* Holly Herschede,* Pres.; Joseph P. Rouse, Treas.; Allison Herschede; Steven Monder; Elizabeth D. Wohlgemuth.
Agent: Fifth Third Bank.
EIN: 311409317
Selected grants: The following grants were reported in 2005.
$35,000 to Cincinnati Symphony Orchestra, Cincinnati, OH.
$15,000 to Beech Acres, Cincinnati, OH.
$15,000 to College of Mount Saint Joseph, Cincinnati, OH.
$15,000 to Literacy Network of Greater Cincinnati, Cincinnati, OH.
$15,000 to Martin Luther King Jr. Performing and Cultural Arts Complex, Columbus, OH.
$13,000 to Cincinnati Nature Center, Milford, OH.
$10,000 to American Red Cross, Akron, OH.
$10,000 to Cincinnati Ballet Company, Cincinnati, OH.
$10,000 to Crayons to Computers, Cincinnati, OH.
$5,000 to Christian Appalachian Project, Lancaster, KY.

7914
Milton A. & Roslyn Z. Wolf Family Foundation ◇
25700 Science Park Dr., Ste. 350
Beachwood, OH 44122

Established in 2002 in OH.
Donors: Roslyn Z. Wolf; Wolf Real Estate.
Foundation type: Independent foundation.
Financial data (yr. ended 12/31/04): Assets, $983,146 (M); gifts received, $901,607; expenditures, $362,804; qualifying distributions, $354,666; giving activities include $355,367 for 9 grants (high: $194,720; low: $1,000).
Fields of interest: Performing arts, music; Arts; Human services; Jewish federated giving programs; Jewish agencies & temples.
Limitations: Giving primarily in Cleveland, OH.
Officers: Milton A. Wolf, Pres.; Michael A. Shemo, V.P.; Caryn Wolf Wechsler, V.P.; Nancy Wolf, Secy.; Sherri Wolf, Treas.
EIN: 030485546
Selected grants: The following grants were reported in 2004.
$274,720 to Jewish Community Federation of Cleveland, Cleveland, OH. 2 grants: $80,000, $194,720
$44,147 to American Austrian Foundation, New York, NY.
$20,000 to Cleveland Orchestra, Cleveland, OH.
$5,000 to Council of American Ambassadors, DC.
$5,000 to Jewish Foundation for the Righteous, New York, NY.

$3,000 to Jewish Federation of Palm Beach County, West Palm Beach, FL.

7915
Wolfe Associates, Inc. ◇
34 S. 3rd St.
Columbus, OH 43215
Contact: Rita J. Wolfe Hoag, V.P.
Application address: 770 Twin Rivers Dr., Columbus, OH 43215, tel.: (614) 460-3782

Incorporated in 1973 in OH.
Donors: The Dispatch Printing Co.; The Ohio Co.; WBNS-TV, Inc.; RadiOhio, Inc.; Video Indiana, Inc.
Foundation type: Company-sponsored foundation.
Financial data (yr. ended 12/31/04): Assets, $16,145,375 (M); gifts received, $2,037,557; expenditures, $1,486,639; qualifying distributions, $1,436,940; giving activities include $1,436,940 for 208 grants (high: $154,291; low: $51).
Purpose and activities: The foundation supports hospitals and organizations involved with arts and culture, education, the environment, health, human services, children and youth, community development, and religion.
Fields of interest: Arts; Secondary school/ education; Higher education; Education; Environment; Hospitals (general); Hospitals (specialty); Health care; Cancer; Children/youth, services; Human services; Community development; Federated giving programs; Religion.
Type of support: General/operating support; Continuing support; Annual campaigns; Building/ renovation; Equipment; Emergency funds; Professorships; Scholarship funds; Matching/ challenge support.
Limitations: Giving primarily in Columbus, OH. No grants to individuals, or for research, demonstration projects, publications, or conferences.
Publications: Application guidelines; Program policy statement.
Application information: Application form not required.
   Initial approach: Letter of inquiry
   Deadline(s): None
   Board meeting date(s): Mar., June, Sept., and Dec.
   Final notification: Following board meetings
Officers and Trustees:* John F. Wolfe, Chair. and Pres.; James H. Gilmour,* V.P. and Treas.; Michael Curtin,* V.P.; Michael J. Fiorile,* V.P.; Rita J. Wolfe Hoag,* V.P.; Nancy Wolfe Lane,* V.P.; Katherine Wolfe Lloyd,* V.P.; Sara Wolfe Perrini,* V.P.; Sherry L. Lewis, Secy.
EIN: 237303111
Selected grants: The following grants were reported in 2004.
$256,548 to United Way of Central Ohio, Columbus, OH. 2 grants: $154,291, $102,257
$64,000 to Ohio Foundation of Independent Colleges, Columbus, OH.
$50,000 to Columbus Association for the Performing Arts, Columbus, OH.
$40,000 to YWCA of Greater Cleveland, Cleveland, OH.
$10,000 to Baldwin-Wallace College, Berea, OH.
$10,000 to Columbus Foundation, Columbus, OH.
$2,500 to Columbus Museum of Art, Columbus, OH.
$2,500 to Ohio State University, Columbus, OH.
$2,500 to YMCA of Central Ohio, Columbus, OH.

7916
Women's Project Foundation ◇
c/o KeyBank N.A.
800 Superior Ave., 4th Fl.
Cleveland, OH 44114 (216) 689-4651
Contact: Karen Potopsky, Trust Off., KeyBank N.A.
Application address: c/o KeyBank N.A., 127 Public Sq., 17th Fl., Cleveland, OH 44114-1306

Established in 1986.
Foundation type: Independent foundation.
Financial data (yr. ended 11/30/05): Assets, $24,973,387 (M); expenditures, $1,228,528; qualifying distributions, $1,127,571; giving activities include $1,127,372 for 6 grants (high: $796,968; low: $5,000).
Purpose and activities: Supports projects for women's and children's issues, including women filmmakers and domestic violence.
Fields of interest: Media, film/video; Visual arts, photography; Arts; Adult/continuing education; Education; Reproductive health, family planning; Alcoholism; Crime/violence prevention, child abuse; Children/youth, services; Women, centers/ services; Minorities/immigrants, centers/services; Foundations (private independent); Minorities; Women.
Type of support: Program development; Research.
Limitations: Giving on a national basis, with emphasis on New York, NY. No grants to individuals.
Application information:
   Initial approach: Proposal
   Deadline(s): None
   Board meeting date(s): Late fall
Trustees: Louise L. Gund; KeyBank N.A.
EIN: 133417304
Selected grants: The following grants were reported in 2003.
$2,924,412 to Goatee Foundation, Cleveland, OH. For unrestricted giving.

7917
Woodruff Foundation
1422 Euclid Ave., Ste. 627
Cleveland, OH 44115 (216) 566-1853
Contact: Allison Rand, Consultant
FAX: (216) 621-8198;
E-mail: arand@fmscleveland.com; *URL:* http:// www.fmscleveland.com/woodruff

Established in 1986 in OH; converted with proceeds from the sale of Woodruff Hospital.
Foundation type: Independent foundation.
Financial data (yr. ended 12/31/05): Assets, $12,494,337 (M); expenditures, $746,831; qualifying distributions, $685,058; giving activities include $573,394 for grants.
Purpose and activities: Giving primarily to support the development and delivery of mental health services in Cuyahoga County, OH. Specifically, the foundation seeks to fund projects that will foster and enhance: the treatment of persons affected by mental disorders and chemical dependency; educational programs related to mental health, the coordination of mental health resources in the community; research into the causes, nature and recurrence of mental illness. High priority areas of interest include encouraging the implementation of innovative prevention and treatment programs and strengthening the effectiveness of existing service delivery systems.
Fields of interest: Substance abuse, services; Mental health/crisis services; Alcoholism.

Type of support: Emergency funds; Program development; Seed money; Research.
Limitations: Giving limited to Cuyahoga County, OH. No grants for scholarships or fellowships, operating expenses, endowments, or annual fundraising campaigns.
Publications: Annual report.
Application information: Please limit the project description to 2 pages. Application form not required.

Initial approach: Proposal
Copies of proposal: 2
Deadline(s): Jan. 2, May 1, and Sept. 1
Board meeting date(s): Feb., June, and Oct.
Final notification: Within 2 weeks

Officers and Trustees:* Oliver C. Henkel, Jr.,* Pres.; David L. Hussey, Ph.D.*, V.P.; Lenora A. Kola, Ph.D.*, Secy.-Treas.; L. Douglas Lenkoski; Myrtle Muntz; Theodore V. Parran, Jr., M.D.; Ann Reichsman; William Sheehan; Mario Tonti.
EIN: 237425631
Selected grants: The following grants were reported in 2005.

$30,900 to Ideastream, Cleveland, OH. For Children's Health: Behavioral Health Awareness program.

$25,000 to Domestic Violence Center, Cleveland, OH. For expanding the Child Therapy program.

$21,000 to Suicide Prevention Education, Cleveland, OH. For expanding Recognizing Adolescent Depression and Suicide Prevention program.

$15,000 to Youth Opportunities Unlimited, Cleveland, OH. For drug prevention services.

$10,350 to Boys and Girls Clubs of Cleveland, Cleveland, OH. For SMART Moves, an alcohol, tobacco and drug prevention program.

7918
The Wuliger Foundation, Inc.
20 Basswood Ln.
Moreland Hills, OH 44022-1377
Contact: Timothy F. Wuliger, Secy.-Treas.

Incorporated in 1956 in OH.
Donor: Ernest M. Wuliger†.
Foundation type: Independent foundation.
Financial data (yr. ended 12/31/04): Assets, $18,465,542 (M); gifts received, $146,776; expenditures, $943,275; qualifying distributions, $827,686; giving activities include $820,370 for 89 grants (high: $525,000; low: $360).
Purpose and activities: Giving for Jewish community organizations; support also for education, health care, and social services for disadvantaged persons.
Fields of interest: Education; Hospitals (general); Health care; Health organizations, association; Crime/violence prevention; Human services; Children/youth, services; Aging, centers/services; Community development; Aging; Economically disadvantaged.
Type of support: General/operating support; Annual campaigns; Capital campaigns; Building/renovation; Emergency funds.

Limitations: Giving primarily in northeastern OH. No grants to individuals.
Application information: Application form not required.

Initial approach: Written proposal (1 or 2 pages)
Copies of proposal: 1
Deadline(s): None
Board meeting date(s): As necessary
Final notification: Within 2 months if possible

Officers and Directors:* E. Jeffrey Wuliger,* Pres.; Gregory Wuliger,* V.P.; Timothy F. Wuliger,* Secy.-Treas.
Number of staff: 1 part-time support.
EIN: 346527281

7919
The Abner and Esther Yoder Charitable Foundation ◇ ☆
P.O. Box 80469
Canton, OH 44708 (330) 478-2100
Contact: Esther Yoder, Secy.

Established in 1991 in OH.
Donor: Stark Truss Co., Inc.
Foundation type: Independent foundation.
Financial data (yr. ended 12/31/05): Assets, $1,214,331 (M); gifts received, $1,200,000; expenditures, $316,000; qualifying distributions, $314,942; giving activities include $314,942 for grants.
Purpose and activities: Giving primarily to evangelical Christian organizations.
Fields of interest: Christian agencies & churches.
Limitations: Giving primarily in OH, OK, and TX. No grants to individuals.
Application information: Application form not required.

Deadline(s): None

Officers: Abner Yoder, Pres.; Esther Yoder, Secy.; Wendy Spillman, Treas.
EIN: 341677646

7920
The Youngstown Foundation
P.O. Box 1162
Youngstown, OH 44501 (330) 744-0320
Contact: G.M. Walsh, Exec. Dir.

Established in 1918 in OH by bank resolution.
Foundation type: Community foundation.
Financial data (yr. ended 12/31/04): Assets, $68,462,443 (M); gifts received, $796,057; expenditures, $3,368,195; giving activities include $2,968,781 for 53+ grants (high: $225,000).
Purpose and activities: The foundation seeks to support local charitable and educational agencies for the betterment of the community; grants for capital purposes, with emphasis on aid to crippled children, community funds, youth agencies, music and cultural programs, and hospitals.
Fields of interest: Visual arts; Museums; Performing arts; Performing arts, music; Historic preservation/historical societies; Arts; Education, association;

Child development, education; Health care; Alcoholism; Recreation; Youth development, services; Children/youth, services; Child development, services; Family services; Residential/custodial care, hospices; Human services; Urban/community development; Leadership development; Disabilities, people with.
Type of support: Continuing support; Capital campaigns; Building/renovation; Equipment.
Limitations: Giving limited to Mahoning County, OH, with emphasis on Youngstown. No grants to individuals (except for scholarships), or for endowment funds, operating budgets, seed money, emergency funds, deficit financing, land acquisition, demonstration projects, publications, fellowships, travel, tours or trips, underwriting of conferences, debt reduction, projects normally the responsibility of government, sabbatical leaves, scholarly research organizations not tax exempt, or matching gifts.
Publications: Application guidelines; Annual report.
Application information: Application form not required.

Initial approach: Proposal
Copies of proposal: 10
Deadline(s): 6 weeks prior to board meeting
Board meeting date(s): Mar., June, Sept., and Nov.
Final notification: 2 months

Officers and Trustees:* Thomas R. Hollern,* Chair.; William Powell,* Vice-Chair.; G.M. Walsh, Exec. Dir.; Cynthia Anderson; Phillip Dennison; Joseph S. Nohra; National City Bank, Northeast.
Number of staff: 2 part-time professional; 1 part-time support.
EIN: 346515788

7921
Zenith Foundation, Inc. ◇
405 Madison Ave., Ste. 1900
Toledo, OH 43604-1207

Established in 1967.
Donors: Richard H. Peters†; Donna M. Peters.
Foundation type: Independent foundation.
Financial data (yr. ended 12/31/05): Assets, $2,555,299 (M); gifts received, $574,050; expenditures, $841,758; qualifying distributions, $833,378; giving activities include $818,772 for 50 grants (high: $162,000; low: $1,000).
Purpose and activities: Giving primarily for health and human services and for the arts.
Fields of interest: Arts; Education; Health care; Human services; Christian agencies & churches.
Type of support: Capital campaigns.
Limitations: Applications not accepted. Giving primarily in Toledo, OH. No grants to individuals.
Application information: Contributes only to pre-selected organizations.

Board meeting date(s): Nov.

Officers and Trustees:* Donna M. Peters,* Pres.; William F. Bates,* V.P. and Secy.; Carol J. Middleton.
EIN: 341018513

OKLAHOMA

7922
8:32, Inc. ✧
P.O. Box 271054
Oklahoma City, OK 73137-1054

Established in 1984 in OK.
Donors: Jack Humphreys; Kent Humphreys; Kirk Humphreys; Heritage Trust Co.
Foundation type: Independent foundation.
Financial data (yr. ended 12/31/03): Assets, $3,584,418 (M); gifts received, $527,792; expenditures, $351,683; qualifying distributions, $324,737; giving activities include $324,737 for 102 grants (high: $94,300; low: $50).
Purpose and activities: Giving primarily for religious activities, particularly Baptist and Christian churches and organizations.
Fields of interest: Higher education; Human services; Christian agencies & churches; Protestant agencies & churches; Religion.
Type of support: General/operating support; Continuing support; Seed money.
Limitations: Applications not accepted. Giving on a national basis, with some emphasis on Oklahoma City, OK, and TX. No grants to individuals.
Application information: Contributes only to pre-selected organizations.
Board meeting date(s): May
Officers: Kirk Humphreys, Pres.; Kent Humphreys, V.P.; Joy Fischer, Secy.
EIN: 731214621
Selected grants: The following grants were reported in 2003.
$94,300 to Northwest Baptist Church, Oklahoma City, OK.
$37,800 to Navigators, The, Colorado Springs, CO.
$1,800 to City Rescue Mission, Oklahoma City, OK.
$600 to Marketplace Ministries, Dallas, TX.
$500 to Lance Armstrong Foundation, Austin, TX.
$500 to Rose State College, Midwest City, OK.
$400 to Cal Farleys Boys Ranch, Amarillo, TX.
$400 to Dallas Theological Seminary, Dallas, TX.
$400 to East-West Ministries International, Dallas, TX.
$400 to Prison Fellowship Ministries, DC.

7923
Larkin Bailey Foundation ✧ ☆
612 S. Denver Ave.
Tulsa, OK 74119-1028 (918) 250-9080
Contact: Roy G. Cartwright, Tr.; Patsy Cravens, Tr.

Established in 1993 in OK.
Donor: Larkin Bailey Trust.
Foundation type: Independent foundation.
Financial data (yr. ended 12/31/05): Assets, $12,685,981 (M); expenditures, $2,386,675; qualifying distributions, $2,175,775; giving activities include $2,175,775 for grants.
Purpose and activities: Giving primarily to human services, youth organizations, and Protestant institutions and churches.
Fields of interest: Historic preservation/historical societies; Education; Substance abuse, treatment; Neighborhood centers; Children/youth, services; Government/public administration; Protestant agencies & churches; Religion.

Type of support: General/operating support; Continuing support; Building/renovation; Land acquisition; Program development; Grants to individuals.
Limitations: Giving primarily in Owasso and Tulsa, OK.
Publications: Annual report; Corporate giving report.
Application information: Application form required.
Initial approach: Letter
Copies of proposal: 2
Deadline(s): None
Board meeting date(s): Monthly and as needed
Final notification: Letter
Trustees: Roy G. Cartwright; Patsy Cravens; Joseph N. Witt.
Number of staff: 3 full-time support; 1 part-time support.
EIN: 731258217
Selected grants: The following grants were reported in 2004.
$20,000 to Jim Riley Outreach, Edmond, OK.
$2,500 to Meals on Wheels, Norman, OK.
$700 to Asbury United Methodist Church, Tulsa, OK.
$500 to Boy Scouts of America, Tulsa, OK.
$500 to Young Life, Oklahoma City, OK.

7924
Florence L. J. and Howard G. Barnett Foundation ✧
6742 S. Evanston
Tulsa, OK 74136
Contact: Howard G. Barnett, Tr.

Established in 1997 in OK.
Donors: Florence L.J. Barnett; Howard G. Barnett.
Foundation type: Independent foundation.
Financial data (yr. ended 12/31/03): Assets, $8,356,647 (M); gifts received, $2,430; expenditures, $495,633; qualifying distributions, $392,781; giving activities include $389,800 for 54 grants (high: $150,000; low: $500).
Fields of interest: Museums (art); Higher education; Higher education, university; Christian agencies & churches.
Limitations: Giving primarily in Tulsa, OK.
Application information: Application form not required.
Initial approach: Proposal
Deadline(s): None
Trustees: Billie Barnett; Florence L.J. Barnett; Howard G. Barnett.
EIN: 736295453
Selected grants: The following grants were reported in 2004.
$50,000 to All Souls Unitarian Church, Tulsa, OK.
$37,500 to Philbrook Museum of Art, Tulsa, OK.
$25,000 to Oklahoma Centennial Commemoration Fund, Oklahoma City, OK.
$25,000 to Salvation Army, Norman, OK.
$25,000 to University of Wisconsin Foundation, Madison, WI.
$10,000 to Center for Individuals with Physical Challenges, Tulsa, OK.
$10,000 to Tulsa Boys Home, Tulsa, OK.
$5,000 to Tulsa Community College Foundation, Tulsa, OK.
$2,500 to Tulsa Historical Society, Tulsa, OK.
$2,500 to YWCA of Tulsa, Tulsa, OK.

7925
Grace & Franklin Bernsen Foundation
15 W. 6th St., No. 1308
Tulsa, OK 74119-5407 (918) 584-4711
FAX: (918) 584-4713; E-mail: gfbernsen@aol.com;
URL: http://www.bernsen.org

Established in 1985 in OK.
Donors: Grace Bernsen†; Franklin Bernsen†.
Foundation type: Independent foundation.
Financial data (yr. ended 9/30/05): Assets, $31,464,224 (M); expenditures, $1,496,350; qualifying distributions, $1,418,360; giving activities include $1,203,524 for 52 grants (high: $205,000; low: $3,024).
Purpose and activities: The foundation was created to provide grants in support of religious, charitable, scientific, literary or educational purposes, or for the prevention of cruelty to children.
Fields of interest: Performing arts, theater; Humanities; Arts; Education; Health care; Health organizations, association; Biomedicine; Medical research, institute; Crime/law enforcement; Human services; Children/youth, services; Biological sciences.
Type of support: Program development; Capital campaigns; Building/renovation; Equipment; Emergency funds; Conferences/seminars; Matching/challenge support.
Limitations: Giving limited to within the city of Tulsa, OK.
Publications: Application guidelines; Annual report; Informational brochure (including application guidelines).
Application information: Application form not required.
Copies of proposal: 1
Deadline(s): 12th of each month
Board meeting date(s): Monthly
Final notification: 30 to 60 days
Officers and Trustees:* W. Bland Williamson,* Secy.; Sandra L. Griffin, Admin.; Donald F. Marlar; Donald E. Pray; John D. Strong, Jr.
Number of staff: 1 full-time professional.
EIN: 237009414
Selected grants: The following grants were reported in 2003.
$260,000 to University of Tulsa, Tulsa, OK.
$205,000 to Saint Johns Medical Center Foundation, Longview, WA. For capital campaign.
$200,000 to Camp Loughridge, Tulsa, OK. For capital support.
$100,000 to Brush Creek Youth Ranch, Tulsa, OK. For capital support.
$100,000 to Family and Childrens Services of Tulsa, Tulsa, OK. For capital support.
$100,000 to Oklahoma Centennial Commemoration Fund, Oklahoma City, OK. For capital dome.
$66,667 to Mental Health Association in Tulsa, Tulsa, OK. For capital support.
$35,833 to Ronald McDonald House, Tulsa, OK. For capital support.
$30,000 to Gilcrease Museum, Tulsa, OK. For program support.
$30,000 to Rogers State University, Claremore, OK. For program support.

7926
Better Days Foundation, Inc. ✧
3030 Northwest Expwy., Ste. 1313
Oklahoma City, OK 73112 (405) 947-6171
Contact: Karen Horton, Exec. Dir.

Established in 1994 in DE and CA.

Donor: Paul G. Heafy.

Foundation type: Independent foundation.

Financial data (yr. ended 11/30/05): Assets, $4,026,550 (M); expenditures, $479,861; qualifying distributions, $423,159; giving activities include $423,159 for 70 grants (high: $172,009; low: $50).

Purpose and activities: Giving primarily for education, health associations, and children, youth and social services.

Fields of interest: Arts; Elementary school/education; Education; Animal welfare; Zoos/zoological societies; Health organizations, association; Food services; Human services; Children/youth, services.

Type of support: General/operating support; Continuing support; Annual campaigns.

Limitations: Giving primarily in Oklahoma City, OK; some giving nationally. No grants to individuals.

Publications: Informational brochure (including application guidelines).

Application information: Application form not required.

  Initial approach: Letter of inquiry

  Deadline(s): None

Officers: Paul G. Heafy, Pres. and Treas.; Rhonda L. Heafy, V.P. and Secy.; Karen Horton, Exec. Dir.

Number of staff: 1 full-time professional.

EIN: 731440536

7927
The Mervin Bovaird Foundation ✧

401 S. Boston Ave., Ste. 3300

Tulsa, OK 74103-4070 (918) 592-3300

Contact: R. Casey Cooper, Pres.

Established in 1955.

Donor: Mabel W. Bovaird†.

Foundation type: Independent foundation.

Financial data (yr. ended 12/31/05): Assets, $46,658,942 (M); expenditures, $2,468,957; qualifying distributions, $2,141,092; giving activities include $1,684,100 for 100 grants (high: $100,000; low: $1,000), and $318,000 for 71 grants to individuals.

Purpose and activities: Support for social services, health, and education; also funds a scholarship program for Tulsa County High School graduating seniors and graduates of Tulsa Community College at the University of Tulsa (not for graduate or professional study).

Fields of interest: Arts; Education; Environment; Health care; Health organizations, association; Human services; Community development.

Type of support: General/operating support; Continuing support; Annual campaigns; Capital campaigns; Building/renovation; Equipment; Endowments; Program development; Conferences/seminars; Curriculum development; Scholarship funds; Research; Matching/challenge support.

Limitations: Giving limited to the Tulsa, OK, area. No grants to individuals (except for scholarships); no loans.

Publications: Program policy statement.

Application information: Scholarship recipients are chosen by Tulsa public high schools and Tulsa Community College based on need and ability to attend Tulsa University. Application form not required.

  Initial approach: Brief letter

  Copies of proposal: 1

Deadline(s): May 1 (or date established by schools selecting a recipient for scholarships); Nov. 15 for grants

  Board meeting date(s): Quarterly

  Final notification: Dec. 15-20

Officers and Trustees:* R. Casey Cooper,* Pres.; David B. McKinney,* V.P. and Treas.; Alinda F. Jones, Secy.; Tilford H. Eskridge; Lance Stockwell; Thomas H. Trower.

Number of staff: 2 part-time professional; 1 part-time support.

EIN: 736102163

7928
H. A. and Mary K. Chapman Charitable Trust ▼ ✧

1 Warren Pl., Ste. 1816

6100 S. Yale

Tulsa, OK 74136 (918) 496-7882

Contact: J. Jerry Dickman, Tr.; Donne W. Pitman, Tr.

Trust established in 1976 in OK.

Donors: H.A. Chapman†; Mary K. Chapman†.

Foundation type: Independent foundation.

Financial data (yr. ended 12/31/05): Assets, $77,879,032 (M); expenditures, $3,919,188; qualifying distributions, $3,478,602; giving activities include $3,291,140 for 97 grants (high: $510,000; low: $145; average: $10,000–$50,000).

Purpose and activities: Grants largely for education, particularly higher education, health, social services, and cultural programs.

Fields of interest: Arts; Higher education; Education; Environment; Animals/wildlife; Health care; Health organizations, association; Human services.

Type of support: General/operating support; Annual campaigns; Capital campaigns; Building/renovation; Program development; Research; Program evaluation; Matching/challenge support.

Limitations: Giving primarily in OK. No grants to individuals, or for endowments or scholarships.

Publications: Application guidelines.

Application information: Proposal form will be sent upon approval of letter of inquiry. Application form required.

  Initial approach: Letter of inquiry

  Copies of proposal: 3

  Deadline(s): None

  Board meeting date(s): Quarterly and as needed

Trustees: J. Jerry Dickman; Donne W. Pitman.

Number of staff: None.

EIN: 736177739

Selected grants: The following grants were reported in 2003.

$250,000 to University of Texas M. D. Anderson Cancer Center, Houston, TX. 2 grants: $125,000 each

$250,000 to University of Tulsa, Tulsa, OK.

$140,000 to Saint John Medical Center Foundation, Tulsa, OK.

$100,000 to Philbrook Museum of Art, Tulsa, OK.

$75,000 to Oklahoma Baptist University, Shawnee, OK.

$50,000 to Cascia Hall Preparatory School, Tulsa, OK.

$50,000 to Childrens Center, Bethany, OK.

$50,000 to Holland Hall School, Tulsa, OK.

$50,000 to Johns Hopkins University, Baltimore, MD. For medical research.

7929
Fulton and Susie Collins Foundation ✧

1924 S. Utica Ave., Ste. 800

Tulsa, OK 74104-6516 (918) 748-9860

Contact: Suzanne M. Collins, Tr.

Established in 1987 in OK.

Donor: G. Fulton Collins III.

Foundation type: Independent foundation.

Financial data (yr. ended 12/31/05): Assets, $15,804,933 (M); gifts received, $5,222,848; expenditures, $1,121,458; qualifying distributions, $1,064,660; giving activities include $1,064,660 for 25 grants (high: $1,000,000; low: $50).

Purpose and activities: Giving primarily for higher education.

Fields of interest: Museums (art); Higher education; Education; Roman Catholic agencies & churches.

Type of support: General/operating support.

Limitations: Giving primarily in Tulsa, OK. No grants to individuals.

Application information: Application form not required.

  Deadline(s): None

Trustees: G. Fulton Collins III; Suzanne M. Collins.

EIN: 731273053

Selected grants: The following grants were reported in 2005.

$1,005,360 to University of Tulsa, Tulsa, OK. 4 grants: $100, $1,000,000, $260, $5,000

$2,500 to Bishop Kelley High School, Tulsa, OK. 2 grants: $1,500, $1,000

7930
George Fulton Collins, Jr. Foundation ✧ ☆

1924 S. Utica Ave., Ste. 800

Tulsa, OK 74104-6516 (918) 748-9860

Established in 1968 in OK.

Foundation type: Independent foundation.

Financial data (yr. ended 12/31/05): Assets, $3,221,572 (M); expenditures, $644,774; qualifying distributions, $631,000; giving activities include $631,000 for 2 grants (high: $625,000; low: $6,000).

Fields of interest: Higher education; Foundations (private grantmaking).

Type of support: General/operating support; Annual campaigns; Capital campaigns; Building/renovation; Scholarship funds.

Limitations: Applications not accepted. Giving primarily in OK. No grants to individuals.

Application information: Contributes only to pre-selected organizations.

Officers: Fulton Collins, Chair.; Suzanne M. Collins, Secy.; Roger B. Collins, Treas.

EIN: 237008179

7931
Communities Foundation of Oklahoma

(formerly Oklahoma Communities Foundation, Inc.)

2932 N.W. 122nd St., Ste. D

Oklahoma City, OK 73120-1955

(405) 488-1450

Contact: Susan R. Graves, Exec. Dir.

FAX: (405) 755-0938; E-mail: sgraves@cfok.org; Additional tel.: (877) 689-7726; URL: http://www.cfok.org

Established in 1992 in OK.

Foundation type: Community foundation.

Financial data (yr. ended 6/30/05): Assets, $13,716,466 (M); gifts received, $7,363,246; expenditures, $2,351,176; giving activities include $1,778,922 for 110 grants, and $209,184 for 82 grants to individuals.

Purpose and activities: The foundation is statewide with primary service to non-metropolitan donors and charities.

Fields of interest: Historic preservation/historical societies; Arts; Education; Animal welfare; Health care; Recreation, community facilities; Human services; Science, research; Women.

Type of support: General/operating support; Endowments; Seed money; Scholarship funds; Technical assistance; Consulting services; Matching/challenge support.

Limitations: Applications not accepted. Giving primarily in OK.

Publications: Financial statement; Grants list; Informational brochure.

Application information:

Board meeting date(s): Quarterly

Officers and Directors:* Richard Ryerson,* Chair.; April Stobbe,* Vice-Chair.; David Boren, Pres.; Richard E. Dixon,* Secy.; Wes Stucky,* Treas.; Susan R. Graves, Exec. Dir.; Malinda Berry Fischer; Jenny Hendrick; Monica McCasland; Jeannine Rainbolt.

Board of Governors: Ed Apple; Steve Beebe; Ron Beer; Terrence Cooksey; Jimmy Cooper; Nancy Ford; Marceda Garrison; Mary Beth Glass; Terry Graham; Jean Harbison; Hon. Robert Henry; James Howard; Bill Humphrey; Craig Knutson; Tom McCasland, Jr.; Melvin Moran; Gene Nelson; Susan Paddack; Steve Poag; H.E. Gene Rainbolt; Larry Roberts; Jim Rodgers; Pam Treadwell; Bruce Von Tungeln.

Number of staff: 2 full-time professional; 2 part-time professional; 2 full-time support; 1 part-time support.

EIN: 731396320

7932

Community Foundation of Ardmore, Inc.

P.O. Box 2597
Ardmore, OK   73402   (580) 223-3883
Contact: Larry A. Pulliam, C.E.O. and Pres.
FAX: (580) 226-0223;
E-mail: lapulliam@sbcglobal.net

Established in 2003 in OK.

Foundation type: Independent foundation.

Financial data (yr. ended 2/28/06): Assets, $12,405,549 (M); expenditures, $533,226; qualifying distributions, $474,849; giving activities include $425,484 for 37 grants (high: $73,626; low: $1,673) and $425,484 for set-asides.

Fields of interest: Education; Health care; Human services.

Type of support: Research; Scholarship funds; Program evaluation; Program development; Land acquisition; Management development/capacity building; General/operating support; Equipment; Emergency funds; Continuing support; Building/renovation; Capital campaigns.

Limitations: Giving primarily in Carter County, OK and adjacent areas, with emphasis on Ardmore. No support for churches and public schools. No grants to individuals.

Application information: Application form required.

Initial approach: Letter

Copies of proposal: 1

Deadline(s): First day of the second month of each calendar quarter

Board meeting date(s): Mar., Jun., Sept., and Dec.

Final notification: 1 week following board meeting

Officers and Trustees:* Albert Riesen, Jr.,* Chair.; Sam Daube,* Vice-Chair.; Larry A. Pulliam, C.E.O. and Pres.; Curtis Davidson,* Secy.-Treas.; Robert M. Bramlett; W. Lee Coffey; J. Robert Dexter; Milliard Ingram; Samuel J. Veazey; Charles F. Williams.

Number of staff: 2 full-time professional; 1 full-time support.

EIN: 200514419

7933

ConocoPhillips Dependent Scholarship Program Trust ◇

(formerly Educational Fund for Children of Phillips Petroleum Company Employees)
1650 PB
Bartlesville, OK   74004
Contact: Ron Stanley, Dir., Educational Funds

Established in 1939 in OK.

Donors: Phillips Petroleum Co.; ConocoPhillips Co.

Foundation type: Company-sponsored foundation.

Financial data (yr. ended 8/31/05): Assets, $0 (M); gifts received, $547,110; expenditures, $642,687; qualifying distributions, $642,687; giving activities include $638,000 for 231 grants to individuals (high: $6,000; low: $1,000).

Purpose and activities: The foundation awards college scholarships to children, adopted children, stepchildren, and fully-dependent wards of present, permanently disabled, and deceased full-time employees of ConocoPhillips and its domestic subsidiaries.

Type of support: Employee-related scholarships.

Limitations: Applications not accepted. Giving on a national basis.

Application information: Contributes only through employee-related scholarships.

Officer: R.J. Stanley, Admin.

Selection Committee: J.R. Morris; R.W. Poole; Peggy Smith.

EIN: 736095141

7934

Crawley Family Foundation ◇ ☆

105 N. Hudson Ave., Ste. 800
Oklahoma City, OK   73102-4803

Donors: James B. Crawley; Mary W. Crawley; JBC Investment Co.

Foundation type: Independent foundation.

Financial data (yr. ended 12/31/05): Assets, $2,138,393 (M); gifts received, $1,050,000; expenditures, $384,851; qualifying distributions, $368,000; giving activities include $368,000 for 30 grants (high: $100,000; low: $1,000).

Fields of interest: Performing arts, orchestra (symphony); Arts; Higher education, university; Business school/education; Theological school/education; Education; Christian agencies & churches.

Limitations: Applications not accepted. Giving primarily in Norman, OK and in TX. No grants to individuals.

Application information: Contributes only to pre-selected organizations.

Officers: James B. Crawley, Pres.; Mary W. Crawley, Secy.; Sara B. Crawley, Treas.

Trustee: Linda S. Crawley.

EIN: 731463271

Selected grants: The following grants were reported in 2005.

$40,000 to University of Oklahoma, Norman, OK. 2 grants: $10,000, $30,000

$12,000 to Girl Scouts of the U.S.A., East Longmeadow, MA.

$10,000 to Opera Colorado, Denver, CO.

$10,000 to Preston Hollow Presbyterian Church, Dallas, TX.

$7,000 to Oklahoma Arts Institute, Oklahoma City, OK.

$5,000 to Community Literacy Centers, Oklahoma City, OK.

$1,000 to Saint Mary of the Woods College, Saint Mary of the Woods, IN.

7935

Ethics & Excellence in Journalism Foundation ◇

210 Park Ave., Ste. 3150
Oklahoma City, OK   73102   (405) 604-5388
Contact: Nancy Woodson, Prog. Off.
FAX: (405) 604-0297;
E-mail: nancy.woodson@journalismfoundation.org;
URL: http://www.journalismfoundation.org

Established in 1982 in OK.

Donor: Edith Kinney Gaylord†.

Foundation type: Independent foundation.

Financial data (yr. ended 6/30/05): Assets, $94,521,364 (M); gifts received, $698,519; expenditures, $4,092,865; qualifying distributions, $4,241,279; giving activities include $3,390,846 for 92 grants (high: $400,000; low: $833), and $48,116 for 41 employee matching gifts.

Purpose and activities: Supports projects designed to improve the quality and ethical standards of journalism in various media.

Fields of interest: Media/communications; Media, journalism/publishing; Higher education.

Type of support: Equipment; Program development; Conferences/seminars; Publication; Curriculum development; Research; Technical assistance.

Limitations: Giving on a national basis, with some emphasis on OK. No grants to individuals.

Publications: Informational brochure (including application guidelines).

Application information: Application process should not be started without prior foundation approval. Application form required.

Initial approach: Letter of inquiry

Copies of proposal: 7

Deadline(s): Apr. 15 and Oct. 15 for letters of inquiry; May 15 and Nov. 15 for approved applications

Board meeting date(s): Jan. and July

Final notification: 3 months

Officers and Directors:* William J. Ross,* Chair.; Robert J. Ross,* C.E.O. and Pres.; David O. Hogan; Andrew W. Roff; J. Hugh Roff, Jr.; Patrick T. Rooney.

Advisory Committee Members: John A. Rieger, Chair.; Janet Cromley; Andrew C. Barth; Marian Cromley; Kay Dyer; John T. Greiner, Jr.

Number of staff: 6 full-time professional; 3 full-time support.

EIN: 731167175

Selected grants: The following grants were reported in 2003.

$71,822 to University of Oklahoma Foundation, Norman, OK. For technological equipment for Journalism Outreach Project.

$64,120 to Radio and Television News Directors Foundation, DC. For Journalism Ethics Project.

$58,000 to Southwestern Oklahoma State University Foundation, Weatherford, OK. For Small Market Media Program.

$50,000 to Oklahoma City University, Oklahoma City, OK. For Edith Kinney Gaylord Interdisciplinary Education Program for Print Journalism Studies.

$30,000 to Manteo High School, Manteo, NC. To purchase five graphics workstations, digital still and video cameras.

$25,000 to Committee to Protect Journalists, New York, NY. For Journalist Security Program.

$25,000 to Minnesota News Council, Minneapolis, MN. For general operating support.

$25,000 to Washington and Lee University, Lexington, VA. To renovate, upgrade and modernize Reid Hall.

$24,000 to National Cowboy and Western Heritage Museum, Oklahoma City, OK.

$15,700 to Colorado College, Department of English, Colorado Springs, CO.

7936
Evergreen Foundation ✦ ☆
15 E. 5th St., Ste. 3200
Tulsa, OK 74103

Established in 1998 in OK.
Donors: Barbara G. Heyman; Stephen J. Heyman.
Foundation type: Independent foundation.
Financial data (yr. ended 12/31/05): Assets, $1,011 (M); gifts received, $404,000; expenditures, $408,040; qualifying distributions, $408,040; giving activities include $408,040 for 8 grants (high: $400,000; low: $500).
Fields of interest: Education; Hospitals (general).
Limitations: Applications not accepted. Giving primarily in Tulsa, OK. No grants to individuals.
Application information: Contributes only to pre-selected organizations.
Officers: Stephen J. Heyman, Pres. and Treas.; Barbara G. Heyman, V.P. and Secy.
EIN: 731535560
Selected grants: The following grants were reported in 2005.
$400,000 to Saint John Medical Center Foundation, Tulsa, OK.
$1,500 to Booker T. Washington Foundation for Excellence, Tulsa, OK.
$1,500 to Oklahoma Foundation for Excellence, Oklahoma City, OK.
$1,500 to University of Tulsa, Tulsa, OK.
$1,040 to Tulsa Global Alliance, Tulsa, OK.
$1,000 to Tulsa Garden Center, Tulsa, OK.
$500 to Foundation for Tulsa Schools, Tulsa, OK.

7937
E. L. and Thelma Gaylord Foundation ▼ ✦
P.O. Box 25125
Oklahoma City, OK 73125
Contact: Christy Gaylord Everest, Tr.

Established in 1994 in OK.
Donors: Edward L. Gaylord; Thelma F. Gaylord.
Foundation type: Independent foundation.
Financial data (yr. ended 12/31/04): Assets, $195,908,424 (M); gifts received, $75,414,890; expenditures, $6,516,599; qualifying distributions, $6,459,205; giving activities include $6,677,000

for 23 grants (high: $3,000,000; low: $500; average: $20,000–$300,000).
Purpose and activities: Funding primarily for education. Some funding also for the Red Cross, and arts and culture.
Fields of interest: Museums (history); Arts; Elementary/secondary education; Higher education; Education; Medical research, institute; Human services; American Red Cross.
Type of support: Building/renovation.
Limitations: Giving primarily in OK. No grants to individuals.
Application information: Application form required.
Initial approach: Proposal (no more than 2 pages)
Copies of proposal: 1
Deadline(s): None
Trustees: Louise Gaylord Bennett; Christine Gaylord Everest; David O. Hogan; Mary Gaylord McClean.
EIN: 731463569
Selected grants: The following grants were reported in 2004.
$3,000,000 to University of Oklahoma Foundation, Norman, OK. For general operating support.
$1,250,000 to National Cowboy and Western Heritage Museum, Oklahoma City, OK. For general operating support.
$1,000,000 to Casady School, Oklahoma City, OK. For general operating support.
$214,000 to Oklahoma Centennial Commemoration Fund, Oklahoma City, OK. For general operating support.
$150,000 to Civic Center Foundation, Oklahoma City, OK. For general operating support.
$100,000 to Asheville School, Asheville, NC. For general operating support.
$40,000 to Oklahoma City Museum of Art, Oklahoma City, OK. For general operating support.
$20,000 to University of Colorado Foundation, Boulder, CO. For general operating support.
$15,000 to Oklahoma City University, Oklahoma City, OK. For general operating support.
$10,000 to Colonial Williamsburg Foundation, Williamsburg, VA. For general operating support.

7938
The Gelvin Foundation ✦
(formerly Lyle M. Gelvin Foundation)
P.O. Box 837
Eufaula, OK 74432
Contact: Terry Doverspike, Tr.; Therese Starr, Tr.
E-mail: lpcstarr@yahoo.com; Additional E-mail: trd@praywalker.com; URL: http://www.gelvinfoundation.org

Established in 1992 in OK.
Donors: Lyle M. Gelvin‡; Lyle Pacific Corp.
Foundation type: Independent foundation.
Financial data (yr. ended 12/31/05): Assets, $8,615,812 (M); expenditures, $464,595; qualifying distributions, $390,390; giving activities include $382,750 for 56 grants.
Purpose and activities: Grants are primarily focused on charitable organizations located within a 30-mile radius of Tulsa or Eufaula, OK, whose programs primarily benefit the citizens of these areas in the fields of civic and cultural, education, family and community service, health care, and religion.
Fields of interest: Education; Hospitals (general); Human services.
Type of support: Capital campaigns; Building/renovation; Equipment; Land acquisition; Program development; Matching/challenge support.

Limitations: Giving primarily in OK, with emphasis within a 30-mile radius of Tulsa or Eufaula. No grants to individuals.
Publications: Application guidelines; Informational brochure (including application guidelines).
Application information: See foundation Web site for application guidelines and procedures. Application form not required.
Initial approach: Letter
Copies of proposal: 2
Deadline(s): Feb. 10, May 10, Aug. 10, and Nov. 10
Board meeting date(s): Mar., June, Sept. and Dec.
Final notification: Varies, usually by end of quarter
Officers and Trustees:* Therese Starr,* Pres. and Treas.; Terry Doverspike,* V.P. and Secy.
EIN: 731419663
Selected grants: The following grants were reported in 2005.
$50,000 to Saint John Medical Center Foundation, Tulsa, OK.
$25,000 to Tulsa Historical Society, Tulsa, OK.
$20,000 to Salvation Army, Norman, OK. 2 grants: $10,000 each
$15,000 to University of Tulsa, Tulsa, OK.
$12,000 to Make-A-Wish Foundation of Oklahoma, Tulsa, OK.
$10,000 to American Red Cross, Tulsa, OK.
$10,000 to Parent Child Center of Tulsa, Tulsa, OK.
$10,000 to Street School, Tulsa, OK.
$5,000 to Tulsa Ballet Theater, Tulsa, OK.

7939
The Charles B. Goddard Foundation Trust ✦
P.O. Box 1485
Ardmore, OK 73402 (580) 226-6040
Contact: William R. Goddard, Jr., Tr.

Established in 1958 in OK.
Donor: Charles B. Goddard‡.
Foundation type: Independent foundation.
Financial data (yr. ended 6/30/05): Assets, $13,831,522 (M); expenditures, $554,168; qualifying distributions, $533,020; giving activities include $533,020 for 34 grants (high: $100,000; low: $100).
Purpose and activities: Giving primarily for education, and health care, particularly a children's medical center and a visiting nurse association; funding also for youth and social services.
Fields of interest: Education; Nursing care; Health care; Human services; Salvation Army; YM/YWCAs & YM/YWHAs; Children/youth, services; Federated giving programs.
Type of support: General/operating support; Continuing support; Annual campaigns; Building/renovation; Equipment; Emergency funds; Seed money; Research.
Limitations: Giving primarily in south central OK, and northern TX. No grants to individuals; no loans.
Application information: Application form not required.
Initial approach: Letter of request
Deadline(s): None
Board meeting date(s): As required
Trustees: Garland Clay; Ann G. Corrigan; William R. Goddard; William R. Goddard, Jr.; William M. Johns.
EIN: 756005868
Selected grants: The following grants were reported in 2005.

$100,000 to Goddard Youth Foundation, Sulphur, OK.

$25,000 to Media Research Center, Alexandria, VA. 2 grants: $5,000, $20,000

$21,000 to Community Childrens Shelter, Ardmore, OK.

$15,000 to Boy Scouts of America, Ardmore, OK.

$5,000 to Austin Street Center, Dallas, TX.

7940
Grace Living Centers Foundation, Inc. ✧
709 Fox Tail Dr.
Edmond, OK 73034

Established in 2000 in OK.
Donors: K. Don Greiner; Shellie Greiner.
Foundation type: Independent foundation.
Financial data (yr. ended 12/31/05): Assets, $1,180,141 (M); gifts received, $210,000; expenditures, $328,146; qualifying distributions, $320,640; giving activities include $320,640 for 13 grants (high: $245,025; low: $25).
Fields of interest: Education; Roman Catholic agencies & churches.
Limitations: Applications not accepted. No grants to individuals.
Application information: Contributes only to pre-selected organizations.
Directors: K. Don Greiner; Shellie Greiner.
EIN: 731596382

7941
Herbert and Roseline Gussman Foundation ✧
15 E. 5th St., Ste. 3200
Tulsa, OK 74103

Established in 1951 in OK.
Donors: Herbert Gussman†; Roseline Gussman†; Barbara Gussman; Ellen Jane Adelson.
Foundation type: Independent foundation.
Financial data (yr. ended 12/31/05): Assets, $11,636,320 (M); expenditures, $694,661; qualifying distributions, $599,534; giving activities include $599,534 for 12 grants (high: $350,000; low: $500).
Purpose and activities: Giving primarily for higher education; funding also for the arts, human services, health associations, and Jewish and other federated giving programs.
Fields of interest: Museums; Museums (art); Performing arts, orchestra (symphony); Arts; Higher education; Education; Health organizations, association; Human services; Federated giving programs; Jewish federated giving programs; Jewish agencies & temples.
Limitations: Applications not accepted. Giving primarily in Tulsa, OK. No grants to individuals.
Application information: Contributes only to pre-selected organizations.
Trustees: Ellen G. Adelson; Barbara G. Heyman.
EIN: 736090063

7942
The Helmerich Foundation ▼
1437 S. Boulder Ave.
Tulsa, OK 74119
Contact: Walter H. Helmerich III, Tr.

Established in 1965 in OK.

Donors: W.H. Helmerich†; Walter H. Helmerich III.
Foundation type: Independent foundation.
Financial data (yr. ended 9/30/05): Assets, $88,410,581 (M); expenditures, $4,919,692; qualifying distributions, $4,341,406; giving activities include $4,299,500 for 44 grants (high: $1,000,000; low: $1,000; average: $10,000–$100,000).
Purpose and activities: Limited to large capital needs in the Tulsa, OK, area for charitable, and educational purposes. Primary areas of interest include community development, higher education, health services, museums, and the performing arts.
Fields of interest: Museums; Performing arts; Arts; Higher education; Education; Health care; Youth, services; Community development.
Type of support: Capital campaigns; Building/renovation; Equipment; Land acquisition.
Limitations: Giving limited to the Tulsa, OK, area. No grants to individuals, or for general support, continuing support, annual campaigns, seed money, emergency funds, deficit financing, matching gifts, scholarships, fellowships, program support, operating budgets, research, demonstration projects, publications, or conferences; generally, no support for endowment funds; no loans.
Publications: Application guidelines; Program policy statement.
Application information: Application form not required.
Initial approach: Letter
Copies of proposal: 1
Deadline(s): None
Board meeting date(s): As required
Final notification: 6 weeks
Trustee: Walter H. Helmerich III.
Number of staff: 2 part-time support.
EIN: 736105607
Selected grants: The following grants were reported in 2005.

$1,000,000 to Oklahoma State University Foundation, Stillwater, OK. For Science Center.

$500,000 to Philbrook Museum of Art, Tulsa, OK. For garden.

$250,000 to Cascia Hall Preparatory School, Tulsa, OK. For Performing Arts Center.

$250,000 to University of Oklahoma Foundation, Norman, OK. For Museum of Art.

$240,000 to Benedictine Sisters of Saint Joseph Monastery, Tulsa, OK. For renovation.

$150,000 to Center for Individuals with Physical Challenges, Tulsa, OK. To purchase property.

$100,000 to Oklahoma County Historical Society, Oklahoma City, OK. For campaign for new Oklahoma History Center.

$60,000 to Wright Christian Academy, Tulsa, OK. For school building project.

$50,000 to Tulsa Day Center for the Homeless, Tulsa, OK. For restroom renovation project.

$30,000 to Eugene Fields Elementary School Foundation, Tulsa, OK. For new gymnasium floor.

7943
Hille Family Charitable Foundation ✧
700 S. Boston Ave., Ste. 210
Tulsa, OK 74119 (918) 592-0079
Contact: Margaret Hille Yar, Exec. Dir.
FAX: (918) 592-4185;
E-mail: info@hillefoundation.org; URL: http://www.hillefoundation.org

Established in 1997 in OK.
Donors: Jo Bob Hille; Mary Ann Hille.

Foundation type: Independent foundation.
Financial data (yr. ended 12/31/05): Assets, $57,922,814 (M); expenditures, $3,074,264; qualifying distributions, $2,813,342; giving activities include $2,591,328 for 96 grants (high: $762,500; low: $200).
Purpose and activities: The foundation was born out of the Christian principle that it is a privilege to serve others. Raising the educational, spiritual, and physical well-being of those helpless or ignored in society is the primary aim of the foundation. Special attention is given to funding research and programming aimed at early onset Alzheimer's Disease; the promotion of education and scholarship; and church projects that benefit the community at large.
Fields of interest: Education; Environment; Alzheimer's disease research; Diabetes research; Recreation, camps; Human services; Children, services; Community development.
Type of support: General/operating support; Continuing support; Annual campaigns; Capital campaigns; Building/renovation; Equipment; Endowments; Program development; Curriculum development; Fellowships; Scholarship funds; Research.
Limitations: Giving primarily in the Tulsa, OK, area. No grants to individuals.
Application information: Application form not required.
Initial approach: Letter
Copies of proposal: 1
Deadline(s): Jan. 1 (for Feb. meeting), May 1 (for June meeting), and Sept. 1 (for Oct. meeting)
Board meeting date(s): Feb., June, and Oct.
Final notification: 4 weeks after board meeting
Officer and Trustees:* Margaret Hille Yar,* Exec. Dir.; Leslie Hille Hamrick; Mary Ann Hille; Sheila Hille Lequerica.
Number of staff: 1 full-time professional; 2 part-time professional.
EIN: 731521975
Selected grants: The following grants were reported in 2004.

$506,500 to Alzheimers Association, Chicago, IL.

$250,000 to Tulsa Educare, Tulsa, OK.

$210,000 to YWCA of Tulsa, Tulsa, OK.

$132,020 to Crosstown Learning Center, Tulsa, OK.

$31,250 to American Lung Association, New York, NY.

$28,534 to Childrens Services Advisory Board, Tulsa, OK.

$25,000 to YMCA.

$15,000 to Oklahoma Foundation for Excellence, Oklahoma City, OK.

$15,000 to Town and Country School, Tulsa, OK.

$15,000 to Tulsa Center for AIDS Resources Education and Support (CARES), Tulsa, OK.

7944
Inasmuch Foundation ▼ ✧
210 Park Ave., Ste. 3150
Oklahoma City, OK 73102 (405) 604-5292
Contact: Nancy Woodson, Prog. Off.
FAX: (405) 604-0297;
E-mail: nancy.woodson@inasmuchfoundation.org;
URL: http://www.inasmuchfoundation.org

Established in 1982 in OK.
Donor: Edith Kinney Gaylord†.
Foundation type: Independent foundation.
Financial data (yr. ended 6/30/05): Assets, $278,116,828 (M); expenditures, $6,365,999;

qualifying distributions, $12,424,815; giving activities include $4,747,212 for 179 grants (high: $300,000; low: $100; average: $5,000–$25,000), $125,006 for 81 employee matching gifts and $7,000,000 for set-asides.

Purpose and activities: Grants are made in the following areas: education, cultural affairs, environmental concerns, the performing arts, human or social services, and historic preservation.

Fields of interest: Performing arts; Arts; Education; Environment; Health care; Health organizations, association; Medical research, institute; Human services.

Type of support: Sponsorships; Capital campaigns; Equipment; Land acquisition; Program development; Conferences/seminars; Seed money; Curriculum development; Research; Program evaluation.

Limitations: Giving primarily in Colorado Springs, CO, and OK. No grants to individuals, or for regular operating expenses or endowments.

Publications: Grants list; Informational brochure (including application guidelines).

Application information: Letter of inquiry must be submitted and approved prior to submitting a full application. Application form is available on the foundation's Web site. Application form required.

Initial approach: Letter of inquiry
Copies of proposal: 2
Deadline(s): Jan. 15 and July 15 for letter of inquiry; Feb. 15 and Aug. 15 for application
Board meeting date(s): Apr. and Oct.
Final notification: 3 months

Officers and Trustees:* William J. Ross,* Chair.; Robert J. Ross,* C.E.O. and Pres.; Richard A. Davis, C.F.O.; David O. Hogan; Andrew W. Roff; J. Hugh Roff, Jr.; Patrick T. Rooney.

Advisory Committee: Barbara L. Yalich, Comm. Chair.; Christine Gaylord Everest; Tricia Everest; Cathy Robbins; Jeanne Hoffman Smith.

Number of staff: 6 full-time professional; 3 full-time support.

EIN: 731167188

Selected grants: The following grants were reported in 2005.

$416,667 to Oklahoma City Museum of Art, Oklahoma City, OK. 2 grants: $166,667 (For acquisition of Dale Chihuly's work), $250,000 (For Presenting Season Sponsor).

$300,000 to University of Central Oklahoma Foundation, Edmond, OK. For Investing in Excellence capital campaign of College of Mathematics and Science.

$200,000 to Tulsa Educare, Tulsa, OK. For early childhood education program.

$166,666 to Variety Health Center, Oklahoma City, OK. For renovation of Lafayette Elementary School into new location of Variety Health Center.

$100,000 to YWCA of Oklahoma City, Oklahoma City, OK. For Crisis Services.

$25,000 to Mount Saint Mary High School, Oklahoma City, OK. For tuition assistance program.

$15,000 to Cherokee National Historical Society, Tahlequah, OK. For Cherokee Humanities Program Initiative.

$10,000 to Hospice of Green Country, Tulsa, OK. For Courtesy Care and Live Alone Programs.

$10,000 to Oklahoma Community Health Services, Oklahoma City, OK. For build-out of Dental Clinic and Laboratory.

7945

The Daisy B. Jackson Charitable Trust ◇ ☆

c/o Hargis, Cotte
944 E. 36th St.
Tulsa, OK 74105 (918) 742-5858
Contact: John Hargis, Tr.; Grace Hargis, Tr.

Foundation type: Independent foundation.

Financial data (yr. ended 12/31/05): Assets, $1,058,283 (M); expenditures, $319,795; qualifying distributions, $318,608; giving activities include $294,746 for 3 grants (high: $200,000; low: $13,666), and $23,862 for 11 grants to individuals (high: $4,000; low: $400).

Fields of interest: Scholarships/financial aid; Education; Christian agencies & churches.

Application information: Application form not required.

Initial approach: Essay
Deadline(s): None

Trustees: Grace Hargis; John Hargis.

EIN: 266017403

7946

Fred and Mary Eddy Jones Foundation ◇

c/o Debbie Melott
9225 Lake Hefner Pkwy., Ste. 200
Oklahoma City, OK 73120 (405) 231-2400
Contact: Debbie Melott

Established in 1991 in OK.

Donor: Mary Eddy Jones.

Foundation type: Independent foundation.

Financial data (yr. ended 6/30/05): Assets, $12,071,326 (M); expenditures, $425,616; qualifying distributions, $346,100; giving activities include $334,950 for 62 grants (high: $150,000; low: $500).

Fields of interest: Higher education, university; Health organizations, association; YM/YWCAs & YM/YWHAs; Economic development; Federated giving programs; Christian agencies & churches.

Limitations: Giving primarily in OK.

Application information:

Initial approach: Letter
Deadline(s): None

Trustees: Brooks Hall, Jr.; Fred Jones Hall; Kirkland Hall; Marilyn Jones Upsher.

EIN: 731404958

7947

Betty and George Kaiser Foundation ▼ ◇

(formerly Betty E. and George B. Kaiser Foundation)
P.O. Box 21468
Tulsa, OK 74121-1468
Contact: Frederic Dorwart, Tr.
Additional address: 124 E. 4th St., Tulsa, OK 74013

Established in 1990 in OK.

Foundation type: Independent foundation.

Financial data (yr. ended 12/31/05): Assets, $609,348 (M); expenditures, $105,707,483; qualifying distributions, $105,657,775; giving activities include $105,657,775 for 16 grants (high: $62,315,782; low: $4; average: $10,000–$8,036,523).

Purpose and activities: Giving primarily for higher education, health care, human services, and Jewish agencies and temples.

Fields of interest: Higher education; Health care; Human services; Jewish agencies & temples.

Limitations: Giving primarily in OK. No grants to individuals.

Application information: Application form not required.

Deadline(s): None

Trustee: Frederic Dorwart.

EIN: 731363237

Selected grants: The following grants were reported in 2005.

$105,127,970 to George Kaiser Family Foundation, Tulsa, OK. 9 grants: $67,605, $708,161, $6,962,634, $7,567,258, $7,687,290, $8,036,523, $62,315,782, $7,717, $11,775,000

$500,000 to Tulsa Community Foundation, Tulsa, OK.

7948

Herman G. Kaiser Foundation ◇

1350 S. Boulder Ave., Ste. 400
Tulsa, OK 74119-3224 (918) 582-8083
Contact: Sheryl Green, Admin. Asst.
E-mail: sherylg@okganesha.com

Established around 1976.

Donor: Herman Kaiser‡.

Foundation type: Independent foundation.

Financial data (yr. ended 6/30/05): Assets, $28,978,004 (M); expenditures, $1,565,330; qualifying distributions, $1,377,367; giving activities include $1,377,367 for 47 grants (high: $510,000; low: $200).

Purpose and activities: Giving primarily to Jewish and Oklahoma organizations for education, health and human services.

Fields of interest: Education; Health organizations, association; Human services; Jewish federated giving programs; Jewish agencies & temples.

Type of support: Continuing support; Annual campaigns; Capital campaigns; Building/renovation; Equipment.

Limitations: Applications not accepted. Giving primarily in Tulsa, OK. No grants to individuals.

Application information: Contributes only to pre-selected organizations.

Board meeting date(s): Thanksgiving weekend

Trustees: Michael S. Nelson; Pamela B. Nelson; Randolph M. Nelson; Timothy B. Nelson.

EIN: 510173653

Selected grants: The following grants were reported in 2005.

$510,000 to Tulsa Community Foundation, Tulsa, OK.

$60,000 to LIFE Senior Services, Tulsa, OK.

$50,000 to Philbrook Museum of Art, Tulsa, OK.

$25,000 to Home of Hope, Vinita, OK.

$25,000 to Sherwin Miller Museum of Jewish Art, Tulsa, OK.

$20,000 to Oklahoma Caring Program for Children, Tulsa, OK.

$12,500 to Gilcrease Museum, Tulsa, OK.

$5,000 to Homelife Association, Tulsa, OK.

$5,000 to Hospice of Green Country, Tulsa, OK.

$2,500 to Tulsa Opera, Tulsa, OK.

7949

The Kerr Foundation, Inc. ✧
12501 N. May Ave.
Oklahoma City, OK   73120   (405) 749-7991
Contact: Cecilia Miller, Admin. Asst.
FAX: (405) 749-2877;
E-mail: ccastle@thekerrfoundation.org; URL: http://www.thekerrfoundation.org/

Incorporated in 1963 in OK, and reincorporated in 1985.
Donor: Grayce B. Kerr Flynn†.
Foundation type: Independent foundation.
Financial data (yr. ended 12/31/05): Assets, $28,440,474 (M); expenditures, $1,984,633; qualifying distributions, $1,229,311; giving activities include $719,664 for grants.
Purpose and activities: Giving primarily for education, the fine arts and other cultural activities, and health. Generally all grants are challenge grants.
Fields of interest: Visual arts; Museums; Performing arts; Arts; Libraries/library science; Education; Health care; Health organizations, association; Human services; Youth, services; Government/public administration.
Type of support: Building/renovation; Equipment; Program development; Professorships; Curriculum development; Fellowships; Internship funds; Research; Program evaluation; In-kind gifts; Matching/challenge support.
Limitations: Giving primarily in AR, CO, Washington, DC, KS, MO, NM, OK, and TX. No grants to individuals, or generally for continuing support.
Publications: Application guidelines; Grants list.
Application information: See foundation Web site for full guidelines and downloadable application form. Application form required.
  Initial approach: Letter
  Copies of proposal: 3
  Deadline(s): July 21
  Board meeting date(s): Quarterly
  Final notification: Next day following receipt of application
Officers and Trustees:* Mrs. Robert S. Kerr,* Chair.; Lou C. Kerr,* Pres.; Steven. S. Kerr, V.P.; Laura K. Ogle, V.P.; Anne Halzdierlein, Secy.; Royce M. Hammons,* Treas.; Cody T. Kerr; Ray Kline; Elmer Staats.
Number of staff: 4 full-time professional; 1 part-time professional.
EIN: 731256122
Selected grants: The following grants were reported in 2004.
$350,000 to Oklahoma Medical Research Foundation, Oklahoma City, OK. 2 grants: $250,000, $100,000
$33,333 to NPR Foundation, DC.
$10,000 to Oklahoma City Art Museum, Oklahoma City, OK.
$8,000 to Cherokee National Historical Society, Tahlequah, OK.

7950

Kerr-McGee Foundation Corporation ✧
(formerly Kerr-McGee Corporation Foundation)
Kerr-McGee Ctr.
123 Robert S. Kerr Ave., MT Plz.
Oklahoma City, OK   73102
Contact: Jon Trudgeon, Community Rels. Coord.

Established in 1996 in OK.
Donor: Kerr-McGee Corp.

Foundation type: Company-sponsored foundation.
Financial data (yr. ended 12/31/05): Assets, $19,672,032 (M); expenditures, $1,918,027; qualifying distributions, $1,836,021; giving activities include $1,836,021 for 434 grants (high: $160,000; low: $25).
Purpose and activities: The foundation supports zoos and organizations involved with arts and culture, education, natural resources, health, human services, and community development.
Fields of interest: Arts; Elementary/secondary education; Higher education; Education; Environment, natural resources; Zoos/zoological societies; Health care; Athletics/sports, Special Olympics; Human services; Community development; Federated giving programs.
Type of support: General/operating support; Continuing support; Annual campaigns; Capital campaigns; Building/renovation; Scholarship funds; Employee matching gifts; Employee-related scholarships.
Limitations: Giving primarily in areas of company and affiliate operations, with emphasis on OK. No grants to individuals (except for employee-related scholarships).
Application information: Application form not required.
  Initial approach: Proposal
  Deadline(s): Nov. 1
  Final notification: 3 months
Officers and Director:* Luke R. Corbett,* Chair. and C.E.O.; Robert M. Wohleber, Sr. V.P.; Gregory F. Pilcher, V.P. and Secy.; John M. Rauh, V.P. and Treas.
EIN: 731496403
Selected grants: The following grants were reported in 2005.
$187,500 to Oklahoma Centennial Commemoration Fund, Oklahoma City, OK. 2 grants: $37,500, $150,000
$160,000 to United Way of Central Oklahoma, Oklahoma City, OK.
$150,000 to Oklahoma City University, Oklahoma City, OK.
$100,000 to Oklahoma City National Memorial Foundation, Oklahoma City, OK.
$65,000 to Allied Arts Foundation, Oklahoma City, OK.
$50,000 to Oklahoma Christian University, Oklahoma City, OK.
$25,000 to United Way of the Texas Gulf Coast, Houston, TX.
$5,000 to United Way of Weld County, Greeley, CO.
$200 to Northwestern University, Evanston, IL.

7951

Kimmell Family Foundation ✧ ☆
52 N.W. 42nd St.
Oklahoma City, OK   73118-8505
(405) 525-6601
Contact: Garman O. Kimmell, Pres.

Donors: Garman O. Kimmell; Tom Hill; Kay Hill.
Foundation type: Operating foundation.
Financial data (yr. ended 12/31/04): Assets, $530,754 (M); gifts received, $840,117; expenditures, $451,257; qualifying distributions, $451,257; giving activities include $451,150 for 54 grants (high: $55,000; low: $100).
Fields of interest: Museums (history); Education; Human services; Children/youth, services; Religious federated giving programs; Christian agencies & churches.

Application information: Application form not required.
  Initial approach: Letter
  Deadline(s): None
Officers: Garman O. Kimmell, Pres.; Thomas A. Hill, Exec. V.P.; Kay Hill, Secy.; David K. Hill, Sr., Treas.
EIN: 731620045

7952

Kirkpatrick Foundation, Inc.
1001 W. Wilshire Blvd., No. 201
Oklahoma City, OK   73116   (405) 608-0934
Contact: Susan McCalmont, Secy.
FAX: (405) 608-0942; URL: http://www.kirkpatrickfoundation.com

Incorporated in 1955 in OK.
Donors: Eleanor B. Kirkpatrick†; John E. Kirkpatrick; Kirkpatrick Oil Co.; Joan E. Kirkpatrick; Kathryn T. Blake†.
Foundation type: Independent foundation.
Financial data (yr. ended 12/31/05): Assets, $34,656,067 (M); expenditures, $2,089,347; qualifying distributions, $1,692,897; giving activities include $1,616,200 for 49 grants (high: $200,500; low: $500).
Purpose and activities: The foundation's mission is to support arts and culture, education, animal concerns, and environmental conservation, primarily in central Oklahoma.
Fields of interest: Visual arts; Museums; Performing arts; Historic preservation/historical societies; Arts; Education; Animals/wildlife, research; Animals/wildlife, preservation/protection.
Type of support: General/operating support; Continuing support; Program development; Seed money; Curriculum development.
Limitations: Giving primarily in central OK. No support for medical and health related causes, social welfare, or lobbying organizations. No grants to individuals or for school trips; no loans.
Publications: Application guidelines.
Application information: Application form required.
  Initial approach: Letter
  Copies of proposal: 1
  Deadline(s): Jan. 15 and July 15
  Board meeting date(s): Mar., June, Sept., and Dec.
Officers and Directors:* John E. Kirkpatrick,* Chair.; Joan E. Kirkpatrick,* Pres.; Christian K. Keesee,* 1st V.P.; Mark Robertson,* 2nd V.P.; Susan McCalmont, Secy.; Joe Howell,* Treas.; John L. Belt; Mischa Gorkuscha; Ann Hoover; Linda Lambert; Anne Hodges Morgan; George Records; Meg Salyer; Laura Warriner; Max Weitzenhoffer.
Number of staff: 3 full-time professional; 1 part-time professional.
EIN: 730701736

7953

The Lyon Foundation ✧
(formerly E. H. and Melody Lyon Foundation, Inc.)
P.O. Box 546
Bartlesville, OK   74005   (918) 336-0066
Contact: James W. Connor, Pres.

Established in 1975 in OK.
Donors: E.H. Lyon†; Melody Lyon†.
Foundation type: Independent foundation.
Financial data (yr. ended 12/31/05): Assets, $24,804,687 (M); expenditures, $1,202,156;

qualifying distributions, $1,088,173; giving activities include $997,277 for 29 grants (high: $300,000; low: $951).

Purpose and activities: Giving primarily for the aged and education as well as civic projects, particularly parks and recreation.

Fields of interest: Arts; Education; Hospitals (general); Recreation; Human services; Children/youth, services; Aging, centers/services; Government/public administration.

Type of support: Capital campaigns.

Limitations: Giving limited to the Bartlesville, OK, area. No grants to individuals.

Publications: Application guidelines.

Application information: Application form required.

  Initial approach: Letter
  Deadline(s): None
  Board meeting date(s): Quarterly

Officers: James W. Connor, Pres. and Mgr.; Walter W. Allison, V.P.; Don Donaldson, V.P.; Charles W. Selby, Secy.; John F. Kane, Treas.

Number of staff: 1 full-time support.

EIN: 237299980

Selected grants: The following grants were reported in 2005.

$149,000 to Oklahoma Wesleyan University, Bartlesville, OK. 2 grants: $5,000, $144,000

$100,000 to Bartlesville, City of, Bartlesville, OK.

$51,125 to Bartlesville Theater Guild, Bartlesville, OK. 2 grants: $7,000, $44,125

$22,640 to Lighthouse Outreach Center, Roseville, MI.

$15,388 to YMCA.

$10,000 to Salvation Army.

7954
The J. E. and L. E. Mabee Foundation, Inc. ▼

401 S. Boston, Ste. 3001
Tulsa, OK 74103-4017   (918) 584-4286
Contact: John H. Conway, Jr., Vice-Chair.
E-mail: mabeefoundation@sbcglobal.net; Additional tel. (for Midland, TX): (432) 682-5902; URL: http://www.mabeefoundation.com

Incorporated in 1948 in DE.

Donors: J.E. Mabee†; L.E. Mabee†.

Foundation type: Independent foundation.

Financial data (yr. ended 8/31/06): Assets, $769,999,802 (M); expenditures, $38,583,991; qualifying distributions, $36,532,800; giving activities include $36,532,800 for grants.

Purpose and activities: Giving to aid Christian religious organizations, charitable organizations, and institutions of higher learning; and to support hospitals and other agencies and institutions engaged in the discovery, treatment, and care of diseases. Grants are limited to building projects and purchase of major medical equipment.

Fields of interest: Higher education; Hospitals (general); Youth development, services; Human services; Youth, services.

Type of support: Capital campaigns; Building/renovation; Equipment.

Limitations: Giving limited to AR, KS, MO, NM, OK, and TX. No support for secondary or elementary education, or tax-supported institutions. No grants to individuals, or for research, endowment funds, scholarships, fellowships, or operating expenses; no loans.

Publications: Application guidelines; Program policy statement.

Application information: Summary statement, found on foundation's Web site, is required as cover page to all grant proposals. Application form not required.

  Initial approach: Proposal
  Copies of proposal: 1
  Deadline(s): Mar. 1, June 1, Sept. 1, and Dec. 1
  Board meeting date(s): Jan., Apr., July, and Oct.
  Final notification: After board meetings

Officers and Directors:* Joe Mabee, Sr.,* Chair.; John H. Conway, Jr.,* Vice-Chair. and Secy.-Treas.; Thomas R. Brett; James L. Houghton; Thomas E. Jones; Joseph Guy Mabee, Jr.; Raymond L. Tullius, Jr.

Number of staff: 1 full-time professional; 6 part-time professional; 6 full-time support.

EIN: 736090162

Selected grants: The following grants were reported in 2005.

$2,000,000 to Saint Edwards University, Austin, TX. For new building construction.

$1,444,000 to Lubbock Christian University, Lubbock, TX. For new building construction.

$1,380,000 to MidAmerica Nazarene University, Olathe, KS. For new building construction.

$1,250,000 to YMCA of Midland, Midland, TX. For new building construction.

$1,000,000 to American Lung Association, Tulsa, OK. For building renovations.

$1,000,000 to Harding University, Searcy, AR. For new building construction.

$1,000,000 to LeTourneau University, Longview, TX. For new building construction.

$1,000,000 to Starlight Theater, Kansas City, MO. For building renovations.

$1,000,000 to Washington University, Saint Louis, MO. For new building construction.

$1,000,000 to YMCA of Greater Oklahoma City, Oklahoma City, OK. For new building construction.

7955
Massey Family Foundation ◇ ☆

c/o John L. Massey
1400 W. Main St.
Durant, OK 74701

Established in 2004 in OK.

Donor: John L. Massey.

Foundation type: Independent foundation.

Financial data (yr. ended 12/31/04): Assets, $625,000 (M); gifts received, $1,000,000; expenditures, $375,000; qualifying distributions, $375,000; giving activities include $375,000 for 1 grant.

Purpose and activities: Giving primarily to a Baptist organization.

Fields of interest: Protestant agencies & churches.

Limitations: Applications not accepted. Giving primarily in OK.

Application information: Contributes only to pre-selected organizations.

Officers: John L. Massey, Pres.; Gregory L. Massey, V.P.

Directors: Steve Burrage; Glen D. Johnson.

EIN: 432065394

7956
McCasland Foundation ◇

McCasland Bldg.
P.O. Box 400
Duncan, OK 73534   (580) 252-6559
Contact: Barbara Braught, Exec. Dir.

Trust established in 1952 in OK.

Donors: T.H. McCasland, Jr.; Mary F. Michaelis; Barbara Braught; Mack Oil Co.; Jath Oil Co.; and members of the McCausland family.

Foundation type: Independent foundation.

Financial data (yr. ended 12/31/04): Assets, $47,361,982 (M); expenditures, $2,468,340; qualifying distributions, $2,150,100; giving activities include $2,141,313 for 76 grants (high: $295,327; low: $710).

Purpose and activities: Support for higher education, cultural organizations, social services, and community improvement.

Fields of interest: Arts, association; Arts councils; Museums (specialized); Arts; Higher education; Hospitals (general); Health organizations, association; Human services; Community development; Public affairs.

Type of support: Employee matching gifts; General/operating support; Building/renovation; Matching/challenge support.

Limitations: Giving primarily in OK.

Application information:

  Initial approach: Letter
  Copies of proposal: 1
  Deadline(s): None
  Board meeting date(s): Varies; usually quarterly
  Final notification: After board meetings

Officer: Barbara Braught, Exec. Dir.

Trustees: T.H. McCasland, Jr.; Mary Frances Michaelis; W.H. Phelps.

EIN: 736096032

Selected grants: The following grants were reported in 2004.

$495,327 to On the Chisholm Trail Association, Duncan, OK. 2 grants: $295,327, $200,000

$245,000 to University of Oklahoma, Norman, OK. 2 grants: $225,000, $20,000

$162,500 to Cameron University Foundation, Lawton, OK.

$100,000 to Oklahoma Medical Research Foundation, Oklahoma City, OK.

$70,000 to Oklahoma Council of Public Affairs, Oklahoma City, OK.

$49,500 to East Central University, Ada, OK.

$10,000 to Oklahoma Heritage Association, Oklahoma City, OK.

$5,000 to Leadership Oklahoma, Oklahoma City, OK.

7957
The McGee Foundation, Inc. ◇

P.O. Box 18127
Oklahoma City, OK 73154
Contact: Marcia McGee Bieber, Pres.

Incorporated in 1963 in OK.

Donor: Dean A. McGee†.

Foundation type: Independent foundation.

Financial data (yr. ended 6/30/05): Assets, $7,901,182 (M); expenditures, $328,008; qualifying distributions, $316,000; giving activities include $315,000 for 13 grants (high: $100,000; low: $2,000).

Fields of interest: Historic preservation/historical societies; Education; Environment, natural resources; Reproductive health, family planning; Children/youth, services; Women.

Type of support: General/operating support; Annual campaigns; Capital campaigns; Building/renovation; Equipment; Land acquisition; Endowments; Professorships; Scholarship funds; Research; Matching/challenge support.

Limitations: Applications not accepted. Giving primarily in CA and OK. No grants to individuals.

Application information: Unsolicited requests for funds not accepted.

 Board meeting date(s): Early May

Officers and Directors:* Marcia McGee Bieber,* Pres.; Patricia McGee Maino,* V.P.; Charles Bieber, M.D.*, Secy.-Treas.; Jerry Love.

Number of staff: 1 part-time support.

EIN: 736099203

Selected grants: The following grants were reported in 2003.

$100,000 to Planned Parenthood Mar Monte, San Jose, CA.

$55,000 to Planned Parenthood of Central Oklahoma, Oklahoma City, OK.

$55,000 to Stanford University, School of Earth Sciences, Stanford, CA.

$20,000 to Oklahoma City Community Foundation, Oklahoma City, OK.

$15,000 to Rose State College, Midwest City, OK.

$10,000 to Lyric Theater of Oklahoma, Oklahoma City, OK.

$10,000 to Wildlife of the American West, National Museum of Wildlife Art, Jackson, WY.

$7,000 to Sugar Creek Camp, Oklahoma City, OK.

$7,000 to YMCA, Okmulgee County Family, Okmulgee, OK.

$6,000 to Boys and Girls Club of Tahlequah, Tahlequah, OK.

7958
Ralph and Frances McGill Foundation ◇

c/o The Trust Co. of Oklahoma
P.O. Box 3627
Tulsa, OK   74101-3627

Established in 2000 in OK.

Foundation type: Independent foundation.

Financial data (yr. ended 12/31/05): Assets, $9,131,744 (M); gifts received, $879,797; expenditures, $877,134; qualifying distributions, $853,910; giving activities include $844,500 for 71 grants (high: $110,000; low: $1,000).

Fields of interest: Education; Human services; Children/youth, services; Community development; Christian agencies & churches.

Limitations: Giving primarily in Tulsa, OK. No grants to individuals.

Application information:

 Initial approach: Letter

 Deadline(s): None

Trustee: The Trust Co. of Oklahoma.

EIN: 731590898

Selected grants: The following grants were reported in 2003.

$40,000 to Saint Catherine Church, Tulsa, OK.

$25,000 to Juvenile Diabetes Research Foundation International, Tulsa, OK.

$22,000 to Saint John Medical Center, Tulsa, OK.

$20,000 to Bishop Kelley High School, Tulsa, OK.

$20,000 to School of Saint Mary, Tulsa, OK.

$20,000 to Trinity Episcopal Church of Tulsa, Tulsa, OK.

$15,000 to University of Oklahoma, Tulsa, OK.

$10,000 to Gilcrease Museum, Tulsa, OK.

$10,000 to Parent Child Center of Tulsa, Tulsa, OK.

$5,000 to Community Food Bank of Eastern Oklahoma, Tulsa, OK.

7959
The McMahon Foundation ◇

P.O. Box 2156
Lawton, OK   73502   (580) 355-4622
Contact: James F. Wood, Dir.

Incorporated in 1940 in OK.

Donors: Eugene D. McMahon‡; Louise D. McMahon‡.

Foundation type: Independent foundation.

Financial data (yr. ended 3/31/05): Assets, $54,347,623 (M); expenditures, $3,050,228; qualifying distributions, $2,634,943; giving activities include $2,577,290 for 21 grants (high: $950,000; low: $500).

Purpose and activities: Support for education, youth and social services organizations, and the arts.

Fields of interest: Performing arts; Arts; Elementary/secondary education; Higher education; Education; Housing/shelter, development; Recreation; Human services; Youth, services; Community development; Federated giving programs.

Type of support: General/operating support; Annual campaigns; Capital campaigns; Building/renovation; Equipment; Land acquisition; Emergency funds; Scholarship funds; Matching/challenge support.

Limitations: Giving limited to OK, with emphasis on Comanche County. No grants to individuals.

Application information: Application form not required.

 Initial approach: Letter

 Copies of proposal: 1

 Deadline(s): None

 Board meeting date(s): Monthly

 Final notification: 2 to 3 days after board meeting

Officers and Trustees:* Charles S. Graybill, M.D.*, Chair.; Manville Redman,* Vice-Chair.; Gale Sadler,* Secy.-Treas.; Kenneth Bridges; Ronald E. Cagle, M.D.; Kenneth E. Easton; Orville D. Smith.

Director: James F. Wood.

Number of staff: 2 full-time professional; 2 full-time support; 2 part-time support.

EIN: 730664314

7960
The Meinders Foundation ◇

4101 Perimeter Center Dr., No. 210
Oklahoma City, OK   73112-5466
(405) 947-2422
Contact: Mo Grotjohn, Exec. Dir.

Established in 1993 in OK.

Donor: Herman Meinders.

Foundation type: Independent foundation.

Financial data (yr. ended 12/31/05): Assets, $4,651,886 (M); expenditures, $1,144,108; qualifying distributions, $1,097,717; giving activities include $1,097,717 for 64 grants (high: $15,000; low: $250).

Purpose and activities: Giving to Christian organizations, and to support education and the environment.

Fields of interest: Arts; Higher education; Education; Health care; Food banks; Housing/

shelter; Human services; Protestant agencies & churches.

Type of support: General/operating support; Annual campaigns; Professorships.

Limitations: Giving primarily in OK. No grants to individuals.

Application information:

 Initial approach: Typewritten letter

 Deadline(s): None

Officers and Trustees:* Herman Meinders,* Pres.; LaDonna Meinders,* V.P.; Robert Meinders,* Secy.; Mo Grotjohn, Treas. and Exec. Dir.; Linda Rice.

EIN: 731438459

7961
Meinig Family Foundation ◇

5810 E. Skelly Dr., Ste. 1650
Tulsa, OK   74135   (918) 664-1914
Contact: Kathryn Geib, Tr.

Established in 1992 in OK.

Donors: Peter C. Meinig; Kathryn Geib.

Foundation type: Independent foundation.

Financial data (yr. ended 12/31/05): Assets, $7,669,725 (M); expenditures, $733,523; qualifying distributions, $539,122; giving activities include $539,122 for 59 grants (high: $100,000; low: $500).

Fields of interest: Arts; Higher education; Hospitals (general); Human services.

Type of support: General/operating support; Continuing support; Annual campaigns; Capital campaigns; Building/renovation; Endowments; Program development; Curriculum development; Scholarship funds.

Limitations: Giving primarily in CO, NY, OK, and TX.

Publications: Application guidelines.

Application information: Currently only funding organizations with which board members have direct involvement. Application form not required.

 Initial approach: Letter

 Copies of proposal: 1

 Deadline(s): Feb. 15, May 15, Aug. 15, and Nov. 15

 Board meeting date(s): Mar., June, Sept., and Dec.

Officer and Trustees:* Kathryn Geib,* Exec. Dir.; Nancy E. Meinig; Peter C. Meinig; Anne Smalling.

Number of staff: 1 full-time professional.

EIN: 731373991

Selected grants: The following grants were reported in 2003.

$33,332 to Marin Montessori School, Corte Madera, CA. For capital campaign.

$25,000 to Boy Scouts of America, Peoria, IL. For capital campaign.

$25,000 to Planned Parenthood of Eastern Oklahoma and Western Arkansas, Tulsa, OK. For capital campaign.

$20,000 to Tulsa Performing Arts Center Trust, Tulsa, OK. For Young at Art Series.

$20,000 to Youth Services of Tulsa County, Tulsa, OK. For capital campaign.

$15,600 to Philbrook Museum of Art, Tulsa, OK. For unrestricted support.

$10,000 to Girl Scouts of the U.S.A., Magic Empire Council, Tulsa, OK. For Juliette Low Leadership Society.

$10,000 to Oklahoma Foundation for Excellence, Oklahoma City, OK. For unrestricted support.

$10,000 to Tulsa Ballet Theater, Tulsa, OK. For Founder's Society.

$10,000 to YWCA of Tulsa, Tulsa, OK. For unrestricted support.

7962

The Merrick Foundation ✧

2932 N.W. 122nd St.
Bradley Sq., Ste. D
Oklahoma City, OK 73120-1955
(405) 755-5571
Contact: Frank W. Merrick, V.P.
FAX: (405) 755-0938;
E-mail: fwmerrick@foundationmanagementinc.com;
Toll free tel.: (877) 689-7726; URL: http://www.foundationmanagementinc.com/default.aspx?page=3

Trust established in 1948 in OK; incorporated in 1968.
Donor: Mrs. Frank W. Merrick†.
Foundation type: Independent foundation.
Financial data (yr. ended 12/31/04): Assets, $12,634,380 (M); expenditures, $645,386; qualifying distributions, $501,544; giving activities include $416,525 for 58 grants (high: $25,000; low: $400).
Purpose and activities: The mission of The Merrick Foundation is to enhance the quality of life of Oklahomans and their communities with primary emphasis on South Central Oklahoma. With this goal in mind, the Merrick Foundation trustees are committed to furthering the philanthropic vision of Ward S. Merrick, Sr. by awarding grants to charitable organizations that foster independence and achievement, and that stimulate educational, economic and cultural growth. Giving for higher education and hospitals; grants also for medical research, youth agencies, and a community fund.
Fields of interest: Higher education; Medical research, institute; Youth, services; Human services.
Type of support: General/operating support; Annual campaigns; Capital campaigns; Building/renovation; Program development; Seed money; Research; Technical assistance; Program evaluation; Matching/challenge support.
Limitations: Giving primarily in OK, with emphasis on southern OK. No grants to individuals, or for endowment funds.
Publications: Annual report; Informational brochure.
Application information: Application form required.
Initial approach: Letter
Copies of proposal: 1
Deadline(s): July 1
Board meeting date(s): May and Nov.
Final notification: Dec. 1
Officers and Trustees:* Ross Coe,* V.P.; Frank W. Merrick,* V.P.; Valda M. Buchanan,* Secy.-Treas.; Robert Bramlett; Michael A. Cawley; Elizabeth Merrick Coe; Charles R. Coe, Jr.; Ward I. Coe; Robert B. Merrick; Ward S. Merrick III; Sally Noble.
EIN: 736111622

7963

The Samuel Roberts Noble Foundation, Inc. ▼ ✧

2510 Sam Noble Pkwy.
P.O. Box 2180
Ardmore, OK 73402 (580) 223-5810
Contact: Michael A. Cawley, C.E.O. and Pres.
Additional tel.: (866) 223-5810; URL: http://www.noble.org

Trust established in 1945 in OK; incorporated in 1952.
Donor: Lloyd Noble†.
Foundation type: Independent foundation.
Financial data (yr. ended 12/31/05): Assets, $1,269,572,071 (M); expenditures, $51,336,881; qualifying distributions, $64,717,385; giving activities include $6,301,730 for 76 grants (high: $1,000,000; low: $5,000; average: $10,000–$200,000), $323,125 for 88 grants to individuals, $204,842 for 74 employee matching gifts, and $53,838,071 for 3 foundation-administered programs.
Purpose and activities: Support through three operating programs for: 1) enabling individual farmers and ranchers to better understand resource management and achieve their goals through consultation, education, research and demonstration; 2) enhancing plant productivity through fundamental research and applied biotechnology; and 3) assisting community service, health research and delivery systems, educational and other selected nonprofit organizations through grants and employee involvement. The foundation also administers a matching gift program for Noble Co. employees.
Fields of interest: Higher education; Health care; Medical research, institute; Human services.
Type of support: General/operating support; Capital campaigns; Building/renovation; Equipment; Endowments; Professorships; Seed money; Research; Program-related investments/loans; Employee matching gifts; Employee-related scholarships; Matching/challenge support.
Limitations: Giving primarily in the Southwest, with emphasis on OK. No grants to individuals (except through Noble Educational Fund and Sam Noble Scholarship Program); no loans (except for program-related investments).
Publications: Application guidelines; Annual report; Grants list; Informational brochure.
Application information: Application form required.
Initial approach: Letter of inquiry
Copies of proposal: 1
Deadline(s): Mar. 1, June 1, Sept. 1, and Dec. 1
Board meeting date(s): Jan., Apr., July, and Oct.
Final notification: 2 weeks after board meetings
Officers and Trustees:* Michael A. Cawley,* C.E.O. and Pres.; Patrick Jones, V.P., C.F.O., and Treas.; Steven Rhines, V.P., General counsel and Dir. of Public Affairs; Elizabeth A. Aldridge, Corp. Secy.; John Mullet, Advisory Tr.; Marianne Rooney, Advisory Tr.; William G. Thurman, Advisory Tr.; Ann Noble Brown; D. Randolph Brown, Jr.; Susan Brown; James C. Day; Sam Dubose; Vivian N. Dubose; William R. Goddard, Jr.; Shelley Dru Mullins; Maria Noble; Rusty Noble.
Number of staff: 130 full-time professional; 170 full-time support.
EIN: 730606209
Selected grants: The following grants were reported in 2005.
$1,200,000 to Oklahoma State University, Stillwater, OK. For Bovine Respiratory Disease research.
$1,000,000 to George West Mental Health Foundation, Atlanta, GA. For Skyland Trail capital campaign.
$1,000,000 to Oklahoma Christian University, Oklahoma City, OK. For construction of science and research center.
$625,000 to Chamber of Commerce Foundation, Ardmore, OK. For Cornerstone Project.

$600,000 to Oklahoma Council of Public Affairs, Oklahoma City, OK. For operating support.
$500,000 to Oklahoma City National Memorial Foundation, Oklahoma City, OK. For Second Decade Campaign.
$300,000 to Ardmore City Schools, Ardmore, OK. For capital improvements at Ardmore High School.
$240,500 to National Cowboy and Western Heritage Museum, Oklahoma City, OK. For renovation of Sam Noble Special Events Center.
$35,000 to Arbuckle Life Solutions, Ardmore, OK. For renewed operating support.
$30,000 to Association of Professional Oklahoma Educators (APOE) Foundation, Norman, OK. For renewed operating support.

7964

Oklahoma City Community Foundation, Inc.

P.O. Box 1146
Oklahoma City, OK 73101-1146
(405) 235-5603
Contact: Nancy B. Anthony, Exec. Dir.
FAX: (405) 235-5612; E-mail: info@occf.org; Additional address: 1300 N. Broadway Dr., Oklahoma City, OK 73103; Additional E-mail: n.anthony@occf.org; URL: http://www.occf.org

Incorporated in 1968 in OK.
Foundation type: Community foundation.
Financial data (yr. ended 6/30/06): Assets, $482,690,313 (M); gifts received, $19,785,912; expenditures, $16,052,234; giving activities include $14,410,000 for 2,485 grants.
Purpose and activities: Giving to serve the charitable needs of the Oklahoma City, OK, area through the development and administration of endowment funds with the goal of preserving capital and enhancing its value for the benefit of the area.
Fields of interest: Arts; Scholarships/financial aid; Education; Environment, beautification programs; Health care; Health organizations, association; Human services; Nonprofit management.
Type of support: General/operating support; Continuing support; Management development/capacity building; Equipment; Program development; Conferences/seminars; Seed money; Scholarship funds; Technical assistance; Consulting services.
Limitations: Giving primarily in the greater Oklahoma City, OK, area. No grants to individuals, or for endowment funds, deficit financing, debt reduction, capital campaigns, development or fundraising campaigns, or academic research projects; no loans.
Publications: Annual report; Grants list; Program policy statement; Program policy statement (including application guidelines).
Application information: Visit foundation Web site for application form and guidelines. Faxed or e-mailed proposals are not accepted. Application form required.
Initial approach: Telephone
Copies of proposal: 15
Deadline(s): Jan. 2, Apr. 1, and July 1
Board meeting date(s): Feb., May, Sept., and Nov.
Final notification: 6 weeks following board meeting
Officers and Trustees:* Kirkland Hall,* Pres.; Paul B. Odom, Jr.,* V.P.; John Belt, Secy. and Genl. Counsel; Stephen Mason,* Treas.; Nancy B. Anthony, Exec. Dir.; James Clark; Nancy L. Coats;

James Daniel; Paul W. Dudman; John Green; Jayne Jayroe; Christian K. Keesee; Judith Love; Harry Merson; J. Larry Nichols; Ronald J. Norick; William Shdeed.

Number of staff: 17 full-time professional; 6 full-time support; 1 part-time support.

EIN: 237024262

Selected grants: The following grants were reported in 2004.

$50,000 to Oklahoma City Beautiful, Oklahoma City, OK. For Adopt-A-Park.

$25,000 to Boys and Girls Club of Oklahoma County, Oklahoma City, OK. To expand to a new facility to serve Hispanic youth.

$23,000 to Rainbow Fleet, Oklahoma City, OK. To improve training for early-childhood and daycare workers.

$20,000 to Women in Need. For follow-up support of women diagnosed with Breast Cancer.

$15,000 to Integris Baptist Medical Center, Center for Mind, Body & Spirit, Oklahoma City, OK. For Rabbi Kusher visit for seminar and public event.

$15,000 to YWCA of Oklahoma City, Oklahoma City, OK. For continuing education for high school students on domestic violence.

$10,000 to City Arts Center, Oklahoma City, OK. For summer arts program in housing projects.

$10,000 to Neighborhood Alliance of Oklahoma City, Oklahoma City, OK. For neighborhood training for leaders.

$7,500 to Possibilities, Inc., Oklahoma City, OK. For training of Hispanic and non-English speaking parents on school readiness.

7965
Oklahoma Gas and Electric Company Foundation, Inc. ✧

P.O. Box 321, M.C. 1100
Oklahoma City, OK   73101-0321
(405) 553-3203
Contact: Steven E. Moore, Pres.

Incorporated in 1957 in OK.
Donor: Oklahoma Gas and Electric Co.
Foundation type: Company-sponsored foundation.
Financial data (yr. ended 12/31/05): Assets, $1,505,330 (M); gifts received, $800,000; expenditures, $938,350; qualifying distributions, $928,494; giving activities include $822,841 for 105 grants (high: $100,000; low: $25), and $105,653 for 47 employee matching gifts.
Purpose and activities: The foundation supports hospitals and organizations involved with arts and culture, higher education, and human services.
Fields of interest: Arts; Higher education; Hospitals (general); Human services.
Type of support: Sponsorships; Capital campaigns; General/operating support; Continuing support; Annual campaigns; Building/renovation; Equipment; Professorships; Scholarship funds; Employee matching gifts.
Limitations: Giving limited to areas of company operations in OK. No grants to individuals; no loans.
Application information: Application form not required.
  Initial approach: Proposal
  Copies of proposal: 1
  Deadline(s): None
  Board meeting date(s): As required
  Final notification: 1 month

Officers and Directors:* Steven E. Moore,* Pres.; J.R. Hatfield,* V.P.; P.B. Delaney,* V.P.; Carla D. Brockman, Secy.-Treas.
EIN: 736093572

7966
The Oklahoman Foundation ✧

P.O. Box 25125
Oklahoma City, OK   73125

Established in 1990 in OK.
Donor: The Oklahoma Publishing Co.
Foundation type: Company-sponsored foundation.
Financial data (yr. ended 12/31/05): Assets, $12,481,309 (M); expenditures, $811,475; qualifying distributions, $796,309; giving activities include $794,700 for 21 grants (high: $200,000; low: $500).
Purpose and activities: The foundation supports organizations involved with arts and culture, education, medical research, human services, and Christianity.
Fields of interest: Museums (art); Museums (history); Arts; Higher education; Education; Medical research; YM/YWCAs & YM/YWHAs; Human services; Federated giving programs; Christian agencies & churches.
Type of support: General/operating support; Building/renovation; Program development.
Limitations: Applications not accepted. Giving limited to Oklahoma City, OK. No grants to individuals.
Application information: Contributes only to pre-selected organizations.
Trustees: Louis Gaylord Bennett; Christine Gaylord Everest; David O. Hogan; Mary Gaylord McClean.
EIN: 731363152
Selected grants: The following grants were reported in 2004.

$200,000 to YMCA of Greater Oklahoma City, Oklahoma City, OK. For general operating support.

$172,500 to United Way of Central Oklahoma, Oklahoma City, OK. 3 grants: $57,500 each (For general operating support).

$40,000 to Allied Arts Foundation, Oklahoma City, OK. For general operating support.

7967
ONEOK Foundation, Inc.

P.O. Box 871
Tulsa, OK   74102-0871   (918) 588-7000
Contact: Ginny Creveling, Exec. Dir.
FAX: (918) 588-7490; *Application address:* 100 W. 5th St., Tulsa, OK 74103

Established in 1997 in OK.
Donor: ONEOK, Inc.
Foundation type: Company-sponsored foundation.
Financial data (yr. ended 12/31/05): Assets, $23,536,799 (M); gifts received, $10,000,000; expenditures, $2,763,791; qualifying distributions, $2,742,877; giving activities include $1,837,588 for 75+ grants (high: $400,000), and $905,289 for employee matching gifts.
Purpose and activities: The foundation supports organizations involved with arts and culture, education, health, human services, and community development.
Fields of interest: Arts; Higher education; Education; Health care; Children/youth, services;

Family services; Human services; Community development; Foundations (community); Federated giving programs.
Type of support: Employee volunteer services; Capital campaigns; Building/renovation; General/operating support; Employee matching gifts.
Limitations: Giving primarily in areas of company operations in KS, OK, and TX. No support for religious or political organizations.
Application information: Application form required.
  Initial approach: Contact foundation for application form
  Copies of proposal: 1
  Deadline(s): The middle of Jan., Apr., July, and Oct.
  Board meeting date(s): Feb., May, Aug., and Nov.
  Final notification: 1 month
Officers and Directors:* David L. Kyle,* Chair., C.E.O., and Pres.; James C. Kneale, Exec. V.P.; Ginny Creveling,* Exec. Dir.; John R. Barker; Samuel Combs III; William R. Cordes; John W. Gibson.
EIN: 731503823

7968
The Oxley Foundation ✧

c/o Krya Prater
1437 S. Boulder, Ste. 770
Tulsa, OK   74119
FAX: (918) 582-9419; *E-mail:* kprater@oxleyfdn.com

Established in 1986 in OK.
Donor: John T. Oxley†.
Foundation type: Independent foundation.
Financial data (yr. ended 12/31/04): Assets, $116,205,372 (M); expenditures, $6,192,179; qualifying distributions, $4,970,663; giving activities include $4,772,515 for 226 grants (high: $250,000; low: $250).
Purpose and activities: Giving primarily for the arts, education, the environment, health associations, recreation, and religion.
Fields of interest: Museums; Museums (art); Arts; Elementary/secondary education; Higher education; Theological school/education; Education; Environment, natural resources; Hospitals (general); Hospitals (specialty); Health organizations, association; Health organizations; Athletics/sports, equestrianism; Recreation; Human services; Children/youth, services; Federated giving programs; Christian agencies & churches; Jewish agencies & temples.
Type of support: General/operating support; Annual campaigns; Capital campaigns; Endowments; Scholarship funds.
Limitations: Applications not accepted. Giving primarily in OK, with emphasis on Tulsa; some giving nationally. No grants to individuals.
Application information: Contributes only to pre-selected organizations.
Trustees: Russell H. Harbaugh, Jr.; John C. Oxley; Mary Jane Tritsch.
EIN: 736224031
Selected grants: The following grants were reported in 2003.

$250,000 to University of Tulsa, Tulsa, OK. For endowed chair for Business Administration Department.

$150,000 to Polo Training Foundation, Lexington, KY. For head umpire instructor.

$106,000 to Nature Conservancy, Oklahoma Center, Tulsa, OK. For Tallgrass Prairie Ecological Research Station.

$105,330 to National Museum of Polo and Hall of Fame, Lake Worth, FL. For endowment fund.

$100,000 to Phillips Theological Seminary, Tulsa, OK. For capital campaign.

$50,000 to Camp Loughridge, Tulsa, OK. For capital campaign.

$50,000 to Monte Cassino School, Tulsa, OK. For The Legacy Capital Campaign.

$30,000 to Miami Valley Christian Academy, Newtown, OH. For projects.

$25,000 to Bacone College, Muskogee, OK. For Current Dollars for Current Scholars campaign.

$25,000 to Brightight Foundation, Herndon, VA. For operating support.

7969
Presbyterian Health Foundation ▼ ✧

655 Research Pkwy., Ste. 500
Oklahoma City, OK 73104-3603
(405) 271-8150
Contact: Dr. Michael D. Anderson, Pres.
FAX: (405) 271-2911; *URL:* http://www.phfokc.com

Established in 1985 in OK; converted from the proceeds of the sale of Presbyterian Hospital to HCA.

Foundation type: Independent foundation.

Financial data (yr. ended 9/30/05): Assets, $210,167,146 (M); gifts received, $16,406; expenditures, $11,661,392; qualifying distributions, $9,203,687; giving activities include $6,529,834 for 28+ grants (high: $2,448,140; average: $125,000–$350,000), and $1,892,190 for 3 loans/program-related investments.

Purpose and activities: Support primarily for health, including medical research and medical education, clinical pastoral education, resource development through medical technology transfer, community health-related programs and to Oklahoma Health Center Institutions.

Fields of interest: Medical school/education; Theological school/education; Medical care, community health systems; Medical research, institute; Engineering/technology.

Type of support: Equipment; Endowments; Program development; Professorships; Research; Program-related investments/loans.

Limitations: Giving primarily in OK. No grants to individuals.

Publications: Annual report; Informational brochure (including application guidelines).

Application information: Application form required.
Initial approach: Letter
Copies of proposal: 18
Deadline(s): Last week in Mar., June, Sept., and Dec.
Board meeting date(s): Quarterly

Officers and Trustees:* Carl Edwards,* Chair.; Michael D. Anderson, Ph.D.*, Pres.; Dennis McGrath,* V.P.; Fred H. Zahn,* Secy.; William M. Beard,* Treas.; Stanton L. Young,* Chair., Emeritus; Jean G. Gumerson,* Pres., Emeritus; William F. Barnes, M.D.; R. Barton Carl, M.D.; Richard G. Dotter, M.D.; Nancy Payne Ellis; Robert S. Ellis, M.D.; Christy Everest; Clyde Ingle; David W. Parke II, M.D.; David Rainbolt; Harry B. Tate, M.D.; Jerry V. Vannata, M.D.

Number of staff: 2 full-time professional; 2 full-time support.

EIN: 730709836

Selected grants: The following grants were reported in 2005.

$2,500,000 to University Hospitals, Oklahoma City, OK. For Children's Hospital atrium project.

$1,000,000 to Oklahoma City Economic Development Foundation, Oklahoma City, OK. For Batell regional bioscience strategy.

$700,000 to University of Oklahoma Foundation, Oklahoma City, OK. 4 grants: $125,000 (For endowed chair in Pediatric Diabetes), $142,000 (For endowed chair in Allied Health), $350,000 (For endowed chair in OB/GYN and Perinatal), $83,000 (For public relations and media support services).

$580,200 to University of Oklahoma Health Sciences Center, Oklahoma City, OK. 3 grants: $37,200 (For College of Medicine's Honors Research Program), $43,000 (For Summer Undergraduate Research Experience Program), $500,000 (For peer-reviewed research for Seed, Bridge, and Equipment Grants Program).

$10,000 to Oklahoma School of Science and Mathematics, Oklahoma City, OK. For faculty awards program.

7970
The Puterbaugh Foundation

P.O. Box 1206
McAlester, OK 74502
Contact: Steven W. Taylor, Chair.
E-mail: jgputerbaugh@sbcglobal.net

Trust established in 1949 in OK.

Donors: Jay Garfield Puterbaugh†; Leela Oliver Puterbaugh†.

Foundation type: Independent foundation.

Financial data (yr. ended 12/31/05): Assets, $12,082,717 (M); expenditures, $931,793; qualifying distributions, $850,124; giving activities include $784,730 for 21 grants (high: $276,580; low: $200).

Purpose and activities: Primary areas of interest include child welfare, community funds, health associations, and higher education.

Fields of interest: Higher education; Education; Health organizations, association; Medical research, institute; Human services; Children/youth, services; Federated giving programs; Biological sciences; Government/public administration.

Type of support: Continuing support; Annual campaigns; Capital campaigns; Building/renovation; Equipment; Endowments; Professorships; Scholarship funds; Exchange programs; Matching/challenge support.

Limitations: Giving primarily in southeastern OK. No grants to individuals.

Publications: Financial statement.

Application information: Budgets are set 1 year in advance of year of payment. Application form not required.
Initial approach: Letter only; no telephone or e-mail
Copies of proposal: 1
Deadline(s): Jan. 15 for payment in Dec.
Board meeting date(s): As necessary

Officer and Trustees:* Steven W. Taylor,* Chair.; Cara Bland; Frank G. Edwards.

Number of staff: None.

EIN: 736092193

Selected grants: The following grants were reported in 2003.

$125,000 to Boys and Girls Club of McAlester, McAlester, OK. For general support.

$30,500 to McAlester Public Schools, McAlester, OK. For general support.

$29,000 to Oklahoma State University Foundation, Stillwater, OK. For scholarships.

$10,000 to American Red Cross, McAlester, OK. For general support.

$8,500 to Eastern Oklahoma State College, Wilburton, OK. For nursing education.

$7,000 to Mercy Health Clinic of McAlester, McAlester, OK. For general support.

$1,700 to Oklahoma Arts Institute, Oklahoma City, OK. For general support.

$1,000 to Oklahoma Heritage Association, Oklahoma City, OK. For scholarships.

$500 to Oklahoma Educational Television Authority, Oklahoma City, OK. For general support.

$500 to Salvation Army, McAlester, OK. For general support.

7971
Robert Glenn Rapp Foundation ✧

2301 W. I-44 Service Rd., Ste. 300
Oklahoma City, OK 73112 (405) 525-8331
Contact: Trustees

Trust established about 1953 in OK.

Donor: Florence B. Clark†.

Foundation type: Independent foundation.

Financial data (yr. ended 12/31/03): Assets, $13,381,877 (M); expenditures, $705,268; qualifying distributions, $570,898; giving activities include $523,283 for 27 grants (high: $50,000; low: $2,000; average: $2,500–$50,000).

Purpose and activities: Giving emphasis is on primary and secondary education.

Fields of interest: Education, research; Secondary school/education; Higher education; Education.

Type of support: Equipment; Capital campaigns; Building/renovation; Endowments; Seed money; Scholarship funds; Matching/challenge support.

Limitations: Giving primarily in OK, with emphasis on Oklahoma City. No grants to individuals, or for operating funds.

Publications: Application guidelines; Informational brochure (including application guidelines).

Application information: Must use application form provided by foundation. Application form required.
Initial approach: Call or write for proposal guidelines
Copies of proposal: 6
Deadline(s): Aug. 31
Board meeting date(s): Annually, usually in the latter part of the year
Final notification: Dec. 31

Trustees: Jilene K. Boghetich; Tony Boghetich; Merry L. Knowles; James H. Milligan; Lois Darlene Milligan; Michael J. Milligan.

Number of staff: 1 part-time support.

EIN: 730616840

7972
The Records-Johnston Family Foundation, Inc. ✧

(formerly Willard Johnston Foundation, Inc.)
c/o George J. Records
P.O. Box 54390
Oklahoma City, OK 73154-1390
(405) 767-7627

Established in 1951 in OK.

Foundation type: Independent foundation.

Financial data (yr. ended 12/31/05): Assets, $36,419,176 (M); gifts received, $7,536,044; expenditures, $2,761,075; qualifying distributions, $2,672,580; giving activities include $2,672,580 for 81 grants (high: $562,500; low: $100).

Fields of interest: Arts; Education; Health care; Human services.

Type of support: General/operating support; Annual campaigns; Capital campaigns; Endowments; Scholarship funds.

Limitations: Applications not accepted. Giving primarily in Oklahoma City, OK. No grants to individuals.

Application information: Contributes only to pre-selected organizations. Unsolicited requests for funds not considered.

Officer: George J. Records, Mgr.

EIN: 736093829

Selected grants: The following grants were reported in 2004.

$204,200 to University of Oklahoma Foundation, Norman, OK. For general support.

$198,500 to Logan School for Creative Learning, Denver, CO. For general support.

$50,000 to United Way, Mile High, Denver, CO. For general support.

$44,796 to Casady School, Oklahoma City, OK. For general support.

$28,000 to Urban Peak, Denver, CO. For general support.

$27,500 to Bright Beginnings, Denver, CO. For general support.

$25,000 to Colorado Ballet Company, Denver, CO. For general support.

$21,860 to Wellesley College, Wellesley, MA. For general support.

$20,000 to Oklahoma Foundation for Excellence, Oklahoma City, OK. For general support.

$12,000 to Rebuilding Together Metro Denver, Denver, CO. For general support.

7973
A. E. and Jaunita Richardson Charitable Foundation ◇ ☆

P.O. Box 432
Nowata, OK 74048

Foundation type: Independent foundation.

Financial data (yr. ended 12/31/05): Assets, $5,288,971 (M); expenditures, $393,481; qualifying distributions, $316,259; giving activities include $316,259 for grants.

Fields of interest: Secondary school/education; Health care, emergency transport services; Christian agencies & churches.

Limitations: Applications not accepted. Giving limited to OK. No grants to individuals.

Application information: Contributes only to pre-selected organizations.

Trustees: Jessie L. Blackwell; Benjamin C. Killion; B.C. Lee; W.E. Maddux; Phyllis Willis.

EIN: 911914497

Selected grants: The following grants were reported in 2003.

$68,500 to Ozark Christian College, Joplin, MO.

$32,606 to Nowata Public Schools, Nowata, OK.

$25,000 to Living Word Family Church, Nowata, OK. For capital support.

$20,000 to First United Methodist Church, Nowata, OK.

$20,000 to University of Oklahoma, Tulsa, OK. For scholarships.

$13,000 to Boys and Girls Club of Nowata, Nowata, OK. For computer equipment.

$11,000 to Cookson Hills Christian School, Kansas, OK.

$8,000 to Rogers State University, Claremore, OK. For scholarships.

$3,089 to Nowata City-County Library, Nowata, OK. For computer equipment.

$2,240 to Nowata Fire Department, Nowata, OK. For equipment.

7974
Sarkeys Foundation

530 E. Main St.
Norman, OK 73071-5823 (405) 364-3703
Contact: Susan C. Frantz, Sr. Prog. Off.
FAX: (405) 364-8191; E-mail: sarkeys@sarkeys.org;
URL: http://www.sarkeys.org

Established in 1962 in OK.

Donor: S.J. Sarkeys†.

Foundation type: Independent foundation.

Financial data (yr. ended 11/30/05): Assets, $100,702,347 (M); expenditures, $4,805,906; qualifying distributions, $4,119,142; giving activities include $2,808,775 for 92 grants (high: $250,000; low: $12; average: $3,000–$50,000), and $181,517 for 4 foundation-administered programs.

Purpose and activities: Giving primarily to improve the quality of life in Oklahoma.

Fields of interest: Arts; Education; Health care; Medical research; Human services.

Type of support: Emergency funds; Capital campaigns; Building/renovation; Equipment; Endowments; Program development; Professorships; Scholarship funds; Research; Program evaluation; Matching/challenge support.

Limitations: Giving limited to OK. No support for direct-to-government agencies or individual public or private elementary or secondary schools, unless they are serving the needs of a special population which are not met elsewhere; generally, no support for hospitals or local programs appropriately financed within the community or for religious institutions and their subsidiaries, or for out of state institutions. No grants to individuals, or for operating support, permanent financing, profitmaking programs, grants which trigger expenditure responsibility, direct mail solicitations, start-up funding for new organizations, feasibility studies, vehicles or for annual campaigns.

Publications: Application guidelines; Annual report (including application guidelines); Informational brochure (including application guidelines); Program policy statement (including application guidelines).

Application information: See foundation Web site for application form. The foundation does not accept faxed or e-mailed proposals. Application form should be downloaded, completed, and mailed to the foundation along with the required attachments. If you cannot access the form please e-mail the foundation and an application will be sent to you. Application form required.

Initial approach: Proposal; telephone calls are encouraged

Copies of proposal: 1

Deadline(s): Feb. 1 and Aug. 1

Board meeting date(s): Jan., Apr., July, and Oct.; grants considered at Apr. and Oct. meetings

Final notification: Varies

Officers and Trustees:* Richard A. Bell,* Pres.; Dan Little,* V.P.; Joseph W. Morris,* Secy.-Treas.; Cheri

D. Cartwright, Exec. Dir.; Teresa B. Adwan; Fred Gipson; Kim Henry; Robert S. Rizley; Terry W. West.

Number of staff: 5 full-time professional; 4 full-time support; 1 part-time support.

EIN: 730736496

Selected grants: The following grants were reported in 2003.

$533,000 to University of Oklahoma Foundation, Norman, OK. For construction of Law Library.

$200,000 to Oklahoma Arts Institute, Oklahoma City, OK. For endowment for Summer Institute scholarships.

$200,000 to Oklahoma School of Science and Mathematics Foundation, Oklahoma City, OK. For construction and naming of dormitory addition.

$150,000 to Assistance League of Norman, Norman, OK. For capital campaign for construction of new headquarters and for Operation School Bell facility, which provides clothing and school supplies to needy children.

$100,000 to Norman Firehouse Art Center, Norman, OK. For capital campaign.

$100,000 to Oklahoma Medical Research Foundation, Oklahoma City, OK. For Sarkey's Chair in Alzheimer's Research.

$100,000 to Special Care, Oklahoma City, OK. For construction of new facility.

$80,000 to Center for Children and Families, Norman, OK. For emergency operating support.

$70,000 to Seminole Junior College Educational Foundation, Seminole, OK. For renovation and expansion of S.J. Sarkeys Dormitory.

$50,000 to Arts and Humanities Council of Tulsa, Tulsa, OK. For capital improvement and endowment campaign.

7975
Charles and Lynn Schusterman Family Foundation ◇

2 W. 2nd St., 20th Fl.
Tulsa, OK 74103-3101 (918) 591-1090
Contact: Sanford R. Cardin, Exec. Dir.
FAX: (918) 591-1758; Mailing address: P.O. Box 51, Tulsa, OK 74101-0051; E-mail: ahughes@schusterman.org; URL: http://www.schusterman.org

Established in 1987 in OK.

Donors: Charles Schusterman†; Lynn Schusterman; LJS Revocable Trust.

Foundation type: Independent foundation.

Financial data (yr. ended 12/31/04): Assets, $89,625,257 (M); gifts received, $3,250,000; expenditures, $3,926,008; qualifying distributions, $3,780,219; giving activities include $3,379,588 for 190 grants (high: $250,000; low: $36; average: $5,000–$100,000).

Purpose and activities: The foundation is dedicated to helping the Jewish people flourish by supporting programs throughout the world that spread Jewish living, giving and learning. The foundation also provides assistance to non-sectarian charitable organizations dedicated to enhancing the quality of life in Tulsa, Oklahoma, especially in the areas of education, child development, and community service.

Fields of interest: Arts; Higher education; Education; Health organizations, association; Crime/violence prevention, child abuse; Human services; Children/youth, services; Community development; Jewish federated giving programs; Jewish agencies & temples.

International interests: Israel; Ukraine.

Type of support: General/operating support; Continuing support; Annual campaigns; Capital campaigns; Building/renovation; Emergency funds; Program development; Conferences/seminars; Professorships; Publication; Seed money; Curriculum development; Fellowships; Internship funds; Scholarship funds; Research; Technical assistance; Consulting services; In-kind gifts; Matching/challenge support.

Limitations: Giving primarily to nonsectarian organizations in OK; giving on a local, national, and international basis for Jewish organizations. No grants to individuals, or for endowment funds, or deficit funds.

Publications: Application guidelines; Grants list.

Application information: The foundation does not accept proposals sent by fax or e-mail. Application form not required.

  Initial approach: Letter
  Copies of proposal: 2
  Deadline(s): None

Officers and Directors:* Lynn Schusterman,* Pres.; Stacy H. Schusterman, V.P. and Treas.; Jerome R. Schusterman, Secy.; Sanford R. Cardin, Exec. Dir.; Steven Dow.

Number of staff: 5 full-time professional.

EIN: 731312965

7976
The Dan & Gloria Schusterman
  Foundation ◇ ☆
2121 S. Columbia Ave., Ste. 650
Tulsa, OK 74114-3506

Established in 1996 in OK.

Donors: Dan Schusterman; Gloria Schusterman.

Foundation type: Independent foundation.

Financial data (yr. ended 12/31/05): Assets, $2,270,968 (M); gifts received, $442,915; expenditures, $430,658; qualifying distributions, $416,696; giving activities include $416,696 for 13 grants (high: $50,196; low: $4,500).

Fields of interest: Jewish federated giving programs.

Limitations: Applications not accepted. Giving primarily in New York, NY. No grants to individuals.

Application information: Contributes only to pre-selected organizations.

Trustees: Dan Schusterman; Gloria Schusterman.

EIN: 731495727

7977
Charles Morton Share Trust ◇ ☆
P.O. Box 21708
Oklahoma City, OK 73156-1708
Application addresses: c/o Dean Linder, 1718 S. 11th St., Alva, OK 73717; c/o Darrell Kline, Northwest Electric, 508 Flynn St., Alva, OK 73717; c/o Jim Holder, Holder Drug Co., 513 Barnes Ave., Alva, OK 73717; and c/o Johnny C. Jones, Rialto Theatre, 516 Flynn St., Alva, OK 73717

Trust established in 1959 in OK.

Donor: Charles Morton Share†.

Foundation type: Independent foundation.

Financial data (yr. ended 6/30/05): Assets, $8,423,779 (M); expenditures, $686,112; qualifying distributions, $454,522; giving activities include $448,255 for 12 grants (high: $242,055; low: $1,200).

Purpose and activities: Giving primarily for family and social services; support also for education and the arts.

Fields of interest: Arts; Education, public education; Libraries/library science; Education; Hospitals (general); Family services; Community development; Military/veterans' organizations.

Type of support: Building/renovation; Equipment; Scholarship funds.

Limitations: Giving primarily in OK. No grants to individuals, or for operating budgets, continuing support, annual campaigns, seed money, emergency or endowment funds, deficit financing, land acquisition, renovations, matching gifts, special projects, research, publications, or conferences; no loans.

Application information: Send copy of application to each trustee. Application form not required.

  Initial approach: Letter
  Copies of proposal: 5
  Deadline(s): None

Trustees: J.R. Holder; Johnny C. Jones; Darrell Kline; Dean Linder; Heritage Trust Co.

EIN: 736090984

Selected grants: The following grants were reported in 2003.

$55,500 to Alva, City of, Alva, OK.

$33,370 to American Legion Childrens Home, Ponca City, OK.

$25,000 to Cherokee Elementary School, Cherokee, OK.

$25,000 to Woods, County of, Alva, OK.

$20,000 to Alva Municipal Cemetery, Alva, OK.

$15,589 to Alva Volunteer Fire Department, Alva, OK.

$15,000 to Northwestern Oklahoma State University, Alva, OK.

$10,000 to Northwestern Oklahoma State University Foundation, Alva, OK.

7978
Silas Foundation ◇
c/o Arvest Trust Co., N.A.
P.O. Box 2248
Bartlesville, OK 74005-2248

Established in 1993 in OK.

Donor: C.J. Silas.

Foundation type: Independent foundation.

Financial data (yr. ended 12/31/05): Assets, $2,111,778 (M); gifts received, $251,310; expenditures, $1,312,226; qualifying distributions, $1,301,000; giving activities include $1,301,000 for 23 grants (high: $1,200,000; low: $1,000).

Fields of interest: Performing arts; Performing arts centers; Mental health, clinics.

Limitations: Giving primarily in OK, with emphasis on Bartlesville.

Application information: Application form not required.

  Initial approach: Letter
  Deadline(s): None

Trustees: C.J. Silas; Theo Silas; Arvest Trust Co., N.A.

EIN: 736260168

7979
Southern Oklahoma Memorial Foundation
P.O. Box 1409
Ardmore, OK 73402-1409   (580) 226-0700
Contact: Larry A. Pulliam, Pres.

FAX: (580) 226-0223;
E-mail: Lapulliam@sbcglobal.net

Established in 1950 in Ardmore, OK.

Donor: Citizens of Southern Oklahoma.

Foundation type: Independent foundation.

Financial data (yr. ended 6/30/06): Assets, $104,549,017 (M); expenditures, $5,769,167; qualifying distributions, $4,868,401; giving activities include $4,618,401 for 50 grants (high: $2,250,000; low: $1,750; average: $20,000– $100,000).

Purpose and activities: Giving primarily for community development, education and health care.

Fields of interest: Education; Hospitals (general); Youth development; Human services; Community development.

Type of support: General/operating support; Continuing support; Annual campaigns; Capital campaigns; Building/renovation; Equipment; Program development; Scholarship funds; Matching/challenge support.

Limitations: Giving limited to OK organizations within a 50-mile radius of Ardmore. No support for churches or political organizations. No grants to individuals.

Publications: Application guidelines; Annual report; Annual report (including application guidelines); Multi-year report; Multi-year report (including application guidelines).

Application information: Application form required.

  Initial approach: Letter to President with brief statement
  Copies of proposal: 1
  Deadline(s): 1st day of the last month of each calendar quarter
  Board meeting date(s): Quarterly
  Final notification: Within 30 days of meeting date

Officer: Larry A. Pulliam, Pres.

Directors: Laura Clay; Bridge Cox; Bill Goddard; Hayden Henry, M.D.; Marilyn Kriet; Phil McAnally; Andre Moore; Henry Roberts; John F. Snodgrass.

Number of staff: 2 full-time professional; 1 full-time support.

EIN: 731300662

Selected grants: The following grants were reported in 2006.

$7,500,000 to Mercy Memorial Health Center Foundation, Ardmore, OK. For patient tower.

$380,000 to Chamber of Commerce Foundation, Ardmore, OK. For Cornerstone Educational Initiative.

$375,000 to Family Health Center of Southern Oklahoma, Tishomingo, OK. For new facility construction.

$285,829 to Southern Oklahoma Technology Center, Ardmore, OK. For Health Science Facility expansion.

$250,000 to Good Shepherd Medical and Dental Clinic Foundation, Ardmore, OK. For operating support.

$225,000 to Ardmore School District I-19, Ardmore, OK. For Science and Technology Project.

$220,000 to Greater Ardmore Scholarship Foundation, Ardmore, OK. For scholarships.

$101,000 to YWCA of Ardmore, Ardmore, OK. For operating support.

$92,500 to HFV Wilson Community Center, Ardmore, OK. For operating support.

$77,026 to Cross Timbers Hospice, Ardmore, OK. For medical records technology upgrade.

7980
Jess L. and Miriam B. Stevens Foundation

4000 One Williams Ctr.
Tulsa, OK 74172-0148
Contact: Joseph J. McCain, Jr., Tr.

Established in 1999 in OK.
Foundation type: Independent foundation.
Financial data (yr. ended 7/31/05): Assets,
$13,434,342 (M); expenditures, $830,745;
qualifying distributions, $704,251; giving activities
include $627,000 for 15 grants (high: $150,000;
low: $2,500), and $45,000 for 8 grants to
individuals (high: $10,000; low: $5,000).
Purpose and activities: Giving primarily to
organizations that benefit education and medical
research, and that contribute to the welfare of needy
persons.
Fields of interest: Higher education.
Type of support: General/operating support;
Continuing support; Capital campaigns; Building/
renovation; Endowments; Scholarship funds;
Scholarships—to individuals.
Limitations: Giving primarily in Tulsa and
northeastern OK.
Application information: Application form not
required.
Initial approach: Letter
Copies of proposal: 2
Deadline(s): None
Trustee: Joseph J. McCain, Jr.
EIN: 731557364
Selected grants: The following grants were reported
in 2004.
$325,000 to University of Tulsa, Tulsa, OK. For
scholarships.
$150,000 to Oklahoma State University
Foundation, Stillwater, OK. For endowed chair in
Agricultural Biotechnology.
$100,000 to American Lung Association, Tulsa, OK.
For research.
$100,000 to Oklahoma Baptist University,
Shawnee, OK. For fine arts renovation project.
$100,000 to Salvation Army of Tulsa, Tulsa, OK.
$50,000 to Camp Loughridge, Tulsa, OK. For capital
campaign.
$50,000 to McCalls Chapel School, Ada, OK. For
academic program.
$35,000 to Easter Seal Society of Oklahoma,
Oklahoma City, OK.
$20,000 to Eagle Family Ministries, Bentonville, AR.
$1,000 to Oklahoma Center for Nonprofits,
Oklahoma City, OK.

7981
Dave & Barbara Sylvan Foundation ✧

1 W. 3rd St., Ste. 918
Tulsa, OK 74103

Donor: Dave R. Sylvan.
Foundation type: Independent foundation.
Financial data (yr. ended 12/31/04): Assets,
$988,532 (M); gifts received, $85,870;
expenditures, $370,535; qualifying distributions,
$370,139; giving activities include $370,327 for 35
grants (high: $77,136; low: $18).
Purpose and activities: Giving for human services,
the arts, and Jewish organizations.
Fields of interest: Arts; Human services; Jewish
federated giving programs; Jewish agencies &
temples.
Limitations: Applications not accepted. Giving
primarily in OK. No grants to individuals.

Application information: Unsolicited requests for
funds not accepted.
Directors: Debra Sylvan de Leeuw; James Framel;
Barbara Sylvan; Dave R. Sylvan.
EIN: 731206320
Selected grants: The following grants were reported
in 2004.
$26,428 to Temple Israel, Tulsa, OK. 2 grants:
$1,000, $25,428
$3,000 to Tulsa Opera, Tulsa, OK.
$500 to Tulsa Historical Society, Tulsa, OK.
$200 to American Jewish Committee, New York, NY.
$200 to Girl Scouts of the U.S.A., Tulsa, OK.
$150 to Dillon International, Tulsa, OK.
$100 to Alzheimers Association, Tulsa, OK.
$100 to Simon Wiesenthal Center, Los Angeles, CA.
$18 to John 316 Mission, Tulsa, OK.

7982
The David E. and Cassie L. Temple Foundation ✧

P.O. Box 35362
Tulsa, OK 74153-0362 (918) 743-9861
Contact: C. Wayne Bland, Chair.

Established in 1995 in OK.
Donors: Cassie L. Temple†; David E. Temple†.
Foundation type: Independent foundation.
Financial data (yr. ended 6/30/05): Assets,
$17,308,372 (M); expenditures, $1,032,737;
qualifying distributions, $803,802; giving activities
include $703,657 for 35 grants (high: $80,000;
low: $1,000).
Purpose and activities: Giving primarily for the
needs of educational service organizations as
determined by the foundation founders.
Fields of interest: Education; Human services.
Limitations: Giving primarily in the Tulsa, OK,
metropolitan area.
Application information: Application form not
required.
Initial approach: Proposal
Copies of proposal: 1
Deadline(s): Nov. 1
Final notification: Between Dec. and May
Officers and Trustees: * C. Wayne Bland,* Chair.;
Betty L. Stephenson,* Secy.; Timothy L. Lyons,*
Treas.
EIN: 731452166
Selected grants: The following grants were reported
in 2005.
$80,000 to Inverness, Village of, Tulsa, OK.
$65,000 to Community Service Council of Greater
Tulsa, Tulsa, OK. For Read Now Program.
$50,952 to Salvation Army of Tulsa, Tulsa, OK. For
A/C system.
$50,000 to University of Tulsa, Tulsa, OK. For
scholarships.
$38,005 to Little Light House, Tulsa, OK. For
software and hardware.
$30,000 to American Red Cross, Tulsa, OK.
$30,000 to Emergency Infant Services, Tulsa, OK.
For Crib and Car Seats.
$25,000 to Camp Loughridge, Tulsa, OK. For
conference center furnishings.
$25,000 to Oral Roberts University, Tulsa, OK. For
scholarships.
$20,000 to Camp Fire USA, Oklahoma Green
Country Council, Tulsa, OK. For mentoring
program.

7983
C. W. Titus Foundation ✧

950 Philtower Bldg., Ste. 950
Tulsa, OK 74103
Application address: 427 S. Boston Ave., No. 950,
Tulsa, OK 74103, tel.: (918) 582-8095

Established in 1968 in OK.
Foundation type: Independent foundation.
Financial data (yr. ended 12/31/05): Assets,
$28,549,673 (M); expenditures, $1,397,824;
qualifying distributions, $1,545,652; giving
activities include $1,301,600 for 66 grants (high:
$250,000; low: $1,000).
Purpose and activities: Giving primarily for health,
and children and social services; support also for
the arts and cultural programs.
Fields of interest: Arts; Education; Hospitals
(general); Health care; Health organizations,
association; Youth development, centers/clubs;
Human services; Children/youth, services.
Type of support: General/operating support;
Building/renovation.
Limitations: Giving primarily in MO and OK. No
grants to individuals.
Application information: Application form not
required.
Initial approach: Letter
Deadline(s): None
Trustee: Timothy T. Reynolds.
EIN: 237016981
Selected grants: The following grants were reported
in 2003.
$500,000 to Advocates for a Healthy Community,
Jordan Valley Community Health Center,
Springfield, MO. For building program.
$150,000 to Child Advocacy Center, Springfield,
MO. For capital campaign.
$50,000 to Community Health Clinic of Joplin,
Joplin, MO. For operating support.
$37,761 to Ozarks Food Harvest, Springfield, MO.
For forklift and Tommy gate.
$30,000 to Ozarks Public Television, Springfield,
MO. For programming support.
$20,000 to Childrens Mercy Hospital, Kansas City,
MO. For Cancer Center.
$12,000 to Salvation Army of Joplin, Joplin, MO. For
Pierce City tornado help.
$10,000 to American Cancer Society, Joplin, MO.
For operating support.
$10,000 to American Cancer Society, Tulsa, OK. For
operating support.
$10,000 to Tulsa Opera, Tulsa, OK. For operating
support.

7984
Tulsa Community Foundation ▼ ✧

7020 S. Yale, Ste. 220
Tulsa, OK 74136 (918) 494-8823
Contact: Phil Lakin, Exec. Dir.
FAX: (918) 494-9826; E-mail: Info@TulsaCF.org;
Additional E-mail: plakin@tulsacf.org; URL: http://
www.tulsacf.org

Established in 1998 in OK.
Foundation type: Community foundation.
Financial data (yr. ended 12/31/05): Assets,
$2,264,564,027 (M); gifts received,
$771,255,479; expenditures, $39,918,942; giving
activities include $29,572,740 for grants.
Purpose and activities: The foundation seeks to
facilitate, assist, and support participating

organizations to the fullest extent possible by growing philanthropy in northeastern OK.

Fields of interest: Education.

Type of support: General/operating support; Annual campaigns; Capital campaigns; Building/renovation; Equipment; Endowments; Emergency funds; Program development; Curriculum development; Fellowships; Scholarship funds; Technical assistance; Consulting services; Program evaluation; Program-related investments/loans; Employee-related scholarships; Scholarships—to individuals; Matching/challenge support.

Limitations: Giving limited to northeastern OK through discretionary funds; donor-advised giving is nationwide.

Publications: Financial statement; Informational brochure (including application guidelines); Occasional report.

Application information: Visit foundation Web site for application information. Application form required.

  Initial approach: Contact foundation
  Copies of proposal: 1
  Deadline(s): None
  Board meeting date(s): 2nd Tues. of Mar., May, Sept., and Nov.

Officers and Trustees:* George B. Kaiser,* Chair.; Phil Lakin, Exec. Dir.; Debbie Allen, Cont.; James Adelson; Sharon J. Bell; Chester Cadieux; Joe Cappy; Terry Carter; David Cleveland; Kathleen Coan; Fred Dorwart; Phil Frohlich; Hans Helmerich; David Kyle; Bill LaFortune; Stan Lybarger; Steve Malcolm; Paula Marshall-Chapman; Tom Maxwell; John C. Oxley; Rose Cellino Reynolds; Stacy Schusterman; Robert Thomas; William Thomas; Henry Will; Andrew Wolov; Jack C. Zarrow.

Number of staff: 2 full-time professional; 2 part-time professional; 1 full-time support.

EIN: 731554474

Selected grants: The following grants were reported in 2004.

$3,554,892 to United Way, Tulsa Area, Tulsa, OK.
$400,000 to Mayo Foundation, Rochester, MN.
$350,000 to Medical Development for Israel, New York, NY.
$338,419 to University of Tulsa, Tulsa, OK.
$324,642 to Tulsa Day Center for the Homeless, Tulsa, OK.
$317,580 to United Way of Metropolitan Atlanta, Atlanta, GA.
$300,000 to Grameen Foundation USA, DC.
$283,750 to Neighbor for Neighbor, Tulsa, OK.
$240,990 to National Christian Charitable Foundation, Atlanta, GA.
$210,774 to United Way, Heart of America, Kansas City, MO.

7985
Sam Viersen Family Foundation, Inc.
P.O. Box 702708
Tulsa, OK 74170 (918) 742-1979
Contact: I.R. Robertson, Exec. Dir.
FAX: (918) 742-1670;
E-mail: rob@viersenoilandgas.com; Application address: 7130 S. Lewis Ave., Ste. 200, Tulsa, OK 74170; tel.: (918) 742-1979

Established in 1988.
Donor: Sam K. Viersen, Jr.‡.
Foundation type: Independent foundation.
Financial data (yr. ended 12/31/05): Assets, $25,106,359 (M); expenditures, $1,264,067;

qualifying distributions, $1,015,250; giving activities include $895,422 for 81 grants.

Fields of interest: Arts; Libraries/library science; Education; Human services; YM/YWCAs & YM/YWHAs; Children/youth, services.

Type of support: General/operating support; Continuing support; Management development/capacity building; Capital campaigns; Building/renovation; Equipment; Land acquisition; Endowments; Emergency funds; Program development.

Limitations: Giving limited to Tulsa and Okmulgee counties, OK. No support for religious or tax funded organizations. No grants to individuals.

Application information: Application form not required.

  Initial approach: Telephone
  Copies of proposal: 1
  Deadline(s): None
  Board meeting date(s): Apr. and Oct.

Officers and Directors:* Maralynn V. Sant,* Pres.; I.R. Robertson, Exec. Dir.; Robert English; Brian C. Johnson; Jill Johnson; Jennifer Miller; Margaret Robinson; Leo M. Sant; Julie Schenk.

Number of staff: 1 full-time professional.

EIN: 731295358

Selected grants: The following grants were reported in 2004.

$2,500,000 to Gilcrease Museum, Tulsa, OK.
$208,674 to YMCA. 2 grants: $8,674, $200,000
$37,440 to Little Light House, Tulsa, OK.
$20,000 to Gilbert and Sullivan Society of Tulsa, Tulsa, OK.
$20,000 to Tulsa Opera, Tulsa, OK.
$10,000 to Hospice of Green Country, Tulsa, OK.
$10,000 to Reaching Hands, Tulsa, OK.
$10,000 to Tulsa Boys Home, Tulsa, OK.
$3,543 to Tulsa Foundation for Architecture, Tulsa, OK.

7986
Warren Charite ✧ ☆
P.O. Box 470372
Tulsa, OK 74147-0372 (918) 492-8100
Contact: W.R. Lissau, V.P.

Established in 1968 in OK.
Donors: William K. Warren; Elizabeth Blankenship; Marilyn Vandever; Jean Warren.
Foundation type: Independent foundation.
Financial data (yr. ended 12/31/05): Assets, $6,462,485 (M); gifts received, $147,590; expenditures, $1,043,905; qualifying distributions, $1,035,200; giving activities include $1,035,200 for 10 grants (high: $500,000; low: $400).

Fields of interest: Higher education; Education; Human services; Children/youth, services.

Type of support: General/operating support.

Limitations: Giving primarily in Tulsa, OK; some funding nationally. No grants to individuals.

Application information: Application form not required.

  Initial approach: Letter
  Deadline(s): None

Officers and Directors:* W.K. Warren, Jr.,* Pres.; W.R. Lissau,* V.P.; R.J. Young, Secy.; M.A. Buntz,* Treas.; D.B. Whitehill.

EIN: 730776064

7987
The William K. Warren Foundation ▼ ✧
P.O. Box 470372
Tulsa, OK 74147-0372
Contact: W.R. Lissau, Vice-Chair.

Incorporated in 1945 in OK.
Donors: William K. Warren†; Mrs. William K. Warren†; N.W. Bryant; P.W. Swindle.
Foundation type: Independent foundation.
Financial data (yr. ended 12/31/04): Assets, $454,511,596 (M); gifts received, $404,940; expenditures, $18,528,777; qualifying distributions, $12,512,274; giving activities include $12,025,113 for 96 grants (high: $4,428,465; low: $100; average: $2,000–$200,000).

Purpose and activities: Grants for local Catholic healthcare facilities, education, and social services; substantial support for a medical research program.

Fields of interest: Education; Health care; Medical research, institute; Human services; Roman Catholic federated giving programs.

Type of support: General/operating support; Building/renovation; Endowments; Program development; Research.

Limitations: Giving primarily in OK. No grants to individuals.

Application information: Application form not required.

  Initial approach: Letter
  Deadline(s): None
  Board meeting date(s): Semiannually

Officers and Directors:* W.K. Warren, Jr.,* Chair.; W.R. Lissau,* Vice-Chair.; John-Kelly C. Warren, Pres.; Stephen K. Warren,* Sr. V.P.; David B. Whitehill,* Secy.; M.A. Buntz, C.F.O. and Treas.; Elizabeth Warren Blankenship; John A. Gaberino, Jr.; Dorothy Warren King; J. Frederick McNeer, M.D.; Patricia Warren Swindle.

Number of staff: 10

EIN: 730609599

Selected grants: The following grants were reported in 2004.

$4,428,465 to William K. Warren Medical Research Center, Tulsa, OK. For general support.
$4,000,000 to University of Notre Dame, Notre Dame, IN. For general support.
$655,000 to Duke University, Durham, NC. For general support.
$565,000 to Montereau, Tulsa, OK. For general support.
$329,155 to Saint Francis Health Systems, Tulsa, OK. For general support.
$301,000 to University of Tulsa, Tulsa, OK. For general support.
$300,000 to University of Oklahoma Foundation, Norman, OK. For general support.
$88,000 to Monte Cassino School, Tulsa, OK. For general support.
$52,000 to Catholic Charities, Tulsa, OK. For general support.
$50,000 to Citizens for a Healthy Oklahoma, Tulsa, OK. For general support.

7988
Waters Charitable Foundation ✧
6846 S. Trenton Ave.
Tulsa, OK 74136 (918) 488-8801

Established in 1988 in OK.
Donors: Thomas J. Carson; Mary L. Carson; Feron Waters; Barbara Waters; Judy Gayle Waters; Cherokee 2000 Investments.

Foundation type: Independent foundation.
Financial data (yr. ended 6/30/05): Assets, $9,501,258 (M); gifts received, $50,000; expenditures, $428,054; qualifying distributions, $367,682; giving activities include $350,150 for 37 grants (high: $52,000; low: $250).
Fields of interest: Libraries/library science; Health care; Human services; Youth, services; Christian agencies & churches.
Limitations: Applications not accepted. Giving primarily in Tulsa, OK. No grants to individuals.
Application information: Contributes only to pre-selected organizations.
Trustees: Pete Adumson III; Barbara Waters; Judy Gayle Waters.
EIN: 731323325
Selected grants: The following grants were reported in 2004.
$67,000 to Heritage Bible Church, Greer, SC.
$41,000 to Glenhaven Youth Ranch, Plainview, AR.
$15,000 to Little Light House, Tulsa, OK.
$15,000 to Salvation Army of Tulsa, Tulsa, OK.
$15,000 to Tulsa Library Trust, Tulsa, OK.
$10,000 to American Red Cross, Tulsa, OK.
$10,000 to Domestic Violence Intervention Services, Tulsa, OK.
$10,000 to Northeastern State University Foundation, Tahlequah, OK.
$10,000 to Oklahoma State University Foundation, Stillwater, OK.
$5,000 to Habitat for Humanity International, Tulsa, OK.

7989

The Williams Companies Foundation, Inc. ✧

1 Williams Ctr., M.D. 45
Tulsa, OK   74172   (918) 573-1190
Contact: Callie J. Mitchell, Pres.
E-mail: communityrelationstulsa@williams.com;
URL: http://www.williams.com/community/foundation.asp

Incorporated in 1974 in OK.
Donor: The Williams Cos., Inc.
Foundation type: Company-sponsored foundation.
Financial data (yr. ended 12/31/05): Assets, $5,337,197 (M); expenditures, $769,914; qualifying distributions, $769,250; giving activities include $769,250 for 18 grants (high: $200,000; low: $2,000).
Purpose and activities: The foundation supports organizations involved with arts and culture, education, health, human services, community development, and civic affairs.
Fields of interest: Media/communications; Museums; Humanities; Arts; Libraries (public); Education; Health care; Family services; Human services; Economic development; Community development; Federated giving programs; Public affairs.
Type of support: General/operating support; Capital campaigns; Building/renovation; Scholarship funds; Research; Employee matching gifts; Employee-related scholarships; Matching/challenge support.
Limitations: Giving primarily in areas of company operations, with emphasis on Tulsa, OK; giving also to statewide and national organizations. No grants to individuals (except for employee-related scholarships).

Application information: Contact foundation for nearest company facility. Application form not required.
Initial approach: Proposal to nearest company facility
Copies of proposal: 1
Deadline(s): None
Board meeting date(s): Varies
Final notification: Approximately 1 month
Officers and Directors:* Michael P. Johnson,* Chair.; Callie J. Mitchell,* Pres.; Brian Shore,* Secy.; Rod Sailor,* Treas.; Alan S. Armstrong*; James J. Bender*; Don R. Chappel*; Ralph Hill*; Bill Hobbs*; Steven J. Malcolm*; Phillip D. Wright*.
EIN: 237413843
Selected grants: The following grants were reported in 2003.
$405,450 to University of Tulsa, Tulsa, OK.
$250,000 to ACHIEVE, Inc. - A Resource Center on Standards, Assessments, Accountability and Technology, Cambridge, MA.
$185,350 to University of Oklahoma Foundation, Norman, OK.
$150,000 to Tulsa Public Schools Foundation, Tulsa, OK.
$140,707 to Oklahoma State University, Stillwater, OK.
$100,000 to Teammates for Kids, Littleton, CO.
$60,000 to Glenbow-Alberta Institute, Calgary, Canada. .
$52,350 to Tulsa Opera, Tulsa, OK.
$50,000 to Family and Childrens Services.
$37,500 to Tulsa Boys Home, Tulsa, OK.

7990

Young Family Foundation ✧

24481 S. Manard Rd.
Fort Gibson, OK   74434-6386
Application address: c/o Joseph P. Rigali, G.W. & Wade, Inc., 62 Walnut St., Wellesley, MA 02481-2109

Established in 2000 in MA.
Donors: Tina B. Young; E. Ryker Young.
Foundation type: Independent foundation.
Financial data (yr. ended 11/30/05): Assets, $6,747,548 (M); expenditures, $365,568; qualifying distributions, $340,610; giving activities include $340,160 for grants.
Fields of interest: Christian agencies & churches.
Limitations: Giving primarily in OK and TN. No grants to individuals.
Trustees: E. Ryker Young; Tina B. Young.
EIN: 043525914
Selected grants: The following grants were reported in 2003.
$275,781 to Crescent Valley Baptist Church, Tahlequah, OK. For general support.
$41,485 to Hand to Hand Ministries, Fort Gibson, OK. For general support.
$3,000 to Fort Gibson Education Foundation, Fort Gibson, OK. For general support.

7991

Zarrow Families Foundation ✧

401 S. Boston Ave., Ste. 900
Tulsa, OK   74103-4012   (918) 295-8004
Contact: Jeanne Gillert
FAX: (918) 295-8049; E-mail: jgillert@zarrow.com;
URL: http://www.zarrow.com/zff.htm

Established in 1987 in OK.
Donors: Henry H. Zarrow; Jack C. Zarrow.
Foundation type: Independent foundation.
Financial data (yr. ended 7/31/05): Assets, $12,046,828 (M); expenditures, $373,373; qualifying distributions, $353,933; giving activities include $330,345 for 93 grants (high: $100,000; low: $100).
Purpose and activities: Giving primarily for Jewish causes and charities' fundraising events.
Fields of interest: Arts; Elementary/secondary education; Health care; Mental health/crisis services; Health organizations, association; Human services; Youth, services; Federated giving programs.
Type of support: General/operating support; Conferences/seminars.
Limitations: Applications not accepted. Giving primarily in the Tulsa, OK, area. No grants to individuals.
Publications: Financial statement; Grants list.
Application information: Contributes only to pre-selected organizations.
Board meeting date(s): May and Nov.
Officers and Trustees:* Henry H. Zarrow,* Pres.; Jack C. Zarrow, Exec. V.P.; Steven B. Cochran, Secy.-Treas.; Judy Z. Kishner; Gail Z. Richards; Scott F. Zarrow; Stuart A. Zarrow.
Number of staff: 1 full-time professional.
EIN: 731332141
Selected grants: The following grants were reported in 2005.
$100,000 to Jewish Federation of Tulsa, Tulsa, OK.
$50,000 to United Way, Tulsa Area, Tulsa, OK.
$12,500 to Temple Israel, Tulsa, OK.
$10,000 to Center for Individuals with Physical Challenges, Tulsa, OK.
$7,250 to University of Tulsa, Tulsa, OK.
$5,500 to LIFE Senior Services, Tulsa, OK.
$2,500 to Street School, Tulsa, OK.
$2,000 to University of Oklahoma Foundation, Norman, OK.
$1,000 to Tulsa Boys Home, Tulsa, OK.
$750 to Jewish Funders Network, New York, NY.

7992

The Maxine and Jack Zarrow Family Foundation ✧

(formerly The Maxine and Jack Zarrow Foundation)
401 S. Boston Ave., Ste. 900
Tulsa, OK   74103-4012   (918) 295-8004
Contact: Jeanne Gillert, Grants Mgr.
FAX: (918) 295-8049; E-mail: jgillert@zarrow.com;
URL: http://www.zarrow.com/mjz.htm

Established in 1988 in OK.
Donor: Jack C. Zarrow.
Foundation type: Independent foundation.
Financial data (yr. ended 12/31/05): Assets, $48,248,400 (M); expenditures, $2,439,352; qualifying distributions, $2,298,870; giving activities include $2,223,819 for 262 grants (high: $200,000; low: $15).
Purpose and activities: The foundation is committed to helping support education, social services, Jewish causes, health programs, medical research and mental health programs. The foundation is also very interested in helping to provide food, clothing, and shelter for the challenged, disadvantaged and homeless, with a geographical preference for the Tulsa, OK, area.

Fields of interest: Museums; Higher education; Health care; Mental health/crisis services; Health organizations, association; Human services; Jewish agencies & temples.

Type of support: General/operating support; Program development.

Limitations: Giving primarily in the Tulsa, OK, area.

Application information: Proposals received after due date will be held until next quarter's meeting. Application form not required.

> *Initial approach:* 2-page request
> *Deadline(s):* Jan. 1, Apr. 1, Aug. 1 or Oct. 1
> *Board meeting date(s):* Quarterly in Feb., May, Sept., and Nov.

Officers and Trustees:* Jack C. Zarrow,* Pres.; Maxine Zarrow,* V.P.; Scott F. Zarrow,* Secy.; Gail Richards,* Treas.; Rebecca Richards.

Number of staff: 1 full-time professional.

EIN: 316640903

Selected grants: The following grants were reported in 2004.

$212,500 to Tulsa Community Foundation, Tulsa, OK. 2 grants: $12,500, $200,000

$125,000 to Thomas Gilcrease Museum Association, Tulsa, OK.

$50,000 to YMCA of Greater Tulsa, Tulsa, OK.

$30,000 to Stanford University, Stanford, CA.

$25,000 to Saint John Medical Center Foundation, Tulsa, OK.

$12,500 to Dean A. McGee Eye Institute Foundation, Oklahoma City, OK.

$5,000 to Tulsa Day Center for the Homeless, Tulsa, OK.

$5,000 to University of Pennsylvania, Philadelphia, PA.

$2,360 to Greenwood Cultural Center, Tulsa, OK.

7993
The Anne and Henry Zarrow Foundation ▼ ✧

401 S. Boston, Ste. 900
Tulsa, OK 74103-4012   (918) 295-8004
Contact: Jeanne Gillert, Grants Mgr.
FAX: (918) 295-8049; E-mail (for Jeanne Gillert): jgillert@zarrow.com; URL: http://www.zarrow.com/ahz.htm

Established in 1986 in OK.

Donor: Henry H. Zarrow.

Foundation type: Independent foundation.

Financial data (yr. ended 12/31/05): Assets, $98,790,967 (M); gifts received, $3,400,000;

expenditures, $6,126,665; qualifying distributions, $5,875,064; giving activities include $5,354,831 for 319 grants (high: $500,000; low: $40; average: $5,000–$50,000), and $394,703 for 101 grants to individuals (high: $21,500; low: $250; average: $1,000–$12,500).

Purpose and activities: Giving primarily for education, social services, Jewish causes, health programs, medical research and mental health programs. The foundation is also very interested in helping to provide food, clothing, and shelter for the challenged, disadvantaged and homeless.

Fields of interest: Arts; Education; Health care; Human services; Aging, centers/services; Federated giving programs; Disabilities, people with.

Type of support: General/operating support; Annual campaigns; Scholarships—to individuals.

Limitations: Giving primarily in the Tulsa, OK, area.

Publications: Application guidelines.

Application information: See foundation's Web site for detailed application information. Application form not required.

> *Initial approach:* Letter
> *Copies of proposal:* 1
> *Deadline(s):* 1st of Jan., Apr., Aug., and Oct.
> *Board meeting date(s):* Feb., Apr., Sept., and Nov.

Officers and Directors:* Henry H. Zarrow,* Pres.; Judith Z. Kishner, Secy.-Treas.; Julie W. Cohen; Jay Wohlgemuth; Stuart A. Zarrow; Ted Zarrow.

Number of staff: 1 full-time professional.

EIN: 731286874

Selected grants: The following grants were reported in 2005.

$500,000 to Mayo Foundation, Rochester, MN. For operating support.

$150,000 to Center for Individuals with Physical Challenges, Tulsa, OK. For operating support.

$125,000 to Oklahoma State University, Stillwater, OK. For operating support.

$100,000 to Habitat for Humanity International, Americus, GA. For operating support.

$50,000 to Jewish Federation of Tulsa, Tulsa, OK. For operating support.

$42,000 to Habitat for Humanity International, Tulsa, OK. For operating support.

$25,000 to Family and Childrens Services of Tulsa, Tulsa, OK. For operating support.

$25,000 to Methodist Home of Enid, Enid, OK. For operating support.

$20,000 to Phillips Theological Seminary, Tulsa, OK. For operating support.

$20,000 to Tulsa Community Foundation, Tulsa, OK. For operating support.

7994
John Steele Zink Foundation

P.O. Box 52910
Tulsa, OK 74152-0910
Contact: Kate Iwata, Fin. Requests Coord.

Established in 1972.

Donors: John Steele Zink†; Jacqueline A. Zink†.

Foundation type: Independent foundation.

Financial data (yr. ended 10/31/05): Assets, $40,694,865 (M); expenditures, $1,966,897; qualifying distributions, $1,852,719; giving activities include $1,805,000 for 78 grants (high: $332,000; low: $1,000).

Purpose and activities: Support for higher education and cultural programs.

Fields of interest: Performing arts; Arts; Higher education; Philanthropy/voluntarism.

Type of support: General/operating support; Continuing support; Annual campaigns; Capital campaigns; Building/renovation; Program development; Curriculum development; Scholarship funds; In-kind gifts; Matching/challenge support.

Limitations: Giving primarily in Tulsa, OK. No grants to individuals.

Application information: Application form not required.

> *Initial approach:* Letter
> *Copies of proposal:* 1
> *Deadline(s):* Aug.

Trustees: Caroline H. Abbott; John E. Barry; Swannie Zink Tarbel; Darton J. Zink.

Number of staff: 1 part-time professional.

EIN: 237246964

Selected grants: The following grants were reported in 2004.

$750,000 to John Zink Foundation, Tulsa, OK.

$105,000 to University of Tulsa, Tulsa, OK. 2 grants: $75,000, $30,000

$90,000 to Tulsa Opera, Tulsa, OK.

$52,500 to Ability Resources, Tulsa, OK.

$35,000 to Tulsa Historical Society, Tulsa, OK. 2 grants: $10,000, $25,000

$27,000 to American Red Cross.

$5,000 to Rogers State University, Claremore, OK.

$5,000 to Tulsa Boys Home, Tulsa, OK.

OREGON

7995
Anna K. Ackerman Trust
c/o U.S. Bank, N.A., Trust Tax Svcs.
P.O. Box 3168
Portland, OR 97208

Established in 1963.
Foundation type: Independent foundation.
Financial data (yr. ended 12/31/05): Assets, $8,859,163 (M); expenditures, $511,428; qualifying distributions, $463,238; giving activities include $450,900 for 48 grants (high: $100,000; low: $1,000).
Purpose and activities: Giving primarily to federated giving programs, recreation, health associations, children and youth services, and human services.
Fields of interest: Higher education; Animal welfare; Zoos/zoological societies; Health organizations, association; Recreation; Boys & girls clubs; Youth development, scouting agencies (general); Human services; YM/YWCAs & YM/YWHAs; Children/youth, services; Family services; Foundations (community); Federated giving programs.
Type of support: General/operating support; Annual campaigns; Building/renovation; Endowments.
Limitations: Giving limited to CO, with emphasis on Colorado Springs. No grants to individuals.
Application information: Application form not required.
   Initial approach: Letter
   Copies of proposal: 3
   Deadline(s): None
Trustee: U.S. Bank, N.A.
EIN: 846032046

7996
Leo Adler Community Trust ✧ ☆
(formerly Leo Adler Trust)
c/o U.S. Bank, N.A.
P.O. Box 3168
Portland, OR 97208-3168
Contact: Marlyn Norquist, Trust Off., U.S. Bank, N.A.

Established in 1993 in OR.
Donor: Leo Adler‡.
Foundation type: Independent foundation.
Financial data (yr. ended 6/30/05): Assets, $25,748,773 (M); expenditures, $1,448,273; qualifying distributions, $1,183,487; giving activities include $1,112,739 for 148 grants to individuals (high: $109,741; low: $30).
Purpose and activities: Giving limited to Baker County, 1) 60 percent scholarships to students who are graduates of high schools located in Baker County, OR, or 2) for North Powder High School in Union County, OR; 40 percent of giving is in the form of community grants to organizations supported by Mr. Adler during his lifetime, primarily in Baker County.
Fields of interest: Community development.
Type of support: Building/renovation; Equipment; Program development; Scholarships—to individuals; Matching/challenge support.
Limitations: Giving limited to North Powder School District or a school district of Baker County, OR (for scholarships); grants for organizations primarily in Baker County, OR.

Publications: Informational brochure.
Application information: Application forms can be obtained at the counseling offices of eligible high schools or at U.S. Bank, Baker City Branch, between Jan. 1 and Mar. 30. Application form required.
   Deadline(s): Apr. 1 for first time applicants; Mar. 1 for renewals. Oct. 1 for community grant application
   Final notification: Aug.
Trustee: U.S. Bank, N.A.
EIN: 936289087
Selected grants: The following grants were reported in 2005.
$109,741 to Eastern Oregon University, La Grande, OR.
$78,598 to Oregon State University, Corvallis, OR.
$50,000 to Saint Elizabeth Health Care Foundation, Baker City, OR.
$41,385 to University of Oregon, Eugene, OR.
$39,465 to Baker County Library District, Baker City, OR.
$23,340 to Pacific University, Forest Grove, OR.
$23,040 to Boise State University, Boise, ID.
$20,980 to Central Oregon Community College, Bend, OR.
$17,414 to Blue Mountain Community College, Pendleton, OR.
$3,660 to College of Southern Idaho, Twin Falls, ID.

7997
The Autzen Foundation ✧
P.O. Box 3709
Portland, OR 97208 (503) 226-6051
Contact: Robin Stewart, Admin.

Incorporated in 1951 in OR.
Donor: Thomas J. Autzen‡.
Foundation type: Independent foundation.
Financial data (yr. ended 12/31/05): Assets, $19,065,567 (M); expenditures, $1,073,276; qualifying distributions, $999,257; giving activities include $949,585 for 208 grants (high: $25,000; low: $1,000; average: $5,000–$10,000).
Purpose and activities: Giving primarily for youth services, education, the arts, and nature.
Fields of interest: Performing arts; Arts; Higher education; Environment; Health care; Human services; Children/youth, services.
Type of support: Continuing support; Building/renovation; Program development; Seed money; Matching/challenge support.
Limitations: Giving primarily in OR, with some emphasis on Portland. Giving limited to the Pacific Northwest region. No grants to individuals, or for scholarships or fellowships; no loans.
Application information: Application form not required.
   Initial approach: Letter
   Copies of proposal: 1
   Deadline(s): Apr. 15, Aug. 15, and Nov. 15
   Board meeting date(s): May, Sept., and Dec.
   Final notification: 3 to 4 months
Officers: Wendy Ulman, Pres.; Christina Grady, Secy.
Directors: Thomas J. Autzen; Kent T. Houser; Robert W. Patton III.
Number of staff: 1 part-time professional.
EIN: 936021333

7998
Charles M. Bair Family Trust
c/o U.S. Bank, N.A, Tax Dept.
P.O. Box 3168
Portland, OR 97208-3168
Application address: c/o U.S. Bank, N.A., 303 N. Broadway, P.O. Box 20678, Billings, MT 59115

Established in 1993 in MT.
Donor: Alberta M. Bair‡.
Foundation type: Independent foundation.
Financial data (yr. ended 4/30/05): Assets, $61,970,488 (M); expenditures, $4,548,274; qualifying distributions, $4,374,505; giving activities include $3,864,406 for 38 grants (high: $1,150,000; low: $1,000).
Purpose and activities: Giving primarily for higher education, the arts, hospitals and organizations providing health services, civic service and human service organizations.
Fields of interest: Museums; Performing arts; Arts; Higher education; Hospitals (general); Health care; Boys & girls clubs; Human services.
Type of support: General/operating support.
Limitations: Giving primarily in MT, with emphasis on Yellowstone, Meagher and Wheatland counties. No support for churches, conventions or associations of churches. No grants to individuals, or for conferences, symposiums, or fundraising events.
Application information: Application form required.
   Copies of proposal: 5
   Deadline(s): Jan. 15 and Aug. 1
Officer and Directors:* Lee B. Rostad,* Vice-Chair.; Brent Cromley; Douglas A. Jenkins.
Trustee: U.S. Bank, N.A.
EIN: 816075761
Selected grants: The following grants were reported in 2005.
$1,150,000 to Alberta Bair Theater, Billings, MT.
$509,704 to Yellowstone Art Museum, Billings, MT.
$95,000 to Billings Symphony Society, Billings, MT.
$20,000 to Billings Studio Theater, Billings, MT.
$10,000 to Western Heritage Center, Billings, MT.

7999
William H. Bauman & Mary L. Bauman Foundation ✧
7991 S.W. Edgewater Dr. E.
Wilsonville, OR 97070

Established in 1991 in OR.
Donor: William H. Bauman‡.
Foundation type: Independent foundation.
Financial data (yr. ended 12/31/05): Assets, $8,863,921 (M); expenditures, $497,123; qualifying distributions, $474,260; giving activities include $461,000 for 16 grants (high: $90,000; low: $1,000).
Purpose and activities: Giving primarily for higher education, and to evangelical Christian churches and organizations.
Fields of interest: Museums (art); Performing arts, ballet; Higher education; Hospitals (general); Salvation Army; Children/youth, services; Protestant agencies & churches.
Limitations: Applications not accepted. Giving primarily in Portland, OR. No grants to individuals.
Application information: Contributes only to pre-selected organizations.
Officer: Paul Schwimdt, Mgr.

Trustees: Clarence Knoepfle; Mary Bauman Mirhady; William Vermillion.
EIN: 936234071

8000
W. Glen Boyd Charitable Foundation ◇
P.O. Box 8128
Portland, OR 97207-8128 (877) 803-8830
Contact: Diana H. Dokos, Prog. Dir.
E-mail: wgbcf@ureach.com; URL: http://www.wgbcf.org

Established in 2000 in OR.
Donor: W. Glen Boyd.
Foundation type: Independent foundation.
Financial data (yr. ended 12/31/05): Assets, $2,054,704 (M); expenditures, $615,271; qualifying distributions, $576,542; giving activities include $475,213 for 38 grants (high: $20,000; low: $5,000).
Purpose and activities: The W. Glen Boyd Charitable Foundation (WGBCF) is a private, grant-making foundation committed to significantly improving the lives of women and children living in violence, poverty or at-risk situations. The WGBCF disperses grants to grassroots and other 501(c)(3) organizations which are committed to empowering women and children through direct service or a blend of direct service and progressive social/systems change.
Fields of interest: Higher education; Education; Youth development, adult & child programs; Youth development; Human services; Children/youth, services; Women, centers/services; Economic development.
Type of support: General/operating support; Emergency funds; Program development; Scholarship funds; Technical assistance; Matching/challenge support.
Limitations: Applications not accepted. Giving primarily in MN and OR. No support for chemical dependency treatment programs, or for healthcare programs. No grants to individuals, or for research, capital or religious campaigns, or for multi-year grants.
Publications: Grants list; Informational brochure.
Application information: The foundation's 2006 grant rounds are on hold until further notice. Foundation limits each grant round to 50-100 invited applicants. Application and deadline information available on foundation Web site.
  Board meeting date(s): 5 times a year
Officers and Trustees:* W. Glen Boyd,* Exec. Dir.; Diana H. Dokos,* Prog. Dir.
Number of staff: 1 full-time professional.
EIN: 931306727
Selected grants: The following grants were reported in 2004.
$147,000 to Self Enhancement, Portland, OR.
$12,500 to Marylhurst University, Marylhurst, OR.
$10,000 to Childrens Home Society and Family Services, Saint Paul, MN.
$10,000 to Day One Center, Saint Paul, MN.
$10,000 to Saint Andrews School, Boca Raton, FL.
$10,000 to Southern Oregon University, Ashland, OR.
$10,000 to Washburn Child Guidance Center, Minneapolis, MN.
$10,000 to Welcome Center, Austin, MN.
$10,000 to YouthCARE, Minneapolis, MN.
$8,000 to Kids 'n Kinship, Apple Valley, MN.

8001
Braemar Charitable Trust ◇
P.O. Box 25442
Portland, OR 97298-0442
Contact: Martha B. Cox, Tr.
E-mail: MaryL@trustmanagementservices.net;
Application address: c/o Mary Lanthrum, Trust Mgmt. Svcs., P.O. Box 1990, Waldport, OR 97394, tel.: (541) 563-7279; FAX: (541) 563-7216; URL: http://www.trustmanagementservices.net

Established in 1993 in OR.
Donors: Hobart M. Bird; Marian A. Bird.
Foundation type: Independent foundation.
Financial data (yr. ended 9/30/05): Assets, $27,487,756 (M); expenditures, $1,358,201; qualifying distributions, $1,242,935; giving activities include $1,184,916 for 146 grants (high: $128,000; low: $807).
Fields of interest: Arts; Education; Human services; Children/youth, services.
Type of support: General/operating support; Building/renovation; Equipment; Program development; Curriculum development.
Limitations: Giving limited to OR. No grants to individuals; or for scholarships, capital campaigns, endowments, debt retirement, operating expenses, salaries, or projects with budgets greater than $50,000.
Publications: Application guidelines.
Application information: Application form required.
  Initial approach: Request application guidelines from Waldport address, or download from Web site
  Copies of proposal: 1
  Deadline(s): Varies by region, refer to Web site
Trustees: Hobart M. Bird; Marian A. Bird; Martha B. Cox; Melanie A. Dawson.
EIN: 936272124
Selected grants: The following grants were reported in 2003.
$12,000 to Umatilla County Special Library District, Pendleton, OR. For Training Wheels program.
$8,000 to Clackamas Womens Services, Milwaukie, OR. For play structure.
$8,000 to Mount Hood Community College, Gresham, OR. For Transitions Retention Program.
$8,000 to Native American Youth Association, Portland, OR. For Clients Special Needs Fund.
$8,000 to Oregon Childrens Foundation, Portland, OR. For Smart Program.
$8,000 to Treasure Valley Community College, Ontario, OR. For WINGS program.
$8,000 to Trinity Lutheran Church, Gresham, OR. For Hispanic outreach program.
$8,000 to Young Audiences of Oregon and Southwest Washington, Portland, OR. For Scholastic Art and Writing Awards.
$5,490 to Friends of Trees, Portland, OR. For equipment for Power Point presentations.
$5,000 to Washington County Historical Society, Portland, OR. For Mobile Museum Project.

8002
The Campbell Foundation ◇
155 B Ave., Ste. 320
Lake Oswego, OR 97034 (503) 675-2781
Contact: Patty Messinger

Established in 1993 in OR.

Donors: J. Duncan Campbell, Jr.; Cynthia A. Campbell; Birdshill, Inc.; United Asset Mgmt.; The Campbell Group.
Foundation type: Independent foundation.
Financial data (yr. ended 12/31/05): Assets, $12,024,375 (M); gifts received, $200,000; expenditures, $888,887; qualifying distributions, $738,339; giving activities include $738,339 for 29 grants (high: $250,000; low: $400).
Purpose and activities: Giving primarily to youth organizations and programs.
Fields of interest: Higher education; Children/youth, services; Foundations (private grantmaking).
Limitations: Giving primarily in Portland, OR. No grants to individuals directly.
Publications: Financial statement.
Application information:
  Initial approach: Letter
  Copies of proposal: 1
  Deadline(s): Dec. 1
  Board meeting date(s): Dec.
Officer: J. Duncan Campbell, Jr., Chair.
Directors: Cynthia A. Campbell; John S. Gilleland.
EIN: 931133917

8003
The Carpenter Foundation
711 E. Main St., Ste. 10
Medford, OR 97504 (541) 772-5851
Contact: Polly Williams, Prog. Off.
FAX: (541) 773-3970;
E-mail: pwilliams@carpenter-foundation.org;
Additional tel.: Polly Williams (541) 772-5732;
URL: http://www.carpenter-foundation.org

Incorporated in 1957 in OR.
Donors: Helen Bundy Carpenter†; Alfred S.V. Carpenter†.
Foundation type: Independent foundation.
Financial data (yr. ended 6/30/05): Assets, $18,132,219 (M); expenditures, $932,752; qualifying distributions, $859,657; giving activities include $766,716 for 87 grants (high: $30,000; low: $1,000).
Purpose and activities: The primary purpose of the Carpenter Foundation is to add opportunity, choice, inclusiveness, enrichment, and a climate for change for those living in the Rogue Valley, OR. Primary areas of interest include the arts, education, public interest, regional planning, and human services, including child welfare and youth.
Fields of interest: Visual arts; Performing arts; Performing arts, theater; Arts; Education, early childhood education; Child development, education; Secondary school/education; Higher education; Adult/continuing education; Adult education—literacy, basic skills & GED; Libraries/library science; Education, reading; Education; Environment, natural resources; Environment; Health care; Substance abuse, services; Mental health/crisis services; Legal services; Housing/shelter, development; Human services; Children/youth, services; Child development, services; Family services; Rural development; Community development; Government/public administration; Economically disadvantaged.
Type of support: General/operating support; Continuing support; Annual campaigns; Capital campaigns; Building/renovation; Equipment; Land acquisition; Program development; Conferences/seminars; Publication; Seed money; Curriculum development; Scholarship funds; Technical

assistance; Consulting services; Program evaluation; Matching/challenge support.

Limitations: Giving limited to Jackson and Josephine counties, OR. No grants to individuals, or for deficit financing.

Publications: Application guidelines; Annual report (including application guidelines); Financial statement; Grants list; Informational brochure (including application guidelines).

Application information: Contact foundation or refer to Web site for latest information. Application form not required.

Initial approach: Letter or telephone for guidelines
Copies of proposal: 1
Deadline(s): Telephone for current deadlines
Board meeting date(s): Quarterly
Final notification: 1 to 2 weeks after board meeting

Officers and Trustees:* Emily C. Mostue,* Pres.; Karen C. Allan, V.P. and Secy.; A. Brian Mostue, Treas.

Public Trustees: Harvey Bennett; Jonathan Gell, M.D.; William Moffat; Sue Naumes; Marc Sirinsky.

Number of staff: 1 part-time professional; 1 part-time support.

EIN: 930491360

Selected grants: The following grants were reported in 2005.

$19,800 to South Medford High School, South Medford, OR.

$14,630 to Central Point High School, Central Point, OR.

$13,750 to Ashland High School, Ashland, OR.

$10,000 to Jacksonville Woodlands Association, Jacksonville, OR.

$10,000 to YMCA.

$5,280 to Rogue River High School, Rogue River, OR.

$3,000 to CARE, Seattle, WA.

8004

Chambers Family Foundation

2295 Coburg Rd., Ste. 304
Eugene, OR 97401 (541) 484-2419
Contact: Carolyn S. Chambers, Tr.

Established in 1999 in OR.
Donor: Carolyn S. Chambers.
Foundation type: Independent foundation.
Financial data (yr. ended 12/31/05): Assets, $19,169,467 (M); expenditures, $958,875; qualifying distributions, $814,909; giving activities include $801,150 for 92 grants (high: $200,000; low: $833).

Purpose and activities: Giving primarily to support and further the arts, education, medical health, and human needs in Lane, Benton and Deschutes counties in OR.

Fields of interest: Arts; Higher education; Medical research; Human services.

Type of support: Management development/ capacity building; General/operating support; Continuing support; Building/renovation; Equipment; Emergency funds; Program development; Seed money; Curriculum development; Research; Matching/challenge support.

Limitations: Giving primarily in Lane, Benton and Deschutes counties, OR. No support for pass through agencies or environmental projects. No grants to individuals or for capital campaigns.

Publications: Informational brochure (including application guidelines).

Application information: Application form required.
Copies of proposal: 1
Deadline(s): Mar. 31 and Sept. 30
Board meeting date(s): Late May and late Nov.
Final notification: 3 months from receipt

Trustees: Carolyn S. Chambers; Elizabeth Chambers; Silva Sullivan.

Number of staff: 1 part-time professional.

EIN: 931266648

Selected grants: The following grants were reported in 2004.

$200,000 to University of Oregon Foundation, Eugene, OR.

$100,000 to Sacred Heart Medical Center Foundation, Eugene, OR.

$25,000 to Volunteers in Medicine Clinic, Eugene, OR.

$18,635 to Relief Nursery, Eugene, OR.

$15,000 to Boys and Girls Clubs of Emerald Valley, Eugene, OR.

$12,000 to Willamette Repertory Theater, Eugene, OR.

$5,000 to Eugene School District 4J, Eugene, OR.

$5,000 to Girl Scouts of the U.S.A., Eugene, OR.

$5,000 to YMCA, Eugene Family, Eugene, OR.

$2,500 to Arts Umbrella, Eugene, OR.

8005

Chiles Foundation ✧

111 S.W. 5th Ave., Ste. 4050
Portland, OR 97204-3643
E-mail: cf@uswest.net

Incorporated in 1949 in OR.
Donors: Eva Chiles Meyer†; Earle A. Chiles†; Virginia H. Chiles†.
Foundation type: Independent foundation.
Financial data (yr. ended 12/31/05): Assets, $13,787,028 (M); expenditures, $2,844,813; qualifying distributions, $2,091,710; giving activities include $1,737,400 for 58 grants (high: $325,500; low: $500).

Purpose and activities: Primary focus is to assist and support higher education, medical research, and the arts.

Fields of interest: Arts; Higher education; Medical research, institute.

Type of support: Scholarship funds; Research.

Limitations: Applications not accepted. No support for projects involving litigation. No grants to individuals, or for deficit financing, mortgage retirement, no loans.

Application information: Unsolicited requests for funds not accepted. Call foundation for application deadlines.

Officers and Trustees:* Earle M. Chiles,* Pres.; Michael Arthur,* Secy.; Pedro Garcia.

Number of staff: 2 full-time professional; 2 part-time professional; 1 full-time support.

EIN: 936031125

Selected grants: The following grants were reported in 2004.

$403,000 to Boston University, Boston, MA. For general support.

$293,500 to Providence Saint Vincent Medical Foundation, Portland, OR. 2 grants: $168,500 (For research programs), $125,000 (For general operating support).

$241,300 to University of Portland, Portland, OR. For building repairs and athletic program support.

$171,500 to Stanford University, Stanford, CA. For general operating support.

$165,000 to Ludwig-Maximilians University, Munich, Germany. For research programs.

$83,000 to High Desert Museum, Bend, OR. For general operating support.

$25,500 to Oregon State University Foundation, Corvallis, OR. For general operating support.

$19,000 to Priest of Holy Cross, Portland, OR. For general operating support.

$16,500 to Major Junior Hockey Education Fund of Oregon, Portland, OR. For general operating support.

8006

The Clemens Foundation ✧

c/o Kelly Howard, Exec. Dir.
P.O. Box 427
Philomath, OR 97370

Incorporated in 1959 in OR.
Donors: Rex Clemens†; Ethel M. Clemens†; Rex Veneer Co.
Foundation type: Independent foundation.
Financial data (yr. ended 12/31/05): Assets, $31,310,787 (M); gifts received, $117; expenditures, $1,919,888; qualifying distributions, $1,764,274; giving activities include $101,387 for 9 grants (high: $25,000; low: $650), and $1,599,385 for 141 grants to individuals (high: $217,358; low: $100).

Purpose and activities: Tuition grants for high school graduates of Philomath, Eddyville, Crane and Alsea, OR to attend college or an accredited vocational school on a full-time basis.

Type of support: Scholarship funds; Scholarships— to individuals.

Limitations: Applications not accepted. Giving limited to residents of Philomath, Eddyville, Crane, and Alsea, OR.

Officers and Trustees:* David Lowther,* Pres.; Steven Lowther, V.P.; Ron Edwards,* Secy.; Fred Lowther,* Treas.; Kelly D. Howard,* Exec. Dir.; Elwood Berklund; Wayne L. Howard; Thad Springer.

Number of staff: 1 full-time professional.

EIN: 936023941

8007

The Collins Foundation ▼ ✧

1618 S.W. 1st Ave., Ste. 505
Portland, OR 97201-5706 (503) 227-7171
Contact: Jerry E. Hudson, Exec. V.P.
FAX: (503) 295-3794;
E-mail: information@collinsfoundation.org;
URL: http://www.collinsfoundation.org

Incorporated in 1947 in OR.
Donor: Members of the Collins family.
Foundation type: Independent foundation.
Financial data (yr. ended 12/31/05): Assets, $185,297,316 (M); expenditures, $8,723,845; qualifying distributions, $8,244,790; giving activities include $8,244,790 for 245 grants (high: $700,000; low: $1,500; average: $5,000– $50,000).

Purpose and activities: Emphasis on higher education, youth, hospices and health agencies, social welfare, and the arts and cultural programs.

Fields of interest: Arts; Higher education; Health care; Human services; Children/youth, services; Religion; Homeless.

Type of support: Capital campaigns; Building/
renovation; Equipment; Research; Matching/
challenge support.
Limitations: Giving limited to OR, with emphasis on
Portland. No support for individual religious
congregations, elementary, secondary or public
higher educational institutions. No grants to
individuals, or for endowments, operational deficits,
financial emergencies, debt retirement, or annual
fundraising activities.
Publications: Annual report; Annual report (including
application guidelines); Grants list; Informational
brochure.
Application information: Do not send proposals
electronically; if applicant's program/project is time
sensitive submitting two months in advance of a
particular trustee meeting is recommended; a
complete description of the application process is
available in the submission guidelines section of the
foundation Web site. Application form not required.
  Initial approach: Call, rather than write, if you have
    questions, otherwise just send complete
    proposal
  Copies of proposal: 1
  Deadline(s): None
  Board meeting date(s): Feb., Apr., June, Aug., Oct.
    and Dec.
  Final notification: 6 to 8 weeks
Officers and Trustees:* Truman W. Collins, Jr.,*
Pres.; Jerry E. Hudson, Exec. V.P.; Ralph Bolliger,*
V.P.; Cherida C. Smith,* V.P.; Cynthia G. Addams,
Secy. and Prog. Dir. and Exec. V.P.- Elect; Timothy R.
Bishop, Treas.; Maribeth W. Collins; Lee Diane
Collins Vest.
Number of staff: 2 full-time professional; 1 full-time
support; 1 part-time support.
EIN: 936021893
Selected grants: The following grants were reported
in 2005.
$750,000 to Willamette University, Salem, OR. For
    renovation of Carnegie Building to house
    university's law program; and renovation of Eaton
    Hall on university's campus, payable over 3
    years.
$475,000 to Portland Center Stage, Portland, OR.
    For acquisition and renovation of Portland Armory
    building for theater's permanent residence, and
    support for artistic programming and operations,
    payable over 3 years.
$350,000 to Foundations for a Better Oregon,
    Portland, OR. For Chalkboard Project.
$245,000 to Oregon Health and Science University
    Foundation, Portland, OR. For creation of clinical
    program to teach physicians how to effectively
    communicate with patients and families during
    difficult situations, payable over 2 years.
$200,000 to Confluences, Vancouver, WA. For
    creation of public artwork projects as part of
    Confluence Project highlighting Corps of
    Discovery, Native Americans, and the
    environment, payable over 2 years.
$160,000 to Ecumenical Ministries of Oregon,
    Portland, OR. For continued support of programs
    and operations.
$55,000 to Oregon Health Access Project, Salem,
    OR. For program assisting medically and
    economically vulnerable Oregonians to facilitate
    access to health services, payable over 2 years.
$35,000 to Campbell Institute for Children,
    Portland, OR. For establishment of Ready for
    School campaign to build public awareness of
    and support for early childhood education.

$25,000 to Human Solutions, Portland, OR. For
    hiring of case manager to serve families eligible
    for subsidized and permanent housing.
$12,000 to Profile Theater Project, Portland, OR. For
    artistic innovation and expansion of theater's
    performances.

8008
Collins McDonald Trust Fund ◇
1618 S.W. 1st Ave., Ste. 500
Portland, OR 97201-5706
Contact: James C. Lynch
Application address: 620 N. 1st St., Lakeview, OR
97630, tel.: (541) 947-2196

Incorporated in 1940 in OR.
Foundation type: Independent foundation.
Financial data (yr. ended 12/31/05): Assets,
$9,763,143 (M); expenditures, $661,673;
qualifying distributions, $652,496; giving activities
include $195,715 for 7 grants (high: $120,041;
low: $900), and $452,695 for 96 grants to
individuals (high: $8,350; low: $1,750).
Purpose and activities: Awards scholarships for
higher education to graduates of local high schools
only; grants also for social and health services.
Fields of interest: Hospitals (general); Disasters,
preparedness/services; Human services.
Type of support: Building/renovation; Equipment;
Scholarships—to individuals.
Limitations: Giving limited to Lake County, OR.
Application information: Application form required
for scholarships.
  Initial approach: Proposal
  Deadline(s): May 1 for scholarships
Trustees: Timothy R. Bishop; Paul Harlan; James E.
Lynch.
EIN: 936021894

8009
Collins Medical Trust
1618 S.W. 1st Ave., Ste. 500
Portland, OR 97201-5706 (503) 227-1219
Contact: Nancy L. Helseth, Admin.

Established in 1956 in OR.
Donor: Truman W. Collins†.
Foundation type: Independent foundation.
Financial data (yr. ended 9/30/05): Assets,
$7,684,361 (M); expenditures, $391,437;
qualifying distributions, $387,775; giving activities
include $386,769 for 13 grants (high: $62,500;
low: $17,287).
Purpose and activities: Grants limited to medical
research and medical education within the state of
Oregon.
Fields of interest: Higher education; Medical
school/education; Nursing school/education;
Cancer; Biomedicine; Medical research, institute;
Cancer research.
Type of support: Equipment; Program development;
Seed money; Scholarship funds; Research;
Matching/challenge support.
Limitations: Giving limited to OR.
Publications: Application guidelines.
Application information: Application form not
required.
  Initial approach: Letter
  Copies of proposal: 5
  Deadline(s): Jan. 1, May 1, and Sept. 1

Board meeting date(s): 3rd Wed. in Jan., May, and
  Sept.
Final notification: 7 days after meeting
Officers: Timothy R. Bishop, Treas.; Nancy L.
Helseth, Admin.
Trustees: Truman W. Collins, Jr.; Elizabeth
Eckstrom, M.D., M.P.H.; Walter J. McDonald, M.D.
EIN: 936021895

8010
Crabby Beach Foundation
P.O. Box 280
Lake Oswego, OR 97034
Contact: Jeanne Becker, Treas.

Established in 2003 in OR.
Donor: Sue D. Cooley.
Foundation type: Independent foundation.
Financial data (yr. ended 12/31/05): Assets,
$18,711,831 (M); expenditures, $804,717;
qualifying distributions, $796,992; giving activities
include $796,992 for 17 grants (high: $125,405;
low: $10,080).
Fields of interest: Arts; Elementary/secondary
education; Education; Environment; Health
organizations, association.
Limitations: Applications not accepted. Giving
primarily in WA. No grants to individuals.
Application information: Unsolicited requests for
funds not accepted.
Officers: Caroline Cooley Browne, Pres.; Jeanne
Becker, Treas.
Directors: David Browne; Sue D. Cooley.
EIN: 300179374

8011
Eiting Foundation ◇
707 S.W. Washington St., Ste. 1500
Portland, OR 97205
Application address: c/o Jack R. Eiting and Marie E.
Eiting, 2015 S.E. Columbia River Dr., Unit 240,
Vancouver, WA 98661

Established in 2002 in OR.
Donors: Jack R. Eiting; Precision Strip, Inc.; Marie
E. Eiting.
Foundation type: Independent foundation.
Financial data (yr. ended 12/31/05): Assets,
$750,208 (M); gifts received, $425,500;
expenditures, $985,560; qualifying distributions,
$973,350; giving activities include $973,350 for 15
grants (high: $257,760; low: $1,000).
Purpose and activities: Giving primarily to Roman
Catholic agencies and churches, and youth
organizations.
Fields of interest: Human services; Children,
services; Roman Catholic agencies & churches.
Limitations: Giving primarily in the U.S., with
emphasis on Portland, OR; giving also in OH and WA.
No grants to individuals.
Application information:
  Initial approach: Letter
  Deadline(s): None
Directors: Jack R. Eiting; Katherine A. Eiting; Marie
E. Eiting.
Trustee: Robert Zagunis.
EIN: 010614397

8012
Fohs Foundation ✧
P.O. Box 1001
Roseburg, OR 97470
Contact: Rose Mary Cooper, Secy.-Treas.

Established in 1937 in NY.
Donors: F. Julius Fohs†; Cora B. Fohs†; Fred & Frances Sohn Charitable Lead Trust.
Foundation type: Independent foundation.
Financial data (yr. ended 12/31/05): Assets, $16,704,345 (M); gifts received, $308,252; expenditures, $795,121; qualifying distributions, $570,974; giving activities include $529,293 for 35 grants (high: $40,000; low: $1,500).
Purpose and activities: To promote science, art, education, health, healthful recreation and good citizenship of children and adults; research in general, charitable, humanitarian, sociological and educational problems; support for Ella Fohs children's and senior citizens' camps in CT; grants for Jewish-sponsored educational institutions, particularly in Israel.
Fields of interest: Arts; Higher education; Education; Recreation; Human services; Children/youth, services; Aging, centers/services; Jewish agencies & temples; Aging.
International interests: Israel.
Type of support: Endowments; Scholarship funds.
Limitations: Giving primarily in OR; some giving also in Israel. No grants to individuals.
Application information: Application form not required.
Initial approach: Letter
Copies of proposal: 1
Deadline(s): Mar. 31
Board meeting date(s): Apr. or May
Officers: Frances F. Sohn, Chair.; Howard F. Sohn, Vice-Chair.; Rose Mary Cooper, Secy.-Treas.
Trustees: Edward F. Sohn; Fred Sohn; Gerard F. Sohn; Mark F. Sohn; Richard F. Sohn; Ruth Sohn.
Number of staff: 1 part-time support.
EIN: 746003165

8013
The Ford Family Foundation ▼
1600 N.W. Stewart Pkwy.
Roseburg, OR 97470 (541) 957-5574
Contact: Norman J. Smith, Pres.
FAX: (541) 957-5720; E-mail: info@tfff.org;
URL: http://www.tfff.org

Incorporated in 1957 in OR.
Donors: Kenneth W. Ford†; Hallie E. Ford.
Foundation type: Independent foundation.
Financial data (yr. ended 3/31/05): Assets, $522,129,631 (M); expenditures, $24,062,830; qualifying distributions, $21,091,475; giving activities include $9,349,445 for 449 grants (high: $100,000; low: $50; average: $5,000–$84,000), $7,457,296 for 850 grants to individuals (high: $45,862; low: $480; average: $5,000–$15,104), $196,612 for 157 employee matching gifts, and $2,370,018 for 2 foundation-administered programs.
Purpose and activities: The mission of the foundation is to help individuals through organized learning opportunities to be contributing and successful citizens, and to enhance the vitality of rural communities. A high percentage of funding is for the benefit of Ford initiatives.
Fields of interest: Education; Human services; Youth, services; Community development.

Type of support: Capital campaigns; Building/renovation; Equipment; Program development; Technical assistance; Employee matching gifts; Scholarships—to individuals; Matching/challenge support.
Limitations: Giving primarily in rural OR, with special interest in Douglas and Coos counties; giving also in Siskiyou County, CA. No grants to individuals (except for scholarships), endowment funds, general fund drives, indirect or overhead expenses, debt retirement or operating expenses, fundraising events, or purchase of art.
Publications: Informational brochure (including application guidelines); Newsletter.
Application information: Accepts pre-applications all year, no deadlines. The foundation will not accept electronic or facsimile submissions. Full applications are by invitation only. Application form required.
Initial approach: Pre-application letter as outlined in brochure or Web site
Copies of proposal: 1
Deadline(s): None
Board meeting date(s): Four times per year
Final notification: Two weeks after decision
Officers and Directors:* Ronald C. Parker,* Chair.; Norman J. Smith, Pres.; Allyn C. Ford,* Secy.-Treas.; Karla S. Chambers; David B. Frohnmayer; Joseph P. Kearns; Carmen R. Phillips; John W. Sweet.
Number of staff: 7 full-time professional; 11 full-time support.
EIN: 936026156
Selected grants: The following grants were reported in 2005.
$1,100,000 to Boys and Girls Clubs of the Umpqua Valley, Roseburg, OR. To purchase, renovate, and expand facility.
$648,516 to Oregon Childrens Foundation, Portland, OR. For Rural County SMART program, payable over 2 years.
$350,000 to La Grande Community Library Foundation, La Grande, OR. For new La Grande Library construction.
$255,000 to Womens Safety and Resource Center, North Bend, OR. For Coddington Place.
$250,000 to Oregon Community Foundation, Portland, OR. For Foundations for a Better Oregon Fund's Chalkboard Project.
$150,000 to Winston Area Community Partnership, Winston, OR.
$10,000 to Pendleton, City of, Pendleton, OR. For Pendleton Convention Center Bleacher Replacement.
$6,000 to Southwestern Oregon Community Action Committee, Coos Bay, OR.
$4,000 to Girl Scouts of the U.S.A., Wester Rivers Council, Eugene, OR.
$3,000 to California State University, Sacramento, CA.

8014
Foreign Mission Foundation
10875 S.W. 89th St.
Tigard, OR 97223-8323

Established around 1982 in OR.
Donors: Eugene L. Davis; Miriam Larson.
Foundation type: Independent foundation.
Financial data (yr. ended 2/28/06): Assets, $7,643,081 (M); gifts received, $987,712; expenditures, $1,799,090; qualifying distributions, $1,385,923; giving activities include $1,301,381 for 56 grants (high: $184,350; low: $100).

Purpose and activities: Giving primarily for missionary programs in the U.S. and India.
Fields of interest: Elementary/secondary education; Christian agencies & churches; Religion.
International interests: India.
Limitations: Applications not accepted. Giving primarily in India. No grants to individuals.
Application information: Contributes only to pre-selected organizations.
Officers and Directors:* Eugene L. Davis,* Pres.; Vivian Davis,* Secy.; Don Chapman; George Hughes; Robert Waymire.
Number of staff: 1 full-time professional; 1 part-time professional.
EIN: 930763215
Selected grants: The following grants were reported in 2003.
$63,243 to Badavo Banjara Phozear. For pastoral training.
$58,550 to Youth With A Mission, Salem, OR. For children's camps.
$15,000 to South Asia Advocates, Kirkland, Asia. For training center.
$10,000 to Mission India, Grand Rapids, MI. For adult literacy.
$5,000 to College Church of the Nazarene, Olathe, KS. For pastoral training.
$2,000 to New Life Fellowship, India. For medical bills.
$2,000 to Youth With A Mission-Honolulu, Honolulu, HI.
$1,500 to InterVarsity Christian Fellowship/USA, Madison, WI. For missionary support.
$1,200 to Samaritans Purse, Boone, NC. For training center.
$1,000 to Taylor University, Upland, IN. For scholarships.

8015
Four Way Community Foundation ✧
P.O. Box 652
Grants Pass, OR 97528-0056
Contact: Phil Hart, Exec. Dir.

Established in 1975 in OR.
Foundation type: Community foundation.
Financial data (yr. ended 6/30/05): Assets, $2,338,124 (M); gifts received, $77,975; expenditures, $1,143,655; giving activities include $1,082,355 for 25+ grants, and $7,859 for grants to individuals.
Purpose and activities: The foundation supports charitable organizations benefiting the residents of Josephine and Western Jackson counties in Oregon.
Fields of interest: Human services; Community development.
Type of support: Capital campaigns; Building/renovation; Equipment; Scholarships—to individuals.
Limitations: Giving limited to Josephine and Western Jackson counties, OR. No support for sectarian religious purposes.
Publications: Application guidelines; Informational brochure (including application guidelines).
Application information: Application form required.
Copies of proposal: 1
Deadline(s): Feb. 1 through Apr. 1
Board meeting date(s): 3rd Tues. of month
Final notification: Mid-May
Officers and Directors:* John Higgins,* Pres.; James Dole,* V.P.; Ann Bauer,* Secy.; Steve Welch,* Treas.; Phil Hart, Exec. Dir.; Brady Adams; Bob Brownell; Giff Gates; Kathy Krauss; Chris

Matthews; Charles Seagraves, Jr.; Barbara Sniffen; Cherryl Walker.
Number of staff: 1 part-time professional.
EIN: 510173092

8016
A. J. Frank Family Foundation ✧
P.O. Drawer 79
Mill City, OR 97360
Contact: Ryan Banning

Incorporated in 1959 in OR.
Donors: A.J. Frank; L.D. Frank; Frank Lumber Co., Inc.; Frank Timber Products, Inc.; and members of the Frank family.
Foundation type: Independent foundation.
Financial data (yr. ended 9/30/05): Assets, $8,306,547 (M); gifts received, $25,000; expenditures, $425,328; qualifying distributions, $321,990; giving activities include $321,990 for 39 grants (high: $45,000; low: $250).
Purpose and activities: Giving primarily to Roman Catholic organizations and schools, as well as for human services.
Fields of interest: Elementary/secondary education; Higher education; Education; Human services; Roman Catholic agencies & churches.
Limitations: Giving primarily in OR. No grants to individuals.
Application information: Application form not required.
  Initial approach: Letter
  Deadline(s): Aug. 15 and Dec. 15
  Final notification: Jan. 15 and Sept. 15
Directors: C.M. Carey; D.D. Frank; J.T. Frank.
EIN: 930523395
Selected grants: The following grants were reported in 2005.
$15,000 to Marion-Polk Food Share, Salem, OR.
$15,000 to Saint Joseph Mission School, San Fidel, NM.
$10,000 to Sisters of Saint Mary, Beaverton, OR.
$10,000 to University of Portland, Portland, OR.
$6,000 to Salvation Army.
$4,000 to Carter Center, Atlanta, GA.
$2,000 to Catholic Charities.
$1,000 to Willamette Valley Hospice, Salem, OR.

8017
Richard and Janet Geary Foundation, Inc.
1211 S.W. 5th Ave., Ste. 2980
Portland, OR 97204
Contact: Janet Geary, Chair.; Richard Geary, Pres.

Established in 1992 in OR.
Donors: Richard Geary; Janet H. Geary.
Foundation type: Independent foundation.
Financial data (yr. ended 12/31/05): Assets, $5,105,014 (M); expenditures, $861,357; qualifying distributions, $790,323; giving activities include $788,975 for 49 grants (high: $200,000; low: $25).
Purpose and activities: Giving for the arts, youth support, healthcare research, higher education and regional and national policy.
Fields of interest: Museums (art); Arts; Higher education; Health care, research.
Limitations: Giving limited to Portland, OR, and Coachella Valley, CA. No grants to individuals.
Application information: Application form not required.

Initial approach: Letter
Copies of proposal: 1
Deadline(s): Varies
Board meeting date(s): Annually
Final notification: Up to 3 months
Officers and Directors:* Janet H. Geary,* Chair.; Richard Geary,* Pres. and Treas.; Suzanne G. Paymar, Secy.
Members: Sarah Geary Gustafson; Brad Paymar.
Trustee: Bank of America, N.A.
Number of staff: None.
EIN: 911748475
Selected grants: The following grants were reported in 2003.
$250,000 to Portland Art Museum, Portland, OR. For general support.
$50,000 to Friends of the Children, Portland, OR. For general support.
$50,000 to John F. Kennedy Center for the Performing Arts, DC. For general support.
$20,000 to Oregon State University Foundation, Portland, OR. For general support.
$20,000 to University of Portland, Portland, OR. For general support.
$5,000 to Oregon Symphony Association, Oregon Symphony, Portland, OR. For general support.
$5,000 to Pacific Legal Foundation, Sacramento, CA. For general support.
$1,500 to Northwest Academy, Portland, OR. For general support.
$1,000 to Boys and Girls Club of Coachella Valley, Palm Desert, CA. For general support.
$1,000 to Childrens Course, Gladstone, OR. For general support.

8018
Rosaria P. Haugland Foundation ☆
1577 Pearl St., Ste. 100
Eugene, OR 97401

Established in 2003 in WA.
Donors: Alexander D. Haugland; Rosaria P. Haugland; Richard P. Haugland; Marina E. Haugland Martin.
Foundation type: Independent foundation.
Financial data (yr. ended 9/30/05): Assets, $22,261,097 (M); gifts received, $3,652,000; expenditures, $1,726,667; qualifying distributions, $1,646,450; giving activities include $1,646,450 for 40 grants (high: $135,000; low: $50).
Purpose and activities: Giving for support of art, education and community institutions to help women and children.
Fields of interest: Performing arts; Performing arts, theater; Performing arts, opera; Higher education.
Type of support: Capital campaigns; Building/renovation; Professorships; Fellowships; Scholarship funds.
Limitations: Applications not accepted. Giving primarily in OR. No support for religious or political organizations. No grants to individuals.
Publications: Annual report.
Application information: Contributes only to pre-selected organizations.
  Board meeting date(s): Annualy
Officers and Directors:* Rosaria P. Haugland,* Pres.; Richard P. Haugland,* V.P.; Alexander D. Haugland; Marina E. Haugland Martin.
Number of staff: None.
EIN: 200270777

8019
Hedinger Family Foundation ✧
1750 N.W. Front Ave., Ste. 106
Portland, OR 97209

Established in 1998 in OR.
Donor: American Industries, Inc.
Foundation type: Company-sponsored foundation.
Financial data (yr. ended 12/31/04): Assets, $2,193,917 (M); gifts received, $1,519,282; expenditures, $606,194; qualifying distributions, $604,157; giving activities include $604,032 for 26 grants (high: $116,550; low: $250).
Purpose and activities: The foundation supports organizations involved with arts and culture, education, health, disaster relief, children and youth, and human services.
Fields of interest: Museums (science/technology); Arts; Education; Hospitals (general); Health care; Disasters, preparedness/services; Children/youth, services; Human services.
Limitations: Applications not accepted. Giving primarily in OR. No grants to individuals.
Application information: Contributes only to pre-selected organizations.
Directors: Hillary H. Clausen; Barkley H. Hedinger; Blake H. Hedinger; Howard H. Hedinger.
EIN: 931255431
Selected grants: The following grants were reported in 2004.
$116,550 to Central Catholic High School, Portland, OR.
$110,000 to Oregon Museum of Science and Industry, Portland, OR.
$100,000 to Mercy Corps, Portland, OR. For Indian Ocean Tsunami relief.
$60,000 to Self Enhancement, Portland, OR.
$40,000 to Oregon College of Art and Craft, Portland, OR.
$30,000 to Dove Lewis Emergency Animal Hospital, Portland, OR.
$26,972 to Okizu Foundation, Novato, CA.
$16,000 to Saint Marys Cathedral, Portland, OR.
$15,000 to Childrens Relief Nursery, Portland, OR.
$15,000 to Guide Dogs for the Blind, Boring, OR.

8020
Charles M. Holmes Foundation ✧
1600 S.W. 4th Ave., Ste 870
Portland, OR 97201 (503) 223-9000
Contact: Terry Bean, Tr.

Established in 2001 in CA.
Donor: Charles M. Holmes Trust.
Foundation type: Independent foundation.
Financial data (yr. ended 12/31/04): Assets, $6,508,267 (M); gifts received, $2,390,440; expenditures, $515,822; qualifying distributions, $487,715; giving activities include $426,096 for 53 grants (high: $150,000; low: $200).
Purpose and activities: Giving primarily to organizations with a focus on the civil and human rights of gay men and lesbians, and AIDS awareness; support also for the arts and education.
Fields of interest: Arts; Education; AIDS; Health organizations; AIDS research; Autism research; Housing/shelter; Human services; Civil rights, gays/lesbians; Women.
Limitations: Giving primarily in CA and OR. No grants to individuals.
Application information: Application form not required.
  Initial approach: Letter or telephone

Trustees: Terrence P. Bean; David Mixner; Amber Stubbs; Shari Williams.
EIN: 943331085

8021
The Honzel Family Foundation ✧
12929 S.W. Forest Meadows Way
Lake Oswego, OR   97034-1593

Established in 1996 in OR.
Donor: Andrew J. Honzel.
Foundation type: Independent foundation.
Financial data (yr. ended 12/31/05): Assets, $22,012,152 (M); expenditures, $1,038,261; qualifying distributions, $984,795; giving activities include $984,795 for 109 grants (high: $127,500; low: $100).
Purpose and activities: Giving primarily for Roman Catholic agencies and churches.
Fields of interest: Education; Health care; Human services; Roman Catholic federated giving programs; Christian agencies & churches; Roman Catholic agencies & churches.
Limitations: Applications not accepted. Giving on a national basis. No grants to individuals.
Application information: Contributes only to pre-selected organizations.
Trustees: Andrew J. Honzel; Beverly J. Honzel.
EIN: 931223928

8022
Intel Foundation ▼
5200 N.E. Elam Young Pkwy., AG6-601
Hillsboro, OR   97124-6497
Contact: Lisa Siewert, Admin.
FAX: (503) 456-1539;
E-mail: intel.foundation@intel.com; URL: http://www.intel.com/community/index.htm

Established in 1988 in OR.
Donors: Intel Corp.; Intel Capital Corp.
Foundation type: Company-sponsored foundation.
Financial data (yr. ended 12/31/05): Assets, $77,744,647 (M); gifts received, $35,000,048; expenditures, $43,414,316; qualifying distributions, $43,105,616; giving activities include $40,360,672 for 1,618 grants (high: $1,813,947; low: $50), and $2,742,277 for 1,837 employee matching gifts.
Purpose and activities: The foundation supports organizations involved with education. Special emphasis is directed toward programs designed to advance math, science, and technical education; improve the effective utilization of technology in classroom teaching; broaden access to technology; and increase the number of people, especially women and minorities, pursuing technical careers.
Fields of interest: Elementary/secondary education; Higher education; Engineering school/education; Education; Science, equal rights; Science, formal/general education; Mathematics; Science; Minorities; African Americans/Blacks; Hispanics/Latinos; Native Americans/American Indians; Women.
Type of support: General/operating support; Program development; Curriculum development; Fellowships; Scholarship funds; Research; Employee volunteer services; Employee matching gifts.
Limitations: Applications not accepted. Giving primarily in Phoenix, AZ, Folsom and Santa Clara, CA, Colorado Springs, CO, Hudson, MA, Albuquerque, NM, Portland, OR, Austin, TX, Riverton, UT, and Dupont, WA; giving also to national organizations. No support for religious, sectarian, fraternal, or political organizations, arts or health care organizations, private schools, or sports teams. No grants to individuals (except for fellowships), or for endowments, capital campaigns, general fund drives, annual campaigns, fundraising events, sporting events, travel or tours, or equipment.
Publications: Corporate giving report.
Application information: Contributes only to pre-selected organizations.
    Board meeting date(s): Semiannually
Officers and Directors:* Craig R. Barrett,* Chair.; Brenda Musilli, Pres.; Patty Murray,* Secy.; Leslie Culbertson,* Treas.; Wendy Hawkins,* Exec. Dir.; Christian Morales.
Number of staff: 1 part-time professional; 1 full-time support.
EIN: 943092928
Selected grants: The following grants were reported in 2004.
$2,460,000 to Science Service, DC. 2 grants: $1,010,000 (For Intel International Science and Engineering Fairs (Intel ISEF)), $1,450,000 (For Intel International Science and Engineering Fairs (Intel ISEF)).
$1,404,324 to United Way, Valley of the Sun, Phoenix, AZ.
$1,041,769 to United Way.
$1,000,000 to Education Development Center, Newton, MA. For evaluation.
$1,000,000 to Institute of Computer Technology, Sunnyvale, CA. 2 grants: $500,000 each (For Intel Teach To the Future (TTF) program).
$44,692 to Arizona State University, Tempe, AZ. For Intel International Science and Engineering Fairs (Intel ISEF).
$40,694 to United Way of Pierce County, Tacoma, WA.
$30,000 to Bernalillo Public Schools, Bernalillo, NM.

8023
J.F.R. Foundation ✧
1211 S.W. 5th Ave., Ste. 2650
Portland, OR   97204

Established in 1993 in OR.
Donor: James F. Rippey.
Foundation type: Independent foundation.
Financial data (yr. ended 12/31/05): Assets, $9,792,553 (M); gifts received, $1,041,310; expenditures, $626,259; qualifying distributions, $623,415; giving activities include $610,000 for 31 grants (high: $45,000; low: $10,000).
Purpose and activities: Giving primarily for higher education.
Fields of interest: Arts; Higher education; Youth development; Human services.
Limitations: Applications not accepted. Giving primarily in OR, with emphasis on Portland. No grants to individuals.
Application information: Contributes only to pre-selected organizations.
Directors: Jan Dimick; Robin R. Holcomb; Jack McCurchie; James F. Rippey; Jeffrey L. Rippey; Shirley K. Rippey; Timothy M. Rippey.
EIN: 943192331

8024
The Jackson Foundation ✧
c/o U.S. Bank, N.A., Trust Group
P.O. Box 3168
Portland, OR   97208   (503) 275-4414
Contact: Robert H. Depew, V.P., U.S. Bank, N.A.
URL: http://www.thejacksonfoundation.com

Trust established in 1960 in OR; Philip Ludwell Jackson Charitable and Residual Trusts were merged into The Jackson Foundation in 1981.
Donor: Maria C. Jackson‡.
Foundation type: Independent foundation.
Financial data (yr. ended 6/30/05): Assets, $13,152,484 (M); expenditures, $676,276; qualifying distributions, $583,587; giving activities include $506,700 for 124 grants (high: $16,000; low: $750).
Purpose and activities: Support for adult care counseling and training, education, children and youth programs, arts and humanities, medical issues, civic affairs and the environment, domestic violence, and food, fuel and shelter.
Fields of interest: Performing arts; Humanities; Arts; Education; Environment; Health care; Substance abuse, services; Health organizations, association; Housing/shelter, development; Human services; Children/youth, services; Aging, centers/services; Women, centers/services; Minorities/immigrants, centers/services; Aging; Disabilities, people with; Minorities; Women.
Type of support: Continuing support; Capital campaigns; Endowments; Research.
Limitations: Giving limited to OR. No support for churches or temples. No grants to individuals, or for matching gifts, scholarships, fellowships, or building or equipment funds for religious organizations; no loans to individuals.
Publications: Annual report.
Application information: Application form required.
    Initial approach: Request for application form
    Copies of proposal: 3
    Deadline(s): Mar. 31, June 30, Sept. 30, and Dec. 31
    Board meeting date(s): Jan., Apr., July, and Oct.
    Final notification: 4 to 6 weeks
Trustees: Milo E. Ormseth; Julie Vigeland; U.S. Bank, N.A.
Number of staff: 3 part-time professional.
EIN: 936020752
Selected grants: The following grants were reported in 2005.
$16,000 to Portland Center Stage, Portland, OR.
$12,000 to Oregon Childrens Foundation, Portland, OR.
$10,000 to Cascade AIDS Project, Portland, OR.
$10,000 to Marylhurst University, Marylhurst, OR.
$10,000 to Northwest Earth Institute, Portland, OR.
$8,000 to Providence Newberg Health Foundation, Newberg, OR.
$7,000 to Portland State University Foundation, Portland, OR.
$5,000 to Hearing and Speech Institute, Portland, OR.
$3,500 to Ecumenical Ministries of Oregon, Portland, OR.
$3,000 to High Desert Museum, Bend, OR.

8025

The Jeld-Wen Foundation ▼ ✧

(formerly Jeld-Wen, Wenco Foundation)
317 S.W. Alder St., Ste. 1100
Portland, OR 97204
Contact: Carol Chestnut
Application address: P.O. Box 1329, Klamath Falls, OR 97601, tel.: (541) 882-3451

Established in 1969.
Donors: Jeld-Wen, Inc.; Jeld-Wen Fiber Products, Inc. of Iowa; Jeld-Wen Co. of Arizona; Wenco, Inc. of North Carolina; Wenco, Inc. of Ohio; Jeld-Wen Holding, Inc.
Foundation type: Company-sponsored foundation.
Financial data (yr. ended 12/31/04): Assets, $52,062,236 (M); gifts received, $4,067,642; expenditures, $5,423,163; qualifying distributions, $5,143,341; giving activities include $5,143,341 for 278 grants (high: $500,000; low: $800).
Purpose and activities: The foundation supports organizations involved with arts and culture, education, health, youth development, human services, and economic development.
Fields of interest: Museums; Arts; Higher education; Education; Health care; Youth development; Children/youth, services; Human services; Economic development; Federated giving programs.
Type of support: General/operating support; Building/renovation; Equipment; Land acquisition; Program development; Seed money; Scholarship funds; Matching/challenge support.
Limitations: Giving primarily in areas of company operations in AZ, FL, IA, KY, NC, OR, SD, and WA. No grants to individuals, or for religious activities or programs that duplicate services provided by other government or private agencies; no loans.
Publications: Application guidelines; Program policy statement.
Application information: Telephone calls are not encouraged. Application form required.
  Initial approach: Contact foundation for application form
  Copies of proposal: 1
  Deadline(s): None
  Board meeting date(s): Generally, quarterly
  Final notification: 2 weeks following board meetings
Trustees: W.B. Early; R.F. Turner; Nancy Wendt; R.C. Wendt; R.L. Wendt.
EIN: 936054272
Selected grants: The following grants were reported in 2004.
$500,000 to Oregon Health and Science University, Portland, OR.
$350,000 to Oregon State University, Department of Wood Science, Corvallis, OR.
$200,000 to Grinnell Regional Medical Center, Grinnell, IA.
$191,836 to YMCA of Klamath County, Klamath Falls, OR.
$100,000 to Oregon Community Foundation, Portland, OR.
$83,000 to Lewis and Clark Bicentennial in Oregon, Portland, OR.
$50,000 to Friends of the Fair Foundation, Central Point, OR.
$50,000 to National Center for Policy Analysis, Dallas, TX.
$50,000 to YMCA of Mount Vernon, Mount Vernon, OH.
$13,600 to Oregon Tech Development Foundation, Klamath Falls, OR. For scholarship.

8026

B. P., Lester and Regina John Foundation ✧

(formerly B. P. John Foundation)
1000 S.W. Vista Ave., Ste. 116
Portland, OR 97205
Contact: Patricia J. Abraham, Pres.

Established in 1971.
Donors: Lester M. John†; Regina M. John.
Foundation type: Independent foundation.
Financial data (yr. ended 12/31/05): Assets, $20,071,567 (M); expenditures, $982,297; qualifying distributions, $935,409; giving activities include $924,265 for 68 grants.
Purpose and activities: Support for Roman Catholic missionary and international relief organizations, Catholic education, and for local church-sponsored and secular health and welfare agencies.
Fields of interest: Education; Health care; Human services; Christian agencies & churches; Roman Catholic agencies & churches; Homeless.
Type of support: Capital campaigns; Endowments; Scholarship funds.
Limitations: Applications not accepted. Giving primarily in Portland, OR. No grants to individuals.
Application information: Contributes only to pre-selected organizations.
  Board meeting date(s): Usually Oct.
Officers and Trustees:* Patricia J. Abraham,* Pres.; Mary Amstad, Secy.; Philip T. Abraham; Melissa Hartnell; Regina M. John.
Number of staff: 1 part-time support.
EIN: 237110263
Selected grants: The following grants were reported in 2004.
$90,000 to Central Catholic High School, Portland, OR.
$50,000 to Trillium Family Services, Portland, OR.
$49,000 to Providence Seaside Hospital, Seaside, OR.
$40,000 to All Saints School, Portland, OR.
$33,000 to Saint Andrew Nativity School, Portland, OR.
$15,000 to Catholic Charities, Portland, OR.
$15,000 to Our Lady of Lourdes School, Vancouver, WA.
$10,000 to Cathedral School, Portland, OR.
$10,000 to Macdonald Center, Portland, OR.
$7,000 to Union Gospel Mission, Portland, OR.

8027

The Samuel S. Johnson Foundation
P.O. Box 356
Redmond, OR 97756-0079 (541) 548-8104
Contact: Elizabeth Hill Johnson, Pres.
FAX: (541) 548-2014; E-mail: mary@tssjf.org

Incorporated in 1948 in CA.
Donors: Samuel S. Johnson†; Elizabeth Hill Johnson; Robert W. Hill†.
Foundation type: Independent foundation.
Financial data (yr. ended 5/31/05): Assets, $9,252,180 (M); expenditures, $461,200; qualifying distributions, $428,978; giving activities include $337,553 for 174 grants (high: $27,500; low: $100), $8,100 for 4 grants to individuals (high: $3,200; low: $1,400), $53,000 for 8 employee matching gifts, and $9,000 for 5 loans to individuals.
Purpose and activities: Giving for education, including adult literacy, mature and returning students, medical education benefiting non-urban

areas, excellence in teaching, music, and distance learning; medical programs, including projects benefiting rural areas, hospice and home health care, promotion of medical ethics and preventive care; domestic violence programs, including shelters and services to victims and families; youth development programs, including scouting, leadership, and reading programs; voluntarism and self-help; emergency food assistance; public safety/crime prevention, including drug and alcohol treatment and prevention programs emphasizing self-discipline; religious organizations, including outreach (but no giving to projects promoting sectarian views); humane societies, including programs for neutering, adoption, and those providing animal companions for elderly, blind and other handicapped people; and historical and museum projects. Support primarily for field of interest grants and emergency, nonrecurring grants primarily to nonprofits located in or benefiting residents of OR.
Fields of interest: Museums; Humanities; Historic preservation/historical societies; Education, early childhood education; Vocational education; Higher education; Dental school/education; Medical school/education; Nursing school/education; Adult education—literacy, basic skills & GED; Education, reading; Reproductive health, family planning; Nursing care; Substance abuse, services; Heart & circulatory diseases; Crime/violence prevention, domestic violence; Human services; Children/youth, services; Family services; Residential/custodial care, hospices; Aging, centers/services; Women, centers/services; Civil liberties, reproductive rights; Rural development; Voluntarism promotion; Science, public education; Leadership development; Religion; Disabilities, people with; Economically disadvantaged.
Type of support: General/operating support; Continuing support; Equipment; Emergency funds; Program development; Publication; Seed money; Scholarship funds; Matching/challenge support; Student loans—to individuals.
Limitations: Giving primarily in OR and southwest WA. No support for foreign organizations. No grants for annual campaigns, deficit financing, construction, sole underwriting of major proposals or projects, or endowments.
Publications: Application guidelines.
Application information: Application form not required.
  Initial approach: Letter
  Copies of proposal: 1
  Deadline(s): May 15 for July meeting, Nov. 15 for Jan. meeting
  Board meeting date(s): Feb. and July
  Final notification: 2 to 3 weeks after board meeting
Officers and Directors:* Elizabeth Hill Johnson,* Pres.; Elizabeth K. Johnson-Helm,* V.P.; Mary A. Krenowicz, Secy.-Treas.; Patricia C. Johnson,* C.F.O.; Karen K. Creason; John C. Helm.
Number of staff: 1 part-time professional.
EIN: 946062478
Selected grants: The following grants were reported in 2004.
$25,000 to Hospice of Redmond, Redmond, OR. For office expansion.
$20,000 to Childrens Cancer Association, Portland, OR. For Caring Cabin construction.
$15,000 to Community Action Team, Saint Helens, OR. For Saint Helens Family Resource Center.
$10,000 to High Desert Museum, Bend, OR. To match Lewis and Clark Bicentennial Grant.

$10,000 to Linfield College, McMinnville, OR. For President's Discretionary Fund.

$10,000 to Oregon Health and Science University, Center for Ethics in Health Care, Portland, OR. For Director's Chair Endowment.

$10,000 to Stop Oregon Litter and Vandalism, Hillsboro, OR. For Best of Oregon program.

$6,000 to Portland State University, Portland, OR. For Simon Benson Awards.

$3,000 to Oregon Food Bank, Portland, OR. For Retail Store Food Rescue Program.

$2,500 to Pacific University, Forest Grove, OR. For SS Johnson Award for Excellence in Teaching.

8028

Jubitz Family Foundation ◇

4380 S.W. MacAdam Ave., Ste. 210
Portland, OR 97201 (503) 274-6255
FAX: (503) 274-6256; URL: http://www.jubitzff.org

Established in 2001 in OR.
Donors: Jubitz Investments, LP; Saybrook, Inc.; M. Albin Jubitz, Jr.
Foundation type: Independent foundation.
Financial data (yr. ended 12/31/05): Assets, $11,509,875 (M); gifts received, $490,000; expenditures, $628,889; qualifying distributions, $576,412; giving activities include $504,130 for 60 grants (high: $70,000; low: $2,000).
Purpose and activities: The foundation supports projects and organizations that enhance the communities in which we live by strengthening families, by respecting the natural environment, and by fostering peace. Areas of interest include early childhood development and youth education, with an emphasis on children at-risk; environmental stewardship, with an emphasis on rivers and their watershed ecosystems; and peacemaking activities, with an emphasis on teaching peace and conflict resolution.
Fields of interest: Museums (children's); Elementary/secondary education; Higher education; Education; Environment, natural resources; Environment; Animals/wildlife, fisheries; Youth development; Human services; Children/youth, services; Family services.
Limitations: Giving primarily in OR.
Publications: Application guidelines; Grants list.
Application information: See foundation Web site for application guidelines and procedures, and application form. Application form required.
Initial approach: 1-page letter of request
Deadline(s): 1st week of April and Oct.
Officers: M. Albin Jubitz, Jr., Pres.; Elizabeth Jubitz Sayler, V.P.; Katherine H. Jubitz, Secy.; Sarah C. Jubitz, Treas.
EIN: 931324016
Selected grants: The following grants were reported in 2004.
$23,800 to Portland State University, Portland, OR.
$12,500 to Portland Schools Foundation, Portland, OR.
$10,000 to Childrens Museum.
$10,000 to Childrens Relief Nursery, Portland, OR.
$10,000 to Friends of the Columbia Gorge, Portland, OR.
$10,000 to Self Enhancement, Portland, OR.
$8,500 to Friends of the Children, Portland, OR.
$7,500 to Boys and Girls Clubs, Hammond, IN.
$5,000 to Audubon Society of Portland, Portland, OR.
$5,000 to Salvation Army.

8029

The Frederick D. & Gail Y. Jubitz Foundation ◇ ☆

33 N.E. Middlefield Rd.
Portland, OR 97211
Application address: c/o BKR Fordham Goodfellow, LLP, 233 S.E. 2nd Ave., Hillsboro, OR 97123

Established in 2001 in OR.
Donors: Fred Jubitz; Gail Jubitz.
Foundation type: Independent foundation.
Financial data (yr. ended 12/31/05): Assets, $3,778,354 (M); gifts received, $399,000; expenditures, $341,517; qualifying distributions, $317,502; giving activities include $317,502 for 10 grants (high: $155,000; low: $2).
Fields of interest: Museums (art); Museums (children's); Secondary school/education; Higher education; Food banks; Human services; Religion.
Limitations: Giving primarily in OR.
Application information:
Initial approach: Letter
Deadline(s): None
Officers: Fred Jubitz, Pres. and Treas.; Gail Jubitz, Secy.
Director: Matthew Jubitz.
EIN: 931326797

8030

Lora L. & Martin N. Kelley Family Foundation Trust

P.O. Box 23503
Eugene, OR 97402

Established in 1990 in OR.
Donors: Martin N. Kelley; Lora L. Kelley‡.
Foundation type: Independent foundation.
Financial data (yr. ended 12/31/04): Assets, $17,433,226 (M); expenditures, $795,847; qualifying distributions, $590,778; giving activities include $549,245 for 32 grants (high: $125,000; low: $900).
Purpose and activities: Giving primarily for the performing arts, education, federated giving programs, the environment and human services.
Fields of interest: Performing arts; Arts; Libraries (public); Education; Environment; Aquariums; Human services; Children, services; Federated giving programs.
Limitations: Applications not accepted. Giving primarily in MT and OR. No grants to individuals.
Application information: Contributes only to pre-selected organizations.
Officers and Trustees:* Bruce R. Kelley,* Vice-Chair.; Kent R. Kelley, Secy.; Craig C. Kelley; Karen D. Kelley; Mark Kelley; Martin N. Kelley; Stephen S. Kelley.
EIN: 476174269

8031

Kinsman Foundation

3727 S.E. Spaulding Ave.
Milwaukie, OR 97267-3938 (503) 654-1668
Contact: Keith Kinsman, C.E.O.
FAX: (503) 654-1759;
E-mail: grants@kinsmanfoundation.org

Established in 1983 in OR.
Donors: Elizabeth T. Kinsman‡; John W. Kinsman‡; Mary S. Mitchell.
Foundation type: Independent foundation.

Financial data (yr. ended 12/31/05): Assets, $32,236,694 (M); gifts received, $850; expenditures, $1,667,111; qualifying distributions, $1,227,353; giving activities include $1,110,149 for 60 grants.
Purpose and activities: Giving for historic preservation, native wildlife rehabilitation and wildlife appreciation, healthcare policy, and arts, culture and the humanities.
Fields of interest: Humanities; Historical activities; Historic preservation/historical societies; Arts; Animals/wildlife; Health care, public policy.
Type of support: General/operating support; Continuing support; Income development; Management development/capacity building; Annual campaigns; Capital campaigns; Building/ renovation; Equipment; Land acquisition; Endowments; Debt reduction; Emergency funds; Program development; Conferences/seminars; Publication; Seed money; Curriculum development; Internship funds; Research; Technical assistance; Consulting services; Program evaluation; Matching/ challenge support.
Limitations: Giving primarily in OR and southern WA. No grants to individuals, or for scholarships.
Publications: Annual report (including application guidelines); Grants list.
Application information: Statement of policies and programs available in foundation's annual report. Application form not required.
Initial approach: Letter of inquiry, including basic information
Copies of proposal: 1
Deadline(s): Aug. 1 for larger grants; no deadline for small grants (under $10,000)
Board meeting date(s): Sept.
Final notification: 7 days to acknowledge receipt; 1-6 weeks for substantive response
Officers and Directors:* Keith Kinsman,* C.E.O. and Pres.; Pamela Reynolds,* V.P., C.F.O. and Treas.; Jack Schwab,* Secy.; Paige Kinsman.
Number of staff: 3 full-time professional.
EIN: 930861885
Selected grants: The following grants were reported in 2004.
$100,000 to Confluences, Vancouver, WA. For creation of artwork by Maya Lin.
$25,000 to Center for Ethics in Health Care, Portland, OR. For program to improve cooperation among Oregon hospitals, nursing homes, and similar facilities.
$25,000 to Columbia River Maritime Museum, Astoria, OR. For Lightship Columbia Restoration.
$25,000 to Mission Mill Museum Association, Salem, OR. For Bell Tower repair and restoration.
$16,500 to American Wildlife Foundation, Molalla, OR. For animal care and facility construction.
$15,000 to Saint Patrick Catholic Church, Independence, OR. For stained glass window restoration.
$10,000 to Wahkiakum County Historical Society, Cathlamet, WA. For Deep River church roof replacement.
$7,000 to Wildlife Rehab Center of the North Coast, Astoria, OR.
$5,000 to Chintimini Wildlife Rehabilitation Center, Portland, OR. For animal food and supplies.
$1,400 to Gilliam County Historical Society, Condon, OR. For cleaning, painting Condon old City Hall and Jail.

8032

Knight Foundation ✧

John McEnroe Bldg.
1 Bowerman Dr.
Beaverton, OR   97005   (503) 671-3500

Established in 1997 in OR.

Donor: Philip H. Knight.

Foundation type: Independent foundation.

Financial data (yr. ended 12/31/05): Assets, $87,061,856 (M); gifts received, $3,500,000; expenditures, $4,917,530; qualifying distributions, $4,902,366; giving activities include $4,900,000 for 4 grants (high: $2,500,000; low: $100,000).

Purpose and activities: Giving primarily for higher and other education, including a graduate school of business.

Fields of interest: Graduate/professional education; Business school/education; Education.

Limitations: Applications not accepted. Giving primarily in Stanford, CA, and OR. No grants to individuals.

Application information: Contributes only to pre-selected organizations.

Officers and Directors:* Philip H. Knight, Pres. and Treas.; Terry Pancoast, V.P. and Secy.; Penelope P. Knight,* V.P.; Travis A. Knight.

EIN: 911791788

Selected grants: The following grants were reported in 2005.

$2,500,000 to Stanford University, Graduate School of Business, Stanford, CA.

$2,000,000 to Oregon Health and Science University Foundation, Portland, OR.

$300,000 to Jesuit High School, Portland, OR.

$100,000 to Stanford University Foundation, Stanford, CA.

8033

Dale Krueger Scholarship ✧

c/o U.S. Bank, N.A.
P.O. Box 3168, Trust Tax Svcs.
Portland, OR   97208   (503) 275-5923
Contact: Jennie Peabody, Trust Account Exec.
FAX: (503) 275-4177;
E-mail: caitlinokeefe@usbank.com; Application address: U.S. Bank, P.O. Box 3168, Charitable Svcs. Group, Portland, OR 97208-3168; e-mail: teresa.ingram@usbank.com; Additional telephones: (503) 275 4400, toll-free tel.: (800) 522 9100; URL: http://www.dalekruegerscholarship.com

Established in 1999 in OR.

Donor: Dale W. Krueger‡.

Foundation type: Independent foundation.

Financial data (yr. ended 7/31/05): Assets, $11,929,869 (M); expenditures, $823,076; qualifying distributions, $618,284; giving activities include $596,002 for 80 grants (high: $98,332; low: $1,000).

Purpose and activities: The foundation awards scholarships to graduates of public high schools located in Gresham-Barlow, Reynolds and Centennial school districts in OR, who at the time of receiving their diploma, are residents of these school districts. Applicants must be graduating seniors, or previous graduates under the age of 21, and must attend a full-time program at an accredited college, university, or trade school.

Fields of interest: Education.

Limitations: Giving primarily in OR.

Application information: Application form available on foundation Web site. Application form required.

Copies of proposal: 1
Deadline(s): Apr. 1
Final notification: May

Trustee: U.S. Bank, N.A.

EIN: 936331222

Selected grants: The following grants were reported in 2005.

$98,332 to Oregon State University, Corvallis, OR.

$82,001 to University of Oregon, Eugene, OR.

$49,002 to Portland State University, Portland, OR.

$36,000 to University of Portland, Portland, OR.

$19,334 to Western Oregon University, Monmouth, OR.

$16,000 to Brigham Young University, Provo, UT.

$12,000 to George Fox University, Newberg, OR.

$10,000 to Willamette University, Salem, OR.

$8,000 to Concordia University, Portland, OR.

$2,000 to Boise State University, Boise, ID.

8034

Marie Lamfrom Charitable Foundation

6600 N. Baltimore Ave.
Portland, OR   97203

Established in 1998 in OR.

Donor: Gertrude Boyle.

Foundation type: Independent foundation.

Financial data (yr. ended 12/31/05): Assets, $6,214,321 (M); gifts received, $1,178,450; expenditures, $941,349; qualifying distributions, $884,834; giving activities include $877,240 for 40 grants (high: $359,000; low: $5,000).

Fields of interest: Education; Hospitals (general); Children/youth, services.

Type of support: General/operating support.

Limitations: Applications not accepted. Giving primarily in OR. No grants to individuals.

Application information: Contributes only to pre-selected organizations.

Trustees: David C. Bany; Sarah A. Bany.

EIN: 931254171

8035

The Lazar Foundation

715 S.W. Morrison St., Ste. 901
Portland, OR   97205-3105   (503) 225-0265
Contact: Irene Vlach
FAX: (503) 225-9620;
E-mail: info@lazarfoundation.org; URL: http://www.lazarfoundation.org

Incorporated in 1956 in DE.

Donors: Jack Lazar‡; Helen B. Lazar‡.

Foundation type: Independent foundation.

Financial data (yr. ended 12/31/04): Assets, $22,542,249 (M); gifts received, $1,000,404; expenditures, $1,728,046; qualifying distributions, $1,085,718; giving activities include $1,085,718 for grants.

Purpose and activities: The foundation focuses on preservation of biological diversity and ecosystems; broadening the environmental movement, and message development.

Fields of interest: Environment.

International interests: Canada.

Type of support: General/operating support; Program development; Seed money.

Limitations: Giving primarily in AK, ID, western MT, OR, and WA in the U.S., and British Columbia in Canada. No support for environmental education, or civic projects. No grants to individuals, or for

endowments, land acquisition, film or video projects, capital campaigns or for computer-related expenses.

Application information: Application form and guidelines available on foundation Web site. Full proposal is upon invitation only. Application form required.

Initial approach: Letter (no more than 2 pages)
Copies of proposal: 1
Deadline(s): Feb. 15, June 15, and Oct. 30
Board meeting date(s): Mar., July, and Nov.

Officers and Trustees:* William B. Lazar,* Pres. and Treas.; Jeanne L. Morency,* Secy.; Michael Morency.

Number of staff: 1 part-time professional; 1 part-time support.

EIN: 136088182

Selected grants: The following grants were reported in 2003.

$50,000 to Southern Environmental Law Center, Charlottesville, VA.

$40,000 to Piedmont Environmental Council, Warrenton, VA.

$25,000 to Wilderness Society, DC.

$20,000 to Alaska Conservation Foundation, Anchorage, AK.

$15,000 to Alaska Wilderness League, DC.

$15,000 to Oregon Natural Desert Association, Bend, OR.

$12,000 to American Rivers, DC.

$10,000 to Conservation Geography, Boise, ID.

$10,000 to Windy Hill Foundation, Middleburg, VA.

$10,000 to World Wildlife Fund, DC.

8036

The E. L. & B. G. Lightfoot Foundation

c/o U.S. Bank, N.A.
P.O. Box 3168
Portland, OR   97208-3168
Contact: Michael W. Sullivan
Application address: P.O. Box 886 Meridian, ID 83642

Established in 1992 in ID.

Donor: Elma Lightfoot Newgen.

Foundation type: Independent foundation.

Financial data (yr. ended 2/28/05): Assets, $21,004,739 (M); gifts received, $6,851,481; expenditures, $982,095; qualifying distributions, $793,528; giving activities include $713,799 for 47 grants (high: $168,383; low: $1,000), and $59,593 for 52 grants to individuals (high: $6,000; low: $93).

Purpose and activities: Giving for education, housing or environmental purposes.

Fields of interest: Education; Environment, natural resources; Housing/shelter; Human services.

Type of support: Grants to individuals.

Limitations: Giving limited to southern ID and eastern OR.

Application information: Application form required.

Initial approach: Letter
Deadline(s): None

Charitable Committee: Elma Lightfoot Newgen, Chair.; Maureen L. Howe; Kathleen D. Mayhew; Sydney L. Mitchell.

Trustee: U.S. Bank, N.A.

EIN: 820454166

8037
Louisiana-Pacific Foundation ✧ ☆
805 S.W. Broadway
Portland, OR 97205 (503) 221-5100
Contact: Mary Jo Kaufman
Application address: c/o Mary Louise Cohn,
Louisiana-Pacific Fdn., 414 Union St., Ste. 2000,
Nashville, TN 37219, tel.: (615) 986-5886

Established in 1973 in OR.
Donor: Louisiana-Pacific Corp.
Foundation type: Company-sponsored foundation.
Financial data (yr. ended 12/31/05): Assets,
$2,367,353 (M); expenditures, $605,257;
qualifying distributions, $604,519; giving activities
include $604,519 for 23 grants (high: $200,000;
low: $414).
Purpose and activities: The foundation supports
organizations involved with education, the
environment, housing, and other areas.
Fields of interest: Education; Environment;
Housing/shelter; General charitable giving.
Type of support: Program development; General/
operating support.
Limitations: Giving primarily in areas of company
operations.
Publications: Application guidelines.
Application information: Application form not
required.
Initial approach: Proposal
Copies of proposal: 1
Board meeting date(s): Quarterly
Officers and Trustees: Mary Louise Cohn,* Chair.
and Pres.; F. Jeff Duncan, Jr.,* V.P.; Nancy A.
Schirmers, Secy.; Russell S. Pattee, Treas.; Russell
L. Carroll; David J. Harvey.
EIN: 237268660
Selected grants: The following grants were reported
in 2004.
$200,000 to Nature Conservancy, Portland, OR.
$150,000 to Portland Art Museum, Portland, OR.
$36,069 to United Way of Wilkes County, North
   Wilkesboro, NC.
$11,654 to Americas Charities, Chantilly, VA.
$10,000 to Izaak Walton League of America,
   Gaithersburg, MD.
$4,913 to United Way of Northeastern Minnesota,
   Chisholm, MN.
$2,430 to United Way of Greater Toledo, Toledo,
   OH.
$1,897 to United Way of Northeast Michigan,
   Alpena, MI.
$1,850 to United Way of Elkhart County, Elkhart, IN.
$520 to United Way of Central Carolinas, Charlotte,
   NC.

8038
Maybelle Clark Macdonald Fund ▼ ✧
5200 S.W. Macadam Ave., Ste. 470
Portland, OR 97239-3836
E-mail: information@mcmfund.org; *URL:* http://
www.mcmfund.org

Established in 1970 in OR.
Donor: Maybelle Clark Macdonald.
Foundation type: Independent foundation.
Financial data (yr. ended 6/30/06): Assets,
$141,247,646 (M); expenditures, $8,681,511;
qualifying distributions, $7,920,793; giving
activities include $7,920,793 for 129 grants (high:
$550,150; low: $500; average: $1,000–
$100,000).

Purpose and activities: Funding primarily for human
services, education, public benefit, medicine and
arts and culture.
Fields of interest: Arts; Elementary/secondary
education; Health care; Medical research; Human
services; Aging, centers/services.
Type of support: General/operating support; Annual
campaigns; Capital campaigns; Building/
renovation; Endowments; Internship funds;
Scholarship funds; Matching/challenge support.
Limitations: Applications not accepted. Giving
primarily in OR. No grants to individuals.
Application information: Contributes only to
pre-selected organizations.
Officers and Directors: Maybelle Clark
Macdonald,* Chair.; Clark C. Munro, Sr.,* Pres.;
Janeen McAninch,* Secy.-Treas.; Christopher A.
Folkestad,* Exec. Dir.; Gary R. Branden; Gene
D'Autremont; Monique M. McCleary; Conrad L.
Moore; Christopher R. Munro; Clark C. Munro, Jr.;
Maurie M. Munro; Warner R. Munro.
Number of staff: 1 part-time professional; 1 full-time
support; 1 part-time support.
EIN: 237108002
Selected grants: The following grants were reported
in 2005.
$790,000 to Faith Enhanced Development
   Enterprises (FEDE), Portland, OR.
$300,000 to Providence Saint Vincent Medical
   Foundation, Portland, OR.
$278,000 to University of Portland, Portland, OR.
$184,332 to Portland Art Museum, Portland, OR.
$175,000 to Central Catholic High School, Portland,
   OR.
$161,500 to Portland State University Foundation,
   Portland, OR.
$160,063 to Loaves and Fishes Centers, Portland,
   OR.
$160,000 to Oregon Historical Society, Portland,
   OR.
$154,000 to Saint Andrew Nativity School, Portland,
   OR.
$150,000 to YWCA of Greater Portland, Portland,
   OR.

8039
Mentor Graphics Foundation ✧
8005 S.W. Boeckman Rd.
Wilsonville, OR 97070 (503) 685-7000
Contact: Sharron Rotty, Pres.
URL: http://www.mentor.com/company/
foundation/index.cfm

Established in 1985 in OR.
Donor: Mentor Graphics Corp.
Foundation type: Company-sponsored foundation.
Financial data (yr. ended 12/31/05): Assets, $0
(M); gifts received, $430,000; expenditures,
$468,299; qualifying distributions, $468,048;
giving activities include $468,048 for 311 grants
(high: $100,779).
Purpose and activities: The foundation supports
organizations involved with arts and culture,
education, health, disaster relief, and human
services.
Fields of interest: Visual arts; Museums; Performing
arts; Arts; Elementary/secondary education;
Education; Health care; Disasters, preparedness/
services; Human services; Science, formal/general
education; Mathematics; Engineering/technology.
Type of support: General/operating support;
Program development; Employee matching gifts.

Limitations: Giving primarily in areas of major
company operations. No support for religious or
animal rights organizations. No grants to individuals,
or for environmental causes, capital campaigns,
building, political campaigns or ballots,
sponsorships of dinners or social events, or
fundraisers.
Publications: Application guidelines; Program policy
statement.
Application information: Application form required.
Initial approach: Download application form and
   mail to foundation
Deadline(s): 3 weeks prior to board meetings
Board meeting date(s): Bimonthly
Officers and Directors: Sharon Rotty,* Pres.; Dean
Freed, Secy.; Twia Bennett; Jim Bores; Diane
Cain-Pozzo; John Issac; Ginney McKee; Debbie
Otterstetter; John Stedman.
EIN: 930870309

8040
Merrill Family Foundation, Inc. ✧
17952 S.W. Parrish Ln.
Sherwood, OR 97140
Application address: c/o Charles W. Merrill, 17980
Kemmer Rd., Beaverton, OR 97007, tel.: (503)
591-5256

Established in 1995 in OR.
Donors: Lenore Merrill; Charles Merrill‡; Kay Merrill.
Foundation type: Independent foundation.
Financial data (yr. ended 12/31/05): Assets,
$10,249,590 (M); gifts received, $5,600;
expenditures, $580,971; qualifying distributions,
$517,258; giving activities include $517,258 for 33
grants (high: $92,000; low: $100).
Purpose and activities: Giving primarily for religious
organizations and scholarships, and a local
historical society.
Fields of interest: Historic preservation/historical
societies; Higher education; Hospitals (general);
Christian agencies & churches.
Type of support: Scholarship funds; Scholarships—
to individuals.
Limitations: Giving primarily in OR.
Application information:
Initial approach: Letter
Deadline(s): None
Officers: Charles Merrill, Pres.; Kay Merrill,
Secy.-Treas.
Directors: Anthony C. Merrill; Lisa K. Sickler.
EIN: 931191941

8041
The Fred Meyer Foundation
(formerly Fred Meyer/Smith Foundation)
3800 S.E. 22nd Ave.
Portland, OR 97202 (503) 797-5605
Contact: Glynda Brockhoff, Coord., Philanthropy
E-mail: foundation@fredmeyer.com; *Additional tel.:*
(800) 858-9202, ext. 5605; *URL:* http://
www.thekrogerco.com/corpnews/
corpnewsinfo_charitablegiving_fredmeyer.htm

Established in 1997 in OR.
Donors: Ronald W. Burkle; Fred Meyer Stores, Inc.
Foundation type: Company-sponsored foundation.
Financial data (yr. ended 2/28/05): Assets,
$3,152,069 (M); gifts received, $1,239,052;
expenditures, $1,230,499; qualifying distributions,

$1,204,747; giving activities include $1,176,930 for 400 grants (high: $50,000; low: $500).

Purpose and activities: The foundation supports organizations involved with hunger and youth development.

Fields of interest: Food services; Youth development.

Type of support: General/operating support; Program development.

Limitations: Applications not accepted. Giving limited to areas of company operations in AK, ID, OR, and WA. No support for national organizations, lobbying organizations, or religious organizations. No grants to individuals, or for capital campaigns, endowments, or conferences.

Publications: Grants list.

Application information: The foundation utilizes an invitation only Request For Proposal (RFP) process. Unsolicited requests are not accepted.

Officers and Directors:* Lynn Marmer,* Pres.; Paul Heldman,* Secy.; Scot Henderson,* Treas.; David Deatherage.

Number of staff: 1 part-time professional; 1 part-time support.

EIN: 931231880

8042
Meyer Memorial Trust ▼

(formerly Fred Meyer Charitable Trust)
425 N.W. 10th Ave., Ste. 400
Portland, OR 97209 (503) 228-5512
Contact: Doug Stamm, Exec. Dir.
E-mail: mmt@mmt.org; URL: http://www.mmt.org

Trust established by will in 1978; obtained IRS status in 1982 in OR.

Donor: Fred G. Meyer†.

Foundation type: Independent foundation.

Financial data (yr. ended 3/31/05): Assets, $528,396,074 (M); expenditures, $29,237,605; qualifying distributions, $27,838,325; giving activities include $24,001,011 for 300 grants (high: $1,110,812; average: $10,000–$100,000), $71,185 for employee matching gifts, and $1,200,000 for 2 loans/program-related investments (high: $700,000; low: $500,000).

Purpose and activities: To invest in people, ideas and efforts that deliver significant social benefit to Oregon and Southwestern WA.

Fields of interest: Museums; Performing arts; Humanities; Historic preservation/historical societies; Arts; Child development, education; Higher education; Education; Environment, natural resources; Environment; Health care; Crime/violence prevention, youth; Housing/shelter, development; Human services; Children/youth, services; Child development, services; Family services; Aging, centers/services; Community development; Aging.

Type of support: Management development/capacity building; General/operating support; Income development; Capital campaigns; Building/renovation; Equipment; Program development; Seed money; Technical assistance; Program-related investments/loans; Employee matching gifts; Matching/challenge support.

Limitations: Giving primarily in OR and Clark County, WA. No support for sectarian or religious organizations for religious purposes. No grants to individuals or for endowment funds, annual campaigns, deficit financing, scholarships, fellowships, or indirect or overhead costs, except as

specifically and essentially related to the grant project.

Publications: Application guidelines; Financial statement.

Application information: All programs accept proposals through an online application only available via the trust's Web site. Special guidelines for Small Grants Program and Support for Teacher Initiatives Program and Program-Related Investment Loans. Application guidelines available on the foundation's Web site. Application form required.

Initial approach: Letter of inquiry
Copies of proposal: 1
Deadline(s): Sept. 1, Feb. 1 and Apr. 1for initial letter of inquiry
Board meeting date(s): Monthly
Final notification: 3 to 5 months for General Purpose proposals that pass first screening; 1 to 2 months for those that do not; 12 to 16 weeks for Small Grants; 12 weeks for Support for Teacher Initiatives

Officers and Trustees:* Gerry Pratt,* Chair.; Wayne G. Pierson, C.F.O. and Treas.; Terry DeBruyne, Compt.; Doug Stamm, Exec. Dir.; Warne Nunn, Tr. Emeritus; Debbie F. Craig; John Emrick; Orcilla Z. Forbes; George J. Puentes.

Number of staff: 14

EIN: 930806316

8043
James E. & Lila G. Miller Charitable Trust ◇ ☆

1805 N.W. Glisan St.
Portland, OR 97209 (503) 295-0580
Contact: Ted M. Miller, Dir.

Established in 1985 in OR.

Donors: James E. Miller; Lila G. Miller.

Foundation type: Independent foundation.

Financial data (yr. ended 5/31/05): Assets, $6,866,173 (M); gifts received, $852,000; expenditures, $443,383; qualifying distributions, $353,437; giving activities include $357,500 for 11 grants (high: $295,000; low: $1,000).

Purpose and activities: Giving primarily for higher education and Christian organizations.

Fields of interest: Higher education; Human services; Salvation Army; Christian agencies & churches.

Type of support: General/operating support; Building/renovation; Scholarship funds.

Limitations: Giving limited to OR and the portion of southwestern WA that is included in the Portland, OR, metropolitan area. No grants to individuals.

Application information:

Initial approach: Proposal
Deadline(s): None
Final notification: Within 2 months

Director: Ted Miller.

Trustees: James E. Miller; Lila G. Miller.

EIN: 936174460

Selected grants: The following grants were reported in 2005.

$25,000 to White Shield Center, Portland, OR.

$5,000 to March of Dimes Birth Defects Foundation, White Plains, NY.

$4,000 to Oregon Independent College Foundation, Portland, OR.

$1,500 to Faith in Practice, Houston, TX.

$1,000 to Mercy Corps, Portland, OR.

8044
Phillip S. Miller Charitable Trust

c/o U.S. Bank, N.A., Tax Svcs.
P.O. Box 3168
Portland, OR 97208-3168
Contact: Deborah J. Smith

Established in 1995 in CO.

Donor: Phillip S. Miller†.

Foundation type: Independent foundation.

Financial data (yr. ended 12/31/05): Assets, $35,764,882 (M); expenditures, $2,309,399; qualifying distributions, $2,119,285; giving activities include $2,100,000 for 8 grants (high: $420,000; low: $42,000).

Purpose and activities: Support primarily for education and hospitals.

Fields of interest: Education; Hospitals (general); Community development.

Limitations: Applications not accepted. Giving limited to CO. No grants to individuals.

Application information: Contributes only to pre-selected organizations. Unsolicited requests not considered.

Trustee: U.S. Bank, N.A.

Number of staff: 9 full-time professional.

EIN: 846290472

Selected grants: The following grants were reported in 2003.

$550,000 to Castle Rock, Town of, Castle Rock, CO. For general support.

$500,000 to Childrens Hospital Foundation, Denver, CO. For general support.

$500,000 to Douglas, County of, Castle Rock, CO. For general support.

$500,000 to Shriners Hospitals for Children, Tampa, FL. For general support.

$250,000 to Douglas County Library, Castle Rock, CO. For general support.

$100,000 to Douglas County High School, Castle Rock, CO. For general support.

$50,000 to Douglas County 4-H Council, Castle Rock, CO. For general support.

$50,000 to Douglas County Fair Association, Castle Rock, CO. For general support.

8045
James F. & Marion L. Miller Foundation ▼ ◇

P.O. Box 8585
Portland, OR 97207
E-mail: info@millerfnd.org; URL: http://www.millerfnd.org

Established in 2002 in OR.

Donor: James F. Miller.

Foundation type: Independent foundation.

Financial data (yr. ended 12/31/05): Assets, $76,277,790 (M); expenditures, $10,924,911; qualifying distributions, $10,289,778; giving activities include $10,248,667 for 66 grants (high: $2,400,000; low: $1,500; average: $10,000–$400,000).

Purpose and activities: Giving to enhance the quality of life of Oregonians through support of the arts and education.

Fields of interest: Arts; Education; Crime/violence prevention, child abuse; Children/youth, services.

Limitations: Giving primarily in OR. Generally no support for propagandizing or influencing elections or legislation or projects of religious organizations that principally benefit their own members. Generally no grants to individuals, or for

endowments, general fund drives, annual appeals, debt retirement, operation deficits, or emergency needs.
Application information: Proposals are not accepted via e-mail. Application form is available on foundation's Web site. Application form required.
Initial approach: Proposal (no more than 5 pages)
Copies of proposal: 5
Deadline(s): None
Final notification: 6 months
Officer: Suzanna McKirdie, Secy.
Directors: William K. Blount; Alice McCartor; Charles H. Putney.
EIN: 030373895
Selected grants: The following grants were reported in 2005.
$2,400,000 to Oregon Symphony Association, Portland, OR. For general support.
$2,000,000 to Lewis and Clark College, Portland, OR. For James F. Miller Scholarship and Grant Programs.
$1,000,000 to Portland State University Foundation, Portland, OR. For scholarships and for music program.
$650,000 to Pacific University, Forest Grove, OR. For new university library and residence hall.
$500,000 to Portland Art Museum, Portland, OR. For North Wing renovation.
$500,000 to Portland Opera, Portland, OR. For leadership challenge grant.
$400,000 to Oregon Public Broadcasting, Portland, OR. For arts and education programming.
$250,000 to George Fox University, Newberg, OR. For baccalaureate nursing degree program.
$50,000 to Pacific Northwest College of Art, Portland, OR. For alumni relations program - 20/20 Campaign.
$30,000 to YMCA of Columbia-Willamette, Portland, OR. For ceramics and digital graphic arts programs.

8046
NIKE Foundation ▼ ✧
(formerly NIKE P.L.A.Y. Foundation)
1 Bowerman Dr.
Beaverton, OR   97005-6453   (888) 448-6453
E-mail: nike.foundation@nike.com; URL: http://www.nike.com/nikebiz/nikefoundation/home.jhtml

Established in 1994 in OR.
Donors: NIKE, Inc.; Michael Jordan.
Foundation type: Company-sponsored foundation.
Financial data (yr. ended 5/31/05): Assets, $24,369,952 (M); gifts received, $6,905,633; expenditures, $5,830,532; qualifying distributions, $5,829,218; giving activities include $5,218,500 for 23 grants (high: $2,200,000; low: $5,000).
Purpose and activities: The foundation supports programs designed to empower and ensure the well-being of adolescent girls in the developing world.
Fields of interest: Elementary/secondary education; Reproductive health; Public health; Health care; Crime/violence prevention; Employment, training; Employment; Youth development, business; Civil rights, alliance; Civil rights; Social entrepreneurship; Community development, small businesses; Leadership development; Girls.
International interests: Bangladesh; Brazil; China; Developing countries; Ethiopia; Zambia.
Type of support: General/operating support; Program development.

Limitations: Applications not accepted. Giving on an international basis, with emphasis on Bangladesh, Brazil, China, Ethiopia, and Zambia; giving also to national organizations. No support for discriminatory organizations. No grants to individuals, or for general operating support for established programs, research or travel, films, television, or radio programs not an integral part of a project, religious programs, endowments or fundraising campaigns, lobbying or political activities, or depreciation or debt reduction.
Application information: Contributes only to pre-selected organizations.
Officers and Directors: Maria Eitel, Pres.; Marcia Stewart, Treas.; Charlie Denson; Philip Knight; Mark Parker; Kirk Stewart; Lindsay D. Stewart.
Executive Team: Jennifer Barsky, Dir., Progs. and Initiatives; Emily Brew, Dir., Social Mtkg.; Lisa MacCallum, Dir., Business Innovation.
EIN: 931159948
Selected grants: The following grants were reported in 2005.
$4,400,000 to Better World Fund, DC. 2 grants: $2,200,000 each (For project, UNF Fund for Adolescent Girls).
$1,000,000 to Charities Aid Foundation (CAF) America, Alexandria, VA. For donor-advised fund.
$300,000 to International Bank for Reconstruction and Development, DC.
$300,000 to International Center for Research on Women, DC. For developing a measurement framework, providing strategic input on and measuring the effectiveness of initiatives aimed at empowering girls in specifically targeted developing countries.
$200,000 to Campaign for Female Education (CAMFED) USA Foundation, San Francisco, CA. To expand educational, economic, and advocacy opportunities to young women living in poverty in rural Africa; and for exchange and understanding between the Nike, Inc. community and young women in Zambia.
$200,000 to JSI Research and Training Institute, Boston, MA. To provide training and support for young women and young men from low-income communities in Rio de Janeiro to develop and carry out a lifestyle social marketing campaign, and a variety of complementary activities, on issues related to gender, sexual and reproductive health, and young women's empowerment in personal and intimate relationships.
$200,000 to Program for Appropriate Technology in Health (PATH), Seattle, WA. To develop and pilot girls' educational and developmental model in selected schools and communities in Guangxi Zhuang Autonomous Region, increase girls' awareness of gender equity, knowledge of reproductive health and self-protection, and life-planning skills in pilot schools, build capacity of local and regional women's federations to develop, implement, and manage a girls' empowerment program.
$125,000 to International Federation of Red Cross and Red Crescent Societies at the UN, New York, NY. For tsunami relief.
$125,000 to Mercy Corps, Portland, OR. For tsunami relief.

8047
Northwest Autism Foundation ✧ ☆
519 15th St.
Oregon City, OR   97045

Established in 1998 in OR.
Donors: Gleason Eakin; Wayne Hamersly.
Foundation type: Operating foundation.
Financial data (yr. ended 12/31/05): Assets, $0 (M); gifts received, $366,529; expenditures, $417,258; qualifying distributions, $365,782; giving activities include $365,782 for grants.
Purpose and activities: Giving primarily to Autism Treatment Network, Lake Oswego, OR, and Massachusetts General Hospital, Boston.
Fields of interest: Autism research.
Limitations: Applications not accepted. Giving primarily in OR and MA. No grants to individuals.
Application information: Contributes only to pre-selected organizations.
Officer: Gleason Eakin, Chair.
Directors: Lynn Hamersly; Wayne Hamersly; Joanne Hazel; David Humphrey; Mary Lynn O'Brien, M.D.
EIN: 931234288

8048
Northwest Health Foundation Fund, II ✧ ☆
1500 S.W. 1st Ave., Ste. 850
Portland, OR   97201

Established in 2000 in OR.
Donor: Kaiser Foundation Health Plan of the Northwest.
Foundation type: Independent foundation.
Financial data (yr. ended 12/31/05): Assets, $28,506,893 (M); gifts received, $81,234; expenditures, $3,608,473; qualifying distributions, $3,465,526; giving activities include $3,060,134 for 15 grants (high: $975,654; low: $10,000).
Fields of interest: Health care; Immigrants/refugees.
Limitations: Applications not accepted. Giving primarily in OR and WA. No grants to individuals.
Application information: Contributes only to pre-selected organizations.
Officers: Mark O. Hatfield, Chair.; Leslie M. Hallick, Vice-Chair.; Thomas D. Aschenbrener, Pres.; M. David Hooff, V.P.; Paul Krissel, Secy.; Richard M. Page, Treas.
Directors: Curtis Bender; Tina Castanares, M.D.; Jacquelyn Gaines; Merwyn R. Greenlick, Ph.D.; James A. Hill, Jr.; and 6 additional directors.
EIN: 931293344

8049
The Oregon Community Foundation ▼ ✧
1221 S.W. Yamhill, Ste. 100
Portland, OR   97205   (503) 227-6846
Contact: Gregory A. Chaille, Pres.; For scholarships: Dianne Causey, Prog. Assoc.
FAX: (503) 274-7771; E-mail: info@ocf1.org;
URL: http://www.ocf1.org

Established in 1973 in OR.
Donors: Richard Reiten; Jon Englund.
Foundation type: Community foundation.
Financial data (yr. ended 12/31/05): Assets, $850,034,138 (M); gifts received, $74,255,623; expenditures, $47,381,948; giving activities include $40,478,757 for grants.
Purpose and activities: The foundation seeks to meet educational, cultural, medical, social and civic needs in all areas and at all levels of society throughout the state of Oregon.
Fields of interest: Arts; Adult education—literacy, basic skills & GED; Education, reading; Education;

Health care; Health organizations, association; Youth development, services; Children/youth, services; Family services; Aging, centers/services; Human services; Community development; Voluntarism promotion; Government/public administration; Leadership development; Aging; Economically disadvantaged.

Type of support: Fellowships; General/operating support; Capital campaigns; Building/renovation; Equipment; Land acquisition; Program development; Seed money; Scholarship funds; Technical assistance; Scholarships—to individuals; Matching/challenge support.

Limitations: Giving limited to OR. No support for religious organizations for religious purposes or projects in individual schools. No grants to individuals (except for scholarships), or for annual fund appeals, sponsorship of one-time events or performances, emergency funding, endowments, annual campaigns, deficit financing, scientific research, publications, films, or conferences, unless so designated by a donor; no loans.

Publications: Application guidelines; Annual report; Informational brochure; Newsletter; Occasional report; Program policy statement.

Application information: Visit foundation Web site for grant application forms and guidelines. Applications sent by fax are not accepted. Scholarship applications are available in high school counseling offices, college financial aid offices, and the OSAC Web site, or by contacting the foundation. Application form required.

Initial approach: Submit application form and attachments
Copies of proposal: 4
Deadline(s): Feb. 1 and Aug. 1
Board meeting date(s): May and Nov.
Final notification: May and Nov.

Officers and Directors:* Eric B. Lindauer,* Chair.; Steve Corey,* Vice-Chair.; Gregory A. Chaille, Pres.; Kathleen Cornett, V.P., Progs.; Brenda VanKanegan, V.P., Finance and Admin.; David Westcott, V.P., Devel.; Laura Winter, V.P., Advised Funds; Mary D. Wilcox,* Secy.; George Bell,* Treas.; Susan Bechtol, Cont.; Duncan Campbell; Jon Englund; Joyce Furman; Scott Gibson; Lynn Hennion; Lynn Loacker; Linda Moore; Gretchen Pierce; Richard G. Reiten.

Investment Managers: Columbia Management Co.; CommonSense Partners; GMO City of London; Harris Associates; Iridian Asset Mgmt.; Pinnacle Associates; Wellington Management; Wells Capital Management.

Number of staff: 27 full-time professional; 3 part-time professional.

EIN: 237315673

Selected grants: The following grants were reported in 2005.

$1,505,207 to Portland Center for the Performing Arts, Friends of the, Portland, OR. For facilitie improvements to Keller Auditorium.

$1,110,180 to E3: Employers for Education Excellence, Portland, OR. For Oregon Small Schools Initiative.

$924,000 to Lincoln County Foundation, Newport, OR. To transfer Noble Alan Carlton Waldport High School Scholarship Fund.

$500,000 to Jefferson Scholars Foundation, Charlottesville, VA. To establish scholarship program for students from Oregon.

$300,000 to Artists Repertory Theater, Portland, OR. For general support.

$250,000 to Sitka Center for Art and Ecology, Otis, OR. For challenge grant, capital campaign to build artists-in-residence living quarters, and studio.

$236,650 to Portland Rotary Charitable Trust, Portland, OR. For Rotary Village Centennial project.

$236,650 to Self Enhancement, Portland, OR. For general purposes.

$200,000 to Loaves and Fishes Centers, Portland, OR. For general support.

$200,000 to Morrison Child and Family Services, Portland, OR. For care coordination, home and community-based outpatient services, and standardization procedures.

8050
PacifiCorp Foundation

(doing business as Pacific Power/Rocky Mountain Power Foundation)
(also known as PacifiCorp Foundation For Learning)
825 N.E. Multnomah St., Ste. 2000
Portland, OR 97232 (503) 813-7257
Contact: Pamela Bradford, Mgr., Grants
FAX: (503) 813-7249;
E-mail: pacificorpfoundation@pacificorp.com;
URL: http://www.pacificorpfoundation.org

Established in 1988 in OR.
Donor: PacifiCorp.
Foundation type: Company-sponsored foundation.
Financial data (yr. ended 3/31/06): Assets, $42,706,706 (M); expenditures, $2,628,552; qualifying distributions, $2,171,117; giving activities include $1,482,525 for 275 grants (high: $50,000; low: $500), and $688,592 for 48 employee matching gifts.
Purpose and activities: The foundation supports organizations involved with arts and culture, education, health, safety education, human services, community development, and civic affairs. Special emphasis is directed toward programs designed to provide sustainable learning initiatives that serve the best aspirations of individuals, organizations, and communities and enhance and develop their capabilities to address significant challenges and opportunities.
Fields of interest: Arts; Education, early childhood education; Education, reading; Education; Health care; Safety, education; Children/youth, services; Human services; Community development; Federated giving programs; Public affairs.
Type of support: General/operating support; Continuing support; Annual campaigns; Emergency funds; Program development; Curriculum development; Scholarship funds; Employee matching gifts.
Limitations: Giving primarily in areas of company operations in northern CA, ID, OR, UT, WA, and WY. No support for political organizations or candidates, religious organizations not of direct benefit to the entire community, or veterans' or fraternal organizations. No grants to individuals, or for endowments, debt reduction, or political campaigns.
Publications: Application guidelines; Informational brochure (including application guidelines).
Application information: Proposals should be no longer than 20 pages. Application form required.

Initial approach: Complete online application form and mail proposal and application form to foundation
Copies of proposal: 1

Deadline(s): Mar. 15 for Education/Research, June 15 for Civic/Community, Sept. 15 for Culture/Arts, and Dec. 15 for Health/Welfare
Board meeting date(s): Mar., June, Sept., and Dec.
Final notification: 3 months following deadlines

Officers and Directors:* A. Richard Walje,* Chair.; Pamela Bradford, Secy.; Bruce Williams, Treas.; Anita Decker; Karen Gilmore; Keith Hartje.
Number of staff: 1 full-time professional; 2 part-time support.
EIN: 943089826
Selected grants: The following grants were reported in 2006.

$25,000 to Guadalupe Center Educational Program, Salt Lake City, UT. For extended learning program for impoverished children.

$25,000 to SMART (Start Making a Reader Today), Portland, OR.

$20,000 to Salt Lake Neighborhood Housing Services, Salt Lake City, UT. For YouthWorks program.

$18,000 to Junior Achievement of Utah, Salt Lake City, UT.

$10,000 to Sue Jorgensen Library Foundation, Casper, WY. For a statewide literacy celebration for first graders.

$7,500 to Self Enhancement, Portland, OR.

$5,000 to Boys and Girls Clubs of the Rogue Valley, Grants Pass, OR. For Project Learn/LEAP.

$5,000 to Habitat for Humanity, Eastern Bighorns, Buffalo, WY. For collaboration with the Buffalo High School Construction Technology Class to build a home.

$5,000 to YMCA of Yakima, Yakima, WA. For ASPIRE (Adult-Student Program to Inspire, Enrich and Relate) to match adult mentors with at-risk students.

$2,500 to Help Inc., Snake River Childrens Advocacy Center, Idaho Falls, ID. For program that coordinates community intervention in child abuse.

8051
PGE Foundation ✧

(formerly PGE-Enron Foundation)
121 S.W. Salmon St.
Portland, OR 97204-2901 (503) 463-7620
Contact: Carole Morse, Pres.
URL: http://www.pgefoundation.org/

Established in 1994 in OR.
Donor: Portland General Electric Co.
Foundation type: Company-sponsored foundation.
Financial data (yr. ended 12/31/04): Assets, $22,283,185 (M); gifts received, $30,777; expenditures, $980,364; qualifying distributions, $897,141; giving activities include $782,084 for 129 grants (high: $95,000; low: $296).
Purpose and activities: The foundation supports organizations involved with arts and culture, health, and human services.
Fields of interest: Museums (art); Arts; Health care; Children/youth, services; Human services; Federated giving programs.
Type of support: General/operating support.
Limitations: Giving primarily in OR. No grants to individuals.
Application information:
Initial approach: Proposal
Deadline(s): None
Officers and Directors:* Gwyneth Gamble-Booth,* Chair.; Carole Morse, Pres.; Rosalie Duron, Secy.;

James J. Diro, Treas.; David K. Carboneau; Carol Dillin; Peggy Y. Fowler; Jerry E. Hudson; Fred D. Miller; Randolph L. Miller; Cindy K. Olson.

EIN: 931138806

Selected grants: The following grants were reported in 2004.

$95,000 to Oregon Independent College Foundation, Portland, OR.

$50,000 to YWCA of Greater Portland, Portland, OR.

$25,000 to Portland State University Foundation, Portland, OR.

$25,000 to Union Gospel Mission, Portland, OR.

$20,000 to Oregon Ballet Theater, Portland, OR.

$20,000 to Oregon Symphony Association, Portland, OR.

$10,000 to Estacada Public Library Foundation, Estacada, OR.

$5,000 to Do Jump Extremely Physical Theater, Portland, OR.

$5,000 to North Salem High School, Salem, OR.

$5,000 to Women in Community Service (WICS), Wilsonville, OR.

8052

Poznanski Foundation ✧

7700 Arbor Lake Ct.
Wilsonville, OR 97070
Contact: Robert Poznanski, Pres.

Established in 1992 in OR.

Donor: Robert Poznanski.

Foundation type: Independent foundation.

Financial data (yr. ended 12/31/05): Assets, $5,930,354 (M); expenditures, $693,668; qualifying distributions, $664,810; giving activities include $664,810 for 33 grants (high: $300,000; low: $1,000).

Purpose and activities: Giving primarily for human services and to Christian organizations.

Fields of interest: Performing arts, theater; Health care; Medical research, institute; Human services; Christian agencies & churches.

Limitations: Giving primarily in OR, with some giving in CA. No grants to individuals.

Publications: Grants list.

Application information: Application form not required.

Initial approach: Letter
Copies of proposal: 1
Deadline(s): None
Board meeting date(s): Yearly
Final notification: None

Officers: Robert Poznanski, Pres.; Dorothy Poznanski, Secy.

Directors: Roberta Keller; Linda Merrihew; Suanne Ramar.

EIN: 943157812

Selected grants: The following grants were reported in 2004.

$500,000 to P.E.O. Foundation, Des Moines, IA.

$35,090 to Friendly House, Portland, OR.

$25,000 to RotaCare Bay Area, Gilroy, CA.

$15,000 to Estrella Family Services, San Jose, CA.

$10,000 to Meridian Park Medical Foundation, Tualatin, OR.

$10,000 to Project PATCH, Clackamas, OR.

$5,000 to Portland Rescue Mission, Portland, OR.

$3,000 to Central City Concern, Portland, OR.

8053

The Renaissance Foundation ✧

(formerly The Levin Family Foundation)
P.O. Box 80516
Portland, OR 97280

Established in 2000 in OR.

Donor: Irving J. Levin.

Foundation type: Independent foundation.

Financial data (yr. ended 12/31/04): Assets, $9,464,287 (M); expenditures, $450,122; qualifying distributions, $410,061; giving activities include $410,061 for 66 grants (high: $46,108; low: $100).

Fields of interest: Education; Human services.

Limitations: Applications not accepted. Giving on a national basis, with some emphasis on Portland, OR. No grants to individuals.

Application information: Contributes only to pre-selected organizations.

Trustees: Stephanie J. Fowler; Irving J. Levin.

EIN: 931306116

Selected grants: The following grants were reported in 2004.

$46,108 to I Have A Dream Foundation, Portland, OR. For general operating support.

$41,200 to Portland Schools Foundation, Portland, OR. For general operating support.

$20,000 to Jewish Federation of Portland, Portland, OR. For general operating support.

$16,500 to Oregon Childrens Foundation, Portland, OR. For general operating support.

$12,000 to Doctors Without Borders USA, New York, NY. For general operating support.

$10,000 to Mercy Corps, Portland, OR. For general operating support.

$10,000 to Nature Conservancy, Arlington, VA. For general operating support.

$10,000 to New Israel Fund, DC. For general operating support.

$10,000 to Save the Children Federation, Westport, CT. For general operating support.

$5,000 to Stand for Children Leadership Center, Portland, OR. For general support.

8054

The Salem Foundation

c/o Pioneer Trust Bank, N.A.
P.O. Box 2305
Salem, OR 97308   (503) 363-3136
Contact: Carol Herman, Trust Admin. Off.
E-mail: salemfoundation@pioneertrustbank.com;
URL: http://www.pioneertrustbank.com

Established in 1930 in OR.

Foundation type: Community foundation.

Financial data (yr. ended 4/30/06): Assets, $13,714,678 (M); gifts received, $1,675,060; expenditures, $1,047,261; giving activities include $907,478 for 114 grants (high: $246,219; low: $218), and $10,035 for 20 grants to individuals (high: $1,803; low: $22).

Purpose and activities: The foundation provides scholarships to local students and distributions for the benefit of the community.

Fields of interest: Elementary/secondary education; Education; Botanical gardens; Health care; Recreation, parks/playgrounds; Youth development; Family services; Human services; Protestant agencies & churches; Roman Catholic agencies & churches.

Limitations: Giving limited to the Salem, OR, area. No grants for capital campaigns (generally).

Publications: Application guidelines; Financial statement; Informational brochure.

Application information: Application form required.

Initial approach: Letter of intent or telephone
Copies of proposal: 1
Deadline(s): May 1 and Dec. 1
Board meeting date(s): 3rd week in Jan. and June
Final notification: 8 to 10 weeks

Trustee: Pioneer Trust Bank, N.A.

EIN: 936018523

8055

The J. Frank Schmidt Family Charitable Foundation ✧ ☆

P.O. Box 189
Boring, OR 97009

Established in 1986 in OR.

Donors: Evelyn Schmidt; J. Frank Schmidt, Jr.

Foundation type: Independent foundation.

Financial data (yr. ended 9/30/05): Assets, $5,603,509 (M); gifts received, $902,014; expenditures, $347,464; qualifying distributions, $321,625; giving activities include $321,625 for grants.

Purpose and activities: Giving primarily to universities and botanical gardens for horticultural research, and to medical associations for medical research.

Fields of interest: Education, research; Higher education; Education; Botanical/horticulture/landscape services; Hospitals (general); Health care; Health organizations, association; Medical research, institute; Agriculture; Human services; Children/youth, services.

Type of support: Continuing support; Annual campaigns; Endowments; Program development; Scholarship funds; Research; Matching/challenge support.

Limitations: Applications not accepted. No grants to individuals.

Publications: Annual report.

Application information: Contributes only to pre-selected organizations.

Trustees: Jan Schmidt Barkley; Norbert Kinen; J. Frank Schmidt, Jr.; J. Frank Schmidt III; Jean Schmidt Webster.

EIN: 931265440

Selected grants: The following grants were reported in 2005.

$51,000 to Oregon Garden Foundation, Silverton, OR.

$10,000 to Friends of Trees, Portland, OR.

$10,000 to Morton Arboretum, Lisle, IL.

$10,000 to Providence Saint Vincent Medical Foundation, Portland, OR.

$7,000 to Clackamas Community College, Oregon City, OR.

$6,000 to Kansas State University, Manhattan, KS.

$5,000 to Hoyt Arboretum, Portland, OR.

$3,800 to Berry Botanic Garden, Portland, OR.

$2,000 to Chemeketa Community College, Salem, OR.

$2,000 to Community Medical Foundation, Fresno, CA.

8056
Harold & Arlene Schnitzer CARE Foundation

P.O. Box 2708
Portland, OR 97208-2708
Contact: Barbara Hall, V.P.

Established in 1994 in OR.
Donors: Harold J. Schnitzer; Arlene Schnitzer.
Foundation type: Independent foundation.
Financial data (yr. ended 12/31/04): Assets, $50,151,073 (M); expenditures, $3,040,027; qualifying distributions, $2,668,777; giving activities include $2,315,837 for 185 grants (average: $50–$500,000), and $157,615 for foundation-administered programs.
Purpose and activities: Giving to arts and culture, education, health and human services, and Jewish organizations; funding also for programs to aid the needy, and to serve youth.
Fields of interest: Arts, multipurpose centers/programs; Museums; Education; Health organizations, association; Boys & girls clubs; Human services; Jewish agencies & temples.
Type of support: General/operating support; Continuing support; Annual campaigns; Capital campaigns; Building/renovation; Equipment; Emergency funds; Scholarship funds; Program-related investments/loans; Matching/challenge support.
Limitations: Giving primarily in OR and southwest WA, with preference given to Portland's metropolitan area. No grants to individuals.
Publications: Application guidelines; Grants list.
Application information: Grant proposals not accepted from organizations that the foundation has not previously supported. Application form not required.
Initial approach: Letter
Copies of proposal: 1
Deadline(s): Feb. 28, May 31, Aug. 31, and Nov. 30
Board meeting date(s): Quarterly
Final notification: Within 2 months of deadline
Officers and Directors:* Arlene Schnitzer,* Chair.; Harold J. Schnitzer,* Exec. V.P.; Thomas E. Eyer,* Sr. V.P. and Secy.; Barbara Hall, V.P.; Theodore P. Malaska, V.P.; Jordan D. Schnitzer,* Treas. and C.I.O.
Number of staff: 1 full-time professional; 1 part-time professional.
EIN: 931159884
Selected grants: The following grants were reported in 2003.
$155,000 to Jewish Federation of Portland, Portland, OR. For general operating support.
$75,000 to Boys and Girls Clubs of Portland Metropolitan Area, Portland, OR. For NightScape Program.
$55,000 to McCallum Theater, Palm Desert, CA. For general operating support.
$44,400 to Northwest Academy, Portland, OR. For scholarships.
$30,000 to De Paul Treatment Centers, Portland, OR. For youth center expansion project.
$30,000 to Hebrew Union College-Jewish Institute of Religion, New York, NY.
$30,000 to Self Enhancement, Portland, OR. For general operating support.
$25,000 to American Diabetes Association, Portland, OR. For Kids Program.
$25,000 to Portland Art Museum, Portland, OR. For general support.

$25,000 to University of Oregon, Eugene, OR. For general operating support for Hillel House.

8057
Schnitzer/Novack Foundation ✧ ☆

c/o Deborah S. Novack
P.O. Box 10047
Portland, OR 97296-0047

Established in 1996.
Foundation type: Independent foundation.
Financial data (yr. ended 12/31/05): Assets, $12,935,458 (M); gifts received, $175,000; expenditures, $689,441; qualifying distributions, $478,012; giving activities include $478,012 for grants.
Purpose and activities: Primary focus on education and health care in the Pacific Northwest with an emphasis on the Portland, OR, area.
Fields of interest: Arts; Education; Health care; Human services; Jewish agencies & temples.
Type of support: Annual campaigns; Capital campaigns; Building/renovation; Program development; Professorships; Research.
Limitations: Applications not accepted. Giving limited to the Pacific Northwest with an emphasis on the Portland, OR, area. No grants to individuals.
Application information: Contributes only to pre-selected organizations.
Trustees: Deborah S. Novack; Kenneth M. Novack; Gilbert Schnitzer; Thelma Schnitzer.
EIN: 931220522

8058
Anne And Eli Shapira Charitable Foundation ✧

7327 S.W. Barnes Rd., No. 124
Portland, OR 97225
Contact: Cathy Thompson, Prog. Dir.
FAX: (877) 586-9416;
E-mail: cathyt@shapirafoundation.org; URL: http://www.shapirafoundation.org

Established in 2000 in OR.
Donor: Elijahu Shapira.
Foundation type: Independent foundation.
Financial data (yr. ended 12/31/05): Assets, $3,934,731 (M); expenditures, $396,351; qualifying distributions, $351,085; giving activities include $321,759 for 16 grants (high: $160,000; low: $200).
Purpose and activities: The focus of the foundation is to provide strong family support including tutoring, mentoring and counseling services to disadvantaged families and individuals, to improve educational opportunities for disadvantaged and/or disabled individuals, and to enhance the healthy development of individuals faced with disadvantages or disabilities that may hinder their quality of life.
Fields of interest: Education, special; Scholarships/financial aid; Youth, services.
Limitations: Giving primarily in OR. No grants to individuals.
Application information: After letter of inquiry is reviewed, foundation will invite full applications. Unsolicited full applications will not be accepted. Application form required.
Initial approach: Letter of inquiry
Copies of proposal: 1

Trustees: Anne L. Shapira; Elijahu Shapira.
EIN: 931306729

8059
Sky View Foundation

P.O. Box 280
Lake Oswego, OR 97034
Contact: Jeanne Becker, Secy.-Treas.

Established in 2003 in OR.
Donor: Sue D. Cooley.
Foundation type: Independent foundation.
Financial data (yr. ended 12/31/05): Assets, $13,144,128 (M); expenditures, $659,542; qualifying distributions, $580,409; giving activities include $580,409 for 5 grants (high: $250,000; low: $43,357).
Fields of interest: Environment, land resources.
Limitations: Applications not accepted.
Application information: Contributes only to pre-selected organizations.
Officers: Robert Cooley-Gilliom, Pres.; Jeanne Becker, Secy.-Treas.
Directors: Sue D. Cooley; Brian Charles Cooley-Gilliom.
EIN: 470927354

8060
Faye & Lucille Stewart Foundation ✧

P.O. Box 11135
Eugene, OR 97440-3335
Application address: c/o Rhett Carlile, 4659 S.E. Meadowcrest Ct., Milwaukie, OR 97222

Donor: Faye H. Stewart†.
Foundation type: Independent foundation.
Financial data (yr. ended 9/30/05): Assets, $8,983,951 (M); gifts received, $300,000; expenditures, $486,566; qualifying distributions, $379,444; giving activities include $349,495 for 32 grants (high: $103,750; low: $250).
Fields of interest: Education; Human services; Foundations (community); Christian agencies & churches.
Limitations: Giving primarily in Eugene, OR.
Application information: Application form required.
Deadline(s): None
Officers: Michael Solomon, Pres. and Secy.; Rhett Carlile, V.P.; Robert Bronson, Treas.
Director: Ronald A. Irvine.
EIN: 930800814
Selected grants: The following grants were reported in 2005.
$15,500 to Food for Lane County, Eugene, OR.

8061
The Swigert Foundation ☆

P.O. Box 3121
Portland, OR 97208 (503) 225-2935
Contact: Robyn E. Brewer
E-mail: robyn.brewer@uboc.com; E-mail: robyn.brewer@uboc.com; URL: http://www.swigertfoundation.org

Established in 1990 in OR.
Donors: Ernest C. Swigert; Henry T. Swigert.
Foundation type: Independent foundation.
Financial data (yr. ended 12/31/05): Assets, $11,407,809 (M); expenditures, $547,562; qualifying distributions, $451,500; giving activities

include $451,500 for 56 grants (high: $50,000; low: $500).

Purpose and activities: Giving primarily in the cultural, medical, religious, educational, and civic areas.

Type of support: General/operating support; Continuing support; Annual campaigns; Capital campaigns; Building/renovation; Equipment; Land acquisition; Emergency funds; Program development; Professorships; Curriculum development; Research; Matching/challenge support.

Limitations: Giving primarily in OR. No grants to individuals.

Application information: Application form not required.

　Initial approach: Letter
　Copies of proposal: 1
　Deadline(s): Feb. 28, May 31, Aug. 31, and Nov. 30
　Board meeting date(s): Semi-annually
　Final notification: 60 days

Officer and Directors:* Ernest C. Swigert,* Pres.; Kate Hall; George C. Spencer; Henry T. Swigert; Elizabeth K. Warren; Wendy Warren.

EIN: 943122667

Selected grants: The following grants were reported in 2004.

$35,500 to De Paul Treatment Centers, Portland, OR. For building campaign.

$26,000 to Portland Art Museum, Portland, OR. For general support for renovation of north building.

$25,000 to Portland State University, Portland, OR. For Center for Engineering.

$15,000 to Boys and Girls Clubs of Southwest Washington, Vancouver, WA. For Youth Guidance Program at Jack, Will, and Rob Center.

$11,000 to World Forestry Center, Portland, OR. For general support.

$10,000 to Albertina Kerr Centers, Portland, OR. To update telecommunication system.

$10,000 to Humane Society of Southwest Washington, Vancouver, WA. For capital campaign.

$10,000 to Oregon Ballet Theater, Portland, OR.

$10,000 to Oregon Health and Science University Foundation, Portland, OR. For Polst Program.

$1,000 to Delta Society, Renton, WA. For program support.

8062
Ann and Bill Swindells Charitable Trust ▼ ✧

1211 S.W. 5th Ave., Ste. 2340
Portland, OR　97204-3723　(503) 222-0689
FAX: (503) 222-0726; E-mail: cdehart@ipns.com;
URL: http://www.swindellstrust.org

Established in 1998 in OR.

Donors: Ann Swindells; William Swindells.

Foundation type: Independent foundation.

Financial data (yr. ended 12/31/05): Assets, $120,941,463 (M); expenditures, $5,696,117; qualifying distributions, $5,126,960; giving activities include $4,984,978 for 73 grants (high: $500,000; low: $500; average: $10,000–$100,000).

Purpose and activities: Giving primarily to organizations whose principal mission is to improve the quality of life of the citizens of Oregon and to assist and sustain the educational, cultural, and scientific endeavors of the state.

Fields of interest: Humanities; Historical activities; Arts; Higher education; Medical school/education; Human services.

Type of support: Capital campaigns; Building/renovation; Equipment; Land acquisition; Program development; Professorships; Scholarship funds; Research; Matching/challenge support.

Limitations: Giving primarily in OR. No support for religious organizations or their capital fund drives or for activist organizations. No grants to individuals, or for annual operating budgets, development office personnel, annual fund raising activities, endowments, operational deficits, financial emergencies or for debt retirements.

Publications: Informational brochure (including application guidelines).

Application information: Application form not required.

　Initial approach: Letter or telephone
　Copies of proposal: 1
　Deadline(s): 30 days prior to board meetings
　Board meeting date(s): Feb. 1, May 1, Aug. 1, and Nov. 1
　Final notification: 15 days after board meetings

Trustees: William Swindells, Managing Tr.; Leslie Ann Ballinger; Ann Swindells; Charles Swindells; William R. Swindells.

Number of staff: 1 full-time support.

EIN: 931246433

Selected grants: The following grants were reported in 2005.

$500,000 to Stanford University, Stanford, CA. For endowment.

$250,000 to Cedars of Marin, Ross, CA. For capital campaign.

$250,000 to Eisenhower Medical Center Foundation, Rancho Mirage, CA. For capital campaign.

$250,000 to Oregon Historical Society, Portland, OR. For Oregon, My Oregon exhibit.

$250,000 to Trillium Family Services, Portland, OR. For capital campaign.

$200,000 to Lucile Packard Foundation for Childrens Health, Palo Alto, CA. For professorship.

$150,000 to Self Enhancement, Portland, OR. For endowment.

$58,253 to Libraries of Eastern Oregon, Cove, OR. To purchase equipment.

$47,900 to Coaster Theater Foundation, Portland, OR. For restoration and capital construction.

$23,500 to Youth Guidance Association, Portland, OR. To repair recreational facilities.

8063
Tektronix Foundation ✧

P.O. Box 5000, M.S. 55-715
Beaverton, OR　97077
Contact: Lisa Aubin

Incorporated in 1952 in OR.

Donor: Tektronix, Inc.

Foundation type: Company-sponsored foundation.

Financial data (yr. ended 12/31/04): Assets, $943,814 (M); gifts received, $700,000; expenditures, $737,206; qualifying distributions, $737,206; giving activities include $611,920 for grants, and $125,286 for employee matching gifts.

Purpose and activities: The foundation supports organizations involved with arts and culture and education. Special emphasis is directed toward programs designed to promote science, math, and engineering education.

Fields of interest: Arts; Elementary/secondary education; Higher education; Education.

Type of support: General/operating support; Continuing support; Annual campaigns; Equipment; Program development; Employee matching gifts.

Limitations: Applications not accepted. Giving primarily in OR. No grants to individuals, or for emergency needs or endowments, demonstration projects, debt reduction, research, publications, or conferences; no loans; no challenge grants.

Application information: Contributes only to pre-selected organizations.

Officers and Trustees:* James F. Dalton,* Chair.; Rich McBee, V.P., Worldwide Sales and Marketing; Barbara Gaffney, V.P., Human Resources.

EIN: 936021540

8064
The Herbert A. Templeton Foundation

1717 S.W. Park Ave.
Portland, OR　97201　(503) 223-0036
Contact: Ruth B. Richmond, Pres.

Incorporated in 1955 in OR.

Donors: Herbert A. Templeton†; and other members of the Templeton family.

Foundation type: Independent foundation.

Financial data (yr. ended 12/31/05): Assets, $17,088,171 (M); gifts received, $561,956; expenditures, $899,305; qualifying distributions, $819,044; giving activities include $750,110 for 110 grants (high: $57,500; low: $1,000).

Purpose and activities: Grants for youth, cultural, and social service organizations operating in OR, or having programs significantly affecting OR residents; present emphasis on program and direct services.

Fields of interest: Arts; Education, early childhood education; Human services; Children/youth, services.

Type of support: General/operating support; Continuing support; Emergency funds; Program development; Seed money.

Limitations: Giving limited to OR. No support for medical services, the aged, or parochial education. No grants to individuals, or for fellowships, building or endowment funds, scientific research or technology, matching gifts, or medical or medically-related programs; no loans or program-related investments.

Publications: Application guidelines; Program policy statement.

Application information: Application form not required.

　Initial approach: Letter or proposal
　Copies of proposal: 1
　Deadline(s): Mar. 15 and Sept. 15
　Board meeting date(s): Feb., May, Aug., and Nov.
　Final notification: May and Nov.

Officers and Trustees:* Ruth B. Richmond,* Pres.; Henry R. Richmond,* V.P.; Terrence R. Pancoast,* Secy.; Loren L. Wyss, Treas.; Jane T. Bryson; Linda McKinley Girard.

Number of staff: 2 part-time professional.

EIN: 930505586

Selected grants: The following grants were reported in 2004.

$40,000 to 1000 Friends of Oregon, Portland, OR.

$40,000 to I Have A Dream Foundation, New York, NY.

$12,500 to Volunteers of America.

$10,000 to Emanuel Childrens Hospital Foundation, Portland, OR.

$10,000 to Kids on the Block Awareness Program, Portland, OR.

$10,000 to Linnton Community Center, Portland, OR.

$10,000 to p:ear, Portland, OR.

$7,500 to Boys and Girls Club.

$5,000 to Oregon Episcopal School, Portland, OR.

$4,000 to Willamette Repertory Theater, Eugene, OR.

8065
Rose E. Tucker Charitable Trust
900 S.W. 5th Ave., Ste. 2600
Portland, OR 97204
Contact: Milo E. Ormseth, Tr.; Terrence R. Pancoast, Tr.
E-mail: Tuckertrust@stoel.com

Trust established in 1976 in OR.
Donors: Rose E. Tucker†; Max and Rose Tucker Foundation.
Foundation type: Independent foundation.
Financial data (yr. ended 6/30/05): Assets, $22,490,042 (M); expenditures, $1,215,074; qualifying distributions, $1,072,100; giving activities include $994,368 for 159 grants (high: $50,000; low: $792).
Fields of interest: Arts; Higher education; Education; Environment; Health care; Human services; Children/youth, services; Community development; Disabilities, people with; Economically disadvantaged.
Type of support: General/operating support; Capital campaigns; Building/renovation; Equipment; Land acquisition; Program development; Scholarship funds; Matching/challenge support.
Limitations: Giving limited to organizations and projects in OR, with emphasis on the metropolitan Portland area. No support for religious purposes, private foundations, or conduit organizations. No grants to individuals, or for fellowships; no loans or program-related investments.
Publications: Application guidelines; Annual report (including application guidelines); Grants list.
Application information: Organizations may only apply once within a 12 month period. Application form not required.
Initial approach: Proposal
Copies of proposal: 2
Deadline(s): None
Board meeting date(s): Approximately every 2 months
Final notification: Within 15 days of board meetings
Trustees: Milo E. Ormseth; Terrence R. Pancoast; U.S. Bank, N.A.
Number of staff: None.
EIN: 936119091
Selected grants: The following grants were reported in 2005.
$50,000 to Reed College, Portland, OR.
$40,000 to Lewis and Clark College, Portland, OR.
$40,000 to Oregon Museum of Science and Industry, Portland, OR.
$35,150 to Lebanon Community Foundation, Lebanon, OR.
$25,000 to Northwest Earth Institute, Portland, OR.
$22,500 to Oregon Childrens Foundation, Portland, OR.
$10,000 to Linfield College, McMinnville, OR.
$3,500 to Audubon Society of Portland, Portland, OR.
$3,500 to Profile Theater Project, Portland, OR.

$3,000 to Ecumenical Ministries of Oregon, Portland, OR.

8066
Nancy J. Wendt Foundation ◇
826 Loma Linda Dr.
Klamath Falls, OR 97601

Established in 1999 in OR.
Donor: Richard Wendt.
Foundation type: Independent foundation.
Financial data (yr. ended 12/31/04): Assets, $18,265 (M); gifts received, $1,543,166; expenditures, $1,898,042; qualifying distributions, $1,895,227; giving activities include $1,895,227 for 26+ grants (high: $1,652,827).
Fields of interest: Arts; Education; Hospitals (general); Health care; Recreation; Human services; YM/YWCAs & YM/YWHAs; Children, services; Public affairs, finance; Protestant agencies & churches.
Limitations: Applications not accepted. Giving primarily in Klamath Falls and Portland, OR. No grants to individuals.
Application information: Contributes only to pre-selected organizations.
Officers: Nancy J. Wendt, Pres.; Richard Wendt, V.P.; Roderick Wendt, Secy.-Treas.
EIN: 931256104

8067
Wessinger Foundation ◇
P.O. Box 474
Portland, OR 97207 (503) 227-2995
Contact: Lynne Siegel, Admin.
URL: http://www.gosw.org/wessinger

Established in 1979.
Donor: Paul Wessinger Trust.
Foundation type: Independent foundation.
Financial data (yr. ended 9/30/05): Assets, $8,688,188 (M); expenditures, $495,531; qualifying distributions, $486,572; giving activities include $465,075 for 46 grants (high: $50,000; low: $1,000).
Purpose and activities: Giving primarily for education, particularly education foundations, arts and culture, health care, including health services for women, youth and social services, and community development.
Fields of interest: Performing arts, theater; Historic preservation/historical societies; Education, single organization support; Education; Health care; Health organizations, association; Disasters, 9/11/01; Recreation, parks/playgrounds; Human services; Youth, services; Community development; Women.
Type of support: Scholarship funds; Program development; Matching/challenge support; Equipment; Capital campaigns; Building/renovation.
Limitations: Giving limited to the Pacific Northwest, with emphasis on the Tri-County, OR, area. No grants to individuals.
Application information:
Initial approach: Letter
Copies of proposal: 1
Deadline(s): None
Board meeting date(s): Quarterly
Officers: Gainor Wessinger Arzt, Pres.; Robert D. Geddes, Secy.; Henry W. Wessinger, Treas.
Directors: Thomas B. Stoel, Emeritus; William W. Wessinger, Emeritus; Anna Boggess; Nancy W.

Kline; Barbara W. Newton; Julie Vigeland; E. Charles Wessinger; Joseph M. Wessinger; Kathryn W. Withers.
EIN: 930754224

8068
Wheeler Foundation ◇
1300 S.W. 5th Ave., Ste. 3009
Portland, OR 97201-5637 (503) 228-0261
Contact: Samuel C. Wheeler, Pres.

Established in 1965 in OR.
Donors: Coleman H. Wheeler†; Coleman H. Wheeler, Jr.†; Cornelia T. Wheeler†.
Foundation type: Independent foundation.
Financial data (yr. ended 12/31/05): Assets, $16,331,160 (M); expenditures, $758,260; qualifying distributions, $697,877; giving activities include $680,000 for 56 grants (high: $35,000; low: $1,000).
Purpose and activities: Giving primarily to cultural institutions.
Fields of interest: Arts; Higher education; Health care; Medical research, institute; Children/youth, services.
Type of support: General/operating support.
Limitations: Giving primarily in OR. No grants to individuals, or for endowment funds.
Application information: Application form not required.
Initial approach: Letter
Copies of proposal: 1
Deadline(s): None
Board meeting date(s): Mar., June, Sept., and Dec.
Officers and Directors:* Samuel C. Wheeler,* Pres.; Charles B. Wheeler,* V.P.; John C. Wheeler,* V.P.; Edward T. Wheeler,* Secy.; Thomas K. Wheeler,* Treas.
EIN: 930553801

8069
Juan Young Trust
c/o Western Division
P.O. Box 91429
Portland, OR 97291
Contact: Antoinette Kienow Arenz, Tr.
E-mail: juanyoungtrust1@msn.com; Eastern Division address: c/o Scott G. Klusmann, 2020 S.W. 8th Ave., PMB252, West Linn, OR 97068; tel.: (503) 722-7080; fax: (503) 650-0259; e-mail: EDJYT@IPNS.com; URL: http://www.gosw.org/juanyoungtrust

Established in 1996 in OR under the will of Juan Young; funded in 1999.
Donor: Juan Young†.
Foundation type: Independent foundation.
Financial data (yr. ended 12/31/05): Assets, $25,529,610 (M); expenditures, $2,039,319; qualifying distributions, $1,956,454; giving activities include $1,672,000 for 48 grants.
Purpose and activities: Giving primarily for the education, health and welfare of children under the age of 21, who reside in OR.
Fields of interest: Education; Health care; Children/youth, services.
Type of support: Capital campaigns; Building/renovation; Equipment; Program development.
Limitations: Giving limited to OR, with emphasis on Portland. No support for religious purposes,

propaganda or to influence legislation, or private foundations. No grants to individuals, or for operating budgets, fund appeals, debt retirement, or to defray deficits; no loans or program-related investments.

Publications: Application guidelines; Informational brochure (including application guidelines).

Application information: See foundation's Web site for additional information. Application form required.

Initial approach: E-mail

Copies of proposal: 2

Deadline(s): Mar. 31, June 30, Sept. 30, and Dec. 31

Board meeting date(s): Jan., Apr., July, and Oct.

Final notification: First week of Feb., May, Aug., and Nov.

Trustees: Antoinette Kienow Arenz; Scott G. Klusmann.

Number of staff: 2 full-time professional.

EIN: 931245000

Selected grants: The following grants were reported in 2004.

$40,000 to Saint Marys Academy, Portland, OR. For High School renovation and Expansion.

$12,000 to Lewis and Clark College, Portland, OR. For annual JYT Scholarship Program.

$12,000 to University of Oregon Foundation, Eugene, OR. For annual JYT Scholarship program.

$10,000 to Christie School, Marylhurst, OR. For medication and medical supplies.

$10,000 to Gales Creek Camp Foundation for Children with Diabetes, Portland, OR. For Youth Camp for Diabetics.

$10,000 to Providence Seaside Hospital Foundation, Seaside, OR. For Update Fetal Monitoring System.

$10,000 to Sisters of Saint Mary, Beaverton, OR. For Athletics Facilities.

$8,000 to Saint Francis School, Sherwood, OR. For Elementary, Renovation, and Expansion.

$7,000 to Childrens Course, Gladstone, OR. For Youth Golf Program.

$5,000 to American Cancer Society, Northwest Division, Portland, OR. For SPEAKOUT Program.

PENNSYLVANIA

8070
1675 Foundation
c/o Pembroke Philanthropy Advisors
16 E. Lancaster Ave., Ste. 102
Ardmore, PA 19003 (610) 896-3868
Contact: Daphne C. Rowe, Exec. Dir.
FAX: (610) 896-3869;
E-mail: drowe@pembrokephilanthropy.net;
Additional e-mail: Jocelyn Arnold, Asst. Dir.:
jarnold@pembrokephilanthropy.net; URL: http://
www.1675foundation.org

Established in 2004 in PA from the reorganization of
The Oxford Foundation into 4 distinct entities.
Foundation type: Independent foundation.
Financial data (yr. ended 12/31/05): Assets,
$18,880,107 (M); gifts received, $82,044;
expenditures, $1,032,386; qualifying distributions,
$909,660; giving activities include $820,857 for 18
grants (high: $400,000; low: $1,000; average:
$5,000–$100,000).
Purpose and activities: The 1675 Foundation is a
private family foundation dedicated to promoting
and supporting excellence in the education, health,
human service, watershed and environmental
issues, and history.
Fields of interest: Historical activities; Education;
Environment, water resources; Environment; Health
care; Human services.
Type of support: Research; Scholarship funds;
Program development; Matching/challenge support;
Endowments; Building/renovation; Annual
campaigns; General/operating support; Capital
campaigns.
Limitations: Giving primarily in Chester County PA;
the greater Boston, MA, area, and southeastern PA.
No grants to individuals; no loans.
Publications: Application guidelines.
Application information: Accepts DVG Common
Grant Application with a foundation cover sheet.
Application form required.
 Copies of proposal: 1
 Deadline(s): Mar. 1, and Oct. 1
 Board meeting date(s): May and Dec.
Officers and Directors:* Carol Ware Gates,* Chair.;
Lisa Rich,* V.P. and Treas.; Daphne C. Rowe,* Exec.
Dir.; Joseph R. Gates; Paul W. Gates; David M. Rich.
Number of staff: 2 part-time professional.
EIN: 201083951

8071
1957 Charity Foundation ✧
c/o Mellon Bank, N.A.
P.O. Box 185
Pittsburgh, PA 15230-0185

Established in 2001 in PA.
Foundation type: Independent foundation.
Financial data (yr. ended 6/30/05): Assets,
$22,594,462 (M); expenditures, $960,699;
qualifying distributions, $837,854; giving activities
include $718,000 for 130 grants (high: $30,000;
low: $1,000).
Purpose and activities: Giving primarily for
education and health care, as well as for children,
youth, families, and for social service programs for
homeless, needy, and aged people.

Fields of interest: Historic preservation/historical
societies; Arts; Elementary/secondary education;
Education; Health care; AIDS; Recreation, camps;
Human services; Children/youth, services; Family
services; Homeless, human services; Community
development, neighborhood development;
Community development; Religion; Aging;
Economically disadvantaged; Homeless.
Limitations: Applications not accepted. Giving
primarily in PA; some giving nationally. No grants to
individuals.
Application information: Contributes only to
pre-selected organizations.
Trustee: Mellon Bank, N.A.
EIN: 233051552

8072
The Aaron Family Foundation ✧ ☆
2401 Pennsylvania Ave., Apt. 5824
Philadelphia, PA 19130

Established in 1998 in PA.
Donor: Daniel Aaron.
Foundation type: Independent foundation.
Financial data (yr. ended 12/31/05): Assets,
$2,517,937 (M); gifts received, $1,012,247;
expenditures, $328,676; qualifying distributions,
$320,384; giving activities include $320,384 for 42
grants (high: $104,243; low: $25).
Fields of interest: Arts; Education; Health
organizations, association; Human services;
Children/youth, services; Jewish federated giving
programs; Jewish agencies & temples.
Limitations: Applications not accepted. Giving
primarily in PA. No grants to individuals.
Application information: Contributes only to
pre-selected organizations.
Trustee: Geraldine Aaron.
EIN: 237996346

8073
The ACE INA Foundation ✧
(formerly ACE USA Foundation)
c/o ACE INA Holdings, Inc.
1601 Chestnut St.
2 Liberty Pl., TL31X
Philadelphia, PA 19103 (215) 640-1737
Contact: Eden M. Kratchman, Exec. Dir.
FAX: (215) 640-5479;
E-mail: eden.kratchman@ace-ina.com; URL: http://
www.acelimited.com/AceLimitedRoot/About+ACE/
ACE+in+the+Community/ACE+INA+Foundation.htm

Established in 1998 in DE.
Donor: ACE USA Inc.
Foundation type: Company-sponsored foundation.
Financial data (yr. ended 12/31/04): Assets,
$163,243 (M); gifts received, $1,618,055;
expenditures, $1,602,288; qualifying distributions,
$1,600,638; giving activities include $1,140,944
for 32 grants (high: $111,111; low: $4,500), and
$459,694 for 621 employee matching gifts.
Purpose and activities: The foundation supports
organizations involved with arts and culture,
education, and human services.
Fields of interest: Arts; Education; Environment;
Children/youth, services; Human services;
Biological sciences.
Type of support: General/operating support;
Program development; Scholarship funds; Employee
volunteer services.

Limitations: Giving primarily in Philadelphia, PA. No
grants to individuals.
Application information: Application form not
required.
 Initial approach: Proposal
 Deadline(s): None
Officer and Trustees:* Eden M. Kratchman, Chair.;
William Curcio; Brian Dowd; Brian Duperreault;
Kewin Gales; Evan Greenberg; Robert Hernandez;
Robert Jefferson; John Lupica; Susan Rivera; Ed
Troy; Keith White.
EIN: 582430571
Selected grants: The following grants were reported
in 2003.
$166,000 to Kimmel Center for the Performing Arts,
 Philadelphia, PA.
$111,111 to Philadelphia Academies, Philadelphia,
 PA. For business curriculum at William Penn
 Business Academy and other high schools in
 Philadelphia.
$50,000 to Boys and Girls Clubs of Delaware,
 Wilmington, DE. For after-school programs.
$50,000 to Philadelphia Cares, Philadelphia, PA.
 For mission of volunteerism to clean, paint, and
 organize Philadelphia public schools.
$33,111 to Business Leadership Organized for
 Catholic Schools, Philadelphia, PA. For
 scholarship programs for underserved youth
 K-12.
$25,000 to National Constitution Center,
 Philadelphia, PA. For public school tours at
 center.
$25,000 to Philadelphia Museum of Art,
 Philadelphia, PA. For Corporate Partners
 Program.
$20,000 to Center for Literacy, Philadelphia, PA. For
 adult literacy and educational programs.
$10,000 to Junior Achievement of Delaware Valley,
 Philadelphia, PA. For educational subjects and
 activities that bridge gap between work and
 school for grades K-12.
$10,000 to Peoples Light and Theater Company,
 Malvern, PA. For To bring theater into classroom
 of students in Philadelphia regional area.

8074
AirCast Foundation, Inc. ✧
5840 Ellsworth Ave., Ste. 304
Pittsburgh, PA 15232 (412) 661-7538
Contact: Susan Pressly Lephart Ph.D., ATC, Exec.
Dir.
FAX: (412) 661-7539;
E-mail: inquiries@aircastfoundation.org; Toll-free
tel.: (800) 720-5516; e-mail:
slephart@aircastfoundation.org (for Susan Pressly
Lephart); URL: http://www.aircastfoundation.org

Established in 1996 in NJ.
Donors: Glenn W. Johnson, Jr.†; Aircast, Inc.
Foundation type: Independent foundation.
Financial data (yr. ended 12/31/05): Assets,
$4,088,862 (M); expenditures, $1,321,133;
qualifying distributions, $1,178,947; giving
activities include $499,255 for grants.
Purpose and activities: Giving to promote scientific
research and education in the area of orthopedic
medicine and science. The foundation is interested
in research proposals that use cellular or molecular
biology, biomechanics, tissue engineering, material
sciences, and clinical trials to enhance knowledge
of human musculoskeletal diseases, and lead to
potential new therapies. Research projects may be
basic science, clinical or translational in design.

Fields of interest: Medical school/education; Orthopedics; Medical research, institute; Orthopedics research.
Type of support: Fellowships; Research.
Limitations: Giving on a national basis.
Publications: Annual report; Grants list.
Application information: Preliminary applications available through the Web site or by contacting the foundation. Preliminary or full applications will only be accepted by U.S. mail, UPS or Fed-Ex, or similar commercial delivery companies. Hand-delivered or faxed materials will not be accepted. Maximum amount of funding available is $100,000, distributed over a 2-year period, with $50,000 available each year. Application form required.
   Initial approach: Complete preliminary application via foundation Web site
   Deadline(s): Feb. 1 for spring preliminary applications; July 1 for fall preliminary applications
   Final notification: Aug. 1 for spring and Dec. 15 for fall
Officers: Glenn W. Johnson III, Pres. and Treas.; Henry J. McVicker, V.P. and Secy.; Susan Pressly Lephart, Ph.D., ATC, Exec. Dir.
Advisory Board: Freddie H. Fu, M.D.; Thay Q. Lee, M.D., Ph.D.; Regis J. O'Keefe, M.D., Ph.D.; Marc R. Safran, M.D.
EIN: 222784475

8075
Alcoa Foundation ▼ ✧
Alcoa Corporate Ctr.
201 Isabella St.
Pittsburgh, PA   15212-5858   (412) 553-2348
E-mail: alcoafoundation@alcoa.com; URL: http://www.alcoa.com/global/en/community/foundation.asp

Trust established in 1952 in PA; incorporated in 1964.
Donors: Aluminum Co. of America; Alcoa Inc.
Foundation type: Company-sponsored foundation.
Financial data (yr. ended 12/31/05): Assets, $550,363,160 (M); gifts received, $500,000; expenditures, $28,240,832; qualifying distributions, $23,934,638; giving activities include $22,749,270 for grants.
Purpose and activities: The foundation supports organizations involved with education, the environment, health, mental health, crime and violence prevention, employment, disabled people, minorities, and women.
Fields of interest: Education, equal rights; Education; Environment, public policy; Environment, forests; Environmental education; Environment; Health care, equal rights; Health care; Mental health/crisis services; Crime/violence prevention, abuse prevention; Employment, equal rights; Employment, training; Employment; Disabilities, people with; Minorities; Women.
International interests: Australia; Brazil; Caribbean; China; Hungary; Italy; Jamaica; Mexico; Netherlands; Spain; Suriname; Wales.
Type of support: General/operating support; Continuing support; Annual campaigns; Building/renovation; Equipment; Emergency funds; Program development; Conferences/seminars; Seed money; Fellowships; Scholarship funds; Research; Program-related investments/loans; Employee matching gifts; Employee-related scholarships; Matching/challenge support.

Limitations: Giving on a national and international basis in areas of company operations; giving also to national and international organizations. No support for political or lobbying organizations, sectarian or religious organizations not of direct benefit to the entire community, private foundations, or trust funds. No grants to individuals (except for fellowships and employee-related scholarships), or for endowments, capital campaigns, debt reduction, or general operating support, fundraising events or sponsorships, trips, conferences, seminars, festivals, one-day events, documentaries, videos, or research projects/programs, or indirect or overhead costs.
Publications: Application guidelines; Annual report (including application guidelines); Corporate giving report; Informational brochure (including application guidelines).
Application information: Proposals should be no longer than 2 pages; letters of inquiry should be no longer than 1 page.
   Initial approach: Complete online application form for national and international organizations; E-mail proposal to nearest company division for organizations located in the U.S.; mail letter of inquiry to nearest company division for organizations located outside the U.S.
   Copies of proposal: 1
   Deadline(s): July 31 for national and international organizations
   Board meeting date(s): Monthly
   Final notification: 1 month for national and international organizations
Officers and Directors:* Meg McDonald,* Pres. and Treas.; Velma Monteiro-Tribble, C.O.O.; Robert Mungo, Cont. and Business Mgr.; Ricardo E. Belda; Earnest J. Edwards; Barbara S. Jeremiah; Joseph C. Muscari; Renata de Camargo Nasicmento; Bernt Reitan; Richard L. Siewart; Paul D. Thomas; Helmut Wieser.
Corporate Trustee: Mellon Financial Corp.
Number of staff: 6 full-time professional; 1 full-time support.
EIN: 251128857
Selected grants: The following grants were reported in 2005.
$3,053,335 to Institute of International Education, New York, NY. For Alcoa Foundation Conservation and Sustainability Fellowship Program.
$1,200,000 to Andy Warhol Museum, Pittsburgh, PA. For exhibit, Andy Warhol: Artist of Modern Life.
$438,000 to ACT, Inc., Iowa City, IA. For required four-year funding for 2005 awards made under Alcoa Foundation Sons and Daughters Scholarship Program.
$350,000 to American Red Cross, National Headquarters, DC. For disaster relief for victims of Hurricane Katrina.
$168,800 to Comune di Portoscuso, Portoscuso, Italy. For creation of community center and development of cultural programs.
$23,000 to K.I.D.S. Foundation, Ballarat, Australia. For school SEE Safety Program.
$20,000 to Greater Pittsburgh Arts Council, Pittsburgh, PA. For Alcoa Foundation Leadership Grants for Arts Managers program.
$20,000 to Louisiana Environmental Educators Association, Baton Rouge, LA. For 05 Louisiana's Environmental Awareness Art and Language Art Contest.
$18,000 to Calhoun County Independent School District, Port Lavaca, TX. For Calhoun County Connection.

$15,000 to Marthas Table, DC. For Martha's Tables First Nine Years Learning Program.

8076
Allegheny Foundation
1 Oxford Ctr.
301 Grant St., Ste. 3900
Pittsburgh, PA   15219-6401   (412) 392-2900
Contact: Matthew A. Groll, Exec. Dir.
URL: http://www.scaife.com/alleghen.html

Incorporated in 1953 in PA.
Donor: Richard M. Scaife.
Foundation type: Independent foundation.
Financial data (yr. ended 12/31/05): Assets, $47,002,956 (M); gifts received, $1,000,000; expenditures, $2,726,049; qualifying distributions, $2,378,527; giving activities include $2,061,500 for 44 grants (high: $250,000; low: $1,000).
Purpose and activities: Giving primarily for historic preservation, education, and community development.
Fields of interest: Historic preservation/historical societies; Education; Youth development; Community development, neighborhood development.
Type of support: General/operating support; Program development; Seed money.
Limitations: Giving primarily in western PA, with emphasis on Pittsburgh. No grants to individuals, or for endowment funds, event sponsorship, capital campaigns, renovations, government agencies, scholarships, or fellowships; no loans.
Publications: Application guidelines; Annual report.
Application information: Application form not required.
   Initial approach: Letter
   Copies of proposal: 1
   Deadline(s): Oct. 1
   Board meeting date(s): Nov.
   Final notification: 4-6 weeks
Officers and Trustees:* Richard M. Scaife,* Chair.; Matthew A. Groll, Exec. Dir.; Joanne B. Beyer; Ralph H. Goettler; Doris O'Donnell; Margaret R. Scaife; George Weymouth; Arthur P. Ziegler, Jr.
Number of staff: 1 part-time professional; 1 full-time support.
EIN: 256012303
Selected grants: The following grants were reported in 2005.
$250,000 to Pennsylvania Trolley Museum, Washington, PA.
$100,000 to Allegheny Institute for Public Policy, Pittsburgh, PA.
$100,000 to Center for the Study of Popular Culture, Los Angeles, CA.
$100,000 to Extra Mile Education Foundation, Pittsburgh, PA.
$50,000 to Crossroads Foundation, Pittsburgh, PA.
$50,000 to Lincoln Institute of Public Opinion Research, Harrisburg, PA.
$40,000 to Boys and Girls Clubs of Western Pennsylvania, Pittsburgh, PA.
$30,000 to Rosedale Block Cluster, Pittsburgh, PA.
$25,000 to Commonwealth Education Organization, Pittsburgh, PA.
$12,000 to Pittsburgh History and Landmarks Foundation, Pittsburgh, PA.

8077

The Allerton Foundation, Inc. ✧

(formerly The Diane Lenfest Myer Foundation, Inc.)
5 Tower Bridge
300 Barr Harbor Dr., Ste. 450
West Conshohocken, PA   19428
(610) 828-4510
Contact: Bruce Melgary, Exec. Dir.

Established in 1999 in PA.
Donor: Diane Lenfest Myer.
Foundation type: Independent foundation.
Financial data (yr. ended 6/30/04): Assets,
$53,588,955 (M); expenditures, $2,966,504;
qualifying distributions, $2,704,138; giving
activities include $2,668,000 for 18 grants (high:
$950,000; low: $2,000; average: $2,000–
$1,000,000).
Purpose and activities: Giving for animal welfare,
and land conservation to preserve animal habitat.
Fields of interest: Environment, land resources;
Animal welfare; Animals/wildlife.
Type of support: General/operating support;
Continuing support; Annual campaigns; Capital
campaigns; Building/renovation; Seed money.
Limitations: Giving primarily in southeastern PA,
southern NJ, and DE. No grants to individuals, or for
event tickets, tables, or sponsorships.
Application information: Application form not
required.
   Initial approach: 2- to 3-page letter
   Copies of proposal: 1
   Deadline(s): None
   Board meeting date(s): As necessary
   Final notification: 3 to 6 months
Officers and Directors:* Diane Lenfest Myer,*
Pres.; Grahame Richards,* Secy.; Joy Tartar, C.F.O.;
Marguerite Lenfest,* Treas.; Bruce Melgary,* Exec.
Dir.
EIN: 233035225
Selected grants: The following grants were reported
in 2005.
$1,000,000 to National Alliance for Autism
   Research, Princeton, NJ.
$950,000 to Conservation Fund, Arlington, VA.
$500,000 to Childrens Hospital Foundation,
   Philadelphia, PA.
$5,000 to Great Valley Nature Center, Devault, PA.

8078

The Alter Family Foundation ✧

c/o Wolf Block Schorr & Solis Cohen
1650 Arch St., 22nd Fl.
Philadelphia, PA   19103-2097

Established in 1998 in PA.
Donors: Dennis Alter; Gisela Alter; Helen Alter;
Dennis Alter Trust.
Foundation type: Independent foundation.
Financial data (yr. ended 12/31/05): Assets,
$7,304,878 (M); gifts received, $141,250;
expenditures, $570,912; qualifying distributions,
$511,250; giving activities include $511,250 for 5
grants (high: $250,000; low: $30,000).
Fields of interest: Museums (art); Performing arts,
theater (musical); Higher education; Athletics/
sports, racquet sports; Human services; Children/
youth, services.
Limitations: Applications not accepted. Giving
primarily in Philadelphia, PA; some giving in NY and
RI. No grants to individuals.
Application information: Contributes only to
pre-selected organizations.

Officers: Dennis Alter, Pres. and Treas.; Gisela Alter,
V.P. and Secy.; William A. Rosoff, V.P.; Michael
Stolper, V.P.
EIN: 232951283
Selected grants: The following grants were reported
in 2004.
$1,125,000 to Temple University, Philadelphia, PA.
$100,000 to Opera Company of Philadelphia,
   Philadelphia, PA.
$81,250 to American Music Theater Festival,
   Philadelphia, PA.

8079

American Eagle Outfitters Foundation ✧

150 Thorn Hill Dr.
Warrendale, PA   15086   (724) 778-3533
Contact: Marcie Eberhart, Dir.
FAX: (724) 779-8182; E-mail: eberhartm@ae.com;
URL: http://www.ae.com/web/corp/
foundation.htm

Established in 1999 in PA.
Donor: American Eagle Outfitters, Inc.
Foundation type: Company-sponsored foundation.
Financial data (yr. ended 12/31/04): Assets, $0
(M); gifts received, $507,551; expenditures,
$514,645; qualifying distributions, $514,626;
giving activities include $509,153 for 114 grants
(high: $132,618; low: $100).
Purpose and activities: The foundation supports
programs designed to foster civic engagement;
render safe and nourishing places for teens;
embrace diversity; and encourage youth/teen
development.
Fields of interest: Youth development; Youth,
services; Civil rights, equal rights; Leadership
development.
Type of support: Employee volunteer services;
General/operating support; Program development.
Limitations: Giving primarily in areas of company
operations, with emphasis on eastern KS, New York,
NY, and southwestern PA, including Pittsburgh;
giving also to regional and national organizations.
No support for organizations not involving American
Eagle business units and/or employees,
organizations not providing regular reports of
financial and program activities, organizations
budgeting over 30 percent of funds for fundraising
purposes, discriminatory organizations, individual
religious organizations, political organizations or
candidates, lobbying organizations, or veterans' or
fraternal organizations. No grants to individuals, or
for fashion shows, political campaigns, medical or
health-related causes, advertising, or capital
campaigns; no non-disaster relief clothing
donations.
Publications: Application guidelines; Financial
statement.
Application information: Proposals should be no
longer than 2 pages. Application form not required.
   Initial approach: Proposal
   Copies of proposal: 1
   Deadline(s): None
   Board meeting date(s): Quarterly
   Final notification: 2 weeks following board
   meetings
Directors: Adam Diamond; Liz Hodges; Joe Kerin;
Kelly Kosheba; Steve Lyman; Susan McGalla.
EIN: 251827476

8080

Harriett Ames Charitable Trust ✧

c/o PNC Advisors
1600 Market St., 19th Fl.
Philadelphia, PA   19103

Trust established in 1952 in NY.
Donor: Harriett Ames†.
Foundation type: Independent foundation.
Financial data (yr. ended 12/31/04): Assets,
$8,686,111 (M); expenditures, $572,843;
qualifying distributions, $549,221; giving activities
include $549,221 for 46 grants (high: $121,577;
low: $1,000; average: $1,000–$25,000).
Purpose and activities: Grants to educational and
charitable organizations, with emphasis on medical
research, education, health associations, and
cultural organizations.
Fields of interest: Visual arts, photography;
Museums; Museums (art); Arts; Education;
Animals/wildlife, preservation/protection; Health
organizations, association; Medical research,
institute; Human services; Community
development; Jewish federated giving programs;
Jewish agencies & temples.
Type of support: General/operating support; Annual
campaigns.
Limitations: Applications not accepted. Giving
primarily in the metropolitan New York, NY, area. No
grants to individuals.
Application information: Contributes only to
pre-selected organizations. Unsolicited requests for
funds not considered.
   Board meeting date(s): Varies
Trustee: Steven Ames.
EIN: 236286757
Selected grants: The following grants were reported
in 2003.
$105,850 to Whitney Museum of American Art, New
   York, NY.
$10,000 to Hospital for Special Surgery Fund, New
   York, NY.
$5,500 to International Center of Photography, New
   York, NY.
$5,000 to Artists Space, New York, NY.
$2,500 to Breast Cancer Research Foundation, New
   York, NY.
$2,500 to Bridgehampton Chamber Music
   Associates, New York, NY.
$2,500 to Mount Sinai Hospital, New York, NY.
$2,500 to Richard Tucker Music Foundation, New
   York, NY.
$1,000 to Studio in a School Association, New York,
   NY.
$1,000 to Studio Museum in Harlem, New York, NY.

8081

AMETEK Foundation, Inc. ✧

37 N. Valley Rd., Bldg. 4
P.O. Box 1764
Paoli, PA   19301-0801
Contact: Kathryn E. Londra

Incorporated in 1960 in NY.
Donor: AMETEK, Inc.
Foundation type: Company-sponsored foundation.
Financial data (yr. ended 12/31/04): Assets,
$7,473,005 (M); expenditures, $1,127,124;
qualifying distributions, $1,115,853; giving
activities include $1,108,368 for 78 grants (high:
$100,648; low: $1,000).
Purpose and activities: The foundation supports
hospitals and organizations involved with arts and

culture, education fundraising, elementary and higher education, environmental conservation, cancer, medical research, human services, and international human rights.

Fields of interest: History/archaeology; Arts; Education, fund raising/fund distribution; Elementary school/education; Higher education; Environment, natural resources; Hospitals (general); Cancer; Cancer research; Medical research; Human services; International human rights; Federated giving programs.

Type of support: General/operating support; Annual campaigns; Building/renovation; Equipment; Endowments; Scholarship funds; Research; Technical assistance; Exchange programs; Matching/challenge support.

Limitations: Giving primarily in areas of company operations. No support for organizations lacking significant employee interest or involvement. No grants to individuals; no loans.

Application information: Application form not required.

   Initial approach: Proposal
   Copies of proposal: 1
   Deadline(s): Feb. 28 and Sept. 1
   Board meeting date(s): Apr. and Oct.

Officers and Directors:* Frank S. Hermance,* Chair. and Pres.; Elizabeth R. Varet,* V.P.; Kathryn E. Londra, Secy.-Treas.; Lewis Cole; Helmut N. Friedlaender.

EIN: 136095939

Selected grants: The following grants were reported in 2004.

$100,648 to Rochester School District, Rochester.

$100,000 to Eagles Youth Partnership, Philadelphia, PA. 2 grants: $50,000 each

$95,452 to Binghamton City School District, Binghamton, NY. For book challenge.

$37,664 to United Way of Southeastern Pennsylvania, Philadelphia, PA.

$35,000 to Paoli Memorial Hospital Foundation, Paoli, PA.

$29,080 to National Merit Scholarship Corporation, Evanston, IL.

$25,108 to United Way of Portage County, Ravenna, OH.

$25,000 to Cornell Cooperative Extension of Broome County, Binghamton, NY.

$25,000 to Memorial Sloan-Kettering Cancer Center, New York, NY.

8082

The Angela Foundation ✧

875 Brackbill Rd.
Gap, PA   17527   (717) 442-0557
Contact: LaWonna Goedhart, Pres.
FAX: (717) 442-0564;
E-mail: theangelafoundation@gmail.com;
URL: http://www.angelafoundation.com

Established in 1998 in PA.

Donors: Anne Beiler; Jonas Beiler; The Coca-Cola Co.

Foundation type: Independent foundation.

Financial data (yr. ended 12/31/05): Assets, $5,248,833 (M); gifts received, $1,921,412; expenditures, $559,591; qualifying distributions, $537,632; giving activities include $519,335 for 39 grants (high: $316,672; low: $84).

Purpose and activities: The Angela Foundation was established to provide financial support for programs and ministries assisting children and families. Giving primarily to Christian counseling

centers who provide services free of charge to women and children.

Fields of interest: Human services; Protestant agencies & churches.

Type of support: General/operating support.

Limitations: Applications not accepted. Giving primarily in the Lancaster County, PA, area. No grants to individuals, or for capital campaigns, equipment, endowments, direct services, or for media productions.

Publications: Annual report.

Application information: Grant application process is currently closed.

Officers and Board Members:* Jonas Beiler,* Chair.; LaWonna Goedhart,* Pres.; Doris Swaim,* Secy.; Anne Belier; LaVale Beiler; Merrill Smucker; Richard Smyth.

EIN: 232985480

8083

The Annenberg Foundation Trust at Sunnylands ▼

150 Radnor-Chester Rd., Ste. A-200
Radnor, PA   19087   (484) 581-1290
Contact: Megan O'Hare, Acct.; Laura Gordon, Fin. Mgr.
FAX: (484) 581-1285;
E-mail: mohare@sunnylandstrust.org; URL: http://www.sunnylands.org

Established in 2001 in PA; reclassified as an operating foundation in 2004.

Donor: The Annenberg Foundation.

Foundation type: Operating foundation.

Financial data (yr. ended 6/30/05): Assets, $262,486,821 (M); expenditures, $10,306,042; qualifying distributions, $15,225,534; giving activities include $4,737,203 for grants, and $5,092,907 for 4 foundation-administered programs.

Purpose and activities: Giving primarily to mental health services, human services, and higher education.

Fields of interest: Higher education; Mental health/crisis services; Children/youth, services.

Type of support: Conferences/seminars; Research.

Limitations: Applications not accepted. Giving primarily in Philadelphia, PA. No grants to individuals.

Application information: Contributes only to pre-selected organizations.

Trustee: Leonore Annenberg.

Director: Kathleen Hall Jamieson.

Number of staff: 2 part-time professional.

EIN: 256774871

Selected grants: The following grants were reported in 2005.

$4,737,203 to University of Pennsylvania, Philadelphia, PA. 3 grants: $2,977,851 (For Civics Education classes), $1,560,653 (For health programs), $198,699 (For public policy programs).

8084

The Annenberg Foundation ▼

Radnor Financial Ctr., Ste. A-200
150 N. Radnor-Chester Rd.
Radnor, PA   19087   (610) 341-9066
Contact: Dr. Gail C. Levin, Exec. Dir.
FAX: (610) 964-8688;
E-mail: info@annenbergfoundation.org; Additional

address (CA office): Center West, Ste. 1605, 10877 Wilshire Blvd., Los Angeles, CA 90024, tel.: (310) 209-4560, FAX: (310) 209-1631; URL: http://www.annenbergfoundation.org

Established in 1989 in PA.

Donor: Hon. Walter H. Annenberg‡.

Foundation type: Independent foundation.

Financial data (yr. ended 6/30/06): Assets, $2,539,268,854 (M); expenditures, $293,947,498; qualifying distributions, $273,414,830; giving activities include $273,414,830 for grants.

Purpose and activities: The foundation exists to advance public well-being through improved communication. As a principal means of achieving this goal, the foundation encourages the development of more effective ways to share ideas and knowledge. The foundation concentrates on four objectives: 1) Expanding educational opportunities; 2) Bolstering arts and cultural and institutions; 3) Fostering good citizenship and strengthening civic life; and 4) Supporting medical centers and continuing medical education.

Fields of interest: Arts education; Visual arts; Performing arts; Humanities; Arts; Education, reform; Education, early childhood education; Elementary/secondary school reform; Higher education; Education; Environment; Animal welfare; Health care; Human services; Community development; Public affairs.

International interests: Africa; Asia; England; France.

Type of support: Program development.

Limitations: Giving nationally with preference for southern CA, greater Philadelphia, PA, and New York, NY; some unsolicited grants to the United Kingdom, France, Africa and Asia. No support for political activities or individual K-12 schools. No grants to individuals, or for scholarships or basic research.

Publications: Application guidelines; Grants list; Multi-year report.

Application information: The letter of inquiry should not include any additional supporting information such as videotapes/compact discs, financial reports, annual reports, or books. Proposals are not accepted unless requested by a representative of the foundation. If sending letter of inquiry via e-mail, please place letter in the body of the e-mail as text. The foundation does not open attachments. Application form not required.

   Initial approach: Letter of inquiry only (no more than 2 pages)
   Copies of proposal: 1
   Deadline(s): See foundation's Web site for additional application information
   Board meeting date(s): Varies
   Final notification: Within 6 months

Officers and Trustees:* Leonore Annenberg,* Chair. and Pres.; Wallis Annenberg,* V.P.; L. Dianne Lomonaco, Secy. and Dir., HR and Risk Mgmt.; Paul J. Manganiello, Treas. and Dir., Finance; David Valentine, Cont.; Lauren Bon; Charles Annenberg Weingarten; Gregory Annenberg Weingarten.

Number of staff: 14 full-time professional; 2 part-time professional; 12 full-time support; 1 part-time support.

EIN: 236257083

Selected grants: The following grants were reported in 2005.

$3,000,000 to University of Pennsylvania, Annenberg Public Policy Center, Philadelphia, PA. For Justice Talking series.

$2,910,195 to American Heart Association, Los Angeles, CA. For Cardiac Life Saver Program which provides fire departments with electrocardiogram equipment.

$1,430,778 to Public Education Network, DC. Toward $4,000,000 commitment to support interrelated projects and strategies that will make public engagement an essential part of national discourse on public school reform, and to disseminate PEN's Annenberg -funded reports on teacher quality, standards and accountability, and school and community services.

$1,000,000 to Delancey Street Foundation, San Francisco, CA. To provide structured educational and living environment for men and women, most of who are ex-felons and substance abusers.

$1,000,000 to Metropolitan Museum of Art, New York, NY. For acquisition of Gilman Collection of Photographs.

$600,000 to George Bush Presidential Library Foundation, College Station, TX. For George Bush Presidential Library.

$340,500 to DreamYard Drama Project, New York, NY. For DreamYard Prep, proposed New York City Public School.

$332,000 to Center for Public Integrity, DC. Payment toward a $500,000 commitment for Charles Lewis Special Projects Fund to allow Center to pursue immediate projects and respond quickly to emerging issues of high national and international significance.

$128,250 to Metropolitan Opera Association, New York, NY. For performances and programs. An additional commitment of $15,000,000 supports Metropolitan Opera's campaign for Saturday afternoon radio broadcasts of live performances, heard throughout the USA and other countries on five continents.

$100,000 to Humane Society of San Diego, San Diego, CA. For general operating support to further the mission of San Diego Humane Society and SPCA to promote humane treatment of animals, prevent cruelty to animals and provide education to enhance human-animal bond.

8085
AO North America, Inc. ✧ ☆
P.O. Box 1658
West Chester, PA   19380   (610) 344-2000
FAX: (610) 344-2001; E-mail: ellisa@aona.org;
Course Info.: c/o AO North America Continuing Medical Education, 1690 Russell Rd., Paoli, PA 19301, tel.: (800) 769-1391 or (610) 695-2459; FAX: (610) 695-2420; E-mail: registrar@aona.org; URL: http://www.aona.org

Established in 1992 in PA.
Donor: AO/ASIF Foundation.
Foundation type: Independent foundation.
Financial data (yr. ended 6/30/05): Assets, $3,354,034 (M); gifts received, $4,977,727; expenditures, $3,671,060; qualifying distributions, $3,662,795; giving activities include $250,646 for 21+ grants (high: $80,000), and $900,000 for 10 grants to individuals (high: $150,000; low: $75,000).
Purpose and activities: The organization is dedicated to the advancement of patient care in orthopedic, craniomaxillofacial, spine, and veterinary surgery. Its mission is to improve the care of patients with musculo-skeletal injuries and their sequelae in North America, through education and research in the principles, practice and results of

treatment. Recipients chosen on the basis of their knowledge of orthopedic medicine for their research ability. Support given to trauma research projects, training in the management and care of teachers, and to visiting professors in the teaching of orthopedic, maxillofacial, spine or veterinary trauma treatment. The organization has also established The Kathryn Cramer Memorial Fellowship to foster medical students, young orthopaedic residents, orthopaedic trauma fellows, and junior orthopedic trauma faculty who are interested in educational and research endeavors in orthopedics (preferably orthopedic trauma).
Fields of interest: Higher education; Medical school/education; Hospitals (general); Medical research, institute; Nerve, muscle & bone research; Orthopedics research.
Type of support: Research.
Limitations: Giving on a national and international basis. No grants for purchase instruments or implants for research, equipment, salaries or travel expenses.
Application information: Grants rarely exceed $5,000 for research projects. Maximum funding for visiting professor program: $3,000 per professor from North America, $6,000 per professor from abroad. Application form required.
  Initial approach: Letter, telephone, or fax for application guidelines, or refer to foundation Web site for guidelines
  Copies of proposal: 10
  Deadline(s): None
  Board meeting date(s): Jan. 15, Apr. 15, July 15, and Oct. 15
Officers: Jack H. Wilber, M.D., Pres.; James E. Gerry, Treas.
EIN: 232701788
Selected grants: The following grants were reported in 2005.
$150,000 to University of Toronto, Toronto, Canada. .
$75,000 to Cleveland Clinic Foundation, Cleveland, OH.
$75,000 to New England Baptist Hospital, Boston, MA.
$75,000 to University of Manitoba, Winnipeg, Canada. .
$75,000 to University of Utah, Salt Lake City, UT.
$10,000 to University of Pittsburgh, Pittsburgh, PA.
$5,000 to Carolinas Medical Center, Charlotte, NC.
$5,000 to Dartmouth College, Hanover, NH.
$5,000 to Massachusetts General Hospital, Boston, MA.
$5,000 to University of Kansas Medical Center, Kansas City, KS.

8086
The Arcadia Foundation ▼
105 E. Logan St.
Norristown, PA   19401-3058
Contact: Marilyn Lee Steinbright, Pres.

Incorporated in 1964 in PA.
Donors: Edith C. Steinbright†; Marilyn Lee Steinbright.
Foundation type: Independent foundation.
Financial data (yr. ended 9/30/06): Assets, $22,204,943 (M); expenditures, $6,027,430; qualifying distributions, $5,877,000; giving activities include $5,877,000 for 31 grants (high: $800,000; low: $2,000; average: $5,000–$500,000).

Purpose and activities: Emphasis on hospitals and hospital building funds, health agencies and services, nursing, hospices, early childhood, adult and higher education, libraries, child development and welfare agencies, youth organizations, and social service and general welfare agencies, including care of the handicapped, aged, and hungry; support also for family services, the environment and conservation, wildlife and animal welfare, religious organizations, historical preservation, and music organizations.
Fields of interest: Performing arts, music; Historic preservation/historical societies; Education, early childhood education; Child development, education; Higher education; Adult/continuing education; Libraries/library science; Education; Environment, natural resources; Environment; Animal welfare; Animals/wildlife, preservation/protection; Hospitals (general); Nursing care; Health care; Health organizations, association; Food services; Human services; Children/youth, services; Child development, services; Family services; Residential/custodial care, hospices; Aging, centers/services; Christian agencies & churches; Protestant agencies & churches; Religion; General charitable giving; Aging; Disabilities, people with; Economically disadvantaged.
Type of support: General/operating support; Continuing support; Annual campaigns; Capital campaigns; Building/renovation; Equipment; Endowments; Program development; Scholarship funds; Research.
Limitations: Applications not accepted. Giving limited to eastern PA organizations whose addresses have zip codes beginning with 18 and 19. Generally, low support for cultural programs. No grants to individuals, or for deficit financing, land acquisition, fellowships, demonstration projects, publications, or conferences; no loans.
Publications: Annual report.
Application information: Contributes only to pre-selected organizations. The foundation has suspended new grantmaking until 2010.
  Board meeting date(s): Nov.
Officers and Directors: * Marilyn Lee Steinbright,* Pres.; Tanya Hashorva,* V.P.; David P. Sandler,* Secy.; Harvey S.S. Miller,* Treas.; Edward L. Jones, Jr.; Dr. Bette E. Landman.
EIN: 236399772
Selected grants: The following grants were reported in 2005.
$750,000 to Montgomery Hospital Foundation, Norristown, PA.
$500,000 to American Red Cross, Southeastern Pennsylvania Chapter, Philadelphia, PA.
$500,000 to Arcadia University, Glenside, PA.
$500,000 to Pennsylvania Academy of the Fine Arts, Philadelphia, PA.
$500,000 to Philadelphia Zoo, Philadelphia, PA.
$23,000 to Philadelphia University, Philadelphia, PA.
$20,000 to Alliance to Protect Life, Wyalusing, PA.
$20,000 to Mennonite Historians of Eastern Pennsylvania, Harleysville, PA.
$15,000 to Easter Seal Society of Southeastern Pennsylvania and Delaware County, Media, PA.
$10,000 to Variety Club of the Delaware Valley, Philadelphia, PA.

8087
Archer Foundation ◇
P.O. Box 418
Upper Darby, PA 19082-0418 (610) 723-0963
Contact: Wayne K. Lynch, Pres.
E-mail: wlynch@advancement.org

Donor: George W. Moffitt, Jr.
Foundation type: Independent foundation.
Financial data (yr. ended 12/31/05): Assets, $619,453 (M); expenditures, $957,141; qualifying distributions, $957,141; giving activities include $953,750 for grants.
Purpose and activities: Giving primarily for evangelical Christian organizations and missionary agencies.
International interests: Africa; Australia; Caribbean; Europe; South America.
Limitations: Giving primarily in PA. No grants to individuals.
Application information: The foundation generally does not accept unsolicited applications.
Application form required.
  Initial approach: E-mail
  Board meeting date(s): Mar. and Sept.
Officers: Wayne K. Lynch, Pres.; H. Eugene Vickers, Secy.; Robert F. Dolan, Treas.
Number of staff: None.
EIN: 236442014

8088
Arete Foundation ◇
1845 Walnut St., 10th Fl.
Philadelphia, PA 19103 (215) 717-3341
Contact: Sue Ann Taylor, Exec. Dir.

Established in 1986 in PA.
Foundation type: Independent foundation.
Financial data (yr. ended 11/30/05): Assets, $29,888,146 (M); gifts received, $3,560,300; expenditures, $718,794; qualifying distributions, $670,942; giving activities include $670,942 for 40 grants (high: $100,124; low: $35; average: $5,000–$25,000).
Fields of interest: Higher education; Medical school/education; Education; Human services; Jewish federated giving programs; Science; Religion.
Type of support: Continuing support; Annual campaigns; Conferences/seminars; Publication; Scholarship funds; Research.
Limitations: Giving primarily in Philadelphia, PA.
Application information: Application form not required.
  Initial approach: Detailed letter
  Copies of proposal: 1
  Deadline(s): None
  Board meeting date(s): Annually
Officer: Sue Ann Taylor, Exec. Dir.
Trustees: Betsy Z. Cohen; Edward E. Cohen.
EIN: 236779271
Selected grants: The following grants were reported in 2003.
$112,000 to National Museum of American Jewish History, Philadelphia, PA.
$100,000 to American Academy in Rome, New York, NY.
$60,000 to Metropolitan Opera Association, New York, NY.
$45,000 to American School of Classical Studies at Athens, Princeton, NJ.

$35,000 to University of Pennsylvania, Philadelphia, PA. For Center for Judaic Studies.
$33,000 to Bryn Mawr College, Bryn Mawr, PA.
$30,000 to Tribeca Organization, New York, NY.
$26,666 to W H Y Y, Philadelphia, PA.
$20,000 to Philadelphia Museum of Art, Philadelphia, PA.
$15,000 to Jewish Federation of Greater Philadelphia, Philadelphia, PA.

8089
Arkema Inc. Foundation
(formerly Atofina Chemicals, Inc. Foundation)
2000 Market St.
Philadelphia, PA 19103-3222 (215) 419-7000
Contact: Diane Milici, Exec. Asst.

Trust established in 1957 in PA.
Donors: Elf Atochem North America, Inc.; Atofina Chemicals, Inc.; Arkema Inc.
Foundation type: Company-sponsored foundation.
Financial data (yr. ended 12/31/04): Assets, $130,699 (M); gifts received, $622,980; expenditures, $573,854; qualifying distributions, $571,067; giving activities include $542,732 for 15 grants (high: $143,193; low: $3,000), and $28,335 for 78 employee matching gifts.
Purpose and activities: The foundation supports organizations involved with arts and culture, education, and government and public administration. Special emphasis is directed toward programs designed to advance elementary school science education.
Fields of interest: Media/communications; Museums; Arts; Elementary school/education; Higher education; Education; Federated giving programs; Science; Government/public administration.
Type of support: General/operating support; Continuing support; Annual campaigns; Building/renovation; Equipment; Emergency funds; Employee matching gifts; Employee-related scholarships; Matching/challenge support.
Limitations: Giving primarily in areas of company operations, with some emphasis on the Philadelphia, PA, area. No support for veterans', fraternal, labor, or sectarian religious organizations. No grants to individuals (except for employee-related scholarships), or for endowments, special projects, research, publications, conferences, courtesy advertising, entertainment promotions, or public education; no loans.
Application information: Application form not required.
  Initial approach: Proposal
  Copies of proposal: 1
  Deadline(s): None
  Board meeting date(s): Mar., June, Sept., and Dec.
  Final notification: 1 to 3 months
Trustees: George Cornelius; Chris Giangrasso; Doug Sharp.
Number of staff: 1 part-time professional.
EIN: 236256818
Selected grants: The following grants were reported in 2003.
$145,000 to Philadelphia Museum of Art, Philadelphia, PA. 2 grants: $120,000, $25,000
$123,233 to Science Teacher Education, Philadelphia, PA.
$18,030 to United Way of Southwest Alabama, Mobile, AL.

$15,000 to Philadelphia Orchestra Association, Philadelphia, PA.
$10,000 to Franklin Institute Science Museum, Philadelphia, PA.
$10,000 to YMCA of Philadelphia and Vicinity, Philadelphia, PA.
$6,310 to United Way of Bucks County, Fairless Hills, PA.
$5,000 to American Council on Science and Health, New York, NY.
$5,000 to W H Y Y-TV, Philadelphia, PA.

8090
Armstrong Foundation ◇
(formerly Armstrong World Industries Charitable Foundation)
2500 Columbia Ave.
Lancaster, PA 17603 (717) 397-0611

Established in 1985 in PA.
Donor: Armstrong World Industries, Inc.
Foundation type: Company-sponsored foundation.
Financial data (yr. ended 12/31/04): Assets, $8,057,916 (M); gifts received, $5,000,000; expenditures, $1,263,490; qualifying distributions, $1,248,920; giving activities include $1,248,920 for 217 grants (high: $500,000; low: $35).
Purpose and activities: The foundation supports organizations involved with higher education, health, human services, and civic affairs.
Fields of interest: Higher education; Health care; Children/youth, services; Family services; Human services; Federated giving programs; Public policy, research; Government/public administration; General charitable giving; Minorities; Economically disadvantaged.
Type of support: Annual campaigns; Building/renovation; Scholarship funds; Employee matching gifts.
Limitations: Applications not accepted. Giving on a national basis. No grants to individuals.
Application information: Contributes only to pre-selected organizations.
Officers: John N. Rigas, Pres.; David A. Frank, Secy.; Barry M. Sullivan, Treas.; Walter T. Gangl, Genl. Counsel.
Directors: Matthew J. Angello; Steven J. Senkowski; Dorothy Brown Smith.
EIN: 232387950
Selected grants: The following grants were reported in 2004.
$500,000 to United Way of Lancaster County, Lancaster, PA.
$400,000 to Goodwill Industries of Middle Georgia, Macon, GA.
$157,340 to National Merit Scholarship Corporation, Evanston, IL.
$25,000 to Franklin and Marshall College, Lancaster, PA.
$18,738 to United Way of Anderson County, Oak Ridge, TN.
$16,798 to Thaddeus Stevens Foundation, Lancaster, PA.
$13,230 to United Way of Central Georgia, Macon, GA.
$12,366 to United Way of Mifflin-Juniata, Lewistown, PA.
$6,048 to United Way of South Central Kentucky, Somerset, KY.
$300 to Cedar Crest College, Allentown, PA.

8091
Asplundh Foundation ✧
708 Blair Mill Rd.
Willow Grove, PA 19090 (215) 784-4200

Incorporated in 1953 in PA.
Donors: Carl H. Asplundh†; Lester Asplundh†.
Foundation type: Independent foundation.
Financial data (yr. ended 12/31/05): Assets, $28,293,614 (M); gifts received, $58,000; expenditures, $1,308,408; qualifying distributions, $1,308,408; giving activities include $1,301,000 for 138 grants (high: $125,000; low: $500).
Purpose and activities: Giving primarily to Christian agencies, churches, and schools.
Fields of interest: Historical activities; Arts; Education; Environment; Hospitals (general); Human services; Christian agencies & churches.
Limitations: Giving primarily in PA; some funding nationally. No grants to individuals.
Application information:
  Initial approach: Letter
  Deadline(s): None
Officers: Edward L. Asplundh, Pres.; Christopher B. Asplundh, V.P.; Kurt H. Asplundh, Secy.-Treas.
EIN: 236297246
Selected grants: The following grants were reported in 2004.
$125,000 to Abington Memorial Hospital Foundation, Abington, PA.
$50,000 to Childrens Hospital of Philadelphia, Philadelphia, PA.
$50,000 to Quaker School at Horsham, Horsham, PA.
$30,000 to Pennypack Ecological Restoration Trust, Huntingdon Valley, PA. 2 grants: $25,000, $5,000
$25,000 to Doylestown Hospital, Doylestown, PA.
$5,000 to Phillips Academy, Andover, MA.
$2,000 to Childrens Hospital Foundation, Philadelphia, PA.
$1,500 to Muhlenberg College, Allentown, PA.
$1,500 to Trust for Public Land, San Francisco, CA.

8092
Dexter F. and Dorothy H. Baker Foundation
c/o Air Products & Chemicals, Inc.
7201 Hamilton Blvd.
Allentown, PA 18195-1526 (610) 481-7537
Contact: Ellen B. Ghelardi, Exec. Dir.

Established in 1986 in PA.
Donors: Dexter F. Baker; Dorothy H. Baker.
Foundation type: Independent foundation.
Financial data (yr. ended 12/31/05): Assets, $17,196,590 (M); expenditures, $1,033,153; qualifying distributions, $919,124; giving activities include $857,811 for 63 grants (high: $100,000; low: $100).
Purpose and activities: Giving primarily for arts and culture, youth, education, and social service initiatives.
Fields of interest: Arts education; Visual arts; Performing arts; Social entrepreneurship; Youth.
Type of support: Film/video/radio; Management development/capacity building; General/operating support; Continuing support; Annual campaigns; Capital campaigns; Equipment; Program development; Conferences/seminars; Curriculum development; Scholarship funds; Technical assistance; Matching/challenge support.

Limitations: Giving primarily in Lehigh, and Northampton counties, PA, trustee endorsed grants in Collier, County FL, Hilton Head, SC, Syracuse, NY, Dallas, TX, San Francisco, CA, and Philadelphia, PA, only. No support for non-Presbyterian religious organizations, for government or for political organizations. No grants to individuals, or for endowment funds or for debt reduction.
Publications: Application guidelines.
Application information: Application form required.
  Initial approach: Request the foundation's letter of intent form, preceded by telephone call with Exec. Dir.
  Copies of proposal: 1
  Deadline(s): Letter of intent deadline: Mar. 15th, if given permission
  Board meeting date(s): Nov.
  Final notification: Dec. 1
Officers and Trustees:* Dexter F. Baker, Chair.; Dorothy H. Baker, Vice-Chair; Ellen Baker Ghelardi,* Exec. Dir.; Carolyn Baker; Leslie Baker Boris; Susan B. Royal.
Number of staff: 1 full-time professional; 1 part-time support.
EIN: 232453230
Selected grants: The following grants were reported in 2005.
$100,000 to Muhlenberg College, Allentown, PA.
$54,165 to Lehigh University, Bethlehem, PA. 2 grants: $11,665, $42,500
$50,000 to Lehigh Valley Community Foundation, Allentown, PA.
$25,000 to Lehigh County Historical Society, Allentown, PA.
$15,000 to Allentown Art Museum, Allentown, PA.
$15,000 to Community Services for Children, Allentown, PA.
$10,000 to Community Action Committee of the Lehigh Valley, Bethlehem, PA.
$6,500 to United Way of the Greater Lehigh Valley, Bethlehem, PA.
$5,000 to Touchstone Theater, Bethlehem, PA.

8093
The Ball Family Foundation ✧
(formerly Russell C. Ball Foundation)
c/o American Manufacturing Corp.
555 Croton Rd., Ste. 300
King of Prussia, PA 19406-3176

Donors: Philadelphia Gear Corp.; American Manufacturing Corp.; Lehigh Consumer Products Corp.; Goddard Systems, Inc.
Foundation type: Company-sponsored foundation.
Financial data (yr. ended 12/31/04): Assets, $109,433 (M); gifts received, $300,000; expenditures, $412,035; qualifying distributions, $409,315; giving activities include $409,220 for 18 grants (high: $231,760; low: $25).
Purpose and activities: The foundation supports organizations involved with education, health, recreation, human services, and religion.
Fields of interest: Elementary/secondary education; Higher education; Education; Health care; Recreation; Human services; Federated giving programs; Religion.
Limitations: Applications not accepted. Giving primarily in PA.
Application information: Contributes only to pre-selected organizations.

Officers and Directors:* Russell C. Ball III,* Pres. and Treas.; Andrew L. Ball,* V.P.; Robert H. Strouse, V.P.; Paul F. Brennan, Secy.
EIN: 516017780
Selected grants: The following grants were reported in 2004.
$231,760 to Haverford School, Haverford, PA.
$76,150 to Baldwin School, Bryn Mawr, PA.
$50,000 to Harvard University, Cambridge, MA.
$5,000 to Bryn Mawr Hospital Foundation, Bryn Mawr, PA.
$5,000 to Childrens Hospital Foundation, Philadelphia, PA.
$2,760 to Baker Industries, Malvern, PA.
$2,200 to Foundation Fighting Blindness, Owings Mills, MD.
$1,875 to Philadelphia Museum of Art, Philadelphia, PA.
$1,500 to American Cancer Society, Atlanta, GA.
$1,000 to Brown University, Providence, RI.

8094
Bannerot-Lappe Foundation ✧
c/o Mellon Bank, N.A.
P.O. Box 185
Pittsburgh, PA 15230-0185 (412) 234-0023
Contact: Laurie A. Moritz, Mellon Financial Corp.

Established in 1994 in PA.
Donor: Joane Lappe Bowman†.
Foundation type: Independent foundation.
Financial data (yr. ended 5/31/05): Assets, $6,362,688 (M); expenditures, $403,033; qualifying distributions, $361,849; giving activities include $349,500 for 8 grants (high: $80,000; low: $9,500).
Fields of interest: Animals/wildlife, special services; Blind/visually impaired.
Limitations: Giving on a national basis. No grants to individuals.
Application information: Application form required.
  Initial approach: Letter to request application form
  Deadline(s): None
Trustee: Mellon Bank, N.A.
EIN: 256440597
Selected grants: The following grants were reported in 2005.
$80,000 to Guiding Eyes for the Blind, Yorktown Heights, NY.
$80,000 to Seeing Eye, Morristown, NJ.
$80,000 to Western Pennsylvania School for Blind Children, Pittsburgh, PA.
$35,000 to Leader Dogs for the Blind, Rochester, MI.
$25,000 to Freedom Guide Dogs for the Blind, Cassville, NY.
$20,000 to Foundation Fighting Blindness, Owings Mills, MD.
$20,000 to Guide Dog Foundation for the Blind, Smithtown, NY.

8095
Barra Foundation, Inc.
8200 Flourtown Ave., Ste. 12
Wyndmoor, PA 19038-7976
Contact: William Harrall III, Pres.
FAX: (215) 836-1033;
E-mail: william.harral@verizon.net

Incorporated in 1963 in DE.

Donor: Robert L. McNeil, Jr.
Foundation type: Independent foundation.
Financial data (yr. ended 12/31/05): Assets, $58,207,772 (M); expenditures, $2,830,649; qualifying distributions, $2,664,977; giving activities include $2,377,864 for grants (high: $500,000; low: $1,000).
Purpose and activities: Giving for the advancement and diffusion of knowledge and its effective application to human needs in certain fields, particularly in 18th Century American art and material culture. Projects must be pilot studies or enterprises requiring foresight, not supported by other agencies or individuals; publication of studies required.
Fields of interest: Humanities; Arts; Education; Health care; Health organizations; Human services; Homeless.
Type of support: Program development; Conferences/seminars; Seed money; Matching/challenge support.
Limitations: Giving limited to organizations in the greater Philadelphia, PA, area. No support for religious organizations, or for environmental or preservation groups. No grants to individuals, or for annual or capital campaigns, building or endowment funds, operating budgets, deficit drives, scholarships, fellowships, ongoing programs, publications, catalogues or exhibitions; no loans.
Publications: Program policy statement.
Application information: Application form required.
　Initial approach: Letter (1 to 2 pages)
　Copies of proposal: 3
　Deadline(s): None
　Board meeting date(s): Nov. and as appropriate
　Final notification: 3 to 6 months
Officers and Directors:* Seymour S. Preston III,* Chair.; William Harrall III,* Pres. and Treas.; A. Louis Denton,* V.P.; Lowell S. Thomas, Jr.,* Secy.; Harry E. Cerino; Robert P. Hauptfuhrer; Herman R. Hutchinson*; Victoria M. LeVine; Joanna M. Lewis; Collin F. McNeil; Robert L. McNeil, Jr.; Robert L. McNeil III.
Number of staff: 1 part-time professional; 1 part-time support.
EIN: 236277885

8096
Bayer Foundation ▼ ✧
(formerly Miles Inc. Foundation)
100 Bayer Rd.
Pittsburgh, PA 15205-9741 (412) 777-2000
Contact: Rebecca Lucore, Exec. Dir.
URL: http://www.bayerus.com/about/community/i_foundation.html

Established in 1985 in PA.
Donor: Bayer Corp.
Foundation type: Company-sponsored foundation.
Financial data (yr. ended 12/31/05): Assets, $46,354,998 (M); gifts received, $3,126,237; expenditures, $6,472,769; qualifying distributions, $6,386,310; giving activities include $6,386,310 for 430 grants (high: $365,000; low: $300).
Purpose and activities: The foundation supports organizations involved with arts and culture, education, the environment, health, employment, human services, science, and civic affairs.
Fields of interest: Arts education; Arts; Education; Environment, natural resources; Environmental education; Health care; Employment; Human services; Science, formal/general education; Science; Public affairs; Youth.

Type of support: Continuing support; Capital campaigns; Program development; Curriculum development.
Limitations: Giving primarily in areas of company operations, with emphasis on Berkeley and Emeryville, CA, West Haven, CT, Elkhart, IN, East Walpole, MA, Kansas City, MO, Research Triangle Park, NC, Morristown, NJ, Tarrytown, NY, Pittsburgh, PA, and New Martinsville, WV. No support for discriminatory, political, or religious organizations. No grants to individuals, or for endowments, debt reduction or general operating support, charitable dinners, events, or sponsorships, community or event advertising, student trips or exchange programs, athletic sponsorships or scholarships, or telephone solicitations.
Publications: Application guidelines; Program policy statement.
Application information: Visit Web site for nearest company facility. Proposals should be no longer than 12 pages. Application form not required.
　Initial approach: Proposal to nearest company facility
　Copies of proposal: 1
　Deadline(s): None; Mar. 15 and Sept. 15 for organizations located in Tarrytown, NY
　Board meeting date(s): Jan. and Sept.
　Final notification: Following board meetings
Officers and Directors:* Attila Molnar,* Pres.; Mark Ryan, V.P.; Tracy Spagnol, Treas.; Rebecca Lucore, Exec. Dir.; Gregory S. Babe; Peg Cherny; Meredith Fischer; Willie Scherf.
EIN: 251508079
Selected grants: The following grants were reported in 2003.
$365,000 to Yale University, New Haven, CT.
$250,000 to University of Pittsburgh, Cathedral of Learning, Pittsburgh, PA.
$135,000 to ASSET, Inc., Pittsburgh, PA.
$118,000 to Carnegie Mellon University, Pittsburgh, PA.
$95,000 to University of New Haven, West Haven, CT. For Bayer Unit Higher Education Alliance.
$90,000 to Massachusetts Institute of Technology, Department of Chemical Engineering, Cambridge, MA.
$75,000 to University of North Carolina, Chapel Hill, NC.
$55,000 to Clayton Cultural Arts Foundation, Clayton, NC.
$51,500 to New Haven Public Schools, New Haven, CT.
$50,000 to Connecticut United for Research Excellence, New Haven, CT. For BioBus.

8097
Helen D. Groome Beatty Trust ✧
c/o Steven Kaplan, Chair., Mellon Mid-Atlantic Charitable Trusts
1735 Market St., 3rd Fl.
Philadelphia, PA 19103 (215) 553-3389
Contact: Yolanda Danean Arnold, Secy., Mellon Mid-Atlantic Charitable Trusts

Trust established in 1951 in PA.
Donor: Helen D. Groome Beatty†.
Foundation type: Independent foundation.
Financial data (yr. ended 12/31/04): Assets, $12,224,671 (M); expenditures, $452,356; qualifying distributions, $435,286; giving activities include $420,356 for 27 grants (high: $58,000; low: $2,500).

Purpose and activities: The foundation focuses on the following giving areas: 1) Extracurricular education and character building programs for children and youth; 2) Support and quality of life enhancement programs for seniors living independently; 3) Women in distress; 4) Food for the hungry; and 5) Programs to benefit the blind and sight impaired.
Fields of interest: Education; Food distribution, groceries on wheels; Children/youth, services; Aging; Blind/visually impaired.
Type of support: General/operating support; Capital campaigns; Building/renovation.
Limitations: Giving limited to the 5-county Philadelphia, PA, area. No grants to individuals, or for endowment funds or operating budgets.
Publications: Application guidelines.
Application information: Application form required.
　Copies of proposal: 2
　Deadline(s): None
　Board meeting date(s): Nov. 15
Trustee: Mellon Bank, N.A.
EIN: 236224798

8098
The Beaver County Foundation
P.O. Box 569
Beaver, PA 15009 (724) 728-1331
Contact: Gloria Cheshier, Exec. Dir.
E-mail: bcfgloria@att.net; *URL:* http://www.beavercounty.com/Service/bcfoundationintro.asp

Established in 1992 in PA.
Foundation type: Community foundation.
Financial data (yr. ended 12/31/04): Assets, $3,134,258 (M); gifts received, $604,200; expenditures, $566,078; giving activities include $455,132 for grants.
Purpose and activities: The foundation seeks to make Beaver County a better place to live, play, work, and worship for generations to follow.
Fields of interest: Pharmacy/prescriptions; Substance abuse, services; Athletics/sports, equestrianism; Community development, neighborhood development; Economic development.
Type of support: General/operating support; Program development; Seed money; Scholarship funds; Research; Scholarships—to individuals.
Limitations: Giving limited to Beaver County, PA; support for pharmacological research or addiction interdiction given nationwide.
Publications: Informational brochure.
Application information: Application form required.
　Initial approach: 2-page letter or e-mail
　Copies of proposal: 1
　Deadline(s): None
　Board meeting date(s): Apr., July, Oct., and Dec.
　Final notification: Within 30 days after board meeting, or dependent on fund advisor meeting date
Officers and Directors:* Charles N. O'Data, Pres.; Carolyn Renninger,* Secy.; Paul Jewell,* Treas.; Gloria Cheshier, Exec. Dir.; Jessica Briggs, Genl. Counsel; Joe Baumann; Richard Blackwood; Richard Canonge; Jeffrey Druzak; Don Flick; Nancy Foster; Del Goedeker; Bernard Logan; Marianne Mantine; Fred Petro; Thomas Reed; Betty Sue Schaughency; Richard L. Shaw; Paul Sweeney; Joe Tosh II; Louise Vochko; Marian Zinkham.
Number of staff: 1 part-time professional.
EIN: 251660309

8099
Claude Worthington Benedum Foundation ▼ ✧
1400 Benedum-Trees Bldg.
223 4th Ave.
Pittsburgh, PA 15222 (412) 288-0360
Contact: William P. Getty, Pres.
FAX: (412) 288-0366; E-mail: info@benedum.org;
URL: http://www.benedum.org

Incorporated in 1944 in PA.
Donors: Michael Late Benedum†; Sarah N. Benedum†.
Foundation type: Independent foundation.
Financial data (yr. ended 12/31/04): Assets, $363,543,766 (M); expenditures, $18,901,008; qualifying distributions, $17,179,345; giving activities include $14,633,436 for 174 grants (high: $558,321; low: $4,000; average: $5,000–$150,000), and $816,000 for 3 loans/program-related investments (high: $500,000; low: $66,000).
Purpose and activities: Grants to WV organizations are in the areas of education, health and human services, and community and economic development. Local initiatives and partnerships are encouraged. In southwestern PA, grants are made primarily to projects for regional economic development, including business development and workforce education. In selected rural counties, grants are made to advance the quality of life for rural populations through a broad range of approaches.
Fields of interest: Education; Health care; Human services; Economic development; Community development.
Type of support: General/operating support; Program development; Seed money; Technical assistance; Program-related investments/loans; Matching/challenge support.
Limitations: Giving limited to southwestern PA and WV. No support for biomedical research, religious activities, national organizations, or individual elementary or secondary schools. No grants to individuals, or for student aid, fellowships, travel, ongoing operating expenses, annual appeals, membership drives, conferences, films, books, or audio-visual productions, unless an integral part of a foundation supported program.
Publications: Application guidelines; Annual report (including application guidelines); Grants list.
Application information: Proposals sent by fax or E-mail are not considered. Application form not required.
  Initial approach: Brief proposal (no longer than 5 pages)
  Copies of proposal: 1
  Deadline(s): None
  Board meeting date(s): Mar., June, Sept., and Dec.
  Final notification: 2 months
Officers and Trustees:* Paul G. Benedum, Jr.,* Chair.; William P. Getty,* Pres.; Dwight M. Keating, V.P. and C.I.O.; Beverly Railey Walter, V.P., Progs.; Rose A. McKee, Secy. and Dir., Admin.; Marcie G. Berry, Treas.; Gov. Gaston Caperton, Honorary Tr.; Hon. Robert E. Maxwell, Honorary Tr.; Paul R. Jenkins, Tr. Emeritus; Gov. Hulett C. Smith, Tr. Emeritus; L. Newton Thomas, Tr. Emeritus; Esther L. Barazzone; Ralph J. Bean, Jr.; G. Nicholas Beckwith III; Lloyd G. Jackson II; G. Randolph Worls.
Number of staff: 7 full-time professional; 4 full-time support.
EIN: 251086799

Selected grants: The following grants were reported in 2004.
$300,000 to Center for the Arts and Sciences of West Virginia, Charleston, WV. For first-year operations in Performance Hall and audience development.
$260,000 to Center for Rural Health Development, Dunbar, WV. For matching grant for West Virginia Rural Health Access Program for loan fund, rural health networking, recruitment and retention, leadership development, and technical assistance.
$250,000 to BIDCO Foundation, Charleston, WV. For start-up funding, including staffing, on behalf of Mid-Atlantic Technology, Research and Innovation Center (MATRIC).
$250,000 to Regional Education Service Agency (RESA I), Beckley, WV. For development of viable distance education model serving middle and high schools in southeast West Virginia through Marshall University and West Liberty State College.
$246,000 to Intermediate Unit I, California, PA. 2 grants: $171,000 (For introduction of robotics curriculum to eighth-grade math and science classes in southwestern Pennsylvania and northern panhandle of West Virginia, in partnership with Carnegie Mellon University), $75,000 (For provision of technical assistance to underperforming districts and creation of peer learning network of Intermediate Unit 1 principals, in partnership with University of Pittsburgh Principals Academy).
$100,000 to Pittsburgh Symphony Society, Pittsburgh, PA. For season support.
$100,000 to Tides Center PA, Pittsburgh, PA. For operating and program support for Sprout Fund.
$100,000 to West Virginia University Foundation, Morgantown, WV. For coordinator position working on integration of CARDIAC and Rural Health Education Partnership, payable over 2 years.

8100
Beneficia Foundation ✧
1 Pitcairn Pl., Ste. 3000
Jenkintown, PA 19046-3593 (215) 887-6700
Contact: Feodor U. Pitcairn, Exec. Secy.

Incorporated in 1953 in PA.
Donor: Members of the Feodor Pitcairn Family.
Foundation type: Independent foundation.
Financial data (yr. ended 4/30/05): Assets, $13,065,533 (M); expenditures, $1,239,446; qualifying distributions, $1,138,230; giving activities include $1,120,000 for 40 grants (high: $125,000; low: $10,000).
Purpose and activities: Giving primarily for natural resource conservation, animals and wildlife, and the arts.
Fields of interest: Performing arts; Arts; Environment, natural resources; Botanical gardens; Animals/wildlife, bird preserves; Animals/wildlife; Christian agencies & churches.
Publications: Informational brochure (including application guidelines).
Application information: Small, innovative projects with limited alternative sources of funding are favored. Application form not required.
  Initial approach: Letter
  Copies of proposal: 1
  Deadline(s): None
  Board meeting date(s): May

Officers and Directors:* Laren Pitcairn,* Pres.; J. Daniel Mitchell,* V.P.; Feodor U. Pitcairn,* Exec. Secy.; Mark J. Pennink,* Treas.; Deana P. Duncan; Miriam P. Mitchell; Eshowe P. Pennink; Kirstin O. Pitcairn; Mary Eleanor Pitcairn; Sharon R. Pitcairn; Heather D. Reynolds.
EIN: 246015630
Selected grants: The following grants were reported in 2004.
$100,000 to Academy of the New Church, Bryn Athyn, PA. For Mitchell Performing Arts Center.
$40,000 to Missouri Botanical Garden, Saint Louis, MO.
$25,000 to Brady Center to Prevent Gun Violence, DC. For unrestricted support.
$25,000 to General Church of the New Jerusalem, Bryn Athyn, PA. For unrestricted support.
$25,000 to Wildlife Conservation Society, Bronx, NY.
$20,000 to Wilderness Society, DC.
$18,050 to Bishop Museum, Honolulu, HI. For unrestricted support.
$15,000 to Abington Art Center, Jenkintown, PA. For unrestricted support.
$15,000 to Bucks County Symphony Society, Doylestown, PA. For unrestricted support.
$10,000 to National Wildlife Refuge Association, DC.

8101
David Berger Foundation ✧ ☆
1515 Market St., Ste. 1700
Philadelphia, PA 19102
Application address: c/o David Berger, 1622 Locust St., Philadelphia, PA 19103

Established in 1965 in PA.
Donor: David Berger.
Foundation type: Independent foundation.
Financial data (yr. ended 12/31/05): Assets, $1,370,800 (M); gifts received, $250,000; expenditures, $336,700; qualifying distributions, $327,495; giving activities include $327,495 for grants.
Purpose and activities: Giving primarily for Jewish organizations and health associations; support also for youth organizations and arts and culture.
Fields of interest: Arts; Higher education; Health organizations, association; Medical research, institute; Children/youth, services; Jewish federated giving programs; Jewish agencies & temples.
Type of support: General/operating support.
Limitations: Giving primarily in Palm Beach, FL, and Philadelphia, PA. No grants to individuals.
Application information:
  Initial approach: Letter
  Deadline(s): None
Officer: David Berger, Pres.
EIN: 236424659
Selected grants: The following grants were reported in 2004.
$100,000 to Duke of Edinburghs Award Scheme, London, England. For unrestricted support.
$35,000 to National Constitution Center, Philadelphia, PA. For unrestricted support.
$25,000 to International Tennis Hall of Fame and Tennis Museum, Newport, RI. For unrestricted support.
$1,435 to Temple Emanu-El. For unrestricted support.
$1,350 to Congregation Mikveh Israel, Philadelphia, PA. For unrestricted support.

$100 to Athenaeum of Philadelphia, Philadelphia, PA. For unrestricted support.

8102
Sybiel B. Berkman Foundation ✧
200 Gateway Twrs.
Pittsburgh, PA 15222

Established in 1965.
Donors: Myles P. Berkman; Jack N. Berkman†.
Foundation type: Independent foundation.
Financial data (yr. ended 12/31/05): Assets, $9,360,812 (M); expenditures, $466,563; qualifying distributions, $456,535; giving activities include $456,535 for 66 grants (high: $100,000; low: $65).
Purpose and activities: Giving primarily for the arts, education, health, children, youth and social services, and Jewish and other federated giving programs.
Fields of interest: Museums (art); Museums (ethnic/folk arts); Arts; Higher education; Education; Hospitals (general); Health organizations; Human services; Children/youth, services; Federated giving programs; Jewish federated giving programs; Jewish agencies & temples.
Limitations: Applications not accepted. Giving primarily in FL, New York, NY, and PA. No grants to individuals.
Application information: Contributes only to pre-selected organizations.
Officers and Trustees:* Myles P. Berkman,* Pres.; David J. Berkman,* V.P. and Secy.; William H. Berkman,* V.P. and Treas.; Monroe E. Berkman,* V.P.; Stephen L. Berkman,* V.P.
EIN: 346566801

8103
Berks County Community Foundation
501 Washington St., Ste. 801
P.O. Box 212
Reading, PA 19603-0212 (610) 685-2223
Contact: Kevin K. Murphy, Pres.; For grants: Richard C. Mappin, V.P., Grantmaking
FAX: (610) 685-2240; E-mail: info@bccf.org; Grant program E-mail: richardm@bccf.org; URL: http://www.bccf.org

Established in 1994 in PA.
Foundation type: Community foundation.
Financial data (yr. ended 6/30/05): Assets, $38,489,236 (M); gifts received, $3,308,704; expenditures, $4,302,847; giving activities include $2,859,068 for 571 grants (high: $500,000; low: $26), and $402,625 for 213 grants to individuals.
Purpose and activities: The mission of the foundation is to promote philanthropy and improve the quality of life for the residents of Berks County, PA.
Fields of interest: Arts, cultural/ethnic awareness; Historic preservation/historical societies; Arts; Higher education; Education; Environment; Animals/wildlife; Health care; Youth development; Community development, neighborhood development; Economic development; Community development; Federated giving programs; Aging.
Type of support: Capital campaigns; Program development; Conferences/seminars; Seed money; Scholarship funds; Research; Consulting services; Program-related investments/loans; Employee-related scholarships; Grants to

individuals; Scholarships—to individuals; Matching/challenge support.
Limitations: Giving limited to Berks County, PA for discretionary funds. No support for religious organizations from discretionary funds. No grants for operational support.
Publications: Application guidelines; Annual report; Financial statement; Grants list; Newsletter.
Application information: Visit foundation Web site for application information. Application form required.
Initial approach: Telephone
Copies of proposal: 1
Deadline(s): Varies
Board meeting date(s): Feb., Apr., June, Aug., Oct., and Dec.
Officers and Directors:* Julia H. Klein,* Chair.; Samuel A. McCullough,* Vice-Chair.; Kevin K. Murphy,* Pres.; Frances Aitken, V.P., Finance and Admin.; Richard C. Mappin, V.P., Grantmaking; J. William Widing III,* Secy.; Daniel B. Boyer III; Hon. Mary Ann Campbell; Nelson DeLeon; P. Michael Ehlerman; Gerard G. Johnson; Sidney D. Kline, Jr.; Thomas D. Leidy; Leon S. Myers; Joni S. Naugle; Paul R. Roedel; Jayne R. Schaeffer; Mary Ann Chelius Smith.
Number of staff: 5 full-time professional; 2 full-time support.
EIN: 232769892

8104
The Philip and Muriel Berman Foundation ▼
1150 S. Cedar Crest Blvd., Ste. 101
Allentown, PA 18103 (610) 433-7497
Contact: Jan Heffner, Admin.
FAX: (610) 437-1435; E-mail: pmbfound@ptd.net

Donors: Philip I. Berman†; Muriel M. Berman†.
Foundation type: Independent foundation.
Financial data (yr. ended 5/31/05): Assets, $25,411,519 (M); gifts received, $31,357,187; expenditures, $6,668,111; qualifying distributions, $6,653,203; giving activities include $6,605,000 for 11 grants (high: $6,500,000; low: $1,000).
Purpose and activities: Giving primarily for arts and culture, education, health and Jewish causes with special focus on eastern PA and Israel.
Fields of interest: Arts, cultural/ethnic awareness; Education; Health care; Jewish agencies & temples.
International interests: Israel.
Type of support: Endowments.
Limitations: Applications not accepted. Giving limited to eastern PA and Israel. No grants to individuals.
Application information: Contributes only to pre-selected organizations.
Officers and Directors:* Nancy Berman Bloch,* Pres. and Exec. Dir.; Jack Kushner,* Secy.; Alan Bloch,* Treas.
EIN: 236270983
Selected grants: The following grants were reported in 2005.
$6,500,000 to Alexander and Louisa Calder Foundation, New York, NY. For Stabile sculpture.
$35,000 to Lehigh University, Bethlehem, PA. 2 grants: $25,000 (For Jewish Studies program), $10,000 (To acquire Segal sculpture).
$25,000 to American Friends of the Israel Museum, New York, NY. For general operating support.
$10,000 to Philadelphia Museum of Art, Philadelphia, PA. For general operating support.

$5,000 to Storm King Art Center, Mountainville, NY. For art catalogue.

8105
Theodora B. Betz Foundation ✧
c/o Bruce Rosenfield
1600 Market St., Ste. 3600
Philadelphia, PA 19103-7212
Application address: c/o Henry Kwiecinski, 1617 John F. Kennedy Blvd., Ste. 1610, Philadelphia, PA, 19103

Established in 1989 in PA.
Foundation type: Independent foundation.
Financial data (yr. ended 4/30/05): Assets, $8,315,016 (M); expenditures, $1,345,180; qualifying distributions, $1,272,046; giving activities include $1,231,585 for 7 grants (high: $397,585; low: $25,000).
Purpose and activities: Giving primarily for cancer research, with emphasis on colo-rectal cancer.
Fields of interest: Higher education; Cancer research.
Type of support: Research.
Limitations: Giving primarily in CA, NH, and PA. No grants to individuals.
Application information: Application form not required.
Initial approach: Letter
Deadline(s): None
Trustees: Henry Kwiecinski; George Nofer.
EIN: 236965187
Selected grants: The following grants were reported in 2004.
$731,445 to Dartmouth College, Hanover, NH. For Dr. Mark Israel's ENC Research.
$541,289 to University of California, San Francisco, CA. 3 grants: $106,000 (For Marvin Sleisenger's Colorectal Cancer Research), $53,000 (For Marvin Sleisenger's Colorectal Cancer Research), $382,289 (For Marvin Sleisenger's Colorectal Cancer Research).
$250,000 to Pennsylvania Hospital of the University of Pennsylvania Health System, Philadelphia, PA. For Joan Karnell Cancer Center.
$25,000 to Foundations Behavioral Health, Doylestown, PA. For general support.

8106
Biesecker Foundation ✧ ☆
c/o Frank Mirabello
1701 Market St.
Philadelphia, PA 19103-2921

Donor: Frederick N. Biesecker.
Foundation type: Independent foundation.
Financial data (yr. ended 12/31/05): Assets, $114,346 (M); gifts received, $494,454; expenditures, $1,334,729; qualifying distributions, $1,308,597; giving activities include $1,308,597 for grants.
Purpose and activities: Giving primarily to a pediatric liver center.
Fields of interest: Health care; Liver disorders; Pediatrics.
Limitations: Applications not accepted. Giving primarily in PA. No grants to individuals.
Application information: Contributes only to pre-selected organizations.

Trustees: Frederick N. Biesecker; Suzanne K. Biesecker.
EIN: 251867942
Selected grants: The following grants were reported in 2004.
$1,000,000 to Childrens Hospital.

8107

The Birmingham Foundation ✧

Brashear Ctr.
2005 Sarah St.
Pittsburgh, PA   15203   (412) 481-2777
Contact: Mary Phan-Gruber, Exec. Dir.
FAX: (412) 481-2727; E-mail: info@bfpgh.org;
URL: http://www.birminghamfoundation.org

Established in 1996 in PA; converted with assets from the sale of The South Side Hospital.
Foundation type: Independent foundation.
Financial data (yr. ended 6/30/05): Assets, $21,020,694 (M); expenditures, $1,142,032; qualifying distributions, $956,740; giving activities include $800,000 for 42 grants (high: $56,000; low: $800).
Purpose and activities: The foundation is dedicated to health and human services, and serves as a change agent for improved health and wellness in South Pittsburgh, PA, through the dynamic use of resources such as grantmaking, information-sharing, partnering and leveraging of assets. Funding priorities include health access and education, strengthening children's well-being, enhancing senior safety and health, building the capacity of local organizations, and improving community life by addressing violence, substance abuse and mental health.
Fields of interest: Health care; Human services.
Type of support: Management development/capacity building; Capital campaigns; General/operating support; Program development; Technical assistance.
Limitations: Giving limited to the south Pittsburgh, PA, area served by the following zip codes: 15203 (South Side), 15210 (Mt. Oliver and Hilltop), and 15211 (Mt. Washington), including in particular the neighborhoods of Allentown, Arlington, Arlington Heights, Beltzhoover, Bon Air, Carrick, Duquesne Heights, Knoxville, Mt. Oliver, Washington, St. Clair Village, and the South Side Flats and Slopes. No grants to individuals, or for operating budgets, deficits, fund-raising, general research, overhead, scholarships, political campaigns; no loans.
Publications: Application guidelines; Biennial report; Grants list; Newsletter.
Application information: Details available on foundation Web site. The foundation suggests use of the Common Grant Application Format developed by Grantmakers of Western PA; see URL: http://www.gwpa.org for copies. Application form required.
   Initial approach: 1- to 3-page letter of intent or call for guidelines. Proposals submitted by fax or E-mail not accepted. Use clips, do not staple or bind proposals
   Copies of proposal: 1
   Deadline(s): 3-4 months prior to board meetings
   Board meeting date(s): Mar., June, and Nov.
Officers and Directors:* Floyd R. Ganassi,* Chair.; Daniel A. Goetz,* Chair. Emeritus; Mihai Marcu,* Vice-Chair., Grants; Terrence L. Wirginis,* Vice-Chair.; Hon. William T. Simmons,* Secy.; H. Don Gordon, Treas.; Mary Phan-Gruber, Exec. Dir.; Mark S. Bibro; Hugo Churchill; Carey A. Harris;

Kenneth McCrory; Jane H. Roesch; Eileen O. Smith; Duane Swager II.
Number of staff: 1 full-time professional; 1 full-time support.
EIN: 250965572
Selected grants: The following grants were reported in 2005.
$56,000 to Mercy Childrens Cedical Center, Pittsburgh, PA. For VAV Warrington Summer Program.
$50,000 to Goodwill Industries of Pittsburgh, Pittsburgh, PA. For non-Custodial Father's project.
$50,000 to YouthWorks, Pittsburgh, PA.
$35,000 to Greater Pittsburgh Community Food Bank, Duquesne, PA. For Pantry Credit Program.
$32,000 to Pittsburgh Action Against Rape, Pittsburgh, PA.
$30,000 to YWCA of Greater Pittsburgh, Pittsburgh, PA. For South Pittsburgh Financial Empowerment Program.
$29,000 to Center for Victims of Violence and Crime, Pittsburgh, PA. For Peace-It Together Program at Phillip Murray.
$25,000 to Animal Rescue League of Western Pennsylvania, Pittsburgh, PA. For Pets for Elderly program.
$24,000 to Lutheran Service Society of Western Pennsylvania, Pittsburgh, PA. For Nutrition Assessment Program Continuation.
$20,000 to Travelers Aid Society of Pittsburgh, Pittsburgh, PA. For Behavioral Health Assistance Program.

8108

Marilyn and J. Robert Birnhak Foundation ✧ ☆

P.O. Box 2300
Fort Washington, PA   19034-2300

Established in 1986 in PA.
Donors: J. Robert Birnhak; Marilyn J. Birnhak; Weight Watchers of Philadelphia, Inc.
Foundation type: Independent foundation.
Financial data (yr. ended 6/30/06): Assets, $405,039 (M); gifts received, $450,000; expenditures, $432,321; qualifying distributions, $430,000; giving activities include $430,000 for grants.
Fields of interest: Jewish federated giving programs; Jewish agencies & temples.
Type of support: General/operating support.
Limitations: Applications not accepted. Giving primarily in Philadelphia, PA. No grants to individuals.
Application information: Contributes only to pre-selected organizations.
Trustees: J. Robert Birnhak; Marilyn J. Birnhak.
EIN: 222779210
Selected grants: The following grants were reported in 2004.
$120,000 to Madlyn and Leonard Abramson Center for Jewish Life, North Wales, PA.
$25,000 to Jewish Federation of Greater Philadelphia, Philadelphia, PA.
$10,000 to American Associates, Ben-Gurion University of the Negev, New York, NY.
$10,000 to Jewish Theological Seminary of America, New York, NY.
$4,000 to National Liberty Museum, Philadelphia, PA.

8109

Black Family Foundation ✧ ☆

100 State St., Ste. 700
Erie, PA   16507-1459
Application address: c/o Samuel P. Black, III, Pres., 121 E. 2nd St., Erie, PA 16507-1501

Established in 1993 in PA.
Donor: 1998 Black Family Charitable Lead Annuity Trust.
Foundation type: Independent foundation.
Financial data (yr. ended 12/31/05): Assets, $2,624,764 (M); gifts received, $90,000; expenditures, $329,845; qualifying distributions, $325,400; giving activities include $325,400 for 31 grants (high: $55,000; low: $1,000).
Purpose and activities: Giving to federated giving programs, health and welfare services, higher education, and the arts.
Fields of interest: Arts; Education; Health organizations, association; Human services; Federated giving programs; Christian agencies & churches.
Limitations: Giving limited to Erie, PA. No grants to individuals.
Application information: Application form required.
   Initial approach: Letter
   Deadline(s): None
   Board meeting date(s): 2nd week of Dec.
Officers: Samuel P. Black III, Pres.; James Cullen, Secy.-Treas.
EIN: 251705824
Selected grants: The following grants were reported in 2004.
$50,000 to Erie Humane Society, Erie, PA. For unrestricted support.
$50,000 to Flagship Niagara League, Erie, PA. For unrestricted support.
$20,000 to Habitat for Humanity, Greater Erie, Erie, PA. For unrestricted support.
$17,480 to Erie Homes for Children and Adults, Erie, PA. For unrestricted support.
$17,000 to Erie Historical Museum, Erie, PA. For unrestricted support.
$16,500 to United Way of Erie County, Erie, PA. For unrestricted support.
$15,000 to Erie Philharmonic, Erie, PA. For unrestricted support.
$14,000 to Ophelia Project, Erie, PA. For unrestricted support.
$3,000 to Community Shelter Services, Erie, PA. For unrestricted support.
$1,000 to Boys and Girls Club of Erie, Erie, PA. For unrestricted support.

8110

Peter P. Blanchard III Trust- Dendroica Foundation ✧

(formerly The Dendroica Foundation)
c/o Mellon Bank, N.A.
P.O. Box 185
Pittsburgh, PA   15230-0185   (412) 234-5892
Application address: c/o Leonard Richards, 1 Mellon Bank Ctr., Ste. 3725, Pittsburgh, PA 15258

Established in 1997 in PA.
Donor: Peter P. Blanchard, Jr.†.
Foundation type: Independent foundation.
Financial data (yr. ended 12/31/05): Assets, $11,737,650 (M); expenditures, $513,476; qualifying distributions, $500,000; giving activities include $500,000 for 1 grant.

Purpose and activities: Giving primarily for the environment.
Fields of interest: Environment, natural resources.
Limitations: Giving primarily in NJ and NY.
Application information:
  Initial approach: Contact foundation for application materials and guidelines
Trustee: Mellon Bank, N.A.
EIN: 237912826
Selected grants: The following grants were reported in 2003.
  $14,831,031 to Greenwood Gardens and Nature Center, Short Hills, NJ. For recreation and conservation.

8111
Arthur F. Blanchard Trust ✧
c/o Mellon Tr. of New England, N.A.
P.O. Box 185
Pittsburgh, PA   15230-0185
Application address: c/o Sandra Brown-Mullen, Mellon Financial Corp., 1 Boston Pl., Boston, MA 02108, tel.: (617) 722-7891

Trust established in 1943 in MA.
Donor: Arthur F. Blanchard†.
Foundation type: Independent foundation.
Financial data (yr. ended 8/31/05): Assets, $19,515,679 (M); expenditures, $785,024; qualifying distributions, $754,806; giving activities include $555,000 for 13+ grants (high: $50,000; low: $30,000), and $68,500 for 64 grants to individuals (high: $5,000).
Purpose and activities: Giving for neighborhood and economic development, health and human services, education, and cultural access. Scholarships are awarded to residents of Boxborough, MA, who had attended the Blanchard Memorial School, and are for the cost of tuition and other expenses related to education.
Type of support: General/operating support; Capital campaigns; Building/renovation; Equipment; Land acquisition; Emergency funds; Program development; Seed money; Research; Scholarships —to individuals; Matching/challenge support.
Limitations: Giving primarily in MA, with strong emphasis on Boston. No grants for endowment funds or fellowships; no loans.
Publications: Application guidelines; Program policy statement.
Application information: Scholarship applicants must apply to principal of Acton High School. Application form not required.
  Initial approach: Letter requesting guidelines
  Deadline(s): June 15
  Board meeting date(s): Mar., June, Sept. and Dec.
  Final notification: 3 to 6 months
Trustee: Mellon Bank, N.A.
EIN: 046093374
Selected grants: The following grants were reported in 2003.
  $100,000 to Goodwill Industries, Morgan Memorial, Boston, MA.
  $50,000 to Childrens Museum, Boston, MA.
  $50,000 to Citizens Schools Committee, Boston, MA. For apprenticeship curriculum in Boston.
  $50,000 to MetroLacrosse, Boston, MA.
  $50,000 to Year Up, Boston, MA. For college expansion project.
  $48,000 to Allston Brighton Media, Allston, MA. For Ida program support.
  $45,000 to Food Project, Lincoln, MA.

$20,000 to Womens Educational and Industrial Union, Boston, MA. For Woman to Woman program.
$1,000 to Johns Hopkins University, Baltimore, MD. For scholarships.
$1,000 to Princeton University, Princeton, NJ. For scholarships.

8112
The Blue Ribbon Foundation of Blue Cross of Northeastern Pennsylvania ✧
(formerly Hospital Service Association of Northeastern Pennsylvania Foundation)
19 N. Main St.
Wilkes Barre, PA   18711   (570) 200-6305
Contact: Jennifer H. Wilson, Grants Mgr.
FAX: (570) 200-6699;
E-mail: jennifer.wilson@bcnepa.com; URL: http://www.bcnepa.com/ceBRFoundation.aspx

Established in 2001 in PA.
Donor: Blue Cross of Northeastern Pennsylvania.
Foundation type: Company-sponsored foundation.
Financial data (yr. ended 12/31/05): Assets, $4,771,246 (M); expenditures, $1,626,926; qualifying distributions, $1,623,416; giving activities include $1,449,500 for 45 grants (high: $190,000; low: $5,000).
Purpose and activities: The foundation supports organizations involved with literacy, health, substance abuse, smoking, depression, cancer, cardiovascular disease, human services, children, senior citizens, disabled people, and women. Special emphasis is directed toward programs designed to prevent rather than treat disease and break the cycle of sickness that impairs lives and makes health care so expensive and programs designed to address critical health issues through creative, community-based, programmatic initiatives; foster collaboration and partnership among community organizations; improve practices impacting the quality and efficacy of health outcomes; and address the root causes of specific diseases and conditions to help moderate escalating health care costs.
Fields of interest: Child development, education; Medical school/education; Education, reading; Health care, equal rights; Medicine/medical care, public education; Pharmacy/prescriptions; Public health; End of life care; Health care; Mental health/crisis services, public education; Substance abuse, prevention; Mental health/crisis services, hot-lines; Mental health, smoking; Mental health, depression; Health organizations, public education; Cancer; Heart & circulatory diseases; Family services; Human services, financial counseling; Human services; Children; Aging; Disabilities, people with; Women; Crime/abuse victims.
Type of support: Program development.
Limitations: Giving limited to Bradford, Carbon, Clinton, Lackawanna, Luzerne, Lycoming, Monroe, Pike, Sullivan, Susquehanna, Tioga, Wayne, and Wyoming counties, PA. No support for schools, parent/teacher organizations, organizations not of direct benefit to the entire community, firefighting organizations, or political organizations. No grants to individuals, or for equipment or fixed assets, tours, trips, or conferences, capital campaigns or building, annual campaigns for hospitals, colleges, universities, or schools, scholarships, endowments, debt reduction, or fundraising.
Publications: Annual report; Grants list.
Application information: Application form required.

Initial approach: Download application form and mail proposal and application form to foundation for Impact Grants and Mini-Grants; download letter of intent form and mail to foundation for Access to Health Care for the Uninsured and Underinsured Initiative
Deadline(s): Feb. 1, May 1, Aug. 1, and Nov. 1 for Impact Grants and Mini-Grants; Apr. 1 for Access to Health Care for the Uninsured and Underinsured Initiative
Board meeting date(s): Apr. 5, June 29, Sept. 26, and Dec. 19
Final notification: 10 business days for Impact Grants and Mini-Grants
Directors: Denise S. Cesare; Judith O. Graziano; Alan S. Hollander; John J. Menapace; John P. Moses; Paul H. Rooney, Jr.
EIN: 233101673

8113
Ross J. Born Family Charitable Trust ✧
c/o Ross J. Born
3571 Catherine Ave.
Allentown, PA   18103

Established in 1991 in PA.
Donors: Ross J. Born; Wendy Born.
Foundation type: Independent foundation.
Financial data (yr. ended 12/31/05): Assets, $4,293,525 (M); gifts received, $69,423; expenditures, $529,490; qualifying distributions, $498,466; giving activities include $497,066 for 51 grants (high: $200,000; low: $300).
Purpose and activities: Giving primarily to charities and agencies that provide services to the needy.
Fields of interest: Education; Health care; Youth development, centers/clubs; Human services; Children/youth, services; Federated giving programs; Jewish federated giving programs; Jewish agencies & temples.
Type of support: General/operating support; Continuing support; Annual campaigns; Capital campaigns; Equipment; Emergency funds; Program development; Seed money.
Limitations: Applications not accepted. Giving primarily in the Lehigh Valley, PA, area. No grants to individuals.
Application information: Contributes only to pre-selected organizations.
Trustee: Ross J. Born.
EIN: 237653033

8114
Bozzone Family Foundation ✧
311 Hillcrest Dr.
Lower Burrell, PA   15068-6701

Established in 1986 in PA.
Donor: Robert P. Bozzone.
Foundation type: Independent foundation.
Financial data (yr. ended 12/31/03): Assets, $8,947,856 (M); expenditures, $964,886; qualifying distributions, $922,082; giving activities include $919,570 for 87 grants (high: $200,000; low: $100).
Purpose and activities: Giving primarily for higher education, as well as for the arts, particularly museums; funding also for children, youth and social services, health care, and to Roman Catholic churches and organizations.

Fields of interest: Museums; Museums (specialized); Performing arts; Performing arts, theater; Higher education; Hospitals (specialty); Boy scouts; Girl scouts; Human services; YM/YWCAs & YM/YWHAs; Children/youth, services; Family services; Roman Catholic agencies & churches.
Type of support: General/operating support.
Limitations: Applications not accepted. Giving primarily in PA, with some emphasis on Pittsburgh. No grants to individuals.
Application information: Contributes only to pre-selected organizations.
Trustee: Robert P. Bozzone.
EIN: 256277066

8115
Joseph G. Bradley Charitable Foundation ◇
c/o Wolf Block
1650 Arch St., 22nd Fl.
Philadelphia, PA 19103

Established in 1990 in PA.
Foundation type: Independent foundation.
Financial data (yr. ended 11/30/05): Assets, $7,826,577 (M); expenditures, $388,193; qualifying distributions, $365,464; giving activities include $356,112 for 3 grants (high: $250,000; low: $50,000).
Purpose and activities: The foundation awards grants to churches, museums, and other organizations for organ restoration.
Fields of interest: Museums (art); Performing arts, music; Protestant agencies & churches; Roman Catholic agencies & churches.
Type of support: Equipment.
Limitations: Giving primarily in Oak Park, IL; giving also in Brooklyn, NY, and Toledo, OH. No grants to individuals.
Application information: Application form not required.
  Deadline(s): None
Trustee: Andrew R. Nehrbas.
EIN: 237647762
Selected grants: The following grants were reported in 2004.
$325,000 to First United Methodist Church, Oak Park, IL. For organ restoration.

8116
Brickman Foundation ◇ ☆
1 Pitcairn Pl., Ste. 3000
Jenkintown, PA 19046

Established in 1994 in PA.
Donors: Sally Brickman; Theodore Brickman; Julie B. Carr; Susan B. McGrath; Scott W. Brickman; Steven G. Brickman.
Foundation type: Independent foundation.
Financial data (yr. ended 12/31/05): Assets, $7,747,766 (M); expenditures, $340,551; qualifying distributions, $318,000; giving activities include $318,000 for grants.
Fields of interest: Arts; Environment; Human services; Foundations (community); Federated giving programs; Christian agencies & churches.
Limitations: Applications not accepted. No grants to individuals.
Application information: Contributes only to pre-selected organizations.

Trustees: Sally Brickman; Scott W. Brickman; Steven G. Brickman; Theodore Brickman; Julie B. Carr; Susan B. McGrath; Pitcairn Trust Co.
EIN: 237790986
Selected grants: The following grants were reported in 2004.
$60,000 to Swedenborg Scientific Association, Bryn Athyn, PA.
$32,000 to Academy of the New Church, Bryn Athyn, PA.
$20,000 to Community Foundation for the National Capital Region, DC.
$10,000 to Abington Memorial Hospital, Abington, PA.
$10,000 to Washington Church of the New Jerusalem, Mitchellville, MD.
$5,000 to Gettysburg College, Gettysburg, PA.
$2,500 to Cure Autism Now Foundation, Los Angeles, CA.
$1,000 to Crohns and Colitis Foundation of America, New York, NY.
$1,000 to National Center for Children and Families, Bethesda, MD.
$1,000 to Washington Area Womens Foundation, DC.

8117
Margaret Briggs Foundation
c/o PNC Advisors
P.O. Box 937
Scranton, PA 18501

Established in 1969 in PA.
Donor: Margaret Briggs†.
Foundation type: Independent foundation.
Financial data (yr. ended 12/31/05): Assets, $10,778,324 (M); expenditures, $551,242; qualifying distributions, $517,705; giving activities include $485,829 for 45 grants (high: $83,556; low: $1,000).
Fields of interest: Museums; Education; Hospitals (general); Medical care, rehabilitation; Health organizations, association; Housing/shelter, development; Youth development, centers/clubs; Human services.
Limitations: Giving limited to the greater Scranton/Lackawanna County, PA, area.
Publications: Application guidelines.
Application information: Application form required.
  Initial approach: Letter
  Copies of proposal: 6
  Deadline(s): None
  Board meeting date(s): Quarterly
  Final notification: Letter
Officers and Directors:* Matthew D. Mackie, Jr.,* Pres.; William J. Calpin,* Secy.; Thomas G. Gallagher; Judith O. Graziano; Kevin E. Rogers.
Trustee: PNC Bank, N.A.
EIN: 232719328

8118
Bristol Fund, Inc.
c/o Michal W. Bristol, Treas.
P.O. Box 206
Carversville, PA 18913

Established in 1962 in NY.
Donors: Brian T. Bristol; Pamela W. Bristol; Edith W. Bristol; Michal W. Bristol.
Foundation type: Independent foundation.

Financial data (yr. ended 12/31/05): Assets, $679,517 (M); gifts received, $447,243; expenditures, $428,161; qualifying distributions, $425,600; giving activities include $425,600 for 141 grants (high: $31,000; low: $50).
Purpose and activities: Giving primarily for higher and other education; support also for music.
Fields of interest: Performing arts, music; Secondary school/education; Higher education; Education.
Type of support: General/operating support; Program development; Scholarship funds; Matching/challenge support.
Limitations: Applications not accepted. No grants to individuals.
Application information: Contributes only to pre-selected organizations in which board members have an active interest. Unsolicited requests for funds not considered or acknowledged.
Officers: Pamela W. Bristol, Pres.; Susannah B. Bristol, V.P.; James D. Bristol, Secy.; Michal W. Bristol, Treas.
EIN: 237209712

8119
The Solomon and Sylvia Bronstein Foundation ◇
c/o Bernard Glassman
1 Logan Sq.
130 N. 18th St.
Philadelphia, PA 19103

Established in 1985 in PA.
Donor: Solomon Bronstein†.
Foundation type: Independent foundation.
Financial data (yr. ended 6/30/05): Assets, $7,022,486 (M); expenditures, $601,157; qualifying distributions, $518,151; giving activities include $511,500 for 37 grants (high: $100,000; low: $1,000).
Purpose and activities: Giving primarily for Jewish organizations.
Fields of interest: Education; Human services; Jewish federated giving programs; Jewish agencies & temples.
Limitations: Applications not accepted. Giving primarily in Philadelphia, PA; some funding also in New York, NY. No grants to individuals.
Application information: Contributes only to pre-selected organizations.
Trustees: Gerald Broker; Marvin Comisky; Rabbi Gerald I. Wolpe.
EIN: 222656339
Selected grants: The following grants were reported in 2004.
$100,000 to Jewish Theological Seminary of America, New York, NY. For general support.
$16,795 to Jewish Federation of Greater Philadelphia, Philadelphia, PA. For general support.
$12,500 to Drexel University, Philadelphia, PA. For general support.
$10,000 to American Friends of the Open University of Israel, New York, NY. For general support.
$10,000 to Har Zion Temple, Narberth, PA. For general support.
$10,000 to Jewish National Fund, Philadelphia, PA. For general support.
$10,000 to University of Pennsylvania, Philadelphia, PA. For general support.
$7,500 to Reconstructionist Rabbinical College, Wyncote, PA. For general support.

$5,000 to Greater Philadelphia Urban Affairs Coalition, Philadelphia, PA. For general support.

$2,500 to Boys Town Jerusalem Foundation of America, Philadelphia, PA. For general support.

8120

The William & Jemima Brossman Charitable Foundation ✧

c/o Ephrata National Bank
31 E. Main St.
P.O. Box 457
Ephrata, PA 17522 (717) 733-6576
Contact: Carl L. Brubaker, V.P. and Trust Off.

Established in 1986 in PA.
Donors: Bertha Brossman Blair†; Anne B. Sweigart Irrevocable Trust.
Foundation type: Independent foundation.
Financial data (yr. ended 10/31/05): Assets, $5,932,844 (M); expenditures, $1,135,880; qualifying distributions, $1,111,123; giving activities include $1,109,475 for 71 grants (high: $300,000; low: $25).
Fields of interest: Performing arts; Arts; Higher education; Theological school/education; Scholarships/financial aid; Education; Health care, alliance; Hospitals (general); Health organizations, association; Youth development, centers/clubs; Youth development, scouting agencies (general); Human services; YM/YWCAs & YM/YWHAs; Federated giving programs; Christian agencies & churches.
Type of support: General/operating support; Capital campaigns; Building/renovation; Scholarship funds.
Limitations: Giving primarily in south central PA. No grants to individuals.
Application information: Application form not required.
Deadline(s): None
Trustee: The Ephrata National Bank.
EIN: 236087844
Selected grants: The following grants were reported in 2005.
$115,000 to Lutheran Theological Seminary at Philadelphia, Philadelphia, PA.
$50,000 to Lancaster Health Alliance, Lancaster, PA.
$50,000 to Lebanon Valley College, Annville, PA.
$50,000 to Rider University, Lawrenceville, NJ.
$46,400 to American Red Cross, Lancaster, PA.
$40,000 to LutherCare, Lititz, PA.
$20,000 to Ephrata Area Community Theater, Ephrata, PA.
$10,000 to Fulton Opera House, Lancaster, PA.
$5,000 to Elizabethtown College, Elizabethtown, PA.
$2,500 to Tabor Community Services, Lancaster, PA.

8121

The Brossman Family Charitable Trust for Scholarships ✧

c/o The Ephrata National Bank
P.O. Box 457
Ephrata, PA 17522-0457
Contact: Carl L. Brubaker, V.P. and Trust Off., The Ephrata National Bank

Established in 1986 in PA.
Donor: William and Jemima Brossman Charitable Foundation.

Foundation type: Independent foundation.
Financial data (yr. ended 10/31/05): Assets, $586 (M); gifts received, $341,000; expenditures, $344,301; qualifying distributions, $344,301; giving activities include $331,000 for 659 grants to individuals (high: $500; low: $500).
Purpose and activities: Scholarship awards to high school graduates of the Ephrata, PA area.
Fields of interest: Higher education.
Type of support: Scholarships—to individuals.
Limitations: Giving limited to residents of the Ephrata, PA, area.
Application information: Student must be a high school graduate and resident of Ephrata area school district, Ephrata, PA, or of a high school served by Denver & Ephrata Telephone & Telegraph Co. Application form required.
Initial approach: Application can be obtained from selection committee
Deadline(s): June 15
Trustee: The Ephrata National Bank.
EIN: 232860047

8122

The W. Dale Brougher Foundation, Inc. ✧

1200 Country Club Rd.
York, PA 17403

Established in 1986 in MD.
Donor: W. Dale Brougher.
Foundation type: Independent foundation.
Financial data (yr. ended 12/31/05): Assets, $5,969,645 (M); expenditures, $487,531; qualifying distributions, $478,607; giving activities include $478,607 for 51 grants (high: $250,000; low: $40).
Purpose and activities: Giving for education, the arts, federated giving programs and for youth services.
Fields of interest: Arts; Education; Animal welfare; Human services; Family services; Federated giving programs.
Limitations: Applications not accepted. Giving primarily in PA, with emphasis on York; some funding nationally. No grants to individuals.
Application information: Contributes only to pre-selected organizations.
Officers: W. Dale Brougher, Pres. and Treas.; Nancy Brougher, V.P. and Secy.
EIN: 521499358
Selected grants: The following grants were reported in 2005.
$30,000 to York College of Pennsylvania, York, PA.
$25,900 to Society of the Four Arts, Palm Beach, FL.
$25,000 to United Way, PA.
$12,500 to York Health Foundation, York, PA.
$11,250 to York County Heritage Trust, York, PA.
$10,000 to Crispus Attucks Association, York, PA.
$10,000 to Peddie School, Hightstown, NJ.
$10,000 to Pennsylvania State University, University Park, PA.
$6,200 to Preservation Foundation of Palm Beach, Palm Beach, FL.
$1,500 to American Red Cross, York, PA.

8123

Caroline Alexander Buck Foundation ✧

1600 Market St., Ste. 3600
Philadelphia, PA 19103 (215) 751-2080
Contact: Bruce A. Rosenfield, Dir.

Established in 1960.
Donors: Caroline A. Churchman†; W. Morgan Churchman.
Foundation type: Independent foundation.
Financial data (yr. ended 12/31/05): Assets, $9,684,406 (M); expenditures, $547,275; qualifying distributions, $487,564; giving activities include $445,120 for 43 grants (high: $100,000; low: $135; average: $5,000–$10,000).
Purpose and activities: Giving primarily for education, including a music school, and social services, including programs aiding children.
Fields of interest: Arts education; Arts; Elementary school/education; Education; Reproductive health, family planning; Health care; Substance abuse, services; Health organizations, association; Human services; Children/youth, services; Minorities/immigrants, centers/services; Christian agencies & churches; Disabilities, people with; Minorities.
Type of support: In-kind gifts.
Limitations: Giving primarily in PA, with emphasis on the greater metropolitan Philadelphia area. No grants to individuals.
Application information: Application guidelines are available upon request. Application form not required.
Initial approach: Letter
Deadline(s): None
Board meeting date(s): Spring and fall
Directors: J. Alexander Churchman; Lee Stirling Churchman; Leidy McIlvaine Churchman; W. Morgan Churchman; George Connell; Gordon L. Keen, Jr.; Wendy Mackey; Beverly McConnell; Bruce A. Rosenfield; Binney H.C. Wietlisbach.
EIN: 236257115

8124

The Buhl Foundation ▼

650 Smithfield St., Ste. 2300
Pittsburgh, PA 15222 (412) 566-2711
Contact: Doreen E. Boyce, Pres.
FAX: (412) 566-2714;
E-mail: buhl@buhlfoundation.org; URL: http://foundationcenter.org/grantmaker/buhl/

Established as a trust in 1927 in PA; reincorporated in 1992.
Donors: Henry Buhl, Jr.†; Henry C. Frick†.
Foundation type: Independent foundation.
Financial data (yr. ended 6/30/06): Assets, $85,005,867 (M); gifts received, $388,643; expenditures, $4,225,533; qualifying distributions, $4,225,533; giving activities include $4,209,353 for grants, and $16,180 for employee matching gifts.
Purpose and activities: Emphasis on developmental or innovative grants to regional institutions, with special interest in education at all levels and in regional concerns, particularly those related to problems of children and youth.
Fields of interest: Education, early childhood education; Child development, education; Elementary school/education; Secondary school/education; Higher education; Adult/continuing education; Libraries/library science; Education; Children/youth, services; Child development, services; Engineering/technology; Science; Minorities.
Type of support: Continuing support; Program development; Seed money; Research; Program-related investments/loans; Employee matching gifts.

Limitations: Giving primarily in southwestern PA, with emphasis on the Pittsburgh area. No support for religious or political activities, or nationally funded organizations. No grants to individuals, or for building funds, overhead costs, accumulated deficits, operating budgets, scholarships, fellowships, fundraising campaigns; no loans (except for program-related investments).
Publications: Annual report; Informational brochure (including application guidelines).
Application information: Submit final proposal upon invitation only. Application form not required.
  Initial approach: Letter of inquiry
  Copies of proposal: 1
  Deadline(s): None
  Board meeting date(s): Monthly
  Final notification: Approximately 3 months
Officers and Directors:* Jean A. Robinson,* Chair.; Helen S. Faison,* Vice-Chair.; Peter F. Mathieson, Vice-Chair.; Doreen E. Boyce, Pres.; Marsha A. Zahumensky, Secy.-Treas.; Frederick W. Thieman.
Number of staff: 2 full-time professional; 1 part-time professional; 2 full-time support.
EIN: 250378910
Selected grants: The following grants were reported in 2004.
$100,000 to Pittsburgh Foundation, Pittsburgh, PA. For completion of Allegheny County Department of Human Services Integration Project.
$100,000 to Pittsburgh Voyager, Pittsburgh, PA. For transitional phase educational programs.
$100,000 to Spectrum Family Network Foundation, Pittsburgh, PA. For technology plan.
$50,000 to Allegheny College, Meadville, PA. To develop technology-based pedagogy.
$50,000 to Carnegie Institute, Carnegie Science Center, Pittsburgh, PA. For SciTech Festival.
$50,000 to Education Policy and Leadership Center, Harrisburg, PA. For activities in southwestern Pennsylvania, payable over 2 years.
$50,000 to Family Hospice and Palliative Care, Pittsburgh, PA. To integrate new information system into working environment.
$50,000 to Greater Pittsburgh Literacy Council, Pittsburgh, PA. For East End Computer Center.
$45,000 to Mattress Factory, Pittsburgh, PA. For school partnerships and teacher professional training. Grant made through Frick Educational Fund, payable over 2 years.
$32,470 to Heartwood Institute, Pittsburgh, PA. To restructure website and establish users group among Pittsburgh teachers. Grant made through Frick Educational Fund.

8125
Buncher Family Foundation ◇
5600 Forward Ave.
Pittsburgh, PA 15217 (412) 422-9900
Contact: Bernita Buncher, Pres.

Established in 1974 in PA.
Donors: Jack G. Buncher‡; The Buncher Co.; Buncher Rail Car Service Co.; Jack G. Buncher Trust.
Foundation type: Independent foundation.
Financial data (yr. ended 11/30/05): Assets, $34,861,602 (M); gifts received, $2,506,307; expenditures, $1,593,266; qualifying distributions, $1,570,784; giving activities include $1,489,276 for 105 grants (high: $675,000; low: $25).
Purpose and activities: Giving primarily for medical research, human services, Jewish federated giving programs, government/public administration, Jewish agencies and temples.

Fields of interest: Education; Medical research, institute; Human services; Jewish federated giving programs; Government/public administration; Jewish agencies & temples.
Limitations: Giving primarily in PA, with emphasis on Pittsburgh. No grants to individuals.
Application information:
  Initial approach: Letter
  Deadline(s): None
  Final notification: Within 3 months from receipt
Officer: Bernita Buncher, Pres.
Number of staff: 1 part-time professional; 1 part-time support.
EIN: 237366998
Selected grants: The following grants were reported in 2004.
$792,459 to United Jewish Federation of Greater Pittsburgh, Pittsburgh, PA.
$55,500 to Childrens Hospital.
$10,000 to United Way of Allegheny County, Pittsburgh, PA.
$1,600 to Pittsburgh Foundation, Pittsburgh, PA.
$1,585 to Grantmakers of Western Pennsylvania, Pittsburgh, PA.
$933 to Heritage Health Foundation, Braddock, PA.

8126
Burke Family Foundation ◇
c/o Comcast Group
1500 Market St., 34th Fl.
Philadelphia, PA 19102

Established in 2001 in PA.
Foundation type: Independent foundation.
Financial data (yr. ended 12/31/05): Assets, $596,339 (M); expenditures, $387,513; qualifying distributions, $375,770; giving activities include $375,770 for 67 grants (high: $100,000; low: $200; average: $1,000–$10,000).
Fields of interest: Arts; Education; Hospitals (general); Human services; Children/youth, services.
Limitations: Applications not accepted. Giving primarily in NY and PA; some giving nationally. No grants to individuals.
Application information: Contributes only to pre-selected organizations.
Trustees: Gretchen Burke; Stephen B. Burke.
EIN: 256699573

8127
The Byers' Foundation ◇
P.O. Box 158
Chalfont, PA 18914-0158
Contact: Joyce F. Byers, Secy.-Treas.

Established in 1986 in PA.
Donor: Byers Choice, Ltd.
Foundation type: Company-sponsored foundation.
Financial data (yr. ended 12/31/05): Assets, $3,337,999 (M); gifts received, $350,000; expenditures, $425,097; qualifying distributions, $403,500; giving activities include $403,500 for grants.
Purpose and activities: The foundation supports hospitals and organizations involved with arts and culture, K-12 and higher education, human services, religion, women, and homeless people.
Fields of interest: Visual arts; Museums; Performing arts; Historic preservation/historical societies; Arts; Elementary/secondary education; Higher education;

Hospitals (general); Youth, services; Women, centers/services; Homeless, human services; Human services; Christian agencies & churches; Protestant agencies & churches; Religion; Women; Homeless.
Type of support: Program development.
Limitations: Giving primarily in southeastern PA, with emphasis on the Doylestown and Philadelphia areas.
Application information: Proposals may be submitted using the Delaware Valley Grantmakers Common Grant Application and Common Report Form. Proposals should be no longer than 1 page. Application form not required.
  Initial approach: Proposal
  Copies of proposal: 1
  Deadline(s): None
  Board meeting date(s): Annually
  Final notification: Within 90 days
Officers and Trustees:* Robert L. Byers,* Pres.; Robert Leslie Byers, Exec. V.P.; Jeffrey D. Byers,* V.P.; Joyce F. Byers,* Secy.-Treas.
EIN: 232406657
Selected grants: The following grants were reported in 2004.
$100,000 to Doylestown Hospital, Doylestown, PA.
$30,000 to American Red Cross, Philadelphia, PA.
$30,000 to Christs Home, Warminster, PA.
$25,000 to Heritage Conservancy, Doylestown, PA.
$10,000 to James A. Michener Art Museum, Doylestown, PA.
$10,000 to Philadelphia Leadership Foundation, Philadelphia, PA.
$7,500 to World Affairs Council of Philadelphia, Philadelphia, PA.
$5,000 to Baker Industries, Malvern, PA.
$5,000 to Lamb Foundation, North Wales, PA.
$2,500 to Boston Rescue Mission, Boston, MA.

8128
Charles Talbot Campbell Foundation ◇
c/o National City Bank
National City Ctr. (25-153)
20 Stanwix St
Pittsburgh, PA 15222-1323 (412) 644-8332
Contact: William M. Schmidt, Sr. V.P., National City Bank

Established in 1975 in PA.
Donor: Charles Talbot Campbell‡.
Foundation type: Independent foundation.
Financial data (yr. ended 1/31/05): Assets, $7,169,995 (M); expenditures, $525,044; qualifying distributions, $516,148; giving activities include $516,000 for 31 grants (high: $80,000; low: $5,000).
Purpose and activities: Emphasis on agencies for the handicapped, youth music programs, and ophthalmological research.
Fields of interest: Performing arts, music; Eye research; Disabilities, people with.
Type of support: General/operating support; Continuing support; Research.
Limitations: Giving primarily in western PA. No support for community funds, including the United Way. No grants to individuals; no loans.
Application information: Grantmakers of Western Pennsylvania Common Grant Application Form required. Application form required.
  Initial approach: Letter
  Copies of proposal: 4
  Deadline(s): Mar. 31 and Aug. 31

Board meeting date(s): Semiannually: Spring (Apr. or May); and fall (Sept. or Oct.)

Final notification: Affirmative replies only

Trustee: National City Bank.

EIN: 251287221

Selected grants: The following grants were reported in 2005.

$80,000 to Eye and Ear Foundation, Pittsburgh, PA.

$50,000 to Goodwill Industries of Pittsburgh, Pittsburgh, PA.

$50,000 to Western Pennsylvania School for the Deaf, Pittsburgh, PA.

$40,000 to Alice Lloyd College, Pippa Passes, KY. 2 grants: $25,000, $15,000

$26,000 to Family Hospice and Palliative Care, Pittsburgh, PA.

$25,000 to West Virginia Wesleyan College, Buckhannon, WV.

$15,000 to Childrens Festival Chorus, Pittsburgh, PA.

$10,000 to Bethlen Home of the Hungarian Reformed Federation of America, Ligonier, PA.

$10,000 to Historical Society of Western Pennsylvania, Pittsburgh, PA.

8129
Cardone Foundation ✧

P.O. Box 45313
Philadelphia, PA 19124
Contact: Luanne Foti

Established in 2002 in PA; as the successor to the Michael Cardone Foundation.

Donor: Michael Cardone Foundation.

Foundation type: Independent foundation.

Financial data (yr. ended 12/31/03): Assets, $5,174,325 (M); gifts received, $606,000; expenditures, $442,778; qualifying distributions, $428,150; giving activities include $428,150 for grants.

Fields of interest: Arts; Education; Health care; Human services; Christian agencies & churches.

Limitations: Applications not accepted. Giving on a national basis, with some emphasis on PA and NJ. No grants to individuals.

Application information: Contributes only to pre-selected organizations.

Officers: Jacqueline Cardone, Pres.; Michael Cardone, Jr., V.P.

Trustees: Michael Cardone III; Ryan D. Cardone; Christin C. McClave; Mark Spuler.

EIN: 300028232

8130
Carnegie Hero Fund Commission

425 6th Ave., Ste. 1640
Pittsburgh, PA 15219-1823
Contact: Walter F. Rutkowski, Exec. Dir.
FAX: (412) 281-5751;
E-mail: carnegiehero@carnegiehero.org; Toll free tel.: (800) 447-8900; URL: http://www.carnegiehero.org/

Established in 1904 in PA.

Donor: Andrew Carnegie†.

Foundation type: Operating foundation.

Financial data (yr. ended 12/31/05): Assets, $35,932,559 (M); gifts received, $150; expenditures, $1,563,160; qualifying distributions, $1,511,295; giving activities include $733,445 for grants to individuals.

Purpose and activities: A private operating foundation established to recognize, with the award of medals and sums of money, heroism voluntarily performed by civilians within the U.S. and Canada in saving or attempting to save the lives of others; and to grant monetary assistance, including scholarship aid, to awardees and to the dependents of those who have lost their lives or who have been disabled in such heroic manner.

Fields of interest: Human services; Voluntarism promotion.

International interests: Canada.

Type of support: Continuing support; Grants to individuals; Scholarships—to individuals.

Limitations: Giving primarily in the U.S.; some giving also in Canada.

Publications: Annual report; Informational brochure; Newsletter.

Application information: Awards by nomination only. Refer to the commission Web site for complete nominating guidelines and form. Application form required.

Initial approach: Letter
Copies of proposal: 1
Deadline(s): Within 2 years of the act for nominations
Board meeting date(s): Feb., Apr., June, Sept., and Dec.
Final notification: Following board meetings

Officers and Trustees:* Mark Laskow,* Pres.; Priscilla J. McCrady,* V.P.; Walter F. Rutkowski, Secy. and Exec. Dir.; James M. Walton,* Treas.; S. Richard Brand; Albert H. Burchfield III; Elizabeth H. Genter; Thomas J. Hilliard, Jr.; David McL. Hillman; Peter F. Mathieson; Christopher R. McCrady; Ann M. McGuinn; Nancy L. Rackoff; Frank Brooks Robinson; Dan D. Sandman; Arthur M. Scully, Jr.; William P. Snyder III; Jerald A. Solot; Sybil P. Veeder; Thomas L. Wentling, Jr.; Alfred W. Wishart, Jr.; Carol A. Word.

Number of staff: 6 full-time professional; 1 part-time professional; 1 full-time support; 1 part-time support.

EIN: 251062730

8131
E. Rhodes & Leona B. Carpenter Foundation ▼ ✧

c/o Joseph A. O'Connor, Jr., Morgan, Lewis & Bockius
1735 Market St., Ste. 3420
Philadelphia, PA 19103-2921 (215) 979-3222

Established in 1975 in VA.

Donors: E. Rhodes Carpenter†; Leona B. Carpenter†.

Foundation type: Independent foundation.

Financial data (yr. ended 12/31/04): Assets, $219,289,858 (M); expenditures, $9,836,943; qualifying distributions, $8,653,734; giving activities include $8,089,305 for 193 grants (high: $1,125,000; low: $1,400; average: $5,000–$250,000).

Purpose and activities: Support for performing arts organizations in the Richmond, VA, area; education, particularly graduate theological educational institutions; museums (including museums associated with colleges and universities) for purchase, restoration, and conservation of Asian art; institutions providing education in the field of Asian art; and organizations providing health care, particularly hospices.

Fields of interest: Arts education; Museums; Performing arts; Arts; Theological school/education; Education; Residential/custodial care, hospices.

Limitations: Giving primarily in areas east of the Mississippi River. No support for private secondary education, or large public charities. No grants to individuals.

Application information: Application form not required.

Initial approach: Letter
Deadline(s): Mar. 15 and Sept. 15
Board meeting date(s): Spring and fall

Officers and Directors:* Ann B. Day,* Pres.; Paul B. Day, Jr.,* V.P. and Secy.; J.A. O'Connor, Jr., Exec. Dir.; M.H. Reinhart.

EIN: 510155772

Selected grants: The following grants were reported in 2004.

$1,125,000 to Carpenter Center for the Performing Arts, Richmond, VA. Toward challenge grant.

$610,000 to Duke University, Durham, NC. 2 grants: $300,000 to Perkins Library (Toward construction of new library space), $310,000 to Perkins Library (Toward construction of new library space).

$250,000 to Peabody Essex Museum, Salem, MA. For construction of upper level of Yin Yu Tang Interpretative Gallery.

$100,000 to Jewish Family and Childrens Service of Greater Philadelphia, Philadelphia, PA. For hospice program.

$75,000 to Peaceable Kingdom Retreat for Children, Temple, TX. Toward construction of Animal Assisted Therapy Program Facility.

$35,000 to Ken-Crest Centers for Exceptional Persons, Plymouth Meeting, PA. Toward training staff to assist with end-of-life care for terminally sick children.

$30,000 to Toledo Museum of Art, Toledo, OH. For exhibition featuring Japanese woodblock prints.

$30,000 to Womens Alliance for Theology Ethics and Ritual (WATER), Silver Spring, MD. To provide assistance to women in graduate theological education.

$20,000 to Wissahickon Hospice, Bala Cynwyd, PA. For Needy Patient Fund.

8132
The Carthage Foundation ▼ ✧

1 Oxford Ctr.
301 Grant St., Ste. 3900
Pittsburgh, PA 15219-6401 (412) 392-2900
Contact: Michael W. Gleba, Treas.
URL: http://www.scaife.com/carthage.html

Incorporated in 1964 in PA.

Donor: Richard M. Scaife.

Foundation type: Independent foundation.

Financial data (yr. ended 12/31/05): Assets, $27,623,535 (M); gifts received, $5,000,000; expenditures, $6,737,818; qualifying distributions, $6,635,776; giving activities include $6,128,500 for 50 grants (high: $550,000; low: $5,000; average: $25,000–$100,000).

Purpose and activities: Grants primarily for public policy research, particularly in the areas of government and international affairs and only to U.S. 501(c)(3) organizations.

Fields of interest: Crime/law enforcement, counterterrorism; International affairs; Political science; Public policy, research; Government/public administration.

Type of support: General/operating support; Conferences/seminars.
Limitations: Giving on a national basis, with some emphasis on CA, and Washington, DC. No grants to individuals. Generally, no grants for event sponsorships, endowments, capital campaigns, or renovations.
Publications: Annual report.
Application information: The foundation does not issue a separate program policy statement or grant application guidelines. The foundation acknowledges receipt of proposals. Application form not required.

Initial approach: Letter
Copies of proposal: 1
Deadline(s): None
Board meeting date(s): Quarterly
Final notification: 1 to 3 weeks

Officers and Trustees:* Richard M. Scaife,* Chair.; R. Daniel McMichael,* Secy.; Michael W. Gleba,* Treas.; Alexis J. Konkol; Roger W. Robinson, Jr.
Number of staff: 2 part-time professional; 2 part-time support.
EIN: 256067979
Selected grants: The following grants were reported in 2005.

$550,000 to Counterterrorism and Security Educational Research Foundation, DC. For Investigation project.
$450,000 to Free Congress Research and Education Foundation, DC. For general operating support and program support.
$250,000 to Landmark Legal Foundation, Kansas City, MO. For general operating support.
$150,000 to Center for Individual Rights, DC. For general operating support.
$150,000 to Institute for Research on the Economics of Taxation, DC. For general operating support and program support.
$125,000 to Center for Individual Freedom Foundation, Alexandria, VA. For project support.
$100,000 to Collegiate Network, Wilmington, DE. For national security and geostrategic training program.
$100,000 to Defenders of Property Rights, DC. For general operating support.
$70,000 to Americas Survival, Owings, MD. For program support.
$65,000 to University of Virginia Law School Foundation, Charlottesville, VA. For National Security Law Summer Institute.

8133
Louis N. Cassett Foundation ◇

1 Penn Ctr., Ste. 1220
Philadelphia, PA 19103-1834   (215) 563-8886
Contact: Malcolm B. Jacobson, Tr.

Trust established in 1946 in PA.
Donor: Louis N. Cassett‡.
Foundation type: Independent foundation.
Financial data (yr. ended 12/31/05): Assets, $8,934,717 (M); expenditures, $532,033; qualifying distributions, $459,062; giving activities include $444,250 for 152 grants (high: $15,000; low: $500).
Purpose and activities: Giving primarily for cultural programs, social service and health agencies, and education; support also for community development, youth agencies, Unitarian churches, and Jewish organizations and temples.
Fields of interest: Arts education; Performing arts centers; Performing arts, theater; Performing arts,

music; Arts; Higher education; Hospitals (general); Health organizations; Cerebral palsy research; Human services; Children/youth, services; Aging, centers/services; Federated giving programs; Jewish federated giving programs; Protestant agencies & churches; Jewish agencies & temples.
Type of support: Annual campaigns; Building/renovation.
Limitations: Giving primarily in Philadelphia, PA, funding also in FL, and New York, NY. No grants to individuals, or for endowment funds.
Application information: Application form not required.

Initial approach: Letter
Copies of proposal: 1
Deadline(s): None
Board meeting date(s): As required

Trustees: William D. Elias; Carol Gerstley; Malcolm B. Jacobson.
EIN: 236274038
Selected grants: The following grants were reported in 2004.

$25,000 to United Cerebral Palsy of New York City, New York, NY.
$15,000 to Jewish Federation of Greater Philadelphia, Philadelphia, PA.
$15,000 to Philadelphia Orchestra Association, Philadelphia, PA.
$15,000 to Saint Andrews School, Boca Raton, FL.
$15,000 to Unity of the Palm Beaches, West Palm Beach, FL.
$4,000 to Association for Developmental Disabilities, Jenkintown, PA.
$3,750 to American Cancer Society, Philadelphia, PA.
$1,750 to Brians House, West Chester, PA.
$1,500 to HMS School for Children with Cerebral Palsy, Philadelphia, PA.
$1,500 to Please Touch Museum, Philadelphia, PA.

8134
Andrea Cavitolo Foundation ◇ ☆

303 W. Lancaster Ave., Ste. 265
Wayne, PA 19087   (800) 832-8026

Established in 1995 in PA.
Donors: Warren Kantor; ACF Holding Co., Inc.
Foundation type: Independent foundation.
Financial data (yr. ended 5/31/05): Assets, $4,994,136 (M); gifts received, $11,752; expenditures, $391,111; qualifying distributions, $341,777; giving activities include $326,832 for 17 grants (high: $154,000; low: $50).
Purpose and activities: Giving primarily for the performing arts, education, children's services, including a children's hospital, and social services, including an eye hospital.
Fields of interest: Performing arts; Performing arts centers; Arts; Education; Hospitals (specialty); Human services; Children, services; Aging, centers/services.
Limitations: Giving primarily in PA, with emphasis on Philadelphia.
Application information: Application form required.

Initial approach: Letter or telephone to request application
Deadline(s): None

Officers: Frank Fontanez, Pres. and Secy.; John Calamari, V.P. and Treas.
EIN: 232818544
Selected grants: The following grants were reported in 2005.

$84,834 to Health Federation of Philadelphia, Philadelphia, PA.
$26,000 to Childrens Hospital.
$16,916 to Temple University, Philadelphia, PA.
$10,700 to Shipley School, Bryn Mawr, PA.
$1,500 to Center for Loss and Bereavement, Skippack, PA.
$1,368 to Pennsylvania Ballet, Philadelphia, PA.
$1,294 to Pennsylvania Academy of the Fine Arts, Philadelphia, PA.

8135
Central Susquehanna Community Foundation

(formerly Administers of the Berwick Health and Wellness Fund)
309 Vine St.
Berwick, PA 18603   (570) 752-3930
Contact: Eric DeWald, Exec. Dir.; For grants: Anne Rupp, Admin. Asst.
FAX: (570) 752-7435;
E-mail: edewald@csgiving.org; Additional E-mail: arupp@csgiving.org; URL: http://www.csgiving.org

Established in 1999 in PA; converted from the sale of Berwick Hospital.
Foundation type: Community foundation.
Financial data (yr. ended 12/31/05): Assets, $31,619,356 (M); gifts received, $629,341; expenditures, $1,955,930; giving activities include $1,353,380 for 116 grants (high: $400,000; low: $75), and $35,100 for 9 grants to individuals (high: $4,100; low: $3,000).
Purpose and activities: The foundation promotes the health and welfare of citizens in the service area of the foundation through donations to charitable and educational institutes.
Fields of interest: Education; Health care; Mental health/crisis services; Human services.
Type of support: General/operating support; Continuing support; Building/renovation; Equipment; Program development; Seed money; Technical assistance; Consulting services; Program-related investments/loans; Scholarships —to individuals; Matching/challenge support.
Limitations: Giving limited to Columbia, Lower Luzerne, Montour, and Northumberland counties, PA. No support for religious purposes. No grants to individuals (except for scholarships).
Publications: Application guidelines; Annual report; Grants list; Newsletter; Occasional report (including application guidelines).
Application information: Visit foundation Web site for application form and guidelines. Prospective applicants may attend an optional, one-hour workshop; telephone foundation for more information. Application form required.

Initial approach: Submit Intent to Apply application form
Copies of proposal: 2
Deadline(s): Mar. 4 for Intent to Apply application form
Board meeting date(s): Quarterly
Final notification: Mar. 25 for Part I (Intent to Apply) determination

Officers and Directors:* John E. DeFinnis, D.D.S.*, Chair.; Al Steward,* Vice-Chair.; Debra Force-Moore,* Secy.; Herbert Woodshick,* Treas.; Eric Dewald,* Exec. Dir.; Freddie Bittenbender; Robert W. Buehner, Jr.; Rev. Frank Demmy; C. James Ferrigno, M.D.; Michael Flock; Michael Goresh, Jr.; Kenneth Hart; Kay Hoosty; Ferne Soberick Krothe; Elmer D. Robinson; David

Saracino; Kevin Tanribilir; Patricia Torsella; Lucille Whitmire; H.W. "Skip" Wieder.
Number of staff: 2 full-time professional; 2 part-time professional.
EIN: 232982141

8136
Centre County Community Foundation, Inc. ✧

2013 Sandy Dr., No. 202
P.O. Box 648
State College, PA   16804-0648   (814) 237-6229
Contact: Barbara Steen, Prog. Coord.
FAX: (814) 237-2624;
E-mail: info@centrecountycf.org; URL: http://www.centrecountycf.org

Established in 1981 in PA.
Foundation type: Community foundation.
Financial data (yr. ended 12/31/04): Assets, $12,251,578 (M); gifts received, $1,536,825; expenditures, $792,350; giving activities include $457,092 for 235 grants (high: $26,500; low: $100).
Purpose and activities: The foundation is a public charity dedicated to meeting changing needs, and assisting individuals, families, and businesses throughout Centre County plan and carry out their charitable giving.
Fields of interest: Arts; Education; Environment; Health care; Disasters, Hurricane Katrina; Human services.
Type of support: General/operating support; Income development; Annual campaigns; Capital campaigns; Building/renovation; Equipment; Emergency funds; Program development; Conferences/seminars; Publication; Seed money; Internship funds; Scholarship funds; Research; Technical assistance; Matching/challenge support.
Limitations: Giving limited to PA, predominantly in Centre County; limited funding also to immediate surrounding counties. No support for religious organizations for sectarian purposes, or government or educational entities with taxing authority. No grants for travel or accommodation services.
Publications: Application guidelines; Annual report (including application guidelines); Informational brochure; Occasional report; Quarterly report.
Application information: Visit foundation Web site for specific application forms and guidelines per grant type. Application form required.
> *Initial approach:* Submit application form and attachments
> *Copies of proposal:* 17
> *Deadline(s):* Mar. 1, June 1, Sept. 1, and Dec. 1 for grants over $1,000; none for grants under $1,000
> *Board meeting date(s):* Last Thurs. of Jan., Apr., July, and Oct.
> *Final notification:* Within 5 days of board meeting
Officers and Directors:* Jeffrey M. Bower,* Chair.; Charles W. Rohrbeck,* 1st Vice-Chair.; Dolores A. Taricani,* 2nd Vice-Chair.; Robert W. Potter,* Pres.; John P. Mandryk,* Secy.; Frances E. Mason,* Treas.; Lydia Abdullah; Ellie Beaver; Edward A. Friedman; Blake Gall; Larry J. Hofer; William A. Jaffe; Alfred Jones, Jr.; Richard L. Kalin; Rodney P. Kirsch; Norman K. Lathbury; Eileen W. Leibowitz; Robert N. Levy; William H. Martin; John R. Miller III; George Moellenbrock, Jr.; Adrian Pratt; James M. Rayback; Karen P. Shute; Thomas F. Songer II; Robert E.

Steward, Jr.; Ralph W. Stewart; James Swistock; Andrew A. Zangrilli.
Number of staff: 2 full-time professional.
EIN: 251782197

8137
The Century Fund Trust

462 Walnut St., Ste. 202
Allentown, PA   18102-5497   (610) 434-4000
Contact: Lisa M. Curran, Exec. Dir.

Established in 1985 in PA.
Foundation type: Independent foundation.
Financial data (yr. ended 12/31/05): Assets, $26,906,002 (M); expenditures, $2,110,909; qualifying distributions, $1,822,885; giving activities include $1,810,885 for 105 grants (high: $130,000; low: $1,000).
Purpose and activities: Giving primarily to arts and cultural programs, education, conservation, human services, and community development in the Lehigh Valley, PA.
Fields of interest: Historic preservation/historical societies; Arts; Education; Environment, natural resources; Animal welfare; Human services; YM/YWCAs & YM/YWHAs; Children/youth, services; Aging, centers/services; Community development.
Type of support: Seed money; General/operating support; Continuing support; Annual campaigns; Capital campaigns; Building/renovation; Equipment; Debt reduction; Program development; Scholarship funds; Matching/challenge support.
Limitations: Giving primarily in the greater Lehigh Valley, PA, area.
Publications: Application guidelines.
Application information: Application form not required.
> *Initial approach:* Proposal
> *Copies of proposal:* 6
> *Deadline(s):* Apr. 1 and Oct. 1
> *Board meeting date(s):* 6-10 times per year
> *Final notification:* 1-2 months
Officers and Trustees:* Alice A. Miller,* Pres.; Rev. Grant E. Harrity,* Secy.; Richard J. Hummel,* Treas.; Lisa M. Curran, Exec. Dir.; David K. Bausch; John Leh II.
Number of staff: 1 part-time professional; 1 part-time support.
EIN: 226404912
Selected grants: The following grants were reported in 2005.
$130,000 to Allentown Symphony Association, Allentown, PA.
$130,000 to Lehigh County Historical Society, Allentown, PA.
$100,000 to Cedar Crest College, Allentown, PA.
$100,000 to Muhlenberg College, Allentown, PA.
$75,000 to DeSales University, Center Valley, PA.
$41,478 to Alliance for Building Communities, Allentown, PA.
$40,000 to East Side Youth Center, Allentown, PA.
$25,000 to Allentown Public Library, Allentown, PA.
$15,000 to Boys and Girls Club.
$5,500 to Allentown Band, Allentown, PA.

8138
Michele and Agnese Cestone Foundation, Inc. ✧

2 PNC Plz., 34th Fl.
620 Liberty Ave.
Pittsburgh, PA   15222   (412) 762-3502
Contact: Bruce Bickel
FAX: (412) 705-1062;
E-mail: bruce.bickel@pncadvisors.com

Established in 1990 in NJ.
Donors: Eclesia J. Cestone; Ralph M. Cestone; The Remvac Group, Inc.; The Marvec Corp.; Macvest Group, Inc.; Maria A. Cestone; Vincent R. Cestone; Michele J. Cestone.
Foundation type: Independent foundation.
Financial data (yr. ended 12/31/05): Assets, $11,887,336 (M); gifts received, $4,372; expenditures, $768,911; qualifying distributions, $706,066; giving activities include $549,980 for 35 grants (high: $157,680; low: $5,000).
Purpose and activities: Giving primarily for the care and welfare of animals.
Fields of interest: Animal welfare.
Type of support: General/operating support; Continuing support; Capital campaigns; Building/renovation; Equipment; Emergency funds; Program development; Seed money; Curriculum development; Scholarship funds; Research; Technical assistance; Scholarships—to individuals; Matching/challenge support; Student loans—to individuals.
Limitations: Giving in the U.S., with some emphasis on NJ and NY.
Publications: Application guidelines.
Application information: Application form not required.
> *Initial approach:* Letter
> *Deadline(s):* Nov. 1
> *Board meeting date(s):* Dec.
> *Final notification:* 30 days
Officers and Trustees:* Michele J. Cestone,* Pres. and Secy.; Vincent R. Cestone II,* V.P.; Michael Krick.
Number of staff: 2 full-time professional.
EIN: 521720903

8139
The Ralph M. Cestone Foundation, Inc. ✧

2 PNC Plz., 30th Fl.
620 Liberty Ave.
Pittsburgh, PA   15222
Contact: Bruce Bickel
FAX: (412) 762-4160;
E-mail: bruce.bickel@pncadvisors.com

Established in 1997 in NJ.
Donors: Maria A. Cestone; Ralph M. Cestone; Vincent R. Cestone; The Marvel Group; The Remvac Group, Inc.
Foundation type: Independent foundation.
Financial data (yr. ended 12/31/05): Assets, $7,273,544 (M); expenditures, $414,936; qualifying distributions, $366,547; giving activities include $348,003 for 17 grants (high: $70,000; low: $2,760), and $1,540 for 1 grant to an individual.
Purpose and activities: Support for education through grants and scholarships to individuals.
Fields of interest: Education.
Type of support: General/operating support; Capital campaigns; Building/renovation; Equipment;

Emergency funds; Curriculum development; Scholarship funds; Research; Technical assistance; Scholarships—to individuals.
Limitations: Giving primarily in NJ, OH, and PA.
Application information: Application form required.
  Initial approach: Letter including necessary historical background
  Copies of proposal: 1
  Deadline(s): Nov. 1
  Board meeting date(s): Dec.
  Final notification: 30 days
Officers and Directors:* Maria A. Cestone,* Pres.; Michele J. Cestone,* Treas.
Number of staff: 2 full-time professional.
EIN: 226703196
Selected grants: The following grants were reported in 2004.
$30,000 to American Red Cross, Plainfield, NJ. For general support.
$30,000 to Metropolitan Opera, New York, NY. For general support.
$30,000 to National Heritage Foundation, Falls Church, VA.
$25,000 to Mount Saint Dominic Academy, Caldwell, NJ. For general support.
$20,000 to Carnegie Hall Society, New York, NY. For general support.
$20,000 to Drew University, Madison, NJ. For general support.
$20,000 to Marylawn of the Oranges High School, South Orange, NJ. For general support.
$16,991 to Saint Johns University, Jamaica, NY. For general support.
$15,000 to Cabrini Mission Foundation, New York, NY. For general support.
$15,000 to Great Swamp Watershed Association, New Vernon, NJ. For general support.

8140
The Chanticleer Foundation ◇
786 Church Rd.
Wayne, PA   19087

Established in 1990 in PA. Classified as a private operating foundation in 1992.
Donor: The Chanticleer Charitable Trust.
Foundation type: Operating foundation.
Financial data (yr. ended 12/31/04): Assets, $13,481,026 (M); gifts received, $2,540,324; expenditures, $2,931,542; qualifying distributions, $2,956,635; giving activities include $475,000 for 2 grants (high: $450,000; low: $25,000), and $2,900,619 for foundation-administered programs.
Purpose and activities: The foundation maintains and operates an arboretum and botanic garden, and makes grants for plant preservation and park maintenance.
Fields of interest: Environment, plant conservation; Botanical gardens.
Type of support: General/operating support.
Limitations: Applications not accepted. Giving primarily in Flagstaff, AZ. No grants to individuals.
Application information: Contributes only to pre-selected organizations.
Officers and Directors:* Edward T. Goodman,* Pres.; Orton P. Jackson, Jr.,* V.P.; Benjamin R. Neilson,* Secy.-Treas.; Cynthia W. Drayton; Christine G. Hayworth; Ann L. Reed; Sabrina Warner.
EIN: 232052829

8141
Chester County Community Foundation
The Lincoln Bldg.
28 W. Market St.
West Chester, PA   19382   (610) 696-8211
Contact: Karen A. Simmons, C.E.O.; For grant applications: Beth Harper Briglia, V.P., Donor Svcs. and Grantmaking
FAX: (610) 696-8213; *E-mail:* info@chescocf.org; Additional E-mail: Karen@chescocf.org; Grant application E-mail: Beth@chescocf.org; URL: http://www.chescocf.org

Established in 1994 in PA.
Foundation type: Community foundation.
Financial data (yr. ended 6/30/06): Assets, $23,986,970 (L); gifts received, $3,098,648; expenditures, $2,644,991; giving activities include $1,310,056 for 352 grants (high: $50,000; low: $25), and $56,518 for 64 grants to individuals (high: $5,000; low: $73).
Purpose and activities: The foundation seeks to maintain and enhance the quality of life in Chester County, PA.
Fields of interest: Arts; Libraries/library science; Scholarships/financial aid; Education, drop-out prevention; Education; Environment; Health care; Youth development; Human services; Community development, neighborhood development; Economic development; Women.
Type of support: Scholarships—to individuals; General/operating support; Management development/capacity building; Capital campaigns; Building/renovation; Endowments; Program development; Conferences/seminars; Scholarship funds; Research; Consulting services; Program evaluation.
Limitations: Giving primarily in Chester County, PA. No grants to individuals (except for scholarships), or for event fundraising or annual meetings.
Publications: Application guidelines; Annual report; Financial statement; Informational brochure; Newsletter.
Application information: Visit foundation Web site for application form and guidelines. Proposals submitted by Sept. 15 will receive priority consideration under all grantmaking programs. Application form required.
  Initial approach: E-mail grant Summary Sheet and proposal
  Copies of proposal: 1
  Deadline(s): Sept. 15 for Unrestricted funds; none for Donor-Advised and Field-of-Interest funds
  Board meeting date(s): Feb., May., Sept., and Nov.
  Final notification: Late Feb. for Unrestricted funds
Officers and Directors:* Madeline Wing Adler, Ph.D.*, Chair.; Alan Elko, Ed.D.*, Vice-Chair.; Scott T. Hattersley,* Vice-Chair.; Matthew D. Kelly,* Vice-Chair.; Karen A. Simmons,* C.E.O. and Pres.; Beth Harper Briglia, V.P., Donor Svcs. and Grantmaking; Henry A. Thorne,* Corp. Secy.-Treas.; Henry A. Jordan, M.D., Chair. Emeritus; Louis J. Beccaria, Ph.D., Dir. Emeritus; John A. Featherman III, Esq., Dir. Emeritus; Carol Ware Gates, Dir. Emeritus; Charles L. Huston III, Dir. Emeritus; Elizabeth R. Moran, Dir. Emeritus; Eva L. Verplanck, Ph.D., Dir. Emeritus; Maj. Genl. Wallace Arnold; Lillian DeBaptiste; Jane H. "Wiggie" Featherman; Thomas Fillippo; David M. Frees III; John H. Hewlett III; Richard I. G. Jones; Michael Karwick; Patrick O'Donnell; Robert A. Portnoy; L. Peter Temple.

Number of staff: 2 full-time professional; 2 part-time professional; 1 full-time support.
EIN: 232773822

8142
The Philip Chosky Charitable & Educational Foundation ◇
610 Ellsworth Pl.
Pittsburgh, PA   15232

Established in 1998 in PA.
Donors: Philip Chosky; Electronic Institutes, Inc.; Electronic Institutes Foundation.
Foundation type: Independent foundation.
Financial data (yr. ended 12/31/05): Assets, $12,514,755 (M); expenditures, $1,069,121; qualifying distributions, $983,362; giving activities include $950,200 for 12 grants (high: $600,000; low: $1,000).
Purpose and activities: Giving primarily for higher education and the arts; funding also for Jewish organizations.
Fields of interest: Arts; Higher education; Scholarships/financial aid; Jewish federated giving programs; Jewish agencies & temples.
Limitations: Applications not accepted. Giving primarily in Pittsburgh, PA. No grants to individuals.
Application information: Contributes only to pre-selected organizations.
Officer: Philip Chosky, Exec. Dir.
Directors: Stanley Barg; Charles Kirshner; Michael O'Malley.
EIN: 232932969
Selected grants: The following grants were reported in 2004.
$400,000 to Jewish Community Center of Greater Pittsburgh, Pittsburgh, PA. For endowment fund.
$271,545 to City Theater Company, Pittsburgh, PA. For general support.
$201,900 to University of Pittsburgh, Pittsburgh, PA. For general support.
$50,000 to United Jewish Federation of Greater Pittsburgh, Pittsburgh, PA. For general support.
$21,000 to Pittsburgh Irish and Classical Theater, Pittsburgh, PA. For general support.
$9,900 to Rosedale Technical Institute, Pittsburgh, PA.
$5,000 to Pittsburgh Symphony Association, Pittsburgh, PA. For general support.
$4,500 to Pittsburgh Musical Theater, Pittsburgh, PA. For general support.
$4,000 to Jewish Theater of Pittsburgh, Pittsburgh, PA. For general support.
$1,000 to Unseam'd Shakespeare Company, Pittsburgh, PA. For general support.

8143
CIGNA Foundation ▼ ◇
1601 Chestnut St., TL06B
Philadelphia, PA   19192-1540
Contact: Arnold W. Wright, Jr., V.P. and Exec. Dir.
E-mail: communityrelations@cigna.com;
URL: http://www.cigna.com/about_us/community/index.html

Incorporated in 1962 in PA.
Donor: CIGNA Corp.
Foundation type: Company-sponsored foundation.
Financial data (yr. ended 12/31/05): Assets, $475,524 (M); gifts received, $3,800,000; expenditures, $3,717,204; qualifying distributions,

$3,931,091; giving activities include $3,523,859 for 63+ grants (high: $1,150,250), and $340,765 for employee matching gifts.

Purpose and activities: The foundation supports organizations involved with arts and culture, higher education, health, cancer, domestic violence, human services, community development, civic affairs, and women. Special emphasis is directed toward programs designed to address preventive health care and well-being, particularly women's health.

Fields of interest: Arts; Higher education; Business school/education; Health care, equal rights; Reproductive health; Reproductive health, prenatal care; Health care, cost containment; Health care; Cancer; Breast cancer; Crime/violence prevention, domestic violence; Human services; Community development, public policy; Community development; Government/public administration; Financial services; Public affairs; Infants/toddlers; Women.

Type of support: General/operating support; Annual campaigns; Program development; Conferences/seminars; Employee volunteer services; Employee matching gifts.

Limitations: Giving primarily in Hartford, CT, and Philadelphia, PA; giving also to national organizations. No support for lobbying, fraternal, or political organizations, religious organizations not of direct benefit to the entire community, or largely United Way-supported organizations or organizations largely supported by other CIGNA-supported federated funding agencies. No grants to individuals, or for capital campaigns, endowments, or hospital improvements or expansions.

Publications: Annual report; Corporate giving report (including application guidelines); Grants list.

Application information: Proposals should be no longer than 5 pages. Application form required.

Initial approach: Download application form and mail proposal and application form to foundation

Copies of proposal: 1

Deadline(s): None

Board meeting date(s): Biannually

Final notification: 6 to 8 weeks

Officers and Directors:* Judith E. Soltz,* Chair.; John Cannon III, Pres.; Mordecai Schwartz, V.P. and Treas.; Arnold W. Wright, Jr., V.P. and Exec. Dir.; Carol J. Ward, Secy.; H. Edward Hanway; John M. Murabito.

EIN: 236261726

Selected grants: The following grants were reported in 2003.

$150,000 to Jacobs Institute of Womens Health, DC.

$77,277 to Susan G. Komen Breast Cancer Foundation, Dallas, TX.

$50,000 to Hartford Action Plan on Infant Health, Hartford, CT.

$40,000 to Maternity Care Coalition of Greater Philadelphia, Philadelphia, PA.

$30,000 to Womens Way, Philadelphia, PA.

$25,000 to American College of Physicians Foundation, Philadelphia, PA.

$25,000 to Institute of Medicine, DC.

$25,000 to Leapfrog Group, DC.

$25,000 to MacPhail Center for Music, Minneapolis, MN.

$25,000 to Rocky Mountain Youth Medical and Nursing Consultants, Denver, CO.

8144
Claneil Foundation, Inc.
2250 Hickory Rd., Ste. 450
Plymouth Meeting, PA   19462-1074
Contact: Cathy M. Weiss, Exec. Dir.
E-mail: cweiss@claneil.com; URL: http://www.claneil.org

Incorporated in 1968 in DE.
Donors: Henry S. McNeil‡; Claneil Enterprises, Inc.
Foundation type: Independent foundation.
Financial data (yr. ended 12/31/05): Assets, $76,266,941 (M); gifts received, $10,562,264; expenditures, $4,828,893; qualifying distributions, $3,903,526; giving activities include $3,903,526 for 259 grants (high: $442,000; low: $3,000; average: $3,000–$442,000).
Purpose and activities: To create healthy communities by supporting organizations that make a difference in the lives of individuals, families and the institutions that support them, and to develop an informed, educated and engaged citizenry, and increase the understanding and appreciation of natural, built and cultural assets.
Fields of interest: Visual arts; Performing arts; Historic preservation/historical societies; Arts; Education, early childhood education; Secondary school/education; Environment, natural resources; Environment, beautification programs; Environment; Reproductive health, family planning; Health care; Crime/violence prevention, domestic violence; Crime/violence prevention, child abuse; Housing/shelter; Youth development; Human services; Family services; Civil liberties, reproductive rights; Community development; Women; Economically disadvantaged.
Type of support: General/operating support; Continuing support; Management development/capacity building; Capital campaigns; Building/renovation; Equipment; Land acquisition; Endowments; Program development; Conferences/seminars; Publication; Seed money; Curriculum development; Scholarship funds; Research; Technical assistance; Consulting services; Program evaluation; Matching/challenge support.
Limitations: Giving primarily in southeastern PA. No support for religion-based programming. No grants to individuals.
Publications: Application guidelines; Informational brochure (including application guidelines).
Application information: Grant requests over $15,000 by invitation only. Full proposals should only be submitted if invited by the foundation. Application form required.
Initial approach: Letter of inquiry due Dec. 15 or June 30
Copies of proposal: 1
Deadline(s): Aug. 15 and Mar. 1
Board meeting date(s): Nov. and June
Final notification: 6 months
Officers and Directors:* Marjorie M. Findlay, Chair.; Gretchen Menzies, Vice-Chair.; Jennifer McNeil, Secy.; Langhorne B. Smith,* Treas.; Cathy M. Weiss, Exec. Dir.; Hathaway F. Jade; Geoffrey T. Freeman; Barbara M. Jordan; Duncan McFarland; Robert D. McNeil.
Number of staff: 1 full-time professional; 1 full-time support.
EIN: 236445450
Selected grants: The following grants were reported in 2003.
$290,000 to Food Trust, Philadelphia, PA. For Feeding Our Children / School Market program.

$125,000 to Westtown School, Westtown, PA. For athletic and community center project.

$45,000 to Nature Conservancy, Boston, MA. For Forest Conservation Project in Westfield River Watershed.

$10,000 to Free Health Clinic of Montgomery County, PA. For medical and dental equipment.

$10,000 to Literacy Council of Norristown, Norristown, PA. For general support.

$10,000 to Maternity Care Coalition of Greater Philadelphia, Philadelphia, PA. For Latina MOMobile.

$8,900 to Woodmere Art Museum, Philadelphia, PA. For technology upgrade.

$5,000 to Darlington Fine Arts Center, Boothwyn, PA. For outreach arts education programming.

$5,000 to Womens Health and Environmental Network, Rosemont, PA. To promote awareness of local environmental health issues.

$3,500 to Asian Arts Initiative, Philadelphia, PA. For youth arts workshop.

8145
The Anne L. and George H. Clapp Charitable and Educational Trust
c/o Mellon Bank, N.A.
1 Mellon Bank Ctr., Rm. 3825
Pittsburgh, PA   15258   (412) 234-1634
Contact: Annette Calgaro, V.P., Mellon Financial Corp.

Established in 1949.
Donor: George H. Clapp‡.
Foundation type: Independent foundation.
Financial data (yr. ended 9/30/05): Assets, $18,597,312 (M); expenditures, $915,983; qualifying distributions, $807,633; giving activities include $758,500 for 97 grants (high: $40,000; low: $1,000).
Purpose and activities: Primary areas of interest include child welfare, education, social services, and community funds; limited support for arts and conservation.
Fields of interest: Arts; Education; Human services; Aging; Economically disadvantaged.
Type of support: General/operating support; Continuing support; Annual campaigns; Capital campaigns; Building/renovation; Endowments; Matching/challenge support.
Limitations: Giving limited to southwestern PA, Richmond, VA, and southwestern NC. No grants to individuals, or for sponsorship of events or trips.
Publications: Application guidelines; Grants list.
Application information: Most grants range from $5,000-$10,000. Application form not required.
Initial approach: Proposal not exceeding 10 pages
Copies of proposal: 3
Deadline(s): May 31
Board meeting date(s): Early Sept.
Final notification: Sept.
Trustee: Mellon Bank, N.A.
EIN: 256018976
Selected grants: The following grants were reported in 2003.
$75,000 to Pittsburgh Symphony Society, Pittsburgh Symphony, Pittsburgh, PA. For First Violin Chair.
$45,000 to Hotchkiss School, Lakeville, CT. 2 grants: $25,000 (For operating support), $20,000 (For operating support).
$45,000 to YMCA of Sewickley Valley, Sewickley, PA. 2 grants: $25,000 (For operating support), $20,000 (For operating support).

$25,000 to Carnegie Institute, Pittsburgh, PA. For operating support.
$20,000 to Childrens Hospital of Pittsburgh, Pittsburgh, PA. For operating support.
$20,000 to Duke University, Durham, NC. For operating support.
$20,000 to Watson Institute, Sewickley, PA. For operating support.
$20,000 to Western Pennsylvania Conservancy, Pittsburgh, PA. For operating support.

8146
Winifred Johnson Clive Foundation ◈ ☆
605 Oliver Bldg.
535 Smithfield St.
Pittsburgh, PA   15222   (412) 355-6416
Contact: Thomas P. Johnson, Jr., Secy.

Established in 1986 in FL.
Donors: Winifred Johnson Clive; Margaret P. Johnson; Thomas P. Johnson; Winifred J. Sharp.
Foundation type: Independent foundation.
Financial data (yr. ended 11/30/05): Assets, $17,862,602 (M); gifts received, $358,157; expenditures, $909,157; qualifying distributions, $757,637; giving activities include $652,250 for 17 grants.
Purpose and activities: Giving primarily for societies to prevent cruelty to animals and preservation of wildlife, and organizations addressing the problem of aging and the aging needy.
Fields of interest: Arts; Education; Environment, natural resources; Animal welfare; Human services; Science; Religion.
Type of support: General/operating support.
Application information:
Initial approach: Letter
Deadline(s): None
Officers and Trustees:* Grace J. Perkins,* Chair.; Thomas P. Johnson, Jr.,* Secy.; Stephanie J. Kewlich; Winifred J. Sharp.
EIN: 256277031
Selected grants: The following grants were reported in 2005.
$200,000 to Bethany College, Bethany, WV.
$67,450 to Pets Unlimited, San Francisco, CA.
$50,000 to A Gift for Teaching, Orlando, FL.
$25,000 to Orlando Museum of Art, Orlando, FL.
$10,000 to Center for Whole Communities, Fayston, VT.
$10,000 to Shakespeare Project, New York, NY.
$5,000 to First Christian Church, New Castle, PA.
$500 to SEED Foundation, DC.

8147
CMS Endowment Foundation ◈
1926 Arch St.
Philadelphia, PA   19103

Established in 1995 in PA.
Donors: Paul Silberberg; Mark Solomon; Kevin Satterthwaite; Rosemary Cataldi; Joseph Lutes; Richard Mitchell; Daniel Melrod; Joseph Melrod; Robert Spivak; William Landman; Brind Lindsay; David Spungen; Ingrid Welch; Morey Goldberg; Michael Sanyour; Russel Holt; Patty Young; Peter Miller; Jeff Rotter; Parkway Corp.
Foundation type: Independent foundation.
Financial data (yr. ended 9/30/05): Assets, $182,250 (M); gifts received, $1,161,320; expenditures, $1,633,668; qualifying distributions,

$1,626,153; giving activities include $1,626,153 for 172 grants (high: $624,113; low: $26).
Fields of interest: Museums (science/technology); Performing arts, orchestra (symphony); Arts; Higher education; Education; Hospitals (general); Health care; Health organizations, association; Human services; Children/youth, services; Federated giving programs; Jewish federated giving programs; Christian agencies & churches.
Limitations: Applications not accepted. Giving primarily in NJ, New York, NY, and Philadelphia, PA; some funding also nationally.
Application information: Unsolicited requests for funds not accepted.
Trustees: Paul Silberg; Mark Solomon.
EIN: 237819212
Selected grants: The following grants were reported in 2005.
$100,000 to New Jersey Performing Arts Center, Newark, NJ.
$94,600 to United Way, PA.
$30,000 to P.E.F. Israel Endowment Funds, New York, NY.
$26,500 to Jewish Heritage Programs, Philadelphia, PA.
$25,000 to Institute for the Advancement of Education in Jaffa, Great Neck, NY.
$25,000 to International Rescue Committee, New York, NY.
$13,167 to Gesu School, Philadelphia, PA.
$5,000 to Jewish Community Center, Scranton, PA.
$5,000 to New Jersey Symphony Orchestra, Newark, NJ.
$1,000 to Jewish Federation of Southern New Jersey, Cherry Hill, NJ.

8148
CMS Foundation ◈ ☆
1926 Arch St.
Philadelphia, PA   19103-1484

Established in 1996 in PA.
Donors: Morey Goldberg; Harry Kammerer; Paul Silberberg; Mark I. Solomon; Patty Young; Joe Lutes; Peter Miller.
Foundation type: Independent foundation.
Financial data (yr. ended 12/31/05): Assets, $144,675 (M); gifts received, $109,830; expenditures, $368,753; qualifying distributions, $361,378; giving activities include $361,363 for 90 grants (high: $75,000; low: $50).
Fields of interest: Higher education; Health organizations, association; Human services; Children/youth, services; Jewish federated giving programs; Jewish agencies & temples.
Limitations: Applications not accepted. Giving primarily in NY and PA, with emphasis on Philadelphia. No grants to individuals.
Application information: Contributes only to pre-selected organizations.
Trustees: Paul Silberberg; Mark I. Solomon.
EIN: 237819211

8149
The Cochran Family Foundation ◈
c/o Glenmede Trust Co., N.A.
1650 Market St., Ste. 1200
Philadelphia, PA   19103-7391

Established in 1998 in DE.
Donor: John R. Cochran III.

Foundation type: Independent foundation.
Financial data (yr. ended 12/31/05): Assets, $1,358,997 (M); gifts received, $1,271; expenditures, $403,216; qualifying distributions, $395,010; giving activities include $395,000 for 6 grants (high: $200,000; low: $10,000).
Purpose and activities: Giving primarily for higher education, with some emphasis on Roman Catholic education.
Fields of interest: Higher education; Education; Health care; Roman Catholic federated giving programs.
Limitations: Applications not accepted. Giving primarily in Baltimore, MD. No grants to individuals.
Application information: Contributes only to pre-selected organizations.
Officers: John R. Cochran III, Pres.; Patricia A. Cochran, V.P.
EIN: 522084405

8150
Colcom Foundation
2 Gateway Ctr., Ste. 1800
Pittsburgh, PA   15222-1402
Contact: Donna Panazzi, V.P.
Tel. for general questions: (412) 765-2400

Established in 1996 in PA.
Donor: C. May.
Foundation type: Independent foundation.
Financial data (yr. ended 12/31/04): Assets, $19,254,094 (M); expenditures, $1,065,530; qualifying distributions, $938,311; giving activities include $886,000 for 18 grants.
Purpose and activities: The mission of the Colcom Foundation is to foster a sustainable environment to ensure quality of life for all Americans by encouraging reasonable US population levels, and by providing grants to organizations whose activities address overpopulation and its adverse effects on natural resources, wildlife habitat and overall quality of life in America. The foundation accords special consideration to opportunities in southwestern PA.
Type of support: General/operating support; Income development; Management development/capacity building; Annual campaigns; Equipment; Land acquisition; Program development; Publication; Seed money; Research; Technical assistance; Program evaluation; Matching/challenge support.
Limitations: Giving on a national basis, in the U.S. only, with emphasis on Pittsburgh, PA for community and economic development. No support for religious organizations. No grants to individuals, or for scholarships; no loans.
Application information: Unsolicited proposals will not be accepted. All proposals will be solicited.
Initial approach: Letter of inquiry
Board meeting date(s): June and Dec.
Officers and Directors:* T. Inglis,* Pres. and Treas.; D. Panazzi,* V.P.; J. Barsotti; M. Strueber.
Number of staff: 3 part-time professional; 3 part-time support.
EIN: 311479839
Selected grants: The following grants were reported in 2003.
$500,000 to Zoological Society of Pittsburgh, Pittsburgh Zoo and PPG Aquarium, Pittsburgh, PA. For capital campaign for International Wildlife Conservation Center.
$225,000 to Oglebay Foundation, Wheeling, WV. For new Master Plan.
$100,000 to Shakertown at Pleasant Hill, Harrodsburg, KY. For general operating support.

$90,000 to Federation for American Immigration Reform (FAIR), DC.

$90,000 to NumbersUSA Education and Research Foundation, Arlington, VA.

$50,000 to Carnegie Institute, Pittsburgh, PA. For Powdermill Nature Reserve's Bird Banding Program.

$50,000 to Pennsylvania Environmental Council, Harrisburg, PA. For Watershed Protection Program.

$40,000 to U.S. Inc., Petoskey, MI.

$40,000 to Western Virginia Land Trust, Roanoke, VA. For general operating support.

$25,000 to Parents Television Council, Los Angeles, CA. For matching grant.

8151
Colonial Oaks Foundation ◇

850 N. Wyomissing Blvd., Ste. 200
Wyomissing, PA 19610
Contact: Kristin E. McGlinn
Application address: P.O. Box 5936, Wyomissing, PA, 19610-5936

Established in 1992 in PA.
Donor: Terrence J. McGlinn, Sr.
Foundation type: Independent foundation.
Financial data (yr. ended 9/30/05): Assets, $17,365,607 (M); expenditures, $920,551; qualifying distributions, $854,452; giving activities include $839,990 for grants.
Fields of interest: Education; Youth development, services; Human services; Family services.
Type of support: General/operating support; Continuing support; Annual campaigns; Capital campaigns; Building/renovation; Emergency funds; Program development.
Limitations: Giving primarily in Berks County, PA. No grants to individuals.
Application information: Application form required.
Initial approach: Letter
Copies of proposal: 1
Deadline(s): None
Officers and Directors:* Terrence J. McGlinn, Sr.,* Chair. and Pres.; Christine M. Auman,* Secy.; Margaret M. Shields,* Treas.; Barbara T. McGlinn; John F. McGlinn II; Terrence J. McGlinn, Jr.; John P. Schreffler.
Number of staff: 1 part-time professional.
EIN: 232705277

8152
The Comcast Foundation ▼ ◇

1500 Market St.
E. Tower, 33rd Fl.
Philadelphia, PA 19102 (215) 665-1700
Contact: Diane Deitz, Exec. Dir.
E-mail for Scholarship Program Administrators: comcast@spaprog.com; URL: http://www.comcast.com/Corporate/About/InTheCommunity/InTheCommunity.html

Established in 1999 in DE.
Donors: Comcast CICG, LP; Comcast QVC, Inc.
Foundation type: Company-sponsored foundation.
Financial data (yr. ended 12/31/05): Assets, $60,021,570 (M); gifts received, $8,230,005; expenditures, $9,759,916; qualifying distributions, $9,555,685; giving activities include $8,202,685 for 614 grants (high: $570,000; low: $500), and

$1,353,000 for 1,353 grants to individuals (high: $1,000; low: $1,000).
Purpose and activities: The foundation supports organizations involved with cultural and ethnic awareness, education, employment, youth leadership, business and industry, and volunteerism and awards college scholarships to high school seniors.
Fields of interest: Arts, cultural/ethnic awareness; Education, ESL programs; Education, reading; Education; Employment, training; Employment; Youth development, services; Business/industry; Voluntarism promotion; Science, formal/general education; Mathematics.
Type of support: Program development; Scholarships—to individuals.
Limitations: Giving primarily in areas of company operations. No support for discriminatory organizations, private foundations, or political organizations. No grants to individuals (except for scholarships), or for marketing sponsorships, sporting events, trips or tours, or capital campaigns.
Publications: Application guidelines; Grants list; IRS Form 990-PF.
Application information: Letters of inquiry should be no longer than 2 pages. Telephone calls during the application process are not encouraged. Contributes only to individuals nominated by high school principals for scholarships. Application form not required.
Initial approach: Mail letter of inquiry to foundation; E-mail nomination to Scholarship Program Administrators for scholarships
Deadline(s): None; Jan. 12 for scholarships
Final notification: 4 to 6 weeks
Officers and Directors:* Ralph J. Roberts,* Chair.; Joseph W. Waz, Jr.,* Pres.; William E. Dordelman,* V.P.; C. Stephen Backstrom,* Secy.; Joe DiTrolio,* Treas.; Diane Deitz,* Exec. Dir.; Dave Breidinger; Julian Brodsky; Steve Burch; David L. Cohen; Brad Dusto; Kerry Knott; John Ridall; Dave Scott; Michael Tallent.
EIN: 510390132

8153
The Community Foundation for the Alleghenies ◇

(also known as The Community Foundation of Greater Johnstown)
116 Market St., Ste. 4
Johnstown, PA 15901 (814) 536-7741
Contact: Mike E. Kane, Exec. Dir.
FAX: (814) 536-5859;
E-mail: cfalleghenies@atlanticbb.net; Additional tel.: (888) 280-7741; URL: http://www.cfalleghenies.org

Established in 1990 in PA.
Foundation type: Community foundation.
Financial data (yr. ended 6/30/05): Assets, $25,130,739 (M); gifts received, $1,707,766; expenditures, $2,849,410; giving activities include $1,429,515 for 231+ grants, and $180,282 for 213 grants to individuals.
Purpose and activities: The foundation seeks to obtain permanent endowments to provide benefits to individuals and organizations located in Bedford, Cambria, Indiana and Somerset counties, PA.
Fields of interest: Humanities; Arts; Education; Environment, natural resources; Health organizations, association; Disasters, Hurricane Katrina; Children/youth; Human services;

Community development; Public affairs; Religion; Children/youth.
Type of support: Continuing support; Equipment; Program development; Program-related investments/loans; Scholarships—to individuals.
Limitations: Giving primarily in Bedford, Cambria, Indiana and Somerset counties, PA.
Publications: Annual report; Grants list; Informational brochure; Newsletter.
Application information: Visit foundation Web site for application form and guidelines; accepts Grantmakers of Western Pennsylvania Common Grant Application Format. Application form required.
Initial approach: Submit application form and attachments
Copies of proposal: 2
Deadline(s): Last Fri. in Jan. and last Fri. in Aug.
Board meeting date(s): Every 2 months
Final notification: Mid-Apr. and Mid-Nov.
Officers and Directors:* Mark E. Pasquerilla,* Chair.; Gary C. Horner,* Secy.; Kim Craig,* Treas.; Michael E. Kane, Exec. Dir.; Robert Allen,* Exec. Dir., Emeritus; Scott Becker; Abe Beerman; G. Henry Cook; Allan Dennison; Raymond DiBattista; Terry K. Dunkle; Robert J. Eyer; Daniel Glosser; William L. Glosser; John M. Kriak; Richard H. Mayer; Renu Narahari; Dan Perkins; Michael Sahlaney; Sara Ann Sargent; Thomas C. Slater; Rev. Robert Swanson; Robert D. Sweet; Donato Zucco.
Number of staff: 2 full-time professional; 1 part-time professional; 1 full-time support; 1 part-time support.
EIN: 251637373

8154
Community Foundation of Warren County

(formerly The Warren Foundation)
P.O. Box 691
Warren, PA 16365-0691 (814) 726-9553
Contact: Charles E. MacKenzie M.D., Exec. Dir.
FAX: (814) 726-7099; E-mail: cfwc@westpa.net; Additional E-mail: info@communityfoundationofwarrencounty.org; URL: http://www.communityfoundationofwarrencounty.org
Alternate URL: http://www.warrenfoundationpa.org

Established in 1949 in PA by declaration of trust.
Foundation type: Community foundation.
Financial data (yr. ended 12/31/05): Assets, $37,704,956 (M); gifts received, $274,633; expenditures, $1,432,925; giving activities include $749,192 for 72 grants (high: $155,781; low: $44; average: $1,000–$15,000), and $517,446 for 788 grants to individuals (high: $5,000; low: $50).
Purpose and activities: The foundation seeks to promote the well-being of local inhabitants. The use of the bulk of funds has been designated by the donors, with distributions for child welfare, church building maintenance, community funds, scholarships, and delinquency and crime prevention.
Fields of interest: Crime/law enforcement; Children/youth, services; Federated giving programs; Protestant agencies & churches.
Type of support: Program development; Matching/challenge support; Equipment; Building/renovation; Continuing support; Capital campaigns; Employee-related scholarships; Scholarships—to individuals.
Limitations: Giving limited to Warren County, PA (except for Donor-Advised funds). No support for religious purposes (unless specified by a donor). No

grants to individuals (except for scholarships), or for administrative expenses or endowment funds.

Publications: Annual report.

Application information: Visit foundation Web site for application form and guidelines. Application form required.

   Initial approach: Telephone or letter

   Copies of proposal: 1

   Deadline(s): None

   Board meeting date(s): 3rd Fri. of each month

   Final notification: 1 to 2 months

Officers and Trustees:* John O. Hanna,* Chair.; Charles E. MacKenzie, M.D., Exec. Dir.; Bernard J. Hessley; Gerald A. Huber; Edward A. Kavanaugh; Murray K. McComas.

Trustee Banks: National City Bank; Northwest Savings Bank; PNC Bank, N.A.

Number of staff: 1 part-time professional; 1 full-time support.

EIN: 251380549

8155
The Community Foundation of Westmoreland County

c/o Chapel Hill Professional Ctr.
126 Mathews St., Ste. 1600
Greensburg, PA 15601 (724) 836-4400
Contact: Kirk Utzinger, Pres.; Jan Fox, Staff Secy.
FAX: (724) 837-5571;
E-mail: kutzinger@cfwestmoreland.org; Additional
E-mail: jfox@cfwestmoreland.org; URL: http://
www.cfwestmoreland.org

Established in 1995 in PA.

Foundation type: Community foundation.

Financial data (yr. ended 6/30/05): Assets, $10,182,208 (M); gifts received, $1,108,003; expenditures, $1,155,937; giving activities include $782,170 for 345 grants (high: $25,000; low: $100; average: $5,000–$10,000).

Purpose and activities: The mission of the foundation is to encourage local residents to become philanthropists, provide grants that support a wide variety of charitable organizations, and serve as a community leader.

Fields of interest: Arts; Education; Environment; Health care; Human services; Community development.

Type of support: Seed money; Management development/capacity building; Capital campaigns; Building/renovation; Equipment; Emergency funds; Program development; Curriculum development; Scholarship funds; Technical assistance.

Limitations: Giving primarily in Westmoreland County, PA.

Publications: Application guidelines; Annual report; Financial statement; Grants list; Informational brochure; Newsletter.

Application information: Visit foundation Web site for application form, guidelines, and deadlines. Faxed or e-mailed applications are not accepted. Application form required.

   Initial approach: Telephone before submitting application

   Copies of proposal: 9

   Deadline(s): Aug. 1 for the Now & Forever unrestricted fund; varies for others

   Board meeting date(s): Feb., May, Aug., and Nov.

   Final notification: Varies

Officers and Directors:* T. Terrance Reese,* Chair.; Vincent J. Quatrini, Jr.,* Vice-Chair.; Kirk Utzinger, Pres.; Martha Medich,* Secy.; Arthur McMullen,*

Treas.; Tina Thoburn, Emeritus; Kathy Jaquette-Tosh; A. Richard Kacin; Nancy Kukovich; Jay R. Mangold; Judith H. O'Toole; Myles D. Sampson; Lou Steiner; J. Robert Stemler; Irvin Tantlinger.

Number of staff: 2 full-time professional; 1 full-time support.

EIN: 251776105

8156
Community Involvement Foundation ◇

139 Freeport Rd., Ste. 100
Pittsburgh, PA 15215-2943
Contact: Christopher Smith, Exec. Dir.
E-mail: info@communityinvolvementfoundation.org;
URL: http://
www.communityinvolvementfoundation.org

Established in 1993 in PA.

Donor: Bruce Weiner.

Foundation type: Independent foundation.

Financial data (yr. ended 12/31/04): Assets, $3,641,345 (M); gifts received, $540,278; expenditures, $655,173; qualifying distributions, $477,185; giving activities include $434,677 for 30 grants (high: $365,050; low: $100).

Purpose and activities: Giving primarily for youth services.

Fields of interest: Youth development; Children/youth, services; Community development.

Type of support: General/operating support; Annual campaigns; Building/renovation; In-kind gifts.

Limitations: Applications not accepted. Giving primarily in PA. No grants to individuals.

Application information: Contributes only to pre-selected organizations.

Officers: Susan Weiner, Pres.; Christopher Smith, Exec. Dir.

Number of staff: 1 part-time professional.

EIN: 251724052

8157
Connelly Foundation ▼

1 Tower Bridge, Ste. 1450
West Conshohocken, PA 19428
(610) 834-3222
Contact: Victoria K. Flaville, V.P., Admin.
FAX: (610) 834-0866; E-mail: info@connellyfdn.org;
URL: http://www.connellyfdn.org

Incorporated in 1955 in PA.

Donors: John F. Connelly‡; Josephine C. Connelly‡.

Foundation type: Independent foundation.

Financial data (yr. ended 12/31/05): Assets, $238,587,066 (M); expenditures, $14,259,213; qualifying distributions, $12,415,651; giving activities include $10,407,555 for 451 grants (high: $1,500,000; low: $100; average: $5,000–$50,000), and $128,000 for 39 employee matching gifts.

Purpose and activities: Giving for education; health and social services; civic and cultural programs to improve the quality of life in the Delaware Valley.

Fields of interest: Arts; Elementary/secondary education; Education, early childhood education; Child development, education; Elementary school/education; Secondary school/education; Higher education; Adult/continuing education; Education; Health care; Substance abuse, services; Alcoholism; Youth development, citizenship; Human services; Children/youth, services; Child

development, services; Aging, centers/services; Women, centers/services; Homeless, human services; Community development; Government/public administration; Welfare policy/reform; Protestant agencies & churches; Roman Catholic agencies & churches; Aging; Disabilities, people with; Minorities; Women; Economically disadvantaged; Homeless.

Type of support: General/operating support; Continuing support; Capital campaigns; Building/renovation; Equipment; Program development; Scholarship funds; Employee matching gifts; Matching/challenge support.

Limitations: Giving in Philadelphia, and surrounding counties of Bucks, Chester, Delaware and Montgomery, PA and Camden, NJ. No support for political or national organizations. No grants to individuals, or for research or annual appeals.

Publications: Application guidelines.

Application information: Applicants may use Delaware Valley Grantmakers Application Form but need to also include all items listed on the foundation's application guidelines. Applicants may be contacted during the proposal review process to request a telephone conference, site visit or presentation. Visits to the foundation office or approaches to staff during the proposal review process are discouraged. Organizations that have received a grant from the Connelly Foundation are required to submit a final report before being considered for a new grant. Final reports need to be submitted under separate cover. Application form not required.

   Initial approach: Proposal

   Copies of proposal: 1

   Deadline(s): None

   Board meeting date(s): Jan., Mar., May, Aug., Nov.

   Final notification: 3 to 6 months after receiving proposal

Officers and Trustees:* Josephine C. Mandeville,* Chair., C.E.O., and Pres.; Emily C. Riley,* Exec. V.P., Progs.; Lewis W. Bluemle,* Sr. V.P.; Victoria K. Flaville,* V.P., Admin. and Secy.; Ira Brind; Craig R. Carnaroli; Christine C. Connelly; Daniele M. Connelly; John F. Connelly, III; Thomas S. Connelly; Caroline M. Crowley; Eleanor L. Davis; Celine C. Delany; Thomas F. Donovan; Scott M. Jenkins; Barbara W. Riley; Thomas A. Riley; Joan M. Willis.

Number of staff: 6 full-time professional; 1 part-time professional; 3 full-time support; 2 part-time support.

EIN: 236296825

Selected grants: The following grants were reported in 2004.

$1,769,363 to Archdiocese of Philadelphia, Philadelphia, PA. 4 grants: $627,125 (For Josephine C. Connelly Achievement Awards), $500,000 (For Josephine C. Connelly Achievement Awards), $639,238 (For Neumann Scholarships), $3,000 (For Cardinal's Christmas Party).

$375,000 to University of Pennsylvania, Philadelphia, PA. For capital support for new Teaching and Research Building to train clinician scientists.

$150,000 to Holy Family Home, Philadelphia, PA. For replacement of windows.

$100,000 to National Museum of American Jewish History, Philadelphia, PA. For capital campaign.

$10,000 to Holy Innocents School, Philadelphia, PA. For partnership with Saint Hugh of Cluny for full-time art teacher.

$7,500 to Montgomery County Association for the Blind, North Wales, PA. For comprehensive services.

$5,000 to Saint Peter the Apostle School, Philadelphia, PA. For needy families.

8158
The Cooper-Siegel Family Foundation ✧
c/o Mellon Financial Corp.
P.O. Box 185
Pittsburgh, PA   15230-0185
Application address: c/o Claire Coffey, 500 Grant St., Ste. 3750, Pittsburgh, PA 15258, tel.: (412) 234-5576

Established in 1996 in PA.
Donors: Eric C. Cooper; Cooper-Siegel Foundation Charitable Lead Trusts; Eric C. Cooper Charitable Lead Trust; Naomi L. Siegel Charitable Lead Trust.
Foundation type: Independent foundation.
Financial data (yr. ended 4/30/05): Assets, $963,124 (M); gifts received, $309,338; expenditures, $677,716; qualifying distributions, $671,184; giving activities include $668,000 for 34 grants (high: $100,000; low: $1,000).
Purpose and activities: Giving primarily for education, health, children's services, including juvenile diabetes and a children's hospital, and social services.
Fields of interest: Media/communications; Education, early childhood education; Higher education; Education, reading; Education; Environment; Hospitals (general); Breast cancer research; Diabetes research; Human services; Children, services; Jewish federated giving programs; Jewish agencies & temples; Economically disadvantaged.
Limitations: Giving primarily in Pittsburgh, PA; some giving in MA and NY. No grants to individuals.
Application information: Application form required.
Initial approach: Letter requesting application form
Deadline(s): None
Directors: Eric C. Cooper; Naomi L. Siegel.
Trustees: E. David Margolis; Mellon Bank, N.A.
EIN: 311537177

8159
Cornerstone Foundation ✧
(formerly GCP Foundation)
4020 Main St.
Elverson, PA   19520

Established in 1989 in PA; funded in 1990.
Foundation type: Independent foundation.
Financial data (yr. ended 12/31/05): Assets, $17,451,682 (M); expenditures, $1,097,680; qualifying distributions, $957,160; giving activities include $957,160 for 17 grants (high: $380,160; low: $2,000).
Purpose and activities: Giving primarily to Baptist organizations, including churches, missions, Bible colleges, and a theological seminary; funding also for Christian organizations, particularly faith-based Christian camps.
Fields of interest: Theological school/education; Recreation, camps; Christian agencies & churches; Protestant agencies & churches.
Type of support: General/operating support.
Limitations: Applications not accepted. Giving on a national basis. No grants to individuals.

Application information: Contributes only to pre-selected organizations.
Officers: Edward H. Cone, Pres. and Treas.; Robert L. Cone, V.P. and Secy.
Directors: Philip Cone; Stephen E. Cone; Derial H. Sanders; Julie Cone Zuber.
EIN: 232593411

8160
The Cotswold Foundation ✧
c/o J. Dowds
2997 Pennview Ave.
Broomall, PA   19008

Established in 1994 in PA.
Donors: I. Wistar Morris III; Martha Morris; Melissa H. Morris; Lydia P. Morris; Eleanor W. Morris; Eleventh Generation, LP.
Foundation type: Independent foundation.
Financial data (yr. ended 12/31/03): Assets, $11,857,974 (M); gifts received, $2,223,606; expenditures, $670,035; qualifying distributions, $630,500; giving activities include $629,500 for 11 grants (high: $400,000; low: $1,000).
Purpose and activities: Giving primarily for education, and human services.
Fields of interest: Museums (art); Medical school/education; Libraries (public); Education; Human services.
Type of support: General/operating support.
Limitations: Applications not accepted. Giving primarily in PA, with emphasis on Philadelphia; some funding nationally. No grants to individuals.
Application information: Contributes only to pre-selected organizations.
Trustees: I. Wistar Morris III; Martha H. Morris.
EIN: 237767257

8161
The Covenant Foundation ✧
723 Clovelly Ln.
Devon, PA   19333-1808

Established in 1990 in PA.
Donors: Dorothy H. Schneider; Arnold Schneider, Jr.
Foundation type: Independent foundation.
Financial data (yr. ended 12/31/05): Assets, $3,798,912 (M); gifts received, $657,415; expenditures, $660,649; qualifying distributions, $657,480; giving activities include $657,480 for 11 grants (high: $584,200; low: $500).
Fields of interest: Christian agencies & churches.
Limitations: Applications not accepted. Giving primarily in PA. No grants to individuals.
Application information: Contributes only to pre-selected organizations.
Trustees: Arnold Schneider, Jr.; Dorothy H. Schneider.
EIN: 237451873

8162
E.R. Crawford Estate Trust Fund "A" ✧
P.O. Box 487
McKeesport, PA   15134-0487   (412) 672-6670
Contact: George F. Young, Jr., Tr.

Trust established in 1936 in PA.
Donor: E.R. Crawford†.
Foundation type: Independent foundation.

Financial data (yr. ended 12/31/05): Assets, $7,186,823 (M); expenditures, $404,875; qualifying distributions, $399,081; giving activities include $350,500 for 106 grants (high: $40,000; low: $500), and $130 for 1 grant to an individual.
Purpose and activities: Giving primarily for Christian, Baptist, Lutheran, Presbyterian and United Methodist churches; funding also for children and youth services, and for social services; funding also to deserving employees or former employees of McKeesport Tin Plate Company, who through illness, accident, other misfortune, or age, have been deprived of the power or opportunity to earn the livelihood formerly enjoyed by them.
Fields of interest: Arts; Libraries/library science; Hospitals (general); Human services; Salvation Army; YM/YWCAs & YM/YWHAs; Children/youth, services; Christian agencies & churches; Protestant agencies & churches.
Type of support: General/operating support; Scholarship funds; Grants to individuals.
Limitations: Giving primarily in PA, with emphasis on Allegheny County.
Application information: Application form required for individuals.
Initial approach: Proposal
Deadline(s): None
Trustees: William H. Johnson; Bernardine H. Kovacs; George F. Young, Jr.
Number of staff: 4
EIN: 256031554
Selected grants: The following grants were reported in 2005.
$40,000 to YMCA of McKeesport, McKeesport, PA.
$25,000 to McKeesport Heritage Center, McKeesport, PA.
$20,000 to Salvation Army, Butler, PA.
$12,500 to Pauline Auberle Foundation, McKeesport, PA.
$12,000 to Community Food Bank, McKeesport, PA.
$5,000 to McKeesport Symphony Society, McKeesport, PA.
$3,000 to A Womans Place, Doylestown, PA.
$1,500 to American Red Cross, Philadelphia, PA.
$1,500 to Ventures in People Program, McKeesport, PA.

8163
The Crels Foundation ✧
5917 Main St.
East Petersburg, PA   17520   (717) 581-8130
Contact: Kenneth N. Burkholder, Chair.

Established in 1953 in PA.
Donor: Edwin B. Nolt†.
Foundation type: Independent foundation.
Financial data (yr. ended 12/31/05): Assets, $15,970,155 (M); expenditures, $856,406; qualifying distributions, $820,030; giving activities include $789,500 for 114 grants (high: $100,000; low: $1,000).
Purpose and activities: Support for hospitals, nursing homes, Mennonite-related religious associations, and parochial elementary education.
Fields of interest: Elementary/secondary education; Education; Hospitals (general); Aging, centers/services; Protestant agencies & churches; Religion; Aging.
Type of support: General/operating support; Capital campaigns; Building/renovation; Equipment; Debt reduction.
Limitations: Giving primarily in the Lancaster County, PA, area. No grants to individuals, or for

endowment funds, research programs, scholarships, fellowships, continuing support, annual campaigns, seed money, emergency funds, land acquisition, renovation projects, publications, conferences, matching gifts, or special projects; no loans.
Application information: Applications not encouraged. Application form not required.
Initial approach: Letter
Copies of proposal: 1
Deadline(s): Sept. 15
Board meeting date(s): Nov. and as required
Officers and Trustees:* Kenneth N. Burkholder,* Chair.; Clarence J. Nelson,* Chair.; Eugene N. Burkholder, Vice-Chair.; J. Michael Burkholder; Leon Ray Burkholder.
Number of staff: 1 part-time professional.
EIN: 236243577

8164
The Davenport Family Foundation ✧
P.O. Box 178
Pocopson, PA   19366-9998

Established in 1997 in PA.
Donor: Peter D. Davenport.
Foundation type: Independent foundation.
Financial data (yr. ended 12/31/05): Assets, $45,886,228 (M); expenditures, $2,738,704; qualifying distributions, $2,482,139; giving activities include $2,332,430 for 30 grants (high: $350,000; low: $1,000; average: $10,000–$100,000).
Purpose and activities: Giving primarily for education, medical research, and human services.
Fields of interest: Arts; Higher education; Education; Medical research, institute; Cancer research; Human services; Children, services.
Limitations: Applications not accepted. Giving primarily in CT, NY, and PA. No grants to individuals.
Application information: Contributes only to pre-selected organizations.
Trustees: Peter D. Davenport; Scott D. Davenport; Christine Senese; Paul Simpson.
EIN: 237871419
Selected grants: The following grants were reported in 2004.
$500,000 to Mercersburg Academy, Mercersburg, PA.
$350,000 to Washington College, Chestertown, MD.
$200,000 to Philadelphia Museum of Art, Philadelphia, PA.
$153,124 to Pennsylvania School for the Deaf, Philadelphia, PA.
$146,000 to Muhlenberg College, Allentown, PA.
$100,000 to Marine Corps Scholarship Foundation, Princeton, NJ.
$59,808 to Childrens Home of Easton, Easton, PA.
$50,000 to Operation Warm, Chadds Ford, PA.
$46,500 to Brians House, West Chester, PA.
$43,862 to Brandywine Conservancy, Chadds Ford, PA.

8165
Elmer R. Deaver Foundation ✧
c/o Wachovia Bank, N.A.
123 S. Broad St., 5th Fl.
Philadelphia, PA   19109

Established in 1996 in PA.

Foundation type: Independent foundation.
Financial data (yr. ended 12/31/05): Assets, $13,355,851 (M); expenditures, $744,445; qualifying distributions, $663,397; giving activities include $654,818 for 15 grants (high: $135,686; low: $968).
Purpose and activities: Giving primarily for higher education.
Fields of interest: Higher education; Scholarships/financial aid.
Type of support: Endowments.
Limitations: Applications not accepted. Giving primarily in PA. No grants to individuals.
Application information: Contributes only to pre-selected organizations.
Trustees: Berthold W. Levy; Wachovia Bank, N.A.
EIN: 237830263

8166
The 1994 Charles B. Degenstein Foundation ▼ ✧
c/o Mellon Bank, N.A.
P.O. Box 185
Pittsburgh, PA   15230-0185
Application address: c/o Sidney Apfelbaum, 43 S. 5th St., Sunbury, PA 17801-2896, tel.: (570) 286-9421

Established in 1996 in PA.
Foundation type: Independent foundation.
Financial data (yr. ended 6/30/05): Assets, $104,093,353 (M); expenditures, $6,131,435; qualifying distributions, $5,372,146; giving activities include $5,110,316 for 134 grants (high: $1,281,318; low: $147; average: $10,000–$50,000).
Purpose and activities: Giving primarily for libraries and YMCA's, as well as for the arts, health, playgrounds, human services, and federated giving programs.
Fields of interest: Arts; Libraries (public); Education; Health care; Disasters, fire prevention/control; Recreation, parks/playgrounds; Human services; YM/YWCAs & YM/YWHAs; Children, services; Federated giving programs.
Type of support: Matching/challenge support.
Limitations: Giving within a 75-mile radius of Sunbury, PA.
Application information: Application form required.
Deadline(s): None
Trustees: Sidney Apfelbaum; Mellon Bank, N.A.
EIN: 237792979
Selected grants: The following grants were reported in 2005.
$1,281,318 to Susquehanna University, Selinsgrove, PA. For grant made in form of stock.
$764,014 to Geisinger Health System Foundation, Danville, PA. 2 grants: $361,872 (For grant made in form of stock), $402,142 (For grant made in form of stock).
$545,327 to Seiple Family Foundation, Sunbury, PA. 2 grants: $400,436 (For grant made in form of stock), $144,891 (For grant made in form of stock).
$330,728 to YMCA, Greater Susquehanna Valley, Sunbury, PA. For grant made in form of stock.
$150,000 to West End Library, Laurelton, PA. For building campaign.
$10,000 to Union County Library System, Lewisburg, PA. For general support.
$8,000 to Family Planning Services of Snyder, Union and Northumberland Counties, Lewisburg, PA.

$2,500 to Second Mile, State College, PA. For student campers.

8167
The Bruno & Lena DeGol Foundation ✧ ☆
c/o The DeGol Organization
3229 Pleasant Valley Blvd.
Altoona, PA   16602

Established in 1994 in PA.
Donors: Bruno DeGol; Lena DeGol.
Foundation type: Independent foundation.
Financial data (yr. ended 12/31/05): Assets, $2,357,522 (M); gifts received, $407,927; expenditures, $748,042; qualifying distributions, $728,022; giving activities include $728,022 for grants.
Purpose and activities: Giving for higher education, community services, Roman Catholic churches and organizations, and for health and human services.
Fields of interest: Education; Human services; Roman Catholic agencies & churches.
Type of support: Annual campaigns; Building/renovation; Endowments.
Limitations: Giving primarily in PA. No grants to individuals.
Application information:
Initial approach: Written request
Deadline(s): None
Board meeting date(s): Monthly
Officers: Bruno DeGol, Pres.; Donald DeGol, V.P.; Dennis DeGol, Secy.; Joseph T. Adams, Treas.
Directors: Gloria DeGol Burgan; Bruno DeGol, Jr.; David DeGol; Lena DeGol.
EIN: 251753903
Selected grants: The following grants were reported in 2003.
$173,562 to Saint Francis University, Loretto, PA.
$11,250 to Easter Seal Society of Central Pennsylvania, Altoona, PA.
$10,000 to Saint Patricks Church, Gallitzin, PA.
$7,500 to Foreman Foundation, Manheim, PA.
$3,400 to Make-A-Wish Foundation, Altoona, PA.
$2,500 to Gallitzin Area Ambulance Service, Gallitzin, PA.
$1,300 to Saint Josephs Church, Bellwood, PA.
$1,050 to Central Pennsylvania Humane Society, Altoona, PA.
$1,000 to Cambria Food Bank, Cresson, PA.
$1,000 to Toys for Tots Foundation, Ebensburg, PA.

8168
Delphi Project Foundation
c/o Charles Denaro
2001 Market St., Ste. 1500
Philadelphia, PA   19103
Contact: Tammy Salvadore, Dir.
E-mail: tammy.salvadore@rsli.com

Established in 1992 in PA.
Donor: Reliance Standard Life Insurance Co.
Foundation type: Operating foundation.
Financial data (yr. ended 12/31/05): Assets, $5,564 (M); gifts received, $400,000; expenditures, $397,416; qualifying distributions, $397,445; giving activities include $350,650 for 3 grants (high: $270,000; low: $35,650).
Purpose and activities: Supports art education programs for Philadelphia, PA, public school students, particularly those residing in impoverished areas of Philadelphia.

Fields of interest: Arts education.
Limitations: Applications not accepted. Giving limited to PA. No grants to individuals.
Application information: Contributes only to pre-selected organizations.
Officers: Larry Daurelle, C.E.O. and Pres.; Charles T. Denaro, Secy.; Janet Bowlby, Treas.
Director: Tammy E. Salvadore.
EIN: 232711230
Selected grants: The following grants were reported in 2004.
$270,000 to Philadelphia Museum of Art, Philadelphia, PA.
$45,384 to Pennsylvania Ballet, Philadelphia, PA.
$35,000 to Philadelphia Zoo, Philadelphia, PA.

8169
G. Fred Dibona, Jr. Memorial Foundation ✧ ☆
(formerly G. Fred & Sylvia Dibona Family Foundation)
1211 Mt. Pleasant Rd.
Villanova, PA   19085

Established in 1996 in PA.
Donors: G. Fred Dibona; Sylvia M. Dibona.
Foundation type: Independent foundation.
Financial data (yr. ended 12/31/05): Assets, $2,599,684 (M); gifts received, $2,310,605; expenditures, $721,004; qualifying distributions, $572,596; giving activities include $572,596 for 1 grant.
Fields of interest: Higher education, university; Education; Federated giving programs.
Limitations: Giving primarily in PA.
Officers: Sylvia M. Dibona, Pres.; G. Fred Dibona III, Treas.; Christine Dibona Lobley, Exec. Dir.
EIN: 232867497
Selected grants: The following grants were reported in 2003.
$43,638 to United Way of Southeastern Pennsylvania, Philadelphia, PA.
$17,000 to Support Center for Child Advocates, Philadelphia, PA.
$10,000 to University of Pennsylvania, Philadelphia, PA.
$7,500 to Encore Series, Philadelphia, PA.
$5,400 to Wellness Community, DC.
$5,000 to Academy of Notre Dame de Namur, Villanova, PA.
$5,000 to La Salle University, Philadelphia, PA.
$1,500 to Peoples Emergency Center, Philadelphia, PA.
$1,500 to Richard J. Caron Foundation, Wernersville, PA.
$1,000 to Saint Maria Goretti High School for Girls, Philadelphia, PA. For annual support.

8170
The Dietrich Foundation, Inc. ✧
P.O. Box 649
Gladwyne, PA   19035-0649   (215) 988-0778
Contact: Daniel W. Dietrich II, Pres.

Incorporated in 1953 in DE.
Donors: Dietrich American Foundation; and members of the Dietrich family.
Foundation type: Independent foundation.
Financial data (yr. ended 12/31/04): Assets, $8,609,445 (M); expenditures, $469,914; qualifying distributions, $391,882; giving activities

include $390,000 for 21 grants (high: $40,000; low: $3,500).
Purpose and activities: Giving primarily for the performing arts, music, visual arts, museums, and cultural programs.
Fields of interest: Arts education; Media, television; Media, journalism/publishing; Visual arts; Museums; Performing arts; Performing arts, music; Historic preservation/historical societies; Arts; Higher education; Buddhism.
Type of support: Continuing support; Program development; Publication.
Limitations: Giving primarily in Philadelphia, PA, and New York, NY; some giving nationally. No grants to individuals.
Application information: Application form not required.
Initial approach: Letter
Copies of proposal: 1
Deadline(s): None
Officers and Directors:* Daniel W. Dietrich II,* Pres. and Treas.; Joseph G.J. Connolly,* Secy.
EIN: 236255134
Selected grants: The following grants were reported in 2003.
$50,000 to University of Pennsylvania, Institute of Contemporary Art, Philadelphia, PA. For exhibition and operating support.
$40,000 to Hamilton College, Clinton, NY. For art gallery, music, and drama.
$35,000 to Philadelphia Museum of Art, Philadelphia, PA. For program and exhibit support.
$30,000 to American Poetry Review, Philadelphia, PA. For operating support.
$30,000 to Theater for the New City Foundation, New York, NY. For operating support.
$22,500 to Tucson Symphony Society, Tucson, AZ. For concert support.
$17,000 to National Academy of Design, New York, NY. For exhibitions.
$16,000 to World Music Institute, New York, NY. For film project.
$15,000 to Network for New Music, Philadelphia, PA. For operating support.
$10,000 to Byerschool Foundation, Philadelphia, PA. For operating support.

8171
William B. Dietrich Foundation, Inc. ✧
P.O. Box 58177
Philadelphia, PA   19102-8177   (215) 979-1919
Contact: William B. Dietrich, Pres.

Incorporated in 1936 in DE.
Donors: Henry D. Dietrich†; Daniel W. Dietrich Foundation, Inc.; Dietrich American Foundation.
Foundation type: Independent foundation.
Financial data (yr. ended 12/31/05): Assets, $15,787,674 (M); expenditures, $882,745; qualifying distributions, $770,959; giving activities include $755,600 for 23 grants (high: $107,650; low: $500).
Purpose and activities: Giving primarily for human services, with emphasis on children and the elderly; funding also for the arts and education.
Fields of interest: Museums; Historic preservation/historical societies; Secondary school/education; Higher education; Education; AIDS; AIDS research; Human services; Children/youth, services; Aging, centers/services.
Type of support: General/operating support; Capital campaigns; Building/renovation; Program

development; Research; Matching/challenge support.
Limitations: Giving primarily in PA. No grants to individuals.
Application information: Application form not required.
Initial approach: Letter
Copies of proposal: 1
Deadline(s): None
Board meeting date(s): Jan., Apr., July, and Oct.
Officers: William B. Dietrich, Pres.; Frank G. Cooper, Secy.
EIN: 231515616
Selected grants: The following grants were reported in 2004.
$280,000 to Philadelphia Museum of Art, Philadelphia, PA. 2 grants: $175,000, $105,000
$60,000 to Curtis Institute of Music, Philadelphia, PA.
$50,000 to Bucks County Historical Society, Doylestown, PA.
$35,480 to Philadelphia Art Alliance, Philadelphia, PA.
$30,000 to Main Line Art Center, Haverford, PA. 2 grants: $15,000 each
$24,420 to Philadelphia University, Philadelphia, PA.
$20,000 to Ambler Theater, Ambler, PA.
$6,000 to Church Farm School, Paoli, PA.

8172
Dolfinger-McMahon Foundation
c/o Duane Morris, LLP
30 S. 17th St.
Philadelphia, PA   19103-4196   (215) 979-1768
Contact: Sharon Renz, Exec. Secy.
FAX: (215) 979-1020;
E-mail: renz@duanemorris.com

Trust established in 1957 in PA, and originally comprised of four separate trusts: T/W of Henry Dolfinger as modified by will of Mary McMahon; 1935 D/T of Henry Dolfinger as modified by will of Caroline D. McMahon; Residuary T/W of Caroline D. McMahon; Dolfinger-McMahon Trust for Greater Philadelphia. In 1986 the 1935 D/T of H. Dolfinger was merged with the residuary T/W of C. McMahon.
Donors: Caroline D. McMahon†; Mary M. McMahon†.
Foundation type: Independent foundation.
Financial data (yr. ended 12/31/05): Assets, $19,757,660 (M); expenditures, $973,840; qualifying distributions, $836,546; giving activities include $756,125 for grants.
Purpose and activities: Primary areas of interest include community development, the disadvantaged, education, the handicapped, and health. Emphasis on experimental, demonstration, or seed money projects in race relations, aid to the handicapped, higher and secondary education, social and urban programs, church programs, and health agencies. Emergency funding will be made rarely and, once made, will disqualify the agency from receiving any additional funding for the succeeding three years.
Fields of interest: Museums; Performing arts; Performing arts, dance; Performing arts, theater; Performing arts, music; Humanities; Arts; Elementary/secondary education; Education, early childhood education; Child development, education; Elementary school/education; Secondary school/education; Vocational education; Higher education; Theological school/education; Adult/continuing

education; Adult education—literacy, basic skills & GED; Education, reading; Education; Environment, natural resources; Environment, energy; Environment; Animal welfare; Hospitals (general); Reproductive health, family planning; Nursing care; Health care; Substance abuse, services; Mental health/crisis services; Health organizations, association; AIDS; Alcoholism; AIDS research; Crime/violence prevention, youth; Legal services; Crime/law enforcement; Employment; Food services; Nutrition; Recreation; Youth development, services; Human services; Children/youth, services; Child development, services; Family services; Aging, centers/services; Women, centers/services; Minorities/immigrants, centers/services; Homeless, human services; Civil rights, race/intergroup relations; Urban/community development; Community development; Voluntarism promotion; Religious federated giving programs; Government/public administration; Transportation; Leadership development; Public affairs; Religion; Aging; Disabilities, people with; Minorities; Women; Economically disadvantaged; Homeless.

Type of support: Emergency funds; Program development; Conferences/seminars; Publication; Seed money; Matching/challenge support.

Limitations: Giving limited to the greater Philadelphia, PA, area. No support for private foundations or special interest advocacy through legislative lobbying or solicitation of government agencies. No grants to individuals, or for endowment funds, physical facilities, ordinary operating expenses, renovations or building repairs, building funds, scholarships, medical or scientific research, or fellowships.

Publications: Application guidelines; Annual report (including application guidelines).

Application information: See guidelines for format required for requests. Grants limited to $10,000 in any one year to a single project or program. Application form not required.

Initial approach: Letter requesting guidelines, followed by proposal

Copies of proposal: 2

Deadline(s): Submit proposal preferably in Mar. or Sept.; must actually be received on or before Apr. 1 or Oct. 1 (or the preceding Fri. if the 1st falls on a weekend)

Board meeting date(s): Late spring, late fall, and as required

Final notification: 2 to 4 weeks following semiannual meeting

Officer: Sharon Renz, Exec. Secy.

Trustees: Sheldon M. Bonovitz; David E. Loder.

EIN: 236207346

8173

Dominion Foundation ▼ ✦

(formerly Consolidated Natural Gas Company Foundation)

625 Liberty Ave.

Pittsburgh, PA 15222-3197 (412) 690-1430

Contact: James C. Mesloh, Exec. Dir.

FAX: (412) 690-7608; E-mail for Dominion Educational Partnership: educational_grants@dom.com; URL: http://www.dom.com/about/community/foundation/index.jsp

Established about 1985 in PA.

Donors: Consolidated Natural Gas Co.; Dominion Resources, Inc.; Peoples Natural Gas Co.; Dominion Energy, Inc.

Foundation type: Company-sponsored foundation.

Financial data (yr. ended 12/31/05): Assets, $1,025,731 (M); gifts received, $8,000,000; expenditures, $9,519,096; qualifying distributions, $9,512,734; giving activities include $7,949,169 for 1,149 grants (high: $500,000; low: $150), and $1,272,203 for 1,409 employee matching gifts.

Purpose and activities: The foundation supports organizations involved with arts and culture, education, the environment, health, human services, community development, and civic affairs.

Fields of interest: Arts; Elementary/secondary education; Education; Environmental education; Environment; Health care; Human services; Economic development; Community development; Science, formal/general education; Mathematics; Public affairs.

Type of support: General/operating support; Continuing support; Annual campaigns; Capital campaigns; Building/renovation; Equipment; Program development; Conferences/seminars; Curriculum development; Employee matching gifts; In-kind gifts; Matching/challenge support.

Limitations: Giving on a national basis in areas of company operations. No support for churches or other sectarian organizations, fraternal, political, advocacy, or labor organizations, or discriminatory organizations. No grants to individuals, or for religious programs, general operating support for individual United Way agencies, fundraising events, golf tournaments or other sporting events, benefit or courtesy advertising, travel or student trips or tours, or memorial campaigns.

Publications: Application guidelines; Informational brochure (including application guidelines).

Application information: A password to access an online application form will be sent following receipt of a passing eligibility quiz.

Initial approach: Complete online eligibility quiz; proposal for Dominion Educational Partnership

Copies of proposal: 1

Deadline(s): None; May 1 for Dominion Educational Partnership

Board meeting date(s): Varies

Officers and Directors:* W.C. Hall, Jr.,* Pres.; M.N. Grier,* V.P.; James C. Mesloh,* Exec. Dir.; T.N. Chewning; T.F. Farrell; E.S. Hardy; J.L. Johnson; Duane Radtke.

Trustee: Mellon Bank, N.A.

Number of staff: 6 full-time professional; 3 full-time support.

EIN: 136077762

Selected grants: The following grants were reported in 2005.

$500,000 to Jamestown-Yorktown Foundation, Williamsburg, VA. For campaign for Jamestown settlement.

$125,000 to Nature Conservancy, Charlottesville, VA.

$120,825 to United Way of Greater Richmond and Petersburg, Richmond, VA. For annual support.

$90,000 to State Council of Higher Education for Virginia, Richmond, VA. For outstanding faculty awards.

$80,000 to Chamber Foundation, Greater Richmond, Richmond, VA. For Imagine a Better Richmond campaign.

$50,000 to Westminster-Canterbury Foundation, Richmond, VA. For capital campaign.

$25,000 to United Way of Allegheny County, Pittsburgh, PA. For corporate pledge.

$15,000 to Friend-in-Deed, Springfield, IL. For support of food, clothing, and shelter.

$15,000 to Pittsburgh Symphony Society, Pittsburgh, PA. For Tiny Tots concert.

$15,000 to Virginia Forestry Educational Foundation, Richmond, VA. For educational programs.

8174

Donahue Family Foundation, Inc. ✦

1001 Liberty Ave., Ste. 850

Pittsburgh, PA 15222

Contact: William Donahue, Pres.

E-mail: bdonahue@thebeechwood.com

Established around 1990.

Donors: John F. Donahue; Rhodora J. Donahue.

Foundation type: Independent foundation.

Financial data (yr. ended 12/31/05): Assets, $7,698,799 (M); gifts received, $386; expenditures, $3,816,840; qualifying distributions, $3,706,840; giving activities include $3,649,078 for 74 grants (high: $1,000,000; low: $500; average: $1,000–$100,000), and $57,762 for 1 foundation-administered program.

Purpose and activities: Giving primarily for education and Roman Catholic organizations.

Fields of interest: Education; Roman Catholic agencies & churches.

Limitations: Giving primarily in Pittsburgh, PA. No grants to individuals.

Application information: Application form not required.

Initial approach: 1-page letter

Copies of proposal: 2

Deadline(s): May 1

Board meeting date(s): June and Dec.

Final notification: 60 days

Officers and Directors:* John F. Donahue,* Chair.; William J. Donahue,* Pres.; Daniel McGrogan,* Secy.-Treas.; Dick K. Barton; Mike Dolan; Ann C. Donahue; Rhodora J. Donahue; Bishop Donald W. Wuerl.

Number of staff: 1 full-time professional.

EIN: 251619351

Selected grants: The following grants were reported in 2005.

$1,000,000 to Ave Maria University, Naples, FL.

$405,000 to Duquesne University, Pittsburgh, PA.

$333,000 to Naples Community Hospital, Naples, FL.

$150,000 to Aquinas Academy, Wildwood, PA.

$100,000 to Fort Ligonier Association, Ligonier, PA.

$80,000 to Holy Family Institute, Pittsburgh, PA.

$25,000 to Basilica of the Assumption Historic Trust, Baltimore, MD.

$20,000 to Commonwealth Education Organization, Pittsburgh, PA.

$10,000 to Foster Care Council of Southwest Florida, Naples, FL.

$2,000 to Summa Health System Foundation, Akron, OH.

8175

The Donley Foundation ✦

c/o Mellon Financial Corp.

P.O. Box 185

Pittsburgh, PA 15230-9897

Application address: c/o Kathy Rock, V.P., Mellon Bank, N.A., 1735 Market St., 2nd Fl., Philadelphia, PA 19101, tel.: (215) 553-1204

Established in 1987 in PA.
Donors: Edward J. Donley; Inez C. Donley.
Foundation type: Independent foundation.
Financial data (yr. ended 12/31/05): Assets, $11,146,481 (M); expenditures, $2,479,479; qualifying distributions, $2,454,013; giving activities include $2,421,568 for 42 grants (high: $1,000,000; low: $1,500).
Purpose and activities: Grants focus on education, human services, and other projects that benefit young persons or disadvantaged people in the spirit of encouraging innovation and community development. The foundation prefers to support projects that provide seed money or have the potential for impact in enhancing education, addressing issues of human needs or encouraging members of disadvantaged communities to work together to overcome adversity.
Fields of interest: Arts; Education; Human services; Youth, services; Community development.
Type of support: General/operating support; Capital campaigns; Building/renovation; Program development; Seed money.
Limitations: Giving primarily in northern IL, NH, York County, the greater Lehigh Valley, and south central PA areas, and White River Junction, VT. No support for religious purposes or civic or agency promotion. No grants to individuals, or for marketing development, publication of annual reports, or fundraising events. Generally, no grants for capital expenditures or endowments.
Publications: Informational brochure (including application guidelines).
Application information: All applications must include proposal cover sheet. Application form required.
  Initial approach: Proposal (no more than 8 pages)
  Copies of proposal: 7.
  Deadline(s): Mar. 15 and Sept. 15
  Board meeting date(s): Apr. and Oct.
  Final notification: 6 weeks after deadline
Trustee: Mellon Bank, N.A.
Number of staff: 1 part-time professional.
EIN: 236859909

8176
Mary J. Donnelly Foundation ◇
650 Smithfield St., Ste. 1810
Pittsburgh, PA   15222-3924
Contact: Thomas J. Donnelly, Tr.

Trust established in 1951 in PA.
Donor: Mary J. Donnelly†.
Foundation type: Independent foundation.
Financial data (yr. ended 6/30/05): Assets, $3,741,464 (M); gifts received, $2,200; expenditures, $474,876; qualifying distributions, $426,200; giving activities include $426,200 for 39 grants (high: $110,000; low: $1,000).
Fields of interest: Secondary school/education; Higher education; Education; Human services; Roman Catholic federated giving programs; Roman Catholic agencies & churches; Religion; Disabilities, people with.
Type of support: General/operating support; Annual campaigns; Capital campaigns; Building/renovation; Program development.
Limitations: Giving primarily in PA. No grants to individuals, or for endowment funds or matching gifts; no loans.
Application information: Application form not required.
  Initial approach: Letter

Copies of proposal: 3
Deadline(s): None
Board meeting date(s): June and Dec.
Trustees: Elizabeth A. Donnelly; Thomas J. Donnelly; Fred N. Egler, Jr.; Ruth D. Egler; C. Holmes Wolfe, Jr.
EIN: 256037469
Selected grants: The following grants were reported in 2004.
$400,000 to Oakland Catholic High School, Pittsburgh, PA. For capital campaign.
$16,000 to DePaul Institute, Pittsburgh, PA. For general support.
$10,000 to Carlow College, Pittsburgh, PA. For general support.
$10,000 to Greater Pittsburgh Literacy Council, Pittsburgh, PA. For general support.
$8,000 to Gregorian University Foundation, New York, NY. For general support.
$6,000 to Marian Manor Nursing Home, Pittsburgh, PA. For general support.
$5,588 to Central Catholic High School, Lawrence, MA. For general support.
$3,000 to Rosemont College, Rosemont, PA. For general support.
$2,500 to Saint Anthony School Programs, Pittsburgh, PA. For general support.
$2,000 to Salvation Army of Pittsburgh, Pittsburgh, PA. For general support.

8177
Drueding Foundation ◇
c/o Mrs. James J. Stokes III
669 Dodds Ln.
Gladwyne, PA   19035

Established in 1986 in PA.
Foundation type: Independent foundation.
Financial data (yr. ended 6/30/05): Assets, $6,945,152 (M); expenditures, $341,401; qualifying distributions, $315,000; giving activities include $315,000 for 37 grants (high: $94,000; low: $200).
Purpose and activities: Giving primarily to hospitals and health organizations, including medical research with emphasis on cancer research.
Fields of interest: Hospitals (general); Health care; Health organizations, association; Cancer research; Medical research; Human services; Children/youth, services.
Limitations: Applications not accepted. Giving primarily in PA. No grants to individuals.
Application information: Contributes only to pre-selected organizations.
Officers: Elizabeth Michener, Pres.; Bernard J. Drueding, Jr., V.P.; James Drueding, Secy.; Patricia D. Stokes, Treas.
Trustees: Albert J. Drueding, Jr.; Diana S. Gifford; Mary E. Lopiccolo; Diana D. Stewart; Mary Grace Synder.
EIN: 232418214
Selected grants: The following grants were reported in 2005.
$15,000 to Abington Memorial Hospital, Abington, PA.
$10,000 to Action AIDS, Philadelphia, PA.
$10,000 to Fox Chase Cancer Center, Philadelphia, PA.
$9,000 to Brockton Hospital, Brockton, MA.
$9,000 to Paralyzed Veterans of America, DC.
$8,000 to NGA, Inc., Warminster, PA.
$5,000 to Aid for Friends, Philadelphia, PA.
$5,000 to Cystic Fibrosis Foundation, Pittsburgh, PA.

$5,000 to Make-A-Wish Foundation, Bellefonte, PA.
$5,000 to Mystic Learning Center, Somerville, MA.

8178
DSF Charitable Foundation ◇
(formerly Scaife Charitable Foundation)
5840 Ellsworth Ave., Ste. 200
Pittsburgh, PA   15232   (412) 362-6000
Contact: J. Nicholas Beldecos, Exec. Dir.

Established in 2000 in PA.
Foundation type: Independent foundation.
Financial data (yr. ended 12/31/05): Assets, $90,384,219 (M); expenditures, $2,789,816; qualifying distributions, $2,521,441; giving activities include $1,925,970 for 15 grants (high: $500,000; low: $5,280; average: $15,000–$250,000).
Purpose and activities: Giving primarily for human services, health, and education.
Fields of interest: Education; Health care; Biomedicine; Neuroscience; Medical research; Human services; Children/youth, services; Residential/custodial care, senior continuing care.
Type of support: General/operating support; Building/renovation; Equipment; Program development; Seed money; Research; Program evaluation; Matching/challenge support.
Limitations: Giving primarily in southwestern PA. No grants to individuals.
Application information: Accepts the Common Grant Application Format of Grantmakers of Western Pennsylvania. Application form not required.
  Initial approach: Letter of inquiry
  Copies of proposal: 1
  Deadline(s): None
  Board meeting date(s): Varies
  Final notification: Following board meeting
Officers and Trustees:* David N. Scaife,* Chair.; Sanford B. Ferguson,* Vice-Chair.; Sara D. Scaife,* Secy.; Edward J. Goncz,* Treas.; J. Nicholas Beldecos, Exec. Dir.; Donald A. Collins; Frances G. Scaife; Joseph C. Walton.
Number of staff: 1 full-time professional; 2 part-time professional; 1 full-time support.
EIN: 251847237

8179
The Eberly Foundation ◇
2 W. Main St., Ste. 600
Uniontown, PA   15401-3448   (724) 438-3789
Contact: Carolyn E. Blaney, Pres. and Treas.

Established in 1963 in PA.
Foundation type: Independent foundation.
Financial data (yr. ended 12/31/05): Assets, $7,808,893 (M); expenditures, $2,768,307; qualifying distributions, $2,661,837; giving activities include $2,495,625 for 33 grants (high: $417,171; low: $100).
Purpose and activities: Giving primarily for higher education, arts and culture; support also for youth, hospitals, and public policy.
Fields of interest: Arts; Higher education; Education; Community development; Public policy, research.
Type of support: Program development; Professorships; Scholarship funds.
Limitations: Giving primarily in PA.
Publications: Annual report.

Application information: Application form not required.

Initial approach: Letter
Copies of proposal: 1
Deadline(s): Aug. 1
Board meeting date(s): Oct.

Officers: Carolyn E. Blaney, Pres. and Treas.; Ruth Ann Carter, V.P. and Secy.

Trustees: Dana Blaney; Carolyn Jill Drost; Paul O. Eberly; Robert E. Eberly, Jr.; Robert E. Eberly III; Patricia H. Miller; Tana M. Shirk.

Number of staff: 2 full-time professional; 1 part-time professional; 2 full-time support.

EIN: 237070246

Selected grants: The following grants were reported in 2005.

$1,400,000 to Pennsylvania State University, University Park, PA.

$500,000 to Fay-Penn Economic Development Council, Uniontown, PA. 2 grants: $250,000 each

$271,647 to Greater Uniontown Heritage Consortium, Uniontown, PA. 4 grants: $76,725, $79,689, $45,456, $69,777

$5,500 to Laurel Highlands School District, Uniontown, PA. 2 grants: $3,000, $2,500

$2,500 to United Negro College Fund, Pittsburgh, PA.

8180

ECOG Research and Education Foundation, Inc. ✧

1818 Market St., Ste. 1100
Philadelphia, PA 19103-3602
Contact: Deborah Deal

Established in 1992 in WI.

Foundation type: Independent foundation.

Financial data (yr. ended 6/30/05): Assets, $11,452,930 (M); gifts received, $7,557,537; expenditures, $2,978,137; qualifying distributions, $2,907,430; giving activities include $2,361,600 for 5 grants (high: $2,044,326; low: $5,000), and $2,983,997 for 4 foundation-administered programs.

Purpose and activities: Giving only for cancer research at academic institutions.

Fields of interest: Health organizations, association; Cancer; Cancer research.

Limitations: Giving primarily in PA and WI. No grants to individuals.

Application information:
Initial approach: Letter
Deadline(s): Varies

Officers: Robert L. Comis, Pres.; Donna Marinucci, Secy.-Treas.; Robert Gray, V.P.

Directors: Janice Dutcher; Thomas Habermann; John Kirkwood.

EIN: 391723095

8181

Eden Charitable Foundation ✧

Strafford Bldg. 2
200 Eagle Rd., Ste. 204
Wayne, PA 19087

Established in 1993 in PA.

Donor: Franklin C. Eden Revocable Trust.

Foundation type: Independent foundation.

Financial data (yr. ended 12/31/05): Assets, $9,927,602 (M); expenditures, $634,456; qualifying distributions, $470,901; giving activities include $374,325 for 86 grants (high: $25,000; low: $500).

Fields of interest: Arts; Education; Health organizations, association; Human services; Christian agencies & churches.

Type of support: General/operating support.

Limitations: Applications not accepted. Giving limited to PA. No grants to individuals.

Application information: Contributes only to pre-selected organizations.

Officer: John M. Kapp, Pres. and Treas.

Trustees: Earl M. Eden; Donald E. Parlee.

EIN: 232706163

Selected grants: The following grants were reported in 2005.

$10,500 to Drexel University, Philadelphia, PA.

$10,500 to Ursinus College, Collegeville, PA.

$10,000 to American Red Cross.

$10,000 to Ebenezer Maxwell Mansion, Philadelphia, PA.

$10,000 to Wynnefield Presbyterian Church, Philadelphia, PA.

$7,000 to Audubon Society, National, New York, NY.

$7,000 to Doylestown Hospital, Doylestown, PA.

$7,000 to Eastern University, Saint Davids, PA.

$5,000 to Community Enrichment Center, Fort Worth, TX.

$700 to Philadelphia Society for the Preservation of Landmarks, Philadelphia, PA.

8182

Eden Hall Foundation ▼ ✧

600 Grant St., Ste. 3232
Pittsburgh, PA 15219 (412) 642-6697
Contact: Sylvia V. Fields, Prog. Dir.
FAX: (412) 642-6698; URL: http://www.edenhallfdn.org

Established in 1984 in PA.

Donor: Eden Hall Farm.

Foundation type: Independent foundation.

Financial data (yr. ended 12/31/05): Assets, $160,987,847 (M); expenditures, $20,068,997; qualifying distributions, $19,480,183; giving activities include $10,028,183 for 100 grants (high: $1,000,000; low: $650; average: $10,000–$300,000).

Purpose and activities: The foundation seeks to improve the quality of life in Pittsburgh and western Pennsylvania through support of organizations whose missions address the needs and concerns of the area. The foundation awards grants over four basic program areas: arts and culture; education; health; and social welfare.

Fields of interest: Arts education; Arts; Higher education; Education; Environment, beautification programs; Health care; Substance abuse, services; Multiple sclerosis; Lupus; Agriculture/food; Recreation, parks/playgrounds; Human services; American Red Cross; YM/YWCAs & YM/YWHAs; Women; Economically disadvantaged.

Type of support: Research; General/operating support; Management development/capacity building; Capital campaigns; Building/renovation; Equipment; Endowments; Program development; Scholarship funds; Program evaluation.

Limitations: Giving limited to southwestern PA. No support for private foundations, sectarian or denominational religious organizations (except those providing direct educational or health care services to the public), or political or fraternal organizations. No grants to individuals, or generally

for operating budgets, endowments, or deficit financing.

Publications: Application guidelines.

Application information: Interviews or visitation may be necessary for additional information. Application form not required.

Initial approach: Letter
Copies of proposal: 5
Deadline(s): None
Board meeting date(s): Quarterly

Officers and Trustees:* George C. Greer,* Chair. and Pres.; Eve H. Shifler,* V.P.; Debora S. Foster,* Secy.; John M. Mazur,* Treas.

Number of staff: 1 full-time professional; 1 full-time support; 1 part-time support.

EIN: 251384468

Selected grants: The following grants were reported in 2005.

$1,000,000 to Carnegie Museum of Natural History, Pittsburgh, PA. For Dinosaurs in Their World.

$1,000,000 to Pittsburgh Parks Conservancy, Pittsburgh, PA. For capital drive.

$500,000 to Pittsburgh Cultural Trust, Pittsburgh, PA. For cabaret theater and restaurant.

$500,000 to Pittsburgh Project, Pittsburgh, PA. For Leaving Footprints expansion and capital campaign.

$500,000 to Sarah Heinz House Association, Pittsburgh, PA. For Building Character capital campaign.

$334,000 to Carnegie Library of Pittsburgh, Pittsburgh, PA. For Library Capital Improvements Program.

$300,000 to Family Resources, Pittsburgh, PA. For Family Retreat Center Capital Campaign.

$100,000 to Mattress Factory, Pittsburgh, PA. For artistic and educational programming and capital building improvements.

$93,000 to Heartwood Institute, Pittsburgh, PA. For development of middle school curriculum.

$50,000 to Veterans Place of Washington Boulevard, Monroeville, PA. For construction of Service Center.

8183

Jerry and Joan Edwards Family Foundation ✧ ☆

1140 Edwards Dr.
St. Thomas, PA 17252-9758

Established in 2003 in PA.

Donors: D. Gerald Edwards; Joan F. Edwards.

Foundation type: Independent foundation.

Financial data (yr. ended 12/31/05): Assets, $3,832 (M); expenditures, $349,147; qualifying distributions, $347,645; giving activities include $347,645 for 8 grants (high: $100,000; low: $1,000).

Fields of interest: Hospitals (general); Human services; Protestant agencies & churches.

Limitations: Applications not accepted. Giving primarily in Chambersburg, PA. No grants to individuals.

Application information: Contributes only to pre-selected organizations.

Officers and Directors:* D. Gerald Edwards,* Pres.; Joan F. Edwards,* Secy.-Treas.

EIN: 200166041

8184
Charles E. Ellis Grant and Scholarship Fund ◇

c/o PNC Advisors
1600 Market St., Tax Dept., 4th Fl.
Philadelphia, PA 19103-7240
Application address: c/o White-Williams Scholars, 215 S. Broad St., 5th Fl., Philadelphia, PA 19102

Established in 1981 in PA.
Donor: Charles E. Ellis†.
Foundation type: Independent foundation.
Financial data (yr. ended 6/30/05): Assets, $35,613,582 (M); expenditures, $1,711,271; qualifying distributions, $1,626,283; giving activities include $1,330,527 for grants.
Purpose and activities: The purpose of the fund is to provide grants and scholarships for the benefit of functionally orphaned girls or for girls from single-parent families, who are living in the 5 county area of southeastern PA, with preference given to girls who are residing in Philadelphia County, PA.
Fields of interest: Secondary school/education; Education; Girls.
Type of support: Scholarship funds; Scholarships—to individuals.
Limitations: Giving limited to Philadelphia County, PA.
Publications: Application guidelines; Informational brochure; Program policy statement.
Application information: Funds paid directly to the educational institution the individual attends. Application form required.
> *Initial approach:* Letter
> *Deadline(s):* None
> *Board meeting date(s):* Apr., May, Aug., and Nov.
> *Final notification:* 2 weeks after each board meeting

Trustee: PNC Bank, N.A.
EIN: 236725618

8185
Elizabeth R. England Trust ◇

c/o Mellon Financial Corp.
P.O. Box 185
Pittsburgh, PA 15230-9897

Established in 1987 in PA.
Foundation type: Independent foundation.
Financial data (yr. ended 6/30/05): Assets, $19,279,920 (M); expenditures, $1,036,322; qualifying distributions, $1,996,727; giving activities include $960,405 for grants to individuals.
Purpose and activities: Giving primarily for education and churches. Scholarships are primarily awarded to art majors who are students at Philadelphia High School for Girls or West Philadelphia High School.
Fields of interest: Arts education; Christian agencies & churches.
Type of support: Grants to individuals; Scholarships—to individuals.
Limitations: Giving limited to residents of Philadelphia, PA.
Application information: Application form not required.
> *Deadline(s):* None

Trustee: Mellon Bank, N.A.
EIN: 236606334

8186
The Samuel Epstein Foundation Trust ◇

c/o National City Bank
20 Stanwix St., Ste. 25 162
Pittsburgh, PA 15222-4801

Established in 1988 in PA.
Donor: Samuel Epstein†.
Foundation type: Independent foundation.
Financial data (yr. ended 12/31/04): Assets, $5,503,765 (M); expenditures, $370,622; qualifying distributions, $346,854; giving activities include $174,250 for 10 grants (high: $17,425; low: $17,425), and $121,975 for 26 grants to individuals (high: $14,279; low: $750).
Purpose and activities: Giving primarily for human services, and Jewish organizations; also awards scholarships to high school students in Warren, PA.
Fields of interest: Human services; Jewish federated giving programs; Jewish agencies & temples.
International interests: Israel.
Type of support: General/operating support; Scholarships—to individuals.
Limitations: Giving primarily in Warren, PA.
Application information: Unsolicited requests for grants not accepted. Application form required for scholarships only.
> *Final notification:* Apr. for scholarships only

Trustee: National City Bank.
EIN: 256311365

8187
Equitable Resources Foundation, Inc. ◇

225 North Shore Dr.
Pittsburgh, PA 15212-5861
Contact: Brian Pietrandrea
URL: http://www.eqt.com/about_EQT/Foundation.asp

Established in 2003 in PA.
Donors: Equitable Production Co.; EQD Holdings Co., LLC.
Foundation type: Company-sponsored foundation.
Financial data (yr. ended 12/31/04): Assets, $35,255,337 (M); gifts received, $18,966,726; expenditures, $1,927,269; qualifying distributions, $1,662,324; giving activities include $1,601,153 for 93+ grants (high: $238,000).
Purpose and activities: The foundation supports organizations involved with arts and culture, education, health, human services, community development, and senior citizens.
Fields of interest: Arts; Elementary/secondary education; Education; Health care; Human services; Community development; Federated giving programs; Aging.
Type of support: General/operating support; Capital campaigns; Program development; Scholarship funds; Sponsorships.
Limitations: Giving primarily in areas of company operations in KY, Pittsburgh, PA, and WV. No support for religious organizations.
Application information: Application form required.
> *Initial approach:* Contact foundation for application form
> *Deadline(s):* None

Officers and Directors:* Charlene Petrelli,* Pres.; Mary Lourdes Gegick, V.P.; Martin A. Fritz, Secy.; James E. Crockard III, Treas.; Murry S. Gerber; Johanna G. O'Loughlin; David L. Porges.
EIN: 043747289

8188
The Erie Community Foundation

127 W. 6th St.
Erie, PA 16501-1001 (814) 454-0843
Contact: Michael L. Batchelor, Pres.; For grants: Amy Cuzzola-Kern Ph.D., V.P., Progs.; Donna Douglass, Prog. Off.
FAX: (814) 456-4965;
E-mail: mbatchelor@cferie.org; Additional E-mails: ackern@cferie.org and ddouglass@cferie.org;
URL: http://www.cferie.org

Established in 1935 in PA as Erie Endowment Foundation; renamed in 1970.
Foundation type: Community foundation.
Financial data (yr. ended 12/31/05): Assets, $121,365,329 (M); gifts received, $6,997,344; expenditures, $8,949,457; giving activities include $7,116,001 for 659 grants (high: $1,356,838; low: $50), and $434,650 for 34 grants to individuals (high: $311,350; low: $500).
Purpose and activities: The foundation primarily provides support for arts, culture, and quality of life, education, human services, community development, health, and nonprofit capacity building.
Fields of interest: Arts; Education; Health care; Human services; Community development.
Type of support: Income development; Management development/capacity building; Capital campaigns; Building/renovation; Equipment; Land acquisition; Emergency funds; Program development; Publication; Curriculum development; Research; Technical assistance; Program evaluation; Scholarships—to individuals; Matching/challenge support.
Limitations: Giving limited to Erie County, PA. No support for sectarian religious activities, fire departments, nursing homes, or school playgrounds. No grants to individuals (except for scholarships), or for fundraising events, programs ads, organization start-up costs, endowments, deficit financing, or operating expenses.
Publications: Application guidelines; Annual report; Financial statement; Grants list; Informational brochure (including application guidelines); Newsletter.
Application information: Visit foundation Web site for application form and guidelines. The foundation strongly suggests applicants attend a technical workshop; visit Web site for details. Application form required.
> *Initial approach:* Telephone or e-mail Prog. Off.
> *Copies of proposal:* 18
> *Deadline(s):* Feb. 1 for Arts, Culture, Quality of Life, and Education, May 1 for Community Development and Human Services, Aug. 1 for Health and Nonprofit Capacity Building, and Nov. 1 for Emergency grant requests and special project RFP's
> *Board meeting date(s):* Mar., June, Sept., and Dec.
> *Final notification:* 4 to 6 weeks

Officers and Trustees:* William M. Hilbert,* Chair.; Michael L. Batchelor,* Pres.; Amy Cuzzola-Kern, Ph.D., V.P., Progs.; Thomas L. Doolin,* Secy.; Edward P. Junker III,* Treas.; James D. Cullen; Kathleen A. Dahlkemper; Geoffrey P. Dunn, M.D.; B.J. Lechner; Ray L. McGarvey; Marne R. Roche; M. Peter Scibetta, M.D.; Philip M. Tredway.
Trustee Banks: Advest, Inc.; First National Bank; LPL Finanacial; Mellon Bank, N.A.; Merrill Lynch Trust Co.; National City Bank; PNC Bank, N.A.

Number of staff: 4 full-time professional; 1 part-time professional; 3 full-time support.
EIN: 256032032
Selected grants: The following grants were reported in 2005.
$55,000 to United Neighborhood Facilities Health Care Corporation, Erie, PA. For WIC program sites.
$30,000 to Early Connections, Erie, PA. For countywide early childhood project in conjunction with United Way of Erie County.
$25,000 to John F. Kennedy Center, Erie, PA. For health equipment.
$20,000 to Bayfront NATO/Martin Luther King Center, Martin Luther King Junior Memorial Center, Erie, PA. For health clinic equipment and renovations.
$20,000 to Community Country Day School, Erie, PA. For new front entrance.
$20,000 to Erie County Historical Society, Erie, PA. For Gift to Our Grandchildren Endowment Campaign.
$20,000 to Friends of the Tom Ridge Center, Erie, PA. For development campaign.
$20,000 to Harborcreek Youth Services, Harborcreek, PA. For management information system.
$17,900 to Gaudenzia Erie, Erie, PA. For new roof.
$14,000 to Roadhouse Theater for Contemporary Arts, Erie, PA. For retractable movie screen and projection system.

8189
Erlbaum Family Foundation ◇
44 W. Lancaster Ave., Ste. 110
Ardmore, PA 19003-1339
Contact: Gary E. Erlbaum, Pres.

Established in 1998 in PA.
Donors: Philip Youtie; Gary E. Erlbaum.
Foundation type: Independent foundation.
Financial data (yr. ended 12/31/05): Assets, $3,579,885 (M); gifts received, $890,800; expenditures, $527,919; qualifying distributions, $509,601; giving activities include $509,601 for 133 grants (high: $75,000; low: $18).
Purpose and activities: Giving primarily for Jewish organizations.
Fields of interest: Health organizations, association; Human services; Jewish federated giving programs; Jewish agencies & temples.
Limitations: Giving primarily in the Philadelphia, PA, area; some funding nationally.
Application information:
Initial approach: Letter
Deadline(s): None
Officer: Gary E. Erlbaum, Pres.
Directors: Daniel A. Erlbaum; Jon L. Erlbaum; Marc N. Erlbaum; Vicki Erlbaum.
EIN: 232962563

8190
ESSA Foundation ◇
(formerly East Stroudsburg Savings Association Foundation)
200 Palmer St.
P.O. Box L
Stroudsburg, PA 18360 (570) 422-0182
Contact: Suzie T. Farley, Exec. Tr.

Established in 1998 in PA.

Donors: East Stroudsberg Savings Assoc.; ESSA Bank & Trust.
Foundation type: Operating foundation.
Financial data (yr. ended 12/31/05): Assets, $182,249 (M); gifts received, $418,931; expenditures, $496,957; qualifying distributions, $496,157; giving activities include $493,932 for 28 grants (high: $100,000; low: $1,140).
Purpose and activities: Giving for family and children services, medical centers and community services, in the greater Pocono, PA, region.
Fields of interest: Education; Health care, research; Children, services; Family services.
Limitations: Giving primarily in the greater Pocono, PA, region. No grants to individuals.
Application information:
Initial approach: Letter
Deadline(s): None
Trustees: Suzie T. Farley, Exec. Tr.; John E. Burrus; Gary S. Olson; Elizabeth B. Weekes.
EIN: 232947729

8191
The Eustace Foundation ◇
c/o Cabrini Asset Mgmt., Inc.
700 S. Henderson Rd., No. 202
King of Prussia, PA 19406
URL: http://foundationcenter.org/grantmaker/eustace

Established in 1985 in PA.
Donor: J. Eustace Wolfington.
Foundation type: Independent foundation.
Financial data (yr. ended 9/30/05): Assets, $19,570,621 (M); expenditures, $854,316; qualifying distributions, $798,878; giving activities include $798,878 for 48 grants (high: $250,000; low: $100).
Purpose and activities: Giving primarily for education, social services, and Roman Catholic organizations located in the Philadelphia, PA, area.
Fields of interest: Elementary/secondary education; Higher education; Human services; Children/youth, services; Christian agencies & churches; Roman Catholic agencies & churches.
Limitations: Applications not accepted. Giving limited to eastern PA. No grants to individuals or for tuition subsidy.
Application information: Contributes only to pre-selected organizations.
Trustees: Tara Guido; Mimi Heany; J. Eustace Wolfington.
EIN: 222664349
Selected grants: The following grants were reported in 2003.
$200,000 to Cabrini College, Radnor, PA.
$50,000 to Legionaries of Christ, Philadelphia, PA.
$34,950 to Magee Rehabilitation Hospital, Philadelphia, PA.
$25,000 to MBF Center, Norristown, PA.
$22,285 to Country Day School of the Sacred Heart, Bryn Mawr, PA.
$17,800 to Malvern Preparatory School, Malvern, PA.
$17,000 to Irish Memorial, Philadelphia, PA.
$12,000 to Alexis de Tocqueville Society, Philadelphia, PA.
$8,000 to SILOAM Ministries, Philadelphia, PA.
$7,500 to Saint Edmonds Home for Crippled Children, Rosemont, PA.

8192
Fair Oaks Foundation, Inc. ◇
(formerly AMPCO-Pittsburgh Foundation II, Inc.)
600 Grant St., Ste. 4600
Pittsburgh, PA 15219-2903 (412) 456-4418
Contact: Rose Hoover, V.P. and Secy.

Established in 1988 in PA.
Donors: Pittsburgh Forgings Foundation; AMPCO-Pittsburgh Foundation.
Foundation type: Company-sponsored foundation.
Financial data (yr. ended 12/31/05): Assets, $5,768,859 (M); expenditures, $362,013; qualifying distributions, $353,480; giving activities include $353,480 for 110 grants (high: $100,000; low: $50).
Purpose and activities: The foundation supports organizations involved with arts and culture, education, health, human services, community development, and religion.
Fields of interest: Arts; Higher education; Education; Health care; Human services; Community development; Federated giving programs; Jewish federated giving programs; Religion.
Type of support: Program development.
Limitations: Giving primarily in PA and VA.
Application information: Application form not required.
Initial approach: Proposal
Deadline(s): Oct. 31
Officers and Trustees:* Louis Berkman,* Chair.; Robert A. Paul,* Pres.; Rose Hoover, V.P. and Secy.; Ernest G. Siddons,* V.P.
EIN: 251576560
Selected grants: The following grants were reported in 2004.
$100,000 to Cornell University, Ithaca, NY.
$50,000 to United Jewish Federation of Greater Pittsburgh, Pittsburgh, PA.
$20,000 to United Way of Allegheny County, Pittsburgh, PA.
$6,000 to Harvard Business School Fund, Boston, MA.
$3,000 to United Way of Central Virginia, Lynchburg, VA.
$2,000 to United Way of Porter County, Valparaiso, IN.
$1,000 to Central Virginia Community College, Lynchburg, VA.
$500 to Carnegie Free Library, Connellsville, PA.
$500 to Extra Mile Education Foundation, Pittsburgh, PA.
$500 to United Negro College Fund, Pittsburgh, PA.

8193
Maurice Falk Fund
(formerly Maurice Falk Medical Fund)
3315 Grant Bldg.
Pittsburgh, PA 15219-2395 (412) 261-2485

Incorporated in 1960 in PA.
Donors: Maurice and Laura Falk Foundation; Jeanette Falk.
Foundation type: Independent foundation.
Financial data (yr. ended 8/31/06): Assets, $19,773,476 (M); gifts received, $9,704; expenditures, $1,248,517; qualifying distributions, $982,733; giving activities include $732,230 for 50 grants (high: $100,000; low: $500), and $27,941 for foundation-administered programs.
Purpose and activities: The grants program primarily focuses on requests for proposals initiated

by the fund, contracts and direct payments for specific work related to conferences, media and publications projects which the fund wishes to produce, and small grants from the Innovation and Development Fund which are limited to the Pittsburgh, PA, area.

Fields of interest: Education; Health care; Employment; Housing/shelter; Civil rights, race/intergroup relations; Civil rights; Public policy, research; Minorities.

Type of support: Program evaluation; Research; Program development; Conferences/seminars; Publication; Seed money; Technical assistance; Consulting services; In-kind gifts.

Publications: Occasional report.

Application information: Application form required.
Initial approach: Letter of inquiry or telephone
Copies of proposal: 2
Deadline(s): Contact foundation for current deadlines
Board meeting date(s): Biannually

Officers and Trustees:* Sigo Falk,* Chair.; Kerry J. O'Donnell, Pres.; Estelle Comay,* Secy.-Treas.; Bertram S. Brown, M.D.; Michelle R. Cooper; Andrew D. Falk; Angela Williams Foster; Eric W. Springer.

Number of staff: 1 full-time professional; 1 full-time support.

EIN: 251099658

8194
Farber Family Foundation ◇

1845 Walnut St., Ste. 800
Philadelphia, PA 19103-4708

Incorporated in 1992 in FL.

Donors: Jack Farber; Ellen B. Kurtzman.

Foundation type: Independent foundation.

Financial data (yr. ended 12/31/05): Assets, $15,093,304 (M); gifts received, $3,167,138; expenditures, $2,721,089; qualifying distributions, $2,662,722; giving activities include $2,652,470 for 24 grants (high: $2,000,000; low: $500).

Purpose and activities: Funding primarily for education, Jewish organizations, and human services.

Fields of interest: Higher education; Human services; Federated giving programs; Jewish federated giving programs; Jewish agencies & temples.

Type of support: General/operating support.

Limitations: Applications not accepted. Giving primarily in PA. No grants to individuals.

Application information: Contributes only to pre-selected organizations.

Officers and Directors:* Jack Farber,* Pres.; Vivian Farber,* V.P. and Secy.; Ellen B. Kurtzman,* V.P. and Treas.; David M. Farber,* V.P.

EIN: 650336266

8195
Farber Foundation, Inc. ◇

1845 Walnut St., Ste. 800
Philadelphia, PA 19103

Contact: Jacqueline A. Tully, Coord., Scholarship Prog.

Established in 1949.

Donor: CSS Industries, Inc.

Foundation type: Company-sponsored foundation.

Financial data (yr. ended 12/31/05): Assets, $2,529,293 (M); expenditures, $393,242;

qualifying distributions, $385,857; giving activities include $221,613 for 37 grants (high: $87,480; low: $50), and $163,832 for 46 grants to individuals (high: $5,000; low: $1,000).

Purpose and activities: The foundation supports performing arts centers and organizations involved with higher education, health, human services, and Judaism.

Fields of interest: Performing arts centers; Higher education; Health care; Children/youth, services; Human services; Federated giving programs; Jewish federated giving programs; Jewish agencies & temples.

Type of support: General/operating support; Employee-related scholarships.

Limitations: Giving primarily in PA, with emphasis on Philadelphia.

Officers: Jack Farber, Chair.; David J.M. Erskine, Pres.; Clifford E. Pietrafitta, V.P.

EIN: 236254221

Selected grants: The following grants were reported in 2004.

$88,500 to American Jewish Committee, New York, NY.

$44,000 to United Way of Southeastern Pennsylvania, Philadelphia, PA.

$30,000 to Kimmel Center for the Performing Arts, Philadelphia, PA.

$10,000 to Committee of Seventy, Philadelphia, PA.

$10,000 to Philadelphia Academies, Philadelphia, PA.

$6,000 to Greater Philadelphia Urban Affairs Coalition, Philadelphia, PA.

$5,000 to Arcadia University, Glenside, PA.

$5,000 to Cedar Crest College, Allentown, PA.

$5,000 to South Kent School, South Kent, CT.

$1,000 to Phillies Charities, Philadelphia, PA.

8196
Federated Investors Foundation, Inc. ◇

Federated Investors Tower
Pittsburgh, PA 15222-3779

Established in 1997.

Donor: Federated Investors, Inc.

Foundation type: Company-sponsored foundation.

Financial data (yr. ended 4/30/03): Assets, $1,157,285 (M); gifts received, $25,000; expenditures, $358,829; qualifying distributions, $358,199; giving activities include $358,050 for 70 grants (high: $65,000; low: $200).

Purpose and activities: The foundation supports organizations involved with arts and culture, education, the environment, medical research, human services, and religion.

Fields of interest: Arts; Education; Environment, natural resources; Medical research, institute; Human services; Federated giving programs; Religion.

Limitations: Applications not accepted. Giving primarily in PA. No grants to individuals.

Application information: Contributes only to pre-selected organizations.

Officers and Directors:* J. Christopher Donahue,* Pres.; John W. McGonigle, Secy.; Thomas R. Donahue, Treas.; John F. Donahue; Thomas J. Donnelly.

EIN: 232913182

Selected grants: The following grants were reported in 2004.

$70,000 to United Way, PA.

$30,000 to Oakland Catholic High School, Pittsburgh, PA.

$25,000 to Americans United for Life, Chicago, IL.

$25,000 to Saint Vincent College, Latrobe, PA.

$15,000 to Morality in Media, New York, NY.

$10,000 to DePaul Institute, Pittsburgh, PA.

$10,000 to Pittsburgh Leadership Foundation, Pittsburgh, PA.

$10,000 to Sisters of Charity of Seton Hill, Greensburg, PA.

$5,000 to Boston College, Chestnut Hill, MA.

$5,000 to National Fatherhood Initiative, Gaithersburg, MD.

8197
Federation Foundation of Greater Philadelphia ◇

2100 Arch St.
Philadelphia, PA 19103

Contact: Richard N. Nassau, Exec. Secy.

Established in 1971 in PA.

Donors: Jonas Brachfeld; Rosalind Brachfeld.

Foundation type: Independent foundation.

Financial data (yr. ended 11/30/03): Assets, $6,512,081 (M); gifts received, $19,860; expenditures, $666,095; qualifying distributions, $619,228; giving activities include $615,013 for grants.

Purpose and activities: The foundation supports services and programs of organizations that contribute to the preservation and enrichment of Jewish life, and it fosters cooperative and constructive relations among the institutions and the other organizations of the Jewish community.

Fields of interest: Higher education; Human services; Jewish agencies & temples.

International interests: Israel.

Type of support: Endowments.

Limitations: Applications not accepted. Giving on a national basis. No grants to individuals.

Application information: Grantees are pre-selected by individual donors of the foundation. Unsolicited requests for funds not considered.

Officers: Andrea Adelman, Chair.; Harold S. Goldman, Pres.; Richard Nassau, Exec. Secy.

Directors: Lawrence S. Chane; Susan Freedman; Howard Glassman; Jay L. Goldberg; Gary D. Kleiman; Robert C. Pozen; Clifford Schlesinger; Rebecca Smolen-Rosenberger; Ralph Snyder; Arthur A. Zatz.

Number of staff: 1 part-time support.

EIN: 237083735

8198
Samuel S. Fels Fund

1616 Walnut St., Ste. 800
Philadelphia, PA 19103-5313 (215) 731-9455
Contact: Helen Cunningham, Exec. Dir.
FAX: (215) 731-9457; URL: http://www.samfels.org

Incorporated in 1935 in PA.

Donor: Samuel S. Fels†.

Foundation type: Independent foundation.

Financial data (yr. ended 12/31/05): Assets, $50,150,458 (M); expenditures, $2,184,687; qualifying distributions, $2,377,518; giving activities include $1,984,119 for 184 grants (high: $166,000; low: $1,000; average: $6,000–$20,000).

Purpose and activities: Grants for projects and organizations that help to prevent, lessen, or resolve contemporary social problems, or that seek to

provide permanent improvements in the provision of services for the improvement of daily life; to increase the stability of arts organizations and enrich the cultural life of the city of Philadelphia, PA.
Fields of interest: Arts; Education; Community development.
Type of support: General/operating support; Continuing support; Building/renovation; Equipment; Program development; Seed money; Curriculum development; Internship funds; Technical assistance; Matching/challenge support.
Limitations: Giving limited to the City of Philadelphia, PA. No support for national organizations, day or after-school care programs, routine social services or counseling, drug and alcohol addiction programs, religious education, private schools, hospitals, programs for animals, or summer recreation programs. No grants for endowment or building funds, travel, research, publications, deficit financing, scholarships, fellowships, purchase of tickets, tables, ads or sponsorships, parties, conferences, fairs and festivals, or disease research.
Publications: Application guidelines; Annual report (including application guidelines); Grants list.
Application information: Applicant must request guidelines before submitting proposals; the fund accepts Delaware Valley Grantmakers Common Grant Application and Common Report Form. Proposal Cover Sheet is available on foundation Web site. Application form required.
  Initial approach: Proposal or telephone requesting guidelines
  Copies of proposal: 1
  Deadline(s): May 15 and Jan. 15 for Arts and Culture; None for others
  Board meeting date(s): Rolling application review, board meets 7 times a year
  Final notification: Usually one or two months
Officers and Directors:* David H. Wice,* Pres.; Sandra Featherman,* V.P.; Helen Cunningham,* Secy. and Exec. Dir.; Ida K. Chen, Treas.; Bro. Daniel Burke, F.S.C.; Phoebe Haddon; David C. Melnicoff; Emmanuel Ortiz; Mindy M. Posoff; Anthony M. Santomero.
Number of staff: 1 full-time professional; 1 full-time support; 1 part-time support.
EIN: 231365325

8199
Ferree Foundation

229 N. Duke St.
Lancaster, PA 17602 (717) 735-8288, ext. 109
Contact: Phillip L. Calhoun, Exec. Dir.
FAX: (717) 735-8291; *URL:* http://www.ferree-foundation.org

Established in 2004 in PA.
Foundation type: Independent foundation.
Financial data (yr. ended 12/31/05): Assets, $18,406,530 (M); gifts received, $770,044; expenditures, $2,016,011; qualifying distributions, $1,899,934; giving activities include $1,827,000 for 71 grants (high: $200,000; low: $25; average: $10,000–$100,000).
Purpose and activities: The foundation is dedicated to promoting and supporting excellence in the arts, culture and history, education, youth engagement, health, human services, and local economic and community development.
Fields of interest: Performing arts; Historical activities; Higher education; Education; Health care; Children/youth, services.

Type of support: Building/renovation; Endowments; Program development; Capital campaigns; Technical assistance; Research; General/operating support; Annual campaigns.
Limitations: Giving primarily in Lancaster County and southeastern PA.
Publications: Application guidelines; Financial statement; Grants list; Program policy statement (including application guidelines).
Application information: Full proposals accepted by invitation only, following positive ruling on letter of inquiry. Delaware Valley Grantmakers application form accepted. Application form required.
  Initial approach: Letter of inquiry
  Copies of proposal: 1
  Deadline(s): Sept. 15th
  Board meeting date(s): Quarterly
  Final notification: Ruling on letter of inquiry within 1 month
Officers and Directors:* Paul W. Ware,* Pres., V.P. and Secy.-Treas.; Phillip L. Calhoun, Exec. Dir.; Layla DeLuria; Julia A. Ware.
Number of staff: 1 part-time professional; 1 part-time support.
EIN: 201060557

8200
Joseph and Marie Field Foundation ◇

c/o E.R. Boynton
2600 1 Commerce Sq.
Philadelphia, PA 19103

Established in 1999 in PA.
Donors: Joseph M. Field; Marie H. Field.
Foundation type: Independent foundation.
Financial data (yr. ended 7/31/05): Assets, $31,892,675 (L); gifts received, $2,179,200; expenditures, $1,674,044; qualifying distributions, $1,650,000; giving activities include $1,650,000 for 8 grants (high: $450,000; low: $100,000).
Fields of interest: Museums; Performing arts centers; Performing arts, music; Performing arts, education; Higher education; Law school/education; Medical research, institute.
Limitations: Applications not accepted. Giving primarily in Philadelphia, PA. No grants to individuals.
Application information: Contributes only to pre-selected organizations.
Officers and Directors:* Joseph M. Field,* Pres. and Treas.; Marie H. Field,* V.P. and Secy.
EIN: 233009586
Selected grants: The following grants were reported in 2003.
$200,000 to Curtis Institute of Music, Philadelphia, PA. For renovation and endowment of concert hall.
$200,000 to National Liberty Museum, Philadelphia, PA. For general operating support.
$200,000 to Settlement Music School, Philadelphia, PA. For construction of chamber music center.
$100,000 to Kimmel Center for the Performing Arts, Philadelphia, PA. For general operating support.
$100,000 to Philadelphia Orchestra Association, Philadelphia, PA. For endowment.
$100,000 to Thomas Jefferson University, Philadelphia, PA. For medical research.
$100,000 to University of Pennsylvania, Philadelphia, PA. For general operating support.

8201
The Fine Family Foundation ☆

(formerly Milton Fine Family Charitable Foundation)
c/o FFC Capital Corp.
Dominion Twr.
625 Liberty Ave., Ste. 3110
Pittsburgh, PA 15222
Contact: Milton Fine, Pres.

Donors: Milton Fine; The Milton Fine Irrevocable Trust of 1998; The Milton Fine Irrevocable Trust of 2000.
Foundation type: Independent foundation.
Financial data (yr. ended 6/30/05): Assets, $300,710 (M); gifts received, $369,200; expenditures, $368,652; qualifying distributions, $368,652; giving activities include $368,652 for grants.
Purpose and activities: Giving primarily to the arts and culture, education, including environmental education, human services, health and Jewish organizations.
Fields of interest: Museums (art); Museums (ethnic/folk arts); Arts; Higher education; Environment; Health care; Human services; Federated giving programs; Jewish federated giving programs; Jewish agencies & temples.
International interests: England.
Type of support: General/operating support; Annual campaigns; Capital campaigns; Building/renovation; Program development; Seed money; Curriculum development; Research; Program evaluation.
Limitations: Giving primarily in MA and Pittsburgh, PA.
Application information: Application form not required.
  Initial approach: Letter
  Deadline(s): None
  Board meeting date(s): Aug. and Nov.
Officer and Directors:* Milton Fine,* Pres. and Secy.-Treas.; David Fine; Sheila Fine; Carolyn Fine Friedman; Sibyl Fine King.
Number of staff: 1 full-time professional.
EIN: 256335329
Selected grants: The following grants were reported in 2005.
$25,000 to National Museum of American Jewish History, Philadelphia, PA.
$18,750 to United Jewish Federation of Greater Pittsburgh, Pittsburgh, PA.
$17,500 to Brandeis University, Waltham, MA.
$10,000 to Forest Watch, Montpelier, VT.
$10,000 to Friends of the Lyric, Stuart, FL.
$10,000 to New England Grassroots Environment Fund, Montpelier, VT.
$5,500 to Combined Jewish Philanthropies of Greater Boston, Boston, MA.
$5,000 to Coalition on the Environment and Jewish Life, New York, NY.
$5,000 to Rachels Network, DC.
$500 to Indian River Community College, Fort Pierce, FL.

8202
First Community Foundation of Pennsylvania ◇

(formerly Williamsport-Lycoming Foundation)
330 Pine St., Ste. 401
Williamsport, PA 17701 (570) 321-1500
Contact: For grants: Dawn M. Linn, Mgr., Progs.

FAX: (570) 321-6434; E-mail: fcfpa@fcfpa.org;
Additional tel.: (866) 901-2372; Grant application
E-mail: dawnl@fcfpa.org; URL: http://www.fcfpa.org

Established in 1916 in PA by bank resolution.
Foundation type: Community foundation.
Financial data (yr. ended 12/31/04): Assets,
$53,282,310 (M); gifts received, $4,361,480;
expenditures, $3,140,207; giving activities include
$1,936,711 for 172 grants (high: $494,053; low:
$24).
Purpose and activities: The foundation serves
Central and Northcentral Pennsylvania by helping
donors make a difference in the community and
making grants to nonprofit organizations in support
of their charitable work.
Fields of interest: Historic preservation/historical
societies; Arts; Higher education; Education;
Environment, natural resources; Environment;
Health care; Recreation; Youth development; Youth,
services; Family services; Human services;
Economic development; Community development.
Type of support: General/operating support;
Continuing support; Capital campaigns; Building/
renovation; Equipment; Land acquisition; Program
development; Conferences/seminars; Seed money;
Scholarship funds; Program-related investments/
loans; Matching/challenge support.
Limitations: Giving primarily in Central and
Northcentral PA. No support for sectarian religious
programs, clubs, sports teams, fire companies, or
research of highly technical or specialized nature.
No grants to individuals (except for scholarships), or
generally for endowment funds, annual campaigns,
event sponsorships, debt reduction, or ongoing
operating support; no loans to individuals.
Publications: Application guidelines; Annual report;
Financial statement; Informational brochure;
Program policy statement.
Application information: Visit foundation Web site
for letter of intent guidelines and instructions.
Based on letter of intent, nonprofit organizations will
be notified of whether they will be invited to submit
a full grant application or whether their proposal has
been denied. Application form required.
  Initial approach: Submit letter of intent
  Copies of proposal: 1
  Deadline(s): June 1 for letter of intent; Aug. 1 for
    full grant application
  Board meeting date(s): Monthly
  Final notification: July 1 for letter of intent
    determination; Oct. 30 for grants
Officers and Directors:* John C. "Jack" Schultz,*
Chair.; Daniel G. Fultz,* Vice-Chair.; Frank J.
Concino, Jr.,* C.E.O. and Pres.; Robert More,*
Secy.-Treas.; Sheryl A. Hoff, C.F.O.; Karen M.
Armstrong; Robert E. Fleck; Barbara B. Hudock;
William J. "Bill" Metzger; Yvonne Morgan; John M.
Young.
Number of staff: 4 full-time professional; 1 part-time
professional; 1 full-time support; 1 part-time
support.
EIN: 246013117

8203
Firstfruits Foundation ◇
P.O. Box 239
Elverson, PA   19520-0239

Established in 1995 in PA.
Donors: Robert L. Cone; Dawn M. Cone.
Foundation type: Independent foundation.

Financial data (yr. ended 12/31/05): Assets,
$13,868,676 (M); expenditures, $760,863;
qualifying distributions, $668,592; giving activities
include $603,670 for 14 grants (high: $118,874;
low: $3,000).
Purpose and activities: Giving primarily to Baptist
churches, schools, and ministries.
Fields of interest: Higher education; Theological
school/education; Education; Protestant agencies
& churches.
Limitations: Applications not accepted. Giving on a
national basis. No grants to individuals.
Application information: Contributes only to
pre-selected organizations.
Officers: Robert L. Cone, Pres. and Treas.; Edward
H. Cone, V.P. and Secy.
Director: Derial H. Sanders.
EIN: 232808624

8204
FISA Foundation
1001 Liberty Ave., Ste. 650
Pittsburgh, PA   15222   (412) 456-5550
Contact: Mary D. Delaney, Exec. Dir.
FAX: (412) 456-5551;
E-mail: info@fisafoundation.org; Additional E-mails:
sue@fisafoundation.org or
kristy@fisafoundation.org or
dee@fisafoundation.org; URL: http://
www.fisafoundation.org/

Established in 1996 in PA; converted from proceeds
received through the sale of Harmaville
Rehabilitation Center to HEALTHSOUTH
Corporation.
Foundation type: Independent foundation.
Financial data (yr. ended 6/30/05): Assets,
$40,698,069 (M); gifts received, $23,844;
expenditures, $1,871,500; qualifying distributions,
$1,678,232; giving activities include $1,380,056
for 71 grants (high: $64,750; low: $200).
Purpose and activities: The foundation's mission is
to build a culture of respect and improve the quality
of life for three populations in southwestern
Pennsylvania: women, girls, and people with
disabilities.
Fields of interest: Medical care, rehabilitation;
Health care; Mental health/crisis services, rape
victim services; Mental health/crisis services;
Autism; Crime/violence prevention, domestic
violence; Crime/violence prevention, sexual abuse;
Employment, vocational rehabilitation; Employment,
sheltered workshops; Recreation; Girl scouts;
Human services; Family services, domestic
violence; Family services, adolescent parents;
Women, centers/services; Human services; Civil
rights, disabled; Civil rights; Mentally disabled;
Women.
Type of support: General/operating support;
Continuing support; Capital campaigns; Building/
renovation; Equipment; Program development;
Conferences/seminars; Seed money; Technical
assistance; Program evaluation; Matching/
challenge support.
Limitations: Giving limited to a 10-county area of
southwestern PA, including: Allegheny, Armstrong,
Beaver, Butler, Greene, Fayette, Indiana, Lawrence,
Washington, and Westmoreland counties. No
support for organizations that lack tax-exempt
status, or for religious purposes. No grants to
individuals, or for scholarships, endowments, travel,
or study.

Publications: Application guidelines; Annual report;
Occasional report.
Application information: Letters must be
accompanied by an application form (available on
the website). Several attachments are specified in
the application form. Application guidelines,
procedures and download of application form are
available on foundation Web site. Unsolicited
inquiries accepted, but unsolicited proposals are
not. Full proposal is by invitation only. Application
form required.
  Initial approach: Letter of inquiry
  Copies of proposal: 1
  Deadline(s): 3-4 months prior to board meeting
  Board meeting date(s): Feb., June and Oct.
  Final notification: Within 2 weeks
Officers and Board Members:* Connie
Mockenhaupt,* Pres.; Laura A. Meaden,* V.P.;
Karyll A. Davis,* Secy.; Angela B. Maher,* Treas.;
Mary D. Delaney, Exec. Dir.; and 15 additional board
members.
Number of staff: 2 full-time professional; 1 full-time
support.
EIN: 250965388
Selected grants: The following grants were reported
in 2004.
  $83,334 to University of Pittsburgh, School of
    Health and Rehabilitation Services, Pittsburgh,
    PA. For endowment.
  $40,709 to Every Child, Pittsburgh, PA. For Healthy
    Infants for Teens and Women with Disabilities
    program.
  $40,000 to Sojourner House, Pittsburgh, PA. For
    capital support for MOMS program.
  $25,000 to Childhood Apraxia of Speech
    Association of North America, Pittsburgh, PA. For
    website update.
  $10,105 to Early Learning Institute, Pittsburgh, PA.
    For new software.
  $5,000 to Health Policy Institute, Pittsburgh, PA. For
    operating support.
  $2,500 to Childrens Institute of Pittsburgh,
    Pittsburgh, PA. For Phyllis Reymer Totten
    Scholarship.
  $2,000 to Grantmakers in Health, DC. For general
    support.
  $1,000 to Working Women with Disabilities,
    Pittsburgh, PA. For awards dinner.
  $700 to Working Order, Pittsburgh, PA. For office
    furnishings.

8205
Audrey Hillman Fisher Foundation ◇
330 Grant St., Ste. 2000
Pittsburgh, PA   15219   (412) 338-3466
Contact: Ronald W. Wertz, V.P. and Exec. Dir.
FAX: (412) 338-3463;
E-mail: foundation@hillmanfo.com

Established in 1986 in DE.
Donors: Audrey Hillman Fisher; Henry Lea Hillman
Charitable Lead Trust.
Foundation type: Independent foundation.
Financial data (yr. ended 12/31/04): Assets,
$8,189,545 (M); expenditures, $443,938;
qualifying distributions, $350,800; giving activities
include $337,800 for 74 grants (high: $25,000;
low: $500; average: $500–$15,000).
Fields of interest: Performing arts; Secondary
school/education; Higher education; Environment;
Health care; Youth development; Children/youth,
services; Human services.

Type of support: General/operating support; Continuing support; Annual campaigns; Capital campaigns; Building/renovation; Equipment; Land acquisition; Endowments; Program development; Seed money.
Limitations: Giving primarily in Santa Barbara, CA, central NH and Pittsburgh, PA. No grants to individuals.
Publications: Application guidelines.
Application information: Application form not required.
> *Initial approach:* Summary letter
> *Copies of proposal:* 1
> *Deadline(s):* None
> *Board meeting date(s):* May and Dec.

Officers and Directors:* Audrey Hillman Fisher,* Pres.; Ronald W. Wertz,* V.P. and Exec. Dir.; Maurice J. White,* Secy.; Eric C. Johnson, Treas.
Number of staff: 1 part-time professional.
EIN: 251536655
Selected grants: The following grants were reported in 2004.
$48,400 to Pittsburgh Parks Conservancy, Pittsburgh, PA. 2 grants: $28,400 (For Spring Hat Luncheon), $20,000 (For programs and campaigns to restore four great parks of Pittsburgh).
$32,600 to Historical Society of Western Pennsylvania, Pittsburgh, PA. 2 grants: $10,000 (For expansion of history center facility), $22,600 (For gala for opening of new Smithsonian Wing and Western Pennsylvania Sports Museum).
$25,000 to Squam Lakes Natural Science Center, Holderness, NH. For Horizon Project Capstone Challenge.
$20,000 to Planned Parenthood of Western Pennsylvania, Pittsburgh, PA. For purchase and renovation of program and administrative facility.
$13,000 to Pittsburgh Cultural Trust, Pittsburgh, PA. For Hillman Cancer Center Benefit for Pittsburgh Cultural Trust at Renaissance Hotel.
$10,000 to New Hampshire Music Festival, Gilford, NH. For establishment of Center for Music.
$10,000 to Shadyside Hospital Foundation, Pittsburgh, PA. For Initiatives for Beckwith Institute for Nursing Innovation.
$10,000 to Speare Memorial Hospital, Plymouth, NH. For capital campaign.

8206
Fleming Foundation ◇ ☆
7661 Beryl Rd.
Zionsville, PA 18092

Established in 1990 in PA.
Donor: Richard Fleming.
Foundation type: Independent foundation.
Financial data (yr. ended 12/31/05): Assets, $8,934,642 (M); expenditures, $448,717; qualifying distributions, $349,895; giving activities include $349,895 for 29+ grants (high: $300,000).
Purpose and activities: Giving primarily for health care, including medical research, emergency relief services, human services, including canine services for the blind, children and youth services, and for community services.
Fields of interest: Animal welfare; Animals/wildlife, special services; Hospitals (general); Health organizations, association; Medical research, institute; Cancer research; Human services; Salvation Army; Children/youth, services; Community development.

Limitations: Applications not accepted. Giving limited to Allentown, PA. No grants to individuals.
Application information: Contributes only to pre-selected organizations.
Trustees: Kathleen Arnold; Richard Fleming; Roberta Fleming.
EIN: 232585510
Selected grants: The following grants were reported in 2005.
$10,000 to Salvation Army.
$10,000 to United Way of the Greater Lehigh Valley, Bethlehem, PA.
$7,000 to Valley Youth House, Allentown, PA.
$2,000 to Allentown Rescue Mission, Allentown, PA.
$1,000 to American Red Cross.
$500 to Canine Partners for Life, Cochranville, PA.

8207
Forney Family Foundation, Inc. ◇ ☆
P.O. Box 549
Unionville, PA 19375-0549

Established in 1997 in DE.
Donor: Robert C. Forney.
Foundation type: Independent foundation.
Financial data (yr. ended 12/31/05): Assets, $16,534 (M); gifts received, $35,000; expenditures, $1,066,820; qualifying distributions, $1,066,055; giving activities include $1,066,055 for 53 grants (high: $1,012,455; low: $250).
Purpose and activities: Giving primarily for education, the arts, environmental causes, social services, and to Lutheran churches.
Fields of interest: Performing arts; Higher education; Education; Environment; Human services; Protestant agencies & churches.
Limitations: Applications not accepted. Giving on a national basis. No grants to individuals.
Application information: Contributes only to pre-selected organizations.
Officers: Robert C. Forney, Pres. and Treas.; Marilyn G. Forney, V.P. and Secy.
Trustees: Barbara D. Forney; Gerald G. Forney.
EIN: 237079172

8208
The Foundation for Enhancing Communities
(formerly The Greater Harrisburg Foundation)
200 N. 3rd St., 8th Fl.
P.O. Box 678
Harrisburg, PA 17108-0678 (717) 236-5040
Contact: Janice R. Black, C.E.O.; For grants: Mary Hall, Prog. Off.
FAX: (717) 231-4463; Grant application E-mail: Mary@tfec.org;; URL: http://www.tfec.org
Scholarships inquiry E-mail: Dawn@tfec.org

Established in 1920 in PA; assets first acquired in 1940; grants first made in the mid-1940's.
Foundation type: Community foundation.
Financial data (yr. ended 12/31/05): Assets, $41,207,227 (M); gifts received, $10,614,720; expenditures, $6,295,728; giving activities include $2,003,957 for 1,058 grants (high: $140,000; low: $20), and $251,535 for 185 grants to individuals (high: $20,000; low: $13).
Purpose and activities: The foundation seeks to make a positive impact on the communities served. Grantmaking areas include education, health,

human services, community development, the arts, and the environment.
Fields of interest: Humanities; Arts; Education; Environment; Health care; Health organizations, association; Human services; Community development; Religion.
Type of support: General/operating support; Equipment; Program development; Publication; Seed money; Scholarship funds; Technical assistance; Scholarships—to individuals; Matching/challenge support.
Limitations: Giving primarily in PA, with emphasis on Cumberland, Dauphin, Franklin, Lebanon, and Perry counties, and also in the Dillsburg area. No support for religious organizations for religious purposes (except from Donor-Advised or Restricted funds), or for private foundations or discretionary funds. No grants to individuals (except for scholarships).
Publications: Application guidelines; Annual report (including application guidelines); Financial statement; Grants list; Informational brochure (including application guidelines); Program policy statement.
Application information: Call Prog. Off. for current application guidelines or visit foundation Web site; copies of application vary per regional fdn.; faxed applications are not accepted. Application form required.
> *Initial approach:* Contact Prog. Off.
> *Copies of proposal:* 13
> *Deadline(s):* Varies
> *Board meeting date(s):* Jan., Mar., June, Sept., and Nov.
> *Final notification:* Approx. 8 weeks after proposal submission

Officers and Directors:* John Oyler,* Chair.; Jonathan Vipond,* Vice-Chair.; Janice R. Black, C.E.O. and Pres.; Velma A. Redmond,* Secy.; Kirk C. Demyan, C.F.O.; Leonardo Herrada,* Treas.; Nancy C. Aronson; John O. Campbell; Susan M. Connell; Linda Hicks; LeRoy D. Kline; William Lehr, Jr.; Harold McInnes; James Mead; Steven H. Neiman; Kiran P. Patel; David A. Schankweiler; Karen Snider; Mary Webber Weston; Carol E. Yon.
Trustee Banks: Citizens Bank of Southern Pennslyvania; Farmers Trust of Carlisle; Financial Trust Services; First National Bank & Trust of Waynesboro; First National Bank of Greencastle; Fulton Financial Advisors, N.A.; GHF, Inc.; Hershey Trust Co.; The Juniata Valley Bank; M&T Bank; Mellon Bank, N.A.; PNC Bank, N.A.; Pennsylvania State Bank; Sentry Trust Co.; Susquehanna Bank; Valley Bank & Trust Co.; Wachovia Bank, N.A.
Number of staff: 6 full-time professional; 3 part-time professional; 4 full-time support.
EIN: 010564355

8209
Fourjay Foundation
2300 Computer Ave., Bldg. G, Ste. 1
Willow Grove, PA 19090-1753
Contact: Ann T. Bucci, Grants Coord.
FAX: (215) 830-0157; E-mail: info@fourjay.org;
URL: http://www.fourjay.org

Established in 1988 in PA.
Donors: Eugene W. Jackson†; Springhouse Realty Co.
Foundation type: Independent foundation.
Financial data (yr. ended 12/31/05): Assets, $21,521,919 (M); expenditures, $1,268,512; qualifying distributions, $1,005,543; giving

activities include $929,046 for 173 grants (high: $100,000; low: $484).

Purpose and activities: The foundation supports education and human services. Its directors believe these two areas of human endeavor offer people the greatest help; education enables people to make the most of their abilities; human services offer a helping hand to the afflicted, the socially disadvantaged, and the financially handicapped.

Fields of interest: Higher education; Adult education —literacy, basic skills & GED; Medical care, rehabilitation; Nursing care; Health care; Substance abuse, services; Mental health/crisis services; Health organizations, association; Cancer; Eye diseases; Ear & throat diseases; Food services; Human services; Children/youth, services; Family services; Residential/custodial care, hospices; Homeless, human services; Disabilities, people with; Economically disadvantaged; Homeless.

Type of support: General/operating support; Continuing support; Building/renovation; Equipment; Endowments; Emergency funds; Program development; Publication; Seed money; Scholarship funds; Matching/challenge support.

Limitations: Giving limited to Philadelphia, Bucks, and Montgomery counties, PA. No support for political or religious organizations, arts and culture, athletic groups, civic associations, elementary or secondary schools, foreign organizations, public broadcasting, libraries, the United Way, or the YMCA. No grants to individuals or multi-year grants.

Publications: Application guidelines; Grants list.

Application information: Telephone calls accepted. Submit 1 complete proposal and 6 copies of cover proposal letter; only 1 application per organization accepted per year. Grant requests lacking appropriate financial information will not be accepted. All requests for foundation guidelines should be submitted in writing on the grantseeking organization's letterhead, with the appropriate return mailing and contact information provided. Copies of current guidelines can be downloaded from the foundation Web site. Unannounced or impromptu visits are not entertained. Application form not required.

Initial approach: Proposal
Copies of proposal: 1
Deadline(s): Mar. 1, June 1, Sept. 1, and Dec. 1
Board meeting date(s): Mar. 15, June 15, Sept. 15, and Dec. 15
Final notification: Generally within 90 days of proposal receipt

Officer and Directors:* Susan Jackson Tressider, Exec. Dir; Geoffrey W. Jackson,* Managing Tr.; Diana Loukedis Doherty; Marie-Louise Jackson; Thomas Lynch; D. O'Connell; Jean Robinson.

Number of staff: 1 part-time professional; 1 part-time support.

EIN: 232537126

Selected grants: The following grants were reported in 2005.

$8,000 to Hannah House, Philadelphia, PA. For general operating support.

$7,500 to Little Brothers - Friends of the Elderly, Philadelphia, PA.

$5,000 to Face to Face, Philadelphia, PA. For Health Center support.

$5,000 to Network of Victim Assistance, Doylestown, PA. For general operating support.

$5,000 to Philadelphia Futures for Youth, Philadelphia, PA. For Sponsor-A-Scholar program.

$5,000 to Wheels of Wellness, Philadelphia, PA.

$4,000 to Literacy Council of Norristown, Norristown, PA. For general operating support.

$4,000 to VNA Community Services, Abington, PA. For RX Support program.

$3,000 to Legal Clinic for the Disabled, Philadelphia, PA. For Legal Services for the Deaf Project.

$2,500 to Child, Home and Community, Doylestown, PA. For general operating support.

8210
The Richard J. Fox Foundation ✧
100 Front St., Ste. 945
West Conshohocken, PA   19428

Established in 1983 in PA.

Donors: Richard J. Fox; Lawrence R. Miller; Patrick A. Gerschel; ADG-L5, LLC; Bovin Family Foundation.

Foundation type: Independent foundation.

Financial data (yr. ended 12/31/05): Assets, $958,336 (M); gifts received, $1,246,250; expenditures, $919,338; qualifying distributions, $899,063; giving activities include $684,993 for 29 grants (high: $187,993; low: $1,000).

Purpose and activities: Giving primarily to museums, higher education, federated giving programs, and Jewish agencies and temples.

Fields of interest: Museums (history); Higher education; Federated giving programs; Jewish agencies & temples.

Limitations: Applications not accepted. Giving primarily in PA. No grants to individuals.

Application information: Contributes only to pre-selected organizations.

Officer: Richard J. Fox, Pres.

Trustee: Harry D. Fox.

EIN: 232267786

Selected grants: The following grants were reported in 2004.

$166,900 to Temple University, Philadelphia, PA. 3 grants: $21,900, $125,000 to Center for Frontier Science, $20,000 to School of Business

$100,000 to Jewish Federation of Greater Philadelphia, Philadelphia, PA.

$100,000 to Lubavitcher Center, Philadelphia, PA.

$75,000 to National Organization for Hearing Research Foundation, Narberth, PA.

$40,000 to United Way of Southeastern Pennsylvania, Philadelphia, PA.

$35,000 to Jewish Policy Center, DC.

$32,500 to National Museum of American Jewish History, Philadelphia, PA.

$10,000 to Center for the Study of Popular Culture, Los Angeles, CA.

8211
Helen Clay Frick Foundation ✧
P.O. Box 185
Pittsburgh, PA   15230-0185

Newly formed in 2002 in PA from The Helen Clay Frick Foundation.

Donor: The Helen Clay Frick Foundation.

Foundation type: Independent foundation.

Financial data (yr. ended 12/31/04): Assets, $23,899,411 (M); expenditures, $1,115,875; qualifying distributions, $1,063,607; giving activities include $1,024,365 for 86 grants (high: $168,500; low: $500).

Fields of interest: Arts; Higher education; Education; Human services.

Limitations: Applications not accepted. Giving on a national basis. No grants to individuals.

Application information: Contributes only to pre-selected organizations.

Officers: Adelaide F. Trafton, Chair.; I. Townsend Burden III, Secy.

Trustees: Peter P. Blanchard III; Childs Frick Burden; Dixon Frick Burden; Frances D. Burden; Henry S. Burden; and 9 additional trustees.

EIN: 300091891

8212
Elsie Lee Garthwaite Memorial Foundation
1234 Lancaster Ave.
P.O. Box 709
Rosemont, PA   19010-0709   (610) 527-8101
Contact: Thomas Kaneda, Secy.

Established in 1943 in PA.

Donor: Albert A. Garthwaite, Jr.†

Foundation type: Independent foundation.

Financial data (yr. ended 12/31/05): Assets, $7,846,601 (M); expenditures, $407,875; qualifying distributions, $352,000; giving activities include $349,200 for 78 grants (high: $5,000; low: $2,000).

Purpose and activities: The foundation has adopted new, more narrowly defined guidelines centered on the children and youth of Lower Montgomery County, PA, and the nearby surrounding communities. Giving primarily to organizations that: 1) provide for the physical and emotional well-being of children and young people; 2) seek to enable young people, particularly the needy, to reach their fullest potential through education, empowerment, and exposure to the arts; and 3) are smaller organizations, with budgets under $1 million per year.

Fields of interest: Arts; Education; Health organizations, association; Children, services; Family services; Homeless, human services; Economically disadvantaged.

Type of support: General/operating support.

Limitations: Giving primarily in Philadelphia, Chester, Montgomery and Delaware counties, PA. No grants to individuals, public, private, or parochial schools, colleges and universities.

Publications: Application guidelines; Grants list.

Application information: The foundation generally does not accept unsolicited applications. Application form required.

Initial approach: Letter of intent 30 days prior to deadlines
Copies of proposal: 1
Deadline(s): Mar. 31 and Aug. 31
Board meeting date(s): Spring and fall
Final notification: Within 10 days following Board meetings

Officers and Trustees:* Diane Garthwaite,* Pres.; John Acuff,* V.P.; Thomas Kaneda,* Secy.; A. Alexander Ridley,* Treas.; and 5 additional trustees.

EIN: 236290877

Selected grants: The following grants were reported in 2004.

$10,000 to Citizen Schools, Boston, MA.

$7,500 to Girard College, Philadelphia, PA.

$6,000 to Urban Bridges at Saint Gabriels, Philadelphia, PA.

$5,000 to Academy of Community Music, Fort Washington, PA.

$5,000 to Daemion House, Berwyn, PA.

$5,000 to Kardon Institute of the Arts, Philadelphia, PA.

$5,000 to Need in Deed, Philadelphia, PA.

$5,000 to Pennsylvania Ballet, Philadelphia, PA.

$5,000 to Peoples Light and Theater Company, Malvern, PA.

$4,000 to Wayne Art Center, Wayne, PA.

8213

Genuardi Family Foundation ◇

470 Norristown Rd., Ste. 300
Blue Bell, PA 19422 (610) 834-2030
Contact: Robert C. Fernandez, Exec. Dir.
FAX: (610) 834-5786;
E-mail: info@genuardifamilyfoundation.org
URL: http://www.genuardifamilyfoundation.org

Established in 2000 in PA.
Donors: Anthony D. Genuardi; Charles A. Genuardi; David T. Genuardi; Dominic S. Genuardi, Jr.; Francis L. Genuardi; Gasper A. Genuardi; James V. Genuardi; Laurence P. Genuardi; Michael A. Genuardi.
Foundation type: Independent foundation.
Financial data (yr. ended 12/31/05): Assets, $30,006,873 (M); expenditures, $1,640,094; qualifying distributions, $1,378,700; giving activities include $1,145,000 for grants (average: $5,000–$50,000).
Purpose and activities: Support for nonprofit agencies and organizations dedicated to promoting education, health, human services and culture in the Delaware Valley.
Fields of interest: Arts; Education; Health care; Human services.
Type of support: General/operating support; Capital campaigns; Equipment; Program development; Conferences/seminars; Scholarship funds; Technical assistance; Program evaluation.
Limitations: Giving primarily in the Delaware Valley, PA, region, with an emphasis on southeastern PA. No support for environmental programs, or for public, private or parochial schools that serve the general public. No grants to individuals, fraternal and civic organizations, political candidates, or to influence legislation; or for fundraising, endowments, debt reduction; other foundations or annual appeals.
Publications: Application guidelines; Informational brochure; Informational brochure (including application guidelines).
Application information: Initial letter of inquiry accepted between June 1 and Sept. 1; if approved, application submitted between Sept. 1 and Oct. 31. Application guidelines available on foundation Web site. Application form not required.
 Initial approach: Letter of inquiry to Exec. Dir.
 Copies of proposal: 1
 Deadline(s): Sept. 1 to Oct. 31
 Final notification: May 1
Officers and Directors:* James V. Genuardi,* Pres.; Michael A. Genuardi,* V.P.; Laurence P. Genuardi,* Secy.; Dominic S. Genuardi, Jr.,* Treas.; Robert C. Fernandez,* Exec. Dir.; Anthony D. Genuardi; Charles A. Genuardi; David T. Genuardi; Francis L. Genuardi; Gasper A. Genuardi.
Number of staff: 1 full-time professional; 1 part-time support.
EIN: 233041300

8214

Giant Eagle Foundation ◇

c/o Giant Eagle, Inc.
101 Kappa Dr.
Pittsburgh, PA 15238 (412) 963-6200

Established around 1955.
Donor: Giant Eagle, Inc.
Foundation type: Company-sponsored foundation.
Financial data (yr. ended 8/31/05): Assets, $32,172,579 (M); gifts received, $3,984,586; expenditures, $1,601,623; qualifying distributions, $1,460,522; giving activities include $1,385,522 for 74 grants (high: $450,000; low: $100), and $75,000 for 75 grants to individuals (high: $1,000; low: $1,000).
Purpose and activities: The foundation supports Jewish agencies and temples and organizations involved with performing arts, higher education, health, human services, and community development.
Fields of interest: Performing arts; Higher education; Health care; Human services; Community development; Jewish federated giving programs; Jewish agencies & temples.
Type of support: General/operating support; Employee-related scholarships.
Limitations: Giving primarily in Pittsburgh, PA. No grants to individuals (except for employee-related scholarships).
Application information:
 Initial approach: Contact foundation for application information
 Board meeting date(s): 4 times per year
Trustees: Gerald Chait; Edward Moravitz; Donald S. Plung; Charles Porter; David Shapira; Norman Weizenbaum.
EIN: 256033905
Selected grants: The following grants were reported in 2005.
$450,000 to Carnegie Mellon University, Pittsburgh, PA.
$215,567 to United Jewish Federation of Greater Pittsburgh, Pittsburgh, PA.
$162,250 to University of Pittsburgh, Pittsburgh, PA.
$25,000 to Jewish Residential Services, Pittsburgh, PA.
$20,000 to Childrens Museum of Pittsburgh, Pittsburgh, PA.
$20,000 to Three Rivers Arts Festival, Pittsburgh, PA.
$15,000 to Jewish Community Federation of Cleveland, Cleveland, OH.
$12,500 to Pittsburgh Opera, Pittsburgh, PA.
$7,000 to Phase 4 Learning Center, West Mifflin, PA.
$5,000 to YMCA of Central Ohio, Columbus, OH.

8215

Addison H. Gibson Foundation

1 PPG Pl., Ste. 2230
Pittsburgh, PA 15222-5401 (412) 261-1611
Contact: Rebecca Wallace, Exec. Dir.
FAX: (412) 261-5733;
E-mail: rwallace@gibson-fnd.org; URL: http://www.gibson-fnd.org

Foundation established in 1937 in PA.
Donor: Addison H. Gibson†.
Foundation type: Independent foundation.
Financial data (yr. ended 12/31/05): Assets, $27,361,800 (M); gifts received, $3,100; expenditures, $1,465,515; qualifying distributions, $2,178,650; giving activities include $1,021,445 for 99 grants (high: $30,000; low: $1,000), and $766,277 for 124 loans to individuals (high: $18,000; low: $2,500).

Purpose and activities: The purpose of the foundation is to help the people of western PA to become productive members of society (through education) or to return to productivity by receiving necessary medical treatment. To this end, the foundation provides limited grants to healthcare providers on behalf of self-supporting residents of western PA who have correctable medical conditions but do not have health insurance or the ability to pay for necessary treatment. The foundation also provides low-interest educational loans to residents of western PA who have successfully completed at least one year of undergraduate or graduate study and continue to be enrolled as full-time students at an accredited college or university.
Fields of interest: Higher education; Health care.
Type of support: Student loans—to individuals.
Limitations: Giving limited to residents of western PA. No grants for building funds, endowments, operating budgets, or special projects.
Application information: Guidelines available on foundation Web site. Medical grants are paid to the healthcare provider treating the approved individual applicant, never directly to the individual. No grants for existing medical bills. Application form required.
 Initial approach: For student loans: e-mail or telephone to determine eligibility and schedule personal interview; for medical assistance: letter or telephone call from referring physician or agency prior to patient interview
 Deadline(s): Ongoing
 Board meeting date(s): 9 times annually
 Final notification: Varies
Officer: Rebecca Wallace, Exec. Dir.
Trustees: Douglas E. Gilbert; Timothy M. Slavish; National City Bank.
Number of staff: 2 full-time professional; 1 full-time support.
EIN: 250965379

8216

Sonia Raiziss Giop Charitable Foundation ◇

c/o Mellon Bank, N.A.
P.O. Box 185
Pittsburgh, PA 15230-9897

Established in 1994 in PA.
Donors: Sonia Giop†; Ines Giop Crut.
Foundation type: Independent foundation.
Financial data (yr. ended 12/31/05): Assets, $4,625,683 (M); expenditures, $330,183; qualifying distributions, $322,858; giving activities include $320,300 for 29 grants (high: $128,100; low: $2,000).
Purpose and activities: Giving primarily for education, the arts, particularly for poetry and other literary organizations, and animal welfare.
Fields of interest: Performing arts, music; Literature; Arts; Higher education; Animal welfare.
Limitations: Applications not accepted. Giving primarily in NY. No grants to individuals.
Application information: Contributes only to pre-selected organizations.
Trustees: Antoinette Denisof; Alfred DePalchi; Mellon Bank, N.A.
EIN: 256453053
Selected grants: The following grants were reported in 2005.
$128,100 to National Italian American Foundation, DC.
$15,000 to Greene Street Friends School, Philadelphia, PA.

$10,000 to Curtis Institute of Music, Philadelphia, PA.
$10,000 to Royal Oak Foundation, New York, NY.
$8,000 to Boa Editions, Rochester, NY.
$5,000 to Academy of American Poets, New York, NY.
$5,000 to Metropolitan Museum of Art, New York, NY.
$5,000 to New York Public Library, New York, NY.
$5,000 to Rudolf Steiner School, New York, NY.
$3,000 to Grace Church School, New York, NY.

8217
The Harvey S. Gitlin Family Foundation ◇
270 New Jersey Dr.
Fort Washington, PA   19034

Established in 1999 in PA.
Donor: Harvey S. Gitlin.
Foundation type: Independent foundation.
Financial data (yr. ended 12/31/05): Assets, $12,446,239 (M); gifts received, $2,000,000; expenditures, $576,874; qualifying distributions, $567,600; giving activities include $567,600 for 9 grants (high: $400,000; low: $1,000).
Fields of interest: Health care; Human services; Jewish agencies & temples.
Limitations: Applications not accepted. Giving primarily in PA. No grants to individuals.
Application information: Contributes only to pre-selected organizations.
Trustee: Harvey S. Gitlin.
EIN: 256645244
Selected grants: The following grants were reported in 2005.
$400,000 to Congregation Beth Or, Springhouse, PA.
$25,000 to Abington Memorial Hospital, Abington, PA.
$25,000 to American Cancer Society, Philadelphia, PA.
$2,600 to Childrens Literacy Initiative, Philadelphia, PA.
$1,000 to Brians House, West Chester, PA.

8218
GlaxoSmithKline Foundation
(formerly SmithKline Beecham Foundation)
1 Franklin Plz., FP2335
P.O. Box 7929
Philadelphia, PA   19101

Established in 1967 in DE.
Donor: SmithKline Beecham Corp.
Foundation type: Company-sponsored foundation.
Financial data (yr. ended 12/31/04): Assets, $3,097,687 (M); gifts received, $4,096,914; expenditures, $4,097,068; qualifying distributions, $4,097,068; giving activities include $370,990 for grants, and $3,725,924 for 14,431 employee matching gifts.
Purpose and activities: The foundation matches contributions made by part-time and full-time employees, directors, and retirees of GlaxoSmithKline to nonprofit organizations.
Type of support: Employee matching gifts.
Limitations: Applications not accepted. Giving primarily in Philadelphia, PA. No grants to individuals.
Application information: Contributes only through employee matching gifts.

Officers and Directors:* Thomas K. Kaney,* Chair.; Judith Lynch,* Secy.-Treas.; Mary Linda Andrews; William Shore.
EIN: 232120418

8219
Glencairn Foundation ◇
1 Pitcairn Pl., Ste. 3000
Jenkintown, PA   19046-3593

Incorporated in 1950 in PA.
Donors: Raymond Pitcairn†; and members of the Pitcairn family.
Foundation type: Independent foundation.
Financial data (yr. ended 12/31/05): Assets, $16,083,947 (M); expenditures, $737,494; qualifying distributions, $675,567; giving activities include $665,799 for 9 grants (high: $324,509; low: $1,000).
Fields of interest: Higher education, college; Science, association; Christian agencies & churches.
Type of support: General/operating support; Building/renovation.
Limitations: Applications not accepted. Giving primarily in Bryn Athyn, PA. No grants to individuals.
Application information: Contributes only to pre-selected organizations.
 Board meeting date(s): As necessary
Officers and Directors:* Laird Pendleton,* Pres.; Lynn Genzlinger, V.P.; Kenneth Schauder,* Secy.-Treas.; Emily Bau-Madsen; Nathaniel Brock; Kim Junge; Alan King; Brant Pitcairn.
EIN: 231429828

8220
Harvey Goodstein Charitable Trust ◇
c/o Sandra Goodstein
540 Pennsylvania Ave., Ste. 323
Fort Washington, PA   19034

Established in 1999 in PA.
Foundation type: Independent foundation.
Financial data (yr. ended 12/31/03): Assets, $7,893,129 (M); expenditures, $487,967; qualifying distributions, $372,159; giving activities include $372,250 for 5 grants (high: $150,000; low: $10,000).
Purpose and activities: Giving primarily to Jewish organizations, as well as to an organization for mentally and physically challenged children; funding also for youth tennis and to a riding academy.
Fields of interest: Athletics/sports, racquet sports; Athletics/sports, equestrianism; Children/youth, services; Jewish agencies & temples.
Limitations: Applications not accepted. Giving primarily in New York, NY, and Devon and Philadelphia, PA. No grants to individuals.
Application information: Contributes only to pre-selected organizations.
Trustees: Sandra Goodstein; Meyer Koplow.
EIN: 237992456
Selected grants: The following grants were reported in 2003.
$150,000 to AMIT Women, Philadelphia, PA. For general support.
$102,250 to Arthur Ashe Youth Tennis and Education, Philadelphia, PA. For general support.
$100,000 to Livnot ULehibanot, Safed, Israel. For general support.

$10,000 to Fox Chase Cancer Center, Philadelphia, PA. For general support.
$10,000 to Pegasus Riding Academy, Philadelphia, PA. For general support.

8221
The Grable Foundation ▼
650 Smithfield St., Ste. 240
Pittsburgh, PA   15222   (412) 471-4550
Contact: Susan H. Brownlee, Exec. Dir.
FAX: (412) 471-2267; E-mail: grable@grablefdn.org;
URL: http://www.grablefdn.org/

Established in 1976 in PA.
Donor: Minnie K. Grable†.
Foundation type: Independent foundation.
Financial data (yr. ended 12/31/05): Assets, $255,898,939 (M); expenditures, $11,804,965; qualifying distributions, $10,396,924; giving activities include $9,215,730 for 259 grants (high: $250,000; low: $500; average: $10,000–$100,000).
Purpose and activities: Giving primarily to organizations that improve educational opportunities, strengthen families and support community efforts that create an environment in which children can succeed.
Fields of interest: Arts education; Elementary/secondary education; Child development, education; Education; Employment, training; Youth, pregnancy prevention; Youth, services.
Type of support: General/operating support; Continuing support; Program development; Conferences/seminars; Seed money; Curriculum development; Research; Technical assistance; Consulting services; Program evaluation; Program-related investments/loans; Matching/challenge support.
Limitations: Giving primarily in southwestern PA. No grants to individuals, or for scholarships or endowment funds.
Publications: Annual report; Grants list.
Application information: Grable Grant Application Cover Sheet required and is available on Web site; applicants may also use Western Pennsylvania Common Grant Application Form, but must still submit Grable Grant Application Cover Sheet. Application form required.
 Initial approach: Letter of inquiry (1-2 pages)
 Copies of proposal: 1
 Deadline(s): Feb. 1, June 1, and Oct. 1
 Board meeting date(s): Mar., July, and Nov.
 Final notification: Generally, following board meetings
Officers and Trustees:* Charles R. Burke, Jr.,* Chair., and Prog. Dir.; Jan Nicholson,* Pres.; Steven E. Burke,* Treas.; Greg Behr, Exec. Dir.; Charles R. Burke, Sr.,* Chair. Emeritus; Susan H. Bcownlee, Sr. Fellow; Patricia Grable Burke; William H. Isler; Barbara Nicholson McFadyen; Marion Grable Nicholson.
Number of staff: 6 full-time professional; 4 full-time support; 1 part-time support.
EIN: 251309888
Selected grants: The following grants were reported in 2005.
$500,000 to Riverlife Task Force, Pittsburgh, PA. For Barges on the Mon, design and construction documents for series of attractions on floating barges along Monongahela Wharf.
$500,000 to University of Pittsburgh, School of Education, Pittsburgh, PA. For endowed chair, Dr. Helen S. Falson Chair in Urban Education.

$250,000 to August Wilson Center for African American Culture, Pittsburgh, PA. For capital campaign.

$200,000 to Hill House Association, Pittsburgh, PA. For Mission Discovery II, collaboration between Hill House and Carnegie Science Center to provide after-school programming for children in grades K-12.

$160,000 to Allegheny Conference on Community Development, Pittsburgh, PA. For Community Development Agenda Development Fund, economic and civic improvement projects in southwestern Pennsylvania.

$150,000 to Tides Center PA, Pittsburgh, PA. For YouthPlaces, network of after-school programs for high-risk teens in area neighborhoods in Allegheny County.

$125,000 to Beginning with Books, Pittsburgh, PA. For operating support, early literacy training for educators, families and volunteers as well as community-wide public awareness campaign.

$100,000 to 3 Rivers Connect, Pittsburgh, PA. For Regional Education Technology Initiative, development and implementation of new ideas and programs in educational technology.

$75,000 to Planned Parenthood of Western Pennsylvania, Pittsburgh, PA. For Peer Education Program, training for peer educators to help reduce teen pregnancy and prevent school dropout in area middle and high schools.

$30,000 to Tickets for Kids Foundation, Pittsburgh, PA. For underprivileged children's attendance at sporting events, museums, cultural events, and other recreational opportunities.

$25,000 to W Q E D Multimedia, Pittsburgh, PA. For OnQ Magazine, education reporting.

$22,136 to Brashear Association, Pittsburgh, PA. For summer youth programming for youth in Saint Clair Village public housing on Pittsburgh's South Side.

$20,000 to Pittsburgh Dance Alloy, Pittsburgh, PA. For Dance Education Initiative, residencies and performances in Pittsburgh public schools.

$10,000 to Afro-American Music Institute, Pittsburgh, PA. For Summer Youth Institute, intensive two-week summer music workshop for middle and high school students.

8222
The Graham Foundation ◇
P.O. Box 1104
York, PA 17405-1104 (717) 849-4001
Contact: William H. Kerlin, Jr., Tr.

Established in 1986 in PA.
Donors: Graham Engineering Corp.; Graham Capital Corp.; Donald C. Graham; Graham Packaging Co., L.P.; Graham Packaging Holdings Co.
Foundation type: Company-sponsored foundation.
Financial data (yr. ended 6/30/05): Assets, $20,881,679 (M); gifts received, $233,333; expenditures, $1,620,582; qualifying distributions, $1,565,150; giving activities include $1,565,150 for 61 grants (high: $1,035,000; low: $100).
Purpose and activities: The foundation supports organizations involved with arts and culture, education, health, and human services.
Fields of interest: Arts; Elementary/secondary education; Higher education; Education; Health care; Human services; Federated giving programs.
Type of support: Sponsorships; Capital campaigns; Annual campaigns; Endowments; General/

operating support; Building/renovation; Debt reduction; Program development.
Limitations: Giving primarily in York, PA. No grants to individuals.
Application information: Application form not required.
> *Initial approach:* Proposal
> *Deadline(s):* None
Trustees: Donald C. Graham; Ingrid A. Graham; William H. Kerlin, Jr.
EIN: 236805421
Selected grants: The following grants were reported in 2004.
$1,000,000 to University of Michigan, Ann Arbor, MI. For Donald C. Graham Endowment Fund.
$248,570 to Burke Mountain Academy, East Burke, VT. For general support.
$60,000 to Strand-Capitol Performing Arts Center, York, PA. For capital campaign.
$59,500 to United Way of York County, York, PA. For general support.
$20,000 to York Foundation, York, PA. For capital campaign.
$10,000 to Boy Scouts of America, York, PA. For capital campaign.
$8,750 to American Red Cross, York, PA. For general support.
$6,000 to Cultural Alliance of York County, York, PA. For capital campaign.
$1,000 to YMCA of York and York County, York, PA. For general support.
$500 to Atkins House, York, PA. For general support.

8223
Grass Family Foundation ◇
1000 N. Front St., Ste. 503
Wormleysburg, PA 17043

Established in 1972.
Donor: Alex Grass.
Foundation type: Independent foundation.
Financial data (yr. ended 11/30/04): Assets, $8,812,787 (M); gifts received, $365,000; expenditures, $830,759; qualifying distributions, $758,860; giving activities include $757,635 for 19 grants (high: $220,000; low: $365).
Purpose and activities: Grants largely for Jewish welfare funds, including those in Israel; some support also for education, and arts and culture.
Fields of interest: Arts; Education; Human services; Federated giving programs; Roman Catholic federated giving programs.
International interests: Israel.
Limitations: Applications not accepted. Giving primarily in FL, Baltimore, MD, New York, NY, and Harrisburg, PA. No grants to individuals.
Application information: Contributes only to pre-selected organizations.
Officers and Directors:* Alex Grass,* Chair.; Linda Grass Shapiro,* Secy.; Elizabeth Grass Weese.
EIN: 237218002

8224
Gray Charitable Trust ◇
c/o Kenneth Gray
1 Town Pl., Ste. 200
Bryn Mawr, PA 19010

Established in 1998 in PA.
Donor: Kenneth B. Gray, Jr.

Foundation type: Independent foundation.
Financial data (yr. ended 12/31/05): Assets, $10,146,621 (M); expenditures, $435,402; qualifying distributions, $422,298; giving activities include $418,000 for 20 grants (high: $210,000; low: $1,000).
Fields of interest: Arts; Education; Human services.
Limitations: Applications not accepted. No grants to individuals.
Application information: Contributes only to pre-selected organizations.
> *Board meeting date(s):* Twice a year
Trustees: Samuel M. Gawthrop; Doreen H. Gray; Kenneth B. Gray, Jr.; Kimberly H. Gray; Meredith L. Gray.
Number of staff: 1 part-time professional.
EIN: 237987964
Selected grants: The following grants were reported in 2004.
$240,000 to White-Williams Foundation, Philadelphia, PA.
$50,000 to Philadelphia Museum of Art, Philadelphia, PA.
$5,000 to Kimmel Center for the Performing Arts, Philadelphia, PA.
$5,000 to Magee Rehabilitation Hospital, Philadelphia, PA.
$3,000 to San Diego Historical Society, San Diego, CA.
$2,000 to Canine Partners for Life, Cochranville, PA.
$2,000 to San Diego Museum of Art, San Diego, CA.
$1,500 to United Way of Cecil County, Elkton, MD.
$1,000 to Lenox Hill Neighborhood House, New York, NY.
$1,000 to Reading is FUNdamental (RIF), DC.

8225
The Daniel B. and Florence E. Green Foundation ◇ ☆
15 E. Ridge Pike, 4th Fl.
Conshohocken, PA 19428
Contact: Daniel B. Green, Tr.

Established in 2005 in PA.
Donors: Rancho Santa Fe Thrift; Firstrust Bank.
Foundation type: Independent foundation.
Financial data (yr. ended 6/30/05): Assets, $3,042,319 (M); gifts received, $4,000,100; expenditures, $1,000,000; qualifying distributions, $1,000,000; giving activities include $1,000,000 for 1 grant.
Fields of interest: Jewish agencies & temples.
Limitations: Giving primarily in Wynnewood, PA.
Trustees: Daniel B. Green; Florence E. Green.
EIN: 201910865

8226
The Mary E. Groff Surgical and Medical Research and Education Charitable Trust ◇ ☆
5 Radnor Corporate Ctr.
100 Malsonford Rd., Ste. 450
Radnor, PA 19087

Established in 1999 in PA.
Donor: Mary E. Groff†.
Foundation type: Independent foundation.
Financial data (yr. ended 12/31/04): Assets, $4,379,944 (M); expenditures, $395,983; qualifying distributions, $365,142; giving activities

include $341,613 for 13 grants (high: $40,625; low: $14,411).

Purpose and activities: Giving primarily for higher education.

Fields of interest: Higher education; Hospitals (general).

Limitations: Applications not accepted. Giving primarily in PA. No grants to individuals.

Application information: Contributes only to pre-selected organizations.

Officer and Trustees:* Manucher Fellahnejad,* Mgr.; Anne M. Cusack; Herbert M. Wallace.

EIN: 232725113

8227

The Grumbacher Family Foundation ✧ ☆

(formerly The Nancy and Tim Grumbacher Family Foundation)
460 Country Club Rd.
York, PA 17403

Established in 1988 in PA.

Foundation type: Independent foundation.

Financial data (yr. ended 1/30/06): Assets, $3,501,857 (M); expenditures, $720,546; qualifying distributions, $720,171; giving activities include $711,136 for 62 grants (high: $130,000; low: $250).

Purpose and activities: Giving primarily for higher education, the arts, human services, YMCAs and to Jewish organizations; funding also for a Presbyterian church.

Fields of interest: Arts; Higher education; Education; Human services; YM/YWCAs & YM/YWHAs; Family services; Federated giving programs; Protestant agencies & churches; Jewish agencies & temples.

Limitations: Applications not accepted. Giving primarily in York, PA. No grants to individuals.

Application information: Contributes only to pre-selected organizations.

Officers and Directors:* M.T. Grumbacher,* Pres.; D.R. Glyn,* Secy.; Thomas Wolf.

EIN: 232524417

8228

The Grundy Foundation

680 Radcliffe St.
P.O. Box 701
Bristol, PA 19007 (215) 788-5460
Contact: Eugene J. Williams, Exec. Dir.
E-mail: info@grundyfoundation.com; URL: http://www.grundyfoundation.com

Established in 1961 in PA.

Donor: Joseph R. Grundy‡.

Foundation type: Independent foundation.

Financial data (yr. ended 12/31/05): Assets, $54,762,975 (M); expenditures, $3,298,776; qualifying distributions, $3,147,196; giving activities include $561,584 for grants, and $1,158,326 for foundation-administered programs.

Purpose and activities: Grants for civic affairs and community planning, social service and youth agencies, a community fund, the arts, higher education, and health. Giving restricted to supported by Mr. Grundy during his lifetime.

Fields of interest: Arts; Higher education; Hospitals (general); Children/youth, services; Community development; Government/public administration.

Type of support: General/operating support; Building/renovation; Equipment; Land acquisition; Program development.

Limitations: Giving limited to Bucks County, PA. No support for religious organizations. No grants to individuals, or for endowment funds, research, scholarships, or fellowships; no loans.

Publications: Application guidelines; Informational brochure (including application guidelines).

Application information: Accepts Delaware Valley Grantmakers Common Application Form. Application form not required.
    Initial approach: Letter
    Copies of proposal: 1
    Deadline(s): None
    Board meeting date(s): Monthly except in Aug.

Trustees: James M. Gassaway; Frederick J.M. LaValley; Thomas F. Praiss; Leonard N. Snyder; Wachovia Bank, N.A.

Number of staff: 2 full-time professional.

EIN: 231609243

Selected grants: The following grants were reported in 2003.

$150,000 to Bristol Riverside Theater, Bristol, PA. 2 grants: $75,000 each

$134,000 to United Way of Bucks County, Fairless Hills, PA. 2 grants: $64,000 (For annual campaign), $70,000 (For annual campaign).

$25,000 to Silver Lake Nature Center, Friends of, Bristol, PA. To renovate residence to provide housing for environmental education interns.

$10,000 to Bucks County Community College Foundation, Newtown, PA. For repair and restoration of the College's greenhouse.

$10,000 to Delaware Valley College, Doylestown, PA. To upgrade Rudley Neumann Gymnasium.

$10,000 to Latino Leadership Alliance of Bucks County, Bristol, PA. For Executive Director position.

$9,000 to Planned Parenthood Association of Bucks County, Bristol, PA. For acquisition of furnishings and equipment for the Bensalem site.

$5,000 to James A. Michener Art Museum, Doylestown, PA. For classroom furniture and equipment at the New Hope site.

8229

The Lloyd V. Guild Charitable Foundation ✧

337 Thomas Rd.
McMurray, PA 15317

Established in 2001 in PA.

Donors: Lloyd V. Guild; SKC Inc.

Foundation type: Independent foundation.

Financial data (yr. ended 12/31/05): Assets, $328 (M); gifts received, $521,703; expenditures, $522,936; qualifying distributions, $522,936; giving activities include $522,208 for 3 grants (high: $320,708; low: $51,000).

Purpose and activities: Grants awarded to spread the work of the Gospel and to provide services to the needy.

Fields of interest: Human services; International relief; Christian agencies & churches.

Limitations: Applications not accepted. Giving to U.S. organizations for national and international benefit. No grants to individuals.

Application information: Contributes only to pre-selected organizations.

Trustees: Daniel L. Guild; Richard L. Guild; Linda Guild Lawler.

EIN: 256794527

8230

The John C. & Chara C. Haas Charitable Trust ✧

c/o Herr, Potts & Herr
175 Strafford Ave., Ste. 314
Wayne, PA 19087-3333

Established in 1989 in PA.

Donors: John C. Haas; Chara C. Haas.

Foundation type: Independent foundation.

Financial data (yr. ended 6/30/05): Assets, $21,690,103 (M); gifts received, $3,750,000; expenditures, $1,131,214; qualifying distributions, $1,045,050; giving activities include $1,035,000 for 38 grants (high: $100,000; low: $5,000).

Purpose and activities: Giving primarily for health associations, including children's health; funding also for education, and social services.

Fields of interest: Arts; Education; Hospitals (specialty); Health organizations; Medical research, institute; Human services; Children/youth, services; Child development, services; Family services; Federated giving programs.

Limitations: Applications not accepted. Giving primarily in PA, with some emphasis on Philadelphia. No grants to individuals.

Application information: Contributes only to pre-selected organizations.

Trustees: Chara C. Haas; John C. Haas; Philip C. Herr II.

EIN: 232587109

Selected grants: The following grants were reported in 2004.

$100,000 to Pathway School, Norristown, PA. For Future Without Limits Campaign.

$54,040 to United Way of Southeastern Pennsylvania, Philadelphia, PA. For Parenting School Readiness Initiative.

$25,000 to Breastcancer.org, Narberth, PA. For general support.

$25,000 to Childrens Hospital of Philadelphia, Philadelphia, PA. For neuroblastoma research fund.

$25,000 to Educating Children for Parenting, Philadelphia, PA. For Building for the Future Campaign.

$15,000 to Living Beyond Breast Cancer, Ardmore, PA. For general support.

$15,000 to Neighborhood Gardens Association - A Philadelphia Land Trust, Philadelphia, PA. For general support.

$10,000 to Bethesda Project, Philadelphia, PA. For general support.

$5,000 to Keystone Hospice, Wyndmoor, PA. For general support.

$5,000 to Urban Tree Connection, Philadelphia, PA. For general support.

8231

The Norman & Elizabeth Hahn Family Foundation ☆

1686 Weaverland Rd.
East Earl, PA 17519

Established in 2002 in PA.

Donors: Norman Hahn; Elizabeth Hahn; Conestoga Wood Specialities Corp.

Foundation type: Independent foundation.

Financial data (yr. ended 12/31/05): Assets, $2,010,907 (M); gifts received, $1,145,000; expenditures, $724,594; qualifying distributions,

$715,067; giving activities include $715,067 for grants.

Fields of interest: Aging, centers/services; Christian agencies & churches.

Limitations: Applications not accepted. Giving primarily in PA. No grants to individuals.

Application information: Unsolicited requests for funds not accepted.

Trustee: Blue Ball National Bank.

Number of staff: None.

EIN: 256818477

8232
Edwin Hall 2nd Charitable Trust ◇

c/o Alexander & Pelli
1 Penn Ctr. Plz., Ste. 1100
Philadelphia, PA 19103-1834

Established in 1996 in PA.

Foundation type: Independent foundation.

Financial data (yr. ended 12/31/05): Assets, $16,663,891 (M); expenditures, $735,640; qualifying distributions, $671,354; giving activities include $653,083 for 2 grants (high: $457,158; low: $195,925).

Fields of interest: Human services.

Limitations: Applications not accepted. Giving limited to PA. No grants to individuals.

Application information: Contributes only to pre-selected organizations.

Trustees: Robert E.J. Curran; Richard B. Goldbeck; William T. Luskus.

EIN: 237892195

8233
The Hamilton Family Foundation ◇

200 Eagle Rd., Ste. 316
Wayne, PA 19087 (610) 975-0517
Contact: Nancy Wingo, Exec. Dir.

Established in 1992 in PA.

Donor: Dorrance H. Hamilton.

Foundation type: Independent foundation.

Financial data (yr. ended 12/31/05): Assets, $43,512,068 (M); expenditures, $2,911,589; qualifying distributions, $2,709,283; giving activities include $2,678,419 for grants.

Purpose and activities: Emphasis is on educational endeavors, including teaching and research with a focus on programs in schooling, conservation, historic preservation, medicine and the arts.

Fields of interest: Historic preservation/historical societies; Arts; Higher education; Education; Environment, natural resources; Hospitals (general); Health care.

Type of support: General/operating support; Annual campaigns; Program development; Scholarship funds; Matching/challenge support.

Limitations: Giving primarily in Philadelphia, PA and surrounding counties. No grants to individuals.

Publications: Application guidelines.

Application information: Proposals accepted only once during a 12-month period. Application form required.

  Initial approach: Proposal
  Copies of proposal: 1
  Deadline(s): Approximately 2 months prior to meeting date
  Board meeting date(s): Quarterly
  Final notification: Within 1 month of meeting

Officers and Directors:* Dorrance H. Hamilton,* Pres.; Nancy Wingo, Exec. Dir.; Barbara R. Cobb; Margaret H. Duprey; Nathaniel P. Hamilton; S. Matthews V. Hamilton, Jr.; Francis J. Mirabello.

Number of staff: 1 full-time professional; 1 full-time support.

EIN: 232684976

Selected grants: The following grants were reported in 2004.

$300,000 to Williamson Free School of Mechanical Trades, Media, PA.

$250,000 to Cabrini College, Radnor, PA.

$100,000 to American Red Cross, Philadelphia, PA.

$100,000 to Peoples Light and Theater Company, Malvern, PA.

$70,000 to Jenkins Arboretum, Devon, PA.

$26,000 to National Constitution Center, Philadelphia, PA. 2 grants: $25,000, $1,000

$2,000 to Foxcroft School, Middleburg, VA.

$1,000 to Episcopal Community Services, Wyndmoor, PA.

$500 to Polly Hill Arboretum, West Tisbury, MA.

8234
Hankin Foundation ☆

(formerly Bernard & Henrietta Hankin Foundation)
707 Eagleview Blvd.
P.O. Box 562
Exton, PA 19341
Contact: Becky Reeves
E-mail: becky.reeves@hankingroup.com

Established in 1984 in PA.

Donors: Bernard Hankin‡; Robert Hankin; Richard Hankin; Henrietta Hankin.

Foundation type: Independent foundation.

Financial data (yr. ended 11/30/05): Assets, $0 (M); gifts received, $279,590; expenditures, $341,972; qualifying distributions, $339,906; giving activities include $339,906 for grants.

Purpose and activities: Giving for health care, human services, and youth services.

Fields of interest: Health care; Human services; YM/YWCAs & YM/YWHAs; Children/youth, services; Federated giving programs.

Type of support: General/operating support; Continuing support; Annual campaigns; Capital campaigns; Building/renovation; Emergency funds; Employee matching gifts; In-kind gifts.

Limitations: Giving primarily in PA. No grants to individuals.

Application information: Application form not required.

  Initial approach: Letter
  Copies of proposal: 1
  Board meeting date(s): Monthly

Officers: Robert S. Hankin, Pres.; Henrietta Hankin, Secy.-Treas.

EIN: 251479501

8235
William Stucki Hansen Foundation ◇

(formerly Hansen Foundation)
2600 Neville Rd., Neville Island
Pittsburgh, PA 15225
Contact: William Gregg Hansen, Pres.

Established in 1984 in PA.

Donors: Gregg Hansen; Hansen, Inc.

Foundation type: Independent foundation.

Financial data (yr. ended 12/31/04): Assets, $487,660 (M); gifts received, $71,250; expenditures, $2,845,047; qualifying distributions, $940,000; giving activities include $940,000 for 13 grants (high: $350,000; low: $500).

Purpose and activities: Giving to public services, higher education, federated giving programs and religion.

Fields of interest: Higher education; Federated giving programs; Religion.

Type of support: General/operating support; Endowments.

Limitations: Giving primarily in western PA; some giving in CO. No grants to individuals.

Application information: Application form not required.

  Deadline(s): None

Directors: Gretchen Hansen; Nancy K. Hansen; William Gregg Hansen; David W. Lendt.

EIN: 251483674

Selected grants: The following grants were reported in 2004.

$250,000 to Family Guidance, Sewickley, PA.

$230,000 to Pittsburgh Leadership Foundation, Pittsburgh, PA.

$200,000 to Navigators, The, Colorado Springs, CO.

$75,000 to Leadership Foundations of America, Pittsburgh, PA.

$75,000 to Neighborhood Academy, Pittsburgh, PA.

$35,000 to Carnegie Institute, Pittsburgh, PA.

$25,000 to Pittsburgh Symphony Society, Pittsburgh, PA.

$10,000 to United Way of Allegheny County, Pittsburgh, PA.

$5,000 to Pittsburgh Experiment, Pittsburgh, PA.

$5,000 to Sewickley Cemetery, Sewickley, PA.

8236
Harsco Corporation Fund ◇

c/o Harsco Corp.
P.O. Box 8888
Camp Hill, PA 17001-8888 (717) 763-7064
Contact: Robert G. Yocum, Chair.

Established in 1956 in PA.

Donor: Harsco Corp.

Foundation type: Company-sponsored foundation.

Financial data (yr. ended 12/31/04): Assets, $2,953,434 (M); expenditures, $1,141,234; qualifying distributions, $1,108,184; giving activities include $1,070,711 for 112 grants (high: $148,470; low: $80), and $37,473 for 42 employee matching gifts.

Purpose and activities: The foundation supports organizations involved with arts and culture, education, health, human services, and community development.

Fields of interest: Arts; Higher education; Education; Hospitals (general); Health care; Human services; Community development; Federated giving programs.

Type of support: General/operating support; Continuing support; Employee matching gifts; Employee-related scholarships.

Limitations: Giving primarily in areas of company operations. No grants to individuals (except for employee-related scholarships), or for special projects, building or endowments, or research; no loans.

Publications: Program policy statement.

Application information: Application form not required.

  Initial approach: Proposal

Deadline(s): None
Board meeting date(s): Apr. and as required
Officers and Trustees:* Robert G. Yocum,* Chair.; Salvatore D. Fazzolari,* Secy.-Treas.; D.C. Hathaway.
EIN: 236278376
Selected grants: The following grants were reported in 2004.
$137,275 to Institute of International Education, New York, NY.
$100,000 to Harrisburg School District, Harrisburg, PA.
$100,000 to North Channel Assistance Ministries, Houston, TX.
$80,070 to National Merit Scholarship Corporation, Evanston, IL.
$30,000 to United Way of the Capital Region, Enola, PA.
$15,000 to YMCA, Harrisburg Area, Harrisburg, PA.
$10,000 to Butler County Community College, Butler, PA.
$1,000 to Children Unlimited, Columbia, SC.
$500 to United States Military Academy, West Point, NY.
$500 to United Way, Claremore Area, Claremore, OK.

8237
The Hassel Foundation ◇
United Plz.
30 S. 17th St., Rm. 1800
Philadelphia, PA   19103   (215) 893-8740
Contact: Michael H. Krekstein, Tr.

Trust established in 1961 in PA.
Donors: Morris Hassel†; Calvin Hassel†.
Foundation type: Independent foundation.
Financial data (yr. ended 12/31/04): Assets, $8,767,020 (M); expenditures, $483,603; qualifying distributions, $405,049; giving activities include $391,500 for 56 grants (high: $100,000; low: $1,000).
Purpose and activities: Support primarily for higher and other education, human services, and the arts; scholarships are awarded annually to graduating seniors of specific high schools.
Fields of interest: Arts; Higher education; Education; Human services; Aging.
Type of support: General/operating support; Building/renovation; Scholarships—to individuals.
Limitations: Giving primarily in PA. No grants to individuals (except for scholarships at specified high schools).
Application information: Application form not required.
   Initial approach: Letter
   Deadline(s): None
   Board meeting date(s): June and as required
Trustees: Andrea Cohen; Barbara Cohen; Elizabeth Cohen; Ellen Cohen; Sarle H. Cohen; Andrew Goldberg; Jay L. Goldberg; Maxine Goldberg; Michael Goldberg; David Khoury; Lisa Khoury; Marilyn Khoury; Michael H. Krekstein; Ephrain Royfe; Merle A. Wolfson.
EIN: 236251862
Selected grants: The following grants were reported in 2004.
$100,000 to University of Pennsylvania, Philadelphia, PA.
$7,500 to Astral Artistic Services, Philadelphia, PA.
$5,000 to After School Activities Partnership, Philadelphia, PA.

$5,000 to Jeanne Ruddy and Dancers, Philadelphia, PA.
$3,000 to Curtis Institute of Music, Philadelphia, PA.
$2,500 to Childrens Crisis Treatment Center, Philadelphia, PA.
$1,000 to Lower Merion Conservancy, Ardmore, PA.

8238
The Hawksglen Foundation
c/o G.F. Partridge, Jr.
3740 1 Mellon Ctr.
Pittsburgh, PA   15258-0001
E-mail: partridge.gf@mellon.com

Established in 2002 in PA.
Donor: Rebecca Barclay Humphrey.
Foundation type: Independent foundation.
Financial data (yr. ended 12/31/05): Assets, $11,637,967 (M); expenditures, $713,556; qualifying distributions, $602,550; giving activities include $602,550 for 86 grants (high: $50,000; low: $1,000).
Fields of interest: Environment, natural resources; Botanical/horticulture/landscape services; Animals/wildlife, preservation/protection.
Limitations: Applications not accepted. Giving on a national basis, with emphasis on PA. No grants to individuals.
Application information: Unsolicited requests for funds not accepted.
Trustees: Rebecca Barclay Humphrey; Mellon Bank, N.A.
Number of staff: None.
EIN: 256820594

8239
The Hayne Foundation ◇
1809 Walnut St.
Philadelphia, PA   19103

Established in 1996 in PA.
Donor: Richard A. Hayne.
Foundation type: Independent foundation.
Financial data (yr. ended 11/30/04): Assets, $1,093,291 (M); expenditures, $1,026,588; qualifying distributions, $1,022,731; giving activities include $1,022,731 for 1 grant.
Fields of interest: Higher education.
Limitations: Applications not accepted. Giving primarily in Philadelphia, PA. No grants to individuals.
Application information: Contributes only to pre-selected organizations.
Officers: Richard A. Hayne, Pres.; Margaret Hayne, V.P.; Freeman Zausner, Secy.
EIN: 232870131

8240
H. J. Heinz Company Foundation ▼ ◇
P.O. Box 57
Pittsburgh, PA   15230-0057   (412) 456-5773
Contact: Tammy B. Aupperle, Dir.
FAX: (412) 442-3227;
E-mail: heinz.foundation@hjheinz.com; *URL:* http://www.heinz.com/Foundation.aspx

Established in 1951 in PA.
Donor: H.J. Heinz Co.
Foundation type: Company-sponsored foundation.

Financial data (yr. ended 4/30/05): Assets, $1,936,672 (M); gifts received, $5,000,000; expenditures, $4,702,630; qualifying distributions, $4,697,861; giving activities include $4,123,097 for 141 grants (high: $425,222; low: $250), and $373,943 for 437 employee matching gifts.
Purpose and activities: The foundation supports organizations involved with arts and culture, education, children's health, nutrition, human services, diversity, and women.
Fields of interest: Arts, association; Arts; Higher education; Education; Health care; Nutrition; Youth, services; Family services; Human services; Civil rights, equal rights; Women.
Type of support: General/operating support; Continuing support; Annual campaigns; Capital campaigns; Building/renovation; Endowments; Emergency funds; Program development; Seed money; Scholarship funds; Technical assistance; Employee matching gifts.
Limitations: Giving primarily in areas of company operations, with emphasis on southwestern PA. No support for religious or political organizations. No grants to individuals, or for debt reduction or land acquisition; no loans.
Publications: Application guidelines; Annual report (including application guidelines); Biennial report (including application guidelines).
Application information: An interview may be requested.
   Initial approach: Contact foundation for application information
   Copies of proposal: 1
   Deadline(s): None
   Board meeting date(s): As necessary
   Final notification: Varies
Officers and Trustees:* J. Runkel,* Chair.; Kristen Clark; Tom Didonato; D. Edward I. Smyth.
Director: Tammy B. Aupperle.
Number of staff: 1 full-time professional; 1 full-time support.
EIN: 300055087
Selected grants: The following grants were reported in 2005.
$425,222 to United Way of Allegheny County, Pittsburgh, PA. For Impact Fund and employee match grant support.
$335,000 to SickKids Foundation, Toronto, Canada. For Sprinkles Research.
$250,000 to Carnegie Museum of Natural History, Pittsburgh, PA. For Dinosaurs in Their World campaign.
$157,500 to International Federation of Red Cross and Red Crescent Societies at the UN, New York, NY. For Tsunami relief in India, Thailand, and Indonesia.
$118,000 to Pittsburgh Symphony Association, Pittsburgh, PA. For operating support and radio broadcast.
$100,000 to Westminster College, New Wilmington, PA. For renovations to Thompson-Clark Hall.
$50,000 to Culinary Institute of America, Hyde Park, NY. For Scholarship Fund.
$50,000 to Helen Keller International, New York, NY. For tsunami relief in Indonesia.
$22,222 to Childrens Miracle Network Foundation, Ontario, Canada. To support hospitals in Canada.
$20,000 to Pittsburgh Civic Light Opera, Pittsburgh, PA. For operating support.

8241
Howard Heinz Endowment ▼
30 Dominion Twr.
625 Liberty Ave.
Pittsburgh, PA 15222-3115 (412) 281-5777
Contact: Maxwell King, Pres.
FAX: (412) 281-5788; E-mail: info@heinz.org;
URL: http://www.heinz.org

Trust established in 1941 in PA; In Jan. 2007, Vira I. Heinz Endowment merged into the Howard Heinz Endowment, and the organization changed its name to The Heinz Endowments.
Donors: Howard Heinz‡; Elizabeth Rust Heinz‡.
Foundation type: Independent foundation.
Financial data (yr. ended 12/31/05): Assets, $948,757,866 (M); expenditures, $48,881,131; qualifying distributions, $39,413,997; giving activities include $39,413,997 for grants.
Purpose and activities: The endowment's mission is to help southwestern Pennsylvania thrive as a whole community—economically, ecologically, educationally, and culturally—while advancing the state of knowledge and practice in the fields in which it works. The endowment funds activities in five program areas: Arts and Culture; Children, Youth, and Families; Economic Opportunity; Education; and the Environment.
Fields of interest: Arts; Education; Environment; Children/youth, services; Family services; Economic development.
Type of support: General/operating support; Continuing support; Management development/capacity building; Capital campaigns; Building/renovation; Equipment; Endowments; Program development; Seed money; Research; Technical assistance; Program evaluation; Program-related investments/loans; Matching/challenge support; Student loans—to individuals.
Limitations: Giving primarily directed to southwestern PA, although in certain cases support may be considered on a national or international basis. No grants to individuals.
Publications: Application guidelines; Annual report; Financial statement; Occasional report; Program policy statement.
Application information: Please do not send additional supporting materials with the initial letter of inquiry. Applicants should not submit full proposals unless they have been asked to do so by a representative of the foundation. Application form not required.
> *Initial approach:* Letter of inquiry or online application available on foundation's Web site
> *Copies of proposal:* 1
> *Deadline(s):* Jan. 15 (for spring board meeting), and Aug. 1 (for fall board meeting)
> *Board meeting date(s):* May and Oct.
> *Final notification:* Within several weeks of board meeting

Officers and Directors:* Teresa F. Heinz,* Chair.; Maxwell King, Pres.; Jack E. Kime, C.F.O.; Ann C. Plunkett, Cont. and Dir., Payroll/Benefits Admin.; Drue Heinz, Dir. Emeritus; Carol R. Brown; Frank V. Cahouet; Judith Davenport; Barbara Robinson DeWitt; Christopher Heinz; H. John Heinz IV; Howard M. Love; Shirley M. Malcom; Frederick W. Thieman; Mallory Walker.
EIN: 251721100
Selected grants: The following grants were reported in 2004.
$4,000,000 to August Wilson Center for African American Culture, Pittsburgh, PA. For capital campaign.

$1,000,000 to Civil Society Institute, Newton Centre, MA. To develop $10 million public-private funding initiative to expand high-quality Pre-K programs throughout Pennsylvania.
$1,000,000 to Port Authority of Allegheny County, Pittsburgh, PA. For Gateway Station project.
$850,000 to Pittsburgh Life Sciences Greenhouse, Pittsburgh, PA. For operating support for entrepreneurial and incubator programs.
$700,000 to United Way of Allegheny County, Pittsburgh, PA. For annual operating support of youth-serving agencies through United Way's Impact Fund and to connect United Way's provider and service data with Allegheny County's HumanServices.net online resource.
$450,000 to Lancaster Osteopathic Health Foundation, Lancaster, PA. For Heinz Challenge for Children in Lancaster County.
$350,000 to Clean Air Task Force, Boston, MA. For Midwest power plant and diesel pollution reduction in southwestern Pennsylvania.
$300,000 to New Century Careers, Pittsburgh, PA. For operating support for regional manufacturing workforce training initiative.
$100,000 to Reading is FUNdamental (RIF), Pittsburgh, PA. For after-school early reading program.
$14,000 to Pittsburgh Symphony Society, Pittsburgh, PA. For general operating support.

8242
Vira I. Heinz Endowment ▼
30 Dominion Twr.
625 Liberty Ave.
Pittsburgh, PA 15222-3115 (412) 281-5777
Contact: Maxwell King, Pres.
FAX: (412) 281-5788; E-mail: info@heinz.org;
URL: http://www.heinz.org

Trust established in 1986 in PA; incorporated in 1995; In Jan. 2007, Vira I. Heinz Endowment merged into the Howard Heinz Endowment. The surviving organization changed its name to The Heinz Endowments.
Donor: Vira I. Heinz‡.
Foundation type: Independent foundation.
Financial data (yr. ended 12/31/05): Assets, $486,147,664 (M); expenditures, $26,336,895; qualifying distributions, $21,904,943; giving activities include $21,904,943 for grants.
Purpose and activities: The endowment's mission is to help southwestern Pennsylvania thrive as a whole community—economically, ecologically, educationally, and culturally—while advancing the state of knowledge and practice in the fields in which it works. The endowment funds activities in 5 program areas: Arts and Culture; Children, Youth, and Families; Economic Opportunity; Education; and the Environment.
Fields of interest: Humanities; Arts; Education; Environment; Children/youth, services; Economic development.
Type of support: General/operating support; Continuing support; Management development/capacity building; Capital campaigns; Building/renovation; Equipment; Endowments; Program development; Seed money; Research; Technical assistance; Program evaluation; Program-related investments/loans; Matching/challenge support.
Limitations: Giving primarily directed to southwestern PA, although in certain cases support may be considered on a national or international basis. No grants to individuals.

Publications: Application guidelines; Annual report; Financial statement; Occasional report; Program policy statement; Quarterly report.
Application information: Please do not send additional supporting materials with the initial letter of inquiry. Applicants should not submit full proposals unless they have been asked to do so by a representative of the foundation. Application form not required.
> *Initial approach:* Letter of inquiry or online application available on foundation's Web site
> *Copies of proposal:* 1
> *Deadline(s):* Jan. 15 (for consideration at spring meeting) and Aug. 1 (for fall meeting)
> *Board meeting date(s):* May. and Oct.
> *Final notification:* Within several weeks of board meeting

Officers and Directors:* James M. Walton,* Chair.; Maxwell King, Pres.; Jack E. Kime, C.F.O.; Ann C. Plunkett, Cont. and Dir., Payroll/Benefits Admin.; Barbara Robinson DeWitt; Franco Harris; Andre T. Heinz; Teresa F. Heinz; Wendy MacKenzie; Konrad M. Weis; S. Donald Wiley.
EIN: 251762825
Selected grants: The following grants were reported in 2004.
$1,000,000 to Pittsburgh Voyager, Pittsburgh, PA. For new vessel and financial stabilization campaign.
$1,000,000 to Point Park University, Pittsburgh, PA. For construction of new building housing dance studios and converted performance space.
$1,000,000 to Saint Vincent College, Latrobe, PA. For construction of Fred Rogers Center.
$568,218 to Pittsburgh Ballet Theater, Pittsburgh, PA. For operating support.
$500,000 to A Plus Schools - Pittsburghs Community Alliance for Public Education, Pittsburgh, PA. For school leadership initiative.
$400,000 to Pittsburgh Life Sciences Greenhouse, Pittsburgh, PA. For operating support for entrepreneurial and incubator programs.
$100,000 to Carnegie Mellon University, Pittsburgh, PA. For federal linkages and resources for regional and CMU initiatives.
$50,000 to Pennsylvania Organization for Watersheds and Rivers, Harrisburg, PA. For Keystone Watershed Monitoring Network project.
$27,000 to Carnegie Institute, Three Rivers Art Festival, Pittsburgh, PA. For Liberty Lab performances.
$20,000 to Negro Educational Emergency Drive (NEED), Pittsburgh, PA. For scholarships.

8243
Heinz Family Foundation ▼ ✧
c/o Jeffrey R. Lewis
3200 Dominion Twr.
625 Liberty Ave.
Pittsburgh, PA 15222
FAX: (412) 497-5790; E-mail (for Jeffrey R. Lewis): jlewis@heinzoffice.org; URL: http://www.hfp.heinz.org/aboutus/philanthropies.html

Established in 1984 in PA; incorporated in 1992.
Donors: Teresa and H. John Heinz III Charitable Trust; H. John Heinz III Charitable and Family Trust.
Foundation type: Independent foundation.
Financial data (yr. ended 12/31/04): Assets, $85,261,568 (M); gifts received, $6,464,430; expenditures, $8,076,243; qualifying distributions, $7,558,526; giving activities include $3,917,817 for 129 grants (high: $1,000,000; low: $100;

average: $5,000–$250,000), $1,027,448 for 19 grants to individuals (high: $250,000; low: $5,556; average: $5,556–$11,764), and $1,678,042 for 4 foundation-administered programs.
Purpose and activities: Giving primarily for the Heinz Awards, environmental organizations, arts and cultural organizations, and women's health and pension.
Fields of interest: Museums; Arts; Education; Environment.
Type of support: Capital campaigns; Building/ renovation; Equipment; Endowments; Grants to individuals.
Limitations: Applications not accepted. Giving only in the U.S. No grants to individuals (except for Heinz Awards).
Application information: Contributes only to pre-selected organizations; unsolicited applications not considered.
Officers and Directors:* Teresa F. Heinz,* Chair. and C.E.O.; Jeffrey R. Lewis, Pres.; Wendy Mackenzie, Secy.; Jack E. Kime, C.F.O.; S. Donald Wiley, Treas.; John R. Taylor, C.I.O.; Andre Heinz.
EIN: 251689382
Selected grants: The following grants were reported in 2004.
$700,000 to Womens Institute for a Secure Retirement, DC. 4 grants: $100,000 (For Women's Health Survey project), $280,000 (For Good Housekeeping insert project, Money and Retirement), $200,000 (For Good Housekeeping insert project, Money and Retirement), $120,000 (For communication services for Massachusetts Women's Pension Laws).
$250,000 to Boston 2004, Boston, MA. For general operating support.
$200,000 to Harvard University, Cambridge, MA. For designated payment by Heinz Award Winner, Public Policy.
$125,000 to West Harlem Environmental Action, New York, NY. For designated payment by Heinz Awards Winner, Environment.
$120,000 to United Negro College Fund, Fairfax, VA. For John Heinz Environmental Fellows program.
$75,000 to University of New Orleans Foundation, New Orleans, LA. For Vietnam War Oral History Project.
$20,000 to Pittsburgh Parks Conservancy, Pittsburgh, PA. For Spring Hat Fund Raising.

8244
Drue Heinz Trust ◇
(formerly H. J. & Drue Heinz Trust)
c/o Mellon Bank. N.A.
P.O. Box 185
Pittsburgh, PA 15230-0185
Application address: c/o Julia V. Shea, P.O. Box 68, FDR Station, New York, NY 10150

Established in 1954 in PA.
Foundation type: Independent foundation.
Financial data (yr. ended 12/31/05): Assets, $29,976,239 (M); expenditures, $2,734,285; qualifying distributions, $2,624,557; giving activities include $2,570,250 for 58 grants (high: $835,000; low: $500).
Purpose and activities: Emphasis on higher education, medical research, conservation, recreation, fine arts, and prevention of cruelty to children and animals.
Fields of interest: Visual arts; Visual arts, architecture; Museums; Performing arts; Arts;

Higher education; Libraries/library science; Children/youth, services.
Type of support: Program development.
Limitations: Giving primarily in NY and PA.
Application information:
Initial approach: Letter or telephone for application guidelines
Board meeting date(s): Nov.
Trustees: James F. Dolan; Drue Heinz; Mellon Bank, N.A.
Number of staff: 1 full-time professional; 1 part-time professional; 1 full-time support.
EIN: 256018930

8245
Henkels Foundation
985 Jolly Rd.
Blue Bell, PA 19422-0900

Established in 1956 in DE and PA.
Donor: Henkels & McCoy, Inc.
Foundation type: Company-sponsored foundation.
Financial data (yr. ended 6/30/05): Assets, $800,838 (M); gifts received, $937,115; expenditures, $843,758; qualifying distributions, $830,277.
Purpose and activities: The foundation supports organizations involved with higher education, human services, and Christianity.
Fields of interest: Higher education; Human services; Christian agencies & churches.
Limitations: Applications not accepted. Giving on a national basis, with some emphasis on PA. No grants to individuals.
Application information: Contributes only to pre-selected organizations.
Officers: Paul M. Henkels, Pres.; Barbara B. Henkels, Secy.-Treas.
Directors: Christopher B. Henkels; Paul M. Henkels, Jr.
EIN: 236235239

8246
J. S. Herr Foundation ◇
P.O. Box 300
Nottingham, PA 19362 (610) 932-9330
Contact: James S. Herr, Pres.

Established in 1990 in PA.
Donors: James S. Herr; Herr Foods, Inc.
Foundation type: Independent foundation.
Financial data (yr. ended 12/31/05): Assets, $1,479,749 (M); gifts received, $264,004; expenditures, $966,193; qualifying distributions, $965,541; giving activities include $964,061 for 76 grants (high: $314,695; low: $1,000).
Purpose and activities: Giving primarily for education and human services.
Fields of interest: Education; Human services; Christian agencies & churches.
Application information:
Initial approach: Letter
Officers and Trustees:* James S. Herr,* Pres.; Miriam Herr,* Secy.; Gene Herr,* Treas.; June Gunden; Edwin Herr; James M. Herr; Martha Thomas.
EIN: 232531170
Selected grants: The following grants were reported in 2005.
$124,366 to Marketplace Ministries, Dallas, TX.
$50,000 to Lancaster Bible College, Lancaster, PA.

$40,000 to International Bible Society, Colorado Springs, CO.
$25,000 to Global Action, Colorado Springs, CO.
$25,000 to Salvation Army, Butler, PA.
$25,000 to Samaritans Purse, Boone, NC.
$23,000 to Navigators, The, Colorado Springs, CO.
$15,000 to Steve Wingfield Ministries, Harrisonburg, VA.
$10,000 to Pennsylvania Family Institute, Harrisburg, PA.
$7,500 to Mission Year, Philadelphia, PA.

8247
Highmark Foundation ◇
120 5th Ave., Ste. 922
Pittsburgh, PA 15222
Contact: Lynne Marchese, Prog. Off.
Application address: 120 5th Ave., Ste. 2628, Pittsburgh, PA 15222; URL: https:// www.highmark.com/hmk2/community/ hmfoundation/index.shtml

Established in 2000 in PA.
Donor: Highmark Inc.
Foundation type: Company-sponsored foundation.
Financial data (yr. ended 12/31/04): Assets, $25,755,511 (M); gifts received, $20,000,000; expenditures, $1,422,766; qualifying distributions, $1,256,466; giving activities include $1,255,886 for 17 grants (high: $206,000; low: $25,000).
Purpose and activities: The foundation supports organizations involved with health and mental health.
Fields of interest: Health care; Mental health/crisis services.
Limitations: Giving primarily in PA.
Application information: Application form not required.
Initial approach: Proposal
Deadline(s): None
Officers and Directors:* Aaron A. Walton,* Chair.; Doris Carson Williams, Vice-Chair.; Elaine B. Krasik, Secy.; Melissa M. Anderson, Treas.; Michael Blackwood; James M. Klingensmith; Thomas J. Rohner, Jr., M.D.
EIN: 251876666

8248
Ruth A. Hill Trust ◇
c/o Mellon Financial Corp.
P.O. Box 185
Pittsburgh, PA 15230
Application address: c/o Marilyn King, 100 State St., Erie, PA 16507, tel.: (814) 874-5209

Foundation type: Independent foundation.
Financial data (yr. ended 12/31/05): Assets, $7,328,953 (M); expenditures, $347,347; qualifying distributions, $342,484; giving activities include $342,037 for 23 grants (high: $160,793; low: $1,130; average: $5,000–$14,530).
Purpose and activities: Support for education, primarily through scholarships to Caucasian residents of Oil City, PA, and African American residents of Venango County, the City of Titusville, or those attending Forest County area vocational-technical schools.
Fields of interest: Vocational education; Higher education; Minorities.
Type of support: General/operating support; Scholarships—to individuals.

Limitations: Giving limited to residents of PA.
Application information: Application form required for scholarships. Application form required.
Deadline(s): Mar. 15 for scholarships
Trustee: Mellon Bank, N.A.
EIN: 256031644

8249
Hillman Foundation ▼ ◇
(formerly The Hillman Foundation, Inc.)
330 Grant St., Ste. 2000
Pittsburgh, PA 15219 (412) 338-3466
Contact: Ronald W. Wertz, Pres.
FAX: (412) 338-3463;
E-mail: foundation@hillmanfo.com

Incorporated in 1951 in DE.
Donors: John Hartwell Hillman, Jr.†; J.H. Hillman & Sons Co.; Hillman Land Co.; and family-owned corporations.
Foundation type: Independent foundation.
Financial data (yr. ended 12/31/04): Assets, $132,092,874 (M); expenditures, $7,811,448; qualifying distributions, $7,455,503; giving activities include $6,243,000 for 69 grants (high: $600,000; low: $4,000; average: $25,000–$100,000).
Purpose and activities: Program areas include cultural advancement and the arts, education, health and medicine, civic affairs, community development, conservation, social welfare, and youth.
Fields of interest: Arts; Higher education; Education; Health care; Health organizations, association; Crime/violence prevention, domestic violence; Human services; Youth, services; Community development; Aging; Disabilities, people with; Women; Economically disadvantaged; Homeless.
Type of support: Continuing support; Capital campaigns; Building/renovation; Equipment; Land acquisition; Endowments; Program development; Professorships; Seed money; Matching/challenge support.
Limitations: Giving primarily in Pittsburgh and southwestern PA. No grants to individuals, or for travel, conferences or seminars; no loans.
Publications: Annual report (including application guidelines).
Application information: Common Grant Application approved by foundation members of Grantmakers of Western PA accepted. Application form required.
Initial approach: Letter
Copies of proposal: 1
Deadline(s): None
Board meeting date(s): Apr., June, Oct., and Dec., and an annual meeting in May
Officers and Directors:* Henry L. Hillman,* Chair.; Ronald W. Wertz,* Pres.; C.G. Grefenstette,* V.P.; Bruce I. Crocker,* Secy.; Eric C. Johnson, Treas.; Elsie H. Hillman.
Number of staff: 3 full-time professional; 2 full-time support.
EIN: 256011462
Selected grants: The following grants were reported in 2005.
$10,000,000 to University of Pittsburgh, Cancer Institute, Pittsburgh, PA. Toward expansion of research and cancer research facilities, clinical research studies, recruitment/retention of faculty, community outreach and education programs, investments in commercial

opportunities and endowment for research, payable over 10 years.
$5,200,000 to Childrens Hospital of Pittsburgh Foundation, Pittsburgh, PA. 2 grants: $5,000,000 to Pediatric Transplantation Institute (Toward construction of new hospital, endowment for clinical and research activities, creation of pediatrics and transplantation institutes and endowed chairs and fellowships, payable over 7 years), $200,000 (Toward innovative initiatives in Pediatric Transplantation, payable over 4 years).
$626,000 to Carnegie Institute, Pittsburgh, PA. 3 grants: $201,000 to Museum of Natural History (Toward purchase of rubies, emeralds, suite of tourmaline crystals and lazurite crystal, payable over 3 years), $200,000 to Museum of Art (Toward purchase of related pieces of furniture designed by Marcel Breuer from Frank House), $225,000 to Museum of Natural History (Toward renovation and expansion of Hillman Hall of Minerals and Gems).
$500,000 to Childrens Home of Pittsburgh, Pittsburgh, PA. Toward construction of new program/administrative facility and program expansion, payable over 5 years.
$300,000 to Westmoreland Museum of American Art, Greensburg, PA. Toward endowment for support of programs, payable over 4 years.
$250,000 to Pittsburgh Symphony Society, Pittsburgh, PA. Toward operations and performances.
$150,000 to Community College of Allegheny County, Pittsburgh, PA. Toward e-learning workforce training program development and implementation, payable over 2 years.

8250
Henry L. Hillman Foundation ▼ ◇
330 Grant St., Ste. 2000
Pittsburgh, PA 15219 (412) 338-3466
Contact: Ronald W. Wertz, Pres.
FAX: (412) 338-3463;
E-mail: foundation@hillmanfo.com

Established in 1964 in PA.
Donor: Henry L. Hillman.
Foundation type: Independent foundation.
Financial data (yr. ended 12/31/04): Assets, $91,410,866 (M); expenditures, $4,742,267; qualifying distributions, $4,186,097; giving activities include $4,143,550 for 100 grants (high: $1,000,000; low: $1,000; average: $1,000–$10,000).
Purpose and activities: Support primarily for art and cultural programs, and higher and secondary education; support also for youth, conservation, civic affairs, community development, social services, and hospitals.
Fields of interest: Arts; Secondary school/education; Higher education; Education; Environment, natural resources; Hospitals (general); Crime/violence prevention, domestic violence; Human services; Children/youth, services; Community development; Government/public administration; Aging; Disabilities, people with; Women; AIDS, people with; Economically disadvantaged; Homeless.
Type of support: General/operating support; Continuing support; Annual campaigns; Capital campaigns; Building/renovation; Equipment; Endowments; Program development; Seed money; Matching/challenge support.

Limitations: Giving primarily in Pittsburgh and southwestern PA. No grants to individuals, or for deficit financing, publications, or conferences; no loans.
Publications: Application guidelines.
Application information: Application form not required.
Initial approach: Letter
Copies of proposal: 1
Deadline(s): None
Board meeting date(s): Mar. and Dec.
Officers and Directors:* Henry L. Hillman,* Chair.; Ronald W. Wertz,* Pres. and Exec. Dir.; Bruce I. Crocker,* Secy.; Eric C. Johnson, Treas.
Number of staff: 1 part-time professional.
EIN: 256065959
Selected grants: The following grants were reported in 2004.
$1,000,000 to Carnegie Institute, Museum of Art, Pittsburgh, PA. Toward endowment and programs as part of capital campaign.
$1,000,000 to Shady Side Academy, Pittsburgh, PA. Toward construction of Hillman Center for the Performing Arts.
$450,000 to Pittsburgh Life Sciences Greenhouse, Pittsburgh, PA. 2 grants: $250,000 (Toward operations and program investments), $200,000 (Toward operations and program investment for research and development of life sciences industry in western Pennsylvania).
$392,125 to University of Pittsburgh Medical Center, Pittsburgh, PA. 4 grants: $57,000 to Cancer Institute (Toward Hillman Foundation Grant: The Immunobiology of Cancer and Aging), $75,000 to Cancer Institute (Toward Hillman Foundation Grant: Targeting Human Papillomavirus E7 Protein for Immunotherapy of Head and Neck Cancer Patients), $75,000 to Cancer Institute (Toward Hillman Foundation Grant: Determinant Spreading in Melanoma Immunotherapy), $185,125 to Cancer Institute (Toward Hillman Foundation Grant: Targeted Imaging of Cancer through Peptide-Guided Magnetic Resonance Imaging Agents).
$50,000 to Catlin Gabel School, Portland, OR. Toward construction of new Upper School Library and modern Language Center.
$50,000 to Taft School, Watertown, CT. Toward endowment of The Lance R. Odden Scholarships.

8251
William Talbott Hillman Foundation ◇
330 Grant St., Ste. 2000
Pittsburgh, PA 15219 (412) 338-3466
Contact: Ronald W. Wertz, V.P. and Exec. Dir.
FAX: (412) 338-3463;
E-mail: foundation@hillmanfo.com

Established in 1986 in DE.
Donors: William Talbott Hillman; Henry Lea Hillman Charitable Lead Trust.
Foundation type: Independent foundation.
Financial data (yr. ended 12/31/04): Assets, $10,561,827 (M); expenditures, $916,506; qualifying distributions, $588,750; giving activities include $575,750 for 94 grants (high: $200,000; low: $1,000).
Fields of interest: Visual arts; Performing arts; Education; Health care; Human services.
Type of support: General/operating support; Continuing support; Annual campaigns; Capital campaigns; Building/renovation; Program development; Seed money.

Limitations: Giving primarily in New York, NY and Pittsburgh, PA. No grants to individuals.
Publications: Application guidelines.
Application information: Application form not required.
Initial approach: Proposal
Copies of proposal: 1
Deadline(s): None
Board meeting date(s): May and Dec.
Officers and Directors:* William Talbott Hillman,* Pres.; Ronald W. Wertz,* V.P. and Exec. Dir.; Maurice J. White,* Secy.; Eric C. Johnson,* Treas.
Number of staff: 1 part-time professional.
EIN: 251536657
Selected grants: The following grants were reported in 2003.
$200,000 to Carnegie Museum of Art, Pittsburgh, PA. Toward endowment of William Talbott Hillman Endowment for Photography.
$10,000 to Gods Love We Deliver, New York, NY. For general support.
$2,500 to Doctors Without Borders USA, New York, NY. For general support.
$2,000 to Metropolitan Museum of Art, New York, NY. For annual support.
$2,000 to Pittsburgh Filmmakers, Pittsburgh, PA. For general support.
$1,500 to Shadyside Hospital Foundation, Pittsburgh, PA. For annual support.
$1,000 to Brooklyn Academy of Music, Brooklyn, NY. For annual support.
$1,000 to Shady Side Academy, Pittsburgh, PA. For annual support.
$1,000 to Solomon R. Guggenheim Museum, New York, NY. For general support.
$500 to Teachers Network, New York, NY. For general support.

8252
Henry Lea Hillman, Jr. Foundation ◇
330 Grant St., Ste. 2000
Pittsburgh, PA 15219 (412) 338-3466
Contact: Ronald W. Wertz, V.P.
FAX: (412) 338-3463;
E-mail: foundation@hillmanfo.com

Established in 1986 in DE.
Donors: Henry Lea Hillman, Jr.; Henry Lea Hillman Charitable Lead Trust.
Foundation type: Independent foundation.
Financial data (yr. ended 12/31/04): Assets, $8,561,563 (M); expenditures, $534,963; qualifying distributions, $433,903; giving activities include $423,710 for 32 grants (high: $50,000; low: $2,500).
Fields of interest: Visual arts; Arts; Higher education; Environment, natural resources; Environment; Health care; Youth development; Economically disadvantaged.
Type of support: General/operating support; Continuing support; Annual campaigns; Capital campaigns; Building/renovation; Program development; Seed money.
Limitations: Giving primarily in Portland, OR. No grants to individuals.
Publications: Application guidelines.
Application information: Application form not required.
Initial approach: Proposal
Copies of proposal: 1
Deadline(s): None
Board meeting date(s): May and Dec.

Officers and Directors:* Henry Lea Hillman, Jr.,* Pres.; Ronald W. Wertz,* V.P.; Maurice J. White,* Secy.; Eric C. Johnson,* Treas.
Number of staff: 1 part-time professional.
EIN: 251536656
Selected grants: The following grants were reported in 2004.
$65,000 to Catlin Gabel School, Portland, OR. 2 grants: $50,000, $15,000
$30,000 to I Have A Dream Foundation, Portland, OR.
$25,000 to Clackamas Community College Foundation, Oregon City, OR.
$20,000 to Estacada Public Library Foundation, Estacada, OR.
$20,000 to Northwest Housing Alternatives, Milwaukie, OR.
$20,000 to Portland Art Museum, Portland, OR.
$15,000 to Head Start of Yamhill County, McMinnville, OR.
$15,000 to Oregon Ballet Theater, Portland, OR.
$12,500 to Carnegie Mellon University, Pittsburgh, PA.

8253
Orris C. Hirtzel and Beatrice Dewey Hirtzel Memorial Foundation ◇
(formerly Elec Material Hirtzel Memorial Foundation)
c/o Mellon Financial Corp.
P.O. Box 185
Pittsburgh, PA 15230
Contact: Laurie Moritz

Established in 1956 in PA.
Donors: Orris C. Hirtzel; Beatrice Dewey Hirtzel.
Foundation type: Independent foundation.
Financial data (yr. ended 12/31/05): Assets, $23,463,075 (M); expenditures, $1,169,249; qualifying distributions, $1,051,363; giving activities include $1,014,000 for 178 grants (high: $250,000; low: $750; average: $1,500–$25,000).
Purpose and activities: Giving primarily for higher education, including scholarships; support also for human services and community funds.
Fields of interest: Higher education; Health care; Medical research, institute; Human services; Community development, neighborhood development; Federated giving programs.
Type of support: General/operating support; Capital campaigns; Building/renovation; Equipment; Fellowships; Research; Scholarships—to individuals.
Limitations: Giving primarily for the Town of Ripley in Chautauqua County, NY and the City of North East in Erie County, PA.
Application information: Application form required.
Initial approach: Letter
Trustees: James S. Bryan; Robert E. Galbraith; James L. Johnson; Douglas P. Moorhead; Mellon Bank, N.A.
EIN: 256018933

8254
Emma Clyde Hodge Memorial Fund ◇
c/o PNC Advisors
620 Liberty Ave., P2-PTPP-10-2
Pittsburgh, PA 15222-2705

Established in 1990 in PA.
Donor: Edwin Hodge, Jr.‡
Foundation type: Independent foundation.

Financial data (yr. ended 6/30/05): Assets, $8,767,546 (M); expenditures, $451,803; qualifying distributions, $427,826; giving activities include $421,200 for 44 grants (high: $36,900; low: $1,500).
Purpose and activities: Giving primarily for the performing arts, as well as to the funding of a casting studio for glass art; funding also for education, children and youth services, including a children's hospital, an avian program, eye disease research, as well as services for people who are blind, and social services.
Fields of interest: Arts, multipurpose centers/ programs; Museums; Performing arts, orchestra (symphony); Higher education; Education; Animals/ wildlife, bird preserves; Hospitals (general); Eye diseases; Eye research; Human services; Children/ youth, services; Women, centers/services; Blind/ visually impaired.
Type of support: Building/renovation.
Limitations: Giving primarily in PA with emphasis on Pittsburgh; funding also in FL; some funding nationally. No grants to individuals.
Application information:
Initial approach: Letter
Deadline(s): None
Trustees: L. Van V. Dauler, Jr.; Anne Gordon Earle; Emma Sarosdy; PNC Bank, N.A.
EIN: 256227653
Selected grants: The following grants were reported in 2005.
$35,000 to Pittsburgh Glass Center, Pittsburgh, PA.
$25,000 to Virginia Military Institute, Lexington, VA.
$20,000 to Thiel College, Greenville, PA.
$20,000 to Valley School of Ligonier, Ligonier, PA.
$10,000 to Guadalupe Center, Immokalee, FL.
$10,000 to Guiding Eyes for the Blind, Yorktown Heights, NY.
$10,000 to Save the Bay, Providence, RI.
$10,000 to Taft School, Watertown, CT.
$8,500 to Moses Brown School, Providence, RI.
$7,000 to Elizabeth Buffum Chace House, Warwick, RI.

8255
The Honickman Foundation ◇
(formerly Lynne & Harold Honickman Foundation)
210 W. Rittenhouse Sq., Ste. 3303
Philadelphia, PA 19103
Contact: Lynne Honickman, Tr.

Established in 1988 in PA.
Donor: Lynne Honickman.
Foundation type: Independent foundation.
Financial data (yr. ended 12/31/05): Assets, $9,247,480 (M); gifts received, $1,776,772; expenditures, $428,047; qualifying distributions, $383,602; giving activities include $349,761 for 111 grants (high: $42,511; low: $50).
Purpose and activities: Giving primarily for photography, poetry, family services (single parents, at-risk children, and homeless), and the Jewish Federation of Greater Philadelphia; wherever possible, the foundation seeks to help the disenfranchised through art and education.
Type of support: Endowments; Program development; Publication; Seed money; Grants to individuals.
Limitations: Applications not accepted. Giving primarily in Philadelphia, PA, and the surrounding 5 counties.
Publications: Grants list.

Application information: Application by invitation only. Unsolicited requests for funds not accepted.
Trustee: Lynne Honickman.
Number of staff: 1 full-time professional.
EIN: 232513138
Selected grants: The following grants were reported in 2005.
$56,500 to Philadelphia Museum of Art, Philadelphia, PA.
$12,000 to Aperture Foundation, New York, NY.
$11,000 to Philadelphia Art Alliance, Philadelphia, PA.
$10,300 to Pennsylvania Ballet, Philadelphia, PA.
$9,500 to American Poetry Review, Philadelphia, PA.
$5,000 to Free Library of Philadelphia, Philadelphia, PA.
$5,000 to Hope Partnership for Education, Philadelphia, PA.
$4,300 to Curtis Institute of Music, Philadelphia, PA.
$3,000 to Alpine Learning Group, River Edge, NJ.
$1,500 to Fabric Workshop and Museum, Philadelphia, PA.

8256
Thorton D. & Elizabeth S. Hooper Foundation ◇
(formerly Elizabeth S. Hooper Foundation)
P.O. Box 7453
St. Davids, PA   19087

Established in 1967.
Donors: Thomas Hooper; Adrian S. Hooper; Bruce H. Hooper; Ralph W. Hooper; Interstate Marine Transport Co.; Interstate Towing Co.; Interstate Ocean Transport Co.; and members of the Hooper family.
Foundation type: Independent foundation.
Financial data (yr. ended 6/30/05): Assets, $14,570,711 (M); expenditures, $2,395,795; qualifying distributions, $2,132,000; giving activities include $2,132,000 for 190 grants (high: $250,000; low: $500).
Purpose and activities: Giving primarily for the arts and historical preservation, education, health associations, youth services, social services, including services for people who are blind, and foreign and public policy research.
Fields of interest: Museums (art); Museums (history); Museums (specialized); Performing arts, music; Historic preservation/historical societies; Libraries (public); Education; Health organizations, association; Human services; Youth, services; International affairs, foreign policy; Foundations (private grantmaking); American studies; Public policy, research; Military/veterans' organizations; Military/veterans.
Type of support: General/operating support; Building/renovation; Emergency funds; Program development; Scholarship funds; Research.
Limitations: Applications not accepted. Giving on a national basis, with emphasis on Washington, DC, MD, and PA. No grants to individuals.
Application information: Contributes only to pre-selected organizations.
Officers and Trustees:* Ralph W. Hooper,* Pres.; Bruce H. Hooper,* V.P.; Morgan R. Jones,* Secy.; John N. Irwin,* Treas.
EIN: 236434997
Selected grants: The following grants were reported in 2003.

$250,000 to United States Naval Academy Foundation, Annapolis, MD.
$75,000 to Independence Seaport Museum, Philadelphia, PA.
$50,000 to Hoover Institution on War, Revolution and Peace, Stanford, CA.
$25,000 to Astronaut Scholarship Foundation, Titusville, FL.
$25,000 to Future Possibilities, New York, NY.
$20,000 to Agnes Irwin School, Rosemont, PA.
$20,000 to Amyotrophic Lateral Sclerosis (ALS) Association, Philadelphia, PA.
$20,000 to Foreign Policy Research Institute, Philadelphia, PA.
$20,000 to Hudson Institute, Indianapolis, IN.
$20,000 to Zoological Society of Philadelphia, Philadelphia, PA.

8257
John M. Hopwood Charitable Trust ◇
2 PNC Plz.
620 Liberty Ave., 25th Fl.
Pittsburgh, PA   15222-2719
Contact: Susan J. Wagner

Established about 1948 in PA.
Donors: John M. Hopwood†; Mary S. Hopwood†; William T. Hopwood; Danforth K. Richardsion; Marge Richardson.
Foundation type: Independent foundation.
Financial data (yr. ended 12/31/04): Assets, $24,862,695 (M); expenditures, $1,620,882; qualifying distributions, $1,400,385; giving activities include $1,333,600 for 36 grants (high: $165,000; low: $1,000).
Purpose and activities: Primary areas of interest include hospitals, education, and the environment.
Fields of interest: Arts; Higher education; Education; Environment, natural resources; Environment, energy; Environment; Hospitals (general); Health organizations, association; Human services; Youth, services; Religion.
Type of support: General/operating support; Continuing support; Annual campaigns; Capital campaigns; Building/renovation; Endowments; Emergency funds; Program development; Conferences/seminars; Seed money; Scholarship funds; Research; Technical assistance; Program-related investments/loans; Matching/challenge support.
Limitations: Applications not accepted. Giving primarily in western PA.
Application information: Unsolicited requests for funds not accepted.
Board meeting date(s): Varies
Trustees: William T. Hopwood; PNC Bank, N.A.
Number of staff: 2 part-time professional.
EIN: 256022634
Selected grants: The following grants were reported in 2004.
$125,000 to Shadyside Hospital Foundation, Pittsburgh, PA.
$100,000 to Indian River Hospital Foundation, Vero Beach, FL.
$100,000 to Northeast Health Foundation, Rockland, ME.
$75,000 to Clean Air Task Force, Boston, MA.
$50,000 to Conservation Law Foundation, Montpelier, VT.
$50,000 to Environmental Defense, Austin, TX.
$50,000 to Nature Conservancy, Brunswick, ME.
$50,000 to Pennsylvania Environmental Council, Pittsburgh, PA.

$26,500 to Allegheny Valley School, Coraopolis, PA.
$25,000 to Mid-Coast Childrens Services, Rockland, ME.

8258
Lawrence L. and Julia Z. Hoverter Charitable Foundation ◇ ☆
320 Market St.
Box 1268
Harrisburg, PA   17108-1268

Established in 1998 in PA.
Donors: Julia Hoverter†; Lawrence Hoverter.
Foundation type: Independent foundation.
Financial data (yr. ended 12/31/05): Assets, $12,662,037 (M); gifts received, $4,035,652; expenditures, $616,633; qualifying distributions, $616,633; giving activities include $478,500 for 13 grants (high: $125,000; low: $5,000).
Fields of interest: Performing arts, orchestra (symphony); Higher education; Medical research; Disasters, fire prevention/control; Girl scouts.
Type of support: General/operating support.
Limitations: Applications not accepted. Giving primarily in PA. No grants to individuals.
Application information: Contributes only to pre-selected organizations.
Officers: H. Craig Watkins, Pres.; Amos Miller, V.P.; Ronald M. Katzman, Secy.
Trustees: Joe Cecere; Rebecca Cecere.
EIN: 232944271
Selected grants: The following grants were reported in 2004.
$50,000 to Bethesda Mission, Harrisburg, PA.
$50,000 to Girl Scouts of the U.S.A., Hemlock Council, Harrisburg, PA.
$50,000 to Millerstown Fire Department and Ambulance League, Millerstown, PA.
$25,000 to Harrisburg Symphony Association, Harrisburg, PA.
$21,830 to Aurora Club, Harrisburg, PA.
$10,000 to Greenwood School District, Millerstown, PA.
$10,000 to Newport School District, Newport, PA.
$10,000 to Pennsylvania State University, University Park, PA.
$5,000 to Susquehanna University, Selinsgrove, PA.
$5,000 to United Way of the Capital Region, Enola, PA.

8259
The Hoyt Foundation ◇
P.O. Box 788
New Castle, PA   16103-1488
Contact: Jaimie Kopp
Lawrence County tel.: (724) 535-3225

Incorporated in 1962 in PA.
Donors: May Emma Hoyt†; Alex Crawford Hoyt.
Foundation type: Independent foundation.
Financial data (yr. ended 10/30/03): Assets, $13,651,986 (M); expenditures, $520,384; qualifying distributions, $336,255; giving activities include $292,237 for 23 grants (high: $61,667; low: $300), and $44,018 for grants to individuals.
Purpose and activities: Emphasis on higher education, including scholarships, and a hospital; some support also for cultural programs.

Fields of interest: Arts; Higher education; Hospitals (general); Human services; Children/youth, services; Economically disadvantaged.

Type of support: Continuing support; Annual campaigns; Capital campaigns; Building/renovation; Seed money; Scholarships—to individuals.

Limitations: Giving limited to residents and organizations in Lawrence County, PA.

Application information: Application form required for scholarships.

> *Copies of proposal:* 1
> *Deadline(s):* June 7 for scholarships
> *Board meeting date(s):* Quarterly

Directors: Debra Lynch; Floyd H. McElwain; Steven Sant; Steven C. Warner.

Number of staff: 1 part-time support.

EIN: 256064468

8260

Milton G. Hulme Charitable Foundation ✧

1146 Old Freeport Rd.
Pittsburgh, PA 15238
Application address: 519 Frick Bldg., Pittsburgh, PA 15219

Established in 1960 in PA.

Donors: Jocelyn H. MacConnell; Natalie H. Curry; Holiday H. Shoup; Glover & MacGregor, Inc.

Foundation type: Independent foundation.

Financial data (yr. ended 12/31/05): Assets, $6,459,574 (M); expenditures, $431,904; qualifying distributions, $423,379; giving activities include $375,000 for 38 grants (high: $40,400; low: $1,000).

Purpose and activities: Giving primarily to health organizations, particularly to hospitals, and for people who are blind; funding also for the arts, children and family services, and social services.

Fields of interest: Museums (art); Performing arts; Arts; Education; Health care; Health organizations, association; Eye diseases; Food banks; Housing/shelter, development; Human services; Children, services; Family services; Christian agencies & churches.

Type of support: General/operating support; Capital campaigns.

Limitations: Giving primarily in Pittsburgh, PA. No grants to individuals.

Application information: Application form not required.

> *Initial approach:* Letter or proposal
> *Copies of proposal:* 1
> *Deadline(s):* June 30
> *Board meeting date(s):* Dec.
> *Final notification:* 2 weeks after application deadline

Trustees: Natalie H. Curry; Aura R. Hulme; Jocelyn H. MacConnell; Holiday H. Shoup.

Number of staff: 2 part-time support.

EIN: 256062896

8261

Roy A. Hunt Foundation ▼

1 Bigelow Sq., Ste. 630
Pittsburgh, PA 15219-3030 (412) 281-8734
Contact: Beatrice C. Carter, Exec. Dir.
FAX: (412) 255-0522; E-mail: info@rahuntfdn.org;
URL: http://www.rahuntfdn.org

Established in 1966 in PA.

Donor: Roy A. Hunt†.

Foundation type: Independent foundation.

Financial data (yr. ended 5/31/05): Assets, $74,007,475 (M); expenditures, $3,922,155; qualifying distributions, $3,776,455; giving activities include $3,331,955 for 485 grants (high: $100,000; low: $500; average: $5,000–$30,000).

Purpose and activities: To improve the quality of life through grants for education, the arts and cultural programs, social services, the environment, health services, community development, and youth violence prevention.

Fields of interest: Arts; Elementary/secondary education; Higher education; Environment; Health care; Crime/violence prevention, youth; Human services; Community development; Religion.

Type of support: General/operating support; Annual campaigns; Capital campaigns; Building/renovation; Endowments.

Limitations: Giving primarily in the Boston, MA, and Pittsburgh, PA, areas, also in CA, ID, NH, ME, and OH. No grants to individuals.

Publications: Application guidelines; Grants list.

Application information: Once invited to submit a proposal (in response to a preliminary inquiry), applicants should follow the proposal guidelines on the foundation Web site, which includes a required application form. Previously funded organizations requesting General grants are only considered in Nov. and do not require a preliminary letter of inquiry, an invitation to submit, or a full proposal. However, previously funded organizations seeking Special Initiative grants should send a letter of inquiry to the foundation's Exec. Dir. and then a full proposal, if invited, is required. Requests for Special Initiative grants are considered in both June and Nov. Foundation accepts application forms from Grantmakers of Western Pennsylvania and Associated Grantmakers. Application form required.

> *Initial approach:* Letter of inquiry (1 page)
> *Copies of proposal:* 2
> *Deadline(s):* General grants: Apr. 15 (June meeting) and Sept.15 (Nov. Meeting); Special Initiative grants: Mar.1 (June meeting) and Aug. 1 (Nov. meeting)
> *Board meeting date(s):* June and Nov.
> *Final notification:* Within 2 months following board meeting

Officer: Beatrice C. Carter, Exec. Dir.

Trustees: Helen Hunt Bouscaren; Susan Hunt Hollingsworth; A. James Hunt; Alexandra K. Hunt; Andrew McQ. Hunt; Caroline H. Hunt; Cathryn J. Hunt; Christopher M. Hunt; Daniel K. Hunt; John B. Hunt; Richard M. Hunt; Roy A. Hunt III; Torrence M. Hunt, Jr.; Torrence W.B. Hunt; William E. Hunt; Marion M. Hunt-Badiner; Rachel Hunt Knowles; Joan F. Scott.

Number of staff: 1 full-time professional; 2 full-time support.

EIN: 256105162

Selected grants: The following grants were reported in 2006.

$75,000 to Riverlife Task Force, Pittsburgh, PA. For Three Rivers Park.

$75,000 to Urban Edge, Roxbury, MA. For Jackson Square Initiative.

$50,000 to Carnegie Institute, Pittsburgh, PA. For capital campaign.

$50,000 to Carnegie Mellon University, Pittsburgh, PA. For Hunt Library Fund in memory of Torrence M. Hunt.

$50,000 to Habitat for Humanity International, Americus, GA. For Tsunami Recovery effort.

$30,000 to Appalachian Mountain Club, Boston, MA. For Maine Woods Initiative.

$20,000 to Childrens Home of Pittsburgh, Pittsburgh, PA. For capital campaign.

$6,000 to Global Greengrants Fund, Boulder, CO.

$5,000 to Centro de Educacion Creativa, Monteverde, Costa Rica. .

$5,000 to National Braille Press, Boston, MA.

8262

Myrtle V. C. Huplits & Woodman E. Huplits Foundation Trust ✧ ☆

2 Davis Dr.
Washington Crossing, PA 18977
(215) 446-8686
Contact: Arnold M. Peskin, Tr.

Established in 1990.

Foundation type: Independent foundation.

Financial data (yr. ended 12/31/05): Assets, $3,655,635 (M); expenditures, $477,927; qualifying distributions, $477,927; giving activities include $425,000 for 5 grants (high: $127,500; low: $21,250).

Fields of interest: Environment, natural resources; Animals/wildlife, alliance; Human services.

Limitations: Giving primarily in PA. No grants to individuals.

Application information:

> *Initial approach:* Letter
> *Deadline(s):* None

Trustees: Arnold M. Peskin; Marni L. Peskin; Todd E. Peskin.

EIN: 237451411

Selected grants: The following grants were reported in 2003.

$81,000 to Philadelphia Zoo, Philadelphia, PA.

$67,500 to Wilderness Society, DC.

$54,000 to Nature Conservancy, Conshohocken, PA.

$54,000 to Sierra Club Foundation, Pittsburgh, PA.

$13,500 to Humane Society, Womans, Bensalem, PA.

8263

The Stewart Huston Charitable Trust ✧

50 S. 1st Ave., 2nd Fl.
Coatesville, PA 19320 (610) 384-2666
Contact: Scott G. Huston, Exec. Dir.
FAX: (610) 384-3396;
E-mail: admin@stewarthuston.org; URL: http://www.stewarthuston.org

Established in 1989 in PA.

Donor: Stewart Huston†.

Foundation type: Independent foundation.

Financial data (yr. ended 12/31/03): Assets, $22,325,922 (M); expenditures, $1,211,584; qualifying distributions, $1,087,872; giving activities include $675,898 for 80 grants (high: $63,898; low: $1,000; average: $1,000–$15,000).

Purpose and activities: Giving primarily for religion, the arts, education, the environment, health care, substance abuse, human services, community development, public affairs, and historic preservation.

Fields of interest: Performing arts; Historic preservation/historical societies; Arts; Education, early childhood education; Education; Environment; Medical care, rehabilitation; Health care; Substance abuse, services; Health organizations, association;

Food services; Housing/shelter, development; Recreation; Youth development, services; Human services; Children/youth, services; Family services; Residential/custodial care, hospices; Aging, centers/services; Homeless, human services; Community development; Public policy, research; Christian agencies & churches; Disabilities, people with; Economically disadvantaged; Homeless.

Type of support: General/operating support; Capital campaigns; Building/renovation; Equipment; Emergency funds; Program development; Seed money; Technical assistance; Matching/challenge support.

Limitations: Giving primarily in the Savannah, GA, area and Coatesville and Chester County, PA. No support for political organizations or volunteer fire companies. No grants to individuals, including scholarships or for endowments.

Publications: Annual report.

Application information: Application guidelines available on trust's Web site. Application form required.

   Initial approach: Letter
   Copies of proposal: 1
   Deadline(s): Apr. 1 (Secular), Mar. 1 and Sept. 1 (Trinitarian-Evangelical)
   Board meeting date(s): May (Trinitarian-Evangelical and Secular) and Nov. (Trinitarian-Evangelical only)
   Final notification: June (Trinitarian-Evangelical and Secular) and Dec. (Trinitarian-Evangelical only)

Officer and Trustees:* Scott G. Huston,* Exec. Dir.; Alex N. Cann, Sr.; Samuel A. Cann; Charles L. Huston III.

Number of staff: 1 full-time professional; 1 full-time support; 1 part-time support.

EIN: 232612599

Selected grants: The following grants were reported in 2003.

$63,898 to Graystone Society, Coatesville, PA. For operating support.

$17,000 to Boy Scouts of America, Chester City Council, West Chester, PA. For operating support.

$8,000 to Lincoln Institute of Public Opinion Research, Harrisburg, PA. For operating support.

$7,500 to Champions of Caring, Villanova, PA. For operating support.

$5,000 to Community Volunteers in Medicine, West Chester, PA. For operating support.

$5,000 to Theater Ariel, Ardmore, PA. For operating support.

$5,000 to YMCA of Savannah, Savannah, GA. For operating support.

$4,500 to Crime Victims Center of Chester County, West Chester, PA. For operating support.

$4,000 to Chester County Womens Services, Thorndale, PA. For operating support.

$2,500 to Coatesville Area Arts Alliance, Coatesville, PA. For operating support.

8264

The Huston Foundation ✧

2 Tower Bridge, Ste. 190
1 Fayette St.
Conshohocken, PA 19428-2064
Contact: Susan B. Heilman, Exec. Asst.
E-mail: hustonfndn@aol.com; Tel./FAX: (610) 832-4949; Additional tel.: (610) 832-4954

Incorporated in 1957 in PA.

Donors: Charles L. Huston, Jr.†; Ruth Huston†.

Foundation type: Independent foundation.

Financial data (yr. ended 12/31/03): Assets, $33,755,319 (M); expenditures, $1,975,014; qualifying distributions, $1,786,636; giving activities include $1,258,800 for 187 grants (high: $25,000; low: $1,000; average: $5,000–$25,000).

Purpose and activities: Giving primarily for religious associations, health organizations, and human service organizations. Also some support for education and the arts.

Fields of interest: Arts; Education; Health care; Human services; Public policy, research; Christian agencies & churches; Protestant agencies & churches.

International interests: Africa; Italy.

Type of support: General/operating support; Annual campaigns; Building/renovation; Equipment; Emergency funds; Program development; Seed money; Research; Technical assistance; Matching/challenge support.

Limitations: Giving primarily in southeastern PA; some funding nationally, particularly in CA. No grants to individuals, or for research programs, endowments, fellowships, capital campaigns or salaries; no loans.

Publications: Application guidelines; Annual report; Informational brochure (including application guidelines).

Application information: Accepts Delaware Valley Grantmakers Common Grant Application and Common Report Form. Application form required.

   Initial approach: Letter of request
   Copies of proposal: 1
   Deadline(s): Apr. 1 and Oct. 1
   Board meeting date(s): May and Nov.

Officers: Nancy Huston Hansen, V.P., Evangelical Rels.; Charles L. Huston III, V.P., Community Rels. and Dir., Opers.; Elinor Huston Lashley, V.P., Arts and Cultural Rels.; Charles L. Huston IV, Treas.

Number of staff: 4 full-time professional; 2 part-time professional.

EIN: 236284125

Selected grants: The following grants were reported in 2003.

$25,000 to Boy Scouts of America, Chester City Council, West Chester, PA. For capital campaign.

$10,000 to Crime Victims Center of Chester County, West Chester, PA. For general support.

$5,000 to Angel Flight PA, Norristown, PA. For general support.

$5,000 to Baker Industries, Malvern, PA. For general support.

$5,000 to Camphill Special School, Glenmoore, PA. For general support.

$5,000 to Community Service Council of Chester County, West Chester, PA. For general support.

$5,000 to Lukens Band, Coatesville, PA. For general support.

$5,000 to Maysies Farm Conservation Center, Philadelphia, PA. For general support.

$2,500 to Pikeville College, Pikeville, KY. For scholarships.

$2,000 to Community Learning Center, Philadelphia, PA. For general operating support.

8265

IKON Office Solutions Foundation, Inc.

(formerly Alco Standard Foundation)
P.O. Box 834
Valley Forge, PA 19482

Established in 1974 in PA.

Donor: IKON Office Solutions, Inc.

Foundation type: Company-sponsored foundation.

Financial data (yr. ended 12/31/05): Assets, $2,995,029 (M); expenditures, $394,073; qualifying distributions, $394,073; giving activities include $394,073 for 236 grants (high: $100,000; low: $25).

Purpose and activities: The foundation supports organizations involved with secondary and higher education.

Fields of interest: Secondary school/education; Higher education.

Type of support: General/operating support; Employee matching gifts.

Limitations: Applications not accepted. Giving primarily in areas of company operations. No grants to individuals.

Application information: Contributes only to pre-selected organizations.

Officers: Bob Woods, Pres.; Kathleen M. Burns, V.P. and Treas.; Mark Hershey, Secy.

EIN: 237378726

Selected grants: The following grants were reported in 2005.

$62,800 to United Way of Southeastern Pennsylvania, Philadelphia, PA. 2 grants: $10,000, $52,800

$33,305 to American Cancer Society, Philadelphia, PA.

$10,000 to College of Saint Rose, Albany, NY.

$7,000 to American Diabetes Association, Alexandria, VA.

$3,000 to Indiana Wesleyan University, Marion, IN.

$2,500 to Purdue University, West Lafayette, IN.

$1,752 to United Way of Central Indiana, Indianapolis, IN.

$1,000 to American Cancer Society, Atlanta, GA.

$100 to Villanova University, Villanova, PA.

8266

Independence Foundation ▼ ✧

200 S. Broad St., Ste. 1101
Philadelphia, PA 19102 (215) 985-4009
Contact: Susan E. Sherman, C.E.O. and Pres.
FAX: (215) 985-3989;
E-mail: artfellowships@independencefoundation.org
; *URL:* http://www.independencefoundation.org

Established in 1932 as International Cancer Research Foundation; incorporated as Donner Foundation in 1945 in DE; divided in 1961 into Independence Foundation and a newly formed William H. Donner Foundation.

Donor: William H. Donner†.

Foundation type: Independent foundation.

Financial data (yr. ended 12/31/05): Assets, $98,043,749 (M); expenditures, $8,598,686; qualifying distributions, $8,057,514; giving activities include $6,564,444 for 327 grants (high: $200,000; low: $250; average: $10,000–$50,000), and $146,600 for 21 grants to individuals (high: $9,000; low: $4,000; average: $5,000–$7,500).

Purpose and activities: The foundation's mission is to support organizations that provide services to people who do not ordinarily have access to them. The current funding agenda includes the following areas of interest: nurse managed health care, culture and the arts, public interest legal services, and health and human services, with special focus on food distribution, housing for the homeless, and services which help people with disabilities to lead independent lives. The foundation also has two special initiatives: Public Interest Law Fellowships and Fellowships for Visual and Performing Artists.

Fields of interest: Visual arts; Performing arts; Arts; Nursing school/education; Nursing care; Health care; Legal services; Legal services, public interest law; Human services.

Type of support: General/operating support; Endowments; Professorships; Fellowships; Scholarship funds; Matching/challenge support.

Limitations: Giving primarily in Philadelphia, PA, and Bucks, Chester, Delaware, and Montgomery counties. No grants to individuals (except for art fellowships), or for building and development funds, travel, research, publications, or matching gifts.

Publications: Application guidelines; Annual report; Grants list; Occasional report.

Application information: Call foundation for category packet or download an application from the foundation's Web site. Exhibit material, if sent, should be in single form. Receipt of proposals is acknowledged. Should the original application prove to be within the scope of the foundation's interests, interviews with the board may be arranged prior to final determination. Application form required.

   Initial approach: Letter
   Copies of proposal: 10
   Deadline(s): Contact foundation for deadline dates
   Board meeting date(s): Varies
   Final notification: Varies

Officers and Directors:* Hon. Phyllis W. Beck,* Chair. and Treas.; Susan E. Sherman,* C.E.O. and Pres.; Andre Dennis,* V. P.; Eugene C. Fish,* V.P.; Andrea L. Mengel, Ph.D., Secy.; Bartain M. Silverman.

Number of staff: 5 full-time professional; 3 full-time support.

EIN: 231352110

Selected grants: The following grants were reported in 2005.

$400,000 to National Nursing Centers Consortium, Philadelphia, PA. For general operating support.

$318,673 to Lebanon Valley College, Annville, PA. For Eugene C. Fish Professorship in Business.

$225,000 to Philadelphia Health Management Corporation, Philadelphia, PA. For Mary Howard Health Center, payable over 2 years.

$225,000 to Philadelphia Mural Arts Advocates, Philadelphia, PA. For general operating support.

$75,000 to Greater Philadelphia Cultural Alliance, Philadelphia, PA. For general operating support, payable over 3 years.

$60,000 to Drexel University, Philadelphia, PA. For 11th Street Family Health.

$59,027 to Friends of Farmworkers, Philadelphia, PA. For Public Interest Law Fellowship.

$30,000 to Act II Playhouse, Ambler, PA. For challenge grant, payable over 3 years.

$28,420 to SeniorLAW Center, Philadelphia, PA. For Public Interest Law Fellowship.

$20,000 to Howard University, School of Law, DC. For scholarships.

8267
Innisfree Foundation of Bryn Mawr, Pennsylvania ◇ ☆

c/o Center Bridge Group, Inc.
300 Conshohocken State Rd., Rm. 210
West Conshohocken, PA   19428

Established in 1989 in PA.
Donor: Harold G. Schaeffer.
Foundation type: Independent foundation.
Financial data (yr. ended 9/30/05): Assets, $809,163 (M); gifts received, $1,028,694;

expenditures, $407,070; qualifying distributions, $406,675; giving activities include $406,273 for 20 grants (high: $110,000; low: $600).
Fields of interest: Performing arts, music; Education; Health care; Health organizations, association; Jewish agencies & temples.
Type of support: Scholarships—to individuals.
Limitations: Applications not accepted. Giving primarily in Philadelphia, PA. No grants to individuals (except for scholarships).
Application information: Contributes only to pre-selected organizations.
Trustees: Adele K. Schaeffer; Anthony L. Schaeffer; Harold G. Schaeffer; James R. Schaeffer; Robert D. Schaeffer.
EIN: 232810871

8268
The Institute for Aegean Prehistory ▼ ◇

3550 Market St., Ste. 100
Philadelphia, PA   19104   (215) 387-4911
Contact: Karen Velucci
FAX: (215) 387-4950; E-mail: instap@hotmail.com;
URL: http://www.aegeanprehistory.net

Established in 1983 in NY.
Donor: Malcolm H. Wiener.
Foundation type: Operating foundation.
Financial data (yr. ended 6/30/05): Assets, $10,523,306 (M); gifts received, $5,013,221; expenditures, $5,330,103; qualifying distributions, $3,972,478; giving activities include $1,423,397 for 68 grants (high: $75,192; low: $2,496; average: $5,000–$50,000), and $2,411,098 for 221 grants to individuals (high: $100,000; low: $250; average: $5,000–$20,000).
Purpose and activities: The Institute for Aegean Prehistory (INSTAP) is a private operating foundation; opportunities to participate in the organization's activities are given only for the purpose of allowing and encouraging persons to study Aegean prehistory with expectation of research publication under the direct supervision of the institute. The goal of the Institute's grant program is to promote knowledge of the Aegean region, and to support archaeological fieldwork and research in that area in the chronological span of the Neolithic Period through to the First Olympiad in 776 BC.
Fields of interest: History/archaeology.
International interests: Greece.
Type of support: Internship funds; Research; Grants to individuals.
Limitations: Giving on a national and international basis, with emphasis on Greece. No grants for students obtaining degrees, travel or maintenance of children or spouses, research expenses incurred before the date of a grant, salaries for researchers, purchase of expensive individual items of equipment such as computers, cameras and video recorders, or general activities of other institutions, or entities including "overhead expenses".
Application information: Application forms are available on the institute's Web site. Application form required.
   Initial approach: Letter
   Deadline(s): Varies
   Final notification: 60 days
Officers and Directors:* Malcolm H. Wiener, Pres. and Treas.; Phillip Betancourt, V.P. and Secy.; Harvey Beker,* V.P.; George E. Crapple,* V.P.; Martin J. Whitman; Carolyn S. Wiener.
EIN: 133137391

Selected grants: The following grants were reported in 2004.

$739,092 to Institute for Aegean Prehistory Study Center for East Crete, New York, NY. 4 grants: $256,075, $135,000, $148,700, $199,317

$83,000 to University of Pennsylvania, Philadelphia, PA. 2 grants: $28,000 to University of Pennsylvania Museum (For Geophysical and Geoarchaeological Project at Priniatikos Pyrgos, Istron), $55,000 to University of Pennsylvania Museum (For salary).

$40,000 to Institute of Nautical Archaeology, College Station, TX. For Uluburun Shipwreck.

$30,000 to British School at Athens, Athens, Greece. For Kythera Island Project.

$30,000 to University of Chicago, Chicago, IL. For Tell Atchana Excavations.

$27,400 to Temple University, Philadelphia, PA. For Hagios Charlambos Excavations.

8269
Fred J. Jaindl Foundation ◇

3150 Coffeetown Rd.
Orefield, PA   18069
Contact: David Jaindl, Tr.

Established in 1988 in PA.
Foundation type: Independent foundation.
Financial data (yr. ended 12/31/04): Assets, $3,616,444 (M); gifts received, $1,934,149; expenditures, $551,578; qualifying distributions, $529,802; giving activities include $529,052 for 77 grants (high: $200,000; low: $100).
Fields of interest: Education; Health organizations, association; Housing/shelter, development; Aging, centers/services; Federated giving programs; Aging; Disabilities, people with.
Limitations: Giving primarily in Lehigh Valley, PA.
Application information: Application form not required.
   Initial approach: Letter
   Deadline(s): 90 days prior to date funds are needed
Trustees: David Jaindl; Mark Jaindl; PNC Bank, N.A.; Wachovia Bank, N.A.
EIN: 232495124
Selected grants: The following grants were reported in 2004.

$200,000 to Sacred Heart Hospital, Allentown, PA.

$100,000 to Diocese of Allentown, Allentown, PA.

$100,000 to Good Shepherd Home and Rehabilitation, Allentown, PA.

$20,000 to Phoebe-Devitt Home, Allentown, PA.

$10,000 to Hillside School, Macungie, PA.

$10,000 to Lehigh Valley Hospital and Health Network, Allentown, PA.

$10,000 to Saint Catherine of Sienna Church, Allentown, PA.

$10,000 to United Way of Lebanon County, Lebanon, PA.

$2,500 to Childrens Home of Easton, Easton, PA.

$1,000 to Allentown Art Museum, Allentown, PA.

8270
The Jake Foundation ◇

311 Edgehill Rd.
Wayne, PA   19087-4716

Established in 1999 in PA.
Donors: Leo W. Pierce, Jr.; Bruce Buckley.
Foundation type: Independent foundation.

Financial data (yr. ended 12/31/04): Assets, $529,552 (M); expenditures, $459,062; qualifying distributions, $450,489; giving activities include $450,000 for 2 grants (high: $250,000; low: $200,000).
Fields of interest: Higher education, university; Education.
Limitations: Applications not accepted. Giving primarily in PA. No grants to individuals.
Application information: Contributes only to pre-selected organizations.
Trustees: Bruce Buckley; Leo W. Pierce, Jr.
EIN: 256638422

8271
Henry Janssen Foundation ◆ ☆
2650 Westview Dr.
Wyomissing, PA 19610

Established in 2005 in PA.
Foundation type: Independent foundation.
Financial data (yr. ended 12/31/05): Assets, $10,675,868 (M); gifts received, $10,428,502; expenditures, $609,198; qualifying distributions, $505,800; giving activities include $488,000 for 32 grants (high: $135,000; low: $2,000).
Fields of interest: Museums; Arts; Elementary/secondary education; Higher education; Hospitals (general); Health organizations; Youth development.
Limitations: Applications not accepted. Giving primarily in PA. No grants for indications.
Application information: Contributes only to pre-selected organizations.
Officers and Trustee:* Elroy P. Master,* Pres.; John W. Bowman, V.P.; Elizabeth B. Rothermel, Secy.; Elsa M. Hoppman, Treas.
EIN: 201812511

8272
The Mary Hillman Jennings Foundation ◆
625 Stanwix St., Ste. 2203
Pittsburgh, PA 15222 (412) 434-5606
Contact: Paul Euwer, Jr., Exec. Dir.

Incorporated in 1968 in PA.
Donor: Mary Hillman Jennings†.
Foundation type: Independent foundation.
Financial data (yr. ended 12/31/04): Assets, $30,819,015 (M); expenditures, $2,941,191; qualifying distributions, $2,456,875; giving activities include $2,072,500 for 118 grants (high: $300,000; low: $1,000).
Purpose and activities: Grants to schools, youth agencies, and hospitals and health associations.
Fields of interest: Education; Hospitals (general); Health care; Health organizations, association; Youth development, services; Children/youth, services.
Type of support: General/operating support; Annual campaigns; Capital campaigns; Building/renovation; Equipment; Endowments; Program development; Curriculum development; Research.
Limitations: Giving primarily in the Pittsburgh, PA, area. No grants to individuals.
Application information: Application form not required.
   Initial approach: Letter
   Copies of proposal: 1
   Deadline(s): May 1 and Oct. 1
   Board meeting date(s): May and Oct.
   Final notification: 3 to 6 months

Officers and Directors:* Evan D. Jennings II,* Pres.; Andrew L. Weil,* Secy.; Irving A. Wechsler,* Treas.; Paul Euwer, Jr.,* Exec. Dir.; Christina Jennings; Cynthia B. Jennings.
Number of staff: 1 full-time professional; 1 part-time support.
EIN: 237002091
Selected grants: The following grants were reported in 2004.
$200,000 to Allegheny Valley School, Coraopolis, PA.
$100,000 to Allegheny General Hospital, Pittsburgh, PA.
$75,000 to Avon Old Farms School, Avon, CT.
$40,000 to Adelphoi, Inc., Latrobe, PA.
$30,000 to YMCA of Pittsburgh, Pittsburgh, PA.
$25,000 to Pennsylvania Trolley Museum, Washington, PA.
$20,000 to Saint Vincent College, Latrobe, PA.
$10,000 to Pittsburgh Mercy Foundation, Pittsburgh, PA.
$5,000 to Kingsley Association, Pittsburgh, PA.
$5,000 to Pittsburgh Arts and Lectures, Pittsburgh, PA.

8273
John Family Foundation ◆
3855 County Line Rd.
Winfield, PA 17889-9661

Established in 1991 in PA.
Donors: Paul R. John; Mildred D. John.
Foundation type: Independent foundation.
Financial data (yr. ended 12/31/05): Assets, $5,321,252 (M); gifts received, $506,524; expenditures, $409,163; qualifying distributions, $395,000; giving activities include $395,000 for 34 grants (high: $200,000; low: $500).
Fields of interest: Higher education; Health organizations, association; Human services; Children/youth, services; Christian agencies & churches.
Type of support: Building/renovation.
Limitations: Giving primarily in PA. No grants to individuals.
Application information:
   Initial approach: Letter
   Deadline(s): None
Officers: Paul R. John, Pres.; Mildred D. John, V.P.
EIN: 232616038

8274
The Thomas Phillips and Jane Moore Johnson Foundation
535 Smithfield St., Ste. 605
Pittsburgh, PA 15222 (412) 261-9008
Contact: Kathleen Sturgeon
Application address: c/o Jane T. Johnson, Tr., The Ayco Co., L.P., 101 State Farm Pl., Ballston Spa, NY 12020

Established in 1990 in PA.
Donors: Thomas Phillips Johnson; Thomas Johnson†.
Foundation type: Independent foundation.
Financial data (yr. ended 12/31/04): Assets, $84,052,012 (M); gifts received, $1,062,496; expenditures, $2,863,474; qualifying distributions, $2,398,427; giving activities include $2,123,810 for 68 grants (high: $300,000; low: $100).

Purpose and activities: Giving primarily for higher education, gay and lesbian services, social services, arts and culture, particularly film-related organizations, and museums.
Fields of interest: Media, film/video; Museums (art); Arts; Higher education; Education; Human services; Civil rights, gays/lesbians; Foundations (community); Public affairs.
Limitations: Applications not accepted. Giving on a national basis. No grants to individuals.
Application information: Unsolicited requests for funds not accepted.
Officers and Trustees:* Thomas P. Johnson,* Chair.; James M. Johnson, Pres.; Asa J. Johnson, Secy.; Jesse D. Johnson; Jane T. Johnson.
EIN: 256357015
Selected grants: The following grants were reported in 2003.
$101,250 to Gay, Lesbian and Straight Education Network (GLSEN), New York, NY. For general support.
$70,000 to Yale University, New Haven, CT. For general support.
$50,000 to Bethany College, Bethany, WV. For general support.
$32,263 to Tides Foundation, San Francisco, CA. For general support.
$25,000 to Gay and Lesbian Alliance Against Defamation (GLAAD), New York, NY. For general support.
$15,000 to Princeton University, Princeton, NJ. For general support.
$11,000 to National Gay and Lesbian Task Force (NGLTF), DC. For general support.
$3,000 to Los Angeles Gay and Lesbian Center, Los Angeles, CA. For general support.
$2,500 to Gay and Lesbian Leadership Institute, DC. For general support.
$1,250 to University of Michigan, Law School, Ann Arbor, MI. For general support.

8275
John Alfred & Oscar Johnson Memorial Trust ◆
c/o M&T Bank
21 E. Market St.
York, PA 17401-1205
Contact: Carole W. Sellstrom, Exec. Dir

Established in 1996 in NY.
Foundation type: Independent foundation.
Financial data (yr. ended 1/31/06): Assets, $6,918,180 (M); expenditures, $447,048; qualifying distributions, $344,425; giving activities include $344,425 for 22 grants (high: $189,300; low: $850).
Purpose and activities: Consideration will be given to applications from charitable, religious, and educational organizations that benefit the citizens of Jamestown, NY and the surrounding area. Consideration will also be given to charitable, religious, and educational organizations which promote the appreciation and enrichment of Swedish heritage.
Fields of interest: Environment, natural resources; Hospitals (general); Health organizations; Human services; Salvation Army; YM/YWCAs & YM/YWHAs; Community development.
Limitations: Giving limited to Jamestown, NY. No grants to individuals.
Application information:
   Initial approach: Proposal
   Deadline(s): None

Trustees: John L. Sellstrom; M&T Bank.
EIN: 166438291
Selected grants: The following grants were reported in 2005.
$184,850 to Salvation Army, Yonkers, NY.
$45,000 to Swedish Council of America, Minneapolis, MN.
$15,000 to Chautauqua Striders Youth Development Coalition, Jamestown, NY.
$10,000 to Moran Eye Center, Salt Lake City, UT.
$5,000 to Meals on Wheels of the Jamestown Area, Jamestown, NY.
$2,500 to Chautauqua Watershed Conservancy, Jamestown, NY.
$2,000 to Chautauqua Region Community Foundation, Jamestown, NY.
$1,500 to United Way of Southern Chautauqua County, Jamestown, NY.
$1,000 to Ice Theater of New York, New York, NY.
$500 to W N E D-TV, Buffalo, NY.

8276

Edith C. Justus Trust ◇ ☆
c/o Kosak & Associates
P.O. Box 374
Oil City, PA   16301   (814) 677-5085

Trust established in 1931 in PA.
Donor: Edith C. Justus‡.
Foundation type: Independent foundation.
Financial data (yr. ended 12/31/05): Assets, $5,662,056 (M); expenditures, $444,003; qualifying distributions, $420,183; giving activities include $386,156 for 41 grants (high: $28,000; low: $25).
Purpose and activities: Giving largely for community development and civic affairs, including public parks, and for social service and health agencies.
Fields of interest: Museums; Arts; Libraries (public); Education; Human services; YM/YWCAs & YM/YWHAs; Family services; Federated giving programs.
Type of support: Program development; Capital campaigns; General/operating support; Continuing support; Annual campaigns; Building/renovation; Equipment; Land acquisition; Debt reduction; Emergency funds; Seed money; Matching/challenge support.
Limitations: Giving restricted to Venango County, PA, with emphasis on Oil City. No grants to individuals, or for endowment funds, matching gifts, scholarships, fellowships, research, publications, or conferences; no loans.
Publications: Application guidelines; Grants list.
Application information: Application form required.
    Initial approach: Letter
    Copies of proposal: 3
    Deadline(s): None
    Board meeting date(s): Apr., June, Oct. and Dec.
    Final notification: 2 months
Trustee: National City Bank.
Number of staff: 1 full-time professional; 1 part-time support.
EIN: 256031057
Selected grants: The following grants were reported in 2004.
$40,000 to Community Services of Venango County, Oil City, PA. For general support.
$28,000 to Family Service and Childrens Aid Society, Oil City, PA. For general support.
$22,500 to Oil City Library, Oil City, PA. For general support.
$20,000 to Grace Learning Center, Franklin, PA. For general support.

$18,900 to Youth Alternatives of Oil City, Oil City, PA. For general support.
$17,075 to Child Development Centers, Franklin, PA. For general support.
$15,000 to Allegheny Valley Trails Association, Franklin, PA. For general support.
$13,500 to Venango Museum of Art, Science and Industry, Oil City, PA. For general support.
$11,520 to Presbyterian Homes in the Presbytery of Lake Erie, Erie, PA. For general support.
$11,000 to Clarion University Foundation, Clarion, PA. For general support.

8277

**Kevy K. & Hortense M. Kaiserman
    Foundation** ◇
201 S. 18th St., Ste. 300
Philadelphia, PA   19103-5921   (215) 546-2665
Contact: Ronald L. Kaiserman, Tr.

Established in 1980 in PA.
Donors: Hortense M. Kaiserman; Kenneth S. Kaiserman; Ronald L. Kaiserman; Kevy K. Kaiserman Marital Trust; Constance Robinson; Kaiserman Enterprises, LP.
Foundation type: Independent foundation.
Financial data (yr. ended 6/30/06): Assets, $976,403 (M); gifts received, $595,000; expenditures, $1,141,464; qualifying distributions, $1,133,500; giving activities include $1,133,500 for 21 grants (high: $550,000; low: $1,000).
Fields of interest: Museums (art); Performing arts; Performing arts, theater; Hospitals (general); Human services; Jewish federated giving programs; Jewish agencies & temples.
International interests: Israel.
Limitations: Applications not accepted. Giving primarily in Philadelphia, PA. No grants to individuals.
Application information: Usually funds same organizations.
    Board meeting date(s): Apr. and Oct.
Trustees: Kenneth S. Kaiserman; Ronald L. Kaiserman; Constance K. Robinson.
EIN: 232299921
Selected grants: The following grants were reported in 2005.
$550,000 to Brandeis University, Waltham, MA.
$25,000 to Jewish Federation of Greater Philadelphia, Philadelphia, PA.
$20,000 to American Music Theater Festival, Philadelphia, PA.
$20,000 to Philadelphia Museum of Art, Philadelphia, PA.
$12,000 to NAACP, Baltimore, MD.
$12,000 to United Way.
$10,000 to American Jewish Committee, New York, NY.
$2,000 to Akiba Hebrew Academy, Merion Station, PA.
$1,000 to Chamah, New York, NY.

8278

The Karabots Foundation ◇
P.O. Box 736
Fort Washington, PA   19034
E-mail: nkarabots@spartanorg.com

Established in 1998 in PA.
Donors: Nicholas Karabots; Athena Karabots; Glendi Publications, Inc.; Kappa Graphics, LP;

Spartan Organization, Inc.; Geopedior Assocs., LP; Kappa Media Group, Inc.
Foundation type: Independent foundation.
Financial data (yr. ended 6/30/06): Assets, $37,669,227 (M); gifts received, $1,246,244; expenditures, $464,697; qualifying distributions, $318,745; giving activities include $318,745 for grants.
Fields of interest: Museums; Libraries (special); Hospitals (general); Recreation, parks/playgrounds.
Type of support: General/operating support.
Limitations: Applications not accepted. Giving primarily in PA. No support for religious organizations. No grants to individuals.
Application information: Contributes only to pre-selected organizations.
Officers: Nicholas Karabots, Chair. and Pres.; Athena Karabots, Vice-Chair. and V.P.; Andrea Duloc, V.P.; Constance Kolkka, V.P.; Despina McNulty, V.P.; William Bonner, Secy.-Treas.
EIN: 232939856

8279

**Samuel and Rebecca Kardon
    Foundation** ◇
c/o Larson Allen Weishair & Co., LLP
18 Sentry Park W., Ste. 300
Blue Bell, PA   19422-2240
Contact: David Kittner, Pres.

Trust established in 1952 in PA.
Donors: Emanuel S. Kardon; American Bag & Paper Corp.
Foundation type: Independent foundation.
Financial data (yr. ended 12/31/04): Assets, $7,136,330 (M); expenditures, $539,858; qualifying distributions, $479,220; giving activities include $479,220 for 58 grants (high: $47,750; low: $200).
Purpose and activities: Emphasis on the musical arts, higher and secondary education, and Jewish organizations; support also for hospitals and social service agencies.
Fields of interest: Museums; Performing arts; Performing arts centers; Higher education; Education; Hospitals (general); Human services; Jewish federated giving programs; Jewish agencies & temples; Disabilities, people with.
Limitations: Giving primarily in PA, with emphasis on Philadelphia, PA. No grants to individuals.
Application information:
    Initial approach: Letter
    Deadline(s): None
Officers and Directors:* David Kittner,* Pres.; Harriet Guin-Kittner,* V.P.; Susan J. Huntting,* V.P.
EIN: 236278123
Selected grants: The following grants were reported in 2003.
$1,000,000 to Constance S. Kittner Foundation, Philadelphia, PA.
$70,000 to Jewish Federation of Greater Philadelphia, Philadelphia, PA.
$31,000 to Settlement Music School, Philadelphia, PA.
$25,000 to Philadelphia Chamber Music Society, Philadelphia, PA.
$25,000 to Thomas Jefferson University, Jefferson Medical College, Philadelphia, PA.
$20,000 to Holy Family University, Philadelphia, PA.
$15,000 to University of North Carolina, Chapel Hill, NC.
$7,500 to Curtis Institute of Music, Philadelphia, PA.

$7,500 to Mann Center for the Performing Arts, Philadelphia, PA.

$5,000 to Akiba Hebrew Academy, Merion Station, PA.

8280

The Harold Katz Family Foundation ✧

c/o G. Daniel Jones
283 2nd St. Pike, Ste. 150
Southampton, PA 18966 (215) 364-0400
Contact: Harold Katz, Pres.

Established in 1986 in PA.
Donors: Harold Katz; Creative Investors L.P.
Foundation type: Independent foundation.
Financial data (yr. ended 12/31/05): Assets, $23,089 (M); gifts received, $330,000; expenditures, $538,154; qualifying distributions, $535,186; giving activities include $535,186 for 18 grants (high: $250,000; low: $100).
Purpose and activities: Giving primarily for kidney research; funding also for health associations and children and social services.
Fields of interest: Higher education; Health organizations, association; Kidney research; Human services; Children, services.
Limitations: Giving primarily in FL and PA, with emphasis on Philadelphia; some funding nationally. No grants to individuals.
Application information:
  Initial approach: Letter
  Deadline(s): None
  Final notification: Within 3 months
Officer: Harold Katz, Pres.
Directors: David Katz; Diane Katz; Marlene Katz; Peggy Katz.
EIN: 232439844

8281

Harry Katz Memorial Fund ✧

c/o Wachovia Bank, N.A.
123 S. Broad St., 5th Fl.
Philadelphia, PA 19109
Contact: Reginald Middleton, V.P., Wachovia Bank, N.A.
E-mail: reginald.middleton@wachovia.com

Established in 1955 in NJ.
Foundation type: Independent foundation.
Financial data (yr. ended 12/31/05): Assets, $2,672,278 (M); expenditures, $378,385; qualifying distributions, $340,750; giving activities include $339,910 for 8 grants (high: $99,250; low: $5,000).
Purpose and activities: Support primarily for Jewish organizations, including education and community and family services.
Fields of interest: Education; Family services; Jewish agencies & temples.
Type of support: General/operating support; Capital campaigns; Equipment; Program development.
Limitations: Giving primarily in Atlantic County, NJ. No grants to individuals.
Application information: Application form not required.
  Initial approach: Letter or proposal
  Copies of proposal: 1
  Deadline(s): Oct. 1
Trustees: Florence K. Bernstein; Wachovia Bank, N.A.

Number of staff: 1 full-time professional; 1 full-time support.
EIN: 510171174
Selected grants: The following grants were reported in 2003.
$50,000 to Trocki Hebrew Academy of Atlantic County, Egg Harbor Township, NJ. For scholarships.
$40,000 to Jewish Community Center of Atlantic County, Margate, NJ. 2 grants: $22,000 (For senior adult program), $18,000 (For fitness program).
$28,000 to BERON Jewish Older Adult Services of Atlantic and Cape May Counties, Atlantic City, NJ.
$10,000 to Board of Jewish Education of Atlantic County, Margate City, NJ.
$5,000 to Jewish Family Service of Atlantic and Cape May Counties, Margate City, NJ. For Elderly Crisis Intervention Program.

8282

T. James Kavanagh Foundation ✧

234 E. State St.
Sharon, PA 16146
Contact: Thomas E. Kavanagh, Tr.

Established in 1968 in PA.
Donor: T. James Kavanagh†.
Foundation type: Independent foundation.
Financial data (yr. ended 12/31/04): Assets, $15,423,019 (M); expenditures, $617,562; qualifying distributions, $484,118; giving activities include $472,512 for 101 grants (high: $50,000; low: $1,000).
Purpose and activities: At least 60 percent of funding for Roman Catholic church support, and religious associations; support also for education, including Roman Catholic schools.
Fields of interest: Arts; Elementary/secondary education; Higher education; Education; Human services; Children/youth, services; Roman Catholic agencies & churches; Religion.
Type of support: General/operating support; Continuing support; Annual campaigns; Equipment; Program development; Scholarship funds; Research.
Limitations: Giving strictly limited to the U.S., with emphasis on southern NJ and PA. No support for private foundations or organizations outside the U.S., including Roman Catholic organizations with missions overseas. No grants to individuals, or for endowment funds, seed money, deficit financing, land acquisition, publications, conferences, scholarships, fellowships, or matching gifts; no loans.
Publications: Application guidelines; Grants list.
Application information: Application guidelines available from the foundation. Application form required.
  Initial approach: Proposal with application form
  Copies of proposal: 1
  Deadline(s): None
  Board meeting date(s): Mar., Aug., and Nov.
  Final notification: End of month preceding board meeting date
Trustees: Melvin Bandzak; Louis J. Esposito; Thomas E. Kavanagh.
Number of staff: 1 full-time professional.
EIN: 236442981
Selected grants: The following grants were reported in 2004.
$50,000 to Buhl Farm Trust, Sharon, PA.

$25,000 to Country Day School of the Sacred Heart, Bryn Mawr, PA.
$25,000 to Prince of Peace Center, Farrell, PA.
$25,000 to Saint Josephs Preparatory School, Philadelphia, PA.
$10,000 to Delaware Valley College, Doylestown, PA.
$7,000 to Saint Michaels School, Greenville, PA.
$5,000 to Cabrini College, Radnor, PA.
$5,000 to United Way of Mercer County, Sharon, PA.
$4,000 to Aid for Friends, Philadelphia, PA.
$4,000 to Drexel Hill School of the Holy Child, Drexel Hill, PA.

8283

Paul E. Kelly Foundation ✧

(formerly Superior-Pacific Fund)
109 Forrest Ave.
Narberth, PA 19072-2212
Contact: Paul E. Kelly, Jr., Pres.

Trust established in 1952 in PA.
Donors: Superior Tube Co.; Pacific Tube Co.; Cawsl Enterprises, Inc.
Foundation type: Independent foundation.
Financial data (yr. ended 12/31/05): Assets, $18,813,682 (M); expenditures, $1,065,140; qualifying distributions, $950,712; giving activities include $836,350 for grants.
Purpose and activities: Grants primarily for Roman Catholic education, community funds, and cultural/arts organizations.
Fields of interest: Arts; Elementary school/education; Secondary school/education; Higher education.
Type of support: General/operating support; Continuing support; Annual campaigns; Capital campaigns; Building/renovation; Endowments.
Limitations: Giving primarily in the Philadelphia, PA, area.
Application information: Application form not required.
  Initial approach: Letter
  Copies of proposal: 1
  Deadline(s): None
  Final notification: Only applications which generate interest will receive a response
Officers and Directors:* Paul E. Kelly, Jr.,* Pres.; Christine K. Kieman,* V.P.; Judith Shea,* V.P.
Number of staff: 1 full-time professional; 1 full-time support.
EIN: 236298237

8284

Kennametal Foundation ✧

P.O. Box 231
Latrobe, PA 15650-0231
Contact: Shirl Latkovic
FAX: (724) 539-5750; Application address: 1600 Technology Way, Latrobe, PA 15650

Established in 1955 in PA.
Donor: Kennametal Inc.
Foundation type: Company-sponsored foundation.
Financial data (yr. ended 6/30/05): Assets, $357,185 (M); gifts received, $500,000; expenditures, $521,153; qualifying distributions, $520,034; giving activities include $520,034 for 132 grants (high: $166,667; low: $25).

Purpose and activities: The foundation supports organizations involved with arts and culture and secondary and higher education.
Fields of interest: Arts; Secondary school/education; Higher education; Minorities.
Type of support: Employee matching gifts; General/operating support; Continuing support; Building/renovation; Equipment; Scholarship funds; Matching/challenge support.
Limitations: Applications not accepted. Giving on a national basis, with emphasis on PA. No support for sectarian or religious organizations, political organizations, private foundations, or trust funds. No grants to individuals, or for endowments, development campaigns, debt reduction, or operating reserves, fundraising events or sponsorships, trips, conferences, seminars, festivals, or one-day events, documents, videos, or research projects/programs, or indirect or overhead costs.
Application information: Contributes only to pre-selected organizations.
Board meeting date(s): Monthly
Officer: Richard P. Gibson, Secy.-Treas.
Trustees: M. Rizwan Chand; Joy Chandler; F. Nicholas Grasberger; David W. Greenfield; Cathy Smith; Markos I. Tambakeras.
EIN: 256036009
Selected grants: The following grants were reported in 2004.
$50,000 to City of Hope, Los Angeles, CA. For general support.
$50,000 to United Way of Westmoreland County, Greensburg, PA. For general support.
$46,956 to Pennsylvania State University, University Park, PA. For general support.
$30,800 to Carnegie Mellon University, Pittsburgh, PA. For general support.
$11,215 to Saint Vincent College, Latrobe, PA. For general support.
$2,090 to Indiana University of Pennsylvania, Indiana, PA. For general support.
$1,735 to Duquesne University, Pittsburgh, PA. For general support.
$1,500 to Chatham College, Pittsburgh, PA. For general support.
$275 to Westminster College, New Wilmington, PA. For general support.
$200 to Grove City College, Grove City, PA. For general support.

8285
Keystone Nazareth Charitable Foundation ✧ ☆
90 Highland Ave.
Bethlehem, PA 18017 (610) 861-5002

Donor: Keystone Nazareth Bank & Trust Co.
Foundation type: Company-sponsored foundation.
Financial data (yr. ended 12/31/04): Assets, $26,787,591 (M); expenditures, $775,621; qualifying distributions, $757,232; giving activities include $749,080 for 249 grants (high: $100,000; low: $250).
Purpose and activities: The foundation supports science museums and organizations involved with historic preservation, education, and children and youth.
Fields of interest: Museums (science/technology); Historic preservation/historical societies; Higher education; Education; YM/YWCAs & YM/YWHAs; Children/youth, services; Federated giving programs.

Type of support: General/operating support; Capital campaigns; Building/renovation; Equipment; Program development; Sponsorships; Scholarship funds.
Limitations: Giving primarily in PA. No grants to individuals.
Application information: Application form not required.
Initial approach: Proposal
Officers and Directors: Jeffrey P. Feather, Pres. and Treas.; Michele A. Linsky, Secy.; Scott V. Fainor; Daniel G. Gambet; R. Charles Stehy.
EIN: 421607170

8286
Keystone Savings Foundation ✧ ☆
c/o Keystone Nazareth Bank & Trust Co.
P.O. Box 25012
Lehigh Valley, PA 18002-5012 (610) 861-5000
Contact: Jefferey P. Feather, Pres.

Established in 1987 in PA.
Donors: Keystone Savings Bank; Keystone Nazareth Bank & Trust Co.
Foundation type: Company-sponsored foundation.
Financial data (yr. ended 12/31/05): Assets, $504,535 (M); expenditures, $827,118; qualifying distributions, $825,109; giving activities include $825,109 for grants.
Purpose and activities: The foundation supports museums and organizations involved with education, health, hunger, housing, human services, and religion.
Fields of interest: Museums; Higher education; Education; Health care; Food distribution, meals on wheels; Housing/shelter; Human services; Religion.
Type of support: General/operating support; Annual campaigns; Capital campaigns; Building/renovation; Equipment; Program development; Scholarship funds; Program evaluation.
Limitations: Giving limited to areas of company operations in Lehigh Valley, PA. No grants to individuals.
Publications: Application guidelines; Annual report.
Application information: Application form not required.
Initial approach: Proposal
Copies of proposal: 1
Deadline(s): Nov. 30
Board meeting date(s): 4th Mon. in Mar., June, Sept., and Dec.
Officers: Jeffery P. Feather, Pres.; R. Charles Stehly, V.P.
EIN: 232407218
Selected grants: The following grants were reported in 2003.
$10,000 to Communities in Schools of the Lehigh Valley, Allentown, PA. For general support.
$10,000 to Good Shepherd Rehabilitation Hospital, Allentown, PA. For general support.
$10,000 to Hispanic American Organization, Allentown, PA. For general support.
$6,000 to YMCA of Bethlehem, Bethlehem, PA. For general support.
$5,000 to Childrens Home of Easton, Easton, PA. For general support.
$2,000 to Adult Literacy Center of the Lehigh Valley, Allentown, PA. For general support.
$2,000 to Lehigh Valley Child Care, Allentown, PA. For general support.
$1,500 to Boys and Girls Clubs of Allentown, Allentown, PA. For general support.

$1,000 to Emmaus Public Library, Emmaus, PA. For general support.
$1,000 to Nazareth Hospital, Philadelphia, PA. For general support.

8287
The James & Agnes Kim Foundation, Inc. ✧
c/o Siana Carr & O'Connor, LLP
1500 E. Lancaster Ave.
Paoli, PA 19301

Established in 1997 in PA.
Donor: James J. Kim.
Foundation type: Independent foundation.
Financial data (yr. ended 12/31/05): Assets, $14,678,893 (M); gifts received, $20,406; expenditures, $2,712,741; qualifying distributions, $2,670,900; giving activities include $2,670,900 for 27 grants (high: $800,000; low: $100).
Purpose and activities: Giving primarily for higher education.
Fields of interest: Elementary/secondary education; Higher education; Education.
Limitations: Applications not accepted. Giving primarily in PA. No grants to individuals.
Application information: Contributes only to pre-selected organizations.
Officers: Agnes C. Kim, Pres.; Susan Y. Kim, Secy.; James J. Kim, Treas.
EIN: 232899799
Selected grants: The following grants were reported in 2004.
$250,000 to Philadelphia Orchestra Association, Philadelphia, PA.
$215,000 to Gesu School, Philadelphia, PA.
$202,000 to Philadelphia Museum of Art, Philadelphia, PA.
$100,000 to National Constitution Center, Philadelphia, PA.
$30,000 to Young Scholars Charter School, Philadelphia, PA.
$15,000 to Pennsylvania Ballet, Philadelphia, PA.
$10,000 to Shipley School, Bryn Mawr, PA.
$5,000 to Hamilton College, Clinton, NY.
$2,500 to Chester County Art Association, West Chester, PA.
$2,500 to Woodlynde School, Strafford, PA.

8288
The Sidney Kimmel Foundation ▼ ✧
1650 Arch St., 22nd Fl.
Philadelphia, PA 19103-2097 (215) 977-2538
Contact: Matthew H. Kamens
FAX: (215) 977-2644;
E-mail: mkamens@wolfblock.com; URL: http://www.kimmel.org
Application address: Kimmel Scholars, Gary Cohen, M.D., Cancer Center GBMC, 6569 N. Charles St., Ste. 203 Baltimore, MD 21204, tel.: (443) 849-3729, E-mail: gcohen@gbmc.org

Established in 1992 in PA.
Donor: Sidney Kimmel.
Foundation type: Independent foundation.
Financial data (yr. ended 7/31/05): Assets, $3,170,529 (M); expenditures, $12,793,568; qualifying distributions, $12,762,336; giving activities include $9,247,589 for 35 grants (high: $5,000,000; low: $100; average: $5,000–

$250,000), and $3,050,000 for grants to individuals.

Purpose and activities: Giving for cancer research and treatment.

Fields of interest: Cancer; Medical research, institute; Cancer research.

Type of support: Scholarships—to individuals.

Limitations: Applications not accepted.

Application information: Unsolicited requests for funds are not accepted.

Officer: Sidney Kimmel, Pres. and Treas.

EIN: 232698492

Selected grants: The following grants were reported in 2005.

$5,000,000 to Memorial Sloan-Kettering Cancer Center, New York, NY.

$3,050,000 to Sidney Kimmel Cancer Center, San Diego, CA.

$1,025,000 to Raymond and Ruth Perelman Jewish Day School, Wynnewood, PA.

$1,000,000 to Jewish Federation of Greater Philadelphia, Philadelphia, PA.

$1,000,000 to Simon Wiesenthal Center, Los Angeles, CA.

$250,000 to Thomas Jefferson University Hospitals, Philadelphia, PA.

$25,000 to Anti-Defamation League of Bnai Brith, Philadelphia, PA.

$25,000 to Madlyn and Leonard Abramson Center for Jewish Life, North Wales, PA.

$15,000 to Food Allergy Initiative, New York, NY.

$10,000 to Temple University, Philadelphia, PA.

8289
Patricia Kind Family Foundation ◇

c/o Glenmede Trust Co.
1650 Market St.
Philadelphia, PA 19103
E-mail: PKFFoundation@comcast.net; Application address: c/o Laura Kind McKenna, Managing Tr., 7707 Pine Rd., Wyndmoor, PA 19038; FAX: (215) 233-2569; URL: http://www.pkffoundation.net

Established in 1996 in PA.

Donors: Hedwig A. van Ameringen†; Louis van Ameringen†.

Foundation type: Independent foundation.

Financial data (yr. ended 12/31/04): Assets, $32,254,829 (M); expenditures, $2,254,680; qualifying distributions, $2,424,506; giving activities include $2,118,250 for 131 grants (high: $40,000; low: $750).

Fields of interest: Education; Health care; Human services.

Type of support: General/operating support; Program development; Curriculum development; Matching/challenge support.

Limitations: Giving primarily in Philadelphia, PA and surrounding counties. No grants to individuals, or for scholarships, international giving activities, or fundraising; no endowments.

Publications: Application guidelines; Annual report (including application guidelines); Financial statement; Grants list; Informational brochure (including application guidelines).

Application information: Application guidelines available on foundation Web site. Application form not required.

Initial approach: Letter requesting application guidelines

Copies of proposal: 1

Deadline(s): None

Board meeting date(s): Jan., Apr., and Aug.

Final notification: Via letter

Trustees: Laura Kind McKenna, Managing Tr.; Christina Kind Baiocchi; Ken Kind; Patricia Kind; Andrew Kindfuller; Valerie Kind-Rubin.

Number of staff: 1 part-time support.

EIN: 237839035

Selected grants: The following grants were reported in 2004.

$40,000 to Compeer of Suburban Philadelphia, Eagleville, PA. For program support.

$40,000 to Juvenile Law Center, Philadelphia, PA.

$30,000 to Community Organization for Mental Health and Retardation (COMHAR), Philadelphia, PA. For general operating support.

$25,000 to Aspira of Pennsylvania, Philadelphia, PA.

$25,000 to Christ Lutheran Church, Upper Darby, PA. For Parish Nurse Community Outreach program.

$25,000 to Hebrew Immigrant Aid Society (HIAS) and Council Migration Service of Philadelphia, Philadelphia, PA. For expansion of services to immigrant survivors of domestics violence through their Pathways to Self-Sufficiency program.

$25,000 to Philadelphia Montgomery Christian Academy, Erdenheim, PA. For financial aid program.

$20,000 to Sunday Breakfast Rescue Mission, Philadelphia, PA. For program support.

$15,000 to Jubilee School, Philadelphia, PA. For program support for student with learning disabilities.

$2,000 to Whosoever Gospel Mission and Rescue Association of Germantown, Philadelphia, PA. For Career Track Learning.

8290
Kinsley Family Foundation ◇

6259 Reynolds Mill Rd.
Seven Valleys, PA 17360
Application address: c/o Anne W. Kinsley, V.P., R.D. 1, Box 131AA, Seven Valleys, PA 17360, (717) 741-8407

Established in 1997 in PA.

Donors: Robert A. Kinsley; Anne W. Kinsley; Kinsley Construction, Inc.; Walton & Co., Inc.; Gettle, Inc.; I.B. Abel, Inc.

Foundation type: Independent foundation.

Financial data (yr. ended 12/31/05): Assets, $5,062,608 (M); gifts received, $347,411; expenditures, $403,713; qualifying distributions, $364,616; giving activities include $364,616 for 36 grants (high: $69,000; low: $3).

Fields of interest: Historic preservation/historical societies; Arts; Education; Health care; Youth development; Human services; Community development; Federated giving programs; Roman Catholic agencies & churches.

Limitations: Giving primarily in PA.

Application information:

Initial approach: Letter

Deadline(s): None

Officers: Robert A. Kinsley, Pres.; Anne W. Kinsley, V.P.; Timothy J. Kinsley, Secy.; Christopher A. Kinsley, Treas.

EIN: 232870170

Selected grants: The following grants were reported in 2005.

$100,000 to Boy Scouts of America, York, PA. 2 grants: $31,000, $69,000

$60,000 to York College of Pennsylvania, York, PA. 2 grants: $10,000, $50,000

$10,000 to Catholic Charities, Princess Anne, MD.

8291
Raymond Klein Charitable Foundation ◇

1700 Market St., Ste. 2600
Philadelphia, PA 19103
Contact: Stephen B. Klein, Pres.

Established in 1988 in PA.

Donor: Raymond Klein.

Foundation type: Independent foundation.

Financial data (yr. ended 10/31/05): Assets, $6,298,531 (M); expenditures, $359,918; qualifying distributions, $343,114; giving activities include $343,114 for 14 grants (high: $110,000; low: $750).

Purpose and activities: Giving primarily for the arts, Jewish organizations, and health associations.

Fields of interest: Arts; Health care; Health organizations, association; Human services; Jewish federated giving programs; Jewish agencies & temples.

Type of support: General/operating support.

Limitations: Giving primarily in Philadelphia, PA. No grants to individuals.

Application information: Application form not required.

Deadline(s): None

Officer and Trustees:* Stephen B. Klein,* Pres.; Miriam K. Klein.

EIN: 232535513

Selected grants: The following grants were reported in 2003.

$200,000 to Kimmel Center for the Performing Arts, Philadelphia, PA. For unrestricted support.

$25,000 to Jewish Federation of Greater Philadelphia, Philadelphia, PA. For unrestricted support.

$10,000 to Thomas Jefferson University Hospitals, Philadelphia, PA. For unrestricted support.

$8,112 to Congregation Adath Jeshurun, Elkins Park, PA. For unrestricted support.

$5,000 to Jewish Community Centers of Greater Philadelphia, Philadelphia, PA. For unrestricted support.

$5,000 to National Museum of American Jewish History, Philadelphia, PA. For unrestricted support.

$2,500 to Boca Raton Community Hospital, Boca Raton, FL. For unrestricted support.

$1,500 to Philadelphia Museum of Art, Philadelphia, PA. For unrestricted support.

$1,100 to United Way of Southeastern Pennsylvania, Philadelphia, PA. For unrestricted support.

$1,000 to Rosenbach Museum and Library, Philadelphia, PA. For unrestricted support.

8292
Charles and Figa Kline Foundation ◇

626 N. Main St.
Allentown, PA 18104
Contact: Fabian I. Fraenkel, Pres. and Treas.

Incorporated in 1957 in PA.

Donors: Charles Kline†; Figa Cohen Kline†.

Foundation type: Independent foundation.

Financial data (yr. ended 10/31/05): Assets, $8,386,870 (M); expenditures, $464,568;

qualifying distributions, $446,600; giving activities include $446,600 for 17 grants (high: $188,000; low: $1,000).

Purpose and activities: Giving largely for Jewish welfare and community service agencies, temple support, and education.

Fields of interest: Education; Human services; Federated giving programs; Jewish federated giving programs; Jewish agencies & temples.

Type of support: Capital campaigns; Building/renovation.

Limitations: Giving primarily in Allentown, PA. No grants to individuals.

Application information: Application form not required.

Deadline(s): Sept. 30

Officers: Fabian I. Fraenkel, Pres. and Treas.; Stewart Furmansky, V.P.; Barnet H. Fraenkel, Secy.

EIN: 236262315

Selected grants: The following grants were reported in 2003.

$185,000 to Jewish Federation of Allentown, Allentown, PA. For unrestricted support.

$74,500 to Jewish Community Center of Allentown, Allentown, PA. For unrestricted support.

$26,000 to Jewish Day School of Allentown, Allentown, PA. For unrestricted support.

$25,000 to Temple Beth El of Allentown, Allentown, PA. For unrestricted support.

$20,000 to United Way in Lehigh County, Allentown, PA. For unrestricted support.

$10,000 to Anti-Defamation League of Bnai Brith, New York, NY. For unrestricted support.

$10,000 to Congregation Keneseth Israel, Allentown, PA. For unrestricted support.

$10,000 to Jewish Family Service of the Lehigh Valley, Allentown, PA. For unrestricted support.

$4,000 to Association for the Blind and Visually Impaired of Lehigh County, Allentown, PA. For unrestricted support.

$4,000 to Boys and Girls Clubs of Allentown, Allentown, PA. For unrestricted support.

8293
Josiah W. and Bessie H. Kline Foundation, Inc. ◇

515 S. 29th St.
Harrisburg, PA 17104 (717) 561-0820
Contact: John A. Obrock, C.P.A.

Incorporated in 1952 in DE.

Donors: Josiah W. Kline†; Bessie H. Kline†.

Foundation type: Independent foundation.

Financial data (yr. ended 12/31/05): Assets, $21,950,911 (M); expenditures, $1,139,223; qualifying distributions, $1,068,181; giving activities include $1,057,568 for 50 grants (high: $50,000; low: $500).

Purpose and activities: Support primarily for higher education, hospitals, and the handicapped; support also for scientific or medical research, educational associations and building funds, health associations, child welfare organizations, historic preservation, and social services.

Fields of interest: Media/communications; Museums; Performing arts; Historic preservation/historical societies; Arts; Higher education; Education; Hospitals (general); Health organizations, association; Medical research, institute; Human services; Children/youth, services; Christian agencies & churches; Disabilities, people with.

Type of support: Continuing support; Annual campaigns; Capital campaigns; Building/renovation; Equipment; Land acquisition; Emergency funds; Curriculum development; Scholarship funds; Research; Matching/challenge support.

Limitations: Giving primarily in south central PA. No grants to individuals, or for endowment funds, operating budgets, special projects, publications, conferences, or fellowships; no loans.

Publications: Application guidelines; Program policy statement.

Application information: Application form required.

Initial approach: Proposal
Copies of proposal: 2
Deadline(s): Contact office for deadline dates
Board meeting date(s): Semiannually
Final notification: 6 months

Officers: Robert F. Nation, Pres.; John A. Obrock, Secy.

Directors: Derek C. Hathaway; James E. Marley; Samuel D. Ross, Jr.; John A. Russell; David A. Smith, M.D.

EIN: 236245783

Selected grants: The following grants were reported in 2004.

$225,000 to Pinnacle Health Foundation, Harrisburg, PA. 2 grants: $75,000, $150,000

$50,000 to Elizabethtown College, Elizabethtown, PA.

$50,000 to Gettysburg College, Gettysburg, PA.

$50,000 to Goodwill Industries of Central Pennsylvania, Harrisburg, PA.

$50,000 to Messiah College, Grantham, PA.

$50,000 to Susquehanna University, Selinsgrove, PA.

$25,000 to ARC of Dauphin and Lebanon Counties, Harrisburg, PA.

$20,000 to Harrisburg Symphony Association, Harrisburg, PA.

$15,000 to American Red Cross, Harrisburg, PA.

8294
Knox Family Foundation ◇

2113 Delancey St.
Philadelphia, PA 19103-6511
Contact: Eleanor G. Nalle, Pres. and Treas.

Incorporated in 1961 in NY.

Donors: Eleanor E. Knox†; Knox Gelatine, Inc.

Foundation type: Independent foundation.

Financial data (yr. ended 12/31/05): Assets, $8,363,478 (M); expenditures, $438,889; qualifying distributions, $390,581; giving activities include $379,750 for 154 grants (high: $20,000; low: $240).

Fields of interest: Secondary school/education; Higher education; Hospitals (general); Human services; Protestant agencies & churches.

Limitations: Applications not accepted. Giving on a national basis. No grants to individuals.

Application information: Contributes only to pre-selected organizations.

Officers and Directors:* Eleanor G. Nalle,* Pres. and Treas.; John K. Graham,* V.P. and Secy.; Nora Armstrong, V.P.; Rose Ann Armstrong,* V.P.; Roseann K. Beaudoin,* V.P.; Rosemary Birchard,* V.P.; Amy Brumley,* V.P.; Kimberly Knox,* V.P.

EIN: 146017797

8295
The Korein Foundation

(formerly Sarah & Isidor Korein Charitable Trust)
c/o Glenmede Trust Co., N.A.
1650 Market St., Ste. 1200
Philadelphia, PA 19103-7391 (215) 419-6144
Contact: Melanie Redmond, Admin.
FAX: (215) 419-6647;
E-mail: melanie.redmond@glenmede.com

Established in 2000 in NY.

Donors: Sarah Korein†; James Korein.

Foundation type: Independent foundation.

Financial data (yr. ended 12/31/05): Assets, $8,833,298 (M); expenditures, $450,103; qualifying distributions, $425,991; giving activities include $385,000 for 38 grants (high: $40,000; low: $3,000; average: $5,000–$10,000).

Fields of interest: Environment; Animals/wildlife.

Limitations: Applications not accepted. Giving on a national basis, with some emphasis on New York, NY. No grants to individuals.

Application information: Contributes only to pre-selected organizations.

Trustees: Lawrence N. Friedland; Beth Korein; James Korein; Jonathan Korein; Julius Korein, M.D.

EIN: 137180474

8296
Hyman Korman Family Foundation ◇

2 Neshaminy Interplex, Ste. 307
Trevose, PA 19053

Trust established in 1947 in PA.

Donors: Members of the Korman family; Hyman Korman, Inc.; I. Barney Moss†.

Foundation type: Independent foundation.

Financial data (yr. ended 12/31/05): Assets, $9,743,857 (M); expenditures, $549,529; qualifying distributions, $467,100; giving activities include $467,100 for 11 grants (high: $100,000; low: $2,100).

Purpose and activities: Giving primarily for Jewish agencies and temples, and for higher education.

Fields of interest: Elementary/secondary education; Higher education; Hospitals (general); Jewish federated giving programs; Jewish agencies & temples.

Limitations: Applications not accepted. Giving primarily in Philadelphia, PA. No grants to individuals.

Application information: Contributes only to pre-selected organizations.

Trustees: Berton E. Korman; Leonard I. Korman; Steven H. Korman.

EIN: 236297326

Selected grants: The following grants were reported in 2004.

$105,000 to Germantown Academy, Fort Washington, PA.

$100,000 to Albert Einstein Medical Center, Philadelphia, PA.

$100,000 to National Museum of American Jewish History, Philadelphia, PA.

$10,000 to Thomas Jefferson University, Philadelphia, PA.

$5,000 to United Way of Bucks County, Fairless Hills, PA.

8297
John Crain Kunkel Foundation ◇
P.O. Box 658
Camp Hill, PA 17001
Application address: c/o J.K. Stark, 2120 Market St., Camp Hill, PA 17011, tel.: (717) 763-1284

Established in 1965 in PA.
Foundation type: Independent foundation.
Financial data (yr. ended 12/31/05): Assets, $13,322,356 (M); expenditures, $723,355; qualifying distributions, $641,984; giving activities include $525,000 for 9 grants (high: $200,000; low: $10,000).
Purpose and activities: Giving primarily for the arts, human services, higher education and health associations, particularly a health foundation.
Fields of interest: Arts; Higher education; Health organizations, association; Human services; Community development.
Type of support: General/operating support.
Limitations: Giving primarily in Harrisburg, PA.
Application information: Application form not required.
>*Initial approach:* Letter
>*Deadline(s):* None

Trustees: Nancy W. Bergert; Elizabeth K. Davis; Deborah L. Facini; John C. Kunkel II; Paul A. Kunkel; Jay W. Stark; John K. Stark; William T. Wright II.
EIN: 237026914

8298
James Annenberg La Vea Charitable Foundation ◇
(formerly James Annenberg Levee Charitable Foundation)
c/o PNC Bank, N.A.
1600 Market St., 29th Fl.
Philadelphia, PA 19103
Contact: Lawrence J. Miller, Tr.

Established in 2000 in FL.
Donors: James Annenberg Levee Charitable Trust; James Annenberg La Vea.
Foundation type: Independent foundation.
Financial data (yr. ended 12/31/04): Assets, $8,479,599 (M); gifts received, $624,057; expenditures, $509,379; qualifying distributions, $377,309; giving activities include $381,456 for 36 grants (high: $17,166; low: $3,815).
Fields of interest: Arts; Health care; Health organizations, association; Medical research; Human services; Children/youth.
Limitations: Applications not accepted. Giving on a national basis, with emphasis on FL and NY. No grants to individuals.
Application information: Contributes only to pre-selected organizations.
Officer: James Annenberg La Vea, Mgr.
Trustee: Lawrence J. Miller.
EIN: 656323823
Selected grants: The following grants were reported in 2004.
$17,165 to Americas Second Harvest, Chicago, IL.
$15,258 to Cancer Research Institute, New York, NY.
$13,350 to Boy Scouts of America National Council, Irving, TX.
$13,350 to Childrens Home Society of Florida, Fort Lauderdale, FL.
$11,443 to Bascom Palmer Eye Institute, Miami, FL.

$11,443 to Buoniconti Fund to Cure Paralysis, Miami, FL.
$11,443 to Kidney and Urology Foundation of America, New York, NY.
$9,536 to Massachusetts Institute of Technology, Cambridge, MA.
$9,536 to National Endowment for the Arts, DC.
$9,536 to Susan G. Komen Breast Cancer Foundation, West Palm Beach, FL.

8299
Robert E. Lamb Foundation, Inc. ◇ ☆
21 Rebel Rd.
Radnor, PA 19087

Established in 2003.
Donors: Robert E. Lamb; Walter E. Lamb Trust.
Foundation type: Independent foundation.
Financial data (yr. ended 12/31/05): Assets, $5,051,976 (M); gifts received, $299,050; expenditures, $826,181; qualifying distributions, $818,507; giving activities include $810,500 for 7 grants (high: $700,000; low: $1,000).
Fields of interest: Higher education; Education; Animal welfare; Civil liberties, reproductive rights; Community development; Foundations (public).
Limitations: Applications not accepted. No grants to individuals.
Application information: Contributes only to pre-selected organizations.
Trustee: Vanguard National Trust Co.
Officer: Robert E. Lamb, Pres.
EIN: 810606210

8300
The Lancaster County Community Foundation
(formerly The Lancaster County Foundation)
53 W. James St., Ste. 101
Lancaster, PA 17603-3046 (717) 397-1629
Contact: Deborah Schattgen, C.E.O.; For grants: Doug Levering, V.P., Progs. and Initiatives
FAX: (717) 397-6877;
E-mail: info@lancastercountyfoundation.org;
Additional E-mail: debbie@lancastercountyfoundation.org; Grant application E-mail: doug@lancastercountyfoundation.org; URL: http://www.lancastercountyfoundation.org
Scholarship E-mail: scholarships@lancastercountyfoundation.org

Established in 1924 in PA.
Foundation type: Community foundation.
Financial data (yr. ended 12/31/05): Assets, $43,325,771 (M); gifts received, $5,060,063; expenditures, $3,084,413; giving activities include $1,051,855 for grants, and $25,000 for 16 grants to individuals (high: $3,000; low: $2,000).
Purpose and activities: The foundation seeks to strengthen the quality of life of county residents by building community capital for today and tomorrow; enhancing the quality of life of citizens engaging people and organizations in philanthropy; convening, planning and working for positive change and supporting and launching new initiatives.
Fields of interest: Arts; Education; Environment; Health care; Housing/shelter, home owners; Children/youth, services; Human services; Community development; Disabilities, people with.

Type of support: Management development/ capacity building; Program development; Publication; Seed money; Scholarship funds; Research; Consulting services; Program-related investments/loans; Scholarships—to individuals; Matching/challenge support.
Limitations: Giving limited to Lancaster County, PA. No support for governmental agencies, umbrella organizations for purposes of re-granting funds, cemetery associations, or sectarian religious purposes. No grants to individuals (except for scholarships), or for operating budgets, continuing support, annual campaigns, deficit financing, land acquisition, endowment funds, fellowships, consulting services, fundraising events, solicitations, multi-year funding for bricks and mortar projects, conferences, trips, or seminars.
Publications: Application guidelines; Annual report; Informational brochure; Newsletter.
Application information: Visit foundation Web site for application form, guidelines, and deadlines. New applicants are encouraged to call or e-mail the foundation before completing an application. Applications must be submitted via e-mail; additional materials may be faxed or mailed. Application form required.
>*Initial approach:* Complete online application form
>*Copies of proposal:* 1
>*Deadline(s):* Varies
>*Board meeting date(s):* 6 times annually
>*Final notification:* Apr. and Nov.

Officers and Directors:* Al Morrison III,* Chair.; Phil Wenger,* Vice-Chair.; Deborah B. Schattgen, C.E.O. and Pres.; Doug Levering, V.P., Progs. and Initiatives; Gene P. Otto,* Secy.; Michael W. Van Belle,* Treas.; Rev. John R. Baldwin; Jill Carson; Buddy Glover; Ellen Arnold Groff; Henry Huffnagle, M.D.; W. Jeffrey Sidebottom; Kae Groshorg Wagner.
Number of staff: 3 full-time professional; 1 full-time support.
EIN: 200874857

8301
Laurel Foundation
2 Gateway Ctr., Ste. 1800
Pittsburgh, PA 15222 (412) 765-2400
Contact: Donna Panazzi, V.P.; Elizabeth Tata, Prog. Dir.

Incorporated in 1951 in PA.
Donor: Cordelia S. May†.
Foundation type: Independent foundation.
Financial data (yr. ended 12/31/04): Assets, $39,403,657 (M); expenditures, $2,067,968; qualifying distributions, $1,868,936; giving activities include $1,700,745 for 85 grants (high: $100,000; low: $1,000).
Purpose and activities: Grants largely to organizations operating in the fields of education, the environment, conservation, family planning, museums and the performing arts, with concentration in the southwestern Pennsylvania area.
Fields of interest: Performing arts; Performing arts, theater; Literature; Arts; Secondary school/ education; Environment, natural resources; Reproductive health, family planning; Health care; Medical research, institute; Human services; Population studies.
Type of support: General/operating support; Capital campaigns; Building/renovation; Equipment; Land acquisition; Program development; Publication; Seed money; Curriculum development; Internship

funds; Technical assistance; Program evaluation; Matching/challenge support.

Limitations: Giving limited to southwestern PA. No support for religious organizations. No grants for scholarships; no loans.

Publications: Annual report (including application guidelines).

Application information: Common Grant Application Form accepted. Application form required.

   Initial approach: Letter of inquiry

   Copies of proposal: 1

   Deadline(s): Apr. 1 and Oct. 1

   Board meeting date(s): June and Dec.

   Final notification: June and Dec.

Officers and Trustees:* T. Inglis,* Pres. and Treas.; D. Panazzi, V.P. and Secy.; J. Barsotti, V.P., Investments; N. Fales; R. Meyer; C. Scaife; T. Schmidt.

Number of staff: 1 full-time professional; 3 part-time professional; 3 part-time support.

EIN: 256008073

Selected grants: The following grants were reported in 2003.

$183,000 to Allegheny Conference on Community Development, Pittsburgh, PA. For film project, The War that Made America.

$100,000 to Pennsylvania Environmental Council, Harrisburg, PA. For Watershed Protection Program.

$60,000 to Westmoreland Museum of American Art, Greensburg, PA. For general operating support.

$50,000 to Carnegie Institute, Pittsburgh, PA. For Hudson River School exhibition.

$50,000 to Phipps Conservatory and Botanical Gardens, Pittsburgh, PA. For general operating support.

$50,000 to Pittsburgh Parks Conservancy, Pittsburgh, PA. For general operating and program support.

$40,000 to Keystone Oaks School District, Pittsburgh, PA. For Project Succeed Program.

$40,000 to Regional Trail Corporation, West Newton, PA. For rehabilitation of Big Savage Tunnel and continued marketing of the trail.

$25,000 to Frick Art and Historical Center, Pittsburgh, PA. For general operating support.

$25,000 to Historical Society of Western Pennsylvania, Pittsburgh, PA. For general operating support.

8302

Jerry Lee Foundation

c/o WBEB FM Radio, Inc.
10 Presidential Blvd.
Bala Cynwyd, PA 19004
Contact: Gloria Dreon, Admin.
E-mail: jerryl@101-FM.com

Established in 1996 in PA.

Donors: David Kurtz‡; Jerry Lee.

Foundation type: Independent foundation.

Financial data (yr. ended 12/31/05): Assets, $87,299 (M); gifts received, $473,272; expenditures, $947,812; qualifying distributions, $947,127; giving activities include $908,500 for grants.

Purpose and activities: Giving limited for research in education and criminology.

Fields of interest: Education, research; Crime/law enforcement, research.

Type of support: Research.

Limitations: Applications not accepted. Giving primarily in the U.S., with some emphasis on

Philadelphia, PA, and the greater metropolitan Washington, DC, area. No grants to individuals.

Application information: Contributes only to pre-selected organizations.

Officer: Gerald Lee, Pres. and Secy.-Treas.

EIN: 232867684

Selected grants: The following grants were reported in 2005.

$868,500 to University of Pennsylvania, Philadelphia, PA. 5 grants: $400,000 to Jerry Lee Center of Criminology (For annual campaign), $31,000 to Jerry Lee Center of Criminology (For administrative expenses for The Campbell Collaboration), $200,000 to Jerry Lee Center of Criminology (For annual support of two Assistant Professorships), $137,500 (For Justice Research Consortium), $100,000 (For Stockholm Prize for Criminology).

$20,000 to University of Maryland-College Park Foundation, Department of Criminology and Criminal Justice, College Park, MD. For Jerry Lee Crime Prevention Symposium.

$10,000 to Gesu School, Philadelphia, PA.

$10,000 to MDRC, Judith Gueron Fund for Methodological Innovation in Social Policy Research, New York, NY. For research on whether and how social programs work.

8303

Lehigh Valley Community Foundation ✧

(formerly Bethlehem Area Foundation)
961 Marcon Blvd., Ste. 300
Allentown, PA 18109-9521   (610) 266-4284
Contact: Carol Dean Henn, Secy.
FAX: (610) 266-4285;
E-mail: lvcf@lehighvalleyfoundation.org;
URL: http://www.lehighvalleyfoundation.org

Established in 1967 in PA.

Foundation type: Community foundation.

Financial data (yr. ended 6/30/05): Assets, $19,784,470 (M); gifts received, $3,054,204; expenditures, $876,351; giving activities include $449,313 for 154 grants (high: $37,769; low: $50).

Purpose and activities: The foundation enables donors, including individuals, families, businesses, private foundations and nonprofit agencies, to establish funds which will serve their charitable intentions temporarily or in perpetuity by providing grants to nonprofit organizations and programs. Giving for arts, culture, and heritage, community development, education, environment and science, health care, and human services.

Fields of interest: Historic preservation/historical societies; Arts; Education; Environment; Health care; Children, services; Family services; Human services; Community development; Science.

Type of support: Capital campaigns; Building/renovation; Equipment; Emergency funds; Program development; Publication; Seed money; Scholarship funds; Matching/challenge support.

Limitations: Giving limited to Lehigh, Monroe, Northampton, and Upper Bucks counties, PA. No support for sectarian religious purposes. No grants for operating budgets, continuing support, annual campaigns, deficit financing, endowments, foundation scholarships, or research; no loans.

Publications: Application guidelines; Annual report (including application guidelines); Grants list; Informational brochure (including application guidelines); Newsletter; Program policy statement.

Application information: Visit foundation Web site for application form and guidelines. Faxed or

e-mailed applications are not accepted. Capital funding: must submit invoice copies when requesting release of funds. Site visits will be made; mid-year and final reports required. Application form required.

   Initial approach: Submit application form and attachments

   Copies of proposal: 7

   Deadline(s): July 1

   Board meeting date(s): Quarterly

   Final notification: Dec. 15

Officers and Board of Governors:* Charles M. Meredith III,* Chair.; Carol Dean Henn, Secy. and Exec. Dir.; Robert D. Romeril,* Treas.; Alan Abraham; Jan Armfield; David K. Bausch; Denise Blew; Walter W. Buckley, Jr.; Hon. Maxwell E. Davison; Marlene O. Fowler; Jean Franz; Gregory E. Grim; Peyton R. Helm, Ph.D.; Frederick Kutteroff; Edward Lentz; Stephen P. Link; Jack H. McNairy; William K. Murphy; David Rabaut, Ph.D.; Elizabeth M. Roberts; Martha Saxton, Ph.D.; John H. Updegrove, M.D.; Robert C. Wood.

Investment Management: The Bank of New York; Dean McDermott & Co.; Bank of America, N.A.; Legg Mason; Merrill Lynch Trust Co.; The Vanguard Group; Wachovia Bank, N.A.

Number of staff: 2 full-time professional; 1 part-time professional; 2 full-time support.

EIN: 231686634

Selected grants: The following grants were reported in 2005.

$37,769 to United Way of the Greater Lehigh Valley, Bethlehem, PA.

$22,500 to Heritage Baptist Church, Jeannette, PA.

$15,000 to Calvary Baptist Church.

$15,000 to Lehigh Valley Charter High School for the Performing Arts, Bethlehem, PA.

$12,100 to Lehigh County Conference of Churches, Allentown, PA.

$10,000 to United Friends School of the Greater Lehigh Valley, Quakertown, PA.

8304

The Brook J. Lenfest Foundation, Inc. ✧

5 Tower Bridge, Ste. 450
300 Barr Harbor Dr.
West Conshohocken, PA 19428
(610) 828-4510
Contact: Bruce Melgary, Exec. Dir.
FAX: (610) 828-0390;
E-mail: lenfestfoundation@lenfestfoundation.org;
URL: http://www.brookjlenfestfoundation.org

Established in 2000 in PA.

Donor: Brook J. Lenfest.

Foundation type: Independent foundation.

Financial data (yr. ended 6/30/05): Assets, $34,211,351 (M); expenditures, $1,294,578; qualifying distributions, $1,540,069; giving activities include $1,127,432 for 25 grants (high: $600,000; low: $2,500).

Purpose and activities: The foundation is dedicated to making people aware of positive life choices and providing support and opportunities for those motivated to pursue them. In keeping with its mission, the foundation will focus mainly on education, job training, mentoring programs, wellness-based health care, and the arts. The foundation also supports the Mastery Charter High School in Philadelphia, PA, whose mission is to ensure all students develop the skills they need to succeed in the 21st century economy with full preparation for college education.

Fields of interest: Arts; Education; Human services.

Type of support: General/operating support; Continuing support; Capital campaigns; Seed money; Scholarship funds.

Limitations: Giving primarily in northern DE, southern NJ, southeastern and south central urban areas of PA, with an emphasis on Philadelphia, as well as Harrisburg. No support for health or religious programs. No grants to individuals, or for medical research, publications or litigation.

Publications: Application guidelines.

Application information: Guidelines on foundation Web site; applications sent by E-mail will not be accepted. Grant requests may be submitted for 1 year only, and not to exceed $25,000. Application form not required.

Initial approach: 2-4 page letter of inquiry
Copies of proposal: 1
Deadline(s): Ongoing
Board meeting date(s): Sept.
Final notification: After June board meeting

Officers and Directors:* Brook J. Lenfest,* Pres.; Dawn Lenfest,* Secy.; Marguerite B. Lenfest,* Treas.; Joy Tartar, C.F.O.; Bruce Melgary, Exec. Dir.

EIN: 233031338

Selected grants: The following grants were reported in 2005.

$600,000 to Mastery Charter High School, Philadelphia, PA.

$30,000 to Philadelphia Futures for Youth, Philadelphia, PA. 2 grants: $10,000, $20,000

$15,000 to Mercy Vocational High School, Philadelphia, PA.

$15,000 to San Miguel School, Camden, NJ.

$10,000 to Pennsylvania School for the Deaf, Philadelphia, PA.

$2,500 to Community Learning Center, Philadelphia, PA.

8305
The Lenfest Foundation, Inc. ▼ ◇

5 Tower Bridge
300 Barr Harbor Dr., Ste. 450
West Conshohocken, PA 19428
(610) 828-4510
Contact: Bruce Melgary, Exec. Dir.
FAX: (610) 828-0390;
E-mail: lenfestfoundation@lenfestfoundation.org;
URL: http://www.lenfestfoundation.org

Established in 1999 in PA.

Donors: H.F. Lenfest; Mrs. H.F. Lenfest.

Foundation type: Independent foundation.

Financial data (yr. ended 6/30/05): Assets, $122,341,875 (M); expenditures, $44,243,947; qualifying distributions, $43,159,278; giving activities include $41,113,700 for 80 grants (high: $10,000,000; low: $2,000; average: $10,000–$1,000,000), and $1,604,107 for 86 grants to individuals.

Purpose and activities: Giving primarily for the foundation's own rural education scholarship programs, major project support initiated by the foundation's founders, and approved by its Board of Directors. Limited number of grants in the areas of education, arts, and the environment.

Fields of interest: Arts; Education; Environment.

Type of support: General/operating support; Continuing support; Annual campaigns; Capital campaigns; Scholarships—to individuals.

Limitations: Giving primarily in northern DE, southern NJ, and southeastern and south central PA. No support for disease research. No grants to

individuals (except Lenfest scholarships), political organizations, religious programs or activities, university presses, tickets, tables or sponsorships or conferences, or organizations that deal with health, physical or mental disabilities; no loans.

Publications: Application guidelines; Informational brochure (including application guidelines).

Application information: Application guidelines available on Web site. Application form not required.

Initial approach: Letter or E-mail (2 - 3 pages)
Copies of proposal: 1
Deadline(s): None
Board meeting date(s): Feb., May, and Oct.
Final notification: Usually 1 - 3 months

Officers and Directors:* H.F. Lenfest,* Chair.; Marguerite Lenfest,* Pres.; Grahame Richards, Secy.; Joy Tarta, C.F.O. and Treas.; Bruce Melgary, Exec. Dir.; T. Douglas Hale; Joseph F. Huber; John Strassburger.

Number of staff: 2 full-time professional; 2 full-time support.

EIN: 233031350

Selected grants: The following grants were reported in 2005.

$5,000,000 to Curtis Institute of Music, Philadelphia, PA. For challenge grant.

$2,000,000 to Mastery Charter High School, Philadelphia, PA. 2 grants: $1,000,000 (For expansion project), $1,000,000 (For challenge grant for expansion project).

$1,100,000 to Pew Charitable Trusts, Philadelphia, PA. 2 grants: $500,000 (For Natural Environmental Trust endangered species work), $600,000 (For Marine Fish Conservation Network Joint Fisheries Campaign).

$1,000,000 to Historic Philadelphia, Philadelphia, PA. For Once Upon A Nation Storytelling Benches.

$100,000 to Benjamin Franklin Tercentenary, Philadelphia, PA. For general operating support.

$75,000 to Generations on Line, Philadelphia, PA. For operating support.

$15,000 to Kids Chance of Pennsylvania, Pottstown, PA. For program support.

$10,000 to American Music Theater Festival, Prince Music Theater, Philadelphia, PA. For youth programs.

8306
Les Oiseaux Foundation ◇

P.O. Box 6056
Pittsburgh, PA 15211

Established in 1999 in PA.

Donor: Kenneth B. Dunn.

Foundation type: Independent foundation.

Financial data (yr. ended 12/31/05): Assets, $2,131,691 (M); expenditures, $671,915; qualifying distributions, $671,850; giving activities include $664,200 for 12 grants (high: $510,000; low: $100).

Fields of interest: Arts; Education; Human services; Protestant agencies & churches.

Limitations: Applications not accepted. Giving primarily in PA. No grants to individuals.

Application information: Contributes only to pre-selected organizations.

Trustees: Amy Dunn; Brett Dunn; Kenneth B. Dunn; Pamela R. Dunn; Chester Spatt.

EIN: 256642155

8307
The Levan Family Foundation ◇

1094 Baltimore Pike
Gettysburg, PA 17325
Contact: David M. Levan, Chair.

Established in 1997 in PA.

Donor: David M. Levan.

Foundation type: Independent foundation.

Financial data (yr. ended 12/31/05): Assets, $568,605 (M); expenditures, $342,616; qualifying distributions, $341,000; giving activities include $341,000 for 23 grants (high: $195,000; low: $250).

Fields of interest: Arts; Elementary/secondary education; Higher education, college; Human services; Children, services; Federated giving programs.

Limitations: Giving primarily in PA. No grants to individuals.

Application information: Application form required.

Initial approach: Letter requesting application
Deadline(s): None

Officers and Directors:* David M. Levan, Chair. and Pres.; Todd M. Levan,* V.P.; Jennifer S. Levan,* Secy.-Treas.

EIN: 232899050

Selected grants: The following grants were reported in 2005.

$100,000 to Gettysburg National Battlefield Museum Foundation, Seven Valleys, PA.

$10,000 to Harrisburg Area Community College Foundation, Harrisburg, PA.

$5,000 to Valley Forge Military Academy, Wayne, PA.

$2,500 to American Heart Association, Philadelphia, PA.

$500 to American Cancer Society, Hershey, PA.

$500 to Arthritis Foundation, Greensburg, PA.

$500 to Ronald McDonald House Charities of Central Pennsylvania, Hershey, PA.

$500 to Susan G. Komen Breast Cancer Foundation, Philadelphia, PA.

8308
Polly A. Levee Charitable Trust A - Krancer Trust ◇

c/o PNC Advisors
1600 Market St., 29th Fl.
Philadelphia, PA 19103

Established in 1993 in PA as partial successor to Polly Annenberg Levee Charitable Trust.

Donor: Polly Annenberg Levee†.

Foundation type: Independent foundation.

Financial data (yr. ended 12/31/05): Assets, $6,450,445 (M); expenditures, $397,619; qualifying distributions, $365,294; giving activities include $365,000 for 17 grants (high: $230,000; low: $1,000).

Purpose and activities: Giving primarily for Jewish and other federated giving programs; funding also for health associations, and social services including canine services for people with physical disabilities.

Fields of interest: Higher education; Hospitals (specialty); Health organizations; Human services; Federated giving programs; Jewish federated giving programs.

Type of support: General/operating support; Annual campaigns.

Limitations: Applications not accepted. Giving primarily in Philadelphia, PA. No grants to individuals.

Application information: Contributes only to
pre-selected organizations. Unsolicited requests for
funds not considered.
Trustees: William J. Henrich; PNC Bank, N.A.
EIN: 232735661
Selected grants: The following grants were reported
in 2004.
$235,000 to Jewish Federation of Greater
Philadelphia, Philadelphia, PA. 2 grants:
$225,000, $10,000
$25,000 to Crohns and Colitis Foundation of
America, Philadelphia, PA.
$25,000 to Jewish Community Centers of Greater
Philadelphia, Philadelphia, PA.
$20,000 to Alexis de Tocqueville Society,
Alexandria, VA. 5 grants: $2,500, $2,500,
$2,500, $2,500, $10,000
$5,000 to Canine Partners for Life, Cochranville, PA.

8309
The Adolph and Rose Levis Family Foundation ◇
c/o Mellon Financial Corp.
P.O. Box 185
Pittsburgh, PA   15230-0185

Established in 1993 in PA.
Donor: Adolph Levis†.
Foundation type: Independent foundation.
Financial data (yr. ended 11/30/05): Assets,
$7,443,165 (M); expenditures, $362,653;
qualifying distributions, $347,357; giving activities
include $342,980 for 10 grants (high: $175,000;
low: $6,000).
Fields of interest: Health organizations,
association; Human services; Residential/custodial
care; Aging, centers/services; Jewish federated
giving programs; Science; Jewish agencies &
temples; Aging.
Limitations: Applications not accepted. Giving
primarily in Boca Raton, FL. No grants to individuals.
Application information: Contributes only to
pre-selected organizations.
Trustee: Mellon Bank, N.A.
EIN: 650211764
Selected grants: The following grants were reported
in 2004.
$150,000 to Jewish Federation of South Palm
Beach County, Boca Raton, FL. For operating
support.
$102,000 to Adolph and Rose Levis Jewish
Community Center, Boca Raton, FL. For operating
support.
$50,000 to Matthew Forbes Romer Foundation,
Boca RAton, FL. For operating support.
$25,000 to American Committee for the Weizmann
Institute of Science, West Palm Beach, FL. For
operating support.
$15,000 to Jewish Association for Residential Care,
Boca Raton, FL. For operating support.
$15,000 to Jewish Community Foundation of Boca
Raton, Boca Raton, FL. For operating support.
$10,000 to Pine Crest School, Fort Lauderdale, FL.
For operating support.
$6,000 to Jewish Adoption and Foster Care Options,
Fort Lauderdale, FL. For operating support.
$2,000 to Elderly Interest Fund, Fort Lauderdale, FL.
For operating support.
$2,000 to Hospice by the Sea, Boca Raton, FL. For
operating support.

8310
Levis Trust ◇
c/o Mellon Financial Corp.
P.O. Box 185
Pittsburgh, PA   15230-0185

Established in 2001 in PA.
Donor: Adolph Levis Trust.
Foundation type: Independent foundation.
Financial data (yr. ended 12/31/05): Assets,
$7,480,851 (M); expenditures, $353,244;
qualifying distributions, $339,242; giving activities
include $334,118 for 9 grants (high: $153,150;
low: $5,000; average: $10,000–$25,000).
Fields of interest: Hospitals (general); Jewish
federated giving programs; Jewish agencies &
temples.
Limitations: Applications not accepted. Giving
primarily Boca Raton, FL and PA. No grants to
individuals.
Application information: Contributes only to
pre-selected organizations.
Trustees: Barbara Brodsky; Mellon Bank, N.A.
EIN: 311631647

8311
Lilliput Foundation ◇
P.O. Box 70
Lederach, PA   19450
Contact: Debbie Maillie
E-mail: dzmaille@comcast.net

Established in 1985 in PA.
Donors: Drew Lewis; Marilyn S. Lewis.
Foundation type: Independent foundation.
Financial data (yr. ended 12/31/04): Assets,
$63,468 (M); gifts received, $10,000;
expenditures, $464,005; qualifying distributions,
$450,613; giving activities include $450,613 for 25
grants (high: $86,637; low: $500).
Purpose and activities: Giving primarily for
education, health, religion, and community
organizations.
Fields of interest: History/archaeology; Arts; Higher
education; Hospitals (general); Recreation;
Children/youth, services; Community development;
Federated giving programs; Christian agencies &
churches.
Type of support: General/operating support;
Building/renovation; Fellowships; Scholarship
funds.
Limitations: Giving primarily in Montgomery County,
PA. No grants to individuals.
Application information: Application form not
required.
Initial approach: Letter (no more than 2 pages)
Copies of proposal: 1
Deadline(s): None
Board meeting date(s): Annually
Final notification: Usually within two months by
letter
Officers and Trustees:* Drew Lewis,* Pres. and
Treas.; Marilyn S. Lewis,* V.P. and Secy.; Andrew L.
Lewis IV; Russell S. Lewis.
Number of staff: 1
EIN: 232385383
Selected grants: The following grants were reported
in 2004.
$88,637 to Richard J. Caron Foundation,
Wernersville, PA.
$30,000 to Fox Chase Cancer Center, Philadelphia,
PA.
$25,000 to High Watch Farm, Kent, CT.

$20,000 to Agnes Irwin School, Rosemont, PA.
$20,000 to Pennsylvania Ballet, Philadelphia, PA.
$10,000 to Marine Corps Heritage Foundation,
Quantico, VA.
$10,000 to Perkiomen School, Pennsburg, PA.
$5,000 to Montgomery County Norristown Public
Library, Norristown, PA.
$1,000 to Alan Ameche Memorial Foundation,
Narberth, PA.

8312
The Lindback Foundation
(also known as Christian R. and Mary F. Lindback
Foundation)
c/o Duane Morris LLP
30 S. 17th St.
Philadelphia, PA   19103-4196   (215) 979-1555
Contact: Sharon M. Renz, Secy.

Established in 1955 in NJ.
Donors: Mary F. Lindback†; Christian R. Lindback†.
Foundation type: Independent foundation.
Financial data (yr. ended 12/31/05): Assets,
$24,538,631 (M); expenditures, $1,419,209;
qualifying distributions, $1,132,413; giving
activities include $1,116,268 for 102 grants (high:
$120,000; low: $1,000).
Purpose and activities: Giving primarily to
universities for distinguished teaching awards,
minority junior faculty awards, and discretionary
grants.
Fields of interest: Museums; Arts; Education;
Hospitals (general).
Type of support: General/operating support; Annual
campaigns; Capital campaigns; Seed money;
Fellowships; Matching/challenge support.
Limitations: Giving primarily in southern NJ, and
southeastern PA. No support for private
organizations. No grants to individuals, or for
building or endowment funds.
Publications: Application guidelines.
Application information: Application form not
required.
Initial approach: Proposal
Copies of proposal: 3
Deadline(s): None
Board meeting date(s): Mar., Aug., and Dec.
Trustees: Sheldon M. Bonovitz; David E. Loder;
Wachovia Bank, N.A.
Number of staff: 1
EIN: 236290348
Selected grants: The following grants were reported
in 2005.
$75,000 to Lincoln University, Lincoln University,
PA. For outstanding minority students
scholarships.
$20,000 to City Year, Philadelphia, PA. For
expanding youth service organization and
strengthening corps member training.
$18,954 to Rutgers, The State University of New
Jersey, New Brunswick, NJ. 2 grants: $4,000 (For
Distinguished Teaching Award), $14,954 (For
Minority Junior Faculty Award).
$15,000 to Philadelphia Orchestra Association,
Philadelphia, PA. For Raising the Invisible Curtain
and other education programs.
$10,000 to Appel Farm Arts and Music Center,
Elmer, NJ. For Community Arts Outreach and
Rising Young Artist Scholarship programs.
$7,500 to Academy of Natural Sciences of
Philadelphia, Philadelphia, PA. For watershed
education program and teachers workshop.

$6,000 to Planned Parenthood Southeastern Pennsylvania, Philadelphia, PA. For Youth First program.

$5,000 to Jewish Family and Childrens Service of Greater Philadelphia, Philadelphia, PA. For senior citizens creative art groups.

$5,000 to Neighbor to Neighbor Community Development Corporation, Sharon Hill, PA. For after-school tutorial and LATCH-On programs.

8313
The Little Family Foundation ◇
c/o Mellon Bank, N.A.
P.O. Box 185
Pittsburgh, PA 15230-0185

Established in 1946 in RI.
Donor: Royal Little†.
Foundation type: Independent foundation.
Financial data (yr. ended 12/31/04): Assets, $26,673,775 (M); expenditures, $1,567,927; qualifying distributions, $1,464,168; giving activities include $1,258,606 for 148+ grants (high: $125,000), and $57,420 for 6 employee matching gifts.
Purpose and activities: Support for scholarship funds at designated business schools; Rhode Island Junior Achievement for programs in secondary schools; and various charities in New England, including youth agencies, cultural programs, and hospitals.
Fields of interest: Performing arts; Performing arts, dance; Performing arts, music; Arts; Elementary/secondary education; Business school/education; Education; Environment, natural resources; Environment; Hospitals (general); Youth, services.
Type of support: General/operating support; Continuing support; Annual campaigns; Building/renovation; Equipment; Emergency funds; Scholarship funds; Matching/challenge support.
Limitations: Applications not accepted. Giving primarily in MA and RI in the New England region, and OR and WA in the Pacific Northwest. No grants to individuals directly, or for seed money or deficit financing; no loans.
Application information: Contributes only to pre-selected organizations.
Board meeting date(s): Quarterly
Trustee: Mellon Bank, N.A.
Number of staff: 1 part-time support.
EIN: 056016740
Selected grants: The following grants were reported in 2003.
$125,000 to Lyford Cay Foundation, New York, NY.
$35,000 to Seattle Academy of Arts and Sciences, Seattle, WA.
$8,000 to Vashon Allied Arts, Vashon, WA.
$7,000 to Bring Me A Book Foundation, Mountain View, CA.
$5,000 to Boys and Girls Clubs of Boston, Boston, MA.
$5,000 to K C T S/Channel 9, Seattle, WA.
$5,000 to Regis College, Weston, MA.
$3,000 to Reed College, Portland, OR.
$3,000 to University of Rhode Island, Providence, RI.
$3,000 to Vashon Youth and Family Services, Vashon, WA.

8314
Karen & Herbert Lotman Foundation ◇
5 Tower Bridge
300 Barr Harbor Dr., Ste. 600
West Conshohocken, PA 19428-1998
(610) 668-6700
Contact: Herbert Lotman, V.P.

Established in 1982 in PA.
Donors: Shelly Lotman Fisher; Herbert Lotman; Jeffrey Lotman; Karen Lotman; Keystone Foods Corp.
Foundation type: Independent foundation.
Financial data (yr. ended 11/30/05): Assets, $11,088,742 (M); expenditures, $1,359,596; qualifying distributions, $1,359,596; giving activities include $1,288,866 for 32 grants (high: $529,966; low: $1,000).
Purpose and activities: Giving primarily for medical research, with emphasis on ophthalmology.
Fields of interest: Arts; Elementary/secondary education; Health organizations, association; Eye research; Human services; Community development.
Limitations: Giving primarily in the U.S., with emphasis on Philadelphia and West Conshohocken, PA; some giving also in Germany.
Application information:
Initial approach: Letter
Deadline(s): Aug. 31
Officers: Karen Lotman, Pres.; Herbert Lotman, V.P.; Shelly Lotman Fisher, Secy.; Jeffrey Lotman, Treas.
EIN: 222429821

8315
The Lubert Family Foundation, Inc. ◇ ☆
2929 Arch St., 16th Fl.
Philadelphia, PA 19104-2868

Established in 2004 in VI.
Donor: Ira M. Lubert.
Foundation type: Independent foundation.
Financial data (yr. ended 12/31/05): Assets, $5,303,065 (M); gifts received, $1,941,672; expenditures, $456,624; qualifying distributions, $427,537; giving activities include $421,037 for 25 grants (high: $102,500; low: $250).
Fields of interest: Higher education, university; Federated giving programs; Jewish agencies & temples.
Limitations: Applications not accepted. Giving primarily in PA. No grants to individuals.
Application information: Contributes only to pre-selected organizations.
Officers: Ira M. Lubert, Pres.; Kristine Lubert, V.P.; Tricia Billings, Secy.; Jonathan Lubert, Treas.
EIN: 660639002

8316
Lutron Foundation ◇
1506 Pleasant View Rd.
Coopersburg, PA 18036

Established around 1985 in PA.
Donors: Joel Spira; Lutron Electronics Co., Inc.
Foundation type: Independent foundation.
Financial data (yr. ended 12/31/04): Assets, $3,032,815 (M); gifts received, $470,000; expenditures, $484,379; qualifying distributions,

$468,538; giving activities include $468,538 for 129+ grants.
Fields of interest: Arts; Higher education; Human services; Federated giving programs; Jewish federated giving programs.
Limitations: Applications not accepted. Giving primarily in PA; some funding nationally, particularly in NY. No grants to individuals.
Application information: Contributes only to pre-selected organizations.
Trustees: Joel Spira; Ruth Spira.
EIN: 232322928

8317
The Luzerne Foundation ◇
613 Baltimore Dr.
Wilkes Barre, PA 18702 (570) 822-5420
Contact: Charles M. Barber, C.E.O.
FAX: (570) 208-9145; E-mail: info@luzfdn.org; Additional tel.: (877) 589-3386; URL: http://www.luzernefoundation.org

Established in 1995 in PA.
Foundation type: Community foundation.
Financial data (yr. ended 12/31/04): Assets, $7,026,186 (M); gifts received, $1,287,050; expenditures, $827,255; giving activities include $498,570 for 305 grants (high: $25,000; low: $9), and $7,670 for 12 grants to individuals (high: $2,500; low: $400).
Purpose and activities: The mission of the foundation is to cultivate measurable community improvement by: 1) serving as a leader, catalyst, and resource for charitable activities; 2) building and administering a permanent reserve of charitable capital for the community's present needs and future opportunities; and 3) making strategic grants in the areas of education, health and human services, the environment, and the arts.
Fields of interest: Arts; Education; Environment; Health care; Health organizations, association; Recreation; Human services; Community development.
Type of support: Endowments; Program development; Scholarship funds; Technical assistance; Consulting services; Scholarships—to individuals.
Limitations: Giving limited to the Luzerne County, PA, area. No grants for annual operating budgets.
Publications: Application guidelines; Annual report; Financial statement; Grants list; Informational brochure (including application guidelines); Newsletter; Program policy statement.
Application information: Visit foundation Web site for application form and guidelines. Application form required.
Initial approach: Submit application form and attachments
Copies of proposal: 10
Deadline(s): Apr. 17 and Oct. 15
Board meeting date(s): Quarterly
Final notification: June 1 and Dec. 15
Officer and Directors: Charles D. "Rusty" Flack, Jr.,* Chair.; Philip G. Decker,* Vice-Chair.; Charles M. Barber, C.E.O. and Pres.; Msgr. Andrew J. McGowan,* Secy.-Treas.; Charie K. Aponick; Stuart M. Bell; Frank H. Bevevino; John R. Bevevino; Daylene T. Burnside; Joseph F. Butcher; Terrence W. Casey; Pat Donohue, Ph.D.; Louis F. Goeringer; Scott Henry; Thomas L. Kennedy; Joseph E. Kluger; Kenneth J. Krogulski; Melanie M. Lumia; Gertrude C. McGowan; Lori A. Nocito; A. Edward Nork; Joseph L.

Persico; Mary R. Siegel; Rhea P. Simms; John T. Yudichak.
Number of staff: 2 full-time professional.
EIN: 232765498

8318
The M & S Foundation ◇
269 Glenmoor Rd.
Gladwyne, PA   19035

Established in 1996 in PA.
Donor: Alfred W. Martinelli.
Foundation type: Independent foundation.
Financial data (yr. ended 12/31/05): Assets, $1,862,134 (M); gifts received, $547,930; expenditures, $1,156,301; qualifying distributions, $1,121,136; giving activities include $1,120,216 for 52 grants (high: $30,000; low: $400).
Fields of interest: Higher education, university; Education; Hospitals (general); Diabetes; Christian agencies & churches; Protestant agencies & churches.
Limitations: Applications not accepted. Giving primarily in PA. No grants to individuals.
Application information: Contributes only to pre-selected organizations.
Directors: A.W. Martinelli; Aline Martinelli; Christine Martinelli; David Martinelli; Bill Shea; Susan Shea.
EIN: 311478148
Selected grants: The following grants were reported in 2004.
$525,000 to Haverford School, Haverford, PA. 3 grants: $100,000, $400,000, $25,000
$150,000 to Paoli Hospital, Paoli, PA.
$80,000 to Philadelphia Zoo, Philadelphia, PA.
$29,500 to Agnes Irwin School, Rosemont, PA. 4 grants: $20,000, $2,000, $2,500, $5,000
$1,000 to Indian River Hospital Foundation, Vero Beach, FL.

8319
Mach-Smjo Foundation ◇
c/o John Cherian
127 Gatehouse
Coraopolis, PA   15108

Established in 2001 in PA.
Donor: John Cherian.
Foundation type: Independent foundation.
Financial data (yr. ended 12/31/04): Assets, $1,279,948 (M); gifts received, $513,520; expenditures, $413,680; qualifying distributions, $403,776; giving activities include $404,247 for 10 grants (high: $234,516; low: $100).
Fields of interest: Christian agencies & churches.
Limitations: Applications not accepted. No grants to individuals.
Application information: Contributes only to pre-selected organizations.
Officers: John Cherian, Pres. and Treas.; Mariamma Cherian, Secy.
EIN: 251890576

8320
The Magee Foundation ◇ ☆
169 Sunken Heights Ave.
Bloomsburg, PA   17815
Contact: Drue A. Magee, Tr.

Established in 1964 in PA.

Donor: Magee Industrial Enterprises.
Foundation type: Independent foundation.
Financial data (yr. ended 10/31/05): Assets, $2,726,046 (M); gifts received, $603,400; expenditures, $639,438; qualifying distributions, $1,617,161; giving activities include $605,161 for 57 grants (high: $500,000; low: $60).
Purpose and activities: Giving primarily for health organizations, children, youth and social services, and federated giving programs; some funding also for the arts.
Fields of interest: Arts; Health organizations, association; Human services; Children/youth, services; Foundations (private operating); Federated giving programs.
Limitations: Applications not accepted. Giving primarily in PA. No grants to individuals.
Application information: Contributes only to pre-selected organizations.
Trustees: Joanne M. Katerman; Audrey R. Magee; Drue A. Magee; James A. Magee; Barbara Paule.
EIN: 236398294

8321
The Maguire Foundation ◇
8405 Flowertown Rd.
Wyndmoor, PA   19038

Established in 2000 in PA.
Donor: James J. Maguire.
Foundation type: Independent foundation.
Financial data (yr. ended 9/30/05): Assets, $22,369,157 (M); expenditures, $761,105; qualifying distributions, $754,395; giving activities include $748,395 for 38+ grants (high: $475,000).
Fields of interest: Arts; Education; Health organizations, association; Human services; Children/youth, services; Roman Catholic federated giving programs; Roman Catholic agencies & churches.
Limitations: Applications not accepted. Giving primarily in Philadelphia, PA. No grants to individuals.
Application information: Contributes only to pre-selected organizations.
Officers: James J. Maguire, Pres.; Frances M. Maguire, Secy.-Treas.
EIN: 233057805

8322
Samuel P. Mandell Foundation ◇
1818 Market St., Ste. 3220
Philadelphia, PA   19103   (215) 979-3404
Contact: Seymour Mandell, Tr.

Established in 1955 in PA.
Donors: Samuel P. Mandell†; Ida S. Mandell†.
Foundation type: Independent foundation.
Financial data (yr. ended 12/31/05): Assets, $21,507,682 (M); expenditures, $1,269,851; qualifying distributions, $1,133,205; giving activities include $1,027,778 for 252 grants (high: $133,850; low: $20).
Purpose and activities: Emphasis on religious funds, hospitals, medical research, health associations and services, higher and other education, the fine arts and other cultural programs, community affairs, and the environment.
Fields of interest: Media/communications; Visual arts; Museums; Performing arts; Arts; Higher education; Libraries/library science; Education;

Environment; Hospitals (general); Health care; Health organizations, association; Cancer; Medical research, institute; Cancer research; Crime/law enforcement; Human services; Jewish federated giving programs; Religious federated giving programs; Government/public administration; Roman Catholic agencies & churches; Disabilities, people with; Minorities.
Type of support: General/operating support; Continuing support; Annual campaigns; Capital campaigns; Building/renovation; Program development; Professorships; Research.
Limitations: Giving primarily in PA. No support for private operating foundations. No grants to individuals.
Application information: Application form not required.
Copies of proposal: 1
Deadline(s): None
Board meeting date(s): Quarterly
Trustees: Gerald Mandell, M.D.; Judith Mandell; Morton Mandell, M.D.; Ronald Mandell; Seymour Mandell.
Number of staff: 2 part-time support.
EIN: 236274709

8323
Maple Hill Foundation ◇
115 Maple Hill Rd.
Gladwyne, PA   19035   (610) 642-5167
Contact: Ella Warren Miller, Dir.

Established in 1986 in PA.
Donors: Paul F. Miller, Jr.; Ella Warren Miller.
Foundation type: Independent foundation.
Financial data (yr. ended 7/31/05): Assets, $5,190,376 (L); expenditures, $515,350; qualifying distributions, $501,200; giving activities include $501,200 for 50 grants (high: $65,950; low: $800).
Fields of interest: Arts; Higher education; Education; Environment, natural resources; Animals/wildlife, preservation/protection.
Limitations: Giving primarily in Palo Alto CA, MA, NH, and Philadelphia, PA. No grants to individuals.
Application information:
Initial approach: Letter on letterhead
Officers and Directors:* Ella Warren Merrill,* Pres.; Katharine S. Miller,* V.P. and Secy.; Paul F. Miller III,* V.P. and Treas.; Ella Warren Miller; Paul F. Miller, Jr.
EIN: 222751182
Selected grants: The following grants were reported in 2005.
$30,000 to National Constitution Center, Philadelphia, PA.
$30,000 to University of Florida Foundation, Gainesville, FL.
$29,000 to Appalachian Mountain Club, Boston, MA. 2 grants: $25,000, $4,000
$25,000 to CARE, Atlanta, GA.
$25,000 to International House of Philadelphia, Philadelphia, PA.
$12,000 to Squam Lakes Natural Science Center, Holderness, NH.
$10,000 to World Wildlife Fund, DC.
$5,000 to University of Pennsylvania Medical Center, Philadelphia, PA.
$1,200 to W G B H Educational Foundation, Boston, MA.

8324

Maplewood Foundation ◇
c/o PNC Advisors, Charitable Trust Comm.
620 Liberty Ave., 25th Fl.
Pittsburgh, PA 15222-2705
Contact: Susan J. Wagner

Established in 1995 in PA.
Foundation type: Independent foundation.
Financial data (yr. ended 6/30/05): Assets, $16,742,303 (M); expenditures, $1,362,549; qualifying distributions, $1,302,421; giving activities include $1,300,000 for 3 grants (high: $1,000,000; low: $100,000).
Purpose and activities: Giving primarily for higher education; support also for an Episcopal church, an Episcopal diocese and Native American causes.
Fields of interest: Higher education; Protestant agencies & churches.
Limitations: Applications not accepted. Giving primarily in Pittsburgh, PA. No grants to individuals.
Application information: Contributes only to pre-selected organizations.
Trustees: G. William Bissell; PNC Bank, N.A.
EIN: 256502637
Selected grants: The following grants were reported in 2004.
$500,000 to Extra Mile Education Foundation, Pittsburgh, PA. For inner-city endowment fund.
$250,000 to Allegheny Cemetery Historical Association, Pittsburgh, PA. For general support.
$250,000 to Carnegie Institute, Carnegie Museum of Natural History, Pittsburgh, PA.
$250,000 to Protestant Episcopal Cathedral Foundation of the District of Columbia, Washington National Cathedral, DC.
$100,000 to Western Pennsylvania Conservancy, Pittsburgh, PA. For watershed stewardship center.
$50,000 to Gettysburg National Battlefield Museum Foundation, Seven Valleys, PA. For general support.

8325

The Maronda Foundation ◇
11 Timberglen Dr.
Imperial, PA 15126-9267 (724) 695-1200
Contact: William J. Wolf, Exec. Dir.

Established in 1979.
Donor: William J. Wolf.
Foundation type: Operating foundation.
Financial data (yr. ended 12/31/04): Assets, $21,522,077 (M); gifts received, $9,777,778; expenditures, $4,147,912; qualifying distributions, $4,489,906; giving activities include $3,066,459 for 21 grants (high: $453,636; low: $910).
Purpose and activities: Giving primarily to Roman Catholic schools for grade school, high school and college scholarships, which will help financially needy students.
Fields of interest: Elementary/secondary education; Higher education; Roman Catholic agencies & churches; Economically disadvantaged.
Type of support: Scholarship funds.
Limitations: Giving primarily in PA. No grants to individuals.
Application information:
Initial approach: Letter
Deadline(s): None
Officers: Ronald W. Wolf, Secy.; William J. Wolf, Exec. Dir.

Director: Mary G. Wolf.
EIN: 251386730

8326

Thomas Marshall Foundation ◇
2593 Wexford-Bayne Rd., Ste. 206
Sewickley, PA 15143-8608 (724) 940-4100
Contact: Janet Stepp, Exec. Dir.
E-mail: jstepp@tmfound.org

Established in 1994 in PA.
Donor: Thomas Marshall.
Foundation type: Independent foundation.
Financial data (yr. ended 12/31/05): Assets, $8,370,376 (M); expenditures, $762,251; qualifying distributions, $613,450; giving activities include $613,450 for grants.
Purpose and activities: Support for improving the quality of life for children.
Fields of interest: Children, services.
Type of support: General/operating support; Annual campaigns; Capital campaigns.
Limitations: Giving primarily in PA.
Application information: Application form required.
Initial approach: Letter
Copies of proposal: 1
Deadline(s): None
Officer: Janet Stepp, Exec. Dir.
Trustee: Sue Marshall Roberts.
Directors: Theresa Marshall; Thomas Marshall; Virginia Marshall.
Agent: PNC Bank, N.A.
Number of staff: 1 part-time professional.
EIN: 256479933

8327

Maslow Family Foundation, Inc. ☆
30 Hayfield Rd.
Shavertown, PA 18708-9748
Contact: Marilyn J. O'Boyle, Exec. Dir.

Established in 1994 in PA.
Donor: Richard Maslow.
Foundation type: Independent foundation.
Financial data (yr. ended 12/31/05): Assets, $8,771,292 (M); gifts received, $155,264; expenditures, $396,720; qualifying distributions, $385,550; giving activities include $385,550 for grants.
Purpose and activities: Giving for the arts, the environment, the special needs of children, and to improve the overall quality of life.
Fields of interest: Arts; Education; Environment; Children, services.
Type of support: Continuing support; Capital campaigns; Building/renovation; Endowments; Program development; Seed money; Scholarship funds; Matching/challenge support.
Limitations: Giving primarily in the greater Wyoming Valley area, in Luzerne County, PA. No grants to individuals.
Application information: Application form not required.
Initial approach: Letter
Deadline(s): Aug. 1
Board meeting date(s): May, July and Sept.
Final notification: 3 months
Trustees: Jennifer Maslow Holtzman; Melanie Maslow Lumia; Allison Maslow; Douglas Maslow; Richard Maslow; Hillary Maslow Naud; Eugene Roth.

Number of staff: 1 part-time support.
EIN: 232791676
Selected grants: The following grants were reported in 2003.
$35,000 to Wilkes University, Wilkes Barre, PA. 2 grants: $20,000 (For Frances and Louis Maslow Scholarship Fund), $15,000 (For Urban Studies Center).
$18,500 to Everhart Museum, Scranton, PA.
$10,000 to Back Mountain Memorial Library Association, Dallas, PA.
$10,000 to F. M. Kirby Center for the Performing Arts, Wilkes Barre, PA.
$10,000 to Jewish Federation of Greater Wilkes-Barre, Wilkes Barre, PA.
$10,000 to Osterhout Free Library, Wilkes Barre, PA.
$5,000 to Saint Josephs Center, Scranton, PA.
$3,206 to Marine Toys for Tots Foundation, Quantico, VA.
$3,000 to Cultural Council of Luzerne County, Wilkes Barre, PA.

8328

Massey Charitable Trust
1370 Washington Pike, Ste. 306
Bridgeville, PA 15017
Contact: Robert M. Connolly, Exec. Dir.

Established in 1968 in PA.
Donors: H.B. Massey†; Doris J. Massey†.
Foundation type: Independent foundation.
Financial data (yr. ended 12/31/05): Assets, $40,386,706 (M); expenditures, $1,939,651; qualifying distributions, $2,027,419; giving activities include $1,878,000 for 123 grants (high: $125,000; low: $100).
Fields of interest: Performing arts; Arts; Higher education; Health care; Health organizations, association; Medical research, institute; Human services; Children/youth, services.
Limitations: Giving primarily in Allegheny County and western PA. No support for political organizations. No grants to individuals.
Application information: Applicants should submit Common Grant Application of Grantmakers of Western Pennsylvania. Application form required.
Initial approach: Letter or telephone
Copies of proposal: 1
Deadline(s): None
Board meeting date(s): May and Sept.
Final notification: Up to 1 year
Officer: Robert M. Connolly, Exec. Dir.
Trustees: Walter J. Carroll; Daniel B. Carroll; Robert M. Entwisle III; Joe B. Massey.
Number of staff: 1 full-time professional.
EIN: 237007897
Selected grants: The following grants were reported in 2005.
$125,000 to Robert Morris University, Pittsburgh, PA.
$75,000 to Atlanta Symphony Orchestra, Atlanta, GA.
$75,000 to Pittsburgh Leadership Foundation, Pittsburgh, PA.
$50,000 to Belmont University, Nashville, TN.
$50,000 to Young Life, Colorado Springs, CO.
$30,000 to Achieva, Pittsburgh, PA.
$15,000 to Catholic Youth Association of Pittsburgh, Pittsburgh, PA.
$10,000 to Greater Pittsburgh Literacy Council, Pittsburgh, PA.
$10,000 to National Black Arts Festival, Atlanta, GA.

$10,000 to YMCA of McKeesport, McKeesport, PA.

8329

McCormick Family Foundation ◇

21 E. Market St.
York, PA 17401-1205
Application address: P.O. Box 2961, Harrisburg, PA 17105

Established in 2003 in PA.
Foundation type: Independent foundation.
Financial data (yr. ended 12/31/05): Assets, $47 (M); gifts received, $605,600; expenditures, $606,127; qualifying distributions, $585,834; giving activities include $585,834 for 50 grants (high: $50,000; low: $1,000).
Fields of interest: Museums (history); Performing arts; Performing arts, music; Education; Human services.
Limitations: Giving primarily in Dauphine, Lebanon, Cumberland, Perry, Lancaster and York counties, PA. No grants to individuals.
Application information:
Initial approach: Letter
Deadline(s): None
Officers: Rick A. Gold, Pres.; Paul B. Shannon, Treas.; Larry A. Hartman, Exec. Dir.
EIN: 300166827

8330

Anne McCormick Trust ◇

c/o M&T Bank, Trust Div.
21 E. Market St., M/C 402-130
York, PA 17401 (717) 255-2045
Contact: Larry A. Hartman, Trust Off., M&T Bank

Donor: Anne McCormick†.
Foundation type: Independent foundation.
Financial data (yr. ended 12/13/05): Assets, $7,964,708 (M); expenditures, $446,780; qualifying distributions, $397,100; giving activities include $39,700 for 1 grant.
Fields of interest: Foundations (public).
Limitations: Giving limited to Cumberland, Dauphin, Franklin, and Perry counties, PA. No grants to individuals.
Application information:
Initial approach: Proposal
Deadline(s): None
Trustee: M&T Bank.
EIN: 236471389

8331

John R. McCune Charitable Trust ▼ ◇

6 PPG Pl., Ste. 750
Pittsburgh, PA 15222 (412) 644-7796
Contact: James M. Edwards, Exec. Dir.

Established in 1972 in PA.
Donor: John R. McCune IV†.
Foundation type: Independent foundation.
Financial data (yr. ended 11/30/04): Assets, $133,777,204 (M); expenditures, $6,897,787; qualifying distributions, $6,706,256; giving activities include $6,400,400 for 145 grants (high: $225,000; low: $5,000; average: $10,000–$100,000).
Purpose and activities: Emphasis on secondary and higher education, health services, church-related institutions, and social services.

Fields of interest: Secondary school/education; Higher education; Health care; Human services; Protestant agencies & churches; Aging.
Type of support: General/operating support; Continuing support; Capital campaigns; Building/renovation; Endowments; Seed money.
Limitations: Giving primarily in southwestern PA.
Publications: Application guidelines.
Application information: Please include an annual report with the proposal. Application form not required.
Initial approach: Brief proposal
Copies of proposal: 1
Deadline(s): Apr. 1
Board meeting date(s): Annually
Final notification: Nov.
Officer: James M. Edwards, Exec. Dir.
Trustee: National City Bank.
Number of staff: 1 full-time professional; 1 part-time professional.
EIN: 256160722
Selected grants: The following grants were reported in 2004.
$225,000 to Colorado State University, Fort Collins, CO. For general support.
$147,000 to Casady School, Oklahoma City, OK. For general support.
$125,000 to Community Homes for Adults, Dallas, TX. For general support.
$125,000 to Educational Foundation for Highland Park Independent School District, Dallas, TX. For general support.
$125,000 to Make-A-Wish Foundation of North Texas, Irving, TX. For general support.
$122,000 to Loomis Chaffee School, Windsor, CT. For general support.
$120,000 to Wednesdays Child Benefit Corporation, Dallas, TX. For general support.
$112,000 to Klingberg Family Centers, New Britain, CT. For general support.
$108,000 to Barrington Christian Academy, Barrington, RI. For general support.
$103,800 to Innovative Media Access Institute, Norman, OK. For general support.

8332

McCune Foundation ▼ ◇

750 6 PPG Pl.
Pittsburgh, PA 15222 (412) 644-8779
Contact: Henry S. Beukema, Exec. Dir.
FAX: (412) 644-8059; *E-mail:* info@mccune.org;
URL: http://www.mccune.org

Established in 1979 in PA.
Donor: Charles L. McCune†.
Foundation type: Independent foundation.
Financial data (yr. ended 9/30/05): Assets, $585,046,089 (M); expenditures, $30,369,927; qualifying distributions, $29,036,963; giving activities include $27,309,409 for 194 grants (high: $2,000,000; low: $1,000; average: $50,000–$500,000).
Purpose and activities: Following the donor's granting interests, the foundation emphasizes two major program areas: independent higher education and human services. The foundation also recognizes the importance of civic, cultural, and community-based organizations that are working to remedy the effects of economic dislocation, while addressing future issues. The foundation is particularly interested in collaborative approaches among groups addressing strategic regional issues

and bringing innovative approaches to traditional challenges.
Fields of interest: Museums; Performing arts; Historic preservation/historical societies; Arts; Higher education; Adult education—literacy, basic skills & GED; Libraries/library science; Health care; Medical research, institute; Employment; Housing/shelter, development; Youth development, services; Human services; Economic development; Urban/community development.
Type of support: Employee matching gifts; Income development; Management development/capacity building; Capital campaigns; Building/renovation; Equipment; Endowments; Program development; Seed money; Technical assistance; Program-related investments/loans.
Limitations: Giving primarily in southwestern PA, with emphasis on the Pittsburgh area. No grants to individuals, or for general operating support.
Publications: Application guidelines; Annual report (including application guidelines).
Application information: Applicants are encouraged to wait at least 3 years after receiving a grant before reapplying. Funding is concentrated in Southwestern PA, mainly the Pittsburgh area. Unsolicited proposals from outside this region are not accepted. Application form required.
Initial approach: Inquiry letter (2 - 3 pages)
Copies of proposal: 1
Deadline(s): None
Board meeting date(s): Mar., June, Sept., and Dec.
Final notification: Minimum 90 days
Officers and Distribution Committee:* James M. Edwards,* Chair.; Henry S. Beukema, Exec. Dir.; Richard D. Edwards,* Chair. Emeritus; Michael M. Edwards; John R. McCune VI.
Trustee: National City Bank.
Number of staff: 4 full-time professional; 2 full-time support.
EIN: 256210269
Selected grants: The following grants were reported in 2005.
$2,000,000 to Pittsburgh Life Sciences Greenhouse, Pittsburgh, PA. To continue and expand biotechnology initiative.
$1,500,000 to Phipps Conservatory and Botanical Gardens, Pittsburgh, PA. For Campaign 2000 Bringing Phipps into Full Flower.
$750,000 to Pittsburgh Partnership for Neighborhood Development, Pittsburgh, PA. For operating support.
$500,000 to Chartiers Valley Partnership, Carnegie, PA. For capital campaign.
$450,000 to Carnegie Institute, Carnegie Museums of Pittsburgh, Pittsburgh, PA. For Dinosaurs in Their World.
$400,000 to Pittsburgh Project, Pittsburgh, PA. For Leaving Footprints expansion campaign.
$390,000 to Hosanna House, Wilkinsburg, PA. For master plan for Sherwood Property and Phase 1 Auditorium.
$150,000 to Lebanese American University, New York, NY. For Gibran Library.
$100,000 to Booker T. Washington High School for the Performing and Visual Arts, The Advisory Board, Dallas, TX. For Arts Magnet Building campaign.
$100,000 to Vietnam Veterans Leadership Program of Western Pennsylvania, Pittsburgh, PA. For housing and urban development programs.

8333
McDonald's Kid's Charities ✧
300 Barr Harbor Dr., Ste. 600
West Conshohocken, PA 19428-2998
(610) 668-6700

Donors: McDonald's Corp.; Richard McCoy; Fibers Nemours; JPMorgan Chase & Co.; HJH Enterprises.
Foundation type: Company-sponsored foundation.
Financial data (yr. ended 7/31/05): Assets, $2,081,358 (M); gifts received, $127,994; expenditures, $8,047,619; qualifying distributions, $1,500,000; giving activities include $1,500,000 for 19+ grants (high: $864,143), and $5,532,959 for foundation-administered programs.
Purpose and activities: The foundation operates the annual McDonald's LPGA Championship golf tournament and supports organizations involved with juvenile diabetes and human services.
Fields of interest: Diabetes; Boys & girls clubs; Boy scouts; Children/youth, services; Human services.
Type of support: Program development; Research.
Limitations: Applications not accepted. Giving primarily in DE, Oak Brook, IL, and PA. No grants to individuals.
Application information: Contributes only to pre-selected organizations.
Officers and Directors: Chris Gabriel,* Co-Chair.; Bill Roberson,* Co-Chair.; Stanley Fronczkowski, Treas.; Alice Miller,* Exec. Dir.
EIN: 232148498
Selected grants: The following grants were reported in 2003.
$1,293,524 to Ronald McDonald House Charities, Oak Brook, IL. For program support.
$150,000 to Juvenile Diabetes Research Foundation International, Philadelphia, PA. For program support.
$130,000 to Ronald McDonald House, Philadelphia, Philadelphia, PA. For program support.
$66,839 to Jeffrey Jay Weinberg Memorial Foundation, Blue Bell, PA. For program support.
$50,000 to Boy Scouts of America, Del-Mar-Va Council, Wilmington, DE. For program support.
$50,000 to Ronald McDonald House of Southern New Jersey, Camden, NJ. For program support.
$43,000 to LPGA Urban Youth Golf Program, Rockland, PA. For program support.
$40,000 to Mary Campbell Center, Wilmington, DE. For program support.
$14,000 to Boy Scouts of America, Chester County Council, West Chester, PA. For program support.
$10,000 to American Red Cross, Southeastern Pennsylvania Chapter, Philadelphia, PA. For program support.

8334
McFeely-Rogers Foundation
1110 Ligonier St., Ste. 300
P.O. Box 110
Latrobe, PA 15650-0110 (724) 537-5588
Contact: James R. Okonak, Exec. Dir.

Incorporated in 1953 in PA.
Donors: James H. Rogers†; Nancy K. McFeely†; Nancy M. Rogers†; Fred M. Rogers†.
Foundation type: Independent foundation.
Financial data (yr. ended 12/31/05): Assets, $21,489,424 (M); expenditures, $1,235,963; qualifying distributions, $935,571; giving activities include $754,110 for 91 grants (high: $85,000; low: $50; average: $1,000–$10,000).

Purpose and activities: Support mainly to local educational and charitable institutions, including civic affairs, community development, recreation programs, Protestant giving, cultural programs, and hospitals.
Fields of interest: Arts; Education; Hospitals (general); Recreation; Human services; Community development; Protestant agencies & churches.
Type of support: General/operating support; Continuing support; Annual campaigns; Capital campaigns; Building/renovation; Equipment; Endowments; Debt reduction; Emergency funds; Program development; Seed money; Scholarship funds; Matching/challenge support.
Limitations: Giving primarily in the Latrobe, PA, area, with some giving in Pittsburgh, PA. No support for political organizations. No grants to individuals, or for scholarships, land acquisition, special projects, research, publications, or conferences; no loans.
Publications: Application guidelines; Program policy statement.
Application information: Application form not required.
  Initial approach: Letter
  Copies of proposal: 2
  Deadline(s): May 1 and Nov. 1
  Board meeting date(s): June and Nov.
  Final notification: 2 weeks after board meeting
Officers and Trustees: Nancy R. Crozier,* Pres.; James R. Okonak,* Secy. and Exec. Dir.; Catherine G. Keefe, Treas.; William P. Barker; Daniel G. Crozier, Jr.; James Brooks Crozier; Douglas R. Nowicki; James B. Rogers; John F. Rogers.
Number of staff: 2 full-time professional.
EIN: 251120947
Selected grants: The following grants were reported in 2004.
$201,600 to Latrobe Foundation, Latrobe, PA.
$87,250 to Saint Vincent College, Latrobe, PA.
$51,300 to Greater Latrobe School District, Latrobe, PA.
$40,000 to American Red Cross, Latrobe, PA.
$30,000 to Pine Springs Camp, Jennerstown, PA.
$30,000 to Saint Vincent Archabbey, Latrobe, PA.
$25,000 to Pittsburgh Youth Symphony Orchestra Association, Pittsburgh, PA.
$25,000 to Westmoreland Museum of American Art, Greensburg, PA.
$1,000 to Salvation Army, Latrobe, PA.
$1,000 to Waynesburg College, Waynesburg, PA.

8335
Gerald E. McGinnis Charitable Foundation ✧
3585 Hills Church Rd.
Export, PA 15632

Established in 1991 in PA.
Donor: Gerald E. McGinnis.
Foundation type: Independent foundation.
Financial data (yr. ended 12/31/04): Assets, $2,169,524 (M); expenditures, $545,158; qualifying distributions, $530,742; giving activities include $530,742 for 5 grants (high: $261,550; low: $10,000).
Fields of interest: Higher education; Recreation, camps.
Limitations: Applications not accepted. Giving primarily in PA. No grants to individuals.
Application information: Contributes only to pre-selected organizations.

Trustee: Gerald E. McGinnis.
EIN: 251671236
Selected grants: The following grants were reported in 2003.
$1,010,505 to Boy Scouts of America, Greater Pittsburgh Council, Pittsburgh, PA. For capital campaign.
$304,960 to Point Park University, Pittsburgh, PA. For general support.
$7,500 to University of Pittsburgh, Pittsburgh, PA.

8336
Lalitta Nash McKaig Foundation ✧
c/o PNC Advisors
620 Liberty Ave.
Pittsburgh, PA 15222-2705 (412) 762-7941
Contact: Robert Dunlap
Application address (Cumberland office): 21 Prospect Sq., Cumberland, MD, 21502, tel.: (301) 777-1515

Established in 1973 in PA.
Foundation type: Independent foundation.
Financial data (yr. ended 9/30/05): Assets, $11,508,365 (M); expenditures, $796,121; qualifying distributions, $766,124; giving activities include $721,170 for 406 grants to individuals.
Fields of interest: Higher education; Higher education, university; Scholarships/financial aid.
Type of support: Scholarships—to individuals.
Limitations: Giving limited to residents who graduated from high schools in Allegany and Garrett counties, MD, Bedford and Somerset counties, PA; and Mineral and Hampshire counties, WV.
Publications: Application guidelines.
Application information: Application forms can be obtained from high school guidance offices in the Cumberland, MD, area, financial aid offices of Frostburg State College and Allegany Community College, the foundation's office in Cumberland, MD, or PNC Bank, N.A. Application form required.
  Deadline(s): May 30
  Board meeting date(s): June
Trustee: PNC Bank, N.A.
EIN: 256071908

8337
Katherine Mabis McKenna Foundation, Inc. ✧
P.O. Box 186
Latrobe, PA 15650 (724) 537-6900
Contact: Linda McKenna Boxx, Chair.

Incorporated in 1969 in PA.
Donor: Katherine M. McKenna†.
Foundation type: Independent foundation.
Financial data (yr. ended 12/31/04): Assets, $73,797,303 (M); expenditures, $3,712,786; qualifying distributions, $3,326,481; giving activities include $3,148,247 for 76 grants (high: $500,000; low: $500; average: $1,000–$50,000).
Purpose and activities: Giving primarily for education, the arts and cultural organizations, philanthropy, and human services. Some support also for environmental organizations and community development.
Fields of interest: Arts; Higher education; Environment, natural resources.
Type of support: General/operating support; Annual campaigns; Capital campaigns; Building/

renovation; Equipment; Land acquisition; Endowments; Program development; Seed money.
Limitations: Giving primarily in Westmoreland County, PA. No grants to individuals; no loans.
Publications: Grants list; Program policy statement.
Application information: Application form not required.
  Initial approach: Letter
  Copies of proposal: 1
  Deadline(s): Submit proposal preferably in Jan. through July; deadline Sept. 1
  Board meeting date(s): Spring and fall
  Final notification: 3 to 6 months
Officers and Directors:* Linda McKenna Boxx,* Chair.; Wilma F. McKenna,* Vice-Chair.; Zan McKenna Rich,* Secy.; T. William Boxx, Treas.
Trustee: Mellon Bank, N.A.
Number of staff: 1 full-time professional.
EIN: 237042752
Selected grants: The following grants were reported in 2004.
$500,000 to Saint Vincent College, Latrobe, PA. For Alex G. McKenna School of Business, Economics and Government.
$200,000 to Gettysburg National Battlefield Museum Foundation, Seven Valleys, PA. For capital campaign.
$90,000 to Westmoreland Trust, Greensburg, PA. For general operating support of Greenburg Garden and Civic Center.
$85,000 to YWCA of Westmoreland County, Greensburg, PA. 2 grants: $25,000 (For general operating support), $60,000 (For capital campaign for Thrift Shop).
$60,000 to Latrobe Foundation, Latrobe, PA. For new field lighting at Latrobe Little League.
$25,000 to Greensburg Central Catholic High School, Greensburg, PA. For capital campaign.
$25,000 to Pennsylvania Parks and Forests, Friends of, Latrobe, PA. For general operating support.
$20,000 to Wild Resource Conservation Fund, Harrisburg, PA. For administrative work on Flight 93 Site.
$15,000 to University of Pittsburgh at Greensburg Foundation, Greensburg, PA. For Route 30 Corridor Project as part of Smart Growth Partnership of Westmoreland County.

8338
Philip M. McKenna Foundation, Inc.
P.O. Box 186
Latrobe, PA 15650 (724) 537-6900
Contact: T. William Boxx, Chair.

Incorporated in 1967 in PA.
Donor: Philip M. McKenna†.
Foundation type: Independent foundation.
Financial data (yr. ended 12/31/04): Assets, $15,544,290 (M); expenditures, $1,225,923; qualifying distributions, $1,158,385; giving activities include $992,275 for 28 grants (high: $300,000; low: $1,000).
Purpose and activities: Support for public policy research, economic education, and other public affairs programs; grants for higher education generally to specified institutions of significance to the donor or in the foundation's local area or for public policy; support locally for community and social service programs.
Fields of interest: Higher education; Economics; Public policy, research.
Limitations: Giving primarily in the Latrobe, PA, area for community and civic programs; grants to PA and

national organizations for public policy research, economic education and public affairs. No grants to individuals, or for matching gifts; no loans.
Publications: Grants list; Program policy statement.
Application information: Application form not required.
  Initial approach: Letter
  Copies of proposal: 1
  Deadline(s): Submit proposal by Apr. 1 for spring meeting; Oct. 1 for fall meeting
  Board meeting date(s): Apr. and Oct.
  Final notification: 3 to 6 months
Officers and Directors:* T. William Boxx,* Chair.; Charles R. Kesler,* Vice-Chair.; Norbert J. Pail,* Secy.; Jonathan C. Hall; Zan M. Rich.
Trustee Bank: Mellon Bank, N.A.
Number of staff: 1 full-time professional.
EIN: 256082635
Selected grants: The following grants were reported in 2003.
$1,520,000 to Saint Vincent College, Latrobe, PA. 2 grants: $1,500,000 to Alex G. McKenna School of Business, Economics, and Government, $20,000 to Center for Economic and Policy Education (For George Washington Fellowship Program, payable over 2 years).
$95,000 to Commonwealth Foundation for Public Policy Alternatives, Harrisburg, PA. For general operating support.
$35,000 to Capital Research Center, DC. For general operating support.
$15,050 to Foundation for Free Enterprise Education, Erie, PA. For scholarships.
$15,000 to Allegheny Institute for Public Policy, Pittsburgh, PA. For general operating support.
$15,000 to Americans for Prosperity Foundation, DC. For general operating support.
$10,000 to Lincoln Institute of Public Opinion Research, Harrisburg, PA. For general operating support.
$10,000 to National Center for Policy Analysis, Dallas, TX. For general operating support.
$10,000 to Social Philosophy and Policy Foundation, Bowling Green, OH. For visiting scholars and doctoral programs.

8339
William V. and Catherine A. McKinney Charitable Foundation ◇
c/o National City Bank
National City Ctr.
20 Stanwix St.
Pittsburgh, PA 15222-1323 (412) 644-8332
Contact: William M. Schmidt, Sr. V.P., National City Bank

Established in 1990 in PA.
Donor: Catherine A. McKinney†.
Foundation type: Independent foundation.
Financial data (yr. ended 3/31/05): Assets, $11,089,561 (M); expenditures, $877,298; qualifying distributions, $821,405; giving activities include $795,000 for 80 grants (high: $35,000; low: $5,000).
Purpose and activities: Giving limited to organizations in western PA whose activities aid the elderly, disadvantaged youth and/or the disabled and support the arts.
Fields of interest: Performing arts; Children/youth, services; Aging, centers/services; Aging; Disabilities, people with.

Type of support: General/operating support; Capital campaigns; Endowments; Program development; Matching/challenge support.
Limitations: Giving limited to western PA. No grants to individuals.
Application information: Use Grantmakers of Western Pennsylvania Common Grant Application form. Application form required.
  Initial approach: Letter
  Copies of proposal: 3
  Deadline(s): Jan., July, and Oct.
  Board meeting date(s): 3 times per year
  Final notification: Affirmative responses only
Trustee: National City Bank.
EIN: 251641619

8340
The McLean Contributionship
945 Haverford Rd., Ste. A
Bryn Mawr, PA 19010 (610) 527-6330
Contact: Sandra L. McLean, Exec. Dir.
FAX: (610) 527-9733; URL: http:// foundationcenter.org/grantmaker/mclean/

Trust established in 1951 in PA.
Donors: William L. McLean, Jr.†; Robert McLean†; William L. McLean III; William Clarke Mason†; William L. McLean IV; Sandra McLean; Lisa McLean; Elizabeth P. McLean; Elizabeth R. McLean; Wendy McLean; Bulletin Co.; Independent Publications, Inc.; Independence Communications, Inc.
Foundation type: Independent foundation.
Financial data (yr. ended 12/31/05): Assets, $53,033,830 (M); gifts received, $109,743; expenditures, $3,229,329; qualifying distributions, $2,881,578; giving activities include $2,789,156 for 100 grants (high: $137,500; low: $1,000).
Purpose and activities: Supports understanding and preservation of the environment, compassionate and cost effective health care and improving the quality of life through capital and other projects. Trustees prefer special projects rather than continuing programs and focus on capital projects: bricks and mortar, endowment, or will provide seed money for purposes falling within the contributorship's guidelines.
Fields of interest: Museums; Performing arts; Historic preservation/historical societies; Libraries/library science; Education; Environment, natural resources; Environmental education; Hospitals (general); Nursing home/convalescent facility; Health care, home services; Medical research, institute; Youth development, services; Children/youth, services; Aging, centers/services.
Type of support: Capital campaigns; Building/renovation; Equipment; Land acquisition; Endowments; Program development; Conferences/seminars; Publication; Seed money; Internship funds; Scholarship funds.
Limitations: Giving primarily in the greater Philadelphia, PA, area; some funding also in Nashua, NH, Du Bois, PA and in central FL. No grants to individuals.
Publications: Application guidelines; Grants list.
Application information: Accepts Delaware Valley Grantmakers Common Grant Application Form, which can be downloaded via foundation Web site. See foundation Web site for application guidelines and procedures. Application form not required.
  Initial approach: Letter
  Copies of proposal: 1
  Deadline(s): 6 weeks prior to board meeting

Board meeting date(s): Quarterly, Mar., June, Sept. and Dec.

Final notification: 2 weeks after board meeting

Officers and Trustees: * William L. McLean III,* Chair.; William L. McLean IV,* Vice-Chair.; Sandra L. McLean, Secy. and Exec. Dir.; Charles E. Catherwood, Treas.; Jean G. Bodine; Joseph K. Gordon; Carolyn M. Raymond.

Advisory Committee: Leila Gordon Dyer; Hunter R. Gordon.

Number of staff: None.

EIN: 236396940

Selected grants: The following grants were reported in 2005.

$137,500 to Lankenau Hospital Foundation, Wynnewood, PA. Toward purchase of da Vinci Surgical System, first surgical robot to be approved by U.S. Food and Drug Administration for performing surgery.

$100,000 to American Philosophical Society, Philadelphia, PA. Toward construction of new Digital Suite of Library Hall.

$100,000 to John J. Tyler Arboretum, Media, PA. Toward endowment to fund part-time Plant Recorder on staff.

$75,000 to YMCA, Upper Main Line, Berwyn, PA. Toward Phase 1 of long range master plan to expand and modernize portion of present facilities.

$50,000 to Bryn Mawr Theater Film Institute, Bryn Mawr, PA. Toward renovation.

$50,000 to Harcum College, Bryn Mawr, PA. Toward equipment needed for expanded nursing program lab.

$50,000 to Tredyffrin Public Library, Strafford, PA. Toward building a state of the art computer lab.

$48,600 to Hawk Mountain Sanctuary Association, Kempton, PA. Toward Raptor Online Learning Center.

$15,000 to Park Place Behavioral Health Care, Kissimmee, FL. Toward purchase of new facility, Children's Home, to house additional children needing behavioral health care.

$10,000 to Police Athletic League, Nashua, Nashua, NH. For outfitting Nashua Police Department Bomb Squad emergency response and command vehicle.

8341
Glen and Diane Meakem Foundation, Inc. ◇

603 Beaver St., Ste. 201
Sewickley, PA 15143

Established in 2000 in PA.

Donors: Glen T. Meakem; Diane B. Meakem; Snowline Partners, LP.

Foundation type: Independent foundation.

Financial data (yr. ended 12/31/05): Assets, $2,043,885 (M); gifts received, $183,810; expenditures, $520,784; qualifying distributions, $401,181; giving activities include $401,181 for 58 grants (high: $80,000; low: $100).

Purpose and activities: Giving primarily for education, as well as for the arts, particularly to museums, including a science center; some funding also for Christian ministries, churches, and schools, and children, youth, and social services, including a women's shelter.

Fields of interest: Museums (history); Museums (science/technology); Performing arts; Historic preservation/historical societies; Arts; Elementary/ secondary education; Higher education; Health

organizations, association; Human services; Children/youth, services; Family services; Community development; Federated giving programs; Christian agencies & churches.

Limitations: Applications not accepted. Giving primarily in PA. No grants to individuals.

Application information: Contributes only to pre-selected organizations.

Officers: Glen T. Meakem, Pres.; Diane B. Meakem, V.P.; Raymond P. Parker, Secy.-Treas.

EIN: 251877307

8342
The Benjamin and Mary Siddons Measey Foundation

225 N. Olive St.
P.O. Box 258
Media, PA 19063

Contact: James C. Brennan, Mgr.

Trust established in 1958 in PA.

Donor: William Maul Measey†.

Foundation type: Independent foundation.

Financial data (yr. ended 12/31/05): Assets, $55,490,258 (M); expenditures, $3,776,146; qualifying distributions, $3,660,844; giving activities include $3,624,500 for grants.

Purpose and activities: Grants to medical schools in Philadelphia for scholarships and fellowships.

Fields of interest: Medical school/education.

Type of support: Fellowships; Scholarship funds.

Limitations: Giving limited to Philadelphia, PA. No grants to individuals.

Publications: Informational brochure.

Application information: Accepts applications only for medical institutions. Scholarship applications should be made to the dean of the particular medical school. Application form not required.

Copies of proposal: 6

Deadline(s): 1 month prior to meeting

Board meeting date(s): 2nd Tues. in Mar., June, Sept., and Dec.

Final notification: 1 month following meeting

Officers: Truman G. Schnabel, M.D., Chair.; Matthew S. Donaldson, Jr., Secy.

Board of Managers: Clyde F. Barker, M.D.; Marshall E. Blume, Ph.D.; James C. Brennan; Stanley Goldfarb, M.D.

Number of staff: 1 part-time support.

EIN: 236298781

8343
The Medleycott Family Foundation ◇ ☆

c/o Leon W. Marchetti
P.O. Box 189
Southampton, PA 18966

Donor: Superpac, Inc.

Foundation type: Independent foundation.

Financial data (yr. ended 12/31/05): Assets, $691,563 (M); expenditures, $669,269; qualifying distributions, $669,027; giving activities include $669,000 for 20 grants (high: $70,000; low: $10,000; average: $25,000–$50,000).

Fields of interest: Hospitals (general); Health care; Christian agencies & churches.

Limitations: Applications not accepted. Giving primarily in PA. No grants to individuals.

Application information: Contributes only to pre-selected organizations.

Trustees: Leon Marchetti; Alice E. Medleycott; Mary E. Medleycott.

EIN: 743101031

8344
R. K. Mellon Family Foundation ◇

P.O. Box 690
Ligonier, PA 15658-0690   (724) 238-5269

Contact: Michael Watson, Dir.

Incorporated in PA in 1978 through consolidation of Landfall, Loyalhanna, Rachelwood, and Cassandra Mellon Henderson foundations.

Donors: Seward Prosser Mellon; Richard P. Mellon; Constance B. Mellon†; Cassandra M. Milbury.

Foundation type: Independent foundation.

Financial data (yr. ended 12/31/04): Assets, $39,301,960 (M); expenditures, $1,815,173; qualifying distributions, $1,671,518; giving activities include $1,469,500 for 75 grants (high: $190,000; low: $500).

Purpose and activities: Grants largely for education, health care, social services, and conservation programs.

Fields of interest: Education; Environment, natural resources; Health care; Human services; Public affairs.

Type of support: General/operating support; Continuing support; Annual campaigns; Capital campaigns; Building/renovation; Equipment; Program development; Seed money; Research.

Limitations: Giving primarily in western PA. No grants to individuals, or for endowment funds, scholarships, fellowships, or matching gifts; no loans.

Publications: Informational brochure (including application guidelines).

Application information: Application form required.

Initial approach: Proposal

Copies of proposal: 1

Deadline(s): Submit proposal preferably Jan. through Mar. or July through Sept.; deadlines Apr. 1 and Oct. 1

Board meeting date(s): June and Dec.

Final notification: 1 to 6 months

Officers and Trustees: * Richard P. Mellon,* Chair.; Scott D. Izzo, Secy.; Robert B. Burr, Jr.,* Treas.; John Turcik, Cont.; Michael Watson,* Dir.; Alison M. Byers; Catharine Mellon Cathey; Richard A. Mellon; Seward Prosser Mellon.

Number of staff: 4 part-time professional; 9 part-time support.

EIN: 251356145

Selected grants: The following grants were reported in 2004.

$190,000 to Valley School of Ligonier, Ligonier, PA.

$75,000 to University of Pittsburgh, Pittsburgh, PA.

$25,000 to Brooklyn Childrens Museum, Brooklyn, NY.

$25,000 to Penikese Island School, Woods Hole, MA.

$25,000 to Quissett Harbor Preservation Trust, Falmouth, MA.

$21,000 to Ruffed Grouse Society, Coraopolis, PA. 2 grants: $9,000, $12,000

$20,000 to Stroud Water Research Center, Avondale, PA.

$15,000 to Gallmann Memorial Foundation, New York, NY.

$10,000 to Pennsylvania Environmental Council, Harrisburg, PA.

8345

Mellon Financial Corporation Fund

(formerly Mellon Financial Corporation Foundation)
1 Mellon Ctr., Ste. 1830
Pittsburgh, PA 15258-0001
Contact: James P. McDonald, Pres.
URL: http://www.mellon.com/aboutmellon/
communityinvolvement/
charitablegivingprogram.html

Established in 1974 in PA.
Donors: Mellon Bank Corp.; Mellon Financial Corp.
Foundation type: Company-sponsored foundation.
Financial data (yr. ended 12/31/05): Assets,
$57,343,856 (M); gifts received, $84,550;
expenditures, $3,728,392; qualifying distributions,
$3,712,901; giving activities include $3,352,771
for 128 grants, and $360,130 for 1,430 employee
matching gifts.
Purpose and activities: The fund supports
organizations involved with arts and culture,
education, human services, and economic
development.
Fields of interest: Arts; Education; Human services;
Economic development.
Type of support: General/operating support;
Building/renovation; Employee matching gifts.
Limitations: Giving primarily in areas of company
operations, with emphasis on Boston, MA, and
Philadelphia and Pittsburgh, PA. No support for
fraternal or religious organizations, United Way
agencies, or national organizations. No grants to
individuals, or for emergency needs, debt reduction,
endowments, equipment, land acquisition,
scholarships, fellowships, research, publications,
travel, conferences, continuing support, or
specialized health campaigns or other highly
specialized projects with little or no positive impact
on communities; no loans.
Publications: Corporate giving report (including
application guidelines).
Application information: Application form not
required.
  Initial approach: Letter of inquiry
  Copies of proposal: 1
  Deadline(s): None
  Board meeting date(s): Quarterly
  Final notification: 2 months
Officers and Trustees: * Rose M. Gabbianelli,*
Chair.; James P. McDonald,* Pres.; Steven G.
Elliott,* Treas.; Walter R. Day III; Carl Krasik; David
B. Kutch; David F. Lamere; James P. Palermo; Lisa
B. Peters.
Number of staff: 2 part-time professional; 1
part-time support.
EIN: 237423500
Selected grants: The following grants were reported
in 2004.
$200,000 to Allegheny Conference on Community
  Development, Pittsburgh, PA.
$150,000 to United Way of Southeastern
  Pennsylvania, Philadelphia, PA.
$124,500 to United Way of Allegheny County,
  Pittsburgh, PA.
$100,000 to Carnegie Mellon University, Pittsburgh,
  PA.
$100,000 to Historical Society of Western
  Pennsylvania, Pittsburgh, PA.
$40,000 to Pittsburgh Partnership for Neighborhood
  Development, Pittsburgh, PA.
$40,000 to YMCA of Pittsburgh, Pittsburgh, PA.
$15,000 to Western Pennsylvania School for the
  Deaf, Pittsburgh, PA.
$10,000 to Operation Warm, Chadds Ford, PA.

$10,000 to Philadelphia Museum of Art,
  Philadelphia, PA.

8346

Richard King Mellon Foundation ▼

1 Mellon Ctr.
500 Grant St., 41st Fl., Ste. 4106
Pittsburgh, PA 15219-2502 (412) 392-2800
Contact: Scott Izzo, Dir.
FAX: (412) 392-2837; *URL:* http://fdncenter.org/
grantmaker/rkmellon

Trust established in 1947 in PA; incorporated in
1971 in PA.
Donor: Richard K. Mellon†.
Foundation type: Independent foundation.
Financial data (yr. ended 12/31/05): Assets,
$1,882,031,732 (M); expenditures, $88,035,160;
qualifying distributions, $76,802,346; giving
activities include $74,356,247 for 193 grants (high:
$7,765,000; low: $1,500; average: $50,000–
$500,000).
Purpose and activities: Local grant programs
emphasize conservation, education, families and
youth, regional economic development, system
reform; support also for conservation of natural
areas and wildlife preservation elsewhere in the
United States.
Fields of interest: Education, early childhood
education; Education; Environment, natural
resources; Environment; Youth development,
services; Human services; Children/youth, services;
Family services; Urban/community development;
Community development.
Type of support: General/operating support;
Continuing support; Capital campaigns; Building/
renovation; Equipment; Land acquisition; Program
development; Seed money; Research; Program
evaluation; Program-related investments/loans;
Matching/challenge support.
Limitations: Giving primarily in PA. No grants to
individuals, or for fellowships or scholarships, or
conduit organizations.
Publications: Annual report (including application
guidelines); Grants list; Informational brochure.
Application information: Application form available
on foundation Web site. The foundation also
accepts the Common Grant Application Format
developed by Grantmakers of Western
Pennsylvania. Electronic requests are not accepted.
Video tapes should not be sent unless specifically
requested. Application form required.
  Initial approach: Proposal
  Copies of proposal: 1
  Deadline(s): None
  Board meeting date(s): Varies
  Final notification: 1 - 6 months
Officers and Trustees: * Richard P. Mellon,* Chair.;
Seward Prosser Mellon,* C.E.O. and Pres.; Michael
Watson, Sr. V.P.; Douglas L. Sisson, V.P.; Ann Marie
Helms, Secy. and Prog. Off.; Robert B. Burr, Jr.,*
Treas.; John J. Turcik, Cont.; Lawrence S. Busch;
Alison M. Byers; W. Russell G. Byers, Jr.; Catharine
Mellon Cathey; Scott D. Izzo; Constance Elizabeth
Mellon Kapp; Armour N. Mellon; Richard A. Mellon.
Number of staff: 3 full-time professional; 7 part-time
professional; 1 full-time support; 14 part-time
support.
EIN: 251127705

8347

Glenn and Ruth Mengle Foundation ✧

c/o First Commonwealth Trust Co.
P.O. Box 1046
Du Bois, PA 15801
Contact: D. Edward Chaplin, V.P., First
Commonwealth Trust Co.

Established in 1956 in PA.
Donors: Glenn A. Mengle†; Ruth E. Mengle Blake†.
Foundation type: Independent foundation.
Financial data (yr. ended 12/31/05): Assets,
$13,659,096 (M); expenditures, $746,598;
qualifying distributions, $746,598; giving activities
include $522,095 for 36 grants (high: $52,000;
low: $500), and $25,000 for 1 employee matching
gift.
Purpose and activities: Giving primarily to public
television, education, hospitals, food services, the
Boy Scouts of America, children's and social
services, the YMCA, federated giving programs, and
Roman Catholic organizations and schools.
Fields of interest: Media, television; Secondary
school/education; Libraries/library science;
Education; Hospitals (general); Food services; Boy
scouts; Human services; YM/YWCAs & YM/YWHAs;
Children, services; Federated giving programs;
Roman Catholic agencies & churches.
Type of support: General/operating support; Capital
campaigns.
Limitations: Giving limited to the Brockway, Du Bois,
and Erie, PA, areas. No grants to individuals.
Application information:
  Initial approach: Letter
  Copies of proposal: 1
  Deadline(s): Sept. 1
Trustees: DeVere L. Sheesley; First Commonwealth
Trust Co.
EIN: 256067616
Selected grants: The following grants were reported
in 2004.
$70,000 to Boy Scouts of America.
$52,000 to YMCA.
$35,000 to United Way.
$20,000 to Girl Scouts of the U.S.A..
$20,000 to YMCA of Erie, Erie, PA.
$15,000 to Salvation Army.

8348

Merchants Fund ✧

(formerly Merchants-Oliver Fund)
P.O. Box 668
Narberth, PA 19072 (610) 949-9270
Contact: Dorothy Darragh, Exec. Dir.
FAX: (610) 949-9412;
E-mail: merchantsfund@comcast.net

Established prior to 1913 in PA.
Donors: Lewis Elkins Fund; Charles Fearon†.
Foundation type: Operating foundation.
Financial data (yr. ended 12/31/05): Assets,
$8,272,372 (M); gifts received, $296,280;
expenditures, $608,635; qualifying distributions,
$541,447; giving activities include $439,761 for 78
grants to individuals (high: $18,000; low: $1,083).
Purpose and activities: Giving to provide relief to
indigent merchants or their widows and families.
Fields of interest: Economically disadvantaged.
Type of support: Grants to individuals.
Limitations: Giving primarily in PA, with emphasis on
Philadelphia; some giving nationally.
Application information: Application form required.

Initial approach: Letter requesting application form
Deadline(s): None
Officers and Directors: * Peter Wilmerding,* Pres.; Bruce Hotaling,* V.P.; George Riter,* Secy.; Dorothy Darragh, Exec. Dir.; Mark Chilutti; Frederic Dittman; Roberta Healey; Stephen J. Peake, Jr.; Patricia Peterson; Stephen G. Voorhees, Jr.
EIN: 231584975

8349
The Merck Genome Research Institute, Inc. ✧
770 Sumneytown Pike
P.O. Box 4, WP44I-206
West Point, PA 19486 (215) 652-8368
Contact: M.J. Finley Austin, Admin. Dir.
FAX: (215) 993-3838; E-mail: mgri@merck.com; URL: http://www.mgri.org

Established in 1996 in NJ.
Donor: Merck & Co., Inc.
Foundation type: Operating foundation.
Financial data (yr. ended 12/31/04): Assets, $3,820 (M); gifts received, $625,000; expenditures, $625,000; qualifying distributions, $625,000; giving activities include $625,000 for 1 grant.
Purpose and activities: The focus of the Institute is to encourage and, where appropriate, sponsor projects which enable scientists to develop assays and methodologies which can be applied broadly across genomics research with the objective of improving the accuracy and speed in which functional associations can be made with sequences of genetic information.
Fields of interest: Higher education; Medical research, institute; Science, research; Biological sciences; Science.
Type of support: Conferences/seminars; Research.
Limitations: Applications not accepted.
Application information: Not accepting pre-proposals or regular proposals at this time.
Officers: Edward M. Scolnick, M.D., Chair.; Anthony W. Ford-Hutchinson, Pres.; Judy C. Lewent, Sr. V.P., Finance; Celia A. Colbert, Secy.; Caroline Dorsa, Treas.; Jayne Kasarda, Cont.
EIN: 223431383

8350
Meshewa Farm Foundation ✧
c/o Mellon Bank, N.A.
P.O. Box 185
Pittsburgh, PA 15230-0185
Contact: Francis R. Grebe, Tr.

Established in 1993 in OH.
Donor: Mary C. LeBlond.
Foundation type: Independent foundation.
Financial data (yr. ended 12/31/03): Assets, $3,765,491 (M); gifts received, $200,578; expenditures, $382,189; qualifying distributions, $370,978; giving activities include $371,500 for 45 grants (high: $50,000; low: $1,000).
Fields of interest: Human services.
Limitations: Applications not accepted. No grants to individuals.
Application information: Contributes only to pre-selected organizations.

Trustees: Francis R. Grebe; Mary Elizabeth Mitsui; Mellon Bank, N.A.
EIN: 237748707

8351
The Dorothy A. Metcalf Charitable Foundation ✧
c/o PNC Advisors, Tax Dept.
1600 Market St.
Philadelphia, PA 19103-7240

Established in 1997 in MD.
Donor: Dorothy A. Metcalf.
Foundation type: Independent foundation.
Financial data (yr. ended 12/31/04): Assets, $34,578 (M); gifts received, $748,858; expenditures, $769,339; qualifying distributions, $769,125; giving activities include $768,500 for 35 grants (high: $250,000; low: $5,000).
Purpose and activities: Giving primarily for historic preservation, wildlife conservation, and health care.
Fields of interest: Museums; Historic preservation/historical societies; Arts; Education; Environment, natural resources; Animal welfare; Animals/wildlife, preservation/protection; Hospitals (general); Human services; Christian agencies & churches.
Limitations: Applications not accepted. Giving on a national basis. No grants to individuals.
Application information: Contributes only to pre-selected organizations.
Trustees: Dorothy A. Metcalf; Robert A. Metcalf; John E. Mullikin.
Agent: PNC Bank, N.A.
EIN: 522053820

8352
Howard E. & Nell E. Miller Charitable Foundation ✧
c/o PNC Advisors, Trust Comm.
620 Liberty Ave., 25th Fl.
Pittsburgh, PA 15222-2719 (412) 762-7076
Contact: Mia Hallett Bernard
Application address: c/o Thomas M. Mulroy, 1106 Frick Bldg., Pittsburgh, PA 15219; FAX: (412) 705-1043

Established in 1988 in PA.
Donor: Nellie E. Miller‡.
Foundation type: Independent foundation.
Financial data (yr. ended 5/31/05): Assets, $6,855,649 (M); expenditures, $418,028; qualifying distributions, $402,536; giving activities include $380,000 for 35 grants (high: $35,000; low: $3,000; average: $10,000–$25,000).
Purpose and activities: Giving primarily for human services and youth services.
Fields of interest: Performing arts, music; Human services; Children/youth, services.
Type of support: General/operating support; Building/renovation; Equipment; Program development; Seed money; Matching/challenge support.
Limitations: Giving primarily in Pittsburgh, PA. No grants to individuals.
Application information: Application form required.
Initial approach: Letter
Copies of proposal: 1
Deadline(s): Apr. 1 and Oct. 1
Trustees: Thomas M. Mulroy; John Pillar; PNC Bank, N.A.
EIN: 256305933

Selected grants: The following grants were reported in 2005.
$35,000 to Pittsburgh Opera Theater, Pittsburgh, PA.
$20,000 to Pittsburgh Symphony Society, Pittsburgh, PA.
$15,000 to Beginning with Books, Pittsburgh, PA.
$15,000 to YMCA of McKeesport, McKeesport, PA.
$10,000 to Bridge to Independence, Braddock, PA.
$10,000 to Girl Scouts of the U.S.A., Pittsburgh, PA.
$10,000 to Greater Pittsburgh Community Food Bank, Duquesne, PA.
$10,000 to Hosanna House, Wilkinsburg, PA.
$10,000 to Merrick Art Gallery Associates, New Brighton, PA.
$10,000 to Pittsburgh Ballet Theater, Pittsburgh, PA.

8353
Mark & Kimberly Miller Charitable Foundation ✧ ☆
142 Justabout Rd.
Venetia, PA 15367

Established in 1999 in PA.
Donor: Mark Miller.
Foundation type: Independent foundation.
Financial data (yr. ended 12/31/05): Assets, $2,071,532 (M); expenditures, $410,686; qualifying distributions, $410,686; giving activities include $409,725 for 21 grants (high: $300,000; low: $25).
Fields of interest: Higher education; Youth, services; Human services; Religion.
Limitations: Giving primarily in PA. No grants to individuals.
Trustees: Kimberley Miller; Mark Miller.
EIN: 256585614
Selected grants: The following grants were reported in 2004.
$100,000 to Alexander-Tharpe Fund, Atlanta, GA.
$20,000 to University of Pittsburgh, Pittsburgh, PA.
$15,000 to Saint Stephens Episcopal School, Bradenton, FL.
$10,000 to YMCA Camp Kon-O-Kwee, Fombell, PA.
$3,000 to Washington County Health Partners, Inc (WCHP), Washington, PA.
$2,000 to Peters Township Police Department, McMurray, PA.
$2,000 to Pittsburgh Pirates Alumni Association, Inc, Pittsburgh, PA.
$1,500 to Holy Cross Greek Orthodox Church, Mount Lebanon, PA.
$1,000 to Bill Bishop Junior Golf Foundation, Sicklerville, NJ.
$500 to Washington Symphony Orchestra, DC.

8354
The Alan B. Miller Family Foundation ✧
57 Crosby Brown Rd.
Gladwyne, PA 19035-1512
Contact: Alan B. Miller, Pres.

Established in 1998 in PA.
Donor: Alan B. Miller.
Foundation type: Independent foundation.
Financial data (yr. ended 1/31/05): Assets, $8,073,264 (M); gifts received, $466,350; expenditures, $680,295; qualifying distributions, $662,875; giving activities include $662,875 for 40 grants (high: $221,875; low: $100).

Purpose and activities: Giving primarily for higher education and Jewish agencies; funding also for the arts, particularly a performing arts center.

Fields of interest: Performing arts centers; Arts; Higher education; Hospitals (general); Eye research; Human services; Jewish federated giving programs; Jewish agencies & temples.

Limitations: Giving primarily in the Philadelphia, PA area. No grants to individuals.

Application information: Application form not required.

Deadline(s): None

Officers and Directors:* Alan B. Miller,* Pres. and Treas.; Jill S. Miller,* Secy.; Abby D. King; Marc D. Miller; Marni E. Spencer.

EIN: 232899896

8355
Marlin Miller, Jr. Family Foundation ◇

211 N. Tulpehocken Rd.
Reading, PA 19601
Contact: Marlin Miller, Jr., Tr.

Established in 1989 in PA.

Donor: Marlin Miller, Jr.

Foundation type: Independent foundation.

Financial data (yr. ended 12/31/03): Assets, $3,364,452 (M); expenditures, $1,044,989; qualifying distributions, $948,550; giving activities include $948,550 for 34 grants (high: $155,000; low: $250).

Purpose and activities: Giving primarily for higher education; funding also for arts and crafts, and human services.

Fields of interest: Museums; Higher education; Education; Human services.

Limitations: Giving primarily in CT, NY and PA. No grants to individuals.

Application information:

Initial approach: Letter
Deadline(s): None

Trustees: Douglas Miller; Eric Miller; James H. Miller; Marlin Miller, Jr.; Regina Miller.

EIN: 232591890

8356
Miller-Worley Charitable Foundation ◇

(formerly The Richard B. Worley and Leslie A. Miller Charitable Trust)
1111 Barberry Rd.
Bryn Mawr, PA 19010 (610) 525-3778
Contact: Richard B. Worley, Tr.; Leslie A. Miller, Tr.

Established in 1996 in PA.

Donor: Richard B. Worley.

Foundation type: Independent foundation.

Financial data (yr. ended 12/31/05): Assets, $10,343,102 (M); expenditures, $970,711; qualifying distributions, $937,663; giving activities include $937,663 for 80 grants (high: $200,000; low: $250).

Purpose and activities: Funding primarily for education and arts and culture. Some funding also for animal welfare and wildlife preservation, and human services.

Fields of interest: Arts; Education; Animals/wildlife; Human services.

Limitations: Giving primarily in the Philadelphia area, PA; some funding nationally. No grants to individuals.

Application information: Application form not required.

Initial approach: Letter
Deadline(s): None

Trustees: Leslie A. Miller; Richard B. Worley.

EIN: 237862650

Selected grants: The following grants were reported in 2003.

$220,000 to Colonial Williamsburg Foundation, Williamsburg, VA. 2 grants: $20,000 (For general support), $200,000 (For general support).

$150,000 to Philadelphia Orchestra Association, Philadelphia, PA. 2 grants: $50,000 (For general support), $100,000 (For general support).

$130,000 to Mount Holyoke College, South Hadley, MA. 2 grants: $100,000 (For general support), $30,000 (For general support).

$65,000 to Kimmel Center for the Performing Arts, Philadelphia, PA. 2 grants: $50,000 (For general support), $15,000 (For general support).

$35,000 to Opera Company of Philadelphia, Philadelphia, PA. For general support.

$20,000 to World Wildlife Fund, DC. For general support.

8357
Mine Safety Appliances Company Charitable Foundation ◇

c/o PNC Advisors
620 Liberty Ave., No. 56222-0
Pittsburgh, PA 15222-2705
Contact: Dennis L. Zeitler, V.P.
Application address: c/o Mine Safety Appliances Co., P.O. Box 426, Pittsburgh, PA 15230, tel.: (412) 967-3000

Established in 1991 in PA as successor to the Mine Safety Appliances Company Charitable Trust.

Donor: Mine Safety Appliances Co.

Foundation type: Company-sponsored foundation.

Financial data (yr. ended 12/31/04): Assets, $1,146,897 (M); gifts received, $13,551; expenditures, $792,614; qualifying distributions, $775,140; giving activities include $775,140 for grants.

Purpose and activities: The foundation supports organizations involved with arts and culture, health, and community development.

Fields of interest: Arts; Hospitals (general); Health care; Community development; Federated giving programs.

Type of support: General/operating support; Continuing support; Annual campaigns; Capital campaigns; Building/renovation; Emergency funds.

Limitations: Giving primarily in Pittsburgh, PA. No grants to individuals.

Application information: Application form not required.

Initial approach: Proposal
Deadline(s): None

Trustee: PNC Bank, N.A.

EIN: 256023104

Selected grants: The following grants were reported in 2004.

$260,000 to United Way of Allegheny County, Pittsburgh, PA.

$55,000 to United Way of Butler County, Butler, PA.

$45,000 to United Way of Westmoreland County, Greensburg, PA.

$19,535 to United Way of Onslow County, Jacksonville, NC.

$18,400 to United Way, Mile High, Denver, CO.

$6,500 to Carnegie Institute, Pittsburgh, PA.

$6,000 to Pittsburgh Opera, Pittsburgh, PA.

$5,000 to Frick Art and Historical Center, Pittsburgh, PA.

$5,000 to Pittsburgh Ballet Theater, Pittsburgh, PA.

$3,000 to North Carolina Symphony, Raleigh, NC.

8358
Ruth Danley & William Enoch Moore Fund ◇ ☆

c/o PNC Advisors
620 Liberty Ave., P2-PTPP-34-1
Pittsburgh, PA 15272-2705 (412) 762-3502
Contact: Bruce Bickel, Mng. Dir.
FAX: (412) 705-1062; E-mail: bruce.bickel@pncadvisors.com

Established in 1992 in PA.

Donor: Grace Danley Moore†.

Foundation type: Independent foundation.

Financial data (yr. ended 12/31/05): Assets, $10,301,584 (M); expenditures, $433,075; qualifying distributions, $339,760; giving activities include $339,760 for grants.

Purpose and activities: Giving for schools educating Indian youth from Indian reservations; support also for the Make A Wish Foundation and the Salvation Army.

Fields of interest: Education; Native Americans/American Indians.

Type of support: Capital campaigns; Building/renovation; Equipment; Program development; Seed money; Scholarship funds.

Application information: Application form required.

Copies of proposal: 1
Deadline(s): Oct.
Board meeting date(s): Nov.
Final notification: 30 days

Trustee: PNC Bank, N.A.

EIN: 256399593

Selected grants: The following grants were reported in 2004.

$50,000 to Red Cloud Indian School, Pine Ridge, SD.

$5,000 to Saint Josephs Indian School, Chamberlain, SD.

$1,124 to Chesapeake College, Wye Mills, MD.

8359
Charles M. Morris Charitable Trust ◇

c/o National City Bank
20 Stanwix St., LOC 25-154
Pittsburgh, PA 15222-1323
Contact: Susan L. Farrell, V.P., National City Bank
FAX: (412) 644-6081;
E-mail: susan.farrell@nationalcity.com; URL: http://www.morrisfoundation.org

Established in 1988 in PA.

Donor: Charles M. Morris†.

Foundation type: Independent foundation.

Financial data (yr. ended 12/31/05): Assets, $30,367,234 (M); expenditures, $1,831,004; qualifying distributions, $1,647,903; giving activities include $1,545,689 for 44 grants (high: $700,000; low: $5,000).

Purpose and activities: Giving primarily to a Jewish home and hospital for the elderly.

Fields of interest: Family services; Aging, centers/services; Homeless, human services; Federated giving programs; Jewish agencies & temples; Religion; Aging; Homeless.

Type of support: General/operating support; Continuing support; Capital campaigns; Building/ renovation; Equipment; Conferences/seminars.
Limitations: Giving primarily in Allegheny County and western PA. No grants to individuals.
Publications: Application guidelines; Grants list; Informational brochure; Multi-year report.
Application information: Application form and guidelines are available on foundation Web site. Application form required.

　　Initial approach: Telephone
　　Copies of proposal: 3
　　Deadline(s): Varies, refer to foundation Web site for current dates
　　Board meeting date(s): Varies
　　Final notification: Following board meetings
Distribution Committee: Arthur C. Fidel; Charles Perlow.
Trustee: National City Bank.
EIN: 256312920
Selected grants: The following grants were reported in 2004.
$715,000 to United Jewish Federation of Greater Pittsburgh, Pittsburgh, PA.
$50,000 to Carnegie Library of Pittsburgh Foundation, Pittsburgh, PA.
$50,000 to City Theater Company, Pittsburgh, PA.
$25,000 to Allegheny Valley School, Coraopolis, PA.
$25,000 to Hillel Academy of Pittsburgh, Pittsburgh, PA.
$25,000 to Lifespan, Homestead, PA.
$25,000 to United Way of Allegheny County, Pittsburgh, PA.
$15,000 to Carnegie Museum of Natural History, Pittsburgh, PA.
$10,000 to Girls Hope of Pittsburgh, Baden, PA.
$10,000 to Pittsburgh Public Theater, Pittsburgh, PA.

8360
Geraldine M. Murray Foundation ◇ ☆

5020 Ritter Rd., Ste. 211
Mechanicsburg, PA　17055-4387
Contact: Jane E. Murray, Tr.

Donor: Geraldine M. Murray†.
Foundation type: Independent foundation.
Financial data (yr. ended 6/30/06): Assets, $872,200 (M); expenditures, $337,970; qualifying distributions, $329,483; giving activities include $329,483 for grants.
Fields of interest: Museums (art); Arts; Higher education, college; Medical research, association; Human services; American Red Cross; Federated giving programs; Christian agencies & churches.
Limitations: Giving primarily in PA.
Application information: Application form not required.

　　Initial approach: Letter
　　Copies of proposal: 1
　　Deadline(s): None
Trustees: Jane E. Murray; Patricia L. Murray.
EIN: 251637471
Selected grants: The following grants were reported in 2005.
$20,000 to Harrisburg Symphony Association, Harrisburg, PA.
$10,000 to Wilson College, Chambersburg, PA.
$7,500 to Mennonite Central Committee, Akron, PA. 2 grants: $5,000, $2,500
$5,000 to International Rescue Committee, New York, NY.

$3,800 to Pinnacle Health Foundation, Harrisburg, PA.
$1,500 to Bethesda Mission, Harrisburg, PA.
$1,000 to Allied Arts Fund, Harrisburg, PA.
$1,000 to CARE, Atlanta, GA.
$1,000 to Yale Alumni Fund, New Haven, CT.

8361
The Warren V. Musser Foundation ◇ ☆

435 Devon Park Dr., No. 500
Wayne, PA　19087　(610) 975-4912
Contact: Diane Swiggard

Established in 1980 in PA.
Donors: Claire V. Sams; Warren V. Musser.
Foundation type: Independent foundation.
Financial data (yr. ended 11/30/05): Assets, $5,796,972 (M); gifts received, $70,500; expenditures, $491,460; qualifying distributions, $350,972; giving activities include $350,972 for grants.
Purpose and activities: Giving primarily for education, human services, and youth development.
Fields of interest: Higher education; Education; Health organizations, association; Food services; Athletics/sports, racquet sports; Youth development, scouting agencies (general); Human services; Youth, services; Jewish federated giving programs.
Limitations: Giving primarily in Philadelphia, PA.
Application information:

　　Initial approach: Letter
　　Deadline(s): None
Trustee: Carl Sempier.
EIN: 232162497
Selected grants: The following grants were reported in 2005.
$30,000 to American Red Cross, Philadelphia, PA.
$15,000 to Community Volunteers in Medicine, West Chester, PA.
$10,000 to National Constitution Center, Philadelphia, PA.
$10,000 to Pennsylvania State University, Malvern, PA.
$8,527 to National Organization for Hearing Research Foundation, Narberth, PA.
$6,000 to American Cancer Society, Philadelphia, PA.
$5,000 to Harrisburg Area Community College, Harrisburg, PA.
$5,000 to Nantucket Cottage Hospital, Nantucket, MA.
$5,000 to Seeing Eye, Morristown, NJ.
$5,000 to Thomas Jefferson University, Philadelphia, PA.

8362
Grace S. & W. Linton Nelson Foundation ◇

West Valley Business Ctr.
940 W. Valley Rd., Ste. 1601
Wayne, PA　19087-1853　(610) 975-9169
Contact: Fred C. Aldridge, Jr., Pres.

Established in 1984 in PA.
Donors: W. Linton Nelson†; William P. Brady; Delaware Management Co.
Foundation type: Independent foundation.
Financial data (yr. ended 12/31/04): Assets, $19,202,015 (M); expenditures, $1,088,257; qualifying distributions, $1,008,601; giving

activities include $568,000 for 80 grants (high: $85,000; low: $1,000), and $323,006 for 14 grants to individuals.
Purpose and activities: Giving for: 1) the unmet needs of children and youth in the areas of shelter, day care, preschool, education, health care, child and drug abuse prevention, after school and summer programs, child advocacy, parenting, and foster care and adoption; 2) The Nelson Foundation Scholarship Program at the Wharton School; and 3) programs fostering leadership and citizenship in youth.
Fields of interest: Child development, education; Youth development, citizenship; Children/youth, services; Child development, services.
Type of support: General/operating support; Equipment; Program development; Seed money.
Limitations: Giving primarily in Philadelphia, PA, and the surrounding counties.
Application information: Application form not required.

　　Initial approach: Letter
　　Copies of proposal: 1
　　Deadline(s): 6 weeks before board meetings in Jan., Apr., July, and Oct.
　　Board meeting date(s): 2nd week of every month; grants reviewed quarterly in Jan., Apr., July, and Oct.
Officers: Fred C. Aldridge, Jr., Pres., Treas. and Mgr.; James P. Schellenger II, V.P. and Secy.
Number of staff: 2 part-time professional.
EIN: 222583922

8363
The Neubauer Foundation ◇

c/o Pressman Ciocca Smith
1800 Byberry Rd., Ste. 1100
Huntingdon Valley, PA　19006-3523

Established in 1998 in PA.
Donor: Joseph Neubauer.
Foundation type: Independent foundation.
Financial data (yr. ended 11/30/05): Assets, $91,550,637 (M); gifts received, $18,142,461; expenditures, $3,959,802; qualifying distributions, $3,942,850; giving activities include $3,942,850 for 28 grants (high: $2,435,875; low: $1,500).
Purpose and activities: Giving primarily for higher education, the arts, and to Jewish organizations.
Fields of interest: Museums; Performing arts; Performing arts, orchestra (symphony); Performing arts, opera; Higher education; Theological school/ education; Education; Hospitals (general); Jewish agencies & temples.
Type of support: Program development.
Limitations: Applications not accepted. Giving primarily in Philadelphia, PA; some funding in Chicago, IL, New York, NY and MA. No grants to individuals.
Application information: Contributes only to pre-selected organizations.
Trustees: Melissa Neubauer Anderson; Joseph Neubauer; Lawrence Neubauer.
EIN: 256627704
Selected grants: The following grants were reported in 2005.
$2,435,875 to University of Chicago, Chicago, IL.
$25,000 to Brandeis University, Waltham, MA.
$5,000 to Lincoln University, Lincoln University, PA.

8364
Yetta Deitch Novotny Charitable Trust ✧
2 Penn Ctr. Plz., Ste. 400
Philadelphia, PA 19102 (215) 564-1300

Established in 1990 in PA.
Donor: Yetta Deitch Novotny‡.
Foundation type: Independent foundation.
Financial data (yr. ended 8/31/05): Assets, $9,231,242 (M); expenditures, $758,805; qualifying distributions, $744,200; giving activities include $744,200 for 24 grants (high: $250,000; low: $500).
Fields of interest: Education; Human services; Jewish federated giving programs; Jewish agencies & temples.
Limitations: Applications not accepted. Giving primarily in New York, NY, and PA. No grants to individuals.
Application information: Contributes only to pre-selected organizations.
Trustees: Andrew Zolot; Stanley L. Zolot.
EIN: 237642807
Selected grants: The following grants were reported in 2004.
$250,000 to University of Pennsylvania, Philadelphia, PA.
$200,000 to Hadassah, Hewlett, NY.
$1,000 to Interfaith Housing Alliance, Frederick, MD.
$1,000 to Jewish National Fund, Philadelphia, PA.
$500 to Kate Svitek Memorial Foundation, Ambler, PA.

8365
Oberkotter Foundation ▼ ✧
1600 Market St., Ste. 3600
Philadelphia, PA 19103-7286 (215) 751-2601
Contact: Bruce A. Rosenfield, Exec. Dir.
FAX: (215) 751-2678;
E-mail: RDIMARTINO@Schnader.com

Established in 1992 in PA.
Donors: Paul Oberkotter‡; Mildred L. Oberkotter.
Foundation type: Independent foundation.
Financial data (yr. ended 11/30/04): Assets, $219,489,274 (M); gifts received, $3,483,053; expenditures, $26,726,016; qualifying distributions, $25,984,739; giving activities include $23,357,154 for 240 grants (high: $507,500; low: $979; average: $20,000–$200,000).
Purpose and activities: The foundation limits its grants to educational institutions and centers for the deaf that use the auditory/oral or auditory/verbal method exclusively; research in the area of hearing-impairment where interdisciplinary resources are used; outreach programs for the treatment of diabetes; and research in the area of diabetes.
Fields of interest: Education, special; Speech/hearing centers; Diabetes; Ear & throat research; Diabetes research.
Type of support: Matching/challenge support; Research; General/operating support.
Limitations: Giving on a national basis.
Application information: Grants usually made on the initiative of the trustees. Telephone inquiries not accepted. Application form not required.
 Copies of proposal: 1
 Deadline(s): None
Officer and Trustees:* Bruce A. Rosenfield,* Exec. Dir.; George H. Nofer, J.D.; Mildred L. Oberkotter.

Number of staff: 1 full-time professional; 1 part-time support.
EIN: 232686151
Selected grants: The following grants were reported in 2004.
$750,000 to University of Washington, Seattle, WA. 2 grants: $375,000 each to Bloedel Hearing Research Center (For deafness research).
$732,500 to Alexander Graham Bell Association for the Deaf, DC. 2 grants: $225,000 (For general support), $507,500 (For general support).
$350,000 to Clarke School Jacksonville, Jacksonville, FL. For school construction.
$325,000 to Clarke School for the Deaf, Northampton, MA. For general support.
$275,000 to Childrens Hospital of Philadelphia, Philadelphia, PA. 2 grants: $200,000 (For early intervention services for children with possible hearing or speech difficulties), $75,000 (For teacher education and training for teachers working with children who have hearing or speech difficulties).
$125,000 to Juvenile Diabetes Research Foundation International, Bala Cynwyd, PA. For diabetes research.
$97,500 to University of Akron, Akron, OH. For early intervention services for children with possible hearing and speech difficulties.

8366
The Ortenzio Family Foundation ✧ ☆
4718 Old Gettysburg Rd., Ste. 405
Mechanicsburg, PA 17055 (717) 972-1305
Contact: Robert A. Ortenzio, Tr.

Established in 1986 in PA.
Donors: Rocco A. Ortenzio; Russell L. Carson.
Foundation type: Independent foundation.
Financial data (yr. ended 12/31/05): Assets, $12,781,810 (M); gifts received, $2,012,464; expenditures, $551,703; qualifying distributions, $520,795; giving activities include $520,795 for grants.
Purpose and activities: Grants are primarily restricted to Roman Catholic educational institutions to provide scholarships or other assistance to qualified students with financial need, with first preference being given to students who are members of St. Ann's Roman Catholic Church, in Steelton, PA.
Fields of interest: Elementary school/education; Secondary school/education; Higher education; Scholarships/financial aid; Residential/custodial care, hospices; Roman Catholic agencies & churches.
Type of support: Scholarship funds.
Limitations: Giving primarily in PA. No grants to individuals.
Application information:
 Initial approach: Letter
 Deadline(s): None
Trustees: John M. Ortenzio; Martin J. Ortenzio; Robert A. Ortenzio; Rocco A. Ortenzio.
EIN: 236805409

8367
The Oxford Area Foundation ✧ ☆
P.O. Box 341
Oxford, PA 19363 (610) 932-4627

Established in 2004 in PA.

Donor: John H. Ware, III Charitable Lead Annuity.
Foundation type: Independent foundation.
Financial data (yr. ended 12/31/05): Assets, $19,646,456 (M); gifts received, $30,624; expenditures, $814,388; qualifying distributions, $697,733; giving activities include $650,000 for 83 grants (high: $75,000; low: $200).
Fields of interest: Education; Human services; Community development; Protestant agencies & churches.
Limitations: Giving primarily in PA.
Application information: No more than 1 grant request per year should be submitted for any given project. Full proposals are by invitation only. Application form not required.
 Initial approach: 2-page letter of inquiry
 Deadline(s): Oct. 15 for letter of inquiry; Nov. 15 for full proposal
 Final notification: Within 1 month for letter of inquiry
Officers and Directors:* John H. Ware IV,* Pres.; Nancy Ware Sapp,* V.P.; Karen Ware,* Secy.; John Charles Ware,* Treas.; Debra Kline.
EIN: 201060782

8368
A. J. & Sigismunda Palumbo Charitable Trust ✧
c/o Smithfield Trust Co.
20 Stanwix St., Ste. 650
Pittsburgh, PA 15222-4801
Contact: Robert Y. Kopf, Jr., C.E.O., Smithfield Trust Co.

Established in 1974 in PA.
Donor: A.J. Palumbo.
Foundation type: Independent foundation.
Financial data (yr. ended 3/31/05): Assets, $29,247,015 (M); expenditures, $1,796,419; qualifying distributions, $1,541,188; giving activities include $1,501,500 for 47 grants (high: $150,000; low: $3,000).
Fields of interest: Higher education; Hospitals (general); Human services; Christian agencies & churches.
Limitations: Giving primarily in western PA.
Application information: Application form required.
 Initial approach: Letter
 Deadline(s): Dec. 31
 Board meeting date(s): Mar. 1
Trustees: E. Rolland Dickson; F.W. Knisley; John W. Kowach; Donald W. Meredith; A.J. Palumbo; P.J. Palumbo; PNC Bank, N.A.
Number of staff: 1 part-time support.
EIN: 256168159
Selected grants: The following grants were reported in 2005.
$50,000 to Forbes Health Foundation, Pittsburgh, PA.
$50,000 to Saint Leo School, Philadelphia, PA.
$30,000 to Salvation Army, Butler, PA.
$25,000 to Cystic Fibrosis Foundation, Pittsburgh, PA.
$25,000 to Mount Aloysius College, Cresson, PA.
$20,000 to First United Presbyterian Church, Du Bois, PA.
$15,000 to Big Brothers and Big Sisters of Greater Pittsburgh, Pittsburgh, PA.
$15,000 to Extra Mile Education Foundation, Pittsburgh, PA.
$10,000 to Jubilee Association, Pittsburgh, PA.
$10,000 to Saint Boniface School, Philadelphia, PA.

8369

The Parmer Family Foundation, Inc. ✧ ☆

c/o George Parmer
911 Grove Rd.
Harrisburg, PA   17111

Established in 2001 in PA.

Donors: Residential Warranty Corp.; Western Pacific Mutual Insurance Co.

Foundation type: Company-sponsored foundation.

Financial data (yr. ended 12/31/05): Assets, $4,413,572 (L); gifts received, $721,033; expenditures, $683,520; qualifying distributions, $680,786; giving activities include $675,150 for 4 grants (high: $500,000; low: $25,150).

Purpose and activities: The foundation supports organizations involved with K-12 and higher education and Christianity.

Fields of interest: Elementary/secondary education; Higher education; Christian agencies & churches.

Type of support: General/operating support.

Limitations: Applications not accepted. Giving limited to PA. No grants to individuals.

Application information: Contributes only to pre-selected organizations.

Officer and Directors:* George A. Parmer,* Pres.; Barbara J. Parmer.

EIN: 251883175

8370

The Peirce Family Foundation, Inc. ✧ ☆

707 Grant St., Ste. 2500
Pittsburgh, PA   15219-1919   (412) 281-7229
Contact: Robert N. Peirce, Jr., Pres.

Established in 1997 in PA.

Donors: Robert N. Peirce, Jr.; Joan Peirce.

Foundation type: Independent foundation.

Financial data (yr. ended 12/31/05): Assets, $10,137,284 (M); gifts received, $3,000,927; expenditures, $526,824; qualifying distributions, $442,450; giving activities include $442,450 for grants.

Purpose and activities: Giving for human services.

Fields of interest: Higher education; Human services.

Limitations: Giving primarily in PA. No grants to individuals.

Application information:
Initial approach: Proposal
Deadline(s): None

Officers: Robert N. Peirce, Jr., Pres.; Joan Peirce, Secy.

EIN: 232903074

8371

The William Penn Foundation ▼

2 Logan Sq., 11th Fl.
100 N. 18th St.
Philadelphia, PA   19103-2757   (215) 988-1830
Contact: Feather O'Connor Houstoun, Pres.
FAX: (215) 988-1823;
E-mail: moreinfo@williampennfoundation.org
URL: http://www.williampennfoundation.org

Incorporated in 1945 in DE.

Donors: Otto Haas†; Phoebe W. Haas†; Otto Haas & Phoebe W. Haas Charitable Trusts.

Foundation type: Independent foundation.

Financial data (yr. ended 12/31/05): Assets, $1,253,208,618 (M); expenditures, $74,042,975; qualifying distributions, $64,641,331; giving activities include $64,641,331 for 381 grants.

Purpose and activities: The foundation strives to improve the quality of life in the Philadelphia region through efforts that foster rich cultural expression, strengthen children's futures, and deepen connections to nature and community.

Fields of interest: Arts, multipurpose centers/programs; Performing arts; Historic preservation/historical societies; Arts; Child development, education; Elementary school/education; Secondary school/education; Elementary/secondary school reform; Environment, natural resources; Environment, beautification programs; Environment; Youth development; Human services; Children/youth, services; Child development, services; Family services; Community development, neighborhood development; Community development, neighborhood associations; Urban/community development; Economically disadvantaged.

Type of support: General/operating support; Capital campaigns; Building/renovation; Equipment; Land acquisition; Program development; Seed money; Technical assistance; Program-related investments/loans; Employee matching gifts; Matching/challenge support.

Limitations: Giving limited to the Greater Philadelphia region. No support for sectarian religious activities, recreational programs, political lobbying or legislative activities, nonpublic schools, pass-through organizations, mental health or retardation treatment programs, or programs focusing on a particular disease, disability, or treatment for addiction, or profit-making enterprises; no support for private foundations. No grants to individuals, or for debt reduction, hospital capital projects, medical research, programs that replace lost government support, housing construction or rehabilitation, scholarships, or fellowships; no loans (except for program-related investments).

Publications: Annual report; Grants list.

Application information: Response time is one month to letter of inquiry. Those applicants encouraged to submit a full proposal will be directed to the Preparing Your Proposal area of the foundation's Web site. Faxed proposals will not be accepted. Application form not required.
Initial approach: All applicants must complete the Letter of Inquiry (LOI) on the foundation's Web site. The LOI can be completed and submitted online, or downloaded, completed and submitted via U.S. Mail
Copies of proposal: 1
Deadline(s): None
Board meeting date(s): Four times per year
Final notification: Approximately 2-3 months

Officers and Directors:* David W. Haas,* Chair.; Frederick R. Haas,* Vice-Chair. and Secy.; Feather O'Connor Houstoun, Pres.; Louise M. Foster, C.F.O.; Kristin Ross, Cont.; Michael Bailin; Christine James Brown; James Gately; Duncan A. Haas; William D. Haas; Gary Hack; Barbara Lawrence; Thomas M. McKenna; Daniel Meyer, M.D.; Hon. Anthony J. Scirica; Lise Yasui.

Number of staff: 17 full-time professional; 4 part-time professional; 4 full-time support.

EIN: 231503488

Selected grants: The following grants were reported in 2005.

$2,283,390 to Nonprofit Finance Fund, New York, NY. Toward dedicated fund investing capital in and providing technical assistance to child care providers for planning, development, and management of facility projects in multi-county region, payable over 2 years.

$1,775,279 to Regional Performing Arts Center, Philadelphia, PA. For final construction and installation stages of Kimmel Center organ, payable over 5 years.

$1,075,000 to Philadelphia Citizens for Children and Youth, Philadelphia, PA. For program and fundraising staff support, payable over 3 years.

$1,000,000 to 10,000 Friends of Pennsylvania, Philadelphia, PA. payable over 3 years.

$1,000,000 to Center City District, Philadelphia, PA. Toward implementing projects enhancing appearance of and access to parks and public spaces, cultural sites, and transportation systems in Center City, payable over 1.50 years.

$1,000,000 to Citizens for Pennsylvanias Future, Harrisburg, PA. Toward promoting state and local policies and investments, payable over 2.50 years.

$1,000,000 to Civil Society Institute, Newton Centre, MA. Toward continued support of Partnership for Quality Pre-Kindergarten, public-private initiative in PA.

$1,000,000 to Greater Philadelphia Tourism Marketing Corporation, Philadelphia, PA. Toward implementing marketing initiative, Think Outside, developed in coordination with regional stakeholders, promoting natural assets and recreational and stewardship opportunities, payable over 2.50 years.

$1,000,000 to Independence Visitor Center Corporation, Philadelphia, PA. Toward completing landscaping and site improvements at Independence Mall, payable over 1.50 years.

$1,000,000 to Pennsylvania Economy League, Philadelphia, PA. Toward developing outcomes-focused public budgets and shared regional agenda in southeastern PA, in collaboration with public and private civic and business leaders, payable over 2 years.

8372

Raymond & Ruth Perelman Community Foundation ✧

225 City Line Ave., Ste. 14
Bala Cynwyd, PA   19004

Established in 1995.

Foundation type: Independent foundation.

Financial data (yr. ended 4/30/05): Assets, $30,003,218 (M); expenditures, $1,444,582; qualifying distributions, $1,325,350; giving activities include $1,325,350 for 14 grants (high: $780,000; low: $100).

Purpose and activities: Giving primarily for arts, health and human services, Jewish federated giving programs, and medical research.

Fields of interest: Arts; Health care; Medical specialty research; Human services; Jewish federated giving programs.

Limitations: Applications not accepted. Giving primarily in FL and PA. No grants to individuals.

Application information: Contributes only to pre-selected organizations.

Trustees: Raymond G. Perelman; Ruth Perelman.

EIN: 232820843

8373
Raymond & Ruth Perelman Education Foundation ◇
225 City Line Ave., Ste. 14
Bala Cynwyd, PA 19004

Established in 1995.
Foundation type: Independent foundation.
Financial data (yr. ended 4/30/05): Assets, $69,321,897 (M); expenditures, $3,938,208; qualifying distributions, $3,190,280; giving activities include $3,190,280 for 23 grants (high: $2,375,000; low: $100).
Purpose and activities: Giving primarily for the arts. Some funding also for human services.
Fields of interest: Museums; Arts; Human services.
Limitations: Applications not accepted. Giving primarily in PA. No grants to individuals.
Application information: Contributes only to pre-selected organizations.
Trustees: Raymond G. Perelman; Ruth Perelman.
EIN: 232819735
Selected grants: The following grants were reported in 2003.
$2,536,851 to Philadelphia Museum of Art, Philadelphia, PA.
$100,000 to Glaucoma Service Foundation to Prevent Blindness, Philadelphia, PA. For medical research.
$25,000 to Federation Allied Jewish Appeal of Philadelphia, Philadelphia, PA. For operating support.
$7,500 to National Museum of American Jewish History, Philadelphia, PA. For operating support.
$4,000 to American Friends of the Israel Museum, New York, NY. For operating support.
$3,500 to Kimmel Center for the Performing Arts, Philadelphia, PA. For operating support.
$3,000 to Dana-Farber Cancer Institute, Boston, MA.
$2,500 to Raymond and Ruth Perelman Jewish Day School, Wynnewood, PA. For operating support.
$2,500 to Temple University, Philadelphia, PA. For operating support.
$2,000 to Adopt-A-Family of the Palm Beaches, West Palm Beach, FL. For operating support.

8374
Raymond & Ruth Perelman Judaica Foundation ◇
225 City Line Ave., Ste. 14
Bala Cynwyd, PA 19004

Established in 1995.
Foundation type: Independent foundation.
Financial data (yr. ended 4/30/05): Assets, $60,746,715 (M); expenditures, $3,429,406; qualifying distributions, $2,438,855; giving activities include $2,438,855 for 15 grants (high: $1,000,000; low: $100).
Purpose and activities: Giving primarily for museums, and to Jewish agencies and temples.
Fields of interest: Museums; Higher education; Jewish federated giving programs; Jewish agencies & temples.
Limitations: Applications not accepted. Giving primarily in PA. No grants to individuals.
Application information: Contributes only to pre-selected organizations.
Trustees: Raymond G. Perelman; Ruth Perelman.
EIN: 232820841

Selected grants: The following grants were reported in 2003.
$1,147,282 to Philadelphia Museum of Art, Philadelphia, PA.
$300,000 to Gratz College, Melrose Park, PA. For operating support.
$210,000 to Kimmel Center for the Performing Arts, Philadelphia, PA. For operating support.
$130,000 to Jewish Federation of Greater Philadelphia, Philadelphia, PA.
$62,480 to Beth Shalom Congregation, Elkins Park, PA. For building support.
$50,000 to Multiple Sclerosis Society, National, New York, NY. For medical research.
$27,500 to Anti-Defamation League of Bnai Brith, Philadelphia, PA. For operating support.
$5,500 to Albert Einstein College of Medicine of Yeshiva University, Bronx, NY. For medical research.
$5,000 to Palm Beach Orthodox Synagogue, Palm Beach, FL.
$3,000 to American Friends of the Israel Museum, New York, NY. For operating support.

8375
Sylvia Perkin Perpetual Charitable Trust ◇
c/o Wachovia Bank, N.A.
P.O. Box 1102
600 Penn St., PA 6497
Reading, PA 19603-1102
Application address: c/o Arnold C. Rapoport, Tr., P.O. Box 443, Allentown, PA 18105-0443

Established in 1986 in PA.
Donor: Sylvia Perkin†.
Foundation type: Independent foundation.
Financial data (yr. ended 4/30/05): Assets, $7,094,209 (M); expenditures, $371,126; qualifying distributions, $332,894; giving activities include $324,090 for 44 grants (high: $40,000; low: $750).
Purpose and activities: Giving primarily for Jewish agencies and federated giving programs, education, human services, and arts and culture.
Fields of interest: Arts; Higher education; Libraries (public); Human services; Jewish federated giving programs; Jewish agencies & temples.
Type of support: General/operating support; Scholarship funds.
Limitations: Giving primarily in Allentown, PA. No grants to individuals.
Application information: Application form not required.
 Deadline(s): None
Trustees: James D. Christie; Arnold C. Rapoport; Wachovia Bank, N.A.
EIN: 236792999
Selected grants: The following grants were reported in 2004.
$42,000 to Jewish Federation of Allentown, Allentown, PA. For general support.
$40,000 to Jewish Community Center of Allentown, Allentown, PA. For general support.
$35,000 to Muhlenberg College, Allentown, PA. For general support.
$30,000 to Cedar Crest College, Allentown, PA. For general support.
$20,000 to Temple Beth El of Allentown, Allentown, PA. For general support.
$10,000 to Allentown Art Museum, Allentown, PA. For general support.
$10,000 to Lehigh County Historical Society, Allentown, PA. For general support.

$10,000 to Lehigh Valley Child Care, Allentown, PA. For general support.
$10,000 to YMCA of Allentown, Allentown, PA. For general support.
$7,500 to Allentown Symphony Association, Allentown, PA. For general support.

8376
The Peterson Foundation ◇
c/o John Iskrant
1600 Market St., Ste. 3600
Philadelphia, PA 19103
Application address: c/o J. Robert Peterson, Tr., 1111 Ritz-Carlton Dr., Residence 1501, Sarasota, FL 34236; tel.: (941) 308-2202

Established in 1986 in PA.
Donors: Lee M. Peterson; J. Robert Peterson.
Foundation type: Independent foundation.
Financial data (yr. ended 12/31/05): Assets, $40,705 (M); gifts received, $877,514; expenditures, $939,388; qualifying distributions, $920,004; giving activities include $845,988 for 127 grants (high: $267,208; low: $150).
Purpose and activities: Giving primarily for medical research, particularly research in schizophrenia and depression; funding also for the arts and for higher education.
Fields of interest: Arts education; Museums; Museums (science/technology); Performing arts; Performing arts centers; Performing arts, theater; Higher education; Environment, natural resources; Mental health, depression; Mental health, schizophrenia; Multiple sclerosis; Diabetes; Medical research; Children/youth, services; Federated giving programs.
Limitations: Giving primarily in CT, FL, and NY; some funding nationally. No grants to individuals.
Application information: Application form not required.
 Initial approach: Proposal
 Deadline(s): None
Trustees: David John Peterson; J. Robert Peterson; Jeffrey R. Peterson; Kane Deglin Peterson; Lee M. Peterson; Janice Peterson Radder; Timothy W. Radder.
EIN: 236766019

8377
The Pew Charitable Trusts
1 Commerce Sq.
2005 Market St., Ste. 1700
Philadelphia, PA 19103-7077 (215) 575-9050
Contact: Rebecca W. Rimel, C.E.O. and Pres.
FAX: (215) 575-4939; E-mail: info@pewtrusts.org;
URL: http://www.pewtrusts.org
Fellowship address: 1608 Walnut St., 18th Fl., Philadelphia, PA 19103, tel.: (267) 350-4920, fax: (267) 350-4997, email: pfa@pcah.us, web site: www.pewarts.org

Established in 1948; the trusts reorganized into a public charity in 2004.
Donors: Mary Ethel Pew†; Mabel Pew Myrin†; J. Howard Pew†; Joseph N. Pew, Jr.†.
Financial data (yr. ended 6/30/05): Revenue, $234,463,454; assets, $197,741,615 (M); gifts received, $232,032,960; expenditures, $224,608,772; program services expenses, $217,524,739; giving activities include $198,031,385 for 453 grants (high: $7,600,000;

low: $2,000), $446,482 for 343 employee matching gifts, and $19,046,872 for 3 foundation-administered programs.

Purpose and activities: The Pew Charitable Trusts support nonprofit activities in the areas of culture, education, the environment, health and human services, public policy and religion. Based in Philadelphia, the trusts make strategic investments to help organizations and citizens develop practical solutions to difficult problems.

Fields of interest: Media, journalism/publishing; Visual arts; Museums; Performing arts; Performing arts, dance; Performing arts, theater; Performing arts, music; Humanities; Historic preservation/historical societies; Arts; Education, research; Child development, education; Education; Environment, natural resources; Environment, energy; Environment; Animals/wildlife, preservation/protection; Public health; Health care; Biomedicine; Employment; Housing/shelter, development; Youth development, services; Youth development, citizenship; Human services; Children/youth, services; Child development, services; Family services; Aging, centers/services; Minorities/immigrants, centers/services; Homeless, human services; Civil rights; Urban/community development; Rural development; Community development; Voluntarism promotion; Biological sciences; Science; Social sciences; Government/public administration; Public affairs, election regulation; Public affairs, citizen participation; Leadership development; Public affairs; Religion, research; Religion, public policy; Minorities; Immigrants/refugees; Economically disadvantaged; Homeless.

International interests: Canada.

Type of support: Continuing support; Program development; Research; Technical assistance; Program-related investments/loans; Employee matching gifts.

Limitations: Giving on a national basis, with a special commitment to the Philadelphia, PA, region. No support for political organizations or government agencies. No grants to individuals, or for endowment funds, capital campaigns, construction, equipment, deficit financing, scholarships, or fellowships (except those identified or initiated by the trusts).

Publications: Application guidelines; Grants list; Occasional report.

Application information: Contact foundation for specific guidelines and limitations or visit the trusts' Web site; applicants should not send full proposals unless requested by trustee representatives. Examples of past work, articles, reports, videos or other material should not be submitted with the letter of inquiry. Application form required.

  Initial approach: Letter of inquiry (2 to 3 pages)
  Copies of proposal: 1
  Deadline(s): None
  Board meeting date(s): Mar., June, Sept., and Dec.
  Final notification: Approximately 4 to 6 weeks

Officers and Board Members:* Rebecca W. Rimel,* C.E.O. and Pres.; Garth B. Seidel, C.F.O.; Henry B. Bernstein, Treas. and Dir., Finance; Karen A. Orth, Cont.; Joy A. Horwitz, Genl. Counsel and Dir., Legal Affairs; Robert H. Campbell; Susan W. Catherwood; Gloria Twine Chisum; Alan J. Davis; Paul F. Miller, Jr.; J. Howard Pew II; J.N. Pew IV, M.D.; Mary Catherine Pew, M.D.; R. Anderson Pew; Sandy Pew; Robert G. Williams; Ethel Benson Wister.

Trustee: The Glenmede Trust Co.

Number of staff: 94 full-time professional; 3 part-time professional; 52 full-time support; 2 part-time support.

EIN: 562307147

Selected grants: The following grants were reported in 2004.

$6,350,000 to George Washington University, DC. 2 grants: $4,450,000 to Graduate School of Political Management (For nonpartisan get-out-the-vote effort designed to significantly increase turnout of young people in 2004 election and to convince political professionals that this is constituency worthy of greater attention), $1,900,000 to Center for Health Services Research and Policy (To improve access to alcohol treatment by working with public- and private-sector health care decision-makers to remove obstacles to treatment).

$4,939,000 to Pew Research Center for the People and the Press, DC. For multination public opinion surveys of attitudes toward democratization, America's role in the world, religion, globalization, terrorism and other issues of abiding global importance.

$3,600,000 to Rutgers, The State University of New Jersey Foundation, New Brunswick, NJ. To provide timely, objective research that informs debate on advancing high-quality prekindergarten for all 3 and 4 year olds at state and national levels.

$3,600,000 to University of California, Center for Health Professions, San Francisco, CA. For research activities of Pew Scholars Program in Biomedical Sciences.

$3,400,000 to Strategies for the Global Environment, Arlington, VA. For Pew Center on Global Climate Change to educate public and policymakers on climate change, and to encourage domestic and international efforts to reduce emissions of greenhouse gases.

$325,000 to Minnesota Public Radio, Saint Paul, MN. For production and distribution of Speaking of Faith, weekly radio program that explores issues in religion and public life.

$250,000 to National Public Radio, DC. For news coverage of religion and public life issues.

$220,000 to Drexel University, Arts Administration Program, Philadelphia, PA. For Pennsylvania Cultural Data Project, which will generate standardized financial and operating data on local arts and cultural organizations.

$80,000 to Dawn Staley Foundation, Philadelphia, PA. For after-school program in North Philadelphia for at-risk girls.

8378

The Philadelphia Foundation ▼ ✧

1234 Market St., Ste. 1800
Philadelphia, PA 19107-3794 (215) 563-6417
Contact: R. Andrew Swinney, Pres.
FAX: (215) 563-6882;
E-mail: parkow@philafound.org; URL: http://www.philafound.org

Established in 1918 in PA by bank resolution.
Donor: 569 different funds.
Foundation type: Community foundation.
Financial data (yr. ended 12/31/05): Assets, $298,515,937 (M); gifts received, $27,677,894; expenditures, $26,754,860; giving activities include $21,074,599 for 1,220+ grants.
Purpose and activities: The foundation seeks to promote charitable, educational, and civic activities;

most of the funds have specific purposes or named beneficiary institutions, with emphasis on capacity-building, empowerment of low-income persons, and health and welfare, including community activities; grants also for education and cultural programs.

Fields of interest: Performing arts, dance; Arts; Education; Health care; AIDS; AIDS research; Legal services; Housing/shelter, development; Family services; Minorities/immigrants, centers/services; Human services; Civil rights; Urban/community development; Community development; Public policy, research; Public affairs; Children; Disabilities, people with; Minorities; Economically disadvantaged.

Type of support: General/operating support; Continuing support; Emergency funds; Program development; Seed money; Scholarship funds; Technical assistance; Matching/challenge support.

Limitations: Giving limited to Bucks, Chester, Delaware, Montgomery, and Philadelphia counties in southeastern PA, except for designated funds. No support for religious purposes; generally, low priority given to national organizations, government agencies, large budget agencies, public or private schools, or umbrella funding organizations. No grants to individuals (except for scholarships), or for annual or capital campaigns, building funds, land acquisition, endowment funds, research, publications, tours or trips, conferences, or deficit financing; no loans.

Publications: Newsletter.

Application information: The foundation will not be accepting grant proposals for the 2006 funding period. The foundation has suspended the May 2006 grant deadline. Visit foundation Web site for details.

  Board meeting date(s): Apr. and Oct.

Officers and Managers:* Ellen P. Foster,* Chair.; Gene Locks,* Vice-Chair.; R. Andrew Swinney, Pres.; Nancy Burd, V.P., Grantmaking Svcs.; Heather Gee, V.P., Devel. Svcs.; Jeff Perkins, V.P., Finance and Admin.; Eric Fraint, Treas.; Peggy Amsterdam; Andrew A. Chirls; Oliver St. C. Franklin; Pamela H. Godwin; Paul C. Heintz; Edward Y. Kung; Frederick J.M. LaValley; Jane M. Mullany; Asuka Nakahara; Eliana Papadakis; R. Duane Perry; Emily C. Riley.

Trustees: The Bryn Mawr Trust Co.; The Glenmede Trust Co.; Mellon Financial Group; Pitcairn Trust Co.; PNC Bank, N.A.; Wachovia Bank, N.A.; Wilmington Trust of Pennsylvania.

Number of staff: 17 full-time professional; 9 full-time support.

EIN: 231581832

Selected grants: The following grants were reported in 2005.

$1,655,743 to Foundations, Inc., Moorestown, NJ. For Pennsylvania High School Coaching Initiative.

$1,066,700 to University of Pennsylvania, Philadelphia, PA. 2 grants: $124,000 (For general operating support), $942,700 to Graduate School of Education (For Penn Literacy Network).

$328,000 to Research for Action, Philadelphia, PA. For Pennsylvania High School Coaching Initiative.

$223,617 to Capital Area Intermediate Unit, Camp Hill, PA. For Phase 1 of Pennsylvania High School Coaching Initiative.

$220,000 to Philadelphia Futures for Youth, Philadelphia, PA. 2 grants: $100,000 (For scholarships), $120,000 (For scholarships).

$210,900 to Cornerstone Christian Academy, Philadelphia, PA. 2 grants: $105,450 each (For scholarships).

$121,250 to Resources for Human Development, Philadelphia, PA. For New Beginnings Nonprofit Incubator.

8379
Philadelphia Health Care Trust ✧
(formerly Graduate Health System, Inc.)
2129 Chestnut St.
Philadelphia, PA 19103

Established in 1976 in PA; assumed current name in 1998.
Foundation type: Independent foundation.
Financial data (yr. ended 6/30/05): Assets, $39,922,089 (M); expenditures, $4,585,018; qualifying distributions, $2,745,106; giving activities include $2,435,166 for 9 grants (high: $760,887; low: $75,000).
Purpose and activities: Giving primarily for education and health care.
Fields of interest: Higher education; Health care.
Limitations: Applications not accepted. Giving primarily in Philadelphia, PA.
Application information: Contributes only to pre-selected organizations.
Officer and Directors:* Marc S. Cornblatt, Secy.; Peter D. Carlino; Harold Cramer; Carol J. Eastwood; Bernard J. Korman*; Russell Kunkel; Janice L. Richter.
EIN: 231985544

8380
Dr. & Mrs. Arthur William Phillips Charitable Trust ✧
229 Elm St.
P.O. Box 316
Oil City, PA 16301-0316 (814) 676-2736
Contact: Berta Winters, Admin. Asst.

Established in 1978 in PA.
Donor: Arthur William Phillips†.
Foundation type: Independent foundation.
Financial data (yr. ended 9/30/04): Assets, $13,613,528 (M); expenditures, $699,799; qualifying distributions, $597,735; giving activities include $580,028 for 27 grants (high: $200,000; low: $1,300).
Purpose and activities: Giving primarily to organizations with medical or educational purposes.
Fields of interest: Arts; Higher education; Education; Hospitals (general); Health organizations, association; Human services; YM/YWCAs & YM/YWHAs; Children/youth, services.
Type of support: Capital campaigns; Building/renovation; Equipment; Program development; Scholarship funds; Matching/challenge support.
Limitations: Giving primarily in northwestern PA. No grants to individuals.
Application information: Application form not required.
  Initial approach: Proposal
  Copies of proposal: 3
  Deadline(s): None
Trustees: Hon. William E. Breene; Edith Gilmore Letcher; William J. McFate.
EIN: 256201015
Selected grants: The following grants were reported in 2005.
$200,000 to Clarion University of Pennsylvania, Clarion, PA.

$50,000 to Pennsylvania State University, Shenango, Sharon, PA.
$25,000 to George Junior Republic, Grove City, PA.
$10,000 to Saint Paul Homes, Greenville, PA.
$7,500 to Community Services of Venango County, Oil City, PA.
$7,000 to United Negro College Fund, Pittsburgh, PA.
$6,800 to Make-A-Wish Foundation, Bellefonte, PA.

8381
Phoenixville Community Health Foundation ☆
1260 Valley Forge Rd., Ste. 102
Phoenixville, PA 19460 (610) 917-9890
Contact: Louis J. Beccaria, C.E.O. and Pres.
FAX: (610) 917-9861; *E-mail:* pchfl@juno.com; *URL:* http://www.pchf1.org/

Established in 1997 in PA; converted from Phoenixville Hospital.
Foundation type: Independent foundation.
Financial data (yr. ended 6/30/05): Assets, $52,394,687 (M); gifts received, $2,000; expenditures, $2,010,232; qualifying distributions, $1,783,254; giving activities include $1,356,134 for 101 grants (high: $6,000; low: $84), $44,000 for 44 grants to individuals (high: $1,000; low: $1,000), and $21,725 for 97 employee matching gifts.
Purpose and activities: The foundation seeks to improve the health and quality of life in the Greater Phoenixville community.
Fields of interest: Medical care, community health systems; Public health; Health care; Mental health/crisis services; Children, services; Youth, services; Human services.
Type of support: Program development; Management development/capacity building; General/operating support; Continuing support; Capital campaigns; Building/renovation; Equipment; Endowments; Seed money; Technical assistance; Program evaluation; Scholarships—to individuals; Matching/challenge support.
Limitations: Giving primarily in the greater Phoenixville, PA, area. No support for fraternal organizations, political parties, or veterans, labor, or civic groups. No grants for benefits, operating deficits, or publications.
Publications: Application guidelines; Annual report; Financial statement; Grants list; Informational brochure (including application guidelines); Newsletter; Program policy statement.
Application information: Application form required.
  Initial approach: Telephone or office visit
  Copies of proposal: 1
  Deadline(s): None
  Board meeting date(s): Jan., Apr., July, and Sept.
  Final notification: 8 weeks
Officers and Directors:* James G. Reading,* Chair.; David M. Frees, Jr.,* Vice-Chair.; Louis J. Beccaria,* C.E.O. and Pres.; Karen Coldwell, Secy.; Eubank T. Travis-Bey, Treas.; Amy Barto; Ronald F. Brien; Frank Cirone; Richard S. Downs; R. John Giannone; Edward Hovick, M.D.; Rev. Cynthia Krommes; John Messing; Debbie Mitchell; Kenneth Winston.
Number of staff: 2 full-time professional; 2 full-time support.
EIN: 232912035
Selected grants: The following grants were reported in 2005.

$67,500 to Open Hearth, Spring City, PA. 2 grants: $42,500, $25,000
$60,000 to Community Volunteers in Medicine, West Chester, PA.
$38,388 to Pennsylvania Association of Non-Profit Organizations, Harrisburg, PA.
$35,000 to Family Service of Chester County, West Chester, PA.
$15,000 to Chester County Futures, West Chester, PA.
$11,600 to Magee Rehabilitation Hospital, Philadelphia, PA.
$10,000 to Moms House, Johnstown, PA.
$9,789 to Chester County Community Foundation, West Chester, PA.
$400 to Holy Family School, Phoenixville, PA.

8382
The L. W. Pierce Family Foundation ✧
8 Tower Bridge, Ste. 1060
161 Washington St.
Conshohocken, PA 19428 (610) 862-2105
Contact: Constance Buckley, Pres.

Established in 1997 in FL.
Donors: Leo W. Pierce, Sr.; Marjorie L. Pierce†.
Foundation type: Independent foundation.
Financial data (yr. ended 12/31/05): Assets, $16,821,601 (M); gifts received, $835,400; expenditures, $717,894; qualifying distributions, $628,726; giving activities include $550,400 for 25 grants (high: $200,000; low: $400; average: $5,000–$10,000).
Purpose and activities: Giving primarily for health, social, and educational services in the areas of alcohol and drug abuse, hospice care and children's welfare.
Fields of interest: Higher education, university; Education; Health care; Health organizations, association; Human services; Homeless, human services.
Type of support: General/operating support; Capital campaigns; Building/renovation; Endowments.
Limitations: Giving limited to the Vero Beach, FL and Philadelphia, PA areas. No grants to individuals.
Publications: Application guidelines; Grants list.
Application information: Application form not required.
  Initial approach: Letter or telephone
  Copies of proposal: 1
  Deadline(s): Mar. 1
  Board meeting date(s): Apr. and Oct.
  Final notification: 2 weeks following board meetings
Officers and Trustees:* Leo W. Pierce, Sr., Chair.; Constance Buckley,* Pres.; Michael Pierce,* Treas.; Kathryn Cox; Eve Pierce; J. Peter Pierce; Karen Pierce; Kathleen F. Pierce; Leo W. Pierce, Jr.; Mary Elizabeth Pierce; Barbara Quinn.
EIN: 597109847

8383
The Pilgrim Foundation ✧
540 Pennsylvania Ave., Ste. 318
Fort Washington, PA 19034
Contact: Gary L. Pilgrim, Pres.
Application address: 5 Great Valley Pkwy., Malvern, PA 19355, tel.: (610) 296-1754

Donor: Gary L. Pilgrim.
Foundation type: Independent foundation.

Financial data (yr. ended 6/30/05): Assets, $8,692,701 (M); expenditures, $392,521; qualifying distributions, $391,961; giving activities include $338,462 for 19 grants (high: $40,000; low: $1,500).
Purpose and activities: Giving primarily to Christian schools; support also for Christian organizations and churches.
Fields of interest: Education; Reproductive health; Family services; Women, centers/services; Christian agencies & churches.
Limitations: Giving primarily in PA.
Application Information:
   Initial approach: Letter
   Deadline(s): None
Officers: Gary L. Pilgrim, Pres.; Suzanne T. Daniel, Exec. V.P.
EIN: 232955610
Selected grants: The following grants were reported in 2004.
$45,000 to Care Center for Christ, West Chester, PA. For general support.
$40,000 to Christian Academy, Media, PA. For general support.
$40,000 to Focus on the Family, Colorado Springs, CO. For general support.
$35,700 to Chester County Womens Services, Thorndale, PA. For general support.
$28,000 to Campus Crusade for Christ International, Orlando, FL. For general support.
$25,000 to Bridge of Hope, Coatesville, PA. For general support.
$15,000 to Amnion Crisis Pregnancy Center, Bryn Mawr, PA. For general support.
$15,000 to Good Works, Coatesville, PA. For general support.
$14,500 to Baptist Bible College and School of Theology, Clarks Summit, PA. For general support.
$10,000 to Delaware County Christian School, Newtown Square, PA. For general support.

8384
The Pincus Charitable Fund ✧
Independence Mall E.
Philadelphia, PA 19106

Established in 1986 in PA.
Donors: David Pincus; Pincus Brothers, Inc.
Foundation type: Independent foundation.
Financial data (yr. ended 11/30/03): Assets, $65,534 (M); gifts received, $330,787; expenditures, $334,675; qualifying distributions, $334,591; giving activities include $334,585 for 95 grants (high: $150,000; low: $50).
Purpose and activities: Giving for health care, children's services, education, and a variety of relief agencies.
Fields of interest: Education; Health care; AIDS; Human services; Children, services; International development; Jewish agencies & temples.
Type of support: General/operating support; Continuing support; Scholarship funds.
Limitations: Applications not accepted. Giving on a national and international basis. No grants to individuals.
Application information: Contributes only to pre-selected organizations.
Officers: David Pincus, Pres.; Gerry Pincus, Secy.; Bruce Fishberg, Treas.
Directors: Alvin Dorsky; Andrew Epstein; Nathan Pincus; Wendy Pincus.
EIN: 222781261

Selected grants: The following grants were reported in 2003.
$150,000 to Israel Sports Center for the Disabled, Ramat Gan, Israel. .
$51,000 to International Rescue Committee, New York, NY.
$35,000 to Penn State Research Foundation, University Park, PA.
$15,000 to National Constitution Center, Philadelphia, PA.
$6,150 to Temple Beth Hillel-Beth El, Wynnewood, PA.
$6,000 to American Friends of the Israel Philharmonic Orchestra, New York, NY.
$6,000 to Jewish Theological Seminary of America, Philadelphia, PA.
$5,000 to Federation Allied Jewish Appeal of Philadelphia, Philadelphia, PA.
$2,000 to Philadelphia Scholars Fund, Philadelphia, PA. For annual support.
$1,250 to United Negro College Fund, Fairfax, VA.

8385
Pine Tree Foundation ✧
120 Righters Mill Rd.
Gladwyne, PA 19035 (610) 649-4601
Contact: A. Morris Williams, Jr., Chair.; Ruth W. Williams, Pres.

Established in 1986 in PA.
Donors: A. Morris Williams, Jr.; Ruth W. Williams.
Foundation type: Independent foundation.
Financial data (yr. ended 7/31/05): Assets, $32,697,162 (L); gifts received, $533,676; expenditures, $1,973,134; qualifying distributions, $1,922,000; giving activities include $1,922,000 for 18 grants (high: $718,000; low: $1,000).
Purpose and activities: Giving primarily for higher education, the arts, and human services, including the Salvation Army and children's services.
Fields of interest: Arts; Higher education; Housing/shelter, services; Human services; Salvation Army; Children/youth, services.
Type of support: General/operating support.
Limitations: Giving primarily in GA, NC, and PA. No grants to individuals.
Application information:
   Initial approach: Letter
   Deadline(s): None
Officers and Directors:* A. Morris Williams, Jr.,* Chair. and Treas.; Ruth W. Williams,* Pres. and Secy.; Susan W. Beltz; Joanne W. Markman.
EIN: 222751187

8386
The Pittsburgh Foundation ▼
5 PPG Pl., Ste. 250
Pittsburgh, PA 15222-5414 (412) 391-5122
Contact: For grant applications: Dr. William E. Trueheart, C.E.O.
FAX: (412) 391-7259; *E-mail:* email@pghfdn.org; Grant application E-mail: trueheartw@pghfdn.org; URL: http://www.pittsburghfoundation.org

Established in 1945 in PA by bank resolution and declaration of trust.
Foundation type: Community foundation.
Financial data (yr. ended 12/31/05): Assets, $690,511,755 (M); gifts received, $56,882,276; expenditures, $36,900,670; giving activities include $31,466,977 for 2,378 grants.

Purpose and activities: The foundation promotes and champions the betterment of the greater Pittsburgh, PA, community and the quality of life for all its citizens by helping a wide variety of donors fulfill their philanthropic interests through providing leadership in identifying and addressing significant community needs. The foundation provides a vehicle to make giving easy, personally satisfying and effective. The foundation is organized for the permanent administration of funds placed in trust for public charitable and educational purposes. Funds are used for programs of regularly established agencies for organizational capacity building, systemic change, improved service delivery, planning and program development, capital and equipment, operating support and community building. Grants are made primarily in the areas of achieving educational excellence and equity; supporting families; fostering economic development; reducing health disparities; and advancing the arts. Unless specified by the donor, grants are generally nonrecurring.
Fields of interest: Arts, cultural/ethnic awareness; Arts; Education; Health care; Disasters, Hurricane Katrina; Youth development; Family services; Community development, public/private ventures; Economic development; Community development.
Type of support: Management development/capacity building; Program development; Seed money; Scholarship funds; Research; Technical assistance; Program-related investments/loans.
Limitations: Giving from unrestricted funds limited to Pittsburgh and Allegheny County, PA. No support for sectarian purposes, private and parochial schools, or hospitals (from unrestricted funds). No grants to individuals (from unrestricted funds except for the Isabel P. Kennedy Award) or for annual campaigns, endowment funds, travel, operating budgets, fellowships, internships, awards, special events or research of a highly technical or specialized nature; no loans (except for program related investments).
Publications: Application guidelines; Annual report; Informational brochure (including application guidelines); Newsletter.
Application information: Visit foundation Web site for application form and guidelines. Program staff will review each letter of inquiry, and contact the organization if additional information, including a complete proposal, is required. Once a full proposal is requested by the foundation, the organization may follow the application guidelines provided by the foundation, or submit the Common Grant Application Form. Proposals should be submitted 2 months prior to board meetings to qualify for possible consideration at the next meeting. Application form required.
   Initial approach: Letter of inquiry
   Copies of proposal: 1
   Deadline(s): None
   Board meeting date(s): Monthly
   Final notification: 7 to 10 days after program committee meetings by correspondence
Officers and Directors:* George A. Davidson, Jr.,* Chair.; Aaron A. Walton,* Vice-Chair.; William E. Trueheart, Ph.D., C.E.O. and Pres.; Richard Reed, Exec. V.P.; John Ellis, V.P., Comms.; Kimberly J. Hammer, V.P., Devel. and Donor Svcs.; Thomas S. Hay, V.P., Finance; Gerri Kay, V.P., Prog. and Policy; Mary Wilson, Cont.; Nancy D. Washington, Ph.D.*, Secy.; Joseph L. Calihan,* Treas.; James Broadhurst, Dir. Emeritus; William J. Copeland, Dir. Emeritus; Douglas D. Danforth, Dir. Emeritus; Arthur J. Edmunds, Dir. Emeritus; Alvin Rogal, Dir.

Emeritus; Dorothy R. Williams, Dir. Emeritus; Robert P. Bozzone; Joanne E. Burley, Ph.D.; Gregory D. Curtis; Linda A. Dickerson; John C. Harmon; Peter F. Mathieson; Mary Lou McLaughlin; Nancy L. Rackoff; James C. Roddey; Edith L. Shapira, M.D.; Gregory R. Spencer; Robert B. Webb.

Trustee Banks: Mellon Bank, N.A.; National City Bank; PNC Bank, N.A.

Number of staff: 34 full-time professional; 2 part-time professional.

EIN: 250965466

Selected grants: The following grants were reported in 2005.

$700,000 to University of Pittsburgh, Pittsburgh, PA. To improve opportunity for reducing and eliminating disparities in health outcomes by addressing critical core infrastructure needs and by expanding Health Empowerment Zone of Healthy Black Family Project.

$425,000 to Family Resources, Pittsburgh, PA. For Beverly Jewel Wall Lovelace Children's Program.

$400,000 to Bay Area Multicultural Arts Initiative, San Francisco, CA. To provide operating support for administrative and grantmaking activities.

$200,500 to Allegheny County Department of Human Services, Pittsburgh, PA. 2 grants: $100,000 (To continue Senior Living Enhancement Project (SLEP) demonstration in partnership with Allegheny County Housing Authority and Pittsburgh Foundation to provide wellness and health promotion/disease prevention services to residents in Allegheny), $100,500 (To continue successful Jail Reintegration Project and match Pennsylvania Commission on Crime and Delinquency, payable over 2 years).

$112,500 to Allegheny Council to Improve Our Neighborhoods (ACTION)-Housing, Pittsburgh, PA. For bridge funding to continue Family Savings Account Program that empowers low-income families to pursue self-sufficiency through asset building and linkages to supportive services.

$100,000 to United Cerebral Palsy of Pittsburgh, Pittsburgh, PA. To introduce Benefit Bank, Internet-based, counselor-assisted program to help low- and moderate-income individuals and families with children apply for benefits and tax credits.

$75,000 to Education Policy and Leadership Center, Harrisburg, PA. For policy work affecting statewide educational reforms to improve Pittsburgh and Allegheny County public school districts.

$50,000 to Pennsylvania State University, McKeesport, PA. To pilot Pathways to Success after-school program in East Allegheny School District.

8387

The Harry Plankenhorn Foundation, Inc. ✧
c/o New Covenant United Church of Christ
202 E. 3rd St.
Williamsport, PA   17701

Incorporated in 1959 in PA.
Donor: Harry Plankenhorn†.
Foundation type: Independent foundation.
Financial data (yr. ended 12/31/04): Assets, $7,791,346 (M); expenditures, $325,011; qualifying distributions, $317,414; giving activities include $315,749 for 18 grants (high: $100,000; low: $1,000).

Purpose and activities: Giving for human services, including programs for the visually handicapped, children and youth, and emergency aid.
Fields of interest: Recreation, camps; Youth development; Human services; Children/youth, services; Human services, emergency aid.
Type of support: General/operating support; Annual campaigns; Building/renovation.
Limitations: Applications not accepted. Giving primarily in Lycoming County, PA. No grants to individuals.
Application information: Unsolicited requests for funds not accepted.
Officers and Board Members:* Charles F. Greevy III,* Pres.; Abram M. Snyder,* V.P.; Nancy Stearns,* Secy.; Fred A. Foulkrod,* Treas.; David Benis; Barbara Ertel; Carl O. Hieber; W. Herbert Poff III; Robert M. Reeder; Carolyn Seifert; Eleanor W. Whiting.
EIN: 246023579

8388

The PNC Foundation ▼
(formerly PNC Bank Foundation)
249 5th Ave., 20th Fl.
1 PNC Plz.
Pittsburgh, PA   15222   (412) 762-7076
Contact: Mia Hallett Bernard, Exec. Dir.
FAX: (412) 705-3584;
E-mail: foundations@pncbank.com; URL: http://www.pnccommunityinvolvement.com/PNCFoundation.htm

Established in 1970 in PA.
Donors: PNC Bank, N.A.; The PNC Financial Services Group, Inc.
Foundation type: Company-sponsored foundation.
Financial data (yr. ended 12/31/05): Assets, $55,401,382 (M); gifts received, $48,197,475; expenditures, $12,054,867; qualifying distributions, $11,982,575; giving activities include $11,194,934 for 897 grants (high: $268,603; low: $40), and $608,777 for employee matching gifts.
Purpose and activities: The foundation supports organizations involved with arts and culture, pre-K and K-12 education, human services, economic development, community development, and economically disadvantaged people.
Fields of interest: Arts education; Arts; Elementary/secondary education; Education, early childhood education; Child development, education; Human services; Economic development; Community development; Economically disadvantaged.
Type of support: General/operating support; Continuing support; Capital campaigns; Building/renovation; Program development; Curriculum development; Program-related investments/loans; Employee matching gifts; Matching/challenge support.
Limitations: Giving primarily in Washington, DC, DE, IN, KY, MD, NJ, OH, PA, and VA. No support for churches or religious organizations. No grants to individuals, or for endowments, conferences, seminars, tickets, or advertising; no loans (except for program-related investments).
Publications: Application guidelines.
Application information: An interview may be requested. Proposals may be submitted using the Delaware Valley Grantmakers, Greater Cincinnati Foundation, or Grantmakers of Western Pennsylvania Common Grant Application. Application form not required.
Initial approach: Proposal

Copies of proposal: 1
Deadline(s): None
Board meeting date(s): Quarterly
Final notification: Approximately 6 weeks
Officers and Trustees:* Eva T. Blum,* Chair.; George P. Long III, Secy.; Samuel R. Patterson, Treas.; Mia Hallett Bernard, Exec. Dir.; Joan Gulley; Joseph C. Guyaux; Neil Hall; Roberta London-Wilson; William C. Mutterperl; Donna C. Peterman; James E. Rohr.
EIN: 251202255
Selected grants: The following grants were reported in 2005.

$268,603 to United Way of Southeastern Pennsylvania, Philadelphia, PA.

$200,000 to Pennsylvania State University, University Park, PA.

$190,000 to Childrens Hospital of Pittsburgh, Pittsburgh, PA.

$143,376 to Pittsburgh Symphony Society, Pittsburgh, PA.

$105,000 to Greater Louisville Inc., Louisville, KY.

$50,000 to Community Services for Children, Allentown, PA.

$37,745 to United Way of Greater Cincinnati, Cincinnati, OH.

$17,500 to Pittsburgh Community Television Corporation, Pittsburgh, PA.

$15,000 to Johnson Technical Institute, Scranton, PA.

$12,300 to Mount Nazareth Center, Pittsburgh, PA.

8389

The Podiatry Foundation of Pittsburgh ✧ ☆
405 Rosslyn Rd.
Carnegie, PA   15106-1057
E-mail: info@podiatryplace.com; URL: http://www.podiatryplace.org
Application address: c/o Joan Abaray, Chair., 534 Woodland Ave., Oakmont, PA 15139, tel.: (412) 828-6616

Foundation type: Independent foundation.
Financial data (yr. ended 6/30/05): Assets, $2,416,354 (M); expenditures, $429,407; qualifying distributions, $421,169; giving activities include $222,202 for 4 grants (high: $147,636; low: $500), and $144,000 for 13 grants to individuals (high: $15,000; low: $8,000).
Purpose and activities: Giving for the study of podiatric medicine.
Fields of interest: Higher education; Hospitals (general); Health care.
Limitations: Giving on a national basis.
Application information: See foundation Web site for grant and scholarship application guidelines. Application form required.
Deadline(s): Nov. 1
Officers: John G. Beering, C.E.O. and Treas.; Jeffrey Nigro, Pres.; Mark L. Unatin, Secy.
Directors: Rachel Berglund; Joan Glunt; Clinton R. Lowery; Nicki Nigro; Michael L. Sparlin; Wayne B. Wolf.
EIN: 251024331

8390

Pollock Foundation ◇ ☆

(formerly S. Wilson & Grace M. Pollock Foundation)
c/o M&T Bank
21 E. Market St., MC 402-130
York, PA 17401-1500
Application address: c/o Heath Allen, P.O. Box
11963, Harrisburg, PA 17108-1963

Established in 1997 in PA.
Donors: Grace Pollock; S. Wilson Pollock.
Foundation type: Independent foundation.
Financial data (yr. ended 4/30/05): Assets,
$9,944,858 (M); expenditures, $532,807;
qualifying distributions, $429,600; giving activities
include $428,100 for 12 grants (high: $150,000;
low: $500).
Fields of interest: Higher education, college
(community/junior); Education; Health
organizations, association; Human services;
Federated giving programs; Protestant agencies &
churches.
Limitations: Giving primarily in PA, with emphasis on
Camp Hill and Harrisburg. No grants to individuals.
Application information:
  Deadline(s): None
Directors: Heath Allen; Courtney Lynn Gordon; David
McLane; Grace M. Pollock; Laureen Elizabeth
Pollock; Lindsay Kathryn Pollock.
Trustee: M&T Bank.
EIN: 237889770

8391

The C. Northop Pond and Alethea Marder
Pond Foundation ◇

c/o PNC Bank, N.A.
1600 Market St., Tax Dept.
Philadelphia, PA 19103-7240
Application address: c/o PNC Bank, N.A., 454 State
Rte. 28, Bridgewater, NJ 08807-2452

Established in 1997 in NJ.
Donor: Alethea Marder Pond†.
Foundation type: Independent foundation.
Financial data (yr. ended 4/30/05): Assets,
$11,049,583 (M); expenditures, $613,049;
qualifying distributions, $522,003; giving activities
include $495,000 for 31 grants (high: $60,000;
low: $5,000).
Purpose and activities: The foundation supports
activities in charity, education, health care,
conservation and the environment.
Fields of interest: Education; Environment; Health
care; Human services; American Red Cross.
Limitations: Giving primarily in NJ.
Application information: Application form not
required.
  Deadline(s): None
Trustees: Grace Pond Fisher; Richard F. Greaves;
Charles N. Pond, Jr.; Donna S. Pond; PNC Bank, N.A.
EIN: 226727894
Selected grants: The following grants were reported
in 2005.
$60,000 to American Red Cross, Plainfield, NJ.
$40,000 to Plainfield Health Center, Plainfield, NJ.
$30,000 to Hospice of Citrus County, Lecanto, FL.
$20,000 to Cape Cod Hospital, Hyannis, MA.
$20,000 to Southfield School, Brookline, MA.
$20,000 to Susan G. Komen Breast Cancer
  Foundation, Summit, NJ.
$15,000 to Crescent Avenue Presbyterian Church,
  Plainfield, NJ.

$10,000 to Best Friends Animal Society, Kanab, UT.
$10,000 to Make-A-Wish Foundation of America,
  Phoenix, AZ.
$10,000 to Smile Train, New York, NY.

8392

Poor Richard's Charitable Trust ◇ ☆

(formerly Lisa S. Roberts & David Seltzer Charitable
Trust)
614 S. 8th St., Ste. 306
Philadelphia, PA 19147

Established in 1997 in PA.
Donor: Lisa S. Roberts.
Foundation type: Independent foundation.
Financial data (yr. ended 12/31/05): Assets,
$11,371,949 (M); gifts received, $52,515;
expenditures, $563,644; qualifying distributions,
$531,450; giving activities include $531,450 for
grants.
Fields of interest: Arts; Elementary/secondary
education; Children, services.
Limitations: Applications not accepted. Giving
primarily in Philadelphia, PA; some giving also in
Crested Butte, CO. No grants to individuals.
Application information: Contributes only to
pre-selected organizations.
Trustees: Lisa S. Roberts; David Seltzer.
EIN: 237909451
Selected grants: The following grants were reported
in 2005.
$138,000 to Atwater Kent Museum, Philadelphia,
  PA. 2 grants: $38,000, $100,000
$100,000 to University of Pennsylvania,
  Philadelphia, PA.
$25,000 to Shipley School, Bryn Mawr, PA. 3 grants:
  $5,000, $10,000, $10,000
$20,000 to StarFinder Foundation, Philadelphia, PA.
  2 grants: $10,000 each
$11,400 to Philadelphia Museum of Art,
  Philadelphia, PA. 2 grants: $1,400, $10,000

8393

Wilbur E. Postles Scholarship Fund ◇ ☆

c/o PNC Bank, N.A.
1600 Market St., Tax Dept.
Philadelphia, PA 19103-7240
Application address: c/o PNC Bank, Delaware,
Attn.: Donald Davis, 222 Delaware Ave., 16th Fl.,
Wilmington, DE 19801

Established in 2002 in DE.
Foundation type: Independent foundation.
Financial data (yr. ended 12/31/05): Assets,
$5,464,262 (M); expenditures, $453,949;
qualifying distributions, $392,841; giving activities
include $375,634 for 38 grants (high: $143,700;
low: $1,000).
Purpose and activities: Scholarship awards to
residents of Delaware who were residents for four
years prior to applying, and who will attend a college,
professional or technical school.
Fields of interest: Scholarships/financial aid.
Type of support: Scholarships—to individuals.
Limitations: Giving limited to residents of DE.
Application information: Application form required.
  Deadline(s): May 9
Trustees: John R. Twombly, Jr.; PNC Bank, N.A.
EIN: 516010602
Selected grants: The following grants were reported
in 2004.

$104,700 to University of Delaware, Newark, DE.
$16,000 to Columbia University, New York, NY. 2
  grants: $8,000 each
$12,000 to College of William and Mary,
  Williamsburg, VA.
$10,000 to Washington College, Chestertown, MD.
$8,000 to Lincoln University, Lincoln University, PA.
$7,550 to Wilmington College, New Castle, DE.
$7,500 to Hartwick College, Oneonta, NY.
$7,500 to New York University, New York, NY.
$7,500 to Syracuse University, Syracuse, NY.

8394

PPG Industries Foundation ▼

1 PPG Pl.
Pittsburgh, PA 15272
Contact: Sue Sloan, Sr. Prog. Off.
URL: http://corporateportal.ppg.com/PPG/topnav/
About/PPG_Ind_Fnd.htm

Incorporated in 1951 in PA.
Donor: PPG Industries, Inc.
Foundation type: Company-sponsored foundation.
Financial data (yr. ended 12/31/04): Assets,
$12,330,415 (M); expenditures, $5,802,948;
qualifying distributions, $5,743,939; giving
activities include $4,072,281 for 806 grants (high:
$575,000; low: $150), and $1,393,795 for 971
employee matching gifts.
Purpose and activities: The foundation supports
organizations involved with arts and culture,
education, the environment, human services,
community development, access to technology, and
civic affairs and awards college scholarships to
minorities and students located in areas of major
PPG facilities.
Fields of interest: Arts, equal rights; Arts;
Elementary/secondary education; Business school/
education; Student services/organizations;
Education; Environment, legal rights; Environmental
education; Youth development, adult & child
programs; Human services; Economic development;
Community development; Science, equal rights;
Science, formal/general education; Public affairs;
Minorities; African Americans/Blacks.
Type of support: General/operating support;
Continuing support; Annual campaigns; Capital
campaigns; Equipment; Emergency funds; Program
development; Scholarship funds; Employee
volunteer services; Employee matching gifts;
Employee-related scholarships; Scholarships—to
individuals.
Limitations: Giving on a national basis in areas of
company operations, with emphasis on the
Pittsburgh, PA, area; giving also to national
organizations. No support for lobbying organizations
or political organizations or religious organizations
not of direct benefit to the entire community. No
grants to individuals (except for scholarships), or for
advertising or sponsorships, endowments, projects
that would directly benefit PPG, special events or
telephone solicitation, or general operating support
for United Way-supported organizations.
Publications: Application guidelines; Annual report
(including application guidelines); Financial
statement; Grants list.
Application information: Proposals should be brief.
An interview may be requested. Application form not
required.
  Initial approach: Proposal to nearest company
    facility; proposal to foundation for national
    organizations
  Copies of proposal: 1

Deadline(s): None
Board meeting date(s): Usually in June and Dec.
Final notification: Following board meetings
Officers and Directors: Charles E. Bunch,* Chair. and C.E.O.; James C. Diggs,* Sr. V.P.; William H. Hernandez,* Sr. V.P.; Lynne D. Schmidt, Exec. Dir.; Charles W. Wise.
Number of staff: 1 full-time professional; 1 part-time professional; 1 part-time support.
EIN: 256037790
Selected grants: The following grants were reported in 2004.
$575,000 to United Way of Allegheny County, Pittsburgh, PA. For operating support.
$550,000 to Zoological Society of Pittsburgh, Pittsburgh Zoo and PPG Aquarium, Pittsburgh, PA.
$452,860 to National Merit Scholarship Corporation, Evanston, IL. For scholarships.
$107,000 to American Chemical Society, DC. For minority scholarships.
$20,000 to Pittsburgh Cultural Trust, Pittsburgh, PA.
$20,000 to United Fund, Shelby, Shelby, NC.
$10,000 to University of Michigan, Department of Chemist, Ann Arbor, MI.
$10,000 to University of South Carolina, Columbia, SC.

8395

The Presser Foundation ◇

385 Lancaster Ave., No. 205
Haverford, PA 19041 (610) 658-9030
Contact: Edith A. Reinhardt

Founded in 1916; incorporated in 1939 in PA.
Donors: Theodore Presser†; Theodore Presser Foundation.
Foundation type: Independent foundation.
Financial data (yr. ended 6/30/05): Assets, $57,489,065 (M); gifts received, $1,747,928; expenditures, $2,948,106; qualifying distributions, $2,906,869; giving activities include $2,459,750 for grants, and $219,371 for grants to individuals.
Purpose and activities: To provide scholarship aid grants to accredited colleges and universities in the field of music; to increase music education in institutions of learning and to popularize the teaching of music as a profession. Grants to individuals limited to providing emergency aid to worthy music teachers in need.
Fields of interest: Arts education; Performing arts, music; Higher education.
Type of support: Building/renovation; Equipment; Program development; Seed money; Fellowships; Scholarship funds; Grants to individuals; Matching/challenge support.
Application information: Application forms available for financial aid to needy music teachers and for scholarships. Application form required.
Deadline(s): None
Officers and Trustees: Robert Capanna, Pres.; Thomas M. Hyndman, Jr.,* V.P.; Bruce Montgomery,* Secy.; William M. Davison IV,* Treas.; Leon Bates; David Boe; Anthony P. Checchia; Jeffrey Cornelius; Robert W. Denious; Herbert P. Evert; Martin A. Hekhscher; Helen Laird; Corey R. Smith; Michael Stairs; Henderson Supplee III; Radclyffe F. Thompson; Vera Wilson.
Number of staff: 1 full-time professional.
EIN: 232164013
Selected grants: The following grants were reported in 2004.

$150,000 to West Chester University of Pennsylvania, West Chester, PA.
$25,000 to Academy of Vocal Arts, Philadelphia, PA.
$25,000 to Settlement Music School, Philadelphia, PA.
$17,000 to Mendelssohn Club, Philadelphia, PA.
$15,000 to Haddonfield Symphony, Haddonfield, NJ.
$4,000 to Manhattan School of Music, New York, NY. For scholarships.
$4,000 to New England Conservatory of Music, Boston, MA. For scholarships.
$4,000 to Western Washington University, Bellingham, WA. For scholarships.
$2,000 to Pennsylvania Academy of Music, Lancaster, PA.
$1,000 to Suburban Music School, Media, PA.

8396

The Pryor Foundation ◇ ☆

c/o Frederic L. Pryor
740 Harvard Ave.
Swarthmore, PA 19081
E-mail: fpryor1@swarthmore.edu

Established in 1947 in MI.
Donors: Mary S. Pryor†; Millard H. Pryor†; Corey Kienholz.
Foundation type: Independent foundation.
Financial data (yr. ended 1/31/06): Assets, $4,209,002 (M); gifts received, $50,001; expenditures, $454,626; qualifying distributions, $415,000; giving activities include $415,000 for grants.
Purpose and activities: Giving to the arts, culture and education.
Fields of interest: Arts; Higher education; Human services; Federated giving programs.
Type of support: Annual campaigns; Capital campaigns; Emergency funds; Consulting services.
Limitations: Applications not accepted. Giving primarily in Hartford, CT, Ann Arbor, MI, Mansfield, OH, and Philadelphia, PA. No support for religious or political organizations. No grants for building funds or land acquisition.
Application information: Contributes to organizations in which Pryor family members are involved.
Board meeting date(s): Nov.
Officer and Trustees: Frederic L. Pryor,* Mgr.; F. Loyal Bemiller; H. Elizabeth Bradley; Daniel A. Pryor; Esther A. Pryor.
Number of staff: None.
EIN: 386056108
Selected grants: The following grants were reported in 2005.
$60,000 to Tougaloo College, Tougaloo, MS. For general support.
$25,000 to Peace Neighborhood Center, Ann Arbor, MI. For general support.
$10,000 to Amistad Foundation, Hartford, CT. For general support.
$10,000 to Asylum Hill Boys and Girls Club Development Association, West Hartford, CT. For general support.
$10,000 to Connecticut Opera Association, Hartford, CT. For general support.
$10,000 to Hartford Symphony Orchestra, Hartford, CT. For general support.
$10,000 to University of Connecticut Foundation, West Hartford, CT. For general support.
$10,000 to Wadsworth Atheneum, Hartford, CT. For general support.

$7,500 to NARAL Pro-Choice America Foundation, DC. For general support.
$5,000 to University of Michigan, Ann Arbor, MI. For general support.

8397

The Psalm 103 Foundation ◇

601 Pembroke Rd.
Bryn Mawr, PA 19010

Established in 1987.
Donor: John M. Templeton, Jr.
Foundation type: Independent foundation.
Financial data (yr. ended 9/30/05): Assets, $4,048,031 (M); gifts received, $252,330; expenditures, $356,528; qualifying distributions, $346,600; giving activities include $346,600 for 10 grants (high: $220,600; low: $300).
Fields of interest: Elementary/secondary education; Higher education; Health care; Health organizations, association; Christian agencies & churches.
Limitations: Applications not accepted. Giving primarily in MD and PA. No grants to individuals.
Application information: Contributes only to pre-selected organizations.
Officers: John M. Templeton, Jr., Pres. and Treas.; Josephine J. Templeton, V.P. and Secy.
EIN: 232500843
Selected grants: The following grants were reported in 2003.
$200,000 to Delaware County Christian School, Newtown Square, PA. For Kingdom Campaign.
$23,000 to American Trauma Society, Upper Marlboro, MD. 3 grants: $14,000 (For trauma prevention research), $5,000 (For membership software), $4,000 (For research).
$9,000 to Esperanza Health Center, Philadelphia, PA. For program support.
$5,000 to Saint John Neumann High School, Philadelphia, PA. To purchase microscopes.
$5,000 to Tufts University, Fletcher School of Law and Diplomacy, Medford, MA. For cultural research.
$5,000 to Women of Excellence, Jacksonville, FL. For transition support.
$4,000 to Boy Scouts of America, Cradle of Liberty Council, Philadelphia, PA. For program support.

8398

PSC Charitable Foundation ◇ ☆

762 W. Lancaster Ave.
Bryn Mawr, PA 19010

Foundation type: Independent foundation.
Financial data (yr. ended 12/31/04): Assets, $83,178 (M); gifts received, $350,000; expenditures, $382,740; qualifying distributions, $382,740; giving activities include $382,720 for 256 grants (high: $30,000; low: $52).
Purpose and activities: Giving primarily for the arts, education, health associations, human services, and YMCAs.
Fields of interest: Performing arts; Arts; Education; Health organizations, association; Human services; YM/YWCAs & YM/YWHAs; Federated giving programs.
Limitations: Applications not accepted. Giving primarily in the Philadelphia, PA, area. No grants to individuals.

Application information: Contributes only to pre-selected organizations.

Directors: Karen Carlson; Nick DeBenedictis; Chris Franklin; Dave Smeltzer; Roy Stahl.

EIN: 232985234

8399

PTS Foundation ◇

c/o Parkland Mgmt. Co.
580 W. Germantown Pike, Ste. 202
Plymouth Meeting, PA 19462
Contact: Thomas H. Oden, Treas.
Application address for HRH Scholarship Program: Scholarship Program Administrators, P.O. Box 23737, Nashville, TN 37202; TN tel.: (615) 292-4379; OH tel.: (216) 479-2200 for other charitable requests (Thomas H. Oden)

Established in 1998 in PA as a follow-up to the Lois U. Horvitz Foundation.

Donors: Lois U. Horvitz Foundation; Pam H. Schneider; Milton S. Schneider.

Foundation type: Independent foundation.

Financial data (yr. ended 12/31/05): Assets, $9,845,996 (M); gifts received, $816,837; expenditures, $429,614; qualifying distributions, $413,123; giving activities include $396,763 for 10 grants (high: $140,000; low: $5,000).

Purpose and activities: Giving primarily for education and health.

Fields of interest: Elementary/secondary education; Higher education; Medical research; Human services.

Type of support: Program development; Scholarship funds.

Limitations: Giving in the U.S., primarily in OH. No support for religious organizations. No grants for operating budgets of established agencies, recurring expenses for direct services, annual appeals, debt reduction campaigns, publications or workshops, travel, or government services.

Application information: Form required for HRH Scholarship Program. Application form required.

   Initial approach: Telephone
   Deadline(s): Apr. 1 for scholarships; none for grants

Officers and Directors:* Pam H. Schneider,* Chair.; Milton S. Schneider,* Pres. and Secy.-Treas.; Thomas H. Oden, Treas.

EIN: 232930670

Selected grants: The following grants were reported in 2004.

$63,638 to HRH Scholarship Fund, Cleveland, OH.

$40,000 to Laurel School, Shaker Heights, OH.

$38,770 to Horvitz Newspapers Charity Fund, Cleveland, OH.

$10,000 to Nature Conservancy, Arlington, VA.

$10,000 to Shipley School, Bryn Mawr, PA.

8400

John G. Rangos Charitable Foundation ◇

1 Trimont Ln., Ste. 230
Pittsburgh, PA 15221-1288
Contact: Nancy Barnhart
URL: http://www.rangosfoundation.org/

Established in 1987 in PA.

Donor: John G. Rangos, Sr.

Foundation type: Independent foundation.

Financial data (yr. ended 6/30/04): Assets, $4,755,291 (M); expenditures, $1,516,368;

qualifying distributions, $1,496,312; giving activities include $1,365,707 for 16 grants (high: $400,000; low: $1,000).

Purpose and activities: The foundation is dedicated to providing children with a springboard to knowledge through education and good health, so that they may build a blue print for life.

Fields of interest: Pediatrics; Youth development; Children/youth, services; Children.

Type of support: Annual campaigns; Program development.

Limitations: Giving primarily in western PA. No grants to individuals.

Application information:

   Initial approach: Letter
   Deadline(s): None

Trustees: Alexander Rangos; Jenica Rangos; Jill Rangos; John G. Rangos, Sr.; John G. Rangos, Jr.

Number of staff: 1 full-time professional.

EIN: 251599198

Selected grants: The following grants were reported in 2003.

$1,000,000 to Childrens Hospital of Pittsburgh, Pittsburgh, PA. For general support.

$800,000 to Johns Hopkins University, Baltimore, MD. For general support.

$100,000 to Carnegie Mellon University, Pittsburgh, PA. For general support.

$70,000 to Congressional Medal of Honor Society, Mount Pleasant, SC. For general support.

$60,000 to International Orthodox Christian Charities, Baltimore, MD. For general support.

$25,000 to Carnegie Institute, Science Center, Pittsburgh, PA.

$10,000 to George W. Bush Childhood Home, Midland, TX. For general support.

$10,000 to Prime Stage Theater, Pittsburgh, PA. For general support.

$6,000 to Leukemia & Lymphoma Society, Pittsburgh, PA. For general support.

$3,000 to American Ireland Fund, Pittsburgh, PA. For general support.

8401

John Nesbit Rees and Sarah Henne Rees Charitable Foundation ◇

314 S. Franklin St., Ste. B
P.O. Box 325
Titusville, PA 16354-0325   (814) 827-1844
Contact: Richard W. Roeder, Tr.
FAX: (814) 827-6620;
E-mail: jnrshrees@stargate.net

Established in 1989 in PA.

Donors: John Nesbit Rees†; Sarah Henne Rees†.

Foundation type: Independent foundation.

Financial data (yr. ended 12/31/05): Assets, $14,589,320 (M); expenditures, $761,025; qualifying distributions, $712,818; giving activities include $676,014 for 47 grants (high: $125,000; low: $100).

Purpose and activities: Giving primarily for local civic causes, the performing arts, and education in the sciences.

Fields of interest: Performing arts; Performing arts, dance; Arts; Higher education; Health care, formal/general education; Health care; Health organizations, association; Youth, services; Science, formal/general education.

Type of support: General/operating support; Continuing support; Annual campaigns; Capital campaigns; Building/renovation; Equipment; Endowments; Program development; Curriculum

development; Scholarship funds; Employee matching gifts; Matching/challenge support.

Limitations: Giving primarily in the Titusville, PA, area, including parts of Forest, Crawford, Venango, and Warren counties. No support for private foundations or for churches. No grants to individuals directly, or for scholarships.

Publications: Application guidelines; Annual report.

Application information: Application and Grant Procedure brochure available upon request. Application form not required.

   Initial approach: Letter
   Copies of proposal: 2
   Deadline(s): None
   Board meeting date(s): Monthly
   Final notification: 2 months

Trustees: Richard W. Roeder; Barbara L. Smith.

Number of staff: 2 part-time professional.

EIN: 256264847

Selected grants: The following grants were reported in 2004.

$125,000 to University of Pittsburgh, School of Medicine, Pittsburgh, PA. For scholarships.

$65,000 to University of Pittsburgh, Titusville, PA. 3 grants: $20,000 (For remodeling dinning hall, Boomers), $25,000 (For operating support), $20,000 (For scholarships).

$45,000 to W Q L N-TV, Public Broadcasting of Northwest Pennsylvania, Erie, PA. For program support.

$42,000 to Erie Area Fund for the Arts, Erie, PA. For program support.

$33,443 to Titusville Area Hospital, Titusville, PA. For annual fund.

$29,000 to YMCA of Brevard County, Titusville, FL. For after-school program.

$20,000 to Genesis Family Center, Titusville, PA. For operating support.

$12,000 to Girl Scouts of the U.S.A., Keystone Tall Tree Council, Kittanning, PA. For program support.

8402

The Reidler Foundation ◇

c/o Bank of America, N.A.
101 W. Broad St.
Hazleton, PA 18201   (570) 454-7654
Contact: Diana L. James, Secy.-Treas.

Incorporated in 1944 in PA.

Donors: John W. Reidler†; Verna C. Reidler†; Howard D. Fegan; Ann B. Fegan.

Foundation type: Independent foundation.

Financial data (yr. ended 10/31/05): Assets, $8,678,226 (M); gifts received, $13,994; expenditures, $513,342; qualifying distributions, $431,333; giving activities include $425,000 for 46 grants (high: $64,500; low: $500).

Fields of interest: Higher education; Environment; Human services; Youth, services; Protestant agencies & churches.

Type of support: General/operating support; Capital campaigns; Building/renovation; Endowments.

Limitations: Giving primarily in the Ashland, Hazleton, and Lehigh Valley, PA, areas. No grants to individuals.

Application information:

   Initial approach: Letter from supervising Principal
   Deadline(s): None
   Board meeting date(s): June and Oct.

Officers and Trustees:* Ann B. Fegan,* Pres.; Robert K. Gicking,* V.P.; Diana L. James,

Secy.-Treas.; Howard D. Fegan; John H. Fegan; Eugene C. Fish; Carl J. Reidler; Paul G. Reidler.
EIN: 246022888

8403
Respironics Sleep and Respiratory Research Foundation ◇
1010 Murry Ridge Ln.
Murrysville, PA 15668-8525

Established in 2003 in PA.
Donor: Respironics, Inc.
Foundation type: Company-sponsored foundation.
Financial data (yr. ended 6/30/05): Assets, $2,502,809 (M); gifts received, $4,000,000; expenditures, $1,566,307; qualifying distributions, $1,566,307; giving activities include $1,565,281 for 4 grants (high: $1,250,000; low: $2,000).
Purpose and activities: The foundation supports programs designed to conduct sleep medicine and respiratory research.
Fields of interest: Higher education; Medical school/education; Health care; Lung research.
Limitations: Applications not accepted. Giving primarily in New England. No grants to individuals.
Application information: Contributes only to pre-selected organizations.
Officers and Directors:* Craig B. Reynolds,* Pres.; James C. Woll,* Treas.; Steven P. Fulton; Gerald E. McGinnis.
EIN: 522421348

8404
Rider-Pool Foundation
1050 S. Cedar Crest Blvd., Ste. 202
Allentown, PA 18103 (610) 770-9346
Contact: Bridget I. Rassler, Admin. Support Mgr.
FAX: (610) 770-9361; E-mail: drpool@ptd.net;
URL: http://www.pooltrust.com/the_rider-pool_foundation.htm

Established in 1957 in PA.
Donor: Dorothy Rider-Pool‡.
Foundation type: Independent foundation.
Financial data (yr. ended 12/31/05): Assets, $10,886,339 (M); expenditures, $519,547; qualifying distributions, $476,311; giving activities include $470,981 for 63 grants (high: $60,000; low: $1,000).
Purpose and activities: To serve as a means to improve the quality of life in the community, to build on the community's strengths and add to its vitality, and to increase the capacity of the community to serve the needs of all its citizens.
Fields of interest: Arts; Education; Health care; Community development.
Type of support: General/operating support; Continuing support; Program development.
Limitations: Giving primarily in the Lehigh Valley, PA, area. No support for fraternal organizations or organizations outside the U.S. or its territories; generally no support for sectarian institutions, religious organizations for religious purposes, hospitals, or United Way member agencies. No grants to individuals, or for fundraising or related advertising, testimonial dinners, subsidization of books, mailings, or articles in professional journals.
Publications: Application guidelines; Biennial report; Financial statement; Grants list; Informational brochure (including application guidelines).

Application information: See foundation Web site for application loan guidelines and procedures. Application form not required.
Initial approach: Letter and proposal
Copies of proposal: 1
Deadline(s): Apr. 1 and Aug. 15
Board meeting date(s): May and Oct.
Final notification: June 1 and Nov. 1
Trustees: Edward Donley; Leon C. Holt, Jr.; John P. Jones III; PNC Bank, N.A.
EIN: 236207356

8405
Gilroy & Lillian P. Roberts Charitable Foundation
101 W. Elm St., Ste. 500
Conshohocken, PA 19428 (610) 862-1998
Contact: Stanley Merves, Mgr.

Established in 1982 in PA.
Donors: Gilroy Roberts‡; Lillian Roberts‡; Segel Foundation.
Foundation type: Independent foundation.
Financial data (yr. ended 6/30/06): Assets, $11,306,307 (M); expenditures, $618,779; qualifying distributions, $548,522; giving activities include $492,548 for 17 grants (high: $200,000; low: $50).
Purpose and activities: Giving primarily for higher education, health, and the arts.
Fields of interest: Arts; Higher education; Hospitals (general); Human services; Jewish federated giving programs; Jewish agencies & temples.
Type of support: Professorships; General/operating support; Continuing support; Annual campaigns; Capital campaigns; Scholarship funds; Program-related investments/loans; Matching/challenge support.
Limitations: Giving primarily in Philadelphia, Montgomery and Delaware counties, PA. No grants to individuals.
Application information: Board of grantseeker organization must have 100 percent participation in grantmaking on a cash basis, annually. Application form not required.
Initial approach: Letter
Copies of proposal: 1
Deadline(s): None
Board meeting date(s): May
Final notification: Varies
Officer and Trustees:* Stanley Merves,* Mgr.; Walter G. Arader; Audrey Merves; Jenifer Merves-Robbins; John T. Roberts.
Number of staff: 1 full-time support; 1 part-time support.
EIN: 232219044
Selected grants: The following grants were reported in 2005.
$25,000 to Bryn Mawr Hospital Foundation, Bryn Mawr, PA.
$20,000 to Pennsylvania Academy of the Fine Arts, Philadelphia, PA.
$18,000 to Harriton Association, Bryn Mawr, PA.
$13,400 to Philadelphia Jewish Archives Center, Philadelphia, PA.
$7,500 to Hillel of Greater Philadelphia, Philadelphia, PA.
$5,000 to American Red Cross, Philadelphia, PA.
$2,500 to Delaware Valley College, Doylestown, PA.
$2,500 to Scheie Eye Institute, Philadelphia, PA.
$2,500 to Settlement Music School, Philadelphia, PA.

$300 to Chapel of Four Chaplains, Philadelphia, PA.

8406
The Aileen K. and Brian L. Roberts Foundation ◇
c/o Comcast Corp.
1500 Market St., 35th Fl.
Philadelphia, PA 19102

Established in 1994 in PA.
Donor: Brian L. Roberts.
Foundation type: Independent foundation.
Financial data (yr. ended 12/31/05): Assets, $3,693,951 (M); gifts received, $226,734; expenditures, $412,750; qualifying distributions, $394,527; giving activities include $394,527 for 71 grants (high: $50,000; low: $50).
Purpose and activities: Giving primarily for the arts, education, and health and human services.
Fields of interest: Arts; Elementary/secondary education; Higher education; Higher education, university; Heart & circulatory diseases; Athletics/sports, amateur leagues; Athletics/sports, racquet sports; Human services; Federated giving programs; Jewish agencies & temples.
Limitations: Applications not accepted. Giving primarily in Philadelphia, PA. No grants to individuals.
Application information: Contributes only to pre-selected organizations.
Officers: Aileen K. Roberts, Pres.; Brian L. Roberts, V.P.
EIN: 232787654
Selected grants: The following grants were reported in 2003.
$150,000 to William Penn Charter School, Philadelphia, PA. For operating support.
$101,000 to University of Pennsylvania, Philadelphia, PA. For operating support.
$50,000 to Kimmel Center for the Performing Arts, Philadelphia, PA. For operating support.
$40,000 to Simon Wiesenthal Center, Los Angeles, CA. For operating support.
$30,000 to Franklin Institute Science Museum, Philadelphia, PA. For operating support.
$25,000 to Jewish Federation of Greater Philadelphia, Philadelphia, PA. For operating support.
$10,349 to Project HOME, Philadelphia, PA.
$5,000 to National Coalition for Cancer Survivorship, Silver Spring, MD. For operating support.
$5,000 to University of Pennsylvania Medical Center of Presbyterian, Philadelphia, PA. For operating support.
$3,050 to Germantown Academy, Fort Washington, PA. For operating support.

8407
Ralph & Suzanne Roberts Foundation ◇
c/o Comcast Corp.
1500 Market St., 35th Fl.
Philadelphia, PA 19102-4735

Established in 1963 in PA.
Donors: Ralph J. Roberts; Suzanne F. Roberts.
Foundation type: Independent foundation.
Financial data (yr. ended 11/30/04): Assets, $24,395,353 (M); gifts received, $1,807,643; expenditures, $936,264; qualifying distributions,

$874,493; giving activities include $874,493 for 93 grants (high: $200,000; low: $100).

Fields of interest: Museums; Performing arts, music; Higher education; Environment, natural resources; Human services.

Limitations: Applications not accepted. Giving primarily in PA. No grants to individuals.

Application information: Grants initiated by trustees.

Trustees: Ralph J. Roberts; Suzanne F. Roberts.

EIN: 237015984

Selected grants: The following grants were reported in 2003.

$200,000 to Brandywine Conservancy, Chadds Ford, PA.

$20,000 to Hedgerow Theater, Media, PA.

$10,000 to Arden Theater Company, Philadelphia, PA.

$10,000 to Simon Wiesenthal Center, Los Angeles, CA.

$5,000 to Franklin Institute Science Museum, Philadelphia, PA.

$5,000 to Rosenbach Museum and Library, Philadelphia, PA.

$1,000 to Shipley School, Bryn Mawr, PA.

$750 to American Music Theater Festival, Prince Music Theater, Philadelphia, PA.

$500 to Variety Club of the Delaware Valley, Philadelphia, PA.

$100 to Amaryllis Theater Company, Philadelphia, PA.

8408
The Rockwell Foundation ✧

c/o PNC Bank, N.A., P2-PTPP-10-2
620 Liberty Ave.
Pittsburgh, PA 15222-2705

Trust established in 1956 in PA.

Donors: Willard F. Rockwell†; and family.

Foundation type: Independent foundation.

Financial data (yr. ended 12/31/04): Assets, $13,249,660 (M); expenditures, $566,781; qualifying distributions, $519,161; giving activities include $502,000 for 58 grants (high: $30,000; low: $2,000).

Purpose and activities: Giving primarily for higher and secondary education; support also for the fine and performing arts, museums, music and dance organizations, child welfare and family services, conservation, hospitals and health agencies, including drug abuse programs, cancer research, mental illness and hospices, biology, science and technology, historic preservation, and religion.

Fields of interest: Museums; Performing arts; Performing arts, dance; Performing arts, music; Historic preservation/historical societies; Arts; Secondary school/education; Higher education; Education; Environment, natural resources; Hospitals (general); Health care; Substance abuse, services; Mental health/crisis services; Health organizations, association; Cancer; Cancer research; Children/youth, services; Family services; Residential/custodial care, hospices; Engineering/technology; Biological sciences; Science; Religion; Disabilities, people with.

Type of support: General/operating support; Continuing support; Annual campaigns; Capital campaigns; Building/renovation; Equipment; Endowments; Seed money; Scholarship funds; Matching/challenge support.

Limitations: Applications not accepted. Giving primarily in PA. No grants to individuals, or for fellowships; no loans.

Application information: Unsolicited requests for funds not accepted.

Board meeting date(s): As required

Trustees: Scott Aiken; G. Peter Rockwell; Russell A. Rockwell; H. Campbell Stuckeman; PNC Bank, N.A.

EIN: 256035975

8409
The Roemer Foundation ✧

(formerly Mary Alice Dorrance Malone Foundation)
c/o B. Rosenfield
1600 Market St., Ste. 3600
Philadelphia, PA 19103-7286

Established in 1996 in PA.

Donor: Mary Alice Dorrance Malone.

Foundation type: Independent foundation.

Financial data (yr. ended 6/30/05): Assets, $8,199,786 (M); gifts received, $333,358; expenditures, $994,224; qualifying distributions, $934,304; giving activities include $930,000 for 34 grants (high: $500,000; low: $500).

Fields of interest: Education; Environment, natural resources.

Limitations: Applications not accepted. Giving primarily in PA. No grants to individuals.

Application information: Contributes only to pre-selected organizations.

Directors: Mary Alice Malone; James L. McCabe.

EIN: 232870277

Selected grants: The following grants were reported in 2004.

$100,000 to Brandywine Conservancy, Chadds Ford, PA.

$100,000 to Fox Chase Cancer Center, Philadelphia, PA.

$5,000 to Elon University, Elon College, NC.

$5,000 to Planned Parenthood of Chester County, West Chester, PA.

$5,000 to Randolph-Macon College, Ashland, VA.

$2,000 to University of Kentucky, Lexington, KY.

$1,000 to Chester County Hospital, West Chester, PA.

$1,000 to Delaware Art Museum, Wilmington, DE.

$1,000 to Sanford School, Hockessin, DE.

$1,000 to Thorncroft Therapeutic Horseback Riding, Malvern, PA.

8410
William G. Rohrer Charitable Foundation ✧

c/o PNC Advisors
1600 Market St., 4th Fl.
Philadelphia, PA 19103-7240
Application address: c/o John C. Watson, V.P., PNC Advisors, Rte. 38 at Eastgate Dr., Moorestown, NJ 08057, tel.: (856) 638-4906

Established in 1990 in NJ.

Foundation type: Independent foundation.

Financial data (yr. ended 12/31/05): Assets, $37,445,282 (M); expenditures, $2,070,253; qualifying distributions, $1,756,976; giving activities include $1,676,500 for 43 grants (high: $500,000; low: $2,500).

Purpose and activities: Giving primarily for higher education, health care, health associations, and human services.

Fields of interest: Higher education; Health care; Health organizations, association; Human services.

Limitations: Giving primarily in NJ. No grants to individuals.

Application information:
Initial approach: Letter
Deadline(s): None

Trustees: Thomas N. Bantivoglio; Daniel J. Ragone; Linda Rohrer; PNC Bank, N.A.

EIN: 226455062

Selected grants: The following grants were reported in 2004.

$130,000 to Rutgers, The State University of New Jersey, Camden, NJ.

$100,000 to Deborah Hospital Foundation, Browns Mills, NJ.

$100,000 to University of Medicine and Dentistry of New Jersey, Newark, NJ.

$50,000 to Coriell Institute for Medical Research, Camden, NJ.

$50,000 to Haddonfield Symphony Society, Haddonfield, NJ.

$25,000 to American Red Cross, Camden, NJ.

$25,000 to South Jersey Performing Arts Center, Camden, NJ.

$20,000 to Union Organization for Social Service, Pennsauken, NJ.

$10,000 to Camden Eye Center, Camden, NJ.

$10,000 to Samaritan Hospice, Marlton, NJ.

8411
The Rorer Foundation, Inc.

761 Newtown Rd.
Villanova, PA 19085
Contact: Gerald B. Rorer, Pres.

Established in 1963.

Donors: Edward C. Rorer; Gerald B. Rorer; Herbert T. Rorer.

Foundation type: Independent foundation.

Financial data (yr. ended 11/30/05): Assets, $9,809,169 (M); expenditures, $509,114; qualifying distributions, $475,500; giving activities include $475,195 for 66 grants (high: $52,000; low: $100).

Purpose and activities: Giving for education, with an emphasis on higher education.

Fields of interest: Higher education, college; Education.

Limitations: Applications not accepted. Giving primarily in New Haven, CT, and the Philadelphia, PA, area. No grants to individuals.

Publications: Annual report.

Application information: Contributes only to pre-selected organizations. Unsolicited requests for funds not accepted.

Officers: Gerald B. Rorer, Pres.; Edward C. Rorer, V.P.; Herbert T. Rorer, Secy.-Treas.

EIN: 516017981

8412
The David M. and Marjorie D. Rosenberg Foundation ✧ ☆

893 Parkes Run Ln.
Villanova, PA 19085 (610) 458-1090
Contact: David M. Rosenberg, Tr.; Marjorie D. Rosenberg, Tr.

Established in 1993.

Donors: David M. Rosenberg; Marjorie D. Rosenberg.

Foundation type: Independent foundation.
Financial data (yr. ended 12/31/05): Assets, $3,000,245 (M); gifts received, $1,145,000; expenditures, $407,386; qualifying distributions, $403,543; giving activities include $397,032 for 43 grants (high: $101,800; low: $100).
Fields of interest: Education; Hospitals (general); Health organizations, association; Human services; Children/youth, services; Jewish federated giving programs.
Limitations: Giving primarily in PA. No grants to individuals.
Application information:
Initial approach: Letter
Deadline(s): None
Trustees: David M. Rosenberg; Marjorie D. Rosenberg.
EIN: 237715847
Selected grants: The following grants were reported in 2005.
$101,800 to Pennsylvania State University, University Park, PA.
$51,000 to Champions of Caring, Villanova, PA.
$50,350 to Childrens Hospital Foundation, Philadelphia, PA.
$22,000 to Chester County Futures, West Chester, PA.
$17,000 to Josephson Institute of Ethics, Marina del Rey, CA.
$15,410 to Temple Shalom, Philadelphia, PA.
$1,500 to Simon Wiesenthal Center, Los Angeles, CA.
$1,000 to Radnor Educational Foundation, Wayne, PA.
$500 to Temple University, Philadelphia, PA.
$100 to Montefiore Medical Center, Bronx, NY.

8413
Mary and Emmanuel Rosenfeld Foundation ✧
c/o Wachovia Bank, N.A.
Broad & Walnut Sts., 5th Fl. - PA1210
Philadelphia, PA 19109 (215) 670-4226
Contact: Reginald Middleton

Established around 1977.
Foundation type: Independent foundation.
Financial data (yr. ended 12/31/05): Assets, $6,043,449 (M); expenditures, $543,867; qualifying distributions, $450,750; giving activities include $450,000 for 60 grants (high: $50,000; low: $500).
Fields of interest: Performing arts; Arts; Higher education; Hospitals (general); Health organizations, association; Food services; Human services; Jewish federated giving programs; Biological sciences; Jewish agencies & temples.
Limitations: Giving primarily in FL and PA. No grants to individuals.
Application information: Unsolicited requests for funds generally not accepted.
Initial approach: Proposal
Deadline(s): None
Trustees: Lester Rosenfeld; Robert Rosenfeld; Rita E. Stein; Wachovia Bank, N.A.
EIN: 236220061

8414
The Ross Loan Fund ✧
c/o M&T Bank
P.O. Box 459
Chambersburg, PA 17201 (717) 261-2833
Contact: Alan B. Rhinehart, M&T Investment Group, M&T Bank

Foundation type: Independent foundation.
Financial data (yr. ended 12/31/05): Assets, $3,637,936 (M); expenditures, $561,682; qualifying distributions, $527,850; giving activities include $520,950 for 77 loans to individuals (high: $6,900; low: $3,450).
Purpose and activities: Student loans to graduates of Chambersburg Area Senior High School. Graduates from other high schools in Franklin County, PA will be considered if funds are available.
Type of support: Student loans—to individuals.
Limitations: Giving limited to Chambersburg, PA.
Application information: Application form required.
Deadline(s): Apr. 15
Trustee: M&T Bank.
EIN: 236262609

8415
Ronald and Marcia J. Rubin Charitable Foundation ✧
200 S. Broad St., 3rd Fl.
Philadelphia, PA 19102

Established in 1988 in PA; funded in 1989.
Donor: Ronald Rubin.
Foundation type: Independent foundation.
Financial data (yr. ended 12/31/05): Assets, $6,677 (M); gifts received, $468,000; expenditures, $513,500; qualifying distributions, $513,500; giving activities include $513,500 for 13 grants (high: $150,000; low: $1,000).
Purpose and activities: Giving primarily to Jewish organizations, including temples, theological education, cultural institutions, and federated giving programs; support also for the performing arts.
Fields of interest: Museums (ethnic/folk arts); Museums (history); Performing arts; Theological school/education; Jewish federated giving programs; Jewish agencies & temples.
Limitations: Applications not accepted. Giving primarily in PA, especially the Philadelphia area; giving also in New York, NY. No grants to individuals.
Application information: Unsolicited requests for funds not accepted.
Trustee: Ronald Rubin.
EIN: 232547416

8416
Ryan Memorial Foundation ✧
P.O. Box 426
Pittsburgh, PA 15230-0426

Established in 1996 in PA.
Foundation type: Independent foundation.
Financial data (yr. ended 12/31/04): Assets, $34,472,809 (M); expenditures, $1,081,519; qualifying distributions, $1,057,419; giving activities include $1,051,849 for 52 grants (high: $216,090; low: $100).
Fields of interest: Performing arts, ballet; Performing arts, orchestra (symphony); Secondary school/education; Higher education; Zoos/zoological societies; Hospitals (general); Hospitals

(specialty); Health care; Youth development, business; International affairs; Federated giving programs; Roman Catholic agencies & churches.
Limitations: Applications not accepted. Giving primarily in PA. No grants to individuals.
Application information: Contributes only to pre-selected organizations.
Trustees: Julia Ryan Parker; Daniel H. Ryan; John T. Ryan III; Mary Irene Ryan; Michael Denis Ryan; William F. Ryan; Irene R. Shaw.
EIN: 251781266
Selected grants: The following grants were reported in 2004.
$216,090 to Extra Mile Education Foundation, Pittsburgh, PA.
$103,048 to Orleans Conservation Trust, East Orleans, MA.
$77,771 to United Way of Allegheny County, Pittsburgh, PA.
$74,862 to Pittsburgh Oratory, Pittsburgh, PA. 2 grants: $32,188, $42,674
$61,760 to Saint Stephens School, Oil City, PA.
$40,235 to Little Sisters of the Poor, Pittsburgh, PA.
$10,600 to Boys and Girls Harbor, New York, NY.
$5,000 to Pennsylvania State University, University Park, PA.
$500 to Western Pennsylvania Conservancy, Pittsburgh, PA.

8417
S & T Bancorp Charitable Foundation ✧
c/o S&T Bank, Trust Dept.
P.O. Box 220
Indiana, PA 15701
Contact: James C. Miller, Pres.
Application address: P.O. Box 190, Indiana, PA 15701, tel.: (724) 465-1443

Established in 1993 in PA.
Donors: S&T Bancorp, Inc.; S&T Bank.
Foundation type: Company-sponsored foundation.
Financial data (yr. ended 12/31/05): Assets, $310,973 (M); gifts received, $612,153; expenditures, $503,150; qualifying distributions, $502,435; giving activities include $461,671 for grants.
Purpose and activities: The foundation supports public libraries, community foundations, and organizations involved with arts and culture, higher education, and cancer.
Fields of interest: Performing arts; Historic preservation/historical societies; Arts; Higher education; Libraries (public); Cancer; Big Brothers/Big Sisters; Boy scouts; Girl scouts; YM/YWCAs & YM/YWHAs; Foundations (community).
Type of support: General/operating support; Capital campaigns; Building/renovation.
Limitations: Giving limited to areas of company operations in PA. No grants to individuals.
Application information:
Initial approach: Proposal
Deadline(s): None
Officers: James C. Miller, Pres.; Edward C. Hauck, V.P.; H. William Klumpp, Treas.
Trustee: S&T Bank.
EIN: 251716950
Selected grants: The following grants were reported in 2004.
$70,000 to Cleveland Clinic, Cleveland, OH. For cancer research.
$29,000 to United Way of Indiana County, Indiana, PA. For general support.

$20,000 to Clarion Hospital Foundation, Clarion, PA. For capital campaign.

$12,000 to United Way, Du Bois Area, Du Bois, PA. For general support.

$6,000 to Jefferson County Area Agency on Aging, Brookville, PA. For capital campaign.

8418

Safeguard Scientifics Foundation ◇

800 The Safeguard Bldg.
435 Devon Park Dr.
Wayne, PA 19087-1945
Contact: Dorie Culp, V.P., Human Resources

Established in 1989 in PA.
Donor: Safeguard Scientifics, Inc.
Foundation type: Company-sponsored foundation.
Financial data (yr. ended 12/31/03): Assets, $4,704 (M); gifts received, $324,792; expenditures, $319,739; qualifying distributions, $319,285; giving activities include $319,740 for 28 grants (high: $200,000; low: $2).
Purpose and activities: The foundation supports organizations involved with arts and culture, health, and education.
Fields of interest: Visual arts; Performing arts; Arts; Education; Health organizations, association; Federated giving programs.
Type of support: General/operating support; Continuing support; Annual campaigns; Capital campaigns; Building/renovation; Employee matching gifts.
Limitations: Applications not accepted. Giving primarily in Philadelphia, PA. No grants to individuals.
Application information: Contributes only to pre-selected organizations.
Officers: Anthony L. Craig, Pres.; Christopher J. Davis, V.P. and Treas.; Tonya L. Zweier, V.P. and Cont.; Deirdre Blackburn, Secy.
EIN: 232571278
Selected grants: The following grants were reported in 2003.

$200,000 to National Business Incubation Association, Athens, OH.

$50,000 to Boy Scouts of America, Cradle of Liberty Council, Philadelphia, PA.

$20,000 to Bournelyf Special Camp, West Chester, PA.

$20,000 to Philadelphia Mural Arts Advocates, Philadelphia, PA.

$7,500 to Community Volunteers in Medicine, West Chester, PA. 2 grants: $2,500, $5,000

$5,000 to West Chester University of Pennsylvania, West Chester, PA.

$3,750 to Philadelphia Orchestra Association, Philadelphia, PA.

$2,500 to City Year, Philadelphia, PA.

$1,500 to Wang Center for the Performing Arts, Boston, MA.

8419

Saint-Gobain Corporation Foundation ◇

(formerly Norton Company Foundation)
P.O. Box 860
Valley Forge, PA 19482
Contact: William C. Seiberlich, Secy.

Trust established in 1953 in MA; incorporated in 1975.
Donor: Norton Co.

Foundation type: Company-sponsored foundation.
Financial data (yr. ended 12/31/04): Assets, $37,111 (M); gifts received, $1,626,239; expenditures, $1,636,758; qualifying distributions, $1,636,758; giving activities include $853,869 for 498 grants (high: $160,000; low: $100), and $782,889 for 2,556 employee matching gifts.
Purpose and activities: The foundation supports organizations involved with arts and culture, education, health, housing for the homeless, human services, and community development.
Fields of interest: Arts; Education; Health care; Housing/shelter; Human services; Community development; Homeless.
Type of support: General/operating support; Continuing support; Annual campaigns; Capital campaigns; Building/renovation; Emergency funds; Program development; Seed money; Employee matching gifts; Matching/challenge support.
Limitations: Giving primarily in areas of company operations, with emphasis on MA and PA. Generally, no support for national organizations, national health agencies, or religious, veterans', or fraternal organizations. No grants to individuals, or for endowments or scholarships; no loans.
Publications: Application guidelines.
Application information: Application form required.
Initial approach: Contact foundation for application form
Copies of proposal: 1
Deadline(s): None
Board meeting date(s): Apr. and Sept.
Final notification: Within 3 weeks
Officers and Directors:* Jean-Francois Phelizon,* Pres.; John J. Sweeney III,* V.P. and Treas.; John R. Mesher, V.P.; M. Shawn Puccio, V.P.; Dorothy C. Wackerman,* V.P.; William C. Seiberlich, Secy.; Dennis Allaire; John K. Donaldson; Carol M. Gray; Thomas G. Kinisky; Thomas P. McDuffee; John P. McKernan; Kermit E. Stahl.
Number of staff: 1 full-time professional.
EIN: 237423043

8420

Saltsgiver Family Foundation ◇

1605 James Rd.
Williamsport, PA 17701

Established in 1995 in PA.
Donors: Thomas M. Saltsgiver; Joann Saltsgiver.
Foundation type: Independent foundation.
Financial data (yr. ended 12/31/04): Assets, $7,502,411 (M); gifts received, $500,455; expenditures, $377,870; qualifying distributions, $372,000; giving activities include $372,000 for 17 grants (high: $167,000; low: $5,000).
Fields of interest: Higher education; Human services; Salvation Army; Religion.
Limitations: Applications not accepted. Giving on a national basis, with emphasis on PA and VA. No grants to individuals.
Application information: Contributes only to pre-selected organizations.
Officers: Thomas M. Saltsgiver, Pres.; Joann Saltsgiver, Secy.-Treas.
EIN: 232803397
Selected grants: The following grants were reported in 2005.

$100,000 to Regent University, Virginia Beach, VA.

$25,000 to Sentinel Group, Lynnwood, WA.

$10,000 to American Red Cross, Philadelphia, PA.

$10,000 to Caring People, Springfield, MO.

$10,000 to Salvation Army, Butler, PA.

$5,000 to Chosen People Ministries, New York, NY.

$2,000 to Focus on the Family, Colorado Springs, CO.

8421

Salvaggio Family Foundation ◇

c/o Norene Salvaggio
1390 Ridgeview Dr., Ste. 300
Allentown, PA 18104

Established in 1998 in PA.
Donors: Norene L. Salvaggio; Anthony Salvaggio.
Foundation type: Independent foundation.
Financial data (yr. ended 12/31/04): Assets, $10,549,902 (M); gifts received, $1,271,000; expenditures, $904,418; qualifying distributions, $883,759; giving activities include $883,759 for 83 grants (high: $500,000; low: $20).
Fields of interest: Education; Human services; Federated giving programs; Christian agencies & churches.
Limitations: Applications not accepted. Giving primarily in PA. No grants to individuals.
Application information: Contributes only to pre-selected organizations.
Trustees: Christy A. Salvaggio; Norene L. Salvaggio; Suzie A. Salvaggio; Thomas A. Salvaggio.
EIN: 256614812

8422

Salvitti Family Foundation ◇

c/o Lovett Bookman Harmon Marks, LLP
5th Ave. Pl., Ste. 2900
Pittsburgh, PA 15222

Established around 1995.
Donors: Constance S. Salvitti; E. Ronald Salvitti, M.D.
Foundation type: Independent foundation.
Financial data (yr. ended 12/31/04): Assets, $7,577,230 (M); gifts received, $245,992; expenditures, $505,903; qualifying distributions, $439,640; giving activities include $439,000 for 50 grants (high: $250,000; low: $500).
Fields of interest: Elementary/secondary education; Higher education; Hospitals (general); Health organizations, association; Cancer; Human services; Community development; Christian agencies & churches.
Limitations: Applications not accepted. Giving primarily in PA, with emphasis on Washington. No grants to individuals.
Application information: Contributes only to pre-selected organizations.
Officers: E. Ronald Salvitti, M.D., Pres.; Constance A. Salvitti, V.P.; Mary Moss, Secy.; Raymond J. Popeck, Treas.
Agent: PNC Bank, N.A.
EIN: 251755617

8423

Myles D. and J. Faye Sampson Family Foundation ◇

100 Sandune Dr.
Pittsburgh, PA 15239

Established in 1993 in PA.
Donors: Myles D. Sampson; J. Faye Sampson; Twila Sampson Foundation; Rimdo Properties Inc.
Foundation type: Independent foundation.

Financial data (yr. ended 12/31/05): Assets, $964,009 (M); expenditures, $392,809; qualifying distributions, $388,408; giving activities include $388,408 for 35 grants (high: $125,000; low: $100).
Purpose and activities: Giving for senior citizen care, youth services, higher education, and public welfare services.
Fields of interest: Arts; Higher education; Hospitals (general); Health organizations, association; Youth development, scouting agencies (general); Human services; YM/YWCAs & YM/YWHAs; International development; Federated giving programs; Protestant agencies & churches.
Limitations: Applications not accepted. Giving primarily in southwestern, PA. No grants to individuals.
Application information: Contributes only to pre-selected organizations.
Trustees: J. Faye Sampson; Myles D. Sampson.
EIN: 256407379
Selected grants: The following grants were reported in 2004.
$153,225 to Bucknell University, Lewisburg, PA.
$32,500 to World Vision, Federal Way, WA.
$15,000 to First Presbyterian Church, Greensburg, PA.
$15,000 to Rocky Mountain Elk Foundation, Missoula, MT.
$500 to Wildlife Works, Kenya. .

8424
Satell Family Foundation ✧
c/o Edward M. Satell
370 Technology Dr.
Malvern, PA 19355

Established in 1995 in PA.
Donors: Edward M. Satell; American Future Systems, Inc.
Foundation type: Independent foundation.
Financial data (yr. ended 12/31/04): Assets, $3,474,390 (M); gifts received, $2,700,000; expenditures, $431,792; qualifying distributions, $425,763; giving activities include $425,748 for 31 grants (high: $200,000; low: $50).
Fields of interest: Education; Federated giving programs; Jewish federated giving programs; Jewish agencies & temples.
Limitations: Applications not accepted. Giving primarily in PA. No grants to individuals.
Application information: Contributes only to pre-selected organizations.
Trustee: Edward M. Satell.
EIN: 237769039
Selected grants: The following grants were reported in 2004.
$26,000 to National Liberty Museum, Philadelphia, PA. 2 grants: $6,000, $20,000
$25,000 to Boy Scouts of America, Philadelphia, PA.
$7,500 to Curtis Institute of Music, Philadelphia, PA.
$1,000 to YMCA, Delaware County, Media, PA.
$400 to Richard J. Caron Foundation, Wernersville, PA.

8425
Sarah Scaife Foundation, Inc. ▼ ✧
1 Oxford Ctr.
301 Grant St., Ste. 3900
Pittsburgh, PA 15219-6401   (412) 392-2900
Contact: Michael W. Gleba, Exec. V.P.
URL: http://www.scaife.com/sarah.html

Trust established in 1941; incorporated in 1959 in PA; present name adopted in 1974.
Donor: Sarah Mellon Scaife†.
Foundation type: Independent foundation.
Financial data (yr. ended 12/31/05): Assets, $289,533,932 (M); expenditures, $18,080,772; qualifying distributions, $17,458,384; giving activities include $15,754,500 for 93 grants (high: $1,000,000; low: $7,500; average: $50,000–$150,000).
Purpose and activities: Grants primarily directed toward public policy programs that address major international and domestic issues.
Fields of interest: Higher education; Education; International affairs; Economics; Political science; Law/international law; International studies; Public policy, research.
Type of support: General/operating support; Continuing support; Program development; Conferences/seminars; Publication; Seed money; Curriculum development; Fellowships; Research.
Limitations: Giving on a national basis. No support for nationally organized fundraising groups or generally for government agencies. No grants to individuals, or generally for event sponsorships, endowments, capital campaigns, or renovations; no loans.
Publications: Annual report (including application guidelines).
Application information: Application form not required.
Initial approach: Letter
Copies of proposal: 1
Deadline(s): None
Board meeting date(s): Feb., May, Sept., and Nov.
Final notification: 2 - 4 weeks
Officers and Trustees:* Richard M. Scaife,* Chair.; Michael W. Gleba,* Exec. V.P.; Barbara L. Slaney, V.P. and Treas.; R. Daniel McMichael,* Secy.; T. Westray Battle III; T. Kenneth Cribb, Jr.; Edwin J. Feulner, Jr.; Allan H. Meltzer, Ph.D.; E. Van R. Milburz; James C. Raddey; Roger W. Robinsin, Jr.; James M. Walton; Arthur P. Ziegler, Jr.
Number of staff: 1 full-time professional; 2 part-time professional; 2 full-time support; 4 part-time support.
EIN: 251113452
Selected grants: The following grants were reported in 2005.
$625,000 to Social Philosophy and Policy Foundation, Bowling Green, OH. For Social Philosophy and Policy Center.
$500,000 to Pittsburgh History and Landmarks Foundation, Pittsburgh, PA. For Wilkinsburg Revolving Fund.
$450,000 to Institute for Foreign Policy Analysis, Cambridge, MA. For general operating support.
$350,000 to Intercollegiate Studies Institute, Wilmington, DE. For general operating support.
$300,000 to Accuracy in Media (AIM), DC. For general operating support.
$300,000 to Tufts University, Fletcher School of Law and Diplomacy, Medford, MA.
$150,000 to Center for the Study of the Presidency, DC. For program support.

$150,000 to Foundation for the Defense of Democracies, DC. For project support.
$150,000 to Independent Womens Forum, Arlington, VA. For general operating support.
$100,000 to Michigan State University, East Lansing, MI. For program support.

8426
Roberta and Ernest Scheller, Jr. Family Foundation ✧ ☆
1 S. Church St.
Hazleton, PA 18201

Established in 1995 in PA.
Donors: Ernest Scheller, Jr.; Roberta Scheller.
Foundation type: Independent foundation.
Financial data (yr. ended 12/31/05): Assets, $475,000 (M); gifts received, $475,000; expenditures, $475,246; qualifying distributions, $445,170; giving activities include $445,170 for grants.
Purpose and activities: Giving for Jewish organizations and higher education.
Fields of interest: Performing arts, orchestra (symphony); Higher education; Liver research; Salvation Army; Federated giving programs; Jewish federated giving programs; Jewish agencies & temples.
Limitations: Applications not accepted. Giving primarily in PA. No grants to individuals.
Application information: Contributes only to pre-selected organizations.
Officer: Ernest Scheller, Jr., Chair.
Trustees: Lisa Jane Peretz; Roberta Scheller.
EIN: 237828732
Selected grants: The following grants were reported in 2004.
$246,200 to Georgia Tech Foundation, Atlanta, GA.
$8,000 to Pennsylvania State University, State College, PA.
$6,100 to Jewish Day School, Lancaster, PA.
$5,000 to Building With Books, Stamford, CT.
$4,000 to DePauw University, Greencastle, IN.
$2,000 to Ball State University, Muncie, IN.
$2,000 to Lehigh University, Bethlehem, PA.
$2,000 to University of Pennsylvania, Philadelphia, PA.
$1,500 to College Misericordia, Dallas, PA.

8427
The Clarence Schock Foundation ✧
(formerly The SICO Foundation)
15 Mount Joy St.
P.O. Box 127
Mount Joy, PA 17552-0127
Contact: Darlene F. Halterman, Corp. Secy.
E-mail: info@sicofoundation.org

Incorporated in 1941 in DE.
Donor: Clarence Schock†.
Foundation type: Independent foundation.
Financial data (yr. ended 5/31/05): Assets, $14,019,477 (M); gifts received, $14,495; expenditures, $899,420; qualifying distributions, $735,016; giving activities include $15,000 for grants, and $433,000 for 8 grants to individuals (high: $127,000; low: $5,000).
Purpose and activities: Scholarships granted to students of public four-year colleges in the service area of the SICO Company.
Fields of interest: Higher education.

Type of support: Scholarships—to individuals; Scholarship funds.
Limitations: Applications not accepted. Giving primarily in PA. No grants to individuals (except for scholarships).
Publications: Informational brochure.
Application information:
Board meeting date(s): 4th Thurs. of Jan., Apr., July and Oct.
Officers and Board Members:* John N. Weidman,* Chair.; Joseph A. Caputo,* Pres.; Darlene F. Halterman, Secy.; Franklin R. Eichler,* Treas.
Directors: Fred S. Engle, Dir. Emeritus; Harrison L. Diehl; Anthony F. Ceddia; David F. Eichler; Carl R. Hallgren; Charles W. Ricedorf; Forrest R. Schaeffer; Helen A. Stine.
Number of staff: 1 full-time support; 4 part-time support.
EIN: 236298332

8428
The Scholler Foundation ◇
1100 One Penn Ctr.
Philadelphia, PA 19103 (215) 568-7500
Contact: E. Brooks Keffer, Jr., Pres.

Trust established in 1939 in PA.
Donor: F.C. Scholler‡.
Foundation type: Independent foundation.
Financial data (yr. ended 12/31/05): Assets, $14,769,147 (M); expenditures, $825,002; qualifying distributions, $692,773; giving activities include $665,295 for 47 grants (high: $40,000; low: $3,750).
Purpose and activities: Giving for the alleviation of poverty and destitution, the promotion of scientific research, including the branches of chemistry, and for other literary, educational, and public purposes; support largely for hospitals, with emphasis on grants for small community hospitals to purchase medical equipment.
Fields of interest: Hospitals (general).
Type of support: General/operating support; Continuing support; Seed money.
Limitations: Giving limited to the Delaware Valley, PA, area. No grants to individuals, or for endowment funds, scholarships, fellowships, or matching gifts; no loans.
Application information: Application form not required.
Initial approach: Proposal
Copies of proposal: 1
Deadline(s): Apr. 1 and Oct. 1
Board meeting date(s): Feb., May, Aug., and Nov.
Officers and Trustees:* E. Brooks Keffer, Jr.,* Pres.; Edwin C. Dreby III,* Secy.; Lawrence R. Brown, Jr.; T. Sergeant Pepper.
EIN: 236245158

8429
J. & L. Schoonmaker - Sewickley Valley Hospital Trust ◇
c/o Mellon Financial Corp.
1 Mellon Ctr.
500 Grant St.
Pittsburgh, PA 15258-0001
Contact: Laurie A. Moritz

Established around 1981.
Foundation type: Independent foundation.

Financial data (yr. ended 9/30/05): Assets, $8,127,279 (M); expenditures, $412,690; qualifying distributions, $403,182; giving activities include $400,700 for grants.
Purpose and activities: Giving limited to those organizations that are of special interest to the donors.
Fields of interest: Arts; Higher education; Hospitals (general); Federated giving programs.
Limitations: Applications not accepted. Giving primarily in Pittsburgh, PA.
Application information: Contributes only to pre-selected organizations.
Board meeting date(s): Feb., and Aug.
Trustee: Mellon Bank, N.A.
EIN: 256016020
Selected grants: The following grants were reported in 2003.
$75,000 to George Washingtons Fredericksburg Foundation, Fredericksburg, VA. For operating support.
$43,000 to Saint Stephens Church, Sewickley, PA. For operating support.
$30,000 to United Way of Allegheny County, Pittsburgh, PA. For operating support.
$25,000 to Boy Scouts of America, Pittsburgh, PA. 2 grants: $12,500 each
$25,000 to Carnegie Library of Pittsburgh, Pittsburgh, PA. For operating support.
$25,000 to Phipps Conservatory and Botanical Gardens, Pittsburgh, PA. For operating support.
$15,000 to Carnegie Museum of Art, Pittsburgh, PA. For operating support.
$15,000 to National Council of Jewish Women, Pittsburgh, PA. For operating support.
$15,000 to Pittsburgh Symphony Society, Pittsburgh, PA. For operating support.

8430
Schwab Rainess Foundation ◇ ☆
(formerly Schwab-Spector-Rainess Foundation)
P.O. Box 5967
Harrisburg, PA 17110-0967
Contact: Israel Schwab, Tr.

Established about 1965 in PA.
Donors: Morris Schwab; D & H Distributing Co.
Foundation type: Independent foundation.
Financial data (yr. ended 12/31/05): Assets, $4,268,864 (M); gifts received, $271,410; expenditures, $370,878; qualifying distributions, $366,541; giving activities include $360,891 for 57 grants (high: $200,000; low: $50).
Purpose and activities: Giving primarily to Jewish agencies and temples.
Fields of interest: Museums; Health organizations, association; Human services; Jewish federated giving programs; Jewish agencies & temples.
Limitations: Giving primarily in Baltimore, MD, New York, NY and Harrisburg, PA.
Application information:
Initial approach: Letter
Deadline(s): None
Trustees: Israel Schwab; Morris Schwab.
EIN: 236401901
Selected grants: The following grants were reported in 2004.
$125,975 to Jewish Federation of Greater Harrisburg, Harrisburg, PA.
$25,000 to Jewish Home of Greater Harrisburg, Harrisburg, PA.
$13,000 to The Associated: Jewish Community Federation of Baltimore, Baltimore, MD.

$3,000 to World Jewish Congress American Section, New York, NY.
$1,250 to Harrisburg Symphony Association, Harrisburg, PA.
$1,000 to Theater Harrisburg, Harrisburg, PA.
$500 to Goodwill Industries of Central Pennsylvania, Harrisburg, PA.
$300 to Whitaker Center for Science and the Arts, Harrisburg, PA.
$100 to ARC of Dauphin and Lebanon Counties, Harrisburg, PA.
$100 to Multiple Sclerosis Society, National, Harrisburg, PA.

8431
The Scranton Area Foundation, Inc. ◇
Bank Towers, Ste. 608
321 Spruce St.
Scranton, PA 18503-1409 (570) 347-6203
Contact: Jeanne A. Bovard, Exec. Dir.
FAX: (570) 347-7587; E-mail: safinfo@safdn.org; Additional E-mail: jab@safdn.org; URL: http://www.safdn.org

Established in 1954 in PA by resolution and declaration of trust; reorganized in 1998.
Foundation type: Community foundation.
Financial data (yr. ended 12/31/04): Assets, $19,754,207 (M); gifts received, $570,584; expenditures, $1,098,802; giving activities include $655,250 for 98 grants (high: $106,086; low: $193).
Purpose and activities: The foundation encourages and helps to build community endowment through grants for new projects and services to address unmet needs. The foundation primarily supports organizations involved with health, education, arts, environment, human services, and civic affairs.
Fields of interest: Historic preservation/historical societies; Arts; Child development, education; Vocational education; Higher education; Libraries/library science; Education; Environment, natural resources; Environment; Animal welfare; Health care; Mental health/crisis services; Health organizations, association; Housing/shelter; Youth development, services; Children/youth, services; Child development, services; Human services; International human rights; Community development; Voluntarism promotion; Leadership development; Public affairs; Religion; Aging.
Type of support: General/operating support; Continuing support; Program development; Conferences/seminars; Publication; Seed money; Curriculum development; Scholarship funds; Research; Technical assistance; Consulting services; Matching/challenge support.
Limitations: Giving limited to Lackawanna County and Scranton, PA, area. No grants for building funds, annual campaigns, deficit financing, or emergency funds.
Publications: Application guidelines; Annual report; Annual report (including application guidelines); Grants list; Informational brochure; Informational brochure (including application guidelines); Newsletter; Occasional report.
Application information: Visit foundation Web site for application guidelines. The foundation strongly recommends submission of letter of intent; immediate response as to the potential for the project will be provided. Application forms may be requested by calling the foundation. Application form required.

Initial approach: Submit letter of intent (1-2 pages maximum)
Copies of proposal: 1
Deadline(s): None
Board meeting date(s): Feb., May, Sept., and Dec.
Final notification: Applications are reviewed quarterly

Officers and Governors: * Austin J. Burke,* Chair.; Kathleen Graff,* Vice-Chair.; William J. Calpin, Secy.; Thomas C. Capezio,* Treas.; Jeanne A. Bovard, Exec. Dir.; Warren T. Acker; Richard S. Bishop; Edward G. Boehm, Ed.D.; Dante A. Cancelli; Karen Clifford; Joanne Cordaro; L. Peter Frieder, Jr.; Carlene R. Gallo; Judith O. Graziano; Cathy Ann Hardaway; George V. Lynett; Patrick J. McMahon; Jane Oppenheim; Carlon E. Preate; James W. Reid; Letha Reinheimer; James A. Ross; Walter L. Schautz; William W. Scranton III; Thomas G. Speicher.
Investment Managers: Penn Security; Smith Barney; Wachovia Securities.
Number of staff: 1 full-time professional; 3 full-time support.
EIN: 232890364

8432
Seiple Family Foundation ◇ ☆

245 Front St.
Northumberland, PA 17857
Application address: c/o Deb Reid, 159 S. 2nd St., Sunbury, PA 17801

Established in 2001 in PA.
Donor: Rachel D. Seiple.
Foundation type: Independent foundation.
Financial data (yr. ended 12/31/05): Assets, $3,048,952 (M); gifts received, $260,245; expenditures, $925,294; qualifying distributions, $775,659; giving activities include $775,659 for grants.
Fields of interest: Recreation, public education; Children.
Type of support: General/operating support.
Limitations: Giving primarily in IN. No grants to individuals.
Application information:
Initial approach: Letter
Deadline(s): None
Trustees: Penn Seiple; Stan Seiple; Northumberland National Bank.
EIN: 256788065

8433
Merle Selfon Memorial Fund Charitable Trust ◇ ☆

c/o Sterling Financial Trust Co.
101 N. Pointe Blvd.
Lancaster, PA 17601-4133

Donors: Merle Selfon†; American Scandia.
Foundation type: Independent foundation.
Financial data (yr. ended 12/31/05): Assets, $7,116,701 (M); gifts received, $106,031; expenditures, $603,408; qualifying distributions, $586,596; giving activities include $582,018 for 1 grant.
Fields of interest: Foundations (community).
Limitations: Applications not accepted. Giving primarily in Lancaster County, PA. No grants to individuals.

Application information: Contributes only to pre-selected organizations.
Trustee: Sterling Financial Trust Co.
EIN: 386814276

8434
The Seraph Foundation ◇

c/o Glenmede Trust Company
1650 Market St., Ste. 1200
Philadelphia, PA 19103-7391
Contact: Carol M. Drummond, Admin.

Established in 1997 in DE.
Donor: Edna Marion Davenport.
Foundation type: Independent foundation.
Financial data (yr. ended 6/30/05): Assets, $44,180,856 (M); expenditures, $2,894,627; qualifying distributions, $2,441,101; giving activities include $2,423,600 for 27 grants (high: $1,000,000; low: $500; average: $15,000–$100,000).
Purpose and activities: Giving primarily for health and education.
Fields of interest: Arts; Education; Environment, natural resources; Environment; Hospitals (general); Cancer; Medical research, association; Medical research, institute; Medical research; Human services; Protestant agencies & churches.
Type of support: Capital campaigns; Building/renovation; Equipment; Land acquisition; Endowments; Professorships; Internship funds; Scholarship funds; Research; Matching/challenge support.
Limitations: Applications not accepted. Giving primarily in the eastern and mid-U.S. No grants to individuals.
Publications: Grants list.
Application information: Contributes only to pre-selected organizations.
Board meeting date(s): Sept., Dec., Mar., and June
Officers and Board Members: * Henry Spire,* Pres. and Treas.; Linda J. Spire,* V.P. and Secy.; Kimberly Spire Folts; William Bruce Spire.
EIN: 522030228
Selected grants: The following grants were reported in 2004.
$1,500,000 to Johns Hopkins University, Sidney Kimmel Comprehensive Cancer Center, Baltimore, MD. For capital support for cancer research auditorium and connector building.
$250,000 to Washington College, Chestertown, MD. 2 grants: $125,000 each (For new science facility).
$100,000 to Lancaster Country Day School, Lancaster, PA. For capital campaign funding for technology initiative.
$100,000 to Memorial Sloan-Kettering Cancer Center, New York, NY. For fellowship in Bioinformatics and Integrative Medicine program.
$100,000 to University of the Cumberlands, Williamsburg, KY. For scholarship aid and service and leadership program.
$83,000 to Cold Spring Harbor Laboratory, Cold Spring Harbor, NY. For cancer research.
$75,000 to Arthritis Foundation, Atlanta, GA. For MAARC initiative.
$51,100 to Chesapeake Bay Maritime Museum, Saint Michaels, MD. For website design.
$50,000 to Academy Art Museum, Easton, MD. For capital campaign.

8435
The Shadyside Academy Fund ◇

c/o PNC Advisors
620 Liberty Ave., P2-PTPP-10-2
Pittsburgh, PA 15222-2705

Established in 2002 in PA.
Donor: Grant M. Shipley†.
Foundation type: Independent foundation.
Financial data (yr. ended 3/31/05): Assets, $5,006,673 (M); expenditures, $4,803,179; qualifying distributions, $4,796,453; giving activities include $4,795,867 for 1 grant.
Purpose and activities: Giving primarily to a school.
Fields of interest: Education, single organization support.
Limitations: Applications not accepted. Giving primarily in Pittsburgh, PA. No grants to individuals.
Application information: Contributes only to pre-selected organizations.
Trustee: PNC Bank, N.A.
EIN: 256817388

8436
Shaffer Family Charitable Trust ◇

3548 Bingen Rd.
Bethlehem, PA 18015
Contact: David N. Shaffer, Tr.

Established in 1987 in PA.
Donors: David Shaffer; Susan Shaffer; Jack M. Shaffer†; Cecile Shaffer; Rose Shaffer.
Foundation type: Independent foundation.
Financial data (yr. ended 12/31/05): Assets, $13,394,029 (M); gifts received, $210,263; expenditures, $927,903; qualifying distributions, $812,275; giving activities include $812,275 for grants.
Purpose and activities: Support for capital operations and special projects not funded through normal income sources to social service agencies serving the at-risk population in the Lehigh Valley, PA, area.
Fields of interest: Human services; Children/youth, services; Aging, centers/services.
Type of support: General/operating support; Capital campaigns; Building/renovation; Endowments; Program development; Seed money.
Limitations: Giving primarily in Lehigh Valley, PA. No grants to individuals.
Application information: Application form not required.
Copies of proposal: 1
Deadline(s): None
Board meeting date(s): Quarterly
Final notification: Following the next quarterly meeting
Trustees: Cecile Shaffer; David Shaffer; Rose Shaffer; Susan Shaffer.
EIN: 232502319

8437
The David S. and Karen A. Shapira Foundation ◇ ☆

101 Kappa Dr.
Pittsburgh, PA 15238

Donors: David S. Shapira; Karen A. Shapira.
Foundation type: Independent foundation.
Financial data (yr. ended 12/31/05): Assets, $3,915,914 (M); gifts received, $307,588;

expenditures, $645,786; qualifying distributions, $631,100; giving activities include $631,100 for grants.

Purpose and activities: Giving primarily for education and Jewish federated giving programs.

Fields of interest: Arts; Higher education; Jewish federated giving programs; Jewish agencies & temples.

Limitations: Giving primarily in Pittsburgh, PA.

Officers and Directors:* Karen A. Shapira,* Pres.; David S. Shapira,* Secy.-Treas.; Laura M. Karet; Deborah B. Shapira; Jeremy M. Shapira.

EIN: 251711993

Selected grants: The following grants were reported in 2005.

$313,100 to United Jewish Federation of Greater Pittsburgh, Pittsburgh, PA.

$110,000 to Carnegie Mellon University, Pittsburgh, PA.

$60,000 to Hillel Academy of Pittsburgh, Pittsburgh, PA.

$50,000 to Jewish National Fund, Philadelphia, PA.

$10,000 to Pittsburgh Cultural Trust, Pittsburgh, PA.

$10,000 to Temple Sinai, Pittsburgh, PA.

$5,000 to Oberlin College, Oberlin, OH.

$2,500 to Stanford University, Stanford, CA.

8438

Shenango Valley Community Foundation ◇

(formerly Shenango Valley Foundation)
33 Chestnut St.
Sharon, PA   16146   (724) 981-5882
Contact: Larry Haynes, Exec. Dir.
FAX: (724) 983-9044; E-mail: larrysvf@adelphia.net;
URL: http://www.sv-foundation.org

Established in PA in 1981.

Donors: Paul O'Brien; Tina O'Brien.

Foundation type: Community foundation.

Financial data (yr. ended 12/31/04): Assets, $25,169,744 (M); gifts received, $1,464,678; expenditures, $1,984,470; giving activities include $1,611,402 for 920 grants (high: $100,000; low: $46), and $1,241,814 for 230 loans to individuals (high: $17,500; low: $1).

Purpose and activities: The foundation seeks to promote the betterment of the Shenango Valley region by enhancing the quality of life for all its citizens through charitable donations to worthy area organizations.

Fields of interest: Education, early childhood education; Higher education; Medical care, rehabilitation; Food services; Homeless, human services; Community development; Aging; Disabilities, people with; Economically disadvantaged.

Type of support: General/operating support; Building/renovation; Equipment; Emergency funds; Program development; Curriculum development; Scholarship funds; Employee-related scholarships; Grants to individuals; Scholarships—to individuals; Matching/challenge support; Student loans—to individuals.

Limitations: Giving limited to the Shenango Valley area, including Trumbull and Mahoning counties, OH, and Mercer and Lawrence counties, PA. No grants for start-up costs or for continuing support.

Publications: Application guidelines; Annual report; Informational brochure.

Application information: Visit foundation Web site for application information. The foundation will request full proposals based on letters of inquiry. Application form required.

Initial approach: Letter of inquiry
Copies of proposal: 1
Deadline(s): None
Board meeting date(s): Quarterly

Officers and Directors:* James A. O'Brien,* Pres.; Robert C. Jazwinski,* Exec. V.P.; Karen Winner Hale,* V.P.; Ronald R. Anderson,* Secy.; Shelly R. Mason, C.F.O.; James E. Feeney,* Treas.; Lawrence E. Haynes, Exec. Dir.; Mel Grata; Paul E. O'Brien; Albert R. Puntureri; William J. Strimbu; James T. Weller, Sr.; James E. Winner, Jr.

Number of staff: 1 full-time professional; 2 part-time professional.

EIN: 251407396

8439

Sherrerd Foundation ◇

(formerly Muirfield Foundation)
c/o Sherrerd and Co.
1 Twr. Bridge, 9th Fl.
West Conshohocken, PA   19428
(610) 940-5020
Contact: John J.F. Sherrerd, Pres.

Established in 1986 in PA.

Donors: John J.F. Sherrerd; Kathleen C. Sherrerd†.

Foundation type: Independent foundation.

Financial data (yr. ended 7/31/05): Assets, $24,119,355 (L); expenditures, $1,270,164; qualifying distributions, $1,155,925; giving activities include $1,155,925 for 65 grants (high: $400,000; low: $200).

Purpose and activities: Giving primarily for education and the arts, with emphasis on museums and music.

Fields of interest: Museums; Arts; Secondary school/education; Higher education; Federated giving programs.

Limitations: Giving primarily in PA, with some emphasis on Philadelphia and Bryn Mawr. No grants to individuals.

Application information:
Initial approach: Letter
Deadline(s): None

Officer and Director:* John J.F. Sherrerd,* Pres.

EIN: 222751186

Selected grants: The following grants were reported in 2003.

$109,350 to Philadelphia Museum of Art, Philadelphia, PA.

$100,000 to Princeton University, Department of Politics, Princeton, NJ. For James Madison Program in American Ideals and Institutions.

$20,000 to Greenwich Academy, Greenwich, CT.

$17,600 to Smith College, Northampton, MA.

$5,000 to Girard College, Philadelphia, PA.

$2,600 to Philadelphia Craft Show, Philadelphia, PA.

$1,000 to Academy of Music of Philadelphia, Philadelphia, PA. For restoration fund.

$1,000 to University of Pennsylvania, University of Pennsylvania Museum, Philadelphia, PA. For Loren Eiseley Society.

$750 to Yale Alumni Fund, New Haven, CT. For annual support.

$500 to Shipley School, Bryn Mawr, PA. For annual support.

8440

Ray S. Shoemaker Trust for Shoemaker Scholarship Fund ◇

c/o Mellon Financial Corp.
2 N. 2nd St., 12th Fl.
Harrisburg, PA   17108
Scholarship application address: c/o Dir. of Admissions, Harrisburg Area Community College, Cameron St., Harrisburg, PA 17108, tel.: (717) 780-2400

Donor: Ray S. Shoemaker.

Foundation type: Independent foundation.

Financial data (yr. ended 9/30/05): Assets, $6,038,725 (M); expenditures, $348,632; qualifying distributions, $341,357; giving activities include $341,357 for 132 grants to individuals.

Purpose and activities: Giving restricted to a scholarship program for graduates of greater Harrisburg, PA, area high schools.

Type of support: Scholarships—to individuals.

Limitations: Giving limited to residents of the greater Harrisburg, PA, area.

Application information: Application form required.
Initial approach: Letter
Deadline(s): Apr. 1

Trustee: Mellon Bank, N.A.

EIN: 236237250

8441

R. P. Simmons Family Foundation ◇

Birchmere, Quaker Hollow Rd.
Sewickley, PA   15143

Established in 1987 in PA.

Donors: Richard P. Simmons; Diamond Investments Corp.

Foundation type: Independent foundation.

Financial data (yr. ended 12/31/05): Assets, $1,760,767 (M); gifts received, $5,000; expenditures, $1,761,091; qualifying distributions, $1,730,400; giving activities include $1,730,400 for 57 grants (high: $250,000; low: $500; average: $1,000–$50,000).

Purpose and activities: Support primarily for arts organizations and education.

Fields of interest: Performing arts, orchestra (symphony); Arts; Higher education; Education; Human services; Children/youth, services; Federated giving programs.

Type of support: General/operating support; Capital campaigns; Endowments; Program development; Professorships; Scholarship funds.

Limitations: Applications not accepted. Giving primarily in PA, with emphasis on Pittsburgh. No grants to individuals.

Application information: Contributes only to pre-selected organizations.

Trustee: Richard P. Simmons.

EIN: 256277068

Selected grants: The following grants were reported in 2004.

$3,827,550 to Massachusetts Institute of Technology, Cambridge, MA. For capital campaign.

$100,000 to Latin School of Chicago, Chicago, IL. For capital campaign.

$80,000 to Pittsburgh Symphony Society, Pittsburgh, PA. For capital campaign.

$50,000 to Andrew Carnegie Free Library and Community Center, Carnegie, PA. For capital campaign.

$50,000 to Childrens Museum of Pittsburgh, Pittsburgh, PA. For general support.

$50,000 to Sewickley Academy, Sewickley, PA. For scholars program.

$25,000 to Carnegie Museum of Natural History, Pittsburgh, PA. For general support.

$25,000 to Gettysburg National Battlefield Museum Foundation, Seven Valleys, PA. For general support.

$25,000 to W Y E P Pittsburgh Community Broadcasting Corporation, WYEP-FM, Pittsburgh, PA. For capital campaign.

$22,000 to Pittsburgh Public Theater, Pittsburgh, PA. For general support.

8442
Juliet L. Hillman Simonds Foundation ✧
330 Grant St., Ste. 2000
Pittsburgh, PA 15219 (412) 338-3466
Contact: Ronald W. Wertz, V.P.
FAX: (412) 338-3463;
E-mail: foundation@hillmanfo.com

Established in 1986 in DE.
Donors: Juliet Lea Hillman Simonds; Henry Lea Hillman Charitable Lead Trust.
Foundation type: Independent foundation.
Financial data (yr. ended 12/31/04): Assets, $10,522,986 (M); expenditures, $269,042; qualifying distributions, $435,028; giving activities include $421,650 for 43 grants (high: $39,000; low: $250).
Fields of interest: Museums; Arts; Secondary school/education; Higher education; Crime/violence prevention, domestic violence; Aging; Disabilities, people with; Women; AIDS, people with; Economically disadvantaged; Homeless.
Type of support: General/operating support; Capital campaigns; Building/renovation; Equipment; Endowments; Program development.
Limitations: Giving primarily in Pittsburgh, PA. No grants to individuals.
Publications: Application guidelines.
Application information: Application form not required.
  Initial approach: Proposal
  Copies of proposal: 1
  Deadline(s): None
  Board meeting date(s): May and Dec.
Officers and Directors:* Juliet Lea Hillman Simonds,* Pres.; Ronald W. Wertz,* V.P.; Maurice J. White,* Secy.; Eric C. Johnson,* Treas.
Number of staff: 1 part-time professional.
EIN: 251536654
Selected grants: The following grants were reported in 2003.
$200,000 to Carnegie Institute, Andy Warhol Museum, Pittsburgh, PA. For capital campaign.
$25,000 to Creative Nonfiction Foundation, Pittsburgh, PA.
$2,000 to Shadyside Hospital Foundation, Pittsburgh, PA.
$1,500 to Pittsburgh Symphony Society, Pittsburgh, PA.
$1,000 to Ellis School, Pittsburgh, PA. For annual fund.
$1,000 to Greater Pittsburgh Community Food Bank, Duquesne, PA.
$1,000 to Ronald McDonald House Charities of Pittsburgh, Pittsburgh, PA.
$1,000 to Saint Edmunds Academy, Pittsburgh, PA. For annual fund.

$1,000 to Womens Center and Shelter of Greater Pittsburgh, Pittsburgh, PA.
$500 to Childrens Institute of Pittsburgh, Pittsburgh, PA.

8443
W. W. Smith Charitable Trust ▼
200 Four Falls Corporate Ctr., Ste. 300
West Conshohocken, PA 19428
(610) 397-1844
Contact: Esther Mallouh, Exec. Dir.
FAX: (610) 397-1680;
E-mail: emallouh@wwsmithchuitabletrust.org;
Additional e-mail for Esther Mallouh:
emallouh@wwsmithcharitabletrust.org; URL: http://www.wwsmithcharitabletrust.org

Trust established in 1976 in PA.
Donor: William Wikoff Smith†.
Foundation type: Independent foundation.
Financial data (yr. ended 6/30/05): Assets, $136,396,599 (M); expenditures, $7,594,119; qualifying distributions, $7,389,933; giving activities include $7,079,611 for 90 grants (high: $504,468; low: $5,000).
Purpose and activities: Support for college financial aid programs for qualified needy undergraduate students at accredited universities and colleges, and for basic scientific medical research programs dealing with cancer, AIDS, and heart disease, and programs of organizations providing shelter, food, and clothing for children and the aged.
Fields of interest: Higher education; Education; Hospitals (general); Health care; Health organizations, association; Cancer; Heart & circulatory diseases; AIDS; Biomedicine; Medical research, institute; Cancer research; Heart & circulatory research; AIDS research; Food services; Housing/shelter, development; Human services; Children/youth, services; Aging, centers/services; Women, centers/services; Minorities/immigrants, centers/services; Homeless, human services; Aging; Minorities; Women; Economically disadvantaged; Homeless.
Type of support: General/operating support; Continuing support; Building/renovation; Equipment; Emergency funds; Program development; Seed money; Scholarship funds; Research; Matching/challenge support.
Limitations: Giving primarily in the Delaware Valley, including Philadelphia, PA, and its six neighboring counties; grants to colleges by invitation only. No grants to individuals, or for deficit financing, capital campaigns, existing endowment funds, or retroactive funding for non-emergencies; no grants over 3 consecutive years; no funding of events such as dinners, golf tournaments, and program ads.
Publications: Biennial report (including application guidelines).
Application information: College financial aid programs by invitation only; applications for medical research grants must be submitted in quadruplicate; seed money support available and application forms required for medical research grants only; accepts Delaware Valley Grantmakers Common Grant Application and Common Report Form.
  Initial approach: Proposal, letter, or telephone requesting guidelines
  Copies of proposal: 1
  Deadline(s): No deadline for food, clothing, and shelter for children and aged; for college scholarships, Apr. 1 by invitation only; for

cancer and AIDS research, June 15; and for heart research, Sept. 15
  Board meeting date(s): For medical care, Mar.; social services, Mar. and Sept.; scholarships, June; cancer and AIDS research, Sept.; heart research, Dec.
  Final notification: 1 month after trustees meet
Officer and Trustees:* Esther Mallouh,* Exec. Dir.; Mary L. Smith; Wachovia Bank, N.A.
Advisors: G. Morris Dorrance; Charles B. Humpton; Deborah J. McKenna; Robert Joe Pierpont.
EIN: 236648841
Selected grants: The following grants were reported in 2005.
$504,468 to Lankenau Hospital Foundation, Wynnewood, PA.
$316,161 to Thomas Jefferson University, Philadelphia, PA.
$291,833 to University of Pennsylvania, Philadelphia, PA. For medical program.
$198,000 to Temple University, Philadelphia, PA.
$151,182 to Fox Chase Cancer Center, Philadelphia, PA.
$100,000 to Habitat for Humanity, Delaware Valley, Philadelphia, PA.
$83,920 to Drexel University, College of Medicine, Philadelphia, PA.
$70,000 to Presbyterian Childrens Village, Rosemont, PA.
$30,000 to Friends Boarding Home of Western Quarterly Meeting, Kennett Square, PA.
$20,000 to Face to Face, Philadelphia, PA. For housing program.

8444
Hoxie Harrison Smith Foundation ✧
(formerly The Smith Foundation)
P.O. Box 665
Downingtown, PA 19335 (610) 269-4802
Contact: Charles P. Barber, Pres.

Incorporated in 1920 in PA.
Donors: W. Hinckle Smith†; H. Harrison Smith†.
Foundation type: Independent foundation.
Financial data (yr. ended 12/31/05): Assets, $8,286,406 (M); expenditures, $451,971; qualifying distributions, $435,858; giving activities include $424,500 for 55 grants (high: $15,000; low: $800).
Purpose and activities: The purpose of the foundation is to support benevolent, charitable and educational undertakings; to further secular and religious education, and to care for the sick, aged and disabled; to minister to the poor and to improve the physical, mental, and moral condition of humanity, and to promote American patriotism.
Fields of interest: Historical activities, war memorials; Education; Hospitals (general); Children/youth, services; Aging, centers/services; Disabilities, people with.
Type of support: General/operating support; Continuing support; Capital campaigns; Building/renovation; Equipment; Program development; Scholarship funds.
Limitations: Giving limited to southeastern PA, including Bucks, Chester, Delaware, Montgomery, and Philadelphia counties. No grants to individuals, or for emergency funds, tickets and tables, special events, multi-year awards, deficit financing, regranting through third parties, replacement of terminating government contracts, or for unfunded government mandates.
Publications: Annual report.

Application information: Delaware Valley Grantmakers Format is accepted. Application form not required.

Initial approach: Letter
Copies of proposal: 2
Deadline(s): Before Sept. 1
Board meeting date(s): Semiannually
Final notification: Positive responses in Dec.; declines in Nov.

Officers and Directors:* Charles P. Barber,* Pres.; William W. Heilig,* V.P.; Mark T. Ledger, V.P.; Joseph H. Barber; James A. Bennett; Bruce M. Brown; Philip C. Burnham; Howard W. Busch; Lee E. Daney; Jack T. Tomarchio.
Custodian: The Vanguard Group.
Number of staff: 1 part-time support.
EIN: 236238148

8445
Ethel Sergent Clark Smith Memorial Fund ✧

c/o Wachovia Bank, N.A.
620 Brandywine Pkwy., PA 5042
West Chester, PA 19380
Contact: Diane O. Stables, V.P. and Sr. Char. Advisor
FAX: (610) 436-7807;
E-mail: diane.stables@wachovia.com

Established in 1977 in PA.
Donor: Ethel Sergeant Clark Smith†.
Foundation type: Independent foundation.
Financial data (yr. ended 5/31/05): Assets, $14,519,487 (M); expenditures, $520,645; qualifying distributions, $479,367; giving activities include $447,300 for 56 grants (high: $50,000; low: $1,500).
Purpose and activities: Giving for health associations and hospitals, education, including early childhood and secondary schools, child welfare and development, social service organizations, libraries, fine and performing arts groups and culture, museums and historical buildings, recreation, music and drama facilities, and programs for women, the handicapped and exceptional persons, and community reinvestment.
Fields of interest: Visual arts; Museums; Performing arts; Performing arts, theater; Performing arts, orchestra (symphony); Historic preservation/historical societies; Arts; Education, early childhood education; Child development, education; Secondary school/education; Higher education; Libraries/library science; Education; Speech/hearing centers; Mental health/crisis services; Health organizations, association; Recreation; Human services; Children/youth, services; Child development, services; Women, centers/services; Community development; Disabilities, people with; Women.
Type of support: General/operating support; Capital campaigns; Building/renovation; Equipment; Emergency funds; Program development; Seed money; Research; Technical assistance; Exchange programs; Matching/challenge support.
Limitations: Giving limited to Delaware County, PA, or to organizations benefiting county residents. No capital funding outside Delaware County, PA. No support for single-disease organizations. No grants to individuals, or for deficit financing, scholarships, or fellowships; no gifts longer than 3 years consecutively; no loans.
Publications: Application guidelines; Informational brochure (including application guidelines).

Application information: Applicant must use our form, and follow guidelines precisely. Application form required.

Initial approach: Letter or e-mail
Copies of proposal: 1
Deadline(s): Mar. 1 and Sept. 1
Board meeting date(s): May and Nov. (Advisory Committee)
Final notification: 2 months after trustee meets with advisory committee

Trustee: Wachovia Bank, N.A.
EIN: 236648857
Selected grants: The following grants were reported in 2005.
$50,000 to Widener University, Chester, PA.
$25,000 to CareLink Community Support Service, Broomall, PA. For facility improvement.
$25,000 to Wayne Art Center, Wayne, PA. For sculpture studio-Kiln room.
$20,000 to CityTeam Ministries, San Jose, CA. For Compass Academy and Career Employment Services.
$20,000 to Mental Health Association of Southeastern Pennsylvania, Philadelphia, PA.
$15,000 to Elwyn, Elwyn, PA.
$10,000 to Court Appointed Special Advocates (CASA)/Youth Advocates, Media, PA. For general operating support.
$10,000 to Delaware County Literacy Council, Chester, PA. For job training.
$10,000 to Opera Company of Philadelphia, Philadelphia, PA. For Sounds of Learning.
$10,000 to West Chester University of Pennsylvania, West Chester, PA. For With Penns In Hand.

8446
Snee-Reinhardt Charitable Foundation

121 Towne Square Way
Pittsburgh, PA 15227 (412) 884-3626
Contact: Karen L. Heasley, Chair.
FAX: (412) 881-4636; E-mail: jperry@ailtd.com;
URL: http://www.snee-reinhardt.org

Established in 1987 in PA.
Donor: Katherine E. Snee†.
Foundation type: Independent foundation.
Financial data (yr. ended 12/31/05): Assets, $20,810,332 (M); expenditures, $1,244,413; qualifying distributions, $1,147,223; giving activities include $1,025,790 for 59 grants (high: $135,000; low: $500).
Fields of interest: Arts; Libraries/library science; Education; Environment; Health care; Substance abuse, services; Health organizations, association; Cancer; Children/youth, services; Aging, centers/services; Community development; Christian agencies & churches; Aging.
Type of support: Building/renovation; Equipment; Program development.
Limitations: Giving primarily in southwestern PA, secondly in northern WV, northern MD, and PA; some giving also throughout the U.S. No support for sectarian or religious organizations or programs that promote, research or support the prevention of life, abortion, the practice of euthanasia, or cruelty to animals, or highly specialized health or medical programs that do not have a specific impact on the community. No grants to individuals, or for capital improvement, endowment funds, or general operating expenses, including salaries and fringe benefits, chairs or professorships.
Publications: Application guidelines; Grants list.

Application information: Application guidelines and procedures are available on foundation Web site. The amount being requested should not exceed $50,000. A request for a greater amount or a request that would be payable over a multiple-year period should not be submitted without first contacting the foundation office. Application form required.

Initial approach: Letter
Copies of proposal: 1
Deadline(s): The 15th of the month prior to the board meeting
Board meeting date(s): Grant review on the second Tues. of May and Sept., and annual meeting on the second Tues. of Nov.
Final notification: 2 weeks after board meeting

Trustee: PNC Bank, N.A.
Number of staff: 1 full-time support.
EIN: 256292908
Selected grants: The following grants were reported in 2006.
$30,000 to Greater Pittsburgh Community Food Bank, Duquesne, PA. To underwrite cost of two truckloads of bulk product.
$15,000 to American Respiratory Alliance of Western Pennsylvania, Cranberry Township, PA. For Camps Huff N' Puff and Breathe-EZ.
$15,000 to Pittsburgh Cultural Trust, Pittsburgh, PA. For presentation of and associated arts education programming for The Joffrey Ballet.
$12,500 to Animal Rescue League of Western Pennsylvania, Pittsburgh, PA. For supplies and equipment for educational programs.
$10,845 to Radio Information Service, Pittsburgh, PA. To produce four documents to improve communication information about programs and services to listeners.
$10,600 to Latrobe Area Hospital Charitable Foundation, Latrobe, PA. For stretchers for emergency room.
$10,000 to Boy Scouts of America, Greater Pittsburgh Council, Pittsburgh, PA. To expand two scouting programs in Mon Valley area.
$10,000 to Senator John Heinz Pittsburgh History Center, Pittsburgh, PA. For educational program materials.
$10,000 to Variety-The Childrens Charity, Pittsburgh, PA. For Kids on the Go! program.

8447
The Snider Foundation ✧

Wachovia Ctr.
3601 S. Broad St.
Philadelphia, PA 19148

Established in 1977 in PA.
Donor: Edward M. Snider.
Foundation type: Independent foundation.
Financial data (yr. ended 4/30/05): Assets, $12,110,919 (M); gifts received, $804,440; expenditures, $1,835,205; qualifying distributions, $1,818,400; giving activities include $1,818,400 for 70 grants (high: $1,000,000; low: $100).
Purpose and activities: Support primarily for Jewish organizations, education, and health; some funding also for the arts.
Fields of interest: Arts; Education; Health organizations, association; Human services; Jewish federated giving programs; Jewish agencies & temples.
Limitations: Applications not accepted. Giving primarily in CA and Philadelphia, PA. No grants to individuals.

Application information: Contributes only to pre-selected organizations.
Officers: Edward M. Snider, Pres.; Sanford Lipstein, Secy.-Treas.
Trustee: Fred A. Shabel.
EIN: 232047668
Selected grants: The following grants were reported in 2005.
$62,500 to Arthur Ashe Youth Tennis and Education, Philadelphia, PA.
$50,000 to Prostate Cancer Foundation, Santa Monica, CA.
$46,500 to National Ethnic Coalition of Organizations, New York, NY.
$25,000 to Brown University, Providence, RI.
$25,000 to Mastery Charter High School, Philadelphia, PA.
$25,000 to National Museum of American Jewish History, Philadelphia, PA.
$25,000 to Simon Wiesenthal Center, Los Angeles, CA.
$10,000 to Santa Barbara International Film Festival, Santa Barbara, CA.
$5,000 to Friends Central School, Wynnewood, PA.
$500 to Susan G. Komen Breast Cancer Foundation, Dallas, TX.

8448
G. Whitney Snyder Charitable Fund
535 Smithfield St., Ste. 1020
Pittsburgh, PA 15222 (412) 471-1331
Contact: Charles E. Ellison, Secy.

Established in 1990 in PA as partial successor to The W. P. Snyder Charitable Fund.
Foundation type: Independent foundation.
Financial data (yr. ended 12/31/05): Assets, $6,114,435 (M); expenditures, $424,133; qualifying distributions, $400,428; giving activities include $371,067 for 32 grants (high: $95,000; low: $500).
Purpose and activities: Giving primarily for education.
Fields of interest: Secondary school/education; Higher education; Health care; Health organizations, association; Human services; Children/youth, services; Protestant agencies & churches.
Type of support: General/operating support; Annual campaigns.
Limitations: Giving primarily in PA.
Application information: Application form not required.
Deadline(s): None
Officer: Charles E. Ellison, Secy.
Trustees: Jean Snyder Armstrong; Linda Snyder Hayes; Carolyn Snyder Miltenberger; G. Whitney Snyder, Jr.
EIN: 251611761
Selected grants: The following grants were reported in 2005.
$25,000 to Sewickley Academy, Sewickley, PA.
$21,000 to Pittsburgh Leadership Foundation, Pittsburgh, PA.
$20,000 to Sewickley Valley Hospital, Sewickley, PA.
$7,500 to YMCA of Sewickley Valley, Sewickley, PA.
$5,000 to Childrens Home Society of New Jersey, Trenton, NJ.
$5,000 to Deerfield Academy, Deerfield, MA.
$5,000 to Elizabethtown College, Elizabethtown, PA.
$5,000 to Princeton Healthcare System Foundation, Princeton, NJ.

$5,000 to Princeton University, Princeton, NJ.
$5,000 to Vanderbilt University, Nashville, TN.

8449
Society for Analytical Chemists of Pittsburgh ✧
300 Penn Ctr. Blvd., Ste. 332
Pittsburgh, PA 15235-5503 (412) 825-3220, ext. 208
Contact: Charles L. Holifield, Chair.
FAX: (412) 825-3224; E-mail: sacpinfo@pitton.org; URL: http://www.sacp.org/

Established in 1971.
Donors: James L. Waters Fund; PGH Conf. on Analytical Chemistry and Applied Spectroscopy.
Foundation type: Independent foundation.
Financial data (yr. ended 6/30/05): Assets, $174,764 (M); gifts received, $459,298; expenditures, $478,723; qualifying distributions, $330,086; giving activities include $273,252 for grants, and $56,834 for 75 grants to individuals (high: $5,000; low: $69).
Purpose and activities: Giving primarily for education and research projects in the field of analytical chemistry and applied spectroscopy.
Fields of interest: Education; Physical/earth sciences.
Type of support: General/operating support; Conferences/seminars; Internship funds; Scholarship funds; Research; Scholarships—to individuals.
Limitations: Giving primarily in the Pittsburgh, PA, area.
Publications: Informational brochure.
Application information: Application form required.
Deadline(s): Varies
Officers: Janeth K. Pifer, Chair.; Walt Sumansky, Chair.-Elect.; Greg Gould, Secy.; Nick Borsic, Treas.
EIN: 256072976

8450
Sordoni Foundation, Inc. ✧
45 Owen St.
Forty Fort, PA 18704-4305 (570) 283-1211
Contact: William B. Sordoni, Pres. and Treas.

Incorporated in 1946 in PA.
Donors: Andrew J. Sordoni, Sr.†; Andrew J. Sordoni, Jr.†; Andrew J. Sordoni III; Mrs. Andrew J. Sordoni, Sr.†; Mrs. Andrew J. Sordoni, Jr.†; Mrs. Andrew J. Sordoni III; Helen Mary Sekera; William B. Sordoni; Margaret F. Sordoni.
Foundation type: Independent foundation.
Financial data (yr. ended 12/31/05): Assets, $12,848,596 (M); expenditures, $823,493; qualifying distributions, $758,937; giving activities include $756,987 for 39 grants (high: $200,000; low: $250).
Purpose and activities: Giving is restricted to civic, cultural, educational, health care and social service organizations located in northeastern Pennsylvania.
Fields of interest: Arts; Education; Environment; Health care; Human services; Economic development.
Type of support: Continuing support; Annual campaigns; Capital campaigns; Building/renovation; Equipment; Program development; Seed money.
Limitations: Giving limited to northeastern PA. No support for organizations that receive support from

governmental agencies. No grants or scholarships will be made to individuals.
Application information: The foundation has discontinued the scholarships to individuals program. No new grants will be awarded. Application form not required.
Initial approach: Letter
Copies of proposal: 1
Deadline(s): None
Board meeting date(s): As required
Final notification: By letter
Officers and Directors:* Andrew J. Sordoni III,* Chair. and Secy.; William B. Sordoni, Pres. and Treas.; Richard Allan; A. William Kelly; John J. Menapace; Patrick J. Solano; Margaret F. Sordoni; Matthew R. Sordoni; Susan F. Sordoni, M.D.; William E. Sordoni.
Number of staff: 1 full-time professional; 1 part-time support.
EIN: 246017505
Selected grants: The following grants were reported in 2004.
$200,000 to United Way of Wyoming Valley, Wilkes Barre, PA.
$60,000 to University of Scranton, Scranton, PA.
$20,000 to Moses Taylor Hospital, Scranton, PA.
$20,000 to National Museum of Industrial History, Bethlehem, PA.
$16,667 to United Way.
$15,000 to Osterhout Free Library, Wilkes Barre, PA.
$3,633 to Wyoming Seminary, Kingston, PA.
$3,421 to Kings College, Wilkes Barre, PA.
$2,500 to College Misericordia, Dallas, PA.
$1,000 to Fine Arts Fiesta, Wilkes Barre, PA.

8451
Sovereign Bank Foundation ✧
c/o Sovereign Bank
1130 Berkshire Blvd.
Wyomissing, PA 19610 (610) 378-6190
Contact: Joseph Schupp, V.P.
Additional application addresses: Mid-Atlantic region: Sovereign Bank, 10-6438-CD2, 601 Penn St., Reading, PA 19601, New England: Sovereign Bank, MA1-SST-0407, 75 State St., Boston, MA 02109; URL: http://www.sovereignbank.com/companyinfo/foundation.asp

Established in 1989 in PA.
Donor: Sovereign Bank.
Foundation type: Company-sponsored foundation.
Financial data (yr. ended 12/31/03): Assets, $0 (M); gifts received, $3,153,131; expenditures, $3,153,131; qualifying distributions, $3,153,131; giving activities include $3,127,066 for 642 grants (high: $200,000; low: $100), $17,500 for 35 grants to individuals (high: $500; low: $500), and $8,550 for 40 employee matching gifts.
Purpose and activities: The foundation supports organizations involved with arts and culture, education, health, youth development, human services, and community development.
Fields of interest: Arts; Education; Reproductive health, family planning; Health care; Health organizations, association; AIDS; AIDS research; Food services; Housing/shelter, development; Youth development; Human services; Urban/community development; Community development.
Type of support: General/operating support; Annual campaigns; Capital campaigns; Building/renovation; Land acquisition; Emergency funds;

Program development; Seed money; Employee matching gifts; Employee-related scholarships.
Limitations: Giving primarily in areas of company operations in CT, MD, MA, NH, NJ, PA, and RI. No support for political candidates or parties or fraternal or labor organizations. No grants to individuals (except for employee-related scholarships), or for athletic events or beauty pageants or sectarian religious purposes.
Publications: Application guidelines; Annual report.
Application information: Submissions of videos and folders or plastic covers are not encouraged. Application form required.
>*Initial approach:* Contact foundation for application form
>*Copies of proposal:* 1
>*Deadline(s):* None
>*Board meeting date(s):* Quarterly

Officers and Directors: * Lawrence M. Thompson, Jr.,* Chair.; John V. Killen, Pres.; Thomas Kennedy, V.P.; Joseph E. Schupp, V.P.; John Merva, Secy.; Brenda Campbell, Treas.; John Hamill.
Number of staff: 1 part-time professional; 1 part-time support.
EIN: 232548113

8452
Spang and Company Charitable Trust ◇
P.O. Box 11422
Pittsburgh, PA 15238 (412) 963-9363
Contact: K.R. McKnight

Established in 1972 in PA.
Donors: Spang and Co.; Magnetics, Inc.; F.E. Rath Trust.
Foundation type: Company-sponsored foundation.
Financial data (yr. ended 12/31/04): Assets, $9,184,382 (M); expenditures, $443,486; qualifying distributions, $366,402; giving activities include $366,402 for 41 grants (high: $125,000; low: $100).
Purpose and activities: The trust supports hospitals and organizations involved with arts and culture, medical research, human services, and community development.
Fields of interest: Arts; Hospitals (general); Medical research; Youth, services; Human services; Community development; Federated giving programs.
Type of support: General/operating support.
Limitations: Giving primarily in the Butler, PA, area. No grants to individuals.
Application information: Application form not required.
>*Initial approach:* Proposal
>*Deadline(s):* 90 days prior to end of calendar quarter
>*Board meeting date(s):* Apr., Aug., and Dec.

Trustees: R.K. Brown; D.F. Rath; Frank E. Rath, Jr.; Robert A. Rath, Jr.
EIN: 256020192
*Selected grants: The following grants were reported in 2004.
$150,000 to Shadyside Hospital Foundation, Pittsburgh, PA. 2 grants: $25,000, $125,000 (For Hillman Cancer Center).
$100,000 to Johns Hopkins Hospital, Patrick C. Walsh Prostate Cancer, Baltimore, MD. For Patrick C. Walsh Prostate Cancer Research Fund.
$25,000 to Phipps Conservatory and Botanical Gardens, Pittsburgh, PA. For capital campaign.
$10,000 to Booneville Development Corporation, Booneville, AR.

$10,000 to Carnegie Institute, Pittsburgh, PA.
$10,000 to Pittsburgh Symphony Society, Pittsburgh, PA. payable over 2 years.
$5,000 to Butler Area Public Library, Butler, PA.
$5,000 to Childrens Hospital of Pittsburgh, Pittsburgh, PA.
$5,000 to Zoological Society of Pittsburgh, Pittsburgh Zoo and PPG Aquarium, Pittsburgh, PA.

8453
Alexander C. & Tillie S. Speyer Foundation ◇ ☆
c/o Mgr.
1202 Benedum Trees Bldg.
Pittsburgh, PA 15222-1783

Established in 1962 in PA.
Donor: Members of the Speyer family.
Foundation type: Independent foundation.
Financial data (yr. ended 12/31/05): Assets, $7,378,968 (M); expenditures, $498,924; qualifying distributions, $317,943; giving activities include $317,943 for grants.
Purpose and activities: Giving primarily for the arts.
Fields of interest: Visual arts; Museums; Arts; Elementary/secondary education; Higher education; Human services; Federated giving programs; Jewish federated giving programs.
Limitations: Giving primarily in Pittsburgh, PA.
Application information: Application form not required.
>*Deadline(s):* None

Trustees: A.C. Speyer, Jr.; Darthea Speyer.
EIN: 256051650
Selected grants: The following grants were reported in 2004.
$21,300 to Carnegie Museum of Art, Pittsburgh, PA.
$17,000 to United Way of Allegheny County, Pittsburgh, PA.
$16,100 to United Jewish Federation of Greater Pittsburgh, Pittsburgh, PA.
$15,000 to Western Pennsylvania Conservancy, Pittsburgh, PA.
$14,000 to Sidwell Friends School, DC.
$12,000 to Jewish Community Center, Scranton, PA.
$8,000 to Pratt Institute, Brooklyn, NY.
$5,000 to Jackson Hole Land Trust, Jackson, WY.
$1,500 to Frick Art and Historical Center, Pittsburgh, PA.
$400 to Salvation Army, Butler, PA.

8454
St. Mary's Catholic Foundation ◇
1935 State St.
St. Marys, PA 15857
Contact: Conrad J. Kogovsek III, Secy.-Treas.

Incorporated in 1960 in PA.
Donors: Benedict R. Reuscher†; Alfred A. Gleixner†; Richard J. Reuscher; R.B. Reuscher; E.H. Gleixner; William E. Reuscher; C.J. Kogovsek III; EB & Assocs.; William P. Gies†; Edward J. Crowe†; Raymond R. Hoffman†.
Foundation type: Independent foundation.
Financial data (yr. ended 11/30/05): Assets, $2,010,391 (M); expenditures, $576,872; qualifying distributions, $533,925; giving activities include $533,925 for 10 grants (high: $241,432; low: $2,500).

Purpose and activities: Grants to local Roman Catholic-sponsored elementary and secondary schools to supplement teachers' salaries and for school equipment in Elk County; support also for Roman Catholic religious associations and organizations of interest to the donor.
Fields of interest: Elementary/secondary education; Secondary school/education; Higher education; Roman Catholic agencies & churches; Religion.
Type of support: General/operating support.
Limitations: Applications not accepted. Giving primarily in the Erie Roman Catholic Diocese of PA, with emphasis on the St. Marys area and Elk County. No grants to individuals, or for endowment funds, scholarships, or fellowships; no loans.
Application information: Contributes only to pre-selected organizations.
>*Board meeting date(s):* Semiannually

Officers and Trustees: * Bishop Donald Troutman,* Chair.; E.H. Gleixner,* Pres.; R.B. Reuscher,* V.P.; C.J. Kogovsek III, Secy.-Treas.; Richard J. Reuscher.
EIN: 256036961

8455
The Donald B. and Dorothy L. Stabler Foundation ◇
c/o M&T Bank
213 Market St.
Harrisburg, PA 17101
Contact: William J. King, Chair.

Established in 1966 in PA.
Donors: Donald B. Stabler; Dorothy L. Stabler; Stabler Cos., Inc.; Work Area Protection Corp.; Eastern Industries, Inc.; Protection Svc., Inc.; Stabler Devel. Co.
Foundation type: Independent foundation.
Financial data (yr. ended 12/31/05): Assets, $14,824,336 (M); gifts received, $2,650; expenditures, $840,431; qualifying distributions, $757,039; giving activities include $749,667 for 60 grants (high: $60,000; low: $500).
Purpose and activities: Giving primarily for education and to Christian agencies and churches.
Fields of interest: Performing arts, music; Higher education; Education; Hospitals (general); Health care; Girls clubs; Youth development, scouting agencies (general); Human services; Protestant agencies & churches; Roman Catholic agencies & churches.
Type of support: General/operating support; Continuing support; Annual campaigns; Building/renovation; Equipment; Endowments; Professorships; Scholarship funds; Matching/challenge support.
Limitations: Giving primarily in PA, with some emphasis on Harrisburg. No grants to individuals, or for seed money, research programs, land acquisition, special projects, publications, conferences, deficit financing, or emergency funds; no loans.
Application information: Application form not required.
>*Initial approach:* Letter
>*Copies of proposal:* 1
>*Deadline(s):* None
>*Board meeting date(s):* Usually in May, Sept., and Oct.
>*Final notification:* 1 month after board meetings

Officers: Cyril C. Dunmire, Jr., Chair.; Sherill T. Moyer, Secy.; Larry Hartman, Exec. Dir.

Directors: David H. Schaper; Paul B. Shannon; Richard A. Zimmerman.
EIN: 236422944

8456
Stackpole-Hall Foundation ◇
44 S. St. Mary's St.
St. Marys, PA   15857-1667   (814) 834-1845
Contact: William C. Conrad, Chair.
FAX: (814) 834-1869;
E-mail: stackpolehall@alltel.net

Trust established in 1951 in PA.
Donors: Lyle G. Hall, Sr.†; J. Hall Stackpole†; Harrison C. Stackpole†; Lyle G. Hall, Jr.; Adelaide Stackpole†.
Foundation type: Independent foundation.
Financial data (yr. ended 12/31/05): Assets, $24,520,703 (M); expenditures, $1,282,116; qualifying distributions, $11,495,000; giving activities include $908,060 for 95 grants (high: $80,000; low: $230).
Purpose and activities: Support for higher and secondary education, and literacy and vocational projects; Christian agencies and churches; social services, including youth and child welfare agencies; the arts and cultural programs; health services, including mental health and drug abuse issues; and community development, including civic affairs and leadership development, conservation concerns, rural development, and voluntarism.
Fields of interest: Education, fund raising/fund distribution; Secondary school/education; Vocational education; Higher education; Adult/continuing education; Adult education—literacy, basic skills & GED; Libraries/library science; Education, reading; Education; Substance abuse, services; Mental health/crisis services; Alcoholism; Youth development, services; Human services; Children/youth, services; Rural development; Community development; Voluntarism promotion; Leadership development; Disabilities, people with.
Type of support: Annual campaigns; Capital campaigns; Building/renovation; Equipment; Program development; Seed money; Matching/challenge support.
Limitations: Giving primarily in Elk County, PA. No grants to individuals, or for scholarships or fellowships; generally, no grants for operating budgets or endowment funds; no loans.
Publications: Application guidelines; Annual report (including application guidelines); Financial statement; Grants list.
Application information: Application form not required.
  Initial approach: Letter
  Copies of proposal: 1
  Deadline(s): None
  Board meeting date(s): Quarterly
Officer and Directors:* William Conrad,* Chair.; Heather Conrad; Douglas Dobson; Francis Grandinetti; Hamlin Johnson; Richard Masson; Deborah Pontzer; John Saalfield; R. Dauer Stackpole; Sara-Jane Stackpole; Laurey Stackpole Turner; Lawrence Whiteman.
Number of staff: 1 full-time professional; 1 full-time support; 1 part-time support.
EIN: 256006650

8457
Staunton Farm Foundation
650 Smithfield St., Ste. 210
Pittsburgh, PA   15222-3907   (412) 281-8020
Contact: Joni Schwager, Exec. Dir.
FAX: (412) 232-3115;
E-mail: jschwager@stauntonfarm.org; URL: http://www.stauntonfarm.org

Incorporated in 1937 in PA.
Donor: Mathilda Staunton Craig McCready†.
Foundation type: Independent foundation.
Financial data (yr. ended 12/31/05): Assets, $50,440,906 (M); expenditures, $1,497,684; qualifying distributions, $1,448,302; giving activities include $1,273,133 for 33 grants (high: $131,500; low: $1,000).
Purpose and activities: Grants limited to local organizations concerned with patient care in the field of mental health.
Fields of interest: Substance abuse, services; Substance abuse, prevention; Substance abuse, treatment; Mental health, treatment; Mental health/crisis services; Crime/violence prevention, domestic violence; Human services; Children/youth, services; Family services; Family services, counseling; Psychology/behavioral science; Homeless.
Type of support: Program development; Seed money; Program evaluation.
Limitations: Giving limited to a ten-county area in southwestern PA: Allegheny, Armstrong, Beaver, Butler, Fayette, Greene, Indiana, Lawrence, Washington, and Westmoreland counties.
Publications: Grants list; Informational brochure (including application guidelines).
Application information: Grantmakers of Western Pennsylvania Common Grant Application Format is preferred. Application form available on foundation Web site. Application form required.
  Initial approach: Letter of intent
  Copies of proposal: 1
  Deadline(s): Refer to foundation Web site for latest deadlines
  Board meeting date(s): Quarterly
  Final notification: Immediately following board meetings
Officers and Directors:* Philip G. Gulley,* Chair., Project Comm.; Thomas J. Wentling, Jr., Chair., Investment Comm. and Treas.; Lee C. Lundback,* Pres.; James E. Knight, V.P.; Richard W. Reed, Jr.,* Secy.; Joni S. Schwager, Exec. Dir.; Ann W. Austin; Sallie Davis; Robert B. Ferree IV; Nancy Gruner; Allen Kukovich; Andrea Torres Mahone; Hadley Matarazzo; Judith Sherry.
Number of staff: 1 full-time professional; 1 part-time support.
EIN: 250965573

8458
James Hale Steinman Foundation ◇
8 W. King St.
P.O. Box 128
Lancaster, PA   17608-0128
Contact: Christine Mellinger
E-mail: cmellinger@lnpnews.com

Established in 1952 in PA.
Donors: James Hale Steinman†; Louise Steinman von Hess†; Lancaster Newspapers, Inc.; and others.
Foundation type: Independent foundation.

Financial data (yr. ended 12/31/05): Assets, $33,457,767 (M); gifts received, $1,000,000; expenditures, $1,543,020; qualifying distributions, $1,407,037; giving activities include $1,405,487 for 70 grants (high: $500,137; low: $500).
Purpose and activities: Giving for the arts and historic preservation, higher and other education (including scholarships to newspaper carriers and children of employees of Steinman Enterprises), youth and social services, health, family planning, and a community fund.
Fields of interest: Performing arts, music; Historic preservation/historical societies; Arts; Secondary school/education; Higher education; Education; Reproductive health, family planning; Health care; Health organizations, association; Human services; Children/youth, services; Federated giving programs.
Type of support: Annual campaigns; Capital campaigns; Building/renovation; Employee-related scholarships; Scholarships—to individuals.
Limitations: Applications not accepted. Giving primarily in Lancaster, PA.
Application information: Unsolicited requests for funds not accepted.
  Board meeting date(s): June and Dec.
Officers: Caroline S. Nunan, Chair.; Beverly R. Steinman, Vice-Chair.; Dennis A. Getz, Secy.; Willis W. Shenk, Treas.
EIN: 236266377
Selected grants: The following grants were reported in 2004.
$75,000 to Virginia Tech Foundation, Blacksburg, VA.
$31,500 to Fulton Opera House, Lancaster, PA.
$10,000 to Project Forward Leap, Philadelphia, PA.
$7,500 to Elizabethtown College, Elizabethtown, PA.
$1,500 to Church Farm School, Paoli, PA.
$1,000 to Rock Ford Foundation, Lancaster, PA.

8459
John Frederick Steinman Foundation ◇
P.O. Box 128
Lancaster, PA   17608-0128
Contact: Christine Mellinger
E-mail: cmellinger@lnpnews.com; Additional address: 8 W. King St., Lancaster, PA 17603

Trust established in 1952 in PA.
Donors: John Frederick Steinman†; Shirley W. Steinman†; Lancaster Newspapers, Inc.; and others.
Foundation type: Independent foundation.
Financial data (yr. ended 12/31/05): Assets, $30,944,947 (M); expenditures, $1,337,154; qualifying distributions, $1,202,300; giving activities include $1,148,750 for 53 grants (high: $50,000; low: $1,000), and $48,000 for grants to individuals.
Purpose and activities: Giving for higher and secondary education, the arts, community funds, family planning and other social services, youth, health services and hospitals, and the handicapped; support also for a fellowship program limited to graduate study in mental health or a related field.
Fields of interest: Arts; Secondary school/education; Higher education; Education; Hospitals (general); Reproductive health, family planning; Health care; Mental health, treatment; Mental health/crisis services; Human services; Children/youth, services; Residential/custodial care,

hospices; Federated giving programs; Psychology/ behavioral science; Disabilities, people with.

Type of support: Emergency funds; General/ operating support; Annual campaigns; Capital campaigns; Building/renovation; Land acquisition; Fellowships.

Limitations: Applications not accepted. Giving primarily in PA, with emphasis on the Lancaster area.

Publications: Informational brochure.

Application information: Unsolicited requests for funds not accepted.

Board meeting date(s): Mar., June, Sept., and Dec.

Officers and Trustees:* Pamela M. Thye,* Chair.; Dennis A. Getz,* Secy.; Willis W. Shenk, Treas.; John M. Buckwalter; Jack S. Gerhart; Henry Pildner, Jr.

EIN: 236266378

8460
The Stewart Foundation ✧ ☆

P.O. Box 902
York, PA   17405

Established in 1986 in PA.

Donors: York Building Products, Inc.; Stewart & March, Inc.; Apple Chevrolet; Stewart & Tate, Inc.

Foundation type: Independent foundation.

Financial data (yr. ended 12/31/05): Assets, $1,558,870 (M); gifts received, $408,280; expenditures, $440,114; qualifying distributions, $433,637; giving activities include $433,637 for 61 + grants (high: $100,000).

Purpose and activities: Giving primarily to a Catholic high school; support also for health care and community development.

Fields of interest: Performing arts centers; Arts; Elementary/secondary education; Secondary school/education; Higher education; American Red Cross; Children/youth, services; Federated giving programs; Roman Catholic agencies & churches; Religion.

Limitations: Applications not accepted. Giving primarily in York, PA. No grants to individuals.

Application information: Contributes only to pre-selected organizations.

Officers: Gary A. Stewart, Pres.; Robert H. Stewart, Jr., V.P.; Terrence S. Stewart, V.P.; Karyl L. Gilbert, Secy.; Dale Voorheis, Treas.

EIN: 222762903

Selected grants: The following grants were reported in 2004.

$100,000 to York Catholic High School, York, PA. For general support.

$39,613 to United Way of York County, York, PA. For general support.

$30,000 to Strand-Capitol Performing Arts Center, York, PA. For general support.

$8,050 to YWCA of York, York, PA. For general support.

$3,000 to YMCA of York and York County, York, PA. For general support.

$2,500 to York Health Foundation, York, PA. For general support.

$2,000 to Valparaiso University, Valparaiso, IN. For general support.

$1,000 to American Red Cross, York, PA. For general support.

$1,000 to Leukemia & Lymphoma Society, Harrisburg, PA. For general support.

$1,000 to York Foundation, York, PA. For general support.

8461
Alexander Stewart, M.D. Foundation ✧

c/o Mellon Financial Corp.
P.O. Box 185
Pittsburgh, PA   15230-9897
Application address: c/o Arnold Johnson, 1735 Market St., Philadelphia, PA 19103, tel.: (215) 553-2295

Established in 1981 in PA.

Foundation type: Independent foundation.

Financial data (yr. ended 6/30/05): Assets, $7,435,216 (M); expenditures, $383,073; qualifying distributions, $351,268; giving activities include $333,385 for 54 grants (high: $20,000; low: $1,000).

Purpose and activities: Giving primarily for human services and mental health. Support also for historical societies and libraries.

Fields of interest: Historic preservation/historical societies; Libraries/library science; Environment, natural resources; Mental health/crisis services; Safety/disasters, volunteer services; Human services; Salvation Army; YM/YWCAs & YM/YWHAs.

Type of support: General/operating support.

Limitations: Giving limited to Shippensburg, PA, and vicinity, including Cumberland, Franklin, Fulton, and Perry counties. No grants to individuals.

Application information:

Initial approach: Proposal
Deadline(s): Apr. 1

Trustee: Mellon Bank, N.A.

EIN: 236732616

8462
James M. and Margaret V. Stine Foundation ✧

c/o Robert J. Weinberg
3000 2 Logan Sq.
Philadelphia, PA   19103-2799

Established in 1996 in PA.

Donors: James M. Stine; Margaret V. Stine.

Foundation type: Independent foundation.

Financial data (yr. ended 12/31/05): Assets, $22,785,518 (M); expenditures, $1,229,071; qualifying distributions, $1,227,517; giving activities include $1,225,000 for 14 grants (high: $500,000; low: $2,500).

Purpose and activities: Giving primarily to Roman Catholic agencies and churches, including a medical foundation.

Fields of interest: Environment, natural resources; Health organizations, association; Federated giving programs; Roman Catholic federated giving programs; Roman Catholic agencies & churches.

Limitations: Applications not accepted. Giving primarily in MD and PA. No grants to individuals.

Application information: Contributes only to pre-selected organizations.

Officers and Directors:* Margaret V. Stine,* Pres. and Treas.; Sarah Igler,* V.P.; Martha Lee Boyd,* Secy.; Michael Boyd; Thomas Igler; David J. Stine; Lindsay Stine.

EIN: 232834787

8463
The Stop & Shop Family Foundation ✧ ☆

1149 Harrisburg Pike
Carlisle, PA   17013
Application address: The Stop & Shop Supermarket Co. LLC, Public Affairs Dept., P.O. Box 55888, Boston, MA 02205-5888, tel.: (617) 770-6050; URL: http://www.stopandshop.com/about/ community.htm

Established in 2002.

Donors: The Stop & Shop Supermarket Co.; The Stop & Shop Supermarket Co. LLC; Ahold Financial Services, LLC.

Foundation type: Company-sponsored foundation.

Financial data (yr. ended 12/31/04): Assets, $767,344 (M); gifts received, $1,402,223; expenditures, $1,921,868; qualifying distributions, $1,789,956; giving activities include $1,789,956 for 382 grants (high: $133,724; low: $251).

Purpose and activities: The foundation supports organizations involved with K-12 education, recreation, and children.

Fields of interest: Elementary/secondary education; Recreation; Children.

Limitations: Giving primarily in areas of company operations in CT, MA, NH, NJ, NY, and RI.

Publications: Application guidelines; Program policy statement.

Application information: Proposals should be submitted using organization letterhead. Application form not required.

Initial approach: Proposal
Deadline(s): At least 6 weeks prior to need

Officers and Directors:* Richard Picariello,* Pres.; Thomas Hippler,* Secy.; Faith Weiner,* Treas.

EIN: 043548392

8464
Strauss Foundation ✧

c/o Wachovia Bank, N.A.
123 S. Broad St., 5th Fl.
Philadelphia, PA   19109
Contact: Reginald Middleton, V.P., Wachovia Bank, N.A.

Trust established in 1951 in PA.

Donor: Maurice L. Strauss.

Foundation type: Independent foundation.

Financial data (yr. ended 12/31/05): Assets, $38,910,150 (M); expenditures, $2,139,690; qualifying distributions, $1,935,114; giving activities include $1,895,150 for grants.

Purpose and activities: Emphasis on Jewish welfare funds in the U.S. and Israel, child welfare and youth agencies, education, hospitals, and cultural programs.

Fields of interest: Arts; Higher education; Education; Hospitals (general); Human services; Children/youth, services; Jewish federated giving programs.

International interests: Israel.

Limitations: Giving primarily in PA and for organizations in Israel. No grants to individuals.

Application information: Unsolicited applications are not encouraged.

Trustees: Henry A. Gladstone; Scott Rosen Isdaner; Sandra S. Krause; Benjamin Strauss; Robert Perry Strauss.

Corporate Trustee: Wachovia Bank, N.A.

EIN: 236219939

8465
Margaret Dorrance Strawbridge Foundation of Pennsylvania I, Inc. ✧
c/o Dechert
Cira Centre
2929 Arch St.
Philadelphia, PA 19104-2808

Established in 1985 in PA.
Donors: George Strawbridge, Jr.; Margaret Dorrance Strawbridge Foundation.
Foundation type: Independent foundation.
Financial data (yr. ended 12/31/05): Assets, $11,656,776 (M); expenditures, $1,053,379; qualifying distributions, $961,667; giving activities include $961,667 for 10 grants (high: $250,000; low: $2,000).
Fields of interest: Museums; Arts; Elementary/secondary education; Higher education; Environment, natural resources; Hospitals (general); Health organizations, association; Medical research, institute.
Limitations: Applications not accepted. Giving on a national basis. No grants to individuals, or for endowment funds.
Application information: Contributes only to pre-selected organizations.
Officers: George Strawbridge, Jr., Pres. and Secy.; Nina S. Strawbridge, V.P.
EIN: 232373081

8466
Margaret Dorrance Strawbridge Foundation of Pennsylvania II, Inc. ✧
2011 Renaissance Blvd., Ste. 102
King of Prussia, PA 19406 (610) 272-0800
Contact: Diana S. Wister, Pres.

Established in 1985 in PA.
Donors: Diana S. Wister; Margaret Dorrance Strawbridge Foundation.
Foundation type: Independent foundation.
Financial data (yr. ended 12/31/04): Assets, $18,717,790 (M); gifts received, $6,000; expenditures, $1,411,707; qualifying distributions, $1,381,780; giving activities include $1,357,780 for 101 grants (high: $100,000; low: $500).
Purpose and activities: Emphasis on higher and secondary education, hospitals and medical research, and the environment. Nearly all grants are for operating expenses.
Fields of interest: Secondary school/education; Higher education; Environment; Hospitals (general); Medical research, institute.
Type of support: General/operating support; Continuing support; Annual campaigns; Research.
Limitations: Giving primarily in the eastern U.S., with emphasis on FL and PA. No grants to individuals, or for capital or endowment funds, scholarships, or fellowships; no loans.
Application information: Application form not required.
  Initial approach: Letter
  Deadline(s): None
Officers and Directors:* Diana S. Wister,* Pres.; William R. Wister, Jr.,* V.P.; Joseph W. Roskos,* Secy.-Treas.
EIN: 232371943
Selected grants: The following grants were reported in 2004.
$100,000 to Campus Crusade for Christ International, Orlando, FL.

$100,000 to Garden Club of America, New York, NY.
$100,000 to Groton School, Groton, MA.
$100,000 to Maine Coast Heritage Trust, Topsham, ME.
$50,000 to Agnes Irwin School, Rosemont, PA.
$40,000 to Society of the Four Arts, Palm Beach, FL.
$20,000 to First Baptist Church, West Palm Beach, FL.
$10,000 to Westover School, Middlebury, CT.
$6,000 to Norton Museum of Art, West Palm Beach, FL.
$5,000 to Island Foundation, Seal Harbor, ME.

8467
Maxwell Strawbridge Foundation ✧
(formerly Maxwell Strawbridge Charitable Trust)
c/o Wolf, Block, Schorr & Solis-Cohen
1650 Arch St., 22nd Fl.
Philadelphia, PA 19103

Established in 1992 in PA.
Donor: Ethel Guy†.
Foundation type: Independent foundation.
Financial data (yr. ended 12/31/05): Assets, $3,907,800 (M); expenditures, $1,125,388; qualifying distributions, $1,108,582; giving activities include $1,097,100 for 152 grants (high: $230,000; low: $250).
Purpose and activities: Giving primarily for Jewish organizations, as well as for the arts, health, and higher education; funding also for children and social services.
Fields of interest: Performing arts; Arts; Higher education; Health care; Health organizations, association; Cancer research; Human services; Children/youth, services; Federated giving programs; Jewish federated giving programs; Jewish agencies & temples.
Limitations: Applications not accepted. Giving primarily in Philadelphia, PA, some funding nationally. No grants to individuals.
Application information: Contributes only to pre-selected organizations.
Trustees: Edward M. Glickman; Charles G. Kopp.
EIN: 232703172
Selected grants: The following grants were reported in 2005.
$230,000 to Thomas Jefferson University, Philadelphia, PA.
$150,000 to Jewish Federation of Greater Philadelphia, Philadelphia, PA.
$50,000 to Childrens Hospital Foundation, Philadelphia, PA.
$35,000 to Gerda and Kurt Klein Foundation, Narberth, PA.
$25,000 to Foundations, Inc., Moorestown, NJ.
$15,000 to American Friends of the Jaffa Institute, Flushing, NY.
$15,000 to Pennsylvania Academy of the Fine Arts, Philadelphia, PA.
$10,500 to American Jewish Committee, Milwaukee, WI.
$3,250 to Federation Early Learning Services, Philadelphia, PA.
$3,000 to Drexel University, Philadelphia, PA.

8468
G. B. Stuart Charitable Foundation
1200 Walnut Bottom Rd., Ste 202
Carlisle, PA 17015 (717) 243-3737
Contact: Keith D. Falconer, Exec. Dir.
FAX: (717) 243-3408; E-mail: kfalc@earthlink.net

Established in 1976.
Donor: George B. Stuart†.
Foundation type: Independent foundation.
Financial data (yr. ended 12/31/05): Assets, $18,165,281 (M); expenditures, $899,415; qualifying distributions, $869,999; giving activities include $737,358 for 39 grants (high: $175,000; low: $500).
Purpose and activities: Support for local concerns, including youth and human services, and charitable, educational and religious purposes.
Limitations: Giving only to PA organizations, primarily in Cumberland County with emphasis on Carlisle. No grants to individuals.
Application information:
  Initial approach: Telephone
  Deadline(s): July 1
  Board meeting date(s): May and Oct.
Officers and Directors:* Barbara E. Falconer,* Pres.; Victoria J. Macauley,* V.P.; Karen E. Faircloth,* Secy.-Treas.; Keith D. Falconer, Exec. Dir.; Alison J. Brockmeyer.
Trustees: M&T Bank; Mellon Bank, N.A.
Number of staff: 1 full-time professional; 1 full-time support.
EIN: 232042245

8469
M. J. Surgala Trust ✧
1210 Wilkins Rd.
Erie, PA 16505 (814) 838-4921
Contact: Mary Lincoln, Exec. Dir.

Established in 2001 in NY.
Donor: M.J. Surgala†.
Foundation type: Independent foundation.
Financial data (yr. ended 12/31/04): Assets, $13,409,248 (M); expenditures, $579,207; qualifying distributions, $578,716; giving activities include $467,600 for 24 grants (high: $325,000; low: $100).
Purpose and activities: Giving primarily in the field of health care.
Fields of interest: Hospitals (general); Health care, home services; Homeless.
Limitations: Giving primarily in New York, NY; some giving also in Erie, PA.
Application information:
  Initial approach: Letter or telephone
  Deadline(s): None
Officer and Trustee:* Mary Lincoln,* Exec. Dir.
EIN: 116556638

8470
Susquehanna Foundation ✧
401 City Line Ave., Ste. 220
Bala Cynwyd, PA 19004

Established in PA.
Donors: Eric Brooks; Arthur Datnchik; Andrew Frost; Joel Greenberg; Jeffrey Yass.
Foundation type: Operating foundation.
Financial data (yr. ended 12/31/04): Assets, $1,530,071 (M); gifts received, $2,789,024;

expenditures, $3,174,578; qualifying distributions, $4,100,347; giving activities include $3,170,848 for 96 grants (high: $525,000; low: $200).

Purpose and activities: Giving primarily for education, hospitals, and children's services.

Fields of interest: Education; Hospitals (general); Children, services.

Type of support: Program-related investments/ loans.

Limitations: Applications not accepted. Giving on a national basis. No support for religious organizations. No grants to individuals.

Application information: Contributes only to pre-selected organizations.

Officers: Arthur Dantchik, Pres.; Eric Brooks, V.P.; Andrew Frost, V.P.; Jeffrey Yass, V.P.; Joel Greenberg, Secy.; Brian Sullivan, Treas.

EIN: 232732477

Selected grants: The following grants were reported in 2003.

$510,000 to Institute for Justice, DC.

$320,000 to Cato Institute, DC.

$278,078 to Childrens Hospital Foundation.

$123,750 to Save the Children Federation, Westport, CT.

$80,000 to Social Security Choice.org Foundation, Evanston, IL.

$60,000 to Gladwyne Montessori School, Gladwyne, PA.

$58,750 to 52nd Street Project, New York, NY.

$50,000 to Don Monti Memorial Research Foundation, Sands Point, NY.

$42,500 to Milton and Rose D. Friedman Foundation, Indianapolis, IN.

$19,355 to Childrens Crisis Treatment Center, Philadelphia, PA.

8471

Susquehanna Pfaltzgraff Foundation ✧

140 E. Market St.
P.O. Box 2026
York, PA   17405-2026   (717) 848-5500
Contact: John L. Finlayson

Established in 1966 in PA.

Donors: Susquehanna Pfaltzgraff Co.; Susquehanna Radio Corp.; The Pfaltzgraff Co.; Susquehanna Cable Co.; York Cable Television Co.

Foundation type: Company-sponsored foundation.

Financial data (yr. ended 12/31/05): Assets, $2,041,063 (L); gifts received, $600,000; expenditures, $594,712; qualifying distributions, $593,850; giving activities include $593,850 for 34 grants (high: $100,000; low: $250).

Purpose and activities: The foundation supports hospitals and organizations involved with arts and culture, education, and human services.

Fields of interest: Arts, multipurpose centers/ programs; Arts; Higher education; Education; Hospitals (general); Human services; Federated giving programs.

Limitations: Giving primarily in the York, PA, area.

Application information: Application form not required.

Initial approach: Proposal
Copies of proposal: 1
Deadline(s): None

Officers: Louis J. Appell, Jr., Pres.; George N. Appell, V.P.; Helen A. Norton, V.P.; William H. Simpson, Secy.

EIN: 236420008

8472

SVF Foundation ✧ ☆

200 Eagle Rd., Ste. 316
Wayne, PA   19087

Established in 1999 in PA.

Donor: Dorrance H. Hamilton.

Foundation type: Operating foundation.

Financial data (yr. ended 12/31/05): Assets, $14,167,268 (M); gifts received, $6,254,672; expenditures, $3,267,417; qualifying distributions, $2,518,063; giving activities include $315,407 for 1 grant.

Fields of interest: Higher education, university; Animals/wildlife, bird preserves.

Limitations: Applications not accepted. Giving primarily in Boston, MA. No grants to individuals.

Application information: Contributes only to pre-selected organizations.

Officer: Dorrance H. Hamilton, Pres.

Directors: Margaret H. Duprey; George W. Moore.

EIN: 256621038

8473

Kenneth and Caroline Taylor Family Foundation ✧

R.R. 1, Box 6B
Wyalusing, PA   18853

Established in 2000 in PA.

Donors: Caroline E. Taylor; Kenneth H. Taylor, Jr.

Foundation type: Independent foundation.

Financial data (yr. ended 12/31/03): Assets, $11,222,874 (M); expenditures, $406,255; qualifying distributions, $362,771; giving activities include $350,167 for 27 grants (high: $204,500; low: $500).

Fields of interest: Higher education; Environment, land resources; Health care; Human services; Protestant agencies & churches.

Limitations: Applications not accepted. Giving primarily in PA and WY. No grants to individuals.

Application information: Contributes only to pre-selected organizations.

Trustees: Caroline E. Taylor; Kenneth H. Taylor, Jr.

EIN: 256742004

Selected grants: The following grants were reported in 2004.

$202,000 to Austin College, Sherman, TX.

$30,000 to Grand Teton Music Festival, Teton Village, WY.

$22,500 to Jackson Hole Land Trust, Jackson, WY.

$5,000 to Dartmouth College, Hanover, NH.

$5,000 to National Museum of Wildlife Art, Jackson, WY.

$5,000 to Wilkes University, Wilkes Barre, PA.

$1,000 to Jackson Hole Conservation Alliance, Jackson, WY.

8474

Tecovas Foundation ✧

c/o Glenmede Trust Co.
1650 Market St., Ste. 1200
Philadelphia, PA   19103-7391

Established in 1999 in TX.

Donor: Caroline Bush Emeny.

Foundation type: Independent foundation.

Financial data (yr. ended 12/31/04): Assets, $3,124,728 (M); gifts received, $185,519; expenditures, $1,270,800; qualifying distributions,

$1,239,229; giving activities include $1,238,500 for 4 grants (high: $1,137,500; low: $1,000; average: $1,000–$50,000).

Fields of interest: Human services.

Limitations: Applications not accepted. Giving primarily in Amarillo, TX. No grants to individuals.

Application information: Contributes only to pre-selected organizations.

Officers and Directors:* Mary T. Emeny,* Chair.; Alicia E. Ingalls,* Secy.; Janet W. Havener, Treas.; Alexander S. Taylor; Mary Wagley.

EIN: 752829989

8475

John Templeton Foundation ▼ ✧

300 Conshohocken State Rd., Ste. 500
West Conshohocken, PA   19428
(610) 941-2828
Contact: Grant Admin.
FAX: (610) 825-1730; E-mail: info@templeton.org;
URL: http://www.templeton.org

Established in 1988 in TN.

Donors: John Marks Templeton; Templeton Religious Trust; Templeton World Charity Foundation.

Foundation type: Independent foundation.

Financial data (yr. ended 12/31/05): Assets, $1,080,335,362 (M); gifts received, $351,356; expenditures, $56,029,033; qualifying distributions, $48,065,952; giving activities include $41,893,755 for 344 grants (high: $3,178,222; low: $135; average: $25,000–$1,220,000), $2,106,444 for 27 grants to individuals (high: $1,529,103; low: $100; average: $3,000–$63,000), $5,500 for 2 employee matching gifts, and $315,565 for 1 foundation-administered program.

Purpose and activities: The mission of the John Templeton Foundation is to pursue new insights at the boundary between theology and science through a rigorous, open-minded and empirically focused methodology, drawing together talented representatives from a wide spectrum of fields of expertise. Using "the humble approach," the foundation typically seeks to focus the methods and resources of scientific inquiry on topical areas which have spiritual and theological significance ranging across the disciplines from cosmology to health care. In the human sciences, the foundation supports programs, competitions, publications, and studies that promote character education and the exploration of positive values and purpose across the lifespan. It supports free enterprise education and development internationally through the Templeton Freedom Awards, new curriculum offerings, and other programs that encourage free-market principles.

Fields of interest: Health care; Youth development; Economic development; Science; Leadership development; Religion.

Type of support: Program development; Conferences/seminars; Publication; Curriculum development; Fellowships; Research; Grants to individuals; Matching/challenge support.

Limitations: Giving on a national and international basis. No grants to individuals, (except for awards chosen by trustees) or for scholarships, endowment funds, building funds, capital campaigns, or artistic productions; no loans.

Publications: Application guidelines; Annual report; Financial statement; Informational brochure; Newsletter.

Application information: Application form not required.

Initial approach: Proposal
Copies of proposal: 4
Deadline(s): None
Board meeting date(s): Varies
Final notification: Varies; 3 to 6 months from date of application

Officers and Trustees:* Sir John Marks Templeton,* Chair.; John Marks Templeton, Jr., M.D.*, Pres.; Arthur J. Schwartz, Exec. V.P.; Charles L. Harper, Jr., Sr. V.P. and Exec. Dir.; Judith Marchand, V.P., Admin. and Special Projects; Pamela Thompson, V.P., Comms.; Valerie K. Martin, C.F.O.; John D. Barrow; Paul C. Davies; George H. Gallup, Jr.; Owen J. Gingerich; Harold G. Koenig, M.D.; Glenn R. Mosley, Ph.D.; David G. Myers; F. Russell Stannard; Handly Templeton; Jennifer A. Templeton; Anne D. Zimmerman.

Number of staff: 12 full-time professional; 6 full-time support.

EIN: 621322826

Selected grants: The following grants were reported in 2005.

$3,584,148 to International Society for Science and Religion, Cambridge, England. For Purpose in Biology Request for Proposals (RFP) Program.

$2,010,000 to Spiritual Enterprise Institute, North Palm Beach, FL. For general support.

$2,000,000 to Cambridge University, Saint Edmund's College, Cambridge, England. For Faraday Projects.

$1,968,701 to Cornell University, Center for the Study of Economy and Society, Ithaca, NY. For research on China's Free Enterprise Economy.

$1,325,000 to Rural Development Institute, Seattle, WA. Toward Global Homestead Program - Exploring the Potential of Homestead Plot Ownership for Improving the Livelihoods of the Poor.

$799,989 to Princeton University, Princeton, NJ. For The Scientific Study of Prayer Using Cognitive and Textual Methods.

$150,000 to University of Chicago, Chicago, IL. For Optimism, Economic Success, and Free Markets.

$125,000 to Institute for Jewish and Community Research, San Francisco, CA. For Research Study of U.S. College Faculty Regarding Their Beliefs About Religion and the Benefits of Business.

$85,274 to University of Portsmouth, Department of Mathematics, Portsmouth, England. Toward a Neo-Patristic Synthesis of Theology and Science.

$27,138 to Oxford University, Nuffield College, Oxford, England. For Austin Farrer Senior Research Project.

8476
The Jean Powell Thompson Charitable Trust ◇

c/o The Glenmede Trust Co.
1650 Market St., Ste. 1200
Philadelphia, PA 19103-7391

Established in 2003 in OH.
Donor: Jean P. Thompson†.
Foundation type: Independent foundation.
Financial data (yr. ended 12/31/04): Assets, $688,487 (M); gifts received, $81,208; expenditures, $397,768; qualifying distributions, $391,951; giving activities include $387,497 for 1 grant.

Fields of interest: Environment, natural resources; Environment, land resources.
Limitations: Applications not accepted. Giving primarily in OH. No grants to individuals.
Application information: Contributes only to pre-selected organizations.
Trustee: The Glenmede Trust Co.
EIN: 546507032

8477
Tippins Foundation

3 Gateway Ctr., Ste. 13E
Pittsburgh, PA 15222
Contact: George R. Knapp, Exec. Dir.

Established in 1987 in PA.
Donors: TMC Investment Co.; Carolyn M. Tippins; George W. Tippins†; Tippins Inc.
Foundation type: Independent foundation.
Financial data (yr. ended 12/31/05): Assets, $1,405,616 (M); gifts received, $750,000; expenditures, $536,416; qualifying distributions, $529,855; giving activities include $529,840 for 63 grants (high: $100,000; low: $500).
Purpose and activities: The foundation supports organizations involved with arts and culture, education, animal welfare, health, medical research, human services, entrepreneurship development, and Christianity.
Fields of interest: Performing arts; Arts; Higher education; Education; Animals/wildlife, research; Animal welfare; Hospitals (general); Health care; Medical research; Salvation Army; Human services; Community development, small businesses; Christian agencies & churches.
Type of support: Annual campaigns; Capital campaigns; Building/renovation.
Limitations: Applications not accepted. Giving primarily in PA. No grants to individuals.
Application information: Contributes only to pre-selected organizations.
Board meeting date(s): Dec.
Officer and Trustees:* George R. Knapp,* Exec. Dir.; Carolyn H. Tippins; John H. Tippins; William H. Tippins.
EIN: 256282382

8478
The Bruce E. and Robbi S. Toll Foundation ◇

(formerly The Bruce E. Toll Foundation)
250 Gibraltar Rd.
Horsham, PA 19044

Established in 1991 in PA.
Donor: Bruce E. Toll.
Foundation type: Independent foundation.
Financial data (yr. ended 1/31/05): Assets, $18,717,020 (M); expenditures, $484,138; qualifying distributions, $425,498; giving activities include $425,498 for 58 grants (high: $128,000; low: $100).
Purpose and activities: Giving primarily for Jewish organizations, including a museum of Jewish history; funding also for arts and culture, higher education, and hospitals.
Fields of interest: Museums (ethnic/folk arts); Performing arts, theater; Arts; Higher education; Hospitals (general); Jewish federated giving programs; Jewish agencies & temples.

Limitations: Applications not accepted. Giving primarily in Philadelphia, PA; funding also in New York, NY. No grants to individuals.
Application information: Contributes only to pre-selected organizations.
Officer: Bruce E. Toll, Pres.
EIN: 232667935

8479
The Robert and Jane Toll Foundation ◇

c/o Toll Brothers, Inc.
250 Gibraltar Rd.
Horsham, PA 19044-2323

Established in 1991 in PA.
Donors: Robert I. Toll; Sylvia S. Toll†.
Foundation type: Independent foundation.
Financial data (yr. ended 12/31/05): Assets, $13,288,524 (M); gifts received, $10,000; expenditures, $483,821; qualifying distributions, $426,843.
Purpose and activities: Giving for Jewish federated giving programs, art and cultural programs, higher education, and for health and human services.
Fields of interest: Higher education; Hospitals (general); Human services; Jewish federated giving programs; Jewish agencies & temples.
Type of support: General/operating support.
Limitations: Applications not accepted. Giving primarily in PA. No grants to individuals.
Application information: Contributes only to pre-selected organizations.
Officer and Director:* Robert I. Toll,* Pres., Treas., and Exec. Dir.
EIN: 232654322

8480
Edith L. Trees Charitable Trust ◇

c/o PNC Bank, N.A.
620 Liberty Ave., 33rd Fl.
Pittsburgh, PA 15222 (412) 762-4133
Contact: M. Bradley Dean, V.P., PNC Bank, N.A.

Established around 1976.
Donor: Edith L. Trees Trust.
Foundation type: Independent foundation.
Financial data (yr. ended 12/31/05): Assets, $69,904,223 (M); gifts received, $2,558,787; expenditures, $4,235,790; qualifying distributions, $4,051,096; giving activities include $3,983,111 for 90 grants (high: $165,000; low: $4,312; average: $10,000–$50,000).
Purpose and activities: Giving solely for the care and welfare of mentally retarded children.
Fields of interest: Children/youth, services; Youth, services; Disabilities, people with.
Type of support: General/operating support; Equipment; Endowments; Debt reduction.
Limitations: Giving primarily in PA. No grants to individuals.
Application information: Application form not required.
Initial approach: Proposal
Deadline(s): Oct. 1
Trustees: J. Murray Egan; PNC Bank, N.A.
EIN: 256026443

8481
Harry C. Trexler Trust ▼ ✧

33 S. 7th St., Ste. 205
Allentown, PA 18101-2406 (610) 434-9645
Contact: Thomas H. Christman, Exec. Dir.

Trust established in 1934 in PA.
Donors: Harry C. Trexler†; Mary M. Trexler†; PPL Corp.; Lehigh Cement Company; Air Products and Chemicals, Inc.; Lehigh Valley Hospital.
Foundation type: Independent foundation.
Financial data (yr. ended 3/31/06): Assets, $116,133,509 (M); gifts received, $1,700; expenditures, $6,163,534; qualifying distributions, $5,683,591; giving activities include $5,369,905 for 98 grants (high: $1,984,905; low: $500; average: $2,500–$100,000), and $6,402 for 1 foundation-administered program.
Purpose and activities: The trust provides that one-fourth of the income shall be added to the corpus, one-fourth paid to the city of Allentown for park purposes, and the remainder distributed to such charitable organizations and objects as shall be of the most benefit to humanity, but limited to Allentown and Lehigh County, PA, particularly for hospitals, churches, institutions for the care of the crippled and orphans, youth agencies, social services, cultural programs, and support of ministerial students at two named Pennsylvania institutions.
Fields of interest: Arts; Higher education; Education; Recreation; Human services; Children/youth, services; Aging, centers/services; Aging; Disabilities, people with; Economically disadvantaged.
Type of support: General/operating support; Continuing support; Capital campaigns; Building/renovation; Equipment; Land acquisition; Program development; Matching/challenge support.
Limitations: Giving limited to Lehigh County, PA. No grants to individuals, or for endowment funds, research, scholarships, or fellowships; no loans.
Publications: Application guidelines; Occasional report.
Application information: Application form not required.
  Initial approach: Letter
  Copies of proposal: 1
  Deadline(s): Dec. 1 for consideration at annual fund distribution
  Board meeting date(s): Monthly; grant distribution takes place annually after Mar. 31
  Final notification: June 1
Officer: Thomas H. Christman, Exec. Dir.
Trustees: Dexter F. Baker; Daniel G. Gambet; Malcolm J. Gross; Kathryn Stephanoff; Robert C. Wood.
Number of staff: 2 full-time professional.
EIN: 231162215
Selected grants: The following grants were reported in 2006.
$2,019,905 to Allentown, City of, Allentown, PA. 2 grants: $1,984,905 (To improve, extend, and maintain parks), $35,000 (For swimming pool).
$300,000 to Sacred Heart Hospital, Allentown, PA. Toward building addition.
$150,000 to DeSales University, Center Valley, PA. For University Center.
$150,000 to Discovery Center of Science and Technology, Bethlehem, PA. For cost of facility.
$125,000 to Good Shepherd Home and Rehabilitation, Allentown, PA. Toward building expansion.

$100,000 to Lehigh Valley Hospital and Health Network, Allentown, PA. For expanded services for adult ambulatory patients.
$30,000 to America On Wheels, Allentown, PA. For alternate fuels exhibit.
$25,000 to Allentown Public Library, Allentown, PA. For after-school programming.
$25,000 to YMCA of Allentown, Allentown, PA. For youth programs.

8482
The Triple T Foundation ✧

c/o Glenmede Trust Co., N.A.
1650 Market St., Ste. 1200
Philadelphia, PA 19103-7391

Established in 1996 in OH.
Donors: Edith J. Bastian; Alison C. Jones; Ellen W. Jones; Theodore T. Jones; Warren Tanner Jones.
Foundation type: Independent foundation.
Financial data (yr. ended 12/31/05): Assets, $8,098,347 (M); gifts received, $59,863; expenditures, $570,338; qualifying distributions, $532,392; giving activities include $526,132 for 71 grants (high: $250,000; low: $250).
Fields of interest: Elementary/secondary education; Higher education; Hospitals (general); Health care; Recreation, camps; Athletics/sports, equestrianism; Human services; Disabilities, people with.
Limitations: Applications not accepted. Giving primarily in OH, with some emphasis on the greater Cleveland area. No grants to individuals.
Application information: Contributes only to pre-selected organizations.
Trustee: Edith Bastian; Alison Jones; Warren Jones; Ellen Nordell.
EIN: 341811968
Selected grants: The following grants were reported in 2004.
$50,000 to Fieldstone Farm Therapeutic Riding Center, Chagrin Falls, OH. 2 grants: $25,000 each
$22,000 to Hathaway Brown School, Shaker Heights, OH. 2 grants: $2,000, $20,000
$11,850 to Charles River School, Dover, MA.
$11,500 to Holden Arboretum, Kirtland, OH. 2 grants: $1,500, $10,000
$7,000 to Fine Arts Council of Trumbull County, Warren, OH.
$2,000 to Massachusetts Eye and Ear Infirmary, Boston, MA.
$1,000 to Western Reserve Historical Society, Cleveland, OH.

8483
Mildred Faulkner Truman Foundation ✧ ☆

c/o M&T Bank, Tax Dept.
21 E. Market St.
York, PA 17401-1205
Application address: c/o Irene C. Graven, Exec. Dir., 195 Front St., P.O. Box 89, Owego, NY 13827-0089, tel.: (607) 687-0225; fax: (607) 687-0268; E-mail: MFTF@clarityconnect.com; URL: http://www.people.clarityconnect.com/webpages3/mftf/

Established in 1985 in NY.
Donor: Mildred Faulkner Truman†.
Foundation type: Independent foundation.
Financial data (yr. ended 8/31/05): Assets, $7,960,877 (M); expenditures, $505,743;

qualifying distributions, $374,897; giving activities include $377,252 for 32 grants (high: $35,535; low: $500).
Purpose and activities: Giving primarily to organizations which enhance the benefit and residents of Tioga County, NY. The foundation wishes to accomplish this mission by encouraging grant requests for critical needs, capital projects, and seed money for new and special projects or programs.
Fields of interest: Historic preservation/historical societies; Higher education; Libraries (public); Education; Human services; Community development, neighborhood development.
Type of support: Capital campaigns; Building/renovation; Equipment; Emergency funds; Program development; Seed money; Scholarship funds; Matching/challenge support.
Limitations: Giving primarily in Owego and Tioga counties, NY. No grants to individuals.
Publications: Annual report (including application guidelines).
Application information: Completed applications can be mailed or deposited in the drop box located in the basement lobby of M&T Bank at the corner of Front and Church Sts., Owego, NY, during normal banking hours. Application guidelines and application form are available on foundation Web site. Application form required.
  Initial approach: Proposal
  Copies of proposal: 11
  Deadline(s): 5 weeks prior to board meeting
  Board meeting date(s): Jan., Apr., June, Sept.
  Final notification: 1 week after board meeting
Officer: Irene C. Graven, Exec. Dir.
Trustee: M&T Bank.
Number of staff: 1 part-time professional.
EIN: 166271201
Selected grants: The following grants were reported in 2005.
$35,535 to Ti-Ahwaga Community Players, Owego, NY.
$24,275 to Coburn Free Library, Owego, NY.
$15,000 to Broome Community College Foundation, Binghamton, NY.
$15,000 to Tompkins Cortland Community College Foundation, Dryden, NY.
$11,500 to Open Door Mission, Rochester, NY.
$10,000 to Catholic Charities of Tompkins-Tioga, Ithaca, NY.
$2,000 to Discovery Center of the Southern Tier, Binghamton, NY.

8484
Turner Family Foundation ✧

9 Horseshoe Ln.
Paoli, PA 19301

Established in 1994 in PA.
Donors: Robert E. Turner, Jr.; Carolyn Turner.
Foundation type: Independent foundation.
Financial data (yr. ended 12/31/03): Assets, $2,768,615 (M); gifts received, $124,500; expenditures, $776,705; qualifying distributions, $741,396; giving activities include $740,020 for 15 grants (high: $575,000; low: $120).
Fields of interest: Higher education; Federated giving programs; Christian agencies & churches.
Limitations: Applications not accepted. No grants to individuals.
Application information: Contributes only to pre-selected organizations.

Officers: Robert E. Turner, Jr., Pres.; Carolyn Turner, Treas.
EIN: 232792012
Selected grants: The following grants were reported in 2003.
$575,000 to Bradley University, Peoria, IL. For general support.
$125,000 to Episcopal Academy, Merion, PA. 2 grants: $100,000 (For general support), $25,000 (For general support).
$13,700 to Paoli Presbyterian Church, Paoli, PA. For general support.
$10,000 to University of Notre Dame, Notre Dame, IN. For general support.
$5,000 to Campus Crusade for Christ International, Orlando, FL. For general support.
$1,000 to Juvenile Diabetes Research Foundation International, New York, NY. For general support.
$500 to Fighting Back Scholarship Program, Devon, PA. For general support.
$500 to Wellness Community, DC. For general support.

8485
Tyco Electronics Foundation ✧
(formerly AMP Foundation)
c/o Tyco Electronics Corp.
P.O. Box 3608, M.S. 140-10
Harrisburg, PA 17105-3608 (717) 592-4869
Contact: Mary J. Rakoczy, Admin.
FAX: (717) 592-4022;
E-mail: mjrakocz@tycoelectronics.com; Application address for overnight delivery: 2901 Fulling Mill Rd., M.S. 140-10, Middletown, PA 17057; URL: http://www.tycoelectronics.com/aboutus/community

Established in 1977 in PA.
Donor: AMP Inc.
Foundation type: Company-sponsored foundation.
Financial data (yr. ended 12/31/05): Assets, $15,356,741 (M); expenditures, $1,287,049; qualifying distributions, $1,159,313; giving activities include $1,159,313 for 160 grants (high: $70,000; low: $20).
Purpose and activities: The foundation supports organizations involved with education. Special emphasis is directed toward organizations with which employees of Tyco Electronics volunteer.
Fields of interest: Elementary/secondary education; Education; Federated giving programs; Science, formal/general education; Mathematics.
Type of support: General/operating support; Program development; Research; Employee volunteer services.
Limitations: Giving primarily in areas of company operations, with emphasis on Menlo Park and northern CA, Boston, MA, Detroit, MI, NC, Harrisburg and central PA, SC, Austin, Dallas, and Houston, TX, and Lynchburg, VA. No support for private foundations, national organizations, service clubs, or fraternal, social, labor, or trade organizations, discriminatory organizations, or religious organizations not of direct benefit to the entire community. No grants to individuals, or for administrative or overhead expenses for research, political campaigns, or programs posing a potential conflict of interest; no loans or investments.
Publications: Application guidelines.
Application information: Organizations receiving support are asked to provide a final report. Application form not required.
Initial approach: Proposal
Copies of proposal: 1

Deadline(s): Mar. 15, June 15, Sept. 15, and Dec. 15
Board meeting date(s): Jan., Apr., July, and Oct.
Final notification: 4 to 6 weeks following board meetings
Trustee: M&T Investment Group.
Number of staff: 1 full-time professional.
EIN: 232022928
Selected grants: The following grants were reported in 2004.
$53,750 to United Way of Central Virginia, Lynchburg, VA.
$50,575 to York Technical College, Rock Hill, SC.
$42,905 to United Way of the Capital Region, Enola, PA.
$40,000 to Council of the Great City Schools, DC.
$40,000 to National Engineers Week Foundation, Alexandria, VA.
$37,385 to United Way of the Bay Area, San Francisco, CA.
$30,000 to MATHCOUNTS Foundation, Alexandria, VA.
$24,027 to Gettysburg College, Gettysburg, PA.
$10,000 to Lehigh University, Bethlehem, PA.
$1,146 to United Way of Johnston County, Smithfield, NC.

8486
United Service Foundation, Inc.
P.O. Box 36
New Holland, PA 17557
Contact: Dale M. Weaver, Pres.

Established in 1969 in PA.
Donors: Janet Newswanger; Larry Newswanger; Dale M. Weaver; Edith M. Weaver†; Irene M. Weaver; Victor F. Weaver†; Dawn Isley; Gregory Newswanger; Kendall Newswanger; Randall Newswanger.
Foundation type: Independent foundation.
Financial data (yr. ended 12/31/05): Assets, $10,498,606 (M); gifts received, $853,480; expenditures, $529,612; qualifying distributions, $489,544; giving activities include $462,710 for 15 grants (high: $150,000; low: $5,000).
Purpose and activities: Giving primarily to Mennonite religious and educational organizations and a camping association. Support for leadership development and microenterprise development.
Fields of interest: Elementary/secondary education; Recreation; Community development; Protestant agencies & churches; Religion; Minorities.
Type of support: General/operating support; Capital campaigns; Building/renovation; Program development; Seed money; Matching/challenge support.
Limitations: Applications not accepted. Giving limited to CA, IL, IN, MD, NC and PA. No grants to individuals.
Application information: Contributes only to pre-selected organizations.
Board meeting date(s): Quarterly
Officers and Trustees:* Dale M. Weaver,* Pres.; Larry W. Newswanger,* Secy.; Janet Newswanger,* Treas.; Greg Newswanger,* Genl. Mgr.
EIN: 237038781

8487
United Space Alliance Foundation ✧
c/o Mellon Financial Corp.
P.O. Box 185
Pittsburgh, PA 15230
Contact: Eileen A. Groves
Application address: 1150 Gemini St., Houston, TX 77058-2708

Established in 2001 in AL, DE, FL, and TX.
Donor: United Space Alliance, LLC.
Foundation type: Company-sponsored foundation.
Financial data (yr. ended 12/31/03): Assets, $16,144 (M); gifts received, $650,000; expenditures, $657,696; qualifying distributions, $657,675; giving activities include $657,667 for 395 grants (high: $160,000; low: $25; average: $500–$5,000).
Purpose and activities: The foundation supports organizations involved with education, health, medical research, human services, and space and aviation.
Fields of interest: Higher education; Education; Health care; Medical research; Children/youth, services; Human services; Space/aviation.
Limitations: Giving on a national basis, with some emphasis on TX.
Application information:
Initial approach: Contact foundation for application information
Directors: Andrew Allen; William Capel; Dennis K. Diemoz; Joseph Hammond; Michael McCulley; Donald K. Reed; Kate B. Kronmiller.
EIN: 760668924

8488
United States Steel Foundation, Inc. ✧
(formerly USX Foundation, Inc.)
600 Grant St., Rm. 639
Pittsburgh, PA 15219-2800 (412) 433-5237
Contact: Susan M. Kapusta, Genl. Mgr.
FAX: (412) 433-2792; URL: http://www.ussteel.com/corp/ussfoundation/ussfound.htm

Incorporated in 1953 in DE.
Donor: United States Steel Corp.
Foundation type: Company-sponsored foundation.
Financial data (yr. ended 11/30/04): Assets, $2,790,243 (M); expenditures, $2,082,590; qualifying distributions, $1,989,296; giving activities include $1,855,000 for 132 grants (high: $125,000; low: $1,000), and $134,296 for 186 employee matching gifts.
Purpose and activities: The foundation supports organizations involved with arts and culture, higher education, the environment, health, violence prevention, safety, human services, and civic affairs.
Fields of interest: Arts; Higher education; Business school/education; Engineering school/education; Environment; Public health; Health care; Crime/violence prevention; Safety, education; Human services; Science; Public affairs.
Type of support: General/operating support; Capital campaigns; Scholarship funds; Employee matching gifts; Employee-related scholarships.
Limitations: Giving on a national basis, with emphasis on areas of company operations. No support for religious organizations for religious purposes, hospitals or nursing homes, or grantmaking foundations. No grants to individuals (except for employee-related scholarships), or for

precollegiate education, individual research projects, economic development, conferences, seminars, or symposia, travel, sponsorship of special events or fundraising events, publication of papers, books, or magazines, production of films, videotapes, or other audio-visual materials, or general operating support for organizations that receive operating funds from United Ways.

Publications: Application guidelines; Annual report (including application guidelines).

Application information: Application form required.

Initial approach: Download application and mail to foundation
Copies of proposal: 1
Deadline(s): Jan. 15 for Public, Cultural, and Scientific Affairs; Apr. 15 for Education; July 15 for Safety, Health, and Human Services
Board meeting date(s): Apr., July, and Oct.
Final notification: Following board meetings

Officers and Trustees:* Thomas W. Sterling,* Chair.; David H. Lohr,* Pres.; Gretchen R. Haggerty,* Exec. V.P.; Larry T. Brockway, V.P. and Treas.; Gary A. Glynn, V.P., Investments; Dan D. Sandman,* Secy. and Genl. Counsel; John P. Surma,* C.F.O.; Larry G. Schultz, Compt.; Susan M. Kapusta,* Genl. Mgr.; Gary W. Walsh, Tax Counsel; John J. Connelly; John H. Goodish.

Number of staff: 1 full-time professional; 1 part-time professional; 2 full-time support.

EIN: 136093185

8489
Thomas and Sandra Usher Charitable Foundation ✧

840 12th St.
Oakmont, PA 15139

Established in 1999 in PA.

Foundation type: Independent foundation.

Financial data (yr. ended 12/31/05): Assets, $40,091,544 (M); gifts received, $8,516,750; expenditures, $831,195; qualifying distributions, $582,000; giving activities include $582,000 for 22 grants.

Fields of interest: Education; Human services; Family services; Christian agencies & churches.

Limitations: Applications not accepted. Giving primarily in Pittsburgh, PA. No grants to individuals.

Application information: Contributes only to pre-selected organizations.

Trustees: Sandra J. Usher; Thomas J. Usher.

EIN: 256681379

8490
The Vanguard Group Foundation ✧

100 Vanguard Blvd.
Malvern, PA 19355 (610) 669-6331
Contact: Tami F. Wise, Mgr.
Application address: P.O. Box 2600 (V38), Valley Forge, PA 19482

Established in 1992 in PA.

Donor: The Vanguard Group, Inc.

Foundation type: Company-sponsored foundation.

Financial data (yr. ended 12/31/05): Assets, $7,419,591 (M); gifts received, $2,994,102; expenditures, $2,954,293; qualifying distributions, $2,949,570; giving activities include $2,929,533 for 632 grants (high: $1,182,500).

Purpose and activities: The foundation supports organizations involved with arts and culture,

education, the environment, health, employment, human services, community development, and civic affairs.

Fields of interest: Media/communications; Museums; Performing arts; Arts; Elementary/secondary education; Higher education; Libraries (public); Education; Environment, natural resources; Environment; Health care; Employment; Human services; Economic development; Community development; Federated giving programs; Public affairs.

Type of support: General/operating support; Employee matching gifts.

Limitations: Giving primarily in the Delaware Valley, PA, area, with emphasis on the greater Philadelphia, PA, metropolitan area. No grants to individuals.

Publications: Application guidelines.

Application information: Telephone calls during the application process are not encouraged. Application form required.

Initial approach: Contact foundation for application form
Deadline(s): None
Board meeting date(s): Quarterly
Final notification: Within 4 to 6 weeks

Officers and Directors:* John J. Brennan,* Chair. and Pres.; Pauline C. Scalvino, Secy.; Ralph K. Packard, Treas.; Tami F. Wise, Mgr.; Tim Buckley; F. William McNabb.

EIN: 232699769

Selected grants: The following grants were reported in 2005.

$1,182,500 to United Way of Southeastern Pennsylvania, Philadelphia, PA.

$105,000 to United Way of Central Carolinas, Charlotte, NC.

$33,865 to Free Library of Philadelphia, Philadelphia, PA.

$28,000 to Boston Latin School Association, Boston, MA.

$12,890 to Saint Josephs University, Philadelphia, PA.

$9,000 to Pottstown School District, Pottstown, PA.

$8,566 to Culver Educational Foundation, Culver, IN.

$5,000 to Triskeles Foundation, Glenmoore, PA.

$260 to Philadelphia Foundation, Philadelphia, PA.

$250 to Saint Katherine Day School, Wynnewood, PA.

8491
Clarence J. Venne Foundation ✧

645 White Ash Dr.
Langhorne, PA 19047-8026

Established in 2000 in PA.

Donors: Clarence J. Venne; Richard A. Venne.

Foundation type: Independent foundation.

Financial data (yr. ended 12/31/05): Assets, $429,266 (M); gifts received, $220,000; expenditures, $414,160; qualifying distributions, $413,753; giving activities include $408,550 for 38 grants (high: $100,000; low: $50).

Fields of interest: Christian agencies & churches.

Limitations: Applications not accepted. Giving primarily in PA. No grants to individuals.

Application information: Contributes only to pre-selected organizations.

Officers: Clarence J. Venne, Pres.; Anne C. Venne, V.P. and Treas.; Ronald Bluestein, V.P.; Margaret Wallick, Secy.

EIN: 233040515

Selected grants: The following grants were reported in 2005.

$25,000 to Saint Alphonsus School, Maple Glen, PA.

$10,250 to Saint Christophers Foundation for Children, Philadelphia, PA.

$3,000 to Cross International Catholic Outreach, Boca Raton, FL.

$2,750 to Grey Nuns of the Sacred Heart, Yardley, PA.

$750 to Sisters of the Immaculate Heart of Mary, Immaculata, PA.

$250 to Saint Charles Borromeo Seminary, Wynnewood, PA.

$250 to Saint Pauls Abbey, Newton, NJ.

$125 to Disabled American Veterans, Cold Spring, KY.

$100 to American Cancer Society, Atlanta, GA.

8492
Anna M. Vincent Trust ✧

c/o Mellon Financial Corp.
P.O. Box 185
Pittsburgh, PA 15230-9897
Application address: c/o Michael L. McGrath, P.O. Box 7899, Philadelphia, PA 19101-7899, tel.: (215) 553-1825

Trust established in 1967 in PA.

Donor: Anna M. Vincent†.

Foundation type: Independent foundation.

Financial data (yr. ended 6/30/05): Assets, $7,582,300 (M); expenditures, $461,389; qualifying distributions, $417,076; giving activities include $394,000 for 117 grants to individuals (high: $5,000; low: $1,000).

Purpose and activities: Scholarships for graduate or undergraduate study at any recognized college, university, or other institution of higher learning.

Fields of interest: Higher education.

Type of support: Scholarships—to individuals.

Limitations: Giving limited to residents of the Delaware Valley, PA, area. No grants for building or endowment funds, operating budgets, or special projects.

Publications: Application guidelines.

Application information: Application forms available at high schools. Application form required.

Initial approach: Letter
Copies of proposal: 1
Deadline(s): Mar. 1
Board meeting date(s): Mar. and Apr.

Trustees: Robert I. Whitelaw; Mellon Bank, N.A.

EIN: 236422666

8493
The Richard C. von Hess Foundation ✧

c/o The Glenmede Trust Co.
1650 Market St., Ste. 1200
Philadelphia, PA 19103-7391 (215) 419-6000

Established in 1989 in PA.

Donor: Richard C. von Hess.

Foundation type: Independent foundation.

Financial data (yr. ended 12/31/03): Assets, $26,142,207 (M); expenditures, $1,559,188; qualifying distributions, $1,455,603; giving activities include $1,339,474 for 32 grants (high: $191,410; low: $5,000).

Purpose and activities: The foundation was created to assist the work of Wright's Ferry Museum, a

---

historic 18th Century house museum in Columbia, PA, as well as to further art education, and other charitable purposes.

Fields of interest: Arts education; Museums (art); Performing arts; Historic preservation/historical societies; Arts.

Limitations: Applications not accepted. Giving primarily in PA; funding also in MD. No grants to individuals.

Application information: Contributes only to pre-selected organizations.

Trustees: Thomas Hills Cook; Anne Genter; Warren A. Reintzel.

EIN: 236962077

Selected grants: The following grants were reported in 2004.

$234,370 to Pennsylvania Academy of the Fine Arts, Philadelphia, PA. 2 grants: $42,960, $191,410

$200,000 to Baltimore Museum of Art, Baltimore, MD. 2 grants: $100,000 each

$166,667 to Walters Art Museum, Baltimore, MD.

$113,910 to University of the Arts, Philadelphia, PA. 4 grants: $9,000, $75,000, $22,910, $7,000

$31,555 to Moore College of Art and Design, Philadelphia, PA.

8494
Wachovia Regional Foundation ◇
(formerly First Union Regional Foundation)
123 S. Broad St., 3rd Fl.
PA4360
Philadelphia, PA   19109   (215) 670-4300
Contact: Denise McGregor Armbrister, Exec. Dir.
FAX: (215) 670-4313; Contact for Neighborhood Implementation and Planning Grants: Kimberly Allen, Prog. Off., tel.: (215) 670-4307, Mailee Walker, Prog. Off., tel.: (215) 670-4311;
URL: http://www.wachovia.com/regionalfoundation

Established in 1998.

Donors: CoreStates Financial Corp; First Union Corp.; Wachovia Corp.

Foundation type: Company-sponsored foundation.

Financial data (yr. ended 12/31/05): Assets, $94,834,472 (M); expenditures, $5,251,793; qualifying distributions, $5,056,879; giving activities include $4,924,500 for 131 grants (high: $117,000; low: $2,500).

Purpose and activities: The foundation supports organizations involved with neighborhood planning and development.

Fields of interest: Urban/community development.

Type of support: Equipment; Program development; Technical assistance; Program evaluation.

Limitations: Giving primarily in the DE, NJ, and eastern PA tri-state area. No support for political organizations or national or international organizations; generally, no support for K-12 private schools, colleges or universities, veterans' or fraternal organizations, arts or cultural organizations, hospitals or medical centers, or health- or disease-related organizations. No grants to individuals, or for general operating support, strategic or business plans, "bricks and mortar" projects, political causes, endowments, capital campaigns, debt reduction, or special events; generally, no grants for religious programs or activities.

Publications: Grants list.

Application information: Application form required.

Initial approach: Complete online application form

Deadline(s): Aug. 31 for Neighborhood Planning Grants; Apr. 13 and Nov. 2 for Neighborhood Implementation Grants

Board meeting date(s): Jan., Apr., July, and Oct.

Officers and Directors: Eleanor V. Horne, Chair.; Ernest E. Jones, Vice-Chair.; Denise McGregor Armbrister, Exec. Dir.; Lillian Escobar Haskins; Judith H. Hoopes; Hugh C. Long; George V. Lynett; Shannon W. McFayden; C. Kent McGuire; Stephanie W. Naidoff; John Petillo; Ralph Smith; Susanne Svizeny.

Number of staff: 4 full-time professional; 1 full-time support.

EIN: 222625990

Selected grants: The following grants were reported in 2004.

$150,000 to Community Builders, Boston, MA. 2 grants: $75,000 each

$125,000 to Congreso de Latinos Unidos, Philadelphia, PA.

$104,000 to West End Neighborhood House, Wilmington, DE.

$100,000 to Alliance for Building Communities, Allentown, PA.

$100,000 to La Casa de Don Pedro, Newark, NJ.

$62,500 to New Community Corporation, Newark, NJ.

$30,000 to New Brunswick Tomorrow, New Brunswick, NJ.

$26,000 to Asociacion de Puertorriquenos en Marcha, Philadelphia, PA.

$21,000 to Partnership CDC, Philadelphia, PA.

8495
The Waldorf Educational Foundation
c/o The Glenmede Trust Co.
1650 Market St., Ste. 1200
Philadelphia, PA   19103-7391   (215) 419-6144
Contact: Melanie Redmond, Fdn. Admin.
FAX: (215) 419-6647;
E-mail: melanie.redmond@glenmede.com

Established in 1951 in PA.

Foundation type: Independent foundation.

Financial data (yr. ended 12/31/04): Assets, $12,004,360 (M); expenditures, $542,147; qualifying distributions, $513,019; giving activities include $489,000 for 17 grants (high: $184,000; low: $2,000).

Purpose and activities: Grants are made for the aid and benefit of the principles and developments of the Waldorf method of Education.

Fields of interest: Education, association; Elementary/secondary education; Higher education.

Type of support: Building/renovation; Program development; Conferences/seminars; Scholarship funds; Research; Matching/challenge support.

Limitations: Giving on a national basis; some funding also in Ontario, Canada. No grants to individuals.

Publications: Application guidelines.

Application information: Application form required.

Initial approach: Letter or E-mail

Deadline(s): Nov. 30

Trustees: David Alsop; Erika V. Asten; Mark Finser; Karin Myrin; Clemens Pietzner; The Glenmede Trust Co.

EIN: 236254206

8496
The Warwick Foundation of Bucks County ◇ ☆
c/o Glenmede Trust Co.
1650 Market St., Ste. 1200
Philadelphia, PA   19103-7391
Contact: Mimi Stauffer, Trust Off.

Established in 2001 in PA; funded in 2003.

Donors: The Warwick Founation; Helen Gemmill.

Foundation type: Independent foundation.

Financial data (yr. ended 12/31/05): Assets, $44,849,082 (M); expenditures, $1,920,385; qualifying distributions, $1,730,956; giving activities include $1,234,000 for 78 grants (high: $250,000; low: $1,000).

Fields of interest: Historic preservation/historical societies; Arts; Education; Animal welfare; Human services.

Limitations: Giving primarily in Bucks County and Delaware Valley, PA. No grants to individuals.

Application information: Application form not required.

Initial approach: Letter

Deadline(s): None

Trustees: Elizabeth H. Gemmill; Helen J. Gemmill; Diana Norris.

EIN: 311789099

8497
Louise Washington Charitable Trust ◇
c/o PNC Bank, N.A., Tax Dept.
1600 Market St.
Philadelphia, PA   19103-7240

Established in 2002 in NJ.

Foundation type: Independent foundation.

Financial data (yr. ended 12/31/05): Assets, $25,677,766 (M); expenditures, $1,591,168; qualifying distributions, $1,430,025; giving activities include $1,430,000 for grants.

Fields of interest: Health care; Eye diseases; Heart & circulatory diseases.

Limitations: Applications not accepted.

Application information: Contributes only to pre-selected organizations.

Trustee: PNC Bank, N.A.

EIN: 226580528

8498
Robert S. Waters Charitable Trust
c/o Mellon Financial Corp.
1 Mellon Ctr., Rm. 151-3825
Pittsburgh, PA   15258   (412) 234-5784
Contact: Barbara Robinson DeWitt, F.V.P., Mellon Financial Corp.

Established in 1952 in PA.

Donor: Robert S. Waters†.

Foundation type: Independent foundation.

Financial data (yr. ended 12/31/04): Assets, $8,310,505 (M); expenditures, $384,912; qualifying distributions, $340,877; giving activities include $322,000 for 24 grants (high: $100,000; low: $1,000).

Fields of interest: Historic preservation/historical societies; Arts; Secondary school/education; Environment, natural resources; Human services.

Limitations: Giving primarily in Johnstown and Pittsburgh, PA. No grants to individuals, or for scholarships or fellowships; no loans.

Application information: Application form required.
Initial approach: Letter
Copies of proposal: 2
Deadline(s): None
Board meeting date(s): May and Nov.
Trustee: Mellon Bank, N.A.
EIN: 256018986

8499
A. H. and Helen L. Weiss Foundation ✧ ☆
c/o Cozen & O'Connor
200 Four Falls Corp. Ctr., Ste. 400
West Conshohocken, PA 19428-2958
(610) 941-2349
Contact: Burton K. Stein

Established about 1956.
Foundation type: Independent foundation.
Financial data (yr. ended 9/30/05): Assets,
$2,413,314 (M); expenditures, $1,118,094;
qualifying distributions, $1,105,711; giving
activities include $1,105,710 for 84 grants (high:
$1,007,710; low: $50).
Purpose and activities: Giving to Jewish agencies,
aging services and medical organizations.
Fields of interest: Elementary/secondary
education; Higher education; Theological school/
education; Hospitals (general); Human services;
Federated giving programs; Jewish agencies &
temples; Religion.
Type of support: General/operating support;
Continuing support; Internship funds.
Limitations: Giving primarily in Philadelphia, PA. No
grants to individuals.
Application information: Application form not
required.
Deadline(s): None
Trustees: Stephen A. Cozen; Philip Nalibotsky; Linda
Saltz.
EIN: 236298302
Selected grants: The following grants were reported
in 2005.
$1,007,710 to Madlyn and Leonard Abramson
Center for Jewish Life, North Wales, PA.
$2,500 to Childrens Hospital Foundation,
Philadelphia, PA.
$250 to Motion Picture and Television Fund,
Woodland Hills, CA.
$200 to Memorial Sloan-Kettering Cancer Center,
New York, NY.
$50 to Planned Parenthood of Los Angeles, Los
Angeles, CA.

8500
The H. O. West Foundation
(also known as The Herman O. West Foundation)
101 Gordon Dr.
Exton, PA 19341 (610) 594-2900
Contact: Richard D. Luzzi, Tr.; Maureen B. Goebel,
Admin.
URL: http://www.westpharma.com/Corporate.asp?
l=8

Established in 1972 in PA.
Donors: The West Co., Inc.; West Pharmaceutical
Services, Inc.
Foundation type: Company-sponsored foundation.
Financial data (yr. ended 12/31/05): Assets,
$1,550,501 (M); gifts received, $450,000;
expenditures, $513,759; qualifying distributions,
$513,759; giving activities include $434,022 for 70

grants (high: $48,189; low: $208), $59,880 for 30
grants to individuals (high: $2,500; low: $1,250),
and $14,975 for 51 employee matching gifts.
Purpose and activities: The foundation supports
organizations involved with arts and culture,
education, health, human services, community
development, and science and technology.
Fields of interest: Arts; Education, fund raising/fund
distribution; Higher education; Education; Hospitals
(general); Pharmacy/prescriptions; Health care;
Human services; Community development;
Federated giving programs; Engineering/technology;
Science.
Type of support: General/operating support;
Continuing support; Annual campaigns; Capital
campaigns; Building/renovation; Emergency funds;
Research; Employee matching gifts;
Employee-related scholarships; Scholarships—to
individuals; Matching/challenge support.
Limitations: Giving primarily in areas of company
operations in AZ, FL, NE, NC, OH, and PA.
Publications: Application guidelines.
Application information: Application form not
required.
Initial approach: Proposal or telephone
Copies of proposal: 1
Deadline(s): 1 week prior to board meetings
Board meeting date(s): Spring and fall
Final notification: Varies
Officer and Trustees:* George R. Bennyhoff, Chair.;
Paula A. Johnson, M.D.; Richard D. Luzzi.
EIN: 383674460

8501
The Wheeler Family Charitable
Foundation ✧
415 N. Center Ave.
Somerset, PA 15501-1401 (814) 445-7188
Contact: Joan M. Wheeler, Chair.

Established in 1997 in PA.
Donors: Harold W. Wheeler; Joan M. Wheeler;
Wheeler Bros., Inc.
Foundation type: Independent foundation.
Financial data (yr. ended 12/31/05): Assets,
$4,608,439 (M); gifts received, $1,940,000;
expenditures, $1,614,595; qualifying distributions,
$1,594,500; giving activities include $1,594,500
for 10 grants (high: $1,000,000; low: $1,000).
Purpose and activities: Giving primarily to a
hospital; funding also for medical research,
children's services, health care, and food
distribution.
Fields of interest: Hospitals (general); Medical
research, institute; Food banks; Food distribution;
meals on wheels; Human services; Children/youth,
services.
Type of support: Continuing support; Annual
campaigns; Capital campaigns; Emergency funds.
Limitations: Giving primarily in Somerset County,
PA. No grants to individuals.
Application information: Application form not
required.
Initial approach: Letter
Deadline(s): None
Board meeting date(s): May and Nov.
Officers and Directors:* Joan M. Wheeler,* Chair.;
Barbara Davies; David L. Wheeler; Harold W.
Wheeler III; Paul J. Wheeler.
Trustee: Somerset Trust Co.
EIN: 232938580

8502
Widener Memorial Foundation in Aid of
Handicapped Children ✧
665 Thomas Rd.
P.O. Box 178
Lafayette Hill, PA 19444-0178 (215) 836-7500
Contact: F. Eugene Dixon, Jr., Pres.

Incorporated in 1912 in PA.
Donors: Peter A.B. Widener†; Widener Memorial
Foundation 2.
Foundation type: Independent foundation.
Financial data (yr. ended 12/31/05): Assets,
$7,240,704 (M); gifts received, $532,220;
expenditures, $656,551; qualifying distributions,
$647,206; giving activities include $642,200 for 22
grants (high: $100,000; low: $3,500).
Purpose and activities: Support for research into
the causes, treatment, and prevention of diseases
and conditions which handicap children
orthopedically; to aid and assist public and private
charitable institutions and associations in the care,
education, and rehabilitation of children so
handicapped.
Fields of interest: Orthopedics; Medical research,
institute; Children/youth, services; Disabilities,
people with.
Type of support: Building/renovation; Equipment;
Program development; Seed money; Research.
Limitations: Giving limited to Delaware Valley, PA.
No grants to individuals, or for endowment funds,
scholarships, fellowships, or matching gifts; no
loans.
Application information: Application form not
required.
Initial approach: Letter
Copies of proposal: 1
Deadline(s): Apr. 15 and Oct. 15
Board meeting date(s): May and Nov.
Final notification: Immediately after board
meetings
Officers and Trustees:* F. Eugene Dixon, Jr.,*
Pres.; Peter M. Mattoon,* V.P.; Edith Robb Dixon,*
Secy.-Treas.; Bruce L. Castor; Michael Clancy, M.D.;
Mark S. DePillis.
EIN: 236267223

8503
Willary Foundation ☆
P.O. Box 283
Scranton, PA 18501-0937 (570) 961-6952
Contact: M. Linda Donovan, Admin. Dir.
FAX: (570) 961-7269; *E-mail:* info@willary.org;
URL: http://www.willary.org

Established in 1968 in PA.
Donors: William W. Scranton; Mary L. Scranton.
Foundation type: Independent foundation.
Financial data (yr. ended 12/31/05): Assets,
$4,681,919 (M); gifts received, $179,400;
expenditures, $452,012; qualifying distributions,
$435,218.
Purpose and activities: The foundation wishes to
promote the special qualities of the people of
northeastern Pennsylvania, and is particularly
interested in projects that support leadership and
the development of leadership in business, the
economy, education, human services, government,
the arts, media and research.
Fields of interest: Arts; Higher education;
Environment; Housing/shelter, volunteer services;

Housing/shelter, development; Human services; Jewish agencies & temples.
Type of support: Program development; Matching/challenge support.
Limitations: Giving primarily in Lackawanna and Luzerne counties, PA. No grants to individuals, or for capital campaigns or annual drives; no loans.
Publications: Application guidelines.
Application information: Application form available on foundation Web site. Application form required.
 Copies of proposal: 6
 Deadline(s): Mar. 25 and Sept. 10
 Board meeting date(s): June and Nov.
Trustees: Susan Scranton Dawson; Joseph C. Scranton; Julien Scranton; Mary L. Scranton; Peter K. Scranton; S. Caitlin Scranton; William W. Scranton; William W. Scranton III; Elizabeth S. Valosek.
EIN: 237014785

8504
Hilda M. Willis Foundation
c/o Mellon Bank
1 Mellon Ctr.
500 Grant St., Ste. 3825
Pittsburgh, PA 15258

Established in 1981 in PA; initial endowment in fiscal 1992.
Donor: Hilda M. Willis†.
Foundation type: Independent foundation.
Financial data (yr. ended 6/30/05): Assets, $13,004,476 (M); expenditures, $526,128; qualifying distributions, $468,907; giving activities include $442,000 for 17 grants (high: $300,000; low: $2,000).
Purpose and activities: Giving primarily for higher education and the arts; special interest in those organizations supported by Mrs. Willis during her lifetime.
Fields of interest: Arts; Elementary/secondary education; Higher education; Medical care, rehabilitation.
Type of support: Capital campaigns; Building/renovation.
Limitations: Giving limited to Allegheny County, PA. No grants to individuals.
Publications: Application guidelines; Grants list.
Application information:
 Initial approach: Contact foundation for application information
 Copies of proposal: 3
 Board meeting date(s): Nov. and Apr.
Trustees: Robert G. Lovett; Alexander M. Minno; Mellon Financial Corp.
Number of staff: None.
EIN: 256371417
Selected grants: The following grants were reported in 2004.
$600,000 to Pittsburgh Opera, Pittsburgh, PA. For operating support.
$135,000 to Chatham College, Pittsburgh, PA. For operating support.
$100,000 to Winchester-Thurston School, Pittsburgh, PA. For operating support.
$20,000 to Pace School, Pittsburgh, PA. For operating support.
$15,000 to Pittsburgh Symphony Society, Pittsburgh, PA. For operating support.
$7,500 to Pittsburgh Public Theater, Pittsburgh, PA. For operating support.
$5,000 to Auberle, McKeesport, PA. For operating support.

$5,000 to Providence Connections, Pittsburgh, PA. For operating support.
$5,000 to Western Pennsylvania School for the Deaf, Pittsburgh, PA. For operating support.
$1,000 to Mendelssohn Choir of Pittsburgh, Pittsburgh, PA. For operating support.

8505
Phillip H. Wimmer and Betty L. Wimmer Family Foundation ◇
1806 Frick Bldg.
Pittsburgh, PA 15219
Contact: Samuel P. Kamin, Tr.

Established in 1997 in PA.
Donor: Betty L. Wimmer†.
Foundation type: Independent foundation.
Financial data (yr. ended 12/31/05): Assets, $6,853,656 (M); expenditures, $379,455; qualifying distributions, $341,540; giving activities include $327,000 for 39 grants (high: $40,000; low: $500).
Fields of interest: Arts; Education; Health care; Jewish federated giving programs; Jewish agencies & temples.
Limitations: Giving primarily in Pittsburgh, PA.
Application information:
 Initial approach: Letter
 Deadline(s): None
Trustee: Samuel P. Kamin.
EIN: 251795161

8506
The Wolf Foundation ◇ ☆
P.O. Box 1267
York, PA 17405-1267 (717) 852-4800
Contact: William B. Zimmerman, Chair.

Established in 1969 in PA.
Donors: Wolf Distributing, Inc.; The Lumber Yard; Thomas W. Wolf.
Foundation type: Company-sponsored foundation.
Financial data (yr. ended 12/31/05): Assets, $6,141 (M); gifts received, $865,081; expenditures, $931,008; qualifying distributions, $922,618; giving activities include $922,618 for grants.
Purpose and activities: The foundation supports organizations involved with arts and culture, health, human services, children and youth services, and community development.
Fields of interest: Arts; Health organizations, association; Human services; Children/youth, services; Community development; Federated giving programs.
Type of support: General/operating support.
Limitations: Giving primarily in York, PA. No grants to individuals.
Application information: Application form not required.
 Initial approach: Proposal
 Deadline(s): None
Officers: William B. Zimmerman, Chair.; Thomas W. Wolf, Pres.; George Hodges, Secy.-Treas.
EIN: 237028494
Selected grants: The following grants were reported in 2005.
$102,500 to YMCA of York and York County, York, PA.
$54,210 to United Way of York County, York, PA.
$33,334 to Habitat for Humanity of York, York, PA.

$22,000 to York College of Pennsylvania, York, PA.
$16,460 to York County Heritage Trust, York, PA.
$15,000 to American Red Cross, York, PA.
$5,000 to Crispus Attucks Association, York, PA.
$3,500 to Historic York, York, PA.
$2,000 to Pennsylvania Partnerships for Children, Harrisburg, PA.
$1,500 to Habitat for Humanity, West Chester, PA.

8507
Women's Aid of Penn Central School ◇
(formerly Women's Aid Scholarship)
c/o Wachovia Bank, N.A.
123 S. Broad St., 5th Fl.
Philadelphia, PA 19109 (215) 209-5054
Contact: Reginald Middleton, V.P.

Established in 1957.
Donor: Conrail Inc.
Foundation type: Company-sponsored foundation.
Financial data (yr. ended 12/31/03): Assets, $2,008,889 (M); expenditures, $372,734; qualifying distributions, $346,175; giving activities include $340,575 for 308 grants to individuals (high: $1,750; low: $125).
Purpose and activities: The foundation awards college scholarships to the children of employees and retirees of Conrail and its predecessor railroads.
Type of support: Employee-related scholarships.
Limitations: Applications not accepted. Giving primarily in areas of company operations.
Application information: Contributes only through employee-related scholarships.
Trustee: Wachovia Bank, N.A.
EIN: 236232572

8508
The Woods Charitable Foundation ◇ ☆
125 E. Lancaster Ave.
Strasburg, PA 17579

Established in 2004 in PA.
Donors: John H. Ware III Charitable Lead Annuity; Marian S. Ware 2003 Charitable Lead Annuity.
Foundation type: Independent foundation.
Financial data (yr. ended 12/31/05): Assets, $19,767,284 (M); gifts received, $164,544; expenditures, $1,163,530; qualifying distributions, $1,023,380; giving activities include $981,400 for 35 grants (high: $250,000; low: $500).
Fields of interest: Education; Human services; Foundations (private grantmaking); Public policy, research.
Limitations: Applications not accepted. Giving on a national basis. No grants to individuals.
Application information: Contributes only to pre-selected organizations.
Officers and Directors:* Marilyn Ware,* Pres.; Scott Strode, V.P.; Mark Strode, Secy.-Treas.; Arthur Johnson; Anthony Terracciano.
EIN: 201060852

8509
The Wyomissing Foundation, Inc. ◇
960 Old Mill Rd.
Wyomissing, PA 19610
Contact: Paul R. Roedel, Treas.
FAX: (610) 372-7626; E-mail: wfbbec@nnl.com

Incorporated in 1929 in DE.

Donors: Ferdinand Thun†; and family.

Foundation type: Independent foundation.

Financial data (yr. ended 12/31/05): Assets, $33,465,395 (M); expenditures, $1,643,939; qualifying distributions, $1,273,948; giving activities include $1,075,636 for 26 grants (high: $220,000; low: $5,000).

Purpose and activities: Primary areas of interest include education, building funds, the environment, and community funds. Giving also for hospitals and health services, higher education, civic affairs, youth and social service agencies, child welfare, and family planning and services; support also for the environment and conservation, and the arts, including performing arts and music.

Fields of interest: Performing arts; Performing arts, music; Arts; Education, fund raising/fund distribution; Higher education; Education; Environment, natural resources; Environment; Hospitals (general); Reproductive health, family planning; Health care; Health organizations, association; Human services; Children/youth, services; Family services; Federated giving programs; Government/public administration.

Type of support: General/operating support; Continuing support; Annual campaigns; Capital campaigns; Building/renovation; Equipment; Endowments; Emergency funds; Seed money; Matching/challenge support.

Limitations: Giving primarily in Berks County, PA, and contiguous counties; limited support also in the mid-Atlantic area. No grants to individuals, or for deficit financing, land acquisition, publications, conferences, scholarships, or fellowships; no loans.

Publications: Application guidelines; Program policy statement.

Application information: Application form not required.

  Initial approach: Proposal (no more than 2 pages, excluding supporting materials)

  Copies of proposal: 1

  Deadline(s): Submit proposal preferably in Feb., May, Aug., or Oct.; deadline 25th of month preceding board meeting

  Board meeting date(s): Mar., June, Sept., and Dec.

  Final notification: 3 months

Officers and Trustees:* Marlin Miller, Jr.,* Pres.; Peter Thun,* V.P.; Ned Diefenderfer,* Secy.; Paul R. Roedel,* Treas.; Tom Beaver; Charlotte Cooper; Alexena Frazee; Sid Kline; Antonia Lake; Hilegard Ryals; Cornelia S. St. John; John P. Weidenhammer.

Number of staff: 1 full-time support; 1 part-time support.

EIN: 231980570

Selected grants: The following grants were reported in 2004.

$124,000 to United Way of Berks County, Reading, PA.

$116,000 to Berks County Community Foundation, Reading, PA.

$42,500 to Girl Scouts of the U.S.A..

$20,000 to Reading Musical Foundation, Reading, PA.

$15,000 to Wood to Wonderful, Bernville, PA.

$5,000 to Berks Business Education Coalition, Reading, PA.

$5,000 to Childrens Literacy Initiative, Philadelphia, PA.

$1,000 to Historical Society of Berks County, Reading, PA.

$500 to Jewish Federation of Reading Pennsylvania, Reading, PA.

8510

Hansjoerg Wyss Foundation ✧

(formerly Hansjoerg Wyss Medical Foundation)
1302 Wrights Lane E.
West Chester, PA 19380
Contact: Joseph M. Fisher, Secy.

Established in 1999 in PA.

Donor: Hansjoerg Wyss.

Foundation type: Independent foundation.

Financial data (yr. ended 12/31/04): Assets, $59,037,508 (M); gifts received, $12,138,060; expenditures, $1,687,012; qualifying distributions, $1,470,060; giving activities include $1,470,060 for 13 grants (high: $549,505; low: $5,000; average: $10,000–$100,000).

Purpose and activities: To fund education and research in the orthopedic field.

Fields of interest: Education; Orthopedics research.

International interests: Germany; Switzerland.

Limitations: Giving on a national and international basis, with emphasis on the U.S. No grants to individuals.

Application information: Application form not required.

  Deadline(s): None

Officers: Hansjoerg Wyss, Chair.; Joseph M. Fisher, Secy.

EIN: 233012622

Selected grants: The following grants were reported in 2003.

$2,000,000 to University of Washington, Seattle, WA.

$1,000,000 to University of Maryland-Baltimore, School of Medicine, Baltimore, MD.

$71,124 to Free University of Berlin, Berlin, Germany. .

$69,168 to Westphalian Wilhelms University, Munster, Germany. .

$50,000 to Ludwig-Maximilians University, Munich, Germany. .

$12,000 to Spine Education and Research Institute, Thornton, CO.

8511

York County Community Foundation ✧

(formerly York Foundation)
20 W. Market St.
York, PA 17401-1203 (717) 848-3733
Contact: For grants: Bryan K. Tate, V.P., Prog.
FAX: (717) 854-7231; E-mail: info@yccf.org;
URL: http://www.yccf.org

Established in 1961 in PA.

Foundation type: Community foundation.

Financial data (yr. ended 12/31/05): Assets, $48,696,720 (M); gifts received, $7,510,725; expenditures, $3,733,192; giving activities include $2,934,615 for 204+ grants.

Purpose and activities: The foundation seeks to promote the betterment of York County, PA, and the enhancement of the quality of life for all its citizens by attracting and managing funds to build a permanent endowment, serving as a leader in responding to community needs, and by serving as a resource and catalyst for charitable activities.

Fields of interest: Arts; Education; Environment, land resources; Environment, energy; Environment; Health care; Child development, services; Human services; Economic development; Community development; Philanthropy/voluntarism, management/technical aid; Public affairs; Youth; Aging.

Type of support: Equipment; Program development; Conferences/seminars; Seed money; Scholarship funds; Technical assistance; Consulting services; Matching/challenge support.

Limitations: Giving primarily in York County, PA. No support for sectarian religious projects. No grants to individuals, or for endowments, capital campaigns, annual appeals, or annual operating expenses of well established organizations, travel, or for research.

Publications: Application guidelines; Annual report; Informational brochure; Newsletter.

Application information: Visit foundation Web site for application forms and specific guidelines per grant type. Applicants are encouraged to attend a Venture grants information session prior to application submission; call foundation for dates. Application form required.

  Initial approach: Telephone V.P., Prog.

  Copies of proposal: 6

  Deadline(s): Mar. 1 and Sept. 15 for venture grants

  Board meeting date(s): Quarterly

  Final notification: June and Dec.

Officers and Directors:* David E. Kennedy,* Chair.; David G. Meckley,* Vice-Chair.; Susan A. Barry, Pres.; Bryan K. Tate, V.P., Prog., Grantmaking and Initiatives; Michael L. Gleim,* Secy.; Donna B. Jones, C.F.O.; Cynthia A. Dotzel,* Treas.; D. Reed Anderson; Louis J. Appell, Jr.; C. Kim Brown; Anthony P. Campisi; R. Joe Crosswhite; Linda B. Davidson; Donald B. Dellinger, Jr.; Wanda D. Filer, M.D.; George H. Glatfelter II; William F. Goodling; Terrence L. Hormel; William H. Kerlin, Jr.; Anne W. Kinsley; Stephen H. Klunk; Melanie A. Lehman; G. Steven McKonly; R. Eric Menzer; Michael F. O'Connor; Robert W. Pullo; Brenda S. Rhinehart; Frederick Uffelman II; Ernest J. Waters; Rose Marie Woodyard; James R. Zarfoss, Jr.

Number of staff: 2 full-time professional; 1 part-time professional; 1 full-time support.

EIN: 236299868

8512

Young Scholars Foundation, Inc. ✧

202 Park West Dr.
Pittsburgh, PA 15275

Established in 2001 in PA.

Donors: Maronda Homes, Inc.; Maronda, Inc.

Foundation type: Independent foundation.

Financial data (yr. ended 12/31/05): Assets, $290,234 (M); gifts received, $693,944; expenditures, $638,564; qualifying distributions, $637,260; giving activities include $637,260 for 62 grants (high: $153,684; low: $400).

Purpose and activities: Giving primarily to Roman Catholic schools, for scholarships.

Fields of interest: Elementary/secondary education; Roman Catholic agencies & churches.

Limitations: Applications not accepted. Giving primarily in PA. No grants to individuals.

Application information: Contributes only to pre-selected organizations.

Officers and Directors:* Ronald W. Wolf,* Pres. and Treas.; William J. Wolf,* C.F.O.

EIN: 311797213

Selected grants: The following grants were reported in 2005.

$103,547 to Saint Joseph School, Collingdale, PA.

$13,450 to Saint James School, Elkins Park, PA.

$5,000 to Saint Anne School, Philadelphia, PA.

$4,600 to Holy Trinity School, Ligonier, PA.

$4,555 to Saint Agnes School, West Chester, PA.

$3,844 to Saint John the Baptist School, Philadelphia, PA.

$3,660 to Saint Teresa of Avila School, Norristown, PA.

$2,300 to Saint Bernard School, Philadelphia, PA.

$2,160 to Saint Joseph Regional School, Port Vue, PA.

$1,295 to Our Lady of Fatima School, Bensalem, PA.

8513
The Zisman Family Foundation ✧ ☆
c/o Michael D. Zisman
311 Orchard Way
Wayne, PA 19087

Established in 2000 in PA.

Donor: Michael D. Zisman.

Foundation type: Independent foundation.

Financial data (yr. ended 12/31/05): Assets, $1,436,091 (M); gifts received, $452,964; expenditures, $521,148; qualifying distributions, $509,620; giving activities include $509,620 for grants.

Fields of interest: Higher education, university; Business school/education; Human services.

Limitations: Applications not accepted. Giving primarily in New York, NY and Philadelphia, PA. No grants to individuals.

Application information: Contributes only to pre-selected organizations.

Officers and Directors:* Linda J. Gamble,* Pres. and Secy.; Michael D. Zisman,* V.P. and Treas.

EIN: 233033239

Selected grants: The following grants were reported in 2003.

$60,000 to Lehigh University, Bethlehem, PA. For general support.

$20,000 to Shipley School, Bryn Mawr, PA. For general support.

$12,800 to Jerry Segal Classic, Philadelphia, PA. For general support.

$10,000 to Peters Place, Berwyn, PA. For general support.

$9,000 to Philadelphia Orchestra Association, Philadelphia, PA. For general support.

$5,000 to Federation Allied Jewish Appeal of Philadelphia, Philadelphia, PA. For general support.

$3,000 to Ronald McDonald House, Philadelphia, Philadelphia, PA. For general support.

PUERTO RICO

8514

FNZ Foundation, Inc.

Box 3425
Carolina, PR   00984-3425
Contact: James D. Klau, Pres.
FAX: (787) 768-9850; E-mail: jdklau@cs.com

Established in 1996 in DE.
Foundation type: Independent foundation.
Financial data (yr. ended 12/31/05): Assets, $0 (M); expenditures, $494,414; qualifying distributions, $445,041; giving activities include $445,041 for 99 grants.
Purpose and activities: Giving primarily for Jewish organizations and temples, youth, health care, animals, education and social action.
Fields of interest: Arts; Education; Animals/wildlife; Health care; Urban League; Youth, services; Jewish agencies & temples.
International interests: Israel; Soviet Union (Former).
Limitations: Giving on a national basis.
Officers: James D. Klau, Pres.; Susan L. Klau, V.P.
EIN: 660535017

8515

Puerto Rico Community Foundation, Inc.

P.O. Box 70362
San Juan, PR   00936-8362   (787) 721-1037
Contact: Juan J. Reyes, Compt.

FAX: (787) 721-1673; E-mail: fcpr@fcpr.og;
URL: http://www.fcpr.org

Incorporated in 1984 in PR; began operations in 1985.
Foundation type: Community foundation.
Financial data (yr. ended 12/31/05): Assets, $26,349,177 (M); gifts received, $4,470,953; expenditures, $3,326,580; giving activities include $661,413 for 116 grants (high: $224,616; low: $426), $110,200 for 49 grants to individuals (high: $7,000; low: $1,000), and $1,522,668 for 4 foundation-administered programs.
Purpose and activities: The foundation seeks to develop the capacities of communities in Puerto Rico to accomplish their social transformation and economic self-sufficiency, stimulating investment in the communities and maximizing the yield of each contribution. The scope of the foundation's program areas, which reflect the area of interest and opportunities available to the community, are community economic development, community development and housing, education, youth, arts and health.
Fields of interest: Arts; Education; Health care; Community development; Economically disadvantaged.
Type of support: General/operating support; Continuing support; Management development/capacity building; Equipment; Emergency funds; Program development; Conferences/seminars; Professorships; Publication; Curriculum development; Research; Technical assistance; Consulting services; Program-related investments/loans; Scholarships—to individuals; In-kind gifts; Matching/challenge support.

Limitations: Giving limited to PR. No grants for annual campaigns, seed money, endowments, deficit financing; generally no grants for building funds.
Publications: Application guidelines; Annual report; Biennial report; Financial statement; Informational brochure (including application guidelines); Newsletter; Occasional report; Program policy statement.
Application information: Visit foundation Web site for application guidelines. Application form required.
   Initial approach: Letter
   Copies of proposal: 2
   Deadline(s): None
   Board meeting date(s): June, Sept., Mar., and Dec.
   Final notification: Within 2 weeks after board meetings
Officers and Directors:* Nelson I. Colon, C.E.O.; Juan Gonzalez Feliciano,* Pres.; Juan J. Reyes, Compt.; Gloria E. Baquero Lleras; Ana Helvia Quintero; Jose Luis Rosado; Carlos Vazquez Rosario; Carlos J. Vazquez.
Number of staff: 11 full-time professional; 3 full-time support.
EIN: 660413230

RHODE ISLAND

8516
The Alperin/Hirsch Family Foundation ✧
(formerly The Alperin Foundation)
327 Pine St.
Pawtucket, RI 02860
Contact: Melvin Alperin, Tr.

Established in 1956 in RI.
Donors: David Hirsch; Hope L. Hirsch; PFI, Inc.; members of the Alperin family.
Foundation type: Independent foundation.
Financial data (yr. ended 4/30/05): Assets, $5,767,814 (M); gifts received, $40,000; expenditures, $426,818; qualifying distributions, $381,476; giving activities include $381,476 for 176 grants (high: $32,000; low: $25).
Purpose and activities: Giving primarily for Jewish organizations, including welfare funds, schools, and temple support; giving also for higher and secondary education and health.
Fields of interest: Museums; Historical activities; Arts; Elementary/secondary education; Higher education; Education; Hospitals (general); Health care; Health organizations, association; Medical research, association; Human services; Children/ youth, services; Jewish federated giving programs; Jewish agencies & temples.
Limitations: Giving primarily in MA, NY, and RI. No grants to individuals.
Application information:
  Initial approach: Letter
  Deadline(s): None
Trustees: Barry Alperin; Melvin Alperin; David Hirsch; Hope L. Hirsch.
EIN: 056008387

8517
Warren Alpert Foundation ✧
27 Warren Way
P.O. Box 72743
Providence, RI 02907
E-mail: lvogel@thecastlegrp.com; URL: http:// www.warrenalpert.org/home/

Established in 1986 in RI.
Donors: Warren Alpert; Warren Equities, Inc.
Foundation type: Independent foundation.
Financial data (yr. ended 12/31/05): Assets, $891,278 (M); gifts received, $4,340,405; expenditures, $4,330,568; qualifying distributions, $4,250,830; giving activities include $4,250,830 for 10 grants (high: $3,935,405; low: $1,000).
Purpose and activities: Support primarily for medical education and research; awards given to individuals for medical research are determined in consultation with a panel of medical experts in concert with the faculties of Harvard Medical School and Albert Einstein School of Medicine.
Fields of interest: Higher education; Medical school/education; Hospitals (general); Medical research, institute; Jewish agencies & temples.
Type of support: Research; Grants to individuals.
Limitations: Applications not accepted. Giving primarily in the Northeast.
Publications: Grants list.
Application information: Unsolicited applications from individuals or organizations not accepted.

Officers: Warren Alpert, Pres.; Edward M. Cosgrove, V.P.; Herbert Kaplan, V.P.; Jeffrey Walker, Secy.; John Dziedzic, Treas.
EIN: 050426623
Selected grants: The following grants were reported in 2005.
$3,935,405 to Mount Sinai Hospital, New York, NY.
$25,000 to Brookings Institution, DC.
$13,200 to Jewish Federation of Rhode Island, Providence, RI.
$5,000 to Chelsea Jewish Nursing Home, Chelsea, MA.
$1,000 to Vermont Academy, Saxtons River, VT.

8518
Amica Companies Foundation
100 Amica Way
Lincoln, RI 02865
Contact: Paul S. Bruno, Banking and Commissions Supvr.

Established in 1997 in RI.
Donor: Amica Mutual Insurance Co.
Foundation type: Company-sponsored foundation.
Financial data (yr. ended 12/31/05): Assets, $15,914,632 (M); gifts received, $505,157; expenditures, $887,448; qualifying distributions, $825,250; giving activities include $825,250 for grants (high: $37,500; low: $250; average: $250– $3,600).
Purpose and activities: The foundation supports organizations involved with arts and culture, education, the environment, health, youth development, human services, community development, and religion.
Fields of interest: Humanities; Arts; Education; Environment; Health care; Youth development; Human services; Community development; Federated giving programs; Religion.
Type of support: General/operating support; Continuing support; Annual campaigns; Capital campaigns; Building/renovation; Endowments; Research; Employee matching gifts; Matching/ challenge support.
Limitations: Giving on a national basis. No support for political or lobbying organizations. No grants to individuals.
Publications: Financial statement; Grants list.
Application information: Application form not required.
  Initial approach: Proposal
  Copies of proposal: 1
  Deadline(s): None
  Board meeting date(s): Bimonthly
Officers and Directors:* Robert A. DiMuccio,* Pres.; Robert K. MacKenzie, Secy.; Mary Q. Williamson, Treas.; Jeffrey P. Aiken; Patricia W. Chadwick; Edward F. DeGraan; Andrew M. Erickson; Barry G. Hittner; Michael D. Jeans; Ronald K. Machtley; Richard A. Plotkin; Donald J. Reaves; Cheryl W. Snead; Thomas A. Taylor.
EIN: 050493445

8519
Bafflin Foundation
1500 Fleet Ctr.
Providence, RI 02903-2319
Contact: Paul A. Silver, Secy.

Established in 1990 in RI.
Donor: Lois Orswell‡.

Foundation type: Independent foundation.
Financial data (yr. ended 12/31/05): Assets, $19,179,894 (M); expenditures, $1,158,149; qualifying distributions, $1,044,380; giving activities include $1,005,500 for 22 grants (high: $391,000; low: $7,000).
Purpose and activities: Giving primarily for the preservation of land and wildlife; some support also for art museums.
Fields of interest: Museums (art); Environment, natural resources; Animals/wildlife, preservation/ protection; Physical therapy; Human services.
Limitations: Giving on a national basis, with some emphasis on the East Coast. No grants to individuals, or for continuing support.
Application information: Application form not required.
  Initial approach: Letter
  Copies of proposal: 2
  Deadline(s): None
  Final notification: 1-5 months
Officers and Directors:* Paul A. Silver,* Secy.; Michael M. Edwards,* Treas.; Joachim A. Weissfeld.
EIN: 050454795
Selected grants: The following grants were reported in 2004.
$300,000 to Westerly Land Trust, Westerly, RI.
$225,000 to Nature Conservancy, Arlington, VA. 2 grants: $100,000, $125,000
$50,000 to Camp Jori, Providence, RI.
$50,000 to Lake Champlain Land Trust, Burlington, VT.
$37,500 to Northern Connecticut Land Trust, Somers, CT.
$30,000 to Nashoba Conservation Trust, Pepperell, MA.
$15,000 to Volunteer Services for Animals, Providence, RI.
$10,500 to Kestrel Trust, Amherst, MA.
$10,000 to Trust for Public Land, San Francisco, CA.

8520
The Harold Brooks Foundation ✧
c/o Bank of America, N.A.
P.O. Box 6767
Providence, RI 02940-6767
Application address: c/o Emma Greene, 100 Federal St., Boston, MA 02110; tel.: (617) 434-0329

Established in 1984 MA.
Donor: Harold Brooks‡.
Foundation type: Independent foundation.
Financial data (yr. ended 12/31/04): Assets, $9,895,767 (M); expenditures, $571,673; qualifying distributions, $545,279; giving activities include $492,559 for 21 grants (high: $200,000; low: $3,000).
Purpose and activities: Giving primarily for social services, with an emphasis on homelessness.
Fields of interest: Health care; Human services; Family services; Family services, domestic violence; Community development.
Type of support: General/operating support; Capital campaigns; Building/renovation; Equipment; Matching/challenge support.
Limitations: Giving limited to MA, with emphasis on the South Shore area. No grants to individuals.
Publications: Application guidelines.
Application information: Application form not required.
  Initial approach: Letter
  Copies of proposal: 1

Deadline(s): None
Board meeting date(s): Mar., June, Sept., and Dec.
Trustees: Arthur R. Connelly; Rev. M. James Workman; Bank of America, N.A.
EIN: 046043983
Selected grants: The following grants were reported in 2004.
$41,000 to Interfaith Housing Partners.
$30,000 to Quincy Interfaith Sheltering Coalition, Quincy, MA.
$20,000 to David Jon Louison Child Center, Brockton, MA.
$20,000 to Neighborhood Housing Services of the South Shore, Quincy, MA.
$15,000 to Homeowners Options for Massachusetts Elders (HOME), Boston, MA.
$15,000 to Project Bread - The Walk for Hunger, Boston, MA.
$15,000 to Quincy Community Action Programs, Quincy, MA.
$15,000 to Wellspring Multi-Service Center, Hull, MA.
$10,000 to Interfaith Social Services, Quincy, MA.
$10,000 to South Shore Community Action Council, Plymouth, MA.

8521

The CARLISLE Foundation

P.O. Box 5549
Wakefield, RI 02880-5549 (401) 284-0368
Contact: Richard A. Goldblatt, Exec. Dir.
FAX: (401) 284-0390;
E-mail: rag@carlislefoundation.org; URL: http://www.carlislefoundation.org

Established in 1991 in MA.
Donors: Helene T. Wilson; Grant M. Wilson.
Foundation type: Operating foundation.
Financial data (yr. ended 11/30/05): Assets, $3,379,055 (M); gifts received, $2,062; expenditures, $1,258,730; qualifying distributions, $1,258,671; giving activities include $976,649 for 48+ grants (high: $236,725).
Purpose and activities: The foundation is dedicated to working in partnership with community coalitions to promote the health and well-being of children and families.
Fields of interest: Substance abuse, services; Mental health/crisis services; Housing/shelter, development; Children/youth, services; Family services; Homeless, human services; Economic development.
Type of support: Program development; Seed money.
Limitations: Giving limited to New England, with emphasis on MA, including the greater Boston area. No grants to individuals.
Publications: Application guidelines; Informational brochure (including application guidelines); Multi-year report.
Application information: Application form required.
Initial approach: 1-page concept paper
Copies of proposal: 1
Deadline(s): None
Officers and Trustees:* Helene T. Wilson,* Pres.; Grant M. Wilson,* Secy.-Treas.; Richard A. Goldblatt, Exec. Dir.; George B. Foote, Jr.; Edward S. Heald; Kirsten Wilson.
Number of staff: 1 full-time professional.
EIN: 046689264
Selected grants: The following grants were reported in 2003.

$100,000 to Brewster Academy, Wolfeboro, NH.
$40,000 to Advocates, Framingham, MA. For Jail Diversion Program.
$40,000 to Framingham Public Schools, Framingham, MA. For Minority Achievement Project.
$40,000 to South Middlesex Opportunity Council (SMOC), Framingham, MA. For Family and Friends for Life Mentoring Program.
$30,000 to Jewish Family Service of Metrowest, Framingham, MA.
$30,000 to Sexual Assault and Trauma Resource Center of Rhode Island, Providence, RI. For Foster Care Family Treatment Program.
$25,000 to Family Health Productions, Gloucester, MA. For evaluation of Alcohol: True Stories.
$20,000 to Fair Tide, Kittery, ME.
$20,000 to Greater Lowell Community Foundation, Lowell, MA. For Substance Abuse Diversion Initiative (SADIL).
$20,000 to Media and Technology Charter High School (MATCH), Boston, MA. For startup support.

8522

The Carter Family Charitable Trust ✧

P.O. Box 41119
Providence, RI 02940-1119
Contact: John S. Carter, Jr., Tr.; Letitia Carter, Tr.

Established in 1991 in RI.
Donors: Letitia M. Carter; John S. Carter, Jr.
Foundation type: Independent foundation.
Financial data (yr. ended 6/30/05): Assets, $13,930,624 (M); gifts received, $5,200,000; expenditures, $2,033,385; qualifying distributions, $1,999,580; giving activities include $1,996,130 for 37 grants (high: $500,000; low: $500).
Purpose and activities: Giving primarily for community development, as well as for education, the arts, and human services.
Fields of interest: Arts; Education; Medical research; Human services; Community development.
Type of support: General/operating support; Continuing support; Annual campaigns; Capital campaigns; Building/renovation; Endowments; Emergency funds; Research; Matching/challenge support.
Limitations: Giving primarily in RI, with emphasis on Providence. No support for religious organizations. No grants to individuals.
Application information: Application form required.
Initial approach: Letter
Copies of proposal: 1
Deadline(s): None
Final notification: 3 months
Trustees: John S. Carter, Jr.; Letitia M. Carter.
EIN: 056093256
Selected grants: The following grants were reported in 2005.
$554,000 to Community Preparatory School, Providence, RI. 2 grants: $500,000 (For general operating support), $54,000 (For scholarships).
$500,000 to Williams College, Williamstown, MA. For John S. Carter Junior Endowment Fund.
$280,000 to Paul Cuffee School, Providence, RI. For general operating support.
$75,000 to Sophia Academy, Cumberland, RI. For tuition assistance.
$75,000 to United Way of Rhode Island, Providence, RI. For impact and philanthropic funds.

$50,000 to Planned Parenthood of Rhode Island, Providence, RI. For general operating support.
$40,000 to Scholarship America, Providence, RI. For scholarships.
$35,000 to Community MusicWorks, Providence, RI. For general operating support.
$35,000 to Rhode Island College, Providence, RI. For Poverty Institute.

8523

The Chace Fund, Inc. ✧

1 Providence Washington Plz.
Providence, RI 02903
Contact: Malcolm G. Chace, Pres.

Established in 1947 in RI.
Donors: Malcolm G. Chace III; Arnold B. Chace; Berkshire Hathaway Inc.; Kathleen Osborne†; Beatrice O. Chace†; Patricia Kent.
Foundation type: Independent foundation.
Financial data (yr. ended 12/31/05): Assets, $4,286,628 (L); gifts received, $728,000; expenditures, $659,170; qualifying distributions, $617,116; giving activities include $617,116 for 46 grants (high: $119,105; low: $100).
Fields of interest: Performing arts, theater; Historic preservation/historical societies; Arts; Education; Environment, natural resources; Human services; Children, services; Women, centers/services; Federated giving programs; Philanthropy/voluntarism; Protestant agencies & churches.
Type of support: General/operating support.
Limitations: Giving primarily in MA, NY, and RI. No grants to individuals.
Application information:
Initial approach: Letter
Deadline(s): None
Officers and Directors:* Malcolm G. Chace,* Pres.; Arnold B. Chace, Jr.,* V.P.; Thomas E. Gardiner, Secy.-Treas.; Malcolm G. Chace, Jr.
EIN: 056008849

8524

The Champlin Foundations ▼

300 Centerville Rd., Ste. 300S
Warwick, RI 02886-0226 (401) 736-0370
Contact: Keith H. Lang, Exec. Dir.
FAX: (401) 736-7248; URL: http://www.foundationcenter.org/grantmaker/champlin

Trusts established in 1932, 1947, and 1975 in DE.
Donors: George S. Champlin†; Florence C. Hamilton†; Hope C. Neaves†.
Foundation type: Independent foundation.
Financial data (yr. ended 12/31/05): Assets, $404,641,686 (M); expenditures, $21,237,279; qualifying distributions, $19,467,708; giving activities include $18,782,633 for 178 grants (high: $3,850,000; low: $1,200; average: $25,000–$75,000).
Purpose and activities: Giving primarily for conservation; higher, secondary, and other education, including libraries; health and hospitals; cultural activities, including historic preservation; scientific activities; and social and family services, including programs for youth and the elderly.
Fields of interest: Historic preservation/historical societies; Arts; Secondary school/education; Higher education; Libraries/library science; Education; Environment, natural resources; Environment; Animal welfare; Hospitals (general); Reproductive

health, family planning; Health care; Health organizations, association; Human services; Youth, services; Engineering/technology; Science.

Type of support: Capital campaigns; Building/renovation; Land acquisition.

Limitations: Giving primarily in RI. No support for churches (with few exceptions) or generally for daycare centers, housing, mental health counseling centers or senior centers. No grants to individuals; or for program or operating expenses, administrative facilities, equipment, books, films, videos, plays, or for multi-year grants.

Publications: Application guidelines; Annual report; Grants list; Program policy statement.

Application information: No grants are awarded on a continuing basis, but applicants may qualify annually. Application form not required.

Initial approach: Brief 1-page letter. Faxed or E-mailed applications will not be accepted

Copies of proposal: 1

Deadline(s): Submit all requests between Mar. 1 and May 31

Board meeting date(s): Nov.

Final notification: After Nov. meeting

Officer and Distribution Committee:* Keith H. Lang,* Exec. Dir.; Jonathan K. Farnum; John Gorham; Timothy Gorham; Louis R. Hampton; Earl W. Harrington, Jr.; Dione D. Kenyon; Robert W. Kenyon; Lisa Koelle; Marie J. Langlois; Rebecca L. Spencer.

Trustee: PNC Bank, N.A.

Number of staff: 2 full-time professional; 1 part-time professional; 1 full-time support; 1 part-time support.

Selected grants: The following grants were reported in 2004.

$2,000,000 to Nature Conservancy of Rhode Island, Providence, RI. For Rhode Island Open Space Conservation Program.

$500,000 to Rhode Island Hospital, Providence, RI. Toward new Emergency Department.

$324,400 to Providence Public Library, Providence, RI. For Americans with Disabilities Act (ADA) improvements to Knight Memorial Library.

$250,000 to Boys and Girls Clubs of East Providence, East Providence, RI. Toward expansion of Williams Avenue Clubhouse.

$250,000 to Meeting Street Center, East Providence, RI. Toward construction of new Meeting Street National Center of Excellence in Providence.

$200,000 to Veterans Memorial Auditorium Foundation, Providence, RI. For construction of elevator in main lobby of Veterans Memorial Auditorium.

$150,000 to Fort Adams Trust, Newport, RI. Toward restoration of roof system over Officers' Quarters at Fort Adams.

$100,000 to University of Rhode Island, Kingston, RI. For Advanced 3d Graphics Laboratory.

$65,000 to Block Island Health Services, Block Island Medical Center, Block Island, RI. For phase I renovations of basement to accommodate space needs of visiting specialists.

$36,480 to Providence Animal Rescue League, Providence, RI. To replace heat and hot water systems.

$33,656 to New England Institute of Technology, Warwick, RI. For Automotive trainers.

$17,936 to Laotian-American Council Corps, North Providence, RI. To purchase computer equipment for English as a Second Language Program in Woonsocket.

$10,000 to Wood-Pawcatuck Watershed Association, Hope Valley, RI. For matching grant towards capital improvements at headquarters building.

$7,020 to Tomaquag Indian Memorial Museum, Exeter, RI. For building improvements.

$3,135 to Warwick Public Library, Warwick, RI. For lockable bookcase for Reference Department.

8525

The Charlesmead Foundation, Inc. ☆

c/o Rex Capital
50 Park Row W., Ste. 113
Providence, RI   02903   (401) 383-5370
Contact: Heather D. Crosby, Exec. Dir.
FAX: (401) 383-5380;
E-mail: hcrosby@rexcapital.com

Established in 1987 in MD.

Donors: Anthony W. Deering; Kathryn R. Deering.

Foundation type: Independent foundation.

Financial data (yr. ended 11/30/05): Assets, $20,839,178 (M); expenditures, $993,713; qualifying distributions, $650,189; giving activities include $622,250 for 59 grants (high: $204,000; low: $250), and $15,000 for 1 loan/program-related investment.

Purpose and activities: Giving for art and cultural programs and education.

Fields of interest: Visual arts; Museums; Performing arts; Elementary/secondary education; Higher education.

Type of support: Program-related investments/loans; General/operating support; Capital campaigns; Annual campaigns.

Limitations: Applications not accepted. Giving primarily in Baltimore, MD. No grants to individuals.

Application information: Unsolicited applications not accepted.

Officers: Anthony W. Deering, Chair.; Kathryn R. Deering, Pres.; Heather D. Crosby, Exec. Dir.

Trustees: Maron Deering; Spencer Deering; John Warren.

EIN: 521550204

Selected grants: The following grants were reported in 2004.

$30,000 to Johns Hopkins University, Peabody Institute, Baltimore, MD.

$25,000 to Center Stage, Baltimore, MD.

$11,000 to Baltimore Museum of Art, Baltimore, MD.

$7,000 to Maryland Citizens for the Arts, Ellicott City, MD.

$5,000 to American Visionary Art Museum, Baltimore, MD.

$5,000 to Drexel University, Philadelphia, PA.

$2,500 to Everyman Theater, Baltimore, MD.

$2,000 to Charleston Museum, Charleston, SC.

$1,500 to Baltimore School for the Arts, Baltimore, MD.

$1,000 to Friends School of Baltimore, Baltimore, MD.

8526

The Charter One Foundation ◇

c/o Citizens Bank of Rhode Island
870 Westminster St.
Providence, RI   02903

Established in 2001 in OH.

Donors: Charter One Bank, F.S.B.; Charter One Bank, N.A.

Foundation type: Company-sponsored foundation.

Financial data (yr. ended 3/31/06): Assets, $0 (M); expenditures, $6,637,317; qualifying distributions, $6,556,658; giving activities include $6,511,000 for 574 grants (high: $300,000; low: $500).

Purpose and activities: The foundation supports organizations involved with arts and culture, education, health, human services, civil rights, community development, and African Americans.

Fields of interest: Museums (art); Performing arts, orchestra (symphony); Arts; Higher education; Education; Health care, clinics/centers; Health care; Human services; Civil rights; Economic development; Community development; Federated giving programs; African Americans/Blacks.

Type of support: General/operating support; Program development; Scholarship funds.

Limitations: Applications not accepted. Giving on a national basis, with emphasis on IL, IN, MI, and OH. No grants to individuals.

Application information: Contributes only to pre-selected organizations.

Trustees: Citizens Bank; Lawrence K. Fish.

EIN: 300005922

Selected grants: The following grants were reported in 2004.

$250,000 to Case Western Reserve University, Cleveland, OH.

$250,000 to Cleveland Clinic Foundation, Cleveland, OH.

$250,000 to John Carroll University, University Heights, OH.

$180,000 to Jewish Federation of Metropolitan Detroit, Bloomfield Hills, MI.

$150,000 to Cleveland Orchestra, Cleveland, OH.

$56,875 to Economic Growth Foundation, Cleveland, OH.

$50,000 to Salvation Army.

$10,000 to Elmhurst College, Elmhurst, IL.

$5,000 to A Cultural Exchange, Cleveland, OH.

$2,000 to United Way.

8527

The Citizens Bank Mid-Atlantic Charitable Foundation ◇

c/o Citizens Bank of Rhode Island
870 Westminster St.
Providence, RI   02903   (401) 282-3836
Contact: Patricia Zeller, Trust Off., Citizens Bank of Rhode Island

Established in 2001 in PA.

Donor: Citizens Financial Group, Inc.

Foundation type: Company-sponsored foundation.

Financial data (yr. ended 3/31/06): Assets, $0 (M); expenditures, $3,719,176; qualifying distributions, $3,655,100; giving activities include $3,598,069 for 393 grants (high: $140,000; low: $263).

Purpose and activities: The foundation supports organizations involved with arts and culture, education, youth development, human services, and community development.

Fields of interest: Arts; Higher education; Education; Youth development; Children/youth, services; Human services; Community development; Federated giving programs; Women.

Application information: Application form not required.

Initial approach: Proposal

Deadline(s): None

Trustees: Donald Gaiter; Bradford Kopp; Stephen Steinour; Citizens Bank of Rhode Island.
EIN: 256795399
Selected grants: The following grants were reported in 2005.
$100,000 to United Way of Southeastern Pennsylvania, Philadelphia, PA. For general support.
$88,000 to Allegheny Conference on Community Development, Pittsburgh, PA. For general support.
$83,334 to Pittsburgh Community Reinvestment Group, Pittsburgh, PA. For general support.
$75,000 to National Constitution Center, Philadelphia, PA. For general support.
$60,000 to Temple University, Philadelphia, PA. For general support.
$50,000 to Greater Philadelphia Urban Affairs Coalition, Philadelphia, PA. For general support.
$50,000 to Pennsylvania Horticultural Society, Philadelphia, PA. For general support.
$50,000 to Philadelphia Safe and Sound, Philadelphia, PA. For general support.
$50,000 to Whitaker Center for Science and the Arts, Harrisburg, PA. For general support.
$46,939 to United Way of Allegheny County, Pittsburgh, PA. For general support.

8528

Cuno Foundation ◇

c/o Bank of America, N.A.
P.O. Box 1802
Providence, RI 02901-1802
Application address: c/o Trudy Magnolia, Secy., Bank of America, N.A., 18 Devon Ct., Meriden, CT 06450

Established in 1948 in CT.
Donor: Frank Davelia†.
Foundation type: Independent foundation.
Financial data (yr. ended 12/31/05): Assets, $9,827,538 (M); gifts received, $153,194; expenditures, $561,622; qualifying distributions, $538,166; giving activities include $219,195 for 36 grants (high: $65,000; low: $1,000), and $263,996 for 118 grants to individuals (high: $2,500; low: $500).
Purpose and activities: Giving primarily to scholarship funds to support students seeking education in CT.
Fields of interest: Higher education; Health care; Human services; Federated giving programs.
Type of support: Scholarship funds; Scholarships—to individuals; Student loans—to individuals.
Limitations: Giving primarily to residents of the Meriden, CT, area.
Application information: Application form required.
Initial approach: Proposal
Trustee: Bank of America, N.A.
EIN: 066033040
Selected grants: The following grants were reported in 2003.
$27,470 to American Red Cross, Wallingford, CT.
$18,526 to YMCA of Meriden, Meriden, CT.
$18,450 to Catholic Family Services, Meriden, CT. For Child Guidance Clinic.
$15,100 to Catholic Family Services, New Haven, CT.
$14,633 to Salvation Army, Meriden, CT.
$12,027 to Boys and Girls Club of Meriden, Meriden, CT.
$10,000 to Meriden Historical Society, Meriden, CT.

$10,000 to New Opportunities for Waterbury, Waterbury, CT.
$5,547 to Kuhn Employment Opportunities, Meriden, CT.
$5,000 to Curtis Home School, Meriden, CT.

8529

CVS/pharmacy Charitable Trust, Inc. ◇

(formerly CVS Charitable Trust, Inc.)
1 CVS Dr.
Woonsocket, RI 02895
URL: http://www.cvs.com/corpInfo/community/charitable_mission.html

Established in 1992 in DE and MA.
Donors: Melville Corp.; CVS Corp.; CVS Pharmacy, Inc.
Foundation type: Company-sponsored foundation.
Financial data (yr. ended 1/1/05): Assets, $81,287,564 (M); gifts received, $39,991,170; expenditures, $6,842,935; qualifying distributions, $6,809,807; giving activities include $5,704,388 for 744 grants (high: $225,000; low: $200), and $558,500 for 184 grants to individuals (high: $5,000; low: $1,000).
Purpose and activities: The trust supports organizations involved with children and youth with physical, developmental, or sensory disabilities.
Fields of interest: Elementary/secondary education; Health care, equal rights; Medicine/medical care, public education; Medical care, rehabilitation; Health care; Children; Youth; Disabilities, people with; Deaf/hearing impaired; Mentally disabled.
Type of support: General/operating support; Program development; Employee volunteer services; Employee-related scholarships.
Limitations: Giving limited to areas of company operations.
Publications: Grants list.
Application information: E-mail messages and telephone calls during the application process are not encouraged. Application form required.
Initial approach: Complete online application form
Deadline(s): May 1 through June 30
Final notification: 10 to 12 weeks
Officers and Directors:* David B. Rickard,* Pres.; Eileen Dunn,* V.P.; Michael K. Golub, V.P.; Zenon P. Lankowsky, Secy.; Larry D. Solberg, Treas.; Thomas M. Ryan.
EIN: 223206973
Selected grants: The following grants were reported in 2005.
$450,000 to United Way of Rhode Island, Providence, RI. 2 grants: $225,000 each (For program support).
$225,000 to Big Picture Company, Providence, RI. For program support.
$125,000 to Landmark Medical Center, Woonsocket, RI. For program support.
$50,000 to Trinity Repertory Company, Providence, RI. For program support.
$25,000 to American Academy of Pediatrics, Elk Grove Village, IL. For program support.
$25,000 to Rhode Island Kids Count, Providence, RI. For program support.
$22,500 to Providence Childrens Museum, Providence, RI. For program support.
$20,000 to Warren G. Harding Middle School, Philadelphia, PA. For program support.
$12,000 to Alliance for Children and Youth, Gastonia, NC. For program support.

8530

The Fred Harris Daniels Foundation, Inc. ◇

c/o Bank of America, N.A.
P.O. Box 1802
Providence, RI 02901-1802
Application address: c/o Brian Hite, Bank of America, N.A., 100 Front St., Worcester, MA 01608

Incorporated in 1949 in MA.
Donors: Fred H. Daniels†; Eleanor G. Daniels†.
Foundation type: Independent foundation.
Financial data (yr. ended 10/31/05): Assets, $18,660,306 (M); expenditures, $1,377,514; qualifying distributions, $1,260,651; giving activities include $1,224,275 for 100 grants (high: $93,375; low: $1,000).
Purpose and activities: Grants for the advancement of the sciences, including marine and medical sciences; support also for secondary and higher education, health services and hospitals, including programs for the mentally ill, community funds, social and family services, including museums, music organizations, historical preservation, libraries, and Protestant giving.
Fields of interest: Museums; Performing arts; Performing arts, music; Historic preservation/historical societies; Arts; Secondary school/education; Higher education; Adult education—literacy, basic skills & GED; Libraries/library science; Education, reading; Education; Hospitals (general); Reproductive health, family planning; Health care; Mental health/crisis services; Health organizations, association; Biomedicine; Medical research, institute; Youth development, services; Human services; Children/youth, services; Family services; Federated giving programs; Marine science; Engineering/technology; Science; Leadership development; Protestant agencies & churches.
Type of support: General/operating support; Continuing support; Annual campaigns; Capital campaigns; Building/renovation; Equipment; Land acquisition; Endowments; Emergency funds; Program development; Scholarship funds; Matching/challenge support.
Limitations: Giving primarily in the Worcester, MA, area. No grants to individuals, or for seed money or deficit financing; no loans.
Application information: Application form not required.
Initial approach: Letter
Copies of proposal: 1
Deadline(s): Mar. 1, June 1, Sept. 1, and Dec. 1
Board meeting date(s): Mar., June, Sept., and Dec.
Final notification: 1 to 3 months after meeting
Officers and Directors:* Fred H. Daniels II,* Pres.; Eleanor D. Hodge,* V.P.; William S. Nicholson,* Secy.; William O. Pettit, Jr.,* Treas.; Jonathan D. Blake; Janet B. Daniels; Amy B. Key; Sarah D. Morse; David A. Nicholson; Meridith D. Wesby.
EIN: 046014333
Selected grants: The following grants were reported in 2005.
$93,375 to YMCA of Greater Worcester, Worcester, MA.
$56,000 to American Antiquarian Society, Worcester, MA. 2 grants: $50,000, $6,000
$50,000 to Tower Hill Botanic Garden, Boylston, MA.
$48,000 to Girls Inc..
$45,000 to Childrens Friend, Worcester, MA.
$40,000 to Bancroft School, Worcester, MA.
$10,000 to Tabor Academy, Marion, MA.

$10,000 to YWCA.

$9,000 to Worcester Youth Center, Worcester, MA.

8531
Dorot Foundation ▼ ✧
439 Benefit St.
Providence, RI 02903 (401) 351-8866
Contact: Michael Hill, Exec. V.P.
FAX: (401) 351-4975; E-mail: info@dorot.org;
URL: http://www.dorot.org

Incorporated in 1958 in NY as Joy and Samuel Ungerleider Foundation.
Donors: Joy G. Ungerleider-Mayerson†; D.S. and R.H. Gottesman Foundation; Yesod Fund.
Foundation type: Independent foundation.
Financial data (yr. ended 3/31/05): Assets, $71,103,871 (M); gifts received, $3,353,788; expenditures, $4,896,538; qualifying distributions, $4,051,272; giving activities include $3,401,314 for 45 grants (high: $800,000; low: $2,500; average: $25,000–$150,000).
Purpose and activities: Grants primarily for informal education; The Dorot Fellowship in Israel; cultural organizations with which the foundation has an existing relationship; and organizations supporting adult education for democratic participation in Israel.
Fields of interest: Arts, cultural/ethnic awareness; Education; Public affairs, citizen participation.
International interests: Israel.
Type of support: General/operating support; Continuing support; Program development; Publication; Seed money; Fellowships; Internship funds; Technical assistance; Program evaluation; Matching/challenge support.
Limitations: Giving primarily in the U.S. and Israel. No support for acquisitions for museums or excavation phase of archaeological work. No grants for endowments, capital campaigns, equipment, debt reduction, consultants or technical assistance, or events.
Publications: Application guidelines; Financial statement; Grants list.
Application information: See foundation's Web site for more application information. Application form not required.
Initial approach: Letter of inquiry (2-3 pages)
Copies of proposal: 1
Deadline(s): 60 days prior to board meetings
Board meeting date(s): Apr./May and Oct./Nov.
Final notification: 4-6 weeks
Officers and Directors:* Ernest S. Frerichs,* Pres.; Michael Hill, Exec. V.P.; Steven Ungerleider,* V.P.; Steven C. Baum, Secy.-Treas.; Jeane Ungerleider.
Number of staff: 3 full-time professional; 1 part-time professional.
EIN: 136116927
Selected grants: The following grants were reported in 2005.
$358,400 to New Israel Fund, DC. To work toward social change in Israel.
$245,000 to Jewish Museum, New York, NY. For Centennial Campaign.
$150,000 to Jewish Womens Archive, Brookline, MA. For Women Who Dared, exhibition in gallery and on-line.
$140,000 to American Jewish World Service, New York, NY. For International Jewish College Corps and for Tsunami relief.
$100,000 to Oregon Health and Science University, Portland, OR. For program support.

$90,000 to Alliance for Justice, DC. For Dorot Fellowships.
$75,000 to Friends of Kol Haneshama, New York, NY. For general operating support.
$65,000 to Israel Exploration Society, Jerusalem, Israel. For general support, and for Journal and Encyclopedia.
$50,000 to Bank Street College of Education, New York, NY. For general operating support.
$50,000 to Hazon, Inc., New York, NY. For New York Jewish Environmental Bike Ride, fundraiser for Hazon.

8532
The Doyle Charitable Foundation ✧
c/o Bank of America, N.A.
P.O. Box 6767
Providence, RI 02940-6767
Application address: c/o Bank of America, N.A., 100 Federal St., MA5-100-20-06, Boston, MA 02110

Established in 1957 in MA.
Foundation type: Independent foundation.
Financial data (yr. ended 12/31/04): Assets, $2,353,037 (M); expenditures, $720,500; qualifying distributions, $710,517; giving activities include $700,000 for 3 grants (high: $600,000; low: $50,000).
Fields of interest: Education; Environment, land resources; Animal welfare.
Type of support: General/operating support; Capital campaigns.
Limitations: Giving primarily in the greater Boston, MA, area. No support for private foundations, national organizations, or projects requiring multi-year commitment. No grants to individuals, or for conferences, film production, travel, research projects, publications, or scholarships; no loans.
Application information: Application form not required.
Initial approach: Proposal
Deadline(s): None
Trustees: Louise I. Doyle; Bank of America, N.A.
EIN: 046010367
Selected grants: The following grants were reported in 2004.
$600,000 to Trustees of Reservations, Beverly, MA. For general support.
$50,000 to Massachusetts Society for the Prevention of Cruelty to Animals, Boston, MA. For general support.
$50,000 to Tufts University, School of Veterinary Medicine, Medford, MA. For general support.

8533
Norman & Rosalie Fain Fund Trust ✧ ☆
505 Central Ave.
Pawtucket, RI 02861

Established in 1964 in RI.
Donor: Norman M. Fain.
Foundation type: Independent foundation.
Financial data (yr. ended 12/31/05): Assets, $6,315,665 (M); expenditures, $468,121; qualifying distributions, $423,460; giving activities include $423,460 for 56 grants (high: $240,000; low: $50).
Purpose and activities: Giving primarily for higher education and for Jewish welfare.

Fields of interest: Secondary school/education; Higher education; Human services; Jewish agencies & temples.
Limitations: Applications not accepted. Giving primarily in RI. No grants to individuals.
Application information: Contributes only to pre-selected organizations.
Trustees: Jonathan D. Fain; Norman M. Fain; Rosalie B. Fain; Wendy F. Feldman.
EIN: 056022655
Selected grants: The following grants were reported in 2005.
$240,000 to Jewish Federation of Rhode Island, Providence, RI.
$350 to United Way of Rhode Island, Providence, RI.

8534
Feinstein Family Fund ✧ ☆
41 Alhambra Cir.
Cranston, RI 02905 (401) 467-5155
Contact: Alan Shawn Feinstein, Pres.

Foundation type: Independent foundation.
Financial data (yr. ended 12/31/05): Assets, $5,190,296 (M); expenditures, $370,435; qualifying distributions, $363,844; giving activities include $363,844 for 12+ grants (high: $50,000).
Officers: Alan Shawn Feinstein, Pres.; Mark Morse, Secy.; Michael S. Finer, Treas.
EIN: 050474981

8535
The Feinstein Foundation, Inc. ✧
41 Alhambra Cir.
Cranston, RI 02905 (401) 467-5155
Contact: Alan Shawn Feinstein, Pres.

Established in 1991 in RI.
Donors: Alan Shawn Feinstein; Fidelity Charitable Gift Fund.
Foundation type: Independent foundation.
Financial data (yr. ended 12/31/03): Assets, $38,126,819 (M); gifts received, $135,881; expenditures, $1,076,289; qualifying distributions, $521,770; giving activities include $521,770 for 10 + grants.
Purpose and activities: Giving primarily for human services.
Fields of interest: Elementary school/education; Secondary school/education; Education; Food banks; Human services.
Application information: Application form not required.
Deadline(s): None
Officers and Directors:* Alan Shawn Feinstein,* Pres.; Thomas West, V.P.; Michael Finer,* Secy.; Edward Walton; Thomas Zammarelli.
EIN: 223142312
Selected grants: The following grants were reported in 2003.
$102,270 to Rhode Island Department of Elementary and Secondary Education, Providence, RI.
$25,475 to University of Rhode Island, Kingston, RI. For Feinstein Memorial Scholarship.
$24,750 to Warwick House of Hope, Warwick, RI.
$20,000 to Rhode Island Community Food Bank Association, Providence, RI.
$15,000 to Youth Caring for Others, Warwick, RI.
$13,566 to Cranston Public Schools, Cranston, RI.

$9,328 to Meals on Wheels of Rhode Island, Providence, RI.

8536
Felicia Fund, Inc. ✧
22 Parsonage St.
Providence, RI 02903
Contact: Pauline C. Metcalf, Pres.

Established in 1985 in RI.
Donor: Pauline C. Metcalf.
Foundation type: Independent foundation.
Financial data (yr. ended 11/30/05): Assets, $7,140,429 (M); gifts received, $300,021; expenditures, $387,435; qualifying distributions, $330,800; giving activities include $330,800 for 42 grants (high: $85,000; low: $500).
Purpose and activities: Giving primarily to fund projects that relate to architecture, decorative art, historic preservation, conservation, and related educational pursuits.
Fields of interest: Visual arts, architecture; Museums (history); Historic preservation/historical societies; Education, formal/general education.
Limitations: Giving primarily in MA, NY, and RI. No grants to individuals.
Application information: Application form not required.
   Deadline(s): None
Officers and Trustees:* Pauline C. Metcalf,* Pres.; Frank Mauran,* Secy.; Paul W. Whyte,* Treas.; Christopher Monkhouse.
EIN: 050420703

8537
FM Global Foundation ✧
(formerly Allendale Insurance Foundation)
1301 Atwood Ave.
P.O. Box 7500
Johnston, RI 02919

Established in 1986 in RI.
Donors: Allendale Mutual Insurance Co.; Factory Mutual Insurance Co.
Foundation type: Company-sponsored foundation.
Financial data (yr. ended 12/31/04): Assets, $5,086,176 (M); expenditures, $2,072,302; qualifying distributions, $1,957,602; giving activities include $1,236,459 for 26 grants (high: $531,316; low: $500), and $721,143 for 1,015 employee matching gifts.
Purpose and activities: The foundation supports organizations involved with arts and culture, education, animals and wildlife, health, fire prevention and control, human services, and community development.
Fields of interest: Arts; Secondary school/education; Higher education; Education; Animals/wildlife; Health care; Disasters, fire prevention/control; Human services; Community development; Federated giving programs.
International interests: Canada.
Type of support: General/operating support; Scholarship funds; Employee matching gifts.
Limitations: Applications not accepted. Giving on a national basis and in Canada. No grants to individuals.
Publications: Financial statement.
Application information: Contributes only to pre-selected organizations.

Officers and Directors: Shivan S. Subramaniam,* Chair., C.E.O. and Pres.; Nelson G. Wester, V.P. and Secy.; William A. Mekrut,* V.P. and Treas.; Roberta H. Butler,* V.P.; Paul E. LaFleche, V.P.; John Lemieux, V.P.
Trustee: JPMorgan Chase Bank, N.A.
Number of staff: 1
EIN: 222773230
Selected grants: The following grants were reported in 2004.
$531,316 to United Way of Rhode Island, Providence, RI.
$275,378 to Educational Testing Service, Princeton, NJ. 2 grants: $253,500, $21,878 (For fees).
$158,191 to United Way of King County, Seattle, WA.
$90,174 to Institute for Business and Home Safety, Tampa, FL.
$24,030 to United Way of Metropolitan Dallas, Dallas, TX.
$21,290 to United Way of Metropolitan Atlanta, Atlanta, GA.
$20,000 to Rhode Island Economic Policy Council, Providence, RI.
$19,370 to United Way of Metropolitan Chicago, Chicago, IL.
$10,592 to United Way of Southeastern Pennsylvania, Philadelphia, PA.

8538
Russell Grinnell Memorial Trust ✧
PO Box 1802
Providence, RI 02901-1802
Contact: Kerry H. Sullivan, Dir., Bank of America, N.A.
E-mail: kerry.h.sullivan@bankofamerica.com

Established in 1998 in RI.
Foundation type: Independent foundation.
Financial data (yr. ended 12/31/05): Assets, $17,740,423 (M); expenditures, $686,881; qualifying distributions, $615,793; giving activities include $563,853 for grants.
Fields of interest: Secondary school/education; Higher education; Libraries (public); Children/youth, services.
Limitations: Applications not accepted. No grants to individuals.
Application information: Contributes only to pre-selected organizations.
Trustee: Bank of America, N.A.
EIN: 311603440

8539
Hasbro Children's Fund ✧
(formerly Hasbro Charitable Trust, Inc.)
c/o Hasbro, Inc.
1027 Newport Ave.
Pawtucket, RI 02862 (401) 727-5429
Contact: Karen Davis, Dir.
URL: http://www.hasbro.org

Established in 1984 in RI.
Donor: Hasbro, Inc.
Foundation type: Company-sponsored foundation.
Financial data (yr. ended 12/25/05): Assets, $560,421 (M); gifts received, $453,317; expenditures, $1,709,722; qualifying distributions, $1,709,356; giving activities include $1,619,140 for 150 grants (high: $450,000).

Purpose and activities: The fund supports programs designed to assist children in triumphing over critical life obstacles; and bring the joy of play into their lives. Special emphasis is directed toward programs designed to provide respite and access to play to terminal and seriously ill children; provide educational programs for children at risk; and address the mental and physical well-being of children in need.
Fields of interest: Elementary/secondary education; Health care; Mental health/crisis services; Recreation; Children, services; Children.
Type of support: General/operating support; Capital campaigns; Building/renovation; Program development; Employee volunteer services; Employee matching gifts.
Limitations: Giving primarily in Springfield, MA, RI, and Renton, WA; giving also to regional, national, and U.S.-based international organizations. No support for religious organizations, political organizations, or schools. No grants to individuals, or for research, scholarships, travel, endowments, advertising, sponsorship of recreational activities, fundraisers, or auctions; no loans; no cash free grants.
Publications: Application guidelines; Corporate giving report; Informational brochure.
Application information: Unsolicited requests from regional, national, and U.S.-based international organizations are not accepted. Contributions to organizations located in Springfield, MA, have been allocated for 2006. Application form required.
   Initial approach: Complete online application form
   Deadline(s): May 1 to May 31
   Board meeting date(s): June
Officers and Directors:* Alan G. Hassenfeld,* Pres.; Alfred J. Verrecchia,* Exec. V.P.; Barry Nagler,* Sr. V.P., Genl. Counsel, and Secy.; David D.R. Hargreaves, Sr. V.P. and C.F.O.; Martin R. Trueb, Sr. V.P. and Treas.; Richard B. Holt, Sr. V.P.
Number of staff: 2 full-time professional; 1 part-time support.
EIN: 222538470

8540
Hassenfeld Foundation ▼ ✧
1011 Newport Ave.
Pawtucket, RI 02861

Established in 1944 in RI.
Donors: Hasbro, Inc.; Stephen Hassenfeld Charitable Lead Trust; and members of the Hassenfeld family.
Foundation type: Independent foundation.
Financial data (yr. ended 12/31/04): Assets, $16,256,899 (M); gifts received, $1,167,005; expenditures, $3,571,859; qualifying distributions, $3,535,793; giving activities include $3,521,346 for 112 grants (high: $673,800; low: $96; average: $1,000–$100,000).
Purpose and activities: Giving primarily for higher education, Jewish federated giving programs, and arts and cultural organizations.
Fields of interest: Arts; Higher education; Jewish federated giving programs.
Limitations: Applications not accepted. No grants to individuals.
Application information: Contributes only to pre-selected organizations.
Officers and Director:* Sylvia K. Hassenfeld,* Pres.; Alan G. Hassenfeld, V.P. and Treas.; Ellen Block, Secy.
EIN: 056015373

Selected grants: The following grants were reported in 2004.

$673,800 to Brandeis University, Waltham, MA. For grant made in form of stock.

$635,201 to University of Pennsylvania, Philadelphia, PA. For grant made in form of stock.

$554,100 to Brown University, Providence, RI. For grant made in form of stock.

$196,850 to Jewish Federation of Rhode Island, Providence, RI. 2 grants: $107,450 (For grant made in form of stock), $89,400 (For grant made in form of stock).

$94,925 to Moses Brown School, Providence, RI. For grant made in form of stock.

$92,075 to Harvard University, Cambridge, MA. For grant made in form of stock.

$77,560 to International Tennis Hall of Fame and Tennis Museum, Newport, RI. For grant made in form of stock.

$76,440 to Jewish Federation of Palm Beach County, West Palm Beach, FL. For grant made in form of stock.

$48,850 to Institute of Contemporary Art, Boston, MA. For grant made in form of stock.

8541
Marion Gardner Jackson Charitable Trust ◇
c/o Bank of America, N.A.
P.O. Box 1802
Providence, RI 02901-1802
Contact: Augusta Haydock, Trust. Off., Bank of America, N.A.
Application address: c/o Bank of America, N.A., 100 Federal St., Boston, MA 02110

Established in 1968 in MA.
Foundation type: Independent foundation.
Financial data (yr. ended 12/31/04): Assets, $10,680,821 (M); expenditures, $799,144; qualifying distributions, $766,653; giving activities include $637,600 for grants.
Fields of interest: Historic preservation/historical societies; Higher education; Crime/violence prevention, abuse prevention; Human services; YM/YWCAs & YM/YWHAs; Family services; Developmentally disabled, centers & services; Federated giving programs.
Type of support: Building/renovation.
Limitations: Giving primarily in Adams County, IL. No grants to individuals.
Application information: Application form not required.
Initial approach: Proposal
Deadline(s): Jan. 15, May 15, and Sept. 15
Trustee: Bank of America, N.A.
EIN: 046010559

8542
Horace A. Kimball and S. Ella Kimball Foundation ◇
130 Woodville Rd.
Hope Valley, RI 02832
Contact: Thomas F. Black III, Pres.
URL: http://www.hkimballfoundation.org

Incorporated in 1956 in DE.
Donor: H. Earle Kimball†.
Foundation type: Independent foundation.
Financial data (yr. ended 10/31/05): Assets, $8,529,602 (M); expenditures, $420,019;

qualifying distributions, $394,852; giving activities include $359,000 for 31 grants (high: $40,000; low: $1,000).
Fields of interest: Arts; Secondary school/education; Education; Environment, natural resources; Environment; Animal welfare; Health care; Health organizations, association; Human services; Children/youth, services; Aging, centers/services; Homeless, human services; Aging; Disabilities, people with; Economically disadvantaged; Homeless.
Type of support: General/operating support; Capital campaigns; Building/renovation; Emergency funds; Seed money; Matching/challenge support.
Limitations: Giving limited to RI, with emphasis on South County. No support for religious organizations. No grants to individuals, or for feasibility studies, capital projects or multi-year commitments.
Publications: Financial statement; Grants list.
Application information: Application form available on foundation Web site. Application form required.
Initial approach: Internet (all applications)
Copies of proposal: 3
Deadline(s): None
Board meeting date(s): Varies
Officers and Trustees: * Thomas F. Black III,* Pres.; Norman D. Baker, Jr.,* Secy.-Treas.; Paul D. Lynch.
Number of staff: 1 part-time support.
EIN: 056006130
Selected grants: The following grants were reported in 2003.

$25,000 to Wood River Health Services, Hope Valley, RI. For capital support.

$20,000 to YMCA, Santa Anita Family, Monrovia, CA. To build playground.

$15,000 to Visiting Nurse Services of Washington County and Jamestown, Wakefield, RI. For matching grant.

$10,500 to Wood-Pawcatuck Watershed Association, Hope Valley, RI. For building repairs and operating expenses.

$10,000 to Big Brothers of Rhode Island, Pawtucket, RI. For operating support.

$10,000 to Chorus of Westerly, Westerly, RI. For capital campaign.

$10,000 to Hope Valley Ambulance Squad, Hope Valley, RI. To purchase a vehicle.

$10,000 to Richmond Senior Services, Staten Island, NY. For operating support.

$10,000 to Salvation Army of Providence, Providence, RI. For capital support.

$8,973 to Big Apple Circus, New York, NY.

8543
Kings Grant Foundation ◇
c/o DFH Mgmt. Corp.
25 Enterprise Ctr.
Middletown, RI 02842

Established in 2001 in RI.
Donor: Dennis Hardiman.
Foundation type: Independent foundation.
Financial data (yr. ended 6/30/05): Assets, $4,089,202 (M); gifts received, $2,072,129; expenditures, $1,380,296; qualifying distributions, $1,349,168; giving activities include $1,349,168 for 7 grants (high: $590,168; low: $4,000).
Fields of interest: Higher education, college; Human services; Christian agencies & churches.
Limitations: Applications not accepted. No grants to individuals.

Application information: Contributes only to pre-selected organizations.
Trustees: Dennis Hardiman; Lisa Hardiman.
EIN: 050520607
Selected grants: The following grants were reported in 2004.

$330,000 to Frontiers, Mesa, AZ. For general support.

$150,000 to Gordon College, Wenham, MA. For general support.

$50,000 to La Salle Academy, Philadelphia, PA. For general support.

$30,000 to Church Planters Training International, Grand Rapids, MI. For general support.

$30,000 to Millennium Relief and Development Services, Bellaire, TX. For general support.

$30,000 to Operation Mobilization, Tyrone, GA. For general support.

$16,725 to Christlike Ministries, Douglasville, GA. For general support.

$5,000 to Jubilee Campaign USA, Fairfax, VA. For general support.

8544
Ida Ballou Littlefield Memorial Trust
1500 Fleet Ctr.
Providence, RI 02903 (401) 274-2000
Contact: Joachim A. Weissfeld, Tr.

Established in 1989 in RI.
Foundation type: Independent foundation.
Financial data (yr. ended 12/31/05): Assets, $8,540,945 (M); expenditures, $569,991; qualifying distributions, $504,676; giving activities include $466,953 for 50 grants (high: $25,000; low: $1,000; average: $5,000–$15,000).
Fields of interest: Museums; Higher education; Hospitals (general); Health care; Health organizations, association; Medical research, institute; Family services.
Type of support: Scholarship funds; Program development; Continuing support; Capital campaigns.
Limitations: Giving primarily in MA and RI. No grants to individuals.
Publications: Application guidelines.
Application information: Application form not required.
Initial approach: Letter
Copies of proposal: 3
Deadline(s): 30 days prior to board meeting
Board meeting date(s): 1st Fri. in May and Nov.
Trustees: William A. Viall; Joachim A. Weissfeld; Citizens Bank.
EIN: 222994936

8545
Henry C. Lord Scholarship Fund Trust ◇
c/o Citizens Bank of NH
870 Westminster St.
Providence, RI 02903
Application address for scholarships: Citizens Bank New Hampshire, attn.: Robert Gerseny, 1 Capital Plz., Concord, NH 03301, tel.: (603) 229-3573

Trust established in 1978 in NH.
Donor: Henry C. Lord†.
Foundation type: Independent foundation.
Financial data (yr. ended 6/30/06): Assets, $11,606,878 (M); expenditures, $820,893; qualifying distributions, $760,127; giving activities

include $706,000 for 189 grants to individuals (high: $6,500; low: $3,000).

Purpose and activities: Awards scholarships for needy residents of Peterborough, NH, and contiguous towns; support also for scholarship funds through a local community foundation.

Fields of interest: Higher education; Scholarships/financial aid.

Type of support: Scholarship funds; Scholarships—to individuals.

Limitations: Giving limited to NH residents. No grants for general support, capital or endowment funds, or matching gifts; no loans.

Application information: Application form required.

  Initial approach: Letter

  Deadline(s): Apr. 30 for 1st time applicants; June 15 each year thereafter

Trustee: Citizens Bank of NH.

EIN: 026051741

8546
The Mann Family Foundation ✧ ☆

50 Channing Ave.
Providence, RI 02906
Contact: Robert Mann, Pres.

Established in 1996 in RI.

Donors: Robert Mann; Leon Mann; Carol Mann; Judith Mann; Inga Mann.

Foundation type: Independent foundation.

Financial data (yr. ended 12/31/05): Assets, $1,278,729 (M); gifts received, $719,457; expenditures, $368,018; qualifying distributions, $367,451; giving activities include $364,081 for 56 grants (high: $100,100; low: $200).

Purpose and activities: Giving for Jewish organizations, health and medical services, and for education.

Fields of interest: Higher education; Education; Hospitals (general); Human services; Federated giving programs; Jewish federated giving programs; Jewish agencies & temples.

Limitations: Giving primarily in RI. No grants to individuals.

Application information: Application form not required.

  Deadline(s): None

Officers and Trustees:* Robert Mann,* Pres. and Treas.; Leon Mann,* Secy.; Carol Mann.

EIN: 050494136

Selected grants: The following grants were reported in 2004.

$66,000 to Moses Brown School, Providence, RI.

$32,035 to Beaumont Foundation, Southfield, MI.

$21,000 to Miriam Hospital Foundation, Providence, RI.

$10,200 to Gordon School, East Providence, RI.

$10,000 to Detroit Institute for Children, Detroit, MI.

$10,000 to Temple Beth El, Providence, RI.

$5,050 to Jewish Federation of Rhode Island, Providence, RI.

$5,000 to Hospice of Michigan, Detroit, MI.

$4,200 to Jewish Federation of Palm Beach County, West Palm Beach, FL.

$1,000 to Planned Parenthood of Rhode Island, Providence, RI.

8547
McAdams Charitable Foundation ✧

320 S. Main St.
Providence, RI 02903

Established in 1992 in RI.

Donors: Norman Estes McCulloch, Jr.; Microfibres, Inc.

Foundation type: Independent foundation.

Financial data (yr. ended 12/31/05): Assets, $16,465,383 (M); expenditures, $1,709,794; qualifying distributions, $1,612,577; giving activities include $1,466,678 for 38 grants (high: $500,000; low: $1,000).

Purpose and activities: Giving primarily for education and to Christian churches; funding also for a theater company, and the United Way.

Fields of interest: Performing arts, theater; Secondary school/education; Higher education; Hospitals (general); Federated giving programs; Christian agencies & churches.

Type of support: General/operating support; Capital campaigns.

Limitations: Applications not accepted. Giving primarily in RI. No grants to individuals.

Application information: Contributes only to pre-selected organizations.

Officers: Norman Estes McCulloch, Jr., Pres. and Treas.; Dorothy R. McCulloch, V.P.

Trustee: Robert S. Davis.

EIN: 050468638

Selected grants: The following grants were reported in 2004.

$1,061,931 to Saint Andrews School, Barrington, RI.

$521,000 to Mount Holyoke College, South Hadley, MA.

$22,000 to Dartmouth College Alumni Fund, Hanover, NH.

$18,000 to Saint Johns Church.

$10,000 to Big Picture Company, Providence, RI.

$10,000 to Community Preparatory School, Providence, RI.

$10,000 to Crestone Charter School, Crestone, CO.

$10,000 to Textron Chamber of Commerce Academy, Providence, RI.

$10,000 to Urban Collaborative Accelerated Program (UCAP), Providence, RI.

8548
Catherine McCarthy Memorial Trust Fund ✧

c/o Bank of America, N.A.
P.O. Box 1802
Providence, RI 02901-1802
Application address: P.O. Box 898, Lawrence, MA 01842-1798

Established in 1984 in MA.

Donor: John J. McCarthy†.

Foundation type: Independent foundation.

Financial data (yr. ended 6/30/06): Assets, $4,797,890 (M); expenditures, $428,070; qualifying distributions, $351,000; giving activities include $351,000 for grants.

Purpose and activities: Giving primarily for health and human services, Roman Catholic churches, and education.

Fields of interest: Performing arts centers; Arts; Higher education; Hospitals (general); Health care; Human services; Children/youth, services; Federated giving programs; Roman Catholic agencies & churches.

Type of support: Capital campaigns; Building/renovation; Equipment; Endowments; Program development; Seed money; Scholarship funds.

Limitations: Giving limited to MA, with emphasis on the greater Lawrence area. No support for national

health organizations or private foundations. No grants to individuals, or for annual campaigns or operating funds for standard educational programs.

Publications: Application guidelines.

Application information: Application form not required.

  Copies of proposal: 1

  Deadline(s): None

Trustees: Thomas F. Caffrey; Bank of America, N.A.

EIN: 222549008

Selected grants: The following grants were reported in 2003.

$30,000 to Merrimack Valley Community Foundation, Andover, MA. 2 grants: $15,000 each (For Ayer Mill Clock Tower restoration).

$14,500 to Lawrence History Center: Immigrant City Archives and Museum, Lawrence, MA. 2 grants: $7,500 (For general operating support), $7,000.

$10,000 to Boys and Girls Club of Lawrence, Lawrence, MA.

$10,000 to Presentation of Mary Academy, Methuen, MA.

$7,500 to Essex County Community Foundation, Danvers, MA. For Lynn Area summer fund.

$6,000 to Merrimack College, North Andover, MA.

$6,000 to YMCA, Merrimack Valley, Lawrence, MA.

$5,000 to Notre Dame Education Center, South Boston, MA.

8549
Jonathan M. Nelson Family Foundation ✧

c/o Providence Equity Partners, Inc.
50 Kennedy Pl., 18th Fl.
Providence, RI 02903

Established in 1999 in RI.

Donor: Jonathan M. Nelson.

Foundation type: Independent foundation.

Financial data (yr. ended 12/31/04): Assets, $32,973,695 (M); gifts received, $13,042,000; expenditures, $890,112; qualifying distributions, $783,750; giving activities include $783,700 for 39 grants (high: $300,000; low: $100).

Fields of interest: Arts; Higher education, university; Education; Jewish agencies & temples.

Limitations: Applications not accepted. Giving primarily in RI. No grants to individuals.

Application information: Contributes only to pre-selected organizations.

Trustees: David K. Duffell; Jane S. Nelson; Jonathan M. Nelson.

EIN: 050504814

Selected grants: The following grants were reported in 2004.

$325,000 to Gordon School, East Providence, RI. 2 grants: $300,000, $25,000

$40,000 to Miriam Hospital Foundation, Providence, RI.

$30,000 to Trinity Repertory Company, Providence, RI. 2 grants: $5,000, $25,000

$20,000 to Harvard Business School Fund, Boston, MA.

$10,200 to Resources for Indispensable Schools and Educators (RISE), San Francisco, CA.

$10,000 to Middlesex School, Concord, MA.

$5,000 to American Friends of Yad Yemin, Brooklyn, NY.

$1,000 to Eleanor Roosevelt Center at Val-Kill, Hyde Park, NY.

8550

Deborah Munroe Noonan Memorial Fund ✧

(formerly Frank M. Noonan Trust)

c/o Bank of America, N.A., Fdn. and Philanthropic Svcs.

P.O. Box 1802

Providence, RI 02901-1802 (617) 434-4846

Contact: Kerry Herlihy Sullivan, Dir., Bank of America, N.A.

E-mail: kerry.h.sullivan@bankofamerica.com;

Application address: c/o Medical Foundation, 95 Berkeley St., Ste. 201, Boston, MA 02116;

Additional tel.: (617) 451-0049; Additional E-mail: research@tmfnet.org

Trust established in 1947 in MA.

Donor: Frank M. Noonan‡.

Foundation type: Independent foundation.

Financial data (yr. ended 9/30/05): Assets, $9,344,265 (M); expenditures, $496,844; qualifying distributions, $467,520; giving activities include $400,000 for 5 grants (high: $80,000; low: $80,000).

Purpose and activities: Grants solely for organizations and hospitals directly serving children with disabilities.

Fields of interest: Hospitals (general); Disabilities, people with.

Type of support: Program development.

Limitations: Giving limited to the greater Boston, MA, area. No grants to individuals, or for scholarships or fellowships; no loans.

Publications: Application guidelines.

Application information: Only 1 proposal per organization may be submitted per 12-month period. No hand deliveries of proposals, or video tapes will be accepted. Application form required.

Initial approach: Proposal with cover sheet

Copies of proposal: 16

Deadline(s): July 7

Board meeting date(s): Distribution committee meets as required

Final notification: Sept.

Trustee: Bank of America, N.A.

EIN: 046025957

Selected grants: The following grants were reported in 2003.

$181,268 to Boston Medical Center, Boston, MA. 2 grants: $103,188 (For general support), $78,080 (For general support).

$78,315 to New England Medical Center, Boston, MA. For general support.

$78,313 to Franciscan Childrens Hospital and Rehabilitation Center, Boston, MA. For general support.

$62,105 to Childrens Hospital Corporation, Boston, MA. For general support.

8551

The Rhode Island Foundation ▼

(also known as The Rhode Island Community Foundation)

1 Union Station

Providence, RI 02903 (401) 274-4564

Contact: Carol Golden, Exec. V.P.

FAX: (401) 331-8085; Artist grants E-mail: celliott@rifoundation.org; URL: http://www.rifoundation.org

Incorporated in 1916 in RI (includes The Rhode Island Community Foundation in 1984).

Foundation type: Community foundation.

Financial data (yr. ended 12/31/05): Assets, $467,942,258 (M); gifts received, $22,021,055; expenditures, $26,994,224; giving activities include $21,301,378 for grants.

Purpose and activities: The foundation seeks to promote educational and charitable activities that tend to improve the living conditions and well-being of the inhabitants of RI; grants for capital and operating purposes principally to agencies working in the fields of education, health care, the arts and cultural affairs, youth, the aged, social services, urban affairs, historic preservation, and the environment. Some restricted grants for scholarships and medical research.

Fields of interest: Performing arts; Historic preservation/historical societies; Arts; Libraries/library science; Education; Environment, natural resources; Environment; Animal welfare; Health care; Health organizations, association; AIDS; Legal services; Housing/shelter; Children/youth, services; Family services; Human services, emergency aid; Minorities/immigrants, centers/services; Homeless, human services; Human services; Nonprofit management; Community development; Voluntarism promotion; Government/public administration; Leadership development; Public affairs; Aging; Minorities; Immigrants/refugees; Economically disadvantaged.

Type of support: General/operating support; Management development/capacity building; Capital campaigns; Building/renovation; Equipment; Land acquisition; Emergency funds; Program development; Conferences/seminars; Film/video/radio; Publication; Seed money; Fellowships; Scholarship funds; Technical assistance; Consulting services; Program evaluation; Grants to individuals; Scholarships—to individuals; Matching/challenge support.

Limitations: Giving through discretionary funds limited to RI. No support for religious organizations for sectarian purposes (except as specified by donors). No grants to individuals (except from Donor-Advised and Designated funds), or for endowment funds, research, hospital equipment, capital needs of health organizations, annual campaigns, deficit financing, or educational institutions for general operating expenses; no loans.

Publications: Application guidelines; Annual report (including application guidelines); Financial statement; Grants list; Informational brochure; Informational brochure (including application guidelines); Newsletter; Occasional report; Program policy statement.

Application information: Organizations are invited to submit a full application after letter of intent is received; visit foundation Web site for guidelines. For scholarship information from the Designated and Donor-Advised funds contact the foundation. Application form required.

Initial approach: Contact Prog. Off. or submit letter of intent

Copies of proposal: 4

Deadline(s): Varies

Board meeting date(s): Varies

Final notification: 1 week after board meeting

Officers and Directors:* George Graboys,* Chair.; Ronald V. Gallo,* C.E.O. and Pres.; Carol Golden, Exec. V.P. and C.O.O.; Michael Jenkinson, Sr. V.P., Finance and Admin. and C.F.O.; Kimberly Butler, Acting V.P., Philanthropic Svcs.; Lance C. Eskelund, V.P., Technology; Rick Schwartz, V.P., Comms.; Jennifer Reid, Cont.; Cynthia Garcia Coll, Ph.D.; Peter S. Damon; Patricia J. Flanagan, M.D.; Hon.

Maureen McKenna Goldberg; Carol Grant; David M. Hirsch; Walter R. Stone; M. Anne Szostak.

Number of staff: 22 full-time professional; 1 part-time professional; 14 full-time support.

EIN: 222604963

Selected grants: The following grants were reported in 2005.

$200,000 to Local Initiatives Support Corporation (LISC), Providence, RI. For core operations and Neighborhood Development Fund that supports Community Development Corporations to revitalize neighborhoods and create affordable housing.

$135,000 to Amos House, Providence, RI. For Amos Culinary Education (ACE) Program and start-up of Amos House Works, for-profit food preparation and delivery enterprise employing ACE Program graduates.

$135,000 to Rhode Island College Foundation, Poverty Institute, Providence, RI. For policy and advocacy work on behalf of low- and moderate-income Rhode Islanders.

$75,000 to Comprehensive Community Action Program, Cranston, RI. To start up new dental program, Westbay Smiles program, to provide dental services to children in Warwick's Head Start programs and public schools.

$55,000 to Grow Smart Rhode Island, Providence, RI. To implement 2004 Housing Act and to promote additional housing initiatives throughout state.

$50,000 to Audubon Society of Rhode Island, Smithfield, RI. To conduct strategic planning.

$50,000 to Rhode Island Childrens Crusade for Higher Education, Providence, RI. To develop comprehensive strategic marketing communications plan.

$40,000 to American Institute for Social Justice, DC. For Association of Community Organizations for Reform Now (ACORN) to organize low- and moderate-income families in Rhode Island's urban areas around areas of education and financial literacy.

$38,000 to Providence Black Repertory Company, Providence, RI. For production and artists' fees for stage productions and staged reading of new play.

$30,000 to Westerly Land Trust, Westerly, RI. For Infrastructure Collaborative, project through which grassroots environmental organizations will share resources such as computer software and personnel.

8552

Roosa Family Foundation Trust ✧

c/o Bank of America, N.A.

P.O. Box 1802

Providence, RI 02901-1802

Application address: c/o Cathy Iacovazzi, 65 LaSalle Rd., West Hartford, CT 06017, tel.: (860) 586-7257

Established in 1994 in CT.

Foundation type: Independent foundation.

Financial data (yr. ended 12/31/04): Assets, $7,931,625 (M); expenditures, $510,317; qualifying distributions, $477,234; giving activities include $415,055 for 66 grants (high: $125,000; low: $105), and $5,000 for 1 employee matching gift.

Purpose and activities: Giving primarily for education, historical preservation, conservation, health associations, children, youth and social

services, economic development, and Baptist and Presbyterian churches.
Fields of interest: Museums; Museums (children's); Higher education; Education; Environment, natural resources; Hospitals (specialty); Health organizations, association; Boys & girls clubs; Human services; Children/youth, services; Economic development; Protestant agencies & churches.
Limitations: Giving primarily in CT and RI.
Application information:
  Initial approach: Proposal
  Deadline(s): None
Trustees: David E. Roosa; Bank of America, N.A.
EIN: 223295175

8553
E. J. & V. M. Routhier Foundation ✧ ☆
(formerly Edward J. & Virginia M. Routhier Foundation)
c/o Citizens Bank
870 Westminster St.
Providence, RI   02903-4024

Established in 1995 in RI.
Foundation type: Independent foundation.
Financial data (yr. ended 12/31/05): Assets, $16,455,110 (M); expenditures, $886,554; qualifying distributions, $832,649; giving activities include $779,000 for 16 grants (high: $365,000; low: $2,000).
Fields of interest: Elementary/secondary education; Animals/wildlife; Foundations (community); Roman Catholic agencies & churches.
Limitations: Applications not accepted. Giving primarily in RI. No grants to individuals.
Application information: Contributes only to pre-selected organizations.
Trustees: Dennis C. Dibennedetto; Phyllis Nigris; Edward J. Routhier; Citizens Bank.
EIN: 050485198
Selected grants: The following grants were reported in 2003.
$300,000 to Rhode Island Foundation/The Rhode Island Community Foundation, Providence, RI. 2 grants: $150,000 (For Routhier Nursing Faculty Endowment Fund), $150,000 (For Routhier Nursing Scholarship Fund).
$50,000 to Boys and Girls Clubs of Warwick, Warwick, RI.
$50,000 to Saint Philomena School, Portsmouth, RI.
$31,000 to Ocean Tides, Narragansett, RI.
$20,000 to South County Center for the Arts, West Kingston, RI.
$2,000 to Saint Mary Star of the Sea Church.
$2,000 to Saint Thomas More Parish, Narragansett, RI.

8554
The Salem Foundation ✧ ☆
(formerly Paul and Navyn Salem Charitable Trust)
c/o Providence Equity Partners
50 Kennedy Pl., 18th Fl.
Providence, RI   02903

Established in 2000 in RI.
Donor: Paul J. Salem.
Foundation type: Independent foundation.
Financial data (yr. ended 12/31/05): Assets, $5,701,936 (M); expenditures, $391,470;

qualifying distributions, $390,400; giving activities include $390,400 for grants.
Fields of interest: Education; Athletics/sports, winter sports; Human services.
Limitations: Applications not accepted. Giving primarily in MA and RI. No grants to individuals.
Application information: Contributes only to pre-selected organizations.
Trustee: Paul J. Salem.
EIN: 137196668

8555
Shaw's Supermarket Charitable Foundation ✧
(formerly Shaw's Market Trust Fund)
P.O. Box 1802
Providence, RI   02901-1802
Application address: c/o Bank of America, 2 Portland Sq., Portland, ME 04104

Trust established in 1959 in ME.
Donor: Shaw's Supermarkets, Inc.
Foundation type: Company-sponsored foundation.
Financial data (yr. ended 7/31/05): Assets, $1,266,341 (M); expenditures, $440,900; qualifying distributions, $436,730; giving activities include $433,000 for 7 grants (high: $400,000; low: $2,500).
Purpose and activities: The foundation supports libraries, hospices, and organizations involved with arts and culture and children and youth.
Fields of interest: Arts; Libraries (public); Youth development; Children/youth, services; Residential/custodial care, hospices; Federated giving programs; Jewish federated giving programs.
Type of support: Capital campaigns; Building/renovation; Emergency funds.
Limitations: Giving limited to areas of company operations in MA, southern ME, and southern NH. No grants to individuals.
Application information: Application form not required.
  Initial approach: Proposal
  Deadline(s): None
Trustee: Bank of America, N.A.
EIN: 016008389

8556
Shriners of Rhode Island Charities Trust ✧
(formerly Palestine Temple Charities Trust)
1 Rhodes Pl.
Cranston, RI   02905   (401) 737-7100
Contact: A. Sheffield Reynolds, Treas.

Established in 1993 in RI.
Donors: Abbey Francis Lawton; Hodges-Lawton Charities.
Foundation type: Independent foundation.
Financial data (yr. ended 12/31/05): Assets, $22,514,899 (M); gifts received, $117,336; expenditures, $1,321,446; qualifying distributions, $1,289,443; giving activities include $1,152,458 for 244 grants (high: $123,564; low: $18).
Purpose and activities: Giving primarily for hospitals; funding also for children and youth services.
Fields of interest: Hospitals (general); Children/youth, services.
Type of support: General/operating support; Scholarships—to individuals.
Limitations: Giving primarily in RI.

Application information:
  Initial approach: Letter with medical information
  Deadline(s): None
Officer and Trustees:* Stephen Carpenter,* Chair.; Robert Williams, Vice-Chair.; Leon Knudsen, Secy.; A. Sheffield Reynolds, Treas.; John Takian, Jr.
EIN: 223191072

8557
Mynde & Gary Siperstein Charitable Foundation ✧ ☆
c/o Gary S. Siperstein
130 Joseph Ct.
Warwick, RI   02886

Established in 2000 in RI.
Donors: Mynde S. Siperstein; Gary S. Siperstein.
Foundation type: Independent foundation.
Financial data (yr. ended 12/31/05): Assets, $1,160,407 (M); gifts received, $195,130; expenditures, $372,321; qualifying distributions, $369,968; giving activities include $369,968 for 20 grants (high: $100,000; low: $100).
Fields of interest: Education; Jewish federated giving programs; Jewish agencies & temples.
Limitations: Applications not accepted. Giving primarily in RI. No grants to individuals.
Application information: Contributes only to pre-selected organizations.
Trustees: Gary S. Siperstein; Mynde S. Siperstein.
EIN: 050514202
Selected grants: The following grants were reported in 2005.
$100,000 to Wheeler School, Providence, RI.
$40,000 to Temple Emanuel, Boston, MA.
$26,000 to Camp Jori, Providence, RI.
$25,500 to Jewish Federation of Rhode Island, Providence, RI.
$25,000 to Emory University, Atlanta, GA.
$12,500 to American Red Cross, Providence, RI.
$7,250 to Community Preparatory School, Providence, RI. 2 grants: $4,875, $2,375
$500 to New England Rabbinical College, Providence, RI.
$500 to Temple Torat Yisrael, Cranston, RI.

8558
Alice I. Sullivan Charitable Trust ✧ ☆
162 Middle St.
Pawtucket, RI   02860

Established in 1997 in RI.
Donor: Collette Travel Service, Inc.
Foundation type: Independent foundation.
Financial data (yr. ended 12/31/05): Assets, $540,037 (M); gifts received, $728,287; expenditures, $379,164; qualifying distributions, $379,164; giving activities include $368,201 for 121 grants (high: $25,000; low: $50).
Purpose and activities: Giving primarily for human services, and for scholarship funds to universities.
Fields of interest: Higher education; Scholarships/financial aid; Health care; Food services; Human services; Children/youth, services; Family services.
Limitations: Giving primarily in RI. No grants to individuals.
Trustees: John Galvin; Daniel J. Sullivan, Jr.
EIN: 050494296
Selected grants: The following grants were reported in 2005.

$49,000 to Salvation Army. 2 grants: $25,000, $24,000

$20,000 to Pawtucket School Department, Pawtucket, RI.

$15,000 to City Year.

$15,000 to Conservation Fund, Arlington, VA.

$15,000 to Hasbro Childrens Hospital, Providence, RI.

$10,000 to Big Brothers/Big Sisters.

$10,000 to Miriam Hospital Foundation, Providence, RI.

$5,000 to Saint Marys Home for Children, North Providence, RI.

$1,000 to Roger Williams University, Bristol, RI.

8559

The Textron Charitable Trust ✧

c/o Textron Inc.
40 Westminster St.
Providence, RI   02903
Contact: Cate M. Roberts, Dir., Community Affairs
URL: http://www.textron.com/profile/ community.html

Trust established in 1953 in VT.
Donor: Textron Inc.
Foundation type: Company-sponsored foundation.
Financial data (yr. ended 12/31/04): Assets, $10,564,988 (M); gifts received, $5,000,000; expenditures, $2,880,800; qualifying distributions, $2,864,791; giving activities include $1,563,023 for 66 grants (high: $110,000; low: $1,000), and $1,131,011 for 868 employee matching gifts.
Purpose and activities: The foundation supports organizations involved with arts and culture, education, and health.
Fields of interest: Arts; Higher education; Education; Hospitals (general); Health care; Federated giving programs.
Type of support: General/operating support; Capital campaigns; Building/renovation; Equipment; Program development; Technical assistance; Employee matching gifts; Employee-related scholarships; Matching/challenge support.
Limitations: Giving on a national basis in areas of company operations. No grants to individuals (except for employee-related scholarships), or for endowments, land acquisition, debt reduction, or demonstration projects; no loans.
Publications: Application guidelines.
Application information: Application form not required.
  Initial approach: Proposal
  Copies of proposal: 1
  Deadline(s): None
  Board meeting date(s): Quarterly
  Final notification: 8 weeks
Officer: Cate M. Roberts, Dir., Community Affairs.
Trustee: U.S. Trust.
Number of staff: 1 full-time professional.
EIN: 256115832
Selected grants: The following grants were reported in 2004.
$200,000 to Textron Chamber of Commerce Academy, Providence, RI.
$110,000 to United Way of Rhode Island, Providence, RI.
$100,000 to Duke University, Durham, NC.
$100,000 to New York Community Trust, New York, NY.
$100,000 to Rhode Island Community Food Bank Association, Providence, RI.

$75,000 to Trinity Repertory Company, Providence, RI.

$50,000 to YMCA of Greater Providence, Providence, RI.

$25,000 to Travelers Aid Society of Rhode Island, Providence, RI.

$17,500 to WaterFire Providence, Providence, RI.

$15,000 to Spring Arbor University, Spring Arbor, MI.

8560

The Irving and Edyth S. Usen Family Charitable Foundation ✧

c/o Bank of America, N.A.
P.O. Box 1802
Providence, RI   02901-1802
Application address: c/o Emma Greene, Bank of America, N.A., 100 Federal St., Boston, MA 02110

Established in 1992 in MA.
Foundation type: Independent foundation.
Financial data (yr. ended 4/30/05): Assets, $3,277,753 (M); expenditures, $429,520; qualifying distributions, $416,856; giving activities include $395,000 for 38 grants (high: $200,000; low: $100), and $9,284 for 9 employee matching gifts.
Purpose and activities: Giving primarily for education, health care and medical research, the arts, human services, and to Jewish organizations.
Fields of interest: Performing arts; Performing arts, orchestra (symphony); Arts; Higher education; Education; Hospitals (specialty); Health organizations, association; Cancer research; Human services; Jewish federated giving programs; Jewish agencies & temples.
Limitations: Giving primarily in the greater Boston, MA, area. No grants to individuals.
Application information:
  Initial approach: Letter
  Deadline(s): None
Trustees: Sumner T. Bernstein; Michael J. Bohnen; Robert Usen.
Agent: Bank of America, N.A.
EIN: 046708737
Selected grants: The following grants were reported in 2003.
$35,000 to Combined Jewish Philanthropies of Greater Boston, Boston, MA.
$20,000 to Hebrew College, Newton Centre, MA.
$20,000 to P.E.F. Israel Endowment Funds, New York, NY.
$10,000 to Boston Center for Jewish Heritage, Boston, MA.
$10,000 to Proctor Academy, Andover, NH. For capital campaign.
$8,500 to United Way of Massachusetts Bay, Boston, MA.
$5,000 to Brigham and Womens Hospital, Boston, MA.
$5,000 to Childrens Hospital Trust, Department of Otolaryngology and Communication Disorders, Boston, MA.
$5,000 to Gann Academy New Jewish High School, Waltham, MA.
$5,000 to Mayo Foundation, Rochester, MN.

8561

van Beuren Charitable Foundation, Inc. ✧

P.O. Box 4098
Middletown, RI   02842   (401) 846-8167
Contact: John A. van Beuren, Chair.
FAX: (401) 849-6859; *E-mail:* vbcfdn@aol.com;
URL: http://www.vbcf.net

Established in 1986 in RI.
Donor: Members of the van Beuren family.
Foundation type: Independent foundation.
Financial data (yr. ended 12/31/05): Assets, $76,015,498 (M); gifts received, $4,462,270; expenditures, $4,043,265; qualifying distributions, $3,616,152; giving activities include $3,514,890 for 54 grants (high: $501,000; low: $50).
Fields of interest: History/archaeology; Environment, land resources; Human services.
Type of support: General/operating support; Capital campaigns; Building/renovation; Land acquisition; Endowments; Program development.
Limitations: Giving primarily in Newport County, RI. No grants to individuals.
Publications: Application guidelines; Annual report (including application guidelines); Grants list.
Application information: Call or write for complete guidelines, or refer to foundation Web site. Application forms can also be downloaded from Web site. Application form required.
  Initial approach: Letter (no more than 2 pages)
  Copies of proposal: 1
  Deadline(s): Proposals accepted between Apr. 15 and June 15 (deadline)
  Board meeting date(s): Fall
Officers and Directors:* John A. van Beuren,* Chair. and Treas.; Barbara van Beuren,* Pres. and Exec. Dir.; Hope Hill van Beuren,* V.P.; Leonard Boehner,* Secy.; Andrea van Beuren; Archbold D. van Beuren.
Number of staff: 1 full-time support.
EIN: 222773769
Selected grants: The following grants were reported in 2005.
$751,000 to Redwood Library and Athenaeum, Newport, RI. 2 grants: $501,000 (For general support), $250,000.
$301,000 to Aquidneck Island Land Trust, Middletown, RI. For general operating support.
$250,500 to Rhode Island Hospital Foundation, Providence, RI. For general support.
$250,000 to Newport Art Museum and Art Association, Newport, RI.
$250,000 to Newport Country Club Preservation Foundation, Newport, RI.
$10,000 to Spence School, New York, NY. For general support.
$1,200 to Newport Hospital Foundation, Newport, RI.
$1,000 to Outward Bound, Garrison, NY.
$900 to Preserve Rhode Island, Providence, RI.

8562

Edward Wagner and George Hosser Scholarship Fund Trust ✧

c/o Citizens Bank of New Hampshire
870 Westminster St.
Providence, RI   02903
Application address: c/o Renee Hall, Citizens Bank New Hampshire, 1 Capital Plz., Concord, NH 03301, tel.: (603) 229-3573

Established in 1964 in NH.

Donor: Ottilie Wagner Hosser†.
Foundation type: Independent foundation.
Financial data (yr. ended 6/30/05): Assets, $5,670,990 (M); expenditures, $475,142; qualifying distributions, $431,703; giving activities include $393,500 for 97 grants to individuals (high: $8,000; low: $3,500).
Purpose and activities: Scholarship grants for college or professional education to worthy boys and young men who wish to pursue an undergraduate program at an accredited school.
Type of support: Scholarships—to individuals.
Limitations: Giving limited to residents of Manchester, NH.
Application information: Application form required.
Initial approach: Letter
Copies of proposal: 1
Deadline(s): May 31
Board meeting date(s): Aug.
Final notification: Approx. the 3rd week in Aug.
Trustee: Citizens Bank of New Hampshire.
EIN: 026005491

8563
The Washington Trust Charitable Foundation ◆
c/o The Washington Trust Co.
23 Broad St.
Westerly, RI 02891
Contact: John C. Warren

Established in 1994 in RI.
Donor: The Washington Trust Co.
Foundation type: Company-sponsored foundation.
Financial data (yr. ended 12/31/05): Assets, $1,321,850 (M); gifts received, $516,264; expenditures, $498,501; qualifying distributions, $493,000; giving activities include $493,000 for 122 grants (high: $100,000; low: $250).
Purpose and activities: The foundation supports hospitals and organizations involved with arts and culture, education, housing, human services, and community development.
Fields of interest: Arts; Higher education; Education; Hospitals (general); Housing/shelter; YM/YWCAs & YM/YWHAs; Human services; Community development; Federated giving programs.
Type of support: General/operating support; Capital campaigns; Building/renovation.
Limitations: Giving primarily in New England, with emphasis on CT and RI. No grants to individuals.
Publications: Annual report.
Application information: Application form not required.
Initial approach: Proposal
Copies of proposal: 1
Deadline(s): Oct. 1
Final notification: Within 3 months
Trustee: The Washington Trust Co.
EIN: 050477294

Selected grants: The following grants were reported in 2004.
$100,000 to Westerly Hospital Foundation, Westerly, RI.
$43,000 to United Way of Rhode Island, Providence, RI.
$20,000 to Habitat for Humanity International. 2 grants: $5,000, $15,000
$20,000 to South County Hospital Healthcare System, Wakefield, RI.
$10,000 to Travelers Aid, New York, NY.
$5,031 to Boston University, Boston, MA.
$5,000 to Kent County Memorial Hospital, Warwick, RI.
$2,500 to Education Partnership, Providence, RI.
$1,000 to Bradford Jonnycake Center, Bradford, RI.

SOUTH CAROLINA

8564
The Abney Foundation ✧
100 Vine St.
Anderson, SC   29621   (864) 964-9201
Contact: Carl T. Edwards, Vice-Chair.
FAX: (864) 964-9209;
E-mail: info@abneyfoundation.org; URL: http://
www.abneyfoundation.org

Trust established in 1957 in SC.
Donors: John S. Abney‡; Susie M. Abney‡.
Foundation type: Independent foundation.
Financial data (yr. ended 12/31/05): Assets,
$49,779,104 (M); gifts received, $11,290,055;
expenditures, $2,389,992; qualifying distributions,
$1,899,730; giving activities include $1,731,500
for 37 grants (high: $400,000; low: $1,000).
Purpose and activities: The mission of the
foundation is to make grants to innovative and
creative projects, and to programs which are
responsive to changing community needs in the
areas of education, health, social services and
cultural affairs. The foundation's primary focus is on
higher education. The foundation also has
scholarship endowments at thirteen colleges and
universities across SC.
Fields of interest: Higher education; Medical
school/education; Health care; Medical research,
institute; Human services; Salvation Army;
Children/youth, services; Residential/custodial
care, hospices; Christian agencies & churches;
Protestant agencies & churches.
Type of support: General/operating support;
Continuing support; Annual campaigns; Building/
renovation; Equipment; Land acquisition;
Endowments; Emergency funds; Professorships;
Seed money; Fellowships; Internship funds;
Scholarship funds; Research.
Limitations: Giving primarily in SC, with emphasis
on the Anderson area. No grants to individuals, or
for operating expenses; no loans.
Publications: Application guidelines.
Application information: See foundation Web site
for application guidelines and procedures, as well as
for scholarship endowment information. Application
form not required.
  Initial approach: Letter
  Copies of proposal: 1
  Deadline(s): Nov. 15
  Board meeting date(s): Dec.
Officers and Trustees:* J.R. Fulp, Jr.,* Chair.; Carl
T. Edwards,* Vice-Chair. and Exec. Dir.; Johnnye K.
Palmer,* Treas.; Lebrena F. Campbell; John R. Fulp
III; Carlette F. Holmes; Edd Sheriff.
Number of staff: 1 full-time professional; 1 part-time
support.
EIN: 576019445
Selected grants: The following grants were reported
in 2005.
$400,000 to Medical University of South Carolina
  (MUSC), Charleston, SC. For Cancer Research
  Scholarship Endowment.
$250,000 to Grace Episcopal Church, Anderson,
  SC. For parking lot project.
$150,000 to Saint Johns United Methodist Church,
  Anderson, SC. For building improvements.
$125,000 to Salvation Army of Anderson, Anderson,
  SC. 2 grants: $100,000 (For Hurricane Katrina
  disaster relief), $25,000 (For general support).

$100,000 to Anderson University, Anderson, IN. For
  scholarship program.
$100,000 to Claflin University, Orangeburg, SC. For
  scholarship endowment.
$100,000 to Presbyterian College, Clinton, SC. For
  scholarship endowment.
$100,000 to Tri-County Technical College,
  Pendleton, SC. For baby and children simulators.
$67,000 to Saint Josephs Catholic School,
  Greenville, SC. For Fine Arts Department and
  chapel seating.

8565
The Arkwright Foundation ✧
P.O. Box 5565
Spartanburg, SC   29304   (864) 585-9213
Contact: Walter S. Montgomery, Jr., Vice-Chair.

Incorporated in 1945 in SC.
Donors: Members of the M.L. Cates family;
members of the W.S. Montgomery family.
Foundation type: Independent foundation.
Financial data (yr. ended 12/31/05): Assets,
$14,524,100 (M); expenditures, $691,514;
qualifying distributions, $631,763; giving activities
include $631,763 for 81 grants (high: $249,845;
low: $50).
Fields of interest: Arts education; Higher education;
Education; Animals/wildlife; Health organizations,
association; Human services; Children/youth,
services; Community development; Protestant
agencies & churches.
Limitations: Giving primarily in SC. No grants to
individuals.
Application information:
  Initial approach: Letter, personal visit, or
    telephone
  Deadline(s): None
Officers: M.L. Cates, Sr., Chair.; Walter S.
Montgomery, Jr., Vice-Chair.
EIN: 576000066

8566
Norman J. Arnold Foundation ☆
(formerly Ben Arnold Memorial Foundation)
800 Gervais St.
Columbia, SC   29201

Foundation type: Independent foundation.
Financial data (yr. ended 12/31/05): Assets,
$2,190,278 (M); expenditures, $624,518;
qualifying distributions, $565,501; giving activities
include $565,501 for 7 grants (high: $250,000;
low: $180).
Fields of interest: Higher education; Jewish
agencies & temples.
Limitations: Applications not accepted. Giving
primarily in SC. No grants to individuals.
Application information: Contributes only to
pre-selected organizations.
Officer: Norman J. Arnold, Mgr.
Trustee: John S. Rainey.
EIN: 576029371

8567
P. S. Bailey and Ouida C. Bailey
Foundation ✧
P.O. Box 494
Clinton, SC   29325

Established in SC.
Donors: Emily F. Bailey; Clinton Investment Co.
Foundation type: Independent foundation.
Financial data (yr. ended 12/31/05): Assets,
$16,402,461 (M); gifts received, $16,367;
expenditures, $850,399; qualifying distributions,
$725,467; giving activities include $721,000 for 7
grants (high: $525,000; low: $6,000).
Purpose and activities: Giving primarily for Christian
agencies and churches; some giving to medical
organizations.
Fields of interest: Human services; Christian
agencies & churches.
Limitations: Applications not accepted. Giving
primarily in SC.
Application information: Unsolicited requests for
funds not accepted.
Officer and Trustees:* Emily F. Bailey,* Chair.;
Bishop Alex D. Dickson; Rev. Charles H. Murphy.
EIN: 570813063

8568
William Barnet III Foundation Trust ✧
(also known as The Barnet Foundation Trust)
507 E. Saint Johns St.
Spartanburg, SC   29302

Established in 1986 in SC.
Donors: William Barnet & Son; William Barnet II.
Foundation type: Independent foundation.
Financial data (yr. ended 9/30/05): Assets,
$2,133,703 (M); gifts received, $3,000;
expenditures, $1,126,050; qualifying distributions,
$1,103,432; giving activities include $1,088,432
for 43 grants (high: $480,000; low: $100).
Purpose and activities: Giving to higher education,
cultural institutes, the arts and public and
community service organizations.
Fields of interest: Arts; Higher education;
Education; Health organizations, association;
Human services; Foundations (community);
Philanthropy/voluntarism.
Limitations: Applications not accepted. Giving
primarily in SC, with emphasis on Spartanburg. No
grants to individuals.
Application information: Contributes only to
pre-selected organizations.
Trustees: Valerie Barnet; William Barnet III; Vernett
Lamp; D. Byrd Miller III.
EIN: 576114255

8569
Mary Black Foundation, Inc.
349 E. Main St., Ste. 100
Spartanburg, SC   29302   (864) 573-9500
Contact: Philip B. Belcher, Pres.
FAX: (864) 573-5805; URL: http://
www.maryblackfoundation.org

Established in 1986 in SC; converted from the
proceeds from the sale of Mary Black Memorial
Hospital in 1996.
Foundation type: Independent foundation.
Financial data (yr. ended 6/30/06): Assets,
$79,670,115 (M); gifts received, $5,000;
expenditures, $4,310,312; qualifying distributions,
$5,730,080; giving activities include $2,689,878
for 61 grants (high: $319,798; low: $300), and
$3,585,781 for foundation-administered programs.

Purpose and activities: The foundation's mission is to improve the health and wellness of the people and communities of Spartanburg County, SC.

Fields of interest: Public health; Health care; Health organizations; public education.

Type of support: General/operating support; Continuing support; Program development; Seed money; Technical assistance; Program evaluation.

Limitations: Giving primarily in Spartanburg County, SC. No support for political organizations. No grants to individuals or for general fundraising solicitations.

Publications: Application guidelines; Annual report; Informational brochure (including application guidelines).

Application information: See foundation Web site for application guidelines and procedures. Application form required.

> *Initial approach:* Telephone call with program staff
> *Copies of proposal:* 1
> *Deadline(s):* Quarterly (Mar. 1, June 1, Sept. 1, and Dec. 1)
> *Board meeting date(s):* 3rd Tues. of Sept., Oct., Nov., Feb., Mar., Apr., May, June
> *Final notification:* Generally within 90 days

Officers and Trustees:* Marvin C. Woodson, Jr., Ph.D.*, Chair.; Karen H. Mitchell,* Vice-Chair.; Philip B. Belcher,* Pres.; Frederick D. Gibbs,* Treas.; Amy D. Herd,* Cont.; H. Walter Barre II; Sheila S. Breitweiser; Bernard E. Brooks; Robert H. Chapman III; Benjamin B. Dunlap, Ph.D.; T. Alexander Evins; John F. Renfro, Jr.; Doris H. Tidwell.

Number of staff: 4 full-time professional; 3 full-time support.

EIN: 570843135

Selected grants: The following grants were reported in 2005.

$297,000 to Palmetto Conservation Foundation, Columbia, SC. 2 grants: $250,000 (For Rails to Trails), $47,000 (For Bike Town Initiative).

$224,000 to Spartanburg County First Steps, Spartanburg, SC. For early education project.

$212,202 to University of South Carolina Research Foundation, Columbia, SC. For BASICSpaces.

$166,000 to Upstate Forever, Greenville, SC. For Upstate Forever's Office of Active Living in Spartanburg.

$110,500 to Partners for Active Living, Spartanburg, SC. For Active Living Program expansion.

$100,000 to Salvation Army of Spartanburg, Spartanburg, SC. For Salvation Army Fitness Trail.

$90,000 to Urban League of the Upstate, Greenville, SC. For parent university and early childhood development.

$73,376 to Spartanburg Nutrition Council, Spartanburg, SC. For active living through community gardens and public markets.

$71,348 to Spartanburg Science Center, Spartanburg, SC. For early childhood health and wellness development.

8570

Blue Cross and Blue Shield of South Carolina Foundation ◈

I-20 at Alpine Rd., Ste. AA270
Columbia, SC 29219-0001
Contact: M. Edward Sellers, Chair.

Donors: Blue Cross and Blue Shield of South Carolina; Companion Healthcare Corp.

Foundation type: Company-sponsored foundation.

Financial data (yr. ended 12/31/05): Assets, $44,414,326 (L); expenditures, $1,618,083;

qualifying distributions, $1,412,677; giving activities include $1,412,677 for 9 grants (high: $500,000; low: $50,000).

Purpose and activities: The foundation supports medical clinics and organizations involved with health.

Fields of interest: Health care, clinics/centers; Health care.

Limitations: Applications not accepted.

Application information: Contributes only to pre-selected organizations.

Officers: M. Edward Sellers, Chair.; Judith M. Davis, Secy.; Robert A. Leichtle, Treas.

Directors: Harry Easterling; James M. Hart; William R. Horton; George L. Johnson; Joseph Sullivan.

EIN: 223847938

8571

Drs. Bruce and Lee Foundation ▼

181 E. Evans St.
BTC Box 022
Florence, SC 29506 (843) 664-2870
Contact: Bradley Callicott, Exec. Dir.
FAX: (843) 664-2815; E-mail: blfound@bellsouth.net

Established in 1995 in SC; converted from the sale of the assets of Carolinas Hospital System to Quorum, Inc.

Foundation type: Independent foundation.

Financial data (yr. ended 12/31/05): Assets, $156,649,893 (M); gifts received, $400; expenditures, $7,580,931; qualifying distributions, $6,974,530; giving activities include $6,193,500 for 14 grants (high: $3,300,000; low: $6,000; average: $50,000–$200,000).

Purpose and activities: The foundation aims to advance the welfare of people in the Florence, SC, area, by providing economic support to organizations and programs which contribute to the area's medical, educational, and cultural resources.

Fields of interest: Arts; Education; Environment; Medical research; Human services.

Type of support: Continuing support; Capital campaigns; Building/renovation; Equipment; Endowments; Debt reduction; Emergency funds; Professorships; Seed money; Scholarship funds; Consulting services; Matching/challenge support.

Limitations: Giving primarily in the Florence, SC, area. No grants to individuals.

Publications: Application guidelines; Annual report (including application guidelines); Grants list; Occasional report.

Application information: Application form required.

> *Initial approach:* Telephone
> *Copies of proposal:* 1
> *Deadline(s):* None
> *Board meeting date(s):* 3rd Tues. monthly except in Dec.
> *Final notification:* Generally within 90 days

Officers and Trustees:* Frank B. Lee, Sr., M.D.*, Chair.; John M. Thomason, M.D.*, Vice-Chair.; Mark Buyck, Jr.,* Secy.; Bradley L. Callicott,* Exec. Dir.; Gordon B. Baker, Jr.; John L. Bruce; C. Edward Floyd, M.D.; Thomas C. Griffin; John W. McGinnis; Robert L. O'Hara; Haigh Porter; Henry Swink.

Number of staff: 2 full-time professional.

EIN: 570902483

Selected grants: The following grants were reported in 2005.

$5,150,000 to Francis Marion University Foundation, Florence, SC. 3 grants: $200,000, $3,300,000, $1,650,000

$590,000 to Florence, County of, Florence, SC. 2 grants: $90,000 (For University of South Carolina), $500,000.

$100,000 to Florence-Darlington Technical College Foundation, Florence, SC.

8572

The Byerly Foundation

P.O. Drawer 1925
Hartsville, SC 29551-1925 (843) 383-2400
Contact: Richard A. Puffer, Exec. Dir.
FAX: (843) 383-0661; E-mail: byerlyfdn@yahoo.com; URL: http://www.byerlyfoundation.org

Established in 1995 in SC; converted from the sale of local hospital.

Foundation type: Independent foundation.

Financial data (yr. ended 9/30/05): Assets, $25,235,451 (M); expenditures, $765,963; qualifying distributions, $385,610; giving activities include $385,610 for 17 grants (high: $134,000; low: $350).

Purpose and activities: The mission of the foundation is to improve the quality of life in Hartsville, SC.

Fields of interest: Education; Economic development; Community development.

Type of support: Curriculum development; General/operating support; Continuing support; Capital campaigns; Building/renovation; Equipment; Program development; Seed money; Technical assistance; Consulting services; Program evaluation; Matching/challenge support.

Limitations: Giving primarily in Hartsville, SC. No support for sectarian religious programs, or intermediate organizations. No grants to individuals, or for debt and existing obligations, lobbying or political campaigns, technical or specialized research, fundraising, teams or special events, advertising, or memorials.

Publications: Annual report; Grants list; Occasional report.

Application information: Refer to foundation Web site for application guidelines. Application form not required.

> *Initial approach:* Letter or telephone
> *Copies of proposal:* 1
> *Deadline(s):* None
> *Board meeting date(s):* Monthly, on the last Tues.
> *Final notification:* 2 months after deadline

Officers and Trustees:* Harris E. DeLoach, Jr.,* Chair.; Howard W. Tucker, Jr.,* Secy.; Vicki Arthur,* Treas.; Richard A. Puffer, Exec. Dir.; Tony Floyd; Lee S. Hicks; Ronnie Holley; Flossie Hopkins; David McFarland; Heather Norwood; Leroy Robinson; Maureen Thomas.

Number of staff: 1 part-time professional; 1 part-time support.

EIN: 570324909

Selected grants: The following grants were reported in 2005.

$134,000 to Hartsville High School, Hartsville, SC.

$25,000 to Black Creek Arts Council, Hartsville, SC.

$5,000 to Hartsville Downtown Development Association, Hartsville, SC.

$1,000 to Christmas in April, Hartsville, SC.

$1,000 to Coker College, Hartsville, SC.

8573
Betsy M. Campbell Foundation ✧
104 Broadus Ave.
Greenville, SC 29601

Established in 1997 in SC.
Foundation type: Independent foundation.
Financial data (yr. ended 12/31/05): Assets, $8,141,253 (M); expenditures, $531,421; qualifying distributions, $380,170; giving activities include $347,500 for 9 grants (high: $110,000; low: $5,000).
Purpose and activities: Giving primarily for higher education and youth programs, including homes for children; funding also for Episcopal churches.
Fields of interest: Higher education; Recreation, camps; Youth development; Protestant agencies & churches.
Limitations: Applications not accepted. Giving primarily in FL and SC. No grants to individuals.
Application information: Contributes only to pre-selected organizations.
Trustee: William W. Brown.
EIN: 586346237

8574
Robert S. Campbell Foundation ✧
104 Broadus Ave.
Greenville, SC 29601

Established in 1995 in SC.
Foundation type: Independent foundation.
Financial data (yr. ended 12/31/05): Assets, $15,155,005 (M); gifts received, $550,053; expenditures, $881,038; qualifying distributions, $656,268; giving activities include $608,100 for 6 grants (high: $289,000; low: $1,000).
Purpose and activities: Funding primarily for higher education; funding also for youth services.
Fields of interest: Higher education; Youth development; Youth, services.
Limitations: Applications not accepted. Giving primarily in SC, some funding also in NC. No grants to individuals.
Application information: Contributes only to pre-selected organizations.
Trustee: William W. Brown.
EIN: 571031564

8575
The Cassels Foundation ✧ ☆
P.O. Box 1691
Columbia, SC 29202

Established in SC.
Foundation type: Independent foundation.
Financial data (yr. ended 12/31/05): Assets, $9,143,420 (M); gifts received, $7,384,121; expenditures, $427,792; qualifying distributions, $422,738; giving activities include $419,250 for 6 grants (high: $125,000; low: $18,750).
Fields of interest: Higher education, college.
Type of support: General/operating support.
Limitations: Applications not accepted. Giving primarily in Lookout Mountain, GA. No grants to individuals.
Application information: Contributes only to pre-selected organizations.
Directors: Charlotte Cassels; W.T. Cassels, Jr.; W.T. Cassels III; Katherine Cassels Wolfe.
EIN: 571029022

8576
Wayland H. Cato, Jr. Foundation, Inc. ✧ ☆
5 Exchange St.
Charleston, SC 29401

Established in 1997 in SC.
Donors: Wayland H. Cato; Wayland H. Cato, Jr.
Foundation type: Independent foundation.
Financial data (yr. ended 12/31/05): Assets, $4,387,492 (M); gifts received, $567,840; expenditures, $722,341; qualifying distributions, $681,870; giving activities include $681,870 for 21 grants (high: $250,000; low: $100).
Purpose and activities: Giving primarily for education and the United Way.
Fields of interest: Arts; Higher education; Federated giving programs; General charitable giving.
Limitations: Applications not accepted. Giving primarily in SC. No grants to individuals.
Application information: Contributes only to pre-selected organizations.
Officers: Wayland H. Cato, Jr., Pres.; Clarice Cato Goodyear, Secy.-Treas.
Directors: Robert G. Berger; Robert W. Bradshaw, Jr.; John P.D. Cato; Thomas E. Cato; Lynn F. Chandler; John J. Kerr.
EIN: 570988435

8577
Central Carolina Community Foundation ✧
P.O. Box 11222
Columbia, SC 29211-1222 (803) 254-5601
Contact: Marjorie L. Gilbert, C.E.O.; For grant application: Joan Fail Hoffman, Dir., Grantmaking and Progs.
FAX: (803) 799-6663;
E-mail: info@yourfoundation.org; Grant application E-mail: joan@yourfoundation.org; URL: http://www.yourfoundation.org

Incorporated in 1984 in SC.
Foundation type: Community foundation.
Financial data (yr. ended 6/30/05): Assets, $67,184,327 (M); gifts received, $10,393,723; expenditures, $6,994,092; giving activities include $5,550,070 for 531 grants (high: $600,000; low: $50).
Purpose and activities: Giving primarily for the arts, education, health services, the disadvantaged, and youth; support also for community development, literacy programs, delinquency and child welfare, child development and family services, family planning, and recreation.
Fields of interest: Performing arts, music; Arts; Education, early childhood education; Child development, education; Elementary school/education; Adult education—literacy, basic skills & GED; Education, reading; Education; Environment; Reproductive health, family planning; Health care; Substance abuse, services; Health organizations, association; AIDS; Crime/violence prevention, youth; Crime/law enforcement; Nutrition; Housing/shelter, development; Recreation; Children/youth, services; Child development, services; Family services; Aging, centers/services; Homeless, human services; Human services; Community development; Government/public administration; Aging; Economically disadvantaged; Homeless.
Type of support: Management development/capacity building; Equipment; Program development; Scholarship funds; Technical assistance; Matching/challenge support.

Limitations: Giving limited to Calhoun, Clarendon, Fairfield, Kershaw, Lee, Lexington, Newberry, Orangeburg, Richland, Saluda, and Sumter counties, SC. No grants to individuals (except for designated awards or prizes), or for endowments, debt reduction, fundraising projects, medical research, publications, annual campaigns, annual appeals, routine operating expenses, or conference travel, underwriting, or sponsorship.
Publications: Annual report; Informational brochure; Newsletter.
Application information: Visit foundation Web site for application guidelines. Applicants must submit a Letter of intent in order to be invited to submit a full proposal. Faxed or e-mailed applications are not accepted. Application form required.
Initial approach: Telephone
Copies of proposal: 1
Deadline(s): Letter of intent: Feb. 15 and Aug. 15; full proposal: Apr. 15 and Oct. 15
Board meeting date(s): Quarterly
Final notification: Within 30 days for letter of intent determination; May and Nov. for full proposals
Officers and Trustees:* Samuel J. Tenenbaum,* Chair.; David C. Sojourner, Jr.,* Vice-Chair.; Marjorie L. Gilbert, C.E.O. and Pres.; Katharine M. Hubbard,* Secy.-Treas.; Russell L. Bauknight; J. Mac Bennett; Carolyn E. Brailsford; Wendy C. Brawley; Michael R. Brenan; Kathleen Fox Creech; Clarence Davis; Paul V. Fant; Frank A. Floyd, Jr.; John S. Goettee; Henry D. Goldberg; D. Christian Goodall; Elizabeth E. Griffith; Daisy W. Harman; R. Thomas Harrell; Robert R. Horger; Bruce W. Hughes; Chris Leevy Johnson; J. Thomas Johnson; D. Michael Kelly; John H. Lumpkin, Jr.; Sally T. McKay; Catherine R. Monetti; Ethan W. Nord; George W. Rogers; F. Xavier Starkes; Thomas E. Suggs; Joe E. Taylor, Jr.; J. Hagood Tighe; Susie H. VanHuss.
Number of staff: 4 full-time professional; 1 full-time support; 1 part-time support.
EIN: 570793960

8578
The Ceres Foundation, Inc. ✧
328 E. Bay St.
Charleston, SC 29401

Established in 1999 in SC.
Donor: Diane D. Terni.
Foundation type: Independent foundation.
Financial data (yr. ended 12/31/05): Assets, $31,414,344 (M); expenditures, $1,621,494; qualifying distributions, $1,237,256; giving activities include $1,094,000 for 100 grants (high: $250,000; low: $500).
Fields of interest: Museums (art); Elementary school/education; Higher education; Education; Environment; Health care, clinics/centers; Reproductive health, family planning; Children, services; International affairs.
Limitations: Applications not accepted. No grants to individuals.
Application information: Contributes only to pre-selected organizations.
Board meeting date(s): Varies
Officer: Diane D. Terni, Pres.
Trustees: Frank J. Gavel, Jr.; Stephen L. Gavel; Linda G. Webb.
Number of staff: 1 full-time support; 1 part-time support.
EIN: 582479387

Selected grants: The following grants were reported in 2003.

$337,500 to Roxbury Land Trust, Roxbury, CT. For general support.

$200,000 to Nature Conservancy, Columbia, SC. For Pine Island conservation.

$60,000 to International Medical Corps, Santa Monica, CA. For programs in Iraq and Afghanistan.

$60,000 to South Carolina Coastal Conservation League, Charleston, SC. 2 grants: $30,000 (For general support), $30,000 (For GIS Center).

$58,000 to Fennell Elementary School, Yemassee, SC. For Aquarium and Literacy Program.

$50,000 to Communities in Schools of South Carolina, Columbia, SC.

$40,000 to Charleston Museum, Charleston, SC. For Redcoats exhibit.

$30,000 to Audubon Society, National, Harleyville, SC. For environmental education for children.

$30,000 to Ducks Unlimited, Charleston, SC. For lowcountry initiative.

8579

Chapin Foundation of Myrtle Beach, South Carolina ✧

P.O. Box 70248
Myrtle Beach, SC 29572
Contact: Claire L. Sprouse, Exec. Dir.
FAX: (843) 449-3895;
E-mail: csprouse@chapinfoundation.org

Trust established in 1943 in SC.
Donor: S.B. Chapin†.
Foundation type: Independent foundation.
Financial data (yr. ended 7/31/05): Assets, $28,769,112 (M); expenditures, $1,533,412; qualifying distributions, $1,493,207; giving activities include $1,350,307 for 29 grants (high: $191,200; low: $10,000).
Purpose and activities: Support for regularly organized religious organizations and their local and foreign missions in Myrtle Beach, SC, that qualify; support also for public libraries, public hospitals, and YM-YWCAs within the city limits and a 1 mile radius.
Fields of interest: Libraries/library science; YM/YWCAs & YM/YWHAs; Christian agencies & churches.
Type of support: General/operating support; Continuing support; Capital campaigns; Building/renovation; Equipment; Emergency funds; Program development; Seed money; Internship funds; Scholarship funds; Technical assistance; Matching/challenge support.
Limitations: Giving limited to the Myrtle Beach, SC, area. No grants to individuals.
Publications: Application guidelines; Informational brochure.
Application information: Application form required.
Initial approach: Letter or proposal
Copies of proposal: 1
Deadline(s): Jan. 1, Apr. 1, July 1 and Oct. 1
Board meeting date(s): Quarterly
Final notification: 90 days
Officers and Directors:* Claude M. Epps,* Chair.; Harold D. Clardy,* Chair. Emeritus; Ruth T. Gore, V.P.; Lawton Benton, Secy.-Treas.; Claire Louise Sprouse, Exec. Dir.; Howell Vaught Bellamy, Jr.; Claire Chapin Cook; Harold Hartshorne, Jr.
Trustee: Bank of America, N.A.

Number of staff: 1 full-time professional.
EIN: 566039453
Selected grants: The following grants were reported in 2004.

$296,700 to First Presbyterian Church, Myrtle Beach, SC. For general support.

$204,750 to Chapin Memorial Library, Myrtle Beach, SC. For general support.

$124,500 to Ocean View Baptist Church, Myrtle Beach, SC. For general support.

$105,000 to First United Methodist Church, Myrtle Beach, SC. For general support.

$60,000 to Humane Society, Grand Strand, Myrtle Beach, SC. For general support.

$35,000 to Trinity Episcopal Church, Myrtle Beach, SC.

$25,000 to Chabad Lubavitch of Myrtle Beach, Myrtle Beach, SC. For general support.

$25,000 to Saint John the Baptist Greek Orthodox Church, Myrtle Beach, SC.

$24,500 to Cornerstone Church of God, Myrtle Beach, SC. For general support.

$20,000 to Cathedral Baptist Church of the Grand Strand, Myrtle Beach, SC. For general support.

8580

The Cline Foundation ✧

c/o N.Q. Cline, Sr.
215 Kilgore Cir.
Simpsonville, SC 29681-4835

Established in 1983 in SC.
Donors: The Cline Co., Inc.; N.Q. Cline, Sr.
Foundation type: Company-sponsored foundation.
Financial data (yr. ended 12/31/05): Assets, $93,203 (M); gifts received, $2,850; expenditures, $336,820; qualifying distributions, $336,520; giving activities include $334,920 for 32 grants (high: $198,870; low: $200).
Purpose and activities: The foundation supports camps and organizations involved with animal welfare.
Fields of interest: Animals/wildlife, preservation/protection; Recreation, camps; Boy scouts.
Type of support: Endowments; Employee matching gifts.
Limitations: Applications not accepted. Giving primarily in Greenville, SC. No grants to individuals.
Application information: Contributes only to pre-selected organizations.
Officers: Martha Cline, Pres.; David M. Cline, Secy.
EIN: 570752730
Selected grants: The following grants were reported in 2004.

$525,000 to Camden Military Academy, Camden, SC.

$135,000 to North Greenville College, Tigerville, SC.

$33,000 to Miracle Hill Ministries, Greenville, SC.

$15,000 to American Red Cross.

$10,000 to Limestone College, Gaffney, SC.

$5,000 to Saint Francis Hospice, Honolulu, HI.

$5,000 to Salvation Army. 2 grants: $4,000, $1,000

$5,000 to Walker Foundation, Spartanburg, SC.

8581

Coastal Community Foundation of South Carolina

(formerly The Community Foundation Serving Coastal South Carolina)
90 Mary St.
Charleston, SC 29403-6230 (843) 723-3635
Contact: For grants: Edie Blaskeslee, Prog. Off.; George C. Stevens, C.E.O.
FAX: (843) 577-3671;
E-mail: gstevens@ccfgives.org; Alternate E-mail: info@ccfgives.org; Grant application E-mail: EBlakeslee@ccfgives.org; URL: http://www.ccfgives.org

Incorporated in 1974 in SC.
Foundation type: Community foundation.
Financial data (yr. ended 6/30/06): Assets, $126,810,507 (M); gifts received, $9,540,873; expenditures, $10,369,392; giving activities include $9,409,368 for 1,313 grants, and $212,322 for 5 grants to individuals.
Purpose and activities: The Coastal Community Foundation is a public grantmaking foundation that fosters philanthropy for the lasting good of the community; giving primarily for education and human services.
Fields of interest: Arts; Child development, education; Education; Environment; Health care; Housing/shelter, development; Children/youth, services; Family services; Homeless, human services; Human services; Civil rights; Rural development; Community development; Minorities; Homeless.
Type of support: General/operating support; Capital campaigns; Building/renovation; Equipment; Land acquisition; Emergency funds; Program development; Publication; Seed money; Scholarship funds; Technical assistance; Consulting services.
Limitations: Giving in eight coastal counties of SC: Beaufort, Berkeley, Charleston, Colleton, Dorchester, Georgetown, Hampton and Jasper. No support for religious activities or private foundations. No grants to individuals (except for designated scholarship funds), or for endowments, deficit financing, dinners or other special one-time events, or generally for building funds.
Publications: Application guidelines; Biennial report; Financial statement; Grants list; Informational brochure (including application guidelines); Newsletter; Occasional report.
Application information: Visit foundation Web site for application forms and additional guidelines per grant type. The foundation's Grants Committee assesses all Open Grants Letters of Intent and then recommends a full proposal be submitted, that a full proposal be submitted with suggested changes, or that the applicant not submit a proposal because the request is not likely to be funded. Faxed or e-mailed Letters of Intent are not accepted. Application form required.
Initial approach: Letter of intent (not to exceed 2 pages excluding attachments)
Copies of proposal: 1
Deadline(s): June 2 for Open Grants Letter of Intent; varies for others
Board meeting date(s): 2nd Wed. of alternate months
Final notification: July 19 for Open Grants Letter of Intent determination; varies for others
Officers and Directors:* John F. Maybank,* Chair.; Burton R. Schools,* Chair.-Elect; George C. Stevens, C.E.O. and Pres.; Richard Hendry, V.P., Progs.; Brian Hussain, V.P., Finance; Paul S.

Saltzman,* Secy.-Treas.; Marguerite Archie-Hudson, Ph.D.; Brad S. Braddock; Kay K. Chitty; George R. Geer, Jr.; Barry D. Gumb; Genl. Walter Johnson; Paul M. Lynch; Elsa F. McDowell; Stephen McLeod-Bryant; George M. Milner; Yvonne T. Orr; Charles G. Rowland III; Richard Stewart; Joseph L. Tamsberg, Jr.; Peter E. Trees; Elizabeth Henry Warner; Fred S. Washington, Jr.; Anita Zucker.

Number of staff: 8 full-time professional; 1 part-time professional; 4 full-time support; 1 part-time support.

EIN: 237390313

Selected grants: The following grants were reported in 2006.

$30,000 to Ronald McDonald House Charities of Charleston, Charleston, SC.

$15,000 to Access Network, Hilton Head Island, SC.

$15,000 to Colleton County Arts Council, Walterboro, SC.

$15,000 to Friends of Caroline Hospice of Beaufort, Port Royal, SC.

$15,000 to Hope Haven of the Lowcountry, Beaufort, SC.

$15,000 to Literacy Volunteers of the Lowcountry, Hilton Head Island, SC.

$15,000 to Lowcountry Food Bank, Charleston, SC.

$15,000 to Second Helpings, Hilton Head Island, SC.

$12,000 to HELP of Beaufort, Beaufort, SC.

$10,000 to Latin American Council of South Carolina, Hilton Head, SC.

8582

Fred Collins Foundation ☆

1341 Rutherford Rd.
Greenville, SC   29609
Contact: Felicia C. Robbins, Tr.

Established in 1986 in SC.
Donor: Fred Collins†.
Foundation type: Independent foundation.
Financial data (yr. ended 12/31/04): Assets, $5,264,343 (M); gifts received, $934,323; expenditures, $503,354; qualifying distributions, $465,183; giving activities include $465,183 for 28 grants (high: $100,000; low: $500).
Fields of interest: Performing arts, orchestra (symphony); Elementary/secondary education; Higher education; Law school/education; Scholarships/financial aid; Crime/law enforcement; Food services; Human services; Foundations (public); Protestant agencies & churches.
Type of support: Scholarship funds.
Limitations: Giving primarily in the Greenville, SC, area. No grants to individuals.
Application information: Application form not required.

Initial approach: Letter
Copies of proposal: 1
Deadline(s): Dec. 15th
Final notification: 2nd week of Jan.

Trustee: Felicia C. Robbins.
EIN: 576107255
Selected grants: The following grants were reported in 2004.

$100,000 to Greenville Hospital System, Greenville, SC.

$100,000 to Salvation Army, Greenwood, SC.

$50,000 to Furman University, Greenville, SC.

$50,000 to Overbrook Baptist Church, Greenville, SC.

$10,000 to Erskine College, Due West, SC.

$10,000 to Greenville Technical College, Greenville, SC.

$10,000 to University of South Carolina, Columbia, SC.

$5,000 to Boys Home of the South, Belton, SC.

$2,000 to College of Charleston, Charleston, SC.

$1,000 to Connie Maxwell Childrens Home, Greenwood, SC.

8583

Community Foundation of Greenville, Inc.

27 Cleveland St., Ste. 101
Greenville, SC   29601   (864) 233-5925
Contact: Robert W. Morris, Pres.
FAX: (864) 242-9292; E-mail: info@cfgreenville.org; Additional Fax: (864) 242-9770; Additional E-mail: rmorris@cfgreenville.org; URL: http://www.cfgreenville.org

Established in 1956 in SC; incorporated in 1970.
Foundation type: Community foundation.
Financial data (yr. ended 12/31/05): Assets, $32,111,953 (M); gifts received, $5,887,854; expenditures, $5,658,466; giving activities include $4,698,494 for 1,199 grants (high: $500,000; low: $6); and $172,205 for 107 grants to individuals (high: $32,000; low: $25).
Purpose and activities: The foundation exists to enhance the quality of life of citizens of Greater Greenville, SC by linking philanthropic leadership, charitable resources and civic influence with needs and opportunities in the community.
Fields of interest: Arts; Education, early childhood education; Higher education; Education; Environment; Health care; Children/youth, services; Human services; Federated giving programs; Christian agencies & churches.
Type of support: Equipment; Emergency funds; Program development; Conferences/seminars; Seed money; Internship funds; Scholarship funds; Technical assistance; In-kind gifts; Matching/challenge support.
Limitations: Giving limited to greater Greenville, SC. No grants to individuals (except for scholarships), or for general operational expenses or existing debts; no multi-year grants.
Publications: Application guidelines; Annual report; Informational brochure; Newsletter; Program policy statement.
Application information: Visit Web site for application form and guidelines. Application form required.

Initial approach: Telephone or letter
Copies of proposal: 2
Deadline(s): Mar. 3
Board meeting date(s): Jan., Mar., May, July, Sept., and Nov.
Final notification: Varies

Officers and Directors:* J. Ernest Lathem,* Chair.; C. Dan Joyner,* Vice-Chair.; Robert W. Morris, Pres.; Pedrick Lowrey, Secy.; Doug Koske, Treas.; J. Tod Hyche, Legal Counsel; Wanda Adams; Steve Brandt; Mark Clary; Randy Fisher; Paul Goldsmith; Rudolph Gordon; Caine Halter; Sean Hartness; Lewis Haselwood, Jr.; Knox Haynsworth, Jr.; Gordon Herring; Fletcher Kirkland; Jeff Lawson; Martha Louise Lewis; Keith Marrero; Glenn Oxner; Louis Oxner; Susan Priester; C. Niles Ray; Cristina Schleifer; Jack Shaw; Susan Shi; James Terry.
Number of staff: 5 full-time professional.
EIN: 576019318
Selected grants: The following grants were reported in 2004.

$1,000,000 to Historic Greenville Foundation, Greenville, SC.

$353,000 to North Greenville College, Tigerville, SC. 2 grants: $120,000, $233,000

$250,000 to Greenville County School District, Fine Arts Center, Greenville, SC.

$50,000 to Buncombe Street United Methodist Church, Greenville, SC.

$25,000 to Hospice House of Greenville, Greenville, SC.

$18,000 to Furman University, Greenville, SC.

$16,000 to Trinity Lutheran Church, Greenville, SC.

$10,000 to Peace Center for the Performing Arts, Greenville, SC.

$10,000 to Thornwell Home and School for Children, Clinton, SC.

8584

Community Foundation of the Lowcountry

(formerly Hilton Head Island Foundation, Inc.)
4 Northridge Dr., Ste. A
P.O. Box 23019
Hilton Head Island, SC   29925-3019
(843) 681-9100
Contact: Denise K. Spencer, C.E.O.
FAX: (843) 681-9101;
E-mail: foundation@cf-lowcountry.org; Additional Address: Oakwood Professional Bldg., 15 Sam's Point Rd., Ste. 103, Beaufort, SC 29907, tel: (843) 525-1325, fax: (843) 522-3471; URL: http://www.cf-lowcountry.org

Established in 1983 in SC; converted to a community foundation in 1994 from the proceeds of the sale of Hilton Head Hospital to AMI.
Foundation type: Community foundation.
Financial data (yr. ended 6/30/05): Assets, $34,552,307 (L); gifts received, $1,904,907; expenditures, $3,591,632; giving activities include $2,329,462 for 244 grants, and $196,100 for 73 grants to individuals.
Purpose and activities: The foundation strengthens the community by connecting people, resources and needs.
Fields of interest: Arts; Education; Environment; Health care; Human services; Community development, neighborhood development.
Type of support: Management development/capacity building; Building/renovation; Equipment; Program development; Seed money; Curriculum development; Technical assistance; Consulting services; Program evaluation; Scholarships—to individuals; Matching/challenge support.
Limitations: Giving limited to Beaufort, Colleton, Hampton and Jasper counties, SC. No support for religious institutions. No grants to individuals (except for scholarships), or for capital campaigns.
Publications: Application guidelines; Annual report; Financial statement; Grants list; Informational brochure; Informational brochure (including application guidelines); Newsletter.
Application information: Visit foundation Web site for application forms and guidelines. Application form required.

Initial approach: Telephone or letter
Copies of proposal: 10
Deadline(s): Apr. 1, Aug. 1, and Dec. 1
Board meeting date(s): Jan., Mar., May, July, Sept., and Nov.
Final notification: Approximately 3 months after deadline

Officers and Trustees:* Joseph B. Fraser III,* Chair.; Robert P. Trask,* Vice-Chair.; Denise K.

Spencer, C.E.O. and Pres.; Peter Parrott, Jr., Treas.; Thomas C. Arnold; Mark L. Baker; Morris C. Campbell; Holly Cork; Eileen M. Fitzgerald; Beryl E. LaMotte; Bernard C. Moscovitz; Susan M. Nimmer; Peggy S. Parker; Anthony I. Poythress; Gail A. Quick; Jonathan G. Verity; Wade J. Webster.
Number of staff: 7 full-time professional; 2 part-time professional; 1 full-time support.
EIN: 570756987

8585
Daniel-Mickel Foundation
(formerly The Daniel Foundation of South Carolina)
P.O. Box 9278
Greenville, SC 29604-9278
Contact: Tamara Lawson, Asst.
E-mail: tamara@thelewiscompany.org; URL: http://www.daniel-mickel-foundation.org

Established in 1978 in SC as partial successor to The Daniel Foundation.
Donors: Daniel International Corp.; Charles E. Daniel†.
Foundation type: Independent foundation.
Financial data (yr. ended 12/31/05): Assets, $17,723,821 (M); expenditures, $899,288; qualifying distributions, $853,498; giving activities include $836,749 for 66 grants (high: $246,500; low: $55).
Purpose and activities: Giving primarily for higher education, art, and upstate SC community development.
Fields of interest: Performing arts, orchestra (symphony); Higher education; Hospitals (general); Human services.
Type of support: Continuing support; Management development/capacity building; Capital campaigns; Building/renovation; Equipment; Endowments; Program development; Seed money; Curriculum development; Program evaluation; Matching/challenge support.
Limitations: Giving primarily in SC. No grants to individuals, or for scholarships.
Publications: Program policy statement.
Application information: Application form available on foundation Web site. Application form not required.
  Initial approach: Detailed letter explaining program for which funds are requested
  Copies of proposal: 1
  Deadline(s): None
  Board meeting date(s): May, Aug., Nov., and Feb.
  Final notification: 4 months
Officers and Trustees:* Minor M. Shaw,* Chair. and Pres.; Buck A. Mickel,* V.P.; Charles Mickel,* V.P.; Ken Lewis,* Secy.-Treas.
EIN: 570673409
Selected grants: The following grants were reported in 2005.
$375,000 to Museum Association, Greenville, SC.
$246,500 to Greenville County Museum of Art, Greenville, SC.
$61,000 to United Way. 2 grants: $50,000, $11,000
$48,980 to Furman University, Greenville, SC.
$44,900 to Christ Church Episcopal School, Greenville, SC.
$25,000 to Converse College, Spartanburg, SC.
$5,000 to Peace Center for the Performing Arts, Greenville, SC.
$4,000 to Washington and Lee University, Lexington, VA.

$1,500 to University of North Carolina Press, Chapel Hill, NC.

8586
The Dintersmith-Hazard Foundation ✧
21 King St.
Charleston, SC 29401

Established in 2000 in MA.
Donor: Ted R. Dintersmith.
Foundation type: Independent foundation.
Financial data (yr. ended 12/31/04): Assets, $4,942,183 (M); expenditures, $367,423; qualifying distributions, $336,056; giving activities include $336,056 for grants.
Fields of interest: Arts; Education; Health care; Human services.
Limitations: Applications not accepted. No grants to individuals.
Application information: Contributes only to pre-selected organizations.
Trustees: Ted R. Dintersmith; Elizabeth S. Hazard.
EIN: 043538497

8587
First Citizens Foundation, Inc. ✧
1225 Lady St.
Columbia, SC 29201
Contact: Peter Bristow, V.P.

Established in 2000 in SC.
Donors: First Citizens Bancorporation of South Carolina, Inc.; First Citizens Bancorporation, Inc.
Foundation type: Company-sponsored foundation.
Financial data (yr. ended 12/31/04): Assets, $11,870,452 (M); gifts received, $885,015; expenditures, $675,870; qualifying distributions, $551,044; giving activities include $549,467 for 66 grants (high: $50,000; low: $800).
Purpose and activities: The foundation supports organizations involved with arts and culture, education, health, human services, children and youth, and community development.
Fields of interest: Arts; Elementary/secondary education; Higher education; Education; Zoos/zoological societies; Health care; Children/youth, services; Human services; Community development; Federated giving programs.
Type of support: Capital campaigns; Annual campaigns; Building/renovation; Endowments; Program development; Scholarship funds; Sponsorships.
Limitations: Giving primarily in SC, with emphasis on Columbia.
Application information: Application form required.
  Initial approach: Contact foundation for application form
  Deadline(s): None
Officers and Directors:* Jim Apple,* Pres.; Peter Bristow,* V.P.; Charles Cook, Secy.; Craig L. Nix, Treas.; Frank B. Holding; W.E. Sellars; Henry F. Sherril.
EIN: 571108547

8588
Foothills Community Foundation ✧
907 N. Main St.
P.O. Box 1228
Anderson, SC 29622 (864) 222-9096
Contact: Robert M. Rainey, Pres.

FAX: (864) 222-9727;
E-mail: rrainey@foothillsfoundation.org; Additional E-mail: ckibler@foothillsfoundation.org; URL: http://www.foothillscommunityfoundation.org

Established in 1999 in SC.
Foundation type: Community foundation.
Financial data (yr. ended 12/31/04): Assets, $9,412,421 (M); gifts received, $2,329,612; expenditures, $1,187,159; giving activities include $1,031,246 for grants.
Purpose and activities: The foundation seeks to retain and nurture the charitable wealth of the community for the perpetual benefit of all in the foundation's service area.
Fields of interest: Education, public education; Higher education, college; Education; Health care; Youth, services; Foundations (community); Federated giving programs.
Type of support: Continuing support; Capital campaigns; Scholarship funds.
Limitations: Giving primarily in Abbeville, Anderson, Oconee, and Pickens counties, SC.
Publications: Occasional report.
Application information: Visit foundation Web site for application information.
  Initial approach: Telephone
Officers and Directors:* Charles Dalton,* Vice-Chair.; Fred L. Foster,* 2nd Vice-Chair.; Robert M. Rainey, Pres.; Mary Anne Douglas Lake,* Secy.; John A. Miller, Jr.,* Treas.; Lamar Bailes; James T. Boseman; Irvin L. Couthen; John M. Greene; John Hamrick; F. Stevon Kay; Manning N. "Nick" Lomax; Jane W. Mudd; William B. Pickens; Cordes G. Seabrook, Jr.; Edward A. Spitz; David Gray Suggs; S. Smith Wham; Robert W. Wilkes.
Number of staff: 1 full-time professional; 1 part-time support.
EIN: 582453349

8589
The Fullerton Foundation, Inc.
515 W. Buford St.
Gaffney, SC 29341 (864) 489-6678
Contact: Walter E. Cavell, Exec. Dir.
Application address: P.O. Box 2208, Gaffney, SC 29342-2208;
E-mail: cjbonner@fullertonfoundation.org

Established in 1954 in NY.
Donor: Alma H. Fullerton†.
Foundation type: Independent foundation.
Financial data (yr. ended 11/30/05): Assets, $46,666,785 (M); expenditures, $2,831,213; qualifying distributions, $2,324,211; giving activities include $2,052,288 for 30 grants (high: $150,000; low: $1,500).
Purpose and activities: Giving primarily for health care and medicine; some support for higher education.
Fields of interest: Higher education; Health care.
Type of support: Program development; Seed money; Matching/challenge support.
Limitations: Giving primarily in NC and SC. No grants to individuals.
Publications: Application guidelines.
Application information: Application form not required.
  Initial approach: Letter requesting guidelines
  Deadline(s): Apr. 1, Aug. 1 and Dec. 1
  Board meeting date(s): 3 times yearly
  Final notification: After each meeting of the Board of Directors

Officers and Directors: * Charles F. Hamrick II,* Chair.; Wylie L. Hamrick,* Vice-Chair.; Lyman W. Hamrick,* Secy.; W. Carlisle Hamrick,* Treas.; Walter E. Cavell, Exec. Dir.; Helen T. Baden; Catherine H. Beattie; Jean H. Haas; A. Wardlaw Hamrick; Volina V. Lyons; Frances R. Ross; Elaine H. Shields.

Number of staff: 1 full-time professional; 1 part-time professional; 1 part-time support.

EIN: 570847444

Selected grants: The following grants were reported in 2005.

$214,236 to Duke University Medical Center, Durham, NC. 2 grants: $100,000 (To implement Patient-Centered Care for Healthcare Professionals), $114,236 (For community nutrition network initiative in the Carolinas).

$190,700 to University of South Carolina, Columbia, SC. 2 grants: $124,505 to School of Medicine (For physician training and biomedical research), $66,195 to School of Medicine (For innovations collaborative for family medicine educators in Carolinas).

$150,000 to Limestone College, Gaffney, SC. For construction of new Physical Education Center.

$125,525 to Medical University of South Carolina (MUSC), Charleston, SC. To elevate level of understanding about Parkinson's Disease in physicians, patients and families across South Carolina.

$110,380 to Senior Centers of Spartanburg County, Spartanburg, SC. For Care Connection, case management service for seniors in Spartanburg, Union and Cherokee Counties.

$110,000 to Carolinas Center for Hospice and End of Life Care, Cary, NC. For Interdisciplinary Education Specialty in End of Life Care.

$100,000 to Providence Hospital, Columbia, SC. To expand Healthy Learners Program into South Carolina counties of Allendale, Dillon and Greenwood.

$50,000 to Gardner-Webb University, Boiling Springs, NC. To equip and expand Athletic Training Program.

8590
Gibbs Charitable Foundation ✧

P.O. Box 1727
Spartanburg, SC 29304-1727

Established in 2002 in SC.

Donors: Jimmy I. Gibbs; Marsha H. Gibbs; Gibbs International, Inc.

Foundation type: Independent foundation.

Financial data (yr. ended 12/31/05): Assets, $21,227 (M); gifts received, $2,685,000; expenditures, $2,294,070; qualifying distributions, $2,293,261; giving activities include $2,293,261 for 53 grants (high: $500,000; low: $100).

Fields of interest: Elementary/secondary education; Higher education; Hospitals (general); Health organizations, association; Human services; Protestant agencies & churches.

Limitations: Applications not accepted. Giving primarily in SC. No grants to individuals.

Application information: Contributes only to pre-selected organizations.

Trustees: Allen O. Clark; Jimmy I. Gibbs; Marsha H. Gibbs; J. Brian Honneycutt; Joe Lesesne; Sidney H. Walker.

EIN: 571111450

8591
Wadley R. Glenn Foundation ✧

c/o W. Raoul Glenn
2041 Cleveland St. Extension
Greenville, SC 29607

Foundation type: Independent foundation.

Financial data (yr. ended 12/31/04): Assets, $13,117,711 (M); expenditures, $682,022; qualifying distributions, $640,000; giving activities include $640,000 for 3 grants (high: $425,000; low: $65,000).

Fields of interest: Higher education; Health care; Children/youth, services.

Limitations: Applications not accepted. Giving primarily in Greenville, SC. No grants to individuals.

Application information: Contributes only to pre-selected organizations.

Officer: W. Raoul Glenn, Jr., Chair.

Trustee: Wadley R. Glenn III.

EIN: 306016104

8592
The W. Hayne Hipp Foundation

135 S. Main St.
Greenville, SC 29601

Established in 1987 in SC.

Donor: W. Hayne Hipp.

Foundation type: Independent foundation.

Financial data (yr. ended 12/31/05): Assets, $13,595,526 (M); expenditures, $1,491,859; qualifying distributions, $1,448,150; giving activities include $1,431,713 for grants.

Purpose and activities: Giving primarily for the arts, education, health associations, social services, YMCAs, community development, and Methodist and Presbyterian churches.

Fields of interest: Arts; Secondary school/education; Higher education; Education; Health organizations, association; Human services; YM/YWCAs & YM/YWHAs; Community development; Foundations (community); Protestant agencies & churches.

Limitations: Applications not accepted. Giving limited to SC and VA. No grants to individuals.

Application information: Contributes only to pre-selected organizations.

Officers: W. Hayne Hipp, Pres.; Martha Williams, Secy.

EIN: 570861526

Selected grants: The following grants were reported in 2004.

$200,000 to Wofford College, Spartanburg, SC. 2 grants: $100,000 each

$100,000 to Mary Baldwin College, Staunton, VA.

$80,000 to Washington and Lee University, Lexington, VA.

$16,000 to Greenville County Museum of Art, Greenville, SC.

$10,000 to Bob Jones University Museum and Gallery, Greenville, SC.

$10,000 to Newberry College, Newberry, SC.

$10,000 to Warehouse Theater, Greenville, SC.

$9,925 to Peace Center for the Performing Arts, Greenville, SC. 2 grants: $7,500, $2,425

8593
Hopewell Foundation, Inc. ✧

P.O. Box 470
Rock Hill, SC 29731-6470

Established in 1985 in SC.

Foundation type: Independent foundation.

Financial data (yr. ended 2/28/06): Assets, $6,772,085 (M); expenditures, $325,775; qualifying distributions, $315,000; giving activities include $315,000 for 11 grants (high: $75,000; low: $10,000).

Purpose and activities: Giving primarily for higher and other education, human services, Christian organizations, as well as to Presbyterian churches and organizations, and to a United Methodist church.

Fields of interest: Higher education; Engineering school/education; Theological school/education; Education; Human services; Christian agencies & churches; Protestant agencies & churches.

Limitations: Applications not accepted. Giving primarily in Rock Hill, SC; some funding nationally. No grants to individuals.

Application information: Contributes only to pre-selected organizations.

Officers and Directors: * Frank S. Barnes, Jr.,* Pres.; E.L. Barnes,* Secy.-Treas.; John M. Barnes, Jr.; L.A. Barnes, Jr.; Robert L. Helmly.

EIN: 570792719

Selected grants: The following grants were reported in 2003.

$100,000 to Reformed Theological Seminary, Charlotte, NC.

$75,000 to Westminster Catawba Christian School, Rock Hill, SC.

$75,000 to York Technical College Foundation, Rock Hill, SC.

$45,000 to Westminster Presbyterian Church, Rock Hill, SC.

$25,000 to Fellowship of Christian Athletes, Kansas City, MO.

$25,000 to Jesus Video Project of South Carolina, Lancaster, SC.

$13,000 to Hospice and Community Care, Rock Hill, SC.

$5,000 to Clemson University Foundation, Clemson, SC.

8594
Dick Horne Foundation ✧ ☆

P.O. Box 306
Orangeburg, SC 29116
Application address: 1360 Russell St. S.E., Orangeburg, SC 29115, tel.: (803) 534-2096

Established in 1966 in SC.

Donor: Amelia S. Horne†.

Foundation type: Independent foundation.

Financial data (yr. ended 12/31/05): Assets, $6,267,372 (M); expenditures, $421,954; qualifying distributions, $365,519; giving activities include $365,519 for grants.

Purpose and activities: Scholarship awards for higher and vocational education for residents within the trading area customarily heretofore served by Horne Motors formerly of Orangeburg, SC and presently adding Calhoun Counties, based on need, character and ability; limited support for community affairs and social services.

Fields of interest: Arts; Elementary/secondary education; Government/public administration.

Type of support: General/operating support; Scholarships—to individuals.

Limitations: Giving primarily in the Orangeburg County, SC, area. No loans or program-related investments.

Application information: Application form required.

Initial approach: Letter
Deadline(s): None
Trustees: W. Louis Griffith; Buster Smith; Bernice W. Tribble.
Number of staff: 1 full-time professional.
EIN: 237015996

8595
Inman-Riverdale Foundation ◇
P.O. Box 207
Inman, SC 29349 (864) 472-2121

Incorporated in 1946 in SC.
Donors: Inman Mills; Chapman High School.
Foundation type: Company-sponsored foundation.
Financial data (yr. ended 11/30/04): Assets, $6,236,139 (M); expenditures, $551,508; qualifying distributions, $512,784; giving activities include $408,788 for 65 grants (high: $251,116; low: $50), and $47,648 for 12 grants to individuals (high: $8,867; low: $400).
Purpose and activities: The foundation supports organizations involved with higher education, health, recreation, children and youth, community development, and Protestantism.
Fields of interest: Higher education; Health care; Recreation; Children/youth, services; Community development; Federated giving programs; Protestant agencies & churches.
Type of support: General/operating support; Employee-related scholarships.
Limitations: Giving primarily in Enoree and Inman, SC.
Application information: Application form not required.
  Initial approach: Proposal
Officers and Trustees:* Robert H. Chapman III,* Chair.; Patricia H. Robbins, Secy.; John F. Renfro, Jr.,* Treas.; Norman H. Chapman; James C. Pace, Jr.
EIN: 576019736

8596
Eugene I. Kane Foundation, Inc. ◇
5 Neptune Ct.
Hilton Head Island, SC 29926
Contact: Mark A. Winters, Tr.
Application address: 2300 T St. N.E., Washington, DC 20002, tel.: (202) 388-6800, ext. 213; E-mail: mwinters@internationallimo.com

Established in 1998.
Donor: Eugene I. Kane‡.
Foundation type: Independent foundation.
Financial data (yr. ended 12/31/05): Assets, $695,526 (M); gifts received, $1,269,101; expenditures, $735,488; qualifying distributions, $735,488; giving activities include $726,500 for 11 grants (high: $500,000; low: $1,000).
Fields of interest: Higher education; Hospitals (general); Roman Catholic agencies & churches.
Type of support: Annual campaigns; Capital campaigns; Building/renovation; Program development; Fellowships; Scholarship funds.
Limitations: Applications not accepted. Giving limited to Washington, DC. No grants to individuals.
Publications: Annual report.
Application information: Contributes only to pre-selected organizations.

Officers and Trustees:* John G. Wharton,* Pres.; Dennis O. Kane,* V.P.; Mark W. Cavanaugh,* Secy.-Treas.
EIN: 522126118

8597
Liberty Corporation Foundation ◇
P.O. Box 502
Greenville, SC 29602 (864) 241-5496
Contact: Sophia G. Vergas, Secy.

Established in 1965 in SC.
Donor: The Liberty Corp.
Foundation type: Company-sponsored foundation.
Financial data (yr. ended 8/31/05): Assets, $116,918 (M); gifts received, $600,000; expenditures, $559,940; qualifying distributions, $557,862; giving activities include $557,862 for 86 + grants (high: $175,000).
Purpose and activities: The foundation supports Christian agencies and churches and organizations involved with arts and culture, education, health, and human services.
Fields of interest: Performing arts; Arts; Education; Health care; Youth, services; Human services; Federated giving programs; Christian agencies & churches; Religion.
Type of support: General/operating support.
Limitations: Giving primarily in SC. No grants to individuals.
Application information: Application form not required.
  Initial approach: Proposal
  Copies of proposal: 1
  Deadline(s): None
  Board meeting date(s): Feb., May, Aug., and Nov.
Officers and Directors:* W. Hayne Hipp,* Chair. and Pres.; Sophia G. Vergas, Secy.; Mark D. Wesson, Treas.; Martha G. Williams.
EIN: 570468195

8598
Lipscomb Family Foundation ◇
P.O. Box 61159
Columbia, SC 29260
Contact: Marshall L. Foster, Secy.
FAX: (803) 256-6039; E-mail: iff@bellsouth.net

Established in 1995 in SC.
Foundation type: Independent foundation.
Financial data (yr. ended 12/31/05): Assets, $15,069,098 (M); gifts received, $7,390; expenditures, $947,494; qualifying distributions, $786,911; giving activities include $732,497 for 85 grants (high: $65,000; low: $200).
Purpose and activities: Giving primarily for programs designed to encourage positive development of youth.
Fields of interest: Higher education, college; Higher education, university; Boys & girls clubs; Youth development; Community development; Protestant agencies & churches.
Limitations: Giving primarily in the midlands of SC, or in areas in which board members reside.
Application information: Application form required.
  Initial approach: Letter
  Board meeting date(s): Feb., June and Oct.
Officers and Trustees:* Guy F. Lipscomb, Jr.,* Pres.; Margaret F. Lipscomb,* V.P.; Marshall L. Foster,* Secy.; Georgia L. Cheek; George C. Fant; Louise L. Howell; Elizabeth L. Tracy.

Number of staff: 1 part-time professional.
EIN: 581368915

8599
Ellison S. & Noel P. McKissick Foundation ◇
(formerly Alice Manufacturing Company, Inc. Foundation)
P.O. Box 369
Easley, SC 29641

Established in 1983.
Donor: Alice Manufacturing Co., Inc.
Foundation type: Company-sponsored foundation.
Financial data (yr. ended 6/30/06): Assets, $6,029,812 (M); expenditures, $487,986; qualifying distributions, $443,278; giving activities include $443,278 for grants.
Purpose and activities: The foundation supports hospices and organizations involved with higher education.
Fields of interest: Higher education; Residential/custodial care, hospices.
Type of support: Scholarship funds; General/operating support.
Limitations: Applications not accepted. Giving primarily in SC. No grants to individuals.
Application information: Contributes only to pre-selected organizations.
Directors: Elizabeth M. Fauntleroy; Caroline McKissick; Ellison Smyth McKissick III.
EIN: 570739969

8600
Rose & Walter Montgomery Foundation ◇
P.O. Box 5565
Spartanburg, SC 29304 (864) 585-9213
Contact: Walter S. Montgomery, Jr., Tr.

Donors: Walter S. Montgomery‡; Rose C. Montgomery Trust A.
Foundation type: Independent foundation.
Financial data (yr. ended 12/31/05): Assets, $18,172,801 (M); expenditures, $1,515,525; qualifying distributions, $1,044,500; giving activities include $1,044,500 for 76 grants (high: $231,000; low: $250).
Purpose and activities: Giving primarily for the arts, social services, and Episcopal churches and organizations.
Fields of interest: Arts education; Performing arts, music; Arts; Higher education; Education; Environment, beautification programs; Environment; Animals/wildlife, preservation/protection; Health care; Human services; Federated giving programs; Protestant agencies & churches.
Limitations: Giving primarily in Spartanburg, SC, and Memphis, TN; some funding nationally. No grants to individuals.
Application information:
  Initial approach: Letter
  Deadline(s): None
Trustees: Rose M. Johnston; Walter S. Montgomery, Jr.
EIN: 570986535

8601
North American Rescue Products Foundation, Inc. ◇ ☆
481 Garlington Rd. Ste A
Greenville, SC 29615-4619

Established in 2005 in SC.
Donor: North American Rescue Products, Inc.
Foundation type: Independent foundation.
Financial data (yr. ended 12/31/05): Assets, $5,263 (M); gifts received, $480,000; expenditures, $474,923; qualifying distributions, $474,804; giving activities include $474,804 for 29 grants (high: $74,782; low: $100).
Fields of interest: Elementary/secondary education; Higher education; Christian agencies & churches.
Limitations: Applications not accepted.
Application information: Unsolicited requests for funds not accepted.
Officers: Robert A. Castellani, Pres.; Curtis W. Stodghill, Secy.-Treas.
EIN: 203128585

8602
Phifer/Johnson Foundation ◇
961 E. Main St.
Spartanburg, SC 29302

Established in 1993 in SC.
Foundation type: Independent foundation.
Financial data (yr. ended 12/31/05): Assets, $29,726,209 (M); expenditures, $1,720,071; qualifying distributions, $1,347,275; giving activities include $1,347,275 for 72 grants (high: $166,600; low: $200).
Purpose and activities: Giving primarily for education, particularly higher education, as well as to a day school, the arts, and Christian agencies and churches; support also for health care.
Fields of interest: Historic preservation/historical societies; Arts; Higher education; Education; Health care; Human services; Christian agencies & churches.
Limitations: Applications not accepted. Giving on a national basis, primarily in FL, NC, and SC. No grants to individuals.
Application information: Contributes only to pre-selected organizations.
Directors: George Dean Johnson, Jr.; George D. Johnson, III; Susan P. Johnson.
EIN: 576153679
Selected grants: The following grants were reported in 2003.
$145,689 to Converse College, Spartanburg, SC.
$31,000 to Spartanburg Day School, Spartanburg, SC.
$25,000 to Washington and Lee University, Lexington, VA.
$20,000 to Wofford College, Spartanburg, SC.
$5,000 to Arts Partnership of Greater Spartanburg, Spartanburg, SC.
$3,500 to Western Piedmont Community College, Morganton, NC.
$2,000 to Davidson College, Davidson, NC.
$1,000 to Music Foundation of Spartanburg, Spartanburg, SC.
$200 to Walker Foundation, Spartanburg, SC.
$100 to YMCA, Spartanburg Family Center, Spartanburg, SC.

8603
Post and Courier Foundation ◇
134 Columbus St.
Charleston, SC 29403-4800
Contact: J. Douglas Donehue, Admin.

Incorporated in 1951 in SC.
Donor: Evening Post Publishing Co.
Foundation type: Company-sponsored foundation.
Financial data (yr. ended 12/31/05): Assets, $8,745,122 (M); gifts received, $394,524; expenditures, $1,098,565; qualifying distributions, $1,046,845; giving activities include $1,046,845 for 82 grants (high: $80,000; low: $200).
Purpose and activities: The foundation supports organizations involved with arts and culture, education, the environment, health, law enforcement, and community development.
Fields of interest: Historic preservation/historical societies; Arts; Education, association; Environment, natural resources; Health care; Crime/law enforcement; Community development.
Type of support: Continuing support; Capital campaigns; Building/renovation; Program-related investments/loans; Employee-related scholarships.
Limitations: Giving primarily in Charleston, SC.
Application information: Application form not required.
  Initial approach: Proposal
  Deadline(s): None
  Board meeting date(s): As needed, usually twice annually
Officers: Rebecca Gilbreth Herres, Pres.; Ivan V. Anderson, Jr., Exec. V.P.; Pierre Manigault, V.P.; James W. Martin, Treas.; Susan Sanders, Exec. Dir.
Number of staff: 1 part-time professional.
EIN: 576020356
Selected grants: The following grants were reported in 2004.
$70,000 to Salvation Army, Greenwood, SC.
$55,000 to College of Charleston Foundation, Charleston, SC. 2 grants: $5,000, $50,000
$50,000 to Spoleto Festival USA, Charleston, SC.
$27,000 to American Sail Training Association, Newport, RI.
$25,000 to Carolina Youth Development Center, North Charleston, SC.
$25,000 to Lowcountry Open Land Trust, Charleston, SC.
$20,000 to Charleston Museum, Charleston, SC.
$20,000 to Friends of the Hunley, Summerville, SC.
$5,000 to National Trust for Historic Preservation, DC.

8604
The Premier Foundation ◇ ☆
116 N. Wynward Pointe Dr.
Salem, SC 29676

Established in 1998 in SC.
Donors: Gary Gentry; Premier Productions, Inc.; Carpenters Home Church; Premier Christian Crusies; Velocity Vending.
Foundation type: Independent foundation.
Financial data (yr. ended 6/30/06): Assets, $0 (M); gifts received, $539,087; expenditures, $564,819; qualifying distributions, $487,199; giving activities include $487,199 for grants.
Purpose and activities: Giving only to ministries directly associated with biblical teachings.
Fields of interest: Media, radio; Christian agencies & churches.

Limitations: Applications not accepted. Giving on a national basis. No grants to individuals.
Application information: Contributes only to pre-selected organizations.
Trustees: Debbie Gentry; Gary Gentry.
EIN: 562066166
Selected grants: The following grants were reported in 2005.
$65,237 to K-Love Radio/K L V M - FM, Sacramento, CA.
$56,572 to Event Ministries, Altamonte Springs, FL.
$26,836 to W C S G Radio, Grand Rapids, MI.
$13,898 to W M H K Radio, Columbia, SC.
$9,798 to K A M Y Radio, Lubbock, TX.
$6,332 to K C B I Radio, Arlington, TX.
$6,000 to W C Q R Radio, Gray, TN.
$2,982 to W I B I Radio, Carlinville, IL.
$2,250 to K R G N Radio, Amarillo, TX.
$1,750 to W A O Y Radio, Gulfport, MS.

8605
Callie & John Rainey Foundation ◇
402nd Blvd.
Anderson, SC 29621 (864) 222-0804
Contact: John S. Rainey, Chair.

Established in 1995 in SC.
Foundation type: Independent foundation.
Financial data (yr. ended 12/31/05): Assets, $7,604,773 (M); expenditures, $1,105,055; qualifying distributions, $936,508; giving activities include $880,328 for 63 grants (high: $250,000; low: $250).
Purpose and activities: Giving primarily for community development, particularly the arts; funding also for education and health organizations.
Fields of interest: Museums; Historical activities; Arts; Education; Botanical/horticulture/landscape services; Medical care, rehabilitation; Community development; Federated giving programs; Protestant agencies & churches.
Limitations: Giving primarily in SC. No grants to individuals.
Application information: Application form not required.
  Initial approach: Letter
  Deadline(s): Sept. 10
Officer and Trustees:* John S. Rainey,* Chair.; Mary R. Belser; Nancy R. Crowley; Robert M. Rainey.
EIN: 570970656
Selected grants: The following grants were reported in 2004.
$135,000 to Arts Partnership of Greater Spartanburg, Spartanburg, SC. 2 grants: $67,500 each
$60,000 to Greenville Associate Reformed Presbyterian Church, Greenville, SC.
$37,000 to Converse College, Spartanburg, SC.
$20,000 to Brookgreen Gardens, Murrells Inlet, SC.
$10,500 to Spartanburg Childrens Shelter, Spartanburg, SC.
$10,500 to United Way of Anderson County, Anderson, SC.
$7,500 to Anderson Free Clinic, Anderson, SC.
$7,200 to Governors School for Science and Math, Columbia, SC.
$2,500 to Saint Johns United Methodist Church, Anderson, SC.

8606

The Reams Foundation, Inc. ✧

216 Confederate Cir.
Charleston, SC 29407

Established in 1994 in IN.
Donor: Fred W. Reams.
Foundation type: Independent foundation.
Financial data (yr. ended 12/31/05): Assets,
$20,625,065 (M); expenditures, $1,127,284;
qualifying distributions, $826,332; giving activities
include $767,900 for 10 grants (high: $450,000;
low: $200).
Fields of interest: Hospitals (general); Health
organizations, association; Housing/shelter,
development; Human services; Foundations
(public).
Limitations: Applications not accepted. Giving
primarily in Columbus and Indianapolis, IN; some
funding nationally. No grants to individuals.
Application information: Contributes only to
pre-selected organizations.
Officers and Directors: * Fred W. Reams,* Pres.;
Karen A. Reams,* V.P.; Karen E. Saboe,* Secy.;
Kristen A. Carter; Kimberly A. Cole; Matthew D.
Reams.
EIN: 351933846

8607

The Roe Foundation

301 N. Main St., Ste. 1735
Greenville, SC 29601 (864) 242-5007
FAX: (864) 242-5014; E-mail: roefdn@aol.com;
Application address: c/o Shirley W. Roe, Chair., 415
Belmont Ave., Greenville, SC 29601

Incorporated in 1968 in SC.
Donor: Thomas A. Roe†.
Foundation type: Independent foundation.
Financial data (yr. ended 12/31/05): Assets,
$35,977,443 (M); expenditures, $1,738,859;
qualifying distributions, $1,461,328; giving
activities include $1,398,000 for 107 grants (high:
$80,000; low: $1,000).
Purpose and activities: Giving to public policy
research organizations which promote the free
market and limited government.
Fields of interest: Education; Public policy,
research.
Type of support: General/operating support;
Continuing support; Annual campaigns; Capital
campaigns; Building/renovation; Equipment; Land
acquisition; Program development; Conferences/
seminars; Publication; Seed money; Research;
Matching/challenge support.
Limitations: Giving on an international basis. No
grants to individuals; no loans.
Publications: Application guidelines.
Application information: Application form not
required.
 Initial approach: Letter
 Copies of proposal: 1
 Deadline(s): Oct. 31
 Board meeting date(s): Jan. or Feb.
 Final notification: 5 months after deadline
Officers and Trustees: * Shirley W. Roe,* Chair. and
Treas.; Edwin J. Feulner, Jr.,* Vice-Chair.; Carl O.
Helstrom; Tracie Sharp; Thomas A. Wilcox.
Number of staff: 1 full-time professional.
EIN: 237011541
Selected grants: The following grants were reported
in 2004.

$160,500 to Fidelity Investments Charitable Gift
 Fund, Boston, MA. For general operating support.
$115,000 to South Carolina Policy Council,
 Columbia, SC. For general operating support.
$75,000 to Heritage Foundation, DC. For general
 operating support.
$65,000 to State Policy Network, Richmond, CA. For
 general operating support.
$50,000 to Intercollegiate Studies Institute,
 Wilmington, DE. For general operating support.
$40,000 to Reason Foundation, Los Angeles, CA.
 For general operating support.
$25,000 to Buckeye Institute for Public Policy
 Solutions, Columbus, OH. For general operating
 support.
$25,000 to Miracle Hill Ministries, Greenville, SC.
 For general operating support.
$20,000 to Atlas Economic Research Foundation,
 Arlington, VA. For general operating support.
$20,000 to Goldwater Institute, Phoenix, AZ. For
 general operating support.

8608

ScanSource Charitable Foundation ✧

6 Logue Ct.
Greenville, SC 29615 (864) 288-2432
Contact: Joan Dilworth, Chair.
E-mail: joan.dilworth@scansource.com; URL: http://
www.scansource.org/

Established in 1998 in SC.
Donors: ScanSource, Inc.; Owings Family
Foundation.
Foundation type: Company-sponsored foundation.
Financial data (yr. ended 12/31/04): Assets,
$1,812,405 (M); gifts received, $808,877;
expenditures, $352,186; qualifying distributions,
$341,888; giving activities include $341,166 for 38
+ grants (high: $125,000).
Purpose and activities: The foundation supports
organizations involved with education and children.
Special emphasis is directed toward programs
designed to ensure that children receive the support
and education they need to grow up safe, happy, and
thriving.
Fields of interest: Education; Children, services.
Type of support: Program development;
Employee-related scholarships.
Limitations: Applications not accepted. Giving
primarily in areas of company operations, with some
emphasis on AZ, FL, GA, SC, TN, and WA. No grants
to individuals (except for employee-related
scholarships).
Application information: Contributes only to
pre-selected organizations.
 Board meeting date(s): 3rd Tue. of every month
Officer: Joan Dilworth, Chair.; Nicki Breon; Sherry
Brian; Kristy Laughter; Joe Leocadio; Cathy
Lundeen; Wendi McMinn; Kristin Robinson; Tony
Sorrentino; Larry Tallant; Bradley Wright.
EIN: 571002959
Selected grants: The following grants were reported
in 2004.

$125,000 to Greenville County School District,
 Greenville, SC.
$15,189 to Habitat for Humanity, Georgetown, SC.
$15,000 to Alliance for Quality Education,
 Greenville, SC.
$5,000 to Cary Center, Greenville, SC.
$4,600 to YMCA, Seneca, SC.
$3,415 to Beaver Ridge Elementary School,
 Norcross, GA.

$1,200 to YMCA of Greater Greenville, Greenville,
 SC.
$1,000 to American Red Cross, Greenville, SC.

8609

Security's Lending Hand Foundation ✧

204 E. Main St.
Spartanburg, SC 29306

Established in 1994 in SC.
Donor: Security Finance Corp.
Foundation type: Company-sponsored foundation.
Financial data (yr. ended 12/31/03): Assets,
$7,580 (M); gifts received, $468,500;
expenditures, $472,150; qualifying distributions,
$471,500; giving activities include $471,500 for 70
grants (high: $150,000; low: $1,000).
Purpose and activities: The foundation supports
hospitals and organizations involved with children
and youth services and religion.
Fields of interest: Hospitals (general); Hospitals
(specialty); Food banks; Food distribution, meals on
wheels; Boys & girls clubs; American Red Cross;
Salvation Army; YM/YWCAs & YM/YWHAs;
Children/youth, services; Children, services;
Residential/custodial care; Residential/custodial
care, hospices; Federated giving programs;
Christian agencies & churches; Protestant agencies
& churches; Roman Catholic agencies & churches;
Religion.
Limitations: Applications not accepted. Giving on a
national basis. No grants to individuals.
Application information: Contributes only to
pre-selected organizations.
Officers: Susan A. Bridges, Chair; Clarence H.
Edwards, Vice-Chair; A.R. Biggs, C.O.O.; A.G.
Williams, Secy.-Treas.
EIN: 571012986

8610

The Self Family Foundation ✧

(formerly The Self Foundation)
P.O. Box 1017
Greenwood, SC 29648-1017 (864) 941-4011
Contact: Frank J. Wideman III, Pres.
FAX: (864) 941-4091;
E-mail: info@selffoundation.org; Application tel.:
(864) 953-2441, e-mail:
application@selffoundation.org; URL: http://
www.selffoundation.org

Incorporated in 1942 in SC.
Donor: James C. Self†.
Foundation type: Independent foundation.
Financial data (yr. ended 12/31/05): Assets,
$34,558,288 (M); expenditures, $3,254,012;
qualifying distributions, $2,988,610; giving
activities include $2,557,074 for 37 grants (high:
$1,495,000; low: $500).
Purpose and activities: Primary interest is in health
care, (K-12) education, and early childhood
development. Support also for civic and community
service, activities for youth and the elderly, and
cultural and historical activities; grants mainly for
programs or special purposes.
Fields of interest: Arts; Education; Health care;
Children/youth, services; Aging, centers/services;
Community development, neighborhood
development; Aging.
Type of support: Equipment; Emergency funds;
Program development; Seed money; Technical

assistance; Consulting services; Matching/ challenge support.

Limitations: Giving limited to SC, with primary emphasis on Greenwood. No support for churches. No grants to individuals, or for endowment funds, land acquisition, operating budgets, continuing support, annual campaigns, deficit financing, publications, conferences, scholarships, fellowships, or research-related programs; no loans.

Publications: Application guidelines; Annual report (including application guidelines); Grants list; Program policy statement.

Application information: E-mail or telephone Prog. Off. prior to submitting proposal. See foundation Web site for application guidelines. Application form not required.

   Initial approach: Proposal (not exceeding 5 pages)
   Copies of proposal: 1
   Deadline(s): Submit proposal preferably in the month prior to board meetings; deadlines, 15th of Feb., May, Aug., and Nov.
   Board meeting date(s): 3rd week in Mar., June, Sept., and Dec.
   Final notification: 10 days after board meeting

Officers and Trustees:* Virginia Preston Self,* Chair.; W.M. Self,* Vice-Chair.; Frank J. Wideman III, Pres.; Sally E. Self, M.D.*, Secy.; J. William Harper, Treas.; Sid G. Johnston; Julian J. Nexsen, Jr.; J.C. Self III; Sam H. Tobert.

Number of staff: 2 full-time professional; 1 full-time support.

EIN: 570400594

Selected grants: The following grants were reported in 2005.

$250,000 to University of South Carolina, Moore School of Business, Columbia, SC. For Business Partnership Foundation.

$60,000 to Arts Council of Greenwood, Greenwood, SC. For annual support.

$50,000 to Greenwood School District No. 50, Greenwood, SC. For integration of Math Out of the Box curriculum.

$30,000 to United Way of Greenwood County, Greenwood, SC. For Neighborhood Development Office.

$25,000 to Museum, The, Greenwood, SC. For revitalization.

$10,000 to ETV Endowment of South Carolina, Columbia, SC.

$10,000 to Greenwood Community Theater, Greenwood, SC. For part-time staff position.

$10,000 to Promised Land Enrichment and Development Center, Greenwood, SC. For summer enrichment program.

$10,000 to Prout School, Wakefield, RI. For computer center.

8611
J. Marion Sims Foundation, Inc. ▼

P.O. Box 818
Lancaster, SC 29721-0868 (803) 286-8772
Contact: James T. Morton, Pres.
FAX: (803) 286-8774; E-mail: grants@jmsims.org;
URL: http://www.jmsims.org

Established in 1994 in SC; converted from sale of Elliott White Springs Memorial Hospital, Inc.

Foundation type: Independent foundation.

Financial data (yr. ended 9/30/05): Assets, $76,900,702 (M); expenditures, $2,997,706; qualifying distributions, $3,938,961; giving activities include $3,471,255 for 149 grants (high: $448,485; low: $157).

Purpose and activities: The foundation supports programs and projects of prevention and education that enhance health and wellness in Lancaster County, SC, and the communities of Great Falls and Fort Lawn.

Fields of interest: Education; Health care.

Type of support: General/operating support; Continuing support; Capital campaigns; Building/ renovation; Equipment; Program development; Seed money; Research; Matching/challenge support.

Limitations: Giving primarily in Lancaster County, Great Falls, and Fort Lawn, SC. No support for political purposes, indigent care, or programs or projects generally considered to be the role of government. No grants to individuals, or for endowments, event tickets, projects of organizations that primarily benefit their own members or adherents, indirect costs (including payments of a percentage of a grant to a local organization's national affiliate), or to retire accumulated debt; no loans.

Publications: Application guidelines; Annual report.

Application information: Application forms and guidelines available on foundation Web site. The foundation will acknowledge receipt of an application by telephone or letter. Application form required.

   Initial approach: Letter or telephone
   Copies of proposal: 1
   Deadline(s): Apr. 15 and Oct. 15
   Board meeting date(s): Monthly (excluding July and Dec.)
   Final notification: Aug. 31 and Feb. 28

Officers and Trustees:* George W. Flanders,* Chair.; Dexter L. Cook, Jr., M.D.*, Vice-Chair.; James T. Morton, Pres.; E. Brown Crenshaw, Jr., V.P., Fin. and Admin.; Coreen B. Khoury,* Secy.; Bruce A. Brumfield,* Treas.; David R. Blackwell; Phyllis B. Bunkley; Miriam M. Boucher; Malcolm Edwards, M.D.; Polly C. Jackson; Stanley D. Johnson; Pamela Y. Temple.

Number of staff: 4 full-time professional; 1 full-time support.

EIN: 570355295

Selected grants: The following grants were reported in 2005.

$448,485 to Lancaster County Council on Aging, Lancaster, SC. For Lancaster Senior Citizens Center Project.

$214,899 to Fort Lawn Community Center, Fort Lawn, SC. For citizenship, workplace, health, and family literacy programs.

$206,540 to Communities in Schools of Lancaster County, Lancaster, SC. For Youthbuild program.

$190,355 to Learning Institute for Tomorrow, Lancaster, SC.

$183,440 to Childrens Council Healthy Mothers/ Healthy Babies, Lancaster, SC. For Skills for Success.

$110,281 to Lancaster Fatherhood Project, Lancaster, SC. For Lancaster and Great Falls Fatherhood Engagement Project.

$82,955 to University of South Carolina, Lancaster, SC. For Project ACCESS, health enhancement program for low-income citizens.

$77,480 to University of South Carolina, School of Medicine, Columbia, SC. For Improving Health Literacy of Health Consumers in Southern Lancaster County.

$39,440 to Multicultural Information Center, Lancaster, SC. For Empowering our Future Today.

$475 to Chester County School District, Chester, SC.

8612
J. E. Sirrine Textile Foundation, Inc. ✧ ☆

c/o Trustees
P.O. Box 929
Greer, SC 29652

Foundation type: Independent foundation.

Financial data (yr. ended 6/30/05): Assets, $3,005,637 (M); expenditures, $3,379,780; qualifying distributions, $6,678,191; giving activities include $3,335,000 for 2 grants (high: $2,800,000; low: $535,000).

Purpose and activities: Support only for textile education, training, and research.

Fields of interest: Higher education, university.

Type of support: Research.

Limitations: Giving primarily in SC. No grants to individuals.

Application information: Application form not required.

   Deadline(s): None

Trustees: Robert H. Chapman III; Wylie L. Hamrick; Lester A. Hudson; Mark B. Kent; Robert C. Lewis; E. Smyth McKissick III; W. Matthew Self.

EIN: 576025551

8613
J. M. Smith Foundation ✧

101 W. St. John St., Ste. 305
Spartanburg, SC 29306

Established in 1996 in SC.

Donor: J M Smith Corp.

Foundation type: Company-sponsored foundation.

Financial data (yr. ended 2/28/05): Assets, $699,981 (M); gifts received, $1,168,176; expenditures, $876,074; qualifying distributions, $872,465; giving activities include $871,038 for 280 grants (high: $38,700; low: $200).

Purpose and activities: The foundation supports Christian agencies and churches and organizations involved with education, health, human services, and children and youth services.

Fields of interest: Higher education; Education; Health care; Children/youth, services; Human services; Federated giving programs; Christian agencies & churches; Protestant agencies & churches.

Limitations: Applications not accepted. Giving on a national basis, with emphasis on NC and SC. No grants to individuals.

Application information: Contributes only to pre-selected organizations.

Officers: Kenneth R. Couch, Pres.; Tammy Devine, Secy.; James C. Wilson, Jr., Treas.

Directors: Henry D. Smith; Russ Weber.

EIN: 571046595

Selected grants: The following grants were reported in 2004.

$42,200 to Boiling Springs First Baptist Church, Boiling Springs, SC. For unrestricted support.

$29,981 to United Way of the Piedmont, Spartanburg, SC. For unrestricted support.

$24,600 to Mobile Meals of Spartanburg County, Spartanburg, SC. For unrestricted support.

$18,500 to Arts Partnership of Greater Spartanburg, Spartanburg, SC. For unrestricted support.

$18,400 to First Baptist Church, Spartanburg, SC. For unrestricted support.

$18,200 to First Presbyterian Church, Spartanburg, SC. For unrestricted support.

$13,000 to Carolina Piedmont Foundation, Spartanburg, SC. For unrestricted support.

$10,000 to YMCA, Spartanburg Family Center, Spartanburg, SC. For unrestricted support.

$5,400 to Spartanburg Methodist College, Spartanburg, SC. For unrestricted support.

$5,000 to Habitat for Humanity of Spartanburg, Spartanburg, SC. For unrestricted support.

8614
Sonoco Foundation ◇
1 N. 2nd St., M.S. A09
Hartsville, SC 29550
Contact: Joyce Beasley

Established in 1983 in SC.
Donor: Sonoco Products Co.
Foundation type: Company-sponsored foundation.
Financial data (yr. ended 12/31/04): Assets, $447,715 (M); gifts received, $1,863,000; expenditures, $1,467,462; qualifying distributions, $1,467,462; giving activities include $1,467,462 for 248 grants (high: $250,000; low: $25).
Purpose and activities: The foundation supports organizations involved with arts and culture, education, health, children and youth, human services, community development, and religion.
Fields of interest: Arts; Higher education; Education; Health care; Children/youth, services; Human services; Community development; Religion.
Type of support: General/operating support; Capital campaigns; Employee matching gifts.
Limitations: Giving primarily in areas of company operations.
Publications: Application guidelines.
Application information: Application form not required.
Initial approach: Contact foundation for application information
Copies of proposal: 1
Deadline(s): None
Board meeting date(s): Quarterly, and as needed
Trustees: C.W. Coker; C.J. Hupfer.
Number of staff: 1 part-time professional.
EIN: 570752950
Selected grants: The following grants were reported in 2004.
$250,000 to Thomas Hart Academy, Hartsville, SC.
$200,000 to University of South Carolina Educational Foundation, Columbia, SC.
$100,000 to Coker College, Hartsville, SC.
$79,000 to United Way of Hartsville, Hartsville, SC.
$60,000 to Boy Scouts of America, Pee Dee Area Council, Florence, SC.
$33,000 to Forum for Corporate Conscience, Charlotte, NC.
$25,000 to Chamber of Commerce, Hartsville, Hartsville, SC. For Hartsville Vista Development Committee.
$25,000 to Florence-Darlington Technical College, Florence, SC.
$20,000 to YMCA, Darlington Family, Darlington, SC.
$15,000 to YMCA of Hartsville, Hartsville, SC.

8615
The South Financial Group Foundation ◇
(formerly Carolina First Foundation)
151 Corley Mill Rd.
Lexington, SC 29072 (803) 996-7406
Contact: G. Bruce Thomas, Exec. Dir.
E-mail: bruce.thomas@carolinafirst.com

Established in 1999 in SC.
Donor: Carolina First Bank.
Foundation type: Company-sponsored foundation.
Financial data (yr. ended 12/31/04): Assets, $10,494,129 (M); expenditures, $814,480; qualifying distributions, $719,977; giving activities include $667,182 for 43 grants (high: $100,000; low: $2,000), and $1,285,000 for 4 foundation-administered programs.
Purpose and activities: The foundation supports organizations involved with arts and culture, education, health, human services, and community development.
Fields of interest: Museums (art); Performing arts centers; Performing arts, orchestra (symphony); Arts; Higher education; Business school/education; Health care; Children/youth, services; Human services; Community development; Federated giving programs.
Type of support: Capital campaigns; Building/renovation; Program development.
Limitations: Giving primarily in areas of company operations in FL, NC, and SC. No support for fraternal, social, labor, or veterans' organizations or religious organizations. No grants to individuals, or for general operating support, educational product development, single-discipline curricula unrelated to comprehensive school reform, charitable dinners, memorials, or recreation.
Application information: Application form required.
Initial approach: Contact foundation for application form
Deadline(s): Quarterly
Officer and Directors:* Bruce Thomas, Exec. Dir.; William Hummers; Elizabeth Stall; Mack Whittle.
EIN: 571077098

8616
The Spartanburg County Foundation
424 E. Kennedy St.
Spartanburg, SC 29302 (864) 582-0138
Contact: John H. Dargan, Pres.; For grant applications: Mary L. Thomas, V.P., Progs.
FAX: (864) 573-5378; *E-mail:* info@spcf.org;
URL: http://www.spcf.org

Incorporated in 1943 in SC.
Foundation type: Community foundation.
Financial data (yr. ended 12/31/05): Assets, $77,436,050 (M); gifts received, $5,099,082; expenditures, $5,926,022; giving activities include $3,744,334 for 362+ grants.
Purpose and activities: The foundation seeks to provide for the mental, moral, intellectual and physical improvement, assistance and relief of the inhabitants of Spartanburg County. Primary areas of interest include local projects in higher and other education, community development, recreation, and health.
Fields of interest: Humanities; Arts; Higher education; Adult/continuing education; Education; Health care; Health organizations, association; Recreation; Children/youth, services; Human services; Community development.
Type of support: Continuing support; Building/renovation; Equipment; Emergency funds; Conferences/seminars; Seed money; Curriculum development; Scholarship funds; Consulting services; Employee-related scholarships; Scholarships—to individuals; In-kind gifts; Matching/challenge support.
Limitations: Giving limited to the Spartanburg County, SC, area. No support for religious

organizations for sectarian purposes. No grants to individuals (except designated scholarship funds), or for operating budgets, annual campaigns, deficit financing, land acquisition, film projects, publication of books or reports, or endowment funds; no loans.
Publications: Application guidelines; Annual report (including application guidelines); Biennial report; Informational brochure; Newsletter.
Application information: Visit foundation Web site for the Project Budget Form and application guidelines. The Grants Review Comm. of the foundation will review each letter of inquiry and extend an invitation to selected organizations to develop the proposed idea into a full request for funding. Application form required.
Initial approach: Submit letter of inquiry (no longer than 2 pages) and Project Budget Form
Copies of proposal: 1
Deadline(s): Jan. 3, May 18, and Aug. 9
Board meeting date(s): Monthly
Final notification: Following board meetings in Mar., Sept., and Dec.
Officers and Trustees:* John Harrill, Jr.,* Chair.; D. Chapman Johnston, Jr.,* Vice-Chair.; John B.H. Dargan, Pres.; Mary L. Thomas, V.P., Progs.; H. Walter "Wally" Barre,* Secy.; Michael DePetris, C.F.O.; Sally D. Foster,* Treas.; Jennifer C. Evins; Thomas E. Hannah; Rev. Dr. Clay H. Turner.
Number of staff: 7 full-time professional.
EIN: 570351398

8617
The Springs Close Foundation, Inc.
(formerly Springs Foundation, Inc.)
1826 Second Baxter Crossing
Fort Mill, SC 29708 (803) 548-2002
Contact: Angela H. McCrae, Exec. Dir.
FAX: (803) 548-1797; *URL:* http://www.thespringsclosefoundation.org

Incorporated in 1942 in DE.
Donors: Elliott W. Springs†; Anne Springs Close; Frances Ley Springs†; members of the Springs and Close families.
Foundation type: Independent foundation.
Financial data (yr. ended 12/31/05): Assets, $41,359,032 (M); gifts received, $1,500; expenditures, $3,575,626; qualifying distributions, $3,206,810; giving activities include $2,928,430 for 100 grants.
Purpose and activities: Support largely for recreation and education, including public schools and student loans (for students living in Lancaster County, Chester, and Fort Mill, SC); support also for community services, health care, and small, rural Christian churches.
Fields of interest: Education, early childhood education; Health care; Family services; Aging, centers/services; Community development; Christian agencies & churches; Economically disadvantaged.
Type of support: General/operating support; Annual campaigns; Capital campaigns; Building/renovation; Equipment; Endowments; Program development; Seed money; Matching/challenge support; Student loans—to individuals.
Limitations: Giving limited to Lancaster County and the townships of Fort Mill and Chester, SC. No grants to individuals (except for student loans), or for travel expenses.
Publications: Application guidelines; Annual report; Annual report (including application guidelines).

Application information: Application form and guidelines available on foundation Web site. Application form required.

Initial approach: Telephone or brief letter
Copies of proposal: 1
Deadline(s): Mar. 15 and Oct. 1
Board meeting date(s): Apr. and Nov.
Final notification: 3 months

Officers and Directors:* Anne Springs Close,* Chair.; William G. Taylor,* Secy.-Treas.; Angela H. McCrae, Exec. Dir.; Crandall Close Bowles; James Bradley; Charles A. Bundy; Derick S. Close; Elliott Springs Close; Frances A. Close; H.W. Close, Jr.; Katherine Anne Close, M.D.; M. Scott Close; James N. Epps, Jr., Ed.D.; Dehler Hart; Robert L. Holcombe, Jr.; Tony E. Pope.

Number of staff: 1 full-time professional; 2 part-time professional; 2 full-time support.

EIN: 570426344

Selected grants: The following grants were reported in 2005.

$525,000 to Leroy Springs and Company, Fort Mill, SC. For operating support.

$134,265 to Catawba Care Coalition, Rock Hill, SC. For expansion program.

$125,000 to Boys and Girls Clubs of York County, York, SC. For relocation of Fort Mill Club.

$81,000 to Childrens Attention Home, Rock Hill, SC. 2 grants: $50,000 (For capital campaign), $31,000 (For supplies for charter school).

$80,000 to Keystone Substance Abuse Services, Rock Hill, SC. For adolescent outreach program.

$51,474 to Lancaster County School District, Lancaster, SC. For homework centers for five middle schools and Lancaster High School.

$50,000 to Lancaster County Partners for Youth, Lancaster, SC. For GEAR UP program.

$36,400 to Anne Springs Close Greenway, Fort Mill, SC.

$25,000 to York County Disabilities and Special Needs Board, Rock Hill, SC. For renovations.

8618
TSC Foundation, Inc. ✧
104 E. Springs St.
Lancaster, SC   29720-2159

Established in 2001 in SC.
Donor: Springs Industries, Inc.
Foundation type: Independent foundation.
Financial data (yr. ended 12/31/05): Assets, $769,117 (M); gifts received, $2,139,900; expenditures, $2,867,015; qualifying distributions, $2,867,015; giving activities include $2,865,429 for 367 grants (high: $100,000; low: $25).
Purpose and activities: Giving primarily to public and community foundations, health associations and medical research, particularly for Lou Gehrig's disease and juvenile diabetes, social services, farmworker legal services, Episcopal churches, and a women's shelter; funding also for children's services, education, and the arts.
Fields of interest: Arts; Elementary school/education; Higher education; Animals/wildlife; Health organizations, association; Medical research, institute; Nerve, muscle & bone research; Diabetes research; Legal services; Food banks; Boy scouts; Human services; American Red Cross; Children, services; Residential/custodial care, hospices; Women, centers/services; Foundations (public); Foundations (community); Protestant agencies & churches.

Limitations: Applications not accepted. Giving primarily in NC and SC. No grants to individuals.
Application information: Contributes only to pre-selected organizations.
Officers: William Taylor, Pres.; Harry Emerson, V.P. and Secy.; Peyton Worley, V.P. and Treas.
EIN: 571124837
Selected grants: The following grants were reported in 2005.
$100,000 to Holy Cross Faith Memorial Episcopal Church, Pawleys Island, SC.
$75,000 to Johns Hopkins University, Baltimore, MD.
$75,000 to Social Justice Fund Northwest, Seattle, WA.
$60,000 to Catholic Medical Mission Board, New York, NY.
$60,000 to Womens Shelter, Columbia, SC.
$50,000 to Ability Beyond Disability, Bethel, CT.
$50,000 to South Carolina Environmental Law Project, Pawleys Island, SC.
$23,500 to Tierra Learning Center, Leavenworth, WA.
$14,200 to Salesian Sisters, Haledon, NJ.
$10,000 to Success by Six of York County, York, SC.

8619
Waccamaw Community Foundation ✧ ☆
507 21st Ave. N.
Myrtle Beach, SC   29577   (843) 916-4483
FAX: (843) 916-8003;
E-mail: jkresken-wcf@sc.rr.com; URL: http://www.waccamawcf.org

Established in 1997 in SC as an affiliate of the Foundation For The Carolinas; became an independent community foundation in 1999.
Foundation type: Community foundation.
Financial data (yr. ended 12/31/03): Assets, $3,857,098 (M); gifts received, $1,244,615; expenditures, $632,089; giving activities include $459,906 for 152 grants (high: $50,000; low: $100).
Purpose and activities: The foundation uses distributions from various funds to award grants to many of the humanitarian, educational and cultural organizations in the community.
Fields of interest: Arts; Education; Environment; Animal welfare; Community development; Children.
Type of support: Scholarship funds.
Limitations: Giving limited to SC.
Publications: Newsletter.
Application information: The foundation is currently not accepting applications while it reevaluates its grant process. See Web site for additional application information and guidelines. Application form required.
Deadline(s): May 5 for Allan Blum Memorial Scholarship; Mar. 31 for Boone Foundation Scholarship Awards
Final notification: June 1 for Boone Foundation Scholarship Awards
Officers and Board Members:* Michael C. Gerald,* Chair.; James J. Johnson,* Vice-Chair.; Thomas C. Stanley,* Secy.; J. Robert Calliham,* Treas.; Helen Andrews; G. David Bishop; James P. Creel; Eric B. Ficken; Laura Jackson Hoy; R.M. Lindsay III; Harold C. Stowe; Gary Wortel.
EIN: 562121992

8620
Wardle Family Foundation ✧
710 Bluefish Rd.
Fripp Island, SC   29920

Established in 1987 in PA.
Donor: Robert V. Wardle.
Foundation type: Independent foundation.
Financial data (yr. ended 12/31/03): Assets, $13,080,541 (M); expenditures, $699,540; qualifying distributions, $592,898; giving activities include $537,000 for grants.
Purpose and activities: Giving primarily for the arts and education; support also for health and human services.
Fields of interest: Arts; Higher education; Human services; YM/YWCAs & YM/YWHAs; Children/youth, services.
Limitations: Applications not accepted. Giving on a national basis. No grants to individuals.
Application information: Contributes only to pre-selected organizations.
Officers and Trustees:* William G. Wardle,* Chair. and Secy.; Corinne G. Wardle,* Vice-Chair.; Megan K. Neary; Douglas G. Wardle; Robert B. Wardle.
EIN: 256290322
Selected grants: The following grants were reported in 2004.
$175,000 to YMCA of Beaufort, Beaufort, SC. For capital campaign.
$129,986 to Saint Peters Catholic Church, Beaufort, SC. For capital campaign.
$40,000 to United Way of Beaufort County, Beaufort, SC. For general support.
$30,000 to United Way, Thomas Jefferson Area, Charlottesville, VA. For general support.
$15,000 to Our Lady of Grace School, Pittsburgh, PA. For computer equipment and library books.
$10,000 to Citizens Opposed To Domestic Abuse, Beaufort, SC. For general support.
$10,000 to New Kensington Summer Youth Programs, Pittsburgh, PA. For general support.
$10,000 to Scholarship America, Saint Peter, MN. For general support.
$10,000 to Waterlines, Santa Fe, NM. For general support.
$5,000 to Shelter for Help in Emergency, Charlottesville, VA. For general support.

8621
Youths' Friends Association, Inc.
P.O. Box 5387
Hilton Head Island, SC   29938
Contact: Walter J. Graver, Secy.-Treas.

Incorporated in 1950 in NY.
Donors: Johan J. Smit‡; Mrs. Johan J. Smit‡.
Foundation type: Independent foundation.
Financial data (yr. ended 12/31/05): Assets, $11,150,710 (M); expenditures, $601,808; qualifying distributions, $575,106; giving activities include $495,000 for 123 grants (high: $35,000; low: $1,000).
Purpose and activities: Grants largely for international relief, and higher and secondary education, through scholarship support earmarked for high school students; support also for social services, youth, health, and cultural programs.
Fields of interest: Arts; Secondary school/education; Higher education; Health care; Health organizations, association; Human services; Children/youth, services; International relief.

Type of support: Seed money; General/operating support; Scholarship funds.
Limitations: Giving on a national basis. No grants to individuals.
Publications: Financial statement.
Application information: Application form not required.
 Initial approach: Letter
 Copies of proposal: 1
 Deadline(s): None
 Board meeting date(s): Semiannually
Officers and Directors:* Sheila Smit,* Pres.; Stephen C. Smit,* V.P.; Walter J. Graver,* Secy.-Treas.; Barbara Graver; Evan Kirchen; Helen Kirchen; Robert Kirchen; Judith Rist; Peta Smit Santos; Lisa Smit.
Number of staff: 1 part-time support.
EIN: 136097828

8622
The Jerry and Anita Zucker Family Foundation, Inc. ✧ ☆
4838 Jenkins Ave.
N Charleston, SC 29405

Established in 1996.
Donor: Jerry Zucker.
Foundation type: Independent foundation.
Financial data (yr. ended 12/31/03): Assets, $4,830,980 (M); expenditures, $443,700; qualifying distributions, $443,575; giving activities include $443,575 for 40 grants (high: $120,000; low: $50).
Purpose and activities: Giving primarily to Jewish organizations, and for education and health care.
Fields of interest: Education; Health care; Jewish agencies & temples.
Limitations: Applications not accepted. Giving primarily in SC. No grants to individuals.
Application information: Contributes only to pre-selected organizations.
Officers: Jerry Zucker, Pres. and Treas.; Jonathan M. Zucker, V.P.; Anita G. Zucker, Secy.
EIN: 571061131
Selected grants: The following grants were reported in 2003.
$54,000 to Charleston Jewish Federation, Charleston, SC.
$33,350 to Israel, State of, Jerusalem, Israel. .
$20,000 to United Way.

$5,000 to American Cancer Society, Atlanta, GA.
$3,500 to College of Charleston Foundation, Charleston, SC.
$3,000 to Jewish Studies Program.
$1,000 to Ashley Hall, Charleston, SC.
$1,000 to South Carolina Aquarium, Charleston, SC.
$180 to Citizens Research Council of Michigan, Livonia, MI.
$50 to Crisis Ministries, Charleston, SC.

SOUTH DAKOTA

8623
Branches Foundation ✧
c/o Dorsey & Whitney Trust
401 E. 8th St., Ste. 319
Sioux Falls, SD 57103

Established in 1999 in MN.
Donors: David O. Christianson; Branches Charitable Annuity Trust.
Foundation type: Independent foundation.
Financial data (yr. ended 12/31/05): Assets, $10,548,626 (M); gifts received, $1,691,881; expenditures, $570,130; qualifying distributions, $473,725; giving activities include $473,700 for 13 grants (high: $148,000; low: $5,000).
Purpose and activities: Giving primarily to Christian churches and organizations.
Fields of interest: Human services; Christian agencies & churches.
Limitations: Applications not accepted. Giving on a national basis, with emphasis on MN. No grants to individuals.
Application information: Contributes only to pre-selected organizations.
Trustees: Todd J. Christianson; Trudy A. Christianson.
EIN: 416463939

8624
Dakota Charitable Foundation, Inc. ✧
P.O. Box 8303
Rapid City, SD 57709

Established in 1992 in SD.
Donors: Margaret Lally; Ray Hillenbrand; and members of the Hillenbrand family.
Foundation type: Independent foundation.
Financial data (yr. ended 12/31/05): Assets, $36,668,829 (M); expenditures, $1,635,515; qualifying distributions, $1,511,958; giving activities include $1,505,500 for 24 grants (high: $800,000; low: $1,000).
Purpose and activities: Giving primarily to education, Roman Catholic agencies and churches, and for human services.
Fields of interest: Arts; Elementary/secondary education; Higher education; Engineering school/education; Human services; YM/YWCAs & YM/YWHAs; Federated giving programs; Roman Catholic agencies & churches.
Limitations: Applications not accepted. Giving primarily in Rapid City, SD, with some giving nationally in Washington, DC. No grants to individuals.
Application information: Contributes only to pre-selected organizations.
Directors: Gretchen Hillenbrand; Heidi Hillenbrand; Margaret Hillenbrand; Ray Hillenbrand.
EIN: 460422869
Selected grants: The following grants were reported in 2004.
$400,000 to Catholic University of America, DC.
$250,000 to Rapid City Catholic Schools, Rapid City, SD.
$200,000 to Dahl Arts Center, Rapid City, SD.
$200,000 to Wildlife Experiences, Rapid City, SD.

$125,000 to United Way of the Black Hills, Rapid City, SD.
$100,000 to South Dakota School of Mines and Technology Foundation, Rapid City, SD.
$100,000 to YMCA of Rapid City, Rapid City, SD.
$60,000 to Catholic Social Services, Rapid City, SD.
$50,000 to Cornerstone Rescue Mission, Rapid City, SD.
$50,000 to Youth and Family Services, Rapid City, SD.

8625
William Mibra Griffith and Bryne Smith Griffith Foundation, Inc. ✧
P.O. Box 1238
Huron, SD 57350

Established in 1991 in SD.
Foundation type: Independent foundation.
Financial data (yr. ended 12/31/05): Assets, $6,784,166 (M); expenditures, $396,184; qualifying distributions, $342,861; giving activities include $341,004 for 7 grants (high: $227,336; low: $1,000).
Fields of interest: Higher education; Salvation Army; Federated giving programs.
Limitations: Applications not accepted. Giving primarily in SD. No grants to individuals.
Application information: Contributes only to pre-selected organizations.
Directors: William Anderson; Thomas Batcheller; Paul Christen; Lynn V. Schneider; Alvin A. Schock; Jane Sebade; Robert T. Wagner.
EIN: 460416533
Selected grants: The following grants were reported in 2005.
$227,336 to South Dakota State University, Brookings, SD.
$80,191 to Beadle County Community Development Fund, Huron, SD.
$10,000 to Huron Regional Medical Center Foundation, Huron, SD.
$10,000 to South Dakota, State of, Pierre, SD.

8626
John D. & Edna Hofer Trust ✧
P.O. Box 1366
Mitchell, SD 57301

Established in 2002 in SD.
Foundation type: Independent foundation.
Financial data (yr. ended 12/31/05): Assets, $16,793,223 (M); expenditures, $988,589; qualifying distributions, $839,865; giving activities include $839,865 for 7 grants (high: $286,365; low: $12,500).
Fields of interest: Human services; Salvation Army; Religion.
Limitations: Applications not accepted. Giving primarily in SD. No grants to individuals.
Application information: Contributes only to pre-selected organizations.
Trustee: First National Bank of South Dakota.
EIN: 466088580
Selected grants: The following grants were reported in 2005.
$286,365 to Salvation Army of Omaha, Omaha, NE.
$190,000 to Society of Saint Vincent de Paul of Sioux Falls, Sioux Falls, SD.
$100,000 to Salem United Church of Christ, Parkston, SD.

$96,000 to Bethany Mennonite Church, Freeman, SD.
$80,000 to Union Gospel Mission, Sioux Falls, SD.
$75,000 to Salem Mennonite Brethren Church, Bridgewater, SD.
$12,500 to Goodwill Industries, Sioux City, IA.

8627
Larson Foundation ✧
2333 Eastbrook Dr.
Brookings, SD 57006-2899
Contact: Maree Larson, Secy.

Established in 1990 in SD.
Donors: O. Dale Larson; Patricia Larson; Maree Larson; Bridget Larson Ennevor; Carmelle Jackson; Larson Manufacturing Co. of SD, Inc.
Foundation type: Independent foundation.
Financial data (yr. ended 4/30/06): Assets, $11,737,221 (M); gifts received, $2,775,000; expenditures, $1,605,941; qualifying distributions, $1,548,408; giving activities include $1,476,674 for 47 grants (high: $1,000,000; low: $100), and $71,734 for 14 employee matching gifts.
Fields of interest: Arts; Higher education; Medical care, rehabilitation; Housing/shelter, development; Recreation, parks/playgrounds; Human services; Children/youth, services; Federated giving programs.
Type of support: Annual campaigns; Building/renovation; Program development; Scholarship funds; Employee matching gifts.
Limitations: Giving primarily in SD, with emphasis on Brookings, and the community of Lake Mills, IA.
Application information: Application form required.
Initial approach: Letter requesting grant request form
Copies of proposal: 7
Deadline(s): Mar. 1 and Sept. 1
Board meeting date(s): Semiannually
Officers: Patricia M. Larson, Pres.; O. Dale Larson, V.P.; Maree Larson, Secy.
EIN: 460412311
Selected grants: The following grants were reported in 2005.
$130,000 to Brookings Foundation, Brookings, SD. For scholarships.
$82,100 to Boys and Girls Club of Black Hills, Hill City, SD. For program support.
$75,000 to Opportunity Village, Clear Lake, IA. For building addition.
$50,000 to Lutheran Social Services of South Dakota, Sioux Falls, SD. For program support.
$50,000 to South Dakota State University Foundation, Brookings, SD. For preschool and daycare program.
$40,000 to Lake Mills Chamber Development Corporation, Lake Mills, IA. For Family Fitness Center.
$28,500 to South Dakota State University, College of Agriculture, Brookings, SD. For Bolivia Project.
$25,000 to Friends of South Dakota Public Broadcasting, Brookings, SD. For Family Reading Program.
$25,000 to Teach for America, Pierre, SD. To expand program.
$25,000 to Youth and Family Services, Rapid City, SD. For program support.

8628
Opus Prize Foundation ✧
(formerly Alpha & Omega Family Foundation)
c/o Adler Mgmt., LLC
401 E. 8th St., Ste. 222
Sioux Falls, SD 57103-7011   (605) 357-8694

Established in 1994 in SD.
Foundation type: Independent foundation.
Financial data (yr. ended 12/31/05): Assets, $28,187,774 (M); expenditures, $1,476,126; qualifying distributions, $1,406,554; giving activities include $1,260,000 for 13 grants (high: $1,000,000; low: $5,000; average: $5,000–$100,000).
Purpose and activities: Giving primarily for human services and Roman Catholic organizations and education.
Fields of interest: Higher education; Education; Human services; Roman Catholic federated giving programs; Roman Catholic agencies & churches; Economically disadvantaged.
International interests: Jamaica; Mexico.
Limitations: Applications not accepted. Giving primarily on a national basis, with emphasis on MN. No grants to individuals.
Application information: Contributes only to pre-selected organizations.
Officers and Directors: Joseph J. Rauenhorst, Pres.; Luz Campa, V.P.; Don Neureuther, Secy. and Exec. Dir.; Jeffrey M. Rauenhorst, Treas.; Thomas J. Mahoney; Susan R. Turner.
EIN: 460434399
Selected grants: The following grants were reported in 2004.
$1,000,000 to Helping Hands for the Poor, Miami, FL. For Ministry programs in Jamaica.
$185,000 to Marquette University, Milwaukee, WI. For general operating support.
$62,500 to Archdiocese of Saint Paul and Minneapolis, Catholic Community Foundation, Saint Paul, MN. For Alpha and Omega Charitable Fund.

8629
Harvey W. Peters Research Foundation ✧ ☆
c/o First Premier Bank Trust Dept.
601 S. Minnesota
Sioux Falls, SD 57101

Established in 1999 in SD.
Donor: Edward Becher Via.
Foundation type: Independent foundation.
Financial data (yr. ended 6/30/05): Assets, $16,115,974 (M); gifts received, $90,000; expenditures, $1,062,175; qualifying distributions, $500,000; giving activities include $500,000 for grants.
Fields of interest: Education.
Limitations: Giving primarily in VA.
Officer: John G. Rocovich, Mgr.
Trustees: David G. Hottman; J. Tracy O'Rourke; Frederick P. Stratton, Jr.
EIN: 460459671

8630
Sioux Falls Area Community Foundation
300 N. Phillips Ave., Ste. 102
Sioux Falls, SD 57104-6035   (605) 336-7055, ext. 20
Contact: Candy Hanson, C.E.O.
FAX: (605) 336-0038; E-mail: chanson@sfacf.org;
URL: http://www.sfacf.org

Established in 1984 in SD.
Foundation type: Community foundation.
Financial data (yr. ended 6/30/05): Assets, $48,728,191 (M); gifts received, $9,912,375; expenditures, $6,529,700; giving activities include $5,578,023 for 1,305 grants (high: $200,000; low: $50; average: $50–$200,000), and $225,765 for 195 grants to individuals (high: $3,000; low: $200).
Purpose and activities: The foundation advances philanthropy in the 4-county area by attracting, managing & distributing charitable funds.
Fields of interest: Museums; Performing arts, dance; Performing arts, theater; Performing arts, music; Humanities; Historic preservation/historical societies; Arts; Libraries/library science; Education; Environment, pollution control; Environment, water pollution; Environment, waste management; Environment, energy; Environment; Animals/wildlife, preservation/protection; Health care; Substance abuse, prevention; Mental health/crisis services; Medical research; Employment, training; Employment; Family services; Human services; Economic development; Community development; Religion; Youth; Aging; Disabilities, people with.
Type of support: General/operating support; Building/renovation; Equipment; Program development; Conferences/seminars; Seed money; Curriculum development; Scholarship funds; Research; Technical assistance; Program evaluation; Employee-related scholarships; Grants to individuals; Matching/challenge support.
Limitations: Giving generally limited to Lincoln, McCook, Minnehaha, and Turner counties and communities within a 25-mile radius of Sioux Falls, SD. No support for educational programs benefiting the work of local community organizations or sectarian religious purposes. No grants to individuals (except for scholarships), or for capital or construction drives, ongoing operating support, reducing or eliminating organizational debts or deficits, computer hardware or software, staff salaries (except in conjunction with a new program), endowments, telephone solicitations, or national fundraising efforts.
Publications: Application guidelines; Annual report (including application guidelines); Financial statement; Grants list; Newsletter.
Application information: Visit foundation Web site for application forms, guidelines, and specific deadlines. Grant requests of under $1,000 do not require an application form. Scholarship application forms available from high school counseling offices or college financial aid offices. Application form required.
Initial approach: Letter or telephone
Copies of proposal: 10
Deadline(s): Feb., Apr., June, Aug., Oct., and Dec. for grants over $1,000; none for grants under $1,000; usually Mar. 15 for scholarships
Board meeting date(s): Bimonthly
Final notification: Within 2 weeks for grants under $1,000; within 6 to 8 weeks for grants over $1,000
Officers and Directors: Mary Pat Sweetman, Chair.; Paul Schiller, Vice-Chair.; Candy Hanson,

C.E.O. and Pres.; Andy Patterson, V.P.; Mary Tidwell, Secy.; Paul W. Peterson, C.F.O.; Jack E. Carmody, Jr., Treas.; Dave Austad; Miles Beacom; Larry Bierman; Richard J. "Dick" Corcoran; Caroline Deinema; Vance Goldammer; Greg Heineman; Arlene Kirby; Kristi Niechwiadowicz; Sandra Pay; Richard Van Denmark.
Number of staff: 5 full-time professional; 2 full-time support; 2 part-time support.
EIN: 311748533
Selected grants: The following grants were reported in 2005.
$70,348 to Sioux Empire Marriage Savers, Sioux Falls, SD. 2 grants: $20,500 (For Sioux Falls Fatherhood Initiative, supporting activities that uphold importance of responsible, involved fathers), $49,848 (For Youth Safety Initiative activities, including support for high school student-led group Straight Forward, which targets safety issues affecting local youth).
$20,000 to South Dakota Symphony Orchestra, Sioux Falls, SD. For free outdoor pops concert at W.H. Lyons Fairgrounds.
$15,000 to Eugene Field Elementary School, Sioux Falls, SD. For art and music program for elementary school students.
$15,000 to Washington Pavilion of Arts and Science, Sioux Falls, SD. 2 grants: $10,000 (To provide teens safe, alcohol-free activity through Pavilion Underground, All Ages Concert Series where they can listen to and perform live alternative music), $5,000 (To complete self-study evaluation required for accreditation by American Association of Museums).
$10,549 to Childrens Home Society of South Dakota, Sioux Falls, SD. To enhance school's fitness program and accommodate growing enrollment with new outdoor fitness center and swing set.
$10,000 to Main Street Sioux Falls, Sioux Falls, SD. For Downtown Economic Development Incentive Fund. Grant made through Citigroup Foundation.
$10,000 to South Dakota Voices for Children, Sioux Falls, SD. To establish citywide task force to achieve high-quality pre-kindergarten and child care for all age levels by launching Action on Early Education and Child Care Project.
$10,000 to South Eastern Development Foundation, Sioux Falls, SD. For 502 Home Loan Partnership Program, which provides loans to low-income families to help them pursue homeownership.

8631
South Dakota Community Foundation ✧
207 E. Capitol Ave.
P.O. Box 296
Pierre, SD 57501-0296   (605) 224-1025
Contact: Bob Sutton, Pres.
FAX: (605) 224-5364;
E-mail: bsutton44@sdcommunityfoundation.org;
Additional tel.: (800) 888-1842; Additional E-mail: stephj16@sdcommunityfoundation.org;
URL: http://www.sdcommunityfoundation.org

Incorporated in 1987 in SD.
Foundation type: Community foundation.
Financial data (yr. ended 12/31/04): Assets, $46,464,530 (M); gifts received, $8,231,344; expenditures, $4,426,436; giving activities include $3,730,166 for 551 grants (high: $1,707,385; low: $5), and $234,649 for 311 grants to individuals (high: $6,665; low: $5).

Purpose and activities: The foundation seeks to promote philanthropy, receive, and administer charitable gifts and invest in a wide range of programs promoting the social and economic well-being of the people of SD.

Fields of interest: Arts; Education; Health care; Health organizations, association; Youth development, citizenship; Human services; Economic development; Community development; Federated giving programs; Public affairs, citizen participation; Minorities; Native Americans/American Indians; Economically disadvantaged.

Type of support: Income development; Capital campaigns; Building/renovation; Endowments; Publication; Seed money; Curriculum development; Research; Technical assistance; Scholarships—to individuals; Matching/challenge support.

Limitations: Giving limited to SD. No grants to individuals (except for scholarships), or for operating expenses; no loans.

Publications: Application guidelines; Annual report; Financial statement; Grants list; Informational brochure; Newsletter; Program policy statement.

Application information: Visit foundation Web site for application form and guidelines. Application form required.

  Initial approach: Telephone
  Copies of proposal: 1
  Deadline(s): None
  Board meeting date(s): May and Nov.
  Final notification: 30-45 days from receipt

Officers and Directors:* John Johnson,* Chair.; Bob Sutton, Pres.; Patricia Adam; Richard Cutler; Rodney Fouberg; Barry Grossenburg; Wayne Gustafson; Noel Hamiel; Nini Hart; Irving Hinderaker; Blake Hoffman; Bob Jostad; Dan Kirby; Jim Means; Mark Mickelson; Earl Nordby; Tom Olsen; Doug Petersen; Charles Riter; Tom Sannes; Thomas Shortbull; Peg Seljeskog; Ann Sigelman; Charlie Thompson.

Number of staff: 2 full-time professional; 1 part-time professional; 1 full-time support.

EIN: 460398115

8632
Gwendolyn L. Stearns Foundation, Inc. ◇

c/o Wells Fargo Bank S.D., N.A.
P.O. Box 1040
Rapid City, SD 57709 (605) 394-3821
Contact: Gary Gunderson

Established in 2001 in SD.

Donor: Gwendolyn L. Stearns†.

Foundation type: Independent foundation.

Financial data (yr. ended 12/31/05): Assets, $6,545,189 (M); expenditures, $376,141;

qualifying distributions, $344,490; giving activities include $344,490 for 25 grants (high: $40,000; low: $4,000).

Fields of interest: Human services; Children/youth, services.

Limitations: Giving primarily in Rapid City, SD.

Application information: Application form required.
  Initial approach: Letter or telephone requesting application
  Deadline(s): None

Officers: William Howard, Pres.; Larry Dahlstrom, V.P.; Phyllis S. Dixon, Secy.; C.J. Dunmire, Treas.

Directors: Hon. Janine Kern; Doris Rudel; Richard Tobias.

EIN: 311737658

Selected grants: The following grants were reported in 2004.

$25,000 to Cornerstone Rescue Mission, Rapid City, SD.

$25,000 to Rural America Initiatives, Rapid City, SD.

$15,000 to Rapid City Fine Arts Council, Rapid City, SD.

$10,000 to Big Brothers/Big Sisters of the Black Hills, Rapid City, SD.

$7,500 to Catholic Social Services, Rapid City, SD.

$6,500 to YMCA of Rapid City, Rapid City, SD.

$5,000 to United Way of the Black Hills, Rapid City, SD.

8633
Via-Bradley College of Engineering, South Dakota ◇

c/o First Premier Bank Trust Co.
601 S. Minnesota Ave.
Sioux Falls, SD 57101

Established in 2002 in SD.

Donor: Edward Via.

Foundation type: Independent foundation.

Financial data (yr. ended 12/31/05): Assets, $21,120,223 (L); gifts received, $180,000; expenditures, $1,867,850; qualifying distributions, $1,601,900; giving activities include $1,601,900 for 2 grants (high: $1,600,000; low: $1,900).

Fields of interest: Higher education, university; Philanthropy/voluntarism.

Limitations: Applications not accepted. Giving primarily in VA.

Application information: Unsolicited requests for funds not accepted.

Officer: John G. Rocovich, Jr.

Director: David Hottman.

Trustees: Frederick P. Stratton, Jr.; J. Tracy O'Rourke.

EIN: 522283401

8634
John T. Vucurevich Foundation ◇

c/o Wells Fargo Bank South Dakota, N.A.
P.O. Drawer 1040
Rapid City, SD 57709 (605) 343-0820
E-mail: jtvfnd@qwest.net; Application address: P.O. Box 170, Rapid City, SD 57709

Established in 1985 in SD.

Donor: John T. Vucurevich.

Foundation type: Independent foundation.

Financial data (yr. ended 12/31/05): Assets, $8,681,482 (M); gifts received, $75; expenditures, $525,288; qualifying distributions, $420,193; giving activities include $324,260 for grants, and $52,498 for foundation-administered programs.

Fields of interest: Human services; Children/youth, services; Federated giving programs.

Type of support: General/operating support; Continuing support; Capital campaigns; Equipment; Emergency funds; Program development; Conferences/seminars; Publication; Scholarship funds; Matching/challenge support.

Limitations: Giving primarily in SD, with emphasis on Rapid City. No grants to individuals.

Application information: Application form required.
  Initial approach: Letter, with cover page
  Copies of proposal: 4
  Deadline(s): Mar. 1, June 1, Sept. 1, and Dec. 1
  Board meeting date(s): Quarterly, and as needed
  Final notification: Within 3 months

Trustee: Wells Fargo Bank South Dakota, N.A.

Advisory Board: Dale Clement; Renee Parker; Alex Vucurevich; Thomas Vucurevich.

EIN: 460359829

Selected grants: The following grants were reported in 2005.

$38,000 to Emmanuel Episcopal Church, Rapid City, SD.

$30,414 to Wellspring, Rapid City, SD.

$30,000 to United Way of the Black Hills, Rapid City, SD.

$30,000 to Working Against Violence, Rapid City, SD.

$25,000 to Saint Elizabeth Seton School, Rapid City, SD.

$21,500 to University of South Dakota Foundation, Vermillion, SD.

$20,000 to Saint Thomas More High School, Rapid City, SD.

$10,000 to Calvary Christian School, Rapid City, SD.

$10,000 to Share South Dakota, Rapid City, SD.

$10,000 to Zion Lutheran School, Rapid City, SD.

TENNESSEE

8635

1939 Foundation ◇
900 S. Gay St., Ste. 1600
Knoxville, TN 37902-1857
Contact: Phillip O. Lawson, V.P.

Established in 1983 in TN.
Donor: F. Rodney Lawler.
Foundation type: Independent foundation.
Financial data (yr. ended 11/30/05): Assets, $5,102,302 (M); expenditures, $1,115,335; qualifying distributions, $1,111,000; giving activities include $1,111,000 for 5 grants (high: $1,100,000; low: $1,000).
Purpose and activities: Giving primarily to a private foundation, as well as for education, children and youth services, social services, and religious purposes.
Fields of interest: Higher education; Human services; Children/youth, services; Foundations (private grantmaking); Christian agencies & churches.
Type of support: General/operating support.
Limitations: Giving primarily in TN, with emphasis on Knoxville. No grants to individuals.
Application information:
Initial approach: Letter
Deadline(s): None
Officers: F. Rodney Lawler, Pres.; Phillip O. Lawson, V.P.; Doris Ballew, Secy.
Directors: Robin L. Gibson; Dell R. Lawler; Jon R. Lawler.
EIN: 621183557

8636

AmSouth/First American Foundation ◇
(formerly First American Foundation)
315 Deaderick St., 4th Fl.
Nashville, TN 37237-0401 (615) 748-2241

Established in 1994 in TN.
Donors: First American National Bank; AmSouth Bank.
Foundation type: Company-sponsored foundation.
Financial data (yr. ended 12/31/03): Assets, $8,932,061 (M); expenditures, $838,205; qualifying distributions, $790,620; giving activities include $789,870 for grants.
Purpose and activities: The foundation supports organizations involved with education and human services.
Fields of interest: Education; Human services; Federated giving programs.
Limitations: Applications not accepted. Giving primarily in TN. No grants to individuals.
Application information: Contributes only to pre-selected organizations.
Officers and Directors:* Beth Mooney,* Chair.; DeVan Ard,* Pres.; Pamela Welch, Secy.; Doug Jackson, Treas.; Donna Cheek; Bernard Werthan; Toby Wilt; Bill Wire; Steve Yoder.
EIN: 582071018

8637

The Aslan Foundation ◇
P.O. Box 550
Knoxville, TN 37901-0550 (865) 637-1440
Contact: Robert S. Young III, V.P.

Established in 1995 in TN.
Donor: Lindsay Young.
Foundation type: Independent foundation.
Financial data (yr. ended 12/31/05): Assets, $13,411,255 (M); expenditures, $675,168; qualifying distributions, $629,058; giving activities include $582,300 for 25 grants (high: $176,300; low: $2,000).
Purpose and activities: Giving for child and family welfare, health care, and for literacy programs.
Fields of interest: Literature; Adult education— literacy, basic skills & GED; Animal welfare; Health care; Children/youth, services; Family services.
Limitations: Giving primarily in east TN.
Application information: Application form required.
Initial approach: Completed application form
Copies of proposal: 5
Deadline(s): None
Board meeting date(s): Mar. and Oct.
Officers and Directors:* Robert S. Young, Jr.,* Pres.; Robert S. Young III,* V.P.; Mark K. Williams,* Secy.; Gregory E. Erickson,* Treas.; Lindsay Y. McDonough.
EIN: 621520208

8638

The Assisi Foundation of Memphis, Inc. ▼
(formerly Assisi Foundation)
515 Erin Dr.
Memphis, TN 38117
Contact: Jan Young, Exec. Dir.
E-mail: jyoung@assisifoundation.org; URL: http://www.assisifoundation.org/

Established in 1994 in TN; converted from the sale of St. Francis Hospital.
Foundation type: Independent foundation.
Financial data (yr. ended 12/31/05): Assets, $216,241,890 (M); expenditures, $13,023,797; qualifying distributions, $11,591,754; giving activities include $11,072,365 for 132 grants (high: $842,230; low: $1,500; average: $15,000–$250,000).
Purpose and activities: Philanthropic investments primarily for health and human services; lifelong learning and education; community enrichment; social justice and ethics.
Fields of interest: Education; Health care; Human services; Community development; Social sciences, ethics; Social sciences, equal rights.
Type of support: General/operating support; Management development/capacity building; Capital campaigns; Equipment; Endowments; Emergency funds; Program development; Conferences/seminars; Publication; Curriculum development; Research; Technical assistance; Consulting services; Program evaluation; Matching/challenge support.
Limitations: Giving primarily in Memphis and Shelby County, TN.
Publications: Application guidelines.
Application information: See foundation's Web site for additional information. Application form required.
Initial approach: Letter on letterhead requesting application
Copies of proposal: 8

Deadline(s): 2006: Feb. 15, May 17, Aug. 16, and Nov. 15; 2007: Feb. 14, May 16, Aug. 15, Nov. 14
Board meeting date(s): 4th Thurs. of Jan., Apr., July, and Oct.
Final notification: Feb. 1, May 1, Aug. 1, and Nov. 1
Officers and Directors:* Forest N. Jenkins,* Chair.; Lee J. Chase III,* Vice-Chair.; Martin F. Thompson,* Secy.; John L. Zoccola,* Treas.; Jan Young, Exec. Dir.; Susan M. Aguillard, M.D.; Franklin P. "Pepper" Allen; Eugene J. Bastedo; Neal S. Beckford, M.D.; Jack A. Belz; Ron Belz; Alison Garrott Braswell; Thomas K. Corona; Fred L. Davis; Thomas C. Farnsworth, III; William E. Frulla; Ethele Hilliard; Charles D. Schaffler; C. Thomas Whitman; Russel L. Wiener, D.D.S.; Becky Wilson; Philip R. Zanone, Jr.
Number of staff: 4 full-time professional; 1 part-time professional; 1 full-time support; 1 part-time support.
EIN: 621558722
Selected grants: The following grants were reported in 2004.
$500,000 to Catholic Memphis Urban Schools, Memphis, TN. For Jubilee Schools Scholarships.
$250,000 to Alzheimers Day Services of Memphis, Memphis, TN. For capital campaign for Adult Day Care Facility.
$250,000 to Christ Community Health Services, Memphis, TN. For Health Center Development.
$200,000 to Bridges, Inc., Memphis, TN. For Bridges Center capital campaign.
$175,000 to Emmanuel Episcopal Center, Memphis, TN. For Community Life Center.
$175,000 to University of Memphis Foundation, Memphis, TN. For Mid-South Reading Alliance.
$150,000 to Saint Agnes Academy-Saint Dominic School, Memphis, TN. For capital endowment.
$133,300 to Partners in Public Education (PIPE), Memphis, TN. For general operations and programs.
$125,000 to Union University, Jackson, TN. For Germantown, TN Campus Nursing Laboratory.
$105,000 to Shelby County Schools Education Foundation, Memphis, TN. For Beginning to Read, Write and Listen.

8639

Atticus Trust ◇
(formerly The Atticus Foundation)
c/o SunTrust Bank
P.O. Box 305110, Mail Code NA6430
Nashville, TN 37230-5110 (615) 748-5813
Contact: Kim Williams, SunTrust Bank

Established in 1986 in TN.
Donor: Sara S. Brown.
Foundation type: Independent foundation.
Financial data (yr. ended 12/31/05): Assets, $14,361,266 (M); expenditures, $745,938; qualifying distributions, $700,430; giving activities include $633,167 for 117 grants (high: $57,000; low: $250).
Purpose and activities: Giving primarily for education as well as for environmental conservation, including an environmental law center; funding also for the arts, health care, including a children's hospital, Christian ministries and organizations, and children, youth, families, and social services, including a soup kitchen.
Fields of interest: Media, television; Media, radio; Visual arts; Museums (art); Performing arts; Historic preservation/historical societies; Arts; Education,

public education; Higher education; Education; Environment, legal rights; Environment, natural resources; Environment; Animals/wildlife; Girl scouts; Human services; Children/youth, services; Family services; Residential/custodial care, hospices; Federated giving programs; Christian agencies & churches.
Limitations: Giving primarily in TN. No grants to individuals.
Application information: Application form not required.
Initial approach: Letter or telephone
Deadline(s): None
Trustee and Trust Committee Members:* Martin S. Brown, Jr.,* Tr.; Mrs. Elizabeth M. Brown; Ms. Elizabeth M. Brown; Martin S. Brown, Sr.; Margaret DeClercq; Susannah Scott-Barnes.
EIN: 581796390

8640
Ayers Foundation ✧ ☆
68 W. Main St., 2nd Fl.
Parsons, TN   38363   (731) 847-4962
Contact: Bernard Clippard, Jr., Pres.

Established in 1999 in TN.
Donors: James W. Ayers; Nancy Sharon Ayers; Jon Ayers.
Foundation type: Independent foundation.
Financial data (yr. ended 12/31/05): Assets, $35,282 (M); gifts received, $768,257; expenditures, $856,091; qualifying distributions, $749,859; giving activities include $749,859 for 29 grants (high: $500,000; low: $250).
Fields of interest: Arts; Higher education, college (community/junior); Education; Cancer; Health organizations; Disasters, preparedness/services; Human services.
Limitations: Giving limited to Decatur and Henderson counties, TN. No grants to individuals.
Application information: Application form not required.
Final notification: None
Officers: James W. Ayers, Chair.; Bernard Clippard, Jr., Pres.; Clay Petrey, Secy.
Director: John Ayers.
EIN: 621773033
Selected grants: The following grants were reported in 2004.
$49,434 to Decatur County Board of Education, Bainbridge, GA. For general operating support.
$25,042 to Nashville State Community College, Nashville, TN. For general operating support.
$13,936 to Columbia State Community College, Columbia, TN. For general operating support.
$12,000 to Public Forum, Nashville, TN. For general operating support.
$4,800 to Tennessee Performing Arts Center, Nashville, TN. For general operating support.
$1,348 to Jackson State Community College, Jackson, TN. For general operating support.
$1,000 to American Diabetes Association, Nashville, TN. For general operating support.
$1,000 to Faith Family Medical Clinic, Nashville, TN. For general operating support.
$1,000 to Fellowship of Christian Athletes, Nashville, TN. For general operating support.
$1,000 to University of Tennessee, Martin, TN. For general operating support.

8641
Wayne G. Basler Charitable Foundation ✧
P.O. Box 2049
Kingsport, TN   37662   (423) 246-4546
Contact: Shari Andrew, Mgr.

Established in 1988 in TN.
Foundation type: Independent foundation.
Financial data (yr. ended 12/31/03): Assets, $10,654,233 (M); expenditures, $580,871; qualifying distributions, $491,170; giving activities include $484,720 for 20 grants (high: $100,000; low: $200).
Purpose and activities: Giving primarily for higher and other education, federated giving programs, the symphony, and to Presbyterian churches; funding also for human services.
Fields of interest: Performing arts, orchestra (symphony); Elementary/secondary education; Higher education; Human services; Federated giving programs; Protestant agencies & churches.
Limitations: Giving primarily in TN; some funding also in IA. No grants to individuals.
Application information:
Initial approach: Letter
Deadline(s): Sept. 30
Officer: Shari L. Andrew, Mgr.
Trustee: Wayne G. Basler.
EIN: 621347054
Selected grants: The following grants were reported in 2004.
$150,000 to East Tennessee State University Foundation, Johnson City, TN. 2 grants: $100,000, $50,000
$115,365 to University of Tennessee, Knoxville, TN. 2 grants: $15,365, $100,000
$50,000 to Cedar Rapids Symphony Orchestra Association, Cedar Rapids, IA.
$50,000 to Tri-Cities Christian Schools, Blountville, TN.
$25,000 to Chamber Foundation of Kingsport, Kingsport, TN.
$15,000 to United Way of Greater Kingsport, Kingsport, TN.
$10,700 to Sullivan North High School, Kingsport, TN. 2 grants: $5,300, $5,400

8642
Alvin and Sally Beaman Foundation ✧
P.O. Box 2408
Brentwood, TN   37024-2408
Contact: Larry T. Thrailkill, Secy.
FAX: (615) 376-3016

Established in 1998 in TN.
Donor: Sally M. Beaman.
Foundation type: Independent foundation.
Financial data (yr. ended 12/31/04): Assets, $19,560,309 (M); expenditures, $988,987; qualifying distributions, $870,500; giving activities include $870,500 for 56 grants (high: $110,000; low: $1,000).
Fields of interest: Zoos/zoological societies; Food banks; Children, services; Family services.
Type of support: General/operating support; Continuing support; Annual campaigns; Capital campaigns; Building/renovation.
Limitations: Applications not accepted. No grants to individuals.
Application information: Contributes only to pre-selected organizations.
Board meeting date(s): Quarterly

Officers and Trustees:* Lee A. Beaman,* Pres.; Kelly S. Beaman,* V.P.; Larry T. Thrailkill,* Secy.
EIN: 621743008

8643
Belz Foundation
100 Peabody Pl., Ste. 1400
Memphis, TN   38103
Contact: Jack A. Belz, Pres.

Incorporated in 1952 in TN.
Donors: Philip Belz†; Martin S. Belz; Ronald A. Belz; Jack A. Belz; Andrew Groveman; Jan B. Groveman.
Foundation type: Independent foundation.
Financial data (yr. ended 12/31/04): Assets, $15,962,584 (M); gifts received, $1,502,800; expenditures, $1,473,135; qualifying distributions, $1,408,806; giving activities include $1,408,786 for 730 grants (high: $225,000; low: $6).
Purpose and activities: Emphasis on Jewish welfare funds, temple support, Israel, education, including higher education and yeshivas, cultural organizations, and health and welfare organizations.
Fields of interest: Arts; Elementary/secondary education; Higher education; Theological school/education; Education; Health care; Health organizations, association; Medical research, institute; Human services; Jewish federated giving programs; Jewish agencies & temples.
International interests: Israel.
Limitations: Applications not accepted. Giving primarily in Memphis, TN. No grants to individuals.
Application information: Contributes only to pre-selected organizations.
Officers and Directors:* Jack A. Belz,* Pres.; Martin S. Belz,* V.P.; Jimmie D. Williams,* Secy.-Treas.; Ronald A. Belz; Andrew Groveman; Jan B. Groveman; Raymond Shainberg.
EIN: 626046715
Selected grants: The following grants were reported in 2003.
$200,000 to Jewish Federation, Memphis, Memphis, TN.
$25,000 to University of Memphis Foundation, Memphis, TN.
$25,000 to Yeshiva University, New York, NY.
$15,500 to Saint Jude Childrens Research Hospital, Memphis, TN.
$6,667 to United Way of the Mid-South, Memphis, TN.
$5,000 to Opera Memphis, Memphis, TN.
$3,000 to Boys and Girls Clubs of Greater Memphis, Memphis, TN.
$1,000 to LeMoyne-Owen College, Memphis, TN.
$500 to Chabads Children of Chernobyl, New York, NY.
$500 to Childrens Museum of Memphis, Memphis, TN.

8644
Benwood Foundation, Inc. ▼ ✧
SunTrust Bank Bldg.
736 Market St., Ste. 1600
Chattanooga, TN   37402   (423) 267-4311
Contact: Corinne Allen, Exec. Dir.

Incorporated in 1944 in DE, and 1945 in TN.
Donor: George Thomas Hunter†.
Foundation type: Independent foundation.
Financial data (yr. ended 12/31/05): Assets, $113,491,850 (M); expenditures, $3,109,997;

qualifying distributions, $2,058,734; giving activities include $1,494,622 for 22 grants (high: $500,000; low: $1,000; average: $1,000–$60,000).

Purpose and activities: Support for secondary and early childhood education, social welfare, health agencies, cultural programs, arts and humanities, including the performing arts, and the environment, including beautification programs.

Fields of interest: Performing arts; Humanities; Arts; Education, early childhood education; Secondary school/education; Environment; Health organizations, association; Human services; Economic development; Urban/community development.

Type of support: Continuing support; Capital campaigns; Building/renovation; Equipment; Program development; Conferences/seminars; Seed money; Scholarship funds; Technical assistance; Matching/challenge support.

Limitations: Giving primarily in the Chattanooga, TN, area. No support for political organizations or causes. No grants to individuals, or for general operating expenses, financial deficits, fundraising, endowments, or multi-year grants; no loans (except for program-related investments).

Publications: Application guidelines.

Application information: Application form required.
Initial approach: Brief 2-page letter
Copies of proposal: 6
Deadline(s): 1st day of month preceding board meetings
Board meeting date(s): Jan., Apr., July, and Oct.
Final notification: 3 weeks after board meeting; board reserves privilege of delaying decision for 3 months

Officers and Trustees:* Sebert Brewer, Jr.,* Chair.; Corinne Allen, Exec. Dir.; Paul K. Brock, Jr.; William H. Chapin; Martha T. Robinson; Robert J. Sudderth, Jr.

Number of staff: 4 full-time professional.

EIN: 620476283

Selected grants: The following grants were reported in 2004.
$1,015,000 to Public Education Foundation, Chattanooga, TN.
$500,000 to Hunter Museum of Art, Chattanooga, TN.
$480,000 to Alexian Brothers of the Southeast, Signal Mountain, TN.
$350,000 to Twenty-First Century Waterfront Trust, Chattanooga, TN.
$225,000 to Community Impact of Chattanooga, Chattanooga, TN.
$200,000 to United Way of Chattanooga, Chattanooga, TN.
$126,500 to Trust for Public Land, San Francisco, CA.
$20,000 to Cumberland University, Lebanon, TN.
$20,000 to Interfaith Hospitality Network of Greater Chattanooga, Chattanooga, TN.
$9,000 to Haystack Mountain School of Crafts, Deer Isle, ME.

8645
The Bornblum Foundation ◇ ☆
100 N. Main St., Ste. 3020
Memphis, TN 38103 (901) 525-5744
Contact: Alvin A. Gordon, Exec. Dir.

Established in 1991 in GA.
Donors: Bert Bornblum; David Bornblum.
Foundation type: Independent foundation.

Financial data (yr. ended 12/31/05): Assets, $200,000 (M); gifts received, $630,300; expenditures, $482,730; qualifying distributions, $482,710; giving activities include $482,710 for grants.
Fields of interest: Education; Jewish agencies & temples.
Limitations: Giving primarily in Memphis, TN. No grants to individuals.
Application information: Application form required.
Deadline(s): None
Officer: Alvin A. Gordon, Exec. Dir.
Directors: Bert Bornblum; David Bornblum; Bruce L. Feldbaum.
EIN: 621448070

8646
The Bridgestone/Firestone Trust Fund ▼
(formerly The Firestone Trust Fund)
535 Marriott Dr., 11th Fl.
Nashville, TN 37214-5092 (615) 937-1415
Contact: Bernice Csaszar, Admin.
FAX: (615) 937-1414;
E-mail: bfstrustfund@bfusa.com; URL: http://www.bridgestone-firestone.com/about/index_citizen.asp?id=trust_main

Trust established in 1952 in OH.
Donors: The Firestone Tire and Rubber Co.; Bridgestone/Firestone, Inc.
Foundation type: Company-sponsored foundation.
Financial data (yr. ended 12/31/05): Assets, $13,198,412 (M); expenditures, $3,504,429; qualifying distributions, $3,426,723; giving activities include $3,143,739 for 431 grants (high: $211,739), and $207,784 for 512 employee matching gifts.
Purpose and activities: The foundation supports museums, public radio and television stations, parks, and organizations involved with arts and culture, education, the environment, children's health, legal issues, safety, and welfare, employment training, youth development, civil rights, voter registration and education, and community development. Special emphasis is directed toward organizations involved with education, the environment, and children and organizations with which employees of Bridgestone Americas volunteer.
Fields of interest: Media, television; Media, radio; Museums; Performing arts; Arts; Elementary/secondary education; Higher education; Adult/continuing education; Libraries/library science; Education; Environment, natural resources; Environment; Health care; Legal services; Employment, training; Safety, education; Recreation, parks/playgrounds; Youth development; Children, services; Child development, services; Civil rights, equal rights; Civil rights, voter education; Civil rights; Community development; Children.
Type of support: General/operating support; Continuing support; Annual campaigns; Capital campaigns; Building/renovation; Endowments; Emergency funds; Program development; Fellowships; Scholarship funds; Research; Sponsorships; Employee matching gifts; Employee-related scholarships; Donated equipment; Exchange programs; Matching/challenge support.
Limitations: Giving on a national basis, with emphasis on areas of company operations; giving also to regional and national organizations. No

support for partisan political organizations, discriminatory organizations, or religious organizations not of direct benefit to the entire community. No grants to individuals (except for employee-related scholarships), or for debt reduction, equipment, land acquisition, or publications; no loans.
Publications: Application guidelines; Corporate giving report; Informational brochure.
Application information: Proposals should be no longer than 2 pages. Application form not required.
Initial approach: Proposal to nearest company facility; proposal to foundation for national organizations
Copies of proposal: 1
Deadline(s): None
Board meeting date(s): As required
Officer and Committee Members:* Christine Karbowiak,* Chair.; David Dumas; Gene Stephens; Ronald Tepner.
Trustee: KeyBank N.A.
Number of staff: 1 full-time support.
EIN: 346505181
Selected grants: The following grants were reported in 2004.
$800,000 to First Tee of Memphis, Memphis, TN.
$195,050 to National Merit Scholarship Corporation, Evanston, IL.
$50,000 to Public Education Partners, Aiken, SC.
$50,000 to WTI Foundation, Laramie, WY.
$45,000 to Aiken Technical College, Aiken, SC.
$45,000 to University of South Carolina, Columbia, SC.
$35,200 to Variety Club of Iowa, Des Moines, IA.
$25,000 to Childrens Advocacy Center, Chattanooga, TN.
$25,000 to Nashville Opera, Nashville, TN.
$25,000 to Tennessee Repertory Theater, Nashville, TN.

8647
Thomas W. Briggs Foundation, Inc. ◇
c/o The Cresent Ctr.
6075 Poplar Ave., Ste. 330
Memphis, TN 38119
Contact: JoAnne Tilley, Exec. Dir.

Established in 1957.
Donor: Thomas W. Briggs Residuary Trust.
Foundation type: Independent foundation.
Financial data (yr. ended 9/30/05): Assets, $14,145,366 (M); expenditures, $716,495; qualifying distributions, $668,053; giving activities include $600,926 for 32 grants (high: $110,000; low: $3,000).
Purpose and activities: Emphasis on youth and education; support also for the arts, and social services.
Fields of interest: Media, television; Museums; Museums (children's); Arts; Education; Human services; Children/youth, services.
Type of support: General/operating support; Capital campaigns; Building/renovation.
Limitations: Giving primarily in the Memphis, TN, area. No support for nationally affiliated organizations. No grants for public and private schools.
Publications: Application guidelines.
Application information: Application form not required.
Initial approach: Letter
Copies of proposal: 1
Deadline(s): Aug. 1 and Feb. 1

Board meeting date(s): Spring and fall
Final notification: May and Nov.
Officers and Directors: Spence Wilson,* Chair.; Buzzy Hussey,* Pres.; James D. Witherington, Jr.,* V.P.; S. Herbert Rhea,* Treas.; JoAnne Tilley, Exec. Dir.; Kathy Blair; Jim Bland, Jr.; William T. Morris; Richard C. Rantzow; Stephen H. Rhea, Jr.; Kenneth S. Robinson.
Number of staff: 1 full-time professional.
EIN: 626039986
Selected grants: The following grants were reported in 2005.
$25,000 to Christian Brothers University, Memphis, TN.
$25,000 to Crichton College, Memphis, TN.
$25,000 to Memphis Zoo, Memphis, TN.
$13,976 to Dixon Gallery and Gardens, Memphis, TN.
$10,700 to Young Life.
$10,000 to University of Memphis, Memphis, TN.
$8,000 to Neighborhood School, Memphis, TN.
$5,000 to Memphis Arts Council, Memphis, TN.
$5,000 to Memphis Athletic Ministries, Memphis, TN.
$5,000 to Young Women Striving for Excellence, Memphis, TN.

8648
Caesars Entertainment Foundation, Inc. ✧
(formerly Park Place Foundation, Inc.)
c/o Corp. Tax Dept.
1023 Cherry Rd.
Memphis, TN 38117-5423
Contact: Brenda O'Boyle, Dir., Community Affairs
Additional application addresses: northern MS: Valerie Morris, Regional Dir., Public Rels. and Community Affairs, Bally's, Sheraton, and Grand Casino Resort, 13615 Old Hwy. 61 N., Tunica Resorts, MS 38644, tel.: (662) 357-3089, southern MS: Susan Walker, Dir., Community Affairs, Mid South Region, 11975 Seaway Rd., Gulfport, MS 39503, tel.: (228) 604-5144, NJ: Redenia Gilliam-Mosee, Sr. V.P., Govt. Rels. and Plan., Bally's Atlantic City, Park Place and the Boardwalk, Atlantic City, NJ 08401, tel.: (609) 340-2108

Established in 2001 in NV.
Donors: Park Place Entertainment Corp.; Caesars Entertainment, Inc.
Foundation type: Company-sponsored foundation.
Financial data (yr. ended 12/31/04): Assets, $668,838 (M); gifts received, $628,245; expenditures, $951,435; qualifying distributions, $951,300; giving activities include $951,300 for 32 grants (high: $100,000; low: $300).
Purpose and activities: The foundation supports organizations involved with education, employment, family services, and community development.
Fields of interest: Education; Employment; Family services; Community development.
Type of support: General/operating support; Building/renovation; Program development; Scholarship funds; Sponsorships.
Limitations: Giving primarily in areas of company operations in MS, NJ, NV, and TN. No support for organizations established less than two years ago, political, labor, or fraternal organizations or civic clubs, religious organizations not of direct benefit to the entire community, or national health organizations or local chapters of national health organizations or research or disease advocacy organizations. No grants for athletic events.
Publications: Application guidelines.

Application information: Contact foundation for nearest company division address. Application form not required.
Initial approach: Mail proposal to nearest company division
Copies of proposal: 1
Deadline(s): None
Board meeting date(s): Quarterly
Final notification: Several months
Officers and Directors: Wallace R. Barr,* Pres.; Bernard E. DeLury, Jr.,* Secy.; Keith R. Holmes,* Treas.; Lorenzo Creighton; Debbie Munch.
EIN: 880513215

8649
Caldwell Foundation, Inc.
c/o SunTrust Bank
SunTrust Bank Bldg.
736 Market St.
Chattanooga, TN 37402 (423) 757-3933
Contact: Barbara Marter
FAX: (423) 757-3388;
E-mail: Barbara.Marter@SunTrust.com

Established about 1960 in TN.
Foundation type: Independent foundation.
Financial data (yr. ended 12/31/05): Assets, $4,899,063 (M); expenditures, $1,432,227; qualifying distributions, $1,420,688; giving activities include $1,419,251 for 90 grants (high: $300,000; low: $1,000).
Purpose and activities: Giving primarily for education, as well as for community environment and beautification programs, Christian organizations, social services with emphasis on children and youth, and health care.
Fields of interest: Museums (art); Arts; Secondary school/education; Higher education; Environment, beautification programs; Boy scouts; Human services; Children/youth, services; Federated giving programs; Christian agencies & churches.
Type of support: General/operating support; Annual campaigns; Capital campaigns; Program development.
Limitations: Giving primarily in TN, with emphasis on Chattanooga.
Application information: Application form required.
Initial approach: Letter (not exceeding 2 pages)
Copies of proposal: 10
Deadline(s): None
Board meeting date(s): Mar., June, Sept., and Dec.
Final notification: 2 weeks after board meeting
Officers and Directors: Robert H. Caldwell,* Pres.; L.H. Caldwell, Jr.,* V.P.; Summer Bryan; Mark A. Caldwell; Robert H. Caldwell, Jr.; Theodore C. Caldwell.
Number of staff: None.
EIN: 620678446
Selected grants: The following grants were reported in 2003.
$1,055,000 to Community Foundation of Greater Chattanooga, Chattanooga, TN. For 21st Century Waterfront Project.
$750,000 to McCallie School, Chattanooga, TN. For capital campaign.
$250,000 to Saint Nicholas School, Chattanooga, TN. For capital campaign.
$110,000 to Center for Youth Issues, National, Chattanooga, TN. For endowment campaign.
$50,000 to Partnership for Families, Children and Adults, Chattanooga, TN. For capital campaign.

$26,232 to Chattanooga Christian Schools, Chattanooga, TN. For scholarships.
$25,000 to Oak Hill School, Nashville, TN. For technology upgrade.
$17,500 to Tennessee River Gardens and Nature Preserve, Lookout Mountain, TN. For environmental education program.
$15,000 to Boy Scouts of America, Cherokee Area Council, Chattanooga, TN. For endowment campaign.
$10,000 to Friends of the Zoo, Chattanooga, TN. For operating support.

8650
Elizabeth Turner Campbell Foundation ✧
30 Burton Hills Blvd., No. 225
Nashville, TN 37215

Donors: Elizabeth Turner Campbell; 1994 Elizabeth Turner Campbell Trust.
Foundation type: Independent foundation.
Financial data (yr. ended 12/31/05): Assets, $22,279,114 (M); expenditures, $1,763,277; qualifying distributions, $1,375,824; giving activities include $1,374,000 for 6 grants (high: $660,000; low: $1,000).
Fields of interest: Recreation, camps; Human services; YM/YWCAs & YM/YWHAs; Christian agencies & churches.
Limitations: Applications not accepted. Giving primarily in FL, KY and Nashville, TN. No grants to individuals.
Application information: Contributes only to pre-selected organizations.
Officers and Directors: Elizabeth Turner Campbell,* Pres.; Jennifer A. Bruner,* V.P.; Croley W. Graham, Jr.,* Secy.-Treas.
EIN: 621833493
Selected grants: The following grants were reported in 2003.
$149,389 to YMCA of Nashville and Middle Tennessee, Nashville, TN. 2 grants: $74,389, $75,000
$80,000 to Christian Benevolent Outreach, Lexington, KY.
$15,000 to Easter Seals Tennessee, Nashville, TN.
$3,000 to Community Action of Southern Kentucky, Bowling Green, KY.
$1,000 to Youth Encouragement Services, Nashville, TN.

8651
Cannon Family Foundation ✧
3251 Poplar Ave., Ste. 115B
Memphis, TN 38111

Donors: Kathryn Gracey Cannon; Robert E. Cannon; Robert Howard Cannon; Katherine Cannon Warren; Timothy Hall Cannon.
Foundation type: Independent foundation.
Financial data (yr. ended 12/31/05): Assets, $686,483 (M); gifts received, $1,242,750; expenditures, $645,009; qualifying distributions, $645,009; giving activities include $628,500 for 1 grant.
Fields of interest: Arts councils.
Limitations: Applications not accepted. Giving primarily in Memphis, TN. No grants to individuals.
Application information: Contributes only to pre-selected organizations.

Officers and Directors:* Robert E. Cannon,* Pres.; Kathryn Gracey Cannon,* V.P.; Henry Patton Doggrell,* Secy.; Richard Prosser Guenther,* Treas.; Robert Howard Cannon; Timothy Hall Cannon; Katherine Cannon Warren.
EIN: 311650513

8652
The Charis Foundation, Inc. ✧
c/o Steiner & Ellis, PLLC
5516 Lonas Dr., Ste. 260
Knoxville, TN 37909
Application address: c/o Todd J. Ellis, P.O. Box 52206, Knoxville, TN 37950-2206

Established in 2001 in TN.
Donors: Cristen G. Haslam; William E. Haslam.
Foundation type: Independent foundation.
Financial data (yr. ended 12/31/05): Assets, $12,309,648 (M); gifts received, $500,000; expenditures, $609,093; qualifying distributions, $520,584; giving activities include $520,584 for 27 grants (high: $110,000; low: $1,000).
Fields of interest: Health care; Children/youth, services; Christian agencies & churches.
Limitations: Giving primarily in eastern TN. No grants to individuals.
Application information:
   Initial approach: Letter
   Deadline(s): June 30 and Dec. 31
Officers and Directors:* William E. Haslam,* Pres.; Cristen G. Haslam,* V.P.; J. Todd Ellis,* Secy.-Treas.
EIN: 621867423
Selected grants: The following grants were reported in 2005.
$110,000 to Historic Tennessee Theater Foundation, Knoxville, TN.
$109,000 to United Way of Greater Knoxville, Knoxville, TN.
$65,000 to Emerald Youth Foundation, Knoxville, TN.
$33,334 to Cedar Springs Presbyterian Church, Knoxville, TN.
$25,000 to East Tennessee Childrens Hospital, Knoxville, TN.
$25,000 to World Vision, Tacoma, WA.
$20,000 to YMCA of Knoxville, Knoxville, TN.
$11,250 to West End Academy, Knoxville, TN.
$10,000 to Webb School of Knoxville, Knoxville, TN.
$9,500 to Knoxville Symphony Orchestra, Knoxville, TN.

8653
The Children's Foundation of Memphis
(formerly Crippled Children's Foundation)
4646 Popular Ave., Ste. 440
Memphis, TN 38117
Contact: Lacy Carpenter

Established in 1982.
Donors: Le Bonheur Health Systems Foundation; Edward H. Little Memorial Trust Fund.
Foundation type: Independent foundation.
Financial data (yr. ended 12/31/04): Assets, $23,474,032 (M); gifts received, $623,430; expenditures, $1,678,936; qualifying distributions, $1,510,448; giving activities include $1,479,626 for 17 grants (high: $500,000; low: $2,500).

Purpose and activities: Giving primarily for children's services, with emphasis on health care and medical research.
Fields of interest: Hospitals (specialty); Medical research, institute; Human services; Children, services.
Limitations: Applications not accepted. Giving primarily in the Memphis, TN, area. No grants to individuals.
Application information: Contributes only to pre-selected organizations.
   Board meeting date(s): Sept., Nov., Jan., and Apr.
Officers: Russell Whitehead, Pres.; Harriet McFadden, 1st. V.P.; Allison Garrott, 2nd V.P.; Suzanne Mallory, Recording Secy.; Ruthie Taylor, Corresponding Secy.; Branden Morrison, Treas.; Co- Melody Taylor, Treas.; Lucia Crenshaw, Co-Grant Chair.; Adele Wellford, Co-Grant Chair.
Number of staff: 1 part-time professional.
EIN: 620560292
Selected grants: The following grants were reported in 2003.
$500,000 to Childrens Foundation of Memphis, Research center, Memphis, TN.
$250,000 to Le Bonheur Childrens Medical Center, Memphis, TN.
$30,000 to Youth Villages, Arlington, TN.
$25,000 to Agape Child and Family Services, Memphis, TN.
$25,000 to Neighborhood School, Memphis, TN.
$10,800 to Boys and Girls Clubs of Greater Memphis, Memphis, TN.
$5,000 to ARC of the Mid-South, Memphis, TN.
$5,000 to Exchange Club Family Center of the Mid-South, Memphis, TN.
$5,000 to Special Kids and Families, Memphis, TN.
$1,800 to Harwood Center, Memphis, TN.

8654
Christy-Houston Foundation, Inc. ▼ ✧
1296 Dow St.
Murfreesboro, TN 37130 (615) 898-1140
Contact: Robert B. Mifflin, Exec. Dir.

Established in 1986 in TN; converted from the sale of Middle Tennessee Medical Center to Mid-State Baptist and Saint Thomas Hospitals.
Foundation type: Independent foundation.
Financial data (yr. ended 12/31/04): Assets, $88,726,697 (M); gifts received, $310; expenditures, $4,321,201; qualifying distributions, $3,712,689; giving activities include $3,507,014 for 17 grants (high: $1,100,000; low: $9,900; average: $50,000–$200,000).
Purpose and activities: Giving primarily for health, education, and arts and culture.
Fields of interest: Hospitals (general); Nursing care; Health care; Health organizations, association; Nutrition; Residential/custodial care, hospices; Community development.
Type of support: Building/renovation; Equipment; Scholarship funds; Matching/challenge support.
Limitations: Giving limited to Rutherford County, TN. No support for religious, political, or veterans' organizations or historical societies. No grants to individuals, operating expenses or endowments.
Publications: Application guidelines; Grants list.
Application information: Application form not required.
   Initial approach: Proposal (less than 5 pages)
   Copies of proposal: 1
   Deadline(s): None
   Board meeting date(s): Varies

Officers and Directors:* Ed Delbridge,* Chair. and Pres.; Larry N. Haynes,* Vice-Chair.; Ed C. Loughry, Jr., Secy.-Treas.; Robert B. Mifflin, Exec. Dir.; Granville S.R. Bouldin; Henry King Butler, M.D.; David C. Davis; Ed Elam; Thomas Hord; William H. Huddleston III; Roger C. Maples; Hubert L. McCullough, Jr.; Matt B. Murfree III.
Number of staff: 1 part-time professional; 1 full-time support.
EIN: 621280998
Selected grants: The following grants were reported in 2004.
$1,100,000 to Vanderbilt University Childrens Hospital, Nashville, TN. For helicopter pad.
$1,000,000 to YMCA of Nashville and Middle Tennessee, Nashville, TN. For North Rutherford County Center.
$628,324 to Middle Tennessee State University, Murfreesboro, TN. For Nursing Education Building.
$200,000 to Cumberland Heights Alcohol and Drug Treatment Center, Nashville, TN. For building program.
$175,000 to Vanderbilt University, Nashville, TN. For nursing scholarships.
$122,222 to Belmont University, Nashville, TN. For occupational and physical therapy equipment.
$75,528 to Salvation Army of Murfreesboro, Murfreesboro, TN. For facility repairs.
$75,500 to Community Helpers, Murfreesboro, TN. For prescriptions for needy.
$50,000 to Linebaugh Public Library, Murfreesboro, TN. For matching grant for book mobile.
$38,000 to Rutherford County Primary Care, Murfreesboro, TN. For equipment.

8655
The Chrysalis Foundation ✧
2444 Broad St.
Chattanooga, TN 37408
Contact: Mary N. Moore, Pres.

Established in 1992 in TN.
Donor: Mary N. Moore.
Foundation type: Independent foundation.
Financial data (yr. ended 12/31/05): Assets, $5,160,163 (M); gifts received, $142,095; expenditures, $952,848; qualifying distributions, $897,042; giving activities include $896,810 for grants.
Fields of interest: Federated giving programs.
Type of support: General/operating support.
Limitations: Giving primarily in TN. No grants to individuals.
Application information: Application form not required.
   Initial approach: 2-page letter or proposal
   Deadline(s): None
   Final notification: 1-3 months
Officers and Director:* Mary N. Moore,* Pres.; William N. Bailey, Secy.; W. Theodore Moore, Treas.
EIN: 621497058
Selected grants: The following grants were reported in 2003.
$70,000 to Elephant Sanctuary in Hohenwald, Hohenwald, TN. For operating support.
$35,630 to Chattanooga Community Kitchen, Chattanooga, TN. For operating support.
$30,000 to Habitat for Humanity of Greater Chattanooga, Chattanooga, TN. For operating support.

$30,000 to Interfaith Hospitality Network of Greater Chattanooga, Chattanooga, TN. For operating support.

$25,000 to Baylor School, Chattanooga, TN. For operating support.

$25,000 to Community Foundation of Greater Chattanooga, Chattanooga, TN. For operating support.

$20,000 to Childrens Medical Mission of Haiti, Chattanooga, TN. For operating support.

$20,000 to New Life Homes, Chattanooga, TN. For operating support.

$20,000 to Tennessee Coalition to Abolish State Killing, Nashville, TN. For operating support.

$20,000 to United Way of Chattanooga, Chattanooga, TN. For operating support.

8656
CIC Foundation, Inc. ✧
2206 21st Ave. S., Ste. 301
Nashville, TN 37212 (615) 386-2296

Established in 2003 in TN.
Donor: Credit Bureau of Nashville, Inc.
Foundation type: Company-sponsored foundation.
Financial data (yr. ended 12/31/04): Assets, $8,416,753 (M); gifts received, $7,550,000; expenditures, $619,410; qualifying distributions, $482,416; giving activities include $240,750 for 27 grants (high: $30,450; low: $300), and $169,150 for 39 grants to individuals (high: $6,000; low: $750).
Purpose and activities: The foundation supports hospitals, hospices, and organizations involved with health and human services and awards college scholarships to students located in Kentucky and Tennessee.
Fields of interest: Hospitals (general); Health care; Residential/custodial care, hospices; Human services.
Type of support: Program development; Scholarships—to individuals; Scholarship funds; General/operating support.
Limitations: Giving primarily in KY and TN.
Application information: Application form required.
  Initial approach: Contact foundation for application information
  Deadline(s): Apr. 1
Officer and Directors: William D. Maxfield,* Chair.; Gary V. Forsythe, Pres.; Charles C. Martin, Secy.; Leslie B. Enoch II; W. Dale Maxfield, Sr.; J. Terry Olive; M. Terry Turner.
EIN: 562348880

8657
Citizens Bank Tri-Cities Foundation, Ltd. ✧ ☆
(formerly Joe LaPorte, Jr. Foundation, Ltd.)
1 Citizens Plz.
302-304 E. Broad St., Ste. 301
Elizabethton, TN 37643-2715 (423) 547-2084
Contact: Sam J. LaPorte, Dir.

Established in 1990 in TN.
Donors: Joseph LaPorte; Sam LaPorte; Citizens Bank; GSC, Inc.; Christopher LaPorte; Stephen LaPorte.
Foundation type: Independent foundation.
Financial data (yr. ended 12/31/05): Assets, $2,974,320 (M); gifts received, $1,253,311; expenditures, $392,808; qualifying distributions,

$376,789; giving activities include $376,789 for 41 grants (high: $129,500; low: $50).
Fields of interest: Higher education; Food banks; Youth development; Federated giving programs; Protestant federated giving programs; Religion.
Limitations: Giving limited to the greater Elizabethton, TN, area. No grants to individuals.
Application information: Application form not required.
  Initial approach: Letter
  Deadline(s): None
Directors: Christopher LaPorte; Joseph LaPorte III; Sam LaPorte; Stephen LaPorte.
EIN: 581914223
Selected grants: The following grants were reported in 2004.
$129,500 to University of Tennessee, Knoxville, TN.
$15,500 to Immanuel Baptist Church, Nashville, TN.
$5,833 to United Way of Greater Kingsport, Kingsport, TN.
$5,674 to United Way of Elizabethton Carter County, Elizabethton, TN.
$2,337 to United Way of Bristol, TN-VA, Bristol, TN.
$643 to United Way, Johnson City Area, Johnson City, TN.

8658
CLARCOR Foundation ✧
840 Crescent Centre Dr., Ste. 600
Franklin, TN 37067
Contact: Pete Nangel, Chair.

Established in 1954 in IL.
Donor: CLARCOR Inc.
Foundation type: Company-sponsored foundation.
Financial data (yr. ended 12/31/04): Assets, $7,743,870 (M); expenditures, $768,930; qualifying distributions, $752,843; giving activities include $752,843 for 54 grants (high: $465,000; low: $80).
Purpose and activities: The foundation supports organizations involved with arts and culture, higher education, health, and human services.
Fields of interest: Museums; Performing arts, theater; Arts; Higher education; Hospitals (general); Health care; YM/YWCAs & YM/YWHAs; Children, day care; Youth, services; Human services; Federated giving programs.
Type of support: General/operating support; Annual campaigns; Capital campaigns; Employee matching gifts.
Limitations: Giving primarily in areas of company operations in IL, KY, NC, NE, OH, OK, and PA, with emphasis on Rockford, IL. No grants to individuals, or for endowments, research, scholarships, or fellowships; no loans.
Publications: Application guidelines; Program policy statement.
Application information: Application form required.
  Initial approach: Contact nearest company facility for application form
  Copies of proposal: 1
  Deadline(s): None
  Board meeting date(s): Feb., May, Aug., and Nov.
Officers and Trustees: David J. Lindsay,* Chair.; Joann Nunez, Secy.; Marybeth Averill; Marcia S. Blaylock; Norman E. Johnson; Brian Keith; Bruce A. Klein; David J. Lindsay.
EIN: 366032573

8659
The Clayton Family Foundation ✧
620 Market St., Ste. 102
Knoxville, TN 37902 (865) 380-3301, ext. 6610
Application address: c/o Jeanne C. Campbell, 3340 Lake View Dr., Knoxville, TN, 37919

Established in 1991 in TN.
Donor: James L. Clayton.
Foundation type: Independent foundation.
Financial data (yr. ended 12/31/05): Assets, $98,888,661 (M); expenditures, $2,042,557; qualifying distributions, $1,974,311; giving activities include $1,974,254 for 136 grants (high: $203,000; low: $100).
Purpose and activities: Giving primarily for higher education, health associations, youth development, the arts, hospitals, and Christian agencies.
Fields of interest: Arts, multipurpose centers/programs; Arts; Higher education; Hospitals (general); Reproductive health, OBGYN/Birthing centers; Health care; Health organizations, association; Human services; Children/youth, services; Foundations (community); Federated giving programs; Christian agencies & churches.
Limitations: Giving primarily in areas of company operations, particularly the Knoxville, TN, area, and the east TN area. No grants to individuals.
Application information: One grant request per calendar year. Application form not required.
  Deadline(s): None
  Final notification: 2 to 3 months following receipt of grant request
Officers and Directors: James L. Clayton,* Pres.; Jeanne C. Campbell,* Secy.; Janice K. Clayton; Ruth B. Clayton; Matthew D. Daniels; Carl Koella.
EIN: 581970851
Selected grants: The following grants were reported in 2003.
$200,500 to University of Tennessee, Knoxville, TN. For Frank H. McClung Museum.
$200,000 to United Way of Greater Knoxville, Knoxville, TN. For general support.
$151,000 to Knoxville Symphony Orchestra, Knoxville, TN. For general support.
$105,000 to Baptist Health System Foundation, Knoxville, TN. For Birthing Center.
$100,000 to Historic Tennessee Theater Foundation, Knoxville, TN. For renovation.
$100,000 to Knoxville Museum of Art, Knoxville, TN. For general support.
$100,000 to Project GRAD Knoxville, Knoxville, TN. For general support.
$100,000 to Webb School of Knoxville, Knoxville, TN. For general support.
$50,000 to Knoxville Zoological Park, Knoxville, TN. For general support.
$25,000 to Knoxvilles Promise - The Alliance for Youth, Knoxville, TN.

8660
The Community Foundation of Greater Chattanooga, Inc. ▼
1270 Market St.
Chattanooga, TN 37402 (423) 265-0586
Contact: Peter T. Cooper, Pres.; For grants: Robin Koch, Prog. Off.
FAX: (423) 265-0587; E-mail: info2@cfgc.org; Additional E-mail: pcooper@cfgc.org; Grant application E-mail: rkoch@cfgc.org; URL: http://www.cfgc.org
Scholarship E-mail: rsmith@cfgc.org

Incorporated in 1963 in TN.

Foundation type: Community foundation.

Financial data (yr. ended 12/31/05): Assets, $61,414,930 (M); gifts received, $16,720,635; expenditures, $18,973,357; giving activities include $18,258,837 for 2,615 grants.

Purpose and activities: The foundation seeks to promote and enhance the well-being of the inhabitants of the greater Chattanooga, TN area. Primary areas of interest include education, community development, youth and child development, the arts, race relations, and literacy development.

Fields of interest: Performing arts; Performing arts, dance; Arts; Education, early childhood education; Child development, education; Elementary school/education; Higher education; Adult education—literacy, basic skills & GED; Education, reading; Education; Environment, natural resources; Environment; Medical care, rehabilitation; Children/youth, services; Child development, services; Family services; Civil rights, race/intergroup relations; Urban/community development; Community development; Minorities; Women.

International interests: Japan.

Type of support: Management development/capacity building; Capital campaigns; Building/renovation; Equipment; Land acquisition; Program development; Seed money; Scholarship funds; Program evaluation; Scholarships—to individuals; Exchange programs.

Limitations: Giving limited to the greater Chattanooga, TN, area. No support for private schools, religious causes, or veterans' or fraternal organizations, public agencies, state, national or regional organizations. No grants to individuals (except for scholarship programs), endowment campaigns, operating support for existing programs, conferences, advertising, telephone solicitations, fundraising expenses, federated fund drives; no loans.

Publications: Application guidelines; Annual report; Biennial report (including application guidelines); Informational brochure; Informational brochure (including application guidelines).

Application information: Visit foundation Web site for application form, guidelines, and specific deadlines. Application form required.

  Initial approach: Telephone program staff

  Copies of proposal: 2

  Deadline(s): 4th Friday of Jan., May, and Sept.

  Board meeting date(s): Quarterly; program committee meets to award grants 3 times per year

  Final notification: Apr., Aug., and Dec.

Officers and Directors:* Spencer McCallie,* Chair.; Ruth S. Holmberg,* Vice-Chair.; Grant Law,* Vice-Chair.; Susan O'Hare,* Vice-Chair.; Peter T. Cooper, Pres.; Marty Robinson, V.P., Donor Rels.; Rebecca Underwood, V.P., Finance and Admin.; Ansley Moses,* Secy.; Nick Decosimo,* Treas.; Max Bahner; Paul Campbell III; Clif Cleveland, M.D.; Ann Coulter; Kathy Hanson; Patsy Hazlewood; Dallas Joseph; Jerry Konahia; Candy Kruesi; Jill Levine; Kristina Montague; Hilda Murray; Chris Ramsey; Lynn Schmissrauter; Pete Serodino; Virginia Anne Sharber; Mary Tanner; Charlesetta Woodard-Thompson.

Number of staff: 5 full-time professional; 2 full-time support.

EIN: 626045999

Selected grants: The following grants were reported in 2005.

$20,000 to East Fifth Street Child Care Center, Chattanooga, TN. For new building.

$20,000 to Sheet Metal Workers Knoxville Area Joint Apprenticeship Training Fund, Knoxville, TN. For new building in Chattanooga.

$20,000 to Tennessee Coalition Against Domestic and Sexual Abuse, Nashville, TN. For DVC Empowerment Project, providing free job skills training for victims of domestic violence.

$20,000 to Woodmore Hall Youth Association, Chattanooga, TN. For football and cheerleading uniforms and equipment.

$19,845 to University of Tennessee, Department of Education, Knoxville, TN. For Music Therapy Gateway in Communication, innovative program providing Neurological Music Therapy sessions to autistic children.

$19,580 to Read Chattanooga, Chattanooga, TN. For Community Outreach and Education Program.

$17,190 to Hamilton County Department of Education, Chattanooga, TN. For project, High School Guidance Counselors Using Technology in Counseling for College, to create college and career center in each high school.

$14,590 to Saint Andrews Center, Chattanooga, TN. For revitalization project providing educational, social, economic, recreational, and cultural opportunities to disadvantaged families in Highland Park and East Chattanooga.

$10,000 to Ballet Tennessee, Chattanooga, TN. For Saint Andrews Center Pilot Dance Program, Creating Learning Environments in Neighborhoods.

$10,000 to Hamilton, County of, Family Justice Alliance, Chattanooga, TN. For strategic planning.

8661
Community Foundation of Greater Memphis ▼

1900 Union Ave.
Memphis, TN 38104 (901) 728-4600
Contact: Gid H. Smith, C.E.O.; For grants and scholarships: Melissa Wolowicz, Dir., Progs.
FAX: (901) 722-0010; E-mail: gsmith@cfgm.org; Tel. for scholarships: (901) 722-0054; E-mail for grants and scholarships: mwolowicz@cfgm.org;
URL: http://www.cfgm.org

Established in 1969 in TN; combined operations with The Memphis-Plough Community Foundation in 1989.

Foundation type: Community foundation.

Financial data (yr. ended 4/30/06): Assets, $280,223,212 (M); gifts received, $29,277,908; expenditures, $36,018,228; giving activities include $32,649,275 for grants.

Purpose and activities: The foundation seeks to provide support for the benefit of the geographic area that the foundation serves, and to strengthen the community through philanthropy.

Fields of interest: Arts; Education; Environment; Health care; Human services; Community development, neighborhood development; Philanthropy/voluntarism; Religion.

Type of support: Research; Management development/capacity building; Program development; Seed money; Scholarship funds; Technical assistance.

Limitations: Giving limited to Crittenden County, AR, DeSoto, Marshall, Tate, and Tunica counties, MS, and Fayette, Shelby, and Tipton counties, TN. No grants to individuals (except for scholarships), or for endowments, capital or building funds, annual campaigns, code enforcement, or core operating costs; no loans.

Publications: Application guidelines; Annual report; Newsletter.

Application information: Visit foundation Web site for grant application guidelines. Community Grants applicants are notified whether or not they are invited to submit a full proposal based on Letter of Intent. The foundation holds a mandatory pre-application workshop; contact foundation to RSVP. Application form required.

  Initial approach: Community Grants Pre-Application Workshop

  Copies of proposal: 1

  Deadline(s): Sept. 5 for Letter of Intent; Nov. 1 for proposals; Apr. 3 for scholarships; and May 15 for Collierville Foundation

  Board meeting date(s): Mar., May, Sept., and Dec.

  Final notification: Dec. 31

Officers and Governors:* Hal D. Crenshaw,* Chair.; Gid H. Smith, C.E.O. and Pres.; Andrea L. Reynolds, Exec. V.P. and Secy.; Mack E. McCaul, Jr., V.P. and C.F.O.; Patti Smith, V.P., Donor Rels., Devel. and Comms.; Sudhir K. Agrawal; Sandra H. Burke; V. Lynn Evans; Robert M. Fockler; Susan H. Foster; Edward J. Goldstein; Robert D. Gooch III; George M. Griesback; Fred D. Johnson; Dorothy Orgill Kirsch; R. Patrick Kruczek; Charles Lee; Yvonne S. Madlock; A. Stephen McDaniel; D. Stephen Morrow; W. Lytle Nichol IV; Ben C. Peternell; R. Michael Potter; Stephen H. Rhea, Jr.; Diane G. Sachs; Dianne A. Shockley-Mall; Robert Smithwick III; Bruce C. Taylor; Linda Tharp; Megan Dunbar Turner; John W. Ueleke; O. Lee Wakeman; Ronald A. Walter; Johnnie B. Watson.

Number of staff: 10 full-time professional; 3 full-time support.

EIN: 581723645

Selected grants: The following grants were reported in 2005.

$3,000,000 to Boys and Girls Clubs of Greater Memphis, Memphis, TN. 2 grants: $2,000,000 (For Vocational Training Facility), $1,000,000 (For operating support for Vocational Training Center).

$1,325,000 to Hope Christian Community Foundation, Memphis, TN. For general operating support.

$1,000,000 to Memphis Arts Council, Memphis, TN. For general operating support.

$675,000 to Alzheimers Day Services of Memphis, Memphis, TN. For general operating support.

$225,000 to Bellevue Baptist Church, Memphis, TN. For Love Offering.

$20,000 to Birthright of Memphis, Memphis, TN. For general operating support.

$17,000 to Childrens Museum of Memphis, Memphis, TN. For general operating support.

$16,244 to Second Presbyterian Church, Memphis, TN. For general operating support.

$15,000 to Saint Marys Episcopal School, Memphis, TN. For general operating support.

8662
Community Foundation of Middle Tennessee, Inc.

(formerly Nashville Community Foundation, Inc.)
3833 Cleghorn Ave., No. 400
Nashville, TN 37215-2519 (615) 321-4939
Contact: Ellen E. Lehman, Pres.

FAX: (615) 327-2746; E-mail: mail@cfmt.org;
Additional tel.: (888) 540-5200; URL: http://
www.cfmt.org

Established in 1991 in TN.
Foundation type: Community foundation.
Financial data (yr. ended 12/31/05): Assets,
$368,437,097 (M); gifts received, $44,710,301;
expenditures, $38,515,616; giving activities
include $35,063,130 for 3,863 grants.
Purpose and activities: The foundation is dedicated
to enriching the quality of life in middle Tennessee.
It serves as a leader, catalyst and resource for
philanthropy, and strives to build a permanent
endowment for the community for now and all time.
Fields of interest: Humanities; Historic
preservation/historical societies; Arts; Education;
Environment, natural resources; Environment;
Animal welfare; Animals/wildlife; Health care;
Health organizations, association; Employment;
Housing/shelter, development; Aging, centers/
services; Human services; Community
development, neighborhood development;
Community development; Aging.
Type of support: Program development.
Limitations: Giving limited to serving the 40
counties comprising the middle TN area. No support
for private foundations, religious or sectarian
purposes, private schools, biomedical or clinic
studies (other than those related to breast cancer),
or fundraising feasibility studies. No grants for
fundraising events, debt retirement, annual and
capital campaigns, endowment campaigns, general
operations, advertising, sponsorships, trips,
conferences, computers or equipment.
Publications: Annual report; Informational brochure;
Newsletter.
Application information: The foundation accepts
unsolicited proposals only for grants from
Unrestricted and Field-of-Interest funds. Visit
foundation Web site for application forms and
guidelines. Faxed or e-mailed applications are not
accepted. Application form required.
   Initial approach: Submit application form and
    attachments
   Copies of proposal: 1
   Deadline(s): May 1 for grants; Apr. 1 for
    scholarships
   Board meeting date(s): Feb., Apr., June, Sept.,
    Nov., and Dec.
   Final notification: Mid-Sept. for grants; May 1 for
    scholarships
Officers and Directors:* Nelson C. Andrews,*
Chair.; Ralph W. Mosley,* Vice-Chair.; Ellen E.
Lehman,* Pres.; Lani Wilkeson, V.P.; Jack B.
Turner,* Secy.; William T. Spitz,* Treas.; Melisa
Currey, Compt.; Charles W. Cook, Jr.; Ben Cundiff;
Kitty Moon Emery; Farzin Ferdowski; Darrell S.
Freeman; Thomas F. Frist, Jr.; Kerry Graham; Francis
Guess; James S. Gulmi; Gordon Inman; Catherine T.
Jackson; William B. King; Hon. William C. Koch, Jr.;
Kevin P. Lavender; Donna D. Nicely; Linda
Rebrovick; Michael D. Schmerling; Susan W.
Simons; Deborah F. Turner; Steve Turner; Betsy
Walkup.
Trustees: Judith Liff Barker; Jack O. Bovender, Jr.;
Betty M. Brown; George N. Bullard; Richard J.
Eskind; Charles O. Frazier; Joel C. Gordon; Aubrey B.
Harwell, Jr.; F.W. Lazenby; John E. Maupin, Jr.; Ben
R. Rechter; Howard L. Stringer; Charles A. Trost;
Jamye C. Williams; Jerry B. Williams; Robert K. Zelle.
Number of staff: 20 full-time professional.
EIN: 621471789

8663
Conwood Charitable Trust ✧
(formerly American Snuff Company Charitable Trust)
c/o Trust Dept., Regions Bank
1100 Ridgeway Loop, 5th Fl.
Memphis, TN 38120
Additional address: c/o Ed Roberson, Conwood Co.,
813 Ridge Lake Blvd., Memphis, TN 38119,
tel.: (901) 761-2050

Established in 1952 in TN.
Donors: American Snuff Co.; Conwood Co.
Foundation type: Company-sponsored foundation.
Financial data (yr. ended 12/31/05): Assets,
$5,756,037 (M); expenditures, $366,402;
qualifying distributions, $341,691; giving activities
include $324,345 for 56 grants (high: $28,000;
low: $845).
Purpose and activities: The trust supports
organizations involved with arts and culture, higher
education, health, human services, community
development, and religion.
Fields of interest: Museums; Arts; Higher
education; Health care; Children/youth, services;
Human services; Community development; Religion.
Limitations: Giving primarily in the Memphis, TN,
area. No grants to individuals.
Application information: Application form not
required.
   Initial approach: Proposal
   Deadline(s): None
Trustees: Ed Roberson; Regions Bank.
EIN: 626036034

8664
The Danner Foundation ✧
2 International Dr., Ste. 510
Nashville, TN 37217-2010
Contact: Raymond L. Danner, Pres.

Established in 1988 in TN.
Donor: Raymond L. Danner.
Foundation type: Independent foundation.
Financial data (yr. ended 12/31/05): Assets,
$6,633,108 (M); expenditures, $616,784;
qualifying distributions, $451,943; giving activities
include $451,943 for 73 grants (high: $78,493;
low: $250; average: $1,000–$10,000).
Purpose and activities: Giving for the arts,
education, and Christian organizations.
Fields of interest: Arts; Secondary school/
education; Higher education; Christian agencies &
churches.
Type of support: Emergency funds; Scholarship
funds.
Limitations: Giving primarily in TN. No grants to
individuals.
Application information: Application form not
required.
   Initial approach: Letter
   Copies of proposal: 1
   Deadline(s): Sept. 30
   Board meeting date(s): Dec.
   Final notification: After Dec.
Officers and Directors:* Raymond L. Danner,* Pres.
and Secy.-Treas.; Judith B. Danner,* V.P.; Gail D.
Greil; Donna D. Wilson.
Number of staff: 2 full-time support.
EIN: 581803926
Selected grants: The following grants were reported
in 2003.
$200,000 to Father Ryan High School, Nashville,
TN.

$13,300 to Arthritis Foundation, Nashville, TN.
$13,300 to Boy Scouts of America, Middle
   Tennessee Council, Nashville, TN.
$10,500 to United Way of Metropolitan Nashville,
   Nashville, TN.
$10,000 to Tennessee Repertory Theater,
   Nashville, TN.
$10,000 to Vanderbilt Bill Wilkerson Center for
   Otolaryngology and Communicative Sciences,
   Nashville, TN.
$7,500 to Waldens Puddle, Joelton, TN.
$6,000 to Frist Center for the Visual Arts
   Foundation, Nashville, TN.
$5,000 to Nashville Zoo, Brentwood, TN.
$1,000 to Ducks Unlimited, Memphis, TN.

8665
Joe C. Davis Foundation ▼
28 White Bridge Rd., Ste. 210
Nashville, TN 37205
Contact: Shannon Barton, Prog. Off.
Application address: 4343 Sneed Rd., Nashville, TN
37215; E-mail: bartonshan@aol.com

Established in 1976 in TN.
Donor: Joe C. Davis‡.
Foundation type: Independent foundation.
Financial data (yr. ended 9/30/05): Assets,
$106,342,684 (M); gifts received, $10,000;
expenditures, $6,879,007; qualifying distributions,
$5,144,880; giving activities include $5,100,500
for 38 grants (high: $2,385,000; low: $500;
average: $1,000–$500,000).
Purpose and activities: Support for all levels of
education; grants also for health, medical research,
and human services.
Fields of interest: Education, early childhood
education; Elementary school/education;
Education; Health care; Substance abuse, services;
Health organizations, association; Cancer;
Alcoholism; Medical research, institute; Cancer
research.
Type of support: Program development; Seed
money; Scholarship funds; Research; Matching/
challenge support.
Limitations: Giving primarily in the Nashville, TN,
area.
Publications: Application guidelines.
Application information: Application form not
required.
   Initial approach: Letter (2-3 pages) sent via e-mail
   Copies of proposal: 1
   Deadline(s): July 1
   Board meeting date(s): Sept. 10
   Final notification: Sept. 30
Trustees: Bond Davis DeLoache; William R.
DeLoache, M.D.; William R. DeLoache, Jr.; Frances
D. Ellison.
Number of staff: 2 part-time support.
EIN: 626125481
Selected grants: The following grants were reported
in 2005.
$2,885,000 to Vanguard Charitable Endowment
   Program, Southeastern, PA. 2 grants:
   $2,385,000, $500,000
$500,000 to Siloam Family Health Center,
   Nashville, TN. For debt reduction and capital
   campaign.
$325,000 to Belmont University, Nashville, TN. 2
   grants: $250,000 (For nursing scholarship
   endowment), $75,000 (For nursing scholarship
   endowment).

$279,000 to Vanderbilt University Medical Center, Department of Urology, Nashville, TN. For Urology fellows.

$250,000 to Montgomery Bell Academy, Nashville, TN. For scholarship endowment.

$100,000 to Nurses for Newborns Foundation, Nashville, TN. For program support.

$75,000 to Harpeth Hall School, Nashville, TN.

$75,000 to Interfaith Dental Clinic of Nashville, Nashville, TN. For expansion campaign.

8666
The Day Foundation ◇
530 Oak Court Dr., Ste. 325
Memphis, TN 38117
Contact: Jean Phebus, Prog. Off.

Established in 1960 in MS.
Donors: Clarence C. Day; Day Cos., Inc.
Foundation type: Independent foundation.
Financial data (yr. ended 12/31/05): Assets, $32,639,074 (M); gifts received, $1,000,000; expenditures, $1,476,327; qualifying distributions, $1,320,361; giving activities include $1,302,287 for 12 grants (high: $482,289; low: $1,000).
Purpose and activities: Funding for education and for community projects in the arts and social services.
Fields of interest: Arts; Education; Youth development, centers/clubs; Children/youth, services.
Type of support: Seed money; Matching/challenge support.
Limitations: Giving primarily in the Memphis, TN, area. No grants to individuals, or for endowment funds, scholarships, fellowships, capital funds, or operating budgets; no loans.
Publications: Application guidelines; Annual report; Informational brochure.
Application information: Write for guidelines. Telephone inquiries are discouraged. Application form not required.
  Initial approach: Concept letter (not to exceed 3 typed pages)
  Copies of proposal: 1
  Deadline(s): None
  Board meeting date(s): As necessary
  Final notification: 2 to 3 months
Officer and Trustees:* Clarence C. Day,* Chair.; David Caywood; William G. Griesbeck.
Number of staff: 1 part-time support.
EIN: 646025122
Selected grants: The following grants were reported in 2005.
$595,400 to Youth Villages, Arlington, TN. 2 grants: $10,400, $585,000
$482,289 to Mississippi State University, Mississippi State, MS.
$66,608 to Rhodes College, Memphis, TN. 2 grants: $4,500, $62,108
$11,399 to Easy K. Foundation, Zion, AR.
$9,191 to University of Memphis, Memphis, TN.
$1,000 to Nature Conservancy, Arlington, VA.

8667
The Terry D. and Rosann B. Douglass
Foundation ◇ ☆
c/o Anne Sale
2035 Lakeside Ctr., Ste. 180
Knoxville, TN 37922
Contact: Terry D. Douglass, Dir.

Established in 1994 in TN.
Donors: Terry D. Douglass; Rosann B. Douglass; Lance Robinson; Deborah Robinson; Norris Hill; Melissa Hill; Dean Douglass; Leslie Douglass.
Foundation type: Independent foundation.
Financial data (yr. ended 12/31/05): Assets, $18,042,623 (M); gifts received, $16,893,432; expenditures, $457,306; qualifying distributions, $431,700; giving activities include $431,700 for 20 grants (high: $332,200; low: $100).
Purpose and activities: Giving to programs that benefit the poor and disadvantaged, youth, education, and/or religion.
Fields of interest: Human services; Youth.
Limitations: Giving primarily in Knoxville, TN. No grants to individuals.
Directors: Rosann B. Douglass; Terry D. Douglass.
EIN: 582068304

8668
Louis R. Draughon Foundation ◇
c/o AmSouth Bank
315 Deaderick St., 4th Fl.
Nashville, TN 37237-0401

Established in 1982 in TN.
Donor: Elizabeth F. Draughon†.
Foundation type: Independent foundation.
Financial data (yr. ended 12/31/05): Assets, $7,941,442 (M); expenditures, $559,487; qualifying distributions, $482,810; giving activities include $472,500 for 30 grants (high: $110,000; low: $1,000).
Purpose and activities: Giving primarily to educational institutions, human services, and Christian agencies, churches, and schools.
Fields of interest: Higher education; Education; Human services; YM/YWCAs & YM/YWHAs; Children, services; Christian agencies & churches.
Type of support: General/operating support.
Limitations: Applications not accepted. Giving primarily in TN. No grants to individuals.
Application information: Contributes only to pre-selected organizations.
Officers and Directors:* James Wilhite,* Pres.; Jeanette Dorris,* V.P.; Robert Newman,* Secy.-Treas.; Bob Andrews; Edith Perry.
Trustee: AmSouth Bank.
EIN: 621147685
Selected grants: The following grants were reported in 2004.
$100,000 to David Lipscomb University, Nashville, TN.
$100,000 to Freed-Hardeman University, Henderson, TN.
$100,000 to Springfield Church of Christ, Springfield, OH.
$25,000 to YMCA.
$10,000 to Association for Guidance, Aid, Placement and Empathy (AGAPE), Nashville, TN.
$10,000 to Rainbow Omega, Eastaboga, AL.
$7,000 to Davidson Academy, Lexington, NC.
$3,500 to Benton Hall School, Nashville, TN.
$3,000 to Columbia Academy, Portland, OR.
$2,500 to Outlook Nashville, Nashville, TN.

8669
Dugas Family Foundation ◇ ☆
(formerly The Laura Jo and Wayne Dugas Family Foundation)
138 2nd Ave. N., Ste. 200
Nashville, TN 37201

Established in 1998 in TN.
Donor: Laura Jo Turner Dugas.
Foundation type: Independent foundation.
Financial data (yr. ended 12/31/04): Assets, $33,136,168 (M); gifts received, $1,839,577; expenditures, $1,914,335; qualifying distributions, $1,894,398; giving activities include $1,857,200 for 7 grants (high: $850,000; low: $1,000).
Fields of interest: Arts; Higher education; Hospitals (general); Human services; Children, services; Protestant agencies & churches.
Limitations: Applications not accepted. Giving primarily in Hammond, LA.
Application information: Unsolicited requests for funds not accepted.
Trustees: Laura Jo Turner Dugas; Stephen H. Dugas; Wayne F. Dugas, Sr.; Wayne F. Dugas, Jr.; William B. Dugas.
EIN: 582426636

8670
H. W. Durham Foundation ◇
5050 Poplar Ave., Ste. 2132
Memphis, TN 38157-2132
Contact: Chris Cooper, Prog. Dir.

Incorporated in 1955 in TN.
Donor: H.W. Durham†.
Foundation type: Independent foundation.
Financial data (yr. ended 12/31/05): Assets, $0 (M); expenditures, $1,127,053; qualifying distributions, $846,953; giving activities include $632,271 for 44 grants (high: $70,000; low: $376).
Purpose and activities: Giving primarily for the elderly and issues relating to the aging process.
Fields of interest: Aging, centers/services; Aging.
Type of support: Program development; Conferences/seminars; Publication; Seed money; Fellowships; Scholarship funds; Research; Technical assistance; Program-related investments/loans.
Limitations: Giving primarily in Memphis and western TN.
Publications: Application guidelines; Informational brochure (including application guidelines).
Application information: Application form required.
  Initial approach: Letter
  Copies of proposal: 5
  Deadline(s): Jan. 15th, Apr. 1st and Aug. 1st
  Board meeting date(s): Feb., May, and Sept.
  Final notification: Immediately after board meeting
Officers: Thomas H. Durham, Jr., Chair.; Jenks E. McCrory, Pres.; John B. Coleman, Jr., V.P.; Kaye D. Brooksbank, Secy.; Larry Boone, Treas.
Directors: Bettie Durham; Evertt Huffard; Hugh McHenry; Linda Nichols.
Number of staff: 2 full-time professional; 1 part-time support.
EIN: 620583854
Selected grants: The following grants were reported in 2003.
$106,003 to Metropolitan Interfaith Council on Affordable Housing, Minneapolis, MN. 2 grants: $31,003, $75,000 (For Expanding Senior Companion Program).

$52,250 to Alzheimers Day Services of Memphis, Memphis, TN. For kitchen equipment for new Southeast Day Care Center.

$36,800 to Memphis Pink Palace Museum, Memphis, TN. 2 grants: $26,946, $9,854

$33,981 to Church Health Center of Memphis, Memphis, TN. For computer upgrade to meet new Medicare requirements.

$24,000 to W K N O-TV 10 Memphis Community Television Foundation, Memphis, TN. For sponsorship of Lawrence Welk TV Program and Live Show.

$17,000 to Memphis/Shelby County Public Library, Memphis, TN. For technical upgrade for radio station.

$15,000 to Brooks Museum of Art, Memphis, TN.

$10,000 to Harding University Graduate School of Religion, Memphis, TN. For Library Fund Endowment.

8671
East Tennessee Foundation
625 Market St., Ste. 1400
Knoxville, TN 37902 (865) 524-1223
Contact: Michael T. McClamroch, C.E.O.
FAX: (865) 637-6039; E-mail: etf@etf.org; Additional tel.: (877) 524-1223; URL: http://www.easttennesseefoundation.org

Incorporated in 1958 in TN.
Foundation type: Community foundation.
Financial data (yr. ended 12/31/04): Assets, $69,436,053 (M); gifts received, $6,805,513; expenditures, $21,468,766; giving activities include $20,238,415 for 772 grants (high: $4,900,000; low: $50), and $400,000 for 2 loans/program-related investments (high: $200,000; low: $200,000).
Purpose and activities: Giving to organizations which strengthen the capacity of existing institutions to reach a broader segment of the community, encourage cooperation, decrease duplication of services, and develop partnerships that can have a synergistic effect; address diversity and positive change; encourage citizen participation in meeting community challenges; demonstrate vision, action, effectiveness, good management and quality; focus on prevention and education; and provides models for replication.
Fields of interest: Arts; Education; Housing/shelter; Children/youth, services; Community development.
Type of support: General/operating support; Building/renovation; Equipment; Program development; Conferences/seminars; Publication; Seed money; Scholarship funds; Technical assistance; Consulting services; Program evaluation; Program-related investments/loans; Matching/challenge support.
Limitations: Giving limited to Knoxville, TN, and its 23 surrounding counties. No grants for annual campaigns, capital fund drives, endowment or general fundraising campaigns, research projects, or general operating budgets.
Publications: Application guidelines; Annual report; Informational brochure (including application guidelines); Newsletter.
Application information: Visit foundation Web site for application guidelines. Application form required.
  Initial approach: E-mail or telephone
  Copies of proposal: 1
  Deadline(s): Varies
  Board meeting date(s): 5 times per year
  Final notification: Varies

Officers and Directors:* Mark K. Williams,* Chair.; Larry B. Martin,* Vice-Chair.; Michael T. McClamroch,* C.E.O. and Pres.; Robert Calloway, V.P., Advancement; Terry Holley, V.P., Progs. and Regional Devel.; Jackie Lane, V.P., Comms.; Carolyn Schwenn,* V.P., Finance & Admin. and Secy.; T. Scott Thompson,* Treas.; Frank M. Addicks; Darrell D. Akins; Marie F. Alcorn; Stephen C. Arnett; Howard Z. Blum; Betsey R. Bush; Vance W. Cheek, Jr.; Edwena L. Crowe; Richard Davies; Frank B. Gray; Peyton T. Hairston, Jr.; Wm. Gregory Hall, Jr.; Jenny L. Hines; Mark A. Jackson; Maribel W. Koella; Sherri P. Lee; James A. Ley; H. Lee Martin; Cheryl Massingale; J.N. McGuire, Jr.; Anne M. McKinney; Alice A. Mercer; Marian E. Oates; Charles M. Peccolo; J. Daniel Pressley; S. Pace Robinson; J. Kenneth Porter; B. Fielding Rolston; Oliver S. Thomas; Carol G. Transou; Lew E. Weems; Paul G. Willson; Annette E. Winston; Margit S. Worsham.
Number of staff: 7 full-time professional; 1 part-time professional; 4 full-time support.
EIN: 620807696

8672
EBS Foundation ◇
c/o Elizabeth Bullard Stadler
2212 Hillsboro Valley Rd.
Brentwood, TN 37027

Established in 1989 in TN.
Donor: Ella Hayes.
Foundation type: Independent foundation.
Financial data (yr. ended 12/31/05): Assets, $8,897,036 (M); gifts received, $205,697; expenditures, $989,962; qualifying distributions, $826,667; giving activities include $776,810 for 215 grants (high: $100,000; low: $100).
Purpose and activities: Giving primarily to Christian organizations, family and children's services, and human services.
Fields of interest: Arts; Education; Environment, natural resources; Boys & girls clubs; Human services; Christian agencies & churches.
Type of support: Continuing support; Annual campaigns.
Limitations: Applications not accepted. Giving primarily in TN. No grants to individuals.
Application information: Contributes only to pre-selected organizations.
Trustee: Elizabeth Bullard Stadler.
EIN: 581797047

8673
The Jane and Richard Eskind and Family Foundation ◇
104 Lynnwood Blvd.
Nashville, TN 37205-2904

Established in 1986 in TN.
Donors: Jane Eskind; Richard Eskind.
Foundation type: Independent foundation.
Financial data (yr. ended 6/30/05): Assets, $6,712,289 (M); expenditures, $1,224,742; qualifying distributions, $1,223,190; giving activities include $1,221,003 for 116 grants (high: $500,000; low: $100).
Purpose and activities: Giving in a wide range of areas, with some emphasis on higher education, human services and the arts.
Fields of interest: Arts; Higher education; Human services; Jewish federated giving programs.

Limitations: Applications not accepted. Giving primarily in Nashville, TN. No grants to individuals.
Application information: Contributes only to pre-selected organizations.
Officers: Jane Eskind, Pres.; Richard Eskind, Secy.
Trustees: William H. Eskind; Ellen E. Lehman.
EIN: 621289998
Selected grants: The following grants were reported in 2005.
$110,700 to Congregation Micah, Brentwood, TN.
$5,000 to Meharry Medical College, Nashville, TN.
$4,000 to Nashville Symphony, Nashville, TN.
$1,500 to Ensworth School, Nashville, TN.
$1,500 to Nashville Public Library, Nashville, TN.
$1,500 to University School of Nashville, Nashville, TN.
$1,000 to Adventure Science Center, Nashville, TN.
$1,000 to American Baptist College, Nashville, TN.
$1,000 to Frist Center for the Visual Arts, Nashville, TN.
$1,000 to Nashville Childrens Theater, Nashville, TN.

8674
The Annette and Irwin Eskind Family Foundation ◇
541 Jackson Blvd.
Nashville, TN 37205-3453

Established in 1986 in TN.
Donors: Annette Eskind; Irwin Eskind; Jeffrey Eskind; Steven Eskind.
Foundation type: Independent foundation.
Financial data (yr. ended 6/30/06): Assets, $4,734,972 (M); expenditures, $1,397,283; qualifying distributions, $1,393,149; giving activities include $1,393,149 for grants.
Fields of interest: Arts; Higher education; Hospitals (general); Human services; Family services; Federated giving programs; Jewish federated giving programs; Jewish agencies & temples.
Limitations: Applications not accepted. Giving primarily in Nashville, TN. No grants to individuals.
Application information: Contributes only to pre-selected organizations.
Officers: Annette Eskind, Pres.; Jeffrey Eskind, Secy.
Director: Steven Eskind.
EIN: 621289997
Selected grants: The following grants were reported in 2004.
$1,000,000 to Vanderbilt University Medical Center, Nashville, TN. 2 grants: $500,000 each
$200,000 to United Way of Metropolitan Nashville, Nashville, TN.
$25,000 to Boston University, Boston, MA.
$1,000 to Brandeis University, Waltham, MA.
$1,000 to Nashville Symphony, Nashville, TN.
$1,000 to Vanderbilt University, Blair School of Music, Nashville, TN.
$1,000 to Watkins College of Art and Design, Nashville, TN.
$300 to Nashville Ballet, Nashville, TN.
$100 to Alive Hospice, Nashville, TN.

8675
The Jeffrey and Donna Eskind Family Foundation ◇ ☆
416 Ellendale Ave.
Nashville, TN 37205-3402

Established in 1986 in TN.
Donors: Jeffrey Eskind; Donna Eskind; Irwin Eskind.
Foundation type: Independent foundation.
Financial data (yr. ended 6/30/05): Assets, $5,618,689 (M); gifts received, $1,506,316; expenditures, $319,787; qualifying distributions, $316,255; giving activities include $316,255 for 73 grants (high: $119,000; low: $50).
Purpose and activities: Giving primarily for education, health care, federated giving programs, Jewish agencies, and temples.
Fields of interest: Arts; Education; Health care; Human services; Jewish agencies & temples.
Limitations: Applications not accepted. Giving primarily in Nashville, TN. No grants to individuals.
Application information: Contributes only to pre-selected organizations.
Officers: Jeffrey Eskind, Pres.; Donna Eskind, Secy.
EIN: 621306904

8676
Ezell Foundation, Inc. ✧
P.O. Box 100957
Nashville, TN 37224
Contact: F. Miles Ezell, Jr., Pres.

Established in 1964.
Donors: F. Miles Ezell, Sr.†; and members of the Ezell family.
Foundation type: Independent foundation.
Financial data (yr. ended 12/31/05): Assets, $13,309,059 (M); expenditures, $2,130,749; qualifying distributions, $1,812,301; giving activities include $1,812,301 for 84 grants (high: $1,234,815; low: $200).
Purpose and activities: Giving primarily to the Church of Christ and related educational programs.
Fields of interest: Education; Christian agencies & churches; Religion.
International interests: Guatemala; Honduras; Nigeria.
Type of support: General/operating support; Continuing support; Capital campaigns; Equipment.
Limitations: Applications not accepted. Giving primarily in TN.
Application information: Unsolicited requests for funds not accepted.
Board meeting date(s): Annually
Officers: F. Miles Ezell, Jr., Pres.; Roy C. Ezell, 1st V.P.; David Thomas, 2nd V.P.; Stanley M. Ezell, Secy.; John W. Ezell, Treas.
EIN: 626046865

8677
First Tennessee Foundation ✧
(formerly Tennessee Charitable Foundation)
c/o First Horizon National Corp.
165 Madison Ave., 8th Fl.
Memphis, TN 38103   (901) 532-4380
Contact: Terry Lee
Additional tel.: (901) 523-4352; FAX: (901) 523-4354

Established in 1993 in TN.
Donors: First Tennessee National Corp.; First Horizon National Corp.
Foundation type: Company-sponsored foundation.
Financial data (yr. ended 12/31/05): Assets, $65,627,627 (M); expenditures, $4,953,676; qualifying distributions, $4,908,676; giving activities include $4,745,011 for grants.

Purpose and activities: The foundation supports organizations involved with arts and culture, higher education, and community development.
Fields of interest: Arts; Higher education; Community development; Federated giving programs.
Limitations: Giving primarily in TN. No grants to individuals.
Application information: Application form not required.
Initial approach: Proposal
Copies of proposal: 1
Deadline(s): None
Officers: Harry A. Johnson III, Chair.; Gregg I. Lansky, Pres. and Treas.; Clyde A. Billings, Jr., Secy.
EIN: 621533987
Selected grants: The following grants were reported in 2004.
$400,000 to Habitat for Humanity International.
$222,500 to Susan G. Komen Breast Cancer Foundation, Dallas, TX.
$219,829 to United Way of the Mid-South, Memphis, TN.
$200,000 to Memphis Tomorrow, Memphis, TN.
$100,000 to Vanderbilt University, Nashville, TN.
$75,000 to Frist Center for the Visual Arts, Nashville, TN.
$65,000 to Girl Scouts of the U.S.A..
$5,000 to Knox Housing Partnership, Knoxville, TN.
$5,000 to United Way of Greater Knoxville, Knoxville, TN.
$2,500 to Ballet Tennessee, Chattanooga, TN.

8678
The Dorothy Cate & Thomas F. Frist Foundation
(formerly The Frist Medical Foundation)
c/o Tracy R. Frazier
1 Burton Hills Blvd., Ste. 300
Nashville, TN 37215

Established in 1989 in TN.
Donors: Thomas F. Frist, Sr.†; Dorothy Cate Frist†.
Foundation type: Independent foundation.
Financial data (yr. ended 11/30/05): Assets, $47,297,277 (M); gifts received, $17,795; expenditures, $2,625,816; qualifying distributions, $2,070,864; giving activities include $2,030,000 for 129 grants (high: $372,681; low: $100).
Fields of interest: Education; Human services.
Type of support: Annual campaigns; Capital campaigns; Building/renovation; Scholarship funds; Research.
Limitations: Applications not accepted. No grants to individuals.
Application information: Contributes only to pre-selected organizations.
Board meeting date(s): 3rd Tues. of Nov.
Officers: Mary Louise Frist Barfield, Pres.; Dorothy Frist Boensch, M.D., V.P.; Robert A. Frist, M.D., V.P.; William H. Frist, M.D., V.P.; Thomas F. Frist, Jr., M.D., Secy.; Tracy R. Frazier, Admin.
Number of staff: 1 part-time professional.
EIN: 621103568
Selected grants: The following grants were reported in 2005.
$133,250 to Ensworth School, Nashville, TN.
$100,000 to YMCA.
$37,000 to Brentwood Academy, Brentwood, TN.
$26,500 to Adventure Science Center, Nashville, TN.
$26,500 to Nashville Public Library, Nashville, TN.
$20,000 to United Way.

$16,000 to Martha OBryan Center, Nashville, TN.
$5,000 to Nashville Alliance for Public Education, Nashville, TN.
$2,000 to American Red Cross.
$1,000 to Tennessee Performing Arts Center, Nashville, TN.

8679
The Frist Foundation
(formerly The HCA Foundation)
3100 West End Ave., Ste. 1200
Nashville, TN 37203   (615) 292-3868
Contact: Peter F. Bird, Jr., C.E.O. and Pres.
FAX: (615) 292-5843;
E-mail: askfrist@fristfoundation.org; URL: http://www.fristfoundation.org

Established in 1982 in TN.
Donors: Hospital Corp. of America; Lee, Danner & Bass, Inc.
Foundation type: Independent foundation.
Financial data (yr. ended 12/31/05): Assets, $196,846,354 (M); gifts received, $7,998; expenditures, $3,994,414; qualifying distributions, $3,046,519; giving activities include $2,405,357 for 296 grants (high: $500,000; low: $800; average: $1,000–$25,000), and $227,053 for 116 employee matching gifts.
Purpose and activities: The foundation supports organizations involved with arts and culture, education, health, human services, youth leadership training, community development, and civic affairs.
Fields of interest: Visual arts; Performing arts; Arts; Education; Health care; Youth development; Human services; Community development; Philanthropy/voluntarism, management/technical aid; Voluntarism promotion; Federated giving programs; Public affairs.
Type of support: Technical assistance; General/operating support; Management development/capacity building; Capital campaigns; Building/renovation; Equipment; Emergency funds; Program development; Curriculum development; Consulting services; Employee matching gifts; Matching/challenge support.
Limitations: Giving primarily in Nashville, TN. No support for national disease-specific organizations, private foundations, religious organizations not of direct benefit to the entire community, hospitals, nursing homes, or retirement homes. No grants to individuals, or for endowments, biomedical or clinical research, social events or similar fundraising events, goodwill advertising, telethons, sponsorships, publications, trips, tours, political activities, or start up needs.
Publications: Application guidelines; Grants list; Informational brochure (including application guidelines).
Application information: An application form is available online. Application form required.
Initial approach: Complete online application form or download application form and mail to foundation
Copies of proposal: 1
Deadline(s): Apr. 1 for Technology Grants Program
Board meeting date(s): Jan., Apr., July, and Oct.
Final notification: Usually within 1 month
Officers and Directors:* Thomas F. Frist, Jr.,* Chair.; Peter F. Bird, Jr.,* C.E.O. and Pres.; Barbara W. Baker, Corp. Secy. and Prog. Asst.; Colette R. Easter, Treas.; Kenneth L. Roberts,* Pres. Emeritus; Frank F. Drowota III; Patricia Frist Elcan; Patricia C. Frist; Thomas F. Frist III; William R. Frist.

Number of staff: 1 full-time professional; 1 part-time professional; 1 full-time support; 1 part-time support.
EIN: 621134070
Selected grants: The following grants were reported in 2004.
$4,539,411 to Frist Center for the Visual Arts Foundation, Nashville, TN. 2 grants: $3,500,000 (For Frist Center for Visual Arts), $1,039,411 (Toward paying off loan which was used to develop center's parking area).
$375,000 to Nashville Symphony Association, Nashville, TN. 2 grants: $250,000 (For construction support of new symphony hall), $125,000 (For special campaign to strengthen orchestra and bring it into national prominence).
$149,000 to United Way of Metropolitan Nashville, Nashville, TN. 3 grants: $49,000 (For support to Community Resource Center), $50,000 (Support for campaign from Ansley Fund), $50,000 (For hardware and other non-operating expenses to initiate 211 service in Nashville).
$125,000 to Saint Lukes Community House, Nashville, TN. 2 grants: $62,500 (For support through Ansley Fund to upgrade and expand facilities), $62,500 (For capital campaign to upgrade and expand facilities).
$50,000 to Nashville Alliance for Public Education, Nashville, TN. For startup support.

8680
Thomas M. Garrott Foundation ◇
c/o SunTrust Bank
850 Ridgelake Blvd., Ste. 101
Memphis, TN 38120
Contact: Arthur Oliver, Trust Off., SunTrust Bank

Established in 1995 in TN.
Donor: Thomas M. Garrott.
Foundation type: Independent foundation.
Financial data (yr. ended 12/31/04): Assets, $6,685,343 (M); expenditures, $518,131; qualifying distributions, $511,461; giving activities include $507,400 for 32 grants (high: $200,000; low: $650).
Purpose and activities: Giving primarily for higher education, health care, including juvenile diabetes research, human services, a Presbyterian church, and to the United Way.
Fields of interest: Elementary/secondary education; Higher education; Education; Health care; Diabetes research; Human services; Federated giving programs; Protestant agencies & churches.
Limitations: Giving on a national basis.
Application information: Application form not required.
 Initial approach: Letter
 Deadline(s): None
Trustee: SunTrust Bank.
EIN: 626289645
Selected grants: The following grants were reported in 2003.
$50,000 to United Way of the Mid-South, Memphis, TN. For general support.
$25,000 to Rhodes College, Development, Memphis, TN.
$20,000 to Second Presbyterian Church, Memphis, TN. For general support.
$20,000 to University of Pennsylvania, Philadelphia, PA. For general support.
$10,000 to Saint Marys Episcopal School, Memphis, TN. For general support.

$6,000 to Beale Street Caravan, Memphis, TN. For general support.
$5,000 to Dixon Gallery and Gardens, Memphis, TN. For general support.
$5,000 to University of Memphis, Memphis, TN. For general support.
$2,500 to Duke University, Durham, NC. For general support.
$1,000 to Hutchison School, Memphis, TN. For general support.

8681
The Bill Gatton Foundation ◇
P.O. Box 1147
Bristol, TN 37621
Contact: Frank Winston, Tr.
Application address: 1000 W. State St., Bristol, TN 37620, tel.: (423) 764-5121

Donors: C.M. Gatton; Customer 1 One, Inc.
Foundation type: Independent foundation.
Financial data (yr. ended 11/30/05): Assets, $46,455,034 (M); gifts received, $1,172,211; expenditures, $2,210,148; qualifying distributions, $2,149,230; giving activities include $2,149,230 for 25 grants (high: $1,217,000; low: $250; average: $1,000–$100,000).
Purpose and activities: Giving primarily for higher education.
Fields of interest: Higher education; Human services.
Limitations: Giving primarily in TN and KY. No grants to individuals.
Application information: Application form not required.
 Initial approach: Proposal
 Deadline(s): None
Trustees: C.M. Gatton; Allan R. Rhodes; Frank Winston.
EIN: 621266284

8682
The Goldsmith Family Foundation, Inc. ◇
(formerly The Goldsmith Foundation)
1900 Union Ave.
Memphis, TN 38104-4029

Incorporated in 1944 in TN.
Donor: Members of the Goldsmith family.
Foundation type: Independent foundation.
Financial data (yr. ended 12/31/05): Assets, $7,213,482 (M); expenditures, $416,951; qualifying distributions, $350,097; giving activities include $350,097 for 139 grants (high: $40,000; low: $35).
Purpose and activities: Giving primarily to Jewish organizations and for education.
Fields of interest: Arts; Higher education; Education; Health care; Health organizations, association; Boys & girls clubs; Human services; Children/youth, services; Federated giving programs; Jewish federated giving programs; Jewish agencies & temples; Religion, interfaith issues.
Limitations: Giving primarily in TN.
Application information:
 Deadline(s): None
Officers and Trustees:* Harry L. Goldsmith,* Pres.; Elvis G. Goldsmith,* V.P.; Fred Goldsmith III,* V.P.; Melvin Goldsmith, V.P.; Thomas B. Goldsmith, V.P.; Sylvia Goldsmith Marks, V.P.; Larry J. Goldsmith,*

Secy.-Treas.; Beth Goldsmith Brown, Jr.; Elise Goldsmith Hicks; Jennifer Entine Matz.
EIN: 626039604
Selected grants: The following grants were reported in 2005.
$40,000 to Jewish Federation, Memphis, Memphis, TN.
$31,350 to Memphis Botanic Garden Foundation, Memphis, TN. 2 grants: $6,350, $25,000
$18,000 to United Way.
$10,000 to Bridges, Inc., Memphis, TN.
$10,000 to Film Arts Foundation, San Francisco, CA.
$10,000 to Lausanne Collegiate School, Memphis, TN.
$1,500 to Boys and Girls Club of Sarasota County, Sarasota, FL.
$500 to Norton Gallery and School of Art, West Palm Beach, FL.
$250 to Monterey Peninsula College, Monterey, CA.

8683
Joel C. and Bernice W. Gordon Family Foundation ◇
c/o Joel C. Gordon, Pres.
3102 West End Ave., Ste. 650
Nashville, TN 37203-1498

Established in 1986 in TN.
Donors: Joel C. Gordon; Bernice W. Gordon; Sherrie Gordon Eisenman; Robert A. Gordon; Frank E. Gordon; Gail E. Gordon.
Foundation type: Independent foundation.
Financial data (yr. ended 6/30/05): Assets, $5,492,619 (M); expenditures, $531,912; qualifying distributions, $523,700; giving activities include $523,536 for 150 grants (high: $200,000; low: $10).
Purpose and activities: Giving primarily to Jewish agencies and temples, as well as for education, and health and social services.
Fields of interest: Visual arts; Arts; Higher education; Libraries/library science; Health care; Health organizations, association; Human services; Federated giving programs; Jewish federated giving programs; Jewish agencies & temples.
Limitations: Applications not accepted. Giving primarily in TN. No grants to individuals.
Application information: Contributes only to pre-selected organizations.
Officers: Joel C. Gordon, Pres.; Bernice W. Gordon, Secy.
Trustees: Alan J. Eisenman; Sherrie Gordon Eisenman; Frank E. Gordon; Gwen L. Gordon; Julie S. Gordon; Robert A. Gordon; Gail Gordon Jacobs; Jeffrey M. Jacobs.
EIN: 621306906

8684
Hamico, Inc. ◇
1715 W. 38th St.
Chattanooga, TN 37409-1248

Incorporated in 1956 in TN.
Donor: Chattem, Inc.
Foundation type: Company-sponsored foundation.
Financial data (yr. ended 12/31/03): Assets, $28,182,768 (M); expenditures, $1,157,212; qualifying distributions, $1,157,212; giving activities include $840,116 for 89+ grants (high: $110,540; average: $1,000–$25,000).

Purpose and activities: The foundation supports organizations involved with arts and culture, K-12 and higher education, health, and recreation.
Fields of interest: Visual arts; Museums; Performing arts; Arts; Elementary/secondary education; Higher education; Hospitals (general); Health care; Athletics/sports, racquet sports; Recreation; Federated giving programs.
Type of support: Continuing support; Endowments.
Limitations: Applications not accepted. Giving primarily in Chattanooga, TN. No grants to individuals.
Application information: Contributes only to pre-selected organizations.
Officers and Directors: * Zan Guerry,* Pres.; Robert E. Bosworth,* Secy.; Herbert Barks; Alexis G. Bogo; John P. Guerry.
EIN: 626040782

8685

The Harrah's Foundation ✧
c/o Harrah's Operating Co., Inc.
1023 Cherry Rd., Corp. Tax Dept.
Memphis, TN 38117-5423
Application address: c/o Scott E. Wiegand, 1 Harrah's Ct., Las Vegas, NV 89119, tel.: (702) 407-6244

Established in 2002 in NV.
Donor: Harrah's Operating Co., Inc.
Foundation type: Company-sponsored foundation.
Financial data (yr. ended 12/31/03): Assets, $366,749 (M); gifts received, $20,036; expenditures, $417,570; qualifying distributions, $417,369; giving activities include $417,000 for 2 grants (high: $217,000; low: $200,000).
Purpose and activities: The foundation supports organizations involved with gambling addiction and housing.
Fields of interest: Mental health, gambling addiction; Housing/shelter.
Limitations: Giving primarily in Reno, NV, and Washington, DC. No grants to individuals.
Application information:
Initial approach: Proposal
Deadline(s): None
Officers and Directors: * Jan Jones,* Pres.; Scott E. Wiegand, Secy.; Anthony D. McDuffie, Treas.; Chuck Atwood; Anthony Sanfilippo; Philip G. Satre; Carlos Tolosa; Tim Wilmott.
EIN: 743050638

8686

Will & Jane Harris Foundation ✧
c/o Mary Lou Drazich, First Tennessee Bank
701 Market St.
Chattanooga, TN 37405

Donor: Jane A. Harris†.
Foundation type: Independent foundation.
Financial data (yr. ended 11/30/05): Assets, $5,912,966 (M); gifts received, $710,293; expenditures, $2,845,130; qualifying distributions, $2,802,524; giving activities include $2,802,524 for 5 grants (high: $1,340,541; low: $50,000).
Purpose and activities: Giving primarily for higher education and to a Presbyterian organization.
Fields of interest: Higher education; Protestant agencies & churches.
Type of support: General/operating support.

Limitations: Applications not accepted. Giving primarily in Chattanooga, TN. No grants to individuals.
Application information: Contributes only to pre-selected organizations.
Officers and Trustees: * Frank A. Brock,* Chair. and Treas.; Don E. Morton,* Secy.; Mary Lou Drazich,* Mgr.; G. Richard Hostetter; Raymond R. Murphy, Jr.
EIN: 581340046

8687

The Haslam Family Foundation, Inc. ✧
P.O. Box 10146
Knoxville, TN 37939-0146 (865) 588-7488
Contact: Todd Ellis, Asst. Secy.
Application address: c/o Todd Ellis, Asst. Secy., P.O. Box 52206, Knoxville, TN 37950-2206; tel.: (865) 212-3800

Established in 1998 in TN.
Donor: James A. Haslam III.
Foundation type: Independent foundation.
Financial data (yr. ended 12/31/04): Assets, $22,800,547 (M); gifts received, $4,000,000; expenditures, $1,323,800; qualifying distributions, $1,124,521; giving activities include $1,119,500 for 47 grants (high: $120,000; low: $1,000).
Purpose and activities: Giving primarily for education, children, youth and social services, health care, and for the arts.
Fields of interest: Performing arts, orchestra (symphony); Historic preservation/historical societies; Arts; Secondary school/education; Education; Health care; Health organizations, association; Boys & girls clubs; Boy scouts; Human services; Children/youth, services; Community development; Federated giving programs.
Limitations: Giving primarily in the eastern TN area. No grants to individuals.
Application information:
Initial approach: Letter
Deadline(s): June 30 and Dec. 31
Officers and Directors: * James A. Haslam II,* Pres.; Ann Haslam Bailey,* V.P.; Natalie L. Haslam,* Secy.; Jim R. Shelby,* Treas.; James A. Haslam III; William E. Haslam.
EIN: 621692007
Selected grants: The following grants were reported in 2003.
$115,000 to United Way of Greater Knoxville, Knoxville, TN.
$100,000 to Knoxville Symphony Orchestra, Knoxville, TN.
$100,000 to University of Tennessee, Knoxville, TN.
$50,000 to East Tennessee Historical Society, Knoxville, TN.
$30,000 to Boys and Girls Clubs of Knoxville, Knoxville, TN.
$25,000 to Child and Family Services of Knox County, Knoxville, TN.
$25,000 to Historic Tennessee Theater Foundation, Knoxville, TN.
$10,000 to YMCA of Knoxville, Knoxville, TN.
$7,500 to Maryville College, Maryville, TN.
$5,000 to Mental Health Association of East Tennessee, Knoxville, TN.

8688

The Haslam Foundation, Inc. ✧
(formerly The Sycamore Foundation, Inc.)
Steiner & Ellis, PLLC
5516 Lonas Dr., Ste. 260
Knoxville, TN 37909 (865) 212-3800
Contact: Susan B. Haslam, Pres.

Established in 2001 in TN.
Donors: James A. Haslam III; Susan B. Haslam.
Foundation type: Independent foundation.
Financial data (yr. ended 12/31/05): Assets, $8,550,826 (M); expenditures, $980,562; qualifying distributions, $892,333; giving activities include $892,333 for grants.
Fields of interest: Arts; Education; Human services; YM/YWCAs & YM/YWHAs; Federated giving programs.
Limitations: Giving primarily in the East TN area.
Application information:
Initial approach: Letter
Deadline(s): June 30 and Dec.31
Officers and Directors: * Susan B. Haslam,* Pres.; James A. Haslam III,* V.P.; J. Todd Ellis,* Secy.-Treas.; Cynthia A. Haslam; Susan W. Haslam.
EIN: 621867421
Selected grants: The following grants were reported in 2004.
$130,000 to United Way of Greater Knoxville, Knoxville, TN.
$86,421 to Emerald Youth Foundation, Knoxville, TN.
$75,000 to Knox Area Rescue Ministries, Knoxville, TN.
$45,000 to Webb School of Knoxville, Knoxville, TN.
$35,000 to YMCA of Knoxville, Knoxville, TN.
$20,000 to Boys and Girls Clubs of Knoxville, Knoxville, TN.
$20,000 to Historic Tennessee Theater Foundation, Knoxville, TN.
$20,000 to Saint Georges Day School, Germantown, TN.
$15,000 to Knoxville Symphony Orchestra, Knoxville, TN.
$5,000 to Boy Scouts of America, Knoxville, TN.

8689

Hawthorn Charitable Foundation ✧ ☆
4094 Hillsboro Park, Ste. 204
Nashville, TN 37215

Established in 1995 in TN.
Donors: W.L. Davis, Jr.; Adelaide Shull Davis; Harrison S. Davis; Florence S. Davis; Virginia A. Davis; W.L. Davis III.
Foundation type: Independent foundation.
Financial data (yr. ended 6/30/05): Assets, $802,329 (M); gifts received, $23,645; expenditures, $396,285; qualifying distributions, $391,965; giving activities include $395,310 for 148 grants (high: $100,000; low: $20).
Purpose and activities: Giving for secondary education, colleges, and youth programs.
Fields of interest: Arts; Higher education; Health care; Recreation; Boy scouts; Human services; Salvation Army; YM/YWCAs & YM/YWHAs; Protestant agencies & churches.
Limitations: Applications not accepted. Giving primarily in TN. No grants to individuals.
Application information: Contributes only to pre-selected organizations.

Trustees: Adelaide Shull Davis; W. Lipscomb Davis, Jr.
EIN: 621624638

8690
The HCA Foundation ▼ ✧
(formerly Columbia/HCA Healthcare Foundation, Inc.)
1 Park Plz., Building 1, 4th Fl. E.
Nashville, TN 37203 (615) 344-2390
Contact: Lois Abrams, Grants Mgr.
FAX: (615) 344-5722;
E-mail: lois.abrams@hcahealthcare.com;
URL: http://www.hcacaring.org/

Established in 1992 in KY.
Donors: Columbia/HCA Healthcare Corp.; HCA—The Healthcare Co.; HCA Inc.
Foundation type: Company-sponsored foundation.
Financial data (yr. ended 12/31/05): Assets, $144,680,687 (M); expenditures, $24,243,454; qualifying distributions, $24,097,258; giving activities include $23,934,875 for grants.
Purpose and activities: The foundation supports organizations involved with child development, health, youth development, and human services. Special emphasis is directed toward programs designed to promote health and well being; and support childhood and youth development in middle Tennessee.
Fields of interest: Child development, education; Health care; Youth development; Child development, services; Philanthropy/voluntarism; Federated giving programs.
Type of support: General/operating support; Annual campaigns; Capital campaigns; Building/renovation; Equipment; Program development; Scholarship funds; Employee matching gifts; Matching/challenge support.
Limitations: Giving primarily in middle TN. No support for political organizations, individual churches or schools, organizations established less than 3 years ago, or organizations involved with arts and culture, athletics, the environment or wildlife, or civic or international affairs. No grants to individuals, or for advertising or sponsorships, or social events or similar fundraising activities.
Publications: Corporate giving report; Informational brochure (including application guidelines); Newsletter.
Application information: Letters of inquiry should be no longer than 1 to 2 pages. Application form not required.
    Initial approach: Letter of inquiry
    Deadline(s): June 16 for capital campaigns; Mar. 24, June 16, and Sept. 8 for general operating support and program development
    Board meeting date(s): Feb., May, Aug., and Nov.
Officers and Directors:* Thomas F. Frist, Jr., M.D.*, Chair.; Jack O. Bovender,* Pres.; Gary Pack, Secy.; David G. Anderson, Treas.* Joanne Pulles,* Exec. Dir.; Peter F. Bird, Jr.; Richard M. Bracken; Milton Johnson; Ray Monroe; Bruce Moore, Jr.; John Steele; Noel Williams.
Number of staff: 1 full-time professional; 1 full-time support.
EIN: 611230563
Selected grants: The following grants were reported in 2004.
$5,014,471 to Ensworth School, Nashville, TN.
$3,005,617 to Frist Center for the Visual Arts, Nashville, TN.

$500,000 to Siloam Family Health Center, Nashville, TN.
$300,000 to Scholarship Program Administrators, Nashville, TN. For scholarships.
$100,000 to YMCA of Nashville and Middle Tennessee, Nashville, TN. To build new North Rutherford County Family YMCA to serve Smyrna and LaVergne communities.
$50,000 to Adventure Science Center, Nashville, TN. For capital support to install Amazing Aging Machine exhibit.
$25,000 to Nashville Public Library Foundation, Nashville, TN. For operating support of Bringing Books to Life initiative.
$20,000 to Easter Seals Tennessee, Nashville, TN. For New Frontiers seniors program.
$17,000 to Monroe Harding Childrens Home, Nashville, TN. For fire recovery and to ensure future safety of youth who live in Scarborough, Grace and Wood Dorm.
$11,000 to Nashville Opera Association, Nashville, TN. For annual tour of OperaNET program.

8691
Willard & Frances Hendrix Foundation
c/o SunTrust Bank
P.O. Box 305110
Nashville, TN 37230-5110
Contact: Melissa Kirkby

Established in 1981 in TN.
Donor: Frances Hendrix.
Foundation type: Independent foundation.
Financial data (yr. ended 4/30/05): Assets, $5,814,514 (M); gifts received, $113,810; expenditures, $476,835; qualifying distributions, $467,142; giving activities include $456,449 for 40 grants (high: $79,184; low: $1,000).
Purpose and activities: Giving primarily for education.
Fields of interest: Elementary/secondary education; Higher education, college; Higher education, university; Education; Youth, services.
Limitations: Applications not accepted. Giving primarily in Nashville, TN.
Application information: Unsolicited requests for funds not accepted.
    Board meeting date(s): Nov.
Trustees: John Anderson; James Gooch; James Hendrix; Richard Holton; Jane Starr; SunTrust Bank.
EIN: 626158855
Selected grants: The following grants were reported in 2004.
$49,500 to Vanderbilt University, Athletic Department, Nashville, TN.
$35,715 to Ensworth School, Nashville, TN.
$19,349 to Bethel College, McKenzie, TN.
$10,000 to Alive Hospice, Nashville, TN.
$10,000 to Boys and Girls Club of Middle Tennessee, Nashville, TN.
$10,000 to Campus for Human Development, Nashville, TN.
$10,000 to Community Foundation of Middle Tennessee, Nashville, TN.
$10,000 to Foundation for Global Community, Palo Alto, CA.
$10,000 to Planned Parenthood of Middle and East Tennessee, Nashville, TN.
$10,000 to YWCA of Nashville and Middle Tennessee, Nashville, TN.

8692
Orion L. & Emma B. Hurlbut Memorial Fund ✧
701 Market St.
Chattanooga, TN 37402
Application address: c/o Kathy Wood, 975 E. 3rd St., Chattanooga, TN 37403

Established in 1937 in TN.
Foundation type: Independent foundation.
Financial data (yr. ended 4/30/05): Assets, $20,291,738 (M); expenditures, $956,156; qualifying distributions, $956,156; giving activities include $724,843 for 23 grants (high: $580,000; low: $95).
Purpose and activities: Giving primarily to a tumor clinic; support also for treatment of indigent cancer patients outside of Hamilton County, TN.
Fields of interest: Cancer; Cancer research; Economically disadvantaged.
Type of support: Grants to individuals.
Limitations: Giving primarily in Chattanooga, TN.
Application information: Applicants should include physicians' detailed expense voucher.
    Initial approach: Letter
    Deadline(s): None
Directors: Stella Anderson; John F. Boxell; C. Windom Kimsey, M.D.
Trustee: First Tennessee Bank, N.A.
EIN: 626034546

8693
Hyde Family Foundations ▼
17 W. Pontotoc Ave., Ste. 200
Memphis, TN 38103 (901) 685-3400
Contact: Teresa Sloyan, Exec. Dir.
FAX: (901) 683-3147;
E-mail: info@hydefamilyfoundations.org;
URL: http://www.hydefamilyfoundations.org

J.R. Hyde Senior Family Foundation and J.R. Hyde III Family Foundation established in TN in 1961 and 1993, respectively.
Donors: J.R. Hyde, Sr.†; J.R. Hyde III; Barbara R. Hyde.
Foundation type: Independent foundation.
Financial data (yr. ended 12/31/04): Assets, $129,922,640 (M); gifts received, $4,918,925; expenditures, $8,476,911; qualifying distributions, $7,245,398; giving activities include $6,440,000 for 255 grants (high: $250,000; low: $35; average: $5,000–$100,000).
Purpose and activities: The Hyde Family Foundations support efforts that improve the quality of life in Memphis, TN and enhance prosperity for all its citizens. The foundations are interested in promoting improved educational opportunities for children and their families, encouraging and empowering new community leadership, and reinforcing a vision of Memphis, TN as a progressive city. The foundations are especially interested in helping stimulate innovation in systems that directly affect the lives of Memphians and impact our community's current well-being and future vitality. They seek to leverage their resources whenever possible, working with both public and private partners.
Fields of interest: Humanities; Arts; Education, reform; Housing/shelter; Community development, neighborhood development.
Type of support: Building/renovation; General/operating support; Capital campaigns; Program

development; Seed money; Technical assistance; Consulting services; Program evaluation; Employee matching gifts; Matching/challenge support.
Limitations: Giving primarily in Memphis, TN. No support for political organizations. No grants to individuals.
Publications: Application guidelines.
Application information: The first step in seeking support from the foundations is to submit a brief concept letter with coversheet (coversheet application must be signed by an authorized representative of the organization). If the project merits further consideration, applicants will be invited to submit a full proposal. Full proposal guidelines will be distributed upon approval of the concept letter. Full proposals postmarked or received in the foundations office by Apr. 15 will be considered at the May meeting. Proposals postmarked or received in the foundations' office by Oct. will be considered at the Nov. meeting. The foundations do not accept concept letters or full proposals by fax or e-mail. Application form not required.
  Initial approach: Concept letter (no more than 3 pages)
  Copies of proposal: 1
  Deadline(s): Concept letter: Feb. 1 and July 15; If invited, full proposals: Apr. 15 and Oct. 1
  Board meeting date(s): May and Nov.
  Final notification: Notification of invitation for full proposal Mar. 15 and Sept. 1; Final funding decision June 1 and Dec. 1
Officers: John Pontius, Treas.; Teresa Sloyan, Exec. Dir.
Trustees: Ruthie Bernabe; Susan Hyde Calhoun; Barbara R. Hyde; J.R. Hyde III; Henry Varnell; Jeanne Varnell.
Number of staff: 3 full-time professional; 3 full-time support.
Selected grants: The following grants were reported in 2004.
$252,700 to Memphis Bioworks Foundation, Memphis, TN. 2 grants: $250,000 (For general operating support), $2,700.
$250,000 to Memphis Tomorrow, Memphis, TN. For Ready, Set, Grow.
$250,000 to Victory Ranch, Bolivar, TN. For capital campaign.
$200,000 to Memphis Brooks Museum of Art, Memphis, TN. For general operating support.
$165,333 to New Leaders for New Schools, Memphis, TN. For start-up support.
$20,000 to Chamber Foundation of Memphis, Memphis, TN. For capital campaign.
$12,500 to Beale Street Caravan, Memphis, TN. For general operating support.
$2,191 to Circles of Success Learning Academy, Memphis, TN.
$1,000 to Memphis Redbirds Baseball Foundation, Memphis, TN.

8694
Martha and Bronson Ingram Foundation ◇
4400 Harding Rd., 9th Fl.
Nashville, TN 37205
Contact: Martha R. Ingram, Pres.

Established in 1988 in TN.
Donors: Martha A. Ingram; The E.B.I. 1994 Charitable Lead Annuity Trust; Ingram Industries Inc.
Foundation type: Independent foundation.
Financial data (yr. ended 12/31/04): Assets, $86,114 (M); gifts received, $860,267;

expenditures, $1,147,116; qualifying distributions, $1,147,114; giving activities include $1,147,114 for 10 grants (high: $594,364; low: $300).
Fields of interest: Historic preservation/historical societies; Arts; Elementary/secondary education; Higher education; Human services; Foundations (community); Federated giving programs.
Limitations: Applications not accepted. Giving primarily in TN. No grants to individuals.
Application information: Unsolicited requests for funds not accepted.
Officers and Trustees:* Martha R. Ingram,* Pres.; Orrin H. Ingram,* V.P.; William P. Morelli, Secy.; John R. Ingram,* Treas.
EIN: 626210987
Selected grants: The following grants were reported in 2003.
$1,175,250 to Community Foundation of Middle Tennessee, Nashville, TN.
$200,970 to United Way of Metropolitan Nashville, Nashville, TN.
$500 to Middleton Place Foundation, Charleston, SC.

8695
The Jeniam Foundation
(also known as The Jeniam Clarkson Foundation)
270 Bremington Pl.
Memphis, TN 38111
Contact: Charlotte G. King, Exec. Dir.

Established in 1992 in TN.
Donors: Andrew M. Clarkson; Carole G. Clarkson.
Foundation type: Independent foundation.
Financial data (yr. ended 12/31/04): Assets, $17,239,472 (M); expenditures, $954,540; qualifying distributions, $802,440; giving activities include $712,222 for 34 grants (high: $153,972; low: $400), and $37,750 for 3 loans/program-related investments (high: $15,000; low: $9,000).
Purpose and activities: The mission of the foundation is to provide venture philanthropy to the arts in Memphis, TN, elder care and education in New Canaan, CT, and national and international conservation.
Fields of interest: Arts, association; Arts, administration/regulation; Museums; Museums (children's); Performing arts, theater; Arts; Higher education; Environment, research; Animals/wildlife, preservation/protection; Human services; Foundations (community); Philanthropy/voluntarism.
Type of support: Capital campaigns; Building/renovation; Equipment; Seed money; Research; Program-related investments/loans; Matching/challenge support.
Limitations: Giving primarily in New Canaan, CT for education and aging, and Memphis, TN, for the performing arts; giving on a national basis for conservation. No grants to individuals, or for ongoing operating support.
Publications: Informational brochure (including application guidelines).
Application information: Contact Exec. Dir. for application guidelines. Application form not required.
  Initial approach: 1- to 2-page letter
  Copies of proposal: 1
  Deadline(s): None
  Board meeting date(s): Varies
Officer: Charlotte G. King, Exec. Dir.

Trustees: Andrew M. Clarkson; Carole G. Clarkson; William M. Clarkson; Jennifer Clarkson Killin.
Number of staff: 1 full-time professional.
EIN: 621516244

8696
George R. Johnson Family Foundation ◇
(formerly George R. Johnson Charitable Trust)
P.O. Box 4558
Cleveland, TN 37320
Contact: Stella Anderson, Trust Off.

Established in 1999 in TN.
Donor: George R. Johnson†.
Foundation type: Independent foundation.
Financial data (yr. ended 12/31/04): Assets, $0 (M); gifts received, $55,500; expenditures, $1,595,165; qualifying distributions, $1,315,461; giving activities include $1,276,490 for grants.
Purpose and activities: The foundation seeks to improve the quality of life in the communities it serves, by supporting programs which improve education, health and general welfare of citizens within the foundation's area.
Limitations: Giving primarily in Catoosa, Dade, Murray and Walker counties, GA, and Bledsoe, Bradley, Grundy, Hamilton, Loudon, Marion, Meigs, Monroe, Polk, Rhea and Sequatchie counties, TN.
Publications: Application guidelines.
Application information: Application form not required.
  Initial approach: Letter
  Deadline(s): Feb. 15, May 15, Aug. 15, and Nov. 15
  Board meeting date(s): Mar., June, Sept., and Dec.
  Final notification: 2 weeks after board meeting
Officer and Trustees:* Janice J. Wilson,* Exec. Dir.; Beverly Johnson; First Tennessee Bank, N.A.
EIN: 626369022
Selected grants: The following grants were reported in 2004.
$150,000 to Boys and Girls Club.
$100,000 to Bethel Bible Village, Hixson, TN.
$100,000 to Lee University, Cleveland, TN.
$55,000 to Hospice of Chattanooga, Chattanooga, TN.
$50,000 to Chattanooga Area Food Bank, Chattanooga, TN.
$30,000 to Bryan College, Dayton, TN.
$30,000 to Hiwassee College, Madisonville, TN.
$24,000 to United Way. 2 grants: $10,000, $14,000
$20,000 to Partnership for Children, Kansas City, MO.

8697
George R. Johnson Family Foundation ◇ ☆
c/o First Tennessee Bank
701 Market St.
Chattanooga, TN 37402-4886
Contact: Janice J. Wilson, Dir.
Application address: P.O. Box 4558, Cleveland, TN 37320-4558, tel.: (423) 614-2393

Established in 2004 in TN.
Donors: George R. Johnson†; Janice J. Wilson; Beverly P. Johnson.
Foundation type: Independent foundation.
Financial data (yr. ended 12/31/05): Assets, $26,798,462 (M); expenditures, $1,690,457;

qualifying distributions, $1,417,179; giving activities include $1,387,073 for 37 grants (high: $150,000; low: $2,000).

Fields of interest: Museums; Performing arts; Higher education; Housing/shelter, development; Youth development; Human services; Federated giving programs.

Type of support: Scholarship funds; Endowments; Equipment; Building/renovation; General/operating support.

Limitations: Giving primarily in Catoosa, Dade, Murray, Walker, and Whitfield counties, GA and in Bradley, Grundy, Hamilton, Loudon, McMinn, Meigs, Monroe, Polk, Rhea, and Sqatchie counties, TN. No grants to individuals.

Application information: Application form not required.

Initial approach: Letter of no more than 2 pages
Deadline(s): None

Trustees: Beverly P. Johnson; Janice J. Wilson; First Tennessee Bank.

EIN: 626401641

8698
Allan Jones Foundation ✧
c/o Jones Mgmt. Svcs., LLC
201 Keith St. S.W., Ste. 80
Cleveland, TN 37311 (423) 756-3000
Contact: W. Allan Jones, Pres.

Established in 2002 in TN.
Donors: Janie P. Jones; W. Allan Jones.
Foundation type: Independent foundation.
Financial data (yr. ended 12/31/05): Assets, $13,580 (M); gifts received, $498,900; expenditures, $920,105; qualifying distributions, $918,598; giving activities include $918,598 for 33 grants (high: $505,903; low: $76).

Fields of interest: Elementary/secondary education; Higher education; Libraries (public); Education; Environment; Human services; Children/youth, services; Community development; Federated giving programs; Christian agencies & churches.

Limitations: Giving primarily in Cleveland, TN.
Application information:

Initial approach: Typed letter (not to exceed 2 pages)
Deadline(s): None

Officers and Directors:* W. Allan Jones,* Pres.; Janie P. Jones,* Secy.; Sandra Rowland, Exec. Dir.; D. Lynn Devault.
EIN: 621859939

8699
Robert E. and Jenny D. Kirkland Foundation ✧ ☆
760 Sanders Chapel Rd.
Union City, TN 38261

Established in 2003 in TN.
Donor: Kirkland 2004 Charitable Foundation.
Foundation type: Independent foundation.
Financial data (yr. ended 12/31/05): Assets, $3,355,905 (M); gifts received, $1,968,940; expenditures, $969,178; qualifying distributions, $951,676; giving activities include $924,166 for grants.

Fields of interest: Elementary/secondary education; Children/youth, services.
Type of support: Scholarship funds.

Limitations: Applications not accepted. Giving primarily in TN. No grants to individuals.
Application information: Contributes only to pre-selected organizations.
Officers and Directors:* Robert E. Kirkland,* Pres.; Christopher Kirkland,* Secy.; Bedford F. Kirkland; Jenny D. Kirkland; Macy D. Swensson.
EIN: 134228589

8700
The Lazarus Foundation, Inc. ▼ ✧
340 Edgemont Ave., Ste. 500
Bristol, TN 37620
Contact: Mary Ann Blessing, Treas.

Established in 1992 in VA.
Donors: John M. Gregory; Joan P. Gregory.
Foundation type: Operating foundation.
Financial data (yr. ended 12/31/05): Assets, $18,970,489 (M); gifts received, $3,600; expenditures, $13,859,288; qualifying distributions, $13,420,164; giving activities include $13,395,500 for 107 grants (high: $1,000,000; low: $611; average: $50,000–$250,000), and $24,664 for 20 grants to individuals.

Purpose and activities: Giving primarily to Christian organizations for family financial distress.
Fields of interest: Food services; Human services; International development; Christian agencies & churches; Economically disadvantaged.
International interests: Developing countries.
Type of support: Grants to individuals.
Limitations: Applications not accepted. Giving primarily in Bristol, TN, and surrounding communities.
Application information: Unsolicited requests for funds not accepted.
Officers and Board Member: John M. Gregory, Pres.; Joan P. Gregory, V.P. and Secy.; Mary Ann Blessing, Treas.; James Gregory.
Number of staff: 1 part-time professional.
EIN: 541654943
Selected grants: The following grants were reported in 2005.

$1,000,000 to Palm Beach Atlantic University, West Palm Beach, FL. For Warren Library.
$750,000 to Peniel Ministries Argentina, Marietta, GA. For matching grant for building fund.
$600,000 to Good News Jail and Prison Ministry, Arlington, VA. 2 grants: $500,000 (To match challenge grant), $100,000 (For matching grant).
$400,000 to City of Refuge, Atlanta, GA. To match challenge grant.
$250,000 to Church of God International, Ministry to Israel, Cleveland, TN.
$175,000 to Children of Promise International, Alma, MO.
$75,000 to Mike Jenkins Evangelistic Association, Gate City, VA. For matching grant.
$50,000 to Focus on the Family, Colorado Springs, CO.
$45,429 to Tri-Cities Christian Schools, Blountville, TN. For matching grant.

8701
LifeWorks Foundation
(formerly George N. Bullard Foundation)
P.O. Box 50276
Nashville, TN 37205 (615) 269-6663
Contact: George Bullard, Dir.

Established in 1967 in TN; reorganized in 1988 in FL; name change in 1990.
Donor: Ella Hayes Trust.
Foundation type: Independent foundation.
Financial data (yr. ended 12/31/05): Assets, $8,228,207 (M); expenditures, $1,058,298; qualifying distributions, $981,525; giving activities include $844,170 for 82 grants (high: $556,000; low: $150), and $13,754 for foundation-administered programs.

Fields of interest: Animals/wildlife; Agriculture; Food services.
Limitations: Applications not accepted. Giving limited to Nashville, TN, and the surrounding area. No support for religious organizations. No grants to individuals.
Publications: Financial statement.
Application information: Unsolicited applications not considered.

Board meeting date(s): Monthly

Director: George Bullard.
Number of staff: 2 full-time professional.
EIN: 621428468

8702
TCH Lindahl Foundation ✧ ☆
c/o SunTrust Bank
P.O. Box 305110
Nashville, TN 37230-5110 (615) 748-5813
Contact: Kim Williams, Trust Off., SunTrust Bank

Established in 2001.
Donor: Evelyn N. Lindahl†.
Foundation type: Independent foundation.
Financial data (yr. ended 12/31/05): Assets, $3,079,627 (M); expenditures, $922,409; qualifying distributions, $909,398; giving activities include $900,000 for 5 grants (high: $250,000; low: $100,000).

Purpose and activities: Giving primarily to Catholic charities, with emphasis on schools.
Fields of interest: Education.
Type of support: General/operating support; Building/renovation.
Limitations: Giving primarily in TN. No grants to individuals; no loans.
Application information: Application form not required.

Initial approach: Letter
Copies of proposal: 4
Deadline(s): Oct. 31
Board meeting date(s): Nov.
Final notification: End of year

Trustee: SunTrust Bank.
EIN: 621838441
Selected grants: The following grants were reported in 2004.

$100,000 to Saint Anns School.
$100,000 to Saint Edwards School.
$50,000 to Dominican Campus, Nashville, TN.

8703
Lyndhurst Foundation ▼
517 E. 5th St.
Chattanooga, TN 37403-1826 (423) 756-0767
Contact: Jack E. Murrah, Pres.
FAX: (423) 756-0770;
E-mail: jmurrah@lyndhurstfoundation.org;
URL: http://www.lyndhurstfoundation.org

Incorporated in 1938 in DE.

Donors: T. Cartter Lupton†; Central Shares Corp.
Foundation type: Independent foundation.
Financial data (yr. ended 12/31/05): Assets, $184,000,000 (M); expenditures, $10,034,774; qualifying distributions, $8,335,664; giving activities include $8,285,664 for 59 grants (high: $1,500,000; low: $1,500; average: $50,000–$250,000), and $50,000 for employee matching gifts.
Purpose and activities: The mission of the foundation is the ongoing revitalization of the Chattanooga area and the conservation of the region surrounding it. Through its funding and partnerships, the foundation will focus on the following six goals: 1) Sustain and strengthen the downtown core as the center of employment, culture institutions, entertainment; maintain appeal to visitors, while accelerating growth in the resident population; 2) Promote urban neighborhoods of choice with rising real estate values, growing population, and favorable social condition; 3) Strengthen the momentum for public education reform that yields higher academic performance throughout the community, while closing the academic gap now linked to race and class; 4) Foster a thriving arts community that has great variety, broad participation, high quality and strong financial support; 5) Bolster the community's identification with green spaces and outdoor recreation, while strengthening Chattanooga's position as a gateway to regional environmental assets and attractions; and 6) Conserve, protect, and restore the region's premier natural assets.
Fields of interest: Arts; Elementary school/education; Secondary school/education; Environment; Community development.
Type of support: General/operating support; Continuing support; Capital campaigns; Building/renovation; Land acquisition; Program development; Seed money; Technical assistance; Employee matching gifts; Matching/challenge support.
Limitations: Giving limited to the southeastern U.S., with emphasis on Chattanooga, TN. No support for political organizations. No grants to individuals.
Publications: Annual report (including application guidelines); Financial statement; Grants list.
Application information: From Jan. 2005 through Dec. 2009, grants will be distributed primarily at the initiative of the foundation through the cultivation of strategic partnerships with nonprofit organizations. Application form not required.
  Initial approach: Letter (no more than 3 pages)
  Copies of proposal: 1
  Deadline(s): Mar., June, Sept., and Dec.; telephone foundation for actual dates
  Board meeting date(s): Feb., May, Aug., and Nov.
  Final notification: 3 months
Officers and Trustees:* Allen L. McCallie,* Chair.; Jack E. Murrah,* Pres.; Benic M. Clark III, V.P. and Secy.-Treas.; Nelson D. Campbell; George R. Fontaine; Margaret L. Gerber; Katherine Crossland Juett; T. Cartter Lupton II; Lasley Thomas Montague; Alice L. Smith.
Number of staff: 4 full-time professional; 1 full-time support.
EIN: 626044177
Selected grants: The following grants were reported in 2005.
$1,500,000 to Twenty-First Century Waterfront Trust, Chattanooga, TN. Toward pledge in support of Waterfront Trust initiative.
$1,265,000 to Chattanooga Neighborhood Enterprise, Chattanooga, TN. For general support and for revitalization activities and housing

incentive programs in targeted urban neighborhoods.
$1,250,000 to Public Education Foundation, Chattanooga, TN. For middle and high school reform initiatives to raise achievement and graduation rates in Hamilton County.
$866,098 to RiverCity Company, Chattanooga, TN. For enhancements to 4th Street in downtown Chattanooga.
$412,500 to Community Impact of Chattanooga, Chattanooga, TN. For continued general support for revitalization strategies in targeted urban neighborhoods.
$250,000 to Baylor School, Chattanooga, TN. For Cartter Lupton Merit Scholarship Fund.
$250,000 to University of Georgia Foundation, Athens, GA. For Music Business Certificate Program at Terry College of Business.
$200,000 to Nature Conservancy, Chattanooga, TN. For joint initiative by Tennessee and Alabama Chapters to expand network of protected areas lying within Southern Cumberland Mountain region.
$128,000 to Tennessee Stand for Children, Nashville, TN. For general support of initiatives to build community support for high performing public schools in Hamilton County.
$50,000 to Chattowah Open Land Trust, Alpharetta, GA. To expand network of working forest, agricultural, and conservation lands in northwest Georgia and northeast Alabama.

8704
The Maclellan Foundation, Inc. ▼ ✧
820 Broad St., Ste. 300
Chattanooga, TN 37402
Contact: Hugh O. Maclellan, Jr., Pres.
E-mail: info@maclellan.net; *URL:* http://www.maclellan.net

Incorporated in 1945 in DE; reincorporated in TN in 1992.
Donors: Robert J. Maclellan†; and members of the Maclellan family.
Foundation type: Independent foundation.
Financial data (yr. ended 12/31/04): Assets, $315,328,617 (M); expenditures, $18,065,589; qualifying distributions, $14,479,926; giving activities include $12,486,779 for grants (high: $12,477,091; low: $100).
Purpose and activities: Grants largely for Protestant missions support and religious organizations.
Fields of interest: Religion, association; Christian agencies & churches; Protestant agencies & churches.
International interests: Africa; Asia; Eastern Europe; Latin America; Middle East.
Type of support: General/operating support; Equipment; Program development; Seed money; Consulting services; Program evaluation.
Limitations: Giving nationally, with emphasis on the Chattanooga, TN, area; giving internationally in Eastern Europe, Asia, Africa, Latin America, and the Middle East. No grants to individuals, or for emergency funds, deficit financing, land acquisition, endowment funds, health services, medical research, publications, or for renovations.
Application information: See foundation's Web site for eligibility quiz and online application. Inquires via fax are not considered. Only online applications will be considered. No unsolicited requests for educational institutions. Application form not required.

Initial approach: Application online required
Copies of proposal: 1
Deadline(s): 6-8 weeks prior to board meetings
Board meeting date(s): 3-4 times per year
Final notification: 1 month after meeting
Officers and Trustees:* Hugh O. Maclellan, Jr.,* Pres.; Thomas H. McCallie III, Exec. V.P., Strategic Initiatives; David Denmark, V.P., Grantmaking; Steve Steele, V.P., Global Strategy and Research; Sandy Barber, Compt.; Daryl Heald,* Sr. Prog. Off.; Mrs. R.L. Maclellan, Tr. Emeritus; Ronald W. Blue; Frank A. Brock; Mrs. Catherine Maclellan Heald; G. Richard Hostetter; Christopher Maclellan; Daniel Maclellan; Robert H. Maclellan; Pat MacMillan; Laurence Powell.
Number of staff: 12 full-time professional; 6 full-time support.
EIN: 626041468
Selected grants: The following grants were reported in 2004.
$12,477,091 to National Christian Charitable Foundation, Atlanta, GA. For church services.
$5,490 to Hope Bible Mission, Morristown, NJ. For Hispanic Initiative.
$1,510 to Chattanooga Resource Foundation, Chattanooga, TN. For operating support.
$1,148 to Generous Giving, Chattanooga, TN. For furnishings.
$1,000 to China Ministries International, Pasadena, CA. For memorial.
$100 to 100 Black Men of Memphis, Memphis, TN. For operating support.

8705
Robert L. and Kathrina H. MacLellan Foundation ✧
820 Broad St., Ste. 300
Chattanooga, TN 37402
Contact: Jan Purdy

Established in 1972 in TN.
Donor: Kathrina H. MacLellan.
Foundation type: Independent foundation.
Financial data (yr. ended 12/31/04): Assets, $41,825,278 (M); gifts received, $5,039,902; expenditures, $1,713,928; qualifying distributions, $1,587,454; giving activities include $1,572,350 for 66 grants (high: $110,000; low: $1,000).
Purpose and activities: Giving primarily to evangelistic Christian educational programs.
Fields of interest: Elementary/secondary education; Education; Christian agencies & churches.
Type of support: General/operating support.
Limitations: Giving primarily in TN.
Application information: Application form required.
  Initial approach: Letter requesting application form
  Deadline(s): None
  Board meeting date(s): May
Officers and Directors:* Kathrina H. MacLellan,* Chair.; Lara Munford Yates, V.P.; Robert H. MacLellan, Pres. and Treas.; Thomas H. McCallie, Secy.; Douglas Daugherty; Donald J. Holwerda; Albert MacMillan.
EIN: 237159802

8706
The Albert Jay Martin Family Foundation ◇ ☆
140 Crescent Dr.
Collierville, TN 38017

Established in 1997 in TN.
Donor: Albert Jay Martin.
Foundation type: Independent foundation.
Financial data (yr. ended 11/30/05): Assets, $887,950 (M); gifts received, $258,165; expenditures, $346,978; qualifying distributions, $337,370; giving activities include $337,370 for 18 grants (high: $50,000; low: $1,000).
Purpose and activities: Giving primarily for education, and to Christian organizations and churches.
Fields of interest: Secondary school/education; Health care; Federated giving programs; Christian agencies & churches.
Limitations: Applications not accepted. No grants to individuals.
Application information: Contributes only to pre-selected organizations.
Trustees and Board Members:* Albert Jay Martin*; Charles A. Pinkham, Jr.*; Henry M. Turley, Jr.*.
EIN: 626345910
Selected grants: The following grants were reported in 2004.
$201,595 to Boys and Girls Club.
$50,000 to United Way.
$25,000 to Volunteers of America.
$10,000 to Junior Achievement.
$7,500 to FedEx Saint Jude Classic, Memphis, TN.
$990 to Youth Villages, Arlington, TN.

8707
R. Brad Martin Family Foundation ◇
(formerly R. Brad & Jean L. Martin Family Foundation)
1025 Cherry Rd.
Memphis, TN 38117

Established in 1994 in TN.
Donors: R. Brad Martin; RBM Shopping Centers, Inc.
Foundation type: Independent foundation.
Financial data (yr. ended 9/30/05): Assets, $1,818,236 (M); gifts received, $1,350,486; expenditures, $607,145; qualifying distributions, $602,684; giving activities include $601,674 for 29 grants (high: $495,100; low: $100).
Purpose and activities: Giving primarily for human services; funding also for education, and United Methodist churches.
Fields of interest: Education; Health organizations, association; Human services; Federated giving programs; Protestant agencies & churches.
Limitations: Applications not accepted. No grants to individuals.
Application information: Contributes only to pre-selected organizations.
Officers and Directors:* R. Brad Martin,* Pres.; Eric Steven Faires,* V.P. and Secy.; Scott Imorde,* V.P.; C.T. Courtenay,* Treas.
EIN: 621548977

8708
The Martin Foundation
P.O. Box 150067
Nashville, TN 37215-6154 (615) 665-6100
Contact: Shannon Presley Martin, Exec. Dir.
FAX: (615) 665-6198;
E-mail: administrator@martinfoundationnashville.org

Established in 1996 in TN.
Donor: Charles N. Martin, Jr.
Foundation type: Independent foundation.
Financial data (yr. ended 12/31/05): Assets, $15,919,458 (M); expenditures, $3,745,416; qualifying distributions, $3,559,588; giving activities include $3,559,588 for 67 grants (high: $575,000; low: $180).
Purpose and activities: Giving primarily for the arts, education, and human services.
Fields of interest: Arts; Education; Health organizations, association; Human services; Children/youth, services.
Type of support: Matching/challenge support; Seed money; General/operating support; Equipment; Debt reduction; Building/renovation; Continuing support; Annual campaigns; Capital campaigns.
Limitations: Giving primarily in TN. No grants to individuals.
Application information:
  Initial approach: Letter of inquiry
  Copies of proposal: 1
  Deadline(s): None
  Board meeting date(s): Annual
  Final notification: 1-month
Officers: Charles N. Martin, Jr., Chair.; Shannon Presley Martin, Exec. Dir.
Trustees: Cathy Faust; Jonathan Harwell.
Number of staff: 1 full-time professional.
EIN: 621679129
Selected grants: The following grants were reported in 2003.
$700,681 to Nashville Symphony, Nashville, TN.
$410,000 to Frist Center for the Visual Arts Foundation, Nashville, TN.
$25,000 to Rape and Sexual Abuse Center of Davidson County, Nashville, TN.
$25,000 to Second Harvest Food Bank of Nashville, Nashville, TN.
$20,000 to Alive Hospice, Nashville, TN.
$15,000 to Oasis Center, Nashville, TN.
$10,000 to Love Helps, Madison, TN.
$10,000 to Nashville Cares, Nashville, TN.
$10,000 to Vanderbilt University, Blair School of Music, Nashville, TN.
$5,000 to Oak Hill School, Nashville, TN.

8709
Jack C. Massey Foundation ◇
(formerly JCM Foundation)
5123 Virginia Way, Ste. B-22
Brentwood, TN 37027

Reincorporated in 1998.
Foundation type: Independent foundation.
Financial data (yr. ended 12/31/05): Assets, $45,051,979 (M); expenditures, $3,587,283; qualifying distributions, $2,995,284; giving activities include $2,993,854 for 143 grants (high: $1,000,000; low: $100).
Purpose and activities: Giving primarily for education, particularly higher education, as well as for health care, children, youth, and social services, and Protestant churches and associations.

Fields of interest: Performing arts; Arts; Elementary/secondary education; Higher education; Education; Environment; Hospitals (general); Health care; Health organizations, association; Medical research, institute; Human services; Children/youth, services; Family services; Residential/custodial care, hospices; Aging, centers/services; Protestant agencies & churches.
Limitations: Applications not accepted. Giving primarily in FL and TN. No grants to individuals.
Application information: Contributes only to pre-selected organizations.
Officers and Directors:* Alyne Massey, Co-Chair.; Barbara M. Rogers, Co-Chair.; Clarence Edmonds,* Pres.; J. Brad Reed,* V.P.
EIN: 621649826
Selected grants: The following grants were reported in 2004.
$1,006,000 to Belmont University, Nashville, TN. 2 grants: $1,000,000, $6,000
$300,000 to Harpeth Hall School, Nashville, TN. 2 grants: $100,000, $200,000
$100,000 to Ensworth School, Nashville, TN.
$50,000 to Society of the Four Arts, Palm Beach, FL. 3 grants: $10,000, $25,000, $15,000
$27,000 to Nashville Symphony, Nashville, TN. 2 grants: $20,000, $7,000

8710
The Master's Table, Inc. ◇
620 Shelby St.
Bristol, TN 37620

Established in 2001 in TN.
Donor: Joseph A. Gregory.
Foundation type: Independent foundation.
Financial data (yr. ended 12/31/05): Assets, $5,596,009 (M); gifts received, $1,020,265; expenditures, $1,188,795; qualifying distributions, $1,170,200; giving activities include $1,170,200 for 26 grants (high: $200,000; low: $1,000; average: $10,000–$25,000).
Fields of interest: Higher education; Christian agencies & churches.
Limitations: Applications not accepted. Giving primarily in TN. No grants to individuals.
Application information: Contributes only to pre-selected organizations.
Officers: Joseph R. Gregory, Pres.; Lucinda J. Gregory, Secy.-Treas.
EIN: 621874715
Selected grants: The following grants were reported in 2004.
$273,000 to Mighty Horn Ministries, Cleveland, TN. 2 grants: $23,000, $250,000
$100,000 to Liberty University, Lynchburg, VA.
$100,000 to Providence Academy, Johnson City, TN.
$50,000 to American Family Association, Tupelo, MS.
$30,000 to Overseas Council International, Indianapolis, IN.
$15,000 to Palm Beach Atlantic University, West Palm Beach, FL.

8711
The Melkus Family Foundation ◇
102 Woodmont Blvd., Ste. 110
Nashville, TN 37205

Established in 1993 in TN.

Donor: Melkus Partners, Ltd.
Foundation type: Independent foundation.
Financial data (yr. ended 12/31/05): Assets, $16,951,626 (M); expenditures, $769,757; qualifying distributions, $658,100; giving activities include $658,100 for 40 grants (high: $185,000; low: $500).
Purpose and activities: Giving primarily for education, particularly to an all girls' school, as well as to the United Way; funding also for the arts, health associations, human services, and Christian churches.
Fields of interest: Arts; Education; Health organizations, association; Human services; Federated giving programs; Christian agencies & churches.
Limitations: Applications not accepted. Giving primarily in Nashville, TN. No grants to individuals.
Application information: Contributes only to pre-selected organizations.
Officers: Kenneth J. Melkus, Pres.; Barbara L. Melkus, Secy.; Lauren E. Melkus, Treas.
EIN: 621518285
Selected grants: The following grants were reported in 2004.
$151,500 to United Way. 2 grants: $150,000, $1,500
$40,000 to Vanderbilt University Childrens Hospital, Nashville, TN.
$21,500 to Habitat for Humanity International. 2 grants: $20,000, $1,500
$10,000 to Doe Fund, New York, NY.
$5,000 to Ronald McDonald House.
$1,500 to Nashville Rescue Mission, Nashville, TN.
$1,000 to Catholic Charities.

8712
The Hermoine and Glen Nelson Foundation ◇
315 Deaderick St., 4th Fl.
Nashville, TN 37237-0401

Established in 1987 in TN.
Donor: Hermoine Corlew Adkisson.
Foundation type: Independent foundation.
Financial data (yr. ended 12/31/05): Assets, $11,977,439 (M); expenditures, $770,572; qualifying distributions, $707,374; giving activities include $705,000 for 17 grants (high: $250,000; low: $10,000).
Purpose and activities: Support primarily for human services and education, including Protestant schools and colleges.
Fields of interest: Elementary/secondary education; Higher education; Cancer; Human services; Children/youth, services; Aging, centers/services; Protestant agencies & churches.
Limitations: Applications not accepted. Giving primarily in TN. No grants to individuals.
Application information: Contributes only to pre-selected organizations.
Officers: Barbara Nelson Lamberson, Pres.; Nelson Lamberson, V.P.; Thomas Lamberson, V.P.
Director: Bob L. Andrews.
EIN: 621317088
Selected grants: The following grants were reported in 2004.
$250,000 to Childrens Hospital.
$50,000 to Fairview Church, Elon College, NC.

8713
No Other Foundation ◇ ☆
c/o John C. Stites, II
1080 S. Willow Ave.
Cookeville, TN 38501

Established in 1999 in TN.
Donors: American Buildings Co.; J&S Construction Co., Inc; John D. Stites II.
Foundation type: Company-sponsored foundation.
Financial data (yr. ended 3/31/06): Assets, $0 (M); gifts received, $382,500; expenditures, $383,700; qualifying distributions, $382,500; giving activities include $382,500 for grants.
Purpose and activities: The foundation supports Christian agencies and churches and organizations involved with higher education and youth development.
Fields of interest: Higher education; Youth development; Christian agencies & churches.
Type of support: General/operating support.
Limitations: Applications not accepted. Giving primarily in NY and TX.
Application information: Contributes only to pre-selected organizations.
Officers and Trustees: John D. Stites II, Pres.; James R. Stites, V.P.; Rosemary T. Stites, Secy.; Donnie Davidson; Sarah Davidson; Mary Stites.
EIN: 621790241

8714
Weldon F. Osborne Foundation, Inc. ◇
Krystal Bldg.
1 Union Sq., Ste. 210
Chattanooga, TN 37402-2501
Application address: c/o Glenn C. Stophel, 2 Union Sq., 1000 Tallan Bldg., Chattanooga, TN 37402, tel.: (423) 757-0227

Established in 1959.
Donors: Osborne Enterprises, Inc.; Osborne Building Corp.
Foundation type: Independent foundation.
Financial data (yr. ended 6/30/05): Assets, $21,125,649 (M); expenditures, $1,531,926; qualifying distributions, $1,006,116; giving activities include $944,805 for 75 grants (high: $100,000; low: $100).
Purpose and activities: Giving for civic, community, education and youth services.
Fields of interest: Education; Human services; Children/youth, services; Federated giving programs; Christian agencies & churches.
Type of support: Capital campaigns; Building/renovation; Seed money; Scholarship funds; Matching/challenge support.
Limitations: Giving primarily in the Chattanooga and Hamilton County, TN, areas. No grants to individuals.
Publications: Application guidelines; Annual report.
Application information: Application form required.
Copies of proposal: 1
Deadline(s): None
Board meeting date(s): 2nd Tues. each quarter; after annual meeting 2nd Tues. in June
Final notification: After next board meeting
Officers and Directors:* Glenn C. Stophel,* Pres.; Gene Burnett,* V.P.; Arch Trimble III,* Secy.; C. Duffy Franck, Jr.; Scott Mattice; Christine B. Smith; Harold S. Wilson.
Number of staff: 1 part-time professional.
EIN: 626026442

8715
Jane L. Pettway Foundation ◇
c/o First Tennessee Bank, N.A., Trust Div.
800 S. Gay St.
Knoxville, TN 37995-1230 (865) 971-2165
Contact: Keith Keisling

Established in 1999 in TN.
Foundation type: Independent foundation.
Financial data (yr. ended 8/31/05): Assets, $8,843,495 (M); expenditures, $439,529; qualifying distributions, $405,622; giving activities include $377,921 for 25 grants (high: $50,000; low: $1,000).
Purpose and activities: Giving primarily for libraries in TN, and/or for the education and training of employees of TN libraries, financially needy women in TN, and Episcopal parishes or ministries in TN.
Fields of interest: Libraries (public); Human services; Christian agencies & churches.
Limitations: Giving primarily in Anderson, Blount, Grainger, Jefferson, Knox, Loudon, Roane, Sevier and Union counties in TN.
Application information: Application may also be hand delivered during normal business hours. Application form required.
Initial approach: Letter
Deadline(s): Mar. 31
Board meeting date(s): Annually, late Apr. or early May
Managers: Larry Frank; David Lantz; Dean John Ross.
Trustee: First Tennessee Bank, N.A.
EIN: 626371465
Selected grants: The following grants were reported in 2005.
$42,135 to Interfaith Health Clinic, Knoxville, TN.
$30,000 to Goodwill Industries - Knoxville, Knoxville, TN.
$18,850 to YWCA of Knoxville, Knoxville, TN.
$12,500 to YMCA of Knoxville, Knoxville, TN.

8716
Louie M. & Betty M. Phillips Foundation ◇
3334 Powell Ave.
P.O. Box 40788
Nashville, TN 37204 (615) 385-5949
Contact: Louie P. Buntin, C.E.O.
FAX: (615) 385-2507;
E-mail: Louie@PhillipsFoundation.org; URL: http://www.phillipsfoundation.org

Established in 1978 in TN.
Donors: Betty M. Phillips†; Louie M. Phillips†.
Foundation type: Independent foundation.
Financial data (yr. ended 12/31/04): Assets, $9,397,324 (M); expenditures, $770,175; qualifying distributions, $659,682; giving activities include $495,750 for 94 grants (high: $55,000; low: $500).
Purpose and activities: Giving primarily for community development.
Fields of interest: Arts; Education; Health care; Human services; Community development.
Type of support: General/operating support; Continuing support; Annual campaigns; Capital campaigns; Building/renovation; Equipment; Endowments; Debt reduction; Seed money; Scholarship funds; Program-related investments/loans; Matching/challenge support.
Limitations: Giving limited to the greater Nashville, TN, area. No support for disease-specific organizations, or for biomedical or clinical research.

No grants to individuals, or for advertising or sponsorships.

Publications: Application guidelines; Grants list; Informational brochure (including application guidelines).

Application information: Application guidelines available on foundation Web site. Application form not required.

> *Initial approach:* Letter (not exceeding two pages) or information request form available on the foundation Web site's grant application page
> *Copies of proposal:* 1
> *Deadline(s):* June 4 and Oct. 29
> *Board meeting date(s):* July 2 and Nov. 26

Officer and Trustees:* Louie P. Buntin,* C.E.O.; Trustmark National Bank.

Number of staff: 1 full-time professional.

EIN: 581326615

Selected grants: The following grants were reported in 2004.
$50,000 to Belmont University, Nashville, TN.
$10,000 to Boys and Girls Club.
$10,000 to Montgomery Bell Academy, Nashville, TN.
$7,750 to Men of Valor, Atlanta, GA.
$5,000 to Currey Ingram Academy, Brentwood, TN.
$5,000 to Nashville Ballet, Nashville, TN.
$5,000 to Nashville Symphony, Nashville, TN.
$5,000 to Tennessee Repertory Theater, Nashville, TN.
$3,000 to Downtown Ministry Center, Nashville, TN.
$3,000 to Nashville Child Advocacy Center, Nashville, TN.

8717
The James W. Pickle Charitable Foundation ◇ ☆

905 Harpeth Valley Pl., Ste. 7057
Nashville, TN 37221 (615) 662-2727
Contact: Lawrence J. Sacks, Pres.
E-mail: debra@sackscpas.com

Established in 2004 in TN.

Donor: James W. Pickle†.

Foundation type: Independent foundation.

Financial data (yr. ended 12/31/05): Assets, $8,790,300 (M); expenditures, $1,065,808; qualifying distributions, $403,954; giving activities include $352,021 for 9 grants (high: $100,000; low: $2,886).

Purpose and activities: Giving for life altering medical care, services and equipment.

Fields of interest: Medicine/medical care, public education.

Application information: Application form required.
> *Initial approach:* Letter or e-mail
> *Deadline(s):* None

Officers: Lawrence J. Sacks, Pres.; Charlene Sanders, Secy.

Trustee: William Boone.

EIN: 200485515

8718
Plough Foundation ▼

6410 Poplar Ave., Ste. 710
Memphis, TN 38119
Contact: Rick C. Masson, Exec. Dir.
FAX: (901) 761-6186; *E-mail:* Masson@plough.org

Established in 1972 in TN.

Donors: Abe Plough†; Jocelyn P. Rudner; Patricia R. Burnham; Diane R. Rudner; Sharon D. Eisenberg; William Rudner.

Foundation type: Independent foundation.

Financial data (yr. ended 12/31/05): Assets, $163,889,361 (M); gifts received, $77,174; expenditures, $9,923,594; qualifying distributions, $8,404,369; giving activities include $7,503,634 for 45 grants (high: $1,250,000; low: $100; average: $50,000–$500,000).

Purpose and activities: Grants to community projects, early childhood and elementary education, crime, health care, economic development, social service agencies, housing and homelessness, and the arts.

Fields of interest: Arts; Education, early childhood education; Elementary school/education; Health care; Crime/violence prevention; Housing/shelter, temporary shelter; Housing/shelter, homeless; Human services; Youth, services; Family services; Economic development.

Type of support: Capital campaigns; Building/renovation; Equipment; Land acquisition; Endowments; Program development; Professorships; Seed money; Curriculum development; Program evaluation; Program-related investments/loans; Matching/challenge support.

Limitations: Giving primarily in Shelby County, TN, with an emphasis on Memphis. No grants to individuals, and generally no grants for annual operating funds.

Publications: Informational brochure (including application guidelines).

Application information: Application form required.
> *Initial approach:* Letter describing project, no more than 3 pages; full application by invitation only
> *Copies of proposal:* 3
> *Deadline(s):* 10th of month prior to board meeting for full application
> *Board meeting date(s):* Feb., May, Aug., and Nov.
> *Final notification:* Generally within 2 days

Officer: Rick C. Masson, Exec. Dir.

Trustees: Patricia R. Burnham; Eugene J. Callahan; Robert A. Compton; D.D. Eisenberg; Diane R. Rudner; Jocelyn P. Rudner; James Springfield; Steve Wishnia; SunTrust Bank.

Number of staff: 3 full-time professional; 1 full-time support.

EIN: 237175983

Selected grants: The following grants were reported in 2005.
$1,250,000 to Memphis Arts Council, Memphis, TN. For endowment.
$1,000,000 to Memphis Zoological Society, Memphis, TN. For capital campaign.
$1,000,000 to Temple Israel, Memphis, TN. For capital campaign.
$500,000 to Le Bonheur Childrens Medical Center Foundation, Memphis, TN. For capital campaign.
$500,000 to University of Memphis, Memphis, TN. For program support.
$300,000 to Jewish Federation, Memphis, Memphis, TN. For annual campaign.
$250,000 to Memphis Bioworks Foundation, Memphis, TN. For program support.
$250,000 to Riverfront Development Corporation, Memphis, TN. For general operating support.
$111,525 to Facing History and Ourselves National Foundation, Memphis, TN. For program support.
$83,334 to Partners in Public Education (PIPE), Memphis, TN. For general operating support.

8719
The Poplar Foundation ▼

(formerly The Longleaf Foundation)
6410 Poplar Ave., Ste. 720
Memphis, TN 38119-4843
Contact: Tom Marino, Exec. Dir.

Established in 1994 in TN.

Donors: O. Mason Hawkins; Joseph L. Ott; Southeastern Asset Management, Inc.

Foundation type: Independent foundation.

Financial data (yr. ended 12/31/04): Assets, $27,795,464 (M); gifts received, $18,155,000; expenditures, $10,617,700; qualifying distributions, $10,589,251; giving activities include $10,589,251 for 67 grants (high: $1,000,000; low: $500; average: $5,000–$100,000).

Purpose and activities: Funding primarily for youth services and education.

Fields of interest: Arts; Education; Health care; Human services; Children/youth, services; Christian agencies & churches.

Limitations: Applications not accepted. Giving primarily in Memphis, TN.

Application information: Unsolicited requests for funds not accepted.

Officers and Directors:* Ann B. Hawkins,* Pres.; G. Staley Cates,* V.P.; Andrew R. McCarroll, Secy.; Joseph L. Ott,* Treas. and Mgr.; O. Mason Hawkins.

EIN: 621586727

Selected grants: The following grants were reported in 2004.
$1,757,206 to Saint Georges Schools Foundation, Germantown, TN. 3 grants: $557,206, $200,000, $1,000,000
$1,163,545 to Urban Youth Initiative, Memphis, TN. 4 grants: $385,125, $320,000, $270,000, $188,420
$1,000,000 to New Hope Christian Academy, Memphis, TN.
$1,000,000 to Trezevant Manor Foundation, Memphis, TN.
$200,000 to Perea Preschool, Memphis, TN.

8720
Justin & Valere Blair Potter Foundation ◇

c/o Bank of America, N.A.
1 Bank of America Plz., Ste. M-7
Nashville, TN 37209-1697 (615) 749-3164
Contact: Polly Lankford, Trust Off., Bank of America, N.A.

Established in 1953.

Foundation type: Independent foundation.

Financial data (yr. ended 12/31/05): Assets, $19,181,327 (M); expenditures, $1,054,869; qualifying distributions, $933,946; giving activities include $925,000 for 11 grants (high: $150,000; low: $25,000).

Fields of interest: Hospitals (general); Health organizations, association; Boys & girls clubs; Human services; Salvation Army.

Limitations: Giving primarily in Nashville, TN.

Application information:
> *Initial approach:* Letter
> *Deadline(s):* None

Trustees: Albert L. Menefee, Jr.; Valere Menefee; Bank of America, N.A.

EIN: 626306577

Selected grants: The following grants were reported in 2003.
$116,431 to Vanderbilt University, Television News Archive, Nashville, TN. For general support.

$100,000 to American Diabetes Association, Alexandria, VA. For general support.
$100,000 to Faith Family Medical Clinic, Nashville, TN. For general support.
$50,000 to Arthritis Foundation, Nashville, TN. For general support.
$50,000 to Easter Seals Tennessee, Nashville, TN. For general support.
$50,000 to Nashville Rescue Mission, Nashville, TN. For general support.
$25,000 to Bootstrap Awards, Nashville, TN. For general support.
$10,000 to Boys and Girls Club of Middle Tennessee, Nashville, TN. For general support.

8721
Promethean Foundation ✧ ☆
624 Reelfoot Ave.
Union City, TN 38261
Application address: c/o Cathy Waggoner 115 W Main St., Union City, TN 38261, tel.: (731) 884-0088

Established in 2004 in TN.
Donor: Robert E. & Jenny D. Kirkland Foundation.
Foundation type: Independent foundation.
Financial data (yr. ended 12/31/05): Assets, $214,322 (M); gifts received, $834,513; expenditures, $633,067; qualifying distributions, $630,614; giving activities include $529,288 for 8 grants (high: $147,275; low: $126).
Purpose and activities: The foundation provides scholarships for qualifying day care to newborns throught school age, with the requirement that their progress be monitored though out their school years. The applicants must live in Union City, TN, and scholarships are only paid to day cares which are approved and monitored by the foundation. The qualifying daycare facility must meet the moral, social, and educational values that the foundation feels are necessary to provide an excellent background for a successful life.
Fields of interest: Children, day care.
Type of support: Scholarship funds.
Limitations: Giving limited to Union City, TN.
Application information: Application form required.
Initial approach: Letter or telephone requesting application form
Deadline(s): Prior to the birth of the child for which the scholarship is being requested
Officers and Directors:* Henry Clay Woods,* Pres.; Gary Houston,* Secy.; Clinton Thorpe Joiner; Robert E. Kirkland; William Martin Sisco; Todd A. Stone.
EIN: 201690784

8722
The Ragsdale Family Foundation ✧
27 Northumberland Dr.
Nashville, TN 37215

Established in 1991 in TN.
Donor: Richard E. Ragsdale.
Foundation type: Independent foundation.
Financial data (yr. ended 12/31/05): Assets, $3,358,628 (M); expenditures, $727,866; qualifying distributions, $707,804; giving activities include $707,022 for 26 grants (high: $250,957; low: $500).
Purpose and activities: Giving primarily for the arts, education, and human services; funding also for a hospice, a cancer center, and a diabetes clinic.

Fields of interest: Performing arts; Arts; Elementary/secondary education; Higher education; Zoos/zoological societies; Hospitals (general); Health organizations, association; Human services; Salvation Army; YM/YWCAs & YM/YWHAs; Children/youth, services; Family services; Residential/custodial care, hospices.
Limitations: Applications not accepted. Giving primarily in Nashville, TN. No grants to individuals.
Application information: Contributes only to pre-selected organizations.
Officers and Directors:* Richard E. Ragsdale,* Pres.; Anne E. Ragsdale,* Secy.; Bethany R. Corrieri; Brett T. Corrieri; Kevin G. Ragsdale; Richard E. Ragsdale II.
EIN: 621481225
Selected grants: The following grants were reported in 2005.
$250,957 to Nashville Symphony Association, Nashville, TN.
$67,000 to Nashville Zoo, Brentwood, TN.
$66,667 to Alice Lloyd College, Pippa Passes, KY.
$46,342 to Nashville Symphony, Nashville, TN.
$20,000 to Maryville College, Maryville, TN.
$20,000 to Nashville Opera Association, Nashville, TN.
$10,000 to Benton Hall School, Nashville, TN.
$10,000 to East Academy, Nashville, TN.
$5,000 to Meharry Medical College, Nashville, TN.

8723
Redbird Foundation ✧
4624 Chambliss Ave.
Knoxville, TN 37919

Established in 1995.
Donors: B. Ray Thompson Charitable Trust; Juanne Thompson Charitable Trust.
Foundation type: Independent foundation.
Financial data (yr. ended 12/31/05): Assets, $8,238,268 (M); expenditures, $448,206; qualifying distributions, $400,000; giving activities include $400,000 for 3 grants (high: $200,000; low: $75,000).
Purpose and activities: Giving primarily to Christian humanitarian organizations.
Fields of interest: Nursing care; Human services; Christian agencies & churches.
Limitations: Applications not accepted. Giving primarily in KY. No grants for endowments or funds to support operating deficits.
Publications: Annual report.
Application information: Contributes only to pre-selected organizations.
Officers and Directors:* Adella Sands Thompson,* Pres.; Sarah Thompson Tarver,* Secy.; Rebekah Thompson Palmer; B. Ray Thompson, Jr.; Catherine Vance Thompson; B. Ray Thompson III; Juanne J. Thompson.
EIN: 621591527
Selected grants: The following grants were reported in 2004.
$100,000 to John Stott Ministries, Carol Stream, IL.
$26,069 to Development Associates International, Colorado Springs, CO.
$25,000 to Frontier Nursing Service, Wendover, KY.
$22,500 to Young Life, Colorado Springs, CO.

8724
The Rust Foundation ✧
c/o Jane C. Rust
373 Old Woodbury Pike
Readyville, TN 37149
Contact: Trustees

Trust established in 1950 in PA.
Donor: The Rust family.
Foundation type: Independent foundation.
Financial data (yr. ended 12/31/05): Assets, $7,012,416 (M); gifts received, $100; expenditures, $468,679; qualifying distributions, $388,200; giving activities include $380,000 for 103 grants (high: $50,000; low: $500).
Purpose and activities: Giving limited to interests of individual trustees, including grants for health care, education, environmental conservation, church support, and community funds.
Type of support: Continuing support; Annual campaigns; Capital campaigns; Building/renovation; Land acquisition; Endowments; Emergency funds; Seed money; Research.
Limitations: Applications not accepted. Giving on a national basis. No grants to individuals.
Application information: Unsolicited requests for funds not accepted.
Board meeting date(s): Late Dec. and early Aug.
Officers and Trustees:* David C. Gillies,* Pres.; Robert B. Rust,* V.P.; James O. Rust, Secy.; John M. Rust,* Treas.; Nancy L. Gillies; Thatcher O. Montgomery; S.M. Rust, Jr.; R. Mark Rust.
EIN: 256049037
Selected grants: The following grants were reported in 2004.
$25,000 to Forman School, Litchfield, CT.
$25,000 to Historical Society of Western Pennsylvania, Pittsburgh, PA.
$15,000 to Habitat for Humanity International.
$10,000 to Audubon Society, Massachusetts, Lincoln, MA.
$10,000 to Cape Cod Foundation, Yarmouth Port, MA.
$10,000 to Gildas Club of Western Pennsylvania, Pittsburgh, PA.
$10,000 to In His Image, Tulsa, OK.
$10,000 to Salvation Army, Butler, PA.
$5,500 to Carlow College, Pittsburgh, PA.
$1,200 to Bowdoin College, Brunswick, ME.

8725
The Schadt Foundation, Inc. ✧
P.O. Box 242049
Memphis, TN 38124-2049

Incorporated in 1958 in TN.
Donors: Charles F. Schadt, Sr.; Harry E. Schadt, Sr.†; Harry E. Schadt, Jr.
Foundation type: Independent foundation.
Financial data (yr. ended 12/31/05): Assets, $5,980,900 (M); expenditures, $451,804; qualifying distributions, $361,000; giving activities include $361,000 for 54 grants (high: $25,000; low: $1,000).
Purpose and activities: Giving primarily for the arts, education, and children, youth, families, and social services.
Fields of interest: Arts councils; Media/communications; Museums; Performing arts, ballet; Arts; Education; Health care; Human services; Salvation Army; YM/YWCAs & YM/YWHAs; Children/youth, services; Family services;

Federated giving programs; Christian agencies & churches.

Limitations: Applications not accepted. Giving limited to Memphis, TN. No grants to individuals.

Application information: Contributes only to pre-selected organizations.

Board meeting date(s): Annually

Officers: Stephen C. Schadt, Sr., Pres.; Lynn Schadt Thomas, Secy.

Directors: Charles F. Schadt, Jr.; Harry E. Schadt; Reid Schadt.

EIN: 626040050

Selected grants: The following grants were reported in 2005.

$20,000 to Memphis Arts Council, Memphis, TN.

$16,000 to Saint Georges Episcopal School, New Orleans, LA.

$10,000 to Bridges, Inc., Memphis, TN.

$10,000 to Hutchison School, Memphis, TN.

$8,000 to Metropolitan Inter-Faith Association, Memphis, TN.

$7,500 to Junior Achievement.

$6,000 to Church of the Holy Communion, Memphis, TN.

$5,000 to Dixon Gallery and Gardens, Memphis, TN.

$5,000 to Rhodes College, Memphis, TN.

$4,000 to Salvation Army.

8726

Scheidt Family Foundation, Inc. ✧

54 S. White Station Rd.
Memphis, TN 38117
Contact: Helen H. Scheidt, Pres.

Established in 1976 in TN.

Donors: Rudi E. Scheidt; Helen H. Scheidt.

Foundation type: Independent foundation.

Financial data (yr. ended 10/31/05): Assets, $5,991,509 (M); gifts received, $740,712; expenditures, $668,021; qualifying distributions, $608,000; giving activities include $608,000 for 10 grants (high: $530,000; low: $1,500).

Purpose and activities: Giving for Jewish organizations, higher education, and the arts.

Fields of interest: Arts; Education; Health care, clinics/centers; Health organizations, association; Jewish agencies & temples.

Limitations: Giving primarily in NY and Memphis, TN. No grants to individuals.

Application information:

Deadline(s): None

Officers: Helen H. Scheidt, Pres.; Susan Scheidt Arney, V.P.; Helen Scheidt Gronauer, V.P.; E. Elkan Scheidt, V.P.; Rudi E. Scheidt, Jr., V.P.; Rudi E. Scheidt, Secy.

EIN: 620989531

Selected grants: The following grants were reported in 2005.

$530,000 to Temple Israel, Memphis, TN.

$27,500 to Germantown Performing Arts Center, Germantown, TN.

$14,750 to Memphis Brooks Museum of Art, Memphis, TN.

$10,000 to American Federation of Arts, New York, NY.

$3,750 to Junior League of Memphis, Memphis, TN.

$3,000 to Santa Fe Opera, Santa Fe, NM.

8727

The Sparks Foundation ✧

775 Ridge Lake Blvd., Ste. 105
Memphis, TN 38120 (901) 766-4600
FAX: (901) 766-8133;
E-mail: info@sparksfoundation.com; URL: http://www.sparksfoundation.com

Established in 2001 in TN.

Donor: Willard D. Sparks.

Foundation type: Independent foundation.

Financial data (yr. ended 12/31/05): Assets, $15,018,624 (M); gifts received, $249,985; expenditures, $911,768; qualifying distributions, $847,000; giving activities include $847,000 for 25 grants (high: $200,000; low: $500).

Fields of interest: Museums (specialized); Higher education, university; Christian agencies & churches.

Limitations: Giving primarily in Memphis, TN, with some giving in MS. No grants to individuals.

Application information: Application form required.

Deadline(s): Mar. 31 and Oct. 31

Final notification: Within 30 days

Trustees: Robert D. Sparks; Willard R. Sparks.

EIN: 237029788

Selected grants: The following grants were reported in 2004.

$100,000 to University of Memphis Foundation, Memphis, TN. 2 grants: $50,000 each

$50,000 to Briarcrest Christian School, Memphis, TN.

$37,500 to University School of Jackson, Jackson, TN.

$30,000 to Memphis Arts Council, Memphis, TN.

$25,000 to Memphis University School, Memphis, TN.

$15,000 to Dixon Gallery and Gardens, Memphis, TN.

$10,000 to National Civil Rights Museum, Memphis, TN.

$10,000 to Opera Memphis, Memphis, TN.

8728

Starfish Foundation ✧

(formerly McInnes Family Foundation)
116 30th Ave. S.
Nashville, TN 37212

Established in 1991 in TN.

Donor: William W. McInnes.

Foundation type: Independent foundation.

Financial data (yr. ended 12/31/05): Assets, $0 (M); gifts received, $377,300; expenditures, $387,969; qualifying distributions, $387,187; giving activities include $387,187 for 20+ grants (high: $219,000).

Purpose and activities: Giving to higher and secondary education, the arts, and human services.

Fields of interest: Arts; Higher education; Higher education, university; Education; Health organizations, association; Youth, services; Federated giving programs.

Limitations: Applications not accepted. Giving limited to Nashville, TN. No grants to individuals.

Application information: Contributes only to pre-selected organizations.

Officers: William W. McInnes, Pres. and Treas.; William V. McInnes, Secy.

Director: Beverly W. McInnes.

EIN: 621459425

Selected grants: The following grants were reported in 2003.

$223,000 to CEO Academy, Nashville, TN. For unrestricted support.

$160,500 to Its About Hope, Nashville, TN. For unrestricted support.

$5,000 to W P L N Educational Foundation, Nashville, TN. For unrestricted support.

$3,000 to Special Olympics Tennessee, Nashville, TN. For unrestricted support.

$1,000 to Angel Heart Farm, Nashville, TN. For unrestricted support.

$1,000 to Land Trust for Tennessee, Nashville, TN. For unrestricted support.

$1,000 to ReConstruct, Nolensville, TN. For unrestricted support.

$1,000 to Salvation Army of Nashville, Nashville, TN. For unrestricted support.

$1,000 to Time to Rise, Nashville, TN. For unrestricted support.

$1,000 to Vanderbilt University, Blair School of Music, Nashville, TN. For unrestricted support.

8729

Stephens Christian Trust ☆

(formerly Stephens Foundation Trust)
6160 Pasquo Rd.
Nashville, TN 37221

Established in 1987 in TN.

Donors: Juanita W. Stephens†; W.E. Stephens, Jr.; Billy C. Pentecost; Helen Richardson.

Foundation type: Independent foundation.

Financial data (yr. ended 7/31/05): Assets, $5,879,772 (M); gifts received, $1,195,470; expenditures, $542,413; qualifying distributions, $384,723; giving activities include $346,617 for 35 grants (high: $169,367; low: $100).

Purpose and activities: Giving primarily for education and Christian schools and churches.

Fields of interest: Elementary/secondary education; Higher education; Children/youth, services; Christian agencies & churches.

Type of support: Capital campaigns; Building/renovation; Seed money; Matching/challenge support.

Limitations: Applications not accepted. Giving primarily in TN. No grants to individuals.

Application information: Contributes only to pre-selected organizations.

Trustees: J. Greg Hardeman; Walter C. Leaver III; Keith Nikolaus; Neika Stephens; W.E. Stephens, Jr.; James Vandiver.

EIN: 626201842

Selected grants: The following grants were reported in 2004.

$81,900 to World Bible Translation Center, Fort Worth, TX. To purchase Bibles.

$42,000 to World Christian Broadcasting, Abilene, TX. For general support.

$18,500 to David Lipscomb University, Nashville, TN. 2 grants: $12,500 (For Bible Building Campaign), $6,000 (For summer celebration).

$10,000 to Brentwood Hills Church of Christ, Nashville, TN. For general support.

$3,000 to Currey Ingram Academy, Brentwood, TN. For endowed scholarships.

$2,500 to Faith Family Medical Clinic, Nashville, TN. For general support.

$2,350 to AGAPE, Nashville, TN. For general support.

$2,000 to ECHO Ministry, Elkin, NC. For general support.

$1,000 to Vanderbilt University, Nashville, TN. For Ross lectures.

8730
The William B. Stokely, Jr. Foundation ✧
620 Campbell Station Rd., Ste. 27
Knoxville, TN 37922-1636 (865) 966-4878
Contact: William B. Stokely III, Pres.

Incorporated in 1951 in IN.
Donor: William B. Stokely, Jr.‡.
Foundation type: Independent foundation.
Financial data (yr. ended 12/31/04): Assets,
$8,391,694 (M); expenditures, $893,479;
qualifying distributions, $893,479; giving activities
include $751,598 for 69 grants (high: $100,000;
low: $200).
Purpose and activities: Giving primarily for
education, health, youth services, and the arts.
Fields of interest: Museums; Arts; Higher
education; Hospitals (general); Health care;
Children/youth, services; Religion.
Type of support: General/operating support;
Continuing support; Annual campaigns; Capital
campaigns; Endowments; Scholarship funds.
Limitations: Giving primarily in eastern TN. No
grants to individuals.
Application information: Application form not
required.
  Initial approach: Letter or proposal
  Copies of proposal: 1
  Deadline(s): None
  Board meeting date(s): Feb., May, Aug., and Nov.
Officers and Directors:* William B. Stokely III,*
Pres.; Kay H. Stokely,* Exec. V.P.; Andrea A.
White-Randall, V.P. and Secy.-Treas.; Stacy S.
Byerly; Clayton F. Stokely; Shelley K. Stokely;
William B. Stokely IV.
Number of staff: 1 full-time professional.
EIN: 356016402
Selected grants: The following grants were reported
in 2003.
$50,000 to Childhelp USA, Knoxville, TN.
$50,000 to First Baptist Church of Concord,
  Concord, TN.
$30,000 to Wellness Community-Knoxville,
  Knoxville, TN.
$25,000 to Knoxville Museum of Art, Knoxville, TN.
$25,000 to Tennessee Theater, Knoxville, TN.
$22,000 to United Way of Greater Knoxville,
  Knoxville, TN.
$20,000 to Maryville College, Maryville, TN.
$15,000 to East Tennessee Childrens Hospital,
  Knoxville, TN.
$10,000 to Helen Ross McNabb Mental Health
  Foundation, Knoxville, TN.
$10,000 to Knoxville Symphony Orchestra,
  Knoxville, TN.

8731
T & T Family Foundation ✧
P.O. Box 101444
Nashville, TN 37224-1444
Contact: Lester L. Turner, Jr., Tr.

Established in 1998 in TN.
Donor: Betty M. Turner‡.
Foundation type: Independent foundation.
Financial data (yr. ended 12/31/05): Assets,
$9,993,033 (M); expenditures, $553,712;
qualifying distributions, $482,075; giving activities
include $482,075 for 113 grants (high: $100,000;
low: $1,000).
Purpose and activities: Giving primarily for
community foundations, health associations, and
human services.

Fields of interest: Arts; Education; Health
organizations, association; Housing/shelter; Boys &
girls clubs; Human services; Children/youth,
services; Foundations (community); Federated
giving programs.
Type of support: Annual campaigns.
Limitations: Giving primarily in Nashville, TN; large
funding also in Abilene, TX.
Application information: Application form not
required.
  Initial approach: Letter
  Copies of proposal: 1
  Deadline(s): Oct.
  Board meeting date(s): Oct.
  Final notification: Up to 1 year
Trustees: Curry Turner Thornton; Lester L. Turner, Jr.
EIN: 626324206

8732
Tennessee Health Foundation, Inc. ✧ ☆
801 Pine St.
Chattanooga, TN 37402
Contact: Beverly Cosley, Mgr.

Established in 2003 in TN.
Donor: BlueCross BlueShield of Tennessee.
Foundation type: Independent foundation.
Financial data (yr. ended 12/31/05): Assets,
$35,654,915 (M); gifts received, $23,300,000;
expenditures, $1,089,842; qualifying distributions,
$1,086,500; giving activities include $1,078,000
for 13 grants (high: $500,000; low: $13,125).
Purpose and activities: Giving primarily for health
care.
Fields of interest: Higher education; Health care,
clinics/centers; Health care; Health organizations,
association; Human services.
Limitations: Giving primarily in TN.
Application information:
  Initial approach: Letter of inquiry
  Deadline(s): 90-day prior to need
Officers: Dewitt Ezell, Jr., Chair.; Lamar J. Partridge,
Vice-Chair.; Vicky Gregg, C.E.O. and Pres.; Shelia
Clemons, Secy.; David Deal, C.F.O. and Treas.;
Beverly Cosley,* Mgr.; Calvin Anderson,* Exec. Dir.
Directors: Hulet Chaney; Betty De Vinney; Gus B.
Denton; J.D. Elliott; John F. Germ; Herbert H.
Hilliard; William H. Latimer III; Gloria Ray; Paul E.
Stanton, M.D.; William R. Walter; Byron B. Winsett,
Jr.
EIN: 200298456

8733
The Thompson Charitable Foundation ✧
P.O. Box 10516
Knoxville, TN 37939
Contact: Monica Luke, Mgr.

Established in 1987 in TN.
Donor: B.R. Thompson, Sr.‡.
Foundation type: Independent foundation.
Financial data (yr. ended 6/30/05): Assets,
$45,331,606 (M); expenditures, $2,606,145;
qualifying distributions, $2,380,502; giving
activities include $2,322,837 for 56 grants (high:
$500,000; low: $1,000).
Purpose and activities: Giving primarily for
education, health, and human services, including
funding for capital and building improvements for
human service organizations and educational

institutions; funding also for youth and Christian
organizations.
Fields of interest: Museums; Historic preservation/
historical societies; Arts; Graduate/professional
education; Education; Environment, water
resources; Hospitals (general); Health care; Cancer;
Autism research; Food services; Housing/shelter,
development; Housing/shelter; Disasters, fire
prevention/control; Human services; YM/YWCAs &
YM/YWHAs; Children/youth, services; Family
services, adolescent parents; Residential/custodial
care, hospices; Community development,
neighborhood development; Christian agencies &
churches.
Type of support: General/operating support; Capital
campaigns; Program development.
Limitations: Giving limited to Bell, Clay, Laurel, and
Leslie counties, KY; Anderson, Blount, Knox, and
Scott counties, TN; and Buchanan and Tazewell
counties, VA. No grants for budget deficits or
endowments.
Application information:
  Initial approach: Letter (no more than 2 pages)
  Deadline(s): Mar. 31, June 30, Sept. 30, and Dec.
  31
Officers: Merle D. Wolfe, Pres.; Monica Luke, Mgr.
Directors: Carl Ensor, Jr.; Greg Erickson; Sylvia M.
Thompson; Lindsay Young.
EIN: 581754763
Selected grants: The following grants were reported
in 2003.
$375,000 to YMCA of Knoxville, Knoxville, TN. For
  capital expansion.
$300,000 to Anderson County Health Department,
  Clinton, TN. For new construction.
$300,000 to Appalachian School of Law, Grundy,
  VA. For capital support.
$150,000 to Southwest Virginia Community
  College, Richlands, VA. For building purchase.
$100,000 to Maryville College, Maryville, TN. For
  capital improvement.
$50,000 to Blount County Public Library Foundation,
  Maryville, TN. For library construction.
$50,000 to Come-Unity Cooperative Care, London,
  KY. For food and medical needs.
$50,000 to Saint Marys Foundation, Knoxville, TN.
  For hospice.
$42,400 to Christian Healthcare Services, Hyden,
  KY.
$40,000 to Hospice and Palliative Care of Virginia,
  Norton, VA.

8734
Tonya Memorial Foundation, Inc. ✧
c/o SunTrust Bank
736 Market St.
Chattanooga, TN 37402

Incorporated in 1949 in DE.
Donor: Burkett Miller‡.
Foundation type: Independent foundation.
Financial data (yr. ended 12/31/05): Assets,
$191,220 (M); expenditures, $1,048,203;
qualifying distributions, $1,047,762; giving
activities include $1,010,000 for 2 grants (high:
$1,000,000; low: $10,000).
Purpose and activities: Grants to new donees
limited to capital projects of a nonsectarian nature;
emphasis on downtown rehabilitation, parks,
hospitals, and educational community projects;
continuing support for a few existing projects
approved during the founder's lifetime.
Fields of interest: Urban/community development.

Type of support: Building/renovation; Equipment; Land acquisition.
Limitations: Giving limited to the Chattanooga, TN, area. No grants to individuals, or for scholarships, endowment funds, or operating budgets; no loans.
Application information:
Initial approach: Letter
Copies of proposal: 5
Deadline(s): Jan. 10, Apr. 10, July 10, and Oct. 10
Board meeting date(s): Jan., Apr., July, and Oct.
Final notification: Following board meetings
Officers and Trustees:* James R. Hedges III,* Chair.; Allen L. McCallie,* Secy.; H. Whitney Durand,* Treas.
Number of staff: 1 part-time professional.
EIN: 626042269

8735
The Tucker Foundation
600 Krystal Bldg.
Chattanooga, TN 37402 (423) 756-1202
Contact: M. Hayne Hamilton, Pres.

Established in 1996.
Donor: S.K. Johnston, Jr.
Foundation type: Independent foundation.
Financial data (yr. ended 12/31/05): Assets, $18,588,507 (M); expenditures, $1,390,094; qualifying distributions, $1,256,861; giving activities include $1,256,861 for 67 grants (high: $500,000; low: $100).
Purpose and activities: Giving primarily for the arts, conservation, education, and social services.
Fields of interest: Arts, multipurpose centers/programs; Museums; Performing arts, theater; Secondary school/education; Higher education, college; Environment; Youth development; Human services.
Type of support: Internship funds; General/operating support; Endowments; Annual campaigns; Capital campaigns; Building/renovation; Land acquisition; Program development; Scholarship funds; Research; Employee-related scholarships.
Limitations: Giving primarily in the Chattanooga, TN metro area, Bradley County, TN and Sheridan, WY. No support for political organizations or start-up organizations.
Application information: Application form not required.
Initial approach: Letter
Deadline(s): None
Board meeting date(s): June and Dec.
Officers and Trustees:* M. Hayne Hamilton,* Pres.; Pamela K. Cuzzort,* Treas.; Andrew G. Cope; Lavinia Johnston; Robert T. Johnston; S.K. Johnston III; Katherine J. Tudor.
Number of staff: 1 full-time professional.
EIN: 621603398
Selected grants: The following grants were reported in 2005.
$100,000 to Baylor School, Chattanooga, TN. For endowment fund.
$50,000 to Girls Preparatory School, Chattanooga, TN. For endowment fund.
$50,000 to Nature Conservancy, Nashville, TN.
$50,000 to Southern Environmental Law Center, Nashville, TN. For general support.
$50,000 to Vanderbilt-Ingram Cancer Center, Nashville, TN. For general support.
$20,000 to Chattanooga Symphony and Opera, Chattanooga, TN. For general support.
$20,000 to YMCA, Cleveland Family, Cleveland, TN. For general support.

$15,000 to Allied Arts of Greater Chattanooga, Chattanooga, TN. For general support.
$10,000 to Lookout Mountain Land Trust, Lookout Mountain, TN.
$10,000 to Museum Center at Five Points, Cleveland, TN. For general support.

8736
James Stephen Turner Charitable Foundation ✧
c/o Cabot Pyle
138 2nd Ave. N., Ste. 200
Nashville, TN 37201

Established in 1997 in TN.
Donor: James Stephen Turner.
Foundation type: Independent foundation.
Financial data (yr. ended 12/31/03): Assets, $26,368,328 (M); gifts received, $22,984,630; expenditures, $2,254,545; qualifying distributions, $2,243,961; giving activities include $2,206,171 for 5 grants (high: $1,042,674; low: $5,000).
Fields of interest: Hospitals (specialty); Human services.
Limitations: Applications not accepted. Giving primarily in TN. No support for private foundations. No grants to individuals, or for travel, seminars, dinner events or telethons; no loans.
Application information: Contributes only to pre-selected organizations.
Trustees: James Stephen Turner, Sr.; James Stephen Turner, Jr.; Judith Payne Turner; Laura Turner.
EIN: 621689256

8737
Laura G. Turner Charitable Foundation, Inc. ✧ ☆
138 Second Ave. N., Rm. 200
Nashville, TN 37201

Established in 1989 in KY.
Donors: Laura Jo Dugas; Cal Turner, Sr.
Foundation type: Independent foundation.
Financial data (yr. ended 12/31/05): Assets, $21,140,982 (M); expenditures, $718,491; qualifying distributions, $547,511; giving activities include $540,489 for 18 grants (high: $139,289; low: $5,000).
Fields of interest: Arts; Human services; Children/youth, services; Federated giving programs.
Limitations: Applications not accepted. Giving primarily in KY, with emphasis on Bowling Green and Scottsville. No grants to individuals.
Application information: Contributes only to pre-selected organizations.
Board meeting date(s): Annually
Officers and Directors:* Laura Jo Dugas,* Pres.; Hubert Craddock,* V.P. and Treas.
Board Members: Katherine Sikora; Laura Turner.
EIN: 611170828
Selected grants: The following grants were reported in 2004.
$30,000 to United Way of Southern Kentucky, Bowling Green, KY.
$25,000 to College Heights Foundation, Bowling Green, KY.
$20,000 to Junior Achievement of South Central Kentucky, Bowling Green, KY.
$3,000 to Ronald McDonald House, Chattanooga, TN.

8738
The Cal Turner Family Foundation ✧
138 2nd Ave. N., Ste. 200
Nashville, TN 37201 (615) 846-4946
Contact: Cabot Pyle

Established in 1991 in TN.
Donors: Cal Turner, Sr.; Gertrude W. Burnett; Cal Turner, Jr.
Foundation type: Independent foundation.
Financial data (yr. ended 12/31/03): Assets, $73,983,993 (M); gifts received, $13,229,494; expenditures, $2,367,191; qualifying distributions, $2,360,199; giving activities include $2,282,370 for 51 grants (high: $250,000; low: $1,000).
Purpose and activities: Giving primarily for health and human services. Funding also for arts and culture, and education.
Fields of interest: Arts; Higher education; Health organizations, association; Human services.
Limitations: Giving primarily in TN. No grants to individuals, or for travel, seminars, government agencies, dinner events, other private foundations, telethons; no loans.
Application information: Application form required.
Deadline(s): None
Trustees: Donnetta H. Turner; H. Calister Turner; Hurley C. Turner III; Margaret B. Turner.
EIN: 626255589
Selected grants: The following grants were reported in 2003.
$250,000 to YWCA of Nashville and Middle Tennessee, Nashville, TN.
$200,000 to Senior Citizens, Nashville, TN.
$195,395 to Alive Hospice, Nashville, TN.
$100,000 to Easter Seals Tennessee, Nashville, TN.
$100,000 to Faith Family Medical Clinic, Nashville, TN.
$100,000 to Nashville Area United Methodist Foundation, Nashville, TN.
$75,000 to Adventure Science Center, Nashville, TN.
$75,000 to Matthew Walker Comprehensive Health Center, Nashville, TN.
$75,000 to Nashville Rescue Mission, Nashville, TN.
$75,000 to Saint Lukes Community House, Nashville, TN.

8739
The Unaka Foundation, Inc. ✧ ☆
(formerly Unaka Scholarship Foundation, Inc.)
P.O. Box 877
Greeneville, TN 37744-0877
Contact: Dominick Jackson, Pres.

Donors: Sopakco Inc.; Unaka Co., Inc.
Foundation type: Company-sponsored foundation.
Financial data (yr. ended 6/30/05): Assets, $1,679 (M); gifts received, $550,035; expenditures, $555,537; qualifying distributions, $555,517; giving activities include $512,367 for 37 grants (high: $450,000; low: $50), $41,500 for 73 grants to individuals (high: $500; low: $500), and $1,650 for 8 employee matching gifts.
Purpose and activities: The foundation supports organizations involved with arts and culture, education, and children.
Fields of interest: Performing arts, orchestra (symphony); Arts; Education; Children, services.

Type of support: General/operating support; Program development; Employee-related scholarships.
Limitations: Giving primarily in SC, TN, and TX. No grants to individuals (except for employee-related scholarships).
Application information: Application form required.
Initial approach: Contact foundation for application form
Deadline(s): None
Officer and Directors: Dominick Jackson,* Pres.; L.A. Yonz, Secy.; Dean A. Nebben; Rayburn H. Tankersley; Harry D. Wade.
EIN: 621530053

8740
Louise B. Wallace Foundation ◇
4400 Harding Rd., Ste. 310
Nashville, TN 37205-5215

Established in 1989 in TN.
Donor: George Newton Bullard Foundation.
Foundation type: Independent foundation.
Financial data (yr. ended 12/31/05): Assets, $14,812,631 (M); expenditures, $615,013; qualifying distributions, $480,434; giving activities include $449,750 for 37 grants (high: $150,000; low: $500).
Fields of interest: Arts; Education; Youth development; Human services; Protestant agencies & churches.
Limitations: Applications not accepted. Giving primarily in Nashville, TN. No grants to individuals.
Application information: Contributes only to pre-selected organizations.
Board meeting date(s): Biannually
Trustees: Elizabeth W. Caldwell; Elena W. Graves; Anne B. Nesbitt; Elizabeth B. Stadler; J. Bransford Wallace, Jr.
EIN: 581797048

8741
Washington Foundation ◇
(formerly Church of Christ Foundation, Inc.)
P.O. Box 159057
Nashville, TN 37215-9057

Incorporated in 1946 in TN.
Donor: G.L. Comer.
Foundation type: Independent foundation.
Financial data (yr. ended 12/31/05): Assets, $11,695,108 (M); expenditures, $530,694; qualifying distributions, $489,954; giving activities include $461,100 for 86 grants (high: $50,000; low: $1,000).
Purpose and activities: Giving primarily to Church of Christ churches, schools, agencies, and homes for the aged.
Fields of interest: Elementary/secondary education; Higher education; Theological school/education; Education; Hospitals (general); Health care; Housing/shelter, aging; Disasters, preparedness/services; Youth development, scouting agencies (general); Human services; Children/youth, services; Family services; Aging, centers/services; Federated giving programs; Protestant agencies & churches.
Type of support: General/operating support.
Limitations: Applications not accepted. Giving primarily in Nashville, TN. No grants to individuals.

Application information: Contributes only to pre-selected organizations.
Trustees: Howard R. Amacher; Andrew Benedict; James N. Denton III; Miles Ezell, Jr.; James Gooch; Paul A. Hargis; Harold Hazelip; E.M. Shepherd; Paschal Young.
Number of staff: 1
EIN: 620649477
Selected grants: The following grants were reported in 2004.
$60,000 to David Lipscomb University, Nashville, TN.
$15,000 to Kings Daughters Day Home, Nashville, TN.
$15,000 to United Way of Metropolitan Nashville, Nashville, TN.
$14,400 to Church of Christ, Henderson, TN. 2 grants: $2,400, $12,000
$12,500 to American Red Cross, Nashville, TN.
$10,000 to Boy Scouts of America.
$5,000 to Franklin Road Academy, Nashville, TN.
$4,000 to Nashville Union Mission, Nashville, TN.
$2,000 to Junior Achievement of Middle Tennessee, Nashville, TN.

8742
West Family Foundation ◇ ☆
4354 Walnut Grove Rd.
Memphis, TN 38117

Established in 2004 in TN.
Donor: Kemmons Wilson†.
Foundation type: Independent foundation.
Financial data (yr. ended 12/31/04): Assets, $2,753,674 (M); gifts received, $2,847,677; expenditures, $358,356; qualifying distributions, $357,494; giving activities include $357,494 for 5 grants (high: $247,590; low: $10,000).
Purpose and activities: Giving primarily to a theological seminary and to a United Methodist church. Support also for day services for people with Alzheimer's disease and for a cancer foundation.
Fields of interest: Theological school/education; Health care, support services; Cancer.
Limitations: Giving primarily in OH and TN.
Officers: Lee West Morris, Pres.; Margaret Hoath West, Secy.; Carole Wilson West, Treas.
EIN: 200901141

8743
Westwood Endowment, Inc.
P.O. Box 4268
Chattanooga, TN 37405 (423) 755-3964
Contact: Thomas H. McCallie III, Pres.
FAX: (423) 755-1640;
E-mail: mccallie60@hotmail.com

Established in 1986 in IN.
Donors: Richard A. West; Florence G. West; Marie G. Byers†; West Baking Co.
Foundation type: Independent foundation.
Financial data (yr. ended 11/30/04): Assets, $12,555,031 (M); gifts received, $240,279; expenditures, $639,749; qualifying distributions, $612,592; giving activities include $603,000 for 29 grants (high: $45,000; low: $5,000).
Purpose and activities: Support for various needs of the Third World through organizations with tax-exempt status.
International interests: Africa; Asia; India.
Type of support: General/operating support.

Limitations: Applications not accepted. Giving primarily to Third World countries.
Application information: The foundation initiates funding for service opportunities in its target fields. Unsolicited requests for funds not considered or acknowledged.
Board meeting date(s): As necessary
Officers and Directors:* Richard A. West,* Chair.; Thomas H. McCallie III,* Pres.; Craig Hammon,* Secy.
Number of staff: 2 part-time support.
EIN: 311197125
Selected grants: The following grants were reported in 2004.
$70,000 to Development Associates International, Colorado Springs, CO. For general support.
$45,000 to MAP International, Brunswick, GA. For general support.
$40,000 to Food for the Hungry, Phoenix, AZ. For general support.
$40,000 to Opportunity International, Oak Brook, IL. For general support.
$25,000 to CURE International, Harrisburg, PA. For general support.
$25,000 to World Relief, Baltimore, MD. For general support.
$20,000 to Partners International, Spokane, WA. For general support.
$20,000 to World Concern, Seattle, WA. For general support.
$20,000 to World Evangelical Alliance, Edmonds, WA. For general support.
$15,000 to Integra Ventures (IVUSA), Arlington Heights, IL. For general support.

8744
The Kemmons Wilson Family Foundation
(formerly Wilson Foundation)
8700 Trail Lake Dr. W., Ste. 300
Memphis, TN 38125 (901) 328-5037
Contact: Lauren Wilson-Young, Exec. Dir.
FAX: (901) 396-3570; E-mail: lyoung@kwilson.com;
Additional e-mail (for S. Wilson): stwilson@kwilson.com; URL: http://www.kwilsonff.com

Established in about 1961 in TN.
Foundation type: Independent foundation.
Financial data (yr. ended 12/31/04): Assets, $33,050,093 (M); gifts received, $33,092,546; expenditures, $12,739,676; qualifying distributions, $12,499,862; giving activities include $12,441,174 for 72 grants (high: $3,502,125; low: $500; average: $1,000–$25,000).
Purpose and activities: The foundation intends to positively impact and transform the Memphis community through grantmaking in the following categories: community outreach, and development advancement of youth, enriching education, faith-based ministries, and health and research related organizations.
Fields of interest: Museums; Elementary/secondary education; Higher education; Hospitals (general); Children/youth, services; Community development; Federated giving programs; Protestant agencies & churches.
Type of support: General/operating support; Continuing support; Annual campaigns; Capital campaigns; Building/renovation; Endowments; Emergency funds; Program development; Seed money; Curriculum development; Scholarship funds; Research; Program evaluation; Matching/challenge support.

Limitations: Giving primarily in the greater Memphis area, TN. No grants to individuals.
Application information: Downloadable grant application on foundation Website. Application form required.
  Initial approach: Letter, E-mail, or telephone
  Copies of proposal: 5
  Deadline(s): 2 months prior to board meeting
  Board meeting date(s): Mar., Aug. and Dec.
  Final notification: 6 weeks
Officers and Directors:* Spence L. Wilson,* Pres.; Charles K. Wilson, Jr.,* Exec., V.P.; Robert A. Wilson,* Exec., V.P.; Lauren Wilson-Young, Exec. Dir; Elizabeth Wilson-Moore; Carol Wilson-West.
Number of staff: 1 full-time professional.
EIN: 626046687
Selected grants: The following grants were reported in 2003.
$200,000 to Hutchison School, Memphis, TN. For capital campaign.
$10,000 to Saint Jude Childrens Research Hospital, Memphis, TN.
$5,000 to Memphis Literacy Council, Memphis, TN.
$2,500 to Memphis Charitable Foundation, Memphis, TN.

$2,500 to University of Tennessee, Memphis, TN.
$2,000 to Young Life of Memphis, Memphis, TN. For operating support.
$1,000 to Boys and Girls Clubs of Greater Memphis, Memphis, TN.
$1,000 to Memphis University School, Memphis, TN. For operating support.
$1,000 to Presbyterian Day School, Memphis, TN.
$1,000 to Youth Villages, Arlington, TN. For operating support.

8745
The Wright-Bentley Foundation ◇
1000 Tallan Bldg.
2 Union Sq.
Chattanooga, TN   37402   (423) 757-0208
Contact: Richard A. Park, Treas.

Established in 1994 in TN.
Donor: Spencer H. Wright.
Foundation type: Independent foundation.
Financial data (yr. ended 12/31/05): Assets, $2,637,480 (M); gifts received, $260,885;

expenditures, $447,464; qualifying distributions, $421,254; giving activities include $415,000 for grants.
Purpose and activities: Giving primarily for higher educational scholarships. Students must attend institutions specified and take twelve or more credit hours per semester, while maintaining a 3.0 average.
Fields of interest: Higher education; Scholarships/financial aid.
Limitations: Giving primarily in Chattanooga, TN.
Application information: Application form not required.
  Initial approach: Proposal for grants; written summary, nominating individuals who are eligible for scholarships
  Deadline(s): None
Officers: Spencer H. Wright, Pres.; J. Nelson Irvine, Secy.; Richard A. Park, Treas.
Director: Donna B. Wright.
EIN: 621585737

TEXAS

8746

The 80/20 Fund ✧ ☆

112 E. Pecan St., Ste. 555
San Antonio, TX   78205-1537
Contact: James E. Irwine, Tr.

Established in 2004 in TX.
Foundation type: Independent foundation.
Financial data (yr. ended 12/31/05): Assets,
$1,753,387 (M); expenditures, $350,276;
qualifying distributions, $350,000; giving activities
include $350,000 for 1 grant.
Application information:
  Initial approach: Letter
Trustee: James Irwine.
EIN: 200683200

8747

A Glimmer of Hope Foundation

4407 Bee Caves Rd., Ste. 301
Austin, TX   78746   (512) 328-9944, ext. 105
Contact: Michael O'Keefe, Comms. Dir.
FAX: (512) 328-8872;
E-mail: inquiries@aglimmerofhope.org; URL: http://
www.aglimmerofhope.org

Established in 2000 in TX.
Donors: Donna Berber; Philip Berber; Eric
Schmidhauser; Lucie Schmidhauser; Leslie Moore;
Kathy Moore; Neil Webber; Ronnie Morgan; Bill
Parrish; Margaret Parrish; Neil Webber; Ernst &
Young; Tim Brosnan; Tony Gannon; Berberfam, Ltd.;
Operation Days Work; Berberfam, Ltd.; Austin
Ethiopian Women Assn.; Lee Portnoi; Mark Stryker;
Oregon Ethiopian Community Organization; Robert
Epstein; Preston Ctr.; The Andrew S. Roddick
Foundation.
Foundation type: Independent foundation.
Financial data (yr. ended 12/31/04): Assets,
$58,021,008 (M); gifts received, $922,452;
expenditures, $5,297,684; qualifying distributions,
$5,151,660; giving activities include $4,691,102
for 3 grants (high: $3,389,509; low: $573,469).
Purpose and activities: The foundation serves to
ease some of the pain and suffering on the planet.
It currently operates a national aid program in
Ethiopia as well as programs for excluded youth in
the U.S. and the U.K.
Fields of interest: Business school/education;
Human services; Children/youth, services;
International relief; International affairs;
Economically disadvantaged.
International interests: England; Ethiopia; Ireland.
Limitations: Applications not accepted. Giving on a
national and international basis, particularly in
Austin, TX, London, England, Ethiopia, and Dublin,
Ireland.
Application information: Contributes only to
pre-selected organizations.
Officers: Donna Berber, Pres.; Philip Berber, V.P.;
Rose Abeyta, Secy.-Treas.
EIN: 311758218

8748

A Glimmer of Hope Foundation - Austin ☆

4407 Bee Caves Rd., Ste. 301
Austin, TX   78746
URL: http://www.aglimmerofhope.org

Donors: Ross Garber; A Glimmer of Hope
Foundation; Silverton Foundation; Austin Athletic
Scholarship Foundation; Cumberland Continental;
Wells Fargo Bank.
Foundation type: Independent foundation.
Financial data (yr. ended 12/31/04): Assets,
$282,106 (M); gifts received, $814,234;
expenditures, $532,768; qualifying distributions,
$532,736; giving activities include $518,388 for 30
grants (high: $28,662; low: $3,222).
Purpose and activities: The foundation is primarily
focused on making a sustainable difference in the
lives of the rural poor in Ethiopia through its
innovative and direct approach to aid and
development.
Fields of interest: International agricultural
development; International economic development;
International relief.
International interests: Ethiopia.
Limitations: Applications not accepted. Giving
primarily in Ethiopia.
Application information: Contributes only to
pre-selected organizations.
Officers: Donna Berber, Pres.; Philip Berber, V.P.;
Rose Abeyta, Secy.-Treas.
EIN: 200733502

8749

Abell-Hanger Foundation ▼

P.O. Box 430
Midland, TX   79702   (432) 684-6655
Contact: David L. Smith, Exec. V.P. and Exec. Dir.
FAX: (432) 684-4474; E-mail: AHF@abell-hanger.org;
URL: http://www.abell-hanger.org

Incorporated in 1954 in TX.
Donors: George T. Abell†; Gladys H. Abell†.
Foundation type: Independent foundation.
Financial data (yr. ended 6/30/06): Assets,
$152,971,966 (M); expenditures, $9,587,900;
qualifying distributions, $8,228,979; giving
activities include $8,042,412 for 195 grants (high:
$727,050; low: $500; average: $20,000–
$200,000), and $186,567 for 222 employee
matching gifts.
Purpose and activities: Support primarily for higher
education, youth activities, cultural programs,
health services, the handicapped, and social
welfare agencies.
Fields of interest: Arts; Higher education; Business
school/education; Nursing school/education;
Nursing care; Health care; Substance abuse,
services; Human services; Children/youth, services;
Family services; Aging, centers/services;
Community development; Voluntarism promotion;
Government/public administration; Aging;
Disabilities, people with; Economically
disadvantaged.
Type of support: General/operating support;
Continuing support; Annual campaigns; Capital
campaigns; Building/renovation; Equipment;
Endowments; Program development; Seed money;
Scholarship funds; Research; Employee matching
gifts; Matching/challenge support.
Limitations: Giving limited to TX, with emphasis
within the Permian Basin. No grants to individuals,

or for individual scholarships or fellowships; no
loans.
Publications: Annual report (including application
guidelines); Financial statement; Grants list.
Application information: First contact with the
foundation should be through the Pre-Application
Summary form which can be obtained through the
foundation Web site. Application form required.
  Initial approach: Letter or e-mail
  Copies of proposal: 1
  Deadline(s): For full grant applications: Feb., May,
   Aug., and Nov. 15; Pre-Application Summary
   forms have no submission deadline, but are
   reviewed by the trustees every 4 to 6 weeks
  Board meeting date(s): Mar., June, Sept., and
   Dec.
  Final notification: 1 month
Officers and Trustees:* Tevis Herd,* Pres.; David L.
Smith,* Exec. V.P. and Exec. Dir.; Herbert L.
Cartwright, V.P., Secy.-Treas., and Compt.; Arlen E.
Edgar; Robert C. Leibrock; Elaine Magruder;
Clarence Scharbauer III; James C. Trott; Wes Perry;
Charles M. Younger, M.D.
Number of staff: 3 full-time professional; 1 full-time
support.
EIN: 756020781
Selected grants: The following grants were reported
in 2005.
$600,000 to Midland Memorial Foundation,
  Midland, TX. For challenge grant for construction
  of Medical Office Building.
$444,500 to Midland College, Midland, TX. 3
  grants: $400,000 (For Legacy scholarship fund),
  $39,500 (For high school Students in
  Philanthropy Program), $5,000 (For Viola
  Coleman Scholarship Fund).
$250,000 to YMCA of Midland, Midland, TX. For
  increased construction costs for Capital
  Campaign.
$200,000 to Midland Community Theater, Midland,
  TX. For challenge grant for construction and
  renovations at Cole Theater.
$170,000 to United Way of Midland, Midland, TX.
  For fundraising campaign to underwrite
  administrative costs.
$35,000 to Permian Basin Womens Resource
  Center, Midland, TX. For unrestricted operating
  support.
$15,000 to American Airpower Heritage Foundation,
  Midland, TX. For matching grant for unrestricted
  operating support.
$15,000 to Visual Aids New Mobile (VAN)-Serving
  the Visually Impaired, Midland, TX. For
  unrestricted operating support.

8750

**Edward & Wilhelmina Ackerman
Foundation** ✧

5956 Sherry Ln., Ste. 1600
Dallas, TX   75225

Established in 1996 in TX.
Donors: Edward M. Ackerman; Wilhelmina
Ackerman.
Foundation type: Independent foundation.
Financial data (yr. ended 12/31/05): Assets,
$9,480,068 (M); gifts received, $345,765;
expenditures, $680,447; qualifying distributions,
$674,574; giving activities include $673,099 for 23
grants (high: $250,000; low: $499).
Purpose and activities: Giving primarily for
education, religion, and community services.

Fields of interest: Education; Medical research, institute; Community development; Foundations (community); Jewish agencies & temples; Religion.
Limitations: Applications not accepted. Giving primarily in TX. No grants to individuals.
Application information: Contributes only to pre-selected organizations.
Directors: David B. Ackerman; Edward M. Ackerman; Wilhelmina Ackerman.
EIN: 752681488

8751

The Judith and Jean Pape Adams Charitable Foundation

105 S. Cherry St.
Fredericksburg, TX 78624 (830) 997-7347
Contact: Marcia Manhart
FAX: (830) 997-9888;
E-mail: mmanhart@jjpafoundation.com

Established in 2003 in OK.
Donor: Jean Pape Adams Trust.
Foundation type: Independent foundation.
Financial data (yr. ended 12/31/05): Assets, $20,496,817 (M); expenditures, $1,319,682; qualifying distributions, $1,019,857; giving activities include $1,019,857 for 51 grants (high: $142,857; low: $500).
Purpose and activities: One-third of giving is reserved for national ALS research. Two-thirds of giving is reserved for Tulsa-area grants for arts/culture, social services, education and health.
Fields of interest: Arts, cultural/ethnic awareness; Education; ALS; Health organizations; Human services.
Type of support: General/operating support; Annual campaigns; Capital campaigns; Building/renovation; Program development; Research; Matching/challenge support.
Limitations: Giving primarily in ALS giving nationally; all other grants exclusively in the Tulsa, OK area. No grants to individuals.
Publications: Annual report; Informational brochure.
Application information: Application form not required.
  Initial approach: Letter or telephone
  Copies of proposal: 1
  Deadline(s): Aug. 15
  Board meeting date(s): May and Nov. or as needed
  Final notification: Dec. 31
Trustees: Katherine G. Coyle; Macia Manhart; U.S. Trust Co.
Number of staff: 1 full-time professional.
EIN: 200189630

8752

The Stanford & Joan Alexander Foundation

c/o Joan Alexander
1400 Post Oak Blvd., Ste. 900
Houston, TX 77056

Established in 1986 in TX.
Donors: Stanford Alexander; Joan Alexander.
Foundation type: Independent foundation.
Financial data (yr. ended 12/31/05): Assets, $43,436,724 (M); gifts received, $1,018,680; expenditures, $2,196,545; qualifying distributions, $2,149,589; giving activities include $2,140,639 for 154 grants (high: $340,000; low: $250).

Fields of interest: Elementary school/education; Secondary school/education; Higher education; Medical school/education; Health care; Mental health/crisis services; Health organizations, association; Medical research, institute; Civil rights; Community development; Government/public administration; Jewish agencies & temples; Religion.
Type of support: General/operating support; Research.
Limitations: Applications not accepted. Giving primarily in Houston, TX. No grants to individuals.
Application information: Contributes only to pre-selected organizations.
Officers and Directors:* Stanford Alexander,* Chair.; Joan Alexander,* Pres. and Treas.; Andrew M. Alexander, Secy.; Melvin Dow; Benjamin Warren.
Number of staff: 1 part-time professional.
EIN: 760204170
Selected grants: The following grants were reported in 2005.
$340,000 to Jewish Federation of Greater Houston, Houston, TX.
$200,000 to Seven Acres Jewish Geriatric Center, Houston, TX.
$125,000 to United Way of the Texas Gulf Coast, Houston, TX.
$104,598 to Texas Childrens Hospital, Houston, TX.
$97,333 to Childrens Museum of Houston, Houston, TX.
$45,000 to Museum of Fine Arts, Houston, Houston, TX.
$30,250 to Baylor College of Medicine, Houston, TX.
$1,500 to Memorial Hermann Foundation, Houston, TX.
$1,000 to Houston Museum of Natural Science, Houston, TX.
$1,000 to United Negro College Fund, Houston, TX.

8753

The Alkek and Williams Foundation ◇

1221 McKinney St., Ste. 4545
Houston, TX 77010-0208 (713) 658-8989
Contact: Charles A. Williams, Tr.

Established in 1996 in TX.
Donor: Margaret M. Alkek.
Foundation type: Independent foundation.
Financial data (yr. ended 12/31/04): Assets, $12,735,055 (M); gifts received, $1,400,000; expenditures, $573,727; qualifying distributions, $525,500; giving activities include $525,500 for 5 grants (high: $200,000; low: $500).
Purpose and activities: Giving primarily for education, as well as to a university's health science center.
Fields of interest: Arts; Elementary/secondary education; Higher education; Medical research, institute.
Limitations: Giving limited to TX, with emphasis on Houston.
Application information:
  Initial approach: Call or write for guidelines
  Deadline(s): None
Trustees: Margaret M. Alkek; Charles A. Williams; Margaret V. Williams; Randa Duncan Williams.
EIN: 766122587
Selected grants: The following grants were reported in 2003.
$200,000 to University of Houston-University Park, Moores School of Music, Houston, TX. For faculty endowment.

$200,000 to University of Texas Health Science Center, Houston, TX. For capital campaign.
$100,000 to River Oaks Baptist School, Houston, TX. For building program.
$25,000 to Houston Music Hall Foundation, Houston, TX. For building program.
$2,000 to Shara Fryer Cancer Research Fund, Houston, TX.
$500 to Baylor College of Medicine, Huffington Center on Aging, Houston, TX. For research.
$500 to Saint Thomas High School, Houston, TX. For scholarships.

8754

Albert and Margaret Alkek Foundation ▼ ◇

1221 McKinney St., Ste. 4525
Houston, TX 77010-2023
Contact: Sandra Bacak, Cont.
FAX: (713) 951-0043; E-mail: info@alkek.org;
URL: http://www.alkek.org

Established in 1996 in TX.
Donors: Albert B. Alkek†; Margaret M. Alkek†.
Foundation type: Independent foundation.
Financial data (yr. ended 12/31/04): Assets, $223,192,908 (M); expenditures, $12,151,725; qualifying distributions, $10,042,319; giving activities include $9,925,000 for 28 grants (high: $7,255,500; low: $1,000; average: $5,000–$200,000).
Purpose and activities: Giving primarily for higher education and medical research.
Fields of interest: Elementary/secondary education; Higher education; Medical school/education; Medical research, institute.
Type of support: General/operating support; Capital campaigns; Building/renovation; Endowments; Seed money; Scholarship funds; Research.
Limitations: Giving limited to TX. No support for political purposes or organizations. No grants to individuals.
Publications: Application guidelines; Grants list.
Application information: Primarily makes contributions to pre-selected charities. Application form not required.
  Initial approach: Brief letter of inquiry
  Copies of proposal: 1
  Deadline(s): None
  Board meeting date(s): Quarterly
  Final notification: Varies
Officers and Directors:* Charles A. Williams,* Pres.; Scott B. Seaman,* Treas. and Exec. Dir.; Sandra Bacak, Cont.; Bobby R. Alford, M.D.; Daniel C. Arnold; Joe M. Bailey; Dan B. Jones, M.D.; Peter G. Traber, M.D.; Margaret Alkek Williams; Randa Duncan Williams.
Number of staff: 1 full-time professional; 1 part-time professional.
EIN: 760491186
Selected grants: The following grants were reported in 2004.
$6,250,000 to Baylor College of Medicine, Houston, TX.
$1,000,000 to University of Texas M. D. Anderson Cancer Center, Houston, TX. For construction of Alkek Hospital.
$150,000 to Texas A & M University System, College Station, TX. For research space and scientific equipment for institute of Bioscience and Technology.

$100,000 to Rice University, Houston, TX. For neuroscience research.

$100,000 to Texas Military Institute, San Antonio, TX. For Alkek Scholars Program.

8755
The Allbritton Foundation
5615 Kirby Dr., Ste. 650
Houston, TX 77005 (713) 522-4921
Contact: Virginia L. White, Secy.

Established in 1958 in TX.
Donor: Joe L. Allbritton.
Foundation type: Independent foundation.
Financial data (yr. ended 11/30/05): Assets, $4,751,168 (M); expenditures, $1,900,366; qualifying distributions, $1,880,485; giving activities include $1,842,822 for 26 grants (high: $1,000,000; low: $100).
Purpose and activities: Giving primarily for education and the arts.
Fields of interest: Arts; Secondary school/education; Higher education; Education; Religion.
Limitations: Giving on a national basis, including national organizations in New York, NY and the greater metropolitan Washington, DC, area.
Publications: Annual report.
Application information: Application form not required.
   Initial approach: Letter
   Copies of proposal: 1
   Deadline(s): Mar. 1
   Board meeting date(s): Mar.
   Final notification: If granted, Apr. 1
Officers and Trustees:* Joe L. Allbritton, Pres.; Barbara Allbritton, V.P.; Robert L. Allbritton, V.P.; Virginia L. White, Secy.; Stephen P. Gibson, Treas.; Charles W. Hall.
Number of staff: 2 part-time support.
EIN: 746051876
Selected grants: The following grants were reported in 2005.
$1,000,000 to Memorial Sloan-Kettering Cancer Center, New York, NY.
$180,000 to Prince of Wales Foundation, DC.
$100,000 to Mississippi Hurricane Recovery Fund, Jackson, MS.
$40,000 to Wesleyan University, Middletown, CT.
$25,100 to Washington Hospital Center, DC.
$25,000 to Foundation for the National Archives, DC.
$25,000 to Ronald Reagan Presidential Foundation, Simi Valley, CA.
$9,500 to Sibley Memorial Hospital, DC.
$5,000 to National Press Foundation, DC.
$4,648 to Folger Shakespeare Library, DC.

8756
The Adrienne Allen Charitable Trust ◇
c/o Jeannine Mason
7521 Twin Oaks Ct.
Garland, TX 75044

Established in 2003.
Donor: Roscoe B. Allen Trust.
Foundation type: Independent foundation.
Financial data (yr. ended 12/31/05): Assets, $8,337 (M); expenditures, $418,375; qualifying distributions, $376,719; giving activities include $376,719 for 1 grant.

Purpose and activities: Giving primarily to an ovarian cancer coalition.
Fields of interest: Cancer.
Limitations: Applications not accepted. Giving primarily in Boca Raton, FL. No grants to individuals.
Application information: Contributes only to pre-selected organizations.
Trustee: Jeannine Mason.
EIN: 756654671

8757
The Carolyn J. and Robert J. Allison, Jr. Family Foundation ◇
1201 Lake Robbins Dr.
The Woodlands, TX 77380

Established in 1997 in TX.
Donors: Carolyn J. Allison; Robert J. Allison.
Foundation type: Independent foundation.
Financial data (yr. ended 12/31/04): Assets, $1,233,185 (M); expenditures, $407,362; qualifying distributions, $392,362; giving activities include $392,362 for grants.
Fields of interest: Salvation Army; Federated giving programs; Protestant agencies & churches.
Limitations: Applications not accepted. Giving primarily in TX. No grants to individuals.
Application information: Contributes only to pre-selected organizations.
Officers: Robert J. Allison, Jr., Pres.; Jane S. Allison, Secy.; Carolyn J. Allison, Treas.
Directors: Ann A. Stanislaw; Amy A. Watkins.
EIN: 760539246
Selected grants: The following grants were reported in 2004.
$40,000 to United Way, TX.
$6,000 to Boy Scouts of America, Houston, TX.
$3,000 to Northwest Assistance Ministries, Houston, TX.
$1,500 to 100 Club, Houston, TX.
$1,200 to American Junior Golf Association, Braselton, GA.
$1,000 to Gideons International, Nashville, TN.
$500 to Disabled American Veterans, Cincinnati, OH.

8758
Amarillo Area Foundation, Inc. ▼
801 S. Fillmore, Ste. 700
Amarillo, TX 79101 (806) 376-4521
Contact: Jim Allison, C.E.O.; For grants: Kathie Grant, Dir., Grants
FAX: (806) 373-3656; *E-mail:* haf@aaf-hf.org; Additional tel.: (806) 373-8353; Additional E-mail: kathie@aaf-hf.org; URL: http://www.aaf-hf.org

Established as a trust in 1957 in TX.
Foundation type: Community foundation.
Financial data (yr. ended 12/31/05): Assets, $163,436,052 (M); gifts received, $3,311,133; expenditures, $7,543,050; giving activities include $5,084,099 for grants.
Purpose and activities: The foundation seeks to improve the quality of life in the TX Panhandle through effective philanthropic efforts.
Fields of interest: Arts; Education; Health care; Disasters, preparedness/services; Recreation, centers; Recreation; Children/youth, services; Aging, centers/services; Human services; Youth; Economically disadvantaged.

Type of support: Management development/capacity building; Emergency funds; Building/renovation; Equipment; Land acquisition; Program development; Seed money; Scholarship funds; Matching/challenge support.
Limitations: Giving limited to the 26 northernmost counties of the Texas Panhandle region. No support for private or parochial schools, national, state, or local fundraising activities, or religious activities or programs that serve or appear to serve specific religious groups, or denominations. No grants to individuals (except for the scholarship program), or generally for operating budgets, annual campaigns, deficit financing, endowment funds, publications, conferences, travel, research projects, or historic preservation; no loans.
Publications: Annual report; Informational brochure; Newsletter.
Application information: Visit Web site for application form and guidelines. Application form required.
   Initial approach: Telephone or letter
   Copies of proposal: 1
   Deadline(s): Jan. 5 and July 6; Feb. 1 for scholarships
   Board meeting date(s): Feb., Apr., June, Aug., Oct., and Dec.; Executive Committee meets bimonthly: Mar., May, July, Sept., and Nov.
   Final notification: Mid-Mar. and mid-Sept.
Officers and Directors:* Richard Ware II,* Chair.; Eddie Bradley,* 1st Vice-Chair.; James Herring,* 2nd Vice-Chair.; Jim Allison,* C.E.O. and Pres.; Angela Lust, Sr. V.P.; Charlotte Rhodes, V.P., Regional Svcs.; Charles King,* Secy.; Allen Durrett,* Treas.; Brent Allen; Julie Attebury; Mark Bivins; Kay Brown; Ben Bruckner; Monte Cluck; Bill Daniel; Mike Engler; Robin Hall; Rick Leverich; Sam Lovelady; Wendy Marsh; Dee Miller; Alice O'Brien; Glen Parkey; Stanley Schaeffer; Joe Street; Robert Steven Urban, M.D.; Deborah D. Welch; Valeri White.
Number of staff: 13 full-time professional.
EIN: 750978220
Selected grants: The following grants were reported in 2005.
$1,192,167 to Globe-News Center for the Performing Arts, Amarillo, TX.
$130,000 to Boys and Girls Club of Maverick, Amarillo, TX.
$51,394 to Amarillo Museum of Art, Amarillo, TX.
$43,912 to Opportunity School, Amarillo, TX. For Parent Education Program at Grand Street Campus.
$33,407 to American Red Cross, Texas Panhandle Chapter, Amarillo, TX.
$30,000 to River Valley Pioneer Museum, Canadian, TX. For facade renovation.
$26,730 to Planned Parenthood of Amarillo and the Texas Panhandle, Amarillo, TX. For implementation of program to educate male juvenile probationers, age 12-16, about male responsibility and teen pregnancy prevention.
$22,132 to Girl Scouts of the U.S.A., Five Star Council, Amarillo, TX.
$20,000 to Panhandle Community Services, Amarillo, TX.
$10,000 to Swisher County Archives and Museum Association, Tulia, TX. To replace heating and air-conditioning units.

8759
Carl C. Anderson, Sr. and Marie Jo Anderson Charitable Foundation ◇

c/o Bank of America, N.A.
P.O. Box 831041
Dallas, TX 75283-1041
Application address: c/o Grant Admin., 1016 La Posada, Ste. 142, Austin, TX 78752, tel.: (512) 485-2285; fax: (512) 452-9055

Donors: Carl C. Anderson, Sr.‡; Marie Jo Anderson.
Foundation type: Independent foundation.
Financial data (yr. ended 12/31/05): Assets, $62,325,088 (M); expenditures, $3,491,259; qualifying distributions, $2,805,180; giving activities include $2,666,761 for 58 grants (high: $500,000; low: $1,500; average: $10,000–$50,000).
Purpose and activities: The mission of the foundation is two-fold: 1) giving medical research grants to qualified institutions within the U.S., with a special emphasis on childhood diseases; 2) funding organizations that provide direct assistance for individuals with special needs, emphasizing organizations which serve young children, youth, and elderly in NM, OK, and TX.
Fields of interest: Arts; Hospitals (specialty); Health care, infants; Health organizations, association; Medical research, institute; Cancer research; Youth development, centers/clubs; Human services; Family services; Aging, centers/services; Developmentally disabled, centers & services; Homeless, human services; Christian agencies & churches.
Type of support: General/operating support; Capital campaigns; Research.
Limitations: Giving primarily in NM, OK, and TX. No support for government agencies or municipalities, or advocacy of indirect support of organizations. No grants to individuals, or for events, seed money, endowments, staff development or for debt reduction.
Application information: Acknowledgment will be sent immediately upon receipt of application. Application form required.
Initial approach: Letter, telephone, or fax requesting application form
Deadline(s): None
Final notification: 4- to 6-months after receipt of application
Trustees: Charles R. Batte III; Jennifer J. Bird; R. Russell Rager; Bank of America, N.A.
EIN: 746078530

8760
Josephine Anderson Charitable Trust ◇

Plz. 1
P.O. Box 1
Amarillo, TX 79105-0001 (806) 378-8342
Contact: James R. Garrison, V.P. and Trust Off.

Established in 1976.
Donor: Josephine Anderson‡.
Foundation type: Independent foundation.
Financial data (yr. ended 2/28/05): Assets, $7,778,882 (M); expenditures, $432,696; qualifying distributions, $350,094; giving activities include $331,100 for 65 grants (high: $20,000; low: $600).
Purpose and activities: Giving primarily for arts, education, health associations, human services, and Christian agencies & churches.

Fields of interest: Performing arts; Arts; Education; Health organizations, association; Food distribution, meals on wheels; Human services; Children/youth, services; Family services; Residential/custodial care; Christian agencies & churches.
Type of support: General/operating support; Building/renovation.
Limitations: Giving primarily in the TX Panhandle, with emphasis on Amarillo. No grants to individuals.
Application information:
Initial approach: Letter
Deadline(s): None
Trustee: Amarillo National Bank.
EIN: 751469596

8761
Rose-Marie and Jack R. Anderson Foundation ◇

16475 Dallas Pkwy., Ste. 735
Addison, TX 75001-0682

Established in 1994 in TX.
Donors: Jack R. Anderson; Rose-Marie Anderson.
Foundation type: Independent foundation.
Financial data (yr. ended 12/31/04): Assets, $43,360,047 (M); gifts received, $1,084,900; expenditures, $1,802,629; qualifying distributions, $1,725,051; giving activities include $1,649,750 for 20 grants (high: $785,000; low: $250).
Purpose and activities: Giving primarily for higher and other education, particularly to a business school and a children's scholarship fund; funding also for health associations, particularly an eye institute, and to federated giving programs.
Fields of interest: Higher education; Business school/education; Education; Health care; Health organizations, association; Human services; Children/youth, services; Foundations (public); Federated giving programs; Public policy, research.
Limitations: Applications not accepted. Giving on a national basis. No grants to individuals.
Application information: Contributes only to pre-selected organizations.
Officers and Directors:* Neil R. Anderson,* Pres. and Treas.; Rose-Marie Anderson,* Secy.; Jack R. Anderson; Gail Anderson Canizares; Barbara Anderson McDonald.
EIN: 752542403
Selected grants: The following grants were reported in 2004.
$250,000 to Childrens Scholarship Fund, New York, NY.
$225,000 to Milton and Rose D. Friedman Foundation, Indianapolis, IN.
$50,000 to Hoover Institution on War, Revolution and Peace, Stanford, CA.
$40,000 to Commonweal Foundation, Silver Spring, MD.
$40,000 to National Center for Policy Analysis, Dallas, TX.
$25,000 to Student Sponsor Partners, New York, NY.
$20,000 to Palmer R. Chitester Fund, Erie, PA.
$5,000 to Greenwich Hospital, Greenwich, CT.
$4,000 to Phoenix Art Museum, Phoenix, AZ.
$250 to Smile Train, New York, NY.

8762
M. D. Anderson Foundation ▼ ◇

P. O. Box 2558
Houston, TX 77252-8037
Contact: Toloria Allen, Secy.-Treas.

Established in 2003 in TX as a successor foundation to the first M.D. Anderson Foundation.
Donor: M.D. Anderson‡.
Foundation type: Independent foundation.
Financial data (yr. ended 12/31/04): Assets, $137,159,049 (M); expenditures, $7,694,363; qualifying distributions, $6,911,778; giving activities include $6,683,000 for 123 grants (high: $350,000; low: $2,500; average: $25,000–$100,000).
Purpose and activities: Giving for the improvement of working class conditions among workers and for the establishment, support and maintenance of hospitals, homes and institutions for the care of the young, sick, the aged and the helpless. Also gives for the improvement of general living conditions and for the promotion of health, science, education and advancement of knowledge.
Fields of interest: Education; Health care; Health organizations; Employment; Youth, services; Aging, centers/services; Human services; Public policy, research; Government/public administration.
Type of support: Building/renovation; Equipment; Seed money; Research; Matching/challenge support.
Limitations: Giving primarily in TX, with emphasis on the Houston area. No grants to individuals, or for operating funds or endowments.
Publications: Application guidelines; Multi-year report.
Application information: Application form required.
Initial approach: Letter
Copies of proposal: 5
Deadline(s): None
Board meeting date(s): 3rd Tues. monthly
Final notification: Within 1 month
Officers: Gibson Gayle, Jr., Pres.; Uriel E. Dutton, V.P.; Charles W. Hall, V.P.; Jack Trotter, V.P.; Toloria Allen, Secy.-Treas.
EIN: 300129656

8763
The Aragona Family Foundation ◇ ☆

(formerly The Sandra and Joseph Aragona Family Foundation)
78 St. Stephens School Rd.
Austin, TX 78746 (512) 328-2178
Contact: Joseph C. Aragona, Pres.

Established in 1997 in TX.
Donors: Joseph C. Aragona; Sandra R. Aragona; Kenneth Deangelis.
Foundation type: Independent foundation.
Financial data (yr. ended 12/31/05): Assets, $2,067,858 (M); gifts received, $8,000; expenditures, $459,624; qualifying distributions, $426,984; giving activities include $414,119 for 25 grants (high: $100,000; low: $400).
Fields of interest: Education; Animals/wildlife, preservation/protection; Hospitals (general); Cancer; Food banks; Children/youth, services; Community development; Philanthropy/voluntarism; Protestant agencies & churches.
Type of support: General/operating support.
Limitations: Giving primarily in Austin, TX.

Application information: Application form not required.

Deadline(s): None

Officers: Joseph C. Aragona, Pres.; Sandra R. Aragona, V.P.

Director: Jeffrey C. Garvey.

EIN: 742833147

Selected grants: The following grants were reported in 2003.

$500,000 to Harvard University, Cambridge, MA.

$245,000 to Lance Armstrong Foundation, Austin, TX.

$25,000 to Saint Stephens Episcopal School, Austin, TX.

$10,000 to Childrens Hospital Foundation of Austin, Austin, TX.

$5,000 to Ballet Austin, Austin, TX.

$5,000 to Junior League of Austin, Austin, TX.

$3,500 to Ronald McDonald House of Central Texas, Austin, TX.

$1,000 to Austin Recovery, Austin, TX.

$1,000 to Jimmy Fund, Boston, MA.

$1,000 to Safeplace, Austin, TX.

8764
Nina Heard Astin Charitable Trust ✧

c/o Wells Fargo Bank, N.A., Trust Dept.
3000 Briarcrest Dr., MAC T5177-020
Bryan, TX 77802 (979) 776-5402
Scholarship application addresses: c/o Bryan High School Counselors, 3401 E. 29th St., Bryan, TX 77802, tel.: (979) 774-3273; c/o A&M Consolidated High School, 701 W. Loop S., College Station, TX 77840, tel.: (979) 696-0544

Established around 1975 in TX.

Foundation type: Independent foundation.

Financial data (yr. ended 3/31/05): Assets, $6,319,613 (M); expenditures, $394,978; qualifying distributions, $381,811; giving activities include $230,667 for 32 grants (high: $30,000; low: $1,000), and $99,917 for grants to individuals.

Purpose and activities: Scholarships limited to graduating seniors attending Bryan High School or A&M Consolidated High School, TX; also giving for the arts, youth services, and Presbyterian agencies and churches.

Fields of interest: Arts; Education; Health care; Health organizations, association; Protestant federated giving programs; Protestant agencies & churches.

Type of support: General/operating support; Program development; Scholarships—to individuals.

Limitations: Giving primarily in TX.

Application information: Application form required for scholarships.

Initial approach: Letter

Deadline(s): May 1 for scholarships; no set deadline for other grant proposals

Trustee: Wells Fargo Bank, N.A.

EIN: 741721901

Selected grants: The following grants were reported in 2005.

$10,000 to United Way.

$8,000 to Brazos County Rape Crisis Center, Bryan, TX.

$6,667 to Childrens Museum of the Brazos Valley, Bryan, TX.

$6,000 to Blinn College, Brenham, TX.

$6,000 to Goodland Presbyterian Childrens Home, Hugo, OK.

$5,000 to Health for All, Sacramento, CA.

$3,000 to Austin Presbyterian Theological Seminary, Austin, TX.

$2,000 to Boy Scouts of America, Anchorage, AK.

$1,500 to University of the Incarnate Word, San Antonio, TX.

$1,000 to American Cancer Society, Atlanta, GA.

8765
AT&T Foundation ▼

(formerly SBC Foundation)
130 E. Travis, Ste. 350
San Antonio, TX 78205 (210) 351-2218
Contact: Laura Sanford, Pres.
FAX: (210) 351-2599;
E-mail: sbcfdn@txmail.sbc.com; Additional tel.: (800) 591-9663; URL: http://att.sbc.com/gen/corporate-citizenship?pid=7736

Established in 1984 in MO; changed name to AT&T Foundation in 2005 following the merger of AT&T Corp. with SBC Communications Inc.

Donors: Southwestern Bell Corp.; SBC Communications Inc.; AT&T Inc.

Foundation type: Company-sponsored foundation.

Financial data (yr. ended 12/31/05): Assets, $194,083,201 (M); expenditures, $48,497,611; qualifying distributions, $47,556,509; giving activities include $47,556,509 for grants.

Purpose and activities: The foundation supports programs designed to enhance education by integrating new technologies and increasing learning opportunities; improve economic development through technology and local initiatives; provide vital assistance to key community-based organizations; support cultural institutions that make a community unique; and advance the goals and meet the needs of diverse populations.

Fields of interest: Arts; Education; Health care; Human services; Civil rights, equal rights; Economic development; Community development; Minorities.

Type of support: Management development/capacity building; Program development; Seed money; Scholarship funds; Technical assistance; Employee matching gifts; Employee-related scholarships; Matching/challenge support.

Limitations: Applications not accepted. Giving primarily in areas of company operations; giving also to statewide, regional, and national organizations. No support for religious organizations not of direct benefit to the entire community, fraternal, veterans', or labor organizations not of direct benefit to the entire community, individual K-12 schools or districts, political organizations, disease-specific organizations, religious schools, or discriminatory organizations. No grants to individuals (except for employee-related scholarships), or for hospital general operating support, capital campaigns, endowments, general operating support for United Way-supported organizations, advertising, ticket or dinner purchases, sports programs or events or cause-related marketing, or political activities; no product or service donations.

Application information: Contributes only to pre-selected organizations.

Board meeting date(s): Twice per year

Officers and Directors:* James W. Cicconi,* Chair.; Laura Sanford, Pres.; Hal Rainbolt, V.P. and Secy.; Jon Klug, V.P. and Treas.; James D. Ellis; Karen E. Jennings; Richard G. Lindner; Forrest E. Miller; Randall L. Stephenson; Rayford Wilkins, Jr.

Number of staff: 5 full-time professional; 1 full-time support.

EIN: 431353948

Selected grants: The following grants were reported in 2005.

$5,000,000 to National Council for Community and Education Partnerships, DC. For GEAR UP, special grants program to provide supplemental educational grant opportunities targeting technological capacity building and academic enrichment programs.

$2,389,854 to Scholarship America, Saint Peter, MN. For new recipient and renewal scholarship awards for SBC Foundation Scholarship Program.

$1,752,836 to American Red Cross, National Headquarters, DC. For relief effort for Hurricane Katrina, to match employee contributions.

$600,000 to United Way of Metropolitan Chicago, Chicago, IL. For annual support.

$584,693 to United Way of the Bay Area, San Francisco, CA. For annual support.

$250,000 to Old Spanish Missions, San Antonio, TX. For Las Misiones capital campaign to restore and preserve four historic San Antonio mission churches and establish permanent endowment fund for future restoration and preservation.

$40,000 to Joint Center for Political and Economic Studies, DC. For Never Again Forum, in cooperation with National Policy Alliance, which will explore ways to ensure that emergency planning for future disasters, whether natural or man-made, is racially inclusive and take into account needs of entire affected populations.

$20,000 to Clinton Association for Rights and Equality, Clinton, OK. For computer learning center to help minorities and low-income persons by providing safe environment with access to mentors and tutors for youth and adults for training programs needed to increase employment opportunities and stability.

$20,000 to Tech Museum of Innovation, San Jose, CA. For Awards program.

$20,000 to United Way, Lubbock Area, Lubbock, TX. For annual support.

8766
The Marilyn Augur Family Foundation

(formerly The Marilyn Augur Foundation)
4209 McKinney Ave., Ste. 202A
Dallas, TX 75205
Contact: Nancy Elizabeth Roberts, V.P.
FAX: (214) 526-0253; E-mail: maff@maugur.com; URL: http://foundationcenter.org/grantmaker/augur/

Established in 1990 in TX; funded in 1991.

Donor: Marilyn Augur.

Foundation type: Independent foundation.

Financial data (yr. ended 12/31/04): Assets, $9,729,986 (M); expenditures, $612,926; qualifying distributions, $500,199; giving activities include $384,678 for 120 grants (high: $50,000; low: $50; average: $1,000–$3,000).

Purpose and activities: Giving primarily for basic human needs (defined by the MAFF Board as food, shelter, clothing, health, and education aimed at transforming lives of those living in poverty or prison. The foundation funds non-profits which provide services for those who are economically, physically, emotionally and spiritually needy as it seeks to accomplish the mission stated in Matthew 25:35-40.

Fields of interest: Hospitals (general); Human services; Children/youth, services; Christian agencies & churches.
Type of support: General/operating support; Continuing support; Annual campaigns; Capital campaigns; Emergency funds; Program development; Scholarship funds.
Limitations: Giving primarily in Dallas, TX. No support for arts and culture. No grants to individuals.
Publications: Application guidelines.
Application information: Eligible organizations will be invited to submit a full proposal. The foundation requests that grantseekers refrain from sending supporting materials with the initial letter. See foundation Web site for complete application guidelines.
   Initial approach: Letter (not exceeding 2 pages)
   Deadline(s): None
   Board meeting date: Spring and fall
Officers and Trustees:* Marilyn Augur,* Pres.; Nancy Elizabeth Roberts, V.P.; Elizabeth T. Jones Turner,* V.P.; P. Mike McCullough,* Secy.; Margaret M. Augur Hancock,* Treas.
Number of staff: 1 part-time professional; 1 part-time support.
EIN: 752358239
Selected grants: The following grants were reported in 2004.
$50,000 to Parkland Foundation, Dallas, TX.
$20,000 to Episcopal Diocese of Dallas, Dallas, TX.
$10,000 to Hockaday School, Dallas, TX.
$7,000 to American Cancer Society, Dallas, TX.
$5,000 to Salvation Army, Plainview, TX.
$5,000 to Wipe Out Kids Cancer, Dallas, TX.
$3,000 to Episcopal Center for Renewal, Dallas, TX.
$2,500 to Texas Womans University Foundation, Denton, TX.
$2,000 to Central Dallas Ministries, Dallas, TX.
$2,000 to Visiting Nurse Association of Texas, Dallas, TX.

8767
Aurora Foundation ◆ ☆
c/o Jeffrey Bronfman
520 Cypress Creek Ln.
Wimberley, TX   78676

Established in 1993 in TX.
Donor: Jeffrey Bronfman.
Foundation type: Operating foundation.
Financial data (yr. ended 9/30/05): Assets, $165,308 (M); gifts received, $565,619; expenditures, $426,804; qualifying distributions, $425,202; giving activities include $396,303 for 17 grants (high: $288,868; low: $450).
Purpose and activities: Giving for projects that embody the strategic efforts for the preservation and protection of planetary ecosystems, (i.e. the environment) as well as efforts that secure the perpetuation and practice of indigenous cultures and ancient religious, spiritual and ceremonial traditions (e.g. certain Native American cultures and their religious traditions).
Fields of interest: Education; Environment.
International interests: Central America; Global programs; South America.
Limitations: Giving on a national and international basis, with emphasis on Santa Fe, NM, Central and South America.
Application information: Application form required.
   Deadline(s): None

Officers and Directors:* Jeffrey Bronfman,* Pres. and Treas.; Duncan E. Osborne,* Secy.; Irvin F. Diamond.
EIN: 742660772
Selected grants: The following grants were reported in 2005.
$12,000 to Earth Restoration Alliance, Englewood, CO.
$11,000 to Wimberley Valley Watershed Association, Wimberley, TX.
$3,600 to Amazon Conservation Team, Arlington, VA.
$2,000 to Collective Heritage Institute, Lamy, NM.
$500 to Life Link, Santa Fe, NM.

8768
Austin Community Foundation for the Capital Area, Inc. ◆
(formerly Austin Community Foundation)
P.O. Box 5159
Austin, TX   78763   (512) 472-4483
Contact: Richard G. Slaughter, Exec. Dir.
FAX: (512) 472-4486;
E-mail: info@austincommunityfoundation.org;
URL: http://www.austincommunityfoundation.org

Established in 1977 in TX.
Foundation type: Community foundation.
Financial data (yr. ended 12/31/04): Assets, $78,252,778 (M); gifts received, $8,897,025; expenditures, $12,602,707; giving activities include $10,134,205 for 2,150 grants (high: $1,000,000; low: $6), and $1,780,945 for 70 foundation-administered programs.
Purpose and activities: The foundation promotes philanthropy in Central Texas to improve the quality of life now and in the future. The foundation provides support for arts and culture, education and training, community development and community services, the environment, health, human services, recreation, and animal-related services.
Fields of interest: History/archaeology; Arts; Child development, education; Education; Environment; Animal welfare; Medical care, rehabilitation; Health care; Disasters, Hurricane Katrina; Recreation; Child development, services; Human services; Community development.
Type of support: Continuing support; Annual campaigns; Capital campaigns; Building/renovation; Equipment; Land acquisition; Program development; Conferences/seminars; Professorships; Publication; Seed money; Research; Technical assistance; Consulting services; Matching/challenge support.
Limitations: Giving limited to Travis County, TX, for discretionary grants. No support for religious organizations for religious purposes. No grants to individuals (except for scholarships), or for deficit financing, emergency funds, endowments, unrestricted general operating expenses, fundraising activities or events, or fellowships; no loans.
Publications: Application guidelines; Annual report; Informational brochure; Newsletter; Program policy statement.
Application information: Visit foundation Web site for Agency Information Sheet and application guidelines. Faxed proposals are not accepted. Application form required.
   Initial approach: Submit Agency Information Sheet and attachments
   Copies of proposal: 1
   Deadline(s): None

Board meeting date(s): At least 9 times per year
Final notification: 4 to 6 months
Officers and Board of Governors:* C. Stephen Saunders,* Pres.; Patty Huffines,* Pres.-Elect; Milo Burdette,* V.P.; JoLynn Free,* Secy.; Christopher Kennedy,* Treas.; Richard G. Slaughter, Exec. Dir.; Sylvia Acevedo; Sam Bryant; Michael L. Cook; Amanda Mayhew Dealey; Mary Margaret Farabee; Gary Farmer; Charles Felger, M.D.; James Flieller; Robert E. Gerrie; Mary Herman; Jan Hughes; Jeff Kodosky; Rosie Mendoza; Patricia C. "Patti" Ohlendorf; Linda Prentice, M.D.; Eugene Sepulveda; Marc Seriff; Max Sherman; Kerry Tate; Geraldine J. Tucker; Kelly White.
Number of staff: 3 full-time professional; 1 part-time professional; 1 full-time support.
EIN: 741934031

8769
B & B Foundation ◆ ☆
8101 Boat Club Rd., No. 330
Fort Worth, TX   76179

Foundation type: Independent foundation.
Financial data (yr. ended 9/30/05): Assets, $515,412 (M); gifts received, $506,750; expenditures, $455,915; qualifying distributions, $438,165; giving activities include $438,165 for 8 grants (high: $400,000; low: $500).
Fields of interest: Higher education; Human services; Protestant agencies & churches.
Type of support: General/operating support; Scholarship funds.
Limitations: Applications not accepted. Giving primarily in TX. No grants to individuals.
Application information: Contributes only to pre-selected organizations.
Officers: Gary J. Baker, Pres.; Deborah L. Baker, Secy.-Treas.
Director: Michael W. Kemp.
EIN: 752813025

8770
B.E.L.I.E.F. Foundation ◆
(formerly Janet Jarie Jensen Foundation)
6500 Beltline Rd., Ste. 170
Irving, TX   75063-6068
Contact: Janet Jarie Jensen, Tr.

Established in 1997 in TX.
Donor: Janet Jarie Jensen.
Foundation type: Independent foundation.
Financial data (yr. ended 12/31/03): Assets, $1,498,876 (M); expenditures, $421,270; qualifying distributions, $413,037; giving activities include $354,700 for 4 grants (high: $302,200; low: $2,500).
Purpose and activities: Giving primarily for education.
Fields of interest: Higher education; Education.
Limitations: Applications not accepted. Giving primarily in TX. No grants to individuals.
Application information: Contributes only to pre-selected organizations.
Trustee: Janet Jarie Jensen.
EIN: 752707934

8771
M D Bailey Foundation ✧ ☆
6060 N. Central Expwy., Ste. 400
Dallas, TX 75206

Established in 2001.
Donor: M D Bailey.
Foundation type: Independent foundation.
Financial data (yr. ended 12/31/04): Assets, $594,212 (M); gifts received, $79,987; expenditures, $317,832; qualifying distributions, $317,290; giving activities include $317,290 for 17 grants (high: $175,365; low: $500).
Purpose and activities: Giving primarily for Protestant youth ministries, Methodist and Presbyterian churches, and Protestant organizations; funding also for education, and social services including a homeless shelter.
Fields of interest: Elementary school/education; Secondary school/education; Human services; Children/youth, services; Children, adoption; Children, foster care; Homeless, human services; Protestant agencies & churches.
Limitations: Giving primarily in Houston, TX.
Directors: Brenda Bailey; Douglas Bailey; Malcolm Bailey, Jr.; Malcolm D. Bailey; Patricia Bailey.
EIN: 760665031

8772
Baker Hughes Foundation ✧
3900 Essex Ln., Ste. 210
Houston, TX 77027-5133   (713) 439-8600
Contact: Isaac C. Kerridge, Exec. Dir.

Established in 1994 in TX.
Donor: Baker Hughes Inc.
Foundation type: Company-sponsored foundation.
Financial data (yr. ended 12/31/04): Assets, $915,642 (M); gifts received, $873,000; expenditures, $638,152; qualifying distributions, $638,111; giving activities include $637,774 for 128 grants (high: $174,486; low: $100).
Purpose and activities: The foundation supports organizations involved with arts and culture, education, health, hunger, and human services.
Fields of interest: Arts; Higher education; Education; Health care; Food services; Boys & girls clubs; American Red Cross; YM/YWCAs & YM/YWHAs; Children/youth, services; Human services; Federated giving programs.
Type of support: Employee matching gifts; Scholarship funds.
Limitations: Giving primarily in the greater Tulsa, OK, and Houston, TX, areas. No support for religious or political organizations or secondary schools.
Application information: Application form not required.
Initial approach: Proposal
Deadline(s): None
Officers and Trustees:* Chad C. Deaton, Chair. and Pres.; G. Stephen Finley,* V.P. and Treas.; Alan R. Crain, Jr.,* V.P.; Greg Nakanishi,* V.P.; Sandra E. Alford, Secy.-Treas.; Isaac C. Kerridge,* Exec. Dir.
EIN: 760441292

8773
Joe Barnhart Foundation ✧
1738 Sunset Blvd.
Houston, TX 77005-1714

Established in 1988 in TX.

Foundation type: Independent foundation.
Financial data (yr. ended 12/31/04): Assets, $23,619,194 (M); expenditures, $1,642,114; qualifying distributions, $1,348,463; giving activities include $766,875 for 25 grants (high: $250,000; low: $1,398), and $451,234 for 4 foundation-administered programs.
Purpose and activities: Giving primarily for education.
Fields of interest: Arts; Education; Youth development, centers/clubs.
Limitations: Applications not accepted. Giving limited to Beeville, TX. No grants to individuals.
Application information: Contributes only to pre-selected organizations.
Officer and Trustees:* Margaret Price,* Exec. Dir.; Jack Bace; Walter S. Baker, Jr.; Margaret Moser; V. Richard Viebig, Jr.
EIN: 760261675
Selected grants: The following grants were reported in 2003.
$250,000 to Beeville Independent School District, Beeville, TX. For technology expansion and improvement.
$180,724 to Beeville Public Library, Beeville, TX. 2 grants: $40,000 (For scholarships), $140,724 (For operating support).
$13,500 to Beeville, City of, Beeville, TX. For general support.
$12,500 to John P. McGovern Museum of Health and Medical Science, Houston, TX. For general support.
$10,000 to Baylor College of Medicine, Houston, TX. For Bronze Hammer Award.
$10,000 to Museum of Fine Arts, Houston, Houston, TX. For general support.
$5,000 to Beeville Vineyard, Beeville, TX. For general support.
$5,000 to Boy Scouts of America, Sam Houston Area Council, Houston, TX. For general support.
$5,000 to Neuhaus Education Center, Bellaire, TX. For general support.

8774
Baron & Blue Foundation ✧ ☆
5950 Deloache Ave.
Dallas, TX 75225   (214) 692-5789
FAX: (214) 750-9092;
E-mail: execdir@baronandbluefdn.org; Application address: c/o Exec. Dir., P.O. Box 25464, Dalles, TX 75225; URL: http://www.baronandbluefdn.org

Established in 2001 in TX.
Donors: Frederick M. Baron; Lisa A. Blue Baron.
Foundation type: Independent foundation.
Financial data (yr. ended 12/31/05): Assets, $5,251,304 (M); gifts received, $673,746; expenditures, $394,365; qualifying distributions, $360,000; giving activities include $360,000 for 21 grants (high: $60,000; low: $5,000).
Purpose and activities: The foundation strives to enhance the function of non-profit organizations in the Dallas Community by assisting to maintain existing programs and further opportunities for grassroots organizations focusing on homelessness, transitional housing and the needs of the underserved.
Fields of interest: Education; Housing/shelter, repairs; Housing/shelter; Human services; Family services.
Application information: See Web site for application request and additional information.

Initial approach: 1-page letter
Deadline(s): Apr. 1st and Oct. 1st
Officers and Directors:* Frederick M. Baron,* Pres.; Lisa A. Blue Baron,* V.P.; Robert M. Greenberg.
EIN: 752965720

8775
Perry and Nancy Lee Bass Corporation ✧
201 Main St., Ste. 2300
Fort Worth, TX 76102-3127

Established in 1989 in TX.
Donor: Perry R. Bass†.
Foundation type: Independent foundation.
Financial data (yr. ended 6/30/05): Assets, $48,173,043 (M); expenditures, $1,094,834; qualifying distributions, $1,053,200; giving activities include $1,053,200 for 11 grants (high: $1,000,000; low: $1,000).
Fields of interest: Museums; Performing arts; Animals/wildlife, preservation/protection.
Type of support: General/operating support.
Limitations: Applications not accepted. Giving primarily in Fort Worth, TX. No grants to individuals.
Application information: Contributes only to pre-selected organizations.
Officers and Directors:* William P. Hallman, Jr., Chair. and Pres.; Nancy Lee Bass,* Vice-Chair. and V.P.; W. Robert Cotham, V.P.; Gary W. Reese, V.P.; Valleau Wilkie, Jr., V.P.; Lee M. Bass,* Secy.-Treas.
EIN: 752308846

8776
Bass Foundation
c/o Valleau Wilkie, Jr.
309 Main St.
Fort Worth, TX 76102   (817) 336-0494

Established in 1963 in TX.
Donors: Perry R. Bass†; Lee M. Bass; Edward P. Bass; Sid Richardson Carbon and Gasoline Co.; Perry R. Bass, Inc.
Foundation type: Independent foundation.
Financial data (yr. ended 12/31/05): Assets, $10,290,900 (M); gifts received, $1,000,000; expenditures, $911,827; qualifying distributions, $816,827; giving activities include $715,000 for 4 grants (high: $550,000; low: $5,000; average: $5,000–$550,000).
Purpose and activities: Giving primarily for the arts and cultural institutions; some support for conservation.
Fields of interest: Arts; Environment, natural resources.
Type of support: General/operating support; Capital campaigns; Building/renovation.
Limitations: Applications not accepted. Giving primarily in Fort Worth, TX.
Application information: Contributes only to pre-selected organizations.
Board meeting date(s): Feb.
Officers and Directors:* Lee M. Bass,* Pres.; Edward P. Bass,* V.P.; Ardon E. Moore, V.P.; Cynthia K. Alexander, Secy.-Treas.; Val Wilkie, Jr., Exec. Dir.
Number of staff: 3 part-time professional.
EIN: 756033983

8777
Harry W. Bass Foundation ✧
4809 Cole Ave., Ste. 250
Dallas, TX 75205 (214) 599-0300
Contact: F. David Calhoun, Exec. Dir.
FAX: (214) 599-0405; E-mail: dcalhoun@hbrf.org;
URL: http://www.harrybassfoundation.org

Established in 1983 in TX.
Donor: Harry W. Bass, Jr.✝.
Foundation type: Independent foundation.
Financial data (yr. ended 12/31/05): Assets,
$59,248,342 (M); expenditures, $1,718,333;
qualifying distributions, $1,536,156; giving
activities include $1,259,966 for 73 grants (high:
$200,100; low: $50).
Purpose and activities: Primary focus is in the areas
of youth and education.
Fields of interest: Arts education; Museums;
Performing arts centers; Historic preservation/
historical societies; Arts; Education, early childhood
education; Child development, education;
Secondary school/education; Adult/continuing
education; Adult education—literacy, basic skills &
GED; Education; Environment, public education;
Botanical gardens; Animals/wildlife; Art & music
therapy; Health care; Mental health/crisis services,
single organization support; Mental health/crisis
services, hot-lines; Mental health/crisis services,
suicide; Mental health, disorders; Mental health,
depression; Cancer; Kidney diseases; Alzheimer's
disease; Diabetes; Kidney research; Lung research;
Liver research; Arthritis research; Pediatrics
research; Medical research; Crime/violence
prevention; Crime/violence prevention, abuse
prevention; Crime/law enforcement; Food banks;
Food distribution, meals on wheels; Housing/
shelter; Disasters, preparedness/services;
Recreation, parks/playgrounds; Human services;
American Red Cross; YM/YWCAs & YM/YWHAs;
Children/youth, services; Children, services; Youth,
services; Child development, services; Family
services; Residential/custodial care, group home;
Aging, centers/services; Community development;
Science; Christian agencies & churches; Religion;
Aging.
Type of support: General/operating support;
Continuing support; Building/renovation;
Equipment; Program development; Research.
Limitations: Giving primarily in the greater Dallas, TX
area. No support for seminaries or private
foundations. No grants to individuals, or for capital
campaigns, fundraisers or conferences.
Application information: Application guidelines
available on foundation Web site. Application form
not required.
   Initial approach: Letter requesting grant
      application guidelines
   Copies of proposal: 1
   Board meeting date(s): Quarterly
   Final notification: 3 months
Officers and Trustees:* Doris L. Bass,* Pres.; F.
David Calhoun,* V.P. and Exec. Dir.; Michael
Calhoun,* V.P.; J. Michael Wylie.
Number of staff: 1 full-time professional; 2 part-time
support.
EIN: 751876307
Selected grants: The following grants were reported
in 2004.
$108,000 to Dallas Museum of Art, Dallas, TX.
$75,000 to Friends of the Katy Trail, Dallas, TX.
$55,000 to Highland Park United Methodist Church,
   Dallas, TX.

$50,000 to Childrens Medical Center of Dallas,
   Dallas, TX.
$50,000 to Dallas Arboretum and Botanical Society,
   Dallas, TX.
$25,000 to Baylor Health Care System Foundation,
   Dallas, TX.
$25,000 to DePelchin Childrens Center, Houston,
   TX.
$25,000 to Family Place, DC.
$10,000 to Kid Net Foundation, Dallas, TX.
$10,000 to Reading and Radio Resource, Dallas,
   TX.

8778
Lee and Ramona Bass Foundation ✧
309 Main St.
Fort Worth, TX 76102 (817) 336-0494
Contact: Valleau Wilkie, Jr., Exec. Dir.
FAX: (817) 332-2176;
E-mail: cjohns@sidrichardson.org; URL: http://
www.leeandramonabass.org

Established in 1994 in TX.
Donor: Lee M. Bass.
Foundation type: Independent foundation.
Financial data (yr. ended 12/31/04): Assets,
$23,341,955 (M); expenditures, $4,433,260;
qualifying distributions, $4,283,604; giving
activities include $4,221,757 for 12 grants (high:
$1,000,000; low: $25,000).
Purpose and activities: The foundation funds grants
in the following categories: 1) Schools, colleges and
universities within Texas, with emphasis placed
upon faculty development and liberal arts programs.
2) Community programs and projects, particularly
related to the arts and the environment, such as
museums, zoos, and educational/research
institutions. 3) National and regional conservation
programs.
Fields of interest: Arts; Higher education;
Environment; Community development.
Type of support: General/operating support;
Building/renovation; Endowments; Curriculum
development.
Limitations: Giving primarily in TX. No grants to
individuals.
Publications: Annual report; Grants list.
Application information: Formal proposals will be
accepted only after the foundation has responded to
the preliminary inquiry.
   Initial approach: Brief letter
   Board meeting date(s): Varies
Officers and Directors:* Lee M. Bass,* Pres. and
Treas.; Ramona S. Bass,* V.P.; William P. Hallman,
Jr.,* Secy.; Valleau Wilkie, Jr.,* Exec. Dir.
Number of staff: 3 full-time support.
EIN: 752495163
Selected grants: The following grants were reported
in 2005.
$3,500,000 to Fort Worth Zoological Association,
   Fort Worth, TX. For general support.
$1,000,000 to Middlesex School, Concord, MA. To
   establish endowment fund, Southern
   Scholarship Fund at Middlesex School.
$825,000 to Intercollegiate Studies Institute,
   Wilmington, DE. 2 grants: $500,000 (For Lee and
   Ramona Bass Pavilion for Western Civilization
   Studies), $325,000 (For Western Civilization
   Project).
$500,000 to Peregrine Fund, Boise, ID. For
   Aplomado Falcon project.
$200,000 to Georgetown University, School of
   Foreign Service, DC.

$150,000 to International Rhino Foundation, Yulee,
   FL. For general support and research.
$75,000 to Princeton University, Department of
   Politics, Princeton, NJ. For James Madison
   Program in American Ideals and Institutions.
$25,000 to Witherspoon Institute, Princeton, NJ. For
   general operating support.

8779
Ruth & Ted Bauer Family Foundation
4400 Post Oak Pkwy., Ste. 2160
Houston, TX 77027
Contact: Carol L. Katrana, Exec. Dir.
E-mail: ckatrana@bauerfoundation.org

Established in 1997 in TX.
Donors: Charles T. Bauer; Ruth J. Bauer.
Foundation type: Independent foundation.
Financial data (yr. ended 12/31/05): Assets,
$13,075,575 (M); expenditures, $575,402;
qualifying distributions, $553,211; giving activities
include $550,500 for 24 grants (high: $155,000;
low: $5,000).
Purpose and activities: Giving primarily for
education, and to address the needs of children.
Fields of interest: Education.
Type of support: General/operating support;
Continuing support; Annual campaigns; Building/
renovation; Scholarship funds.
Limitations: Applications not accepted. No grants to
individuals.
Application information: Contributes only to
pre-selected organizations.
Officers: Charles T. Bauer, Pres. and Treas.; Ruth J.
Bauer, Exec. V.P. and Secy.; Charles Douglas Bauer,
V.P.; Carol L. Katrana, Exec. Dir.
EIN: 760537473
Selected grants: The following grants were reported
in 2005.
$155,000 to Southern Methodist University, Dallas,
   TX.
$30,000 to Houston Arboretum and Nature Center,
   Houston, TX.
$30,000 to Small Steps Nurturing Center, Houston,
   TX.
$25,000 to Boys and Girls Harbor, Houston, TX.
$25,000 to Kinkaid School, Houston, TX.
$25,000 to Project Yes, Houston, TX.
$25,000 to Saint Johns School, Houston, TX.
$25,000 to Texas Childrens Hospital, Houston, TX.
$15,000 to Houston Grand Opera Association,
   Houston, TX.
$12,500 to Houston Symphony Society, Houston,
   TX.

8780
Charles T. Bauer Foundation ✧ ☆
11 Greenway Plz., Ste. 2600
Houston, TX 77046

Established in 2004 in TX.
Donor: Charles T. Bauer✝.
Foundation type: Independent foundation.
Financial data (yr. ended 12/31/05): Assets,
$64,701,172 (M); gifts received, $3,868,950;
expenditures, $828,508; qualifying distributions,
$564,174; giving activities include $450,000 for 5
grants (high: $250,000; low: $5,000).
Fields of interest: Higher education; Education.
Limitations: Applications not accepted. Giving on a
national basis. No grants to individuals.

Application information: Contributes only to pre-selected organizations.
Trustees: Theodore Wingate Bauer; Janet Bauer Hartman; Darren Wolfman.
EIN: 206284839

8781

Eula Mae and John Baugh Foundation ◇ ☆
1321 Park Bayou Dr., Apt. B301
Houston, TX 77077

Established in 1995 in TX.
Donors: Eula Mae Baugh; John F. Baugh.
Foundation type: Independent foundation.
Financial data (yr. ended 12/31/05): Assets, $17,149,990 (M); expenditures, $1,595,130; qualifying distributions, $1,526,430; giving activities include $1,511,839 for 14 grants (high: $700,000; low: $5,000).
Fields of interest: Higher education; Theological school/education; Education; Christian agencies & churches.
Limitations: Applications not accepted. Giving primarily in TX. No grants to individuals.
Application information: Contributes only to pre-selected organizations.
Officers: Barbara Baugh, Pres.; Jaqueline Morrison Moore, V.P.; Julia Morrison Ortiz, Secy.; Douglas C. Chiles, Treas. and Exec. Dir.
Trustees: Eula Mae Baugh; John F. Baugh; E. James Lowrey.
EIN: 760457820
Selected grants: The following grants were reported in 2005.
$700,000 to Baptist University of the Americas, San Antonio, TX.
$225,839 to Baptist General Convention of Texas, Dallas, TX. 2 grants: $33,750, $192,089
$100,000 to University of Mary Hardin-Baylor, Belton, TX.
$81,000 to Tallowood Baptist Church, Houston, TX. 2 grants: $26,000, $55,000
$50,000 to Baylor University, Waco, TX.
$50,000 to Central Baptist Theological Seminary, Kansas City, KS.

8782

Baumberger Endowment ◇
P.O. Box 6067
San Antonio, TX 78209-0067

Trust established in 1973 in TX.
Donor: Charles Baumberger, Jr.†.
Foundation type: Independent foundation.
Financial data (yr. ended 12/31/05): Assets, $28,688,736 (M); expenditures, $1,038,166; qualifying distributions, $910,825; giving activities include $715,075 for grants to individuals.
Purpose and activities: Scholarships only for Bexar County high school seniors to attend TX colleges and universities.
Fields of interest: Higher education.
Type of support: Scholarships—to individuals.
Limitations: Giving limited to residents of Bexar County, TX.
Publications: Application guidelines; Program policy statement.
Application information: Contact high school counselor for guidelines; student must pick up application at high school counselor's office; no applications will be mailed. The endowment will only consider applications from Bexar County, TX; all other applications will not be considered. Application form required.
Deadline(s): Feb. 15 for filing financial aid form, high school transcript, and application form
Board meeting date(s): Mar., June, Sept., and Dec.
Final notification: May
Officers: Jerome F. Weynand, Chair.; Ronald Schmidt, Vice-Chair.; Stanley H. Schmidt, Secy.; Cynthia A. Guyon, Exec. Dir.
Trustees: Frank W. Burk.
Number of staff: 1 full-time professional; 1 full-time support.
EIN: 237225925

8783

The Beal Foundation ◇
c/o American State Bank
P.O. Box 1401
c/o Spencer E. Beal, Tr., 104 S. Pecos St., Midland, TX 79701
Lubbock, TX 79401 (915) 682-3753
Additional address: c/o Spencer E. Beal, 104 S. Pecos St., Midland, TX 79701, tel.: (915) 682-3753

Incorporated in 1962 in TX.
Donors: Carlton Beal; Keleen H. Beal; W.R. Davis.
Foundation type: Independent foundation.
Financial data (yr. ended 12/31/04): Assets, $10,863,222 (M); expenditures, $1,086,669; qualifying distributions, $808,000; giving activities include $808,000 for 60 grants (high: $75,000; low: $3,000).
Purpose and activities: Emphasis on education, social services, including programs for women and children, youth agencies, health associations and a community fund.
Fields of interest: Arts; Elementary/secondary education; Education; Hospitals (general); Health organizations, association; Human services; Children/youth, services; Women, centers/services; Federated giving programs.
Type of support: General/operating support.
Limitations: Giving primarily in the Midland, TX, area.
Application information: First time applicants must complete longer application form. Application form required.
Deadline(s): 1 month before meetings for first time applicants; 2 weeks for repeat applicants
Board meeting date(s): Apr. 1 and Nov. 1
Officers: Carlton E. Beal, Jr., Chair.; Bill J. Hill, Secy.-Treas.
Trustees: Barry A. Beal; Keleen H. Beal; Kelly S. Beal; Spencer E. Beal; Larry Bell; Robert J. Cowen; Karlene Beal Garber; Steven C. Hofer; Ray Poage; Jane B. Ramsland.
EIN: 756034480
Selected grants: The following grants were reported in 2003.
$100,000 to YMCA of Midland, Midland, TX. For operating support.
$20,000 to Hillcrest School, Midland, TX. For operating support.
$12,000 to Big Brothers Big Sisters of Midland, Midland, TX. For operating support.
$10,000 to Boys and Girls Club of Midland, Midland, TX. For operating support.
$10,000 to Midland College Foundation, Midland, TX. For operating support.
$10,000 to Midland Rape Crisis and Childrens Advocacy Center, Midland, TX. For operating support.
$8,000 to Bynum School, Midland, TX. For operating support.
$8,000 to Centers for Children and Families, Midland, TX. For operating support.
$6,000 to Community Childrens Clinic, Midland, TX. For operating support.
$6,000 to Midland Teen Court, Midland, TX. For operating support.

8784

Theodore and Beulah Beasley Foundation, Inc. ◇
3811 Turtle Creek Blvd., Ste. 940
Dallas, TX 75219-4490

Incorporated in 1957 in TX.
Donor: Theodore P. Beasley.
Foundation type: Independent foundation.
Financial data (yr. ended 12/31/05): Assets, $19,446,975 (M); gifts received, $4,576,414; expenditures, $1,004,319; qualifying distributions, $723,167; giving activities include $637,600 for 68 grants (high: $100,000; low: $1,000).
Fields of interest: Higher education; Health care; Goodwill Industries; Human services; American Red Cross; YM/YWCAs & YM/YWHAs; Children/youth, services; Christian agencies & churches.
Type of support: General/operating support; Capital campaigns; Building/renovation.
Limitations: Applications not accepted. Giving primarily in the Dallas, TX, area. No grants to individuals.
Application information: Contributes only to pre-selected organizations.
Officers: Robert R. Beasley, Pres.; Vicki Vanderslice, V.P.; Linda Tinney, Secy.; Samuel Dashefsky, Treas. and Exec. Dir.
EIN: 756035806

8785

Behmann Brothers Foundation ◇
P.O. Box 271486
Corpus Christi, TX 78427-1486
Contact: Charles L. Kosarek, Jr., Pres.

Established in 1979.
Donors: Arno W. Behmann†; Herman W. Behmann†.
Foundation type: Independent foundation.
Financial data (yr. ended 6/30/05): Assets, $7,168,616 (M); expenditures, $463,642; qualifying distributions, $379,505; giving activities include $372,000 for 95 grants (high: $40,000; low: $300).
Purpose and activities: Primary areas of interest are farming, education, health, and youth programs.
Fields of interest: Arts; Higher education; Education; Health care; Health organizations, association; Agriculture, farmlands; Human services; Children/youth, services; Community development; Christian agencies & churches.
Type of support: Program development.
Limitations: Giving primarily in southern TX. No grants to individuals.
Application information:
Initial approach: Proposal
Deadline(s): May 1
Final notification: June, positive replies only

Officers and Directors:* Charles L. Kosarek, Jr.,* Pres.; Frances R. Kosarek,* V.P.; John Lloyd Bluntzer,* Secy.; Willie J. Kosarek,* Treas.; T. Mark Anderson; Karen K. Clark; Joshua Kosarek; Ross Mitchon.
EIN: 742146739
Selected grants: The following grants were reported in 2005.
$40,000 to Texas Agricultural Experiment Station, College Station, TX. For program support.
$17,500 to Bandina Christian Youth Camp, Wharton, TX. For program support.
$17,500 to Boles Childrens Home, Quinlan, TX. For program support.
$15,000 to Del Mar College Foundation, Corpus Christi, TX. For program support.
$10,000 to South Texas Public Broadcasting System, Corpus Christi, TX. For program support.
$10,000 to Texas A & M University, Corpus Christi, TX. For program support.
$10,000 to Womens Shelter of South Texas, Corpus Christi, TX. For program support.
$8,000 to Palmer Drug Abuse Program of Corpus Christi, Corpus Christi, TX. For program support.
$5,000 to Texas State Aquarium Association, Corpus Christi, TX. For program support.
$1,000 to Lymphoma Research Foundation, New York, NY. For program support.

8786
Bell Trust
660 Preston Forest Ctr.
P.O. Box 289
Dallas, TX 75230-2718 (972) 788-4151
Contact: Barry D. Packer, Exec. Tr.
FAX: (972) 788-4181;
E-mail: barrypacker@belltrust.org; URL: http://www.belltrust.org

Trust established in 1956 in TX.
Donors: R.S. Bell†; Katharine Bell†.
Foundation type: Independent foundation.
Financial data (yr. ended 12/31/05): Assets, $19,063,240 (M); gifts received, $13,197; expenditures, $1,320,289; qualifying distributions, $1,203,710; giving activities include $1,159,626 for 102 grants (high: $50,000; low: $2,400).
Purpose and activities: Grants to the Church of Christ organization.
Fields of interest: Christian agencies & churches.
Type of support: General/operating support.
Limitations: Giving on a national and international basis. No grants to individuals, or for building or endowment funds, scholarships, fellowships, or matching gifts; no loans.
Application information: Application guidelines available on the trust's Web site. Application form not required.
Initial approach: Letter from Church of Christ
Copies of proposal: 1
Deadline(s): Feb. 15, May 15, Aug. 15, and Nov. 15
Board meeting date(s): The 1st Tues. of Mar., June, Sept., and Dec.
Trustees: Barry D. Packer, Exec. Tr.; Betty Bell Muns; James N. Muns; John B. Muns; Barbara Bell Packer; C. Philip Slate; Harold Taylor; Robert T. Waldron.
Number of staff: 1 full-time professional.
EIN: 756020180

8787
The Belo Foundation ◇
(formerly A. H. Belo Corporation Foundation)
P.O. Box 655237
Dallas, TX 75265-5237 (214) 977-6661
Contact: Amy M. Meadows, V.P., Secy., and Exec. Dir.
URL: http://www.belo.com/about/foundation.x2

Established in 1995 in TX as successor to the Dallas Morning News-WFAA Foundation, established in 1952.
Donors: A.H. Belo Corp.; Belo Corp.
Foundation type: Company-sponsored foundation.
Financial data (yr. ended 12/31/04): Assets, $43,784,384 (M); gifts received, $800,000; expenditures, $1,767,034; qualifying distributions, $1,259,935; giving activities include $1,135,762 for 31 grants (high: $500,000; low: $2,000), and $2,500 for 1 employee matching gift.
Purpose and activities: The foundation supports organizations involved with college-level journalism education, city planning and public improvement, urban parks, and civic affairs.
Fields of interest: Media, journalism/publishing; Higher education; Recreation, parks/playgrounds; Community development; Government/public administration; Public affairs.
Type of support: General/operating support; Continuing support; Capital campaigns; Endowments; Professorships; Scholarship funds.
Limitations: Giving primarily in areas of company operations.
Publications: Application guidelines; Informational brochure.
Application information: Application form not required.
Initial approach: Telephone foundation
Copies of proposal: 1
Deadline(s): None
Board meeting date(s): Twice annually
Final notification: Varies
Officers and Trustees:* Robert W. Decherd,* Chair.; Marian Spitzberg,* Pres.; Amy M. Meadows, V.P., Secy., and Exec. Dir.; Ward L. Huey, Jr.; James M. Moroney, Jr.; Burl Osborne.
Number of staff: 1 part-time professional; 1 full-time support.
EIN: 752564365
Selected grants: The following grants were reported in 2004.
$280,000 to United Way of Metropolitan Dallas, Dallas, TX. For general support.
$250,000 to Dallas Bar Foundation, Dallas, TX. For Belo Mansion expansion.
$200,000 to Southern Newspaper Publishers Association Foundation, Atlanta, GA. For endowment campaign.
$111,939 to Dallas, City of, Parks and Recreation Department, Dallas, TX. For Lubben Plaza annual maintenance and wall renovation project.
$40,900 to Southern Methodist University, Dallas, TX. For Central University Library conservation project.
$26,000 to United Way of Metropolitan Tarrant County, Fort Worth, TX. For general support.
$25,000 to Committee to Protect Journalists, New York, NY. For general support.
$25,000 to Dallas Symphony Association, Dallas, TX.
$25,000 to University of Dallas, Irving, TX. For lecture series endowment.
$19,553 to McKinney Avenue Contemporary, Dallas, TX. For Belo Sculptures Series.

8788
Grace and Tom Benson Charitable Foundation ◇
100 Sandau, Ste. 210
San Antonio, TX 78216 (210) 349-6200
Contact: R. Tom Roddy, Dir.

Established in 2002 in TX.
Donors: Bensco, Inc.; Benson Football, LLC.
Foundation type: Independent foundation.
Financial data (yr. ended 12/31/05): Assets, $1,051,730 (M); gifts received, $5,000; expenditures, $463,000; qualifying distributions, $463,000; giving activities include $463,000 for 8 grants (high: $100,000; low: $33,000).
Fields of interest: Museums; Museums (marine/maritime); Higher education; Education; Heart & circulatory diseases; Children, adoption; Children, services.
Limitations: Giving primarily in FL, LA and TX.
Application information: Application form not required.
Deadline(s): None
Officer: Tom Benson, Pres.
Directors: Carol Baskin; Larry Benson; Renee Benson; Miriam Walker Peake; R. Tom Roddy; Stanley Rosenberg; Susan Walker.
EIN: 426631533

8789
Bergman-Davison-Webster Charitable Trust ◇
2301 Israel Rd.
Livingston, TX 77351-2531 (936) 327-8642
Contact: Carolyn Davison Nixon, Tr.

Established in 1996 in TX.
Foundation type: Independent foundation.
Financial data (yr. ended 6/30/05): Assets, $8,623,320 (M); expenditures, $603,214; qualifying distributions, $538,069; giving activities include $429,480 for 6 grants (high: $142,000; low: $10,000), and $47,854 for 28 grants to individuals (high: $3,000; low: $780).
Purpose and activities: Giving to promote, assist, and further the cultural, artistic, educational, literary, recreational, charitable, and historical activities and facilities carried on, or maintained by, the cities of Corrigan and Livingston, TX, and Polk County, TX, for their residents.
Fields of interest: Arts; Education; Human services.
Type of support: Scholarships—to individuals.
Limitations: Giving limited to the cities of Corrigan and Livingston as well as Polk County, TX.
Application information: Application form not required.
Deadline(s): None
Trustees: Gene Bush; Carolyn Davison Nixon; Anthony Page.
EIN: 760521612

8790
Bickel & Brewer Legal Foundation ◇ ☆
1717 Main St., Ste. 4800
Dallas, TX 75201

Foundation type: Operating foundation.
Financial data (yr. ended 12/31/05): Assets, $41,793 (M); gifts received, $1,067,641; expenditures, $1,042,929; qualifying distributions,

$377,875; giving activities include $377,875 for 41 grants (high: $65,000; low: $100).

Fields of interest: Performing arts, orchestra (symphony); Higher education, university; Medical care, in-patient care; Diabetes; Human services; Christian agencies & churches.

Type of support: General/operating support.

Limitations: Applications not accepted. No grants to individuals.

Application information: Contributes only to pre-selected organizations.

Officers: John W. Bickel II, Pres.; William A. Brewer III, V.P.; James S. Renard, Secy.-Treas.

EIN: 752625364

Selected grants: The following grants were reported in 2003.

$64,704 to Saint Marks School of Texas, Dallas, TX.

$60,000 to New York University, New York, NY.

$10,650 to Crystal Charity Ball, Dallas, TX.

$10,000 to Dallas Symphony Orchestra, Dallas, TX.

$10,000 to Puerto Rican Legal Defense and Education Fund, New York, NY.

$5,000 to Dallas Theater Center, Dallas, TX.

$2,500 to Dallas Historical Society, Dallas, TX.

$1,350 to Hispanic Chamber of Commerce, Denver, CO.

$1,250 to Southern Methodist University, Dallas, TX.

$1,000 to Hockaday School, Dallas, TX.

8791
The Bookout Family Foundation ✧ ☆
c/o John F. Bookout, Jr.
P. O. Box 61369
Houston, TX   77208

Established in 1996 in TX.

Donors: John F. Bookout, Jr.; Carolyn C. Bookout.

Foundation type: Independent foundation.

Financial data (yr. ended 12/31/05): Assets, $2,401,450 (M); gifts received, $718,590; expenditures, $762,605; qualifying distributions, $708,302; giving activities include $708,302 for grants.

Purpose and activities: Giving for art and cultural programs, museums, federated giving programs, children's services, and religion.

Fields of interest: Museums (art); Arts; Education; Human services; Foundations (private grantmaking); Religion.

Limitations: Applications not accepted. Giving primarily in TX.

Application information: Contributes only to pre-selected organizations.

Officers and Directors: * John F. Bookout, Jr.,* Pres.; John F. Bookout III,* V.P.; Beverly Von Kurnatowski,* Secy.-Treas.; Carolyn C. Bookout; Adair Stevenson.

EIN: 760508684

Selected grants: The following grants were reported in 2005.

$550,000 to Methodist Hospital, Houston, TX.

$31,335 to Kinkaid School, Houston, TX.

$30,000 to Baylor College of Medicine, Houston, TX.

$15,000 to Vanderbilt University, Nashville, TN.

$1,500 to Rice University, Houston, TX.

8792
Bosque Foundation ✧
(formerly Bosque Charitable Foundation)
5950 Cedar Springs Blvd., Ste. 210
Dallas, TX   75235-6803
Contact: Louis A. Beecherl, Jr., Tr.

Established in 1983 in TX.

Donors: Julia T. Beecherl; Louis A. Beecherl, Jr.

Foundation type: Independent foundation.

Financial data (yr. ended 12/31/05): Assets, $2,616,582 (M); expenditures, $371,619; qualifying distributions, $370,850; giving activities include $370,850 for 48 grants (high: $50,000; low: $500).

Purpose and activities: Giving primarily for education.

Fields of interest: Higher education, university; Education; Salvation Army; YM/YWCAs & YM/YWHAs; Christian agencies & churches.

Type of support: Capital campaigns; Building/renovation; Research.

Limitations: Giving primarily in TX. No grants to individuals.

Application information: Application form not required.

Initial approach: Letter

Deadline(s): None

Board meeting date(s): As required

Trustees: John T. Beecherl; Julia T. Beecherl; Louis A. Beecherl, Jr.; Louis A. Beecherl III; William C. Beecherl; Julianna Beecherl Davis; Mary Beecherl Dillard.

EIN: 756380232

8793
George W. Brackenridge Foundation ✧
711 Navarro St., Ste. 535
San Antonio, TX   78205   (210) 224-1011

Trust established in 1920 in TX.

Donor: George W. Brackenridge†.

Foundation type: Independent foundation.

Financial data (yr. ended 12/31/05): Assets, $25,639,370 (M); expenditures, $1,423,727; qualifying distributions, $1,332,779; giving activities include $1,289,659 for 50 grants (high: $250,350; low: $100).

Purpose and activities: Giving primarily to the support of accredited educational institutions.

Fields of interest: Arts education; Museums; Arts; Secondary school/education; Higher education; Education.

Type of support: Endowments; Program development; Scholarship funds; Research.

Limitations: Giving limited to TX. No grants to individuals, or for general purposes, continuing support, seed money, emergency funds, land acquisition, renovation projects, building funds, operating budgets, annual campaigns, deficit financing, or matching gifts; no loans.

Application information:

Initial approach: Letter of request, on organization letterhead

Deadline(s): None

Board meeting date(s): Mar., June, Sept., and Dec.

Trustees: Leroy G. Denman, Jr.; Emily D. Thuss.

EIN: 746034977

Selected grants: The following grants were reported in 2005.

$233,000 to University of the Incarnate Word, San Antonio, TX.

$132,500 to Trinity University, San Antonio, TX.

$49,705 to Saint Pauls Episcopal Church, Waco, TX.

$38,678 to San Antonio Museum of Art, San Antonio, TX.

$37,500 to Saint Marys University, San Antonio, TX.

$35,000 to Arts San Antonio, San Antonio, TX.

$20,000 to Keystone School, San Antonio, TX.

$20,000 to Witte Museum, San Antonio, TX.

$10,000 to Carver Academy, San Antonio, TX.

$10,000 to Say Si, San Antonio, TX.

8794
C. B. and Anita Branch Trust ✧
103 Ranger Creek Rd.
Boerne, TX   78006

Established in 1995 in TX.

Donors: C.B. Branch†; Anita Branch.

Foundation type: Independent foundation.

Financial data (yr. ended 12/31/05): Assets, $11,953,226 (M); gifts received, $180,000; expenditures, $556,494; qualifying distributions, $487,475; giving activities include $479,015 for 33 grants (high: $300,000; low: $15).

Purpose and activities: Giving primarily for education, human services, and to Roman Catholic agencies and churches, including missionary work, and schools.

Fields of interest: Education; Human services; Children/youth, services; Roman Catholic agencies & churches.

Limitations: Applications not accepted. Giving primarily in TX, with emphasis on Boerne and San Antonio; some funding nationally. No grants to individuals.

Application information: Contributes only to pre-selected organizations.

Trustees: Anita Branch; C. Stephen Fritsch.

EIN: 746431994

Selected grants: The following grants were reported in 2005.

$320,000 to Saint Peter the Apostle Catholic Church, Boerne, TX. 2 grants: $20,000, $300,000

$22,000 to Boerne Independent School District, Boerne, TX. 2 grants: $7,000, $15,000

$5,000 to Bernardine Franciscan Sisters, King of Prussia, PA.

$5,000 to School Sisters of Saint Francis, Milwaukee, WI.

8795
The Bridge Foundation, Inc. ✧
c/o Bruce Petty
201 Main St., Ste. 600
Fort Worth, TX   76102
Contact: Marguerite M. Gordon, Pres.

Established in NM.

Donor: Anna Melissa Gordon.

Foundation type: Independent foundation.

Financial data (yr. ended 12/31/05): Assets, $9,520,979 (M); expenditures, $481,893; qualifying distributions, $460,000; giving activities include $460,000 for 5 grants (high: $250,000; low: $15,000).

Fields of interest: Animal welfare.

Limitations: Applications not accepted. Giving on a national basis, with some emphasis on NM. No grants to individuals.

Application information: Contributes only to pre-selected organizations.
Officers: Marguerite M. Gordon, Pres.; Anna Melissa Gordon, V.P. and Treas.; Bruce Petty, Secy.
EIN: 850476426

8796
Bridgeway Charitable Foundation ✧
5615 Kirby Dr., Ste. 518
Houston, TX 77005

Established in 2000 in TX.
Donor: Bridgeway Capital Management, Inc.
Foundation type: Company-sponsored foundation.
Financial data (yr. ended 12/31/04): Assets, $1,273,769 (M); gifts received, $922,352; expenditures, $992,889; qualifying distributions, $988,892; giving activities include $945,948 for 92 grants (high: $75,000; low: $300).
Purpose and activities: The foundation supports organizations involved with education, human services, and religion.
Fields of interest: Education; Environment, radiation control; Disasters, preparedness/services; American Red Cross; Human services; Religion.
Type of support: Scholarship funds; Program development; Emergency funds; General/operating support.
Limitations: Applications not accepted. Giving primarily in TX. No grants to individuals.
Application information: Contributes only to pre-selected organizations.
Officers and Directors:* John N.R. Montgomery,* Pres.; Ann M. Montgomery,* V.P.; Joanna R. Schima Barnhill,* Secy.
EIN: 760666069
Selected grants: The following grants were reported in 2004.
$75,000 to Tahirih Justice Center, Falls Church, VA.
$60,000 to Joy Development School, Houston, TX.
$35,000 to Foundation for Worldwide Mercy and Sharing, Aspen, CO.
$30,000 to ACCION Texas, San Antonio, TX.
$20,000 to Alamo Childrens Advocacy Center, San Antonio, TX.
$20,000 to Childrens Bereavement Center of South Texas, San Antonio, TX.
$20,000 to Fifth Ward Enrichment Program, Houston, TX.
$20,000 to Row House Community Development Corporation, Houston, TX.
$10,000 to Houston Symphony Society, Houston, TX.
$5,000 to Westview School, Houston, TX.

8797
The J. S. Bridwell Foundation ✧
807 8th St., 2nd Fl.
Wichita Falls, TX 76301-3365

Incorporated in 1949 in TX.
Donors: J.S. Bridwell†; Margaret B. Bowdle.
Foundation type: Independent foundation.
Financial data (yr. ended 12/31/05): Assets, $42,221,895 (M); expenditures, $2,407,889; qualifying distributions, $2,252,230; giving activities include $2,220,730 for 87 grants (high: $500,000; low: $500).
Purpose and activities: Giving primarily for arts, culture, health, and volunteer fire departments;

funding also for human services, children and youth services, and federated giving programs.
Fields of interest: Museums; Arts; Hospitals (general); Health care; Health organizations, association; Disasters, fire prevention/control; Human services; YM/YWCAs & YM/YWHAs; Children/youth, services; Foundations (community); Federated giving programs.
Type of support: General/operating support; Building/renovation; Equipment; Program development.
Limitations: Applications not accepted. Giving primarily in TX, with emphasis on Wichita Falls. No grants to individuals, or for endowment funds.
Application information: Contributes only to pre-selected organizations.
Officers: Mac W. Cannedy, Jr., Pres. and Treas.; Paul Schoppa, Jr., Secy.
Directors: Ralph S. Bridwell; Thomas E. Knight; Terry M. Walker.
EIN: 756032988
Selected grants: The following grants were reported in 2004.
$502,500 to Midwestern State University, Wichita Falls, TX. 2 grants: $2,500, $500,000
$500,000 to Wichita County Heritage Society, Wichita Falls, TX.
$402,500 to United Regional Health Care Foundation, Wichita Falls, TX. 2 grants: $400,000, $2,500
$150,000 to Wichita Falls Area Community Foundation, Wichita Falls, TX. 2 grants: $100,000, $50,000
$20,000 to Drury University, Springfield, MO.
$5,000 to Wichita Falls Symphony Orchestra, Wichita Falls, TX.
$2,000 to Texas Scottish Rite Hospital for Children, Dallas, TX.

8798
T. J. Brown and C. A. Lupton Foundation, Inc. ✧
c/o Charles L. Geren
P.O. Box 1629
Fort Worth, TX 76101-1629

Incorporated in 1942 in TX.
Donors: T.J. Brown†; C.A. Lupton†; V.J. Earnhart; J.A. Gooch.
Foundation type: Independent foundation.
Financial data (yr. ended 12/31/05): Assets, $36,394,967 (M); expenditures, $1,897,937; qualifying distributions, $1,710,935; giving activities include $1,624,000 for 35 grants (high: $625,000; low: $1,000).
Purpose and activities: Giving primarily to arts/cultural areas especially museums, symphony, and opera; children services; and higher education.
Fields of interest: Performing arts; Arts; Higher education; Health organizations, association; Christian agencies & churches.
Limitations: Applications not accepted. Giving primarily in Fort Worth, TX. No grants to individuals, or for scholarships, prizes, or similar benefits; no loans.
Application information: Contributes only to pre-selected organizations.
Board meeting date(s): Quarterly
Officer and Directors:* Sam P. Woodson III,* Pres.; Tav Holmes Berry; Whitfield J. Collins; Charles Lupton Geren; Kit Tennison Moncrief; Lee Lupton Tennison; William E. Tucker.

Number of staff: 1 full-time professional; 1 part-time professional.
EIN: 750992690
Selected grants: The following grants were reported in 2004.
$600,000 to Texas Christian University, Fort Worth, TX. For scholarships and baseball stadium.
$200,000 to Fort Worth Zoological Association, Fort Worth, TX.
$150,000 to Modern Art Museum of Fort Worth, Fort Worth, TX.
$125,000 to Fort Worth Symphony Orchestra, Fort Worth, TX.
$100,000 to Amon Carter Museum of Western Art, Fort Worth, TX.
$100,000 to Fort Worth Museum of Science and History, Fort Worth, TX.
$70,000 to Texas Ballet Theater, Fort Worth, TX.
$50,000 to All Saints Health Foundation, Fort Worth, TX.
$50,000 to Cook Childrens Medical Center, Fort Worth, TX.
$20,000 to Performing Arts Center, Fort Worth, TX.

8799
The Brown Foundation, Inc. ▼ ✧
2217 Welch Ave.
Houston, TX 77019 (713) 523-6867
Contact: Nancy Pittman, Exec. Dir.
FAX: (713) 523-2917;
E-mail: bfi@brownfoundation.org; Application address: P.O. Box 130646, Houston, TX 77219-0646; URL: http://www.brownfoundation.org

Incorporated in 1951 in TX.
Donors: Herman Brown†; Margarett Root Brown†; George R. Brown†; Alice Pratt Brown†.
Foundation type: Independent foundation.
Financial data (yr. ended 6/30/06): Assets, $1,223,019,722 (M); expenditures, $73,085,661; qualifying distributions, $69,392,177; giving activities include $68,356,805 for grants.
Purpose and activities: Support principally for the encouragement of and assistance to education, the arts and community service. The projects selected for funding most likely will have the potential for long-lasting significant impact in the community. The foundation's current emphasis is in the field of public education at the primary and secondary levels. It will focus on finding and supporting nontraditional and innovative approaches designed to improve public education primarily within the state of Texas. Other areas of interest continue to be the visual and performing arts, and also include community service projects focused upon the needs of children and youth, especially in the Houston area.
Fields of interest: Arts; Education; Human services; Science; Public affairs.
Type of support: General/operating support; Continuing support; Annual campaigns; Capital campaigns; Building/renovation; Land acquisition; Program development; Professorships; Curriculum development; Scholarship funds; Research; Employee matching gifts; Matching/challenge support.
Limitations: Giving primarily in TX, with emphasis on Houston. No support for political organizations, private foundations, or religious organizations for religious purposes. No grants to individuals, or for operating deficits, debt retirement, testimonial dinners, marketing or fundraising events; no loans.

Publications: Application guidelines; Annual report (including application guidelines); Informational brochure (including application guidelines).
Application information: Grant proposal guidelines and proposal summary form are available upon request. Will consider one grant proposal per 12-month period from an organization. Application form required.

Initial approach: Proposal should be submitted a minimum of 4 months before funds are needed
Copies of proposal: 1
Deadline(s): None
Board meeting date(s): Feb., May, Sept., and Nov.
Final notification: 3 months

Officers and Trustees: Maconda Brown O'Connor,* Chair.; Louisa Stude Sarofim,* Pres.; Isabel Brown Wilson,* 1st. V.P.; Nancy Brown Negley,* V.P.; Herman L. Stude,* V.P.; John F. Fort III,* Secy.; William N. Mathis,* Treas.; Nancy Pittman, Exec. Dir.; Leslie Negley; John H. O'Connor; Christopher B. Sarofim; M.S. Stude.
Number of staff: 3 full-time professional; 1 part-time professional; 4 full-time support; 1 part-time support.
EIN: 746036466
Selected grants: The following grants were reported in 2005.

$10,000,000 to Houston Downtown Park Corporation, Houston, TX. For land acquisition and park development.
$9,000,000 to Houston Symphony Society, Houston, TX. For Margarett and Alice Brown Endowment Fund for Education.
$2,000,000 to KIPP (Knowledge is Power Program) Academy, Houston, TX. For Campaign for KIPP, SHINE Preparatory.
$1,741,550 to University of Texas M. D. Anderson Cancer Center, Houston, TX. For Proton Therapy Center Educational and Indigent Care Initiatives, Nurse-Oncologist Award, and capital campaign.
$1,500,000 to Center for Big Bend Studies, Friends of, Alpine, TX. For Trans-Pecos Archaeological Program.
$55,000 to Korima Foundation of the Big Bend Ranch, Houston, TX. For Texas Inner City Youth Work-Study Program.
$25,000 to Childrens Defense Fund, Austin, TX. For Texas Early Childhood Education Coalition.
$25,000 to Healthcare for the Homeless, Houston, Houston, TX. For operating support.
$25,000 to Ragtown Historical Project, Ransom Canyon, TX. For capital campaign.
$15,000 to Friends of Hudson River Park, New York, NY. For operating support.

8800
The Brumley Foundation ✧
P.O. Box 9294
Amarillo, TX 79105-9294   (806) 376-1555
Contact: Marilyn C. Ault, Secy.-Treas.

Established in 1986 in TX.
Donors: Dixie Holland†; Frank J. Warren†; Vivian Warren†.
Foundation type: Independent foundation.
Financial data (yr. ended 12/31/05): Assets, $16,269,684 (M); expenditures, $861,626; qualifying distributions, $697,531; giving activities include $697,531 for 36 grants (high: $45,000; low: $1,000).
Purpose and activities: Giving primarily for human services. Scholarship requests are accepted only from 501(c)(3) organizations. The preference is to

help persons to help themselves: needy, students, aged, ill or disabled, day care, and youth programs.
Fields of interest: Recreation, community facilities; Human services; Children/youth, services; Family services; Aging; Economically disadvantaged.
Type of support: General/operating support; Capital campaigns; Equipment; Scholarship funds; Matching/challenge support.
Limitations: Giving limited to the upper 26 counties of the Texas Panhandle, with preference to the population center (Amarillo) and Moore County. No grants to individuals, directly.
Application information: Application form not required.

Initial approach: Letter
Copies of proposal: 1
Deadline(s): None
Board meeting date(s): As necessary
Final notification: Letter following board meeting

Officers and Directors: Dayle Tipton,* Pres.; Bruce Burnett,* V.P.; Marilyn C. Ault,* Secy.-Treas.; Dennis Beene; Kurt Gehring; Ida Mae Gorsline.
EIN: 752089705
Selected grants: The following grants were reported in 2005.

$90,000 to High Plains Food Bank, Amarillo, TX. 3 grants: $45,000, $20,000, $25,000
$40,000 to Frank Phillips College, Borger, TX.
$30,000 to Marthas Home, Amarillo, TX.
$25,357 to Girl Scouts of the U.S.A., Amarillo, TX.
$20,000 to Another Chance House, Amarillo, TX.
$17,800 to Opportunity Plan, Canyon, TX.
$15,000 to Amarillo Opera, Amarillo, TX.
$3,500 to Amarillo Little Theater, Amarillo, TX.

8801
The Burnett Foundation ▼ ✧
(formerly The Burnett-Tandy Foundation)
801 Cherry St., Unit 16
Fort Worth, TX 76102-6881   (817) 877-3344
Contact: V. Neils Agather, Exec. Dir.

Established in 1978 in TX.
Donors: Anne Burnett Tandy†; Dee Kelly Foundation.
Foundation type: Independent foundation.
Financial data (yr. ended 12/31/04): Assets, $220,948,780 (M); expenditures, $22,264,655; qualifying distributions, $19,213,289; giving activities include $18,542,106 for 38 grants (high: $2,660,000; low: $5,000; average: $25,000–$1,000,000), and $70,607 for foundation-administered programs.
Purpose and activities: Support primarily for major museum projects and other cultural institutions, social service agencies, community development groups, and educational institutions.
Fields of interest: Museums; Arts; Education; AIDS; Human services; Community development, neighborhood development.
Type of support: General/operating support; Capital campaigns; Program development; Seed money; Technical assistance; Program-related investments/loans.
Limitations: Applications not accepted. Giving primarily in the Fort Worth, TX, area.
Application information: Unsolicited requests not accepted.

Board meeting date(s): Generally in June and Nov.

Officers and Trustees: Anne W. Marion,* Pres.; Thomas F. Beech, Exec. V.P.; Edward R. Hudson, Jr.,* V.P. and Secy.-Treas.; V. Neils Agather, Exec.

Dir.; Benjamin J. Fortson; Anne Windfohr Grimes; John L. Marion.
Number of staff: 1 full-time professional; 2 full-time support.
EIN: 751638517
Selected grants: The following grants were reported in 2004.

$2,410,000 to Fort Worth Art Association, Fort Worth, TX. For operating support.
$2,250,000 to Georgia OKeeffe Museum, Santa Fe, NM. 2 grants: $1,575,000 (For operating support), $675,000 (For endowment fund).
$2,000,000 to Fordham University, Bronx, NY. For endowment of John L. Marion Professorship in Art History.
$1,000,000 to All Saints Episcopal School, Fort Worth, TX. For Building for Character Saints United Capital Campaign.
$1,000,000 to George Bush Presidential Library Foundation, College Station, TX. For library.
$600,000 to Site Santa Fe, Santa Fe, NM. For operating support.
$300,000 to National Cowgirl Museum and Hall of Fame, Fort Worth, TX. For operating support.
$250,000 to Santa Fe Art Institute, Santa Fe, NM. For operating support.
$250,000 to Texas Wesleyan University, Fort Worth, TX. For renovations for the Law Library.

8802
Sarah & Ernest Butler Family Fund
7601 Rustling Rd.
Austin, TX 78731
URL: http://www.butlerfamilyfund.com

Established in 1997 in TX.
Donors: Ernest C. Butler; Sarah Butler; Linda E. Butler; Robert E. Butler.
Foundation type: Independent foundation.
Financial data (yr. ended 12/31/05): Assets, $18,299,119 (M); expenditures, $1,519,518; qualifying distributions, $1,513,200; giving activities include $1,513,200 for 7 grants (high: $250,000; low: $10,000).
Purpose and activities: Giving for educational and arts organizations.
Fields of interest: Museums (art); Performing arts, ballet; Performing arts, orchestra (symphony); Higher education.
Limitations: Applications not accepted. Giving limited to Austin and central TX. No grants to individuals.
Application information: Contributes only to pre-selected organizations.

Board meeting date(s): Jan.

Officer: Ernest C. Butler, Pres.
Trustees: Linda E. Butler; Robert E. Butler; Sarah Butler.
EIN: 742852289
Selected grants: The following grants were reported in 2003.

$626,700 to Austin Museum of Art, Austin, TX. 3 grants: $26,700, $300,000, $300,000 (For endowment fund).
$129,100 to Austin Symphony Orchestra, Austin, TX. 3 grants: $100,000 (For endowment), $9,100, $20,000.
$105,000 to Ballet Austin, Austin, TX.
$29,000 to University of Texas, Austin, TX.
$25,000 to Baylor University, Waco, TX.
$6,000 to Austin Lyric Opera, Austin, TX.

8803
The Charles Butt Foundation ✧
P.O. Box 839999
San Antonio, TX 78283

Established in 2001 in TX.
Donor: Charles C. Butt.
Foundation type: Independent foundation.
Financial data (yr. ended 12/31/04): Assets, $90,340 (M); expenditures, $1,586,781; qualifying distributions, $1,585,656; giving activities include $1,584,906 for 90 grants (high: $333,333; low: $200).
Fields of interest: Museums; Performing arts; Higher education; Environment, natural resources; Hospitals (general); Health care; Cancer research.
Type of support: General/operating support.
Limitations: Applications not accepted. No grants to individuals.
Application information: Contributes only to pre-selected organizations.
Trustee: Charles C. Butt.
EIN: 316674532
Selected grants: The following grants were reported in 2004.
$50,000 to Houston Grand Opera, Houston, TX.
$50,000 to Texans Care for Children, Austin, TX.
$35,500 to Menil Collection, Houston, TX.
$26,000 to Museum of Fine Arts, Houston, Houston, TX.
$25,000 to World Vision, Federal Way, WA.
$20,000 to Maine Coast Heritage Trust, Topsham, ME.
$15,000 to Friends of Acadia, Bar Harbor, ME.
$10,000 to Natural Resources Council of Maine, Augusta, ME.
$10,000 to Synergos Institute, New York, NY.
$5,000 to Maine Lighthouse Museum, Rockland, ME.

8804
H. E. Butt Foundation
c/o Howard E. Butt, Jr.
P.O. Box 290670
Kerrville, TX 78029-0670
FAX: (830) 257-3137; URL: http://www.hebuttfoundation.org

Incorporated as a company-sponsored operating foundation in 1933 in TX.
Donors: Howard E. Butt, Sr.†; Howard E. Butt, Jr.; H.E. Butt Grocery Co.
Foundation type: Operating foundation.
Financial data (yr. ended 12/31/05): Assets, $53,340,298 (M); gifts received, $5,746,184; expenditures, $4,875,861; qualifying distributions, $4,697,087; giving activities include $381,484 for 15 grants (high: $179,506; low: $1,000), and $1,345,083 for 2 foundation-administered programs.
Purpose and activities: The foundation supports camps in Texas used by qualifying organizations related to church renewal, summer Christian youth camps, and organizations involved with lay theological education and mental health.
Fields of interest: Theological school/education; Mental health/crisis services; Recreation, camps; Christian agencies & churches; Youth.
Type of support: General/operating support.
Limitations: Applications not accepted. Giving limited to TX. No grants to individuals, or for building or endowments.

Application information: Contributes only to pre-selected organizations.
Board meeting date(s): Dec.
Officers and Directors:* Howard E. Butt, Jr.,* Pres.; David M. Rogers,* Exec. V.P.; F. Dwight Lacy,* Sr. V.P.; Barbara Dan Butt,* V.P. and Secy.-Treas.; Deborah Butt Rogers,* V.P.; Jennifer D. Hargrave, Cont.
EIN: 741239819

8805
C.I.O.S. ▼ ✧
P.O. Box 20815
Waco, TX 76702

Incorporated about 1952 in TN; corporation liquidated into a charitable trust in 1987.
Donors: Paul P. Piper, Sr.; Mrs. Paul P. Piper; Paul P. Piper, Jr.; Piper Industries, Inc.
Foundation type: Independent foundation.
Financial data (yr. ended 6/30/05): Assets, $137,334,795 (M); expenditures, $6,482,524; qualifying distributions, $9,803,735; giving activities include $5,028,175 for 46 grants (high: $1,965,809; low: $300; average: $10,000–$150,000), and $4,713,460 for 22 loans/program-related investments (high: $1,000,000; low: $9,000).
Purpose and activities: Grants for Protestant church support and religious programs, including Christian education, evangelism, welfare, and support for foreign missions.
Fields of interest: Theological school/education; Human services; Christian agencies & churches; Protestant agencies & churches.
Type of support: Program-related investments/loans.
Limitations: Applications not accepted. Giving on a national basis. No grants to individuals.
Application information: Contributes only to pre-selected organizations.
Board meeting date(s): Monthly
Trustees: Mary J. Piper; Paul Piper, Jr.; Polly Piper Rickard.
EIN: 742472778
Selected grants: The following grants were reported in 2005.
$1,965,809 to Waco Community Development Corporation, Waco, TX. For program support.
$300,000 to Buckner Baptist Benevolences, Dallas, TX. For operating support.
$300,000 to Mission Society for United Methodists, Decatur, GA. For operating support.
$250,000 to Haggai Institute for Advanced Leadership Training, Atlanta, GA. For missions.
$200,000 to Alabama Baptist Convention, Mobile, AL. For hurricane disaster relief.
$200,000 to Florida Baptist Convention, Jacksonville, FL. For hurricane disaster relief and missions.
$150,000 to Baptist Childrens Home Ministries, San Antonio, TX. For missions.
$150,000 to Baptist General Convention of Texas, Dallas, TX. For Piper Institute, organization focused on planting churches in Latin America, and missions.
$150,000 to Cooperative Baptist Fellowship. For tsunami disaster relief.
$33,200 to Springs Baptist Church, San Antonio, TX. For operating support.

8806
Kathleen Cailloux Family Foundation ✧
c/o JPMorgan Chase Bank, N.A.
P.O. Box 50
Austin, TX 78767 (512) 479-2684
Contact: Cecilia Rohloff

Established in 1998 in TX.
Donor: Kathleen C. Cailloux.
Foundation type: Independent foundation.
Financial data (yr. ended 12/31/04): Assets, $17,219,283 (M); expenditures, $1,078,472; qualifying distributions, $1,023,000; giving activities include $1,023,000 for 3 grants (high: $511,500; low: $255,750).
Purpose and activities: Giving primarily for higher education, hospitals, and health associations; support also for social service agencies and youth organizations.
Fields of interest: Education; Animal welfare; Hospitals (general); Health organizations, association; Human services.
Limitations: Giving primarily in Galveston and Kerr counties, TX.
Application information:
Deadline(s): None
Board meeting date(s): Mar.
Trustees: Robert S. Andresakis; Kenneth F. Cailloux; Paula L. Heileman; JPMorgan Chase Bank, N.A.
EIN: 742857513

8807
The Cailloux Foundation ✧
(also known as Floyd A. & Kathleen C. Cailloux Foundation)
P.O. Box 291276
Kerrville, TX 78029-1276 (830) 895-5222
Contact: Barbara Gaither, Exec. Asst.
FAX: (830) 895-5212;
E-mail: info@caillouxfoundation.org; URL: http://www.caillouxfoundation.org

Established in 1994 in TX.
Donors: Floyd A. Cailloux†; Kathleen C. Cailloux.
Foundation type: Independent foundation.
Financial data (yr. ended 12/31/05): Assets, $60,369,774 (M); expenditures, $3,686,117; qualifying distributions, $3,576,938; giving activities include $2,826,709 for 38 grants (high: $250,000; low: $3,500).
Purpose and activities: To better individual lives, with emphasis on the needs of disadvantaged children.
Fields of interest: Education; Health care; Health organizations; Children/youth, services; Family services; Community development.
Type of support: General/operating support; Continuing support; Annual campaigns; Capital campaigns; Building/renovation; Equipment; Land acquisition; Emergency funds; Program development; Seed money; Scholarship funds; Technical assistance; Program evaluation; Matching/challenge support.
Limitations: Giving primarily in the TX Hill Country region. No support for seminaries for construction, projects normally funded by governmental entities or church-related entities that do not meet foundation guidelines. No grants to individuals, or for fund raisers, conferences, membership drives or competitions; no loans.

Publications: Application guidelines; Financial statement; Program policy statement (including application guidelines).

Application information: Letter of inquiry may be submitted online via the foundation Web site. The foundation only reviews grant proposals from applicants whose written or online letter of inquiry has been approved. Application available on foundation Web site. Application form required.

> *Initial approach:* Letter of inquiry
> *Copies of proposal:* 1
> *Deadline(s):* None
> *Board meeting date(s):* Quarterly
> *Final notification:* Within 4 weeks

Officers and Directors:* Kenneth F. Cailloux,* Chair. and Pres.; Stephen Andresakis,* V.P.; Paula Heileman,* V.P.; Sandy Cailloux,* Exec. Dir.; Steve Ables; David Jackson.

Number of staff: 2 full-time professional; 1 part-time professional; 1 full-time support.

EIN: 746422979

8808

The Effie and Wofford Cain Foundation ▼ ◇

4131 Spicewood Springs Rd., Ste. A-1
Austin, TX 78759 (512) 346-7490
Contact: Lynn Fowler, Secy.-Treas. and Exec. Dir.

Incorporated in 1952 in TX.

Donors: Effie Marie Cain†; R. Wofford Cain†.

Foundation type: Independent foundation.

Financial data (yr. ended 10/31/05): Assets, $128,227,077 (M); expenditures, $5,497,171; qualifying distributions, $4,797,537; giving activities include $4,308,225 for 113 grants (high: $670,000; low: $500).

Purpose and activities: Giving primarily to scientific, medical, and educational institutions.

Fields of interest: Elementary/secondary education; Secondary school/education; Higher education; Law school/education; Health care; Medical research, institute; Protestant agencies & churches.

Type of support: Endowments; Professorships; Scholarship funds; Research.

Limitations: Giving primarily in TX. No grants to individuals or organizations on behalf of specific individuals.

Publications: Application guidelines.

Application information: Organizations may re-apply for funding every other fiscal year. The foundation provides grants and contributions, on a highly selective basis, primarily to scientific/medical institutions and educational institutions. Substantially all of the grants and contributions are made to organizations with which the foundation has an existing historical relationship. Application form required.

> *Initial approach:* Telephone call or letter requesting guidelines
> *Copies of proposal:* 1
> *Deadline(s):* None; budget usually fully committed by early July
> *Board meeting date(s):* Oct. (annual meeting); 6 to 8 interim meetings (dates vary)
> *Final notification:* Varies

Officers and Directors:* Franklin W. Denius,* Pres.; James B. Cain,* Sr. V.P.; John C. Cain,* V.P.; F. Wofford Denius,* V.P.; Charmaine D. McGill,* V.P.; Lynn Fowler, Secy.-Treas. and Exec. Dir.

Number of staff: 3 full-time professional.

EIN: 756030774

Selected grants: The following grants were reported in 2005.

$670,000 to University of Texas Southwestern Medical Center, Dallas, TX. For research endowment.

$500,000 to Baylor College of Medicine, Houston, TX. For research endowment.

$500,000 to University of Texas System, Austin, TX. For facility enhancements.

$405,000 to University of Texas, Austin, TX. 2 grants: $175,000 (For acquisition of painting), $230,000 (For documentary expenses).

$200,000 to Southern Methodist University, Dallas, TX. For scholarships.

$150,000 to Daughters of Charity of Saint Vincent de Paul, Austin, TX. For hospital endowment.

$50,000 to Austin College, Sherman, TX. For scholarships.

$30,000 to Childrens Burn Foundation, Sherman Oaks, CA. For medical care and services.

$30,000 to First Cavalry Division Association Museum Foundation, Copperas Cove, TX. For scholarships.

8809

The Gordon and Mary Cain Foundation ▼

8 Greenway Plz., Ste. 702
Houston, TX 77046
Contact: James D. Weaver, Pres.

Established in 1988 in TX.

Donors: Gordon A. Cain; Mary H. Cain.

Foundation type: Independent foundation.

Financial data (yr. ended 12/31/05): Assets, $123,364,899 (M); expenditures, $6,835,290; qualifying distributions, $5,739,784; giving activities include $5,632,754 for 111 grants (high: $607,754; low: $1,000; average: $10,000–$250,000).

Purpose and activities: Giving primarily for higher and secondary education, social services, health associations, arts, and denominational giving.

Fields of interest: Visual arts; Museums; Performing arts; Performing arts, dance; Performing arts, music; Historic preservation/historical societies; Arts; Education, association; Education, fund raising/fund distribution; Elementary school/education; Secondary school/education; Higher education; Medical school/education; Adult education—literacy, basic skills & GED; Education, reading; Education; Environment, natural resources; Environment; Hospitals (general); Reproductive health, family planning; Nursing care; Substance abuse, services; Health organizations, association; Cancer; Heart & circulatory diseases; AIDS; Alcoholism; Medical research, institute; Cancer research; Heart & circulatory research; AIDS research; Youth development, services; Human services; Children/youth, services; Family services; Homeless, human services; Chemistry; Economics; Leadership development; Disabilities, people with; Economically disadvantaged; Homeless.

Type of support: General/operating support; Continuing support; Annual campaigns; Capital campaigns; Building/renovation; Professorships; Scholarship funds; Research.

Limitations: Giving primarily in Houston, TX. No grants to individuals.

Publications: Application guidelines.

Application information: Application form not required.

> *Initial approach:* Proposal
> *Copies of proposal:* 1
> *Deadline(s):* None
> *Board meeting date(s):* Apr., Sept., and Dec.

Officers and Trustees:* James D. Weaver,* Pres.; Mary H. Cain, V.P.; William A. McMinn, V.P.; Margaret W. Oehmig, V.P.; Sharyn A. Weaver, V.P.; William C. Oehmig, Secy.-Treas.; Gordon R. Cain.

Number of staff: 1 full-time professional.

EIN: 760251558

Selected grants: The following grants were reported in 2005.

$757,754 to Rice University, Houston, TX. 2 grants: $607,754 (For general support for Cain Project in Engineering and Professional Communication), $150,000 (For Center for Education).

$500,000 to Baylor College of Medicine, Department of Nephrology, Houston, TX. To establish Cain Chair in Nephrology.

$390,000 to University of Houston-Downtown, Houston, TX. For scholarships.

$250,000 to Brookwood Community, Brookshire, TX. For staff salary enhancement.

$250,000 to Houston Downtown Park Conservancy, Houston, TX. For project.

$250,000 to TIRR Foundation, Houston, TX. For Mission Connect Phase II.

$200,000 to Houston Museum of Natural Science, Houston, TX. For annual fund.

$50,000 to Briarwood School, Houston, TX. For capital campaign.

$15,000 to Mill Mountain Theater, Roanoke, VA. For project.

8810

The Callaway Foundation ◇

(formerly Central Texas Scholarship Foundation)
605 W. Park Ave.
Temple, TX 76501-1641 (254) 771-7409
Contact: Kevin J. Koch, Tr.

Established in 2002 in TX.

Donor: J.L. Callaway, Jr.

Foundation type: Independent foundation.

Financial data (yr. ended 12/31/05): Assets, $10,661,121 (M); expenditures, $613,117; qualifying distributions, $549,000; giving activities include $549,000 for 19 grants (high: $150,000; low: $1,725).

Fields of interest: Higher education.

Limitations: Giving primarily in TX. No grants to individuals.

Application information: Application form not required.

> *Deadline(s):* None

Trustee: Kevin J. Koch.

EIN: 331010957

8811

Flora Cameron Foundation ◇

5701 Broadway, Ste. 106
San Antonio, TX 78209 (210) 824-8301
Contact: Flora C. Atherton, Pres.

Established in 1952 in TX.

Donor: Flora C. Atherton.

Foundation type: Independent foundation.

Financial data (yr. ended 8/31/04): Assets, $1,042,822 (M); expenditures, $348,881; qualifying distributions, $336,483; giving activities

include $334,850 for 10 grants (high: $201,000; low: $150).

Purpose and activities: Giving primarily for education, the arts, and human services.

Fields of interest: Museums (art); Libraries (public); Biomedicine research; Human services.

Type of support: General/operating support.

Limitations: Giving primarily in TX; with some giving in Richmond, VA. No grants to individuals.

Application information:

Initial approach: Proposal on organization's letterhead

Deadline(s): None

Officers: Flora C. Atherton, Pres. and Treas.; John H. Crichton, V.P.; Gloria Labatt, Secy.

EIN: 746038681

8812

Harry S. and Isabel C. Cameron Foundation ◇

c/o Bank of America, N.A.
P.O. Box 2518
Houston, TX 77252-2518

Established in 1966 in TX.

Donor: Isabel C. Cameron†.

Foundation type: Independent foundation.

Financial data (yr. ended 6/30/05): Assets, $32,908,570 (M); expenditures, $2,209,242; qualifying distributions, $1,901,046; giving activities include $1,870,666 for 155 grants (high: $200,000; low: $500).

Purpose and activities: Giving primarily for elementary, secondary, and higher education, religious organizations, and human services.

Fields of interest: Elementary school/education; Secondary school/education; Higher education; Nursing care; Health care; Substance abuse, services; Mental health/crisis services; Health organizations, association; AIDS; AIDS research; Food services; Human services; Youth, services; Residential/custodial care, hospices; Aging, centers/services; Homeless, human services; Roman Catholic federated giving programs; Roman Catholic agencies & churches; Aging; Homeless.

Type of support: General/operating support; Building/renovation; Equipment; Research.

Limitations: Applications not accepted. Giving primarily in TX, with emphasis on Houston. No grants to individuals, or for operating support, endowment funds, or matching gifts; no loans.

Application information: Contributes only to pre-selected organizations.

Board meeting date(s): Apr., Aug., and Dec.

Trustees: Priscilla Bomet; David Cameron; Sylvia Cameron; Estelle Cameron Maloney; Frances Cameron Miller; Bank of America, N.A.

EIN: 746073312

Selected grants: The following grants were reported in 2004.

$125,000 to University of Saint Thomas, Houston, TX.

$26,000 to Saint Ambrose School, Houston, TX.

$25,000 to Avondale House, Houston, TX.

$7,000 to Star of Hope Mission, Houston, TX.

$5,000 to Texas A & M University, Kingsville, TX.

$3,000 to Gathering Place, Houston, TX.

$2,500 to Bo's Place, Houston, TX.

$2,000 to Covenant House Texas, Houston, TX.

$2,000 to Literacy Advance of Houston, Houston, TX.

$2,000 to University of Houston-University Park, Houston, TX.

8813

The Campbell Foundation ◇

P.O. Box 297
Abilene, TX 79604-0297
Contact: T.C. Campbell, Tr.

Established in 1978 in TX.

Donors: T.C. Campbell; Clara G. Campbell.

Foundation type: Independent foundation.

Financial data (yr. ended 12/31/05): Assets, $3,247,071 (M); expenditures, $432,884; qualifying distributions, $428,429; giving activities include $428,000 for 2 grants (high: $427,000; low: $1,000).

Fields of interest: Higher education.

Type of support: Continuing support.

Limitations: Giving primarily in the Abilene, TX, area. No grants to individuals.

Application information: Application form not required.

Initial approach: Letter

Copies of proposal: 1

Deadline(s): Nov. 1

Board meeting date(s): Annually

Final notification: Dec.

Trustees: Clara G. Campbell; Sarah C. Campbell; T.C. Campbell; Howard Wilkins.

Number of staff: 1 part-time support.

EIN: 756256881

Selected grants: The following grants were reported in 2003.

$77,000 to Rice University, Houston, TX. For operating support.

$4,000 to Center for Contemporary Arts, Abilene, TX. For operating support.

$2,000 to Abilene Christian University, Abilene, TX. For operating support.

$2,000 to McMurry University, Abilene, TX. For operating support.

$2,000 to Sears Methodist Retirement System, Abilene, TX. For operating support.

$1,500 to American Red Cross, Abilene, TX. For operating support.

$1,000 to Food Bank of Abilene, Abilene, TX. For operating support.

$1,000 to Girl Scouts of the U.S.A., West Texas Council, Abilene, TX. For operating support.

$1,000 to Hendrick Medical Center Foundation, Abilene, TX. For operating support.

$1,000 to University of the South, Sewanee, TN. For operating support.

8814

Caris Foundation ◇

(formerly Halbert Walling Family Foundation)
c/o David D. Halbert
5215 N. O'Connor Blvd., Ste. 2650
Irving, TX 75039-4421

Established in 2002 in TX.

Donors: David D. Halbert; Kathryn Ann Halbert; JoAnn Walling Halbert Trust.

Foundation type: Independent foundation.

Financial data (yr. ended 12/31/05): Assets, $27,096,104 (M); gifts received, $1,647,690; expenditures, $2,495,197; qualifying distributions, $2,195,188; giving activities include $1,787,542 for 28 grants (high: $1,000,000; low: $300).

Fields of interest: Higher education; Education; Christian agencies & churches.

Type of support: General/operating support.

Limitations: Applications not accepted. Giving primarily in TX. No grants to individuals.

Application information: Contributes only to pre-selected organizations.

Officers and Directors:* David D. Halbert,* Pres.; Kathryn Ann Halbert,* V.P.; Christopher Harmon, V.P.; Laurie Johnansen, Secy.; Kristen S. Halbert,* Treas.; Carroll Osburn, Exec. Dir.; Patrick Helbert.

EIN: 460510753

Selected grants: The following grants were reported in 2005.

$1,012,000 to Abilene Christian University, Abilene, TX. 3 grants: $1,000,000, $10,000, $2,000

$89,772 to Healing Hands International, Abilene, TX.

$24,283 to Family Health Ministries, Chapel Hill, NC.

$20,000 to Augusta State University Foundation, Augusta, GA.

$1,000 to Communities Foundation of Texas, Dallas, TX.

$500 to Abilene Independent School District, Abilene, TX.

8815

The Carlson Foundation ◇

c/o Clint D. Carlson
2100 McKinney Ave., Ste. 1600
Dallas, TX 75201

Established in 2002 in TX.

Donor: Clint D. Carlson.

Foundation type: Independent foundation.

Financial data (yr. ended 12/31/05): Assets, $3,268,927 (M); gifts received, $1,000,000; expenditures, $640,252; qualifying distributions, $602,750; giving activities include $600,000 for 4 grants (high: $250,000; low: $50,000).

Fields of interest: Performing arts centers; Performing arts, ballet; Zoos/zoological societies.

Limitations: Applications not accepted. Giving primarily in TX.

Application information: Unsolicited requests for funds not accepted.

Directors: Keith T. Anderson; Clint D. Carlson; Nancy Packer Carlson.

EIN: 270005700

Selected grants: The following grants were reported in 2003.

$250,000 to Fort Worth Dallas Ballet, Fort Worth, TX.

8816

Amon G. Carter Foundation ▼ ◇

201 Main St., Ste. 1945
Fort Worth, TX 76102 (817) 332-2783
Contact: John H. Robinson, Exec. V.P., Grant Admin.
FAX: (817) 332-2787; *E-mail:* jrobinson@agcf.org;
Application address: P.O. Box 1036, Fort Worth, TX 76101; URL: http://www.agcf.org/

Incorporated in 1945 in TX.

Donors: Amon G. Carter†; N.B. Carter†; Star-Telegram Employees Fund; Carter Foundation Production Co.

Foundation type: Independent foundation.

Financial data (yr. ended 12/31/04): Assets, $354,672,832 (M); expenditures, $23,606,203; qualifying distributions, $19,747,637; giving activities include $17,812,168 for 219 grants (high: $8,148,000; low: $1,000; average: $5,000–$750,000).

Purpose and activities: Grants primarily for arts, education, health care and medical services, social service and youth agencies, programs for youth and the elderly, and civic and community endeavors that enhance the quality of life. The foundation sponsors and largely supports the Amon Carter Museum.

Fields of interest: Museums; Performing arts; Arts; Higher education; Education; Hospitals (general); Health care; Human services; Youth, services; Aging, centers/services; Government/public administration; Aging.

Type of support: General/operating support; Continuing support; Annual campaigns; Capital campaigns; Building/renovation; Equipment; Land acquisition; Endowments; Emergency funds; Program development; Professorships; Seed money; Scholarship funds; Research; Matching/challenge support.

Limitations: Giving largely restricted to Fort Worth and Tarrant County, TX. No grants to individuals, or for ongoing operating budgets, deficit financing, publications, or conferences; no loans.

Publications: Application guidelines; Financial statement; Grants list; Program policy statement.

Application information: Grants outside local geographic area usually initiated by board. The foundation does not currently accept grant applications via e-mail. Application form not required.

> *Initial approach:* Letter
> *Copies of proposal:* 1
> *Deadline(s):* None
> *Board meeting date(s):* Apr., Sept., and Dec.
> *Final notification:* Within 10 days of board meeting

Officers and Directors:* Ruth Carter Stevenson,* Pres.; W. Patrick Harris, Exec. V.P., Investments; John H. Robinson, Exec. V.P., Grant Admin.; Robert W. Brown, M.D.*, V.P.; Sheila B. Johnson,* Secy.; Mark L. Johnson,* Treas.; Kathy A. King, Cont.; Kate Johnson.

Number of staff: 3 full-time professional; 2 full-time support.

EIN: 756000331

Selected grants: The following grants were reported in 2004.

$8,148,000 to Amon Carter Museum of Western Art, Fort Worth, TX. For operating support.

$1,000,000 to Carter BloodCare, Bedford, TX. For capital support.

$750,000 to All Saints Episcopal School, Fort Worth, TX. 2 grants: $500,000 (For capital support), $250,000 (For capital support).

$750,000 to Harris Methodist Health Foundation, Fort Worth, TX. For capital support.

$500,000 to All Church Home for Children, Fort Worth, TX. For capital support.

$500,000 to Texas Wesleyan University, Fort Worth, TX. For capital support.

$280,000 to Tarrant County Youth Collaboration, Fort Worth, TX. For special program.

$175,000 to Fort Worth Public Library Foundation, Fort Worth, TX. For technology support.

$150,000 to Fort Worth Academy of Fine Arts, Fort Worth, TX. For capital support.

8817
Amon G. Carter Star-Telegram Employees Fund ✧

P.O. Box 17480
Fort Worth, TX 76102 (817) 332-3535
Contact: Nenetta Carter Tatum, Pres.

Established in 1945 in TX.

Donors: Fort Worth Star-Telegram; Amon G. Carter†; KXAS-TV; WBAP Radio.

Foundation type: Company-sponsored foundation.

Financial data (yr. ended 4/30/05): Assets, $25,929,797 (M); expenditures, $1,202,457; qualifying distributions, $1,138,949; giving activities include $648,980 for 54 grants (high: $175,000; low: $1,000), and $416,092 for 227 grants to individuals (high: $7,352; low: $70).

Purpose and activities: The foundation supports organizations involved with arts and culture, education, health, youth development, children and youth, and human services.

Fields of interest: Performing arts; Arts; Education; Hospitals (general); Health care; Youth development; Children/youth, services; Human services.

Type of support: General/operating support; Building/renovation; Employee-related scholarships; Grants to individuals.

Limitations: Giving primarily in Tarrant County, TX. No grants to individuals (except for employee-related scholarships and employee assistance grants).

Application information: Application form not required.

> *Initial approach:* Letter of inquiry
> *Copies of proposal:* 1
> *Deadline(s):* None
> *Board meeting date(s):* Apr. and June

Officers: Nenetta Carter Tatum, Pres.; Mark L. Johnson, V.P.; John H. Robinson, Secy.-Treas.

Number of staff: 1 part-time professional; 1 part-time support.

EIN: 756014850

8818
Castle Hills Schools Foundation, Inc. ✧ ☆

4228 N. Central Expwy., Ste. 300
Dallas, TX 75206-6534

Donors: Castle Hills Development Corp.; Weekley Homes, L.P.; Wyndsor Custom Homes; Highland Homes; Darling Homes; Sanders; Lewis and Early; Landstar Homes; Shelly Malone Custom Builders; Garvey Homes.

Foundation type: Independent foundation.

Financial data (yr. ended 12/31/05): Assets, $1,935,005 (M); gifts received, $783,954; expenditures, $411,047; qualifying distributions, $393,938; giving activities include $272,177 for 4 grants (high: $10,360; low: $863), and $121,761 for 75 grants to individuals (high: $2,000; low: $760).

Purpose and activities: Giving primarily for education and religious schools.

Fields of interest: Theological school/education; Education; Christian agencies & churches.

Limitations: Applications not accepted. Giving primarily in TX. No grants to.

Application information: Unsolicited requests for funds not accepted.

Officers: Christopher R. Bright, Pres. and Treas.; Clay V.N. Bright, V.P.

Directors: Margaret Bright Vonder Hoya; Carol Bright Hunter.

EIN: 752732689

Selected grants: The following grants were reported in 2003.

$34,253 to Hebron High School, Carrollton, TX. For projectors, laptops and laptops.

$25,000 to Creek Valley Middle School, Carrollton, TX. For equipment and staff development.

$11,000 to Prince of Peace Christian School, Carrollton, TX. For library.

$7,300 to Carrollton Christian Academy, Carrollton, TX. For software.

$6,700 to Prestonwood Christian Academy, Plano, TX. For videos and scanner.

$5,000 to Prince of Peace Catholic School, Lewisville, TX. For general support.

$5,000 to Trinity Christian Academy, Addison, TX. For broadcast studio.

$1,000 to Castle Hills Elementary School, Lewisville, TX. For Best Teacher in Texas award.

8819
Catto Charitable Foundation ✧

c/o Jessica Hobby Catto
200 Navarro St., Ste. 200
San Antonio, TX 78205

Established in 1967.

Foundation type: Independent foundation.

Financial data (yr. ended 12/31/05): Assets, $27,832,303 (M); expenditures, $1,546,577; qualifying distributions, $1,381,778; giving activities include $1,352,346 for 111 grants (high: $348,666; low: $250).

Purpose and activities: Funding primarily for environmental conservation and education; funding also for arts and culture, and children, youth, and social services.

Fields of interest: Museums; Arts; Higher education; Education; Environment, natural resources; Environment; Animal welfare; Health organizations, association; Children/youth, services.

Limitations: Applications not accepted. Giving on a national basis, with some emphasis on TX, particularly San Antonio, and Washington, DC, and CO. No grants to individuals.

Application information: Contributes only to pre-selected organizations.

Officers and Directors:* Jessica Hobby Catto,* Pres.; Henry E. Catto, Jr.,* V.P.; Susan R. Fammond, Secy.-Treas.

EIN: 742773632

Selected grants: The following grants were reported in 2004.

$476,000 to Aspen Center for Environmental Studies, Aspen, CO.

$228,666 to Conservation Fund, Arlington, VA. 2 grants: $166,666, $62,000

$200,000 to Environmental Defense, Boulder, CO.

$158,900 to National Parks Conservation Association, DC.

$75,000 to Aspen Institute, Queenstown, MD.

$26,000 to Aspen Institute, DC.

$10,000 to International Center for Research on Women, DC.

$10,000 to Trust for Public Land, New York, NY.

$2,450 to Aspen Institute, Aspen, CO.

8820
John & Mildred Cauthorn Charitable Trust

P.O. Box 678
Sonora, TX 76950
Contact: Jessie Kerbow, Secy.

Established in 1985 in TX.

Donor: Mildred Cauthorn†.

Foundation type: Independent foundation.

Financial data (yr. ended 12/31/05): Assets, $9,766,306 (M); expenditures, $1,471,918; qualifying distributions, $966,300; giving activities include $604,066 for 14 grants (high: $313,907; low: $500).
Purpose and activities: Giving primarily for health and human services.
Fields of interest: Secondary school/education; Health care; Youth, services; Federated giving programs; Protestant agencies & churches.
Type of support: General/operating support; Scholarship funds.
Limitations: Giving limited to Sutton County, TX. No grants to individuals.
Application information: Application form not required.
  Initial approach: Letter
  Copies of proposal: 1
  Deadline(s): None
  Board meeting date(s): 1st Tues. monthly
Officer: Jessie Kerbow, Secy.
Trustees: Milton Cavaness; Michael V. Hale; Jo Ann Jones; Nelda Mayfield; Bob Teaff.
Number of staff: 1 part-time support.
EIN: 751977779

8821
CEMEX Foundation ✧
(formerly Southdown Foundation)
P.O. Box 1500
Houston, TX 77251-1500
Application address: c/o Human Resources, CEMEX Inc., 840 Gessner, Ste. 1400, Houston, TX 77024, tel.: (713) 650-6200

Established in 1993.
Donor: Medusa Corp.
Foundation type: Company-sponsored foundation.
Financial data (yr. ended 12/31/04): Assets, $812,824 (M); expenditures, $586,966; qualifying distributions, $581,775; giving activities include $581,775 for 187 grants (high: $200,000; low: $24).
Purpose and activities: The foundation supports Christian agencies and churches, foundations, and organizations involved with arts and culture, education, health, human services, and civic affairs.
Fields of interest: Arts; Education; Environment; Health care; Human services; Foundations (public); Government/public administration; Christian agencies & churches.
Type of support: General/operating support.
Limitations: Giving on a national basis in areas of company operations. No grants to individuals.
Application information:
  Initial approach: Proposal
  Deadline(s): None
Officers and Trustees:* Gilberto Perez,* Chair. and Pres.; Leslie S. White, Secy.-Treas.; R. Frank Craddock, Jr.; Stephen R. Miley; Andrew Miller*.
EIN: 346505254
Selected grants: The following grants were reported in 2003.
$200,000 to Ready Mixed Concrete Research Foundation, Silver Spring, MD.
$150,000 to Texas A & M Research Foundation, College Station, TX.
$15,000 to Day Spring, Louisville, KY. For spring ball.
$5,000 to Rocks Build America Foundation, DC.
$1,000 to Blue Lake Academy, Eustis, FL. For fundraiser.

$1,000 to Crippled Childrens Foundation, Birmingham, AL.
$783 to University of Pittsburgh, Pittsburgh, PA.
$635 to Colgate University, Hamilton, NY.
$200 to Boys and Girls Clubs of Stanton, Stanton, CA.
$68 to Houston Repertoire Ballet, Houston, TX.

8822
CFP Foundation ✧
P.O. Box 1063
Houston, TX 77251 (713) 830-3400
Contact: Patricia N. Lewis, Exec. Dir.

Established in 1997 in TX.
Donors: Gary T. Crum; Sylvie P. Crum.
Foundation type: Independent foundation.
Financial data (yr. ended 12/31/05): Assets, $18,853,308 (M); gifts received, $6,810,725; expenditures, $682,761; qualifying distributions, $481,210; giving activities include $399,500 for 32 grants (high: $100,000; low: $2,000).
Purpose and activities: Giving primarily for education.
Fields of interest: Elementary/secondary education; Higher education; Education.
Type of support: General/operating support; Continuing support; Annual campaigns; Capital campaigns; Building/renovation.
Limitations: Applications not accepted. Giving primarily in TX.
Application information: Unsolicited requests for funds not accepted.
Officers: Gary T. Crum, Pres. and Treas.; Sylvie P. Crum, Exec. V.P.; Carol L. Drawe, V.P. and Secy.; Patricia N. Lewis, Exec. Dir.
EIN: 760537479
Selected grants: The following grants were reported in 2005.
$100,000 to Southern Methodist University, Dallas, TX.
$25,000 to Bo's Place, Houston, TX.
$25,000 to Saint Johns School, Houston, TX.
$20,000 to Episcopal High School, Bellaire, TX.
$20,000 to Texas Childrens Hospital, Houston, TX.
$15,000 to Dress for Success Houston, Houston, TX.
$10,000 to Camp for All Foundation, Houston, TX.
$10,000 to Small Steps Nurturing Center, Houston, TX.
$10,000 to Teach for America, Houston, TX.
$10,000 to Zina Garrison All Court Tennis Academy, Houston, TX.

8823
The CH Foundation ▼ ✧
P.O. Box 94038
Lubbock, TX 79493-4038 (806) 792-0448
Contact: Kay Sanford, Pres.

Established in 1976 in TX.
Donor: Christine DeVitt†.
Foundation type: Independent foundation.
Financial data (yr. ended 12/31/05): Assets, $113,623,896 (M); expenditures, $7,307,225; qualifying distributions, $5,307,599; giving activities include $5,151,606 for 83 grants (high: $550,000; low: $16; average: $5,000–$75,000).
Purpose and activities: Giving primarily for education, arts and cultural organizations, health, and human services.

Fields of interest: Museums; Elementary/secondary education; Higher education; Medical school/education; Nursing school/education; Hospitals (general); Crime/violence prevention, domestic violence; Human services; Aging; Disabilities, people with; Women; Economically disadvantaged.
Type of support: General/operating support; Annual campaigns; Capital campaigns; Building/renovation; Equipment; Publication; Curriculum development; Scholarship funds; Research; Matching/challenge support.
Limitations: Giving primarily in Lubbock, TX and surrounding counties.
Publications: Application guidelines; Grants list.
Application information: Application form not required.
  Initial approach: Proposal
  Copies of proposal: 1
  Deadline(s): May 1
  Board meeting date(s): As necessary
Officers and Trustees:* Kay Sanford,* Pres. and Grants Admin.; Louise Willson Arnold,* V.P.; Don Graf,* Secy. and Exec. Dir.; Kevin G. McMahon,* Treas.; Nelda Thompson, Tr. Emeritus; Kathy Gilbreath.
Number of staff: 1 full-time professional; 1 part-time professional.
EIN: 751534816
Selected grants: The following grants were reported in 2005.
$1,000,000 to Texas Tech University, Lubbock, TX. 2 grants: $500,000 each to College of Human Sciences
$550,000 to Covenant Health System Foundation, Lubbock, TX.
$325,000 to Louise Hopkins Underwood Center for the Arts, Lubbock, TX.
$274,940 to Texas Tech University Health Sciences Center, Lubbock, TX. 2 grants: $222,000 to Garrison Institute on Aging, $52,940 to Department of Pharmacology and Neuroscience
$208,800 to YWCA of Lubbock, Lubbock, TX.
$57,482 to Lubbock Christian University, Lubbock, TX. For Core Knowledge Center for area schools.
$25,000 to Hospice of Lubbock, Lubbock, TX.
$23,950 to Buddy Holly Center, Lubbock, TX.

8824
The Charitable Foundation of the Frost
National Bank of San Antonio ✧
c/o Frost National Bank
P.O. Box 2950
San Antonio, TX 78299 (210) 220-4353
Contact: Melissa Adams
Application address: c/o Exec. Comm., The Frost National Bank, 100 W. Houston St., San Antonio, TX 78205

Established around 1979 in TX.
Donor: The Frost National Bank.
Foundation type: Company-sponsored foundation.
Financial data (yr. ended 12/31/05): Assets, $863,894 (M); gifts received, $950,000; expenditures, $798,007; qualifying distributions, $790,250; giving activities include $790,250 for 82 grants (high: $226,000; low: $1,000).
Purpose and activities: The foundation supports organizations involved with arts and culture, education, medical research, and human services.
Fields of interest: Arts; Education; Medical research, institute; Human services; Federated giving programs.

Limitations: Giving primarily in San Antonio, TX. No grants to individuals.
Application information:
  Initial approach: Proposal
  Deadline(s): None
Trustee: Frost National Bank.
EIN: 742058155

8825
Chatham Hill Foundation ✧
3322 Shorecrest, Ste. 235
Dallas, TX   75235

Established in 1994 in TX.
Donors: The Florida Co.; Joe C. Thompson, Jr.
Foundation type: Independent foundation.
Financial data (yr. ended 12/31/04): Assets, $4,263,905 (M); gifts received, $1,645,520; expenditures, $380,548; qualifying distributions, $376,222; giving activities include $376,222 for 39 grants (high: $25,000; low: $250).
Fields of interest: Religion.
Limitations: Giving primarily in TX. No grants to individuals.
Application information:
  Deadline(s): None
Officers: Joe C. Thompson, Jr., Pres.; Joe C. Thompson III, V.P.; Dorothy K. Thompson, Treas.
EIN: 752532557
Selected grants: The following grants were reported in 2004.
$35,000 to Media Research Center, Alexandria, VA.
$25,000 to Focus on the Family, Colorado Springs, CO.
$25,000 to Franciscan Foundation for the Holy Land, DC.
$15,000 to Family Research Council, DC.
$10,000 to Christian Community Action, Lewisville, TX.
$10,000 to Highlands School, Irving, TX.
$10,000 to Zale Lipshy University Hospital, Dallas, TX.
$2,500 to Joni and Friends, Dallas, TX.
$1,500 to Rise School of Dallas, Dallas, TX.

8826
The Al and Lenore Chilton Foundation ✧
(formerly The Chilton Foundation Trust)
c/o Bank of America, N.A.
P.O. Box 830241
Dallas, TX   75283-1041   (214) 209-9446
Contact: Alice Rahlfs, Sr. V.P., Bank of America, N.A.

Established in 1945 in TX.
Donors: Arthur L. Chilton†; Leonore Chilton†.
Foundation type: Independent foundation.
Financial data (yr. ended 12/31/05): Assets, $10,839,992 (M); expenditures, $531,323; qualifying distributions, $462,045; giving activities include $453,850 for 29 grants (high: $125,000; low: $500).
Fields of interest: Medical school/education; Hospitals (general); Health care; Human services; Children/youth, services; Religion.
Limitations: Giving primarily in Dallas County, TX. No grants to individuals.
Application information: Application form not required.
  Deadline(s): None
  Board meeting date(s): As necessary
  Final notification: 2 months

Trustee: Bank of America, N.A.
EIN: 756006996
Selected grants: The following grants were reported in 2003.
$130,000 to Southwestern Medical Foundation, Dallas, TX. For unrestricted support.
$100,000 to Lovers Lane United Methodist Church, Dallas, TX. For Shipp Chapel Project.
$52,500 to Parish Day School of the Episcopal Church of the Transfiguration, Dallas, TX. For program support.
$35,000 to Crystal Charity Ball, Dallas, TX. For unrestricted support.
$35,000 to Fellowship of Christian Athletes, Dallas, TX. For unrestricted support.
$18,500 to Salesmanship Club Youth and Family Centers, Dallas, TX. For unrestricted support.
$10,000 to Dallas Theological Seminary, Dallas, TX. For professorships.
$10,000 to Goodwill Industries of Dallas, Dallas, TX. For capital project.
$5,000 to University of Arkansas at Fayetteville Foundation, Fayetteville, AR. For Chilton Foundation Endowment Award.
$2,500 to Trinity Christian Academy, Addison, TX. For unrestricted support.

8827
Chinquapin Foundation ✧
(formerly MJR Fund)
2801 Turtle Creek Blvd., Ste. 4E
Dallas, TX   75219   (214) 350-7434
Contact: Margaret J. Rogers, Pres.

Donor: Margaret J. Rogers.
Foundation type: Independent foundation.
Financial data (yr. ended 12/31/03): Assets, $6,108,911 (M); gifts received, $5,000; expenditures, $445,270; qualifying distributions, $373,475; giving activities include $364,670 for 9 grants (high: $200,000; low: $1,500).
Purpose and activities: Giving primarily for education.
Fields of interest: Higher education; Education; Hospitals (general); Cancer; Marine science.
Limitations: Giving primarily in CA. No grants to individuals.
Application information: Application form not required.
  Initial approach: Letter
  Deadline(s): None
Officers: Margaret J. Rogers, Pres.; Laura Charlton Cole, V.P.; Emily Charlton Corrigan, Secy.; Erik Allen Charlton, Treas.
EIN: 752052571
Selected grants: The following grants were reported in 2003.
$200,000 to Monterey Bay Aquarium, Monterey, CA.
$100,000 to Southwestern Medical Foundation, Dallas, TX.
$18,170 to Lamplighter School, Dallas, TX.
$12,500 to Hockaday School, Dallas, TX.
$10,000 to Pacific Legal Foundation, Sacramento, CA.
$10,000 to Stanford Hospital and Clinics, Stanford, CA.
$7,500 to Southern Methodist University, Dallas, TX.
$5,000 to Saint Phillips School, Dallas, TX.
$1,500 to Neighbors United for Quality Education, East Dallas Community School, Dallas, TX.

8828
Christian Mission Concerns ✧
P.O. Box 20815
Waco, TX   76702

Established in 1984 in TX.
Donors: Paul Piper, Sr.; Paul Piper, Jr.; Kent Reynolds; Mrs. Kent Reynolds.
Foundation type: Independent foundation.
Financial data (yr. ended 12/31/05): Assets, $20,689,709 (M); gifts received, $20,000; expenditures, $1,259,392; qualifying distributions, $1,136,200; giving activities include $1,033,981 for 67 grants (high: $200,000; low: $100).
Purpose and activities: Giving primarily to Baptist churches and organizations.
Fields of interest: Human services; Protestant agencies & churches.
Type of support: Program-related investments/ loans.
Limitations: Applications not accepted. Giving primarily in Waco, TX. No grants to individuals.
Application information: Contributes only to pre-selected organizations.
Officers and Directors:* Kent Reynolds,* Pres.; Paul Piper, Jr.,* V.P.; H.H. Reynolds,* Secy.; J.D. Hudson,* Treas.
EIN: 742317938
Selected grants: The following grants were reported in 2005.
$84,836 to Cedar Crest Foundation, Belton, TX.
$39,000 to Habitat for Humanity International.
$38,500 to Cross Culture Experiences, Waco, TX.
$37,000 to Waco Community Baptist Church, Waco, TX.
$35,000 to Central Texas Senior Ministry, Waco, TX.
$25,000 to Waco Community Development Corporation, Waco, TX.
$16,000 to El Paso Baptist Clinic, El Paso, TX.
$15,000 to First Baptist Church.
$10,000 to Compassion Ministries, Harare, Zimbabwe. .
$10,000 to Texas Baptist Childrens Home, Round Rock, TX.

8829
Circle Bar Foundation ✧ ☆
P.O. Box 791000
San Antonio, TX   78279-1000

Established in 1964 as John H. & Dela W. White Fund.
Donors: John H. White; Dela W. White.
Foundation type: Independent foundation.
Financial data (yr. ended 12/31/05): Assets, $7,759,053 (M); gifts received, $390,000; expenditures, $431,882; qualifying distributions, $359,665; giving activities include $359,665 for 26 grants (high: $44,000; low: $1,000).
Purpose and activities: Support for secondary education, support also for programs for child welfare.
Fields of interest: Secondary school/education; Human services; Children/youth, services; Disabilities, people with.
Limitations: Applications not accepted. Giving primarily in San Antonio, TX. No grants to individuals.
Application information: Contributes only to pre-selected organizations.
Manager: Dela W. White.
Trustees: John H. White, Jr.; Tuleta C. White.
EIN: 746063672

Selected grants: The following grants were reported in 2005.

$80,000 to Childrens Shelter of San Antonio, San Antonio, TX. 2 grants: $40,000 each

$44,000 to San Antonio Public Library Foundation, San Antonio, TX.

$17,865 to Warm Springs Rehabilitation Hospital, San Antonio, TX.

$15,000 to Child Advocates San Antonio, San Antonio, TX.

$10,000 to Texas Burn Survivor Society, San Antonio, TX.

$6,000 to ARC of San Antonio, San Antonio, TX.

$6,000 to YMCA.

$5,000 to Assistance League of San Antonio, San Antonio, TX.

$5,000 to Elf Louise, San Antonio, TX.

8830
The Clayton Fund, Inc. ✧

c/o JPMorgan Chase Bank, N.A.
600 Travis St., 7th Fl.
Houston, TX 77002 (713) 216-4513
Contact: Charlene Slack

Trust established in 1952 in TX.
Donors: William L. Clayton†; Susan V. Clayton†.
Foundation type: Independent foundation.
Financial data (yr. ended 12/31/03): Assets, $41,911,128 (M); expenditures, $2,365,411; qualifying distributions, $2,057,651; giving activities include $2,020,000 for 79 grants (high: $250,000; low: $5,000).
Purpose and activities: Giving primarily for higher and other education, the environment, health associations and family planning, children, youth and social services, and community foundations.
Fields of interest: Performing arts, opera; Elementary/secondary education; Higher education; Education; Environment, natural resources; Hospitals (general); Reproductive health, family planning; Health organizations, association; Human services; YM/YWCAs & YM/YWHAs; Children/youth, services; Family services; Foundations (community).
Type of support: General/operating support; Continuing support; Building/renovation; Program development; Scholarship funds.
Limitations: Giving primarily in TX. No grants to individuals.
Publications: Application guidelines.
Application information: Request application guidelines. Application form not required.
   Copies of proposal: 5
   Deadline(s): Feb. 1, May 1, Aug. 1, and Nov. 1
   Board meeting date(s): Mar., June, Sept., and Dec.
   Final notification: In writing
Officer: William L. Garwood, Jr., Pres.
Trustees: Burdine C. Johnson; JPMorgan Chase Bank, N.A.
Number of staff: 1 full-time professional; 1 full-time support.
EIN: 760285764
Selected grants: The following grants were reported in 2003.

$250,000 to Chesapeake Bay Foundation, Annapolis, MD.

$125,000 to Planned Parenthood of Houston and Southeast Texas, Houston, TX.

$37,500 to Texas Tech University, Lubbock, TX. For scholarships.

$25,000 to Good Neighbor Health Care Center, Houston, TX.

$20,000 to University of Washington, School of Nursing, Seattle, WA.

$15,000 to Katy Prairie Conservancy, Houston, TX.

$10,000 to Brigids Place, Houston, TX.

$10,000 to United Cerebral Palsy of Greater Houston, Houston, TX.

$5,000 to Bo's Place, Houston, TX.

$5,000 to Trees for Houston, Houston, TX.

8831
Clear Channel Communications Foundation ✧

200 E. Basse Rd.
San Antonio, TX 78209

Established in 1999 in TX.
Donors: Clear Channel Communications, Inc.; J. Walter Thompson USA, Inc.
Foundation type: Company-sponsored foundation.
Financial data (yr. ended 12/31/03): Assets, $5,176,497 (M); gifts received, $7,972; expenditures, $348,020; qualifying distributions, $347,842; giving activities include $336,343 for 46 grants (high: $75,000; low: $100).
Purpose and activities: The foundation supports organizations involved with arts and culture, health, youth development, and human services.
Fields of interest: Arts; Health organizations, association; Disasters, 9/11/01; Youth development; Human services; American Red Cross; Salvation Army; Federated giving programs.
Limitations: Applications not accepted. Giving primarily in San Antonio, TX. No grants to individuals.
Application information: Contributes only to pre-selected organizations.
Officers and Directors:* L. Lowry Mays,* Pres.; Mark P. Mays,* V.P. and Secy.; Randall T. Mays,* V.P. and Treas.
EIN: 742908486

8832
Clements Foundation ✧

1901 N. Akard St.
Dallas, TX 75201 (214) 720-0337
Contact: Shirley Warren

Established in 1968 in TX.
Foundation type: Independent foundation.
Financial data (yr. ended 12/31/05): Assets, $14,223,340 (M); expenditures, $410,071; qualifying distributions, $328,500; giving activities include $328,500 for 124 grants (high: $50,000; low: $100), and $1,842 for foundation-administered programs.
Purpose and activities: Support primarily for youth groups and higher education; giving also for cultural institutions. The foundation supports courses of study involving the history of the state of TX, the greater Southwest, and related matters of historical value.
Fields of interest: Museums; History/archaeology; Historic preservation/historical societies; Arts; Elementary/secondary education; Higher education; Theological school/education; Health care; Human services; Children/youth, services.
Type of support: General/operating support.
Limitations: Giving primarily in the Dallas, TX, area. No grants to individuals.

Application information:
   Deadline(s): None
Officers: William P. Clements, Jr., Pres.; B. Gill Clements, V.P.; Nancy Clements Seay, V.P.
EIN: 756065076
Selected grants: The following grants were reported in 2003.

$360,000 to Episcopal Diocese of Dallas, Dallas, TX.

$100,000 to University of Texas Southwestern Medical Center, Dallas, TX.

$50,000 to Southern Methodist University, Dallas, TX.

$10,200 to Highland Park Independent School District, Dallas, TX.

$10,000 to Friends of Zale Lipshy University Hospital, Dallas, TX.

$10,000 to United Way of Metropolitan Dallas, Dallas, TX.

$5,200 to Old City Park, Dallas, TX.

$1,250 to Kidney Texas, Dallas, TX.

$1,000 to Southwestern Diabetic Foundation, Gainesville, TX.

$1,000 to Southwestern Medical Foundation, Dallas, TX.

8833
Coastal Bend Community Foundation

The Six Hundred Bldg.
600 Leopard St., Ste. 1716
Corpus Christi, TX 78473 (361) 882-9745
FAX: (361) 882-2865;
E-mail: kwilliams@cbcfoundation.org; URL: http://www.cbcfoundation.org

Established in 1981 in Texas.
Foundation type: Community foundation.
Financial data (yr. ended 12/31/05): Assets, $37,963,881 (M); gifts received, $3,097,404; expenditures, $4,208,094; giving activities include $3,137,343 for grants.
Purpose and activities: The foundation serves as leader, catalyst, and resource for philanthropy in the Coastal Bend region, TX. The foundation strives to provide a better quality of life for the residents of the Coastal Bend by promoting philanthropy, matching community needs with donors wishing to support the programs that meet those needs, and managing a growing investment to assure that changing community needs will be met into the future.
Fields of interest: Museums; History/archaeology; Arts; Higher education; Adult education—literacy, basic skills & GED; Libraries/library science; Education, reading; Education; Environment; Animal welfare; Hospitals (general); Health care; Substance abuse, services; Alcoholism; Food services; Children/youth, services; Homeless, human services; Human services; Community development; Economically disadvantaged; Homeless.
Type of support: General/operating support; Equipment; Program development; Seed money; Fellowships; Scholarship funds.
Limitations: Giving limited to Aransas, Bee, Jim Wells, Kleberg, Nueces, Refugio, and San Patricio counties, TX. No support for religious purposes, athletic teams, school groups, school districts, or elementary or secondary schools, or federal, state, county, or municipal governments. No grants to individuals (except for scholarships), or for trips.
Publications: Application guidelines; Annual report; Grants list; Informational brochure.

Application information: Visit foundation Web site for application Cover Form and guidelines. Application form required.

Initial approach: Submit application Cover Form and attachments
Copies of proposal: 1
Deadline(s): June 30 to Aug. 31
Board meeting date(s): Feb., May, Aug., and Nov.
Final notification: 2nd week of Nov.

Officers and Directors:* Patricia M. Eisenhauer,* Chair.; Tom Dobson,* Vice-Chair.; Kent Williams, C.E.O. and Pres.; Dick Messbanger,* Secy.; Fred J. Nemec,* Treas.; Harry Lee "Butch" Adams, Jr.; Deborah A. Bauer; Jeff Bell, Jr.; Nancy Johnson Bellows; Lola L. Bonner; Roberto Bosquez, M.D.; Gene Bouligny; John Chapman; Lawrence Cornelius; Laura Fischer; Paul R. Haas; Wes Hoskins; Leon S. Loeb; Lou Adele May; Josephine Miller; T.D. Sells, Jr.; F. John Shepherd III; Jean Claire Turcotte; Norman P. Wilcox; C. Ivan Wilson; Dale Wilson.

Number of staff: 3 full-time professional; 1 part-time professional; 1 full-time support.

EIN: 742190039

Selected grants: The following grants were reported in 2004.

$16,775 to Texas A & M University, Corpus Christi, TX.

$11,000 to Boys and Girls Club of Corpus Christi, Corpus Christi, TX.

$10,960 to Avance Family Support and Education Program-San Antonio, San Antonio, TX.

$10,000 to Texas A & M University, Kingsville, TX.

$10,000 to Womens Shelter of South Texas, Corpus Christi, TX.

8834

Elizabeth Huth Coates Charitable Foundation of 1992 ✧

c/o Broadway National Bank
P.O. Box 17001
San Antonio, TX   78217-0001
Contact: Nancy F. May, V.P. and Trust Off., Broadway National Bank

Established in 1993 in TX.
Donor: Elizabeth Huth Coates†.
Foundation type: Independent foundation.
Financial data (yr. ended 12/31/04): Assets, $36,319,048 (M); expenditures, $1,622,100; qualifying distributions, $1,563,949; giving activities include $1,539,173 for 35 grants (high: $279,950; low: $3,500).
Purpose and activities: Giving for the arts, private education and medical research.
Fields of interest: Museums; Arts; Higher education; Medical research, institute.
Type of support: General/operating support; Continuing support; Annual campaigns; Capital campaigns; Building/renovation; Program development; Curriculum development; Research.
Limitations: Giving primarily in San Antonio, TX. No grants to individuals.
Publications: Application guidelines.
Application information: Application form not required.

Initial approach: Letter
Copies of proposal: 1
Deadline(s): Dec. 31
Board meeting date(s): Feb.
Final notification: Feb.-Mar.

Trustee: Broadway National Bank.

Number of staff: 2
EIN: 746399782
Selected grants: The following grants were reported in 2004.

$279,950 to Hill Country Arts Foundation, Ingram, TX. For unrestricted support.

$120,000 to Starr County Memorial Hospital, Rio Grande City, TX. For education expenses for medical student.

$113,000 to Daughters of the Republic of Texas, San Antonio, TX. For unrestricted support.

$100,000 to Texas A & M University-Kingsville Foundation, Kingsville, TX. For Caesar Kleberg Wildlife Research Institute.

$80,000 to Marion Koogler McNay Art Museum, San Antonio, TX. For unrestricted support.

$66,150 to Texas State Historical Association, Austin, TX. For unrestricted support.

$50,431 to Communities in Schools of San Antonio, San Antonio, TX. For unrestricted support.

$50,000 to Childrens Shelter of San Antonio, San Antonio, TX. For unrestricted support.

$50,000 to San Antonio Academy of Texas, San Antonio, TX. For unrestricted support.

$25,000 to San Antonio Botanical Center, San Antonio, TX. For unrestricted support.

8835

The Cockrell Foundation ▼ ✧

1000 Main St., Ste. 3250
Houston, TX   77002-7348   (713) 209-7500
Contact: M. Nancy Williams, Exec. V.P.
E-mail: foundation@cockrell.com; URL: http://www.cockrell.com/foundation

Trust established in 1957 in TX; incorporated in 1966.
Donors: Dula Cockrell†; Ernest Cockrell, Jr.†; Virginia H. Cockrell†.
Foundation type: Independent foundation.
Financial data (yr. ended 12/31/05): Assets, $141,666,110 (M); expenditures, $7,441,814; qualifying distributions, $6,436,164; giving activities include $6,436,164 for 29 grants (high: $2,937,279; low: $1,000; average: $5,000–$50,000).
Purpose and activities: The foundation gives only one higher education grant to the University of Texas Engineering Foundation. Giving primarily for cultural programs, social services, youth services, and health care.
Fields of interest: Museums; Arts; Higher education; Hospitals (general); Crime/violence prevention, domestic violence; Human services; Children/youth, services; Christian agencies & churches; Aging; Disabilities, people with; Women.
Type of support: General/operating support; Annual campaigns; Capital campaigns; Building/renovation; Land acquisition; Endowments; Program development; Professorships; Fellowships; Scholarship funds; Research; Matching/challenge support.
Limitations: Giving primarily in Houston, TX. No grants to individuals, or for medical or scientific research projects, or mass appeal solicitations.
Publications: Informational brochure (including application guidelines).
Application information: The foundation does not accept grant requests via fax or e-mail. Application form not required.

Initial approach: Brief proposal
Copies of proposal: 1
Deadline(s): None

Board meeting date(s): Spring and fall
Final notification: 6 weeks

Officers and Directors:* Ernest H. Cockrell,* Pres.; M. Nancy Williams, Exec. V.P.; Milton T. Graves,* V.P. and Assoc. Dir.; Douglas E. Bryant, Secy.-Treas.; David A. Cockrell, Advisory Dir.; Ernest D. Cockrell II; Janet S. Cockrell; Carol Cockrell Curran; Richard B. Curran; J. Webb Jennings; Laura Jennings Turner.

EIN: 746076993

Selected grants: The following grants were reported in 2004.

$2,100,000 to University of Texas, Austin, TX.

$2,047,000 to Methodist Hospital Foundation, Houston, TX. For Distinguished Clinical Chair in Medical Research.

$218,500 to Childrens Educational Opportunity Foundation (CEO Foundation), Houston, TX. For scholarships.

$100,000 to Greater Houston Community Foundation, Houston, TX. For TexGen - a Collaborative Genetic Research Project in the Texas Medical Center.

$15,000 to Barbara Bush Foundation for Family Literacy, DC. For A Celebration of Reading Gala.

$10,000 to I Have A Dream Foundation, Houston, TX. For Aloha Gala.

8836

College First Foundation ✧

6500 Belt Line Rd., Ste 200
Irving, TX   75063   (972) 999-4560
Contact: Toppy Cantrell, Admin.

Established in 1996 in TX.
Donors: Ronald L. Jensen; Alliance for Affordable Healthcare Association, Inc.
Foundation type: Independent foundation.
Financial data (yr. ended 12/31/05): Assets, $626,102 (M); gifts received, $480,655; expenditures, $482,264; qualifying distributions, $480,656; giving activities include $435,764 for 161 grants to individuals (high: $4,000; low: $500).
Purpose and activities: Only children of active employees or agents of participating companies and associations are eligible for the scholarships.
Type of support: Scholarships—to individuals.
Limitations: Applications not accepted. Giving on a national basis.
Application information: Unsolicited requests for funds not accepted.
Officers and Directors:* Jeff Jensen,* Pres.; Lou Anne Jensen,* V.P.; Burton C. Eisenpruch,* Secy.-Treas.; Vantisa Hudson, Admin.; Janet Jensen.
EIN: 752638941

8837

Calvert K. Collins Family Foundation, Inc. ✧

(formerly Calvert K. Collins Foundation, Inc.)
1701 N. Hampton Rd., Ste. C
DeSoto, TX   75115-2387

Incorporated in 1962 in TX.
Donor: Carr P. Collins.
Foundation type: Independent foundation.
Financial data (yr. ended 12/31/03): Assets, $11,807,930 (M); expenditures, $1,406,993; qualifying distributions, $1,129,330; giving activities include $878,714 for 60 grants (high:

$481,000; low: $40), and $33,294 for 1 foundation-administered program.

Purpose and activities: Giving primarily to federated giving programs and for philanthropy; funding also for the arts, education, and children, youth, and social services. The foundation also has an investment in an 1872 registered historic property, the House of the Seasons, in Jefferson, TX. The foundation is involved in preserving this historic property, promoting and increasing the visibility of Jefferson, TX, and other historic homes, buildings and monuments, while providing information and education to the public regarding the historic city of Jefferson.

Fields of interest: Historic preservation/historical societies; Arts; Secondary school/education; Higher education; Education; Human services; Children/youth, services; Community development; Federated giving programs; Roman Catholic federated giving programs; Philanthropy/voluntarism.

Type of support: General/operating support; Building/renovation; Research.

Limitations: Applications not accepted. Giving primarily in Dallas, TX; funding also in Jefferson. No grants to individuals.

Application information: Contributes only to pre-selected organizations.

Board meeting date(s): Annually

Officers and Directors:* Calvert K. Collins,* Pres.; Richard H. Collins,* V.P. and Treas.

Number of staff: 1 full-time professional.

EIN: 756011615

Selected grants: The following grants were reported in 2003.

$511,000 to Today Foundation, Dallas, TX. 2 grants: $481,000, $30,000

$100,000 to CooperRiis, Mill Spring, NC.

$76,030 to Southern Methodist University, Dallas, TX.

$58,402 to Childrens Scholarship Fund, New York, NY.

$37,342 to Catholic Foundation, Dallas, TX.

$10,000 to Media Research Center, Alexandria, VA.

$5,000 to Cushing Academy, Ashburnham, MA.

$2,000 to Muscular Dystrophy Association, Tucson, AZ.

$1,000 to Education is Freedom Foundation, Dallas, TX.

8838
The James M. Collins Foundation ✧

8115 Preston Rd., Ste. 680
Dallas, TX 75225

Established in 1964 in TX.

Donor: James M. Collins†.

Foundation type: Independent foundation.

Financial data (yr. ended 12/31/03): Assets, $19,796,787 (M); expenditures, $1,075,762; qualifying distributions, $1,016,096; giving activities include $1,011,288 for 76 grants (high: $301,100; low: $100).

Fields of interest: Museums (art); Arts; Higher education; Education; Health organizations, association; Human services; Salvation Army; Economic development.

Limitations: Giving primarily in TX. No grants to individuals; no loans.

Application information: Application form not required.

Initial approach: Letter

Deadline(s): None

Officers: Dorothy Dann Collins Torbett, Pres.; Michael J. Collins, V.P.; Dorothy Collins Weaver, Secy.

EIN: 756040743

Selected grants: The following grants were reported in 2004.

$201,500 to Southern Methodist University, Dallas, TX.

$200,250 to Wellesley College, Wellesley, MA.

$150,000 to Phillips Academy, Andover, MA.

$50,475 to Smithsonian Institution, DC.

$50,000 to Old Red Courthouse, Dallas, TX.

$20,000 to Booker T. Washington High School for the Performing and Visual Arts, Dallas, TX. For building fund.

$17,950 to Dallas Museum of Art, Dallas, TX.

$15,000 to United Way of Metropolitan Dallas, Dallas, TX.

$12,500 to Baylor Health Care System Foundation, Dallas, TX.

$12,500 to Harvard University, Cambridge, MA.

8839
Communities Foundation of Texas, Inc. ▼ ✧

5500 Caruth Haven Ln.
Dallas, TX 75225-8146 (214) 750-4222
Contact: Jeverley R. Cook Ph.D., V.P., Grants; For grants: Leslie Parks, Grants Admin.
FAX: (214) 750-4210; E-mail: Jcook@cftexas.org; Grant application E-mail: LParks@cftexas.org; URL: http://www.cftexas.org

Established in 1953 in TX; incorporated in 1960.

Foundation type: Community foundation.

Financial data (yr. ended 6/30/06): Assets, $699,873,000 (M); gifts received, $73,397,000; expenditures, $75,172,000; giving activities include $59,931,000 for grants.

Purpose and activities: Grants from unrestricted funds are generally for education, health, social services, youth activities, civic improvement, and arts and culture.

Fields of interest: Arts; Higher education; Education; Environment, natural resources; Hospitals (general); Health care; Health organizations, association; Disasters, Hurricane Katrina; Youth, services; Human services.

Type of support: Scholarships—to individuals; Capital campaigns; Building/renovation; Equipment; Land acquisition; Emergency funds; Program development; Seed money; Scholarship funds; Research; Technical assistance; Matching/challenge support.

Limitations: Giving primarily in the Dallas, TX, area (for grants from unrestricted funds). No support for religious purposes from general fund or organizations which redistribute funds to other organizations. No grants to individuals (except for scholarships), or for continuing support, media projects or publications, deficit financing, endowment funds, fellowships, salaries, annual campaigns, or operational expenses of well-established organizations.

Publications: Application guidelines; Annual report; Financial statement; Newsletter; Program policy statement.

Application information: Visit foundation Web site for application guidelines. Proposals sent by fax are not accepted. Application form not required.

Initial approach: Submit proposal

Copies of proposal: 1

Deadline(s): Jan. 16 and Sept. 15

Board meeting date(s): Distribution committee for unrestricted funds meets in Mar. and Nov.

Final notification: 1 week after distribution committee meeting

Officers and Trustees:* Charles J. Wyly, Jr.,* Chair.; Milton P. Levy, Jr.,* Vice-Chair.; Brent E. Christopher, C.E.O. and Pres.; Dwight D. Clasby, V.P., External Affairs; Jeverley R. Cook, Ph.D., V.P., Grants; Marcia Williams Godwin, V.P., Admin.; J. Steven Orr, V.P., Investments; J. Michael Redfearn, V.P., Finance and C.F.O.; Linda Pitts Custard, Secy.; Philip O'Bryan Montgomery III,* Treas.; Kris Thomas, Cont.; Ebby Halliday Acers, Tr. Emeritus; Ruth Sharp Altshuler; Daniel W. Cook III; Joseph M. "Jody" Grant, Ph.D.; Jack M. Kinnebrew; Linda Brack McFarland; Lydia Haggar Novakov; Jere W. Thompson; Gifford Touchstone; Joel T. Williams III.

Number of staff: 10 full-time professional; 1 part-time professional; 15 full-time support; 4 part-time support.

EIN: 750964565

Selected grants: The following grants were reported in 2005.

$5,905,959 to Wichita Falls Area Community Foundation, Wichita Falls, TX. For program support.

$4,251,400 to Southwestern Medical Foundation, Dallas, TX. For program support.

$4,063,850 to Dallas Center for the Performing Arts Foundation, Dallas, TX. For program support.

$3,320,000 to Oklahoma State University Foundation, Stillwater, OK. For program support.

$1,975,000 to Leadership Network, Dallas, TX. For religious activities.

$87,720 to SEI Giving Fund, Oaks, PA.

$40,541 to Dallas Theological Seminary, Dallas, TX.

$37,780 to American Film Institute, Los Angeles, CA.

$25,050 to Equest, Dallas, TX.

$24,000 to Catholic Foundation, Dallas, TX.

8840
Community Foundation of Abilene

500 Chestnut, Ste. 1634
P.O. Box 1001
Abilene, TX 79604 (325) 676-3883
Contact: Nancy E. Jones, C.E.O.; For grants: Leigh Black, Dir., Grants
FAX: (325) 676-4206; E-mail: cfa@abilene.com; Additional E-mail: cfa.jmundy@abilene.com; Grant application E-mail: cfa.lblack@abilene.com; URL: http://www.cfabilene.org

Incorporated in 1985 in TX.

Foundation type: Community foundation.

Financial data (yr. ended 6/30/05): Assets, $44,044,934 (M); gifts received, $4,921,027; expenditures, $4,119,748; giving activities include $3,573,418 for 179 grants (high: $408,650; low: $550).

Purpose and activities: The mission of the foundation is to provide charitable endowments to promote local philanthropy, and to address local challenges and opportunities.

Fields of interest: Museums; Arts; Education; Animals/wildlife; Health care; Cancer; Children/youth, services; Family services, domestic violence; Human services; Community development.

Type of support: General/operating support; Building/renovation; Equipment; Conferences/seminars; Publication; Seed money; Scholarship funds; Technical assistance; Consulting services; Matching/challenge support.

Limitations: Giving limited to the Abilene, TX, area. No support for sectarian religious purposes. No grants to individuals (except for scholarships), or for continuing support, capital debt reduction, medical or scholar research, fundraising events, travel, operating or maintenance expenses, membership fees, or endowment funds; no loans or program-related investments, or multi-year grants (generally).

Publications: Application guidelines; Annual report; Newsletter.

Application information: Visit foundation Web site or call for grant guidelines and deadline information. The foundation's Grant Distribution Committee reviews Letters of Intent and determines which organizations are invited to submit a grant proposal. Application form required.

   Initial approach: Letter of Intent (no more than 2 pages)
   Copies of proposal: 15
   Deadline(s): Feb. 1 and Sept. 1 for Letter of Intent
   Board meeting date(s): 1st Tues. of Feb., Apr., June, Aug., Oct., and Dec.
   Final notification: 1 month after proposal submission

Officers and Trustees:* Lee Caldwell,* Chair.; George Nichols,* Vice-Chair.; Nancy E. Jones, C.E.O. and Pres.; Billye Proctor-Shaw,* Corp. Secy.; Mark Hudson,* Treas.; Tom Allen; Lynn Anderson; Paul Cannon; Tom Choate; Gil DeShazo; Bob Eagle; Don Fitzgibbons; Bobbie Gee; Joseph Johnson; Leigh King; Kathy Merrill.

Number of staff: 5 full-time professional.
EIN: 752045832

8841
Community Foundation of North Texas
(formerly The Community Foundation of Metropolitan Tarrant County)
Fort Worth Club Bldg.
306 W. 7th St., Ste. 306
Fort Worth, TX 76102 (817) 877-0702
Contact: Homer M. Dowd, Pres.
FAX: (817) 877-1215; E-mail: hdowd@cfntx.org;
URL: http://www.cfntx.org

Established in 1981 in TX as a program of the United Way; status changed to independent community foundation in 1989.

Foundation type: Community foundation.
Financial data (yr. ended 12/31/04): Assets, $121,707,823 (M); gifts received, $6,844,584; expenditures, $9,528,545; giving activities include $8,119,917 for 681 grants (high: $1,500,000; low: $20).

Purpose and activities: The foundation provides stewardship for many individual charitable funds. With its specialized services, the foundation gives donor efficient charitable fund administration. Support for community development, social services, education, youth, health, and arts and cultural programs; emphasis on one-time grants to new and innovative programs.

Fields of interest: Arts; Education; Health care; Health organizations, association; AIDS; AIDS research; Children/youth, services; Human services; Community development; Aging; Disabilities, people with; Women; Economically disadvantaged; Homeless.

Type of support: General/operating support; Equipment; Program development; Seed money; Scholarship funds; Technical assistance.

Limitations: Applications not accepted. Giving primarily in northern TX. No grants to individuals, or for deficit financing, endowments or emergency funds, matching grants, publications, research, continuing support, or conferences and seminars.

Publications: Annual report; Grants list; Informational brochure; Newsletter.

Application information: The foundation is not presently accepting applications for discretionary grants; visit foundation Web site for updates.

   Board meeting date(s): Mar., June, Sept., and Dec.

Officers and Directors:* Tom Cravens,* Chair.; Marty V. Leonard,* Vice-Chair.; Homer M. Dowd,* Pres.; Melissa Saniuk, V.P., Finance; Martha S. Williams,* V.P., Distribs.; Mrs. Carol W. Dunaway,* Secy.; Mark L. Walton,* Treas.; Jeff Alexander; L.O. Brightbill III; Robert W. Brown, M.D.; Crawford H. Edwards; L. Allen Hodges III; Phillip W. McCrury; Wade T. Nowlin; J. Russell Reid; Edgar H. Schollmaier; John M. Stevenson; Clifford A. Taylor, Jr.; Philip C. Williamson; David A. York.

Number of staff: 2 full-time professional; 2 full-time support.
EIN: 752267767

8842
Community Foundation of the Texas Hill Country ✧
(formerly Kerrville Area Community Trust)
P.O. Box 291354
Kerrville, TX 78029-1354 (830) 896-8811
Contact: Rick McManigle, Exec. Dir.
FAX: (830) 792-5956;
E-mail: lpl@communityfoundation.net; Additional E-mail: rick@communityfoundation.net; URL: http://www.communityfoundation.net

Established in 1981 in TX.
Donors: Mary Bright†; Alma Dietert†; Ollie Mittack†; Joe Foy.

Foundation type: Community foundation.
Financial data (yr. ended 12/31/04): Assets, $6,593,782 (M); gifts received, $604,547; expenditures, $760,750; giving activities include $553,954 for 134+ grants (high: $223,086).

Purpose and activities: Giving primarily to arts, education, human services, youth services, and community services. The foundation seeks to respond to area needs by providing stewardship of donations, and funding worthwhile community projects.

Fields of interest: Arts; Education; Health care; Children/youth, services; Family services; Human services; Community development; Youth; Aging.

Type of support: General/operating support; Capital campaigns; Building/renovation; Equipment; Endowments; Program development; Publication; Seed money; Scholarship funds; Technical assistance; Employee matching gifts; Matching/challenge support.

Limitations: Giving limited to the area generally known as the Texas Hill Country, including Center Point, Comfort, Fredericksburg, Hunt, Ingram, Kerrville and Medina. No support for religious activities. No grants to individuals, or for debt reduction or operating budgets of established organizations.

Publications: Application guidelines; Annual report; Financial statement; Grants list; Informational brochure; Newsletter.

Application information: Visit foundation Web site for application form and guidelines. Application form required.

   Initial approach: Submit application form and attachments
   Copies of proposal: 3
   Deadline(s): None
   Board meeting date(s): 4 to 5 times annually, as required
   Final notification: 6 to 8 weeks

Officers and Directors:* Sharon Joseph,* Pres.; Gary Lindner,* V.P.; Paul Urban,* Treas.; Rick McManigle, Exec. Dir.; Carroll Butler; Sue Cummings; Charlotte Daniels; Billie Davis; Joan Dell Dolce; Judy Ferguson; Sherrie Gold; Bill Johnston; Louis Romero; Bryant Williams; Victoria Wilson.

Number of staff: 1 full-time professional; 1 part-time professional.
EIN: 742225369

8843
The Constantin Foundation
4809 Cole Ave., LB 127
Dallas, TX 75205-3578 (214) 522-9300
Contact: Catherine I. Doyle, Exec. Dir.
FAX: (214) 521-7023;
E-mail: constantinfdn@sbcglobal.net

Trust established in 1947 in TX.
Donors: E. Constantin, Jr.†; Mrs. E. Constantin, Jr.†.

Foundation type: Independent foundation.
Financial data (yr. ended 12/31/05): Assets, $50,118,116 (M); expenditures, $2,748,119; qualifying distributions, $2,259,784; giving activities include $2,215,000 for 28 grants (high: $500,000; low: $7,250).

Purpose and activities: Emphasis on higher and other education; some support for cultural programs, social service and youth agencies, and hospitals and health, including alcohol and drug abuse programs.

Fields of interest: Museums; Performing arts, music; Humanities; Arts; Secondary school/education; Vocational education; Higher education; Adult/continuing education; Libraries/library science; Education; Hospitals (general); Medical care, rehabilitation; Health care; Substance abuse, services; Health organizations, association; Crime/violence prevention, youth; Housing/shelter, development; Human services; Children/youth, services; Disabilities, people with; Economically disadvantaged.

Type of support: Capital campaigns; Building/renovation; Equipment; Land acquisition; Program development; Matching/challenge support.

Limitations: Giving limited to Dallas County, TX. No support for state schools, theater groups, churches, or state supported institutions. No grants to individuals, or for research, special events, fundraisers, or second party requests; no loans.

Publications: Application guidelines.

Application information: Application form not required.

   Initial approach: Letter (up to 3 pages)
   Copies of proposal: 1
   Deadline(s): Sept. 30 for letters of inquiry; grants reviewed at quarterly meetings; grant meeting in Dec.
   Board meeting date(s): Feb., May, Aug., Nov., and Dec.
   Final notification: Following review

Officer: Catherine I. Doyle, Exec. Dir.

Trustees: Henry C. Beck, Jr.; Gene H. Bishop; Harvey Berryman Cash; Roy Gene Evans; Patrick McEvoy, Jr.; Joseph Boyd Neuhoff; Joel T. Williams, Jr.
Number of staff: 1 full-time professional; 1 part-time support.
EIN: 756011289
Selected grants: The following grants were reported in 2003.
$500,000 to YMCA Camp Grady Spruce, Dallas, TX. For capital support.
$325,000 to Childrens Medical Center of Dallas, Dallas, TX. For program support.
$150,000 to Visiting Nurse Association of Texas, Dallas, TX. For equipment.
$100,000 to Dallas Methodist Hospitals Foundation, Dallas, TX. For capital support.
$50,000 to Habitat for Humanity, Dallas Area, Dallas, TX. For capital support.
$50,000 to Rise School of Dallas, Dallas, TX. For program support.
$33,000 to Genesis Womens Shelter, Dallas, TX. For building renovations.
$25,000 to Saint Philips School and Community Center, Dallas, TX. For scholarships.
$20,000 to Girl Scouts of the U.S.A., Texas-Tejas Council, Dallas, TX. For capital support.
$15,000 to Suicide and Crisis Center of Dallas, Dallas, TX. For program support.

8844
The Convergence Institute ✧
4544 S. Lamar Blvd., Ste. G300
Austin, TX 78745-1500

Established in 1998 in TX.
Donors: Mary K. Martin; Thomas B. Martin, Jr.
Foundation type: Independent foundation.
Financial data (yr. ended 12/31/03): Assets, $4,894,528 (M); expenditures, $566,450; qualifying distributions, $355,889; giving activities include $355,941 for 12 grants (high: $125,000; low: $250).
Purpose and activities: Giving to educational, medical, and religious organizations.
Fields of interest: Education; Health care; Human services; Christian agencies & churches.
Limitations: Applications not accepted. Giving primarily in TX. No grants to individuals.
Application information: Contributes only to pre-selected organizations.
Officers: Mary K. Martin, Pres.; Peg Ferrier, Secy.
Director: Thomas B. Martin.
EIN: 742871700
Selected grants: The following grants were reported in 2003.
$151,700 to Austin Waldorf School, Austin, TX. 2 grants: $125,000 (For construction), $26,700 (For computer lab).
$76,084 to First Tee of Greater Austin, Austin, TX. 2 grants: $13,584 (For general support), $62,500 (For capital campaign).
$75,000 to Austin Lyric Opera, Austin, TX. For general support.
$40,924 to Schoenstatt Movement of Austin, Austin, TX. For general operating support.
$7,083 to University of Texas Longhorn Foundation, Austin, TX. For general support.
$3,000 to Brown University, Providence, RI. For general support.
$750 to University of Texas, McDonald Observatory, Austin, TX. For general support.
$250 to Austin Area Interreligious Ministries, Austin, TX. For general support.

8845
Kelly Gene Cook, Sr. Charitable Foundation, Inc. ✧
232 Warrenton Dr.
Houston, TX 77024

Incorporated in 1986 in TX.
Donors: Kelly G. Cook†; Peggy Cook Pool.
Foundation type: Independent foundation.
Financial data (yr. ended 12/31/05): Assets, $31,413,883 (M); gifts received, $1,020; expenditures, $1,555,194; qualifying distributions, $1,397,105; giving activities include $663,788 for 26 grants (high: $200,000; low: $500), and $593,778 for 91 grants to individuals (high: $44,041; low: $50).
Purpose and activities: Support primarily for higher education, including student aid provided through scholarship funds at Millsaps College, the University of Mississippi, Mississippi State University, and the University of Southern Mississippi.
Fields of interest: Higher education.
Type of support: Endowments; Professorships; Scholarship funds; Scholarships—to individuals; Matching/challenge support.
Limitations: Giving primarily in LA, MS, and TX.
Application information: Apply to the financial aid office at Millsaps College, the University of Mississippi, Mississippi State University, or the University of Southern Mississippi; the foundation makes final selection of recipients. Application form required.
    Copies of proposal: 5
    Deadline(s): Apr. 15
    Board meeting date(s): Oct.
Officers and Directors:* Peggy Cook Pool,* Pres.; Deborah Rochelle,* V.P.; JoAnn Mikell,* Secy.; Robert Kneppler, Jr.
Number of staff: 1 full-time professional; 1 part-time support.
EIN: 760201807

8846
Cooper Industries Foundation ✧
P.O. Box 4446
Houston, TX 77210-4446 (713) 209-8800
Contact: Victoria B. Guennewig, V.P., Public Affairs
FAX: (713) 209-8982;
E-mail: info@cooperindustries.com; URL: http://www.cooperindustries.com/common/aboutCooper/corporateGiving.cfm

Incorporated in 1964; absorbed Crouse-Hinds Foundation in 1982; absorbed McGraw-Edison Foundation in 1985.
Donors: Cooper Industries, Inc.; Gerda Kaudisch†.
Foundation type: Company-sponsored foundation.
Financial data (yr. ended 12/31/05): Assets, $8,662,233 (M); expenditures, $2,036,325; qualifying distributions, $2,020,099; giving activities include $1,402,969 for 164 grants (high: $177,500; low: $250), and $617,130 for 615 employee matching gifts.
Purpose and activities: The foundation supports organizations involved with arts and culture, education, the environment, health, safety, human services, and community development.
Fields of interest: Museums; Performing arts; Arts; Vocational education; Higher education; Education; Environment; Health care; Safety, education; Youth, services; Human services; Community development.
Type of support: General/operating support; Continuing support; Annual campaigns; Capital campaigns; Building/renovation; Emergency funds; Program development; Scholarship funds; Employee volunteer services; Employee matching gifts; Employee-related scholarships; In-kind gifts.
Limitations: Giving primarily in areas of company operations in AL, AR, CA, CO, CT, GA, IL, ME, MI, MO, MS, NC, NV, NY, OH, PA, SC, TX, and WI, with emphasis on Houston, TX. No support for United Way-supported organizations, national or state organizations, religious, veterans', political, labor, or lobbying organizations, hospitals, or primary or secondary schools. No grants to individuals (except for employee-related scholarships).
Publications: Application guidelines; Corporate giving report.
Application information: Requests may be forwarded by the foundation to other Cooper Industries locations when appropriate. Application form not required.
    Initial approach: Proposal to nearest company division; proposal to foundation for organizations located in the Houston, TX, metropolitan area
    Copies of proposal: 1
    Deadline(s): None
    Board meeting date(s): Feb. and Nov.
    Final notification: Within 90 days
Officers and Trustees:* H. John Riley, Jr.,* Chair.; Victoria B. Guennewig,* Pres.; Terry A. Klebe, Treas.; D.K. Schumacher.
Number of staff: 1 full-time support.
EIN: 316060698
Selected grants: The following grants were reported in 2005.
$88,535 to United Way of the Texas Gulf Coast, Houston, TX. 2 grants: $45,251, $43,284
$70,000 to Alley Theater, Houston, TX.
$25,000 to Museum of Fine Arts, Houston, Houston, TX.
$15,525 to National Merit Scholarship Corporation, Evanston, IL.
$15,320 to American Red Cross, Goldsboro, NC.
$5,809 to United Way of Washington County, Springdale, AR.
$645 to Channel 10/36 Friends, Milwaukee, WI.
$350 to American Red Cross, Houston, TX.
$310 to Ohio Northern University, Ada, OH.

8847
Covenant Foundation, Inc. ▼
8122 Datapoint Dr., Ste. 1000
San Antonio, TX 78229-3270
Contact: David Craven, Pres.

Established in 1991 in TX.
Donors: James R. Leininger; Cecelia A. Leininger.
Foundation type: Independent foundation.
Financial data (yr. ended 12/31/05): Assets, $33,729,727 (M); expenditures, $11,983,709; qualifying distributions, $10,804,087; giving activities include $10,804,087 for 163 grants (high: $4,822,320; low: $300; average: $10,000–$100,000).
Purpose and activities: Giving primarily to Christian agencies and churches.
Fields of interest: Elementary/secondary education; Public affairs; Christian agencies & churches.
Type of support: General/operating support; Continuing support; Publication; Seed money; Internship funds.

Limitations: Applications not accepted. Giving primarily in TX. No grants to individuals.
Application information: Contributes only to pre-selected organizations.
Board meeting date(s): Quarterly
Officers and Directors:* Franklin B. Stagg,* Pres.; Thomas W. Lyles, Jr., Secy.; Charles A. Staffel,* Treas.; David Craven; Tracy M. Craven; Brian C. Leininger; Cecelia A. Leininger; James R. Leininger; Kelly C. Welch; Richard H. Welch; Robert Welch.
Number of staff: 1 full-time professional.
EIN: 742622129
Selected grants: The following grants were reported in 2005.
$4,822,320 to Christian Academy of San Antonio, San Antonio, TX. For general support.
$1,150,000 to Rafiki Foundation, San Antonio, TX. For general support.
$1,074,705 to Childrens Educational Opportunity Foundation (CEO Foundation), San Antonio, TX. For general support.
$500,000 to Patrick Henry College, Purcellville, VA. For general support.
$188,900 to Campus Crusade for Christ. For general support.
$115,000 to Touch the World. For general support.
$60,000 to Advocates International, Fairfax, VA. For general support.
$20,000 to Mercy Ships, Garden Valley, TX. For general support.
$10,000 to Alliance of Christian Home Education Leadership, Brooks, GA. For general support.
$10,000 to Wall Builder Presentations, San Antonio, TX. For general support.

8848
Louetta M. Cowden Foundation ◇
c/o Bank of America, N.A.
P.O. Box 831041
Dallas, TX   75283-1041
Application address: c/o James J. Mueth, Bank of America, P.O. Box 419119, Kansas City, MO 64141-6119, tel.: (816) 979-7405

Trust established in 1964 in MO.
Donor: Louetta M. Cowden‡.
Foundation type: Independent foundation.
Financial data (yr. ended 12/31/05): Assets, $13,786,517 (M); expenditures, $701,378; qualifying distributions, $618,989; giving activities include $575,000 for 11 grants (high: $150,000; low: $10,000).
Purpose and activities: Support for children's welfare and hospitals, with emphasis on capital fund grants.
Fields of interest: Hospitals (general); Youth development, centers/clubs; Human services; Children/youth, services; Family services.
Type of support: Capital campaigns; Building/renovation; Equipment; Land acquisition; Emergency funds; Program development; Seed money.
Limitations: Giving limited to MO, with an emphasis on the metropolitan Kansas City area. No grants to individuals, or for endowment funds, scholarships, fellowships, or matching gifts; no loans.
Publications: Application guidelines.
Application information: Application form not required.
Initial approach: Letter (no more than 3 pages)
Copies of proposal: 1
Deadline(s): None

Board meeting date(s): Mar., June, Sept., and Dec.
Final notification: 2 months
Trustees: Arthur Bowen; Bank of America, N.A.
Number of staff: 1 full-time professional.
EIN: 436052617
Selected grants: The following grants were reported in 2003.
$100,000 to Childrens Mercy Hospital, Kansas City, MO. For Destiny Expansion Program.
$100,000 to Starlight Theater Association, Kansas City, MO. To purchase Paciolan software.
$60,000 to Cornerstones of Care, Kansas City, MO. For Healthy Kansas City program.
$50,000 to Harvesters-The Community Food Network, Kansas City, MO. To purchase new distribution center.
$50,000 to K C P T-Kansas City Public Television Channel 19, Kansas City, MO. For capital campaign.
$50,000 to National Association of Basketball Coaches, Overland Park, KS. For Headquarters relocation.
$33,000 to Kansas City Ballet Association, Kansas City, MO. For capital campaign.
$25,000 to Fellowship of Christian Athletes, Kansas City, MO. For capital campaign.
$25,000 to Girl Scouts of the U.S.A., Mid-Continent Council, Kansas City, MO. For capital campaign.
$25,000 to Kansas City Repertory Theater, Kansas City, MO. For Spencer Theater Reseating Project.

8849
The Jerry & Kay Cox Foundation ◇
c/o Jerry S. Cox
6-C Lacewood Ln.
Houston, TX   77024-7412

Established in 1996 in TX.
Donor: Jerry S. Cox.
Foundation type: Independent foundation.
Financial data (yr. ended 12/31/05): Assets, $5,822,267 (M); expenditures, $438,127; qualifying distributions, $388,333; giving activities include $388,333 for 4 grants (high: $333,333; low: $10,000).
Purpose and activities: Giving primarily for education, and to a Christian church.
Fields of interest: Education; Human services; Christian agencies & churches.
Limitations: Applications not accepted. Giving primarily in TX. No grants for endowments, individual scholarships, political expenditures and lobbying activities, or deficit funding.
Application information: Unsolicited requests for funds not accepted.
Board meeting date(s): Quarterly
Officers and Directors:* Jerry S. Cox,* Pres. and Treas.; Kay Cox,* V.P. and Secy.; Courtney Ellen Cox; Joshua Paul Cox.
EIN: 760511052

8850
John and Maurine Cox Foundation ◇
P.O. Box 2217
Midland, TX   79702-2217

Established in 1994 in TX.
Donor: John L. Cox.
Foundation type: Independent foundation.

Financial data (yr. ended 12/31/05): Assets, $13,419,938 (M); gifts received, $1,000,000; expenditures, $710,281; qualifying distributions, $593,200; giving activities include $593,200 for 24 grants (high: $150,000; low: $300).
Purpose and activities: Giving primarily for health associations and children's services.
Fields of interest: Museums; Cancer; Boy scouts; Residential/custodial care, hospices; Federated giving programs.
Limitations: Applications not accepted. Giving limited to TX. No grants to individuals.
Application information: Contributes only to pre-selected organizations.
Trustees: Kelly Cox; Maurine T. Cox.
EIN: 752536459
Selected grants: The following grants were reported in 2004.
$150,000 to PB Charity Golf Classic, Midland, TX. For unrestricted support.
$130,000 to Texas Christian University, Fort Worth, TX. For unrestricted support.
$51,000 to Midland Memorial Foundation, Midland, TX. For unrestricted support.
$50,000 to High Sky Childrens Ranch, Midland, TX. For unrestricted support.
$50,000 to Petroleum Museum, Midland, TX. For unrestricted support.
$30,000 to Rice University, Houston, TX. For unrestricted support.
$25,000 to City of Midland Aquatics, Midland, TX. For unrestricted support.
$25,000 to Palmer Drug Abuse Program Midland Texas, Midland, TX. For unrestricted support.
$15,000 to Gladney Fund, Fort Worth, TX. For unrestricted support.
$10,000 to Midland Childrens Rehabilitation Center, Midland, TX. For unrestricted support.

8851
The Crain Foundation ◇
P.O. Box 2146
Longview, TX   75606-2146   (903) 758-8276
Contact: Ann Lacy Crain, Pres.

Established in 1997 in TX.
Foundation type: Independent foundation.
Financial data (yr. ended 12/31/05): Assets, $10,766,309 (M); gifts received, $2,400,000; expenditures, $514,622; qualifying distributions, $442,500; giving activities include $442,500 for 24 grants (high: $140,000; low: $500).
Purpose and activities: Giving for higher education, Christian and Protestant churches and organizations, art and cultural programs, and for medical services.
Fields of interest: Higher education; Students, sororities/fraternities; Education; Christian agencies & churches; Protestant agencies & churches.
Application information:
Initial approach: Proposal
Deadline(s): None
Final notification: Within 2 months of request
Officers and Directors:* Ann Lacy Crain,* Pres.; Rogers L. Crain,* V.P. and Secy.; B. Walter Crain III,* V.P. and Treas.; Ann Lacy Crain II,* V.P.; Neal Hawthorn, V.P.
EIN: 752698267
Selected grants: The following grants were reported in 2005.
$140,000 to First Presbyterian Church, Kerrville, TX.
$64,000 to Episcopal High School, Houston, TX.

$25,000 to Saint Johns School, Houston, TX.

$21,000 to River Oaks Baptist School, Houston, TX.

$17,000 to Lawrenceville School, Lawrenceville, NJ.

$10,000 to Trinity-Pawling School, Pawling, NY.

$10,000 to Washington and Lee University, Lexington, VA.

$5,000 to Crisman Preparatory School, Longview, TX.

$5,000 to Neuhaus Education Center, Bellaire, TX.

$1,000 to Colgate University, Hamilton, NY.

8852
James R. Crane Foundation ✧ ☆
15350 Vickery Dr.
Houston, TX   77032

Established in 1999 in TX.
Donor: James R. Crane.
Foundation type: Independent foundation.
Financial data (yr. ended 12/31/04): Assets, $1,938,292 (M); gifts received, $1,226,000; expenditures, $1,374,510; qualifying distributions, $1,319,240; giving activities include $1,319,240 for grants.
Fields of interest: Museums; Arts; Human services.
Limitations: Applications not accepted. Giving primarily in Houston, TX. No grants to individuals.
Application information: Contributes only to pre-selected organizations.
Directors: James R. Crane; Ronald Franklin; Douglas Seckel.
EIN: 760626224

8853
Mark Cuban Foundation ✧ ☆
P.O. Box 12388
Dallas, TX   75225
Application address for the Fallen Patriot Fund: c/o Bank of America Private Bank, TX 1-492-19-09, P.O. Box 832409, Dallas, TX 75283-2409, tel.: (214) 658-7125, fax: (214) 696-6310, e-mail: info@fallenpatriotfund.org

Established in TX.
Donors: Michael Jones; Diane Jones; Rod Sanders; Nancy Sanders; Michael Goodwin; Mark Cuban; Michael Thesman; Abell-Hanger Foundation; White Party Benefit; The Isaac I Foundation; McKinney/Pearl Restaurant Partners, L.P.; Horizon Casino Resort; Rippey Commercial LLC; SFX-American Century; Folsom Ford; American Century Companies; Glenstone Foundation; Belz Enterprizes; Keatara Investments.
Foundation type: Independent foundation.
Financial data (yr. ended 12/31/04): Assets, $1,435,882 (M); gifts received, $1,206,186; expenditures, $590,480; qualifying distributions, $589,173; giving activities include $10,000 for 1 grant, and $574,000 for 28 grants to individuals (high: $60,000; low: $2,500).
Purpose and activities: Giving primarily for living assistance for families of U.S. military personnel killed or seriously wounded in Operation Iraqi Freedom. The foundation will also proactively contact families of U.S. military personnel who were killed or seriously injured during the same military operation.
Fields of interest: Military/veterans.
Application information:
  Deadline(s): None

Officers: Mark Cuban, Pres.; Martin Woodall, V.P.; Robert Hart, Secy.
Director: Brian Cuban.
EIN: 260063142

8854
The Cullen Foundation ▼
601 Jefferson St., 40th Fl.
Houston, TX   77002
Contact: Alan M. Stewart, Treas.
E-mail: salexander@cullenfdn.org; URL: http://www.cullenfdn.org

Trust established in 1947 in TX.
Donors: Hugh Roy Cullen†; Lillie Cullen†.
Foundation type: Independent foundation.
Financial data (yr. ended 12/31/05): Assets, $245,442,830 (M); expenditures, $13,308,535; qualifying distributions, $11,223,095; giving activities include $10,922,950 for 58 grants (high: $2,150,000; low: $5,000; average: $50,000–$250,000).
Purpose and activities: Giving for charitable, educational, medical, and other eleemosynary purposes; grants for hospitals, medical research, including eye research, and higher education; support also for music, the performing arts, social services, drug abuse prevention, community funds, and conservation.
Fields of interest: Arts; Education; Hospitals (general); Health care; Health organizations, association; Medical research, institute; Human services; Homeless.
Type of support: General/operating support; Annual campaigns; Capital campaigns; Building/renovation; Equipment; Land acquisition; Endowments; Debt reduction; Program development; Professorships; Curriculum development; Fellowships; Scholarship funds; Research; Matching/challenge support.
Limitations: Giving limited to TX, with emphasis on Houston. No support for religious organizations directly. No grants to individuals, or for underwriting or sponsorship of fundraising events; no loans.
Publications: Application guidelines.
Application information: Application form not required.
  Initial approach: Proposal, letter, or telephone
  Copies of proposal: 1
  Deadline(s): None
  Board meeting date(s): Usually in Jan., Apr., July, Oct., and as required
  Final notification: Varies
Officers and Directors:* Roy Henry Cullen,* Pres.; Isaac Arnold, Jr.,* V.P.; Wilhelmina E. Robertson,* Secy.; Alan M. Stewart, Treas. and Exec. Dir.; Bert L. Campbell; William H. Drushel, Jr.
Number of staff: 3 full-time professional.
EIN: 760647361
Selected grants: The following grants were reported in 2005.
$2,150,000 to University of Texas Health Science Center, Houston, TX. For New Frontiers Campaign for Institute of Molecular Medicine for the Prevention of Human Diseases.
$1,400,000 to Museum of Fine Arts, Houston, Houston, TX. For new museum building and renovation of existing one.
$1,000,000 to Houston Downtown Park Corporation, Houston, TX. 2 grants: $500,000 each (For new Central Park).

$500,000 to Project GRAD Houston, Bellaire, TX. To implement Enriched High School Program in all Project Grad high schools.
$300,000 to Saint Lukes Episcopal Hospital, Houston, TX. For Health, Hope and the Human Spirit capital campaign.
$250,000 to Alley Theater, Houston, TX. For The Cullen Terrace, naming opportunity for Staging the Future capital and endowment campaign.
$200,000 to Fay School, Houston, TX. For final phase of construction to complete Campus Master Plan.
$150,000 to TIRR Foundation, Houston, TX. For Mission Connect.
$62,500 to Houston Ballet Foundation, Houston, TX.

8855
The Dallas Foundation ▼ ✧
900 Jackson St., Ste. 150
Dallas, TX   75202   (214) 741-9898
Contact: Mary M. Jalonick, Exec. Dir.; For grants: Shelley Fuld Nasso, Dir., Community Philanthropy
FAX: (214) 741-9848;
E-mail: info@dallasfoundation.org; Additional E-mail: mjalonick@dallasfoundation.org; Grant request E-mail: sfuldnasso@dallasfoundation.org;
URL: http://www.dallasfoundation.org

Established in 1929 in TX.
Foundation type: Community foundation.
Financial data (yr. ended 12/31/05): Assets, $119,878,256 (M); gifts received, $43,426,266; expenditures, $20,996,292; giving activities include $20,147,983 for grants.
Purpose and activities: The foundation serves as a resource, leader, and catalyst for philanthropy by providing donors with flexible means of making gifts to charitable causes that enhance the community.
Fields of interest: Arts; Education; Animal welfare; Health care; Health organizations, association; Crime/violence prevention, child abuse; Disasters, Hurricane Katrina; Recreation, parks/playgrounds; Human services; Community development, neighborhood development; Aging; Disabilities, people with; African Americans/Blacks; Economically disadvantaged.
Type of support: General/operating support; Capital campaigns; Building/renovation; Equipment; Scholarship funds; Employee-related scholarships; Matching/challenge support.
Limitations: Giving limited to the City and County of Dallas, TX. No support for religious purposes from discretionary funds. No grants to individuals from discretionary funds, or for endowments, research, operating budgets, annual campaigns, debt retirement, or underwriting of fundraising events; generally no multi-year grants.
Publications: Application guidelines; Annual report; Financial statement; Grants list; Newsletter.
Application information: Visit foundation Web site for application guidelines per grant type. The foundation will invite selected organizations to submit Unrestricted fund full proposals based on letters of inquiry. Application form required.
  Initial approach: Letter of inquiry for Unrestricted fund
  Copies of proposal: 1
  Deadline(s): Aug. 1 for Unrestricted fund letters of inquiry; Oct. 2 for Unrestricted fund full proposals. Apr. 17 for Field-of-Interest application

Board meeting date(s): Mar., June, Sept., and Dec.

Final notification: June for Field-of-Interest funds and Dec. for Unrestricted funds

Officers and Governors:* John R. Castle,* Chair.; Elizabeth A. Lang-Miers,* Vice-Chair.; Regen H. Fearon,* Secy.; William T. Solomon, Jr., C.F.O.; Mary M. Jalonick, Exec. Dir.; Gary W. Garcia, Cont.; Henry C. Beck III; Mary McDermott Cook; David R. Corrigan; Lisbeth F. Minyard; Robert R. Penn; Philip J. Ritter; John D. Solana; John L. Ware.

Trustee Banks: Bank of America, N.A.; Compass Bank; JPMorgan Chase Bank, N.A.

Number of staff: 7 full-time professional; 1 full-time support.

EIN: 752890371

Selected grants: The following grants were reported in 2005.

$1,000,000 to Dallas Center for the Performing Arts Foundation, Dallas, TX. For general operating support.

$1,000,000 to Parkland Foundation, Dallas, TX. For Ambulatory Surgery Center.

$1,000,000 to Southwestern Medical Foundation, Dallas, TX. For Community Health Initiatives.

$350,000 to Foundation for Community Empowerment, Dallas, TX. 2 grants: $250,000 (For general operating support), $100,000 (For general operating support).

$186,560 to Gateway Church, Southlake, TX. For general operating support.

$150,000 to YWCA of Metropolitan Dallas, Dallas, TX. To pilot Nurse-Family Partnership program in Dallas.

$125,000 to Texas Christian University, Fort Worth, TX. For Professor of Contemporary Art/Annual Fund.

$25,000 to Dallas Institute of Humanities and Culture, Dallas, TX. For Hiett Prize and Summer Program.

$25,000 to Eastern European Mission, Houston, TX. For Faces of Russia Campaign.

8856
Sidney and Charline Dauphin Foundation ✧

(formerly Texas Home Health, Inc.)
4140 Gladys Ave., Ste. 101
Beaumont, TX 77706

Established in 2001 in TX.

Foundation type: Independent foundation.

Financial data (yr. ended 12/31/05): Assets, $5,903,957 (L); expenditures, $1,175,523; qualifying distributions, $1,001,000; giving activities include $1,001,000 for 9 grants (high: $350,000; low: $25,000).

Fields of interest: Health organizations, association; Breast cancer; Medical research, institute; Cancer research; Human services; Protestant agencies & churches.

Limitations: Applications not accepted. Giving primarily in TX. No grants to individuals.

Application information: Contributes only to pre-selected organizations.

Officers: Charline Dauphin, Pres. and Secy.; Robin Dauphin, Treas.

Trustee: Dorothy Modisette.

EIN: 237009052

8857
Carl A. Davis & Lois E. Davis Religious & Charitable Trust ✧

2700 Post Oak Blvd., Ste. 1050
Houston, TX 77056-5709

Established in 1990 in TX.

Donors: Carl A. Davis; Lois E. Davis.

Foundation type: Independent foundation.

Financial data (yr. ended 12/31/04): Assets, $1,064,650 (M); expenditures, $408,835; qualifying distributions, $407,810; giving activities include $408,400 for 14 grants (high: $319,900; low: $1,000).

Purpose and activities: Giving primarily for human services and religious organizations.

Fields of interest: Human services; Civil liberties, right to life; Foundations (private grantmaking); Christian agencies & churches; Roman Catholic agencies & churches.

Limitations: Applications not accepted. Giving on a national basis, with emphasis on Houston, TX. No grants to individuals.

Application information: Contributes only to pre-selected organizations.

Trustee: Carl A. Davis.

EIN: 766066429

Selected grants: The following grants were reported in 2003.

$150,000 to Walsingham Foundation, Houston, TX.

$12,000 to Eternal Word Television Network, Birmingham, AL.

$5,000 to American Center for Law and Justice, Virginia Beach, VA.

$5,000 to Focus on the Family, Colorado Springs, CO.

$5,000 to Right to Life Committee Educational Fund, Texas, Houston, TX.

$5,000 to Saint Andrews Episcopal Church, Fort Worth, TX.

$3,000 to Alliance Defense Fund, Scottsdale, AZ.

$3,000 to Samaritans Purse, Boone, NC.

$2,500 to Saint Pauls Anglican Church, Midland, TX.

$2,500 to Star of Hope Mission, Houston, TX.

8858
Ed & Birdie Dawley Educational Trust ✧

c/o Robert L. Bucher II
1006 Crossroad Dr.
Houston, TX 77079-5018

Established in 2001 in TX.

Donor: Birdie Dawley†.

Foundation type: Independent foundation.

Financial data (yr. ended 9/30/04): Assets, $72,195 (M); expenditures, $786,463; qualifying distributions, $785,807; giving activities include $775,059 for 6 grants (high: $367,681; low: $2,000).

Fields of interest: Secondary school/education; Higher education; Scholarships/financial aid.

Limitations: Applications not accepted. Giving primarily in Houston, TX. No grants to individuals.

Application information: Contributes only to pre-selected organizations.

Trustees: Haidee D. Bucher; Robert L. Bucher II; Leonard Radoff; Lisel Radoff; Albert Valentas; Rosemary Valentas.

EIN: 316662973

Selected grants: The following grants were reported in 2004.

$367,681 to HSPVA Friends, Houston, TX. For scholarships.

$238,167 to Brookwood Community, Brookshire, TX. For scholarships.

$90,000 to First Book, DC. For children's books.

$71,211 to Saint Thomas High School, Houston, TX. For scholarships.

$6,000 to Casa Juan Diego, Houston, TX. For educational materials.

$2,000 to Holy Name School, Houston, TX. For scholarships.

8859
Matias De Llano Charitable Trust ✧ ☆

c/o International Bank of Commerce
1200 San Bernardo Ave.
Laredo, TX 78042-1359

Established in 2003 in TX.

Donor: Matias De Llano†.

Foundation type: Independent foundation.

Financial data (yr. ended 12/31/05): Assets, $9,995,894 (M); gifts received, $7,417; expenditures, $477,923; qualifying distributions, $420,800; giving activities include $420,800 for 9 grants (high: $100,000; low: $10,000).

Fields of interest: Higher education; Human services; Children/youth; services.

Limitations: Giving primarily in Laredo, TX.

Trustee: International Bank of Commerce.

EIN: 743013012

8860
Katrine Menzing Deakins Charitable Trust

c/o Bank of America, N.A.
P.O. Box 1317
Fort Worth, TX 76101-1317 (817) 390-6714
Contact: William D. Huhn, S.V.P., Bank of America, N.A.

Established in 1987 in TX.

Foundation type: Independent foundation.

Financial data (yr. ended 3/31/06): Assets, $7,236,427 (M); expenditures, $419,541; qualifying distributions, $332,860; giving activities include $325,750 for 28 grants (high: $84,000; low: $500).

Fields of interest: Arts; Education; Health care; Mental health, treatment; Health organizations, association; Human services.

Type of support: General/operating support.

Limitations: Giving limited to TX, with emphasis on Fort Worth. No grants to individuals.

Publications: Annual report (including application guidelines).

Application information:
Initial approach: Letter
Deadline(s): Sept. 30

Trustee: Bank of America, N.A.

EIN: 756370503

8861
The Deason Foundation ✧

2828 N. Haskell, 10th Fl.
Dallas, TX 75204

Established in 1997 in TX.

Donor: Darwin Deason.

Foundation type: Independent foundation.

Financial data (yr. ended 12/31/05): Assets, $7,711,272 (M); expenditures, $370,751; qualifying distributions, $362,000; giving activities

include $362,000 for 8 grants (high: $180,000; low: $1,000).
Fields of interest: Education; Protestant agencies & churches.
Limitations: Applications not accepted. Giving primarily in TX. No grants to individuals.
Application information: Contributes only to pre-selected organizations.
Officers: Darwin Deason, Pres. and Treas.; Star Chen, V.P. and Secy.; Douglas Deason, V.P.
EIN: 752715549

8862
Andrew Delaney Foundation
5406 Western Hills Dr.
Austin, TX 78731-4824
Contact: Janet Delaney, V.P. and Tr.
E-mail: jld215@sbcglobal.net

Established in 1988 in TX.
Donor: Andrew Delaney.
Foundation type: Independent foundation.
Financial data (yr. ended 12/31/04): Assets, $4,051,471 (M); gifts received, $8,122; expenditures, $499,131; qualifying distributions, $488,067; giving activities include $440,990 for 23 grants (high: $333,206; low: $500).
Purpose and activities: Giving to education, and to family, youth and community services.
Fields of interest: Museums; Higher education; Environment, natural resources; Animal welfare; Health care, research; Health organizations, association; Human services; Protestant agencies & churches.
Type of support: General/operating support.
Limitations: Applications not accepted. Giving primarily in TX. No support for political organizations. No grants to individuals.
Application information: Contributes only to pre-selected organizations.
  Board meeting date(s): Varies
Officers and Trustees:* Andrew Delaney,* Pres.; Janet L. Delaney,* V.P. and Secy.-Treas.; Pauline M. Delaney; James P. Lee; Antoinette R. Stapper.
Number of staff: 1 part-time support.
EIN: 760265537
Selected grants: The following grants were reported in 2005.
$6,325 to Emerson Unitarian Church, Houston, TX. For operating support.
$2,500 to Planned Parenthood of Houston and Southeast Texas, Houston, TX. For operating support.
$2,200 to American Heritage Education Foundation, Houston, TX. For operating support.
$2,000 to American Red Cross, Houston, TX. For operating support.
$2,000 to Big Brothers Big Sisters of Greater Houston, Houston, TX. For operating support.
$1,500 to Foundation for the Retarded, Houston, TX. For operating support.
$1,500 to Houston Public Library, Houston, TX. For operating support.
$1,250 to Best Friends Animal Society, Kanab, UT. For operating support.
$1,000 to Houston Museum of Natural Science, Houston, TX. For operating support.
$500 to Salvation Army of Houston, Houston, TX. For operating support.

8863
The Michael and Susan Dell
Foundation ▼ ✧
P.O. Box 163867
Austin, TX 78716-3867
URL: http://www.msdf.org/

Established in 1999 in TX.
Donors: Michael Dell; Susan Dell.
Foundation type: Independent foundation.
Financial data (yr. ended 12/31/05): Assets, $1,226,020,349 (M); expenditures, $62,985,921; qualifying distributions, $61,302,619; giving activities include $56,238,527 for 272 grants (high: $4,573,128; low: $100; average: $50,000–$2,000,000).
Purpose and activities: The foundation's mission is to fund initiatives that seek to foster active minds, healthy bodies and a safe environment where children can thrive. It proactively seeks out opportunities to support or develop programs that address five essential focus areas: children's health, education, safety, youth development and early childhood care.
Fields of interest: Elementary/secondary education; Elementary/secondary school reform; Education; Health care, HMOs; Health care, clinics/centers; Health care, infants; Health care; Health care, patient services; Crime/violence prevention, abuse prevention; Crime/violence prevention, child abuse; Youth development; Children/youth, services; Children, day care; Community development.
Limitations: Giving on a local, regional, national and international basis. No support for medical research. No grants to individuals, or for fundraisers, sponsorships, or endowments.
Publications: Grants list.
Application information: See foundation Web site for guidelines and requirements. Unsolicited full proposals are not accepted. If the foundation finds that the preliminary grant request fulfills its mission, grant seekers will be notified and provided a password to access official grant application forms through its Web site.
  Initial approach: Submit preliminary grant request online
Officers and Directors:* Michael Dell,* Pres.; Susan Dell,* 1st V.P.; Alexander Dell,* 2nd V.P.; Marc Lisker, Secy.; Tricia Teegardin, Treas.; Janet Mountain, Exec. Dir.
EIN: 364336415
Selected grants: The following grants were reported in 2004.
$25,833,628 to Daughters of Charity Health Services of Austin, Austin, TX. 2 grants: $25,000,000 (For Dell Children's Medical Center of Central Texas), $833,628 (For insure a kid School Outreach).
$2,114,060 to Advanced Placement Strategies, Dallas, TX. For Texas High School Projects.
$2,000,000 to Fund for Public Schools, New York, NY. For NYC Leadership Academy.
$1,638,733 to Austin Community Foundation for the Capital Area, Austin, TX. 2 grants: $998,873 (For Project ADVANCE which provides coaching to students applying for college), $639,860 (For Project SMART, Science, Math and Reading Tutorials).
$1,000,000 to Harlem Childrens Zone, New York, NY. For Harlem Gems Head Start Expansion.
$765,000 to LAs BEST (Better Educated Students for Tomorrow), Los Angeles, CA. For after-school care.

$545,082 to University of Texas-Pan American, Edinburg, TX. For Advancement via Individual Determination (AVID).
$488,000 to Seton Fund of the Daughters of Charity of Saint Vincent de Paul, Austin, TX. For insure a kid.

8864
The Dell Foundation ✧
1 Dell Way
Round Rock, TX 78682
Contact: Lisa Huddleson, Secy.
E-mail: the_dell_foundation@dell.com; *URL:* http://www.dell.com/dellfoundation

Established in 1995.
Donors: Dell Computer Corp.; Dell Inc.; Dell USA.
Foundation type: Company-sponsored foundation.
Financial data (yr. ended 1/28/05): Assets, $12,245,768 (M); gifts received, $2,503,912; expenditures, $2,281,905; qualifying distributions, $1,987,514; giving activities include $1,826,714 for 300+ grants (high: $625,000).
Purpose and activities: The foundation supports organizations involved with education, health, human services, and technology access. Special emphasis is directed toward programs designed to benefit children and youth, newborn to 18 years of age.
Fields of interest: Education, reading; Education; Health care; Children/youth, services; Children, services; Human services; Computer science; General charitable giving.
Type of support: General/operating support; Employee volunteer services.
Limitations: Giving primarily in Twin Falls County, ID, Forsyth and Guilford counties, NC, Butler and Hamilton counties, OH, Oklahoma County, OK, Douglas County, OR, Davidson and Wilson counties, TN, and Bell, McLennan, Travis, and Williamson counties, TX. No support for civic, religious, or political organizations or sports organizations. No grants to individuals, or for academic or research projects, school fundraisers, capital campaigns or endowments, sponsorships, marketing opportunities, or event fundraisers, or sports events.
Publications: Application guidelines; Grants list.
Application information: The next cycle of Healthy Communities grants begins in 2008. Application form required.
  Initial approach: Download application form and E-mail to foundation
  Copies of proposal: 1
  Deadline(s): None for Open Grants; May 15 for Literate Communities grants; July 14 for Connected Communities grants
  Board meeting date(s): Apr., July, Oct., and Jan.
  Final notification: 2 to 14 weeks for Open Grants; June 19 for Literate Communities grants; Aug. 28 for Connected Communities grants
Officers and Directors: Paul McKinnon, Chair. and Pres.; Lisa Huddleson,* Secy.; Brian MacDonald,* Treas.; Dick Hunter; Pat Nathan; Susan Sheskey; Carl Stolle; Karen Quintos; Thurmond Woodard.
Number of staff: 1 full-time professional; 1 full-time support.
EIN: 742732496
Selected grants: The following grants were reported in 2005.
$2,000,000 to American Red Cross, National Headquarters, DC. For relief efforts for Hurricane Katrina.

$26,000 to Big Brothers/Big Sisters. 2 grants: $25,000, $1,000
$25,000 to Austin Public Library Foundation, Austin, TX.
$25,000 to Communities in Schools, Alexandria, VA.
$25,000 to Girl Scouts of the U.S.A..
$25,000 to Junior Achievement.
$25,000 to Salvation Army.
$25,000 to Youth and Family Alliance, Austin, TX.
$1,000 to Family Eldercare, Austin, TX.

8865
Enrico & Sandra di Portanova Charitable Foundation ◇ ☆
P.O. Box 27285
Houston, TX   77227-7285

Established in 1993 in TX.
Foundation type: Independent foundation.
Financial data (yr. ended 12/31/05): Assets, $7,268,870 (M); expenditures, $513,083; qualifying distributions, $350,000; giving activities include $350,000 for 45 grants (high: $25,000; low: $500).
Purpose and activities: Giving primarily for children, youth, and social services.
Fields of interest: Education, early childhood education; Health care; Human services; Children/ youth, services; Roman Catholic federated giving programs; Mentally disabled; Crime/abuse victims; Economically disadvantaged.
Type of support: General/operating support.
Limitations: Applications not accepted. Giving primarily in TX. No grants to individuals.
Application information: Contributes only to pre-selected organizations.
Officers: Lewis M. Linn, Pres.; Esther M. Perrine,* Secy.-Treas.
Director: Jennifer Hovas.
EIN: 760408460
Selected grants: The following grants were reported in 2004.
$25,000 to Community Family Centers, Houston, TX. For Early Childhood Education Program.
$25,000 to Houston Community Health Centers, Houston, TX. For renovation.
$15,000 to Child Advocates, Houston, TX. For court program.
$15,000 to Greater Houston Community Foundation, Houston, TX.
$12,000 to Amigos de las Americas, Houston, TX. For general operating support.
$10,000 to Exchange Club Center for the Prevention of Child Abuse of Houston, Escape Family Resource Center, Houston, TX. For program support.
$10,000 to Houston Achievement Place, Houston, TX. For Project Class Early Childhood Initiative.
$10,000 to Pro-Vision Ministries, Houston, TX. For general operating support.
$10,000 to Rise School of Houston, Houston, TX. For operating support.
$5,000 to Justice for Children, Houston, TX. For children's rights and protection from abuse.

8866
The Raymond Dickson Foundation ◇
P.O. Box 406
Hallettsville, TX   77964-0406   (361) 798-2531

Established in 1958 in TX.
Donors: Raymond Dickson†; Alton C. Allen†.
Foundation type: Independent foundation.
Financial data (yr. ended 12/31/05): Assets, $12,997,161 (M); expenditures, $821,490; qualifying distributions, $686,031; giving activities include $686,031 for 40 grants (high: $150,000; low: $1,000).
Purpose and activities: Primary areas of interest include education, medical research, and medical facilities.
Fields of interest: Arts; Elementary/secondary education; Higher education; Education; Hospitals (general); Medical research, institute; Biomedicine research; Human services; Children/youth, services.
Type of support: General/operating support; Building/renovation; Scholarship funds.
Limitations: Giving limited to TX. No grants to individuals, or for building funds.
Publications: Application guidelines; Program policy statement.
Application information: Application form not required.
Initial approach: Proposal
Copies of proposal: 1
Board meeting date(s): Oct. or Nov.
Trustees: Jessie L. Allen; Wilbur Baber, Jr.; Curtis Gunn, Jr.; Dunham F. Jewett; Curtis T. Vaughan III.
EIN: 746052983
Selected grants: The following grants were reported in 2003.
$100,000 to Lavaca Exposition Association, Hallettsville, TX. For general operating support.
$100,000 to Neurological Research Foundation, Houston, TX. For research.
$45,000 to Sacred Heart School, Hallettsville, TX. For computers and communication equipment.
$42,500 to Lavaca Medical Center, Hallettsville, TX. For general operating support.
$25,000 to Saint Johns School, Houston, TX. For general operating support.
$25,000 to Texas A & M University Development Foundation, College Station, TX. For scholarships.
$20,000 to Southwest Foundation for Biomedical Research, San Antonio, TX. For general operating support.
$20,000 to Witte Museum, San Antonio, TX. For general operating support.
$10,000 to James Dick Foundation for the Performing Arts, Round Top, TX. For general operating support.
$10,000 to Lavaca County Senior Citizens, Hallettsville, TX. For general operating support.

8867
Robert and Michelle Diener Foundation ◇ ☆
10710 Strait Ln.
Dallas, TX   75229-5427
Contact: Robert B. Diener, Dir.
FL tel.: (305) 358-8333

Established in 2001 in TX.
Donors: Robert B. Diener; Michelle S. Diener.
Foundation type: Independent foundation.
Financial data (yr. ended 12/31/05): Assets, $36,682,443 (M); expenditures, $1,150,718; qualifying distributions, $818,776; giving activities include $818,776 for grants.

Purpose and activities: Giving primarily for Jewish education, agencies and temples; funding also for human services.
Fields of interest: Museums (children's); Education; Hospitals (general); Human services; Jewish federated giving programs; Jewish agencies & temples.
Limitations: Giving primarily in FL.
Application information: Application form not required.
Deadline(s): None
Directors: Michelle S. Diener; Robert B. Diener; David S. Litman.
EIN: 752919060
Selected grants: The following grants were reported in 2004.
$129,500 to Hillel Community Day School, North Miami Beach, FL.
$26,100 to Miami Childrens Museum, Miami, FL.
$10,000 to High School in Israel, North Miami, FL.
$1,500 to Tulane University, New Orleans, LA.
$1,200 to Vizcayans, The, Miami, FL.
$1,000 to Israel Project, DC.
$1,000 to Victory School, Aventura, FL.

8868
Dodge Jones Foundation ▼ ◇
P.O. Box 176
Abilene, TX   79604-0176   (325) 673-6429
Contact: Lawrence E. Gill, V.P. and Grants Admin.

Incorporated in 1954 in TX.
Donors: Ruth Leggett Jones†; and others.
Foundation type: Independent foundation.
Financial data (yr. ended 12/31/04): Assets, $127,532,036 (M); expenditures, $10,500,614; qualifying distributions, $7,763,907; giving activities include $7,516,263 for 144 grants (high: $620,000; low: $600; average: $5,000–$50,000).
Purpose and activities: Support for education, the arts, health, community funds, and youth programs.
Fields of interest: Arts; Education; Health care; Health organizations, association; Youth, services; Federated giving programs.
Type of support: General/operating support.
Limitations: Giving primarily in Abilene, TX. No grants to individuals.
Application information: Application form not required.
Initial approach: Letter
Copies of proposal: 1
Deadline(s): None
Board meeting date(s): Varies
Final notification: Varies; negative responses are immediate
Officers and Directors:* Julia Jones Matthews, Pres.; Joseph E. Canon,* Exec. V.P. and Exec. Dir.; Thomas R. Allen, V.P. and C.F.O.; Lawrence E. Gill, V.P. and Grants Admin.; Linda Buckner, Secy.-Treas.; Joe B. Matthews; Kade L. Matthews; Jill Matthews Wilkinson.
Number of staff: 1 full-time professional; 1 part-time professional; 3 part-time support.
EIN: 756006386
Selected grants: The following grants were reported in 2004.
$620,000 to Down Home Ranch, Elgin, TX. For capital campaign.
$600,000 to Abilene Independent School District, Abilene, TX. For administration building.
$507,562 to Advanced Placement Strategies, Dallas, TX. For advanced placement incentive program in Abilene Independent School District.

$500,262 to West Texas Rehabilitation Center Foundation, Abilene, TX. For endowment campaign.

$500,000 to Hendrick Medical Center Foundation, Abilene, TX. To construct new nursing school facility.

$500,000 to West Texas Rehabilitation Center, Abilene, TX. For endowment campaign.

$487,500 to Taylor County Historical Foundation, Abilene, TX. For Texas Forts Trail Visitors Center.

$125,000 to House That Kerry Built, The Center for Medically Fragile Children, Abilene, TX. For operating support.

$100,000 to College for All Texans Foundation Closing the Gaps, Austin, TX. For Closing the Gap campaign.

$25,000 to Commemorative Air Force, Midland, TX. To create Texas Medal of Honor memorial sculpture.

8869
The M. S. Doss Foundation, Inc. ▼ ✧
P.O. Box 1677
Seminole, TX 79360-1677 (915) 758-2770
Contact: Joe K. McGill, Pres.

Established in 1985 in TX.
Donors: M.S. Doss†; Meek Lane Doss†; Twin Mountain Supply, Inc.
Foundation type: Independent foundation.
Financial data (yr. ended 12/31/05): Assets, $69,620,458 (M); expenditures, $4,645,893; qualifying distributions, $3,971,108; giving activities include $3,735,574 for 55 grants (high: $550,077; low: $166; average: $25,000–$50,000), and $75,537 for 4 foundation-administered programs.
Purpose and activities: Support primarily for family and youth services, clubs, and centers; support also for scholarships for higher education.
Fields of interest: Higher education; Youth development, centers/clubs; Children/youth, services; Family services; Residential/custodial care; Community development.
Type of support: General/operating support; Building/renovation; Equipment; Endowments; Scholarship funds.
Limitations: Giving primarily in the eastern NM and western TX area; giving limited to Gaines County, TX, for scholarships. No grants to individuals directly.
Application information: Scholarship payments made directly to the college on behalf of named recipient. Application form required.
   Initial approach: Letter of inquiry
   Copies of proposal: 1
   Deadline(s): None
   Board meeting date(s): Feb. and as required
   Final notification: Following board meeting
Officers and Trustees:* Joe K. McGill,* Chair. and Pres.; Richard Spraberry,* V.P.; Billie Thompson,* Secy.; Stuart Robertson,* Treas.; Julia Narvarte Romanow.
Number of staff: 1 full-time professional; 1 full-time support; 1 part-time support.
EIN: 751945227
Selected grants: The following grants were reported in 2005.

$550,077 to University Medical Center Foundation, Lubbock, TX. For medical equipment and repairs.

$500,000 to Civic Development Foundation, Weatherford, TX. For building renovations.

$300,000 to University of Texas M. D. Anderson Cancer Center, Houston, TX. For radiology equipment.

$298,622 to Covenant Health System Foundation, Lubbock, TX. For equipment.

$220,000 to Texas Scottish Rite Hospital for Children, Dallas, TX. For building renovations.

$136,545 to M. S. Doss Youth Center, Seminole, TX. For endowment, operating support, and equipment.

$75,000 to Day Nursery of Abilene, Abilene, TX. For capital campaign.

$50,000 to Texas A & M Foundation, College Station, TX. For scholarship endowment.

$34,305 to Helen Keller International, New York, NY. For equipment.

$31,350 to Family Outreach, Lubbock, Lubbock, TX. For equipment.

8870
James R. Dougherty, Jr. Foundation, Inc
P.O. Box 640
Beeville, TX 78104-0640
Contact: Daren R. Wilder, Treas.

Established in 1950. Incorporated in 2002 in TX.
Foundation type: Independent foundation.
Financial data (yr. ended 12/31/05): Assets, $6,244,869 (M); expenditures, $404,126; qualifying distributions, $337,882; giving activities include $320,645 for 114 grants (high: $25,000; low: $100).
Type of support: General/operating support; Continuing support; Income development; Management development/capacity building; Annual campaigns; Capital campaigns; Building/renovation; Equipment; Endowments; Program development; Seed money; Curriculum development; Scholarship funds; Research; Technical assistance; Program evaluation; Matching/challenge support.
Application information:
   Initial approach: Letter
   Copies of proposal: 1
   Deadline(s): Mar. 1 and Sept. 1
   Board meeting date(s): Spring and fall
   Final notification: 3 to 4 weeks after Board meeting
Officer: Daren R. Wilder, Treas.
Trustees: Rachael Carr Magennis; Beatrice Rossi-Landi; Frances Carr Tapp; Ben F. Vaughan III; Genevieve Vaughan; Rachael Pauley.
Number of staff: 1 part-time professional; 2 part-time support.
EIN: 020583552

8871
The Duda Family Foundation ✧
1 Galleria Twr.
13355 Noel Rd., LB3, Ste. 1315
Dallas, TX 75240-6603 (972) 934-2244
Contact: Steven F. Tabor

Established in 1997.
Donors: Fritz L. Duda; Mrs. Fritz L. Duda.
Foundation type: Independent foundation.
Financial data (yr. ended 12/31/05): Assets, $18,397,721 (M); expenditures, $877,407; qualifying distributions, $755,589; giving activities include $755,589 for 100 grants (high: $150,000; low: $200; average: $1,000–$10,000).

Purpose and activities: Giving primarily to Roman Catholic churches, and for education, including Roman Catholic higher and secondary education; some funding also for children, youth, and social services.
Fields of interest: Performing arts; Arts; Elementary/secondary education; Higher education; Education; Zoos/zoological societies; Hospitals (general); Hospitals (specialty); Health organizations, association; Cancer research; Human services; Children/youth, services; Roman Catholic agencies & churches.
Limitations: Giving primarily in CA and TX; some giving nationally. No grants to individuals.
Application information:
   Initial approach: Letter
   Deadline(s): Oct. 31
Trustees: Fritz L. Duda; Fritz L. Duda, Jr.; James F. Duda; Mary L. Duda; Leigh A. Duda Scott; Lendy D. Duda Vail.
EIN: 436765664

8872
John S. Dunn Research Foundation ▼ ✧
3355 W. Alabama St., Ste. 720
Houston, TX 77098-1718
Contact: Lloyd J. Gregory, Jr. M.D., Exec. V.P. and Medical Advisor

Established in 1985 in TX.
Donor: John S. Dunn, Sr.†.
Foundation type: Independent foundation.
Financial data (yr. ended 12/31/04): Assets, $106,000,989 (M); gifts received, $150; expenditures, $6,193,618; qualifying distributions, $5,116,890; giving activities include $4,874,840 for 30 grants (high: $650,000; low: $5,000; average: $10,000–$100,000).
Purpose and activities: Giving limited to health and medical-related organizations, especially hospitals; support also for cancer, other medical research, and freestanding clinics.
Fields of interest: Hospitals (general); Health care; Health organizations, association; Cancer; Medical research, institute; Cancer research; Biological sciences.
Type of support: Endowments; Professorships; Research; Matching/challenge support.
Limitations: Giving limited to TX. No grants to individuals, or for multi-year or seed money grants.
Publications: Application guidelines; Informational brochure (including application guidelines).
Application information: Application form not required.
   Initial approach: Letter
   Copies of proposal: 1
   Deadline(s): None
   Board meeting date(s): Full board meets quarterly; Executive Committee meets on the 4th Wed. of each month
   Final notification: Written notice 1 week following meeting
Officers and Trustees:* John S. Dunn, Jr.,* Pres.; Lloyd J. Gregory, Jr., M.D.*, Exec. V.P. and Medical Advisor; C. Harold Wallace,* V.P. and Secy.; Dagmar Dunn Pickens Gipe,* V.P.; Charles W. Hall,* V.P.; J. Dickson Rogers,* V.P.
Number of staff: 1 full-time professional; 2 full-time support.
EIN: 741933660
Selected grants: The following grants were reported in 2003.

$649,947 to University of Texas M. D. Anderson Cancer Center, Houston, TX. For budgetary support.
$500,000 to Saint Lukes Episcopal Hospital, Houston, TX. For CV MRI for research.
$350,000 to University of Texas Health Science Center, Houston, TX. 2 grants: $100,000 (For mouse models of human disease and cancer), $250,000 (For Chair in Physiology and Medicine).
$300,000 to Greater Houston Partnership, Health Services Steering Committee, Houston, TX. For salaries for nursing programs.
$250,000 to Baylor College of Medicine, Baylor Heart Clinic, Houston, TX. For JSD Chair and Clinical Echo Research.
$250,000 to Saint Joseph Hospital Foundation, John S. Dunn, Sr. Emergency Care Center, Houston, TX.
$200,000 to Texas Heart Institute, Houston, TX. For research, education, and patient care.
$107,714 to Shriners Hospitals for Children, Houston, TX. For salaries.
$100,000 to San Jose Clinic, Houston, TX. To continue support for dentist.

8873
Devary Durrill Foundation, Inc. ◇
615 S. Upper Broadway
Corpus Christi, TX 78401

Established in 1984 in TX.
Donor: William R. Durrill.
Foundation type: Independent foundation.
Financial data (yr. ended 12/31/03): Assets, $9,254,935 (M); gifts received, $564,715; expenditures, $1,411,731; qualifying distributions, $1,123,221; giving activities include $1,084,060 for grants (high: $637,349).
Fields of interest: Arts; Higher education; Human services.
Limitations: Applications not accepted. Giving limited to Corpus Christi, TX. No grants to individuals.
Application information: Contributes only to pre-selected organizations.
Officers: William R. Durrill, Pres.; Shirley R. Durrill, Secy.-Treas.
Directors: Ginger Durrill; Melissa Durrill; Michele Durrill; William R. Durrill, Jr.
EIN: 742370613
Selected grants: The following grants were reported in 2003.
$637,349 to Art Center of Corpus Christi, Corpus Christi, TX. For building construction costs.
$446,057 to Texas A & M University, Corpus Christi, TX. For construction of artwork on college campus.

8874
Dynegy Foundation, Inc. ◇
1000 Louisiana St., Ste. 5800
Houston, TX 77002 (713) 767-0092

Established in 2001.
Donor: Dynegy Corp.
Foundation type: Company-sponsored foundation.
Financial data (yr. ended 12/31/03): Assets, $0 (M); gifts received, $37,279; expenditures, $829,675; qualifying distributions, $829,675; giving activities include $829,675 for 1 grant.

Purpose and activities: The foundation supports organizations involved with education, health, youth development, and community development.
Fields of interest: Higher education; Education; Health organizations, association; Youth development; Community development.
Limitations: Applications not accepted. Giving primarily in IL and TX. No grants to individuals.
Application information: Contributes only to pre-selected organizations.
Officers and Directors:* Deborah A. Fiorito,* Chair.; Sara Speer Selber, Pres.; Carla Truitt, Secy.; Mariam M. Davenport; Alec G. Dreyer; Stephen A. Fubacher; Michael R. Mott; Blake R. Young.
EIN: 760686959

8875
J. Tom Eady Charitable Trust ◇
c/o Corsicana National Bank & Trust
P.O. Box 624
Corsicana, TX 75151
Contact: Les Leskoven, Sr. V.P. and Trust Off., Corsicana National Bank & Trust

Established in 2000 in TX.
Donor: John Thomas Eady‡.
Foundation type: Independent foundation.
Financial data (yr. ended 12/31/05): Assets, $9,532,967 (M); expenditures, $501,844; qualifying distributions, $468,765; giving activities include $402,350 for 31 grants (high: $60,000; low: $950), and $62,500 for 14 grants to individuals (high: $7,500; low: $2,500).
Fields of interest: Arts; Education; Youth development; Human services; Community development; Christian agencies & churches.
Type of support: General/operating support; Continuing support; Annual campaigns; Capital campaigns; Building/renovation; Equipment; Program development; Scholarships—to individuals; Matching/challenge support.
Limitations: Giving limited to Navarro County, TX.
Application information: Application form not required.
  Initial approach: Letter
  Deadline(s): None
  Board meeting date(s): Jan., Apr., July, and Oct.
  Final notification: 3 month or less, depending on time of receipt
Trustee: Corsicana National Bank.
EIN: 756604134
Selected grants: The following grants were reported in 2004.
$50,000 to First United Methodist Church, Corsicana, TX. For operating support.
$50,000 to United Way of Navarro County, Corsicana, TX. For operating support.
$50,000 to YMCA of Corsicana, Corsicana, TX. For operating support.
$35,000 to Corsicana, City of, Corsicana, TX. For operating support.
$30,255 to Chamber Foundation, Corsicana Area, Corsicana, TX. For operating support.
$15,000 to Corsicana Youth Baseball, Corsicana, TX. For capital projects.
$13,500 to Camp Fire USA, Corsicana Council, Corsicana, TX. For operating support.
$7,500 to James L. Collins Catholic School, Corsicana, TX. For operating support.
$7,500 to Pregnancy Counseling Service of Abilene, Abilene, TX.
$5,000 to Food Pantry Ministry, Corsicana, TX. For operating support.

8876
East Texas Communities Foundation, Inc. ◇
(formerly East Texas Area Foundation)
315 N. Broadway, Ste. 210
Tyler, TX 75702 (903) 533-0208
Contact: Kyle L. Penney, Pres.
FAX: (903) 533-0258; E-mail: etcf@etcf.org;
Additional tel.: (866) 533-3823; URL: http://www.etcf.org

Established in 1989 in TX.
Foundation type: Community foundation.
Financial data (yr. ended 12/31/03): Assets, $17,585,117 (M); gifts received, $5,638,202; expenditures, $1,371,549; giving activities include $1,101,288 for 195 grants (high: $102,300; low: $50).
Purpose and activities: The foundation seeks to promote charitable giving which enhances the quality of life. The foundation does this by: 1) serving as a flexible and cost-effective vehicle for donors to invest in the community; 2) promoting philanthropy in all its forms; and 3) building permanent endowments for the region's changing issues and opportunities. Primary areas of grantmaking include arts and humanities, education, health, and human services.
Fields of interest: Humanities; Historic preservation/historical societies; Arts; Education; Hospitals (general); Health care; Youth, services; Human services; Community development; Engineering/technology.
Type of support: Endowments; Scholarship funds; In-kind gifts; Matching/challenge support.
Limitations: Giving primarily in eastern TX. No support for private schools, or religious or sectarian purposes. No grants to individuals (except for scholarships), or for budget deficits, debt retirement, or restructuring, conferences, or travel, capital campaigns, general operating expenses, endowments or reserve funds, or scholarly research, biomedical, or clinical studies.
Publications: Annual report; Informational brochure; Newsletter.
Application information: Visit foundation Web site for application guidelines. Application form required.
  Initial approach: Letter
  Copies of proposal: 15
  Deadline(s): Oct. 2
  Board meeting date(s): 3rd Tues., monthly
  Final notification: Dec.
Officers and Directors:* Whit Riter,* Chair.; Scott Terry,* Vice-Chair. and Investment Comm. Chair.; Kyle L. Penney, Pres.; W. Fred Smith,* Secy.; Thomas A. Lowery, M.D.*, Treas.; Michelle Brookshire, Mktg. Comm. Chair.; John Payne,* Policy Comm. Chair.; Allen Burt, Dir. Emeritus; F. William Martin, Dir. Emeritus; H.T. Smith, Dir. Emeritus; Craig S. Adams; Timothy F. Alexander; James Richard Allen; Michael D. Allen; Lawrence L. Anderson, M.D.; Carl E. Bochow, Sr.; Jeff Buford; Herbert Buie; Wendy W. Gerard; Richard W. Jett, Jr.; Melvin B. Lovelady; Gordon L. Northcutt; James I. Perkins; Sam Roosth; Sandy Shepard*; Linda Ryan Thomas; Kenneth W. Threlkeld; Laura Koenig Young.
Number of staff: 1 full-time professional; 2 part-time support.
EIN: 752309138

8877
The EDS Foundation ✧

5400 Legacy Dr., H3-6F-47
Plano, TX 75024 (972) 605-8429
Contact: Diane Spradlin, Exec. Dir.
E-mail: diane.spradlin-eds@eds.com; URL: http://www.eds.com/about/community/foundation

Established in 2000 in TX.
Donor: Electronic Data Systems Corp.
Foundation type: Company-sponsored foundation.
Financial data (yr. ended 12/31/05): Assets, $6,276,022 (M); expenditures, $648,031; qualifying distributions, $632,141; giving activities include $547,157 for 24 grants (high: $49,968; low: $5,000).
Purpose and activities: The foundation supports organizations involved with arts and culture, education, health, human services, and bridging the digital divide.
Fields of interest: Arts education; Arts; Education; Health care, equal rights; Reproductive health, prenatal care; Public health; Public health, communicable diseases; Health care; Youth development, adult & child programs; Children, day care; Human services; Computer science.
Type of support: Continuing support; General/operating support; Program development.
Limitations: Giving on a national and international basis. No support for pass-through foundations, athletic teams, fraternal, social, or labor organizations, political or partisan organizations, private foundations, or discriminatory organizations, or organizations lacking a current employee volunteer partnership with EDS. No grants to individuals, or for debt reduction, sponsorships, trips or tours, athletic events, or journal or program advertising.
Publications: Application guidelines; Annual report; Grants list; Program policy statement.
Application information: Multi-year funding is not automatic. Application form required.
Initial approach: Download application form and mail proposal and application form to foundation
Copies of proposal: 1
Deadline(s): Feb. 26, June 25, and Oct. 15
Board meeting date(s): Apr. 30, Aug. 27, and Dec. 10
Officers and Directors: Richard H. Brown, Pres.; Troy W. Todd, V.P.; Janice Jones, Secy.; Scott J. Krenz, Treas.; Diane Spradlin, Exec. Dir.; Albert J. Edmonds; Ray L. Hunt; Tom Mattia; Steve Smith; Myrna B. Vance.
Number of staff: 2 part-time professional.
EIN: 752859297
Selected grants: The following grants were reported in 2004.
$62,808 to John C. Ford Program, Dallas, TX.
$51,631 to Hoop Dreams Scholarship Fund, DC.
$51,469 to Cerebral Palsy Research Foundation of Kansas, Wichita, KS.
$49,506 to Focus: Hope, Detroit, MI.
$44,254 to Special Olympics of Indiana, Indianapolis, IN.
$42,600 to Wake Education Partnership, Raleigh, NC.
$38,893 to Mayors Time, Detroit, MI.
$30,364 to Plano Symphony Orchestra, Plano, TX.
$24,974 to BestPrep, Brooklyn Park, MN.
$15,986 to Big Brothers and Big Sisters of Green County, Tulsa, OK.

8878
Educational Advancement Foundation ✧

c/o Grant Committee
2303 Rio Grande St.
Austin, TX 78705 (512) 469-1700
E-mail: info@educationaladvancementfoundation.org; URL: http://www.educationaladvancementfoundation.org

Established in 1969 in TX.
Donors: Harry Lucas, Jr.; Louis Beecherl; Gayle Ball; William Mahavier; E. Paul Mosbo; David Murphy; Allen Stenger; Larry Wadle; Kenneth Whipple; Kodosky Foundation; Lucas Petroleum Group.
Foundation type: Independent foundation.
Financial data (yr. ended 12/31/05): Assets, $1,330,826 (M); gifts received, $982,412; expenditures, $613,496; qualifying distributions, $579,465; giving activities include $319,432 for 14 grants (high: $103,646; low: $1,325).
Fields of interest: Elementary/secondary education; Higher education; Education; Mathematics.
Type of support: Endowments; Seed money; Research; Grants to individuals.
Limitations: Giving primarily in TX.
Publications: Application guidelines; Informational brochure.
Application information: See foundation Web site for downloadable grant application package, application guidelines and procedures. Application form required.
Initial approach: Proposal
Deadline(s): None
Officer: Fain Bock, Treas.
Trustees: Hamilton Beazley; Edward Burger; Earl C. Lairson; Alfred E. Leiser, M.D.; Terry Lester; Harry Lucas, Jr.
Advisory Committee: Greg Cotter; Bob Lawless; Carol Lucas.
Number of staff: 1 part-time support.
EIN: 237001761

8879
Bryant Edwards Foundation, Inc. ✧

807 8th St., 2nd Fl.
Wichita Falls, TX 76301-3381

Established in 1959.
Donors: Bryant Edwards†; Dorothy B. Edwards†.
Foundation type: Independent foundation.
Financial data (yr. ended 10/31/05): Assets, $16,888,738 (M); gifts received, $569,000; expenditures, $706,285; qualifying distributions, $565,280; giving activities include $553,030 for 10 grants (high: $250,000; low: $1,000).
Fields of interest: Arts; Elementary school/education; Higher education; Education; Youth development.
Limitations: Applications not accepted. Giving primarily in Wichita Falls, TX. No grants to individuals.
Application information: Contributes only to pre-selected organizations.
Officers and Directors:* Mac W. Cannedy, Jr.,* Pres.; Dennis D. Cannedy,* V.P.; Erwin Davenport,* Secy.; John W. Barfield,* Treas.
EIN: 756012973

8880
J. E. S. Edwards Foundation

4413 Cumberland Rd. N.
Fort Worth, TX 76116 (817) 737-6924
Contact: Jareen E. Schmidt, Pres.

Established in 1976 in TX.
Donor: Jareen E. Schmidt.
Foundation type: Independent foundation.
Financial data (yr. ended 7/31/05): Assets, $6,788,221 (M); gifts received, $100,000; expenditures, $375,689; qualifying distributions, $324,000; giving activities include $324,000 for 34 grants (high: $25,000; low: $500).
Purpose and activities: Grants largely for social services, including programs for women, hunger, the disadvantaged, and child welfare; support also for health and youth agencies, and Christian missionary programs.
Fields of interest: Child development, education; Adult/continuing education; Health care; Cancer; Medical research, institute; Cancer research; Food services; Human services; Youth, services; Child development, services; Women, centers/services; Christian agencies & churches; Religion; Women; Economically disadvantaged.
Type of support: General/operating support; Capital campaigns; Equipment; Emergency funds; Research.
Limitations: Giving primarily in Fort Worth, TX. No grants to individuals, or for scholarships.
Application information: Grant requests outside of the Fort Worth, TX, area considered only if program is not available within Fort Worth. Application form not required.
Initial approach: Letter
Copies of proposal: 1
Deadline(s): June 1
Board meeting date(s): June
Officers: Jareen E. Schmidt, Pres.; Stace Sewell, V.P.; Sheryl E. Bowen, Secy.-Treas.
EIN: 510173260
Selected grants: The following grants were reported in 2005.
$25,000 to Breedlove Dehydrated Foods, Lubbock, TX.
$25,000 to Texas Baptist Men, Dallas, TX.
$15,000 to American Cancer Society, Fort Worth, TX.
$15,000 to Hawaii Baptist Academy, Honolulu, HI.
$14,000 to World Hunger Relief, Elm Mott, TX.
$10,000 to Catholic Charities of the Diocese of Fort Worth, Fort Worth, TX.
$10,000 to Mental Health Mental Retardation of Tarrant County, Fort Worth, TX.
$10,000 to Mercy Ships, Garden Valley, TX.
$10,000 to Romanian Missionary Society, Wheaton, IL.
$5,000 to Cenikor Foundation, Fort Worth, TX.

8881
El Paso Community Foundation ▼

310 N. Mesa, 10th Fl.
P.O. Box 272
El Paso, TX 79943 (915) 533-4020
Contact: Janice W. Windle, Pres.
FAX: (915) 532-0716; *E-mail:* info@epcf.org; URL: http://www.epcf.org

Incorporated in 1977 in TX.
Foundation type: Community foundation.
Financial data (yr. ended 12/31/05): Assets, $94,004,567 (M); gifts received, $7,252,351;

expenditures, $11,252,629; giving activities include $7,608,712 for 900 grants (high: $946,922; low: $100).

Purpose and activities: The foundation seeks to establish permanent charitable endowments; provide a vehicle for donors' varied interests; promote local philanthropy; and provide leadership and resources in addressing local challenges and opportunities. Primary areas of interest include education, human services, health and disabilities, arts and humanities, the environment and animals, and community development.

Fields of interest: Humanities; Arts; Education; Environment; Animal welfare; Health care; Human services; Community development.

International interests: Mexico.

Type of support: General/operating support; Continuing support; Program development; Seed money; Scholarship funds; Technical assistance; Matching/challenge support.

Limitations: Giving limited to the El Paso, TX, area. No support for medical or academic research, or religious purposes. No grants to individuals (except for scholarships), or for deficit financing, annual campaigns, travel, capital campaigns, fundraising events, endowments, or ongoing support.

Publications: Application guidelines; Annual report; Informational brochure; Newsletter.

Application information: Visit foundation Web site for Letter of Inquiry and application guidelines. Based upon review of the Letter of Inquiry, the foundation will decide whether to invite the organization to submit a full proposal. Application form required.

> *Initial approach:* Complete online Letter of Inquiry (no longer than 2 pages)
> *Copies of proposal:* 1
> *Deadline(s):* Feb. 1 and Aug. 1 for Letter of Inquiry
> *Board meeting date(s):* May and Nov.
> *Final notification:* Following board consideration

Officers and Directors: * Roger Ortiz, D.D.S.,* Chair.; Susan Gray Kisler,* Vice-Chair.; Tom Porter,* Vice-Chair.; Janice W. Windle, Pres.; Virginia Martinez, Exec. V.P.; Carmen Castorena, V.P., Finance; Cathy Hill, V.P., Donor Rels.; Eric Pearson, V.P., Exec. Office; Nestor Valencia, V.P., Planning; Carl E. Ryan, Secy.; Carolyn R. Chambers,* Treas.; Richard Harlan "Rickie" Feuille; Ramiro Guzman; Guillermo Avila; Frances R. Axelson; Leigh V. Bloss; Patricia Saucedo Burdick; Tommye Duncan; Mabel Fayant; Steve Hoy; Sharon Smith Kidd; Margie Melby.

Number of staff: 7 full-time professional; 1 part-time professional; 4 full-time support.

EIN: 741839536

Selected grants: The following grants were reported in 2005.

$2,419,000 to Plaza Theater Performing Arts Center, El Paso, TX.

$100,000 to Greater New Orleans Foundation, New Orleans, LA.

$32,000 to El Paso Symphony Orchestra Association, El Paso, TX.

$30,000 to Mascarenas Foundation, El Paso, TX.

$18,000 to Border WaterWorks, Santa Fe, NM.

$15,000 to International AIDS Empowerment Project, El Paso, TX.

$15,000 to Planned Parenthood Center of El Paso, El Paso, TX.

$10,000 to Opportunity Center for the Homeless, El Paso, TX.

$5,000 to Nonprofit Enterprise Center, El Paso, TX.

$4,500 to Center Against Family Violence, El Paso, TX.

8882
El Paso Corporate Foundation ▼ ◇
(formerly El Paso Energy Foundation)
P.O. Box 2511
Houston, TX 77252-2511 (713) 420-2878
Contact: Gloria Moritz, Sr. Coord., Community Rels.
Application address: 1001 Louisiana St., Houston, TX 77002

Established in 1992 in TX.

Donors: El Paso Natural Gas Co.; El Paso Energy Corp.; El Paso Corp.

Foundation type: Company-sponsored foundation.

Financial data (yr. ended 12/31/04): Assets, $15,536,035 (M); expenditures, $3,519,858; qualifying distributions, $3,494,854; giving activities include $3,228,958 for 151 grants (high: $617,323; low: $500), $7,000 for 3 grants to individuals (high: $3,500; low: $1,750), and $258,896 for 199 employee matching gifts.

Purpose and activities: The foundation supports organizations involved with education, mental health, human services, and community development.

Fields of interest: Higher education; Business school/education; Education; Substance abuse, services; Mental health, treatment; Mental health/ crisis services, hot-lines; Crime/violence prevention; Recreation, parks/playgrounds; Youth development, services; Children/youth, services; Family services; Aging, centers/services; Women, centers/services; Human services; Community development, neighborhood development; Community development; Federated giving programs; Minorities; Women.

Type of support: Scholarships—to individuals; General/operating support; Continuing support; Annual campaigns; Building/renovation; Program development; Curriculum development; Employee volunteer services; Employee matching gifts; Donated equipment.

Limitations: Giving limited to areas of company operations. No support for religious organizations not of direct benefit to the entire community, political, youth sports, athletic, veterans', or fraternal organizations, national health organizations or the local chapters of national health organizations, or hospitals. No grants to individuals (except for scholarships), or for endowments, fundraising events, medical research, national or statewide initiatives, computers, or computer-related projects; no loans.

Publications: Application guidelines; Informational brochure (including application guidelines); Program policy statement.

Application information: Application form required.

> *Initial approach:* Contact foundation for application form
> *Deadline(s):* Jan. 31, May 31, and Sept. 30
> *Final notification:* 4 months

Officers and Directors: * Douglas L. Foshee,* Chair.; Bruce L. Connery, Pres.; Jeffrey I. Beason, Sr. V.P. and Cont.; Katherine A. Murray, Sr. V.P.; Susan B. Ortenstone,* Sr. V.P.; Robert W. Baker,* Exec. V.P. and Genl. Counsel; D. Dwight Scott,* Exec. V.P. and C.F.O.; David L. Siddall, V.P. and Secy.; John J. Hopper, V.P. and Treas.; Fayr L. Stallings, V.P.; John W. Somerhalder II; Lisa Stewart.

Number of staff: 2 full-time professional; 1 full-time support.

EIN: 742638185

Selected grants: The following grants were reported in 2004.

$617,323 to United Way of the Texas Gulf Coast, Houston, TX. For annual campaign.

$500,000 to Rice University, Houston, TX. For El Paso Energy Trading Room.

$134,356 to United Way of Central Alabama, Birmingham, AL. For annual campaign.

$120,690 to National Merit Scholarship Corporation, Evanston, IL. For scholarships.

$100,000 to YMCA of the Greater Houston Area, Houston, TX. For capital campaign.

$78,000 to Houston Music Hall Foundation, Houston, TX. For Executive Match grant.

$60,000 to United Way of Gloucester County, Woodbury, NJ. For campaign.

$50,000 to Houston Grand Opera, Houston, TX. For Performing Arts Safety Initiative.

$15,000 to University of Houston Law Foundation, Houston, TX. For Institute for Energy, Law, and Enterprise at Bauer College of Business.

$10,000 to Lighthouse for the Blind of Houston, Houston, TX. For Center for Education and Adaptive Technology.

8883
Margaret & James A. Elkins, Jr. Foundation
1166 First City Twr.
1001 Fannin St.
Houston, TX 77002

Established in 1956 in TX.

Foundation type: Independent foundation.

Financial data (yr. ended 10/31/05): Assets, $32,032,350 (M); gifts received, $4,040,031; expenditures, $1,515,736; qualifying distributions, $1,255,000; giving activities include $1,255,000 for 17 grants (high: $310,000; low: $5,000).

Purpose and activities: Grants primarily for charitable, religious, scientific, or educational and literacy programs, including public safety testing, and the prevention of cruelty to children and animals.

Fields of interest: Child development, education; Elementary school/education; Secondary school/ education; Higher education; Medical school/ education; Education; Hospitals (general); Health organizations, association; Medical research, institute; Safety/disasters; Children/youth, services; Child development, services; Engineering/ technology; Biological sciences; Science; Christian agencies & churches; Religion.

Type of support: Capital campaigns; Building/ renovation; Equipment; Endowments; Emergency funds; Program development; Research.

Limitations: Giving primarily in the metropolitan Houston, TX area. No grants to individuals, or for deficit financing; generally no grants for continuing operating support.

Application information: Application form not required.

> *Initial approach:* Letter
> *Copies of proposal:* 1
> *Deadline(s):* Aug. 31
> *Board meeting date(s):* Varies

Trustees: James A. Elkins III; Margaret Elise Elkins Joseph; Leslie Keith Elkins Sasser; Robert A. Seale, Jr.

EIN: 746051746

Selected grants: The following grants were reported in 2005.

$310,000 to Rice University, Houston, TX.

$200,000 to Christ Church Cathedral, Houston, TX.

$150,000 to Saint Johns School, Houston, TX.

$100,000 to Episcopal Diocese of Texas, Houston, TX.

$75,000 to Menil Foundation, Houston, TX.

$50,000 to Episcopal High School, Bellaire, TX.

$50,000 to Parish School, Houston, TX.

$50,000 to Princeton University, Princeton, NJ.

$30,000 to Barbara Bush Foundation for Family Literacy, DC.

$5,000 to Houston Museum of Natural Science, Houston, TX.

8884
The Ellwood Foundation ✧
P.O. Box 550049
Houston, TX 77255-0049 (713) 785-5507
Contact: H. Wayne Hightower, Tr.

Trust established in 1958 in TX.
Donors: D.C. Ellwood†; Irene L. Ellwood†.
Foundation type: Independent foundation.
Financial data (yr. ended 9/30/05): Assets, $37,598,272 (M); expenditures, $1,986,298; qualifying distributions, $1,750,000; giving activities include $1,750,000 for 54 grants (high: $120,000; low: $10,000).
Purpose and activities: Giving primarily for medical research and mental health.
Fields of interest: Secondary school/education; Education, special; Higher education; Medical school/education; Hospitals (general); Health care; Mental health/crisis services; Biomedicine; Medical research, institute; Human services; Children/youth, services.
Type of support: General/operating support; Scholarship funds; Research.
Limitations: Giving primarily in the Houston, TX, area.
Application information: Application form not required.
Initial approach: Letter
Deadline(s): None
Trustees: H. Wayne Hightower; H. Wayne Hightower, Jr.; Raybourne Thompson, Jr.
EIN: 746039237
Selected grants: The following grants were reported in 2003.
$150,000 to University of Texas M. D. Anderson Cancer Center, Houston, TX. 2 grants: $75,000 (For prostate cancer research), $75,000 (For breast cancer research).
$100,000 to Briarwood School, Houston, TX.
$100,000 to Brookwood Community, Brookshire, TX.
$100,000 to University of Texas Medical School, Houston, TX. For Neuroscience Center.
$50,000 to Child Advocates, Houston, TX.
$50,000 to Parish School, Houston, TX. For program support.
$50,000 to Texas Heart Institute, Houston, TX. For cardiology research.
$40,000 to Texas Childrens Hospital, Houston, TX. For capital campaign.
$40,000 to Texas Christian University, Fort Worth, TX. For upgrade pre-medical program.

8885
The Roger and Rosemary Enrico Foundation ✧ ☆
3831 Turtle Creek Blvd., No. 23B
Dallas, TX 75219

Established in 2000 in TX.
Donor: Roger A. Enrico.
Foundation type: Independent foundation.
Financial data (yr. ended 12/31/05): Assets, $22,460,014 (M); expenditures, $1,191,463; qualifying distributions, $906,024; giving activities include $906,024 for grants.
Fields of interest: Health care; Roman Catholic agencies & churches.
Type of support: General/operating support.
Limitations: Applications not accepted. Giving primarily in TX. No grants to individuals.
Application information: Contributes only to pre-selected organizations.
Officer: Terence C. Sullivan, Treas.
Directors: Aaron J. Enrico; Roger A. Enrico; Rosemary Enrico.
EIN: 752871636

8886
Esping Family Foundation ✧
2828 Routh St., Ste. 500
Dallas, TX 75201 (214) 849-9808
Contact: Sherrye Willis, Exec. Dir.
FAX: (214) 849-9807;
E-mail: sherrye@espingfamilyfoundation.org;
URL: http://www.espingfamilyfoundation.org

Established in 1997 in TX.
Donor: Perry E. Esping†.
Foundation type: Independent foundation.
Financial data (yr. ended 12/31/04): Assets, $10,332,122 (M); expenditures, $584,400; qualifying distributions, $478,887; giving activities include $435,000 for 16 grants (high: $60,000; low: $10,000).
Purpose and activities: The mission of the Esping Family Foundation is "to help others help themselves" by supporting active programs with strong leadership and entrepreneurial activity. The foundation gives priority to projects that target 3 primary program areas: children and the families, youth development, and minority communities.
Fields of interest: Education; Health care; Human services; Children/youth, services; Family services; Christian agencies & churches.
Type of support: Continuing support; Equipment; Program development; Curriculum development; Scholarship funds; Research.
Limitations: Giving limited to the Dallas - Fort Worth, TX, metroplex. No support for school sports or bands. No grants for individual scholarships, underwriting for charity balls, endowment or permanent funds, or capital campaigns; no loans.
Application information: Application form not required.
Initial approach: Letter
Copies of proposal: 1
Deadline(s): April 1 (for consideration at the May boarding meeting); Oct 1 (for consideration at the Nov. board meeting)
Board meeting date(s): May and Nov.
Officers and Directors:* Heather H. Esping,* Pres.; Jennifer E. Kirtland,* V.P. and Secy.; Julie E. Blanton,* V.P. and Treas.; Darren Blanton; Kathryn R. Esping; William P. Esping; John E. Kirtland.
Number of staff: 2 part-time support.
EIN: 752702676

8887
Essar Foundation ✧
P.O. Box 1310
Beaumont, TX 77704-8311

Established in 1984 in TX.
Donor: S.J. Rogers.
Foundation type: Independent foundation.
Financial data (yr. ended 12/31/04): Assets, $203,364 (M); expenditures, $348,971; qualifying distributions, $348,035; giving activities include $348,121 for 15 grants (high: $204,572; low: $1,500).
Purpose and activities: Giving for health associations, Jewish organizations, youth services, the arts, and education.
Fields of interest: Arts; Higher education; Health organizations, association; Cancer; Children/youth, services; Jewish agencies & temples.
Limitations: Applications not accepted. Giving primarily in Beaumont, Hitchcock, and Houston, TX. No grants to individuals.
Application information: Contributes only to pre-selected organizations.
Trustee: Jordan Rogers.
EIN: 760101655
Selected grants: The following grants were reported in 2004.
$204,572 to National Philanthropic Trust, Jenkintown, PA. For unrestricted support.
$50,000 to University of Texas M. D. Anderson Cancer Center, Houston, TX. For unrestricted support.
$15,500 to American Diabetes Association, Austin, TX. For unrestricted support.
$11,000 to National Parkinson Foundation, Miami, FL. For unrestricted support.
$10,500 to American Cancer Society, Beaumont, TX. For unrestricted support.
$5,000 to Any Baby Can, Austin, TX. For unrestricted support.
$5,000 to Julie Rogers Gift of Life Free Mammogram Program, Beaumont, TX. For unrestricted support.
$5,000 to Special Olympics, DC. For unrestricted support.
$3,850 to Greater Houston Community Foundation, Houston, TX. For unrestricted support.
$1,750 to Houston Grand Opera, Houston, TX. For unrestricted support.

8888
Estill Foundation ✧
4022 Lowman St.
Corpus Christi, TX 78411-3133
Contact: Jeannette Holloway, Pres.

Established in 1976.
Donors: Gentry Estill†; Jeannette Holloway.
Foundation type: Independent foundation.
Financial data (yr. ended 9/30/05): Assets, $1,684,422 (M); expenditures, $481,713; qualifying distributions, $335,641; giving activities include $335,641 for 15 grants (high: $127,381; low: $15).
Purpose and activities: Giving primarily for higher education.
Fields of interest: Higher education; Education; Animal welfare; Health care; Boys & girls clubs; Boy scouts; Human services; YM/YWCAs & YM/YWHAs; Federated giving programs; Protestant agencies & churches; Mormon agencies & churches.

Limitations: Giving primarily in TX. No grants to individuals.
Application information:
Initial approach: Letter
Deadline(s): None
Officers: Jeannette Holloway, Pres.; Mary Ann Madrigal, V.P.
EIN: 741892894

8889
ExxonMobil Foundation ▼

(formerly ExxonMobil Education Foundation)
5959 Las Colinas Blvd.
Irving, TX 75039-2298 (972) 444-1104
Contact: Gerald W. McElvy, Pres.
URL: http://www.exxonmobil.com/community

Incorporated in 1955 in NJ as Esso Education Foundation; name changed to Exxon Education Foundation in 1972; name changed to ExxonMobil Foundation in 1999.
Donors: Exxon Corp.; Exxon Mobil Corp.
Foundation type: Company-sponsored foundation.
Financial data (yr. ended 12/31/05): Assets, $110,612,415 (M); gifts received, $75,750,074; expenditures, $64,441,279; qualifying distributions, $63,957,068; giving activities include $36,929,383 for 597 grants (high: $7,360,500; low: $100), and $26,731,582 for employee matching gifts.
Purpose and activities: The foundation supports organizations involved with education, the environment, endangered species and habitats, health, medical research, human services, community development, and civic affairs. Special emphasis is directed toward programs designed to provide mathematics, engineering, science, and technology education.
Fields of interest: Higher education; Engineering school/education; Education, reading; Education; Environment, natural resources; Environment; Animals/wildlife, endangered species; Health care; Medical research; Human services; Economic development; Community development; Science, formal/general education; Mathematics; Public policy, research; Public affairs.
International interests: Developing countries.
Type of support: General/operating support; Program development; Employee volunteer services; Employee matching gifts.
Limitations: Applications not accepted. Giving primarily in Baldwin and Mobile counties, AL, Anchorage, Fairbanks, Juneau, and North Slope, AK, Santa Barbara County and Torrance, CA, Cortez and Rio Blanco County, CO, Washington, DC, LaGrange, GA, Joliet, IL, Kingman and Stevens County, KS, Baton Rouge, Chalmette, Grand Isle, Gueydan, and Kaplan, LA, Detroit, MI, Billings, MT, Clinton and Paulsboro, NJ, Lee County, NM, Rochester, NY, Akron, OH, Shawnee and Texas County, OK, Exton, PA, Baytown, Beaumont, Dallas, Fort Worth, Houston, Longview, Midland, Odessa, and Tyler, TX, San Juan County, UT, Fairfax County and northern VA, and Lincoln, Sublette, and Sweetwater counties, WY; giving also in developing countries. No support for political or religious organizations or youth sports organizations. No grants to individuals, or for institutional scholarship or fellowship programs, capital campaigns, land acquisition, equipment, renovation projects, endowments, athletics, or scholarships; no loans.
Publications: Annual report; Corporate giving report; Grants list.

Application information: Contributes only to pre-selected organizations.
Officers and Trustees:* K.P. Cohen,* Chair.; Gerald W. McElvy, Pres.; T. Plemenos, Secy.; C.M. FitzGerald, Treas.; R.E. Harayda, Cont.; Andre Madec, Exec. Dir.; F.W. Bass; P.B. Henretty; Donald D. Humphreys; B.G. Macklin; S.K. Stuewer; P.A. Wetz.
Number of staff: 4 full-time professional; 2 full-time support.
EIN: 136082357
Selected grants: The following grants were reported in 2005.
$3,000,000 to Save the Children Federation, Westport, CT. For Tsunami Disaster Relief.
$2,081,000 to United Nations Foundation, DC. For Africa Health Institute to purchase mosquito nets and for logistical support for mosquito net campaigns in Nigeria and Angola.
$1,000,000 to Agency for International Development (USAID), DC. For President's Malaria Initiative in Luanda.
$500,000 to Medicines for Malaria Venture, Geneva, Switzerland. For Africa Health Initiative: Malaria Initiative.
$375,000 to Centre for Development and Population Activities, DC. For Global Women in Management Program.
$350,000 to Leuser International Foundation, Indonesia. For Leuser Ecosystem Preservation.
$300,000 to Southeastern Consortium for Minorities in Engineering (SECME), Atlanta, GA. For SECME Scholars and General Support.
$170,000 to HealthStore Foundation, Alexandria, VA. For Kenya Pilot Project to Convert Malaria Medications.
$125,000 to JHPIEGO, Baltimore, MD. For Improving Women's Livelihoods.
$100,000 to Uplift International, Seattle, WA. For Tsunami Disaster Relief.

8890
Fain Foundation ◇ ☆

807 8th St., 2nd Fl.
Wichita Falls, TX 76301-3381

Established in 1942 in TX.
Donor: Minnie Rhea Wood.
Foundation type: Independent foundation.
Financial data (yr. ended 12/31/05): Assets, $1,238,142 (M); expenditures, $401,493; qualifying distributions, $398,750; giving activities include $396,500 for 22 grants (high: $150,000; low: $1,000).
Fields of interest: Arts; Higher education; Human services; YM/YWCAs & YM/YWHAs; Foundations (community); Federated giving programs; Protestant agencies & churches.
Type of support: General/operating support; Capital campaigns; Program development.
Limitations: Applications not accepted. Giving primarily in Wichita Falls, TX. No grants to individuals.
Application information: Contributes only to pre-selected organizations.
Officers and Directors:* Martha Fain,* Pres. and Treas.; Mac W. Cannedy, Jr.,* V.P. and Secy.; Dennis D. Cannedy; John M. Kelly; Ann K. Thompson.
EIN: 756016679
Selected grants: The following grants were reported in 2005.
$150,000 to Presbyterian Manor, Wichita Falls, TX.

$10,000 to River Bend Nature Works, Wichita Falls, TX.
$5,500 to Wichita Falls Symphony Orchestra, Wichita Falls, TX.
$5,000 to Hospice of Wichita Falls, Wichita Falls, TX.
$5,000 to Wichita County Heritage Society, Wichita Falls, TX.
$1,000 to Salvation Army, Plainview, TX.
$1,000 to Wichita Falls Ballet Theater, Wichita Falls, TX.

8891
The R. W. Fair Foundation ◇

P.O. Box 689
Tyler, TX 75710 (903) 592-3811
Contact: James Fair, Pres.

Established in 1936; incorporated in 1959 in TX.
Donors: R.W. Fair‡; Mattie Allen Fair‡.
Foundation type: Independent foundation.
Financial data (yr. ended 12/31/04): Assets, $10,401,902 (M); expenditures, $1,007,906; qualifying distributions, $369,640; giving activities include $369,100 for 52 grants (high: $56,000; low: $200).
Purpose and activities: Grants largely for Protestant church support and church-related programs, and for secondary and higher education. Some support for hospitals, youth and social service agencies, libraries, and cultural activities.
Fields of interest: Arts; Education, fund raising/fund distribution; Secondary school/education; Higher education; Libraries/library science; Education; Hospitals (general); Cancer; Heart & circulatory diseases; Cancer research; Heart & circulatory research; Human services; Youth, services; Protestant agencies & churches.
Type of support: Building/renovation; Equipment; Endowments; Program development; Seed money; Research; Matching/challenge support.
Limitations: Giving primarily in the Southwest, with emphasis on TX. No grants to individuals, or for operating budgets.
Publications: Application guidelines.
Application information: Application form required.
Initial approach: Letter
Copies of proposal: 1
Deadline(s): Mar. 1, June 1, Sept. 1, and Dec. 1
Board meeting date(s): Mar., June, Sept., and Dec.
Final notification: 3 months
Officers and Directors:* James W. Fair,* Pres.; John R. (Bob) Garrett,* V.P.; Mel Lovelady,* V.P.; Barbara King Fair,* Secy.-Treas.; Harold Beaird; B.G. Hartley; Will A. Knight.
Number of staff: 2 part-time professional.
EIN: 756015270
Selected grants: The following grants were reported in 2003.
$70,000 to University of Texas Health Science Center, Tyler, TX.
$25,000 to University of Texas M. D. Anderson Cancer Center, Houston, TX.
$10,050 to Texas College, Tyler, TX.
$5,000 to First Presbyterian Church, Tyler, TX.
$2,500 to Arthritis Foundation, North Texas Chapter, Dallas, TX.
$2,500 to Literacy Council of Tyler, Tyler, TX.
$1,500 to Troup Public Library, Troup, TX.
$1,000 to Regional East Texas Food Bank, Tyler, TX.
$1,000 to Southern Methodist University, Dallas, TX.

$1,000 to Tyler Museum of Art, Tyler, TX.

8892
The Fant Foundation ◆
9219 Katy Freeway, Ste. 161
Houston, TX 77024
Contact: Kelley Williams, Dir.

Established in 1994 in TX.
Donors: Alta Fay Fant†; Fant Properties; Land and Gravel Pit.
Foundation type: Operating foundation.
Financial data (yr. ended 12/31/03): Assets, $845,186 (M); gifts received, $258,000; expenditures, $350,288; qualifying distributions, $339,522; giving activities include $293,550 for 34 grants (high: $100,000; low: $500), and $46,177 for 7 grants to individuals.
Purpose and activities: Giving for support and assistance to impoverished, distressed, and disadvantaged individuals and families who seek to improve their present living conditions.
Fields of interest: Economically disadvantaged.
Type of support: Scholarships—to individuals.
Limitations: Giving primarily to residents of TX.
Application information:
  Initial approach: Letter requesting application
  Deadline(s): None
Directors: Richard E. Fant; Phil O. Kelley; Sheldon E. Richie; Kelley Williams.
EIN: 760443413
Selected grants: The following grants were reported in 2004.
$250,000 to University of Texas, Austin, TX.
$25,000 to American Red Cross, Houston, TX.
$21,500 to Boy Scouts of America, Houston, TX.
$5,000 to Best Buddies International, Houston, TX.
$5,000 to Brookwood Community, Brookshire, TX.
$2,500 to Kinkaid School, Houston, TX.

8893
The Harold Farb Foundation ◆ ☆
P.O. Box 27741
Houston, TX 77227-7741

Established in 1980 in TX.
Foundation type: Independent foundation.
Financial data (yr. ended 11/30/05): Assets, $249,850 (M); expenditures, $342,196; qualifying distributions, $340,535; giving activities include $340,535 for 37 grants (high: $111,000; low: $25).
Purpose and activities: Giving primarily for medical research and Jewish organizations.
Fields of interest: Arts; Education; Hospitals (general); Health organizations, association; Medical research; Human services; Jewish federated giving programs; Jewish agencies & temples.
Limitations: Applications not accepted. Giving primarily in Houston, TX. No grants to individuals.
Application information: Contributes only to pre-selected organizations.
Trustee: Harold Farb.
EIN: 742150068

8894
The William Stamps Farish Fund ▼
1100 Louisiana, Ste. 2200
Houston, TX 77002
Contact: William Stamps Farish, Pres.

Incorporated in 1951 in TX.
Donor: Libbie Rice Farish†.
Foundation type: Independent foundation.
Financial data (yr. ended 6/30/04): Assets, $181,182,684 (M); expenditures, $9,370,819; qualifying distributions, $9,065,198; giving activities include $9,000,000 for 124 grants (high: $600,000; low: $5,000; average: $10,000–$200,000).
Purpose and activities: Giving primarily for basic education and basic medical research.
Fields of interest: Education; Medical research; Human services.
Type of support: Equipment; Program development; Research.
Limitations: Giving primarily in Houston, TX. No grants to individuals, or for annual campaigns, deficit financing, operating budgets, exchange programs, consulting services, or endowment funds; no loans.
Publications: Application guidelines.
Application information: Application form not required.
  Initial approach: Proposal
  Copies of proposal: 1
  Deadline(s): None
  Board meeting date(s): Annually
  Final notification: 1 year
Officers and Trustees:* William Stamps Farish, Pres.; Martha Farish Gerry,* V.P.; Caroline P. Rotan, Secy.; Terry W. Ward, Treas.; Laura Farish Chadwick; Cornelia Gerry Corbett.
Number of staff: 1 full-time professional.
EIN: 746043019
Selected grants: The following grants were reported in 2004.
$300,000 to Saint Pauls School, Concord, NH. For E.H. Gerry Chair for Professional Development.
$275,000 to Saint Johns School, Houston, TX. For annual giving and capital campaign.
$250,000 to Markey Cancer Foundation, Lexington, KY. To establish chair.
$250,000 to Saint Timothys School, Stevenson, MD. For capital campaign.
$250,000 to University of Texas Health Science Center, Houston, TX. For capital campaign for Institute for Molecular Medicine.
$250,000 to Vassar College, Poughkeepsie, NY. For capital campaign.
$210,000 to W. Oscar Neuhaus Memorial Foundation, Bellaire, TX. For teaching reading methods to teachers.
$200,000 to Hermann Eye Fund, Houston, TX. For chair in clinical research.
$125,000 to Independent Day School, Tampa, FL. For training of area teachers.
$100,000 to Aucilla Christian Academy, Monticello, FL. For teacher salaries.

8895
The Fasken Foundation ◆
P.O. Box 162786
Austin, TX 78716-2786 (512) 708-1003
Contact: Andrew C. Elliot, Jr., Dir.

Incorporated in 1955 in TX.
Donors: Andrew A. Fasken†; Helen Fasken House†; Vickie Mallison†; Howard Marshall Johnson†; Ruth Shelton†.
Foundation type: Independent foundation.
Financial data (yr. ended 12/31/05): Assets, $24,225,161 (M); expenditures, $1,689,864; qualifying distributions, $1,314,396; giving

activities include $1,149,095 for 71 grants (high: $125,000; low: $500; average: $10,000–$40,000), and $114,311 for 43 grants to individuals (high: $8,000; low: $1,498; average: $1,650–$3,300).
Purpose and activities: Support for higher education, including scholarships to TX institutions for graduates of Midland County public high schools and Midland Community College; support also for health and social services, including hospices and programs for drug abuse and rehabilitation.
Fields of interest: Higher education; Education; Health care; Substance abuse, services; Human services; Children/youth, services; Residential/custodial care, hospices.
Type of support: General/operating support; Scholarships—to individuals.
Limitations: Giving limited to the Midland, TX, area. No grants to individuals (except scholarships limited to graduates of Midland County, TX, public high schools and junior college); no loans.
Publications: Application guidelines.
Application information: Application form required.
  Initial approach: Letter
  Copies of proposal: 1
  Deadline(s): None; grants reviewed quarterly
  Board meeting date(s): Feb., May, Aug., and Nov.
  Final notification: 6 months
Officers: Steven Fasken, Pres.; F. Andrew Fasken, V.P.
Trustees: Andrew C. Elliott; Murray T. Fasken; William P. Franklin; Susan Fasken Hartin; Tevis Herd; B.L. Jones; Thomas E. Kelly; Gerald C. Nobles, Jr.
Director: Andrew C. Elliot, Jr.
Number of staff: 1 full-time professional; 1 part-time support.
EIN: 756023680

8896
The Faulconer Scholarship Programs ◆
3600 Old Bullard Rd., No. 501
Tyler, TX 75701
Contact: Ron Gleason, V.P. and Secy.
E-mail: info@faulconerscholars.org; URL: http://www.faulconerscholars.org
E-mail address for Ron Gleason:
rgleason@faulconerscholars.org

Donor: Vernon E. Faulconer.
Foundation type: Independent foundation.
Financial data (yr. ended 12/31/05): Assets, $168,182 (M); gifts received, $650,000; expenditures, $672,042; qualifying distributions, $668,035; giving activities include $453,647 for 16 grants to individuals (high: $193,772; low: $2,500).
Purpose and activities: The programs award scholarships to African-American and Hispanic-American graduating seniors who have earned at least a 2.5 GPA while in high school and who are enrolled in schools within the Tyler Junior College District in East TX. The Tyler Junior College District includes the Independent School Districts in Chapel Hill, Grand Saline, Lindale, Tyler, Van, and Winona, TX.
Fields of interest: Higher education.
Type of support: Scholarships—to individuals.
Limitations: Giving primarily in TX.
Application information: Application form available on foundation Web site. See foundation Web site for application guideline procedures, and downloading of application form. Applications must be mailed.

E-mailed, faxed or hand-delivered applications will not be accepted. Application form required.

Deadline(s): Mar. 1

Officers: Vernon E. Faulconer, Pres.; Ron Gleason, V.P. and Secy.; Tom Markel, Treas.

EIN: 010752611

8897
The Favrot Fund

1770 Saint James Pl., Ste. 510
Houston, TX 77056-3405
Contact: Julie Richardson

Established in 1952 in TX.

Foundation type: Independent foundation.

Financial data (yr. ended 12/31/05): Assets, $21,962,272 (M); expenditures, $1,437,905; qualifying distributions, $1,265,207; giving activities include $1,222,200 for 41 grants (high: $120,000; low: $500).

Fields of interest: Arts; Education; Animals/wildlife; Human services.

Type of support: General/operating support; Management development/capacity building; Building/renovation; Program development; Conferences/seminars; Research; Program evaluation.

Limitations: Applications not accepted. Giving primarily in CA and TX.

Application information: Unsolicited requests for funds not accepted.

Board meeting date(s): 3rd quarter

Officers and Trustees:* Laurence Favrot,* Pres.; Romelia Favrot,* Treas.; Celestine Favrot Arndt; Leo M. Favrot; Lenior M. Josey; Jeanette F. Peterson.

Number of staff: 1 part-time professional.

EIN: 760638639

8898
Feinberg Foundation, Inc. ◇ ☆

4855 N. Mesa St., Ste. 120
El Paso, TX 79912
Contact: Stephen L. Feinberg, Pres.

Established in 1971.

Donors: Milton D. Feinberg†; Stephen L. Feinberg; David C. Feinberg; William I. Feinberg.

Foundation type: Independent foundation.

Financial data (yr. ended 12/31/05): Assets, $4,815,272 (M); gifts received, $4,622; expenditures, $340,333; qualifying distributions, $340,333; giving activities include $315,200 for 28 + grants (high: $65,300).

Fields of interest: Performing arts, dance; Arts; Higher education; Health organizations, association; YM/YWCAs & YM/YWHAs; Jewish federated giving programs; Jewish agencies & temples.

Limitations: Giving primarily in Santa Fe, NM, El Paso, TX and WA.

Application information: Application form not required.

Deadline(s): None

Officers: Stephen L. Feinberg, Pres.; Jack T. Chapman, V.P.; Andrew Feinberg, V.P.; Elisa Varela, Secy.-Treas.

Number of staff: None.

EIN: 746039246

Selected grants: The following grants were reported in 2004.

$40,000 to Saint Johns College, Annapolis, MD.

$31,850 to American Jewish Committee, New York, NY.

$12,000 to Site Santa Fe, Santa Fe, NM.

$10,000 to Santa Fe Institute, Santa Fe, NM.

$5,000 to Seattle Jewish Film Festival, Seattle, WA.

$2,500 to Texas Tech University, Lubbock, TX.

8899
Leland Fikes Foundation, Inc. ◇

500 N. Akard St., Ste. 1919
Dallas, TX 75201-3322 (214) 754-0144
Contact: Nancy J. Solana, V.P., Research and Grant Admin.

Incorporated in 1952 in DE.

Donors: Leland Fikes†; Catherine W. Fikes†.

Foundation type: Independent foundation.

Financial data (yr. ended 12/31/04): Assets, $77,820,965 (M); expenditures, $5,592,224; qualifying distributions, $3,656,561; giving activities include $3,345,800 for 59 grants (high: $650,000; low: $1,000; average: $5,000–$100,000).

Purpose and activities: Giving primarily for medical research, health, and social services, family planning, public interest groups, and education; grants also for population research and cultural programs.

Fields of interest: Museums; Performing arts; Performing arts, music; Arts; Elementary school/education; Secondary school/education; Higher education; Medical school/education; Adult education—literacy, basic skills & GED; Education, reading; Education; Environment; Reproductive health, family planning; Health care; Mental health/crisis services; Health organizations, association; Medical research, institute; Crime/violence prevention, domestic violence; Legal services; Food services; Housing/shelter, development; Human services; Children/youth, services; Family services; Homeless, human services; Civil liberties, reproductive rights; Community development, neighborhood development; Philanthropy/voluntarism, management/technical aid; Philanthropy/voluntarism; Science; Population studies; Public policy, research; Public affairs.

Type of support: General/operating support; Continuing support; Annual campaigns; Capital campaigns; Building/renovation; Equipment; Endowments; Emergency funds; Program development; Seed money; Research; Program evaluation; Matching/challenge support.

Limitations: Giving primarily in the Dallas, TX, area. No grants to individuals; no loans.

Publications: Application guidelines.

Application information: Application form not required.

Initial approach: Letter on organization letterhead
Copies of proposal: 1
Deadline(s): None
Board meeting date(s): Bimonthly
Final notification: By letter, usually within 1-3 months

Officers and Trustees:* Lee Fikes,* Pres. and Treas.; Nancy J. Solana, V.P., Research and Grant Admin., and Secy.; Amy L. Fikes,* V.P.; Catherine F. Lavie,* Prog. Off.; Brendan J. Fikes.

Number of staff: 1 full-time professional; 2 part-time professional; 1 part-time support.

EIN: 756035984

Selected grants: The following grants were reported in 2004.

$725,000 to University of Texas Southwestern Medical Center, Dallas, TX. 2 grants: $75,000 (For study on Genetic Disease Phenotypes), $650,000 (For research projects).

$250,000 to Dallas Symphony Association, Dallas, TX. For European Tour.

$200,000 to Dallas Center for the Performing Arts Foundation, Dallas, TX. For building.

$100,000 to Old Red Courthouse, Dallas, TX. To develop Old Red Museum.

$100,000 to Texas Freedom Network Education Fund, Austin, TX. For general support.

$80,000 to Dallas County Community College District Foundation, Dallas, TX. For Rising Star Scholarship Program.

$50,000 to University of California, Berkeley, CA. For general support for Medical Products and Services Division of Center for Entrepreneurship in International Health and development of School of Public Health.

$40,000 to Family Gateway, Dallas, TX. For general support.

$25,000 to North Dallas Shared Ministries, Dallas, TX. To renovate space for medical and dental clinic.

8900
Jerry and Nanette Finger Foundation ◇ ☆

520 Post Oak Blvd., Ste. 750
Houston, TX 77027

Established in 1986 in TX.

Donors: Jerry E. Finger; Nanette B. Finger; and other members of the Finger family.

Foundation type: Independent foundation.

Financial data (yr. ended 12/31/05): Assets, $2,365,539 (M); gifts received, $413,585; expenditures, $362,245; qualifying distributions, $354,635; giving activities include $354,635 for 285 grants (high: $20,000; low: $10).

Purpose and activities: Giving for theatrical arts, Jewish organizations, food services, and health and medical services.

Fields of interest: Museums; Arts; Higher education; Education; Aging, centers/services; Jewish federated giving programs; Jewish agencies & temples; Aging.

Type of support: General/operating support; Annual campaigns; Building/renovation; Endowments; Scholarship funds.

Limitations: Applications not accepted. Giving primarily in Aspen, CO, and Houston, TX. No grants to individuals.

Application information: Contributes only to pre-selected organizations.

Officers: Jerry E. Finger, Pres.; Nanette B. Finger, V.P.; Walter G. Finger, Secy.-Treas.; Jonathan S. Finger, Mgr.

EIN: 760209018

Selected grants: The following grants were reported in 2003.

$20,000 to Inprint, Houston, TX. For Poets and Writers Ball.

$10,000 to Williston Northampton School, Easthampton, MA. For annual support.

$6,397 to Aspen Institute, Aspen, CO.

$6,000 to Alley Theater, Houston, TX. For The Wild Things.

$5,000 to Susan Smith Blackburn Prize, Houston, TX.

$3,000 to Aspen Art Museum, Aspen, CO. For membership.

$2,500 to Saint Pius X High School, Houston, TX. For Veritas Table.

$1,250 to Young Audiences of Houston, Houston, TX. For Conducting the Future.

$1,000 to Holocaust Museum Houston, Houston, TX.

$100 to Art and Environmental Architecture, Houston, TX.

8901
Ben & Maytee Fisch Foundation

P.O. Box 132821
Tyler, TX 75713
Contact: Ben Fisch, Pres.

Established in 1997 in TX.
Donors: Ben Fisch; Maytee R. Fisch†.
Foundation type: Independent foundation.
Financial data (yr. ended 5/31/05): Assets, $33,832,773 (M); expenditures, $1,832,725; qualifying distributions, $1,711,918; giving activities include $1,709,993 for 53 grants (high: $650,000; low: $1,000).
Fields of interest: Adult education—literacy, basic skills & GED; Education; Mental health/crisis services; Food banks; Housing/shelter; Human services; Children/youth, services; Residential/custodial care, hospices.
Type of support: Matching/challenge support; General/operating support; Continuing support; Annual campaigns; Capital campaigns; Building/renovation; Equipment; Program development; Professorships; Scholarship funds; Research.
Limitations: Giving primarily in east TX. No support for public or private elementary or secondary schools. No grants for debt retirement, reserve funding, endowments or conferences.
Publications: Application guidelines.
Application information: Application form required.
Initial approach: Letter
Copies of proposal: 1
Board meeting date(s): Quarterly
Final notification: 60-90 days
Officers: Ben Fisch, Pres.; Martee F. Fuerst, V.P.
Director: Jan F. Fuerst.
Number of staff: 1 part-time support.
EIN: 752732192

8902
Ray C. Fish Foundation ◇

2001 Kirby Dr., Ste. 1005
Houston, TX 77019 (713) 522-0741
Contact: Paula Hooton, Exec. Admin.
URL: http://www.raycfishfoundation.org

Incorporated in 1957 in TX.
Donors: Raymond Clinton Fish†; Mirtha G. Fish†.
Foundation type: Independent foundation.
Financial data (yr. ended 6/30/05): Assets, $27,145,226 (M); gifts received, $69,950; expenditures, $1,613,348; qualifying distributions, $1,241,880; giving activities include $962,500 for 135 grants (high: $200,000; low: $500).
Purpose and activities: To support, establish or advance educational, scientific or other charitable activities.
Fields of interest: Performing arts; Arts; Higher education; Libraries (special); Education; Hospitals (general); Medical research, institute; Human services; Children/youth, services.

Type of support: General/operating support; Continuing support; Annual campaigns; Capital campaigns; Building/renovation; Endowments; Program development; Professorships; Seed money; Scholarship funds; Research; Matching/challenge support.
Limitations: Giving primarily in TX, with emphasis on Houston. No grants to individuals.
Publications: Application guidelines; Informational brochure (including application guidelines).
Application information: See foundation Web site for complete guidelines. Application form not required.
Initial approach: Letter
Copies of proposal: 1
Deadline(s): Feb. 28, June 30, Sept. 30, and Dec. 31
Board meeting date(s): Quarterly
Final notification: By mail; May, Sept., Dec., and Feb.
Officers and Trustees:* Barbara F. Daniel,* Pres.; Robert J. Cruikshank,* V.P. and Treas.; Christopher J. Daniel,* V.P.; James L. Daniel, Jr.,* V.P.; Catherine Daniel Kaldis, V.P.; Paula Hooton,* Exec. Admin.
Number of staff: 1 full-time professional; 1 part-time professional.
EIN: 746043047
Selected grants: The following grants were reported in 2004.
$101,500 to University of Texas M. D. Anderson Cancer Center, Houston, TX. For teen room and pediatric programs.
$100,000 to Texas Heart Institute, Houston, TX. For capital campaign.
$26,500 to Houston READ Commission, Houston, TX. For literacy program.
$25,000 to Foundation for Financial Literacy, Houston, TX. For training project.
$25,000 to Post Oak School, Bellaire, TX. For general operating support.
$15,000 to American Heart Association, Houston, TX. For general operating support.
$15,000 to YMCA of the Greater Houston Area, Houston, TX. For after-school programs.
$10,700 to Good Samaritan Foundation, Houston, TX. For nursing scholarships.
$10,000 to Fay School, Houston, TX. For capital campaign.
$10,000 to Rose, The, Houston, TX. For capital campaign.

8903
Fleming Endowment ◇ ☆

1330 Post Oak Blvd., Ste. 3030
Houston, TX 77056-3019

Established in 1997 in TX.
Donor: George M. Fleming.
Foundation type: Independent foundation.
Financial data (yr. ended 10/31/05): Assets, $16,300,304 (M); expenditures, $1,635,126; qualifying distributions, $1,510,179; giving activities include $1,499,977 for 22 grants (high: $552,062; low: $200).
Fields of interest: Higher education; Boy scouts; Human services; Community development; Christian agencies & churches.
Limitations: Applications not accepted. Giving primarily in TX. No grants to individuals.
Application information: Contributes only to pre-selected organizations.

Trustees: George M. Fleming; Scott Fleming.
EIN: 760555849
Selected grants: The following grants were reported in 2004.
$130,000 to OConnell High School, Galveston, TX.
$101,000 to University of Texas Medical Branch, Galveston, TX.
$29,000 to Briarwood School, Houston, TX.
$25,000 to Catholic Charities, El Paso, TX.
$11,000 to Saint Francis Episcopal Day School, Houston, TX.
$4,650 to Boys and Girls Harbor, Houston, TX.
$1,000 to 100 Club, Houston, TX.
$1,000 to Baylor Bear Foundation, Waco, TX.
$1,000 to Neuhaus Education Center, Bellaire, TX.
$1,000 to University of Texas Law School Foundation, Austin, TX.

8904
The Fleming Foundation ◇

500 W. 7th St., Ste. 1007
Fort Worth, TX 76102-4732
Contact: G. Malcolm Louden, V.P.

Incorporated in 1936 in TX.
Donor: William Fleming†.
Foundation type: Independent foundation.
Financial data (yr. ended 12/31/05): Assets, $2,426,255 (M); expenditures, $548,948; qualifying distributions, $474,000; giving activities include $474,000 for 3 grants (high: $250,000; low: $4,000).
Purpose and activities: Giving primarily for Protestant church support and church-related activities, higher and secondary education, and the arts.
Fields of interest: Performing arts; Elementary/secondary education; Higher education; Hospitals (general); Human services; Protestant agencies & churches.
Type of support: General/operating support; Continuing support; Annual campaigns; Emergency funds; Program development; Professorships; Research.
Limitations: Giving primarily in TX, with emphasis on Fort Worth. No grants to individuals, or for deficit financing, building or endowment funds, land acquisition, matching or challenge grants, scholarships, fellowships, exchange programs, publications, or conferences; single-year grants only; no loans.
Application information: Application form not required.
Initial approach: Proposal
Copies of proposal: 1
Deadline(s): None
Board meeting date(s): 1st Wed. in April
Final notification: 2 months
Officers: Mary D. Walsh, Pres.; G. Malcolm Louden, V.P. and Mgr.; F. Howard Walsh, Jr., Secy.-Treas.
Director: Gary Goble.
EIN: 756022736

8905
Folsom Charitable Foundation, Inc. ◇

16475 Dallas Pkwy., Ste. 800
Addison, TX 75001-6856

Established in 1984 in TX.
Donors: Margaret D. Folsom; Robert S. Folsom.
Foundation type: Independent foundation.

Financial data (yr. ended 12/31/05): Assets, $979,937 (M); expenditures, $436,873; qualifying distributions, $436,723; giving activities include $431,978 for 27 grants (high: $250,000; low: $5).
Purpose and activities: Giving primarily for education, health, and human services; funding also for a United Methodist church.
Fields of interest: Arts; Higher education; Hospitals (general); Health care; Medical research, institute; Human services; Children/youth, services; Protestant agencies & churches.
Limitations: Applications not accepted. Giving primarily in TX, with emphasis on Dallas. No grants to individuals.
Application information: Contributes only to pre-selected organizations.
Officers and Trustees:* Robert S. Folsom,* Pres.; Margaret D. Folsom,* V.P.; Robert Stephen Folsom,* V.P.; Diane Folsom Frank,* V.P.; Debra Folsom Jarma,* V.P.; Haddon O. Winckler, Secy.-Treas.
EIN: 751862254

8906
The Fondren Foundation ▼
P.O. Box 2558
Houston, TX 77252-8037 (713) 216-4513
Contact: Martie Herrick

Established in 1948 in TX.
Donor: Mrs. W.W. Fondren, Sr.†.
Foundation type: Independent foundation.
Financial data (yr. ended 10/31/05): Assets, $200,265,130 (M); expenditures, $11,308,370; qualifying distributions, $9,775,010; giving activities include $9,620,833 for 100 grants (high: $1,266,907; low: $5,000; average: $25,000–$100,000).
Purpose and activities: Emphasis on higher and secondary education, social service and youth agencies, cultural organizations, and health.
Fields of interest: Arts; Secondary school/education; Higher education; Health care; Human services; Youth, services.
Type of support: General/operating support; Continuing support; Capital campaigns; Building/renovation; Program development.
Limitations: Giving primarily in TX, with emphasis on Houston. No grants to individuals, or for annual or operating fund drives.
Publications: Application guidelines.
Application information: Application form not required.
  Initial approach: Letter
  Copies of proposal: 1
  Deadline(s): Feb. 1, May 1, Aug. 1, Nov. 1
  Board meeting date(s): Mar., June, Sept., and Dec.
  Final notification: 3 to 6 months
Officers and Trustees:* Walter W. Fondren IV,* Chair.; David M. Underwood, Jr.,* Vice-Chair.; Carrie Trammell Sturges,* Secy.-Treas.; Doris Fondren Allday; R. Edwin Allday; Laura Trammell Baird; Ellanor Allday Beard; Celia Whitfield Crank; Bentley B. Fondren; Leland T. Fondren; Robert E. Fondren; Walter W. Fondren III; Marie Fondren Hall; Catherine Underwood Murray; Michael W. Springer; Ann Gordon Trammell; Harper B. Trammell; David M. Underwood; Duncan K. Underwood; Lynda Knapp Underwood; Sue Trammell Whitfield; Susan T. Whitfield; W. Trammell Whitfield; William F.

Whitfield, Sr.; William F. Whitfield, Jr.; Frances Fondren Wilson.
EIN: 746042565
Selected grants: The following grants were reported in 2005.
$2,000,000 to Methodist Hospital, Houston, TX. To establish research institute.
$1,500,000 to Houston Downtown Park Corporation, Houston, TX. For creating a new central park for Houston.
$1,266,907 to Houston Katrina/Rita Relief Fund, Houston, TX. To aid Hurricane Katrina victims.
$1,000,000 to KIPP (Knowledge is Power Program) Academy, Houston, TX. For construction of KIPP Houston High School and KIPP SHINE Prep.
$550,000 to Houston Museum of Natural Science, Houston, TX. For capital campaign to add lot to lease with city of Houston.
$300,000 to Chinquapin School, Highlands, TX. For Lead Scholarship Gift to underwrite 6th grade programs.
$300,000 to University of Texas Medical Branch Hospitals, School of Medicine, Galveston, TX. For construction of Galveston National Laboratory.
$300,000 to Yellowstone Academy, Houston, TX. For program support.
$250,000 to Neuhaus Education Center, Bellaire, TX. For annual teacher scholarships and Lenox Reed Endowment scholarship.
$100,000 to Jack S. Blanton Museum of Art, Austin, TX. For capital campaign.

8907
Ershel Franklin Charitable Trust
P.O. Box 790
Post, TX 79356
Contact: Giles C. McCrary, Tr.

Established in 1985 in TX.
Foundation type: Independent foundation.
Financial data (yr. ended 12/31/05): Assets, $8,840,221 (M); expenditures, $346,635; qualifying distributions, $346,635; giving activities include $336,435 for 133 grants (high: $30,000; low: $25).
Fields of interest: Education, research; Higher education; Business school/education; Medical school/education; Education; Hospitals (general); Nursing care; Cancer; Alcoholism; Biomedicine; Medical research, institute; Cancer research; Government/public administration; Religion.
Type of support: Endowments; Scholarship funds; Research.
Limitations: Applications not accepted. Giving primarily in TX. No grants to individuals.
Application information: Contributes only to pre-selected organizations.
  Board meeting date(s): As needed
Trustee: Giles C. McCrary.
EIN: 756305761

8908
Franklin Family Foundation ◇
P.O. Box 269
San Antonio, TX 78291-0269

Established in 1999 in TX.
Donors: Larry D. Franklin; Charlotte A. Franklin.
Foundation type: Independent foundation.
Financial data (yr. ended 12/31/05): Assets, $1,706,205 (M); gifts received, $509,480;

expenditures, $1,533,143; qualifying distributions, $1,520,342; giving activities include $1,520,342 for 33 grants (high: $774,000; low: $300).
Purpose and activities: Giving primarily for youth related health services, arts, education, child welfare and music organizations; some Christian agencies and churches funding.
Fields of interest: Museums (children's); Health care, research; Diabetes; Medical research, institute; Youth development, public education; Youth development, services; Christian agencies & churches.
Limitations: Applications not accepted. Giving primarily in TX; limited funding nationally, primarily in Washington, DC. No grants to individuals.
Application information: Contributes only to pre-selected organizations.
Officers and Directors:* Larry D. Franklin,* Pres. and Treas.; Charlotte A. Franklin,* V.P. and Secy.; Kristi Franklin Borchardt; Kelly Leigh Hardwick.
EIN: 742921587
Selected grants: The following grants were reported in 2004.
$202,616 to International Foundation, DC. 2 grants: $58,916, $143,700
$166,000 to Victory Outreach, San Antonio, TX.
$133,893 to Victory Fellowship, San Antonio, TX.
$114,180 to Carver Academy, San Antonio, TX. 2 grants: $79,180 (For scholarship), $35,000 (For scholarship).
$103,578 to Southwest Foundation for Biomedical Research, Houston, TX.
$25,000 to Gathering, The, Tyler, TX.
$10,000 to International Center for Religion and Diplomacy, DC.
$4,500 to Juvenile Diabetes Research Foundation International, San Antonio, TX.

8909
The Frees Foundation
1770 St. James Pl., Ste. 616
Houston, TX 77056
Contact: Nancy Frees Fountain, Managing Dir.
FAX: (713) 623-6509;
E-mail: freesfoundation@msn.com; URL: http://www.freesfoundation.org

Established in 1983 in TX.
Donors: C. Norman Frees†; Shirley B. Frees.
Foundation type: Independent foundation.
Financial data (yr. ended 12/31/05): Assets, $10,093,494 (M); expenditures, $679,810; qualifying distributions, $587,002; giving activities include $420,000 for 44 grants (high: $35,000; low: $2,500).
Purpose and activities: The mission is to assist vulnerable and underserved populations achieve self-sufficiency.
Fields of interest: Education; Health care; Housing/shelter, development; Children/youth, services; Family services; Community development; Women; Homeless.
Type of support: General/operating support; Continuing support; Program development.
Limitations: Giving primarily in Houston, TX. No support for art programs. No grants to individuals, or for deficit financing, endowments, capital campaigns, or fundraising events.
Publications: Application guidelines; Grants list; Multi-year report.
Application information: Application form required.
  Initial approach: Letter of inquiry
  Copies of proposal: 1

Deadline(s): Feb. 15 and Aug. 15
Board meeting date(s): Apr. 15 and Oct. 15
Final notification: 1 month
Officers and Directors:* Edmund M. Fountain, Jr.,*
Pres. and Treas.; Nancy Frees Fountain,* Secy. and
Managing Dir.; Shirley B. Frees, Chair. Emeritus;
Esther M. Perrine.
Number of staff: 1 full-time professional; 1 full-time
support.
EIN: 760053200
Selected grants: The following grants were reported
in 2005.
$20,000 to Catholic Charities of the Archdiocese of
Galveston-Houston, Houston, TX.
$15,000 to Bering Omega Community Services,
Houston, TX.
$15,000 to Collaborative for Children, Houston, TX.
$15,000 to Exchange Club Center for the Prevention
of Child Abuse of Houston, Houston, TX.
$10,000 to Houston Area Womens Center,
Houston, TX.
$10,000 to Interfaith Caring Ministries, League City,
TX.
$10,000 to Mercy Ships, Garden Valley, TX.
$5,000 to American Lung Association, Houston, TX.
$5,000 to Child Advocates, Houston, TX.
$5,000 to Muscular Dystrophy Association,
Houston, TX.

8910
Pat and Tom Frost Foundation ✧ ☆
c/o Frost Financial Mgmt. Svcs.
P.O. Box 2950
San Antonio, TX 78299

Established in 1994 in TX.
Donors: Patricia H. Frost; Thomas C. Frost.
Foundation type: Independent foundation.
Financial data (yr. ended 12/31/05): Assets,
$6,258,531 (M); expenditures, $366,250;
qualifying distributions, $343,333; giving activities
include $343,333 for grants.
Purpose and activities: Giving for education,
environmental conservation, youth services and for
health services.
Fields of interest: Museums; Higher education;
Religion.
Type of support: Research; Capital campaigns.
Limitations: Applications not accepted. Giving
primarily in San Antonio, TX. No grants to individuals.
Application information: Contributes only to
pre-selected organizations.
Trustees: Patricia H. Frost; Thomas C. Frost.
EIN: 742699577
Selected grants: The following grants were reported
in 2004.
$55,000 to Texas Military Institute, San Antonio, TX.
For repairs to TMI-Frost Athletic Center.
$50,000 to Cibolo Nature Center, Boerne, TX.
$50,000 to University of Texas, San Antonio, TX. 2
grants: $5,000, $45,000 (For UTeach Program).
$8,333 to YMCA of San Antonio and the Hill Country,
San Antonio, TX. For Roberts Ranch Youth Camp.
$5,000 to Baptist Child and Family Services, San
Antonio, TX.
$5,000 to Carver Academy, San Antonio, TX.
$5,000 to K L R N-TV, San Antonio, TX.
$5,000 to Southwest Foundation for Biomedical
Research, San Antonio, TX.

8911
The John D. Furst Foundation ✧
200 Crescent Ct., Rm. 1600
Dallas, TX 75201

Established in 1997 in TX.
Donor: Jack D. Furst.
Foundation type: Independent foundation.
Financial data (yr. ended 12/31/05): Assets,
$2,053,568 (M); gifts received, $292,000;
expenditures, $432,870; qualifying distributions,
$432,475; giving activities include $432,475 for 23
grants (high: $250,000; low: $25; average:
$1,000–$5,000).
Purpose and activities: Giving primarily to Christian
churches; some giving also for children and youth
services.
Fields of interest: Boy scouts; Children/youth,
services; Christian agencies & churches.
Limitations: Applications not accepted. Giving
primarily in TX. No grants to individuals.
Application information: Contributes only to
pre-selected organizations.
Officer: John D. Furst, Chair.
Directors: Debra L. Furst; John S. Furst; Robert S.
Furst.
EIN: 752724923
Selected grants: The following grants were reported
in 2003.
$500,000 to Cross Timbers Community Church,
Argyle, TX.
$300,000 to Liberty Christian High School, Dallas,
TX.
$5,000 to Boy Scouts of America National Council,
Circle Ten Council, Irving, TX.
$5,000 to National Cowgirl Museum and Hall of
Fame, Fort Worth, TX.
$4,500 to Boy Scouts of America, TX.
$2,500 to National Foundation for Advancement in
the Arts, Miami, FL.
$1,500 to Senior Citizens of Greater Dallas, Dallas,
TX.
$1,000 to H. Lee Moffitt Cancer Center and
Research Institute Foundation, Tampa, FL.
$500 to Revlon Run/Walk for Women, New York,
NY.
$100 to Arizona State University, Tempe, AZ.

8912
Futureus Foundation ✧ ☆
P.O. Box 2907
Corpus Christi, TX 78403 (361) 888-7708
Contact: Gary Mize, Tr.

Donor: Manti Operating Co., Inc.
Foundation type: Independent foundation.
Financial data (yr. ended 10/31/05): Assets, $0
(M); gifts received, $1,969,725; expenditures,
$532,383; qualifying distributions, $480,829;
giving activities include $480,829 for 39 grants
(high: $373,284; low: $100).
Fields of interest: Education; Human services;
Children/youth, services.
Limitations: Giving primarily in Corpus Christi, TX.
Application information: Each applicant should
submit a youth education scholarship application, a
copy of their most recent high school or college
transcript and a letter of recommendation from a
current teacher, former teacher, or a community
leader. Application form required.
Trustees: Lee Barberito; Kenton McDonald; Gary
Mize.
EIN: 270004671

8913
The Gale Foundation ✧
2615 Calder St., Ste. 630
Beaumont, TX 77702

Donor: Edwin Gale.
Foundation type: Independent foundation.
Financial data (yr. ended 4/30/06): Assets,
$8,917,207 (M); expenditures, $497,077;
qualifying distributions, $497,077; giving activities
include $443,360 for 48 grants (high: $117,500;
low: $75).
Purpose and activities: Giving primarily for Jewish
organizations, as well as for education, health, and
human services.
Fields of interest: Arts; Higher education, university;
Medical school/education; Theological school/
education; Education; Health organizations; Human
services; Family services; Jewish federated giving
programs; Jewish agencies & temples.
Limitations: Applications not accepted. Giving
primarily in TX; some funding also in NY. No grants
to individuals.
Application information: Contributes only to
pre-selected organizations.
Trustee: Rebecca S. Gale.
EIN: 760009604
Selected grants: The following grants were reported
in 2006.
$117,500 to University of Texas Medical Branch,
Galveston, TX.
$59,560 to Temple Emanuel, Beaumont, TX.
$50,545 to American Jewish Committee, New York,
NY.
$50,000 to Ner Israel Rabbinical College,
Baltimore, MD.
$7,980 to University of Texas System, Austin, TX.
$5,000 to Center for Equal Opportunity, Sterling, VA.
$200 to Union for Reform Judaism, New York, NY.

8914
Garvey Texas Foundation, Inc. ✧
P.O. Box 9600
Fort Worth, TX 76147-2600
Contact: Shirley F. Garvey, Pres.

Incorporated in 1962 in TX.
Donors: James S. Garvey; Shirley F. Garvey; Garvey
Foundation.
Foundation type: Independent foundation.
Financial data (yr. ended 12/31/04): Assets,
$9,171,961 (M); expenditures, $481,943;
qualifying distributions, $405,645; giving activities
include $405,645 for 93 grants (high: $50,000;
low: $100).
Purpose and activities: Giving primarily for
secondary and higher education, the arts, and to
youth organizations, Protestant agencies and
churches, and federated giving programs.
Fields of interest: Arts, association; Museums;
Performing arts; Historic preservation/historical
societies; Arts; Elementary school/education;
Higher education; Health care; Health organizations,
association; Human services; Children/youth,
services; Residential/custodial care; Federated
giving programs; Protestant agencies & churches.
Type of support: Capital campaigns;
Program-related investments/loans.
Limitations: Giving primarily to organizations
operating in the immediate geographic area of the
foundation. No grants, scholarships or loans to
individuals.
Application information: Application form required.

Initial approach: Letter
Copies of proposal: 1
Deadline(s): None
Officers: Shirley F. Garvey, Pres.; Carol G. Sweat, V.P.; Richard F. Garvey, Secy.; Reece Pettigrew, Treas.
EIN: 756031547

8915
Gayden Family Foundation ◆ ☆
13727 Noel Rd., Ste. 500
Dallas, TX 75240
Contact: Laura McElroy

Established in 1999 in TX.
Donors: William K. Gayden; Mrs. William Gayden.
Foundation type: Independent foundation.
Financial data (yr. ended 12/31/05): Assets, $7,212,282 (M); gifts received, $2,448,382; expenditures, $326,861; qualifying distributions, $316,500; giving activities include $314,900 for 29 grants (high: $65,000; low: $1,000).
Fields of interest: Arts; Education; Health organizations, association; Human services; Federated giving programs; Science; Christian agencies & churches.
Limitations: Giving primarily in Dallas, TX; giving also in Washington, DC. No grants to individuals.
Application information:
Initial approach: Letter
Deadline(s): None
Directors: Cynthia N. Gayden; William K. Gayden; Katherine G. Keenan; Elizabeth G. Williams.
EIN: 756563143

8916
The George Foundation ▼ ◆
310 Morton St., PMB Ste. C
Richmond, TX 77469 (281) 342-6109
Contact: Dee Koch, Grants Off.
FAX: (281) 341-7635; Additional address: 215 Morton St., Richmond, TX 77469; E-mail: dkoch@thegeorgefoundation.org; URL: http://www.thegeorgefoundation.org

Trust established in 1945 in TX.
Donors: A.P. George†; Mamie E. George†.
Foundation type: Independent foundation.
Financial data (yr. ended 12/31/05): Assets, $220,943,530 (M); expenditures, $8,838,156; qualifying distributions, $6,170,966; giving activities include $3,789,771 for 71 grants (high: $666,667; low: $250; average: $15,000–$82,500), and $1,329,011 for foundation-administered programs.
Purpose and activities: Giving primarily for human services, education, health care and for community enhancement.
Fields of interest: Historic preservation/historical societies; Education, early childhood education; Child development, education; Elementary school/education; Adult education—literacy, basic skills & GED; Education, reading; Education; Health care; AIDS; Human services; Children/youth, services; Child development, services; Family services; Economically disadvantaged.
Type of support: General/operating support; Capital campaigns; Program development; Seed money; Scholarship funds; Matching/challenge support.
Limitations: Giving primarily in Fort Bend County, TX. No support for religious, fraternal, or regranting

organizations. No grants to individuals; or for travel, conferences, conventions, group meetings, or seminars, research or studies, films, videos, books or other media projects, direct mail campaigns, no loans.
Publications: Application guidelines; Grants list; Informational brochure.
Application information: The foundation acknowledges receipt of proposals within two weeks. During the review process, interviews and site visits are requested to better evaluate the proposal. The foundation will not consider a grant application from the same applicant, whether granted or denied, more frequently than once every twelve month period. Application form not required.
Initial approach: Letter
Copies of proposal: 1
Deadline(s): Jan. 15, Apr. 15, July 15, and Oct. 15 (for capital proposals)
Board meeting date(s): Monthly; grants reviewed quarterly
Final notification: Approximately 6 months
Officers and Trustees:* Charles H. Herder,* Chair.; Sandra G. Thompson, C.F.O.; Roland C. Adamson, Exec. Dir.; Bill Jameson; Dean Leaman; Gene Reed; Mike Wells.
Number of staff: 3 full-time professional; 9 full-time support.
EIN: 746043368
Selected grants: The following grants were reported in 2005.
$666,667 to Polly Ryon Memorial Hospital, Richmond, TX. For expansion of Intensive Care Unit and construction of Cancer Care Unit.
$303,178 to Memorial Hermann Foundation, Houston, TX. For medical services for underserved populations in Fort Bend County.
$150,000 to Project Yes, Houston, TX. For replication of YES College Preparatory School in Richmond and Rosenberg area.
$145,500 to University of Texas Health Science Center, Houston, TX. 2 grants: $100,000 (For second phase of construction on Brown Foundation Institute for Molecular Medicine), $45,500 (For nursing scholarships for Fort Bend County residents).
$130,000 to YMCA of the Greater Houston Area, Houston, TX. 2 grants: $100,000 (For matching grant for renovations to T.W. Davis Family YMCA in Fort Bend County), $30,000 (For after-school, summertime tutorial and recreational programs for underserved Fort Bend County youth).
$110,000 to Fort Bend Family Health Center, Richmond, TX. For oral health services for Fort Bend County residents.
$106,825 to Fort Bend County Museum Association, Richmond, TX. 2 grants: $24,325 (To expand marketing strategies for George Ranch Historical Park), $82,500 (For public programs at George Ranch Historical Park).

8917
GHS Foundation ◆
2900 Weslayan St., Ste. B
Houston, TX 77027

Established in 2000 in TX.
Donors: Gerald H. Smith; Fidelity Charitable Gift Trust.
Foundation type: Independent foundation.
Financial data (yr. ended 2/28/06): Assets, $11,927,145 (M); gifts received, $1,683,907; expenditures, $742,705; qualifying distributions,

$741,200; giving activities include $741,200 for 7 grants (high: $544,275; low: $1,000).
Purpose and activities: Giving primarily for higher education and health associations.
Fields of interest: Higher education, university; Health organizations, association; Human services.
Limitations: Giving primarily in TX. No grants to individuals; no loans or scholarships.
Application information: Application form not required.
Deadline(s): None
Officers: Gerald H. Smith, Pres.; Nancy Hamlin Cooke, V.P. and Secy.-Treas.; Robert E. Hutson, V.P.
EIN: 760628970
Selected grants: The following grants were reported in 2003.
$216,600 to Sam Houston State University, Huntsville, TX. For scholarships.
$20,000 to Acadian Baptist Center, Eunice, LA. For general support.
$5,000 to Friends of Scouting, Houston, TX. For general support.
$5,000 to Interfaith CarePartners, Houston, TX. For general support.
$1,000 to American Cancer Society, Trinity, TX. For general support.
$1,000 to March of Dimes Birth Defects Foundation, Houston, TX. For general support.
$1,000 to University of Texas M. D. Anderson Cancer Center, Houston, TX. For general support.

8918
Mary Rodes Gibson Hemostasis-Thrombosis Foundation ◆ ☆
1707 Broadmoor, No. 103
Bryan, TX 77802-5219

Established in 2001 in TX.
Donor: Mary R. Gibson†.
Foundation type: Independent foundation.
Financial data (yr. ended 12/31/05): Assets, $8,880,566 (M); gifts received, $982,833; expenditures, $401,675; qualifying distributions, $334,000; giving activities include $334,000 for grants.
Fields of interest: Higher education, university.
Limitations: Applications not accepted. Giving primarily in Houston, TX. No grants to individuals.
Application information: Contributes only to pre-selected organizations.
Officer: Larry G. Holt, Chair.
Trustees: William Price; Edwin Sandhop, Jr.
EIN: 743015534

8919
Pauline Allen Gill Foundation ◆
1901 N. Akard St.
Dallas, TX 75201 (214) 521-7243
Contact: Pauline Allen Gill Sullivan, Pres.

Established in 1975 in TX.
Donor: Pauline Allen Gill Sullivan.
Foundation type: Independent foundation.
Financial data (yr. ended 12/31/05): Assets, $20,963,515 (M); expenditures, $1,121,107; qualifying distributions, $770,495; giving activities include $770,495 for 38 grants (high: $750,000; low: $30).
Purpose and activities: Giving primarily for education, health associations, social services, children and youth services, community

development, and federated giving programs; some funding also for Episcopal organizations, as well as to a Presbyterian church, and to an art museum.

Fields of interest: Museums (art); Education; Hospitals (general); Health care; Health organizations, association; Human services; Children/youth, services; Community development; Federated giving programs; Protestant agencies & churches.

Type of support: General/operating support; Capital campaigns; Building/renovation; Program development.

Limitations: Applications not accepted. Giving primarily in Dallas, TX. No grants to individuals.

Application information: Contributes only to pre-selected organizations.

Officers and Trustees:* Pauline Allen Gill Sullivan,* Pres.; B. Gill Clements,* V.P. and Treas.; Nancy Clements Seay,* V.P.; Pauline A. Seay Neuhoff, Secy.

Number of staff: 1 part-time support.

EIN: 237431528

Selected grants: The following grants were reported in 2004.

$500,000 to Southwestern Medical Foundation, Dallas, TX.

$205,000 to Dallas Museum of Art, Dallas, TX.

$100,000 to Presbyterian Healthcare Foundation, Dallas, TX.

$36,235 to Episcopal School of Dallas, Dallas, TX.

$10,000 to Neighbors United for Quality Education, Dallas, TX.

$2,500 to Parkland Foundation, Dallas, TX.

$2,000 to Educational First Steps, Dallas, TX.

$2,000 to Mi Escuelita Preschool, Dallas, TX.

$1,000 to Reading and Radio Resource, Dallas, TX.

$100 to Colorado Childrens Chorale, Denver, CO.

8920
The Goldsbury Foundation ▼ ✧

P.O. Box 460567
San Antonio, TX   78246-0567
Contact: Suzanne Mead Feldmann, Mgr.
E-mail: info@goldsbury-foundation.org; Application address: 5121 Broadway, San Antonio, TX 78209, tel.: (210) 930-1251, ext. 12; FAX: (210) 930-2482; Additional e-mail (for Suzanne Mead Feldmann): sfeldmann@goldsbury-foundation.org; URL: http://www.goldsbury-foundation.org

Established in 1996 in TX.

Donors: Christopher Goldsbury, Jr.; Goldsbury Charitable Trust.

Foundation type: Independent foundation.

Financial data (yr. ended 12/31/04): Assets, $10,088,270 (M); expenditures, $4,364,251; qualifying distributions, $4,239,416; giving activities include $4,191,684 for 47 grants (high: $1,000,000; low: $1,000; average: $5,000–$274,000).

Purpose and activities: The foundation's main emphasis is on preventing substance abuse in children, including through after-school programs, youth mentoring, education and drop-out prevention. The foundation is involved in furthering the interests of Latin American culture, including museums, exhibits, educational programs, and the performing arts.

Fields of interest: Arts; Elementary/secondary education; Education; Substance abuse, prevention; Crime/violence prevention, child abuse; Children/youth, services; Homeless, human services.

Type of support: General/operating support; Program development; Matching/challenge support.

Limitations: Giving primarily in San Antonio, TX. No support for research. No grants to individuals, or for capital campaigns or conferences.

Application information: Application form not required.

Initial approach: 2-3 page letter of inquiry
Copies of proposal: 1
Deadline(s): None
Board meeting date(s): Quarterly
Final notification: 30 days for letter of inquiry

Officers and Directors:* Christopher Goldsbury, Jr.,* Pres.; Rodney J. Sands,* V.P. and Treas.; William Scanlon, Jr.,* Secy.; Suzanne Mead Feldmann, Mgr.; Richard A. Longoria Derby; Angela Aboltin Goldsbury; Ron A. Lichtenfeld.

Number of staff: 1 part-time professional.

EIN: 742780083

Selected grants: The following grants were reported in 2004.

$1,000,000 to University of Texas Health Science Center, Houston, TX. For cardiovascular research.

$600,000 to Childrens Shelter of San Antonio, San Antonio, TX. For emergency shelter for abused and neglected children.

$274,000 to Hidalgo Foundation of Bexar County, San Antonio, TX. For child abuse and neglect court programming.

$250,000 to San Antonio Food Bank, San Antonio, TX. For program support.

$225,000 to Daughters of Charity Services of San Antonio, San Antonio, TX. For program support.

$203,000 to KIPP Foundation, San Antonio, TX. For programming at KIPP Aspire Academy.

$150,000 to Big Brothers Big Sisters of South Texas, San Antonio, TX. For general support.

$70,000 to Girl Scouts of the U.S.A., San Antonio Area Council, San Antonio, TX. To expand scouting into public housing projects.

$50,000 to San Antonio Metropolitan Ministry, SAMMINISTRIES, San Antonio, TX. For general support.

$10,000 to Healy-Murphy Center, San Antonio, TX. For Child Development Center for infants of children attending Healy-Murphy.

8921
Goodman-Abell Foundation ✧

2550 N. Loop W., Ste. 750
Houston, TX   77092-8980

Established in 1998 in TX.

Donors: G. Hughes Abell; Betsy G. Abell; Nelson Abell Foundation.

Foundation type: Independent foundation.

Financial data (yr. ended 2/29/04): Assets, $2,263,310 (M); gifts received, $180,922; expenditures, $939,612; qualifying distributions, $905,965; giving activities include $905,962 for 32 grants (high: $420,000; low: $100).

Purpose and activities: Giving primarily for the arts, education, including an Episcopal school, children and youth services, and the United Way.

Fields of interest: Museums; Arts; Elementary/secondary education; Higher education; Education; Children/youth, services; Federated giving programs.

Limitations: Applications not accepted. Giving primarily in Austin, TX. No grants to individuals.

Application information: Contributes only to pre-selected organizations.

Officers: Betsy G. Abell, Pres.; G. Hughes Abell, V.P.

EIN: 742869876

Selected grants: The following grants were reported in 2003.

$300,000 to United Way Capital Area, Austin, TX.

$40,000 to Center for Social and Emotional Education, New York, NY.

$32,800 to University of Texas, Austin, TX.

$26,000 to Saint Andrews Episcopal School, Austin, TX.

$10,000 to Saint Davids Episcopal Church, Austin, TX.

$10,000 to Vanderbilt University, Nashville, TN.

$6,000 to Austin Museum of Art, Austin, TX.

$5,000 to Houston Achievement Place, Houston, TX.

$5,000 to Texas Book Festival, Austin, TX.

$5,000 to United Cerebral Palsy Association of Texas, Austin, TX.

8922
The Gorman Foundation ✧

7373 Broadway, Ste. 508
San Antonio, TX   78209
Application address: c/o Frances S. Coker, 4040 Broadway, San Antonio, TX 78209

Established in 1997.

Foundation type: Independent foundation.

Financial data (yr. ended 12/31/05): Assets, $6,614,909 (M); expenditures, $417,576; qualifying distributions, $417,576; giving activities include $412,150 for 53 grants (high: $100,000; low: $100).

Purpose and activities: Giving primarily for education and to a Christian evangelistic fund, as well as for health and children's and social services.

Fields of interest: Education; Health care; Human services; Children, services; Christian agencies & churches.

Limitations: Giving primarily in San Antonio, TX.

Application information:

Initial approach: Letter (2-3 pages)
Deadline(s): None

Officers: James W. Gorman, Jr., Pres.; Rowena C. Gorman, V.P.; Frances M. Coker, Secy.; David A. Gorman, Treas.

Director: Michael A. Schott.

EIN: 742822598

Selected grants: The following grants were reported in 2004.

$100,000 to University of the Incarnate Word, San Antonio, TX.

$10,000 to United Way of San Antonio and Bexar County, San Antonio, TX.

$5,000 to YMCA of San Antonio and the Hill Country, San Antonio, TX.

$2,500 to Junior Achievement of South Texas, San Antonio, TX.

$1,000 to Catholic Charities, El Paso, TX.

$300 to Young Life of San Antonio, San Antonio, TX.

$250 to Guadalupe Community Center, San Antonio, TX.

$250 to Witte Museum, San Antonio, TX.

8923

Helen Greathouse Charitable Trust ◇
c/o Wells Fargo Bank, N.A.
P.O. Box 41629
Austin, TX 78704-9926 (432) 685-5300
Application address: c/o Wells Fargo Bank, N.A.,
Trust Dept., P.O. Box 1959, Midland, TX 79702

Established in 1997 in TX.
Foundation type: Independent foundation.
Financial data (yr. ended 12/31/05): Assets,
$47,522,914 (M); expenditures, $2,791,659;
qualifying distributions, $2,435,000; giving
activities include $2,435,000 for 118 grants (high:
$125,000; low: $2,000).
Purpose and activities: Funds are available for
charitable, religious, scientific, literary or
educational purposes and to organizations that work
with children and persons who must overcome
physical and mental changes.
Fields of interest: Arts; Education; Human services.
Type of support: General/operating support.
Limitations: Giving primarily in Midland County, TX.
No grants to individuals.
Application information: Application form required.
  Initial approach: Request formal application
  Deadline(s): Apr. 15 and Oct. 15
  Final notification: June and Dec.
Advisory Committee: Joan Baskin; Frank K.
Cahoon; Joann Foster; Vicky Jay; Paul Morris.
Trustee: Wells Fargo Bank, N.A.
EIN: 752691859
Selected grants: The following grants were reported
in 2005.
$125,000 to Manor Park, Midland, TX.
$100,000 to Midland Childrens Rehabilitation
  Center, Midland, TX.
$100,000 to Midland College, Midland, TX.
$40,000 to Commemorative Air Force, Midland, TX.
$30,000 to Community Childrens Clinic, Midland,
  TX.
$28,000 to Boys Club of Midland, Midland, TX.
$25,000 to Midland Fair Havens, Midland, TX.
$20,000 to Buckner Children and Family Services,
  Longview, TX.
$20,000 to University of Texas of the Permian
  Basin, Odessa, TX.
$10,000 to Junior Achievement of West Texas,
  Midland, TX.

8924

Greathouse Foundation ◇
P.O. Box 3739
Abilene, TX 79604
Contact: Dewayne E. Chitwood, Exec. Dir.

Established in 1997 in TX.
Donor: Wes-Tex Drilling Co.
Foundation type: Independent foundation.
Financial data (yr. ended 12/31/05): Assets,
$11,556,659 (M); expenditures, $421,873;
qualifying distributions, $380,678; giving activities
include $376,503 for 51 grants (high: $30,000;
low: $200).
Purpose and activities: Giving primarily for children,
youth and social services, including support for
programs for local firefighters; funding also for
services for the elderly, as well as Christian
organizations and churches.
Fields of interest: Higher education; Human
services; Children/youth, services; Aging, centers/
services; Christian agencies & churches.

Type of support: General/operating support;
Continuing support; Emergency funds; Program
development.
Limitations: Giving primarily in Abilene, TX.
Application information: Application form not
required.
  Initial approach: Letter
  Deadline(s): None
  Board meeting date(s): Quarterly
Officers and Directors: Marcella Greathouse,
Pres.; Carl S. Cook, Jr., Secy.; Sharon Mcdonald,*
Treas.; Dewayne E. Chitwood,* Exec. Dir.; Micah
Greathouse.
EIN: 752710208
Selected grants: The following grants were reported
in 2005.
$50,000 to University of Oklahoma, Norman, OK.
$30,000 to Diamondback Charity Classic, Abilene,
  TX.
$26,000 to Abilene Boys Ranch, Abilene, TX.
$23,000 to First Christian Church, Arlington, TX.
$10,000 to YMCA of Abilene, Abilene, TX.
$9,950 to Volunteer Services Council, Harlingen,
  TX.
$7,500 to Sears Methodist Foundation, Abilene, TX.
$5,000 to Love and Care Ministries, Abilene, TX.
$2,500 to Abilene Christian University, Abilene, TX.
$1,000 to Harmony Family Services, Abilene, TX.

8925

The Neil and Elaine Griffin Foundation ◇
P.O. Box 291910
Kerrville, TX 78029-1910 (830) 896-6667
Contact: Richard D. Griffin, Dir.
E-mail: rgriffin@ktc.com

Established in 1994 in TX.
Donor: F. O'Neil Griffin.
Foundation type: Independent foundation.
Financial data (yr. ended 9/30/05): Assets,
$6,187,480 (M); expenditures, $676,694;
qualifying distributions, $605,420; giving activities
include $40,954 for 3 grants (high: $25,000; low:
$3,454), and $562,803 for 56 grants to individuals
(high: $18,000; low: $2,000).
Fields of interest: Higher education; Animal welfare;
Cancer; Human services.
Type of support: Building/renovation; Scholarships
—to individuals.
Limitations: Giving limited to Kerrville, TX.
Application information: Scholarships are restricted
to Kerr County High School graduates only.
Application form required.
  Deadline(s): None
Directors: F. O'Neil Griffin; Richard D. Griffin.
EIN: 742729281

8926

Gulf Coast Medical Foundation
P.O. Box 30
Wharton, TX 77488 (979) 532-0904
Contact: Melissa M. Burnham, Exec. V.P.
FAX: (979) 532-0904;
E-mail: mburnham1@houston.rr.com

Established in 1983 in TX; converted from Caney
Valley Memorial Hospital and Gulf Coast Medical
Center.
Foundation type: Independent foundation.
Financial data (yr. ended 12/31/05): Assets,
$18,001,798 (M); gifts received, $50;

expenditures, $927,332; qualifying distributions,
$761,957; giving activities include $716,300 for 50
grants (high: $62,500; low: $300).
Fields of interest: Higher education; Medical
school/education; Nursing care; Health care;
Mental health/crisis services; Children/youth,
services.
Type of support: General/operating support; Capital
campaigns; Building/renovation; Equipment;
Endowments; Program development; Matching/
challenge support.
Limitations: Giving primarily in Wharton, Matagorda,
Jackson, Colorado, Fort Bend, and Brazoria
counties, TX. No support for national fundraising
organizations. No grants to individuals.
Application information: Application form required.
  Initial approach: Letter, telephone, or E-mail
  Copies of proposal: 1
  Deadline(s): Dec. 15, Mar. 15, June 15, and Sept.
   15
  Board meeting date(s): Quarterly
  Final notification: 6-8 weeks
Officers and Trustees: Clive Runnells III,* Pres.;
Melissa M. Burnham, Exec. V.P.; Jeffrey Blair, V.P.;
Jack Moore,* Secy.; Charles Davis,* Treas.; Guy F.
Stovall III; and 7 additional trustees.
Number of staff: 1 part-time professional.
EIN: 741285242

8927

D. D. Hachar Charitable Trust Fund ◇
c/o The Laredo National Bank
P.O. Box 59
Laredo, TX 78042-0059 (956) 723-1151, ext.
2297

Established in 1980 in TX.
Donor: Lamar Bruni Vergara Trust.
Foundation type: Independent foundation.
Financial data (yr. ended 4/30/05): Assets,
$27,512,904 (M); gifts received, $182,145;
expenditures, $1,283,899; qualifying distributions,
$952,512; giving activities include $557,134 for 7
grants (high: $400,000; low: $2,500), and
$348,825 for 271 grants to individuals (high:
$4,000; low: $250).
Purpose and activities: Grants for higher and other
education; some support for youth groups; awards
to individuals for higher education, primarily through
scholarships and loans.
Fields of interest: Elementary school/education;
Higher education; Children/youth, services.
Type of support: General/operating support;
Scholarships—to individuals; Student loans—to
individuals.
Limitations: Giving limited to Laredo and Webb
County, TX, and surrounding areas.
Publications: Application guidelines; Annual report;
Informational brochure; Program policy statement.
Application information: Application form required
for scholarships. Grants to organizations are limited.
Application form required.
  Initial approach: Letter or telephone
  Deadline(s): Last Fri. in Apr. and Oct. for
   scholarships
Advisor: Joaquin Gonzales Cigarroa, Jr., M.D.
Trustee: The Laredo National Bank.
Number of staff: 2 full-time professional.
EIN: 742093680

8928
Hackett Family Foundation
3372 Del Monte Dr.
Houston, TX 77019-3104
Contact: James T. Hackett, Pres.

Established in 1996 in TX.
Donors: James T. Hackett; Maureen Hackett; H. Patrick Hackett, Jr.
Foundation type: Independent foundation.
Financial data (yr. ended 12/31/05): Assets, $3,113,240 (M); gifts received, $1,460,550; expenditures, $807,142; qualifying distributions, $783,577; giving activities include $783,577 for 105 grants (high: $182,550; low: $42).
Purpose and activities: Giving primarily for education, and health and human services.
Fields of interest: Elementary/secondary education; Higher education; Health organizations, association; Human services; Children/youth, services; Residential/custodial care, hospices; Federated giving programs; Christian agencies & churches.
Limitations: Applications not accepted. Giving primarily in Houston, TX. No grants to individuals.
Application information: Contributes only to pre-selected organizations.
 Board meeting date(s): July
Officers and Directors:* James T. Hackett,* Pres.; Maureen O'Gara Hackett,* Secy.; H. Patrick Hackett, Jr.; Kevin Hickey; Nellie O'Gara.
EIN: 760522431
Selected grants: The following grants were reported in 2003.
$88,543 to Saint Agnes Academy, Houston, TX. For gala sponsor.
$50,000 to Villanova University, Villanova, PA. For unrestricted support.
$33,763 to Loyola Academy, Wilmette, IL.
$25,300 to Mental Health Association of Greater Houston, Houston, TX. For unrestricted support.
$25,000 to Georgetown University, DC. For GSB Fund.
$15,000 to Harvard University, Cambridge, MA. For unrestricted support.
$14,300 to United Way of the Texas Gulf Coast, Houston, TX. For unrestricted support.
$10,000 to Alley Theater, Houston, TX. For Resident Company Society.
$10,000 to Catholic Charities of the Archdiocese of Galveston-Houston, Houston, TX. For annual fund.
$10,000 to New York University, New York, NY. For Ghana project.

8929
Haggar Corp. Foundation ✧ ☆
11511 Luna Rd.
Dallas, TX 75234 (214) 953-4311
Contact: Marcia Heath, Admin.

Established in 1944 in TX.
Donor: Haggar Clothing Co.
Foundation type: Company-sponsored foundation.
Financial data (yr. ended 6/30/05): Assets, $1,739,658 (M); gifts received, $254,710; expenditures, $402,647; qualifying distributions, $390,910; giving activities include $390,910 for grants.
Purpose and activities: The foundation supports organizations involved with higher education, health, and human services.

Fields of interest: Higher education; Health care; Health organizations, association; Big Brothers/Big Sisters; Youth, services; Family services; Human services.
Limitations: Applications not accepted. Giving primarily in TX, with emphasis on Dallas. No grants to individuals.
Application information: Contributes only to pre-selected organizations.
 Board meeting date(s): Quarterly
Directors: Frank Bracken; Joe Haggar III.
EIN: 752620906
Selected grants: The following grants were reported in 2003.
$108,000 to University of North Texas Foundation, Denton, TX. For scholarships.
$23,500 to Salesmanship Club of Dallas, Dallas, TX.
$20,000 to Saint Jude Childrens Research Hospital, Irving, TX.
$15,000 to Project Shelter, Dallas, TX.
$13,000 to Big Brothers Big Sisters of Northern Texas, Dallas, TX.
$10,000 to Presbyterian Healthcare Foundation, Dallas, TX.
$6,000 to Boy Scouts of America, Greater New York Council, New York, NY.
$4,000 to Alzheimers Association, Dallas, TX.
$3,000 to Alliance for Children, Fort Worth, TX.
$2,500 to American Jewish Committee, New York, NY.

8930
Ed Haggar Family Foundation ✧
3198 Royal Ln., Ste. 100-B
Dallas, TX 75229 (469) 335-0110
Contact: Patricia J. Haggar, Pres.

Established in 1995 in TX.
Foundation type: Independent foundation.
Financial data (yr. ended 12/31/05): Assets, $7,022,813 (M); expenditures, $671,206; qualifying distributions, $531,750; giving activities include $531,750 for 54 grants (high: $60,000; low: $1,000).
Purpose and activities: The foundation gives to a wide variety of organizations, including charities, education, health, and human services.
Fields of interest: Higher education; Education; Hospitals (general); Health care; Health organizations, association; Medical research, institute; Roman Catholic agencies & churches.
Limitations: Giving primarily in Dallas, TX, Denver, CO and the Coachella Valley, CA area. No grants to individuals.
Application information:
 Initial approach: Letter
 Deadline(s): None
Directors: E.R. Haggar; John D. Haggar; Patricia A. Haggar; Patricia J. Haggar.
EIN: 752565413
Selected grants: The following grants were reported in 2004.
$50,600 to University of Notre Dame, Notre Dame, IN.
$30,000 to Dallas Center for the Performing Arts, Dallas, TX.
$20,500 to Eisenhower Medical Center Foundation, Rancho Mirage, CA.
$20,000 to Habitat for Humanity International, Americus, GA.
$17,500 to University of Dallas, Irving, TX.
$10,000 to Kidney Texas, Dallas, TX.

$10,000 to Saint Jude Childrens Research Hospital, Memphis, TN.
$9,100 to Alzheimers Association, Dallas, TX.
$5,000 to Saint Elizabeth Catholic School, Dallas, TX.
$5,000 to Texas Stampede, Dallas, TX.

8931
The J. M. Haggar, Jr. Family Foundation ✧
(formerly The J. M. Haggar, Jr. Charitable Foundation)
16300 Addison Rd., Ste. 290
Addison, TX 75001
Application address: c/o Gail Peisach, 8111 Preston Rd., Ste. 925, Dallas, TX 75225, tel.: (214) 365-9374

Established in 1997.
Donor: Joseph M. Haggar, Jr.
Foundation type: Independent foundation.
Financial data (yr. ended 12/31/04): Assets, $7,905,584 (M); expenditures, $434,841; qualifying distributions, $321,067; giving activities include $321,067 for 63 grants (high: $30,000; low: $500).
Purpose and activities: Giving primarily for the arts, education, and health and human services.
Fields of interest: Arts education; Performing arts centers; Arts; Secondary school/education; Higher education; Education; Environment; Hospitals (general); Health care; Health organizations, association; Medical research, institute; Human services; Children/youth, services; Roman Catholic federated giving programs; Roman Catholic agencies & churches.
Limitations: Giving primarily in Dallas, TX. No grants to individuals.
Application information: Application form not required.
 Initial approach: Letter
 Deadline(s): None
Directors: Marian H. Bryan; Isabell Haggar; J.M. Haggar, Jr.; J.M. Hagger III; Lydia H. Novakov.
EIN: 752565414
Selected grants: The following grants were reported in 2004.
$30,000 to University of Dallas, Irving, TX.
$25,000 to Bishop Lynch High School, Dallas, TX.
$20,000 to Dallas Center for the Performing Arts, Dallas, TX.
$20,000 to Presbyterian Hospital, Kaufman, TX.
$10,000 to United Way, TX.
$5,650 to Crystal Charity Ball, Dallas, TX.
$5,000 to Equest, Dallas, TX.
$3,000 to Junior League of Dallas, Dallas, TX.
$2,500 to Hockaday School, Dallas, TX.
$2,000 to Dallas Museum of Art, Dallas, TX.

8932
The Patrick and Beatrice Haggerty Foundation
(formerly Haggerty Foundation)
P.O. Box 7027
Dallas, TX 75209
Contact: Patrick E. Haggerty, Jr., Chair.

Established in 1968 in TX.
Donors: Patrick E. Haggerty†; Beatrice M. Haggerty†.
Foundation type: Independent foundation.

Financial data (yr. ended 12/31/05): Assets, $16,188,394 (M); gifts received, $1,500,000; expenditures, $751,338; qualifying distributions, $577,573; giving activities include $567,500 for grants.
Purpose and activities: Giving primarily for the arts, education, and human services.
Fields of interest: Arts; Education; Health care; Human services; Roman Catholic agencies & churches.
Type of support: Matching/challenge support; Equipment; General/operating support; Capital campaigns; Building/renovation; Scholarship funds; Research.
Limitations: Giving primarily in Dallas County, TX. No grants to individuals.
Application information: Application form not required.
   Initial approach: Letter
   Copies of proposal: 1
   Deadline(s): Oct. 1
   Board meeting date(s): Nov.
Officers: Patrick E. Haggerty, Jr., Chair.; Michael G. Haggerty, Secy.-Treas.
Trustees: Kathleen Haggerty; Teresa Haggerty Parravano; Sheila Haggerty Turner.
Number of staff: 1 part-time professional; 1 part-time support.
EIN: 752076387

8933
Jon and Linda Halbert Family Foundation ✧ ☆
c/o Jon S. Halbert
4245 N. Central Expwy., Ste. 505
Dallas, TX 75205
Contact: Carol Cashman

Donors: Jon S. Halbert; Linda M. Halbert; Jo Ann Walling Halbert†; Jo Ann Walling Halbert Trust.
Foundation type: Independent foundation.
Financial data (yr. ended 12/31/05): Assets, $12,877,306 (M); gifts received, $267,517; expenditures, $2,255,203; qualifying distributions, $2,153,325; giving activities include $2,146,536 for 10 grants (high: $2,000,000; low: $500).
Fields of interest: Christian agencies & churches.
Limitations: Giving primarily in TX. No grants to individuals.
Application information:
   Initial approach: Letter
   Deadline(s): None
Officers: Jon S. Halbert, Pres. and Treas.; Linda M. Halbert, V.P. and Secy.
EIN: 470929091

8934
G. A. C. Halff Foundation ✧
745 E. Mulberry Ave., Ste. 400
San Antonio, TX 78212-3166   (210) 735-3300
Contact: Thomas F. Bibb, V.P

Incorporated in 1951 in TX.
Donor: G.A.C. Halff†.
Foundation type: Independent foundation.
Financial data (yr. ended 2/28/06): Assets, $6,921,574 (M); expenditures, $464,498; qualifying distributions, $408,122; giving activities include $408,000 for 61 grants (high: $30,000; low: $2,000).

Purpose and activities: Giving primarily for human services.
Fields of interest: Arts; Human services; Children/youth, services; Community development; Federated giving programs.
Type of support: Continuing support.
Limitations: Giving limited to TX, primarily in San Antonio. No grants to individuals.
Publications: Application guidelines.
Application information: Application form not required.
   Initial approach: Letter
   Copies of proposal: 1
   Deadline(s): May 15
   Board meeting date(s): End of June
Officers and Trustees: * Hugh Halff, Jr.,* Chair.; Thomas F. Bibb,* V.P. and Treas.; Catherine H. Edson; Thomas H. Edson; Marie M. Halff; Jerry O. Street; Stephanie H. Street.
EIN: 746042432
Selected grants: The following grants were reported in 2005.
$30,000 to United Way.
$10,000 to Cancer Therapy and Research Center, San Antonio, TX.
$10,000 to Family Service.
$10,000 to Hill Country Montessori School, Boerne, TX.
$10,000 to Nonprofit Resource Center of Texas, San Antonio, TX.
$10,000 to Respite Care of San Antonio, San Antonio, TX.
$10,000 to Witte Museum, San Antonio, TX.
$10,000 to Youth Alternatives, Portland, ME.
$5,000 to Christian Senior Services, San Antonio, TX.
$5,000 to Saint Philips College, San Antonio, TX.

8935
Halliburton Foundation, Inc. ✧
2601 E. Belt Line Rd.
Carrollton, TX 75006-5401
Contact: Margaret E. Carriere, V.P. and Secy.
Application address: 4100 Clinton Dr., Bldg. 1, 7th Fl., Houston, TX 77020, tel.: (713) 676-3717

Incorporated in 1965 in TX.
Donors: Halliburton Co.; Brown & Root, Inc.
Foundation type: Company-sponsored foundation.
Financial data (yr. ended 12/31/04): Assets, $14,868,815 (M); gifts received, $1,000,001; expenditures, $2,080,443; qualifying distributions, $1,995,392; giving activities include $1,085,605 for grants, and $909,787 for employee matching gifts.
Purpose and activities: The foundation supports organizations involved with education.
Fields of interest: Education.
Type of support: General/operating support; Continuing support; Annual campaigns; Program development; Conferences/seminars; Research; Employee matching gifts; Employee-related scholarships.
Limitations: Giving primarily in the Southwest, with emphasis on TX. No grants to individuals (except for employee-related scholarships), or for start-up needs, emergency needs, debt reduction, building, land acquisition, renovation projects, endowments, scholarships, fellowships, demonstration projects, or publications; no loans.
Application information: Application form not required.
   Initial approach: Proposal

Copies of proposal: 1
Deadline(s): None
Board meeting date(s): Quarterly
Final notification: Within 3 months
Officers and Trustees: * David J. Lesar,* Pres.; Margaret E. Carriere,* V.P. and Secy.; Jerry H. Blurton, V.P. and Treas.; D.L. Foshee; Susan S. Keith; Gary V. Morris.
EIN: 751212458
Selected grants: The following grants were reported in 2003.
$100,000 to Oklahoma Centennial Commemoration Fund, Oklahoma City, OK.
$100,000 to University of Texas M. D. Anderson Cancer Center, Houston, TX.
$32,000 to University of Texas, Engineering School, Austin, TX. For annual support.
$30,000 to Junior Achievement of Southeast Texas, Houston, TX.
$15,000 to Texas A & M University, Business School, College Station, TX.
$10,000 to Boy Scouts of America, Sam Houston Area Council, Houston, TX.
$5,000 to Montana Tech Foundation, Butte, MT.
$5,000 to Star of Hope Mission, Houston, TX.
$5,000 to University of Oklahoma, Business School, Norman, OK.
$400 to Youth Services of Stephens County, Duncan, OK.

8936
The Ewing Halsell Foundation ▼ ✧
711 Navarro St., Ste. 537
San Antonio, TX 78205

Trust established in 1957 in TX.
Donors: Ewing Halsell†; Mrs. Ewing Halsell†; Grace F. Rider†.
Foundation type: Independent foundation.
Financial data (yr. ended 6/30/05): Assets, $110,034,155 (M); expenditures, $5,805,055; qualifying distributions, $4,766,810; giving activities include $4,734,279 for 39 grants (high: $1,100,000; low: $1,000; average: $20,000–$50,000).
Purpose and activities: Grants primarily for education, cultural programs, health organizations, and social service and youth agencies.
Fields of interest: Museums (art); Performing arts, orchestra (symphony); Arts; Higher education; Libraries (public); Education; Health organizations, association; Medical research, institute; Girl scouts; Human services; Youth, services.
Type of support: Annual campaigns; Building/renovation; Equipment; Land acquisition; Publication; Seed money; Research; Technical assistance.
Limitations: Giving limited to TX, with emphasis on southwestern TX, particularly San Antonio. No grants to individuals, or for deficit financing, emergency funds, general endowments, matching gifts, scholarships, fellowships, demonstration projects, general purposes, or conferences; no loans.
Publications: Biennial report (including application guidelines); Program policy statement.
Application information: Application form not required.
   Initial approach: Letter or proposal
   Copies of proposal: 1
   Deadline(s): None
   Board meeting date(s): Quarterly
   Final notification: 3 months

Trustees: Edward H. Austin, Jr.; Jean Deacy; Leroy G. Denman, Jr.; Hugh A. Fitzsimmons, Jr.
Number of staff: 1 full-time professional; 2 part-time support.
EIN: 746063016
Selected grants: The following grants were reported in 2005.
$1,100,000 to San Antonio Botanical Center Society, San Antonio, TX. For project support.
$1,000,000 to University of Texas Health Science Center, Houston, TX. Toward cardiovascular data project.
$800,000 to Carver Academy, San Antonio, TX. Toward completion of new classrooms.
$400,000 to Texas Military Institute, San Antonio, TX. Toward Knowledge is Power Program (KIPP) Scholarship.
$300,000 to Saint Marys Hall, San Antonio, TX. Toward rebuilding of lower and middle schools.
$238,300 to San Antonio Museum of Art, San Antonio, TX. For museum operations.
$200,000 to Southwest School of Art and Craft, San Antonio, TX. Toward plan for historic preservation.
$50,000 to Daughters of the Republic of Texas, San Antonio, TX. Toward new fire suppression system.
$50,000 to Mission Road Ministries, San Antonio, TX. Toward day care renovations.
$15,000 to Seton Home, San Antonio, TX. Toward maternity home.

8937
The Hamill Foundation ▼
1160 Dairy Ashford, Ste. 250
Houston, TX   77079-3014   (281) 556-9581
Contact: Charlie H. Read, C.E.O.
FAX: (281) 556-0456;
E-mail: cread__hamill@sbcglobal.net

Established in 1969 in TX.
Donors: Marie G. Hamill†; Claud B. Hamill†.
Foundation type: Independent foundation.
Financial data (yr. ended 12/31/05): Assets, $97,840,866 (M); expenditures, $6,179,167; qualifying distributions, $4,731,803; giving activities include $4,480,000 for 62 grants (high: $250,000; low: $10,000; average: $25,000–$200,000).
Purpose and activities: Giving primarily to education, health associations, medical research, human services, children and youth services, and Christian agencies and churches.
Fields of interest: Museums; Higher education; Education; Health organizations, association; Medical research, institute; Human services; Children/youth, services; Christian agencies & churches.
Type of support: General/operating support; Annual campaigns; Capital campaigns; Emergency funds; Scholarship funds; Research.
Limitations: Applications not accepted. Giving primarily in Houston, TX. No grants to individuals.
Application information: Contributes only to pre-selected organizations.
Board meeting date(s): Four or five times a year
Officers and Directors:* Charles D. McMurrey,* Chair.; Charlie H. Read,* C.E.O., Pres., and Treas.; Thomas H. Brown,* V.P., Secy., and Dir., Grants; Charles W. Snider,* V.P.; William T. Miller.
Number of staff: 1 full-time professional; 1 part-time professional; 2 full-time support.
EIN: 237028238

Selected grants: The following grants were reported in 2005.
$250,000 to University of Texas Foundation, Austin, TX. For research at M. D. Anderson Cancer Center and for capital campaign.
$200,000 to Houston Museum of Natural Science, Houston, TX. For program support.
$200,000 to Northwest Assistance Ministries, Houston, TX. For operating support.
$200,000 to Saint Lukes Episcopal Hospital, Houston, TX. For capital campaign.
$200,000 to Texas Heart Institute Foundation, Houston, TX. For operating support, research and Heart Information Center.
$100,000 to Council on Alcohol and Drugs Houston, Houston, TX. For substance abuse treatment programs.
$100,000 to University of Houston-University Park, Houston, TX. For capital campaign and program support.
$75,000 to Alzheimers Association, Houston and Southeast Texas Chapter, Houston, TX. For program support.
$50,000 to Billy Graham Evangelistic Association, Minneapolis, MN. For Capital Campaign.
$50,000 to Memorial Assistance Ministries, Houston, TX. For operating support and capital campaign.

8938
George and Mary Josephine Hamman Foundation
3336 Richmond, Ste. 310
Houston, TX   77098-3022   (713) 522-9891
Contact: E. Alan Fritsche, Exec. Dir.
FAX: (713) 522-9693;
E-mail: HammanFdn@aol.com; URL: http://www.hammanfoundation.org

Incorporated in 1954 in TX.
Donors: Mary Josephine Hamman†; George Hamman†.
Foundation type: Independent foundation.
Financial data (yr. ended 12/31/05): Assets, $72,364,193 (M); expenditures, $4,173,714; qualifying distributions, $3,692,409; giving activities include $2,585,000 for 193 grants (high: $125,000; low: $1,000; average: $10,000–$25,000), $618,000 for 212 grants to individuals (high: $3,000; low: $1,500; average: $1,500–$3,000), and $150,035 for foundation-administered programs.
Purpose and activities: Giving for construction and operation of hospitals, medical treatment, and research organizations and programs; grants to churches and affiliated religious organizations (nondenominational); individual scholarship program for local high school students; grants to building programs or special educational projects at colleges and universities, mostly local; contributions also to cultural programs, social services, and youth agencies.
Fields of interest: Arts; Higher education; Education; Hospitals (general); Health care; Medical research, institute; Human services; Children/youth, services; Religion.
Type of support: General/operating support; Continuing support; Annual campaigns; Capital campaigns; Building/renovation; Equipment; Scholarship funds; Research; Scholarships—to individuals; Matching/challenge support.
Limitations: Giving only in the state of TX for grants. Scholarships to high school seniors is limited to the

immediate Houston area. No support for postgraduate education. No grants to individuals (except for scholarships).
Publications: Application guidelines; Financial statement; Grants list.
Application information: Grant Application form and Grant follow-up reports must be completed for grantseekers. Application and financial qualification statement must be completed for scholarships. Forms can also be downloaded from foundation Web site. Requests by fax or E-mail will not be accepted. Application form required.
Initial approach: Application
Copies of proposal: 1
Deadline(s): Feb. 28 for scholarships, none for grants
Board meeting date(s): Monthly
Final notification: 60 days
Officers and Directors:* Henry R. Hamman,* Pres.; Anne H. Shepherd,* Secy.; Charles D. Milby, Jr.,* Treas.; E. Alan Fritsche, Exec. Dir.; Mary M. Brown; Russell R. Hamman.
Number of staff: 1 full-time professional; 1 full-time support.
EIN: 746061447

8939
The Curtis & Doris K. Hankamer Foundation ✧
9039 Katy Freeway, Ste. 530
Houston, TX   77024

Established in 1981 in TX.
Donors: Doris K. Hankamer†; Earl Curtis Hankamer, Jr.†.
Foundation type: Independent foundation.
Financial data (yr. ended 12/31/04): Assets, $16,371,548 (M); expenditures, $811,758; qualifying distributions, $660,407; giving activities include $635,000 for 16 grants (high: $160,000; low: $5,000).
Purpose and activities: Giving primarily for services for the elderly, particularly in the areas of medical research and ministry programs.
Fields of interest: Medical school/education; Hospitals (general); Medical research, institute; Cancer research; Food distribution, meals on wheels; Protestant agencies & churches; Roman Catholic agencies & churches; Aging.
Type of support: General/operating support; Fellowships.
Limitations: Applications not accepted. Giving primarily in Houston, TX. No grants to individuals.
Application information: Contributes only to pre-selected organizations.
Trustees: S. Terry Bracken; Earl Curtis Hankamer III; H. Scott Hunsaker.
EIN: 760022687
Selected grants: The following grants were reported in 2003.
$300,000 to Baylor College of Medicine, Houston, TX. For heart research.
$115,000 to Interfaith Ministries for Greater Houston, Houston, TX. For Meals on Wheels program.
$75,000 to Stehlin Foundation for Cancer Research, Houston, TX.
$60,000 to Saint Dominic Villa, Houston, TX.
$50,000 to Baylor University, Waco, TX.
$50,000 to Saint Joseph Hospital Foundation, Houston, TX. For medical services for the elderly.
$20,000 to Christ the King Evangelical Lutheran Church, Houston, TX. For elderly ministry.

$10,000 to American Cancer Society, Atlanta, GA. For research.

$10,000 to Inner City Youth, Houston, TX.

$10,000 to Saint Francis Cathedral, Santa Fe, NM. For elderly ministry.

8940

The Bryant & Nancy Hanley Foundation ◇

5455 Northbrook Dr.

Dallas, TX 75220 (214) 665-1900

Contact: Bryant M. Hanley, Jr., Pres.

Established in 1996 in TX.

Donors: Bryant M. Hanley; Nancy Hanley.

Foundation type: Independent foundation.

Financial data (yr. ended 12/31/05): Assets, $1,613,369 (M); expenditures, $676,779; qualifying distributions, $674,990; giving activities include $673,860 for 83 grants (high: $430,000; low: $250).

Purpose and activities: Giving primarily for education and the arts.

Fields of interest: Museums (art); Performing arts; Arts; Higher education; Education; Environment; Animals/wildlife; Reproductive health, family planning; Human services; Children/youth, services; Federated giving programs.

Limitations: Giving primarily in Dallas, TX. No grants to individuals.

Application information: Application form required.

Initial approach: Letter

Deadline(s): None

Officers and Directors:* Bryant M. Hanley, Jr.,* Pres.; Nancy C. Hanley,* Secy.-Treas.; Sarah E. Hanley; Barbara Hanley-Caldas.

EIN: 752683075

8941

Halbert Harmon Foundation ◇ ☆

(formerly Halbert Harmon Foundation, Inc.)

c/o David S. Halbert, Pres.

5215 N. O'Connor Blvd., Ste. 2650

Irving, TX 75039

Application address: 917 N. 13th St., Abilene, TX 79601

Established in 2003 in TX.

Donor: David S. Halbert.

Foundation type: Independent foundation.

Financial data (yr. ended 12/31/05): Assets, $2,444,819 (M); gifts received, $277,190; expenditures, $1,363,129; qualifying distributions, $1,290,695; giving activities include $1,290,695 for 7 grants (high: $1,000,000; low: $2,000).

Purpose and activities: Giving for Christian education and ministries.

Fields of interest: Higher education; Children/youth, services; Christian agencies & churches.

Limitations: Applications not accepted. No grants to individuals.

Application information: Contributes only to pre-selected organizations.

Officers and Directors:* David S. Halbert,* Pres.; Belinda Jo Harmon,* V.P.; Jon Mark Harmon,* V.P.; Robert G. Harmon,* V.P.; Christopher Robert Harmon,* Secy.; David Todd Harmon.

EIN: 200214688

8942

The Hartman Foundation, Inc. ◇

10711 Burnet Rd., Ste. 331

Austin, TX 78758

Established in 1999 in TX.

Donors: David A. Hartman; Claudette L. Hartman; Douglas M. Hartman.

Foundation type: Operating foundation.

Financial data (yr. ended 5/31/05): Assets, $4,449,666 (M); gifts received, $2,325; expenditures, $775,713; qualifying distributions, $722,792; giving activities include $517,138 for 18 grants (high: $90,000; low: $500), and $125,320 for 1 foundation-administered program.

Purpose and activities: Giving for human services, education, public policy, and the arts; funding also for a weekly newsletter devoted exclusively to coverage of Texas politics and government.

Fields of interest: Arts; Higher education; Education; Human services; Economics; Public affairs.

Type of support: General/operating support.

Limitations: Applications not accepted. Giving on a national basis, with some emphasis on TX. No grants to individuals.

Publications: Newsletter.

Application information: Contributes only to pre-selected organizations.

Officers and Directors:* David A. Hartman,* Chair.; Douglas M. Hartman,* Pres.; Claudette L. Hartman,* V.P.; Shirley Wolfe, Secy.-Treas.; John E. Hartman; Wayne P. Hartman.

EIN: 582471439

Selected grants: The following grants were reported in 2003.

$58,034 to Rockford Institute, Rockford, IL. 2 grants: $50,000, $8,034 (For Academic Speakers Bureau).

$50,000 to Howard Center for Family, Religion and Society, Rockford, IL.

$40,886 to Austin Symphony Orchestra, Austin, TX.

$39,930 to Institute for Policy Innovation, Lewisville, TX. For project support.

$33,300 to Austin Community Development Corporation, Austin, TX.

$25,000 to Intercollegiate Studies Institute, Wilmington, DE. For civic literacy project.

$20,000 to Texas Public Policy Foundation, Austin, TX.

$10,000 to Austin S.D.A. Junior Academy, Austin, TX. For endowment fund.

$10,000 to Heritage Foundation, DC.

8943

Hawn Foundation, Inc. ◇

5949 Sherry Ln., Ste. 775

Dallas, TX 75225-8043 (214) 696-6595

Contact: Joe V. Hawn, Jr., Pres.

Incorporated in 1962 in TX.

Donors: Mildred Hawn†; W.R. Hawn†; Mary C. Hawn†.

Foundation type: Independent foundation.

Financial data (yr. ended 8/31/05): Assets, $43,779,580 (M); expenditures, $2,549,524; qualifying distributions, $2,202,041; giving activities include $2,069,433 for 76 grants (high: $250,000; low: $100).

Purpose and activities: Giving primarily for health care, and to organizations providing direct assistance to needy individuals.

Fields of interest: Arts; Education; Hospitals (general); Health care; Medical research, institute; Human services.

Limitations: Giving primarily in the metropolitan area of Dallas, TX.

Application information: Application form not required.

Initial approach: Detailed letter

Copies of proposal: 1

Deadline(s): None

Board meeting date(s): Aug. and as necessary

Final notification: Aug. 31

Officers and Directors:* Joe V. Hawn, Jr.,* Pres. and Treas.; William Russell Hawn, Jr.,* V.P.; Edward A. Copley,* Secy.; Janey F. Bateman; Margaret Hawn; Cynthia Krause; John Ward.

Number of staff: 2 part-time professional.

EIN: 756036761

Selected grants: The following grants were reported in 2004.

$200,000 to Southwestern Medical Foundation, Dallas, TX.

$100,000 to Highland Park Presbyterian Church, Dallas, TX.

$50,000 to Arthritis Foundation, North Texas Chapter, Dallas, TX.

$50,000 to West Dallas Community School, Dallas, TX.

$30,000 to American Red Cross, Dallas, TX.

$25,000 to Dallas Museum of Art, Dallas, TX.

$25,000 to Scripps Foundation for Medicine and Science, San Diego, CA.

$15,000 to Victims Outreach, Dallas, TX.

$10,000 to Tyler Street Christian Academy, Dallas, TX.

$2,500 to Park Cities Presbyterian Church, Dallas, TX.

8944

Healthcare and Nursing Education Foundation ◇

(formerly Visiting Nurse Association of Houston Foundation)

3815 Montrose Blvd., Ste. 200

Houston, TX 77006-4665 (713) 802-7865

FAX: (713) 868-2619; E-mail: info@hnef.org; Leslie Winesett tel.: (713) 802-7870; URL: http://www.hnef.org

Established in 1994 in TX.

Donor: Vaughn Nelson Investment Mgmt.

Foundation type: Independent foundation.

Financial data (yr. ended 6/30/05): Assets, $7,955,757 (M); gifts received, $3,000; expenditures, $503,269; qualifying distributions, $415,357; giving activities include $337,762 for 19 grants (high: $35,500; low: $1,713), and $32,000 for 7 grants to individuals (high: $6,000; low: $4,000).

Purpose and activities: It is the foundation's mission to address unmet healthcare needs in the greater Houston, TX community through the provision of educational scholarships in nursing and community grants supporting the delivery of health care. Scholarships are awarded to students who have graduated from high school and will be attending an accepted undergraduate program in preparation for entry into an accredited college program leading to a bachelor's degree in nursing, who have been accepted into an accredited bachelor's-level nursing program, or who have been accepted into an accredited graduate-level nursing program leading to a master's degree in nursing, or to a Nurse Practitioner degree.

Fields of interest: Higher education; Nursing school/education; Scholarships/financial aid; Nursing care; Health care, home services.

Type of support: Continuing support; Program development; Seed money; Scholarships—to individuals.

Limitations: Giving primarily in the greater Houston, TX, area.

Publications: Application guidelines; Grants list.

Application information: See Web site for application information regarding nursing scholarships. The foundation is currently not accepting grant proposals.

Board meeting date(s): Quarterly

Officers: Donald S. Huge, M.D., Pres.; Willy Kuehn, Pres.-Elect; Geri Wood, Ph.D, Secy.; Noel Graubart, Treas.

Directors: Lewis E. Brazelton; Alan Fisherman, MD., R.N.; Shirley Gee Henry, R.N., Ph.D.; Gloria Herman; Karen S. Ho; Shirley F. Hutchinson; Ann P. Kaufman, Ph.D.; David Lummis; Edward K. Muraski; Marylou Robins, Ph.D.; Renae Schuman; Elsa Tansey, Ph.D.; Nancy Yuill, Ph.D.

EIN: 760454511

8945
The Gary & Diane Heavin Community Fund Inc. ◇

(formerly The Curves Community Fund, Inc.)
100 Ritchie Rd.
Waco, TX 76712

Established in 2001 in TX.

Donors: Curves International, Inc.; Gary Heavin.

Foundation type: Company-sponsored foundation.

Financial data (yr. ended 4/30/05): Assets, $19,296,403 (M); gifts received, $6,586,139; expenditures, $4,937,808; qualifying distributions, $4,907,442; giving activities include $4,870,339 for grants, and $37,103 for grants to individuals.

Purpose and activities: The fund supports organizations involved with radio, health, cancer, human services, and Christianity.

Fields of interest: Media, radio; Hospitals (general); Reproductive health, prenatal care; Health care; Cancer; Family services; Human services; Christian agencies & churches.

Type of support: General/operating support; Scholarships—to individuals.

Limitations: Applications not accepted. Giving primarily in TX.

Application information: Contributes only to pre-selected individuals and organizations.

Officers: Gary Heavin, Pres.; Diane Heavin, V.P.

EIN: 743003293

Selected grants: The following grants were reported in 2004.

$2,000,000 to Thomas Edison State College.

$250,000 to American Center for Law and Justice, DC.

$100,000 to Focus on the Family, Colorado Springs, CO.

$100,000 to Salvation Army.

$99,000 to Mission Waco, Waco, TX.

$50,359 to American Cancer Society, Atlanta, GA.

$50,000 to Heidi Group, Austin, TX.

$16,185 to March of Dimes Birth Defects Foundation, White Plains, NY.

$13,650 to Midway United Methodist Church, Lexington, NC.

$5,755 to Alzheimers Association, Chicago, IL.

8946
Wilton & Effie Mae Hebert Foundation ◇
P.O. Box 908
Port Neches, TX 77651 (409) 727-2345
Application address: c/o Pauline Womack, 802 West Dr., Port Neches, TX 77651

Established in 1992 in TX.

Donors: Wilton P. Hebert†; Effie Mae Hebert†.

Foundation type: Independent foundation.

Financial data (yr. ended 12/31/05): Assets, $13,142,747 (M); expenditures, $886,737; qualifying distributions, $671,124; giving activities include $636,281 for 27 grants (high: $125,000; low: $1,000).

Purpose and activities: Giving primarily for children and youth services, as well as for hospitals and health associations; funding also for education, social services, and Roman Catholic organizations and churches.

Fields of interest: Education; Hospitals (general); Substance abuse, prevention; Health organizations, association; Muscular dystrophy; Human services; Children/youth, services; Roman Catholic agencies & churches.

Type of support: General/operating support; Building/renovation.

Limitations: Giving primarily in TX. No grants to individuals.

Application information: Application form required.

Copies of proposal: 6

Deadline(s): None

Board meeting date(s): Mar., June, Sept., and Dec.

Officer and Directors:* Pauline Womack,* Admin.; James Black; Joe Hebert; Ed Hughes; Joe Vernon.

Number of staff: 1 full-time professional; 1 part-time professional.

EIN: 760065521

8947
The Helm Foundation, Inc. ◇
8 Greenway Plz., Rm. 718
Houston, TX 77046

Established in 1993 in TX.

Donors: Glora Bee Helm; Tair, Ltd.

Foundation type: Independent foundation.

Financial data (yr. ended 12/31/04): Assets, $8,097,826 (M); expenditures, $457,686; qualifying distributions, $337,807; giving activities include $336,085 for 13+ grants (high: $165,075).

Purpose and activities: Giving primarily to a United Methodist church and to an Episcopal school.

Fields of interest: Education; Human services; Protestant agencies & churches.

Limitations: Applications not accepted. Giving primarily in TX. No grants to individuals.

Application information: Contributes only to pre-selected organizations.

Officers and Directors:* Glora Bee Helm,* Chair.; Cyrus Vard Helm,* Pres.; Susan Helm, Secy.

EIN: 760419884

Selected grants: The following grants were reported in 2004.

$165,075 to First United Methodist Church, Houston, TX.

$110,000 to Saint James Episcopal School, Austin, TX.

$20,660 to Wesley Academy, Houston, TX.

$20,250 to Saint Stephens Episcopal School, Austin, TX.

$11,000 to Star of Hope Mission, Houston, TX.

$3,000 to Duke University, Durham, NC.

$1,000 to Crested Butte Academy, Crested Butte, CO.

$1,000 to Homes of Saint Marks, Houston, TX.

$900 to Room to Grow, New York, NY.

$100 to City Wide Club of Clubs, Houston, TX.

8948
Bob L. Herd Foundation ◇
P.O. Box 9340
Tyler, TX 75711
Application address: c/o: Janice Thompson, 3901 Manhattan, Tyler, TX 75701, tel.: (903) 509-3456, ext. 104

Established in 1994 in TX.

Donor: Bob L. Herd.

Foundation type: Independent foundation.

Financial data (yr. ended 12/31/05): Assets, $19,843,026 (M); gifts received, $6,000,000; expenditures, $626,532; qualifying distributions, $550,804; giving activities include $462,412 for 63 grants (high: $110,000; low: $100).

Purpose and activities: Giving primarily for health and human services.

Fields of interest: Arts; Education; Health organizations; Human services; Children/youth, services; Federated giving programs.

Limitations: Giving primarily in Tyler, TX. No grants to individuals.

Application information:

Initial approach: Letter

Deadline(s): None

Officers: Bob L. Herd, Pres.; Patsy L. Herd, V.P.; Janice Thompson, Secy.-Treas.

EIN: 752530305

8949
Albert & Ethel Herzstein Charitable Foundation ◇
6131 Westview Dr.
Houston, TX 77055-5421 (713) 681-7868
Contact: L. Michael Hajtman, Pres.
FAX: (713) 681-3652;
E-mail: albertandethel@herzsteinfoundation.org;
URL: http://www.herzsteinfoundation.org

Established in 1965 in TX.

Donors: Albert H. Herzstein†; Ethel Avis Herzstein†; Sadie Herzstein Smith†; and members of the Herzstein family.

Foundation type: Independent foundation.

Financial data (yr. ended 12/31/04): Assets, $69,037,899 (M); expenditures, $3,714,745; qualifying distributions, $3,319,179; giving activities include $3,037,119 for 178 grants (high: $500,000; low: $500; average: $5,000–$50,000).

Purpose and activities: The trust was organized and shall be operated exclusively for religious, charitable, scientific, literary and/or educational purposes.

Fields of interest: Arts; Education, community/ cooperative; Education; Environment; Health care; Youth development; Human services; Community development, civic centers; Community development.

Type of support: General/operating support; Continuing support; Annual campaigns; Capital campaigns; Building/renovation; Equipment; Land acquisition; Endowments; Debt reduction; Seed money; Scholarship funds; Research.

Limitations: Giving primarily in TX. No grants to individuals.
Publications: Application guidelines; Grants list; Informational brochure (including application guidelines).
Application information: Only one proposal may be submitted in any twelve month period. Application form not required.
 Initial approach: Letter or proposal
 Copies of proposal: 1
 Deadline(s): None
 Final notification: 90 days
Officers: Nathan H. Topek, M.D., Chair.; L. Michael Hajtman, Pres.; Paul Van Gilder, Cont.
Directors: David L. Nelson, Advisory Dir.; Richard J. Loewenstern; George W. Strake, Jr.
Number of staff: 1 full-time professional; 3 full-time support.
EIN: 746070484
Selected grants: The following grants were reported in 2004.
$500,000 to Emery/Weiner Center for Jewish Education, Houston, TX.
$400,000 to Houston Symphony Society, Houston, TX.
$200,000 to Jewish Community Center of Houston, Houston, TX.
$110,000 to Alley Theater, Houston, TX. 2 grants: $100,000, $10,000
$100,000 to University of Saint Thomas, Houston, TX.
$50,000 to Museum of New Mexico Foundation, Santa Fe, NM.
$15,000 to Boys and Girls Country of Houston, Hockley, TX.
$10,000 to Incarnate Word Academy, Houston, TX.
$5,000 to Nehemiah Center, Houston, TX.

8950
Walter Hightower Foundation ☆
c/o El Paso Community Foundation
310 N. Mesa, 10th Fl.
El Paso, TX 79901 (915) 533-4020
Contact: Virginia Martinez, Exec. V.P.
FAX: (915) 532-0716; E-mail: grants@epcf.org

Incorporated in 1987 in TX.
Donor: Walter H. Hightower†.
Foundation type: Independent foundation.
Financial data (yr. ended 12/31/05): Assets, $9,736,516 (M); expenditures, $592,560; qualifying distributions, $479,452; giving activities include $468,950 for 2 grants (high: $461,000; low: $7,950).
Purpose and activities: The foundation provides funding for medical care and treatment of crippled children in far west Texas and southern New Mexico.
Type of support: General/operating support; Continuing support; Capital campaigns; Building/ renovation; Equipment.
Limitations: Giving primarily in southern NM and far west TX. No support for religious or political organizations. No grants to individuals or for debt reduction or endowments.
Application information:
 Initial approach: Letter of Inquiry
 Deadline(s): Feb. 1
 Board meeting date(s): June
 Final notification: 4-5 months
Officers and Directors:* Lillian Crouch,* Pres.; Roger Ortiz, D.D.S.*, V.P.; Virginia Martinez, Exec. V.P.; Guillermo Avila,* Secy.; Carl Ryan, Secy.; Carmen Maria Castorena, Treas.; Joe Alcantar;

Margaret Varner Bloss; Mabel Fayant; Rickie Feuille; Ramiro Guzman; Susan Gray Kisler; Jose Manuel Mascarenas; Margie Melby.
Agent: Bank of the West.
EIN: 300176957

8951
Hildebrand Foundation
P.O. Box 1308
Houston, TX 77251-1308 (713) 965-9046
Contact: Myra Williams
FAX: (713) 622-2732;
E-mail: myrawilliams@hilhouse.com

Established in 2001 in TX.
Donors: Jeffrey D. Hildebrand; Melinda B. Hildebrand.
Foundation type: Independent foundation.
Financial data (yr. ended 12/31/05): Assets, $7,175,809 (M); expenditures, $433,241; qualifying distributions, $433,241; giving activities include $397,200 for 25 grants (high: $75,000; low: $1,000).
Purpose and activities: Giving for the poor and needy through faith-based organizations.
Fields of interest: Religion.
Limitations: Giving primarily in Houston, TX. No grants to individuals.
Application information: Application form not required.
 Initial approach: Written request on organization's letterhead
 Copies of proposal: 3
 Deadline(s): Ongoing
 Board meeting date(s): Triannually
 Final notification: Two weeks after board meeting
Officers: Jeffrey D. Hildebrand, Pres.; Melinda B. Hildebrand, V.P.
Director: Jean-Paul Budinger.
EIN: 760699250
Selected grants: The following grants were reported in 2004.
$100,000 to River Oaks Baptist School, Houston, TX.
$21,000 to Casa Juan Diego, Houston, TX.
$12,500 to Houston Music Hall Foundation, Houston, TX.
$10,000 to Small Steps Nurturing Center, Houston, TX.
$5,000 to Holy Cross Chapel, Houston, TX.
$4,100 to Saint Michael Catholic Church, Houston, TX.

8952
Hillcrest Foundation ▼ ✧
c/o Bank of America, N.A.
P.O. Box 830241
Dallas, TX 75283-1041 (214) 209-1965
Contact: Daniel Kelly, Sr. V.P., Bank of America, N.A.

Trust established in 1959 in TX.
Donor: Mrs. W.W. Caruth, Sr.†.
Foundation type: Independent foundation.
Financial data (yr. ended 5/31/05): Assets, $145,657,074 (M); expenditures, $8,099,243; qualifying distributions, $6,625,213; giving activities include $6,488,000 for 123 grants (high: $323,500; low: $3,000; average: $10,000–$100,000).
Purpose and activities: To relieve poverty, advance education, and promote health; support for higher

and other education, health and hospitals, social services, including programs for youth and child welfare, drug abuse, rehabilitation and housing.
Fields of interest: Secondary school/education; Vocational education; Higher education; Business school/education; Adult/continuing education; Education; Hospitals (general); Dental care; Medical care, rehabilitation; Health care; Substance abuse, services; Health organizations, association; Cancer; Medical research, institute; Food services; Housing/shelter, development; Human services; Children/youth, services; Aging, centers/services; Aging; Disabilities, people with.
Type of support: Capital campaigns; Building/ renovation; Equipment; Land acquisition; Program development; Matching/challenge support.
Limitations: Giving limited to TX, with emphasis on Dallas County. No grants to individuals, or for endowment funds, scholarships, or fellowships; no loans.
Publications: Application guidelines; Informational brochure (including application guidelines).
Application information: Application form required.
 Initial approach: Letter
 Copies of proposal: 2
 Deadline(s): End of Mar., Aug., and Nov.
 Board meeting date(s): As required, usually 3 times annually; Feb., May, and Oct.
 Final notification: Within 30 days after meeting
Trustees: D. Harold Byrd, Jr.; W.W. Caruth III; Sandra Estess; Charles P. Storey; Bank of America, N.A.
Number of staff: 1 part-time professional; 2 part-time support.
EIN: 756007565
Selected grants: The following grants were reported in 2005.
$323,500 to Childrens Medical Center Foundation, Dallas, TX. For capital campaign to expand pediatric pathology laboratory.
$250,000 to Parkland Foundation, Dallas, TX. To construct new Ambulatory Surgery Center at Parkland Health and Hospital System.
$250,000 to Southern Methodist University, Cox School of Business, Dallas, TX. To construct new James M. Collins Executive Education Center.
$250,000 to YMCA of Metropolitan Dallas, Dallas, TX. For capital campaign to build, renovate, and expand branches.
$130,000 to Sky Ranches, Van, TX. To construct new cabin for youth and families.
$125,000 to Old Red Courthouse, Dallas, TX. To create exhibits for opening of Museum of Dallas County History and Culture.
$100,000 to Happy Hill Farm Childrens Home and Academy, Granbury, TX. To construct new Academic Complex.
$100,000 to Presbyterian Healthcare Foundation, Dallas, TX. For capital campaign for expansion of Presbyterian Hospital of Allen.
$30,000 to Our Lady of Perpetual Help School, Dallas, TX. To replace roof and for other renovations.
$25,000 to Promise House, Dallas, TX. For computer equipment.

8953
Hirsch Family Foundation ✧ ☆
3811 Turtle Creek Blvd., Ste. 250
Dallas, TX 75201 (214) 245-5000
Contact: Rachel Gallini

Established in 2004 in TX.
Donors: Laurence Hirsch; Susan Hirsch.

Foundation type: Independent foundation.
Financial data (yr. ended 12/31/05): Assets, $26,332,817 (M); gifts received, $8,172,500; expenditures, $1,114,965; qualifying distributions, $907,250; giving activities include $907,250 for 41 grants (high: $200,000; low: $250).
Fields of interest: Arts; Elementary/secondary education; Higher education; Education; Human services; Children/youth, services; Federated giving programs; Jewish federated giving programs; Jewish agencies & temples.
Limitations: Giving primarily in TX.
Application information:
  Initial approach: Letter
  Deadline(s): None
Directors: Bradford Hirsch; Daria Lee Hirsch; Laurence Hirsch; Susan Hirsch.
EIN: 201225862

8954
Hobby Family Foundation ◇
2131 San Felipe
Houston, TX   77019-5620   (713) 521-1163
Contact: Jennifer Cole, Secy.

Established in 1995 in TX.
Donor: W.P. Hobby.
Foundation type: Independent foundation.
Financial data (yr. ended 12/31/03): Assets, $19,056,246 (M); gifts received, $620,050; expenditures, $1,804,499; qualifying distributions, $1,711,396; giving activities include $1,710,330 for 146 grants (high: $350,000; low: $100).
Purpose and activities: Giving primarily for the arts, health care, community development and social services.
Fields of interest: Performing arts, orchestra (symphony); Humanities; Elementary school/education; Higher education; Environment, natural resources; Health care, clinics/centers; Medical research, institute; Human services; American Red Cross; Children/youth, services; Community development; Protestant agencies & churches.
Limitations: Giving primarily in TX. No grants to individuals.
Application information: Application form not required.
  Deadline(s): None
Officers and Trustees:* W.P. Hobby,* Pres.; Laura H. Beckworth,* V.P.; Diana P. Hobby,* V.P.; Paul W. Hobby, V.P.; Jennifer Cole, Secy.; Cathy Leeson, Treas.
EIN: 760489862
Selected grants: The following grants were reported in 2004.
$215,000 to Palmer Memorial Episcopal Church, Houston, TX. 2 grants: $15,000, $200,000
$200,000 to Saint Johns School, Houston, TX.
$100,000 to College Foundation of the University of Virginia, Charlottesville, VA.
$50,000 to Center for Public Policy Priorities, Austin, TX.
$50,000 to Kinkaid School, Houston, TX.
$25,000 to Houston Grand Opera, Houston, TX.
$10,000 to Saint Lukes United Methodist Church, Houston, TX.
$5,000 to Saint Albans School, DC.
$5,000 to Susan Smith Blackburn Prize, Houston, TX.

8955
Hoblitzelle Foundation ▼
5956 Sherry Ln., Ste. 901
Dallas, TX   75225-6522   (214) 373-0462
Contact: Paul W. Harris, Exec. V.P.
FAX: (214) 750-7412;
E-mail: pharris@hoblitzelle.org; URL: http://www.hoblitzelle.org

Trust established in 1942 in TX; incorporated in 1953.
Donors: Karl St. John Hoblitzelle†; Esther T. Hoblitzelle†; Karl Hoblitzelle Trust.
Foundation type: Independent foundation.
Financial data (yr. ended 4/30/06): Assets, $127,287,680 (M); gifts received, $27,106; expenditures, $7,220,029; qualifying distributions, $6,682,854; giving activities include $6,151,687 for 61 grants (high: $500,000; low: $2,000; average: $25,000–$125,000).
Purpose and activities: Grants for higher, secondary, vocational, scientific and medical education, hospitals and health services, youth agencies, cultural programs, social services, and community development.
Fields of interest: Visual arts; Performing arts; Historic preservation/historical societies; Arts; Secondary school/education; Vocational education; Higher education; Medical school/education; Adult/continuing education; Adult education—literacy, basic skills & GED; Education, reading; Education; Hospitals (general); Medical care, rehabilitation; Health care; AIDS; Alcoholism; Housing/shelter, development; Human services; Children/youth, services; Aging, centers/services; Community development; Science; Aging; Minorities; Economically disadvantaged.
Type of support: Capital campaigns; Building/renovation; Equipment; Land acquisition; Program development; Seed money; Matching/challenge support.
Limitations: Giving limited to TX, primarily Dallas. No support for religious organizations (except for sectarian purposes). No grants to individuals; only occasional board-initiated support for operating budgets, debt reduction, research, scholarships, media productions, publications, or endowments; no loans (except for program-related investments).
Publications: Application guidelines; Annual report (including application guidelines); Grants list; Newsletter; Program policy statement.
Application information: Application form not required.
  Initial approach: Letter
  Copies of proposal: 1
  Deadline(s): Jan. 15, May 15, and Sept. 15
  Board meeting date(s): Latter part of Feb., June, and Oct.
  Final notification: After next board meeting
Officers and Directors:* Gerald W. Fronterhouse,* Chair.; George A. Shafer,* C.E.O. and Pres.; Paul W. Harris, Exec. V.P.; Donna C. Berry, Secy.; Caren H. Prothro,* Treas.; Linda P. Custard; Jerry Farrington; Kern Wildenthal, M.D., Ph.D.; J. McDonald Williams; William T. Solomon*.
Number of staff: 1 full-time professional; 1 full-time support.
EIN: 756003984
Selected grants: The following grants were reported in 2005.
$1,500,000 to Southwestern Medical Foundation, Karl and Esther Hoblitzelle Fund/Children's Medical Center, Dallas, TX. For capital

construction for Pediatric Neurology Science Area.
$500,000 to Hockaday School, Dallas, TX. Toward renovation of Academic Center.
$350,000 to Carter BloodCare, Bedford, TX. Toward expanded facilities.
$250,000 to Presbyterian Healthcare Foundation, Dallas, TX. Toward new emergency services area.
$200,000 to Jesuit College Preparatory School, Dallas, TX. For window replacement.
$120,000 to Collin County Community College District, Nursing Program, Plano, TX. Toward state-of-the-art patient service equipment.
$100,000 to Bishop Lynch High School, Dallas, TX. For campus improvements.
$100,000 to Dallas Summer Musicals, Dallas, TX. For improvements to sound system at Majestic Theater.
$100,000 to University of Texas at Dallas, Center for Brain Health, Richardson, TX. Toward renovation, furnishings and equipment.
$70,000 to Dallas Opera, Dallas, TX. Toward set construction and costuming costs.

8956
The Hoglund Foundation
5910 N. Central Expwy., Ste. 255
Dallas, TX   75206   (214) 987-3605
Contact: Kelly H. Compton, Secy.-Treas.
FAX: (214) 363-6507;
E-mail: info@hoglundfoundation.org; URL: http://www.hoglundfoundation.org

Established in 1989 in TX.
Donor: Forrest E. Hoglund.
Foundation type: Independent foundation.
Financial data (yr. ended 12/31/05): Assets, $62,116,571 (M); gifts received, $1,055,420; expenditures, $2,481,341; qualifying distributions, $2,184,496; giving activities include $2,030,996 for 136 grants (high: $250,000; low: $400).
Purpose and activities: To promote interests and entities in education, health science and services, social services, and children's health and development.
Fields of interest: Education; Health care; Health organizations, association; Human services; Child development, services.
Type of support: General/operating support; Annual campaigns; Capital campaigns; Building/renovation; Equipment; Endowments; Program development; Scholarship funds; Research; Matching/challenge support.
Limitations: Giving primarily to organizations that are located in and focused on the Houston and Dallas, TX metropolitan areas. No grants to individuals.
Publications: Application guidelines.
Application information: Application guidelines available on foundation Web site. Application form not required.
  Initial approach: Brief letter of inquiry
  Copies of proposal: 1
  Deadline(s): 30 days prior to quarter end
  Board meeting date(s): Apr., July, Oct., and Dec.
  Final notification: Within 4 months
Officers and Trustees:* Forrest E. Hoglund,* Chair. and Pres.; Sally R. Hoglund,* V.P.; Kelly H. Compton,* Secy.-Treas. and Exec. Dir.; Shelly H. Dee; Kristy H. Robinson.
Number of staff: 1 full-time professional; 1 part-time professional.
EIN: 752300978

Selected grants: The following grants were reported in 2003.

$200,000 to University of Texas M. D. Anderson Cancer Center, Houston, TX. Toward basic science research building.

$50,000 to Texas Childrens Hospital, Cancer Center, Houston, TX. For pediatric brain tumor research.

$15,000 to Girls Inc. of Metropolitan Dallas, Dallas, TX. For general operating support.

$10,000 to Saint Anthony School, Dallas, TX. For general operating support.

$10,000 to Saint Marks School of Texas, Dallas, TX. For Charlene Sullivan Compton Scholarship Fund.

$10,000 to Senior Citizens of Greater Dallas, Dallas, TX. For general operating support.

$7,500 to Womens Home, Houston, TX. For general operating support.

$5,000 to Hockaday School, Dallas, TX. For general operating support.

$5,000 to Houston Hospice and Palliative Care System, Houston, TX. For general operating support.

$5,000 to Suicide and Crisis Center, Dallas, TX. For general operating support.

8957
Don L. & Julie Holden Foundation, Inc. ◇ ☆

(formerly Don L. Holden Foundation, Inc.)
1002 N. Llano St.
Fredericksburg, TX 78624 (830) 997-4489
Contact: Merilee Hazelett, Secy.

Established in TX.
Donor: Don L. Holden.
Foundation type: Independent foundation.
Financial data (yr. ended 11/30/05): Assets, $8,102,835 (M); gifts received, $8,165,689; expenditures, $1,782,699; qualifying distributions, $1,550,000; giving activities include $1,550,000 for 18 grants (high: $1,000,000; low: $500).
Fields of interest: Health care, single organization support; Hospitals (general); Cancer research; Human services; Federated giving programs.
Limitations: Giving primarily in TX. No grants to individuals.
Application information:
  Initial approach: Letter
  Deadline(s): None
Officers and Trustees:* Robert Jones,* Pres.; Travis Davis,* V.P.; Merilee Hazelett,* Secy.; Ray Geistweidt,* Treas.; J.D. Davis; Richard Hoerster.
EIN: 746048619

8958
Holt Foundation ◇
P.O. Box 207916
San Antonio, TX 78220-7916

Established in 1994 in TX.
Donors: Benjamin D. Holt, Jr.; Holt Companies.
Foundation type: Independent foundation.
Financial data (yr. ended 12/31/05): Assets, $1,156,942 (M); gifts received, $381,236; expenditures, $383,764; qualifying distributions, $376,358; giving activities include $376,358 for 43 grants (high: $120,000; low: $100).
Fields of interest: Museums (specialized); Higher education; Libraries (public); Cancer research; Christian agencies & churches.

Limitations: Applications not accepted. Giving primarily in San Antonio, TX. No grants to individuals.
Application information: Contributes only to pre-selected organizations.
Officers and Directors:* Peter M. Holt,* Pres.; Kenneth R. Kamp, V.P. and Secy.; David C. Hennessee, Treas.; Anne Holt; Benjamin D. Holt, Jr.; Benjamin D. Holt III.
EIN: 742728633
Selected grants: The following grants were reported in 2003.
$120,000 to Texas A & M University, College Station, TX.
$32,500 to Texas State Aquarium Association, Corpus Christi, TX.
$25,000 to Texas Public Policy Foundation, Austin, TX.
$17,000 to Cancer Therapy and Research Center, San Antonio, TX.
$12,500 to Southwest Foundation for Biomedical Research, San Antonio, TX.
$5,000 to American Red Cross, San Antonio, TX.
$5,000 to Baptist Health System Foundation, San Antonio, TX.
$5,000 to San Antonio Council on Alcohol and Drug Abuse, San Antonio, TX.
$3,000 to South Texas Blood and Tissue Center, San Antonio, TX.
$2,500 to Childrens Bereavement Center of South Texas, San Antonio, TX.

8959
The Holthouse Foundation for Kids ◇
c/o Michael Holthouse
1800 West Loop S., Ste. 1875
Houston, TX 77027 (713) 626-5511
Contact: Paula Barnes, Exec. Dir.
FAX: (713) 626-5521; E-mail: pbarnes@hffk.org;
URL: http://hffk.org

Established in 2000 in TX.
Donors: Colleen Holthouse; Michael H. Holthouse.
Foundation type: Independent foundation.
Financial data (yr. ended 12/31/04): Assets, $20,080,186 (M); expenditures, $805,163; qualifying distributions, $652,308; giving activities include $585,835 for 32 grants (high: $161,952; low: $200).
Purpose and activities: Giving primarily for an Episcopal day school, and social services.
Fields of interest: Performing arts; Education; Hospitals (general); Diabetes; Diabetes research; Recreation; Boys & girls clubs; Human services; Family services; Federated giving programs.
Limitations: Applications not accepted. Giving primarily in Houston, TX. No grants to individuals.
Application information: Contributes only to pre-selected organizations.
Officers: Michael H. Holthouse, Pres.; Richard H. Stein, Secy.-Treas.; Paula Barnes, Exec. Dir.
Board Members: Colleen Holthouse; Lisa Holthouse.
EIN: 760620426
Selected grants: The following grants were reported in 2004.
$161,952 to Boys and Girls Clubs of Greater Houston, Houston, TX.
$30,000 to Laguna Beach Community Clinic, Laguna Beach, CA.
$27,500 to River Oaks Baptist School, Houston, TX.
$15,000 to Orange Show Center for Visionary Art, Houston, TX.

$5,000 to American Friends of the Louvre, New York, NY.
$5,000 to Houston Ballet, Houston, TX.
$5,000 to KIPP (Knowledge is Power Program) Academy, Houston, TX.
$5,000 to Reasoning Mind, Houston, TX.
$5,000 to Saint Francis Episcopal Day School, Houston, TX.
$5,000 to University of Texas Foundation, Austin, TX.

8960
Greater Houston Community Foundation
c/o Linda Gardner
4550 Post Oak Pl., Ste. 100
Houston, TX 77027-3106 (713) 333-2200
Contact: Robert W. Paddock, V.P., Devel.
FAX: (713) 333-2220; E-mail: lgardner@ghcf.org;
URL: http://www.ghcf.org

Established in 1971 in TX.
Foundation type: Community foundation.
Financial data (yr. ended 12/31/05): Assets, $199,126,686 (M); gifts received, $152,970,092; expenditures, $111,578,495; giving activities include $102,983,648 for 2,755 grants, and $6,160,827 for grants to individuals.
Purpose and activities: The foundation grows effective philanthropy by connecting donors to the causes they care about, provides excellent stewardship of assets entrusted to them, and convenes resources to address important community needs.
Type of support: General/operating support; Continuing support; Income development; Management development/capacity building; Annual campaigns; Capital campaigns; Building/renovation; Equipment; Land acquisition; Endowments; Debt reduction; Emergency funds; Program development; Conferences/seminars; Professorships; Publication; Seed money; Curriculum development; Fellowships; Internship funds; Scholarship funds; Research; Technical assistance; Consulting services; Program evaluation; Program-related investments/loans; Employee matching gifts; Employee-related scholarships; Exchange programs; In-kind gifts; Matching/challenge support.
Limitations: Applications not accepted. Giving primarily in Houston, TX area. No grants to individuals (except for disaster relief funds).
Publications: Financial statement; Grants list; Informational brochure.
Application information: The foundation does not issue requests for proposals or take grant applications.
  Board meeting date(s): 5 times a year
Officers and Directors:* Stephen M. Kaufman,* Chair.; Emily Attwell Crosswell,* Chair.-Elect; Stephen D. Maislin, C.E.O. and Pres.; Domingo Barrios, V.P., Community Investment; Robert W. Paddock, V.P., Devel.; William F. Galtney, Jr.,* Secy.; George Martinez,* Treas.; Ed Padar, Cont.; Morrie K. Abramson; Ric Campo; Ernest H. Cockrell; Gus H. Comiskey, Jr.; Robert E. Corder; Musa A. Dakri; Robert D. Duncan; Nancy Frees Fountain; Saundria Chase Gray; Maureen Hackett; Joseph A. Hafner, Jr.; Bernard A. Harris, Jr.; Paul W. Hobby; Lee W. Hogan; Ned S. Holmes; Walter E. Johnson; James L. Ketelsen; R. Stan Marek; Rodney H. Margolis; Anne C. Mendelsohn; Randall Meyer; Steven L. Miller; Michael C. Morgan; Paul B. Murphy, Jr.; Wilhelmina E. "Beth" Robertson; Mark A.

Wallace; J.C. "Rusty" Walter III; David M. Weekley; William H. White.
Number of staff: 4 full-time professional; 10 full-time support.
EIN: 237160400

8961
Houston Endowment Inc. ▼
600 Travis, Ste. 6400
Houston, TX 77002-3000 (713) 238-8100
FAX: (713) 238-8101;
E-mail: info@houstonendowment.org; URL: http://www.houstonendowment.org

Incorporated in 1937 in TX.
Donors: Jesse H. Jones†; Mrs. Jesse H. Jones†.
Foundation type: Independent foundation.
Financial data (yr. ended 12/31/05): Assets, $1,512,185,118 (M); expenditures, $63,288,117; qualifying distributions, $51,642,096; giving activities include $47,479,881 for 565 grants (high: $5,000,000; low: $1,000; average: $20,000–$200,000), $3,889,500 for 322 grants to individuals, and $272,715 for employee matching gifts.
Purpose and activities: For the support of any charitable, educational or religious undertaking.
Fields of interest: Arts; Education; Health care; Human services.
Type of support: General/operating support; Continuing support; Annual campaigns; Capital campaigns; Building/renovation; Equipment; Land acquisition; Endowments; Program development; Conferences/seminars; Professorships; Publication; Curriculum development; Fellowships; Scholarship funds; Research; Employee matching gifts.
Limitations: Giving primarily in Houston, TX; no grants outside the continental U.S. No support for religious organizations for religious purposes, or organizations that are the responsibility of the government. No grants to individuals (except for scholarships); or generally for fundraising activities including galas, grantmaking organizations or charities operated by service clubs, testimonial dinners, or advertising; or the purchase of uniforms, equipment or trips for school related organizations; no loans.
Publications: Application guidelines; Annual report; Financial statement; Grants list; Informational brochure (including application guidelines).
Application information: Proposal materials that are bound or inserted in protective sleeves are discouraged. Grant applications are not accepted by electronic mail. For organizations that have received a multi-year grant, the foundation prefers to receive applications only after all payments of that grant have been made. The foundation prefers not to consider applications from an organization more frequently than once every twelve months, whether a previous application was approved or denied. The foundation also prefers not to consider second requests for a capital project for which a grant was previously made. Application form not required.
Initial approach: Letter
Copies of proposal: 1
Deadline(s): None
Board meeting date(s): 9 to 10 times per year
Final notification: 3 to 6 months
Officers and Directors:* D. Kent Anderson,* Chair.; Larry R. Faulkner,* Pres.; Sheryl L. Johns, Exec. V.P.; Peggy J. Howell, Cont.; Anthony W. Hall, Jr.;

Melissa A. Jones; David Louis Mendez; Harold Metts; Paul B. Murphy, Jr.; Laurence E. Simmons.
Number of staff: 9 full-time professional; 10 full-time support.
EIN: 746013920
Selected grants: The following grants were reported in 2005.
$5,000,000 to Houston Zoo, Houston, TX. Toward African Forest master plan.
$3,000,000 to Childrens Museum of Houston, Houston, TX. Toward expanding museum's exhibition and office spaces.
$3,000,000 to Houston Downtown Park Corporation, Houston, TX. Toward acquiring land and designing, developing, and operating active urban park in downtown Houston.
$2,600,000 to Neighborhood Centers, Houston, TX. Toward community center in Gulfton that will improve delivery of social services and encourage economic development in area.
$2,500,000 to Prairie View A & M University, Prairie View, TX. Toward technology infrastructure for new College of Nursing facility.
$2,423,000 to Harris, County of, Public Health and Environmental Services, Houston, TX. Toward reducing childhood obesity and improving long-term health by implementing health programs in Harris County elementary schools.
$164,000 to Texas Southern University, Houston, TX. Toward College of Education graduate fellowship fund.
$100,000 to Community Clinic, Oak Ridge North, TX. Toward free dental care for low-income, uninsured people in Montgomery County.
$90,000 to Greater Texas Community Partners, Dallas, TX. Toward helping abused and neglected children in Houston through volunteer support for Children Protective Services caseworkers.
$70,500 to Cultural Arts Council of Houston, Houston, TX. Toward study to assess contributions of arts and culture to economy and quality of life in Houston.

8962
The M. R. & Evelyn Hudson Foundation ◇
P.O. Box 2110
Keller, TX 76244

Established in 1992 in KS.
Donors: M.R. Hudson; Murdock Hudson†.
Foundation type: Independent foundation.
Financial data (yr. ended 12/31/05): Assets, $78,949,262 (M); gifts received, $2,150,000; expenditures, $4,511,888; qualifying distributions, $3,918,195; giving activities include $3,073,887 for 111 grants (high: $250,000; low: $33), $33 for in-kind gifts, and $754 for foundation-administered programs.
Purpose and activities: Giving primarily for community development, and medical research; funding also for the arts, education, and children, youth and family services.
Fields of interest: Visual arts; Museums; Museums (art); Performing arts; Arts; Elementary/secondary education; Higher education; Medical school/education; Libraries (public); Education; Hospitals (general); Health care, support services; Cancer research; Human services; Children/youth, services; Community development.
Type of support: In-kind gifts; Scholarship funds.
Limitations: Applications not accepted. Giving primarily in TX; some giving nationally. No grants to individuals.

Application information: Contributes only to pre-selected organizations.
Officers and Directors:* Marshall K. Larson,* C.E.O. and Pres.; John D. Hooser, V.P. Admin.; Jesse Larson, V.P. Operations; Kristal Brown; C. Wally Hooser.
EIN: 481107753
Selected grants: The following grants were reported in 2005.
$100,000 to Johnson County Community College, Overland Park, KS.
$100,000 to Rensselaerville Institute, Rensselaerville, NY.
$90,000 to Center for Nonprofit Management, Dallas, TX.
$55,000 to Dallas Childrens Theater, Dallas, TX.
$55,000 to Interfaith Housing Coalition, Dallas, TX.
$50,000 to Coterie Theater, Kansas City, MO.
$50,000 to University of Texas M. D. Anderson Cancer Center, Houston, TX.
$25,000 to Trinity River Mission, Dallas, TX.
$15,000 to Community Enrichment Center, Fort Worth, TX.
$15,000 to Saint Joseph Institute for the Deaf, Overland Park, KS.

8963
Huffington Foundation
700 Louisiana St., Ste. 2400
Houston, TX 77002 (713) 753-1001
Contact: Roy Huffington, Tr.
FAX: (713) 651-0119; Additional address: P.O. Box 4337, Houston, TX 77210-4337

Established in 1987 in TX.
Donors: Terry L. Huffington; Michael Huffington; Roy M. Huffington.
Foundation type: Independent foundation.
Financial data (yr. ended 12/31/05): Assets, $26,279,887 (M); expenditures, $1,583,360; qualifying distributions, $1,245,750; giving activities include $1,245,750 for 48 grants (high: $475,000; low: $1,000).
Purpose and activities: Giving primarily for medical school education, as well as regular education; funding also for the arts, health associations and human services.
Fields of interest: Museums (art); Performing arts centers; Arts; Higher education; Medical school/education; Education; Environment, natural resources; Hospitals (general); Health organizations, association; Cancer; Children, services.
Type of support: Building/renovation; General/operating support; Annual campaigns; Endowments; Scholarship funds.
Limitations: Applications not accepted. Giving primarily in Houston, TX. No grants to individuals.
Application information: Contributes only to pre-selected organizations.
Board meeting date(s): Quarterly
Trustees: Ralph E. Dittman, M.D.; Roy M. Huffington; Terry L. Huffington.
EIN: 766040840

8964
Elizabeth A. Hull Charitable Trust ◇
c/o Bank of America, N.A.
P.O. Box 831041
Dallas, TX 75283-1041 (800) 357-7094

Established in 1996 in MO.
Donor: A. & M. Janesky Unitrust.
Foundation type: Independent foundation.
Financial data (yr. ended 12/31/05): Assets, $36,420,351 (M); gifts received, $696; expenditures, $1,875,204; qualifying distributions, $1,644,715; giving activities include $1,625,246 for 6 grants (high: $413,975; low: $195,492; average: $203,156–$203,156).
Fields of interest: Media, radio; Higher education; Hospitals (specialty); Eye diseases; Human services; Christian agencies & churches.
Limitations: Applications not accepted. Giving on a national basis. No grants to individuals.
Application information: Contributes only to pre-selected organizations.
Trustee: Bank of America, N.A.
EIN: 436345246

8965
The Humphreys Foundation ✧
P.O. Box 550
Liberty, TX 77575-0550 (936) 336-3321
Contact: Doris Peters, Mgr.

Incorporated in 1957 in TX.
Donor: Geraldine Davis Humphreys†.
Foundation type: Independent foundation.
Financial data (yr. ended 9/30/05): Assets, $14,561,516 (M); expenditures, $701,553; qualifying distributions, $515,169; giving activities include $498,000 for 7 grants (high: $135,000; low: $4,000).
Purpose and activities: Giving for production costs of plays and performances in the field of dramatic arts. The foundation also makes some of its grants to colleges and universities which, in turn, use the grant money to award scholarships to students studying drama or dance under the supervision of the grantee educational institutions.
Fields of interest: Performing arts; Performing arts, theater; Higher education.
Limitations: Giving limited to TX. No grants to individuals, or for building funds; no loans.
Publications: Application guidelines.
Application information: Application form required.
  Initial approach: Letter or proposal
  Copies of proposal: 4
  Deadline(s): Applications accepted between July 1 and Aug. 15
  Board meeting date(s): Sept.
Officers: Linda Bertman, Pres. and Treas.; Claude C. Roberts, V.P. and Secy.; Louis B. Paine, V.P.
Number of staff: 1 full-time support.
EIN: 746061381
Selected grants: The following grants were reported in 2003.
$125,000 to Theater Under the Stars, Houston, TX. For production of Jekyll and Hyde.
$80,000 to Houston Grand Opera, Houston, TX. For production of The Merry Widow.
$50,000 to Alley Theater, Houston, TX. For production of Proof.
$50,000 to Valley Players of Ligonier, Ligonier, PA. For production of The Toys Take Over Christmas.
$30,000 to Society for the Performing Arts, Houston, TX. For Merce Cunningham Dance Company.
$10,000 to Houston Ballet, Houston, TX. For production of Cinderella.
$6,000 to Grand 1894 Opera House, Galveston, TX. For production of Kiss Me Kate.

$5,000 to Sam Houston State University, Huntsville, TX. For Drama scholarships.
$5,000 to University of Houston-University Park, Houston, TX. For production of Rosencrantz and Guildenstern are Dead.
$4,000 to Lamar University, Beaumont, TX. For Drama scholarships.

8966
The Hunt Family Foundation ✧
(formerly The Cimarron Foundation)
4401 N. Mesa St.
El Paso, TX 79902-1150 (915) 533-1122
Contact: Marcus J. Hunt

Established in 1987 in TX.
Donor: Woody L. Hunt.
Foundation type: Independent foundation.
Financial data (yr. ended 12/31/05): Assets, $2,663,862 (M); expenditures, $671,804; qualifying distributions, $621,181; giving activities include $613,047 for 91 grants (high: $95,000; low: $250).
Purpose and activities: Giving primarily for higher education.
Fields of interest: Higher education; Health care; Cancer; Human services; YM/YWCAs & YM/YWHAs; Federated giving programs.
Type of support: General/operating support; Capital campaigns; Building/renovation; Research.
Limitations: Giving primarily in El Paso, TX. No grants to individuals.
Application information: Application form required.
  Initial approach: Letter
  Deadline(s): None
Officers and Trustees: * Woody L. Hunt,* Pres.; Gayle G. Hunt,* V.P.
EIN: 742489868

8967
Imaca Education Foundation ✧
P.O. Box 16279
Fort Worth, TX 76162-0279

Foundation type: Independent foundation.
Financial data (yr. ended 12/31/05): Assets, $244,851 (M); expenditures, $763,353; qualifying distributions, $474,730; giving activities include $474,370 for grants.
Purpose and activities: The purpose of the foundation is to fund programs to train technicians to modify older style automotive air conditioning systems to use newer EPA approved coolants.
Fields of interest: Employment, training; Employment, retraining.
Limitations: Applications not accepted. Giving on a national basis.
Application information: Contributes only to pre-selected organizations.
Officers: Jimmy Tice, Pres.; Brian Jordan, V.P.; Jack Rieke, Treas.; Frank Allison, Mgr.
Directors: Mike Gratton; Jorge Vivar.
EIN: 752825170

8968
Interdenominational Christian Missions, Inc. ✧
30260 Saratoga Dr.
Fair Oaks Ranch, TX 78015

Established in 1997 in TX.
Donors: Ralph E. Fair, Jr.; Michael Clark; Carole Clark; First Baptist Church.
Foundation type: Operating foundation.
Financial data (yr. ended 12/31/05): Assets, $6,746 (M); gifts received, $722,419; expenditures, $727,322; qualifying distributions, $727,322; giving activities include $657,205 for 27 grants (high: $430,522; low: $200).
Purpose and activities: Giving to Christian organizations performing evangelistic, social and human services, and operating orphanages.
Fields of interest: Christian agencies & churches.
International interests: Central America; Costa Rica; Honduras; Nicaragua; Peru; South America.
Limitations: Giving on a national and international basis, including Costa Rica, Honduras, Nicaragua, and Peru.
Officers: Ralph E. Fair, Jr., Pres.; Douglas J. Richardson, V.P.; Suzanne F. Richardson, Secy.-Treas.
EIN: 742798861

8969
David & Sharon Jamail Family Foundation ✧
2303 River Hills Rd.
Austin, TX 78733

Established in 1997 in TX.
Foundation type: Independent foundation.
Financial data (yr. ended 12/31/03): Assets, $3,366,160 (M); expenditures, $464,015; qualifying distributions, $462,115; giving activities include $462,115 for 46 grants (high: $80,000; low: $25).
Purpose and activities: Giving primarily for health, children, youth and social services, and Christian churches and organizations.
Fields of interest: Health organizations, association; Medical research, institute; Recreation, camps; Human services; Children/youth, services; Christian agencies & churches.
Limitations: Applications not accepted. Giving primarily in TX, with emphasis on Austin; some funding nationally. No grants to individuals.
Application information: Contributes only to pre-selected organizations.
Officers: David G. Jamail, Pres. and Treas.; Sharon Jamail, V.P. and Secy.
Trustee: Brian M. Wallace.
EIN: 742854045
Selected grants: The following grants were reported in 2003.
$80,000 to Westlake Bible Church, Austin, TX.
$68,250 to Young Life, Austin, TX.
$67,000 to Medical Institute for Sexual Health, Austin, TX.
$16,000 to Navigators, The, Colorado Springs, CO.
$12,500 to Girl Scouts of the U.S.A., Lone Star Council, Austin, TX.
$6,000 to YMCA of Austin, Austin, TX.
$4,000 to World View Academy, New Braunfels, TX.
$3,900 to Frontiers, Mesa, AZ.
$400 to Watchman Fellowship, Arlington, TX.
$25 to American Heart Association, Austin, TX.

8970
The Joseph D. and Lillie H. Jamail Foundation ◇
1200 Smith St., Ste. 1135
Houston, TX 77002 (713) 650-8544
Contact: Robert L. Jamail, Secy.-Treas.

Established in 1986 in TX.
Donors: Joseph D. Jamail; Lillie H. Jamail.
Foundation type: Independent foundation.
Financial data (yr. ended 12/31/05): Assets, $15,311,115 (M); expenditures, $519,276; qualifying distributions, $457,500; giving activities include $457,500 for 31 grants (high: $68,500; low: $1,000).
Purpose and activities: Giving to tax exempt 501 (c) (3) organizations located in the state of Texas only.
Fields of interest: Museums (art); Arts; Higher education; Education; Human services; Children/youth, services; Christian agencies & churches.
Type of support: General/operating support; Capital campaigns; Endowments; Scholarship funds.
Limitations: Giving limited to TX. No grants to individuals or to organizations which are professional fundraisers.
Application information: No videos accepted. Application form not required.
　Initial approach: Letter on organization letterhead
　Deadline(s): None
　Board meeting date(s): Dec.
Officers: Lee H. Jamail, Pres.; Joseph D. Jamail III, V.P.; Randall Hage Jamail, V.P.; Robert Lee Jamail, Secy.-Treas.; Denise S. Davidson, Secy.
EIN: 760181247

8971
Jenesis Group ◇
P.O. Box 637
Hurst, TX 76054 (972) 999-4554
Contact: Julie Jensen, Tr.
FAX: (972) 999-4599; E-mail: ktanner@jenesis.org;
URL: http://www.jenesis.org

Established in 1986 in TX.
Donor: R.J. Jensen.
Foundation type: Independent foundation.
Financial data (yr. ended 12/31/05): Assets, $15,524,450 (M); expenditures, $6,589,598; qualifying distributions, $6,383,936; giving activities include $6,150,679 for 46+ grants (high: $1,760,000), and $81,607 for 2 employee matching gifts.
Purpose and activities: Support limited to grass-roots organizations with annual budgets below $500,000 that sponsor programs which serve children under 18 years of age, provide some type of leadership training, teach entrepreneurial skills, and/or help children develop self-esteem and self reliance. Provides funds for development of preventive social service programs, their expansion, and materials needed.
Fields of interest: Education, early childhood education; Child development, education; Youth development, services; Human services; Children/youth, services; Child development, services; Minorities/immigrants, centers/services; Leadership development; Minorities.
Type of support: General/operating support; Continuing support; Program development; Seed money; Technical assistance; Matching/challenge support.

Limitations: Applications not accepted. Giving on a national basis. No grants to individuals, or for buildings or building maintenance, transportation of clients to programs, refreshments, or media presentations.
Application information: The foundation is not accepting unsolicited applications for the remainder of 2006. Check foundation Web site in 2007 for updated status on application procedures.
　Board meeting date(s): Varies
Officer: Kim Tanner, Admin.
Trustees: Julie Jensen; and 4 additional trustees.
EIN: 756349718
Selected grants: The following grants were reported in 2004.
$200,000 to Latin American Youth Center, DC. For general operating support.
$150,000 to Stages of Learning, Brooklyn, NY. For capacity building.
$141,700 to Youth Radio, Berkeley, CA. For CS Seminar and Marketing materials.
$53,250 to Legal Outreach, New York, NY. For College Bound Program.
$50,565 to Hamilton Community Foundation, Hamilton, OH. For construction of Phillips Community.
$50,000 to Dallas Leadership Foundation, Dallas, TX. For general operating support.
$49,000 to College Summit, DC.
$42,500 to Still Creek Boys Ranch, Bryan, TX. For general operating support.
$25,000 to Rocky Mountain Wildlife Conservation Center, Keenesburg, CO. For general operating support.
$23,933 to Eagle Flight Squadron, East Orange, NJ. For general operating support.

8972
The Willard and Ruth Johnson Charitable Foundation ◇
P.O. Box 27727
Houston, TX 77227

Established in 1992 in TX.
Donor: Ruth Johnson†.
Foundation type: Independent foundation.
Financial data (yr. ended 12/31/04): Assets, $23,115,697 (M); gifts received, $394,392; expenditures, $1,089,733; qualifying distributions, $952,166; giving activities include $950,139 for 67 grants (high: $140,000; low: $150).
Purpose and activities: Giving primarily for education, children and youth services, social services, and to a United Methodist church, as well as to Episcopal churches and organizations.
Fields of interest: Higher education; Education; Human services; Children/youth, services; Protestant agencies & churches.
Limitations: Applications not accepted. Giving primarily in Houston and Midland, TX. No grants to individuals.
Application information: Contributes only to pre-selected organizations.
Trustees: David M. Johnson; John W. Johnson; Mary Anne Johnson Lindley.
EIN: 760386599

8973
The Burdine Johnson Foundation ◇
P.O. Box 1230
Buda, TX 78610 (512) 312-1336
Contact: Robert C. Giberson, Tr.

Established in 1960 in TX.
Donors: Burdine C. Johnson; J.M. Johnson.
Foundation type: Independent foundation.
Financial data (yr. ended 12/31/05): Assets, $32,443,751 (M); expenditures, $1,875,924; qualifying distributions, $1,599,350; giving activities include $1,599,350 for 37 grants (high: $150,000; low: $2,500).
Purpose and activities: Giving primarily for the performing arts and education; some funding for human services.
Fields of interest: Performing arts; Performing arts, music; Elementary/secondary education; Higher education; Education; Human services.
Limitations: Giving primarily in TX. No grants to individuals.
Application information: Application form not required.
　Initial approach: Proposal
　Deadline(s): None
Trustees: Robert C. Giberson; William T. Johnson; Martha L. Mattox.
EIN: 746036669
Selected grants: The following grants were reported in 2004.
$250,000 to James Dick Foundation for the Performing Arts, Round Top, TX. 2 grants: $150,000 (For operating support), $100,000 (For construction work in Concert Hall).
$225,000 to Saint Stephens Episcopal School, Wimberley, TX. 2 grants: $75,000 (For operating support), $150,000 (For operating support).
$150,000 to Nature Conservancy of Texas, San Antonio, TX.
$75,000 to Hays Consolidated Independent School District, Kyle, TX. For two Kodaly music teachers and equipment.
$60,000 to Childrens Medical Center Foundation of Central Texas, Austin, TX. For building costs of new children's hospital.
$50,000 to Planned Parenthood Center of the Texas Capital Region, Austin, TX. For program support.
$40,000 to Texas State University Development Foundation, San Marcos, TX. For Katherine Anne Porter Young Writer's Program.
$25,000 to YMCA of Austin, Austin, TX. For capital support.

8974
M. G. and Lillie A. Johnson Foundation, Inc.
P.O. Box 2269
Victoria, TX 77902
Contact: Robert Halepeska, Exec. V.P.
E-mail: mgljf@sbcglobal.net; Tel./Fax: (361) 575-7970

Incorporated in 1958 in TX.
Donors: M.G. Johnson†; Lillie A. Johnson†.
Foundation type: Independent foundation.
Financial data (yr. ended 11/30/05): Assets, $56,223,766 (M); expenditures, $2,875,858; qualifying distributions, $2,423,590; giving activities include $2,412,707 for 41 grants (high: $225,000; low: $3,954).
Purpose and activities: Primary emphasis on medical and allied health purposes and institutions

of higher education located on the Texas Gulf Coast in the 14 counties surrounding Victoria County.
Fields of interest: Higher education; Nursing school/education; Education; Hospitals (general); Nursing care; Health care; Health organizations, association; Human services; Aging, centers/services; Community development.
Type of support: Capital campaigns; Building/renovation; Equipment; Land acquisition; Scholarship funds.
Limitations: Giving limited to TX. Recent giving exclusively to the Texas Gulf Coast area, including Matagorda, Wharton, Colorado, Lavaca, Jackson, Calhoun, Victoria, DeWitt, Gonzales, Karnes, Bee, Goliad, Refugio, Aransas, and Waller counties. No support for most religious and political organizations, and large nation wide charities. No grants to individuals, or for general support, operating budgets, endowment funds, fellowships, research, special projects, publications, or conferences; no loans.
Publications: Application guidelines.
Application information: Application form not required.
Initial approach: Proposal
Copies of proposal: 1
Deadline(s): Submit proposal 1 month before meetings; no set deadline
Board meeting date(s): Mar., July, Oct.
Final notification: Following board meetings
Officers and Trustees:* M.H. Brock,* Pres.; Robert Halepeska, Exec. V.P.; Munson Smith,* V.P.; Jack R. Morrison, Secy.; James Bouligny; Dick Koop; Terrell Mullins.
Number of staff: 1 full-time professional; 1 part-time support.
EIN: 746076961
Selected grants: The following grants were reported in 2003.
$250,000 to Wharton County Junior College, Wharton, TX. To purchase instructional equipment for academic programs in the Allied Health Division.
$100,750 to Jackson County Hospital, Edna, TX. To purchase a chemistry analyzer.
$100,000 to El Campo Medical Foundation, El Campo, TX. To purchase a Telemetry System for El Campo Hospital.
$100,000 to El Campo, City of, El Campo, TX. For constructioni of swimming pool.
$100,000 to Lavaca Exposition Association, Hallettsville, TX. To construct a covered youth facility.
$88,532 to Brownson Home, Victoria, TX. To purchase two vehicles, to purchase various pieces of equipment, and for improvements to its facility.
$75,000 to Habitat for Humanity, Victoria, Victoria, TX. For challenge grant to puchase a building.
$60,000 to Texas Settlement Trails, Victoria, TX. For La Salle Odyssey project.
$50,000 to Perpetual Help Home, Victoria, TX. For renovation to its new home.
$50,000 to Wharton, City of, Wharton, TX. To purchase a chassis and module remount on an ambulance.

8975
Helen Jones Foundation, Inc. ▼ ✧
P.O. Box 53665
Lubbock, TX 79453
Contact: James C. Arnold, Pres.

Application address: 4608 89th St., Lubbock, TX 79424, tel.: (806) 794-8899

Established about 1984 in TX.
Donor: Helen DeVitt Jones.
Foundation type: Independent foundation.
Financial data (yr. ended 12/31/05): Assets, $111,336,751 (M); expenditures, $6,656,344; qualifying distributions, $5,078,463; giving activities include $4,969,427 for 79 grants (high: $1,050,000; low: $222; average: $20,000–$250,000).
Purpose and activities: Giving primarily for religious, charitable, scientific, testing for public safety, literary or educational purposes.
Fields of interest: Museums; Arts; Higher education; Human services; Science; Religion.
Type of support: General/operating support; Equipment; Scholarship funds; Research.
Limitations: Giving primarily in Lubbock, TX. No grants to individuals.
Application information: Application form not required.
Initial approach: Letter
Deadline(s): None
Officers and Directors:* James C. Arnold,* Pres.; Marianna Markham,* V.P.; Randy L. Wright,* Treas.; Stephen Michael Briggs; Barbara Bush.
EIN: 751977748
Selected grants: The following grants were reported in 2004.
$1,750,000 to Texas Tech University, Lubbock, TX. 3 grants: $500,000 to College of Human Sciences (For child development building), $500,000 to College of Human Sciences (For children center), $750,000 to College of Visual and Performing Arts (For building support).
$500,000 to Lubbock Symphony Orchestra, Lubbock, TX. For education endowment.
$275,000 to Museum of Texas Tech University, Lubbock, TX. 2 grants: $250,000 (For archeology collection) and $25,000 (For Davies Gallery opening).
$83,500 to Lubbock Christian University, College of Education, Lubbock, TX. For core knowledge center.
$44,000 to Volunteer Services Council for Lubbock State School, Lubbock, TX.
$10,000 to Success by Six, Lubbock, TX. For mentor program.
$10,000 to YWCA of Lubbock, Lubbock, TX. For summer programs scholarship.

8976
Walter S. and Evan C. Jones Testamentary Trust ✧
c/o Bank of America, N.A.
P.O. Box 831041
Dallas, TX 75283-1041
Application address: c/o Rudy Wrenick, Bank of America, N.A., P.O. Box 88, Topeka, KS 66601-0088, tel.: (785) 295-3463

Foundation type: Independent foundation.
Financial data (yr. ended 6/30/05): Assets, $49,735,631 (M); expenditures, $3,301,078; qualifying distributions, $2,450,294; giving activities include $2,420,616 for 19 grants (high: $1,000,000; low: $4,018).
Purpose and activities: Giving primarily for education, youth and community services.
Fields of interest: Higher education; Recreation, parks/playgrounds; Youth development, centers/

clubs; Community development, public/private ventures; Foundations (private grantmaking).
Limitations: Giving limited to Lyon, Coffey and Osage counties, KS. No grants to individuals.
Application information: Application form not required.
Initial approach: Letter
Deadline(s): None
Board meeting date(s): 2nd Tues. quarterly
Advisory Committee: Ken Calhoun; Arnold Graham; Max Stewart, Jr.; Thomas D. Thomas.
Trustee: Bank of America, N.A.
EIN: 480674648
Selected grants: The following grants were reported in 2005.
$425,000 to Emporia Granada Theater Alliance, Emporia, KS.
$384,041 to Emporia State University Foundation, Emporia, KS.
$67,500 to Flint Hills Community Health Center, Emporia, KS.
$34,000 to Wichita State University Foundation, Wichita, KS.

8977
The Philip R. Jonsson Foundation ✧
5781 Keller Springs Rd.
Dallas, TX 75248 (972) 380-6123
Contact: Theresa Miller
Application address: c/o Terri Mahan, 2400 Cottondale Ln., Little Rock, AR 72202, tel.: (501) 664-9410

Established in 1977 in TX.
Donors: Philip R. Jonsson; The Jonsson Foundation.
Foundation type: Independent foundation.
Financial data (yr. ended 12/31/05): Assets, $7,224,379 (M); expenditures, $680,479; qualifying distributions, $556,495; giving activities include $556,495 for 57 grants (high: $99,645; low: $1,000).
Purpose and activities: Giving primarily for education, health, and children, youth and social services.
Fields of interest: Arts; Higher education; Education; Reproductive health, family planning; Health organizations; Cancer research; Human services; Children/youth, services.
Type of support: General/operating support; Continuing support; Annual campaigns; Capital campaigns; Building/renovation; Equipment; Curriculum development; Scholarship funds; Research; Matching/challenge support.
Limitations: Giving primarily in TX, with emphasis on Dallas; some funding nationally, particularly in AR and CA. No grants to individuals.
Application information: Application form not required.
Initial approach: Proposal
Copies of proposal: 1
Board meeting date(s): Annually in the fall
Officers: Suzanne E. Jonsson, Pres.; Christina A. Jonsson, 1st V.P.; Kenneth B. Jonsson, 2nd V.P.; Eileen J. Lewis, Secy.; Steven W. Jonsson, Treas.; Philip R. Jonsson, Pres. Emeritus.
EIN: 751552642

8978
K. H. Jordan Foundation
4242 Lomo Alto, No. N110
Dallas, TX 75219
Contact: Kathryn H. Jordan, Tr.

Established in 1999 in TX.
Donor: Kathryn H. Jordan.
Foundation type: Independent foundation.
Financial data (yr. ended 12/31/05): Assets,
$7,763,920 (M); gifts received, $86,338;
expenditures, $373,921; qualifying distributions,
$351,100; giving activities include $351,100 for 21
grants (high: $210,000; low: $1,000).
Purpose and activities: Giving primarily to a
Unitarian church and to health organizations.
Fields of interest: Arts; Health organizations,
association; Human services.
Limitations: Giving primarily in TX. No grants to
individuals.
Application information: Unsolicited requests for
funds generally not accepted; applicants should
have already established personal contact with the
foundation.
 Initial approach: Proposal
 Deadline(s): None
Trustee: Kathryn H. Jordan.
EIN: 752851443
Selected grants: The following grants were reported
in 2005.
$5,000 to American Heart Association, Dallas, TX.
$5,000 to Dallas Symphony Orchestra, Dallas, TX.
$2,500 to American Red Cross.
$2,500 to Museum of New Mexico Foundation,
 Santa Fe, NM.
$1,000 to Arthritis Foundation, San Antonio, TX.
$1,000 to Dallas Womens Foundation, Dallas, TX.
$1,000 to Lawrence University, Appleton, WI.
$200 to American Red Cross, Albuquerque, NM.

8979
Jane and John Justin Foundation ◇
1300 S. University, Ste. 400
Fort Worth, TX 76107

Donor: Jane C. Justin†.
Foundation type: Independent foundation.
Financial data (yr. ended 12/31/05): Assets,
$129,705,785 (M); gifts received, $411,000;
expenditures, $3,025,099; qualifying distributions,
$5,933,068; giving activities include $2,072,500
for 7 grants (high: $1,000,000; low: $35,000).
Fields of interest: Higher education; Hospitals
(specialty); Cancer; Human services.
Limitations: Applications not accepted. Giving
primarily in TX. No grants to individuals.
Application information: Contributes only to
pre-selected organizations.
Officers: J.T. Dickenson, Pres.; Roy B. Topham,
Secy.-Treas. and Exec. Dir.
Directors: Mary C. Justin; Dee J. Kelly; Robert Watt.
EIN: 752442749

8980
Fannie and Stephen Kahn Charitable Foundation ◇
5950 Berkshire Ln., Ste. 1050
Dallas, TX 75225 (214) 369-6202
Contact: Sherian Minczewski, V.P.

Established in TX.

Donor: Stephen S. Kahn†.
Foundation type: Independent foundation.
Financial data (yr. ended 12/31/05): Assets,
$8,583,855 (M); expenditures, $572,821;
qualifying distributions, $455,360; giving activities
include $324,600 for 66 grants (high: $25,000;
low: $250).
Fields of interest: Museums; Performing arts;
Elementary/secondary education; Higher education;
Hospitals (general); Medical research; Human
services; Jewish agencies & temples; Women.
Type of support: Endowments; Annual campaigns;
Scholarship funds; Program development; General/
operating support.
Limitations: Giving primarily in Dallas, TX; giving
also in Washington, DC. No grants to individuals.
Officers: Sallie A. Scanlan, Pres.; Sherian
Minczewski, V.P.; Susan S. Cameron, Secy.
EIN: 752873734
Selected grants: The following grants were reported
in 2004.
$25,000 to Childrens Medical Center of Dallas,
 Dallas, TX. For We Promise Campaign.
$25,000 to Womens Research and Education
 Institute, DC. For Women in Military program.
$15,000 to Dallas Symphony Orchestra, Dallas, TX.
 For Hans Kreissig Society.
$10,000 to Museum of Modern Art, New York, NY.
 For program publication support.
$10,000 to Texas Scottish Rite Hospital for
 Children, Dallas, TX.
$10,000 to Winston School, Dallas, TX. For
 scholarship fund.
$7,500 to Genesis Womens Shelter, Dallas, TX.
$6,000 to Dallas Womens Foundation, Dallas, TX.
 For annual fund.
$5,000 to American Red Cross, National
 Headquarters, DC. For hurricane victims support.
$5,000 to Women in Military Service for America
 Memorial Foundation, Arlington, VA. For
 unrestricted support.

8981
The Ann & Stephen Kaufman Family Foundation ◇ ☆
c/o Stephen M. Kaufman
3 Riverway, Ste. 1350
Houston, TX 77056-1982

Established in 1996 in TX.
Donor: Jean Kaufman.
Foundation type: Independent foundation.
Financial data (yr. ended 11/30/05): Assets,
$104,551 (M); expenditures, $644,507; qualifying
distributions, $585,375; giving activities include
$585,375 for 7 grants (high: $585,000; low: $25).
Fields of interest: Arts; Hospitals (specialty); Health
organizations, association; Cancer research;
Residential/custodial care, senior continuing care;
Foundations (community); Jewish agencies &
temples.
Limitations: Applications not accepted. Giving
primarily in Houston, TX. No grants to individuals.
Application information: Contributes only to
pre-selected organizations.
Trustees: Ann P. Kaufman; Stephen M. Kaufman.
EIN: 760524143

8982
Ben E. Keith Foundation Trust ◇
c/o JPMorgan Chase Bank, N.A.
600 Bailey Ave., TX1-3434
Fort Worth, TX 76107
Application address: c/o Robert Lansford, JPMorgan
Chase Bank, N.A., NA-420 Throckmorton St., Fort
Worth, TX 76102, tel.: (817) 884-4151

Established in 1951 in TX.
Foundation type: Independent foundation.
Financial data (yr. ended 6/30/05): Assets,
$15,530,881 (M); expenditures, $892,849;
qualifying distributions, $841,033; giving activities
include $837,755 for grants.
Fields of interest: Museums; Performing arts,
orchestra (symphony); Arts; Higher education;
Education; Health care; Recreation, parks/
playgrounds; Recreation; Human services;
Children/youth, services; Community development;
Federated giving programs.
Type of support: General/operating support;
Continuing support; Annual campaigns; Capital
campaigns; Building/renovation; Equipment; Land
acquisition; Endowments; Debt reduction;
Emergency funds; Seed money; Matching/challenge
support.
Limitations: Giving limited to TX. No grants to
individuals, or for scholarships or fellowships; no
loans.
Application information:
 Initial approach: Letter
 Deadline(s): Sept.
 Board meeting date(s): Jan., Mar., June, and Oct.
Trustee: JPMorgan Chase Bank, N.A.
EIN: 756013955

8983
Roy and Cindy Keithley Family Foundation ◇ ☆
3736 Bee Caves Rd., Rm 4-173
Austin, TX 78746
Contact: Roy Keithley, Pres.

Established in 2001 in OH.
Donors: Cynthia O. Keithley; Roy F. Keithley; Nancy
Keithley Charitable Lead Trust.
Foundation type: Independent foundation.
Financial data (yr. ended 12/31/05): Assets,
$32,959 (M); gifts received, $178,046;
expenditures, $952,521; qualifying distributions,
$945,000; giving activities include $945,000 for 10
grants (high: $550,000; low: $10,000).
Fields of interest: Education; Animals/wildlife,
preservation/protection; Breast cancer; Human
services; Children/youth, services; Christian
agencies & churches; Roman Catholic agencies &
churches.
Application information:
 Initial approach: Letter
 Deadline(s): None
Officers: Roy F. Keithley, Pres.; Cynthia O. Keithley,
Secy.-Treas.
Trustee: James Cameron.
EIN: 341931360

8984
Joan and Herb Kelleher Charitable Foundation

P.O. Box 829
San Antonio, TX 78293
Contact: Ruth K. Agather, Tr.
FAX: (210) 223-3512;
E-mail: tina.pawelek@paisanocattle.com

Established in 1997 in TX.
Donors: Herbert D. Kelleher; Joan N. Kelleher.
Foundation type: Independent foundation.
Financial data (yr. ended 12/31/05): Assets, $13,250,841 (M); gifts received, $1,000; expenditures, $759,456; qualifying distributions, $612,145; giving activities include $577,490 for 60 grants (high: $100,000; low: $1,200).
Fields of interest: Historic preservation/historical societies; Arts; Environment; Youth development; Human services.
Type of support: General/operating support; Capital campaigns; Building/renovation.
Limitations: Giving primarily in Bexar, Brewster and Presidio counties, TX, and Jackson, WY.
Publications: Application guidelines.
Application information: Application form not required.
  Initial approach: Letter or e-mail requesting application guidelines
  Copies of proposal: 1
  Deadline(s): None
  Board meeting date(s): Varies
  Final notification: Varies
Trustees: Ruth K. Agather; David N. Kelleher; Herbert D. Kelleher; J. Michael Kelleher; Joan N. Kelleher; Julia K. Stacy.
EIN: 742833381

8985
The Boyd and Joan Kelley Charitable Foundation ✧

4600 Taft Blvd., Ste. 229
Wichita Falls, TX 76308

Established in 1998 in TX.
Donor: Joan Kelley.
Foundation type: Independent foundation.
Financial data (yr. ended 12/31/04): Assets, $3,617,446 (M); expenditures, $421,119; qualifying distributions, $391,474; giving activities include $391,474 for 33 grants (high: $55,000; low: $200).
Fields of interest: Hospitals (general); Salvation Army; Protestant agencies & churches.
Type of support: General/operating support.
Limitations: Applications not accepted. Giving primarily in TX. No grants to individuals.
Application information: Contributes only to pre-selected organizations.
Officer and Trustee:* Joan Kelley,* Mgr.
EIN: 742897733
Selected grants: The following grants were reported in 2004.
$55,000 to Navigators, The, Colorado Springs, CO.
$21,000 to Salvation Army, Plainview, TX.
$20,200 to Presbyterian Manor, Wichita Falls, TX.
$20,000 to Alliance Defense Fund, Scottsdale, AZ.
$20,000 to Every Home for Christ, Colorado Springs, CO.
$20,000 to World Neighbors, Oklahoma City, OK.
$15,200 to Hospice of Wichita Falls, Wichita Falls, TX.

$10,000 to Christian Freedom International, DC.
$5,000 to Frontiers, Mesa, AZ.
$2,750 to Campus Crusade for Christ, Miami, FL.

8986
W. D. Kelley Foundation ✧

(formerly W. D. Kelley Charitable Trust)
c/o Grants Committee
707 Rock St.
Georgetown, TX 78626
Contact: Dale Illig, Exec. Dir.

Established in 1996 in TX.
Foundation type: Independent foundation.
Financial data (yr. ended 12/31/05): Assets, $7,615,661 (M); expenditures, $519,577; qualifying distributions, $342,113; giving activities include $342,113 for grants.
Purpose and activities: Funding for projects directed at youth and family, with preference given to faith-based programs.
Fields of interest: Education; Health care; Recreation; Human services; Children/youth, services; Family services; Religion.
Limitations: Giving primarily within 50 miles of Georgetown, TX. No grants to individuals, or for endowments, capital campaigns, events or galas.
Application information: Application form not required.
  Initial approach: Letter or telephone for guidelines
  Copies of proposal: 2
  Board meeting date(s): May and Nov.
  Final notification: July and Dec.
Officer: Dale Illig, Exec. Dir.
Number of staff: 1 part-time support.
EIN: 743007226
Selected grants: The following grants were reported in 2005.
$9,500 to Faith Lutheran Church, Bellaire, TX.
$5,000 to Southwestern University, Georgetown, TX.
$4,000 to Grace Episcopal Church, Galveston, TX.
$1,500 to Cedar Crest College, Allentown, PA.
$1,500 to Concordia Seminary, Saint Louis, MO.
$1,250 to Austin College, Sherman, TX.
$1,000 to Nature Conservancy of Texas, San Antonio, TX.
$1,000 to Peace Lutheran Church, Palm Bay, FL.

8987
Harris and Eliza Kempner Fund, Inc.

2201 Market St., Ste. 601
Galveston, TX 77550-1529 (409) 762-1603
Contact: Barbara K. Crews, Exec. Dir.
FAX: (409) 762-5435;
E-mail: information@kempnerfund.org; *URL:* http://www.kempnerfund.org

Established in 1946 in TX; incorporated in 2001.
Donor: Various interests and members of the Kempner family.
Foundation type: Independent foundation.
Financial data (yr. ended 12/31/04): Assets, $42,384,897 (M); gifts received, $10,458; expenditures, $2,084,008; qualifying distributions, $1,842,896; giving activities include $1,276,492 for 123 grants (high: $301,998; low: $500), and $259,855 for 551 employee matching gifts.
Purpose and activities: Support primarily for human services, arts and humanities, education, community development, and Jewish issues in the

Galveston, TX, area, and a small allocation for international issues.
Fields of interest: Visual arts; Museums; Performing arts; Performing arts, dance; Performing arts, theater; Humanities; History/archaeology; Historic preservation/historical societies; Arts; Education, early childhood education; Child development, education; Elementary school/education; Secondary school/education; Higher education; Medical school/education; Adult education—literacy, basic skills & GED; Education, reading; Education; Environment, natural resources; Environment; Reproductive health, family planning; Health care; Substance abuse, services; Mental health/crisis services; Health organizations, association; Cancer; Heart & circulatory diseases; Biomedicine; Medical research, institute; Cancer research; Heart & circulatory research; Crime/law enforcement; Food services; Housing/shelter, development; Youth development, services; Human services; Youth, services; Child development, services; Residential/custodial care, hospices; Minorities/immigrants, centers/services; Homeless, human services; Civil rights, race/intergroup relations; Community development; Federated giving programs; Economics; Population studies; Leadership development; Jewish agencies & temples; Disabilities, people with; Minorities; Native Americans/American Indians; Economically disadvantaged; Homeless.
International interests: Africa; Mexico; South America.
Type of support: Employee matching gifts; General/operating support; Continuing support; Annual campaigns; Capital campaigns; Building/renovation; Equipment; Emergency funds; Program development; Conferences/seminars; Professorships; Publication; Seed money; Curriculum development; Fellowships; Scholarship funds; Research; Matching/challenge support.
Limitations: Giving primarily in Galveston County, TX. No support for non-U.S. based organizations. No grants to individuals, or for fundraising benefits or direct mail solicitations.
Publications: Annual report (including application guidelines).
Application information: Computerized solicitations not considered. Application form not required.
  Initial approach: Letter requesting guidelines
  Copies of proposal: 1
  Deadline(s): For grant program: Mar. 15 and Oct. 15
  Board meeting date(s): Usually in Apr., July, Dec., and as required
  Final notification: 8 weeks
Officers and Directors:* Barbara Weston Sasser,* Pres.; Lyda Ann Thomas, V.P.; Patricia Gray,* Secy.; John Campbell, Treas.; Barbara K. Crews, Exec. Dir.; Rhoda Thompson Ezell; Hetta Towler Kempner*; Daniel W. Hamilton; Elizabeth K. McFarland; Eliza K. Quigley.
Number of staff: 1 full-time professional; 1 full-time support; 1 part-time support.
EIN: 760680130

8988
Dr. and Mrs. Hugh A. Kennedy Foundation ✧

802 N. Carancahua St., Ste. 1270
Corpus Christi, TX 78470-0400

Established in 2001 in TX.
Donors: Hugh A. Kennedy†; Margaret T. Kennedy†.

Foundation type: Independent foundation.
Financial data (yr. ended 12/31/05): Assets, $11,770,709 (M); gifts received, $25,551; expenditures, $760,458; qualifying distributions, $560,736; giving activities include $560,736 for 10 grants (high: $143,184; low: $20,000; average: $25,000–$100,000).
Fields of interest: Higher education; Health care; Human services; Roman Catholic agencies & churches; Homeless.
Limitations: Applications not accepted. Giving primarily in TX; some funding in WI. No grants to individuals.
Application information: Contributes only to pre-selected organizations.
Officers and Directors:* Martin C. Davis,* Pres.; Mrs. Avalee Byrd,* V.P.; James Roach,* Secy.; Linda R. Cadigan,* Treas.
EIN: 742983794

8989
The Keown Charitable Foundation ✧ ☆
c/o Wells Fargo Bank Texas, N.A.
P.O. Box 913
Bryan, TX   77805-0913   (979) 776-3267

Established in 1993 in TX.
Foundation type: Independent foundation.
Financial data (yr. ended 6/30/05): Assets, $7,593,205 (M); gifts received, $181,360; expenditures, $476,979; qualifying distributions, $444,657; giving activities include $409,092 for 36 grants (high: $33,000; low: $1,000).
Fields of interest: Higher education; Education; Human services; Protestant agencies & churches.
Limitations: Applications not accepted. No grants to individuals.
Application information: Contributes only to pre-selected organizations.
Trustees: Ira Betts; Laverne Klenk; Mitchell Koop; Kenneth Loke; Charles Wendt.
EIN: 742668057

8990
KFFH, Inc. ✧
4211B Southwest Fwy.
Houston, TX   77027

Established in 2000 in TX.
Donor: Frost Family.
Foundation type: Independent foundation.
Financial data (yr. ended 3/31/05): Assets, $3,905 (M); expenditures, $641,683; qualifying distributions, $636,247; giving activities include $636,247 for 7 grants (high: $500,000; low: $1,000).
Fields of interest: Education; Human services; Children/youth, services; Christian agencies & churches.
Limitations: Applications not accepted. Giving primarily in TX. No grants to individuals.
Application information: Contributes only to pre-selected organizations.
Officers: Mark Klein, Pres.; Timothy Klein, V.P.; Kathryn Klein, Secy.
EIN: 760657129

8991
William S. & Lora Jean Kilroy Foundation ✧
3700 Buffalo Speedway, Ste. 750
Houston, TX   77098

Established in 1985 in TX.
Donors: William S. Kilroy†; Lora Jean Kilroy.
Foundation type: Independent foundation.
Financial data (yr. ended 12/31/05): Assets, $10,056,804 (M); expenditures, $527,620; qualifying distributions, $470,494; giving activities include $456,548 for grants.
Fields of interest: Museums; Performing arts; Higher education; Education; Community development.
Type of support: General/operating support; Annual campaigns; Capital campaigns.
Limitations: Giving primarily in TX, with emphasis on Houston. No grants to individuals.
Application information: Donations made only to organizations known to trustees. Application form not required.
  Initial approach: Letter
  Deadline(s): None
Trustee: Lora Jean Kilroy; William S. Kilroy, Jr.; Mari Angela Kilroy.
EIN: 760169904

8992
Kimberly-Clark Foundation, Inc. ▼
351 Phelps Dr.
Irving, TX   75038-6507
Contact: Carolyn A. Mentesana, V.P.
URL: http://www.kimberly-clark.com/aboutus/kc_foundation.asp

Incorporated in 1952 in WI.
Donor: Kimberly-Clark Corp.
Foundation type: Company-sponsored foundation.
Financial data (yr. ended 12/31/05): Assets, $5,409,450 (M); gifts received, $7,129,449; expenditures, $6,045,004; qualifying distributions, $6,040,008; giving activities include $4,499,012 for 48 grants (high: $1,892,500; low: $250), and $1,347,243 for employee matching gifts.
Purpose and activities: The foundation supports organizations involved with arts and culture, education, the environment, health, human services, community development, and minorities. Special emphasis is directed toward programs designed to strengthen families, with a focus on health and hygiene issues.
Fields of interest: Museums; Performing arts; Arts; Education; Environment, natural resources; Environment; Health care; Children/youth, services; Human services; Community development; Minorities.
Type of support: Sponsorships; Program development; Curriculum development; General/operating support; Continuing support; Employee volunteer services; Employee matching gifts; Employee-related scholarships.
Limitations: Applications not accepted. Giving primarily in areas of company operations; giving also to national organizations. No support for religious or political organizations. No grants to individuals (except for employee-related scholarships), or for sports or athletic activities; no loans.
Publications: Corporate giving report; Financial statement.

Application information: Contributes only to pre-selected organizations.
Officers and Director: Tina S. Barry, Pres.; Mark A. Buthman, V.P.; Carolyn A. Mentesana, V.P.; Timothy C. Everett, Secy.; Jolene L. Varney, Treas.; Ronald D. McCray.
Number of staff: 1 full-time professional; 1 full-time support.
EIN: 396044304
Selected grants: The following grants were reported in 2005.
$1,892,500 to Bright Futures Scholarship Program, Irving, TX.
$1,376,000 to Community Partners, Los Angeles, CA.
$200,000 to Visiting Nurse Association of Texas, Dallas, TX.
$150,000 to American Red Cross, Mobile, AL.
$100,000 to American Red Cross, National Headquarters, DC.
$50,000 to Citizens Foundation USA, Lincolnshire, IL.
$25,000 to Make-A-Wish Foundation of North Texas, Irving, TX.
$25,000 to Paris Living, A Community Development Corporation, Paris, TX.
$25,000 to Texans Can, Dallas, TX. For capital and operating support.
$10,000 to Childrens Medical Center Foundation, Dallas, TX.

8993
The Kincaid Foundation
1085 Texan Trail, No. 500
Grapevine, TX   76051
Contact: Richard Jones, Tr.; Thomas R. Kincaid, Tr.
Mailing Address: P.O. Box 1747, Grapevine, TX 76099

Established in 1997 in TX.
Donor: Thomas R. Kincaid.
Foundation type: Independent foundation.
Financial data (yr. ended 12/31/05): Assets, $468,279 (M); expenditures, $614,683; qualifying distributions, $597,717; giving activities include $276,250 for 3+ grants (high: $200,000), and $303,093 for grants to individuals.
Purpose and activities: Giving to private schools for operations and scholarships to attendees of special education schools.
Fields of interest: Student services/organizations; Scholarships/financial aid.
Application information: Application form required.
  Initial approach: Letter
  Deadline(s): Mar. 31
Trustees: Richard Jones; Thomas R. Kincaid.
EIN: 752687930

8994
Kinder Foundation ▼ ✧
(formerly Richard D. Kinder Foundation, Inc.)
P.O. Box 130776
Houston, TX   77219-0776
Contact: Nancy G. Kinder, Pres.

Established in 1994 in TX.
Donor: Richard D. Kinder.
Foundation type: Independent foundation.
Financial data (yr. ended 12/31/05): Assets, $24,640,374 (M); expenditures, $4,043,270; qualifying distributions, $3,947,565; giving

activities include $3,942,844 for 57 grants (high: $2,000,000; low: $100; average: $5,000–$50,000).

Purpose and activities: Giving primarily for education including teacher appreciation, and children's issues. Some giving also for the environment, health, and religious organizations.

Fields of interest: Arts; Higher education; Environment; Zoos/zoological societies; Hospitals (general); Health organizations, association; Human services; Children, services; Civil rights, race/intergroup relations; Federated giving programs; Religion.

Type of support: General/operating support; Continuing support; Annual campaigns; Capital campaigns; Building/renovation; Endowments; Program development; Professorships.

Limitations: Applications not accepted. Giving primarily in TX. No grants to individuals.

Application information: Contributes only to pre-selected organizations.

Board meeting date(s): Unscheduled

Officers: Richard D. Kinder, Chair.; Nancy G. Kinder, Pres.; Katherine Kinder Howes, V.P. and Secy.-Treas.

Number of staff: None.

EIN: 760519073

Selected grants: The following grants were reported in 2005.

$2,000,000 to Houston Downtown Park Corporation, Houston, TX. For general support.

$300,200 to University of Texas M. D. Anderson Cancer Center, Houston, TX. For general support.

$230,200 to Museum of Fine Arts, Houston, Houston, TX. For general support.

$205,000 to Texas Childrens Hospital, Houston, TX. For general support.

$200,000 to University of Texas Health Science Center, Institute of Molecular Medicine, Houston, TX. For general support.

$182,000 to KIPP (Knowledge is Power Program) Academy, Houston, TX. For general support.

$50,000 to Houston Grand Opera, Houston, TX. For general support.

$29,350 to Houston Center for Contemporary Craft, Houston, TX. For general support.

$14,300 to Park People Endowment Foundation, Houston, TX. For general support.

$10,000 to Teach for America, Houston, TX. For general support.

8995
Carl B. and Florence E. King Foundation

2929 Carlisle St., Ste. 222
Dallas, TX   75204   (214) 750-1884
Contact: Michelle D. Monse, Pres.
FAX: (214) 750-1651;
E-mail: michellemonse@kingfoundation.com;
URL: http://www.kingfoundation.com

Incorporated in 1966 in TX.

Donors: Carl B. King‡; Florence E. King‡; Dorothy E. King‡.

Foundation type: Independent foundation.

Financial data (yr. ended 12/31/05): Assets, $51,487,899 (M); expenditures, $3,166,912; qualifying distributions, $2,509,666; giving activities include $1,894,110 for 52 grants (high: $200,000; low: $1,750).

Purpose and activities: The King Foundation is committed to the highest standards of philanthropy and to honoring the intent of the generous founders, Carl B. and Florence E. King. The foundation's work

is guided by the following principles: commitment to high ethical standards, adherence to strict financial guidelines, selection of appropriate and mission-focused grantees, evaluation and assessment of the grants, and clear and timely communications with all constituents. Grants are made in Texas and Arkansas in the following areas: aging, children and youth, education, the indigent and medical and scientific research. More detailed information on each category is available on the foundation Web site.

Fields of interest: Education, public education; Elementary school/education; Higher education; Adult education—literacy, basic skills & GED; Education, ESL programs; Education; Public health; Health care; Human services; Children/youth, services; Child development, services; Aging, centers/services; Human services; Homeless.

Type of support: Capital campaigns; Building/renovation; Equipment; Land acquisition; Program development; Research; Program evaluation.

Limitations: Giving statewide in AR and in the Dallas-Fort Worth area, the Permian Basin, and rural areas in TX. No support for religious organizations, or to non-exempt organizations. No grants to individuals directly, or for construction of churches or seminaries, or for religious programs (except for those that are social serviced based initiatives) or for ongoing operating expenses or funds to offset operating losses. No grants for loan financing; endowments; professional conferences or symposia; or balls, events, or for galas benefiting charitable organizations.

Publications: Financial statement; IRS Form 990-PF; Program policy statement (including application guidelines).

Application information: Application information available on foundation Web site. Proposals will be invited only after a letter of inquiry has been submitted. Contact foundation for grant application requirements. Some forms required. Application form not required.

Initial approach: Letter of inquiry (see foundation Web site for required elements)
Copies of proposal: 1
Deadline(s): Fall cycle: letter of inquiry due June 30; invited proposals are due Aug. 31; spring cycle: letter of inquiry due last business day before Dec. 24; invited proposals are due Feb. 28
Board meeting date(s): June and Dec.
Final notification: Early June and Dec.

Officers: John Martin Davis, Chair.; Michelle D. Monse, Pres.; Brian E. McManus, V.P.; Michael Phillips, V.P.; Patricia A. Porter, V.P.; Robert E. Weiss, V.P.; Ann C. Fielder, Secy.; Anthony W. Atkiss, Treas.

Number of staff: 1 full-time professional; 1 part-time professional; 1 full-time support.

EIN: 756052203

Selected grants: The following grants were reported in 2004.

$120,000 to K E R A/K D T N, Dallas, TX. For underwriting of Sesame Street.

$65,000 to Dickinson Place Charitable Corporation, Dallas, TX. For new elevator in apartments for low-income elderly.

$50,000 to Dallas County Community College District Foundation, Dallas, TX. For scholarships for graduates of Dallas County high schools to attend community College.

$50,000 to Sul Ross State University, Museum of the Big Bend, Alpine, TX. Toward construction of museum.

$25,000 to Booker T. Washington High School for the Performing and Visual Arts, Dallas, TX. Toward construction of new high school.

$10,000 to Wilkinson Center, Dallas, TX. For emergency assistance program.

8996
The Klabzuba Family Foundation ✧

930 W. 1st St.
Fort Worth, TX   76102
Contact: Hank Akin, V.P., Business Opers.

Established in 2002 in TX.

Donor: Robert Klabzuba.

Foundation type: Independent foundation.

Financial data (yr. ended 12/31/05): Assets, $1,122,079 (M); gifts received, $1,175,000; expenditures, $1,541,423; qualifying distributions, $1,541,423; giving activities include $1,533,333 for 11 grants (high: $866,666; low: $1,000).

Purpose and activities: The mission of the foundation is to enhance the quality of life through education, health care, and culture. The foundation seeks to recognize and support organizations and programs that serve others through generosity, compassion, good citizenship, and philanthropy.

Type of support: Scholarships—to individuals; Scholarship funds; Research; Program development; Professorships; Matching/challenge support; Equipment; Endowments; Capital campaigns; Building/renovation.

Limitations: Giving primarily in cities in which Klabzuba family members or businesses are located, with emphasis on TX and OK.

Application information: Application information and form available on foundation Web site. Application form required.

Initial approach: Internet/Web site
Copies of proposal: 1
Deadline(s): Feb. 1 and Sept. 1
Board meeting date(s): Mar. and Oct.
Final notification: 60 days

Officers and Directors:* Robert Klabzuba,* Pres.; Hank Akin,* V.P., Business Opers.; Doris Klabzuba,* V.P.; Judy Park,* V.P.; Janet Stevens,* V.P.; Jane Korman,* Secy.; John Klabzuba,* Treas.; Melinda Klabzuba; Josh Korman; Alice Park; Byron Searcy; E.R. Sidwell; Jackie Stevens.

EIN: 912136476

8997
The KLE Foundation ✧

P.O. Box 163991
Austin, TX   78716-3991

Established in 1997 in TX.

Donors: Lorraine Clasquin; Eric Harslem.

Foundation type: Independent foundation.

Financial data (yr. ended 12/31/05): Assets, $23,621,590 (M); expenditures, $1,027,973; qualifying distributions, $988,318; giving activities include $988,318 for 10 grants (high: $625,000; low: $500).

Fields of interest: Education; Environment.

Limitations: Applications not accepted. Giving on a national basis. No grants to individuals.

Application information: Contributes only to pre-selected organizations.

Officers and Directors:* Lorraine Clasquin,* Pres.; Eric Harslem,* V.P. and Secy.; Kate Harslem.

EIN: 742860436

8998
Caesar Kleberg Foundation for Wildlife Conservation ◇

711 Navarro St., Ste. 535
San Antonio, TX   78205   (361) 592-7174
Contact: Leroy G. Denman, Jr., Tr.

Trust established about 1951 in TX.
Donor: Caesar Kleberg‡.
Foundation type: Independent foundation.
Financial data (yr. ended 12/31/05): Assets, $45,838,697 (M); expenditures, $2,752,595; qualifying distributions, $2,255,875; giving activities include $2,121,000 for 5 grants (high: $2,047,000; low: $1,000).
Purpose and activities: Funding for wildlife conservation and studies.
Fields of interest: Animals/wildlife, research; Animals/wildlife, preservation/protection.
Limitations: Giving on a national basis. No grants to individuals, or for building or endowment funds, scholarships, fellowships, or matching gifts; no loans.
Application information: Application form not required.
  Initial approach: Letter
  Copies of proposal: 3
  Deadline(s): None
  Board meeting date(s): As required
  Final notification: 3 months
Trustees: Leroy G. Denman, Jr.; Stephen J. Kleberg; Duane M. Leach.
EIN: 746038766

8999
Robert J. Kleberg, Jr. and Helen C. Kleberg Foundation ▼ ◇

700 N. St. Mary's St., Ste. 1200
San Antonio, TX   78205   (210) 271-3691
Contact: Robert L. Washington, Grants Coord.

Incorporated in 1950 in TX.
Donors: Helen C. Kleberg‡; Robert J. Kleberg, Jr.‡.
Foundation type: Independent foundation.
Financial data (yr. ended 12/31/05): Assets, $209,934,754 (M); expenditures, $11,063,901; qualifying distributions, $9,633,405; giving activities include $9,577,107 for 36 grants (high: $3,000,000; low: $7,000; average: $20,000–$500,000).
Purpose and activities: Giving on a national basis for medical research, veterinary and animal sciences, wildlife research and preservation, health services, higher education, and arts and humanities; support also for local community organizations.
Fields of interest: Arts; Higher education; Animals/wildlife, preservation/protection; Health care; Health organizations, association; Medical research, institute; Biological sciences.
Type of support: Building/renovation; Equipment; Conferences/seminars; Research; Matching/challenge support.
Limitations: Giving on a national basis. No support for organizations limited by race or religion. No grants for endowments, or for normal operating functions.
Publications: Application guidelines; Annual report.
Application information: Application form not required.
  Initial approach: Letter on organization letterhead
  Copies of proposal: 1

Deadline(s): None
Board meeting date(s): Usually in June and Dec.
Final notification: 6 months
Officers and Directors:* Helen K. Groves,* Pres.; John D. Alexander, Jr.,* V.P. and Secy.; Emory G. Hamilton,* V.P. and Treas.; Helen C. Alexander,* V.P.; Henrietta K. Alexander; Caroline R. Forgason; Dorothy A. Matz; H. Virgil Sherrill.
Number of staff: 1 full-time professional.
EIN: 746044810
Selected grants: The following grants were reported in 2005.
$3,000,000 to University of Texas M. D. Anderson Cancer Center, Houston, TX. For molecular marker program.
$1,000,000 to Baylor College of Medicine, Houston, TX. For pediatric cancer center.
$752,795 to University of Texas Health Science Center, San Antonio, TX. For South Texas virology research.
$737,300 to University of Texas, San Antonio, TX. For aging brain research program.
$500,000 to San Antonio Zoological Society, San Antonio, TX. For African exhibit.
$500,000 to Texas A & M University, College Station, TX. For Phase II of Bovine Genome project.
$500,000 to University of Texas Medical Branch, Galveston, TX. For Biocontainment Lab Construction.
$386,600 to Webb-Waring Institute for Cancer, Aging and Antioxidant Research, Denver, CO. For breast cancer and tuberculosis research.
$378,000 to Southwest Foundation for Biomedical Research, San Antonio, TX. For support for Monodelphis Colony.
$300,000 to Howard Florey Biomedical Foundation, San Antonio, TX. For neuroendocrinology research.

9000
The Kodosky Foundation ◇

22 Cousteau Ln.
Austin, TX   78746
Contact: Gail T. Kodosky, V.P. and Secy.
E-mail: kodoskyfoundation@austin.rr.com

Established in 1996 in TX.
Donors: Gail T. Kodosky; Jeffrey L. Kodosky.
Foundation type: Independent foundation.
Financial data (yr. ended 12/31/04): Assets, $15,120,475 (M); expenditures, $1,236,971; qualifying distributions, $1,196,137; giving activities include $1,194,000 for 34 grants (high: $386,000; low: $1,000).
Purpose and activities: Giving primarily for the performing arts and science education.
Fields of interest: Performing arts; Performing arts, ballet; Performing arts, orchestra (symphony); Performing arts, opera; Higher education; Science, formal/general education.
Type of support: General/operating support; Continuing support; Annual campaigns; Capital campaigns; Building/renovation; Endowments; Program development; Conferences/seminars; Seed money; Curriculum development; Scholarship funds; Matching/challenge support.
Limitations: Applications not accepted. Giving primarily in TX. No grants to individuals.
Application information: Contributes only to pre-selected organizations.

Officers and Directors:* Jeffrey L. Kodosky,* Pres. and Treas.; Gail T. Kodosky,* V.P. and Secy.; Karen K. Tips; Laura L. Walterman.
EIN: 742802674

9001
Marcia & Otto Koehler Foundation

c/o Bank of America, N.A.
P.O. Box 121
San Antonio, TX   78291-0121
Contact: Thomas Killion, Sr. V.P., Bank of America, N.A.
FAX: (210) 270-5520;
E-mail: thomas.k.killion@bankofamerica.com

Established in 1980 in TX.
Donor: Marcia Koehler‡.
Foundation type: Independent foundation.
Financial data (yr. ended 7/31/05): Assets, $8,410,928 (M); expenditures, $554,933; qualifying distributions, $432,500; giving activities include $432,500 for 42 grants (high: $50,000; low: $2,000).
Fields of interest: Arts; Higher education; Nursing school/education; Human services; Youth, services; Aging; Disabilities, people with; Economically disadvantaged.
Type of support: Capital campaigns; Building/renovation; Equipment; Debt reduction; Emergency funds; Program development; Curriculum development; Research; Technical assistance; Matching/challenge support.
Limitations: Giving limited to Bexar County, TX. No grants to individuals.
Publications: Application guidelines; Annual report.
Application information: Application form required.
  Initial approach: Letter or e-mail requesting application form
  Copies of proposal: 11
  Deadline(s): June 1
  Board meeting date(s): July 31
  Final notification: Aug.
Trustee: Bank of America, N.A.
EIN: 742131195

9002
Albert & Bessie Mae Kronkosky Charitable Foundation ▼

112 E. Pecan, Ste. 830
San Antonio, TX   78205   (210) 475-9000
Contact: Palmer Moe, Managing Dir.
FAX: (210) 354-2204;
E-mail: kronfndn@kronkosky.org; Additional tel.: (888) 309-9001; URL: http://www.kronkosky.org

Established in 1991 in TX.
Donors: Albert Kronkosky‡; Bessie Mae Kronkosky.
Foundation type: Independent foundation.
Financial data (yr. ended 12/31/05): Assets, $278,260,896 (M); expenditures, $14,596,843; qualifying distributions, $13,134,266; giving activities include $11,717,955 for 203 grants (high: $500,000; low: $136; average: $10,000–$100,000), and $128,810 for foundation-administered programs.
Purpose and activities: To produce profound good that is tangible and measurable in Bandera, Bexar, Comal, and Kendall counties in Texas by implementing the Kronkosky's charitable purposes.
Fields of interest: Arts, multipurpose centers/programs; Museums; Libraries (public); Animal

welfare; Animals/wildlife, sanctuaries; Zoos/zoological societies; Medical research, institute; Crime/violence prevention, child abuse; Recreation, parks/playgrounds; Youth development, centers/clubs; Family services, parent education; Aging; Disabilities, people with.

Type of support: General/operating support; Continuing support; Management development/capacity building; Capital campaigns; Building/renovation; Equipment; Land acquisition; Endowments; Debt reduction; Emergency funds; Program development; Seed money; Research; Technical assistance; Consulting services; Program evaluation; Matching/challenge support.

Limitations: Giving limited to Bandera, Bexar, Comal, and Kendall counties, TX. No support for religious or political activities, private or public education, or for economic development. No grants to individuals, scholarships, annual funds, or for galas and other events.

Publications: Application guidelines; Annual report; Grants list.

Application information: Proposal package supplied with acceptance of letter of inquiry. See foundation's Web site for more detailed information. Application form required.

   Initial approach: Letter of Inquiry
   Copies of proposal: 3
   Deadline(s): None
   Board meeting date(s): 6 times annually
   Final notification: Within 10 days of receipt of letter of inquiry and within 1 week of Dist. Comm. meeting, upon decision

Officer: Palmer Moe, Managing Dir.

Trustee: Bank of America, N.A.

Number of staff: 3 full-time professional; 3 full-time support; 2 part-time support.

EIN: 746385152

Selected grants: The following grants were reported in 2005.

$500,000 to YMCA of San Antonio and the Hill Country, San Antonio, TX. For Vision 2010 Capital Campaign.

$400,000 to San Antonio Food Bank, San Antonio, TX. For Meeting the Need: Capital Campaign.

$350,000 to McKenna Healthcare Foundation, New Braunfels, TX. For McKenna Children's Museum.

$250,000 to Christian Senior Services, San Antonio, TX. For Meals on Wheels.

$250,000 to San Antonio Public Library Foundation, San Antonio, TX. For Bookend Collection.

$125,000 to South Texas Blood and Tissue Center, San Antonio, TX. For Texas Cord Blood Bank.

$65,000 to New Braunfels Art League, New Braunfels, TX. For building renovations.

$53,061 to Saint Peter the Apostle Catholic Church, Boerne, TX. For Positive Parenting Collaborative.

$50,000 to Medical Equipment Network for the Disabled, San Antonio, TX. For operating support.

$30,750 to Universal City Public Library, Universal City, TX. For KCF Small Library Initiative.

9003
Ernest L. Kurth, Jr. Charitable Foundation ◇

c/o Bank of America, N.A.
P.O. Box 831041
Dallas, TX 75283-1041
Contact: Wyatt Leinart, Tr.
Application address: P.O. Box 1506, Lufkin, TX 75902-1506, tel.: (936) 632-6450

Established in 1983.

Donor: Ernest L. Kurth‡.

Foundation type: Independent foundation.

Financial data (yr. ended 12/31/05): Assets, $26,227,012 (M); expenditures, $1,403,470; qualifying distributions, $1,227,061; giving activities include $1,225,565 for 29 grants (high: $142,000; low: $5,000; average: $30,000–$100,000).

Purpose and activities: Supports institutions and organizations that give promise of producing significant advances in the areas of education, health, community and social service, and cultural arts and the humanities.

Fields of interest: Museums; Elementary/secondary education; Human services; Family services; Government/public administration.

Limitations: Giving primarily in Angelina County, TX. No grants to individuals.

Application information: Application form required.

   Initial approach: 1-page letter
   Deadline(s): None

Directors: Martha Chandler; J.C. Clement, Jr.; Lynn Fisher; Sandra G. Kurth; Joe McElroy; Thomas Moore; Terry Morrow; Donna Mulholland.

Trustees: Wyatt Leinart; Bank of America, N.A.

EIN: 751862248

9004
Lantana Education Charitable Foundation ◇ ☆

8401 N. Central Expwy., Ste. 350
Dallas, TX 75225 (214) 292-3400
Contact: Richard Strauss, Pres.

Established in 2000 in TX.

Donor: Rayzor Ranch.

Foundation type: Independent foundation.

Financial data (yr. ended 12/31/05): Assets, $486,566 (M); gifts received, $703,888; expenditures, $597,078; qualifying distributions, $575,274; giving activities include $575,274 for 12 grants (high: $323,640; low: $250).

Fields of interest: Education; Health organizations; Human services; Children/youth, services.

Limitations: Giving primarily in TX. No grants to individuals.

Application information: Application form not required.

   Initial approach: Letter
   Deadline(s): None

Officers and Directors:* Richard C. Strauss,* Pres.; John P. Wagner,* V.P.; Mark R. Wagner,* V.P.; Paul Farr,* Secy.-Treas.

EIN: 752882214

9005
Mary Potishman Lard Trust ◇

c/o JPMorgan Chase Bank, N.A.
600 Bailey Ave.
Fort Worth, TX 76107
Application address: c/o Walker C. Friedman, 604 E. 4th St., Ste. 200, Fort Worth, TX 76102

Trust established in 1968 in TX.

Donor: Mary P. Lard‡.

Foundation type: Independent foundation.

Financial data (yr. ended 12/31/04): Assets, $13,413,295 (M); expenditures, $719,373; qualifying distributions, $586,815; giving activities include $566,917 for 64 grants (high: $144,000; low: $750).

Fields of interest: Arts; Education; Health care; Youth development; Human services; Children/youth, services.

Limitations: Giving primarily in TX, with emphasis on Fort Worth. No grants to individuals.

Application information:

   Initial approach: Letter
   Deadline(s): None
   Board meeting date(s): Generally in June or July, and Dec.
   Final notification: Within 2 weeks of meeting

Trustees: Alan D. Friedman; Walker C. Friedman.

Agent: JPMorgan Chase Bank, N.A.

Number of staff: 1 full-time professional.

EIN: 756210697

Selected grants: The following grants were reported in 2004.

$144,000 to Texas Christian University, Fort Worth, TX.

$25,000 to All Saints Health Foundation, Fort Worth, TX.

$25,000 to Modern Art Museum of Fort Worth, Fort Worth, TX.

$10,000 to Gill Childrens Services, Fort Worth, TX.

$10,000 to Score a Goal in the Classroom, Fort Worth, TX.

$5,000 to American Heart Association, Dallas, TX.

$5,000 to Childrens Medical Center of Dallas, Dallas, TX.

$5,000 to Fort Worth Opera, Fort Worth, TX.

$3,000 to Cancer Care Services, Fort Worth, TX.

$2,500 to YMCA.

9006
Caroline Wiess Law Foundation ◇

c/o Houston Trust Co.
1001 Fannin St., Ste. 700
Houston, TX 77002-6707

Established in 1983 in TX.

Donor: Caroline Wiess Law.

Foundation type: Independent foundation.

Financial data (yr. ended 12/31/05): Assets, $1,099,708 (M); expenditures, $16,762,178; qualifying distributions, $16,707,934; giving activities include $16,694,603 for 2 grants (high: $15,289,297; low: $1,405,306).

Fields of interest: Museums (art).

Type of support: General/operating support; Building/renovation; Research.

Limitations: Applications not accepted. Giving limited to Houston, TX. No grants to individuals.

Application information: Contributes only to pre-selected organizations.

   Board meeting date(s): Dec. or as needed

Officers and Trustees:* Caroline Wiess Law,* Pres.; Jo Marsh,* V.P.; Peter C. Marzio,* V.P.; James A. Elkins III,* Secy.-Treas.

EIN: 760077285

Selected grants: The following grants were reported in 2005.

$16,694,603 to Museum of Fine Arts, Houston, Houston, TX. 2 grants: $1,405,306 (For operating endowment), $15,289,297 (For operating endowment).

9007
Martha, David & Bagby Lennox Foundation ◇
228 6th St. S.E.
Paris, TX 75460
Application address: c/o William P. Streng, Bracewell & Giuliani LLP, 711 Louisiana St., Ste. 2300, Houston, TX 77002-2770

Established in 1985 in TX.
Donors: Martha Lennox†; David Lennox†; Bagby Lennox†.
Foundation type: Independent foundation.
Financial data (yr. ended 12/31/05): Assets, $13,842,546 (M); expenditures, $934,635; qualifying distributions, $666,137; giving activities include $650,455 for 34 grants (high: $108,000; low: $2,500).
Purpose and activities: Giving primarily for education, natural resource conservation, and historical preservation.
Fields of interest: Historic preservation/historical societies; Higher education; Education; Environment, natural resources; Human services; Children/youth, services; Family services.
Limitations: Giving primarily in the northeast TX area. No grants to individuals.
Publications: Application guidelines.
Application information:
  Initial approach: Letter
  Deadline(s): None
  Board meeting date(s): Varies
Officers: William P. Streng, Pres.; Sam L. Hocker, V.P.
Director: Mary Clark.
EIN: 760157945

9008
The Levant Foundation ◇ ☆
c/o Jamal Daniel
600 Travis St., Ste. 6800
Houston, TX 77002-3010

Established in 1999 in TX.
Donors: Jamal Daniel; Rania Daniel.
Foundation type: Independent foundation.
Financial data (yr. ended 12/31/05): Assets, $8,203 (M); gifts received, $704,000; expenditures, $712,583; qualifying distributions, $583,584; giving activities include $583,584 for 13 grants (high: $300,000; low: $1,850).
Fields of interest: Education; Health organizations, association; Foundations (community).
Limitations: Applications not accepted. Giving primarily in Lebanon and Geneva, Switzerland as well as in Houston, TX. No grants to individuals.
Application information: Contributes only to pre-selected organizations.
Officers and Directors:* Jamal Daniel,* Chair. and Pres.; John Howland,* Treas.
EIN: 311637973
Selected grants: The following grants were reported in 2004.
$100,037 to Foundation de Recherches et du Dialogues Interreligieux, Geneva, Switzerland. To acquire facilities for educational purposes.
$100,000 to Awty International School, Houston, TX. For capital support.
$25,000 to Encyclopedia Iranica, New York, NY. For encyclopedia about Iran.

$6,647 to University of Houston-University Park, Conrad Hilton College of Hotel and Restaurant Management, Houston, TX. For tuition books.
$2,000 to Texas Premier FC, Houston, TX.
$500 to Christian Hope Baptist Church, Houston, TX.

9009
Joe Levit Family Foundation ◇
P.O. Box 14200
Houston, TX 77221-4200

Established in 1968 in TX.
Donors: Max S. Levit; Milton H. Levit; Grocers Supply Co.
Foundation type: Independent foundation.
Financial data (yr. ended 12/31/04): Assets, $21,570,421 (M); gifts received, $100; expenditures, $991,676; qualifying distributions, $938,711; giving activities include $938,711 for 251 grants (high: $330,000; low: $35).
Purpose and activities: Support primarily for Jewish organizations and temples; funding also for higher and other education, children and family services, the arts, social services, and health associations.
Fields of interest: Arts; Elementary/secondary education; Higher education; Education; Hospitals (general); Health organizations, association; Human services; Children/youth, services; Family services; Aging, centers/services; Jewish federated giving programs; Jewish agencies & temples.
Limitations: Applications not accepted. Giving primarily in Houston, TX. No grants to individuals.
Application information: Contributes only to pre-selected organizations.
Directors: Leah S. Levit; Max S. Levit; Milton H. Levit; Rochelle Levit.
EIN: 746103403

9010
The Morris L. Lichtenstein, Jr. Foundation ◇ ☆
615 N. Upper Broadway, Ste. 800
Corpus Christi, TX 78477
Application address: c/o Harry L. Marks, P.O. Box 2888, Corpus Christi, TX 78403, tel.: (361) 884-1961

Established in 1995 in TX.
Donor: Morris L. Lichtenstein, Jr.†.
Foundation type: Independent foundation.
Financial data (yr. ended 12/31/05): Assets, $10,596,530 (M); expenditures, $1,438,922; qualifying distributions, $458,429; giving activities include $393,432 for 16 grants (high: $200,000; low: $1,000).
Purpose and activities: Grants given primarily to public charities in south TX for medical research, the arts, education, historical landmarks, care of animals, and mental health.
Type of support: General/operating support; Research.
Limitations: Giving primarily in Corpus Christi, TX. No support for private foundations. No grants to individuals.
Application information: Application form not required.
  Initial approach: Proposal
  Deadline(s): None

Trustees: Harry L. Marks; Marcia Marks; Charles W. Thomasson.
EIN: 742757309
Selected grants: The following grants were reported in 2005.
$200,000 to Del Mar College Foundation, Corpus Christi, TX.
$47,500 to Corpus Christi Symphony Society, Corpus Christi, TX.
$15,000 to Womens Shelter of South Texas, Corpus Christi, TX.
$5,000 to Palmer Drug Abuse Program of Corpus Christi, Corpus Christi, TX.
$3,000 to American Diabetes Association, Dallas, TX.
$3,000 to Food Bank of Corpus Christi, Corpus Christi, TX.
$2,500 to Ronald McDonald House, Corpus Christi, TX.

9011
Jack H. & William M. Light Charitable Trust ◇
c/o Broadway National Bank
P.O. Box 17001
San Antonio, TX 78217
Contact: Nancy F. May, V.P. and Trust Off., Broadway National Bank

Established in 1998 in TX.
Donors: Jack H. Light†; William M. Light†.
Foundation type: Independent foundation.
Financial data (yr. ended 12/31/05): Assets, $8,454,138 (M); expenditures, $490,296; qualifying distributions, $417,735; giving activities include $411,500 for 43 grants (high: $26,000; low: $2,500).
Purpose and activities: Giving primarily for health and human services for the benefit of children.
Fields of interest: Human services.
Type of support: Continuing support; Annual campaigns; Capital campaigns; Building/renovation; Equipment; Endowments; Emergency funds; Program development; Curriculum development; Research.
Limitations: Giving primarily in Houston and San Antonio, TX. No grants to individuals.
Publications: Application guidelines.
Application information: Application form not required.
  Initial approach: Letter
  Copies of proposal: 1
  Deadline(s): Apr. 30th and Oct. 31st
  Board meeting date(s): May and Nov.
  Final notification: June and Dec.
Trustee: Broadway National Bank.
EIN: 742874941
Selected grants: The following grants were reported in 2005.
$26,000 to Sunshine Cottage School for Deaf Children, San Antonio, TX.
$20,000 to Bo's Place, Houston, TX.
$20,000 to DePelchin Childrens Center, Houston, TX.
$17,500 to TIRR Foundation, Houston, TX. 2 grants: $5,000, $12,500
$15,000 to Childrens Fund, Houston, TX.
$10,000 to Camp for All Foundation, Houston, TX.
$10,000 to Good Samaritan Foundation, Houston, TX.
$10,000 to Park People, Houston, TX.
$5,000 to Mission Road Ministries, San Antonio, TX.

9012
Lightner Sams Foundation, Inc.
5400 Lyndon B. Johnson Freeway, Ste. 515
Dallas, TX 75240 (972) 458-8811
Contact: Larry F. Lightner, Pres.
FAX: (972) 458-8812;
E-mail: foundation@lightnersams.org

Established in 1994 in TX.
Foundation type: Independent foundation.
Financial data (yr. ended 12/31/05): Assets,
$14,735,854 (M); expenditures, $992,436;
qualifying distributions, $715,013; giving activities
include $569,360 for 62 grants (high: $42,000;
low: $1,000).
Fields of interest: Education; Health organizations,
association; Medical research, institute; Human
services; Children/youth, services; Community
development; Aging; Women.
Type of support: Matching/challenge support;
General/operating support; Annual campaigns;
Capital campaigns; Building/renovation;
Equipment; Debt reduction; Program development;
Research.
Limitations: Giving limited to the Dallas, TX,
metroplex. The only exception is when one of the
foundation trustees is actively involved or familiar
with a nonprofit organization outside of Dallas, TX.
No grants to individuals, or for fundraising events,
unless one of the foundation trustees is closely
involved with a nonprofit organization.
Publications: Application guidelines.
Application information: Organizations should
submit only 1 grant request per year. Application
form not required.
Initial approach: Letter
Copies of proposal: 1
Deadline(s): Feb. 1, June 1, and Oct. 1
Board meeting date(s): Late Mar., late July, and
late Nov.
Final notification: Within 10 days after board
meeting
Officers and Trustees:* Larry F. Lightner,* Pres.;
Sue B. Lightner,* V.P.; Charles Derek Adleta,
Psy.D.; Earl Sams Lightner, Sr.; Robin H. Lightner;
Kamala Lightner-Scammahorn.
Number of staff: 1 full-time professional; 1 part-time
professional; 1 full-time support.
EIN: 752555622

9013
The Link Foundation ✧ ☆
c/o H. David Hughes
111 Congress Ave., Ste. 1400
Austin, TX 78701 (512) 472-5456
Contact: Joe W. Bratcher III, Pres.

Established in 1985 in TX.
Donor: Joe W. Bratcher III.
Foundation type: Independent foundation.
Financial data (yr. ended 12/31/05): Assets,
$1,885,851 (M); gifts received, $173,120;
expenditures, $417,338; qualifying distributions,
$410,223; giving activities include $408,333 for 15
grants (high: $85,000; low: $5,000).
Purpose and activities: Giving primarily to human
services, medical, and relief organizations.
Fields of interest: Arts; Hospitals (general); Health
organizations, association; Food banks; Human
services; Children/youth, services; Family services,
domestic violence; International relief; International
human rights; Federated giving programs.

Limitations: Giving on a national basis, with some
emphasis on Austin, TX. No grants to individuals.
Application information:
Initial approach: Letter
Deadline(s): Sept. 30
Officers: Joe W. Bratcher III, Pres. and Treas.; Brigid
Anne Cockrum, V.P. and Secy.
Director: Elizbieta Szoka.
EIN: 742387802
Selected grants: The following grants were reported
in 2005.
$68,333 to Orpheon, The Little Orchestra Society,
New York, NY.
$40,000 to Mount Sinai Medical Center, New York,
NY.
$35,000 to UNICEF, New York, NY.
$15,000 to Human Rights Watch, New York, NY.
$15,000 to Safe Place, Dumas, TX.
$12,500 to Ronald McDonald House, Corpus
Christi, TX.
$5,000 to American Red Cross, Dallas, TX.
$5,000 to Austin Child Guidance Center, Austin, TX.
$5,000 to Center for Attitudinal Healing, Austin, TX.

9014
Helen Irwin Littauer Educational Trust ✧
c/o Bank of America, N.A.
P.O. Box 831041
Dallas, TX 75283-1041
Contact: Linda M. Metcalf, V.P., Bank of America,
N.A.
Application address: P.O. Box 1317, Fort Worth, TX
76101, tel.: (817) 390-6921

Established in 1969 in TX.
Foundation type: Independent foundation.
Financial data (yr. ended 4/30/05): Assets,
$7,772,506 (M); expenditures, $405,430;
qualifying distributions, $348,902; giving activities
include $337,510 for 37 grants (high: $71,000;
low: $1,000).
Fields of interest: Performing arts; Performing arts,
theater; Arts; Education; Health organizations,
association; Human services; Children/youth,
services; Christian agencies & churches.
Limitations: Giving primarily in TX. No grants to
individuals.
Application information: Application form not
required.
Initial approach: Proposal
Deadline(s): Mar. 31 and Sept. 30
Trustee: Bank of America, N.A.
EIN: 237029857
Selected grants: The following grants were reported
in 2005.
$71,000 to Presbyterian Night Shelter of Tarrant
County, Fort Worth, TX.
$25,000 to Harris Methodist Health Foundation,
Fort Worth, TX.
$20,000 to Fort Worth Opera Association, Fort
Worth, TX.
$15,000 to Cancer Care Services, Fort Worth, TX.
$15,000 to Child Advocates, Houston, TX.
$12,750 to Guardianship Services, Fort Worth, TX.
$11,000 to I Have A Dream Foundation, Houston,
TX.
$10,000 to Alliance for Children, Fort Worth, TX.
$10,000 to Alzheimers Association, Dallas, TX.
$10,000 to United Community Centers, Fort Worth,
TX.

9015
Lockheed Martin Missiles and Fire Control Employee Charity Fund ✧
(formerly Lockheed Martin Vought Systems
Employee Charity Fund)
P.O. Box 650003, PT 42
Dallas, TX 75265-0003
Contact: Brent Berryman, Treas.

Established in 1994 in TX.
Donor: Lockheed Martin Corp.
Foundation type: Company-sponsored foundation.
Financial data (yr. ended 12/31/04): Assets,
$363,692 (M); gifts received, $544,052;
expenditures, $469,004; qualifying distributions,
$469,004; giving activities include $425,004 for 46
grants (high: $206,019; low: $200), and $44,000
for 25 grants to individuals (high: $5,000; low:
$500).
Purpose and activities: The fund supports food
banks and organizations involved with women and
awards emergency grants to employees of Lockheed
Martin Missiles and Fire Control for accidents,
illness, or other catastrophes.
Fields of interest: Food banks; Women, centers/
services.
Type of support: General/operating support;
Continuing support; Annual campaigns; Emergency
funds; Research; Grants to individuals.
Limitations: Giving primarily in Dallas, Fort Worth,
and Lufkin, TX, and Camden, AR.
Application information: Application form not
required.
Initial approach: Proposal
Copies of proposal: 1
Deadline(s): None
Officers: James F. Berry, Pres.; G.D. Troxel, Secy.;
Brent Berryman, Treas.
Director: Tom Cunningham.
EIN: 752528901
Selected grants: The following grants were reported
in 2004.
$206,019 to United Way of Metropolitan Tarrant
County, Fort Worth, TX.
$45,000 to United Way of Collin County, Dallas, TX.
$22,500 to United Way of Clark County,
Arkadelphia, AR.
$20,500 to North Texas Food Bank, Dallas, TX.
$8,500 to American Cancer Society, Dallas, TX.
$8,000 to American Heart Association, Dallas, TX.
$2,500 to United Way of Angelina County, Lufkin,
TX.
$1,600 to United Way of Southwest New Mexico,
Las Cruces, NM.
$1,000 to Alzheimers Association, Dallas, TX.
$1,000 to Cystic Fibrosis Foundation, Bethesda,
MD.

9016
The Looper Foundation ✧
11757 Katy Freeway, Ste. 1400
Houston, TX 77079

Established in 1997 in TX.
Donors: Doris Looper; Terry Looper.
Foundation type: Independent foundation.
Financial data (yr. ended 6/30/05): Assets,
$3,059,471 (M); gifts received, $100,000;
expenditures, $1,198,822; qualifying distributions,
$1,186,774; giving activities include $1,179,996
for 34 grants (high: $240,000; low: $600).
Purpose and activities: Giving primarily to human
services.

Fields of interest: Secondary school/education; Human services; Religion; Economically disadvantaged.
Limitations: Applications not accepted. Giving primarily in Colorado Springs, CO. No grants to individuals.
Application information: Contributes only to pre-selected organizations.
Officers: Terry Looper, Pres. and Treas.; Doris Looper, V.P. and Secy.
EIN: 760330594

9017

Carrie J. Loose Trust ◇

c/o Bank of America, N.A.
P.O. Box 831041
Dallas, TX 75283-1041
E-mail: grants@gkccf.org; Application address: c/o Greater Kansas City Community Foundation, Grants Mgr., 1055 Broadway, Ste. 130, Kansas City, MO 64105, tel.: (816) 842-0944

Trust established in 1927 in MO.
Donors: Harry Wilson Loose†; Carrie J. Loose†.
Foundation type: Independent foundation.
Financial data (yr. ended 12/31/05): Assets, $15,920,213 (M); expenditures, $1,089,334; qualifying distributions, $975,999; giving activities include $925,000 for 6 grants (high: $300,000; low: $50,000).
Purpose and activities: Grants to established local educational, health, and welfare institutions; support for research into the community's social and cultural needs and for experimental and demonstration projects. A member trust of the Kansas City Association of Trusts and Foundations.
Fields of interest: Museums; Higher education; Crime/violence prevention, gun control; Human services; Children/youth, services; Community development; Foundations (community).
Limitations: Applications not accepted. Giving limited to Kansas City, MO. No grants to individuals, business start-up or reduction, or annual appeals.
Application information: Unsolicited grant requests not accepted.
   Board meeting date(s): Quarterly
Trustee: Bank of America, N.A.
Number of staff: 43
EIN: 446009246
Selected grants: The following grants were reported in 2004.
$175,000 to Greater Kansas City Community Foundation, Kansas City, MO.
$75,000 to Saint Teresas Academy, Kansas City, MO.

9018

Grogan Lord Foundation, Inc. ◇

P.O. Box 649
Georgetown, TX 78627 (512) 930-4554
Contact: R. Griffin Lord, Pres.

Established in 1992 in TX.
Donors: Sharon Lord Caskey; R. Griffin Lord; Grogan Lord; Ruth Joyce Hite.
Foundation type: Independent foundation.
Financial data (yr. ended 12/31/05): Assets, $3,727,607 (M); gifts received, $617,127; expenditures, $425,847; qualifying distributions, $425,000; giving activities include $425,000 for 6 grants (high: $250,000; low: $25,000).

Fields of interest: Higher education; Health care, clinics/centers; Human services; Children/youth, services; Christian agencies & churches.
Limitations: Giving primarily in TX.
Application information: Application form required.
   Deadline(s): None
Officers: R. Griffin Lord, Pres.; Sharon Lord Caskey, V.P. and Secy.-Treas.
EIN: 742623948
Selected grants: The following grants were reported in 2004.
$250,000 to Southwestern University, Georgetown, TX.
$50,000 to Methodist Mission Home, San Antonio, TX.
$50,000 to Saint Edwards University, Austin, TX.
$50,000 to University of Mary Hardin-Baylor, Belton, TX.
$20,000 to Gladney Fund, Fort Worth, TX.
$15,000 to Georgetown Community Clinic, Georgetown, TX.
$10,000 to Peaceable Kingdom Retreat for Children, Temple, TX.

9019

The Lord's Fund ◇ ☆

c/o Momentum Sports Group, LLC
8122 Datapoint Dr., Ste. 830
San Antonio, TX 78229 (210) 593-1012
Contact: Larry Berkman, Secy.-Treas.
FAX: (210) 614-8033; E-mail: LARGENT@Texas.NET

Established in 1997 in TX.
Donor: William Lance Berkman.
Foundation type: Independent foundation.
Financial data (yr. ended 12/31/05): Assets, $838,861 (M); gifts received, $1,090,408; expenditures, $1,197,788; qualifying distributions, $1,197,680; giving activities include $1,192,430 for 15 grants (high: $519,030; low: $1,200), and $5,250 for foundation-administered programs.
Purpose and activities: Support for missionary and charitable programs.
Fields of interest: Christian agencies & churches.
Type of support: General/operating support.
Limitations: Giving primarily in TX.
Application information: Application form not required.
   Initial approach: Proposal
   Deadline(s): None
Officers and Directors:* William Lance Berkman,* Pres.; Cynthia Ann Berkman,* V.P.; Larry Berkman, Secy.-Treas.; Jason Baker; Jason Walton.
EIN: 742879125

9020

Lowe Foundation

1005 Congress Ave., No. 895
Austin, TX 78701 (512) 322-0041
Contact: Clayton Maebius, Tr.
FAX: (512) 322-0061;
E-mail: info@thelowefoundation.org; URL: http://www.thelowefoundation.org

Established in 1988 in TX.
Donors: Erma Lowe†; Maralo, Inc.; Mary Ralph Lowe.
Foundation type: Independent foundation.
Financial data (yr. ended 12/31/05): Assets, $34,743,021 (M); gifts received, $2,290,414; expenditures, $1,793,861; qualifying distributions,

$1,475,000; giving activities include $1,475,000 for 48 grants (high: $300,000; low: $5,000).
Purpose and activities: Support for organizations that serve the health and educational needs of women and children.
Fields of interest: Arts; Education; Health care; Human services; Children/youth, services; Family services; Women, centers/services; Women.
Type of support: General/operating support; Capital campaigns; Building/renovation; Professorships; Research.
Limitations: Giving limited to the Dallas-Fort Worth-Midland and Austin-San Antonio, TX, areas. No grants to individuals.
Publications: Application guidelines.
Application information: Application guidelines and pre-proposal form available on foundation Web site. All requests are pre-screened to evaluate whether the project falls within the foundation's guidelines. If it does meet the criteria, then a full written proposal will be requested by the foundation. Application form required.
   Initial approach: Submit pre-proposal application
   Copies of proposal: 1
   Deadline(s): Dec. 31
   Board meeting date(s): Apr.
   Final notification: Funding occurs in May
Officers and Trustees:* Mary Ralph Lowe,* Pres.; Diana Strauss,* V.P.; Barbara Hendry, Secy.; Geoffrey Perrin, Treas.; Patricia Fleming; Clayton Maebius.
Number of staff: None.
EIN: 760262645

9021

Lubbock Area Foundation, Inc.

1655 Main St., Ste. 202
Lubbock, TX 79401 (806) 762-8061
Contact: Kathleen Stocco, Exec. Dir.
FAX: (806) 762-8551;
E-mail: contact@lubbockareafoundation.org; Grant application E-mail: tami@lubbockareafoundation.org; URL: http://www.lubbockareafoundation.org

Incorporated in 1980 in TX.
Foundation type: Community foundation.
Financial data (yr. ended 12/31/05): Assets, $13,132,341 (M); gifts received, $730,812; expenditures, $847,773; giving activities include $562,867 for 110+ grants (high: $100,000), and $154,649 for foundation-administered programs.
Purpose and activities: The foundation is a permanent charitable institution dedicated to the South Plains community. Giving primarily for education, arts, environment, health, civic affairs, and social services.
Fields of interest: Historic preservation/historical societies; Arts; Adult education—literacy, basic skills & GED; Education, reading; Education; Environment; Animal welfare; Health care; Health organizations, association; Children/youth, services; Family services; Human services; Community development.
Type of support: General/operating support; Continuing support; Capital campaigns; Building/renovation; Equipment; Emergency funds; Program development; Seed money; Scholarship funds; Matching/challenge support.
Limitations: Giving limited to Lubbock, TX, and the surrounding South Plains counties. No grants to individuals (except for scholarships), or for debt retirement; no loans.

Publications: Application guidelines; Annual report; Financial statement; Grants list; Informational brochure; Newsletter.
Application information: Visit foundation Web site for application form and guidelines. Application form required.
 Initial approach: Telephone or letter
 Copies of proposal: 10
 Deadline(s): Jan. 1, Mar. 1, May 1, July 1, Sept. 1, and Nov. 1
 Board meeting date(s): Jan., Mar., May, July, Sept., and Nov.
 Final notification: 2 months
Officers and Directors:* Samuel Hawthorne,* Pres.; Frank Stogner,* Pres.-Elect; Sammie Prather,* V.P., Donor Rels.; Joe Tombs,* Secy.-Treas.; Kathleen Stocco, Exec. Dir.; Brent Brown; Terri Cash; Adrienne Cozart; Jim Earsley; Larry Fryer; Sonny Garza; Larry Harvey; Chuck Heinz; Regina Johnston; Jay Matsler; Velma Medina; Phil Price; Don Rushing; Ted Rushing; Benji Snead; Joe Stettheimer; Gwen Titus; Terry Williams.
Number of staff: 2 full-time professional; 2 part-time professional.
EIN: 751709180
Selected grants: The following grants were reported in 2005.
$7,025 to Boys and Girls Club of Lubbock, Lubbock, TX. For remodeling of John W. Wilson branch.
$5,400 to South Plains Food Bank, Lubbock, TX. For GRUB (Growing Recruits for Urban Business) Program.
$5,000 to Backyard Mission, Lubbock, TX. For building supplies.
$5,000 to Lockney Youth Activity Center, Lockney, TX. For Youth Activities Coordinator.
$5,000 to Lubbock Arts Alliance, Lubbock, TX. For art opportunities for children at annual Lubbock Arts Festival.
$5,000 to YMCA of Plainview, Plainview, TX. For renovation of pool and pool room.
$4,335 to Goodwill Industries of Lubbock, Lubbock, TX. For Connected4Success.
$4,000 to Family Guidance & Outreach Center of Lubbock, Lubbock, TX. For Shaken Baby Syndrome educational materials.
$2,500 to Muleshoe Heritage Foundation, Muleshoe, TX. For irrigation system and landscaping.
$2,100 to Childrens Advocacy Center of the South Plains Texas, Lubbock, TX. For intensive forensic interviewer training.

9022
The Luchsinger Family Foundation ✧ ☆
2121 Kirby Dr., Apt. 27N
Houston, TX 77019

Established in 1988 in TX.
Donors: Amelia D. Luchsinger; John W. Luchsinger.
Foundation type: Independent foundation.
Financial data (yr. ended 12/31/05): Assets, $1,686,467 (M); gifts received, $500,249; expenditures, $609,643; qualifying distributions, $604,950; giving activities include $604,200 for grants.
Purpose and activities: Giving primarily for education, religion and for children's services.
Fields of interest: Museums; Higher education; Education; Hospitals (general); Health organizations, association; Christian agencies & churches.

Limitations: Applications not accepted. Giving primarily in TX. No grants to individuals.
Application information: Contributes only to pre-selected organizations.
Officers and Trustees:* Amelia D. Luchsinger,* Pres.; Mary L. Castaneda,* V.P.; Patricia L. Ward,* V.P.; John W. Luchsinger,* Secy.-Treas.
EIN: 760254155
Selected grants: The following grants were reported in 2003.
$25,000 to First Presbyterian Church School, Houston, TX.
$15,000 to Junior League of Houston, Houston, TX.
$15,000 to Texas Childrens Hospital, Houston, TX.
$10,000 to DePelchin Childrens Center, Houston, TX.
$10,000 to Hobby Center for the Performing Arts, Houston, TX.
$6,250 to Childrens Museum of Houston, Houston, TX.
$5,000 to Literacy Volunteers of America, Atlanta, GA.
$3,000 to Davidson College, Davidson, NC.
$3,000 to United Cerebral Palsy of Greater Houston, Houston, TX.
$2,500 to BEAR Be a Resource for CPS Kids, Houston, TX.

9023
Rachel Lyman Charitable Trust ✧
c/o Bank of America, N.A.
P.O. Box 831041
Dallas, TX 75283-1041

Established in 2000 in TX.
Donor: Rachel Lyman†.
Foundation type: Independent foundation.
Financial data (yr. ended 7/31/05): Assets, $12,219,018 (M); gifts received, $250,000; expenditures, $489,726; qualifying distributions, $416,051; giving activities include $406,542 for 30 grants (high: $60,981; low: $813).
Purpose and activities: Giving primarily for health associations, including children's health, and human services, including services for people who are blind; funding also for higher education.
Fields of interest: Higher education; Hospitals (general); Health care; Health organizations, association; Human services; Children, services.
Limitations: Applications not accepted. Giving on a national basis, with emphasis on AZ, CA, TN, and TX. No grants to individuals.
Application information: Contributes only to pre-selected organizations.
Trustee: Bank of America, N.A.
EIN: 527114493
Selected grants: The following grants were reported in 2005.
$60,981 to University of the South, Sewanee, TN.
$40,654 to Guide Dogs for the Blind, San Rafael, CA.
$40,654 to High Sky Childrens Ranch, Midland, TX.
$40,654 to Saint Jude Childrens Research Hospital, Memphis, TN.
$40,654 to West Texas Boys Ranch, San Angelo, TX.
$24,392 to Saint Lukes Episcopal Hospital, Houston, TX.
$20,327 to Calvary Baptist Church, San Angelo, TX.
$16,668 to Midland College Foundation, Midland, TX.
$11,383 to Gladney Center, Fort Worth, TX.

$4,065 to Midland Memorial Foundation, Midland, TX.

9024
The Lyons Foundation ✧
1202A Dairy Ashford St.
Houston, TX 77079-3004   (281) 497-0332, ext. 102
Contact: R.A. Seale, Jr., Pres.

Established in 1961 in TX.
Donors: Richard T. Lyons†; Sammie Lyons†; Magalou W. Hestand Trust.
Foundation type: Independent foundation.
Financial data (yr. ended 12/31/05): Assets, $13,038,446 (M); expenditures, $668,314; qualifying distributions, $552,493; giving activities include $548,000 for 54 grants (high: $35,000; low: $5,000).
Purpose and activities: Giving primarily for education and health and human services.
Fields of interest: Secondary school/education; Higher education; Health care; Human services; Children/youth, services; Family services; Developmentally disabled, centers & services.
Type of support: General/operating support; Continuing support; Annual campaigns; Capital campaigns; Building/renovation; Equipment; Endowments; Emergency funds; Program development; Professorships; Internship funds; Exchange programs; Matching/challenge support.
Limitations: Giving limited to Harris, Fort Bend, Montgomery and Galveston counties, TX.
Publications: Application guidelines.
Application information: Application form required.
 Initial approach: Letter
 Copies of proposal: 2
 Deadline(s): Nov. 1
 Board meeting date(s): Dec.
Officers: R.A. Seale, Jr., Pres.; Flo McGee, V.P.; John W. Storms, V.P.; James S. Prentice, Secy.-Treas.
EIN: 746038717
Selected grants: The following grants were reported in 2003.
$70,000 to Child Advocates, Houston, TX. For general operating support.
$40,000 to Casa de Esperanza de los Ninos, Houston, TX. For general operating support.
$30,000 to Ronald McDonald House of Houston, Houston, TX. For general operating support.
$30,000 to Star of Hope Mission, Houston, TX. For Children's Critical Care Project.
$25,000 to Regis School of the Sacred Heart, Houston, TX. For capital campaign.
$25,000 to Saint Joseph Hospital Foundation, Houston, TX. For general operating support.
$20,000 to Episcopal High School, Bellaire, TX. For capital campaign.
$20,000 to Saint Thomas High School, Houston, TX. For general operating support.
$20,000 to San Jose Clinic, Houston, TX. For capital campaign.
$20,000 to Texas Childrens Hospital, Houston, TX. For capital campaign.

9025
MacDonald-Peterson Foundation ✧
1 Riverway, Ste. 1000
Houston, TX 77056   (713) 579-2310
Contact: Wm. Nathan Cabaniss, V.P. and Treas.

Established in 1995 in TX.

Foundation type: Independent foundation.

Financial data (yr. ended 12/31/04): Assets, $6,927,206 (M); expenditures, $410,241; qualifying distributions, $351,164; giving activities include $356,000 for 28 grants (high: $60,000; low: $1,000).

Purpose and activities: Giving primarily for health and human services.

Fields of interest: Performing arts, orchestra (symphony); Higher education; Health organizations; Medical research, institute; Human services; Children, services; Community development; Federated giving programs.

Limitations: Giving primarily in TX. No grants to individuals, or for scholarships; no loans.

Application information: Application form not required.

Deadline(s): None

Officers: Philip M. Peterson, Pres.; William Nathan Cabaniss, V.P. and Treas.; William T. Miller, Secy.

Directors: Diana MacDonald Moore; Erik G. Peterson.

EIN: 760430319

Selected grants: The following grants were reported in 2005.

$30,000 to Houston Food Bank, Houston, TX.

$20,000 to Princeton University, Princeton, NJ.

$20,000 to Saint Martins Episcopal Church, Houston, TX.

$15,000 to Assistance League of Houston, Houston, TX.

$15,000 to Christian Community Service Center, Houston, TX.

$10,000 to Art and Environmental Architecture, Houston, TX.

$10,000 to Police Athletic League, Dallas, TX.

$5,000 to Ronald McDonald House of Houston, Houston, TX.

$4,000 to University of Texas Medical School, Houston, TX.

$2,500 to Boy Scouts of America, Houston, TX.

9026

Thomas G. & Nancy J. Macrini Foundation ✧ ☆

8607 Stable Crest Blvd.
Houston, TX   77024

Established in 2000 in TX.

Donors: Nancy J. Macrini; Thomas G. Macrini.

Foundation type: Independent foundation.

Financial data (yr. ended 12/31/05): Assets, $7,185,345 (M); gifts received, $353,700; expenditures, $331,100; qualifying distributions, $326,076; giving activities include $324,750 for 7 grants (high: $124,700; low: $14,000).

Fields of interest: Education; Christian agencies & churches.

Limitations: Applications not accepted. Giving primarily in Houston, TX. No grants to individuals.

Application information: Contributes only to pre-selected organizations.

Officers: Thomas G. Macrini, Pres.; Nancy J. Macrini, V.P. and Secy.

Director: John A. Macrini.

EIN: 760641778

Selected grants: The following grants were reported in 2003.

$25,000 to Dennis W. Holder Scholarship Fund, Houston, TX. For scholarships.

$25,000 to Saint Mary Cathedral Basilica, Galveston, TX. For renovations.

$20,000 to West Houston Assistance Ministries, Houston, TX. For general support.

$15,000 to Childrens Educational Opportunity Foundation (CEO Foundation), Houston, TX. For general support.

$15,000 to Saint James Episcopal School, Houston, TX. For general support.

9027

The Mankoff Family Foundation ✧

(formerly The Mankoff Charitable Foundation)
c/o Joy S. Mankoff
5950 Berkshire Ln., Ste. 550
Dallas, TX   75225

Established in 1997 in TX.

Donors: Joy S. Mankoff; Ronald M. Mankoff; Douglas F. Mankoff.

Foundation type: Independent foundation.

Financial data (yr. ended 12/31/03): Assets, $10,534,853 (M); expenditures, $897,510; qualifying distributions, $757,199; giving activities include $715,676 for 136 grants (high: $200,000; low: $15).

Purpose and activities: Giving primarily for the arts, health associations, particularly to a Crohn's and colitis foundation, Jewish organizations and temples, and to services for women.

Fields of interest: Performing arts centers; Performing arts, opera; Arts; Reproductive health, family planning; Health organizations; Federated giving programs; Jewish federated giving programs; Religion, interfaith issues; Religion; Women.

Type of support: Annual campaigns; Capital campaigns; Building/renovation; Program-related investments/loans; Matching/challenge support.

Limitations: Applications not accepted.

Application information: Contributes only to pre-selected organizations.

Board meeting date(s): Varies

Directors: Douglas F. Mankoff; Jeffrey W. Mankoff; Joy S. Mankoff; Ronald M. Mankoff.

EIN: 752739184

Selected grants: The following grants were reported in 2003.

$200,000 to Dallas Center for the Performing Arts, Dallas, TX. For annual support.

$5,000 to Foundation for Jewish Camping, New York, NY. For general support.

$2,500 to American Jewish Committee, Dallas, TX. For general support.

$1,000 to Dallas Womens Foundation, Dallas, TX. For annual campaign.

$250 to Genesis Womens Shelter, Dallas, TX. For general support.

$250 to National Council of Jewish Women, Dallas, TX. For Hannah's List.

$100 to League of Women Voters of Dallas Education Fund, Dallas, TX. For general support.

$100 to National Museum of Women in the Arts, DC. For general support.

$25 to Dallas Home for Jewish Aged, Dallas, TX. For general support.

$25 to Jewish Federation of Greater Dallas, Dallas, TX. For general support.

9028

Marathon Oil Company Foundation ▼ ✧

P.O. Box 3128
5555 San Felipe
Houston, TX   77253
Contact: Jennifer L. Evans, Mgr., Philanthropy and Community Affairs
E-mail: jlevans@marathonoil.com; Additional E-mail: philanthropy@marathonoil.com; URL: http://www.marathon.com/Our_Values/Philanthropy/

Established in 2001 in TX.

Donors: Marathon Oil Co.; Marathon Ashland Petroleum LLC.

Foundation type: Company-sponsored foundation.

Financial data (yr. ended 11/30/04): Assets, $3,986,658 (M); gifts received, $3,649,726; expenditures, $3,170,356; qualifying distributions, $3,144,036; giving activities include $2,259,386 for 316 grants (high: $219,114; low: $500), and $884,650 for 1,199 employee matching gifts.

Purpose and activities: The foundation supports organizations involved with arts and culture, higher education, the environment, health, human services, community development, and civic affairs.

Fields of interest: Performing arts; Arts; Higher education; Business school/education; Engineering school/education; Environment; Health care; Human services; Business/industry; Community development; Science; Public policy, research; Public affairs.

Type of support: General/operating support; Continuing support; Management development/capacity building; Annual campaigns; Capital campaigns; Program development; Scholarship funds; Research; Employee volunteer services; Program evaluation; Employee matching gifts; Matching/challenge support.

Limitations: No support for religious, fraternal, political, or veterans' organizations, United Way agencies, or primary or secondary educational institutions. No grants to individuals, or for special events, memberships, or emergency needs.

Application information: Application form not required.

Initial approach: Proposal
Copies of proposal: 1
Deadline(s): Dec.
Board meeting date(s): Quarterly
Final notification: 2 weeks to 2 months

Officers and Directors:* C.P. Cazalot, Jr.,* Pres.; J.T. Mills,* V.P.; W.F. Schwind, Jr.,* Secy.; J. Howard,* Treas.; J.M. Trevino, Business Mgr.; E.M. Campbell; G.D. Golder; G.R. Heminger; S.B. Hinchman; G.L. Peiffer; J.T. Mills; W.M. Stanfield.

EIN: 760694751

Selected grants: The following grants were reported in 2004.

$269,114 to United Way of the Texas Gulf Coast, Houston, TX. 2 grants: $219,114 (For operating support), $50,000 (For operating support).

$100,000 to Blanchard Valley Health Foundation, Findlay, OH. For capital support.

$100,000 to Colorado School of Mines, Golden, CO. For operating support.

$75,000 to American Red Cross, National Headquarters, DC. For operating support.

$75,000 to La Roche College, Pittsburgh, PA. For Pacem in Terris Institute.

$62,500 to Houston Museum of Natural Science, Houston, TX. For operating support.

$50,000 to Rice University, Baker Institute for Public Policy, Houston, TX.

$25,000 to Supporters of Civil Society in Russia, DC. For operating support.

$10,400 to Texas A & M University System, College Station, TX. For Marathon Scholars program.

9029
The Edward and Betty Marcus Foundation ◇ ☆
8222 Douglas Ave., Ste. 680
Dallas, TX 75225-5937 (214) 361-4681
Contact: M'Lou Bancroft, Exec. Dir.
FAX: (214) 941-3103; E-mail: bancroft@flash.net

Established about 1984 in TX.
Donor: Betty B. Marcus†.
Foundation type: Independent foundation.
Financial data (yr. ended 12/31/05): Assets, $10,002,883 (M); expenditures, $592,112; qualifying distributions, $453,755; giving activities include $453,755 for grants.
Purpose and activities: Support primarily for innovative programs in visual arts education for both youth and adults, especially those which involve the cooperation of two or more institutions.
Fields of interest: Arts education; Visual arts; Museums; Arts.
Type of support: Program development; Seed money; Curriculum development; Matching/challenge support.
Limitations: Giving limited to TX. No grants to individuals, or for capital campaigns, operating support, or endowment funds.
Publications: Application guidelines; Biennial report.
Application information: Application form not required.
  Initial approach: Proposal
  Copies of proposal: 1
  Deadline(s): Mar. 1; proposals may be submitted throughout the year
  Board meeting date(s): 1st Tues. in Feb., May, and Oct.
  Final notification: Mid-May
Officers: Melba Davis Whatley, Chair.; Carolyn Levy Clark, Secy.-Treas.; M'Lou Bancroft, Exec. Dir.
Trustees: Norine Haynes; Cary Shel Marcus; Richard C. Marcus; Susan Russell Marcus.
Number of staff: 1 part-time professional.
EIN: 751989529
Selected grants: The following grants were reported in 2003.
$106,690 to University of North Texas, School of Visual Arts, Denton, TX. For Marcus Fellows.
$59,075 to Grace Museum, Abilene, TX. For initiative visual arts education in rural west Texas.
$28,250 to Old Jail Art Center, Albany, TX. For Albany Arts.
$10,000 to Arts Foundation, San Antonio, TX. For visual literacy program expansion.

9030
Marti Foundation ◇
1501-D N. Main St.
Cleburne, TX 76033 (817) 558-0079
Contact: Hoylene Harris, Mgr.

Established in 1988 in TX.
Donors: George W. Marti; Jo C. Marti.
Foundation type: Independent foundation.
Financial data (yr. ended 12/31/05): Assets, $9,859,623 (M); gifts received, $30,000; expenditures, $428,977; qualifying distributions, $419,488; giving activities include $51,215 for 7 grants (high: $14,000; low: $863), and $368,273 for 185 grants to individuals (high: $4,500; low: $85; average: $1,500–$2,500).
Purpose and activities: Provides educational scholarships and loans to residents of TX; support also for scholarship funds and youth agricultural programs.
Fields of interest: Scholarships/financial aid; Youth development, agriculture.
Type of support: Scholarship funds; Scholarships—to individuals; Student loans—to individuals.
Limitations: Giving primarily to residents of Johnson County, TX.
Application information: Application form required.
  Deadline(s): 60 days prior to beginning of semester
Officer: George W. Marti, Pres.
Director: Michelle Marti.
EIN: 752265837

9031
Martin Foundation, Inc. ◇ ☆
c/o Lendell Martin
7037 Brittmoore Rd.
Houston, TX 77041-3210

Established in 2001 in TX.
Donor: AllStyle Coil Co., L.P.
Foundation type: Company-sponsored foundation.
Financial data (yr. ended 12/31/05): Assets, $526,728 (M); gifts received, $406,009; expenditures, $652,153; qualifying distributions, $615,932; giving activities include $615,932 for grants.
Purpose and activities: The foundation supports Christian agencies and churches and organizations involved with human services.
Fields of interest: Human services; Christian agencies & churches.
Limitations: Applications not accepted. Giving primarily in TX. No grants to individuals.
Application information: Contributes only to pre-selected organizations.
Trustees: Lawanna S. Martin; Lendell Martin; Roger D. Martin.
EIN: 760671303

9032
The Guadalupe and Lilia Martinez Foundation ◇
c/o Guadalupe Martinez
361 Pine Valley Dr.
Fairview, TX 75069

Established in 2002 in TX.
Donors: Guadalupe Martinez; Lilia Martinez.
Foundation type: Independent foundation.
Financial data (yr. ended 12/31/05): Assets, $2,913,792 (M); gifts received, $1,600,000; expenditures, $843,851; qualifying distributions, $843,851; giving activities include $815,100 for 11 grants (high: $275,000; low: $100).
Purpose and activities: The foundation provides support for charitable and religious organizations and for scientific testing for public safety, literacy, health, and education primarily for the benefit of the people of Webb and Zapata counties in Texas.
Fields of interest: Elementary/secondary education; Higher education; Human services.
Type of support: Annual campaigns; Capital campaigns; Building/renovation; Scholarship funds.
Limitations: Giving primarily in Webb and Zapata counties, TX. No grants to individuals.
Application information: Application form required.
  Initial approach: Letter of request
  Copies of proposal: 2
  Deadline(s): None
  Board meeting date(s): 3-4 times annually, as determined by board
  Final notification: After the next board meeting
Officers and Directors:* Guadalupe Martinez,* Pres.; Maria Louisa Sandlin,* V.P.; Shirley Gonzalez,* Secy.; Robert Gonzalez,* Treas.; Larry Sandlin.
EIN: 743005930
Selected grants: The following grants were reported in 2005.
$114,000 to Blessed Sacrament Church, Laredo, TX.
$100,000 to Diocese of Laredo, Laredo, TX.
$100,000 to Laredo Community College, Laredo, TX.
$85,000 to Boy Scouts of America, Corpus Christi, TX.
$30,000 to Laredo Philharmonic, Laredo, TX.
$5,000 to Ruth B. Cowl Rehabilitation Center, Laredo, TX.

9033
The Frank W. & Sue Mayborn Foundation ◇
(formerly The Frank and Anyse Sue Mayborn Foundation)
10 S. 3rd St.
Temple, TX 76501-7619

Established in 1965 in TX.
Donors: Anyse Sue Mayborn; Anyse Sue Mayborn Charitable Lead Annuity Trust.
Foundation type: Independent foundation.
Financial data (yr. ended 12/31/05): Assets, $19,734,574 (M); gifts received, $5,165,168; expenditures, $1,394,426; qualifying distributions, $1,392,923; giving activities include $1,190,147 for 22 grants (high: $800,000; low: $500), and $200,000 for 1 employee matching gift.
Purpose and activities: Giving primarily to a community foundation; support also for higher education.
Fields of interest: Higher education; Foundations (community).
Type of support: General/operating support; Capital campaigns; Building/renovation; Endowments; Scholarship funds.
Limitations: Applications not accepted. Giving primarily in the central TX area. No grants to individuals.
Application information: Contributes only to pre-selected organizations.
Officers and Directors:* Anyse Sue Mayborn,* Pres. and Treas.; Jerry L. Arnold,* Secy.; Jim D. Bowmer; Frank M. Burke, Jr.
EIN: 746067859
Selected grants: The following grants were reported in 2003.
$2,500,000 to University of Mary Hardin-Baylor, Belton, TX. For Frank and Sue Mayborn Center.
$500,000 to Temple College, Temple, TX.
$150,000 to Saint Marys School, Temple, TX.

$100,000 to Communities Foundation of Texas, Dallas, TX. For general support.

$27,971 to Baylor University, Waco, TX. 2 grants: $12,000 (For Mayborn Scholar Program), $15,971 (For Poage Legislative Library/Mayborn Washington Program).

9034
Oliver Dewey Mayor Foundation
P.O. Box 1088
Sherman, TX 75091-1088 (903) 813-5105
Contact: Regina D. Pruitt, Asst. V.P.
FAX: (903) 813-5121; E-mail: rpruitt@mail.bokf.com

Established in 1983 in TX.
Donor: Oliver Dewey Mayor†.
Foundation type: Independent foundation.
Financial data (yr. ended 6/30/05): Assets, $24,948,496 (M); expenditures, $1,708,238; qualifying distributions, $1,272,243; giving activities include $1,231,596 for 82 grants (high: $120,000; low: $382).
Purpose and activities: Support for education, community development, youth, and social and health services; support also for the construction of an outdoor theater.
Fields of interest: Education; Health care; Human services; Youth, services; Community development.
Type of support: General/operating support; Building/renovation; Research; Matching/challenge support.
Limitations: Giving limited to Mayes County, OK and Grayson County, TX. No grants to individuals.
Publications: Application guidelines.
Application information: Application form required.
  Initial approach: Proposal
  Copies of proposal: 9
  Deadline(s): Feb. 15, May 15, Aug. 15, and Nov. 15
  Board meeting date(s): Mar. 15, June, Sept. 15, and Dec. 15
Board of Governors: Tracey Dean; Samuel W. Graber; Nash Lamb; Jim Pledger; Regina D. Pruitt; Marien Stinson; Vickie White.
EIN: 751864630
Selected grants: The following grants were reported in 2004.
$156,616 to Mayes County Commissioners, Pryor, OK. For fairgrounds improvement.
$41,667 to Grayson County Womens Crisis Line, Sherman, TX. Toward new shelter building.
$25,000 to Austin College, Sherman, TX. For general support.
$25,000 to Rogers State University Foundation, Claremore, OK. For Oliver Dewey Mayor Endowed Chair.
$15,000 to Denison Public Library, Denison, TX. For Read to Win program.
$10,000 to Denison Helping Hands, Denison, TX.
$7,200 to Junior Achievement of Grayson County, Denison, TX. For Junior Achievement for Golden Rule Elementary.
$1,348 to Grayson County Shelter, Denison, TX. For new heater and air conditioner units.
$1,158 to Denison Independent School District Education Foundation, Denison, TX. For Denison High School dual credit courses.
$1,000 to Home Hospice of Grayson County, Sherman, TX. For Light Up a Light project.

9035
Mays Family Foundation ✧
200 E. Basse Rd.
San Antonio, TX 78209

Established around 1994 in TX.
Donors: L. Lowry Mays; Mark Mays; Randall Mays; Mays Family 2000 Charitable Lead Annuity Trust.
Foundation type: Independent foundation.
Financial data (yr. ended 12/31/05): Assets, $51,586,857 (M); gifts received, $1,255,000; expenditures, $2,724,235; qualifying distributions, $2,702,711; giving activities include $2,626,496 for 73 grants (high: $1,000,000; low: $30).
Purpose and activities: Giving primarily for the arts particularly to art museums, to education and for health, children, and social services.
Fields of interest: Museums; Museums (art); Museums (specialized); Elementary/secondary education; Libraries (special); Education; Health care; Health organizations, association; Cancer; Human services; Children/youth, services; Federated giving programs; Christian agencies & churches.
Limitations: Applications not accepted. Giving primarily in San Antonio, TX. No grants to individuals.
Application information: Contributes only to pre-selected organizations.
Officers and Directors:* Peggy P. Mays,* Pres.; Kathryn M. Johnson,* V.P.; L. Lowry Mays,* Treas.; Mark P. Mays; Randall T. Mays; Linda M. McCaul.
EIN: 742691624
Selected grants: The following grants were reported in 2004.
$515,792 to San Antonio Museum of Art, San Antonio, TX.
$400,000 to George Bush Presidential Library Foundation, College Station, TX.
$200,185 to San Antonio Zoological Society, San Antonio, TX.
$50,000 to Alamo Heights School Foundation, San Antonio, TX.
$11,000 to Saint Marys Hall, San Antonio, TX.
$10,000 to San Antonio Public Library Foundation, San Antonio, TX.
$10,000 to Witte Museum, San Antonio, TX.
$5,000 to Wellesley College, Wellesley, MA.
$2,000 to Bat Conservation International, Austin, TX.
$1,450 to Southwest School of Art and Craft, San Antonio, TX.

9036
Mays Foundation ✧
914 S. Tyler St.
Amarillo, TX 79101
Contact: Troy M. Mays, Pres.

Established in 1965.
Donor: W.A. Mays and Agnes Mays Trust.
Foundation type: Independent foundation.
Financial data (yr. ended 7/31/05): Assets, $8,657,345 (M); gifts received, $46,422; expenditures, $556,306; qualifying distributions, $373,851; giving activities include $369,901 for 93 grants (high: $90,000; low: $125).
Fields of interest: Elementary/secondary education; Higher education; Government/public administration; Protestant agencies & churches.
Type of support: Continuing support; Annual campaigns; Capital campaigns; Internship funds.
Limitations: Giving primarily in TX. No grants to individuals.

Publications: Newsletter.
Application information: Application form not required.
  Initial approach: Letter
  Copies of proposal: 1
  Deadline(s): None
  Board meeting date(s): Jan.
Officer and Trustees:* Troy M. Mays,* Pres.; Karra Mays Hill; Stacy Mays Sharp.
Number of staff: 1 part-time support.
EIN: 751213346
Selected grants: The following grants were reported in 2004.
$131,307 to Wayland Baptist University, Plainview, TX.
$109,800 to Baylor University, Waco, TX.
$30,000 to Hawaii Baptist Academy, Honolulu, HI.
$7,667 to Don and Sybil Harrington Regional Medical Center, Amarillo, TX.
$7,500 to Amarillo Symphony, Amarillo, TX.
$5,000 to Don Harrington Discovery Center, Amarillo, TX.
$2,500 to Newton County Library System, Covington, GA.
$2,000 to Amarillo College Foundation, Amarillo, TX.
$1,000 to Boy Scouts of America, Golden Spread Council, Amarillo, TX.
$1,000 to Samaritan Pastoral Counseling Center, Amarillo, TX.

9037
McCombs Foundation, Inc. ▼ ✧
755 E. Mulberry, Ste. 600
San Antonio, TX 78212 (210) 821-6523
Contact: Gary V. Woods, Secy.-Treas.

Established in 1981 in TX.
Donors: Gary V. Woods; McCombs Family Charitable Lead Trust; and members of the McCombs family.
Foundation type: Independent foundation.
Financial data (yr. ended 12/31/05): Assets, $96,346,710 (M); expenditures, $8,809,703; qualifying distributions, $8,651,491; giving activities include $7,000,000 for 231 grants (high: $6,000,000; low: $100; average: $1,000–$25,000).
Purpose and activities: Giving primarily for higher education, athletic programs, and historic preservation.
Fields of interest: Historic preservation/historical societies; Arts; Higher education; Medical research, institute; Athletics/sports, school programs; Recreation; Youth development, centers/clubs; Philanthropy/voluntarism.
Limitations: Giving primarily in TX. No grants to individuals.
Publications: Annual report.
Application information: Application form not required.
  Initial approach: Letter
  Copies of proposal: 1
  Deadline(s): None
  Final notification: 2 weeks
Officers: Marsha M. Shields, Pres.; Gary V. Woods, Secy.-Treas.
Directors: Lynda G. McCombo; Connie M. McNab.
EIN: 742204217
Selected grants: The following grants were reported in 2004.
$6,000,000 to University of Texas, Austin, TX.
$333,333 to Southwestern University, Georgetown, TX.

$70,000 to Carver Academy, San Antonio, TX. 2
grants: $20,000, $50,000
$50,000 to Saint Lukes Episcopal School, San
Antonio, TX.
$50,000 to San Antonio Academy of Texas, San
Antonio, TX.
$50,000 to Southwest Foundation for Biomedical
Research, San Antonio, TX.
$50,000 to Texas State University, San Marcos, TX.
$25,000 to United Way of San Antonio and Bexar
County, San Antonio, TX.
$20,000 to Buckner Fanning Christian Schools at
Mission Springs, San Antonio, TX.

9038
Emmett and Miriam McCoy Foundation ◇
P.O. Box 1028
San Marcos, TX   78667-1028

Established in 1993 in TX.
Donors: Emmett F. McCoy; Miriam M. McCoy.
Foundation type: Independent foundation.
Financial data (yr. ended 12/31/05): Assets,
$7,118,912 (M); expenditures, $575,474;
qualifying distributions, $557,774; giving activities
include $553,635 for 24 grants (high: $150,000;
low: $100).
Purpose and activities: Giving primarily to an animal
shelter and for community service.
Fields of interest: Environment; Animals/wildlife;
Diabetes; Women.
Limitations: Applications not accepted. Giving
primarily in TX. No grants to individuals.
Application information: Contributes only to
pre-selected organizations.
Officers and Directors:* Emmett F. McCoy,* Pres.;
Miriam M. McCoy,* V.P. and Treas.; Brenda M.
Remme,* Secy.
EIN: 742686146

9039
James N. McCoy Foundation ◇
5001 Ditto Ln.
Wichita Falls, TX   76302-3501   (940) 767-4334
Contact: Carolyn Hays, Pres.

Established in 1995 in TX.
Donor: James N. McCoy.
Foundation type: Independent foundation.
Financial data (yr. ended 12/31/05): Assets,
$16,113,135 (M); gifts received, $2,000,000;
expenditures, $609,946; qualifying distributions,
$609,122; giving activities include $601,355 for 45
grants (high: $75,000; low: $2,000).
Fields of interest: Education; Human services;
Foundations (community); Roman Catholic agencies
& churches.
Limitations: Giving primarily in OK and TX. No grants
to individuals.
Application information:
Initial approach: Letter
Deadline(s): None
Officers and Trustees:* Carolyn Hays,* Pres.; Mark
McCoy,* V.P.; R. Ken Hines,* Secy.-Treas.; Robert
W. Goff, Jr.
EIN: 752587034
Selected grants: The following grants were reported
in 2004.
$90,750 to Wichita Falls Area Community
Foundation, Wichita Falls, TX. 2 grants: $70,750,
$20,000

$40,000 to Midwestern State University, Wichita
Falls, TX.
$35,000 to United Regional Health Care
Foundation, Wichita Falls, TX. 2 grants: $10,000,
$25,000
$20,000 to YMCA of Wichita Falls, Wichita Falls, TX.
$12,500 to Patsys House Childrens Advocacy
Center, Wichita Falls, TX.
$10,500 to Camp Fire USA, Wichita Falls, TX.
$10,000 to Happy Hands Education Center, Tulsa,
OK.
$10,000 to Young Life, Dallas, TX.

9040
McCrea Foundation ◇ ☆
c/o Phoebe Muzzy
5005 Woodway Dr., Ste. 220
Houston, TX   77056

Established in 1960 in VA.
Donor: Mary Corling McCrea†.
Foundation type: Independent foundation.
Financial data (yr. ended 2/28/06): Assets,
$6,810,562 (M); expenditures, $358,421;
qualifying distributions, $321,625; giving activities
include $317,500 for 49 grants (high: $25,000;
low: $1,000).
Purpose and activities: Giving primarily for
education and health, including a children's
hospital; funding also for human services and
religion.
Fields of interest: Museums; Secondary school/
education; Education; Animal welfare; Hospitals
(specialty); Cancer research; Human services;
Children/youth, services; Residential/custodial
care, hospices; Community development; Religion.
Type of support: General/operating support;
Scholarship funds.
Limitations: Applications not accepted. Giving
primarily in Minden, NV, Portland, OR, and Houston,
TX. No grants to individuals.
Application information: Contributes only to
pre-selected organizations.
Board meeting date(s): Generally in May
Officers: Mrs. John L. Welsh, Pres.; Phoebe W.
Muzzy, V.P. and Treas.; David D. Welsh, V.P.; John
L. Welsh III, V.P.; Edward C. Welsh, Secy.
Agent: The Northern Trust Co.
EIN: 546052010

9041
Ralph H. & Ruth J. McCullough Foundation
c/o Joseph W. Royce
1300 Post Oak Blvd., 20th Fl.
Houston, TX   77056-8000

Established in 1981 in TX.
Donors: Ralph H. McCullough†; Ruth J.
McCullough†.
Foundation type: Independent foundation.
Financial data (yr. ended 12/31/05): Assets,
$15,942,767 (M); expenditures, $770,199;
qualifying distributions, $668,762; giving activities
include $517,500 for 42 grants (high: $100,000;
low: $1,000).
Purpose and activities: Support primarily for higher
education; some support also for medical services,
welfare, religion and the arts.
Fields of interest: Higher education; Health care;
Human services.

Type of support: General/operating support;
Endowments; Scholarship funds.
Limitations: Applications not accepted. Giving
primarily in TX. No support for political organizations.
No grants to individuals.
Publications: Annual report.
Application information: Contributes only to
pre-selected organizations.
Board meeting date(s): Quarterly
Officers and Trustees:* Joe E. Coleman,* Pres. and
Treas.; James T. McCullough,* V.P.; Joseph W.
Royce, Secy.; Jack H. Hooper; Dee S. Osborne; Anne
M. Shallenberger; H. Michael Tyson.
EIN: 742177193

9042
McDaniel Charitable Foundation
P.O. Box 2968
Texas City, TX   77592   (409) 942-1910
Contact: Rachel Smith, Exec. Asst.
FAX: (409) 944-0120;
E-mail: rsmith@mainlandbank.com

Established in 1999 in TX.
Foundation type: Independent foundation.
Financial data (yr. ended 12/31/04): Assets,
$9,400,599 (M); expenditures, $625,542;
qualifying distributions, $514,330; giving activities
include $420,325 for grants (high: $66,000; low:
$500).
Purpose and activities: Giving primarily for higher
education.
Fields of interest: Higher education.
Limitations: Applications not accepted. Giving
primarily in TX. No grants to individuals.
Application information: Contributes only to
pre-selected organizations.
Officers: Mark A. Lyons, Pres.; Michelle Lyons-Spier,
V.P.; Melissa Lyons-Gardner, Secy.
Directors: Stewart Campbell; William H. Frazier;
Randall Harris; John W. Lyons, Jr.
EIN: 760538313
Selected grants: The following grants were reported
in 2005.
$60,000 to Texas A & M University, Galveston, TX.
$51,000 to Texas A & M Research Foundation,
College Station, TX.
$11,422 to First United Methodist Church,
Dickinson, TX.
$5,200 to First United Methodist Church, La
Marque, TX.

9043
The Eugene McDermott Foundation ▼ ◇
3808 Euclid Ave.
Dallas, TX   75205-3102   (214) 521-2924
Contact: Mary McDermott Cook, Pres.

Incorporated in 1972 in TX; absorbed The
McDermott Foundation in 1977.
Donors: Eugene McDermott†; Mrs. Eugene
McDermott.
Foundation type: Independent foundation.
Financial data (yr. ended 8/31/05): Assets,
$104,928,640 (M); expenditures, $5,335,942;
qualifying distributions, $5,053,990; giving
activities include $5,004,000 for 98 grants (high:
$500,000; low: $1,000; average: $5,000–
$100,000).

Purpose and activities: Support primarily for cultural programs, higher and secondary education, health, and general community interests.

Fields of interest: Museums; Historic preservation/historical societies; Arts; Education, early childhood education; Elementary school/education; Secondary school/education; Higher education; Education; Hospitals (general); Health care; Health organizations, association; Medical research, institute; Children/youth, services; International human rights; Community development; Federated giving programs; Government/public administration; Minorities.

Type of support: General/operating support; Continuing support; Annual campaigns; Capital campaigns; Building/renovation; Equipment; Land acquisition; Endowments; Program development; Professorships; Seed money; Curriculum development; Scholarship funds; Research; Matching/challenge support.

Limitations: Giving primarily in Dallas, TX. No grants to individuals.

Application information: No printed material available. Application form not required.

  Initial approach: Letter
  Copies of proposal: 1
  Deadline(s): None
  Board meeting date(s): Quarterly
  Final notification: Prior to Aug. 31

Officers and Trustees:* Mary McDermott Cook,* Pres.; Charles E. Cullum,* V.P.; J.H. Cullum Clark; Mrs. Eugene McDermott; C.J. Thomsen.

Agent: Bank of America, N.A.

Number of staff: 2 part-time professional.

EIN: 237237919

Selected grants: The following grants were reported in 2005.

$1,000,000 to University of Texas Southwestern Medical Center, Dallas, TX. 2 grants: $500,000 each (For refurbishing of medical school).

$750,000 to University of Texas at Dallas, Richardson, TX. 2 grants: $250,000 (For Center for BrainHealth), $500,000 (For capital campaign).

$500,000 to Friends of the Katy Trail, Dallas, TX. For Plaza at Reverchon Park.

$300,000 to Stanford University, Stanford, CA. For Mary Cook Scholarship.

$250,000 to University of Texas, Austin, TX. For Jack S. Blanton Museum of Art.

$100,000 to Dallas Black Dance Theater, Dallas, TX. For operating support.

$50,000 to Dallas Public Library, Dallas, TX. For programs.

$25,000 to Arts District Friends, Dallas, TX. For operating support and marketing.

9044
John P. McGovern Foundation ▼

2211 Norfolk St., Ste. 900
Houston, TX 77098-4044 (713) 661-4808
Contact: John P. McGovern M.D., Pres.

Established in 1961 in TX.

Donor: John P. McGovern, M.D.

Foundation type: Independent foundation.

Financial data (yr. ended 8/31/05): Assets, $182,011,442 (M); gifts received, $360,000; expenditures, $9,647,084; qualifying distributions, $9,434,946; giving activities include $9,017,652 for 543 grants (high: $300,000; low: $55; average: $10,000–$100,000).

Purpose and activities: To carry on the charitable interests of the donor to support the activities of established nonprofit organizations, which are of importance to human welfare with special focus on children and family health education and promotion, treatment and disease prevention.

Fields of interest: Education; Health care; Children/youth, services; Family services; Community development, neighborhood development.

Type of support: General/operating support; Continuing support; Building/renovation; Endowments; Emergency funds; Conferences/seminars; Professorships; Publication; Curriculum development; Scholarship funds; Research; Matching/challenge support.

Limitations: Giving primarily in TX, with emphasis on Houston; giving also in the Southwest. No grants to individuals.

Application information:

  Board meeting date(s): Usually on or before Aug. 31

Officers and Directors:* John P. McGovern, M.D.*, Pres.; Kathrine G. McGovern,* V.P.; Gay Collette, Secy.; Orville L. Story,* Treas.

Number of staff: 1 part-time professional; 6 part-time support.

EIN: 746053075

Selected grants: The following grants were reported in 2004.

$750,000 to National Health Museum, DC.

$250,000 to Harris County Childrens Protective Services Fund, Houston, TX. For Caring for our Kids capital campaign.

$250,000 to University of Houston-University Park, Houston, TX. For M.D. Anderson Library/Honor College challenge grant.

$150,000 to Salvation Army of Houston, Houston, TX.

$100,000 to Barbara Bush Foundation for Family Literacy, DC. For gala.

$100,000 to John P. McGovern Museum of Health and Medical Science, Houston, TX. For general operating fund.

$100,000 to Ronald Reagan Presidential Foundation, Simi Valley, CA. For Air Force One pavilion reception area.

$100,000 to Texas Medical Center, Houston, TX. For VA Fisher House project.

$75,000 to Star of Hope Mission, Houston, TX. For challenge grant.

$60,000 to Association for Community Television, ACT for 8, Houston, TX. For Women's Health Conference.

9045
Robert E. and Evelyn McKee
Foundation ◇ ☆

5835 Cromo Dr., Ste. 1
El Paso, TX 79913-5501 (915) 581-4025
Contact: Louis B. McKee, Pres.
FAX: (915) 833-3714;
E-mail: mckeefoundation@direcway.com;
Application address: P.O. Box 220599, El Paso, TX 79913-2599; *URL:* http://www.mckeefoundation.org

Incorporated in 1952 in TX.

Donors: Robert E. McKee†; Evelyn McKee†; Robert E. McKee, Inc.; The Zia Co.

Foundation type: Independent foundation.

Financial data (yr. ended 12/31/05): Assets, $7,341,682 (M); gifts received, $200; expenditures, $709,299; qualifying distributions,

$539,300; giving activities include $539,300 for grants.

Purpose and activities: Emphasis on local hospitals, community funds, and rehabilitation and the handicapped; grants also for religious organizations, higher and other education, youth agencies, child welfare, and medical research.

Fields of interest: Higher education; Education; Hospitals (general); Medical care, rehabilitation; Medical research, institute; Children/youth, services; Federated giving programs; Religion; Disabilities, people with.

Type of support: General/operating support; Continuing support; Annual campaigns; Capital campaigns; Building/renovation; Equipment; Emergency funds; Program development; Conferences/seminars; Seed money; Scholarship funds; Research; In-kind gifts.

Limitations: Giving primarily in TX, with emphasis on El Paso. No support for organizations limited by race or ethnic origin, other private foundations (except for a local community foundation), religious organizations (except local Episcopal churches), or attempts to influence legislation. No grants to individuals, or for endowment funds or deficit financing; no loans.

Publications: Application guidelines; Annual report (including application guidelines); Program policy statement.

Application information: Application guidelines available on foundation Web site. Application form not required.

  Initial approach: Proposal
  Copies of proposal: 1
  Deadline(s): Dec. 15
  Board meeting date(s): June
  Final notification: After Feb. 28

Officers and Trustees:* Louis B. McKee,* Pres. and Treas.; Helen Lund Yancey,* V.P. and Secy.; Charlotte McKee Cohen,* V.P.; Sharon Hays Herrera,* V.P.; David C. McKee,* V.P.; Susan J. McKee,* V.P.; Linda Hays Gunter, V.P.; Carolyn McKee Hughes; C. Steven McKee; F. James McKee; James T. McKee; John S. McKee, Jr.; Philip Russell McKee; R. Brian McKee; Robert E. McKee IV; H.A. Woods.

Number of staff: 1 part-time professional; 1 part-time support.

EIN: 746036675

Selected grants: The following grants were reported in 2005.

$25,000 to El Paso Community Foundation, El Paso, TX.

$25,000 to Rescue Mission of El Paso, El Paso, TX.

$13,000 to New Mexico State University, Las Cruces, NM. 2 grants: $5,000, $8,000

$8,000 to University of New Mexico, Albuquerque, NM.

$7,500 to El Paso Lighthouse for the Blind, El Paso, TX.

$5,000 to United Way of El Paso County, El Paso, TX.

$2,500 to Prevent Blindness Texas, El Paso, TX.

$2,000 to Candlelighters of the El Paso Area, El Paso, TX.

$2,000 to Center Against Family Violence, El Paso, TX.

9046
Bruce McMillan, Jr. Foundation, Inc. ◇

P.O. Box 9
Overton, TX 75684 (903) 834-3148
Contact: Ralph Ward, Jr., Pres.

Trust established in 1951 in TX.
Donors: V. Bruce McMillan, M.D.†; Mary Moore McMillan†.
Foundation type: Independent foundation.
Financial data (yr. ended 6/30/05): Assets, $18,627,466 (M); expenditures, $1,344,898; qualifying distributions, $830,785; giving activities include $681,373 for 43 grants (high: $138,912; low: $200), and $33,500 for 9 grants to individuals (high: $12,000; low: $500).
Purpose and activities: Grants largely for higher education, including a scholarship program for graduates of 9 specific high schools in the immediate Overton, TX, area; support also for Protestant churches, youth agencies, agricultural conservation, and medical research.
Fields of interest: Higher education; Health care; Medical research, institute; Cancer research; Agriculture; Human services; Children/youth, services; Family services; Protestant agencies & churches.
Type of support: General/operating support; Program development; Scholarship funds; Scholarships—to individuals.
Limitations: Giving primarily in the Overton, TX, area.
Publications: Application guidelines.
Application information: Application form required.
  Initial approach: Letter
  Deadline(s): May 1 for churches and noneducational institutions; June 15 for scholarship applications
  Board meeting date(s): June and Oct.
  Final notification: July 1 (for scholarships)
Officers and Directors:* Drew R. Heard, Chair. and V.P.; John Rodgers Pope,* Vice-Chair. and V.P.; Ralph Ward, Jr., Pres. and Treas.; Pamela M. Merritt, Secy.
Number of staff: 2 full-time professional; 4 full-time support.
EIN: 750945924
Selected grants: The following grants were reported in 2004.
$126,700 to Kilgore College, Kilgore, TX.
$57,500 to Baylor University, Waco, TX.
$42,000 to University of Texas M. D. Anderson Cancer Center, Houston, TX.
$40,000 to Buckner Children and Family Services of North Texas, Dallas, TX.
$27,000 to Texas A & M University, College Station, TX.
$10,000 to Presbyterian Childrens Home and Service Agency, Austin, TX.
$10,000 to Stewart Blood Bank Center, Tyler, TX.
$9,500 to University of Texas, Tyler, TX.
$9,000 to Tyler Junior College, Tyler, TX.
$3,000 to Literacy Council of East Texas, Longview, TX.

9047
The Robert and Janice McNair Foundation ▼ ◇
Reliant Stadium
Two Reliant Park
Houston, TX 77054-1573 (832) 667-2014
Contact: Joanie Haley, Exec. Dir.
FAX: (832) 667-2057;
E-mail: jhaley@mcnairfoundation.org; URL: http://mcnairfoundation.org/

Established in 1988 in TX.
Donors: Robert McNair; Janice McNair.
Foundation type: Independent foundation.

Financial data (yr. ended 12/31/04): Assets, $16,445,849 (M); gifts received, $864,826; expenditures, $11,422,167; qualifying distributions, $10,547,904; giving activities include $10,419,560 for grants.
Purpose and activities: Giving primarily for education and the arts.
Fields of interest: Performing arts, opera; Arts; Higher education; Education; Community development.
Type of support: Program development; Curriculum development; Scholarship funds.
Limitations: Giving primarily in Houston, TX. No grants to individuals.
Publications: Informational brochure.
Application information:
  Initial approach: 1-page synopsis
  Deadline(s): None
  Board meeting date(s): Varies, usually quarterly
Officer: Joanie Haley, Exec. Dir.
Trustees: Janice McNair; Robert McNair.
Number of staff: 1 full-time professional; 2 full-time support.
EIN: 766050185
Selected grants: The following grants were reported in 2003.
$1,750,000 to Rice University, Houston, TX.
$1,140,000 to University of South Carolina Educational Foundation, Columbia, SC.
$501,500 to Houston Baptist University, Houston, TX.
$431,162 to Sigma Chi Foundation, Evanston, IL.
$300,000 to All Saints Episcopal School, Fort Worth, TX.
$260,000 to Baylor College of Medicine, Houston, TX.
$215,958 to Houston Independent School District, Houston, TX.
$205,000 to University of Texas Health Science Center, Houston, TX.
$146,479 to Austin College, Sherman, TX.
$118,863 to Houston Grand Opera, Houston, TX.

9048
Amy Shelton McNutt Charitable Trust ◇
153 Treeline Park, Ste. 300
San Antonio, TX 78209-1880
Contact: Trust Secy.

Established about 1983 in TX.
Donor: Amy Shelton McNutt†.
Foundation type: Independent foundation.
Financial data (yr. ended 9/30/05): Assets, $14,895,623 (M); expenditures, $704,193; qualifying distributions, $644,099; giving activities include $577,500 for 138 grants (high: $53,555; low: $40), and $10,000 for employee matching gifts.
Fields of interest: Museums (art); Arts; Higher education; Education; Environment, natural resources; Animal welfare; Zoos/zoological societies; Human services; Foundations (private grantmaking); Christian agencies & churches.
Type of support: General/operating support; Capital campaigns; Building/renovation; Matching/challenge support.
Limitations: Giving primarily in TX. No grants to individuals.
Application information: Unsolicited applications from outside of the San Antonio and Corpus Christi, TX, metropolitan areas will not be considered. Application form not required.

Initial approach: Letter of application, not to exceed 3 pages
Deadline(s): Feb. 28 and July 31
Board meeting date(s): Mar. and Aug.
Trustees: R.B. Cutlip; Jack Guenther; Courtney J. Walker.
EIN: 742298675

9049
The Meadows Foundation, Inc. ▼
Wilson Historic District
3003 Swiss Ave.
Dallas, TX 75204-6049 (214) 826-9431
Contact: Bruce H. Esterline, V.P., Grants
FAX: (214) 827-7042; E-mail: grants@mfi.org; Additional tel.: (800) 826-9431; URL: http://www.mfi.org

Incorporated in 1948 in TX.
Donors: Algur Hurtle Meadows†; Virginia Meadows†.
Foundation type: Independent foundation.
Financial data (yr. ended 12/31/05): Assets, $876,650,177 (M); expenditures, $48,907,441; qualifying distributions, $35,433,061; giving activities include $26,038,090 for grants, $623,797 for 2 foundation-administered programs and $663,000 for 6 loans/program-related investments.
Purpose and activities: Support for the arts, social services, community and rural development, health including mental health, education, and civic and cultural programs. Operates a historic preservation investment-related program using a cluster of Victorian homes as offices for nonprofit agencies.
Fields of interest: Media/communications; Visual arts, architecture; Museums; Humanities; History/archaeology; Historic preservation/historical societies; Arts; Education, public education; Education, early childhood education; Child development, education; Medical school/education; Adult/continuing education; Adult education—literacy, basic skills & GED; Libraries/library science; Education, reading; Education; Environment, natural resources; Environment; Animals/wildlife, preservation/protection; Dental care; Medical care, rehabilitation; Nursing care; Health care; Substance abuse, services; Mental health/crisis services; AIDS; Alcoholism; AIDS research; Crime/violence prevention, abuse prevention; Crime/violence prevention, domestic violence; Crime/violence prevention, child abuse; Crime/law enforcement; Employment; Agriculture; Nutrition; Housing/shelter, development; Housing/shelter, homeless; Safety/disasters; Recreation; Youth development, services; Human services; Children/youth, services; Child development, services; Family services; Residential/custodial care, hospices; Aging, centers/services; Homeless, human services; Civil rights, race/intergroup relations; Urban/community development; Rural development; Community development; Voluntarism promotion; Government/public administration; Transportation; Leadership development; Public affairs; Aging; Economically disadvantaged; Homeless.
Type of support: General/operating support; Continuing support; Income development; Management development/capacity building; Capital campaigns; Building/renovation; Equipment; Land acquisition; Debt reduction; Emergency funds; Program development; Publication; Seed money; Curriculum development;

Research; Technical assistance; Consulting services; Program evaluation; Program-related investments/loans; Employee matching gifts; Matching/challenge support.

Limitations: Giving limited to TX. No grants to individuals; generally, no grants for annual campaigns, fundraising events, professional conferences and symposia, travel expenses for groups to perform or compete outside of TX, or construction of churches and seminaries.

Publications: Application guidelines; Annual report (including application guidelines); Financial statement.

Application information: An online grant application form is available on the foundation's Web site. Please do not attempt to attach files to online applications. Application form not required.

  Initial approach: Proposal
  Copies of proposal: 1
  Deadline(s): None
  Board meeting date(s): Grants review committee
    meets monthly; full board meets 2 or 3 times
    a year
  Final notification: 3 to 4 months

Officers and Directors:* Robert A. Meadows,* Chair. and V.P.; Linda P. Evans,* C.E.O. and Pres.; Michael E. Patrick, V.P. and C.I.O.; Paula Herring, V.P. and Treas.; Bruce H. Esterline, V.P., Grants; Robert E. Weiss, V.P., Admin.; Emily J. Jones, Corp. Secy.; Evelyn Meadows Acton, Dir. Emeritus; Sally R. Lancaster, Dir. Emeritus; Curtis W. Meadows, Jr., Dir. Emeritus; Sally Cheney Miller, Dir. Emeritus; Eloise Meadows Rouse, Dir. Emeritus; Dorothy Cheney Wilson, Dir. Emeritus; John W. Broadfoot; Daniel H. Chapman; Judy Broadfoot Culbertson; John A. Hammack; Virginia Wilson Hanson; George Lancaster; P. Mike McCullough; Eric R. Meadows; John M. Meadows; Karen Meadows; William A. Nesbitt; G. Tomas Rhodus; Amy Miller Whiting.

Number of staff: 22 full-time professional; 1 part-time professional; 18 full-time support; 2 part-time support.

EIN: 756015322

Selected grants: The following grants were reported in 2004.

$3,000,000 to Childrens Medical Center of Dallas, Dallas, TX. Toward constructing new surgery center as part of multi-phased expansion of hospital, payable over 3 years.

$1,300,000 to Southern Methodist University, Dallas, TX. 2 grants: $600,000 (Toward mounting temporary exhibits and acquiring painting Saint Vincent Ferrer by Joan Reixach, payable over 2 years), $700,000 (Toward exhibitions and acquisitions fund at Meadows Museum).

$1,000,000 to Frontiers of Flight Museum, Dallas, TX. Toward designing and installing key exhibits, payable over 2 years.

$750,000 to Methodist Hospitals of Dallas, Dallas, TX. Toward renovating and expanding neonatal intensive care unit to serve more premature and critically-ill infants.

$515,000 to Foundation for Community Empowerment, Dallas, TX. Toward increasing number of low-income children receiving language-rich and research-based early childhood curriculum, payable over 3 years.

$420,000 to Fair Park, Friends of, Dallas, TX. Toward improving capacity of Fair Park museums and opening ice rink at Coliseum in order to increase number of visitors to Fair Park, payable over 2 years.

$401,000 to Science Place, Dallas, TX. Toward hiring new science educators to enhance educational programming and quality of visitor's experience, payable over 2 years.

$333,000 to University of Texas, Vaughn Gross Center for Reading and Language Arts, Austin, TX. Toward developing and implementing teacher-training materials for children with reading difficulties in grades four through seven, payable over 3 years.

$300,000 to Alternative Community Development Service, Dallas, TX. Toward furnishing and equipping new Education and Youth Center in order to expand school and youth outreach program, payable over 2 years.

9050
Mechia Foundation ✧ ☆
P.O. Box 1310
Beaumont, TX 77704-1310

Established in 1978.

Donors: Ben J. Rogers†; Julie Rogers†; Regina Rogers.

Foundation type: Independent foundation.

Financial data (yr. ended 12/31/05): Assets, $5,487,577 (M); expenditures, $429,021; qualifying distributions, $407,017; giving activities include $381,688 for 44 grants (high: $75,000; low: $180).

Fields of interest: Museums (specialized); Arts; Higher education; Hospitals (general); Health organizations, association; Cancer; Human services; Children/youth, services; Community development; Jewish federated giving programs; Jewish agencies & temples.

Limitations: Applications not accepted. Giving primarily in Beaumont and Houston, TX. No grants to individuals.

Application information: Contributes only to pre-selected organizations.

  Board meeting date(s): June 15 and Dec. 15
Trustee: Regina Rogers.
Number of staff: 1 part-time professional.
EIN: 741948840

Selected grants: The following grants were reported in 2004.

$70,000 to M. D. Anderson Cancer Center Outreach Corporation, Houston, TX. 2 grants: $20,000 (For capital campaign), $50,000 (For Health Disparities Initiative).

$35,000 to Julie Rogers Gift of Life Free Mammogram Program, Beaumont, TX. 2 grants: $20,000, $15,000

$30,000 to Temple Emanuel, Beaumont, TX.

$20,000 to Holocaust Museum Houston, Houston, TX.

$18,000 to Lamar University, Beaumont, TX. For I Have A Dream Program.

$12,500 to University of Texas M. D. Anderson Cancer Center, Houston, TX. For endowment.

$10,000 to Community Development Properties Lancaster, Inc, Lancaster, PA. For Hotel Beaumont Restoration.

$10,000 to Southeast Texas Family Resource Center, Beaumont, TX.

9051
Medallion Foundation, Inc. ✧
1407 Fannin St.
Houston, TX 77002-7613 (713) 654-0144

Established in 1984 in TX.
Donor: H.S. Finkelstein.
Foundation type: Independent foundation.
Financial data (yr. ended 9/30/05): Assets, $5,606,436 (M); gifts received, $4,025,524; expenditures, $974,558; giving activities include $764,266 for 21 grants (high: $200,000; low: $806).

Fields of interest: Medical school/education; Education; Health organizations, association; Biomedicine; Medical research, institute.

Limitations: Giving primarily in TX. No grants to individuals.

Application information:
  Initial approach: Letter or telephone
  Deadline(s): None

Officers and Directors:* Mark I. Entman,* Pres.; Jerald E. McQueen,* V.P.; Robert J. Pilegge,* V.P.; Harry Reay,* Secy.

EIN: 760141071

Selected grants: The following grants were reported in 2003.

$100,000 to Baylor College of Medicine, Houston, TX. For research.

$55,800 to Texas Neurofibromatosis Foundation, Houston, TX. For unrestricted support.

9052
Bhupat and Jyott Mehta Family Foundation ✧
738 Hwy. 6 S.
Houston, TX 77079-4033
Application address: c/o Janet Bertolino, U.S. National Bank, 2201 Market St., Galveston, TX 77553, tel.: (409) 770-7165

Established in 1996 in TX.
Donor: Rahul Mehta.
Foundation type: Independent foundation.
Financial data (yr. ended 9/30/05): Assets, $14,896,773 (M); expenditures, $766,048; qualifying distributions, $734,835; giving activities include $733,067 for 17 grants (high: $670,000; low: $250).

Purpose and activities: Giving primarily for education, human services, and to a community foundation; funding for scholarships to TX residents who are U.S. citizens and full-time students at an accredited university.

Fields of interest: Education; Human services; Foundations (community).

Limitations: Giving primarily in Houston, TX.

Application information: Application form required.
  Initial approach: Write or telephone to request
    application
  Deadline(s): Jan. 1 to Mar. 31

Directors: Bhupat J. Mehta; Isah B. Mehta; Jainesh Mehta; Rahul B. Mehta.

EIN: 760522455

Selected grants: The following grants were reported in 2005.

$670,000 to Greater Houston Community Foundation, Houston, TX.

$7,200 to DePelchin Childrens Center, Houston, TX.

$5,000 to United States Fund for UNICEF, Houston, TX.

$2,500 to Ronald McDonald House, Corpus Christi, TX.

$2,000 to Daya, Inc., Houston, TX.

$1,500 to Muscular Dystrophy Association, Houston, TX.

$1,000 to American Cancer Society, Baltimore, MD.

9053
Trini and O. C. Mendenhall Foundation ◇
8835 Stable Ln.
Houston, TX 77024

Established in 1998 in TX.
Foundation type: Independent foundation.
Financial data (yr. ended 12/31/03): Assets, $194,016 (M); gifts received, $425,000; expenditures, $346,646; qualifying distributions, $346,513; giving activities include $338,750 for 17 grants (high: $75,000; low: $250).
Fields of interest: Arts; Higher education; Human services; Federated giving programs; Christian agencies & churches.
Limitations: Applications not accepted. Giving primarily in TX. No grants to individuals.
Application information: Contributes only to pre-selected organizations.
Officers: Trinidad V. Mendenhall, Chair.; Oniel Mendenhall, Jr., Secy.
EIN: 760530965

9054
Meredith Foundation ◇
P.O. Box 117
Mineola, TX 75773

Trust established in 1958 in TX.
Donor: Harry W. Meredith†.
Foundation type: Independent foundation.
Financial data (yr. ended 12/31/05): Assets, $18,152,065 (M); expenditures, $852,034; qualifying distributions, $722,296; giving activities include $708,780 for 11 grants (high: $195,008; low: $1,000).
Purpose and activities: Giving primarily for civic projects; support also for educational and cultural projects and a library.
Fields of interest: Arts; Libraries/library science; Education; Children/youth, services; Community development, civic centers; Government/public administration.
Type of support: General/operating support; Equipment; Scholarship funds.
Limitations: Applications not accepted. Giving limited to the Mineola, TX, area. No grants to individuals.
Publications: Program policy statement.
Application information: Contributes only to pre-selected organizations.
  Board meeting date(s): Monthly
Officers: James Dear, Chair.; J. Carl Norris, Vice-Chair.; Ray Williams, Secy.-Treas.; Coulter Templeton, Exec. Dir.
Trustee: Lou Wagner.
EIN: 756024469

9055
Merrick Family Foundation ◇
3625 Greenbrier
Dallas, TX 75225

Established in 1999 in TX.
Donors: Nicholas A. Merrick; Leslie T. Merrick.
Foundation type: Independent foundation.
Financial data (yr. ended 12/31/05): Assets, $691,659 (M); gifts received, $670,534; expenditures, $374,634; qualifying distributions, $352,305; giving activities include $352,305 for 19

grants (high: $90,000; low: $50; average: $1,000–$10,000).
Fields of interest: Education; Human services; Christian agencies & churches; Roman Catholic agencies & churches.
Limitations: Applications not accepted. Giving primarily in Dallas, TX; some funding nationally. No grants to individuals.
Application information: Contributes only to pre-selected organizations.
Officers: Nicholas A. Merrick, Pres.; Leslie T. Merrick, Secy.
Director: Judith L. Merrick.
EIN: 752851383
Selected grants: The following grants were reported in 2005.
$90,000 to Providence Christian School of Texas, Dallas, TX.
$50,000 to Catholic Community Appeal, Dallas, TX.
$34,500 to Park Cities Presbyterian Church, Dallas, TX.
$25,000 to Eagle Ranch, Chestnut Mountain, GA.
$20,500 to Young Life, Colorado Springs, CO.
$10,000 to American Life League, Stafford, VA.
$10,000 to Dallas Theological Seminary, Dallas, TX.
$5,690 to Crystal Charity Ball, Dallas, TX.
$1,000 to Ronald McDonald House of Dallas, Dallas, TX.
$100 to Carelift International, Bala Cynwyd, PA.

9056
The Mevatek Foundation ◇ ☆
(formerly The Milagro Foundation)
5707 Bent Tree Ct.
Colleyville, TX 76034-3145

Established in 2000 in AL.
Donor: Nancy E. Archuleta.
Foundation type: Independent foundation.
Financial data (yr. ended 12/31/05): Assets, $2,643,121 (M); gifts received, $1,796,064; expenditures, $472,663; qualifying distributions, $478,338; giving activities include $432,338 for 29 grants (high: $57,698; low: $400).
Purpose and activities: Giving primarily to Roman Catholic agencies, churches, and schools.
Fields of interest: Elementary/secondary education; Higher education; Boy scouts; American Red Cross; Roman Catholic federated giving programs; Roman Catholic agencies & churches.
Limitations: Applications not accepted. Giving primarily in Huntsville, AL. No grants to individuals.
Application information: Contributes only to pre-selected organizations.
Officers: Nancy E. Archuleta, Pres.; Daniel R. Archuleta, V.P.; Gina A. Morgan, Secy.-Treas. and Exec. Dir.
Trustees: Joseph A. Lujan; Jessica R. Mayer; Gabriel A. Nieto; Robert Joseph Nieto.
EIN: 311738252

9057
Paul & Jane Meyer Family Foundation ◇
(formerly Paul J. Meyer Family Foundation)
P.O. Box 7411
Waco, TX 76714

Established in 1985 in TX.
Donors: Paul J. Meyer, Sr.; Jane Meyer; Japale, Ltd.; SMI International, Inc.; L-K Marketing.
Foundation type: Independent foundation.

Financial data (yr. ended 12/31/04): Assets, $43,488,364 (M); gifts received, $7,949,877; expenditures, $3,563,976; qualifying distributions, $2,439,259; giving activities include $2,432,892 for grants.
Purpose and activities: Giving primarily for Christian organizations, as well as for education, human services, and community development.
Fields of interest: Higher education; Education; Health organizations, association; Boys & girls clubs; Human services; Community development, neighborhood development; Philanthropy/voluntarism; Astronomy; Christian agencies & churches.
Limitations: Giving primarily in Waco, TX. No grants to individuals.
Application information:
  Initial approach: Typed statement
  Deadline(s): None
Officers and Directors:* Paul J. Meyer, Sr.,* Pres.; Terry Irwin,* V.P.; Alice Jane Meyer,* V.P.; Joe Baxter,* Secy.-Treas.
EIN: 742357421

9058
Morton H. Meyerson Family Foundation ◇ ☆
3401 Armstrong Ave.
Dallas, TX 75205

Foundation type: Independent foundation.
Financial data (yr. ended 12/31/04): Assets, $37,796 (M); expenditures, $851,668; qualifying distributions, $850,000; giving activities include $850,000 for 1 grant.
Fields of interest: Jewish federated giving programs.
Limitations: Giving primarily in Dallas, TX.
Application information:
  Initial approach: Letter
  Deadline(s): None
Trustee: Morton H. Meyerson.
EIN: 756535613

9059
MFI Foundation ◇
(formerly Meredith Private Foundation)
P.O. Box 163597
Austin, TX 78716

Established in 1998 in TX.
Donors: Lynn M. Meredith; Thomas J. Meredith.
Foundation type: Independent foundation.
Financial data (yr. ended 12/31/04): Assets, $26,693,559 (M); expenditures, $1,217,887; qualifying distributions, $1,091,304; giving activities include $1,091,304 for 36 grants (high: $201,000; low: $200).
Purpose and activities: Giving primarily to Roman Catholic education.
Fields of interest: Museums (art); Museums (children's); Elementary/secondary education; Higher education; Environment, natural resources; Community development; Roman Catholic agencies & churches.
Limitations: Applications not accepted. Giving on a national basis, with some emphasis on Austin, TX. No grants to individuals.
Application information: Contributes only to pre-selected organizations.

Directors: Lynn M. Meredith; Thomas J. Meredith; Scott M. Mullen.
EIN: 742882442
Selected grants: The following grants were reported in 2004.
$251,000 to Saint Stephens and Saint Agnes School, Alexandria, VA.
$50,000 to Austin Idea Network, Austin, TX.
$25,000 to Austin Film Society, Austin, TX.
$25,000 to New York University, New York, NY.
$25,000 to Youth and Family Alliance, Austin, TX.
$15,000 to Clark Fork Coalition, Missoula, MT.
$10,000 to Five Valleys Land Trust, Missoula, MT.
$7,054 to Austin Childrens Museum, Austin, TX.
$5,000 to American Indian Institute, Bozeman, MT.
$5,000 to Austin Project, Austin, TX.

9060
The Miles Foundation, Inc. ✧ ☆
200 Highland Cir.
Argyle, TX 76226

Established in 1999 in TX.
Donors: Ellison Miles†; Miles Production, Co., Inc.
Foundation type: Independent foundation.
Financial data (yr. ended 12/31/05): Assets, $11,115,244 (M); gifts received, $9,859,125; expenditures, $648,047; qualifying distributions, $620,682; giving activities include $610,700 for 9 grants (high: $389,000; low: $1,000).
Purpose and activities: Giving primarily for higher education.
Fields of interest: Museums (specialized); Elementary/secondary education; Higher education.
Limitations: Applications not accepted. Giving primarily in TX. No grants to individuals.
Application information: Contributes only to pre-selected organizations.
Officers and Directors: * Mike Russ,* Pres.; Jack Burdett,* V.P. and Treas.; Sherry Wilson,* Secy.; Richard Macomb.
EIN: 752739180
Selected grants: The following grants were reported in 2003.
$32,000 to Dallas County Community College District Foundation, Dallas, TX. For program support.
$25,000 to Texas College of Osteopathic Medicine Foundation, Fort Worth, TX. For program support.
$20,000 to Frontiers of Flight Museum, Dallas, TX. For educational assistance and program support.
$10,000 to Northwest Educational Foundation, Fort Worth, TX. For program support.
$5,000 to Bridgeport ISD Education Foundation, Bridgeport, TX. For program support.
$2,400 to Argyle ISD Education Foundation, Argyle, TX. For program support.
$2,000 to Jacksboro High School, Jacksboro, TX. For scholarships.
$1,000 to Bridgeport High School, Bridgeport, TX. For scholarships.

9061
The Arnold and Suzanne Miller Foundation ✧ ☆
5701 Woodway Dr., Ste. 324
Houston, TX 77057-1505

Donors: Bertha Gordon Miller; I.L. and Bertha Gordon Miller Foundation.
Foundation type: Independent foundation.

Financial data (yr. ended 3/31/06): Assets, $28,450 (M); expenditures, $1,297,937; qualifying distributions, $1,295,176; giving activities include $1,293,650 for grants.
Fields of interest: Museums; Arts; Education; Health organizations, association; Human services; Jewish agencies & temples.
Limitations: Applications not accepted. Giving primarily in Houston, TX. No grants to individuals.
Application information: Contributes only to pre-selected organizations.
Officers and Trustees: * Arnold M. Miller,* Pres.; Arnold M. Miller, Jr.,* V.P. and Secy.; Suzanne S. Miller,* Treas.
EIN: 760314951

9062
Steven and Sheila Miller Foundation ✧ ☆
501 Crawford St., Ste. 500
Houston, TX 77002-2113

Established in 2002 in TX.
Donors: Sheila M. Miller; Steven L. Miller.
Foundation type: Independent foundation.
Financial data (yr. ended 12/31/05): Assets, $5,341,954 (M); expenditures, $662,648; qualifying distributions, $635,240; giving activities include $616,850 for 53 grants (high: $264,900; low: $100).
Fields of interest: Arts; Higher education, university; Education; Human services; Youth, services; Federated giving programs; Christian agencies & churches.
Type of support: General/operating support.
Limitations: Applications not accepted. Giving primarily in Houston, TX. No grants to individuals.
Application information: Contributes only to pre-selected organizations.
Officers and Directors: * Steven L. Miller,* Pres. and Treas.; Sheila M. Miller,* V.P.; Steven L. Miller, Jr.,* Secy.; Ashley Miller.
EIN: 820576089
Selected grants: The following grants were reported in 2004.
$50,000 to University of Illinois Foundation, Urbana, IL. For general support.
$9,000 to Museum of Fine Arts, Houston, Houston, TX. For general support.
$5,181 to United Way. For general support.
$5,000 to Barbara Bush Texas Fund for Family Literacy, Houston, TX. For general support.
$5,000 to Rice University, Jesse H. Jones Graduate School of Management, Houston, TX. For general support.
$3,000 to Houston Public Library, Houston, TX. For general support.
$3,000 to Texas Southern University Foundation, Houston, TX. For general support.
$1,000 to Boys and Girls Clubs of Greater Houston, Houston, TX. For general support.
$1,000 to Houston Symphony Orchestra, Houston, TX. For general support.
$210 to University of Texas, School of Nursing, Austin, TX. For general support.

9063
The Walter M. Mischer & Mary A. Mischer Foundation ✧
9 Greenway Plz., Ste. 2900
Houston, TX 77046 (713) 869-7800
Contact: Sheryl Taylor, Secy.

Additional tel.: (713) 293-3517

Established in 1998 in TX.
Donors: Mary A. Mischer; Walter M. Mischer.
Foundation type: Independent foundation.
Financial data (yr. ended 12/31/05): Assets, $4,970,551 (M); expenditures, $349,299; qualifying distributions, $320,000; giving activities include $320,000 for 4 grants (high: $200,000; low: $20,000).
Purpose and activities: Giving primarily for education, with emphasis on health care and medical research.
Fields of interest: Education; Health care; Cancer research; Prostate cancer research.
Limitations: Giving primarily in Houston, TX. No grants to individuals.
Application information: Application form required.
Initial approach: Request application form
Deadline(s): Nov. 1
Officers: Mary A. Mischer, Pres.; John W. Storms, V.P.; Sheryl Taylor, Secy.
Directors: Walter M. Mischer, Jr.; Paula Mischer.
EIN: 760574194

9064
The Cynthia & George Mitchell Foundation ✧
10077 Grogan's Mill Rd., Ste. 475
The Woodlands, TX 77380 (512) 474-8887
Contact: Meredith Mitchell Dreiss, Dir.
Application address: P.O. Box 5708, Austin, TX 78763-5708

Established in 1981 in TX.
Donors: Cynthia W. Mitchell; George P. Mitchell.
Foundation type: Independent foundation.
Financial data (yr. ended 12/31/05): Assets, $147,392,395 (M); expenditures, $6,766,656; qualifying distributions, $6,753,158; giving activities include $6,618,500 for 28 grants (high: $4,000,000; low: $500; average: $10,000–$250,000).
Purpose and activities: Giving primarily for higher education.
Fields of interest: Arts; Higher education; Science.
Limitations: Giving limited to TX.
Application information:
Initial approach: Letter
Deadline(s): None
Officers and Directors: * George P. Mitchell, Chair.; Meredith L. Dreiss, Pres. and Treas.; Pamela Mitchell Maguire,* V.P.; Brian Gregory Mitchell,* Secy.; Meredith Mitchell Dreiss; Sheridan Mitchell Lorenz; Carleton Grant Mitchell; George Scott Mitchell; Jeffrey Todd Mitchell; John Kirk Mitchell; Mark Douglas Mitchell; Michael Kent Mitchell.
EIN: 742170127
Selected grants: The following grants were reported in 2005.
$4,000,000 to University of Houston-University Park, Houston, TX.
$2,000,000 to University of Texas M. D. Anderson Cancer Center, Houston, TX.
$70,000 to University of Texas, Austin, TX. 3 grants: $10,000, $30,000, $30,000.
$10,000 to E.E. Waddell High School, Charlotte, NC.
$5,000 to University of Arkansas for Medical Sciences, Little Rock, AR.
$2,500 to American YouthWorks, Austin, TX.
$2,000 to Pacific Bridge Institute, Sebastopol, CA.
$500 to Austin Public Library, Austin, TX.

9065
The Mitchell Foundation ◇
3900 Dallas Pkwy., Ste. 500
Plano, TX 75093
Contact: Keri Chorba

Established in 1998 in TX.
Donors: Lee Roy Mitchell; Tandy Mitchell.
Foundation type: Independent foundation.
Financial data (yr. ended 12/31/04): Assets, $29,716,219 (M); gifts received, $30,044,738; expenditures, $1,147,031; qualifying distributions, $1,116,000; giving activities include $1,116,000 for 28 grants (high: $200,000; low: $200).
Fields of interest: Health care; Medical research; Human services; Religion.
Limitations: Giving primarily in TX. No grants to individuals.
Application information:
Initial approach: Letter
Deadline(s): None
Officers: Lee Roy Mitchell, Pres.; Robert Copple, V.P.; Tandy Mitchell, Secy.
EIN: 752769798
Selected grants: The following grants were reported in 2004.
$300,000 to Champions for Life, Dallas, TX. 3 grants: $100,000 each
$205,000 to Young Life, Colorado Springs, CO. 2 grants: $5,000, $200,000
$200,000 to Dallas Theological Seminary, Dallas, TX.
$50,000 to National Jewish Medical and Research Center, Denver, CO.

9066
Richard Warren Mithoff Family Charitable Foundation ◇
500 Dallas St., Ste. 3450
Houston, TX 77002-4800

Established in 1984 in TX.
Donors: Richard Warren Mithoff; Virginia Mithoff.
Foundation type: Independent foundation.
Financial data (yr. ended 12/31/04): Assets, $663,800 (M); gifts received, $369,336; expenditures, $354,650; qualifying distributions, $352,117; giving activities include $349,742 for 52 grants (high: $125,000; low: $800).
Fields of interest: Museums; Museums (science/technology); Performing arts; Arts; Higher education, university; Human services; Children, services.
Type of support: General/operating support.
Limitations: Applications not accepted. Giving primarily in Houston, TX. No grants to individuals.
Application information: Contributes only to pre-selected organizations.
Officers: Richard Warren Mithoff, Jr., Chair.; Virginia Mithoff, Secy.
Directors: Caroline Mithoff; Michael Mithoff; V. Richard Viebig, Jr.
EIN: 760094136
Selected grants: The following grants were reported in 2004.
$125,000 to El Paso Museum of Art, El Paso, TX.
$9,405 to Houston Grand Opera, Houston, TX.
$5,670 to Houston Ballet, Houston, TX.
$4,750 to Alley Theater, Houston, TX.
$4,700 to Houston Public Library, Houston, TX.
$4,675 to Teach for America, Houston, TX.
$4,250 to Orange Show Center for Visionary Art, Houston, TX.

$2,800 to Houston Museum of Natural Science, Houston, TX.
$2,400 to Childrens Museum of Houston, Houston, TX.
$1,000 to Communities in Schools, Bay Area, Houston, TX.

9067
Roy F. and Joann Cole Mitte Foundation
1008 West Ave.
Austin, TX 78701   (512) 233-5599
Contact: Cheryl Nolting, Exec. Dir.
FAX: (512) 233-5542;
E-mail: info@mittefoundation.org; URL: http://www.mittefoundation.org

Established in 1994 in TX.
Donors: Roy F. Mitte; Joann Cole Mitte.
Foundation type: Independent foundation.
Financial data (yr. ended 12/31/05): Assets, $32,736,001 (M); expenditures, $4,785,698; qualifying distributions, $4,041,070; giving activities include $3,955,083 for 31 grants (high: $949,703; low: $350).
Purpose and activities: Giving primarily to universities to support scholarships. Additional support toward for a community giving program localized to the Central Texas area.
Fields of interest: Arts; Higher education, university; Scholarships/financial aid; Education; Housing/shelter; Aging, centers/services; Community development.
Type of support: General/operating support; Continuing support; Annual campaigns; Capital campaigns; Building/renovation; Equipment; Endowments; Program development; Professorships; Curriculum development; Fellowships; Scholarship funds; Research.
Limitations: Giving primarily in the central TX area. Generally, no support for religious or political organizations, private foundations, community foundations, or the United Way. No grants to individuals, indirect costs, or loans or program-related investments.
Publications: Application guidelines; Newsletter.
Application information: See foundation Web site for more application information, including acceptable proposal formats. Application form required.
Initial approach: Letter of inquiry (by mail or E-mail)
Copies of proposal: 2
Deadline(s): Sept. 15
Board meeting date(s): Twice a year
Final notification: Up to 6 months following deadline
Officers and Directors:* Roy F. Mitte,* Pres.; Joann Cole Mitte,* Exec. V.P.; M. Scott Mitte,* Sr. V.P.; William Skipping,* Secy.; Jim Weitzul, Ph.D., Treas.; Cheryl Nolting, Exec. Dir.; Kent Dove; Cathy Supple; Denise Trauth.
Number of staff: 3 full-time professional; 1 part-time professional.
EIN: 742766058
Selected grants: The following grants were reported in 2003.
$1,007,000 to Texas State University Development Foundation, San Marcos, TX. For scholarships.
$368,965 to Ohio State University, Columbus, OH. For scholarships.
$358,175 to Texas A & M University Development Foundation, College Station, TX. For scholarships.

$318,750 to Pennsylvania State University, University Park, PA. For scholarships.
$135,000 to University of Texas, Austin, TX. 2 grants: $50,000 (For general support), $85,000 (For scholarships).
$81,750 to Family Eldercare, Austin, TX. For general support.
$50,000 to Saint Edwards University, Austin, TX. For scholarships.
$25,000 to Mexic-Arte Museum, Austin, TX. For general support.

9068
Mike Modano Foundation, Inc. ◇
P.O. Box 192291
Dallas, TX 75219
Contact: Monica Long, Exec. Dir.
E-mail: foundation@mikemodano.com; URL: http://www.mikemodano.com/thefoundation/thefoundation.asp?titleid=4

Established in 1999 in TX.
Donors: Mark Cuban; Reebok International Ltd.; Bob's Steak & Chop House; CIBC; Italian Club of Dallas; Southwest Sports Group; Heroes Celebrity Baseball.
Foundation type: Independent foundation.
Financial data (yr. ended 12/31/03): Assets, $56,755 (M); gifts received, $419,261; expenditures, $516,153; qualifying distributions, $516,024; giving activities include $465,820 for 3 grants (high: $465,313; low: $250).
Purpose and activities: Giving to improve the quality of life for at-risk and underserved children in the Dallas, TX, area. The foundation's primary focus is to serve children who have been abused (either physically, emotionally, or both), abandoned or neglected. In addition, the foundation provides funding for organizations whose purpose is to offer education to children and families suffering from the devastation of abuse, to help break the cycle of abuse.
Fields of interest: Crime/violence prevention, child abuse; Human services; Children/youth, services; Family services, domestic violence.
Application information: The foundation does not accept unsolicited proposals. Upon review of letter of inquiry, the applicant will be contacted if there is interest from the foundation.
Initial approach: Letter of inquiry
Officer and Directors:* Mike Cramer, Chair.; Bob Sambol,* Pres.; Michael T. Modano,* V.P.; Donald T. Hess, Secy.-Treas.; Monica Long, Exec. Dir.; John Carlisle; Jeff Fronterhouse; Kevin Healy; Charlie McKinney; Kit Sawers.
EIN: 311662114

9069
William A. and Elizabeth B. Moncrief Foundation ◇
Moncrief Bldg.
950 Commerce St.
Fort Worth, TX 76102   (817) 336-7232
Contact: W.A. Moncrief, Jr., Pres.

Established in 1954.
Donors: W.A. Moncrief†; Elizabeth B. Moncrief†; W.A. Moncrief, Jr.
Foundation type: Independent foundation.
Financial data (yr. ended 9/30/05): Assets, $19,173,686 (M); expenditures, $547,866;

qualifying distributions, $499,700; giving activities include $499,700 for 33 grants (high: $102,500; low: $500; average: $1,000–$25,000).

Fields of interest: Museums (art); Museums (specialized); Arts; Higher education; Education; Zoos/zoological societies; Hospitals (general); Human services; Federated giving programs.

Type of support: General/operating support.

Limitations: Giving primarily in TX. No grants to individuals.

Application information:
Initial approach: Letter
Deadline(s): None

Officers: W.A. Moncrief, Jr., Pres. and Mgr.; R.W. Moncrief, V.P.; C.B. Moncrief, Secy.-Treas.

EIN: 756036329

Selected grants: The following grants were reported in 2005.

$26,000 to University of Texas Southwestern Medical Center, Dallas, TX.

$25,000 to Jewel Charity Ball, Fort Worth, TX.

$17,000 to All Saints Health Foundation, Fort Worth, TX.

$15,000 to Texas Independent College Fund, Fort Worth, TX.

$10,000 to Cato Institute, DC.

$10,000 to National Center for Policy Analysis, Dallas, TX.

$2,000 to Fort Worth Country Day School, Fort Worth, TX.

$1,500 to Score a Goal in the Classroom, Fort Worth, TX.

9070
The Moody Foundation ▼ ✧
2302 Post Office St., Ste. 704
Galveston, TX 77550 (409) 797-1500
Contact: Peter M. Moore, Dir., Grants
FAX: (409) 763-5564; E-mail: info@moodyf.org;
Additional tel. (for Dallas office): (866) 742-1133;
Additional e-mail (for grants): grants@moodyf.org;
URL: http://www.moodyf.org

Trust established in 1942 in TX.

Donors: William Lewis Moody, Jr.‡; Libbie Shearn Moody‡.

Foundation type: Independent foundation.

Financial data (yr. ended 12/31/05): Assets, $1,158,543,467 (M); gifts received, $19,344,000; expenditures, $22,035,611; qualifying distributions, $19,887,713; giving activities include $15,803,315 for 56 grants (high: $4,421,996; low: $2,381; average: $6,500–$2,534,794).

Purpose and activities: Funds to be used for historic restoration projects, performing arts organizations, and cultural programs; promotion of health, science, and education; community and social services; and the field of religion.

Fields of interest: Performing arts; Arts; Medical school/education; Education; Environment; Health care; AIDS; Medical research, institute; AIDS research; Youth development; Human services; Community development; Engineering/technology; Science; Religion; Aging; Disabilities, people with; Economically disadvantaged.

Type of support: Capital campaigns; Building/renovation; Equipment; Land acquisition; Program development; Conferences/seminars; Publication; Seed money; Scholarship funds; Research; Technical assistance; Grants to individuals; Matching/challenge support.

Limitations: Giving limited to TX. No grants to individuals (except for students covered by one

scholarship program in Galveston County), or for operating budgets (except for start-up purposes), continuing support, annual campaigns, or deficit financing; no loans or program-related investments.

Publications: Application guidelines; Annual report; Grants list.

Application information: Foundation will send application guidelines if project is of interest. For scholarship application form and submission deadlines contact Sandy Griffin. Application form not required.
Initial approach: Letter or telephone
Copies of proposal: 1
Deadline(s): 6 weeks prior to board meetings
Board meeting date(s): Quarterly
Final notification: 3 weeks after board meetings

Officers and Trustees:* Robert L. Moody, Sr.,* Chair.; Harold C. MacDonald, Compt.; Frances A. Moody-Dahlberg,* Exec. Dir.; Ross R. Moody.

Number of staff: 10 full-time professional; 5 full-time support.

EIN: 741403105

Selected grants: The following grants were reported in 2004.

$5,821,661 to Moody Gardens, Galveston, TX. 3 grants: $2,186,867 (For operating support), $1,100,000 (Toward non-recurring administrative support), $2,534,794 (For operating support).

$1,000,000 to Trinity Episcopal School, Galveston, TX. For capital campaign to construct new Middle School builiding, playground and parking lot.

$400,000 to Moody Scholars Program, Galveston, TX. 3 grants: $100,000 (For college scholarships for Dallas County residents), $200,000 (For college scholarships for Galveston County residents), $100,000 (For college scholarships for Dallas County residents).

$96,651 to University of Texas Medical Branch, School of Allied Health Sciences Department of Physical Therapy, Galveston, TX. For continued support of research project improving movement efficiency in individual with acquired brain injury.

$91,877 to Saint Andrews Episcopal School, Austin, TX. Toward Learning Specialist position.

$55,000 to Planned Parenthood Center of the Texas Capital Region, Austin, TX. Toward constructing Education and Volunteer Resource Center component of new south Austin clinic, and fundraising event.

9071
Allen Lovelace Moore and Blanche Davis Moore Foundation ✧
700 Everhart Rd., Ste. J-21
Corpus Christi, TX 78411 (361) 814-6700
Contact: Gary Leach, Dir.

Established in 1993 in TX.

Donor: Blanche Davis Moore‡.

Foundation type: Independent foundation.

Financial data (yr. ended 12/31/04): Assets, $14,884,518 (M); expenditures, $1,257,368; qualifying distributions, $899,507; giving activities include $899,507 for 49 grants.

Purpose and activities: Support primarily for projects benefiting children and youth under 18 years of age, in the Coastal Bend area of TX.

Fields of interest: Higher education; Athletics/sports, training; Human services; Salvation Army; YM/YWCAs & YM/YWHAs; Children/youth, services; Christian agencies & churches.

Limitations: Giving primarily in the Corpus Christi, TX area. No grants to individuals.

Application information: Application form required.
Deadline(s): Sept. 1

Directors: Rev. Joseph Homer Davis, Jr.; Lorine Jones; Gary Leach; Paul C. Pearson III.

EIN: 742675281

9072
The W. T. & Louise J. Moran Foundation ✧
3843 N. Braeswood Blvd., Ste. 200
Houston, TX 77025-3001
Contact: R. Robert Mullins, Tr.

Established in 1997 in TX.

Donor: Mrs. W.T. Moran.

Foundation type: Independent foundation.

Financial data (yr. ended 12/31/04): Assets, $19,256,851 (M); expenditures, $921,614; qualifying distributions, $816,715; giving activities include $751,700 for 36 grants (high: $100,000; low: $900).

Fields of interest: Museums; Health organizations, association; Federated giving programs.

Limitations: Applications not accepted. Giving primarily in Houston, TX. No grants to individuals.

Application information: Contributes only to pre-selected organizations.

Trustees: Randall E. Evans; Allen L. Jogerst; R. Robert Mullins; C.W. Sunday.

EIN: 760513027

Selected grants: The following grants were reported in 2004.

$100,000 to Houston Museum of Natural Science, Houston, TX.

$40,000 to Christian Community Service Center, Houston, TX.

$30,000 to Childrens Museum of Houston, Houston, TX.

$25,000 to Medical Bridges, Houston, TX.

$10,000 to Star of Hope Mission, Houston, TX.

$2,000 to 100 Club, Houston, TX.

$2,000 to Houston Area Womens Center, Houston, TX.

$2,000 to Salvation Army.

$2,000 to YMCA.

$1,000 to Search, Bangalore, India. .

9073
Morgan Charitable Foundation, Inc. ✧
801 Laurel St.
Beaumont, TX 77701-2228 (409) 838-1000
Contact: Glen W. Morgan, Pres.

Established in 1998 in TX.

Donor: Glen W. Morgan.

Foundation type: Independent foundation.

Financial data (yr. ended 12/31/04): Assets, $3,881,888 (M); gifts received, $6,500,000; expenditures, $3,136,623; qualifying distributions, $3,135,375; giving activities include $3,135,375 for 20 grants (high: $2,500,000; low: $10,000).

Purpose and activities: Giving primarily to a Baptist church, as well as to Christian organizations; funding also for human services.

Fields of interest: Human services; Salvation Army; Children/youth, services; Christian agencies & churches; Protestant agencies & churches.

Limitations: Giving primarily in Beaumont, TX.

Application information: Application form not required.

Deadline(s): None
Officer: Glen W. Morgan, Pres.
EIN: 760589391
Selected grants: The following grants were reported in 2003.

$860,000 to Calvary Baptist Church, Beaumont, TX. For unrestricted support.

$75,000 to Young Life Ministries, Beaumont, TX. For unrestricted support.

$50,000 to Salvation Army of Beaumont, Beaumont, TX. Fo unrestricted support.

$40,000 to Hampton Road Ministries, Chesapeake, VA. For unrestricted support.

$30,000 to Jay Strack Evangelical Association, Fort Worth, TX. For unrestricted support.

$20,000 to Court Appointed Special Advocates (CASA) of Southeast Texas, Beaumont, TX. For unrestricted support.

$15,000 to American Cancer Society, Beaumont, TX. For unrestricted support.

$10,000 to Some Other Place, Beaumont, TX. For unrestricted support.

$2,000 to Monsignor Kelly High School, Beaumont, TX. 2 grants: $1,000 each (For unrestricted support).

9074
Morgan Foundation ✧
4400 Post Oak Pkwy., Ste. 1450
Houston, TX 77027

Established in 2002 in TX.
Donor: Portcullis Partners, L.P.
Foundation type: Company-sponsored foundation.
Financial data (yr. ended 12/31/04): Assets, $15,901,324 (M); expenditures, $1,305,473; qualifying distributions, $1,100,000; giving activities include $1,100,000 for 2 grants (high: $1,050,000; low: $50,000).
Purpose and activities: The foundation supports family and community foundations.
Fields of interest: Foundations (private independent); Foundations (community).
Type of support: General/operating support.
Limitations: Applications not accepted. Giving primarily in Houston, TX. No grants to individuals.
Application information: Contributes only to pre-selected organizations.
Officers and Directors:* Michael C. Morgan,* Pres.; William V. Morgan,* Secy.-Treas.; Catherine A. Morgan; Christine R. Morgan; Sara S. Morgan.
EIN: 223886549

9075
The Morning Star Family Foundation ✧
3628 Beverly Dr.
Dallas, TX 75205-2868

Established in 1996 in TX.
Donors: John D. McStay; Mrs. John D. McStay; The Morning Star Family Limited Partnership.
Foundation type: Independent foundation.
Financial data (yr. ended 12/31/05): Assets, $10,104,311 (M); gifts received, $175,000; expenditures, $697,902; qualifying distributions, $691,085; giving activities include $675,150 for 31 grants (high: $151,000; low: $500).

Purpose and activities: Giving for education, youth programs, and Christian organizations and ministries.
Fields of interest: Education; Housing/shelter; Children/youth, services; Christian agencies & churches.
Limitations: Applications not accepted. Giving primarily in Dallas, TX. No grants to individuals.
Application information: Contributes only to pre-selected organizations.
Officers and Trustees:* Ellen McStay,* Pres.; John McStay,* Secy.; Dee Devlin; Eric Devlin; Judge McStay.
EIN: 752682211
Selected grants: The following grants were reported in 2004.

$115,000 to Special Camps for Special Kids, Dallas, TX. For youth programs.

$90,000 to Highland Park Presbyterian Church, Dallas, TX. For general operating support.

$75,000 to Saint Philips School and Community Center, Dallas, TX. For general operating support.

$61,000 to Union Gospel Mission, Dallas, TX. For general operating support.

$20,385 to First Baptist Church, Hico, TX. For recreational building.

$14,500 to Young Life, North Central Texas Region, Dallas, TX. For general operating support.

$10,000 to Childrens Medical Center of Dallas, Dallas, TX. For Circle of Care Campaign.

$10,000 to Dallas Theological Seminary, Dallas, TX. For scholarships.

$10,000 to Wilkinson Center, Dallas, TX. For general operating support.

$10,000 to Youth Believing in Change, Dallas, TX. For general operating support.

9076
The Morris Foundation ✧
4545 Bellaire Dr. S., Ste. 3
Fort Worth, TX 76109-1811

Established in 1986 in TX.
Donors: Jack B. Morris; Linda C. Morris.
Foundation type: Independent foundation.
Financial data (yr. ended 12/31/04): Assets, $95,229,819 (M); gifts received, $57,305,470; expenditures, $2,259,073; qualifying distributions, $2,198,680; giving activities include $2,198,680 for 73 grants (high: $400,000; low: $50).
Purpose and activities: Giving primarily for social services, including child development and welfare; support also for educational programs, health associations, and to a United Methodist church.
Fields of interest: Child development, education; Higher education; Education; Health organizations; Human services; Children/youth, services; Child development, services; Protestant agencies & churches.
Limitations: Applications not accepted. Giving primarily in Fort Worth, TX. No grants to individuals.
Application information: Contributes only to pre-selected organizations.
Officer: Joseph A. Monteleone, Exec. Dir.
Trustees: Jack B. Morris; Linda C. Morris.
EIN: 752137184
Selected grants: The following grants were reported in 2003.

$160,000 to Austin College, Sherman, TX. For scholarship funds.

$50,000 to Child Study Center Foundation, Fort Worth, TX. For Patient Care Fund and Program Endowment.

$34,000 to All Saints Episcopal School, Fort Worth, TX. For scholarship funds.

$30,000 to Safe Haven of Tarrant County, Arlington, TX. For Children's program.

$30,000 to Tarrant County AIDS Interfaith Network, Fort Worth, TX. For operating support.

$30,000 to Tarrant County Samaritan Housing, Fort Worth, TX. For operating support.

$20,000 to Harris Methodist Health Foundation, Fort Worth, TX. For Indigent Mammography Fund.

$20,000 to Meals on Wheels of Tarrant County, Fort Worth, TX. For operating support.

$20,000 to Presbyterian Night Shelter of Tarrant County, Fort Worth, TX. For operating support.

$10,000 to Cassata High School, Fort Worth, TX. For scholarships and teacher salary.

9077
Mosbacher Foundation, Inc. ✧
c/o Mosbacher Properties
712 Main St., Ste. 2200
Houston, TX 77002

Incorporated in 1948 in NY.
Donors: Emil Mosbacher; Gertrude Mosbacher; Emil Mosbacher, Jr.†; Barbara Mosbacher; Robert A. Mosbacher, Jr.; A.W. Downing Mears, Jr.; Diane Mosbacher; Kathryn Mosbacher; Lisa M. Mears; Robert A. Mosbacher.
Foundation type: Independent foundation.
Financial data (yr. ended 12/31/04): Assets, $988 (M); gifts received, $532,662; expenditures, $541,837; qualifying distributions, $541,812; giving activities include $541,812 for 120 grants (high: $53,000; low: $100).
Purpose and activities: Giving primarily for the arts, education, health and medical research, and children, youth, and social services.
Fields of interest: Museums (art); Performing arts; Arts; Elementary/secondary education; Higher education; Education; Health organizations, association; Human services; Family services; Public affairs; Religion.
Limitations: Applications not accepted. Giving primarily in Houston, TX; some giving nationally. No grants to individuals.
Application information: Contributes only to pre-selected organizations. Unsolicited requests for funds not considered.
Officers and Directors:* Robert A. Mosbacher, Jr.,* Pres. and Treas.; A.W. Downing Mears, Jr.,* V.P. and Secy.; W.R. Smith.
EIN: 136155392

9078
Harry S. Moss Heart Trust ✧
c/o Bank of America, N.A.
P.O. Box 831041
Dallas, TX 75283-1041 (214) 209-1965

Trust established in 1973 in TX.
Donors: Harry S. Moss†; Florence M. Moss†.
Foundation type: Independent foundation.
Financial data (yr. ended 9/30/05): Assets, $35,014,462; expenditures, $2,578,778; qualifying distributions, $2,336,153; giving activities include $2,304,194 for 9 grants (high: $455,000; low: $50,000).
Purpose and activities: Support for the cure and research of heart disease.

Fields of interest: Heart & circulatory diseases; Medical research, institute; Heart & circulatory research.
Type of support: Annual campaigns; Capital campaigns; Building/renovation; Equipment; Endowments; Research.
Limitations: Giving limited to TX, with emphasis on Dallas County.
Publications: Application guidelines; Program policy statement.
Application information: Application form not required.
  Initial approach: Proposal
  Copies of proposal: 1
  Deadline(s): None
  Board meeting date(s): As required
  Final notification: 30 days
Trustee: Bank of America, N.A.
Number of staff: 1 part-time professional; 1 part-time support.
EIN: 756147501

9079
Peach Mott Foundation, Inc. ✧
P.O. Box 2549
Victoria, TX 77902-2549 (361) 573-4383
Contact: Rayford L. Keller, V.P.

Established in 1994 in TX.
Donor: Michael Scott Anderson.
Foundation type: Independent foundation.
Financial data (yr. ended 11/30/04): Assets, $8,040,417 (M); expenditures, $622,661; qualifying distributions, $622,558; giving activities include $622,558 for 21 grants (high: $150,000; low: $500).
Fields of interest: Education; Health organizations, association; Children/youth, services; Roman Catholic agencies & churches.
Limitations: Giving primarily in TX.
Officers: Michael Scott Anderson, Pres.; Rayford L. Keller, V.P.; Thomas L. Keller, Secy.-Treas.
EIN: 742730037
Selected grants: The following grants were reported in 2004.
$150,000 to Saint Monica Catholic Church, Santa Monica, CA.
$125,000 to Saint Marks School of Texas, Dallas, TX.
$105,000 to Hockaday School, Dallas, TX.
$50,000 to Meals on Wheels, Victoria, TX.
$20,000 to Grameen Foundation USA, DC.
$20,000 to Texas Scottish Rite Hospital for Children, Dallas, TX.
$15,000 to Victoria Christian Assistance Ministry, Victoria, TX.
$15,000 to VNA and Hospice of South Texas, San Antonio, TX.
$10,000 to Habitat for Humanity, Victoria, Victoria, TX.
$10,000 to Victims Outreach, Dallas, TX.

9080
The Mundy Family Foundation ✧
11150 S. Wilcrest Dr., Ste. 300
Houston, TX 77099

Established in 1996 in TX.
Donors: Joe S. Mundy; John T. Mundy.
Foundation type: Independent foundation.

Financial data (yr. ended 12/31/05): Assets, $10,373,883 (M); gifts received, $308,417; expenditures, $717,817; qualifying distributions, $636,870; giving activities include $636,870 for 18 grants (high: $260,000; low: $1,000).
Purpose and activities: Giving primarily for religion, community, education, and arts and culture.
Fields of interest: Arts; Education; Human services; Community development; Religion.
Limitations: Giving primarily in TX. No grants to individuals.
Application information:
  Initial approach: Letter
  Deadline(s): None
Trustees: John T. Mundy; Marion E. Mundy; Sue E. Mundy.
EIN: 760520888
Selected grants: The following grants were reported in 2004.
$105,000 to Westbury Christian School, Houston, TX.
$100,000 to Lifeline Chaplaincy, Houston, TX.
$40,000 to Crime Stoppers of Houston, Houston, TX.
$30,000 to Saint Martins Episcopal Church, Houston, TX.
$25,000 to Free Enterprise Institute, Houston, TX.
$10,000 to Boston University, Boston, MA.
$10,000 to Brookwood Community, Brookshire, TX.
$10,000 to Museum of Fine Arts, Houston, Houston, TX.
$5,000 to Holocaust Museum Houston, Houston, TX.
$5,000 to Petroleum Museum, Midland, TX.

9081
The Ginger Murchison Foundation ✧
5949 Sherry Ln., Ste. 1225
Dallas, TX 75225

Established in 1993 in TX.
Donor: Virginia L. Murchison†.
Foundation type: Independent foundation.
Financial data (yr. ended 12/31/04): Assets, $61,373,028 (M); expenditures, $2,448,490; qualifying distributions, $1,521,357; giving activities include $1,478,800 for 90 grants (high: $200,000; low: $200).
Purpose and activities: Giving primarily for health and human services.
Fields of interest: Higher education; Health organizations, association; Human services; Community development.
Limitations: Applications not accepted. Giving primarily in TX. No grants to individuals.
Application information: Contributes only to pre-selected organizations.
Officers and Directors:* Don Wills,* Pres. and Treas.; Don Jackson,* V.P.; Rusty Workman,* Secy.; Joe Warren.
EIN: 752482261
Selected grants: The following grants were reported in 2004.
$200,000 to Cain Center, Athens, TX. For refurbishing, remodeling, and renewing of equipment and facilities.
$181,000 to National Christian Charitable Foundation, Atlanta, GA. For unrestricted support.
$130,000 to Athens Independent School District, Athens, TX.
$57,000 to Athens, City of, Athens, TX. For soccer fields upgrades at Coleman Park.

$55,000 to United Way of Henderson County, Athens, TX. For unrestricted support.

9082
J. Campbell Murrell Fund ✧
8113 Hickory Creek Dr.
Austin, TX 78735

Established in 1997 in TX.
Donor: J. Campbell Murrell.
Foundation type: Independent foundation.
Financial data (yr. ended 12/31/05): Assets, $13,827,545 (M); expenditures, $655,576; qualifying distributions, $649,873; giving activities include $647,686 for 38 grants (high: $210,780; low: $416).
Purpose and activities: Giving primarily to Presbyterian agencies and churches; giving also to other religious organizations and for human services.
Fields of interest: Education; Human services; Religion.
Limitations: Applications not accepted. Giving primarily in Fort Worth, TX. No grants to individuals.
Application information: Contributes only to pre-selected organizations.
Officer: Melinda M. Grace, Pres.
Director: Guy Grace.
EIN: 752694405
Selected grants: The following grants were reported in 2003.
$503,801 to Regents School of Austin, Austin, TX. For grant made in form of stock.
$51,118 to Fellowship of Christian Athletes, Austin, TX. For grant made of stock.
$16,975 to Saint Margarets Episcopal School, San Juan Capistrano, CA. 2 grants: $1,470 (For general support), $15,505 (For grant made in form of stock).
$15,783 to Young Life, Austin, TX. For grant made in form of stock.
$5,000 to Life Care Pregnancy, Austin, TX. For general support.
$2,000 to Riverbend Christian School, Austin, TX. For general support.
$1,000 to Gathering, The, Tyler, TX. For general support.
$250 to Association of Small Foundations, DC. For general support.
$150 to Keith-Ann Wagner Hope Relay, Arlington, TX. For general support.

9083
The Muse Educational Foundation ✧
200 Crescent Ct., Ste. 1600
Dallas, TX 75201 (214) 965-7911
Contact: John R. Muse, Pres.

Established in 1999 in TX.
Donors: John R. Muse; Lyn R. Muse.
Foundation type: Independent foundation.
Financial data (yr. ended 12/31/03): Assets, $7,116,052 (M); expenditures, $443,200; qualifying distributions, $440,674; giving activities include $439,877 for 25 grants (high: $200,000; low: $25).
Fields of interest: Education.
Limitations: Giving primarily in TX.
Application information:
  Initial approach: Letter
  Deadline(s): None

Officers and Directors:* John R. Muse,* Pres. and Treas.; Lyn R. Muse, Exec. V.P.; Thomas O. Hicks; H. Rand Reynolds.
EIN: 752824936
Selected grants: The following grants were reported in 2004.
$500,000 to Saint Philips School and Community Center, Dallas, TX. 2 grants: $250,000 each
$120,000 to Saint Marks School of Texas, Dallas, TX. 3 grants: $10,000, $100,000 (For Muse Family Middle Income Scholarship Fund), $10,000 (For Summer Enrichment Program).
$30,000 to Hockaday School, Dallas, TX. For Hockaday Tomorrow campaign.
$20,000 to American School in London Foundation, London, England. For capital campaign.
$20,000 to West Chester University of Pennsylvania, West Chester, PA. For Elisa A. Triano Biology Research Fund.
$7,888 to Dallas Center for the Performing Arts Foundation, Dallas, TX. For campaign to build Dallas Center for the Performing Arts.
$1,000 to Prevent Blindness, Dallas, TX. For Eye Ball.

9084
The NAH Foundation ✧
1445 Ross at Field, Ste. 1500
Dallas, TX   75202-2785

Established in 2001 in TX.
Donors: Ray L. Hunt; Nancy Ann Hunt.
Foundation type: Independent foundation.
Financial data (yr. ended 12/31/03): Assets, $1,636,866 (M); gifts received, $1,000,392; expenditures, $1,137,710; qualifying distributions, $1,137,710; giving activities include $1,122,368 for 12 grants (high: $350,000; low: $10,000).
Purpose and activities: Giving primarily to a telephone counseling, crisis prevention, intervention and referral and emergency aid service; support also for a center for the homeless, an organization that provides shelter, food, and clothing for runaway homeless youth, services for women, and for a ministry.
Fields of interest: Education; Mental health/crisis services, hot-lines; Housing/shelter, homeless; Human services; Youth, services; Christian agencies & churches; Women.
Limitations: Applications not accepted. Giving primarily in Dallas, TX. No grants to individuals.
Application information: Contributes only to pre-selected organizations.
Officers and Directors:* Nancy Ann Hunt,* Pres.; Christoper W. Kleinert,* Secy.; Hunter L. Hunt,* Treas.
EIN: 752945062
Selected grants: The following grants were reported in 2003.
$350,000 to Austin Street Center, Dallas, TX. For general support.
$342,368 to CONTACT Crisis Line, Dallas, TX. For general support.
$100,000 to Shelter Ministries of Dallas, Dallas, TX. For general support.
$50,000 to Genesis Womens Shelter, Dallas, TX. For general support.
$35,000 to Boy Scouts of America, Circle Ten Council, Dallas, TX. For general support.
$35,000 to New Friends New Life, Dallas, TX. For general support.
$30,000 to Methodist Mission Home, San Antonio, TX. For general support.

$20,000 to Dallas Womens Foundation, Dallas, TX. For general support.
$15,000 to Promise House, Dallas, TX. For general support.
$15,000 to Winston School, Dallas, TX. For general support.

9085
The Ted Nash Long Life Foundation ✧
510 N. Valley Mills Dr., Ste. 600
Waco, TX   76710
Contact: Daniel A. Palmer, Dir.

Donor: Theodore E. Nash†.
Foundation type: Independent foundation.
Financial data (yr. ended 12/31/04): Assets, $9,728,516 (M); gifts received, $8,881,658; expenditures, $698,086; qualifying distributions, $500,000; giving activities include $500,000 for 5 grants (high: $100,000; low: $100,000).
Fields of interest: Medical school/education; Health care; Medical research.
Limitations: Giving primarily in TX.
Application information: Cover page required. Application form not required.
   Initial approach: Brief summary (250 words) followed by description (1000 words)
   Deadline(s): Oct. 1
Directors: J. Bond Browder; Daniel A. Palmer; C. Nick Pace; John M. Wilkinson.
EIN: 742875627

9086
The Nasher Foundation
8080 N. Central Expwy., Ste. 830
Dallas, TX   75206-1838

Established in 1996 in TX.
Donor: Raymond D. Nasher.
Foundation type: Operating foundation.
Financial data (yr. ended 12/31/03): Assets, $64,113,166 (M); gifts received, $26,754,695; expenditures, $2,612,896; qualifying distributions, $26,818,305; giving activities include $528,957 for 14 grants (high: $200,000; low: $500), and $24,565,268 for foundation-administered programs.
Purpose and activities: Funding primarily for the construction and subsequent operation of a sculpture gallery and garden.
Fields of interest: Visual arts, sculpture.
Limitations: Applications not accepted. Giving primarily in Dallas, TX. No grants to individuals.
Application information: Contributes only to pre-selected organizations.
Officers: Raymond D. Nasher, Chair. and Pres.; Byron A. Parker, Treas.; Elliot R. Cattarulla, Exec. Dir.
EIN: 752674048
Selected grants: The following grants were reported in 2003.
$200,000 to Boston Latin School, Boston, MA. For general support.
$200,000 to Southwestern Medical Foundation, Dallas, TX. For cancer research.
$29,143 to Nasher Sculpture Center, Dallas, TX. For general support.
$28,314 to Temple Emanu-El, Dallas, TX. For capital campaign.
$25,000 to American Assembly, New York, NY. For general support.

$13,000 to Dallas Symphony Orchestra, Dallas, TX. For general support.
$10,000 to Raleigh Tavern Society, Williamsburg, VA. For general support.
$10,000 to World Affairs Council of Greater Dallas, Dallas, TX. For general support.
$1,000 to Hoff-Barthelson Music School, Scarsdale, NY. For general support.
$500 to Arts District Friends, Dallas, TX. For general support.

9087
Nation Foundation (Corporation) ✧
P.O. Box 180849
Dallas, TX   75218   (214) 388-5751
Contact: James H. Nation, Dir.

Established in 1999 in TX.
Donors: Oslin Nation; James Nation; Merle Nation.
Foundation type: Independent foundation.
Financial data (yr. ended 1/31/05): Assets, $5,061,740 (M); gifts received, $257,000; expenditures, $374,806; giving activities include $110,170 for 5 grants (high: $50,000; low: $1,000), and $264,628 for 63 grants to individuals (high: $25,679; low: $500).
Purpose and activities: Giving primarily for education; support also for Protestant churches.
Fields of interest: Performing arts, orchestra (symphony); Education; Protestant agencies & churches.
Type of support: Scholarships—to individuals.
Application information:
   Initial approach: Letter
   Deadline(s): None
Directors: Frieda Ashworth; James H. Nation; Sally Nation.
EIN: 752791965

9088
National Instruments Foundation ✧ ☆
11500 N. Mopac Expwy., Bldg. A
Austin, TX   78759   (218) 279-5000
Contact: Ray Almgren

Established in 2002 in TX.
Donor: National Instruments Corp.
Foundation type: Company-sponsored foundation.
Financial data (yr. ended 12/31/05): Assets, $2,163,084 (M); expenditures, $827,998; qualifying distributions, $817,097; giving activities include $817,097 for grants.
Purpose and activities: The foundation supports organizations involved with science and engineering higher education.
Fields of interest: Higher education; Engineering school/education; Science.
Limitations: No support for religious organizations. No grants to individuals.
Application information: Application form not required.
   Initial approach: Proposal
   Deadline(s): None
Officers and Directors:* James Truchard,* Pres.; Raymond Almgren,* V.P. and Treas.; David Hugley, Secy.; Howard Neal; Melodie Zamora Summersett.
EIN: 383667781
Selected grants: The following grants were reported in 2004.
$100,000 to Southern Methodist University, Dallas, TX.

$62,100 to Stanford University, Stanford, CA. 3 grants: $26,550, $9,000, $26,550
$57,000 to Massachusetts Institute of Technology, Cambridge, MA. 2 grants: $50,000, $7,000
$11,800 to Tufts University, Medford, MA.
$10,148 to Hands On Technology, Leipzig, Germany. .
$10,000 to Rensselaer Polytechnic Institute, Troy, NY.
$7,500 to Institute of Electrical and Electronics Engineers (IEEE) Foundation, Piscataway, NJ.

9089
Navarro Community Foundation ◇
P.O. Box 1035
Corsicana, TX 75151 (903) 874-4301
Contact: Bruce Robinson, Exec. Secy.-Treas.

Established in 1938 in TX.
Donor: Frank N. Drane†.
Foundation type: Independent foundation.
Financial data (yr. ended 12/31/05): Assets, $18,660,472 (M); expenditures, $841,344; qualifying distributions, $763,905; giving activities include $757,619 for 37 grants (high: $118,570; low: $6,000).
Purpose and activities: Support largely for public schools, higher education, community development, and a community fund; grants also for Christian church support, child welfare, youth agencies, a hospital, a library, and cultural programs.
Fields of interest: Arts; Education; Human services; Community development; Christian agencies & churches.
Type of support: General/operating support; Annual campaigns; Capital campaigns; Building/ renovation; Seed money; Scholarship funds; Matching/challenge support.
Limitations: Giving limited to Navarro County, TX. No grants to individuals, or for research, conferences, endowment funds, publications, or special projects; no loans.
Application information: Application form not required.
  Initial approach: Proposal
  Copies of proposal: 2
  Deadline(s): Jan. 1, Apr. 1, July 1, and Oct. 1
  Board meeting date(s): Jan., Apr., July, and Oct.
Officers: C. David Campbell, M.D., Chair.; O.L. Albritton, 1st Vice-Chair.; Lynn Cooper, 2nd Vice-Chair.; Bruce Robinson, Exec. Secy.-Treas.
Trustees: Gioia Keeney; Bill Maupin; Billie Love McFerran; Ellen McKeown; Melissa Means; Scott Middleton; John B. Stroud; Kim Wyatt.
Number of staff: 1 full-time professional; 1 part-time professional.
EIN: 750800663

9090
John and Florence Newman Foundation ◇
112 E. Pecan St., Ste. 2222
San Antonio, TX 78205 (210) 226-0371

Established in 1988 in TX.
Donor: Florence B. Newman.
Foundation type: Independent foundation.
Financial data (yr. ended 12/31/04): Assets, $13,681,864 (M); expenditures, $671,570; qualifying distributions, $479,305; giving activities include $418,234 for 16 grants (high: $100,000; low: $400).

Purpose and activities: Giving primarily for the arts and education.
Fields of interest: Media/communications; Museums; Arts; Libraries/library science; Education; Environment; Community development; Foundations (community).
Type of support: General/operating support; Equipment; Scholarship funds.
Limitations: Applications not accepted. Giving primarily in San Antonio, TX. No grants to individuals.
Application information: Contributes only to pre-selected organizations.
Directors: Ann J. Newman; John E. Newman, Jr.; Thomas R. Semmes.
EIN: 742525348

9091
The Nightingale Code Foundation ◇
1001 McKinney St., Ste. 1900
Houston, TX 77002-6411 (713) 265-0270
Contact: Michael Zilkha, Pres.

Established in 1998 in TX.
Donor: Michael Zilkha.
Foundation type: Independent foundation.
Financial data (yr. ended 12/31/05): Assets, $7,416,363 (M); gifts received, $4,651,511; expenditures, $1,295,767; qualifying distributions, $1,295,627; giving activities include $1,295,627 for 58 grants (high: $200,000; low: $100).
Purpose and activities: Giving primarily for education and the arts in Houston, TX.
Fields of interest: Arts; Education; Health organizations, association; Human services; Jewish agencies & temples.
Limitations: Applications not accepted. Giving primarily in New York, NY, and TX.
Officers: Michael Zilkha, Pres.; Joseph Romano, Secy.
Director: Cornelia O'Leary Zilkha.
EIN: 760574572
Selected grants: The following grants were reported in 2004.
$441,435 to British Schools and Universities Foundation, New York, NY.
$195,000 to Contemporary Arts Museum Houston, Houston, TX. 2 grants: $70,000 (For general support), $125,000 (For endowment fund).
$184,557 to Museum of Fine Arts, Houston, Houston, TX. For Heiting collection.
$83,000 to Menil Foundation, Houston, TX. For Menil collection.
$57,000 to Chinquapin School, Highlands, TX. For general support.
$50,000 to Jewish Federation of Greater Houston, Houston, TX. For general support.
$50,000 to United Jewish Campaign, Houston, TX. For general support.
$25,000 to Houston Symphony Orchestra, Houston, TX. For general support.
$20,000 to Dia Art Foundation, New York, NY. To purchase Boetti's Victoria Boogie Woogie.

9092
Mary Moody Northen Endowment ◇
P.O. Box 1300
Galveston, TX 77553-1300 (409) 765-9770
Contact: Betty Massey, Exec. Dir.

Established in 1964.
Donor: Mary Moody Northen†.

Foundation type: Independent foundation.
Financial data (yr. ended 12/31/04): Assets, $70,265,215 (M); expenditures, $4,288,000; qualifying distributions, $1,626,442; giving activities include $679,966 for 20 grants (high: $484,500; low: $1,000), and $2,623,399 for 3 foundation-administered programs.
Purpose and activities: Support for educational institutions, community development and civic affairs, and wildlife and the environment. The foundation has completed restoration of the W.L. Moody residence and currently operates it as a house museum. The foundation also conducts research of the history of 20th century Texas.
Fields of interest: Museums; History/archaeology; Historic preservation/historical societies; Education, research; Higher education; Education; Environment, natural resources; Environment; Animals/wildlife, preservation/protection; Community development.
Type of support: General/operating support; Continuing support; Capital campaigns; Building/ renovation; Program development; Curriculum development; Consulting services.
Limitations: Giving limited to TX and VA.
Application information: Application form not required.
  Initial approach: Letter
  Copies of proposal: 1
  Deadline(s): None
  Board meeting date(s): Monthly
  Final notification: Grants are usually made in the 2nd quarter of each year
Officers and Directors:* Edward L. Protz,* Pres.; G. William Rider,* V.P. and Treas.; Robert L. Moody,* Secy.; Betty Massey, Exec. Dir.
Number of staff: 1 full-time professional; 1 full-time support; 1 part-time support.
EIN: 751171741

9093
Notsew Orm Sands Foundation ☆
50 Briar Hollow Ln., Ste. 590E
Houston, TX 77027

Established around 1995.
Donor: Charles Burnett III.
Foundation type: Independent foundation.
Financial data (yr. ended 12/31/04): Assets, $2,155,096 (M); expenditures, $700,114; qualifying distributions, $653,771; giving activities include $638,574 for 19 grants (high: $462,582; low: $200).
Purpose and activities: Giving primarily for animal welfare, including search and rescue organizations; support also for medical education and research.
Fields of interest: Medical school/education; Animal welfare; Disasters, search/rescue; Human services.
Limitations: Applications not accepted. Giving on a national and international basis, with some emphasis on Houston, TX, and the United Kingdom. No grants to individuals.
Application information: Contributes only to pre-selected organizations.
Officers: Charles Burnett III, Pres. and Secy.; Miriam W. Burnett, V.P. and Treas.
Directors: Garfield Mitchell; Graham Weston.
EIN: 760455176

9094
The O'Connor & Hewitt Foundation ✧
(formerly Dorothy O'Connor Foundation)
1 O'Connor Plz., Ste. 1100
Victoria, TX 77901-6549
Contact: Robert J. Hewitt, Pres.

Established in 1989 in TX.
Donors: Dorothy Hanna O'Connor‡; Dennis O'Connor‡; Robert J. Hewitt.
Foundation type: Independent foundation.
Financial data (yr. ended 12/31/05): Assets, $19,333,814 (M); gifts received, $2,791,275; expenditures, $743,871; qualifying distributions, $732,941; giving activities include $732,941 for 111 grants (high: $239,272; low: $99).
Fields of interest: Performing arts; Arts; Education; Recreation; Human services; Children/youth, services; Protestant agencies & churches.
Type of support: General/operating support; Continuing support; Annual campaigns; Building/renovation.
Limitations: Giving generally limited to the south TX area. No grants to individuals or for matching gifts; no loans.
Publications: Annual report.
Application information: Application form not required.
> *Initial approach:* Letter
> *Copies of proposal:* 2
> *Deadline(s):* None
> *Board meeting date(s):* As required

Officers: Robert J. Hewitt, Pres.; Robert J. Hewitt, Jr., V.P.; Robert L. Coffey, Secy.-Treas.
EIN: 742527227
Selected grants: The following grants were reported in 2003.
$414,027 to Six Flags Humane Society, Victoria, TX.
$40,000 to Refugio, County of, Refugio, TX.
$24,500 to Trinity Episcopal School, Victoria, TX.
$13,500 to Trinity Episcopal Church, Victoria, TX.
$10,500 to Saint Joseph High School, Victoria, TX.
$6,000 to Victoria, City of, Victoria, TX. For Texas Zoo.
$5,000 to American Cancer Society, Victoria, TX.
$5,000 to Victoria College, Victoria, TX. For Museum Coastal Bend.
$4,500 to Victoria Community Theater, Victoria, TX.
$4,000 to Victoria Symphony Society, Victoria, TX.

9095
The Kathryn O'Connor Foundation ✧
1 O'Connor Plz., Ste. 1100
Victoria, TX 77901
Contact: D.H. Braman, Jr., Pres.

Incorporated in 1951 in TX.
Donors: Kathryn S. O'Connor‡; Tom O'Connor, Jr.‡; Dennis O'Connor‡; Mary O'Connor Braman‡; The O'Connor & Hewitt Foundation.
Foundation type: Independent foundation.
Financial data (yr. ended 12/31/05): Assets, $6,521,933 (M); gifts received, $10,000; expenditures, $472,020; qualifying distributions, $432,608; giving activities include $432,608 for 29 grants (high: $117,500; low: $500).
Purpose and activities: Support for institutions for the advancement of religion, education, and the relief of poverty; grants also for hospitals. The foundation also operates and maintains a church.
Fields of interest: Elementary/secondary education; Secondary school/education; Higher education; Libraries/library science; Hospitals

(general); Cancer; Cancer research; Residential/custodial care, hospices; Christian agencies & churches; Roman Catholic agencies & churches; Religion.
Type of support: General/operating support; Continuing support; Annual campaigns; Building/renovation.
Limitations: Giving limited to southern TX, with emphasis on Victoria and Refugio counties and surrounding area. No support for political organizations. No grants to individuals, or for matching gifts; no loans.
Publications: Annual report.
Application information: Application form not required.
> *Initial approach:* Letter
> *Deadline(s):* None
> *Board meeting date(s):* As required

Officers: D.H. Braman, Jr., Pres.; Kathryn Counts, V.P.; Louise O'Connor, V.P.; Venable B. Proctor, Secy.; Ralph R. Gilster III, Treas.
EIN: 746039415
Selected grants: The following grants were reported in 2004.
$117,500 to Saint Joseph High School, Victoria, TX. For operating support.
$90,539 to Saint Dennis Church, Victoria, TX. For operating support.
$19,600 to Nazareth Academy, Victoria, TX. For operating support.
$19,600 to Our Lady of Victory School, Victoria, TX. For operating support.
$19,600 to Trinity Episcopal School, Victoria, TX. For operating support.
$10,000 to Diocese of Victoria, Victoria, TX. For operating support.
$10,000 to Junior League of Victoria, Victoria, TX. For restoration of historic building.
$10,000 to Mid-Coast Family Services, Victoria, TX. For operating support.
$10,000 to Refugio County Memorial Hospital, Refugio, TX. For operating support.
$10,000 to Victoria Christian Assistance Ministry, Victoria, TX. For operating support.

9096
O'Donnell Foundation ▼ ✧
100 Crescent Ct., Ste. 1660
Dallas, TX 75201-1884 (214) 871-5800
Contact: Carolyn R. Bacon, Exec. Dir.
E-mail: info@odf.org; URL: http://www.odf.org

Incorporated in 1957 in TX.
Donors: Peter O'Donnell, Jr.; Edith Jones O'Donnell.
Foundation type: Independent foundation.
Financial data (yr. ended 11/30/04): Assets, $142,906,726 (M); gifts received, $1,100,000; expenditures, $9,793,258; qualifying distributions, $9,171,988; giving activities include $8,812,668 for 21 grants (high: $2,000,000; low: $1,000; average: $1,000–$200,000).
Purpose and activities: The foundation primarily supports engineering, science, and mathematics education at the graduate level. The foundation also supports Advanced Placement programs (math, science, English, art) as well as arts programs in higher education.
Fields of interest: Arts; Higher education; Education; Mathematics; Engineering; Science.
Limitations: Giving primarily in TX. No grants to individuals, or for scholarships, fellowships, or prizes; no loans.

Application information: Application form not required.
> *Initial approach:* Letter with brief proposal
> *Deadline(s):* None
> *Board meeting date(s):* As required

Officers and Directors: * Peter O'Donnell, Jr.,* Pres.; Rita Clements,* V.P.; Edith Jones O'Donnell,* Secy.-Treas.; Carolyn R. Bacon, Exec. Dir.; Duncan E. Boeckman; Edward A. Copley; Tom Luce; Philip Montgomery, Jr., M.D.; Ruth O'Donnell Mutch.
Number of staff: 4 full-time professional.
EIN: 756023326
Selected grants: The following grants were reported in 2003.
$6,350,000 to University of Texas, Austin, TX. For education and research.
$917,479 to Advanced Placement Strategies, Dallas, TX.
$300,000 to National Academy of Sciences, DC.
$159,181 to National Center for Educational Accountability, Just for the Kids, Austin, TX. For operating support and research.
$100,000 to Southern Methodist University, Dallas, TX. For building fund.
$50,000 to Cisco Junior College, Cisco, TX.
$25,000 to Georgia Tech Foundation, Atlanta, GA.
$25,000 to Rice University, Houston, TX. For operating support for Texas Academy of Science, Engineering, and Medicine.
$12,600 to National Merit Scholarship Corporation, Evanston, IL. For scholarships.
$10,152 to Rowlett High School, Rowlett, TX. For advanced placement curriculum.

9097
John M. O'Quinn Foundation ✧
(formerly The O'Quinn Foundation)
3518 Travis St., Ste. 200
Houston, TX 77002
Contact: John M. O'Quinn, Pres.
Application address: 440 Louisiana St., Houston, TX 77002, tel.: (713) 236-2659

Established in 1986 in TX.
Donor: John M. O'Quinn.
Foundation type: Independent foundation.
Financial data (yr. ended 12/31/05): Assets, $5,947,778 (M); expenditures, $25,633,916; qualifying distributions, $25,594,935; giving activities include $25,579,500 for 15 grants (high: $25,000,000; low: $2,000).
Purpose and activities: Giving primarily for higher education, including a school of music, as well as for health care, including medical research, an Episcopal hospital; and other health associations, as well as for children, youth, women, and social services including sports programs for youth.
Fields of interest: Higher education; Law school/education; Health organizations, association; Cancer research; Athletics/sports, Special Olympics; Recreation; Human services; Children/youth, services; Residential/custodial care, hospices; Women, centers/services; Protestant agencies & churches.
Limitations: Giving primarily in TX, with emphasis on Houston. No grants to individuals.
Application information: Application form not required.
> *Initial approach:* Letter
> *Deadline(s):* None

Officers: John M. O'Quinn, Pres.; Robert C. Wilson, Secy.-Treas.

Trustee: David Griffis.

EIN: 760206844

Selected grants: The following grants were reported in 2003.

$2,625,000 to Childrens Assessment Center Foundation, Houston, TX. For general support.

$220,000 to Houston Area Womens Center, Houston, TX. For general support.

$150,000 to M. D. Anderson Cancer Center Outreach Corporation, Houston, TX. For general support.

$97,800 to University of Houston Law Foundation, Houston, TX. For general support.

$72,300 to South Texas College of Law, Houston, TX. For general support.

$67,000 to University of Houston-University Park, Houston, TX. For general support.

$50,000 to Baylor College of Medicine, Houston, TX. For general support.

$30,000 to Valley Alliance of Mentors for Opportunities and Scholarships, McAllen, TX. For general support.

9098
The O'Sullivan Foundation ✧ ☆

6800 W. Gate Blvd., Ste. 132
P.O. Box 123
Austin, TX   78745

Established in 1999 in MA.

Donor: Sean M. O'Sullivan.

Foundation type: Independent foundation.

Financial data (yr. ended 12/31/04): Assets, $9,903,085 (M); gifts received, $4,548,723; expenditures, $1,070,544; qualifying distributions, $985,700; giving activities include $985,700 for 4 grants (high: $975,700; low: $2,500).

Fields of interest: Human services; International development; International relief.

Limitations: Applications not accepted. Giving on a national basis, with some emphasis on GA. No grants to individuals.

Application information: Contributes only to pre-selected organizations.

Trustees: Anne S. O'Sullivan; Marie T. O'Sullivan; Sean M. O'Sullivan.

EIN: 066487034

9099
The Oehmig Foundation ✧ ☆

8 Greenway Plz., Ste. 702
Houston, TX   77046   (713) 877-8257
Contact: William C. Oehmig, C.E.O.

Established in 1988 in TX.

Donors: William C. Oehmig; Margaret W. Oehmig.

Foundation type: Independent foundation.

Financial data (yr. ended 12/31/05): Assets, $738,327 (M); expenditures, $825,407; qualifying distributions, $816,970; giving activities include $816,970 for 5 grants (high: $773,970; low: $8,000).

Purpose and activities: Giving for education and religion.

Fields of interest: Higher education; Human services; Foundations (community); Christian agencies & churches.

Type of support: General/operating support.

Limitations: Giving primarily in KY, MD, MS, TN and TX. No grants to individuals.

Application information:

Initial approach: Letter
Deadline(s): None

Officers and Trustees:* William C. Oehmig, C.E.O.; Gordon D. Oehmig,* Pres.; Randolph D. Oehmig,* V.P. and Secy.; William B. Oehmig, Treas.

EIN: 760260014

Selected grants: The following grants were reported in 2004.

$50,000 to Kinkaid School, Houston, TX.

$10,000 to Baylor School, Chattanooga, TN.

$10,000 to Transylvania University, Lexington, KY.

$4,750 to Neuhaus Education Center, Bellaire, TX.

9100
Oldham Little Church Foundation ✧

5177 Richmond Ave., Ste. 1030
Houston, TX   77056-6701
Contact: Louis E. Finlay, Pres.

Trust established in 1949 in TX.

Donor: Morris Calvin Oldham‡.

Foundation type: Independent foundation.

Financial data (yr. ended 12/31/04): Assets, $26,286,173 (M); expenditures, $1,634,599; qualifying distributions, $1,364,638; giving activities include $1,057,500 for 222 grants (high: $50,000; low: $2,000).

Purpose and activities: Giving limited to small Protestant churches and organizations with emphasis on Baptist churches.

Fields of interest: Education; Protestant agencies & churches.

Type of support: Building/renovation; Equipment; Program development.

Limitations: Giving on a national basis. No grants to individuals, or for operating budgets, endowments, or deficit financing.

Application information: Application form required.

Initial approach: Letter
Copies of proposal: 1
Deadline(s): None
Board meeting date(s): Monthly
Final notification: Usually within 60 days

Officers: Louis E. Finlay, Pres.; David Chavanne, V.P.; Raymond E. Hankamer, V.P.; Carloss Morris, Jr., V.P.; Stewart Morris, Jr., V.P.; James S. Riley, V.P.; Stewart Morris, Sr., Secy.

Trustees: Linda R. Dunham; Sadie Hodo.

Number of staff: 1 part-time professional; 1 full-time support; 1 part-time support.

EIN: 760465633

Selected grants: The following grants were reported in 2003.

$44,950 to College of Biblical Studies-Houston, Houston, TX. For scholarships.

$4,800 to Woodfield Park Baptist Church, Columbia, SC. For building renovations and repairs.

$4,500 to Old Hickory Baptist Church, Hattieville, AR. For building renovations and repairs.

$4,300 to Friendship Baptist Church, La Porte, IN. For building renovations and repairs.

$4,300 to Pleasant Grove Baptist Church, Rosebud, TX. For building renovations and repairs.

$4,000 to Fairview Baptist Church, Anamosa, IA. For building renovations and repairs.

$4,000 to Valley View Church of the Nazarene, Kamiah, ID. For building renovations and repairs.

$3,900 to Blessed Hope Baptist Church, Tenino, WA. For building renovations and repairs.

$3,300 to Adirondack Church of the Nazarene, Lake Placid, NY. For building renovations and repairs.

$2,500 to Arbor Grove Congregational Church, Jackson, MI. For building renovations and repairs.

9101
Once Upon A Time Foundation ✧

(formerly Will E. Coyote Foundation)
301 Commerce St., Ste. 3200
Fort Worth, TX   76102-4175

Established in 1998 in TX.

Donor: Geoffrey P. Raynor.

Foundation type: Independent foundation.

Financial data (yr. ended 12/31/05): Assets, $22,651,327 (M); expenditures, $3,114,667; qualifying distributions, $3,114,667; giving activities include $2,517,556 for 104 grants (high: $100,000; low: $50), and $217,500 for 4 employee matching gifts.

Purpose and activities: Support primarily for the arts, especially toward the construction of a modern art museum facility and the performing arts; giving also for health care and animal welfare.

Fields of interest: Arts, multipurpose centers/ programs; Museums (art); Performing arts; Education; Animal welfare; Hospitals (general); Health care; Health organizations, association.

Type of support: General/operating support; Capital campaigns; Building/renovation; Equipment; Program development; Employee matching gifts.

Limitations: Applications not accepted. Giving primarily in the Fort Worth/Dallas, TX area; some funding nationally. No grants to individuals.

Application information: Contributes only to pre-selected organizations.

Officers and Directors:* Sam Lett, Pres. and Treas.; Noel Nesser, Secy.; Kim Baldi; William Cunningham; Randy Eisenman; Edward Nelson, Jr., M.D.; Geoffrey P. Raynor; Tom Rogers, Jr., M.D.

EIN: 752765224

Selected grants: The following grants were reported in 2004.

$562,500 to Dallas Center for the Performing Arts, Dallas, TX. 2 grants: $375,000, $187,500

$463,000 to Texas Ballet Theater, Fort Worth, TX. 2 grants: $288,000, $175,000

$250,000 to Tiger Woods Foundation, Los Alamitos, CA.

$80,000 to Kinderplatz of Fine Arts, Fort Worth, TX. 2 grants: $30,000, $50,000

$25,000 to Dallas Mavericks Foundation, Dallas, TX.

$10,000 to Yale University, New Haven, CT.

$9,500 to National Cowgirl Museum and Hall of Fame, Fort Worth, TX.

9102
The Robert R. and Kay M. Onstead Foundation ✧

600 Travis St., Ste. 6475
Houston, TX   77002-3007   (713) 227-5884
Contact: Robert R. Onstead, Pres.

Established in 1993 in TX.

Donors: Robert R. Onstead; Kay M. Onstead.

Foundation type: Independent foundation.

Financial data (yr. ended 12/31/03): Assets, $29,155,174 (M); gifts received, $1,092,182; expenditures, $960,000; qualifying distributions, $960,000; giving activities include $960,000 for 16 grants (high: $350,000; low: $5,000).

Purpose and activities: Giving for religious, charitable, scientific, literacy, and educational purposes.
Fields of interest: Education; Science; Religion.
Limitations: Giving primarily in TX. No grants to individuals.
Application information: Application form not required.
   Initial approach: Letter
   Deadline(s): None
Officers and Board Members:* Robert R. Onstead, Pres.; Kay M. Onstead,* V.P.; Ann Onstead Hill.
Trustees: Charles M. Onstead; Mary Onstead; R. Randall Onstead, Jr.
EIN: 760417998
Selected grants: The following grants were reported in 2003.
$350,000 to University of Texas M. D. Anderson Cancer Center, Houston, TX.
$200,000 to Boles Childrens Home, Quinlan, TX.
$125,000 to Houston Music Hall Foundation, Houston, TX.
$50,000 to Texas Childrens Hospital, Houston, TX.
$50,000 to United Way of the Texas Gulf Coast, Houston, TX.
$25,000 to Second Baptist Church, Houston, TX.
$10,000 to Barbara Bush Texas Fund for Family Literacy, Houston, TX.
$10,000 to Theater Under the Stars, Houston, TX.
$10,000 to Westbury Christian School, Houston, TX.
$5,000 to Medina Childrens Home, Medina, TX.

9103
Onward & Upward Initiative Charitable Trust ◇ ☆
6500 N. Belt Line Rd., Ste. 170
Irving, TX   75063-6068

Established in 1997 in TX.
Donor: James J. Jensen.
Foundation type: Independent foundation.
Financial data (yr. ended 12/31/05): Assets, $1,936,109 (M); gifts received, $923,260; expenditures, $354,907; qualifying distributions, $392,177; giving activities include $390,270 for 8 grants (high: $200,000; low: $2,500).
Purpose and activities: Giving primarily for educational and religious purposes.
Fields of interest: Education; Human services; International agricultural development; Community development; Christian agencies & churches.
Type of support: Scholarship funds.
Limitations: Applications not accepted. Giving on a national basis.
Application information: Contributes only to pre-selected organizations.
Trustee: James J. Jensen.
EIN: 752707910

9104
Oshman Foundation ◇ ☆
P.O. Box 27969
Houston, TX   77227-7969

Established in 1958.
Donors: Oshman's Sporting Goods, Inc.; Jeanette Oshman Efron.
Foundation type: Company-sponsored foundation.
Financial data (yr. ended 11/30/05): Assets, $5,853,773 (M); expenditures, $322,000;

qualifying distributions, $315,336; giving activities include $315,336 for grants.
Purpose and activities: The foundation supports Jewish agencies and temples and organizations involved with arts and culture, higher education, and children and youth services.
Fields of interest: Museums (art); Museums (specialized); Arts; Higher education; Children/youth, services; Jewish agencies & temples.
Limitations: Applications not accepted. Giving primarily in Houston, TX. No grants to individuals.
Application information: Contributes only to pre-selected organizations.
Officers: Jeanette Oshman, Pres.; Marilyn Oshman, V.P. and Secy.; Judy O. Margolis, V.P. and Treas.
EIN: 746039864
Selected grants: The following grants were reported in 2004.
$50,000 to Houston Jewish Geriatric Foundation, Houston, TX.
$25,000 to Robert M. Beren Academy, Houston, TX.
$20,000 to Asia Society/Houston, Houston, TX.
$15,000 to Fay School, Houston, TX.
$12,200 to Congregation Emanu-El, Houston, TX.
$10,000 to Orange Show Center for Visionary Art, Houston, TX.
$2,500 to Houston Museum of Natural Science, Houston, TX.

9105
Otter Island Foundation ◇
700 Louisiana St., Ste. 5000
Houston, TX   77002-2767

Established in 1993 in TX.
Donors: Matthew R. Simmons; Ellen C.L. Simmons.
Foundation type: Independent foundation.
Financial data (yr. ended 12/31/05): Assets, $4,917,964 (M); expenditures, $685,855; qualifying distributions, $677,920; giving activities include $677,920 for 156 grants (high: $50,000; low: $25).
Purpose and activities: Giving primarily for the arts, education, and health and human services.
Fields of interest: Arts; Education; Environment; Health organizations, association; Human services.
Limitations: Applications not accepted. No grants to individuals.
Application information: Contributes only to pre-selected organizations.
Officers and Director:* Matthew R. Simmons,* Pres.; Ellen C.L. Simmons, V.P. and Treas.; Shelly K. Daughtrey, Secy.
EIN: 760421104
Selected grants: The following grants were reported in 2003.
$50,000 to National Trust for Historic Preservation, DC. For Barn Again.
$25,000 to Annunciation Orthodox School, Houston, TX.
$25,000 to Initiative for a Competitive Inner-City (ICIC), Boston, MA. For annual fund.
$20,000 to Rice University, Jones Graduate School of Management, Houston, TX.
$20,000 to University of Texas M. D. Anderson Cancer Center, Houston, TX. For George and Cynthia Mitchell Basic Sciences Research Building.
$12,500 to Sears House Association, Boston, MA. For annual fund.
$10,000 to Island Institute, Rockland, ME. For annual fund.

$10,000 to Northfield Mount Hermon School, Northfield, MA. For annual fund.
$10,000 to Robert E. Lee Memorial Association, Stratford Hall Plantation, Stratford, VA.
$10,000 to Vanderbilt University, Peabody Library, Nashville, TN. For group study room.

9106
Dian Graves Owen Foundation
400 N. Pine St., Ste. 1000
Abilene, TX   79601

Established in 1996 in TX.
Donor: Dian Graves Owen Stai.
Foundation type: Independent foundation.
Financial data (yr. ended 12/31/04): Assets, $35,138,932 (M); gifts received, $1,540,200; expenditures, $2,185,272; qualifying distributions, $1,888,662; giving activities include $1,822,067 for 173 grants (high: $250,000; low: $50).
Purpose and activities: Giving primarily for the arts, education, health, human services, and federated giving programs.
Fields of interest: Performing arts; Performing arts, opera; Historic preservation/historical societies; Arts; Higher education; Education; Hospitals (general); Hospitals (specialty); Health care; Health organizations, association; Cancer; Boys & girls clubs; Human services; Children/youth, services; Family services; Foundations (community); Federated giving programs; Christian agencies & churches.
Limitations: Applications not accepted. Giving primarily in Abilene, TX. No grants to individuals.
Application information: Contributes only to pre-selected organizations.
Officers and Directors:* Dian Graves Owen Stai,* Chair. and Treas.; Tucker S. Bridwell,* Pres.; Diane K. Nichols, Secy.; Deborah O. Carson.
EIN: 752682536
Selected grants: The following grants were reported in 2003.
$135,000 to Taylor County Historical Foundation, Abilene, TX.
$33,333 to McMurry University, Abilene, TX.
$25,000 to Abilene Boys Ranch, Ben Richey Boys Ranch, Abilene, TX.
$25,000 to United Way of Abilene, Abilene, TX.
$15,000 to Houston Grand Opera, Houston, TX.
$12,500 to Cisco Junior College, Cisco, TX.
$10,000 to Abilene Philharmonic Orchestra Association, Abilene, TX.
$5,000 to Food Bank of Abilene, Abilene, TX.
$1,500 to West Texas Rehabilitation Center, Abilene, TX.
$1,000 to M. D. Anderson Cancer Center Outreach Corporation, Houston, TX.

9107
B. B. Owen Trust ◇ ☆
P.O. Box 830068
Richardson, TX   75083
Contact: Monty J. Jackson, Tr.

Established in 1974 in TX.
Donor: B.B. Owen†.
Foundation type: Independent foundation.
Financial data (yr. ended 9/30/05): Assets, $20,807,586 (M); expenditures, $857,290; qualifying distributions, $420,000; giving activities include $420,000 for grants.

Purpose and activities: Giving primarily for education and human services, with emphasis on children and youth, and for local government facilities.

Fields of interest: Education; Hospitals (specialty); Health organizations, association; Legal services; Boy scouts; Human services; American Red Cross; Salvation Army; Children/youth, services; Public affairs, government agencies; Christian agencies & churches.

Type of support: General/operating support; Capital campaigns; Building/renovation; Equipment; Program development.

Limitations: Giving primarily in the Dallas, TX, area. No grants to individuals.

Application information: Application form not required.

  Initial approach: Letter

  Deadline(s): None

  Board meeting date(s): As necessary

  Final notification: 3 to 4 months

Trustees: Spencer Carver; Monty J. Jackson; Wendell W. Judd.

Number of staff: 1 full-time professional.

EIN: 751385809

Selected grants: The following grants were reported in 2003.

$1,500,000 to YMCA of Metropolitan Dallas, Dallas, TX. For land for future site expansion.

$50,000 to Texas Scottish Rite Hospital for Children, Dallas, TX.

$25,000 to Camp El Har, Dallas, TX. For program support.

$25,000 to Fannin County Family Crisis Center, Bonham, TX. For facilities.

$15,000 to Hope Cottage Pregnancy and Adoption Center, Dallas, TX. For program support.

$10,000 to Boys and Girls Club of Collin County, McKinney, TX. For program support.

$10,000 to Collin County Childrens Advocacy Center, Plano, TX. For program support.

$10,000 to Collin County Committee on Aging, McKinney, TX. For facilities repair.

$10,000 to Heard Natural Science Museum and Wildlife Sanctuary, McKinney, TX. For program support.

$10,000 to Maurice Barnett Geriatric Wellness Center, Plano, TX.

9108
Alvin and Lucy Owsley Foundation ◇
65 Briar Hollow Ln.
Houston, TX 77027
Contact: Alvin M. Owsley, Jr., Tr.

Trust established in 1950 in TX.

Donors: Alvin M. Owsley†; Lucy B. Owsley†.

Foundation type: Independent foundation.

Financial data (yr. ended 12/31/05): Assets, $7,869,330 (M); expenditures, $468,461; qualifying distributions, $440,631; giving activities include $427,527 for 60 grants (high: $100,000; low: $100).

Purpose and activities: Giving primarily for the arts, education and human services.

Fields of interest: Arts; Medical school/education; Education; Animal welfare; Reproductive health, family planning; Biomedicine; Medical research, institute; Human services; Children/youth, services; Civil liberties, reproductive rights.

Type of support: General/operating support; Continuing support; Annual campaigns; Building/

renovation; Emergency funds; Seed money; Scholarship funds; Matching/challenge support.

Limitations: Giving limited to TX. No grants to individuals, or for endowment funds; no loans.

Publications: Application guidelines.

Application information: Application form not required.

  Initial approach: Letter not exceeding 2 pages (no enclosures)

  Copies of proposal: 1

  Deadline(s): Submit proposal preferably in months when board meets; no set deadline

  Board meeting date(s): Mar., June, Sept., and Dec.

  Final notification: 2 months, positive responses only

Trustees: Wendy Garrett; Alvin M. Owsley, Jr.; David T. Owsley.

EIN: 756047221

Selected grants: The following grants were reported in 2004.

$101,856 to Dallas Museum of Art, Dallas, TX. For general operating support.

$42,000 to Baylor College of Medicine, Houston, TX. For general operating support.

$40,000 to Fort Worth Public Library Foundation, Fort Worth, TX. For general operating support.

$25,000 to Boy Scouts of America, Sam Houston Area Council, Houston, TX. For general operating support.

$25,000 to Texas Christian University, Fort Worth, TX. For general operating support.

$24,500 to Houston Ballet, Houston, TX. For general operating support.

$11,000 to Botanical Research Institute of Texas, Fort Worth, TX. For general operating support.

$10,000 to Boys and Girls Harbor, Houston, TX. For general operating support.

$10,000 to Volunteer Houston, Houston, TX. For general operating support.

$7,750 to Saint Johns School, Houston, TX. For general operating support.

9109
Fred & Mabel R. Parks Foundation
12926 Dairy Ashford Rd., Ste. 130
Sugar Land, TX 77478-3102 (281) 313-6464
Contact: James G. McClellan, Tr.
FAX: (281) 313-6466;
E-mail: jimmcclellan@alltel.net

Established in 1984 in TX.

Donor: Fred Parks†.

Foundation type: Independent foundation.

Financial data (yr. ended 12/31/05): Assets, $29,199,069 (M); gifts received, $12,662,728; expenditures, $6,861,213; qualifying distributions, $809,028; giving activities include $785,000 for 28 grants (high: $250,000; low: $10,000; average: $20,000–$50,000).

Purpose and activities: Giving primarily for health and education.

Fields of interest: Higher education; Education; Health care.

Type of support: Continuing support; General/operating support.

Limitations: Giving primarily in Houston, TX area. No support for political organizations. No grants to individuals.

Application information: Application form required.

  Initial approach: Letter

  Copies of proposal: 1

  Deadline(s): None

  Board meeting date(s): Summer

  Final notification: 3 months

Officers and Trustees:* James G. McClellan,* Pres.; Virginia McClintock,* V.P. and Secy.; Debra Marfin,* V.P. and Treas.; Sloan B. Blair,* V.P.; Ann Parks Stallings,* V.P.

Number of staff: 1 part-time professional; 4 part-time support.

EIN: 760122692

Selected grants: The following grants were reported in 2004.

$2,115,263 to South Texas College of Law, Houston, TX. For general support.

$1,072,632 to Texas Heart Institute, Houston, TX. For general support.

$230,527 to Texas Aviation Hall of Fame, Galveston, TX. For general support.

$210,526 to Judge John R. Brown Scholarship Foundation, Houston, TX. For general support.

$210,526 to Rice University, Houston, TX. For general support.

$210,526 to Texas Childrens Hospital, Houston, TX. For general support.

$105,000 to Juvenile Diabetes Research Foundation International, Fort Worth, TX. For general support.

$10,000 to Trinity Valley School, Fort Worth, TX. For endowment.

$10,000 to University of Houston-University Park, Houston, TX. To create public lecture series.

9110
The Partnership Foundation ◇
5430 LBJ Freeway, Ste. 900
Dallas, TX 75240
Contact: Jay Wagley

Established in 1999 in TX.

Foundation type: Independent foundation.

Financial data (yr. ended 12/31/05): Assets, $10,737,878 (M); expenditures, $542,124; qualifying distributions, $502,160; giving activities include $490,000 for 22 grants (high: $50,000; low: $2,500).

Purpose and activities: Giving primarily for social services, food services, and for natural resource conservation, including conservation law.

Fields of interest: Performing arts, theater; Environment, natural resources; Environment; Legal services; Food banks; Housing/shelter; Human services.

Limitations: Applications not accepted. No grants to individuals.

Application information: Contributes only to pre-selected organizations.

Officers and Directors:* Anne Paxton Wagley,* Pres.; B. Allyn Copp,* V.P.; James F.P. Wagley,* V.P.; Mary Wagley Copp,* Secy.; Sue Wagley,* Treas.

EIN: 752796975

9111
Paso del Norte Health Foundation ▼ ◇ ☆
1100 N. Stanton, Ste. 510
El Paso, TX 79902 (915) 544-7636
Contact: Ann G. Pauli, C.E.O. and Pres.
FAX: (915) 544-7713; *E-mail:* apauli@pdnhf.org;
URL: http://www.pdnhf.org

Established in 1995 in TX; converted from sale of the assets of Providence Memorial Hospital.

Foundation type: Independent foundation.
Financial data (yr. ended 12/31/04): Assets, $192,024,199 (M); expenditures, $11,008,493; qualifying distributions, $9,019,858; giving activities include $7,143,409 for 147 grants (high: $400,000; low: $500), and $4,124,679 for 4 foundation-administered programs.
Purpose and activities: The foundation's mission is to effect long-term improvement in the health status of the Paso Del Norte region through education and prevention.
Fields of interest: Education, public education; Health care, support services; Health care; Mental health/crisis services; Nutrition; Youth development; Human services.
Limitations: Giving limited to the Paso del Norte Region, including eastern TX and southern NM. No support for political organizations. No grants to individuals, building/renovation, or for research.
Publications: Annual report; Newsletter.
Application information: Unsolicited applications not accepted.
   Board meeting date(s): Jan., Mar., May, July, Sept., and Nov.
Officers and Directors:* Jackson Curlin,* Chair.; Dwayne Aboud, M.D.*, Vice-Chair.; Ann G. Pauli, C.E.O. and Pres.; Gilbert Alvarado, C.I.O.; Alan R. Abbott; Jack Chapman; Martini De Groat; Victor A. Diaz; Bert Mijares; David W. Osborn.
Number of staff: 8 full-time professional; 5 full-time support; 1 part-time support.
EIN: 741143071
Selected grants: The following grants were reported in 2004.
$400,000 to Education Service Center Region 19, El Paso, TX. For Coordinated Approach to Child Health (CATCH) School Year.
$189,526 to Child Crisis Center of El Paso, El Paso, TX. For Begin at Birth, Organizing Agency.
$150,000 to Nonprofit Enterprise Center, El Paso, TX. For technical assistance for Action for Youth program.
$150,000 to University of Texas, El Paso, TX. For Coordinated Approach to Child Health (CATCH) After-School Program's Diabetes Prevention Demonstration.
$137,400 to American Cancer Society, El Paso, TX. For Smoke Free Paso del Norte.
$70,649 to American Lung Association of Texas, El Paso, TX. For Smoke-Free Coalition, Not on Tobacco, and Healthy Beginnings.
$50,000 to Project Vida, El Paso, TX. For Border Diabetes Healthy Lifestyles Program.
$49,858 to Programa Companeros, Ciudad Juarez, Mexico. For Healthy Communities.
$46,740 to Wayside Cafe Ministries, El Paso, TX. For Action for Youth-East side Youth connection.
$25,000 to Techo Communitario, Juarez, Mexico. For Begin at Birth.

9112
The Paulos Foundation ✧ ☆
6708 Ashbrook Dr.
Fort Worth, TX   76132

Established in 1990 in TX.
Donor: James J. Paulos.
Foundation type: Independent foundation.
Financial data (yr. ended 12/31/05): Assets, $4,318,320 (M); expenditures, $676,622; qualifying distributions, $671,773; giving activities include $670,400 for 87 grants (high: $250,000; low: $250).

Purpose and activities: Giving for arts, education, youth services and religion.
Fields of interest: Media/communications; Performing arts; Arts; Education; Environment, natural resources; Zoos/zoological societies; Health organizations, association; Human services; YM/YWCAs & YM/YWHAs; Children/youth, services; Protestant federated giving programs; Protestant agencies & churches; Religion.
Limitations: Applications not accepted. Giving limited to Dallas, TX. No grants to individuals.
Application information: Contributes only to pre-selected organizations.
Officers: Flora P. Brewer, Chair. and Pres.; Angela D. Paulos, V.P. and Secy.
Directors: John J. Paulos; Sam G. Paulos.
EIN: 752353196
Selected grants: The following grants were reported in 2003.
$40,000 to Overton Park United Methodist Church Foundation, Fort Worth, TX.
$30,000 to United Way of Metropolitan Tarrant County, Fort Worth, TX. For YWCA.
$25,000 to Tarrant County College Foundation, Fort Worth, TX. 2 grants: $10,000 (For Cowtown Trinity Duck Stampede), $15,000 (For Cowtown Trinity Duck Stampede).
$20,000 to Fort Worth Academy for the Education of Children and Youth, Fort Worth, TX. For performing arts studio.
$20,000 to Southeast Fort Worth, Fort Worth, TX.
$10,000 to Leadership 100, New York, NY.
$6,000 to Nonprofit Service Center of Tarrant County, Fort Worth, TX.
$5,000 to Austin Christian Educational Foundation, Saint Francis School, Austin, TX.
$5,000 to Church World Service, Elkhart, IN.

9113
Pearle Vision Foundation, Inc. ✧
2465 Joe Field Rd.
Dallas, TX   75229   (972) 277-6191
Contact: Trina Parasiliti, Admin.
FAX: (972) 277-6422;
E-mail: trinaparasiliti@pearlevision.com;
URL: http://www.pearlevision.com/webapp/wcs/ stores/servlet/PearleVision/StoreContent/about/ community.jsp

Established as a company-sponsored operating foundation in 1986 in CA.
Donor: Pearle Vision, Inc.
Foundation type: Operating foundation.
Financial data (yr. ended 1/1/05): Assets, $658,072 (M); gifts received, $450,422; expenditures, $465,169; qualifying distributions, $461,670; giving activities include $375,420 for 72 grants (high: $30,000; low: $675; average: $3,000–$6,000), and $38,660 for 19 grants to individuals (high: $3,274; low: $820).
Purpose and activities: The foundation supports programs designed to conduct research to find better treatments and cures for vision threatening diseases and disorders; provide vision education through optometric educational institutions; and conduct research on and provide treatment for diabetic eye diseases.
Fields of interest: Medical school/education; Eye diseases; Diabetes; Eye research; Diabetes research.
Type of support: Program development; Research.
Limitations: Giving on a national basis. No grants for endowments or general operating support.

Publications: Application guidelines; Newsletter.
Application information: Application form required.
   Initial approach: Download application form and mail to foundation
   Copies of proposal: 1
   Deadline(s): Postmarked by Dec. 31 and June 30
   Board meeting date(s): Feb., May, Aug., and Nov.
   Final notification: Mid-Mar. and mid-Sept.
Officers and Directors:* Jeff Smith,* Chair.; Scott Stoelting, V.P.; Beth Serraino, Treas.; Stanley C. Pearle, Exec. Dir.; James Benning, O.D.; Koula Callas; Dan Griffin; Barbara McAninch.
Number of staff: 1 part-time professional.
EIN: 752173714
Selected grants: The following grants were reported in 2005.
$25,000 to University of Medicine and Dentistry of New Jersey, Foundation of the, Newark, NJ. For Telehealth Technology Vision Research Project.
$25,000 to University of Texas Southwestern Medical Center, Dallas, TX. For research project for improvement of contact lens safety.
$19,640 to Retina Foundation of the Southwest, Dallas, TX. For research project, The Link Between Accommodation and Convergency: In Search of Risk Factors for Accommodative Esotropia.
$15,000 to University of California, Berkeley, CA. For Suitcase Clinic.
$10,000 to Glaucoma Service Foundation to Prevent Blindness, Philadelphia, PA. For research to refine and expand AARV.
$10,000 to Medical College of Wisconsin, Milwaukee, WI. To purchase Heidelberg Retina Flowmeter.
$10,000 to Saint Jude Childrens Research Hospital, Memphis, TN. For research to test new chemotherapy drugs against Retinoblastoma.
$5,000 to Lighthouse International, New York, NY. For testing and clinical development of Degraded Texture Discrimination Test.
$5,000 to University of Alabama, Department of Opthalmology, Tuscaloosa, AL. For Project Impact: Educating the Older African American Community About the Importance of Routine Eye Care.

9114
Pema Foundation ▼ ✧
3555 Timmons Ln., Ste. 800
Houston, TX   77027

Established in 2002 in IL.
Donors: Pritzker's Foundation; Pritzker's Cousin Foundation.
Foundation type: Independent foundation.
Financial data (yr. ended 12/31/04): Assets, $27,540,213 (M); gifts received, $6,251; expenditures, $6,911,123; qualifying distributions, $6,630,593; giving activities include $6,595,660 for 7 grants (high: $5,000,000; low: $97,000).
Purpose and activities: The foundation supports initiatives that are socially constructive.
Fields of interest: Human services; Community development, real estate; Foundations (community); Philanthropy/voluntarism; Financial services.
Type of support: Program-related investments/ loans.
Limitations: Applications not accepted. Giving primarily in San Francisco, CA; some funding nationally. No grants to individuals.
Application information: Contributes only to pre-selected organizations.

Officers: Linda Pritzker, Pres.; Lewis M. Linn, Secy.-Treas.
Directors: Roland B. Pritzker; Rosemary Pritzker.
EIN: 300039844
Selected grants: The following grants were reported in 2004.

$5,000,000 to RSF Global Community Fund, San Francisco, CA. To support socially constructive initiatives.

$800,000 to RSF Community Investment Fund, San Francisco, CA. To support socially constructive initiatives.

$400,000 to Academy for the Love of Learning, Sedona, AZ. For real estate.

$298,660 to Rudolf Steiner Foundation, San Francisco, CA. 3 grants: $98,660 (To support socially constructive initiatives), $100,000 to Advisory Support Fund (For general operating support), $100,000 to Operations (To support socially constructive initiatives).

$97,000 to Tai Sophia Institute, Columbia, MD. For project support at university.

9115
J. C. Penney Company Fund, Inc. ✧
P.O. Box 10001
Dallas, TX 75301-4317   (972) 431-1349
Contact: Jeannette M. Siegel, V.P.
FAX: (972) 431-1355;
E-mail: jsiegel@jcpenney.com; URL: http://www.jcpenney.net/company/commrel/index.htm

Established in 1984 in NY.
Donors: J.C. Penney Co., Inc.; J.C. Penney Corp., Inc.
Foundation type: Company-sponsored foundation.
Financial data (yr. ended 1/29/05): Assets, $5,632,125 (M); gifts received, $3,000,000; expenditures, $989,292; qualifying distributions, $989,292; giving activities include $989,292 for grants.
Purpose and activities: The foundation supports organizations involved with K-12 and business education, disaster relief, youth development, afterschool initiatives, human services, minorities, and women.
Fields of interest: Elementary/secondary education; Business school/education; Disasters, preparedness/services; Youth development; Children, day care; Human services; Minorities; Women.
Type of support: General/operating support; Annual campaigns; Program development; Employee volunteer services.
Limitations: Giving primarily in areas of company operations. No support for individual K-12 schools lacking a community partnership with J.C. Penney, PTOs or PTAs, higher education institutions lacking a business or recruiting relationship with J.C. Penney, or membership, religious, political, labor, or fraternal organizations. No grants to individuals, or for door prizes, gift certificates, or other giveaways, fundraising or special events, proms or graduations, scholarships for colleges lacking a recruiting relationship with J.C. Penney, conferences or seminars, capital campaigns, multi-year or long-term support, or film or video projects or research projects; no merchandise donations; no employee matching gifts.
Publications: Application guidelines; Corporate giving report; Financial statement.

Application information: Additional information may be requested at a later date. Telephone calls are not encouraged. Application form not required.
Initial approach: Letter of inquiry
Copies of proposal: 1
Deadline(s): None
Final notification: 6 to 8 weeks
Officers: Robin M. Caldwell, Pres. and Exec. Dir.; Jeannette M. Siegel, V.P.; Bob Hood, Secy.; W. Alcorn, Treas. and Cont.
EIN: 133274961
Selected grants: The following grants were reported in 2005.

$182,000 to American Red Cross, National Headquarters, DC.

$178,998 to United Way of Metropolitan Dallas, Dallas, TX. 3 grants: $168,498 (For annual campaign), $8,000 (For campaign associate support), $2,500 (For legislative forum sponsorship).

$35,000 to Four-H Council, National, Chevy Chase, MD.

$34,500 to National Minority Supplier Development Council, New York, NY. For general support.

$15,000 to Womens Business Enterprise National Council, DC. For general support.

$10,000 to Council on Foundations, DC. For general support.

$10,000 to Texas A & M University, College Station, TX. For Center for Retail Studies.

$2,000 to Junior Achievement of Delaware, Wilmington, DE. For Job Shadowing Program.

$1,000 to Boys and Girls Clubs of Metropolitan Phoenix, Phoenix, AZ. For afterschool program.

9116
Perkins-Prothro Foundation ▼ ✧
2304 Midwestern Pkwy., Ste. 200
Wichita Falls, TX 76308-2334   (940) 723-7163

Established in 1967.
Donors: Lois Perkins†; Charles N. Prothro; Elizabeth P. Prothro.
Foundation type: Independent foundation.
Financial data (yr. ended 12/31/04): Assets, $38,632,556 (M); gifts received, $1,952,944; expenditures, $5,609,526; qualifying distributions, $5,270,800; giving activities include $5,219,646 for 85 grants (high: $1,005,802; low: $50; average: $2,000–$100,000).
Purpose and activities: Emphasis on higher education, Protestant organizations, youth development, and social services.
Fields of interest: Higher education; Aquariums; Camp Fire; Human services; Protestant agencies & churches.
Type of support: General/operating support; Building/renovation; Endowments.
Limitations: Applications not accepted. Giving limited to TX, with emphasis on Wichita Falls. No grants to individuals.
Application information: Contributes only to pre-selected organizations.
Officers and Trustees:* Joe N. Prothro,* Pres.; Elizabeth P. Prothro,* V.P.; Kathryn Prothro Yeager,* V.P.; K. Elizabeth Edwards,* Secy.; Mark H. Prothro,* Treas.; David H. Prothro.
EIN: 751247407
Selected grants: The following grants were reported in 2004.

$1,005,802 to Sweet Briar College, Sweet Briar, VA. For unrestricted support.

$518,007 to University of Texas, Austin, TX. 2 grants: $512,847 to Henry Ransom Humanities Research Center (For facilities enhancement fund), $5,160 (For general support).

$497,426 to Hospice of Wichita Falls, Wichita Falls, TX. For Trust Fund.

$494,235 to Dallas Center for the Performing Arts, Dallas, TX. For building design and construction.

$349,041 to River Bend Nature Works, Wichita Falls, TX. For capital campaign.

$221,850 to United Regional Health Care Foundation, Wichita Falls, TX. For general support.

$37,780 to Wichita Falls Symphony Orchestra, Wichita Falls, TX. For annual fund.

$10,731 to Methodist Childrens Home, Waco, TX. For annual Christmas program.

$10,000 to North Central Texas Community Health Care Center, Wichita Falls, TX. For building fund.

9117
Permian Basin Area Foundation
550 W. Texas Ave., Ste. 1260
Midland, TX 79701   (432) 682-4704
Contact: John D. Swallow, C.E.O.; Guy McCrary, V.P.
FAX: (432) 617-0151; E-mail: gmccrary@pbaf.org;
URL: http://www.pbaf.org

Incorporated in 1989 in TX.
Foundation type: Community foundation.
Financial data (yr. ended 12/31/05): Assets, $37,423,408 (M); gifts received, $3,639,484; expenditures, $2,897,172; giving activities include $2,239,322 for 276+ grants.
Purpose and activities: The foundation seeks to provide a vehicle through which donors may make gifts for charitable, religious, scientific, and educational uses. The ultimate goals are to improve the quality of life of the communities' residents, promote equality of opportunity, and assist those in need or at risk in the Permian Basin.
Fields of interest: Humanities; Arts; Education; Health care; Housing/shelter; Human services; Community development; Public affairs.
Type of support: Emergency funds; Program development; Seed money; Scholarship funds; Matching/challenge support.
Limitations: Giving primarily in the Permian Basin area of western TX, with consideration to southeastern NM. No grants to individuals (except for scholarships), or for ongoing operating expenses, basic research, endowment funds, deficit financing, or fundraising campaigns; generally no multi-year grants.
Publications: Application guidelines; Annual report; Newsletter.
Application information: Visit foundation Web site for application form and guidelines. Based on Pre-Application Summary form, applicants will be notified that they are encouraged to submit a full application or that their project is unlikely to be funded. Application form required.
Initial approach: Submit Pre-Application Summary form
Copies of proposal: 1
Deadline(s): Apr. 1 and Oct. 1 for pre-application summary
Board meeting date(s): Feb., Apr., June, Aug., Oct., and Dec.
Final notification: Approx. 30 days for pre-application determination; June 30 and Dec. 30 for grants

Officers and Governors: * Tracy Elms,* Chair.; W. Scott Ryburn,* Vice-Chair.; John D. "Jack" Swallow, C.E.O. and Pres.; Guy McCrary, V.P. and C.O.O.; Suzy Boldrick,* Secy.; Rodney Robinson,* Treas.; Steve Barron; John Bergman; A.J. Brune III; Sondra Eoff; G. William Fowler; Hiram Hubert; Grace King; LaDoyce Lambert; Robert McKnight, Jr.; Richard McMillan; Jimmy Stallings.
Number of staff: 5 full-time professional; 2 full-time support.
EIN: 752295008

9118
The Perot Foundation ▼ ✧
P.O. Box 269014
Plano, TX   75026   (972) 788-3000
Contact: Carolyn P. Rathjen, V.P.

Established in 1969 in TX.
Donor: H. Ross Perot.
Foundation type: Independent foundation.
Financial data (yr. ended 12/31/05): Assets, $45,710,911 (M); gifts received, $10,143,823; expenditures, $12,243,423; qualifying distributions, $12,234,212; giving activities include $11,955,571 for 195 grants (high: $3,960,000; low: $44; average: $5,000–$400,000), and $137,761 for 30 grants to individuals (high: $29,851; low: $12; average: $5,000–$13,950).
Purpose and activities: Support primarily for higher education, a Salvation Army training school, and a Presbyterian church.
Fields of interest: Higher education; Human services; Religious federated giving programs; Protestant agencies & churches.
Type of support: Grants to individuals.
Limitations: Applications not accepted. Giving primarily in TX.
Application information: Contributes only to pre-selected organizations. Unsolicited requests for funds not considered. The scholarship program for children of graduates of the class of 1953 of the United States Naval Academy is no longer active.
Officers and Directors: * H. Ross Perot,* Pres.; Carolyn P. Rathjen,* V.P. and Exec. Dir.; J. Thomas Walter,* Secy.; J.Y. Robb III, Treas.; Katherine P. Flanagan; Suzanne P. McGee; Nancy P. Mulford; Bette Perot; H. Ross Perot, Jr.; Margot B. Perot.
EIN: 756093258
Selected grants: The following grants were reported in 2005.
$3,960,000 to Operation Homecoming USA, Branson, MO. For tribute to Vietnam Veterans.
$1,668,258 to University of Texas Southwestern Medical Center, Dallas, TX. 4 grants: $400,000 (For medical research), $423,000 (For medical research), $422,500 (For medical research), $422,758 (For medical research).
$200,000 to Marine Corps Heritage Foundation, Quantico, VA. For Building Fund for Marine Corps Heritage Center and National Museum.
$150,000 to Armed Forces Foundation, DC. To underwrite annual Veteran's Ball, raising funds for programs benefiting veterans.
$100,000 to Mount Vernon Ladies Association, Mount Vernon, VA. To educate Americans about George Washington.
$25,000 to Dallas Museum of Art, Dallas, TX. For Annual Fund.
$10,000 to Congressional Medal of Honor Society, Mount Pleasant, SC. To underwrite Patriots Award Dinner.

9119
The Sarah and Ross Perot, Jr.
Foundation ✧ ☆
P.O. Box 269014
Plano, TX   75026

Established in 2002 in TX.
Donor: Henry Ross Perot, Jr.
Foundation type: Independent foundation.
Financial data (yr. ended 12/31/05): Assets, $2,027,934 (M); gifts received, $2,695,000; expenditures, $719,145; qualifying distributions, $719,145; giving activities include $719,145 for 61 grants (high: $200,000; low: $100).
Fields of interest: Performing arts; Arts; Education; Human services; Christian agencies & churches.
Type of support: Capital campaigns; Building/renovation; General/operating support.
Limitations: Applications not accepted.
Application information: Contributes only to pre-selected organizations.
Officers and Trustees: * Henry Ross Perot, Jr.,* Pres. and Treas.; Sarah F. Perot,* V.P. and Secy.; Darcy Glen Anderson; J.Y. Robb III.
EIN: 431964344
Selected grants: The following grants were reported in 2005.
$200,000 to Dallas Center for the Performing Arts, Dallas, TX.
$80,000 to Episcopal School of Dallas, Dallas, TX. 2 grants: $40,000 each
$75,000 to Saint Marks School of Texas, Dallas, TX. 2 grants: $50,000, $25,000
$30,167 to Wycliffe Seed Company, Arlington, TX.
$25,000 to Dallas Symphony Orchestra, Dallas, TX.
$25,000 to Vice Presidents Residence Foundation, DC.
$20,000 to Vanderbilt University, Nashville, TN.
$8,333 to Presbyterians for Renewal, Louisville, KY.

9120
Hal & Charlie Peterson Foundation ✧
P.O. Box 293870
Kerrville, TX   78029-3871
Contact: John Mosty, Secy.-Treas.
FAX: (830) 896-2283; E-mail: hepfdn@ktc.com

Established in 1944 in TX.
Donors: Hal Peterson†; Charlie Peterson†.
Foundation type: Independent foundation.
Financial data (yr. ended 12/31/05): Assets, $50,314,034 (M); gifts received, $20,180; expenditures, $3,928,035; qualifying distributions, $3,690,306; giving activities include $3,432,386 for 44 grants (high: $2,000,000; low: $390).
Purpose and activities: A major portion of funding is allocated for a local charitable hospital; support also for higher, secondary, and elementary education.
Fields of interest: Elementary school/education; Secondary school/education; Higher education; Hospitals (general).
Type of support: General/operating support; Building/renovation; Equipment; Seed money; Matching/challenge support.
Limitations: Giving limited to Kerr County, TX, and adjacent counties, and to state or national organizations with a local chapter in this area. No support for religious purposes. No grants to individuals, or for operating budgets, debt retirement, media productions, publications, or endowments; no loans.

Publications: Application guidelines; Informational brochure (including application guidelines); Program policy statement.
Application information: Application form required.
Initial approach: Letter
Copies of proposal: 1
Deadline(s): None
Board meeting date(s): Monthly
Officers and Directors: * Scott Parker,* Pres.; W.H. Cowden, Jr.,* V.P.; John Mosty,* Secy.-Treas.; Lynn Lemeilleur; Nowlin McBryde; Kyle Priour; James Stehling.
Number of staff: 1 full-time professional; 1 full-time support.
EIN: 741109626
Selected grants: The following grants were reported in 2005.
$2,010,100 to Sid Peterson Memorial Hospital, Kerrville, TX. 2 grants: $10,100, $2,000,000
$223,000 to Schreiner University, Kerrville, TX.
$110,586 to Kimble County Hospital District, Junction, TX.
$22,552 to Notre Dame Catholic School, Wichita Falls, TX.
$1,000 to Raphael Community Free Clinic, Kerrville, TX.

9121
Petrello Family Foundation ✧ ☆
515 W. Greens Rd., Ste. 1200
Houston, TX   77067

Established in 2001 in DE.
Donor: Anthony G. Petrello.
Foundation type: Independent foundation.
Financial data (yr. ended 6/30/06): Assets, $4,774,436 (M); gifts received, $1,086,957; expenditures, $1,467,052; qualifying distributions, $1,461,800; giving activities include $1,461,800 for grants.
Fields of interest: Performing arts, theater; Arts; Elementary/secondary education.
Limitations: Applications not accepted. Giving primarily in TX. No grants to individuals.
Application information: Contributes only to pre-selected organizations.
Directors: Anthony G. Petrello; Cynthia A. Petrello.
EIN: 010559509
Selected grants: The following grants were reported in 2005.
$82,350 to Houston Grand Opera, Houston, TX.
$60,000 to Yale University, New Haven, CT.
$50,000 to Camp for All, Houston, TX.
$25,000 to Exploring the Arts, New York, NY.
$25,000 to YMCA of Stamford, Stamford, CT.
$19,250 to KIPP (Knowledge is Power Program) Academy, Houston, TX.
$8,750 to Parkside School, New York, NY.
$8,548 to Alley Theater, Houston, TX.
$5,000 to Franciscan Life Center, Sylvania, OH.
$2,655 to Museum of Fine Arts, Houston, Houston, TX.

9122
Phillips Family Foundation ✧
P.O. Box 17149
Sugar Land, TX   77496

Established in 2001 in TX.
Donors: D. Martin Phillips; Liane M. Phillips.
Foundation type: Independent foundation.

Financial data (yr. ended 12/31/05): Assets, $1,132,177 (M); gifts received, $1,967,206; expenditures, $936,837; qualifying distributions, $936,433; giving activities include $936,433 for 16 grants (high: $510,000; low: $100).

Fields of interest: Children/youth, services; Human services; Science; Biological sciences; Protestant agencies & churches; Women.

Limitations: Applications not accepted. Giving primarily in Houston, TX. No grants to individuals.

Application information: Contributes only to pre-selected organizations.

Trustees: Gary R. Petersen; D. Martin Phillips; Liane M. Phillips.

EIN: 750590214

Selected grants: The following grants were reported in 2004.

$230,000 to Memorial Drive Presbyterian Church, Houston, TX.

9123

The Pine Foundation ✧ ☆

111 Congress Ave., Ste. 1400
Austin, TX 78701 (512) 472-5456
Contact: Brigid Anne Cockrum, Pres.; H. David Hughes

Established in 1985 in TX.
Donor: Brigid Anne Cockrum.
Foundation type: Independent foundation.
Financial data (yr. ended 12/31/05): Assets, $1,149,764 (M); gifts received, $25,000; expenditures, $470,146; qualifying distributions, $466,200; giving activities include $463,000 for 5 grants (high: $311,500; low: $1,500).
Purpose and activities: Giving primarily for education, human services, and youth programs.
Fields of interest: Arts; Elementary/secondary education; Education; Human services; Children/youth, services.
Limitations: Giving limited to the central TX area. No grants to individuals.
Application information: Application form not required.
  Initial approach: Proposal
  Deadline(s): Sept. 30
Officer: Brigid Anne Cockrum, Pres.
Director: Wendy Albrecht.
EIN: 742387801
Selected grants: The following grants were reported in 2004.
$128,000 to Book Boosters, Cibolo, TX.

9124

Minnie Stevens Piper Foundation ✧

1250 N.E. Loop 410, Ste. 810
San Antonio, TX 78209-1539 (210) 525-8494
Contact: Joyce M. Ellis, Secy. and Exec. Dir.
FAX: (210) 341-6627; E-mail: mspf@mspf.org;
URL: http://www.mspf.org

Incorporated in 1950 in TX.
Donors: Randall G. Piper‡; Minnie Stevens Piper‡.
Foundation type: Independent foundation.
Financial data (yr. ended 12/31/05): Assets, $22,717,812 (M); gifts received, $861; expenditures, $1,780,931; qualifying distributions, $1,745,156; giving activities include $102,000 for 38 grants (high: $5,000; low: $500), $466,250 for grants to individuals, $475,137 for loans to

individuals, and $368,443 for foundation-administered programs.

Purpose and activities: Giving especially to contribute toward the education of worthy students. The foundation administers a student loan fund, annual Piper Professor Awards to recognize teaching excellence at the college level, Piper Scholar Awards of four-year college scholarships to outstanding high school graduates in TX, a student aid library and information center, and a scholarship clearinghouse. Grants to individuals as educational loans, scholarships, and teaching awards are made only through the programs operated by the foundation.

Fields of interest: Higher education; Education.
Type of support: Scholarships—to individuals; Student loans—to individuals.
Limitations: Giving limited to TX; student loans limited to U.S. citizens residing in TX and attending TX educational institutions. No grants for building or endowment funds.
Publications: Application guidelines; Occasional report; Program policy statement.
Application information: Recipients of scholarship and professorship award programs must be nominated; nomination not necessary for student loans. See foundation Web site for current information. Application form not required.
  Initial approach: Letter
  Deadline(s): None
  Board meeting date(s): Mar., June, Sept., and Dec.; student loan committee meets monthly
Officers and Directors: John H. Wilson II,* Pres.; J. Burleson Smith,* V.P.; Joyce M. Ellis,* Secy. and Exec. Dir.; Martin R. Harris,* Treas.; Paul T. Curl; Lewis M. Fox; Kenneth Shumate.
Number of staff: 5 full-time professional; 5 full-time support; 1 part-time support.
EIN: 741292695

9125

The Plus Valia Foundation ✧ ☆

1400 W. 6th St.
Austin, TX 78703 (650) 592-1521

Established in CA.
Donor: T.M. Scruggs.
Foundation type: Independent foundation.
Financial data (yr. ended 12/31/05): Assets, $0 (M); gifts received, $526,880; expenditures, $526,880; qualifying distributions, $526,880; giving activities include $525,000 for 1 grant.
Purpose and activities: Giving primarily to a center for economic and policy research.
Fields of interest: Economics; Public policy, research.
Limitations: Giving primarily in Washington, DC.
Officers: T.M. Scruggs, C.E.O.; Laura Graham, Secy.; Tony Choban, Mgr.
EIN: 943064462

9126

The Pogue Family Foundation ✧

P.O. Box 1920
Dallas, TX 75221

Established in 2000 in TX.
Donors: Jeffrey Blake Pogue; David Brent Pogue; Blair Matthew Pogue; A. Mack Pogue.
Foundation type: Independent foundation.

Financial data (yr. ended 12/31/03): Assets, $24,263,582 (M); gifts received, $471,000; expenditures, $1,382,058; qualifying distributions, $1,153,550; giving activities include $1,152,000 for 3 grants (high: $500,000; low: $152,000).

Purpose and activities: Giving primarily for medical centers, including a children's medical center.
Fields of interest: Hospitals (general); Children, services; Federated giving programs.
Limitations: Applications not accepted. Giving primarily in Dallas, TX. No grants to individuals.
Application information: Contributes only to pre-selected organizations.
Officer: Nancy Davis, Secy.
Directors: William C. Cooper; B. Jack Pogue; Blair Matthew Pogue; David Brent Pogue; Jean Pogue; Jeffrey Blake Pogue; Mack Pogue; Robert C. Taylor.
EIN: 752894071

9127

Pollock Foundation ✧

2626 Howell St., Ste. 895
Dallas, TX 75204
Contact: Robert G. Pollock, Tr.

Established in 1955 in TX.
Donors: Lawrence S. Pollock, Sr.‡; Lawrence S. Pollock, Jr.‡.
Foundation type: Independent foundation.
Financial data (yr. ended 12/31/05): Assets, $20,741,459 (M); gifts received, $43,152; expenditures, $1,174,842; qualifying distributions, $998,224; giving activities include $998,224 for 23 grants (high: $334,000; low: $1,250).
Fields of interest: Arts; Public health school/education; Libraries/library science; Nursing care; Youth development, centers/clubs; Human services; Jewish agencies & temples.
Limitations: Giving primarily in Dallas, TX.
Application information: Application form required.
  Initial approach: Letter
  Copies of proposal: 1
  Deadline(s): None
  Board meeting date(s): Apr. and Oct.
Trustees: Lawrence S. Pollock III; Richard Pollock; Robert G. Pollock; Shirley Pollock.
EIN: 756011985
Selected grants: The following grants were reported in 2003.
$336,137 to University of Texas Southwestern Medical Center, Dallas, TX. 2 grants: $236,137 (For general operating support), $100,000 (For Pollock Center for Research).
$100,000 to Dallas Symphony Association, Dallas, TX. For general operating support.
$50,000 to Temple Emanu-El, Dallas, TX. For endowment.
$20,000 to Visiting Nurse Association of Texas, Dallas, TX. For general operating support.
$13,698 to Advanced Placement Strategies, Dallas, TX. For general operating support.
$5,000 to Community Homes for Adults, Dallas, TX. For general operating support.
$5,000 to Vogel Alcove Childcare Center for the Homeless, Dallas, TX. For general operating support.
$3,500 to National Council of Jewish Women, Dallas, TX. For general operating support.
$2,500 to Shakespeare Festival of Dallas, Dallas, TX. For general operating support.

9128
The Powell Foundation
2121 San Felipe, Ste. 110
Houston, TX 77019-5600 (713) 523-7557
Contact: Caroline J. Sabin, Exec. Dir.
FAX: (713) 523-7553;
E-mail: info@powellfoundation.org; URL: http://
www.powellfoundation.org

Established in 1967 in TX.
Donors: Ben H. Powell, Jr.†; Kitty King Powell.
Foundation type: Independent foundation.
Financial data (yr. ended 12/31/05): Assets,
$20,729,125 (M); expenditures, $1,091,599;
qualifying distributions, $989,687; giving activities
include $833,076 for 128 grants (high: $45,000;
low: $250).
Purpose and activities: The foundation distributes
funds for public charitable purposes, principally for
the support, encouragement, and assistance to
education, health, conservation, and the arts with a
direct impact within the foundation's geographic
zone of interest: Harris, Travis, & Walker counties,
in TX.
Fields of interest: Arts; Education, early childhood
education; Higher education; Education;
Environment; Health care; Human services;
Minorities; Economically disadvantaged.
Type of support: General/operating support;
Management development/capacity building;
Program development; Curriculum development;
Scholarship funds; Matching/challenge support.
Limitations: Giving primarily for public education in
Houston, Austin, and Huntsville, TX. No support for
private foundations, or religious organizations for
religious purposes. No grants for testimonial
dinners, building funds, fundraising events,
advertising, or for debt retirement.
Publications: Application guidelines; Annual report
(including application guidelines); Grants list.
Application information: Application guidelines and
proposal form available on Web site. Application
form required.
  Initial approach: Letter
  Copies of proposal: 1
  Deadline(s): Varies - ongoing
  Board meeting date(s): Spring and fall
  Final notification: Positive replies only
Officers and Trustees:* Nancy Powell Moore,* Pres.
and Treas.; Albert S. Tabor,* V.P. and Secy.; Ben H.
Powell V,* V.P.; Marian P. Harrison; Katherine P.
Hill; Molly N. Kidd; Harvin C. Moore; Kitty King
Powell.
Number of staff: 1 full-time professional; 1 part-time
professional; 1 part-time support.
EIN: 746104592
Selected grants: The following grants were reported
in 2005.
$45,000 to Collaborative for Children, Houston, TX.
$24,000 to Project Yes, Houston, TX. 2 grants:
  $20,000, $4,000
$20,000 to KIPP (Knowledge is Power Program)
  Academy, Houston, TX.
$15,000 to Families Under Urban and Social Attack,
  Houston, TX.
$10,000 to Environmental Defense, Austin, TX.
$10,000 to Houston Symphony Society, Houston,
  TX.
$5,000 to Armand Bayou Nature Center Foundation,
  Houston, TX.
$5,000 to Association for Community Television,
  Houston, TX.
$5,000 to Christian Community Service Center,
  Houston, TX.

9129
The Prairie Foundation ◇
303 W. Wall Ave., Ste. 1901
Midland, TX 79701-5116
Contact: Lynda James, Grants Comm.

Established in 1957 in TX.
Donors: David Fasken Special Trust; Barbara
Fasken.
Foundation type: Independent foundation.
Financial data (yr. ended 12/31/05): Assets,
$8,330,025 (M); expenditures, $433,057;
qualifying distributions, $400,225; giving activities
include $400,000 for 32 grants (high: $80,500;
low: $1,000).
Fields of interest: Arts; Education; Health
organizations, association; Housing/shelter,
development; Boy scouts; Human services;
Children/youth, services; Residential/custodial
care, hospices; Community development; Federated
giving programs.
Limitations: Giving primarily in the San Francisco
Bay Area, CA, and Midland, Laredo, and Odessa, TX.
Publications: Application guidelines.
Application information: Application form required.
  Initial approach: Letter or telephone requesting
    application guidelines
  Copies of proposal: 1
  Deadline(s): None
  Board meeting date(s): As needed
  Final notification: Responses sent to all
    organizations submitting completed grant
    request
Officers and Directors:* Robert T. Dickson,* Pres.;
Norbert J. Dickman,* V.P.; Benjamin L. Blake,* 2nd
V.P.; Lynda James, Secy.
EIN: 756012458
Selected grants: The following grants were reported
in 2005.
$80,500 to Thacher School, Ojai, CA.
$25,000 to Friends of San Rafael, San Rafael, CA.
$15,000 to Safe Place, Dumas, TX.
$12,500 to Texas Migrant Council, Laredo, TX.
$10,000 to Boy Scouts of America, Midland, TX.
$10,000 to Girl Scouts of the U.S.A., Odessa, TX.
$10,000 to High Sky Childrens Ranch, Midland, TX.
$10,000 to Saint Anthony Foundation, San
  Francisco, CA.
$7,500 to Midland Community Theater, Midland, TX.
$5,000 to Museum of the Southwest, Midland, TX.

9130
Robert & Ruby Priddy Charitable Trust ◇
c/o Robert T. Priddy
807 8th St., Ste. 600
Wichita Falls, TX 76301

Established in 2000 in TX.
Donors: Robert T. Priddy; Mrs. Robert T. Priddy.
Foundation type: Independent foundation.
Financial data (yr. ended 12/31/05): Assets,
$17,693,032 (M); gifts received, $2,683,390;
expenditures, $7,669,882; qualifying distributions,
$7,582,679; giving activities include $7,323,524
for 8 grants (high: $2,010,000; low: $3,000;
average: $837,105–$1,450,846).
Purpose and activities: Giving primarily for higher
education.
Fields of interest: Higher education.
Type of support: Scholarship funds.
Limitations: Applications not accepted. Giving
primarily in TX. No grants to individuals.

Application information: Contributes only to
pre-selected organizations.
Officers: Robert T. Priddy, Chair.; Berneice R. Leath,
Secy.; John Bridgman, Exec. Dir.
Trustees: Richard H. Bundy; G. Murphy Davis; Betsy
Priddy; Joseph N. Sherrill, Jr.; David Wolverton.
EIN: 752924748
Selected grants: The following grants were reported
in 2005.
$2,010,000 to Hendrix College, Conway, AR. For
  scholarship funds.
$1,507,311 to Rhodes College, Memphis, TN. For
  scholarship funds.
$1,450,846 to Colorado College, Colorado Springs,
  CO. For scholarship funds.
$1,087,270 to Southwestern University,
  Georgetown, TX. For scholarship funds.
$837,105 to Oklahoma City University, Oklahoma
  City, OK. For scholarship funds.
$424,992 to University of North Texas Foundation,
  Denton, TX. For scholarship funds.
$3,000 to Duke University, Durham, NC. For
  scholarship funds.
$3,000 to Fund for Theological Education, Atlanta,
  GA. For honorarium.

9131
The Priddy Foundation
807 8th St., Ste. 1010
Wichita Falls, TX 76301 (940) 723-8720
Contact: Debbie C. White, Dir., Grants
FAX: (940) 723-8656; E-mail: info@priddyfdn.org;
URL: http://www.priddyfdn.org

Established in 1963 in TX.
Donors: Ashley H. Priddy†; Robert T. Priddy;
Swannanoa H. Priddy†; Walter M. Priddy†.
Foundation type: Independent foundation.
Financial data (yr. ended 12/31/05): Assets,
$84,235,732 (M); expenditures, $4,648,716;
qualifying distributions, $4,209,866; giving
activities include $3,796,232 for 78 grants (high:
$500,000; low: $100; average: $5,000–$50,000).
Purpose and activities: The foundation is dedicated
to the support of programs in human services,
education, the arts, and health, which offer
significant potential for individual development and
community improvement.
Fields of interest: Arts; Education; Health care;
Youth development; Human services; Community
development.
Type of support: Management development/
capacity building; General/operating support;
Capital campaigns; Building/renovation;
Equipment; Program development; Scholarship
funds; Matching/challenge support.
Limitations: Giving primarily in Archer, Baylor,
Childress, Clay, Cottle, Foard, Hardeman, Haskell,
Jack, King, Knox, Montague, Stonewall,
Throckmorton, Wichita, Wilbarger, Wise, and Young
counties, TX; and Carter, Comanche, Cotton, Garvin,
Jackson, Jefferson, Love, Murray, Stephens, and
Tillman counties, OK. No support for individual
public elementary or secondary schools, or religious
institutions (except for non-sectarian, human
service programs offered on a non-discriminatory
basis). No grants to individuals, or for endowments,
operating deficits, debt retirement, start-up funding,
basic or applied research, fundraising programs or
events, conferences or other educational events
(except through an organizational development
grant), media productions or publications, or school
trips.

Publications: Application guidelines; Financial statement; Grants list; Informational brochure (including application guidelines); Program policy statement.

Application information: See foundation's Web site for more application information. The preliminary and formal applications must be submitted online at the foundation's Web site. Application form required.

Initial approach: Brief preliminary application online through the website

Copies of proposal: 1

Deadline(s): Feb. 1 and Aug. 1 for preliminary application; Mar. 1 and Sept. 1 for formal application

Board meeting date(s): May and Nov.

Final notification: Within two weeks of board meeting

Officer and Trustees:* David Wolverton,* Pres.; Julia Whitmire,* V.P.; Robert T. Priddy, Tr. Emeritus; Paul Clark; Bill Daniel; David Flack; Ralph Harvey III; Alice Huang; Jerry Johnson; Berneice R. Leath; Martin Litteken*; Nancy Marks; Rick Schleider.

Number of staff: 3 full-time professional; 1 full-time support.

EIN: 756029882

Selected grants: The following grants were reported in 2005.

$1,600,000 to Advanced Placement Strategies, Dallas, TX.

$79,000 to Association for Retarded Citizens, Wichita Falls, TX. For respite assistance program.

$62,500 to Boys and Girls Club of Vernon, Vernon, TX. 3 grants: $20,000 (To support after-school and summer outreach program), $30,000 (For fee assistance program), $12,500 (For fee assistance program).

$54,568 to Wichita Falls Area Food Bank, Burkburnett Boys and Girls Club, Wichita Falls, TX. For the Kids' Cafe.

$50,000 to Friendly Door, Iowa Park, TX. For meals and transportation.

$41,524 to First Step of Wichita Falls, Wichita Falls, TX. For renovations and repairs of emergency shelter.

$28,000 to Nonprofit Management Center of Wichita Falls, Wichita Falls, TX. For Summer Institute training.

$18,500 to Armed Services YMCA, Lawton Chapter, Lawton, OK. For childcare scholarships.

$16,350 to Wichita Falls Ballet Theater, Wichita Falls, TX. For technical and rental support, and organizational development.

9132
Hahl Proctor Charitable Trust ◇
c/o Bank of America, N.A.
P.O. Box 831041
Dallas, TX 75283-1041

Established in 1987 in TX.

Foundation type: Independent foundation.

Financial data (yr. ended 4/30/05): Assets, $5,915,513 (M); expenditures, $415,362; qualifying distributions, $335,781; giving activities include $329,000 for 43 grants (high: $24,000; low: $1,000).

Purpose and activities: Giving primarily for education, health associations, crime and violence prevention, children, youth and social services.

Fields of interest: Performing arts, theater; Education; Hospitals (general); Substance abuse, treatment; Health organizations, association;

Crime/violence prevention, abuse prevention; Crime/law enforcement; Housing/shelter; Human services; Children/youth, services; Human services; Aging, centers/services; Community development; Economically disadvantaged.

Limitations: Giving primarily in Midland, TX. No grants to individuals.

Application information: Application form not required.

Deadline(s): May 15

Officers: Bill Hill, Pres.; John Peterson, V.P.; Jeff Morton, Secy.; Joe Julian, Treas.

Trustee: Bank of America, N.A.

EIN: 756382699

Selected grants: The following grants were reported in 2004.

$24,000 to United Way of Midland, Midland, TX.

$15,000 to High Sky Childrens Ranch, Midland, TX.

$15,000 to YMCA of Midland, Midland, TX.

$14,000 to Casa de Amigos of Midland, Midland, TX.

$14,000 to Safe Place of the Permian Basin, Midland, TX.

$12,000 to Boys and Girls Club of Midland, Midland, TX.

$10,000 to Midland College, Midland, TX.

$10,000 to Palmer Drug Abuse Program Midland Texas, Midland, TX.

$5,000 to Big Brothers Big Sisters of Midland, Midland, TX.

$5,000 to Communities in Schools of the Permian Basin, Midland, TX.

9133
Progress Foundation ◇
P.O. Box 2950
San Antonio, TX 78299

Established in 1997 in TX.

Donors: Carlos Enrique Alvarez; Maria de Guadalupe Alvarez.

Foundation type: Independent foundation.

Financial data (yr. ended 9/30/05): Assets, $12,486,082 (M); expenditures, $640,110; qualifying distributions, $550,943; giving activities include $550,943 for 5 grants (high: $343,333; low: $10,000).

Purpose and activities: Giving primarily for education.

Fields of interest: Secondary school/education; Higher education.

Type of support: General/operating support; Capital campaigns.

Limitations: Applications not accepted. Giving in the U.S., primarily in Davidson, NC, and San Antonio, TX. No grants to individuals.

Application information: Contributes only to pre-selected organizations.

Trustee: Frost National Bank.

EIN: 746449471

Selected grants: The following grants were reported in 2004.

$250,000 to School Year Abroad, Lawrence, MA. To purchase building.

$200,000 to Childrens Shelter of San Antonio, San Antonio, TX.

$47,633 to United Way of San Antonio and Bexar County, San Antonio, TX.

$20,000 to Sammy Tippit Ministries, San Antonio, TX.

$10,000 to Davidson College, Davidson, NC. For capital support.

$10,000 to San Antonio Zoological Society, San Antonio, TX. For Africa Live.

9134
Vin & Caren Prothro Foundation ◇
PMB 377
25 Highland Park Village, No. 100
Dallas, TX 75205-2785

Established in 2000 in TX.

Donor: Caren H. Prothro.

Foundation type: Independent foundation.

Financial data (yr. ended 12/31/05): Assets, $20,928,402 (M); expenditures, $2,455,450; qualifying distributions, $2,312,499; giving activities include $2,280,700 for 48 grants (high: $1,000,000; low: $500).

Fields of interest: Arts; Education; Human services.

Limitations: Applications not accepted. Giving primarily in TX. No grants to individuals.

Application information: Contributes only to pre-selected organizations.

Officers: Caren H. Prothro, Pres.; Vincent H. Prothro, V.P.; Nita C. Clark, Secy.; J.H. Cullum Clark, Treas.

EIN: 752911958

Selected grants: The following grants were reported in 2004.

$1,000,000 to Dallas Center for the Performing Arts, Dallas, TX.

$152,500 to Episcopal School of Dallas, Dallas, TX. 2 grants: $50,000, $102,500

$100,000 to Dallas Museum of Art, Dallas, TX.

$12,500 to Southern Methodist University, Dallas, TX.

$10,000 to Saint Marks School of Texas, Dallas, TX.

$10,000 to World Monuments Fund, New York, NY.

$5,000 to Dallas Theater Center, Dallas, TX.

$5,000 to Stanford University, Stanford, CA.

$4,700 to Dallas Historical Society, Dallas, TX.

9135
Providence Journal Charitable Foundation ◇
c/o Board of Trustees
400 S. Record St.
Dallas, TX 75202
Application address: 75 Fountain St., Providence, RI 02902

Trust established in 1956 in RI.

Donor: The Providence Journal Co.

Foundation type: Company-sponsored foundation.

Financial data (yr. ended 12/31/05): Assets, $554 (M); expenditures, $1,461,033; qualifying distributions, $701,000; giving activities include $701,000 for grants.

Purpose and activities: The foundation supports hospitals and organizations involved with arts and culture and education.

Fields of interest: Arts; Higher education; Education; Hospitals (general); Federated giving programs.

Type of support: General/operating support; Capital campaigns.

Limitations: Giving primarily in RI, with emphasis on Providence. No grants to individuals.

Application information:

Initial approach: Proposal

Copies of proposal: 1

Deadline(s): Quarterly

Board meeting date(s): Monthly

Trustees: Sandra J. Radcliffe; Mark Ryan; Henry D. Sharpe, Jr.; Howard G. Sutton; John W. Wall.
EIN: 056015372
Selected grants: The following grants were reported in 2003.
$100,000 to Providence Public Library, Providence, RI.
$50,000 to United Way of Rhode Island, Providence, RI.
$30,000 to Salve Regina University, Newport, RI.
$30,000 to Women and Infants Hospital of Rhode Island, Providence, RI.
$27,000 to Rhode Island Philharmonic Orchestra, Providence, RI.
$25,000 to Memorial Hospital, Pawtucket, RI.
$25,000 to Providence Performing Arts Center, Providence, RI.
$25,000 to Rhode Island College Foundation, Providence, RI.
$25,000 to Roger Williams University, Bristol, RI.
$25,000 to University of Rhode Island Foundation, Providence, RI.

9136
Myra Stafford Pryor Charitable Trust
c/o Frost National Bank
P.O. Box 1600
San Antonio, TX 78296 (210) 220-4353
Contact: Melissa Adams, Sr. V.P., Frost National Bank
Application address: c/o Frost National Bank, San Antonio, TX 78296

Established in 1993.
Foundation type: Independent foundation.
Financial data (yr. ended 12/31/05): Assets, $24,321,480 (M); expenditures, $1,372,212; qualifying distributions, $1,161,193; giving activities include $1,161,193 for grants.
Fields of interest: Arts; Education; Hospitals (general); Human services; Religion.
Type of support: Capital campaigns; Building/ renovation; Equipment.
Limitations: Giving primarily in San Antonio, TX.
Application information: Application form not required.
  Initial approach: Letter on organization's letterhead
  Copies of proposal: 1
  Deadline(s): Mar. 31, July 31, and Oct. 31
Trustee: Frost National Bank.
EIN: 746417499
Selected grants: The following grants were reported in 2004.
$40,000 to United Way of San Antonio and Bexar County, San Antonio, TX. 2 grants: $10,000, $30,000
$25,000 to Centro Alameda, San Antonio, TX.
$20,000 to San Antonio Public Library Foundation, San Antonio, TX.
$15,000 to Hill Country Mission for Health, Bandera, TX.
$15,000 to Rainbow House, San Antonio, TX.
$10,000 to Baptist Child and Family Services, San Antonio, TX.
$10,000 to Carver Academy, San Antonio, TX.
$10,000 to Texas Public Radio, San Antonio, TX.
$9,600 to San Antonio Eye Bank, San Antonio, TX.

9137
The PSH Foundation ◇
P.O. Box 2888
Wimberley, TX 78676

Established in 2001 in TX.
Donor: Patti S. Harrison.
Foundation type: Independent foundation.
Financial data (yr. ended 5/31/06): Assets, $9,999,929 (M); expenditures, $522,335; qualifying distributions, $453,299; giving activities include $408,413 for 23 grants (high: $92,730; low: $500).
Fields of interest: Arts; Education; Health care; Housing/shelter, development; Residential/ custodial care.
Type of support: General/operating support; Equipment; Scholarship funds.
Limitations: Applications not accepted. No grants to individuals.
Application information: Contributes only to pre-selected organizations.
Officer: Patti S. Harrison, Pres.
Directors: Dale A. Dossey; Thomas Locerbie; Teresa Ann Ward; Barbara Willard.
EIN: 760683559
Selected grants: The following grants were reported in 2006.
$25,083 to Houston Livestock Show and Rodeo, Houston, TX.
$20,500 to Habitat for Humanity International. 2 grants: $500, $20,000
$20,000 to American Cancer Society, Atlanta, GA.
$20,000 to Austin Plastic Surgery Foundation-Austin Smiles, Austin, TX.
$1,000 to Association of Small Foundations, DC.
$1,000 to Intrepid Fallen Heroes Fund, New York, NY.

9138
Ed Rachal Foundation ◇
500 N. Shoreline Blvd., Ste. 1002
Corpus Christi, TX 78471-1016 (361) 881-9040
Contact: Paul D. Altheide, C.E.O.
FAX: (361) 881-9885; E-mail: info@edrachal.org;
URL: http://www.edrachal.org

Established in 1965 in TX.
Donor: Ed Rachal†.
Foundation type: Independent foundation.
Financial data (yr. ended 8/31/05): Assets, $41,278,780 (M); expenditures, $1,717,689; qualifying distributions, $1,731,987; giving activities include $1,120,641 for 57 grants (high: $100,000; low: $305), and $635,258 for 1 foundation-administered program.
Fields of interest: Higher education; Libraries/ library science; Health organizations, association; Human services; Christian agencies & churches.
Type of support: General/operating support; Capital campaigns; Building/renovation; Equipment; Emergency funds.
Limitations: Giving limited to TX. No grants to individuals, or for multi-year commitments.
Publications: Application guidelines; Annual report; Grants list.
Application information: Applications sent by fax will not be accepted. It is not necessary to place application in folder or binder. Application form required.
  Initial approach: Application form via foundation Web site
  Copies of proposal: 1

Deadline(s): None
Board meeting date(s): Jan., Apr., July, and Oct.
Officers and Directors:* John D. White,* Chair.; Robert L. Walker,* Vice-Chair.; Paul D. Altheide,* C.E.O. and Secy.; Richard Schendel,* Treas.
Number of staff: 1 full-time professional; 1 full-time support.
EIN: 741116595
Selected grants: The following grants were reported in 2003.
$299,500 to Texas A & M University, College Station, TX. 2 grants: $250,000 (For series on Nautical Archaeology), $49,500.
$150,000 to Texas A & M Research Foundation, College Station, TX.
$100,000 to Institute of Nautical Archaeology, College Station, TX. For Denbigh Project.
$75,000 to Bo's Place, Houston, TX. For building blocks.
$50,000 to Bandina Christian Youth Camp, Wharton, TX. For Vision for Youth capital campaign.
$49,795 to Fort Worth Christian School, North Richland Hills, TX. For Let the Little Children Come program.
$31,880 to Texas A & M International University, Laredo, TX. For Child Development Center.
$25,000 to HALO-Flight, Corpus Christi, TX. For new helicopter capital campaign.
$25,000 to South Texas Public Broadcasting System, Corpus Christi, TX. For digital conversion.

9139
Howard Earl Rachofsky Foundation ☆
c/o Regal Asset Mgmt.
8201 Preston Rd., Ste. 400
Dallas, TX 75225
Contact: Dina H. Bardi, Secy.

Established in 1993 in TX.
Donor: Howard Earl Rachofsky.
Foundation type: Independent foundation.
Financial data (yr. ended 3/31/05): Assets, $6,914 (M); gifts received, $510,288; expenditures, $476,194; qualifying distributions, $436,565; giving activities include $432,920 for 42 grants (high: $102,500; low: $250).
Fields of interest: Museums (art); Arts; Elementary/ secondary education; Education, early childhood education; Higher education; Human services; Children/youth, services; Jewish federated giving programs; Jewish agencies & temples.
Type of support: Emergency funds; General/ operating support; Continuing support; Annual campaigns; Capital campaigns; Building/ renovation; Equipment; Endowments; Program development; Research; Matching/challenge support.
Limitations: Giving limited to Dallas, TX. No support for political organizations. No grants or student loans to individuals, no support for conferences/ seminars or professorships or funds for internships.
Application information: Must be a 501(c)(3) organization. Application form not required.
  Initial approach: Letter
  Copies of proposal: 1
  Deadline(s): None
  Board meeting date(s): Annually, and as necessary
  Final notification: 2 weeks

Officers and Directors:* Howard Earl Rachofsky,* Pres.; Dina H. Bardi, Secy.; Margueritte Hoffman; Cindy Rachofsky; Sharon Young.
EIN: 752481321

9140
Randall & Dewey Foundation, Inc. ✦ ☆
74 Wincrest Falls Dr.
Cypress, TX   77429-5154

Established in 2004 in TX.
Donors: Jack P. Randall; Beverly Randall.
Foundation type: Independent foundation.
Financial data (yr. ended 12/31/05): Assets, $149,152 (M); expenditures, $417,202; qualifying distributions, $416,600; giving activities include $416,600 for 6 grants (high: $300,000; low: $1,600).
Fields of interest: Education; Medical research.
Limitations: Applications not accepted. Giving on a national basis. No grants to individuals.
Application information: Contributes only to pre-selected organizations.
Officers: Jack P. Randall, C.E.O. and Pres.; Kenneth W. Dewey, V.P.; Samuel S. Griffin III, Secy.
EIN: 202002269

9141
Bernard and Audre Rapoport Foundation ✦
5400 Bosque Blvd., 245
Waco, TX   76710   (254) 741-0510
Contact: Carole Jones, Fdn. Coord.
FAX: (254) 741-0092;
E-mail: rapoport@rapoportfdn.org; URL: http://www.rapoportfdn.org

Established in 1988 in TX.
Donors: Audre Rapoport; Bernard Rapoport; Patricia Rapoport; Ronald B. Rapoport.
Foundation type: Independent foundation.
Financial data (yr. ended 12/31/05): Assets, $59,834,828 (M); expenditures, $3,607,544; qualifying distributions, $2,942,681; giving activities include $2,690,287 for 46 grants (high: $438,842; low: $225).
Purpose and activities: Giving primarily for early childhood education as well as for higher education. Support also for the arts, community building, health care, human services, and Jewish organizations.
Fields of interest: Media, television; Media, radio; Performing arts, orchestra (symphony); Higher education; Education, reading; Education; Health organizations; Human services; Salvation Army; Children/youth, services; Family services; Aging, centers/services; Foundations (community); Jewish federated giving programs; Economics; Public affairs.
Type of support: Seed money; Program development; Matching/challenge support.
Limitations: Giving primarily within a 30 mile radius of Waco, TX. No grants to individuals.
Publications: Application guidelines; Annual report.
Application information: Contact foundation for guidelines. Application form not required.
  Initial approach: Letter (no more than 4 pages, double-spaced, about 1,000 words)
  Copies of proposal: 1
  Deadline(s): None
  Board meeting date(s): Twice a year
Officers and Trustees:* Ronald B. Rapoport,* Chair.; Audre Rapoport,* Vice-Chair.; Bernard

Rapoport,* Pres.; Larry D. Jaynes, Secy.-Treas.; Margaret M. McCarthy, Exec. Dir.; Rick Battistoni; James D. Chesney; William A. Nesbitt; Lyndon Olson; Abby Rapoport; Emily Rapoport; Patricia Rapoport; Joel Schwartz.
Number of staff: 2 full-time professional.
EIN: 742479712
Selected grants: The following grants were reported in 2004.
$424,999 to University of Texas, Austin, TX. For scholarships.
$300,000 to Avance Family Support and Education Program-Waco, Waco, TX. For program support.
$250,000 to YMCA of Central Texas, Waco, TX.
$212,500 to Jerusalem Foundation, Jerusalem, Israel. For annual fund.
$212,500 to UJA-Federation of New York, New York, NY. For annual fund.
$100,000 to Library of Congress, DC. For Jewish exhibit.
$100,000 to Oberlin College, Oberlin, OH. For scholarships.
$50,000 to Institute for Americas Future, DC. For general support.
$45,000 to Carter BloodCare, Bedford, TX. For donor coach.
$45,000 to World Hunger Relief, Elm Mott, TX. For program support.

9142
Norman H. Read 1985 Charitable Trust ✦
c/o Amarillo National Bank
P.O. Box 1
Amarillo, TX   79105-0001

Established in 1994 in TX.
Foundation type: Independent foundation.
Financial data (yr. ended 6/30/05): Assets, $21,868,239 (M); expenditures, $1,428,962; qualifying distributions, $1,068,674; giving activities include $1,055,305 for 4 grants (high: $455,430; low: $49,900).
Purpose and activities: Giving primarily for medical research, and to educational organizations.
Fields of interest: Education; Health care; Medical research, institute.
Limitations: Applications not accepted. Giving primarily in Boston and Salem, MA. No grants to individuals.
Application information: Contributes only to pre-selected organizations.
Trustees: Nile L. Albright, M.D.; Amarillo National Bank.
EIN: 752622754

9143
The Reaud Charitable Foundation, Inc. ✦
801 Laurel St.
Beaumont, TX   77701   (409) 838-1000
Contact: Wayne A. Reaud, Dir.

Established in 1989 in TX.
Donor: Wayne A. Reaud.
Foundation type: Independent foundation.
Financial data (yr. ended 12/31/04): Assets, $34,308,332 (M); gifts received, $1,700,000; expenditures, $1,984,942; qualifying distributions, $1,837,990; giving activities include $1,837,990 for 45 grants (high: $342,650; low: $180).
Fields of interest: Performing arts, theater; Elementary/secondary education; Hospitals

(general); Cancer; Youth development, services; Human services; Aging, centers/services; Christian agencies & churches.
Limitations: Giving primarily in Beaumont, TX. No grants to individuals directly.
Application information: Application form not required.
  Deadline(s): None
Officer: Jon A. Reaud, Exec. Dir.
Director: Wayne A. Reaud.
EIN: 760291657
Selected grants: The following grants were reported in 2003.
$253,786 to Beaumont Civic Center, Beaumont, TX. For Bibles and Bikes.
$179,000 to Lamar University, Beaumont, TX.
$160,000 to Salvation Army of Beaumont, Beaumont, TX.
$75,000 to Catholic Charities of the Diocese of Beaumont, Beaumont, TX.
$75,000 to Nutrition and Services for Seniors, Beaumont, TX.
$75,000 to Some Other Place, Beaumont, TX.
$35,000 to Southeast Texas Food Bank, Beaumont, TX.
$24,714 to University of Texas, Law School, Austin, TX.
$20,000 to Buckner Childrens Home, Beaumont, TX.
$10,000 to Girls Haven, Beaumont, TX.

9144
Reliant Resources Foundation ✦
(formerly Reliant Energy Foundation)
P.O. Box 148
Houston, TX   77002-0148   (713) 207-5155
Contact: Cyndy Garza-Roberts

Established in 1997 in TX.
Donors: Reliant Energy, Inc.; Reliant Energy Ventures, Inc.; Lynn Culmer; Mark Jacobs; Shawn McFarlane; Carla Mitcham.
Foundation type: Company-sponsored foundation.
Financial data (yr. ended 12/31/05): Assets, $6,838,042 (M); gifts received, $69,966; expenditures, $1,925,008; qualifying distributions, $1,899,300; giving activities include $1,899,300 for 61 grants (high: $594,700; low: $1,000).
Purpose and activities: The foundation supports public charities and organizations involved with higher education, housing repair, youth, family services, senior citizens, disabled people, and economically disadvantaged people.
Fields of interest: Higher education; Housing/shelter, repairs; Youth, services; Family services; Foundations (public); Federated giving programs; Aging; Disabilities, people with; Economically disadvantaged.
Type of support: General/operating support.
Limitations: Giving primarily in TX. No grants to individuals.
Application information: Application form not required.
  Initial approach: Proposal
  Deadline(s): None
Officers and Directors:* Joel V. Staff,* Chair.; James B. Robb, Pres.; James Ajello, V.P.; David S. Freysinger, V.P.; Mark M. Jacobs, V.P.; Suzanne Kupiec, V.P.; Brian Landrum, V.P.; David Roylance, V.P.; Karen D. Taylor, V.P.; Judith Tink, V.P.; Michael L. Jines, Secy.; Daniel H. Hannon, Treas.; Robert W. Harvey.
EIN: 760537222

9145
Alice Kleberg Reynolds Foundation ✧
(also known as Alice Kleberg Reynolds Meyer Foundation)
c/o Frost National Bank
P.O. Box 2127
Austin, TX 78768 (512) 473-4803
Contact: Sherry McGillicuddy, Exec. V.P., Frost National Bank
FAX: (512) 473-4835;
E-mail: smcgillicuddy@frostbank.com; URL: http://www.akrfoundation.org

Established in 1978 in TX.
Donor: Alice K. Meyer‡.
Foundation type: Independent foundation.
Financial data (yr. ended 12/31/05): Assets, $23,553,549 (M); expenditures, $1,154,828; qualifying distributions, $1,065,000; giving activities include $1,065,000 for 72 grants (high: $75,000; low: $4,500).
Purpose and activities: Grants to qualified non-profit organizations for arts and culture, charitable, educational, literary, medical, and scientific purposes.
Fields of interest: Visual arts; Performing arts; Arts; Education; Medical research, institute.
Type of support: General/operating support; Capital campaigns; Building/renovation; Equipment; Endowments; Program development; Curriculum development; Fellowships; Research.
Limitations: Giving limited to 50 specified counties in south central TX, (Aransas, Atascosa, Bandera, Bee, Bexar, Blanco, Brooks, Caldwell, Calhoun, Cameron, Colorado, Comal, DeWitt, Dimmit, Duval, Fayette, Frio, Goliad, Gonzalez, Guadalupe, Harris, Hays, Hidalgo, Jackson, Jim Hogg, Jim Wells, Karnes, Kendall, Kenedy, Kleberg, LaSalle, Lavaca, Live Oak, Matagorda, Maverick, McMullen, Medina, Nueces, Rufugio, San Patricio, Starr, Travis, Uvalde, Victoria, Webb, Wharton, Willacy, Wilson, Zapata and Zavala). No support for religious organizations. No grants to individuals, or for scholarships or salaries.
Publications: Application guidelines; Grants list.
Application information: Application guidelines and form available on foundation Web site. Application form required.
Initial approach: Proposal
Copies of proposal: 1
Deadline(s): Throughout the year
Board meeting date(s): Varies
Final notification: Nov. 30
Trustee: Frost National Bank.
EIN: 742847652
Selected grants: The following grants were reported in 2004.
$100,000 to Greater Austin Performing Arts Center, Austin, TX.
$30,000 to Peoples Community Clinic, Austin, TX.
$25,000 to Fuerza Unida, San Antonio, TX.
$25,000 to San Antonio Urban Ministries, San Antonio, TX.
$15,000 to Alpha Home, San Antonio, TX.
$15,000 to University of Texas Health Science Center, San Antonio, TX.
$10,000 to Alamo Area Rape Crisis Center, San Antonio, TX.
$10,000 to Womens Shelter of South Texas, Corpus Christi, TX.
$3,278 to Saint Andrews Episcopal School, Austin, TX.
$2,500 to Hope Stone, Houston, TX.

9146
RGK Foundation ✧
1301 W. 25th St., Ste. 300
Austin, TX 78705-4236
Contact: Suzanne Haffey, Grants Assoc.
FAX: (512) 474-7281; E-mail: shaffey@rgkfoundation.org; URL: http://www.rgkfoundation.org

Incorporated in 1966 in TX.
Donors: George Kozmetsky‡; Ronya Kozmetsky.
Foundation type: Independent foundation.
Financial data (yr. ended 12/31/04): Assets, $126,025,003 (M); expenditures, $4,605,284; qualifying distributions, $3,426,952; giving activities include $3,015,853 for 106 grants (high: $500,000; low: $2,000).
Purpose and activities: Grants to education, community, and medicine/health.
Fields of interest: Education, formal/general education; Higher education; Health care, equal rights; Medical research; Crime/violence prevention, abuse prevention; Crime/violence prevention, domestic violence; Crime/violence prevention, child abuse; Family services, domestic violence; Women.
Type of support: Program development; Conferences/seminars; Research; Matching/challenge support.
Limitations: Giving on a national basis. No support for organizations limited by race or religion. No grants to individuals, or for deficit financing, building or endowment funds, indirect costs, special events, disaster relief funds, student research projects, political lobbying, or equipment; no loans.
Publications: Grants list.
Application information: Unsolicited full proposals will not be accepted. Proposals will be invited by the foundation following positive response to Letter if Inquiry. Application form required.
Initial approach: Submit an electronic letter of inquiry form availablre on foundation Web site
Copies of proposal: 1
Deadline(s): None
Board meeting date(s): Mar., June and Oct.
Final notification: Decision on Letter of Inquiry within two weeks
Officers and Trustees:* Gregory A. Kozmetsky,* Chair., Pres. and Treas.; Christina C. Collier, Exec. V.P.; Cynthia H. Kozmetsky,* V.P. and Secy.; Nadya Kozmetsky Scott,* V.P.; Coleith Molstad, Cont.; Lois J. Cox; Aaron W. Kozmetsky; Ronya Kozmetsky; Michael E. Patrick; Mary Beth Rogers; G. Taylor Scott.
Number of staff: 4 full-time professional; 1 part-time professional; 1 full-time support.
EIN: 746077587
Selected grants: The following grants were reported in 2004.
$787,500 to University of Texas, Austin, TX. 3 grants: $37,500 (For operating program support for RGK Center for Philanthropy and Community Service), $250,000 (For RGK Center for Philanthropy and Community Service), $500,000 (For RGK Center for Philanthropy and Community Service).
$221,381 to University of Texas Health Science Center, San Antonio, TX. For research project, The Role of Hyaluronic Molecular Size in the Stiffness of Fibromyalgia Syndrome.
$125,000 to Austin Independent School District, Austin, TX. For technology and leadership team to direct and monitor The Austin Blueprint: To Leave Behind no Child designed to raise student achievement in chronically under-performing and low-performing schools.
$100,000 to KIPP Austin College Preparatory School, Austin, TX. For Computer Lab in honor of Barbara and Charles Hurwitz.
$86,250 to Santa Monica-Malibu Education Foundation, Santa Monica, CA. For Institute for Learning's New Instructional Leadership Program to build instructional capacity within the district.
$75,000 to Greenlights for Nonprofit Success, Austin, TX. For capacity building.
$68,461 to Center for Child Protection and Family Support, DC. For Bridge project.
$65,000 to Para Los Ninos, Los Angeles, CA. For SPIN/Video Interactive Guidance training program for Child Development Center and after-school program teachers.

9147
Sid W. Richardson Foundation ▼
309 Main St.
Fort Worth, TX 76102 (817) 336-0494
Contact: Valleau Wilkie, Jr., Exec. V.P.
FAX: (817) 332-2176; URL: http://www.sidrichardson.org

Established in 1947 in TX.
Donors: Sid W. Richardson‡; and associated companies.
Foundation type: Independent foundation.
Financial data (yr. ended 12/31/05): Assets, $372,996,901 (M); expenditures, $14,101,755; qualifying distributions, $13,983,227; giving activities include $10,754,360 for 111 grants (high: $500,000; low: $2,000; average: $5,000–$75,000), and $782,242 for 1 foundation-administered program.
Purpose and activities: Giving primarily for education, health, the arts, and social service programs.
Fields of interest: Performing arts; Arts; Higher education; Education; Health care; Health organizations, association; Human services.
Type of support: General/operating support; Continuing support; Building/renovation; Equipment; Land acquisition; Endowments; Program development; Conferences/seminars; Publication; Seed money; Research; Matching/challenge support.
Limitations: Giving limited to TX, with emphasis on Fort Worth for the arts and human services, and statewide for health and education. No support for religious organizations. No grants to individuals, or for scholarships or fellowships; no loans (except for program-related investments).
Publications: Annual report (including application guidelines); Financial statement; Grants list.
Application information: Application form required.
Initial approach: Letter
Copies of proposal: 1
Deadline(s): Jan. 15
Board meeting date(s): Spring and fall
Final notification: Varies
Officers and Directors:* Edward P. Bass,* Pres.; Valleau Wilkie, Jr., Exec. V.P.; Lee M. Bass,* V.P. and Treas.; Sid R. Bass,* V.P.; Dee Steer, Secy.; M.E. Chappell,* Treas.; Nancy Lee Bass, V.P. Emeritus.
Number of staff: 5 full-time professional.
EIN: 756015828
Selected grants: The following grants were reported in 2004.

$1,250,000 to Fort Worth Symphony Orchestra Association, Fort Worth, TX. 3 grants: $250,000 (For additional support), $500,000 (For Fort Worth Symphony Concerts), $500,000 (For general support for Fort Worth Symphony Concerts).

$1,000,000 to Cook Childrens Medical Center, Fort Worth, TX. For construction of new patient pavilion.

$300,000 to Van Cliburn Foundation, Fort Worth, TX. For Cliburn Competition.

$265,000 to University of Texas Southwestern Medical Center, Dallas, TX. For establishment of clinic at Moncrief Cancer Center in Fort Worth for evaluation and treatment of cancer pain in collaboration with existing program in Dallas.

$250,000 to Fort Worth Art Association, Fort Worth, TX. For operating support for Modern Art Museum.

$250,000 to Texas Wesleyan University, School of Law, Fort Worth, TX. Toward expansion of law school library.

$200,000 to Scott and White Memorial Hospital and Scott, Sherwood and Brindley Foundation, Temple, TX. For establishment of computerized radiology network for medical care in rural Central Texas.

$175,000 to Baylor College of Medicine, Houston, TX. For program in internal medicine.

9148

The Riddle Foundation ◆ ☆
9400 FM 1960 Rd. W.
Houston, TX 77070-6211 (281) 444-9090
Contact: Don R. Riddle, Pres.

Established in 1994 in TX.
Donor: Don R. Riddle.
Foundation type: Independent foundation.
Financial data (yr. ended 12/31/05): Assets, $298,411 (M); expenditures, $532,260; qualifying distributions, $530,000; giving activities include $530,000 for grants.
Purpose and activities: Giving for community development and education.
Fields of interest: Higher education; Education; Human services; Community development; Foundations (private grantmaking).
Type of support: General/operating support; Scholarship funds.
Limitations: Giving primarily in Houston, TX.
Application information:
  Initial approach: Letter
  Deadline(s): Oct. 1
Officers and Directors: * Don R. Riddle,* Pres.; Jenny L. Riddle,* V.P.; Stacy Riddle-Baumgartner,* Secy.; Todd Arlis Riddle,* Treas.
EIN: 760455477

9149

A. W. Riter, Jr. Family Foundation ◆ ☆
110 N. College, Ste. 1406
Tyler, TX 75702-7244

Established in 1997 in TX.
Donors: A.W. Riter, Jr.; Betty Jo B. Riter.
Foundation type: Independent foundation.
Financial data (yr. ended 12/31/05): Assets, $9,255,514 (M); expenditures, $735,762; qualifying distributions, $530,250; giving activities

include $530,250 for 31 grants (high: $130,000; low: $1,000).
Purpose and activities: Giving primarily for education.
Fields of interest: Elementary/secondary education; Higher education; Medical research; Human services; Children/youth, services.
Type of support: General/operating support.
Limitations: Applications not accepted. Giving primarily in Tyler, TX. No grants to individuals.
Application information: Contributes only to pre-selected organizations.
Officers: A.W. Riter III, Pres.; Betty Jo B. Riter, V.P.; Melvin B. Lovelady, Secy.-Treas.
Director: Cynthia S. Riter.
EIN: 752707712
Selected grants: The following grants were reported in 2005.
$50,000 to Regional East Texas Food Bank, Tyler, TX.
$20,100 to Advanced Placement Strategies, Dallas, TX.
$15,000 to Azleway Boys Ranch, Tyler, TX.
$10,000 to Tyler Museum of Art, Tyler, TX.
$10,000 to University of Texas System, Austin, TX.
$6,500 to Brook Hill School, Bullard, TX.
$5,950 to Literacy Council of Tyler, Tyler, TX.
$1,200 to All Saints Episcopal School, Tyler, TX.
$1,000 to New Mexico Military Institute, Roswell, NM.
$1,000 to Tyler Junior College, Tyler, TX.

9150

The Roach Foundation, Inc. ◆
100 Throckmorton St., Ste. 480
Fort Worth, TX 76102

Established in 1999 in TX.
Donors: John V. Roach; Jean W. Roach.
Foundation type: Independent foundation.
Financial data (yr. ended 12/31/04): Assets, $4,495,566 (M); gifts received, $500,000; expenditures, $467,166; qualifying distributions, $325,481; giving activities include $325,481 for 98 grants (high: $152,350; low: $25).
Purpose and activities: Giving primarily for higher education.
Fields of interest: Performing arts, orchestra (symphony); Arts; Higher education; Education; Health care; Human services; Children/youth, services; Christian agencies & churches.
Limitations: Applications not accepted. Giving primarily in TX. No grants to individuals.
Application information: Contributes only to pre-selected organizations.
Officers: John V. Roach, Pres.; Jean W. Roach, V.P.; Amy Roach Callaway, Secy.; Lori Anne Roach, Treas.; Lou Ann Blaylock, Exec. Dir.
EIN: 752848244

9151

Dora Roberts Foundation
c/o JPMorgan Chase Bank, N.A.
P.O. Box 2050
Fort Worth, TX 76113 (817) 884-4772
Contact: Konnie Darrow, Off., JPMorgan Chase Bank, N.A.
FAX: (817) 884-4294;
E-mail: konnie.darrow@jpmorgan.com

Established in 1948 in TX.

Donor: Dora Roberts†.
Foundation type: Independent foundation.
Financial data (yr. ended 6/30/05): Assets, $43,501,259 (M); expenditures, $2,512,062; qualifying distributions, $2,058,410; giving activities include $2,011,500 for 38 grants (high: $200,000; low: $5,000).
Fields of interest: Arts; Education; Health care; Human services.
Type of support: General/operating support.
Limitations: Giving limited to TX, with emphasis on Big Spring.
Application information: Application form not required.
  Initial approach: Proposal
  Copies of proposal: 1
  Deadline(s): Sept. 30
  Board meeting date(s): Annually in Oct. or Nov.
  Final notification: End of Dec.
Advisory Board: J.P. Taylor, Chair.; Lisa Canter; Mrs. Horace Garrett; Bob Moore; Sue Garrett Partee; R.H. Weaver.
Trustee: JPMorgan Chase Bank, N.A.
EIN: 756013899
Selected grants: The following grants were reported in 2004.
$200,000 to Salvation Army of Big Spring, Big Spring, TX.
$190,000 to Howard College, Big Spring, TX.
$65,000 to University of Texas of the Permian Basin, Odessa, TX.
$60,500 to YMCA of Big Spring, Big Spring, TX.
$50,000 to Rape Crisis Services of Big Spring, Big Spring, TX.
$50,000 to YMCA of Midland, Midland, TX.
$30,000 to Boy Scouts of America, Buffalo Trail Council, Big Spring, TX.
$25,000 to Midland College Foundation, Midland, TX.
$10,000 to Big Brothers Big Sisters of Midland, Midland, TX.
$10,000 to High Sky Childrens Ranch, Midland, TX.

9152

The David Robinson Foundation ◆
P.O. Box 691207
San Antonio, TX 78269
FAX: (210) 696-7754; *URL:* http://www.theadmiral.com/drf.htm

Established in 1992 in TX.
Donors: David Robinson; Valerie Robinson; William E. Simon Foundation.
Foundation type: Independent foundation.
Financial data (yr. ended 8/31/05): Assets, $1,312,170 (M); gifts received, $488,370; expenditures, $1,265,109; qualifying distributions, $1,261,538; giving activities include $1,258,000 for 6 grants.
Purpose and activities: Support primarily to local organizations that aid the spiritual needs of families, feed the hungry, and provide mothers with baby supplies.
Fields of interest: Agriculture; Human services; Family services, single parents.
Limitations: Applications not accepted. Giving primarily in San Antonio, TX.
Application information: Contributes only to pre-selected organizations.
Directors: David Robinson; Valerie H. Robinson.
EIN: 742644713
Selected grants: The following grants were reported in 2003.

$845,679 to Carver Academy, San Antonio, TX. 4
grants: $359,516, $100,000, $321,214,
$64,949

$500,000 to Carver Development Board, San
Antonio, TX.

$100,000 to Mana Christian Ohana, Kamuela, HI.

$100,000 to Oak Hills Church of Christ, San
Antonio, TX.

$100,000 to United States Naval Academy
Foundation, Annapolis, MD.

$6,000 to Community Recreation Center, Mount
Pleasant, MI.

$1,000 to Palo Alto College, San Antonio, TX.

9153
The Rockjensen Foundation, Inc. ✧ ☆
76 Golden Scroll Cir.
The Woodlands, TX 77382

Established in 2004 in TX.
Donors: Douglas Rock; Julie Rock.
Foundation type: Operating foundation.
Financial data (yr. ended 12/31/05): Assets,
$7,620,828 (M); expenditures, $406,000;
qualifying distributions, $406,000; giving activities
include $406,000 for 12 grants (high: $300,000;
low: $1,000).
Fields of interest: Human services; Christian
agencies & churches.
Limitations: Applications not accepted. Giving
primarily in TX. No grants to individuals.
Application information: Contributes only to
pre-selected organizations.
Directors: Gary M. Howell; Douglas Rock; Julie
Rock.
EIN: 201823029

9154
Rockwell Fund, Inc. ▼
770 S. Post Oak Ln., Ste. 525
Houston, TX 77056 (713) 629-9022
Contact: Judy Ahlgrim, Grants Admin.
FAX: (713) 629-7702;
E-mail: jahlgrim@rockfund.org; URL: http://
www.rockfund.org

Trust established in 1931; incorporated in 1949 in
TX; merged with Rockwell Brothers Endowment, Inc.
in 1981.
Donor: Members of the James M. Rockwell family.
Foundation type: Independent foundation.
Financial data (yr. ended 12/31/04): Assets,
$115,996,973 (M); gifts received, $1,000;
expenditures, $5,900,557; qualifying distributions,
$4,967,527; giving activities include $4,158,880
for 125 grants (high: $100,000; low: $500;
average: $15,000–$50,000), and $146,389 for 3
loans/program-related investments.
Purpose and activities: Giving primarily for
charitable, human services, educational, health,
arts and humanities, environmental, historic
preservation, and civic purposes.
Fields of interest: Visual arts; Museums; Performing
arts; Historic preservation/historical societies; Arts;
Education, early childhood education; Child
development, education; Elementary school/
education; Secondary school/education; Adult
education—literacy, basic skills & GED; Libraries/
library science; Education, reading; Education;
Environment; Hospitals (general); Medical care,
rehabilitation; Nursing care; Health care; Health

organizations, association; AIDS; Crime/violence
prevention, youth; Human services; Children/youth,
services; Child development, services; Homeless,
human services; Aging; Disabilities, people with;
Homeless.
Type of support: General/operating support;
Continuing support; Management development/
capacity building; Capital campaigns; Building/
renovation; Equipment; Land acquisition;
Endowments; Program development;
Professorships; Seed money; Curriculum
development; Fellowships; Scholarship funds;
Technical assistance; Program evaluation;
Program-related investments/loans; Matching/
challenge support.
Limitations: Giving primarily in Houston, TX. No
grants to individuals or for medical or scientific
research projects, underwriting benefits, dinners,
galas, and fundraising special events, or mass
appeal solicitations; grants primarily awarded on a
year-to-year basis only.
Publications: Application guidelines; Grants list.
Application information: Please refer to the
foundation's Web site. Applicants should not submit
more than 1 proposal per year. Application form
required.
  Initial approach: Full proposal
  Copies of proposal: 1
  Deadline(s): None
  Board meeting date(s): Quarterly
  Final notification: After each quarterly meeting
Officers and Trustees:* R. Terry Bell,* C.E.O. and
Pres.; Margaret E. McConn,* V.P. and C.F.O.;
Barbara Bellatti,* Secy.; Bennie Green,* Treas.;
Gene Graham*.
Number of staff: 4 full-time professional; 2 full-time
support.
EIN: 746040258
Selected grants: The following grants were reported
in 2004.
$126,000 to South Texas College of Law, Houston,
TX. For expansion of general civil clinic and pro
bono work.
$115,000 to Inwood North Community Outreach
Program, Houston, TX. For executive director and
program director.
$100,000 to Briarwood-Brookwood, Brookshire, TX.
For continuing care program/facility.
$100,000 to Saint Agnes Academy, Houston, TX.
For centennial campaign.
$75,000 to Houston Community Health Centers,
Houston, TX. For renovation of Hahlo Street Clinic
and Robert Woods Johnson match.
$50,000 to Admiral Nimitz Foundation,
Fredericksburg, TX. For renovation of Nimitz Hotel
for museum.
$30,000 to Learning Center of North Texas, Fort
Worth, TX. For professional training for public
school educators.
$30,000 to Montrose Clinic, Houston, TX. For
Specialty Clinics Program.
$25,000 to Seniors Place, Houston, TX. For general
operating support.
$20,000 to Miller Theater Advisory Board, Houston,
TX. For Miller Outdoor Theater concession facility.

9155
The Rogers Foundation ✧
601 Chase Dr.
Tyler, TX 75701-9431
Contact: Robyn M. Rogers, Pres.
Application address: P.O. Box 8799, Tyler, TX
75711-8799

Established in 1986 in TX.
Donors: Robert M. Rogers†; Rogers Children's
Heritage Trust One; Rogers Children's Heritage Trust
Two; Rogers Granchildren's Heritage Trust.
Foundation type: Independent foundation.
Financial data (yr. ended 12/31/05): Assets,
$46,232,169 (M); gifts received, $420,000;
expenditures, $2,652,564; qualifying distributions,
$2,322,902; giving activities include $2,196,446
for 66 grants (high: $300,000; low: $1,000).
Purpose and activities: To promote education by
providing funds for schools, educational programs,
scholarships, and scholarship funds; support also
for Protestant organizations.
Fields of interest: Arts; Education, fund raising/fund
distribution; Elementary/secondary education;
Elementary school/education; Higher education;
Health care; Protestant agencies & churches;
Religion.
Type of support: General/operating support;
Building/renovation; Scholarship funds.
Limitations: Giving primarily in ID and TX. No grants
to individuals.
Publications: Informational brochure (including
application guidelines).
Application information: Application form required.
  Initial approach: Letter
  Copies of proposal: 1
  Deadline(s): Oct. 1
Officers and Directors:* Robyn M. Rogers,* Pres.;
Sheryl Rogers Palmer,* V.P.; Paul W. Powell,*
Treas.
Number of staff: 1 part-time professional.
EIN: 752143064
Selected grants: The following grants were reported
in 2005.
$300,000 to Hospice of East Texas, Tyler, TX.
$200,000 to Texas Christian University, Fort Worth,
TX.
$175,000 to Tyler Museum of Art, Tyler, TX.
$150,000 to East Texas Symphony Orchestra
Association, Tyler, TX.
$130,000 to Meals on Wheels Ministry, Tyler, TX.
$125,546 to East Texas Crisis Center, Tyler, TX.
$10,000 to Advocates for Survivors of Domestic
Violence, Hailey, ID.
$10,000 to American Red Cross, Tyler, TX.
$10,000 to University of Mary Hardin-Baylor, Belton,
TX.
$7,500 to Tyler Rose Museum, Tyler, TX.

9156
Russell H. Rogers Fund for the Arts ✧
(formerly Russell Hill Rogers Fund for the Arts)
c/o Bank of America, N.A.
P.O. Box 831041
Dallas, TX 75283-1041
Application address: c/o Jean Winchell, 4040
Broadway, Ste. 605, San Antonio, TX 78209,
tel.: (210) 826-8781

Established in 1986.
Foundation type: Independent foundation.
Financial data (yr. ended 12/31/05): Assets,
$15,012,293 (M); expenditures, $911,308;
qualifying distributions, $727,920; giving activities
include $720,000 for 27 grants (high: $105,716;
low: $1,000).
Purpose and activities: Support for the
encouragement and preservation of the creative and
performing arts.
Fields of interest: Museums; Performing arts; Arts.

Limitations: Giving limited to the San Antonio, TX, metropolitan area. No grants to individuals.
Application information: Application form not required.
  Deadline(s): None
Trustees: Frank P. Christian; Barbara S. Condos; Robert Lende; Allan G. Paterson, Jr.; Jean Rogers Winchell; Bank of America, N.A.
EIN: 742403914
Selected grants: The following grants were reported in 2005.
$100,000 to San Antonio Museum of Art, San Antonio, TX.
$97,550 to Lyric Opera of San Antonio, San Antonio, TX.
$45,000 to Arts San Antonio, San Antonio, TX.
$45,000 to Carver Development Board, San Antonio, TX.
$39,404 to San Antonio Symphony, San Antonio, TX.
$22,300 to San Antonio Chamber Music Society, San Antonio, TX.
$17,000 to Cactus Pear Music Festival, San Antonio, TX.
$13,000 to San Antonio International Keyboard Competition, San Antonio, TX.
$10,000 to Magik Childrens Theater, San Antonio, TX.
$7,900 to Childrens Fine Arts Series, San Antonio, TX.

9157
Marcus & Ann Rosenberg Foundation ◇
12020 Excelsior Way
Dallas, TX 75230-2243 (214) 934-1809

Established in 1986 in TX.
Donors: Ann Rosenberg; Marcus Rosenberg†; Steve Rosenberg.
Foundation type: Independent foundation.
Financial data (yr. ended 12/31/04): Assets, $2,278,290 (M); gifts received, $348,091; expenditures, $478,772; qualifying distributions, $448,996; giving activities include $436,801 for 14 + grants (high: $200,000).
Fields of interest: Historical activities; Elementary/secondary education; Higher education; Jewish federated giving programs; Jewish agencies & temples.
Limitations: Giving primarily in New York, NY, and Dallas, TX. No grants to individuals.
Application information: Application form not required.
  Initial approach: Letter
  Deadline(s): None
Officers and Directors:* Ann Rosenberg,* V.P.; Steve Rosenberg,* V.P.
EIN: 752141473

9158
The Rosewood Foundation ◇
500 Crescent Ct., Ste. 300
Dallas, TX 75201
Contact: C.W. Howell

Established in 2000 in TX.
Donor: The Rosewood Corp.
Foundation type: Independent foundation.
Financial data (yr. ended 12/31/04): Assets, $11,246 (M); gifts received, $965,000; expenditures, $976,631; qualifying distributions,

$977,366; giving activities include $977,366 for 180 grants (high: $100,000; low: $25).
Fields of interest: Arts; Education; Environment; Human services; Children/youth, services.
Type of support: General/operating support; Continuing support; Annual campaigns; Capital campaigns; Building/renovation; Program development; Research; Program evaluation; Employee matching gifts; Matching/challenge support.
Limitations: Applications not accepted. Giving primarily in TX. No support for direct funding of churches or schools. No grants to individuals.
Application information:
  Board meeting date(s): 4 times per year
Officers and Trustees:* Laurie Sands Harrison,* Pres.; Don W. Crisp,* V.P.; Schuyler B. Marshall IV; David K. Sands; Patrick B. Sands; Stephen H. Sands.
Number of staff: 1 part-time professional.
EIN: 752827470
Selected grants: The following grants were reported in 2003.
$142,857 to Dallas Center for the Performing Arts Foundation, Dallas, TX. For general support.
$100,625 to University of Texas Southwestern Medical Center, Dallas, TX. For general support.
$65,865 to Dallas Museum of Art, Dallas, TX. For general support.
$40,000 to Nature Conservancy of Texas, San Antonio, TX. For general support.
$12,000 to Parkland Foundation, Dallas, TX. For general support.
$5,000 to Junior Achievement of Dallas, Richardson, TX. For general support.
$1,250 to Turtle Creek Association, Dallas, TX. For general support.
$1,000 to Bryans House, Dallas, TX. For general support.
$1,000 to Wheatland Community Learning Center, Dallas, TX. For general support.
$300 to YMCA of Metropolitan Dallas, Dallas, TX. For general support.

9159
The Dale and Deborah Ross Foundation ◇
P.O. Box 17149
Sugar Land, TX 77496-7149

Established in 1997 in TX.
Donors: Deborah H. Ross; R. Dale Ross.
Foundation type: Independent foundation.
Financial data (yr. ended 12/31/05): Assets, $970,739 (M); gifts received, $1,310,062; expenditures, $513,433; qualifying distributions, $508,600; giving activities include $508,600 for 15 grants (high: $180,600; low: $500).
Fields of interest: Museums (art); Elementary/secondary education; Education, early childhood education; Higher education; Education; Protestant agencies & churches.
Limitations: Applications not accepted. Giving primarily in Houston, TX. No grants to individuals.
Application information: Contributes only to pre-selected organizations.
Officers: R. Dale Ross, Pres.; David J. Ross, V.P.; Michael A. Ross, V.P.; Deborah H. Ross, Secy.-Treas.
EIN: 760551779
Selected grants: The following grants were reported in 2005.
$100,000 to Young Life, Colorado Springs, CO.

$35,000 to Northland Christian School, Houston, TX.
$22,000 to Lifeline Chaplaincy, Houston, TX.
$1,000 to Tulane University, New Orleans, LA.

9160
Rowling Foundation ◇
420 Decker Dr.
Irving, TX 75062

Established in 2003 in TX.
Donors: Robert B. Rowling; Terry H. Rowling; TRT Holdings, Inc.
Foundation type: Independent foundation.
Financial data (yr. ended 12/31/05): Assets, $10,188,003 (M); gifts received, $10,980,401; expenditures, $2,043,188; qualifying distributions, $2,042,244; giving activities include $2,042,244 for 37 grants (high: $1,046,000; low: $100).
Fields of interest: Higher education; Human services; Christian agencies & churches.
Limitations: Applications not accepted. Giving primarily in TX, with some emphasis on Dallas. No grants to individuals.
Application information: Contributes only to pre-selected organizations.
Trustees: James D. Caldwell; William C. Dunlap; Robert B. Rowling; Robert B. Rowling, Jr.; Terry H. Rowling; Travis Blake Rowling.
EIN: 736351612

9161
RSMIS Foundation ◇
(formerly Robert S. and Marilyn I. Silverthorn Foundation)
c/o Frost Financial Services
P.O. Box 1315
Houston, TX 77251-1315
Application address: c/o Frost National Bank, P.O. Box 2845, Houston, TX, 77252; tel.: (713) 388-7854

Established in 1994 in TX.
Donors: Cody Carlson; Barbara Carlson; Kenneth Wahl Hatfield; James Floyd Allen; Fred J. Curry, Jr.; Sandra Hatfield; Sugar Creek Baptist Church.
Foundation type: Independent foundation.
Financial data (yr. ended 11/30/05): Assets, $7,870,376 (M); gifts received, $1,017,694; expenditures, $1,292,366; qualifying distributions, $1,275,008; giving activities include $1,222,000 for 6 grants (high: $562,000; low: $5,000).
Fields of interest: Higher education; Human services; Christian agencies & churches.
Limitations: Giving primarily in Houston, TX. No grants to individuals.
Application information:
  Initial approach: Proposal
  Deadline(s): None
Officers: Robert S. Silverthorn, Pres.; Marilyn Silverthorn, V.P.
Directors: Doug Hodo; Daniel L. Mark.
EIN: 760421802
Selected grants: The following grants were reported in 2003.
$500,000 to Houston Baptist University, Houston, TX. For general support.
$422,535 to Campus Crusade for Christ International, Orlando, FL. For general support.
$205,000 to Houston Livestock Show and Rodeo, Houston, TX. For scholarships.

$146,945 to Alzheimers Association, Houston, TX. For general support.

$140,000 to Campus Crusade for Christ, Newport News, VA. For general support.

$120,250 to Campus Crusade for Christ, Houston, TX. For general support.

$96,758 to Girls Inc. of Metropolitan Dallas, Dallas, TX. For general support.

$60,000 to Focus on the Family, Colorado Springs, CO. For general support.

$25,000 to Alliance Defense Fund, Scottsdale, AZ. For general support.

$25,000 to Precept Ministries International, Chattanooga, TN. For general support.

9162

The Jerry and Maury Rubenstein Foundation ◇ ☆

2330 Holmes Rd.
Houston, TX 77051

Established in 2000 in TX.

Donor: Texas Pipe & Supply Co., Inc.
Foundation type: Independent foundation.
Financial data (yr. ended 5/31/06): Assets, $4,731,692 (M); gifts received, $1,491,137; expenditures, $353,200; qualifying distributions, $350,200; giving activities include $350,200 for grants.
Fields of interest: Cancer research; Crime/law enforcement, single organization support; Children/youth, services; Family services; Jewish agencies & temples.
Limitations: Applications not accepted. Giving primarily in Houston, TX. No grants to individuals.
Application information: Contributes only to pre-selected organizations.
Trustees: Jerry Rubenstein; Maury Rubenstein.
EIN: 316645608
Selected grants: The following grants were reported in 2005.

$85,000 to M. D. Anderson Cancer Center Outreach Corporation, Houston, TX.

$50,000 to University of Texas Health Science Center, Houston, TX.

$25,000 to Baylor College of Medicine, Houston, TX. For pediatric urology research program.

$20,000 to Jewish Federation of Greater Houston, Houston, TX. For general support.

$8,500 to Bellaire Police Assistance Program, Bellaire, TX. For general support.

$4,124 to Bellaire Police Department, Bellaire, TX. For general support.

$2,600 to Child Advocates, Houston, TX. For general support.

$2,500 to Family to Family Network, Houston, TX. For general support.

$1,000 to Texas Childrens Hospital, Houston, TX. For general support.

$500 to Houston Fire Museum, Houston, TX. For general support.

9163

Earl C. Sams Foundation, Inc. ◇

101 N. Shoreline Dr., Ste. 602
Corpus Christi, TX 78401 (361) 888-6485
Contact: Bruce S. Hawn, C.E.O.
FAX: (361) 884-4241; URL: http://www.ecsams.org

Incorporated in 1946 in NY; reincorporated in 1988 in TX.

Donor: Earl C. Sams†.
Foundation type: Independent foundation.
Financial data (yr. ended 12/31/04): Assets, $30,172,621 (M); expenditures, $1,486,723; qualifying distributions, $1,206,111; giving activities include $956,100 for 45 grants (high: $103,000; low: $2,000).
Purpose and activities: Giving support for health care, youth and community development, and the environment.
Fields of interest: Environment; Health care; Children/youth, services; Community development.
Type of support: General/operating support; Continuing support; Annual campaigns; Building/renovation; Equipment; Program development; In-kind gifts; Matching/challenge support.
Limitations: Giving primarily in southern TX. No grants to individuals.
Publications: Application guidelines; Grants list; Program policy statement (including application guidelines).
Application information: Application form available from foundation Web site. Application form required.
  Initial approach: Proposal
  Copies of proposal: 1
  Deadline(s): 4 weeks prior to board meeting
  Board meeting date(s): Mar., June, and Nov.
Officers and Directors:* Susan Hawn Yuras,* Chair. and V.P.; Bruce Sams Hawn,* C.E.O. and Pres.; Susan Ohnmacht, Secy. and Admin. Mgr.; Nancy E. Hawn.
Number of staff: 4 full-time professional.
EIN: 741463151

9164

San Angelo Area Foundation ☆

2201 Sherwood Way, Ste. 205
San Angelo, TX 76901 (325) 947-7071
Contact: Matt Lewis, C.E.O.
FAX: (325) 947-7322;
E-mail: infosaaf@saafound.org; Additional E-mail: mlewis@saafound.org; URL: http://www.saafound.org

Established in 2002 in TX by the San Angelo Health Foundation, a private foundation.

Foundation type: Community foundation.
Financial data (yr. ended 12/31/05): Assets, $17,548,272 (M); gifts received, $5,124,961; expenditures, $810,328; giving activities include $512,036 for 66 grants (high: $25,000; low: $360).
Purpose and activities: The foundation seeks to improve quality of life in the San Angelo, Texas, area by awarding grants to nonprofits and scholarships to individuals.
Fields of interest: Arts; Elementary/secondary education; Higher education; Human services; Community development.
Type of support: Scholarships—to individuals.
Limitations: Giving limited to the 17-county San Angelo, TX, area: Concho, Coke, Crockett, Glasscock, Irion, Kimble, Llano, Mason, McCullough, Menard, Reagan, Runnels, San Saba, Schleicher, Sterling, Sutton, and Tom Green. No support for umbrella funding organizations for distribution of the requested funds at their own discretion. No grants for endowments, debt retirement, deficit financing, reduction of an operating deficit or liquidation of debt, or replenishment of resources used to pay for such purposes; or for courtesy advertising, benefit tickets, telephone solicitations.

Publications: Annual report; Informational brochure; Newsletter.
Application information: Visit foundation Web site for full application guidelines and requirements, including downloadable application form for invited formal proposal. Application form required.
  Initial approach: Mail or e-mail 1- to 2-page executive summary
  Copies of proposal: 1
  Deadline(s): Sept. 1 for executive summary; Sept. 30 for invited formal proposal; Mar. 15 for scholarships
  Board meeting date(s): Quarterly, 1st Thurs. of 2nd month of quarter
  Final notification: Dec. 1
Officers and Board Members:* Frank Rose,* Chair.; James Carter,* Vice-Chair.; Matt Lewis, C.E.O. and Pres.; J. Michael Anderson, Secy.-Treas.; Sonny Cleere; Gary Cox; Al Elliott; James Hindman; Katie Mertz Johnson; Deanna Mayfield; Betty Miller; Richey Oliver; Bob Pfluger; Allen Price; Doris Rousselot; F.L. "Steve" Stephens.
Number of staff: 2 full-time professional; 1 full-time support.
EIN: 731634145

9165

San Angelo Health Foundation

P.O. Box 3550
San Angelo, TX 76902-3550 (325) 486-0185
Contact: Tom Early, Pres.
FAX: (325) 486-1125;
E-mail: sahf.tx@sahfoundation.org; URL: http://www.sahfoundation.org

Established in 1995 in TX.

Foundation type: Independent foundation.
Financial data (yr. ended 12/31/05): Assets, $0 (M); expenditures, $2,975,829; qualifying distributions, $2,740,661; giving activities include $2,280,528 for 37 grants (high: $600,000; low: $400), and $215,000 for 2 employee matching gifts.
Purpose and activities: The foundation seeks to enhance the quality of life for the people of the San Angelo, TX, area.
Fields of interest: Community development.
Type of support: General/operating support; Capital campaigns; Building/renovation; Equipment; Land acquisition; Emergency funds; Program development; Conferences/seminars; Seed money; Research; Technical assistance; Program evaluation; Matching/challenge support.
Limitations: Giving limited to San Angelo and the Concho Valley, TX, area. No support for religious organizations for religious purposes. No grants to individuals, or for fundraising events, operating deficits or debt retirement.
Publications: Annual report.
Application information: See foundation Web site for application guidelines. Application form not required.
  Initial approach: Proposal
  Copies of proposal: 2
  Deadline(s): 3 to 4 months prior to when funds are needed
  Board meeting date(s): Quarterly
  Final notification: 1 to 3 months
Officers and Trustees:* T. Richey Oliver,* Chair.; Robert S. Patyrak, M.D., Vice-Chair.; Tom Early, Pres.; Mike Boyd,* Secy.; Hugh Lamar Stone III, Treas.; Marilyn Aboussie; George Alexander; Rick Dehoyos; O. Sterling Gillis, M.D.; Sande Vincent

Harrison; Karen Pfluger; Joanne Rice; F.L. Stephens; Joe B. Wilkinson, M.D.
Number of staff: 2 full-time professional.
EIN: 751315145
Selected grants: The following grants were reported in 2004.
$500,000 to YMCA of San Angelo, San Angelo, TX.
$308,393 to Angelo State University, San Angelo, TX. 3 grants: $79,047, $219,106, $10,240
$125,000 to San Angelo Area Foundation, San Angelo, TX.
$87,462 to Adult Day Care of San Angelo, San Angelo, TX. 2 grants: $21,882, $65,580
$80,000 to Library Club of Menard, Menard, TX.
$70,000 to Volunteer Services Council, Harlingen, TX.
$3,500 to Salvation Army, Plainview, TX.

9166
San Antonio Area Foundation
110 Broadway, Ste. 230
San Antonio, TX 78205 (210) 225-2243
Contact: Clarence R. "Reggie" Williams, C.E.O.; For grant applications: Lydia Rodriguez, Prog. Off., Discretionary Funds
FAX: (210) 225-1980; E-mail: info@saafdn.org; Grant application tel.: (210) 228-3753 and E-mail: lrodriguez@saafdn.org; URL: http://www.saafdn.org

Established in 1964 in TX.
Foundation type: Community foundation.
Financial data (yr. ended 12/31/05): Assets, $123,604,277 (M); gifts received, $18,628,820; expenditures, $16,510,392; giving activities include $13,816,348 for grants, and $658,876 for 329 grants to individuals (high: $25,310; low: $250).
Purpose and activities: The foundation seeks to help donors achieve their charitable goals for the greater benefit of the community.
Fields of interest: Media/communications; Visual arts; Museums; Performing arts; Performing arts, dance; Performing arts, theater; Historic preservation/historical societies; Arts; Education, research; Education, early childhood education; Child development, education; Higher education; Medical school/education; Nursing school/ education; Adult/continuing education; Adult education—literacy, basic skills & GED; Education, reading; Education; Environment, natural resources; Environment; Animal welfare; Animals/wildlife, preservation/protection; Reproductive health, family planning; Medical care, rehabilitation; Health care; Substance abuse, services; Health organizations, association; Cancer; Heart & circulatory diseases; Alcoholism; Diabetes; Medical research, institute; Cancer research; Heart & circulatory research; AIDS research; Crime/ violence prevention, domestic violence; Disasters, Hurricane Katrina; Children/youth, services; Child development, services; Family services; Residential/custodial care, hospices; Aging, centers/services; Homeless, human services; Human services; Community development; Computer science; Religion.
Type of support: General/operating support; Continuing support; Annual campaigns; Building/ renovation; Equipment; Land acquisition; Emergency funds; Program development; Professorships; Publication; Seed money; Curriculum development; Scholarship funds; Research; Program-related investments/loans;

Scholarships—to individuals; Matching/challenge support.
Limitations: Giving limited to Bexar County, TX, and surrounding counties, except when otherwise specified by donor. No support for individual churches, congregations, or parishes (unless projects benefit community at large). No grants to individuals (except for designated scholarship funds), or for debt reduction, operating deficits, endowment funds, or salaries for full-time regular employees.
Publications: Application guidelines; Annual report; Financial statement; Grants list; Informational brochure; Newsletter.
Application information: Visit foundation Web site for applications and specific guidelines per grant type. The foundation offers grant information meetings; reservations must be made via e-mail. Faxed applications are not accepted. Scholarship applications must be submitted to Bexar County Scholarship Clearinghouse, unless specifically designated by donor. Application form required.
Initial approach: Complete online application and submit hard copy application packet
Copies of proposal: 12
Deadline(s): Nov. 15
Board meeting date(s): Bimonthly
Final notification: May
Officers and Directors:* Pat L. Wilson,* Chair.; C. Nanette Clare, M.D.*, Vice-Chair.; Clarence R. "Reggie" Williams, C.E.O. and Pres.; J. Robert Mehall,* Secy.; Joe Lozano,* Treas.; Michelle Cox, Cont.; Richard E. Goldsmith, Legal Counsel; William Fisher, Legal Counsel; Mindi Alterman; J. David Bamberger; John E. Banks, Jr.; William T. Bayern; Raymond Carvajal; Charles Cotrell, Ph.D.; Sarah Harte; Edward B. Kelley; Claudia Ladensohn; Joe Linson; Laura McNutt; Conrad J. Netting IV; Ommy Strauch.
Trustee Banks: Bank of America, N.A.; Bank One, Texas, N.A.; Broadway National Bank; Frost National Bank; Jefferson State Bank; JPMorgan Chase Bank, N.A.; Wells Fargo Bank, N.A.; Merrill Lynch Trust Co.
Number of staff: 11 full-time professional; 2 full-time support.
EIN: 746065414

9167
Don A. Sanders Family Foundation ◇ ☆
3100 Chase Twr.
Houston, TX 77002 (713) 250-4213

Established in 1997 in TX.
Donor: Don A. Sanders.
Foundation type: Independent foundation.
Financial data (yr. ended 12/31/05): Assets, $167,071 (M); gifts received, $533,514; expenditures, $512,975; qualifying distributions, $509,350; giving activities include $509,350 for grants.
Purpose and activities: Giving for Christian churches and organizations, children's services, education, and for health and human services.
Fields of interest: Arts; Elementary/secondary education; Higher education; Hospitals (specialty); Recreation; Human services; American Red Cross; Children/youth, services; Philanthropy/voluntarism; Christian agencies & churches.
Limitations: Applications not accepted. Giving primarily in Houston, TX. No grants to individuals.
Application information: Contributes only to pre-selected organizations.

Officers: Don A. Sanders, Pres.; Ben T. Morris, V.P.; Walter P. Zivley, Secy.; Jay F. Rea, Treas.
EIN: 760537031
Selected grants: The following grants were reported in 2003.
$25,000 to Kinkaid School, Houston, TX.
$15,000 to Texas Childrens Hospital, Houston, TX.
$10,000 to Houston Ear Research Foundation, Houston, TX.
$10,000 to Rise School of Houston, Houston, TX.
$10,000 to Sam Houston State University, Huntsville, TX.
$10,000 to Special Olympics of Texas, Austin, TX.
$10,000 to University of Louisiana at Lafayette Foundation, Lafayette, LA.
$7,500 to Child Advocates, Houston, TX.
$7,000 to Citizens for Animal Protection, Houston, TX.
$5,000 to Emery/Weiner Center for Jewish Education, Houston, TX.

9168
Sarofim Foundation ▼ ◇
P.O. Box 52830
Houston, TX 77052-2830 (713) 654-4484
Contact: Fayez Sarofim, Tr.

Established in 1968 in TX.
Donors: Fayez Sarofim; Louisa Stude Sarofim.
Foundation type: Independent foundation.
Financial data (yr. ended 6/30/05): Assets, $21,966,341 (M); gifts received, $165,079; expenditures, $3,905,409; qualifying distributions, $3,896,100; giving activities include $3,896,100 for 9 grants (high: $1,000,000; low: $8,000).
Purpose and activities: Giving primarily for education and art museums.
Fields of interest: Museums (art); Higher education, university; Education; Cancer.
Type of support: Building/renovation.
Limitations: Giving primarily in NY and Houston, TX. No grants to individuals, or for scholarships programs.
Application information: Application form not required.
Initial approach: Letter
Deadline(s): None
Trustees: Christopher B. Sarofim; Fayez Sarofim; Raye G. White.
EIN: 237065248
Selected grants: The following grants were reported in 2005.
$2,000,000 to Rumsey Hall School, Washington Depot, CT. For capital campaign.
$500,000 to Baylor Medical Foundation, Department of Pediatrics, Houston, TX. For Texas Children's Cancer Center.
$200,000 to Archdiocese of Galveston-Houston, Houston, TX. For capital campaign.
$200,000 to Awty International School, Houston, TX. For capital campaign.
$200,000 to Harvard University, Business School, Cambridge, MA. For Fellowship Fund.
$200,000 to University of Houston-University Park, Houston, TX.
$150,000 to Saint Thomas High School, Houston, TX. For capital campaign.
$100,000 to Arbor School, Houston, TX.
$25,000 to Saint Georges School, Newport, RI. For Fund Drive.
$10,000 to Regis School of the Sacred Heart, Houston, TX. For capital campaign.

9169
Louisa Stude Sarofim Foundation ✧
1001 Fannin St., Ste. 4700
Houston, TX 77002

Established in 1991.
Foundation type: Independent foundation.
Financial data (yr. ended 12/31/03): Assets, $25,812,097 (M); expenditures, $1,175,530; qualifying distributions, $1,130,562; giving activities include $1,110,000 for 11 grants (high: $310,000; low: $25,000).
Purpose and activities: Giving primarily for the arts.
Fields of interest: Performing arts, dance; Performing arts, opera; Arts; Education; Eye diseases; Christian agencies & churches.
Limitations: Applications not accepted. Giving primarily in NM, NY, and TX. No grants to individuals.
Application information: Contributes only to pre-selected organizations.
Trustees: Mary L. Porter; Allison Sarofim; Christopher Sarofim; Louisa S. Sarofim.
EIN: 760347329

9170
Scaler Foundation, Inc. ✧
800 Gessner Rd., Ste. 1260
Houston, TX 77024-4276

Incorporated in 1954 in TX.
Donor: Eric Boissonnas.
Foundation type: Independent foundation.
Financial data (yr. ended 12/31/05): Assets, $23,409,238 (M); expenditures, $1,423,091; qualifying distributions, $1,092,179; giving activities include $1,092,179 for 7 grants (high: $477,961; low: $15,000).
Purpose and activities: Giving primarily for arts and culture, and for children and social services.
Fields of interest: Arts; Higher education; Hospitals (general); Human services; Children, services; Federated giving programs.
International interests: France.
Type of support: General/operating support; Continuing support; Program development; Seed money.
Limitations: Applications not accepted. Giving primarily in the U.S. and France. No grants to individuals, or for building or endowment funds, research, scholarships, fellowships, or matching gifts; no loans.
Application information: Contributes only to pre-selected organizations.
Officers and Directors:* Catherine B. Coste,* Pres.; Nicolas N. Boissonnas,* V.P.; Marvin A. Wurzer,* Secy.-Treas.; Jacques C. Boissonnas.
EIN: 746036684

9171
Scarborough-Linebery Foundation ✧
(formerly Tom & Evelyn Linebery Foundation)
c/o A.M. Nunley
3300 N. A St., Ste. 8-125
Midland, TX 79705 (915) 682-0357

Established in 1976 in TX.
Donors: Tom Linebery; Evelyn Linebery.
Foundation type: Independent foundation.
Financial data (yr. ended 6/30/03): Assets, $12,792,116 (M); gifts received, $1,391,896; expenditures, $8,201,136; qualifying distributions,

$8,082,652; giving activities include $8,082,652 for 43 grants (high: $2,970,357; low: $300; average: $15,000–$125,000).
Purpose and activities: Giving primarily for health associations.
Fields of interest: Health organizations, association.
Type of support: General/operating support.
Limitations: Giving primarily in NM and western TX. No grants to individuals.
Publications: Informational brochure (including application guidelines).
Application information:
   Initial approach: Letter
   Deadline(s): None
   Board meeting date(s): Mar., June, Sept., and Dec.
Officers and Directors:* Doug Grimes,* Pres.; Bill Humphries,* V.P.; C.C. Matthews; Billy Tankersley; Joe Max Walker.
Number of staff: 1 full-time professional.
EIN: 510187878

9172
Schollmaier Foundation ✧
3904 Arlan Ln.
Fort Worth, TX 76109-4705

Established in 1978.
Donors: Edgar H. Schollmaier; Rama L. Schollmaier.
Foundation type: Independent foundation.
Financial data (yr. ended 12/31/05): Assets, $10,841,551 (M); gifts received, $139,013; expenditures, $999,034; qualifying distributions, $992,728; giving activities include $981,000 for 42 grants (high: $200,000; low: $500).
Purpose and activities: Giving primarily for education, arts and culture, and health care.
Fields of interest: Arts; Higher education; Education; Hospitals (general); Human services; Children/youth, services.
Limitations: Applications not accepted. Giving primarily in Fort Worth, TX. No grants to individuals.
Application information: Contributes only to pre-selected organizations.
Officers and Directors:* Rama L. Schollmaier, Pres. and Treas.; Edgar H. Schollmaier,* V.P.; Harry M. Brants.
EIN: 751577328

9173
Victor E. & Caroline Schutte Foundation ✧
c/o Bank of America, N.A.
P.O. Box 831041
Dallas, TX 75283-1041
Application address: c/o James J. Mueth, Bank of America, N.A., P.O. Box 419119, Kansas City, MO 64141-6119, tel.: (816) 979-7405

Established in 1993 in MO.
Donor: Caroline Schutte†.
Foundation type: Independent foundation.
Financial data (yr. ended 12/31/05): Assets, $15,768,155 (M); expenditures, $835,673; qualifying distributions, $726,565; giving activities include $641,668 for 13 grants (high: $400,000; low: $8,334).
Purpose and activities: Giving primarily for the arts, as well as for education, and health and social services.

Fields of interest: Arts; Education; Hospitals (general); Health organizations, association; Cancer, leukemia; Children/youth, services.
Type of support: Capital campaigns; Building/renovation; Endowments.
Limitations: Giving primarily in Kansas City, MO; some funding also in KS.
Application information:
   Initial approach: Letter (not exceeding 3 pages)
   Deadline(s): None
Trustees: Bank of America, N.A.; Stinson Morrison Hecker, LLP.
EIN: 431661684

9174
William E. Scott Foundation
801 Cherry St., Ste. 2000
Fort Worth, TX 76102
Contact: Raymond B. Kelly III, Pres.

Incorporated in 1960 in TX.
Donor: William E. Scott†.
Foundation type: Independent foundation.
Financial data (yr. ended 5/31/06): Assets, $20,052,464 (M); expenditures, $1,118,243; qualifying distributions, $958,060; giving activities include $945,000 for 51 grants (high: $87,500; low: $1,000).
Purpose and activities: Giving for programs in the arts, education, health, and human services.
Fields of interest: Performing arts; Arts; Child development, education; Elementary school/education; Secondary school/education; Health care; Health organizations, association; Children/youth, services; Child development, services.
Type of support: Continuing support; Annual campaigns; Capital campaigns; Building/renovation; Equipment; Program development.
Limitations: Giving limited to TX, with special emphasis on the Fort Worth-Tarrant County, TX, area. No grants to individuals or for endowments or debt reduction.
Publications: Application guidelines.
Application information: Application form not required.
   Initial approach: Letter
   Copies of proposal: 1
   Deadline(s): None
   Board meeting date(s): As required
   Final notification: By mail, within 60-90 days
Officer and Director:* Raymond B. Kelly III,* Pres.
Number of staff: 1 part-time support.
EIN: 756024661
Selected grants: The following grants were reported in 2005.
$105,000 to All Saints Health Foundation, Fort Worth, TX.
$100,000 to Fort Worth Academy for the Education of Children and Youth, Fort Worth, TX.
$75,000 to All Church Home for Children, Fort Worth, TX.
$75,000 to All Saints Episcopal School, Fort Worth, TX.
$50,000 to Fort Worth Symphony Orchestra, Fort Worth, TX.
$35,000 to Alliance for Children, Fort Worth, TX.
$25,000 to Lena Pope Home, Fort Worth, TX.
$20,000 to Van Cliburn Foundation, Fort Worth, TX.
$10,000 to Fort Worth Academy of Fine Arts, Fort Worth, TX.
$5,000 to National Jewish Medical and Research Center, Denver, CO.

9175
Scurlock Foundation
3355 W. Alabama St., Ste. 630
Houston, TX 77098
Contact: Kathy Munger, Admin.
FAX: (713) 222-0419; *URL:* http://
www.scurlockfoundation.org

Incorporated in 1954 in TX.
Donors: E.C. Scurlock†; Mrs. E.C. Scurlock†;
Scurlock Oil Co.; D.E. Farnsworth†; Jack S. Blanton,
Sr.; Mrs. Jack S. Blanton†; and other members of
the Blanton family.
Foundation type: Independent foundation.
Financial data (yr. ended 12/31/04): Assets,
$38,637,498 (M); gifts received, $1,227,096;
expenditures, $2,385,124; qualifying distributions,
$2,066,760; giving activities include $2,036,447
for 224 grants.
Purpose and activities: Emphasis on hospitals,
secondary and higher education, church-related
institutions, and arts and cultural programs; support
also for health agencies, social services, and youth
agencies.
Fields of interest: Museums; Performing arts; Arts;
Elementary/secondary education; Higher education;
Education; Hospitals (general); Health care; Health
organizations, association; Medical research,
institute; Human services; Children/youth, services;
Public affairs; Protestant agencies & churches;
Religion.
Type of support: General/operating support;
Continuing support; Annual campaigns; Capital
campaigns; Building/renovation; Land acquisition;
Endowments; Emergency funds; Research;
Matching/challenge support.
Limitations: Giving primarily in TX, with emphasis on
the Houston area. No grants to individuals, or for
scholarships or fellowships; no loans.
Publications: Application guidelines; Financial
statement.
Application information: Funds heavily committed.
Application form not required.
   Initial approach: Letter on organization letterhead
   Copies of proposal: 1
   Deadline(s): Quarterly: Feb. 28, May 30, Aug. 30,
   and Nov. 1
   Board meeting date(s): Quarterly
Officers and Directors:* Jack S. Blanton, Jr.,* Pres.;
Elizabeth B. Wareing,* V.P.; Eddy S. Blanton,*
Secy.-Treas.; Jack S. Blanton, Sr.
Number of staff: 1 part-time professional.
EIN: 741488953
Selected grants: The following grants were reported
in 2004.
$200,000 to Greater Houston Community
   Foundation, Houston, TX. 2 grants: $100,000
   each
$180,000 to Lon Morris College, Jacksonville, TX.
$85,000 to Saint Johns School, Houston, TX. 2
   grants: $5,000, $80,000
$70,000 to Museum of Fine Arts, Houston,
   Houston, TX.
$51,000 to TIRR Foundation, Houston, TX.
$50,000 to A.D. Players, Houston, TX.
$50,000 to Texas Childrens Hospital, Houston, TX.
$2,500 to Childrens Museum of Houston, Houston,
   TX.

9176
The Search Foundation ✧
(formerly The Sophia Foundation)
800 Gessner, Ste. 1260
Houston, TX 77024

Established in 1996 in TX.
Donor: Fondation Ventose.
Foundation type: Independent foundation.
Financial data (yr. ended 12/31/05): Assets,
$9,215,616 (M); expenditures, $559,748;
qualifying distributions, $489,892; giving activities
include $489,892 for 9 grants (high: $254,554;
low: $7,239).
Fields of interest: History/archaeology;
Philanthropy/voluntarism.
International interests: France; Ukraine.
Type of support: General/operating support;
Program development.
Limitations: Applications not accepted. Giving on a
national and international basis, primarily in TX and
the United Kingdom, particularly London, England;
funding also in Melbourne, Australia, and Paris,
France. No grants to individuals.
Application information: Contributes only to
pre-selected organizations.
Officers and Directors:* Roger Coste,* Chair.;
Catherine B. Coste,* Pres.; Bertrand Coste,* Sr.
V.P.; Stephane Coste,* V.P.; Marvin A. Wurzer,
Secy.-Treas.
EIN: 760520202
Selected grants: The following grants were reported
in 2004.
$245,211 to Fondation de France, Paris, France. .
$50,000 to Howard Florey Biomedical Foundation,
   San Antonio, TX.

9177
Sei Burning Bush Fund One ✧
2626 Cole Ave., Ste. 900
Dallas, TX 75204

Established in 1999 in TX.
Donors: James M. Seneff; The Anschutz
Foundation; Buford Foundation.
Foundation type: Operating foundation.
Financial data (yr. ended 12/31/05): Assets,
$191,238 (M); gifts received, $975,000;
expenditures, $946,515; qualifying distributions,
$894,110; giving activities include $717,000 for 16
grants (high: $75,000; low: $30,000), and
$228,127 for foundation-administered programs.
Purpose and activities: Giving primarily to aid and
encourage the growth and expansion of Christian
organizations that appear to have strong potential
for effectively spreading the Gospel of Jesus Christ
and helping large numbers of people, but that lack
financial or other resources to expand on to
maintain their operation.
Fields of interest: Christian agencies & churches.
Limitations: Applications not accepted. Giving on a
national basis. No grants to individuals.
Application information: Contributes only to
pre-selected organizations.
Officers: Robert P. Buford, Pres.; Dave Travis,
Secy.-Treas.
Director: Jeff Thomasson.
EIN: 311680251
Selected grants: The following grants were reported
in 2004.
$78,000 to Joy Leadership Center, Glendale, AZ.
$52,000 to Fellowship Bible Church North,
   Richardson, TX.

$50,000 to Fellowship Associates, Little Rock, AR.

9178
The Abe and Annie Seibel Foundation ✧
c/o Frost National Bank
P.O. Box 179
Galveston, TX 77553 (409) 770-5665
Contact: Janet L. Bertiolino, V.P. and Trust Off., Frost
National Bank

Trust established in 1960 in TX.
Donors: Abe Seibel†; Annie Seibel†.
Foundation type: Independent foundation.
Financial data (yr. ended 7/31/05): Assets,
$45,113,911 (M); expenditures, $4,669,470;
qualifying distributions, $4,255,145; giving
activities include $3,859,590 for loans to
individuals.
Purpose and activities: Interest-free loans to needy
and worthy full-time undergraduate students
enrolled in four-year higher educational institutions.
Type of support: Student loans—to individuals.
Limitations: Giving limited to graduates of TX high
schools attending TX colleges and universities.
Publications: Application guidelines; Informational
brochure (including application guidelines).
Application information: Application form required.
   Initial approach: Telephone or letter
   Deadline(s): Feb. 28
Directors: Ellen Druss; Katherine Konkel; Rabbi of
Temple B'Nai Israel.
Trustee: Frost National Bank.
EIN: 746035556

9179
Semmes Foundation, Inc.
800 Navarro St., Ste. 210
San Antonio, TX 78205-1877
Contact: Thomas R. Semmes, Pres.
URL: http://www.semmesfoundation.org

Incorporated in 1952 in TX.
Donors: Douglas R. Semmes†; Julia Yates
Semmes†.
Foundation type: Independent foundation.
Financial data (yr. ended 12/31/05): Assets,
$20,670,944 (M); gifts received, $45,739;
expenditures, $1,178,328; qualifying distributions,
$997,174; giving activities include $958,495 for 15
grants (high: $500,000; low: $450).
Purpose and activities: Support for museums and
nonprofit organizations involved with education and
health.
Fields of interest: Museums; Education; Health
care.
Limitations: Giving primarily in the San Antonio, TX,
area. No grants to individuals; no loans.
Publications: Application guidelines; IRS Form
990-PF.
Application information: The overwhelming majority
of grants are initiated by the directors of the
foundation. Application form not required.
   Initial approach: Proposal via regular mail
   Copies of proposal: 1
   Deadline(s): None
   Board meeting date(s): Annually, and as required
   Final notification: Within 6 months
Officers and Directors:* Thomas R. Semmes,*
Pres.; Douglas R. Semmes, Jr.,* V.P.; Carol Duffell,
Secy.-Treas.; Lucian L. Morrison; Patricia A.
Semmes.

Number of staff: 1 part-time professional.
EIN: 746062264

9180
Ruth C. and Charles S. Sharp Foundation, Inc. ✧
P.O. Box 560397
The Colony, TX   75056-0397

Incorporated in 1965 in TX.
Donors: Charles S. Sharp; Ruth Collins Sharp; Henry J. Smith; Carr P. Collins Foundation.
Foundation type: Independent foundation.
Financial data (yr. ended 12/31/05): Assets, $19,547,880 (M); expenditures, $1,442,766; qualifying distributions, $1,249,520; giving activities include $1,217,705 for 126 grants (high: $221,750; low: $75).
Purpose and activities: Giving primarily for higher education, human services, and the arts.
Fields of interest: Museums; Performing arts centers; Arts; Higher education; Hospitals (general); Health organizations; Human services; Children/youth, services; Community development; Foundations (public); Federated giving programs; Protestant agencies & churches.
Type of support: General/operating support.
Limitations: Applications not accepted. Giving primarily in Dallas, TX. No grants to individuals.
Application information: Contributes only to pre-selected organizations.
Officers and Directors:* Ruth Sharp Altshuler,* Pres.; Sally S. Harris,* V.P.; Susan S. McAdam.
EIN: 756045366
Selected grants: The following grants were reported in 2005.
$221,750 to Dallas Center for the Performing Arts, Dallas, TX.
$76,000 to Southern Methodist University, Dallas, TX.
$76,000 to Southwestern Medical Foundation, Dallas, TX.
$50,500 to Highland Park United Methodist Church, Dallas, TX.
$32,250 to Salvation Army, Plainview, TX.
$30,000 to Albert Schweitzer Fellowship, Boston, MA.
$15,000 to Saint James Episcopal Church, Great Barrington, MA.
$5,000 to Womens Board of the Dallas Opera, Dallas, TX.
$2,500 to Dallas Bethlehem Center, Dallas, TX.
$2,500 to Latin School of Chicago, Chicago, IL.

9181
Shell Oil Company Foundation ▼ ✧
(formerly Shell Companies Foundation, Inc.)
1 Shell Plz., P.O. Box 4749
Houston, TX   77210-4749
Contact: S.B. Hopkins, V.P.
FAX: (713) 241-3329;
E-mail: scofoundation@shellus.com

Incorporated in 1953 in NY.
Donor: Shell Oil Co.
Foundation type: Company-sponsored foundation.
Financial data (yr. ended 12/31/04): Assets, $47,443,328 (M); gifts received, $9,055,265; expenditures, $10,193,796; qualifying distributions, $9,287,433; giving activities include $7,462,657 for 101 grants (high: $2,523,389; low: $48), and $2,217,424 for employee matching gifts.
Purpose and activities: The foundation supports organizations involved with arts and culture, education, the environment, health, children and youth, human services, community development, civic affairs, disabled people, minorities, and economically disadvantaged people. Special emphasis is directed toward specific educational, environmental, and quality-of-life programs that are aligned with clearly defined educational and social concerns.
Fields of interest: Visual arts; Museums; Performing arts; Performing arts, dance; Performing arts, theater; Performing arts, music; Arts; Education, association; Elementary school/education; Secondary school/education; Higher education; Business school/education; Law school/education; Engineering school/education; Libraries/library science; Education; Environment, natural resources; Environment, energy; Environment; Animals/wildlife, preservation/protection; Hospitals (general); Health care; Substance abuse, services; Cancer; Medical research, institute; Cancer research; Children/youth, services; Residential/custodial care, hospices; Minorities/immigrants, centers/services; Human services; Business/industry; Community development; Federated giving programs; Chemistry; Mathematics; Engineering/technology; Computer science; Engineering; Science; Economics; Public policy, research; Government/public administration; Public affairs, citizen participation; Disabilities, people with; Minorities; Economically disadvantaged.
Type of support: Scholarships—to individuals; Employee-related scholarships; General/operating support; Continuing support; Annual campaigns; Capital campaigns; Program development; Professorships; Publication; Curriculum development; Fellowships; Scholarship funds; Research; Consulting services; Employee matching gifts; Matching/challenge support.
Limitations: Giving on a national basis in areas of company operations. No support for religious institutions, city, state, or federal government departments or entities, political organizations or entities, labor unions, or fraternal, veterans', or service organizations. No grants to individuals (except for scholarships), or for events, fundraising, or sport-related events.
Publications: Annual report; Corporate giving report (including application guidelines).
Application information: Application form not required.
Initial approach: Proposal
Copies of proposal: 1
Deadline(s): Sept. prior to funding year
Board meeting date(s): Mar. and Dec.
Final notification: 1 month
Officers and Directors:* L.L. Eisenhans,* Pres.; S.B. Hopkins, V.P.; T.J. Garland, Secy.; D. Campbell, Treas.; T.T. Coles; G.M. Cowan; R.J. Decyk; V.M. Hanafin; M.F. Keeth; Cathy A. Lamboley; R.M. Restucci.
Number of staff: 7
EIN: 136066583
Selected grants: The following grants were reported in 2004.
$2,773,389 to United Way of the Texas Gulf Coast, Houston, TX. 2 grants: $250,000, $2,523,389
$590,000 to Rice University, Houston, TX.
$423,927 to National Merit Scholarship Corporation, Evanston, IL. For Shell Companies Merit Scholarships.
$375,000 to Texas Southern University Foundation, Houston, TX.
$316,718 to United Way for the Greater New Orleans Area, New Orleans, LA.
$311,125 to Educational Testing Service, Princeton, NJ. For Alliance Scholars Program.
$250,000 to Points of Light Foundation, DC.
$136,945 to United Way, Capital Area, Baton Rouge, LA.
$134,002 to Scholarship America, Saint Peter, MN. For Los Angeles Scholars.

9182
Shelton Family Foundation ▼ ✧
P.O. Box 2791
Abilene, TX   79604   (325) 676-7724
Contact: David L. Copeland, Pres.

Established in 1997 in TX.
Donor: Andrew B. Shelton†.
Foundation type: Independent foundation.
Financial data (yr. ended 6/30/05): Assets, $159,422,395 (M); expenditures, $5,576,839; qualifying distributions, $5,297,703; giving activities include $4,979,488 for 98 grants (high: $1,000,000; low: $200; average: $1,000–$50,000).
Purpose and activities: Giving primarily for education, hospitals, children and youth services, and Christian organizations and churches; funding also for a Baptist church.
Fields of interest: Arts; Higher education; Education; Hospitals (general); Medical care, rehabilitation; Health organizations, association; Salvation Army; Children/youth, services; Foundations (community); Christian agencies & churches; Protestant agencies & churches.
Limitations: Giving primarily in the west central TX area. No grants to individuals.
Application information: Application form not required.
Initial approach: Letter requesting guidelines
Deadline(s): None
Officers and Directors:* David L. Copeland,* Pres. and Treas.; Larry D. Franklin,* V.P. and Secy.; Stanley P. Wilson,* V.P.; Andrew D. Durham, Advisory Dir.; Wendy H. Durham, Advisory Dir.; C. Christine Nicols, Advisory Dir.; David R. Durham; Sindy Shelton Durham; Leonard R. Hoffman; Shay Shelton Hoffman; Ruby W. Shelton.
EIN: 752655885
Selected grants: The following grants were reported in 2006.
$2,000,000 to Hendrick Medical Center, School of Pharmacy, Abilene, TX. For land acquisitions and facility construction.
$750,000 to Hardin-Simmons University, Health Science Academy, Abilene, TX. For construction.
$500,000 to Carver Academy, San Antonio, TX. For construction of faculty housing.
$500,000 to McMurry University, Abilene, TX. For renovations to Bynum Band Hall.
$300,000 to Community Action Program of Taylor County, Abilene, TX. For matching grant for Financial Resources for Economic Empowerment Program, and Assets Building Program.
$175,000 to Community Foundation of Abilene, Abilene, TX. 2 grants: $25,000 (For Ruby Shelton Donor Advised Fund), $150,000 (For Shay Hoffman Donor Advised Fund).
$5,000 to Callahan County Aging Services, Baird, TX.
$4,800 to Abilene Arts Alliance, Abilene, TX.

$1,000 to Kenley School, Abilene, TX.

9183
Shield-Ayres Foundation ✧
115 E. Travis St., Ste. 1445
San Antonio, TX 78205-1693   (210) 224-8839
Contact: Patricia Shield Ayres, Pres.

Established in 1977 in TX.
Donors: Fred W. Shield†; Robert M. Ayres, Jr.;
Patricia Shield Ayres.
Foundation type: Independent foundation.
Financial data (yr. ended 12/31/05): Assets,
$18,529,695 (M); expenditures, $1,460,442;
qualifying distributions, $1,151,500; giving
activities include $1,151,500 for 91 grants (high:
$60,000; low: $500).
Purpose and activities: Giving primarily for human
services.
Fields of interest: Human services; Children/youth,
services.
Type of support: General/operating support; Annual
campaigns; Capital campaigns; Building/
renovation; Land acquisition; Emergency funds;
Program development; Matching/challenge support.
Limitations: Giving primarily in Austin and San
Antonio, TX. No grants to individuals.
Publications: Annual report (including application
guidelines).
Application information: Application form not
required.
   Initial approach: Letter
   Deadline(s): Oct. 1 and Mar. 1
   Board meeting date(s): Spring and fall
Officer and Trustees:* Patricia Shield Ayres,* Pres.;
Margaret Bowers Ayres; Robert Atlee Ayres; Robert
M. Ayres, Jr.; Vera Ayres Bowen.
EIN: 741938157
Selected grants: The following grants were reported
in 2004.
$50,000 to Nature Conservancy of Texas, San
   Antonio, TX.
$25,000 to Boy Scouts of America, San Antonio, TX.
$25,000 to San Antonio Food Bank, San Antonio,
   TX.
$20,000 to Environmental Defense, Austin, TX.
$20,000 to Texans Care for Children, Austin, TX.
$15,000 to ACCION Texas, San Antonio, TX.
$10,000 to Bexar Land Trust, San Antonio, TX.
$10,000 to Foundation for the Homeless, Austin,
   TX.
$10,000 to Land Trust for Tennessee, Nashville,
   TN.
$10,000 to United States Fund for UNICEF,
   Houston, TX.

9184
Shivers Cancer Foundation ✧ ☆
P.O. Box 98
Austin, TX 78767

Foundation type: Independent foundation.
Financial data (yr. ended 12/31/05): Assets,
$10,175,143 (M); gifts received, $14,804;
expenditures, $1,589,486; qualifying distributions,
$1,037,063; giving activities include $1,037,063
for 7 grants (high: $500,000; low: $40,000).
Fields of interest: Medical research, institute;
Cancer research.
Limitations: Applications not accepted. Giving
primarily in Austin, TX. No grants to individuals.

Application information: Contributes only to
pre-selected organizations.
Officers: Clarke Heidrick, Chair.; Arthur Dilly,
Vice-Chair.; Britt Steffensen, Secy.
Directors: Mary Lou Adams, R.N., Ph.D.; Robert E.
Askew, M.D.; Jack Gray; Charles E. Lemaistre, M.D.;
Barbara Jean Olsen.
EIN: 741715889
Selected grants: The following grants were reported
in 2003.
$138,300 to Daughters of Charity Health Services
   of Austin, Austin, TX. For general support.
$123,952 to Peoples Community Clinic, Austin, TX.
   For cancer screening, diagnosis, and treatment.
$100,000 to Seton Fund of the Daughters of Charity
   of Saint Vincent de Paul, Austin, TX. For floor
   renovation.
$50,000 to Wonders and Worries, Austin, TX. For
   general support.
$25,000 to Austin Community Foundation for the
   Capital Area, Austin, TX. For Hope Fund.

9185
The Sidhu-Singh Family Foundation ✧
2301 N. Greenville Ave., Ste. 150
Richardson, TX   75082

Established in 1999 in TX.
Donors: Sanjiv Sidhu; Lekha Singh.
Foundation type: Independent foundation.
Financial data (yr. ended 12/31/05): Assets,
$2,119,204 (M); expenditures, $567,605;
qualifying distributions, $565,020; giving activities
include $565,020 for 14 grants (high: $189,000;
low: $1,000).
Fields of interest: Education; Health care; Human
services; Children/youth, services; Women,
centers/services.
International interests: Canada.
Limitations: Applications not accepted. Giving
primarily in Dallas, TX. No grants to individuals.
Application information: Contributes only to
pre-selected organizations.
Directors: Michael Held; Sanjiv Sidhu; Lekha Singh.
EIN: 752849866

9186
Silverton Foundation, Inc. ✧
1000 Rio Grande St.
Austin, TX 78701   (512) 472-6262
Contact: Andrew S. White, Exec. Dir.
URL: http://www.silvertonfoundation.org

Established in 1999 in TX.
Donor: Silverton Partners, LP.
Foundation type: Independent foundation.
Financial data (yr. ended 12/31/05): Assets,
$14,046,886 (M); expenditures, $1,053,187;
qualifying distributions, $694,664; giving activities
include $613,437 for 38 grants (high: $197,500;
low: $500).
Purpose and activities: Support for underserved
and disadvantaged populations through
empowerment and self help programs in the areas
of health, education, social services and economic
development in central Texas and Australia.
Fields of interest: Education; Health care; Human
services; Economic development.
Limitations: Giving in Australia, East Timor, and the
U.S., with primary emphasis on central TX.
Publications: Annual report.

Application information: Application guidelines
available on foundation Web site. Application form
not required.
   Initial approach: Letter
Officers: Pamela M. Ryan, Chair.; William P. Wood,
Pres.; Andrew S. White, Exec. Dir.
EIN: 742936881
Selected grants: The following grants were reported
in 2003.
$175,000 to Issues Deliberation Australia,
   Australia. .
$50,000 to Brown University, Providence, RI.
$50,000 to University of Texas, Austin, TX.
$27,991 to Austin Community Foundation for the
   Capital Area, Austin, TX.
$25,000 to Austin Community Development
   Corporation, Austin, TX.
$20,000 to Breakthrough, Austin, TX.
$5,000 to Heart House Austin, Austin, TX.
$5,000 to Manos de Cristo, Austin, TX.
$500 to Cook Childrens Medical Center, Fort Worth,
   TX.
$500 to Leukemia & Lymphoma Society, White
   Plains, NY.

9187
The Virginia and L. E. Simmons Family
Foundation ☆
6600 JPMorgan Chase Twr.
Houston, TX   77002-3007

Established in 1994 in TX.
Donors: L.E. Simmons; Virginia W. Simmons.
Foundation type: Independent foundation.
Financial data (yr. ended 12/31/05): Assets,
$9,220,703 (M); expenditures, $474,320;
qualifying distributions, $450,203; giving activities
include $449,528 for 89 grants (high: $133,333;
low: $50).
Purpose and activities: Giving primarily for health
associations, and children and youth services;
funding also for human services.
Fields of interest: Arts; Education; Environment;
Hospitals (general); Health organizations,
association; Pediatrics; Cancer research; Boy
scouts; Human services; Children/youth, services;
Family services; Community development, women's
clubs; Foundations (private grantmaking); Federated
giving programs.
Limitations: Applications not accepted. Giving
primarily in Houston, TX. No grants to individuals.
Application information: Contributes only to
pre-selected organizations.
Officers: L.E. Simmons, Pres.; Virginia W. Simmons,
V.P.; Anthony F. DeLuca, Secy.-Treas.
EIN: 760453177
Selected grants: The following grants were reported
in 2005.
$25,000 to Community Foundation of Jackson Hole,
   Jackson, WY.
$21,000 to Boy Scouts of America, Anchorage, AK.
   2 grants: $20,000, $1,000
$10,000 to Camp for All, Houston, TX.
$10,000 to Center for Houstons Future, Houston,
   TX.
$10,000 to Kinkaid School, Houston, TX.
$7,240 to Texas Childrens Hospital, Houston, TX.
$5,000 to Jackson Hole Land Trust, Jackson, WY.
$4,550 to Foundation for the Retarded, Houston,
   TX.
$4,000 to Alexis de Tocqueville Society, Alexandria,
   VA.

9188
Harold Simmons Foundation ◇
3 Lincoln Ctr.
5430 LBJ Fwy., Ste. 1700
Dallas, TX 75240-2697 (972) 233-2134
Contact: Lisa Simmons Epstein, Pres.

Incorporated in 1988 in TX.
Donors: Contran Corp.; NL Industries, Inc.
Foundation type: Company-sponsored foundation.
Financial data (yr. ended 12/31/05): Assets,
$18,786,656 (M); gifts received, $6,950,000;
expenditures, $8,033,967; qualifying distributions,
$8,007,058; giving activities include $7,950,058
for 225 grants (high: $1,500,000; low: $1,000),
and $57,000 for employee matching gifts.
Purpose and activities: The foundation supports
organizations involved with arts and culture, child
development education, literacy, health, medical
research, housing, human services, community
development, minorities, and women.
Fields of interest: Arts; Child development,
education; Education, reading; Health care; Medical
research; Housing/shelter; Children/youth,
services; Human services; Community
development; Minorities; Women.
Type of support: General/operating support;
Continuing support; Income development;
Management development/capacity building;
Annual campaigns; Capital campaigns; Building/
renovation; Equipment; Land acquisition;
Emergency funds; Program development;
Conferences/seminars; Professorships;
Publication; Seed money; Curriculum development;
Fellowships; Internship funds; Scholarship funds;
Research; Technical assistance; Consulting
services; Program evaluation; Program-related
investments/loans; Matching/challenge support.
Limitations: Giving primarily in the Dallas and Fort
Worth, TX, area. No grants to individuals, or for
endowments; no loans to individuals.
Publications: Application guidelines.
Application information: Application form not
required.
  Initial approach: Proposal
  Copies of proposal: 1
  Deadline(s): None
  Board meeting date(s): As needed
  Final notification: 3 months
Officers and Directors:* Harold C. Simmons,*
Chair.; Lisa Simmons Epstein,* Pres.; Steven L.
Watson,* V.P. and Secy.; Eugene K. Anderson,
Treas.; Keith A. Johnson, Cont.
Number of staff: 2 full-time professional; 1 part-time
professional; 1 full-time support.
EIN: 752222091

9189
The Simmons Foundation
109 N. Post Oak Ln., Ste. 220
Houston, TX 77024 (713) 268-8099
Contact: Linda K. May, Pres.
FAX: (713) 580-1850;
E-mail: lmay@thesimmonsfoundation.org;
URL: http://www.thesimmonsfoundation.org

Established in 1993.
Donor: Gay A. Roane.
Foundation type: Independent foundation.
Financial data (yr. ended 12/31/04): Assets,
$20,350,352 (M); gifts received, $10,076,319;
expenditures, $1,428,490; qualifying distributions,

$1,419,800; giving activities include $1,419,800
for 134 grants (high: $50,000; low: $400).
Purpose and activities: Giving to help people to help
themselves by supporting programs that improve
education, develop healthy lifestyles and promote
economic and leadership opportunities.
Fields of interest: Education; Health care; Human
services; Children/youth, services; Women,
centers/services; Community development.
Type of support: General/operating support;
Continuing support; Capital campaigns; Building/
renovation; Endowments; Program development;
Seed money; Matching/challenge support.
Limitations: Giving primarily in Harris County and
Houston, TX. No support for religious organizations
for religious purposes, major arts organizations or
political organizations. No grants for galas/social
fundraisers, major medical research projects, or
annual giving campaigns.
Publications: Application guidelines; Annual report;
Annual report (including application guidelines);
Grants list.
Application information: Application form available
on foundation Web site. Application form required.
  Initial approach: Proposal (in required format
    found on foundation Web site)
  Copies of proposal: 1
  Deadline(s): None
  Board meeting date(s): Quarterly
  Final notification: 4 weeks after being presented
    to board
Officers and Directors:* Linda K. May,* Pres.; David
Shindeldecker,* V.P.; David L. Solomon,* V.P.;
Amanda Cloud, Secy.-Treas.; Gay A. Roane; George
Grant Roane IV*.
Number of staff: 2 full-time professional; 1 full-time
support.
EIN: 760398915
Selected grants: The following grants were reported
in 2004.
$50,000 to Houston Area Womens Center,
  Houston, TX. For capital campaign for new facility
  for abused women and their children.
$25,000 to Rose, The, Houston, TX. For capital
  campaign.
$25,000 to San Jose Clinic, Houston, TX.
$25,000 to YMCA of the Greater Houston Area,
  Houston, TX. For capital campaign.
$20,000 to Houston Achievement Place, Houston,
  TX.
$20,000 to New Hope Housing, Houston, TX. For
  capital campaign.
$20,000 to Project Yes, Houston, TX.
$20,000 to Teach for America, Houston, TX.
$20,000 to Yellowstone Academy, Houston, TX.
$15,000 to Project GRAD USA, Houston, TX.

9190
The Sixty Four Foundation ◇ ☆
5205 N. O'Connor Blvd.
Irving, TX 75039

Foundation type: Independent foundation.
Financial data (yr. ended 12/31/05): Assets,
$3,365,633 (M); gifts received, $2,160,573;
expenditures, $1,358,335; qualifying distributions,
$1,358,335; giving activities include $1,358,335
for grants.
Fields of interest: Scholarships/financial aid;
Health care; Cancer.
Limitations: Giving primarily in TX. No grants to
individuals.

Officers and Directors:* V. Prem Wasta,* Pres.;
Ronald Schokking, V.P. and Treas.; Robbert Hartog;
Eric Salsberg.
EIN: 980364976

9191
Clara B. and W. Aubrey Smith Charitable Foundation ◇
c/o Bank of America, N.A.
P.O. Box 831041
Dallas, TX 75283-1041
Application address: c/o Bank of America, N.A.,
Attn.: Dan Kelly, 901 Main St., 19th Fl., Dallas, TX
75202, tel.: (214) 209-1965

Established in 1985 in TX.
Donor: Clara Blackford Smith†.
Foundation type: Independent foundation.
Financial data (yr. ended 6/30/05): Assets,
$17,462,121 (M); expenditures, $1,276,729;
qualifying distributions, $1,144,965; giving
activities include $1,119,781 for 66 grants (high:
$200,000; low: $250).
Purpose and activities: Giving primarily for health
care, education and human services.
Fields of interest: Historic preservation/historical
societies; Arts; Higher education; Education; Health
care; Human services; Children/youth, services;
Family services; Aging, centers/services;
Community development; Federated giving
programs; Religion; Economically disadvantaged.
Type of support: Capital campaigns; Building/
renovation; Equipment; Program development.
Limitations: Giving primarily in Grayson County, TX
and the surrounding areas.
Application information: Application form required.
  Initial approach: Letter
  Copies of proposal: 6
  Deadline(s): None
  Board meeting date(s): Quarterly
Officer: Gary Melle, Chair.
Directors: Ronnie Cole; Jerry Culpepper; Wayne E.
Delaney, M.D.; Jack Lilley.
Trustee: Bank of America, N.A.
EIN: 756314114
Selected grants: The following grants were reported
in 2003.
$175,000 to Austin College, Sherman, TX.
$60,000 to Grayson County Shelter, Denison, TX.
$23,572 to Grayson County College, Denison, TX.
$16,000 to Child Guidance Clinic of Grayson
  County, Sherman, TX.
$15,000 to Denison Public Library, Denison, TX.
$10,000 to Girls Club of Denison, Denison, TX.
$10,000 to United Way of Grayson County,
  Sherman, TX.
$7,500 to North Texas Food Bank, Dallas, TX.
$1,000 to Denison Helping Hands, Denison, TX.
$1,000 to Salvation Army of Grayson County,
  Sherman, TX.

9192
Lester H. Smith Charitable Foundation ◇
1001 Fannin, Ste. 3800
Houston, TX 77002

Established in 2002 in TX.
Donor: Lester H. Smith.
Foundation type: Independent foundation.
Financial data (yr. ended 12/31/04): Assets,
$2,345,425 (M); gifts received, $2,970,091;

expenditures, $6,343,276; qualifying distributions, $6,101,389; giving activities include $5,721,491 for 18 grants (high: $4,501,491; low: $500).

Fields of interest: Museums (science/technology); Medical research, institute; Cancer research; Breast cancer research; Prostate cancer research.

Limitations: Applications not accepted. No grants to individuals.

Application information: Contributes only to pre-selected organizations.

Officers and Trustees:* Lester H. Smith,* Pres.; Sue Ashcraft Smith,* V.P.; Sharin A. Scott, Secy.; Martha E. Leggett,* Treas.; Michelle Smith Hendry; Stuart M. Smith.

EIN: 270040023

9193
Vivian L. Smith Foundation for Neurological Research ✧

(formerly Vivian L. Smith Foundation for Restorative Neurology)
1900 W. Loop S., Ste. 1050
Houston, TX 77027 (713) 622-8611
Contact: Amy M. Meckel

Established in 1981 in TX.

Donor: Vivian L. Smith†.

Foundation type: Independent foundation.

Financial data (yr. ended 6/30/05): Assets, $12,540,354 (M); expenditures, $855,414; qualifying distributions, $735,128; giving activities include $585,075 for 1 grant, and $139,490 for 1 foundation-administered program.

Purpose and activities: To develop therapies to improve the outcome of patients with 1) acute brain injury, 2) spinal cord injury, 3) chronic brain injury, 4) chronic spinal cord injury, 5) epilepsy.

Fields of interest: Biomedicine; Medical research, institute.

Type of support: Research.

Application information: Application form not required.

Initial approach: Proposal
Copies of proposal: 1
Deadline(s): None
Board meeting date(s): Varies

Officers and Trustees:* R.A. Seale, Jr.,* Pres.; Suzanne R. Benson,* V.P. and Treas.; Steven H. Gerdes,* Secy.; Sandra Smith Dompier; Dee S. Osborne.

EIN: 742139770

9194
Bob and Vivian Smith Foundation ✧

1900 W. Loop S., Ste. 1050
Houston, TX 77027-3207 (713) 986-8030
Contact: Amy Meckel

Established about 1969.

Donors: R.E. Smith†; Vivian L. Smith†.

Foundation type: Independent foundation.

Financial data (yr. ended 12/31/05): Assets, $10,725,938 (M); expenditures, $493,288; qualifying distributions, $430,000; giving activities include $420,000 for 21 grants (high: $50,000; low: $5,000; average: $10,000–$25,000).

Purpose and activities: Emphasis on medical research and secondary education; support also for higher education.

Fields of interest: Secondary school/education; Higher education; Medical research, institute.

Type of support: General/operating support; Continuing support; Annual campaigns; Capital campaigns.

Limitations: Giving primarily in Houston and Harris County, TX. No grants to individuals; no program-related investments.

Publications: Application guidelines.

Application information: Application form not required.

Initial approach: Proposal
Copies of proposal: 1
Deadline(s): Oct. 15
Board meeting date(s): Around Nov. 15
Final notification: After board meeting

Officer: Suzanne R. Benson,* Pres.; H. Devon Graham, Jr,* V.P.; Amy M. Meckel,* Secy.-Treas.

Trustees: Bobby Smith Cohn; Sandra Smith Dompier.

EIN: 237029052

Selected grants: The following grants were reported in 2003.

$150,000 to Houston Farm and Ranch Club, Houston, TX.

$50,000 to Saint Lukes Episcopal Hospital, Houston, TX. For nurse fellowship program.

$30,000 to Texas Childrens Hospital, Houston, TX. 2 grants: $25,000 to Cancer Center, $5,000

$25,000 to Cancer Answers, Houston, TX.

$25,000 to Chinquapin School, Highlands, TX.

$25,000 to CHRISTUS Spohn Health System Corporation, Corpus Christi, TX.

$25,000 to Houston Museum of Natural Science, Houston, TX.

$25,000 to Texas Institute for Behavioral Medicine and Neurosciences, Bellaire, TX. For free clinic for women.

$10,000 to Texas A & M University, College of Veterinary Medicine, College Station, TX.

9195
Dr. Bob and Jean Smith Foundation

(formerly Bob Smith, M.D. Foundation)
3811 Turtle Creek Ctr.
No. 200, LB 53
Dallas, TX 75219 (214) 521-3461
Contact: Sally S. Mashburn

Established in 1989 in TX.

Foundation type: Independent foundation.

Financial data (yr. ended 9/30/05): Assets, $27,456,400 (M); expenditures, $1,729,529; qualifying distributions, $1,335,875; giving activities include $1,123,807 for 21 grants (high: $506,000; low: $200).

Purpose and activities: Giving for higher education, medical education and research, and health.

Fields of interest: Arts; Education; Health care.

Type of support: Program development; Endowments; Equipment; General/operating support; Continuing support; Annual campaigns; Capital campaigns; Building/renovation; Scholarship funds; Research; Matching/challenge support.

Limitations: Giving primarily in the Dallas, TX, area. No grants to individuals.

Publications: Application guidelines.

Application information: Application form not required.

Initial approach: Letter
Copies of proposal: 1
Deadline(s): None
Board meeting date(s): Quarterly
Final notification: Via letter

Officers and Directors:* Jean K. Smith,* Chair.; Patty A. Smith,* Pres., C.F.O. and Treas.; Sally Smith, Secy.; Marty S. Kelley; George A. Nicoud, Jr.; Scott R. Smith; Robert West.

Number of staff: 3 full-time professional; 1 full-time support.

EIN: 510137245

Selected grants: The following grants were reported in 2004.

$915,000 to University of Texas Southwestern Medical Center, Dallas, TX. 3 grants: $400,000 to Center of Development Biology (For unrestricted support), $500,000 to Department of Neurology (For unrestricted support), $15,000 (For unrestricted support).

$500,000 to Laura Bush Foundation for Americas Libraries, DC. For unrestricted support.

$25,000 to Crystal Charity Ball, Dallas, TX. For unrestricted support.

$25,000 to Juliette Fowler Homes, Dallas, TX. For unrestricted support.

$10,000 to Austin Street Center, Dallas, TX. For unrestricted support.

$10,000 to Easter Seals of Greater Dallas, Carrollton, TX. For general support.

$10,000 to Southwestern Diabetic Foundation, Gainesville, TX. For unrestricted support.

$10,000 to Zale Lipshy University Hospital, Dallas, TX. For unrestricted support.

9196
Ralph L. Smith Foundation ✧

c/o Bank of America, N.A.
P.O. Box 831041
Dallas, TX 75283-1041
Application address: c/o James J. Mueth, Bank of America, P.O. Box 419119, Kansas City, MO, 64141-6119, tel.: (816) 979-7405

Trust established in 1952 in MO.

Donors: Harriet T. Smith†; Ralph L. Smith†.

Foundation type: Independent foundation.

Financial data (yr. ended 12/31/05): Assets, $20,202,048 (M); expenditures, $1,311,279; qualifying distributions, $1,189,244; giving activities include $1,139,000 for 129 grants (high: $97,500; low: $500).

Fields of interest: Arts; Higher education; Education; Environment, natural resources; Health care; Human services; Children/youth, services; Women, centers/services; Community development, neighborhood development; Women.

Limitations: Giving primarily in the metropolitan Kansas City, MO, area. No grants to individuals.

Application information: Applications for grants will not be acknowledged.

Initial approach: Telephone followed by 3-page letter
Copies of proposal: 1
Deadline(s): None
Board meeting date(s): Quarterly
Final notification: 2 months

Managers: Neil T. Dauthat; Harriet H. Dennison; Neil T. Smith.

Trustee Bank: Bank of America, N.A.

EIN: 446008508

Selected grants: The following grants were reported in 2005.

$97,500 to Greater Kansas City Community Foundation, Kansas City, MO.

$55,000 to Orme School, Mayer, AZ.

$40,000 to Barstow School, Kansas City, MO.

$29,000 to Mano a Mano, Salem, OR.

$13,000 to Raindrops to Refuge, Sherwood, OR.
$10,000 to Coast Range Association, Corvallis, OR.
$10,000 to Nelson-Atkins Museum of Art, Kansas City, MO.
$5,000 to Georgia Council on Economic Education, Atlanta, GA.
$5,000 to Jeffrey Foundation, Los Angeles, CA.
$5,000 to Tucson Museum of Art, Tucson, AZ.

9197
Vivian L. Smith Foundation
1900 W. Loop S., Ste. 1050
Houston, TX 77027-3207 (713) 986-8030
Contact: Amy Meckel, Tr.

Established in 1981 in TX.
Donor: Vivian L. Smith‡.
Foundation type: Independent foundation.
Financial data (yr. ended 12/31/05): Assets, $81,642,634 (M); expenditures, $4,283,109; qualifying distributions, $3,619,556; giving activities include $3,580,891 for 90 grants (high: $467,391; low: $2,000).
Purpose and activities: Giving primarily for arts and cultural programs, education, medical research, and religious agencies and churches.
Fields of interest: Arts; Education; Medical research; Christian agencies & churches.
Type of support: General/operating support; Continuing support; Annual campaigns; Capital campaigns; Building/renovation; Equipment; Research.
Limitations: Giving primarily to Harris County and Houston, TX. No grants to individuals.
Publications: Application guidelines; Annual report.
Application information: Application form not required.
  Initial approach: Letter or proposal
  Copies of proposal: 1
  Deadline(s): Feb. 15, May 15, Aug. 15, and Oct. 25
  Board meeting date(s): Approximately Apr. 15, July 15, Oct. 15, and Nov. 15
  Final notification: 3 weeks after meeting
Officers and Trustees:* Suzanne R. Benson,* Pres.; H. Devon Graham, Jr., V.P.; Janice R. Smith, Secy.-Treas.; H.L. Brown, Jr.; Bobby Smith Cohn; Sandra Smith Dompier; James A. Elkins III; Amy M. Meckel; Richard H. Skinner; Jack T. Trotter.
Number of staff: None.
EIN: 760101380
Selected grants: The following grants were reported in 2004.
$300,000 to University of Texas Health Science Center, Houston, TX. 2 grants: $50,000 (For faculty teaching grant), $250,000 (For Surgical Stimulation Room).
$150,000 to University of Texas M. D. Anderson Cancer Center, Houston, TX. For general support.
$100,000 to Communities in Schools, Bay Area, Houston, TX. For general support.
$100,000 to South Campus Sports Association, Houston, TX. For general support.
$100,000 to TexGen Research, Houston, TX. For general support.
$35,000 to Houston Parks Board, Houston, TX. For general support.
$25,000 to Stehlin Foundation for Cancer Research, Houston, TX. For general support.
$25,000 to Sunshine Kids Foundation, Houston, TX. For general support.
$16,000 to Educational and Research Foundation for the American Academy of Facial Plastic and Reconstructive Surgery, Alexandria, VA. For general support.

9198
The William A. and Madeline Welder Smith Foundation ◇
P.O. Box 2558
Houston, TX 77252-8037

Established in 1992 in TX.
Donor: William A. Smith‡.
Foundation type: Independent foundation.
Financial data (yr. ended 6/30/05): Assets, $18,218,581 (M); expenditures, $818,983; qualifying distributions, $713,775; giving activities include $593,200 for 30 grants (high: $100,000; low: $1,000).
Purpose and activities: Giving primarily for higher and other education, medical research, including a cancer center, youth and social services, the arts, and federated giving programs.
Fields of interest: Performing arts; Arts; Education, early childhood education; Higher education; Libraries/library science; Education; Medical research, institute; Cancer research; Eye research; Human services; Youth, services; Federated giving programs.
Type of support: General/operating support; Capital campaigns; Scholarship funds.
Limitations: Applications not accepted. Giving primarily in TX, with emphasis on Houston. No grants to individuals.
Application information: Contributes only to pre-selected organizations.
Trustees: Joe E. Coleman; Jack Hooper; Joseph W. Royce; H. Michael Tyson; JPMorgan Chase Bank, N.A.
EIN: 766076267
Selected grants: The following grants were reported in 2005.
$100,000 to Baylor University, Waco, TX.
$35,000 to Schreiner University, Kerrville, TX.
$35,000 to Victoria Performing Arts Center, Victoria, TX.
$25,000 to Texas Childrens Hospital, Houston, TX.
$20,000 to Houston Livestock Show and Rodeo, Houston, TX. 2 grants: $10,000 each
$20,000 to Incarnate Word Academy, Houston, TX.
$20,000 to University of Saint Thomas, Houston, TX.
$15,000 to Phi Delta Theta Educational Foundation, Oxford, OH.
$15,000 to University of Mary Hardin-Baylor, Belton, TX.

9199
Nancy and John Snyder Foundation ◇ ☆
(formerly Nancy and John Foundation)
201 Main St., Ste. 1450
Fort Worth, TX 76102-3105

Established in 1980.
Donor: John C. Snyder.
Foundation type: Independent foundation.
Financial data (yr. ended 12/31/05): Assets, $10,002,683 (M); expenditures, $664,952; qualifying distributions, $345,938; giving activities include $345,938 for grants.
Purpose and activities: Giving primarily for community funds and Christian religious organizations; support also to individuals to alleviate personal hardship.
Fields of interest: Human services; Federated giving programs; Christian agencies & churches; General charitable giving.
Type of support: General/operating support; Grants to individuals.
Limitations: Applications not accepted. Giving primarily in Fort Worth, TX.
Application information: Contributes primarily to pre-selected organizations and individuals.
Officers and Directors:* John C. Snyder,* Pres.; Nancy T. Snyder,* V.P.; Linda Gosdin,* Secy.-Treas.; Dudley R. Snyder; Marcus M. Snyder; Wesley V. Snyder.
EIN: 751737014
Selected grants: The following grants were reported in 2004.
$26,100 to Christ Chapel Bible Church, Fort Worth, TX.
$25,000 to All Saints Episcopal School, Fort Worth, TX.
$25,000 to All Saints Health Foundation, Fort Worth, TX.
$10,000 to Young Life Foundation, Colorado Springs, CO.
$6,500 to Union Gospel Mission, Dallas, TX.
$6,300 to Campus Crusade for Christ, Miami, FL.
$3,400 to Search Ministries, Fort Worth, TX.
$2,400 to Christian Legal Society, Annandale, VA.
$2,400 to Navigators, The, Colorado Springs, CO.
$1,500 to Success Through Academic Readiness (STAR) Sponsorship Program, Fort Worth, TX.

9200
The Sooch Foundation ◇ ☆
c/o Navdeep Sooch
P.O. Box 160904
Austin, TX 78716-0904

Donors: Janet Harman; Navdeep S. Sooch.
Foundation type: Independent foundation.
Financial data (yr. ended 12/31/05): Assets, $12,081,926 (M); gifts received, $1,627; expenditures, $628,548; qualifying distributions, $525,000; giving activities include $525,000 for grants.
Fields of interest: Education; Boys & girls clubs; Protestant agencies & churches.
Limitations: Applications not accepted. Giving primarily in the Austin, TX area. No grants to individuals.
Application information: Contributes only to pre-selected organizations.
Officers: Navdeep S. Sooch, Pres. and Treas.; Janet E. Harman, V.P. and Secy.
Trustee: David R. Welland.
EIN: 200399480

9201
South Texas Charitable Foundation ◇
P.O. Box 2549
Victoria, TX 77902-2549 (361) 573-4383
Contact: Rayford L. Keller, Secy.-Treas.

Established in 1981 in TX.
Donor: Maude O'Connor Williams.
Foundation type: Independent foundation.
Financial data (yr. ended 11/30/04): Assets, $7,329,377 (M); expenditures, $468,147; qualifying distributions, $458,858; giving activities

include $458,858 for 19 grants (high: $70,000; low: $2,500).

Purpose and activities: Giving primarily for education, health care, including a neurological institute, social services particularly services for the elderly, and Roman Catholic churches.

Fields of interest: Arts; Elementary school/ education; Education; Hospitals (specialty); Health care; Neuroscience research; Food services; Human services; YM/YWCAs & YM/YWHAs; Children, services; Aging, centers/services; Roman Catholic agencies & churches.

Limitations: Giving primarily in TX, with emphasis on Victoria. No grants to individuals.

Application information: Application form not required.

> *Deadline(s):* None

Officers: Ann O.W. Harithas, Pres.; Michael S. Anderson, V.P.; Rayford L. Keller, Secy.-Treas.

EIN: 742148107

Selected grants: The following grants were reported in 2004.

$110,000 to Our Lady of Victory Cathedral, Victoria, TX. 2 grants: $70,000 (For building, maintenance, and repair fund), $40,000 (For Pastor's Emergency Fund).

$50,000 to Affectionate Arms, Victoria, TX.

$50,000 to Barrow Neurological Institute, Phoenix, AZ.

$50,000 to Christs Kitchen, Victoria, TX.

$50,000 to Texas Childrens Hospital, Houston, TX.

$30,000 to Nazareth Academy, Victoria, TX.

$28,631 to Refugio County Elderly Services, Refugio, TX.

$15,727 to FotoFest, Houston, TX.

$15,000 to Saint Joseph Elementary School, Yoakum, TX.

9202
Thomas & Lillian Sowell Charitable Trust ◇ ☆

c/o Bank Of America, N.A.
P.O. Box 831041
Dallas, TX   75283-1041

Established in 2005 in TX.

Donor: Lillian K. Sowell†.

Foundation type: Independent foundation.

Financial data (yr. ended 9/30/05): Assets, $12,866,422 (M); gifts received, $13,131,535; expenditures, $670,631; qualifying distributions, $606,842; giving activities include $600,815 for 4 grants (high: $240,326; low: $30,041).

Purpose and activities: Giving primarily to the United Way, a Presbyterian church, and a healthcare foundation.

Fields of interest: Health care; Federated giving programs; Protestant agencies & churches.

Limitations: Applications not accepted. Giving primarily in Dallas, TX.

Application information: Contributes only to pre-selected organizations.

Trustee: Bank of America, N.A.

EIN: 597247352

9203
James E. Sowell Foundation ◇ ☆

c/o Keith Martin
1601 Elm St., Ste. 300
Dallas, TX   75201

Established in 1997 in TX.

Donor: James E. Sowell.

Foundation type: Independent foundation.

Financial data (yr. ended 12/31/05): Assets, $14,073,524 (M); gifts received, $6,140,728; expenditures, $755,797; qualifying distributions, $429,693; giving activities include $428,524 for 1 grant.

Fields of interest: Education; Human services.

Type of support: General/operating support.

Limitations: Applications not accepted. Giving primarily in TX. No grants to individuals.

Application information: Contributes only to pre-selected organizations.

Officers: James E. Sowell, Pres.; Keith Martin, Secy.-Treas.

Directors: Larry James; Elizabeth Sowell.

EIN: 752641436

9204
The Sparrow Charitable Foundation ◇

211 N. Record St., Ste. 222
Dallas, TX   75202

Established in 2003 in TX.

Donors: Marydel Harris; Raymond Harris.

Foundation type: Independent foundation.

Financial data (yr. ended 12/31/05): Assets, $2,001,582 (M); gifts received, $3,000,000; expenditures, $1,136,726; qualifying distributions, $1,135,200; giving activities include $1,134,250 for 36 grants (high: $186,000; low: $200).

Fields of interest: Higher education; Theological school/education; Education; Cancer; Human services; Christian agencies & churches.

Limitations: Applications not accepted. Giving primarily in TX. No grants to individuals.

Application information: Contributes only to pre-selected organizations.

Directors: Elizabeth A. Harris; Marydel Harris; Raymond Harris; Stephen R. Harris.

EIN: 200488561

9205
The Sparrow Foundation ◇ ☆

12850 Hillcrest Rd., Ste. 200
Dallas, TX   75230

Established in 2004 in TX.

Donor: Jean Ann Brock.

Foundation type: Independent foundation.

Financial data (yr. ended 12/31/05): Assets, $730,685 (M); expenditures, $521,110; qualifying distributions, $521,000; giving activities include $521,000 for 5 grants (high: $250,000; low: $1,000).

Fields of interest: Cancer; Women, centers/ services.

Limitations: Applications not accepted. Giving primarily in TX. No grants to individuals.

Application information: Contributes only to pre-selected organizations.

Officers and Directors:* Jean Ann Brock,* Pres.; Steve Brock,* V.P.; Michael W. Moore, Secy.-Treas. and C.F.O.; Rodger M. Sanders.

EIN: 200253717

9206
Victor E. Speas Foundation ◇

c/o Bank of America, N.A.
P.O. Box 831041
Dallas, TX   75283-1041   (800) 357-7094
Contact: David P. Ross, Sr. V.P., Bank of America, N.A.
Application address: c/o James J. Mueth, Bank of America, N.A., P.O. Box 419119, Kansas City, MO 64141-6119, tel.: (816) 979-7405

Trust established in 1947 in MO.

Donors: Effie E. Speas†; Victor E. Speas†; Speas Co.; Alice J. Speas Unitrust.

Foundation type: Independent foundation.

Financial data (yr. ended 12/31/05): Assets, $33,813,971 (M); gifts received, $783,428; expenditures, $2,057,721; qualifying distributions, $1,774,463; giving activities include $1,677,531 for 30 grants (high: $289,000; low: $2,500).

Purpose and activities: Giving restricted to improving the quality of health care in the Kansas City, MO, area. Support mainly for medically-related higher education, including loans for medical students at the University of Missouri at Kansas City, preventive health care, and medical research; grants also for agencies serving the healthcare needs of the elderly, youth, and the handicapped.

Fields of interest: Medical school/education; Hospitals (general); Dental care; Medical care, rehabilitation; Health care; Substance abuse, services; Mental health/crisis services; Cancer; Heart & circulatory diseases; AIDS; Alcoholism; Medical research, institute; Cancer research; Heart & circulatory research; AIDS research; Safety/ disasters; Children/youth, services; Residential/ custodial care, hospices; Aging, centers/services; Women, centers/services; Voluntarism promotion; Aging; Disabilities, people with; Women.

Type of support: General/operating support; Capital campaigns; Building/renovation; Equipment; Emergency funds; Program development; Seed money; Research; Matching/challenge support; Student loans—to individuals.

Limitations: Giving limited to Jackson, Clay, Platte, and Cass counties, MO. No grants for endowment funds or scholarships; no loans (except to medical students at the University of Missouri at Kansas City).

Publications: Application guidelines; Program policy statement.

Application information: Application form not required.

> *Initial approach:* Letter (no longer than 3 pages)
> *Copies of proposal:* 1
> *Deadline(s):* None
> *Board meeting date(s):* Bimonthly
> *Final notification:* 2 months

Trustee: Bank of America, N.A.

Number of staff: 1 full-time professional.

EIN: 446008340

Selected grants: The following grants were reported in 2003.

$225,000 to Community Resource Network, Kansas City, MO. For program support.

$115,000 to Cabot Westside Health Center, Kansas City, MO. For capital campaign.

$107,500 to Camp Fire USA, Kansas City, MO. For ecommerce and customer fulfillment projects.

$101,000 to Ozanam Home for Boys, Kansas City, MO. For mapping service project.

$85,535 to Niles Home for Children, Kansas City, MO.

$73,809 to Energy Services, Madison, WI. For technology upgrade.

$62,000 to Della Lamb Community Services, Kansas City, MO. For equipment.

$59,000 to Project AIM, Raytown, MO. For operating support.

$50,000 to Westside Agency Collaborative, Kansas City, MO. To purchase real estate.

$50,000 to William Jewell College, Liberty, MO. To purchase of scientific equipment.

9207
John W. and Effie E. Speas Memorial Trust ◇
c/o Bank of America, N.A.
P.O. Box 831041
Dallas, TX 75283-1041 (800) 357-7094
Application address: c/o Spence Heddens, Bank of America, N.A., P.O. Box 419119, Kansas City, MO 64141-6119, tel.: (816) 979-7304

Trust established in 1947 in MO.
Donors: Effie E. Speas†; Victor E. Speas†; Speas Co.
Foundation type: Independent foundation.
Financial data (yr. ended 12/31/05): Assets, $32,274,540 (M); expenditures, $1,742,861; qualifying distributions, $1,443,198; giving activities include $1,387,815 for 48 grants (high: $175,000; low: $100).
Purpose and activities: Giving primarily for hospitals and health services, including support for mental health services, higher education in the health professions, and medical research, including cancer research.
Fields of interest: Education; Hospitals (general); Health care; Medical research, institute; Family services; Nonprofit management.
Type of support: General/operating support; Equipment; Program development; Seed money; Research.
Limitations: Giving limited to the greater bi-state metropolitan Kansas City area.
Application information: Application form not required.
   Initial approach: Letter of 3 pages or fewer
   Copies of proposal: 1
   Deadline(s): None
   Board meeting date(s): Biweekly
   Final notification: Within 2 months
Trustee: Bank of America, N.A.
Number of staff: 1 full-time professional.
EIN: 446008249
Selected grants: The following grants were reported in 2003.

$262,000 to Resource Development Institute, Kansas City, MO. For Mental Health Information Network.

$244,138 to University of Kansas Medical Center, Kansas City, KS.

$221,250 to Archdiocese of Kansas City, Kansas City, KS. For Gardner Institute.

$175,000 to Childrens Mercy Hospital, Kansas City, MO. For Destiny Expansion Program.

$100,000 to Model Cities Health Corporation of Kansas City, Swope Health Services, Kansas City, MO.

$100,000 to Park University, Parkville, MO. For expanded health care training program.

$75,000 to El Centro, Kansas City, KS. For capital campaign.

$72,500 to Community Living Opportunities, Kansas City, MO. For monitoring technology project.

$64,500 to TLC for Children and Families, Olathe, KS.

$57,000 to Saint Joseph Health Center Foundation, Kansas City, MO.

9208
The Stanzel Family Foundation, Inc. ◇
P.O. Box 6
Schulenburg, TX 78956
Contact: Robert R. Stanzel, Pres.

Established in 1989 in TX; funded in 1990.
Donors: Joseph Stanzel†; Victor Stanzel†.
Foundation type: Independent foundation.
Financial data (yr. ended 7/31/05): Assets, $16,132,333 (M); gifts received, $36,043; expenditures, $1,990,251; qualifying distributions, $1,790,000; giving activities include $321,999 for 12 grants (high: $100,000; low: $200), and $208,778 for 134 grants to individuals (high: $2,000; low: $264).
Purpose and activities: Scholarships only to graduating high school seniors who reside within a 30-mile radius of Schulenburg, or Weimar independent school districts, TX, and who plan to enroll at any institution of higher education after graduation; support also for medical research.
Fields of interest: Scholarships/financial aid; Medical research, public policy.
Type of support: Research; Scholarships—to individuals.
Limitations: Giving limited to Schulenburg and Weimar, TX.
Application information: Application form required.
   Deadline(s): Mar. 31
   Board meeting date(s): Jan., Mar., May, July, Sept. and Nov.
Officers: Robert R. Stanzel, Pres.; Theodore E. Stanzel, V.P.; Ginger Bosl, Secy.; Helen Niesner, Treas.
Board Member: Melinda Barneycastle.
EIN: 742579827

9209
Nelda C. and H. J. Lutcher Stark Foundation
P.O. Box 909
Orange, TX 77631-0909 (409) 883-3513
Contact: Grant Dept.
FAX: (409) 883-3530;
E-mail: stark@starkadmin.org; Address for physical delivery: 601 W. Green Ave. Orange, TX 77630-5718; URL: http://www.starkfoundation.org

Incorporated in 1961 in TX.
Donors: H.J. Lutcher Stark†; Nelda C. Stark†.
Foundation type: Independent foundation.
Financial data (yr. ended 12/31/05): Assets, $468,244,322 (M); gifts received, $85,649,318; expenditures, $16,741,847; qualifying distributions, $16,043,523; giving activities include $4,441,021 for 35 grants (high: $1,227,943; low: $900; average: $10,000–$50,000), $49,340 for 13 grants to individuals (high: $20,000; low: $1,500; average: $2,000–$5,000), $10,685,018 for 4 foundation-administered programs and $128,250 for 1 loan/program-related investment.

Purpose and activities: Grants primarily for education, health, and human services. Operating programs include a western art museum, an historical home, a theater for the performing arts, and a botanical/nature classroom.
Fields of interest: Education; Health care; Human services.
Type of support: Continuing support; Management development/capacity building; Capital campaigns; Building/renovation; Equipment; Program development; Publication; Curriculum development; Program evaluation; Grants to individuals; In-kind gifts; Matching/challenge support.
Limitations: Giving primarily in southeastern TX. No grants to individuals (except local contest award winners), or for endowment funds or operating budgets.
Publications: Application guidelines; Annual report.
Application information: Faxed or e-mailed letters of proposal are not accepted; application guidelines available on foundation Web site. Application form not required.
   Initial approach: Letter of proposal
   Copies of proposal: 1
   Deadline(s): Mar. 1, June 1 and Oct. 1
   Board meeting date(s): Quarterly
   Final notification: 2 months
Officers and Trustees:* Laurence R. David,* Chair.; Ruby J. Wimberley,* Vice-Chair.; W.G. Riedel III,* C.E.O. and Pres.; Roy S. Wingate,* Secy.; Clyde V. McKee III,* C.F.O, V.P. and Treas.; Eunice R. Benckenstein, Dir. Emeritus; R. Frederick Gregory, M.D.; John Cash Smith.
Number of staff: 13 full-time professional; 3 part-time professional; 45 full-time support; 37 part-time support.
EIN: 746047440
Selected grants: The following grants were reported in 2005.

$77,936 to Capland Center for Communication Disorders, Port Arthur, TX. For matching grant for new facility construction.

$75,400 to Orange Texas Police Department, Orange, TX. For matching grant for Homeland Security.

$75,000 to Julie Rogers Gift of Life Free Mammogram Program, Beaumont, TX. For mammogram and prostate screening.

$58,500 to Orange County Association for Retarded Citizens, Orange, TX. For new engraver for workshop and lost revenues due to Hurricane Rita.

$50,000 to United Way of Orange County, Orange, TX. For assistance for local nonprofits.

$40,000 to West Orange-Cove Consolidated Independent School District, Orange, TX. For assistance for UIL Competitions.

$35,000 to K V L U - FM, Beaumont, TX. For public radio-APM affiliation and program fees.

$35,000 to Triangle AIDS Network (TAN), Beaumont, TX. For supplemental food cards and copays.

$25,000 to Samaritan Counseling Center of Southeast Texas, Port Arthur, TX. For counseling for indigent persons in Orange County.

$20,000 to Self-Help Housing of East Texas, Newton, TX. To assist in qualifying for grant from USDA Rural Development for Self-Help Housing Program.

9210
Dorothy Richard Starling Foundation

P.O. Box 66709
Houston, TX 77266
Contact: Dunham F. Jewett, Tr.
Application address: 2727 Allen Pkwy., Ste. 1700,
Houston, TX 77019-2125

Foundation established in 1969 in TX.
Donor: Frank M. Starling‡.
Foundation type: Independent foundation.
Financial data (yr. ended 12/31/04): Assets,
$31,311,310 (M); expenditures, $1,680,945;
qualifying distributions, $1,507,071; giving
activities include $1,468,333 for 21 grants (high:
$125,000; low: $15,000).
Purpose and activities: Support for classical violin
discipline, teaching, and scholarships made through
institutions.
Fields of interest: Performing arts, music.
Type of support: General/operating support;
Endowments; Professorships; Fellowships;
Scholarship funds.
Publications: Annual report.
Application information: Program must relate to
classical violin at highest levels. Application form
not required.
　Initial approach: Letter
　Copies of proposal: 3
　Deadline(s): None
　Board meeting date(s): Feb.
　Final notification: Within 60 days
Trustees: Dunham F. Jewett; Melinda M. Kacal;
Alexander C. Speyer, Jr.
Number of staff: 1 part-time professional.
EIN: 746121656

9211
Stemmons Foundation ✧

P.O. Box 143127
Irving, TX 75014-3127
Contact: Mary Lee J. Virden, Secy.-Treas.

Established in 1963 in TX.
Foundation type: Independent foundation.
Financial data (yr. ended 12/31/04): Assets,
$34,226,648 (M); expenditures, $1,476,172;
qualifying distributions, $1,416,458; giving
activities include $1,415,800 for 59 grants (high:
$500,000; low: $3,500).
Fields of interest: Performing arts, music; Arts;
Education; Human services; Children/youth,
services.
Type of support: Capital campaigns; Building/
renovation; Equipment; Program development;
Curriculum development; Technical assistance.
Limitations: Giving primarily in Dallas, TX. No grants
to individuals, or for scholarships; no loans.
Publications: Application guidelines.
Application information: Application form not
required.
　Initial approach: Proposal
　Copies of proposal: 1
　Deadline(s): Apr. 1 and Oct. 1
　Board meeting date(s): May and Nov.
　Final notification: 10 days after board meeting
Officers: Allison S. Simon, Pres.; Heinz K. Simon,
V.P.; Jean H. Rose, V.P.; Mary Lee J. Virden,
Secy.-Treas. and Mgr.
Number of staff: 1 part-time support.
EIN: 756039966

Selected grants: The following grants were reported
in 2004.
$600,000 to Dallas Center for the Performing Arts,
　Dallas, TX. 2 grants: $100,000, $500,000
$110,000 to International Exotic Feline Sanctuary,
　Boyd, TX. 2 grants: $10,000, $100,000
$50,000 to Booker T. Washington High School for
　the Performing and Visual Arts, Dallas, TX.
$25,000 to Agnes Scott College, Decatur, GA.
$16,000 to West Dallas Community School, Dallas,
　TX.
$15,000 to Dallas Opera, Dallas, TX.
$15,000 to Dallas Symphony Association, Dallas,
　TX.
$10,000 to Dallas Summer Musicals, Dallas, TX.

9212
Sterling-Turner Foundation ✧

(formerly Turner Charitable Foundation)
815 Walker St., Ste. 1543
Houston, TX 77002-5724 (713) 237-1117
Contact: Patricia Moser, Exec. Asst.
FAX: (713) 223-4638;
E-mail: patricia@sterlingturnerfoundation.org;
URL: http://sterlingturnerfoundation.org

Incorporated in 1960 in TX.
Donors: Isla Carroll Turner‡; P.E. Turner‡.
Foundation type: Independent foundation.
Financial data (yr. ended 12/31/04): Assets,
$46,716,781 (M); expenditures, $3,250,732;
qualifying distributions, $3,111,006; giving
activities include $3,001,700 for 63 grants (high:
$800,000; low: $1,000).
Purpose and activities: Giving for higher and
secondary education, social services, youth, the
elderly, fine and performing arts groups and other
cultural programs, Catholic, Jewish, and Protestant
church support and religious programs, hospitals,
health services, AIDS research, hospices, programs
for women and children, minorities, the homeless,
the handicapped, urban and community
development, civic and urban affairs, libraries, and
conservation programs.
Fields of interest: Visual arts; Museums; Performing
arts; Performing arts, theater; Historic preservation/
historical societies; Arts; Education, association;
Education, research; Education, fund raising/fund
distribution; Elementary/secondary education; Child
development, education; Secondary school/
education; Higher education; Adult education—
literacy, basic skills & GED; Libraries/library
science; Education, reading; Education;
Environment, natural resources; Hospitals (general);
Medical care, rehabilitation; Health care; Substance
abuse, services; Mental health/crisis services;
Cancer; Heart & circulatory diseases; AIDS; Cancer
research; Heart & circulatory research; AIDS
research; Crime/violence prevention, domestic
violence; Food services; Recreation; Children/youth,
services; Child development, services; Family
services; Residential/custodial care, hospices;
Minorities/immigrants, centers/services;
Homeless, human services; Community
development, business promotion; Community
development; Protestant agencies & churches;
Roman Catholic agencies & churches; Jewish
agencies & temples; Religion; Children; Youth;
Aging; Minorities; African Americans/Blacks;
Hispanics/Latinos; Women; AIDS, people with;
Homeless.
Type of support: General/operating support; Annual
campaigns; Capital campaigns; Building/

renovation; Equipment; Land acquisition;
Endowments; Debt reduction; Emergency funds;
Program development; Conferences/seminars;
Professorships; Publication; Seed money;
Curriculum development; Fellowships; Scholarship
funds; Research; Matching/challenge support.
Limitations: Giving limited to Travis, Harris, Kerr,
Fort Bend, and Tom Greene counties, TX. No grants
to individuals.
Publications: Application guidelines; Financial
statement.
Application information: Guidelines can be found on
Web site. Application form available on foundation
Web site. Application form required.
　Initial approach: On-line application
　Copies of proposal: 1
　Deadline(s): Mar. 1 at 5PM
　Board meeting date(s): First Tues. in Apr.
Officers and Trustees:* T.R. Reckling III,* Pres.;
Bert F. Winston, Jr.,* V.P.; Christiana R. McConn,*
Secy.; Isla C. Reckling,* Treas.; Eyvonne Moser,
Exec. Dir.; Carroll R. Goodman; Chaille W. Hawkins;
James S. Reckling; John B. Reckling; Stephen M.
Reckling; T.R. "Cliff" Reckling IV; Thomas K.
Reckling; Blake W. Winston; L. David Winston; Bert
F. Winston III.
Number of staff: 2 full-time professional.
EIN: 741460482
Selected grants: The following grants were reported
in 2003.
$400,000 to Saint Joseph Hospital Foundation,
　Houston, TX.
$300,000 to Brookwood Community, Brookshire,
　TX.
$200,000 to Saint Thomas High School, Houston,
　TX.
$180,000 to University of Houston System,
　Houston, TX.
$105,000 to Kinkaid School, Houston, TX.
$100,000 to Episcopal High School, Bellaire, TX.
$90,000 to Schreiner University, Kerrville, TX.
$60,000 to Texas Childrens Hospital, Houston, TX.
$50,000 to Girl Scouts of the U.S.A., San Jacinto
　Council, Houston, TX.
$50,000 to Star of Hope Mission, Houston, TX.

9213
The Marlene and J. O. Stewart, Jr. Foundation ✧ ☆

124 W. Castellano, Ste. 100
El Paso, TX 79912
Contact: Ron F. Acton, Pres.

Established in 2000 in TX.
Donors: Marlene Stewart; James O. Stewart, Jr.
Foundation type: Independent foundation.
Financial data (yr. ended 12/31/05): Assets,
$4,101,945 (M); expenditures, $431,988;
qualifying distributions, $346,317; giving activities
include $346,317 for grants.
Purpose and activities: Giving primarily for Christian
agencies and churches.
Fields of interest: Arts; Health organizations,
association; Human services; Christian agencies &
churches.
Limitations: Giving primarily in TX. No grants to
individuals.
Application information:
　Initial approach: Letter
　Deadline(s): None

Officers and Directors:* Ron F. Acton,* Pres.;
Myron Brown,* V.P.; James O. Stewart, Jr.,* V.P.;
James O. Stewart III,* V.P.; Marlene Stewart,* V.P.
EIN: 742958268
Selected grants: The following grants were reported
in 2003.
$25,000 to University of Texas, El Paso, TX. For
Music Department.
$20,000 to Luis Palau Evangelistic Association,
Portland, OR. To support gatherings.
$10,000 to El Paso Opera Company, El Paso, TX.
$7,000 to Kings Kids El Paso, El Paso, TX.
$5,000 to Hospice of El Paso, El Paso, TX. For
cancer patients.
$5,000 to Lydia Patterson Institute of the Methodist
Church, El Paso, TX. To support work scholarship
program for needy children.
$5,000 to Pastoral Counseling Service of El Paso,
El Paso, TX.
$5,000 to Revival Tabernacle Assembly of God,
Highland Park, MI. For general support.
$5,000 to Rick Renner Ministries, Tulsa, OK.
$3,000 to Gathering, The, Tyler, TX.

9214
Gayle and Paul Stoffel Foundation ◇
5949 Sherry Ln., Ste. 1465
Dallas, TX 75225

Established in 1997 in TX.
Donors: Paul Stoffel; Gayle Stoffel.
Foundation type: Independent foundation.
Financial data (yr. ended 12/31/04): Assets,
$83,647 (M); expenditures, $535,214; qualifying
distributions, $535,064; giving activities include
$533,439 for 52 grants (high: $310,000; low: $25).
Purpose and activities: Giving primarily for the arts.
Fields of interest: Performing arts, orchestra
(symphony); Arts.
Type of support: General/operating support.
Limitations: Applications not accepted. Giving
primarily in Dallas, TX. No grants to individuals.
Application information: Contributes only to
pre-selected organizations.
Officers: Paul Stoffel, Pres.; Gayle Stoffel, V.P.
EIN: 311542757
Selected grants: The following grants were reported
in 2004.
$310,000 to Episcopal School of Dallas, Dallas, TX.
$101,800 to Dallas Museum of Art, Dallas, TX.
$10,000 to Dallas Symphony Association, Dallas,
TX.
$5,300 to Aspen Art Museum, Aspen, CO. 2 grants:
$5,000, $300
$5,000 to Educational First Steps, Dallas, TX.
$5,000 to Harvard Business School Fund, Boston,
MA.
$855 to Nasher Sculpture Center, Dallas, TX.
$750 to TACA, Dallas, TX.
$335 to Music Associates of Aspen, Aspen, CO.

9215
Strake Foundation
712 Main St., Ste. 3300
Houston, TX 77002-3210 (713) 216-2400
Contact: George W. Strake, Jr., Pres.
E-mail: foundation@strake.org

Trust established in 1952 in TX; incorporated in
1983.

Donors: George W. Strake, Sr.†; Susan K. Strake†;
George W. Strake, Jr.; Susan S. Dilworth†;
Georganna S. Parsley†.
Foundation type: Independent foundation.
Financial data (yr. ended 12/31/05): Assets,
$52,350,742 (M); expenditures, $2,694,341;
qualifying distributions, $2,409,000; giving
activities include $2,224,780 for 363 grants (high:
$100,000; low: $500).
Purpose and activities: Giving primarily to hospitals,
medical research, and secondary and higher
educational institutions, cultural and social
services, including programs for youth.
Fields of interest: Secondary school/education;
Higher education; Hospitals (general); Health care;
Medical research, institute; Human services;
Children/youth, services; Roman Catholic agencies
& churches; Religion; Disabilities, people with;
Minorities.
Type of support: General/operating support;
Continuing support; Annual campaigns; Capital
campaigns; Building/renovation; Equipment;
Program development; Professorships; Scholarship
funds; Research; Matching/challenge support.
Limitations: Giving primarily in TX, especially
Houston; no grants outside the U.S. No support for
elementary schools or federally funded institutions
of higher learning. No grants to individuals, or for
deficit financing, consulting services or technical
assistance; no loans.
Publications: Application guidelines; Annual report
(including application guidelines); Informational
brochure.
Application information: Application form required.
Initial approach: Brief written proposal
Copies of proposal: 1
Deadline(s): Submit proposal before Apr. 1 or Oct.
1
Board meeting date(s): May and Nov.
Final notification: Within 45 days
Officers and Director:* George W. Strake, Jr.,*
Pres. and Treas.; Paul L. Robison, Jr., Exec. Dir.
Number of staff: 3 part-time professional.
EIN: 760041524

9216
Roy and Christine Sturgis Charitable and Educational Trust ◇
c/o Bank of America, N.A.
P.O. Box 830241
Dallas, TX 75283-0241 (214) 209-1965
Contact: Daniel J. Kelly, Sr. V.P., Bank of America,
N.A.

Established in 1981 in AR.
Donor: Christine Sturgis†.
Foundation type: Independent foundation.
Financial data (yr. ended 9/30/05): Assets,
$48,197,000 (M); expenditures, $3,341,992;
qualifying distributions, $2,845,825; giving
activities include $2,700,000 for 58 grants (high:
$700,000; low: $5,000; average: $25,000–
$50,000).
Purpose and activities: Support primarily for
charitable, scientific, literary, and educational
organizations.
Fields of interest: Arts; Libraries/library science;
Education; Hospitals (general); Health care; Health
organizations, association; Medical research,
institute; Food services; Human services;
Homeless, human services; Engineering/

technology; Science; Economically disadvantaged;
Homeless.
Type of support: General/operating support; Capital
campaigns; Building/renovation; Equipment;
Endowments; Program development; Scholarship
funds; Research; Matching/challenge support.
Limitations: Giving primarily in AR and the Dallas,
TX, area. No grants to individuals or for seminars;
no loans.
Publications: Application guidelines; Program policy
statement.
Application information: No personal interviews
granted prior to receipt of application. After
application is received, a Sturgis consultant will
contact the organization to arrange a site visit.
Application form required.
Initial approach: Letter
Copies of proposal: 2
Deadline(s): Dec. 31
Board meeting date(s): Apr.
Final notification: May
Trustee Bank: Bank of America, N.A.
Number of staff: 1 part-time professional; 1
part-time support.
EIN: 756331832
Selected grants: The following grants were reported
in 2005.
$700,000 to William J. Clinton Presidential
Foundation, Little Rock, AR.
$200,000 to Henderson State University,
Arkadelphia, AR.
$100,000 to Francis A. Allen School for Exceptional
Children, Little Rock, AR.
$75,000 to Dallas Center for the Performing Arts
Foundation, Dallas, TX.
$50,000 to Baylor University, Waco, TX.
$50,000 to Our House, Little Rock, AR.
$45,000 to Mi Escuelita Preschool, Dallas, TX.
$25,000 to Captain Hopes Kids, Dallas, TX.
$20,000 to Centers for Youth and Families, Little
Rock, AR.
$20,000 to Dallas Museum of Natural History,
Dallas, TX.

9217
The Summerlee Foundation
5956 Sherry Ln., Ste. 610
Dallas, TX 75225-8017 (214) 363-9000
Contact: John W. Crain, Pres.
FAX: (214) 363-1941; *E-mail:* info@summerlee.org;
Animal Protection Program Address: c/o Melanie A.
Lambert, Prog. Dir., 716 N. Tejon, Ste. 9, Colorado
Springs, CO, 80903; tel.: (800) 265-7515, FAX:
(719) 266-5459; URL: http://www.summerlee.org/

Established in 1988 in TX.
Donor: Annie Lee Roberts†.
Foundation type: Independent foundation.
Financial data (yr. ended 6/30/05): Assets,
$55,077,059 (M); gifts received, $4,100;
expenditures, $2,727,611; qualifying distributions,
$2,183,081; giving activities include $1,441,965
for 62 grants (high: $356,000; low: $2,000).
Purpose and activities: Giving limited to 1) the
alleviation of pain and suffering and the prevention
of cruelty to animals; and 2) for the study,
promotion, preservation, and documentation of all
facets of TX history.
Fields of interest: History/archaeology; Historic
preservation/historical societies; Animal welfare;
Animals/wildlife, preservation/protection.
International interests: Canada; Mexico.

Type of support: Film/video/radio; Professorships; Capital campaigns; Building/renovation; Equipment; Land acquisition; Endowments; Program development; Conferences/seminars; Publication; Seed money; Curriculum development; Fellowships; Internship funds; Research; Technical assistance; Matching/challenge support.
Limitations: Giving primarily in TX for historical preservation; National and international giving for animal welfare program. No support for religious purposes. No grants to individuals.
Publications: Application guidelines; Grants list.
Application information: See foundation Web site for programs, and application guidelines including deadlines and procedures. Faxed or E-mailed applications will not be accepted. Application form not required.
> *Initial approach:* Telephone or letter (no more than two pages)
> *Copies of proposal:* 1
> *Deadline(s):* Deadlines vary every year. See Foundation Web site.
> *Board meeting date(s):* Quarterly
> *Final notification:* 3 months

Officers and Directors:* John W. Crain,* Pres. and Prog. Dir., TX history; Hon. David D. Jackson,* V.P. and Treas.; Melanie A. Lambert,* V.P. and Prog. Dir., Animal Protection; Lynne K. Starnes, Corp. Secy.; Martha Benson; Ron Tyler.
Number of staff: 2 full-time professional; 1 part-time professional; 1 full-time support.
EIN: 752252355
Selected grants: The following grants were reported in 2005.
$356,000 to Spay-Neuter Assistance Program, Houston, TX.
$100,000 to Old Red Courthouse, Dallas, TX.
$75,000 to Frontiers of Flight Museum, Dallas, TX.
$70,000 to Witte Museum, San Antonio, TX.
$50,000 to Austin College, Sherman, TX.
$30,000 to Southern Methodist University, Dallas, TX.
$28,300 to Kittico Cat Rescue, Dallas, TX.
$20,000 to Galveston Historical Foundation, Galveston, TX.
$15,000 to Saint Josephs Indian School, Chamberlain, SD.
$7,500 to Trumpeter Swan Society, Maple Plain, MN.

9218
Hatton W. Sumners Foundation for the Study and Teaching of Self-Government, Inc. ✧

(formerly Hatton W. Sumners Foundation)
325 N. Saint Paul St., Ste. 3920
Dallas, TX 75201-3821 (214) 220-2128
Contact: Hugh C. Akin, Exec. Dir.
FAX: (214) 953-0737;
E-mail: info@hattonsumners.org; Additional E-mail: hugh@hattonsumners.org; URL: http://www.hattonsumners.org

Trust established in 1949 in TX, became a Texas nonprofit corporation in 1998.
Foundation type: Independent foundation.
Financial data (yr. ended 12/31/05): Assets, $61,629,432 (M); gifts received, $23,420; expenditures, $4,000,845; qualifying distributions, $2,845,410; giving activities include $2,250,526 for 45 grants (high: $300,000; low: $2,500), and $120,000 for 3 employee matching gifts.

Purpose and activities: Giving for youth organizations, higher education and others for the study and teaching of the science of self-government.
Fields of interest: Higher education; Law school/education; Teacher school/education; Big Brothers/Big Sisters; Boy scouts; YM/YWCAs & YM/YWHAs; Youth, services; Foundations (community); Social sciences, public policy; Political science; Government/public administration.
Type of support: General/operating support; Continuing support; Endowments; Program development; Conferences/seminars; Curriculum development; Fellowships; Internship funds; Scholarship funds; Research; Matching/challenge support.
Limitations: Giving primarily in TX and the southwestern states. No support for religious organizations. No grants to individuals directly.
Publications: Application guidelines; Grants list; Informational brochure (including application guidelines).
Application information: Summary Grant Application form required. One of the copies of the proposal must be unbound. Application information and form available on foundation Web site. Separate application guidelines for challenge grants. Scholarships are controlled by various universities administering the program. Applications sent via E-mail or fax are not accepted. Application form required.
> *Initial approach:* Letter
> *Copies of proposal:* 2
> *Deadline(s):* Aug. 1
> *Board meeting date(s):* Varies
> *Final notification:* Early Nov.

Officers and Trustees:* James Cleo Thompson, Jr.,* Chair.; Alfred Paul Murrah, Jr.,* Vice-Chair.; William C. Pannell,* Secy.; Thomas Slater Walker,* Treas.; Hugh Clark Akin,* Exec. Dir.; Gordon R. Carpenter; Laura L. Cross; David G. Drumm; David B. Long; William W. Meadows; Charles L. Moore; Jerry D. Reis; Christy Thompson; Lon R. Williams, Jr.
Number of staff: 1 full-time professional; 2 full-time support.
EIN: 752734032
Selected grants: The following grants were reported in 2004.
$300,000 to National Center for Policy Analysis, Dallas, TX.
$75,000 to Bill of Rights Institute, Arlington, VA.
$75,000 to Oklahoma Council of Public Affairs, Oklahoma City, OK.
$75,000 to University of North Texas, Denton, TX.
$75,000 to YMCA of Metropolitan Fort Worth, Fort Worth, TX.
$63,000 to YMCA of Greater Oklahoma City, Oklahoma City, OK.
$55,000 to New Mexico First, Albuquerque, NM.
$50,000 to Oklahoma Christian University, Oklahoma City, OK.
$50,000 to YMCA of Metropolitan Dallas, Dallas, TX.
$10,000 to Espanola Valley High School, Espanola, NM.

9219
Sunnyside Foundation, Inc. ✧

(formerly Sunnyside, Inc.)
8222 Douglas Ave., Ste. 501
Dallas, TX 75225 (214) 692-5686
Contact: Peggy Hueffner, Exec. Dir.

FAX: (214) 692-1968;
E-mail: sunnysidetexas@sbcglobal.net

Established in 1928 in TX.
Donors: I. Jalonick†; K. Jalonick†.
Foundation type: Independent foundation.
Financial data (yr. ended 12/31/05): Assets, $27,856,892 (M); gifts received, $4,116; expenditures, $1,670,796; qualifying distributions, $1,335,479; giving activities include $1,253,796 for grants to individuals.
Purpose and activities: Giving exclusively to members of the Christian Science faith for education, camp, Christian Science care and general assistance.
Type of support: Emergency funds; Grants to individuals; Scholarships—to individuals.
Limitations: Giving limited to residents of TX.
Publications: Application guidelines; Informational brochure (including application guidelines); Program policy statement (including application guidelines).
Application information: Application form required.
> *Initial approach:* Application can be mailed, faxed or e-mailed
> *Deadline(s):* 1 week before board meeting
> *Board meeting date(s):* Last Fri. of each month
> *Final notification:* 2-3 days after board meeting

Officers: Greg McLane, Pres.; Tony Givins, V.P.; Chris Slaughter, Treas.; Peggy Heuffner, Exec. Dir.
Trustees: Sharon Wootton; Peggy Williams.
Number of staff: 1 full-time professional; 1 part-time support.
EIN: 756037004

9220
Susman Family Foundation ✧

c/o Ellen Susman
2001 Kirby Dr., Ste. 702
Houston, TX 77019 (713) 653-7839

Established in 1998 in TX.
Donor: Stephen D. Susman.
Foundation type: Independent foundation.
Financial data (yr. ended 3/31/05): Assets, $5,054,938 (M); expenditures, $473,985; qualifying distributions, $429,156; giving activities include $425,645 for 68 grants (high: $50,000; low: $100).
Purpose and activities: Giving for higher education and for Jewish organizations.
Fields of interest: Museums (art); Arts; Higher education, university; Human services; Jewish agencies & temples.
Limitations: Applications not accepted. Giving primarily in NY and TX.
Application information: Contributes only to pre-selected organizations.
Officers: Ellen Susman, Pres.; Harry P. Susman, V.P. and Secy.; Stacy M. Kuhn, V.P. and Treas.; Stephen D. Susman, V.P.
EIN: 760569093
Selected grants: The following grants were reported in 2004.
$55,000 to Alley Theater, Houston, TX.
$10,000 to Congregation Beth Israel, Houston, TX.
$10,000 to United Way of the Texas Gulf Coast, Houston, TX.
$10,000 to Yale University, New Haven, CT.
$5,000 to National Foundation for Jewish Culture, New York, NY.
$3,000 to University of Texas, Austin, TX.
$2,500 to Glassell School of Art, Houston, TX.

$1,000 to Emery/Weiner Center for Jewish Education, Houston, TX.
$1,000 to Kinkaid School, Houston, TX.
$100 to Chinquapin School, Highlands, TX.

9221
Ralph & Eileen Swett Foundation ◇
1114 Lost Creek Blvd., Ste. 200
Austin, TX 78746
E-mail: mswett@swettfoundation.org; URL: http://www.swettfoundation.org

Established in 1999 in NV.
Donors: Ralph Swett; Eileen Swett.
Foundation type: Independent foundation.
Financial data (yr. ended 5/31/05): Assets, $5,633,293 (M); expenditures, $591,676; qualifying distributions, $475,174; giving activities include $456,131 for 12 grants (high: $102,500; low: $6,000).
Purpose and activities: The foundation's mission is to make a positive difference in the lives of individuals. It has identified 1)the assistance of orphaned children including the promotion of their adoption and 2)intervention in the lives of troubled youths as two areas of interest to which it expects to direct a portion of its funding each year. Funding, however, is by no means limited to these areas.
Fields of interest: Health care; Human services; Children, adoption; International relief; Roman Catholic agencies & churches.
Limitations: Applications not accepted. Giving on a national basis. No grants to individuals.
Application information: Contributes only to pre-selected organizations. See foundation Web site for application information.
Officer: Robin Swett Wooten, Pres.
Directors: Eileen Swett; Jeffrey Swett; Michael Swett; Ralph Swett; Timothy Swett.
EIN: 742940596

9222
Edward F. Swinney Trust ◇
c/o Bank of America, N.A.
P.O. Box 831041
Dallas, TX 75283-1041
Application address: c/o Greater Kansas City Comm. Fdn.,1055 Broadway, Ste. 130, Kansas City, MO 64105, tel.: (816) 842-0944; Fax: (816) 842-8079; e-mail: grants@gkccf.org

Trust established in 1946 in MO; affiliated trust of the Greater Kansas City Community Foundation and its Affiliated Trusts.
Donor: Edward F. Swinney†.
Foundation type: Independent foundation.
Financial data (yr. ended 12/31/05): Assets, $21,017,602 (M); expenditures, $738,369; qualifying distributions, $738,369; giving activities include $675,000 for 3 grants (high: $300,000; low: $125,000).
Purpose and activities: To further and develop local charitable and educational purposes; grants for mental health, higher education, hospitals, rehabilitation, and other health and welfare and community action programs; support for consolidation and monitoring of present arts and humanities projects. Giving for demonstration and experimental projects, extension and improvement of human services, with preference in the voluntary sector, planning and cooperation among voluntary

agencies and between public and private agencies, and for education and training in community service.
Fields of interest: Arts; Mental health/crisis services; Health organizations, association; Human services; Children/youth, services; Urban/community development; Community development; Foundations (community).
Type of support: Continuing support; Equipment; Program development; Seed money; Technical assistance; Program evaluation; Matching/challenge support.
Limitations: Giving limited to Kansas City, MO. No grants to individuals, business start-up, debt reduction or annual appeals.
Publications: Application guidelines; Annual report; Grants list; Newsletter.
Application information: Application guidelines available upon request. See also Greater Kansas City Community Foundation Web site: http://www.gkccf.org, for application information. Application form not required.
Initial approach: Letter or proposal
Copies of proposal: 1
Deadline(s): None
Board meeting date(s): Quarterly
Final notification: Quarterly
Officers and Directors:* Richard C. Green,* Chair.; Laura A. Cray,* Vice-Chair.; Drue Jennings,* Vice-Chair.; William C. Nelson,* Vice-Chair.; Janice C. Kreamer, Pres.; David F. Oliver,* Secy.; Sandra A.J. Lawrence,* Treas.; and 19 additional directors.
Trustee: Bank of America, N.A.
Number of staff: 13 full-time professional; 1 part-time professional; 8 full-time support; 1 part-time support.
EIN: 446009264

9223
The Tapeats Fund ◇
P.O. Box 1063
Houston, TX 77251 (713) 830-3400
Application address: c/o Patricia N. Lewis, 11 Greenway Plz., Ste. 2600, Houston, TX 77046, tel.: (713) 830-3400

Established in 1993 in TX.
Donors: Robert H. Graham; Laurel A.W. Graham.
Foundation type: Independent foundation.
Financial data (yr. ended 12/31/05): Assets, $14,915,634 (M); gifts received, $483,339; expenditures, $823,609; qualifying distributions, $686,087; giving activities include $581,000 for 59 grants (high: $44,400; low: $2,500).
Purpose and activities: Support for organizations which benefit the health, education, and general welfare of children; support also for zoos, animal shelters and wildlife associations, and organizations which preserve or enrich the environment; and for civic revitalization in Houston, TX.
Fields of interest: Education; Environment; Animals/wildlife; Health care; Human services; Children/youth, services; Federated giving programs.
Type of support: General/operating support; Continuing support; Annual campaigns; Capital campaigns; Building/renovation; Equipment.
Limitations: Giving primarily in TX, with emphasis on Houston.
Publications: Application guidelines.
Application information: Application form not required.
Initial approach: Letter

Copies of proposal: 1
Deadline(s): None
Board meeting date(s): 4th quarter
Officers: Robert H. Graham, Pres. and Treas.; Laurel A. Graham, Exec. V.P. and Secy.; David R. Graham, V.P.; Patricia N. Lewis, Exec. Dir.
Trustee: Spencer R. Graham; Whitney Laurel Graham.
Number of staff: 6 full-time support.
EIN: 760412011

9224
Hope Pierce Tartt Scholarship Fund ◇
P.O. Box 1964
Marshall, TX 75671-1964
Contact: E.N. Smith, Jr., Chair.

Established in 1978 in TX.
Donor: Hope Pierce Tartt†.
Foundation type: Independent foundation.
Financial data (yr. ended 5/31/05): Assets, $11,006,803 (M); expenditures, $615,511; qualifying distributions, $540,048; giving activities include $507,000 for 14 grants (high: $185,000; low: $4,000).
Purpose and activities: To assist in providing education for east TX students attending a tax exempt school in TX or Centenary College of Louisiana.
Fields of interest: Higher education.
Type of support: Scholarship funds.
Limitations: Giving primarily in Harrison, Panola, Marion, Gregg, and Upshur counties, TX. No support for tax supported colleges or universities. No grants to individuals.
Publications: Application guidelines; Program policy statement.
Application information: Students must contact financial aid offices of participating schools for application. Foundation does not select individuals for grants. Application form required.
Initial approach: Letter
Copies of proposal: 1
Deadline(s): Varies
Board meeting date(s): Feb. and as required
Final notification: Varies
Officers: E.N. Smith, Jr., Chair.; Robert L. Duvall, Secy.-Treas.
Directors: Joel D. McMahon III; Bushe Morgan.
Number of staff: 1 part-time support.
EIN: 756263272

9225
The Charles W. Tate & Judy Spence Tate Charitable Foundation ◇
3640 Del Monte
Houston, TX 77019
Contact: Judy S. Tate, Tr.
Additional address: 4646 Hwy. 6 S., Ste. 345, Sugarland, TX 77478

Established in 1994.
Donor: Charles W. Tate.
Foundation type: Independent foundation.
Financial data (yr. ended 12/31/05): Assets, $2,468,583 (M); expenditures, $381,738; qualifying distributions, $368,990; giving activities include $367,500 for 6 grants (high: $100,000; low: $5,000).
Purpose and activities: Giving primarily for higher and other education.

Fields of interest: Higher education; Education; Christian agencies & churches.
Type of support: General/operating support; Continuing support; Capital campaigns; Building/renovation; Program development; Research.
Limitations: Giving primarily in Houston, TX.
Application information: Application form not required.
  Initial approach: Letter
  Copies of proposal: 1
  Deadline(s): None
Trustees: Charles W. Tate; Judy Spence Tate.
EIN: 137047916
Selected grants: The following grants were reported in 2004.
$250,000 to Kinkaid School, Houston, TX.
$200,000 to Texas State Historical Association, Austin, TX.
$10,000 to West Texas Boys Ranch, San Angelo, TX.
$5,000 to Childrens Museum of the Brazos Valley, Bryan, TX.
$5,000 to Womens Fund for Health Education and Research, Houston, TX.

9226
Taylor County Historical Foundation ◆
400 Pine St., Ste. 1000
Abilene, TX 79601-5142

Established in 1999 in TX.
Donors: Dian Graves Owen Foundation; Dodge Jones Foundation; First National Bank of Abilene.
Foundation type: Independent foundation.
Financial data (yr. ended 12/31/04): Assets, $834 (M); gifts received, $1,057,475; expenditures, $1,583,906; qualifying distributions, $1,583,906; giving activities include $1,582,706 for 3 grants (high: $1,338,073; low: $32,475).
Fields of interest: Museums; Museums (specialized); Community development.
Limitations: Applications not accepted. Giving primarily in Abilene, TX. No grants to individuals.
Application information: Contributes only to pre-selected organizations.
Officers: Tucker S. Bridwell, Pres.; Dian G. Stai, V.P.; H.C. Zachary, Secy.; Joseph E. Canon, Treas.
EIN: 752802500
Selected grants: The following grants were reported in 2003.
$894,400 to Frontier Texas, Abilene, TX. For Exhibits and Sculptures.
$203,128 to Abilene, City of, Abilene, TX. For Frontier Texas Building.
$33,970 to Grady McWhiney Research Foundation, Abilene, TX. To establish public historical museum.

9227
T. L. L. Temple Foundation ▼
109 Temple Blvd., Ste. 300
Lufkin, TX 75901
Contact: M.F. "Buddy" Zeagler, Deputy Exec. Dir.

Trust established in 1962 in TX.
Donors: Georgie T. Munz‡; Katherine S. Temple‡.
Foundation type: Independent foundation.
Financial data (yr. ended 11/30/05): Assets, $354,397,952 (M); expenditures, $16,103,186; qualifying distributions, $15,127,476; giving

activities include $14,772,983 for 154 grants (high: $3,379,657; low: $100).
Purpose and activities: Support for education, health, and community and social services; support also for civic affairs and cultural programs.
Fields of interest: Arts; Elementary school/education; Higher education; Adult/continuing education; Education; Animal welfare; Hospitals (general); Medical care, rehabilitation; Health care; Substance abuse, services; Mental health/crisis services; Human services; Residential/custodial care, hospices; Community development; Government/public administration; Economically disadvantaged.
Type of support: Professorships; General/operating support; Capital campaigns; Building/renovation; Equipment; Emergency funds; Program development; Scholarship funds; Research; Program-related investments/loans; Employee matching gifts; Matching/challenge support.
Limitations: Giving primarily in counties in TX constituting the East Texas Pine Timber Belt. No support for private foundations. No grants to individuals, or for deficit financing.
Publications: Application guidelines; Program policy statement.
Application information: Application form required.
  Initial approach: Letter
  Copies of proposal: 1
  Deadline(s): None
  Board meeting date(s): As required
  Final notification: 2 - 3 months
Officers and Trustees:* Arthur Temple III,* Chair.; M.F. Zeagler, Cont.; A. Wayne Corley, Exec. Dir.; Ward R. Burke; Phillip M. Leach; H.J. Shands III; Charlotte Temple; W. Temple Webber, Jr.; W. Temple Webber III; Charles N. Wilson.
Number of staff: 4 full-time professional; 2 part-time professional; 1 part-time support.
EIN: 756037406
Selected grants: The following grants were reported in 2005.
$6,232,041 to Memorial Medical Center of East Texas, Lufkin, TX. 2 grants: $3,379,657 (For cancer center), $2,852,384 (For information systems).
$1,000,000 to University of Texas Health Science Center, Houston, TX. For New Frontiers Campaign- Molecular Medicine.
$787,188 to Diboll Independent School District, Diboll, TX. For new classrooms, auditorium, parking.
$724,015 to East Texas Behavioral Resources, Lufkin, TX. For construction and renovation of facility in Livingston.
$656,471 to Angelina College, Lufkin, TX. 2 grants: $654,581 (To purchase property), $1,890.
$125,000 to Salvation Army of Lufkin, Lufkin, TX. For general support.
$93,750 to Angelina County and Cities Health District, Lufkin, TX. For pharmaceutical program.
$200 to Knights Templar Eye Foundation, Springfield, IL.

9228
Temple-Inland Foundation ▼ ◆
1300 S. Mopac Expwy.
Austin, TX 78749 (936) 829-1721
Contact: M. Richard Warner, V.P.

Established in 1985 in TX.
Donors: Temple-Inland Inc.; Temple-Inland Forest Products Corp.

Foundation type: Company-sponsored foundation.
Financial data (yr. ended 6/30/05): Assets, $725,879 (M); gifts received, $4,835,770; expenditures, $5,364,474; qualifying distributions, $5,344,348; giving activities include $5,172,687 for 1,771 grants (high: $209,164), and $153,000 for 154 grants to individuals (high: $1,000; low: $500).
Purpose and activities: The foundation supports organizations involved with arts and culture, education, health, youth development, human services, and Christianity and awards college scholarships to valedictorians and salutatorians of high schools located in areas of company operations.
Fields of interest: Museums; Performing arts; Arts; Elementary/secondary education; Higher education; Education; Medical care, rehabilitation; Health care; Youth development, centers/clubs; Children/youth, services; Human services; Christian agencies & churches.
Type of support: General/operating support; Research; Employee matching gifts; Employee-related scholarships; Scholarships—to individuals.
Limitations: Giving primarily in areas of company operations. No grants to individuals (except for scholarships).
Application information:
  Initial approach: Proposal; contact foundation for application form for scholarships
  Copies of proposal: 1
  Deadline(s): Mar. 15 for scholarships
  Board meeting date(s): Quarterly
  Final notification: June 1 for new scholarship applications; Aug. 15 for renewals
Officers and Directors:* Doyle R. Simmons,* Pres.; Roger B. Smart, V.P.; Jack C. Sweeny,* V.P.; M. Richard Warner,* V.P.; Evonne Nerren, Secy.-Treas.; Kenneth R. Dubuque; Kenneth M. Jastrow II; Harold C. Maxwell; Terry R. Rodgers; Arthur Temple III.
EIN: 751977109
Selected grants: The following grants were reported in 2005.
$209,164 to United Way Capital Area, Austin, TX.
$175,000 to Diboll, City of, Diboll, TX.
$156,023 to Ronald McDonald House of Central Texas, Austin, TX.
$100,600 to Beth and Horace Stubblefield Learning Center, Lufkin, TX.
$90,000 to Diboll Boosters Club, Diboll, TX.
$78,795 to Boys and Girls Clubs of Deep East Texas, Nacogdoches, TX.
$56,921 to American Cancer Society, Lufkin, TX.
$48,428 to United Way of Angelina County, Lufkin, TX.
$25,500 to Bogalusa, City of, Bogalusa, LA.
$15,181 to Texas A & M University, College Station, TX.

9229
Tenet Healthcare Foundation ▼ ◆
13737 Noel Rd., Ste. 100
Dallas, TX 75240 (469) 893-6502
Contact: Maria Martineau Plankinton, Exec. Dir.
FAX: (469) 893-2605;
E-mail: foundation@tenethealth.com; URL: http://www.tenethealth.com/TenetHealth/TenetFoundation

Established in 1998 in DE.
Donor: Tenet Healthcare Corp.
Foundation type: Company-sponsored foundation.

Financial data (yr. ended 12/31/05): Assets, $14,925,259 (M); gifts received, $1,293,192; expenditures, $8,324,120; qualifying distributions, $7,658,415; giving activities include $4,801,422 for 1,118 grants (high: $272,424; low: $50), $1,198,940 for 589 grants to individuals (high: $2,000; low: $390), and $1,658,053 for 7,694 employee matching gifts.
Purpose and activities: The foundation supports organizations involved with arts and culture, education, health, human services, community development, civic affairs, and minorities.
Fields of interest: Humanities; Arts; Education; Public health; Health care; Human services; Community development; Public affairs; Minorities.
Type of support: General/operating support; Annual campaigns; Capital campaigns; Building/renovation; Equipment; Program development; Scholarship funds; Employee volunteer services; Sponsorships; Employee matching gifts; Employee-related scholarships; Grants to individuals; Scholarships—to individuals.
Limitations: Giving on a national basis, with emphasis on areas of company operations. No support for fraternal, labor, political, or veterans' organization. No grants to individuals (expect for scholarships and disaster relief grants), or for direct funding for hospital operations, religious activities not of direct benefit to the entire community, or travel expenses or culture exchange programs.
Publications: Application guidelines; Annual report; Program policy statement.
Application information: Application form required.
   Initial approach: Download application form and mail proposal and application form to foundation
   Copies of proposal: 1
   Deadline(s): None
   Board meeting date(s): Quarterly
   Final notification: 6 to 8 weeks
Officer and Directors: Harold O. Anderson, Pres.; Jeff Sherman, Treas.; Maria Martineau Plankinton, Exec. Dir.; Trevor Fetter; Cathy Fraser; John Holland; Caitlin Larsen; Bob Smith.
Number of staff: 2 full-time professional.
EIN: 742873537
Selected grants: The following grants were reported in 2004.
$502,000 to Philadelphia Health and Education Corporation, Philadelphia, PA. For Center for the Study of Nosocomial Infections.
$305,600 to Scholarship America, Saint Peter, MN. Toward scholarships for employees' children.
$272,635 to Florida Atlantic University Foundation, College of Nursing, Boca Raton, FL. For accelerated career entry and BSN programs for nursing.
$206,914 to Georgia State University Research Foundation, Atlanta, GA. For accelerated career entry and BSN programs for nursing.
$179,280 to Texas Womans University, Houston Center, Denton, TX. For accelerated career entry and BSN programs for nursing.
$153,322 to University of Texas, El Paso, TX. For accelerated career entry and BSN programs for nursing.
$128,333 to TELACU Education Foundation, Los Angeles, CA. For nursing scholarships, program outreach, and to promote healthcare careers in secondary schools.
$73,010 to National Merit Scholarship Corporation, Evanston, IL. For merit scholarship.
$62,530 to Drexel University, College of Nursing and Health Professions, Philadelphia, PA. For

faculty positions to develop leadership and technology skills program for nursing management, registered nurses and supportive, assistive staff.
$60,000 to Teach for America, Los Angeles, CA. For recruitment, selection, training, and placement of corps members in Tenet's major sites.

9230
Tennessee Titans Foundation ✧ ☆
P.O. Box 844
Houston, TX 77001
Contact: K.S. Adams, Jr., Pres.

Established in 1999 in TN.
Donors: Tennessee Football, Inc.; K.S. Adams, Jr.
Foundation type: Company-sponsored foundation.
Financial data (yr. ended 12/31/04): Assets, $1,410,626 (M); gifts received, $190,659; expenditures, $471,636; qualifying distributions, $375,103; giving activities include $375,103 for 13 + grants (high: $125,000).
Purpose and activities: The foundation supports organizations involved with arts and culture, education, health, housing, human services, disaster relief, and community development.
Fields of interest: Humanities; Historic preservation/historical societies; Arts; Education; Health care; Housing/shelter; Safety/disasters; Human services; Community development.
Type of support: Annual campaigns; Capital campaigns; Building/renovation; Equipment; Land acquisition; Program development.
Limitations: Giving limited to TN. No grants to individuals.
Application information: Application form not required.
   Initial approach: Proposal
   Copies of proposal: 1
   Deadline(s): None
Officers and Directors: * K.S. Adams, Jr.,* Pres.; John Adams Barrett,* V.P. and Treas.; Nancy N. Adams,* V.P.; Susan C. Lewis; Susan Adams Smith; Amy Adams Strunk.
EIN: 760611503

9231
The Terry Foundation ✧ ☆
3104 Edloe St., Ste. 300
Houston, TX 77027-6038

Established in 1986 in TX.
Donors: Howard L. Terry; Nancy M. Terry.
Foundation type: Independent foundation.
Financial data (yr. ended 12/31/05): Assets, $124,110,133 (M); gifts received, $401,870; expenditures, $8,234,180; qualifying distributions, $7,811,799; giving activities include $7,263,500 for 4 grants (high: $3,035,500; low: $403,000).
Fields of interest: Higher education; Scholarships/financial aid.
Type of support: Scholarship funds.
Limitations: Applications not accepted. Giving limited to TX. No grants to individuals (directly).
Application information: Contributes only to pre-selected organizations.
Officers and Directors: * Rhett Campbell,* Chair.; Edward T. Cotham,* Pres.; James Davis; Yvonne R. Moody; Carter Overton; John W. Storms; H.L. Terry; Nancy M. Terry.
EIN: 311551093

9232
Texas Instruments Foundation ▼ ✧
12500 TI Blvd., M.S. 8656
Dallas, TX 75243 (214) 480-6873
Contact: Ann Pomykal, Dir., Corp. and Fdn. Giving
FAX: (214) 480-6820; *E-mail:* giving@ti.com;
Application address: P.O. Box 660199, M.S. 8656, Dallas, TX 75265-0199, tel.: (214) 480-3221;
URL: http://www.ti.com/giving

Trust established in 1951 in TX; incorporated in 1964.
Donor: Texas Instruments Inc.
Foundation type: Company-sponsored foundation.
Financial data (yr. ended 12/31/05): Assets, $33,567,551 (M); gifts received, $12,067,862; expenditures, $7,237,937; qualifying distributions, $7,004,240; giving activities include $5,963,365 for 46 grants (high: $1,300,000; low: $1,000), $988,419 for employee matching gifts, and $52,456 for foundation-administered programs.
Purpose and activities: The foundation supports organizations involved with arts and culture, education, health, human services, business, community development, civic affairs, minorities, and women.
Fields of interest: Arts; Elementary/secondary education; Secondary school/education; Education; Health care; Human services; Business/industry; Community development; Science, formal/general education; Mathematics; Public affairs; Minorities; Women.
Type of support: General/operating support; Continuing support; Annual campaigns; Capital campaigns; Building/renovation; Program development; Scholarship funds; Research; Employee matching gifts.
Limitations: Giving primarily in Attleboro, Austin, Dallas, Houston, Hunt Valley, Lubbock, and Sherman, TX. No support for private foundations, sectarian, denominational, or religious organizations, political parties or candidates, veterans', fraternal, or labor organizations, or sport teams. No grants to individuals, or for sponsorships, endowments, political activities, courtesy advertising, program books, yearbooks, entertainment events, scholarships, or conferences, sporting events, golf tournaments, or travel or tours; no product donations.
Publications: Application guidelines; Program policy statement.
Application information: Application form required.
   Initial approach: Complete online application form
   Deadline(s): None
   Board meeting date(s): Mar., June, Sept., and Dec.
   Final notification: 3 weeks following board meetings
Officers and Directors: * Jack E. Swindle,* Pres.; Terri West,* V.P.; Bart Thomas, Secy.; Kevin P. March,* Treas.; Thomas Engibous; Steve Leven; Venu Menon; Phil Ritter; Shaunna Sowell.
Number of staff: 1 full-time professional.
EIN: 756038519
Selected grants: The following grants were reported in 2004.
$1,300,000 to United Way of Metropolitan Dallas, Dallas, TX.
$515,000 to Dallas Black Dance Theater, Dallas, TX.
$440,535 to Advanced Placement Strategies, Dallas, TX.
$354,950 to Dallas Independent School District, Dallas, TX. For Advanced Placement Program.

$350,000 to Southern Methodist University, School of Engineering, Dallas, TX.

$300,000 to University of Texas Southwestern Medical Center, Dallas, TX.

$250,000 to University of Texas, El Paso, TX.

$200,000 to Childrens Medical Center of Dallas, Dallas, TX.

$200,000 to Dallas Center for the Performing Arts, Dallas, TX.

$200,000 to United Way of Eastern New England, Attleboro, MA.

9233
Texas Pioneer Foundation ✧ ☆
215 W. San Antonio St. 2001
San Marcos, TX   78666

Foundation type: Independent foundation.
Financial data (yr. ended 6/30/05): Assets, $44,974,811 (M); gifts received, $36,242,366; expenditures, $563,784; qualifying distributions, $520,644; giving activities include $344,842 for 8 grants (high: $125,000; low: $5,000).
Fields of interest: Higher education; Education.
Limitations: Applications not accepted. Giving primarily in TX. No grants to individuals.
Application information: Contributes only to pre-selected organizations.
Officers: Fred J. Markham, Pres.; Leland Wilson, V.P.; Margaret Lindsey, Secy.; Clifford D. Bandy, Treas.
Board Member: Mary Borm.
EIN: 741966306

9234
The Billie and Gillis Thomas Family Foundation ✧ ☆
(formerly The Thomas Foundation)
8333 Douglas Ave., Ste. 1414
Dallas, TX   75225-5821
Contact: Gillis Thomas, Pres.

Established in 1997 in TX.
Donors: H. Gillis Thomas; Billie D. Thomas.
Foundation type: Independent foundation.
Financial data (yr. ended 12/31/05): Assets, $7,027,239 (M); gifts received, $1,200,000; expenditures, $374,694; qualifying distributions, $353,887; giving activities include $352,725 for 14 grants (high: $100,000; low: $5,000).
Fields of interest: Education; Human services.
Limitations: Giving primarily in Dallas, TX.
Application information: Application form required.
Deadline(s): Varies
Officers and Trustees:* Gillis Thomas,* Pres.; Billie D. Thomas,* V.P.; Robyn T. Conlon,* Secy.; Walter T. Shank, Treas.
EIN: 752721588

9235
The Tobin Endowment ✧
P.O. Box 90869
San Antonio, TX   78209   (210) 930-5160
Contact: J. Bruce Bugg, Jr., Tr.

Established in 1999 in TX.
Donors: J. Bruce Bugg, Jr.; Robert L.B. Tobin†; Robert Batts Tobin Trust.
Foundation type: Independent foundation.

Financial data (yr. ended 12/31/03): Assets, $58,324,983 (M); gifts received, $340,000; expenditures, $2,916,030; qualifying distributions, $2,215,585; giving activities include $1,859,886 for 16 grants (high: $512,431; low: $29).
Purpose and activities: Giving primarily for the arts and culture.
Fields of interest: Museums (art); Arts; Cancer research; Foundations (private operating); Federated giving programs; Religion, interfaith issues.
Limitations: Giving primarily in TX, with emphasis on San Antonio. No grants to individuals.
Application information:
Initial approach: Proposal on organization letterhead
Deadline(s): None
Officer and Trustees:* J. Bruce Bugg, Jr.,* Chair.; Leroy G. Denman, Jr.
EIN: 746478848
Selected grants: The following grants were reported in 2003.

$512,431 to Santa Fe Opera, Santa Fe, NM. For general support.

$500,000 to Tobin Endowment, San Antonio, TX. For operating support.

$150,000 to Southwest Foundation for Biomedical Research, San Antonio, TX. For building campaign support.

$101,150 to Historical Centre Foundation, San Antonio, TX. For renovation of the Tobin reservation chapel.

$100,000 to K L R N-TV, San Antonio, TX. For Robert L. B. Tobin studio.

$80,000 to Marion Koogler McNay Art Museum, San Antonio, TX. For Tobin Collection of Theater Arts.

$50,000 to Saint Marys Hall, San Antonio, TX. For Tobin Center of the Performing Arts.

$38,600 to Metropolitan Opera, New York, NY. For Margaret Batts Tobin award.

$25,000 to United Way of San Antonio and Bexar County, San Antonio, TX. For general support.

$5,000 to Charity Ball Association of San Antonio, San Antonio, TX. For general support.

9236
Tocker Foundation
3814 Medical Pkwy.
Austin, TX   78756-4002   (512) 452-1044
Contact: Darryl Tocker, Exec. Dir.
FAX: (512) 452-7690; E-mail: grants@tocker.org;
URL: http://www.tocker.org

Established in 1964 in TX.
Donors: Phillip Tocker†; Mrs. Phillip Tocker†.
Foundation type: Independent foundation.
Financial data (yr. ended 11/30/05): Assets, $31,801,711 (M); expenditures, $2,040,157; qualifying distributions, $1,678,831; giving activities include $1,554,178 for grants.
Purpose and activities: Giving primarily for the support, encouragement of and assistance to, small, rural libraries in TX, which serve populations of 12,000 or less.
Fields of interest: Libraries/library science.
Type of support: Management development/capacity building; Equipment; Program development; Conferences/seminars.
Limitations: Giving primarily in TX. No grants to individuals, or for debt service, endowment funds, salaries or employee benefits.
Publications: Informational brochure (including application guidelines).

Application information: Application guidelines available on foundation Web site. Application form required.
Initial approach: Letter
Copies of proposal: 1
Deadline(s): Jan. 15 and June 1 (short extensions can be obtained by contacting the foundation via fax letter, or e-mail)
Final notification: 45-60 days after the application deadline
Officers and Directors:* Robert Tocker,* Chair.; Darryl Tocker, Exec. Dir.; Mel Kunze; Brooke Sheldon; Barbara Tocker; Terry Tocker.
Number of staff: 1 full-time professional.
EIN: 756037871

9237
The Tolleson Family Foundation ✧
5500 Preston Rd., Ste. 250
Dallas, TX   75205-1241

Established in 1994.
Foundation type: Independent foundation.
Financial data (yr. ended 12/31/04): Assets, $1,064,742 (M); expenditures, $403,589; qualifying distributions, $392,510; giving activities include $394,746 for 50 grants (high: $75,000; low: $100).
Purpose and activities: Giving primarily for children, youth and social services, health associations, YMCAs, and to Protestant organizations and churches; funding also for the arts.
Fields of interest: Arts; Higher education; Health organizations, association; Human services; YM/YWCAs & YM/YWHAs; Children/youth, services; Homeless, human services; Federated giving programs; Protestant agencies & churches.
Limitations: Applications not accepted. Giving primarily in TX. No grants to individuals.
Application information: Contributes only to pre-selected organizations.
Officers: Debra J. Tolleson, Pres.; John C. Tolleson, V.P.; Eric W. Bennett, Secy.-Treas.
EIN: 752567318
Selected grants: The following grants were reported in 2004.

$90,000 to Episcopal School of Dallas, Dallas, TX. 2 grants: $75,000, $15,000

$55,880 to Southern Methodist University, Dallas, TX. 3 grants: $4,480, $1,400, $50,000

$15,000 to United Way, TX.

$5,000 to Salvation Army, Plainview, TX.

$4,800 to Episcopal School of Dallas Parents Association, Dallas, TX.

$4,650 to Salvation Army of Dallas, Dallas, TX.

$1,000 to Child Care Group, Dallas, TX.

9238
Topfer Family Foundation ▼ ✧
(formerly The Morton & Angela Topfer Family Foundation)
5000 Plz. on the Lake, Ste. 170
Austin, TX   78746
Contact: Julie Hudnall, Grants Admin.
FAX: (512) 329-6462;
E-mail: info@topferfoundation.org; URL: http://www.topferfamilyfoundation.org

Established in 2000 in TX.
Donors: Angela Topfer†; Morton Topfer.
Foundation type: Independent foundation.

Financial data (yr. ended 12/31/04): Assets, $60,831,535 (M); expenditures, $6,071,450; qualifying distributions, $5,996,130; giving activities include $5,577,306 for 153 grants (high: $1,023,056; low: $100; average: $1,000–$500,000).

Purpose and activities: The foundation is committed to helping people connect to the tools and resources needed to build self-sufficient and fulfilling lives.

Fields of interest: Education, drop-out prevention; Health care, infants; Pediatrics; Crime/violence prevention, child abuse; Employment, services; Employment, job counseling; Employment, training; Housing/shelter, aging; Youth development; Children/youth, services; Family services, parent education; Family services, adolescent parents; Economically disadvantaged.

Type of support: General/operating support; Continuing support; Capital campaigns; Building/renovation; Program development; Matching/challenge support.

Limitations: Giving primarily in the greater metropolitan areas of Chicago, IL and Austin, TX. No support for political campaigns or purposes, academic or scientific research. No grants to individuals, advertising, dinner, gala, or raffle tickets, school fundraisers or events; no loans.

Publications: Application guidelines.

Application information: Applications available on the foundation's Web site. Application form required.

  Initial approach: Online grant application with required documents
  Copies of proposal: 1
  Deadline(s): None
  Board meeting date(s): Mar., June, Sept., and Dec.

Officers and Directors:* Morton Topfer,* Chair., Pres., and Treas.; Alan Topfer,* V.P.; Richard Topfer,* Secy.; Anne Cohn Donnelly; Patricia Hayes, Ph.D.; Jacqueline Hynek; Bonnie Vozar.

Number of staff: 2 full-time professional; 1 part-time professional.

EIN: 742961304

Selected grants: The following grants were reported in 2004.

$1,023,056 to Seton Fund of the Daughters of Charity of Saint Vincent de Paul, Austin, TX. For Seton Community Clinic Endowment.

$250,000 to Outreach Community Ministries, Wheaton, IL. For expansion of transitional shelter care program for young single mothers and their children.

$250,000 to Youth and Family Alliance, LifeWorks, Austin, TX. For capital campaign to build Resource Center and to expand shelter.

$175,000 to Jane Addams Juvenile Court Foundation, Chicago, IL. For child welfare and juvenile court reform through strengthening relationships and collaborations with community partners and by improving court systems and procedures.

$125,000 to Juvenile Protective Association, Chicago, IL. For collaborative project with Chicago Children's Advocacy Center (CCAC) to improve mental health services for victims of sexual and severe physical abuse.

$75,000 to Urban League, Austin Area, Austin, TX. For summer and school year educational programs for disadvantaged youth.

$40,000 to Lifelink Corporation, Bensenville, IL. For Healthy Families, providing child abuse

prevention services for non-English speaking teen parents.

$25,000 to Community Care Options, Berwyn, IL. For case management services for seniors.

$25,000 to Easter Seals Central Texas, Austin, TX. For medical rehabilitative services for children.

$24,000 to Fund for Child Care Excellence, Austin, TX. For job training for child-care workers.

9239

The Triad Hospitals Private Foundation ☆

c/o Mktg. and Public Affairs Dept., Admin. Asst.
5800 Tennyson Pkwy.
Plano, TX 75024 (214) 473-3762
URL: http://www.triadhospitals.com/TriadFoundation/default

Established in 2000 in DE.

Donor: Triad Hospitals, Inc.

Foundation type: Company-sponsored foundation.

Financial data (yr. ended 12/31/05): Assets, $1,600,751 (M); gifts received, $506,959; expenditures, $383,985; qualifying distributions, $383,245; giving activities include $383,245 for grants.

Purpose and activities: The foundation supports programs designed to train future health care workers; and benefit the health and well being of the community and the health care industry as a whole. Special emphasis is directed toward organizations with which employees of Triad Hospitals are involved.

Fields of interest: Medical school/education; Nursing school/education; Health care.

Type of support: General/operating support; Equipment; Scholarship funds; Employee volunteer services.

Limitations: Giving primarily in areas of company operations. No support for private foundations. No grants to individuals, or for controversial, precedent-setting purposes, political activities, advertising or event sponsorships, social or fundraising events, or disaster relief.

Publications: IRS Form 990-PF.

Application information: Application form required.

  Initial approach: Download application form and mail proposal and application form to foundation
  Copies of proposal: 1

Officer and Directors:* Michael J. Parsons,* Chair.; Patricia G. Ball; James R. Bedenbaugh; Susan Bolger; Thomas H. Frazier; Robert P. Frutiger; Rebecca Hurley; W. Stephen Love.

EIN: 752865869

9240

The Trull Foundation

404 4th St.
Palacios, TX 77465 (361) 972-5241
Contact: E. Gail Purvis, Exec. Dir.
FAX: (361) 972-1109; *E-mail:* trullfdn@wcnet.net;
URL: http://www.trullfoundation.org

Established in 1967 in TX.

Donors: R.B. Trull†; Florence M. Trull†; Gladys T. Brooking; Jean T. Herlin†; Laura Shiflett.

Foundation type: Independent foundation.

Financial data (yr. ended 12/31/05): Assets, $25,563,146 (M); expenditures, $1,581,730; qualifying distributions, $1,310,602; giving

activities include $1,210,360 for 250 grants (high: $25,000; low: $500).

Purpose and activities: For over 39 years, the foundation has been actively interested in various educational, religious, cultural and social programs, the majority of which have been in TX. The foundation supports, but is not limited to Presbyterian interests. The foundation is also concerned with people, and improving the quality of life for those living in poor or repressed conditions. Additional interests of the foundation include local health care, children and families, people suffering from substance abuse, and a concern for the coastal TX environment.

Fields of interest: Museums; History/archaeology; Elementary/secondary education; Child development, education; Elementary school/education; Secondary school/education; Higher education; Theological school/education; Adult education—literacy, basic skills & GED; Libraries/library science; Education; Environment; Substance abuse, services; Food services; Human services; Children/youth, services; Child development, services; Family services; Minorities/immigrants, centers/services; Homeless, human services; International relief; International peace/security; Community development; Protestant federated giving programs; Population studies; Protestant agencies & churches; Religion; Minorities; Hispanics/Latinos; Immigrants/refugees; Economically disadvantaged; Homeless.

Type of support: General/operating support; Continuing support; Annual campaigns; Building/renovation; Equipment; Program development; Conferences/seminars; Publication; Seed money; Curriculum development; Scholarship funds; Technical assistance; Matching/challenge support.

Limitations: Giving primarily in rural southern TX, with emphasis on the Palacios and Matagorda County areas. No grants to individuals directly, or for capital building campaigns, endowment funds; no loans.

Publications: Application guidelines; Biennial report (including application guidelines); Newsletter.

Application information: Proposals submitted by fax or e-mail not considered. Telephone inquiries about proposals and grants will be answered Mon.-Fri., from 8:00am-12:00pm. Application guidelines and proposal fact sheet available on foundation Web site. Please do not send 990s, audits, CDs, videos, information concerning staff, Board of Dirs., plaques or certificates of appreciation. Application form required.

  Initial approach: Proposal
  Copies of proposal: 4
  Deadline(s): None
  Board meeting date(s): Usually twice a year; contributions committee meets monthly and as required
  Final notification: 3 months

Officers and Trustees:* Colleen Claybourn,* Chair.; Rose C. Lancaster,* Vice-Chair.; J. Fred Huitt,* Secy.-Treas.; E. Gail Purvis, Exec. Dir.; Cara P. Herlin, Advisory Tr.; Susan Herlin, Advisory Tr.; Sarah H. Olfers; R. Scott Trull.

Number of staff: 1 full-time professional; 1 full-time support.

EIN: 237423943

Selected grants: The following grants were reported in 2004.

$20,000 to Friends of Elder Citizens, Palacios, TX.

$10,000 to Boys and Girls Clubs of America, Palacios, TX.

$8,000 to Nature Center of Matagorda County, Bay City, TX.

$7,000 to Ministry of Challenge, Austin, TX.

$5,000 to Bay City Baptist Harvest Reapers Mission, Bay City, TX.

$5,000 to Palmer Drug Abuse Program of Corpus Christi, Corpus Christi, TX.

$5,000 to Phoenix House, Austin, TX.

$5,000 to Planned Parenthood of San Antonio and South Central Texas, San Antonio, TX.

$5,000 to University of Houston-Victoria, Victoria, TX.

$3,500 to Teen Court of Maragorda County, Bay City, TX.

$3,000 to Friends of the Colorado River Foundation, Austin, TX.

9241
Courtney S. Turner Charitable Trust ◇

c/o Bank of America, N.A.
P.O. Box 831041
Dallas, TX 75283-1041
Contact: Spence Heddens, Bank of America, N.A.
Application address: c/o Bank of America, P.O. Box 419119, Kansas City, MO, 64141-6119, tel.: (816) 979-7304

Established in 1986 in MO.
Donor: Courtney S. Turner.
Foundation type: Independent foundation.
Financial data (yr. ended 12/31/05): Assets, $33,046,922 (M); expenditures, $1,962,333; qualifying distributions, $1,812,508; giving activities include $1,672,579 for 42 grants (high: $255,000; low: $3,000).
Purpose and activities: Giving primarily for higher education, the arts, and human services.
Fields of interest: Arts; Higher education; Education; Hospitals (general); Health care, clinics/centers; Human services; Children/youth, services; Community development.
Type of support: Capital campaigns; Program development; Seed money; Matching/challenge support.
Limitations: Giving primarily in Atchison KS, and Kansas City, MO.
Application information: Application form not required.
  Initial approach: Letter (not exceeding 3 pages)
  Deadline(s): None
Trustees: Daniel C. Weary; Bank of America, N.A.
EIN: 436316904
Selected grants: The following grants were reported in 2005.
$255,000 to Benedictine College, Atchison, KS.
$100,000 to Saint Lukes Hospital Foundation, Kansas City, MO.
$75,000 to Atchison, City of, Atchison, KS.
$75,000 to Westminster College, Fulton, MO.
$73,334 to Bishop Spencer Place, Kansas City, MO.
$50,000 to Childrens Mercy Hospital, Kansas City, MO.
$50,000 to Operation Breakthrough, Kansas City, MO.
$50,000 to Powell Gardens, Kingsville, MO.
$50,000 to Unicorn Theater, Kansas City, MO.
$30,000 to Friends of Chamber Music, Kansas City, MO.

9242
Turner Construction Company Foundation ◇ ☆

901 Main St., Ste. 4900
Dallas, TX 75202

Established in 1980 in NY.
Donor: Turner Construction Co.
Foundation type: Company-sponsored foundation.
Financial data (yr. ended 12/31/05): Assets, $452,801 (M); gifts received, $338,776; expenditures, $440,151; qualifying distributions, $322,138; giving activities include $322,138 for grants.
Purpose and activities: The foundation supports organizations involved with arts and culture, health, and children and youth.
Fields of interest: Arts; Health care; Disasters, 9/11/01; Children/youth, services.
Type of support: General/operating support; Scholarship funds.
Limitations: Applications not accepted. Giving primarily in Chicago, IL. No grants to individuals.
Application information: Contributes only to pre-selected organizations.
Officer and Directors: Donald G. Sleeman, Pres. and Treas.; Lori V. Willox, Secy.; Peter J. Davoren; Thomas C. Leppert; Rodney J. Michalka.
EIN: 133072570
Selected grants: The following grants were reported in 2004.
$50,000 to After School Matters, Chicago, IL.
$7,000 to Rebuilding Together Metro Chicago, Chicago, IL.
$6,000 to Horizons for Youth, Chicago, IL.
$6,000 to Womens Business Development Center, Chicago, IL.
$1,000 to Community Health, Chicago, IL.

9243
Unkefer Foundation ◇ ☆

750 N. Saint Paul St., 10th Fl.
Dallas, TX 75201

Established in 1999 in TX.
Donors: Ronald A. Unkefer; Terry L. Unkefer.
Foundation type: Independent foundation.
Financial data (yr. ended 12/31/05): Assets, $4,663,373 (M); gifts received, $3,500,000; expenditures, $498,592; qualifying distributions, $495,241; giving activities include $495,241 for 20 grants (high: $250,000; low: $100).
Fields of interest: Boys & girls clubs; Human services; Christian agencies & churches.
Type of support: General/operating support.
Limitations: Applications not accepted. No grants to individuals.
Application information: Contributes only to pre-selected organizations.
Officers: Ronald A. Unkefer, Pres.; Terry L. Unkefer, Secy.
Director: Gary M. Lawrence.
EIN: 752794083
Selected grants: The following grants were reported in 2004.
$32,532 to Boys and Girls Clubs of Greater Dallas, Dallas, TX.
$23,500 to Cattle Barons Ball, Dallas, TX.
$10,406 to Texas Stampede, Dallas, TX.
$10,000 to Girls Inc. of Metropolitan Dallas, Dallas, TX.
$10,000 to Highland Park Independent School District, Dallas, TX.

$4,425 to Gildas Club North Texas, Dallas, TX.
$1,000 to La Fiesta de las Seis Banderas, Dallas, TX.
$400 to Salvation Army of Dallas, Dallas, TX.
$250 to YMCA of Metropolitan Dallas, Dallas, TX.
$125 to Juvenile Diabetes Research Foundation International, Dallas, TX.

9244
The Charles and Betty Urschel Foundation ◇

153 Treeline Park, Ste. 300
San Antonio, TX 78209-1880

Established in 1960 in TX.
Donors: Elizabeth H. Urschel†; Jack Guenther; Valerie Urschel Guenther.
Foundation type: Independent foundation.
Financial data (yr. ended 7/31/05): Assets, $9,821,092 (M); gifts received, $3,001,251; expenditures, $529,373; qualifying distributions, $512,049; giving activities include $505,000 for 2 grants (high: $500,000; low: $5,000).
Purpose and activities: Giving primarily for health care and medical research.
Fields of interest: Museums (art); Hospitals (specialty); Cancer; Cancer research.
Type of support: General/operating support; Building/renovation.
Limitations: Applications not accepted. Giving primarily in the San Antonio, TX, area. No grants to individuals.
Application information: Contributes only to pre-selected organizations.
Officers: Valerie Urschel Guenther, Pres.; Abigail G. Kampmann, V.P.; Jack Guenther, Secy.; Jack E. Guenther, Jr., Treas.
EIN: 746053172
Selected grants: The following grants were reported in 2004.
$500,000 to Cancer Therapy and Research Center, San Antonio, TX. For building construction.

9245
The USAA Foundation, Inc. ◇ ☆

P.O. Box 690286
San Antonio, TX 78269-0286

Established in 2004 in TX as successor to the USAA Foundation, a Charitable Trust.
Donor: The USAA Educational Foundation.
Foundation type: Company-sponsored foundation.
Financial data (yr. ended 6/30/05): Assets, $152,336,576 (M); gifts received, $200,000; expenditures, $651,100; qualifying distributions, $651,100; giving activities include $651,100 for 52 grants (high: $104,000; low: $100).
Purpose and activities: The foundation supports organizations involved with arts and culture, education, health, human services, and economic development.
Fields of interest: Arts; Education; Health care; Human services; Economic development.
Type of support: General/operating support.
Limitations: Applications not accepted. Giving primarily in San Antonio, TX, and Norfolk, VA.
Application information: Contributes only to pre-selected organizations.
Officers and Directors:* Robert G. Davis,* Chair.; Barbara B. Gentry,* Vice-Chair. and Pres.; Steven Alan Bennett,* Exec. V.P.; Josue Robles, Jr.,* Exec.

V.P.; Kenneth W. Smith, Sr. V.P.; Amy D. Cannefax, V.P.; Kristi A. Matus; Wendi E. Strong; Joseph H. Wehrle, Jr.
EIN: 202303140

9246
The Vale-Asche Foundation
2001 Kirby Dr., Ste. 1010
Houston, TX 77019-6081   (713) 520-7334, ext. 7

Incorporated in 1956 in DE.
Donors: Ruby Vale†; Fred B. Asche†.
Foundation type: Independent foundation.
Financial data (yr. ended 11/30/05): Assets, $18,559,526 (M); expenditures, $847,557; qualifying distributions, $804,000; giving activities include $804,000 for 35 grants (high: $100,000; low: $2,000).
Purpose and activities: Giving primarily for education, health, social services, and children services.
Fields of interest: Secondary school/education; Higher education; Medical school/education; Teacher school/education; Education; Health organizations, association; Ear & throat diseases; Nerve, muscle & bone diseases; Alzheimer's disease; Food banks; Youth development, scouting agencies (general); Human services; American Red Cross; Children, services.
Type of support: Technical assistance; Publication; Equipment; Program development; Research.
Limitations: Giving primarily in Harris County or Houston, TX. No grants to individuals, or for operating funds.
Application information: Requests reviewed mid-Aug. through Oct. Application form not required.
   Initial approach: Letter
   Copies of proposal: 1
   Deadline(s): Aug. 15
   Board meeting date(s): Early Sept. and early Oct.
   Final notification: Varies depending on when received
Officers: Mrs. Vale Asche Russell, Pres.; Asche Ackerman, V.P.; Anna B. Leonard, V.P.; William E. Blummer, Secy.-Treas.
EIN: 516015320
Selected grants: The following grants were reported in 2006.
$50,000 to University of Texas Medical Branch, Galveston, TX. For establishing fellowship in Infectious Disease Research.
$35,000 to Child Advocates, Houston, TX. For volunteer training programs.
$30,000 to Casa de Esperanza de los Ninos, Houston, TX.
$30,000 to Rose, The, Houston, TX. For purchase of mammography system and service contract.
$20,000 to AIDS Foundation Houston, Houston, TX. For camp programs for HIV-positive youth and their families.
$15,000 to American Lung Association, Houston, TX. For programs to help local youth stop smoking.
$15,000 to Nehemiah Center, Houston, TX. For Academic Enrichment Program.
$15,000 to Periwinkle Foundation, Houston, TX. For program support.
$10,000 to Bayou Preservation Association, Houston, TX.
$10,000 to Planned Parenthood of Houston and Southeast Texas, Houston, TX. For reproductive health and sexuality education programs.

9247
Valero Energy Foundation ▼ ✧
(formerly Ultramar Diamond Shamrock Foundation)
1 Valero Way
P.O. Box 696000
San Antonio, TX 78269-6000
Contact: Letitia Rutan, Exec. Dir.
E-mail: letitia.rutan@valero.com; *URL:* http://www.valero.com/Community/

Established in 1999 in TX.
Donors: Ultramar Diamond Shamrock Corp.; Valero Energy Corp.
Foundation type: Company-sponsored foundation.
Financial data (yr. ended 12/31/04): Assets, $10,170,677 (M); gifts received, $19,163,638; expenditures, $11,355,240; qualifying distributions, $10,421,785; giving activities include $10,421,785 for 399 grants (high: $2,970,554; low: $25).
Purpose and activities: The foundation supports organizations involved with arts and culture, education, muscular dystrophy, human services, children and youth, civic affairs, and religion.
Fields of interest: Arts; Elementary/secondary education; Higher education; Education; Muscular dystrophy; Children/youth, services; Human services; Federated giving programs; Government/public administration; Religion.
Type of support: Employee matching gifts; Sponsorships; Program development; General/operating support.
Limitations: Giving primarily in areas of company operations, with emphasis on TX. No grants to individuals.
Publications: Application guidelines.
Application information: Application form not required.
   Initial approach: E-mail proposal to foundation
Officers: William E. Greehey, Pres.; Keith D. Booke, Exec. V.P.; Mary Rose Brown, Sr. V.P.; Jay D. Browning, V.P. and Secy.; Clayton E. Killinger, V.P. and Cont.; T. Wyatt Stripling, V.P. and Tax Dir.; Donna M. Titzman, Treas.; Letitia Rutan, Exec. Dir.
EIN: 742904514
Selected grants: The following grants were reported in 2004.
$2,970,554 to United Way of San Antonio and Bexar County, San Antonio, TX. For fundraising activities.
$1,185,216 to Muscular Dystrophy Association, Tucson, AZ. For fundraising activities.
$517,655 to Saint Marys University, San Antonio, TX. For fundraising activities.
$199,182 to American Red Cross, San Antonio, TX. For fundraising activities.
$50,000 to Boys and Girls Club of Live Oak County, George West, TX. For youth mentoring program.
$20,000 to Boys and Girls Club of Paulsboro, Paulsboro, NJ. For youth mentoring program.
$15,000 to National Hemophilia Foundation, Baton Rouge, LA. For fundraising activities.

9248
Vanberg Family Foundation ✧
25 Highland Park Village, Ste. 100
P.O. Box 506
Dallas, TX 75205-2785

Established in 1990 in TX.
Donors: Harold E. Vanberg, Sr.†; Anne M. Vanberg; Harold Vanberg Charitable Lead Trust.
Foundation type: Independent foundation.

Financial data (yr. ended 12/31/04): Assets, $13,975,564 (M); expenditures, $2,465,085; qualifying distributions, $2,388,000; giving activities include $2,388,000 for 46 grants (high: $200,000; low: $500).
Fields of interest: Performing arts; Education; Human services; Community development; Christian agencies & churches.
Type of support: General/operating support; Capital campaigns; Building/renovation; Land acquisition; Conferences/seminars; Matching/challenge support.
Limitations: Applications not accepted. Giving primarily in Dallas, TX; some funding nationally. No grants to individuals.
Application information: Contributes only to pre-selected organizations.
Officers: Anne M. Vanberg, Pres.; Nancy Brooks, Secy.
Director: Elizabeth R. Anthony.
EIN: 752342463
Selected grants: The following grants were reported in 2003.
$275,000 to Child Evangelism Fellowship, Warrenton, MO.
$250,000 to Fellowship for the Performing Arts, Morristown, NJ.
$100,000 to Urban Alternative, Dallas, TX.
$75,000 to Reach International, Omaha, NE.
$5,000 to Shared Table, Taos, NM.
$2,500 to Young Life, Colorado Springs, CO.
$1,500 to Living Bank International, Houston, TX.
$1,000 to Boy Scouts of America, Circle Ten Council, Dallas, TX.
$1,000 to Youth-Reach Houston, Houston, TX.
$500 to Salvation Army of Dallas, Dallas, TX.

9249
Rosemary Haggar Vaughan Family Foundation ✧
12830 Hillcrest Rd., Ste. 111
Dallas, TX 75230

Established in 1996.
Foundation type: Independent foundation.
Financial data (yr. ended 12/31/05): Assets, $7,118,951 (M); expenditures, $521,565; qualifying distributions, $509,875; giving activities include $374,250 for 51 grants (high: $25,000; low: $500).
Purpose and activities: Giving primarily for education, health associations including hospitals, the arts, and human services.
Fields of interest: Museums (art); Performing arts; Arts; Elementary/secondary education; Education; Hospitals (general); Hospitals (specialty); Health care; Health organizations, association; Eye research; Diabetes research; Human services; Salvation Army; YM/YWCAs & YM/YWHAs; Children/youth, services; Christian agencies & churches; Religion.
Limitations: Applications not accepted. Giving primarily in Dallas, TX. No grants to individuals.
Application information: Contributes only to pre-selected organizations.
Officers: Rosemary Vaughan, Pres.; Mary Lynn Vaughan, V.P.; Vicki Miller, Secy.-Treas.
EIN: 752577797
Selected grants: The following grants were reported in 2005.
$35,000 to Episcopal School of Dallas, Dallas, TX. 2 grants: $10,000, $25,000

$20,000 to Southwestern Diabetic Foundation, Gainesville, TX.
$15,000 to Austin Museum of Art, Austin, TX.
$10,000 to Bishop Lynch High School, Dallas, TX.
$10,000 to Camp Summit, Dallas, TX.
$10,000 to Saint Marks School of Texas, Dallas, TX.
$10,000 to Salvation Army, Plainview, TX.
$5,000 to TACA, Dallas, TX.
$5,000 to Wipe Out Kids Cancer, Dallas, TX.

9250
Susan Vaughan Foundation, Inc. ✧

(formerly McAshan Foundation, Inc.)
c/o JPMorgan Chase Bank, N.A.
600 Travis St., 7th Fl.
Houston, TX   77002   (713) 216-4513
Contact: Jennifer Grosvner

Trust established in 1952 in TX; reorganized in 1991 under current name.
Donors: Susan C. McAshan; Susan Vaughan Clayton Trust No. 1.
Foundation type: Independent foundation.
Financial data (yr. ended 12/31/03): Assets, $25,864,298 (M); expenditures, $1,361,080; qualifying distributions, $1,121,124; giving activities include $1,087,266 for 42 grants (high: $185,000; low: $2,500).
Purpose and activities: Emphasis on education, conservation, and the arts.
Fields of interest: Museums (art); Arts; Higher education; Education; Environment, natural resources; Reproductive health, family planning; Human services.
Type of support: General/operating support; Annual campaigns; Capital campaigns; Building/renovation; Matching/challenge support.
Limitations: Giving primarily in Houston and Austin, TX.
Publications: Application guidelines.
Application information: Application form not required.
  Initial approach: Letter
  Copies of proposal: 1
  Deadline(s): None
  Board meeting date(s): Quarterly (Feb., May, Aug., and Nov.)
  Final notification: Within 3 months
Trustees: Susan Clayton Garwood; Duncan E. Osborne; Elizabeth B. Osborne; JPMorgan Chase Bank, N.A.
EIN: 760285765
Selected grants: The following grants were reported in 2003.
$185,000 to University of Texas, Austin, TX.
$145,000 to Museum of Fine Arts, Houston, Houston, TX.
$85,000 to Planned Parenthood of Houston and Southeast Texas, Houston, TX.
$20,000 to University of Houston-University Park, Houston, TX.
$15,000 to Scenic Houston, Houston, TX.
$15,000 to Trees for Houston, Houston, TX.
$10,000 to Ecology Action of Texas, Austin, TX.
$10,000 to Nature Conservancy of Texas, Houston, TX.
$7,500 to Writers in the Schools, Houston, TX.
$2,500 to Baylor College of Medicine, Houston, TX.

9251
Jim M. Vaughn Foundation ✧

(formerly The Vaughn Foundation)
c/o Marc Irvin
P.O. Box 2558
Houston, TX   77252-8037
Contact: Jim M. Vaughn, Dir.
Application address: 830 S. Beckham Ave., Tyler, TX 75701-1904, tel.: (903) 597-7652

Established in 1952 in TX.
Donors: Edgar H. Vaughn†; Lillie Mae Vaughn†; John Willie Bell Crut.
Foundation type: Independent foundation.
Financial data (yr. ended 12/31/05): Assets, $8,512,914 (M); expenditures, $781,499; qualifying distributions, $742,886; giving activities include $719,775 for 104 grants (high: $100,000; low: $25).
Purpose and activities: Giving primarily for higher education, health associations and hospitals, and Baptist, Christian and Methodist churches and organizations, as well as for an Episcopal school; funding also for the arts, children, youth, and social services, and federated giving programs.
Fields of interest: Performing arts, theater; Performing arts, orchestra (symphony); Arts; Elementary school/education; Higher education; Hospitals (general); Health organizations, association; Human services; Children/youth, services; Federated giving programs; Christian agencies & churches; Protestant agencies & churches.
Limitations: Giving primarily in Tyler, TX. No grants to individuals.
Application information: Application form not required.
  Initial approach: Letter
  Copies of proposal: 1
  Deadline(s): None
Directors: Jim M. Vaughn; James M. Vaughn, Jr.; JPMorgan Chase Bank, N.A.
Number of staff: 1 part-time support.
EIN: 756008953

9252
Andrew F. & Barbara Veres Charitable Trust ✧

2715 Quenby St.
West University Place, TX   77005

Established in 2000 in TX.
Donors: Andrew F. Veres; Barbara Veres.
Foundation type: Independent foundation.
Financial data (yr. ended 12/31/05): Assets, $0 (M); gifts received, $580,000; expenditures, $590,270; qualifying distributions, $590,000; giving activities include $590,000 for 2 grants (high: $500,000; low: $90,000).
Fields of interest: Higher education; Nerve, muscle & bone research.
Limitations: Applications not accepted. Giving primarily in Dayton, OH and TX. No grants to individuals.
Application information: Contributes only to pre-selected organizations.
Trustee: Andrew F. Veres.
EIN: 766166971
Selected grants: The following grants were reported in 2003.
$100,000 to Hepatitis Support Association, Houston, TX.

$50,000 to University of Dayton, Dayton, OH.
$5,000 to Houston Golf Association, Houston, TX. For Birdies for Charity program.
$1,000 to Christophers, New York, NY.
$1,000 to Glenmary Home Missioners, Cincinnati, OH.
$1,000 to Paulist National Catholic Evangelization Association, DC.
$100 to University of Saint Thomas, Houston, TX.

9253
Lamar Bruni Vergara Trust ▼ ✧

106 Del Ct.
Laredo, TX   78041

Established in 1990 in TX.
Donor: Lamar Bruni Vergara†.
Foundation type: Independent foundation.
Financial data (yr. ended 12/31/05): Assets, $55,114,583 (M); expenditures, $4,182,433; qualifying distributions, $3,589,541; giving activities include $3,589,237 for 17 grants (high: $1,798,130; low: $5,000; average: $20,000–$344,738).
Purpose and activities: Giving primarily for education; funding also for the arts, and children, youth and social services.
Fields of interest: Performing arts; Elementary school/education; Secondary school/education; Education; Boys & girls clubs; Human services; Children/youth, services; Christian agencies & churches.
Limitations: Giving primarily in Laredo, TX. No grants to individuals.
Application information: Application form not required.
  Deadline(s): None
Trustees: Solomon Casseb, Jr.; J.C. Martin III.
EIN: 746374699
Selected grants: The following grants were reported in 2005.
$1,798,130 to United Day School, Laredo, TX.
$658,152 to Diocese of Laredo, Laredo, TX.
$344,738 to Texas A & M International University, Laredo, TX.
$262,115 to Sacred Heart Childrens Home, Laredo, TX.
$261,852 to Bethany House of Laredo, Laredo, TX.
$50,000 to Laredo Migrant Council, Laredo, TX.
$26,250 to Saint Peters Memorial School, Laredo, TX.
$20,000 to Mary Help of Christians Catholic School, Laredo, TX.
$15,000 to American Red Cross, Webb County Chapter, Laredo, TX.
$10,000 to San Luis Rey Church, Laredo, TX.

9254
E. F. Von Seggern Charitable Foundation

c/o Dwight E. Saur, Jr.
P.O. Box 154193
Irving, TX   75015   (214) 559-3944

Established in 1994 in TX.
Donor: E.F. Von Seggern†.
Foundation type: Independent foundation.
Financial data (yr. ended 12/31/05): Assets, $11,748,217 (M); expenditures, $715,146; qualifying distributions, $567,247; giving activities include $307,000 for 4 grants (high: $250,000;

low: $2,000), and $165,000 for 5 employee matching gifts.

Purpose and activities: Giving limited to the opera, symphony, and ballet, primarily the Dallas Symphony Orchestra and the Dallas Opera.

Fields of interest: Performing arts, orchestra (symphony); Performing arts, opera.

Type of support: Matching/challenge support.

Limitations: Applications not accepted. Giving limited to Dallas, TX. No grants to individuals.

Application information: Contributes only to pre-selected organizations.

Board meeting date(s): Quarterly

Trustee and Directors:* Dwight E. Saur, Jr.,* Tr.; Charles Campbell; Ronald Daniel; John Fisher, M.D.; Rogene Russell.

Number of staff: 1 full-time professional; 1 part-time professional.

EIN: 752304039

9255
The Waco Foundation
900 Austin Ave., Ste. 1000
Waco, TX 76701-1949 (254) 754-3404
Contact: Tom H. Collins, Jr., Exec. Dir.
FAX: (254) 753-2887;
E-mail: info@wacofoundation.org; Additional E-mail: tomc@wacofoundation.org; URL: http://www.wacofoundation.org

Established in 1958 in TX.

Foundation type: Community foundation.

Financial data (yr. ended 3/31/05): Assets, $45,088,326 (M); gifts received, $3,157,479; expenditures, $3,159,249; giving activities include $1,573,557 for 420 grants (high: $250,000; low: $25).

Purpose and activities: The foundation seeks to make a positive difference in the lives and future of the people in Waco and McLennan County through grantmaking, promotion of community philanthropy, and support of the nonprofit sector.

Fields of interest: Arts; Education; Environment; Medical research, institute; Children/youth, services; Children, day care; Family services; Women, centers/services; Human services; Community development; Women; Economically disadvantaged.

Type of support: Building/renovation; Equipment; Emergency funds; Program development; Seed money; Scholarship funds; Matching/challenge support.

Limitations: Giving limited to McLennan County, TX. No support for religious activities. No grants to individuals (except for scholarships), or for annual campaigns, continuing support, deficit financing, endowments, operating budgets, student loans, or technical assistance.

Publications: Application guidelines; Annual report; Grants list; Informational brochure; Program policy statement.

Application information: Visit foundation Web site for application form and guidelines. Application form required.

Initial approach: Letter or telephone
Copies of proposal: 12
Deadline(s): Apr. 1 and Sept. 1
Board meeting date(s): 4th Wed. of each month
Final notification: Mid-June and mid-Nov.

Officers and Directors:* Nancy Callan,* Chair.; Louis Englander,* Vice-Chair.; Tom Salome,* Secy.; Tom H. Collins, Jr.,* Exec. Dir.; David Horner; Beth

Mayfield; William R. Pakis; Art Pertile; Nelwyn Reagan; Maggie Davis Stinnett.

Number of staff: 3 full-time professional; 2 full-time support.

EIN: 746054628

9256
Crystelle Waggoner Charitable Trust ◊
c/o Bank of America, N.A.
P.O. Box 831041
Dallas, TX 75283-1041
Application address: c/o Darlene Mann, Sr. V.P., Bank of America, N.A., P.O. Box 1317, Fort Worth, TX 76101; tel.: (817) 390-6114

Established in 1982 in TX.

Donor: Crystelle Waggoner†.

Foundation type: Independent foundation.

Financial data (yr. ended 6/30/05): Assets, $15,255,389 (M); expenditures, $1,490,724; qualifying distributions, $1,179,149; giving activities include $1,154,100 for 82 grants (high: $150,000; low: $1,250), and $12,500 for 2 employee matching gifts.

Purpose and activities: Giving to charitable organizations in existence before Jan. 24, 1982, including health associations and services, the performing arts and other cultural programs, and social services including services for the deaf.

Fields of interest: Museums; Museums (art); Performing arts; Arts; Higher education; Law school/education; Libraries/library science; Education; Zoos/zoological societies; Hospitals (general); Health care; Health organizations, association; Cancer; Food distribution, meals on wheels; Housing/shelter, development; Boys & girls clubs; Human services; Neighborhood centers; Children/youth, services; Residential/custodial care; Women, centers/services; Federated giving programs.

Type of support: General/operating support; Continuing support; Annual campaigns; Capital campaigns; Building/renovation; Equipment; Endowments; Emergency funds; Program development; Professorships; Publication; Seed money; Curriculum development; Scholarship funds; Research.

Limitations: Giving limited to TX, especially Fort Worth and Decatur. No grants to individuals, or for consulting services, deficit financing, or conferences; no loans.

Publications: Annual report (including application guidelines).

Application information: Application form not required.

Initial approach: Letter
Copies of proposal: 1
Deadline(s): June 30 and Dec. 31
Board meeting date(s): Jan. and July
Final notification: 6 months

Trustee: Bank of America, N.A.

EIN: 751881219

Selected grants: The following grants were reported in 2003.

$40,000 to Fort Worth Dallas Ballet, Fort Worth, TX. To underwrite Nutcracker.

$25,000 to All Church Home for Children, Fort Worth, TX.

$25,000 to Boys and Girls Club of Vernon, Vernon, TX. For playground project.

$25,000 to Fort Worth Art Association, Fort Worth, TX. For capital support.

$25,000 to Fort Worth Opera, Fort Worth, TX.

$25,000 to Van Cliburn Foundation, Fort Worth, TX. For program support.

$20,000 to Lena Pope Home, Fort Worth, TX. For operating support.

$18,800 to Big Brothers and Sisters of Tarrant County, Fort Worth, TX. For program support.

$16,500 to Boys and Girls Clubs of Greater Fort Worth, Fort Worth, TX. For program support.

$10,000 to Arts Council of Fort Worth and Tarrant County, Fort Worth, TX.

9257
E. Paul and Helen Buck Waggoner Foundation, Inc. ◊
P.O. Box 2130
Vernon, TX 76385 (940) 552-2521
Contact: Gene W. Willingham, Secy.-Treas.

Incorporated in 1966 in TX.

Donors: E. Paul Waggoner†; Helen Buck Waggoner†.

Foundation type: Independent foundation.

Financial data (yr. ended 4/30/05): Assets, $6,170,268 (M); expenditures, $328,694; qualifying distributions, $325,252; giving activities include $325,252 for 36 grants (high: $75,000; low: $500).

Purpose and activities: Giving for higher education, including agricultural research and scholarship funds; grants also for youth agencies, museums, and human services.

Fields of interest: Museums; Higher education; Boys & girls clubs; Protestant agencies & churches.

Type of support: Building/renovation; Scholarship funds; Research.

Limitations: Giving primarily in TX; some giving also in FL.

Application information:

Initial approach: Letter
Deadline(s): None

Officers: Helen Willingham, Pres.; Electra Moulder, V.P.; Gene W. Willingham, Secy.-Treas.

Director: Bill Moulder.

EIN: 751243673

Selected grants: The following grants were reported in 2004.

$88,000 to Saint Margarets Episcopal Church, Green Cove Springs, FL. For Organ Fund.

$75,000 to All Saints Episcopal School, Fort Worth, TX. For building fund.

$32,200 to Boys and Girls Club of Vernon, Vernon, TX. For building fund.

$20,000 to Rolling Plains Technical Foundation, Sweetwater, TX. For Library Fund.

$19,500 to Vernon College, Vernon, TX. For scholarships.

$15,000 to Midwestern State University, Wichita Falls, TX. For scholarships.

$6,000 to Red River Valley Museum, Vernon, TX. For general support.

$5,000 to Southeastern Foundation, Durant, OK. For scholarships.

$3,300 to Tarleton State University, Stephenville, TX. For scholarships.

$2,500 to Texas Heritage, Fort Worth, TX. For general support.

9258
The Waggoners Foundation ◊ ☆
6605 Cypresswood Dr., Ste. 250
Spring, TX 77379-7740

Established in 1993 in TX.
Donors: J. Virgil Waggoner; June Waggoner.
Foundation type: Independent foundation.
Financial data (yr. ended 12/31/05): Assets, $5,620,037 (M); expenditures, $744,187; qualifying distributions, $615,000; giving activities include $615,000 for grants.
Purpose and activities: Giving primarily for higher education and health and human services.
Fields of interest: Higher education; Health organizations, association; Human services.
Type of support: Scholarship funds.
Limitations: Applications not accepted. Giving primarily in Houston, TX. No grants to individuals.
Application information: Contributes only to pre-selected organizations.
Officers and Directors: J. Virgil Waggoner,* Chair.; June Waggoner,* Vice-Chair.; Kevin Quisenberry, Exec. Admin.; Liz Quisenberry.
EIN: 760404981

9259
Todd Wagner Foundation ◇
3008 Taylor St.
Dallas, TX 75226 (214) 752-9119
Contact: Kevin Parke, Pres.
FAX: (214) 752-7085;
E-mail: info@toddwagnerfoundation.org;
URL: http://www.toddwagnerfoundation.org

Established in 2000 in TX.
Donor: Todd R. Wagner.
Foundation type: Independent foundation.
Financial data (yr. ended 12/31/05): Assets, $7,652,544 (M); gifts received, $4,704,528; expenditures, $3,448,069; qualifying distributions, $3,476,020; giving activities include $1,379,481 for 15 grants (high: $1,000,000; low: $2,000), $1,839,787 for 1 foundation-administered program and $100,000 for 1 loan/program-related investment.
Purpose and activities: Giving primarily to support athletic, educational and computer technology programs for young people.
Fields of interest: Education; Recreation; Children/youth, services; Computer science.
Type of support: Program-related investments/loans.
Limitations: Giving primarily in CA and TX. No grants to individuals.
Application information: See foundation Web site for program information and for their respective E-mail contacts.
Initial approach: Letter
Officers and Directors: Todd R. Wagner,* Chair. and C.E.O.; Kevin Parke, Pres.; Matthew J. Dolan, Secy.; Leslie W. McMahon,* Treas.; Brian Dameris, Exec. Dir.
EIN: 912028112

9260
Wal-Dot Foundation
7557 Rambler Rd., Ste. 1425
Dallas, TX 75231
Contact: Walter Neustadt, Jr., Pres.
FAX: (214) 891-5979; *E-mail:* neuwalter@aol.com

Established in 1993 in OK.
Donors: Walter Neustadt, Jr.; Dolores K. Neustadt.
Foundation type: Independent foundation.

Financial data (yr. ended 12/31/05): Assets, $7,815,669 (M); gifts received, $29,014; expenditures, $413,276; qualifying distributions, $406,283; giving activities include $356,500 for 47 grants (high: $25,000; low: $350).
Purpose and activities: Giving primarily for education and human services.
Fields of interest: Arts education; Museums; Elementary/secondary education; Higher education; Education; Human services; American Red Cross; Children/youth, services; Family services; Residential/custodial care, hospices.
Type of support: Continuing support; Annual campaigns; Capital campaigns; Emergency funds; Professorships; Scholarship funds; Research.
Limitations: Applications not accepted. Giving primarily in TX. No grants to individuals.
Application information: Contributes only to pre-selected organizations.
Board meeting date(s): Jan. and July
Officers and Directors: Walter Neustadt, Jr.,* Pres.; Dolores K. Neustadt,* V.P.
EIN: 731414803
Selected grants: The following grants were reported in 2004.
$34,563 to Temple Emanu-El, Dallas, TX.
$25,000 to Vogel Alcove Childcare Center for the Homeless, Dallas, TX.
$15,000 to VNA Care Network, Danvers, MA.
$8,000 to American Red Cross, Dallas, TX.
$6,000 to Dallas Childrens Theater, Dallas, TX.
$5,000 to American Red Cross of Central Baltimore, Baltimore, MD.
$5,000 to Beaver Country Day School, Chestnut Hill, MA.
$5,000 to Greenhill School, Addison, TX.
$5,000 to Jewish Family Service, Houston, TX.
$1,750 to Dallas Museum of Art, Dallas, TX.

9261
Walsh Foundation ◇
500 W. 7th St., Ste. 1007
Fort Worth, TX 76102 (817) 335-3741
Contact: G. Malcolm Louden, Mgr.

Established in 1956 in TX.
Donors: Mary D. Walsh; F. Howard Walsh, Sr.
Foundation type: Independent foundation.
Financial data (yr. ended 12/31/05): Assets, $4,453,634 (M); gifts received, $47,125; expenditures, $712,963; qualifying distributions, $662,000; giving activities include $662,000 for 13 grants (high: $561,000; low: $1,500).
Purpose and activities: Emphasis on cultural programs, including those for youth; support also for elementary and higher education and a Baptist church.
Fields of interest: Performing arts; Elementary school/education; Higher education; Children/youth, services; Protestant agencies & churches.
Type of support: General/operating support; Continuing support; Annual campaigns; Equipment; Program development.
Limitations: Giving primarily in Fort Worth, TX. No grants to individuals.
Application information:
Initial approach: Letter
Deadline(s): None
Board meeting date(s): 1st Wed. in Apr.
Officers: Mary D. Walsh, Pres.; G. Malcolm Louden, Mgr.
Director: Gary Goble.
EIN: 756021726

9262
The Ward Family Foundation ◇ ☆
5949 Sherry Ln., Ste. 1735
Dallas, TX 75225

Established in 1993 in TX.
Donors: William C. Ward; Cynthia R. Ward.
Foundation type: Independent foundation.
Financial data (yr. ended 12/31/05): Assets, $7,584,833 (M); expenditures, $477,927; qualifying distributions, $384,038; giving activities include $379,893 for 22 grants (high: $200,000; low: $100).
Purpose and activities: Giving primarily for education and the developmentally disabled.
Fields of interest: Museums (art); Elementary/secondary education; Education; Food banks; Human services; Children/youth, services; Developmentally disabled, centers & services.
Type of support: Capital campaigns.
Limitations: Applications not accepted. Giving primarily in TX. No grants to individuals.
Application information: Contributes only to pre-selected organizations.
Officers: William C. Ward, Pres.; Cynthia R. Ward, V.P. and Secy.; Katherine J. Ward, Treas.
EIN: 752514341
Selected grants: The following grants were reported in 2004.
$205,250 to June Shelton School and Evaluation Center, Dallas, TX. 6 grants: $4,750, $500, $15,000, $106,000, $50,000, $29,000
$28,000 to American Red Cross, National Headquarters, DC.
$25,000 to Peaceable Kingdom Retreat for Children, Temple, TX.
$23,750 to Parish Day School of the Episcopal Church of the Transfiguration, Dallas, TX.
$1,750 to Southeastern Guide Dogs, Palmetto, FL.

9263
Mamie McFaddin Ward Heritage Foundation ◇
P.O. Box 3928
Beaumont, TX 77704-3928
Application address: c/o Hibernia National Bank, 510 Park, Beaumont, TX, 77701; tel: (409) 838-0234

Established in 1976 in TX.
Donor: Mamie McFaddin Ward‡.
Foundation type: Independent foundation.
Financial data (yr. ended 12/31/04): Assets, $28,826,782 (M); expenditures, $1,309,386; qualifying distributions, $1,242,034; giving activities include $929,301 for 19 grants (high: $718,905; low: $1,000).
Purpose and activities: Support for the Mamie McFaddin Ward Heritage Museum and other cultural programs, education, and human services.
Fields of interest: Humanities; Historic preservation/historical societies; Arts; Education; Health care; Human services; Children/youth, services.
Type of support: Capital campaigns; Building/renovation; Equipment; Seed money.
Limitations: Giving limited to Jefferson County, TX. No grants to individuals.
Publications: Application guidelines.
Application information: Application form required.
Initial approach: Letter
Copies of proposal: 9

Deadline(s): Aug. 31
Final notification: Nov.
Trustees: Eugene H.B. McFaddin; James L.C. McFaddin, Jr.; Ida M. Pyle; Rosine M. Wilson; Hibernia National Bank.
EIN: 746260525

9264
The Ware Foundation ✧
c/o Amarillo National Bank-Trust
P.O. Box 1
Amarillo, TX   79105-0001

Established in 1996 in TX.
Donors: B.T. Ware II; Richard C. Ware II; Mary S. Ware.
Foundation type: Independent foundation.
Financial data (yr. ended 12/31/05): Assets, $5,344,155 (M); gifts received, $1,207,644; expenditures, $742,625; qualifying distributions, $669,096; giving activities include $669,096 for 45 grants (high: $109,000; low: $100).
Purpose and activities: Giving primarily for health care, education, religion, and human services.
Fields of interest: Education; Health care; Health organizations, association; Human services; Religion.
Limitations: Applications not accepted. Giving primarily in TX. No grants to individuals.
Application information: Contributes only to pre-selected organizations.
Officer: B.T. Ware II, Pres.
Directors: Mary S. Ware; Richard C. Ware II; W.R. Ware.
EIN: 752662421

9265
The Waste Management Charitable Foundation ✧
(formerly Wheelabrator Technologies Rust International Charitable Foundation, Inc.)
c/o Waste Management, Inc.
1001 Fannin St., Ste. 4000
Houston, TX   77002   (713) 512-6200
Contact: Debbie Sigueras-Cano

Established in 1990 in TX.
Donors: Wheelabrator Technologies Inc.; Waste Management, Inc.
Foundation type: Company-sponsored foundation.
Financial data (yr. ended 12/31/04): Assets, $7,121,434 (M); gifts received, $957,447; expenditures, $1,026,071; qualifying distributions, $962,115; giving activities include $962,115 for 92 grants (high: $150,000; low: $500).
Purpose and activities: The foundation supports organizations involved with arts and culture, education, the environment, children and youth services, human services, and community development.
Fields of interest: Arts; Education; Environment; Children/youth, services; Human services; Community development.
International interests: Canada.
Type of support: General/operating support; Annual campaigns; Emergency funds; Program development; Seed money.
Limitations: Giving on a national basis and in Canada, with some emphasis on TX. No grants to individuals.
Publications: Occasional report.

Application information: Application form not required.
  Initial approach: Proposal
  Copies of proposal: 1
  Deadline(s): Last day of Mar., June, Sept., and Dec.
  Board meeting date(s): Annually
  Final notification: Within 30 days following board meetings
Officers and Directors: * Barry Caldwell,* Pres.; Linda Smith, V.P. and Secy.; Ron Jones, V.P. and Treas.; Marilyn Brown, V.P.; Jimmy LaValley, V.P.; Cherie Rice, V.P.; Robert Simpson, V.P.; David Steiner,* V.P.
EIN: 043073733
Selected grants: The following grants were reported in 2003.
$150,000 to After School Matters, Chicago, IL. For salute to Historic Soldier Field.
$25,000 to Houston Symphony Orchestra, Houston, TX. For general support.
$15,000 to Baylor College of Medicine, Houston, TX. For general support.
$7,700 to Toronto Symphony, Toronto, Canada. For general support.
$5,500 to Franklin Educational Foundation, Franklin, WI. For general support.
$5,000 to Keep Texas Beautiful, Austin, TX. For general support.
$5,000 to Whiz Kids Tutoring, Denver, CO. For general support.
$2,500 to Brooklyn Animal Resources Coalition, Brooklyn, NY. For general support.
$2,500 to Leadership Houston, Houston, TX. For general support.
$2,500 to Trees for Houston, Houston, TX. For general support.

9266
Watson Family Foundation ✧ ☆
P.O. Box 56389
Houston, TX   77256
Contact: Charles L. Watson, Pres.

Established in 1994 in TX.
Donors: Charles L. Watson; Kim R. Watson.
Foundation type: Independent foundation.
Financial data (yr. ended 12/31/05): Assets, $1,074,552 (M); gifts received, $400,000; expenditures, $480,097; qualifying distributions, $472,763; giving activities include $472,763 for 32 grants (high: $140,000; low: $100).
Purpose and activities: Giving primarily to a Presbyterian church, as well as, for the arts, education, health, children, youth and social services, and federated giving programs.
Fields of interest: Arts, cultural/ethnic awareness; Arts; Secondary school/education; Health organizations, association; Human services; Children/youth, services; Federated giving programs; Protestant agencies & churches.
Limitations: Giving primarily in Houston, TX.
Application information:
  Deadline(s): End of 3rd quarter
Officers: Charles L. Watson, Pres.; Kim R. Watson, V.P. and Secy.-Treas.
Director: Billie M. Hogan.
EIN: 760420732

9267
The Gil and Dody Weaver Foundation ✧
1845 Woodall Rodgers Freeway, Ste. 1275
Dallas, TX   75201   (214) 999-9497
Contact: William R. Weaver M.D., Tr.
FAX: (214) 999-9496

Established in 1980 in TX.
Donors: Galbraith McF. Weaver; Elizabeth Eudora Weaver.
Foundation type: Independent foundation.
Financial data (yr. ended 9/30/05): Assets, $17,864,278 (M); expenditures, $1,250,855; qualifying distributions, $787,293; giving activities include $774,300 for 89 grants (high: $50,000; low: $500).
Purpose and activities: Primary areas of interest include women, children and youth, the elderly, and the handicapped.
Fields of interest: Human services; Children/youth, services; Child development, services; Aging, centers/services; Aging; Disabilities, people with; Economically disadvantaged.
Type of support: General/operating support; Continuing support; Annual campaigns; Scholarship funds.
Limitations: Giving primarily in TX; some giving also in LA and OK. No grants to individuals.
Publications: Application guidelines.
Application information: Application form not required.
  Initial approach: Letter including organizational information
  Copies of proposal: 1
  Deadline(s): May 31
  Final notification: Sept. 30
Trustee: William R. Weaver, M.D.
EIN: 751729449
Selected grants: The following grants were reported in 2005.
$100,000 to Episcopal Diocese of Dallas, Dallas, TX.
$85,000 to Southwestern Diabetic Foundation, Gainesville, TX. 2 grants: $45,000, $40,000
$50,000 to Dallas Theological Seminary, Dallas, TX.
$50,000 to Parents Television Council, Los Angeles, CA.
$35,000 to Salvation Army, Plainview, TX.
$15,000 to American Family Association, Tupelo, MS.
$7,500 to Cancer Care Services, Fort Worth, TX.
$3,000 to Learning Center of North Texas, Fort Worth, TX.
$2,500 to Salvation Army, Saint Petersburg, FL.

9268
William M. Weaver Foundation ✧ ☆
c/o Lamesa National Bank
P.O. Box 301
Lamesa, TX   79331
Contact: Elwood Freeman, Trust Off., Lamesa National Bank

Established in 2003 in TX.
Donor: William M. Weaver Charitable Trust.
Foundation type: Independent foundation.
Financial data (yr. ended 12/31/05): Assets, $10,351,127 (M); expenditures, $493,412; qualifying distributions, $442,316; giving activities include $378,821 for 6 grants (high: $139,850; low: $7,500).
Purpose and activities: Giving primarily for community development.

Fields of interest: Community development; Protestant agencies & churches.
Limitations: Giving primarily in Dawson County, TX.
Application information:
  Initial approach: Proposal
  Deadline(s): None
Admin. Board: Dwaine Brown; Janet Eveheart; John Farris; Sam Saleh; Ray Stephens; Mike C. Tyler.
Trustee: Lamesa National Bank.
EIN: 300140386

9269
The Webber Family Foundation
P.O. Box 550
Austin, TX 78767
FAX: (512) 479-2656;
E-mail: info@webberfoundation.org; Additional address: c/o JPMorgan Chase Bank, N.A., Attn.: Cynthia Scovel, 700 Lavaca St., Austin, TX 78701-3101; URL: http://www.webberfoundation.org

Established in 1999 in TX.
Donors: Neil Webber; Noelie Alito.
Foundation type: Independent foundation.
Financial data (yr. ended 12/31/05): Assets, $11,649,932 (M); gifts received, $50,000; expenditures, $918,283; qualifying distributions, $854,287; giving activities include $835,747 for 36 grants (high: $40,000; low: $5,000).
Purpose and activities: Giving primarily for youth and education.
Fields of interest: Education; Youth, services.
Limitations: Giving primarily to the Washington, DC, area, and the surrounding MD and VA communities, as well as to Austin and central TX. No support for religious organizations. No grants to individuals, or for capital campaigns, recurring expenses, endowments, or fundraisers.
Publications: Application guidelines; Grants list.
Application information: See foundation Web site for full application guidelines and requirements, including downloadable form. Application form required.
  Initial approach: Online or letter of inquiry
  Copies of proposal: 4
  Deadline(s): None
  Board meeting date(s): As needed
  Final notification: Generally within 60 days
Officer and Directors:* Neil Webber,* Chair.; Jessica S. D'Arcy; Adrian Webber; Arthur L. Webber.
Trustee: JPMorgan Chase Bank, N.A.
EIN: 742927126
Selected grants: The following grants were reported in 2005.
$52,861 to Imagination Stage, Bethesda, MD.
$35,000 to Heart House Austin, Austin, TX.
$30,695 to University of Texas Foundation, Austin, TX.
$30,420 to Westcave Preserve Corporation, Round Mountain, TX.
$30,000 to Columbia Center for Theatrical Arts, Columbia, MD.
$30,000 to Foundation Communities, Austin, TX.
$25,000 to Austin Film Festival, Austin, TX.
$25,000 to Community Family Life Services, DC.
$25,000 to Girlstart, Austin, TX.
$25,000 to Zachary Scott Theater Center, Austin, TX.

9270
The Wedge Foundation ✧
1415 Louisiana St., Ste. 3000
Houston, TX 77002-7351

Established in 2001 in TX.
Foundation type: Independent foundation.
Financial data (yr. ended 12/31/05): Assets, $99,896 (M); gifts received, $2,444,975; expenditures, $1,421,727; qualifying distributions, $1,419,527; giving activities include $1,419,527 for 4 grants (high: $750,000; low: $200,000).
Purpose and activities: Giving primarily for art scholarships, as well as for a university's endowment for the creation of a lecture series on Lebanese and Eastern Mediterranean studies.
Fields of interest: Arts, formal/general education; Higher education, university; Scholarships/financial aid.
Limitations: Applications not accepted. Giving primarily in MA and TX.
Application information: Contributes only to pre-selected organizations.
Officers: F.I. Fares, Pres.; R.E. Blohm, Jr., Secy.; J.M. Tidwell, Treas.
EIN: 760533546

9271
David Weekley Family Foundation ✧
1111 N. Post Oak Rd.
Houston, TX 77055

Established in 1990.
Donors: David M. Weekley; Bonnie S. Weekley.
Foundation type: Independent foundation.
Financial data (yr. ended 12/31/04): Assets, $51,776,868 (M); gifts received, $11,500,000; expenditures, $2,871,232; qualifying distributions, $2,721,724; giving activities include $2,542,354 for 55 grants (high: $723,495; low: $100; average: $1,000–$100,000).
Purpose and activities: Giving primarily to cancer, youth services, and Christian agencies and churches.
Fields of interest: Health organizations, association; Youth, services; Christian agencies & churches.
Type of support: General/operating support; Annual campaigns; Capital campaigns.
Limitations: Applications not accepted. Giving primarily in Houston, TX. No grants to individuals.
Application information: Contributes only to pre-selected organizations.
Officers: David M. Weekley, Pres.; Weldon T. Weekley, V.P.; Bonnie S. Weekley, Secy.
EIN: 760324538
Selected grants: The following grants were reported in 2003.
$210,000 to Living Water International, Sugar Land, TX. For general support.
$105,000 to Houston Achievement Place, Houston, TX. For general support.
$102,500 to Star of Hope Mission, Houston, TX. For general support.
$75,000 to Casa de Esperanza de los Ninos, Houston, TX. For general support.
$49,000 to Memorial Drive Presbyterian Church, Houston, TX. For general support.
$43,750 to YMCA of the Greater Houston Area, Houston, TX. For general support.
$30,000 to New Covenant Presbytery Church, Houston, TX. For Barnabas Ministry.

$10,000 to American Heart Association, Houston, TX. For general support.
$10,000 to Boys and Girls Country of Houston, Hockley, TX. For general support.

9272
The Weiser Foundation ✧
c/o John M. Weiser
5925 Cypress Point Dr.
Fort Worth, TX 76132 (817) 390-8876

Established in 1994 in TX.
Donor: John M. Weiser.
Foundation type: Independent foundation.
Financial data (yr. ended 12/31/05): Assets, $2,693,958 (M); gifts received, $3,501,635; expenditures, $1,198,920; qualifying distributions, $1,197,874; giving activities include $1,197,000 for 11 grants (high: $382,000; low: $8,000).
Purpose and activities: Giving primarily for Christian education and organizations.
Fields of interest: Theological school/education; Christian agencies & churches.
Limitations: Applications not accepted. Giving primarily in TX.
Application information: Unsolicited requests for funds not accepted.
Officers: John M. Weiser, Pres.; R. Douglas Wallace, V.P.; Terri L. Weiser, Secy.
EIN: 752561493
Selected grants: The following grants were reported in 2003.
$232,000 to Westminster Theological Seminary, Glenside, PA.
$230,000 to Reformed University Fellowship, Lawrenceville, GA.
$100,000 to Christian Counseling and Educational Foundation, Laverock, PA.
$15,000 to North Texas Presbyterian, TX.
$10,000 to West Dallas Community School, Dallas, TX.

9273
The Robert A. Welch Foundation ▼
5555 San Felipe, Ste. 1900
Houston, TX 77056-2732
Contact: Norbert Dittrich, Pres.
E-mail: dittrich@welch1.org; URL: http://www.welch1.org

Established in 1954 in TX as a private foundation.
Donor: Robert A. Welch†.
Foundation type: Independent foundation.
Financial data (yr. ended 8/31/05): Assets, $611,141,615 (M); expenditures, $31,955,362; qualifying distributions, $28,130,851; giving activities include $26,407,362 for 463 grants (high: $500,000; low: $4,795; average: $15,000–$75,000), $797,944 for grants to individuals, and $188,053 for 2 foundation-administered programs.
Purpose and activities: The general policy of the foundation is to support fundamental chemical research at colleges and universities within the state of Texas.
Fields of interest: Chemistry.
Type of support: Research.
Limitations: Giving limited to TX.
Publications: Application guidelines; Annual report; Newsletter.
Application information: To be eligible for consideration, an applicant must be a university,

college or other educational institution within the state of TX. Application form required.

Initial approach: Written application
Copies of proposal: 1
Deadline(s): Feb. 1 for regular research grant program and for Robert A. Welch Award in Chemistry
Board meeting date(s): As needed
Final notification: Approximately 2 months

Officers and Directors:* J. Evans Attwell,* Chair.; Dennis R. Hendrix,* Vice-Chair.; Norbert Dittrich, Pres.; Wilhelmina E. Robertson,* Secy.; Ernest H. Cockrell,* Treas.; Peter J. Fluor.
Number of staff: 8 full-time professional.
EIN: 760343128
Selected grants: The following grants were reported in 2005.

$4,400,000 to University of Texas, Austin, TX. 3 grants: $500,000 (For Chair in Chemistry), $400,000 (For Chair in Chemistry), $3,500,000 (For Texas Institute for Drug and Diagnostic Development).

$1,620,000 to University of Texas Health Science Center, Houston, TX. For Gulf Coast Consortia.

$720,000 to Rice University, Houston, TX. 3 grants: $240,000 (For research project, Chemistry of carbon nanomaterials), $240,000 (For research project, Genetic regulatory proteins structure-function relationships), $240,000 (For research project, Chemical mechanisms of ligand binding to heme proteins).

$330,000 to University of Texas at Dallas, Richardson, TX. 2 grants: $180,000 (For research project, Lanthanide-DOTA-Tetraamide Complexes as Biological Sensors), $150,000 (For general methodology to develop peptidomimetics of large peptide hormones).

$150,000 to University of Texas Health Science Center, San Antonio, TX. For research project, Ligand-Receptor Interactions in the TGF-beta Superfamily.

9274
The West Endowment ✧
P.O. Box 491
Houston, TX 77001
Contact: Grants Coord.

Established in 1995 in TX.
Foundation type: Independent foundation.
Financial data (yr. ended 12/31/05): Assets, $13,782,977 (M); expenditures, $714,512; qualifying distributions, $684,012; giving activities include $682,000 for grants.
Purpose and activities: Giving primarily for education and health organizations.
Fields of interest: Secondary school/education; Higher education; Education; Health care, formal/general education; Health organizations, association; Eye diseases; Boy scouts; Human services; Children/youth, services; Federated giving programs; Social sciences, public education.
Limitations: Giving primarily in TX, with emphasis on Harris County. No grants to individuals.
Application information:
Initial approach: Letter
Deadline(s): None
Officers and Directors:* W.R. Lloyd, Jr.,* Pres.; James A. Reichert,* V.P.; Ronald S. Webster,* Secy.; Barbara Keyes, Treas.; William West Lloyd.
EIN: 760481204
Selected grants: The following grants were reported in 2004.

$150,000 to Hermann Eye Fund, Houston, TX.
$50,000 to Rumsey Hall School, Washington Depot, CT.
$50,000 to Saint John the Divine Episcopal Church, Houston, TX.
$50,000 to Strake Jesuit College Preparatory, Houston, TX.
$25,000 to Rise School of Houston, Houston, TX.
$25,000 to Shumla School, College Station, TX.
$25,000 to Texas Womans University, Denton, TX.
$15,000 to Casa de Esperanza de los Ninos, Houston, TX.
$15,000 to Strand Street Theater, Galveston, TX.
$5,000 to Gathering Place, Houston, TX.

9275
West Foundation ✧
c/o Reece A. West
P.O. Box 1675
Wichita Falls, TX 76307-1675

Established in 1973 in TX.
Donors: Gordon T. West†; Ellen B. West†; Gordon T. West, Jr.
Foundation type: Independent foundation.
Financial data (yr. ended 9/30/05): Assets, $19,719,556 (M); gifts received, $25,000; expenditures, $948,229; qualifying distributions, $921,341; giving activities include $739,553 for 17 grants (high: $147,039; low: $4,639), and $100,000 for 20 grants to individuals (high: $5,000; low: $5,000).
Purpose and activities: Support limited to education, through excellence in teaching awards to public school teachers and scholarship and other educational programs on the public school and university levels.
Fields of interest: Higher education; Education.
Type of support: Scholarship funds; Grants to individuals.
Limitations: Applications not accepted. Giving limited to the Wichita Falls, TX, area.
Application information: Unsolicited requests for funds not accepted.
Officers and Trustees:* Reece A. West,* Pres.; Joseph N. Sherrill, Jr.,* V.P.; Gordon T. West, Jr.,* V.P.
Number of staff: 1 full-time professional; 2 part-time support.
EIN: 237332105
Selected grants: The following grants were reported in 2005.

$220,315 to Wichita Falls Independent School District, Wichita Falls, TX. 5 grants: $68,595, $68,000, $26,851, $27,861, $29,008
$186,599 to Midwestern State University, Wichita Falls, TX. 3 grants: $20,000, $19,560, $147,039
$100,000 to Trinity University, San Antonio, TX.
$100,000 to Wellesley College, Wellesley, MA.

9276
Neva and Wesley West Foundation ✧
P.O. Box 7
Houston, TX 77001
Contact: Stuart W. Stedman, Tr.

Trust established in 1956 in TX.
Donors: Wesley West†; Mrs. Wesley West; Neva Watkins West.
Foundation type: Independent foundation.

Financial data (yr. ended 12/31/04): Assets, $23,464,245 (M); gifts received, $5,000,000; expenditures, $842,318; qualifying distributions, $605,000; giving activities include $605,000 for 38 grants (high: $110,000; low: $500).
Purpose and activities: Giving primarily for the arts, education, health care, and medical research.
Fields of interest: Arts; Higher education; Education; Health care; Health organizations, association; Medical research, institute.
Type of support: General/operating support; Capital campaigns; Building/renovation; Professorships; Research.
Limitations: Applications not accepted. Giving primarily in TX. No grants to individuals, or for scholarships or fellowships; no loans.
Application information: Unsolicited requests for funds not accepted.
Trustees: Randolph L. Pullin; Betty Ann West Stedman; Stuart West Stedman.
EIN: 746039393
Selected grants: The following grants were reported in 2003.

$210,000 to Texas A & M University, Caesar Kleberg Wildlife Research Institute, Kingsville, TX. For operating support.
$60,000 to Texas Childrens Hospital, Houston, TX. For operating support.
$42,850 to Museum of Fine Arts, Houston, Houston, TX. For operating support.
$35,000 to Houston Grand Opera, Houston, TX. For operating support.
$7,500 to Phi Beta Kappa Alumni Association, Houston, TX. For operating support.
$7,500 to United Cerebral Palsy of Greater Houston, Houston, TX. For operating support.
$5,000 to March of Dimes Birth Defects Foundation, Houston, TX. For operating support.
$2,500 to Houston Museum of Natural Science, Houston, TX. For operating support.
$1,500 to Society for the Performing Arts, Houston, TX. For operating support.
$1,500 to Womens Fund for Health Education and Research, Houston, TX. For operating support.

9277
The Clarence Westbury Foundation ✧
(formerly The Scaler Westbury Foundation)
800 Gessner Rd., Ste. 1260
Houston, TX 77024-4273

Established in 1996 in TX.
Donor: Jacques C. Boissonnas.
Foundation type: Independent foundation.
Financial data (yr. ended 12/31/05): Assets, $10,660,539 (M); expenditures, $2,843,009; qualifying distributions, $2,608,965; giving activities include $2,608,965 for 11 grants (high: $2,005,800; low: $3,600).
Fields of interest: Museums; Health organizations, association.
International interests: France.
Limitations: Applications not accepted. Giving primarily in Paris, France; giving also in the U.S. No grants to individuals.
Application information: Contributes only to pre-selected organizations.
Officers and Directors:* Jacques C. Boissonnas,* Pres.; Nicolas N. Boissonnas,* V.P.; Catherine B. Coste,* V.P.; Marvin A. Wurzer, Secy.-Treas.
EIN: 760507294

9278
Westcott Foundation ✧
100 Crescent Ct., Ste. 1620
Dallas, TX 75201-1884 (214) 777-5015
Contact: Jack T. Smith, Pres.

Established in 1989 in TX.
Donors: Carl Westcott; Jimmy Westcott.
Foundation type: Independent foundation.
Financial data (yr. ended 12/31/05): Assets,
$3,245,240 (M); expenditures, $1,183,958;
qualifying distributions, $1,163,275; giving
activities include $1,152,533 for 50 grants (high:
$500,000; low: $227).
Purpose and activities: Giving primarily for higher
education, and federated giving programs; funding
also for hospitals, and human services.
Fields of interest: Arts; Higher education;
Education; Health organizations; Athletics/sports,
golf; Boys & girls clubs; Human services; Children,
services; Federated giving programs.
Type of support: General/operating support.
Limitations: Giving primarily in Dallas, TX.
Application information: Application form required.
> *Initial approach:* Letter requesting application
> form
> *Copies of proposal:* 1
> *Deadline(s):* None

Officers: Carl Westcott, Chair.; Jack T. Smith, Pres.;
Jimmy Westcott, V.P.; Judy Ledoux, Secy.-Treas.
Directors: Diane Adler; Court Westcott.
Number of staff: 1 part-time support.
EIN: 752304233

9279
G. R. White Trust ✧
c/o JPMorgan Chase Bank, N.A.
600 Bailey Ave., TX1-3434
Fort Worth, TX 76107
Application address: c/o JPMorgan Chase Bank,
attn.: Don Smith, Trust Off., 420 Throckmorton St.,
Fort Worth, TX 76102, tel.: (817) 884-4165

Established in 1965.
Donor: G.R. White†.
Foundation type: Independent foundation.
Financial data (yr. ended 9/30/05): Assets,
$7,746,181 (M); expenditures, $567,841;
qualifying distributions, $359,014; giving activities
include $352,483 for 30 grants (high: $15,955;
low: $2,000).
Fields of interest: Museums (history); Higher
education; Libraries/library science; Environment;
Disasters, fire prevention/control; Human services;
Community development; Christian agencies &
churches.
Type of support: General/operating support;
Building/renovation; Equipment; Professorships;
Scholarship funds.
Limitations: Giving limited to TX. No grants to
individuals.
Application information: Application form not
required.
> *Initial approach:* Letter
> *Copies of proposal:* 1
> *Deadline(s):* Sept.
> *Board meeting date(s):* Fall

Trustee: JPMorgan Chase Bank, N.A.
EIN: 756094930
Selected grants: The following grants were reported
in 2003.

$120,000 to University of Texas, Austin, TX. 3
grants: $40,000 each (For G. Rollie White
teaching excellence chair).
$82,457 to Texas A & M University, College Station,
TX. 2 grants: $62,457, $20,000
$50,000 to Texas and Southwestern Cattle Raisers
Foundation, Fort Worth, TX.
$21,600 to Saint Stephens Episcopal School,
Austin, TX. For expeditions and equipment.
$20,000 to Texas Baptist Men, Dallas, TX. 2 grants:
$10,000 each
$4,000 to Southwestern Baptist Theological
Seminary, Fort Worth, TX. For G. Rollie White
Scholarship Fund.

9280
Wichita Falls Area Community Foundation
807 8th St., Ste. 750
Wichita Falls, TX 76301 (940) 766-0829
Contact: Teresa Pontius, Exec. Dir.
FAX: (940) 766-2861;
E-mail: pontiustx@sbcglobal.net; Additional E-mail:
info@wfacf.org; URL: http://www.wfacf.org

Established in 1999 in TX.
Foundation type: Community foundation.
Financial data (yr. ended 12/31/04): Assets,
$13,828,127 (M); gifts received, $3,534,729;
expenditures, $1,565,027; giving activities include
$1,181,732 for 127 grants (high: $576,500; low:
$20), and $63,009 for 25 grants to individuals
(high: $7,000; low: $500).
Purpose and activities: The foundation seeks to
provide charitable means for area residents to leave
a legacy for the future benefit of their communities;
to build agency endowments; and to promote
philanthropy.
Fields of interest: Historic preservation/historical
societies; Arts; Higher education; Education;
Environment; Health organizations, association;
Recreation, community facilities; Children/youth,
services; Human services; Community
development, neighborhood development;
Federated giving programs.
Type of support: Technical assistance; Seed money;
Program development; Matching/challenge support;
Fellowships; Capital campaigns; Building/
renovation; Scholarships—to individuals.
Limitations: Giving primarily to TX, particularly the
metropolitan Wichita Falls area. No support for
private foundations, religious activities, or for
organizations which redistribute funds to other
organizations. No grants to individuals (except for
scholarships), or for endowments, operating
expenses of well-established organizations, annual
fund drives, deficit financing, basic research, or
fundraising campaigns; no multi-year grants.
Publications: Annual report; Informational brochure;
Newsletter; Occasional report.
Application information: Visit foundation Web site
for application checklist, summary form, and
guidelines. Letter of intent is required before
submitting a full grant application; applicants will be
notified that they are encouraged to submit a full
application or that their project is unlikely to be
funded based on letter of intent. Application form
required.
> *Initial approach:* Letter of intent 30 days prior to
> grant proposal deadline
> *Deadline(s):* Feb. 25 and Sept. 25; Mar. 15 for
> scholarships
> *Board meeting date(s):* Feb., May, Aug., and Dec.
> *Final notification:* May and Dec.

Officers and Directors:* John Hirschi,* Chair.; Pat
Morgan,* Vice-Chair.; David Wolverton,*
Secy.-Treas.; Teresa Pontius, Exec. Dir.; D. Phil
Bolin,* Emeritus; Ray Clymer,* Emeritus; Robert T.
Priddy,* Emeritus; Joe Sherrill,* Emeritus; Kay
Yeager,* Emeritus; Warren Ayres; Darrell Coleman;
Barry Donnell; Elizabeth Edwards; Martha Fain; Carol
Carlson Gunn; Reno Gustafson; Ralph Harvey;
Berneice Leath; Jim McCoy; Charles B. Prothro; Gary
H. Shores; Danny Taylor; Sara Jane Wood.
Number of staff: 1 full-time professional; 1 full-time
support.
EIN: 752817894

9281
Cecilia Young Willard Helping Fund ✧
c/o Broadway National Bank
P.O. Box 17001
San Antonio, TX 78217
Contact: Nancy F. May, C.T.F.A., V.P. and Trust Off.,
Broadway National Bank

Established in 1987 in TX.
Donor: Cecilia Young Willard Trust.
Foundation type: Independent foundation.
Financial data (yr. ended 5/31/06): Assets,
$5,598,644 (M); expenditures, $406,490;
qualifying distributions, $351,883; giving activities
include $351,883 for 24 grants (high: $50,000;
low: $5,000).
Purpose and activities: Support primarily for a
Presbyterian church, higher and other education,
and a children's home.
Fields of interest: Higher education; Education;
Children/youth, services; Protestant agencies &
churches.
Type of support: General/operating support;
Continuing support; Annual campaigns; Capital
campaigns; Building/renovation; Emergency funds;
Curriculum development; Research.
Limitations: Giving primarily in MD, NC, and TX. No
grants to individuals.
Application information: Funding limited primarily to
those organizations that Dr. Willard contributed to
during her lifetime. Grant requests are reviewed.
Application form not required.
> *Initial approach:* Letter
> *Copies of proposal:* 1
> *Deadline(s):* May 31
> *Board meeting date(s):* Between June and Oct.
> *Final notification:* Oct. or Nov.

Trustee: Broadway National Bank.
EIN: 746350893
Selected grants: The following grants were reported
in 2006.
$50,000 to Greater Baltimore Medical Center
Foundation, Baltimore, MD.
$30,000 to Hospice of Baltimore, Baltimore, MD.
$24,779 to First Presbyterian Church, Hickory, NC.
$17,368 to Grandfather Home for Children, Banner
Elk, NC.
$15,000 to Fund for Johns Hopkins Medicine,
Baltimore, MD.
$15,000 to Maryland Historical Society, Baltimore,
MD.
$14,868 to Crossnore School, Crossnore, NC.
$14,868 to Lees-McRae College, Banner Elk, NC.
$10,000 to Baltimore Symphony Orchestra,
Baltimore, MD.
$10,000 to Family and Childrens Services of Central
Maryland, Baltimore, MD.

9282
J. L. Williams Foundation, Inc. ✧ ☆
P.O. Box 797464
Dallas, TX 75379
Contact: Julia Underwood, Secy.-Treas.

Established in 2000 TX.
Donors: J.L. Williams†; The Barbara Barton Trust.
Foundation type: Independent foundation.
Financial data (yr. ended 12/31/05): Assets,
$20,026,676 (M); expenditures, $907,873;
qualifying distributions, $487,912; giving activities
include $451,100 for 17 grants (high: $120,000;
low: $1,000), and $17,000 for 1 grant to an
individual.
Fields of interest: Health care; Food banks; Human
services; Christian agencies & churches; Homeless.
Limitations: Giving primarily in Dallas, TX.
Application information: Application form not
required.
   Initial approach: Letter
   Deadline(s): None
Officers and Trustees:* R.J. Pipes,* Chair.; Jonell
H. Williams,* Pres.; Julia Underwood,* Secy.-Treas.
EIN: 752671320
Selected grants: The following grants were reported
in 2005.
$200,000 to Dallas Morning News Charities,
   Dallas, TX. 2 grants: $100,000 each
$10,000 to American Red Cross, Dallas, TX.
$10,000 to Dallas Leadership Foundation, Dallas,
   TX.
$10,000 to Genesis Womens Shelter, Dallas, TX.
$10,000 to North Texas Food Bank, Dallas, TX.
$10,000 to Wilkinson Center, Dallas, TX.
$1,000 to Guide Dogs of Texas, San Antonio, TX.
$1,000 to YMCA of Metropolitan Dallas, Dallas, TX.

9283
Lester & Beatrice Williams Foundation
P.O. Box 809
Cameron, TX 76520 (254) 605-0275
Contact: Mike Zajicek, Tr.
FAX: (254) 605-0274; E-mail: mikez@vvm.com

Established in 1997 in TX.
Donor: Beatrice Williams†.
Foundation type: Operating foundation.
Financial data (yr. ended 12/31/04): Assets,
$11,721,822 (M); gifts received, $104,645;
expenditures, $929,263; qualifying distributions,
$452,325; giving activities include $452,325 for 21
grants (high: $70,000; low: $500).
Purpose and activities: A private operating
foundation, giving primarily for education and
community organizations.
Fields of interest: Education; Health care; Food
services; Boy scouts; Girl scouts; Children/youth,
services; Community development; Protestant
agencies & churches.
Limitations: Giving primarily in Cameron, TX. No
grants to individuals.
Application information: Generally contributes to
pre-selected organizations. Application form not
required.
   Initial approach: Letter
   Copies of proposal: 3
   Deadline(s): None
Trustees: Amy Poe; Mike Zajicek.
EIN: 742847229

9284
The William and Marie Wise Family
Foundation ✧ ☆
c/o Nancy Palmieri
10223 Broadway, Ste. P257
Pearland, TX 77584

Established in 1998 in TX.
Donor: William A. Wise.
Foundation type: Independent foundation.
Financial data (yr. ended 12/31/05): Assets,
$2,039,023 (M); gifts received, $4,495;
expenditures, $509,047; qualifying distributions,
$504,464; giving activities include $504,464 for 16
grants (high: $305,000; low: $100).
Purpose and activities: Giving primarily for higher
education, and social services.
Fields of interest: Museums (art); Higher education;
Education; Health organizations, association;
Human services; YM/YWCAs & YM/YWHAs;
Federated giving programs.
Type of support: General/operating support.
Limitations: Giving primarily in Boulder, CO, and
Houston, TX. No grants to individuals.
Officers: Marie Figge Wise, Pres. and Treas.; William
A. Wise, V.P. and Secy.; Genevieve Wise Evans,
Exec. Dir.
EIN: 311519664
Selected grants: The following grants were reported
in 2005.
$12,500 to Mental Health Association of Greater
   Houston, Houston, TX.
$11,000 to University of Saint Thomas, Houston,
   TX.
$10,000 to Texas Childrens Hospital, Houston, TX.
$5,000 to Council on Alcohol and Drugs Houston,
   Houston, TX.
$5,000 to Girl Scouts of the U.S.A., Houston, TX.
$5,000 to Vanderbilt University, Nashville, TN.
$2,500 to Hobby Center for the Performing Arts,
   Houston, TX.
$100 to Covenant House Texas, Houston, TX.

9285
Watson W. Wise Foundation ✧
(formerly Watson W. Wise Foundation & Charitable
Trust)
110 N. College, Ste. 1002
Tyler, TX 75702 (903) 531-9615

Established around 1967.
Donor: Watson W. Wise†.
Foundation type: Independent foundation.
Financial data (yr. ended 12/31/05): Assets,
$11,058,995 (M); expenditures, $629,623;
qualifying distributions, $523,299; giving activities
include $485,500 for grants.
Fields of interest: Museums; Arts; Higher
education; Education; Health care; Health
organizations, association; Human services;
Children/youth, services; Federated giving
programs; Christian agencies & churches.
Limitations: Giving primarily in TX, with emphasis on
Tyler. No grants to individuals.
Application information: Application form not
required.
   Deadline(s): None
Officers: Will A. Knight, Pres.; Calvin Clyde, Jr., V.P.
Trustees: Herman A. Engel; Emma F. Wise.
EIN: 756064539

9286
Kalman & Ida Wolens Foundation
5430 Glen Lakes Dr., Ste. 116
Dallas, TX 75231
Contact: Joe W. Milkes, Pres.

Established in 1972 in TX.
Donor: Louis Wolens†.
Foundation type: Independent foundation.
Financial data (yr. ended 7/31/05): Assets,
$8,253,228 (M); expenditures, $680,750;
qualifying distributions, $646,606; giving activities
include $644,653 for 12 grants (high: $300,000;
low: $1,500).
Fields of interest: Education; Human services;
Children/youth, services; Jewish agencies &
temples.
International interests: Israel.
Type of support: Endowments; Program
development; Scholarship funds; Research.
Limitations: Applications not accepted. Giving
primarily in TX. No grants to individuals.
Application information: Funds fully committed;
unsolicited requests for funds not accepted.
   Board meeting date(s): Feb., May, Aug., and Nov.
Officers and Directors:* Joe W. Milkes,* Pres. and
Treas.; Bette Miller,* Secy.; Marjorie Milkes; Cheryl
Jerome Moore.
EIN: 237222516
Selected grants: The following grants were reported
in 2003.
$500,000 to Legacy Senior Communities, Dallas,
   TX.
$166,667 to Alzheimers Research Center, Augusta,
   GA.
$10,000 to United Way of Navarro County,
   Corsicana, TX.
$500 to YMCA of Corsicana, Corsicana, TX.
$250 to Home Instruction Program for Preschool
   Youngsters (HIPPY), New York, NY.

9287
Wolf Mountain Foundation ✧ ☆
c/o Dan Kerst
P.O. Box 2207
Fredericksburg, TX 78624

Established in 1999 in CO.
Donor: Pierce Mangurian.
Foundation type: Independent foundation.
Financial data (yr. ended 12/31/05): Assets,
$6,373,464 (M); expenditures, $599,518;
qualifying distributions, $315,000; giving activities
include $315,000 for grants.
Fields of interest: Children/youth, services.
Limitations: Applications not accepted. No grants to
individuals.
Application information: Contributes only to
pre-selected organizations.
Officers and Director:* Pierce Mangurian,* Pres.
and Treas.; Dan Kerst, Secy.
EIN: 841524399
Selected grants: The following grants were reported
in 2004.
$50,000 to Smile Train, New York, NY.
$10,000 to Boles Childrens Home, Quinlan, TX.
$10,000 to Cal Farleys Boys Ranch, Amarillo, TX.
$10,000 to Cherokee Home for Children, Cherokee,
   TX.
$10,000 to Childrens Home of Lubbock, Lubbock,
   TX.
$10,000 to High Plains Childrens Home and Family
   Services, Amarillo, TX.

$10,000 to Medina Childrens Home, Medina, TX.
$10,000 to Texas Baptist Childrens Home, Round Rock, TX.
$10,000 to Tiny Tim Center, Longmont, CO.
$5,000 to Boysville, Converse, TX.

9288
Cyvia and Melvyn Wolff Foundation ◇
P.O. Box 219169
Houston, TX 77218

Established in 1997 in TX.
Donors: Curtis Wolff; Cyvia G. Wolff; Melvyn L. Wolff.
Foundation type: Independent foundation.
Financial data (yr. ended 11/30/05): Assets, $1,997,357 (M); expenditures, $355,711; qualifying distributions, $332,977; giving activities include $331,875 for 45 grants (high: $63,600; low: $250).
Fields of interest: Museums (art); Performing arts, orchestra (symphony); Education; Health care, clinics/centers; Cancer; Human services; Federated giving programs; Jewish agencies & temples.
Limitations: Applications not accepted. Giving primarily in Houston, TX. No grants to individuals.
Application information: Contributes only to pre-selected organizations.
Officers: Melvyn L. Wolff, Pres. and Treas.; Cyvia G. Wolff, V.P. and Secy.
Trustee: Curtis Wolff.
EIN: 760556526

9289
The Pauline Sterne Wolff Memorial Foundation ◇
c/o Texan Bldg.
333 W. Loop N., 4th Fl.
Houston, TX 77024
Application address: c/o Carol Rusciano, JPMorgan Chase Bank, N.A. P.O. Box 2558, Houston, TX 77252, tel.: (713) 216-1451

Incorporated in 1922 in TX.
Donor: Henry J.N. Taub.
Foundation type: Independent foundation.
Financial data (yr. ended 12/31/03): Assets, $24,803,470 (M); gifts received, $1,000; expenditures, $1,470,050; qualifying distributions, $1,258,113; giving activities include $1,154,700 for 7 grants (high: $730,000; low: $5,000).
Purpose and activities: Giving primarily for Jewish welfare organizations, especially a home for the elderly; support also for medical education and research and hospitals.
Fields of interest: Medical school/education; Hospitals (general); Medical research, institute; Human services; Jewish federated giving programs.
Limitations: Giving limited to TX, with emphasis on Harris County. No grants to individuals.
Application information:
  Initial approach: Letter
  Deadline(s): Nov. 1
Officers: Henry J.N. Taub II, Pres.; Henry J.N. Taub, V.P. and Secy.-Treas.; Jenard M. Gross, V.P.; Regina J. Rogers, V.P.; Marc J. Shapiro, V.P.
EIN: 741110698
Selected grants: The following grants were reported in 2003.
$730,000 to Seven Acres Jewish Geriatric Center, Houston, TX.

$209,700 to Jewish Community Center of Houston, Houston, TX.
$125,000 to Jewish Family Service, Houston, TX.
$30,000 to Baylor College of Medicine, Houston, TX.
$30,000 to Goldberg Bnai Brith Towers, Houston, TX.
$25,000 to Texas Childrens Hospital, Houston, TX.
$5,000 to DePelchin Childrens Center, Houston, TX.

9290
The Wolslager Foundation ◇
P.O. Box 1191
San Angelo, TX 76902
Contact: Shirley Rogers, Secy.-Treas.

Established in 1993.
Donors: J.W. Wolslager; Josephine S. Wolslager†.
Foundation type: Independent foundation.
Financial data (yr. ended 12/31/05): Assets, $25,998,616 (M); expenditures, $4,436,143; qualifying distributions, $3,866,900; giving activities include $3,866,900 for 73 grants (high: $350,000; low: $1,500; average: $10,000–$300,000).
Purpose and activities: The foundation was established to improve the quality of life for individuals within the areas where the Wolslager family owned and operated their Coca-Cola business through Dec. 31, 1998. This goal is being met by providing support for many educational opportunities, making grants for medical facilities and services, supporting child development programs, and providing services for our elderly citizens.
Fields of interest: Health care; Geriatrics; Food services, congregate meals; Youth development, centers/clubs; Boys & girls clubs; Residential/custodial care, group home.
Type of support: General/operating support; Capital campaigns; Building/renovation; Equipment; Program development; Scholarship funds; Matching/challenge support.
Limitations: Applications not accepted. Giving limited to Tom Green, Irion, Runnels, McCulloch, Mills, Schleicher, El Paso, Concho, Sterling, Brown, Coke, Crockett, Culberson, and Hudspeth counties, TX, Dona Ana and Sierra counties, NM, and Pima, Cochise, and Santa Cruz counties, AZ. No support for religious and political organizations or for historical restoration. No grants to individuals.
Application information: Unsolicited requests for funds not accepted.
  Board meeting date(s): Dec. 1
Officers and Trustees:* J.W. Wolslager, Jr., Pres.; Stephen J. Wolslager, V.P.; Shirley M. Rogers,* Secy.-Treas.; James A. Carter; J.W. Wolslager III.
Number of staff: 2 full-time professional; 1 part-time support.
EIN: 752493763
Selected grants: The following grants were reported in 2003.
$475,000 to YWCA El Paso Del Norte Region, El Paso, TX.
$190,000 to Boys and Girls Clubs of Tucson, Tucson, AZ.
$100,000 to Boys and Girls Clubs of El Paso, El Paso, TX.
$90,000 to Child Crisis Center of El Paso, El Paso, TX.
$75,000 to Assistance League of Tucson, Tucson, AZ.

$52,400 to Four-H Youth Foundation, Arizona, Tucson, AZ.
$40,000 to Boys and Girls Clubs of San Angelo, San Angelo, TX.
$35,000 to Assistance League of El Paso, El Paso, TX.
$33,600 to Meals for the Elderly, San Angelo, TX.
$30,000 to Casa de Peregrinos, Las Cruces, NM.

9291
The Works of Grace Foundation ☆
100 Congress Ave., Ste. 2200
Austin, TX 78701
Contact: Vicki Browne
E-mail: vicki@worksofgracefoundation.org;
URL: http://www.worksofgracefoundation.org/

Established in 2000 in TX.
Donor: Theresa Castellano-Wood.
Foundation type: Independent foundation.
Financial data (yr. ended 12/31/04): Assets, $7,759,212 (M); expenditures, $500,407; qualifying distributions, $425,930; giving activities include $371,132 for 20 grants (high: $151,000; low: $100).
Purpose and activities: The foundation's mission is to provide support and inspiration to individuals, programs and organizations that make a difference in the lives of children and families. The foundation also supports a scholarship program for children of Blaine County, ID, teachers.
Fields of interest: Arts; Education; Children/youth, services; Family services.
Type of support: General/operating support; Continuing support; Income development; Annual campaigns; Capital campaigns; Building/renovation; Program development; Curriculum development; Scholarship funds; Program evaluation.
Limitations: Applications not accepted. Giving primarily in ID and TX. No grants to individuals.
Application information: Unsolicited applications accepted only for college scholarship program; applications from organizations by invitation only.
Officers: Benjamin David Wood, Pres.; Theresa Castellano-Wood, V.P.; Elizabeth Schurig, Secy.; Carolyn Beckett, Treas.
Number of staff: 1 part-time support.
EIN: 752906814
Selected grants: The following grants were reported in 2003.
$50,000 to Crystal Charity Ball, Dallas, TX. For general support.
$48,098 to Sun Valley Center for the Arts, Sun Valley, ID. For general support.
$25,650 to Highland Park United Methodist Church, Dallas, TX. For general support.
$12,813 to Gildas Club North Texas, Dallas, TX. For general support.
$10,925 to Episcopal School of Dallas Parents Association, Dallas, TX. For general support.
$10,000 to Wildaid, Phnom Penh, Cambodia. For general support.
$7,000 to Company of Fools, Hailey, ID. For general support.
$5,000 to Childrens Medical Center of Dallas, Dallas, TX. For general support.
$4,966 to Sawtooth Botanical Garden, Sun Valley, ID. For general support.
$200 to Campfire Foundation, Ketchum, ID. For general support.

9292
The Wortham Foundation ▼ ✧

2727 Allen Pkwy., Ste. 1570
Houston, TX 77019-2125 (713) 526-8849
Contact: Barbara J. Snyder, Grants Admin.
FAX: (713) 526-7222; E-mail: bsnyder@wortham.org

Trust established in 1958 in TX.
Donors: Gus S. Wortham†; Lyndall F. Wortham†.
Foundation type: Independent foundation.
Financial data (yr. ended 9/30/05): Assets, $222,659,337 (M); expenditures, $12,257,483; qualifying distributions, $11,079,860; giving activities include $10,739,431 for 70 grants (high: $3,400,000; low: $3,500), and $122,593 for foundation-administered programs.
Purpose and activities: Support primarily for the arts, including the performing arts and museums, and community improvement, including civic beautification projects that benefit the citizens of Houston and Harris County, TX.
Fields of interest: Museums; Performing arts; Historic preservation/historical societies; Arts; Environment, beautification programs.
Type of support: General/operating support; Continuing support; Annual campaigns; Capital campaigns; Endowments; Emergency funds; Seed money; Matching/challenge support.
Limitations: Giving limited to Houston and Harris County, TX. Generally, no grants to colleges, universities, or hospitals. No grants to individuals.
Publications: Annual report; Informational brochure (including application guidelines).
Application information: Please do not send bound copies of proposal. Application form required.
    Initial approach: Letter
    Copies of proposal: 1
    Deadline(s): Submit unbound proposal preferably by the 2nd week of Jan., Apr., July, or Oct.
    Board meeting date(s): Feb., May, Aug., and Nov.
    Final notification: 3 months
Officers and Trustees:* Brady F. Carruth,* Chair.; R.W. Wortham III,* Pres.; Fred C. Burns,* Secy.-Treas.; William V.H. Clarke, Cont.; James A. Elkins III.
Number of staff: 2 full-time support.
EIN: 741334356
Selected grants: The following grants were reported in 2005.
$3,400,000 to Houston Downtown Park Corporation, Houston, TX. For capital support.
$1,000,000 to Houston Symphony Society, Houston, TX. For general operating support.
$750,000 to Houston Grand Opera, Houston, TX. For general operating support.
$750,000 to Houston Museum of Natural Science, Houston, TX. For capital support.
$474,431 to University of Saint Thomas, Houston, TX. For capital support.
$375,000 to Buffalo Bayou Partnership, Houston, TX. For capital support.
$150,000 to Parks and Wildlife Foundation of Texas, Dallas, TX. For capital support.
$60,000 to Trees for Houston, Houston, TX. For general operating support.
$25,000 to Miller Theater Advisory Board, Houston, TX. For general operating support.
$25,000 to University of Texas Medical Branch, Galveston, TX. For capital support.

9293
William Wright Family Foundation ✧ ☆

P.O. Box 4517
Wichita Falls, TX 76308-0517

Established in 1998 in TX.
Donors: William E. Wright; William Dan Wright.
Foundation type: Independent foundation.
Financial data (yr. ended 12/31/05): Assets, $6,273,142 (M); expenditures, $364,027; qualifying distributions, $354,000; giving activities include $354,000 for 7 grants (high: $150,000; low: $2,000).
Fields of interest: Higher education, university; Genetics/birth defects research; Recreation; Boys & girls clubs; Foundations (public); Christian agencies & churches.
Limitations: Applications not accepted. Giving primarily in La Jolla, CA, and Vernon, TX. No grants to individuals.
Application information: Contributes only to pre-selected organizations.
Officers and Directors:* William D. Wright,* Pres.; Betty J. Wright,* V.P.; William E. Wright,* Secy.-Treas.; Betty Duane Bolton; James L. Bolton; Patricia L. Wright.
EIN: 752743584
Selected grants: The following grants were reported in 2003.
$90,000 to University of California at San Diego Foundation, La Jolla, CA.
$30,000 to Boys and Girls Club of Vernon, Vernon, TX.
$2,000 to First Baptist Church, Vernon, TX.
$1,000 to First Presbyterian Church of Vernon, Vernon, TX.
$1,000 to Sundt Memorial Foundation, La Jolla, CA.
$500 to Christmas in April, Wichita Falls, TX.

9294
Lola Wright Foundation, Inc. ✧

612 Toledo Trail
Georgetown, TX 78628 (512) 869-2574
Contact: Sandra O'Donnell
Austin, TX, tel.: (512) 255-5353

Incorporated in 1954 in TX.
Donor: Johnie E. Wright†.
Foundation type: Independent foundation.
Financial data (yr. ended 12/31/05): Assets, $22,480,487 (M); expenditures, $1,206,441; qualifying distributions, $940,033; giving activities include $890,370 for grants.
Purpose and activities: Emphasis on social services, including drug and alcohol abuse programs, family services and planning, organizations providing assistance to minorities, the aged and youth, legal services, community funds, and health services and hospitals, including rehabilitation programs, AIDS research, diseases of the heart, and organizations serving the handicapped. Support also for the arts and culture, including fine and performing arts, early childhood, adult, higher, and other education, media and communications, and the environment.
Fields of interest: Media/communications; Visual arts; Museums; Performing arts; Arts; Education, association; Education, early childhood education; Child development, education; Higher education; Adult/continuing education; Adult education—literacy, basic skills & GED; Education, reading; Education; Environment; Reproductive health, family planning; Medical care, rehabilitation; Health care;

Substance abuse, services; Health organizations, association; Heart & circulatory diseases; AIDS; Alcoholism; Heart & circulatory research; AIDS research; Legal services; Human services; Children/youth, services; Child development, services; Family services; Residential/custodial care, hospices; Aging, centers/services; Minorities/immigrants, centers/services; Homeless, human services; Federated giving programs; Aging; Disabilities, people with; Minorities; Homeless.
Type of support: Continuing support; Building/renovation; Equipment; Program development; Research; Matching/challenge support.
Limitations: Giving limited to within a 50-mile radius of Austin, TX. No grants to individuals; generally no support for operating budgets.
Publications: Application guidelines.
Application information: Application form not required.
    Initial approach: Letter
    Copies of proposal: 9
    Deadline(s): Feb. 28 and Aug. 31
    Board meeting date(s): May and Nov.
    Final notification: May 15 and Nov. 15
Officers and Directors:* Wilford Flowers,* Pres.; Paul Hilgers, V.P.; Ron Oliveira, Secy.; Adrian Fowler; Carole Keeton; James Meyers; Shelley E. Todd.
EIN: 746054717
Selected grants: The following grants were reported in 2004.
$29,650 to Greater East Austin Youth Association, Austin, TX. For Baseball, Football, and cheerleader items.
$27,765 to Hospice Austin, Austin, TX. For Cadd pumps and patient transfer chair.
$25,000 to James Dick Foundation for the Performing Arts, Round Top, TX. For Library and Museum.
$22,523 to Capital Area Food Bank of Texas, Austin, TX. To replace computer network equipment.
$21,954 to Austin Child Guidance Center, Austin, TX. For computers, email accounts, phone and database.
$20,000 to Any Baby Can, Austin, TX. For Bridge fund.
$19,992 to Peoples Community Clinic, Austin, TX. For technology upgrades.
$18,320 to Caritas of Austin, Austin, TX. For kitchen equipment.
$18,000 to Georgetown Community Service Center, Georgetown, TX. Toward new truck.
$17,500 to Settlement Club, Austin, TX. For used van.

9295
George & Fay Young Foundation, Inc.

5520 Lyndon B. Johnson Freeway, Ste. 540
Dallas, TX 75240 (972) 404-4001
Contact: Carol Young Marvin, Pres.
FAX: (972) 385-8990;
E-mail: info@gfyfoundation.org; URL: http://www.gfyfoundation.org

Established in 1993 in TX as successor to George & Fay Young Charitable Foundation.
Donors: George Young†; Fay Cameron Young†.
Foundation type: Independent foundation.
Financial data (yr. ended 11/30/05): Assets, $53,936,304 (M); gifts received, $1,008,310; expenditures, $2,674,440; qualifying distributions, $2,275,968; giving activities include $2,188,750 for 72 grants (high: $300,000; low: $1,000).

Purpose and activities: Giving primarily in the following areas: 1) Youth and Family Intervention: programs that work to break destructive cycles, and help indigent individuals to better themselves and create successful lives; 2) Strengthening Community and Human Relationships: programs advocating healthy family interaction within a community environment, providing and teaching positive solutions for negative situations; 3) Education: practices and programs that focus on both traditional and non-traditional ways of providing keys to academic achievement or creating greater opportunities and practices for TX youth; 4) Arts and Culture: youth programs emphasizing hands-on participation, education and appreciation; 5) Healthcare Services: providing service aid to those who are unable to provide proper care for themselves or their family; 6) Religious Organizations: support is not restricted to those promoting the beliefs of a particular denomination; 7) Environmental Preservation, and 8) Animal Rescue.

Fields of interest: Education; Health care; Human services; Children/youth, services; Family services; Aging, centers/services; Religion.

Type of support: General/operating support; Continuing support; Annual campaigns; Capital campaigns; Building/renovation; Endowments; Program development; Curriculum development; Scholarship funds; Matching/challenge support.

Limitations: Giving primarily in Dallas and Fort Worth, TX. No support for political organizations or research requests. No grants to individuals or start-ups less than 3 yrs. old.

Publications: Application guidelines.

Application information: Gifts exceeding $50,000 may be considered for multi-year status to be given over a 3-year period. Binders and notebooks are not accepted with applications submitted via mail. Application guidelines and Grant Proposal Summary available on foundation Web site. Application form not required.

  Initial approach: Proposal
  Copies of proposal: 1
  Deadline(s): Apr. 15 and Sept. 15
  Board meeting date(s): Oct. and May
  Final notification: June and Nov.

Officers and Directors: Carol Young Marvin,* Pres.; Richard L. Ripley,* Secy.; L. Edward Marvin,* Treas.; John C. Franklin; John T. Green.

Number of staff: 1 full-time support.

EIN: 752478225

Selected grants: The following grants were reported in 2004.

$300,000 to Ouachita Baptist University, Arkadelphia, AR.

$150,000 to Presbyterian Healthcare Foundation, Dallas, TX.

$100,000 to American Foundation for the Blind, Dallas, TX.

$75,000 to Austin College, Sherman, TX.

$75,000 to Kittico Cat Rescue, Dallas, TX.

$63,439 to Baylor Health Care System, Dallas, TX.

$40,000 to Texas Tech University, Lubbock, TX.

$25,000 to Dallas Symphony Association, Dallas, TX.

$25,000 to Richardson Symphony, Richardson, TX.

$16,000 to Guide Dogs of Texas, San Antonio, TX.

9296
The Zachry Foundation

310 S. Saint Mary's St., Ste. 2000
San Antonio, TX 78205   (210) 258-2663
Contact: Amy Dameron Phipps, Exec. Dir.
FAX: (210) 258-2670;
E-mail: foundation@zachry.com; URL: http://www.zachryfoundation.org

Incorporated in 1960 in TX.

Donors: H.B. Zachry Co.; Zachry Construction Corp.; Capitol Aggregates.

Foundation type: Independent foundation.

Financial data (yr. ended 12/31/05): Assets, $9,874,871 (M); gifts received, $1,300,000; expenditures, $6,021,078; qualifying distributions, $5,988,759; giving activities include $5,983,189 for 46 grants (high: $5,152,898; low: $1,000; average: $5,000–$125,000).

Purpose and activities: The areas of primary interest include: education, arts and humanities, and health and social services throughout San Antonio, TX.

Fields of interest: Humanities; Arts; Elementary/secondary education; Higher education; Health care; Human services; Engineering/technology.

Type of support: Annual campaigns; Capital campaigns; Equipment; Program development; Research; Matching/challenge support.

Limitations: Giving limited to San Antonio, TX, except for higher education grants, which are available to all of Texas. No grants to individuals, or for endowments.

Publications: Application guidelines.

Application information: Application form available on foundation Web site. Application form required.

  Initial approach: Letter following format found on foundation Web site
  Copies of proposal: 1
  Deadline(s): Feb. 15
  Board meeting date(s): Twice in the summer
  Final notification: Aug.

Officers and Trustees: J.P. Zachry,* Pres.; Murray L. Johnston, Jr.,* Secy.; Charles Ebrom,* Treas.; Amy Dameron Phipps, Exec. Dir.; Cathy Obriotti Green; Anne Zachry Rochelle; H.B. Zachry, Jr.; Mollie Steves Zachry.

Number of staff: 1 full-time professional.

EIN: 741485544

Selected grants: The following grants were reported in 2004.

$250,000 to Childrens Shelter of San Antonio, San Antonio, TX.

$50,000 to Historical Centre Foundation, San Antonio, TX.

$35,000 to Barrio Comprehensive Family Health Care Center, San Antonio, TX.

$25,000 to Old Spanish Missions, San Antonio, TX.

$25,000 to South Texas Blood and Tissue Center, San Antonio, TX.

$25,000 to University of Texas Law School Foundation, Austin, TX.

$25,000 to Youth Orchestras of San Antonio, San Antonio, TX.

$12,500 to Guadalupe Cultural Arts Center, San Antonio, TX.

$11,000 to Catholic Charities.

$7,000 to Daughters of Charity Services of San Antonio, San Antonio, TX.

9297
M. B. and Edna Zale Foundation

(formerly The Zale Foundation)
3102 Maple Ave., Ste. 225
Dallas, TX 75201   (214) 855-0627
Contact: Leonard R. Krasnow, Pres.
FAX: (214) 720-7252;
E-mail: mail@zalefoundation.org; URL: http://www.zalefoundation.org

Incorporated in 1951 in TX.

Donor: Members of the Zale family.

Foundation type: Independent foundation.

Financial data (yr. ended 12/31/05): Assets, $31,905,194 (M); gifts received, $229,071; expenditures, $2,194,710; qualifying distributions, $1,930,986; giving activities include $1,655,132 for 341 grants (high: $100,453; low: $100).

Purpose and activities: The foundation honors the tradition of its founders through grants that stimulate change. To accomplish this mission, the foundation acts as a catalyst for collaboration and makes grants in communities where the directors live or have an interest. Primary areas of interest include programs aiding the homeless with particular emphasis on children of the homeless, and other social services, including child welfare and programs for the disadvantaged.

Fields of interest: Education; Hospitals (general); Human services; Children/youth, services; Homeless, human services; Jewish agencies & temples; Economically disadvantaged; Homeless.

Type of support: General/operating support; Seed money; Technical assistance.

Limitations: Giving primarily in the communities of Dallas and Houston, TX, Boca Raton, FL, Portland, OR, and New York, NY (including Long Island). No grants to individuals, or for annual campaigns, emergency funds, deficit financing, renovation projects, endowment funds, conferences, study, films, publications, land acquisition, matching gifts, or continuing support; no loans. No grants for periods of more than 3 to 5 years.

Publications: Application guidelines; Annual report; Grants list.

Application information: Application form not required.

  Initial approach: Letter and proposal (not more than 2 or 3 pages)
  Copies of proposal: 1
  Deadline(s): 2 months prior to board meeting; see Web site for exact dates
  Board meeting date(s): Semiannually
  Final notification: 3 months

Officers and Trustees: Donald Zale,* Chair.; Sheryl Bogen, Vice-Chair.; Leonard R. Krasnow, Pres.; George Tobolowsky, Secy.-Treas.; David Fields; Leo Fields; Gloria Landsberg; Jeff Landsberg; Margie Plough; Michael F. Romaine; Ruth Suzman; Julie Tobolowsky; Barry Zale; David Zale; Stanley Zale.

Number of staff: 1 full-time professional; 1 full-time support; 1 part-time support.

EIN: 756037429

Selected grants: The following grants were reported in 2005.

$50,000 to Greater Dallas Jewish Community Capital Campaign for the 21st Century, Dallas, TX.

$24,000 to Project Renewal, New York, NY.

$6,000 to Dallas Jewish Coalition for the Homeless, Dallas, TX.

$5,200 to New York Cares, New York, NY.

$5,000 to Christians Reaching Out to Society Ministries, West Palm Beach, FL.

$5,000 to YWCA of Metropolitan Dallas, Dallas, TX.
$600 to City Harvest, New York, NY.

9298
Roger L. and Laura D. Zeller Charitable Foundation ✧
P.O. Box 13430
San Antonio, TX 78213 (210) 344-9211
Contact: Ronald J. Herrmann, Tr.

Established in 1991 in TX.
Donors: Laura D. Zeller†; Roger L. Zeller; Zeller Living Trust.
Foundation type: Independent foundation.
Financial data (yr. ended 12/31/05): Assets, $28,283 (M); gifts received, $480,000; expenditures, $473,590; qualifying distributions, $473,120; giving activities include $472,650 for 3 grants (high: $26,000; low: $1,000).
Purpose and activities: Giving is limited to the following areas: health care, zoo and animal welfare, promotion of education, and charities related to the sport of bowling.
Fields of interest: Education; Animal welfare; Health care; Cancer; Cancer research; Recreation; Human services; Christian agencies & churches.
Type of support: General/operating support; Capital campaigns; Endowments.
Limitations: Giving limited to Bexar County, TX, with emphasis on San Antonio. No grants to individuals.
Application information: Application form required.
  Initial approach: Letter or proposal
  Copies of proposal: 1
  Deadline(s): None
Trustees: David S. Herrmann; Karen H. Herrmann; Ronald J. Herrmann.
EIN: 742610755

9299
Zephyr Foundation ✧ ☆
4006 FM 1035
Wellington, TX 79095
Contact: Valerie White, Pres.

FAX: (806) 447-5440; E-mail: vpwhite@count.net

Established in 1996 in TX.
Donors: Dave Swalm; Beth Swalm.
Foundation type: Independent foundation.
Financial data (yr. ended 12/31/05): Assets, $10,461,674 (M); gifts received, $3,000,000; expenditures, $573,683; qualifying distributions, $567,325; giving activities include $567,325 for 11 grants (high: $300,000; low: $4,000).
Purpose and activities: Giving for public education, hospital equipment, youth programs, food services, and educational scholarships.
Fields of interest: Education; Children, services; Family services; Community development; Aging.
Type of support: General/operating support; Continuing support; Capital campaigns; Building/renovation; Equipment; Scholarship funds; Matching/challenge support.
Limitations: Giving primarily in Collingsworth County, TX, and surrounding counties in the TX Panhandle.
Officers: Valerie White, Pres.; Pat White, V.P. and Secy.; Charles W. Darter, Jr., V.P.
EIN: 752647195

9300
Zimmer Family Foundation ✧
5803 Glenmont Dr.
Houston, TX 77081-1701 (713) 295-7200
Contact: Noemi Warren, Chair.
Application address: 40650 Encyclopedia Cir., Fremont, CA 94538, tel.: (800) 777-8580

Established in 1992 in TX.
Donors: George Zimmer; Donna Zimmer; Robert E. Zimmer.
Foundation type: Independent foundation.
Financial data (yr. ended 12/31/05): Assets, $2,848,511 (M); gifts received, $1,595,320; expenditures, $1,752,956; qualifying distributions, $1,704,596; giving activities include $1,155,300 for 61 grants (high: $100,000; low: $170), and $516,180 for grants to individuals.

Purpose and activities: Giving primarily for education, Jewish agencies, hospitals, and Jewish federated giving programs.
Fields of interest: Education; Hospitals (general); Jewish federated giving programs; Jewish agencies & temples.
Type of support: General/operating support; Scholarships—to individuals.
Limitations: Giving primarily in CA and TX.
Application information:
  Initial approach: Letter
  Deadline(s): None
Officers: George Zimmer, Chair.; David Edwab, Vice-Chair.; Kirk Warren, V.P.; Michael Conlon, Secy.; Gary Ckodre, Treas.
Trustees: Lynn Zimmer; Robert E. Zimmer.
EIN: 760370782
Selected grants: The following grants were reported in 2003.
$200,000 to Eisenhower Medical Center, Rancho Mirage, CA.
$20,000 to Chabad of San Francisco, San Francisco, CA.
$12,500 to Alta Bates Summit Foundation, Berkeley, CA.
$10,250 to Agape Foundation, San Francisco, CA.
$10,000 to California Institute of Integral Studies, San Francisco, CA.
$5,000 to Holy Names University, Oakland, CA.
$5,000 to UJA-Federation of New York, New York, NY.
$5,000 to Washington University, Saint Louis, MO.
$2,000 to I Have A Dream Foundation, Houston, TX.
$1,000 to Anti-Defamation League of Bnai Brith Foundation, New York, NY.

UTAH

9301
The ALS Foundation ✧
584 S. State St.
Orem, UT 84058

Established in 1994 in UT.
Donor: Katherine Swim†.
Foundation type: Independent foundation.
Financial data (yr. ended 6/30/05): Assets, $27,700,616 (M); expenditures, $1,862,914; qualifying distributions, $1,570,295; giving activities include $1,558,000 for 7 grants (high: $900,000; low: $5,000).
Purpose and activities: Giving primarily to a community foundation, as well as for children, youth and social services, and education; funding also for the Church of Jesus Christ of Latter-day Saints.
Fields of interest: Education; Human services; Children/youth, services; Foundations (community); Social sciences, public policy; Mormon agencies & churches.
Type of support: General/operating support; Building/renovation; Equipment; Scholarship funds.
Limitations: Applications not accepted. Giving primarily in UT, with emphasis on Provo and Salt Lake City. No grants to individuals.
Application information: Contributes only to pre-selected organizations.
Officers: Victoria M. Rose, Pres.; Roger C. Swim, Secy.
Trustees: Paul Mero; Douglas W. Morrison; Lauralyn B. Swim.
EIN: 870514581
Selected grants: The following grants were reported in 2005.
$900,000 to Foundation for the American West, Orem, UT. For general support.
$250,000 to Children First Utah, Salt Lake City, UT. For general support.
$223,000 to Howard Center for Family, Religion and Society, Rockford, IL. For general support.
$150,000 to Sutherland Institute, Murray, UT. For general support.
$25,000 to Brigham Young University, Benson Institute, Provo, UT. For general support.

9302
The ALSAM Foundation ▼
6190 S. Moffat Farm Ln.
Salt Lake City, UT 84121
Contact: Ronny L. Cutshall, Pres.

Established in 1984.
Donor: L.S. Skaggs.
Foundation type: Independent foundation.
Financial data (yr. ended 12/31/05): Assets, $117,364,091 (M); gifts received, $7,500,025; expenditures, $4,096,555; qualifying distributions, $3,718,802; giving activities include $3,209,544 for 9 grants (high: $2,500,000; low: $10,000; average: $25,000–$200,000).
Purpose and activities: Giving primarily for education, religion, animal welfare, medical research, and human services.
Fields of interest: Arts education; Theological school/education; Scholarships/financial aid; Education; Animals/wildlife, preservation/

protection; Medical research, institute; Food services; Housing/shelter; Human services; Homeless, human services; Roman Catholic federated giving programs; Science, research; Religion; General charitable giving; Economically disadvantaged; Homeless.
Type of support: Building/renovation; Scholarship funds.
Limitations: Applications not accepted. No grants to individuals.
Application information: Contributes only to pre-selected organizations.
Board meeting date(s): Varies
Officers and Trustees:* Ronny L. Cutshall,* Pres.; Msgr. George Davich,* V.P.; Claudia Skaggs Luttrell,* Secy.; Lynda Sue Skaggs Balukoff; George L. Moosman; Don L. Skaggs; Mark S. Skaggs; The Northern Trust Co.
Number of staff: 1 full-time professional.
EIN: 742364289
Selected grants: The following grants were reported in 2005.
$2,500,000 to Moran Eye Center, Salt Lake City, UT. For general support.
$245,000 to Scripps Foundation for Medicine and Science, San Diego, CA. 2 grants: $45,000 (For general support), $200,000 (For fellowship in melanoma surgery).
$219,970 to Idaho Falls, City of, Idaho Falls, ID. For Tautphaus Park Zoo.
$150,000 to Idaho Youth Ranch, Boise, ID. For general support.
$39,574 to Ducks Unlimited, Vancouver, WA. For general support.
$25,000 to MCPAWS, McCall, ID. For general support.
$20,000 to English Language Center of Cache Valley, Logan, UT. For general support.
$10,000 to University of Colorado, School of Pharmacy, Denver, CO.

9303
The Ashton Family Foundation
251 River Park Dr., Ste. 350
Provo, UT 84604
Contact: Ralph Rasmussen, Exec. Dir.

Established in 1993 in UT.
Donor: Alan C. Ashton.
Foundation type: Independent foundation.
Financial data (yr. ended 12/31/04): Assets, $15,989,069 (M); gifts received, $40,000; expenditures, $2,124,119; qualifying distributions, $1,922,568; giving activities include $1,922,568 for 68 grants (high: $1,310,000; low: $1,000).
Purpose and activities: Support for religious institutions, as well as education, the arts and health.
Fields of interest: Arts; Education; Health organizations, association; Mormon agencies & churches.
Type of support: Program development; Equipment; General/operating support.
Limitations: Giving primarily in UT.
Publications: Application guidelines.
Application information:
Initial approach: Letter
Copies of proposal: 1
Deadline(s): 15th of month prior to meeting
Board meeting date(s): Quarterly
Final notification: Varies
Officer: Ralph Rasmussen, Exec. Dir.

Trustees: Alan C. Ashton; Brigham Ashton; Elizabeth Ashton; Erma Ashton; Karen Ashton; Melissa Ashton; Morgan Ashton; Samuel Ashton; Spencer Ashton; Stephanie Ashton; Stephen Ashton; Traci Ashton; Emily Ann Eddington; Paul Eddington; Allison Norton; Toby Norton; Eliza Smith; Michael Smith; Heath Westfall; Rebekah Westfall; Amy Jo Young; Chad Young.
Number of staff: 1 part-time support.
EIN: 870480108
Selected grants: The following grants were reported in 2004.
$1,310,000 to Brigham Young University, Provo, UT. For unrestricted support.
$192,145 to Church of Jesus Christ of Latter Day Saints, Provo, UT. For unrestricted support.
$15,000 to Utah Shakespearean Festival, Cedar City, UT. For unrestricted support.
$15,000 to Utah Symphony and Opera, Salt Lake City, UT. For unrestricted support.
$11,000 to Alpine School District, American Fork, UT. For unrestricted support.
$10,000 to Caring Foundation for Children, Salt Lake City, UT. For unrestricted support.
$10,000 to Uintah Basin Medical Center, Roosevelt, UT. For unrestricted support.

9304
The B. Attitudes Foundation ✧
P.O. Box 767
Farmington, UT 84025-0767

Established in 2003 in UT.
Donor: Brent L. Bishop.
Foundation type: Independent foundation.
Financial data (yr. ended 12/31/05): Assets, $6,452,099 (M); gifts received, $27,100; expenditures, $437,546; qualifying distributions, $435,496; giving activities include $322,649 for 29 grants (high: $82,999; low: $100).
Fields of interest: Education; Human services; Mormon agencies & churches.
Limitations: Applications not accepted. Giving primarily in UT.
Application information: Unsolicited requests for funds will not be accepted.
Officer and Director:* Brent L. Bishop,* Pres. and Treas.
EIN: 550828666

9305
Ruth Eleanor Bamberger and John Ernest Bamberger Memorial Foundation ✧
136 S. Main St., Ste. 418
Salt Lake City, UT 84101-1690 (801) 364-2045
Contact: Eleanor Roser, Member
E-mail: bambergermemfdn@qwest.net; URL: http://www.ruthandjohnbambergermemorialfdn.org

Incorporated in 1947 in UT.
Donors: Ernest Bamberger†; Eleanor F. Bamberger†.
Foundation type: Independent foundation.
Financial data (yr. ended 12/31/05): Assets, $26,024,592 (M); expenditures, $1,103,426; qualifying distributions, $965,720; giving activities include $754,147 for 79 grants (high: $125,000; low: $1,000), and $152,469 for 5 grants to individuals (high: $76,162; low: $9,668).
Purpose and activities: Support for secondary education, especially undergraduate scholarships

for student nurses, and for schools, hospitals and health agencies, youth and child welfare agencies; occasional loans for medical education.

Fields of interest: Elementary/secondary education; Higher education; Medical school/ education; Nursing care; Health care; Human services; Children/youth, services.

Type of support: General/operating support; Continuing support; Equipment; Scholarship funds; Scholarships—to individuals.

Limitations: Giving limited to UT. No grants to individuals, except for scholarships to local students (which are not paid directly), or for endowment or building funds, research, or matching gifts.

Application information: Application form not required.

> *Initial approach:* Letter
> *Copies of proposal:* 6
> *Deadline(s):* Check foundation Web site for deadlines; application deadlines are updated each December for the following year
> *Board meeting date(s):* Bimonthly beginning in Feb.
> *Final notification:* 2 months

Members: Clarence Bamberger, Jr.; Julie Barrett; Clark P. Giles; Carol Olwell; Eleanor Roser.

Number of staff: None.

EIN: 876116540

9306
M. Bastian Family Foundation ✧
51 W. Center St., Ste. 305
Orem, UT 84057 (801) 225-2455
Contact: McKay S. Matthews, Tr.

Established in 1993 in UT.

Donor: Melanie L. Bastian.

Foundation type: Independent foundation.

Financial data (yr. ended 12/31/05): Assets, $3,228,485 (L); expenditures, $346,255; qualifying distributions, $346,255; giving activities include $333,300 for 24 grants (high: $40,000; low: $1,300).

Purpose and activities: Giving primarily for education, health care and medical research, and children's health services.

Fields of interest: Media, television; Media, radio; Performing arts, orchestra (symphony); Secondary school/education; Higher education; Education; Health care; Health organizations, association; Medical research, institute; Cystic fibrosis research; AIDS research; Diabetes research; Food services; Housing/shelter, homeless; Children, services; Women, centers/services; Federated giving programs.

Limitations: Applications not accepted. Giving primarily in UT. No grants to individuals.

Application information: Unsolicited requests for funds not accepted.

Trustees: Melanie L. Bastian; McKay S. Matthews.

EIN: 876225255

Selected grants: The following grants were reported in 2005.

$30,000 to Center for Women and Children in Crisis, Provo, UT.

$25,000 to American Diabetes Association, Alexandria, VA.

$5,000 to Gina Bachauer International Piano Foundation, Salt Lake City, UT.

$2,000 to Crossroads Urban Center, Salt Lake City, UT.

$2,000 to South Valley Sanctuary, West Jordan, UT.

$1,300 to Box Elder Family Support Center, Brigham City, UT.

9307
The B. W. Bastian Foundation ✧
51 W. Center St., Ste. 755
Orem, UT 84057

Established in 1997 in UT.

Foundation type: Independent foundation.

Financial data (yr. ended 12/31/04): Assets, $14,838,206 (M); expenditures, $729,916; qualifying distributions, $723,242; giving activities include $673,700 for 47 grants (high: $107,500; low: $1,000).

Purpose and activities: Giving primarily for the arts and for hospices.

Fields of interest: Performing arts, ballet; Performing arts, orchestra (symphony); Arts; Residential/custodial care, hospices; Civil rights; AIDS, people with.

Limitations: Applications not accepted. Giving primarily in UT. No grants to individuals.

Application information: Contributes only to pre-selected organizations.

Officer and Trustees:* Michael S. Marriott,* Exec. Dir.; Bruce W. Bastian; Brent Erklens; Rich Ith.

EIN: 841378232

Selected grants: The following grants were reported in 2003.

$75,000 to Ballet West, Salt Lake City, UT.

$35,000 to Utah Symphony and Opera, Salt Lake City, UT.

$17,000 to Utah AIDS Foundation, Salt Lake City, UT. For general operating support.

$10,000 to American Red Cross, Salt Lake City, UT.

$10,000 to Utah Arts Festival, Salt Lake City, UT. For general operating support.

$10,000 to Utah Valley State College, Orem, UT. For scholarships.

$2,500 to Crossroads Urban Center, Salt Lake City, UT. For general operating support.

$2,500 to Salt Lake Symphony, Salt Lake City, UT. For general operating support.

$2,000 to University of Utah, School of Music, Salt Lake City, UT. For general operating support.

$1,500 to Salt Lake County Aging Services, Salt Lake City, UT. For general operating support.

9308
Val A. Browning Charitable Foundation
c/o Wells Fargo Bank Northwest, N.A.
299 S. Main St., MAC S4035-014
Salt Lake City, UT 84111
Application address: c/o Nathan D. Felix, P.O. Box 9936, Ogden, UT 84409, tel.: (801) 246-1446

Established in 1975 in UT.

Donor: Val A. Browning.

Foundation type: Independent foundation.

Financial data (yr. ended 12/31/05): Assets, $29,605,969 (M); expenditures, $1,794,178; qualifying distributions, $1,663,043; giving activities include $1,618,648 for 32 grants (high: $248,000; low: $3,000).

Purpose and activities: Giving primarily to secondary school and higher education; and human services.

Fields of interest: Secondary school/education; Higher education; Human services.

Type of support: Continuing support; Annual campaigns; Capital campaigns; Building/ renovation; Endowments; Program development.

Limitations: Giving primarily in UT.

Application information: Application form not required.

> *Initial approach:* Letter
> *Copies of proposal:* 1
> *Deadline(s):* Preferably by Sept. 30

Board Members: Bruce W. Browning; John A. Browning; Carol Browning Dumke; Judith B. Jones.

Trustee: Wells Fargo Bank Northwest, N.A.

EIN: 876167851

Selected grants: The following grants were reported in 2005.

$248,000 to University of Utah, Salt Lake City, UT.

$170,000 to Utah State University, Logan, UT.

$35,000 to Island School, Bainbridge Island, WA.

$35,000 to Union Station Foundation, Ogden, UT.

$20,000 to Eccles Community Art Center, Ogden, UT.

$7,500 to Community Library, Ketchum, ID.

$3,000 to Weber State University, Ogden, UT.

9309
R. Harold Burton Foundation
709 E. South Temple St.
P.O. Box 58477
Salt Lake City, UT 84158
Contact: Richard G. Horne, Exec. Dir.
FAX: (801) 364-6783; Address for hand delivery or Fed. Ex.: 709 E. South Temple St., Salt Lake City, UT 84102; Richard G. Horne, Exec. Dir., tel.: (801) 715-7140; URL: http:// www.rharoldburtonfoundation.org

Established in 1987 in UT.

Donor: Robert Harold Burton†.

Foundation type: Independent foundation.

Financial data (yr. ended 12/31/05): Assets, $34,875,483 (M); expenditures, $1,792,553; qualifying distributions, $1,596,550; giving activities include $1,395,229 for 83 grants (high: $125,000; low: $2,720).

Purpose and activities: Giving primarily for education, and health.

Fields of interest: Secondary school/education; Higher education; Health care; Health organizations, association.

Type of support: Continuing support; Annual campaigns; Building/renovation; Equipment; Emergency funds; Program development; Fellowships; Scholarship funds; Research; Matching/challenge support.

Limitations: Giving primarily in the greater Salt Lake metropolitan area in UT. No grants for overhead expenses, or endowments.

Publications: Application guidelines.

Application information: After submitting application, telephone the foundation at the 7141 number, to make an appointment to review application. Application form required.

> *Initial approach:* Use application form on foundation's Web site, which should be printed on white paper
> *Copies of proposal:* 1
> *Deadline(s):* Feb. 15 and July 15
> *Board meeting date(s):* Apr. and Sept.
> *Final notification:* After May 1 and Nov. 1

Board Members: Frederick A. Moreton, Jr.; Mike Moreton; Judith Burton Moyle; Rebecca Moyle; Wood Moyle.

Trustee: Wells Fargo Bank Northwest, N.A.

Number of staff: 1 full-time professional; 1 part-time professional.
EIN: 742425567
Selected grants: The following grants were reported in 2005.
$125,000 to Western Folklife Center, Elko, NV.
$100,000 to Community Services Council, Salt Lake City, UT. 2 grants: $15,000, $85,000
$100,000 to Westminster College, Salt Lake City, UT.
$35,000 to Guadalupe Schools, Salt Lake City, UT.
$15,000 to Utah Symphony and Opera, Salt Lake City, UT.
$12,500 to English Skills Learning Center, Salt Lake City, UT.
$10,000 to Museum of Utah Art and History, Salt Lake City, UT.
$10,000 to South Valley Sanctuary, West Jordan, UT.
$10,000 to Spy Hop Productions, Salt Lake City, UT.

9310
Marie Eccles Caine Charitable Foundation ✧
c/o Wells Fargo Bank Northwest, N.A.
299 S. Main St., MAC S4035-014
Salt Lake City, UT   84111

Established in 1981 in UT.
Donor: Marie Eccles Caine†.
Foundation type: Independent foundation.
Financial data (yr. ended 5/31/05): Assets, $25,406,929 (M); expenditures, $1,415,217; qualifying distributions, $1,328,143; giving activities include $1,293,374 for 36 grants (high: $280,531; low: $2,800).
Purpose and activities: Giving for the advancement of the fine arts, particularly at Utah State University, for other programs at that university which were of interest to the donor, and for other charitable purposes, including historical preservation and educational research.
Fields of interest: Visual arts; Performing arts; Historic preservation/historical societies; Education, research; Business school/education.
Type of support: General/operating support; Continuing support; Program development; Curriculum development; Scholarship funds.
Limitations: Applications not accepted. Giving primarily in Logan and Cache County, UT. No grants to individuals.
Application information: Contributes only to pre-selected organizations.
  Board meeting date(s): Varies
Committee Members: Dan C. Russell; Manon C. Russell; Marie Russell Shaw; George Ralph Wanlass; Kathryn C. Wanlass; Ralph Wanlass.
Trustee: Wells Fargo Bank Northwest, N.A.
EIN: 942764258
Selected grants: The following grants were reported in 2004.
$539,331 to Utah State University, Logan, UT. 5 grants: $221,646 to Art/Harrison Museum, $33,100 to Department of English, $11,900 to Interior Design Department, $141,585 to Department of Music, $131,100 to Department of Theater
$65,000 to Utah Festival Opera Company, Logan, UT.
$47,300 to Utah Symphony and Opera, Salt Lake City, UT.
$44,000 to Cache Valley Center for the Arts, Logan, UT.

$15,000 to Ballet West, Salt Lake City, UT.
$5,890 to Brigham City Fine Arts Council, Brigham City, UT.

9311
Harold & Ruth Dance Charitable Foundation ✧ ☆
1044 N. 1600 E.
Logan, UT   84341-3044

Donors: Harold W. Dance; Ruth B. Dance.
Foundation type: Independent foundation.
Financial data (yr. ended 12/31/05): Assets, $392,354 (M); gifts received, $156; expenditures, $356,813; qualifying distributions, $356,500; giving activities include $356,500 for 2 grants.
Fields of interest: Higher education; Aging.
Limitations: Applications not accepted. Giving limited to Logan, UT. No grants to individuals.
Application information: Contributes only to pre-selected organizations.
Trustees: Harold W. Dance; Ruth B. Dance.
EIN: 870440689

9312
Stephen G. and Susan E. Denkers Family Foundation ✧
5210 Skyline Dr.
Ogden, UT   84403

Established in 2000 in UT.
Donors: Stephen G. Denkers; Susan E. Denkers.
Foundation type: Independent foundation.
Financial data (yr. ended 9/30/05): Assets, $12,900,350 (M); expenditures, $682,871; qualifying distributions, $606,970; giving activities include $593,100 for 31 grants (high: $100,000; low: $5,000).
Fields of interest: Arts; Education; Human services; Community development; Federated giving programs.
Limitations: Applications not accepted. Giving primarily in UT and WA. No grants to individuals.
Application information: Contributes only to pre-selected organizations.
Trustees: Ashley Nicole Bishop; Kelli Sue Denkers; Stephen E. Denkers; Stephen G. Denkers; Susan E. Denkers; Julie Denkers-Bishop.
EIN: 870659552
Selected grants: The following grants were reported in 2005.
$100,000 to United Way of Northern Utah, Ogden, UT.
$40,000 to Ogden School Foundation, Ogden, UT.
$25,000 to Junior League of Ogden, Ogden, UT.
$25,000 to Road Home, Salt Lake City, UT.
$25,000 to Ronald McDonald House.
$23,000 to Utah Museum of Natural History, Salt Lake City, UT.
$15,000 to Nature Conservancy of Idaho, Hailey, ID.
$10,000 to Weber Pathways, Ogden, UT.
$5,000 to Box Elder Family Support Center, Brigham City, UT.
$5,000 to Henrys Fork Foundation, Ashton, ID.

9313
Dialysis Research Foundation ✧
5575 S. 500 E.
Ogden, UT   84405   (801) 479-0351

Established in 1984.
Foundation type: Independent foundation.
Financial data (yr. ended 12/31/05): Assets, $4,615,963 (M); expenditures, $1,407,511; qualifying distributions, $919,831; giving activities include $843,310 for 55 grants (high: $500,000; low: $6; average: $1,000–$14,500), and $65,121 for 40 grants to individuals (high: $2,750; low: $27).
Purpose and activities: Giving limited to renal disease research and treatment, and for non-profit kidney disease foundations.
Fields of interest: Medical research, institute.
Type of support: Research.
Limitations: Giving primarily in UT.
Application information: The foundation no longer awards grants to individual patients.
  Initial approach: Letter
  Deadline(s): None
Officers and Board Members:* Fred Galvez,* Pres.; Leo N. Harris,* V.P.; Mark Lindsay,* Secy.-Treas.; Mardee Hagen,* Exec. Dir.; Adhish Agarwal; Kelvin Jackson; Lee L. Miles; H.J. Orme; Phil K. Robinson; Todd Schenck; Harry Senekjian, M.D.
EIN: 942819009

9314
Dreamweaver Foundation ✧
6440 S. Wasatch Blvd., Ste. 105
Salt Lake City, UT   84121   (801) 365-4010
Contact: John B. Benear II, Tr.

Established in 2000 in UT.
Donor: John B. Benear.
Foundation type: Independent foundation.
Financial data (yr. ended 12/31/04): Assets, $2,376,362 (M); expenditures, $389,715; qualifying distributions, $376,838; giving activities include $373,164 for 1 grant.
Purpose and activities: Giving primarily to a medical foundation which assists in the transfer of medical supplies to medical mission agencies.
Fields of interest: Health care; Health organizations, association; Human services.
Limitations: Giving primarily in Salt Lake City, UT.
Application information:
  Initial approach: Proposal
  Deadline(s): Aug. 31
Manager: William C. Klintworth.
Directors: Bradford Bond; John B. Benear.
EIN: 870648469

9315
Dr. Ezekiel R. and Edna Wattis Dumke Foundation ✧
P.O. Box 776
Kaysville, UT   84037   (801) 497-9474
Contact: Denise R. Johnsen, Office Mgr.
E-mail: erd@fndtn.org

Incorporated in 1959 in UT.
Foundation type: Independent foundation.
Financial data (yr. ended 12/31/05): Assets, $13,423,135 (M); expenditures, $745,083; qualifying distributions, $632,882; giving activities include $619,404 for 10 grants (high: $201,404; low: $5,000).
Purpose and activities: Support for organizations involved with arts and culture, education, the environment, and health and human services.

Fields of interest: Arts; Higher education; Environment, natural resources; Hospitals (general); Health care; Children/youth, services.
Type of support: Equipment; Land acquisition; Technical assistance; Matching/challenge support.
Limitations: Giving limited to the western region of the U.S., with emphasis on MT, NM, UT, and WY. No support for religious or political organizations. No grants to individuals or for scholarships.
Publications: Application guidelines.
Application information: Application form required.
  Initial approach: Telephone, e-mail, or letter requesting application form and deadline
  Copies of proposal: 4
  Deadline(s): Varies by year
  Board meeting date(s): Approx. Apr. and Aug.
  Final notification: Within 6 weeks after board meeting
Directors: Andrea Dumke Manship; Claire Dumke Ryberg; Nancy Healy Schwanfelder; Betsy Thornton.
EIN: 876199783

9316
The Katherine W. Dumke and Ezekiel R. Dumke, Jr. Foundation ✧
P.O. Box 776
Kaysville, UT 84037 (801) 544-4626
Contact: Denise R. Johnsen, Off. Mgr.
E-mail: kwd@fndtn.org

Established in 1988 in UT.
Donor: Ezekiel R. Dumke, Jr.
Foundation type: Independent foundation.
Financial data (yr. ended 12/31/05): Assets, $22,738,010 (M); expenditures, $1,143,808; qualifying distributions, $1,060,493; giving activities include $1,037,827 for 34 grants (high: $171,300; low: $500; average: $1,000–$25,000).
Purpose and activities: Giving primarily to higher education, health care, health organizations, and child and youth services.
Fields of interest: Higher education; Health care; Health organizations; Children/youth, services.
Type of support: Equipment; Program development; Technical assistance; Matching/challenge support.
Limitations: Giving limited to the intermountain area, with emphasis on UT. No grants to individuals or for scholarships.
Publications: Application guidelines.
Application information: Application form required.
  Initial approach: Letter, e-mail or telephone requesting application
  Copies of proposal: 4
  Deadline(s): Generally Feb. 1 and July 1. Call for exact deadlines
  Board meeting date(s): Spring and fall
  Final notification: 6 weeks after board meeting
Officers and Trustees:* Katherine W. Dumke,* Pres.; Katherine E. Thornton,* V.P.; Ezekiel R. Dumke, Jr.,* Secy.-Treas.
Grants Committee: Andrea S. Dumke.
EIN: 870461899
Selected grants: The following grants were reported in 2003.
$145,000 to University of Utah, Salt Lake City, UT. 3 grants: $25,000 to College of Humanities (To upgrade student computing lab to video conferencing classroom), $100,000 to John A. Moran Eye Center (To build clinic patient recreation area), $20,000 to Museum of Fine Arts (To sponsor traveling exhibit, Edward Hopper and Urban Realism).

$125,000 to Girl Scouts of the U.S.A., Utah Council, Salt Lake City, UT. To build new dining hall on Trefoil Ranch.
$100,000 to Westminster College, Theater Department, Salt Lake City, UT. To build Dumke Student Theater.
$66,000 to Community Services Council, Salt Lake City, UT. To install new locks, doors, warehouse lighting, and a model superpantry/kids cafe.
$50,000 to Nature Conservancy, Salt Lake City, UT. To build visitor's center at Great Salt Lake Shore Lands Preserve.
$42,000 to Yellowstone Historic Center, West Yellowstone, MT.
$11,000 to Ronald McDonald House Charities of the Intermountain Area, Salt Lake City, UT. To purchase new phone system.
$10,000 to United Way of Salt Lake, Salt Lake City, UT.

9317
Willard L. Eccles Charitable Foundation
P.O. Box 58198
Salt Lake City, UT 84158-0198 (801) 582-4483
FAX: (801) 582-2955; E-mail: steve@wleccles.org;
URL: http://www.wleccles.org

Established in 1981 in UT.
Foundation type: Independent foundation.
Financial data (yr. ended 3/31/06): Assets, $37,829,852 (M); expenditures, $2,144,804; qualifying distributions, $2,061,793; giving activities include $1,822,185 for 48 grants (high: $240,000; low: $1,000), and $7,093 for 2 in-kind gifts.
Purpose and activities: Grants primarily for the environment, medical education, human services, medical research, and health organizations.
Fields of interest: Medical school/education; Environment; Health care; Health organizations, association; Biomedicine; Medical research, institute.
Type of support: General/operating support; Capital campaigns; Building/renovation; Equipment; Land acquisition; Fellowships; Scholarship funds; Research; Matching/challenge support.
Limitations: Giving primarily in UT, with emphasis in the Ogden area. No grants to individuals.
Application information: Please note that the foundation is not accepting new applications at this time. New grant guidelines will be available in Jan., 2007. Applications are also accepted through the foundation Web site; application form available on the foundation Web site. Application form required.
  Initial approach: None
  Copies of proposal: 8
  Deadline(s): Apr. 1 and Oct. 1
  Board meeting date(s): Quarterly
  Final notification: Following meeting
Officer & Committee Members:* Stephen E. Denkers,* Exec. Dir.; Julie E. Denkers Bishop; Barbara E. Coit; Susan Coit; William E. Coit, M.D.; Stephen G. Denkers; Susan E. Denkers; Ann Goss.
Trustee: Wells Fargo Bank Northwest, N.A.
Number of staff: 1 full-time support.
EIN: 942759395
Selected grants: The following grants were reported in 2005.
$250,000 to Nature Conservancy, Oregon Chapter, Portland, OR.
$225,000 to Nature Conservancy, Salt Lake City, UT.

$200,000 to Midtown Community Health Center, Ogden, UT.
$190,000 to University of Utah, Salt Lake City, UT. 2 grants: $40,000 to College of Pharmacy, $150,000 (For Honors Program).
$164,000 to Utah State University, Logan, UT. 3 grants: $50,000 to School of the Arts, $54,000 to College of Science, $60,000 (For scholarships).
$100,000 to Grand Canyon Trust, Flagstaff, AZ.
$100,000 to University Hospital Foundation, Salt Lake City, UT.

9318
Eccles Family Foundation ✧
(formerly Spencer F. & Cleone P. Eccles Family Foundation)
c/o Wells Fargo Bank, NA
299 S. Main St., MAC S4035-014
Salt Lake City, UT 84111

Established in 1993 in UT.
Donors: Spencer F. Eccles; Hope Eccles Behlf†.
Foundation type: Independent foundation.
Financial data (yr. ended 6/30/05): Assets, $23,335,718 (M); gifts received, $5,728,599; expenditures, $627,568; qualifying distributions, $606,467; giving activities include $600,000 for 2 grants (high: $500,000; low: $100,000).
Purpose and activities: Giving primarily for higher education.
Fields of interest: Higher education; Hospitals (general).
Limitations: Applications not accepted. Giving primarily in Salt Lake City, UT; some giving also in Salinas, CA. No grants to individuals.
Application information: Contributes only to pre-selected organizations.
Trustee: Wells Fargo Bank, N.A.
EIN: 876227329

9319
George S. and Dolores Dore Eccles Foundation ▼ ✧
79 S. Main St., 12th Fl.
Salt Lake City, UT 84111 (801) 246-5340
Contact: Lisa Eccles, Exec. Dir.
FAX: (801) 350-3510; E-mail: gse@gseccles.org;
URL: http://www.gsecclesfoundation.org

Incorporated in 1958 in UT; absorbed Lillian Ethel Dufton Charitable Trust in 1981.
Donor: George S. Eccles†.
Foundation type: Independent foundation.
Financial data (yr. ended 12/31/05): Assets, $546,685,083 (M); gifts received, $575,518; expenditures, $29,408,381; qualifying distributions, $26,063,006; giving activities include $12,208,099 for 343 grants (high: $1,200,000; low: $100; average: $15,000–$150,000), and $13,370,946 for 32 in-kind gifts.
Purpose and activities: The foundation is dedicated to serving the people of the state of Utah by carrying forth the philanthropic interests and goals of its founders. The foundation supports projects and programs that have the potential to make a significant difference in bettering Utah's communities and enriching the quality of life of its citizens, granting funds in the following areas: arts and culture, social services, education, health care, and preservation and conservation.

Fields of interest: Visual arts; Performing arts; Arts; Higher education; Environment; Hospitals (general); Health care; Medical research, institute; Human services; Children/youth, services; Economics.

Type of support: General/operating support; Annual campaigns; Capital campaigns; Building/renovation; Equipment; Program development; Professorships; Scholarship funds; Research; Program-related investments/loans; Matching/challenge support.

Limitations: Giving primarily in the intermountain area, particularly UT. No support for private foundations or conduit organizations. No grants to individuals, or for endowment funds, contingencies, deficits, debt reduction, conferences, seminars, or medical research.

Application information: Application form required.
Initial approach: Letter of inquiry or complete the online grant application form request on foundation's Web site
Copies of proposal: 3
Deadline(s): None
Board meeting date(s): Quarterly
Final notification: Following meeting

Officers and Directors:* Spencer F. Eccles,* Pres.; Alonzo W. Watson, Jr.,* V.P., Secy., and Genl. Counsel; Robert M. Graham,* Treas.; Lisa Eccles,* Exec. Dir.

Number of staff: 1
EIN: 876118245

Selected grants: The following grants were reported in 2005.

$1,998,943 to Childrens Museum of Utah, Salt Lake City, UT. For in-kind gift of stock for new Children's Museum Discovery Center.

$1,787,169 to University of Utah, Salt Lake City, UT. 2 grants: $617,748 (For in-kind gift of stock John A. Moran Eye Center to help in center construction; for college of Education to support reading program entitled, When Basic Intervention Isn't Enough, Helping Students with Dyslexia; for Department of History to help establish Dean L. May Fellowship in Graduate Studies of Utah and the American West), $1,169,421 (For in-kind gift of stock for David Eccles School of Business).

$1,200,000 to Westminster College, Salt Lake City, UT. For capital campaign to construct Health, Wellness, and Athletic Center to house health-related academic programs, including School of Nursing and student health clinic.

$997,253 to Nature Conservancy, Salt Lake City, UT. For in-kind gift of stock to support Living Lands and Waters campaign.

$336,209 to Road Home, Salt Lake City, UT. For in-kind gift of stock for services for homeless individuals and families at Salt Lake Community Shelter and Midvale Community Winter Shelter.

$50,000 to Utah Valley State College, Orem, UT. For general operating support of library.

$30,000 to ARTS, Inc., Salt Lake City, UT. For ABC the ART and ME! program, providing arts program to elementary school children in Utah.

$25,000 to Gentle Ironhawk Shelter, Blanding, UT. For salary and benefits for executive director.

$25,000 to Salt Lake Donated Dental Services, Salt Lake City, UT. For Pediatric Dental Program and Preventative Education and Restorative Care programs.

9320
Marriner S. Eccles Foundation ◇
79 S. Main St., Ste. 701
Salt Lake City, UT 84111
Contact: Anne Watson, Exec. Dir.
E-mail: mseccles@xmission.com

Established in 1973 in Utah.
Donor: Marriner S. Eccles‡.
Foundation type: Independent foundation.
Financial data (yr. ended 3/31/06): Assets, $33,902,605 (M); expenditures, $1,837,997; qualifying distributions, $1,692,504; giving activities include $1,610,001 for 138 grants (high: $85,000; low: $2,000).
Purpose and activities: Giving primarily for higher education; health, hospitals, and medical research; arts and culture, including the performing arts, fine arts, and museums; and family and social services, including programs for rehabilitation, the elderly, drug and alcohol abuse and prevention, youth, women, the disabled, and the homeless.
Fields of interest: Visual arts; Museums; Performing arts; Performing arts, dance; Performing arts, theater; Humanities; Arts; Higher education; Medical school/education; Hospitals (general); Reproductive health, family planning; Medical care, rehabilitation; Nursing care; Health care; Substance abuse, services; Mental health/crisis services; Health organizations, association; AIDS; Alcoholism; Biomedicine; Medical research, institute; Cancer research; Food services; Housing/shelter, development; Human services; Children/youth, services; Family services; Aging, centers/services; Women, centers/services; Homeless, human services; Aging; Disabilities, people with; Women; Economically disadvantaged; Homeless.
Type of support: General/operating support; Continuing support; Program development; Internship funds; Scholarship funds; Research; Matching/challenge support.
Limitations: Giving limited to UT. No support for religious organizations, government agencies, or conduit organizations. No grants to individuals, or for capital campaigns, K-12 education, trips, tours or travel, or endowments.
Publications: Application guidelines.
Application information: Guidelines revised annually, e-mail for revised guidelines in Nov. Application form required.
Initial approach: Letter of inquiry via mail or e-mail
Copies of proposal: 2
Deadline(s): Early spring
Board meeting date(s): 2 meetings annually
Final notification: Fall

Officers and Committee Members:* Spencer F. Eccles, Chair.; Alonzo W. Watson, Jr.,* Secy.; Anne Watson, Exec. Dir.; C. Hope Eccles; James M. Steele; Elmer D. Tucker.
Trustee: Wells Fargo Bank, N.A.
Number of staff: 1 part-time professional.
EIN: 237185855

Selected grants: The following grants were reported in 2004.

$32,500 to Utah State University, College of Agriculture, Logan, UT. For biomedical research.

$24,000 to University of Utah, Lowell Bennion Community Service Center, Salt Lake City, UT. For student-directed community service programs.

$20,000 to Planned Parenthood Association of Utah, Salt Lake City, UT.

$20,000 to YWCA of Salt Lake City, Salt Lake City, UT. For residency program for pregnant and parenting teens.

$18,000 to Road Home, Salt Lake City, UT.

$10,000 to Central Utah Food Sharing, Provo, UT. For general operating support and salaries.

$10,000 to Salt Lake Acting Company, Salt Lake City, UT. For general support.

$10,000 to Treehouse Childrens Museum, Ogden, UT. For Alphabet Soup program designed to help three to ten year olds learn to read.

$7,500 to Association of Utah Community Health, UT. To supply living stipends for Americorps and medically underserved in Utah members who are providing services to the rural community.

$5,000 to Big Brothers Big Sisters of Great Salt Lake, Salt Lake City, UT.

9321
Esther Foundation, Inc. ◇
1716 N. Meadowlark Rd.
Orem, UT 84057
Contact: L. Graig Taylor, Pres.

Established in 1994 in UT.
Donors: United Way of Utah County; Holmes Holmes and Associates; Salisbury Development L.C.
Foundation type: Independent foundation.
Financial data (yr. ended 6/30/05): Assets, $1,855,658 (M); gifts received, $14,089,292; expenditures, $13,992,534; qualifying distributions, $13,962,007; giving activities include $13,181,170 for 67 grants (high: $12,833,380; low: $100; average: $1,000–$10,000).
Purpose and activities: Giving primarily for the arts, education, human services, and health care.
Fields of interest: Historical activities; Arts; Education; Health care; Human services.
Type of support: General/operating support; Building/renovation; Equipment; Program development; Conferences/seminars; Publication; Seed money; Curriculum development; Scholarship funds; Program-related investments/loans; Grants to individuals; Matching/challenge support.
Limitations: Applications not accepted. Giving primarily in UT.
Application information: Unsolicited requests for funds not accepted.
Board meeting date(s): As needed
Officers: L. Graig Taylor, Pres.; Varden Hadfield, V.P.; Bud Bate, Secy.; Rob Bennett, Treas.
EIN: 870532890

9322
The Force for Good Foundation ◇
c/o Nu Skin Enterprises, Inc.
75 W. Center St.
Provo, UT 84601-4432
URL: http://www.forceforgood.org

Established in 1998 in UT.
Donors: Diamond Technology Partners Inc.; Nu Skin Enterprises, Inc.
Foundation type: Company-sponsored foundation.
Financial data (yr. ended 12/31/04): Assets, $1,062,019 (M); gifts received, $1,202,473; expenditures, $1,082,133; qualifying distributions, $928,808; giving activities include $928,808 for grants.

Purpose and activities: The foundation support programs designed to improve human life; preseve indigenous cultures; and protect fragile environments.

Fields of interest: Arts, cultural/ethnic awareness; Environment, natural resources; Human services.

Limitations: Giving on a national and international basis. No support for fraternal organizations or religious organizations. No grants to individuals, or for capital campaigns, start-up needs, administrative costs, or advertising.

Application information:
  Initial approach: Mail letter of inquiry to foundation
  Deadline(s): None
Officers: Blake M. Roney, Chair. and Pres.; Sandra N. Tillotson, V.P.; Steven J. Lund, Secy.; Brooke Roney, Treas.; Shannon Anderson, Compt.
EIN: 870577244
Selected grants: The following grants were reported in 2003.
$161,802 to Seacology, Berkeley, CA.
$45,000 to Malawi Project, Indianapolis, IN.
$22,250 to University of Michigan, Ann Arbor, MI.
$20,000 to KinderVision Foundation, Peru, IN.
$20,000 to New York Botanical Garden, Bronx, NY.
$11,000 to Opportunity International, Oak Brook, IL. For operations in Kenya.
$10,000 to Deseret International Foundation, Provo, UT.
$10,000 to Enterprise Mentors International, Chesterfield, MO.
$10,000 to World Vision, Federal Way, WA.
$2,100 to Charity Anywhere, Twin Falls, ID.

9323
Sterling and Shelli Gardner Foundation ◇ ☆
610 Westfield Rd.
Alpine, UT 84004
Application address: c/o Megan White, 810 S. Plumtree Dr., Kanab, UT 84741, tel.: (435) 644-3360

Established in 2002 in UT.
Donors: Sterling Gardner; Shelli Gardner.
Foundation type: Independent foundation.
Financial data (yr. ended 12/31/05): Assets, $18,252 (M); gifts received, $330,000; expenditures, $658,922; qualifying distributions, $657,648; giving activities include $657,648 for 38 grants (high: $345,000; low: $200).
Fields of interest: Performing arts, orchestra (symphony); Environment; YM/YWCAs & YM/YWHAs; Children/youth, services.
Limitations: Giving primarily in UT.
Application information:
  Initial approach: Letter
Trustees: Shelli Gardner; Sterling Gardner.
EIN: 870686202

9324
The GFC Foundation ◇ ☆
584 S. State St.
Orem, UT 84058

Established in 1994 in UT.
Donors: Katherine Swim; The ALS Foundation.
Foundation type: Independent foundation.
Financial data (yr. ended 6/30/05): Assets, $41,800,601 (M); gifts received, $11,631,324;

expenditures, $655,770; giving activities include $389,409 for 13 grants (high: $300,000; low: $2,500).
Purpose and activities: Giving primarily for historical preservation, education, and economics.
Fields of interest: Historic preservation/historical societies; Education; Economics; Protestant agencies & churches.
Limitations: Applications not accepted. Giving primarily in UT, with emphasis on Orem.
Application information: Contributes only to pre-selected organizations.
Trustees: Alan Funk; Brent McKinley; Lauralyn B. Swim.
EIN: 870529248
Selected grants: The following grants were reported in 2005.
$300,000 to Sutherland Institute, Murray, UT.
$20,000 to Aspen Grove Family Camp, Provo, UT.
$10,000 to Toward Tradition, Mercer Island, WA.
$2,500 to Philanthropy Roundtable, DC.
$2,500 to State Policy Network, Richmond, CA.

9325
The D. Forrest Greene & Gerda M. Greene Foundation ◇
1456 Penrose Dr.
Salt Lake City, UT 84103

Established in 2000 in UT.
Donors: Gloria Pitt; David H. Greene; Susan Parkinson; Randi Greene; Enid Greene.
Foundation type: Independent foundation.
Financial data (yr. ended 12/31/03): Assets, $563,945 (M); gifts received, $550,000; expenditures, $595,207; qualifying distributions, $595,200; giving activities include $595,200 for 37 grants (high: $50,000; low: $500).
Fields of interest: Education; Health care; Human services; Mormon agencies & churches; Religion.
Limitations: Applications not accepted. Giving primarily in UT.
Application information: Contributes only to pre-selected organizations.
Trustees: Enid Greene; Mark S. Hawkes; Susan Parkinson.
EIN: 943382293

9326
The Alan and Jeanne Hall Foundation ◇
4155 Harrison Blvd., Ste. 300
Ogden, UT 84403

Established in 1999 in UT.
Donors: Alan E. Hall; Jeannie Hall; Betty Nowak; Henry Nowak; Hall Family Investments, LLC.
Foundation type: Independent foundation.
Financial data (yr. ended 12/31/05): Assets, $14,270,991 (M); gifts received, $6,404,456; expenditures, $553,942; qualifying distributions, $494,998; giving activities include $487,604 for 13 + grants (high: $150,500).
Fields of interest: Higher education, university; Federated giving programs.
Limitations: Applications not accepted. Giving primarily in Ogden, UT. No grants to individuals.
Application information: Contributes only to pre-selected organizations.
Officer: Alan E. Hall, Pres.

Trustees: Aaron Hall; Adam Hall; Eric Hall; Jeannie Hall; Laura West.
EIN: 870644251

9327
Hayward Family Foundation ◇
(formerly Nancy Eccles & Homer M. Hayward Foundation)
c/o Wells Fargo Bank Northwest, N.A.
P.O. Box 25491
Salt Lake City, UT 84125

Established in 1993 in UT.
Donors: Nancy Eccles Hayward†; Hope Eccles Behle†; Homer M. Hayward; Wendy A. Hayward.
Foundation type: Independent foundation.
Financial data (yr. ended 6/30/05): Assets, $10,936,758 (M); gifts received, $2,225,000; expenditures, $548,127; qualifying distributions, $530,070; giving activities include $527,640 for 25 grants (high: $200,000; low: $1,000).
Fields of interest: Botanical gardens; Recreation.
Type of support: General/operating support; Continuing support; Building/renovation; Research; Program evaluation; Matching/challenge support.
Limitations: Applications not accepted. Giving on a national basis. No grants to individuals.
Application information: Contributes only to pre-selected organizations. Unsolicited requests for funds not accepted.
  Board meeting date(s): Varies
Trustee: Wells Fargo Bank Northwest, N.A.
EIN: 876227330

9328
The Richard K. and Shirley S. Hemingway Foundation ◇
P.O. Box 11026
Salt Lake City, UT 84147 (801) 363-5227
Contact: Brianne Johnson, Admin.
FAX: (801) 863-6157;
E-mail: briannej@xmission.com; URL: http://www.HemingwayFoundation.org

Established in 1987 in UT.
Donors: Richard Keith Hemingway; Shirley Stranquist Hemingway.
Foundation type: Independent foundation.
Financial data (yr. ended 12/31/04): Assets, $15,418,304 (M); gifts received, $327,592; expenditures, $860,008; qualifying distributions, $758,176; giving activities include $708,346 for 87 grants (high: $100,000; low: $200).
Purpose and activities: The foundation gives primarily in the following areas: Fostering Self-Reliance Among Disadvantaged Populations: The foundation sets out to help economically, culturally, and physically disadvantaged populations so that they may become self-reliant and able to provide for their own needs. It is interested in preventative, results-oriented programs that encourage personal development, spiritual development, community involvement and affordable housing. Promoting and Encouraging Environmental Stewardship: The foundation has a strong commitment to the natural world and a sustainable human environment. It supports nature education, environmental protection, environmental advocacy, and the acquisition and preservation of open space. Protecting and Nurturing Young Children and Teens: The foundation believes that all

young people deserve a good start in life. It therefore invests in programs that emphasize early childhood education, good parenting skills, basic child medical care, positive activities for teens and at-risk children, and healthy, safe environments for children of all ages. Encouraging or Inspiring Involvement in the Arts: The foundation believes that the arts contribute immeasurably to quality of life and character. It therefore funds programs that provide opportunities for under privileged individuals to experience and participate in the arts. It also provides support to certain organizations with a history of providing outstanding arts programming to the community at large. It gives preference to programs, which have a direct and substantial human benefit over funding of capital campaigns or ordinary operations and focuses their resources upon projects that serve communities in ID and UT.

Fields of interest: Arts; Higher education; Children/youth, services; Government/public administration.

Type of support: General/operating support; Continuing support; Building/renovation; Equipment; Emergency funds; Program development; Conferences/seminars; Curriculum development; Research; Consulting services; In-kind gifts.

Limitations: Giving limited to ID and UT. No support for religious organizations. No grants to individuals, or for general operating expenses or building funds.

Application information: 2 copies of all additional forms/info. Application form required.

  Initial approach: Letter or telephone for application form or download from Web site
  Copies of proposal: 2
  Deadline(s): Mar. 1 and Sept. 1, unless otherwise posted on Web site
  Board meeting date(s): Apr. and Oct.

Officers and Trustees:* Jane Hemingway Mason, Chair.; Helen Hemingway Cardon,* Pres.; Ann Hemingway,* Secy.; Henry S. Hemingway.

Number of staff: 1 full-time professional.

EIN: 876205846

9329
The Jon and Karen Huntsman Foundation ▼ ✧
500 Huntsman Way
Salt Lake City, UT 84108-1235

Established in 1988 in UT.

Donors: Jon M. Huntsman; Ellis Ivory.

Foundation type: Independent foundation.

Financial data (yr. ended 12/31/04): Assets, $5,829,707 (M); gifts received, $10,000; expenditures, $7,759,151; qualifying distributions, $7,645,176; giving activities include $7,642,423 for 9 grants (high: $5,500,000; low: $16,667; average: $30,756–$100,000).

Purpose and activities: Giving primarily for music, education, health care, science, and Christian agencies and churches.

Fields of interest: Performing arts, music; Education; Health care; Science; Christian agencies & churches.

Type of support: Program-related investments/loans.

Limitations: Applications not accepted. Giving on a national basis. No grants to individuals.

Application information: Contributes only to pre-selected organizations.

Officers and Trustees:* Jon M. Huntsman,* Pres.; J. Kimo Esplin, V.P. and Treas.; Christena Durham,* V.P.; David Gardner,* V.P.; Kathleen Huffman,*

V.P.; David H. Huntsman,* V.P.; James H. Hunstman,* V.P.; Karen H. Huntsman,* V.P.; Paul C. Huntsman,* V.P.; Jennifer H. Parkin,* V.P.

EIN: 742521914

Selected grants: The following grants were reported in 2004.

$6,500,000 to University of Pennsylvania, Philadelphia, PA. 2 grants: $5,500,000 to Wharton School of Business (For Strategic Initiatives Fund and building fund), $1,000,000 to Wharton School of Business (For international studies and business programs).

$720,000 to Huntsman Cancer Foundation, Salt Lake City, UT. For cancer research and treatment.

$229,167 to University of Utah, Salt Lake City, UT. 3 grants: $100,000, $112,500 (For scholarships), $16,667.

$100,000 to Idaho State University Foundation, Pocatello, ID. For scholarships.

$62,500 to Huntsman World Senior Games, Salt Lake City, UT.

$30,756 to Armenia, Government of, Yerevan, Armenia. For urban development project.

9330
Emma Eccles Jones Foundation ▼ ✧
c/o Clark P. Giles
P.O. Box 45385
Salt Lake City, UT 84145-0385 (801) 532-1500

Established in 1972 in UT.

Donor: Emma Eccles Jones†.

Foundation type: Independent foundation.

Financial data (yr. ended 8/31/05): Assets, $109,659,515 (M); expenditures, $4,730,588; qualifying distributions, $4,455,397; giving activities include $4,273,000 for 34 grants (high: $1,500,000; low: $2,000; average: $10,000–$100,000).

Purpose and activities: Giving primarily to education. Giving also to human services and arts and culture.

Fields of interest: Arts; Education; Human services; YM/YWCAs & YM/YWHAs.

Type of support: General/operating support; Continuing support; Building/renovation.

Limitations: Applications not accepted. Giving primarily in UT.

Application information: Unsolicited requests for funds not accepted. No grants will be made to unsolicited requests until 2010.

  Board meeting date(s): 3 times per year

Officers and Committee Members:* Clark P. Giles,* Chair.; Horace T. Clemm,* Vice-Chair.; Robert A. Hatch,* Secy.; Spencer F. Eccles; Frederick Q. Lawson.

Trustee Bank: Wells Fargo Bank Northwest, N.A.

EIN: 876155073

Selected grants: The following grants were reported in 2005.

$1,615,000 to University of Utah, Salt Lake City, UT. 2 grants: $115,000, $1,500,000

$1,350,000 to Westminster College, Salt Lake City, UT.

$429,000 to Utah State University, Logan, UT.

$300,000 to Utah Museum of Natural History, Salt Lake City, UT.

$100,000 to Utah Symphony and Opera, Salt Lake City, UT.

$50,000 to Ballet West, Salt Lake City, UT.

$50,000 to Salt Lake Acting Company, Salt Lake City, UT.

$30,000 to Utah Shakespearean Festival, Cedar City, UT.

$25,000 to Guadalupe Schools, Salt Lake City, UT.

9331
Frederick Q. Lawson Foundation ✧
P.O. Box 45385
Salt Lake City, UT 84145-0385

Established around 1991 in UT.

Donors: Emma Eccles Jones†; Frederick Q. Lawson.

Foundation type: Independent foundation.

Financial data (yr. ended 12/31/04): Assets, $13,540,958 (M); expenditures, $643,454; qualifying distributions, $580,765; giving activities include $580,000 for 10 grants (high: $390,000; low: $5,000).

Purpose and activities: Giving primarily to a cathedral; support also for the fine and performing arts.

Fields of interest: Visual arts; Performing arts, theater; Performing arts, opera; Christian agencies & churches.

Type of support: General/operating support.

Limitations: Applications not accepted. Giving primarily in Salt Lake City, UT. No grants to individuals.

Application information: Contributes only to pre-selected organizations.

Advisory Committee and Trustees:* Frederick Q. Lawson,* Advisor; Herbert C. Livsey,* Advisor.

EIN: 870481510

Selected grants: The following grants were reported in 2003.

$125,000 to Saint Marks Cathedral, Salt Lake City, UT. For general support.

$63,000 to Utah Symphony and Opera, Salt Lake City, UT. For general support.

$38,000 to Ballet West, Salt Lake City, UT.

$30,000 to Salt Lake Acting Company, Salt Lake City, UT. For general support.

$16,000 to Ulster Project of Utah, Salt Lake City, UT. For general support.

$11,700 to Utah State University, Nora Eccles Harrison Museum of Art, Logan, UT. For general support.

$6,000 to Plan B Theater Company, Salt Lake City, UT. For general support.

$5,000 to Platinum Pro Foundation, Fort Collins, CO. For general support.

$2,500 to Utah Arts Council Museum Foundation, Salt Lake City, UT. For general support.

$1,000 to Madeleine Choir School, Salt Lake City, UT. For general support.

9332
Janet Q. Lawson Foundation ✧
P.O. Box 45385
Salt Lake City, UT 84145-0385

Established around 1991 in UT.

Donors: Emma Eccles Jones†; Janet Q. Lawson.

Foundation type: Independent foundation.

Financial data (yr. ended 12/31/03): Assets, $15,982,018 (M); expenditures, $766,696; qualifying distributions, $738,707; giving activities include $725,000 for 3 grants (high: $450,000; low: $75,000).

Purpose and activities: Giving primarily for arts and culture.

Fields of interest: Performing arts, ballet; Performing arts, orchestra (symphony); Arts; Zoos/zoological societies.

Limitations: Applications not accepted. Giving limited to UT, with emphasis on Salt Lake City. No grants to individuals.

Application information: Contributes only to pre-selected organizations.

Advisory Committee and Trustees:* Frederick Q. Lawson, Advisor; Janet Q. Lawson,* Advisor; Peter Q. Lawson, Advisor; Herbert C. Livsey,* Advisor.

EIN: 870481508

Selected grants: The following grants were reported in 2003.

$450,000 to Utah Symphony and Opera, Salt Lake City, UT. For general support.

$200,000 to Utahs Hogle Zoo, Salt Lake City, UT. For general support.

$75,000 to Ballet West, Salt Lake City, UT. For general support.

9333
Lockwood Family Foundation ◇ ☆

P.O. Box 1240
Park City, UT 84060

Established in 1999 in NY.

Donor: Christopher J. Lockwood.

Foundation type: Independent foundation.

Financial data (yr. ended 12/31/05): Assets, $427,364 (M); gifts received, $116,530; expenditures, $355,172; qualifying distributions, $347,320; giving activities include $344,220 for 13 grants (high: $262,000; low: $500).

Fields of interest: Education; Human services; Family services.

Type of support: General/operating support.

Limitations: Applications not accepted. Giving primarily in NY. No grants to individuals.

Application information: Contributes only to pre-selected organizations.

Officers: Susan E. Lockwood, Pres.; Kristen M. Lockwood, Secy.; Christopher J. Lockwood, Treas.

EIN: 134094392

Selected grants: The following grants were reported in 2005.

$262,000 to Family Service League of Suffolk County, Huntington, NY.

$9,220 to Sundance Institute, Beverly Hills, CA.

$5,000 to Literacy Volunteers of America, Elmsford, NY.

$1,000 to Cinema Arts Centre, Huntington, NY.

$1,000 to Hospital for Special Surgery Fund, New York, NY.

$500 to Huntington Hospital, Huntington, NY.

9334
McGillis Charitable Foundation ◇

3068 S. 1030 W.
Salt Lake City, UT 84119-3343

Established in 1986 in UT.

Donors: Richard L. McGillis; Joanne S. McGillis.

Foundation type: Independent foundation.

Financial data (yr. ended 12/31/05): Assets, $1,740,881 (M); gifts received, $604,455; expenditures, $560,689; qualifying distributions, $559,127; giving activities include $559,127 for 19 grants (high: $451,080; low: $25).

Purpose and activities: Giving for Jewish agencies, higher education and cultural organizations.

Fields of interest: Higher education; Human services; Jewish federated giving programs; Jewish agencies & temples.

Limitations: Applications not accepted. Giving primarily in Salt Lake City, UT. No grants to individuals.

Application information: Contributes only to pre-selected organizations.

Trustees: Roger McGillis; Mary Ann O'Connell; Evan R. Terry.

EIN: 870437797

9335
Larry H. Miller Education Foundation ◇

9350 S. 150 E., Ste. 1000
Sandy, UT 84070-2721

Established in 1996 in UT.

Donors: Karen G. Miller; Lawrence H. Miller.

Foundation type: Operating foundation.

Financial data (yr. ended 12/31/05): Assets, $0 (M); gifts received, $662,058; expenditures, $689,806; qualifying distributions, $689,806; giving activities include $677,808 for 228 grants to individuals.

Purpose and activities: Giving to provide employee-related scholarships to individuals for post high school education at accredited institutions. The scholarships are for the dependents of employees only.

Type of support: Scholarships—to individuals.

Limitations: Applications not accepted. Giving limited to residents of Murray, UT.

Application information: Unsolicited requests for funds not accepted. Scholarships are for employees' dependents only.

Officers: Karen G. Miller, Pres.; Larry H. Miller, Secy.-Treas.

Trustees: Gregory S. Miller; Roger L. Miller; G. Stephen Tarbet.

EIN: 870560678

9336
The Ray and Tye Noorda Foundation ▼ ◇

(formerly The Worth of a Soul Foundation)
P.O. Box 434
Orem, UT 84058-0434

Established in 2000 in UT.

Donor: Dialogic Systems Corp.

Foundation type: Independent foundation.

Financial data (yr. ended 12/31/05): Assets, $113,270,252 (M); expenditures, $7,414,783; qualifying distributions, $6,728,292; giving activities include $6,719,000 for 16 grants (high: $1,001,000; low: $1,000; average: $100,000–$500,000).

Purpose and activities: Giving primarily for education, human services, and housing.

Fields of interest: Education; Housing/shelter; Human services.

Limitations: Applications not accepted. Giving primarily in Provo, UT. No grants to individuals.

Application information: Contributes only to pre-selected organizations.

Trustee: Lewena "Tye" Noorda.

EIN: 870649164

Selected grants: The following grants were reported in 2005.

$1,001,000 to Brigham Young University, Provo, UT.

$1,001,000 to University of Utah, Salt Lake City, UT.

$1,000,000 to Primary Childrens Medical Center, Salt Lake City, UT.

$600,000 to Food and Care Coalition, Provo, UT.

$585,000 to Saint Josephs Hospital Foundation.

$500,000 to Center for Women and Children in Crisis, Provo, UT.

$500,000 to Habitat for Humanity of Utah County, Provo, UT.

$500,000 to Kids on the Move, Orem, UT.

$300,000 to Make-A-Wish Foundation of Utah, Murray, UT.

$225,000 to Utah Valley State College, School of Business, Orem, UT.

9337
The Louis Scowcroft Peery Charitable Foundation ◇

P.O. Box 45385
Salt Lake City, UT 84145-0385

Established in 1990 in UT.

Donors: Louis S. Peery; Janet P. Peery.

Foundation type: Independent foundation.

Financial data (yr. ended 12/31/04): Assets, $38,266,830 (M); gifts received, $2,600,000; expenditures, $1,678,192; qualifying distributions, $1,317,977; giving activities include $1,271,558 for 19 grants (high: $400,000; low: $3,000).

Fields of interest: Environment, land resources; Animals/wildlife; Recreation; Human services; Children/youth, services.

Limitations: Applications not accepted. Giving primarily in Ogden and Salt Lake City, UT.

Application information: Contributes only to pre-selected organizations.

Board Members: Leslie Peery Howa, Chair.; Herbert C. Livsey; Gerald T. Snow; Scott C. Ulbrich; David B. Wirthlin.

EIN: 870483734

Selected grants: The following grants were reported in 2004.

$200,000 to McKay-Dee Foundation, Ogden, UT.

$96,300 to Spy Hop Productions, Salt Lake City, UT.

$75,000 to Community Services Council, Salt Lake City, UT.

$60,000 to Childrens Center, Salt Lake City, UT.

$60,000 to Heart and Soul, Salt Lake City, UT.

$54,000 to Utah Youth Village, Salt Lake City, UT.

$25,000 to Summit County Friends of Animals, Park City, UT.

$10,000 to Utah Symphony and Opera, Salt Lake City, UT.

$6,000 to Intermountain Therapy Animals, Salt Lake City, UT.

$5,000 to United Way of Salt Lake, Salt Lake City, UT.

9338
S. J. & Jessie E. Quinney Foundation ▼ ◇

P.O. Box 45385
Salt Lake City, UT 84145-0385
Contact: Herbert C. Livsey, Dir.

Established about 1982 in UT.

Donor: S.J. Quinney‡.

Foundation type: Independent foundation.

Financial data (yr. ended 12/31/04): Assets, $73,999,122 (M); expenditures, $4,537,393; qualifying distributions, $4,290,299; giving activities include $4,250,833 for 94 grants (high:

$2,061,000; low: $300; average: $5,000–$50,000).

Purpose and activities: Giving primarily for higher and other education; support also for social services, cultural programs, including performing arts, and Protestant churches.

Fields of interest: Performing arts; Arts; Elementary/secondary education; Higher education; Environment; Medical care, in-patient care; Health organizations, association; Human services; Christian agencies & churches.

Type of support: General/operating support.

Limitations: Applications not accepted. Giving limited to UT. No grants to individuals.

Application information: Contributes only to pre-selected organizations.

Directors: Ellen S. Erlingsson; James W. Freed; Clark P. Giles; Frederick Q. Lawson; Janet Q. Lawson; Peter Q. Lawson; Herbert C. Livsey; Stephen B. Nebeker; David E. Quinney, Jr.; Alonzo W. Watson, Jr.

EIN: 870389312

Selected grants: The following grants were reported in 2004.

$2,272,583 to University of Utah, Salt Lake City, UT. 3 grants: $3,250 to David Eccles School of Business (For general support), $208,333 (For general support for Fort Douglas Heritage Commons), $2,061,000 to S.J. Quinney College of Law (For general support).

$730,000 to Utah State University, Logan, UT. For general support.

$258,000 to Nature Conservancy, Salt Lake City, UT. For general support.

$103,500 to Utah Symphony and Opera, Salt Lake City, UT. For general support.

$81,000 to Alf Engen Ski Museum Foundation, Salt Lake City, UT. For general support.

$41,000 to Guadalupe Schools, Salt Lake City, UT. For Early Learning Center.

$10,000 to Black Mesa Trust, Flagstaff, AZ. For general support.

$5,000 to Utah Symphony Society, Salt Lake City, UT. For general support.

9339
Raymond Family Foundation ◇

c/o Wells Fargo Bank Northwest, N.A.
P.O. Box 25491
Salt Lake City, UT 84125 (801) 246-1436
Contact: David L. Buchman

Established in 1996 in UT.

Donors: Mary R. Redmond; Mary R. Raymond Charitable Lead Trust; Robert Raymond Foundation, Inc.

Foundation type: Independent foundation.

Financial data (yr. ended 12/31/04): Assets, $12,426,557 (M); gifts received, $187,500; expenditures, $574,399; qualifying distributions, $532,762; giving activities include $510,200 for 107 grants (high: $23,500; low: $250).

Fields of interest: Arts; Higher education; Libraries (public); Education; Animals/wildlife; Hospitals (general); Reproductive health, family planning; Human services; Federated giving programs.

Limitations: Applications not accepted. Giving on a national basis, with emphasis on CA, ME, NY, PA, and UT.

Application information: Contributes only to pre-selected organizations.

Trustee: Wells Fargo Bank Northwest, N.A.

EIN: 566502391

Selected grants: The following grants were reported in 2003.

$50,000 to Bucknell University, Lewisburg, PA.

$25,000 to Future Wave, Santa Fe, NM.

$25,000 to San Francisco Chamber Orchestra, San Francisco, CA.

$17,600 to Berkeley Public Library Foundation, Berkeley, CA.

$10,000 to Chez Panisse Foundation, Berkeley, CA.

$10,000 to Oakland Museum of California Foundation, Oakland, CA.

$10,000 to Planned Parenthood of Central North Carolina, Chapel Hill, NC.

$10,000 to Planned Parenthood of Metropolitan New Jersey, Montclair, NJ.

$10,000 to United States Ski Team Foundation, Park City, UT.

$10,000 to Utah Food Bank, Salt Lake City, UT.

9340
The Neal & Sherrie Savage Family Foundation ◇ ☆

6340 S. 3000 E., Ste. 600
Salt Lake City, UT 84121

Established in 2000 in UT.

Donors: Savage Industries, Inc.; Savage Services Corp.

Foundation type: Company-sponsored foundation.

Financial data (yr. ended 12/31/05): Assets, $1,088,882 (M); gifts received, $5,000,000; expenditures, $5,937,361; qualifying distributions, $5,908,500; giving activities include $5,908,500 for grants.

Purpose and activities: The foundation supports food banks and organizations involved with education, medical research, and human services.

Fields of interest: Education; Cystic fibrosis; Medical research, institute; Medical research; Food banks; Human services; Federated giving programs.

Limitations: Applications not accepted. Giving primarily in New York, NY, and Salt Lake City, UT. No grants to individuals.

Application information: Contributes only to pre-selected organizations.

Officers and Trustees:* Gregory James Savage,* Pres.; Nathan Neal Savage,* Secy.-Treas.; Anna Savage Benedict; Melissa Ann Clayton; Malinda Savage Melville; Emilee Jayne Savage.

EIN: 870651828

9341
Semnani Foundation ◇

P.O. Box 11623
Salt Lake City, UT 84147-0623 (801) 321-7725
Contact: Khosrow B. Semnani, Tr.

Established in 1991 in UT.

Donor: Khosrow B. Semnani.

Foundation type: Independent foundation.

Financial data (yr. ended 12/31/04): Assets, $29,813,534 (M); gifts received, $3,949,207; expenditures, $1,642,189; qualifying distributions, $1,584,310; giving activities include $1,470,095 for grants.

Purpose and activities: Giving primarily for social services, with emphasis on Islamic charity services. Support also for an Iranian encyclopedia and other Iranian causes.

Fields of interest: Arts, cultural/ethnic awareness; Hospitals (specialty); Health organizations,

association; Human services; American Red Cross; Children/youth, services; International relief; Islam.

Limitations: Giving primarily in UT. No grants to individuals.

Application information:
Initial approach: Letter
Deadline(s): None

Trustees: Nolan Karras; Shirin Kia; Ghazelah Semnani; Khosrow B. Semnani.

EIN: 742639794

Selected grants: The following grants were reported in 2004.

$114,000 to Museum of Utah Art and History, Salt Lake City, UT.

$112,160 to University of Utah, Salt Lake City, UT.

$42,000 to Wheelchair Foundation, Danville, CA.

$25,830 to United Way, UT.

$10,700 to Westminster College, Salt Lake City, UT.

$5,000 to Utah State University, Logan, UT.

$2,500 to Weber State University, Ogden, UT.

$2,000 to Association for the Retention of Cultural Heritages, Provo, UT.

$1,000 to Art Works for Kids, Salt Lake City, UT.

$1,000 to Childrens Center, Salt Lake City, UT.

9342
Simmons Family Foundation ◇

722 W. Shepherd Ln., No. 103
Farmington, UT 84025 (435) 655-3818
Contact: Elizabeth W. Gerner, Exec. Dir.
E-mail: elizabeth@simmonsfoundation.org

Established in 1986 in UT.

Donor: Roy W. Simmons.

Foundation type: Independent foundation.

Financial data (yr. ended 11/30/05): Assets, $15,359,488 (M); gifts received, $1,088,200; expenditures, $582,560; qualifying distributions, $577,105; giving activities include $516,750 for 38 grants (high: $28,000; low: $1,000).

Fields of interest: Higher education; Human services; Children/youth, services.

Type of support: General/operating support; Emergency funds; Program development; Scholarship funds; Research; Matching/challenge support.

Limitations: Giving limited to UT. No grants to individuals, or for capital campaigns, or endowments.

Publications: Application guidelines.

Application information: The foundation will not accept proposals between the periods of Feb. 15 to Apr. 30, and Sept. 15 to Nov. 30. Application information available on foundation Web site. Application form required.
Initial approach: Letter on organization letterhead
Copies of proposal: 1
Deadline(s): Feb. 15 and Sept. 15
Board meeting date(s): Apr. 15 and Nov. 15

Officer: Elizabeth W. Gerner, Exec. Dir.

Trustees: Elizabeth S. Hoke; David E. Simmons; Harris H. Simmons; L.E. Simmons; Matthew R. Simmons; Julia S. Watkins.

Number of staff: 1 full-time professional.

EIN: 133420599

Selected grants: The following grants were reported in 2005.

$35,000 to Pioneer Theater Company, Salt Lake City, UT.

$28,000 to University of Utah, Salt Lake City, UT.

$25,000 to Treehouse Childrens Museum, Ogden, UT.

$25,000 to Weber State University, Ogden, UT.

$20,000 to American Indian Services, Provo, UT.

$20,000 to Utah State University, Logan, UT.

$15,000 to Community Nursing Services, Salt Lake City, UT.

$10,000 to Utah Shakespearean Festival, Cedar City, UT.

$7,000 to Caring Foundation for Children, Salt Lake City, UT.

$5,000 to Utah Youth Village, Salt Lake City, UT.

9343
The Sorenson Legacy Foundation ✧

2511 S. West Temple St.

Salt Lake City, UT 84115-3060 (801) 461-9700

Contact: Gloria Smith

Established in 2001 in UT.

Donors: James LeVoy Sorenson; Sorenson Devel., Inc.

Foundation type: Independent foundation.

Financial data (yr. ended 12/31/05): Assets, $14,051 (M); gifts received, $4,877,278; expenditures, $4,872,369; qualifying distributions, $4,872,369; giving activities include $4,867,846 for 37 grants (high: $2,083,501; low: $1,000).

Fields of interest: Elementary school/education; Health organizations, association; Human services; Children/youth, services; Foundations (private grantmaking).

Limitations: Giving primarily in Salt Lake City, UT.

Application information: Submissions early in the year have a better chance for funding. Application form not required.

Initial approach: Letter

Trustees: Carol S. Smith; Beverly T. Sorenson; James LeVoy Sorenson.

EIN: 870669065

9344
Pauline and Edgar Stern Foundation ✧ ☆

P.O. Box 3179

Park City, UT 84060

Established in 2002 in UT.

Donors: Edgar B. Stern, Jr.; Pauline S. Stern.

Foundation type: Independent foundation.

Financial data (yr. ended 12/31/05): Assets, $2,642,943 (M); gifts received, $209,969; expenditures, $352,924; qualifying distributions, $345,390; giving activities include $345,390 for 12 grants (high: $115,000; low: $100).

Fields of interest: Performing arts, theater; Animal welfare.

Type of support: General/operating support.

Limitations: Applications not accepted. Giving primarily in Friday Harbor, WA; giving also in New Orleans, LA. No grants to individuals.

Application information: Contributes only to pre-selected organizations.

Officers and Directors: Edgar B. Stern, Jr.,* Pres.; Pauline S. Stern,* V.P.; Gil S. Williams,* Secy.-Treas.; Samuel P. Guyton.

EIN: 470867448

9345
Stewart Education Foundation ✧

(formerly Donnell B. and Elizabeth Dee Shaw Stewart Educational Foundation)

c/o Wells Fargo Bank Northwest, N.A.

299 S. Main St., MAC S4035-014

Salt Lake City, UT 84111

Contact: Mary Barker, Secy. for applications

Application address: c/o Wells Fargo Bank, N.A., P.O. Box 9936. Ogden, UT 84409, tel.: (801) 626-9531

Established in 1977 in UT.

Donor: Elizabeth D.S. Stewart†.

Foundation type: Independent foundation.

Financial data (yr. ended 12/31/04): Assets, $87,586,222 (M); expenditures, $2,656,445; qualifying distributions, $2,500,393; giving activities include $2,317,025 for 37 grants (high: $1,889,585; low: $25).

Fields of interest: Higher education, college; Education; Hospitals (general); Health organizations, association; Human services.

Type of support: Annual campaigns; Capital campaigns; Building/renovation; Equipment; Endowments; Professorships; Scholarship funds; Research; Matching/challenge support.

Limitations: Giving primarily in UT.

Application information: Application form required.

Initial approach: Letter

Copies of proposal: 1

Deadline(s): None, but Sept. 30 is preferred

Board meeting date(s): Apr., June, Sept., and Dec.

Officers: Jack D. Lampros, Chair.; Dean W. Hurst, Vice-Chair.; C.W. Stromberg, Vice-Chair.

Members: Mary L. Barker; Orville Rex Child; Kristen Hurst-Hyde; Jamie Shenefelt; Richard Stromberg.

Trustee: Wells Fargo Bank Northwest, N.A.

EIN: 876179880

Selected grants: The following grants were reported in 2005.

$3,397,858 to Weber State University, Ogden, UT. For grant made in form of stock.

$90,300 to Ogden Symphony-Ballet Association, Ogden, UT.

$50,500 to Utah State University, Logan, UT.

$50,000 to Utah Symphony and Opera, Salt Lake City, UT.

$42,000 to Treehouse Childrens Museum, Ogden, UT.

$36,050 to American Red Cross, Ogden, UT.

$30,000 to South High School Alumni Association, Salt Lake City, UT.

$20,100 to Rotary Club of Ogden Foundation, Ogden, UT.

$12,000 to Ogden School Foundation, Ogden, UT.

$10,000 to Saint Joseph Catholic Schools, Ogden, UT.

9346
Dr. W. C. Swanson Family Foundation, Inc. ▼ ✧

2955 Harrison Blvd., Ste. 201

Ogden, UT 84403 (801) 392-0360

Contact: Lynda Murphy, Grants Admin.

FAX: (801) 392-0429; E-mail: SFF@swanfound.org; Additional tel.: (801) 530-0360; E-mail (for Lynda Murphy): lynda@swanfound.org

Established in 1977; incorporated in 1999.

Donor: W.C. Swanson†.

Foundation type: Independent foundation.

Financial data (yr. ended 12/31/05): Assets, $37,488,751 (M); gifts received, $46,897; expenditures, $6,921,829; qualifying distributions, $5,632,794; giving activities include $967,014 for 66 grants (high: $292,885; low: $200; average: $1,000–$25,000), $2,417,438 for 48 in-kind gifts, and $1,672,368 for 10 foundation-administered programs.

Purpose and activities: Giving primarily for education, arts and culture, human services, and the prevention of cruelty to children and animals.

Fields of interest: Media/communications; Arts; Education; Animal welfare; Children/youth, services; Homeless, human services.

International interests: Mongolia.

Type of support: General/operating support; Continuing support; Equipment; Emergency funds; Program development; Conferences/seminars; Scholarship funds; Research; In-kind gifts; Matching/challenge support.

Limitations: Giving primarily in UT, with emphasis on Weber County and Ogden City. No grants to individuals, or for salaries and benefits, "bricks and mortar," or capital campaigns.

Publications: Application guidelines; Newsletter.

Application information: Must complete application and provide all requested information. Application form required.

Initial approach: Letter

Copies of proposal: 1

Deadline(s): End of the quarter/prior to the quarter when grant request will be considered. Contact Grants Admin. for specific deadline dates, they may vary year to year

Board meeting date(s): Quarterly

Advisory Board and Directors: W. Charles Swanson,* Chair. and C.E.O.; Cindy Purcell, Pres.; Annabel Hofer,* Exec. V.P.; Kim Dohrer; Michael Fosmark; Marcy Korgenski; Robert Marguardt; Tami Swanson.

Number of staff: 4 full-time professional; 4 part-time professional; 14 full-time support; 4 part-time support.

EIN: 870578540

Selected grants: The following grants were reported in 2004.

$447,531 to Ogden Rescue Mission, Ogden, UT. For general support.

$340,378 to National Center on Shaken Baby Syndrome, Ogden, UT. For general support.

$192,107 to Ogden School Foundation, Ogden, UT. 2 grants: $45,750 (For mini-grant program), $146,357 (For in-kind grant of quilts and blankets, coats, gloves, and hats for Rainbow Bus and Community of Caring programs).

$100,800 to Ogden City Police Department, Ogden, UT. For Operation Sustain Hope and for Cops, Kids, and Christmas.

$65,750 to Treehouse Childrens Museum, Ogden, UT. For architectural fees.

$51,400 to Weber County School District, Ogden, UT. For new marquee, mini-grant program and fundraiser.

$39,464 to Friends of Time Society, Orem, UT. For in-kind grant of miscellaneous equipment and supplies.

$25,000 to Utah Symphony and Opera, Salt Lake City, UT. For educational outreach programs.

$23,900 to Weber State University, Ogden, UT. For Teachers Assistants Path to Teaching program and family literacy program.

9347
Tanner Charitable Trust ✧
1930 S. State St.
Salt Lake City, UT 84115 (801) 486-2430

Incorporated in 1965 in UT.
Donor: Obert C. Tanner.
Foundation type: Independent foundation.
Financial data (yr. ended 12/31/05): Assets, $6,400,374 (M); gifts received, $2,473,630; expenditures, $1,929,623; qualifying distributions, $1,922,203; giving activities include $1,914,784 for 79 grants (high: $200,000; low: $50).
Purpose and activities: Giving primarily for arts, education, and social services.
Fields of interest: Performing arts; Performing arts, orchestra (symphony); Arts; Higher education; Environment, natural resources; Health organizations, association; Human services; Federated giving programs.
Limitations: Applications not accepted. Giving primarily in Salt Lake City, UT. No grants to individuals.
Application information: Contributes only to pre-selected organizations.
Officer and Trustees:* Carolyn T. Irish,* Chair.; Kent H. Murdock.
EIN: 876125059
Selected grants: The following grants were reported in 2004.
$130,000 to Utah Community Foundation, Salt Lake City, UT.
$100,000 to Nature Conservancy, Salt Lake City, UT.
$30,000 to YWCA of Salt Lake City, Salt Lake City, UT.
$26,000 to Salvation Army of Salt Lake City, Salt Lake City, UT.
$25,000 to Multicultural Services of Utah, Provo, UT.
$25,000 to Road Home, Salt Lake City, UT.
$15,000 to United Way of Salt Lake, Salt Lake City, UT.
$14,500 to University of Utah, Lowell Bennion Community Service Center, Salt Lake City, UT.
$10,000 to Hearing Help Foundation, Salt Lake City, UT.
$10,000 to Quest for the Gift of Life Foundation, Salt Lake City, UT.

9348
Thrasher Research Fund
15 W. South Temple St., Ste. 1650
Salt Lake City, UT 84101 (801) 240-4753
Contact: Aaron V. Pontsler, Research Mgr.
FAX: (801) 240-1625;
E-mail: thrasherinfo@thrasherresearch.org;
Additional E-mail: pontslerav@thrasherresearch.org;
URL: http://www.thrasherresearch.org

Established in 1977 in UT.
Donor: E.W. "Al" Thrasher.
Foundation type: Independent foundation.
Financial data (yr. ended 12/31/04): Assets, $92,903,337 (M); expenditures, $5,228,732; qualifying distributions, $4,044,992; giving activities include $4,044,992 for grants.
Purpose and activities: The fund seeks to foster an environment of creativity and discovery aimed at finding solutions to children's health problems. The fund awards grants for research that offers substantial promise for meaningful advances in prevention and treatment of children's diseases,

particularly research that offers broad-based applications. Emphasis is placed on projects with potential findings that would be clinically applicable in a relatively short period of time for the prevention, diagnosis and/or treatment of pediatric medical problems.
Fields of interest: Medical research, institute; Pediatrics research.
Type of support: Research.
Limitations: Giving on a national and international basis. No support for research using fetal tissue, other funding organizations, behavioral science research, or educational programs. No grants for general operations, construction or renovation of facilities, student aid, or scholarships; no loans.
Publications: Application guidelines; Biennial report (including application guidelines); Informational brochure (including application guidelines).
Application information: Guidelines are available on Web site, and should be viewed before submitting any applications. Applicants whose concept papers are approved will receive an invitation to submit a full proposal as well as an electronic application kit. Application form required.
Initial approach: Concept paper
Copies of proposal: 1
Deadline(s): Revolving
Board meeting date(s): Quarterly
Final notification: 6 to 9 months from initial consultation
Officers and Advisory Committee:* Keith B. McMullin,* Co-Chair.; Charlotte G. Neumann, M.D.*, Co-Chair.; A. Dean Byrd, Ph.D., Pres.; Janet A. Englund, M.D.; Elena Fuentes-Afflick, M.D.; Donald L. Granger, M.D.; Kurt T. Hegman, M.D.; Ray M. Merrill, Ph.D.; Mark R. Palmert, M.D., Ph.D.; Joseph B. Stanford, M.D.; John A. Widness, M.D.
Number of staff: 4 full-time professional; 1 full-time support; 1 part-time support.
EIN: 876179851

9349
Wadman Foundation ✧ ☆
4111 N. 250 W.
Pleasant View, UT 84414
Contact: V. Jay Wadman

Established in 1998 in UT.
Donor: V. Jay Wadman.
Foundation type: Independent foundation.
Financial data (yr. ended 12/31/05): Assets, $236,795 (M); gifts received, $620,593; expenditures, $833,465; qualifying distributions, $828,870; giving activities include $828,870 for 23 + grants (high: $500,000).
Fields of interest: Elementary/secondary education; Higher education; Youth development; Mormon agencies & churches.
Limitations: Giving primarily in UT. No grants to individuals.
Application information:
Initial approach: Letter
Deadline(s): None
Officer: V. Jay Wadman, Pres.
EIN: 841392243
Selected grants: The following grants were reported in 2005.
$500,000 to Church of Jesus Christ, San Diego, CA.
$2,500 to Ogden Rescue Mission, Ogden, UT.
$2,500 to Saint Annes Center, Ogden, UT.
$1,200 to Rocky Mountain Elk Foundation, Missoula, MT.
$1,000 to American Red Cross.

$1,000 to Boy Scouts of America, Anchorage, AK.

9350
C. Scott and Dorothy E. Watkins Charitable Foundation ✧
1935 E. Vine St., Ste. 260
Salt Lake City, UT 84121

Established in 1992.
Foundation type: Independent foundation.
Financial data (yr. ended 12/31/05): Assets, $5,412,453 (M); expenditures, $452,700; qualifying distributions, $450,000; giving activities include $450,000 for grants.
Purpose and activities: Giving primarily for medical research and health care.
Fields of interest: Higher education; Hospitals (general); Food services; Human services; Religion.
Limitations: Applications not accepted. Giving primarily in UT. No grants to individuals.
Application information: Contributes only to pre-selected organizations.
Trustees: Alonzo A. Hinckley; Jay Rasmussen; Gary Watkins.
EIN: 876218993
Selected grants: The following grants were reported in 2005.
$35,000 to Utah Food Bank, Salt Lake City, UT.
$16,000 to Primary Childrens Medical Center, Salt Lake City, UT.
$15,000 to Huntsman Cancer Institute, Salt Lake City, UT.
$15,000 to Road Home, Salt Lake City, UT.
$12,000 to Salvation Army.
$10,000 to American Red Cross.
$8,000 to American Heart Association, Dallas, TX.
$5,000 to American Diabetes Association, Alexandria, VA.
$5,000 to Huntsman World Senior Games, Salt Lake City, UT.
$5,000 to Utah Youth Village, Salt Lake City, UT.

9351
Steven J. Wideman Family Foundation ✧ ☆
3421 N. 825 E.
North Ogden, UT 84414

Established in 2003 in UT.
Donor: Steven J. Wideman.
Foundation type: Independent foundation.
Financial data (yr. ended 12/31/05): Assets, $5,617 (M); gifts received, $360,300; expenditures, $405,149; qualifying distributions, $404,155; giving activities include $404,155 for 5 grants (high: $403,319; low: $10).
Fields of interest: Christian agencies & churches.
Limitations: Applications not accepted. No grants to individuals.
Application information: Contributes only to pre-selected organizations.
Director: Steven J. Wideman.
Trustee: Kenneth R. Burton.
EIN: 270059376

9352

The H. R. Wing Family Benevolent Agency ◇ ☆

180 N. 1440 E.
Springville, UT 84663 (801) 489-3684
Application address: c/o Wing Family Benevolent Agency Review Committee, 1325 W. Industrial Cir., Springville, UT 84663

Established in 2004 in UT.
Donor: Wing Enterprises, Inc.
Foundation type: Independent foundation.
Financial data (yr. ended 12/31/04): Assets, $13,959 (M); gifts received, $1,070,945; expenditures, $1,056,986; qualifying distributions, $1,056,243; giving activities include $881,852 for 19+ grants (high: $535,500), and $174,391 for grants to individuals (high: $43,000).
Fields of interest: Higher education, university; Human services; Children/youth, services; Community development; Mormon agencies & churches; Disabilities, people with.
Type of support: General/operating support; Scholarship funds.
Limitations: Giving primarily in UT.
Application information: Application form required.
  Initial approach: Letter
  Deadline(s): None
Officer: Harold R. Wing, Pres.
EIN: 300235381

9353

Robert I. Wishnick Foundation ◇

(formerly The Witco Foundation)
P.O. Box 681869
Park City, UT 84068
Contact: William Wishnick, Pres.

Incorporated in 1951 in IL.
Donor: William Wishnick.
Foundation type: Independent foundation.

Financial data (yr. ended 12/31/05): Assets, $7,401,792 (M); expenditures, $375,187; qualifying distributions, $343,052; giving activities include $341,620 for 67 grants (high: $49,250; low: $25).
Purpose and activities: Giving primarily to Jewish organizations and federated giving programs; some funding also for the arts, education, the environment, children and youth services, health associations, and social services, including a Native American organization.
Fields of interest: Performing arts; Arts; Elementary/secondary education; Higher education; Education; Environment, natural resources; Environment; Animal welfare; Animals/wildlife; Hospitals (general); Reproductive health, family planning; Health organizations, association; Athletics/sports, winter sports; Recreation; Human services; Children/youth, services; Jewish federated giving programs; Jewish agencies & temples; Native Americans/American Indians.
Type of support: General/operating support; Annual campaigns; Capital campaigns; Endowments; Research.
Limitations: Applications not accepted. Giving on a national basis. No grants to individuals.
Application information: Contributes only to pre-selected organizations.
  Board meeting date(s): 4 to 5 times a year
Officers and Directors:* William Wishnick,* Pres.; Lisa Wishnick,* V.P.; Ami Jo Gibson; Gina Grossman.
EIN: 136068668

9354

The Zions Bancorporation Foundation ◇

1 S. Main St., Ste. 1142
Salt Lake City, UT 84111-1909

Established in 1997 in UT.
Donor: Zions Bancorporation.

Foundation type: Company-sponsored foundation.
Financial data (yr. ended 12/31/04): Assets, $3,148,688 (M); expenditures, $425,591; qualifying distributions, $424,391; giving activities include $424,391 for 38 grants (high: $35,000; low: $1,000).
Purpose and activities: The foundation supports organizations involved with arts and culture, education, human services, and community development.
Fields of interest: Performing arts, theater; Performing arts, orchestra (symphony); Arts; Higher education, university; Education; Human services; Community development; Federated giving programs.
Type of support: General/operating support.
Limitations: Applications not accepted. Giving limited to areas of company operations. No grants to individuals.
Application information: Contributes only to pre-selected organizations.
Officer and Trustee:* Harris Simmons,* Pres.
EIN: 841411938
Selected grants: The following grants were reported in 2004.
$35,000 to United Way of Salt Lake, Salt Lake City, UT.
$25,000 to Utah Symphony and Opera, Salt Lake City, UT.
$24,000 to Road Home, Salt Lake City, UT.
$16,666 to Utah Museum of Natural History, Salt Lake City, UT.
$15,000 to Ballet West, Salt Lake City, UT.
$15,000 to Neighborhood Housing Services of Orange County, Anaheim, CA.
$10,000 to Alpha Project for the Homeless, San Diego, CA.
$10,000 to East County Economic Development Council, El Cajon, CA.
$10,000 to Money Management International, Houston, TX.
$10,000 to Northwest Tempe Neighborhoods CDC, Tempe, AZ.

VERMONT

9355
Ben & Jerry's Foundation, Inc. ✧
30 Community Dr.
South Burlington, VT 05403 (802) 846-1500
Contact: Debby Kessler, Admin. Asst.
URL: http://www.benjerry.com/foundation/index.html

Established in 1985 in NY.
Donor: Ben & Jerry's Homemade Inc.
Foundation type: Company-sponsored foundation.
Financial data (yr. ended 12/31/03): Assets, $4,994,526 (M); gifts received, $1,148,262; expenditures, $2,010,799; qualifying distributions, $1,904,072; giving activities include $1,878,201 for 337 grants (high: $150,000; low: $200), and $25,871 for 160 employee matching gifts.
Purpose and activities: The foundation supports organizations involved with early childhood development, the environment, AIDS, employment, agriculture, housing, youth citizenship, civil rights, community development, citizen participation, minorities, Native Americans, women, gays and lesbians, immigrants, economically disadvantaged people, and homeless people. Special emphasis is directed toward programs designed to facilitate progressive social change/justice.
Fields of interest: Child development, education; Environment, natural resources; Environment; AIDS; Employment, labor unions/organizations; Employment; Agriculture; Housing/shelter; Youth development, citizenship; Civil rights, race/intergroup relations; Civil rights; Community development; Public affairs, citizen participation; Minorities; Native Americans/American Indians; Women; LGBTQ; Immigrants/refugees; Economically disadvantaged; Homeless.
Type of support: General/operating support; Program development; Seed money; Matching/challenge support.
Limitations: Giving on a national basis and to U.S. territories. No support for state agencies, basic or direct service organizations, or universities. No grants to individuals, or for research projects, discretionary support or emergency needs, international or foreign programs, scholarships, or religious projects.
Publications: Application guidelines; Annual report; Grants list.
Application information: The NNG Common Grant Application is accepted; contact foundation before submitting. Application form required.
Initial approach: Download application form and mail letter of inquiry and application form to foundation
Copies of proposal: 2
Deadline(s): Mar. 1, July 1, and Nov. 1 for proposals; 10 weeks prior to proposal deadlines for letters of inquiry and application forms
Officers and Trustees:* Jerry Greenfield,* Pres.; Elizabeth Bankowski,* Secy.; Jeffrey Furman,* Treas.
Number of staff: 2 part-time professional; 1 part-time support.
EIN: 030300865
Selected grants: The following grants were reported in 2004.
$50,000 to Ruckus Society, Berkeley, CA.

$13,500 to Environmental Justice Fund, Oakland, CA. For Climate Justice Corps, a campaign to provide leadership development for young organizers and researchers from disproportionately affected communities in the U.S. and to invigorate a new constituency for climate action.
$13,500 to Great Old Broads for Wilderness, Durango, CO. For Healthy Lands Project, which will train citizen volunteers to collect field data to bridge a serious policy information gap addressing the use and impacts of Off-Highway Vehicles (OHV) on public lands.
$13,500 to San Luis Obispo Mothers for Peace, Pismo Beach, CA. For efforts to educate the public and elected officials on the importance of making aging nuclear power plants safer and more secure in the face of terrorist and seismic threats.
$13,500 to Save Our Cumberland Mountains Resource Project, Lake City, TN. For Mountaintop Removal Organizing Project which engages local community members to organize to prevent the permitting of specific MTR mining operations and will implement a statewide campaign to pressure the governor to stop the spread of MTR.
$12,500 to Dakota Rural Action, Brookings, SD. For Stop Factory Farms Campaign focused on halting the influx of huge industrial dairies into the state using the right of citizens referendums where necessary.
$12,500 to Global Community Monitor, San Francisco, CA. To expand use of Bucket Brigades into non-refinery communities that are over-burdened by chemical pollution, including from hazardous waste incinerators, landfills, pulp and paper mills, pesticide production and power plants.
$12,500 to Institute for Social Ecology, Plainfield, VT. For grassroots initiative for biotechnology activism, committed to expanding public debate around genetic engineering and other biotechnologies through grassroots education and action, internationally recognized public events, and the development of democratic, community-based activist networks to challenge corporate agribusiness and advocate for ecological and equitable local food systems.
$10,000 to Calumet Project for Industrial Jobs, Hammond, IN. For Coalition for a Clean Environment in East Chicago, which is fighting a proposed Confined Disposal Facility to be sited near two schools.
$10,000 to Concerned Citizens for a Better Tunica County, Tunica, MS. For general support for youth leadership development, education policy organizing, environmental racism work, community democracy work, organizational development trainings and to enhance their use of technology for organizing.

9356
General Education Fund, Inc. ✧
c/o Merchants Trust Co.
P.O. Box 8490
Burlington, VT 05402
Application address: c/o Scholarship-NEW, VSAC Scholarship Program, P.O. Box 2000, Champlain Mill, Winooski, VT, 05404-2601

Incorporated in 1918 in VT.
Donors: Emma Eliza Curtis†; Lorenzo E. Woodhouse†.

Foundation type: Independent foundation.
Financial data (yr. ended 7/31/05): Assets, $31,346,556 (M); gifts received, $6,653; expenditures, $1,490,306; qualifying distributions, $1,329,890; giving activities include $1,308,467 for 901 grants to individuals.
Purpose and activities: Provides undergraduate scholarships to VT high school graduates.
Type of support: Scholarships—to individuals.
Limitations: Giving limited to VT residents. No grants for building or endowment funds, operating budgets, or special projects.
Application information: Applicants must apply through Vermont Student Assistance Corp. Application form required.
Copies of proposal: 1
Deadline(s): July 31 for New Award Scholarships; July 1 for Scholarship Renewals.
Officer: Geoffrey Hesslink, Pres.
Trustees: Joseph Boutin; Michael Tuttle.
EIN: 036009912

9357
Frank M. & Olive E. Gilman Foundation ✧
220 Holiday Dr., No. 27
White River Junction, VT 05001 (802) 295-3358
Contact: Reginald H. Jones, Pres.

Established in 1991 in VT; funded in 1992.
Donors: Frank Gilman†; Olive Gilman†.
Foundation type: Independent foundation.
Financial data (yr. ended 12/31/05): Assets, $11,550,825 (M); expenditures, $845,782; qualifying distributions, $738,536; giving activities include $730,000 for 1 grant.
Purpose and activities: Giving primarily for educational assistance in Orange and Windsor counties, VT.
Fields of interest: Education.
Limitations: Giving limited to Grafton County, NH, and Orange and Windsor counties, VT. No grants to individuals.
Application information:
Initial approach: Letter
Deadline(s): None
Board meeting date(s): Varies
Officers: Reginald H. Jones, Pres.; Brenda Jones, V.P.; Elizabeth Jones, Secy.-Treas.
EIN: 030330527
Selected grants: The following grants were reported in 2005.
$730,000 to Vermont Student Assistance Corporation, Winooski, VT.

9358
Green Mountain Coffee Roasters Foundation ✧ ☆
33 Coffee Ln.
P.O. Box 607
Waterbury, VT 05676 (802) 244-5621
Contact: Michael Dupee, Admin.
URL: http://www.greenmountaincoffeefoundation.org

Established in 2000 in VT.
Donor: Robert J. Stiller.
Foundation type: Company-sponsored foundation.
Financial data (yr. ended 9/30/06): Assets, $143,967 (M); gifts received, $469,934; expenditures, $492,928; qualifying distributions,

$457,842; giving activities include $457,842 for grants.
Purpose and activities: The foundation supports organizations involved with secondary education, the environment, health, and human services.
Fields of interest: Secondary school/education; Environment; Health care; Children/youth, services; Human services.
Limitations: Giving on a national basis.
Application information:
  Initial approach: Contact foundation for application information
  Deadline(s): None
Officers: Robert Stiller, Pres.; Paul Comey, V.P.; Michael Dupee, Admin.
EIN: 030341004
Selected grants: The following grants were reported in 2005.
$100,000 to Revitalizing Waterbury, Waterbury, VT.
$83,000 to 01 Expert Systems, Winooski, VT.
$25,000 to Media Rights Foundation, Albuquerque, NM.
$19,500 to Family Television, Concord, CA.
$10,000 to Institute of Noetic Sciences, Petaluma, CA.

9359
Lintilhac Foundation ◇
886 N. Gate Rd.
Shelburne, VT   05482   (802) 985-4106
Contact: Crea S. Lintilhac, Pres.
FAX: (802) 985-3725; URL: http://www.lintilhacfoundation.org

Established in 1975.
Donors: Claire Malcolm Lintilhac†; Claire D. Lintilhac Annuity Trust I; Claire D. Lintilhac Annuity Trust II.
Foundation type: Independent foundation.
Financial data (yr. ended 6/30/06): Assets, $17,426,871 (M); expenditures, $959,041; qualifying distributions, $892,740; giving activities include $854,801 for grants.
Purpose and activities: Support for medical education programs at specified institutions in VT; support also for health services, community development, civic projects and educational institutions.
Fields of interest: Medical school/education; Education; Environment; Reproductive health, family planning; Health care; Family services; Community development; Marine science; Government/public administration.
Type of support: General/operating support; Continuing support; Building/renovation; Equipment; Land acquisition; Program development; Conferences/seminars; Professorships; Seed money; Curriculum development; Fellowships; Scholarship funds; Matching/challenge support.
Limitations: Giving primarily in north central VT, including Chittenden, Lamoille, and Washington counties. No grants to individuals.
Publications: Biennial report.
Application information: Application form not required.
  Initial approach: Proposal
  Copies of proposal: 4
  Deadline(s): None
  Board meeting date(s): Quarterly
Officers and Directors:* Crea S. Lintilhac,* Pres.; Philip M. Lintilhac,* V.P. and Secy.; Raeman P. Sopher,* Treas.

Number of staff: 1 full-time support; 1 part-time support.
EIN: 510176851
Selected grants: The following grants were reported in 2004.
$139,925 to University of Vermont, Burlington, VT. 2 grants: $99,925 to Department of Botany (For continued support of project: Reproductive Differentiation in Plants: A Structural Mathematical Analysis), $40,000 to School of Natural Resources (For Aiken project).
$50,000 to Fletcher Allen Health Care, Burlington, VT. To create new birthing center.
$50,000 to Shelburne Museum, Shelburne, VT. For Brick House preservation and program support.
$17,000 to Middlebury College, Middlebury, VT. For Geology department equipment.
$13,500 to Shelburne Community School, Shelburne, VT. For educational partnership with Shelburne Craft School.
$2,500 to Visiting Nurse Association of Chittenden and Grand Isle Counties, Colchester, VT. For staff development and address the shortage of nurses.
$2,386 to Burke Mountain Academy, East Burke, VT. For electrical update in library.
$1,000 to Noise Pollution Clearinghouse, Montpelier, VT. For unrestricted support.
$1,000 to Vermont Stage Company, Burlington, VT. For unrestricted support.

9360
George W. Mergens Foundation
P.O. Box 633
Milton, VT   05468   (802) 862-6770
Contact: Paul Mergens, Pres.; Bill Wiltshire, Dir., Opers.
FAX: (802) 863-5968;
E-mail: info@mergensfoundation.org

Established in 1994 in VT.
Donors: Paul Mergens; Mary Mergens-Loughran.
Foundation type: Independent foundation.
Financial data (yr. ended 8/31/05): Assets, $11,689,094 (M); expenditures, $740,532; qualifying distributions, $615,137; giving activities include $550,288 for 32 grants (high: $150,000; low: $500).
Purpose and activities: Giving primarily for educational, cultural, medical and general welfare needs of children in VT.
Fields of interest: Arts; Elementary/secondary education; Education; Boys & girls clubs; Boy scouts; Human services; Christian agencies & churches.
Type of support: General/operating support; Continuing support; Income development; Annual campaigns; Building/renovation; Equipment; Program development; Scholarship funds; Program-related investments/loans; Matching/challenge support.
Limitations: Giving primarily in VT. No grants to individuals.
Publications: Application guidelines.
Application information: Application form required.
  Initial approach: Letter requesting grant guidelines and information, including a brief introduction of the applicant
  Copies of proposal: 1
  Deadline(s): None
Officers: Paul Mergens, Pres.; Lenora Mergens, V.P.; Mary Mergens-Loughran, Secy.

Number of staff: 2 full-time support.
EIN: 030345055
Selected grants: The following grants were reported in 2005.
$275,000 to Saint Francis Xavier School, Winooski, VT. 3 grants: $65,000 (For general operating support), $60,000 (For general operating support), $150,000 (For general operating support).
$62,000 to Boy Scouts of America, Waterbury, VT. 3 grants: $15,000 to Green Mountain Council (For general operating support), $35,000 (For general operating support for program in Burlington, VT), $12,000 to Green Mountain Council (For general operating support).
$33,969 to Rice Memorial High School, South Burlington, VT. For general operating support.
$10,000 to Flynn Center for the Performing Arts, Burlington, VT. For general operating support.
$8,679 to Birds of Vermont Museum, Huntington, VT. For general operating support.
$5,000 to Vermont Studio Center, Johnson, VT. For general operating support.

9361
Vermont Community Foundation
3 Court St.
P.O. Box 30
Middlebury, VT   05753   (802) 388-3355
Contact: Julie Cadwallader-Staub, V.P., Community Grantmaking
FAX: (802) 388-3398; *E-mail:* info@vermontcf.org;
Additional E-mails: jcstaub@vermontcf.org and mconlon@vermontcf.org; URL: http://www.vermontcf.org

Established in 1986 in VT.
Foundation type: Community foundation.
Financial data (yr. ended 12/31/05): Assets, $100,910,052 (M); gifts received, $17,822,311; expenditures, $8,973,357; giving activities include $6,718,567 for grants.
Purpose and activities: As a developer of resources, the foundation seeks to build a permanent accessible endowment of funds for charitable purposes, and to increase charitable capital for VT.
Fields of interest: Humanities; Historic preservation/historical societies; Arts; Education, early childhood education; Child development, education; Elementary school/education; Secondary school/education; Higher education; Adult/continuing education; Libraries/library science; Education; Environment, natural resources; Environment; Reproductive health, family planning; Health care; Substance abuse, services; Mental health/crisis services; AIDS; Alcoholism; Health organizations; Food services; Housing/shelter; Children/youth, services; Youth, services; Child development, services; Family services; Minorities/immigrants, centers/services; Homeless, human services; Human services; Civil rights; Economic development; Community development; Public affairs; Children; Aging; Disabilities, people with; Economically disadvantaged.
Type of support: General/operating support; Continuing support; Income development; Management development/capacity building; Building/renovation; Emergency funds; Program development; Conferences/seminars; Publication; Seed money; Curriculum development; Scholarship funds; Research; Technical assistance; Consulting services; Program evaluation; Program-related

investments/loans; Grants to individuals; Scholarships—to individuals.

Limitations: Giving limited to VT. No support for religious purposes. No grants for annual campaigns, or for building funds, continuing support, debt reduction, equipment and materials, general endowments, or for operating budgets.

Publications: Application guidelines; Annual report; Financial statement; Grants list; Informational brochure; Newsletter; Occasional report.

Application information: Visit foundation Web site for application cover sheets, additional guidelines per grant type, and specific deadlines. The foundation's staff holds a series of grantseeker forums for those individuals interested in learning more about applying for a grant from the VCF Community Fund; visit Web site for specific dates and to register. Application form required.

Initial approach: Submit cover sheet, proposal, and attachments
Copies of proposal: 3

Deadline(s): Varies
Board meeting date(s): 4 times annually
Final notification: Varies

Officers and Directors:* Vicky Young,* Chair.; Kathy Hoyt,* Vice-Chair.; Brian T. Byrnes,* C.E.O. and Pres.; Faith Brown, V.P., Finance and Opers.; Julie Cadwallader-Staub, V.P., Community Grantmaking; Scott McArdle, V.P., Donor Svcs. and Comms.; Robert Woolmington,* Secy.; Deborah W. Granquist,* Treas.; Richard C. White, Emeritus; Kevin Harper; Robert D. Ide; Ellen Kahler; Lisa Lorimer; Lawrence H. Mandell; Patricia P. Motch; Albert Perry; Ernest A. Pomerleau; Rose Pulliam; J. Alvin Wakefield.

Number of staff: 13 full-time professional; 1 part-time professional; 5 full-time support.

EIN: 222712160

Selected grants: The following grants were reported in 2005.

$10,000 to Alliance for Building Community, Dummerston, VT.

$10,000 to Blue Cross Blue Shield of Massachusetts Foundation for Expanding Healthcare Access, Boston, MA.

$10,000 to Burlington Community Land Trust, Burlington, VT.

$10,000 to Central Vermont Early Childhood Council, Barre, VT.

$10,000 to Chittenden Emergency Food Shelf, Burlington, VT.

$10,000 to Committee on Temporary Shelter, Burlington, VT.

$10,000 to King Street Youth Center, Burlington, VT.

$10,000 to People of Addison County Together (PACT), Middlebury, VT.

$10,000 to Spectrum Youth and Family Services, Burlington, VT.

$10,000 to Visiting Nurse Association of Chittenden and Grand Isle Counties, Colchester, VT.

VIRGIN ISLANDS

9362
Bartner Family Foundation Trust ✧
c/o Young & Moriwaki, LLP
P.O. Box 25259
Gallows Bay Station
St. Croix, VI   00824

Established in 2000 in CT.
Donors: Robert G. Bartner; Beverly D.N. Bartner.
Foundation type: Independent foundation.
Financial data (yr. ended 12/31/05): Assets, $335,133 (M); expenditures, $530,374; qualifying distributions, $528,548; giving activities include $525,673 for 26 grants (high: $125,000; low: $250).
Purpose and activities: Giving primarily for the arts; funding also for human services.
Fields of interest: Performing arts; Arts; Education; Hospitals (general); Human services; Children/youth, services.
Limitations: Applications not accepted. Giving primarily in CT and NY; some funding in the U.S. Virgin Islands. No grants to individuals.
Application information: Contributes only to pre-selected organizations.
Trustees: Beverly D.N. Bartner; Robert G. Bartner; Nicole Bartner Graff; Arabella Bartner Higgins; Jennifer Bartner Indeck.
EIN: 137235081

9363
Community Foundation of the Virgin Islands ✧
(also known as CFVI)
c/o Royal Dane Mall
30 Dronningens Gade, Ste. 2C
P.O. Box 11790
St. Thomas, VI   00801   (340) 774-6031
Contact: Dee Baecher-Brown, Pres.

FAX: (340) 774-3852; E-mail: info@cfvi.net;
Additional E-mail: dbrown@cfvi.net; URL: http://www.cfvi.net/

Established in 1990 in the U.S. Virgin Islands.
Foundation type: Community foundation.
Financial data (yr. ended 12/31/04): Assets, $3,723,478 (M); gifts received, $2,016,000; expenditures, $1,265,000; giving activities include $1,108,000 for grants, and $70,000 for 31 grants to individuals.
Purpose and activities: The Community Foundation of the Virgin Island (CFVI) was created to serve both donors and nonprofit organizations of the Virgin Islands that want to ensure the highest quality of life for both present and future generations. Its primary goal is to build a growing collection of permanent funds, the income from which will be used to enhance the educational, physical, social, cultural and environmental well-being of the islands' people.
Fields of interest: Education; Health care; Children/youth, services; Child development, services; Family services; Community development.
Type of support: Grants to individuals.
Limitations: Giving limited to St. Croix, St. Thomas, St. John, and Water Island, VI.
Application information: Visit the foundation Web site for full application guidelines, specific deadlines, and requirements, including downloadable forms for mini-grants program and scholarships. Application form required.
  Initial approach: Submit application form
  Deadline(s): Mar. for mini-grants program
  Board meeting date(s): Monthly
Officers and Directors:* Ricardo Charaf,* Chair.; Catherine L. Mills,* 1st Vice-Chair.; John deJongh, Jr.,* 2nd Vice-Chair.; Dee Baecher-Brown, Pres.; Ruth H. Beagles,* Secy.; Sebastiano Paiewonsky Cassinelli,* Treas.; Henry L. Feuerzeig, Emeritus; Penny Feuerzeig, Emeritus; Charlotte Kimelman, Emeritus; Henry L. Kimelman, Emeritus; Pamela B. Berkowsky; Vivek A. Daswani; Sharon E.A. Hupprich; Randolph H. Knight; Hurdle H. "Trip" Lea III; Ishmael A. Meyers; Steven D. Morton; Trudie J. Prior; Suzanne Robinson; Betty Saks; Edward E. Thomas;

Marie E. ThomasGriffith; Thelma Ruth Watson-Comissiong; Henry U. Wheatley.
Number of staff: 1 part-time professional.
EIN: 660470703

9364
Prosser ICC Foundation, Inc. ✧
P.O. Box 1730
Christiansted, VI   00821-1730   (340) 713-8998
Contact: Bernice D. Knight, Admin.

Established in VI.
Foundation type: Independent foundation.
Financial data (yr. ended 12/31/05): Assets, $237,008 (M); gifts received, $500,000; expenditures, $369,670; qualifying distributions, $369,510; giving activities include $349,039 for 39 grants (high: $28,428; low: $210).
Fields of interest: Arts; Animal welfare; Athletics/sports, amateur leagues; Athletics/sports, golf; Boy scouts; Women, centers/services.
Limitations: Giving primarily in the Virgin Islands.
Application information: Application form required.
  Deadline(s): None
Officers: Dawn E. Prosser, Pres.; Adrian Prosser, V.P.; Luz Highfield, Secy.; Bernice D. Knight, Admin.
Director: Dwain Ford.
Trustee: Lillian Ebbesen.
EIN: 660565727
Selected grants: The following grants were reported in 2005.
$35,000 to Saint Croix Country Day School, Saint Croix, VI.
$28,428 to Good Hope School, Frederiksted, VI.
$25,000 to United Way of Saint Thomas-Saint John, Saint Thomas, VI.
$20,000 to Saint Croix Landmarks Society, Frederiksted, VI.
$20,000 to Womens Coalition of Saint Croix, Saint Croix, VI.
$10,000 to Humane Society of Saint Thomas, Saint Thomas, VI.
$5,000 to Pistarckle Theater, Saint Thomas, VI.
$2,622 to Antilles School, Saint Thomas, VI. 2 grants: $1,622, $1,000

VIRGINIA

9365
The 118 Foundation ✧
(formerly webMethods Foundation)
1350 Beverly Rd., No. 115-325
McLean, VA 22101 (703) 338-5948
E-mail: grants@webmethods.org; URL: http://www.webmethods.org/index.html

Established in 2000 in VA.
Donors: Caren DeWitt; Phillip Merrick; Will Dunbar.
Foundation type: Independent foundation.
Financial data (yr. ended 3/31/05): Assets, $761,475 (M); gifts received, $32,322; expenditures, $569,168; qualifying distributions, $441,974; giving activities include $383,634 for 27 grants (high: $100,000; low: $250).
Purpose and activities: The mission of The 118 Foundation is to support organizations that play a key role in making communities better in the areas of housing, education, and healthcare. The foundation has also expanded its outreach internationally to support organizations that also fight poverty, create jobs, and transform lives.
Fields of interest: Education; Health care; Housing/shelter.
Type of support: Management development/capacity building.
Limitations: Applications not accepted. Giving limited to the greater Washington, DC, area and Santa Clara and Alameda counties, CA. No support for organizations lacking 501(c)(3) status. No grants to individuals, or for endowments, capital campaigns, scholarships, or medical research.
Application information: Contributes only to pre-selected organizations.
Officers and Directors: * Caren DeWitt,* Chair.; Diane Tollefson, Exec. Dir.; Garland Hall; James M. "Marty" Irving; Phillip Merrick; Eric Morse.
EIN: 542005915
Selected grants: The following grants were reported in 2004.
$40,000 to Association of Clinicians for the Underserved, McLean, VA. For dental health education program for doctors and other clinicians.
$37,500 to In2Books, DC. For expansion of literacy focus, penal program for ten thousand DC public school children.
$35,000 to CASA of Maryland, Takoma Park, MD. For Salud es Vida (Health is Life) outreach program.
$30,000 to Community of Hope, DC. For general operating support for relocation of health clinic.
$30,000 to Healthy Babies Project, DC. For program support.
$25,000 to Bill Wilson Center, Santa Clara, CA. For health education and wellness program for homeless and at-risk youth.
$25,000 to Center for Multicultural Human Services, Falls Church, VA. For Graduate Internship Field Training (GIFT) program.
$25,000 to Community Health Partnership of Santa Clara County, San Jose, CA. To fund publication of third edition of the Women's Health Resource Directory.
$10,000 to N Street Village, DC. For Wellness Center program.
$7,500 to Volunteer Fairfax, Fairfax, VA.

9366
Jessie & Hertha Adams Charitable Trust ✧
c/o BB&T
P.O. Box 268
Alexandria, VA 22313

Established in 2003 in MD.
Foundation type: Independent foundation.
Financial data (yr. ended 12/31/05): Assets, $17,595,864 (M); gifts received, $47,373; expenditures, $1,088,975; qualifying distributions, $882,740; giving activities include $882,740 for 31 grants (high: $44,137; low: $11,034).
Purpose and activities: Giving primarily for children with disabilities.
Fields of interest: Hospitals (specialty); Human services; Children, services; Developmentally disabled, centers & services; Protestant agencies & churches.
Limitations: Applications not accepted. No grants to individuals.
Application information: Contributes only to pre-selected organizations.
Trustees: Carole S. Brudin; BB&T; Burke & Herbert Bank and Trust Co.
EIN: 256821173

9367
The Alleghany Foundation
450 W. Main St.
P.O. Box 1176
Covington, VA 24426 (540) 962-0970
FAX: (540) 962-1170; E-mail: allegfnd@aol.com

Established in 1995 in VA; converted from the sale of Alleghany Regional Hospital Corporation to Columbia/HCA Healthcare Corp. The foundation awarded its first grants in Nov. 1996.
Foundation type: Independent foundation.
Financial data (yr. ended 5/31/05): Assets, $57,230,467 (M); expenditures, $1,221,714; qualifying distributions, $717,039; giving activities include $652,850 for grants.
Purpose and activities: The foundation awards grants to organizations serving the Alleghany County, Covington, and Clifton Forge areas of VA, with an emphasis on new and different programs that improve the community's quality of life. The foundation awarded its first grants in Nov. 1996.
Fields of interest: Community development.
Type of support: Continuing support; Capital campaigns; Building/renovation; Equipment; Land acquisition; Program development; Publication; Curriculum development; Consulting services; Matching/challenge support.
Limitations: Giving primarily in Alleghany County, Covington, and Clifton Forge, VA. No support for debt reduction, endowment funds, ongoing general operating expenses, or existing deficits. No grants to individuals, or to religious organizations.
Publications: Application guidelines; Annual report; Informational brochure (including application guidelines).
Application information: Application form not required.
Initial approach: Letter
Copies of proposal: 13
Deadline(s): Mar. 1 and Sept. 1
Board meeting date(s): Quarterly
Final notification: June 1 and Dec. 1
Officers and Directors: * James D. Snyder,* Pres.; James I. Dill,* V.P.; Patrick H. Winston, Jr.,* Secy.; Charles Kahle,* Treas.; Ward H. Robons, Jr., Exec.

Dir.; Harrison L. Fridley, Jr.; Jack A. Hammond; George J. Kostel; Wallace C. Nunley; John G. Sanders; William J. Withrow; Anne L. Wright.
Number of staff: 2 part-time support.
EIN: 541027400

9368
American Woodmark Foundation, Inc. ☆
3102 Shawnee Dr.
Winchester, VA 22601-4282 (540) 665-9100
Contact: Brenda K. Dupont, Secy.-Treas.
E-mail: awfoundation@woodmark.com; URL: http://www.americanwoodmark.com/about.asp?iAreaID=1&iSectionID=7

Established in 1995 in VA.
Donor: American Woodmark Corp.
Foundation type: Company-sponsored foundation.
Financial data (yr. ended 4/30/06): Assets, $646,389 (M); gifts received, $355,910; expenditures, $343,258; qualifying distributions, $341,700; giving activities include $341,700 for grants.
Purpose and activities: The foundation supports organizations involved with education, domestic violence, housing, and public safety.
Fields of interest: Education; Crime/violence prevention, domestic violence; Housing/shelter; Disasters, preparedness/services.
Type of support: General/operating support; Continuing support; Annual campaigns; Capital campaigns; Building/renovation; Equipment; Curriculum development.
Limitations: Giving limited to areas of company operations in AZ, GA, IN, KY, MD, MN, OK, TN, VA, and WV. No support for private foundations or political organizations. No grants to individuals.
Application information: Application form not required.
Initial approach: Proposal
Copies of proposal: 1
Deadline(s): None
Board meeting date(s): Jan., Apr., July, and Oct.
Final notification: Within 3 months
Officers and Directors: * David Blount,* Chair.; Brenda K. Dupont,* Secy.-Treas.; Alan S. Davis.
EIN: 541759773
Selected grants: The following grants were reported in 2004.
$30,000 to Glass-Glen Burnie Museum, Winchester, VA. For construction of the Museum of Shenandoah Valley.
$15,353 to Winchester Day Nursery, Winchester, VA. For capital improvements and repairs.
$10,000 to Blue Ridge Hospice, Winchester, VA. For operating support.
$10,000 to Hardy County Parks and Recreation Commission, Brighton Park, Moorefield, WV.
$9,500 to Our Health, Winchester, VA. For cabinets.
$8,700 to New Life Alumni and Friends, Winchester, VA. To purchase furniture.
$7,500 to Leary Educational Foundation, Winchester, VA. For construction of Adventure Challenge Ropes Course.
$5,500 to Henry and William Evans Home for Children, Winchester, VA. To purchase cabinets.
$5,000 to Moorefield Volunteer Fire Company, Moorefield, WV. For operating support.
$3,000 to Cookson Hills Community Action Foundation, Tahlequah, OK. For operating support.

9369
AMERIGROUP Foundation ✧
4425 Corporation Ln.
Virginia Beach, VA 23462-3103 (757) 490-6900
Contact: Amy Sheyer
FAX: (757) 222-2360; URL: http://
www.amerigroupcorp.com/Foundation/

Donor: AMERIGROUP Corp.
Foundation type: Company-sponsored foundation.
Financial data (yr. ended 12/31/04): Assets,
$2,644,144 (M); gifts received, $2,000,000;
expenditures, $837,676; qualifying distributions,
$837,132; giving activities include $719,456 for
236 grants (high: $25,000; low: $100).
Purpose and activities: The foundation supports
organizations involved with education, health,
human services, community development, disabled
people, and economically disadvantaged people.
Fields of interest: Arts, cultural/ethnic awareness;
Education; Health care, research; Health care,
public policy; Health care, equal rights; Health care;
YM/YWCAs & YM/YWHAs; Human services;
Community development; Federated giving
programs; Disabilities, people with; Economically
disadvantaged.
Type of support: General/operating support.
Limitations: Giving primarily in FL, IL, MD, NJ, NY,
TX, VA, and Washington, DC. No support for private
foundations, fraternal, social, athletic, labor, or
veterans' organizations, political parties or
candidates, or for organizations not of direct benefit
to the entire community. No grants to individuals, or
for endowments, capital campaigns, tickets, tables,
benefits, raffles, souvenir programs, fundraising
dinners, golf outings, trips, tours, or similar events.
Application information: Application form required.
   Initial approach: Download application form and
      mail or fax to foundation
   Deadline(s): None
Officers and Directors:* Jeffrey L. McWaters,*
Chair. and Pres.; Stanley F. Baldwin,* V.P. and
Secy.; Sherri E. Lee, V.P. and Treas.; Scott Anglin,
V.P.; Nancy L. Grden,* V.P.; John E. Littel,* V.P.;
Richard C. Zoretic,* V.P.
EIN: 542014061
Selected grants: The following grants were reported
in 2003.
$60,000 to National Association for Elimination of
   Health Disparities, DC.
$5,000 to March of Dimes Birth Defects Foundation,
   Dallas, TX.
$5,000 to Sickle Cell Disease Association of
   America, Culver City, CA.
$2,500 to Cancer Institute of New Jersey, New
   Brunswick, NJ.
$1,500 to Plainfield Health Services, Plainfield, NJ.
$1,000 to Cure Autism Now Foundation, Los
   Angeles, CA.
$1,000 to Saint Petersburg Free Clinic, Saint
   Petersburg, FL.
$1,000 to Trinitas Hospital, Elizabeth, NJ.
$500 to Family Health Centers of Baltimore,
   Baltimore, MD.
$500 to Healthy Mothers, Healthy Babies Coalition
   of Palm Beach County, Boynton Beach, FL.

9370
K. C. Ames Foundation ✧
(formerly Sleeper Vision Mission Supporting
Organization)
c/o Sterling Foundation Mgmt.
11921 Freedom Dr., Ste. 730
Reston, VA 20190 (703) 437-9720

Established in 2004 in VA.
Foundation type: Independent foundation.
Financial data (yr. ended 12/31/04): Assets,
$25,207 (M); expenditures, $531,968; qualifying
distributions, $531,968; giving activities include
$525,000 for 20 grants (high: $200,000; low:
$5,000).
Fields of interest: Higher education; Science, public
education; Social sciences, public policy; Public
policy, research; Public affairs.
Limitations: Giving on a national basis, with some
emphasis on CA, Washington, DC, and NY. No
grants to individuals.
Application information: Application form not
required.
   Initial approach: Letter
   Deadline(s): None
Officer and Director:* Roger Silk,* Pres.
EIN: 522287599

9371
Arlington Community Foundation ✧
2525 Wilson Blvd.
Arlington, VA 22201 (703) 243-4785
Contact: Patricia A. E. Rodgers, Exec. Dir.
FAX: (703) 243-4796; URL: http://www.arlcf.org

Established in 1991 in VA.
Foundation type: Community foundation.
Financial data (yr. ended 6/30/05): Assets,
$7,026,892 (M); gifts received, $580,023;
expenditures, $924,574; giving activities include
$486,720 for 60 grants (high: $10,000; low: $100),
and $186,500 for 112 grants to individuals (high:
$5,000; low: $500).
Purpose and activities: The foundation provides
support for the arts, education, hospitals, human
services, community development, and public
administration.
Fields of interest: Performing arts; Humanities;
Arts; Adult education—literacy, basic skills & GED;
Education, reading; Education; Environment; Health
care; Food services; Housing/shelter; Disasters,
Hurricane Katrina; Safety/disasters; Children/
youth, services; Aging, centers/services;
Minorities/immigrants, centers/services; Human
services; Community development; Government/
public administration; Aging; Minorities; Native
Americans/American Indians; Women; Economically
disadvantaged.
Type of support: General/operating support;
Continuing support; Management development/
capacity building; Emergency funds; Program
development; Seed money; Curriculum
development; Scholarship funds; Technical
assistance; Consulting services; Grants to
individuals.
Limitations: Giving limited to the Arlington, VA, area.
No support for religious purposes. No grants to
individuals (except for specific awards by
nomination), or for endowments, capital campaigns
or for debts.
Publications: Application guidelines; Annual report;
Financial statement; Grants list; Informational

brochure; Multi-year report; Newsletter; Program
policy statement.
Application information: Visit foundation Web site
for application form and guidelines. Application form
required.
   Initial approach: Letter or telephone
   Copies of proposal: 1
   Deadline(s): Sept. for general grants
   Board meeting date(s): Feb., Apr., June, Aug.,
      Oct., and Dec.
   Final notification: 1 week
Officers and Trustees:* Hon. William T. Newman,
Jr.,* Pres.; John P. Andelin,* V.P.; Christine T.
Milliken,* Secy.; Sidney G. Simmonds,* Treas.;
Patricia A. E. Rodgers, Exec. Dir.; Nancy A. Albrittain;
Richard Anderson; Charles Bean; Ellen M. Bozman;
Pauline A. Ellison; Todd Endo; Julian Fore; Pamela
Y. Galloway-Tabb; Leni Gonzalez; Robert H.
Hawthorne; Linda E. Henderson; Fernanda Howard;
Jonathan C. Kinney; Donald O. Manning; John R.
Maxwell; Scott O'Gorman, Jr.; Susan S. Prominski;
Lola C. Reinsch; Libby Ross; Diane M. Smith; Marion
Spraggins; Keegan Stroup; Michael Timpane;
Audrey Wyatt.
Number of staff: 1 full-time professional; 2 part-time
professional.
EIN: 541602838

9372
The Bansal Foundation ✧
1861 International Dr.
McLean, VA 22102
Contact: Sanjeev K. Bansal, Tr.

Established in 1998 in MA and VA.
Donor: Sanjeev K. Bansal.
Foundation type: Independent foundation.
Financial data (yr. ended 12/31/04): Assets,
$11,472,162 (M); expenditures, $634,403;
qualifying distributions, $545,670; giving activities
include $545,670 for 8 grants (high: $400,000;
low: $1,000).
Purpose and activities: Giving primarily to a
charitable gift fund, as well as to other public and
community foundations; funding also for the arts.
Fields of interest: Media, radio; Performing arts;
Foundations (public); Foundations (community).
Limitations: Giving on a national basis. No grants to
individuals.
Application information: Application form required.
   Initial approach: Letter
   Deadline(s): None
Trustee: Sanjeev K. Bansal.
EIN: 541933631
Selected grants: The following grants were reported
in 2004.
$400,000 to Fidelity Investments Charitable Gift
   Fund, Boston, MA.
$100,000 to American University, DC. For WAMU
   88.5FM radio station.
$20,000 to Upakar, The Indo-American Community
   Foundation, Reston, VA.
$11,170 to Wolf Trap Foundation for the Performing
   Arts, Vienna, VA.
$10,000 to Inova Health System Foundation, Falls
   Church, VA.
$2,500 to Leukemia & Lymphoma Society, White
   Plains, NY.
$1,000 to American Indian Foundation, New York,
   NY.
$1,000 to Holy Transfiguration Society of Saint
   John, Eagle Harbor, MI.

9373
The D. N. Batten Foundation ✧
(also known as The Batten-Rolph Foundation)
P.O. Box 360
Keswick, VA 22947

Established in 1997 in VA.
Donor: Dorothy B. Rolph.
Foundation type: Independent foundation.
Financial data (yr. ended 12/31/04): Assets, $2,843,971 (M); expenditures, $561,605; qualifying distributions, $550,000; giving activities include $550,000 for 5 grants (high: $200,000; low: $50,000).
Purpose and activities: Giving primarily for education and the arts.
Fields of interest: Arts; Education; Environment.
Limitations: Applications not accepted. Giving primarily in VA. No grants to individuals.
Application information: Contributes only to pre-selected organizations.
Officer: Dorothy N. Batten, Pres.
Director: Frank Batten, Jr.
EIN: 541864288

9374
The Batten Foundation ✧
150 W. Brambleton Ave.
Norfolk, VA 23510-2018

Established in 1988 in VA.
Donor: Frank Batten.
Foundation type: Independent foundation.
Financial data (yr. ended 6/30/05): Assets, $43,989,541 (M); expenditures, $748,984; qualifying distributions, $650,000; giving activities include $650,000 for 8 grants (high: $350,000; low: $10,000).
Purpose and activities: Giving primarily for higher education, including colleges and foundations.
Fields of interest: Higher education; Business school/education; Education; Human services; Federated giving programs.
Limitations: Applications not accepted. Giving primarily in VA. No grants to individuals.
Application information: Contributes only to pre-selected organizations.
Officer: Frank Batten, Pres.
EIN: 541451569
Selected grants: The following grants were reported in 2004.
$1,000,000 to Mariners Museum, Newport News, VA. For general support.
$100,000 to Hollins University, Roanoke, VA. For general support.
$50,000 to Old Dominion University Educational Foundation, Norfolk, VA. For general support.
$40,000 to Culver Educational Foundation, Culver, IN. For general support.
$40,000 to W H R O-FM TV, Norfolk, VA. For general support.
$25,000 to Chrysler Museum, Norfolk, VA. For general support.
$25,000 to Norfolk Academy, Norfolk, VA. For general support.
$25,000 to Raleigh Tavern Society, Williamsburg, VA. For general support.
$5,000 to Chesapeake Bay Academy, Virginia Beach, VA. For general support.
$5,000 to Miller Center Foundation, Charlottesville, VA. For general support.

9375
Aimee & Frank Batten, Jr. Foundation ▼ ✧
150 W. Brambleton Ave.
Norfolk, VA 23510

Established in 1998 in VA.
Donor: Frank Batten, Jr.
Foundation type: Independent foundation.
Financial data (yr. ended 12/31/04): Assets, $56,374,497 (M); expenditures, $4,317,604; qualifying distributions, $3,981,500; giving activities include $3,981,500 for 51 grants (high: $1,000,000; low: $1,000; average: $5,000–$100,000).
Purpose and activities: Giving primarily for Christian causes.
Fields of interest: Arts; Human services; Christian agencies & churches.
Limitations: Applications not accepted. No grants to individuals.
Application information: Contributes only to pre-selected organizations.
Officer and Director:* Frank Batten, Jr.,* Pres. and Secy.-Treas.
EIN: 541879266
Selected grants: The following grants were reported in 2003.
$1,745,000 to Norfolk Christian Schools, Norfolk, VA. 4 grants: $620,000 (For general support), $125,000 (For general support), $875,000 (For general support), $125,000 (For general support).
$1,000,000 to Wycliffe Bible Translators, Orlando, FL. For general support.
$500,000 to Samaritans Purse, Boone, NC. For general support.
$100,000 to Salvation Army of Hampton Roads, Norfolk, VA. For general support.
$60,000 to Project Light, Norfolk, VA. For general support.
$60,000 to Regent University, Virginia Beach, VA. For general support.
$60,000 to Tabernacle Church of Norfolk, Norfolk, VA. For general support.

9376
Beazley Foundation, Inc.
3720 Brighton St.
Portsmouth, VA 23707-1788 (757) 393-1605
Contact: Hon. Richard S. Bray, Pres.
FAX: (757) 393-4708;
E-mail: info@beazleyfoundation.org; E-mail for Donna M. Russell, Assoc. Dir.: donna@beazleyfoundation.org; URL: http://www.beazleyfoundation.org/index.html

Incorporated in 1948 in VA.
Donors: Fred W. Beazley†; Marie C. Beazley†; Fred W. Beazley, Jr.†.
Foundation type: Independent foundation.
Financial data (yr. ended 12/31/05): Assets, $64,237,265 (M); expenditures, $4,327,757; qualifying distributions, $3,990,990; giving activities include $3,002,245 for 74 grants (high: $335,878; low: $50; average: $5,000–$100,000), and $355,752 for foundation-administered programs.
Purpose and activities: To further the causes of charity, education, and religion. Support also for higher, secondary and medical education, youth agencies, community development, the aged, and other general charities, including health organizations and hospitals, the homeless, religion, and recreation.
Fields of interest: Secondary school/education; Higher education; Medical school/education; Education; Hospitals (general); Health care; Health organizations, association; Recreation; Youth, services; Aging, centers/services; Homeless, human services; Community development; Religion; Aging; Homeless.
Type of support: General/operating support; Capital campaigns; Building/renovation; Equipment; Endowments; Program development; Scholarship funds; Matching/challenge support.
Limitations: Giving primarily in the South Hampton Roads area, VA. No support for environmental, cultural, media, international or national programs. No grants to individuals.
Publications: Annual report; Biennial report; Financial statement; Grants list; Program policy statement.
Application information: Application information and form available on foundation Web site. Application form required.
Initial approach: Letter or telephone
Copies of proposal: 1
Deadline(s): 1st of the month preceding board meeting. See foundation Web site for current dates
Board meeting date(s): Feb., Apr., July, and Nov.
Final notification: Within 2 weeks
Officers and Trustees:* Hon. Richard S. Bray,* Pres.; Diane Pomeroy Griffin,* V.P.; P. Ward Robinett, Jr.,* Secy.; Leroy T. Canoles, Jr.; Hon. William H. Hodges; Lawrence W. I'Anson, Jr.; W. Ashton Lewis; Whitney G. Saunders.
Number of staff: 3 full-time professional.
EIN: 540550100
Selected grants: The following grants were reported in 2005.
$200,000 to Portsmouth Community Health Center, Portsmouth, VA.
$180,000 to Virginia Foundation for Independent Colleges, Richmond, VA.
$125,000 to YMCA of Portsmouth, Portsmouth, VA.
$105,000 to Virginia Wesleyan College, Virginia Beach, VA.
$100,000 to Eastern Virginia Medical School, Norfolk, VA.
$56,000 to United Way of South Hampton Roads, Norfolk, VA. 2 grants: $50,000, $6,000
$50,000 to YMCA of South Hampton Roads, Norfolk, VA.
$25,000 to An Achievable Dream, Newport News, VA.
$25,000 to YWCA of South Hampton Roads, Norfolk, VA.

9377
Eric and Marianne Billings Foundation, Inc. ✧
1001 19th St., 18th Fl.
Arlington, VA 22209

Established in 1993 in VA.
Donors: Eric Billings; Marianne Billings.
Foundation type: Independent foundation.
Financial data (yr. ended 6/30/05): Assets, $25,401 (M); gifts received, $75,000; expenditures, $603,810; qualifying distributions, $603,309; giving activities include $603,309 for 25 grants (high: $246,125; low: $200).

Purpose and activities: Giving primarily to children and youth organizations with emphasis on education, health and social services.

Fields of interest: Higher education; Education; Health care; Boys & girls clubs; Human services; Children/youth, services.

Limitations: Applications not accepted. Giving primarily in MA, MD, and Washington, DC. No grants to individuals.

Application information: Contributes only to pre-selected organizations.

Directors: Eric Billings; Marianne Billings; Ned S. Scherer.

EIN: 521853715

9378
Blue Dot Foundation ◇

(formerly Satori Foundation)
8404 Parham Ct.
McLean, VA 22102

Established in 1994 in VA.
Donor: Steven M. Rales.
Foundation type: Independent foundation.
Financial data (yr. ended 12/31/05): Assets, $10,395,497 (M); expenditures, $3,010,802; qualifying distributions, $2,963,821; giving activities include $2,961,500 for 16 grants (high: $2,000,000; low: $2,500).
Fields of interest: Higher education, university; Christian agencies & churches.
Limitations: Applications not accepted. Giving primarily in Washington, DC. No grants to individuals.
Application information: Contributes only to pre-selected organizations.
Officers and Director:* Steven M. Rales,* Chair.; Michael G. Ryan, Pres.; Joseph O. Bunting III, V.P.; Teresa L.C. Baldwin, Secy.-Treas.
EIN: 541739160

9379
Blue Moon Fund, Inc. ◇

(formerly W. Alton Jones Foundation, Inc.)
433 Park St.
Charlottesville, VA 22902-5178
(434) 295-5160
FAX: (434) 295-6894;
E-mail: info@bluemoonfund.org; URL: http://www.bluemoonfund.org

Incorporated in 1944 in NY as W. Alton Jones Foundation. Underwent restructure in 2001, and was renamed Blue Moon Fund (retaining original EI number) and two new funds were created, Oak Hill Fund and Edgerton Foundation.
Donor: W. Alton Jones†.
Foundation type: Independent foundation.
Financial data (yr. ended 12/31/04): Assets, $189,776,311 (M); expenditures, $7,296,675; qualifying distributions, $6,467,856; giving activities include $3,994,308 for 38 grants (high: $634,000; low: $50; average: $50,000–$250,000), and $25,619 for 1 foundation-administered program and $875,000 for 1 loan/program-related investment.
Purpose and activities: The fund supports initiatives that elevate the human condition by comprehensively addressing human consumption, the natural world, and economic advancement,

including sponsoring a fellows program aimed at cultivating cutting-edge approaches to these issues.
Fields of interest: Environment, natural resources; Environment, energy; Urban/community development.
Type of support: Program-related investments/loans; Matching/challenge support; General/operating support; Program development; Fellowships.
Limitations: Giving in the Americas and Asia. No grants for lobbying, advertising, dissertations, thesis and other academic work.
Application information: The fund is an initiative-based organization and generally does not take unsolicited proposals. Staff review letters of inquiry submitted through the foundation's Web site and invite proposals.
Initial approach: Eligibility quiz on foundation Web site
Board meeting date(s): Apr. and Nov.
Officers and Directors:* Diane Edgerton Miller,* C.E.O. and Pres.; Ethan A. Miller,* V.P. and Secy.; Adrian Forsyth, Ph.D., V.P., Progs.; Ji-Qiang Zhang, V.P., Progs.; Diane Schmidt, C.F.O.; Patricia Jones Edgerton,* Treas.; Beverly Lamb, Compt.; Jaime Yordan.
EIN: 136034219
Selected grants: The following grants were reported in 2004.
$500,000 to Energy Foundation, San Francisco, CA.
$260,000 to Natural Resources Defense Council, New York, NY.
$200,000 to World Wildlife Fund, DC.
$190,000 to Conservation International, DC.
$160,000 to Worldwatch Institute, DC.
$150,000 to Enterprise Foundation, New York, NY.
$130,000 to Nature Conservancy, Charlottesville, VA.
$120,000 to New Jersey Institute of Technology, Newark, NJ.
$115,000 to WildAid, San Francisco, CA.
$100,000 to University of Cincinnati, Cincinnati, OH.

9380
The Bryant Foundation ◇

P.O. Box 1239
Stephens City, VA 22655 (540) 868-2183
Contact: Arthur H. Bryant II, Pres.

Established about 1949.
Donor: J.C. Herbert Bryant†.
Foundation type: Independent foundation.
Financial data (yr. ended 12/31/05): Assets, $8,624,419 (M); expenditures, $1,527,742; qualifying distributions, $1,446,521; giving activities include $1,446,521 for 46 grants (high: $500,000; low: $100).
Purpose and activities: Giving for higher and other education, health and human services, historic preservation, amateur sports groups and civic affairs.
Fields of interest: Historic preservation/historical societies; Elementary school/education; Higher education; Education; Health care; Athletics/sports, amateur leagues; Government/public administration.
Type of support: Employee matching gifts.
Limitations: Giving primarily in VA. No grants to individuals.
Application information: Application form not required.

Initial approach: Letter or telephone
Deadline(s): None
Officers: Arthur H. Bryant II, Pres. and Treas.; Arthur H. Bryant, Jr., Secy.
Trustee: James T. Holland.
EIN: 546032840

9381
The Robert G. Cabell III and Maude Morgan Cabell Foundation ▼

901 E. Cary St., Ste. 1402
Richmond, VA 23219-4037 (804) 780-2050
Contact: John B. Werner, Exec. Dir.

Incorporated in 1957 in VA.
Donors: Robert G. Cabell III†; Maude Morgan Cabell†.
Foundation type: Independent foundation.
Financial data (yr. ended 12/31/05): Assets, $91,914,800 (M); expenditures, $3,844,901; qualifying distributions, $3,589,000; giving activities include $3,589,000 for 36 grants (high: $400,000; low: $10,000; average: $50,000–$100,000).
Purpose and activities: Grants primarily for higher education, health care, historic preservation, the arts and cultural projects, community development, and social welfare.
Fields of interest: Historic preservation/historical societies; Arts; Higher education; Human services; Community development.
Type of support: Capital campaigns; Building/renovation; Equipment; Endowments; Matching/challenge support.
Limitations: Giving limited to VA. No support for special interest groups. No grants to individuals, or for operating programs, or research projects.
Publications: Application guidelines; Informational brochure (including application guidelines).
Application information: Application form not required.
Initial approach: Letter
Copies of proposal: 1
Deadline(s): Apr. 1 and Oct. 1
Board meeting date(s): Mar., May, and Nov.
Final notification: Promptly following spring and fall board grant review meetings
Officers and Directors:* J. Read Branch,* Pres. and Treas.; Charles L. Cabell,* Secy.; John B. Werner, Exec. Dir.; Joseph L. Antrim III; J. Read Branch, Jr.; Patteson Branch, Jr.; John B. Cabell; Elizabeth Cabell Jennings; Mary Z. Zeugner.
Number of staff: 1 part-time professional; 1 part-time support.
EIN: 546039157
Selected grants: The following grants were reported in 2004.
$300,000 to Randolph-Macon College, Ashland, VA. For restoration and expansion of Thomas Branch Hall.
$250,000 to Association for the Preservation of Virginia Antiquities, Richmond, VA. For museum construction and Jamestown Island Richmond.
$250,000 to Montpelier Foundation, Montpelier Station, VA. For restoration of mansion.
$250,000 to University of Virginia, Charlottesville, VA. For restoration of Ranges room.
$200,000 to Hollins University, Roanoke, VA. For renovation of Presser Hall.
$150,000 to Maymont Foundation, Richmond, VA. For restoration of Maymont House basement.

$100,000 to Ferrum College, Ferrum, VA. For classroom construction.

$90,000 to Bridgewater College, Bridgewater, VA. For renovations and equipment for Writing Center Lab.

$54,000 to Ladies Memorial Association of Petersburg, Petersburg, VA. For New Lexan screening of Tiffany windows.

$50,000 to Apple Ridge Farm, Roanoke, VA. For construction and expansion of facilities.

9382
Camp Foundation ◇
P.O. Box 813
Franklin, VA 23851
Contact: Bobby B. Worrell, Exec. Dir.

Incorporated in 1942 in VA.
Donors: James L. Camp†; P.D. Camp†; and their families.
Foundation type: Independent foundation.
Financial data (yr. ended 12/31/05): Assets, $19,760,245 (M); expenditures, $866,841; qualifying distributions, $824,091; giving activities include $610,775 for 67 grants, and $90,000 for 28 grants to individuals.
Purpose and activities: To provide or aid in providing, in or near the town of Franklin, VA, parks, playgrounds, recreational facilities, libraries, hospitals, clinics, homes for the aged or needy, refuge for delinquent, dependent or neglected children, training schools, or other like institutions or activities. Grants also to select organizations statewide, with emphasis on youth agencies, safety programs, hospitals, mental illness, and nursing programs, higher and secondary education, including scholarships filed through high school principals, recreation, the environment, historic preservation, and cultural programs.
Fields of interest: Historic preservation/historical societies; Arts; Secondary school/education; Higher education; Libraries/library science; Education; Environment; Hospitals (general); Nursing care; Health care; Mental health/crisis services; Safety/disasters; Recreation; Children/youth, services; Aging, centers/services; Government/public administration; Aging.
Type of support: Annual campaigns; Building/renovation; Equipment; Land acquisition; Emergency funds; Seed money; Scholarship funds; Research; Scholarships—to individuals; Matching/challenge support.
Limitations: Giving primarily in the city of Franklin, and Southampton and Isle of Wight counties, VA.
Publications: Application guidelines.
Application information: 4-year scholarships awarded to graduating high school seniors who are residents of the City of Franklin or the counties of Southampton and Isle of Wight. Application form not required.
Initial approach: Proposal
Copies of proposal: 7
Deadline(s): Submit proposal between June and Aug.; deadline Sept. 1. Scholarship application deadline is Feb. 26 for filing with high school principals
Board meeting date(s): May and Nov.
Final notification: 3 months
Officers and Directors:* Robert C. Ray,* Chair.; Sol W. Rawls, Jr.,* Pres.; Westbrook Parker,* V.P.; John M. Camp, Jr.,* Treas.; Bobby B. Worrell,* Exec. Dir.; John M. Camp III; W.M. Camp, Jr.; William W. Cutchins; Randy B. Drake; John R. Marks; Paul

Camp Marks; J. Edward Moyler, Jr.; John D. Munford; S. Waite Rawls, Jr.; Richard E. Ray; Toy D. Savage, Jr.
Number of staff: 2 full-time professional; 1 part-time support.
EIN: 546052488

9383
Ruth and Henry Campbell Foundation
c/o Wachovia Bank, N.A.
1021 E. Cary St.
Richmond, VA 23219
Contact: Karen N. Buchanan, V.P., Char. Svcs., Wachovia Bank

Established in 1957.
Foundation type: Independent foundation.
Financial data (yr. ended 12/31/05): Assets, $13,713,401 (M); expenditures, $815,756; qualifying distributions, $639,056; giving activities include $606,934 for 78 grants (high: $112,500; low: $500).
Fields of interest: Arts; Elementary/secondary education; Higher education; Disasters, preparedness/services; Government/public administration.
Type of support: Annual campaigns; Capital campaigns; Building/renovation; Scholarship funds.
Limitations: Giving primarily in VA.
Application information: Application form not required.
Initial approach: Letter
Deadline(s): None
Directors: John M. Camp, Jr.; Paul D. Camp III; Paul Camp Marks; Harry W. Walker III.
Trustee: Wachovia Bank, N.A.
EIN: 546031023

9384
CAP Charitable Foundation USA ◇ ☆
1160 Pepsi Pl., Ste. 206
Charlottesville, VA 22901-0807
(434) 964-1588
Contact: Fran Hardey, Exec. Asst.
FAX: (434) 964-1589; *E-mail:* franh@ronbrown.org

Established in 1986 in DE.
Donor: CAP America Trust.
Foundation type: Independent foundation.
Financial data (yr. ended 12/31/05): Assets, $101,611 (M); gifts received, $1,928,075; expenditures, $1,834,802; qualifying distributions, $816,665; giving activities include $816,665 for grants.
Purpose and activities: Giving primarily college scholarships to African-American high school seniors through a scholarship program. Students must be U.S. citizens or have a permanent resident Visa card, attend a 4-year college or university in the U.S., and demonstrate financial need.
Type of support: Scholarships—to individuals.
Limitations: Giving on a national basis.
Publications: Application guidelines; Informational brochure; Newsletter.
Application information: Application guidelines and downloadable application form available on Web site. Faxed submissions will not be accepted. Application form required.
Initial approach: By mail
Deadline(s): Jan. 9 for scholarships
Final notification: Apr. 15

Officer: Michael Mallory, Pres.
Number of staff: 2 full-time professional; 1 full-time support; 1 part-time support.
EIN: 541832314

9385
The CarMax Foundation ◇
12800 Tuckahoe Creek Pkwy.
Richmond, VA 23238 (804) 747-0422
E-mail: kmxfoundation@carmax.com; *URL:* http://www.carmaxcares.com

Established in 2003 in VA.
Donor: CarMax Auto Superstores, Inc.
Foundation type: Company-sponsored foundation.
Financial data (yr. ended 2/28/05): Assets, $127,884 (M); gifts received, $1,193,384; expenditures, $1,127,741; qualifying distributions, $1,127,717; giving activities include $1,024,154 for 43 grants (high: $150,000; low: $500), and $14,697 for 93 employee matching gifts.
Purpose and activities: The foundation supports organizations involved with education, disaster relief, automobile safety, and youth leadership.
Fields of interest: Elementary/secondary education; Vocational education; Education; Disasters, preparedness/services; Safety, automotive safety; Youth development; Children.
Type of support: General/operating support; Program development; Employee volunteer services; Employee matching gifts; Grants to individuals.
Limitations: Giving primarily in areas of company operations, with emphasis on the greater Richmond, VA, area; giving also to national organizations. No support for discriminatory organizations, organizations posing a conflict of interest with CarMax's mission, goals, programs, or products, fraternal, athletic, or social organizations, or veterans', labor, or political organizations. No grants for debt reduction, political campaigns, or capital campaigns, endowments, event sponsorships, or scholarships; no vehicle donations.
Publications: Annual report; IRS Form 990-PF.
Application information: Application form required.
Initial approach: Mail letter of inquiry to foundation; complete online application form
Deadline(s): None
Board meeting date(s): Quarterly
Final notification: Mar. 31, June 30, Sept. 30, and Dec. 31
Officers and Directors:* Joseph Kunkel,* Pres.; Mike Dolan,* V.P.; Scott Rivas,* V.P.; Thomas Reedy,* Treas.
Number of staff: 1 full-time professional.
EIN: 383681796

9386
Alexander Berkeley Carrington, Jr. and Ruth S. Carrington Charitable Trust ◇
c/o American National Bank and Trust Co.
P.O. Box 191
Danville, VA 24543-0191
Contact: E. Budge Kent, Jr.

Established in 1985 in VA.
Donors: Alexander Berkeley Carrington†; Ruth Simpson Carrington†.
Foundation type: Independent foundation.
Financial data (yr. ended 2/28/05): Assets, $20,092,591 (M); expenditures, $1,250,150;

qualifying distributions, $1,006,930; giving activities include $997,950 for 43 grants (high: $124,940; low: $500).

Purpose and activities: Giving primarily to cultural and educational institutions and to Christian agencies and churches.

Fields of interest: Arts; Higher education; Health care; Human services; Christian agencies & churches.

Limitations: Applications not accepted. Giving primarily in Danville, VA. No grants to individuals.

Application information: Contributes only to pre-selected organizations. Unsolicited requests for funds not accepted.

Trustees: Kirk B. Echols; James W. Perkinson; R. Lee Yancey; American National Bank and Trust Co.

EIN: 546223108

Selected grants: The following grants were reported in 2005.

$374,819 to Sweet Briar College, Sweet Briar, VA.

$50,000 to Averett University, Danville, VA.

$41,646 to Salvation Army.

$18,997 to Danville Area Association for the Arts and Humanities, Danville, VA. 2 grants: $3,997, $15,000

$15,000 to Danville Museum of Fine Arts and History, Danville, VA.

$6,000 to YMCA.

9387
The Beirne Carter Foundation ✧

1802 Bayberry Ct., Ste. 401
Richmond, VA   23226-3773   (804) 521-0272
FAX: (804) 521-0274; E-mail: bcarterfn@aol.com;
URL: http://www.bcarterfdn.org

Established in 1986 in VA.

Donor: Beirne B. Carter‡.

Foundation type: Independent foundation.

Financial data (yr. ended 12/31/04): Assets, $27,870,483 (M); expenditures, $1,624,182; qualifying distributions, $1,277,009; giving activities include $1,163,997 for 55 grants (high: $500,000; low: $250).

Purpose and activities: Support primarily for education, the environment, human services, housing, arts and culture, youth development, and health care.

Fields of interest: History/archaeology; Arts; Education; Environment, natural resources; Environment; Health care; Health organizations, association; Children/youth, services.

Type of support: Capital campaigns; Building/renovation; Equipment; Matching/challenge support.

Limitations: Giving primarily in VA. No support for churches, public secondary schools and colleges and local municipalities. No grants to individuals; endowment funds, existing deficits or debt reduction.

Publications: Informational brochure (including application guidelines).

Application information: See foundation Web site for application form and for list of items needed in preliminary proposal. Application form required.

Initial approach: 2-page letter

Copies of proposal: 4

Deadline(s): Feb. 1 and Aug. 1, for preliminary proposals; Apr. 14 and Oct. 16, by 12:00 PM, for formal applications

Board meeting date(s): Apr. and Oct.

Final notification: Following board meeting

Officers: Mary Ross Carter Hutcheson, Pres.; Kenneth Laughon, V.P.; Talfourd H. Kemper, Secy.-Treas.

Number of staff: 2 part-time professional.

EIN: 541397827

Selected grants: The following grants were reported in 2004.

$153,000 to Saint Christophers School, Richmond, VA. 3 grants: $3,000, $100,000, $50,000

$50,000 to Corporation for Jeffersons Poplar Forest, Forest, VA.

$25,000 to Science Museum of Western Virginia, Roanoke, VA.

$25,000 to Shenandoah Resource Conservation and Development Council, Verona, VA.

$25,000 to YMCA, Alleghany Highlands, Covington, VA.

$15,000 to Saint Francis of Assisi Service Dog Foundation, Roanoke, VA.

$5,000 to Chesapeake Bay Foundation, Annapolis, MD.

$5,000 to Science Museum of Virginia Foundation, Richmond, VA.

9388
Cartledge Charitable Foundation, Inc. ✧

4235 Electric Rd. S.W., Ste. 100
Roanoke, VA   24014   (540) 776-7000
Contact: George B. Cartledge, Jr., Chair.

Established in 1960 in VA.

Donors: Olive M. Cartledge; Grand Piano and Furniture Co.

Foundation type: Independent foundation.

Financial data (yr. ended 8/31/05): Assets, $202,846 (M); gifts received, $444,474; expenditures, $324,984; qualifying distributions, $321,896; giving activities include $321,896 for 113 grants (high: $50,000; low: $20).

Purpose and activities: Giving primarily for the arts and culture, higher and other education, social services, health associations, and youth organizations.

Fields of interest: Museums (specialized); Performing arts; Performing arts, theater; Arts; Higher education; Education; Health organizations, association; Human services; YM/YWCAs & YM/YWHAs; Children/youth, services; Community development; Protestant agencies & churches.

Type of support: General/operating support.

Limitations: Giving primarily in VA, with emphasis on Roanoke.

Application information:

Initial approach: Letter

Deadline(s): None

Officers: George B. Cartledge, Jr., Chair.; George B. Cartledge III, Pres.; Robert G. Bennett, Exec. V.P.; Randall Lundy, Secy.

Director: Pat Bennett.

EIN: 546044831

Selected grants: The following grants were reported in 2005.

$56,500 to Hampden-Sydney College, Hampden Sydney, VA. 2 grants: $50,000, $6,500

$20,000 to Virginia Museum of Transportation, Roanoke, VA.

$20,000 to YMCA, Roanoke Valley Family Center, Roanoke, VA.

$16,667 to Second Presbyterian Church, Richmond, VA.

$10,000 to Virginia Episcopal School, Lynchburg, VA.

$9,500 to Mill Mountain Theater, Roanoke, VA. 2 grants: $7,500, $2,000

$5,000 to Virginia Tech Foundation, Blacksburg, VA.

$1,000 to American Red Cross, Roanoke, VA.

9389
Roy R. Charles Charitable Trust Two ✧

951 E. Byrd St., Ste. 930
Richmond, VA   23219
Contact: Thomas N.P. Johnson III, Tr.

Established in 1999 in VA.

Donors: Roy R. Charles Trust; Roy Charles Interim Trust.

Foundation type: Independent foundation.

Financial data (yr. ended 12/31/05): Assets, $13,789,794 (M); gifts received, $410,000; expenditures, $780,026; qualifying distributions, $617,432; giving activities include $617,432 for 15 grants (high: $100,000; low: $10,000).

Fields of interest: Arts; Education; Health care; Human services; Children/youth, services.

Limitations: Giving primarily in VA. No grants to individuals.

Application information:

Initial approach: Letter

Deadline(s): None

Distribution Committee: Margaret Johnson; Wade L. Johnson.

Trustees: Angie Newman Johnson; Karen B. Johnson, Jr.; Thomas N.P. Johnson III.

EIN: 546445977

Selected grants: The following grants were reported in 2004.

$100,000 to Woodberry Forest School, Woodberry Forest, VA. For football stadium.

$75,000 to Comfort Zone Camp, Richmond, VA.

$50,000 to Corporation for Jeffersons Poplar Forest, Forest, VA. For capital campaign.

$50,000 to Thomas Jefferson Memorial Foundation, Charlottesville, VA. For general support.

$50,000 to Virginia Health Care Foundation, Richmond, VA.

$50,000 to Virginia State Golf Association Foundation, Richmond, VA. For general support.

$35,000 to Peninsula Fine Arts Center, Newport News, VA. For annual support.

$25,000 to Learning Bridge Richmond, a Breakthrough Program, Richmond, VA.

$25,000 to YMCA of Greater Richmond, Richmond, VA. For general support.

$17,700 to Camp Holiday Trails, Charlottesville, VA. For scholarships.

9390
Charlottesville Area Community Foundation ✧

(formerly Charlottesville-Albemarle Community Foundation)
114 4th St. S.E.
P.O. Box 1767
Charlottesville, VA   22902-1767
(434) 296-1024
FAX: (434) 296-2503; E-mail: cacf@cacfonline.org;
URL: http://www.cacfonline.org

Established in 1967 in VA.

Foundation type: Community foundation.

Financial data (yr. ended 12/31/04): Assets, $29,466,441 (M); gifts received, $4,964,651;

expenditures, $2,848,418; giving activities include $2,279,068 for grants.

Purpose and activities: The mission of the foundation is to improve the quality of life for those living and working in the city of Charlottesville, VA and the surrounding counties of Albemarle, Buckingham, Fluvanna, Greene, Louisa, Nelson, and Orange.

Fields of interest: Humanities; Arts; Education; Environment; Health care; Human services; Community development.

Type of support: General/operating support; Seed money; Scholarship funds; Matching/challenge support.

Limitations: Giving limited to the Charlottesville, VA, area, including the City of Charlottesville and the counties of Albemarle, Greene, Orange, Louisa, Fluvanna, Buckingham, and Nelson east of the Blue Ridge Mountains. No support for religious programs. No grants to individuals, or for endowments, deficit reduction, fundraising events, or annual appeals of well-established organizations.

Publications: Application guidelines; Annual report; Newsletter.

Application information: Visit foundation Web site for Grant Proposal Cover Sheet and application guidelines. Faxed or E-mailed proposals are not accepted. Application form required.

> *Initial approach:* Submit Grant Proposal Cover Sheet and proposal (no more than 3 pages)
> *Copies of proposal:* 3
> *Deadline(s):* Apr. 1 and Oct. 1
> *Board meeting date(s):* Twice annually
> *Final notification:* Sept. and Mar.

Officers and Board of Governors: * Ralph L. Feil,* Chair.; Alan N. Culbertson,* Vice-Chair.; John R. Redick,* Pres.; Arthur G. Kiser, V.P. and C.F.O.; Jane Shields, Exec. Dir. Emeritus; Hovey S. Dabney, Emeritus; Lockwood Frizzell,* Emeritus; Robert P. Hodous,* Emeritus; James B. Murray, Jr.,* Emeritus; Jean Printz,* Emeritus; Mrs. Frederic W. Scott,* Emeritus; Charles T. Baber; William L. Bickley; Julian M. Bivins, Jr.; Daniel M. Brody; Edward H. Brownfield, Jr.; Louise M. Dudley; Linda K. Ford; Joe H. Gieck; Carlton S. Gregory; J. Dawn Heneberry; Kat Imhoff; Lawrence J. Martin; Christopher McLean; Susan K. Payne; Charles M. Rotgin, Jr.; Joseph T. Samuels; Zan Short; Constance M. Waite; Elizabeth H. Woodard.

Number of staff: 2 full-time professional; 1 part-time professional; 2 full-time support.

EIN: 541506312

9391
Chase Foundation of Virginia ◇
300 Preston Ave., Ste. 403
Charlottesville, VA 22902 (434) 293-9104
Contact: Derwood S. Chase, Jr., Tr.

Established in 1995 in VA.

Donors: Derwood S. Chase, Jr.; Johanna B. Chase.

Foundation type: Independent foundation.

Financial data (yr. ended 12/31/05): Assets, $10,410,001 (M); expenditures, $587,144; qualifying distributions, $583,805; giving activities include $578,000 for 47 grants (high: $35,000; low: $2,000).

Fields of interest: Social sciences, research; Social sciences, public policy; Public affairs.

Type of support: General/operating support.

Limitations: Giving on a national basis. No grants to individuals.

Application information: Application form not required.

> *Deadline(s):* None

Trustees: Alejandro A. Chafuen; Cheryl O. Chase; Derwood S. Chase, Jr.; Gabriela C. Chase; Johanna B. Chase; Stuart F. Chase; John C. Goodman; Walter E. Williams.

EIN: 541770697

Selected grants: The following grants were reported in 2004.

$37,820 to Atlas Economic Research Foundation, Arlington, VA.

$37,820 to National Center for Policy Analysis, Dallas, TX.

$35,380 to Institute for Justice, DC.

$30,500 to Heartland Institute, Chicago, IL.

$25,620 to Acton Institute for the Study of Religion and Liberty, Grand Rapids, MI.

$15,860 to National Journalism Center, DC.

$13,000 to Locke Institute, Fairfax, VA.

$10,980 to John Locke Foundation, Raleigh, NC.

$10,000 to Alliance for School Choice, Phoenix, AZ.

$10,000 to Fund for American Studies, DC.

9392
Circuit City Foundation ◇
9950 Mayland Dr.
Richmond, VA 23233-1464 (804) 527-4000
Contact: Jane Gurganus

Established in 1962 in VA as a company-sponsored operating foundation.

Donors: Circuit City Stores, Inc.; Wards Co., Inc.

Foundation type: Operating foundation.

Financial data (yr. ended 2/28/05): Assets, $2,295,796 (M); gifts received, $2,000,000; expenditures, $1,892,146; qualifying distributions, $1,891,825; giving activities include $1,635,828 for 430 grants (high: $500,000; low: $25), and $192,950 for 150 grants to individuals.

Purpose and activities: The foundation supports organizations involved with K-12 education reform.

Fields of interest: Education, reform; Education, public education; Education.

Type of support: General/operating support; Annual campaigns; Employee matching gifts; Employee-related scholarships.

Limitations: Giving limited to areas of company operations. No support for national organizations. No grants to individuals (except for employee-related scholarships).

Application information: Unsolicited requests are accepted but not encouraged.

> *Board meeting date(s):* Spring and fall

Officer and Trustees: Cassandra O. Stoddart, Exec. Dir.; W. Stephen Cannon.

Number of staff: 1 part-time professional; 1 full-time support.

EIN: 546048660

Selected grants: The following grants were reported in 2004.

$1,000,000 to Boys and Girls Clubs of America, Atlanta, GA. 2 grants: $500,000 each

$80,000 to United Way of Greater Richmond and Petersburg, Richmond, VA.

$50,000 to Boy Scouts of America, Robert E. Lee Council, Richmond, VA.

$50,000 to Boys and Girls Clubs of Richmond, Richmond, VA.

$40,000 to Jewish Community Federation of Richmond, Richmond, VA.

$25,000 to An Achievable Dream, Newport News, VA.

$20,000 to Visual Arts Center of Richmond, Richmond, VA.

$10,000 to Richmond Renaissance, Richmond, VA.

$10,000 to University of Kentucky, Lexington, KY.

9393
The Gladys and Franklin Clark Foundation ◇
P.O. Box 47
Williamsburg, VA 23187

Established in 1992 in VA.

Donor: Gladys & Franklin Clark Revocable Trust.

Foundation type: Independent foundation.

Financial data (yr. ended 12/31/04): Assets, $8,086,041 (M); expenditures, $490,479; qualifying distributions, $357,506; giving activities include $329,800 for 5 grants (high: $200,000; low: $17,500).

Fields of interest: Media/communications; Museums; Historical activities; Higher education; Children, services; Residential/custodial care, hospices.

Limitations: Applications not accepted. Giving primarily in VA, with emphasis on Williamsburg. No grants to individuals.

Application information: Contributes only to pre-selected organizations.

Officers and Directors: * Gilbert A. Bartlett,* Pres.; L. Alvin Garrison,* Secy.; Joseph W. Montgomery,* Treas.

EIN: 541640751

Selected grants: The following grants were reported in 2004.

$200,000 to Jamestown-Yorktown Foundation, Williamsburg, VA.

$72,300 to Colonial Williamsburg Foundation, Williamsburg, VA.

$20,000 to Virginia Living Museum, Newport News, VA.

$17,500 to Child Development Resources, Norge, VA.

9394
Claws Foundation ◇ ☆
c/o Sterling Foundation Mgmt., LLC
11921 Freedom Dr., Rm. 730
Reston, VA 20190 (703) 437-9720

Established in 2005 in VA.

Donor: Arthur Dantchik.

Foundation type: Independent foundation.

Financial data (yr. ended 12/31/05): Assets, $9,988 (M); gifts received, $2,185,000; expenditures, $2,175,012; qualifying distributions, $2,175,000; giving activities include $2,175,000 for 5 grants (high: $2,000,000; low: $25,000).

Fields of interest: Hospitals (general); Community development.

Limitations: Giving primarily in PA. No grants to individuals.

Application information:

> *Initial approach:* Letter
> *Deadline(s):* None

Directors: Arthur Dantchik; Alan P. Dye; Jeff Yass.

EIN: 201658710

9395
The Colburn Family Foundation ✧
c/o Sterling Foundation Mgmt., LLC
11921 Freedom Dr., Ste. 730
Reston, VA 20190
Contact: Barry Bondroff

Established in 1998 in VA.
Donors: David Colburn; Kathleen Colburn.
Foundation type: Independent foundation.
Financial data (yr. ended 12/31/05): Assets,
$7,722,969 (M); expenditures, $1,279,792;
qualifying distributions, $1,167,162; giving
activities include $1,167,162 for grants.
Purpose and activities: Giving primarily to Jewish
agencies, temples, and schools; funding also for a
community center.
Fields of interest: Elementary/secondary
education; Neighborhood centers; Jewish federated
giving programs; Jewish agencies & temples.
Limitations: Applications not accepted. No grants to
individuals.
Application information: Contributes only to
pre-selected organizations.
Officers: Kathleen Colburn, Chair.; David Colburn,
Pres. and Secy.-Treas.
EIN: 541923880

9396
The Cole Family Foundation, Inc. ✧ ☆
P.O. Box 478
Washington, VA 22747-0478
Contact: Margaret B. Cole, Dir.

Established in 1997 in FL.
Donors: David C. Cole; Margaret B. Cole.
Foundation type: Independent foundation.
Financial data (yr. ended 11/30/05): Assets,
$641,259 (M); gifts received, $445,850;
expenditures, $486,464; qualifying distributions,
$431,120; giving activities include $431,120 for
grants.
Purpose and activities: Giving primarily for the
environment, education, and the arts.
Fields of interest: Arts; Education; Environment,
natural resources.
Limitations: Giving primarily in Washington, DC, HI,
MD, NY, and VA.
Application information: Application form not
required.
  Deadline(s): None
Directors: David C. Cole; Margaret B. Cole.
EIN: 541835269
Selected grants: The following grants were reported
in 2003.
$100,000 to In2Books, DC.
$28,000 to University of California, Donald Bren
  School of Environmental Science &
  Management, Santa Barbara, CA.
$24,850 to Crossroads Resource Center,
  Minneapolis, MN.
$20,000 to National Gallery of Art, DC. For art
  acquisition.
$20,000 to National Museum of Women in the Arts,
  DC.
$13,000 to Sesame Workshop, New York, NY.
$10,000 to American Farmland Trust, DC.
$10,000 to Environmental Working Group, DC.
$5,000 to Meridian International Center, DC. For
  general support.
$4,750 to Headwaters, The Rappahannock County
  Public Education Foundation, Washington, VA.

9397
Quincy Cole Trust ✧
c/o Bank of America, N.A.
P.O. Box 26606
Richmond, VA 23261-6606
Application address: Rita Smith c/o Bank of America,
N.A., P.O. Box 26903, Richmond, VA 23261,
tel.: (804) 788-2143

Established in 1969 in VA.
Donor: Quincy Cole†.
Foundation type: Independent foundation.
Financial data (yr. ended 6/30/05): Assets,
$4,858,428 (M); expenditures, $713,879;
qualifying distributions, $586,649; giving activities
include $583,499 for 23 grants (high: $83,499;
low: $5,000).
Fields of interest: Arts; Education; Human services.
Limitations: Giving limited to the metropolitan
Richmond, VA, area.
Application information: Applicants should submit
the following:.
  Initial approach: Letter
  Deadline(s): Apr. 20
  Board meeting date(s): June
Trustee: Bank of America, N.A.
EIN: 546086247
Selected grants: The following grants were reported
in 2004.
$82,476 to Windsor Foundation, Richmond, VA. For
  upkeep and maintenance of house.
$60,000 to Virginia Performing Arts Foundation,
  Richmond, VA. For general support.
$50,000 to Richmond Symphony, Richmond, VA. For
  general support.
$30,000 to Saint Christophers School, Richmond,
  VA. For general operating support.
$25,000 to Arts Council of Richmond, Richmond,
  VA. For general support.
$25,000 to Richmond Better Housing Coalition,
  Richmond, VA. For general support.
$25,000 to Riverside School, Richmond, VA. For
  general support.
$20,000 to William Byrd Community House,
  Richmond, VA. For general support.
$15,000 to Memorial Child Guidance Clinic,
  Richmond, VA. For general support.
$7,000 to Good Samaritan Ministries, Richmond,
  VA. For general support.

9398
The Collis/Warner Foundation, Inc. ✧ ☆
201 N. Union St., Ste. 300
Alexandria, VA 22314

Established in 1997 in VA.
Donors: Lisa D. Collis; Mark R. Warner.
Foundation type: Independent foundation.
Financial data (yr. ended 12/31/05): Assets,
$6,693,450 (M); expenditures, $615,793;
qualifying distributions, $595,500; giving activities
include $595,500 for grants.
Purpose and activities: Giving primarily for
education, health care, and children and family
services. The foundation also administers a
partnership between historically black colleges and
universities; support also for high technology
community in VA, in order to develop curriculum and
a hardware/software infrastructure that will produce
technologically proficient to assist students in
technology-related careers.
Fields of interest: Education; Environment, natural
resources; Health care; Crime/violence prevention,

child abuse; Children/youth, services; Family
services; Computer science; Public affairs.
Type of support: General/operating support.
Limitations: Applications not accepted. Giving
primarily in VA, with emphasis on Alexandria and
Richmond. No grants to individuals.
Application information: Contributes only to
pre-selected organizations.
Directors: Lisa D. Collis; Mark R. Warner.
EIN: 541854416
Selected grants: The following grants were reported
in 2005.
$100,000 to Old Presbyterian Meeting House,
  Alexandria, VA.
$50,000 to Virginia Union University, Richmond, VA.
$25,000 to Nature Conservancy, Charlottesville, VA.
$6,500 to American Heart Association, VA.
$5,000 to Extra Hands for ALS, Saint Louis, MO.
$2,500 to Scholarship Fund of Alexandria,
  Alexandria, VA.
$2,500 to Virginia College Fund, Richmond, VA.

9399
The Columbus Phipps Foundation ✧
P.O. Box 26606
Richmond, VA 23261-6606
Application address: c/o Paul D. Buchanan, P.O. Box
1145, Clintwood, VA 24228, tel.: (540) 926-8152

Established in 1993 in VA.
Donor: Beulah G. Phipps†.
Foundation type: Independent foundation.
Financial data (yr. ended 3/31/06): Assets,
$11,633,931 (M); expenditures, $641,779;
qualifying distributions, $551,469; giving activities
include $533,659 for 54 grants (high: $103,500;
low: $500).
Purpose and activities: Support for local cultural
and educational activities, including scholarships to
high school graduates of Dickenson County.
Fields of interest: Arts, multipurpose centers/
programs; Performing arts; Elementary/secondary
education; Higher education.
Type of support: General/operating support;
Building/renovation; Scholarships—to individuals.
Limitations: Giving limited to Dickenson County, VA.
Application information: Application form required.
  Deadline(s): May 15; June 15 for renewal
  applications
Trustees: Carol P. Buchanan; Paul D. Buchanan;
William R. McFall.
Advisory Committee: Rita F. Justice; Betty Jo
Dodson; Rick Mullins.
EIN: 546338751
Selected grants: The following grants were reported
in 2005.
$23,000 to Virginia Intermont College, Bristol, VA.
  3 grants: $8,500, $6,000, $8,500
$13,000 to Shenandoah University, Winchester, VA.
  2 grants: $6,500 each
$12,000 to Pikeville College, Pikeville, KY. 2 grants:
  $6,000 each
$10,500 to Emory and Henry College, Emory, VA. 2
  grants: $5,250 each
$2,500 to Liberty University, Lynchburg, VA.

9400
The Community Foundation of
Harrisonburg and Rockingham County ✧
(formerly Harrisonburg Rockingham Community
Foundation)
P.O. Box 1068
Harrisonburg, VA 22801 (540) 432-3863
Contact: Stephanne S. Byrd, Exec. Dir.
E-mail: foundation@ntelos.net; URL: http://
www.the-community-foundation.org

Established in VA.
Foundation type: Community foundation.
Financial data (yr. ended 6/30/05): Assets,
$7,288,090 (M); gifts received, $4,459,340;
expenditures, $561,488; giving activities include
$478,392 for 45 grants (high: $100,000; low:
$1,000).
Purpose and activities: The foundation seeks to
enrich the quality of life in the Harrisonburg and
Rockingham County, VA, community by developing
and managing permanent endowments to respond
to changing community needs.
Fields of interest: Historic preservation/historical
societies; Arts; Education; Environment; Health
care; Human services; Community development;
Religion; Children; Aging.
Type of support: Scholarships—to individuals.
Limitations: Giving limited to Harrisonburg and
Rockingham County, VA.
Publications: Annual report; Informational brochure.
Application information: Visit foundation Web site
for scholarship information. Application form not
required.
Initial approach: Telephone
Board meeting date(s): 3rd Wed. of Feb., May,
Aug., and Nov.
Officers and Directors: Ellen H. Brodersen,* Pres.;
Michael E. Fiore,* V.P. and Chair., Nom. Comm.;
Betty B. Martin,* Secy.; Stephanne S. Byrd, Exec.
Dir.; David W. Driver,* Chair., Distrib. Comm.;
George W. Pace,* Chair., Aud. Comm.; Christopher
S. Runion,* Chair., P.R.; Richard A. Baugh; Kathleen
M. Graves; W. Michael Heatwole III; Lawrence H.
Hoover, Jr.; Andrew M. Huggins; Brenda Lenhart;
Susanne Myers; Esteban Nieto; Ramona D. Rogers;
C. Douglas Wine.
Number of staff: 1 part-time professional; 1
part-time support.
EIN: 541920746

9401
Community Foundation of the Dan River
Region
(formerly DPC Community Foundation)
530 Main St., Ste. 302
P.O. Box 1039
Danville, VA 24543 (434) 793-0884
Contact: Debra L. Dodson, Exec. Dir.
FAX: (434) 793-6489;
E-mail: communityfoundation@gamewood.net;
Additional E-mail:cfdrr@gamewood.net; URL: http://
www.cfdrr.org

Established in 1996 in VA.
Foundation type: Community foundation.
Financial data (yr. ended 6/30/05): Assets,
$11,857,508 (M); gifts received, $582,221;
expenditures, $1,394,297; giving activities include
$1,208,831 for 32+ grants.

Purpose and activities: The foundation helps
donors meet community needs through endowment
funds.
Type of support: Scholarship funds; Scholarships—
to individuals.
Limitations: Giving primarily in Caswell County, NC,
and Danville and Pittsylvania County, VA, as well as
southern VA and northern NC.
Publications: Application guidelines; Annual report;
Grants list; Informational brochure; Newsletter.
Application information: Visit foundation Web site
for application guidelines. Organizations wishing to
be added to the foundation's mailing list for grant
applications should contact the foundation's office.
Application forms for scholarships are sent to
guidance offices of public high schools in early
spring. Application form required.
Initial approach: Preliminary grant request letter
Copies of proposal: 1
Deadline(s): June
Board meeting date(s): 4th Mon. of Mar., June,
and Sept., and 2nd Mon. of Dec.
Final notification: Jan.
Officers and Directors: Connie Fletcher,* Pres.;
John E. Herndon, Jr.,* V.P.; Bonnie Cooper,* Secy.;
Vaden Wright,* Treas.; Debra L. Dodson, Exec. Dir.;
Rubie Archie; Richard Barkhouser; Wilson Carter;
Kirk Echols; Nan Freed; Harry L. Goodrich; Lee
Goodrich; H.F. Haymore; Samuel A. Kushner;
Kenneth Miller; H. Victor Millner, Jr.; Kelvin G. Perry;
Betty Sartin; Carroll Thackson; Jack C. Tuner.
Number of staff: 2 full-time professional.
EIN: 541823141

9402
The Community Foundation Serving
Richmond & Central Virginia ▼ ✧
(formerly Greater Richmond Community Foundation)
7501 Boulders View Dr., Ste. 110
Richmond, VA 23225 (804) 330-7400
Contact: Darcy S. Oman, C.E.O.; For grants: Susan
Hallett, Prog. Off.; For grants: Elaine Summerfield,
Prog. Off.
FAX: (804) 330-5992; E-mail: info@tcfrichmond.org;
Additional E-mail: doman@tcfrichmond.org; Grant
application E-mails: shallett@tcfrichmond.org and
esummerfield@tcfrichmond.org; URL: http://
www.tcfrichmond.org

Established in 1968 in VA.
Foundation type: Community foundation.
Financial data (yr. ended 12/31/05): Assets,
$297,707,558 (M); gifts received, $55,285,395;
expenditures, $9,728,335; giving activities include
$7,887,857 for grants.
Purpose and activities: The purpose of the
foundation is to solve problems, preserve legacies
and to build permanent endowments to enhance the
lives of the citizens of central VA.
Fields of interest: Arts; Education; AIDS; Housing/
shelter, development; Youth development;
Children/youth, services; Community development.
Type of support: Grants to individuals; General/
operating support; Continuing support; Equipment;
Emergency funds; Program development; Seed
money; Technical assistance; Scholarships—to
individuals; Matching/challenge support.
Limitations: Giving limited to residents of
metropolitan Richmond, the tri-cities area, including
Hopewell, Colonial Heights, and Petersburg, and
Chesterfield, Hanover, and Henrico counties, VA. No

grants for annual campaigns, deficit financing, land
acquisition, or building funds.
Publications: Application guidelines; Annual report;
Biennial report.
Application information: Visit foundation Web site
for additional guidelines per grant type. The
foundation will invite organizations to submit a full
proposal based on their letter of intent. Faxed or
e-mailed letters of intent are not accepted. R.E.B.
Awards for Teaching Excellence forms available in
Jan. from participating schools. Application form
required.
Initial approach: Preliminary letter of intent (no
more than 2 pages)
Copies of proposal: 2
Deadline(s): May 5 and Nov. 5 for letter of intent;
Jan. 5 and July 5 for proposals
Board meeting date(s): Quarterly
Final notification: May 19 and Nov. 19 for full
proposal invitation; 3rd week of Mar. and Sept.
for grant decision
Officers and Board of Governors: Fred T.
Tattersall,* Chair.; Walter S. Robertson III,*
Vice-Chair.; Darcy S. Oman,* C.E.O. and Pres.;
Barbara B. Ukrop,* Secy.; Beverley W. Armstrong,*
Treas.; William L.S. Rowe,* Genl. Counsel; A.
Marshall Acuff, Jr.; Farhad Aghdami; Joseph L.
Antrim III; Thomas D. Byer; Denise P. Dickerson;
Waller H. Horsley; Katherine N. Markel; Michele A.W.
McKinnon; E. Bryson Powell; John Sherman, Jr.; E.
Lee Showalter; Richard G. Tilghman; Jane G.
Watkins; Erwin H. Will, Jr.
Number of staff: 10 full-time professional; 1
part-time professional; 4 full-time support.
EIN: 237009135
Selected grants: The following grants were reported
in 2005.
$156,000 to Sussex County Public Schools,
Sussex, VA. To meet requirements of Qualified
Zone Academy Bond Program and for educational
improvements within district. Grant made
through Garland and Agnes Taylor Gray
Foundation.
$125,000 to Vernon J. Harris East End Community
Health Center, Richmond, VA. To provide salary
support for full-time dentist and dental assistant.
Grant made through Jenkins Foundation.
$100,000 to Daily Planet, Richmond, VA. To expand
and enhance access to mental health services
for homeless population. Grant made through
Jenkins Foundation.
$60,000 to Freedom House, Richmond, VA. To
provide respite for high-risk homeless
populations in need of continued medical or
mental health treatment. Grant made through
Jenkins Foundation.
$50,000 to Saint Johns Church Foundation,
Richmond, VA. For educational programs and
interpretive exhibits on Second Virginia
Convention held at historic Saint John's Church
in 1775. Grant made through Garland and Agnes
Taylor Gray Foundation.
$50,000 to University of Richmond, Richmond, VA.
For maintenance and improvement of
ConnectRichmond network, providing multiple
Web-based tools and resources for area
nonprofits.
$32,500 to Fan Free Clinic, Richmond, VA. For
program support. Grant made through Jenkins
Foundation.
$30,000 to Big Brothers and Big Sisters Services,
Richmond, VA. To provide salary support for
part-time Enrollment Specialist and Match
Support Specialist.

$25,000 to Riverside School, Richmond, VA. For Riverside School Teachers Training Program, preparing public school teachers to work with students with learning disabilities.

$25,000 to Virginia Home for Boys and Girls, Richmond, VA. To open residential cottage for at-risk girls.

9403
The Connors Foundation, Inc. ✧
P.O. Box 7317
Alexandria, VA 22307-0317 (703) 683-4367
Contact: Julia B. Connors, V.P.
E-mail: JConnors@aol.com

Established in 1999.
Donors: Michael M. Connors; Julia B. Connors.
Foundation type: Independent foundation.
Financial data (yr. ended 12/31/04): Assets, $8,398,846 (M); expenditures, $672,680; qualifying distributions, $666,271; giving activities include $644,358 for 35 grants (high: $254,215; low: $50).
Purpose and activities: Giving primarily for children's health and development, environmental protection and development, and the arts.
Fields of interest: Museums (art); Performing arts; Environment, natural resources; Health care; Children/youth, services.
Limitations: Applications not accepted. Giving primarily in Washington, DC. No grants to individuals.
Application information: Unsolicited requests for funds not accepted.
Board meeting date(s): 4 times per year
Officers: Michael M. Connors, Pres.; Julia B. Connors, V.P.
Directors: Gregory Connors; Patrick E. Connors; Kathleen C. Mueller.
EIN: 522204597
Selected grants: The following grants were reported in 2004.
$254,215 to Community Foundation for the National Capital Region, DC.
$100,000 to John F. Kennedy Center for the Performing Arts, DC. 2 grants: $50,000 each
$36,250 to National Museum of Women in the Arts, DC. 2 grants: $20,000, $16,250
$25,000 to Childrens Hospital Foundation, DC.
$25,000 to National Opera Institute, DC.
$25,000 to National Symphony Orchestra, DC.
$20,000 to Washington Performing Arts Society, DC.
$15,000 to Gods Love We Deliver, New York, NY.

9404
The Constitution Foundation ✧
(formerly The Saylor Foundation)
1861 International Dr.
McLean, VA 22102 (703) 848-8600
Contact: Michael J. Saylor, Tr.

Established in 1998 in MA.
Donor: Michael J. Saylor.
Foundation type: Operating foundation.
Financial data (yr. ended 12/31/04): Assets, $14,177,229 (M); expenditures, $716,358; qualifying distributions, $700,485; giving activities include $700,485 for 7 grants (high: $630,000; low: $110).

Purpose and activities: Giving primarily to a national donor-advised fund; some funding also for the arts and human services.
Fields of interest: Performing arts; Arts; Human services; Children, services; Philanthropy/voluntarism.
Limitations: Giving primarily in Boston, MA; funding also in the greater Washington, DC, area, including VA.
Application information:
Initial approach: Letter
Trustee: Michael J. Saylor.
EIN: 541933630

9405
Jack Kent Cooke Foundation
44325 Woodridge Pkwy.
Lansdowne, VA 20176 (703) 723-8000
Contact: Matthew J. Quinn, Exec. Dir.
FAX: (703) 723-8030;
E-mail: jkc@jackkentcookefoundation.org;
URL: http://www.jackkentcookefoundation.org
Application address: Jack Kent Cooke Foundation, ACT, P.O. Box 4030, Iowa City, IA 52243

Established in 1997 in VA. The foundation became active in 2000.
Donor: Jack Kent Cooke†.
Foundation type: Independent foundation.
Financial data (yr. ended 5/31/06): Assets, $637,795,172 (M); expenditures, $24,719,836; qualifying distributions, $15,759,958; giving activities include $15,759,958 for grants.
Purpose and activities: The purpose of the foundation is to help young people of exceptional promise reach their full potential through education.
Fields of interest: Education.
Type of support: General/operating support; Scholarship funds; Grants to individuals; Scholarships—to individuals; Student loans—to individuals.
Limitations: Giving on a national basis.
Publications: Application guidelines; Financial statement; Grants list; Informational brochure.
Application information: Application guidelines available on foundation Web site. Application form required.
Deadline(s): Feb. 1 for Undergraduate Transfer Scholarship program; Feb. 16 for September 11th Grants; Mar. 15 for Graduate Scholarship program; and May 7 for Young Scholars program
Officers and Directors:* Stuart A. Haney,* Pres.; Joshua S. Wyner, V.P., Progs.; Wanda G. Wiser,* Secy.; Mark Birmingham, C.F.O. and Treas.; Matthew J. Quinn, Exec. Dir.; John Kent Cooke, Sr.; Gregory R. Dillon; Linda J. King; Mark Pollak; Howard B. Soloway.
Number of staff: 24 full-time professional; 2 full-time support; 1 part-time support.
EIN: 541896244
Selected grants: The following grants were reported in 2005.
$460,500 to University of Virginia, Center for Undergraduate Excellence, Charlottesville, VA. For State Level support for College Access Program through Virginia College Access Network (VCAN).
$425,000 to KIPP (Knowledge is Power Program) Foundation, San Francisco, CA. For program expansion as part of Young Scholars Pipeline.

$304,500 to From the Top, Boston, MA. For Young Scholars Pipeline, initiative to identify young people with exceptional musical talent.
$250,000 to Citizen Schools, Boston, MA. For Young Scholars Pipeline Program, initiative to expand number of cities and students served.
$170,000 to Breakthrough Collaborative, San Francisco, CA. To expand summer and out-of-school programs as part of Young Scholars Pipeline Program.
$130,853 to University of Massachusetts, Boston, MA. For Community College Transfer Initiative.
$75,000 to Ryman Arts, Los Angeles, CA. To expand opportunities to talented urban youth.
$50,000 to Alliance for Young Artists and Writers, New York, NY. For Young Scholars Pipeline Program, initiative to increase outreach to underserved students with artistic promise.
$28,000 to Kennedy Krieger Institute, Baltimore, MD. For scholarships.
$6,000 to MusicLink Foundation, Arlington, VA. For program expansion as part of Young Scholars Pipeline.

9406
The Dalis Foundation ✧
c/o Goodman & Co.
1 Commercial Pl., Ste. 800
Norfolk, VA 23510

Established in 1956.
Donor: M. Dan Dalis†.
Foundation type: Independent foundation.
Financial data (yr. ended 5/31/05): Assets, $9,110,389 (M); expenditures, $378,883; qualifying distributions, $337,495; giving activities include $337,495 for 6 grants (high: $250,000; low: $1,000).
Fields of interest: Performing arts; Education; Reproductive health, family planning; Reproductive health, fertility; Medical research, institute; Athletics/sports, water sports; Human services; Children/youth, services; Jewish agencies & temples.
Limitations: Applications not accepted. Giving primarily in Norfolk, VA; funding also in Boston, MA. No grants to individuals.
Application information: Contributes only to pre-selected organizations.
Officer: Joan W. Dalis, Pres. and Treas.
Directors: Matthew R. Norment; Michael H. Norment.
EIN: 546046229
Selected grants: The following grants were reported in 2005.
$250,000 to Jones Institute for Reproductive Medicine, Norfolk, VA.
$50,000 to Planned Parenthood.
$20,000 to Hurrah Players, Norfolk, VA.
$10,495 to Norfolk Rowing Center, Norfolk, VA.
$6,000 to University of North Carolina, Chapel Hill, NC. For Hillel.
$1,000 to Old Dominion University, Norfolk, VA. For Rowing Club.

9407
Datatel Scholars Foundation ✧
4375 Fair Lakes Ct.
Fairfax, VA 22033 (703) 968-9000, ext. 4549
FAX: (703) 968-4625;
E-mail: scholars@datatel.com; Additional tel.: (800)

486-4332; URL: http://www.datatel.com/global/scholarships/

Established in 1990 in VA.
Donor: Datatel, Inc.
Foundation type: Company-sponsored foundation.
Financial data (yr. ended 12/31/03): Assets, $143,435 (M); gifts received, $431,890; expenditures, $478,333; qualifying distributions, $478,125; giving activities include $478,100 for 361 grants to individuals (high: $2,500; low: $700).
Purpose and activities: The foundation awards college and graduate scholarships to students attending an institution of higher learning that uses Datatel's software.
International interests: Bermuda; Canada.
Type of support: Scholarships—to individuals.
Limitations: Giving on a national and international basis.
Publications: Application guidelines.
Application information: Application form required.
Initial approach: Complete online application form
Deadline(s): Jan. 31
Board meeting date(s): Spring
Final notification: May 1
Officers and Directors:* Bryant L. Cureton; Thomas R. Davidson; Robert E. Dunker; Geraldine A. Evans; Leonardo de la Garza; H. Russell Griffith; Vernon R. Hollidge; Ronald R. Ingle; E.G. Kendrick, Jr.; Margaret McKenna; Nancy B. Moody; David Rues; Elaine Ryan; William Segura; Karen A. Stout; Edwin H. Welch.
EIN: 541604129

9408
de Beaumont Foundation, Inc.
P.O. Box 1021
McLean, VA 22101-1021 (703) 714-0777
Contact: James B. Sprague M.D., Chair.
FAX: (703) 935-5655;
E-mail: info@deBeaumont.org; URL: http://www.deBeaumont.org

Established in 1999 in MA.
Donor: Pierre de Beaumont.
Foundation type: Independent foundation.
Financial data (yr. ended 10/31/05): Assets, $8,177,610 (M); expenditures, $565,690; qualifying distributions, $512,239; giving activities include $426,205 for 3 grants (high: $176,205; low: $125,000).
Purpose and activities: Areas of focus include bioterrorism preparedness, immunology, and entrepreneurial approaches to public health.
Fields of interest: Public health; Public health, communicable diseases; Public health, epidemiology; Public health, bioterrorism; Health care; Immunology; Disasters, preparedness/services.
Type of support: Seed money; Research; Program development; Professorships; General/operating support; Fellowships.
Limitations: Applications not accepted. Giving limited to the U.S. No support for religious or political organizations.
Publications: Financial statement; Grants list.
Application information: Proposals by invitation only.
Board meeting date(s): Feb., May, Aug., and Oct.
Officers: James B. Sprague, M.D., Chair. and C.E.O.; Murray Brennan, V.P.; Leroy Parker, Secy.-Treas.
Directors: Richard Burnes; Carol Miller.

Number of staff: 1 full-time support.
EIN: 043467074

9409
The DeLaski Family Foundation ◇
(formerly The Donald and Nancy L. DeLaski Foundation)
605 Deerfield Pond Ct.
Great Falls, VA 22066

Established in 1998 in VA.
Donors: Donald DeLaski; Nancy L. DeLaski.
Foundation type: Independent foundation.
Financial data (yr. ended 12/31/05): Assets, $32,061,329 (M); gifts received, $25,786,408; expenditures, $1,278,331; qualifying distributions, $1,187,737; giving activities include $1,187,737 for 23 grants (high: $383,000; low: $1,000).
Purpose and activities: Giving primarily for health care and the arts.
Fields of interest: Museums (art); Performing arts, opera; Medical care, in-patient care; Health organizations, association.
Limitations: Applications not accepted. Giving on a national basis. No grants to individuals.
Application information: Contributes only to pre-selected organizations.
Officers and Directors:* Donald DeLaski,* Pres.; Nancy L. DeLaski,* Secy.-Treas.
EIN: 541902570
Selected grants: The following grants were reported in 2004.
$434,000 to George Mason University Foundation, Fairfax, VA.
$119,000 to Patricia M. Sitar Center for the Arts, DC.
$62,000 to Mount Vernon Ladies Association, Mount Vernon, VA.
$22,500 to Arena Stage, DC.
$20,000 to Langley School, McLean, VA.
$16,000 to Duke University, Durham, NC.
$5,000 to Hoover Institution on War, Revolution and Peace, Stanford, CA.
$4,500 to National Gallery of Art, DC.
$3,000 to Tenley Study Center, DC.
$1,000 to John F. Kennedy Center for the Performing Arts, DC.

9410
The Charles Delmar Foundation ◇
5203 Leesburg Pike, Ste. 1304
Falls Church, VA 22041
Contact: Mareen D. Hughes, Pres.

Established in 1957 in DC.
Donors: Charles Delmar†; Roland H. Delmar†; Elizabeth A. Delmar†; Mareen D. Hughes.
Foundation type: Independent foundation.
Financial data (yr. ended 12/31/05): Assets, $8,411,446 (M); expenditures, $393,599; qualifying distributions, $382,929; giving activities include $375,250 for 165 grants (high: $14,000; low: $250; average: $1,000–$5,000).
Purpose and activities: Special interests include inter-American studies, higher, secondary, elementary, and other education, underprivileged youth, the disadvantaged, the aged, the homeless and housing issues, general welfare organizations, and fine and performing arts.
Fields of interest: Visual arts; Museums; Performing arts; Performing arts, theater; Performing arts,

music; Historic preservation/historical societies; Elementary school/education; Secondary school/education; Higher education; Adult education—literacy, basic skills & GED; Education, reading; Environment, natural resources; Hospitals (general); Reproductive health, family planning; Substance abuse, services; Health organizations, association; Cancer research; Housing/shelter, development; Human services; Children/youth, services; Family services; Residential/custodial care, hospices; Aging, centers/services; Homeless, human services; Civil rights, race/intergroup relations; Aging; Disabilities, people with; Native Americans/American Indians; Economically disadvantaged; Homeless.
International interests: Latin America.
Type of support: Continuing support; Annual campaigns; Capital campaigns; Conferences/seminars; Seed money; Internship funds; Scholarship funds.
Limitations: Giving primarily in the Washington, DC area; some giving also nationally and in Latin America. No grants to individuals, or for building or endowment funds, or matching gifts; no loans.
Application information: Application form not required.
Initial approach: Letter
Copies of proposal: 1
Deadline(s): None
Board meeting date(s): As required
Officers and Trustees:* Mareen D. Hughes,* Pres.; R. Bruce Hughes,* Secy.-Treas.
EIN: 526035345
Selected grants: The following grants were reported in 2005.
$8,000 to College of Charleston, Charleston, SC.
$8,000 to College of Wooster, Wooster, OH.
$5,000 to Maryland Public Broadcasting Foundation, Owings Mills, MD.
$4,000 to American University of Paris, Paris, France. .
$4,000 to Dumbarton Concerts, DC.
$3,000 to Saint Anns Infant and Maternity Home, Hyattsville, MD.
$2,000 to Chillum Youth Project, Mount Rainier, MD.
$2,000 to Columbia Lighthouse for the Blind, DC.
$2,000 to Reading Connection, Arlington, VA.
$2,000 to Washington Concert Opera, DC.

9411
The Dorothy-Ann Foundation ☆
c/o Vernon Geddy III
1177 Jamestown Rd.
Williamsburg, VA 23185

Established in 1999 in VA.
Donors: Darwin O'Ryan Curtis; Darwin O'Ryan Curtis Charitable Lead Annuity Trust.
Foundation type: Independent foundation.
Financial data (yr. ended 12/31/05): Assets, $2,126,596 (M); gifts received, $179,789; expenditures, $516,286; qualifying distributions, $494,401; giving activities include $490,723 for 10 grants (high: $282,723; low: $8,000).
Purpose and activities: Giving primarily for international health and environmental conservation.
Fields of interest: Environment, natural resources; Health care.
International interests: Africa; Latin America.

Type of support: General/operating support; Program development; Seed money; Matching/challenge support.
Limitations: Applications not accepted. Giving on an international basis. No grants to individuals.
Publications: Occasional report.
Application information: Contributes only to pre-selected organizations.
Board meeting date(s): Fall
Officer: Vernon M. Geddy III, Secy.-Treas.
Number of staff: None.
EIN: 541965966

9412
Doudera Family Foundation ✧
2940 N. Lynnhaven Rd., Ste. 200
Virginia Beach, VA 23452

Established in 1996 VA.
Donor: Ralph J. Doudera.
Foundation type: Independent foundation.
Financial data (yr. ended 12/31/04): Assets, $6,220,021 (M); gifts received, $1,238,165; expenditures, $1,118,401; qualifying distributions, $1,609,400; giving activities include $804,700 for 3 grants (high: $700,000; low: $4,700).
Purpose and activities: Giving primarily to promote fundamentalist Christianity, and for human services.
Fields of interest: Family services; Homeless, human services; Protestant agencies & churches.
Limitations: Applications not accepted. Giving on a national basis. No grants to individuals.
Application information: Contributes only to pre-selected organizations.
Officers and Director:* Ralph J. Doudera,* Pres. and Secy-Treas.; Richard C. Mapp III, V.P.
EIN: 541817654
Selected grants: The following grants were reported in 2003.
$1,700,000 to Jesus Film Project.
$1,000,000 to Haggai Institute for Advanced Leadership Training, Atlanta, GA.
$100,000 to CURE International, Harrisburg, PA.
$9,700 to TMCJ International.

9413
Dreyfus Foundation ✧ ☆
106B 83rd St.
Virginia Beach, VA 23451

Established in 1997 in VA.
Donor: Mark Dreyfus.
Foundation type: Independent foundation.
Financial data (yr. ended 12/31/05): Assets, $2,211,019 (M); gifts received, $493,795; expenditures, $507,863; qualifying distributions, $505,900; giving activities include $505,900 for grants.
Purpose and activities: Giving for education and community organizations.
Fields of interest: Education; Community development.
Limitations: Applications not accepted. Giving primarily in VA. No grants to individuals.
Application information: Contributes only to pre-selected organizations.
Officers and Directors:* Alfred Dreyfus,* Pres.; Mildred Dreyfus,* Secy.; Mark Dreyfus,* Treas.; Claudia Dreyfus Levi.
EIN: 541851411

9414
W. C. English Foundation ✧
P.O. Box P7000
Lynchburg, VA 24505
Contact: Beverley E. Dalton, Tr.
Application address: c/o English Construction Co., P.O. Box P7000, Lynchburg, VA 24505

Established in 1954 in VA.
Donor: Members of the English family.
Foundation type: Independent foundation.
Financial data (yr. ended 5/31/05): Assets, $22,060,648 (M); expenditures, $1,464,514; qualifying distributions, $1,102,650; giving activities include $1,100,500 for 32 grants (high: $120,000; low: $1,000), and $69,361 for 1 loan/program-related investment.
Purpose and activities: Giving primarily for higher and other education, human services, YMCAs, and Baptist and Christian organizations, including a program which provides facilities to a Christian elementary and middle school.
Fields of interest: Historic preservation/historical societies; Elementary/secondary education; Higher education; Education; Alzheimer's disease research; Housing/shelter, development; Human services; Salvation Army; YM/YWCAs & YM/YWHAs; Community development; Christian agencies & churches; Religion, interfaith issues.
Limitations: Giving primarily in SC and VA. No grants to individuals.
Application information:
Initial approach: Letter
Deadline(s): None
Trustees: Joan E. Allen; Beverley E. Dalton; Louise T. English; Margaret E. Lester; Suzanne E. Morse.
EIN: 546061817
Selected grants: The following grants were reported in 2005.
$120,000 to Faith Christian Academy, Hurt, VA.
$100,000 to Clemson University Foundation, Clemson, SC.
$100,000 to Oak Hill Academy, Mouth of Wilson, VA.
$100,000 to YMCA, Altavista Area, Altavista, VA.
$75,000 to Fork Union Military Academy, Fork Union, VA.
$40,000 to Anderson Interfaith Ministries, Anderson, SC.
$30,000 to Clemson Community Care, Clemson, SC.
$30,000 to Womens Center of Fayetteville, Fayetteville, NC.
$30,000 to YMCA, Martinsville and Henry County Family, Martinsville, VA.
$25,000 to YMCA, Seneca, SC.

9415
Estes Foundation ✧
5607 Grove Ave.
Richmond, VA 23226
Contact: Controller

Established in 1969 in VA.
Donor: C.E. Estes.
Foundation type: Independent foundation.
Financial data (yr. ended 12/31/05): Assets, $13,871,841 (M); expenditures, $728,975; qualifying distributions, $600,000; giving activities include $600,000 for 14+ grants (high: $516,000).
Purpose and activities: Giving primarily for education.

Fields of interest: Child development, education; Higher education; Human services; Protestant agencies & churches.
Type of support: General/operating support.
Limitations: Applications not accepted. Giving primarily in VA. No grants to individuals.
Application information: Contributes only to pre-selected organizations.
Officers: C.E. Estes, Pres. and Treas.; Barbara Dodson, Secy.
Director: Martha E. Grover.
EIN: 237045252

9416
Edward P. Evans Foundation ✧ ☆
P.O. Box 46, Rte. 602
Casanova, VA 20139
Contact: Edward P. Evans, Tr.

Established in 1983 in VA.
Donor: Edward P. Evans.
Foundation type: Independent foundation.
Financial data (yr. ended 11/30/05): Assets, $3,760,458 (M); expenditures, $476,841; qualifying distributions, $463,906; giving activities include $463,906 for grants.
Fields of interest: Secondary school/education; Environment; Hospitals (general); Health care; Health organizations, association.
Type of support: General/operating support.
Limitations: Giving primarily in MA and VA. No grants to individuals.
Application information: Application form not required.
Deadline(s): None
Trustees: Edward P. Evans; Dorsey R. Gardner.
Number of staff: None.
EIN: 256232129
Selected grants: The following grants were reported in 2004.
$49,800 to Washington Ballet, DC.
$15,000 to Fauquier Society for the Prevention of Cruelty to Animals, Warrenton, VA.
$10,000 to Piedmont Environmental Council, Warrenton, VA.
$4,750 to Memorial Sloan-Kettering Cancer Center, Society of, New York, NY.
$1,000 to Chase Wildlife Foundation, New York, NY.
$500 to Mount Carmel House, DC.
$500 to Museum of the City of New York, New York, NY.
$425 to East Side Settlement House, New York, NY.
$200 to Citizens for Fauquier County, Warrenton, VA.
$165 to Meadows Outdoors Foundation, The Plains, VA.

9417
The Flagler Foundation ✧
(formerly The Clisby Charitable Trust)
8100 Three Chopt Rd., Ste. 125
Richmond, VA 23229 (804) 285-4581
Contact: Fleet Roberts, Asst. Secy.
Application address: c/o SunTrust Bank Endowments & Foundations, P.O. Box 26665, Richmond, VA 23261-6665, tel.: (804) 782-5280; FAX: (804) 285-6560

Incorporated in 1963 in VA.
Donor: Jessie Kenan Wise†.
Foundation type: Independent foundation.

Financial data (yr. ended 12/31/05): Assets, $20,098,151 (M); expenditures, $2,497,987; qualifying distributions, $2,358,198; giving activities include $2,312,200 for 32 grants (high: $1,000,000; low: $5,000).
Purpose and activities: Support largely for higher and secondary education, human services and cultural programs.
Fields of interest: Arts; Elementary/secondary education; Higher education; Human services.
Type of support: General/operating support; Continuing support; Capital campaigns; Building/renovation; Endowments; Emergency funds; Professorships; Seed money; Curriculum development; Scholarship funds; Matching/challenge support.
Limitations: Giving in the central VA area. No grants to individuals.
Publications: Informational brochure (including application guidelines).
Application information: Receipt of proposals acknowledged. Application form not required.
  Initial approach: Proposal
  Copies of proposal: 5
  Deadline(s): Mar. 1
  Board meeting date(s): Oct.
  Final notification: Dec. 31
Officers and Directors:* Louise L. Foster,* Pres.; Bradford B. Sauer,* V.P. and Treas.; Lewis B. Pollard, V.P.; Kenan Lewis White, Secy.; William Hill Brown III; Catherine Gray Hathaway; Janet Lewis Sauer; B. Briscoe White III.
Number of staff: 1 part-time professional.
EIN: 546051282
Selected grants: The following grants were reported in 2005.
$1,000,000 to Flagler College, Saint Augustine, FL.
$100,000 to Virginia Home for Boys and Girls, Richmond, VA.
$50,000 to Highland School, Warrenton, VA.
$50,000 to Saint Christophers School, Richmond, VA.
$47,400 to International Hospital for Children, Richmond, VA.
$35,000 to Westminster-Canterbury Foundation, Richmond, VA.
$27,000 to Salvation Army, Hayes, VA.
$25,000 to Freedom House, Richmond, VA.
$25,000 to Hospice of the Piedmont, High Point, NC.
$20,000 to Noahs Children, Richmond, VA.

9418
The Lee and Juliet Folger Fund ✧
(formerly The Folger Fund)
c/o Anne L. Stone & Assocs., LLC
6862 Elm St., Ste. 740
McLean, VA 22101 (703) 847-1350

Incorporated in 1955 in DC.
Donors: Eugenia B. Dulin†; Kathrine Dulin Folger†; Lee Merritt Folger.
Foundation type: Independent foundation.
Financial data (yr. ended 8/31/05): Assets, $55,165,099 (M); expenditures, $3,305,756; qualifying distributions, $3,130,196; giving activities include $3,081,250 for 113 grants (high: $350,000; low: $250).
Purpose and activities: Giving primarily for the arts and education; funding also for human services.
Fields of interest: Museums; Performing arts; Historic preservation/historical societies; Secondary school/education; Higher education;

Education; Hospitals (general); Health organizations, association; Human services.
Type of support: General/operating support; Building/renovation; Endowments; Scholarship funds.
Limitations: Applications not accepted. Giving primarily in Washington, DC, and MA; some funding nationally. No grants to individuals.
Publications: Annual report.
Application information: Contributes only to pre-selected organizations.
Officers: Lee Merritt Folger, Pres. and Treas.; Juliet C. Folger, V.P.; John Dulin Folger, Secy.
EIN: 520794388
Selected grants: The following grants were reported in 2005.
$300,000 to National Gallery of Art, DC.
$250,000 to Saint Albans School, DC.
$200,000 to Washington National Cathedral, DC.
$150,000 to National Geographic Society, DC.
$100,000 to John F. Kennedy Center for the Performing Arts, DC.
$100,000 to North Haven Conservation Partners, North Haven, ME.
$50,000 to Asia Society, New York, NY.
$25,000 to Center for Strategic and International Studies, DC.
$5,000 to Capital Partners for Education, DC.
$5,000 to National Building Museum, DC.

9419
Foundation for Roanoke Valley, Inc. ✧
310 1st St., Ste. 1150
P.O. Box 1159
Roanoke, VA 24006 (540) 985-0204
Contact: Alan E. Ronk, Exec. Dir.
FAX: (540) 982-8175;
E-mail: alan@foundationforroanokevalley.org;
URL: http://www.foundationforroanokevalley.org

Established in 1988 in VA; funded in 1990.
Foundation type: Community foundation.
Financial data (yr. ended 6/30/05): Assets, $20,734,677 (M); gifts received, $1,094,823; expenditures, $1,588,368; giving activities include $1,073,114 for 628+ grants.
Purpose and activities: The foundation seeks to foster positive change on behalf of the community by: 1) enabling donors to carry out their charitable intent through prudently administered permanent endowment funds; 2) offering a comprehensive array of services to encourage, advance and educate concerning effective philanthropy; 3) making creative grants to meet continuing and emerging community needs and opportunities; and 4) providing leadership in identifying and assessing community issues and acting as a catalyst to initiate specific responses.
Fields of interest: Arts; Education; Health care; Health organizations, association; Children/youth, services; Family services; Human services.
Type of support: General/operating support; Equipment; Emergency funds; Program development; Seed money; Scholarship funds.
Limitations: Giving primarily in the greater Roanoke Valley, VA, area, with emphasis on Roanoke, Botetourt, Craig, Franklin and Rockbridge counties, VA. No support for sectarian, religious, or fraternal organizations. No grants to individuals, or for deficit reduction, capital campaigns or endowments, fundraising events, or celebration events.
Publications: Annual report; Informational brochure; Newsletter.

Application information: Visit foundation Web site for grant information. Application form required.
  Initial approach: Letter or telephone
  Copies of proposal: 1
  Deadline(s): Varies by fund, but primarily Aug. 1 and Feb. 1
  Board meeting date(s): Quarterly
  Final notification: Usually within 60 days
Officers and Governors:* William A. Nash,* Chair.; Nancy Howell Agee,* Vice-Chair.; R. Steve Blanks, Treas.; Alan E. Ronk, Exec. Dir.; Robert A. Archer; Dotsy S. Clifton; Nan L. Coleman; Edwin R. Feinour; John R. Francis; Jan B. Garrett; Clydenne R. Glenn; Maryellen F. Goodlatte; Mason Haynesworth; Robert C. Lawson, Jr.; John C. Parrott II; Charlotte K. Porterfield; Harry S. Rhodes; Frank W. Rogers III; Kenneth D. Tuck, M.D.; John B. Williamson III; Jack F. Wright, Jr.
Number of staff: 2 full-time professional; 1 part-time professional.
EIN: 541959458

9420
The Horace G. Fralin Charitable Trust ✧
P.O. Box 20069
Roanoke, VA 24018
Contact: W. Heywood Fralin, Tr.

Established in 1989 in VA.
Foundation type: Independent foundation.
Financial data (yr. ended 12/31/05): Assets, $45,522,373 (L); expenditures, $2,022,687; qualifying distributions, $1,876,955; giving activities include $1,876,955 for 26 grants (high: $1,753,783; low: $250).
Purpose and activities: The trust primarily provides grants to qualified charitable organizations in Roanoke Valley, VA for the purchase, construction, renovation or expansion of buildings, equipment and other capital assets of a long-term nature that help the organizations to further their goals.
Fields of interest: Museums (art); Performing arts; music; Arts; Higher education; Education; Environment, natural resources; Human services; Children/youth, services.
Type of support: Building/renovation; Equipment; Land acquisition.
Limitations: Giving primarily in Roanoke, VA. No support for private foundations. No grants to individuals, or for multi-year commitments, sponsorships, scholarships or fund-raisers.
Application information: Videos will not be accepted. Application form not required.
  Initial approach: Written proposal
  Deadline(s): None
Officer and Trustee:* W. Heywood Fralin,* Mgr.
Number of staff: 1 part-time support.
EIN: 541509505
Selected grants: The following grants were reported in 2004.
$1,889,023 to Art Museum of Western Virginia, Roanoke, VA.
$5,000 to River Foundation, Roanoke, VA.
$2,000 to Mill Mountain Theater, Roanoke, VA.
$1,000 to Blue Ridge Public Television, Roanoke, VA.
$500 to History Museum and Historical Society of Western Virginia, Roanoke, VA.
$500 to Opera Roanoke, Roanoke, VA.
$250 to Arts Council of the Blue Ridge, Roanoke, VA.

9421
Franklin Southampton Charities ◇
P.O. Box 276
Franklin, VA 23851 (757) 569-1611
Contact: G. Elliott Cobb, Jr., Dir.

Established in 2000 in VA.
Donors: Old Hospital Corp.; Southampton Memorial Hospital Endowment Fund.
Foundation type: Independent foundation.
Financial data (yr. ended 12/31/04): Assets, $31,061,590 (M); expenditures, $1,692,361; qualifying distributions, $1,454,115; giving activities include $1,426,262 for 65 grants (high: $90,744; low: $1,750).
Fields of interest: Education; Health organizations, association; Children/youth, services; Community development.
Limitations: Giving primarily in the city of Franklin, and Southampton County, VA.
Application information:
Initial approach: Letter
Deadline(s): Apr. 1 and Aug. 30
Officers and Directors:* Asa B. Johnson,* Chair.; E. Warren Beale, Jr.,* Vice-Chair.; G. Elliott Cobb, Jr.,* Secy.; Robert L. Putze, M.D.*, Treas.; Glenn P. Bidwell, Jr., M.D.; William M. Birdsong, Jr.; Ernest Cloud, Jr.; Anita T. Felts; Edna R. King; William A. Peak; Sol W. Rawls, Jr.; James J. Vasoti; W. Elliott Whitfield.
EIN: 311613116
Selected grants: The following grants were reported in 2003.
$112,000 to Paul D. Camp Community College, Franklin, VA. For equipment for RN program and independent RN program support.
$79,740 to Childrens Center, Franklin, VA. For Ready to Learn scholarships for low-income families.
$55,000 to Boys and Girls Clubs of America, Norfolk, VA.
$34,000 to Franklin, City of, Franklin, VA. For local economic revitalization project.
$24,815 to Southampton, County of, Courtland, VA. To upgrade self-contained breathing apparatus for Sourtland Volunteer Fire Department.
$20,580 to United Way, Franklin/Southampton Area, Franklin, VA. For admin expenses.
$16,000 to Hunterdale Volunteer Fire Department, Franklin, VA. For back-up power generator.
$14,486 to Franklin City School, Franklin, VA. For equipment, uniforms, and fees for indigent students in Health and Medical Sciences Program.
$13,500 to Boy Scouts of America, Colonial Virginia Council, Newport News, VA. For summer camp programs for local scouts.
$10,000 to Planned Parenthood of Southeastern Virginia, Hampton, VA. For family life/pregnancy prevention program for local schools.

9422
Freddie Mac Foundation ▼ ◇
8250 Jones Branch Dr.
M.S. A-40
McLean, VA 22102 (703) 918-8888
Contact: Tia Waller-Pryde, Mgr.
FAX: (703) 918-8895;
E-mail: freddiemac_foundation@freddiemac.com;
URL: http://www.freddiemacfoundation.org

Established in 1991 in VA.
Donor: Federal Home Loan Mortgage Corp.

Foundation type: Company-sponsored foundation.
Financial data (yr. ended 12/31/05): Assets, $206,483,808 (M); gifts received, $150; expenditures, $28,233,119; qualifying distributions, $28,015,846; giving activities include $22,363,126 for grants.
Purpose and activities: The foundation supports organizations involved with pre-K-12 education, human services public education, children and youth, and families.
Fields of interest: Elementary/secondary education; Education, early childhood education; Human services, public education; Children/youth, services; Children, foster care; Child development, services; Family services; Family services, parent education.
Type of support: General/operating support; Continuing support; Capital campaigns; Program development; Conferences/seminars; Publication; Seed money; Research; Technical assistance; Consulting services; Employee volunteer services; Program evaluation; Employee matching gifts.
Limitations: Giving primarily in the metropolitan Washington, DC, area, with emphasis on Washington, DC, Charles, Frederick, Howard, Montgomery, and Prince George's counties, MD, and Alexandria, Arlington County, Fairfax County, Falls Church, Leesburg, Loudoun County, Manassas Park, and Prince William County, VA; giving also to statewide organizations in MD and VA and national organizations. No support for discriminatory organizations. No grants to individuals, or for training in or promotion of religious doctrine, debt reduction, or endowments.
Publications: Application guidelines; Annual report; Grants list; Informational brochure.
Application information: Application form required.
Initial approach: Complete online application form
Deadline(s): Mar. 1 and Sept. 6
Board meeting date(s): 1st Thurs. in Mar., June, Sept., and Dec.
Final notification: May 15 and Nov. 15
Officers and Directors:* Ralph F. Boyd, Jr.,* Chair.; Maxine B. Baker,* C.E.O. and Pres.; Dionisia Bejarano Coffman; Michelle Engler; Tracy Hagen Mooney; Ronald F. Poe; Dwight P. Robinson; Richard F. Syron; Clarice Dibble Walker.
Number of staff: 11 full-time professional.
EIN: 541573760
Selected grants: The following grants were reported in 2005.
$1,500,000 to Boys and Girls Clubs of Greater Washington, Silver Spring, MD. For Education Initiative for DC area clubs and to enable children to attend Camp Brown.
$1,500,000 to National Center for Children and Families, Bethesda, MD. 2 grants: $500,000 (For academic enrichment activities and social support services that enhance lives of students and their families at J.C. Nalle Community School located in DC), $1,000,000 (For construction of Youth Activity Center, to address needs of children and youth who are homeless and/or at risk of delinquency, and homeless families in DC area).
$550,000 to Center for Multicultural Human Services, Falls Church, VA. To provide homeless families who are language and cultural minorities with transitional housing and support services that prepare them to move to permanent and affordable housing in Fairfax County, VA.
$500,000 to Doorways for Women and Families, Arlington, VA. To rebuild Emergency Family Shelter for homeless families in Arlington County,

VA, improve level of service and increase bed capacity.
$500,000 to Higher Achievement Program, DC. For after-school program that improves academic performance and creates culture that values achievements of disadvantaged youth in DC.
$100,000 to Coalition for the Homeless, DC. To enhance transitional housing program in DC by upgrading security system and by installing basketball court for homeless children residing in program.
$50,000 to Marys Center for Maternal and Child Care, DC. For Healthy Families programs that offer home visitation, long-term partnership with families, and linkages with community resources to ensure children are healthy, safe, and ready for school.
$30,000 to Heads Up: A University Neighborhood Initiative, DC. To provide daily academic and social support to low-income elementary school students.
$25,000 to National Organization of Concerned Black Men, DC. To provide tutoring in math and reading to students at Kramer Middle School located in Ward 6 of DC.

9423
Fredericksburg Savings Charitable Foundation ◇
P.O. Box 783
400 George St.
Fredericksburg, VA 22404
Contact: Samuel C. Harding, Jr., Dir.

Established in 1998 in DE and VA.
Donor: Virginia Capital Bancshares, Inc.
Foundation type: Company-sponsored foundation.
Financial data (yr. ended 12/31/04): Assets, $16,212,821 (M); expenditures, $831,768; qualifying distributions, $813,376; giving activities include $812,500 for 87 grants (high: $75,000; low: $500).
Purpose and activities: The foundation supports programs designed to expand home ownership opportunities; and contribute to the quality of life in communities where Fredericksburg Savings Bank operates.
Fields of interest: Housing/shelter; Human services; Community development.
Limitations: Giving primarily in VA. No grants to individuals.
Application information: Application form required.
Initial approach: Contact foundation for application form
Deadline(s): Varies
Directors: William M. Anderson, Jr.; Samuel C. Harding, Jr.; Duval Q. Hicks, Jr.; Peggy J. Newman; William B. Young.
EIN: 541913172

9424
The Freedom Forum, Inc. ▼
1101 Wilson Blvd.
Arlington, VA 22209-2248 (703) 528-0800
Contact: Charles L. Overby, Chair.
FAX: (703) 284-3770;
E-mail: news@freedomforum.org; URL: http://www.freedomforum.org

Incorporated in 1991 in VA.
Foundation type: Operating foundation.

Financial data (yr. ended 12/31/05): Assets, $1,071,127,819 (M); expenditures, $62,213,150; qualifying distributions, $108,428,633; giving activities include $28,112,737 for 225 grants (high: $22,286,105; low: $100; average: $1,000–$175,000), $212,969 for 184 grants to individuals (high: $25,000; low: $56; average: $1,100–$12,500), $42,750 for 45 employee matching gifts, and $10,350,311 for 4 foundation-administered programs.

Purpose and activities: The Freedom Forum is a nonpartisan foundation dedicated to free press, free speech and free spirit for all people. The foundation focuses on three funding priorities: the Newseum, First Amendment and newsroom diversity.

Type of support: Employee matching gifts; Grants to individuals.

Limitations: Applications not accepted. Giving on a national and international basis.

Publications: Annual report; Occasional report.

Application information: Unsolicited requests for funds not accepted.

Board meeting date(s): Quarterly

Officers and Trustees:* Charles L. Overby,* Chair., C.E.O., and Pres.; Alberto Ibarguen, Chair., Newseum; Peter S. Prichard,* Pres., Newseum; Nicole F. Mandeville, Sr. V.P., Finance, C.F.O. and Treas.; Joe Urschel, Sr. V.P. and Exec. Dir., Newseum; Mary Kay Blake, Sr. V.P., Partnership and Initiatives; Jack Hurley, Sr. V.P., Broadcasting; Christine Wells, Sr. V.P., International Initiatives and Free Spirit Progs.; Constance Aguayo, V.P., Human Resources; Pamela Y. Galloway-Tabb, V.P., Genl. Svcs.; Max Page, V.P., and Deputy Dir., Newseum; Rod Sandeen, V.P., Admin. and Publications; Jim Updike, V.P., Technology; James C. Duff, Secy.; John E. Heselden, Sr. Advisory Tr.; Allen H. Neuharth, Sr. Advisory Tr.; Martin F. Birmingham, Advisory Tr.; Bernard B. Brody, M.D., Advisory Tr.; Genl. Harry W. Brooks, Jr., Advisory Tr.; Brian Mulroney, Advisory Tr.; John C. Quinn, Advisory Tr.; John Seigenthaler, Advisory Tr.; James W. Abbott; Howard H. Baker, Jr.; Louis D. Boccardi; Tom Daschle; Michael G. Gartner; Gordon Gee; Felix F. Gutierrez; Charlene Drew Jarvis; Madelyn P. Jennings; Robert Khayat; Malcolm R. Kirschenbaum; Bette Bao Lord; Robert MacNeil; Wilma P. Mankiller; Jan Neuharth; H. Wilbert Norton, Jr.; Kenneth A. Paulson; Orage Quarles III; Timothy J. Russert; Gary Sisco; Michael I. Sovern; Ronald Townsend; Mark Trahant; Judy C. Woodruff.

Number of staff: 111 full-time professional; 6 part-time professional; 45 full-time support; 5 part-time support.

EIN: 541604427

9425
Friedman, Billings & Ramsey Charitable Foundation, Inc. ✧
1001 19th St. N., 20th Fl.
Arlington, VA 22209 (703) 469-1121
Contact: Richard O. Walker III, V.P., Corp. Giving
FAX: (703) 312-9757; E-mail: dwalker@fbr.com; URL: http://www.fbr.com/company/charitable-giving

Established in 1992 in DE and DC.

Donors: Friedman, Billings, Ramsey & Co., Inc.; Emanuel Friedman; Kindy French; Eric Billings; Marianne Billings; Eric Generous.

Foundation type: Company-sponsored foundation.

Financial data (yr. ended 9/30/04): Assets, $138,059 (M); gifts received, $591,400; expenditures, $465,750; qualifying distributions,

$462,265; giving activities include $462,265 for 70 grants (high: $83,950; low: $100).

Purpose and activities: The foundation supports organizations involved with arts and culture, education, health, at-risk youth, families, and human services.

Fields of interest: Arts; Education; Health care; Youth development; Family services; Human services.

Type of support: General/operating support.

Limitations: Applications not accepted. Giving primarily in the Washington, DC, area, including MD and VA. No grants to individuals.

Application information: Contributes only to pre-selected organizations.

Directors: Eric Billings; Emanuel Friedman.

EIN: 521802675

Selected grants: The following grants were reported in 2005.

$88,600 to Black Student Fund, DC.

$50,000 to Fidelity Investments Charitable Gift Fund, Boston, MA.

$50,000 to Public Education Partnership Fund, DC.

$31,000 to Capital Partners for Education, DC.

$25,370 to Georgetown University, DC.

$25,000 to Boys and Girls Clubs of Greater Washington, Silver Spring, MD.

$25,000 to Imagination Stage, Bethesda, MD.

$25,000 to Washington Performing Arts Society, DC.

$20,100 to National Foundation for Teaching Entrepreneurship, DC.

$800 to Lehigh University, Bethlehem, PA.

9426
The Funger Foundation, Inc. ✧
1650 Tysons Blvd., No. 820
McLean, VA 22102

Established in 1998 in MD.

Donors: Morton Funger; Norma Lee Funger; Yetta K. Cohen†.

Foundation type: Independent foundation.

Financial data (yr. ended 12/31/05): Assets, $5,731,099 (M); gifts received, $201,548; expenditures, $834,596; qualifying distributions, $776,668; giving activities include $776,668 for 48 grants (high: $155,000; low: $100).

Purpose and activities: Giving primarily to a children's medical center, as well as for arts and culture, and higher education; funding also for health associations, social services, and Jewish organizations.

Fields of interest: Museums (art); Museums (specialized); Performing arts; Performing arts centers; Higher education; Hospitals (general); Health organizations, association; Human services; Jewish federated giving programs; Jewish agencies & temples.

Limitations: Applications not accepted. Giving primarily in the eastern U.S., with emphasis on Washington, DC and MD. No grants to individuals.

Application information: Contributes only to pre-selected organizations.

Officers: Morton Funger, Pres.; Norma Lee Funger, Secy.-Treas.

Directors: C. Richard Beyda; Keith Parker Funger; William Scott Funger; Lydia Joy McClain; Melanie Nichols.

EIN: 541893307

Selected grants: The following grants were reported in 2004.

$100,000 to Childrens National Medical Center, DC.

$65,000 to National Gallery of Art, DC.

$60,020 to John F. Kennedy Center for the Performing Arts, DC.

$50,000 to Jewish Federation of Greater Washington, Rockville, MD.

$50,000 to Smithsonian American Art Museum, DC.

$23,334 to Duke University Medical Center, Durham, NC.

$20,000 to University of Pennsylvania, Philadelphia, PA.

$20,000 to Washington Performing Arts Society, DC.

$17,000 to National Symphony Orchestra, DC.

$10,000 to University of Virginia, Charlottesville, VA.

9427
The Galbraith Foundation ✧ ☆
c/o SunTrust Bank
402 Park St.
Charlottesville, VA 22903
Contact: Stephen Campbell

Donor: John W. Galbraith.

Foundation type: Independent foundation.

Financial data (yr. ended 12/31/05): Assets, $13,777,044 (M); gifts received, $10,000; expenditures, $583,436; qualifying distributions, $559,450; giving activities include $550,000 for 3 grants (high: $400,000; low: $50,000).

Fields of interest: Higher education; Public affairs.

Limitations: Applications not accepted. No grants to individuals.

Application information: Contributes only to pre-selected organizations.

Officers and Directors:* John W. Galbraith,* Pres. and Treas.; Rosemary Patricia Galbraith,* V.P. and Secy.; Rebecca Louise Galbraith; Rachel Leah Galbraith Watson.

EIN: 201371321

9428
Gannett Foundation, Inc. ▼
(formerly Gannett Communities Fund)
7950 Jones Branch Dr.
McLean, VA 22107
Contact: Pat Lyle, Mgr.
FAX: (703) 854-2167;
E-mail: foundation@gannett.com; URL: http://www.gannettfoundation.org

Established in 1991 in VA.

Donor: Gannett Co., Inc.

Foundation type: Company-sponsored foundation.

Financial data (yr. ended 12/31/04): Assets, $15,822,067 (M); gifts received, $3,584,667; expenditures, $4,044,576; qualifying distributions, $4,001,070; giving activities include $3,967,514 for 431+ grants (high: $950,000).

Purpose and activities: The foundation supports organizations involved with arts and culture, education, the environment, health, housing, human services, community development, and disadvantaged populations. Grants and employee matching gifts are also made through the Gannett Foundation Fund at the Rochester Area Community Foundation and the Community Foundation of Louisville, Inc.

Fields of interest: Media/communications; Media, journalism/publishing; Arts; Vocational education; Adult education—literacy, basic skills & GED; Education, reading; Education; Environment, natural resources; Environment; Health care; Housing/shelter; Youth, services; Human services; Civil rights, aging; Community development; Voluntarism promotion; Aging; Disabilities, people with; Asians/Pacific Islanders; African Americans/Blacks; Hispanics/Latinos; Native Americans/American Indians; Women; AIDS, people with; LGBTQ; Immigrants/refugees; Economically disadvantaged; Homeless.

International interests: United Kingdom.

Type of support: General/operating support; Capital campaigns; Building/renovation; Equipment; Program development; Conferences/seminars; Employee matching gifts; Employee-related scholarships.

Limitations: Giving primarily in areas of company daily newspaper and television station operations, including in the United Kingdom. No support for religious organizations, elementary or secondary schools (except for special initiatives not provided for by regular school budgets), fraternal, political, or veterans' organizations, athletic teams, bands, volunteer fire departments, or national or international organizations (except for journalism education/training grants). No grants to individuals (except for employee-related scholarships), or for endowments, multiple-year pledge campaigns, or medical or other research.

Publications: Application guidelines; Annual report; Informational brochure (including application guidelines).

Application information: Unsolicited requests for non-journalism education/training grants from national and international organizations are not accepted. Application form required.

Initial approach: Download application form and mail proposal and application form to nearest company daily newspaper or television station

Copies of proposal: 1

Deadline(s): Contact nearest company daily newspaper or television station for deadlines

Board meeting date(s): 3 times per year from Feb. to Sept.

Final notification: Approximately 2 to 3 months

Officers and Director:* Douglas H. McCorkindale,* Chair.; Daniel S. Ehrman, V.P.; Gracia C. Martore, V.P.; Todd Mayman, Secy.; Michael Hart, Treas.; Tara Connell, Exec. Dir.

Number of staff: 1 full-time professional; 1 full-time support.

EIN: 541568843

9429
The Glenstone Foundation ✧
8404 Parham Ct.
McLean, VA 22102

Established in 1995 in VA.

Donors: Mitchell P. Rales; The Mnuchin Foundation.

Foundation type: Independent foundation.

Financial data (yr. ended 12/31/04): Assets, $62,600,871 (M); gifts received, $20,000; expenditures, $2,738,852; qualifying distributions, $2,464,079; giving activities include $2,457,945 for 38 grants (high: $440,725; low: $250).

Purpose and activities: Giving primarily for art museums and to health association; funding also for education and human services.

Fields of interest: Museums (art); Elementary/secondary education; Education; Hospitals (specialty); Health organizations, association; Human services; Children, services; Foundations (private grantmaking).

Limitations: Applications not accepted. Giving on a national basis, with some emphasis on the greater metropolitan Washington, DC, area. No grants to individuals.

Application information: Contributes only to pre-selected organizations.

Officers and Director:* Mitchell P. Rales,* Chair.; Michael G. Ryan, Pres.; Joseph O. Bunting III, V.P.; Teresa L.C. Baldwin, Secy.-Treas.

EIN: 541739159

Selected grants: The following grants were reported in 2004.

$615,725 to National Gallery of Art, DC. 2 grants: $175,000, $440,725

$600,000 to SEED Foundation, DC. 2 grants: $100,000, $500,000

$200,000 to Bullis School, Potomac, MD.

$144,800 to Fight for Children, DC. 2 grants: $44,800, $100,000

$50,000 to Mark Cuban Foundation, Dallas, TX.

$20,000 to Shakespeare Society, New York, NY.

$15,000 to Solomon R. Guggenheim Museum, New York, NY.

9430
The Sam and Marion Golden Helping Hand Foundation, Inc. ✧ ☆
(formerly Virginia Scrap Iron & Metal Co. Charitable Foundation, Inc.)
P.O. Box 8278
Roanoke, VA 24014 (540) 343-3667
Contact: Mary Ann Ward, Pres.

Donors: Virginia Scrap Iron & Metal Co., Inc.; Industrial & Mill Suppliers, Inc.; Robin Wohlleban; Samuel Golden.

Foundation type: Company-sponsored foundation.

Financial data (yr. ended 12/31/05): Assets, $16,063,755 (M); gifts received, $14,276,241; expenditures, $781,821; qualifying distributions, $753,016; giving activities include $750,000 for 50 grants (high: $170,000; low: $100).

Purpose and activities: The foundation supports organizations involved with arts and culture, education, health, youth development, human services, and Judaism.

Fields of interest: Arts; Education; Health care, clinics/centers; Health care; Youth development; Salvation Army; Homeless, human services; Human services; Jewish agencies & temples; Religion.

Type of support: General/operating support.

Limitations: Giving primarily in VA. No grants to individuals.

Application information: Application form not required.

Initial approach: Proposal

Deadline(s): None

Officers and Directors: Mary Ann Ward, Pres.; John Lichenstein; David Tenzer.

EIN: 546050920

9431
Gottwald Foundation ✧
P.O. Box 955
Goochland, VA 23063

Established in 1957.

Donors: Floyd D. Gottwald, Sr.†; Floyd D. Gottwald, Jr.; Ann Gottwald†.

Foundation type: Independent foundation.

Financial data (yr. ended 12/31/04): Assets, $14,117,047 (M); gifts received, $30,000; expenditures, $564,245; qualifying distributions, $540,141; giving activities include $540,141 for 53 grants (high: $315,641; low: $100).

Purpose and activities: Giving primarily for education, health associations, and human services.

Fields of interest: Historic preservation/historical societies; Education; Health organizations, association; Human services; Federated giving programs.

Type of support: General/operating support; Capital campaigns; Scholarship funds.

Limitations: Applications not accepted. Giving primarily in VA, with emphasis on Richmond. No grants to individuals.

Application information: Contributes only to pre-selected organizations.

Officers: Floyd D. Gottwald, Jr., Pres.; James T. Gottwald, V.P.; Bruce C. Gottwald, Secy.-Treas.

EIN: 546040560

Selected grants: The following grants were reported in 2003.

$322,051 to Lewis Ginter Botanical Gardens, Richmond, VA. For Phase One Conservancy.

$75,000 to Virginia Military Institute Foundation, Lexington, VA. For Gottwald Scholars Program and Les German Science Chair.

$50,000 to Richmond Hill, Richmond, VA. For capital campaign.

$10,000 to Delta Waterfowl Foundation, Bismarck, ND. For Tidewater Virginia Scholar.

$10,000 to People Assisting the Homeless (PATH), Los Angeles, CA. For operating support.

$10,000 to Virginia Home, Richmond, VA. For operating support.

$6,500 to Virginia Foundation for Independent Colleges, Richmond, VA. For operating support.

$6,000 to American Red Cross, Richmond, VA. For operating support.

$5,000 to Christian Childrens Fund, Richmond, VA. For general support.

$5,000 to United Way of Greater Richmond and Petersburg, Richmond, VA.

9432
Harry and Harriet Grandis Family Foundation ✧
c/o Grandis Properties
P.O. Box 3029
Glen Allen, VA 23058

Established in 1998 in VA.

Donors: Sophia Gumenick; Harry Grandis; Harriet Grandis.

Foundation type: Independent foundation.

Financial data (yr. ended 1/31/05): Assets, $5,577,376 (M); expenditures, $462,578; qualifying distributions, $459,377; giving activities include $459,377 for 50 grants (high: $160,000; low: $1,000).

Purpose and activities: Giving primarily for health associations and health care, human services, and to Jewish organizations and temples; funding also for the arts.

Fields of interest: Museums; Museums (art); Museums (children's); Performing arts, orchestra (symphony); Arts; Education; Health care; Health organizations, association; Human services; Foundations (private grantmaking); Jewish federated giving programs; Jewish agencies & temples.

Limitations: Applications not accepted. Giving primarily in Richmond, VA. No grants to individuals.

Application information: Contributes only to pre-selected organizations.

Officers and Directors:* Harry Grandis,* Pres. and Treas.; Betty G. Lepage,* V.P.; Nancy Grandis White,* Secy.

EIN: 541922209

Selected grants: The following grants were reported in 2005.

$160,000 to Virginia Museum of Fine Arts, Richmond, VA.

$59,877 to Medical College of Virginia Foundation, Richmond, VA.

$50,000 to Jewish Community Federation of Richmond, Richmond, VA.

$10,000 to Richmond Ballet, Richmond, VA.

$5,000 to Collegiate School, Richmond, VA.

$5,000 to Richmond Symphony, Richmond, VA.

$1,000 to Historic Richmond Foundation, Richmond, VA.

9433

Elizabeth Ireland Graves Charitable Trust ◇

1853 Glenarvon Dr.
Bremo Bluff, VA   23022-2157

Established in 1998 in VA.

Foundation type: Independent foundation.

Financial data (yr. ended 12/31/05): Assets, $13,080,734 (M); expenditures, $857,048; qualifying distributions, $857,048; giving activities include $839,645 for 32 grants (high: $313,258; low: $500).

Purpose and activities: Giving primarily for animal welfare, as well as for the arts, education, social services, and to a Baptist church.

Fields of interest: Museums; Historic preservation/historical societies; Arts; Elementary/secondary education; Higher education; Education; Animal welfare; Human services; Protestant agencies & churches.

Type of support: General/operating support; Equipment; Program development; Publication.

Limitations: Applications not accepted. Giving primarily in VA; some funding nationally. No grants to individuals.

Application information: Contributes only to pre-selected organizations.

Trustee: Sayre O. Graves.

EIN: 546421160

Selected grants: The following grants were reported in 2004.

$264,002 to Grace Episcopal Church, The Plains, VA.

$200,000 to Virginia Center for the Creative Arts, Amherst, VA.

$50,000 to Virginia Tech Foundation, Blacksburg, VA.

$10,000 to Salvation Army, Hayes, VA.

$2,000 to Maymount Foundation, Richmond, VA.

$2,000 to Wildlife Center of Virginia, Waynesboro, VA.

$500 to American Friends Service Committee, Philadelphia, PA.

$500 to Virginia Museum of Fine Arts, Richmond, VA.

9434

The Guilford Foundation ◇

P.O. Box 13439
Richmond, VA   23225-8439

Established in 1987 in VA.

Donors: Ann K. Kirby‡; Roger H.W. Kirby; Annette S. Kirby; Wade H.O. Kirby; James W. Kirby, Jr.

Foundation type: Independent foundation.

Financial data (yr. ended 12/31/05): Assets, $13,382,830 (M); expenditures, $743,592; qualifying distributions, $644,925; giving activities include $644,500 for 20 grants (high: $150,000; low: $5,000).

Purpose and activities: Giving primarily for education and health care.

Fields of interest: Museums; Higher education; Health care; Human services.

International interests: England.

Limitations: Applications not accepted. Giving in the U.S., with emphasis on VA; some giving also in England. No grants to individuals.

Application information: Contributes only to pre-selected organizations.

Officers and Directors:* Wade H.O. Kirby, Pres.; Roger H.W. Kirby,* V.P.; Annette S. Kirby,* Secy.; Frank C. Page,* Exec. Dir.; James P. Flore; Alexandra Louise Kirby; Linda T. Kirby; James R. Landrigan.

EIN: 541423873

Selected grants: The following grants were reported in 2004.

$100,000 to Hampden-Sydney College, Hampden Sydney, VA.

$100,000 to Saint Christophers School, Richmond, VA.

$50,000 to Community Foundation of New Jersey, Morristown, NJ.

$50,000 to Medical College of Virginia Foundation, Richmond, VA.

$50,000 to Sacred Heart Center, Richmond, VA.

$25,000 to Childrens Hospital, Richmond, VA.

$20,000 to Doe Fund, New York, NY.

$15,000 to South Carolina Historical Society, Charleston, SC.

$15,000 to Valley Hospital Foundation, Ridgewood, NJ.

$10,000 to Media Research Center, Alexandria, VA.

9435

Richard and Caroline T. Gwathmey Memorial Trust

c/o Bank of America, N.A.
P.O. Box 26688
Richmond, VA   23261   (804) 788-3698

Established in 1981 in VA.

Donor: Elizabeth G. Jeffress‡.

Foundation type: Independent foundation.

Financial data (yr. ended 6/30/05): Assets, $14,813,852 (M); expenditures, $853,291; qualifying distributions, $748,475; giving activities include $730,500 for grants.

Purpose and activities: Giving primarily to the arts, cultural institutions, and for education.

Fields of interest: Museums; Historic preservation/historical societies; Arts; Education; Human services.

Type of support: Capital campaigns; Building/renovation; Equipment; Program development; Matching/challenge support.

Limitations: Giving limited to VA. No grants to individuals or for operating expenses.

Publications: Informational brochure (including application guidelines).

Application information: Application form not required.

Initial approach: Letter requesting guidelines
Copies of proposal: 1
Deadline(s): Mar. 1 and Sept. 1
Board meeting date(s): Nov. and May
Final notification: Immediately following meeting at which proposal was considered

Trustee: Bank of America, N.A.

Advisor: Richard B. Brandt, Ph.D.

Allocations Committee: William G. Broaddus; Richard C. Franson; William A. Hazel, Jr.; Brenda O. Mead; R. Gordon Smith.

Number of staff: 1 part-time professional; 1 part-time support.

EIN: 546191586

Selected grants: The following grants were reported in 2004.

$30,000 to J. Sargeant Reynolds Community College, Richmond, VA. For general support.

$25,000 to Virginia Historical Society, Richmond, VA. For general support.

$20,000 to Bluefield College, Bluefield, VA. For general support.

$16,000 to Virginia State University, Petersburg, VA. For general support.

$15,000 to Northstar Academy, Richmond, VA. For general support.

$15,000 to Virginia Foundation for Architecture, Richmond, VA. For general support.

$10,000 to Randolph-Macon Womans College, Lynchburg, VA. For general support.

$10,000 to Riverside School, Richmond, VA. For general support.

$7,725 to Neighborhood School of the Arts, Richmond, VA. For general support.

$7,300 to 1708 Gallery, Richmond, VA. For general support.

9436

Harrison Family Foundation, Inc. ◇

1000 Flowerdew Hundred Rd.
Hopewell, VA   23860

Established in 1993 in VA.

Donors: David A. Harrison III‡; Mary A. Harrison.

Foundation type: Independent foundation.

Financial data (yr. ended 9/30/05): Assets, $67,550,621 (M); expenditures, $3,560,608; qualifying distributions, $3,100,000; giving activities include $3,100,000 for 42 grants (high: $972,500; low: $2,500).

Purpose and activities: Giving for education, human services, and Protestant organizations.

Fields of interest: Education; Hospitals (general); Human services; Protestant agencies & churches.

Limitations: Applications not accepted. Giving primarily in VA. No grants to individuals.

Application information: Contributes only to pre-selected organizations.

Officers and Directors:* George A. Harrison,* Chair.; David A. Harrison IV, Pres.; Marjorie H. Webb,* Treas.; Ann L.H. Armstrong; Mary T.H. Keevil.

EIN: 541692935

9437

Herndon Foundation ✧
P.O. Box 995
Goochland, VA 23063

Established in 1965 in VA.
Donor: Floyd D. Gottwald, Jr.
Foundation type: Independent foundation.
Financial data (yr. ended 12/31/04): Assets, $21,611,799 (M); expenditures, $414,436; qualifying distributions, $362,356; giving activities include $362,356 for 54 grants (high: $166,667; low: $25).
Purpose and activities: Giving primarily for the arts, health associations, children, youth and social services, education, federated giving programs, a botanical garden, a game fish association, and to a Baptist church.
Fields of interest: Museums; Historic preservation/historical societies; Arts; Higher education; Botanical gardens; Health organizations, association; Recreation; Human services; Children/youth, services; Federated giving programs; Protestant agencies & churches.
Type of support: General/operating support; Endowments; Scholarship funds.
Limitations: Applications not accepted. Giving primarily in the Richmond, VA, area. No grants to individuals.
Application information: Contributes only to pre-selected organizations.
Officer: James T. Gottwald, Jr., Mgr.
Trustees: Floyd D. Gottwald, Jr.; William Gottwald.
EIN: 546060809
Selected grants: The following grants were reported in 2003.
$2,000,000 to Collegiate School, Richmond, VA. payable over 7 years.
$1,500 to Childrens Hospital, Richmond, VA. For annual support.
$1,000 to Virginia Union University, Richmond, VA. For annual support.
$500 to Maymont Foundation, Richmond, VA. For annual support.
$500 to Virginia Home, Richmond, VA. For annual support.
$300 to American Cancer Society, Richmond, VA. For annual support.
$300 to Carpenter Center for the Performing Arts, Richmond, VA. For annual support.
$300 to Historic Richmond Foundation, Richmond, VA. For annual support.
$300 to Meals on Wheels of Greater Richmond, Richmond, VA. For annual support.
$200 to American Lung Association of Virginia, Richmond, VA. For annual support.

9438

Houff Foundation ✧ ☆
P.O. Box 220
Weyers Cave, VA 24486
Contact: Dwight E. Houff, Secy.

Established in 1979 in VA.
Donors: Cletus E. Houff†; Houff Transfer, Inc.; Charlotte R. Houff†.
Foundation type: Independent foundation.
Financial data (yr. ended 12/31/05): Assets, $5,331,606 (M); expenditures, $321,187; qualifying distributions, $317,450; giving activities include $317,450 for 38 grants (high: $50,000; low: $500).

Purpose and activities: Giving primarily for health care and youth services; some giving for social services and Christian organizations.
Fields of interest: Arts; Health care; Boys & girls clubs; Human services; Youth, services; Federated giving programs; Christian agencies & churches.
Limitations: Giving primarily in the Shenandoah Valley, VA, area. No grants to individuals.
Application information: Application form not required.
Deadline(s): None
Officers: Roxie White, Pres.; Douglas Houff, V.P.; Dwight E. Houff, Secy.
EIN: 540236893

9439

HRH Charitable Foundation ✧
c/o Tax Dept.
4951 Lake Brook Dr., Ste. 500
Glen Allen, VA 23060
URL: http://www.hrh.com/pages/about/charitableFoundation.asp

Established in 1995 in VA.
Donor: Hilb, Rogal and Hamilton Co.
Foundation type: Company-sponsored foundation.
Financial data (yr. ended 12/31/03): Assets, $387,760 (M); gifts received, $570,388; expenditures, $447,886; qualifying distributions, $447,525; giving activities include $285,000 for 2 grants (high: $250,000; low: $35,000), and $162,525 for 8 grants to individuals (high: $53,525; low: $5,000).
Purpose and activities: The foundation supports organizations involved with arts and culture, housing, disaster relief, and human services.
Fields of interest: Arts; Housing/shelter, development; Safety/disasters; Children/youth, services; Human services.
Type of support: Scholarships—to individuals; Emergency funds.
Limitations: Applications not accepted. Giving primarily in VA.
Application information: Contributes only to pre-selected organizations and individuals.
Officers and Directors:* Martin L. Vaughan III, Pres.; Timothy J. Korman,* V.P.; Walter L. Smith,* Secy.; Carolyn Jones, Treas.
EIN: 541757380

9440

The Cecil and Irene Hylton Foundation, Inc. ✧
5593 Mapledale Plz.
Dale City, VA 22193-4527
Contact: Malcolm W. Cook, Treas.

Established in 1989 in VA.
Donors: Cecil D. Hylton†; The First Grandchildren's Charitable Trust; The Second Grandchildren's Charitable Trust; Irene V. Hylton Charitable Lead Trust; The Second Childrens Charitable Trust.
Foundation type: Independent foundation.
Financial data (yr. ended 12/31/04): Assets, $62,406,370 (M); gifts received, $4,888,282; expenditures, $3,004,988; qualifying distributions, $2,831,425; giving activities include $2,771,425 for 16 grants (high: $850,000; low: $2,500; average: $5,000–$500,000).
Purpose and activities: Giving primarily to a forest conservation fund, as well as to a hospital and a

Christian chapel; funding also for education and human services.
Fields of interest: Secondary school/education; Higher education; Environment, natural resources; Hospitals (general); Human services; Christian agencies & churches.
Type of support: General/operating support; Capital campaigns; Land acquisition.
Limitations: Giving primarily in Prince William County, VA; funding also in northern VA, and metropolitan Washington County; giving on a national basis for land conservation and ecology. No grants to individuals.
Application information:
Initial approach: Letter
Deadline(s): None
Officers and Directors:* Conrad C. Hylton,* Pres.; George A. Halfpap,* Secy.; Malcolm W. Cook,* Treas.; Cecilia M. Hylton.
EIN: 521633658

9441

The Jackson Foundation ✧
104 Shockoe Slip, Ste. 2B
Richmond, VA 23219-4125 (804) 644-5735
Contact: Patricia M. Asch, Exec. Dir.
FAX: (804) 644-5736; *E-mail:* pat@jacksonf.org;
URL: http://www.jacksonf.org

Established in 1981 in VA.
Donor: Andrew J. Asch, Jr.†.
Foundation type: Independent foundation.
Financial data (yr. ended 11/30/05): Assets, $14,572,416 (M); expenditures, $1,533,187; qualifying distributions, $1,386,448; giving activities include $1,386,448 for 52 grants (high: $75,000; low: $500).
Purpose and activities: Giving for the betterment of education and the environment in the metropolitan Richmond, VA, area; support also for education of economically disadvantaged children and historical preservation.
Fields of interest: Historic preservation/historical societies; Education; Environment; Children/youth, services; Economically disadvantaged.
Type of support: Building/renovation; Seed money; Matching/challenge support.
Limitations: Giving limited to VA, with emphasis on the Richmond, VA, metropolitan area. No grants to individuals or for endowment funds.
Publications: Informational brochure (including application guidelines).
Application information: See foundation Web site for guidelines; preference given to organizations in the Richmond, VA, metropolitan area. Application form not required.
Initial approach: Grant request with required information
Copies of proposal: 3
Deadline(s): 2nd Fri. of Jan. and 2nd Fri. of June, by noon
Final notification: 2nd Fri. of May and 2nd Fri. of Nov.
Officers and Directors:* Anthony James Asch,* Pres. and Treas.; Thomas A. Asch,* Secy.; Patricia M. Asch, Exec. Dir.; Linda Buchanan; W. Birch Douglass III.
Number of staff: 2 part-time professional.
EIN: 541186114

9442
Thomas F. and Kate Miller Jeffress Memorial Trust ✧

c/o Bank of America, N.A.
P.O. Box 26606
Richmond, VA   23261-6606
Contact: Richard B. Brandt, Advisor, Bank of America, N.A.
Application address: c/o Bank of America, N.A., Private Bank, P.O. Box 26688, Richmond, VA 23261-6688, tel.: (804) 788-3698; additional application address: c/o Bank of America, N.A., Private Bank, 1111 E. Main St., 12th Fl., Richmond, VA 23219

Established in 1981 in VA.
Donor: Robert M. Jeffress†.
Foundation type: Independent foundation.
Financial data (yr. ended 6/30/05): Assets, $31,098,241 (M); expenditures, $1,790,956; qualifying distributions, $1,666,074; giving activities include $1,613,340 for 86 grants (high: $30,000; low: $9,920).
Purpose and activities: Grants to VA colleges and universities for research activities.
Fields of interest: Higher education; Biomedicine; Medical research, institute; Science; Physical/earth sciences; Chemistry.
Type of support: Research.
Limitations: Giving limited to VA. No support for clinical research. No grants to individuals.
Publications: Informational brochure (including application guidelines).
Application information: Application form not required.
  Copies of proposal: 6
  Deadline(s): Mar. 1 and Sept. 1
  Board meeting date(s): May and Nov.
  Final notification: After meeting at which proposal has been considered
Officer: Sarah Kay, Secy.
Trustee: Bank of America, N.A.
Advisor: Richard B. Brandt, Ph.D.
Allocations Committee: Lawrence Blanchard; Cary "Thomas" Gresham; W. David Harless; Thomas Hass; Austin L. Roberts.
Number of staff: 1 part-time professional; 1 part-time support.
EIN: 546094925
Selected grants: The following grants were reported in 2004.
  $30,000 to College of William and Mary, Williamsburg, VA. For research.
  $30,000 to James Madison University, Harrisonburg, VA. For research.
  $30,000 to Old Dominion University, Norfolk, VA. For research.
  $30,000 to Sweet Briar College, Sweet Briar, VA. For research.
  $30,000 to Virginia Commonwealth University, Richmond, VA. For research.
  $29,000 to Roanoke College, Salem, VA. For research.
  $27,320 to Bridgewater College, Bridgewater, VA. For research.
  $20,000 to University of Virginia, Charlottesville, VA. For research.
  $10,000 to University of Richmond, Richmond, VA. For research.
  $10,000 to Virginia Polytechnic Institute and State University, Blacksburg, VA. For research.

9443
The Joco Foundation ✧

312 Burruss Hall 0142, Virginia Tech.
Blacksburg, VA   24061   (540) 231-5751
Contact: Raymond D. Smoot, Jr., Treas.

Established in 1990 in VA.
Donor: Reid Jones, Jr.†.
Foundation type: Independent foundation.
Financial data (yr. ended 12/31/05): Assets, $86,645 (M); expenditures, $1,123,386; qualifying distributions, $1,114,740; giving activities include $1,114,740 for 7 grants (high: $541,400; low: $10,000).
Fields of interest: Education; Human services; Foundations (private grantmaking).
Limitations: Giving primarily in VA.
Application information:
  Initial approach: Proposal
  Deadline(s): None
Officers and Directors:* Margaret J. Irvin,* Pres.; John G. Rocovich, Jr.,* Secy.; Raymond D. Smoot, Jr.,* Treas.; W.E. Skelton.
EIN: 541552388

9444
Sheila C. Johnson Foundation, Inc. ✧

(formerly Geron P. Johnson Foundation, Inc.)
P.O. Box 1767
Middleburg, VA   20118
Contact: Merline Murray

Established in 1991 in VA.
Donors: Robert Johnson; Black Entertainment, Inc.; Sheila Johnson.
Foundation type: Independent foundation.
Financial data (yr. ended 12/31/05): Assets, $27,159,960 (M); gifts received, $1,423,450; expenditures, $2,826,336; qualifying distributions, $2,624,566; giving activities include $2,624,566 for grants.
Purpose and activities: Giving primarily to provide access to the arts for disadvantaged children in the U.S. and to work for the freedom of missing and exploited children worldwide. The foundation is committed to providing opportunities for children in the U.S.A. to express their innate creativity through the arts, specifically music, design and the visual arts. Priority is given to programs that create ongoing structures for children to have access to arts education and to initiatives that incorporate the arts as an essential element in basic educational curricula. The foundation is also committed to addressing the cause of missing and exploited children worldwide, and to working for their freedom and well being. Specific focus is on ending child pornography and sexual exploitation through supporting innovative programs and institutions that make a measurable difference in the lives of the children caught in the cycle of poverty and violence.
Fields of interest: Arts; Elementary/secondary education; Human services.
Limitations: Applications not accepted. Giving on a national basis. No grants to individuals.
Application information: Unsolicited requests for funds not accepted.
Officer: Sheila Johnson, Pres.
EIN: 521755871

9445
Kanter Family Foundation ✧

8000 Towers Crescent Dr., Ste. 1300
Vienna, VA   22182-2700   (703) 448-7688
Contact: Joel S. Kanter, Pres.

Established in 1989 in IL.
Donors: Burton W. Kanter†; Joshua S. Kanter; Joel S. Kanter.
Foundation type: Independent foundation.
Financial data (yr. ended 10/31/05): Assets, $8,182,746 (M); expenditures, $804,188; qualifying distributions, $732,795; giving activities include $732,795 for 43 grants (high: $248,312; low: $250).
Purpose and activities: Giving primarily for the arts, education, and Jewish organizations and temples.
Fields of interest: Visual arts; Museums; Performing arts; Performing arts, theater; Arts; Higher education; Education; Public policy, research; Jewish agencies & temples.
Type of support: Annual campaigns; Capital campaigns; Building/renovation; Endowments; Program development; Scholarship funds; Matching/challenge support.
Limitations: Giving primarily in Washington, DC, Chicago, IL, and VA. No grants to individuals.
Publications: Annual report.
Application information: Application form not required.
  Initial approach: Proposal
  Copies of proposal: 1
  Deadline(s): None
  Board meeting date(s): Varies
Officers: Joel S. Kanter, Pres. and Treas.; Joshua S. Kanter, V.P.; Janis Kanter, Secy.
Number of staff: 1 part-time professional.
EIN: 363682199

9446
Cyrus Katzen Foundation, Inc. ✧ ☆

P.O. Box 1040
Baileys Crossroads, VA   22041-0040
Contact: Cyrus Katzen, Tr.
Application address: 6031 Leesburg Pike, Falls Church VA 22041-2203; tel.: (703) 578-4000

Established in 1991 in MD.
Donors: Cyrus Katzen; Jay Katzen; Lynn Katzen; United Mortgage & Invest. Corp.; Mozel Development Corp.; Culmore Realty Co.
Foundation type: Independent foundation.
Financial data (yr. ended 11/30/05): Assets, $7,050,882 (M); gifts received, $1,642,519; expenditures, $3,445,976; qualifying distributions, $3,417,165; giving activities include $3,417,165 for 13 grants (high: $3,140,000; low: $125).
Fields of interest: Visual arts, art conservation; Museums (art); Higher education; Education; Jewish agencies & temples.
Limitations: Giving primarily in Washington, DC. No grants to individuals.
Application information:
  Initial approach: Letter
  Deadline(s): None
Trustee: Cyrus Katzen.
EIN: 521756979

9447

Kaufman Americana Foundation ✧
480 World Trade Ctr.
Norfolk, VA 23510 (757) 625-1627
Contact: Linda Kaufman, Pres.

Established in 1977 in VA. Classified as a private operating foundation in 1982.
Donors: George M. Kaufman†; Linda H. Kaufman.
Foundation type: Operating foundation.
Financial data (yr. ended 11/30/05): Assets, $22,054,458 (M); gifts received, $302,035; expenditures, $623,117; qualifying distributions, $524,501; giving activities include $513,000 for 3 grants (high: $500,000; low: $1,000).
Purpose and activities: Awards are generally made for the encouragement, promotion and enhancement of the study of American decorative arts or design, or related items; funding also for medical research, particularly health foundations.
Fields of interest: Arts; Medical research, institute.
Type of support: General/operating support.
Limitations: Giving on a national basis.
Application information: Application form not required.
  Initial approach: Letter
  Deadline(s): None
Officers and Directors:* Linda H. Kaufman,* Pres.; Betty Cloud, Secy.-Treas.; Luke Beckerdite; Claire K. Benjack; Wendy A. Cooper; Thomas G. Johnson, Jr.; Edward G. Kaufman; Mark Leithauser.
EIN: 510217081

9448

The J. Henry Kegley Foundation ✧
P.O. Box 1689
Bristol, VA 24203-1689

Established in 2000 in VA.
Donors: J. Henry Kegley†; The Frances E., Kegley Trust; The J. Henry Kegley Trust.
Foundation type: Independent foundation.
Financial data (yr. ended 12/31/05): Assets, $422,825 (M); gifts received, $390,080; expenditures, $395,052; qualifying distributions, $392,396; giving activities include $390,150 for 8 grants (high: $257,150; low: $2,500).
Purpose and activities: Giving for education, culture and the arts, civic and community improvements, and human services.
Fields of interest: Arts; Education; Human services; Community development.
Limitations: Giving limited to bi-state counties in east TN and southwest VA of Bristol, Washington and Sullivan. No support for political causes; religious, veterans' or fraternal organizations; private clubs; pre-college level private schools; national or international organizations; or intermediary organizations that distribute funds to other organizations. No grants to individuals, or for capital projects, travel, or conferences.
Application information:
  Initial approach: Letter (not to exceed 2 pages)
  Copies of proposal: 2
  Deadline(s): None
Trustees: Homer A. Jones, Jr.; George M. Warren, Jr.
EIN: 546445584

9449

The Kellar Family Foundation ✧
P.O. Box 1178
Alexandria, VA 22313-1178

Established in 1997 in VA.
Donor: Arthur Kellar.
Foundation type: Independent foundation.
Financial data (yr. ended 2/28/05): Assets, $27,652,331 (M); expenditures, $888,011; qualifying distributions, $739,944; giving activities include $710,346 for 13 grants (high: $300,000; low: $50).
Purpose and activities: Giving primarily for the arts, hospitals and health associations, children, youth and social services, family services, and federated giving programs.
Fields of interest: Performing arts; Performing arts, opera; Arts; Higher education; Hospitals (general); Substance abuse, services; Mental health/crisis services; Health organizations, association; Cancer; Human services; Children/youth, services; Family services; Residential/custodial care, hospices; Foundations (community); Federated giving programs.
Limitations: Applications not accepted. Giving primarily in VA. No grants to individuals.
Application information: Contributes only to pre-selected organizations.
Officers: Arthur Kellar, Pres.; Elizabeth Kellar, Secy.; Peter Keefe, Treas.
Directors: Judith C. Kellar Box; Nathan Box; Mary K. Kellar.
EIN: 522026425
Selected grants: The following grants were reported in 2003.
$500,000 to Inova Health System, Falls Church, VA. 2 grants: $300,000 to Inova Kellar Center (For operating support), $200,000 to Inova Kellar Center (For capital campaign).
$100,000 to Youth for Tomorrow New Life Center, Bristow, VA. For general support.
$50,000 to Fairfax Symphony Orchestra, Annandale, VA. For general support.
$50,000 to Raymond F. Kravis Center for the Performing Arts, West Palm Beach, FL. For general support.
$50,000 to Wolf Trap Foundation for the Performing Arts, Vienna, VA. For general support.
$33,000 to Center for the Arts, Manassas, VA. For general support.
$25,000 to Palm Beach Opera, Palm Beach, FL. For general support.
$15,000 to Volunteer Emergency Families for Children, Richmond, VA. For general support.
$10,000 to Armory Art Center, West Palm Beach, FL. For general support.

9450

The Kington Foundation, Inc. ✧
201 N. Union St., Ste. 300
Alexandria, VA 22314-2642 (703) 519-3036
Contact: Mark J. Kington, Pres. and Treas.

Established in 1997 in VA.
Donors: Ann A. Kington; Mark J. Kington.
Foundation type: Independent foundation.
Financial data (yr. ended 11/30/05): Assets, $390,364 (M); expenditures, $442,698; qualifying distributions, $439,333; giving activities include $439,333 for 18 grants (high: $310,000; low: $1,000).

Purpose and activities: Support for religious, educational, humanitarian and arts programs in the southeastern regions of the U.S., particularly in TN and VA.
Fields of interest: Museums (art); Historic preservation/historical societies; Education; Environment.
Type of support: Annual campaigns; Building/renovation.
Limitations: Giving primarily in TN and VA, as well as in the southeastern U.S. region.
Application information: Application form required.
  Initial approach: Letter
  Deadline(s): None
Officers and Directors:* Mark J. Kington,* Pres. and Treas.; Allison W. Cryor,* Secy.; Ann A. Kington; Helen J. Kington.
EIN: 541831668
Selected grants: The following grants were reported in 2005.
$310,000 to National Gallery of Art, DC.
$33,333 to Virginia Historical Society, Richmond, VA.
$20,000 to Saint Stephens and Saint Agnes School, Alexandria, VA.
$12,500 to National Trust for Historic Preservation, DC.
$10,000 to Potomac School, McLean, VA.
$5,000 to Montpelier Foundation, Montpelier Station, VA.
$5,000 to Mount Vernon Ladies Association, Mount Vernon, VA.

9451

The Kluge-Moses Foundation ✧ ☆
(formerly The Patricia M. Kluge Foundation)
100 Grand Cru Dr.
Charlottesville, VA 22902-7734
Application address: c/o Patricia M. Kluge, Albemarle House, 3414 Ellerslie Dr., Charlotte, VA 22902, tel.: (434) 961-9009

Established in 1995 in VA.
Donor: Patricia M. Kluge.
Foundation type: Independent foundation.
Financial data (yr. ended 12/31/05): Assets, $847,850 (M); expenditures, $422,415; qualifying distributions, $391,207; giving activities include $391,207 for grants.
Purpose and activities: Giving primarily for education and human services.
Fields of interest: Education; Human services; Christian agencies & churches.
Limitations: Giving primarily in Charlottesville, VA. No grants to individuals.
Application information: Application form not required.
  Initial approach: Letter
  Deadline(s): None
  Final notification: Within 60 days
Officer and Directors:* Patricia M. Kluge,* Pres.; Robert M. Huff; John Kluge, Jr.; Gerald McCarthy; William Moses.
EIN: 541803094

9452

The Robert P. and Arlene R. Kogod Family Foundation ✧
2345 Crystal Dr., 10th Fl.
Arlington, VA 22202

Established in 1998 in VA.
Donors: Arlene R. Kogod; Robert P. Kogod; Charles E. Smith Mgmt., Inc.
Foundation type: Independent foundation.
Financial data (yr. ended 12/31/05): Assets, $8,331,259 (M); expenditures, $418,506; qualifying distributions, $401,198; giving activities include $345,450 for 56 grants (high: $100,000; low: $250), and $51,998 for 1 foundation-administered program.
Purpose and activities: Funding for a scientific research program. Giving also to a youth center.
Fields of interest: Museums; Elementary/secondary education; Vocational education, post-secondary; Higher education; Higher education, college; Youth, services; Jewish agencies & temples.
Type of support: Scholarship funds.
Limitations: Applications not accepted. No grants to individuals.
Application information: Contributes only to pre-selected organizations.
Officers and Directors: Robert P. Kogod,* Pres.; Menachem Gottlieb, V.P. and Treas.; Arlene R. Kogod,* Secy.
EIN: 541813660
Selected grants: The following grants were reported in 2004.
$100,000 to Latin American Youth Center, DC.
$10,000 to American Jewish Committee, New York, NY.
$10,000 to Center for Mind-Body Medicine, DC.
$10,000 to Middle East Media Research Institute, DC.
$5,000 to Contemporary Jewish Museum, San Francisco, CA.
$5,000 to Filipino Community Support, San Jose, CA.
$5,000 to Urban League.
$3,000 to American Federation of Arts, New York, NY.
$2,500 to American Friends of the Tel Aviv Museum, New York, NY.
$2,500 to Jewish Historical Society of Greater Washington, DC.

9453
Lucille and Bruce Lambert Charitable Foundation, Inc. ✧ ☆
2100 Powhatan St.
Falls Church, VA 22043-1940 (703) 333-5370
Contact: J.T. Butler, Pres.

Established in 1999 in VA.
Foundation type: Independent foundation.
Financial data (yr. ended 12/31/05): Assets, $7,813,663 (M); gifts received, $500,000; expenditures, $620,347; qualifying distributions, $358,889; giving activities include $358,889 for grants.
Purpose and activities: Giving primarily for higher education, and to volunteer fire departments.
Fields of interest: Higher education; Disasters, fire prevention/control; Human services; Christian agencies & churches.
Limitations: Giving on a national basis. No grants to individuals.
Officer and Directors: J.T. Butler,* Pres.; George P. Levendis; Jay C. Brockman; Cynthia I. Butler; Harold M. Lambert.
EIN: 541898273

9454
LandAmerica Foundation ✧
(formerly Lawyers Title Foundation)
P.O. Box 27567
Richmond, VA 23261 (804) 267-8330
Contact: Helen Parham, Tr.

Established in 1952 as Richmond Corporation Foundation.
Donor: Lawyers Title Insurance Corp.
Foundation type: Company-sponsored foundation.
Financial data (yr. ended 12/31/04): Assets, $1,749,119 (M); gifts received, $1,504,875; expenditures, $1,028,657; qualifying distributions, $1,028,657; giving activities include $1,028,657 for 1,349 grants (high: $76,342).
Purpose and activities: The foundation supports organizations involved with arts and culture, education, health, human services, and religion.
Fields of interest: Arts; Higher education; Education; Hospitals (general); Health care; Children/youth, services; Human services; Federated giving programs; Religion.
Type of support: Annual campaigns; Capital campaigns; Employee matching gifts.
Limitations: Giving primarily in areas of company operations. No support for alumni groups. No grants for subscriptions or religious building.
Application information: Application form required.
   Initial approach: Contact foundation for application form
   Deadline(s): None
   Board meeting date(s): Quarterly
Trustees: Theodore L. Chandler; Ross Dorneman; Charles H. Foster, Jr.; Helen Parham; Linda Rehak; William Thornton.
EIN: 546031167
Selected grants: The following grants were reported in 2003.
$63,703 to United Way of Richmond County, Rockingham, NC.
$5,000 to University of Maryland-College Park, College Park, MD.
$1,100 to University of Washington, Seattle, WA.
$1,000 to Bates College, Lewiston, ME.
$750 to Fordham University, Bronx, NY.
$500 to Colgate University, Hamilton, NY.
$400 to Sweet Briar College, Sweet Briar, VA.
$200 to Harvard University, Cambridge, MA.
$150 to Western Washington University, Bellingham, WA.
$50 to New York University, New York, NY.

9455
Landmark Communications Foundation ✧
(formerly Landmark Charitable Foundation)
150 W. Brambleton Ave.
Norfolk, VA 23510 (757) 446-2010
Contact: Linda Hyatt Wilson, V.P.
FAX: (757) 446-2489;
E-mail: lwilson@lcimedia.com; URL: http://www.landmarkcom.com/about/community.php

Incorporated in 1953 in VA.
Donors: Landmark Communications, Inc.; The Virginian-Pilot; Greensboro News Co.; Times-World Corp.; KLAS-TV; WTVF-News Channel 5 Network; Capital Gazette Communications, Inc.
Foundation type: Company-sponsored foundation.
Financial data (yr. ended 12/31/04): Assets, $62,960,694 (M); gifts received, $890,720; expenditures, $2,876,324; qualifying distributions,

$2,506,098; giving activities include $2,309,997 for 141 grants (high: $210,000; low: $500).
Purpose and activities: The foundation supports organizations involved with arts and culture, education, youth development, human services, and leadership development.
Fields of interest: Arts; Education; Youth development; Human services; Leadership development.
Type of support: Annual campaigns; Capital campaigns; Building/renovation; Equipment; Emergency funds; Program development; Professorships; Seed money; Curriculum development; Scholarship funds; Technical assistance; Program-related investments/loans; In-kind gifts; Matching/challenge support.
Limitations: Giving primarily in areas of company operations in Greensboro, NC, Las Vegas, NV, Nashville, TN, and the Hampton Roads and Roanoke, VA, areas. No support for health-related organizations. No grants to individuals, or for debt reduction.
Publications: Application guidelines.
Application information: Application form required.
   Initial approach: Letter of inquiry or telephone for application form
   Copies of proposal: 1
   Deadline(s): None
   Board meeting date(s): As required
   Final notification: Within 3 months
Officers and Directors: Frank Batten,* Chair.; Frank Batten, Jr., Pres.; Linda S. Hyatt,* V.P. and Exec. Dir.; Richard F. Barry III,* V.P. and Treas.; Decker Anstrom,* V.P.; Guy Friddell,* Secy.; D.R. Carpenter III; R. Bruce Bradley; L. Govan King; Emily Neilson; Donald H. Patterson, Jr.; Deborah Turner; Wendy Zomparelli.
Number of staff: 1 full-time professional; 1 part-time support.
EIN: 546038902
Selected grants: The following grants were reported in 2004.
$210,000 to Norfolk State University Foundation, Norfolk, VA.
$200,000 to Old Dominion University, Norfolk, VA.
$200,000 to Tidewater Community College, Portsmouth, VA.
$195,000 to United Way of South Hampton Roads, Norfolk, VA.
$113,000 to Business Consortium for Arts Support, Norfolk, VA.
$60,000 to Virginia Sports Hall of Fame, Portsmouth, VA.
$50,000 to Chesapeake Service Systems, Chesapeake, VA.
$50,000 to Chrysler Museum, Norfolk, VA.
$40,000 to Apple Ridge Farm, Roanoke, VA.
$25,000 to Elizabeth River Project, Norfolk, VA.

9456
Minnie & Bernard Lane Foundation
c/o Mrs. Bernard Lane
414 Washington St.
Altavista, VA 24517
Contact: Cindy Jester, Admin. Asst.
Mailing address: P.O. Box 359, Altavista, VA 24517

Established in 1957 in VA.
Donors: Bernard B. Lane†; Minnie B. Lane.
Foundation type: Independent foundation.
Financial data (yr. ended 3/31/06): Assets, $7,093,061 (M); gifts received, $354,909; expenditures, $940,615; qualifying distributions,

$854,410; giving activities include $854,410 for 110 grants (high: $250,247; low: $30).
Purpose and activities: Giving primarily for a food distribution program; support also for Methodist churches and other Christian organizations, social and human services, and international giving, including relief and missionary programs. Support is for U.S.-based organizations only, and primarily for projects in Campbell County, VA.
Fields of interest: Food services; Human services; International relief; Christian agencies & churches; Protestant agencies & churches.
Type of support: Seed money; Matching/challenge support.
Limitations: Applications not accepted. Giving primarily in Campbell County, VA, for new projects. No support for foreign organizations. No grants to individuals; no loans.
Application information: Unsolicited requests for funds not accepted; funds fully committed.
Trustees: Minnie B. Lane; R.L. Short.
Number of staff: 1 part-time professional.
EIN: 546052404
Selected grants: The following grants were reported in 2003.
$156,436 to YMCA, Altavista Area, Altavista, VA.
$100,000 to Virginia Historical Society, Richmond, VA.
$51,000 to Princeton University, Princeton, NJ.
$50,000 to Altavista, Town of, Altavista, VA.
$50,000 to Project Concern International, San Diego, CA.
$40,000 to Habitat for Humanity, Altavista Area/ Campbell County, Altavista, VA.
$25,000 to Virginia Episcopal School, Lynchburg, VA.
$20,000 to Austin College, Sherman, TX.
$12,000 to Avoca Museum and Historical Society, Altavista, VA.
$10,000 to National D-Day Memorial Foundation, Bedford, VA.

9457
Lind Lawrence Foundation ◇
4132 Innslake Dr.
Glen Allen, VA 23060
Contact: Lee P. Martin, Jr., Tr.

Established in 1973 in VA.
Donor: Lind Lawrence†.
Foundation type: Independent foundation.
Financial data (yr. ended 9/30/05): Assets, $7,360,038 (M); expenditures, $418,833; qualifying distributions, $358,246; giving activities include $355,375 for 16 grants (high: $135,000; low: $2,500).
Purpose and activities: Giving primarily for neurosurgical research; funding also for youth, family and social services.
Fields of interest: Neuroscience research; Human services; Youth, services; Family services; Community development.
Type of support: General/operating support; Capital campaigns; Building/renovation; Research.
Limitations: Giving primarily in Richmond, VA.
Application information:
Initial approach: Letter
Deadline(s): July 31
Trustees: Fred J. Bernhardt, Jr.; Lee P. Martin, Jr.
EIN: 237310359
Selected grants: The following grants were reported in 2005.
$15,000 to Elk Hill Farm, Goochland, VA.

$10,000 to American Red Cross, Richmond, VA.
$7,500 to Good Neighbor Village, Richmond, VA.
$5,000 to Richmond House, Richmond, VA.
$3,000 to Sacred Heart Center, Richmond, VA.

9458
The Lincoln-Lane Foundation ◇
207 Granby St., Ste. 302
Norfolk, VA 23510 (757) 622-2557
Contact: Edith G. Grandy, Secy.-Treas.
FAX: (757) 623-2698;
E-mail: lincolnlane@earthlink.net

Incorporated in 1928 in VA.
Donor: John H. Rogers†.
Foundation type: Independent foundation.
Financial data (yr. ended 7/31/05): Assets, $8,726,031 (M); gifts received, $3,000; expenditures, $581,241; qualifying distributions, $474,430; giving activities include $379,500 for 173 grants to individuals (high: $4,000; low: $500).
Purpose and activities: Giving limited to awards for college scholarships to individuals.
Type of support: Scholarships—to individuals.
Limitations: Giving limited to permanent residents of the Tidewater, VA, area. No grants for endowment or building programs, operating budgets, special projects, or annual fundraising campaigns; no loans.
Publications: Application guidelines; Program policy statement.
Application information: New applications available starting Sept. 1. Application form required.
Initial approach: Letter requesting application form
Copies of proposal: 1
Deadline(s): Oct. 1 through Oct. 31. Letters requesting applications must be postmarked no later than Oct. 15
Board meeting date(s): Apr., May, Oct., and Dec.
Final notification: Apr.
Officers and Directors:* Charles E. Jenkins II,* Pres.; Edith G. Grandy,* V.P., Secy.-Treas., and Exec. Dir.; Ruth P. Acra; John M. Ankerson; Patricia P. Cavender; Walter M. Moore IV.
Number of staff: 1 part-time professional; 1 part-time support.
EIN: 540601700

9459
The Lipman Foundation ◇ ☆
(formerly The Eric and Jeanette Lipman Foundation)
c/o Trust Company of Virginia
9030 Stony Point Pkwy.
Richmond, VA 23235

Established in 1985 in VA.
Donors: Eric M. Lipman†; Jeanette S. Lipman.
Foundation type: Independent foundation.
Financial data (yr. ended 12/31/05): Assets, $8,157,126 (M); expenditures, $677,895; qualifying distributions, $340,400; giving activities include $340,400 for grants.
Fields of interest: Museums; Education; Jewish agencies & temples.
Limitations: Applications not accepted. Giving primarily in Richmond, VA. No grants to individuals.
Application information: Contributes only to pre-selected organizations.
Officers: Jeanette S. Lipman, Pres.; W. Birch Douglass III, V.P.
EIN: 541360375

9460
The Jesse & Rose Loeb Foundation, Inc. ◇
P.O. Box 803
Warrenton, VA 20188 (540) 428-1960
Contact: Thomas H. Kirk, Exec. Dir.
FAX: (540) 428-1961;
E-mail: tkirk@loebfoundation.org; URL: http://www.loebfoundation.org

Established in 1991 in VA.
Donor: Rose Loeb.
Foundation type: Independent foundation.
Financial data (yr. ended 9/30/05): Assets, $9,490,630 (M); expenditures, $577,988; qualifying distributions, $540,512; giving activities include $464,224 for 21 grants (high: $55,000; low: $3,900), and $39,226 for 8 grants to individuals (high: $5,000; low: $5,000).
Purpose and activities: Giving primarily for human services and community development. Funding also for scholarships to student graduates of Liberty High School in Fauquier County, VA, who are pursuing higher education in the state of VA.
Fields of interest: Education; Human services; Community development.
Limitations: Giving primarily in the Fauquier County, VA, region. No grants to.
Publications: Application guidelines.
Application information: Application guidelines and form available on foundation Web site. Application form required.
Initial approach: Application form
Deadline(s): None for community grant applications; mid-Apr. for scholarship applications
Officers and Directors:* Sue Ann Meek,* Pres.; Fred G. Wayland, Jr.,* Secy.-Treas.; Thomas H. Kirk; Donald R. Yowell.
EIN: 541604839
Selected grants: The following grants were reported in 2005.
$50,000 to Fauquier Hospital, Warrenton, VA.
$20,000 to Fauquier Family Shelter Services, Warrenton, VA.
$10,000 to James Madison University, Harrisonburg, VA. 2 grants: $5,000 each
$5,000 to College of William and Mary, Williamsburg, VA.
$5,000 to Old Dominion University, Norfolk, VA.
$5,000 to University of Virginia, Charlottesville, VA.
$5,000 to Virginia Commonwealth University, Richmond, VA.
$2,115 to Northern Virginia Community College, Annandale, VA.
$2,111 to Mary Washington College, Fredericksburg, VA.

9461
Luck Stone Foundation, Inc. ◇
c/o Luck Stone Mktg. Dept.
P.O. Box 29682
Richmond, VA 23242 (800) 898-5825
Contact: Charles S. Luck III, Pres.
FAX: (804) 784-6390;
E-mail: ltissiere@luckstone.com; URL: http://www.luckstone.com/about/foundation.php

Established in 1966 in VA.
Donor: Luck Stone Corp.
Foundation type: Company-sponsored foundation.
Financial data (yr. ended 10/31/05): Assets, $9,684,104 (M); gifts received, $2,199,000; expenditures, $573,494; qualifying distributions,

$515,982; giving activities include $515,982 for 62 grants (high: $120,000; low: $100).

Purpose and activities: The foundation supports organizations involved with education, the environment, health, and safety, and community development.

Fields of interest: Education; Environment; Health care; Crime/law enforcement, police agencies; Disasters, fire prevention/control; Community development.

Type of support: General/operating support; Program development.

Limitations: Giving primarily in VA. No support for religious organizations. No grants to individuals, or for national disease-related fundraising, event sponsorships, or political campaigns.

Application information: Application form required.

Initial approach: Download application form and mail proposal and application form to foundation

Deadline(s): None

Officers: Charles S. Luck III, Pres.; Joseph Andrews, Jr., Secy.; J.H. Parker III, Treas.

EIN: 546064982

Selected grants: The following grants were reported in 2005.

$72,000 to Saint Christophers School, Richmond, VA.

$60,000 to Collegiate School, Richmond, VA.

$35,000 to Saint Catherines School Foundation, Richmond, VA.

$20,000 to Childrens Museum of Richmond, Richmond, VA.

$20,000 to Mary Baldwin College, Staunton, VA.

$10,000 to National D-Day Memorial Foundation, Bedford, VA.

$10,000 to Richmond Ballet, Richmond, VA.

$7,313 to Jamestown-Yorktown Foundation, Williamsburg, VA.

$5,000 to Virginia Foundation for Independent Colleges, Richmond, VA.

$3,000 to Virginia Historical Society, Richmond, VA.

9462

Ludington, Inc. ✧

P.O. Box 12641
Roanoke, VA 24027

Established in 1984 in KY.

Foundation type: Independent foundation.

Financial data (yr. ended 12/31/05): Assets, $5,589,179 (M); expenditures, $370,240; qualifying distributions, $363,451; giving activities include $360,000 for 3 grants (high: $270,000; low: $40,000).

Purpose and activities: Giving primarily for natural resource conservation, and family planning.

Fields of interest: Environment, natural resources.

Limitations: Applications not accepted. No grants to individuals; no loans.

Application information: Contributes only to pre-selected organizations.

Officer and Directors:* Philip Abbey,* Pres.; Emily Parrino; Greta Tisdale.

EIN: 311128833

9463

Greater Lynchburg Community Trust ✧

P.O. Box 714
Lynchburg, VA 24505-0714 (434) 845-6500
Contact: George H. Murphy, Pres.

FAX: (434) 845-6530; E-mail: challglct@ntelos.net; URL: http://www.lynchburgtrust.org

Established as a community trust in 1972 in VA.

Foundation type: Community foundation.

Financial data (yr. ended 9/30/04): Assets, $20,984,945 (M); gifts received, $1,392,072; expenditures, $1,082,818; giving activities include $917,371 for 137 grants (high: $324,429; low: $83), and $12,750 for grants to individuals.

Purpose and activities: Needs served are broad in scope including human services to children, youth, the needy, and the elderly; education; health; the arts; and the humanities.

Fields of interest: Humanities; Arts; Libraries/library science; Education; Health care; Food services; Youth development, services; Children/youth, services; Family services; Aging, centers/services; Women, centers/services; Homeless, human services; Human services; Nonprofit management; Community development; Social sciences; Youth; Aging; Disabilities, people with; Women; Economically disadvantaged; Homeless.

Type of support: Capital campaigns; Building/renovation; Equipment; Emergency funds; Program development; Seed money; Scholarship funds; Technical assistance; Employee-related scholarships; Scholarships—to individuals; Matching/challenge support.

Limitations: Giving limited to Lynchburg and Bedford City, and Amherst, Bedford, and Campbell counties, VA. No support for religious organizations for sectarian or religious purposes. No grants to individuals (except for designated scholarship funds), or for routing operating expenses, continuing support, annual campaigns, deficit financing, employee matching gifts, or non-grant support; no loans or multiple-year grants.

Publications: Application guidelines; Annual report; Informational brochure; Newsletter; Program policy statement.

Application information: Visit foundation Web site for grant application information sheet and guidelines. Application form required.

Initial approach: Submit grant information sheet and attachments

Copies of proposal: 10

Deadline(s): Mar. 15 and Sept. 15

Board meeting date(s): June, Sept., Dec., Feb., and Apr.

Final notification: June and Dec.

Officers and Directors:* Terry Hall Jamerson,* Chair.; John P. Eckert,* Chair., Distribs. Comm.; Yuille Holt III,* Vice-Chair.; George H. Murphy,* Pres.; William F. Quillian, Jr., Advisor; Elliot S. Schewel, Advisor; Stuart J. Turille, Advisor; Kenneth S. White, Advisor; W. Starke Camden; Samuel P. Cardwell; William E. Gayle, Jr.; Robert H. Gilliam; Joyce Houck; Joseph C. Knakal, Jr.; Amy Ray; John F. Richards; Irma Seiferth; Benny R. Shrader; John A. Watts, Jr.; T. Ashby Watts III.

Trustee Banks: Bank of America, N.A.; BB&T; SunTrust Bank; Wachovia Bank, N.A.

Number of staff: 1 full-time professional; 1 part-time professional; 1 part-time support.

EIN: 546112680

9464

The M.E. Foundation ✧

44180 Riverside Pkwy.
Lansdowne, VA 20176
Contact: Kelli R. Morris, Dir.
VA tel.: (703) 478-0100

Established in 1966 in NY.

Donors: Margaret Brown Trimble†; Frances Carroll Brown†.

Foundation type: Independent foundation.

Financial data (yr. ended 12/31/05): Assets, $10,089,902 (M); expenditures, $1,704,299; qualifying distributions, $1,624,620; giving activities include $1,579,291 for 101 grants (high: $335,000; low: $1,000; average: $10,000–$20,000).

Purpose and activities: Grants to organizations in the U.S. and abroad for evangelistic missionary work and Bible studies.

Fields of interest: Christian agencies & churches.

Limitations: Giving on a national and international basis. No grants to individuals.

Application information: Application form not required.

Initial approach: Proposal

Deadline(s): None

Board meeting date(s): May and Dec.

Officer and Directors:* Charles W. Colson,* Chair. and Pres.; Sharon Berry, M.D.; Calvin E. Howe; Grace McCrane; Kelli R. Morris.

EIN: 136205356

Selected grants: The following grants were reported in 2003.

$338,000 to Prison Fellowship Ministries, DC.

$97,000 to Prison Fellowship International, DC.

$53,000 to Campus Crusade for Christ International, Orlando, FL.

$50,000 to LeTourneau University, Longview, TX.

$44,000 to International Cooperating Ministries, Hampton, VA. 2 grants: $22,000 each

$32,500 to Ravi Zacharias International Ministries, Norcross, GA.

$20,000 to Crossroad Bible Institute, Grandville, MI.

$20,000 to Good News Jail and Prison Ministry, Richmond, VA.

$16,500 to Foundation for Reformation, Orlando, FL.

9465

The Malek Family Charitable Trust ✧

1259 Crest Ln.
McLean, VA 22101

Established in 1995 in VA.

Donor: Frederic V. Malek.

Foundation type: Independent foundation.

Financial data (yr. ended 12/31/04): Assets, $1,724,286 (M); gifts received, $125,000; expenditures, $402,261; qualifying distributions, $371,411; giving activities include $373,330 for 113 grants (high: $50,000; low: $20).

Fields of interest: Performing arts; Arts; Health organizations, association; Cancer; Cancer research; Human services; Children/youth, services.

Limitations: Applications not accepted. Giving on a national basis. No grants to individuals.

Application information: Contributes only to pre-selected organizations.

Trustees: Frederic V. Malek; Frederic W. Malek; Marlene Malek; Michelle Malek.

EIN: 546373070

9466
The Mars Foundation ✧
6885 Elm St.
McLean, VA 22101-3810 (703) 821-4900
Contact: Susan Martin, Asst. Secy.

Incorporated in 1956 in IL.
Donor: Mars, Inc.
Foundation type: Company-sponsored foundation.
Financial data (yr. ended 12/31/05): Assets, $9,398,006 (M); gifts received, $600,000; expenditures, $896,320; qualifying distributions, $830,383; giving activities include $812,000 for 91 grants (high: $100,000; low: $1,000).
Purpose and activities: The foundation supports organizations involved with arts and culture, education, natural resources, animal welfare, health, and human services.
Fields of interest: Historic preservation/historical societies; Arts; Education; Environment, natural resources; Animals/wildlife, preservation/protection; Health care; Children/youth, services; Human services.
Type of support: Continuing support; Annual campaigns; Building/renovation; Equipment; Endowments; Research; Matching/challenge support.
Application information: Application form required.
  Initial approach: Contact foundation for application form
  Copies of proposal: 1
  Deadline(s): Oct. 15
  Board meeting date(s): May and Dec.
  Final notification: Jan.
Officers: Jacqueline B. Mars, Pres.; Forrest E. Mars, Jr., V.P.; John F. Mars, V.P.; Otis O. Otih, Secy.-Treas.
EIN: 546037592
Selected grants: The following grants were reported in 2003.
$100,000 to Fort Ticonderoga Association, Ticonderoga, NY. For program support.
$100,000 to World Wildlife Fund, DC. For traveling exhibition and education project.
$20,000 to Student Conservation Association, Charlestown, NH.
$20,000 to Zoological Society of Philadelphia, Philadelphia, PA. For living classroom to educate the public.
$15,000 to Achievement Rewards for College Scientists (ARCS) Foundation, McLean, VA. For scholarships.
$15,000 to Planned Parenthood of New York City, New York, NY. For general support.
$15,000 to Planned Parenthood, Virginia League, Richmond, VA. For A Better Today for a Brighter Tomorrow program.
$15,000 to Virginia Foundation for Independent Colleges, Richmond, VA. For Scholars program.
$12,000 to National Opera Institute, DC. For productions and programs.
$11,000 to Hotchkiss School, Lakeville, CT. For annual support.

9467
Massey Foundation
4 N. 4th St., Ste. 100
Richmond, VA 23219
Contact: William E. Massey, Jr., Pres.

Established in 1958 in VA.
Foundation type: Independent foundation.

Financial data (yr. ended 11/30/05): Assets, $57,668,920 (M); expenditures, $3,147,992; qualifying distributions, $2,822,545; giving activities include $2,755,000 for 61 grants (high: $1,000,000; low: $5,000).
Purpose and activities: Giving primarily for higher and secondary education; some support for hospitals and health services, cultural programs, and social services.
Fields of interest: Arts; Secondary school/education; Higher education; Hospitals (general); Health care; Human services.
Type of support: General/operating support; Annual campaigns.
Application information:
  Initial approach: Letter
  Deadline(s): None
  Board meeting date(s): Annually
  Final notification: Apr.
Officers and Directors:* William E. Massey, Jr.,* Pres.; E. Morgan Massey,* Treas.; Craig L. Massey; William Blair Massey, Jr.
Number of staff: None.
EIN: 546049049
Selected grants: The following grants were reported in 2003.
$750,000 to Medical College of Virginia, Richmond, VA. For Massey Cancer Center.
$140,000 to University of Virginia Foundation, Department of Engineering, Charlottesville, VA. For general support.
$130,000 to Lewis Ginter Botanical Gardens, Richmond, VA. For general support.
$100,000 to American Red Cross, Richmond, VA. Fo general support.
$100,000 to University of Richmond, Richmond, VA. For general support.
$100,000 to Virginia Institute of Marine Science, Gloucester Point, VA. For general support.
$50,000 to Blue Ridge School, Dyke, VA. For general support.
$50,000 to Hampden-Sydney College, Hampden Sydney, VA. For general support.
$50,000 to Marshall University, Huntington, WV. For general support.
$50,000 to New Community School, Richmond, VA. For general support.

9468
John J. McDonald, Jr. & Marian J. McDonnell Charitable Foundation ✧ ☆
7984 Georgetown Pike
McLean, VA 22102-1426

Established in 1996 in VA.
Donors: John J. McDonnell, Jr.; Marian J. McDonnell.
Foundation type: Independent foundation.
Financial data (yr. ended 11/30/04): Assets, $1,226,203 (M); gifts received, $71,150; expenditures, $449,532; qualifying distributions, $427,574; giving activities include $427,574 for grants.
Fields of interest: Arts; Higher education; Human services.
Limitations: Applications not accepted. Giving primarily in VA. No grants to individuals.
Application information: Contributes only to pre-selected organizations.
Officers and Directors:* John J. McDonnell, Jr.,* Pres.; Marian J. McDonnell,* V.P. and Secy.
EIN: 541828698

9469
The McGlothlin Foundation
1005 Glenway Ave.
Bristol, VA 24201 (276) 645-5370
Contact: Thomas D. McGlothlin, Pres.

Established in 1998 in VA.
Donor: Woodrow W. McGlothlin‡.
Foundation type: Independent foundation.
Financial data (yr. ended 12/31/05): Assets, $23,940,060 (M); gifts received, $162,565; expenditures, $1,449,818; qualifying distributions, $1,196,563; giving activities include $1,094,240 for 10 grants (high: $451,000; low: $1,240).
Purpose and activities: Giving to worthy causes in higher education, health care, and the arts.
Fields of interest: Arts; Higher education; Health care; Human services.
Type of support: Building/renovation; Equipment; Land acquisition; Program development.
Limitations: Giving in the southeastern U.S., with special emphasis to eastern KY, southwest VA, and northeast TN.
Publications: Informational brochure.
Application information: Application form not required.
  Initial approach: Letter (not exceeding 2 pages)
  Copies of proposal: 1
  Deadline(s): Apr. 30 of each year
  Board meeting date(s): June and Dec.
  Final notification: Dec.
Officers: Thomas D. McGlothlin, Pres.; Michael D. McGlothlin, Secy.; James W. McGlothlin, Treas.
Number of staff: 1 part-time professional; 1 full-time support.
EIN: 541907305

9470
The McGue Millhiser Family Trust ✧ ☆
P.O. Box 1535
Richmond, VA 23218-1535 (804) 788-8732
Contact: Thomas McNally Millhiser, Tr.

Donors: Thomas McNally Millhiser; Ross R. Millhiser‡.
Foundation type: Independent foundation.
Financial data (yr. ended 12/31/05): Assets, $11,292,392 (M); expenditures, $534,022; qualifying distributions, $505,000; giving activities include $505,000 for 17 grants (high: $120,000; low: $1,000).
Fields of interest: Performing arts, dance; Performing arts, theater; Arts; Higher education, university; Education; Human services; Jewish agencies & temples.
Application information: Application form not required.
  Deadline(s): None
Trustees: Mary McGue Millhiser; Ross R. Millhiser, Jr.; Thomas Mcnally Millhiser; Timothy McGue Millhiser.
EIN: 306068869

9471
MCI Education Foundation ✧ ☆
(doing business as MCI Foundation)
(formerly WorldCom Education Foundation)
22001 Loudoun County Pkwy.
Bldg. G1-3-110
Ashburn, VA 20147
Contact: Laura Lott

Established in 1986 in DC.
Donors: MCI Communications Corp.; MCI WORLDCOM, Inc.; WorldCom, Inc.; MCI, Inc.
Foundation type: Company-sponsored foundation.
Financial data (yr. ended 12/31/05): Assets, $2,660,918 (M); gifts received, $3,518,296; expenditures, $1,228,738; qualifying distributions, $1,201,725; giving activities include $1,201,725 for 4 grants (high: $330,000; low: $269,225).
Purpose and activities: The foundation supports organizations involved with education and technology integration. Special emphasis is directed toward programs designed to integrate technology into K-12 education.
Fields of interest: Elementary/secondary education; Education; Science.
Type of support: General/operating support; Program development; Curriculum development; Research; Technical assistance; Program evaluation; In-kind gifts.
Limitations: Applications not accepted. No grants to individuals, or for capital campaigns or endowments; no employee matching gifts.
Publications: Occasional report.
Application information: The foundation utilizes an invitation only Request For Proposal (RFP) process. Unsolicited requests are not accepted.
   Board meeting date(s): Quarterly
Directors: Vinton G. Cerf; Jennifer McGarey.
EIN: 510294683

9472
Gerald and Paula McNichols Family Foundation, Inc. ✧
23349 Parsons Rd.
Middleburg, VA 20117-2817 (540) 687-4164

Established in 2000 in VA.
Donor: Gerald R. McNichols.
Foundation type: Independent foundation.
Financial data (yr. ended 12/31/04): Assets, $5,549,927 (M); expenditures, $450,395; qualifying distributions, $450,395; giving activities include $447,113 for 15 grants (high: $50,000; low: $500).
Fields of interest: Performing arts; Arts; Education; Human services.
Limitations: Giving primarily in AL and VA.
Application information:
   Initial approach: Letter
   Deadline(s): None
Directors: Melissa S. Cardon; Katherine L. Loftis; Gerald R. McNichols; Gerald R. McNichols, Jr.; Paula A. McNichols.
EIN: 541973996

9473
James A. Meador Foundation ✧
305 Blvd.
Salem, VA 24153
Application addresses: c/o Guidance Office, Staunton River High School, Rte. 4, Box 732, Moneta, VA 24121, tel.: (540) 947-2867; c/o Salem High School, 400 Spartan Dr., Salem, VA 24153, tel.: (540) 387-2437; c/o Glenvar High School, 4549 Malus Dr., Salem, VA 24153, tel.: (540) 387-6536

Foundation type: Independent foundation.
Financial data (yr. ended 12/31/05): Assets, $9,275,533 (M); expenditures, $640,261;

qualifying distributions, $536,400; giving activities include $536,400 for 21 grants (high: $75,000; low: $400).
Purpose and activities: Scholarships to seniors at Staunton River High School, Salem High School or Glenvar High School, VA, who plan to attend college. Grants also for health associations, human services, federated giving programs, Christian organizations and churches, and to a fire department.
Fields of interest: Health organizations, association; Disasters, fire prevention/control; Human services; Federated giving programs; Christian agencies & churches.
Type of support: Scholarships—to individuals.
Limitations: Giving primarily in VA, with emphasis on Moneta and Roanoke.
Application information: Application forms available at each high school. Application form required.
   Deadline(s): May 15
Officers: S.M. Meador, Pres.; Susan Tinsley, V.P.; C.M. Thomas, Secy.-Treas.
EIN: 540795438

9474
The Memorial Foundation for Children ✧
c/o SunTrust Bank
P.O. Box 26665
Richmond, VA 23261-6665 (804) 782-7114
Contact: Karl McTaggart, Grants Admin.

Established about 1934 in VA.
Donors: Alexander S. George†; Elizabeth Strother Scott†.
Foundation type: Independent foundation.
Financial data (yr. ended 12/31/05): Assets, $15,748,072 (M); gifts received, $300; expenditures, $851,853; qualifying distributions, $807,908; giving activities include $805,784 for 48 grants (high: $100,000; low: $500).
Purpose and activities: Aid to nonprofit groups for the care and education of Richmond, VA, area children 18 years of age and under.
Fields of interest: Arts; Child development, education; Education; Human services; Children/youth, services; Child development, services; Disabilities, people with; Economically disadvantaged.
Type of support: General/operating support; Equipment; Program development; Seed money; Curriculum development; Scholarship funds.
Limitations: Giving limited to the Richmond, VA, area. No grants to individuals, or for capital or endowment funds, annual campaigns, emergency funds, deficit financing, matching gifts, publications, conferences, scholarships, or fellowships; no loans.
Publications: Informational brochure (including application guidelines).
Application information: Grants not made for greater than 2 years in succession. Application form required.
   Initial approach: Letter or proposal
   Copies of proposal: 2
   Deadline(s): May 31
   Board meeting date(s): Mar., May, Oct., and Nov.
   Final notification: By Dec.
Officers: Mrs. Paul B. Cosentino, Pres.; Mrs. James M. Glave, V.P.; Mrs. Michael Jarvis, Corresponding Secy.; Mrs. Rupert Winfree, Recording Secy.; Mrs. Cotesworth Pinckney, Treas.
Number of staff: 1 part-time support.
EIN: 540536103

Selected grants: The following grants were reported in 2003.
$165,000 to Lewis Ginter Botanical Gardens, Richmond, VA.
$45,000 to Charity Family Life, Richmond, VA.
$40,000 to Cross-Over Ministry, Richmond, VA.
$35,000 to Irvin Gammon Craig Health Center, Richmond, VA.
$30,000 to Central Virginia Foodbank, Richmond, VA.
$30,000 to Northstar Academy, Richmond, VA.
$20,000 to Boys and Girls Clubs of Richmond, Richmond, VA.
$20,000 to New Community School, Richmond, VA.
$20,000 to Richmond Ballet, Richmond, VA.
$18,000 to Jacobs Ladder, Urbanna, VA.

9475
Tim Miller Foundation ✧ ☆
5301 Cleveland St.
Virginia Beach, VA 23462

Established in 2002 in VA.
Donor: ACS Systems & Engineering, Inc.
Foundation type: Independent foundation.
Financial data (yr. ended 12/31/05): Assets, $0 (M); expenditures, $1,194,158; qualifying distributions, $438,785; giving activities include $438,785 for 21 grants (high: $145,000; low: $500).
Fields of interest: YM/YWCAs & YM/YWHAs; Children, services; Family services.
Limitations: Applications not accepted. Giving primarily in VA. No grants to individuals.
Application information: Contributes only to pre-selected organizations.
Officers and Directors:* Timothy S. Miller,* Pres.; Troy Clifton, V.P.; Mitchell Murphy, Secy.; Mark A. Benson; Robert G. Bielat; Thomas R. Frantz; Rosann O. Runte, Ph.D.
EIN: 571136563

9476
Mitsubishi Electric America Foundation
1560 Wilson Blvd., Ste. 1150
Arlington, VA 22209 (703) 276-8240
FAX: (703) 276-8260; *URL:* http://www.meaf.org

Established in 1991 in DC.
Donor: Mitsubishi Electric Corp.
Foundation type: Company-sponsored foundation.
Financial data (yr. ended 12/31/04): Assets, $19,667,353 (M); gifts received, $300; expenditures, $1,349,977; qualifying distributions, $1,174,469; giving activities include $840,420 for 114+ grants (high: $145,000).
Purpose and activities: The foundation supports programs designed to advance the independence, productivity, and community of young people with disabilities. Special emphasis is directed toward programs designed to have a national scope and impact.
Fields of interest: Education, equal rights; Recreation, equal rights; Youth; Disabilities, people with.
Type of support: General/operating support; Program development; Publication; Seed money; Curriculum development; Employee volunteer services; Employee matching gifts.
Limitations: Giving on a national basis, with emphasis on areas of company operations; giving

also to national organizations. No support for religious organizations not of direct benefit to the entire community, intermediary organizations, fraternal, labor, political, or lobbying organizations, discriminatory organizations, or individual schools or school districts. No grants to individuals, or for endowments, capital campaigns, equipment or devices for individual users, fundraising events, controversial social or political issues, or local activities without national impact; no loans.

Publications: Application guidelines; Biennial report (including application guidelines); Grants list; Informational brochure (including application guidelines); Multi-year report.

Application information: Telephone calls during the application process are not encouraged. Proposals should be no longer than 3 to 4 pages. Application form not required.

  Initial approach: Mail or fax proposal to foundation or complete online application form
  Copies of proposal: 1
  Deadline(s): June 1
  Board meeting date(s): Fall
  Final notification: 10 to 12 weeks

Officers and Directors:* Akira Tasaki,* Pres.; Shoji Hibara, Treas.; Rayna Aylward,* Exec. Dir.; Darla Achey; Roger Barna; Cayce Blanchard; Bruce Brenizer; Mike DeLano; Art Lewis; Perry Pappous; David Rebmann; Billy Schatzle; Setsuhiro Shimomura; Richard C. Waters.

Number of staff: 2 full-time professional; 1 full-time support.

EIN: 521700855

9477
Modzelewski Charitable Trust ✧
c/o Sterling Foundation Mgmt., LLC
11921 Freedom Dr.
Reston, VA 20190

Established in 1996 in NJ.
Donor: Stephen Modzelewski.
Foundation type: Independent foundation.
Financial data (yr. ended 9/30/05): Assets, $34,912,525 (M); gifts received, $1,825,000; expenditures, $1,721,864; qualifying distributions, $1,691,570; giving activities include $1,571,900 for 35 grants (high: $650,000; low: $100).
Purpose and activities: Giving primarily for civil liberties and education.
Fields of interest: Elementary school/education; Higher education; Hospitals (general); Health organizations, association; Human services; Civil liberties, advocacy; Federated giving programs; Public affairs, research; Public affairs.
Limitations: Applications not accepted. Giving on a national basis, with some emphasis on Washington, DC, CA, NJ, PA, and VA. No grants to individuals.
Application information: Contributes only to pre-selected organizations.
Trustee: Stephen Modzelewski.
EIN: 137098625
Selected grants: The following grants were reported in 2004.
$400,000 to Vanguard Charitable Endowment Program, Southeastern, PA.
$325,000 to Institute for Justice, DC.
$152,600 to Reason Foundation, Los Angeles, CA.
$102,750 to Cato Institute, DC.
$50,300 to Princeton Day School, Princeton, NJ.
$40,000 to Shady Side Academy, Pittsburgh, PA.
$35,000 to Center for Individual Rights, DC.
$30,000 to Competitive Enterprise Institute, DC.

$10,000 to Foundation for Economic Education, Irvington, NY.
$10,000 to Palmer R. Chitester Fund, Erie, PA.

9478
The Claude Moore Charitable Foundation
11350 Random Hills Rd., Ste. 520
Fairfax, VA 22030-7429 (703) 934-1147
Contact: J. Hamilton Lambert, Exec. Dir.
FAX: (703) 273-0152;
E-mail: claudemoore@patriot.net; *URL:* http://www.claudemoorefoundation.org

Established in 1987 in VA.
Donor: Claude Moore†.
Foundation type: Independent foundation.
Financial data (yr. ended 12/31/05): Assets, $167,080,098 (M); expenditures, $6,772,583; qualifying distributions, $5,747,620; giving activities include $3,789,080 for 33 grants (high: $2,000,000; low: $5,000).
Purpose and activities: Giving primarily for the enhancement of educational opportunities, including higher education for young people.
Fields of interest: Museums (specialized); Higher education; Medical school/education; Nursing school/education; Teacher school/education; Adult education—literacy, basic skills & GED; Education; Health care, formal/general education; Boy scouts.
Type of support: Continuing support; Building/renovation; Endowments; Program development; Conferences/seminars; Scholarship funds; Matching/challenge support.
Publications: Application guidelines.
Application information: See foundation Web site for application guidelines and application form. Application form required.
  Initial approach: Letter on organization letterhead
  Copies of proposal: 10
  Deadline(s): Sept. 1
  Board meeting date(s): Monthly
  Final notification: 3 months
Officer: J. Hamilton Lambert, Exec. Dir.
Trustees: Peter A. Arntson; Guy M. Gravett; Leigh B. Middleditch, Jr.; Verlin W. Smith; Jesse B. Wilson III.
EIN: 521558571

9479
Marietta McNeill Morgan & Samuel Tate Morgan, Jr. Foundation ✧
c/o Bank of America, N.A.
P.O. Box 26606
Richmond, VA 23261-6606
Contact: Elizabeth D. Seaman, Advisor

Trust established in 1967 in VA.
Donors: Marietta McNeill Morgan†; Samuel T. Morgan, Jr.†.
Foundation type: Independent foundation.
Financial data (yr. ended 6/30/05): Assets, $19,600,262 (M); expenditures, $1,376,399; qualifying distributions, $1,186,893; giving activities include $1,173,000 for 43 grants (high: $75,000; low: $5,000).
Purpose and activities: Grants for specific capital projects only.
Fields of interest: Museums; Historic preservation/historical societies; Arts; Higher education; Health care; Cancer research; Human services; Foundations (private grantmaking).
Type of support: Building/renovation; Equipment.

Limitations: Giving limited to VA. No support for private foundations or individual churches or congregations. No grants to individuals, or for scholarships, endowment funds, multi-year grants, production of videos, movies, radio or TV programs, or for any purposes except capital projects; no loans.
Publications: Informational brochure (including application guidelines).
Application information: Application form not required.
  Initial approach: Letter
  Copies of proposal: 1
  Deadline(s): Submit proposal preferably in Feb., Mar., Sept. or Oct.; deadlines May 1 and Nov. 1
  Board meeting date(s): Dec. and June
  Final notification: After board meeting by written notification only
Trustee: Bank of America, N.A.
Advisor: Elizabeth Seaman.
EIN: 546069447
Selected grants: The following grants were reported in 2004.
$65,000 to Boys and Girls Clubs of Richmond, Richmond, VA. Toward construction of capital one boys and girls club.
$50,000 to University of Richmond, Richmond, VA. Toward renovation of Gottwald Science Center.
$35,000 to Virginia University of Lynchburg, Lynchburg, VA. For roof replacement on Humbles Hall.
$25,000 to John Singleton Mosby Foundation, Warrenton, VA. For exterior renovation and repair.
$25,000 to Virginia Quality Life, Kilmarnock, VA. Toward construction of YMCA and American Red Cross facilities.
$22,500 to Habitat for Humanity, Richmond Metropolitan, Richmond, VA. For construction of houses in Henrico County.
$20,000 to Boys Home, Covington, VA. Toward construction of staff residence.
$20,000 to Northampton Free Library, Friends of the, Nassawadox, VA. Toward construction of new library building.
$10,000 to All Saints Catholic School, Richmond, VA. For new playground equipment.
$10,000 to Fauquier Family Shelter Services, Warrenton, VA. For expansion of haven shelter.

9480
The Mousetrap Foundation ✧
c/o Sterling Foundation Mgmt., LLC
11921 Freedom Dr.
Reston, VA 20190 (703) 437-9720

Established in 2002 in VA.
Donor: Judith Randal Hines.
Foundation type: Independent foundation.
Financial data (yr. ended 12/31/05): Assets, $12,715,184 (M); gifts received, $1,551,948; expenditures, $510,161; qualifying distributions, $397,250; giving activities include $335,000 for 4 grants (high: $145,000; low: $50,000).
Fields of interest: Environment, natural resources; Health care, clinics/centers; Legal services; International development.
Limitations: Giving on a national basis, with some emphasis on VA. No grants to individuals.
Application information: Application form not required.
  Initial approach: Letter
  Deadline(s): None

Officers: Judith Randal Hines, Pres.; Georgia H. Herbert, V.P. and Secy.
Director: Rosina Bierbaum.
EIN: 522285383
Selected grants: The following grants were reported in 2004.
$131,000 to Piedmont Environmental Council, Warrenton, VA.
$100,000 to Innocence Project, New York, NY.
$50,000 to Catoctin Foundation, Waterford, VA.

9481
Mustard Seed Foundation, Inc. ▼

3330 N. Washington Blvd., Ste. 100
Arlington, VA   22201   (703) 524-5620
Contact: Brian Bakke, Regional Dir., North America
FAX: (703) 524-5643; URL: http://www.msfdn.org

Established in 1983 in SC.
Donors: Eileen Harvey Bakke; Dennis W. Bakke; Warren Harvey; and members of the Bakke and Harvey families.
Foundation type: Independent foundation.
Financial data (yr. ended 12/31/05): Assets, $12,481,866 (M); expenditures, $6,946,188; qualifying distributions, $5,785,384; giving activities include $3,440,971 for 673 grants (high: $200,000; low: $325; average: $3,000–$15,000), $2,267,000 for 1,659 grants to individuals, and $77,413 for employee matching gifts.
Purpose and activities: To advance the Kingdom of God through granting and scholarships. Provides grants to churches and Christian organizations worldwide engaged in ministries such as outreach, discipleship, and empowerment. Provides scholarships to Christians pursuing advanced education in non-western theological studies or under-represented fields.
Fields of interest: Theological school/education; Christian agencies & churches.
Type of support: Seed money; Fellowships; Scholarship funds; Employee matching gifts; Scholarships—to individuals.
Limitations: Giving on a national basis in San Francisco and Los Angeles, CA, Washington, DC, Miami, FL, Chicago, IL, Detroit, MI, New York City, NY, Philadelphia, PA, and Houston, TX, and internationally in large urban centers. No grants for general purposes, buildings, land purchases, small towns or rural projects, administrative costs or for ongoing operations, projects without local church financial support, or scholarships to undergraduate programs.
Publications: Application guidelines; Annual report.
Application information: Please submit one copy of application for grants and four copies for Harvey Fellows. Application form required.
   Initial approach: Letter or E-mail
   Deadline(s): Grants - revolving; Harvey Fellows - Nov. 1
   Board meeting date(s): Every 7 or 8 weeks
   Final notification: Up to 3 months from submission date
Officers and Directors:* Dennis W. Bakke, Co-Chair.; Eileen Harvey Bakke,* Co-Chair.; Paul O. Pearson,* Treas.; Duane Grobman, Exec. Dir.; Andrea Bakke; Lowell B. Bakke; Raymond J. Bakke; Helen C. Harvey; W. Brantley Harvey, Jr.; Warren Harvey; Helen Laffitte; Todd Pearson; Margaret Thompson.
Number of staff: 13 full-time professional.
EIN: 570748914

Selected grants: The following grants were reported in 2003.
$15,000 to Evangelical Church of the 19th District, Paris, France. For start-up salary of a pastor to reach North African refugees and asylum seekers.
$10,000 to Bernal Heights Faith Community, San Francisco, CA. For salary of pastor to establish cell based house churches.
$10,000 to Primitive Christian Church, Brooklyn, NY. For salary of new youth outreach minister.
$10,000 to Saint John Coptic Orthodox Church, Cairo, Egypt. For final payment on multi-year grant to equip new church in greater church serving large Christian urban-poor population.
$7,000 to Moscow Orthodox Parish, Moscow, Russia. To establish new church-based holistic physical and spiritual outreach to drug addicted people.
$6,000 to Confidential, China. For final payment on grant to establish Christian pre-school in one of the largest cities in southern China.
$5,000 to Confidential, Almaty, Kazakhstan. To equip young local church lay leaders to reach indigenous people and establish local churches among them.
$3,200 to Catholic Youth for Chastity, Ouagadougou, Burkina Faso. For church-based youth AIDS awareness and evangelistic outreach.
$3,000 to Philadelphia Christian Fellowship, Manila, Philippines. For initial payment on multi-year grant to enable Filipino couple to serve as cross-cultural missionaries in Bangkok, Thailand.
$2,500 to Christian Revival Center, Johannesburg, South Africa. For salary for church-based youth worker and mentor.
$1,600 to Dombibili Church of the Nazarene, India. For initial payment on multi-year grant to start Christian pre-school, adult literacy and tailoring outreach ministry in Santoshi Nagar slums of greater Mumbai.

9482
The N.E.W. Charitable Foundation, Inc. ✧ ☆

(formerly The N.E.W. Relief Fund, Inc.)
22660 Executive Dr., Ste. 122
Sterling, VA   20166-9535

Established in 2001.
Donors: N.E.W. Customer Service Cos., Inc.; AIG Warranty Guard; National Electronics Warranty Corp.
Foundation type: Company-sponsored foundation.
Financial data (yr. ended 3/31/06): Assets, $366,805 (M); gifts received, $355,779; expenditures, $384,790; qualifying distributions, $384,790; giving activities include $381,945 for 30 grants (high: $105,000; low: $500).
Purpose and activities: The foundation supports organizations involved with arts and culture, health, housing, and human services.
Fields of interest: Arts; Hospitals (specialty); Health care; Breast cancer; Housing/shelter; Children/youth, services; Human services; Federated giving programs.
Type of support: General/operating support.
Limitations: Applications not accepted. Giving primarily in MD and VA. No grants to individuals.
Application information: Contributes only to pre-selected organizations.
Officers and Directors:* Frederick Schaufeld,* Chair. and Pres.; Martin Bloom,* V.P.; Anthony

Nader,* V.P.; Karen Schaufeld,* Secy.; Clifford A. White,* Treas.
EIN: 542055525

9483
Nirman Foundation ✧

600 N. Pickett St.
Alexandria, VA   22304

Established in 1994 in VA.
Donor: Chandrakant C. Shroff.
Foundation type: Independent foundation.
Financial data (yr. ended 6/30/05): Assets, $1,763,493 (M); expenditures, $496,482; qualifying distributions, $475,280; giving activities include $475,280 for 12 grants (high: $380,000; low: $1,900).
Purpose and activities: Giving primarily for higher education.
Fields of interest: Higher education, university.
Limitations: Applications not accepted. Giving primarily in India. No grants to individuals.
Application information: Contributes only to pre-selected organizations.
Officer: Chandrakant C. Shroff, Pres.
EIN: 541740988

9484
The Norfolk Foundation ▼

1 Commercial Pl., Ste 1410
Norfolk, VA   23510-2103   (757) 622-7951
Contact: Angelica D. Light, C.E.O.; For grants: Leigh Evans Davis, Dir., Prog. and Donor Svcs.
FAX: (757) 622-1751;
E-mail: info@norfolkfoundation.org; Additional E-mails: alight@norfolkfoundation.org and ldavis@norfolkfoundation.org; URL: http://www.norfolkfoundation.org

Established in 1950 in VA by resolution and declaration of trust; the foundation was incorporated in 2002.
Foundation type: Community foundation.
Financial data (yr. ended 12/31/05): Assets, $192,374,269 (M); gifts received, $10,810,891; expenditures, $7,753,913; giving activities include $6,654,080 for 525 grants (high: $400,000; low: $500).
Purpose and activities: The foundation seeks to make grants that transform the quality of life and inspire philanthropy in Southeastern Virginia. Support for post-secondary educational institutions, family and child welfare agencies, cultural and civic programs, and environmental organizations.
Fields of interest: Museums; Historic preservation/historical societies; Arts; Child development, education; Higher education; Medical school/education; Adult/continuing education; Adult education—literacy, basic skills & GED; Libraries/library science; Education, reading; Education; Environment, natural resources; Environment; Animal welfare; Health care; Substance abuse, services; Mental health/crisis services; Health organizations, association; Medical research, institute; Youth development, services; Children/youth, services; Child development, services; Family services; Aging, centers/services; Homeless, human services; Human services; Community development; Aging; Disabilities, people with; Economically disadvantaged; Homeless.

Type of support: Management development/
capacity building; Capital campaigns; Building/
renovation; Equipment; Land acquisition;
Emergency funds; Program development; Seed
money; Curriculum development; Scholarship funds;
Technical assistance; Consulting services;
Matching/challenge support.
Limitations: Giving limited to southeastern VA. No
support for national or international organizations
(except for those with offices in southeastern VA),
or religious organizations for religious purposes,
fraternal activities, hospitals and similar health care
facilities, or projects normally the responsibility of
the government. No grants to individuals (except for
donor-designated scholarships), or for operating
budgets, annual campaigns, endowment funds,
fundraising events, ongoing operating support,
scholarly research, travel, or deficit financing.
Publications: Application guidelines; Annual report
(including application guidelines); Financial
statement; Grants list; Informational brochure;
Newsletter.
Application information: Visit foundation Web site
for concept proposal cover sheet and application
guidelines. If proposal is selected for further
consideration, a foundation staff member will
contact the organization to discuss additional
materials required for a full application and the
deadline for submission. Application form required.
  Initial approach: Submit Concept Proposal form
    and attachments
  Copies of proposal: 2
  Deadline(s): None for concept proposal
  Board meeting date(s): 4 times a year
  Final notification: Within 2 weeks for initial
    response
Officers and Directors:* Joshua P. Darden, Jr.,*
Chair.; Toy D. Savage, Jr.,* Vice-Chair.; Angelica D.
Light,* C.E.O. and Pres.; Nan C. Edgerton, V.P.,
Devel.; John O. Wynne,* Treas.; Paul O. Hirschbiel,
Jr.; Mary Louis Lehew; Harry Lester; Kurt M.
Rosenbach.
Number of staff: 4 full-time professional; 3 part-time
professional; 1 full-time support.
EIN: 542035996
Selected grants: The following grants were reported
in 2004.
$394,500 to Business Consortium for Arts Support,
  Norfolk, VA. For combined fund to support area
  cultural groups.
$329,022 to Old Dominion University Educational
  Foundation, Norfolk, VA. To establish Clinical
  Research Center within Health Sciences and to
  purchase a concert piano for Constant Center.
  Grant made through E.K. Sloane Fund.
$300,000 to Saint Marys Home for Disabled
  Children, Norfolk, VA. For capital campaign to
  build new facility.
$250,000 to Jamestown-Yorktown Foundation,
  Williamsburg, VA. To build replicas of Godspeed
  and Discovery that brought original settlers to
  Jamestown.
$190,000 to Endependence Center, Norfolk, VA. To
  purchase and renovate new headquarters.
$150,000 to United Jewish Federation of Tidewater,
  Norfolk, VA. For new home for Jewish Family
  Service of Tidewater on Sandler Family Campus
  of Tidewater Jewish Community.
$100,000 to Tidewater Community College
  Educational Foundation, Norfolk, VA. For
  multi-media classrooms on campuses.
$90,000 to United Way of South Hampton Roads,
  Norfolk, VA. For seed funding of Raising a Reader
  program.

$79,200 to Child and Family Services, Norfolk, VA.
  For technology upgrades associated with merger
  and Building Excellence grant for strategic
  planning.
$75,000 to ForKids, Inc., Norfolk, VA. For expansion
  of Morgan Place transitional housing facility.

9485
Norfolk Southern Foundation ✧
P.O. Box 3040
Norfolk, VA 23514-3040 (757) 629-2881
Contact: Deborah H. Wyld, Exec. Dir.
E-mail: deborah.wyld@nscorp.com; URL: http://
www.nscorp.com/nscorp/application?
pageid=About%20NS&category=About%
20NS&contentId=english/nscorp/about_ns/
ns_foundation.html

Established in 1983 in VA.
Donors: Norfolk Southern Corp.; The Cincinnati,
New Orleans and Texas Pacific Railway Co.; Rail
Investment Co.
Foundation type: Company-sponsored foundation.
Financial data (yr. ended 12/31/05): Assets,
$4,345,796 (M); gifts received, $3,001,133;
expenditures, $4,367,780; qualifying distributions,
$4,323,097; giving activities include $3,166,697
for 221 grants (high: $155,000; low: $200), and
$1,134,329 for employee matching gifts.
Purpose and activities: The foundation supports
organizations involved with arts and culture, higher
education, and natural resources.
Fields of interest: Museums; Performing arts; Arts;
Higher education; Environment, natural resources;
Federated giving programs.
Type of support: General/operating support;
Continuing support; Annual campaigns; Capital
campaigns; Building/renovation; Equipment;
Emergency funds; Program development; Seed
money; Scholarship funds; Employee matching gifts;
Employee-related scholarships; In-kind gifts;
Matching/challenge support.
Limitations: Giving on a national basis in areas of
company operations. No support for religious,
fraternal, social, or veterans' organizations, political
or lobbying organizations, public or private
elementary or secondary schools, sports or athletic
organizations, community or private foundations or
pass-through organizations, or disease-related
organizations, hospitals, or social services
organizations. No grants to individuals (except for
employee-related scholarships), or for fundraising
events, telethons, races, or benefits or sports or
athletic activities.
Publications: Application guidelines; Annual report;
Program policy statement.
Application information: Application form not
required.
  Initial approach: Proposal
  Copies of proposal: 1
  Deadline(s): From July 15 to Sept. 30
  Board meeting date(s): As needed
  Final notification: By Dec. 31
Officers: David R. Goode, Chair., C.E.O., and Pres.;
Henry D. Light, V.P.; Mark D. Manion, V.P.; Kathryn
B. McQuade, V.P.; L.I. Prillaman, Jr., V.P.; Stephen
C. Tobias, V.P.; Henry C. Wolf, V.P.; Reginald J.
Chaney, Secy.; Thomas Hurlbut, Treas.; Deborah H.
Wyld, Exec. Dir.
Number of staff: 1 full-time professional.
EIN: 521328375

9486
Northern Virginia Community Foundation
8283 Greensboro Dr.
McLean, VA 22102 (703) 917-2600
Contact: Eileen M. Ellsworth, Pres.
FAX: (703) 902-3564;
E-mail: ellsworth_eileen@ne.bah.com; URL: http://
www.novacf.org

Incorporated in 1978 in VA.
Foundation type: Community foundation.
Financial data (yr. ended 6/30/05): Assets,
$25,060,425 (M); gifts received, $5,101,928;
expenditures, $1,947,505; giving activities include
$948,734 for 145 grants (high: $110,000; low:
$250), and $78,500 for 39 grants to individuals
(high: $3,000; low: $500).
Purpose and activities: The foundation provides
support for community improvement for the benefit
of citizens of northern VA, including health, the arts,
education, and youth, scholarship, nonprofit, and
charitable programs.
Fields of interest: Arts; Education; Health care;
Children/youth, services; Community development;
Youth.
Type of support: General/operating support;
Continuing support; Equipment; Endowments;
Emergency funds; Program development;
Scholarship funds; Employee-related scholarships;
Scholarships—to individuals; In-kind gifts;
Matching/challenge support.
Limitations: Giving limited to northern VA.
Publications: Annual report; Financial statement;
Grants list; Informational brochure; Informational
brochure (including application guidelines);
Newsletter; Occasional report.
Application information: Visit foundation Web site
for application form and guidelines. Application form
required.
  Initial approach: Submit application form and
    attachments
  Copies of proposal: 1
  Deadline(s): Grant proposals accepted during
    Sept.; deadline Sept. 30
  Board meeting date(s): Quarterly
  Final notification: Within 120 days
Officers and Directors:* George F. Albright,* Chair.;
Eileen M. Ellsworth,* Pres.; Robert Y. Hottle,*
Treas.; Dennis Belcher,* Genl. Counsel; C.G.
Appelby; Leigh-Alexandra Basha; Lavern J. Chatman;
John J. Dillon; Richard Duvall; Robert A. Hickey;
David P. Johnson; Dan A. Krevere; Cathy Lange; A.
Paul Lanzillotta; George P. Levendis; Rodney W.
Mateer; Fred McNair; Marsha Peters; Valerie C.
Robbins; Dean Umemoto; Paul G. Veith; James M.
Wordsworth.
Number of staff: 2 full-time professional; 3 part-time
professional.
EIN: 510232459

9487
**The O'Shaughnessy-Hurst Memorial
  Foundation, Inc.** ✧
87 Lee Hwy., Ste. 23
Warrenton, VA 20186

Established in VA.
Donor: Mary Hurst O'Shaughnessy†.
Foundation type: Independent foundation.
Financial data (yr. ended 12/31/04): Assets,
$8,599,722 (M); expenditures, $571,840;
qualifying distributions, $402,028; giving activities

include $391,500 for 11 grants (high: $300,000; low: $1,000).

Fields of interest: Higher education; Hospitals (general); Cancer research; Athletics/sports, school programs.

Limitations: Applications not accepted. Giving primarily in Warrenton, VA. No grants to individuals.

Application information: Contributes only to pre-selected organizations.

Officers: William Soza, Chair.; Deborah Dech Piland, Pres.; Richard Piland, V.P.; Stephanie Marsh, Secy.; Kathleen Poorbaugh, Treas.

EIN: 541394736

9488
Oak Hill Fund

P.O. Box 1624
Charlottesville, VA 22902
Contact: Jeff Adams, C.F.O
E-mail: info@oakhillfund.org; Additional E-mails: ESAD Program: esadinfo@oakhillfund.org; Something Ventured Program: svinfo@oakhillfund.org; URL: http://www.oakhillfund.org

Established in 2002 in VA as part of the restructure of the W. Alton Jones Foundation (now known as Blue Moon Fund).

Donor: Blue Moon Fund, Inc.

Foundation type: Independent foundation.

Financial data (yr. ended 3/31/06): Assets, $98,775,346 (M); expenditures, $6,559,800; qualifying distributions, $5,237,021; giving activities include $4,364,158 for 169 grants (high: $434,000; low: $50).

Purpose and activities: The mission of the fund is to promote the well-being of mankind through effective and inspiring grantmaking. The fund currently has three programs: 1) to focus on the promotion of the principles of sustainable development into the design of affordable construction, with a primary focus on residential housing; 2) empowering women and girls through the initiatives of education and leadership, health and vitality, and self-determination; and 3) a local program that addresses quality of life issues within the greater Charlottesville community, including the areas of health and safety, grassroots environment, volunteerism and community leadership, and the creative arts.

Fields of interest: Arts; Environment, natural resources; Health care; Crime/violence prevention, domestic violence; Housing/shelter, development; Safety, education; Girls clubs; Community development, neighborhood development; Economic development; Voluntarism promotion; Women.

Limitations: Giving limited to the southeastern U.S., including AL, DE, FL, GA, KY, MD, MS, NC, TN, SC, VA, WV, and Washington, DC. The fund's local program is limited to the Thomas Jefferson Planning District, in the foothills of central VA's Blue Ridge Mountains; the district includes the city of Charlottesville and the counties of Albemarle, Greene, Louisa, Fluvanna, and Nelson. No support for organizations lacking 501(c)(3) status. No grants to individuals, or for capital campaigns, endowments, bricks and mortar projects, books, or films; no general operating support.

Publications: Application guidelines.

Application information: The fund uses an online application process; see fund Web site for

application guidelines and requirements. Application form not required.

> *Initial approach:* E-mail letter of inquiry
> *Copies of proposal:* 1
> *Deadline(s):* None
> *Final notification:* 30 days from receipt

Officers: William A. Ederton, Pres.; Liza T. Ederton, V.P.; Robert W. Hurst, Exec. Dir.; Jeff Adams, C.F.O.

Number of staff: 5 full-time professional; 6 part-time professional.

EIN: 311810011

Selected grants: The following grants were reported in 2005.

$520,573 to homeWORD, Missoula, MT.

$122,350 to Rector and Visitors of the University of Virginia, Charlottesville, VA.

$60,000 to Appalachian Sustainable Development, Abingdon, VA.

$58,168 to Family Pathways of Colorado, Wheat Ridge, CO.

$52,276 to Red Feather Development Group, Bozeman, MT.

$50,000 to Advocates for Youth, DC.

$35,000 to Jefferson Area Board for Aging, Charlottesville, VA.

$26,375 to Virginia Blood Services, Richmond, VA.

$17,600 to Denver Public Schools Foundation, Denver, CO.

$1,050 to Dogwood Alliance, Asheville, NC.

9489
The Ochsman Foundation, Inc. ✧

1650 Tysons Blvd., Ste. 820
McLean, VA 22102

Established in 1998 in MD.

Donors: Ralph Ochsman; Meurice C. Ochsman; Yetta K. Cohen†.

Foundation type: Independent foundation.

Financial data (yr. ended 12/31/05): Assets, $7,994,234 (M); gifts received, $1,548; expenditures, $480,993; qualifying distributions, $403,795; giving activities include $403,795 for 44 grants (high: $204,415; low: $30).

Purpose and activities: Giving primarily to Jewish organizations and health associations, particularly for Tourettes syndrome; funding also for education and social services.

Fields of interest: Education; Animal welfare; Hospitals (general); Health organizations, association; Health organizations; Human services; Jewish federated giving programs; Jewish agencies & temples.

Limitations: Applications not accepted. Giving primarily in the eastern U.S., with emphasis on Washington, DC, MD, and New York, NY, NC, and VA. No grants to individuals.

Application information: Contributes only to pre-selected organizations.

Officers: Ralph Ochsman, Pres.; Jeffrey Wayne Ochsman, V.P.; Michael Paul Ochsman, V.P.; Bruce David Ochsman, Secy.

EIN: 541893317

Selected grants: The following grants were reported in 2004.

$204,700 to Washington Hebrew Congregation, DC.

$25,000 to Jewish Federation of Greater Washington, Rockville, MD.

$10,000 to Washington Hospital Center Foundation, DC.

$5,000 to Hebrew Home of Greater Washington, Rockville, MD.

$110 to Childrens Hospital Foundation, DC.

9490
The George and Carol Olmsted Foundation ✧

150 S. Washington St., Ste. 403
Falls Church, VA 22046-2921
Contact: RADM. Larry R. Marsh, Pres.
FAX: (703) 536-5020;
E-mail: scholars@olmstedfoundation.org; Toll-free tel.: (877) 656-7833; URL: http://www.olmstedfoundation.org

Incorporated in 1960 in VA.

Donor: George Olmsted†.

Foundation type: Independent foundation.

Financial data (yr. ended 12/31/05): Assets, $51,134,306 (M); expenditures, $2,657,899; qualifying distributions, $2,297,060; giving activities include $1,535,108 for grants.

Purpose and activities: The primary objective of the foundation is to support programs designed to contribute to the nation's security by providing potential leaders with a comprehensive education, knowledge and depth of understanding of the political, economic and military factors involved in international relations. To this end, the foundation funds the Olmsted Scholar Program, through which career officers are awarded grants for study in a foreign country.

Fields of interest: Education; Military/veterans' organizations.

Type of support: General/operating support; Scholarships—to individuals.

Limitations: Giving on a national basis. No grants to individuals (except for Olmsted Scholars).

Publications: Annual report; Informational brochure.

Application information: Qualified military officers apply through their respective Military Service. Applicants are encouraged to take the candidate qualifications survey, which is available on the foundation Web site.

> *Initial approach:* Grant requests should be sent to the foundation for forwarding to the Board of Directors. Requests for grants considered when initiated by a member of the Board of Directors
> *Board meeting date(s):* Apr.

Officers and Directors:* Brig. Genl. Anthony A. Smith, Chair.; RADM. Larry R. Marsh,* C.E.O. and Pres.; Col. Robert Yablonski,* Exec. V.P.; Joseph McManus, Secy.-Treas.; Genl. George Lee Butler; RADM William D. Crowder; Col. David G. Estep; Lt. Genl. Emerson Gardner; Brig. Genl. Silvanus Gilbert; Col. Peter A. Henry; RADM Deborah Ann Loewer; Maj. Genl. Bruce K. Scott; Genl. Henry Viccellio, Jr.

Number of staff: 1 full-time professional; 1 part-time professional; 1 full-time support.

EIN: 546049005

Selected grants: The following grants were reported in 2003.

$350,000 to United States Air Force Academy Association of Graduates, Colorado Springs, CO. 2 grants: $300,000 (For Tri-Service Academy program), $50,000 (For AFROTC Overseas Travel Program).

$325,000 to Association of Graduates of the United States Military Academy, West Point, NY. 2 grants: $300,000 (For Tri-Service Academy program), $25,000 (For Foreign Affairs Conference).

$325,000 to United States Naval Academy, Annapolis, MD. 2 grants: $300,000 (For Tri-Service Academy program), $25,000 (For Foreign Affairs Conference).

$150,000 to Saint James School, Saint James, MD. For construction of Holloway Hall.

$50,000 to Boy Scouts of America, National Capital Area Council, Bethesda, MD. For operation and maintenance of Camp Olmsted.

$20,900 to Virginia Military Institute, Lexington, VA. For Cadet overseas travel.

$20,000 to Society of the Cincinnati, DC. For museum functions.

9491
Elis Olsson Memorial Foundation ✧
c/o Dennis I. Belcher
P.O. Box 397
Richmond, VA 23218-0397
Application address: P.O. Box 151, West Point, VA 23181; tel.: (804) 843-9066

Established in 1966 in VA.
Donors: Inga Olsson Nylander†; Signe Maria Olsson†.
Foundation type: Independent foundation.
Financial data (yr. ended 12/31/04): Assets, $23,735,748 (M); gifts received, $18,981; expenditures, $1,132,555; qualifying distributions, $1,033,339; giving activities include $950,179 for 81 grants (high: $200,000; low: $250).
Purpose and activities: Giving primarily for higher and other education, Roman Catholic churches, and the arts, particularly historical activities; funding also for hospitals and health associations, including services for people who are blind, children, youth and social services, and volunteer and fire departments.
Fields of interest: Museums; Historic preservation/historical societies; Arts; Elementary/secondary education; Higher education; Education; Environment, natural resources; Hospitals (general); Health organizations, association; Food services; Disasters, fire prevention/control; Human services; Children/youth, services; Residential/custodial care, group home; Foundations (community); Marine science; Roman Catholic agencies & churches; Economically disadvantaged.
Type of support: Professorships; Fellowships.
Limitations: Giving primarily in VA. No grants to individuals.
Application information:
 Initial approach: Letter
 Deadline(s): None
 Board meeting date(s): Oct. 1
Officers and Directors:* Sture G. Olsson,* Chair.; C. Elis Olsson,* Pres.; Shirley C. Olsson,* V.P.; Lisa O. Armstrong,* Secy.-Treas.; Thelma L. Downey, Exec. Dir.; Anne O. Loebs; Inga O. Rogers.
Number of staff: 1 part-time professional.
EIN: 546062436
Selected grants: The following grants were reported in 2004.
$200,000 to Episcopal Diocese of Virginia, Richmond, VA. For general support.
$200,000 to University of Virginia, School of Engineering and Applied Science, Charlottesville, VA. For general support.
$100,000 to National D-Day Memorial Foundation, Bedford, VA. For general support.
$50,000 to Virginia Historical Society, Richmond, VA. For general support.
$50,000 to Virginia Institute of Marine Science, Gloucester Point, VA. For general support.
$25,000 to American Red Cross, Richmond, VA. For general support.

$25,000 to Christchurch School, Christchurch, VA. For general support.
$25,000 to Foundation for Historic Christ Church, Irvington, VA. For general support.
$25,000 to Walkerton Community Fire Association, Walkerton, VA. For general support.
$25,000 to West Point Volunteer Fire Department and Rescue Squad, West Point, NY. For general support.

9492
Parker Foundation ✧
500 Forest Ave.
Richmond, VA 23229 (804) 285-5416
Contact: Malcolm J. Myers, V.P.
FAX: (804) 285-5410;
E-mail: mmyers@parkerfoundation.org; URL: http://www.parkerfoundation.org

Established in 1995 in VA.
Donors: Clark N. Hogan; Craig Harmon.
Foundation type: Independent foundation.
Financial data (yr. ended 12/31/05): Assets, $2,113,195 (M); gifts received, $205,139; expenditures, $2,258,949; qualifying distributions, $2,220,023; giving activities include $1,910,871 for 63 grants.
Purpose and activities: The mission is to support, through counsel and grants, well-conceived strategies to redeem individuals and societies for Jesus Christ, throughout the United States.
Fields of interest: International affairs; Christian agencies & churches.
Type of support: Employee matching gifts.
Limitations: Giving on a national basis. No support for denominational concerns, organizations targeting domestic localities (with the exception of Richmond, VA), organizations of which the Staff or Board of the foundation have no previous personal knowledge, or organizations expecting the foundation to be sustaining donors. No grants to individuals.
Publications: Application guidelines.
Application information: Applications submitted without prior contact will not be accepted. Application guidelines and form available on foundation Web site.
 Initial approach: Telephone call
Officers and Directors:* R. Jerry Parker, Jr.,* Pres.; Malcolm J. Myers,* V.P.; Deana A. Parker,* Secy.-Treas.; Fritz Kling, Exec. Dir.
EIN: 541770265
Selected grants: The following grants were reported in 2004.
$166,667 to University of Virginia, Charlottesville, VA.
$50,000 to CARE for Children, Bradford, PA.
$50,000 to Chicago Hope Academy, Chicago, IL.
$50,000 to Ethics and Public Policy Center, DC.
$50,000 to Robin Hood Foundation, New York, NY. 2 grants: $25,000 each
$50,000 to Scripture Union, USA, Wayne, PA.
$35,000 to Care Net, Sterling, VA.
$30,000 to Lynchburg College, Lynchburg, VA.
$25,000 to Global Mapping International, Colorado Springs, CO.

9493
The Mary Morton Parsons Foundation ▼
901 E. Cary St., Ste. 1404
Richmond, VA 23219-4037
Contact: Hugh K. Leary, Exec. Dir.

Established in 1988 in VA.
Donor: Mary Morton Parsons†.
Foundation type: Independent foundation.
Financial data (yr. ended 12/31/05): Assets, $90,721,094 (M); expenditures, $4,723,543; qualifying distributions, $4,307,375; giving activities include $4,307,375 for 57 grants (high: $500,000; low: $5,000; average: $25,000–$150,000).
Purpose and activities: Support primarily for museums and historical groups, institutions concerned with education, and social services or welfare.
Fields of interest: Museums; History/archaeology; Historic preservation/historical societies; Arts; Education; Human services.
Type of support: Capital campaigns; Building/renovation; Equipment.
Limitations: Giving primarily in VA, with an emphasis on Richmond. No grants to individuals, or for debt reduction, endowments, research, or general operating expenses.
Publications: Informational brochure (including application guidelines).
Application information: Application form not required.
 Initial approach: Letter
 Copies of proposal: 1
 Deadline(s): Mar. 15 and Sept. 15
 Board meeting date(s): May and Nov.
Officers and Directors:* Joseph L. Antrim III,* Pres. and Treas.; Charles F. Witthoefft,* V.P. and Secy.; Hugh K. Leary, Exec. Dir.; William C. Day; Mrs. Palmer P. Garson; Thurston R. Moore.
Number of staff: 1 part-time professional.
EIN: 541530891
Selected grants: The following grants were reported in 2005.
$500,000 to Virginia Museum of Fine Arts, Richmond, VA. For annual fund.
$300,000 to Montpelier Foundation, Montpelier Station, VA. For annual fund.
$300,000 to Thomas Jefferson Memorial Foundation, Charlottesville, VA. For annual fund.
$150,000 to Hollins University, Roanoke, VA. For annual fund.
$150,000 to Virginia Wesleyan College, Virginia Beach, VA. For annual fund.
$125,000 to Maymont Foundation, Richmond, VA. For annual fund.
$100,000 to Westminster-Canterbury Corporation, Richmond, VA. For annual fund.
$50,000 to Commonwealth Catholic Charities, Richmond, VA. For annual fund.
$50,000 to Virginia Intermont College, Bristol, VA. For annual fund.
$10,000 to Senior Connections, The Capital Area Agency on Aging, Richmond, VA. For annual fund.

9494
The Pauley Family Foundation ✧ ☆
c/o S.F. Pauley
314 Saint David's Ln.
Richmond, VA 23221

Established in 1993 in VA.
Donors: Stanley F. Pauley; Dorothy A. Pauley.

Foundation type: Independent foundation.
Financial data (yr. ended 12/31/05): Assets, $28,141,157 (M); expenditures, $1,612,729; qualifying distributions, $1,181,622; giving activities include $1,157,750 for 12 grants (high: $1,025,000; low: $2,250).
Purpose and activities: Giving primarily for education and the arts.
Fields of interest: Museums; Performing arts; Higher education; Animal welfare; Health care.
Limitations: Applications not accepted. Giving primarily in Richmond, VA. No grants to individuals.
Application information: Contributes only to pre-selected organizations.
Officers and Directors: * Stanley F. Pauley,* Chair.; Dorothy A. Pauley,* Pres. and Treas.; Katharine Pauley Hickok,* V.P.; Lorna Pauley Jordan,* V.P.; W. Birch Douglass III, Secy.
EIN: 541685158

9495
Perry Foundation, Inc. ◇
P.O. Box 558
Charlottesville, VA   22902   (434) 977-5679
Contact: Francis H. Fife, Pres.; Stephanie Leech

Incorporated in 1946 in VA.
Donors: Hunter Perry†; Lillian Perry Edwards†.
Foundation type: Independent foundation.
Financial data (yr. ended 12/31/05): Assets, $23,889,465 (M); expenditures, $1,304,971; qualifying distributions, $1,119,961; giving activities include $1,091,104 for 30 grants (high: $311,600; low: $100).
Purpose and activities: Support for higher and secondary education; grants also for human services, and aid to the handicapped.
Fields of interest: Arts; Education, fund raising/fund distribution; Secondary school/education; Higher education; Education; Hospitals (general); Human services; Aging, centers/services; Federated giving programs; Disabilities, people with.
Type of support: Annual campaigns; Building/ renovation; Equipment; Matching/challenge support.
Limitations: Giving primarily in VA, with emphasis on Albemarle County and Charlottesville. No grants to individuals, or for operating budgets.
Application information: Application form not required.
  Initial approach: Letter
  Copies of proposal: 8
  Deadline(s): First of the month prior to the months of board meetings
  Board meeting date(s): Quarterly
Officers and Trustees: * Francis H. Fife,* Pres.; Gary C. Mcgee,* V.P.; Susan Cabell-Mains,* Secy.; Edward D. Tayloe II,* Treas.; Roberta F. Brownfield; Suzanne S. Brooks; Wade Tremblay.
Number of staff: 1 part-time support.
EIN: 546036446
Selected grants: The following grants were reported in 2005.
$311,600 to Jefferson Area Board for Aging, Charlottesville, VA.
$100,000 to Hospice of the Piedmont, Charlottesville, VA.
$93,000 to Legal Aid Justice Center, Charlottesville, VA.
$80,000 to Charlottesville Contemporary Arts, Charlottesville, VA.
$65,000 to United Way, Thomas Jefferson Area, Charlottesville, VA.

$52,000 to Blue Ridge Area Food Bank, Verona, VA.
$35,000 to Salvation Army, Hayes, VA.
$25,000 to Senior Center, Charlottesville, VA.
$20,000 to Camp Holiday Trails, Charlottesville, VA.
$15,000 to Charlottesville-Albemarle Rescue Squad, Charlottesville, VA.

9496
Patricia and Douglas Perry Foundation ◇
P.O. Box 869
Virginia Beach, VA   23451-2521

Established in 1993 in VA.
Donors: J. Douglas Perry; Patricia W. Perry.
Foundation type: Independent foundation.
Financial data (yr. ended 12/31/04): Assets, $3,722,606 (M); gifts received, $618,057; expenditures, $1,055,944; qualifying distributions, $1,048,896; giving activities include $1,048,896 for 24 grants (high: $507,500; low: $200).
Purpose and activities: Giving primarily for the arts and education in the Hampton Roads, VA, area.
Fields of interest: Arts; Elementary/secondary education; Higher education, university; Salvation Army; Federated giving programs; Protestant agencies & churches.
Type of support: Scholarships—to individuals.
Limitations: Applications not accepted. Giving limited to residents of Virginia Beach and Norfolk, VA.
Application information: Contributes only to pre-selected organizations.
Officers: Patricia W. Perry, Pres.; Brandon D. Perry, V.P.; J. Christopher Perry, V.P.; Paige Perry, V.P.; J. Douglas Perry, Treas.
EIN: 541691140
Selected grants: The following grants were reported in 2003.
$844,602 to Old Dominion University, Norfolk, VA.
$87,500 to Chesapeake Bay Academy, Virginia Beach, VA.
$36,000 to Salvation Army of Hampton Roads, Norfolk, VA.
$20,000 to Sugar Plum Bakery, Virginia Beach, VA.
$10,000 to Alexis de Tocqueville Society, Alexandria, VA.
$10,000 to Hope House Foundation, Norfolk, VA.
$10,000 to Park Place School, Norfolk, VA.
$7,500 to Business Consortium for Arts Support, Norfolk, VA.
$7,500 to Cape Henry Collegiate School, Virginia Beach, VA.
$1,000 to Virginia College Fund, Richmond, VA.

9497
Peterson Family Foundation, Inc. ◇
12500 Fair Lakes Cir., Ste. 400
Fairfax, VA   22033
Contact: Blanca Rosa Ramos

Established in 1998 in VA.
Donors: Lauren P. Fellows; Jon M. Peterson; Milton V. Peterson; Steven B. Peterson; William E. Peterson.
Foundation type: Independent foundation.
Financial data (yr. ended 12/31/05): Assets, $5,475,312 (M); gifts received, $3,543,931; expenditures, $2,328,974; qualifying distributions, $2,315,289; giving activities include $2,315,289 for 122+ grants, and $359,781 for 4 foundation-administered programs.

Purpose and activities: Giving primarily for education, health associations, human services, and religious purposes.
Fields of interest: Education; Health organizations, association; Human services; Residential/custodial care, hospices; Federated giving programs; Religion.
Type of support: In-kind gifts.
Limitations: Applications not accepted. Giving primarily in Prince George's County, MD, and in VA, with emphasis on Fairfax.
Application information: Unsolicited requests for funds not accepted.
Officers: Milton V. Peterson, Pres.; Lauren P. Fellows, Secy.; William E. Peterson, Treas.
Directors: Carolyn S. Peterson; Jon M. Peterson; Steven B. Peterson.
Number of staff: 1 full-time professional.
EIN: 541870812
Selected grants: The following grants were reported in 2003.
$133,974 to Saint Stephens and Saint Agnes School, Alexandria, VA. For general support.
$109,000 to Life with Cancer, Falls Church, VA. For general support.
$106,000 to Flint Hill School, Oakton, VA. 2 grants: $30,000 (For general support), $76,000 (For general support).
$105,000 to George Mason University Foundation, Fairfax, VA. For general support.
$50,000 to Northern Virginia Transportation Alliance, Vienna, VA. For general support.
$33,000 to Youth for Tomorrow New Life Center, Bristow, VA. For general support.
$28,700 to Northern Virginia Family Service, Oakton, VA. For general support.
$15,000 to Burke United Methodist Church, Burke, VA. For general support.
$10,000 to Westmoreland Davis Memorial Foundation, Leesburg, VA. For general support.

9498
The Portsmouth Community Foundation
360 Crawford St.
Portsmouth, VA   23704   (757) 397-5424
Contact: Judith E. Luffman, Exec. Dir.
FAX: (757) 397-7948; E-mail: office@thepcf.org; Additional E-mail: luffmanj@thepcf.org; URL: http:// www.thepcf.org

Established in 1965 in VA.
Foundation type: Community foundation.
Financial data (yr. ended 12/31/05): Assets, $5,988,862 (M); gifts received, $1,098,510; expenditures, $846,946; giving activities include $647,154 for grants.
Purpose and activities: Primary areas of interest include community development, community funds, hospital building funds, and general charitable giving. Support also for museums, music, and other arts groups, libraries, public and civic affairs, recreational programs, medical, and education, including higher, secondary, adult education, and programs for minorities.
Fields of interest: Museums; Performing arts, music; Arts; Secondary school/education; Higher education; Medical school/education; Adult/ continuing education; Libraries/library science; Education; Hospitals (general); Health care, patient services; Health care; Recreation; Human services; Economic development; Community development; Federated giving programs; Marine science; Government/public administration; Public affairs; Minorities.

Type of support: Building/renovation; General/operating support; Continuing support; Annual campaigns; Capital campaigns; Equipment; Scholarship funds.

Limitations: Giving limited to within a 50 mile radius of Portsmouth, VA. No support for religious purposes or any agency which has received a discretionary grant from the Portsmouth Community Foundation within the preceding year. No grants to individuals (except for scholarships), or for deficit financing.

Publications: Application guidelines; Annual report (including application guidelines); Financial statement; Grants list; Informational brochure; Newsletter.

Application information: Visit foundation Web site for application form and guidelines. Application form required.

   Initial approach: Telephone
   Copies of proposal: 2
   Deadline(s): Mar. 15 and Sept. 15
   Board meeting date(s): Last Wed. in Feb., May, Aug., and Nov.
   Final notification: 7 weeks

Officers and Directors:* Patrick S. Callahan,* Pres.; Phillip M. Rudisill,* V.P.; Kurt W. Taves,* Treas.; Judith E. Luffman, Exec. Dir.; Donald W. Comer, Jr.; Gloria M. Creecy; Carl L. Hardee; Louis L. Hibbitts, Jr.; Jerold L. Miller; Albert J. Taylor; Lynn M. Wiggins; Robert T. Williams; Thomas E. Wood; Nancy G. Wren.

Trustee Banks: Bank of America, N.A.; BB&T; Old Dominican Trust Co./AMG Guaranty Trust; SunTrust Bank; Wachovia Securities.

Number of staff: 1 full-time professional; 2 part-time support.

EIN: 546062589

Selected grants: The following grants were reported in 2003.

$10,000 to ACCESS College Foundation, Norfolk, VA.

$10,000 to Virginia Arts Festival, Norfolk, VA.

$7,500 to Academy of Music, Norfolk, VA.

$5,000 to Citizens Committee to Protect the Elderly, Virginia Beach, VA.

$5,000 to Hampton Roads Youth Center, Virginia Beach, VA.

$5,000 to Hoffler Creek Wildlife Foundation, Portsmouth, VA.

$5,000 to Senior Services of Southeastern Virginia, Norfolk, VA.

$4,755 to Medication Access Program, VA.

$2,000 to Genieve Shelter, Suffolk, VA.

$1,500 to Special Olympics Virginia, Richmond, VA.

9499
Portsmouth General Hospital Foundation

360 Crawford St.
Portsmouth, VA 23704   (757) 391-0000
Contact: Alan E. Gollihue, C.E.O. and Pres.; Patricia Clifford Irwin, Exec. Asst.
FAX: (757) 391-0004;
E-mail: office@pghfoundation.org; URL: http://www.pghfoundation.org

Established in 1987 in VA as the Seller's Trust; converted through the sale of Portsmouth General Hospital, Inc. to Tidewater Health Care, Inc.; funded in 1988.

Foundation type: Independent foundation.

Financial data (yr. ended 6/30/06): Assets, $15,221,580 (M); gifts received, $3,850; expenditures, $912,198; qualifying distributions,

$792,873; giving activities include $503,665 for 46 grants (high: $68,000; low: $50).

Purpose and activities: Giving to promote and support innovative as well as established healthcare programs in the city of Portsmouth, VA. A major focus of the foundation is on issues dealing with children's health (newborn to 5 years old).

Fields of interest: Public health school/education; Health care, infants; Reproductive health, family planning; Health care; Substance abuse, services; Youth, pregnancy prevention.

Type of support: Program development; Seed money; Technical assistance.

Limitations: Giving limited to healthcare programs in Portsmouth, VA. No support for political activities. No grants to individuals, scholarships, building funds, elimination of deficits, travel, research and development, or capital campaigns.

Publications: Application guidelines; Grants list.

Application information: See foundation Web site for application guidelines and downloading of Common Application Form. Application form required.

   Initial approach: Letter of intent and/or telephone call
   Copies of proposal: 1
   Deadline(s): Jan. 1 (for Mar. meeting), and Jul. 1 (for Sept. meeting)
   Board meeting date(s): 1st Wed. of Mar., June, Sept. and Dec.; grant review only at Mar. and Sept. meetings
   Final notification: 1-2 weeks

Officers and Directors:* Karl S. Morrisette,* Chair.; Demetria M. Lindsay, M.D.*, Vice-Chair.; Alan E. Gollihue, C.E.O and Pres.; Burle U. Stromberg,* Secy.; Dia DuVernet,* Treas.; Patricia Fisher, Ph.D.; Gina H. Harris; Christopher K. Hersh, M.D.; Starr Oliver; Harry L. "Hal" Short; Randy Webb; Nancy G. Wren*.

Number of staff: 2 full-time professional.

EIN: 541463392

Selected grants: The following grants were reported in 2006.

$68,000 to Child and Family Services, Norfolk, VA. For Healthy Families Program.

$25,000 to Chesapeake Service Systems, Chesapeake, VA. For Vocational Habitation Program for people with disabilities.

$20,500 to Childrens Resources-Hampton Roads, Chesapeake, VA. For Adolescent Anger Management Services.

$20,000 to Catholic Charities of Southeast Virginia, Portsmouth, VA. For Money Management Bill Payer Program.

$18,000 to Medication Access Program, VA. For Medication Assistance Plan.

$16,300 to Portsmouth Circuit Court, Portsmouth, VA. For Portsmouth Adult Drug Treatment Court Program.

$15,000 to Planned Parenthood of Southeastern Virginia, Hampton, VA. For Real Life, Real Talk Sex Education Program.

$11,000 to Boys and Girls Clubs of Southeast Virginia, Chesapeake, VA. For Smart Smiles Dental Care Program.

$10,000 to Alzheimers Association, Southeastern Virginia Chapter, Norfolk, VA. For community outreach and support program.

$10,000 to Citizens Committee to Protect the Elderly, Virginia Beach, VA. For program support.

9500
The Praxis Foundation ✧

(formerly The James B. and Bruce R. Murray, Jr. Foundation)
O Court Sq.
Charlottesville, VA   22902-5144
(434) 971-8080
Contact: James B. Murray, Jr., Pres.

Established in 1996 in VA.

Donors: James B. Murray, Jr.; Bruce R. Murray.

Foundation type: Independent foundation.

Financial data (yr. ended 12/31/05): Assets, $1,644,431 (M); gifts received, $514,910; expenditures, $649,669; qualifying distributions, $632,733; giving activities include $628,200 for 36 grants (high: $502,000; low: $100; average: $1,000–$5,000).

Fields of interest: Education; Hospitals (general); Health care, clinics/centers; Human services; Foundations (community).

Limitations: Giving primarily in VA. No grants to individuals.

Application information:
   Initial approach: Letter
   Deadline(s): None

Officers and Directors:* James B. Murray, Jr.,* Pres.; Bruce R. Murray,* Secy.

EIN: 541830546

9501
The Ratner Family Foundation ✧

1577 Spring Hill Rd., Ste. 500
Vienna, VA   22182-2223

Established in 1990 in VA.

Donors: Creative Hairdressers, Inc.; and its subsidiaries.

Foundation type: Independent foundation.

Financial data (yr. ended 12/31/04): Assets, $85,356 (M); gifts received, $424,367; expenditures, $577,577; qualifying distributions, $574,469; giving activities include $574,469 for 9 + grants (high: $509,269).

Purpose and activities: Giving primarily to Jewish institutes and culture, including a Jewish museum.

Fields of interest: Museums (ethnic/folk arts); Higher education; Cancer; Human services; Jewish federated giving programs; Jewish agencies & temples.

Limitations: Applications not accepted. Giving primarily in the metropolitan Washington, DC, area, and MD. No grants to individuals.

Application information: Contributes only to pre-selected organizations.

Officers: Dennis F. Ratner, Pres.; Warren A. Ratner, Secy.

EIN: 541527670

9502
The Reinhart Foundation

c/o The Community Foundation
7501 Boulders View Dr., Ste. 100
Richmond, VA   23225

Established in 2000 in VA.

Donor: Myron H. Reinhart.

Foundation type: Independent foundation.

Financial data (yr. ended 12/31/05): Assets, $14,030,160 (M); expenditures, $685,485; qualifying distributions, $523,327; giving activities

include $484,765 for 32 grants (high: $100,805; low: $1,000).

Fields of interest: Higher education; Crime/violence prevention, domestic violence; Boys & girls clubs; Children/youth; services; Foundations (private grantmaking); Foundations (community).

Limitations: Applications not accepted. Giving primarily in New York, NY and Richmond, VA. No grants to individuals.

Application information: Contributes only to pre-selected organizations.

Officer: Myron H. Reinhart, Chair.

Directors: William L. Reinhart; Cynthia R. Richards.

EIN: 542001451

9503
Richard S. Reynolds Foundation ◇
1403 Pemberton Rd., Ste. 102
Richmond, VA 23233-4474 (804) 740-7350
Contact: Victoria Pitrelli
FAX: (804) 740-7807; E-mail: VPRSRFDN@aol.com

Incorporated in 1955 in VA.

Donors: David P. Reynolds; Julia L. Reynolds†; David P. Reynolds Irrevocable Trust.

Foundation type: Independent foundation.

Financial data (yr. ended 6/30/05): Assets, $36,461,002 (M); gifts received, $41,646; expenditures, $2,127,865; qualifying distributions, $1,666,673; giving activities include $1,610,642 for 35 grants (high: $251,642; low: $1,000).

Purpose and activities: Support for higher and secondary education, health, arts and culture, human services, and historic preservation.

Fields of interest: Museums; Performing arts; Historic preservation/historical societies; Secondary school/education; Higher education; Education; Health organizations, association; Boys & girls clubs; Human services; American Red Cross; Foundations (private grantmaking); Protestant agencies & churches.

Type of support: General/operating support; Annual campaigns; Capital campaigns; Building/renovation; Endowments; Professorships; Scholarship funds; Research.

Limitations: Giving primarily in VA. No grants to individuals.

Application information: Application form not required.

Initial approach: Letter
Copies of proposal: 1
Deadline(s): Apr. 30 and Oct. 31
Board meeting date(s): Mid-May and Mid-Nov.
Final notification: 2 weeks after board meeting

Officers: Richard S. Reynolds III, Pres.; Mrs. Glenn R. Martin, V.P.; Dorothy R. Brotherton, Secy.; Randolph N. Reynolds, Treas.

Number of staff: 1 full-time professional.

EIN: 546037003

Selected grants: The following grants were reported in 2005.

$200,000 to Virginia Historical Society, Richmond, VA.

$82,500 to Richmond Ballet, Richmond, VA. 2 grants: $50,000, $32,500

$60,000 to Boys and Girls Club.

$35,000 to Virginia, Commonwealth of, Richmond, VA.

$25,000 to Longwood University, Farmville, VA.

$25,000 to Richmond Symphony, Richmond, VA.

$10,000 to Gunston Hall, Lorton, VA.

$7,000 to Maymont Foundation, Richmond, VA.

9504
The Rice Family Foundation ◇
4378 Montreux Rd.
Warrenton, VA 20187

Established in 2001 in VA.

Donors: Paul Rice; Gina Rice.

Foundation type: Independent foundation.

Financial data (yr. ended 12/31/05): Assets, $9,541,724 (M); gifts received, $9,254,257; expenditures, $1,212,831; qualifying distributions, $1,184,749; giving activities include $1,184,749 for 5 grants (high: $1,000,000; low: $1,000).

Purpose and activities: Giving primarily for education, including an organization for children's music education.

Fields of interest: Arts education; Elementary/secondary education; Education; Protestant agencies & churches.

Limitations: Applications not accepted. Giving limited to VA. No grants to individuals.

Application information: Contributes only to pre-selected organizations.

Officers: Gina Rice, Pres. and Treas.; Paul Rice, V.P. and Secy.

EIN: 542055867

Selected grants: The following grants were reported in 2004.

$428,227 to Highland School, Warrenton, VA.

$60,000 to Warrenton Presbyterian Church, Warrenton, VA. For general operating support.

$28,586 to Fauquier Hospital Auxiliary, Warrenton, VA. For general operating support.

$27,000 to Sweet Briar College, Sweet Briar, VA.

$21,000 to American Children of SCORE (String, Choral, Orff and Recorder Ensemble), Warrenton, VA. 2 grants: $20,000 (For general operating support), $1,000 (For general operating support).

$2,500 to Piedmont Regional Orchestra, Warrenton, VA. For general operating support.

$1,000 to Fauquier Society for the Prevention of Cruelty to Animals, Warrenton, VA. For general operating support.

$500 to Fauquier Family Shelter Services, Warrenton, VA. For general operating support.

9505
The Riverside Foundation Charitable Trust
305 Harrison St. S.E., 3rd Fl.
Leesburg, VA 20175
Contact: Kelli R. Morris, Admin. Dir.

Established in 1998.

Donor: The Trimble Revocable Living Trust.

Foundation type: Independent foundation.

Financial data (yr. ended 12/31/05): Assets, $11,430,945 (M); expenditures, $1,961,635; qualifying distributions, $1,837,995; giving activities include $1,792,266 for 45 grants (high: $662,000; low: $1,500; average: $2,000–$10,000).

Purpose and activities: The trust supports organizations that participate in religious ministry to the handicapped community.

Fields of interest: Human services; Religion.

Limitations: Giving on a national basis. No grants to individuals.

Application information: Applicants should submit statement describing how organization has participated in religious ministry to the handicapped. Application form required.

Initial approach: Proposal

Copies of proposal: 1
Deadline(s): None

Officers and Directors:* Daniel D. Smith,* Pres.; Sharon R. Berry,* V.P.; Charles W. Colson,* Treas.; Joni Erickson Tada; Ralph Veerman.

EIN: 546417931

Selected grants: The following grants were reported in 2004.

$518,594 to Joni and Friends, Agoura Hills, CA.

$50,000 to Young Life, Colorado Springs, CO.

$25,000 to CURE International, Harrisburg, PA.

$13,000 to American Leprosy Missions, Greenville, SC.

$10,000 to Rainbow Acres, Camp Verde, AZ.

$4,000 to Echoing Hills Village Foundation, Warsaw, OH.

9506
Robins Foundation ▼
1021 E. Cary St., 8th Fl.
Richmond, VA 23219 (804) 697-6917
Contact: William L. Roberts, Jr., Exec. Dir.
Application address: P.O. Box 1124, Capitol Station Richmond, VA 23218-1124; URL: http://www.robins-foundation.org

Established in 1957 in VA.

Donor: E. Claiborne Robins†.

Foundation type: Independent foundation.

Financial data (yr. ended 12/31/04): Assets, $122,218,206 (M); expenditures, $6,958,514; qualifying distributions, $5,918,755; giving activities include $5,655,818 for 80 grants (high: $1,000,000; low: $2,500; average: $5,000–$200,000).

Purpose and activities: Gives to a broad range of causes in the Richmond area.

Fields of interest: Arts; Human services; Children/youth, services.

Type of support: Matching/challenge support; Program development; Land acquisition; Income development; Capital campaigns; Building/renovation; Equipment; Endowments; Consulting services; Program evaluation.

Limitations: Giving primarily in Richmond, VA. No grants to individuals, or for annual funds or special events.

Publications: Application guidelines; Annual report; Grants list.

Application information: See foundation's Web site for additional application information. Application form required.

Initial approach: Request guidelines and submit preliminary proposal
Copies of proposal: 1
Deadline(s): Feb., May, July, and Oct.
Final notification: June and Dec.

Officers and Directors:* E. Claiborne Robins, Jr.,* Pres.; Lewis T. Booker, V.P.; Ann Carol Marchant,* Secy.; Reginald N. Jones,* Treas.; William L. Roberts, Jr., Exec. Dir.; E. Bruce Heilman*; Robert E. Marchant; Sheryl Robins Nolt; Betty Robins Porter; Gregory C. Robins; Lora M. Robins; Robin R. Shield; Juliet E. Shield-Taylor.

Number of staff: 1 full-time professional; 1 full-time support.

EIN: 540784484

Selected grants: The following grants were reported in 2005.

$276,000 to North Richmond Partnership for Families, Richmond, VA. 2 grants: $58,000 (For Partnership for Families Northside), $218,000 (For Partnership for Families Northside).

$250,000 to Healing Place, Richmond, VA. For capital campaign for new building, operating support and endowment.

$250,000 to Valentine Richmond History Center, Richmond, VA. For Phase II of Second Century Campaign.

$150,000 to Family Life Line, Richmond, VA. For Communities in Schools Program.

$110,000 to CrossOver Ministry, Richmond, VA. For strategic technology planning.

$100,000 to Virginia State Golf Association Foundation, Richmond, VA. For Junior Programs at Independence Golf Club.

$75,000 to Fan Free Clinic, Richmond, VA. For positions of Medical Assistant and Medical Case Manager.

$50,000 to Commonwealth Public Broadcasting, Richmond, VA. For Ready to Learn Project.

$40,000 to Jamestown-Yorktown Foundation, Williamsburg, VA. For Powhatan Indian Village.

9507
The Roller-Bottimore Foundation ◇

c/o Bank of America, N.A.
P.O. Box 26688, VA2-300-12-99
Richmond, VA 23261-6688 (804) 788-2963
Contact: Elizabeth D. Seaman, Trust Off., Bank of America, N.A.

Established in 1981.
Donor: Elizabeth R. Bottimore†.
Foundation type: Independent foundation.
Financial data (yr. ended 12/31/05): Assets, $8,474,009 (M); expenditures, $439,142; qualifying distributions, $382,742; giving activities include $379,400 for 8 grants (high: $100,000; low: $10,000; average: $25,000–$50,000).
Purpose and activities: Giving for capital projects and specific programs of an educational, historical or charitable nature, primarily to organizations in central VA; primary interests are historic preservation and Virginia history.
Fields of interest: Historic preservation/historical societies.
Type of support: Building/renovation; Program development; Matching/challenge support.
Limitations: Giving primarily in central VA. No grants to individuals, or for endowments, debt reduction, national fund drives, scholarship funds or general operating expenses.
Publications: Informational brochure (including application guidelines).
Application information: Application form not required.
Initial approach: Request guidelines
Copies of proposal: 1
Deadline(s): May 1 and Nov. 1
Board meeting date(s): June and Dec.
Final notification: After board meetings
Officers and Directors:* Henry Spalding, Jr.,* Pres.; Lucy P. Summerell,* V.P.; John Thomas King,* Treas.
EIN: 541201084

9508
The Marion & Robert Rosenthal Family Foundation ◇

c/o Donald Bavely
1100 S. Glebe Rd.
Arlington, VA 22204 (703) 553-4300
Contact: Robert M. Rosenthal, Pres.

Established in 1995 in VA.
Donors: Marion Rosenthal; Robert M. Rosenthal.
Foundation type: Independent foundation.
Financial data (yr. ended 12/31/04): Assets, $8,903,145 (M); expenditures, $424,293; qualifying distributions, $361,533; giving activities include $361,533 for 36 grants (high: $50,000; low: $500).
Purpose and activities: Giving primarily for the arts and education; support also for Jewish agencies and temples.
Fields of interest: Museums (art); Performing arts, orchestra (symphony); Elementary/secondary education; Higher education; Jewish federated giving programs; Jewish agencies & temples; Women.
Type of support: General/operating support; Program development; Scholarship funds; Research.
Limitations: Applications not accepted. Giving primarily in the Washington, DC area, including MA and VA. No grants to individuals.
Application information: Contributes only to pre-selected organizations.
Officers and Directors:* Robert M. Rosenthal,* Pres.; Jane R. Cafritz,* V.P.; Marion Rosenthal,* V.P.; Nancy Rosenthal,* Secy.; Brooke R. Peterson,* Treas.
EIN: 541740285

9509
Sacharuna Foundation

P.O. Box 130
The Plains, VA 20198
Contact: Lori Udall, Prog. Dir.

Established in 1985 in NY.
Donor: Lavinia Currier.
Foundation type: Independent foundation.
Financial data (yr. ended 12/31/04): Assets, $13,048,279 (M); expenditures, $941,754; qualifying distributions, $853,397; giving activities include $752,570 for 21 grants (high: $360,000; low: $570).
Purpose and activities: Giving primarily for conservation, environmental, and wildlife organizations, and indigenous peoples' issues; some support for education, and historic and cultural preservation.
Fields of interest: Environment; Animals/wildlife, preservation/protection; Indigenous people.
Type of support: General/operating support.
Limitations: Applications not accepted. No grants to individuals.
Application information: Contributes only to pre-selected organizations.
Trustee: Lavinia Currier.
Number of staff: 1 part-time professional.
EIN: 133264132
Selected grants: The following grants were reported in 2004.
$360,000 to Conservation Fund, Arlington, VA.
$25,000 to Chesapeake Bay Foundation, Annapolis, MD.
$20,000 to Sierra Madre Alliance, Tucson, AZ.
$14,000 to Halawa Valley Land Trust, Kaunakakai, HI.
$12,500 to Ruckus Society, Berkeley, CA.
$10,000 to World Wildlife Fund, DC.
$7,500 to San Juan Citizens Alliance, Durango, CO.
$3,000 to Endangered Species Coalition, DC.
$2,000 to Bluemont Concert Series, Leesburg, VA.

9510
Samberg Family Foundation ▼

3101 Wilson Blvd., Suite 220
Arlington, VA 22201
Contact: Jerry Levine, Co-Dir.; Laura J. Samberg, Co-Dir.
Telephone for Jerry Levine: (703) 351-9405

Established in 1996.
Donor: Arthur Samberg.
Foundation type: Independent foundation.
Financial data (yr. ended 11/30/05): Assets, $74,791,812 (M); expenditures, $5,072,421; qualifying distributions, $4,821,947; giving activities include $4,266,868 for 21 grants (high: $1,000,000; low: $5,000; average: $20,000–$100,000).
Purpose and activities: Giving primarily for children, youth and families; health; and Jewish issues.
Fields of interest: Museums; Education; Health care; Children/youth, services; Family services; Jewish federated giving programs.
Type of support: General/operating support; Continuing support; Management development/capacity building; Program development; Conferences/seminars; Seed money; Curriculum development; Research; Technical assistance; Program evaluation; Matching/challenge support.
Limitations: Applications not accepted. Giving primarily in NY. No grants to individuals.
Application information: Unsolicited requests for funds not accepted.
Officers: Jerry Levine, Co-Dir.; Laura J. Samberg, Co-Dir.
Trustees: Arthur Samberg; Rebecca Samberg.
Number of staff: 2 full-time professional.
EIN: 066439895
Selected grants: The following grants were reported in 2005.
$1,000,000 to Harlem Childrens Zone, New York, NY.
$500,000 to College Summit, DC.
$500,000 to UJA-Federation of New York, New York, NY.
$490,601 to New York-Presbyterian Hospital, New York, NY. 4 grants: $93,000 to Morgan Stanley Childrens Hospital of New York, $134,444 to Morgan Stanley Childrens Hospital of New York, $100,000 to Morgan Stanley Childrens Hospital of New York, $163,157 to Morgan Stanley Childrens Hospital of New York
$206,305 to Open Door Family Medical Center, Ossining, NY.
$150,000 to Spark-Partnership for Service, Baltimore, MD.
$100,000 to Center for Jewish History, New York, NY.
$100,000 to Jewish Outreach Institute, New York, NY.

9511
Art and Annie Sandler Foundation, Inc. ◇

448 Viking Dr., Ste. 220
Virginia Beach, VA 23452

Established in 1996 in VA.
Donor: Arthur B. Sandler.
Foundation type: Independent foundation.
Financial data (yr. ended 6/30/05): Assets, $859,634 (M); gifts received, $57,015; expenditures, $555,740; qualifying distributions, $549,925; giving activities include $549,925 for 17 grants (high: $275,000; low: $2,500).

Purpose and activities: Giving primarily for Jewish agencies and temples; funding also for education.
Fields of interest: Elementary/secondary education; Higher education; Higher education, university; Jewish federated giving programs; Jewish agencies & temples.
Limitations: Giving primarily in MA, and Norfolk and Virginia Beach, VA.
Officers: Arthur B. Sandler, Pres.; Steven B. Sandler, V.P.; Annie L. Sandler, Secy.
EIN: 541850741
Selected grants: The following grants were reported in 2004.
$456,076 to United Jewish Federation of Tidewater, Norfolk, VA.
$175,000 to Brandeis University, Waltham, MA.
$75,000 to Norfolk Collegiate School, Norfolk, VA.
$55,000 to American Israel Education Foundation (AIEF), DC.
$25,000 to Jewish Federation, Raleigh-Cary, Raleigh, NC.
$15,025 to Congregation Beth El, Norfolk, VA.
$13,800 to Temple Israel, Norfolk, VA.
$10,000 to Virginia Wesleyan College, Virginia Beach, VA.
$5,000 to Norfolk Academy, Norfolk, VA.
$924 to Jewish Community Center of Tidewater Virginia, Norfolk, VA.

9512

Steve and Toni Sandler Foundation, Inc. ✧
448 Viking Dr., Ste. 220
Virginia Beach, VA   23452

Established in 1996 in VA.
Donors: Steven B. Sandler; Arthur & Annie Sandler Foundation.
Foundation type: Independent foundation.
Financial data (yr. ended 6/30/06): Assets, $1,743,843 (M); expenditures, $471,664; qualifying distributions, $461,500; giving activities include $461,500 for grants.
Fields of interest: Elementary/secondary education; Higher education; Dental care; Jewish federated giving programs; Jewish agencies & temples.
Limitations: Giving primarily in VA.
Officers: Steven B. Sandler, Pres.; Arthur B. Sandler, V.P.; Toni Sandler, Secy.
EIN: 541850740
Selected grants: The following grants were reported in 2004.
$365,076 to United Jewish Federation of Tidewater, Norfolk, VA.
$85,500 to Norfolk Collegiate School, Norfolk, VA.
$40,000 to Boston University, Boston, MA.
$28,995 to Temple Israel, Norfolk, VA.
$27,500 to Washington and Lee University, Lexington, VA.
$25,000 to Beth Sholom Home of Eastern Virginia, Virginia Beach, VA.
$25,000 to College of Charleston Foundation, Charleston, SC.
$25,000 to Johns Hopkins University, Baltimore, MD.
$25,000 to University of North Carolina, Wilmington, NC.
$6,900 to Hebrew Academy, Virginia Beach, VA.

9513

The William H., John G., and Emma Scott Foundation
901 E. Cary St., Ste. 1406
Richmond, VA   23219-4037
Contact: Hugh K. Leary, Exec. Dir.

Incorporated in 1956 in VA.
Donors: John G. Scott†; Emma Scott Taylor†.
Foundation type: Independent foundation.
Financial data (yr. ended 9/30/05): Assets, $10,893,733 (M); expenditures, $640,500; qualifying distributions, $548,500; giving activities include $548,500 for 22 grants (high: $100,000; low: $6,000).
Purpose and activities: Giving primarily to support programs which alleviate human suffering, and improve the health of those families, individuals and children in need of aid and/or education. A portion of the grants may be applied to support the needs of church schools in the Episcopal Diocese of VA, and private elementary and secondary education. To a lesser degree, grants may be available in support of the arts and humanities.
Fields of interest: Museums; Education; Human services; Christian agencies & churches.
Type of support: Capital campaigns; Building/ renovation; Equipment; Program development; Seed money; Program evaluation.
Limitations: Giving primarily in the Richmond, VA, metropolitan area. No grants to individuals, or for endowment funds, operating budgets, research, national fund drives, or debt reduction.
Publications: Application guidelines; Informational brochure (including application guidelines).
Application information: Scholarship program has been discontinued. Application form not required.
Initial approach: Letter
Copies of proposal: 1
Deadline(s): July 31
Board meeting date(s): Sept.
Final notification: 1 year
Officers and Trustees:* C. Cotesworth Pinckney,* Pres.; E. Bryson Powell,* V.P.; Susanne B. Crump,* Secy.; Hugh K. Leary, Treas. and Exec. Dir.; W. Hill Brown III; Charles M. Guthridge; Robert F. Norfleet, Jr.
Number of staff: 1 part-time professional.
EIN: 540648772
Selected grants: The following grants were reported in 2005.
$100,000 to Saint Margarets School, Tappahannock, VA.
$35,000 to Orchard House School, Richmond, VA.
$30,000 to ESI Connections, Richmond, VA.
$25,000 to CrossOver Ministry, Richmond, VA.
$25,000 to Free Clinic of Goochland, Manakin Sabot, VA.
$25,000 to Interfaith Housing Corporation, Richmond, VA.
$25,000 to Little Sisters of the Poor, Richmond, VA.
$25,000 to Saint Christophers School, Richmond, VA.
$25,000 to Saint Josephs Villa, Richmond, VA.
$15,000 to Neighborhood Resource Center, Norfolk, VA.

9514

The Edward W. and Betty Knight Scripps Foundation ▼ ✧
1405 Eagle Hill Farm
Charlottesville, VA   22901   (434) 973-3345
Contact: Gregory A. Robbins, V.P., Fin.

Established in 1987 in VA.
Donors: Betty K. Scripps; Scripps League Newspapers, Inc.
Foundation type: Independent foundation.
Financial data (yr. ended 4/30/06): Assets, $713,563 (M); gifts received, $1,570,000; expenditures, $2,612,508; qualifying distributions, $2,596,352; giving activities include $2,570,000 for 4 grants (high: $1,000,000; low: $250,000).
Purpose and activities: Giving primarily for education and human services.
Fields of interest: Arts; Higher education; Medical research, institute.
Type of support: Annual campaigns; Research.
Limitations: Giving on a national basis. No grants to individuals.
Application information: Requests are considered in May/June annually. Application form required.
Initial approach: Letter
Copies of proposal: 1
Board meeting date(s): Mar. or Apr. and Oct. or Nov.
Officers: Betty K. Scripps, Chair., Pres. and Treas.; Gregory A. Robbins, V.P., Fin. and Secy.
Directors: Charles H. Ewald; Joseph E. Killory, Jr.; Jack C. Morgan.
Number of staff: 1 full-time professional.
EIN: 541426826
Selected grants: The following grants were reported in 2005.
$1,500,000 to Scripps Foundation for Medicine and Science, San Diego, CA.
$1,301,000 to Washington Opera, DC.
$320,000 to Miller Center Foundation, Charlottesville, VA.
$250,000 to Mayo Foundation, Rochester, MN.
$100,000 to Thomas Jefferson Memorial Foundation, Charlottesville, VA.
$50,000 to American Center for Wine, Food and the Arts, Napa, CA.
$50,000 to Anti-Defamation League of Bnai Brith, New York, NY.
$35,000 to Friends of Lincoln Theater, Yountville, CA.

9515

The Sharp Foundation ✧
P.O. Box 42333
Richmond, VA   23242-2333

Established in 1989 in VA.
Donor: Richard L. Sharp.
Foundation type: Independent foundation.
Financial data (yr. ended 12/31/04): Assets, $8,312,910 (M); expenditures, $504,966; qualifying distributions, $480,660; giving activities include $479,873 for 81 grants (high: $55,000; low: $50).
Purpose and activities: Giving to Christian agencies and churches, and higher education.
Fields of interest: Higher education; Health care; Health organizations, association; Federated giving programs; Christian agencies & churches.

Limitations: Applications not accepted. Giving primarily in Richmond, VA; some giving nationally. No grants to individuals.
Application information: Contributes only to pre-selected organizations.
Officers: Richard L. Sharp, Pres. and Treas.; Elizabeth J. Girard, Secy.
EIN: 541526891
Selected grants: The following grants were reported in 2003.
$275,000 to Elijah House Academy, Richmond, VA.
$5,000 to Carpenter Center for the Performing Arts, Richmond, VA.
$5,000 to Virginia One to One: The Mentoring Partnership, Richmond, VA.
$1,500 to Richmond Symphony, Richmond, VA. For annual campaign.
$1,000 to Heritage Foundation, DC.
$1,000 to Theater IV, Richmond, VA.
$750 to Fellowship of Christian Athletes, Kansas City, MO.
$500 to Lewis Ginter Botanical Gardens, Richmond, VA.
$500 to Riverside School, Richmond, VA. For annual campaign.
$100 to March of Dimes Birth Defects Foundation, Arlington, VA.

9516
Silver Foundation ◇ ☆
1201 Central Park Blvd.
Fredericksburg, VA 22401

Established in 1990 in VA.
Donors: Carl D. Silver; Larry D. Silver.
Foundation type: Independent foundation.
Financial data (yr. ended 4/30/06): Assets, $608 (M); gifts received, $371,108; expenditures, $390,981; qualifying distributions, $390,632; giving activities include $390,632 for grants.
Fields of interest: Federated giving programs; Economically disadvantaged.
Limitations: Giving primarily in VA. No grants to individuals.
Directors: Paul S. Elkin; Carl D. Silver; Larry D. Silver.
EIN: 541556341

9517
Charles E. Smith Family Foundation ▼ ◇
2345 Crystal Dr.
Arlington, VA 22202

Established in 1963 in VA.
Donors: Charles E. Smith†; Robert H. Smith; Robert P. Kogod; Charles E. Smith Trust.
Foundation type: Independent foundation.
Financial data (yr. ended 2/28/05): Assets, $77,914,182 (M); gifts received, $1,920; expenditures, $5,674,956; qualifying distributions, $5,585,760; giving activities include $5,578,850 for 32 grants (high: $1,500,000; low: $2,500; average: $5,000–$200,000).
Purpose and activities: Support primarily for a Jewish welfare fund and other Jewish organizations.
Fields of interest: Human services; Jewish federated giving programs; Jewish agencies & temples.
Limitations: Applications not accepted. Giving primarily in the greater Washington, DC, area, MD, VA, NJ, and NY. No grants to individuals.

Application information: Contributes only to pre-selected organizations.
Officers: Robert H. Smith, Pres.; Arlene R. Kogod, V.P.; Clarice R. Smith, V.P.; Robert P. Kogod, Secy.-Treas.
EIN: 311570183
Selected grants: The following grants were reported in 2004.
$1,000,000 to Jewish Federation of Greater Washington, Rockville, MD.
$500,000 to Charles E. Smith Jewish Day School of Greater Washington, Rockville, MD.
$500,000 to Jewish Day School, DC.
$300,000 to Hebrew Home of Greater Washington, Rockville, MD.
$250,000 to American Friends of Shalom Hartman Institute, New York, NY.
$250,000 to Israel, State of, Jerusalem, Israel. .
$250,000 to University of Maryland-College Park, College Park, MD.
$231,000 to American Friends of the Hebrew University, DC. For the National Institute of Psychobiology of Israel.
$200,000 to Capital Camps, Rockville, MD.
$200,000 to Jewish Community Center of Greater Washington, Rockville, MD.

9518
Robert H. Smith Family Foundation ◇
2345 Crystal Dr.
Arlington, VA 22202

Established in 1987 in VA.
Donors: Robert H. Smith; Clarice R. Smith; CES Mgmt., Inc.; RCS II, LLC.
Foundation type: Independent foundation.
Financial data (yr. ended 11/30/05): Assets, $15,188,416 (M); gifts received, $7,289,625; expenditures, $539,245; qualifying distributions, $529,828; giving activities include $527,078 for grants.
Fields of interest: Museums; Performing arts, opera; Historic preservation/historical societies; Arts; Higher education; Education; Environment; Hospitals (general); Jewish agencies & temples.
Limitations: Applications not accepted. Giving primarily in Washington, DC. No grants to individuals.
Application information: Contributes only to pre-selected organizations.
Officers: Robert H. Smith, Pres. and Treas.; Clarice R. Smith, V.P. and Secy.
Directors: David B. Smith; Michelle Smith.
EIN: 521502273

9519
The Smithfield-Luter Foundation, Inc. ◇ ☆
c/o Hamill, C.P.A.
P.O. Box 6010
Norfolk, VA 23508

Established in 2001 in VA and NC.
Donor: Joseph W. Luter III.
Foundation type: Independent foundation.
Financial data (yr. ended 11/30/05): Assets, $4,320,007 (M); gifts received, $11,965; expenditures, $668,997; qualifying distributions, $651,833; giving activities include $651,833 for grants.
Fields of interest: Higher education.

Officers: Joseph W. Luter III, Chair.; Richard J.M. Poulson, Secy.; Joseph W. Luter IV, Treas.
EIN: 542062029
Selected grants: The following grants were reported in 2004.
$60,000 to Iowa State University, Ames, IA.
$60,000 to Virginia Polytechnic Institute and State University, Blacksburg, VA.
$25,000 to Isle of Wight Academy, Isle of Wight, VA.
$25,000 to Johnson and Wales University, Providence, RI.
$25,000 to Nansemond-Suffolk Academy, Suffolk, VA.
$6,431 to University of Wisconsin, Milwaukee, WI.

9520
Snead Family Foundation ◇
103 Lockgreen Pl.
Richmond, VA 23226 (804) 354-3510
Contact: Thomas G. Snead, Jr., Dir.

Established in 2004 in VA.
Donors: Thomas G. Snead, Jr.; Vickie M. Snead.
Foundation type: Independent foundation.
Financial data (yr. ended 12/31/05): Assets, $2,727,358 (M); gifts received, $1,310,462; expenditures, $409,043; qualifying distributions, $380,780; giving activities include $378,525 for 38 grants (high: $251,000; low: $200; average: $1,000–$5,000).
Purpose and activities: The foundation focuses on projects that improve health, human services, and education.
Fields of interest: Arts; Higher education; Hospitals (general); Medical research; Human services.
Limitations: Giving primarily in Richmond, VA. No grants to individuals.
Application information: Application form not required.
Initial approach: Letter
Deadline(s): None
Directors: Christen E. Snead; Thomas G. Snead, Jr.; Vickie M. Snead.
EIN: 201037290

9521
Staunton Augusta Waynesboro Community Foundation ◇
(doing business as Community Foundation of the Central Blue Ridge)
(also known as SAW Community Foundation)
27 Stone Ridge Dr.
Waynesboro, VA 22980 (540) 932-7878
Contact: Joi E. Brown, Exec. Dir.
FAX: (540) 932-7539;
E-mail: communityfoundation@ntelos.net;
URL: http://www.cfw.com/~sawfdtn
Additional URL: http://www.communityfoundationCBR.org

Established in 1992 in VA.
Donor: H.D. "Buz" Dawbarn†.
Foundation type: Community foundation.
Financial data (yr. ended 12/31/05): Assets, $7,838,184 (M); gifts received, $680,559; expenditures, $526,948; giving activities include $417,546 for grants.
Purpose and activities: The foundation provides support for the arts, education, and human services.
Fields of interest: Arts; Education; Environment; Health care; Youth, services; Family services;

Community development, neighborhood development.

Type of support: Equipment; Program development; Curriculum development; Program evaluation.

Limitations: Giving limited to Augusta County, Nelson County, Staunton, and Waynesboro, VA. No support for sectarian, fraternal, or religious organizations. No grants for start-up operations, deficit reduction, capital campaigns, endowments, or events.

Publications: Application guidelines; Annual report; Grants list; Informational brochure.

Application information: Application form required.

Initial approach: Telephone requesting application and describing project

Copies of proposal: 1

Deadline(s): Dec. 15

Board meeting date(s): 3rd Mon. of every odd number month

Final notification: Apr. or May

Officers and Directors:* Carl G. Lind,* Pres.; Douglas L. Guynn,* V.P.; N. Douglas Noland, Jr.,* Secy.-Treas.; Joi E. Brown, Exec. Dir.; A. Tracy Aitcheson; C. Phillip Barger; Kenneth S. Cleveland III; David Deering; Barbara R. Gibb; Timothy C. Hess; Andrew Hodson; Pamela T. Huggins; Deborah T. Metz; P. William Moore, Jr.; Beverly S. "Cheri" Moran; E. Ray Murphy; Richard Schilling; Phillip R. Winter.

Number of staff: 2 full-time professional.

EIN: 541647385

9522
Stern Family Fund ✧

(formerly Philip M. Stern Family Fund)

P.O. Box 100670

Arlington, VA 22210-0890 (703) 527-6692

Contact: Elizabeth Collaton, Exec. Dir.

FAX: (703) 527-5775;

E-mail: sternfund@verizon.net; URL: http://www.sternfund.org

Established in 1959 in DC; reorganized in 1994.

Donor: Philip M. Stern†.

Foundation type: Independent foundation.

Financial data (yr. ended 6/30/04): Assets, $1,133,474 (M); expenditures, $607,996; qualifying distributions, $591,797; giving activities include $545,000 for 26 grants (high: $75,000; low: $10,000).

Purpose and activities: Support for systemic reform efforts that attack the root causes of problems rather than providing direct services; projects that strive for a more equitable distribution of political and economic power; and action-oriented projects with the potential for significant regional and national impact.

Fields of interest: Public affairs.

Type of support: General/operating support; Program development; Seed money; Matching/challenge support.

Limitations: Giving limited to the U.S. No support for international programs or domestic programs dealing with international issues, the performing arts, universities, hospitals, museums, or social service programs offering ongoing or direct delivery of service. No grants for building or endowment funds, capital campaigns, academic research, scholarships, land acquisition, films, or benefits.

Publications: Application guidelines; Grants list; Informational brochure (including application guidelines).

Application information: The fund's popular Public Interest Pioneer program was discontinued. Telephone inquiries and FAX submissions are discouraged; each proposal for the Strategic Opportunity Grants must be accompanied by a cover page format provided by NNG Common Grant Application section I cover page, see foundation Web site for copy; Questions and letter of introduction may be sent by mail, E-mail, or fax, but proposals must be submitted by mail. Application form required.

Initial approach: Letter or proposal

Copies of proposal: 3

Deadline(s): Aug. 15 for Strategic Opportunity Grants

Board meeting date(s): Semiannually

Final notification: Nov. for Strategic Opportunity Grants

Officers and Directors:* David M. Stern,* Pres.; Tracey Hughes,* V.P. and Secy.; Elizabeth Collaton, Exec. Dir.; Michael Caudell-Feagan; Alan Morrison; Sidney Wolfe.

Number of staff: 1 part-time professional.

EIN: 526037658

Selected grants: The following grants were reported in 2004.

$150,000 to Proteus Fund, Amherst, MA. 2 grants: $75,000 each

$100,000 to Mississippi Center for Justice, Jackson, MS. 3 grants: $20,000, $50,000, $30,000

$20,000 to Maine Citizen Leadership Fund, Portland, ME.

$20,000 to Midwest States Center, Prairie Farm, WI.

$15,000 to Center for Voting and Democracy, Takoma Park, MD.

$15,000 to New Hampshire Citizens Alliance, Concord, NH.

$10,000 to Media Access Project, DC.

9523
SunTrust Foundation MidAtlantic ▼ ✧

(formerly Crestar Foundation)

c/o SunTrust Banks, Inc.

919 E. Main St.

Richmond, VA 23219 (804) 782-7907

Contact: Brenda L. Skidmore, Pres.

Established in 1973 in VA.

Donors: Crestar Bank; SunTrust Bank.

Foundation type: Company-sponsored foundation.

Financial data (yr. ended 12/31/05): Assets, $6,809,679 (M); gifts received, $3,750,000; expenditures, $3,576,696; qualifying distributions, $3,575,739; giving activities include $3,574,739 for 775 grants (high: $123,750; low: $50).

Purpose and activities: The foundation supports organizations involved with arts and culture, higher education, the environment, health, and business and industry.

Fields of interest: Arts; Higher education; Environment; Health care; Business/industry; Federated giving programs.

Type of support: Annual campaigns; Capital campaigns; Building/renovation; Equipment; Professorships; Employee matching gifts.

Limitations: Giving limited to areas of company operations, with emphasis on VA. No support for government-supported, political, religious, or national organizations. No grants to individuals, or for research, scholarships, or fellowships; no loans.

Publications: Informational brochure.

Application information: Application form not required.

Initial approach: Proposal

Copies of proposal: 1

Deadline(s): Before Oct.

Board meeting date(s): Semiannually, and as required

Officers: Brenda L. Skidmore, Pres.; Jane A. Markins, Secy.-Treas.

Number of staff: 2 full-time professional.

EIN: 237336418

Selected grants: The following grants were reported in 2005.

$123,750 to United Way Services. For general support.

$55,000 to Habitat for Humanity International. For general support.

$55,000 to Virginia Foundation for Independent Colleges, Richmond, VA. For general support.

$40,000 to Business Consortium for Arts Support, Norfolk, VA. For general support.

$35,000 to Richmond Renaissance, Richmond, VA. For general support.

$25,000 to Mercy Medical Center, Baltimore, MD. For general support.

$22,000 to Jewish Community Foundation. For general support.

$16,666 to Saint Pauls College, Lawrenceville, VA. For general support.

$15,000 to B and O Railroad Museum, Baltimore, MD. For general support.

$12,500 to Baltimore Neighborhood Collaborative, Baltimore, MD. For general support.

9524
The Taubman Foundation ✧

(formerly Arthur & Grace W. Taubman Foundation, Inc.)

2965 Colonnade Dr., Ste. 300

Roanoke, VA 24018

Established around 1958.

Donors: Nicholas F. Taubman; Advance Stores Co., Inc.

Foundation type: Independent foundation.

Financial data (yr. ended 12/31/05): Assets, $55,196 (M); gifts received, $910,000; expenditures, $501,331; qualifying distributions, $501,331; giving activities include $501,307 for 23 grants (high: $250,000; low: $250).

Purpose and activities: Giving primarily for the arts, education and health associations.

Fields of interest: Museums (art); Performing arts, opera; Historic preservation/historical societies; Education; Health care, clinics/centers; Health organizations, association; Federated giving programs; Jewish agencies & temples.

Limitations: Applications not accepted. Giving on a national basis, with emphasis on Roanoke, VA.

Application information: Unsolicited requests for funds not accepted.

Officers: Nicholas F. Taubman, Pres. and Secy.-Treas.; Eugenia L. Taubman, V.P.

EIN: 546052861

9525
Three Swallows Foundation ✧

12608 Wyclow Dr.

Clifton, VA 20124

Established in 1981 in VA.

Foundation type: Independent foundation.
Financial data (yr. ended 10/31/04): Assets, $2,154,458 (M); expenditures, $1,696,251; qualifying distributions, $473,197; giving activities include $368,104 for 44 grants (high: $148,000; low: $25).
Fields of interest: Education; Health organizations, association; Neuroscience research; International development; Federated giving programs; Science, research; Christian agencies & churches.
Type of support: Research.
Limitations: Applications not accepted. Giving on a national basis, with some emphasis on CO. No grants to individuals; no program-related investments.
Application information: Contributes only to pre-selected organizations.
Officers and Directors:* Paul N. Temple, Pres.; Steven Greenberg,* Treas.; D. Barry Abell; Marc Abell; Pamela T. Abell; Rebecca Abell; James Brown; Monique Brown; Thomas Brown; Lise Temple Greenberg; G. Michael Moore; Diane E. Temple; Nancy L. Temple; Robin R. Temple; Thomas D. Temple.
EIN: 521234546
Selected grants: The following grants were reported in 2003.
$220,750 to International Foundation, DC. For general support.
$90,000 to Institute of Noetic Sciences, Petaluma, CA. For general support.
$38,615 to All Season Chalice Church, Longmont, CO. For general support.
$20,000 to Kaleida Health Foundation, Buffall General Hospital, Buffalo, NY. For Jacobs Neurological Institute.
$20,000 to Marin Academy, San Rafael, CA. For general support.
$20,000 to Rockwood Leadership Program, Berkeley, CA. For general support.
$7,000 to Rocky Mountain Peace and Justice Center, Boulder, CO. For general support.
$6,000 to American Friends of the British Museum, New York, NY. For general support.
$6,000 to Child and Family Advocacy Program, Blue Sky Bridge, Boulder, CO. For general support.
$1,000 to Hospice of Boulder County, Lafayette, CO. For general support.

9526
The Edgar A. Thurman Charitable Foundation for Children ✧
c/o SunTrust Bank
P.O. Box 27385
Richmond, VA 23261-7385
Contact: Carolyn McCoy
Application address: c/o SunTrust Bank, P.O. Box 13888, Roanoke, VA 24038, tel.: (540) 982-3076

Trust established in 1952 in VA.
Donor: Edgar A. Thurman‡.
Foundation type: Independent foundation.
Financial data (yr. ended 6/30/05): Assets, $6,724,021 (M); expenditures, $470,222; qualifying distributions, $442,511; giving activities include $424,540 for 58 grants (high: $22,000; low: $1,000).
Purpose and activities: To provide maintenance, care, and education for needy children; support for orphanages, youth agencies, preschool education, and social service agencies.
Fields of interest: Education, early childhood education; Human services; Children/youth,

services; Christian agencies & churches; Economically disadvantaged.
Limitations: Giving limited to VA, with emphasis on the Roanoke area. No grants to individuals, or for building or endowment funds, salaries, or deficit financing.
Publications: Application guidelines; Program policy statement.
Application information: Application form required.
Initial approach: Letter
Copies of proposal: 1
Deadline(s): Dec.
Board meeting date(s): Annually
Final notification: 3 months from receipt
Trustee: SunTrust Bank.
EIN: 546113281

9527
The Titmus Foundation, Inc.
3516 Whippernock Farm Rd.
Sutherland, VA 23885-8720 (804) 265-5834
Contact: Edward B. Titmus, Pres.; Edward H. Titmus III, Exec. V.P.
FAX: (804) 265-5203; *E-mail:* tfound@aol.com;
Mailing address: P.O. Box 10, Sutherland, VA 23885-0010

Incorporated in 1945 in VA.
Donors: Edward Hutson Titmus, Sr.‡; Edward Hutson Titmus, Jr.‡; Edward B. Titmus; Edward H. Titmus III.
Foundation type: Independent foundation.
Financial data (yr. ended 1/31/06): Assets, $25,266,196 (M); expenditures, $1,285,677; qualifying distributions, $1,178,588; giving activities include $978,494 for 137 grants (high: $50,000; low: $425), and $109,068 for 10 employee matching gifts.
Purpose and activities: Emphasis on Baptist church support and religious organizations, higher education, health, cancer research, and child welfare. Also giving for the United Methodist Church and two cancer-research centers. The foundation makes grants to organizations outside its normal giving area whenever there is a disaster such as the Gulf Coast disaster in 2005. This has been done on several occasions.
Fields of interest: Arts; Education; Health care; Health organizations, association; Cancer; Medical research, institute; Cancer research; Crime/violence prevention, domestic violence; Human services; Children/youth, services; Christian agencies & churches; Protestant agencies & churches; Religion; General charitable giving.
Type of support: General/operating support; Annual campaigns; Capital campaigns; Building/renovation; Equipment; Land acquisition; Endowments; Emergency funds; Professorships; Scholarship funds; Research; Matching/challenge support.
Limitations: Giving primarily in VA; some funding also to various parts of NC. No support for a political party, or a specific politician regardless of their stand on any issue, or political organizations having anything to do with lobbyists. No grants to individuals; non tax-exempt organizations or organizations without a physical address.
Publications: Application guidelines.
Application information: No applications should be submitted in Jan. and Feb. Please check application guidelines for acceptable formats. Applications submitted by E-mail not accepted. Application form required.

Initial approach: Request guidelines
Copies of proposal: 1
Deadline(s): None
Board meeting date(s): Aug.
Final notification: Within 1 month prior to annual meeting
Officers: Edward B. Titmus, Pres.; Edward H. Titmus III, Exec. V.P.; William D. Allen II, V.P.; Andrew J. White, V.P.; William A. Young, Jr., V.P.; Kimberly T. Przybyl, Secy.; John J. Muldowney, Treas.
Number of staff: 1 full-time professional; 2 full-time support.
EIN: 546051332
Selected grants: The following grants were reported in 2005.
$100,000 to Petersburg Urban Ministries, Petersburg, VA.
$25,000 to Alleghany Memorial Hospital, Sparta, NC.
$25,000 to Christian Childrens Fund, Richmond, VA.
$20,000 to Bluefield College, Bluefield, VA.
$20,000 to College of William and Mary, Williamsburg, VA.
$15,000 to North Carolina Wesleyan College, Rocky Mount, NC.
$10,000 to Emory and Henry College, Emory, VA.
$5,000 to American Red Cross, Richmond, VA.
$5,000 to Free Clinic of Danville, Danville, VA.
$5,000 to Lynchburg College, Lynchburg, VA.

9528
The Truland Foundation ✧
1900 Oracle Way, Ste. 700
Reston, VA 20190 (703) 516-2600
Contact: Robert W. Truland, Tr.
E-mail: rtruland@truland.com

Established in 1954 in VA.
Donor: Truland Systems Corp.
Foundation type: Company-sponsored foundation.
Financial data (yr. ended 3/31/04): Assets, $1,466,757 (M); expenditures, $373,204; qualifying distributions, $363,068; giving activities include $361,912 for 48 grants (high: $50,000; low: $20).
Purpose and activities: The foundation supports organizations involved with arts and culture, education, health, children and youth services, human services, and community development.
Fields of interest: Arts; Higher education; Education; Environment, natural resources; Hospitals (general); Health organizations, association; Children/youth, services; Human services; Community development.
Type of support: Continuing support; Publication; Matching/challenge support.
Limitations: Giving primarily in VA. No grants to individuals.
Application information: Application form not required.
Initial approach: Proposal
Deadline(s): None
Officers: Robert W. Truland, Pres.; Mary W. Truland, V.P.; Ingrid A. Moini, Secy.; Marc L. Freeman, Treas.
EIN: 546037172

9529
The Ukrop Foundation ✧
600 Southlake Blvd.
Richmond, VA 23236-3922
Contact: Gail Long

Application address: 111 Virginia St., Ste. 200, Richmond, VA 23219

Established in 1983 in VA.

Donor: Ukrop's Super Markets, Inc.

Foundation type: Company-sponsored foundation.

Financial data (yr. ended 6/30/05): Assets, $13,672,327 (M); gifts received, $329,832; expenditures, $1,042,098; qualifying distributions, $945,522; giving activities include $941,895 for 157 grants (high: $80,000; low: $25).

Purpose and activities: The foundation supports organizations involved with arts and culture, education, health, children and youth services, community development, and religion.

Fields of interest: Museums (children's); Arts; Higher education; Education; Health care; YM/YWCAs & YM/YWHAs; Children/youth, services; Human services; Community development; Federated giving programs; Religion.

Type of support: General/operating support; Annual campaigns; Capital campaigns; Program development; Employee matching gifts.

Limitations: Giving primarily in the greater Richmond, VA, area. No support for national or state-supported organizations or health or disease research or treatment organizations (except for memorials). No grants to individuals.

Publications: Informational brochure (including application guidelines).

Application information: Application form not required.

> *Initial approach:* Proposal
> *Deadline(s):* Nov. 1
> *Final notification:* Dec. 31

Officers and Directors: * James E. Ukrop,* Pres.; Robert S. Ukrop,* V.P.; David J. Naquin,* Secy.-Treas.

Number of staff: 1 full-time support.

EIN: 541206389

9530
The United Company Charitable Foundation ✦

(formerly United Coal Company Charitable Foundation)
1005 Glenway Ave.
Bristol, VA 24201-3473

Established in 1986 in VA.

Donors: United Coal Co., Inc.; Burton Fletcher; The Summit Fund, LLC.

Foundation type: Company-sponsored foundation.

Financial data (yr. ended 12/31/05): Assets, $51,752,024 (M); expenditures, $2,905,180; qualifying distributions, $2,813,481; giving activities include $2,560,877 for 68 grants (high: $500,000; low: $300), and $132,683 for 2 foundation-administered programs.

Purpose and activities: The foundation supports organizations involved with arts and culture, education, health, youth development, and human services.

Fields of interest: Arts; Higher education; Medical school/education; Education; Health care; Youth development; YM/YWCAs & YM/YWHAs; Human services.

Type of support: General/operating support; Annual campaigns; Capital campaigns; Building/renovation; Program development; Scholarship funds; Sponsorships.

Limitations: Applications not accepted. Giving primarily in TN and VA. No grants to individuals.

Application information: Contributes only to pre-selected organizations.

Officers and Directors: * James W. McGlothlin,* Chair.; Martha Gayle, Pres.; Nicholas Street, Secy.; Lois A. Clarke, Treas.; Frances McGlothlin; David Street; Fay Street.

EIN: 541390453

9531
Universal Leaf Foundation ✦

Hamilton and Broad Sts.
P.O. Box 25099
Richmond, VA 23260 (804) 359-9311
Contact: Todd Haymore, V.P.

Established in 1975 in VA.

Donor: Universal Leaf Tobacco Co., Inc.

Foundation type: Company-sponsored foundation.

Financial data (yr. ended 6/30/06): Assets, $17,299,787 (M); expenditures, $1,180,744; qualifying distributions, $926,932; giving activities include $926,932 for 440 grants (high: $80,000; low: $25).

Purpose and activities: The foundation supports organizations involved with arts and culture, education, health, multiple sclerosis, human services, and community development.

Fields of interest: Museums (science/technology); Historic preservation/historical societies; Arts; Elementary/secondary education; Higher education; Business school/education; Education; Health care; Multiple sclerosis; American Red Cross; YM/YWCAs & YM/YWHAs; Children/youth, services; Human services; Business/industry; Community development; Federated giving programs.

Type of support: General/operating support; Annual campaigns; Capital campaigns; Endowments; Emergency funds; Program development.

Limitations: Giving primarily in Richmond, VA. No grants to individuals.

Publications: Financial statement.

Application information: Application form not required.

> *Initial approach:* Letter of inquiry
> *Deadline(s):* None
> *Final notification:* 3 to 4 weeks

Officers and Directors: * A.B. King,* Pres.; Todd Haymore, V.P.; Julian Keevil, V.P.; Catherine H. Claiborne, Secy.; Karen M.L. Whelan, Treas.; George C. Freeman III, Genl. Counsel; C.A. Lelong, Jr.; D.C. Moore; J.S. Rowe; H.B. Smith; J.H. Starkey III; W.L. Taylor.

Number of staff: 1 full-time professional; 1 part-time support.

EIN: 510162337

9532
The Virginia Beach Foundation

P.O. Box 4629
Virginia Beach, VA 23454 (757) 422-5249
Contact: Debra R. Steiger, Exec. Dir.
FAX: (757) 422-1849;
E-mail: mainoffice@vabeachfoundation.org;
Hand-delivered application address: 1604 W. Hilltop Exec. Ctr., Ste. 214A, Virginia Beach, VA 23451;
URL: http://www.vabeachfoundation.org

Incorporated in 1987 in VA.

Foundation type: Community foundation.

Financial data (yr. ended 9/30/05): Assets, $12,318,997 (M); gifts received, $1,262,777;

---

expenditures, $1,763,708; giving activities include $1,562,886 for 101 grants (high: $50,000; low: $325; average: $1,000–$2,500).

Purpose and activities: The foundation seeks to: 1) stimulate the establishment of endowments to serve the people of Virginia Beach, VA, now and in the future; 2) respond to changing, emerging community needs; 3) provide a vehicle and a service for donors with varied interests; and 4) serve as a resource, broker, catalyst and leader in the community.

Fields of interest: Humanities; Arts; Education; Environment; Animals/wildlife; Health care; Crime/violence prevention, domestic violence; Children/youth, services; Human services; Aging; Disabilities, people with; Economically disadvantaged; Homeless.

Type of support: Emergency funds; Program development; Scholarship funds; Technical assistance; In-kind gifts; Matching/challenge support.

Limitations: Giving primarily in Virginia Beach, VA. No support for religious purposes, hospitals or similar healthcare facilities, national or international organizations or purposes, or primary or secondary schools or academies (for special needs). No grants to individuals, or for general operating support, ongoing operating support, event underwriting, multi-year awards, endowment building, research, annual fund drives, debt reduction, seed money, conferences, seminars, fellowships, or travel.

Publications: Application guidelines; Annual report; Financial statement; Grants list; Informational brochure; Newsletter; Occasional report.

Application information: The foundation conducts an annual grant cycle that normally commences in Jan. with an announcement that proposals are being accepted; visit foundation Web site for application form and guidelines. Fax or e-mail submissions are not accepted. Project report and site visit for evaluation required. Application form required.

> *Initial approach:* Submit application form and attachments
> *Copies of proposal:* 2
> *Deadline(s):* Mid-Mar.
> *Board meeting date(s):* Semi-annually
> *Final notification:* Mid-May

Officers and Directors: * Mrs. Robin D. Ray,* Chair.; Morris H. Fine,* Vice-Chair.; William D. Sessoms, Jr.,* 1st Vice-Chair.; Margaret G. Campbell,* Secy.; Dennis R. Deans,* Treas.; Debra R. Steiger, Exec. Dir.; Ted Clarkson,* Assoc. Dir.; and 69 additional directors.

Distribution Committee: John F. Malbon, Chair.; Macon F. Brock; Thomas C. Broyles; Lynne G. Farrell; Andrew S. Fine; Susan Hirschbiel.

Number of staff: 1 full-time professional; 1 full-time support; 1 part-time support.

EIN: 541553631

9533
VuBay Foundation ✦

P.O. Box 13109
Norfolk, VA 23506-3109 (757) 466-0464
Contact: Cyrus A. Dolph IV, Asst. Secy.

Established in 1997 in VA.

Donor: Gertrude S. Dixon.

Foundation type: Independent foundation.

Financial data (yr. ended 6/30/05): Assets, $7,921,050 (M); expenditures, $438,801; qualifying distributions, $424,500; giving activities

include $424,500 for 20 grants (high: $95,000; low: $5,000).

Fields of interest: Museums; Arts; Elementary/secondary education; Higher education; Human services; Foundations (public).

Type of support: General/operating support.

Limitations: Giving primarily in VA.

Application information: Application form required.

Initial approach: Letter requesting application

Deadline(s): Sept. 30

Officers: Ann D. Wallace, Pres.; Robert F. Shuford, V.P. and Secy.; James R. Chisman, Treas.

EIN: 541840750

Selected grants: The following grants were reported in 2005.

$50,000 to Virginia Living Museum, Newport News, VA.

$10,000 to College of William and Mary, Williamsburg, VA.

$10,000 to Hampton University, Hampton, VA.

$10,000 to Norfolk State University, Norfolk, VA.

$10,000 to Old Dominion University Educational Foundation, Norfolk, VA.

$10,000 to Peninsula Catholic High School, Newport News, VA.

$10,000 to Tidewater Community College, Portsmouth, VA.

$10,000 to Virginia College Fund, Richmond, VA.

$5,000 to Christopher Newport University, Newport News, VA.

$5,000 to Virginia Foundation for Independent Colleges, Richmond, VA.

9534
Washington Forrest Foundation

2300 9th St. S., Ste. GR-1
Arlington, VA 22204 (703) 920-3688
Contact: Deborah G. Lucckese, V.P.
FAX: (703) 920-0130; E-mail: washforr@aol.com

Incorporated in 1968 in VA.

Donors: Benjamin M. Smith†; Charlotte Smith Gravett†; Virginia N. Smith†.

Foundation type: Independent foundation.

Financial data (yr. ended 6/30/05): Assets, $15,792,802 (M); expenditures, $862,053; qualifying distributions, $625,357; giving activities include $566,393 for 105 grants (high: $20,000; low: $500).

Purpose and activities: Emphasis on youth programs; support also for the arts, education, health, community welfare and human services.

Fields of interest: Arts; Education; Health organizations, association; Human services; Children/youth, services; Religion.

Type of support: General/operating support; Continuing support; Annual campaigns; Capital campaigns; Building/renovation; Equipment; Endowments; Emergency funds; Program development; Seed money; Scholarship funds; Matching/challenge support.

Limitations: Giving primarily in northern VA, with emphasis on South Arlington. The foundation defines northern VA as the counties of Arlington, Fairfax and Prince William, and the cities of Alexandria, Fairfax and Falls Church. Generally, no support for national programs, or foreign programs. No grants to individuals, or for fellowships or multi-year pledges.

Publications: Grants list; Program policy statement.

Application information: The foundation uses the WG Common Grant Application (modified for small proposals). Application form required.

Initial approach: Letter or telephone

Copies of proposal: 1

Deadline(s): Aug. 1, Nov. 1, Feb. 1, and May 1

Board meeting date(s): Mar., June, Sept., and Dec.

Final notification: 2 weeks after Board meeting

Officers and Directors:* Margaret S. Peete,* Pres.; Deborah Lucckese,* V.P.; Leslie Ariail,* Secy.; Benjamin M. Smith, Jr.,* Treas.; Allison Erdle; Benjamin C. Gravett; Rachel Mrad; David D. Peete, Jr.

Number of staff: 1 part-time professional.

EIN: 237002944

Selected grants: The following grants were reported in 2005.

$20,000 to LArche Washington, DC, DC.

$18,000 to Alexandria Neighborhood Health Services, Alexandria, VA.

$15,000 to Hispanics Against Child Abuse and Neglect, Falls Church, VA.

$15,000 to Marymount University, Arlington, VA.

$10,000 to CrisisLink, Arlington, VA.

$7,500 to Community Lodgings, Alexandria, VA.

$7,500 to Fairfax Symphony Orchestra, Annandale, VA.

$7,500 to Northern Virginia Area Health Education Center, Annandale, VA.

$6,000 to Virginia College Fund, Richmond, VA.

$5,000 to Womens Center, Vienna, VA.

9535
Weil Foundation ✧

c/o Murphy Deane & Co.
3400 Franklin Manor Ct.
Fairfax, VA 22033 (703) 796-1040
Contact: Kenneth M. Weil, Secy.-Treas.

Established in 1998 in OH.

Donors: Kenneth M. Weil; Audrey York Weil.

Foundation type: Independent foundation.

Financial data (yr. ended 6/30/05): Assets, $6,887,607 (M); gifts received, $298; expenditures, $405,862; qualifying distributions, $326,402; giving activities include $328,760 for 13 grants (high: $195,000; low: $100).

Purpose and activities: Giving primarily for higher education and human services, including a center for support and education for older adults.

Fields of interest: Museums; Higher education; Education; Human services; Aging, centers/services; Federated giving programs.

Type of support: General/operating support.

Limitations: Giving primarily in NC, NV, and OH. No grants to individuals.

Application information:

Initial approach: Letter

Deadline(s): None

Officers: Audrey York Weil, Pres.; Kenneth M. Weil, Secy.-Treas.

EIN: 311627660

Selected grants: The following grants were reported in 2003.

$125,000 to United Way of Central Ohio, Columbus, OH. For operating support.

$25,000 to Smithsonian Institution, Hirshhorn Museum and Sculpture Garden, DC. For operating support.

$20,000 to Columbus Academy, Gahanna, OH. For scholarships.

$12,500 to New Albany Community Foundation, New Albany, OH. For operating support.

$10,000 to American Foundation for AIDS Research (AMFAR), New York, NY. For research.

$5,000 to Accelerate Brain Cancer Cure, DC. For research.

$5,000 to Queen of the Valley Hospital, Napa, CA. For operating support.

$2,000 to Wexner Center for the Arts, Columbus, OH. For operating support.

$1,500 to COSI Columbus, Columbus, OH. For operating support.

$1,000 to Phoenix Theater Circle, Columbus, OH. For program support.

9536
Weissberg Foundation

1901 N. Moore St., Ste. 803
Arlington, VA 22209
Contact: Ilene C. Trachtenberg, Exec. Dir.
FAX: (703) 276-1770;
E-mail: ilene@weissbergcorp.com

Established in 1988 in DE.

Donor: Marvin F. Weissberg.

Foundation type: Independent foundation.

Financial data (yr. ended 12/31/05): Assets, $6,522,380 (M); gifts received, $610,678; expenditures, $771,967; qualifying distributions, $728,284; giving activities include $584,720 for 86 grants (high: $15,000; low: $500; average: $3,000–$5,000).

Purpose and activities: The foundation funds activities that address the underlying causes of distress in vulnerable communities within the metropolitan Washington, D.C. area. The foundation supports well-managed and fiscally responsible community-based programs that advance social justice, combat poverty, improve health, and enrich the arts. The foundation has particular interest in the following areas: 1) education and youth development, particularly for in-school, pre-school, after-school and summer programs, as well as tutoring, arts for children, and environmental conservation programs for youth; 2) theaters that are members of the League of Washington Theatres, particularly for substantive outreach programs and small theater support; 3) health, particularly for clinics, mental health, violence prevention and family planning; and 4) human services, particularly for homelessness, job training, immigrant services and human rights.

Fields of interest: Performing arts, theater; Education; Health care; Youth development; Human services.

Type of support: General/operating support; Continuing support; Management development/capacity building; Equipment; Program development; Publication; Seed money; Curriculum development; Fellowships; Scholarship funds; Technical assistance; Consulting services; Program evaluation; Matching/challenge support.

Limitations: Giving limited to the metropolitan Washington, DC, area. No support for programs that promote religious doctrine, or programs that receive Federal faith-based funding. No grants to individuals, or for special events or capital campaigns.

Publications: Application guidelines; Grants list.

Application information: Priority will be given to organizations with budgets of less than $5 million. Application form not required.

Initial approach: Proposal, or e-mail to request guidelines

Copies of proposal: 1

Deadline(s): Mar. 15 for theater, education and youth development programs; Sept. 15 for health and human services proposals

Board meeting date(s): Biannually: spring for education, youth development and theater; fall for health and human services

Final notification: June 30 for spring proposals, and Dec. 31 for fall proposals

Officers and Directors:* Marvin F. Weissberg,* Pres.; Nina V. Weissberg,* V.P.; Barbara T. Napolitano,* Secy.; Martin Heyert,* Treas.; Ilene C. Trachtenberg,* Exec. Dir.; Wallace K. Babington; Weslie M. Weissberg.

Number of staff: 2 full-time professional.

EIN: 541475954

9537
The Wellspring Foundation ✧

(formerly The Stone Foundation)
c/o Investors Records Corp.
614 E. High St.
Charlottesville, VA 22902
Contact: Russell J. Bell, Secy.

Established in 1985 in NY.

Donors: Diana B. Clark; James Clark‡.

Foundation type: Independent foundation.

Financial data (yr. ended 12/31/03): Assets, $3,281,375 (M); gifts received, $39,022; expenditures, $381,663; qualifying distributions, $326,350; giving activities include $330,000 for 21 grants (high: $40,000; low: $5,000).

Fields of interest: Media, film/video; Education; Environment.

Limitations: Giving primarily in New York, NY. No grants to individuals.

Application information: Application form not required.

Initial approach: Letter or proposal
Deadline(s): Nov. 1
Board meeting date(s): Early Dec.
Final notification: Jan. 31

Officers: Russell J. Bell, Secy.; Benjamin Brewster, Treas.

Trustees: Ashley S. Pettus; Brewster W. Pettus; Elise S. Pettus.

Number of staff: 1 part-time support.

EIN: 133457878

Selected grants: The following grants were reported in 2003.

$40,000 to Primary Source, Watertown, MA. For general support.

$20,000 to Arts Engine, New York, NY. For general support.

$20,000 to Columbia University, School of Journalism, New York, NY. For general support.

$20,000 to Human Rights Watch, New York, NY. For general support.

$20,000 to Museum of Modern Art, New York, NY. For general support.

$15,000 to Educational Video Center, New York, NY. For general support.

$10,000 to Arts Company, Cambridge, MA. For general support.

$10,000 to Childrens Museum of Manhattan, New York, NY. For general support.

$10,000 to Girls Club of New York, Lower East Side, New York, NY. For general support.

$10,000 to Women Make Movies, New York, NY. For general support.

9538
WestWind Foundation ✧

232 E. High St.
Charlottesville, VA 22902 (434) 977-5762
Contact: Heidi Binko, Prog. Off.
FAX: (434) 977-3176;
E-mail: info@westwindfoundation.org; Additional E-mail: binko@westwindfoundaiton.org (Heidi Binko, Prog. Off.); URL: http://www.westwindfoundation.org

Established in 1987 in DC.

Donors: Edward M. Miller; WWF, Ltd.

Foundation type: Independent foundation.

Financial data (yr. ended 12/31/05): Assets, $16,208,943 (M); gifts received, $4,303,955; expenditures, $2,238,431; qualifying distributions, $2,101,200; giving activities include $2,101,200 for 104 grants (high: $195,000; low: $100).

Purpose and activities: The foundation is dedicated to protecting the integrity of natural ecosystems and the health of human communities through its grantmaking programs. WestWind tends to provide more general support grants, but the foundation will also provide grants for project or program specific requests.

Fields of interest: Education; Environment, land resources; Environment, forests; Environment; Reproductive health, family planning; Youth development; Human services.

International interests: Caribbean; Latin America.

Type of support: General/operating support; Continuing support; Land acquisition; Program development; Conferences/seminars; Matching/challenge support.

Limitations: Giving on a national level, with emphasis on the Southeast, New England and AK, for environment program. Giving is primarily targeted toward Latin America and the Caribbean for Reproductive Health and Rights program, although domestic support is available. No grants to individuals, or for capital campaigns, endowments, or brick and mortar projects; no multi-year grants.

Publications: Application guidelines; Grants list.

Application information: Organizations that have never received a grant from the foundation before, must first submit an online letter of inquiry 60 days before program deadline. Proposal submission is by invitation only. See foundation Web site for application guidelines and procedures. Currently, letters of inquiry are not being accepted for the Environmental Program. The foundation expects to hold 2 environmental grant cycles in 2006. The foundation tends to provide more general support grants, but the foundation will also provide grants for project or program specific requests. Application form required.

Initial approach: Letter of inquiry online via foundation Web site
Copies of proposal: 1
Deadline(s): Reproductive Health and Rights grants deadline is Apr.
Board meeting date(s): May and Nov.
Final notification: Late June for Reproductive Health and Rights Program

Trustees: Edward M. Miller; Janet H. Miller.

Number of staff: 1 full-time professional.

EIN: 526358830

Selected grants: The following grants were reported in 2003.

$185,000 to Planned Parenthood Federation, International, Western Hemisphere Region, New York, NY.

$100,000 to Southern Environmental Law Center, Charlottesville, VA.

$60,000 to Rainforest Alliance, New York, NY.

$50,000 to Lehigh University, Bethlehem, PA.

$35,000 to Center for International Environmental Law, DC.

$25,000 to Global Forest Watch, DC.

$25,000 to Land Trust Alliance, DC.

$25,000 to NARAL Pro-Choice America Foundation, DC.

$20,000 to Alaska Center for the Environment, Anchorage, AK.

$1,000 to Ethel Walker School, Simsbury, CT.

9539
The Nettie L. Wiley and Charles L. Wiley Foundation ✧

P.O. Box 126
Irvington, VA 22480
Application address: c/o Thomas A. Gosse, Pres., P.O. Box 420, Irvington, VA 22480-0420

Established in 1981 in VA.

Donor: Nettie L. Lokey Wiley‡.

Foundation type: Independent foundation.

Financial data (yr. ended 12/31/05): Assets, $9,180,448 (M); expenditures, $365,188; qualifying distributions, $348,584; giving activities include $320,000 for 17 grants (high: $125,000; low: $1,000), and $11,540 for 7 grants to individuals (high: $3,000; low: $540).

Purpose and activities: Giving scholarship awards to students living in the northern neck of VA interested in teaching and working with young people.

Fields of interest: Education; Health care, clinics/centers; Youth development; Human services.

Type of support: Scholarship funds; Scholarships—to individuals.

Limitations: Giving primarily in VA.

Application information: Application form not required.

Deadline(s): None

Officers: Thomas A. Gosse, Pres.; Gloria C. Conley, V.P.; Catherine B. Moore, Secy.; B.H.B. Hubbard III, Treas.

EIN: 521231771

Selected grants: The following grants were reported in 2005.

$125,000 to Virginia Quality Life, Kilmarnock, VA.

$5,000 to Rappahannock Community College, Warsaw, VA.

$5,000 to Salvation Army, Hayes, VA.

$3,500 to Lancaster Community Library, Kilmarnock, VA.

$3,000 to Rappahannock General Hospital, Kilmarnock, VA.

$2,000 to Mary Washington College, Fredericksburg, VA.

9540
Vincent Wilkinson Foundation ✧

8045 Leesburg Pike, Ste. 650
Vienna, VA 22182-2737

Established in 2002 in VA.

Donor: AW Family Limited Partnership.

Foundation type: Independent foundation.

Financial data (yr. ended 12/31/05): Assets, $9,002,283 (M); expenditures, $1,155,067; qualifying distributions, $1,037,801; giving

activities include $1,030,109 for 32 grants (high: $300,000; low: $620; average: $5,000–$25,000).
Fields of interest: Performing arts; Elementary/secondary education; Law school/education; Public policy, research.
Type of support: General/operating support.
Limitations: Applications not accepted. Giving primarily in the greater metropolitan Washington, DC, area, including MD and VA, and the New York, NY, area. No grants to individuals.
Application information: Contributes only to pre-selected organizations.
Officers and Directors:* Anthony Welters,* Chair. and Pres.; Beatrice W. Welters,* Secy.
EIN: 527318075
Selected grants: The following grants were reported in 2004.
$600,000 to New York University, New York, NY. 2 grants: $300,000 each
$250,000 to Maret School, DC.
$220,000 to Langley School, McLean, VA.
$131,982 to Brookings Institution, DC. 2 grants: $50,000, $81,982
$68,825 to John F. Kennedy Center for the Performing Arts, DC. 2 grants: $43,825, $25,000
$25,000 to Washington Jesuit Academy, DC.
$12,000 to Jazz at Lincoln Center, New York, NY.

9541
Williamsburg Community Health Foundation ☆
516-A S. Henry St.
Williamsburg, VA 23185-4151 (757) 345-0912
Contact: Kerry C. Mellette, Pres. and C.E.O.
FAX: (757) 345-0913; E-mail: info@wchf.com;
URL: http://www.wchf.com

Established in 1996 in VA; converted from the partnership between the Williamsburg Community Hospital and Sentara Health System.
Foundation type: Independent foundation.
Financial data (yr. ended 12/31/05): Assets, $127,631,000 (M); expenditures, $6,447,000; qualifying distributions, $5,073,832; giving activities include $5,073,832 for 56 grants.
Purpose and activities: Giving to organizations that demonstrate health benefits to Williamsburg area residents.
Fields of interest: Medical care, in-patient care; Medical care, community health systems; Health care; Substance abuse, services; Substance abuse, prevention; Substance abuse, treatment; Pediatrics; Residential/custodial care, hospices; Aging.
Type of support: General/operating support; Continuing support; Program development; Conferences/seminars; Seed money; Scholarship funds; Technical assistance; Program evaluation; Matching/challenge support.
Limitations: Giving limited to James City County and the greater Williamsburg, VA, area. No support for organizations limiting services to an exclusive membership. No grants to individuals.
Publications: Application guidelines; Annual report; Newsletter.
Application information: Application form not required.
Initial approach: Letter of intent
Copies of proposal: 1
Deadline(s): May 5 and Nov. 5 for letter of intent; Jan. 10 and July 10 for proposal

Board meeting date(s): Quarterly
Final notification: Nov. 15 and May 15
Officers and Trustees:* F. Roger Thaler,* Chair.; Gilbert A. Bartlett, Vice-Chair.; Kerry C. Mellette, Pres., C.E.O., and Secy.; Gwen Williams, Treas.; Carol A. Beers; Jean C. Bruce; Howard J. Busbee; Virginia McLaughlin, Ph.D.; Jeffrey Smith; and 13 additional trustees.
Number of staff: 4 full-time professional; 2 part-time professional; 2 full-time support; 1 part-time support.
EIN: 541822359

9542
Mark and Catherine Winkler Foundation ◇
4900 Seminary Rd., Ste. 900
Alexandria, VA 22311 (703) 998-0400
Contact: Lynne S. Ball, Asst. Treas.

Established about 1964 in VA.
Donors: Catherine Winkler; Mark Winkler†; Catherine W. Herman.
Foundation type: Independent foundation.
Financial data (yr. ended 12/31/04): Assets, $547,684 (M); gifts received, $700,000; expenditures, $854,513; qualifying distributions, $849,917; giving activities include $742,993 for 24 grants (high: $251,000; low: $700).
Purpose and activities: Giving primarily for higher education, social services, particularly for aid to single parents, environmental projects, conservation, and medical research.
Fields of interest: Higher education; Environment, natural resources; Health care; Human services; Children/youth, services; Community development.
Type of support: General/operating support; Annual campaigns; Capital campaigns; Building/renovation; Equipment; Endowments; Emergency funds; Program development; Conferences/seminars; Professorships; Seed money; Fellowships; Research; Matching/challenge support.
Limitations: Giving on a national basis, with some emphasis on the metropolitan Washington, DC, area.
Publications: Application guidelines.
Application information: Accepts Washington Grantmakers Common Grant Application Format. Application form required.
Initial approach: Proposal or letter
Copies of proposal: 1
Deadline(s): None
Board meeting date(s): Nov.
Officers: Catherine W. Herman, Chair.; Kathleen W. Wennesland, Pres.; Margaret Hecht, V.P.; Corolyn W. Thomas, Secy.
Director: Kim S. Wennesland.
Number of staff: 1 part-time professional; 1 part-time support.
EIN: 546054383
Selected grants: The following grants were reported in 2004.
$251,000 to Colorado College, Colorado Springs, CO.
$60,000 to American Friends Service Committee, Philadelphia, PA.
$50,000 to Child and Family Network Centers, Alexandria, VA.
$50,000 to Potomac School, McLean, VA.
$10,000 to Computer CORE, Alexandria, VA.
$1,000 to Berea College, Berea, KY.

9543
The Bob Wiser Charitable Foundation Trust ◇
3849 Pickett Rd.
Fairfax, VA 22031-3605

Established in 1994 in VA.
Donor: Bob Wiser.
Foundation type: Independent foundation.
Financial data (yr. ended 6/30/05): Assets, $4,578,334 (M); gifts received, $500,000; expenditures, $1,113,300; qualifying distributions, $1,097,300; giving activities include $1,096,700 for 6 grants (high: $1,076,000; low: $500).
Fields of interest: Youth, services.
Limitations: Applications not accepted. Giving primarily in VA. No grants to individuals.
Application information: Contributes only to pre-selected organizations.
Trustees: Irving L. Greenspon; Rhonda J. MacDonald; Nancy B. Padgett.
EIN: 546372531

9544
Woodbury Fund, Inc. ◇
(formerly Do'lkyte Foundation)
21570 Schoolhouse Ct.
Ashburn, VA 20148-5018

Established in 1993 in DC.
Donors: Daniel Solomon; Lillian Cohen Solomon Trust.
Foundation type: Independent foundation.
Financial data (yr. ended 12/31/04): Assets, $13,734,504 (M); expenditures, $923,541; qualifying distributions, $854,726; giving activities include $752,265 for 51 grants (high: $200,000; low: $240).
Fields of interest: Education, public education; International human rights; Jewish federated giving programs; Jewish agencies & temples.
Limitations: Applications not accepted. Giving primarily in Washington, DC; some funding in CA and NY. No grants to individuals.
Application information: Contributes only to pre-selected organizations.
Officers and Directors:* Daniel Solomon,* Pres.; Jane Solomon,* V.P.; Thomas R. Asher,* Secy.; Liza Albright, Treas.
EIN: 043198227
Selected grants: The following grants were reported in 2004.
$200,000 to Shefa Fund, Philadelphia, PA.
$100,000 to Community Foundation for the National Capital Region, DC.
$90,325 to Coalition for DC Representation in Congress Education Fund, DC.
$50,000 to Proteus Fund, Amherst, MA.
$35,000 to Sustainable Community Initiatives, DC.
$25,000 to Tides Foundation, San Francisco, CA.
$20,000 to Center for Economic Justice, Albuquerque, NM.
$10,000 to Jews United for Justice, DC.
$5,000 to Center for Progressive Leadership, DC.
$5,000 to Peace Development Fund, Amherst, MA.

9545
Wrinkle in Time Foundation, Inc.
P.O. Box 306
The Plains, VA 20198-0306

Established in 1980 in NY.
Donor: Andrea B. Currier.
Foundation type: Independent foundation.
Financial data (yr. ended 12/31/05): Assets, $10,003,701 (M); expenditures, $845,154; qualifying distributions, $748,719; giving activities include $748,000 for 12 grants (high: $460,000; low: $2,500).
Purpose and activities: Support primarily for improving the rural and urban environment; including wildlife and wilderness preservation; as well as to gather, preserve and disseminate information about the environment, make productive contributions to either the rural or urban surroundings; restore and maintain historic buildings, sites and antiquities; or encourage, promote and popularize art or design which enhances the rural or urban environment.
Fields of interest: Education; Environment, natural resources; Environment; Animals/wildlife, preservation/protection; Rural development.
Type of support: General/operating support; Capital campaigns; Program development; Seed money.
Limitations: Applications not accepted. Giving primarily in VA. No grants to individuals; no loans.
Application information: Unsolicited requests for funds not accepted.
Board meeting date(s): Jan., Apr., July, and Oct.

Officer and Board Member:* Andrea B. Currier,* Chair. and Pres.
Number of staff: None.
EIN: 222351518
Selected grants: The following grants were reported in 2004.
$260,000 to Buxton School, Williamstown, MA.
$50,000 to Piedmont Environmental Council, Warrenton, VA.
$47,300 to Bull Run Mountains Conservancy, Broad Run, VA.
$40,000 to Fauquier Housing Corporation, Warrenton, VA.
$10,000 to Fauquier Hospital Foundation, Warrenton, VA.

WASHINGTON

9546
444S Foundation
(also known as 444 Sierra Foundation)
P.O. Box 1128
Bellevue, WA 98009-1128
Contact: Peggy Ford, Fdn. Admin.
FAX: (425) 453-0844; E-mail: 444s@kamutlake.net

Established in 1998 in WA.
Donor: G. James Roush.
Foundation type: Independent foundation.
Financial data (yr. ended 12/31/05): Assets, $33,697,263 (M); gifts received, $802,059; expenditures, $1,782,084; qualifying distributions, $1,544,490; giving activities include $1,400,000 for 29 grants (high: $412,000; low: $3,000).
Purpose and activities: Giving to support environmental, wildlands and wildlife protection efforts.
Fields of interest: Environment, natural resources; Animals/wildlife, preservation/protection.
International interests: Canada.
Type of support: General/operating support; Program development; Matching/challenge support.
Limitations: Applications not accepted. Giving primarily for the benefit of the Pacific Northwest, including western Canada and AK. No grants to individuals.
Application information: Contributes only to pre-selected organizations. Foundation will solicit proposals. Unsolicited requests for funds not accepted.
　Board meeting date(s): Varies
Trustees: Del Langbauer; G. James Roush; William Morgan Roush; James Sheldon; Cynthia Wayburn.
Number of staff: 1 full-time professional; 1 part-time support.
EIN: 916468421
Selected grants: The following grants were reported in 2004.
$532,000 to Wilderness Society, DC.
$100,000 to Earthjustice, Oakland, CA.
$100,000 to Partnership Project, DC.
$60,000 to National Wildlife Federation, Anchorage, AK.
$50,000 to Nature Conservancy of Montana, Helena, MT.
$50,000 to Trustees for Alaska, Anchorage, AK.
$50,000 to Wildlands Center for Preventing Roads, Missoula, MT.
$40,000 to Alaska Wilderness League, DC.
$40,000 to Montana Wilderness Association, Helena, MT.
$15,000 to Predator Conservation Alliance, Bozeman, MT.

9547
Ginger and Barry Ackerley Foundation
1301 5th Ave., Ste. 3525
Seattle, WA 98101-2634
Contact: Kimberly Cleworth, Exec. Dir.
FAX: (206) 623-7853;
E-mail: kcleworth@ackerley.com; URL: http://www.ackerleyfoundation.org

Established in 1997 in WA.
Donors: Barry A. Ackerley; Gail A. Ackerley.

Foundation type: Independent foundation.
Financial data (yr. ended 12/31/04): Assets, $15,819,294 (M); expenditures, $1,177,960; qualifying distributions, $1,066,217; giving activities include $944,526 for grants.
Purpose and activities: Grants to public and private institutions around Puget Sound that sponsor core programs enhancing the education of young learners. Support opportunities such as skills support, literacy development, mentoring relationships and programs that connect school and home.
Fields of interest: Secondary school/education; Education; Economically disadvantaged.
Type of support: Matching/challenge support; Scholarship funds; Capital campaigns; Building/renovation; Endowments; Program development; Curriculum development.
Limitations: Giving primarily in the greater Puget Sound, WA region. No support for religious organizations. No grants to individuals, or for debt retirement, operating deficits, team sponsorship, individual athletic endeavors, travel expenses, or annual fund drives; no loans.
Publications: Application guidelines; Grants list; Informational brochure (including application guidelines).
Application information: See foundation Web site for application guidelines, procedures and restrictions. Grant request summary sheet can be downloaded on foundation Web site. Application form required.
　Initial approach: 2-page letter
　Copies of proposal: 1
　Deadline(s): Jan. 1 and Aug. 1; Jan. 1 for capital requests
　Board meeting date(s): 1st and 3rd quarters
　Final notification: Within 90 days
Officers: Kim Cleworth, Pres. and Exec. Dir.; Christopher Ackerley, V.P.; Edward Ackerley, V.P.
Directors: Barry A. Ackerley; Gail A. Ackerley.
Number of staff: 1 full-time professional; 1 part-time support.
EIN: 911800463

9548
Moss Adams Foundation ◇ ☆
1001 4th Ave., 31st Fl.
Seattle, WA 98154-1199

Established in 1994 in WA.
Donors: Moss Adams, LLP; Robert Bunting; Roger Peterson; Arthur Miles; Chris Schmidt; Rick Anderson; Joe Karas; Tony Maki; Russ Wilson.
Foundation type: Independent foundation.
Financial data (yr. ended 12/31/05): Assets, $385,952 (L); gifts received, $570,724; expenditures, $545,292; qualifying distributions, $545,265; giving activities include $545,265 for 27 grants (high: $83,505; low: $200).
Purpose and activities: Giving primarily for education.
Fields of interest: Higher education; Human services.
Type of support: General/operating support.
Limitations: Applications not accepted. Giving primarily in the Northwest. No grants to individuals.
Application information: Contributes only to pre-selected organizations.
Officers: Russ Wilson, Pres.; Randy Fenich, Secy.; Gary Grimstad, Treas.

Directors: Corinne Baughman; Tina Caratan; Robert Ryker; Chris Schmidt; Trace Skopil.
EIN: 911496816
Selected grants: The following grants were reported in 2005.
$83,505 to World Vision, Federal Way, WA.
$68,700 to University of Washington Foundation, Seattle, WA.
$53,334 to California State University, Fullerton, CA.
$42,920 to Gonzaga University, Spokane, WA.
$41,300 to Western Washington University Foundation, Bellingham, WA.
$35,000 to Seattle Pacific University, Seattle, WA.
$12,022 to Eastern Washington University, Cheney, WA.
$9,150 to University of Oregon, Eugene, OR.
$6,600 to University of Idaho Foundation, Moscow, ID.
$6,000 to California State University, Sacramento, CA.

9549
Akibene Foundation ◇
177 107th Ave. N.E., Ste. 2004
Bellevue, WA 98004

Established in 2002 in WA.
Donors: John Bennett; Marie Bennett.
Foundation type: Independent foundation.
Financial data (yr. ended 12/31/03): Assets, $834,372 (M); expenditures, $667,957; qualifying distributions, $665,365; giving activities include $665,365 for 5 grants (high: $195,000; low: $56,216).
Purpose and activities: Giving primarily for higher education. Support also for a magnetism and malaria project and to assist impoverished children.
Limitations: Applications not accepted. Giving primarily in VA and WA. No grants to individuals.
Application information: Contributes only to pre-selected organizations.
Directors: John Bennett; Marie Bennett.
EIN: 431954012

9550
The Paul G. Allen Family Foundation ☆
505 5th Ave. S, Ste. 900
Seattle, WA 98104 (206) 342-2030
Contact: Katherine Killebrew, Grant Asst.
FAX: (206) 342-3030;
E-mail: info@pgafamilyfoundation.org; URL: http://www.pgafamilyfoundation.org

Established in 2005 in WA. In 2004, The Paul G. Allen Charitable Foundation, along with The Allen Foundation for the Arts, The Paul G. Allen Foundation for Medical Research, The Paul G. Allen Forest Protection Foundation, The Allen Foundation for Music, and The Paul G. Allen Virtual Education Foundation, were consolidated into a new foundation, The Paul G. Allen Family Foundation.
Donors: Paul G. Allen; The Paul G. Allen Foundation for Medical Research; The Paul G. Allen Virtual Education Foundation; The Allen Foundation for Music.
Foundation type: Independent foundation.
Financial data (yr. ended 12/31/05): Assets, $17,212,262 (M); expenditures, $23,694,382; qualifying distributions, $23,683,669; giving activities include $23,683,669 for grants.

Purpose and activities: The mission of the foundation is to transform lives and strengthen communities by fostering innovation, creating knowledge, and promoting social programs. The foundation advances its mission through focusing on the following key areas: arts and culture, community development, innovations in science and technology and youth engagement.

Fields of interest: Education; Health care; Human services; Youth, services; Family services.

Type of support: Capital campaigns; Building/renovation; Program development; Matching/challenge support.

Limitations: Giving primarily in the Pacific Northwest, including AK, ID, MT, OR and WA. No support for sectarian or religious organizations whose principle activity is for the benefit of their own members or adherents, or for organizations whose policies or practices discriminate on the basis of ethnic, origin, gender, race, religion, or sexual orientation. No grants to individuals or for general operating support, annual appeals, federated campaigns, general fund drives, scholarships, special events or sponsorships, or for projects not aligned with the foundation's specified program areas; no loans.

Publications: Grants list.

Application information: Unsolicited letters of inquiry and proposals are not accepted innovations in science and technology grants. Full proposals by invitation only. Application form not required.

   Initial approach: Online letter of inquiry preferred, using submittal tool on foundation Web site; for a postal LOI, print and complete a copy of the foundation's LOI form

   Copies of proposal: 1

   Deadline(s): No deadline for Letters of Inquiry. Deadlines for invited full proposals: Mar. 15 (corresponding LOI due Feb. 15) and Aug. 15 (corresponding LOI due July 15)

   Final notification: 30 days after submission of letter of inquiry applicants will be notified whether or not a full proposal is invited; up to six minths after submittal of full proposal for funding decision

Officers and Directors:* Paul G. Allen,* Pres.; Gregory P. Landis,* V.P. and Secy.; Jo Allen Patton,* V.P.; Nathaniel T. Brown,* V.P.; Allen D. Israel.

Number of staff: 6 full-time professional.

EIN: 943082532

9551
Anderson Foundation
9420 N.E. 27th St.
Bellevue, WA 98004-1702

Established in 1952 in WA.
Donors: Charles M. Anderson†; Dorothy I. Anderson; William Anderson; Barbara A. Lawrence.
Foundation type: Independent foundation.
Financial data (yr. ended 6/30/05): Assets, $31,179,875 (M); gifts received, $12,217,842; expenditures, $1,802,559; qualifying distributions, $1,667,000; giving activities include $1,667,000 for 29 grants (high: $200,000; low: $5,000).
Purpose and activities: Giving primarily for education, health care, including a pediatric center and a research institute, and to Protestant churches.
Fields of interest: Museums; Elementary/secondary education; Higher education; Libraries (public); Education; Hospitals (general); Hospitals (specialty); Health care, infants; Speech/hearing

centers; Health organizations, association; Medical research, institute; Cancer research; Human services; YM/YWCAs & YM/YWHAs; Children/youth, services; Protestant agencies & churches.
Type of support: Building/renovation; Equipment; Professorships; Scholarship funds; Research.
Limitations: Applications not accepted. Giving primarily in WA, with emphasis on Seattle. No grants to individuals, or for endowment funds or matching gifts; no loans.
Application information: Contributes only to pre-selected organizations.
   Board meeting date(s): Annually
Officers: Barbara A. Lawrence, Pres.; Katherine C. Murray, Secy.-Treas.
Number of staff: 2 part-time support.
EIN: 916031724
Selected grants: The following grants were reported in 2005.
$200,000 to Pacific Lutheran University, Tacoma, WA.
$200,000 to Pediatric Interim Care Center, Kent, WA.
$200,000 to Whitman College, Walla Walla, WA.
$110,000 to Childhaven, Seattle, WA.
$100,000 to Valley of the Moon Childrens Foundation, Santa Rosa, CA.
$75,000 to Salvation Army, WA.
$50,000 to Independent Colleges of Washington, Seattle, WA.
$50,000 to Overlake Hospital Foundation, Bellevue, WA.
$10,000 to Bellevue Schools Foundation, Bellevue, WA.
$10,000 to Boyer Childrens Clinic, Seattle, WA.

9552
Apex Foundation
P.O. Box 245
Bellevue, WA 98009
Contact: Craig W. Stewart, Pres.

Established in 1999 in WA.
Donors: Bruce R. McCaw; The McCaw Foundation.
Foundation type: Independent foundation.
Financial data (yr. ended 12/31/04): Assets, $143,056,742 (M); expenditures, $4,568,124; qualifying distributions, $2,505,366; giving activities include $2,142,630 for 142 grants (high: $230,000; low: $250; average: $1,000–$20,000), and $11,017 for 39 employee matching gifts.
Purpose and activities: To support programs that help children and families reach their highest potential.
Fields of interest: Museums (specialized); Education; Medical research, institute.
Type of support: Employee matching gifts.
Limitations: Applications not accepted. Giving primarily in Seattle, WA. No grants to individuals.
Application information: Contributes only to pre-selected organizations.
   Board meeting date(s): As needed
Officers and Directors:* Bruce R. McCaw,* Co-Chair.; Jolene M. McCaw, Co-Chair.; Craig W. Stewart,* Pres.; Charles E. Hill, Secy.-Treas.
Number of staff: 1 part-time professional; 1 part-time support.
EIN: 911950397

9553
Norman Archibald Charitable Foundation
c/o Wells Fargo Bank, N.A.
P.O. Box 21927, MAC P6540-144
Seattle, WA 98111
Contact: Chuck Viele, Secy., Wells Fargo Bank, N.A.

Established in 1976 in WA.
Donor: Norman Archibald†.
Foundation type: Independent foundation.
Financial data (yr. ended 9/30/05): Assets, $9,272,217 (M); expenditures, $544,519; qualifying distributions, $479,150; giving activities include $453,000 for 76 grants (high: $36,000; low: $1,000).
Purpose and activities: Support youth and child development programs; support also for higher education and libraries, museums and the performing arts, family and social services, and federated giving programs.
Fields of interest: Museums (specialized); Performing arts; Arts; Education; Human services; Children/youth, services; Family services; Federated giving programs.
Type of support: Capital campaigns; Building/renovation; Equipment; Land acquisition; Research; Seed money.
Limitations: Giving in the Puget Sound region of WA. No support for government entities, private foundations, or religious organizations for religious purposes. No grants to individuals, or for ongoing operational or program support, deficit financing, endowment funds, or scholarships; no loans.
Publications: Application guidelines; Annual report.
Application information: Application form not required.
   Initial approach: Letter
   Copies of proposal: 3
   Deadline(s): None
   Board meeting date(s): Varies
   Final notification: 4 months
Advisors: Robert L. Gerth; Shan J. Mullin; Stuart H. Prestrud; Charles W. Viele.
Trustee: Wells Fargo Bank, N.A.
EIN: 911098014
Selected grants: The following grants were reported in 2003.
$30,000 to Fred Hutchinson Cancer Research Center, Seattle, WA.
$25,000 to Seattle Center Foundation, Seattle, WA.
$25,000 to United Ways of Washington, Seattle, WA.
$25,000 to Woodland Park Zoological Society, Seattle, WA.
$20,000 to Museum of Flight, Seattle, WA.
$20,000 to Seattle Opera, Seattle, WA.
$15,000 to Pacific Northwest Ballet, Seattle, WA.
$15,000 to Seattle Symphony Orchestra, Seattle, WA.
$12,500 to Mary Bridge Childrens Hospital and Health Center, Tacoma, WA.
$12,500 to Salvation Army of Seattle, Seattle, WA. For Hope Campaign.

9554
Aven Foundation ⟡
c/o John W. Stanton
P.O. Box 53508
Bellevue, WA 98015-3508

Established in 1999 in WA.
Donors: John W. Stanton; Theresa E. Gillespie.
Foundation type: Independent foundation.

Financial data (yr. ended 12/31/05): Assets, $40,991,633 (M); gifts received, $4,592,044; expenditures, $1,434,558; qualifying distributions, $1,390,000; giving activities include $1,390,000 for 7 grants (high: $750,000; low: $10,000).
Purpose and activities: Support primarily for education, and children and youth services, including a center for emotionally and developmentally challenged children and youth to help them lead normal and productive lives.
Fields of interest: Elementary/secondary education; Higher education; Mental health/crisis services; Children/youth, services; Developmentally disabled, centers & services.
Type of support: General/operating support.
Limitations: Giving primarily in Seattle and Walla Walla, WA. No grants to individuals.
Application information: Application form not required.
   Deadline(s): None
Trustees: Theresa E. Gillespie; John W. Stanton.
EIN: 912009458

9555
Bas Family Foundation ✧ ☆
P.O. Box 3831
Bellevue, WA   98009

Established in 2002 in WA.
Donor: Brad A. Silverberg.
Foundation type: Independent foundation.
Financial data (yr. ended 12/31/05): Assets, $7,330,698 (M); expenditures, $378,343; qualifying distributions, $339,003; giving activities include $333,283 for 18 grants (high: $80,000; low: $1,000).
Fields of interest: Higher education; Higher education, university.
Limitations: Applications not accepted. Giving primarily in WA, with some giving in OR. No grants to individuals.
Application information: Contributes only to pre-selected organizations.
Trustees: Brad A. Silverberg; Robert F. Trenner.
EIN: 916557030
Selected grants: The following grants were reported in 2004.
$150,834 to University of Washington, Seattle, WA.
$65,000 to Oregon Health and Science University, Portland, OR.
$50,000 to Carver Academy, San Antonio, TX.
$29,000 to Lance Armstrong Foundation, Austin, TX.
$5,000 to Childrens Hospital and Health System Foundation, Milwaukee, WI.
$5,000 to Northwest Harvest, Seattle, WA.
$1,500 to Washington Women in Need, Bellevue, WA.
$1,000 to American Friends of Whistler, Seattle, WA.

9556
Benaroya Foundation ✧
1100 Olive Way, Ste. 1700
Seattle, WA   98101   (206) 343-4750
Contact: Jack A. Benaroya, Chair.

Established in 1984 in WA.
Donors: Jack A. Benaroya; Larry R. Benaroya; Rebecca B. Benaroya; Sherry-Lee Benaroya.
Foundation type: Independent foundation.

Financial data (yr. ended 11/30/05): Assets, $8,562,015 (M); expenditures, $1,080,958; qualifying distributions, $1,067,000; giving activities include $1,067,000 for 2 grants (high: $867,000; low: $200,000).
Purpose and activities: Support primarily for a symphony orchestra and for diabetes research.
Fields of interest: Performing arts, orchestra (symphony); Diabetes.
Type of support: General/operating support; Building/renovation; Research.
Limitations: Giving primarily in Seattle, WA.
Application information:
   Initial approach: Proposal
   Deadline(s): None
Officers: Jack A. Benaroya, Chair.; Larry R. Benaroya, Pres.; Rebecca B. Benaroya, V.P.; Joel Benoliel, Secy.; Sherry-Lee Benaroya, Treas.
EIN: 911280516
Selected grants: The following grants were reported in 2003.
$327,150 to Juvenile Diabetes Research Foundation International, Seattle, WA.

9557
Bezos Family Foundation ✧ ☆
c/o Lorri A. Dunsmore
1201 3rd Ave., Ste. 4800
Seattle, WA   98101-3099

Established in 2000 in WA.
Donors: Miguel A. Bezos; Jacklyn G. Bezos.
Foundation type: Independent foundation.
Financial data (yr. ended 12/31/05): Assets, $11,892,507 (M); gifts received, $2,031,672; expenditures, $494,671; qualifying distributions, $488,111; giving activities include $475,263 for 36 grants (high: $48,213; low: $49).
Fields of interest: Children/youth, services; International exchange; Children/youth.
Limitations: Applications not accepted. Giving primarily in NY and WA; some funding nationally. No grants to individuals.
Application information: Contributes only to pre-selected organizations.
Directors: Jacklyn G. Bezos; Jeffrey P. Bezos; Lisa Bezos; Mackenzie T. Bezos; Mark S. Bezos; Miguel A. Bezos; Lorri A. Dunsmore; Christina Bezos Poore; Stephen S. Poore.
EIN: 912073258
Selected grants: The following grants were reported in 2003.
$184,000 to Global Nomads Group, New York, NY. For operating support.
$20,000 to KidsQuest Childrens Museum, Bellevue, WA.
$10,000 to Childrens Aid Society, New York, NY.
$10,000 to Save the Children Federation, Westport, CT.
$9,659 to Program for Early Parent Support (PEPS), Seattle, WA. For general support.

9558
Blakemore Foundation ✧
c/o Perkins Coie LLP
1201 3rd Ave., Ste. 4800
Seattle, WA   98101-3266   (206) 359-8778
Contact: Griffith Way, Board Member; For inquiries: Cathy Scheibner, Admin. Asst.

FAX: (206) 359-9778;
E-mail: blackmore@perkinscoie.com; URL: http://www.blakemorefoundation.org

Established in 1990 in WA.
Donors: Thomas L. Blakemore†; Frances L. Blakemore†.
Foundation type: Independent foundation.
Financial data (yr. ended 12/31/05): Assets, $11,972,477 (M); gifts received, $1,000,000; expenditures, $1,416,812; qualifying distributions, $1,291,027; giving activities include $214,710 for 19 grants (high: $25,000; low: $2,100), and $972,747 for 56 grants to individuals (high: $39,250; low: $1,581).
Purpose and activities: Grants to individuals pursuing academic, business, or professional careers involving East or Southeast Asia for advanced study of East or Southeast Asian languages at institutions in Asia. Grants to museums, universities and other educational or art-related institutions in the United States who have programs, exhibits or publications dealing with the fine arts of Northeast, East and Southeast Asia.
Fields of interest: Museums; Language (foreign); Arts; Higher education; Education.
Type of support: Program development; Conferences/seminars; Publication; Fellowships; Scholarships—to individuals.
Limitations: Giving limited to U.S. organizations for art grants; giving limited to U.S. citizens or permanent residents for language grants. No grants for undergraduate students, or for endowments, general operating expenses, capital projects, or general administrative expenses.
Application information: Application form required for language grants to individuals and are available on foundation Web site. No application form required for art grants.
   Initial approach: See Web site for forms and eligibility requirements
   Copies of proposal: 1
   Deadline(s): Dec. 30 for language grants; May 15 and Nov. 1 for art grants
   Board meeting date(s): Biannually, usually June and Dec.
   Final notification: Late Mar. or early Apr. for language grants; 4-6 weeks after deadlines for art grants
Board Members: Charles T. Cross; William E. Franklin; Thomas W. Gething; R. Kent Guy; Heng-Pin "Ping" Kiang; Eugene Lee; William J. Rathbun; Griffith Way.
Trustee: Eleanor M. Hadley.
EIN: 911505735

9559
Blue Mountain Community Foundation ✧
(formerly Blue Mountain Area Foundation)
8 S. 2nd, Ste. 618
P.O. Box 603
Walla Walla, WA   99362-0015   (509) 529-4371
Contact: Lawson F. Knight, Exec. Dir.
FAX: (509) 529-5284;
E-mail: bmcf@bluemountainfoundation.org;
URL: http://www.bluemountainfoundation.org

Incorporated in 1984 in WA.
Foundation type: Community foundation.
Financial data (yr. ended 6/30/05): Assets, $21,632,098 (M); gifts received, $263,417; expenditures, $1,201,187; giving activities include $649,560 for 147 grants (high: $30,932; low: $50),

and $241,618 for 159 grants to individuals (high: $7,717; low: $80).

Purpose and activities: The foundation promotes effective philanthropy by fostering private charitable giving, providing management of funds, and financially supporting students and charitable organizations to improve the quality of life in the community.

Fields of interest: Visual arts; Performing arts; Humanities; Historic preservation/historical societies; Arts; Higher education; Adult education—literacy, basic skills & GED; Education; Animal welfare; Reproductive health, family planning; Health care; Children/youth, services; Child development, services; Family services; Residential/custodial care, hospices; Aging, centers/services; Homeless, human services; Human services.

Type of support: General/operating support; Continuing support; Management development/capacity building; Equipment; Endowments; Program development; Curriculum development; Fellowships; Internship funds; Technical assistance; Scholarships—to individuals.

Limitations: Giving limited to Umatilla County, OR, and Benton, Columbia, Franklin, Garfield, and Walla Walla counties, WA. No support for sectarian religious organizations. No grants for seed money, multi-year grants, operating expenses, annual fund drives, field trips, or travel to or in support of conferences.

Publications: Application guidelines; Annual report; Grants list; Informational brochure; Newsletter.

Application information: Visit foundation Web site for application form and guidelines. Application form required.

> *Initial approach:* Submit application summary and attachments
> *Copies of proposal:* 10
> *Deadline(s):* July 1 for grants; Mar. 1 for scholarships
> *Board meeting date(s):* Monthly
> *Final notification:* Oct. for grants; June 1 for scholarships

Officers and Trustees:* Ellen Wolf,* Pres.; James Hobkirk,* V.P.; Jane Kreitzberg,* Secy.; W.W. "Pete" Peery,* Treas. and Legal Counsel; Lawson F. Knight, Exec. Dir.; Tom Baker; Leslie Brown; Megan F. Clubb; Deborah D. Frol; Peter Harvey; James K. Hayner; Tom Madsen; Carol Varga Morgan; Terry Nealey; Dan Reid; Mark Thompson; Rick Wylie.

Number of staff: 1 full-time professional; 1 full-time support.

EIN: 911250104

9560
The Boeing Company Charitable Trust ✧ ☆

c/o The Boeing Co.
P.O. Box 34345
Seattle, WA 98124-1345
FAX: (206) 655-2133; URL: http://www.boeing.com/companyoffices/aboutus/community/index.html

Trust established in 1964 in WA as successor to the Boeing Airplane Company Charitable Trust, established in 1952.

Donor: The Boeing Co.

Foundation type: Company-sponsored foundation.

Financial data (yr. ended 12/31/05): Assets, $47,445,305 (M); gifts received, $2,622,430; expenditures, $4,007,684; qualifying distributions,

$3,863,967; giving activities include $3,863,967 for grants.

Purpose and activities: The foundation supports organizations involved with arts and culture, education, the environment, health, and human services.

Fields of interest: Arts; Elementary/secondary education; Higher education; Higher education, college (community/junior); Business school/education; Education; Environment; Health care; Human services; Federated giving programs; Space/aviation; Mathematics; Engineering/technology; Science.

Type of support: Seed money; Research; Program evaluation; Sponsorships; Equipment; Capital campaigns; Building/renovation; Program development; Professorships; Curriculum development; Matching/challenge support.

Limitations: Giving on a national and international basis in areas of company operations, including in Australia and Canada. No support for political organizations. No grants to individuals, or for memorials or endowments, travel, athletic events or athletic group sponsorships (except for the Special Olympics), door prizes, raffles, or school-affiliated orchestras, bands, choirs, drama groups, yearbooks, or class parties, religious activities, or medical research.

Publications: Annual report (including application guidelines); Corporate giving report.

Application information: Application form required.

> *Initial approach:* Complete online application form
> *Deadline(s):* Visit Web site for deadlines

Trustee: Bank of America, N.A.

EIN: 916056738

9561
The Brainerd Foundation

1601 2nd Ave., Ste. 610
Seattle, WA 98101 (206) 448-0676
Contact: Ann Krumboltz, Exec. Dir.
FAX: (206) 448-7222; E-mail: info@brainerd.org;
URL: http://www.brainerd.org

Established in 1995 in WA.

Donor: Paul Brainerd.

Foundation type: Independent foundation.

Financial data (yr. ended 12/31/05): Assets, $41,200,000 (M); gifts received, $26,473; expenditures, $3,217,742; qualifying distributions, $2,943,379; giving activities include $2,745,000 for grants, and $10,683 for foundation-administered programs.

Purpose and activities: The foundation's mission is to protect the environmental quality of the Northwest and to build citizen support for environmental protection. This is accomplished in part by making grants within three program areas: Conservation Policy, Place-based Conservation and Conservation Capacity.

Fields of interest: Environment, natural resources.

Type of support: General/operating support; Continuing support; Income development; Management development/capacity building; Emergency funds; Program development; Conferences/seminars; Seed money; Technical assistance; Matching/challenge support.

Limitations: Giving in AK, ID, MT, OR, WA, British Columbia, and the Yukon Territory. No support for for-profit organizations, or for candidates or lobbying. No grants to individuals, or for school education campaigns, land purchases or easements, endowments, capital campaigns, debt

reduction, basic research, fellowships, or books and videos that are not components of a broader strategy.

Publications: Application guidelines; Financial statement; Grants list; Program policy statement.

Application information: Proposals are accepted by invitation only. Publications available on foundation Web site only. Please see Web site for complete application instructions. Application form required.

> *Initial approach:* Letter of inquiry
> *Copies of proposal:* 1
> *Deadline(s):* None
> *Board meeting date(s):* Mar., June, and Nov.
> *Final notification:* Usually less than 1 month

Officers and Directors:* Paul Brainerd,* Pres. and Treas.; Sherry Brainerd,* V.P. and Secy.; Ann Krumboltz, V.P. and Exec. Dir., Comms. and Capacity Building.

Number of staff: 2 full-time professional; 1 part-time professional; 2 full-time support.

EIN: 911675591

Selected grants: The following grants were reported in 2003.

$100,000 to Montana Wilderness Association, Helena, MT.

$100,000 to Wilderness Society, DC.

$83,000 to Oregon Natural Resources Council, Portland, OR.

$71,500 to Northern Plains Resource Council, Billings, MT.

$50,000 to Earthjustice, Oakland, CA.

$35,000 to Center for Environmental Citizenship, DC.

$20,000 to National Wildlife Federation, Reston, VA.

$15,000 to Alaska Conservation Foundation, Anchorage, AK.

$15,000 to Oregon Natural Desert Association, Bend, OR.

$10,000 to Sierra Club of British Columbia Foundation, Victoria, Canada. .

9562
Brotman Family Foundation ✧ ☆

999 Lake Dr., Ste. 300
Issaquah, WA 98027

Established in 2001 in WA.

Donors: Jeffrey H. Brotman; Susan T. Brotman.

Foundation type: Independent foundation.

Financial data (yr. ended 12/31/05): Assets, $618,960 (M); expenditures, $3,400,094; qualifying distributions, $3,400,000; giving activities include $3,400,000 for 2 grants (high: $1,900,000; low: $1,500,000).

Fields of interest: Higher education.

Limitations: Applications not accepted. Giving primarily in Seattle, WA. No grants to individuals.

Application information: Contributes only to pre-selected organizations.

Officers: Susan T. Brotman, Pres. and Treas.; Jeffrey H. Brotman, V.P. and Secy.

EIN: 522364320

9563
The Bullitt Foundation ▼

1212 Minor Ave.
Seattle, WA 98101-2825 (206) 343-0807
Contact: Denis Hayes, Pres.
FAX: (206) 343-0822; E-mail: info@bullitt.org;
URL: http://www.bullitt.org

Incorporated in 1952 in WA.

Donors: Dorothy S. Bullitt†; Members of the Bullitt Family.

Foundation type: Independent foundation.

Financial data (yr. ended 12/31/05): Assets, $114,821,362 (M); gifts received, $31; expenditures, $6,092,750; qualifying distributions, $7,692,896; giving activities include $4,682,700 for 150 grants, $148,083 for 154 employee matching gifts, and $2,099,813 for 2 loans/program-related investments (high: $2,000,000; low: $99,813).

Purpose and activities: To protect, maintain, and restore the natural physical environment of the Pacific Northwest for present and future generations.

Fields of interest: Environment, radiation control; Environment, toxics; Environment, global warming; Environment, natural resources; Environment, water resources; Environment, land resources; Environment, energy; Environment; Animals/wildlife; Agriculture/food, management/technical aid; Agriculture, soil/water issues; Transportation.

International interests: Canada.

Type of support: Management development/capacity building; General/operating support; Continuing support; Income development; Equipment; Emergency funds; Program development; Seed money; Technical assistance; Program-related investments/loans; Employee matching gifts; Matching/challenge support.

Limitations: Giving exclusively in the Pacific Northwest. No support for political organizations. No grants to individuals, or for capital campaigns.

Publications: Application guidelines.

Application information: Applications sent by fax or other electronic applications are not accepted. Application form required.

Initial approach: Proposal or telephone call
Copies of proposal: 1
Deadline(s): May 1 and Nov. 1
Board meeting date(s): Mar./Apr. and Sept./Oct.
Final notification: 5 months

Officers and Trustees:* Maggie Walker,* Chair.; Harriet Bullitt,* Vice-Chair.; Denis Hayes,* Pres.; David Buck, Secy.; Anne Fennessy,* Treas.; Jabe Blumenthal; Estella Leopold; Hubert G. Locke, Ph.D.; Tomoko Moriguchi-Matsuno; James Youngren.

Number of staff: 5 full-time professional.

EIN: 916027795

Selected grants: The following grants were reported in 2005.

$85,000 to Natural Resources Defense Council, New York, NY. For Northwest energy, climate, toxics, forestlands and aquatic programs.

$35,000 to Audubon Society of Portland, Portland, OR. For Oregon ocean campaign.

$35,000 to Cook Inlet Keeper, Homer, AK. To protect watershed.

$25,000 to Craighead Environmental Research Institute, Bozeman, MT. For conservation design for inland Cedar-Hemlock Forest.

$20,000 to Coalition for a Livable Future, Portland, OR. For regional equity project.

$20,000 to Environmental Coalition of South Seattle, Seattle, WA. For multicultural outreach program.

$16,000 to Farm Folk/City Folk Society, Vancouver, Canada. For Farmland Watch Network.

$15,000 to Idaho Conservation League, Boise, ID. For voter education and outreach.

$10,000 to Bellevue Community College, Bellevue, WA. For sustainable agriculture.

9564
The Burning Foundation ◇

c/o Northwest Grantmaking Resources
6723 Sycamore Ave. N.W.
Seattle, WA 98117 (206) 781-3472
Contact: Therese Ogle, Grants Consultant
FAX: (206) 784-5987; E-mail: OgleFounds@aol.com;
URL: http://foundationcenter.org/grantmaker/burning/

Established in 1997 in WA.

Donor: David Weise.

Foundation type: Independent foundation.

Financial data (yr. ended 12/31/05): Assets, $11,278,727 (M); gifts received, $2,392,920; expenditures, $679,735; qualifying distributions, $456,176; giving activities include $439,000 for 51 grants (high: $30,000; low: $1,000).

Purpose and activities: Giving in the following areas: to protect the region's rivers, forest, native fish, and land; to help low-income youth become environmental stewards; and to address the impact of overpopulation and to develop effective pregnancy prevention strategies for teens.

Fields of interest: Environment, natural resources; Environment, water resources; Environment, land resources; Environment, forests; Environmental education; Animals/wildlife, fisheries; Youth, pregnancy prevention; Youth, services.

Type of support: General/operating support; Program development.

Limitations: Giving limited to OR and WA for environmental requests, and the Puget Sound area for conservation programs for youth and teen pregnancy prevention programs. No support for private schools. No grants to individuals for research or scholarships, or for capital campaigns for building construction or renovations, computer, software, or office equipment purchases, or book, video, film, or home-page productions, unless the production is an essential component of the funded project.

Publications: Application guidelines; Grants list.

Application information: See foundation Web site for complete application guidelines. Accepts Philanthropy Northwest Common Grant Application Form. Materials submitted by fax or E-mail not considered. Groups who have received funding 3 out of the previous 5 years may apply for a 3-year grant.

Initial approach: 1- to 2-page letter or inquiry; submission of full proposals is by invitation only
Deadline(s): Spring cycle: 3rd Wed. of Jan. for letter, 1st Wed. of Mar. for invited proposal; Fall cycle: 3rd Wed. of Aug for letter, 1st Wed. of Oct. for invited proposal
Final notification: 1st Wed. of May and 4th Wed. of Nov.

Officers: David Weise, Pres.; Virginia Howlett, V.P.; Alisa Weise, Secy.

EIN: 911815335

Selected grants: The following grants were reported in 2005.

$12,000 to Klamath-Siskiyou Wildlands Center, Williams, OR. For conservation program.

$10,000 to Cascade Land Conservancy, Seattle, WA. For general operating support.

$10,000 to Deaconess Childrens Service, Everett, WA. For Teen Advocacy program.

$10,000 to Friends of Opal Creek, Mill City, OR. For educational program to inspire understanding of ancient forest ecosystems, and to protect Opal Creek area.

$10,000 to Skagit Land Trust, Mount Vernon, WA. For general support.

$8,000 to People for Puget Sound, Seattle, WA. For saving Puget Sounds Shorelines program.

$6,000 to Gifford Pinchot Task Force, Vancouver, WA. For general operating support.

$6,000 to Inland Northwest Land Trust, Spokane, WA. For general operating support.

$6,000 to Power of Hope, Bellingham, WA. For Wild Hope program in collaboration with North Cascades Institute.

$5,000 to Mid-Puget Sound Fisheries Enhancement Group, Seattle, WA. For general operating support.

9565
John A. and Helen M. Cartales Foundation ◇

8710 S.E. Porter Cir.
Vancouver, WA 98664-2866

Established in 1998 in WA.

Donors: John A. Cartales; Helen M. Cartales.

Foundation type: Independent foundation.

Financial data (yr. ended 6/30/05): Assets, $8,143,874 (M); expenditures, $402,351; qualifying distributions, $349,157; giving activities include $350,000 for 3 grants (high: $125,000; low: $100,000).

Purpose and activities: Giving primarily for children's medical care; support also for children's education.

Fields of interest: Education; Hospitals (specialty); Pediatrics.

Limitations: Applications not accepted. Giving primarily in OR. No grants to individuals.

Application information: Contributes only to pre-selected organizations.

Trustees: Helen M. Cartales; John A. Cartales.

EIN: 911940389

9566
Casey Family Programs

1300 Dexter Ave. N., 3rd Fl.
Seattle, WA 98109-3547
URL: http://www.casey.org

Established in 1966. Classified as a private operating foundation in 1972.

Foundation type: Operating foundation.

Financial data (yr. ended 12/31/05): Assets, $2,265,711,291 (M); gifts received, $9,367,962; expenditures, $95,969,658; qualifying distributions, $88,442,484; giving activities include $8,129,176 for 25 grants (high: $6,000,000; low: $6,000; average: $10,000–$400,000), $119,538 for in-kind gifts, and $86,253,956 for foundation-administered programs.

Purpose and activities: Serves children, youth, and families. Primary focus is on children who cannot live safely within their own home.

Fields of interest: Substance abuse, services; Mental health/crisis services; Children, foster care.

Type of support: General/operating support; Continuing support; Program development; Scholarship funds; Research; Technical assistance; Program evaluation.

Limitations: Applications not accepted. No grants to individuals.

Publications: Informational brochure.

Application information: Unsolicited requests for funds will not be accepted.

Officers and Trustees: * Gary Severson,* Chair.; Joan B. Poliak, Vice-Chair.; William C. Bell, C.E.O. and Pres.; David Berns,* Exec. V.P., Child and Family Svcs.; Ann Holmes, Exec. V.P., Admin. and Chief Prog. Counsel; Renee Kaplan, Exec. V.P., Public Affairs and Comms.; David Sanders, Exec. V.P., Systems Improvement; Dave Danielson,* C.F.O.; Joseph A. Boateng, C.I.O.; Shelia Evans-Tranum; Dennis Hightower; Irene M. Ibarra; Sharon L. McDaniel-Lowe; Gloria Reeg.

Number of staff: 273 full-time professional; 6 part-time professional; 71 full-time support; 29 part-time support.

EIN: 910793881

Selected grants: The following grants were reported in 2004.

$962,000 to Three Affiliated Tribes, New Town, ND. 2 grants: $400,000, $562,000

$420,000 to Denver Indian Family Resource Center, Lakewood, CO.

$176,409 to Foster Family Programs of Hawaii, Honolulu, HI. 2 grants: $100,000, $76,409

$120,000 to Childrens Home Society of Washington, Seattle, WA. 2 grants: $70,000, $50,000

$79,528 to American Public Human Services Association, DC.

$37,694 to Missoula Youth Homes, Missoula, MT.

$5,000 to Washington, State of, Olympia, WA.

9567
Marguerite Casey Foundation ▼

(formerly Casey Family Grants Program)
1300 Dexter Ave. N., Ste. 115
Seattle, WA 98109-3542 (206) 691-3134
Contact: Kathleen Baca, Sr. Comms. Off.
FAX: (206) 286-2725; E-mail: info@caseygrants.org;
TTY: (206) 273-7395; URL: http://www.caseygrants.org/

Established in 2001 in WA.

Donor: Casey Family Programs.

Foundation type: Independent foundation.

Financial data (yr. ended 12/31/05): Assets, $663,183,945 (M); expenditures, $34,288,971; qualifying distributions, $31,989,391; giving activities include $27,580,930 for 159 grants, $106,470 for 51 employee matching gifts, and $865,671 for 1 foundation-administered program.

Purpose and activities: The foundation is dedicated to improving the lives of families, youth and children. Grants are designed to assist families (including parents, caregivers and youth) in reaching their full potential as active, engaged, and empowered members of society. Grantmaking is focused in three categories: education, advocacy, and activism.

Fields of interest: Youth development; Children/youth, services; Family services; Economic development; Community development.

Type of support: Employee matching gifts; General/operating support; Income development; Management development/capacity building; Program development; Research; Technical assistance; Program evaluation.

Limitations: Applications not accepted. Giving primarily in four regions of the U.S.: CA; the Southwest, including the U.S./Mexico border; the deep south; the Midwest, beginning in Chicago, IL; and WA state. No support for religious purposes. No grants to individuals, or for capital campaigns, endowments, fundraising drives, litigation, or film and video production.

Publications: Annual report; Financial statement; Grants list; Informational brochure; Program policy statement.

Application information: The foundation does not accept unsolicited proposals or letters of intent.
Board meeting date(s): Quarterly

Officers and Directors: * Freeman A. Hrabowski III,* Chair.; Patricia Schroeder,* Vice-Chair.; Luz Vega-Marquis, C.E.O. and Pres.; William H. Foege,* Secy.; Douglas X. Patino,* Treas.; William Bell, CEO & Pres. Casey Family Programs; Joan B. Poliak; Gary R. Severson.

Number of staff: 7 full-time professional; 8 full-time support; 1 part-time support.

EIN: 912062197

Selected grants: The following grants were reported in 2005.

$1,500,000 to Association of Community Organizations for Reform Now (ACORN), Brooklyn, NY. To continue and expand community mobilization work in West, Midwest and Deep South regions.

$1,125,000 to American Institute for Social Justice, New Orleans, LA. For ACORN's Earned Income Tax Credit campaign.

$1,000,000 to Hispanics in Philanthropy, San Francisco, CA. For Funders Collaborative for Strong Latino Communities.

$1,000,000 to Tides Center, Economic Justice Fund, San Francisco, CA. For general support.

$333,333 to Massachusetts Department of Social Services, Boston, MA. For efforts to fundamentally revise the nature of its child welfare practice to incorporate a family-centered approach at all levels of the organization.

$300,000 to Parents for Public Schools, Jackson, MS. To expand the membership base of low-income parents and to increase parent influence in public school improvement issues by forming statewide networks in at least three southern states by 2007.

$150,000 to Coalition of Immokalee Workers, Immokalee, FL. For grassroots organizing and activism of workers to hold low-wage industries, including day labor, construction and tourism-related services and agricultural corporations accountable to basic worker justice and dignity.

$100,000 to ARISE Por el Rio, Pharr, TX. For education programs and to conduct additional outreach work among women and families who have recently immigrated to the Rio.

$100,000 to Peoples Institute for Survival and Beyond, New Orleans, LA. To strengthen the organization's anti-racist organizing capacity, expand training and curricula and implement a national People's Institute Youth Agenda.

$54,000 to Revisioning New Mexico, Albuquerque, NM. To expand the capacity of Latino and other low-income families to further public policies that will protect and promote the opportunities of working families.

9568
Channel Foundation ✧ ☆

P.O. Box 24524
Seattle, WA 98124-0524
Application address: 601 Stewart St., Ste. 415, Seattle, WA 98101, tel.: (206) 621-5447

Established in 1998 in WA.

Donor: Elaine M. Nonneman.

Foundation type: Independent foundation.

Financial data (yr. ended 12/31/05): Assets, $7,059,667 (M); gifts received, $1,220,213; expenditures, $444,178; qualifying distributions, $407,671; giving activities include $105,699 for 14 grants (high: $43,000; low: $250), and $209,840 for 11 grants to individuals (high: $35,000; low: $4,000).

Purpose and activities: Giving primarily for human services in developing nations.

Fields of interest: Housing/shelter, public housing; Housing/shelter; Women, centers/services; International affairs, equal rights; International development; International agricultural development; International economic development; International human rights; Civil rights, women.

Application information:
Deadline(s): Jan.1-Mar. 23

Officer: Katrin Wilde, Exec. Dir.

Trustee: Elaine M. Nonneman.

EIN: 916478055

Selected grants: The following grants were reported in 2004.

$35,000 to London School of Hygiene and Tropical Medicine, London, England. .

$35,000 to Nature Conservancy, Seattle, WA.

$25,000 to Brandeis University, Waltham, MA.

$25,000 to Global Fund for Women, San Francisco, CA.

$25,000 to Program for Appropriate Technology in Health (PATH), Seattle, WA.

$8,000 to Harvard University, Cambridge, MA.

$6,000 to Potlatch Fund, Seattle, WA.

$5,500 to University of Warwick, Coventry, England. .

$159 to University of East Anglia, Norwich, England. .

9569
Ben B. Cheney Foundation ✧

3110 Ruston Way, Ste. A
Tacoma, WA 98402-5307 (253) 572-2442
Contact: Bradbury F. Cheney, Exec. Dir.
E-mail: info@benbcheneyfoundation.org;
URL: http://www.benbcheneyfoundation.org

Incorporated in 1955 in WA.

Donors: Ben B. Cheney‡; Marian Cheney Olrogg‡.

Foundation type: Independent foundation.

Financial data (yr. ended 12/31/04): Assets, $75,587,900 (M); expenditures, $3,620,424; qualifying distributions, $4,103,727; giving activities include $2,727,578 for 150 grants (high: $100,000; low: $1,000; average: $10,000–$25,000).

Purpose and activities: The foundation prefers to fund projects that develop new and innovative approaches to community problems, facilitate the improvement of services or programs, and invest in equipment or facilities that will have a long-lasting impact on community needs. The foundation organizes its grantmaking into eight categories: 1) Charity: Programs providing for basic needs such as food, shelter, and clothing; 2) Civic: Programs improving the quality of life in a community as a whole such as museums and recreation facilities; 3) Culture: Programs encompassing the arts; 4) Education: Programs supporting capital projects and scholarships, primarily for fourteen pre-selected colleges and universities in the Pacific Northwest; 5) Elderly: Programs serving the social, health, recreational, and other needs of older people; 6) Health: Programs related to providing health care; 7) Social Services: Programs serving people with physical or mental disabilities or other special needs; and 8) Youth: Programs helping young people to gain the skills needed to become responsible and productive adults.

Fields of interest: Museums; Arts; Higher education; Education; Hospitals (general); Health care; Health organizations, association; Human services; Youth, services; Aging, centers/services; Aging; Disabilities, people with.

Type of support: Employee matching gifts; General/operating support; Capital campaigns; Building/renovation; Equipment; Emergency funds; Program development; Seed money; Scholarship funds.

Limitations: Giving limited to portions of Del Norte, Humboldt, Lassen, Shasta, Siskiyou, and Trinity counties in CA, southern OR, particularly in the Medford area, Tacoma and Pierce County, and southwestern WA. No support for religious organizations for sectarian purposes. No grants to individuals, or for general operating budgets, basic research, endowment funds, conferences or seminars, book, film, or video production, or school-related tours, no loans.

Publications: Annual report; Grants list; Informational brochure (including application guidelines).

Application information: Application deadline and final notification provided with application; may take 6 - 9 months from the receipt of a proposal letter to consideration of a grant application by the board. Proposal letters submitted via E-mail will not be reviewed. Application form required.

Initial approach: Proposal letter (2 to 3 pages)
Copies of proposal: 1
Deadline(s): Based upon meeting or site visit with applicant
Board meeting date(s): Apr., June, Sept., and Dec.
Final notification: Proposal letters responded to within 2 - 3 weeks

Officers and Directors: Bradbury F. Cheney,* Pres. and Exec. Dir.; Elgin E. Olrogg,* V.P.; John F. Hansler,* Secy.; Piper Cheney,* Treas.; Carolyn J. Cheney; Allan L. Undem.

Number of staff: 2 full-time professional; 1 full-time support.

EIN: 916053760

Selected grants: The following grants were reported in 2005.

$250,000 to Harold E. LeMay Museum, Tacoma, WA. To build major car museum in Pierce County.

$150,000 to Greater Tacoma Community Foundation, Tacoma, WA. To establish Elgin Olrogg Endowment for criminal justice scholarships.

$100,000 to Charles Wright Academy, Tacoma, WA. To complete lower school.

$75,000 to Rogue Valley Medical Center Foundation, Medford, OR. For campaign for new hospital tower.

$50,000 to American Lake Veterans Golf Course, Lakewood, WA. To improve access for disabled golfers.

$50,000 to Catholic Social Service, Northern Valley, Redding, CA. To assist community campaign for new service center.

$50,000 to Linfield College, McMinnville, OR. To build new music building.

$50,000 to Mary Bridge Childrens Foundation, Tacoma, WA. For 50th Anniversary campaign.

$50,000 to Pacific University, Forest Grove, OR. To build new library.

$45,000 to American Red Cross, Tacoma, WA. For Senior Emergency Grant Fund.

9570
Community Foundation for Southwest Washington

(formerly Clark County Community Foundation)
1053 Officers Row
Vancouver, WA 98661 (360) 694-2550
Contact: Nancy E. Hales, Pres.; For grant applications: Anne Digenis, Prog. Off.
FAX: (360) 737-6335; E-mail: director@cfsww.org; Grant application E-mail: anne@cfsww.org;
URL: http://www.cfsww.org

Incorporated in 1984 in WA.
Foundation type: Community foundation.
Financial data (yr. ended 12/31/05): Assets, $49,129,817 (M); gifts received, $8,379,702; expenditures, $8,591,781; giving activities include $7,818,659 for 402 grants (high: $3,000,000; low: $25).

Purpose and activities: The foundation seeks to enrich the quality of life in southwestern WA, by supporting the needs of the local region and sustaining existing organizations through grants made in the areas of health and human services, education, conservation, and the arts.

Fields of interest: Humanities; Arts; Education; Environment; Health care; Disasters, Hurricane Katrina; Children, services; Human services; Community development.

Limitations: Giving primarily in southwest WA, serving Clark, Cowlitz, and Skamania counties. No support for sectarian or religious programs, private schools, specific research or medical projects, or re-granting purposes. No grants to individuals (except for scholarships), or for endowment funds, capital campaigns, debt reduction, or travel expenses for individuals or groups such as bands, sports teams, or classes.

Publications: Annual report; Informational brochure; Newsletter.

Application information: Visit foundation Web site for Form of Inquiry and guidelines. Full applications are only accepted if requested in writing by the foundation, in response to Form of Inquiry. Application form required.

Initial approach: Submit Form of Inquiry
Copies of proposal: 8
Deadline(s): Aug. 18 for Form of Inquiry; Sept. 29 for full application
Board meeting date(s): Quarterly
Final notification: Mid-Feb.

Officers and Directors: Susan Keil,* Chair.; Russ Tennant,* Vice-Chair.; Nancy E. Hales, Pres.; Sarah Nevue, V.P., Devel.; Allan Kirkwood,* Secy.; Mary Pringle, C.F.O.; Bob Kirchner,* Treas.; Holly Bard; Don Fuesler, M.D.; Jo Marie Hansen; Steve Hix; Lee Kearney; Greg Kubicek; Jim McClaskey; Rick Melching; Art Miles; David Nierenberg; Jan Oliva.

Number of staff: 4 full-time professional; 2 full-time support; 1 part-time support.

EIN: 911246778

9571
Community Foundation of North Central Washington

(formerly Greater Wenatchee Community Foundation)
P.O. Box 3332
Wenatchee, WA 98807-3332 (509) 663-7716
Contact: Beth A. Stipe, Exec. Dir.; For grants: Lila Edlund, Prog. and Office Mgr.

FAX: (509) 667-2208; E-mail: foundaton@cfncw.org; Additional E-mails: beth@cfncw.org and judy@cfncw.org; Grant inquiry E-mail: lila@cfncw.org; URL: http://www.cfncw.org

Incorporated in 1986 in WA.
Foundation type: Community foundation.
Financial data (yr. ended 6/30/06): Assets, $26,547,435 (M); gifts received, $2,345,682; expenditures, $1,734,532; giving activities include $966,685 for 586 grants (high: $20,000; low: $1,000), and $269,250 for 169 grants to individuals (high: $16,000; low: $175).

Purpose and activities: The foundation makes a difference by serving as a bridge between donors and the broader community. Primary areas of interest include the arts, education, the environment, and the disadvantaged, with emphasis on child welfare and the elderly.

Fields of interest: Media/communications; Visual arts; Museums; Performing arts; Performing arts, theater; Performing arts, music; Humanities; History/archaeology; Historic preservation/historical societies; Arts; Education, early childhood education; Child development, education; Elementary school/education; Higher education; Adult/continuing education; Adult education—literacy, basic skills & GED; Libraries/library science; Education, reading; Education; Environment, natural resources; Environment; Animal welfare; Animals/wildlife, preservation/protection; Hospitals (general); Reproductive health, family planning; Medical care, rehabilitation; Health care; Substance abuse, services; Mental health/crisis services; AIDS; Alcoholism; Food services; Housing/shelter, development; Safety/disasters; Recreation; Children/youth, services; Child development, services; Family services; Residential/custodial care, hospices; Aging, centers/services; Women, centers/services; Minorities/immigrants, centers/services; Homeless, human services; Human services; Community development, neighborhood development; Community development; Voluntarism promotion; Aging; Disabilities, people with; Minorities; Women; Economically disadvantaged; Homeless.

Type of support: Capital campaigns; Building/renovation; Equipment; Land acquisition; Program development; Seed money; Technical assistance; Scholarships—to individuals; Matching/challenge support.

Limitations: Giving limited to north central WA, especially Chelan, Douglas, and Okanogan counties. No support for religious sectarian purposes. No grants to individuals (except for designated scholarships), or for continuing support, fundraising, endowments, annual campaigns, general operating budgets, concerts or theater productions, travel, or conferences.

Publications: Application guidelines; Annual report; Grants list; Informational brochure; Informational brochure (including application guidelines); Newsletter; Occasional report.

Application information: Visit foundation Web site for application information and guidelines. Application form not required.

Initial approach: Telephone or letter
Copies of proposal: 1
Deadline(s): Feb. 1 and Oct. 1 for Community grants; Mar. 1 for scholarships
Board meeting date(s): 6 times annually
Final notification: Within 90 days

Officers and Trustees:* Christopher Stahler, M.D.*, Chair.; Mall Boyd,* Vice-Chair.; Mary C. Murphy,* Secy.-Treas.; Beth A. Stipe, Exec. Dir.; Judy A. Cleveland, C.F.O.; Jim Baxter; Faviola Contreras; L. Courtney Cox; Frank J. Kuntz; Judith A. Lurie; Kenneth J. Martin; Brian S. Nelson; Maria Reyes; Christine E. Scull, M.D.; Kris Taylor; Jacki Thomas; Robert L. White; Wayne Wright.
Number of staff: 1 full-time professional; 1 part-time professional; 1 part-time support.
EIN: 911349486

9572
John & Kathy Connors Foundation ◆ ☆
P.O. Box 94
Medina, WA 98039

Established in 2004 in WA.
Donors: John Connors; Kathy Connors.
Foundation type: Independent foundation.
Financial data (yr. ended 12/31/05): Assets, $2,043,645 (M); gifts received, $1,002,009; expenditures, $660,044; qualifying distributions, $632,129; giving activities include $629,231 for 18 grants (high: $166,667; low: $100).
Fields of interest: Higher education; Education; Environment, natural resources; Health organizations, association; Public affairs.
Limitations: Applications not accepted. Giving primarily in Bellevue and Seattle, WA. No grants to individuals.
Application information: Contributes only to pre-selected organizations.
Officers: John Connors, Pres.; Ross Connors, V.P.; Shannon Connors, V.P.; Sean Connors, Secy.; Mick Connors, Treas.
EIN: 202015301

9573
Viola Vestal Coulter Foundation, Inc. ◆
3004 Viewcrest Dr., N.E.
Bremerton, WA 98310
Contact: Mary Lynn Braun, Secy.

Established in 1935.
Donor: Mabel Munro Coulter†.
Foundation type: Independent foundation.
Financial data (yr. ended 12/31/05): Assets, $7,207,885 (M); expenditures, $463,495; qualifying distributions, $379,036; giving activities include $110,000 for 9 grants (high: $35,000; low: $5,000), and $221,750 for grants to individuals (high: $10,000; low: $500).
Purpose and activities: Support for higher education, including funding scholarships at specifically designated colleges and universities in the western U.S. for undergraduate and graduate programs.
Fields of interest: Higher education; Nursing school/education; Engineering school/education; Medical research, institute; Engineering.
Type of support: General/operating support; Research.
Limitations: Applications not accepted. Giving primarily in CO. No grants to individuals directly.
Application information: Applications available at financial aid offices at pre-selected universities; unsolicited requests for funds not considered; grants do not go directly to individuals.
Officers and Trustees:* Harold A. Norblom,* Chair.; Bruce T. Buell,* Pres.; Judy G. Ward,* V.P.; Mary

Lynne Braun,* Secy.; Pamela L. Saxton,* Treas.; Priscilla Ann Barsotti; Allan D. Buell; James Gutshall; Robert L. Klingensmith; Ellen M. Vestal.
EIN: 846029641
Selected grants: The following grants were reported in 2004.
$67,000 to Colorado School of Mines, Golden, CO. 3 grants: $35,000 (For Coulter Memorial Chair in Mineral Economics), $16,000 (For W. Coulter Instructorship in Mineral Economics), $16,000 (For Wm. J. Coulter Instructorship in Mineral Economics).
$11,000 to Regis University, Denver, CO.
$11,000 to University of Nevada, Mackay School of Mines, Reno, NV. For scholarships.
$11,000 to Washington State University, Pullman, WA.
$10,000 to National Jewish Hospital and Research Center, Denver, CO.
$10,000 to University of Colorado Health Sciences Center, Denver, CO.
$6,600 to University of Denver, College of Business, Denver, CO. For Karl Mayer Memorial Scholarship.
$5,500 to University of Idaho, Moscow, ID.

9574
Harriet Cheney Cowles Foundation, Inc. ◆
999 W. Riverside Ave., Rm. 626
Spokane, WA 99201

Incorporated in 1944 in WA.
Donors: Spokane Chronicle Co.; Cowles Publishing Co.; Inland Empire Paper Co.
Foundation type: Independent foundation.
Financial data (yr. ended 12/31/05): Assets, $14,645,541 (M); expenditures, $732,629; qualifying distributions, $660,000; giving activities include $660,000 for 3 grants (high: $400,000; low: $10,000).
Fields of interest: Performing arts, orchestra (symphony); Higher education; Hospitals (general).
Type of support: Capital campaigns; Endowments.
Limitations: Applications not accepted. Giving primarily in Spokane, WA. No grants to individuals.
Application information: Contributes only to pre-selected organizations.
Officers: E.A. Cowles, Pres.; W.S. Cowles, V.P.; S.R. Rector, Secy.
EIN: 910689268
Selected grants: The following grants were reported in 2004.
$425,000 to Spokane Symphony, Spokane, WA.
$100,000 to Salvation Army of Spokane, Spokane, WA.
$25,000 to North Idaho College, Coeur d Alene, ID.
$25,000 to University of Montana Foundation, Missoula, MT.
$13,000 to Childrens Museum of Spokane, Spokane, WA.

9575
William H. Cowles Foundation, Inc. ◆
999 W. Riverside Ave., Rm. 626
Spokane, WA 99201

Incorporated in 1952 in WA.
Foundation type: Independent foundation.
Financial data (yr. ended 12/31/05): Assets, $4,433,954 (M); expenditures, $425,208;

qualifying distributions, $400,000; giving activities include $400,000 for 1 grant.
Purpose and activities: Giving primarily for education.
Fields of interest: Higher education; Education.
Type of support: Endowments.
Limitations: Applications not accepted. Giving primarily in CA and CT. No grants to individuals.
Application information: Contributes only to pre-selected organizations.
Officers and Trustees:* W.S. Cowles,* Pres.; S.R. Rector,* Secy.; E.A. Cowles.
EIN: 916020496
Selected grants: The following grants were reported in 2004.
$400,000 to Thacher School, Ojai, CA.

9576
Crystal Springs Foundation ◆
c/o Ahrens & DeAngeli
1001 4th Ave., Ste. 4333
Seattle, WA 98154-1142

Established in 1999 in WA.
Donors: Michael R. Murray; Joyce B. Murray.
Foundation type: Independent foundation.
Financial data (yr. ended 12/31/04): Assets, $45,423,105 (M); expenditures, $2,447,605; qualifying distributions, $2,053,868; giving activities include $1,832,330 for 34 grants (high: $250,000; low: $1,000).
Purpose and activities: Giving primarily for education, children, youth, families, and social services, and for Mormon ministries and organizations.
Fields of interest: Elementary/secondary education; Higher education; Education; Animals/wildlife; Hospitals (general); Health organizations, association; Human services; Children/youth, services; Family services; Aging, centers/services; International relief, 2004 tsunami; Economic development; Economics; Mormon agencies & churches; Economically disadvantaged.
Limitations: Applications not accepted. No grants to individuals.
Application information: Contributes only to pre-selected organizations.
Officers and Directors:* Michael R. Murray,* Pres. and Treas.; Joyce B. Murray,* V.P. and Secy.
Number of staff: 1 full-time support.
EIN: 912008832
Selected grants: The following grants were reported in 2003.
$259,450 to Unitus, Inc., Redmond, WA. For operating support.
$146,058 to Friends of the Children of King County, Seattle, WA. For general support.
$100,000 to ACCION International, DC. For general support.
$41,377 to Open Arms, Tigard, OR. 2 grants: $40,983 (For equipment for Kakinada Hospital), $394 (For general support).
$10,000 to Quest Scholars Program, Palo Alto, CA. For general support.
$5,000 to Ashesi University Foundation, Seattle, WA. For general support.
$5,000 to Families Northwest, Bellevue, WA. For general support.
$5,000 to Stanford University, Stanford, CA. For general support.
$64 to Church of Jesus Christ of Latter Day Saints, Salt Lake City, UT. For general support.

9577
The F. Danz Foundation ✧
P.O. Box 91723
Bellevue, WA 98009-1723

Established in 1998 in WA.
Donor: Frederic A. Danz.
Foundation type: Independent foundation.
Financial data (yr. ended 12/31/05): Assets, $12,759 (M); gifts received, $450,000; expenditures, $451,706; qualifying distributions, $451,692; giving activities include $451,667 for 5 grants (high: $200,000; low: $10,000).
Fields of interest: Museums (children's); Higher education; Hospitals (general); Medical research, institute; Heart & circulatory research.
Limitations: Applications not accepted. Giving primarily in Bellevue and Seattle, WA. No grants to individuals.
Application information: Contributes only to pre-selected organizations.
Trustees: Alison Danz; Frederic A. Danz; William F. Danz.
EIN: 916477156

9578
De Falco Family Foundation
c/o Santina De Falco
2205 55th St. Ct. N.W.
Gig Harbor, WA 98335
Additional address: 3125 N. 33rd St., Tacoma, WA 98407

Established in 1992 in CA.
Foundation type: Independent foundation.
Financial data (yr. ended 9/30/05): Assets, $7,416,617 (M); expenditures, $473,109; qualifying distributions, $405,000; giving activities include $405,000 for 62 grants (high: $38,500; low: $1,500).
Fields of interest: Arts; Scholarships/financial aid; Zoos/zoological societies; Aquariums; Medical care, in-patient care; Health care; Pediatrics; Food distribution, meals on wheels; Recreation, parks/playgrounds; Children/youth, services; Homeless, human services; Homeless.
Type of support: General/operating support; Continuing support; Annual campaigns; Scholarship funds; Research.
Limitations: Applications not accepted. Giving primarily in Phoenix, AZ, San Diego, CA, and WA. No grants to individuals.
Application information: Contributes only to pre-selected organizations.
    Board meeting date(s): June and Sept.
Officers and Trustees:* Santina De Falco,* Pres.; Victoria J. Shrewsbury, V.P.; Darrell F. Johnson, Secy.; David A. Johnson, Treas.
EIN: 330526533
Selected grants: The following grants were reported in 2004.
$35,000 to Multicare Health Foundation, Tacoma, WA. For equipment fund.
$25,000 to Point Defiance Zoo and Aquarium, Tacoma, WA. For Pavilion Carousel.
$20,000 to Zoological Society of San Diego, San Diego, CA. For Heart of Zoo Pledge.
$10,000 to Childrens Hospital and Health Center, San Diego, CA. For Circle of Caring.
$10,000 to Kids Included Together San Diego, San Diego, CA. For general support.
$10,000 to Kids Turn San Diego, Fallbrook, CA. For Psycho-Education program.

$10,000 to Mercy Hospital Foundation, San Diego, CA. For Heart Care center.
$10,000 to San Diego Museum of Man, San Diego, CA. For education program.
$6,000 to California Center for the Arts, Escondido, CA. For education program.
$5,000 to Andre House of Arizona, Phoenix, AZ. For general support.

9579
The Dimmer Family Foundation
1019 Pacific Ave., Ste. 916
Tacoma, WA 98402-4492
Contact: Diane C. Dimmer, Exec. Dir.

Established in 1994.
Donor: John C. Dimmer.
Foundation type: Independent foundation.
Financial data (yr. ended 12/31/05): Assets, $11,919,462 (M); expenditures, $708,446; qualifying distributions, $573,424; giving activities include $511,823 for 237 grants (high: $50,000; low: $100).
Purpose and activities: Giving primarily for the arts, education, and for health care and human services.
Fields of interest: Museums; Arts; Higher education; Education; Animal welfare; Hospitals (general); Health care; Medical research, institute; Youth development, centers/clubs; Human services.
Type of support: General/operating support; Continuing support; Annual campaigns; Capital campaigns; Building/renovation; Equipment; Endowments; Program development; Scholarship funds; Research; Matching/challenge support.
Limitations: Applications not accepted. Giving primarily in Tacoma, WA.
Publications: Grants list; Informational brochure.
Application information: Unsolicited requests for funds not accepted.
    Board meeting date(s): 4-6 weeks after each deadline
Officers: John C. Dimmer, Pres.; Carolyn Dimmer, V.P.; Marilyn Dimmer, V.P.; Diane C. Dimmer, Secy. and Exec. Dir.; John B. Dimmer, Treas.
Number of staff: 1 part-time professional.
EIN: 911622059
Selected grants: The following grants were reported in 2005.
$25,000 to University of Oregon Foundation, Eugene, OR.
$15,000 to Mary Bridge Childrens Foundation, Tacoma, WA.
$10,000 to Childrens Museum of Tacoma, Tacoma, WA.
$5,000 to American Cancer Society, Tacoma, WA.
$5,000 to American Red Cross, Tacoma, WA.
$3,000 to Toy Rescue Mission, Tacoma, WA.
$2,500 to Tacoma Art Museum, Tacoma, WA.
$2,000 to Puget Sound Blood Center, Seattle, WA.
$1,000 to University of Puget Sound, Tacoma, WA.
$500 to Arthritis Foundation, Seattle, WA.

9580
Edwards Mother Earth Foundation
P.O. Box 16225
Seattle, WA 98116-0225
Contact: Sonia E. Baker, Pres.
E-mail: psnow@foundationsource.com; Toll free tel.: (800) 839-1754; e-mail for Sharon Schneider:

sschneider@foundationsource.com; URL: http://www.fsrequests.com/EMEF

Established in 1997 in WA.
Donors: Bob Edwards†; Jane Edwards†.
Foundation type: Independent foundation.
Financial data (yr. ended 12/31/05): Assets, $30,996,124 (M); expenditures, $1,527,326; qualifying distributions, $1,428,510; giving activities include $1,306,000 for 41 grants (average: $10,000–$100,000).
Purpose and activities: The purpose of the foundation is to enhance a sustainable quality of life on earth by supporting organizations that strengthen the interconnectedness of the human community with each other and the environment. The foundation is interested in: Sustainable building practices; environmental biodiversity in oceans, rainforests, renewable energy, populations; and local environmental justice through the people most directly involved.
Fields of interest: Environment, reform; Environment, public education; Environment, pollution control; Environment, air pollution; Environment, water pollution; Environment, noise pollution; Environment, toxics; Environment, waste management; Environment, recycling; Environment, global warming; Environment, natural resources; Environment, water resources; Environment, land resources; Environment, energy; Environment, forests; Environment, plant conservation; Health care; Community development; Youth.
International interests: China; Ecuador; Indonesia.
Type of support: General/operating support; Continuing support; Management development/capacity building; Equipment; Land acquisition; Program development; Technical assistance; Matching/challenge support.
Limitations: Giving in the Pacific Northwest in the U.S., and in Ecuador, China, and Indonesia. No support for organizations that are not nationally-based. No grants to individuals.
Application information: Applications are by invitation only. Letter of intent form is available on foundation Web site and must be sent electronically. Application form required.
    Initial approach: Letter of intent form sent electronically (Jan. 1 - Mar. 31)
    Copies of proposal: 1
    Deadline(s): Following invitation, Sept. 15 for applications
    Board meeting date(s): 3rd weekend in Oct.; last Fri.-Sat. in Apr.
    Final notification: Nov. 15
Officers: Sonia E. Baker, Pres. and Gen. Mgr.; Jonathan D. Edwards, V.P.; Kendall Baker, Secy.; Eric Rayl, Treas.
Directors: Andrew Bell; Johanna Bell; Otis Bell; Marcy Edwards; Ruth Edwards; Frank Martin; Kristie Rayl.
Number of staff: 1 part-time professional; 1 part-time support.
EIN: 911789783
Selected grants: The following grants were reported in 2004.
$150,000 to Nature Conservancy, Seattle, WA. 2 grants: $50,000, $100,000
$100,000 to Marine Conservation Biology Institute, Redmond, WA.
$75,000 to Nature Conservancy, Anchorage, AK.
$40,000 to Friends of the Earth, DC.
$30,000 to Camp Fire USA, Seattle, WA.
$30,000 to Natural Resources Defense Council, New York, NY.

$30,000 to Salish Sea Expeditions, Bainbridge Island, WA.

$25,000 to Population Communications International, New York, NY.

$25,000 to Population Connection, DC.

9581
Tom and Sue Ellison Foundation ✧ ☆
400 112th Ave. N.E., Ste. 230
Bellevue, WA 98004
Contact: Cathi Metcalf

Established in 2002 in WA.
Donors: Thomas A. Ellison; Maureen Sue Ellison.
Foundation type: Independent foundation.
Financial data (yr. ended 12/31/05): Assets, $3,063,555 (M); gifts received, $1,011,791; expenditures, $409,828; qualifying distributions, $384,185; giving activities include $381,885 for 28 grants (high: $166,667; low: $100).
Fields of interest: Higher education; Education; Hospitals (general); Medical research; Federated giving programs.
Application information:
Initial approach: Letter
Officers: Thomas A. Ellison, Pres.; Maureen Sue Ellison, V.P.
EIN: 916557865
Selected grants: The following grants were reported in 2005.
$2,500 to American Heart Association, Dallas, TX.
$2,500 to Seattle Art Museum, Seattle, WA.
$1,500 to Newport High School, Newport, OR.
$1,108 to Rainier Scholars, Seattle, WA.
$1,000 to Boy Scouts of America, Anchorage, AK.

9582
The Everard Family Foundation ✧ ☆
15824 S.E. 296th St.
Kent, WA 98042 (253) 631-4737
Contact: Lloyd D. Everard, Tr.

Established in 2000 in WA.
Donors: Lloyd D. Everard; Glenda C. Everard.
Foundation type: Independent foundation.
Financial data (yr. ended 12/31/05): Assets, $433,941 (M); expenditures, $380,445; qualifying distributions, $366,616; giving activities include $366,616 for grants.
Fields of interest: Human services; Christian agencies & churches; Religion.
Application information: Application form not required.
Deadline(s): None
Trustees: Donald Everard; Glenda C. Everard; Lloyd D. Everard; Alan Gray; Deanne Sandvold.
EIN: 911998779

9583
Evertrust Foundation ✧
(formerly Everett Mutual Savings Bank Foundation)
P.O. Box 1245
Everett, WA 98206

Established in 1993.
Donor: Everett Mutual Savings Bank.
Foundation type: Company-sponsored foundation.
Financial data (yr. ended 12/31/04): Assets, $10,708,642 (M); expenditures, $616,848; qualifying distributions, $442,904; giving activities

include $442,904 for 95 grants (high: $50,000; low: $15).
Purpose and activities: The foundation supports organizations involved with arts and culture, education, health, youth development, human services, and community development.
Fields of interest: Arts; Education; Health care; Athletics/sports, amateur leagues; Boys & girls clubs; Youth development; Human services; Community development; Federated giving programs.
Type of support: General/operating support; Continuing support; Building/renovation; Program development; Scholarship funds; Sponsorships.
Limitations: Applications not accepted. Giving limited to the Everett, WA, area. No grants to individuals.
Application information: Contributes only to pre-selected organizations.
Officers and Directors: Margaret Bavasi, Pres.; Mary B. Sievers,* Secy. and Exec. Dir.; Tom Collins; Michael Deller; Thomas J. Gaffney; Larry Hanson; George Newland; Harry Stuchell.
EIN: 911510567
Selected grants: The following grants were reported in 2004.
$52,500 to Boys and Girls Clubs of Snohomish County, Everett, WA. 2 grants: $50,000, $2,500
$42,500 to Providence General Foundation, Everett, WA. 2 grants: $2,500, $40,000
$40,000 to Volunteers of America, Everett, WA.
$14,339 to Everett Community College Foundation, Everett, WA. 2 grants: $12,424, $1,915
$8,250 to United Way, WA.
$2,500 to Greater Everett Community Foundation, Everett, WA.
$2,100 to Cocoon House, Everett, WA.

9584
The Martin Fabert Foundation ✧
c/o Foundation Mgmt. Group, LLC
1000 2nd Ave., 34th Fl.
Seattle, WA 98104

Established in 2001 in IL.
Donors: Martin Foundation; Elizabeth Martin.
Foundation type: Independent foundation.
Financial data (yr. ended 6/30/05): Assets, $11,857,867 (M); expenditures, $619,343; qualifying distributions, $500,131; giving activities include $497,591 for 32 grants (high: $100,000; low: $2,250).
Fields of interest: Arts; Environment; Animals/wildlife.
Limitations: Applications not accepted. Giving on a national basis. No grants to individuals.
Application information: Contributes only to pre-selected organizations.
Officers: Elizabeth Martin, Pres. and Treas.; Kenneth Fabert, V.P.; Daniel Asher, Secy.
Director: Geraldine Martin.
EIN: 364437950
Selected grants: The following grants were reported in 2004.
$87,000 to Organic Center for Education and Promotion, Greenfield, MA.
$25,000 to Conservation Northwest, Bellingham, WA.
$25,000 to Nature Conservancy, Seattle, WA.
$15,000 to Environmental Law and Policy Center of the Midwest, Chicago, IL.
$12,500 to Institute for Environmental Research and Education, Vashon, WA.

$10,000 to Hoosier Environmental Council, Indianapolis, IN.
$10,000 to International Snow Leopard Trust, Seattle, WA.
$5,000 to Sound Experience, Port Townsend, WA.
$2,500 to Marine Science Society of the Pacific Northwest, Poulsbo, WA.
$2,500 to Northwest Maritime Center, Port Townsend, WA.

9585
The Hugh and Jane Ferguson Foundation ✧
701 5th Ave., Ste. 6770
Seattle, WA 98104 (206) 781-3472
Contact: Therese Ogle, Prog. Off.
E-mail: OgleFounds@aol.com; *URL:* http://foundationcenter.org/grantmaker/ferguson/

Established in 1986 in WA.
Donors: Hugh S. Ferguson; Jane Avery Ferguson†.
Foundation type: Independent foundation.
Financial data (yr. ended 9/30/05): Assets, $1,095,834 (M); gifts received, $260,000; expenditures, $1,016,818; qualifying distributions, $1,001,107; giving activities include $979,700 for 59 grants (high: $200,000; low: $400).
Purpose and activities: The foundation is dedicated to the preservation and restoration of nature, including wildlife and their required habitats. It also supports the institutions that present nature and the cultural heritage of the greater Puget Sound area to the public—museums, libraries, aquariums, zoos and public media.
Fields of interest: Museums; Higher education; Libraries (public); Education; Environment, natural resources; Zoos/zoological societies; Aquariums; Animals/wildlife; Human services; Federated giving programs.
Type of support: General/operating support; Continuing support; Capital campaigns; Land acquisition; Program development; Seed money; Technical assistance.
Limitations: Giving primarily in AK, OR, and WA, with emphasis on WA. No support for social service agencies, schools or government agencies or collaborations between nonprofits and government agencies in which the government provides majority funding or leadership. No grants to individuals or for research projects, book publications, web or video/film productions, capital campaigns, curriculum development, or scholarships.
Publications: Application guidelines; Grants list.
Application information: The foundation accepts the Common Application Form developed by the Pacific Northwest Grantmakers Forum. See Web site for application guidelines and procedures. Application form not required.
Initial approach: Telephone, E-mail, or submit 2-page pre-application letter
Copies of proposal: 1
Deadline(s): Pre-application letter: Jan. 15 and July 15; Full proposal (if requested): Feb. 15 and Aug. 15
Board meeting date(s): Mar. and Sept.
Final notification: Mar. and Sept.
Officers and Directors:* Hugh S. Ferguson,* Pres.; Ellen Lee Ferguson,* Secy.
EIN: 911357603

9586
Forest Foundation
820 A St., Ste. 345
Tacoma, WA 98402 (253) 627-1634
Contact: Brian F. Boyd, Exec. Dir.

Incorporated in 1962 in WA.
Donors: C. Davis Weyerhaeuser†; William T. Weyerhaeuser.
Foundation type: Independent foundation.
Financial data (yr. ended 10/31/05): Assets, $29,532,861 (M); expenditures, $1,753,424; qualifying distributions, $1,523,492; giving activities include $1,302,300 for 81 grants (high: $250,000; low: $2,000).
Purpose and activities: Giving primarily for arts and culture, exercising stewardship of natural resources, human services, and community building and development.
Fields of interest: Arts; Environment, natural resources; Human services; Community development.
Type of support: General/operating support; Capital campaigns; Building/renovation; Matching/challenge support.
Limitations: Giving primarily in southwestern WA, with emphasis on Pierce County. Grants given for capital projects only in Clallum, Cowlitz, Clark, Grays Harbor, Jefferson, Kitsap, Lewis, Mason, Pacific, Skamania, Thurston and Wahkiakum counties. No support for religious organizations to promulgate religion. No grants to individuals, or for endowment funds, debt retirement, annual appeals, research, scholarships, films, publications, or fellowships; no loans.
Publications: Application guidelines.
Application information: Application form required.
  Initial approach: 2- to 3-page letter of inquiry, 2 copies required
  Copies of proposal: 6
  Deadline(s): Check guidelines for specific dates
  Board meeting date(s): 6 times a year
  Final notification: 60 to 90 days
Officers and Directors:* Gail T. Weyerhaeuser,* Pres. and Treas.; Annette B. Weyerhaeuser,* V.P.; Nicholas C. Spika, Secy.; Brian F. Boyd, Exec. Dir.; William T. Weyerhaeuser.
EIN: 916020514
Selected grants: The following grants were reported in 2005.
$250,000 to Charles Wright Academy, Tacoma, WA.
$115,000 to Greater Tacoma Community Foundation, Tacoma, WA. 2 grants: $50,000, $65,000
$75,000 to Tacoma Art Museum, Tacoma, WA.
$60,000 to Washington Womens Employment and Education, Seattle, WA.
$50,000 to Good Samaritan Foundation, Puyallup, WA.
$50,000 to Vassar College, Poughkeepsie, NY.
$30,000 to Helping Hand House, Puyallup, WA.
$15,000 to Associated Ministries of Tacoma-Pierce County, Tacoma, WA.
$15,000 to Broadway Center for the Performing Arts, Tacoma, WA.

9587
Fortune Family Foundation ◇
914 164 St. S.E., Ste. 1682
Mill Creek, WA 98012 (800) 914-2687
Contact: Kathleen Shaw

E-mail to request application form: application@fortunefoundation.org; URL: http://www.fortunefoundation.org

Established in 1998 in WA.
Donor: Cathryn R. Fortune.
Foundation type: Independent foundation.
Financial data (yr. ended 12/31/05): Assets, $3,435,307 (M); expenditures, $650,001; qualifying distributions, $639,565; giving activities include $639,565 for 4 grants (high: $161,912; low: $15,000).
Purpose and activities: Giving primarily for capacity building in the Puget Sound, WA, area; fund raising capacity building for nonprofits that serve the homeless, domestic and child abuse, and early education.
Fields of interest: Cancer; Crime/violence prevention, domestic violence; Crime/violence prevention, child abuse; Housing/shelter; Human services; YM/YWCAs & YM/YWHAs; Homeless.
Type of support: Income development; Management development/capacity building; Capital campaigns; Building/renovation; Conferences/seminars; Consulting services.
Limitations: Giving limited to the Puget Sound, WA, region, with priority on the greater Seattle area. No grants to individuals or programs.
Application information: Application form available on Web site. Application form required.
  Copies of proposal: 1
  Deadline(s): None
Officers and Directors:* Cathryn R. Fortune,* Pres.; John C. Shimer,* V.P.; Reginald S. Koehler III,* Secy.; Robert A. Underhill,* Treas.; Scott R. Thomson.
EIN: 911913219

9588
The Foster Foundation ◇
601 Union St., Ste. 3707
Seattle, WA 98101 (206) 726-1815
Contact: Jill Goodsell, Admin.
FAX: (206) 903-0628;
E-mail: info@thefosterfoundation.org; URL: http://www.thefosterfoundation.org

Established in 1984 in WA.
Donors: Evelyn W. Foster†; Albert O. Foster†; Michael Foster†.
Foundation type: Independent foundation.
Financial data (yr. ended 12/31/05): Assets, $87,790,931 (M); gifts received, $1,056,648; expenditures, $5,552,719; qualifying distributions, $5,317,329; giving activities include $2,515,262 for 73 grants (high: $1,750,000; low: $5,000; average: $5,000–$270,000).
Purpose and activities: Giving to enhance the quality of life in the Pacific Northwest and in AK, through support of qualified needs in the areas of arts and culture, medical research, treatment and care, education, and human welfare.
Fields of interest: Performing arts; Arts; Higher education; Education; Health care; Health organizations, association; AIDS; Pediatrics; Medical research; Human services; YM/YWCAs & YM/YWHAs; Children/youth, services; Homeless, human services; Federated giving programs.
Type of support: Building/renovation; Equipment; Program development; Seed money; Scholarship funds; Research; Matching/challenge support.
Limitations: Giving primarily in the Pacific Northwest, with emphasis on Seattle, WA. No grants

to individuals directly, or for fundraising, endowment funds, or unrestricted operating funds; no loans.
Application information: Application form required.
  Initial approach: Submit grant form via foundation web site
  Deadline(s): Aug. 31
  Board meeting date(s): Dec.
  Final notification: 3 months
Trustees: Michael G. Foster, Jr.; Shalisan Lee Foster.
EIN: 911265474
Selected grants: The following grants were reported in 2005.
$1,750,000 to University of Washington, Seattle, WA. For general support.
$1,500,000 to Childrens Hospital and Medical Center, Seattle, WA. For general support.
$291,952 to Seattle Foundation, Seattle, WA. For general support.
$63,000 to New Beginnings for Battered Women and Their Children, Seattle, WA. For general support of homeless service programs.
$50,000 to Pike Market Medical Clinic, Seattle, WA. For general support.

9589
Foundation Northwest
(formerly Spokane Inland Northwest Community Foundation)
Old City Hall
221 N. Wall St., Ste. 624
Spokane, WA 99201-0826 (509) 624-2606
Contact: Mark Hurtubise, C.E.O.
FAX: (509) 624-2608;
E-mail: admin@foundationw.org; Additional tel.: (888) 267-5606; URL: http://www.foundationnw.org

Incorporated in 1974 in WA.
Foundation type: Community foundation.
Financial data (yr. ended 6/30/05): Assets, $40,382,031 (M); gifts received, $2,229,787; expenditures, $3,789,258; giving activities include $3,066,137 for 419 grants (high: $726,280; low: $100).
Purpose and activities: The foundation seeks to foster vibrant and sustainable communities in the Inland Northwest. Primary areas of interest include the arts, humanities, education, community development, and human services.
Fields of interest: Humanities; Historic preservation/historical societies; Arts; Education; Medical care, rehabilitation; Health care; Youth, services; Aging, centers/services; Human services; Economic development; Community development; Government/public administration; Aging.
Type of support: Matching/challenge support; General/operating support; Management development/capacity building; Capital campaigns; Building/renovation; Equipment; Program development; Seed money; Scholarship funds; Technical assistance; Program evaluation; Employee-related scholarships.
Limitations: Giving limited to the Inland Northwest: Benewah, Bonner, Boundary, Clearwater, Idaho, Kootenai, Latah, Lewis, Nez Perce, and Shoshone counties, ID, and Adams, Asotin, Columbia, Ferry, Garfield, Lincoln, Pend Oreille, Spokane, Stevens, and Whitman counties, WA. No support for sectarian religious purposes, or programs addressing specific disease or health conditions. No grants to individuals (except for scholarship awards), or for deficit financing, debt reduction, conferences

(including travel), endowments, publications and film production, private or parochial education, academic or scientific research, or replacement of government funding.

Publications: Application guidelines; Annual report; Biennial report; Informational brochure (including application guidelines); Newsletter.

Application information: Visit foundation Web site for application guidelines. Faxed or e-mailed applications are not accepted. Final proposal is invited based on the foundation's evaluation of organization's preliminary application. Scholarship awards are paid to educational institutions. Application form required.

> *Initial approach:* Submit a preliminary application (1 page letter)
> *Copies of proposal:* 1
> *Deadline(s):* Feb. 1 and Sept. 15 for preliminary application; Mar. 1 for scholarships
> *Board meeting date(s):* Sept. through June
> *Final notification:* 3 months

Officers and Directors: * Roger D. Woodworth, * Chair.; Patricia A. Dahmen-Ray, * Vice-Chair.; Mark Hurtubise, C.E.O. and Pres.; Michael C. Ormsby, * Secy.; Jeffrey J. Bell; Richard W. Boutz; Nancy M. Collins-Warner; Priscilla L. Gilkey; Michael D. Nowling; Mary Lou Reed; Donald Z. Ting; Brenda E. Tudor.

Number of staff: 5 full-time professional; 1 full-time support.

EIN: 910941053

Selected grants: The following grants were reported in 2004.

$20,000 to Citizens Utility Alliance of Washington, Spokane, WA.

$12,000 to Peaceful Valley Home Front Association, Spokane, WA. For Single Family Homeownership Program.

$10,000 to Neighborhood Alliance of Spokane County, Spokane, WA. For general support.

$10,000 to Northwest EcoBuilding Guild, Inland Northwest and Southeast BC Chapter, Tukwila, WA. For Green Building Education.

$10,000 to Odyssey Youth Center, Spokane, WA. For Youth Leadership and Community Organizing Project.

$7,500 to Northwest Museum of Arts and Culture, Spokane, WA. For American-Indian Collection Preservation and Program project.

$5,000 to Idaho Nonprofit Development Center, Boise, ID. For operating support for North Idaho TA programs.

$5,000 to Lands Council, Spokane, WA. For Watershed and Aquifer Protection Program.

$5,000 to Second Harvest Food Bank of the Inland Northwest, Spokane, WA. For Cereal and Vegetables.

$4,000 to Cutter Theater, Metaline Falls, WA. For operating support.

9590
The Gottfried & Mary Fuchs Foundation

c/o Union Bank of California, N.A.
1501 Commerce St.
Tacoma, WA 98402
Contact: Alison J. Yeager, V.P., Tacoma Trust Manager

Trust established in 1960 in WA.
Donors: Gottfried Fuchs†; Mary Fuchs†; Gottfried Fuchs Trust.
Foundation type: Independent foundation.

Financial data (yr. ended 12/31/05): Assets, $22,870,578 (M); expenditures, $1,223,585; qualifying distributions, $1,045,679; giving activities include $999,500 for 60 grants (high: $45,000; low: $500).

Purpose and activities: Support for charitable, educational, or cultural activities in Pierce County, WA, not normally financed by tax funds. Prefers funding services projects rather than operating budgets.

Fields of interest: Arts; Higher education; Education.

Type of support: General/operating support; Continuing support; Annual campaigns; Capital campaigns; Building/renovation; Equipment; Emergency funds; Program development; Research; Technical assistance; Consulting services; Matching/challenge support.

Limitations: Giving limited to Pierce County, WA. No grants to individuals.

Publications: Application guidelines.

Application information: Applications from outside the Pierce County, WA, area, not accepted. Request application form from: dawn.bell@UBOC.com. Application form required.

> *Initial approach:* Letter
> *Copies of proposal:* 6
> *Deadline(s):* Mar. 15, Sept. 15, and Dec. 15
> *Board meeting date(s):* Apr., Sept., and Dec.
> *Final notification:* Approx. 6 weeks

Trustee: Union Bank of California, N.A.
Number of staff: 1 part-time professional.
EIN: 916022284

9591
Bill & Melinda Gates Foundation ▼

(formerly William H. Gates Foundation)
P.O. Box 23350
Seattle, WA 98102 (206) 709-3100
Contact: Grant Inquiry Coord.
FAX: (206) 709-3180;
E-mail: info@gatesfoundation.org; URL: http://www.gatesfoundation.org

Established in 1994 in WA; name changed in Aug. 1999. The Gates Learning Foundation merged into the foundation Jan. 1, 2000; May 1, 2006 the foundation reorganized its grantmaking programs; In 2006, Warren Buffett pledged a significant portion of his Berkshire Hathaway Inc. stock (valued at $31 billion) to the Bill & Melinda Gates Foundation to be paid out on a yearly basis. The annual giving of the foundation is expected to rise sharply in the immediate future as a result; The foundation is restructuring and has decided to create a separate organization, the Bill & Melinda Gates Foundation Trust, to oversee the foundation's assets in 2007. Its eventual closure is planned for 50 years after the deaths of its three current trustees - Bill and Melinda Gates, and Warren Buffett.

Donors: William H. Gates III; Melinda French Gates; Warren E. Buffett.
Foundation type: Independent foundation.
Financial data (yr. ended 12/31/05): Assets, $29,153,508,829 (M); gifts received, $357,602,750; expenditures, $1,768,043,736; qualifying distributions, $1,484,020,392; giving activities include $1,355,371,860 for 957 grants (high: $150,000,000; low: $75), $878,432 for 460 employee matching gifts, and $37,919,314 for foundation-administered programs.

Purpose and activities: Guided by the belief that every life has equal value, the Bill & Melinda Gates

Foundation works to reduce inequities and improve lives around the world. In developing countries, it focuses on improving health, reducing extreme poverty, and increasing access to technology in public libraries. In the United States, the foundation seeks to ensure that all people have access to a great education and to technology in public libraries. In its local region, it focuses on improving the lives of low-income families.

Fields of interest: Libraries/library science; Education; Reproductive health, family planning; Public health; Health care; AIDS; Nutrition; Human services; International development; Telecommunications, electronic messaging services.

International interests: Africa; Asia; Europe; South America.

Type of support: General/operating support; Continuing support; Annual campaigns; Capital campaigns; Building/renovation; Program development; Publication; Scholarship funds; Research; Technical assistance; Program-related investments/loans; Employee matching gifts; In-kind gifts; Matching/challenge support.

Limitations: Giving on a national and international basis to support initiatives in health and learning; the foundation also supports community giving in the Pacific Northwest. No support for religious purposes. No grants to individuals.

Publications: Application guidelines; Annual report; Financial statement; Grants list; Informational brochure; Newsletter; Occasional report; Program policy statement.

Application information: Review funding guidelines and eligibility overview on foundation's Web site before initial contact with foundation; proposals should not be submitted without prior invitation by the foundation. Application form not required.

> *Initial approach:* Letter of inquiry (not exceeding 2 pages and only accepted in Global Health and Pacific Northwest giving programs); submit formal funding proposal upon invitation from foundation
> *Deadline(s):* None
> *Final notification:* 6-8 weeks

Officers and Trustees: * Melinda French Gates, * Co-Chair.; William H. Gates III, * Co-Chair.; William H. Gates, Sr., Co-Chair.; Patricia Q. Stonesifer, C.E.O.; Cheryl Scott, C.O.O.; Allan C. Golston, Pres., U.S. Prog.; Sylvia M. Mathews, Pres., Global Devel. Prog.; Tadataka Yamada, Pres., Global Health Prog.; Connie Collingsworth, Genl. Counsel; Warren E. Buffett.

Number of staff: 260 full-time professional; 6 part-time professional; 68 full-time support.

EIN: 911663695

Selected grants: The following grants were reported in 2005.

$186,541,084 to Program for Appropriate Technology in Health (PATH), Seattle, WA. 4 grants: $2,917,213 (To accelerate access to safe and effective microbicides, payable over 3 years), $107,626,290 (For clinical development of RTS,S, malaria vaccine, payable over 6 years), $997,581 (To accelerate access to HPV vaccines in developing countries), $75,000,000 (For Pneumococcal Vaccine Solutions, portfolio of pneumococcal vaccine projects, payable over 5 years).

$100,000,000 to Medicines for Malaria Venture, Geneva, Switzerland. To further develop and accelerate antimalarial discovery and development projects, payable over 5 years.

$60,000,000 to Save the Children Federation, Westport, CT. To test and evaluate critical set of newborn health care tools and technologies, payable over 6 years.

$58,003,043 to United Negro College Fund, Fairfax, VA. For graduate scholarships in Public Health in Gates Millennium Scholars program.

$40,000,000 to Lakeside School, Seattle, WA. For endowment campaign, payable over 5 years.

$450,000 to Give2Asia, San Francisco, CA. To disseminate AIDS prevention messages to Chinese public.

$180,000 to Atlanta-Fulton Public Library, Atlanta, GA. To provide sustainable public access computer hardware and software upgrades, payable over 3 years.

9592
Geneva Foundation ✧

8701 Madrona Ln.
Edmonds, WA 98026-8653
Contact: Wanda Kamahele, Tr.

Established in 1964 in WA.
Donor: Genevieve Albers†.
Foundation type: Independent foundation.
Financial data (yr. ended 6/30/05): Assets, $5,616,473 (M); expenditures, $1,397,793; qualifying distributions, $1,357,371; giving activities include $1,248,258 for 36 grants (high: $257,500; low: $100), and $18,895 for 1 employee matching gift.
Purpose and activities: Giving primarily for human services; funding also for education, and Roman Catholic schools and organizations.
Fields of interest: Education; Health organizations, association; Food banks; Human services; Children/youth, services; Roman Catholic agencies & churches.
Type of support: General/operating support.
Limitations: Giving primarily to HI and to the West Coast of the U.S., with emphasis on WA. No grants to individuals.
Publications: Annual report.
Application information:
Initial approach: Letter
Deadline(s): None
Trustee: Wanda J. Kamahele.
Number of staff: 1
EIN: 916056767
Selected grants: The following grants were reported in 2005.
$257,500 to Northwest Harvest, Seattle, WA.
$150,000 to Saint James Cathedral, Seattle, WA.
$121,500 to Catholic Community Services, Tacoma, WA.
$100,000 to Polynesian Voyaging Society, Honolulu, HI.
$63,503 to Pacific American Foundation, Honolulu, HI. 3 grants: $18,895, $19,000, $25,608
$50,000 to Communities in Schools of Peninsula, Vaughn, WA.
$43,300 to Lynnwood Food Bank, Lynnwood, WA.
$5,000 to Snohomish County Center for Battered Women, Everett, WA.

9593
GLA Foundation ✧ ☆

c/o Irwin L. Treiger
1420 5th Ave., No. 400
Seattle, WA 98101-1307
Application address: c/o Daniel Russo, V.P., 949 S. Coast Dr., No. 600, Costa Mesa, CA 92626

Established in 1990 in WA.
Donors: Hardball-I, LP; George L. Argyros.
Foundation type: Independent foundation.
Financial data (yr. ended 3/31/06): Assets, $5,073,281 (M); expenditures, $328,669; qualifying distributions, $327,494; giving activities include $326,512 for 2 grants (high: $200,000; low: $126,512).
Fields of interest: Higher education; Foundations (private independent).
Limitations: Giving primarily in CA.
Application information:
Initial approach: Letter
Officers: George L. Argyros, Pres. and Treas.; Daniel Russo, V.P. and Secy.
Director: Irwin L. Treiger.
EIN: 931029890
Selected grants: The following grants were reported in 2003.
$164,611 to Argyros Foundation, Costa Mesa, CA.
$100,000 to California Institute of Technology, Pasadena, CA.
$50,000 to Richard M. Nixon Center for Peace and Freedom, DC.

9594
Glaser Foundation, Inc. ✧

P.O. Box 6548
Bellevue, WA 98008-0548

Incorporated in 1952 in WA.
Donor: Paul F. Glaser†.
Foundation type: Independent foundation.
Financial data (yr. ended 11/30/05): Assets, $14,252,781 (M); expenditures, $859,152; qualifying distributions, $767,772; giving activities include $734,140 for 109 grants.
Purpose and activities: Major focus on direct-line service agencies serving children, youth, the handicapped, the aged, and the indigent; support also for substance abuse and health services.
Fields of interest: Vocational education; Medical care, rehabilitation; Health care; Substance abuse, services; Mental health/crisis services; Health organizations, association; Alcoholism; Biomedicine; Medical research, institute; Crime/violence prevention, youth; Employment; Human services; Children/youth, services; Family services; Residential/custodial care, hospices; Aging, centers/services; Homeless, human services; Aging; Disabilities, people with; Minorities; Economically disadvantaged; Homeless.
Type of support: Program development; Seed money; Matching/challenge support.
Limitations: Giving limited to within King County, WA, and immediately adjoining areas. No grants to individuals, or for endowment funds, scholarships, fellowships, publications, or conferences; no loans.
Publications: Application guidelines.
Application information: Application form required.
Initial approach: Letter
Copies of proposal: 2
Deadline(s): None

Board meeting date(s): Jan., Mar., May, July, Sept., and Nov.
Final notification: Last day in month of board meeting
Officers: R.N. Brandenburg, Pres.; Janet Politeo, V.P.; R. William Carlstrom, Secy.; Walter Smith, Treas.
Board Members: Matt Carlson; Linda Hughes; R. Thomas Olson.
Number of staff: 1 part-time professional.
EIN: 916028694

9595
Glaser Progress Foundation
(formerly The Glaser Foundation)
P.O. Box 91123
Seattle, WA 98111 (206) 728-1050
Contact: Melessa Rogers, Operations Mgr.
FAX: (206) 728-1123;
E-mail: grants@glaserprogress.org; URL: http://www.glaserprogress.org

Established in 1993 in WA.
Donor: Robert D. Glaser.
Foundation type: Independent foundation.
Financial data (yr. ended 12/31/05): Assets, $31,265,068 (M); expenditures, $2,307,454; qualifying distributions, $2,295,874; giving activities include $1,937,500 for 40 grants (high: $150,000; low: $1,000).
Purpose and activities: The foundation focuses on four program areas: 1) Measuring Progress: build a more equitable and sustainable world by improving our understanding and measurement of human progress, 2) Animal Advocacy: make animal treatment a crucial consideration in business, policy and personal decision-making, 3) Independent Media: strengthen democracy by making independent voices heard, 4) Global HIV/AIDS: to identify and implement programs that provide support for and fulfillment of the goals of the Global Fund to Fight AIDS, tuberculosis, and malaria.
Fields of interest: Media/communications; Animals/wildlife, equal rights; Animal welfare; AIDS; Civil rights; Community development.
Type of support: General/operating support; Program development; Technical assistance; Matching/challenge support.
Limitations: Giving on a national basis. No grants to individuals.
Publications: Application guidelines.
Application information: Guidelines available on Web site. Application form not required.
Initial approach: Letter or e-mail
Copies of proposal: 1
Deadline(s): None
Board meeting date(s): Approx. 6 months after receipt of application letter to staff and board review
Officers: Martin Collier, Exec. Dir.; Robert D. Glaser, Mgr.
Number of staff: 3 full-time professional.
EIN: 911626010
Selected grants: The following grants were reported in 2005.
$500,000 to Columbia University, New York, NY.
$150,000 to Democracy Now Productions, New York, NY.
$104,000 to Yale University, New Haven, CT.
$100,000 to American Civil Liberties Union Foundation, New York, NY.
$100,000 to Habitat for Humanity International, Americus, GA.

$100,000 to Media Matters for America, DC.
$75,000 to American Constitution Society for Law and Policy, DC.
$75,000 to Humane Society of the United States, DC.
$50,000 to Free Press, Northampton, MA.
$25,000 to Pasados Safe Haven, Sultan, WA.

9596
Marsha and Jay Glazer Foundation ✧
(formerly Marsha Sloan Glazer Philanthropic Fund)
P.O. Box 997
Mercer Island, WA   98040   (206) 230-8969
Contact: Marsha S. Glazer, Pres.

Established in 1991.
Donors: Marsha Sloan Glazer; Jay M. Glazer.
Foundation type: Independent foundation.
Financial data (yr. ended 12/31/05): Assets, $1,993,934 (M); expenditures, $417,975; qualifying distributions, $416,684; giving activities include $416,684 for 23 grants (high: $87,500; low: $1,000).
Purpose and activities: Giving primarily for Jewish organizations, as well as for higher education, arts and culture, and to children's hospitals.
Fields of interest: Performing arts, theater; Arts; Higher education; Hospitals (specialty); Human services; Federated giving programs; Jewish federated giving programs; Jewish agencies & temples.
Type of support: Annual campaigns; Capital campaigns; Building/renovation; Program-related investments/loans.
Limitations: Giving primarily in the Peoria, IL, area and the greater Seattle, WA, area.
Application information: Application form not required.
Initial approach: Letter
Copies of proposal: 1
Deadline(s): Apr. 1, for funding made in May, and Oct. 1, for funding made in Nov.
Board meeting date(s): Apr. and Oct.
Final notification: May and Nov.
Officers: Marsha Sloan Glazer, Pres. and Treas.; Jay M. Glazer, V.P. and Secy.
Number of staff: 1 full-time support.
EIN: 943146475
Selected grants: The following grants were reported in 2003.
$150,000 to Indiana University Foundation, Indianapolis, IN. 2 grants: $75,000 each
$100,000 to Seattle Repertory Theater, Seattle, WA. 2 grants: $50,000 each
$88,000 to University of Washington, Seattle, WA. 2 grants: $75,000, $13,000
$75,000 to Jewish Federation of Greater Santa Barbara, Santa Barbara, CA.
$40,000 to Jewish Federation of Greater Seattle, Seattle, WA.
$25,000 to United Way of King County, Seattle, WA.
$15,000 to Bradley University, Peoria, IL.

9597
Grays Harbor Community Foundation
707 J St.
P.O. Box 615
Hoquiam, WA   98550   (360) 532-1600
Contact: Stan Pinnick, Pres.
FAX: (360) 532-8111; E-mail: info@gh-cf.org;
URL: http://www.gh-cf.org

Established in 1994 in WA.
Foundation type: Community foundation.
Financial data (yr. ended 12/31/05): Assets, $12,981,689 (M); gifts received, $3,021,559; expenditures, $567,866; giving activities include $414,644 for grants, and $82,417 for grants to individuals.
Purpose and activities: The foundation aims to improve the quality of life in communities throughout Grays Harbor County by promoting philanthropy at all levels of giving; seeking permanent endowment funds and other contributions from a diverse and ever-widening group of donors; helping donors achieve their charitable and financial goals by offering services that make charitable giving easy, effective and satisfying; providing responsible and effective financial management; distributing earnings from investments according to community needs and donor intent; and championing good works in every community served. Grantmaking priorities include arts and culture, education, health, human services, and community development.
Fields of interest: Arts; Libraries/library science; Scholarships/financial aid; Education; Health care; Family services, domestic violence; Human services; Community development.
Type of support: General/operating support; Income development; Management development/capacity building; Capital campaigns; Building/renovation; Equipment; Land acquisition; Emergency funds; Program development; Seed money; Curriculum development; Scholarships—to individuals; Matching/challenge support.
Limitations: Giving primarily to residents of Grays Harbor County, WA, area. No support for religious organizations for religious purposes, or for government agencies. No grants to individuals (except for scholarships), or for endowments, debt retirement, fundraising events, advertising, or conferences.
Publications: Application guidelines; Annual report; Financial statement; Grants list; Informational brochure.
Application information: Visit foundation Web site for grant application cover sheet and guidelines. The foundation welcomes phone calls and letters of inquiry at all times. Application form required.
Initial approach: Submit application cover sheet and attachments
Copies of proposal: 8
Deadline(s): Jan. 1, Apr. 1, July 1, and Oct. 1
Board meeting date(s): 3rd Thurs. of alternating months
Final notification: Quarterly
Officers and Directors:* Robert M. Wiggins,* Chair.; Scott Weatherwax,* Vice-Chair.; Stan Pinnick,* Pres.; Dick Warren,* V.P.; Eileen Sterling,* Secy.; Bob Preble,* Treas.; Jim Daly, Exec. Dir.; Donald J. Arima; Jane Goldberg; John C. Hughes; Ernie Ingram; Todd Lindley; John Mertz; Wes Peterson; Randy Rust; Rich Vroman.
Number of staff: 1 full-time professional; 1 part-time support.
EIN: 911607005

9598
Joshua Green Foundation, Inc. ✧
P.O. Box 21829
Seattle, WA   98111-3829   (206) 622-2809
Contact: Sandra Spurlock, Secy.
Application address: 1425 4th Ave., Seattle, WA 98101

Established in 1956 in WA.
Donors: Joshua Green†; Mrs. Joshua Green†; Charles P. Burnett III; Joshua Green III; Jennifer Carter; Frances Davidson; Laura Gowen; Herbert Gowen; William C. Gowen; Louisa Gowen; Shirley Burnett; William Burnett; Vivian Burnett; William Burnett, Jr.
Foundation type: Independent foundation.
Financial data (yr. ended 12/31/05): Assets, $38,746,914 (M); gifts received, $483,350; expenditures, $1,945,937; qualifying distributions, $1,912,550; giving activities include $1,912,550 for 81 grants (high: $200,000; low: $500).
Purpose and activities: Giving primarily for the arts, particularly to museums, as well as for higher and other education, health care, including a children's hospital, social services, including homeless veterans, and for Christian ministries and education.
Fields of interest: Museums (art); Museums (science/technology); Performing arts, orchestra (symphony); Arts; Elementary/secondary education; Higher education; Environment; Hospitals (general); Human services; Family services; Federated giving programs; Christian agencies & churches.
Type of support: Capital campaigns; Building/renovation; Land acquisition; Emergency funds.
Limitations: Giving primarily in the King County, WA, area. No grants to individuals, or for scholarships or fellowships; no loans.
Publications: Application guidelines.
Application information: Application form required.
Initial approach: Letter or telephone
Copies of proposal: 1
Deadline(s): None
Board meeting date(s): Mar., June, Sept., and Dec.
Final notification: Within 1 week
Officers and Trustees:* Joshua Green III,* Pres.; Charles P. Burnett III,* V.P.; Sandra Spurlock, Secy.; Steven E. Carlson, Treas.; Jennifer Carter; Louisa Malatos; Charles E. Riley.
EIN: 916050748

9599
Saul and Dayee G. Haas Foundation, Inc.
1818 Westlake Ave. N.
Seattle, WA   98109
Contact: Bonnie B. Hilory, Exec. Dir.
FAX: (206) 352-1203;
E-mail: bhilory@haasfoundation.org; Additional
E-mail: staff@haasfoundation.org; URL: http://www.haasfoundation.org

Incorporated in 1972 in WA.
Donors: Saul Haas†; Dayee G. Haas†.
Foundation type: Independent foundation.
Financial data (yr. ended 6/30/05): Assets, $9,041,126 (M); gifts received, $19,250; expenditures, $460,565; qualifying distributions, $417,734; giving activities include $289,458 for 398 grants (high: $33,400; low: $5), and $46,896 for 204 employee matching gifts.
Purpose and activities: Emphasis on a school-administered fund to aid at-risk and low-income secondary school students in WA completing their education. Also sponsors a local university lecture series on broadcasting.
Fields of interest: Secondary school/education; Education; Human services; Minorities; Economically disadvantaged.
Type of support: Matching/challenge support; Emergency funds.

Limitations: Giving limited to WA. No support for religious organizations, or political organizations. No grants to individuals, or for equipment, land acquisition, renovation projects, or endowment funds.

Publications: Annual report; Grants list; Informational brochure; Newsletter; Program policy statement.

Application information: Applicant must be a WA school, serve 7th - 12th grade students, and understand the foundation's strategic plan and goals, which are to help the immediate needs of a child. Schools are added as funding becomes available. Application form not required.

   Initial approach: E-mail staff
   Copies of proposal: 1
   Deadline(s): June 30th annually. Check Web site for further details.
   Board meeting date(s): As necessary
   Final notification: Aug.

Officers and Directors: * Roger Percy,* Pres.; Carver Gayton,* V.P.; Deesa Haas,* Secy.; Bonnie B. Hilory, Exec. Dir.; Dan Barritt; Jon Bowman; Artie Buerk; Emory Bundy; Hon. Betty Fletcher; Jody Foster; Ruth Gerberding; R. Danner Graves; Jock W. Groen; Frank S. Hanawalt; Kate Janeway; Hon. Charles V. Johnson; Laura Kohn; John L. MacKenzie; Dick McCormick; Jim Menzies; Lee Miller; George P. Moynihan.

Number of staff: 1 full-time professional; 2 part-time professional; 1 part-time support.

EIN: 237189670

Selected grants: The following grants were reported in 2004.

$10,000 to Washington State University, Pullman, WA.

$500 to Emerald Ridge High School, South Hill, WA.

$500 to Enumclaw Senior High School, Enumclaw, WA.

$400 to Capital High School, Olympia, WA.

$400 to Omak Middle School, Omak, WA.

$388 to Cedarcrest Junior High School, Spanaway, WA.

$375 to Centralia High School, Centralia, WA.

$350 to Fort Vancouver High School, Vancouver, WA.

$200 to Bremerton High School, Bremerton, WA.

$100 to Aberdeen High School, Aberdeen, WA.

9600
Harder Foundation ◇

401 Broadway, Ste. 303
Tacoma, WA 98402
Contact: Mary G. Martin, Off. Mgr.
FAX: (253) 593-2122;
E-mail: grants@theharderfoundation.org;
URL: http://www.theharderfoundation.org

Incorporated in 1955 in MI.

Donor: Delmar S. Harder‡.

Foundation type: Independent foundation.

Financial data (yr. ended 12/31/05): Assets, $34,771,287 (M); gifts received, $123,010; expenditures, $1,909,494; qualifying distributions, $1,592,292; giving activities include $1,350,000 for 59 grants (high: $120,000; low: $3,500).

Purpose and activities: The foundation is dedicated to the preservation of an American quality of life that includes clean air and drinking water, unpolluted lakes and rivers, and healthy forests, parks, and wildland. It has a special concern for the protection of wildlife populations and the habitats on which they depend. Projects funded by the foundation

typically involve efforts to achieve long-term protection of specific public forests and wildlands, rivers, near shore marine ecosystems, and estuaries.

Fields of interest: Environment, natural resources; Environment.

Type of support: General/operating support; Continuing support; Annual campaigns; Endowments; Seed money; Matching/challenge support.

Limitations: Giving limited to AK, CO, FL, ID, MT, NV, OR, UT, WA, and WY. No grants to individuals, or for deficit financing, building funds, equipment, renovation projects, scholarships, fellowships, research, publications, or conferences; no loans.

Publications: Application guidelines; Annual report; Grants list.

Application information: Proposals accepted only from WA, or ID, MT, NV, WY, UT, CO, AK. Proposals from FL accepted by invitation only. Application form not required.

   Initial approach: Letter of inquiry
   Copies of proposal: 1
   Deadline(s): Late May and late Aug.
   Board meeting date(s): Feb.
   Final notification: 2 months

Officers and Trustees: * Del Langbauer,* Pres.; Jay A. Herbst,* Secy.; Robert Langbauer,* Treas.; John Driggers; William H. Langbauer.

Number of staff: 2 full-time professional; 1 full-time support.

EIN: 386048242

Selected grants: The following grants were reported in 2005.

$120,000 to Sierra Club Foundation, San Francisco, CA.

$100,000 to Wilderness Society, DC. 2 grants: $60,000, $40,000

$74,000 to Alaska Conservation Foundation, Anchorage, AK. 2 grants: $25,000, $49,000

$50,000 to Western Resource Advocates, Boulder, CO.

$35,000 to National Wildlife Federation, DC.

$32,500 to Idaho Conservation League, Boise, ID.

$25,000 to Trout Unlimited, Portland, OR.

$18,000 to Water Watch of Oregon, Portland, OR.

9601
John and Wauna Harman Foundation ◇

P.O. Box 10572
Yakima, WA 98909

Established in 1999 in WA.

Donor: Wauna Harman.

Foundation type: Independent foundation.

Financial data (yr. ended 12/31/05): Assets, $9,525,527 (M); expenditures, $2,435,758; qualifying distributions, $2,428,178; giving activities include $2,428,178 for 5 grants (high: $2,218,178; low: $25,000).

Purpose and activities: Giving primarily for human services and long-term care for the aging.

Limitations: Applications not accepted. Giving primarily in Yakima, WA. No grants to individuals.

Application information: Contributes only to pre-selected organizations.

Officers: Barry W. Harman, Pres.; Dawn Cook, V.P.; Elaine Harmon, Secy.

EIN: 911999241

9602
Harvest Foundation

P.O. Box 75554
Seattle, WA 98175-0554
Contact: Marjorie Ringness, Secy.-Treas.
FAX: (206) 299-9850; E-mail: info@harvestf.org;
URL: http://www.harvestf.org

Established in 2000 in WA.

Donors: Edward Ringness; Marjorie Ringness.

Foundation type: Independent foundation.

Financial data (yr. ended 12/31/05): Assets, $10,407,068 (M); expenditures, $583,452; qualifying distributions, $508,380; giving activities include $500,000 for 27 grants (high: $50,000; low: $10,000).

Purpose and activities: The foundation was created to provide funding primarily in the areas of social services and education. It is specifically interested in organizations that promote economic self-sufficiency through education and training of youth or families with children; it also supports organizations that serve the elderly by providing services to help senior citizens live independently. Grants for education are made in 2 areas: 1) teacher training in technology and curriculum development; and 2) supporting arts programs.

Fields of interest: Arts education; Human services.

Type of support: General/operating support; Continuing support; Capital campaigns; Building/renovation; Program development; Conferences/seminars; Seed money; Curriculum development.

Limitations: Giving primarily in AK, ID, MT, OR, and WA. No grants to individuals.

Publications: Application guidelines; Annual report; Annual report (including application guidelines); Grants list.

Application information: Unsolicited applications are not accepted but letters of inquiry are accepted. Application information available on foundation Web site.

   Initial approach: 1-page letter or e-mail
   Copies of proposal: 1
   Deadline(s): Apr. 15 and Oct. 15
   Board meeting date(s): Varies
   Final notification: May 31 and Nov. 30

Officers and Directors: * Edward Ringness,* Pres.; Marjorie Ringness,* Secy.-Treas.

EIN: 912065635

Selected grants: The following grants were reported in 2005.

$50,000 to Puget Sound Center Foundation for Teaching, Learning and Technology, Bothell, WA. For Teach the Teachers program.

$20,000 to Bainbridge Island Arts and Humanities Council, Bainbridge Island, WA.

$20,000 to Boys and Girls Clubs of South Puget Sound, Tacoma, WA. For Building Opportunity Through Technology (BOTT) program.

$20,000 to FareStart, Seattle, WA.

$20,000 to Seattle Education Access, Seattle, WA. For general operating support.

$20,000 to Seattle Goodwill, Seattle, WA. For Support and Training Result in Valuable Employees (STRIVE) program.

$20,000 to Whatcom Literacy Council, Bellingham, WA. For general operating support.

$15,000 to REUSE WORKS, Bellingham, WA. For Jobs Training Business program.

$10,000 to Arts Corps, Seattle, WA.

9603
Richard P. Haugland Foundation
(formerly Haugland Foundation)
2103 Harrison Ave. N.W., PMB 2602
Olympia, WA 98502

Established in 1996.
Foundation type: Independent foundation.
Financial data (yr. ended 9/30/05): Assets,
$23,336,290 (M); gifts received, $3,085,000;
expenditures, $1,705,689; qualifying distributions,
$1,619,009; giving activities include $1,619,009
for 9 grants (high: $1,000,000; low: $500).
Purpose and activities: Giving primarily for the arts,
education, and human services.
Fields of interest: Arts; Education; Human services;
Children/youth, services.
Type of support: General/operating support.
Limitations: Applications not accepted. Giving
primarily in OR. No support for religious
organizations. No grants to individuals.
Application information: Contributes only to
pre-selected organizations.
Officers: Richard P. Haugland, Pres.; Rosaria P.
Haugland, V.P.; Alexander D. Haugland, Secy.-Treas.
EIN: 931220478

9604
The Elizabeth Hebert and Donald Guthrie
Charitable Foundation ✧ ☆
425 Lagoon Pt. Rd.
Greenbank, WA 98253

Established in 1999 in WA.
Donors: Elizabeth Herbert; Donald Guthrie.
Foundation type: Independent foundation.
Financial data (yr. ended 12/31/05): Assets,
$4,149,689 (M); gifts received, $1,223,800;
expenditures, $390,124; qualifying distributions,
$353,508; giving activities include $353,508 for
grants.
Fields of interest: Education; Cancer research;
Human services; YM/YWCAs & YM/YWHAs.
Limitations: Giving primarily in WA.
Application information: Application form not
required.
  Deadline(s): None
Officers: Elizabeth Hebert, Pres.; Donald Guthrie,
V.P. and Secy.-Treas.
EIN: 912010848
Selected grants: The following grants were reported
in 2004.
$12,000 to Conservation Northwest, Bellingham,
  WA.
$11,000 to Seattle Arts and Lectures, Seattle, WA.
  For Writers in the Schools program.
$10,000 to United Way of King County, Seattle, WA.
$5,000 to Virginia Mason Medical Foundation,
  Seattle, WA.
$5,000 to YWCA of Seattle-King-Snohomish County,
  Seattle, WA. For capital campaign.
$5,000 to Zion Preparatory Academy, Seattle, WA.
$2,500 to Powerful Schools, Seattle, WA.
$1,500 to Seattle Repertory Theater, Seattle, WA.
$1,000 to American Red Cross of King and Kitsap
  Counties, Seattle/King County Chapter, Seattle,
  WA.
$1,000 to Arboretum Foundation, Seattle, WA.

9605
The Helstrom Foundation ✧
4550 3rd Ave. S.E., Ste. 104
Lacey, WA 98503
URL: http://www.helstromfoundation.org

Established in 1991 in WA.
Donors: Norris Helstrom; Robert L. Helstrom.
Foundation type: Operating foundation.
Financial data (yr. ended 6/30/05): Assets,
$5,986,396 (M); gifts received, $23,295;
expenditures, $945,276; qualifying distributions,
$346,138; giving activities include $343,011 for 17
grants (high: $115,308; low: $100).
Purpose and activities: Giving to Protestant
agencies and churches, and for higher education.
Fields of interest: Higher education; Protestant
agencies & churches.
Limitations: Applications not accepted. Giving on a
national basis, primarily in ID, KS, MO, and WA. No
grants to individuals directly.
Application information: Unsolicited requests for
funds not accepted.
Officers: Robert L. Helstrom, Pres.; Brian L.
Helstrom, V.P.; Yvonne E. Helstrom, Secy.; Phillip G.
Harris, Treas.
EIN: 943124662

9606
Robert G. Hemingway Foundation ✧
c/o U.S. Bank, N.A.
1420 5th Ave., Ste. 2100
Seattle, WA 98101
Contact: Lisa Carlson, Grants Coord.

Established in 1967 in UT.
Donor: Susan G. Hemingway†.
Foundation type: Independent foundation.
Financial data (yr. ended 4/30/05): Assets,
$7,269,500 (M); expenditures, $1,952,615;
qualifying distributions, $1,934,265; giving
activities include $1,907,000 for 5 grants (high:
$1,000,000; low: $7,000).
Purpose and activities: Giving primarily for
education and human services.
Fields of interest: Child development, education;
Higher education; Education; Mental health/crisis
services; Health organizations, association; Medical
research, institute; Crime/law enforcement; Human
services; Children/youth, services; Child
development, services; International human rights;
Biological sciences; Religion; Economically
disadvantaged.
Type of support: General/operating support;
Continuing support; Annual campaigns; Building/
renovation; Equipment; Endowments; Emergency
funds; Program development; Curriculum
development; Internship funds; Scholarship funds;
Research; Technical assistance.
Limitations: Giving limited to the U.S., with
preference given to the Northwest region. No grants
to individuals.
Application information: Phone requests will not be
honored. Application form not required.
  Initial approach: Letter on organization letterhead
    requesting guidelines
  Copies of proposal: 1
  Deadline(s): The final business day of the
    calendar year
  Board meeting date(s): Varies
  Final notification: Apr. 30
Officer: Craig Caviezel, Admin. Dir.

Trustee: U.S. Bank, N.A.
EIN: 876176774
Selected grants: The following grants were reported
in 2004.
$150,000 to Prosthetics Outreach Foundation,
  Bellevue, WA. For general support.
$75,000 to Sacramento Valley School, Sacramento,
  CA. For general support.
$30,000 to Zion Preparatory Academy, Seattle, WA.
  For general support.
$25,000 to Hunger Project, New York, NY. For
  general support.
$20,000 to Pendulum Project, Cambridge, MA. For
  general support.
$15,000 to Neighborhood House, Seattle, WA. For
  general support.
$12,000 to Diablo Valley School, Concord, CA. For
  general support.
$7,500 to Family and Adult Service Center, Seattle,
  WA. For general support.
$5,750 to K R C L-FM Listeners Community Radio of
  Utah, Salt Lake City, UT. For general support.
$5,000 to Bread of Life Mission, Seattle, WA. For
  general support.

9607
Heritage Valley Foundation ✧
18697 Hickox Rd.
Mount Vernon, WA 98273-9007

Donors: Jim Youngsman; Ruth Youngsman.
Foundation type: Independent foundation.
Financial data (yr. ended 12/31/05): Assets,
$1,181,205 (M); gifts received, $923,096;
expenditures, $330,837; qualifying distributions,
$319,100; giving activities include $319,100 for 35
+ grants (high: $43,000).
Fields of interest: Children/youth, services;
Christian agencies & churches.
Limitations: Applications not accepted. Giving
primarily in WA; some giving nationally. No grants to
individuals.
Application information: Contributes only to
pre-selected organizations.
Managers: Jim Youngsman; Ruth Youngsman.
EIN: 911784775
Selected grants: The following grants were reported
in 2003.
$42,000 to Partners International, Spokane, WA.
$32,600 to Youth Dynamics, Burlington, WA.
$30,496 to Enterprise Development International,
  Fairfax, VA.
$27,000 to International Institute for Christian
  Studies, Overland Park, KS.
$25,000 to Families Northwest, Bellevue, WA.
$24,500 to Latin American Mission, Miami, FL.
$22,800 to SIM USA, Charlotte, NC.
$18,000 to Prison Fellowship Ministries, DC.
$15,000 to Wycliffe Bible Translators, Orlando, FL.
$14,400 to Prison Impact, Kalispell, MT.

9608
Horizons Foundation
4020 E. Madison St., Ste. 322
Seattle, WA 98112 (206) 323-8061
Contact: Ralph R. Hadac, Exec. Dir.
E-mail: rhadac@aol.com

Established in 1990 in WA as partial successor to
the McAshan Foundation, Inc.
Donor: The McAshan Foundation, Inc.

Foundation type: Independent foundation.
Financial data (yr. ended 12/31/05): Assets, $20,757,353 (M); expenditures, $1,075,943; qualifying distributions, $1,031,181; giving activities include $960,800 for 113 grants (high: $100,000; low: $500).
Purpose and activities: Giving primarily to address the social and environmental problems of the Pacific Northwest. Emphasis is on the prevention of problems through educational projects, and citizen education programs aimed at improving the quality of the environment; some support also for the arts.
Fields of interest: Environment, natural resources; Environment; Reproductive health, family planning; Crime/violence prevention, domestic violence; Human services; Youth, pregnancy prevention; Family services, domestic violence; Family services, adolescent parents; Family services, counseling; Human services, emergency aid; Women, centers/services.
Type of support: General/operating support; Capital campaigns; Land acquisition; Emergency funds; Program development.
Limitations: Giving primarily in WA. No support for religious organizations. No grants to individuals, or for scholarships, debt retirement, operating deficits, endowment funds; no loans.
Publications: Application guidelines; Program policy statement.
Application information: Full proposal required if foundation accepts synopsis. Application form required.
  Initial approach: 2-page synopsis
  Copies of proposal: 4
  Deadline(s): None
  Board meeting date(s): Monthly
  Final notification: 10 days after board meeting
Officers and Directors:* Lucy J. Hadac,* Pres.; Jerald Forster,* V.P.; Stephen Hadac,* Secy.; Ralph R. Hadac,* Treas. and Exec. Dir.
Number of staff: 1 full-time professional.
EIN: 911493424

9609
Howard Charitable Foundation ◇ ☆
4616 25th N.E., Ste. 617
Seattle, WA 98105
Contact: Richard D. Newell, Secy.-Treas.

Established in 1999 in WA.
Donor: Robert S. Howard.
Foundation type: Independent foundation.
Financial data (yr. ended 12/31/04): Assets, $105,051,104 (M); expenditures, $6,114,457; qualifying distributions, $5,469,709; giving activities include $5,389,050 for 20 grants (high: $2,500,000; low: $5,000; average: $50,000–$200,000).
Purpose and activities: Giving primarily to health care, educational, and domestic humanitarian charities.
Fields of interest: Education; Health care; Human services.
Limitations: Giving primarily in San Diego, CA. No grants to individuals.
Application information:
  Initial approach: Letter of request
  Deadline(s): None
Officers: Robert S. Howard, Pres.; Richard D. Newell, Secy.-Treas.
EIN: 911952040
Selected grants: The following grants were reported in 2004.

$2,500,000 to Scripps Memorial Hospital, San Diego, CA.
$500,000 to Indiana University, Bloomington, IN.
$200,000 to Interfaith Community Services, Escondido, CA.
$200,000 to Oceanside Museum of Art, Oceanside, CA.
$120,000 to Womens Resource Center, Oceanside, CA.
$100,000 to Brother Benno Foundation, Oceanside, CA.
$50,000 to North County Solutions for Change, Vista, CA.
$50,000 to Salvation Army, Redding, CA.
$10,000 to Childrens Initiative, San Diego, CA.
$5,000 to Vista Community Clinic, Vista, CA.

9610
The John C. & Karyl Kay Hughes Foundation ◇
2323 Eastlake Ave. E.
Seattle, WA 98102-3305

Established in 1984 in WA.
Donor: Karyl Kay Hughes.
Foundation type: Independent foundation.
Financial data (yr. ended 11/30/05): Assets, $31,411,375 (M); expenditures, $1,895,890; qualifying distributions, $1,703,868; giving activities include $1,663,000 for 27 grants (high: $368,000; low: $1,000).
Purpose and activities: Giving primarily for human services, and to Christian agencies; funding also for a Baptist church, Christian Scientist churches, and the United Way.
Fields of interest: Human services; Federated giving programs; Christian agencies & churches; Protestant agencies & churches.
Limitations: Applications not accepted. Giving primarily in Seattle, WA. No grants to individuals.
Application information: Contributes only to pre-selected organizations. Unsolicited requests for funds not considered.
Trustee: Christopher R. Hughes.
EIN: 911286019
Selected grants: The following grants were reported in 2004.

$300,000 to United Way, WA. 2 grants: $239,000, $61,000
$225,000 to Church Council of Greater Seattle, Seattle, WA.
$100,000 to Carter Center, Atlanta, GA.
$80,000 to Habitat for Humanity, Wapato, WA.
$20,000 to Habitat for Humanity International, Americus, GA.
$2,000 to United Way of San Juan County, Friday Harbor, WA.

9611
The Hussey Foundation ◇ ☆
c/o Jeffrey S. Hussey
5131 N.E. Laurelcrest Ln.
Seattle, WA 98105

Established in 1999 in WA.
Donor: Jeffrey S. Hussey.
Foundation type: Independent foundation.
Financial data (yr. ended 12/31/05): Assets, $12,713,099 (M); gifts received, $12,450; expenditures, $464,550; qualifying distributions,

$443,000; giving activities include $443,000 for grants.
Fields of interest: Human services; Christian agencies & churches.
Limitations: Applications not accepted. Giving primarily in FL and WA. No grants to individuals.
Application information: Contributes only to pre-selected organizations.
Directors: Jeffrey S. Hussey.
EIN: 912013522

9612
The Hyder Family Foundation ◇ ☆
23292 N.E. 16th Pl.
Sammamish, WA 98074-4448

Established in 2001.
Donors: Ifrah Hyder; Jameel Hyder.
Foundation type: Independent foundation.
Financial data (yr. ended 12/31/05): Assets, $1,417,681 (M); gifts received, $430,000; expenditures, $424,316; qualifying distributions, $422,900; giving activities include $422,900 for grants.
Purpose and activities: Grants to promote Islamic education and communities.
Fields of interest: Islam.
International interests: Canada; India; Pakistan.
Limitations: Applications not accepted. Giving on a national and international basis.
Application information: Contributes only to pre-selected organizations.
Directors: Ifrah Hyder; Jameel Hyder; Rizwan Hyder.
EIN: 912159711
Selected grants: The following grants were reported in 2003.

$50,000 to Al Rasool Center, Denver, CO.
$25,000 to Faiz-e-Aam Trust, Karachi, Pakistan. .
$25,000 to Zehra Girls Home, India. .
$5,000 to Islamic Education Center of Seattle, Mountlake Terrace, WA.

9613
Islands Fund ◇
c/o John Munn
6523 California Ave., S.W., Ste. 137
Seattle, WA 98136-1833
Contact: Sarah R. Werner, Dir.

Established in 1995.
Foundation type: Independent foundation.
Financial data (yr. ended 12/31/05): Assets, $108,219,325 (M); expenditures, $5,746,175; qualifying distributions, $5,350,000; giving activities include $5,350,000 for 62 grants (high: $800,000; low: $2,500; average: $10,000–$100,000).
Purpose and activities: Giving primarily for conservation and the environment.
Fields of interest: Education; Environment, natural resources; Children/youth, services.
Limitations: Applications not accepted. No grants to individuals.
Application information: Contributes only to pre-selected organizations.
Directors: E. Leeds Gulick; George G. Gulick; Rick S. Werner; Sarah R. Werner.
EIN: 911663838
Selected grants: The following grants were reported in 2004.

$1,450,000 to Future Generations, Franklin, WV. 2 grants: $450,000, $1,000,000

$1,230,000 to Aloha Foundation, Fairlee, VT. 3 grants: $320,000, $310,000, $600,000

$645,000 to Ecotrust, Portland, OR. 2 grants: $45,000, $600,000

$300,000 to Overlake School, Redmond, WA.

$65,000 to Open Window School, Bellevue, WA.

$10,000 to Odea High School, Seattle, WA.

9614
The Jones Family Foundation, Inc. ☆
c/o Betty Corbett
P.O. Box 2019
Eastsound, WA 98245-2019

Established in 1993 in GA.
Donor: Peggy Dutton Jones†.
Foundation type: Independent foundation.
Financial data (yr. ended 12/31/04): Assets, $473,474 (M); gifts received, $800; expenditures, $943,865; qualifying distributions, $925,703; giving activities include $925,703 for grants.
Fields of interest: Foundations (private grantmaking).
Limitations: Applications not accepted. Giving primarily in Dalton, GA. No grants to individuals.
Application information: Contributes only to pre-selected organizations. Unsolicited requests for funds not accepted.
Officers: Betty Bardsley Corbett, Chair.; Rick Anda, Treas.
EIN: 582023255

9615
The Herbert B. Jones Foundation ✧
c/o EverTrust Asset Mgmt.
505 5th Ave. S., Ste. 170
Seattle, WA 98104
Contact: Michael P. Bauer, Tr.
URL: http://www.hbjfoundation.com

Established in 1989 in WA.
Donor: Herbert B. Jones.
Foundation type: Independent foundation.
Financial data (yr. ended 8/31/05): Assets, $11,468,539 (M); expenditures, $551,809; qualifying distributions, $535,155; giving activities include $474,689 for 12 grants (high: $97,087; low: $7,820; average: $20,000–$50,000).
Purpose and activities: The foundation promotes small-business entrepreneurism through programs managed by post-secondary educational institutions.
Fields of interest: Higher education; Business school/education; Education.
Limitations: Giving primarily in Seattle, WA. No grants to individuals, or for equipment, capital projects, gifts, endowments or food costs.
Application information: Application guidelines available on foundation Web site. Application form required.
   Copies of proposal: 7
   Deadline(s): Apr. 1
   Final notification: Within 8 weeks
Trustees: Michael P. Bauer; Tom Crha; Bill Erwert; Judy Klinkham; Gary Kuhar; Nancy Lemke; Terry Smith; Janet Woods.
EIN: 943124801
Selected grants: The following grants were reported in 2004.

$93,636 to Seattle Pacific University, Seattle, WA. For entrepreneurship and mentor programs.

$57,851 to Northwest School for Hearing-Impaired Children, Seattle, WA. For endowment.

$46,563 to Eastern Washington University, Cheney, WA. For resource center.

$45,019 to Whitworth College, Spokane, WA. For Center for Entrepreneurship.

$43,300 to University of Washington, Seattle, WA. For speaker series.

$37,282 to Seattle University, Seattle, WA. For Entrepreneur 2001.

$37,000 to Gonzaga University, Spokane, WA. For coordinator.

$30,998 to Washington State University, Pullman, WA. For international entrepreneurship.

$30,000 to Green River Community College, Auburn, WA. For small business assistance center.

$19,900 to Heritage University, Toppenish, WA. For internships.

9616
Kaleidoscope Foundation ✧
c/o Richard Leeds
227 Bellevue Way N.E., Ste. 543
Bellevue, WA 98004

Established in 1997 in WA.
Donors: Gerard Leeds; Liselotte Leeds; Richard Leeds.
Foundation type: Independent foundation.
Financial data (yr. ended 11/30/05): Assets, $13,656,944 (M); gifts received, $400,000; expenditures, $3,194,072; qualifying distributions, $3,144,405; giving activities include $3,045,966 for 63 grants (high: $1,100,000; low: $100).
Purpose and activities: Giving for conservation and wildlife, education, children's services, and the arts.
Fields of interest: Museums; Performing arts; Higher education; Education; Environment; Animals/wildlife; Human services; Children/youth, services.
Limitations: Applications not accepted. Giving primarily in WA, with emphasis on Seattle; some funding nationally. No grants to individuals.
Application information: Unsolicited requests for funds not accepted.
Officers: Anne F. Kroeker, Co-Pres.; Richard Leeds, Co-Pres.; Robert H. Blais, Secy.
EIN: 911874926
Selected grants: The following grants were reported in 2005.

$1,100,000 to Cascade Land Conservancy, Seattle, WA.

$550,000 to Nature Conservancy, Cold Spring Harbor, NY.

$102,000 to Ecotrust, Portland, OR.

$100,400 to Museum of Flight, Seattle, WA.

$87,500 to Bellevue Schools Foundation, Bellevue, WA.

$75,000 to Childhaven, Seattle, WA.

$56,000 to Museum of Glass, Tacoma, WA.

$50,000 to Bainbridge Graduate Institute, Bainbridge Island, WA.

$38,000 to Youth Theater Northwest, Mercer Island, WA.

$10,000 to Hopelink, Redmond, WA.

9617
The Forest C. & Ruth V. Kelsey Foundation ✧
P.O. Box 404
Montesano, WA 98563
Contact: Charles Caldwell, Pres.

Established in 1999 in WA.
Donors: Forest Kelsey†; Ruth Kelsey; Eda Esses†.
Foundation type: Independent foundation.
Financial data (yr. ended 12/31/05): Assets, $11,675,612 (M); gifts received, $139,690; expenditures, $964,998; qualifying distributions, $856,465; giving activities include $412,359 for 20 grants (high: $65,000; low: $1,000), and $444,106 for 258 grants to individuals (high: $2,500; low: $1,000; average: $1,500–$2,000).
Purpose and activities: Scholarships awarded to residents of Grays Harbor County or businesses within the county or serving county residents.
Fields of interest: Scholarships/financial aid; Education.
Type of support: Scholarships—to individuals.
Limitations: Giving limited to residents of Grays Harbor County, WA.
Application information: Application form required.
   Deadline(s): July 15, Nov. 15, and Mar. 15 for grants; None for scholarships
Officers: Charles Caldwell, Pres.; Larry James "Jim" Hliboki, V.P.; Linda Caldwell, Secy.; Joann Hliboki, Treas.
Trustees: Loni Crass; Teresa Frafjord.
EIN: 912013369

9618
The Kerry and Linda Killinger Foundation ✧ ☆
The Highlands
Seattle, WA 98177

Established in 2004 in WA.
Donors: Kerry Killinger; Linda Killinger.
Foundation type: Independent foundation.
Financial data (yr. ended 12/31/05): Assets, $3,037,617 (M); gifts received, $105,681; expenditures, $670,090; qualifying distributions, $665,000; giving activities include $665,000 for grants.
Fields of interest: Federated giving programs.
Limitations: Applications not accepted. Giving primarily in Seattle, WA. No grants to individuals.
Application information: Contributes only to pre-selected organizations.
Trustees: Kerry Killinger; Linda Killinger.
EIN: 276018254

9619
Klorfine Foundation ✧
1450 Madrona Dr.
Seattle, WA 98122-3518
Contact: Leonard Klorfine, Tr.
E-mail: lklor@comcast.net

Established in 1993 in PA.
Donors: Leonard Klorfine; Norma E. Klorfine.
Foundation type: Independent foundation.
Financial data (yr. ended 11/30/05): Assets, $17,483,698 (M); gifts received, $1,663,712; expenditures, $799,329; qualifying distributions, $749,515; giving activities include $749,515 for 29 grants (high: $251,500; low: $50).

Purpose and activities: Giving for the arts, medicine, fire prevention, political research, and the environment.

Fields of interest: Arts; Environment; Health care, formal/general education; Disasters, fire prevention/control; Recreation, camps.

Type of support: General/operating support; Continuing support; Annual campaigns; Capital campaigns; Building/renovation; Endowments; Emergency funds.

Limitations: Applications not accepted. Giving primarily in Philadelphia, PA and Seattle, WA. No grants to individuals.

Publications: Annual report.

Application information: Unsolicited requests for funds not accepted.

Board meeting date(s): Monthly

Trustees: Leonard Klorfine; Norma E. Klorfine.

EIN: 227743385

Selected grants: The following grants were reported in 2004.

$200,459 to Main Line Art Center, Haverford, PA. For general support.

$76,400 to Pilchuck Glass School, Seattle, WA. For general support.

$66,400 to Woodmere Art Museum, Philadelphia, PA. For general support.

$65,750 to Philadelphia Museum of Art, Philadelphia, PA. For general support.

$58,000 to Bellevue Art Museum, Bellevue, WA. For general support.

$25,000 to IslandWood, Bainbridge Island, WA. For general support.

$15,000 to Seattle Art Museum, Seattle, WA. For general support.

$3,000 to Heritage Foundation, DC. For general support.

$2,000 to Philadelphia Citizens for Children and Youth, Philadelphia, PA. For general support.

$1,000 to University of Washington Foundation, Seattle, WA. For general support.

9620
Kongsgaard-Goldman Foundation ✧

1932 1st Ave., Ste. 602
Seattle, WA 98101 (206) 448-1874
Contact: Martha Kongsgaard, Pres.
FAX: (206) 448-1973;
E-mail: kgf@kongsgaard-goldman.org; URL: http://www.kongsgaard-goldman.org

Established in 1988 in WA.

Donors: Peter Goldman; Martha Kongsgaard.

Foundation type: Independent foundation.

Financial data (yr. ended 12/31/05): Assets, $86,658 (M); gifts received, $838,191; expenditures, $883,039; qualifying distributions, $879,653; giving activities include $777,249 for grants.

Purpose and activities: Primary areas of interest include the arts (in WA only), human rights and civic developments, the environment, and technical assistance.

Fields of interest: Visual arts; Museums; Performing arts; Performing arts, theater; Performing arts, music; Arts; Child development, education; Adult education—literacy, basic skills & GED; Education; Environment; Reproductive health, family planning; AIDS; Child development, services; Women, centers/services; International peace/security; Civil rights, race/intergroup relations; Civil rights; Community development; Jewish federated giving

programs; Economics; Jewish agencies & temples; Women; LGBTQ; Immigrants/refugees.

International interests: Canada.

Type of support: General/operating support; Continuing support; Annual campaigns; Equipment; Land acquisition; Emergency funds; Program development; Conferences/seminars; Seed money; Technical assistance; Matching/challenge support.

Limitations: Giving limited to AK, ID, MT, OR, and WA, with emphasis on Missoula, MT, Portland, OR, and Seattle, WA; giving also in British Columbia, Canada. No support for institutions of higher learning or medical institutions. No grants to individuals, or for scholarships, fellowships, medical research or general animal welfare; no direct services in the human services sector, or for land acquisition.

Publications: Grants list; Informational brochure (including application guidelines).

Application information: Accepts Philanthropy Northwest Common Grant Application Form; eligible organizations will be invited to send a full proposal; foundation does not accept faxed letters of intent or full proposals; discourages the use of express mail and the use of folders, plastic binders and videos, but encourages the use of express mail and the use of recycled paper, double sided paper and re-used envelopes. Refer to foundation Web site for application guidelines. Application form not required.

Initial approach: Letter of intent
Copies of proposal: 1
Deadline(s): Letter of intent due Mar. 16 and Sept. 16; full proposal Apr. 30 and Oct. 31
Board meeting date(s): Contributions made in Feb. and Aug.
Final notification: Feb. and Aug.

Officers and Directors:* Martha Kongsgaard,* Pres.; Peter Goldman,* V.P.

Number of staff: 1 full-time professional.

EIN: 943088217

9621
Kreielsheimer Remainder Foundation ✧

c/o Foundation Management Group, LLC
1000 2nd Ave., Ste. 3400
Seattle, WA 98104-1022

Established in 2000 in WA.

Donor: Kreielsheimer Foundation.

Foundation type: Independent foundation.

Financial data (yr. ended 12/30/05): Assets, $10,578,402 (M); expenditures, $458,025; qualifying distributions, $382,508; giving activities include $374,383 for 20 grants (high: $51,215; low: $3,977).

Purpose and activities: Support for the arts, with emphasis on fine and performing arts institutions.

Fields of interest: Visual arts; Museums; Performing arts; Performing arts, theater; Performing arts, orchestra (symphony).

Limitations: Applications not accepted. Giving primarily in Seattle, WA. No grants to individuals.

Application information: Contributes only to pre-selected organizations.

Officers: William P. Gerberding, Chair.; Irwin L. Treiger, Pres.; James F. Tune, V.P. and Secy.

Directors: Peter F. Donnelly; Susan B. Trapnell.

EIN: 912064061

Selected grants: The following grants were reported in 2003.

$3,026,470 to Cornish College of the Arts, Seattle, WA.

$49,840 to INTIMAN Theater Company, Seattle, WA.

$49,455 to A Contemporary Theater (ACT), Seattle, WA.

$47,127 to Washington Art Consortium, Bellingham, WA.

$25,311 to Alaska Native Heritage Center, Anchorage, AK.

$20,000 to Book-It Repertory Theater, Seattle, WA.

$17,270 to Empty Space Theater, Seattle, WA.

$17,270 to Northwest Chamber Orchestra, Seattle, WA.

$12,336 to Pilchuck Glass School, Seattle, WA.

$12,336 to Seattle Youth Symphony Orchestras, Seattle, WA.

9622
Jean K. Lafromboise Foundation ✧ ☆

c/o Deyonne Tegman
10510 N.E. Northup Way, Ste. 150
Kirkland, WA 98033

Established in 1988 in WA.

Donor: Jean K. Lafromboise.

Foundation type: Independent foundation.

Financial data (yr. ended 12/31/05): Assets, $8,943,922 (M); gifts received, $5,000; expenditures, $465,849; qualifying distributions, $350,000; giving activities include $350,000 for grants.

Purpose and activities: Giving to West Seattle High School and Roosevelt High School, WA, for their scholarship programs. Giving also for rowing activities.

Fields of interest: Higher education.

Type of support: Scholarship funds.

Limitations: Giving primarily in Seattle, WA. No grants to individuals.

Application information:

Initial approach: Letter
Deadline(s): Mar. 31

Officers: Frank Coyle, Pres.; Deyonne Tegman, V.P. and Secy.; Leo Sheehan, Treas.

EIN: 911416209

Selected grants: The following grants were reported in 2004.

$71,500 to University of Washington, Seattle, WA. 3 grants: $15,000, $25,000, $31,500

$20,000 to Ronald McDonald House Charities of Western Washington, Seattle, WA.

$7,000 to Whitworth College, Spokane, WA.

$5,000 to Bellevue Christian School, Clyde Hill, WA.

$5,000 to Northwest Maritime Center, Port Townsend, WA.

$3,500 to Seattle University, Seattle, WA.

$2,500 to Forgotten Childrens Fund, Seattle, WA.

$2,500 to Pacific Northwest Ballet, Seattle, WA.

9623
Laird Norton Family Fund ✧

801 2nd Ave., Ste. 1600
Seattle, WA 98104
Contact: Kathryn Sullivan, Treas.

Established in 1963 in MN.

Donors: Laird Norton Trust Co.; Patrick S. de Freitas; Douglas Gardner; Jill Gardner; The Quiet Harbor Trust; Carl Helmholz; Elizabeth Helmholz; Laird Norton Co. LLC; Lanoga Corp.

Foundation type: Company-sponsored foundation.

Financial data (yr. ended 12/31/04): Assets, $341,619 (M); gifts received, $637,176;

expenditures, $726,531; qualifying distributions, $723,483; giving activities include $718,568 for 314 grants (high: $67,000; low: $9).
Purpose and activities: The fund supports food banks and organizations involved with arts and culture, education, health, housing, and children and youth.
Fields of interest: Performing arts, theater; Arts; Higher education; Education; Health care; Food banks; Housing/shelter; Children/youth, services.
Type of support: General/operating support; Continuing support; Capital campaigns.
Limitations: Applications not accepted. Giving on a national basis. No grants to individuals.
Publications: Annual report.
Application information: Contributes only to pre-selected organizations.
Officers and Director:* Bruce Reed,* Pres.; Mary Alice Parks, V.P.; Dawn Teufel, Secy.; Kathryn Sullivan, Treas.
EIN: 916048373

9624
The Larson Family Charitable Foundation ◇ ☆
14224 168th Ave. N.E.
Woodinville, WA 98072

Established in 1997 in WA.
Donors: Dale Larson; Phyllis Larson.
Foundation type: Independent foundation.
Financial data (yr. ended 12/31/05): Assets, $1,834,341 (M); expenditures, $442,094; qualifying distributions, $438,095; giving activities include $438,095 for 55 grants (high: $184,360; low: $24).
Purpose and activities: Giving primarily to Christian agencies and churches and to health associations.
Fields of interest: Health organizations, association; Human services; Christian agencies & churches.
Limitations: Applications not accepted. Giving primarily in WA. No grants to individuals.
Application information: Contributes only to pre-selected organizations.
Officers: Dale Larson, Pres.; Phyllis Larson, Secy.
EIN: 911875867
Selected grants: The following grants were reported in 2005.
$60,000 to Shared Hope International, Vancouver, WA.
$5,600 to Prisoners for Christ Outreach Ministries, Kirkland, WA.
$4,800 to New Horizons Ministries, Seattle, WA.
$3,300 to World Concern, Seattle, WA.
$2,200 to Bridges for Peace, Tulsa, OK.
$600 to Salvation Army, WA.
$285 to Vine, The, Seattle, WA.
$100 to Focus on the Family, Colorado Springs, CO.
$100 to Harvest Bible Chapel, Rolling Meadows, IL.
$65 to Campus Crusade for Christ, Miami, FL.

9625
The Laurel Foundation
911 N. 145th St.
Seattle, WA 98133
Contact: Catherine Smits, Fdn. Admin.

Established in 1995 in WA.
Donor: Julia Larson Calhoun.
Foundation type: Independent foundation.

Financial data (yr. ended 12/31/04): Assets, $7,687,369 (M); gifts received, $7,578,200; expenditures, $577,085; qualifying distributions, $574,751; giving activities include $568,800 for 37 grants (high: $140,000; low: $1,000), and $1,225 for 6 employee matching gifts.
Purpose and activities: Giving primarily to children and human services.
Fields of interest: Youth development; Human services; Family services.
Type of support: General/operating support; Continuing support; Capital campaigns; Program development.
Limitations: Applications not accepted. Giving primarily in King County, WA. No grants to individuals.
Application information: Contributes only to pre-selected organizations.
Board meeting date(s): Quarterly
Officers: Julia Larson Calhoun, Pres.; Christopher Larson, V.P.; Larry Bailey, Secy.; Catherine Smits, Fdn. Admin.
EIN: 911689238

9626
Paul Lauzier Charitable Foundation ◇
117 Basin St. N.W.
P.O. Box 1230
Ephrata, WA 98823-1230 (509) 754-3209
Contact: Michael Rex Tabler, Tr.
FAX: (509) 754-8481; *E-mail:* info@lauzier.org;
URL: http://www.lauzier.org/foundation/index.htm

Established in 1997 in WA.
Foundation type: Independent foundation.
Financial data (yr. ended 12/31/05): Assets, $10,881,348 (M); expenditures, $750,091; qualifying distributions, $522,427; giving activities include $434,100 for 22 grants (high: $130,000; low: $1,000), and $18,000 for 1 employee matching gift.
Purpose and activities: Giving primarily for higher and other education, as well as for health care and hospitals, including a children's hospital, food services, children, youth and social services, as well as to services and centers for senior citizens; funding also for Christian and Roman Catholic churches.
Fields of interest: Education, early childhood education; Higher education; Education; Hospitals (general); Health care; Health organizations; Agriculture; Food services; Human services; Children/youth, services; Aging, centers/services; Community development, neighborhood development; Christian agencies & churches; Roman Catholic agencies & churches.
Limitations: Giving primarily in WA, with emphasis on Ephrata, Moses Lake, and Pullman.
Application information: Application information available on foundation Web site. Application form not required.
Initial approach: 1-page proposal
Deadline(s): Before Mar. 1
Trustee: Michael Rex Tabler.
EIN: 911701539

9627
Paul Lauzier Scholarship Foundation ◇
P.O. Box 1230
Ephrata, WA 98823-1230
Contact: Michael Rex Tabler, Tr.

Established in 1997.
Foundation type: Independent foundation.
Financial data (yr. ended 12/31/05): Assets, $10,881,348 (M); expenditures, $706,824; qualifying distributions, $491,062; giving activities include $408,833 for 200 grants to individuals.
Purpose and activities: Awards scholarships to graduates from Grant County, WA high schools who have resided in the county for not less than 2 years prior to graduation, to further their education at institutions in Washington.
Fields of interest: Higher education.
Type of support: Scholarships—to individuals.
Limitations: Giving limited to Grant County, WA. No grants to individuals directly.
Application information: Applicants can obtain an application through the Grant County high school that they are attending or from which they have graduated. Application form required.
Initial approach: Completed application submitted to high school
Deadline(s): Before Mar. 1
Trustee: Michael Rex Tabler.
EIN: 911701545

9628
The Lematta Foundation ◇
201 N.E. Park Plz. Dr., Ste. 244
Vancouver, WA 98684 (360) 750-6884
Contact: Nancy Lematta, Secy.-Treas.

Established in 1998 in WA.
Donors: Wes Lematta; Nancy Lematta.
Foundation type: Independent foundation.
Financial data (yr. ended 12/31/05): Assets, $1,410,132 (M); gifts received, $2,133,218; expenditures, $1,509,115; qualifying distributions, $1,492,535; giving activities include $1,492,535 for 29 grants (high: $500,035; low: $2,000).
Purpose and activities: Giving primarily for education and health associations, including a children's hospital foundation; funding also for family and social services, and aeronautic museums.
Fields of interest: Museums (specialized); Higher education; Hospitals (specialty); Health care; Health organizations, association; Human services; Family services; Federated giving programs.
Limitations: Giving primarily in Portland, OR and WA.
Application information: Application form not required.
Initial approach: Letter
Deadline(s): None
Officers and Directors:* Wes Lematta,* Pres.; Nancy Lematta,* Secy.-Treas.; Greg Damico; Bart Lematta; Betsy Lematta; Marci Ann Lematta-Abel.
EIN: 911914392
Selected grants: The following grants were reported in 2004.
$100,000 to Meridian Park Medical Foundation, Tualatin, OR.
$50,000 to Doernbecher Childrens Hospital Foundation, Portland, OR.
$25,000 to Arthur Academy, Portland, OR.
$25,000 to Pearson Air Museum, Vancouver, WA.
$25,000 to United Way of the Columbia-Willamette, Portland, OR.
$25,000 to Vancouver School District Foundation, Vancouver, WA.
$10,104 to YMCA of Clark County, Vancouver, WA.
$10,000 to Oregon Museum of Science and Industry, Portland, OR.
$10,000 to Portland Art Museum, Portland, OR.

$10,000 to Providence Child Center, Portland, OR.

9629

The Gunnar and Ruth Lie Foundation ◊ ☆
9309 Olympic View Dr.
Edmonds, WA 98020-2397

Established in 2000 in WA.
Donors: Gunnar Lie; Ruth Lie.
Foundation type: Independent foundation.
Financial data (yr. ended 12/31/05): Assets,
$4,661,798 (M); expenditures, $432,881;
qualifying distributions, $416,000; giving activities
include $416,000 for grants.
Fields of interest: Human services; Children/youth,
services; Christian agencies & churches.
Limitations: Applications not accepted. Giving
primarily in FL and WA. No grants to individuals.
Application information: Contributes only to
pre-selected organizations.
Directors: Elizabeth Lie; Gunnar Lie; Kirsten Lie;
Ruth Lie.
EIN: 912090480
Selected grants: The following grants were reported
in 2004.
$104,500 to City Church, Kirkland, WA.
$25,000 to Christian Outreach International, Vero
Beach, FL.
$10,000 to Keolahou Congregational Hawaiian
Church, Kihei, HI.
$1,000 to Everett Gospel Mission, Everett, WA.
$1,000 to Youth for Christ, Tacoma, WA.

9630

The Lochland Foundation ◊
90 Cascade Key
Bellevue, WA 98006

Established in 2002 in WA.
Donor: Exotic Metals Forming Co., LLC.
Foundation type: Independent foundation.
Financial data (yr. ended 12/31/05): Assets,
$5,337,541 (M); expenditures, $377,237;
qualifying distributions, $375,825; giving activities
include $372,900 for 8 grants (high: $144,000;
low: $5,000; average: $10,000–$50,000).
Fields of interest: Education; Human services; YM/
YWCAs & YM/YWHAs.
Limitations: Applications not accepted. Giving
primarily in WA.
Application information: Unsolicited requests for
funds not accepted.
Officers: Phyllis Lindsey, Pres.; Mark Lindsey, V.P.;
Katherine Binder, Secy.-Treas.
EIN: 510420961

9631

**Byron W. and Alice L. Lockwood
Foundation**
P.O. Box 4
Mercer Island, WA 98040
Contact: Lee Kraft, Exec. Dir.

Established in 1968 in WA.
Foundation type: Independent foundation.
Financial data (yr. ended 12/31/04): Assets,
$22,657,905 (M); expenditures, $1,037,696;
qualifying distributions, $840,139; giving activities
include $684,300 for 50 grants (high: $61,500;
low: $100).

Purpose and activities: Giving primarily for
education, health care, and human services in King
County, WA.
Fields of interest: Higher education; Education;
Hospitals (general); Health organizations,
association; Medical research, institute; Housing/
shelter; Human services.
Type of support: General/operating support;
Continuing support; Equipment; Emergency funds;
Professorships; Scholarship funds; Research.
Limitations: Giving limited to King County, WA. No
support for religious organizations. No grants to
individuals.
Application information: E-mail for application
guidelines at: lockwoodfdn@earthlink.net. Only
requests for application guidelines will be accepted
at this E-mail address. Application form required.
Initial approach: Letter or proposal
Copies of proposal: 1
Deadline(s): Oct. 31
Board meeting date(s): Dec.
Final notification: Dec. 31 to Jan. 31
Officers and Trustee:* Paul R. Cressman, Sr.,*
Pres.; Paul R. Cressman, Jr., V.P.; Lee Kraft,
Secy.-Treas. and Exec. Dir.
Number of staff: 1 part-time professional.
EIN: 910833426
Selected grants: The following grants were reported
in 2003.
$56,000 to Museum of Flight, Seattle, WA.
$55,000 to University of Washington, Seattle, WA.
$51,000 to Bellevue Community College, Bellevue,
WA.
$30,000 to Puget Sound Blood Center, Seattle, WA.
$10,000 to Millionair Club, Seattle, WA.
$10,000 to Northwest Burn Foundation, Seattle,
WA.
$10,000 to Overlake Hospital Foundation, Bellevue,
WA.
$10,000 to Swedish Medical Center Foundation,
Seattle, WA.
$5,000 to Camp Brotherhood, Bellevue, WA.
$5,000 to Childhaven, Seattle, WA.

9632

The Lucky Seven Foundation
2366 Eastlake Ave. E., Ste. 312
Seattle, WA 98102-3399
Contact: John T. Backus, Pres.
URL: https://online.foundationsource.com/public/
home/luckyseven

Established in 1996 in WA.
Donors: Frances A. Backus†; Manson Backus†.
Foundation type: Independent foundation.
Financial data (yr. ended 4/30/05): Assets,
$17,196,788 (M); gifts received, $1,777,287;
expenditures, $890,907; qualifying distributions,
$842,559; giving activities include $842,559 for 72
grants (high: $75,000; low: $1,100).
Purpose and activities: Giving primarily for
education, children, family and social services.
Fields of interest: Higher education; Education;
Human services; Children/youth, services; Family
services.
Type of support: Seed money; Program-related
investments/loans; Program evaluation; Program
development; Equipment; Debt reduction;
Curriculum development; Capital campaigns;
Building/renovation; Annual campaigns; General/
operating support.
Limitations: Giving primarily in WA, with emphasis
on the Puget Sound Basin. No grants to individuals.

Application information:
Initial approach: Check foundation Web site
Deadline(s): None
Board meeting date(s): Feb., June, and Sept.
Officers: John T. Backus, Pres.; Edward A. Backus,
V.P.; Susan B. Stoller, Secy.-Treas.
Directors: Carol S. Backus; Valerie F. Backus;
Robert Fisko; Willard Steckel; Philip Stoller.
EIN: 911722000

9633

Elizabeth A. Lynn Foundation
13300 Bothell Everett Hwy.
PMB 6159
Mill Creek, WA 98012-5312 (425) 334-9215
Contact: Diane Titch, Grant Admin.

Established in 1981 in WA.
Donor: Elizabeth A. Lynn†.
Foundation type: Independent foundation.
Financial data (yr. ended 11/30/05): Assets,
$7,023,061 (M); expenditures, $383,771;
qualifying distributions, $329,750; giving activities
include $329,750 for 63 grants (high: $15,000;
low: $4,750).
Fields of interest: Elementary/secondary
education; Health care; Mental health/crisis
services, volunteer services; Substance abuse,
treatment; Mental health, treatment; Medical
research; Employment; Housing/shelter; Youth
development; Human services; Roman Catholic
agencies & churches; Religion.
Type of support: General/operating support; Capital
campaigns; Building/renovation; Equipment;
Program development; Scholarship funds;
Research.
Limitations: Giving primarily in WA, with preference
on the Puget Sound corridor. No grants to
individuals.
Publications: Application guidelines; Financial
statement.
Application information: Application form required.
Initial approach: Letter of inquiry or telephone to
request guidelines
Copies of proposal: 5
Deadline(s): Jan. 15, May 15, and Sept. 15
Board meeting date(s): 3 times annually
Final notification: Mar. 31, July 31, and Nov. 30.
Trustees: Jeff Lynn; Traci Lynn; Jody Moss; Thomas
J. Stephens.
EIN: 911156982
Selected grants: The following grants were reported
in 2005.
$15,000 to Sojourner Place, Seattle, WA.
$5,000 to American Red Cross.
$5,000 to Bailey-Boushay House, Seattle, WA.
$5,000 to Big Brothers/Big Sisters.
$5,000 to Childrens Hospital.
$5,000 to Family and Adult Service Center, Seattle,
WA.
$5,000 to FareStart, Seattle, WA.
$5,000 to Seattle Education Access, Seattle, WA.
$5,000 to Shared Housing Services, Tacoma, WA.
$5,000 to Youth Tutoring Program, Seattle, WA.

9634

Charlotte Y. Martin Foundation Trust
c/o Union Bank of California
P.O. Box 3123
Seattle, WA 98114 (206) 587-3621
Contact: Linda Pancheri

E-mail: info@charlottemartin.org; URL: http://www.charlottemartin.org

Established in 1988 in WA.
Donor: Charlotte Y. Martin†.
Foundation type: Independent foundation.
Financial data (yr. ended 3/31/06): Assets, $23,034,090 (M); expenditures, $1,215,136; qualifying distributions, $1,125,560; giving activities include $994,489 for 83 grants (high: $179,238; low: $500).
Purpose and activities: Support for: 1) education of youth through the establishment of permanent scholarship funds at several pre-selected educational institutions; 2) youth organizations and organizations providing youth-related programs designed to educate and develop young people's cultural awareness and athletic skills beyond the basics of a formal classroom education; and 3) organizations and agencies dedicated to the preservation, protection, and perpetuation of fish and wildlife and/or their habitats.
Fields of interest: Visual arts; Performing arts; Elementary/secondary education; Higher education; Environment, natural resources; Animals/wildlife, fisheries; Animals/wildlife, sanctuaries; Athletics/sports, school programs; Children/youth.
Type of support: General/operating support; Continuing support; Building/renovation; Equipment; Land acquisition; Program development; Seed money; Curriculum development; Matching/challenge support.
Limitations: Giving primarily in the Pacific Northwest. No support for private foundations or for social services. No grants to individuals, or for multi-year grants.
Publications: Application guidelines; Annual report; Grants list; Program policy statement.
Application information: Application form and information available on Web site. Applications only accepted via foundation Web site. No mailed in applications are accepted. Application form required.
  Initial approach: All applications accepted by Web site only. No applications or letter of intent accepted by mail
  Deadline(s): None
  Board meeting date(s): Quarterly
  Final notification: 1-6 months
Board Members: Tom Campbell; Joan Gagliardi; Peter Galloway; Sheila Kelly; Bonnie Sachatello-Sawyer.
Trustee: Union Bank of California, N.A.
Number of staff: 1 part-time professional.
EIN: 916294504

9635
Edmund F. Maxwell Foundation ◇
P.O. Box 22537
Seattle, WA 98122-0537
Contact: Jane Thomas, Admin.
E-mail: admin@maxwell.org; URL: http://www.maxwell.org

Established in 1992 in WA.
Foundation type: Independent foundation.
Financial data (yr. ended 12/31/05): Assets, $9,887,975 (M); expenditures, $469,222; qualifying distributions, $401,432; giving activities include $346,675 for 102 grants to individuals (high: $3,500; low: $527).
Purpose and activities: Scholarships for residents of western Washington attending accredited

independent colleges or universities. Grants are dependent on financial need, as determined by the college or university attended.
Type of support: Scholarships—to individuals.
Limitations: Giving limited to students residing in western WA attending accredited private colleges and universities. No grants to individuals directly.
Publications: Informational brochure (including application guidelines).
Application information: Application forms available on Web site. Scholarship funds will be paid to the educational institution which the student will be attending. Application form required.
  Initial approach: Letter, e-mail requesting application form, or see Web site
  Deadline(s): Apr. 30
  Board meeting date(s): Varies
  Final notification: June
Officer: Jane Thomas, Admin.
Trustees: David G. Johansen; David D. Lewis; Alan T. Robertson.
Number of staff: 2 part-time professional.
EIN: 916181008

9636
Keith & Mary Kay McCaw Family Foundation ◇ ☆
201 Terry Ave. N., Ste. A
Seattle, WA 98109

Established in 1995 in WA.
Donors: Keith McCaw; Mary Kay McCaw.
Foundation type: Independent foundation.
Financial data (yr. ended 12/31/05): Assets, $21,244,620 (M); gifts received, $9,000,000; expenditures, $700,213; qualifying distributions, $565,932; giving activities include $562,749 for 13 grants (high: $330,649; low: $100).
Fields of interest: Performing arts; Federated giving programs.
Limitations: Applications not accepted. Giving primarily in Seattle, WA. No grants to individuals.
Application information: Contributes only to pre-selected organizations.
  Board meeting date(s): 1st Tues. in Nov.
Officers and Directors:* Mary Kay McCaw,* Pres.; Debra Tawney Stroh,* V.P.; Joseph D. Weinstein, Secy.; Steven M. Setser, Treas.
EIN: 911920617
Selected grants: The following grants were reported in 2004.
$411,752 to United Way.
$335,562 to Epiphany School, Seattle, WA.
$200,000 to Museum of Flight, Seattle, WA.
$76,383 to Alliance for Education, Seattle, WA.
$500 to Rice University, Houston, TX.
$200 to Treehouse Fund, Seattle, WA.
$150 to Lazarus Day Center, Seattle, WA.
$100 to American Heart Association, Seattle, WA.
$100 to Catholic Community Services, Tacoma, WA.

9637
The Craig and Susan McCaw Foundation ▼ ◇
P.O. Box 2908
Kirkland, WA 98083-2908

Established in 1998 in WA.
Donor: Craig O. McCaw.
Foundation type: Independent foundation.

Financial data (yr. ended 12/31/04): Assets, $45,104,112 (M); gifts received, $38,382,500; expenditures, $6,294,641; qualifying distributions, $6,042,967; giving activities include $6,035,783 for 14 grants (high: $5,000,012; low: $1,500).
Purpose and activities: Giving primarily for community development and community organizations.
Fields of interest: Higher education; Health care; Community development.
Limitations: Applications not accepted. Giving primarily in Seattle, WA. No grants to individuals.
Application information: Contributes only to pre-selected organizations.
Officers and Directors:* Craig O. McCaw,* Pres.; Susan R. McCaw,* Secy.
EIN: 911943269
Selected grants: The following grants were reported in 2004.
$5,000,012 to Stanford University, Stanford, CA. For general operating support.
$733,750 to Seattle Foundation, Seattle, WA. For general operating support.
$250,000 to Alliance for Education, Seattle, WA. For general operating support.
$10,500 to University of Washington, Seattle, WA. For Team Read scholarship.
$2,500 to Pacific University, Forest Grove, OR. For Team Read scholarship.
$1,500 to Arizona State University, Tempe, AZ. For Team Read scholarship.
$1,500 to Lake Washington College Foundation, Kirkland, WA. For Team Read scholarship.
$1,500 to Multnomah Bible College and Seminary, Portland, OR. For Team Read scholarship.
$1,500 to New School, New York, NY. For Team Read scholarship.
$1,500 to Seattle University, Seattle, WA. For Team Read scholarship.

9638
D. V. & Ida McEachern Charitable Trust ◇
(formerly Ida J. McEachern Charitable Trust)
c/o Union Bank of California, N.A.
P.O. Box 3123
Seattle, WA 98114 (206) 781-3472
Contact: Therese Ogle, Grants Consultant
E-mail: OgleFounds@aol.com; URL: http://foundationcenter.org/grantmaker/mceachern/

Trust established in 1966 in WA.
Donors: Ida J. McEachern†; D.V. McEachern†.
Foundation type: Independent foundation.
Financial data (yr. ended 8/31/05): Assets, $18,544,582 (M); expenditures, $853,831; qualifying distributions, $760,571; giving activities include $708,000 for 87 grants (high: $75,000; low: $500).
Purpose and activities: Giving exclusively for capital funding of youth agencies serving children under the age of 18, where the purpose is to give a better start in life, both physically and mentally, to all children. Prefers organizations in existence at least five years and whose operational funding comes generally from a non-tax-based source.
Fields of interest: Performing arts; Education; Health organizations, association; Recreation; Children/youth, services.
Type of support: Capital campaigns; Building/renovation; Equipment.
Limitations: Giving limited to the Puget Sound area of WA, particularly King, Pierce, and Snohomish counties. Generally no support for organizations

established less than five years (absent indications of community leadership and reputation, offering unique enrichment programs for children), or for religious institutions. No grants to individuals, or for endowment funds, scholarships, fellowships, operating budgets, continuing support, annual campaigns, seed money, deficit financing, publications, conferences, research programs, or matching gifts; no loans.

Publications: Application guidelines.
Application information: See foundation Web site for full application guidelines. Application form not required.
 Initial approach: Proposal (narrative not to exceed 4 pages)
 Copies of proposal: 1
 Deadline(s): Mar. 8, Sept. 8, and Dec. 8
 Board meeting date(s): Usually in May and Oct.
Trustee: Union Bank of California, N.A.
EIN: 916063710
Selected grants: The following grants were reported in 2004.

$60,000 to Delridge Neighborhoods Development Association, Seattle, WA. For capital campaign to create a community arts center, low-income housing, and a community center.

$40,000 to Camp Fire USA, Central Puget Sound Council, Seattle, WA. For capital campaign, Spark the Future.

$30,000 to Boys and Girls Clubs of King County, Seattle, WA. For capital campaign for Youth Development Center for teens in Federal Way.

$25,000 to Wing Luke Asian Museum, Seattle, WA. For capital campaign for new museum in historic building in International District.

$20,000 to FareStart, Seattle, WA. For Futures Rising capital campaign.

$20,000 to Springboard Alliance, Redmond, WA. For capital campaign.

$15,000 to Center for Wooden Boats, Seattle, WA. To purchase a cedar longboat for youth programs.

$15,000 to Highline Community Hospital Foundation, Tukwila, WA. For children's area of new cancer center.

$10,000 to Encompass Northwest, North Bend, WA. For exterior and interior re-painting.

$7,000 to Providence General Foundation, Everett, WA. For Universal Newborn Hearing Screening equipment.

9639
The Robert B. McMillen Foundation ◇
1495 N.W. Gilman Blvd., Rm. 4J
Issaquah, WA 98027 (509) 668-0366
Contact: Erin McMillen, Secy.
FAX: (509) 888-0180;
E-mail: erin@mcmillenfoundation.org; URL: http://www.mcmillenfoundation.org

Established in 2004 in WA.
Donor: Robert B. McMillen†.
Foundation type: Independent foundation.
Financial data (yr. ended 12/31/05): Assets, $12,462,252 (M); expenditures, $854,580; qualifying distributions, $771,028; giving activities include $562,208 for 20 grants (high: $323,100; low: $5,000).
Purpose and activities: The foundation is dedicated to providing funding for medical research in the areas of lipid, organ transplant and cardiology; supporting education at the university and college

level in states of Washington and Alaska, and providing funding for social service organizations.
Fields of interest: Medical school/education; Health organizations, research; Heart & circulatory diseases; Human services.
Type of support: Scholarships—to individuals; Scholarship funds.
Limitations: Giving primarily in AK and WA.
Application information: See Web site for scholarship guidelines and deadline information. Application form required.
 Initial approach: Check Web site
Officers and Directors:* Mike McMillen,* Pres.; Sue Walker,* V.P.; Erin McMillen, Secy.; Marilyn Delucia.
EIN: 200011616

9640
Medina Foundation ▼
1300 Northon Bldg.
801 2nd Ave., Ste. 1300
Seattle, WA 98104 (206) 652-8783
Contact: Patricia G. McKay, Exec. Dir.
FAX: (206) 652-8791;
E-mail: info@medinafoundation.org; Additional tel.: (206) 652-8783; URL: http://www.medinafoundation.org

Incorporated in 1947 in WA.
Foundation type: Independent foundation.
Financial data (yr. ended 12/31/05): Assets, $93,327,838 (M); expenditures, $4,851,520; qualifying distributions, $4,362,777; giving activities include $3,906,035 for 155 grants (high: $100,000; low: $3,000; average: $10,000–$50,000).
Purpose and activities: The foundation is a family foundation that works to foster positive change in the greater Puget Sound area. In honoring the vision of its founder, Norton Clapp, the foundation strikes to improve the human condition of supporting organizations that provide critical services to those in need.
Fields of interest: Education; Mental health/crisis services; Human services; Children/youth, services; Community development; Disabilities, people with; Economically disadvantaged.
Type of support: Matching/challenge support; Income development; General/operating support; Capital campaigns; Building/renovation; Equipment; Emergency funds; Seed money; Technical assistance; Program evaluation.
Limitations: Giving limited to the greater Puget Sound, WA, area, with emphasis on the counties of Clallam, Grays Harbor, Island, Jefferson, King, Kitsap, Mason, Pacific, Pierce, San Juan, Skagit, Snohomish Thurston, and Whatcom. No support for public institutions. No grants to individuals, or for endowment funds, research, or scholarships.
Publications: Application guidelines; Grants list.
Application information: The foundation will provide a grant application via E-mail to selected organizations upon review of initial letter. If your organization received funding from the foundation within the last year, please wait at least twelve months from receipt of last grant before submitting another letter of inquiry. Application form required.
 Initial approach: Letter (1-2 pages)
 Copies of proposal: 1
 Deadline(s): None
 Board meeting date(s): Monthly
 Final notification: 30 to 60 days

Officers and Trustees:* Gail Gant,* Pres.; Elizabeth Williams,* V.P.; Patricia Henry, Secy.; Gary MacLeod,* Treas.; Patricia G. McKay, Exec. Dir.; James N. Clapp II; Margaret Clapp; Matthew N. Clapp, Jr.; Paula Clapp; Tamsin Clapp; Jean Gardner; Marion Hand; Piper Henry-Keller.
Number of staff: 3 full-time professional; 1 full-time support.
EIN: 910745225
Selected grants: The following grants were reported in 2004.

$100,000 to Treehouse Fund, Seattle, WA. For program support for Tutoring Program and Fostering Futures Campaign.

$82,500 to Plymouth Housing Group, Seattle, WA. For general operating support.

$60,000 to First Place, Seattle, WA. For program support for Library and Information Systems Initiative.

$50,000 to Abused Deaf Womens Advocacy Services, Seattle, WA. For A Place of Our Own Capital Campaign.

$50,000 to Powerful Schools, Seattle, WA. For general operating support.

$25,000 to Saint Martin de Porres Shelter, Seattle, WA. For general operating support.

$22,000 to Olympia Child Care Center, Olympia, WA. For capital funds to expand Westside Center.

$20,000 to Big Brothers Big Sisters of King and Pierce Counties, Seattle, WA. For program support school-based mentoring program.

$20,000 to Rainier Scholars, Seattle, WA. For general operating support.

$15,000 to Boys and Girls Club of Whatcom, Bellingham, WA. For clubs in Lummi Island, Lynden and Blaine.

9641
Gary E. Milgard Family Foundation ▼
(formerly Gary & Carol Milgard Family Foundation)
1701 Commerce St.
Tacoma, WA 98402 (253) 274-0121
Contact: Christine Zemanek, V.P.
FAX: (253) 274-0478; URL: http://www.garymilgardfamilyfoundation.org

Established in 2000 in WA.
Foundation type: Independent foundation.
Financial data (yr. ended 12/31/05): Assets, $95,144,078 (M); expenditures, $4,447,093; qualifying distributions, $3,903,921; giving activities include $3,741,858 for 61 grants (high: $1,000,000; low: $2,000; average: $10,000–$200,000).
Purpose and activities: The goal of the foundation is to support the work of a wide variety of organizations that serve our community. The foundation believes this is a way for the family to give back and continue to educate their descendants in the value of community service.
Fields of interest: Education; Health care; Human services; Children/youth, services.
Type of support: Matching/challenge support; Scholarship funds; Program development; Equipment; Endowments; Capital campaigns; Building/renovation; Annual campaigns; General/operating support.
Limitations: Giving primarily in Pierce County and the greater Puget Sound, WA, area. No support for political organizations or religious organizations where funds would be used to further a religious purpose. No grants for deficit reduction.
Publications: Grants list.

Application information: See foundation's Web site for more details. Application form is available on foundation's Web site. Application form required.
Initial approach: Application
Copies of proposal: 1
Deadline(s): Mar. 1, June 1, Sept. 1, and Dec. 1
Board meeting date(s): Jan., Apr., July, and Oct.
Final notification: 60 days
Officers and Directors:* Carol B. Milgard,* Pres.; Christine Zemanek, V.P. and Exec. Dir.; Cari Milgard-De Goede,* V.P.; Lori Migord-Rivera,* V.P.; Mark Milgard,* V.P.
EIN: 912074073
Selected grants: The following grants were reported in 2004.
$1,100,000 to Boys and Girls Clubs of South Puget Sound, Tacoma, WA. 2 grants: $1,000,000 (For Lakewood Project directed costs and Tacoma regional programs), $100,000 (For Campaign for Kids).
$1,000,000 to University of Washington, Tacoma, WA. For Milgard School of Business.
$250,000 to Good Samaritan Foundation, Puyallup, WA. To develop cancer resource center.
$200,000 to Charles Wright Academy, Lower School, Tacoma, WA.
$200,000 to Horatio Alger Association of Distinguished Americans, Alexandria, VA. For awards activities.
$150,000 to Girl Scouts of the U.S.A., Pacific Peaks Council, Tumwater, WA. For capital campaign.
$100,000 to Pierce College Foundation, Tacoma, WA. For child care center.
$20,000 to Metropolitan Development Council, Tacoma, WA. To equip low-income Lakewood fathers with resources.
$20,000 to R. Merle Palmer Minority Scholarship Foundation, Fircrest, WA. For scholarships.

9642
Pendleton and Elisabeth Carey Miller Charitable Foundation
1910 Fairview Ave. E., Ste. 102
Seattle, WA 98102-3019 (206) 329-1019
Contact: Frank D. Minton, Secy.-Treas.
FAX: (206) 329-8230; E-mail: fminton@pgcalc.com

Established in 1995 in WA.
Donor: Elisabeth Miller‡.
Foundation type: Independent foundation.
Financial data (yr. ended 12/31/05): Assets, $13,466,494 (M); expenditures, $479,769; qualifying distributions, $382,502; giving activities include $357,142 for 11 grants (high: $154,413; low: $1,000).
Purpose and activities: Giving primarily for horticulture, education, and Northwest history.
Fields of interest: Museums; Museums (art); Higher education; Higher education, university; Botanical/ horticulture/landscape services.
Type of support: Continuing support; Equipment; Endowments; Program development; Conferences/ seminars; Publication; Seed money; Internship funds; Research; Technical assistance; Program evaluation; Program-related investments/loans; Matching/challenge support.
Limitations: Giving primarily in WA.
Publications: Application guidelines; Informational brochure (including application guidelines); Occasional report.
Application information: Application form not required.

Initial approach: Letter
Copies of proposal: 1
Deadline(s): None
Board meeting date(s): May and Nov.
Final notification: Apr. 15 and Oct. 15
Officers and Trustees:* Winlock W. Miller,* Pres.; Geoffrey G. Revelle, V.P.; Frank D. Minton,* Secy.-Treas.; Christopher Bailey; Elisabeth A. Bottler; Richard A. Brown; W. Howarth Meadowcroft; Carey K. Miller; Malcolm Moore.
Number of staff: 2 part-time professional.
EIN: 911671814
Selected grants: The following grants were reported in 2003.
$163,032 to University of Washington, Seattle, WA. 2 grants: $106,339, $56,693 to Elisabeth C. Miller Library.
$45,000 to Seattle Parks Foundation, Seattle, WA.
$43,000 to Elisabeth Carey Miller Botanical Garden, Seattle, WA.
$25,000 to Childrens Home Society of Washington, Seattle, WA.
$20,000 to Fort Nisqually Association, Tacoma, WA.
$11,000 to Seattle Garden Club, Seattle, WA.
$10,000 to Rhododendron Species Foundation, Federal Way, WA. For botanical garden.
$10,000 to Woodland Park Zoological Society, Seattle, WA.
$7,500 to Pacific Horticultural Foundation, Oakland, CA.
$6,000 to Pacific Science Center, Seattle, WA.
$2,000 to Phillips Academy, Andover, MA.
$2,000 to Yale University, New Haven, CT.

9643
Moccasin Lake Foundation ◇
1405 42nd Ave. E.
Seattle, WA 98112 (206) 329-8899
E-mail: mlfoundation@moccasinlake.org;
URL: http://www.moccasinlake.org

Established in 1991 in WA.
Donors: James C. Pigott; Gaye T. Pigott; Maureen Pigott; Paul Pigott; Mark Kranwinkle; Sara Kranwinkle; Lisa Anderson; Michael Anderson; Julie Gould; Frederick Beau Gould.
Foundation type: Independent foundation.
Financial data (yr. ended 12/31/04): Assets, $2,229,963 (M); gifts received, $1,515,248; expenditures, $1,545,854; qualifying distributions, $1,517,369; giving activities include $1,514,334 for 89 grants (high: $501,020; low: $100).
Fields of interest: Arts; Education; Environment, natural resources; Animals/wildlife, preservation/ protection; Hospitals (general); Reproductive health, family planning; Cancer; Multiple sclerosis; Human services; Religion.
Limitations: Giving primarily in WA. No grants to individuals.
Application information: Application Guidelines and Concept Paper available on foundation Web site.
Initial approach: Concept paper
Deadline(s): None
Board meeting date(s): Quarterly
Final notification: 6 months
Officers and Directors:* Michael Anderson,* Pres.; Frederick Beau Gould,* Secy.; James C. Pigott,* Treas.; Lisa Anderson; Julie Gould; Mark Kranwinkle; Sara Kranwinkle; Gaye T. Pigott; Maureen "Dina" Pigott; Paul Pigott.
EIN: 911545081
Selected grants: The following grants were reported in 2003.

$63,500 to Canterbury School, New Milford, CT.
$12,000 to Epiphany School, Seattle, WA.
$10,443 to Seattle Girls Middle School, Seattle, WA. For financial aid fund.
$10,099 to Cascades Conservation Partnership, Seattle, WA.
$5,141 to Lakeside School, Seattle, WA. For annual fund.
$5,141 to Northwest School of the Arts, Humanities and Environment, Seattle, WA.
$5,000 to Methow Valley Community School, Winthrop, WA.
$5,000 to Methow Valley Education Foundation, Twisp, WA.
$5,000 to Powerful Schools, Seattle, WA.
$4,000 to Childhaven, Seattle, WA.

9644
M. J. Murdock Charitable Trust ▼
703 Broadway, Ste. 710
Vancouver, WA 98660 (360) 694-8415
Contact: John B. Van Zytveld Ph.D, Sr. Prog. Dir.
FAX: (360) 694-1819; Mailing address: P.O. Box 1618, Vancouver, WA 98668; URL: http:// www.murdock-trust.org

Trust established in 1975 in WA.
Donor: Melvin Jack Murdock‡.
Foundation type: Independent foundation.
Financial data (yr. ended 12/31/05): Assets, $758,617,116 (M); expenditures, $46,561,341; qualifying distributions, $29,707,690; giving activities include $25,977,150 for 293 grants (high: $1,250,000; low: $3,300); $199,533 for 170 employee matching gifts, and $530,000 for foundation-administered programs.
Purpose and activities: To strengthen and enrich the educational and cultural environment of the Pacific Northwest by providing grants to organizations that seek the same with creative and sustainable approaches. Emphasis is placed on higher education and scientific research.
Fields of interest: Museums; Arts; Higher education; Education; Human services; Family services; Science, research; Physical/earth sciences; Science.
Type of support: Building/renovation; Equipment; Program development; Seed money; Research; Employee matching gifts; Matching/challenge support.
Limitations: Giving primarily in the Pacific Northwest (AK, ID, MT, OR, and WA). No support for government programs; projects common to many organizations without distinguishing merit; sectarian or religious organizations whose principal activities are for the benefit of their own members; no organizations which in policy or practice unfairly discriminate against race, ethnic origin, sex, creed, or religion. No grants to individuals, or for deficit financing, debt retirement, political activities, generally no grants for annual campaigns, general support, continuing support, endowments, or emergency funds; no loans.
Publications: Application guidelines; Annual report (including application guidelines); Grants list; Informational brochure (including application guidelines).
Application information: Application form required.
Initial approach: Letter of inquiry (no longer than 2 pages)
Copies of proposal: 8
Deadline(s): None

Board meeting date(s): Quarterly
Final notification: 6 to 9 months
Officers and Trustees: * Julie D. Cieloha, C.F.O.; James R. Martin, C.I.O.; Steven G. W. Moore, Exec. Dir.; John W. Castles; Lynwood W. Swanson, Ph.D.; Neal O. Thorpe, Ph.D.
Number of staff: 9 full-time professional; 1 part-time professional; 8 full-time support.
EIN: 237456468
Selected grants: The following grants were reported in 2005.
$650,000 to Confluences, Vancouver, WA. For Lewis & Clark Bicentennial LandBridge construction and education outreach to connect Fort Vancouver with Columbia River.
$600,000 to Museum of the Rockies, Bozeman, MT. For Dinosaurs Under the Big Sky exhibit.
$591,500 to Montana State University, Bozeman, MT. For Cold Chamber Laboratory Facilities for science and engineering studies in low temperature environments.
$512,500 to University of Oregon Foundation, Eugene, OR. For acquisition of equipment for research in materials science to support nanoscience studies.
$500,000 to Wing Luke Memorial Foundation, Seattle, WA. For museum expansion project to educate visitors about art, history and culture of Asian Pacific Americans.
$480,000 to Sheldon Jackson College, Sitka, AK. For renovation of historic Allen Memorial Hall for college and community use.
$475,500 to Washington State University Foundation, Pullman, WA. For acquisition of Biosciences Research Equipment to support transgenic and targeting studies.
$455,000 to University of Washington, Seattle, WA. For acquisition of Engineering Research Instrumentation for support of materials science studies.
$450,000 to Union Gospel Mission, Portland, OR. For new building construction to expand LifeChange program.
$419,000 to University of Idaho, Moscow, ID. For acquisition of mass spectrometer for research in proteomics and natural product chemistry.

9645
Murr Family Foundation ◇
105 S. 3rd Ave.
Walla Walla, WA 99362
Application address: c/o Dr. Neil Follett, 1040 Southview Dr., Walla Walla, WA 99362, tel.: (509) 525-1555

Established in 1992 in WA.
Donors: Eva Murr; Michael Murr.
Foundation type: Independent foundation.
Financial data (yr. ended 6/30/04): Assets, $24,291 (M); gifts received, $1,236,137; expenditures, $1,295,350; qualifying distributions, $1,294,000; giving activities include $1,294,000 for 7 grants (high: $1,000,000; low: $2,500).
Fields of interest: Arts, alliance; Higher education; Scholarships/financial aid; Environment, land resources; Animals/wildlife, preservation/ protection; Foundations (community).
Limitations: Giving primarily in Walla Walla, WA, with some giving in NY. No grants to individuals.
Application information:
Initial approach: Letter
Deadline(s): None

Officers: Neil Follett, Pres.; William Bieloh, V.P.; William Fleenor, Secy.-Treas.
EIN: 911568178

9646
Natan Foundation ◇ ☆
1155 N. 130th St., Ste 310
Seattle, WA 98133

Established in 2003 in WA.
Donors: Larry J. Sundquist; Steve Balas; Nathan Sundquist; Kristi Sundquist; David Sundquist.
Foundation type: Independent foundation.
Financial data (yr. ended 12/31/05): Assets, $949,824 (M); gifts received, $1,091,130; expenditures, $366,936; qualifying distributions, $338,011; giving activities include $338,011 for 11 grants (high: $160,000; low: $500).
Fields of interest: Education; Human services; Christian agencies & churches.
Limitations: Applications not accepted. Giving on a national and international basis, particularly in WA and in India. No grants to individuals.
Application information: Contributes only to pre-selected organizations.
Officers and Directors: * Larry J. Sundquist,* Pres.; Kristina M. Sundquist,* V.P.; Diane Y. Sundquist,* Secy.; Roger Lageschulte, Treas.
EIN: 830380273

9647
Nesholm Family Foundation ◇
120 Lakeside Ave., Ste. 340
Seattle, WA 98122 (206) 324-3339
Contact: Nancy Cochran, Grants Admin.

Established in 1987 in WA.
Donor: Elmer J. Nesholm†.
Foundation type: Independent foundation.
Financial data (yr. ended 12/31/05): Assets, $72,099,625 (M); expenditures, $3,638,392; qualifying distributions, $3,464,223; giving activities include $3,293,145 for 120 grants (high: $350,000; low: $600).
Purpose and activities: Giving primarily for the performing arts, health and human services, and education.
Fields of interest: Performing arts; Education; Health care; Health organizations, association; Human services.
Type of support: Matching/challenge support; Equipment; Building/renovation; Capital campaigns; Program development.
Limitations: Giving limited to Seattle, WA. No support for conduit organizations, i.e., tax-exempt organizations that pass funds on to organizations not tax-exempt in their own right, organizations that carry on propaganda or attempt to influence legislation or elections, institutions that in policy or practice unfairly discriminate against race, ethnic origin, sex, or creed, or for activities of sectarian or religious organizations that principally benefit their own members or adherents. No grants for ongoing normal operations or operating deficits, debt retirement or endowment funds, general fund drives, annual appeals, federated campaigns, scholarships and fellowships, or the benefit of specific individuals or for basic science research; no loans.
Publications: Application guidelines; Annual report; Grants list; Program policy statement.
Application information: Application form required.

Initial approach: Application form, with 1-2 page letter signed by Exec. Dir, including project budget
Copies of proposal: 7
Deadline(s): Call office for next deadline
Board meeting date(s): 8-10 times yearly
Officer: Laurel Nesholm, Exec. Dir.
Directors: Joseph M. Gaffney; Edgar K. Marcuse, M.D., M.P.H; Erika J. Nesholm; John F. Nesholm; Kirsten Nesholm.
Agent: Bank of America, N.A.
Number of staff: 1 full-time professional.
EIN: 943055422
Selected grants: The following grants were reported in 2003.
$600,000 to Alliance for Education, Seattle, WA. For Kids in the Middle Literacy and for staff development in middle schools.
$200,000 to Seattle Opera, Seattle, WA. For production of Norma.
$50,000 to Childhaven, Seattle, WA. For new facility for abused children.
$50,000 to Pacific Northwest Ballet, Seattle, WA. For production of Amazed in Burning Dreams.
$25,000 to Transitional Resources for Young Adults, Seattle, WA. For affordable housing for the mentally ill.
$15,000 to Downtown Emergency Service Center, Seattle, WA. For housing program for disabled homeless.
$15,000 to Langston Hughes Cultural Arts Center, Seattle, WA. For summer youth theater project.
$10,000 to Seattle Arts and Lectures, Seattle, WA. For Writers in the Schools program.
$10,000 to Seattle Youth Symphony Orchestras, Seattle, WA. For season concert.
$5,000 to Washington Adult Day Services, Seattle, WA. For training program for eldercare workers.

9648
Nestle Scholarship Foundation ◇
(formerly Carnation Company Scholarship Foundation)
c/o Bank of America, N.A.
P.O. Box 34345
Seattle, WA 98124-1345

Established in 1952 in CA.
Donors: Carnation Co.; Nestle USA, Inc.
Foundation type: Company-sponsored foundation.
Financial data (yr. ended 12/31/05): Assets, $11,353,283 (M); expenditures, $560,718; qualifying distributions, $492,085; giving activities include $477,000 for 1 grant.
Purpose and activities: The foundation awards college scholarships to the children of employees of Nestle USA. The program is administered by Scholarship America, Inc.
Type of support: Employee-related scholarships.
Limitations: Applications not accepted.
Application information: Contributes only through employee-related scholarships.
Advisory Committee: Peter D. Argentine; Kenneth W. Bentley; Mrs. Carn Starrett.
Trustee Bank: Bank of America, N.A.
EIN: 956118622

9649
Neukom Family Foundation ◇
2120 Waverly Way E.
Seattle, WA 98112

Established in 1998 in WA.
Donor: William H. Neukom.
Foundation type: Independent foundation.
Financial data (yr. ended 3/31/05): Assets, $51,374,113 (M); gifts received, $5,780,900; expenditures, $2,020,665; qualifying distributions, $1,316,766; giving activities include $1,316,766 for 13 grants (high: $451,781; low: $194).
Fields of interest: Higher education; Environment; Reproductive health, family planning; Human services.
Limitations: Applications not accepted. No grants to individuals.
Application information: Contributes only to pre-selected organizations.
Directors: Gillian Neukom; John McMakin Neukom; Josselyn Neukom; Samantha Neukom; William H. Neukom.
EIN: 911737888

9650
The Norcliffe Foundation ▼ ✧
(formerly The Norcliffe Fund)
999 3rd Ave., Ste. 1006
Seattle, WA 98104 (206) 682-4820
Contact: James C. Pigott, Pres.
FAX: (206) 682-4821;
E-mail: arline@thenorcliffefoundation.com;
URL: http://www.thenorcliffefoundation.com/

Incorporated in 1952 in WA.
Donors: Theiline M. McCone†; Mary Ellen Hughes; Mary Pigott; Lee W. Rolfe; Theiline P. Scheumann; Ann Pigott Wyckoff; Christy Wyckoff.
Foundation type: Independent foundation.
Financial data (yr. ended 11/30/05): Assets, $244,673,338 (M); gifts received, $782,612; expenditures, $11,634,480; qualifying distributions, $11,387,744; giving activities include $11,280,602 for 281 grants (high: $1,000,000; low: $275; average: $10,000–$100,000).
Purpose and activities: Giving for the arts and cultural activities, Roman Catholic church support and religious associations, hospitals, early childhood, higher and secondary education, and historic preservation; support also for medical research and health associations, hospices, the environment and conservation, and social services, including programs for the disabled, the homeless, child welfare, youth agencies, wildlife organizations, and the aged.
Fields of interest: Visual arts; Visual arts, architecture; Performing arts; Performing arts, theater; Performing arts, music; Historic preservation/historical societies; Arts; Education, association; Education, fund raising/fund distribution; Elementary/secondary education; Vocational education; Higher education; Adult education—literacy, basic skills & GED; Libraries/library science; Education, reading; Education; Environment, natural resources; Environment; Animals/wildlife, preservation/protection; Hospitals (general); Dental care; Health care; Substance abuse, services; Mental health/crisis services; Health organizations, association; Cancer; AIDS; Alcoholism; Biomedicine; Medical research, institute; Cancer research; AIDS research; Legal services; Employment; Food services; Nutrition; Housing/shelter, development; Recreation; Human services; Children/youth, services; Child development, services; Family services; Residential/custodial care, hospices; Community development; Voluntarism promotion; Federated

giving programs; Mathematics; Computer science; Christian agencies & churches; Aging; Disabilities, people with; Minorities; Native Americans/American Indians; Women; Economically disadvantaged; Homeless.
Type of support: Scholarship funds; General/operating support; Annual campaigns; Capital campaigns; Building/renovation; Equipment; Endowments; Program development; Professorships; Curriculum development; Fellowships; Research; Matching/challenge support.
Limitations: Giving in the Puget Sound region of WA, with emphasis in and around Seattle. No grants to individuals, or for deficit financing, matching gifts, or scholarships; no loans.
Publications: Application guidelines; Program policy statement.
Application information: An application form is available on the foundation Web site. Application form not required.
Initial approach: Telephone or submission based on guidelines
Copies of proposal: 1
Deadline(s): None
Board meeting date(s): As required
Final notification: 3 to 6 months
Officers and Trustees:* James C. Pigott,* Pres.; Mary Ellen Hughes,* V.P.; Arline Hefferline, Secy.; Ann Pigott Wyckoff, Treas.; Lisa Anderson; Kevin Hughes; Charles M. Pigott; Dana Pigott; Mary Pigott; Susan Pohl; Theiline P. Scheumann.
Number of staff: 1 full-time professional.
EIN: 916029352
Selected grants: The following grants were reported in 2005.
$1,000,000 to Convent of the Sacred Heart, Bellevue, WA. To construct new chapel and high school.
$500,000 to Fulcrum Foundation, Seattle, WA. For capital campaign for endowment.
$500,000 to Plymouth Housing Group, Seattle, WA. To purchase and renovate historic buildings and new construction project for the homeless.
$496,270 to Childhaven, Seattle, WA. For capital campaign.
$333,333 to Seattle Center Foundation, Seattle, WA. For construction of McCaw Hall.
$300,000 to Seattle Art Museum, Seattle, WA. For pledge.
$200,000 to Seattle Central Community College, Seattle, WA. For Clinical Laboratory for Dental Hygiene Program.
$15,000 to Archdiocese of Seattle, Seattle, WA. For Annual Catholic Appeal.
$10,000 to ArtsFund, Seattle, WA. For Peter Donnelly Merit Fund.
$10,000 to Atlantic Street Center, Seattle, WA. For summer school, grades K-7, for students falling behind.

9651
North Pacific Marine Science Foundation ✧
1900 W. Emerson Pl., Ste. 205
Seattle, WA 98119-1649 (206) 281-1667
FAX: (206) 283-2387; E-mail: info@npmsf.org;
URL: http://www.npmsf.org

Established in 1993 in WA.
Donor: National Oceanic & Atmospheric Administration.
Foundation type: Independent foundation.

Financial data (yr. ended 3/31/06): Assets, $30,380 (M); gifts received, $2,658,711; expenditures, $2,711,678; qualifying distributions, $2,711,678; giving activities include $2,668,361 for 7 grants (high: $2,129,633; low: $28,683).
Purpose and activities: The foundation's mission is dedicated to fostering a better understanding of the interaction between marine life and fisheries. Giving primarily for independent research conducted on marine mammals and their habitat. The foundation's first priority continues to be the funding of the work of North Pacific Universities Marine Mammal Research Consortium.
Fields of interest: Higher education; Marine science.
Limitations: Applications not accepted. Giving limited to the Pacific Northwest. No grants to individuals.
Application information: Contributes only to pre-selected organizations.
Officers and Directors:* Dave Hanson,* Pres.; Glenn Reed,* V.P.; James Brenner,* Treas.; Dave Benton; Douglas C. Forsyth; Simon Kinneen; Paul MacGregor; Eric A. Olson; Brent Paine.
EIN: 911582669

9652
O'Donnell Family Charitable Foundation ✧
c/o Jim O'Donnell
1326 5th Ave., 703 Skinner Bldg.
Seattle, WA 98101

Established in 1996 in WA.
Donors: Harry J. O'Donnell; Mariette E. O'Donnell.
Foundation type: Independent foundation.
Financial data (yr. ended 12/31/04): Assets, $895,732 (M); gifts received, $1,337,625; expenditures, $443,038; qualifying distributions, $442,544; giving activities include $442,134 for 34 grants (high: $280,000; low: $50).
Fields of interest: Performing arts; Literature; Arts; Elementary school/education; Multiple sclerosis; AIDS; Housing/shelter; Boys & girls clubs; Human services; Children/youth, services.
Limitations: Giving primarily in Seattle, WA. No grants to individuals.
Application information:
Initial approach: Letter
Officers: Harry J. O'Donnell, Jr., Pres.; Mariette E. O'Donnell, Secy.-Treas.
EIN: 911712175

9653
The Oki Foundation ✧
(formerly The Oki Charitable Foundation)
1416 112th Ave. N.E.
Bellevue, WA 98004 (425) 454-2800
Contact: Laurie Oki, Pres.

Established in 1988 in WA.
Donors: Laurie Oki; Scott Oki.
Foundation type: Independent foundation.
Financial data (yr. ended 12/31/04): Assets, $164,463 (M); gifts received, $848,712; expenditures, $750,269; qualifying distributions, $726,022; giving activities include $724,332 for 46 grants (high: $205,190; low: $50).
Purpose and activities: Giving primarily for children's health and welfare issues in King County, WA.

Fields of interest: Education; Hospitals (specialty); Children, services.
Type of support: Continuing support; Annual campaigns; Capital campaigns.
Limitations: Applications not accepted. Giving limited to King County, WA. No grants to individuals.
Application information: Unsolicited requests for funds not accepted.
Officers: Laurie Oki, Pres. and Treas.; Scott Oki, V.P. and Secy.
EIN: 911394156

9654
OneFamily Foundation ◇
(formerly Wood Family Foundation)
6723 Sycamore Ave. N.W.
Seattle, WA 98117 (206) 781-3472
Contact: Therese Ogle, Grants Mgr.
E-mail: OgleFounds@aol.com; URL: http://www.foundationcenter.org/grantmaker/onefamily

Established in 1997 in WA.
Donors: Bill Morgan; Sara Morgan; Brenda Wood.
Foundation type: Independent foundation.
Financial data (yr. ended 12/31/05): Assets, $10,603,227 (M); gifts received, $35,332; expenditures, $592,033; qualifying distributions, $529,126; giving activities include $445,900 for 46 grants (high: $75,000; low: $1,000), and $73,973 for 4 foundation-administered programs.
Purpose and activities: To provide resources to enhance the lives of women living in poverty, and of at-risk youth; to support services for abused women, and to aid efforts to end violence and sexual assault against women and children.
Fields of interest: Education; Hospitals (general); AIDS; Human services; Family services, domestic violence; Women, centers/services.
Limitations: Giving limited to King and Snohomish counties, WA, and the Olympic Peninsula. No grants to individuals, or for scholarships, research, summer camps, multi-year grants, athletic events, video/film/homepage productions, or book publications.
Publications: Application guidelines; Grants list.
Application information: Multi-year requests not considered. Application form not required.
Initial approach: Letter or telephone
Copies of proposal: 2
Deadline(s): 3rd Fri. of Mar., July and Nov. for pre-application; 2nd Fri. of Jan., May, and Sept. for full proposal
Final notification: 4th Fri. of Feb., June, and Oct.
Officers: Brenda K. Wood, Pres.; Donald R. Wood III, V.P.; Brandon C. Wood, Secy.
EIN: 911722889
Selected grants: The following grants were reported in 2004.
$20,000 to Low Income Housing Institute, Seattle, WA.
$17,500 to Neighborhood House, Seattle, WA.
$15,000 to Boys and Girls Clubs of King County, Seattle, WA.
$15,000 to New Beginnings for Battered Women and Their Children, Seattle, WA.
$12,000 to Noel House, Seattle, WA.
$10,000 to Domestic Abuse Womens Network (DAWN), Tukwila, WA.
$10,000 to Family Works, Seattle, WA.
$9,000 to Childrens Home Society of Washington, Seattle, WA.
$8,000 to Pike Market Medical Clinic, Seattle, WA.
$8,000 to YouthNet.

9655
Opportunities for Education Foundation
P.O. Box 33159
Seattle, WA 98133-0159

Established in 2000 in WA.
Donor: Chris Larson.
Foundation type: Independent foundation.
Financial data (yr. ended 12/31/04): Assets, $5,488,490 (M); gifts received, $102,850; expenditures, $1,395,860; qualifying distributions, $1,365,437; giving activities include $1,364,000 for 3 grants (high: $1,164,000; low: $100,000).
Fields of interest: Elementary/secondary education; Higher education; Education; Youth development, formal/general education.
Limitations: Applications not accepted. Giving primarily in Seattle, WA. No grants to individuals.
Application information: Contributes only to pre-selected organizations.
Officers: Chris Larson, Pres.; Julia Calhoun, V.P. and Treas.; Lawrence B. Bailey, Secy.
EIN: 912091348
Selected grants: The following grants were reported in 2003.
$1,614,001 to New School Foundation, Seattle, WA. For New School at South Shore.
$400,000 to University of Washington, Seattle, WA. For professor John Bransford start-up costs and endowment.
$50,000 to Rainier Scholars, Seattle, WA. For general operating support.
$15,000 to Choices Education Group, Seattle, WA. For school districts in Everett, Arlington, and Wenatchee.
$10,000 to Catholic Community Services of Western Washington, Seattle, WA. For youth tutoring program.

9656
PACCAR Foundation ◇
c/o PACCAR Inc
P.O. Box 1518
Bellevue, WA 98009 (425) 468-7546
Contact: John Waggoner, V.P. and Genl. Mgr.
E-mail: foundation@paccar.com; URL: http://www.paccar.com/foundation.asp

Incorporated in 1951 in WA.
Donor: PACCAR Inc.
Foundation type: Company-sponsored foundation.
Financial data (yr. ended 12/31/05): Assets, $8,165,992 (M); gifts received, $7,167,327; expenditures, $4,813,386; qualifying distributions, $4,797,531; giving activities include $4,797,531 for 247 grants (high: $750,000).
Purpose and activities: The foundation supports children's hospitals, regional college associations, and organizations involved with cultural advancement and economic education.
Fields of interest: Arts; Education, association; Higher education; Hospitals (specialty); Human services, financial counseling; Federated giving programs; Children.
Type of support: Annual campaigns; Capital campaigns; Building/renovation; Employee matching gifts.
Limitations: Giving primarily in areas of company operations, with emphasis on King County, WA. No grants to individuals, or for scholarships or fellowships, program development, general operating support, or fundraising events.

Application information: Application form not required.
Initial approach: Proposal
Copies of proposal: 1
Deadline(s): None
Board meeting date(s): Quarterly; dates vary
Final notification: 2 to 4 months
Officers and Directors:* Charles M. Pigott,* Pres.; John Waggoner, V.P. and Genl. Mgr.; Mark C. Pigott,* V.P.; Janice M. D'Amato,* Secy.; Andrew J. Wold, Treas.; William G. Reed, Jr.
EIN: 916030638

9657
PAH Foundation ◇
600 Washington Ave. S.
Kent, WA 98032-5707
Contact: Thomas H. Oden, Treas.
Scholarship applications: c/o HRH Scholarship Program, Scholarship Prog. Admins., P.O. Box 23737, Nashville, TN 37202-3737, tel.: (615) 627-3834

Established in 1998 in WA as a follow-up to the Lois U. Horvitz Foundation.
Donor: Lois U. Horvitz Foundation.
Foundation type: Independent foundation.
Financial data (yr. ended 12/31/05): Assets, $4,764,991 (M); expenditures, $1,167,993; qualifying distributions, $1,158,331; giving activities include $1,145,297 for 31 grants (high: $200,000; low: $2,500).
Purpose and activities: Giving primarily for the arts, particularly to an art museum, and a ballet company; funding also for education, human services, and health associations. Scholarships awarded to high school seniors who either are presently attending a high school in Lake, Lorain, Richland, and Tuscarawas counties in OH, or Rensselaer County, NY, or any direct descendants (including adopted children, but not step children), of a person who by Aug. 1, 1987, had been a full-time employee of either The Mansfield News Journal, The Lorain Journal, The Luke County News Herald, The Dover/New Philadelphia Times Reporter, The Troy Times Record, or The Multi-Channel TV Cable Co., for at least two years.
Fields of interest: Museums (art); Performing arts, ballet; Arts; Higher education; Education; Hospitals (general); Health organizations, association; Human services; Federated giving programs; Jewish federated giving programs.
Type of support: Scholarships—to individuals.
Limitations: Giving on a national basis with an emphasis on communities where foundation members reside. No grants to individuals (except for scholarships), operating budgets, recurring expenses for direct services or administrative costs, annual appeals, debt reduction, campaigns, religion, publications, seminars or workshops, travel, or governmental services.
Application information: Contact Scholarship Program Admin., Inc., for scholarship application. Application form not required.
Initial approach: Letter, for grants
Copies of proposal: 1
Deadline(s): None for grants; Apr. 1 for scholarships
Final notification: May 1 for scholarships
Officers and Trustee:* Peter A. Horvitz,* Pres.; Margaret A. O'Meara, V.P.; Peter A. Kuhn, Secy. and Exec. Dir.; Thomas H. Oden, Treas.
EIN: 911866138

Selected grants: The following grants were reported in 2005.

$325,000 to Pacific Northwest Ballet, Seattle, WA. 2 grants: $75,000, $250,000

$66,763 to HRH Scholarship Fund, Cleveland, OH.

$50,000 to Jewish Federation of Greater Seattle, Seattle, WA.

$50,000 to Performing Arts Center Eastside, Bellevue, WA.

$33,334 to Seattle Art Museum, Seattle, WA.

$32,500 to United Way of King County, Seattle, WA. 2 grants: $12,500, $20,000

$30,000 to Bellevue Art Museum, Bellevue, WA.

$5,000 to Renton Technical College Foundation, Renton, WA.

9658
Paulus Family Foundation ◆
P.O. Box 178
Bow, WA 98232

Established in 2003 in WA.
Foundation type: Independent foundation.
Financial data (yr. ended 12/31/04): Assets, $628 (M); gifts received, $466,500; expenditures, $466,087; qualifying distributions, $465,500; giving activities include $465,500 for 6 grants (high: $275,000; low: $10,000).
Fields of interest: Education; Animal welfare; Animals/wildlife, fisheries.
Limitations: Giving primarily in WA. No grants to individuals.
Application information: Contributes only to pre-selected organizations.
Officers: Werner K. Paulus, Pres.; Paula E. Paulus, V.P.; C. Michelle Paulus, Secy.
EIN: 200351925

9659
Peach Foundation ◆ ☆
1601 2nd Ave., Ste. 615
Seattle, WA 98101

Established in 2001 in WA.
Donor: Priscilla B. Collins.
Foundation type: Independent foundation.
Financial data (yr. ended 12/31/05): Assets, $10,924,370 (M); gifts received, $4,406,407; expenditures, $577,555; qualifying distributions, $553,879; giving activities include $549,664 for 63 grants (high: $25,000; low: $85).
Fields of interest: Performing arts, music; Environment, formal/general education; Environment.
Limitations: Applications not accepted. Giving primarily in Seattle, WA. No grants to individuals.
Application information: Contributes only to pre-selected organizations.
Officers and Directors:* Jean Gardner,* Pres.; Delphine Haley,* Secy.; Gail Ransom,* Treas.
EIN: 912094325

9660
PEMCO Foundation ◆
325 Eastlake Ave. E.
Seattle, WA 98109
Contact: Stan W. McNaughton, Treas.

Established in 1965 in WA.

Donors: Gladys McLaughlin†; PEMCO Corp.; Washington School Employees Credit Union; Evergreen Bank, N.A.; Evergreenbancorp, Inc.; Teachers Foundation; PEMCO Technology Services, Inc.
Foundation type: Company-sponsored foundation.
Financial data (yr. ended 6/30/05): Assets, $3,153,303 (M); gifts received, $646,055; expenditures, $573,956; qualifying distributions, $571,958; giving activities include $415,358 for 96 grants (high: $55,000; low: $50), and $156,600 for 246 grants to individuals (high: $2,500; low: $200).
Purpose and activities: The foundation supports organizations involved with education, health, children and youth, and human services and awards college scholarships to high school students located in Washington.
Fields of interest: Media/communications; Elementary/secondary education; Higher education; Education; Health care; Boys & girls clubs; Children/youth, services; Human services; Federated giving programs.
Type of support: General/operating support; Scholarship funds; Research; Scholarships—to individuals.
Limitations: Giving primarily in WA, with emphasis on Seattle; giving limited to WA for scholarships.
Application information: Application form not required.
Initial approach: Letter from school principal stating academic qualifications for scholarships
Deadline: None
Final notification: 2 months for scholarships
Officers and Trustees:* Astrid I. Thompson,* Pres.; Sandra Kurack,* V.P.; Denice M. Town, Secy.; Stan W. McNaughton,* Treas.; Brian McNaughton.
EIN: 916072723

9661
James B. Pendleton Charitable Trust ◆
P.O. Box 50005
Bellevue, WA 98015-0005
Contact: David E. Ellison, Tr.

Established in 1992 in CA.
Donor: James B. Pendleton†.
Foundation type: Independent foundation.
Financial data (yr. ended 12/31/05): Assets, $26,893,776 (M); expenditures, $1,608,591; qualifying distributions, $1,174,445; giving activities include $1,027,557 for 5 grants (high: $506,395; low: $17,162).
Purpose and activities: Giving solely for basic research on causes, cures, and prevention of AIDS/HIV.
Fields of interest: AIDS research.
Type of support: Research.
Limitations: Giving on a national basis, with preference for the western U.S. No grants to individuals.
Application information: Application form not required.
Initial approach: Letter
Copies of proposal: 2
Deadline(s): None
Final notification: Upon review of proposal
Officers and Trustees:* David E. Ellison,* C.E.O. and Dir., Investments; Dayle G. Ellison,* Grants Dir.
Number of staff: 1 full-time professional; 1 part-time professional.
EIN: 956944277

9662
The Peterson Family Foundation ◆ ☆
203 S.E. Park Plz. Dr., Ste. 270
Vancouver, WA 98684

Established in 1996 in WA.
Donors: Claudia J. Peterson; Kenneth D. Peterson, Jr.; Columbia Ventures Corp.
Foundation type: Independent foundation.
Financial data (yr. ended 12/31/05): Assets, $33,945 (M); gifts received, $1,025,000; expenditures, $1,167,810; qualifying distributions, $1,167,061; giving activities include $1,166,277 for 21 grants (high: $900,000; low: $150).
Purpose and activities: Giving primarily for higher education, and human services.
Fields of interest: Higher education; Law school/education; Human services.
Limitations: Applications not accepted. Giving primarily in OR. No grants to individuals.
Application information: Contributes only to pre-selected organizations.
Officers: Kenneth D. Peterson, Jr., Pres.; Claudia J. Peterson, Secy.-Treas.
EIN: 911746622
Selected grants: The following grants were reported in 2004.

$43,000 to Washington Policy Center, Seattle, WA.

$14,000 to Project PATCH, Clackamas, OR.

$5,000 to Evergreen Freedom Foundation, Olympia, WA.

$4,000 to Cascade Policy Institute, Portland, OR.

$1,000 to Oregon Museum of Science and Industry, Portland, OR.

$1,000 to Portland Art Museum, Portland, OR.

$1,000 to Portland Baroque Orchestra, Portland, OR.

$1,000 to Reason Foundation, Los Angeles, CA.

$875 to Loaves and Fishes.

$354 to International Childrens Care, Vancouver, WA.

9663
Paul Pigott Scholarship Foundation ◆ ☆
P.O. Box 1518
Bellevue, WA 98009 (425) 468-7890
Contact: Jerry Huffman

Established in 1961 in WA.
Foundation type: Independent foundation.
Financial data (yr. ended 12/31/05): Assets, $2,049,339 (M); expenditures, $489,615; qualifying distributions, $488,225; giving activities include $488,225 for grants.
Purpose and activities: Scholarship awards to children of employees of PACCAR, Inc. and its subsidiaries for the first college year.
Type of support: Employee-related scholarships.
Limitations: Giving on a national basis.
Application information: Application form required.
Initial approach: Request application form
Deadline(s): Nov. 1
Officer: G.V. Huffman, Mgr.
Directors: M.C. Pigott; T.E. Plimpton; M.A. Tembreull.
EIN: 916030639

9664
The Positive Transitions Foundation
P.O. Box 77818
Seattle, WA 98177-0818

Established in 2000 in WA.
Donor: Julia Calhoun.
Foundation type: Independent foundation.
Financial data (yr. ended 12/31/04): Assets, $7,058,684 (M); gifts received, $8,692,100; expenditures, $1,638,011; qualifying distributions, $1,636,818; giving activities include $1,635,625 for 12 grants (high: $586,000; low: $1,000; average: $25,000–$350,000).
Purpose and activities: Giving primarily for children and youth services, as well as for social services.
Fields of interest: Housing/shelter; Human services; Children/youth, services.
Type of support: General/operating support.
Limitations: Applications not accepted. Giving primarily in King County, WA. No grants to individuals.
Application information: Contributes only to pre-selected organizations.
Officers: Julia Calhoun, Pres.; Chris Larson, V.P. and Treas.; Lawrence B. Bailey, Secy.
EIN: 912091347

9665
Potlatch Foundation for Higher Education
601 W. Riverside Ave., Ste. 1100
Spokane, WA 99201
Contact: Sharon Pegau, Corp. Progs. and Board Admin.
E-mail: foundation@potlatchcorp.com; URL: http://www.potlatchcorp.com/scholarship

Incorporated in 1952 in DE.
Donors: Potlatch Corp.; Potlach Foundation II.
Foundation type: Company-sponsored foundation.
Financial data (yr. ended 12/31/05): Assets, $20,531 (M); gifts received, $341,018; expenditures, $344,730; qualifying distributions, $343,025; giving activities include $327,658 for 499 grants to individuals (high: $700; low: $700).
Purpose and activities: The foundation awards college scholarships to undergraduate students located in certain areas of company operations of Potlatch Corporation.
Type of support: Scholarships—to individuals.
Limitations: Giving limited to areas of company operations, with emphasis on AR, ID, and MN. No grants for general operating support, building or endowments, or research; no loans; no employee matching gifts; no graduate school scholarships.
Publications: Informational brochure (including application guidelines).
Application information: Application form required.
  Initial approach: Download application form
  Deadline(s): Feb. 15 for new applications; July 1 for renewals
  Board meeting date(s): Apr.
  Final notification: May 1 for new applications
Officers and Trustees:* L. Pendleton Siegel,* Pres.; Douglas D. Spedden,* V.P. and Treas.; Michael S. Gadd, Secy.; A.L. Alford, Jr.; Jack A. Buell; John B. Frazer, Jr.; John L. Hogan; Sally J. Ihne; John M. Richards.
EIN: 826005250

9666
Quest for Truth Foundation ✧
c/o DeLancey B. Lewis
10507 S.E. 28th St.
Beaux Arts, WA 98004

Established in 1982 in WA.
Foundation type: Independent foundation.
Financial data (yr. ended 9/30/05): Assets, $6,551,733; expenditures, $360,077; qualifying distributions, $351,500; giving activities include $351,500 for 18 grants (high: $100,000; low: $1,500).
Purpose and activities: Grants for research and publication of papers dealing with history, geography, politics, economics, sociology, health care and related subjects without restriction as to geographic areas or political jurisdiction, for the education of the reading public. Grants generally through organizations.
Fields of interest: History/archaeology; Anthropology/sociology; Economics; Political science.
Type of support: Publication; Research.
Limitations: Applications not accepted. Giving primarily in CA, and the Pacific Northwest.
Application information: Unsolicited requests for funds not accepted.
Officers and Directors:* DeLancey B. Lewis,* Pres.; Bradley F. Henke,* V.P.; Paul K. Scripps,* V.P.; Roxanne D. Greene; Marion W. Roozen.
EIN: 911190760
Selected grants: The following grants were reported in 2003.
$50,000 to Museum of the Rockies, Bozeman, MT. For Relive Lewis and Clark exhibit.
$50,000 to Puget Sound Blood Center, Seattle, WA.
$50,000 to Skagit Valley College Foundation, Mount Vernon, WA.
$50,000 to University of California at San Diego Foundation, La Jolla, CA. For research project, Susceptibility of San Diego Beaches.
$30,000 to Northwest School for Hearing-Impaired Children, Seattle, WA.
$20,000 to Museum of Flight Foundation, Seattle, WA.
$20,000 to Thomas Burke Memorial Washington State Museum, Seattle, WA. For program support.
$15,000 to San Diego Historical Society, San Diego, CA.
$10,000 to Columbia River Maritime Museum, Astoria, OR. For Footsteps in History project.
$10,000 to Northwest Railway Museum, Snoqualmie, WA. For renovation.

9667
Quixote Foundation, Inc. ✧
5703 20th Ave. N.W.
Seattle, WA 98107-3027   (206) 783-5554
Contact: Lenore M. Hanisch, Exec. Dir.
FAX: (206) 783-1815;
E-mail: lenore@quixotefoundation.org; URL: http://www.quixotefoundation.org

Established in 1998 in WI.
Donor: Arthur S. Hanisch‡.
Foundation type: Independent foundation.
Financial data (yr. ended 12/31/04): Assets, $23,500,614 (M); gifts received, $63,153; expenditures, $1,775,615; qualifying distributions, $1,530,708; giving activities include $1,120,000 for 33 grants (high: $102,000; low: $2,000).
Purpose and activities: To advance progressive causes through the action, education and policy work of dynamic nonprofit groups. Current interests of the foundation are: 1) protecting reproductive rights; 2) developing effective message strategies to safeguard the world's natural environment; 3)

reforming media coverage and promoting public awareness of economic inequality; and 4) restoring U.S. democracy by making sure every vote is counted as cast.
Fields of interest: Environment; Civil liberties, reproductive rights; Civil rights.
Type of support: General/operating support; Continuing support; Income development; Management development/capacity building; Equipment; Land acquisition; Emergency funds; Program development; Conferences/seminars; Professorships; Publication; Seed money; Curriculum development; Fellowships; Research; Technical assistance; Consulting services; Program evaluation; Program-related investments/loans; In-kind gifts; Matching/challenge support.
Limitations: No support for partisan efforts, in general or religious organizations. No grants to individuals, or for endowments, in general, and bricks and mortar campaigns.
Application information: Unsolicited applications are not accepted. Proposals are by invitation only.
  Initial approach: 1-page letter of inquiry
  Board meeting date(s): Winter, spring, summer, and fall (dates determined yearly)
Officers: Erik M. Hanisch, Chair. and Pres.; Richard J. Langer, V.P.; Martha Vukelich-Austin, Secy.-Treas.; Lenore M. Hanisch, Exec. Dir.
Number of staff: 1 full-time professional.
EIN: 391916960
Selected grants: The following grants were reported in 2003.
$101,318 to University of Wisconsin Foundation, Madison, WI. For general support.
$100,000 to Wilderness Society, Center for Landscape Analysis, DC. For general support.
$40,000 to Institute for Agriculture and Trade Policy, Minneapolis, MN. For antibiotic testing program.
$30,000 to Media Education Foundation, Northampton, MA. For Free Press National Conference on Media Reform.
$30,000 to Midwest Environmental Advocates, Madison, WI. For general support.
$25,000 to Alliance for Justice, DC. For general operating support.
$25,000 to Headwaters Foundation for Justice, Minneapolis, MN. For endowment.
$25,000 to Natural Resources Defense Council, New York, NY. For BioGems program.
$25,000 to Planned Parenthood of Wisconsin, Milwaukee, WI. For general support.
$25,000 to Urban Justice Center, New York, NY. For planning conference on inequality.

9668
Raikes Family Foundation ✧
1500 4th Ave., Ste. 600
Seattle, WA 98101

Established in 2001 in WA.
Donors: Jeffrey S. Raikes; Patricia M. Raikes.
Foundation type: Independent foundation.
Financial data (yr. ended 12/31/04): Assets, $20,554,433 (M); gifts received, $13,861,225; expenditures, $540,684; qualifying distributions, $530,877; giving activities include $501,338 for 57 grants (high: $202,504; low: $25).
Purpose and activities: Giving primarily for education, and children, youth and social services; funding also for the arts.
Fields of interest: Arts; Child development, education; Higher education; Education; Human services.

Limitations: Applications not accepted. Giving primarily in WA. No grants to individuals.
Application information: Contributes only to pre-selected organizations.
Directors: J.J. Leary, Jr.; Jeffrey S. Raikes; Patricia M. Raikes.
EIN: 912173492

9669
Rainier Pacific Foundation

P.O. Box 11628
Tacoma, WA 98411-6628
Contact: Rachelle Keenan
E-mail: rkeenan@rainierpac.com; URL: http://www.rainierpac.com/content.asp?chapterID=47&subchapterID=55&pageid=247#Rainier-Pacific-Foundation-Washington-Bank-Rainier-Pacific

Established in 2003.
Donor: Rainier Pacific Financial Group, Inc.
Foundation type: Company-sponsored foundation.
Financial data (yr. ended 12/31/04): Assets, $9,945,228 (M); expenditures, $468,625; qualifying distributions, $468,625; giving activities include $443,781 for 63 grants (high: $30,000; low: $500).
Purpose and activities: The foundation supports organizations involved with education, health, and community development.
Fields of interest: Education; Health care; Community development.
Type of support: Capital campaigns; Annual campaigns; General/operating support; Building/renovation; Program development; Scholarship funds; Employee volunteer services; Sponsorships; Employee matching gifts.
Limitations: Giving primarily in Federal Way, Pierce County, and Tacoma, WA.
Publications: Application guidelines; Annual report.
Application information: Gifts are grants less than $5,000; Basic Grants are grants from $5,000 to $25,000; Major Grants are grants greater than $25,000. Application form not required.
　Initial approach: Proposal
　Copies of proposal: 1
　Deadline(s): None
　Board meeting date(s): 2nd Thur. of each month
　Final notification: 1 to 2 months
Officers and Trustees:* John A. Hall,* Chair.; Dalen Harrison,* Secy.; Vic Toy,* Treas.; Peter Grignon; Carol Thomas.
EIN: 200327633

9670
Raven Trust Fund ◇

1000 2nd Ave., No. 3700
Seattle, WA 98104

Established in 1997 in WA.
Donors: John Standford Endowment; Tom A. Alberg.
Foundation type: Independent foundation.
Financial data (yr. ended 12/31/05): Assets, $12,427,095 (M); expenditures, $842,347; qualifying distributions, $674,630; giving activities include $556,933 for 81 grants (high: $65,000; low: $500).
Purpose and activities: Giving for the arts, education, and environmental conservation.
Fields of interest: Museums (art); Arts; Elementary/secondary education; Higher education; Law

school/education; Education; Environment; Aquariums; Hospitals (general); Health organizations, association; Medical research, institute; Recreation; Human services; Children/youth, services; Foundations (private grantmaking).
Limitations: Applications not accepted. Giving primarily in WA, with emphasis on Seattle. No grants to individuals.
Application information: Contributes only to pre-selected organizations.
Officers and Trustee:* Tom A. Alberg, Pres. and Treas.; Judith Beck,* V.P. and Secy.
EIN: 911816037
Selected grants: The following grants were reported in 2004.
$80,000 to Seattle Foundation, Seattle, WA.
$60,000 to Discovery Institute, Seattle, WA.
$25,000 to Explorer West - An Independent Middle School, Seattle, WA.
$20,000 to INTIMAN Theater Company, Seattle, WA.
$16,000 to Seattle Aquarium Society, Seattle, WA.
$15,000 to FareStart, Seattle, WA.
$10,000 to Treehouse Fund, Seattle, WA.
$10,000 to United Way of King County, Seattle, WA.
$8,500 to Pacific Science Center, Seattle, WA.
$5,650 to Washington Womens Foundation, Seattle, WA.

9671
W. Razore Family Foundation ◇

3927 Lake Washington Blvd. N.E.
Kirkland, WA 98033-7867 (425) 822-1996
Contact: Jeffrey A. Williamson, V.P.

Established in 1998 in WA.
Donor: Mary Razore Maron.
Foundation type: Independent foundation.
Financial data (yr. ended 4/30/05): Assets, $2,557,487 (M); expenditures, $503,493; qualifying distributions, $468,000; giving activities include $468,000 for 6 grants (high: $250,000; low: $500).
Purpose and activities: Giving primarily for health services.
Fields of interest: Health care.
Limitations: Giving primarily in Denver, CO. No grants to individuals.
Application information:
　Deadline(s): None
Officers: Mary Razore Maron, Pres.; Robert S. Jaffe, V.P. and Secy.; Jeffrey A. Williamson, V.P. and Treas.
EIN: 911939131
Selected grants: The following grants were reported in 2005.
$250,000 to Ronald McDonald House.
$5,000 to Family Law CASA of King County, Seattle, WA.
$2,500 to Swedish Medical Center Foundation, Seattle, WA.
$500 to American Cancer Society, Seattle, WA.

9672
RealNetworks Foundation ◇

c/o RealNetworks, Inc.
P.O. Box 91123
Seattle, WA 98111-9223 (206) 892-6644
FAX: (206) 956-8249;
E-mail: info@realfoundation.org; URL: http://www.realfoundation.org/

Established in 2000 in WA.

Donor: RealNetworks, Inc.
Foundation type: Company-sponsored foundation.
Financial data (yr. ended 12/31/05): Assets, $189,377 (M); gifts received, $288,561; expenditures, $380,319; qualifying distributions, $346,532; giving activities include $346,532 for grants.
Purpose and activities: The foundation supports programs designed to enhance the quality of life in areas of company operations; and enable alternative voices or foster the right of free speech throughout the world.
Fields of interest: Arts; Health care; Family services; Human services; Civil liberties, first amendment; Community development; Telecommunications, electronic messaging services; African Americans/Blacks; Economically disadvantaged.
International interests: Czech Republic; England; France.
Type of support: General/operating support; Employee matching gifts.
Limitations: Applications not accepted. Giving on a national and international basis, with some emphasis on areas of company operations. No grants to individuals.
Publications: Grants list.
Application information: Contributes only to pre-selected organizations.
Officers and Director: Eileen Quigley, Pres. and Treas.; Rob Glaser, V.P.; Kelly Jo MacArthur, Secy.; Sid Ferrales.
EIN: 912033075

9673
The Russell Family Foundation ◇

P.O. Box 2567
Gig Harbor, WA 98335 (253) 858-5050
Contact: Stephanie Anderson, Grants Mgr.
FAX: (253) 851-0460; E-mail: info@trff.org; Toll Free tel.: (888) 252-4331; URL: http://www.trff.org

Established in 1994 in WA.
Donors: George F. Russell, Jr.; Jane T. Russell‡.
Foundation type: Independent foundation.
Financial data (yr. ended 12/31/04): Assets, $138,555,257 (M); gifts received, $20,475,000; expenditures, $13,956,802; qualifying distributions, $13,013,906; giving activities include $11,996,240 for grants.
Purpose and activities: The foundation seeks to contribute to innovative community impact, build quality relationships with partners and have an outstanding work culture.
Fields of interest: Education; Environment.
Type of support: Grants to individuals; Fellowships; General/operating support; Program development; Employee matching gifts.
Limitations: Giving primarily in the Puget Sound region of WA. No support for lobbying, city or county government programs, work on water quantity or water rights, watershed planning, or corporate development of new products or services. No grants for capital construction or purchases of land.
Application information: All letters of inquiry are acknowledged within two weeks of receipt at the foundation. Full proposals are accepted by invitation only. Application form required.
　Initial approach: Letter of inquiry
　Copies of proposal: 1
　Deadline(s): Jan. 17 and July 1
　Board meeting date(s): June 10 and Nov 11
　Final notification: Following board meeting

Officers: Richard Woo, C.E.O.; Sarah Cavanaugh, Pres.; George Russell, Jr., V.P.; Dion Rurik, Secy.; Eric Russell, Treas.
Directors: Tim Cavanaugh; Gun Denhart; John O'Neil; Jileen Russell; Richard Russell.
Number of staff: 5 full-time professional.
EIN: 911663336
Selected grants: The following grants were reported in 2004.
$3,950,000 to Vanguard Charitable Endowment Program, Southeastern, PA.
$1,000,000 to Nuclear Threat Initiative, DC. For general operating support.
$600,000 to EastWest Institute, New York, NY. 2 grants: $300,000 each (For general operating support).
$500,000 to National Bureau of Asian Research, Seattle, WA. 2 grants: $200,000 (For general operating support), $300,000 (For general operating support).
$145,000 to Business Humanitarian Forum, Geneva, Switzerland. For reconstruction and development programs.
$125,000 to Environmental Education Association, Olympia, WA. For comprehensive plan and operational development.
$40,000 to Ecotrust, Portland, OR. For general operating support.
$13,170 to Council on Foundations, DC. For membership.

9674
Sage Foundation ◇
14311 Stehr Rd.
Arlington, WA   98223

Established in 2003 in WA.
Donor: Edmund W. Littlefield, Jr.
Foundation type: Independent foundation.
Financial data (yr. ended 12/31/04): Assets, $460,510 (M); gifts received, $1,473,977; expenditures, $1,452,638; qualifying distributions, $1,428,775; giving activities include $1,428,775 for 145 grants (high: $100,000; low: $500).
Fields of interest: Museums; Education; Environment, natural resources; Environment; Animals/wildlife; Hospitals (general); Human services.
Limitations: Applications not accepted. No grants to individuals.
Application information: Contributes only to pre-selected organizations.
Officers: E.W. Littlefield, Jr., Pres. and Treas.; Julia W. Derby, V.P. and Secy.
EIN: 200404771

9675
Samis Foundation
208 James St., Ste. C
Seattle, WA   98104
Contact: Eddie I. Hasson, Co-Chair.
FAX: (206) 622-4918;
E-mail: grantsadministrator@samis.com;
URL: http://www.samis.com/foundation/index.html

Established in 1979.
Donor: Samuel Israel.
Foundation type: Independent foundation.
Financial data (yr. ended 12/31/05): Assets, $135,242,308 (M); expenditures, $17,034,382;

qualifying distributions, $2,755,556; giving activities include $2,470,078 for grants.
Purpose and activities: Support primarily for Jewish giving, with emphasis on education in WA; giving also for general support in Israel, including Jewish welfare, archaeology, wildlife and scholarships.
Fields of interest: History/archaeology; Elementary/secondary education; Animals/wildlife, preservation/protection; Jewish agencies & temples; Religion.
International interests: Israel.
Type of support: Matching/challenge support; General/operating support; Continuing support; Building/renovation; Emergency funds; Program development; Publication; Seed money; Scholarship funds; Research; Technical assistance; Exchange programs.
Limitations: Giving primarily in WA for Jewish organizations; some giving also in Israel. No grants to individuals.
Publications: Application guidelines; Grants list; Informational brochure (including application guidelines).
Application information: Application form required.
  Initial approach: Letter
  Copies of proposal: 2
  Deadline(s): Mar. 1
  Board meeting date(s): Quarterly
  Final notification: July 1
Officers and Directors:* Eddie I. Hasson,* Co-Chair. and Pres.; Albert S. Maimon,* Co-Chair. and V.P.; Irwin L. Treiger,* Secy.; Morris Piha, Tr. Emeritus; Victor D. Alhadeff; Eli J. Almo; David Azose; Jerome O. Cohen; Barry D. Ernstoff; David Friedenberg; Eli Genauer; Rabbi William Greenberg; Mike Israel; Lucy Pruzan; Martin Selig; Ernest Sherman; Alex Sytman.
Number of staff: 2 full-time professional; 1 part-time professional; 1 full-time support.
EIN: 911641746
Selected grants: The following grants were reported in 2003.
$4,120,395 to Seattle Hebrew Academy, Seattle, WA.
$893,315 to Northwest Yeshiva High School, Mercer Island, WA.
$755,813 to Jewish Day School of Metropolitan Seattle, Bellevue, WA.
$356,593 to Menachem Mendel Seattle Cheder, Seattle, WA.
$316,964 to Seattle Jewish Community School, Seattle, WA.
$85,000 to Jewish Federation of Greater Seattle, Jewish Education Council, Seattle, WA.
$19,000 to Congregation Ezra Bessaroth, Seattle, WA.
$13,000 to Sephardic Religious School, Mercer Island, WA.
$12,000 to National Conference of Synagogue Youth, Jewish Student Network, Los Angeles, CA.
$12,000 to Washington State Holocaust Education Resource Center, Seattle, WA.

9676
The Herman and Faye Sarkowsky Family Charitable Foundation ◇
(formerly Sarkowsky Family Charitable Foundation)
700 5th Ave., Ste. 6100
Seattle, WA   98104-5004

Established in 1991 in WA.
Donors: Herman Sarkowsky; Faye Sarkowsky.
Foundation type: Independent foundation.

Financial data (yr. ended 12/31/05): Assets, $3,093,289 (M); gifts received, $2,749,182; expenditures, $477,470; qualifying distributions, $475,354; giving activities include $475,104 for 49 grants (high: $200,000; low: $75).
Purpose and activities: Giving primarily for the arts, education, health, children and youth services, and the United Way.
Fields of interest: Performing arts; Arts; Higher education; Education; Hospitals (general); Health organizations, association; Medical research; Children/youth, services; Federated giving programs; Jewish federated giving programs; Jewish agencies & temples.
Limitations: Applications not accepted. Giving primarily in WA. No grants to individuals.
Application information: Contributes only to pre-selected organizations.
Officers: Faye Sarkowsky, Pres.; Herman Sarkowsky, V.P. and Treas.; Cathy Sarkowsky, V.P.; Steve Sarkowsky, V.P.; Louis Treiger, Secy.
EIN: 911479527
Selected grants: The following grants were reported in 2005.
$200,000 to United Way of King County, Seattle, WA.
$82,200 to Seattle Art Museum, Seattle, WA.
$25,000 to Eisenhower Medical Center Foundation, Rancho Mirage, CA.
$14,000 to Palm Springs Art Museum, Palm Springs, CA.
$10,000 to Washington Womens Foundation, Seattle, WA.
$5,000 to Seattle Opera, Seattle, WA.
$3,000 to Washington State Holocaust Education Resource Center, Seattle, WA.
$2,500 to Northwest Film Forum, Seattle, WA.
$1,900 to Washington News Council, Seattle, WA.
$550 to Childrens Hospital Foundation, Seattle, WA.

9677
Satterberg Foundation ◇
810 Securities Bldg.
1904 3rd Ave.
Seattle, WA   98101
Contact: Peter F. Helsell, Treas.
FAX: (206) 374-9336; E-mail: info@satterberg.org;
URL: http://www.satterberg.org

Established in 1990 in WA.
Donors: Virginia S. Helsell†; Judy P. Swenson; William A. Helsell.
Foundation type: Independent foundation.
Financial data (yr. ended 12/31/05): Assets, $4,580,969 (M); gifts received, $500,000; expenditures, $561,466; qualifying distributions, $514,059; giving activities include $489,783 for 51 grants (high: $115,000; low: $750; average: $2,000–$10,000).
Purpose and activities: Giving primarily to organizations that support the communities of members of Board of Directors.
Fields of interest: Education; Health care; Housing/shelter, development; Youth development, centers/clubs; Human services; Children/youth, services; Family services.
Type of support: Income development; Management development/capacity building.
Limitations: Giving primarily in CA and WA. No support for evangelical groups. No grants to individuals.
Application information: Application guidelines for capacity-building only, may be obtained by writing to

the foundation or from the Web site. Application form required.

Initial approach: Letter or E-mail
Copies of proposal: 1
Deadline(s): Available on request
Board meeting date(s): Quarterly
Final notification: Quarterly

Officers and Directors:* Peter F. Helsell,* Treas.; Mary Pigott,* Exec. Dir.; Christine Helsell; Frank P. Helsell; David Lazarus; Katherine Lazarus; Michael J. Pigott; Judy P. Swenson.

EIN: 911501066

Selected grants: The following grants were reported in 2005.

$115,000 to Northwest Maritime Center, Port Townsend, WA.

$20,000 to Catholic Charities, Spokane, WA.

$20,000 to Fremont Public Association, Seattle, WA.

$20,000 to Seattle Childrens Theater, Seattle, WA.

$15,000 to Sunnyvale Community Services, Sunnyvale, CA.

$12,500 to IslandWood, Bainbridge Island, WA.

$5,000 to Port Townsend Aero Museum, Chimacum, WA.

$5,000 to Wooden Boat Foundation, Port Townsend, WA.

$2,000 to Eastside Baby Corner, Issaquah, WA.

$2,000 to Trust for Public Land, Seattle, WA.

9678

Schuler Family Foundation ✧ ☆
(formerly Force Schuler Family Foundation)
P.O. Box 2438
Seattle, WA 98111

Established in 2002 in WA.

Donor: Jean A. Schuler.

Foundation type: Independent foundation.

Financial data (yr. ended 12/31/05): Assets, $5,625,721 (M); expenditures, $385,489; qualifying distributions, $361,125; giving activities include $361,125 for 15 grants (high: $113,125; low: $1,000).

Fields of interest: Higher education; Hospitals (general); Human services; Child development, services; Family services; Family services, domestic violence.

Limitations: Applications not accepted. Giving primarily in WA. No grants to individuals.

Application information: Contributes only to pre-selected organizations.

Trustees: Jean A. Schuler; Keith R. Vernon.

EIN: 916557029

9679

Schultz Family Foundation ✧
108 S. Washington St., Ste. 300
Seattle, WA 98104
Contact: Loren D. Hostek, Tr.

Established in 1996 in WA.

Donors: Howard D. Schultz; Sheri K. Schultz.

Foundation type: Independent foundation.

Financial data (yr. ended 6/30/05): Assets, $6,541,215 (M); expenditures, $1,754,965; qualifying distributions, $1,754,965; giving activities include $1,752,940 for 24 grants (high: $993,500; low: $500).

Purpose and activities: Giving primarily for federated giving programs, education, social services, and Jewish agencies and temples.

Fields of interest: Museums (specialized); Higher education; Education; Health organizations, association; Human services; Federated giving programs; Jewish federated giving programs; Jewish agencies & temples.

Limitations: Giving primarily in Seattle, WA. No grants to individuals.

Application information:
Initial approach: Letter
Deadline(s): None

Trustees: Georgette Essad; Loren D. Hostek; Sheri Kersch-Schultz; Howard D. Schultz.

EIN: 911746414

Selected grants: The following grants were reported in 2004.

$733,872 to United Ways of Washington, Seattle, WA. For grant made in form of stock.

$50,000 to Kline Galland Center, Seattle, WA.

$40,000 to Seattle Hebrew Academy, Seattle, WA.

$10,000 to Northwest Yeshiva High School, Mercer Island, WA.

$10,000 to P.E.F. Israel Endowment Funds, New York, NY.

$10,000 to Pratt Fine Arts Center, Seattle, WA. For capital campaign.

$10,000 to Seattle Theater Group, Seattle, WA.

$5,000 to American Cancer Society, Seattle, WA.

$2,500 to Childhaven, Seattle, WA.

$2,500 to Lake Forest Academy, Lake Forest, IL.

9680

The Seattle Foundation ▼
1200 5th Ave., Ste. 1300
Seattle, WA 98101-3151 (206) 622-2294
Contact: Phyllis J. Campbell, C.E.O.; For grants: Ceil Erickson, Dir., Community Grantmaking Prog.
FAX: (206) 622-7673;
E-mail: info@seattlefoundation.org; Grant information E-mails: grantmaking@seattlefoundation.org and ceil@seattlefoundation.org; URL: http://www.seattlefoundation.org

Incorporated in 1946 in WA.

Foundation type: Community foundation.

Financial data (yr. ended 12/31/05): Assets, $473,444,919 (M); gifts received, $60,596,389; expenditures, $52,027,804; giving activities include $45,948,620 for 4,861 grants.

Purpose and activities: The foundation seeks to improve the quality of life in the greater Seattle, WA, area by facilitating and acting as a catalyst for charitable giving; administering charitable funds, trusts, gift annuities and bequests; pooling assets where possible to respond to community needs; distributing grants to nonprofit organizations that are making a positive difference in the community; responding as a positive force to the changing needs of the community in a creative, sensitive and timely manner.

Fields of interest: Media, film/video; Performing arts, dance; Performing arts, music; Humanities; Literature; Historic preservation/historical societies; Arts; Education, early childhood education; Adult/continuing education; Education, ESL programs; Libraries (public); Education; Environment, public education; Environment, air pollution; Environment, water pollution; Environment; Animals/wildlife; Health care; Mental health/crisis services; Health organizations,

association; Housing/shelter; Recreation; Youth development; Children/youth, services; Homeless, human services; Human services; Economic development; Community development, small businesses; Community development; Public affairs.

Type of support: General/operating support; Management development/capacity building; Capital campaigns; Building/renovation; Equipment; Emergency funds; Program development; Scholarship funds; Technical assistance.

Limitations: Giving limited to Seattle-King County, WA. No support for religious purposes. No grants to individuals, or for endowment funds, debt reduction, fundraising events, fundraising feasibility projects, conferences or seminars, film or video production, publications, or operating expenses for public or private elementary and secondary schools, colleges, and universities.

Publications: Application guidelines; Annual report; Financial statement; Grants list; Informational brochure; Informational brochure (including application guidelines); Newsletter; Program policy statement.

Application information: Visit foundation Web site for application Cover Sheet and guidelines. Faxed applications are not accepted. Application form required.

Initial approach: Submit application Cover Sheet and attachments
Copies of proposal: 1
Deadline(s): None
Board meeting date(s): Mar., June, Sept., and Dec.
Final notification: 6 weeks to 2 months

Officers and Trustees:* Stewart M. Landefeld,* Chair.; Bill Lewis,* Vice-Chair.; Robert A. Watt,* Vice-Chair.; Phyllis J. Campbell,* C.E.O. and Pres.; Molly Stearns, Sr. V.P.; Roberta Goodnow, V.P., Gift Planning; Bill Sperling, V.P., Fdn. Affairs; Jared Watson, V.P., Prog. and Donor Svcs.; Susan G. Duffy,* Secy.; Jeffrey Rudd, C.F.O.; Rick Fox,* Treas.; Tom A. Alberg; Martha Choe; Steve Davis; Jose Gaitan; Gerald Grinstein; Valerie Hood; Peter Horvitz; Katherine Ann Janeway; Gary S. Kaplan, M.D.; Carolyn Kelly; Donna Lou; Don Nielsen; Mary Pugh; Constance W. Rice, Ph.D.; Steve Rotella; Judy Runstad; Bradford L. Smith; Patty Stonesifer; Al J. Thompson, M.D.; Irwin L. Treiger; Margaret Walker; Robert C. Wallace; Jan Whitsitt; Grace T. Yuan.

Number of staff: 15 full-time professional; 9 full-time support.

EIN: 916013536

Selected grants: The following grants were reported in 2005.

$1,000,000 to Institute for Systems Biology, Seattle, WA. For general support.

$1,000,000 to Palm Springs Art Museum, Palm Springs, CA. For general support.

$1,000,000 to University of Washington Foundation, Seattle, WA. For Founders Pool.

$750,000 to Cascade Land Conservancy, Seattle, WA. To leverage regional conservation.

$750,000 to New Tribes Mission, Sanford, FL. To provide support for Kodiak Aircraft.

$350,000 to United Way of King County, Seattle, WA. For general support.

$250,000 to Saint Vincent de Paul Society, Indianapolis, IN. For purchase of Pratt Building and to begin capital campaign.

$200,000 to Ashoka: Innovators for the Public, Arlington, VA. For general support.

$20,000 to Seattle Public Library Foundation, Seattle, WA. For construction of new library branch in South Park.

$19,584 to Sanscha Community and Cultural Centre Foundation, Sidney, Canada. For general support.

9681
Sequoia Foundation

820 A St., Ste. 345
Tacoma, WA 98402 (253) 627-1634
Contact: Brian F. Boyd, Exec. Dir.

Established in 1982 in WA.
Donors: W. John Driscoll; C. Davis Weyerhaeuser†; F.T. Weyerhaeuser; William T. Weyerhaeuser.
Foundation type: Independent foundation.
Financial data (yr. ended 10/31/05): Assets, $36,058,120 (M); gifts received, $1,273,741; expenditures, $3,704,476; qualifying distributions, $3,420,575; giving activities include $3,232,500 for 35 grants (high: $1,235,000; low: $2,500).
Purpose and activities: The foundation is designed to serve the philanthropic goals of its trustees.
Fields of interest: Higher education; Education; Philanthropy/voluntarism.
Limitations: Applications not accepted. Giving primarily in the Pacific Northwest.
Application information: The foundation solicits proposals at its sole discretion. Unsolicited proposals are not considered.
Officers and Directors:* William T. Weyerhaeuser,* Pres. and Treas.; Gail T. Weyerhaeuser,* V.P.; Nicholas C. Spika, Secy.; Brian F. Boyd, Exec. Dir.; Annette B. Weyerhaeuser.
Number of staff: None.
EIN: 911178052

9682
Tillie and Alfred Shemanski Testamentary Trust

c/o Bank of America, N.A.
P.O. Box 24565, No. WA1-102-22-16
Seattle, WA 98124-8824 (206) 358-0912
Application Address: c/o Bank of America, Philanthropic Management, Attn: Nancy L.D. Atkinson, 701 Fifth Ave., Ste. 2200, Seattle, WA 98104

Trust established in 1974 in WA.
Donors: Alfred Shemanski†; Tillie Shemanski†.
Foundation type: Independent foundation.
Financial data (yr. ended 12/31/05): Assets, $8,168,250 (M); expenditures, $430,122; qualifying distributions, $383,381; giving activities include $354,100 for 18 grants (high: $78,500; low: $2,500).
Purpose and activities: Giving primarily for education, religious respect and tolerance, caring for those in need, and strengthening the Jewish community.
Fields of interest: Higher education; Hospitals (general); Health organizations, association; Human services; Children/youth, services; Youth, services; Jewish federated giving programs; Jewish agencies & temples; Religion.
Limitations: Giving primarily in the greater Seattle, WA, area. No grants to individuals.
Application information: Telephone inquiries will not be acknowledged. Application form not required.
Initial approach: Letter

Copies of proposal: 1
Deadline(s): Oct. 15th
Board meeting date(s): End of Nov.
Final notification: Late Dec. or early Jan.
Trustee: Bank of America, N.A.
EIN: 916196855
Selected grants: The following grants were reported in 2005.
$78,500 to Temple De Hirsch Sinai, Seattle, WA.
$74,000 to Seattle University, Seattle, WA.
$20,000 to Childrens Hospital.
$16,000 to Jewish Federation of Greater Seattle, Seattle, WA.
$10,000 to American Jewish Committee, New York, NY.
$4,500 to Childrens Home Society.
$2,500 to Multifaith Works, Seattle, WA.

9683
Sherwood Trust ◇

P.O. Box 1855
Walla Walla, WA 99362
Contact: George M. Edwards, Pres.

Established in 1991 in WA.
Donors: Donald Sherwood†; Virginia Sherwood†.
Foundation type: Independent foundation.
Financial data (yr. ended 12/31/05): Assets, $33,466,432 (M); expenditures, $1,683,992; qualifying distributions, $1,412,595; giving activities include $1,382,599 for 22 grants (high: $300,000; low: $500).
Fields of interest: Performing arts; Higher education, college; Education, services; Human services; International relief; Community development; Economically disadvantaged.
Type of support: General/operating support; Management development/capacity building; Capital campaigns; Building/renovation; Land acquisition; Technical assistance.
Limitations: Giving limited to the Walla Walla, WA, area. No grants to individuals.
Publications: Application guidelines; Program policy statement.
Application information: Application form not required.
Copies of proposal: 2
Deadline(s): Mar. 1
Board meeting date(s): Monthly
Final notification: 1-2 months from receipt
Officers: Joanne Martin, Chair.; George M. Edwards, Pres.; Leona M. Clarno, Secy.-Treas.
Directors: James F. Aylward; Allan Gillespie.
Number of staff: 2 part-time support.
EIN: 916337526
Selected grants: The following grants were reported in 2004.
$130,000 to Camp Fire USA, Walla Walla, WA. 2 grants: $1,000, $129,000
$125,000 to Blue Mountain Action Council, Walla Walla, WA. 3 grants: $20,000, $91,000, $14,000
$10,000 to Walla Walla Community Hospice, Walla Walla, WA.
$5,000 to YWCA of Walla Walla, Walla Walla, WA.
$2,000 to Walla Walla Senior Citizens Center, Walla Walla, WA.
$500 to American Red Cross, Tacoma, WA.
$500 to Salvation Army, WA.

9684
The Jon and Mary Shirley Foundation ◇

c/o Lawrence B. Bailey
300 E. Pine St.
Seattle, WA 98122

Established in 1992 in WA.
Donors: Jon A. Shirley; E. Mary Shirley.
Foundation type: Independent foundation.
Financial data (yr. ended 9/30/05): Assets, $43,639,420 (M); expenditures, $1,998,308; qualifying distributions, $1,967,377; giving activities include $1,958,067 for 63 grants (high: $1,000,000; low: $100; average: $1,000–$200,000).
Purpose and activities: Giving primarily for the arts, with emphasis on support for art museums.
Fields of interest: Museums; Museums (art); Museums (specialized); Arts; Higher education; Education; Health organizations; Human services; Federated giving programs.
Type of support: General/operating support; Annual campaigns.
Limitations: Applications not accepted. Giving primarily in WA. No grants to individuals.
Application information: Contributes only to pre-selected organizations.
Directors: E. Mary Shirley; Jon A. Shirley.
EIN: 943163120

9685
Alex Shulman Family Foundation ◇ ☆

4201 6th Ave. S.
Seattle, WA 98108-1702

Established in 2001 in WA.
Donor: Alex Shulman.
Foundation type: Independent foundation.
Financial data (yr. ended 12/31/05): Assets, $8,043,676 (M); expenditures, $458,654; qualifying distributions, $398,842; giving activities include $384,817 for 35 grants (high: $100,000; low: $250).
Purpose and activities: Giving primarily to Reform Jewish causes.
Fields of interest: Arts; Education; Human services; Jewish federated giving programs.
Limitations: Applications not accepted. Giving primarily in Seattle, WA. No grants to individuals.
Application information: Contributes only to pre-selected organizations.
Officers and Directors:* Richard Loeb,* Chair. and V.P.; Francine Loeb,* Pres. and Treas.; Daniel M. Asher, Secy.; Barry Shulman.
EIN: 912100817
Selected grants: The following grants were reported in 2004.
$201,000 to Jewish Federation of Greater Seattle, Seattle, WA.
$10,000 to Bertschi School, Seattle, WA.
$2,500 to Pomona College, Claremont, CA.
$2,500 to University Preparatory Academy, Seattle, WA.

9686
Charles Simonyi Fund for Arts and Sciences ◇

500 108th Ave. N.E., Ste. 1050
Bellevue, WA 98004 (425) 467-1440
Contact: Susan Hutchison, Exec. Dir.

FAX: (425) 467-6601;
E-mail: susan@simonyifund.org; URL: http://www.simonyifund.org/

Established in 2003 in WA.
Donor: Charles Simonyi.
Foundation type: Independent foundation.
Financial data (yr. ended 12/31/04): Assets, $43,095,577 (M); expenditures, $4,682,020; qualifying distributions, $4,370,324; giving activities include $4,213,250 for 31 grants (high: $2,014,750; low: $1,000; average: $5,000–$200,000).
Purpose and activities: The foundation which distributes funds to worthy organizations that demonstrate excellence in the arts, sciences and education.
Fields of interest: Arts; Education; Science, public education; Science.
Limitations: Applications not accepted. Giving primarily in Seattle, WA. No grants to individuals.
Application information: Contributes only to pre-selected organizations.
Officer: Susan Hutchison, Exec. Dir.
Director: Charles Simonyi.
EIN: 550846712
Selected grants: The following grants were reported in 2004.
$500,000 to Seattle Public Library, Seattle, WA.
$200,000 to Metropolitan Opera, New York, NY.
$110,000 to Museum of Flight, Seattle, WA.
$102,500 to Childrens Hospital Guild Association, Seattle, WA.
$25,500 to Seattle Art Museum, Seattle, WA.
$25,000 to Taproot Theater, Seattle, WA.
$15,000 to American Hungarian Foundation, New Brunswick, NJ.
$12,000 to Textile Museum, DC.
$8,500 to Seattle University, Seattle, WA.
$5,000 to Bertschi School, Seattle, WA.

9687
The Sloan Foundation ◇
1301 5th Ave., Ste. 3000
Seattle, WA   98101

Established in 1997 in WA.
Donor: Stuart M. Sloan.
Foundation type: Independent foundation.
Financial data (yr. ended 12/31/05): Assets, $6,960,561 (M); gifts received, $487,940; expenditures, $518,471; qualifying distributions, $516,207; giving activities include $513,940 for 9 grants (high: $333,914; low: $1,000; average: $5,000–$26,268).
Purpose and activities: Giving primarily for education.
Fields of interest: Education; Jewish federated giving programs.
Limitations: Applications not accepted. Giving primarily in CA and WA. No grants to individuals.
Application information: Contributes only to pre-selected organizations.
Officers: Stuart M. Sloan, Pres.; Adam D. Sloan, V.P.; Scott J. Sloan, Secy.
EIN: 911799087
Selected grants: The following grants were reported in 2004.
$330,411 to New School Foundation, Seattle, WA.
$1,000 to Camp Ronald McDonald for Good Times, Los Angeles, CA.
$1,000 to Guide Dogs for the Blind.

$1,000 to Pancreatic Cancer Action Network, El Segundo, CA.
$1,000 to YMCA of Greater Seattle, Seattle, WA.

9688
Orin Smith Family Foundation ◇ ☆
4963 N.E. 85th St.
Seattle, WA   98115-3913

Established in 2004 in WA.
Donor: Orin C. Smith.
Foundation type: Independent foundation.
Financial data (yr. ended 12/31/05): Assets, $18,932,261 (M); gifts received, $700,000; expenditures, $502,349; qualifying distributions, $401,682; giving activities include $400,000 for 2 grants (high: $200,000; low: $200,000).
Fields of interest: Higher education.
Limitations: Applications not accepted. Giving primarily in WA.
Application information: Contributes only to pre-selected organizations.
Directors: Kevin Smith; Orin C. Smith.
EIN: 200477535

9689
Frost and Margaret Snyder Foundation ◇
c/o KeyBank N.A., Trust Div.
P.O. Box 11500, M.S. WA 31-01-0210
Tacoma, WA   98411-5052
Contact: Mollie Determan, Trust Off., KeyBank N.A.

Trust established in 1957 in WA.
Donors: Frost Snyder†; Margaret Snyder†.
Foundation type: Independent foundation.
Financial data (yr. ended 12/31/05): Assets, $12,669,170 (M); expenditures, $733,157; qualifying distributions, $650,601; giving activities include $622,000 for 15 grants (high: $100,000; low: $20,000).
Purpose and activities: Giving primarily for education.
Fields of interest: Secondary school/education; Higher education; Education; Human services; Roman Catholic agencies & churches.
Limitations: Giving primarily in WA. No grants to individuals.
Application information: Application form not required.
 Initial approach: Letter
 Deadline(s): Sept.
 Board meeting date(s): Aug.
Trustees: Margaret S. Cunningham; Andrea S. Gernon; Robert Mallon; KeyBank N.A.
EIN: 916030549

9690
The Starbucks Foundation
c/o Starbucks Corp.
2401 Utah Ave. S.
Seattle, WA   98134
Contact: Catherine Bachy, Prog. Mgr.
E-mail: foundationgrants@starbucks.com;
URL: http://www.starbucks.com/aboutus/foundation.asp

Established in 1997 in WA.
Donors: Starbucks Corp.; Starbucks Coffee Co.
Foundation type: Company-sponsored foundation.

Financial data (yr. ended 9/30/05): Assets, $11,514,408 (M); gifts received, $12,732,626; expenditures, $2,697,966; qualifying distributions, $2,688,463; giving activities include $2,688,463 for 96 grants (high: $800,000; low: $2,500).
Purpose and activities: The foundation supports programs designed to serve young people by providing them access to arts and culture, education, literacy, and environmental education. Special emphasis is directed toward programs designed to intergrate the support of Starbucks stores, employees, and customers; and encourage learning in innovative ways.
Fields of interest: Arts; Elementary/secondary education; Education, reading; Education; Environmental education; Youth.
International interests: Canada.
Type of support: Program development.
Limitations: Giving on a national basis and in Canada. No support for political organizations or religious organizations. No grants to individuals, or for neighborhood clean-ups or tree plantings, wildlife conservation projects, capital campaigns, capital expenditures or land acquisition, school bands or orchestras or non-literacy art programs, fundraising events, one-time events or programs, event sponsorships, adventure travel, league sports programs, scholarships or fellowships, expeditions, political campaigns, the production of marketing material promoting Starbucks, the production of products to sell in Starbucks stores, or endowments.
Publications: Application guidelines; Corporate giving report; Grants list; Informational brochure (including application guidelines).
Application information: Application form required.
 Initial approach: Complete online application form
 Deadline(s): Mar. 1 and Sept. 1
 Final notification: 12 weeks
Officers and Directors:* Orin Smith,* Pres.; Paula E. Boggs,* Secy.; Donna Brooks,* Treas.; Lauren Moore, Exec. Dir.; Martin Coles; Margie Giuntini; Jonathan Greenblatt; Dub Hay; Gregg Johnson; Elise McClure; David M. Olsen; David A. Pace; Sandra Taylor; Peter Thum.
Number of staff: 1 full-time professional; 2 part-time professional; 1 part-time support.
EIN: 911795425

9691
The Stewardship Foundation ▼
P.O. Box 1278
Tacoma, WA   98401-1278
Contact: Cary Paine, Exec. Dir.
E-mail: info@stewardshipfdn.org; URL: http://www.stewardshipfdn.org

Trust established in 1962 in WA.
Donor: C. Davis Weyerhaeuser Irrevocable Trust.
Foundation type: Independent foundation.
Financial data (yr. ended 12/31/04): Assets, $119,535,338 (M); expenditures, $7,164,946; qualifying distributions, $6,286,901; giving activities include $5,814,876 for 178 grants (high: $500,000; low: $225; average: $10,000–$100,000).
Purpose and activities: The foundation provides resources to Christ-centered organizations whose mission is to share their faith in Jesus Christ with people throughout the world. The foundation will consider making grants to organizations that promote: 1) Leadership - preparation and training of leaders for the church and marketplace; and

mentoring and discipleship of indigenous leaders in the least evangelized world. 2) Poverty - community development (i.e. health, agriculture, water, education); and economic development primarily in the developing world. 3) Reconciliation and Justice - advocacy and intervention on behalf of people suffering injustice, oppression and persecution; protection for refugees and displaced people around the world, and efforts which seek to end the conditions that create displacement; promotion of reconciliation and healing among current and historic enemies; and advocacy and promotion of religious liberty. 4) Relational Evangelism - building relationships and friendships with people for the purpose of introducing them to Jesus Christ. 5) Cultural Engagement - addressing issues faced by youth and families. 6) Organizational Enhancement - support for organizations which serve other organizations working in areas of the themes above; and promoting collaboration and partnership among organizations.

Fields of interest: Youth development, services; Youth development, religion; Youth, services; International economic development; International peace/security; Community development; Leadership development; Christian agencies & churches.

Type of support: General/operating support; Continuing support; Program development; Matching/challenge support.

Limitations: Giving internationally, nationally and in western WA, especially in Tacoma and Pierce County and the Puget Sound Region. No support for churches (except for religious support to Christian parachurch organizations and Christian-Evangelical purposes). No grants to individuals, or for seed money, endowment funds, deficit financing, research, videos, media time or program production.

Publications: Application guidelines.

Application information: Application limited to once a year. Applicants should not submit full proposals unless requested to do so by the foundation. Application form required.

  Initial approach: Letter of inquiry (1-2 pages)
  Copies of proposal: 1
  Deadline(s): Jan. 1, Apr. 1, July 1, and Oct. 1
  Board meeting date(s): Mar., June, Sept., and Dec.
  Final notification: 90 days

Officers and Directors:* William T. Weyerhaeuser,* Chair.; Annette B. Weyerhaeuser,* Vice-Chair. and Treas.; Cary Paine, Exec. Dir.; Wesley J. Anderson; Kerry L. Dearborn; Susan S. Hutchison; Donald W. Mowat.

Number of staff: 1 full-time professional.

EIN: 916020515

Selected grants: The following grants were reported in 2004.

$500,000 to Whitworth College, Spokane, WA. For academic building.

$453,333 to Young Life, Colorado Springs, CO. 2 grants: $333,333 (For Malibu Club Hydro project), $120,000 (For Northwest indigenous leadership project).

$105,441 to Fuller Theological Seminary, Pasadena, CA. For Center for Ministry to Youth and Their Families.

$100,000 to International Justice Mission, Alexandria, VA. For general operating support.

$100,000 to Presbytery of North Puget Sound, Everett, WA. For Skagit Hispanic Ministries for establishment of ecumenical center.

$30,000 to Advocates International, Fairfax, VA. For development of web site.

$25,000 to Compassion International, Colorado Springs, CO. For Haiti Child Survival program.

$25,000 to InterVarsity Christian Fellowship/USA, Madison, WI. For International Fellowship of Evangelical Students program.

$20,000 to R. Merle Palmer Minority Scholarship Foundation, Fircrest, WA. For scholarship assistance for low-income minority students.

9692

T.E.W. Foundation ✧

506 2nd Ave., Ste. 2900
Seattle, WA 98104-2343

Established in 1997 in WA.

Donor: T. Evans Wyckoff†.

Foundation type: Independent foundation.

Financial data (yr. ended 12/31/05): Assets, $8,881,327 (M); expenditures, $474,114; qualifying distributions, $416,005; giving activities include $407,776 for 43 grants (high: $20,000; low: $500).

Purpose and activities: Giving primarily for education.

Fields of interest: Elementary/secondary education; Secondary school/education; Higher education, university; Environment, natural resources; Human services; Roman Catholic agencies & churches.

Limitations: Applications not accepted. Giving primarily in WA. No grants to individuals.

Application information: Contributes only to pre-selected organizations.

Officers: Alison Wyckoff Milliman, Co-Chair.; Paul L. Wyckoff, Co-Chair.

Trustees: Theiline Wyckoff Cramer; Susan Wyckoff Pohl; Ann Pigott Wyckoff; Martha Wyckoff-Byrne; Sheila Wyckoff-Dickey.

EIN: 911817398

Selected grants: The following grants were reported in 2004.

$90,000 to Wyckoff House and Association, Brooklyn, NY.

$25,000 to Bishop Blanchet High School, Seattle, WA.

$20,000 to Puget Sound Community School, Seattle, WA.

$13,300 to Community Assessment, Referral and Education (CARE), Fraser, MI.

$10,000 to American Red Cross.

$10,000 to Chief Seattle Club, Seattle, WA.

$10,000 to University of Washington Foundation, Seattle, WA.

$5,000 to Hamlin Robinson School, Seattle, WA.

$5,000 to Northwest Maritime Center, Port Townsend, WA.

$3,000 to University of Redlands, Redlands, CA.

9693

The Greater Tacoma Community Foundation

950 Pacific Ave., Ste. 1200
P.O. Box 1995
Tacoma, WA 98401-1995 (253) 383-5622
Contact: For grants: Kristen Corning, Community Progs. Coord.; For grants: Sherrana Kempton, Office Mgr.

FAX: (253) 272-8099; E-mail: kcorning@gtcf.org; Grant application E-mail: sherrana@gtcf.org; URL: http://www.tacomafoundation.org

Incorporated in 1977 in WA.

Foundation type: Community foundation.

Financial data (yr. ended 6/30/06): Assets, $59,001,732 (M); gifts received, $4,597,650; expenditures, $4,907,275; giving activities include $2,339,429 for grants.

Purpose and activities: The foundation improves the quality of life in the community by promoting private giving, maximizing donor benefits and grantmaking for the public good.

Fields of interest: Arts education; Museums; Performing arts; Performing arts, theater; Humanities; Historic preservation/historical societies; Arts; Child development, education; Higher education; Adult/continuing education; Libraries/library science; Education; Environment, natural resources; Environment; Animal welfare; Hospitals (general); Health care; Substance abuse, services; Mental health/crisis services; Health organizations, association; AIDS; AIDS research; Food services; Housing/shelter, development; Recreation; Youth development, services; Children/ youth, services; Child development, services; Family services; Residential/custodial care, hospices; Aging, centers/services; Homeless, human services; Human services; Community development; Voluntarism promotion; Government/ public administration; Leadership development; Aging; Disabilities, people with; Economically disadvantaged; Homeless.

Type of support: Scholarships—to individuals; General/operating support; Continuing support; Management development/capacity building; Capital campaigns; Building/renovation; Equipment; Land acquisition; Emergency funds; Program development; Seed money; Technical assistance; Consulting services; Program-related investments/loans; Matching/challenge support.

Limitations: Giving limited to Pierce County, WA. No support for religious organizations for sacramental/ theological purposes. No grants to individuals (except for scholarships), or for annual campaigns, fellowships, seminars, meetings or travel, fundraising events or fundraising feasibility projects, endowments or debt reduction, or publications, unless specified by donor.

Publications: Application guidelines; Annual report; Financial statement; Informational brochure; Informational brochure (including application guidelines); Newsletter.

Application information: Visit foundation Web site for application forms and guidelines. A letter of intent is required prior to submitting a full grant request. Faxed or e-mailed applications are not accepted. Application form required.

  Initial approach: Letter of intent (1 page)
  Copies of proposal: 2
  Deadline(s): Jan. 15 and July 15 for letter of intent; Feb. 15 and Aug. 15 for grant proposal
  Board meeting date(s): 6 times yearly
  Final notification: Within 10 days for letter of intent determination; June and Dec. for grants

Officers and Directors:* James L. Walton,* Chair.; Wendy Gray,* Vice-Chair.; Rose Lincoln, Pres.; John Lantz,* Secy.; Francie Carr, C.F.O.; Terry Stone,* Treas.; Shirley Brockmann, Cont.; Albert S. Bacon III; James Brown; Tammis Greene; Linda Gutmann; Dennis E. Hanberg; Tom Hosea; John S. Larsen; Amy Lewis; Claude A. Remy; Joan Watt.

Number of staff: 6 full-time professional; 1 full-time support.
EIN: 911007459

9694
Talaris Research Institute ✧
P.O. Box 45040
Seattle, WA 98145
FAX: (206) 529-6899; E-mail: info@talaris.org;
URL: http://www.talaris.org

Donor: Apex Foundation.
Foundation type: Independent foundation.
Financial data (yr. ended 12/31/03): Assets, $513,863 (M); gifts received, $2,025,397; expenditures, $1,863,811; qualifying distributions, $1,448,631; giving activities include $392,194 for 2 grants (high: $306,194; low: $86,000).
Purpose and activities: Giving to advance knowledge of early brain development for all who nurture children.
Fields of interest: Health care, infants; Brain research.
Limitations: Applications not accepted. Giving primarily in WA. No grants to individuals.
Application information: Contributes only to pre-selected organizations.
Officers: Bruce R. McCaw, Co-Chair.; Jolene M. McCaw, Co-Chair.; Samuel H. Smith, Ph.D., Pres.; Bridgett Chandler, V.P. and Chief Prog. Off.
Directors: Roberta R. Katz, Ph.D.; Donald P. Nielsen; Craig W. Stewart.
EIN: 912011024
Selected grants: The following grants were reported in 2003.
$306,194 to Relationship Research Institute, Seattle, WA. For early childhood development research.
$86,000 to University of Washington, Seattle, WA. For early childhood development research.

9695
The Tamaki Foundation ✧ ☆
4616 25th Ave. N.E., PMB #37
Seattle, WA 98105

Established in 1988 in WA.
Donor: Meriko Tamaki.
Foundation type: Independent foundation.
Financial data (yr. ended 12/31/05): Assets, $4,270,930 (M); gifts received, $89,000; expenditures, $361,069; qualifying distributions, $335,757; giving activities include $333,000 for 8 grants (high: $145,000; low: $2,000).
Purpose and activities: Giving primarily for education and social services.
Fields of interest: Higher education; Crime/law enforcement; Human services; Roman Catholic agencies & churches.
Limitations: Giving on a national basis, with emphasis on CA; also some giving internationally.
Application information:
Initial approach: Letter
Deadline(s): None
Officers: Meriko Tamaki, Pres.; Fr. John Martin, V.P.; Kozo Yamamura, Secy.; John H. Hopkins, Treas.
EIN: 943099647
Selected grants: The following grants were reported in 2003.
$166,676 to University of Washington, Jackson School of International Studies, Seattle, WA.

Toward project in conjunction with Maryland University.
$40,000 to Giarretto Institute, San Jose, CA.
$15,000 to Youth Services Program, San Jose, CA.
$12,000 to Friends of the Poor, La Jolla, CA.
$300 to Paralyzed Veterans of America, Wilton, NH.

9696
Lawrence True and Linda Brown Foundation ✧
614 W. Prospect St.
Seattle, WA 98119-3627
Contact: Linda Brown, Secy.

Established in 1997 in VA.
Donors: Lawrence True; Linda Brown.
Foundation type: Independent foundation.
Financial data (yr. ended 12/31/05): Assets, $14,258,582 (M); gifts received, $100; expenditures, $692,699; qualifying distributions, $674,750; giving activities include $672,750 for 14 grants (high: $250,000; low: $750).
Purpose and activities: Giving primarily for medical and other education, as well as for medical research; funding also for social services, and legal services.
Fields of interest: Arts; Medical school/education; Education; Health organizations, association; Cancer research; Prostate cancer research; Pathology research; Legal services; Economically disadvantaged.
Type of support: Program development; Curriculum development; Research.
Limitations: Giving on a national basis, with emphasis on Washington, DC, and Seattle, WA.
Application information: Application form not required.
Deadline(s): None
Officers: Lawrence True, Pres.; Linda Brown, Secy.
EIN: 911817055
Selected grants: The following grants were reported in 2003.
$200,000 to Legal Aid for Washington Fund, Seattle, WA. 2 grants: $100,000 each.
$100,000 to Endowment for Equal Justice, Seattle, WA.
$100,000 to University of Washington, Medical School, Department of Pathology, Seattle, WA.
$75,000 to Saint Albans School, DC.
$25,000 to Fred Hutchinson Cancer Research Center, Seattle, WA. For prostate cancer research.
$15,000 to Pike Market Senior Center, Seattle, WA.
$5,000 to Downtown Emergency Service Center, Seattle, WA.
$5,000 to Jubilee Womens Center, Seattle, WA.
$3,500 to Memorial Sloan-Kettering Cancer Center, New York, NY. For breast cancer research.

9697
The UNOVA Foundation ✧
(formerly The Western Atas Foundation)
6001 36th Ave. W.
Everett, WA 98203-1264 (425) 265-2465
Contact: Cathy D. Younger, Pres.

Established in 1993.
Foundation type: Independent foundation.
Financial data (yr. ended 12/31/05): Assets, $19,538,027 (M); expenditures, $1,039,068;

qualifying distributions, $963,541; giving activities include $915,260 for 206 grants.
Purpose and activities: Giving primarily for education; funding also for the Boy Scouts of America, a performing arts center, and the United Way.
Fields of interest: Performing arts centers; Elementary/secondary education; Higher education; Education; Boy scouts; YM/YWCAs & YM/YWHAs; Federated giving programs.
Type of support: Employee matching gifts.
Limitations: Giving primarily in CA, IA, MI, and WA; some giving also in OH.
Application information:
Initial approach: Letter
Deadline(s): None
Officer: Cathy D. Younger, Pres.
Directors: Dan S. Bishop; Larry Brady; Michael E. Keane.
EIN: 954453230
Selected grants: The following grants were reported in 2004.
$97,610 to National Merit Scholarship Corporation, Evanston, IL.
$28,254 to United Way of Snohomish County, Everett, WA.
$25,000 to Northwestern University, Evanston, IL.
$25,000 to University of Southern California, Los Angeles, CA.
$13,828 to United Way of Greater Cincinnati, Cincinnati, OH.
$10,000 to Don Bosco Technical Institute, Rosemead, CA.
$5,360 to Latin School of Chicago, Chicago, IL.
$5,277 to Saint Chrysostoms Day School, Chicago, IL.
$3,334 to United Way of Rock River Valley, Rockford, IL.
$2,000 to Memorial Junior High School, South Euclid, OH.

9698
Vidalakis Family Foundation ✧ ☆
101 Stewart St., Ste. 1111
Seattle, WA 98101

Established in 1999 in WA.
Donors: Nick S. Vidalakis; Nancy G. Vidalakis.
Foundation type: Independent foundation.
Financial data (yr. ended 12/31/05): Assets, $29,218 (M); gifts received, $103,991; expenditures, $1,277,814; qualifying distributions, $1,274,450; giving activities include $1,274,450 for 17 grants (high: $1,000,000; low: $100).
Fields of interest: Higher education, college; Higher education, university; Protestant agencies & churches; Roman Catholic agencies & churches.
Limitations: Applications not accepted. No grants to individuals.
Application information: Contributes only to pre-selected organizations.
Officers: Nick S. Vidalakis, Pres.; Perry N. Vidalakis, Exec. V.P. and Secy.; John N. Vidalakis, Exec. V.P. and Treas.; Nancy G. Vidalakis, Sr. Exec. V.P.; George N. Vidalakis, V.P.; Nicole N. Vidalakis, V.P.
EIN: 911997816
Selected grants: The following grants were reported in 2004.
$55,250 to Holy Trinity Greek Orthodox Church.
$38,400 to Stanford University, Stanford, CA.
$27,750 to University of Washington, Seattle, WA. For Dr. Nick and Nancy Vidalakis Family Endowed Professorship.

$13,000 to Hellenic Cultural Foundation, Saint Louis, MO.

$10,000 to Greek Orthodox Cathedral of the Ascension, Oakland, CA.

$10,000 to Leadership 100, New York, NY.

$1,000 to Archons of the Ecumenical Patriarchate, New York, NY.

$1,000 to Bread of Life Mission, Seattle, WA.

$1,000 to Community Breast Health Project, Palo Alto, CA.

$1,000 to IOCC, Baltimore, MD.

9699
Vista Hermosa ☆
1111 Fishhook Park Rd.
Prescott, WA 99348
Contact: Suzanne Broetje, Exec. Dir.
URL: http://www.vista-hermosa.org

Established in 1990 in WA.
Donors: Broetje Orchards; Cheryl Broetje; Ralph Broetje.
Foundation type: Independent foundation.
Financial data (yr. ended 12/31/04): Assets, $13,213,805 (M); gifts received, $5,483,182; expenditures, $1,362,417; qualifying distributions, $1,160,277; giving activities include $679,485 for 6 grants (high: $659,294; low: $585), $73,205 for 23 grants to individuals (high: $19,228; low: $148), and $423,756 for 3 foundation-administered programs.
Purpose and activities: The foundation was established for the purpose of using proceeds from Broetje Orchards to serve children and underserved communities, both at home and around the world. The foundation also provides FirstFruits Scholarships for children of Broetje Orchards' employees, and community service scholarships for low-income, first-generation students.
Fields of interest: Education; Nutrition; Agriculture/food; Housing/shelter, development; International relief; Community development.
International interests: Haiti; India; Jamaica; Kenya; Mexico.
Type of support: Program development; Seed money; Scholarships—to individuals; Matching/challenge support.
Limitations: Giving on a national and international basis. No grants to individuals (except for scholarships), or endowments, professorships; no student loans, or loans to individuals.
Publications: Application guidelines; Grants list; Informational brochure; Newsletter.
Application information: See foundation Web site for application guides and procedures, and downloading of application form. Application form required.
Initial approach: Letter of inquiry
Copies of proposal: 2
Deadline(s): None
Board meeting date(s): Monthly
Final notification: 4 weeks
Officers: Cheryl Broetje, Pres.; Teresa Morton, Secy.; Sandra Gamble, Treas.; Suzanne Broetje, Exec. Dir.
Directors: Ralph Broetje; Sara Broetje.
Number of staff: 7 full-time professional; 2 part-time professional; 23 full-time support; 9 part-time support.
EIN: 911491438
Selected grants: The following grants were reported in 2006.

$87,000 to Food for the Poor, Jamaica. For housing and agricultural development in Falmouth.

$62,000 to Methodist Church, Marimanti Rural Training Center, Kenya. For farmer training.

$50,000 to Bread for the World, DC. For Latino Community Organizer and advocacy on hunger.

$50,000 to International Justice Mission, Alexandria, VA. For eradication of forced prostitution in Mumbai.

$50,000 to Shared Hope International, Home of Hope, Vancouver, WA. For care of sex trafficking victims in Jamaica.

$46,500 to Catholic Relief Services, Mexico. For Just Market for Small Farmers in Chihuahua.

$30,000 to Catholic Relief Services, India. For education of child laborers in Andhra Pradesh.

$25,000 to Beyond Borders, Norristown, PA. For environmental education campaign.

$25,000 to Harambee Ministries, Harambee Prep School, Pasadena, CA. For fundraising and development.

$25,000 to Voices of Hope, Kenya. For education and leadership development of Maasai girls.

9700
Robert C. and Nani S. Warren Foundation ✦ ☆
82 Swigert Rd.
Washougal, WA 98671-7636
Contact: Jack B. Schwartz, Dir.

Established in 1994 in WA and OR.
Donor: Nani S. Warren.
Foundation type: Independent foundation.
Financial data (yr. ended 12/31/05): Assets, $10,898,594 (M); gifts received, $11,744; expenditures, $457,158; qualifying distributions, $405,780; giving activities include $405,780 for grants.
Fields of interest: Arts; Higher education; Education; Health organizations, association; Human services; Roman Catholic agencies & churches; Religion.
Limitations: Applications not accepted. No grants to individuals.
Application information: Contributes only to pre-selected organizations.
Officer: Penny Guest, Treas.
Directors: Jack B. Schwartz; Elizabeth Warren; Nani S. Warren.
EIN: 931083078
Selected grants: The following grants were reported in 2005.

$100,000 to Portland Art Museum, Portland, OR. 2 grants: $50,000 each

$50,000 to Oregon Health and Science University Foundation, Portland, OR.

$36,133 to Catlin Gabel School, Portland, OR. 2 grants: $2,800, $33,333

$33,634 to Jack, Will and Rob Kids Foundation, Camas, WA.

$21,000 to Orcas Theater and Community Center, Eastsound, WA.

$14,900 to American Federation of Arts, New York, NY.

$5,000 to Portland State University Foundation, Portland, OR.

$500 to National Trust for Historic Preservation, DC.

9701
Washington Research Foundation ✦
2815 Eastlake Ave. E., Ste. 300
Seattle, WA 98102
Contact: Amy McCormick, Office Mgr.
FAX: (206) 336-5615;
E-mail: amccormi@wrfseattle.org; URL: http://www.wrfseattle.org

Established in 1981 in WA.
Foundation type: Independent foundation.
Financial data (yr. ended 6/30/05): Assets, $64,903,736 (M); expenditures, $24,079,919; qualifying distributions, $7,139,078; giving activities include $5,041,423 for 60 grants (high: $142,000; low: $125), and $1,358,027 for loans/program-related investments.
Purpose and activities: The foundation's mission is to capture and enhance the value of intellectual property, arising from Washington State research institutions, to support research and scholarship.
Fields of interest: Science, research.
Type of support: Seed money; Research; Program-related investments/loans.
Limitations: Applications not accepted. Giving limited to research institutions in WA. No grants to individuals.
Publications: Annual report; Informational brochure.
Application information: Contributes only to pre-selected organizations.
Board meeting date(s): Jan., Apr., July, and Oct.
Officers and Directors:* Thomas J. Cable,* Chair.; Ronald S. Howell,* Pres.; C. Kent Carlson, Secy.; Paul Bialek; Barry Forman; Calvert Knudsen; Sally Narodick; W. Hunter Simpson; George I. Thomas, M.D.
Number of staff: 8 full-time professional; 3 full-time support.
EIN: 911160492
Selected grants: The following grants were reported in 2005.

$2,200,000 to University of Washington, Seattle, WA. 10 grants: $250,000, $187,500, $200,000, $250,000, $250,000, $62,500, $250,000, $250,000, $250,000, $250,000

9702
Washington Women in Need ✦
1849 114th Ave. N.E.
Bellevue, WA 98004 (425) 451-8838
Contact: Colleen M. Crowley, Exec. Dir.

Established in 1992 in WA.
Donor: Julia L. Pritt.
Foundation type: Operating foundation.
Financial data (yr. ended 6/30/05): Assets, $2,137,563 (M); gifts received, $1,227,757; expenditures, $931,295; qualifying distributions, $907,726; giving activities include $532,852 for grants to individuals.
Purpose and activities: Grants for healthcare services, educational assistance, and emergency services to low-income women residing in Washington state.
Fields of interest: Women, centers/services; Women; Economically disadvantaged.
Type of support: Grants to individuals.
Limitations: Giving limited to female residents of WA state.
Application information: Application form required.
Deadline(s): None

Officers: Malia Reid-Radford, Pres.; Patricia Dye, V.P.; Christopher Johnson, Secy.; Susan Bohman, Treas.; Colleen M. Crowley, Exec. Dir.
Directors: Karen Bloomquist; Beth Calkins; Robin Carey; Carmel Duer; Nancy Duncan; Eric Flaten; Dena Gregory; Donna Linn; Shawn McCord; Kathleen Miller; Barbara Porter; Kristen M. Schuerlein.
EIN: 911559848

9703
Weyerhaeuser Company Foundation ▼
CH 1K36
P.O. Box 9777
Federal Way, WA 98063-9777 (253) 924-3159
Contact: Elizabeth A. Crossman, Pres.
FAX: (253) 924-3658; URL: http://www.weyerhaeuser.com/citizenship/philanthropy/weyerfoundation.asp

Incorporated in 1948 in WA.
Donor: Weyerhaeuser Co.
Foundation type: Company-sponsored foundation.
Financial data (yr. ended 12/25/05): Assets, $21,584,328 (M); gifts received, $4,100,000; expenditures, $11,294,431; qualifying distributions, $10,787,003; giving activities include $9,941,515 for 1,253 grants (high: $500,000; low: $45), and $319,624 for employee matching gifts.
Purpose and activities: The foundation supports organizations involved with the environment, housing, neighborhood safety, and the forest products industry.
Fields of interest: Environment, research; Environment, public policy; Environment, natural resources; Environment, forests; Environmental education; Housing/shelter, temporary shelter; Housing/shelter; Safety, education; Business/industry; Children.
Type of support: Employee volunteer services; General/operating support; Capital campaigns; Building/renovation; Equipment; Land acquisition; Emergency funds; Program development; Conferences/seminars; Publication; Seed money; Curriculum development; Research; Technical assistance; Employee matching gifts; Employee-related scholarships.
Limitations: Giving on a national and international basis, with emphasis on areas of company operations. No support for religious organizations not of direct benefit to the entire community; generally, no support for disease-specific organizations. No grants to individuals (except for employee-related scholarships), or for political campaigns, lobbying activities, general operating support for organizations indirectly receiving Weyerhaeuser Foundation support through a federated organization or combined campaign, tickets or tables, or activities providing benefits to Weyerhaeuer or employees of Weyerhaeuser; generally, no grants for services the public sector should be reasonably expected to provide, endowments or memorials, research or conferences unrelated to the forest products industry, hospital capital campaigns resulting in higher costs to health care users, or debt reduction.
Publications: Application guidelines; Biennial report (including application guidelines).
Application information: Application form required.
Initial approach: Download application form and mail proposal and application form to foundation
Copies of proposal: 1

Deadline(s): Aug. 31
Board meeting date(s): Feb. and mid-year
Final notification: 2 to 3 months
Officers and Trustees:* Ernesta Ballard,* Chair.; Elizabeth A. Crossman, Pres.; Karen L. Veitenhans, V.P. and Secy.; Jeffrey W. Nitta, Treas.; Steven J. Hillyard, Cont.; Patricia M. Bedient; Marvin D. Cooper; Daniel S. Fulton; Richard E. Hanson; Mike Jackson; James R. Keller; Sandy D. McDade; Susan M. Mersereau; Craig D. Neeser; Edward P. Rogel; Steven R. Rogel; Richard J. Taggart; George H. Weyerhaeuser, Jr.
Number of staff: 4 full-time professional; 2 full-time support.
EIN: 916024225
Selected grants: The following grants were reported in 2005.
$500,000 to American Red Cross, National Headquarters, DC. For relief efforts for Hurricane Katrina.
$400,000 to University of Washington Foundation, Seattle, WA.
$350,000 to Habitat for Humanity International, Americus, GA.
$179,400 to United Way of Pierce County, Tacoma, WA.
$75,591 to American Forest Foundation, DC.
$22,000 to HomeAid Houston, Houston, TX.
$20,303 to University of New Brunswick, Faculty of Forestry and Environmental Management, Fredericton, Canada. .
$15,000 to United Way of Garland County, Hot Springs, AR.
$12,500 to Oregon Independent College Foundation, Portland, OR.
$12,000 to Little Swift Creek Volunteer Fire Department, Ernul, NC.

9704
Wiancko Charitable Foundation, Inc. ✦ ☆
P.O. Box 1964
Vashon Island, WA 98070

Established in 1989 in WY.
Donors: Thomas H. Wiancko; Sibyl S. Wiancko.
Foundation type: Independent foundation.
Financial data (yr. ended 12/31/05): Assets, $14,463,841 (M); expenditures, $836,556; qualifying distributions, $704,746; giving activities include $699,813 for grants.
Purpose and activities: Giving primarily for environmental and wildlife conservation.
Fields of interest: Environment, natural resources; Environment; Animals/wildlife, preservation/protection; Reproductive health, family planning.
Limitations: Applications not accepted. Giving on a national basis. No grants to individuals.
Application information: Contributes only to pre-selected organizations.
Officers: R. Dennis Wiancko, Pres.; Anna K. Wiancko-Chasman, V.P.; Judith W. Parker, Secy.-Treas.
Trustees: Paul Chasman; Bradley Parker; Anna K. Wiancko-Chasman; Thomas H. Wiancko.
EIN: 830291490

9705
The Wilburforce Foundation ▼ ✦
3601 Fremont Ave. N., Ste. 304
Seattle, WA 98103 (206) 632-2325
Contact: Timothy Greyhavens, Exec. Dir.

FAX: (206) 632-2326;
E-mail: grants@wilburforce.org; Additional address (Montana office): P.O. Box 296, Bozeman, MT 59771-0296, tel.: (406) 586-9796, FAX: (406) 586-3076, E-mail: jennifer@wilburforce.org; Additional tel.: (800) 201-0148 (Seattle office), (800) 317-8180 (Montana office); URL: http://www.wilburforce.org

Established in 1990 in WA.
Donors: James Letwin; Rosanna W. Letwin.
Foundation type: Independent foundation.
Financial data (yr. ended 12/31/04): Assets, $11,779,654 (M); gifts received, $19,333,035; expenditures, $10,424,888; qualifying distributions, $10,211,055; giving activities include $8,885,528 for 235 grants (high: $1,051,212; low: $200; average: $5,000–$250,000).
Purpose and activities: The foundation is dedicated to protecting nature's richness and diversity through funding programs that help to preserve our remaining wild places.
Fields of interest: Environment, natural resources; Environment.
International interests: Canada.
Type of support: General/operating support; Capital campaigns; Equipment; Program development; Seed money; Technical assistance; Consulting services; Matching/challenge support.
Limitations: Giving primarily in the western U.S. and western Canada, particularly AK, AZ, NM, OR, UT, WA, WY, British Columbia, and the Yellowstone to Yukon region of U.S.-Canada. No support for schools or universities, or governmental agencies. No grants to individuals, or for fellowships or scholarships, endowment funds, operating budgets, or deficit financing or indirect costs; no loans.
Publications: Grants list.
Application information: Application form required.
Initial approach: Telephone
Copies of proposal: 1
Deadline(s): Given upon invitation
Board meeting date(s): Spring, summer, and fall
Final notification: 4 months
Officers and Directors:* Rosanna W. Letwin,* Chair. and Treas.; Stephanie Nichols-Young,* Pres.; Timothy Greyhavens, Secy. and Exec. Dir.; Gary Austin.
Number of staff: 9 full-time professional.
EIN: 943137894
Selected grants: The following grants were reported in 2004.
$1,051,212 to Nature Conservancy, Arlington, VA. For program support.
$650,000 to Training Resources for the Environmental Community, Santa Fe, NM. 2 grants: $325,000 (For general support to increase confidence, knowledge, and skills of Wilburforce grantees and their organizational leaders to carry out their missions and effectively manage change), $325,000 (For general support to increase confidence, knowledge, and skills of Wilburforce grantees and organizational leaders to carry out their missions and effectively manage change).
$350,000 to Earthworks, DC. For general support to protect West's pristine landscapes by promoting reform of U.S. mining industry.
$100,000 to Earthjustice, Oakland, CA. To protect pristine public lands and habitat for endangered species throughout western U.S.
$100,000 to Raincoast Conservation Foundation, Tofino, Canada. For Raincoast Wolf Project, to complete critical genetics research and conduct

sophisticated, multi-organization conservation campaign to generate and activate public interest in British Columbia's coastal wolves and their habitat, as well as leverage major change in North American wildlife management and forestry policies.

$90,000 to Wildlife Conservation Society, Bronx, NY. For carnivore conservation in Southern Rocky Mountains and Greater Yellowstone Ecosystem towards scientific research to study wildlife movement.

$84,000 to Center for Biological Diversity, Tucson, AZ. For general support to protect endangered species throughout the West.

$25,000 to Craighead Environmental Research Institute, Bozeman, MT. To map core grizzly bear habitat and connectivity over large region centered on Greater Yellowstone Ecosystem, and to provide information for conservation activities on areas of priority for connectivity beyond Grizzly Bear Recovery Zone.

$25,000 to Nevada Conservation League Education Fund, Las Vegas, NV. For general support and capacity building to strengthen conservation organizations and empower individuals to protect air, land, and water resources.

9706
Williams, Kastner & Gibbs Foundation in Memorial of J. K. McMullin & W. H. Robertson ✧ ☆
1121 39th Ave. E.
Seattle, WA 98112

Established in 1994.
Foundation type: Independent foundation.
Financial data (yr. ended 12/31/05): Assets, $129,354 (M); expenditures, $336,102; qualifying distributions, $333,350; giving activities include $333,350 for grants.
Fields of interest: Health care.
Limitations: Applications not accepted. Giving primarily in Seattle, WA. No grants to individuals.
Application information: Contributes only to pre-selected organizations.
Directors: Robert Betts; Teresa Bigelow; Anne Kirk; Sara Robertson.
EIN: 911461348

9707
Howard S. Wright Family Foundation ✧
(formerly Howard S. Wright Foundation)
1264 Eastlake Ave. E.
Seattle, WA 98102 (425) 323-3686
Contact: Sally S. Wright, Pres.

Established in 1984 in WA.
Donor: Howard S. Wright†.
Foundation type: Independent foundation.
Financial data (yr. ended 12/31/05): Assets, $7,427,078 (M); expenditures, $468,344; qualifying distributions, $406,138; giving activities include $400,000 for 20 grants (high: $150,000; low: $7,000).

Purpose and activities: Primary areas of interest include the arts, education, and health.
Fields of interest: Arts; Higher education; Education; Environment; Health care; Health organizations, association; Christian agencies & churches.
Type of support: Annual campaigns; Capital campaigns; Building/renovation; Endowments.
Limitations: Applications not accepted. Giving primarily in the Pacific Northwest, with emphasis on Seattle, WA. No support for religious organizations. No grants to individuals.
Publications: Annual report.
Application information: Unsolicited requests for funds not accepted.
 Board meeting date(s): Quarterly
Officers and Directors:* Sally S. Wright,* Pres.; Katherine A. Janeway,* Treas.; Theiline W. Rolfe; Korynne H. Wright.
Number of staff: 1 part-time support.
EIN: 911276047
Selected grants: The following grants were reported in 2004.
$100,000 to A Contemporary Theater (ACT), Seattle, WA.
$45,000 to Seattle Center Foundation, Seattle, WA.
$30,000 to Summer Search Seattle, Seattle, WA.
$25,000 to Camp Fire USA, Seattle, WA.
$12,000 to Living Desert Reserve, Palm Desert, CA.
$7,300 to Seattle Art Museum, Seattle, WA.
$5,000 to Pacific Northwest Ballet Association, Seattle, WA.
$1,000 to Palm Springs Air Museum, Palm Springs, CA.
$1,000 to Seattle Repertory Theater, Seattle, WA.
$1,000 to Woodland Park Zoological Society, Seattle, WA.

9708
The Bagley Wright Family Fund ✧
407 Dexter Ave. N.
Seattle, WA 98109-4704
Contact: Jan Day

Established in 2001 in WA.
Donor: Bill True.
Foundation type: Independent foundation.
Financial data (yr. ended 12/31/05): Assets, $37,543,295 (M); expenditures, $1,780,369; qualifying distributions, $1,419,986; giving activities include $1,323,512 for grants, and $50,968 for foundation-administered programs.
Purpose and activities: Giving primarily for arts and culture.
Fields of interest: Museums (art); Performing arts; Performing arts, opera; Arts.
Type of support: Capital campaigns.
Limitations: Applications not accepted. Giving primarily in Seattle, WA. No grants to individuals.
Application information: Contributes only to pre-selected organizations.
Trustees: Robin Wright Moll; C. Bagley Wright; Charles B. Wright III; Merrill Wright; Prentice B. Wright; Virginia B. Wright.
EIN: 916526097

Selected grants: The following grants were reported in 2004.
$250,000 to Seattle Art Museum, Seattle, WA.
$250,000 to Seattle Opera, Seattle, WA.
$250,000 to Seattle Repertory Theater, Seattle, WA.
$50,000 to Childrens Museum, Seattle, WA.
$50,000 to Dia Center for the Arts, New York, NY.
$50,000 to On the Boards, Seattle, WA.
$50,000 to San Francisco Museum of Modern Art, San Francisco, CA.
$25,000 to IslandWood, Bainbridge Island, WA.

9709
Wyman Youth Trust ✧
104 30th Ave. S.
Seattle, WA 98144
Contact: Board of Trustees

Trust established in 1951 in WA.
Donor: Members of the Wyman family.
Foundation type: Independent foundation.
Financial data (yr. ended 12/31/05): Assets, $5,438,972 (M); expenditures, $433,314; qualifying distributions, $383,109; giving activities include $369,157 for grants.
Purpose and activities: Support primarily for youth-oriented projects, civic and cultural development, and special community endeavors; support also for schools and health services.
Fields of interest: Arts; Education; Health care; Children/youth, services; Government/public administration.
Limitations: Applications not accepted. Giving primarily in York, Custer and Lancaster counties, NE, and King, Pierce, and Snohomish counties, WA, with emphasis on King County. No grants to individuals, or for scholarships, capital funds or aggregate donors.
Application information: Unsolicited requests for funds not accepted.
 Board meeting date(s): Mar., June, Sept., and Dec.
Trustees: David E. Wyman; Hal Wyman; Virginia Wyman.
Number of staff: 1 part-time professional.
EIN: 916031590
Selected grants: The following grants were reported in 2004.
$52,250 to Bush School, Seattle, WA.
$50,000 to Museum of Flight, Seattle, WA.
$30,275 to Pratt Fine Arts Center, Seattle, WA.
$20,000 to Seattle Center Foundation, Seattle, WA.
$15,000 to Seattle Academy of Arts and Sciences, Seattle, WA.
$15,000 to YWCA of San Diego County, San Diego, CA.
$11,000 to University of Washington Press, Seattle, WA.
$10,000 to YMCA.
$3,000 to K C T S/Channel 9, Seattle, WA.
$2,000 to Family and Adult Service Center, Seattle, WA.

WEST VIRGINIA

9710
BB&T West Virginia Foundation
(formerly One Valley Bank Foundation, Inc.)
c/o BB&T Corp., Trust Dept.
P.O. Box 1793
Charleston, WV 25326-1793   (304) 348-7000
Contact: John M. Barry

Established in 1954 in WV.
Donors: One Valley Bank, N.A.; BB&T Corp.; OVB
Charitable Trust.
Foundation type: Company-sponsored foundation.
Financial data (yr. ended 12/31/05): Assets,
$10,832,978 (M); gifts received, $100,000;
expenditures, $609,868; qualifying distributions,
$599,540; giving activities include $599,540 for
105 grants (high: $83,000; low: $350).
Purpose and activities: The foundation supports
organizations involved with arts and culture,
education, health, and human services.
Fields of interest: Arts; Higher education;
Education; Hospitals (general); Health care;
Children/youth, services; Human services;
Federated giving programs.
Type of support: General/operating support.
Limitations: Giving limited to WV. No grants to
individuals.
Application information: Application form not
required.
  Initial approach: Proposal
  Copies of proposal: 1
  Deadline(s): None
  Board meeting date(s): As needed
  Final notification: In calendar quarter of receipt of
    proposal
Trustees: Phyllis H. Arnold; Nelle Ratrie Chilton; J.
Holmes Morrison; Brent Robinson; Steven M. Rubin;
K. Richard Sinclair; Edwin H. Welch.
EIN: 556017269

9711
Ethel N. Bowen Foundation ◇
c/o First Century Bank, N.A.
500 Federal St.
Bluefield, WV 24701   (304) 325-8181

Established about 1968 in WV.
Donor: Ethel N. Bowen†.
Foundation type: Independent foundation.
Financial data (yr. ended 12/31/04): Assets,
$10,948,563 (M); gifts received, $1,000;
expenditures, $544,691; qualifying distributions,
$497,047; giving activities include $209,413 for 78
grants (high: $25,000; low: $50), and $276,808 for
477 grants to individuals (high: $3,595; low: $184).
Purpose and activities: Giving primarily for
scholarships to further the education of students in
southern WV and southwestern VA; support also for
higher, secondary, and other education, and a
municipality.
Fields of interest: Secondary school/education;
Higher education; Education; Government/public
administration.
Type of support: General/operating support;
Scholarship funds; Scholarships—to individuals.
Limitations: Giving limited to residents of
southwestern VA and southern WV.

Application information: Students required to
submit transcript. Application form not required.
  Initial approach: Letter
  Copies of proposal: 1
  Deadline(s): Prior to beginning of academic year
    for scholarships.
  Board meeting date(s): Monthly
Officers and Directors: Richard W. Wilkinson,*
Pres.; Basil L. Jackson, Jr.,* V.P.; Frank W.
Wilkinson,* Secy.; B.K. Satterfield,* Treas.; Henry
Bowen; Jeffrey L. Forlines.
Trustee: First Century Bank, N.A.
EIN: 237010740

9712
Carter Family Foundation ◇
c/o United Bank
129 Main St.
Beckley, WV 25801
Application address: c/o Dianna Hunt, United Bank
Trust Dept., P.O. Box 1269, Beckley, WV
25802-1269

Established in 1981 in WV.
Donors: Bernard E. Carter†; Georgia Carter†; Leslie
R. Carter†.
Foundation type: Operating foundation.
Financial data (yr. ended 6/30/05): Assets,
$16,373,959 (M); expenditures, $835,992;
qualifying distributions, $762,287; giving activities
include $762,287 for 76 grants (high: $250,000;
low: $1,000).
Purpose and activities: The foundation provides
scholarships and student loans to individuals willing
to continue their education and teaching profession
within WV.
Fields of interest: Higher education; Hospitals
(specialty); Health organizations, association;
Human services; Children/youth, services; Christian
agencies & churches; Protestant agencies &
churches.
Type of support: Program development; Scholarship
funds; Scholarships—to individuals; Student loans
—to individuals.
Limitations: Giving limited to WV, with emphasis on
Raleigh County residents for scholarships.
Application information: Application form not
required.
  Initial approach: Letter and resume
  Deadline(s): None
Trustee: United Bank.
EIN: 550606479
Selected grants: The following grants were reported
in 2005.
$275,000 to Alderson-Broaddus College, Philippi,
  WV. 2 grants: $25,000, $250,000
$191,667 to Concord University, Athens, WV. 2
  grants: $25,000, $166,667
$26,000 to West Virginia University Foundation,
  Morgantown, WV.
$25,000 to Appalachian Bible College, Bradley, WV.
$25,000 to Mountain State University, Beckley, WV.
$25,000 to West Virginia Wesleyan College,
  Buckhannon, WV.
$10,000 to Southern West Virginia Community and
  Technical College, Mount Gay, WV.

9713
James B. Chambers Memorial ◇
P.O. Box 3047
Wheeling, WV 26003
Contact: Emily Schramm-Fisher, Admin. Asst.
Tel./fax: (304) 243-9373

Established in 1924 in WV.
Foundation type: Independent foundation.
Financial data (yr. ended 12/31/05): Assets,
$11,859,670 (M); expenditures, $443,440;
qualifying distributions, $408,081; giving activities
include $385,366 for 16 grants (high: $258,336;
low: $100).
Purpose and activities: Emphasis on youth,
including recreation and education, social services,
a YMCA, and community development.
Fields of interest: Education; Recreation; Human
services; YM/YWCAs & YM/YWHAs; Youth,
services; Community development; Economically
disadvantaged.
Type of support: Capital campaigns; Building/
renovation; Equipment; Program development; Seed
money; Technical assistance; Scholarships—to
individuals; Matching/challenge support.
Limitations: Giving limited to the greater Wheeling,
WV, area.
Application information: Application form required.
  Initial approach: Letter or telephone
  Copies of proposal: 7
  Deadline(s): None
  Board meeting date(s): Bimonthly
Officers and Trustees: Thomas L. Thomas,* Pres.;
James E. Altmeyer,* V.P.; Edward G. Sloane, Jr.,
Secy.-Treas.; E. Lee Jones; Brian E. Joseph; Arthur
Recht; C. Jack Savage.
Number of staff: 2 part-time professional.
EIN: 550360517
Selected grants: The following grants were reported
in 2004.
$233,336 to YMCA of Wheeling, Wheeling, WV. For
  building fund.
$50,000 to Wheeling, City of, Wheeling, WV. For
  maintenance.
$20,000 to Saint Vincent de Paul Church, Wheeling,
  WV. For youth program.
$16,000 to Laughlin Community Center, Wheeling,
  WV. For clothing project.
$6,300 to Ball Field Complex, Wheeling, WV. For
  maintenance.
$5,000 to Linsly School, Wheeling, WV. For building
  fund.
$5,000 to Wheeling Symphony Orchestra, Wheeling,
  WV. For Young Peoples concert.
$3,000 to Wheeling-Ohio County Health
  Department, Wheeling, WV. For Fit Kids Project.
$2,500 to House of the Carpenter, Wheeling, WV.
  For Youth Summer camp.
$2,500 to Young Life of Wheeling, Wheeling, WV. For
  summer camp.

9714
Clay Foundation, Inc. ▼
1426 Kanawha Blvd. E.
Charleston, WV 25301
Contact: Charles M. Avampato, Pres.

Incorporated in 1986 in WV.
Donors: Lyell B. Clay; Buckner W. Clay†; Mrs.
Buckner W. Clay.
Foundation type: Independent foundation.
Financial data (yr. ended 10/31/05): Assets,
$61,342,313 (M); expenditures, $8,504,825;

qualifying distributions, $7,832,116; giving activities include $7,560,592 for 15 grants (high: $5,028,825; low: $57).
Purpose and activities: Giving primarily for education, the arts, and human services.
Fields of interest: Arts; Education; Human services.
Type of support: Building/renovation; Program development; Seed money; Research.
Limitations: Giving limited to WV, with emphasis on the greater Kanawha Valley area. No support for religious purposes or private functions. No grants to individuals, or for operating expenses, deficit financing, annual campaigns, ongoing normal operations, or debt retirement.
Application information: Application form not required.
  Initial approach: Letter
  Copies of proposal: 1
  Deadline(s): No set deadline; 30 working days should be allowed for review of preliminary letter
  Board meeting date(s): Jan., Apr., July, and Oct.
  Final notification: 10 days after board meeting
Officers and Directors: * Hamilton G. Clay,* Co-Chair.; Lyell B. Clay,* Co-Chair.; Charles M. Avampato,* Pres.; Adryon H. Clay,* V.P.; James K. Brown,* Secy.; Whitney Clay Diller,* Treas.; Louis S. Southwerth II.
Number of staff: 1 full-time professional; 2 full-time support.
EIN: 550670193
Selected grants: The following grants were reported in 2005.
$5,028,825 to Clay Center for the Arts and Sciences, Charleston, WV.
$1,000,000 to College Foundation of the University of Virginia, Charlottesville, VA. For endowment.
$1,000,000 to University of Charleston, Charleston, WV. For new residence hall.
$130,000 to West Virginia Symphony Orchestra, Charleston, WV. For annual campaign.
$85,000 to Avampato Discovery Museum, Charleston, WV. 2 grants: $25,000 (For development consultant), $60,000 (For Partners in Education).
$65,000 to Fund for the Arts, Charleston, WV. For annual campaign.

9715

Lyell B. & Patricia K. Clay Foundation
1426 Kanawha Blvd. E.
Charleston, WV 25301
Contact: Charles M. Avampato, Pres.

Established in 1992 in WV.
Donor: Lyell B. Clay.
Foundation type: Independent foundation.
Financial data (yr. ended 10/31/05): Assets, $8,321,010 (M); expenditures, $475,207; qualifying distributions, $329,784; giving activities include $329,017 for 34 grants (high: $100,000; low: $805).
Purpose and activities: Giving primarily to universities and high school music departments.
Fields of interest: Performing arts, music; Performing arts, education; Higher education.
Type of support: Program development; Seed money; Technical assistance.
Limitations: Giving primarily in WV. No support for religious organizations. No grants to individuals or for scholarships or national fundraising events or for debt-retirement.

Application information: Application form not required.
  Initial approach: Letter of inquiry
  Copies of proposal: 1
  Deadline(s): None
  Board meeting date(s): Quarterly
  Final notification: 3 months from receipt
Officers: Lyell B. Clay, Chair.; Charles M. Avampato, Pres.
Director: Louis S. Southworth II.
Number of staff: None.
EIN: 550723844
Selected grants: The following grants were reported in 2005.
$100,000 to Kanawha Players, Charleston, WV.
$32,617 to Kanawha County Schools, Charleston, WV. 2 grants: $31,812, $805
$20,000 to YWCA of Charleston, Charleston, WV.
$5,973 to South Charleston High School, South Charleston, WV.
$2,132 to Sissonville Middle School, Sissonville, WV.
$1,292 to Clay Center for the Arts and Sciences, Charleston, WV. For music equipment.
$1,011 to George Washington High School, Charleston, WV.

9716

The Community Foundation for the Ohio Valley, Inc.
70 12th St.
P.O. Box 3048
Wheeling, WV 26003 (304) 242-3144
Contact: Zoe Metcalf, Exec. Dir.
FAX: (304) 234-4753; *E-mail:* director@cfov.org;
URL: http://www.cfov.org

Established in 1972 in WV.
Foundation type: Community foundation.
Financial data (yr. ended 5/31/06): Assets, $21,889,350 (M); expenditures, $1,252,564; giving activities include $1,180,558 for grants.
Purpose and activities: The mission of the foundation is to respond to the charitable needs of the Upper Ohio Valley area and to contribute to the quality of life in this region.
Fields of interest: Arts; Education; Health care; Recreation; Human services.
Type of support: Building/renovation; Equipment; Land acquisition; Program development; Conferences/seminars; Seed money; Scholarship funds; Technical assistance; Scholarships—to individuals; Matching/challenge support.
Limitations: Giving in the Upper Ohio Valley area: Brooke, Marshall, Ohio, Tyler and Wetzel counties, WV, and Belmont, Guernsey and Monroe counties, OH; emphasis on WV. No support for sectarian religious purposes. No grants to individuals (except for scholarships), or for endowment campaigns, or general operating or maintenance expenses for established organizations; no loans.
Publications: Application guidelines; Annual report (including application guidelines); Grants list; Informational brochure; Newsletter.
Application information: Visit foundation Web site for application form and guidelines. Application form required.
  Initial approach: Telephone or letter
  Copies of proposal: 7
  Deadline(s): Mar. 15 and Sept. 15; Mar. 30 for scholarships

Board meeting date(s): Jan., Apr., July, and Oct.
Final notification: June and Dec. for grants
Officers and Directors: * C.J. Kaiser, Jr.,* Pres.; Edward "Ted" Gompers,* V.P.; David B. Dalzell, Jr.,* Secy.; Jerome B. Schmitt,* Treas.; Zoe Metcalf, Exec. Dir.; Joseph W. Boutaugh, Emeritus Member; Frances "Pinkie" Williams, Emeritus Member; Joseph J. Buch; Ray A. Byrd; Sue Seibert Farnsworth; Mark C. Ferrell; Roland L. Hobbs; Carlos Jimenez, M.D.; John N. Kramer; Mark A. McKeen; William O. Nutting; Lee C. Paull III; Denise Penz; Bob Robinson; Fredrick Dean Rohrig; James G. Squibb, Jr.; Ruth K. Wagner; William J. Yaeger, Jr.
Trustee Banks: BB&T; JPMorgan Chase Bank, N.A.; Security National Trust Co.; Sky Bank; WesBanco Trust & Investment Services, Inc.; United Bank.
Number of staff: 1 full-time professional; 1 full-time support.
EIN: 310908698
Selected grants: The following grants were reported in 2005.
$5,000 to Harmony House Childrens Advocacy Center, Wheeling, WV. For facility expansion.
$5,000 to West Virginia Independence Hall Foundation, Wheeling, WV. For conservation project.
$600 to Childs Place CASA, Wellsburg, WV. For training support.

9717

The Daywood Foundation, Inc.
1600 Bank One Ctr.
Charleston, WV 25301 (304) 345-8900
Contact: William W. Booker, Secy.-Treas.
Application address: 1500 Bank One Ctr., Charleston, WV 25301, tel.: (304) 343-4841

Incorporated in 1958 in WV.
Donor: Ruth Woods Dayton†.
Foundation type: Independent foundation.
Financial data (yr. ended 12/31/04): Assets, $21,013,090 (M); expenditures, $1,119,643; qualifying distributions, $980,618; giving activities include $974,500 for 55 grants (high: $310,000; low: $1,500).
Purpose and activities: Giving primarily for community service organizations focusing on the arts, and health and human services.
Fields of interest: Museums; Arts; Higher education; Education; Human services; American Red Cross; Children/youth, services; Family services; Community development.
Type of support: Debt reduction; Continuing support; General/operating support; Annual campaigns; Capital campaigns; Building/renovation; Equipment; Emergency funds; Seed money; Matching/challenge support.
Limitations: Giving limited to Barbour, Greenbrier and Kanawha counties, WV. No grants to individuals, or for endowment funds, research, individual scholarships, or fellowships; no loans.
Publications: Application guidelines.
Application information: Application form not required.
  Initial approach: Letter
  Copies of proposal: 1
  Deadline(s): Sept. 15
  Board meeting date(s): Oct. and Dec.
  Final notification: Dec. 30
Officers: L. Newton Thomas, Jr., Pres.; Richard E. Ford, V.P.; William Satterfield, V.P.; William W. Booker, Secy.-Treas.

Number of staff: 1 part-time support.
EIN: 556018107
Selected grants: The following grants were reported in 2004.
$310,000 to Clay Center for the Arts and Sciences, Charleston, WV. For capital campaign.
$50,000 to Greenbrier County Library, Lewisburg, WV. For capital campaign.
$50,000 to United Way of Central West Virginia, Charleston, WV. For program support.
$50,000 to West Virginia University Foundation, Morgantown, WV. For Rosenbaum Family House.
$25,000 to Charleston Regatta Commission, Charleston, WV. For Festiv-All start-up.
$20,000 to University of Charleston, Charleston, WV. For nursing scholarships.
$15,000 to Covenant House, Charleston, WV. For Emergency Assistance Program.
$13,000 to Girl Scouts of the U.S.A., Black Diamond Council, Charleston, WV. For camping program.
$12,500 to West Virginia Symphony Orchestra, Charleston, WV. For concert season.
$5,000 to Heart and Hand House, Philippi, WV. For housing and food assistance.

9718
August J. & Thelma S. Hoffmann Foundation ✧
83 Edgington Ln.
Wheeling, WV   26003-1541
Contact: Robert J. Krall, Secy.
E-mail: RKRALL@HMHY.com

Established in 2000 in WV.
Donor: Thelma S. Hoffman†.
Foundation type: Independent foundation.
Financial data (yr. ended 12/31/05): Assets, $7,581,728 (M); expenditures, $393,131; qualifying distributions, $362,317; giving activities include $330,000 for 20 grants (high: $50,000; low: $5,000).
Purpose and activities: Giving primarily to Roman Catholic organizations and schools.
Fields of interest: Education; Roman Catholic agencies & churches.
Application information: Application form required.
   Deadline(s): None
Officer: Robert J. Krall, Secy.
Trustees: Ross C. Gaudoin; Harold J. Roth; William J. Yaeger.
EIN: 550769742
Selected grants: The following grants were reported in 2005.
$50,000 to Soup Kitchen of Greater Wheeling, Wheeling, WV.
$50,000 to Wheeling Catholic Elementary School, Wheeling, WV.
$20,000 to Gabriel Project of West Virginia, Wheeling, WV.
$15,000 to Salvation Army of Wheeling, Wheeling, WV.
$10,000 to Catholic Community Services, Morgantown, WV.
$10,000 to West Virginia Northern Community College, Weirton, WV.
$10,000 to YWCA of Wheeling, Wheeling, WV.
$8,000 to Youth Services System, Wheeling, WV.
$5,000 to Archdiocese of New Orleans, New Orleans, LA.

9719
Hollowell Foundation, Inc.
(formerly Hollowell-Ford Foundation, Inc.)
103 E. Washington St.
Lewisburg, WV   24901
Contact: Jesse O. Guills, Jr., Pres.

Established in 1975 in WV.
Donors: Margaret F. Hollowell†; John R. Dawkins†; Otto Hollowell Unitrust.
Foundation type: Independent foundation.
Financial data (yr. ended 6/30/05): Assets, $7,574,890 (M); expenditures, $486,276; qualifying distributions, $378,151; giving activities include $376,300 for 43 grants (high: $50,000; low: $500).
Purpose and activities: Giving primarily for community improvement and renovation projects.
Fields of interest: Arts; Higher education; Human services; Community development.
Type of support: Capital campaigns; General/operating support; Building/renovation; Matching/challenge support.
Limitations: Giving limited to Greenbrier County, WV. No grants to individuals.
Application information: Application form required.
   Initial approach: Letter
   Copies of proposal: 1
   Deadline(s): Apr. 1
   Board meeting date(s): Jan., Apr., June, and Sept.
Officers: Jesse O. Guills, Jr., Pres.; Thomas G. McMillan, V.P.; Marshall Musser, Secy.; Allen Carson, Treas.
Number of staff: 1 part-time professional.
EIN: 510183517
Selected grants: The following grants were reported in 2004.
$50,000 to Carnegie Hall, A Corporation, Lewisburg, WV. For staffing, data transition and management.
$50,000 to Greenbrier County Library, Lewisburg, WV. Toward new library.
$50,000 to Greenbrier Repertory Theater Company, Lewisburg, WV. For education programs.
$16,500 to Greenbrier Community College Foundation, Lewisburg, WV. For scholarships and endowment fund.
$7,500 to Shepherds Center of Greenbrier Valley, Lewisburg, WV. For Gwens Meals program.
$5,000 to Greenbrier County Child and Youth Advocacy Center, Lewisburg, WV. For general support.
$5,000 to Lewisburg Foundation, Lewisburg, WV. For horticulture program.
$3,000 to Ronceverte Public Library, Ronceverte, WV. For books.
$2,000 to Southeastern Appalachian Rural Alliance, Lewisburg, WV. For tools and equipment.
$1,000 to Appalachian by Design, Lewisburg, WV. For online software.

9720
The H. P. and Anne S. Hunnicutt Foundation, Inc. ✧
P.O. Box 309
Princeton, WV   24740-0309
Contact: William Stafford II, Secy.

Established in 1987 in WV.
Donors: H.P. Hunnicutt; Anne S. Hunnicutt†.
Foundation type: Independent foundation.
Financial data (yr. ended 6/30/05): Assets, $42,610,875 (M); expenditures, $2,224,952;

qualifying distributions, $2,145,920; giving activities include $2,133,400 for 18 grants (high: $1,602,500; low: $191).
Fields of interest: Education, administration/regulation; Secondary school/education; Education; Human services; Salvation Army; Foundations (community); Christian agencies & churches; Protestant agencies & churches.
Limitations: Giving limited to southern WV.
Application information:
   Initial approach: Letter
   Deadline(s): None
Officers: William P. Stafford, Pres.; James H. Sarver, V.P.; William Stafford II, Secy.; James H. Sarver II, Treas.
Trustee: First Community Bank, Inc.
EIN: 550670462
Selected grants: The following grants were reported in 2005.
$1,602,500 to Community Foundation of the Virginias, Bluefield, WV.
$150,000 to Mercer County Composite Squadron, Bluefield, WV.
$105,000 to Salvation Army of Princeton, Princeton, WV.
$98,000 to First United Methodist Church, Princeton, WV.
$60,000 to Bluefield, City of, Bluefield, WV.
$30,000 to Tender Mercies, Princeton, WV.
$25,000 to Mercer County Board of Education, Princeton, WV.
$24,000 to Johnston Chapel Baptist Church, Princeton, WV.
$16,000 to Athens School, Athens, WV.

9721
The Huntington Foundation, Inc. ✧ ☆
P.O. Box 2548
Huntington, WV   25726
Contact: Glenna J. Smoot, Exec. Secy.
Application address: 401 11th St., Ste 306, Huntington, WV 25701, tel.: (304) 522-0611

Established 1986 in WV.
Foundation type: Independent foundation.
Financial data (yr. ended 12/31/05): Assets, $6,802,248 (M); expenditures, $412,414; qualifying distributions, $345,990; giving activities include $339,466 for 15 grants (high: $90,653; low: $2,250).
Purpose and activities: Grants given toward encouraging institutional change or to help grant recipients make more effective use of resources they generate from other sources. The Foundation also promotes strong public-private collaborative efforts to meet community needs and foster volunteer efforts wherever possible.
Fields of interest: Arts; Higher education; Human services; Federated giving programs.
Type of support: General/operating support; Equipment; Land acquisition.
Limitations: Giving primarily in WV. No grants to individuals.
Application information: Application form required.
   Initial approach: Letter or telephone
   Copies of proposal: 6
   Deadline(s): None
   Board meeting date(s): Quarterly in Jan., Apr., July and Oct.
   Final notification: 3-6 months from receipt
Officers: Cecil H. Underwood, Pres.; Frank E. Hanshaw, Jr., V.P.; Kermit E. McGinnis, Secy.-Treas.
Directors: John E. Jenkins, Jr.; Joseph B. Touma.

Number of staff: 1 part-time support.
EIN: 550370129
Selected grants: The following grants were reported in 2005.
$90,653 to Childrens Home Society of West Virginia, Charleston, WV.
$72,526 to YMCA of Huntington, Huntington, WV.
$33,000 to Huntington Museum of Art, Huntington, WV.
$30,000 to Hospice of Huntington, Huntington, WV.
$20,933 to Rotary Club of Huntington, Huntington, WV.
$15,000 to American Red Cross, Huntington, WV.
$7,880 to Kiwanis Day Care Center, Huntington, WV.

9722

Bernard H. and Blanche E. Jacobson Foundation ✧

c/o BB&T, Trust Dept.
P.O. Box 1793
Charleston, WV 25326
Application address: c/o John L. Ray, Tr., 109 Capitol St., Ste. 700, Charlotte, WV 25301, tel.: (304) 342-1141

Established in 1954 in WV.
Donors: Bernard H. Jacobson; Blanche E. Jacobson.
Foundation type: Independent foundation.
Financial data (yr. ended 12/31/05): Assets, $7,360,119 (M); expenditures, $469,303; qualifying distributions, $445,306; giving activities include $437,750 for 25 grants (high: $155,000; low: $500).
Purpose and activities: Giving primarily for a center for arts and sciences, as well as for education, health, social services, and Jewish organizations.
Fields of interest: Arts; Education; Health care; Human services; Children/youth, services; Federated giving programs; Jewish federated giving programs.
Limitations: Giving primarily in WV, with emphasis on the Kanawha Valley and Charleston areas.
Application information: Application form not required.
    Deadline(s): None
Trustees: John L. Ray; Christopher J. Winton; Christopher J. Winton; BB&T.
EIN: 556014902
Selected grants: The following grants were reported in 2004.
$100,000 to Clay Center for the Arts and Sciences, Charleston, WV.
$55,000 to United Way of Central West Virginia, Charleston, WV.
$31,250 to BIDCO Foundation, Charleston, WV.
$25,000 to Library Foundation of Kanawha County, Charleston, WV.
$25,000 to West Virginia Symphony Orchestra, Charleston, WV.
$20,000 to University of Charleston, Charleston, WV.
$10,000 to Avampato Discovery Museum, Charleston, WV.
$10,000 to Snowshoe Institute, Charleston, WV.
$10,000 to West Virginia Independent Colleges and Universities, Charleston, WV.
$2,500 to Charleston Ballet, Charleston, WV.

9723

The Greater Kanawha Valley Foundation

1600 Huntington Sq.
900 Lee St. E.
Charleston, WV 25301 (304) 346-3620
Contact: Rebecca Ceperley, C.E.O.; For grants: Kim Barber Tieman, Sr. Prog. Off.; For grants: Christina Williams, Receptionist
FAX: (304) 346-3640; E-mail: tgkvf@tgkvf.org; Additional address: P.O. Box 3041, Charleston, WV 25331; Additional tel.: (800) 467-5909; Grant application E-mails: ktieman@tgkvf.org and cwilliams@tgkvf.org; URL: http://www.tgkvf.org

Established in 1962 in WV.
Foundation type: Community foundation.
Financial data (yr. ended 12/31/05): Assets, $123,485,938 (M); gifts received, $5,639,206; expenditures, $9,262,720; giving activities include $7,599,635 for grants, and $750,499 for grants to individuals.
Purpose and activities: The foundation seeks to enrich the lives of those it services - contributors, beneficiaries, and the community - by being the premier provider of philanthropic and charitable services for all citizens in the region. Primary areas of interest include higher and other education, youth, recreation, the arts, and the social sciences. Support also for child welfare and family services, women, housing, the medical sciences, including research on AIDS, heart disease, and cancer, ecology and the environment, and community development programs.
Fields of interest: Museums; Performing arts; Performing arts, dance; Humanities; Historic preservation/historical societies; Arts; Education, early childhood education; Elementary school/education; Higher education; Libraries/library science; Education; Environment, natural resources; Environment; Dental care; Nursing care; Health care; Substance abuse, services; Housing/shelter, development; Recreation; Children/youth, services; Family services; Residential/custodial care, hospices; Women, centers/services; Homeless, human services; Human services; Economic development; Community development; Social sciences; Disabilities, people with; Women; Homeless.
Type of support: Continuing support; Capital campaigns; Building/renovation; Equipment; Emergency funds; Program development; Publication; Seed money; Scholarship funds; Research; Technical assistance; Program evaluation; Scholarships—to individuals; Matching/challenge support.
Limitations: Giving limited to the greater Kanawha Valley, WV, area, except scholarships which are limited to residents of WV. No support for religious activities of religious organizations. No grants to individuals (except for designated scholarship funds), or for general operating budgets for established organizations, annual campaigns, membership drives, travel, uniforms, ongoing support for the same project, staff costs, consultants, consultant fees, conferences, workshop speakers, student aid or fellowships, or endowments; no loans.
Publications: Application guidelines; Annual report (including application guidelines); Financial statement; Grants list; Informational brochure; Occasional report.
Application information: Visit foundation Web site for application form and guidelines. The foundation offers free grant writing sessions; visit Web site for details. Application form required.
    Initial approach: Letter, telephone, fax or e-mail
    Copies of proposal: 4
    Deadline(s): Feb. 1 for Education, Arts, & Culture, May 1 for Health and Human Svcs., and Aug. 1 for Recreation & Land Use; Feb. 15 for scholarships
    Board meeting date(s): Quarterly, usually in Mar., June, Sept., and Dec.
    Final notification: Immediately after board action
Officers and Trustees:* Mary Ann Michael,* Chair.; Henry Harmon,* Vice-Chair.; Rebecca Ceperley, C.E.O. and Pres.; Patricia Majic, C.F.O.; Susan L. Basile; Jr. Hazo Carter; Nelle Ratrie Chilton; T. Randolph Cox; Stephen R. Crislip; Kimberly Thomas Foster; Melvin Jones; Dr. Jamal H. Khan; Judith N. McJunkin; Ron L. Potesta; Troy Stallard; Arthur M. Standish.
Advisory Committee: Paul Arbogast; G. Thomas Battle; Frederick H. Belden, Jr.; Charles L. Capito, Jr.; Elsie P. Carter; William D. Chambers; Elizabeth E. Chilton; William M. Davis; Deborah A. Faber; Rebecca B. Goldman; Charles R. McElwee; Thomas N. McJunkin; Harry S. Moore; Rick Morgan; William E. Mullett, Ph.D.; Sandra Murphy; David Rollins; Barbara Rose; Virginia Rugeley; Mark H. Schaul; Dolly Sherwood; K. Richard C. Sinclair; Olivia R. Singleton; Louis B. Southworth; L. Newton Thomas, Jr.; Adeline J. Voorhees.
Trustee Banks: City National Bank of Charleston; BB&T; The Huntington National Bank; JPMorgan Chase Bank, N.A.; United Bank; WesBanco Bank, Inc.
Number of staff: 7 full-time professional; 3 part-time support.
EIN: 556024430

9724

George A. Laughlin Trust ✧

c/o WesBanco Bank, Inc., Trust Dept.
1 Bank Plz.
Wheeling, WV 26003 (304) 234-9428
Contact: Lea Ridenhour, Trust Off., WesBanco Bank, Inc.

Established in 1936 in WV.
Foundation type: Independent foundation.
Financial data (yr. ended 12/31/05): Assets, $13,944,810 (M); expenditures, $728,122; qualifying distributions, $664,362; giving activities include $613,082 for 109 grants to individuals (high: $90,900; low: $89; average: $1,861–$3,700), and $51,280 for 4 foundation-administered programs.
Purpose and activities: Awards non-interest-bearing home loans to local area low-income individuals.
Fields of interest: Housing/shelter; Economically disadvantaged.
Type of support: Program-related investments/loans; Student loans—to individuals.
Limitations: Giving limited to Ohio County, WV, residents.
Application information: Application form required.
    Initial approach: Letter or telephone
    Deadline(s): May 1 to May 31
Trustee: WesBanco Bank, Inc.
EIN: 556016889

9725
Maier Foundation, Inc.
(formerly Sarah & Pauline Maier Foundation)
P.O. Box 6190
Charleston, WV 25362 (304) 343-2201
Contact: Edward H. Maier, Chair.
E-mail: edhmaier@genrlcorp.com; URL: http://
www.maierfoundation.org

Established in 1958 in WV.
Donors: William J. Maier, Jr.†; Pauline Maier†;
General Corporation.
Foundation type: Independent foundation.
Financial data (yr. ended 10/31/05): Assets,
$20,468,958 (M); gifts received, $200,000;
expenditures, $1,649,076; qualifying distributions,
$1,239,452; giving activities include $1,238,000
for 13 grants (high: $400,000; low: $6,000).
Purpose and activities: Giving for higher education
in WV and other educationally-related pursuits in
Kanawha County, WV.
Fields of interest: Higher education; Education.
Type of support: General/operating support; Annual
campaigns; Capital campaigns; Building/
renovation; Equipment; Endowments; Program
development; Professorships; Scholarship funds;
Matching/challenge support.
Limitations: Giving limited to WV. No support for
religious or political organizations. No grants to
individuals.
Publications: Application guidelines; Program policy
statement.
Application information: Application form required.
  Initial approach: Letter
  Copies of proposal: 11
  Deadline(s): Oct. 1
  Board meeting date(s): 1st Fri. in Dec.
  Final notification: Dec. 31
Officers and Board Members:* Edward H. Maier,*
Chair. and Pres.; W.J. Maier III,* V.P.; Sandra D.
Thomas,* Secy.; Sara M. Rowe,* Treas.; John T.
Copenhaver; Charles I. Jones, Jr.; J. Holmes
Morrison; Bradley M. Rowe; Thomas W. Rowe; J.
Randy Valentine.
Number of staff: None.
EIN: 556023833
Selected grants: The following grants were reported
in 2005.
$400,000 to Clay Center for the Arts and Sciences,
  Charleston, WV. For building campaign.
$300,000 to West Virginia University Foundation,
  Morgantown, WV. For endowed chair for Law
  School.
$200,000 to Marshall University Foundation,
  Huntington, WV. For Biotech Center.
$100,000 to Kanawha Players, Charleston, WV. For
  Building Campaign.
$70,000 to Charleston Area Medical Center
  Foundation, Charleston, WV. For simulator
  challenge.
$50,000 to Randolph-Macon Womans College,
  Lynchburg, VA. For scholarship endowment.
$50,000 to West Virginia Independent Colleges and
  Universities, Charleston, WV. For private West
  Virginia colleges.
$25,000 to Fund for the Arts, Charleston, WV.
$10,000 to College Summit West Virginia,
  Charleston, WV. For operating support.
$10,000 to Concord University, Athens, WV. For
  Entrepreneurial Studies Scholarship.

9726
Bernard McDonough Foundation, Inc. ✧
311 4th St.
Parkersburg, WV 26101 (304) 424-6280
FAX: (304) 424-6281; URL: http://
www.mcdonoughfoundation.org/

Incorporated in 1961 in WV.
Donor: Bernard P. McDonough†.
Foundation type: Independent foundation.
Financial data (yr. ended 12/31/05): Assets,
$37,980,082 (M); expenditures, $1,879,469;
qualifying distributions, $1,757,448; giving
activities include $1,442,009 for 100 grants (high:
$83,000; low: $200), and $15,500 for 3 employee
matching gifts.
Purpose and activities: Support for higher and other
education, including building funds; civic and public
affairs, community funds, and leadership
development programs; the humanities and cultural
programs; and health and social service agencies,
including rehabilitation programs for the
handicapped and drug abuse, hospital building
funds, and the elderly.
Fields of interest: Performing arts centers; Arts;
Higher education; Medical school/education;
Education; Hospitals (general); Hospitals
(specialty); Health care; Health organizations,
association; Boys & girls clubs; Youth development,
services; Human services; YM/YWCAs & YM/
YWHAs; Children/youth, services; Foundations
(community); Federated giving programs;
Leadership development; Public affairs; Aging;
Disabilities, people with; Economically
disadvantaged.
Type of support: General/operating support; Annual
campaigns; Capital campaigns; Building/
renovation; Equipment; Emergency funds; Program
development; Employee matching gifts; Matching/
challenge support.
Limitations: Giving primarily in WV. No support for
religious organizations. No grants to individuals.
Publications: Application guidelines.
Application information: Application form not
required.
  Initial approach: Letter
  Copies of proposal: 1
  Deadline(s): None
  Board meeting date(s): Feb., May, Aug. and Oct.
  Final notification: 2 to 4 weeks
Officers and Directors:* Robert W. Stephens, Jr.,
Ed.D.*, Exec. V.P.; Mary Riccobene,* V.P.; Katrina
A. Valentine, Secy.; F.C. McCusker,* Treas.; Robert
S. Boone; Dale A. Knight; George F. Partridge.
Number of staff: 2 full-time professional.
EIN: 556023693
Selected grants: The following grants were reported
in 2004.
$200,000 to American Red Cross, Parkersburg, WV.
$184,983 to Ohio Valley University, Vienna, WV. 2
  grants: $30,000 (For software system),
  $154,983 (For scholarships and equipment).
$50,000 to West Virginia Independent Colleges and
  Universities, Charleston, WV.
$50,000 to Wheeling Jesuit University, Wheeling,
  WV.
$41,000 to Smoot Theater Corporation,
  Parkersburg, WV.
$40,000 to Artsbridge, Parkersburg, WV.
$40,000 to Childrens Home Society of West
  Virginia, Charleston, WV.
$30,000 to Jackson General Hospital, Ripley, WV.
$26,000 to Wood County Senior Citizens
  Association, Parkersburg, WV.

9727
Hazel Ruby McQuain Charitable Trust ✧
(formerly H. L. Robinson Charitable Trust)
P.O. Box 683
Morgantown, WV 26505

Established in 1989 in WV.
Donors: Hazel Ruby McQuain†; Hazel Ruby McQuain
Trust.
Foundation type: Independent foundation.
Financial data (yr. ended 12/31/05): Assets,
$139,504,344 (M); gifts received, $116,127,941;
expenditures, $5,629,153; qualifying distributions,
$5,461,437; giving activities include $5,226,126
for 53 grants (high: $2,000,500; low: $100).
Fields of interest: Performing arts; Higher
education, university; Boy scouts; Human services;
American Red Cross; Federated giving programs;
Christian agencies & churches.
Limitations: Applications not accepted. Giving
primarily to Morgantown, WV. No grants to
individuals.
Application information: Contributes only to
pre-selected organizations.
Trustees: Charles D. Dunbar; George R. Farmer, Jr.;
Stephen B. Farmer; Robert A. Toepfer.
EIN: 346899181
Selected grants: The following grants were reported
in 2005.
$2,000,500 to Monongalia General Hospital,
  Morgantown, WV. For general support.
$1,200,000 to Monongalia County Schools
  Foundation, Morgantown, WV. For general
  support.
$1,100,000 to West Virginia University Foundation,
  Morgantown, WV. 2 grants: $800,000 (For
  wrestling facility at Mountaineer Athletic Club),
  $300,000 (For Alumni Center).
$300,000 to Morgantown, City of, Morgantown, WV.
  To acquire Borsey's Knob Park.
$27,500 to Mountain Heart Foundation, Star City,
  WV. For general support.
$25,000 to Morgantown Health Right, Morgantown,
  WV. For general support.
$25,000 to Trinity Christian School, Morgantown,
  WV. For general support.
$24,576 to Mon Home Corporation, Sundale
  Nursing Home, Morgantown, WV. For general
  support.
$15,000 to Mon River Trails Conservancy,
  Morgantown, WV. For general support.

9728
The Mylan Charitable Foundation ✧
P.O. Box 4310
781 Chestnut Ridge Rd.
Morgantown, WV 26504-4310

Established in 2002 in PA and WV.
Donor: Mylan Laboratories Inc.
Foundation type: Company-sponsored foundation.
Financial data (yr. ended 12/31/05): Assets,
$5,899,386 (M); expenditures, $665,002;
qualifying distributions, $654,000; giving activities
include $654,000 for grants.
Purpose and activities: The foundation supports
organizations involved with education, health,
human services, and community development.
Fields of interest: Education; Health care; Cancer,
leukemia research; Human services; Community
development.
Limitations: Applications not accepted. Giving
primarily in PA and WV. No grants to individuals.

Application information: Contributes only to pre-selected organizations.
Officers: Milan Puskar, Pres.; C.B. Todd, Treas.
Director: Robert Coury.
EIN: 431954390
Selected grants: The following grants were reported in 2004.
$25,000 to Allegheny Conference on Community Development, Pittsburgh, PA.
$10,000 to West Virginia Independent Colleges and Universities, Charleston, WV.
$7,500 to Greater Morgantown Community Trust, Morgantown, WV.

9729
The Nutting Foundation ✧
1500 Main St.
Wheeling, WV 26003

Donors: Robert M. Nutting; William O. Nutting.
Foundation type: Independent foundation.
Financial data (yr. ended 12/31/05): Assets, $13,330,441 (M); expenditures, $512,829; qualifying distributions, $424,396; giving activities include $424,371 for 22 grants (high: $70,000; low: $1,871).
Fields of interest: Arts; Education.
Limitations: Applications not accepted. Giving primarily in WV. No grants to individuals.
Application information: Contributes only to pre-selected organizations.
Officers: Robert M. Nutting, Pres.; William O. Nutting, Secy.
EIN: 311683582

9730
Parkersburg Area Community Foundation
501 Avery St.
P.O. Box 1762
Parkersburg, WV 26102-1762 (304) 428-4438
Contact: Judy Sjostedt, Exec. Dir.; Marian Clowes, Prog. and Devel. Off.; Sarah Holt, Prog. and Devel. Off.
FAX: (304) 428-1200; E-mail: info@pacfwv.com; Additional tel.: (866) 428-4438; Additional E-mails: marian.clowes@pacfwv.com and sarah.holt@pacfwv.com; URL: http://www.pacfwv.com

Established in 1963 in WV.
Donors: Albert Wolfe†; The Keystone Foundation; members of the Wolfe family.
Foundation type: Community foundation.
Financial data (yr. ended 6/30/05): Assets, $17,708,600 (M); gifts received, $6,304,024; expenditures, $1,033,740; giving activities include $496,149 for 359 grants, and $207,950 for 207 grants to individuals (high: $5,000; low: $130).
Purpose and activities: The foundation's mission is to serve the people of the Parkersburg, WV, area by building permanent resources to meet the community's broad charitable needs, managing these assets efficiently, and using them effectively in response to the area's changing needs and opportunities.
Fields of interest: Arts, alliance; Museums; Historic preservation/historical societies; Arts; Child development, education; Higher education; Adult education—literacy, basic skills & GED; Libraries/library science; Education, reading; Education; Animal welfare; Health care; Mental health/crisis

services; Health organizations, association; Recreation; Children/youth, services; Child development, services; Family services; Human services; Economic development; Community development; Disabilities, people with.
Type of support: Management development/capacity building; Capital campaigns; Building/renovation; Equipment; Emergency funds; Program development; Seed money; Scholarship funds; Scholarships—to individuals; Matching/challenge support.
Limitations: Giving limited to the Mid-Ohio Valley communities of Calhoun, Doddridge, Gilmer, Jackson, Mason, Pleasants, Ritchie, Roane, Wirt, and Wood counties, WV, and Washington County, OH. No support for sectarian religious purposes. No grants for travel, meetings, seminars, conferences, student exchange programs, annual campaigns, endowment funds, operating expenses for ongoing programs, debt reduction, or maintenance needs.
Publications: Application guidelines; Annual report; Informational brochure; Newsletter.
Application information: Visit foundation Web site for application form and guidelines; may also e-mail, telephone, or send letter for guidelines. Application form required.
Initial approach: Mail application form and attachments
Copies of proposal: 10
Deadline(s): Mar. 1 and Sept. 1 for local grants; Mar. 23 for scholarships; will consider emergency grants at other times only from WV organizations
Board meeting date(s): 3rd Fri. in Jan., Mar., May, Sept., and Nov.
Final notification: May and Nov.
Officers and Governors:* Sheryl Holdren, Chair.; James Crews, Vice-Chair.; Judy Sjostedt,* Exec. Dir.; Edwin L.D. Dils,* Chair., Advisory Council; Walt Auvil; Diane Brown Balderson; Marie E. Caltrider; Bill Crites; Earl Daughtery; Barbara N. Fish; Richard Hudson; Becky Ingram; Linda McLean; Ronald N. Roberts; Harry L. Shannon; Judy Sheppard; Frederick H. Shipley; Amy Strobl; Dave Underwood; Jerry L. Villers; David Vincent; Thomas Weyer; Daniel B. Wharton.
Trustee Banks: BB&T; Peoples Bank; United Bank, N.A.; WesBanco Bank, Inc.
Number of staff: 4 full-time professional; 1 full-time support.
EIN: 556027764

9731
Board of Trustees of the Prichard School ✧
c/o JPMorgan Chase Bank, N.A.
P.O. Box 179
Huntington, WV 25706
Application address: c/o Steven P. Hatten, 2122 Holswade Dr., Huntington, WV 25705

Established in 1923 in WV.
Foundation type: Independent foundation.
Financial data (yr. ended 12/31/05): Assets, $9,673,884 (M); expenditures, $618,821; qualifying distributions, $590,334; giving activities include $588,000 for 23 grants (high: $60,000; low: $2,000).
Purpose and activities: Giving primarily for education, the arts, and youth services.
Fields of interest: Arts; Elementary/secondary education; Higher education; Boys clubs; Big Brothers/Big Sisters; Children/youth, services.

Type of support: General/operating support; Scholarship funds.
Limitations: Giving primarily in VA and WV. No grants to individuals.
Application information: Application form not required.
Deadline(s): None
Officers and Directors:* Steven P. Hatten,* Pres.; Marc W. Wild,* V.P.; Paul W. McCreight, Secy.; Margaret C. Breece, Treas.; Edward W. Morrison; John F. Speer; Ann Todd.
EIN: 550435910

9732
The Albert Schenk III & Kathleen H. Schenk Charitable Trust No. 1
1031 National Rd.
Wheeling, WV 26003 (304) 243-5440
Contact: Frank A. Jackson

Established in 1998 in WV.
Foundation type: Independent foundation.
Financial data (yr. ended 12/31/05): Assets, $61,067 (M); gifts received, $820,267; expenditures, $816,072; qualifying distributions, $750,215; giving activities include $750,215 for 38 grants (high: $106,000; low: $106).
Purpose and activities: Giving to promote philanthropic causes in WV and around Wheeling, WV.
Fields of interest: Arts; Higher education; Education; Health care; Mental health, treatment; Human services; Children/youth, services; Religion; Economically disadvantaged.
Type of support: Capital campaigns; Building/renovation; Equipment; Program development; Seed money; Scholarship funds.
Limitations: Giving limited to Ohio and Marshall counties, WV. No grants to individuals or for operating expenses or general overhead.
Application information: Application form required.
Initial approach: Letter
Copies of proposal: 9
Deadline(s): None
Board meeting date(s): Monthly
Final notification: Generally within 90 days
Officer: Mary S. Hamilton, Chair.
Trustees: Frank Bonacci; Kathleen S. Bonacci; Heidi S. Bruhn; Nancy S. Casey; Louise S. DeFelice; William N. Hogan, Jr.; Karen S. Sligar.
EIN: 550764535
Selected grants: The following grants were reported in 2005.
$106,000 to YMCA of Wheeling, Wheeling, WV. For capital improvements.
$78,500 to Laughlin Community Center, Wheeling, WV. For capital improvements.
$65,000 to Russell Nesbitt Services, Wheeling, WV. For capital improvements.
$55,000 to West Virginia University Foundation, Morgantown, WV. For scholarships.
$50,000 to Wheeling Catholic Elementary School, Wheeling, WV. For program support.
$50,000 to Wheeling Jesuit University, Wheeling, WV. For program support and equipment.
$30,000 to Catholic Community Services of the Diocese of Wheeling-Charleston, Wheeling, WV. For program support.
$20,000 to Central Catholic High School, Wheeling, WV. For equipment.
$18,000 to Mount de Chantal Visitation Academy, Wheeling, WV. For scholarships.

$14,080 to Walter Long Teen Challenge for a New Life, Wheeling, WV. For program support.

9733
Hugh I. Shott, Jr. Foundation ✧
c/o First Century Bank, N.A.
500 Federal St.
P.O. Box 1559
Bluefield, WV 24701
Contact: Richard W. Wilkinson, Pres.

Established in 1985 in WV.
Donor: Hugh I. Shott, Jr.✝.
Foundation type: Independent foundation.
Financial data (yr. ended 12/31/05): Assets, $35,117,132 (M); expenditures, $1,879,070; qualifying distributions, $1,664,497; giving activities include $1,635,516 for 19 grants (high: $500,000; low: $5,000).
Purpose and activities: Giving primarily for secondary and higher education, including business education and building funds for schools; some support also for the arts, community development, and health.
Fields of interest: Arts; Secondary school/education; Higher education; Education; Health care; Children/youth, services; Community development; Government/public administration.
Type of support: Annual campaigns; Capital campaigns; Building/renovation.
Limitations: Giving limited to southwestern VA and southern WV. No grants to individuals.
Application information: Application form required.
   Deadline(s): None
Officers: R.W. Wilkinson, Pres.; Scott H. Shott, V.P.; John C. Shott, Secy.; B.K. Satterfield, Treas.
Directors: John H. Shott; W. Chandler Swope; Frank W. Wilkinson.
Trustee: First Century Bank, N.A.
Number of staff: 1 part-time professional.
EIN: 550650833
Selected grants: The following grants were reported in 2004.
$500,000 to Bluefield Regional Medical Center, Bluefield, WV.
$450,000 to Concord College Foundation, Athens, WV.
$138,900 to Bluefield College, Bluefield, VA. 2 grants: $38,900, $100,000
$100,000 to Blanchette Rockefeller Neurosciences Institute, Morgantown, WV.
$76,775 to Bluefield, City of, Bluefield, WV.
$25,000 to Bland County Medical Clinic, Bastian, VA.
$20,000 to Graham Intermediate School, Bluefield, VA.
$10,000 to Mercer County Board of Education, Princeton, WV.
$2,000 to Montcalm High School, Montcalm, WV.

9734
O. J. Stout Scholarship Fund ✧
c/o Unizan Bank, N.A.
P.O. Box 1508
Parkersburg, WV 26102
Contact: Seth Cumberledge, Trust Off., Unizan Bank, N.A.
Application address: c/o Unizan Bank N.A., Trust Dept., 514 Market St., Parkersburg, WV 26101

Established around 1973 in WV.

Foundation type: Independent foundation.
Financial data (yr. ended 12/31/05): Assets, $11,346,691 (M); expenditures, $478,243; qualifying distributions, $493,807; giving activities include $337,600 for 151 grants to individuals (high: $4,000; low: $800), and $84,400 for 151 loans to individuals (high: $1,000; low: $200).
Purpose and activities: Awards scholarships and loans to male high school graduates residing in Wood County, WV, and adjacent WV counties. Preference given to applicants studying for the ministry at West Virginia Wesleyan College in Buckhannon, WV.
Fields of interest: Theological school/education.
Type of support: Scholarships—to individuals; Student loans—to individuals.
Limitations: Giving limited to residents of WV from Wood and adjacent counties.
Application information: Application form required.
   Initial approach: Completed scholarship application
   Deadline(s): Apr. 1
Trustee: Laura Knight.
EIN: 556029015

9735
The James H. and Alice Teubert Charitable Trust ✧
P.O. Box 2131
Huntington, WV 25722-2131 (304) 525-6337
Contact: Jimelle Bowen, Exec. Dir.
E-mail: teubert@accessmountain.net

Established in 1987 in WV.
Donor: WV Culture and Arts Grant.
Foundation type: Independent foundation.
Financial data (yr. ended 9/30/05): Assets, $20,755,845 (M); expenditures, $1,332,933; qualifying distributions, $1,241,337; giving activities include $1,166,432 for 10 grants (high: $850,683; low: $750).
Purpose and activities: Support for organizations which provide aid to the blind in Cabell and Wayne Counties in WV.
Fields of interest: Eye diseases; Disabilities, people with.
Limitations: Giving primarily in Cabell and Wayne counties, WV. No grants to individuals.
Publications: Application guidelines; Informational brochure.
Application information: Application form required.
   Initial approach: Letter
   Copies of proposal: 8
   Deadline(s): Mar. 1 for Apr. awards and Oct. 1 for Nov. awards
   Board meeting date(s): Apr. and Nov.
Officers and Trustees:* Grant McGuire,* Chair.; Jimelle Bowen, Exec. Dir.; Betty Bruce; Michael A. Fiery; David H. Lunsford; Michael Nuce; Sue Richardson; Matthew A. Rohrbach.
Number of staff: 1 part-time professional.
EIN: 556101813
Selected grants: The following grants were reported in 2005.
$850,683 to Cabell Wayne Association of the Blind, Huntington, WV.
$200,000 to American Foundation for the Blind, New York, NY.
$32,000 to West Virginia University Foundation, Morgantown, WV. For aid to the blind.
$25,769 to West Virginia School for the Blind, Romney, WV.

$21,000 to Faith in Action of the River Cities, Huntington, WV. For aid to the blind.
$18,430 to YMCA of Huntington, Huntington, WV. For aid to the blind.
$6,600 to Ebenezer Medical Outreach, Huntington, WV.
$5,000 to Little League of Barboursville, Barboursville, WV.
$750 to Western Pennsylvania Hospital, Pittsburgh, PA.

9736
Tucker Community Endowment Foundation
P.O. Box 491
Parsons, WV 26287 (304) 478-2930
Contact: Robert Burns, Exec. Dir.
E-mail: tcef@frontiernet.net; Additional tel.: (304) 478-3533

Established in 1988 in WV.
Foundation type: Community foundation.
Financial data (yr. ended 12/31/05): Assets, $15,611,534 (M); gifts received, $189,708; expenditures, $557,460; giving activities include $399,870 for 35 grants (high: $364,820; low: $150), and $36,550 for 30 grants to individuals (high: $5,000; low: $350).
Purpose and activities: Scholarships for local community services, including playgrounds, art and cultural programs, and for fire and medical services.
Fields of interest: Visual arts; Performing arts; Libraries/library science; Education; Health care; Recreation.
Type of support: Technical assistance; Seed money; Scholarships—to individuals; Program development; General/operating support; Employee-related scholarships; Curriculum development; Continuing support; Endowments; Scholarship funds.
Limitations: Giving limited to Barbour, Grant, Pocahontas, Preston, Randolph, and Tucker Counties, WV. No support for annual fund campaigns, deficit financing or debt retirement, fraternal organizations, religious organizations for sectarian purposes, scientific research, or political organizations or campaigns. No grants to individuals, except for selected scholarships.
Publications: Annual report.
Application information: Application form required for scholarships. Application form required.
   Initial approach: Letter or telephone
   Copies of proposal: 6
   Deadline(s): Apr. for scholarships; Sept. for grants
   Board meeting date(s): Jan., May, and Oct.
   Final notification: May and Oct.
Officers and Directors:* Diane Beall,* Pres.; Dan Bucher,* V.P.; Mariwyn McClain Smith,* Secy.; Marvin Parsons,* Treas.; Robert A. Burns, Exec. Dir.; Jane H. Barb; Pamela A. Chenoweth; Beth Clevenger; David Cooper; James C. Cooper III; Mark Doak; Nancy K. Dotson; Amy Fiorini; Sam Goughnour; Arvin Harsh; Janie Hedrick; Shawn Nichols; Milan Nypl; Donna Patrick; Walt Ranalli; Randall R. Reed; Vidia Ross; Robin Steffl; Ann Wardwell.
Number of staff: 1 full-time professional.
EIN: 550687098

9737

Jack Whittaker Foundation, Inc. ▼ ✧

2 Smiley Dr.
St. Albans, WV 25177 (304) 755-6162
Contact: Andrew J. Whittaker, Pres.

Established in 2003 in WV.
Donor: Jack Whittaker.
Foundation type: Independent foundation.

Financial data (yr. ended 12/31/04): Assets, $1,169,168 (M); gifts received, $2,200,000; expenditures, $8,615,580; qualifying distributions, $8,247,785; giving activities include $8,247,785 for 45 grants (high: $4,766,139; low: $100; average: $1,000–$280,000).
Purpose and activities: Established to help charities operated by the Church of God in WV.

Fields of interest: Human services; Children/youth, services; Christian agencies & churches.
Limitations: Giving primarily in WV. No grants to individuals.
Application information:
 Initial approach: Letter
 Deadline(s): None
Officers: Andrew J. Whittaker, Pres.; Ginger Bragg McMahan, V.P.; Jewell K. Whittaker, Secy.-Treas.
EIN: 753094074

WISCONSIN

9738
1923 Fund ◇

c/o U.S. Bank, N.A.
P.O. Box 2043
Milwaukee, WI 53201-9668

Established in 1994 in IL.
Donors: David A. Cofrin; Mary Ann Cofrin.
Foundation type: Independent foundation.
Financial data (yr. ended 12/31/05): Assets,
$51,081,113 (M); expenditures, $2,045,062;
qualifying distributions, $1,981,027; giving
activities include $1,930,440 for 11 grants (high:
$400,000; low: $10,000; average: $10,000–
$200,000).
Purpose and activities: Giving primarily for
education and hospitals.
Fields of interest: Higher education; Medical
school/education; Hospitals (general).
Limitations: Applications not accepted. Giving
primarily in FL, NY and WI. No grants to individuals.
Application information: Contributes only to
pre-selected organizations.
Trustee: U.S. Bank, N.A.
Advisors: David A. Cofrin, Chief Advisor; Steven P.
Dhein, Exec. Co-Advisor.
EIN: 367070455

9739
Acuity Charitable Foundation, Inc. ◇ ☆

2800 S. Taylor Dr.
P.O. Box 58
Sheboygan, WI 53082-0058 (920) 458-9131
Contact: Lynn Yunger

Established in 2003 in WI.
Donor: Acuity Mutual Insurance Co.
Foundation type: Company-sponsored foundation.
Financial data (yr. ended 12/31/05): Assets,
$6,081,789 (M); gifts received, $2,000,000;
expenditures, $2,169,959; qualifying distributions,
$2,156,041; giving activities include $2,156,041
for grants.
Purpose and activities: The foundation supports
public libraries and organizations involved with arts
and culture, higher education, and health.
Fields of interest: Arts; Higher education; Libraries
(public); Health care.
Type of support: Program development; General/
operating support; Sponsorships.
Limitations: Giving primarily in Sheboygan, WI.
Application information: Proposals should be
submitted using organization letterhead. Application
form not required.
Initial approach: Proposal
Officers and Directors:* Benjamin M. Salzmann,*
Pres. and C.E.O.; Richard A. Waldhart,* V.P.; Laura
J. Conklin,* Secy.; Wendy R. Schuler,* Treas.;
Thomas C. Gast; Robert H. Hanlon; Sara E. Larsen.
EIN: 200354193

9740
Alexander Charitable Foundation, Inc.

1 Port Plz.
Port Edwards, WI 54469
Contact: John A. Casey, Pres.

Incorporated in 1955 in WI.
Donor: John E. Alexander‡.
Foundation type: Independent foundation.
Financial data (yr. ended 12/31/05): Assets,
$17,527,909 (M); gifts received, $200;
expenditures, $1,018,611; qualifying distributions,
$992,042; giving activities include $888,202 for 38
grants (high: $338,000; low: $1,000), and
$100,119 for foundation-administered programs.
Purpose and activities: Emphasis on community
centers, Protestant church support, and hospitals.
Fields of interest: Hospitals (general); Human
services; Family services; Community development;
Protestant agencies & churches; Religion.
Limitations: Applications not accepted. Giving
primarily in WI. No grants to individuals.
Application information: Contributes only to
pre-selected organizations.
Board meeting date(s): Semiannually
Officers and Directors:* John A. Casey,* Pres.;
Leslie V. Arendt,* V.P.; Charles R. Lester,* V.P.;
Inez Krohn, Secy.-Treas.; Thomas J. McCormick; Tim
Wright.
Number of staff: 1 part-time professional.
EIN: 396045140

9741
Judd S. Alexander Foundation, Inc.

500 3rd St., Ste. 320
P.O. Box 2137
Wausau, WI 54402-2137 (715) 845-4556
Contact: Gary W. Freels, Pres.
FAX: (715) 848-9336; URL: http://
www.juddsalexanderfoundation.org

Incorporated in 1973 in WI.
Donor: Anne M. Alexander‡.
Foundation type: Independent foundation.
Financial data (yr. ended 6/30/05): Assets,
$69,902,724 (M); expenditures, $2,134,385;
qualifying distributions, $2,134,906; giving
activities include $1,510,043 for 80 grants (high:
$500,000; low: $193), and $220,000 for loans/
program-related investments.
Purpose and activities: Giving for the direct benefit
of residents of Marathon County, WI; primary areas
of interest include community development, social
services, youth, educational programs, economic
development, arts and human services.
Fields of interest: Arts; Education, early childhood
education; Elementary school/education; Higher
education; Adult/continuing education; Education;
Health care; Crime/law enforcement; Recreation;
Human services; Children/youth, services;
Economic development; Community development.
Type of support: Program development; Capital
campaigns; Building/renovation; Equipment; Land
acquisition; Emergency funds; Seed money;
Technical assistance; Program-related
investments/loans; Matching/challenge support.
Limitations: Giving limited to Marathon County, WI,
or to organizations directly benefiting the residents
of Marathon County. No support for religion, or for
medical research, or for organizations or projects
whose mission is to prevent, eradicate and/or
alleviate the effects of a specific disease, requests
from hospitals (unless they are for community wide
capital campaigns with a slated goal and beginning
and ending dates), or charities operated by service
clubs. No grants to individuals, or for endowment
funds, fellowships, fundraising campaigns,
research, publications, film, videos, television
programs, travel, conferences, the writing or

publication of books, private businesses, or annual
operating support.
Publications: Application guidelines.
Application information: Application information is
available on foundation Web site. Fax or e-mail
proposals are not accepted. Proposals should not
be bound or placed in protective covers or other
presentation formats. Application form not required.
Initial approach: Letter, proposal, or telephone
Copies of proposal: 6
Deadline(s): None
Board meeting date(s): Monthly
Final notification: 60 days
Officers and Directors:* Stanley F. Staples, Jr.,*
Chair.; Gary W. Freels,* Pres.; Richard D. Dudley,*
V.P.; John F. Michler,* Secy.-Treas.; Dwight E. Davis.
EIN: 237323721
Selected grants: The following grants were reported
in 2004.
$950,000 to Marathon County Development
Corporation (MCDEVCO), Wausau, WI.
$81,181 to North Central Technical College
Foundation, Wausau, WI. For Salvation Army
Outreach.
$73,221 to Girl Scouts of the U.S.A., Birth Trails
Council, Wausau, WI. For Camp Del O' Claire.
$42,472 to Chamber Foundation, Wausau Area,
Wausau, WI. For Marathon County Partners in
Education.
$32,500 to Wausau Area Hmong Mutual
Association, Wausau, WI. For Fresh Start.
$25,000 to United Way of Marathon County,
Wausau, WI. For Ready to Read.
$15,000 to Leigh Yawkey Woodson Art Museum,
Wausau, WI. For restoration.
$10,700 to YMCA of Wausau Foundation, Wausau,
WI. For camperships.
$10,000 to Junior Achievement of Wisconsin,
Milwaukee, WI. For Pyramid of Strength.
$10,000 to Marathon County Child Development
Agency, Wausau, WI. For Free to Grow Program.

9742
Alliant Energy Foundation, Inc. ◇

(formerly Wisconsin Power and Light Foundation,
Inc.)
4902 N. Biltmore Ln.
P.O. Box 77007
Madison, WI 53707-1007 (608) 458-4483
Contact: Jo Ann Healy, Prog. Mgr.
FAX: (608) 458-4820;
E-mail: foundation@alliantenergy.com; Additional
tel.: (800) 255-4268, ext. 458-4483; URL: http://
www.alliantenergy.com/docs/groups/public/
documents/pub/p014350.hcsp

Established in 1984 in WI.
Donors: Wisconsin Power and Light Co.; Alliant
Energy Corp.
Foundation type: Company-sponsored foundation.
Financial data (yr. ended 12/31/03): Assets,
$26,389,664 (M); gifts received, $500,000;
expenditures, $2,058,739; qualifying distributions,
$1,902,534; giving activities include $1,249,777
for 849 grants (high: $117,466; low: $50), and
$508,073 for 2,629 employee matching gifts.
Purpose and activities: The foundation supports
organizations involved with arts and culture,
education, the environment, employment, housing,
youth development, human services, and
community development.
Fields of interest: Arts, equal rights; Humanities;
Arts; Vocational education; Higher education;

Education; Environment, natural resources; Environment, energy; Environment; Employment, training; Employment; Housing/shelter; Youth development; Human services; Economic development; Community development; Minorities. **Type of support:** Research; General/operating support; Continuing support; Annual campaigns; Capital campaigns; Building/renovation; Equipment; Emergency funds; Program development; Seed money; Scholarship funds; Employee matching gifts; Employee-related scholarships. **Limitations:** Giving limited to areas of company operations in IA, IL, MN, and WI. No support for religious, social, or fraternal organizations. No grants to individuals (except for employee-related scholarships), or for advertising, door prizes, raffles, dinner tables, golf outings, travel, endowments, fundraising, tours, or "bricks and mortar" projects. **Publications:** Annual report (including application guidelines); Informational brochure (including application guidelines). **Application information:** Application form required. *Initial approach:* Download application form and mail to foundation or nearest company facility *Copies of proposal:* 1 *Deadline(s):* Varies *Board meeting date(s):* Quarterly *Final notification:* Feb. **Officers:** Barbara Swan, Pres.; Eliot Protsch,* V.P.; Tim Heinrich, Secy. and Exec. Dir.; Janet Nebel, Treas. **Directors:** Thomas L. Aller; Erroll B. Davis, Jr.; William D. Harvey; James E. Hoffman. **Number of staff:** 3 full-time professional; 3 part-time professional. **EIN:** 391444065

9743
AnnMarie Foundation ✧
c/o Phillips Plastics Technology Ctr.
N4660 1165th St.
P.O. Box 185
Prescott, WI 54021-7644 (715) 262-8000
Contact: Lori Feiten
FAX: (715) 262-8080;
E-mail: AnnMarieFoundation@phillipsplastics.com;
URL: http://www.phillipsplastics.com/corporateoverview/community.html

Established in 1973 in WI.
Donors: Phillips Plastics Corp.; Mike Litvinoff Memorial; Robert Cervenka; Debbie Cervenka.
Foundation type: Company-sponsored foundation.
Financial data (yr. ended 4/30/06): Assets, $4,508,859 (M); gifts received, $116,006; expenditures, $419,970; qualifying distributions, $395,841; giving activities include $322,763 for 205 grants (high: $8,732; low: $150), and $73,078 for 81 grants to individuals (high: $2,078; low: $500).
Purpose and activities: The foundation supports organizations involved with arts and culture, education, health, and youth and awards college scholarships to students pursuing education in a plastics-related field.
Fields of interest: Arts; Libraries (public); Education; Health care; Big Brothers/Big Sisters; Youth development, scouting agencies (general); Youth, services.
Type of support: General/operating support; Scholarships—to individuals.

Limitations: Giving primarily in areas of company operations in WI.
Application information: Unsolicited requests for scholarships are not accepted. Application form required.
Initial approach: Contact foundation for application form
Deadline(s): None
Members: Nancy Bieraguel; Duane Dingmann; Charlie Krueger; Brian Kulas; Kaye Omnien; Vickie Petrashek; Tim Popp; Tami Satre.
EIN: 237301323
Selected grants: The following grants were reported in 2003.
$7,148 to Eau Claire Area School District, Eau Claire, WI.
$5,000 to Eau Claire Regional Arts Council, Eau Claire, WI.
$4,000 to Big Brothers Big Sisters of Northwestern Wisconsin, Eau Claire, WI.
$4,000 to Chippewa Valley Museum, Eau Claire, WI.
$4,000 to Menomonie Area Public Schools, Menomonie, WI.
$3,100 to Girl Scouts of the U.S.A., Council of Saint Croix Valley, Saint Paul, MN.
$3,037 to Carpenter Saint Croix Valley Nature Center, Hastings, MN.
$2,500 to Big Brothers/Big Sisters of Price County, Phillips, WI.
$2,500 to West Central Wisconsin Community Action Agency, Glenwood City, WI.
$2,000 to Dunn County Interfaith Volunteer Caregivers, Menomonie, WI.

9744
Anon Charitable Trust ✧
c/o U.S. Bank, N.A.
P.O. Box 2043
Milwaukee, WI 53201-9116
Application address: Donald S. Buzard c/o U.S. Bank, P.O. Box 3194, Milwaukee, WI 53201-3194

Established in 1993 in WI.
Donor: Clarice Turer.
Foundation type: Independent foundation.
Financial data (yr. ended 12/31/04): Assets, $4,762,340 (M); gifts received, $43; expenditures, $450,354; qualifying distributions, $397,722; giving activities include $391,500 for 23 grants (high: $100,000; low: $500).
Purpose and activities: Giving primarily for children and Jewish centers.
Fields of interest: Youth development, centers/clubs; Boys & girls clubs; Human services; Children/youth, services; Jewish federated giving programs; Jewish agencies & temples.
Limitations: Giving primarily in Milwaukee, WI. No grants to individuals.
Application information:
Initial approach: Proposal
Deadline(s): None
Trustees: Bert L. Bilsky; Donald S. Buzard; Wayne R. Lueders.
EIN: 391771579
Selected grants: The following grants were reported in 2004.
$100,000 to United Way, WI.
$95,000 to Boys and Girls Clubs of Greater Milwaukee, Milwaukee, WI. 3 grants: $15,000, $45,000, $35,000.
$8,000 to Big Brothers/Big Sisters of Metropolitan Milwaukee, Milwaukee, WI.

$5,000 to United Performing Arts Fund, Milwaukee, WI.
$4,250 to First Stage Childrens Theater, Milwaukee, WI. 2 grants: $1,000, $3,250
$2,000 to Skylight Opera Theater, Milwaukee, WI.
$500 to Milwaukee Symphony Orchestra, Milwaukee, WI.

9745
Antioch Foundation ✧
c/o North Central Trust Co.
230 Front St. N.
La Crosse, WI 54601
Contact: Darwin Isaacson, Trust Off., North Central Trust Co.

Established in 1998 in WI.
Donors: Jill Swanson; Scott Zietlow; Donald Zietlow; Lavonne Zietlow.
Foundation type: Independent foundation.
Financial data (yr. ended 12/31/05): Assets, $7,983,162 (M); gifts received, $4,977,404; expenditures, $597,253; qualifying distributions, $574,900; giving activities include $573,950 for 19 grants (high: $124,000; low: $450).
Purpose and activities: Giving primarily for education and to Lutheran churches and organizations.
Fields of interest: Scholarships/financial aid; Education; Protestant agencies & churches.
Type of support: General/operating support.
Limitations: Giving primarily in the Rochester, MN, and La Crosse, WI, areas. No grants to individuals.
Application information: Application form not required.
Deadline(s): None
Trustees and Directors:* Dan Kunz*; Vicki Kunz*; Amy Zietlow*; Jill Zietlow*; Scott Zietlow*; Steve Zietlow*; North Central Trust Co.
EIN: 363779525

9746
Jacqueline G. Archer Charitable Trust ✧
c/o JPMorgan Chase Bank, N.A.
P.O. Box 1308
Milwaukee, WI 53201

Established in 2002 in CO.
Foundation type: Independent foundation.
Financial data (yr. ended 12/31/05): Assets, $15,298,486 (M); expenditures, $885,877; qualifying distributions, $805,824; giving activities include $781,428 for 104 grants (high: $39,070; low: $1,954).
Fields of interest: Education; Animal welfare; Youth development, services; Human services; Christian agencies & churches.
Limitations: Applications not accepted. Giving primarily in CO; some funding nationally. No grants to individuals.
Application information: Contributes only to pre-selected organizations.
Trustee: JPMorgan Chase Bank, N.A.
EIN: 686218949

9747
The Argosy Foundation ▼ ✧

(formerly The Abele Family Charitable Trust)
555 E. Wells St., Ste. 1650
Milwaukee, WI 53202
Contact: Jeff Snell, C.O.O.
E-mail: info@argosyfnd.org; Tel./FAX: (414)
721-0021

Established in 1993 in MA. Over the next few years, the Abele family plans to more than double the foundation's endowment, which would make it one of the larger foundations in the nation with assets eventually approaching $2 billion.

Donor: John E. Abele.
Foundation type: Independent foundation.
Financial data (yr. ended 12/30/05): Assets, $91,157,023 (M); expenditures, $13,623,798; qualifying distributions, $12,606,663; giving activities include $12,606,663 for 300 grants.
Purpose and activities: The foundation's mission is to support people and programs that make our society a better place to live. The method is to support creative, entrepreneurial approaches that help people to help themselves. These programs should have the potential to become self-sustaining whenever possible, to build teams and communities, to be replicated, and to motivate and inspire others to contribute in their own ways.
Fields of interest: Performing arts, music; Arts; Education; Environment, public education; Environment; Housing/shelter, services; Human services.
Type of support: General/operating support; Scholarship funds.
Limitations: Applications not accepted. Giving on a national basis, with emphasis on Milwaukee, WI, Boston, MA, Boulder, CO and VT. No grants to individuals.
Application information: Contributes only to pre-selected organizations.
Officer: Jeffrey T. Snell.
Trustees: Alexander T. Abele; Christopher S. Abele; Jennifer L. Abele; John E. Abele; Mary S. Abele.
EIN: 046752868
Selected grants: The following grants were reported in 2004.
$746,300 to Boys and Girls Clubs of America, Atlanta, GA. 2 grants: $250,000, $496,300 (For grant made in form of stock).
$641,130 to Milwaukee Symphony Orchestra, Milwaukee, WI. For grant made in form of stock.
$300,426 to United Community Center, Milwaukee, WI. For grant made in form of stock.
$193,795 to Colorado Conservation Trust, Boulder, CO. For grant made in form of stock.
$125,000 to University of Michigan, Regents, Ann Arbor, MI.
$113,040 to Childrens Hospital Corporation, Boston, MA. For grant made in form of stock.
$35,000 to Preserve Our Parks, Milwaukee, WI.
$20,000 to University of Wyoming Foundation, Cheyenne, WY.
$15,000 to Junior Achievement of Wisconsin, Milwaukee, WI.
$15,000 to Sacramento Philharmonic Orchestra, Sacramento, CA.

9748
Assurant Health Foundation ✧

(formerly Fortis Health Foundation, Inc.)
501 W. Michigan St.
Milwaukee, WI 53203-2706   (414) 299-1358
Contact: Rob Guilbert, Pres.
FAX: (414) 299-6749;
E-mail: rob.guilbert@assurant.com

Established in 1973 in WI.
Donors: Time Insurance Co.; Fortis Insurance Co.
Foundation type: Company-sponsored foundation.
Financial data (yr. ended 12/31/04): Assets, $10,110,522 (M); gifts received, $6,000,000; expenditures, $569,709; qualifying distributions, $515,167; giving activities include $438,000 for 35 grants (high: $50,000; low: $1,000), and $77,167 for employee matching gifts.
Purpose and activities: The foundation supports organizations involved with education, health, children and youth, and community development.
Fields of interest: Education; Medical care, community health systems; Health care, clinics/centers; Health care, patient services; Health care; Children/youth, services; Community development, neighborhood development; Federated giving programs.
Type of support: General/operating support; Continuing support; Program development; Professorships; Seed money; Consulting services; Employee matching gifts; Employee-related scholarships; In-kind gifts; Matching/challenge support.
Limitations: Applications not accepted. Giving primarily in southeastern WI. No support for political, labor, or religious organizations.
Publications: Annual report; Financial statement; Grants list; Informational brochure.
Application information: The foundation utilizes an invitation only Request For Proposal (RFP) process. Unsolicited requests are not accepted.
Board meeting date(s): Quarterly
Officers: Rob Guilbert, Pres.; Mary Brown, V.P.; Jennifer Kopps-Wagner, Secy.; Howard Miller, Treas.
Trustees: Tom Brophy; Laree Daniel; Kay Kerlin; Howard Miller; Kim Pollard.
EIN: 237346436
Selected grants: The following grants were reported in 2004.
$50,000 to Galen Institute, Alexandria, VA.
$30,000 to National Center for Policy Analysis, Dallas, TX.
$26,500 to United Way of Greater Milwaukee, Milwaukee, WI. 2 grants: $25,000, $1,500
$20,000 to Heartland Institute, Chicago, IL.
$15,000 to Skylight Opera Theater, Milwaukee, WI.

9749
Helen Bader Foundation, Inc. ▼ ✧

233 N. Water St., 4th Fl.
Milwaukee, WI 53202   (414) 224-6464
Contact: Daniel J. Bader, Pres.
FAX: (414) 224-1441; E-mail: info@hbf.org;
URL: http://www.hbf.org

Established in 1991 in WI.
Donors: Daniel Bader Charitable Trust; David Bader Charitable Trust.
Foundation type: Independent foundation.
Financial data (yr. ended 8/31/05): Assets, $5,149,599 (M); gifts received, $14,400,000; expenditures, $13,445,672; qualifying distributions, $13,883,200; giving activities include $11,329,781 for 299 grants (high: $1,488,625; low: $500; average: $10,000–$100,000), $99,793 for foundation-administered programs and $500,779 for 3 loans/program-related investments (high: $200,779; low: $150,000).
Purpose and activities: The foundation's mission is to support innovative projects and programs which advance the well-being of people and promote successful relationships with their families and communities. The foundation currently concentrates grantmaking in five program areas: Alzheimer's Disease and dementia; economic development; early childhood development in Israel; Jewish life and learning; and Sankofa-youth development. The foundation prefers funding programs that demonstrate results, are coordinated with other community programs, and can be replicated.
Fields of interest: Alzheimer's disease; Medical research, institute; Youth development; Human services; Children/youth, services; Economic development; Community development; Jewish federated giving programs; Jewish agencies & temples; Religion.
International interests: Israel.
Type of support: General/operating support; Annual campaigns; Capital campaigns; Building/renovation; Debt reduction; Program development; Conferences/seminars; Seed money; Scholarship funds; Research; Technical assistance; Program-related investments/loans.
Limitations: Giving primarily in the greater Milwaukee, WI, area for education and economic development; giving locally and nationally for Alzheimer's disease and dementia; giving in Israel for early childhood development. No grants to individuals.
Publications: Application guidelines; Annual report (including application guidelines); Grants list.
Application information: The foundation also accepts the Donor's Forum of Wisconsin Common Application Form. After receipt of the preliminary application form, the foundation will respond in writing regarding the status of the application. If a full proposal is requested, an on-site visit will also be required. Full proposals may not be submitted via fax or E-mail. Application form required.
Initial approach: Preliminary application form
Copies of proposal: 1
Deadline(s): Preliminary application: Jan. 22 and July 17; Full proposal: Feb. 27 and Aug. 14
Board meeting date(s): May and Nov.
Final notification: Within 2 weeks
Officers and Directors:* Jere D. McGaffey,* Chair. and Secy.-Treas.; Daniel J. Bader,* Pres.; David M. Bader,* V.P.; Lisa G. Hiller, V.P., Admin.; Robin B. Mayrl, V.P., Prog. Devel.; Linda C. Bader; Michelle Berrong; Deirdre H. Britt; Frances Klitsner Wolff.
Number of staff: 7 full-time professional; 2 part-time professional; 3 full-time support; 1 part-time support.
EIN: 391710914
Selected grants: The following grants were reported in 2005.
$1,000,000 to Jewish Federation, Milwaukee, WI. For Jewish Community Capital Campaign, payable over 2 years.
$333,459 to University of Wisconsin Foundation, Milwaukee, WI. For Center for Jewish Studies Implementation Plan, payable over 5 years.
$270,000 to Alzheimers Association, Green Bay, WI. For Blue Cross Blue Shield Match for Rural Program, payable over 3 years.
$255,000 to Local Initiatives Support Corporation (LISC), Milwaukee, WI. For Milwaukee

Partnership for Community Development, payable over 3 years.

$200,000 to Company for Centers of Culture and Sport for Youth and Adults, Jerusalem, Israel. For Early Childhood Development Centers, payable over 2 years.

$200,000 to Legacy Redevelopment Corporation, Milwaukee, WI. For expansion of revolving community loan fund, payable over 3 years.

$180,000 to Alzheimers Disease and Related Disorders Association, South Central Wisconsin Chapter, Madison, WI. For Blue Cross Blue Shield Match, payable over 3 years.

$150,000 to Association for the Development of Welfare Services in Lod, Lod, Israel. For Mashal Rehabilitation Center and Rosenwald Early Childhood Center in Lod, payable over 3 years.

$150,000 to Friends of Lubavitch, Milwaukee, WI. For lay leadership and administrative transformation, payable over 3 years.

$150,000 to Milwaukee Center for Independence, Milwaukee, WI. For capital campaign, payable over 3 years.

9750

Robert W. Baird and Company Foundation, Inc. ✧

c/o James D. Bell
777 E. Wisconsin Ave.
Milwaukee, WI 53202

Established in 1967 in WI.
Donor: Robert W. Baird and Co.
Foundation type: Company-sponsored foundation.
Financial data (yr. ended 12/31/04): Assets, $9,186,084 (M); gifts received, $2,150,000; expenditures, $1,364,919; qualifying distributions, $1,359,236; giving activities include $1,322,753 for 417 grants (high: $95,000; low: $100), and $36,483 for 87 employee matching gifts.
Purpose and activities: The foundation supports hospitals and organizations involved with arts and culture, education, health, youth development, human services, and religion.
Fields of interest: Performing arts; Arts; Higher education; Education; Hospitals (general); Health care; Youth development; Children/youth, services; Human services; Federated giving programs; Religion.
Type of support: General/operating support; Capital campaigns.
Limitations: Applications not accepted. Giving primarily in WI. No grants to individuals.
Application information: Contributes only to pre-selected organizations.
Officers and Directors: G. Frederick Kasten, Jr., Chair.; Paul Purcell, Pres. and C.E.O.; Glenn Hackmann, Secy.; Leonard M. Rush,* C.F.O.; Paul J. Carbone; Patrick S. Lawton; William W. Mahler; Terrance P. Maxwell; Michael J. Schroeder; Mary Ellen Stanek; Robert J. Venable.
EIN: 396107937

9751

Pat and Jay Baker Foundation, Inc. ▼ ✧

6350 N. Lake Dr.
Whitefish Bay, WI 53217

Established in 1993 in WI.
Donor: Jay H. Baker.
Foundation type: Independent foundation.

Financial data (yr. ended 12/31/05): Assets, $5,180,343 (M); gifts received, $6,431,400; expenditures, $6,770,374; qualifying distributions, $6,704,500; giving activities include $6,701,000 for 11 grants (high: $3,200,000; low: $1,000).
Purpose and activities: Giving primarily for the performing arts and higher education.
Fields of interest: Museums (art); Performing arts; Higher education, university; Libraries (public); Federated giving programs; Protestant agencies & churches.
Limitations: Applications not accepted. Giving primarily in Milwaukee, WI. No grants to individuals.
Application information: Contributes only to pre-selected organizations.
Officers and Directors:* Jay H. Baker,* Pres. and Treas.; Pat Good Baker,* V.P. and Secy.; Peter M. Sommerhauser.
EIN: 391776268
Selected grants: The following grants were reported in 2005.
$3,200,000 to Naples Jewish Community Fund, Naples, FL.
$2,050,000 to Educational Foundation for the Fashion Industries, New York, NY.
$1,000,000 to NCH Healthcare System, Naples, FL.
$10,000 to Seacrest Country Day School, Naples, FL.

9752

Banta Corporation Foundation, Inc. ✧

P.O. Box 8003
Menasha, WI 54952-8003 (920) 751-7777
Contact: Frank W. Rudolph, Pres.

Incorporated in 1953 in WI.
Donor: Banta Corp.
Foundation type: Company-sponsored foundation.
Financial data (yr. ended 12/31/05): Assets, $336,230 (M); gifts received, $600,000; expenditures, $411,897; qualifying distributions, $411,897; giving activities include $300,475 for 78 grants (high: $62,500; low: $125), $90,000 for 38 grants to individuals (high: $2,500; low: $1,500), and $8,223 for 42 employee matching gifts.
Purpose and activities: The foundation supports organizations involved with arts and culture and higher education. Special emphasis is directed toward programs designed to engage in literary scholarship or educational endeavors.
Fields of interest: Performing arts; Arts; Higher education.
Type of support: General/operating support; Continuing support; Annual campaigns; Building/renovation; Equipment; Land acquisition; Debt reduction; Emergency funds; Program development; Seed money; Employee matching gifts; Employee-related scholarships; Matching/challenge support.
Limitations: Giving limited to areas of company operations, with emphasis on WI. No support for religious organizations. No grants to individuals (except for employee-related scholarships), raffle tickets or door prizes, endowments, or political actions or lobbying efforts.
Application information: Proposals should be submitted using organization letterhead. Application form not required.
Initial approach: Proposal
Deadline(s): Nov. 1
Board meeting date(s): Apr.
Final notification: Within 30 days following board meeting

Officers: Frank W. Rudolph, Pres.; Stephanie A. Streeter, V.P.; Robert T. Michel, Secy.; Ronald D. Kneezel, Treas.
EIN: 396050779

9753

Edward & Helen Bartlett Foundation ✧

(formerly Edward E. Bartlett & Helen Turner Bartlett Foundation)
c/o JPMorgan Chase Bank, N.A.
P.O. Box 1308
Milwaukee, WI 53201
Application address: Mike Bartel c/o JPMorgan Chase Bank, N.A., P.O. Box 1, Tulsa, OK 74193

Established in 1961 in OK.
Donor: Edward E. Bartlett‡.
Foundation type: Independent foundation.
Financial data (yr. ended 12/31/05): Assets, $28,286,391 (M); expenditures, $1,528,688; qualifying distributions, $1,353,753; giving activities include $1,313,565 for 49 grants (high: $438,465; low: $1,000).
Fields of interest: Higher education; Education; Health organizations, association; Boy scouts; Human services; Children/youth, services.
Limitations: Giving limited to OK. No grants to individuals directly.
Application information: Application form not required.
Initial approach: Letter
Deadline(s): None
Trustees: Harry C. Freeman; JPMorgan Chase Bank, N.A.
EIN: 736092250

9754

Theodore W. Batterman Family Foundation, Inc.

1017 W. Glen Oaks Ln., Ste. 209
Mequon, WI 53092
Contact: Carmen Witt, Exec. Dir.

Established in 1990 in WI.
Donors: Theodore W. Batterman; Spacesaver Corp.
Foundation type: Independent foundation.
Financial data (yr. ended 12/31/05): Assets, $52,368,019 (M); gifts received, $112,500; expenditures, $3,043,702; qualifying distributions, $2,519,119; giving activities include $2,459,717 for 55 grants (high: $530,000; low: $2,100).
Purpose and activities: Giving primarily for Christian faith advancement and education.
Fields of interest: Education; Protestant agencies & churches.
Limitations: Applications not accepted. Giving limited to WI. No grants to individuals, or for endowments.
Application information: Contributes only to pre-selected organizations.
Officers and Directors:* Theodore W. Batterman,* Pres. and Treas.; Marilyn H. Batterman,* V.P. and Secy.; Carmen Witt, Exec. Dir.; Christopher T. Batterman; Eric D. Batterman; Linda C. Batterman Johnson; Andrew R. Lauritzen; Laura G. Batterman Wilkins.
EIN: 391688812
Selected grants: The following grants were reported in 2004.
$150,000 to Salvation Army of Janesville, Janesville, WI.

$100,000 to Lakeside Lutheran High School, Lake Mills, WI.

$92,200 to Community Foundation of Southern Wisconsin, Janesville, WI.

$50,000 to Janesville Performing Arts Center, Janesville, WI.

$50,000 to Kandu Industries, Janesville, WI.

$50,000 to Salvation Army.

$50,000 to Wisconsin Lutheran Chapel and Student Center, Madison, WI.

$40,500 to Acacia Theater Company, Milwaukee, WI.

$37,025 to Wisconsin Academic Decathlon Foundation, Green Bay, WI.

$20,000 to Wisconsin Conservatory of Music, Milwaukee, WI.

9755
Lucy & Emily Beasley Charitable Trust ✧ ☆
c/o JPMorgan Chase Bank, N.A.
P.O. Box 1308
Milwaukee, WI 53201
Application address: c/o Thomas Barsody, JPMorgan Chase Bank, N.A., 50 S. Main St., Akron, OH 44308

Established in 1981 in OH.
Donor: Robert P. Beasley Trust.
Foundation type: Independent foundation.
Financial data (yr. ended 9/30/05): Assets, $7,906,095 (M); gifts received, $1,147; expenditures, $410,758; qualifying distributions, $325,000; giving activities include $325,000 for grants.
Fields of interest: Education; Health care; Substance abuse, treatment; Goodwill Industries; Human services; American Red Cross.
Limitations: Giving primarily in Akron, OH.
Application information:
  Initial approach: Letter
  Deadline(s): None
Advisory Committee: Robert E. Hissong; A. Russell Smith.
Trustee: Howard W. Cable, Jr.
Agent: JPMorgan Chase Bank, N.A.
EIN: 341350747
Selected grants: The following grants were reported in 2003.
$50,000 to Interval Brotherhood Homes Corporation, Akron, OH. For general support.
$50,000 to University of Akron Foundation, Akron, OH. For general support.
$30,000 to Summa Health System, Akron, OH. For general support.
$25,000 to Access, Akron, OH. For general support.
$25,000 to Goodwill Industries of Akron, Akron, OH. For general support.
$25,000 to H.M. Life Opportunity Services, Akron, OH. For general support.
$20,000 to Ardmore Foundation, Akron, OH. For general support.
$15,000 to Battered Womens Shelter, Akron, OH. For general support.
$15,000 to Gennesaret, Akron, OH. For general support.
$10,000 to American Red Cross, Akron, OH. For general support.

9756
Bell Family Charitable Foundation, Inc. ✧
(formerly WCN Bancorp—Bell Charitable Foundation, Inc.)
181 2nd St. S.
Wisconsin Rapids, WI 54494

Established in 1992 in WI.
Donors: Steven C. Bell; Margaret L. Bell; Wood County National Bank; WCN Bancorp; Paula J. Bell; Wood County Trust Co.
Foundation type: Company-sponsored foundation.
Financial data (yr. ended 11/30/03): Assets, $2,161,038 (M); gifts received, $300,000; expenditures, $330,661; qualifying distributions, $323,113; giving activities include $323,000 for 13 grants (high: $150,000; low: $500).
Purpose and activities: The foundation supports organizations involved with historic preservation, K-12 and higher education, health, and families.
Fields of interest: Historical activities; Elementary/secondary education; Higher education; Health care; YM/YWCAs & YM/YWHAs; Family services.
Limitations: Applications not accepted. Giving primarily in WI. No grants to individuals.
Application information: Contributes only to pre-selected organizations.
Officers and Directors:* Chad D. Kane,* Pres.; Paula J. Bell,* V.P.; Margaret L. Bell,* Secy.; Steven C. Bell,* Treas.; David W. Kumm.
EIN: 396572208
Selected grants: The following grants were reported in 2005.
$17,000 to Lincoln High School, Wisconsin Rapids, WI.
$15,000 to Family Center, Wisconsin Rapids, WI.
$11,739 to YMCA of South Wood County, Port Edwards, WI. 2 grants: $10,000, $1,739
$10,000 to Wisconsin Rapids Public Schools, Wisconsin Rapids, WI.
$8,250 to Opportunity Development Centers, Wisconsin Rapids, WI.
$5,000 to United Way of South Wood County, Wisconsin Rapids, WI.
$2,500 to Assumption High School, Wisconsin Rapids, WI. 2 grants: $2,000, $500
$2,000 to University of Wisconsin, Madison, WI.

9757
Beloit Foundation, Inc. ✧
2870 Riverside Dr.
Beloit, WI 53511-1506 (608) 368-1300
Contact: Gary G. Grabowski, Exec. Dir.

Incorporated in 1959 in WI.
Donor: Elbert H. Neese, Sr.‡.
Foundation type: Independent foundation.
Financial data (yr. ended 12/31/05): Assets, $11,358,934 (M); expenditures, $680,761; qualifying distributions, $506,080; giving activities include $447,873 for 15 grants (high: $272,051; low: $1,000).
Purpose and activities: Giving only to local community organizations for special projects and new program development; support also for education, with emphasis on a local college; family and social services, including children and youth services; building funds and community development.
Fields of interest: Arts; Higher education; Human services; Children/youth, services; Family services; Community development, neighborhood development.

Type of support: Capital campaigns; Building/renovation; Equipment; Program development; Seed money; Matching/challenge support.
Limitations: Giving limited to the local Stateline area, including South Beloit, Rockton, Roscoe, IL and Beloit, WI. No grants to individuals, or for endowment funds, research, direct scholarships, fellowships, or nationally organized fundraising campaigns.
Application information: Application form required.
  Initial approach: Letter requesting application form
  Copies of proposal: 10
  Deadline(s): None
  Board meeting date(s): May and Sept.
Officers and Directors:* Alonzo A. Neese, Jr.,* Pres.; Kim M. Kotthaus, Secy.; Gary G. Grabowski,* Treas. and Exec. Dir.; Diane Hendricks; Laura N. Malik; Harry C. Moore, Jr.; Gordon C. Neese; Walter K. Neese; Jane Petit-Moore.
Number of staff: 1 part-time professional; 1 part-time support.
EIN: 396068763
Selected grants: The following grants were reported in 2005.
$110,750 to Family Service Association, Beloit, WI. 2 grants: $83,250, $27,500
$72,863 to Beloit College, Beloit, WI. 2 grants: $60,000, $12,863
$33,000 to Merrill Community Center, Beloit, WI.
$15,584 to School District of Beloit, Beloit, WI.
$14,027 to Beloit Janesville Symphony Orchestra, Beloit, WI. 2 grants: $7,281, $6,746
$12,000 to Wisconsin Center for Academically Talented Youth, Madison, WI.
$10,000 to Tellurian UCAN, Madison, WI.

9758
Charles E. Benidt Foundation, Inc. ✧ ☆
115 N. Elm Grove Rd., Ste. D
Brookfield, WI 53005-6228

Established in 2003 in WI.
Donor: Charles E. Benidt.
Foundation type: Independent foundation.
Financial data (yr. ended 12/31/05): Assets, $87,824 (M); gifts received, $300,000; expenditures, $345,460; qualifying distributions, $335,200; giving activities include $335,200 for grants.
Fields of interest: Human services; Protestant agencies & churches.
Limitations: Applications not accepted. Giving primarily in Milwaukee, WI.
Application information: Contributes only to pre-selected organizations.
Officers and Directors :* Charles E. Benidt,* Pres.; Beatrice A. Benidt,* V.P.; Reuben W. Peterson, Jr.
EIN: 364522803

9759
A. G. Bishop Charitable Trust ✧
c/o JPMorgan Chase Bank, N.A.
P.O. Box 1308
Milwaukee, WI 53201
Application address: c/o JPMorgan Chase Bank, N.A., 111 E. Court St., Ste. 100, Flint MI, 48502, tel.: (810) 237-3836

Trust established in 1944 in MI.
Donor: Arthur Giles Bishop‡.

Foundation type: Independent foundation.
Financial data (yr. ended 12/31/05): Assets, $11,408,295 (M); expenditures, $655,156; qualifying distributions, $581,547; giving activities include $554,473 for 50 grants (high: $120,000; low: $1,500).
Purpose and activities: Giving primarily for education, the arts, and to youth and social services.
Fields of interest: Arts; Higher education; Human services; YM/YWCAs & YM/YWHAs; Children/youth, services; Federated giving programs.
Type of support: General/operating support; Continuing support; Annual campaigns; Building/renovation; Equipment; Land acquisition; Debt reduction; Emergency funds; Seed money; Research.
Limitations: Giving limited to the Flint and Genesee County, MI, community. No grants to individuals, or for endowment funds, scholarships, fellowships, or matching gifts; no loans.
Publications: Application guidelines.
Application information: Application form not required.
  Initial approach: Letter
  Copies of proposal: 3
  Deadline(s): None
  Board meeting date(s): 2 to 3 times per year
  Final notification: 6 months
Trustees: Robert J. Bellairs, Jr.; Elizabeth B. Wentworth; JPMorgan Chase Bank, N.A.
EIN: 386040693

9760
Bleser Family Foundation, Inc. ◇
c/o Marsha E. Huff
P.O. Box 328
Shawano, WI 54166

Established in 1986 in WI.
Donor: Clarence P. Bleser‡.
Foundation type: Independent foundation.
Financial data (yr. ended 12/31/05): Assets, $30,777,465 (M); expenditures, $1,653,291; qualifying distributions, $1,442,450; giving activities include $1,438,000 for 42 grants (high: $250,000; low: $1,000).
Fields of interest: Higher education; Education; Environment; Health organizations, association; Human services.
Limitations: Applications not accepted. Giving primarily in WI. No grants to individuals.
Application information: Contributes only to pre-selected organizations.
Officers and Directors:* Mary B. Hayes,* Pres.; Carol A. Bleser,* V.P. and Secy.; James F. Bleser,* Treas.
EIN: 391585269

9761
Bless Foundation, Inc. ◇
5718 52nd St.
Kenosha, WI 53144-2237 (262) 658-4114
Contact: Robert Block, Treas.

Established in 1987.
Donor: Laminated Products, Inc.
Foundation type: Independent foundation.
Financial data (yr. ended 12/31/05): Assets, $1,584,964 (M); gifts received, $1,985,982; expenditures, $1,028,956; qualifying distributions,

$1,013,200; giving activities include $1,013,200 for 4 grants (high: $1,000,000; low: $200).
Fields of interest: Christian agencies & churches.
Type of support: Building/renovation; Equipment.
Limitations: Giving on a national basis. No grants to individuals.
Application information:
  Initial approach: Letter or telephone
  Deadline(s): None
Officers: Mark Hess, Pres.; Milton Hess, V.P.; Gail Hess, Secy.; Robert Block, Treas.
EIN: 391574310
Selected grants: The following grants were reported in 2003.
$300,000 to India Gospel Outreach, Rancho Cucamonga, CA. For operating support.
$95,000 to Lakeshore Tabernacle. For operating support.
$57,000 to Give Kids the World, Kissimmee, FL. For operating support.
$40,000 to Crusades International, Kenosha, WI. For operating support.
$20,000 to Haiti Gospel Ministries, Haiti. For operating support.
$11,000 to Edgewood Childrens Center, Saint Louis, MO. For operating support.
$10,000 to Make-A-Wish Foundation of Wisconsin, Butler, WI. For Chip Allen Memorial Endowment Fund.
$5,000 to PACE Center for Girls of Jacksonville, Jacksonville, FL. For operating support.
$3,000 to Blue Ridge Autism. For operating support.

9762
Eugenie Mayer Bolz Family Foundation ◇
P.O. Box 8100
Madison, WI 53708-8100

Established in 1976 in WI and IL.
Donors: Eugenie M. Bolz; Eugenie M. Bolz Charitable Lead Trust.
Foundation type: Independent foundation.
Financial data (yr. ended 12/31/05): Assets, $4,095,695 (M); expenditures, $538,687; qualifying distributions, $850,593; giving activities include $486,400 for 39 grants (high: $300,000; low: $1,000).
Purpose and activities: Giving primarily to arts organizations; some support also for higher education and social services.
Fields of interest: Museums; Performing arts; Arts; Higher education; Education; Environment, natural resources; Food services; Youth development; Human services; Children/youth, services; Residential/custodial care, hospices; Foundations (community).
Type of support: General/operating support.
Limitations: Applications not accepted. Giving primarily in Madison, WI. No grants to individuals.
Application information: Contributes only to pre-selected organizations.
Officers: Robert M. Bolz, Pres.; Julia M. Bolz, V.P.; Sara L. Bolz, V.P.; John A. Bolz, Secy.-Treas.
EIN: 237428561

9763
The Lynde and Harry Bradley Foundation, Inc. ▼
1241 N. Franklin Pl.
Milwaukee, WI 53202-2901 (414) 291-9915
Contact: Daniel P. Schmidt, V.P., Progs.

FAX: (414) 291-9991; URL: http://www.bradleyfdn.org

Incorporated in 1942 in WI as the Allen-Bradley Foundation, Inc.; adopted present name in 1985.
Donors: Harry L. Bradley‡; Caroline D. Bradley‡; Margaret B. Bradley‡; Margaret Loock Trust; Allen-Bradley Co.; Michael Keiser; Mrs. Michael Keiser.
Foundation type: Independent foundation.
Financial data (yr. ended 12/31/05): Assets, $755,894,000 (M); gifts received, $3,307,000; expenditures, $40,995,079; qualifying distributions, $34,737,079; giving activities include $34,737,079 for grants.
Purpose and activities: Support for projects that cultivate a renewed, healthier, and more vigorous sense of citizenship, at home and abroad. Projects will reflect the assumption that free men and women are genuinely self-governing, personally responsible citizens, able to run their daily affairs without the intrusive therapies of the bureaucratic, social service state. Consequently, they will seek to reinvigorate and revive the authority of the traditional institutions of civil society - families, schools, churches, neighborhoods, and entrepreneurial enterprises - that cultivate and provide room for the exercise of citizenship, individual responsibility, and strong moral character. Projects reflecting this view of citizenship and civil society may be demonstrations with national significance; public policy research in economics, politics, culture, or foreign affairs; or media and public education undertakings. Local support is directed toward cultural programs, education, social services, medical and health programs, and public policy research.
Fields of interest: Humanities; History/archaeology; Arts; Education, research; Higher education; Education; Youth development, citizenship; International affairs, foreign policy; International affairs; Economics; Political science; Public policy, research; Public affairs, citizen participation; Public affairs.
Type of support: General/operating support; Continuing support; Annual campaigns; Building/renovation; Equipment; Program development; Conferences/seminars; Professorships; Publication; Curriculum development; Fellowships; Internship funds; Scholarship funds; Research; Program-related investments/loans; Matching/challenge support.
Limitations: Giving primarily in Milwaukee, WI; giving also on a national and international basis. No support for strictly denominational projects. No grants to individuals (except for Bradley Prizes), or for endowment funds.
Publications: Application guidelines; Annual report; Grants list; Occasional report (including application guidelines).
Application information: Application form not required.
  Initial approach: Letter of inquiry
  Copies of proposal: 1
  Deadline(s): Mar. 1, June 1, Sept. 1, and Dec. 1
  Board meeting date(s): Feb., May or June, Aug., and Nov.
  Final notification: 3 to 5 months
Officers and Directors:* Thomas L. Rhodes,* Chair.; David V. Uihlein, Jr.,* Vice-Chair.; Michael W. Grebe,* C.E.O. and Pres.; Cynthia K. Friauf, V.P., Finance and Treas.; R. Michael Lempke, V.P., Investments; Daniel P. Schmidt, V.P., Progs.; Thomas L. Smallwood,* Secy.; Mandy L. Hess,

Cont.; William L. Armstrong; Terry Considine; Pierre S. duPont IV; Robert P. George; Dennis J. Kuester; San W. Orr, Jr.; Br. Bob Smith; Pat Toomey.
Number of staff: 9 full-time professional; 8 full-time support; 3 part-time support.
EIN: 396037928
Selected grants: The following grants were reported in 2005.
$1,500,000 to Charter School Growth Fund, Broomfield, CO. For general program support.
$1,175,000 to Encounter for Culture and Education, Milwaukee, WI. For general operating support.
$400,000 to American Enterprise Institute for Public Policy Research, DC. For Foreign and Defense Policy Studies, survey dissemination, and Bradley Lectures.
$400,000 to National Strategy Information Center, DC. For general operating support and Special Project to Enhance U.S. Intelligence.
$400,000 to Wisconsin Policy Research Institute, Mequon, WI. For general operating support.
$325,000 to Center for the Study of Popular Culture, Los Angeles, CA. For general operating support.
$300,000 to Intercollegiate Studies Institute, Wilmington, DE. For Civic Liberty Program.
$265,000 to Federalist Society for Law and Public Policy Studies, DC. For general operating support, Sovereignty Project, and conference on legacy of Chief Justice William Rehnquist.
$250,000 to Black Alliance for Educational Options, DC. For general operating support.
$250,000 to Freedom House, DC. For general program support.

9764
Bradshaw-Knight Foundation, Inc.
(formerly Cavaliere Foundation, Inc.)
712 Harrison St.
Madison, WI 53711
Contact: James A. Knight, Pres.
E-mail: bkfd@mac.com; *URL:* http://www.bkfnd.org

Established in 1999 in WI.
Donor: James A. Knight, Sr.†.
Foundation type: Independent foundation.
Financial data (yr. ended 12/31/05): Assets, $6,295,024 (M); expenditures, $532,535; qualifying distributions, $468,411; giving activities include $391,644 for 14 grants (high: $80,000; low: $100).
Purpose and activities: Giving primarily for environmental education, environmental justice, ecological restoration, and religious approaches to environmental problems.
Fields of interest: Environment, ethics; Environment, natural resources; Environment.
Type of support: Emergency funds; Curriculum development; General/operating support; Equipment; Program development; Conferences/ seminars; Seed money; Research.
Limitations: Giving primarily in the West Slope of CO, and the Upper Midwest Region of IA, IL, MI and WI. No grants to individuals.
Publications: Grants list; Program policy statement.
Application information: Application form required.
  Initial approach: Letter or e-mail
  Copies of proposal: 7
  Deadline(s): Sept. 15
  Board meeting date(s): Oct. 15
  Final notification: 2 months
Officers and Directors:* James A. Knight,* Pres.; Renee Miller Knight, Exec. Dir.; Kathe Conn; Mike Heck; Ed Marston; Warren Porter; Vern Visick.

Number of staff: 1 part-time professional.
EIN: 391960035

9765
Briggs & Stratton Corporation Foundation, Inc. ✧
12301 W. Wirth St.
Wauwatosa, WI 53222   (414) 259-5496
Contact: Robert F. Heath, Secy.-Treas.
Application address: P.O. Box 702, Milwaukee, WI 5320; Additional tel.: (414) 259-5333

Incorporated in 1953 in WI.
Donor: Briggs & Stratton Corp.
Foundation type: Company-sponsored foundation.
Financial data (yr. ended 11/30/05): Assets, $23,337,351 (M); gifts received, $2,000,000; expenditures, $2,371,279; qualifying distributions, $2,358,500; giving activities include $2,323,900 for 122 grants (high: $330,000; low: $500), and $34,000 for grants to individuals.
Purpose and activities: The foundation supports organizations involved with arts and culture and education.
Fields of interest: Performing arts; Arts; Education; Federated giving programs.
Type of support: General/operating support; Annual campaigns; Capital campaigns; Building/ renovation; Program development; Employee-related scholarships.
Limitations: Giving primarily in areas of company operations in Auburn, AL, Statesboro, GA, Murray, KY, Poplar Bluff and Rolla, MO, and Milwaukee, WI. No support for religious organizations. No grants to individuals (except for employee-related scholarships).
Application information: Application form not required.
  Initial approach: Proposal
  Copies of proposal: 1
  Deadline(s): None
  Board meeting date(s): June and Nov.
  Final notification: Nov. 30
Officers and Directors:* Frederick P. Stratton, Jr.,* Pres.; John S. Shiely,* V.P.; Robert F. Heath, Secy.-Treas.; Michael D. Hamilton.
EIN: 396040377
Selected grants: The following grants were reported in 2005.
$330,000 to United Way of Greater Milwaukee, Milwaukee, WI.
$152,500 to United Performing Arts Fund, Milwaukee, WI.
$100,000 to Childrens Hospital of Wisconsin, Milwaukee, WI.
$100,000 to Milwaukee Symphony Orchestra, Milwaukee, WI.
$75,000 to Taliesin Preservation Commission, Spring Green, WI.
$60,000 to Notre Dame Middle School, Milwaukee, WI.
$50,000 to Hoover Institution on War, Revolution and Peace, Stanford, CA.
$20,000 to Milwaukee Repertory Theater, Milwaukee, WI.
$10,000 to Americans for Prosperity Foundation, DC.
$8,000 to Murray State University Foundation, Murray, KY.

9766
Brookbank Foundation, Inc. ✧
P.O. Box 84
Grafton, WI 53024-0084

Established in 1984 in WI.
Donors: Orion Corp.; CPL Industries, Inc.
Foundation type: Independent foundation.
Financial data (yr. ended 10/31/05): Assets, $10,002,263 (M); gifts received, $700,000; expenditures, $372,458; qualifying distributions, $370,130; giving activities include $350,880 for 48 grants (high: $50,000; low: $1,000).
Purpose and activities: Giving primarily for art, education, human services, and to Serbian Orthodox churches.
Fields of interest: Museums (art); Performing arts; Arts; Higher education; Human services; Orthodox Catholic agencies & churches.
Type of support: General/operating support; Capital campaigns.
Limitations: Applications not accepted. Giving primarily in WI, with emphasis on Milwaukee. No grants to individuals.
Application information: Contributes only to pre-selected organizations.
Officers: Mary Ann LaBahn, Pres.; Charles P. LaBahn, Exec. V.P. and Secy.; Ridge A. Braunschweig, V.P. and Treas.
EIN: 391516196

9767
Frank G. and Frieda K. Brotz Family Foundation, Inc. ✧
(formerly Frank G. Brotz Family Foundation, Inc.)
3518 Lakeshore Rd.
Sheboygan, WI 53083-2903   (920) 458-2121
Contact: Grants Comm.

Incorporated in 1953 in WI.
Donor: Plastics Engineering Co., Inc.
Foundation type: Independent foundation.
Financial data (yr. ended 9/30/05): Assets, $24,593,087 (M); expenditures, $1,194,406; qualifying distributions, $1,128,460; giving activities include $1,127,050 for 63 grants (high: $100,000; low: $250).
Purpose and activities: Giving primarily for the arts, education, health, and human services.
Fields of interest: Museums (marine/maritime); Performing arts, theater; Arts; Elementary/ secondary education; Higher education; Education; Hospitals (general); Food banks; Boys & girls clubs; Big Brothers/Big Sisters; Christian agencies & churches.
Type of support: Building/renovation.
Limitations: Giving primarily in WI. No grants to individuals.
Application information:
  Initial approach: Detailed letter
  Deadline(s): None
  Board meeting date(s): Periodically
Officers and Trustees:* Stuart W. Brotz,* Pres.; Ralph R. Brotz,* Secy.-Treas.; Adam T. Brotz; Roland M. Neumann.
EIN: 396060552

9768

The Edwin E. and Janet L. Bryant Foundation, Inc. ✧ ☆

(formerly BGB Foundation)
c/o June Bunting
P.O. Box 600
Stoughton, WI 53589-0600
Application address: 3039 Shadyside Dr., Stoughton
WI, 53589-0600; tel.: (608) 873-4378

Established in 1993 in WI.
Foundation type: Independent foundation.
Financial data (yr. ended 12/31/05): Assets, $7,908,898 (M); expenditures, $482,527; qualifying distributions, $336,403; giving activities include $336,403 for grants.
Fields of interest: Education; Hospitals (general); Boy scouts; Human services; Christian agencies & churches.
Limitations: Giving primarily in Madison and Stoughton, WI. No grants to individuals.
Application information: Application form required.
Initial approach: Letter requesting application form
Deadline(s): None
Officers: Rockne G. Flowers, Pres.; David W. Bjerke, V.P.; June C. Bunting, Secy. and Exec. Dir.; Jerry A. Gryttenholm, Treas.
EIN: 391746858
Selected grants: The following grants were reported in 2005.
$30,000 to Stoughton, City of, Stoughton, WI.
$10,000 to Aldo Leopold Nature Center, Monona, WI.
$3,000 to American Cancer Society, Milwaukee, WI.
$2,000 to Wisconsin Chamber Orchestra, Madison, WI.

9769

William and Catherine Bryce Memorial Fund ✧

c/o JPMorgan Chase Bank, N.A.
P.O. Box 1308
Milwaukee, WI 53201
Application address: c/o JPMorgan Chase Bank, N.A., 420 Throckmorton St., Fort Worth, TX 76102, tel.: (817) 884-4151

Established in 1944 in TX.
Foundation type: Independent foundation.
Financial data (yr. ended 9/30/05): Assets, $16,208,854 (M); expenditures, $767,054; qualifying distributions, $627,562; giving activities include $589,500 for 31 grants (high: $100,000; low: $2,500).
Fields of interest: Performing arts; Performing arts, orchestra (symphony); Arts; Child development, education; Secondary school/education; Higher education; Health care; Health organizations, association; Human services; YM/YWCAs & YM/YWHAs; Children/youth, services; Child development, services; Government/public administration; Protestant agencies & churches.
Limitations: Giving limited to TX, with emphasis on the Fort Worth area. No grants to individuals.
Application information:
Initial approach: Letter
Copies of proposal: 1
Deadline(s): Sept.
Board meeting date(s): Nov.
Trustee: JPMorgan Chase Bank, N.A.
EIN: 756013845

9770

William J. & Gertrude R. Casper Foundation ✧

c/o U.S. Bank, N.A.
P.O. Box 2043
Milwaukee, WI 53201-9116 (715) 723-6618
Contact: M. Berry
Application address: c/o The Edward Rutledge Charity, Betty Manning, 404 N. Bridge St., Chippewa Falls, WI 54729

Established in 1988 in WI.
Donors: William J. Casper†; Gertrude R. Casper†.
Foundation type: Independent foundation.
Financial data (yr. ended 5/31/04): Assets, $17,186,591 (M); expenditures, $820,734; qualifying distributions, $774,677; giving activities include $647,527 for 87 grants (high: $50,000; low: $120), and $95,800 for 109 grants to individuals (high: $800; low: $300).
Purpose and activities: Scholarships awards to students who are residents of the Chippewa Falls; grants to organizations that improve the quality of life for residents of the Chippewa Falls, WI, area.
Fields of interest: Higher education; Human services; Children/youth, services.
Type of support: General/operating support; Scholarships—to individuals.
Limitations: Giving limited to residents of the Chippewa Falls, WI, area.
Application information: Application form required.
Initial approach: Letter requesting an application for scholarship; Proposals for community based organizations for grants
Deadline(s): None
Trustee: U.S. Bank, N.A.
EIN: 396484669

9771

Chapman Foundation ✧

312 E. Wisconsin Ave., Ste. 402
Milwaukee, WI 53202-4305

Established in 1944 in WI.
Donors: Laura Isabelle Miller†; G.M. Chester; William M. Chester, Jr.; Marion C. Read; John Chapman Chester.
Foundation type: Independent foundation.
Financial data (yr. ended 12/31/05): Assets, $3,790,435 (M); gifts received, $5,000; expenditures, $676,476; qualifying distributions, $673,255; giving activities include $673,255 for 210 grants (high: $109,750; low: $25).
Purpose and activities: Giving primarily for arts and culture, particularly museums, funding also for higher education, health associations, social services, and children and youth services.
Fields of interest: Museums; Museums (art); Arts; Higher education; Education; Health care; Health organizations, association; Human services; Children/youth, services; Federated giving programs.
Type of support: General/operating support; Annual campaigns; Capital campaigns; Building/renovation.
Limitations: Applications not accepted. Giving primarily in Milwaukee, WI. No grants to individuals.
Application information: Contributes only to pre-selected organizations.
Board meeting date(s): Varies

Officers: William M. Chester, Jr., Pres. and Treas.; Verne R. Read, V.P. and Secy.; John Chapman Chester, V.P.; Marion C. Read, V.P.
EIN: 396059569
Selected grants: The following grants were reported in 2004.
$108,750 to University School of Milwaukee, Milwaukee, WI. For general support.
$102,700 to Girl Scouts of the U.S.A., Greater Milwaukee Area Council, Milwaukee, WI. For general support.
$100,000 to Lawrence University, Appleton, WI. For general support.
$64,250 to Milwaukee Public Museum, Milwaukee, WI. 2 grants: $34,250 (For annual support), $30,000 (For Quest Exhibit).
$40,000 to Junior League of Milwaukee, Milwaukee, WI. For general support.
$25,250 to Citizens for Juvenile Justice, Boston, MA. For general support.
$25,000 to Florentine Opera Company, Milwaukee, WI.
$21,200 to Corcoran School of Art, DC. For general support.
$18,000 to United Performing Arts Fund, Milwaukee, WI. For general support.

9772

Charter Manufacturing Company Foundation, Inc. ✧

411 E. Wisconsin Ave., Ste. 2040
Milwaukee, WI 53202-4497

Established in 1984 in WI.
Donor: Charter Manufacturing Co., Inc.
Foundation type: Company-sponsored foundation.
Financial data (yr. ended 12/31/05): Assets, $3,523,526 (M); gifts received, $1,988,812; expenditures, $1,288,295; qualifying distributions, $1,288,237; giving activities include $1,288,237 for 42 grants (high: $310,664; low: $100).
Purpose and activities: The foundation supports art museums and organizations involved with theater, higher, medical, and engineering education, family planning, hemophilia research, and women.
Fields of interest: Museums (art); Performing arts, theater; Higher education; Medical school/education; Engineering school/education; Reproductive health, family planning; Hemophilia research; Boy scouts; YM/YWCAs & YM/YWHAs; Federated giving programs; Women.
Type of support: General/operating support; Annual campaigns; Capital campaigns; In-kind gifts.
Limitations: Applications not accepted. Giving primarily in Milwaukee, WI. No grants to individuals.
Application information: Contributes only to pre-selected organizations.
Officers and Directors:* Linda T. Mellowes,* Pres.; John A. Mellowes,* V.P. and Treas.; Henry J. Loos,* Secy.; Charles A. Mellowes; John W. Mellowes.
EIN: 391486363
Selected grants: The following grants were reported in 2004.
$203,250 to Medical College of Wisconsin, Milwaukee, WI.
$100,000 to Milwaukee School of Engineering, Milwaukee, WI.
$60,500 to Greater Milwaukee Foundation, Milwaukee, WI.
$5,500 to University School of Milwaukee, Milwaukee, WI.
$2,400 to Milwaukee Foundation Womens Fund, Milwaukee, WI.

$1,500 to Saint Francis Childrens Center, Glendale, WI.

$1,000 to Kenyon College, Gambier, OH.

9773
Emory T. Clark Family Foundation ✧

P.O. Box 2043
Milwaukee, WI 53201-9668
Application address: c/o Linda Hansen 125 N. Executive Dr., Ste. 363, Brookfield, WI 53005. (414) 765-5118

Established in 1982 in WI.
Donor: Emory T. Clark†.
Foundation type: Independent foundation.
Financial data (yr. ended 3/31/06): Assets, $9,915,349 (M); expenditures, $493,121; qualifying distributions, $488,932; giving activities include $452,900 for 22 grants.
Purpose and activities: Giving primarily for the arts, education, health, and human services.
Fields of interest: Arts; Education, fund raising/fund distribution; Higher education; Adult/continuing education; Education; Hospitals (general); Children/youth, services.
Type of support: Capital campaigns; Building/renovation; Equipment; Scholarship funds; Research.
Limitations: Giving primarily in WI.
Publications: Application guidelines; Informational brochure.
Application information: Application form required.
Initial approach: Proposal
Copies of proposal: 1
Deadline(s): None
Board meeting date(s): Nov.
Final notification: Dec. 1
Trustee: Gerald E. Connolly; Helen Ruth La Badie; Marjorie J. Takton; U.S. Bank, N.A.
EIN: 391410324
Selected grants: The following grants were reported in 2005.
$50,000 to Congregational Home, Brookfield, WI.
$50,000 to Marquette University, Milwaukee, WI.
$30,000 to American Cancer Society, Pewaukee, WI.
$25,000 to Big Brothers/Big Sisters of Metropolitan Milwaukee, Milwaukee, WI.
$25,000 to Humane Society, Elm-Brook, Brookfield, WI.
$25,000 to Ronald McDonald House, Marshfield, WI.
$15,315 to Womens Center, Waukesha, WI.
$3,400 to Sinsinawa Dominicans, Sinsinawa, WI.

9774
Cleary-Kumm Foundation, Inc. ✧

(formerly Cleary Foundation)
310 Sky Harbour Dr.
La Crosse, WI 54603 (608) 783-7500
Contact: Gail K. Cleary, Pres.

Established in 1982 in WI; merged with the Kumm Foundation in 2000.
Donors: Gail K. Cleary; Russell G. Cleary†; Lillian H. Kumm†.
Foundation type: Independent foundation.
Financial data (yr. ended 11/30/05): Assets, $12,511,670 (M); expenditures, $622,432; qualifying distributions, $462,871; giving activities

include $437,702 for 103 grants (high: $100,150; low: $15).
Fields of interest: Arts; Higher education; Human services; Children/youth, services; Federated giving programs.
Type of support: Annual campaigns; Capital campaigns; Endowments; Scholarship funds.
Limitations: Giving primarily in the La Crosse, WI, area. No grants to individuals.
Publications: Annual report.
Application information: Application form not required.
Initial approach: Letter
Copies of proposal: 1
Deadline(s): None
Board meeting date(s): May, July, Sept., and Oct.
Final notification: Normally 1 month or less
Officer and Directors:* Gail K. Cleary,* Pres.; Kristine H. Cleary; Sandra G. Cleary.
Number of staff: 1 part-time professional; 2 part-time support.
EIN: 391426785
Selected grants: The following grants were reported in 2005.
$100,150 to Gundersen Lutheran Medical Foundation, La Crosse, WI.
$65,200 to Boys and Girls Club of La Crosse, La Crosse, WI.
$30,000 to La Crosse Rotary Foundation, La Crosse, WI.
$20,204 to YMCA, La Crosse Area Family, La Crosse, WI.
$7,200 to Boy Scouts of America, La Crosse, WI.
$6,500 to American Red Cross, La Crosse, WI.
$6,100 to Salvation Army, WI.
$1,000 to Mayo Foundation, Rochester, MN.

9775
David & Ruth Coleman Charitable Foundation, Inc. ✧

1610 N. Prospect Ave., Ste. 701
Milwaukee, WI 53202 (414) 226-2209
Contact: Ruth Coleman, Pres.

Established in 1993 in WI.
Donors: Ruth Coleman; Ida Soref.
Foundation type: Independent foundation.
Financial data (yr. ended 12/31/05): Assets, $8,198,693 (M); expenditures, $977,632; qualifying distributions, $920,000; giving activities include $920,000 for 6 grants (high: $400,000; low: $10,000).
Purpose and activities: Giving primarily to a heart research foundation, and to a Jewish elementary school; funding also for social services, a medical college, a dance theater, and Jewish and other federated giving programs.
Fields of interest: Performing arts, dance; Elementary school/education; Higher education; Medical school/education; Education; Heart & circulatory research; Human services; Jewish federated giving programs; Jewish agencies & temples.
Limitations: Giving primarily in Milwaukee, WI. No grants to individuals.
Application information: Application form not required.
Deadline(s): None
Officers and Directors:* Ruth Coleman,* Pres.; Mark Sklar,* V.P.; Roberta Gorenstein Caraway,* Secy.; Maggie Glezer,* Treas.
EIN: 391772862

Selected grants: The following grants were reported in 2003.
$175,000 to Milwaukee Heart Research Foundation, Milwaukee, WI. For Milwaukee Heart Project.
$109,000 to Cardinal Stritch University, Milwaukee, WI. For operating support.
$100,000 to Jewish Home and Care Center Foundation, Milwaukee, WI. For operating support.
$100,000 to Yeshiva Elementary School, Milwaukee, WI. For operating support.
$25,000 to Habad, Friends of, Milwaukee, WI. For operating support.
$10,000 to Chabad Intown, Atlanta, GA. For operating support.
$10,000 to Coast Guard Foundation, Stonington, CT. For educational program support.
$10,000 to Helios Dance Theater, Malibu, CA. For operating support.
$10,000 to Milwaukee Public Library Foundation, Milwaukee, WI. For operating support.
$10,000 to Planned Parenthood of Wisconsin, Milwaukee, WI. For program support.

9776
Community Foundation for the Fox Valley Region, Inc.

4455 W. Lawrence St.
P.O. Box 563
Appleton, WI 54912-0563 (920) 830-1290
Contact: Curt S. Detjen, C.E.O.; Tammy Williams, V.P., Comms.; Jeff Johnson, V.P., Donor Svcs.
FAX: (920) 830-1293; E-mail: cffvr@cffoxvalley.org; Grant application E-mail: jjohnson@cffoxvalley.org; URL: http://www.cffoxvalley.org

Organized in 1986 in Appleton, WI.
Foundation type: Community foundation.
Financial data (yr. ended 6/30/05): Assets, $145,301,022 (M); gifts received, $44,338,793; expenditures, $15,294,948; giving activities include $13,347,247 for 1,778 grants (high: $1,000,000; low: $10; average: $500–$10,000), and $1,077,843 for foundation-administered programs.
Purpose and activities: The foundation exists to enhance the quality of life for all citizens of the Fox Valley region by using funds entrusted to the foundation's stewardship to address community problems and opportunities.
Fields of interest: Arts; Education; Environment; Health care; Substance abuse, services; AIDS; Alzheimer's disease; Diabetes; Children/youth, services; Human services; Community development; Women.
Type of support: Technical assistance; Management development/capacity building; Emergency funds; Program development; Conferences/seminars; Seed money; Scholarship funds; Employee-related scholarships; Scholarships —to individuals; Matching/challenge support.
Limitations: Giving limited to Calumet, Outagamie, Waupaca and northern Winnebago counties, WI. No support for sectarian or religious purposes, or medical projects. No grants for annual fund drives, deficit financing, endowment funds, travel expenses, capital construction, ongoing operating expenses, or research.
Publications: Annual report; Grants list; Informational brochure (including application guidelines); Newsletter.

Application information: Upon receipt of Letter of Intent, the foundation will determine if the project merits further consideration in light of available resources and grantmaking priorities. The foundation's staff will then contact the organization to schedule a meeting or phone conference. Visit foundation Web site for guidelines. Application form required.

> *Initial approach:* Complete Letter of Intent online
> *Copies of proposal:* 1
> *Deadline(s):* Submit Letter of Intent no later than 1 month prior to application proposal deadline; Jan. 10, Apr. 10, July 10, and Sept. 30 for proposals
> *Board meeting date(s):* Feb., May, Aug., Oct., Nov., and Dec.
> *Final notification:* Mar., June, Sept., and Nov.

Officers and Directors: * Wyon Wiegratz,* Chair.; Richard Bergstrom,* Vice-Chair.; Ray Durkee,* Vice-Chair.; Ralph Evans,* Vice-Chair.; Mark Johannsen,* Vice-Chair.; Walter S. Rugland,* Vice-Chair.; Curt S. Detjen,* C.E.O. and Pres.; Jeff Johnson, V.P., Donor Svcs.; Cathryn Mutschler, V.P., Foundation Svcs.; Terri Towle, V.P., Finance and Admin.; Tammy Williams, V.P., Comms. and Mktg.; Greg Curry III,* Secy.; Katherine Westover,* Treas.; Kay E. Abel; Jocye Bytof; Kathy Davis; Dr. Natalie Gehringer; Doug Hahn; Patrick Hawley; Gerald A. Henseler; Adalia Jansen; Mary Kabacinski; Robert Keller; Steve Morton; Keith Spritz; Rollie Stephenson; Marie Uhrich; Allan Williamson.

Number of staff: 12 full-time professional; 1 part-time professional; 4 full-time support.

EIN: 391548450

9777
Community Foundation of North Central Wisconsin, Inc. ✧

(formerly Wausau Area Community Foundation, Inc.)
500 3rd St., Ste. 310
Wausau, WI 54403-4857 (715) 845-9555
Contact: Jean C. Tehan, Exec. Dir.; For grants: Sue E. Nelson, Prog. Mgr.
FAX: (715) 845-5423; E-mail: info@cfoncw.org; Additional tel.: (888) 845-9223; Community Arts application E-mail: sue@cfoncw.org; URL: http://www.cfoncw.org

Incorporated in 1987 in WI.
Foundation type: Community foundation.
Financial data (yr. ended 12/31/04): Assets, $19,579,866 (M); gifts received, $1,514,831; expenditures, $1,491,285; giving activities include $1,118,845 for 245 grants.
Purpose and activities: The foundation is a nonprofit community corporation, created by and for the people of north central Wisconsin. The foundation devotes special emphasis to programs enriching life in five distinct areas: education, the arts, health, social services, and the conservation and preservation of resources, including historical and cultural.
Fields of interest: Historic preservation/historical societies; Arts; Education; Environment, natural resources; Health care; Health organizations, association; Housing/shelter, development; Human services; Community development.
Type of support: Capital campaigns; Building/renovation; Equipment; Program development; Curriculum development.
Limitations: Giving limited to the greater Wausau, WI, area, including Marathon County. No support for sectarian causes. No grants to individuals (except

for designated scholarships), or for annual campaigns, endowments, debt retirement, or routine operating expenses.
Publications: Application guidelines; Annual report; Informational brochure (including application guidelines); Newsletter.
Application information: Visit foundation Web site for application forms and additional guidelines per grant type. Application form required.

> *Initial approach:* Letter or telephone
> *Copies of proposal:* 11
> *Deadline(s):* Quarterly; Apr. 1 and Oct. 1 for Community Arts grants
> *Board meeting date(s):* Monthly

Officers and Directors: * Ginger Alden,* Pres.; Todd R. Nicklaus,* V.P.; George A. Evenhouse,* Secy.; Sidney C. Sczygelski,* Treas.; Jean C. Tehan, Exec. Dir.; Beverly B. Abbott; Chip Burgett; John W. Dunn; Stewart L. Etten; John M. Hattenhauer; Nancy Hessert; Glen Moberg; Brad Peck; Linda E. Prehn; Linda F. Semling; James F. Veninga.

Number of staff: 3 full-time professional; 1 part-time professional.

EIN: 391577472

9778
Community Foundation of Portage County, Inc. ✧ ☆

(formerly Stevens Point Area Foundation, Inc.)
1501 Clark St.
P.O. Box 968
Stevens Point, WI 54481-0968 (715) 342-4454
Contact: John Jury, Exec. Dir.
FAX: (715) 342-5560;
E-mail: foundation@cfpcwi.org; URL: http://www.cfpcwi.org

Established in 1982 in WI.
Foundation type: Community foundation.
Financial data (yr. ended 6/30/05): Assets, $3,330,090 (M); gifts received, $716,698; expenditures, $492,223; giving activities include $348,302 for grants.
Purpose and activities: The foundation seeks to help make the Portage County community a better place to grow, work, play, and retire by helping people, enhancing education, enriching culture, contributing to wellness, and improving the environment through financial management of gifts and grants from individuals and organizations.
Fields of interest: Arts; Education; Environment; Health care; Human services; Women.
Type of support: Continuing support; Building/renovation; Equipment; Land acquisition; Program development; Conferences/seminars; Seed money; Curriculum development; Scholarship funds; Research; Matching/challenge support.
Limitations: Giving limited to Portage County, WI. No support for sectarian causes. No grants to individuals (except for scholarships), or for annual campaigns, debt retirement, endowment funds, staff salaries, or operation losses.
Publications: Application guidelines; Annual report; Informational brochure; Newsletter.
Application information: Visit foundation Web site for application form and guidelines. Application form required.

> *Initial approach:* Telephone or e-mail
> *Copies of proposal:* 10
> *Deadline(s):* Mar. 1
> *Board meeting date(s):* Monthly
> *Final notification:* May

Officers and Directors: * Hark Ilten,* Pres.; Beth Hoffman,* V.P.; Leslie Rusek,* Secy.; Robert Taylor,* Treas.; John Jury, Exec. Dir.; Paul Adamski; Anton Anday; Brant Bergeron; John Buzza; Amy Eddy; Karen Engelhard; James Firninhac; Brian Formella; Helen Godfrey; Angie Heuck-Diekroeger; Ben Katz; Christine Klessig; George May; Paul Munck; Heidi Okray; David Quick; Bill Schierl; Paula Schlice; Cheri Smith; Jim Schuh; Bob Spoerl; Yang Pao Thao.

Number of staff: 1 part-time professional; 1 part-time support.

EIN: 390827885

9779
Community Foundation of South Wood County, Inc. ✧

478 E. Grand Ave.
P.O. Box 444
Wisconsin Rapids, WI 54495-0444
(715) 423-3863
Contact: Kelly Lucas, C.E.O.; For grants: Mary Wirtz, V.P., Progs.
FAX: (715) 423-3019; E-mail: info@cfswc.org; Grant request E-mail: mlwirtz@cfswc.org; URL: http://www.cfswc.org

Established in 1994 in WI.
Foundation type: Community foundation.
Financial data (yr. ended 6/30/05): Assets, $18,785,306 (M); gifts received, $3,379,119; expenditures, $3,583,095; giving activities include $2,669,919 for grants, and $109,700 for 142 grants to individuals (high: $1,000).
Purpose and activities: The foundation is entrusted with the responsibility to enhance the quality of life of the residents of South Wood County, WI. It serves as a resource and catalyst for giving, attracts and manages a growing endowment for the area's future, provides a flexible vehicle and quality service for donors with varied philanthropic interests, and identifies and effectively responds to emerging and changing community needs through strategic grantmaking.
Fields of interest: Museums (art); Performing arts; Performing arts, theater; Historic preservation/historical societies; Arts; Elementary/secondary education; Higher education; Education; Hospitals (general); Health care; Health organizations; Disasters, preparedness/services; Boys & girls clubs; Youth development; Children/youth, services; Family services; Aging, centers/services; Human services; Community development.
Type of support: Building/renovation; Equipment; Emergency funds; Program development; Seed money; Scholarship funds; Technical assistance; Scholarships—to individuals; Matching/challenge support.
Limitations: Giving limited to South Wood County, WI, and the Town of Rome. No support for religious organizations for sectarian purposes. No grants to individuals (except for scholarships), or for debt retirement, deficit financing, fundraising activities, endowment funds, operating expenses for United Way agencies, routine operating needs, annual fundraising, capital fund drives, or for umbrella funding.
Publications: Application guidelines; Annual report; Grants list; Informational brochure; Newsletter.
Application information: Visit foundation Web site for application form and guidelines. Application form required.

> *Initial approach:* Telephone, e-mail, or letter of inquiry

Copies of proposal: 1
Deadline(s): Feb. 28, May 31, Aug. 31, and Nov. 30 for grants over $1,000; none for grants under $1,000
Board meeting date(s): Quarterly
Final notification: 4 to 6 weeks
Officers and Trustees:* Jake Close,* Chair.; Patrick Brennan,* Vice-Chair.; Kelly Lucas, C.E.O. and Pres.; Mary Olson, V.P., Donor Rels. and Comms.; M. Jill Thornburg, C.P.A., V.P. Finance and Opers.; Mary Wirtz, V.P., Progs.; Deborah Hickey, Secy.; Dennis Conway,* Treas.; Guadalupe Ancel; Leslie V. Arendt; Helen Jungwirth; Gilbert Mead, Ph.D.; Dawn Neuman; Francis Podvin; Fred Siemers.
Number of staff: 5 full-time professional; 4 part-time support.
EIN: 391772651

9780
Community Foundation of Southern Wisconsin, Inc.

(formerly United Community Foundation, Inc.)
111 N. Main St.
Janesville, WI 53545 (608) 758-0883
Contact: Sue S. Conley, Exec. Dir.
FAX: (608) 758-8551; E-mail: info@cfsw.org; Additional tel.: (800) 995-CFSW; Additional E-mail: sconley.cfsw@sbcglobal.net; URL: http://www.cfsw.org

Established in 1991 in WI.
Foundation type: Community foundation.
Financial data (yr. ended 6/30/05): Assets, $20,017,240 (M); gifts received, $2,013,434; expenditures, $2,360,959; giving activities include $1,093,602 for 557 grants (high: $59,430; low: $25), and $590,400 for 447 grants to individuals (high: $6,000; low: $200).
Purpose and activities: The foundation primarily supports the arts, the environment, education, health, human services, and historic preservation in Grant, Green, Iowa, Jefferson, Lafayette, Rock, and Walworth counties, WI.
Fields of interest: Historic preservation/historical societies; Arts; Education; Environment; Health care; Disasters, Hurricane Katrina; Recreation; Human services.
Type of support: Building/renovation; Equipment; Endowments; Emergency funds; Conferences/seminars; Seed money; Curriculum development; Scholarships—to individuals; In-kind gifts; Matching/challenge support.
Limitations: Giving limited to Grant, Green, Iowa, Lafayette, Jefferson, Rock, and Walworth counties, WI. No grants for regular operating expenses, capital campaigns, or for redundant programs.
Publications: Application guidelines; Annual report; Informational brochure (including application guidelines); Newsletter.
Application information: Visit foundation Web site for application form and guidelines. Scholarship applications accepted through recipient school districts only. Application form required.
Initial approach: Letter of inquiry or telephone
Copies of proposal: 6
Deadline(s): Mar. 1 and Sept. 1
Board meeting date(s): Quarterly
Final notification: May and Nov.
Officers and Directors:* Ronald M. Spielman,* Chair.; Linda Heckert,* Vice-Chair.; Jim Cripe,* Secy.; Tina Lorenz,* Treas.; Sue S. Conley, Exec. Dir.; Clara B. McFall, Cont.; George Brunner; Bob

Collins; Barbara Daus; Richard Gruber; Rhonda Hartwig; Robert Lisser; David MacDougall; Mike Sanders; Frank Scott; Cere Turner.
Number of staff: 1 full-time professional; 3 part-time professional; 1 full-time support; 3 part-time support.
EIN: 391711388

9781
Cornerstone Foundation of Northeastern Wisconsin, Inc.

111 N. Washington St., Ste. 450
Green Bay, WI 54301 (920) 490-8290
Contact: Sheri Prosser, Exec. Dir.
FAX: (920) 490-8620;
E-mail: cornerstone@cfnew.org

Incorporated in 1953 in WI.
Foundation type: Independent foundation.
Financial data (yr. ended 12/31/05): Assets, $25,981,658 (M); expenditures, $1,706,863; qualifying distributions, $1,515,154; giving activities include $1,280,820 for 62 grants (high: $250,000; low: $100).
Purpose and activities: Emphasis on education, cultural programs, and social service and youth agencies; support also for healthcare facilities.
Fields of interest: Education, association; Education, fund raising/fund distribution; Adult education—literacy, basic skills & GED; Health care; Human services; Youth, services; Disabilities, people with; Economically disadvantaged.
Type of support: General/operating support; Continuing support; Annual campaigns; Capital campaigns; Building/renovation; Equipment; Endowments; Debt reduction; Emergency funds; Program development; Matching/challenge support.
Limitations: Giving primarily in Brown County, WI. No grants to individuals.
Publications: Application guidelines.
Application information: Application form not required.
Initial approach: Telephone
Copies of proposal: 12
Deadline(s): Feb. 15 and Sept. 1
Board meeting date(s): Mar. and Oct.
Final notification: Normally within 7 to 10 days following meeting
Officers and Directors:* Paul J. Schierl,* Pres.; Sheri Prosser, V.P., Secy., and Exec. Dir.; James J. Schoshinski,* V.P. and Treas.; John W. Hickey,* V.P.; Robert E. Manger,* V.P.; Thomas L. Olson, V.P.; Carol A. Schierl,* V.P.; Michael J. Schierl,* V.P.
Number of staff: 1 full-time professional; 1 part-time support.
EIN: 362761910
Selected grants: The following grants were reported in 2005.
$225,000 to Boys and Girls Club of Green Bay, Green Bay, WI. 2 grants: $150,000, $75,000
$210,000 to New Community Shelter, Green Bay, WI. 3 grants: $200,000, $5,000, $5,000
$50,000 to Saint Vincent Hospital, Green Bay, WI.
$25,000 to Ecumenical Partnership for Housing, Green Bay, WI.
$15,159 to Salvation Army, WI. 2 grants: $5,000, $10,159
$7,000 to Encompass Child Care, Green Bay, WI.

9782
A. G. Cox Charity Trust ✧

c/o JPMorgan Chase Bank, N.A.
P.O. Box 1308
Milwaukee, WI 53201
Application address: c/o JPMorgan Chase Bank, N.A., Attn.: Sandra M. Wallick, 70 W. Madison St., Chicago, IL 60670

Established in 1924 in IL.
Foundation type: Independent foundation.
Financial data (yr. ended 12/31/04): Assets, $15,762,810 (M); expenditures, $687,484; qualifying distributions, $671,651; giving activities include $667,668 for grants.
Purpose and activities: Giving primarily for education and human services.
Fields of interest: Higher education; Hospitals (general); Health care; Health organizations, association; Cancer; Human services; American Red Cross; Children/youth, services.
Limitations: Giving primarily in Chicago, IL. No grants to individuals.
Application information:
Initial approach: Letter
Deadline(s): None
Trustee: JPMorgan Chase Bank, N.A.
EIN: 366011498

9783
Joe and Jessie Crump Fund ✧

c/o JPMorgan Chase Bank, N.A.
P.O. Box 1308
Milwaukee, WI 53202

Trust established in 1965 in TX.
Foundation type: Independent foundation.
Financial data (yr. ended 9/30/05): Assets, $23,463,448 (M); expenditures, $1,609,511; qualifying distributions, $1,219,032; giving activities include $1,211,911 for 27 grants (high: $309,658; low: $5,000).
Purpose and activities: Giving primarily for an Episcopal theological seminary; support also for cancer research, aid to handicapped children, and the Episcopal church.
Fields of interest: Theological school/education; Medical care, rehabilitation; Cancer; Medical research, institute; Cancer research; Protestant agencies & churches; Disabilities, people with.
Type of support: Curriculum development; Scholarship funds; Research; Program-related investments/loans.
Limitations: Applications not accepted. Giving primarily in TX. No grants to individuals, or for building or endowment funds, matching gifts, or general purposes.
Application information: Contributes only to pre-selected organizations.
Board meeting date(s): As required
Trustee: JPMorgan Chase Bank, N.A.
EIN: 756045044

9784
The Cudahy Foundation ▼ ✧

(formerly Michael J. Cudahy Foundation)
9100 N. Swan Rd.
Milwaukee, WI 53224
Contact: Kevin L. Lindsey, Tr.

Established in 1999 in WI.

Donor: Michael J. Cudahy.
Foundation type: Independent foundation.
Financial data (yr. ended 12/31/04): Assets, $62,242,487 (M); expenditures, $8,801,044; qualifying distributions, $8,658,397; giving activities include $8,634,300 for 27 grants (high: $6,900,000; low: $1,000; average: $1,000–$230,645).
Purpose and activities: Giving primarily for education, youth development, and for human services.
Fields of interest: Education; Health care; Housing/shelter, development; Human services; Children/youth, services.
Limitations: Applications not accepted. Giving primarily in Milwaukee, WI. No grants to individuals.
Application information: Contributes only to pre-selected organizations.
Trustees: Julia A. Cudahy; Joanna D. Hamadi; Kevin L. Lindsey; John W. Linnen.
EIN: 396720806
Selected grants: The following grants were reported in 2004.
$6,900,000 to Pier Wisconsin, Milwaukee, WI.
$800,000 to Pabst Theater Foundation, Milwaukee, WI.
$75,000 to United Performing Arts Fund, Milwaukee, WI.
$17,000 to Discovery World: The James Lovell Museum of Science, Economics and Technology, Milwaukee, WI.
$10,000 to Milwaukee Art Museum, Milwaukee, WI.
$10,000 to Wisconsin Conservatory of Music, Milwaukee, WI.
$1,000 to Milwaukee School of Engineering, W M S E Radio, Milwaukee, WI.
$1,000 to Wisconsin Area Music Industry, Milwaukee, WI.

9785
Patrick and Anna M. Cudahy Fund ◆
c/o Godfrey & Kahn, S.C.
780 N. Water St.
Milwaukee, WI 53202 (414) 271-6020
E-mail: secretary@cudahyfund.org; IL address: c/o Judith Borchers, 1609 Sherman Ave., Ste. 207, Evanston, IL, 60201; IL tel.: (847) 866-0760; fax: (847) 475-0679; URL: http://www.cudahyfund.org

Incorporated in 1949 in WI.
Donor: Michael F. Cudahy‡.
Foundation type: Independent foundation.
Financial data (yr. ended 12/31/05): Assets, $19,438,410 (M); expenditures, $1,719,042; qualifying distributions, $1,587,047; giving activities include $1,441,340 for 180 grants (high: $200,000; low: $500).
Purpose and activities: Primary areas of interest include the arts, education, youth, international relief, and social services. Support for the homeless, family services, and international development programs; support also for national programs concerned with environmental and public interest issues, and cultural and civic affairs programs.
Fields of interest: Arts; Adult/continuing education; Adult education—literacy, basic skills & GED; Education, reading; Education; Environment; Food services; Housing/shelter, development; Human services; Youth, services; Family services; Homeless, human services; International economic development; International relief; International human rights; Rural development; Public affairs;

Roman Catholic agencies & churches; Aging; Disabilities, people with; Women; Immigrants/refugees; Economically disadvantaged; Homeless.
International interests: Africa.
Type of support: General/operating support; Continuing support; Annual campaigns; Building/renovation; Equipment; Program development; Seed money; Technical assistance; Matching/challenge support.
Limitations: Giving limited to Chicago, IL, and WI for local programs and for international (U.S.-based) programs. No grants to individuals, or for endowments; no loans.
Publications: Application guidelines; Grants list.
Application information: The fund does not accept proposals via fax. Applications guidelines, procedures and form are available on the fund's Web site. Application form required.
  Initial approach: Proposal
  Copies of proposal: 1
  Deadline(s): Varies annually, specific dates are available upon written request.
  Board meeting date(s): Usually in Mar., June, Sept., and Dec.
  Final notification: 2 weeks after meetings
Officers and Directors: Richard D. Cudahy,* Chair.; Janet S. Cudahy, M.D.*, Pres.; Dudley J. Godfrey, Jr.,* Secy.-Treas.; Judith L. Borchers, Exec. Dir.; James Bailey; Molly Cudahy; Patrick G. Cudahy; Jean Holtz; Annette Stoddard-Freeman.
Number of staff: 1 part-time professional; 1 part-time support.
EIN: 390991972
Selected grants: The following grants were reported in 2004.
$48,200 to Maryknoll Sisters of Saint Dominic, Maryknoll, NY. 2 grants: $18,700 (For Philippines Rehabilitation Center), $29,500 (For Brazil AFYA Women's Holistic Health Center).
$20,000 to Catholic Theological Union at Chicago, Chicago, IL. For capital campaign.
$20,000 to Habitat for Humanity International, Milwaukee, WI. For anniversary building program.
$19,430 to Special Olympics of Wisconsin, Madison, WI. For Athlete Recognition Awards.
$15,000 to Association House of Chicago, Chicago, IL. For Listo after-school program.
$15,000 to Center for Deaf-Blind Persons, Milwaukee, WI. For rehabilitation training.
$15,000 to Oxfam America, Boston, MA. For program support.
$10,000 to Alverno College, Milwaukee, WI. For nursing equipment for students.
$10,000 to Saint Ann Center for Intergenerational Care, Milwaukee, WI. For operating support.

9786
CUNA Mutual Group Foundation, Inc. ◆
(formerly CUNA Mutual Insurance Group Charitable Foundation, Inc.)
5910 Mineral Point Rd.
Madison, WI 53705
Contact: Steven A. Goldberg, Exec. Dir.
Application address: P.O. Box 391, Madison, WI 53701; URL: http://www.cunamutual.com/cmg/freeFormDetail/0,1248,888,00.html

Incorporated in 1967 in WI.
Donor: CUNA Mutual Insurance Society.
Foundation type: Company-sponsored foundation.
Financial data (yr. ended 12/31/03): Assets, $408,785 (M); gifts received, $662,005; expenditures, $779,256; qualifying distributions,

$771,223; giving activities include $771,223 for 181 grants (high: $271,000; low: $25).
Purpose and activities: The foundation supports organizations involved with education, health, hunger, housing, human services, community development, and economically disadvantaged people.
Fields of interest: Education; Health care; Food services; Housing/shelter; Human services; Community development; Economically disadvantaged.
Type of support: Continuing support; Capital campaigns; Emergency funds; Program development; Scholarship funds; Research; Employee matching gifts; Matching/challenge support.
Limitations: Giving primarily in IA and WI. No grants to individuals, or for debt reduction, land acquisition, endowments, or publications; no loans.
Application information:
  Initial approach: Letter of inquiry
Officers: Loretta M. Bard, Pres.; Michael B. Kitchen, Secy.-Treas. and Exec. Off.; Steven A. Goldberg, Exec. Dir.
EIN: 396105418
Selected grants: The following grants were reported in 2005.
$280,000 to United Way of Dane County, Madison, WI.
$227,000 to National Credit Union Foundation, Madison, WI.
$30,000 to Boys and Girls Club.
$25,000 to YWCA of Madison, Madison, WI.
$20,000 to Big Brothers/Big Sisters.
$20,000 to Boys and Girls Club of Dane County, Madison, WI.
$20,000 to Urban League.
$16,000 to United Way.
$7,000 to American Red Cross.
$7,000 to Community Coordinated Child Care, Madison, WI.

9787
Davis Foundation ◆
c/o JPMorgan Chase Bank, N.A.
P.O. Box 1308
Milwaukee, WI 53201

Established in OH.
Donor: David Davis†.
Foundation type: Independent foundation.
Financial data (yr. ended 12/31/04): Assets, $33,518,353 (M); gifts received, $400,000; expenditures, $1,977,849; qualifying distributions, $1,439,438; giving activities include $1,430,500 for 15 grants (high: $530,000; low: $1,000).
Purpose and activities: Giving primarily to Evangelical Christian agencies and churches; funding also for Christian higher education.
Fields of interest: Higher education; Theological school/education; Human services; YM/YWCAs & YM/YWHAs; Christian agencies & churches.
Limitations: Giving primarily in OH; some funding nationally.
Application information:
  Initial approach: Letter
  Deadline(s): None
Trustee: JPMorgan Chase Bank, N.A.
EIN: 346566892

9788
Gretchen & Andrew Dawes Charitable Trust ✧

c/o Provident Trust Co.
N16 W23217 Stone Ridge Dr.
Waukesha, WI 53188

Established in 2003 in WI.
Foundation type: Independent foundation.
Financial data (yr. ended 12/31/05): Assets, $4,277,616 (M); gifts received, $118,059; expenditures, $910,314; qualifying distributions, $864,410; giving activities include $837,000 for 20 grants (high: $100,000; low: $5,000).
Fields of interest: Arts; Animal welfare; Health organizations, association.
Limitations: Applications not accepted. Giving primarily in Milwaukee, WI. No grants to individuals.
Application information: Contributes only to pre-selected organizations.
Trustees: Stephen M. Fisher; Max E. Grefig; Janis C. Lenz.
EIN: 367407807

9789
DeAtley Family Foundation, Inc. ✧ ☆

c/o William B. DeAtley
1440 County Rd. JG
Mount Horeb, WI 53572-2992

Established in 1997.
Donor: William B. DeAtley.
Foundation type: Independent foundation.
Financial data (yr. ended 12/31/05): Assets, $3,619,339 (M); gifts received, $1,256,250; expenditures, $344,777; qualifying distributions, $340,500; giving activities include $340,500 for grants.
Purpose and activities: Giving primarily to children's services.
Fields of interest: Environment, natural resources; Muscular dystrophy; Housing/shelter, development; Human services; Children/youth, services; Family services; Protestant agencies & churches.
Limitations: Applications not accepted. Giving on a national basis. No grants to individuals.
Application information: Contributes only to pre-selected organizations.
Officers: William B. DeAtley, Chair. and Treas.; Janine B. DeAtley, Secy.
Trustees: Brantner M. DeAtley; Leesa D. Schlimgen.
EIN: 061496358
Selected grants: The following grants were reported in 2003.
$100,000 to Habitat for Humanity International, Americus, GA.
$30,000 to Madison Community Health Center, Madison, WI.
$10,000 to VSA Arts of Wisconsin, Madison, WI. For general support.
$5,000 to CARE, Atlanta, GA. For general support.
$5,000 to Habitat for Humanity, Madison, WI. For general support.
$5,000 to Nature Conservancy, Arlington, VA. For general support.
$5,000 to Save the Children Federation, Westport, CT. For general support.
$5,000 to Smile Train, New York, NY.
$5,000 to Southbury-Middlebury Youth and Family Services, Southbury, CT. For general support.
$1,000 to Madison Childrens Museum, Madison, WI. For general support.

9790
Nelson B. Delavan Foundation ✧

c/o JPMorgan Chase Bank, N.A.
P.O. Box 1308
Milwaukee, WI 53201
Application address: c/o Janis Mosher, 130 S. Main St., Canandaigua, NY 14424-1904, tel.: (315) 394-7675

Established in 1983 in NY.
Foundation type: Independent foundation.
Financial data (yr. ended 12/31/05): Assets, $6,059,503 (M); expenditures, $518,138; qualifying distributions, $487,949; giving activities include $478,077 for grants.
Purpose and activities: Primary areas of interest include the performing arts and other cultural programs, health, and social services.
Fields of interest: Performing arts; Arts; Medical school/education; Animal welfare; Health care; Health organizations, association; Human services; Children/youth, services; Women, centers/services; International affairs; Women.
Type of support: General/operating support.
Limitations: Giving primarily in NY, with emphasis on the Seneca Falls region. No grants to individuals.
Application information: Application form not required.
  Initial approach: Letter
  Copies of proposal: 2
  Deadline(s): None
Trustee: JPMorgan Chase Bank, N.A.
EIN: 166260274

9791
Mae E. Demmer Charitable Trust

c/o JPMorgan Chase Bank, N.A.
P.O. Box 1308
Milwaukee, WI 53201
Application address: c/o JPMorgan Chase Bank, N.A., 111 E. Wisconsin Ave., Milwaukee, WI 53202, tel.: (414) 977-2000

Established in 1998 in WI.
Donor: Mae E. Demmer‡.
Foundation type: Independent foundation.
Financial data (yr. ended 12/31/05): Assets, $9,092,132 (M); expenditures, $498,307; qualifying distributions, $450,005; giving activities include $375,000 for 25 grants (high: $50,000; low: $5,000).
Purpose and activities: Giving primarily for the arts, and health and human services.
Fields of interest: Arts education; Museums; Performing arts, orchestra (symphony); Performing arts, opera; Arts; Elementary/secondary education; Higher education; Medical school/education; Environmental education; Environment; Zoos/zoological societies; Hospitals (general); Cerebral palsy; Eye diseases; Eye research; Food services; Human services; Children/youth, services; Family services; Foundations (public); Federated giving programs; Protestant agencies & churches.
Limitations: Giving primarily in Milwaukee, WI.
Application information:
  Initial approach: Proposal and completed grant application form
  Copies of proposal: 2
  Deadline(s): Apr. 1, Aug. 1, and Nov. 15
  Board meeting date(s): May, Aug., and Dec.
Trustees: Richard Goisman; Harrold McComas; JPMorgan Chase Bank, N.A.
EIN: 311576907

9792
Dudley Foundation, Inc. ☆

P.O. Box 2137
Wausau, WI 54402-2137 (715) 849-5729
Contact: Ann Dudley Shannon, Pres.
Application address: 500 3rd St., Ste. 208-216, Wausau, WI 54403

Established in 2000 in WI.
Donor: Richard D. Dudley.
Foundation type: Independent foundation.
Financial data (yr. ended 6/30/06): Assets, $5,607,597 (M); expenditures, $449,719; qualifying distributions, $376,730; giving activities include $376,730 for grants.
Purpose and activities: Support for organizations benefiting WI, with emphasis on Marathon County, WI.
Fields of interest: Arts; Education; Environment; Health care, home services; Housing/shelter; Safety/disasters, public education; Safety/disasters; Recreation; Human services; Children, services; Economic development.
Type of support: General/operating support; Capital campaigns; Building/renovation; Equipment; Land acquisition; Emergency funds; Program development; Seed money; Technical assistance; Program evaluation; Matching/challenge support.
Limitations: Giving primarily in WI, with emphasis on Marathon County, WI. No grants to individuals or private businesses.
Application information: Application form required.
  Initial approach: Proposal
  Copies of proposal: 8
  Deadline(s): 1 month before board meeting
  Board meeting date(s): Mar., June, Sept., and Dec.
  Final notification: 2 months from receipt
Officers: Richard D. Dudley, Chair.; Ann Dudley Shannon, Pres.; John D. Dudley, V.P.; Paul C. Schlindwein II, Secy.; Gary W. Freels, Treas.
Directors: Mary C. Dudley; Robert J. Dudley II.
Number of staff: None.
EIN: 392003427
Selected grants: The following grants were reported in 2005.
$15,000 to Saint Anthony Retreat Center, Marathon, WI.
$10,000 to Community Foundation of North Central Wisconsin, Wausau, WI.
$10,000 to Junior Achievement of Wisconsin, Milwaukee, WI.
$10,000 to Performing Arts Foundation, Wausau, WI.
$8,500 to Boys and Girls Club of the Wausau Area, Wausau, WI.
$6,300 to Wausau and Marathon County Parks Foundation, Wausau, WI.
$6,000 to Habitat for Humanity, Madison, WI.
$5,000 to Wausau Area Hmong Mutual Association, Wausau, WI.
$2,500 to Childrens Service Society of Wisconsin, Wausau, WI.
$2,000 to Center for the Visual Arts, Wausau, WI.

9793
Louise Head Duncan Trust ✧ ☆
(also known as The Peyton Samuel Head Family Trust)
c/o JPMorgan Chase Bank, N.A.
P.O. Box 1308
Milwaukee, WI 53201
Application address: c/o The Peyton Samuel Head Family Trust, P.O. Box 248, LaGrange, KY 40031

Established in 1991.
Donor: Louise Head Duncan†.
Foundation type: Independent foundation.
Financial data (yr. ended 12/31/05): Assets, $9,461,700 (M); expenditures, $552,317; qualifying distributions, $462,652; giving activities include $430,041 for 31 grants (high: $65,990; low: $1,250).
Purpose and activities: Giving for the overall improvement of the quality of life of the people of Oldham County, KY.
Fields of interest: Historic preservation/historical societies; Education; Environment, natural resources; Housing/shelter; Disasters, fire prevention/control; Recreation, parks/playgrounds; Recreation; Human services; American Red Cross; Children/youth, services; Community development; Federated giving programs; Christian agencies & churches.
Type of support: General/operating support.
Limitations: Giving limited to Oldham County, KY. No grants to individuals.
Application information: One request per year per organization. Include cover letter with application. Application form required.
  Copies of proposal: 3
  Board meeting date(s): July and Nov.
Advisory Committee: Thomas W. Gaines, Jr.; Joseph William Hall; Annette Paine.
Trustee: JPMorgan Chase Bank, N.A.
EIN: 616183556

9794
Eastman Chemical Company Foundation, Inc. ✧
c/o JPMorgan Chase Bank, N.A.
P.O. Box 1308
Milwaukee, WI 53201 (423) 229-1413
Contact: Paul Montgomery, V.P.
Application address: P.O. Box 511, Kingsport, TN 37662-5075

Established in 1996 in TN.
Donor: Eastman Chemical Co.
Foundation type: Company-sponsored foundation.
Financial data (yr. ended 12/31/05): Assets, $5,822,927 (M); expenditures, $1,761,788; qualifying distributions, $1,753,280; giving activities include $1,750,455 for 361 grants (high: $200,000; low: $50).
Purpose and activities: The foundation supports organizations involved with arts and culture, education, health, and human services.
Fields of interest: Arts; Elementary/secondary education; Higher education; Health care; Children/youth, services; Human services; Federated giving programs.
Limitations: Giving on a national basis in areas of company operations. No support for labor, veterans', fraternal, social, religious, political, or national health organizations or teams. Generally, no grants to individuals.

Application information: Application form not required.
  Initial approach: Proposal
  Deadline(s): None
Officers and Directors:* Norris Sneed,* Pres.; Paul Montgomery,* V.P.; Brian L. Henry, Secy.; Mary Hall,* Treas.; Richard Lorraine.
EIN: 621614800
Selected grants: The following grants were reported in 2003.
$75,000 to Wellmont Foundation, Kingsport, TN.
$50,000 to East Tennessee State University Foundation, Johnson City, TN. For Roan Scholars Leadership Endowment.
$50,000 to Junior Achievement of Kingsport, Kingsport, TN.
$36,555 to United Way of Greater Kingsport, Kingsport, TN.
$33,625 to Chemical Educational Foundation, Arlington, VA.
$25,000 to Good Shepherd Medical Center, Longview, TX. For capital campaign.
$23,772 to Research Foundation of the State University of New York, Albany, NY.
$20,000 to Tennessee Sports Hall of Fame, Nashville, TN.
$10,000 to Northeast State Technical Community College, Blountville, TN.
$10,000 to University of Arkansas Community College Morrilton, Morrilton, AR.

9795
Eastman Kodak Charitable Trust ▼ ✧
c/o JPMorgan Chase Bank, N.A.
P.O. Box 1308
Milwaukee, WI 53201
Application address: 343 State St., Rochester, NY 14650, tel.: (585) 724-2434

Trust established in 1952 in NY.
Donor: Eastman Kodak Co.
Foundation type: Company-sponsored foundation.
Financial data (yr. ended 12/31/05): Assets, $1,060,635 (M); gifts received, $3,850,000; expenditures, $3,001,983; qualifying distributions, $3,000,160; giving activities include $2,999,300 for 132 grants (high: $500,000; low: $500).
Purpose and activities: The trust supports organizations involved with arts and culture, education, and the environment.
Fields of interest: Arts; Higher education; Education; Environment; Federated giving programs; Minorities.
Type of support: General/operating support; Continuing support; Fellowships; Scholarship funds.
Limitations: Giving primarily in areas of company operations, with emphasis on Windsor, CO, Rochester, NY, and Kingsport, TN; giving on a national and international basis for higher education. No grants to individuals; low priority for building or endowments; no loans; no matching gifts.
Publications: Corporate giving report.
Application information: Application form not required.
  Initial approach: Proposal
  Deadline(s): None
  Board meeting date(s): Monthly
Trustee: JPMorgan Chase Bank, N.A.
EIN: 166015274
Selected grants: The following grants were reported in 2004.

$1,850,000 to United Way of Greater Rochester, Rochester, NY. 3 grants: $925,000, $462,500, $462,500
$325,000 to University of Rochester, Rochester, NY. For imaging research.
$250,000 to Rochester Institute of Technology, Rochester, NY. For Partnership for Success.
$200,000 to Clarkson University, Potsdam, NY. For Campaign for Clarkson.
$200,000 to Monroe Community College, Rochester, NY. For EKC Center for Teaching and Learning.
$100,000 to Achieve, Palo Alto, CA. For general support.
$100,000 to World Wildlife Fund, DC. For Windows on the Wild.
$75,000 to Nazareth College of Rochester, Rochester, NY. For expansion.

9796
Clyde R. Evans Charitable Trust ✧
c/o JPMorgan Chase Bank, N.A.
P.O. Box 1308
Milwaukee, WI 53201

Established in 1997 in OK.
Foundation type: Independent foundation.
Financial data (yr. ended 6/30/05): Assets, $10,376,510 (M); expenditures, $572,952; qualifying distributions, $531,651; giving activities include $515,000 for 23 grants (high: $65,000; low: $2,000).
Purpose and activities: Giving primarily for education, human services, and health care, with emphasis on children.
Fields of interest: Education; Hospitals (general); Hospitals (specialty); Medical research, institute; Human services; Children/youth, services.
Limitations: Applications not accepted. Giving primarily in Oklahoma City, OK. No grants to individuals.
Application information: Contributes only to pre-selected organizations.
Trustees: Roy W. Chandler; Gordon Henderson; David C. Johnston; JPMorgan Chase Bank, N.A.
EIN: 736296082
Selected grants: The following grants were reported in 2004.
$60,000 to Oklahoma Baptist Homes for Children, Oklahoma City, OK.
$57,500 to Oklahoma Medical Research Foundation, Oklahoma City, OK.
$57,500 to Salvation Army of Oklahoma City, Oklahoma City, OK.
$40,000 to Oklahoma City University, Oklahoma City, OK.
$15,000 to Boys and Girls Club of Oklahoma County, Oklahoma City, OK.
$10,000 to Childrens Center, Bethany, OK.
$10,000 to Childrens Medical Research Institute, Oklahoma City, OK.
$10,000 to Family Life, Little Rock, AR.
$10,000 to Fellowship of Christian Athletes, Oklahoma City, OK.
$10,000 to Oklahoma City Public Schools Foundation, Oklahoma City, OK.

9797
The Evjue Foundation, Inc.
1901 Fish Hatchery Rd.
P.O. Box 8060
Madison, WI 53708
Contact: Arlene Hornung, Exec. Dir.
E-mail: ahornung@madison.com; URL: http://
www.madison.com/captimes/evjue

Incorporated in 1958 in WI.
Donor: William T. Evjue†.
Foundation type: Community foundation.
Financial data (yr. ended 2/28/05): Assets,
$24,060,789 (M); gifts received, $1,490,021;
expenditures, $2,109,544; giving activities include
$1,986,810 for 156 grants (high: $200,000; low:
$300).
Purpose and activities: Support for education,
including higher education; grants also for mental
health, youth, and social service agencies, and for
cultural programs.
Fields of interest: Media, journalism/publishing;
Arts; Higher education; Education; Animal welfare;
Hospitals (general); Reproductive health, family
planning; Substance abuse, services; Mental
health/crisis services; Alcoholism; Food services;
Children/youth, services; Family services; Aging,
centers/services; Human services; Aging.
Type of support: General/operating support;
Continuing support; Emergency funds; Program
development; Professorships; Publication; Seed
money; Internship funds.
Limitations: Giving primarily in Dane County, WI. No
support for medical or scientific research. No grants
to individuals, or for building funds, equipment,
endowment funds, land acquisition, renovation
projects, or operating expenses; no loans.
Publications: Application guidelines; Informational
brochure (including application guidelines); Program
policy statement.
Application information: Visit foundation Web site
for application form, guidelines, and specific
deadlines. Application form required.
   Initial approach: Letter or telephone inquiry
   Copies of proposal: 1
   Deadline(s): Submit proposal preferably in Mar.,
     Apr., or Oct.
   Board meeting date(s): Apr., May, Nov., and as
     required
   Final notification: 3 months
Officers and Directors:* John H. Lussier,* Pres.;
Nancy Brooke Gage,* V.P.; Clayton Frink,*
Secy.-Treas.; Arlene Hornung, Exec. Dir.; Marion F.
Brown; Daniel Erdman; W. Jerome Frautschi; Virginia
Henderson; James D. Lussier; Laura J. Lussier-Lee;
Steve Mixtacki; Marianne D. Pollard; Carmen
Skilton; Andrew A. Wilcox; John Wiley; Dave Zweifel.
Number of staff: 1 part-time support.
EIN: 396073981

9798
Harvey Firestone, Jr. Foundation ◇
c/o JPMorgan Chase Bank, N.A.
P.O. Box 1308
Milwaukee, WI 53201
Application address: Charles D'Arcy c/o JPMorgan
Chase Bank, N.A., 50 S. Main St., Akron, OH 44308,
tel.: (330) 972-1872

Established in 1983 in OH.
Foundation type: Independent foundation.
Financial data (yr. ended 12/31/05): Assets,
$21,987,575 (M); expenditures, $1,092,840;

qualifying distributions, $915,105; giving activities
include $900,000 for 81 grants (high: $151,000;
low: $500).
Purpose and activities: Emphasis on hospitals and
education; support also for cultural programs, social
services, and Christian churches and organizations.
Fields of interest: Arts; Education; Hospitals
(general); Human services; Christian agencies &
churches.
Type of support: General/operating support.
Limitations: Giving primarily in the eastern U.S. No
grants to individuals.
Application information: Application form not
required.
   Deadline(s): None
Trustees: Anne F. Ball; Martha F. Ford; JPMorgan
Chase Bank, N.A.
EIN: 341388254

9799
Fleck Foundation ◇
(formerly Fleckenstein Family Foundation)
16655 W. Bluemound Rd., Ste. 290
Brookfield, WI 53005 (262) 860-1680
Contact: Andrew J. Fleckenstein, Tr.
FAX: (262) 860-1683;
E-mail: info@fleckfoundation.org; URL: http://
www.fleckfoundation.org

Established in 1996 in WI.
Donor: Andrew J. Fleckenstein.
Foundation type: Independent foundation.
Financial data (yr. ended 12/31/05): Assets,
$11,480,762 (M); gifts received, $500,000;
expenditures, $3,493,403; qualifying distributions,
$3,418,425; giving activities include $3,308,114
for 104 grants (high: $435,000; low: $300), and
$25,000 for 1 employee matching gift.
Purpose and activities: The mission of the
foundation is to offer educational opportunities for
people who would otherwise not be able to afford
them in the city of Milwaukee, WI. Also provides
assistance to men and women recovering from
alcohol addiction.
Fields of interest: Elementary school/education;
Secondary school/education; Education; Substance
abuse, treatment; Mental health, transitional care;
Civil rights, race/intergroup relations.
Type of support: General/operating support; Capital
campaigns; Building/renovation; Seed money;
Scholarship funds; Matching/challenge support.
Limitations: Giving primarily in Milwaukee, WI. No
grants to individuals.
Publications: Application guidelines; Annual report.
Application information: Application form required.
   Initial approach: Letter
   Copies of proposal: 1
   Deadline(s): Complete applications received by
     Dec. 1, Mar. 1, June 1 or Sept. 1 will be
     considered at the next board meeting.
     Applications received after these dates will be
     considered at the next board meeting if a
     complete review can be made.
   Board meeting date(s): Jan., Apr., July, and Oct.
Officer and Trustees:* Jay Scott,* Exec. Dir.;
Andrew J. Fleckenstein.
Board Members: Nate Cunniff; Carolyn Scott; Jim
Stern.
Number of staff: 2 full-time professional.
EIN: 391832464

9800
Fond du Lac Area Foundation ◇
384 N. Main St., Ste. 4
Fond du Lac, WI 54935 (920) 921-2215
Contact: Sandi Braun Roehrig, Exec. Dir.
FAX: (920) 921-1036;
E-mail: info@fdlareafoundation.com; URL: http://
www.fdlareafoundation.com

Established as a trust in 1975 in WI.
Foundation type: Community foundation.
Financial data (yr. ended 12/31/04): Assets,
$14,806,102 (M); gifts received, $1,405,249;
expenditures, $2,216,578; giving activities include
$1,686,332 for 374 grants (high: $351,781; low:
$26), and $129,480 for 160 grants to individuals
(high: $4,000; low: $100).
Purpose and activities: The foundation's purpose is
to accept, manage, and distribute charitable
contributions that will fulfill the needs and enhance
the present and future quality of life within the Fond
du Lac, WI, community.
Fields of interest: Arts; Education; Environment;
Health care; Youth, services; Human services;
Community development.
Type of support: Emergency funds; Program
development; Seed money; Scholarship funds;
Grants to individuals.
Limitations: Giving limited to the Fond du Lac, WI,
area. No support for religious organizations for
religious purposes. No grants to individuals (except
for scholarships), or for ongoing operating expenses
or building funds, capital campaigns, endowments,
debt reduction, scholarly research, fund drives, or
for travel.
Publications: Application guidelines; Annual report
(including application guidelines); Financial
statement; Grants list; Informational brochure
(including application guidelines); Newsletter.
Application information: Visit foundation Web site
for application guidelines; contact the foundation to
receive an application form. Application form
required.
   Initial approach: Telephone or letter
   Copies of proposal: 1
   Deadline(s): Jan. 15 and July 31
   Board meeting date(s): Quarterly
   Final notification: June 30 and Dec. 4
Officers and Directors:* Ann E. Blamey,* Chair.;
Thomas H. Tobin, Jr.,* Vice-Chair.; Nancy Witkowski,
Secy.; David M. Klumpyan,* Treas.; Sandi Braun
Roehrig, Exec. Dir.; John E. Ahern; Tom D. Baker;
Dale G. Brooks; Brian P. Johnson; James W.
Neumann; Mimi Sager; John St. Peter.
Number of staff: 3 full-time professional.
EIN: 510181570

9801
Fort Atkinson Community Foundation ◇
c/o Premier Bank
244 N. Main St.
Fort Atkinson, WI 53538 (920) 563-3210
E-mail: facf@idcnet.com; URL: http://
www.fortfoundation.org

Established in 1974 in WI.
Foundation type: Community foundation.
Financial data (yr. ended 6/30/05): Assets,
$15,770,300 (M); gifts received, $448,755;
expenditures, $533,053; giving activities include
$260,174 for 29 grants (high: $106,820; low: $88),
and $176,988 for 81 grants to individuals (high:
$7,500; low: $500).

Purpose and activities: The purpose of the foundation is to receive and accept property exclusively for educational, cultural, charitable or benevolent purposes for the benefit and improvement of residents of the Fort Atkinson, Wisconsin, metropolitan area in such a way that the quality of life shall be enhanced.

Fields of interest: Arts; Education; Environment, beautification programs; Recreation; Human services; Community development.

Type of support: General/operating support; Scholarships—to individuals.

Limitations: Giving limited to the Fort Atkinson, WI, area. No support for sectarian or religious purposes. No grants to individuals (except through award or pre-established scholarship fund), or for endowment funds, debt retirement, or operating expenses (in response to annual fund drives or to eliminate previously incurred deficits).

Application information: Visit foundation Web site for application information. Application form required.

Initial approach: Contact foundation for application form
Deadline(s): Mar. 15, June 15, Sept. 15, and Dec. 15 for grants; varies for scholarships
Board meeting date(s): Jan., Apr., July, and Oct.
Final notification: Following board meetings

Officers and Directors:* Rick Klopcic,* Pres.; Phillip Jones,* V.P.; James J. Vance,* Secy. and Legal Counsel; Gordon "Chip" Day, Jr.; Laurette Greenhalgh; Don V. Henning; Randy Knox.

Trustee: Premier Bank.

EIN: 396220899

9802
The Fotsch Foundation ✧
13965 W. Burleigh Rd., Rm. 101
Brookfield, WI   53005

Established in 1967 in IL.

Donors: Abina D. Fotsch; William E. Fotsch; Baush Machine Tool Co.; BMT Corp.; JFC Enterprises; Tridan Industries.

Foundation type: Independent foundation.

Financial data (yr. ended 11/30/05): Assets, $11,271,893 (M); gifts received, $160,000; expenditures, $503,924; qualifying distributions, $476,700; giving activities include $476,700 for 34 grants (high: $60,000; low: $1,000).

Purpose and activities: Giving primarily to higher education, health and human services.

Fields of interest: Media/communications; Arts; Higher education; Medical school/education; Cancer; Health organizations; Cancer research; Alzheimer's disease research; Human services; American Red Cross; Salvation Army; Federated giving programs; Roman Catholic agencies & churches.

Limitations: Applications not accepted. Giving primarily in IL and WI. No grants to individuals.

Application information: Contributes only to pre-selected organizations.

Officer: William E. Fotsch, Pres.

EIN: 366190007

Selected grants: The following grants were reported in 2004.
$60,000 to Marquette University, Milwaukee, WI.
$36,000 to American Red Cross.
$33,500 to Salvation Army.
$25,000 to American Cancer Society, Atlanta, GA.
  2 grants: $21,000, $4,000
$14,000 to United Way.

$12,000 to Alzheimers Association, Chicago, IL.
$4,250 to Channel 10/36 Friends, Milwaukee, WI.

9803
The Four-Four Foundation, Inc. ✧
c/o Provident Trust Co.
N16 W23217 Stone Ridge Dr., Ste. 310
Pewaukee, WI   53072
Contact: Sally S. Manegold, Pres.

Established in 1994 in WI.

Foundation type: Independent foundation.

Financial data (yr. ended 12/31/05): Assets, $27,439,472 (M); expenditures, $1,351,429; qualifying distributions, $1,171,334; giving activities include $1,162,000 for 55 grants (high: $101,000; low: $2,000).

Fields of interest: Arts; Education; Environment, natural resources; Medical care, rehabilitation; Public health.

Type of support: Continuing support; Annual campaigns; Capital campaigns; Building/renovation; Endowments; Professorships.

Limitations: Applications not accepted. Giving primarily in Milwaukee, WI. No grants to individuals.

Application information: Contributes only to pre-selected organizations. Unsolicited requests for funds not accepted.

Board meeting date(s): Between June and Sept.

Officers and Directors:* Sally S. Manegold,* Pres.; Robert H. Manegold,* V.P. and Treas.; Katherine M. Biersach,* Secy.; Joan M. Dukes; Lynn M. Rix.

EIN: 391867243

9804
John J. Frautschi Family Foundation, Inc. ✧
303 Lakewood Blvd.
Madison, WI   53704

Established in 1986 in WI.

Donors: John J. Frautschi; members of the Frautschi family.

Foundation type: Independent foundation.

Financial data (yr. ended 12/31/03): Assets, $4,072,253 (M); gifts received, $590,155; expenditures, $468,285; qualifying distributions, $468,285; giving activities include $465,500 for 62 grants (high: $155,000; low: $1,000).

Purpose and activities: Giving primarily for education, the arts, health associations, human services, and to a Presbyterian church.

Fields of interest: Museums; Performing arts, theater; Arts; Elementary school/education; Higher education; Environment, natural resources; Health organizations, association; Cancer research; Human services; Federated giving programs; Protestant agencies & churches.

Type of support: General/operating support.

Limitations: Applications not accepted. Giving primarily in WI. No grants to individuals.

Application information: Contributes only to pre-selected organizations. Unsolicited requests for funds not considered.

Board meeting date(s): Annually

Officers and Directors:* John J. Frautschi,* Pres.; Elizabeth J. Frautschi,* V.P.; Christopher J. Frautschi,* Secy.-Treas.; Peter W. Frautschi,* Secy.-Treas.

EIN: 391561017

Selected grants: The following grants were reported in 2003.
$155,000 to Webcrafters-Frautschi Foundation, Madison, WI.
$100,000 to Madison Country Day School, Waunakee, WI.
$50,000 to University of Wisconsin Foundation, Madison, WI.
$5,000 to Edgewood College, Madison, WI.
$5,000 to Madison Symphony Orchestra, Madison, WI.
$1,000 to Beloit College, Beloit, WI.
$1,000 to Madison Opera, Madison, WI.
$1,000 to Northland College, Sigurd Olson Environmental Institute, Ashland, WI.
$1,000 to Wisconsin Academy of Sciences, Arts and Letters, Madison, WI.
$1,000 to Wisconsin Chamber Orchestra, Madison, WI.

9805
Glover-Crask Charitable Trust ✧
c/o JPMorgan Chase Bank, N.A.
P.O. Box 1308
Milwaukee, WI   53201   (716) 258-5169

Established in 1998 in NY.

Foundation type: Independent foundation.

Financial data (yr. ended 12/31/05): Assets, $14,436,362 (M); expenditures, $859,531; qualifying distributions, $766,310; giving activities include $749,790 for 32 grants (high: $150,000; low: $1,500).

Fields of interest: Performing arts, orchestra (symphony); Higher education; Student services/organizations; Cancer; Eye research; Food services; Human services; Children, services; Christian agencies & churches.

Limitations: Applications not accepted. Giving primarily in Rochester, NY. No grants to individuals.

Application information: Contributes only to pre-selected organizations.

Trustees: George F. Harris; JPMorgan Chase Bank, N.A.

EIN: 166478709

9806
Raymond and Marie Goldbach Foundation, Inc. ✧
(formerly Goldbach Charitable Foundation, Inc.)
304 East St.
Marathon, WI   54448
Contact: John L. Skoug, Pres.

Established in 1997 in WI.

Donors: Marie S. Goldbach Life Trust; Marathon Cheese Corp.; Packaging Tape, Inc.

Foundation type: Independent foundation.

Financial data (yr. ended 12/31/05): Assets, $10,441,044 (M); gifts received, $3,250,000; expenditures, $397,096; qualifying distributions, $362,390; giving activities include $352,390 for 19 grants (high: $220,000; low: $40), and $10,000 for 10 grants to individuals (high: $1,000; low: $1,000).

Purpose and activities: Giving for education, athletics, and community.

Fields of interest: Elementary/secondary education; Education; Athletics/sports, water sports; Foundations (community).

Type of support: General/operating support; Building/renovation; Grants to individuals.
Limitations: Applications not accepted. Giving primarily in WI.
Application information: Unsolicited requests for funds not accepted.
Officers: John L. Skoug, Pres. and Treas.; Marie S. Goldbach, V.P.
Director: Rev. Joseph G. Diermeier.
EIN: 391877824
Selected grants: The following grants were reported in 2004.
$160,000 to Marathon Area Swim Association, Marathon, WI.
$5,000 to Thomas Aquinas College, Santa Paula, CA.
$2,000 to Junior Achievement of Wausau, Wausau, WI.
$1,200 to American Life League, Stafford, VA.
$500 to Life Legal Defense Foundation, Napa, CA.
$200 to Human Life International, Front Royal, VA.
$50 to Disabled American Veterans, Cincinnati, OH.
$50 to Sacred Heart Southern Missions, Walls, MS.
$35 to American Institute of Philanthropy, Chicago, IL.

9807
Goodman's, Inc. ✧ ☆
P.O. Box 8100
Madison, WI 53708-8100 (608) 257-6761
Contact: Irwin A. Goodman, Pres. and Treas.

Established in 1961 in WI.
Donors: Irwin A. Goodman; Robert D. Goodman.
Foundation type: Independent foundation.
Financial data (yr. ended 8/31/05): Assets, $3,504,690 (M); gifts received, $922,000; expenditures, $1,975,078; qualifying distributions, $1,974,000; giving activities include $1,974,000 for 5 grants (high: $1,776,000; low: $300).
Purpose and activities: Giving primarily for federated giving programs.
Fields of interest: Federated giving programs; Jewish agencies & temples.
Limitations: Giving primarily in Madison, WI. No grants to individuals.
Application information:
Initial approach: Letter
Deadline(s): None
Officers: Irwin A. Goodman, Pres. and Treas.; Robert D. Goodman, V.P. and Secy.
Directors: Robert Pricer; E.G. Shramka; Howard A. Sweet; Mark Vitense.
EIN: 396056619
Selected grants: The following grants were reported in 2005.
$1,776,000 to Madison Parks Foundation, Madison, WI.
$150,000 to United Way of Dane County, Madison, WI.

9808
Gertrude S. Gordon Foundation ✧
c/o North Central Trust Co.
230 Front St. N.
La Crosse, WI 54601

Established in WI.
Foundation type: Independent foundation.
Financial data (yr. ended 12/31/05): Assets, $10,112,297 (M); expenditures, $514,917;

qualifying distributions, $435,847; giving activities include $432,847 for 10 grants (high: $123,096; low: $22,237).
Fields of interest: Libraries (public); Education; Animal welfare; Hospitals (general); Boys & girls clubs; Human services; Foundations (public); Foundations (community); Federated giving programs; Protestant agencies & churches.
Limitations: Applications not accepted. Giving primarily in La Crosse, WI. No grants to individuals.
Application information: Contributes only to pre-selected organizations.
Trustee: North Central Trust Co.
EIN: 316672080
Selected grants: The following grants were reported in 2004.
$109,489 to La Crosse Community Foundation, La Crosse, WI.
$95,414 to Gundersen Lutheran Medical Foundation, La Crosse, WI.
$50,197 to Boys and Girls Club of La Crosse, La Crosse, WI.
$27,333 to La Crosse Public Library, La Crosse, WI.
$26,672 to La Crosse Public Education Foundation, La Crosse, WI.
$26,460 to Salvation Army, WI.

9809
Edward S. Gould Charitable Trust ✧
c/o JPMorgan Chase Bank, N.A.
P.O. Box 1308
Milwaukee, WI 53201

Established in 1997 in CA.
Foundation type: Independent foundation.
Financial data (yr. ended 12/31/05): Assets, $665,558 (M); expenditures, $632,724; qualifying distributions, $600,000; giving activities include $600,000 for grants.
Fields of interest: Higher education; Human services; LGBTQ.
Limitations: Applications not accepted. Giving primarily in CA. No grants to individuals.
Application information: Contributes only to pre-selected organizations.
Trustees: Frederick O. Nelson; JPMorgan Chase Bank, N.A.
EIN: 367183706

9810
Greater Green Bay Community Foundation, Inc. ✧
310 W. Walnut St., Ste. 350
Green Bay, WI 54303 (920) 432-0800
Contact: Steve Schmeisser, Finance Off.; For grants: Martha Ahrendt Ph.D., Prog. Off.
FAX: (920) 432-5577; E-mail: steve@ggbcf.org;
Grant application E-mail: martha@ggbcf.org;
URL: http://www.ggbcf.org

Established in 1991 in WI.
Foundation type: Community foundation.
Financial data (yr. ended 6/30/04): Assets, $38,902,169 (M); gifts received, $2,564,475; expenditures, $2,505,636; giving activities include $1,749,766 for 225 grants (high: $152,000; low: $100; average: $100–$152,000), and $254,350 for 55 grants to individuals (high: $40,000; low: $350; average: $350–$40,000).
Purpose and activities: The foundation enhances the community by: providing donors the immediate

flexibility of personal charitable gift funds and the philanthropic legacy of endowment funds; working with clients to distribute charitable gifts across the breadth of nonprofit organizations; acting as a prudent manager of the community's philanthropic assets; and serving as a leader on community issues by bringing together donors and promising solutions from the nonprofit world. A major part of the foundation's effort to fulfill its mission centers around the distribution of charitable grants to worthy nonprofit organizations serving the people of the Greater Green Bay, WI, area.
Fields of interest: Arts, cultural/ethnic awareness; Historic preservation/historical societies; Arts; Education; Environment; Health care; Alzheimer's disease; Diabetes; Youth development; Residential/custodial care, hospices; Human services; Community development, neighborhood development; Community development; Aging.
Type of support: Continuing support; Equipment; Emergency funds; Program development; Seed money; Curriculum development; Scholarship funds; Technical assistance; Program evaluation; Scholarships—to individuals; Matching/challenge support.
Limitations: Giving limited to Brown, Door, Kewaunee and Oconto counties, WI. No support for religious programs for religious purposes. No grants to individuals (except scholarships), annual or capital campaigns, or debt retirement.
Publications: Application guidelines; Annual report; Financial statement; Informational brochure.
Application information: Visit foundation Web site for grant application form and guidelines. Faxed applications are not accepted. Required scholarship application forms available through Northeast WI high schools; scholarship recipients must be residents of Brown, Door, Kewaunee or Oconto counties, WI. Application form required.
Initial approach: Telephone
Copies of proposal: 1
Deadline(s): Jan. 1, Apr. 1, July 1, and Oct. 1
Board meeting date(s): Mar., June, Sept., and Dec.
Final notification: Within 4 weeks of application deadline
Officers and Board Members: Jeff Ottum,* Chair.; Kenneth D. Strmiska, C.E.O. and Pres.; George Hartmann,* V.P.; Donna Scattergood,* V.P.; Bill Van Ess,* Secy.; Kenneth Krueger,* Treas.; Julie Ariens; Nancy Armburst; Mike Calawerts; Tim Cisler; Diane Conway; Susan Finco; Diane Ford; Wes Garner; Gary Johnson; Lindi Kuritz; Ken Larsen; Larry Lindsley; Kathy Reinke; Kramer Rock; Fred Schmidt; Satinder Sundlass; Ron Van Den Heuvel; Julie Van Straten.
Number of staff: 3 full-time professional; 2 part-time professional; 2 part-time support.
EIN: 391699966

9811
Joseph & Sally Handleman Charitable Foundation Trust C ✧
c/o JPMorgan Chase Bank, N.A.
P.O. Box 1308
Milwaukee, WI 53201
Contact: Gary W. Gomoll, Mgr., JPMorgan Chase Bank
Application address: c/o JPMorgan Chase Bank, N.A., 3399 PGA Blvd., Ste. 100, Palm Beach Gardens, FL 33410, tel.: (561) 799-1135

Foundation type: Independent foundation.

Financial data (yr. ended 12/31/05): Assets, $627,359 (M); expenditures, $415,532; qualifying distributions, $353,486; giving activities include $335,000 for 16 grants (high: $60,000; low: $5,000).
Purpose and activities: Giving primarily for health care, including medical research and hospices, environmental conservation, Jewish organizations, education, and children, youth, and human services.
Fields of interest: Education, special; Education; Environment, natural resources; Animal welfare; Medical research, institute; Human services; Salvation Army; Children/youth, services; Jewish agencies & temples.
Limitations: Giving primarily in Washington, DC, FL and NY. No grants to individuals.
Application information: Application form not required.
  Initial approach: Proposal
  Deadline(s): None
Trustees: Joyce Ann Muller; JPMorgan Chase Bank, N.A.
EIN: 656263328

9812
Harley-Davidson Foundation, Inc. ✧
3700 W. Juneau Ave.
Milwaukee, WI 53208 (414) 343-4001
Contact: Mary Ann Martiny

Established in 1994 in WI.
Donor: Harley-Davidson, Inc.
Foundation type: Company-sponsored foundation.
Financial data (yr. ended 12/31/05): Assets, $21,229,947 (M); gifts received, $4,467,093; expenditures, $3,565,067; qualifying distributions, $3,419,505; giving activities include $3,419,505 for 339 grants (high: $1,000,000; low: $13).
Purpose and activities: The foundation supports organizations involved with arts and culture, education, youth development, and human services.
Fields of interest: Arts; Education; Hospitals (general); Youth development, scouting agencies (general); Youth development; Human services; Federated giving programs.
Limitations: Giving primarily in AL, MO, PA, and WI.
Application information: The Milwaukee Area Funders Common Application Form is accepted. Application form required.
  Initial approach: Contact foundation for application form; mail application form to foundation
  Deadline(s): Mar. 26, June 4, Aug. 13, Oct. 1, and Dec. 10
Officers and Directors:* James L. Ziemer, Pres.; Gail A. Lione, V.P. and Secy.; James M. Brostowitz, V.P. and Treas.; Jeffrey L. Bleustein; Kathleen A. Lawler; Harold A. Scott.
EIN: 391769946
Selected grants: The following grants were reported in 2003.
$250,000 to Bradley Technology and Trade School Foundation, Milwaukee, WI. For program support.
$220,094 to United Way of Greater Milwaukee, Milwaukee, WI. For program support.
$150,000 to Habitat for Humanity International, Milwaukee, WI. 2 grants: $50,000 (For program support), $100,000 (For program support).
$84,000 to Boys and Girls Clubs of Greater Milwaukee, Milwaukee, WI. For program support.
$83,420 to United Way of York County, York, PA. For program support.

$50,000 to Hunger Task Force of Milwaukee, Milwaukee, WI. For program support.
$50,000 to Next Door Foundation, Milwaukee, WI. For program support.
$50,000 to YMCA of Metropolitan Milwaukee, Milwaukee, WI. For program support.
$25,000 to Urban Day School, Milwaukee, WI. For program support.

9813
Evan and Marion Helfaer Foundation ✧
P.O. Box 147
Elm Grove, WI 53122 (262) 784-9778
Contact: Thomas L. Smallwood, Admin.

Established in 1971 in WI.
Donor: Evan P. Helfaer†.
Foundation type: Independent foundation.
Financial data (yr. ended 7/31/05): Assets, $23,927,046 (M); expenditures, $1,654,414; qualifying distributions, $1,353,500; giving activities include $1,235,060 for 130 grants (high: $200,000; low: $400).
Purpose and activities: Support for higher education, cultural programs, youth and social service agencies, and health.
Fields of interest: Museums; Museums (art); Arts; Higher education; Education; Environment, natural resources; Hospitals (general); Health organizations, association; Crime/violence prevention, child abuse; Youth development, scouting agencies (general); Human services; Children/youth, services; Family services; Community development; Federated giving programs; Social sciences, public policy; Blind/visually impaired; Deaf/hearing impaired.
Type of support: Building/renovation; Professorships; Curriculum development; Research.
Limitations: Giving limited to WI. No grants to individuals.
Application information: Application form not required.
  Initial approach: Letter
  Deadline(s): None
  Board meeting date(s): Periodically
  Final notification: Within 90 days after end of fiscal year
Trustees: William T. Gaus; Thomas L. Smallwood; Marshall & Ilsley Bank.
Number of staff: 1
EIN: 396238856
Selected grants: The following grants were reported in 2004.
$200,000 to Southeastern Wisconsin Professional Baseball Park District, WI.
$100,000 to Marquette University, John P. Raynor, SJ Library, Milwaukee, WI.
$100,000 to Milwaukee Art Museum, Milwaukee, WI.
$25,000 to Milwaukee School of Engineering, Milwaukee, WI.
$20,000 to Boys and Girls Clubs of Greater Milwaukee, Milwaukee, WI.
$20,000 to United Way of Greater Milwaukee, Milwaukee, WI.
$10,000 to HeartLove Place, Milwaukee, WI.
$10,000 to Milwaukee Center for Independence, Milwaukee, WI.
$10,000 to Milwaukee Public Library, Milwaukee, WI.
$10,000 to YMCA of Metropolitan Milwaukee, Milwaukee, WI.

9814
The Herma Family Foundation ✧ ☆
1260 Overhill Rd.
Elm Grove, WI 53122

Established in 1993 in WI.
Foundation type: Independent foundation.
Financial data (yr. ended 12/31/05): Assets, $5,541,404 (M); expenditures, $1,344,482; qualifying distributions, $1,311,782; giving activities include $1,311,782 for grants.
Purpose and activities: Giving primarily for pediatric health care, specializing in congenital heart disease.
Limitations: Applications not accepted. Giving primarily in WI, with emphasis on Milwaukee. No grants to individuals.
Application information: Contributes only to pre-selected organizations.
Officers and Directors:* John E. Herma,* Pres. and Treas.; Susan M. Herma,* V.P. and Secy.; Peter M. Sommerhauser.
EIN: 391776108

9815
The Richard & Ethel Herzfeld Foundation, Inc. ✧
219 N. Milwaukee St., 7th Fl.
Milwaukee, WI 53202
Contact: Mark Warhus, Prog. Mgr.
E-mail: mail@herzfeldfoundation.org

Established around 1973 in WI.
Donors: Ethel D. Herzfeld†; Richard P. Herzfeld†.
Foundation type: Independent foundation.
Financial data (yr. ended 12/31/04): Assets, $77,500,773 (M); expenditures, $3,837,147; qualifying distributions, $3,709,426; giving activities include $3,254,867 for 104 grants (high: $350,000; low: $250).
Purpose and activities: Giving primarily to museums, arts organizations, and education.
Fields of interest: Museums; Arts; Education.
Type of support: General/operating support; Continuing support; Capital campaigns; Building/renovation; Program development.
Limitations: Giving primarily in WI, with emphasis on the greater Milwaukee area. No grants to individuals.
Publications: Application guidelines.
Application information: Application form required.
  Initial approach: E-mail foundation to request inquiry form
  Copies of proposal: 1
  Deadline(s): Feb. 1, May 1, and Aug. 1
  Board meeting date(s): Spring, summer, and fall
  Final notification: Approximately 3 months
Officer: F. William Haberman, Pres. and Treas.
Directors: Edward Hinshaw; Gordon Miller.
Number of staff: 1 full-time professional; 2 part-time professional.
EIN: 237230686

9816
Myrtle E. & William G. Hess Charitable Trust ✧
c/o JPMorgan Chase Bank, N.A.
P.O. Box 1308
Milwaukee, WI 53201
Contact: Matthew Wasmund

Application address: c/o JPMorgan Chase Bank, N.A., 611 Woodward Ave., Ste. MI1-8113, Detroit, MI 48226-3408, tel.: (313) 225-3454, FAX: (313) 225-3948

Established in 1984 in MI.
Donor: Myrtle E. Hess†.
Foundation type: Independent foundation.
Financial data (yr. ended 9/30/05): Assets, $7,877,329 (M); expenditures, $420,229; qualifying distributions, $398,763; giving activities include $390,000 for 27 grants (high: $100,000; low: $5,000).
Purpose and activities: Giving only to Roman Catholic institutions and agencies located in Oakland County, MI, including Roman Catholic hospitals and schools, or to those institutions that received grants during the donor's lifetime or that were designated for support in donor's will.
Fields of interest: Elementary/secondary education; Child development, education; Education; Hospitals (general); Alcoholism; Recreation; Human services; Child development, services; Roman Catholic federated giving programs; Roman Catholic agencies & churches; Religion.
Type of support: General/operating support; Annual campaigns; Building/renovation; Endowments; Program development; Scholarship funds.
Limitations: Giving limited to Oakland County, MI.
Application information: Application form not required.
  Initial approach: Proposal
  Copies of proposal: 2
  Deadline(s): Mar. 1
  Board meeting date(s): Mar.
Trustees: Thomas W. Payne; JPMorgan Chase Bank, N.A.
EIN: 382617770
Selected grants: The following grants were reported in 2003.
$100,000 to Saint Patrick Catholic Church. For general support.
$45,000 to Angels Place, Southfield, MI. For general support.
$25,000 to Archdiocese of Detroit, Detroit, MI. For general support.
$20,000 to Dominican Sisters of Oxford, Oxford, MI. For general support.
$15,000 to Guest House, Lake Orion, MI. For general support.
$10,000 to Camp Sancta Maria Trust, Gaylord, MI. For general support.
$10,000 to Lighthouse of Oakland County, Pontiac, MI. For general support.
$10,000 to Marygrove College, Detroit, MI. For general support.
$10,000 to Saint Joseph Mercy Hospital, Ann Arbor, MI. For emergency center.
$5,000 to Academy of the Sacred Heart, Bloomfield Hills, MI. For after school learning center.

9817
Jerome J. and Dorothy H. Holz Family Foundation ◇
10400 Innovation Dr.
Milwaukee, WI 53226 (414) 774-1031
Contact: Don Tushas, Fdn. Admin.

Established in 2001 in WI.
Foundation type: Independent foundation.
Financial data (yr. ended 8/31/05): Assets, $8,899,243 (M); gifts received, $850,000;

expenditures, $863,007; qualifying distributions, $798,964; giving activities include $771,500 for 22 grants (high: $600,000; low: $500).
Purpose and activities: To give back to the community that supported the founder's business.
Fields of interest: Arts; Higher education; Engineering school/education; Zoos/zoological societies; Children/youth, services; Community development.
Type of support: Continuing support; General/operating support; Capital campaigns; Building/renovation; Equipment; Scholarship funds.
Limitations: Giving primarily in Hales Corners, WI and the surrounding area. No support for political organizations. No grants to individuals, or for fundraisers.
Application information: Application form required.
  Initial approach: Letter or telephone for application
  Copies of proposal: 7
  Deadline(s): May 15th
  Board meeting date(s): May and Aug.
Officers and Trustees:* Jerome J. Holz,* Pres.; Dorothy Holz,* Exec. V.P.; Loraine Schuffler,* V.P.; Barbara Holz Weis,* Secy.; Judith Holz Stathas,* Treas.; J.J. Weis; Traci Weis.
EIN: 367368506
Selected grants: The following grants were reported in 2005.
$600,000 to Wisconsin Masonic Home, Dousman, WI.
$30,000 to Milwaukee School of Engineering, Milwaukee, WI.
$6,000 to Center for Blind and Visually Impaired Children, Milwaukee, WI.
$5,000 to ARC Milwaukee, Wauwatosa, WI.
$2,000 to Marquette University, Milwaukee, WI.
$2,000 to Milwaukee SCORES, Milwaukee, WI.

9818
The Hyde Family Charitable Fund ◇ ☆
c/o James J. Malczweski
491 S. Washburne St., Ste. 100
Oshkosh, WI 54904-6733

Established in 1996 in NY.
Donor: Charles F. Hyde, Jr.
Foundation type: Independent foundation.
Financial data (yr. ended 12/31/05): Assets, $2,278,382 (M); gifts received, $96,700; expenditures, $333,335; qualifying distributions, $325,360; giving activities include $325,360 for 17 grants (high: $250,000; low: $100).
Fields of interest: Museums (art); Performing arts, orchestra (symphony); Education; Housing/shelter, development; Boys & girls clubs; Human services.
Limitations: Applications not accepted. Giving primarily in Buffalo, NY. No grants to individuals.
Application information: Contributes only to pre-selected organizations.
Trustees: Charles F. Hyde, Jr.; Douglas W. Hyde; Joyce W. Hyde; Thomas R. Hyde; Margaret H. Wachtel.
EIN: 161502229

9819
Charles D. Jacobus Family Foundation ◇ ☆
11815 W. Bradley Rd.
Milwaukee, WI 53224 (414) 577-0252
Contact: Missy MacLeod, Pres.

FAX: (414) 359-1357;
E-mail: quickinfo@jacobusenergy.com; Mailing address: P.O. Box 13009, Milwaukee, WI 53213-0009; Additional tel.: 1 (800) JACOBUS ext. 252; URL: http://www.cdjff.org

Established in 1986 in WI.
Donors: Charles D. Jacobus; Eugenia T. Jacobus; Jacobus Co.
Foundation type: Independent foundation.
Financial data (yr. ended 12/31/05): Assets, $5,521,690 (M); expenditures, $432,705; qualifying distributions, $314,871; giving activities include $314,871 for grants.
Purpose and activities: Giving primarily for youth development in the areas of preventive programs, positive youth activities, strengthening families and research; also funding for scholarships to children of employees of Jacobus Investments and Subs.
Fields of interest: Arts; Education, early childhood education; Children/youth, services; Family services; Federated giving programs.
Type of support: Continuing support; Annual campaigns; Capital campaigns; Building/renovation; Program development; Publication; Research; Technical assistance; Program evaluation; Scholarships—to individuals.
Limitations: Giving limited to southeastern WI, with emphasis on Milwaukee. No support for religious organizations. No grants to individuals, or for scholarships (except employee-related), tuition, seminars, fundraisers, travel, legislative or lobbying activities, or for benefits (sponsoring tables, buying auction items, etc.), competitions, parades, or camps.
Application information: Application guidelines and forms available on Web site.
  Initial approach: Letter
  Deadline(s): Apr. 5 (for Special Program Grants pre-application form); May 3 (foundation notifies qualifying organizations); June 1 (site visit sign-up and final application for qualifying organizations); Nov. 1 (for general operating and capital funding)
  Board meeting date(s): Sept. and Nov.
  Final notification: Sept. 29
Officers and Directors:* Missy MacLeod,* Pres.; Eugenia Jacobus,* V.P. and Secy.; Eugene Jacobus,* Treas.; Charles D. Jacobus, Jr.
Number of staff: 1 part-time professional.
EIN: 391559892
Selected grants: The following grants were reported in 2004.
$20,454 to United Way of Greater Milwaukee, Milwaukee, WI.
$15,000 to Childrens Hospital.
$15,000 to Girl Scouts of the U.S.A..
$15,000 to United Migrant Opportunity Services, Milwaukee, WI.
$15,000 to Wisconsin Council on Children and Families, Madison, WI.
$14,000 to Milwaukee Art Museum, Milwaukee, WI. 2 grants: $10,000, $4,000
$10,000 to Alverno College, Milwaukee, WI.
$10,000 to Wisconsin Womens Business Initiative Corporation, Milwaukee, WI.
$5,000 to Donors Forum of Wisconsin, Milwaukee, WI.

9820

Janesville Foundation, Inc.

121 N. Parker Dr.
P.O. Box 8123
Janesville, WI 53547-8123 (608) 752-1032
Contact: Bonnie Lynne Robinson, Pres. and Exec. Dir.

Incorporated in 1944 in WI.
Donor: The Parker Pen Co.
Foundation type: Independent foundation.
Financial data (yr. ended 12/31/05): Assets, $7,771,026 (M); gifts received, $6,476; expenditures, $522,432; qualifying distributions, $461,360; giving activities include $263,655 for 6 grants (high: $118,925; low: $500), $57,749 for 32 grants to individuals (high: $3,500; low: $1,000), and $40,000 for 1 employee matching gift.
Purpose and activities: Primary areas of interest include secondary and elementary education, including scholarships for current graduating Janesville public high school students; emphasis on capital and community development. All giving must impact the Janesville, WI, area.
Fields of interest: Elementary/secondary education; Education; Youth, services; Community development.
Type of support: Capital campaigns; Land acquisition; Program development; Conferences/seminars; Seed money; Scholarships—to individuals; Matching/challenge support.
Limitations: Giving limited to grants that impact the local Janesville, WI, area; scholarships limited to Janesville public high school students. No support for programs that do not impact the local Janesville, WI, area, or for religious or partisan organizations. No grants to individuals (except for scholarships), or for operating budgets or endowment and investment funds, medical research or non-501(c)(3) organizations.
Publications: Informational brochure (including application guidelines).
Application information: Application guidelines available. Application form not required.
Initial approach: Letter of inquiry
Copies of proposal: 2
Deadline(s): No deadlines for funding. Letters of interest are reviewed on an ongoing basis
Board meeting date(s): Varies
Final notification: After board meetings
Officers and Directors:* Alan W. Dunwiddie,* Chair.; Bonnie Lynne Robinson,* Pres. and Exec. Dir.; Roger E. Axtell,* V.P.; Rowland J. McClellan,* V.P.; Dolores M. Dilley, Secy.; Ronald K. Ochs,* Treas.; Dennis L. Hansch.
Number of staff: 1 full-time professional; 2 part-time support.
EIN: 396034645
Selected grants: The following grants were reported in 2004.
$181,075 to Rotary Gardens, Janesville, WI. For capital campaign for Education Center.
$50,000 to Janesville Performing Arts Center, Janesville, WI. For capital campaign for performing arts center.
$10,000 to Janesville School District, Janesville, WI. For planning grant for International Charter School.
$1,300 to Aldo Leopold Nature Center, Monona, WI. For environmental training for Janesville public school teachers.

9821

Jeffris Family Foundation, Ltd. ✧

P.O. Box 650
Janesville, WI 53547-0650 (608) 757-1039
Contact: Thomas M. Jeffris, Pres.

Established in 1977.
Donor: Thomas M. Jeffris.
Foundation type: Independent foundation.
Financial data (yr. ended 12/31/05): Assets, $24,746,658 (M); expenditures, $2,335,252; qualifying distributions, $2,021,289; giving activities include $2,021,289 for 6 grants (high: $1,000,000; low: $5,000).
Purpose and activities: Provides funds for the publishing of books on historic preservation and decorative arts.
Fields of interest: Historic preservation/historical societies; Community development.
Type of support: Building/renovation; Matching/challenge support.
Limitations: Applications not accepted. Giving primarily in WI. No grants to individuals, or for endowments or compensation.
Publications: Informational brochure.
Application information: Contributes only to pre-selected organizations.
Board meeting date(s): Fall
Officers and Directors:* Thomas M. Jeffris,* Pres.; Charles R. Rydberg,* V.P.; Marion M. Schumacher,* Secy.-Treas.; Henry E. Fuldner.
EIN: 391281879

9822

The JKO Foundation Charitable Trust ✧ ☆

c/o Mr. & Mrs. Kenneth Ozinga
1580 Thorofare Rd.
P.O. Box 169
Minocqua, WI 54548

Established in 1999 in IL.
Donors: Kenneth J. Zinga; Judith A. Zinga.
Foundation type: Independent foundation.
Financial data (yr. ended 12/31/05): Assets, $327,132 (M); gifts received, $711,464; expenditures, $783,050; qualifying distributions, $778,000; giving activities include $778,000 for 8 grants (high: $385,000; low: $1,000).
Fields of interest: Elementary/secondary education; Theological school/education; Medical care, community health systems; Christian agencies & churches.
Type of support: General/operating support.
Limitations: Applications not accepted. Giving primarily in IL, MI, WA, and WI. No grants to individuals.
Application information: Contributes only to pre-selected organizations.
Trustees: Charles J. Ozinga; Judith A. Ozinga; Kenneth J. Ozinga.
EIN: 367293190
Selected grants: The following grants were reported in 2004.
$100,000 to Advocate Charitable Foundation, Park Ridge, IL. For unrestricted support.
$100,000 to Christ Church of Oak Brook, Oak Brook, IL. For unrestricted support.
$25,000 to Calvin College, Grand Rapids, MI. For unrestricted support.

9823

Johnson Controls Foundation ▼ ✧

5757 N. Green Bay Ave.
P.O. Box 591
Milwaukee, WI 53201-0591 (414) 524-2296
Contact: Valerie Adisek, Coord.
URL: http://www.johnsoncontrols.com/corpvalues/foundation.htm

Trust established in 1952 in WI.
Donor: Johnson Controls, Inc.
Foundation type: Company-sponsored foundation.
Financial data (yr. ended 12/31/05): Assets, $43,297,836 (M); expenditures, $6,859,004; qualifying distributions, $6,670,094; giving activities include $6,668,394 for 1,225 grants (high: $1,000,000).
Purpose and activities: The foundation supports organizations involved with arts and culture, education, the environment, health, justice and law, safety, human services, civil rights, community development, and civic affairs.
Fields of interest: Media, television; Media, radio; Visual arts; Museums; Performing arts; Literature; Arts; Higher education; Adult/continuing education; Libraries (public); Education; Environment; Hospitals (general); Health care; Crime/law enforcement; Safety, education; Youth, services; Human services, financial counseling; Human services; Civil rights, equal rights; Civil rights; Urban/community development; Community development; Federated giving programs; Public affairs, citizen participation; Public affairs.
Type of support: General/operating support; Continuing support; Annual campaigns; Capital campaigns; Building/renovation; Emergency funds; Seed money; Employee matching gifts; Employee-related scholarships.
Limitations: Giving primarily in areas of company operations. No support for political or lobbying organizations, public or private pre-schools, elementary or secondary schools, sectarian institutions or organizations not of direct benefit to the entire community, foreign-based institutions, fraternal or veterans' organizations, or private foundations. No grants to individuals (except for employee-related scholarships), or for testimonial dinners, fundraising events, tickets to benefits, shows, advertising, travel or tours, seminars or conferences, book or magazine publication, media productions, specific medical or scientific research projects, or endowments; no equipment, product, or labor donations.
Publications: Application guidelines.
Application information: Telephone calls and personal visits are not encouraged. Multi-year funding is not automatic. Additional information may be requested at a later date. Application form not required.
Initial approach: Proposal
Copies of proposal: 1
Deadline(s): None
Board meeting date(s): Usually Mar. and Sept.
Final notification: Up to 120 days
Trustee: U.S. Bank, N.A.
Advisory Board Members: John Barth; Robert Cornog; James H. Keyes; Blaine Rieke; Denise Zutz.
Number of staff: 1 full-time professional.
EIN: 396036639
Selected grants: The following grants were reported in 2005.
$1,000,000 to American Red Cross. For general support.

$696,909 to Holland Rescue Mission, Holland, MI. For general support.

$408,157 to United Way, Plymouth Community, Plymouth, MI. For general support.

$350,000 to United Performing Arts Fund, Milwaukee, WI. For general support.

$225,672 to United Way of Greater Milwaukee, Milwaukee, WI. For general support.

$100,000 to Marquette University, Milwaukee, WI. For general support.

$20,949 to United Way of the Bluegrass, Lexington, KY. For general support.

$20,000 to Cornerstone Schools, Detroit, MI. For general support.

$20,000 to Detroit Symphony Orchestra, Detroit, MI. For general support.

$20,000 to YMCA of Metropolitan Milwaukee, Milwaukee, WI. For general support.

9824

Johnson Family Foundation ✧ ☆

555 Main St., Ste. 500
Racine, WI 53403

Established in 1995 in WI.
Foundation type: Independent foundation.
Financial data (yr. ended 12/31/05): Assets, $14,669,806 (M); gifts received, $10,000,000; expenditures, $725,430; qualifying distributions, $692,000; giving activities include $692,000 for 19 grants (high: $218,000; low: $500).
Fields of interest: Higher education; Education; Youth, services; Christian agencies & churches.
Limitations: Applications not accepted. Giving primarily in Racine, WI. No grants to individuals.
Application information: Contributes only to pre-selected organizations.
Officer: Winifred J. Marquart, Pres.
Trustees: H. Fisk Johnson; Imogene P. Johnson; Helen Johnson-Leipold; S. Curtis Johnson.
EIN: 367092273
Selected grants: The following grants were reported in 2004.
$108,000 to Norfolk Academy, Norfolk, VA. For unrestricted support.
$5,500 to YWCA of Racine, Racine, WI. For unrestricted support.
$5,000 to Latin School of Chicago, Chicago, IL. For unrestricted support.
$5,000 to University of Chicago, Chicago, IL. For unrestricted support.
$4,000 to Mayo Clinic and Foundation, Rochester, MN. For unrestricted support.
$3,000 to Next Generation Now, Racine, WI. For unrestricted support.
$2,500 to Nashville Predators Foundation, Nashville, TN. For unrestricted support.
$2,200 to Racine Area Soccer Association, Racine, WI. For unrestricted support.
$2,000 to Herbert F. Johnson Museum of Art, Ithaca, NY. For unrestricted support.
$2,000 to Virginia Arts Festival, Norfolk, VA. For unrestricted support.

9825

Lester & Frances Johnson Foundation, Inc. ✧

c/o Frances Johnson
6209 Mineral Point Rd., Ste. 805
Madison, WI 53705

Established in 2000 in WI.
Donors: Frances M. Johnson; Lester O. Johnson.
Foundation type: Operating foundation.
Financial data (yr. ended 12/31/04): Assets, $10,922,383 (M); expenditures, $582,151; qualifying distributions, $577,000; giving activities include $577,000 for 22 grants (high: $200,000; low: $1,000).
Purpose and activities: Giving primarily for medical research and health associations, particularly cancer research; funding also for social services, Lutheran churches and Christian organizations.
Fields of interest: Health organizations, association; Medical research, institute; Cancer research; Human services; Christian agencies & churches; Protestant agencies & churches.
Limitations: Applications not accepted. Giving on a national basis, with some emphasis on Madison, WI. No grants to individuals.
Application information: Contributes only to pre-selected organizations.
Officers: Lester O. Johnson, Pres.; Frances M. Johnson, V.P.; Aubrey R. Fowler, Secy.; Michael R. Heald, Treas.
Directors: Robert W. Anderson; Graham L. Johnson; Jeffery L. Kuchenbecker.
EIN: 391988285

9826

SC Johnson Fund, Inc. ▼ ✧

(formerly SC Johnson Wax Fund Inc.)
1525 Howe St.
Racine, WI 53403 (262) 260-4855
Contact: Colleen Cribari, Prog. Admin.
URL: http://www.scjohnson.com/community

Incorporated in 1959 in WI.
Donors: S.C. Johnson & Son, Inc.; JohnsonDiversey, Inc.
Foundation type: Company-sponsored foundation.
Financial data (yr. ended 6/30/05): Assets, $8,087,628 (M); gifts received, $9,614,235; expenditures, $10,215,728; qualifying distributions, $10,186,235; giving activities include $8,423,196 for 75 grants (high: $1,550,000; low: $500), and $1,506,572 for employee matching gifts.
Purpose and activities: The foundation supports organizations involved with arts and culture, education, the environment, human services, community development, and civic affairs.
Fields of interest: Arts; Higher education; Business school/education; Education; Environment; Health care; Human services; Community development; Government/public administration.
Type of support: General/operating support; Annual campaigns; Capital campaigns; Building/renovation; Equipment; Program development; Seed money; Fellowships; Scholarship funds; Employee matching gifts; Employee-related scholarships; Scholarships—to individuals.
Limitations: Giving primarily in Racine, WI. No support for political, religious, social, athletic, veterans', labor, or fraternal organizations, United Way-supported organizations, or national health organizations. No grants to individuals (except for scholarships and fellowships), or for staff or administrative payrolls or national health fund drives.
Publications: Annual report.
Application information: Application form not required.
Initial approach: Proposal

Copies of proposal: 1
Deadline(s): Mar. 1, July 1, and Nov. 1
Board meeting date(s): Feb., June, and Oct.
Final notification: 4 months
Officers and Trustees: * H. Fisk Johnson,* Chair. and Pres.; S. Curtis Johnson,* Vice-Chair. and Pres.; Helen P. Johnson-Leipold,* Vice-Chair.; Jane M. Hutterly, Exec. V.P.; Thomas J. Reigle,* V.P., Secy., and Exec. Dir.; Jeffrey M. Waller,* Treas.; Kim B. Adriano; Gregory F. Clark; J. Gary Raley; William A. Schiller.
Number of staff: 2 full-time professional; 2 part-time professional; 2 part-time support.
EIN: 396052089
Selected grants: The following grants were reported in 2005.
$1,550,000 to Cornell University, Ithaca, NY. For Ornithology Lab and Johnson School of Management.
$1,061,610 to Racine Charter One, Racine, WI. For start-up support.
$1,000,000 to Prairie School, Racine, WI. For construction of new Field House.
$414,740 to Scholarship America, Saint Peter, MN. For Sons and Daughters Scholarship Program.
$330,000 to Sustainable Racine, Racine, WI. For general support.
$293,693 to Downtown Racine Corporation, Racine, WI. For Downtown Refinement Plan.
$250,000 to Conservation International, DC. For unrestricted support.
$175,000 to Nature Conservancy, Wisconsin Chapter, Madison, WI. For marketing campaign.
$165,000 to Racine County Economic Development Corporation, Sturtevant, WI. To develop brand strategy for Racine County.
$100,000 to Opportunities Industrialization Center of Racine County, Racine, WI. For YouthBuild Racine Project II.

9827

Jones Family Foundation ✧ ☆

481 E. Division St., Ste. 800
P.O. Box 1167
Fond du Lac, WI 54936-1167

Established in 1989 in WI.
Donors: Donald Jones; Terri Jones.
Foundation type: Independent foundation.
Financial data (yr. ended 12/31/05): Assets, $127,610 (M); expenditures, $481,302; qualifying distributions, $458,785; giving activities include $452,500 for 3 grants (high: $400,000; low: $2,500).
Fields of interest: Higher education.
Type of support: General/operating support.
Limitations: Applications not accepted. Giving primarily in Fond du Lac, WI. No grants to individuals.
Application information: Contributes only to pre-selected organizations.
Trustees: Donald Jones.
EIN: 396501525

9828

Joy Global Foundation, Inc. ✧

(formerly Harnischfeger Industries Foundation)
P.O. Box 554
Milwaukee, WI 53201-0554
Contact: Sandy McKenzie

Established in 1989 in WI.

Donors: Harnischfeger Industries, Inc.; Joy Global Inc.
Foundation type: Company-sponsored foundation.
Financial data (yr. ended 10/31/05): Assets, $10,618,421 (M); expenditures, $883,552; qualifying distributions, $829,488; giving activities include $829,488 for 105 grants (high: $110,000; low: $500).
Purpose and activities: The foundation supports organizations involved with arts and culture, education, health, medical research, and community development.
Fields of interest: Visual arts; Museums; Performing arts; Arts; Libraries/library science; Education; Health care; Medical research; Community development, neighborhood development; Community development; Government/public administration.
Type of support: General/operating support; Continuing support; Annual campaigns; Program development.
Limitations: Giving primarily in areas of company operations in WI. No grants to individuals.
Publications: Application guidelines.
Application information: Personal visits and telephone calls are not encouraged. Application form not required.
Initial approach: Proposal
Copies of proposal: 1
Board meeting date(s): 2nd Mon. in Dec.
Officers and Directors:* John N. Hanson, Pres.; James A. Chokey,* V.P.; Don Roof, V.P.; Dennis Winkleman, V.P.; Eric Fonstad, Secy.; Ken Stark,* Treas.
EIN: 391659070
Selected grants: The following grants were reported in 2005.
$110,000 to United Performing Arts Fund, Milwaukee, WI.
$65,000 to Milwaukee Womens Center, Milwaukee, WI.
$56,662 to United Way of Greater Milwaukee, Milwaukee, WI.
$50,000 to Milwaukee Symphony Orchestra, Milwaukee, WI.
$45,000 to Boys and Girls Clubs of Greater Milwaukee, Milwaukee, WI.
$30,000 to American Cancer Society, Pewaukee, WI.
$20,000 to Milwaukee Public Museum, Milwaukee, WI.
$20,000 to Milwaukee School of Engineering, Milwaukee, WI.
$7,500 to Latino Community Center, Milwaukee, WI.
$5,000 to Betty Brinn Childrens Museum, Milwaukee, WI.

9829
Halbert & Alice Kadish Foundation ◇
3057 E. Newport Ct.
Milwaukee, WI 53211

Established in 1994 in WI.
Donor: Alice B. Kadish.
Foundation type: Independent foundation.
Financial data (yr. ended 12/31/04): Assets, $5,236,713 (M); expenditures, $998,367; qualifying distributions, $985,889; giving activities include $944,334 for 28 grants (high: $124,875; low: $125).
Purpose and activities: Giving primarily for the arts and community services.

Fields of interest: Arts; Boys & girls clubs; Human services; Community development.
Limitations: Applications not accepted. Giving primarily in WI. No grants to individuals.
Application information: Contributes only to pre-selected organizations.
Officers: Adelbert L. Bertschy, Pres.; Dorothy Bertschy, V.P.; Nancy Lidecker, V.P.; Robert H. Lidecker, V.P.; Paul F. Meissner, Secy.
EIN: 391770402

9830
Kelben Foundation, Inc. ◇
225 E. Mason St., Ste. 800
Milwaukee, WI 53202   (262) 242-4794
Contact: Mary Kellner, Pres.
Additional tels.: Judy Shane (262) 241-4563; Janet Larscheid (262) 241-4086; Patty Schuyler (262) 354-7968; FAX: (262) 242-4760;
E-mail: kellner@ameritech.net

Established in 1983.
Donors: Ted D. Kellner; Jack W. Kellner; Jack F. Kellner†; Fiduciary Management, Inc.
Foundation type: Independent foundation.
Financial data (yr. ended 12/31/05): Assets, $22,335,688 (M); gifts received, $1,597,614; expenditures, $1,249,622; qualifying distributions, $1,190,013; giving activities include $1,123,362 for grants, and $49,000 for grants to individuals.
Purpose and activities: Giving primarily for higher education, including scholarships to graduating seniors from the Milwaukee Public School System, WI, who rank in the top 50 percent of their class and intend to pursue a four-year college degree.
Fields of interest: Higher education; Education; Hospitals (general); Health care.
Type of support: General/operating support; Continuing support; Annual campaigns; Capital campaigns; Building/renovation; Debt reduction; Emergency funds; Program development; Seed money; Curriculum development; Scholarship funds; Scholarships—to individuals.
Limitations: Giving limited to WI. No support for political organizations.
Application information: Application form required.
Initial approach: Letter
Copies of proposal: 1
Deadline(s): Apr. 1 for scholarships
Final notification: May 10
Officers: Mary Kellner, Pres.; Ted D. Kellner, Treas.
Number of staff: 1 part-time professional.
EIN: 391494625
Selected grants: The following grants were reported in 2004.
$1,325,000 to University of Wisconsin Foundation, Madison, WI.
$241,900 to United Way of Greater Milwaukee, Milwaukee, WI.
$130,000 to Next Door Foundation, Milwaukee, WI.
$70,000 to YMCA.
$50,000 to University of Wisconsin Foundation, Milwaukee, WI.
$25,000 to Nehemiah Project, Milwaukee, WI.
$19,000 to Cornerstone Achievement Academy, Milwaukee, WI.
$10,000 to United Way.
$2,000 to Partners Advancing Values in Education (PAVE), Milwaukee, WI.
$400 to Center for the Deaf and Hard of Hearing, Brookfield, WI.

9831
Keller Foundation, Inc. ◇ ☆
3003 W. Breezewood Ln.
P.O. Box 368
Neenah, WI 54957-0368

Established in 1990 in WI.
Donor: J.J. Keller & Associates, Inc.
Foundation type: Company-sponsored foundation.
Financial data (yr. ended 12/31/05): Assets, $3,231,603 (M); gifts received, $9,600; expenditures, $476,250; qualifying distributions, $464,920; giving activities include $464,920 for 93 grants (high: $59,500; low: $25).
Purpose and activities: The foundation supports organizations involved with arts and culture, education, medical research, youth, and religion.
Fields of interest: Arts; Education; Medical research; Boy scouts; American Red Cross; Salvation Army; Youth, services; Philanthropy/voluntarism; Religion.
Type of support: General/operating support.
Limitations: Applications not accepted. No grants to individuals.
Application information: Contributes only to pre-selected organizations.
Directors: Brian Keller; James J. Keller; John J. Keller; Robert L. Keller; Marne Keller-Krikava; Marion Murvine; Ronald Phillips.
EIN: 391683437
Selected grants: The following grants were reported in 2003.
$35,000 to Youthfutures, Appleton, WI.
$10,000 to Wisconsin Motor Carriers Association Foundation, Madison, WI.
$9,500 to University of Wisconsin, Eau Claire, WI.
$9,500 to University of Wisconsin, Whitewater, WI.
$9,500 to University of Wisconsin-Stout, Menomonie, WI.
$7,500 to Murray State University Foundation, Murray, KY.
$7,000 to Marquette University, Milwaukee, WI.
$7,000 to University of Wisconsin, Stevens Point, WI.
$7,000 to University of Wisconsin, Superior, WI.
$7,000 to University of Wisconsin-Platteville Foundation, Platteville, WI.

9832
The Kellogg Family Foundation, Inc. ◇
c/o Godfrey & Kahn
780 N. Water St.
Milwaukee, WI 53202

Established in 1993 in WI.
Donor: William S. Kellogg.
Foundation type: Independent foundation.
Financial data (yr. ended 12/31/04): Assets, $23,590,874 (M); expenditures, $3,193,303; qualifying distributions, $7,712,806; giving activities include $1,364,000 for 10 grants (high: $1,000,000; low: $7,000), and $5,291,527 for 2 loans/program-related investments.
Purpose and activities: Giving primarily for human services, especially to a center for people who are deaf and hard of hearing, as well as for health associations, particularly for juvenile diabetes; funding also for children and youth services, a Lutheran church, and the United Way.
Fields of interest: Health organizations, association; Diabetes research; Human services; Children/youth, services; Federated giving

programs; Protestant agencies & churches; Deaf/hearing impaired.

Type of support: Program-related investments/loans.

Limitations: Applications not accepted. Giving primarily in Milwaukee, WI. No grants to individuals.

Application information: Contributes only to pre-selected organizations.

Officers and Directors:* William S. Kellogg,* Pres. and Treas.; Madeleine Kellogg,* V.P. and Secy.; Peter M. Sommerhauser.

EIN: 391775567

9833

Kenosha Community Foundation ✧

600 52nd St., Ste. 110
Kenosha, WI 53140 (262) 654-2412
Contact: Peter Walcott, Exec. Dir.
FAX: (262) 654-2615;
E-mail: email@kenoshafoundation.org; Additional
E-mail: pwalcott@kenoshafoundation.org;
URL: http://www.kenoshafoundation.org

Established in 1926 in WI.
Foundation type: Community foundation.
Financial data (yr. ended 12/31/04): Assets, $3,266,715 (M); gifts received, $915,090; expenditures, $955,274; giving activities include $731,554 for grants.
Purpose and activities: The foundation seeks to provide philanthropic leadership to address the changing needs of the people of Greater Kenosha in order to enhance their quality of life. The foundation is structured to receive charitable gifts of any size to advance civic, cultural, educational, health, and welfare causes.
Fields of interest: Historic preservation/historical societies; Arts; Education; Environment; Health care; Human services; Public affairs.
Type of support: General/operating support; Seed money; Scholarship funds; Matching/challenge support.
Limitations: Giving primarily in Kenosha County, WI. No support for sectarian religious programs. No grants to individuals (except for scholarships), or for endowment funds, annual campaigns, debt retirement, or emergency funding.
Publications: Application guidelines; Annual report; Grants list; Informational brochure.
Application information: Visit foundation Web site for application form and guidelines. Application form required.
Initial approach: Telephone or letter of intent
Copies of proposal: 12
Deadline(s): Mar. 24
Board meeting date(s): Quarterly
Officers and Directors:* Alan R. Schaefer,* Pres.; Kenneth L. Fellman,* V.P.; Victor N. Weiler,* Secy.-Treas.; Peter Walcott, Exec. Dir.; Constance M. Ferwerda, Grants Co-Chair.; Neil F. Guttormsen, Grants Co-Chair.; Cathryn S. Bothe; Howard J. Brown; Elynor Chemerow; Jack S. Harris.
Board of Advisors: Mary Frost Ashley; George R. Connolly; Robert A. Cornog; Mary P. Enroth; Jerold P. Franke; A. Allan Jankus; Samuel Seavitte; James D. Seymour; Gene F. Soens; Ralph J. Tenuta.
Number of staff: 1 full-time professional; 1 part-time support.
EIN: 396045289

9834

The Kern Family Foundation, Inc. ▼

W305 S4239 Brookhill Rd.
Waukesha, WI 53189
Contact: Robert Tweed, Exec. Dir.
E-mail: rtweed@centurytel.net

Established in 1998 in WI.
Donors: Robert D. Kern; Patricia E. Kern.
Foundation type: Independent foundation.
Financial data (yr. ended 12/3/05): Assets, $75,965,599 (M); gifts received, $27,515,345; expenditures, $10,004,677; qualifying distributions, $9,790,996; giving activities include $8,194,090 for 107 grants.
Purpose and activities: The foundation's purpose is to seek to enhance and encourage religious values, family and community competitive educational structures, and moral and ethical values in society. The foundation supports the promotion of religious values in religious ministry and promotes the study and enhancement of competitive educational structures in the U.S.
Fields of interest: Youth development; Protestant agencies & churches.
Type of support: Program development; Scholarship funds.
Limitations: Giving primarily in the Midwest. No support for individual public or private K-12 schools. No grants to individuals, or for endowments, indirect costs as part of the grant request, debt reduction, or annual fund drives for sustaining support.
Publications: Application guidelines.
Application information: Contact the foundation for application form and guidelines. Limited unsolicited applications. Application form not required.
Initial approach: 1-2 page letter
Deadline(s): None
Board meeting date(s): Jan., Apr., July, and Oct.
Officers: Patricia E. Kern, Pres.; Robert D. Kern, V.P.; Richard Van Deuten, Secy.; Michael Senske, C.F.O.; Robert Tweed, Exec. Dir.
Number of staff: 4 full-time professional; 1 full-time support.
EIN: 391923558
Selected grants: The following grants were reported in 2004.
$800,000 to Green Lake Conference Center, Green Lake, WI. 2 grants: $200,000 (For general operating support), $600,000 (For capital campaign).
$100,000 to Leadership, Education and Development (LEAD) Program in Business, New York, NY. For general support.

9835

The Virginia W. Kettering Foundation ✧ ☆

c/o JPMorgan Chase Bank, N.A.
P.O. Box 1308
Milwaukee, WI 53201
Application address: c/o JPMorgan Chase Bank, N.A., P.O. Box 1103, Dayton, OH 45401

Established in 2003 in OH.
Donor: Virginia W. Kettering‡.
Foundation type: Independent foundation.
Financial data (yr. ended 4/30/05): Assets, $6,799,741 (M); gifts received, $1,000,286; expenditures, $468,949; qualifying distributions, $432,706; giving activities include $422,482 for 29 grants (high: $50,000; low: $2,000).
Fields of interest: Performing arts, theater; Performing arts, orchestra (symphony); Performing

---

arts, opera; Arts; Reproductive health, family planning; AIDS; Big Brothers/Big Sisters; Human services; American Red Cross; YM/YWCAs & YM/YWHAs; Women, centers/services.
Limitations: Giving primarily in Dayton, OH.
Application information:
Initial approach: Proposal
Deadline(s): None
Trustee: JPMorgan Chase Bank, N.A.
EIN: 316570701

9836

Kikkoman Foods Foundation, Inc. ✧

P.O. Box 69
Walworth, WI 53184 (262) 275-6181
Contact: Robert V. Conover, Dir.

Established in 1993 in WI.
Donor: Kikkoman Foods, Inc.
Foundation type: Company-sponsored foundation.
Financial data (yr. ended 12/31/05): Assets, $8,013,570 (M); gifts received, $500,000; expenditures, $440,225; qualifying distributions, $423,084; giving activities include $423,004 for 75 grants (high: $100,000; low: $349).
Purpose and activities: The foundation supports organizations involved with arts and culture, education, disaster relief, human services, and intergroup and race relations.
Fields of interest: Performing arts; Arts; Higher education; Education; Disasters, preparedness/services; Human services; Civil rights, race/intergroup relations.
Type of support: General/operating support; Annual campaigns; Scholarship funds; Sponsorships.
Limitations: Giving primarily in WI. No support for private organizations, political organizations, religious or sectarian organizations, or discriminatory organizations. No grants to individuals, or for raffle tickets or product purchases, non-food-related scientific or development research, travel or lodging, or promotional events.
Application information: Application form not required.
Initial approach: Proposal
Deadline(s): None
Board meeting date(s): Monthly
Directors: Robert V. Conover; Kuniki Hatayama; Masaaki Hirose; Karl N. Keane; Daniel P. Miller; Yuzaburo Mogi; Milton E. Neshek; Yoshiyuki Nogi; Mitsuo Someya; Shigeomi Ushijima.
EIN: 391763633

9837

Herbert H. Kohl Charities, Inc. ✧

825 N. Jefferson St., Ste. 350
Milwaukee, WI 53202

Established in 1977 in WI.
Donors: Herbert H. Kohl; Mary Kohl.
Foundation type: Independent foundation.
Financial data (yr. ended 6/30/05): Assets, $8,047,853 (M); expenditures, $891,477; qualifying distributions, $873,110; giving activities include $870,716 for 765 grants (high: $200,000; low: $100).
Purpose and activities: Giving primarily for higher and other education, health associations, children, youth and social services, arts and culture, federated giving programs, and community

development; some funding also for Christian organizations and churches, and Jewish organizations.

Fields of interest: Museums (art); Arts; Higher education; Education; Health organizations, association; Medical research, institute; Boys & girls clubs; Human services; Children/youth, services; Community development; Federated giving programs; Christian agencies & churches; Jewish agencies & temples.

Limitations: Applications not accepted. Giving primarily in WI, with strong emphasis on Milwaukee. No grants to individuals.

Application information: Contributes only to pre-selected organizations.

Officers and Directors:* Herbert H. Kohl,* Pres.; Allen D. Kohl,* V.P.; Sidney A. Kohl,* Secy.; Dolores K. Kohl,* Treas.

EIN: 391300476

Selected grants: The following grants were reported in 2005.

$200,000 to Marquette University, Milwaukee, WI.

$64,958 to United Way of Greater Milwaukee, Milwaukee, WI.

$50,000 to Milwaukee Art Museum, Milwaukee, WI.

$50,000 to Safe and Sound, Milwaukee, WI.

$48,208 to Midwest Athletes Against Childhood Cancer, Milwaukee, WI.

$40,000 to Naismith Memorial Basketball Hall of Fame, Springfield, MA.

$750 to United Way, Oshkosh Area, Oshkosh, WI.

$300 to Rock County Historical Society, Janesville, WI.

$300 to Wisconsin Academic Decathlon Foundation, Green Bay, WI.

$250 to Center Against Sexual and Domestic Abuse, Superior, WI.

9838
Herb Kohl Educational Foundation ◇
825 N. Jefferson St.
Milwaukee, WI 53202
URL: http://www.kohleducation.org
Scholarship address: c/o Greg Doyle, Wisconsin Dept. of Public Instruction, P.O. Box 7841, Madison, WI 53707-7841, tel.: (608) 266-1098, E-mail: greg.doyle@dpi.state.wi.us

Established in 1989 in WI.

Donors: Herbert H. Kohl; Herbert H. Kohl Charities, Inc.

Foundation type: Independent foundation.

Financial data (yr. ended 12/31/05): Assets, $2,372,487 (M); expenditures, $634,431; qualifying distributions, $608,071; giving activities include $305,000 for 107 grants (high: $100,000; low: $1,000), and $287,000 for 287 grants to individuals (high: $1,000; low: $1,000).

Purpose and activities: Awards scholarships to graduating seniors of public and private WI high schools; also awards fellowships for teachers of public and private WI schools. Giving also for elementary and secondary education.

Fields of interest: Elementary school/education; Secondary school/education.

Type of support: General/operating support; Grants to individuals; Scholarships—to individuals.

Limitations: Giving primarily in WI.

Application information: Teaching awards by nomination. Application form required.

Deadline(s): Feb. 1 for scholarships and teaching awards

Officers and Directors:* Herbert H. Kohl,* Pres.; Allen D. Kohl,* V.P.; Sidney A. Kohl,* Secy.; Dolores Kohl.

EIN: 391661743

9839
Charlotte & Walter Kohler Charitable Trust
P.O. Box 1065
Sheboygan, WI 53082-1065
Contact: Roberta Childs, Grants Off.

Established in 1995 in WI.

Donor: Charlotte M. Kohler‡.

Foundation type: Independent foundation.

Financial data (yr. ended 12/31/04): Assets, $6,140,719 (M); expenditures, $1,470,626; qualifying distributions, $1,425,464; giving activities include $1,382,144 for 12 grants (high: $300,000; low: $20,000).

Fields of interest: Public policy, research.

Type of support: Income development; Capital campaigns; Equipment; Endowments; Program development; Conferences/seminars; Professorships; Research; Matching/challenge support.

Limitations: Applications not accepted. Giving on a national basis with an emphasis on WI. No support for projects financed partially by public tax funds or programs involving worship. No grants to individuals or for operating support.

Application information: Unsolicited requests for funds not accepted.

Board meeting date(s): May and Oct.

Trustees: Michael W. Grebe; Roland M. Neumann, Jr.; Wells Fargo Bank, N.A.

EIN: 391834766

9840
Kohler Foundation, Inc. ◇
725 Woodlake Rd., Ste. X
Kohler, WI 53044 (920) 458-1972
Contact: Terri Yoho, Exec. Dir.
FAX: (920) 458-4280;
E-mail: terri.yoho@kohler.com; URL: http://www.kohlerfoundation.org

Incorporated in 1940 in WI.

Donors: Herbert V. Kohler‡; Marie C. Kohler‡; Evangeline Kohler‡; Lillie B. Kohler‡; O.A. Kroos‡.

Foundation type: Independent foundation.

Financial data (yr. ended 12/31/04): Assets, $182,352,508 (M); expenditures, $8,044,875; qualifying distributions, $7,997,717; giving activities include $195,134 for 34 grants (high: $44,000; low: $500; average: $1,000–$5,000), $210,793 for 90 grants to individuals (high: $7,500; low: $250; average: $1,250–$6,250), and $6,191,477 for 19 in-kind gifts.

Purpose and activities: Supports education and the arts in WI. Annual program funds provide scholarships for students graduating from Sheboygan County high schools. All scholarship recipients are chosen by their schools. The Distinguished Guest Series, a performing arts series, is presented as a cultural benefit to the community.

Fields of interest: Visual arts; Performing arts; Arts; Higher education; Education.

Type of support: Scholarships—to individuals; Capital campaigns; Building/renovation; Equipment; Endowments; Program development;

Conferences/seminars; Publication; Seed money; Scholarship funds; Matching/challenge support.

Limitations: Giving limited to WI. No support for health care or medical programs. No grants to individuals (except for scholarships), or for operating budgets or annual fundraising drives; no loans.

Application information: Application guidelines available upon request. Application form not required.

Initial approach: Letter

Copies of proposal: 1

Deadline(s): Submit proposal preferably between Jan. and Apr., or June. and Oct. Deadlines May 1 and Nov. 1

Board meeting date(s): June, Dec. and as required

Final notification: 1 week after contributions meetings

Officers and Directors:* Ruth DeYoung Kohler II,* C.O.O. and Pres.; Jeffrey P. Cheney,* V.P. and Treas.; Natalie A. Black,* V.P.; Paul H. Ten Pas,* Secy.; Terri Yoho, Exec. Dir.; Tryg Jacobson.

Number of staff: 1 full-time professional; 5 part-time professional; 1 full-time support.

EIN: 390810536

9841
Krause Family Foundation
(formerly Charles A. Krause Foundation)
c/o Krause Consultants, Ltd.
700 N. Water St., Ste. 1246
Milwaukee, WI 53202-4206
Contact: Charles A. Krause III, Secy.-Treas.

Incorporated in 1952 in WI.

Foundation type: Independent foundation.

Financial data (yr. ended 12/31/05): Assets, $6,683,354 (M); expenditures, $419,156; qualifying distributions, $334,538; giving activities include $321,500 for 59 grants (high: $50,000; low: $500), and $13,037 for 30 employee matching gifts.

Fields of interest: Museums; Arts; Secondary school/education; Higher education; Education; Environment, natural resources.

Type of support: General/operating support; Continuing support; Annual campaigns; Capital campaigns; Building/renovation; Endowments.

Limitations: Giving limited to southeastern WI. No grants to individuals, or for medical research.

Application information: Employee-related scholarship program has been discontinued. Previous commitments honored; no new awards to individuals. Application form not required.

Initial approach: Letter

Copies of proposal: 1

Deadline(s): Nov. 15

Board meeting date(s): Mid-Dec.

Officers and Directors:* Carol Krause Wythes,* Pres.; Charles A. Krause III,* Secy.-Treas.; Victoria K. Mayer.

EIN: 396044820

Selected grants: The following grants were reported in 2005.

$20,000 to Milwaukee Public Museum, Milwaukee, WI.

$18,000 to International Crane Foundation, Baraboo, WI.

$15,000 to Salvation Army.

$10,000 to Zoological Society of Milwaukee County, Milwaukee, WI.

$6,000 to Boys and Girls Club.

$5,000 to Partners Advancing Values in Education (PAVE), Milwaukee, WI.

$4,000 to Neighborhood House of Milwaukee, Milwaukee, WI.
$3,000 to Our Next Generation, Milwaukee, WI.
$3,000 to Skylight Opera Theater, Milwaukee, WI.
$2,000 to Medical College of Wisconsin, Milwaukee, WI.

9842
Krause Foundation, Inc. ◇
P.O. Box 335
Iola, WI 54945
Application address: c/o Patricia Klug, 175 Pine St., Iola, WI 54945, tel.: (715) 445-2338

Established in 1987 in WI.
Donors: Krause Publications, Inc.; Chester L. Krause.
Foundation type: Independent foundation.
Financial data (yr. ended 12/31/04): Assets, $1,674,331 (M); gifts received, $250,000; expenditures, $397,972; qualifying distributions, $397,972; giving activities include $391,850 for 28 grants (high: $250,000; low: $250), and $6,000 for 6 grants to individuals (high: $1,000; low: $1,000).
Purpose and activities: Funding primarily for youth programs, scholarships, and various health and community services agencies.
Fields of interest: Media, television; Arts; Health organizations, association; Human services; Children/youth, services; Community development.
Type of support: General/operating support; Annual campaigns; Capital campaigns; Building/renovation; Emergency funds; Research; Employee-related scholarships; Scholarships—to individuals; In-kind gifts.
Limitations: Giving primarily in central WI.
Application information:
Initial approach: Letter
Deadline(s): None
Board meeting date(s): Quarterly
Officers: Chester L. Krause, Pres.; Patricia Klug, V.P.; Patricia Krause, V.P.; Bruce J. Meagher, Secy.-Treas.
EIN: 391571437

9843
Helen and Rudy Krejci Trust ◇ ☆
1905 Hollister Ave.
Tomah, WI 54660
Contact: Robert Steele, Tr.

Foundation type: Independent foundation.
Financial data (yr. ended 12/31/05): Assets, $27,679 (M); expenditures, $564,416; qualifying distributions, $554,500; giving activities include $542,500 for 19 grants (high: $70,000; low: $2,000), and $12,000 for 27 grants to individuals (high: $500; low: $350).
Purpose and activities: Scholarship awards to students attending a 2- or 4-year college on a full time basis.
Fields of interest: Historic preservation/historical societies; Libraries (public); Education; Environment; Boys & girls clubs.
Type of support: General/operating support; Scholarships—to individuals.
Limitations: Giving limited to Monroe County, WI.
Application information: Application form required.
Deadline(s): Feb. 26

Trustees: Harold Gehrke; Leone Gehrke; Kevin McCoy; Arlys Steele; Robert Steele.
EIN: 396643512

9844
The George Kress Foundation, Inc.
c/o Green Bay Packaging
P.O. Box 19017
Green Bay, WI 54307
Application address: John F. Kress c/o Green Bay Packaging Co., 1700 N. Webster Ave., Green Bay, WI 54301

Incorporated in 1953 in WI.
Donor: Green Bay Packaging, Inc.
Foundation type: Independent foundation.
Financial data (yr. ended 12/31/05): Assets, $7,792,218 (M); gifts received, $4,000,125; expenditures, $1,836,139; qualifying distributions, $1,800,816; giving activities include $1,800,816 for grants.
Purpose and activities: Giving primarily to federated giving programs, libraries, Christian agencies and churches, and higher education; funding also for arts and culture, historical preservation, hospitals, health associations, recreation, particularly local sporting events, children and youth services, social and family services, community development, and the United Way.
Fields of interest: Historic preservation/historical societies; Arts; Higher education; Libraries (public); Education; Hospitals (general); Health organizations, association; Recreation; Boys & girls clubs; Human services; YM/YWCAs & YM/YWHAs; Children/youth, services; Family services; Community development; Federated giving programs; Christian agencies & churches.
Type of support: Continuing support; Annual campaigns; Capital campaigns; Building/renovation; Program development; Professorships; Scholarship funds; Research.
Limitations: Giving primarily in Green Bay and Madison, WI.
Application information: Application form not required.
Initial approach: Letter
Copies of proposal: 1
Deadline(s): None
Officers: James F. Kress, V.P.; John F. Kress, Secy.
Trustee: Associated Banc-Corp.
Number of staff: 1 full-time professional; 1 part-time support.
EIN: 396050768

9845
La Crosse Community Foundation
(formerly La Crosse Foundation)
300 2nd St. N., Ste. 320
La Crosse, WI 54601
Contact: Sheila Garrity, Exec. Dir.
E-mail: lacrosscommfound@centurytel.net;
URL: http://www.laxcommfoundation.com

Established in 1930 in WI.
Foundation type: Community foundation.
Financial data (yr. ended 12/31/05): Assets, $23,827,733 (M); gifts received, $625,554; expenditures, $1,216,456; giving activities include $859,555 for grants.
Purpose and activities: The purpose of the foundation is to enrich the quality of life in the

greater La Crosse area by: 1) attracting charitable gifts promoting community philanthropy; 2) serving as a steward for entrusted funds and using these precious resources wisely and efficiently; 3) supporting programs and activities of economic, educational, social and cultural nonprofit organizations; 4) providing leadership by serving as a convenor/catalyst in identifying problems and opportunities and shaping effective responses to them; and 5) being a community resource and providing services to donors, nonprofit agencies and the community-at-large.
Fields of interest: Arts; Higher education; Children/youth, services; Family services; Human services; Government/public administration.
Type of support: General/operating support; Continuing support; Capital campaigns; Program development; Seed money; Curriculum development; Scholarship funds; Scholarships—to individuals; Matching/challenge support.
Limitations: Giving primarily in La Crosse County, WI, and surrounding area. No support for sectarian or religious purposes. No grants to individuals (except for scholarships), or for operating expenses of well-established organizations, deficit financing, endowment funds, travel, land acquisition, consulting services, or technical assistance; no loans.
Publications: Annual report (including application guidelines).
Application information: Visit foundation Web site for application information; contact foundation for initial application form and guidelines. Proposals are reviewed in cycles according to quarterly focus. Application form required.
Initial approach: Letter
Copies of proposal: 15
Deadline(s): Submit proposal by the 15th of Jan., Apr., July, and Oct.
Board meeting date(s): Feb., May, Aug., and Nov.
Final notification: Within 1 month of committee meetings
Officers and Directors: * Brad Sturm,* Chair.; Roger Le Grand,* Vice-Chair.; Sue Durtsche,* Secy. and Chair., Community Needs Comm.; Sheila Garrity, Exec. Dir.; David Morrison, C.P.A.*, Chair., Investment Comm.; Sue Christopherson; Pauline Jackson, M.D.; Duane Ring, Jr.; Chip Schilling; Richard Swantz; John Wabaunsee; John Wettstein.
Trustee: North Central Trust Co.
Number of staff: 1 full-time professional; 1 full-time support.
EIN: 396037996

9846
Ladish Company Foundation ◇
P.O. Box 8902
Cudahy, WI 53110-8902
Contact: Ronald O. Wiese, Tr.

Established in 1952 in WI.
Donor: Ladish Co., Inc.
Foundation type: Company-sponsored foundation.
Financial data (yr. ended 11/30/05): Assets, $28,795,564 (M); expenditures, $1,493,200; qualifying distributions, $1,483,600; giving activities include $1,480,000 for 127 grants (high: $300,000; low: $500).
Purpose and activities: The foundation supports organizations involved with arts and culture, education, health, youth development, human services, community development, and Catholicism.

Fields of interest: Arts; Higher education; Education; Hospitals (general); Health care; Youth development; Children/youth, services; Human services; Community development; Federated giving programs; Roman Catholic agencies & churches.
Type of support: General/operating support; Annual campaigns; Capital campaigns; Endowments; Scholarship funds; Research.
Limitations: Applications not accepted. Giving primarily in WI. No grants to individuals.
Application information: Contributes only to pre-selected organizations.
 Board meeting date(s): Oct.
Trustees: Wayne E. Larsen; Ronald O. Wiese; Kerry Woody.
EIN: 396040489
Selected grants: The following grants were reported in 2004.
$221,000 to Wisconsin Foundation for Independent Colleges and Universities, Milwaukee, WI. 2 grants: $21,000 (For general support for 21 Club), $200,000 (For scholarships).
$50,000 to Saint Marcus Lutheran School, Milwaukee, WI. For capital campaign.
$50,000 to United Way of Greater Milwaukee, Milwaukee, WI. For general support.
$50,000 to YMCA of Metropolitan Milwaukee, South Shore, Cudahy, WI. For capital campaign.
$25,000 to Childrens Hospital of Wisconsin, Milwaukee, WI. For general support.
$25,000 to Hunger Task Force of Milwaukee, Milwaukee, WI. For emergency food pantries.
$20,000 to Center for Deaf-Blind Persons, Milwaukee, WI. For Communication Access Program.
$20,000 to Milwaukee School of Engineering, Milwaukee, WI. For scholarships.
$15,000 to Americas Second Harvest of Wisconsin, Milwaukee, WI. For Food for the Hungry.

9847
Herman W. Ladish Family Foundation, Inc. ✧
13255 W. Bluemound Rd., Ste. 201A
Brookfield, WI 53005 (262) 780-9640
Contact: William J. Ladish, Pres.

Incorporated in 1956 in WI.
Donor: Herman W. Ladish†.
Foundation type: Independent foundation.
Financial data (yr. ended 6/30/05): Assets, $11,348,353 (M); expenditures, $835,617; qualifying distributions, $788,141; giving activities include $706,000 for 44 grants (high: $200,000; low: $1,000).
Purpose and activities: Giving primarily for education, with emphasis on Roman Catholic schools, health care, and the arts.
Fields of interest: Arts; Elementary/secondary education; Higher education; Education; Hospitals (general); Health care; Health organizations, association; Roman Catholic agencies & churches.
Limitations: Giving primarily in WI, with strong emphasis on Milwaukee. No grants to individuals.
Application information: Application form not required.
 Deadline(s): None
 Board meeting date(s): 2 times per year
Officers and Directors:* William J. Ladish,* Pres.; Laura L. Jacobson,* V.P.; Robert T. Stollenwerk,* Secy.-Treas.; Margaret L. Exner; Mary L. Selander.
EIN: 396063602

Selected grants: The following grants were reported in 2005.
$55,000 to Medical College of Wisconsin, Milwaukee, WI.
$30,000 to Froedtert Memorial Lutheran Hospital, Milwaukee, WI.
$30,000 to Lyric Opera of Chicago, Chicago, IL.
$20,000 to Cardinal Stritch University, Milwaukee, WI.
$15,000 to Chicago Historical Society, Chicago, IL.
$10,000 to Elmbrook Memorial Hospital, Brookfield, WI.
$10,000 to Old Saint Patricks Church, Chicago, IL.
$10,000 to Saint John Vianney Parish, Janesville, WI.
$10,000 to University of Miami, Miami, FL.
$10,000 to Waukesha Memorial Hospital, Waukesha, WI.

9848
The Lakeview Foundation, Inc.
P.O. Box 253
Thiensville, WI 53092-2053
Contact: William H. Foshag, Dir.

Established in 1996 in WI.
Foundation type: Independent foundation.
Financial data (yr. ended 7/31/05): Assets, $12,108,534 (M); expenditures, $796,982; qualifying distributions, $632,000; giving activities include $632,000 for 8 grants (high: $200,000; low: $17,000).
Purpose and activities: Giving primarily for programs benefiting youth in the inner city of Milwaukee, WI.
Fields of interest: Education; Boys & girls clubs.
Type of support: Equipment; Curriculum development; Capital campaigns; Building/renovation.
Limitations: Applications not accepted. Giving primarily in the inner city of Milwaukee, WI. No grants to individuals.
Application information: Unsolicited requests for funds not accepted.
 Board meeting date(s): Quarterly
Officers and Directors:* William J. Haese,* Pres.; John H. Woodin,* V.P.; Charles J. Osborn,* Secy.; David A. Grant,* Treas.; Fred J. Bartkowski; Robert H. Brogan; William H. Foshag; Robert R. Magliocco; Ron Perri; E. Thomas Sheahan; Vernon H. Swanson.
EIN: 391857646
Selected grants: The following grants were reported in 2004.
$240,000 to Nativity Jesuit Middle School, Milwaukee, WI. 2 grants: $40,000 to Central City Teaching (For general support), $200,000 (For general support).
$100,000 to Notre Dame Middle School, Milwaukee, WI. For general support.
$75,000 to Messmer High School, Milwaukee, WI. For general support.
$41,000 to Saint Joan Antida High School, Milwaukee, WI. For general support.
$25,000 to Boys and Girls Clubs of Greater Milwaukee, Milwaukee, WI. For general support.
$25,000 to Midwestern University, Downers Grove, IL. For general support.
$17,000 to Milwaukee Childrens Choir, Wauwatosa, WI. For general support.

9849
Louise Briley Leake Charitable Trust ✧ ☆
c/o JPMorgan Chase Bank, N.A.
P.O. Box 1308
Milwaukee, WI 53201

Established in 1996 in ID.
Donor: Louise Briley Leake†.
Foundation type: Independent foundation.
Financial data (yr. ended 12/31/05): Assets, $519,587 (M); expenditures, $655,151; qualifying distributions, $647,621; giving activities include $646,021 for 2 grants (high: $622,988; low: $23,033).
Purpose and activities: Giving primarily to children's services and religious organizations.
Fields of interest: Children/youth, services; Residential/custodial care; Protestant agencies & churches.
Limitations: Applications not accepted. Giving limited to LA. No grants to individuals.
Application information: Contributes only to pre-selected organizations.
Trustee: JPMorgan Chase Bank, N.A.
EIN: 726166273

9850
Phoebe R. & John D. Lewis Foundation ✧
9729 N. Lake Dr.
Milwaukee, WI 53217
Contact: John D. Lewis, Treas.

Established in 1995 in WI and OH.
Donors: Phoebe R. Lewis; John D. Lewis.
Foundation type: Independent foundation.
Financial data (yr. ended 12/31/04): Assets, $9,728,093 (M); expenditures, $490,145; qualifying distributions, $413,240; giving activities include $411,750 for 69 grants (high: $80,000; low: $500).
Fields of interest: Arts, formal/general education; Museums; Higher education; Higher education, college; Higher education, university; Federated giving programs.
Type of support: Building/renovation; Professorships; Curriculum development.
Limitations: Applications not accepted. Giving on a national basis, with some emphasis on WI. No grants to individuals.
Application information: Contributes only to pre-selected organizations.
 Board meeting date(s): Varies
Officers: Phoebe R. Lewis, Pres.; Graham D. Lewis, V.P.; Thelka Metz, Secy.; John D. Lewis, Treas.
EIN: 311401478

9851
The Lubar Family Foundation, Inc. ✧
700 N. Water St.
Milwaukee, WI 53202-4206

Established in 1968 in WI.
Donor: Members of the Lubar family.
Foundation type: Independent foundation.
Financial data (yr. ended 12/31/05): Assets, $15,715,996 (M); gifts received, $782,524; expenditures, $2,029,884; qualifying distributions, $2,019,159; giving activities include $2,019,159 for 88 grants (high: $823,900; low: $25).
Fields of interest: Performing arts; Arts; Higher education; Health care; Human services; Family

services; Jewish federated giving programs; Jewish agencies & temples.

Type of support: Capital campaigns; Endowments.
Limitations: Applications not accepted. Giving primarily in WI. No grants to individuals.
Application information: Contributes only to pre-selected organizations.
Officers: Sheldon B. Lubar, Chair.; Marianne S. Lubar, Pres.; Mary Beth Wisniewski, Treas.
Director: David J. Lubar.
EIN: 391098690
Selected grants: The following grants were reported in 2003.

$99,400 to United Way of Greater Milwaukee, Milwaukee, WI. For unrestricted support.

$80,550 to Milwaukee Public Museum, Milwaukee, WI. For unrestricted support.

$72,689 to Florentine Opera Company, Milwaukee, WI. For unrestricted support.

$50,000 to Minneapolis Federation for Jewish Service, Minnetonka, MN. For unrestricted support.

$37,500 to Milwaukee Jewish Day School, Milwaukee, WI. For unrestricted support.

$25,300 to Milwaukee Art Museum, Milwaukee, WI. For unrestricted support.

$25,000 to Shalom Hartman Institute of Judaic Studies, Jerusalem, Israel. For unrestricted support.

$25,000 to University of Wisconsin Foundation, Madison, WI. For Lubar Scholarships.

$16,735 to Congregation Sinai, Milwaukee, WI. For unrestricted support.

$12,860 to Temple Israel. For unrestricted support.

9852
Lunda Charitable Trust
620 Gebhardt Rd.
Black River Falls, WI   54615-0669
Contact: Carl Holmquist, Tr.

Established in 1988 in WI.
Donor: Milton Lunda.
Foundation type: Independent foundation.
Financial data (yr. ended 12/31/05): Assets, $17,242,474 (M); gifts received, $300,000; expenditures, $749,194; qualifying distributions, $671,014; giving activities include $644,756 for 68 grants (high: $100,000; low: $350).
Purpose and activities: Giving primarily for community services. Funding priority will be given to perpetuating existing Lunda family endeavors (Lunda Theater, Lunda Park, and Lunda Center).
Fields of interest: Arts; Education; Health care; Recreation.
Type of support: Capital campaigns; Building/renovation; Equipment; Land acquisition; Seed money; Scholarship funds; Matching/challenge support.
Limitations: Giving primarily in Jackson County, WI. No grants to individuals.
Publications: Financial statement.
Application information: Application form required.
  Initial approach: Letter
  Copies of proposal: 1
  Deadline(s): Applications accepted July 1 through July 31
  Board meeting date(s): Varies
  Final notification: 3 months
Trustees: Carl Holmquist; Larry Lunda; Lydia Lunda; Milton Lunda; Marlee Slifka; Mary van Gorden; Bill Waughtal.

Number of staff: 2 part-time professional; 1 part-time support.
EIN: 396491037

9853
Charles J. Lynn Trust ◇
c/o JPMorgan Chase Bank, N.A.
P.O. Box 1308
Milwaukee, WI   53201

Established in IN.
Foundation type: Independent foundation.
Financial data (yr. ended 12/31/05): Assets, $59,393,699 (M); expenditures, $1,543,958; qualifying distributions, $1,342,993; giving activities include $1,275,172 for 7 grants (high: $382,551; low: $127,517; average: $127,517).
Fields of interest: Higher education; Health care; YM/YWCAs & YM/YWHAs; Residential/custodial care, senior continuing care.
Limitations: Applications not accepted. Giving primarily in IN.
Application information: Contributes only to pre-selected organizations.
Trustee: JPMorgan Chase Bank, N.A.
EIN: 356009281

9854
Madison Community Foundation ▼ ◇
2 Science Ct.
P.O. Box 5010
Madison, WI   53705-0010   (608) 232-1763
Contact: Kathleen Woit, Pres.; For grant application: Tom M. Linfield, V.P., Grantmaking and Comm.
FAX: (608) 232-1772;
E-mail: frontdesk@madisoncommunityfoundation.org; Additional E-mail: acasey@madisoncommunityfoundation.org; Grant application E-mail: tlinfield@madisoncommunityfoundation.org;
URL: http://www.madisoncommunityfoundation.org

Established in 1942 in WI.
Foundation type: Community foundation.
Financial data (yr. ended 12/31/05): Assets, $118,108,867 (M); gifts received, $20,929,980; expenditures, $10,612,553; giving activities include $10,624,060 for grants.
Purpose and activities: The foundation seeks to enhance the quality of life in Dane County, WI, in the areas of arts and culture, economic and community development, the environment, the elderly, families, and youth. The foundation makes capacity-building grants to area nonprofits to hire key personnel or expand the core business of the organization.
Fields of interest: Performing arts; Arts; Child development, education; Education; Environment; Employment; Housing/shelter, services; Youth development, services; Children, day care; Children, services; Youth, services; Family services; Residential/custodial care, senior continuing care; Aging, centers/services; Community development, neighborhood development; Economic development; Community development, business promotion; Community development; Leadership development; Youth; Aging.
Type of support: Management development/capacity building; Building/renovation; Equipment; Land acquisition; Program development; Seed money; Technical assistance; Matching/challenge support.

Limitations: Giving limited to Dane County, WI. No support for religious organizations for religious purposes, health care services, including mental health, or substance abuse treatment. No grants to individuals, or for annual campaigns, endowment funds, debt retirement, short-term events (such as conferences, festivals, celebrations and fund raising functions), or scholarships; no capital grants to support ongoing maintenance.
Publications: Annual report; Annual report (including application guidelines); Financial statement; Newsletter.
Application information: Visit foundation Web site for applications and guidelines. A full grant proposal will be invited based on the foundation's determination of the organization's Letter of Inquiry. The foundation encourages grant seekers to complete the online Letter of Inquiry, although paper copies are accepted (via mail only). Application form required.
  Initial approach: Submit Letter of Inquiry
  Copies of proposal: 1
  Deadline(s): Jan. 15 and July 15 for Letter of Inquiry; Mar. 1 and Sept. 1 for full grant proposals
  Board meeting date(s): 6 times a year
Officers and Board of Governors:* George Nelson,* Chair.; Dave Reinecke,* Vice-Chair.; Kathleen Woit, Pres.; Ann Casey, V.P., Finance and Planned Giving; Tom M. Linfield, V.P., Grantmaking and Community Initiatives; Amy T. Overby, V.P., Donor Rels.; Phyllis Lovrien,* Treas.; Martha Vukelich Austin; Darrell Bazzell; James E. Burgess; Dan Erdman; Clayton Frink; Richard Lynch; Sonya Newenhouse; John Pollock; Toni Sikes; Jerry Smith; Gary Wolter.
Number of staff: 4 full-time professional; 2 part-time professional; 3 full-time support; 1 part-time support.
EIN: 396038248
Selected grants: The following grants were reported in 2005.

$150,000 to Henry Vilas Park Zoological Society, Madison, WI. For leadership gift to support additional indoor and outdoor classrooms for animal education and conservation programs as part of Zoo's Discovery Center.

$100,000 to East Madison Community Center, Madison, WI. To create Performing Arts and Wellness Center.

$100,000 to Madison Metropolitan School District, Madison, WI. For first grade math intervention program, payable over 2 years.

$100,000 to Madison Museum of Contemporary Art, Madison, WI. For new facility's opening exhibition focused on Madison's history, culture, and people.

$100,000 to Wexford Ridge Neighborhood Center, Madison, WI. For innovative model establishing community partnership with comprehensive coordinated programs for people of all ages.

$80,000 to YMCA of Dane County, Madison, WI. To construct and furnish Preschool Center at Northeast Branch YMCA, to greatly expand family programs and services for low-income families.

$75,000 to Attic Angels Association, Madison, WI. Toward construction of Memory Care Unit, for full range of care under one roof for those with dementia.

$60,000 to United Way of Dane County, Madison, WI. For improvement of pre-literacy skills of students through Preschools of Hope, payable over 3 years.

$40,000 to Porchlight, Inc., Madison, WI. To develop Porchlight Products, social enterprise to manufacture and sell locally produced foods and create training and employment opportunities for people with disabilities.

$35,000 to Kanopy Dance Theater, Madison, WI. To create dance and movement center.

9855
Madison Gas and Electric Foundation, Inc. ✧
P.O. Box 1231
Madison, WI 53701-1231 (608) 252-7024

Established in 1966 in WI.
Donor: Madison Gas and Electric Co.
Foundation type: Company-sponsored foundation.
Financial data (yr. ended 12/31/03): Assets, $10,174,763 (M); gifts received, $750,000; expenditures, $352,948; qualifying distributions, $318,353; giving activities include $318,353 for 67 grants (high: $77,376; low: $75).
Purpose and activities: The foundation supports organizations involved with arts and culture, education, health, community development, minorities, and other areas.
Fields of interest: Arts; Education; Health care; Community development; Federated giving programs; General charitable giving; Minorities.
Type of support: General/operating support; Capital campaigns; Scholarship funds; Employee-related scholarships.
Limitations: Giving limited to areas of company operations.
Application information:
   Initial approach: Proposal
Officers and Directors:* Gary J. Wolter, Pres.; Lynn K. Hobbie, V.P.; Thomas R. Krull, V.P.; Terry A. Hanson, Secy.-Treas.
EIN: 396098118

9856
Make a Mark Foundation, Inc. ✧
1145 Clark St.
Stevens Point, WI 54481

Established in 2003 in WI.
Donor: Travel Guard Group, Inc.
Foundation type: Operating foundation.
Financial data (yr. ended 12/31/05): Assets, $133,136 (M); gifts received, $596,033; expenditures, $595,665; qualifying distributions, $358,004; giving activities include $358,004 for 104 grants (high: $85,339; low: $25).
Fields of interest: Arts; Human services; Salvation Army; Children/youth, services; Children, adoption; International development.
Limitations: Applications not accepted. Giving in the U.S., primarily in Stevens Point, WI, and internationally in Kenya. No grants to individuals.
Application information: Contributes only to pre-selected organizations.
Officers and Directors:* John M. Noel,* Pres.; Dan McGinnity,* Secy. and Exec. Dir.; Patricia D. Noel,* Secy.; James L. Koziol,* Treas.
EIN: 364518995

9857
Managed Health Services, Inc.
(doing business as Elizabeth A. Brinn Foundation)
890 Elm Grove Rd., Ste. 210
Elm Grove, WI 53122 (262) 821-0400
Contact: Richard Wiederhold, Pres.

Established in 1999 in WI.
Foundation type: Independent foundation.
Financial data (yr. ended 12/31/05): Assets, $22,206,852 (M); expenditures, $3,794,642; qualifying distributions, $3,288,346; giving activities include $3,288,346 for 201 grants (high: $106,000; low: $45).
Purpose and activities: Giving primarily to organizations that help disadvantaged and underprivileged children.
Fields of interest: Museums (children's); Arts; Libraries (public); Crime/violence prevention, domestic violence; Human services; Children, services; Community development; Christian agencies & churches; Roman Catholic agencies & churches.
Type of support: General/operating support; Continuing support; Annual campaigns; Capital campaigns; Building/renovation; Debt reduction; Emergency funds; Program development; Seed money; Scholarship funds.
Limitations: Giving primarily in Milwaukee, WI.
Publications: Grants list.
Application information: Application form not required.
   Initial approach: Letter
   Copies of proposal: 1
   Deadline(s): None
   Board meeting date(s): 6 times annually
   Final notification: 1 to 3 months
Officers and Directors:* Richard Wiederhold,* Pres. and Treas.; William P. Jollie,* V.P.; Samuel E. Bradt,* Secy. and C.I.O.; Raymond C. Brinn; Claire W. Johnson.
Number of staff: 1 full-time professional; 3 part-time support.
EIN: 391509757
Selected grants: The following grants were reported in 2003.
$150,000 to Family House, Milwaukee, WI. For expansion to add 18-bed facility.
$30,000 to New Beginnings Are Possible, Milwaukee, WI. For general operating support.
$15,000 to Hope Street, Milwaukee, WI. For general support.
$15,000 to Milwaukee Leadership Training Center, Milwaukee, WI. For general operating support.
$10,000 to Holton Youth Center, Milwaukee, WI. For general operating support.
$10,000 to Safe and Sound, Milwaukee, WI. For general support.
$5,000 to Latino Community Center, Milwaukee, WI. For general support.
$5,000 to Our Next Generation, Milwaukee, WI. For general support.
$2,500 to Milwaukee Careers Cooperative, Milwaukee, WI. To help ex-offenders secure employment.
$1,000 to Partners with Youth, Milwaukee, WI. For general support.

9858
Manpower Foundation, Inc. ✧
5301 N. Ironwood Rd.
Milwaukee, WI 53201 (414) 961-1000

Established in 1953 in WI.
Donor: Manpower Inc.
Foundation type: Company-sponsored foundation.
Financial data (yr. ended 12/31/04): Assets, $481,746 (M); gifts received, $328,000; expenditures, $338,230; qualifying distributions, $338,193; giving activities include $331,650 for 25 grants (high: $80,000; low: $500), and $6,000 for 3 grants to individuals (high: $2,000; low: $2,000).
Purpose and activities: The foundation supports organizations involved with arts and culture, higher education, health, youth development, human services, and community development.
Fields of interest: Museums; Performing arts, theater; Arts; Higher education; Health organizations, association; Youth development; Human services; Community development; Federated giving programs.
Type of support: General/operating support; Employee-related scholarships.
Limitations: Giving primarily in Milwaukee, WI.
Application information: Application form not required.
   Initial approach: Proposal
Officers and Directors:* Jeffrey A. Joerres,* Pres.; Julie Krey, V.P.; Michael J. Van Handel,* Secy.-Treas.
EIN: 396052810
Selected grants: The following grants were reported in 2005.
$297,000 to United Way of Greater Milwaukee, Milwaukee, WI.
$92,500 to United Performing Arts Fund, Milwaukee, WI.
$65,000 to NAACP, Baltimore, MD.
$30,000 to YMCA. 2 grants: $15,000 each
$4,000 to Milwaukee Art Museum, Milwaukee, WI.
$1,000 to Walkers Point Youth and Family Center, Milwaukee, WI.
$100 to Milwaukee Youth Symphony Orchestra, Milwaukee, WI.

9859
Marcus Corporation Foundation, Inc. ✧
100 E. Wisconsin Ave., Ste. 1900
Milwaukee, WI 53202-4125
Contact: Stephen H. Marcus, Pres. and Treas.

Established in 1961 in WI.
Donor: The Marcus Corp.
Foundation type: Company-sponsored foundation.
Financial data (yr. ended 12/31/05): Assets, $3,553,863 (M); gifts received, $2,639,722; expenditures, $833,707; qualifying distributions, $832,607; giving activities include $803,765 for 112 grants (high: $100,000; low: $80).
Purpose and activities: The foundation supports organizations involved with arts and culture, education, health, and human services.
Fields of interest: Arts; Medical school/education; Education; Health care; Recreation, fairs/festivals; Children/youth, services; Human services; Federated giving programs.
Type of support: Program development; Research.
Limitations: Giving limited to Milwaukee, WI. No grants to individuals.
Application information: Application form not required.
   Initial approach: Proposal
   Deadline(s): None
   Board meeting date(s): Dec.

Officers and Directors:* Stephen H. Marcus,* Pres. and Treas.; Thomas F. Kissinger,* Secy.; Gregory S. Marcus.
EIN: 396046268
Selected grants: The following grants were reported in 2004.
$153,885 to United Way of Greater Milwaukee, Milwaukee, WI.
$100,000 to Medical College of Wisconsin, Milwaukee, WI.
$40,000 to Childrens Hospital and Health System Foundation, Milwaukee, WI.
$15,000 to Milwaukee World Festival, Milwaukee, WI.
$12,500 to Betty Brinn Childrens Museum, Milwaukee, WI.
$12,500 to HeartLove Place, Milwaukee, WI.
$3,000 to Waukesha Memorial Hospital, Waukesha, WI.
$2,475 to Urban League.
$1,100 to Creative SHARP Presentations, Mequon, WI.
$700 to Saint Francis Childrens Center, Glendale, WI.

9860
Marshall & Ilsley Foundation, Inc.
(formerly Marshall & Ilsley Bank Foundation, Inc.)
770 N. Water St.
Milwaukee, WI 53202 (414) 765-7835
Contact: Meg Sullivan, Asst. Secy.

Incorporated in 1958 in WI.
Donor: Marshall & Ilsley Corp.
Foundation type: Company-sponsored foundation.
Financial data (yr. ended 12/31/05): Assets, $8,153,497 (M); gifts received, $11,272,732; expenditures, $3,215,551; qualifying distributions, $3,214,900; giving activities include $3,125,450 for 151 grants (high: $250,000; low: $1,000), and $89,450 for 61 grants to individuals (high: $1,500; low: $450).
Purpose and activities: The foundation supports hospitals and organizations involved with arts and culture, education, youth development, human services, and Christianity.
Fields of interest: Museums; Arts; Elementary/secondary education; Higher education; Education; Hospitals (general); Youth development; Children/youth, services; Human services; Christian agencies & churches.
Type of support: Scholarship funds; Capital campaigns; Program development; Employee-related scholarships.
Limitations: Giving primarily in WI. No grants to individuals (except for employee-related scholarships).
Application information: Application form not required.
Initial approach: Proposal
Copies of proposal: 1
Deadline(s): None
Board meeting date(s): As necessary
Final notification: Varies
Officers and Directors:* James B. Wigdale,* Pres.; Dennis J. Kuester,* V.P.; Margaret A. Hamell, Secy.-Treas.; Richard A. Abdoo; Mark F. Furlong; Bruce E. Jacobs; Robert J. O'Toole; George E. Wardeberg.
Trustee: Marshall & Ilsley Bank.
EIN: 396043185

9861
Marshfield Area Community Foundation ☆
P.O. Box 456
Marshfield, WI 54449
Contact: Dean Markwardt, Exec. Dir.
E-mail: dean@marshfieldareacommunityfoundation.org; *URL:* http://marshfieldareacommunityfoundation.org/

Established in 1993 in WI.
Donors: Harry Chronquist†; Gladys Chronquist†; G. Stanley Custer†; Violet Custer†; Leonard L. Hartl†; Margaret Quirt Heck†; Melvin A. Hintz†; LaVerne R. Kohs†; Patrice LeGrand†; J.P. Leonard†; George Mac Kinnon†; Anne Adler; Bette Adler; Joseph Lang†; Floyd Hamus; Pat Hamus.
Foundation type: Community foundation.
Financial data (yr. ended 12/31/05): Assets, $2,710,074 (M); gifts received, $598,272; expenditures, $459,277; giving activities include $360,162 for 66 grants (high: $89,498; low: $57), and $51,430 for 47 grants to individuals (high: $2,835; low: $287).
Purpose and activities: The purpose of the foundation is to receive and accept property exclusively for educational, recreational, artistic/cultural, conservation, community development, charitable or benevolent purposes for the benefit and improvement of residents of the Marshfield, WI, area.
Fields of interest: Arts; Education; Environment; Recreation; Community development, neighborhood development; Community development.
Type of support: Continuing support; Annual campaigns; General/operating support; Equipment; Endowments; Program development; Conferences/seminars; Publication; Scholarship funds; Technical assistance; Grants to individuals; Scholarships—to individuals; In-kind gifts.
Limitations: Giving limited to Marshfield, WI and surrounding areas. No grants for capital campaigns or debt reduction.
Publications: Application guidelines; Annual report; Financial statement; Grants list; Informational brochure; Informational brochure (including application guidelines); Newsletter.
Application information: Application form required.
Initial approach: Letter (no more than 2 pages)
Copies of proposal: 7
Deadline(s): Sept. 1
Board meeting date(s): Last Tues. in Jan., Mar., May, July, Sept., and Nov.
Final notification: Following Sept. board meeting
Officers and Trustees:* Brenda Dillenburg,* Chair.; James Bartelt,* Chair., Internal Opers.; Jane Wagner,* Chair., Community Rels.; Steve Yorder,* Chair., Donor Rels.; Deborah Janz,* Vice-Chair.; Terri Malueg,* Secy.; Dean Markwardt, Exec. Dir.; Anne Adler; E.B. Adler; Pat Anderson; Matt Berrier; Alan Billings; Michelle Boernke; John Bujalski; Dennis DeVetter; Randy Gershman; Rev. Dean Pingle; Keith Strey.
Number of staff: 1 part-time professional; 1 part-time support.
EIN: 396578767

9862
Martin Family Foundation ◇
2601 W. Cedar Ln.
Milwaukee, WI 53217-1138
Contact: Vincent L. Martin, Tr.

Established around 1994.

Donors: Janet Dowler Martin; Vincent L. Martin.
Foundation type: Independent foundation.
Financial data (yr. ended 7/31/05): Assets, $6,561,901 (M); expenditures, $379,270; qualifying distributions, $336,500; giving activities include $336,500 for 29 grants (high: $150,000; low: $1,000).
Purpose and activities: Giving primarily for higher education and the arts; funding also for a Presbyterian church.
Fields of interest: Performing arts, theater; Arts; Higher education; Education; Federated giving programs; Protestant agencies & churches.
Limitations: Applications not accepted. Giving primarily in WI. No grants to individuals.
Application information: Contributes only to pre-selected organizations.
Trustees: Janet Dowler Martin; Vincent L. Martin.
EIN: 396584789

9863
B. A. Mason Trust ◇ ☆
1251 1st Ave.
Chippewa Falls, WI 54729-1408
Contact: William Scobie, Tr.

Trust established about 1953.
Donor: Mason Shoe Manufacturing Co.
Foundation type: Independent foundation.
Financial data (yr. ended 12/31/05): Assets, $291,951 (M); gifts received, $425,900; expenditures, $402,380; qualifying distributions, $400,050; giving activities include $400,050 for grants.
Purpose and activities: Giving primarily for a cultural association, a youth sports association, and a park.
Fields of interest: Arts; Elementary/secondary education; Environment, natural resources; Athletics/sports, training; Community development.
Limitations: Giving primarily in Chippewa Falls, WI.
Application information:
Initial approach: Letter
Deadline(s): None
Trustees: Jane Mason Lubs; Rosemary Scobie; William M. Scobie; Marshall & Ilsley Bank.
EIN: 396075816

9864
Faye McBeath Foundation ◇
1020 N. Broadway, Ste. 112
Milwaukee, WI 53202-3157 (414) 272-2626
Contact: Scott E. Gelzer, Exec. Dir.
FAX: (414) 272-6235;
E-mail: info@fayemcbeath.org; *URL:* http://www.fayemcbeath.org

Trust established in 1964 in WI.
Donor: Faye McBeath†.
Foundation type: Independent foundation.
Financial data (yr. ended 12/31/05): Assets, $11,051,151 (M); gifts received, $2,000; expenditures, $1,849,479; qualifying distributions, $1,811,256; giving activities include $1,651,896 for 90 grants (high: $100,000; low: $1,000).
Purpose and activities: To benefit the people of WI by providing homes and care for elderly persons, promoting education in medical science and public health, providing medical, nursing, and hospital care for the sick and disabled, promoting the welfare of children, and promoting research in civics and

government, directed towards improvement in the efficiency of local government.

Fields of interest: Education, early childhood education; Elementary school/education; Secondary school/education; Medical school/education; Dental care; Nursing care; Health care; Substance abuse, services; Mental health/crisis services; Health organizations, association; AIDS; Alcoholism; Biomedicine; Nutrition; Youth development, citizenship; Human services; Children/youth, services; Child development, services; Family services; Residential/custodial care, hospices; Aging, centers/services; Public policy, research; Government/public administration; Public affairs, citizen participation; Aging.

Type of support: General/operating support; Continuing support; Program development; Seed money; Technical assistance; Matching/challenge support.

Limitations: Giving limited to WI, with emphasis on the greater Milwaukee area, including Milwaukee, Ozaukee, Waukesha and Washington counties. No grants to individuals, or for annual campaigns, capital projects, scholarships, fellowships, or specific medical or scientific research projects; grants rarely for emergency funds; no loans.

Publications: Application guidelines; Annual report; Grants list; Program policy statement.

Application information: Formal proposals are to be submitted by invitation only. Invitees are to use the Milwaukee-area Common Grant Application Form, which can be downloaded from the foundation Web site. Application form required.

Initial approach: 1- to 2-page letter of intent
Copies of proposal: 1
Deadline(s): Deadlines are established upon discussion with foundation staff
Board meeting date(s): Feb., May, Sept., Dec.
Final notification: 10 days after meeting

Officers and Trustees:* Steven J. Smith,* Chair.; Sara E. Aster,* Vice-Chair.; P. Michael Mahoney,* Secy.; Scott E. Gelzer, Exec. Dir.; Mary T. Kellner; Gregory Wesley.

Number of staff: 1 part-time professional; 1 part-time support.

EIN: 396074450

Selected grants: The following grants were reported in 2005.

$100,000 to Marquette University, Milwaukee, WI.
$50,000 to Milwaukee Symphony Orchestra, Milwaukee, WI.
$45,000 to Alverno College, Milwaukee, WI.
$40,000 to Milwaukee Center for Independence, Milwaukee, WI.
$30,000 to Milwaukee County Department on Aging, Milwaukee, WI.
$30,000 to Milwaukee Public Theater, Milwaukee, WI.
$30,000 to Neighborhood House of Milwaukee, Milwaukee, WI.
$25,000 to Creative SHARP Presentations, Mequon, WI.
$25,000 to Next Door Foundation, Milwaukee, WI.
$25,000 to Strive Media Institute, Milwaukee, WI.

9865
McDonough Foundation, Inc. ✧

780 N. Water St.
Milwaukee, WI 53202-3590
Contact: Richard Bliss

Established in 1987 in WI.

Donors: John J. McDonough; Midwest Dental Products Corp.

Foundation type: Independent foundation.

Financial data (yr. ended 9/30/05): Assets, $8,621 (M); gifts received, $321,463; expenditures, $340,449; qualifying distributions, $338,462; giving activities include $336,586 for 19 grants (high: $75,000; low: $200).

Purpose and activities: Giving primarily for arts and culture and for diabetes organizations.

Fields of interest: Arts; Education; Health organizations, association; Diabetes; Human services.

Limitations: Applications not accepted. Giving primarily in IL; some giving in NY. No grants to individuals.

Application information: Contributes only to pre-selected organizations.

Officers and Directors:* Allison McDonough,* Pres.; John J. McDonough,* Treas.; Marilyn N. McDonough.

EIN: 391627844

Selected grants: The following grants were reported in 2003.

$206,950 to Juvenile Diabetes Research Foundation International, Chicago, IL. For general support.
$77,100 to Juvenile Diabetes Research Foundation International, New York, NY. 2 grants: $38,500 (For general support), $38,600 (For general support).
$30,000 to University of Chicago, Chicago, IL. For scholarships.
$10,000 to Juvenile Diabetes Research Foundation International, Johnston, IA. For general support.
$7,500 to Mill, The, Rockford, IL. For general support.
$5,000 to Juvenile Diabetes Research Foundation International, Palm Beach, FL. For general support.
$5,000 to Juvenile Diabetes Research Foundation International, Houston, TX. For general support.
$5,000 to Rosecrance Foundation, Rockford, IL. For general support.
$3,000 to University of Illinois, Rockford, IL. For scholarships.

9866
Adeline and George McQueen
Foundation ✧

c/o JPMorgan Chase Bank, N.A.
P.O. Box 1308
Milwaukee, WI 53201
Application address: c/o JPMorgan Chase Bank, N.A., P.O. Box 2050, Fort Worth, TX 76113

Established in 1960 in TX.

Foundation type: Independent foundation.

Financial data (yr. ended 6/30/05): Assets, $17,641,102 (M); expenditures, $1,365,339; qualifying distributions, $1,093,467; giving activities include $1,084,500 for 62 grants (high: $100,000; low: $1,000).

Purpose and activities: Giving primarily for the arts, education, and children, youth and social services.

Fields of interest: Arts, association; Performing arts centers; Arts; Higher education; Theological school/education; Education; Health organizations, association; Boys & girls clubs; Big Brothers/Big Sisters; Human services; Children/youth, services; Youth, services.

Limitations: Giving primarily in Fort Worth, TX. No grants to individuals.

Application information: Application form not required.

Initial approach: Proposal
Copies of proposal: 1
Deadline(s): None
Board meeting date(s): Nov.

Trustee: JPMorgan Chase Bank, N.A.

EIN: 756014459

Selected grants: The following grants were reported in 2004.

$100,000 to Dallas Theological Seminary, Dallas, TX.
$100,000 to Fort Worth Museum of Science and History, Fort Worth, TX.
$100,000 to Ronald McDonald House of Dallas, Dallas, TX.
$50,000 to All Saints Health Foundation, Fort Worth, TX. For Heritage Awards Dinner.
$15,000 to Child Advocates of Tarrant County, Fort Worth, TX.
$15,000 to Kids Who Care, Fort Worth, TX.
$15,000 to Young Life, Fort Worth, TX. For general operating support.
$10,000 to Alliance for Children, Fort Worth, TX. For The Great Conversation Dinner.
$10,000 to University of Texas, Arlington, TX.
$5,000 to University of North Texas, Denton, TX. For Hazel Harvey Peace Professorship Campaign.

9867
Mead Witter Foundation, Inc. ✧

(formerly Consolidated Papers Foundation, Inc.)
P.O. Box 39
Wisconsin Rapids, WI 54495-0039
(715) 424-3004
Contact: Susan A. Feith, Pres.

Incorporated in 1951 in WI.

Donors: Consolidated Papers, Inc.; and members of the George W. Mead family.

Foundation type: Independent foundation.

Financial data (yr. ended 12/31/05): Assets, $67,151,671 (M); expenditures, $3,201,144; qualifying distributions, $2,961,282; giving activities include $2,825,404 for 117 grants (high: $1,700,000; low: $30).

Purpose and activities: Giving for local community causes, and youth and social service agencies in communities where Mead Witter Inc. conducts operations; higher education grants generally limited to those in WI; support also for the fine and performing arts and other cultural programs.

Fields of interest: Visual arts; Performing arts; Performing arts, theater; Historic preservation/historical societies; Arts; Higher education; Medical school/education; Engineering school/education; Education; Hospitals (general); Human services; Youth, services.

Type of support: General/operating support; Continuing support; Annual campaigns; Capital campaigns; Building/renovation; Equipment; Endowments; Emergency funds; Professorships; Seed money; Scholarship funds; Employee matching gifts.

Limitations: Giving primarily in WI, usually near areas of company operations. No grants to individuals, or for deficit financing, research, or conferences; no loans.

Publications: Informational brochure (including application guidelines).

Application information: Full proposal is by invitation only. Application form not required.

Initial approach: 1-page letter of inquiry

Copies of proposal: 1
Deadline(s): None
Board meeting date(s): June and Dec.
Final notification: Following June and Dec.
  meetings
Officers: George W. Mead, Chair. and Treas.; Susan A. Feith, Pres.; Emily B. McKay, Secy.
Director: Helen B. Ambuel.
Number of staff: 1 part-time professional; 1 full-time support.
EIN: 396040071
Selected grants: The following grants were reported in 2005.
$205,738 to United Way of South Wood County, Wisconsin Rapids, WI.
$130,000 to Milwaukee School of Engineering, Milwaukee, WI.
$125,000 to 21st Century Urban Schools, Chicago, IL.
$57,925 to National Merit Scholarship Corporation, Evanston, IL.
$37,000 to Lawrence University, Appleton, WI.
$36,000 to Beloit College, Beloit, WI.
$26,000 to Opera for the Young, Madison, WI.
$12,000 to Minnesota Ballet, Duluth, MN.
$6,000 to Vassar College, Poughkeepsie, NY.
$750 to Sharon Lynne Wilson Center for the Arts, Brookfield, WI.

9868
Meehan Family Foundation, Inc. ◇
(formerly Daniel E. Meehan Foundation, Inc.)
1473 E. Goodrich Ln.
Fox Point, WI 53217-2950
Contact: Daniel E. Meehan, Chair.

Established in 1983 in WI.
Donor: Daniel E. Meehan.
Foundation type: Independent foundation.
Financial data (yr. ended 12/31/05): Assets, $6,765,541 (M); gifts received, $3,902,973; expenditures, $560,913; qualifying distributions, $554,489; giving activities include $487,102 for 28 grants (high: $55,590; low: $341).
Purpose and activities: Support for higher and secondary education, and social services. Also awards scholarships to children of employees of Meehan Seaway Service.
Fields of interest: Secondary school/education; Higher education; Human services; Religion.
Type of support: Scholarship funds; Employee-related scholarships.
Publications: Application guidelines.
Application information: Individual scholarships are awarded only to children or grandchildren of employees of Meehan Seaway Service. Foundation is currently accepting applications from organizations. Application form required.
Initial approach: Letter or inter-company mail
Deadline(s): May 15
Board meeting date(s): June and Nov.
Officers: Daniel E. Meehan, Chair.; Theresa Meehan-Felknor, Pres.; Henry Loos, Secy.; Eileen Meehan, Treas.
EIN: 391445333

9869
Menasha Corporation Foundation ◇
P.O. Box 367
Neenah, WI 54957-0367   (920) 751-1000
Contact: Kevin Schuh, Treas.

Established in 1953 in WI.
Donor: Menasha Corp.
Foundation type: Company-sponsored foundation.
Financial data (yr. ended 12/31/03): Assets, $690,060 (M); gifts received, $300,000; expenditures, $416,491; qualifying distributions, $412,243; giving activities include $296,717 for 215 grants (high: $25,000; low: $50), $50,625 for 51 grants to individuals (high: $1,125; low: $500), and $59,118 for 130 employee matching gifts.
Purpose and activities: The foundation supports organizations involved with arts and culture, education, the environment, health, human services, and community development. The foundation also provides employee-related scholarships and an employee matching gift program.
Fields of interest: Media/communications; Arts; Higher education; Business school/education; Education; Environment, natural resources; Environment; Hospitals (general); Health care; Health organizations, association; Human services; Community development; Federated giving programs; Economics.
Type of support: General/operating support; Continuing support; Annual campaigns; Capital campaigns; Building/renovation; Equipment; Emergency funds; Program development; Curriculum development; Fellowships; Scholarship funds; Research; Employee matching gifts; Employee-related scholarships; Matching/challenge support.
Limitations: Giving primarily in areas of company operations. No grants to individuals (except for fellowships and employee-related scholarships).
Publications: Application guidelines.
Application information: Application form required.
Initial approach: Contact foundation for application form
Copies of proposal: 1
Deadline(s): None
Board meeting date(s): Feb., May, Sept., and Dec.
Officers and Directors:* Oliver C. Smith,* Chair.; Anne Des Marais Vought,* Co-Pres.; Julie Shepard White,* Co-Pres.; Angie Burns, Secy.; Kevin Schuh, Treas.; Katherine Gosin Ganser; Katharine Holzman; Edward Norris; Thomas J. Prosser; James J. Sarosiek; Nancy B. Sensenbrenner; Charles E. Shepard; Kim Smith; Lydia B. Smith; Marc Vaccaro; Lucas Vought; Margie Weiss, Ph.D.
EIN: 396047384

9870
John and Engrid Meng, Inc. ◇
428 N. Superior St., Ste. 202
De Pere, WI 54115

Established in 1982 in WI.
Donors: Engrid Meng; John C. Meng.
Foundation type: Independent foundation.
Financial data (yr. ended 12/31/04): Assets, $8,746,721 (M); gifts received, $558,000; expenditures, $504,806; qualifying distributions, $379,511; giving activities include $382,808 for 77 grants (high: $149,374; low: $15).
Purpose and activities: Giving for education, mental health services, women, and the economically disadvantaged.
Fields of interest: Education; Mental health/crisis services; Women; Economically disadvantaged.
Limitations: Applications not accepted. Giving limited to northeastern WI, with emphasis on Green Bay and Brown County. No grants to individuals.

Application information: Contributes only to pre-selected organizations.
Officers: Engrid Meng, Pres.; John C. Meng, V.P. and Treas.; Gerald C. Condon, Jr., Secy.
EIN: 391432568

9871
Mercy Works Foundation, Inc. ◇
200 S. Executive Dr., Ste. 101
Brookfield, WI 53005

Established in 2002 in WI; as a successor to the Mercy Works Foundation, 1996; formerly known as The Follett Family Foundation, 1991.
Donor: Mercy Works Foundation.
Foundation type: Independent foundation.
Financial data (yr. ended 12/31/03): Assets, $51,099,281 (M); gifts received, $3,177,992; expenditures, $3,180,525; qualifying distributions, $2,386,757; giving activities include $2,386,757 for 105 grants, and $1,000,000 for 1 loan/program-related investment.
Fields of interest: Education; Human services; Christian agencies & churches.
Type of support: Program-related investments/loans.
Limitations: Applications not accepted. Giving primarily in WI. No grants to individuals.
Application information: Contributes only to pre-selected organizations.
Officers and Directors:* Sally S. Follett, Pres.; Brian Follett, V.P.; Bob Follett, Secy.; Joseph Malone,* Treas.; Mark Follett; Scott S. Follett.
EIN: 431954871
Selected grants: The following grants were reported in 2004.
$254,000 to Catholic Relief Services, Baltimore, MD. 3 grants: $109,000, $20,000, $125,000
$212,000 to Missionaries of the Poor, Jamaica. 2 grants: $62,000, $150,000.
$110,000 to Salvatorian Mission Warehouse, New Holstein, WI.
$100,120 to Ave Maria University, Naples, FL.
$50,000 to Mount Carmel Academy, New Orleans, LA.
$35,000 to Holy Apostles College and Seminary, Cromwell, CT.
$30,000 to Catholic Foundation of the Diocese of Green Bay, Green Bay, WI.

9872
The Merrill Foundation, Inc. ◇ ☆
312 E. Wisconsin Ave., Ste. 402
Milwaukee, WI 53202

Established in 1997 in WI.
Donor: Marion C. Read.
Foundation type: Independent foundation.
Financial data (yr. ended 12/31/05): Assets, $1,776,611 (M); gifts received, $99,909; expenditures, $335,150; qualifying distributions, $318,200; giving activities include $318,200 for 27 grants (high: $100,000; low: $500).
Fields of interest: Museums; Arts; Higher education, university; Environment, natural resources; Botanical gardens; Zoos/zoological societies; Christian agencies & churches.
Limitations: Applications not accepted. Giving primarily in Milwaukee, WI.
Application information: Contributes only to pre-selected organizations.

Officers and Directors:* Marion Merrill Chester Read,* Pres.; Verne R. Read,* V.P.; Alice E. Read,* Secy.; V. Ross Read III,* Treas.; Alexander R. Read; Thomas Merrill Read.
EIN: 391892801
Selected grants: The following grants were reported in 2004.
$26,000 to Bat Conservation International, Austin, TX. For general support.
$25,000 to Girl Scouts of the U.S.A., Greater Milwaukee Area Council, Milwaukee, WI. For general support.
$3,000 to EAA Aviation Foundation, Oshkosh, WI. For general support.
$2,000 to American Alpine Club, Golden, CO. For general support.
$1,500 to Milton Academy, Milton, MA. For general support.
$1,500 to Milwaukee Symphony Orchestra, Milwaukee, WI. For general support.
$1,000 to 1000 Friends of Wisconsin Land Use Institute, Madison, WI. For general support.
$1,000 to Harvard Law School Association, Cambridge, MA. For general support.
$1,000 to Lyric Opera of Chicago, Chicago, IL. For general support.
$1,000 to Neighborhood House of Milwaukee, Milwaukee, WI. For general support.

9873
Walter L. Merten Charitable Trust ◇
402 Pine Terr.
Oconomowoc, WI 53066

Donor: Walter L. Merten.
Foundation type: Independent foundation.
Financial data (yr. ended 12/31/05): Assets, $3,225,712 (M); expenditures, $1,566,923; qualifying distributions, $1,489,884; giving activities include $1,489,884 for 31 grants (high: $1,000,000; low: $30).
Fields of interest: Theological school/education; Human services; Residential/custodial care, hospices.
Limitations: Applications not accepted. No grants to individuals.
Application information: Contributes only to pre-selected organizations.
Trustees: Clifford Brooks; Michael Gallagher; Grace M. Merten.
EIN: 391976901
Selected grants: The following grants were reported in 2005.
$325,000 to Family Service of Waukesha, Waukesha, WI.
$25,000 to Interfaith Caregiving Network, Waukesha, WI.
$5,000 to Christian Foundation for Children and Aging, Kansas City, KS.
$5,000 to Sharon Lynne Wilson Center for the Arts, Brookfield, WI.
$1,000 to Habitat for Humanity International.
$1,000 to Michael Fields Agricultural Institute, East Troy, WI.
$1,000 to Sisters of the Divine Savior, Milwaukee, WI.
$1,000 to University of Dayton, Dayton, OH.
$200 to Valley of Our Lady Monastery, Prairie du Sac, WI.

9874
Dale R. & Ruth L. Michels Family Foundation ◇
P.O. Box 414
Brownsville, WI 53006-0414

Established in 1999 in WI.
Donors: Ruth L. Michels; Patrick D. Michels; Michels Corp.
Foundation type: Independent foundation.
Financial data (yr. ended 12/31/03): Assets, $3,505,252 (M); gifts received, $500,000; expenditures, $683,979; qualifying distributions, $662,500; giving activities include $662,500 for 51 grants (high: $250,000; low: $200).
Purpose and activities: Giving primarily for education, children, youth and social services, and for Roman Catholic churches.
Fields of interest: Higher education; Education; Youth development; Human services; Children/youth, services; Roman Catholic agencies & churches.
Limitations: Giving primarily in WI.
Trustees: Kevin P. Michels; Patrick D. Michels; Ruth L. Michels; Steven R. Michels; Timothy J. Michels.
EIN: 391949453

9875
The Steve J. Miller Foundation ☆
111 E. Kilbourn Ave., 4th Fl., Ste. 200
Milwaukee, WI 53202
Contact: Michael J. Sheldon, Secy.-Treas.

Established about 1946 in WI.
Donors: Steve J. Miller‡; Central Cheese Co., Inc.
Foundation type: Independent foundation.
Financial data (yr. ended 12/31/05): Assets, $3,764,607 (M); expenditures, $414,962; qualifying distributions, $373,000; giving activities include $373,000 for 52 grants (high: $50,000; low: $1,000).
Purpose and activities: Funding primarily for education and children's services.
Fields of interest: Arts; Education; Health care; Human services; Children/youth, services.
Type of support: General/operating support; Continuing support; Income development; Annual campaigns; Capital campaigns; Building/renovation; Equipment; Endowments; Debt reduction; Emergency funds; Program development; Conferences/seminars; Curriculum development; Fellowships; Scholarship funds; Research; Consulting services; Matching/challenge support.
Publications: Application guidelines.
Application information: Application form required.
   Initial approach: Full proposal required
   Copies of proposal: 1
   Deadline(s): Apr. 1
   Board meeting date(s): June
Officers: Norman C. Miller, Pres.; Michael J. Sheldon, Secy.-Treas.
Directors: Paulina Miller; Theodore W. Miller; Kurt Spreyer.
Number of staff: None.
EIN: 396051879
Selected grants: The following grants were reported in 2005.
$30,000 to Opportunity Development Centers, Wisconsin Rapids, WI.
$20,000 to Lura Turner Homes, Phoenix, AZ.
$12,000 to Cornucopia Institute, Cornucopia, WI.
$12,000 to Northland College, Ashland, WI.

$10,000 to Americas Second Harvest of Wisconsin, Milwaukee, WI.
$10,000 to Citizens for Safe Water Around Badger, Merrimac, WI.
$10,000 to Clean Wisconsin, Madison, WI.
$10,000 to River Alliance of Wisconsin, Madison, WI.
$6,000 to International Rivers Network, Berkeley, CA.
$5,000 to ARC Milwaukee, Wauwatosa, WI.

9876
Greater Milwaukee Foundation ▼
(formerly Milwaukee Foundation)
1020 N. Broadway, Ste. 112
Milwaukee, WI 53202 (414) 272-5805
Contact: Douglas M. Jansson, Pres.
FAX: (414) 272-6235;
E-mail: info@greatermkefdn.org; Additional address: N16 W23250 Stoneridge Dr., Ste. 6, Waukesha, WI 53188, tel.: (262) 522-8350, FAX: (262) 544-9301; Additional E-mail: info@greatermkefdn.org; URL: http://www.greatermilwaukeefoundation.org

Established in 1915 in WI by declaration of trust.
Foundation type: Community foundation.
Financial data (yr. ended 12/31/05): Assets, $435,664,187 (M); gifts received, $24,030,680; expenditures, $31,026,289; giving activities include $26,235,640 for grants.
Purpose and activities: Present funds include many discretionary funds and some funds designated by the donors to benefit specific institutions or for special purposes, including educational institutions, arts and cultural programs, community development, social services, and health care; support also for conservation and historic preservation.
Fields of interest: Visual arts; Performing arts; Performing arts, dance; Historic preservation/historical societies; Arts; Education, early childhood education; Child development, education; Elementary school/education; Secondary school/education; Higher education; Adult/continuing education; Education; Environment, natural resources; Environment; Reproductive health, family planning; Health care; Substance abuse, services; Mental health/crisis services; Health organizations, association; AIDS; Alcoholism; Crime/violence prevention, youth; Legal services; Employment, training; Employment; Food services; Nutrition; Housing/shelter, development; Recreation; Youth development; Children/youth, services; Child development, services; Family services; Aging, centers/services; Women, centers/services; Homeless, human services; Human services; Civil rights, race/intergroup relations; Urban/community development; Community development; Public policy, research; Government/public administration; Aging; Disabilities, people with; Minorities; Girls; Economically disadvantaged.
Type of support: Capital campaigns; Building/renovation; Equipment; Land acquisition; Program development; Seed money; Technical assistance; Program evaluation; Matching/challenge support.
Limitations: Giving primarily in Milwaukee, Ozaukee, Washington, and Waukesha, WI. No support for the general use of churches or for sectarian religious purposes, or for specific medical or scientific projects, except from components of the foundation established for such purposes. No grants to individuals (except for established awards), or for

operating budgets, continuing support, annual campaigns, endowment funds, or deficit financing.

Publications: Application guidelines; Annual report (including application guidelines); Grants list; Informational brochure; Informational brochure (including application guidelines); Newsletter; Occasional report; Program policy statement.

Application information: Visit foundation Web site for online letter of inquiry and application guidelines. The foundation's staff will invite selected applicants to submit full proposals based on letter of inquiry. Capital requests are reviewed at Dec. board meeting. Application form required.

  Initial approach: Contact foundation Prog. Off.
  Copies of proposal: 1
  Deadline(s): None for letter of inquiry; Jan. 4, Mar. 14, June 13, and Sept. 12 for full grant application
  Board meeting date(s): Mar., June, Sept., Dec., and as needed
  Final notification: 1 week after board meetings

Officers and Directors:* Frederick P. Stratton, Jr.,* Chair.; Judy Jorgenson,* Vice-Chair.; Douglas M. Jansson, Pres., Secy., and Exec. Dir.; James A. Marks, V.P. and Dir., Grants Prog.; Patti Dew, C.F.O.; Ned W. Bechthold; Peter W. Bruce; John W. Daniels; Janine P. Geske; Franklyn F. Gimbel; David J. Lubar; Patricia McKeithan; Linda T. Mellowes; Joan Marie Prince, Ph.D.; Thomas L. Spero.

Trustees: JPMorgan Chase Bank, N.A.; Marshall & Ilsley Bank; U.S. Bank, N.A.; The Northern Trust Co.

Number of staff: 24 full-time professional; 1 part-time professional; 5 full-time support.

EIN: 396036407

Selected grants: The following grants were reported in 2005.

$1,595,000 to Tides Foundation, San Francisco, CA. For Environment Fund.

$452,898 to Mount Mary College, Milwaukee, WI. For Caroline Scholars.

$250,000 to Milwaukee Art Museum, Milwaukee, WI. For capital campaign.

$243,000 to West Bend High School, West Bend, WI. For scholarships.

$200,000 to United Performing Arts Fund, Milwaukee, WI. For campaign.

$150,000 to YMCA of Metropolitan Milwaukee, South Shore, Cudahy, WI. For construction of Special Needs/Family Locker Rooms.

$40,000 to Sierra Madre Alliance, Tucson, AZ. For sustaining support.

$25,000 to COA Youth and Family Centers, Milwaukee, WI. For Development of Citywide Teen Center.

$20,000 to Turner Ballroom Preservation Trust, Milwaukee, WI.

$17,500 to Boys and Girls Club, West Bend, West Bend, WI. For Digital Explorers Computer Education Program/Jacks.

9877
MMG Foundation, Inc. ✧
702 Eisenhower Dr., Ste. B
Kimberly, WI 54136

Established around 1994 in WI.
Donor: Cynthia F. Moeller Stiehl.
Foundation type: Independent foundation.
Financial data (yr. ended 12/31/05): Assets, $6,167,332 (M); expenditures, $631,536; qualifying distributions, $560,225; giving activities include $560,225 for 61 grants (high: $80,000; low: $200).

Fields of interest: Arts; Higher education; Human services; YM/YWCAs & YM/YWHAs; Protestant agencies & churches.

Limitations: Applications not accepted. Giving primarily in WI. No grants to individuals.

Application information: Contributes only to pre-selected organizations.

Officers: Cynthia F. Moeller Stiehl, Pres.; William D. Calkins, Secy.; Daniel J. Peterich, Treas.

EIN: 396571237

Selected grants: The following grants were reported in 2005.

$159,250 to Lawrence University, Appleton, WI. 4 grants: $50,000, $50,000, $34,250, $25,000

$75,000 to Birch Creek Music Center, Egg Harbor, WI.

$25,000 to Fox Cities Performing Arts Center, Appleton, WI.

$15,000 to American Red Cross, Appleton, WI. 2 grants: $5,000, $10,000

$10,000 to YMCA of the Fox Cities, Appleton, WI.

$1,000 to Door County Maritime Museum, Sturgeon Bay, WI.

9878
The Modine Manufacturing Company Foundation, Inc.
1500 DeKoven Ave.
Racine, WI 53403
Contact: Lori Stafford, Mgr., Corp. Comms.

Established in 1995 in WI.
Donor: Modine Manufacturing Co.
Foundation type: Company-sponsored foundation.
Financial data (yr. ended 3/31/04): Assets, $223,006 (M); gifts received, $460,957; expenditures, $426,822; qualifying distributions, $426,802; giving activities include $426,759 for 40 grants (high: $130,452; low: $300).

Purpose and activities: The foundation supports organizations involved with arts and culture, education, health, human services, community development, and civic affairs.

Fields of interest: Arts; Higher education; Education; Health care; Human services; Community development; Federated giving programs; Public affairs.

Type of support: Employee-related scholarships; Employee volunteer services; Continuing support; Capital campaigns; Building/renovation; Program development; Scholarship funds; Scholarships—to individuals; Matching/challenge support.

Limitations: Giving limited to areas of company operations, with emphasis on Racine, WI. No support for religious or political organizations, organizations lacking a business plan, political parties or candidates, or discriminatory organizations. No grants for travel.

Application information: Support is limited to 3 years. Application form not required.

  Initial approach: Proposal
  Copies of proposal: 1
  Deadline(s): None
  Board meeting date(s): Every other month
  Final notification: 1 to 2 months

Officer: David B. Rayburn, C.E.O. and Pres.

EIN: 391818362

9879
The Elizabeth Morse Charitable Trust ✧
c/o JPMorgan Chase Bank, N.A.
P.O. Box 1308
Milwaukee, WI 53201
Contact: James L. Alexander
Application address: c/o Camille M. Jozsi, Grants Admin./Prog. Assoc., 79 W. Monroe St., Ste. 905, Chicago, IL 60603, tel.: (312) 739-0326; URL: http://www.morsetrust.org

Established in 1992.
Donor: Richard M. Genius, Jr.
Foundation type: Independent foundation.
Financial data (yr. ended 12/31/04): Assets, $47,713,691 (M); expenditures, $2,484,502; qualifying distributions, $2,175,314; giving activities include $1,690,089 for 64 grants (high: $400,000; low: $1,500).

Purpose and activities: Giving primarily to the arts, particularly for theater, as well as for human services, and children and youth services.

Fields of interest: Performing arts, theater; Performing arts, opera; Arts; Health organizations, association; Human services; Children/youth, services.

Type of support: General/operating support; Continuing support; Program development; Seed money; Technical assistance; Program evaluation; Matching/challenge support.

Limitations: Giving primarily in the Chicago, IL, metropolitan area. No support for religious or political organizations. No grants to individuals, or for scholarships, capital campaigns, endowments, or for benefits; no loans.

Publications: Application guidelines.

Application information: See trust Web site for application guidelines and procedures. Letter of Inquiry must be mailed or hand delivered, no faxed Letters of Inquiry are accepted. Full proposals are by invitation only. Application form not required.

  Initial approach: Letter of inquiry
  Copies of proposal: 1
  Deadline(s): None

Trustees: James L. Alexander; JPMorgan Chase Bank, N.A.

Number of staff: 3 full-time professional; 1 part-time support.

EIN: 366999365

Selected grants: The following grants were reported in 2004.

$400,000 to Fourth Presbyterian Church, Chicago, IL. For capital campaign, A Light in the City: Sharing God's Grace, and to support Center for Older Adults.

$125,000 to Chicago Historical Society, Chicago, IL. 2 grants: $50,000 (For Teen Chicago Initiative, a research and development project and exhibition on American youth culture), $75,000 (For Out: Exploring the LGBT Past exhibition and to diversify CHS's audience and educate the public about the LGBT community).

$110,000 to Lyric Opera of Chicago, Chicago, IL. For sponsorship support for Anniversary concert.

$78,825 to Music and Dance Theater Chicago, Chicago, IL. For genera operating support.

$70,000 to Horizons Community Services, Chicago, IL. For operating support.

$50,000 to Goodman Theater, Chicago, IL. For program support.

$36,000 to Civic Orchestra of Chicago, Chicago, IL. For scholarships.

$30,000 to Chicago Community Trust, Chicago, IL. For Arts Education: Every Child, Every School.

$25,000 to Chicago Architecture Foundation, Chicago, IL. For equipment and technology upgrades for new studio.

9880

W. B. Munson Foundation ✧
c/o JPMorgan Chase Bank, N.A.
P.O. Box 1308
Milwaukee, WI 53201
Application address: c/o JPMorgan Chase Bank, N.A., 8111 Preston Rd., Dallas, TX 75225, tel.: (214) 360-4391

Trust established in 1943 in TX.
Foundation type: Independent foundation.
Financial data (yr. ended 12/31/05): Assets, $7,777,487 (M); expenditures, $454,772; qualifying distributions, $394,499; giving activities include $364,246 for 26 grants (high: $50,000; low: $1,000), and $17,000 for 22 grants to individuals (high: $1,000; low: $500).
Purpose and activities: Support for a hospital, the arts, and scholarships for high school graduates of Denison, TX, only.
Fields of interest: Performing arts; Arts; Higher education; Libraries (public); Education; Hospitals (general); Reproductive health, family planning; Recreation, camps; Athletics/sports, school programs; Human services; American Red Cross; Salvation Army; Children/youth, services; Community development.
Type of support: Employee matching gifts; General/operating support; Building/renovation; Equipment; Endowments; Scholarships—to individuals.
Limitations: Giving limited to Grayson County, TX.
Application information: Applications not accepted for scholarships. Application form required.
Initial approach: Letter
Copies of proposal: 7
Deadline(s): 10 days prior to meeting
Board meeting date(s): Quarterly
Trustee: JPMorgan Chase Bank, N.A.
EIN: 756015068

9881

The Nelson Family Foundation, Inc. ✧
P.O. Box 447
Hudson, WI 54016-0447

Established in 1996 in WI.
Donors: Carol J. Nelson; Grant E. Nelson.
Foundation type: Independent foundation.
Financial data (yr. ended 12/31/04): Assets, $57,630,787 (M); expenditures, $2,467,612; qualifying distributions, $2,120,000; giving activities include $2,120,000 for 14 grants (high: $500,000; low: $10,000).
Purpose and activities: Giving primarily for education and religious purposes.
Fields of interest: Education; Christian agencies & churches; Religion.
Limitations: Applications not accepted. Giving primarily in MN; some funding nationally. No grants to individuals.
Application information: Contributes only to pre-selected organizations.
Officers and Directors:* Grant E. Nelson,* Pres.; Carol J. Nelson,* Exec. V.P.; Sarah Curtis,* V.P. and Secy.; Rodney G. Nelson,* V.P. and Treas.; Marybeth Nelson; Curtis D. Curtis.
EIN: 391868979

Selected grants: The following grants were reported in 2003.
$500,000 to English Language Institute in China, San Dimas, CA. For general support.
$500,000 to Heritage Christian Academy, Maple Grove, MN. For building improvement.
$300,000 to Evangelical Free Church of America, Bloomington, MN. For general support.
$300,000 to Joni and Friends, Agoura Hills, CA. 2 grants: $250,000 (For building improvement), $50,000 (For general support).
$150,000 to Asian Access Life Ministries, San Dimas, CA.
$138,000 to Healing Waters, Golden, CO. For general support.
$100,000 to Lakewood Evangelical Free Church, White Bear Lake, MN. For building improvements.
$100,000 to National Prayer Committee, Colorado Springs, CO. For National Broadcast Concert.
$60,000 to Habitat for Humanity, Saint Croix Valley, River Falls, WI.

9882

Victor and Mary D. Nelson Scholarship Fund ✧
c/o Marshall & Ilsley Bank
P.O. Box 2980
Milwaukee, WI 53201-2980
Application address: c/o William Retinstrand, Superior Senior High School, 2600 Catlin Ave., Superior, WI 54880, tel.: (715) 384-0271

Established in 1973 in WI.
Donor: Mary D. Nelson†.
Foundation type: Independent foundation.
Financial data (yr. ended 6/30/05): Assets, $5,265,957 (M); expenditures, $400,868; qualifying distributions, $369,505; giving activities include $366,305 for 220 grants to individuals (high: $21,055; low: $666; average: $1,250–$2,000).
Purpose and activities: Awards scholarships for higher and vocational education to graduates of Superior High School in WI.
Fields of interest: Vocational education; Higher education; Education.
Type of support: Scholarships—to individuals.
Limitations: Giving limited to Superior, WI.
Application information: Applications available at school counseling offices. Application form required.
Deadline(s): Apr. 15
Trustee: Marshall & Ilsley Bank.
EIN: 396184729

9883

Nicholas Family Foundation ✧
10309 N. River Rd.
Mequon, WI 53092 (262) 242-3040
Contact: Lynn S. Nicholas, Tr.

Established in 1993 in WI.
Foundation type: Independent foundation.
Financial data (yr. ended 12/31/05): Assets, $32,733,709 (M); expenditures, $1,658,624; qualifying distributions, $1,609,747; giving activities include $1,546,680 for 73 grants (high: $250,000; low: $2,180).
Purpose and activities: Giving primarily for education and human services.

Fields of interest: Arts; Higher education; Health care; Human services; Children/youth, services; Foundations (community).
Limitations: Giving primarily in WI, with emphasis on Milwaukee. No grants to individuals.
Application information:
Initial approach: Typewritten letter
Deadline(s): None
Trustees: Susan N. Fasciano; Albert O. Nicholas; David O. Nicholas; Lynn S. Nicholas; Nancy J. Nicholas.
EIN: 396589261
Selected grants: The following grants were reported in 2004.
$318,000 to University of Wisconsin Foundation, Madison, WI.
$100,000 to United Way of Greater Milwaukee, Milwaukee, WI.
$50,000 to American Red Cross, Milwaukee, WI.
$50,000 to Boys and Girls Clubs of Greater Milwaukee, Milwaukee, WI.
$25,000 to Saint Johns Home of Milwaukee, Milwaukee, WI.
$25,000 to Salvation Army, WI.
$20,000 to Center for Blind and Visually Impaired Children, Milwaukee, WI.
$16,500 to Milwaukee Public Museum, Milwaukee, WI.
$15,000 to Ronald McDonald House, Wauwatosa, WI.
$10,000 to Ten Chimneys Foundation, Genesee Depot, WI.

9884

Northwestern Mutual Foundation ▼ ✧
(formerly Northwestern Mutual Life Foundation)
720 E. Wisconsin Ave.
Milwaukee, WI 53202 (414) 665-2904
Contact: Gilbert R. Llanas
E-mail: nmfoundation@northwesternmutual.com;
URL: http://www.nmfn.com/tn/aboutus—fd_intro

Established in 1992 in WI.
Donor: The Northwestern Mutual Life Insurance Co.
Foundation type: Company-sponsored foundation.
Financial data (yr. ended 6/30/05): Assets, $64,803,728 (M); expenditures, $13,544,847; qualifying distributions, $13,271,697; giving activities include $10,073,609 for 749 grants (high: $750,000; low: $100), and $3,055,738 for 2,452 employee matching gifts.
Purpose and activities: The foundation supports organizations involved with arts and culture, education, health, mental health, medical research, employment, hunger, housing, human services, community development, disabled people, minorities, economically disadvantaged people, and homeless people.
Fields of interest: Media, television; Media, radio; Museums; Performing arts; Arts; Elementary/secondary education; Higher education; Business school/education; Education; Health care; Substance abuse, services; Mental health/crisis services; Cancer; Heart & circulatory diseases; AIDS; Alcoholism; Cancer research; Heart & circulatory research; Medical research; Employment; Food services; Housing/shelter; Children/youth, services; Family services; Homeless, human services; Human services; Urban/community development; Community development; Federated giving programs; Disabilities, people with; Minorities; Economically disadvantaged; Homeless.

Type of support: General/operating support; Continuing support; Annual campaigns; Capital campaigns; Building/renovation; Emergency funds; Scholarship funds; Research; Employee volunteer services; Employee matching gifts; Matching/challenge support.
Limitations: Giving primarily in the greater Milwaukee, WI, area. No grants to individuals.
Publications: Biennial report.
Application information: Application form required.
 Initial approach: Contact foundation for application form
 Copies of proposal: 1
 Deadline(s): Mar. 15 is recommended
 Board meeting date(s): Bimonthly
 Final notification: Varies
Officers and Directors: * Edward J. Zore,* Pres.; Frederic H. Sweet, Exec. V.P.; Scott J. Morris, Secy.; Gary M. Hewitt, Treas.; Edward F. Barr; Pierre "Pete" S. Du Pont; Patricia Albjerg Graham; Daniel F. McKeithan, Jr.; Brenda F. Skelton; Peter M. Sommerhauser.
Number of staff: 3 full-time professional; 1 full-time support.
EIN: 391728908
Selected grants: The following grants were reported in 2005.
$750,000 to National Public Radio, DC.
$575,000 to United Way of Greater Milwaukee, Milwaukee, WI.
$537,500 to United Performing Arts Fund, Milwaukee, WI.
$386,325 to Scholarship America, Saint Peter, MN. 2 grants: $191,025, $195,300
$250,000 to American Red Cross, National Headquarters, DC.
$25,000 to Milwaukee Repertory Theater, Milwaukee, WI.
$15,000 to Consortium for Graduate Study in Management, Saint Louis, MO.
$15,000 to Greater Milwaukee Foundation, Milwaukee, WI.
$15,000 to Salvation Army, WI.

9885
Oshkosh Area Community Foundation

(formerly Oshkosh Foundation)
404 N. Main St., Ste. 205
Oshkosh, WI 54901
Contact: Eileen Connolly-Keesler, Exec. Dir.
FAX: (920) 426-6997;
E-mail: info@oshkoshareaf.org; URL: http://www.oshkoshareacf.org

Established in 1928 in WI by declaration of trust.
Foundation type: Community foundation.
Financial data (yr. ended 6/30/05): Assets, $52,335,480 (M); gifts received, $12,957,777; expenditures, $4,450,070; giving activities include $3,713,835 for 567 grants (high: $680,000; low: $50), and $10,600 for 17 grants to individuals (high: $2,000; low: $100).
Purpose and activities: The foundation seeks to address and anticipate community needs by providing leadership and coordination through grantmaking and fund development.
Fields of interest: Arts; Higher education; Education; Environment; Recreation; Children/youth, services; Community development; Youth; Aging; Women; Girls.
Type of support: Conferences/seminars; General/operating support; Continuing support; Capital campaigns; Building/renovation; Equipment;

Endowments; Seed money; Scholarship funds; Scholarships—to individuals; Matching/challenge support.
Limitations: Giving limited to Green Lake, Waukesha and Winnebago, counties, WI. No grants to individuals (except for scholarships), or for deficit financing, research, or publications; no loans.
Publications: Application guidelines; Annual report; Financial statement; Informational brochure; Newsletter.
Application information: Visit foundation Web site for application forms, guidelines, and specific deadlines. Applications not accepted unless residency requirements are met. Application form required.
 Initial approach: Submit application form and attachments
 Copies of proposal: 12
 Deadline(s): Varies
 Board meeting date(s): 8 times a year
 Final notification: 12 weeks
Officers and Board of Governors: * William Wyman,* Chair.; Patrick Seubert,* Vice-Chair.; Marcy Coglianese,* Secy.; Sam Sundet,* Treas.; Eileen Connolly-Keesler, Exec. Dir.; Nancy Albright; John Bermingham, Jr.; Lawrence Bittner; Willard Carlson; Tom Harenburg; Mark Lasky; Jack Schloesser; Jack Sullivan; Dave Vierthaler.
Trustees: Associated Banc-Corp; Great Lakes; JPMorgan Chase Bank, N.A.; Legg Mason; Marshall & Ilsley Bank; Reinhart-Mahony; Sound Capital; Sound Capital Vanguard; U.S. Bank, N.A.
Number of staff: 5 full-time professional; 1 part-time professional.
EIN: 396041638

9886
Oshkosh B'Gosh Foundation, Inc. ✧

c/o U.S. Bank, N.A.
P.O. Box 300
Oshkosh, WI 54902 (920) 231-8800
Contact: David Omachinski, V.P.
Application address: c/o Cheryl Fowler, Prog. Dir., Oshkosh Area Community Fdn., 404 N. Main St., Ste. 205, Oshkosh, WI 54901; tel.: (920) 426-3993, FAX: (920) 426-6997

Established in 1985 in WI.
Donor: Oshkosh B'Gosh, Inc.
Foundation type: Company-sponsored foundation.
Financial data (yr. ended 12/31/05): Assets, $0 (M); gifts received, $350,000; expenditures, $1,456,194; qualifying distributions, $1,452,084; giving activities include $1,452,084 for grants.
Purpose and activities: The foundation supports organizations involved with education and children and youth and awards college scholarships to high school graduates in areas of company operations.
Fields of interest: Higher education; Education; Children/youth, services; Federated giving programs.
Type of support: General/operating support; Capital campaigns; Scholarships—to individuals.
Limitations: Giving primarily in WI.
Application information: An application form is required for scholarships.
 Initial approach: Contact foundation for application form for scholarships
 Deadline(s): Contact high school for deadlines for scholarships

Officers and Directors: * William Wyman,* Pres.; Doug Hyde,* V.P. and Secy.; David Omachinski,* V.P. and Treas.
EIN: 391525020
Selected grants: The following grants were reported in 2003.
$57,294 to United Way, Oshkosh Area, Oshkosh, WI. For general support.
$53,000 to YMCA, Oshkosh Community, Oshkosh, WI. For general support.
$47,500 to Paine Art Center and Arboretum, Oshkosh, WI. For general support.
$16,500 to Boys and Girls Club of Oshkosh, Oshkosh, WI. For general support.
$13,555 to Mercy Medical Center Foundation of Oshkosh, Oshkosh, WI. For general support.
$13,409 to United Way of Sumner County, Gallatin, TN. For general support.
$10,000 to Childrens Hospital and Health System Foundation, Milwaukee, WI. For general support.
$5,635 to American Cancer Society, Appleton, WI. For general support.
$5,000 to Grand Opera House Guild of Oshkosh, Oshkosh, WI. For general support.
$2,000 to Auburn University, Auburn, AL. For general support.

9887
Oshkosh Truck Foundation, Inc. ✧

2307 Oregon St.
P.O. Box 2566
Oshkosh, WI 54902-2566
Contact: Robert G. Bohn, Pres.

Incorporated in 1960 in WI.
Donor: Oshkosh Truck Corp.
Foundation type: Company-sponsored foundation.
Financial data (yr. ended 9/30/05): Assets, $1,078,457 (M); gifts received, $602,900; expenditures, $319,717; qualifying distributions, $319,571; giving activities include $316,657 for 49 grants (high: $78,500; low: $100).
Purpose and activities: The foundation supports community foundations and organizations involved with arts and culture, education, health, youth development, and human services.
Fields of interest: Performing arts centers; Arts; Education; Health care; Boys & girls clubs; Youth development; YM/YWCAs & YM/YWHAs; Human services; Foundations (community); Federated giving programs.
Type of support: General/operating support; Continuing support; Annual campaigns; Building/renovation; Equipment; Emergency funds; Employee-related scholarships.
Limitations: Giving primarily in Oshkosh and the Winnebago County, WI, area. No grants for start-up needs, debt reduction, land acquisition, special projects, research, publications, conferences, or endowments; no loans; no matching gifts.
Application information: Application form not required.
 Initial approach: Proposal
 Copies of proposal: 1
 Deadline(s): None
 Board meeting date(s): Mar., June, Sept., and Dec.
Officers and Trustees: * Robert G. Bohn,* Pres.; Bryan J. Blankfield,* V.P. and Secy.; Charles L. Szews,* V.P. and Treas.; Matthew J. Zolnowski, V.P.
EIN: 396062129
Selected grants: The following grants were reported in 2005.

$78,500 to United Way, WI.

$46,500 to United Way, Oshkosh Area, Oshkosh, WI.

$30,000 to Fox Cities Performing Arts Center, Appleton, WI.

$5,000 to YMCA Community Center of Neenah-Menasha, Neenah, WI.

$5,000 to YMCA of the Fox Cities, Appleton, WI.

$5,000 to YMCA, Oshkosh Community, Oshkosh, WI.

$2,700 to American Red Cross, Appleton, WI.

$2,150 to Salvation Army, WI.

$1,000 to United Way of Manatee County, Bradenton, FL.

$250 to Fox Valley Symphony, Appleton, WI.

9888
Outagamie Charitable Foundation, Inc. ✧
100 W. Lawrence St.
P.O. Box 727
Appleton, WI 54912-0727

Established in 1985 in WI.
Donor: Fox Valley Corp.
Foundation type: Independent foundation.
Financial data (yr. ended 3/31/05): Assets, $6,251,371 (M); expenditures, $351,532; qualifying distributions, $315,000; giving activities include $315,000 for 15 grants (high: $75,000; low: $5,000).
Purpose and activities: Giving primarily for the arts, education, nature conservancy, human services, children and youth services, federated giving programs, and the YMCA.
Fields of interest: Arts; Higher education; Environment, natural resources; Human services; YM/YWCAs & YM/YWHAs; Federated giving programs.
Limitations: Applications not accepted. Giving on a national basis. No grants to individuals.
Application information: Contributes only to pre-selected organizations.
Officers and Directors: * Lynn Fey,* Pres.; John Buchanan,* V.P.; Rita Vitalis,* V.P.; Lyle H. Richter, Secy.-Treas.; Barbara Aalfs; Charlie Buchanan; Caroline Fey; Emily Lehto; Susan Lenfestey; Patrick McLoughlin.
EIN: 391526589
Selected grants: The following grants were reported in 2003.
$200,000 to Fox Cities Performing Arts Center, Appleton, WI. 2 grants: $100,000 each (For operating support).
$90,000 to Claremont School of Theology, Center for Process Studies, Claremont, CA. For operating support.
$57,500 to Women at the Courthouse (WATCH), Minneapolis, MN. For operating support.
$30,000 to Cornwall Child Center, West Cornwall, CT. For operating support.
$30,000 to National Ability Center of Park City, Park City, UT. For operating support.
$25,000 to University of Utah, Salt Lake City, UT. For operating support.
$10,000 to Happytime Nursery School, Pismo Beach, CA. For operating support.
$5,000 to Environmental Media Association, Los Angeles, CA. For operating support.
$2,500 to Park City Historical Society and Museum, Park City, UT. For operating support.

9889
Overture Foundation ▼ ✧
1 S. Pinckney St., Ste. 816
Madison, WI 53703
Contact: Sandy Derer, Admin.
FAX: (608) 294-9076;
E-mail: info@overturefoundation.com

Established in 1996.
Donor: W. Jerome Frautschi.
Foundation type: Independent foundation.
Financial data (yr. ended 12/31/05): Assets, $28,938,913 (M); gifts received, $21,361,302; expenditures, $38,570,932; qualifying distributions, $37,750,723; giving activities include $37,750,723 for 34 grants (high: $4,247,740; low: $250; average: $535,000–$2,300,000).
Purpose and activities: Giving primarily to arts and cultural programs, and education.
Fields of interest: Arts; Education.
Limitations: Giving primarily in Madison, and Dane County, WI.
Application information: Specific guidelines will be sent with the application form. Application form required.
Initial approach: Letter
Deadline(s): None
Officers and Directors: * W. Jerome Frautschi,* Chair.; George E. Austin, Pres.; Rhona E. Vogel, Secy.; Grant J. Frautschi; Lance A. Frautschi.
Number of staff: 1 full-time professional; 1 full-time support.
EIN: 391855130
Selected grants: The following grants were reported in 2004.
$31,373,277 to Overture Development Corporation, Madison, WI. 10 grants:
$3,525,661 (For Overture Center construction),
$2,075,826 (For Overture Center construction),
$5,478,559 (For Overture Center construction),
$2,263,976 (For Overture Center construction),
$600,000 (For Overture Center construction),
$2,917,922 (For Overture Center construction),
$3,516,197 (For Overture Center construction),
$3,249,846 (For Overture Center construction),
$4,130,277 (For Overture Center construction),
$3,615,013 (For Overture Center construction).

9890
The Palmer Foundation
1025 56th St.
Kenosha, WI 53140
Contact: Diane Pavela, Admin. Asst.
FAX: (262) 842-0069;
E-mail: thepalmerfoundation@tds.net; *URL:* http://www.thepalmerfoundation.org

Established in 1990 in IL.
Donors: Rogers Palmer†; Mary Palmer†; Mary P. Enroth.
Foundation type: Independent foundation.
Financial data (yr. ended 12/31/05): Assets, $13,512,692 (M); gifts received, $100,000; expenditures, $714,241; qualifying distributions, $667,338; giving activities include $604,908 for 50 grants (high: $35,000; low: $2,000).
Purpose and activities: The trustees believe in honest, open communication, creativity, education and individual empowerment. With these values in mind, the foundation seeks to empower young people (up to age 25) to reach their potential to become responsible contributors to their families and communities.

Fields of interest: Arts; Education; Health care; Human services; International affairs.
International interests: Guatemala; Mexico.
Type of support: Program development; Matching/challenge support.
Limitations: Giving limited to the Midwest states: IL, IN, IA, MI, MN, OH, and WI, and the Mid Atlantic states: DE, MD, NJ, NC, PA, VA, WV, and in Washington, DC. No support for lobbying, sectarian religious purposes, individual medical purposes, or for scientific research. No grants to individuals, or for multi-year grants, endowment drives, operational support, annual campaigns, or salaries.
Publications: Application guidelines; Annual report; Grants list; Program policy statement.
Application information: Letter of intent form must be filled out on foundation Web site. Full proposals will only be accepted upon invite from foundation. Application form required.
Initial approach: Letter of intent
Copies of proposal: 7
Board meeting date(s): Apr. and Oct.
Final notification: After board meeting
Officers and Directors: * Mary P. Enroth,* Pres.; Karen E. Lischick,* V.P.; Jay L. Owen,* Secy.-Treas.; John Allen; Susan Enroth.
Number of staff: 1 part-time support.
EIN: 363700897

9891
Pamida Foundation ✧
P.O. Box 19060
Green Bay, WI 54307-9060   (402) 339-2400
Contact: Robert C. Hafner, V.P.
URL: http://www.pamida.com/foundation/foundation.asp

Established in 1983 in NE.
Donor: Pamida, Inc.
Foundation type: Company-sponsored foundation.
Financial data (yr. ended 1/31/05): Assets, $106,887 (M); gifts received, $906,160; expenditures, $959,264; qualifying distributions, $659,288; giving activities include $659,288 for 1,054 grants (high: $36,665; low: $5).
Purpose and activities: The foundation supports organizations involved with education, children and youth services, human services, and community development.
Fields of interest: Higher education; Education; Children/youth, services; Human services; Community development; Federated giving programs.
Type of support: General/operating support.
Limitations: Giving limited to areas of company operations. No support for religious organizations. No grants to individuals, or for solicitations or advertising.
Application information: Application form required.
Initial approach: Complete online application form
Deadline(s): None
Board meeting date(s): Varies
Officers and Trustees: * Michael J. Hopkins,* Pres.; Robert C. Hafner,* V.P.
EIN: 470656225
Selected grants: The following grants were reported in 2005.
$52,625 to Multiple Sclerosis Society, Edmonton, Canada. 2 grants: $15,960, $36,665.
$20,000 to United Way.
$5,500 to United Way of Central Indiana, Indianapolis, IN.

$2,500 to Southern Sudan Community Association, Omaha, NE.

$2,000 to United Way of Crawford County, Pittsburg, KS.

$1,000 to Garfield Memorial Library, Clare, MI.

$500 to American Cancer Society, Atlanta, GA.

$500 to Green Hills Community Action Agency, Trenton, MO.

$265 to Platte County School District No. 1, Wheatland, WY.

9892
The Pangburn Foundation ◇
c/o JPMorgan Chase Bank, N.A.
P.O. Box 1308
Milwaukee, WI 53201
Application address: c/o JPMorgan Chase Bank, N.A., Attn.: Robert Lansford, P.O. Box 2050, Fort Worth, TX 76113

Established in 1962 in TX.
Foundation type: Independent foundation.
Financial data (yr. ended 3/31/06): Assets, $7,617,044 (M); expenditures, $478,733; qualifying distributions, $407,000; giving activities include $407,000 for grants.
Purpose and activities: Emphasis on cultural programs, especially music and the performing arts; funding also for education and human services.
Fields of interest: Museums; Performing arts; Performing arts, ballet; Performing arts, theater; Performing arts, opera; Education; Human services.
Limitations: Giving primarily in the Fort Worth, TX, area. No grants to individuals.
Application information:
    Initial approach: Letter
    Copies of proposal: 1
    Deadline(s): Sept. 30
    Board meeting date(s): Oct. or Nov.
Trustee: JPMorgan Chase Bank, N.A.
EIN: 756042630
Selected grants: The following grants were reported in 2005.
$50,000 to Fort Worth Opera Association, Fort Worth, TX.
$21,000 to Van Cliburn Foundation, Fort Worth, TX.
$16,000 to Texas Christian University, Fort Worth, TX.
$15,000 to Cornerstone Assistance Network, North Richland Hills, TX.
$15,000 to Kids Who Care, Fort Worth, TX.
$6,000 to Open Arms Home, Fort Worth, TX.
$5,000 to Ballet Concerto, Fort Worth, TX.
$5,000 to Bruce Wood Dance Company, Fort Worth, TX.
$5,000 to Texas Girls Choir, Fort Worth, TX.
$5,000 to Texas Wesleyan University, Fort Worth, TX.

9893
Martha Sue Parr Trust ◇ ☆
c/o JPMorgan Chase Bank, N.A.
P.O. Box 1308
Milwaukee, WI 53201
Application address: JPMorgan Chase Bank, N.A.; Attn.: Don Smith, 420 Throckmorton, Fort Worth, TX 76102

Donor: Martha Sue Parr†.
Foundation type: Independent foundation.

Financial data (yr. ended 3/31/05): Assets, $20,482,070 (M); gifts received, $10,307,237; expenditures, $770,744; qualifying distributions, $593,717; giving activities include $552,500 for 5 grants (high: $200,000; low: $5,000).
Purpose and activities: Giving primarily to health foundations; support also for a children's home, an Episcopal diocese, and some giving to a theater.
Fields of interest: Performing arts, theater; Health care, association; Children, services; Residential/custodial care; Protestant agencies & churches.
Limitations: Giving primarily in TX.
Application information:
    Initial approach: Letter
    Deadline(s): None
Trustee: JPMorgan Chase Bank, N.A.
EIN: 416519559

9894
Milton and Lillian Peck Foundation, Inc. ◇
c/o Komisar Brady & Co., LLP
633 W. Wisconsin Ave., Ste. 900
Milwaukee, WI 53203-1907

Established in 1958.
Donors: Peck Meat Packing Corp.; Emmber Brands, Inc.; Gibbon Packing, Inc.; Moo-Battue, Inc.
Foundation type: Independent foundation.
Financial data (yr. ended 12/31/03): Assets, $10,260,064 (M); expenditures, $696,758; qualifying distributions, $654,598; giving activities include $647,333 for 62 grants (high: $307,000; low: $400).
Purpose and activities: Giving primarily to a zoological society, and for social services and health associations, including services for people who are blind or deaf; funding also for children's services, the arts and education.
Fields of interest: Arts; Higher education; Animal welfare; Health organizations; Human services; Children, services.
Type of support: General/operating support; Building/renovation; Scholarship funds.
Limitations: Applications not accepted. Giving primarily in Milwaukee, WI. No grants to individuals.
Application information: Contributes only to pre-selected organizations.
Officers and Directors:* Karen Peck Katz,* Pres.; Miriam Peck,* V.P.; William L. Komisar, Secy.-Treas.; Harvey Alligood; Bernard Peck; Jodi Peck.
EIN: 396051782

9895
Peck Foundation, Milwaukee, Ltd. ☆
(formerly Miriam & Bernard Peck Foundation, Ltd.)
P.O. Box 441
Milwaukee, WI 53201-0441
Contact: Karen Peck Katz, Co-Pres.

Established in 1985 in WI.
Donors: Jodi Peck; Miriam Peck; Bernard Peck; Karen Peck Katz.
Foundation type: Independent foundation.
Financial data (yr. ended 12/31/05): Assets, $13,500,885 (M); expenditures, $810,547; qualifying distributions, $750,031; giving activities include $732,515 for 85 grants (high: $200,000; low: $100).
Purpose and activities: Giving for education, health, human services, and Jewish organizations.

Fields of interest: Museums (art); Arts; Education; Health organizations, association; Human services; Jewish federated giving programs; Jewish agencies & temples.
Type of support: General/operating support; Capital campaigns; Annual campaigns.
Limitations: Applications not accepted. Giving primarily in Fort Lauderdale, FL and Milwaukee, WI. No grants for political organizations.
Application information: Unsolicited requests for funds not accepted.
    Board meeting date(s): Sept.
Officers and Directors:* Karen Peck Katz,* Co-Pres.; Jodi Peck,* Co-Pres.; William Komisar,* Secy.-Treas.; Harvey Alligood; Bernard Peck; Miriam Peck.
EIN: 391519687
Selected grants: The following grants were reported in 2005.
$50,000 to Broward Performing Arts Foundation, Fort Lauderdale, FL.
$27,500 to Concert Association of Florida, Miami Beach, FL.
$15,000 to Medical College of Wisconsin, Milwaukee, WI.
$15,000 to Planned Parenthood of Wisconsin, Milwaukee, WI.
$10,000 to American Jewish Committee, Milwaukee, WI.
$7,500 to Milwaukee Womens Center, Milwaukee, WI.
$3,000 to Jewish Home and Care Center, Milwaukee, WI.
$3,000 to Wisconsin Conservatory of Music, Milwaukee, WI.
$3,000 to Zink the Zebra Foundation, Mequon, WI.
$2,000 to Milwaukee School of Engineering, Milwaukee, WI.

9896
Fred J. Peterson Foundation, Inc.
41 N. 3rd Ave.
Sturgeon Bay, WI 54235-2413
Contact: Ellsworth L. Peterson, Pres.

Incorporated in 1962 in WI.
Donors: Ellsworth L. Peterson; Fred J. Peterson†; Irene Peterson†; Peterson Builders, Inc.
Foundation type: Independent foundation.
Financial data (yr. ended 9/30/05): Assets, $2,386,603 (M); expenditures, $907,631; qualifying distributions, $891,138; giving activities include $891,138 for 108 grants (high: $600,000; low: $34).
Purpose and activities: Giving to organizations working to improve the quality of life for WI citizens, with priority given to Door County organizations; grants for higher education, including scholarships through Rotary International, and various colleges, cultural programs, youth, and community development.
Fields of interest: Performing arts; Arts; Higher education; Children/youth, services; Residential/custodial care, hospices; Community development.
Type of support: Scholarship funds; Debt reduction; General/operating support; Continuing support; Annual campaigns; Capital campaigns; Building/renovation; Equipment; Endowments; Program development.
Limitations: Giving primarily in Door County, WI. No grants to individuals.

Application information: All scholarship decisions made by Rotary International or individual colleges. Application form not required.

Initial approach: Letter or telephone
Copies of proposal: 1
Deadline(s): None
Board meeting date(s): As needed
Final notification: Sept. 10

Officers and Trustees:* Ellsworth L. Peterson,* Pres.; Fred Peterson,* V.P.; Marsha L. Kerley,* Secy.

EIN: 396075901

Selected grants: The following grants were reported in 2004.

$200,000 to United States Merchant Marine Academy Foundation, Kings Point, NY.

$50,000 to Door County Memorial Hospital, Sturgeon Bay, WI.

$25,000 to YMCA of Door County, Sturgeon Bay, WI.

$10,000 to United Way of Door County, Sturgeon Bay, WI.

$7,200 to Wisconsin Foundation for Independent Colleges and Universities, Milwaukee, WI.

$5,000 to Door Community Auditorium, Fish Creek, WI.

$5,000 to Humane Society, Door County, Sturgeon Bay, WI.

$3,000 to American Maritime History Project, Kings Point, NY.

$3,000 to Help of Door County, Sturgeon Bay, WI.

$1,500 to Door County Maritime Museum, Sturgeon Bay, WI.

9897
Jane Bradley Pettit Foundation ▼ ◇
(formerly Jane and Lloyd Pettit Foundation, Inc.)
c/o Cook & Franke
660 E. Mason St., 5th Fl.
Milwaukee, WI 53202 (414) 227-1266
Contact: Cecelia I. Gore, Prog. Off.
URL: http://www.jbpf.org

Incorporated in 1986 in WI.

Donor: Jane Bradley Pettit†.

Foundation type: Independent foundation.

Financial data (yr. ended 12/31/04): Assets, $50,979,147 (M); gifts received, $11,309,545; expenditures, $5,265,780; qualifying distributions, $4,987,401; giving activities include $4,561,550 for 122 grants (high: $500,000; low: $450; average: $10,000–$50,000).

Purpose and activities: The foundation will provide funds to initiate and sustain projects in the Greater Milwaukee, WI, community. The foundation will focus on programs and projects that serve low-income and disadvantaged individuals, women, children and the elderly. The foundation will support charitable organizations that address these concerns through arts and culture, community and social development, education and health.

Fields of interest: Secondary school/education; Higher education; Hospitals (general); Health care; Health organizations, association; Human services; Children/youth, services; Children, services; Aging, centers/services; Women, centers/services.

Type of support: General/operating support; Annual campaigns; Capital campaigns; Building/ renovation; Program development; Research.

Limitations: Giving primarily in the greater Milwaukee, WI, area. No grants to individuals.

Publications: Application guidelines.

Application information: The foundation will not consider requests for additional support for the period in which an organization currently has a grant in effect. Requests for capital projects will only be considered in the Jan. 15 grant cycle.

Initial approach: Letter of inquiry (no more than 2 pages)
Copies of proposal: 1
Deadline(s): Jan. 15, May 15, and Sept. 15
Board meeting date(s): Varies
Final notification: Following board meeting

Officers and Directors:* Francis R. Croak,* Pres.; Margaret T. Lund,* V.P.; JoAnn C. Youngman,* Secy.-Treas.

EIN: 391574123

Selected grants: The following grants were reported in 2004.

$500,000 to Alverno College, Milwaukee, WI. For capital support.

$500,000 to Milwaukee Public Market, Milwaukee, WI. For capital support.

$500,000 to Riveredge Nature Center, Newburg, WI. For capital support.

$250,000 to Mount Mary College, Milwaukee, WI. For capital support.

$200,000 to Milwaukee Center for Independence, Milwaukee, WI. For capital support.

$175,000 to Pettit National Ice Center, Milwaukee, WI. For capital support.

$105,000 to Channel 10/36 Friends, Milwaukee, WI. For operating support.

$15,000 to Hunger Task Force of Milwaukee, Milwaukee, WI. For operating support.

$15,000 to Latino Community Center, Milwaukee, WI. For operating support.

$15,000 to Strive Media Institute, Milwaukee, WI. For operating support.

9898
William H. Phipps Foundation ◇
P.O. Box 653
Hudson, WI 54016

Incorporated in 1946 in WI.

Donors: Helen Clark Phipps†; Stephen C. Phipps†; John Harding†.

Foundation type: Independent foundation.

Financial data (yr. ended 4/30/05): Assets, $7,650,472 (M); expenditures, $478,751; qualifying distributions, $418,629; giving activities include $412,950 for 15 grants (high: $190,000; low: $1,450).

Purpose and activities: Support primarily for an arts center, as well as for education, and youth, family and social services. The foundation may also make grants to the Hudson, WI, school district for scholarships to graduating seniors.

Fields of interest: Arts, multipurpose centers/ programs; Secondary school/education; Education; Youth development, scouting agencies (general); Human services; Children/youth, services; Family services.

Type of support: Building/renovation; Curriculum development; Scholarship funds.

Limitations: Giving limited to the Hudson, WI, area. No grants to individuals.

Application information: Application form not required.

Initial approach: Letter outlining request
Copies of proposal: 1
Deadline(s): None
Board meeting date(s): May 1 and as needed
Final notification: 3 months

Officers and Directors:* Hugh G. Bryce,* Pres.; John Clymer, Secy.; Hugh F. Gwin,* Treas.; Gordon Anderson; Frederick E. Nagel; James Steel.

EIN: 396043312

Selected grants: The following grants were reported in 2004.

$180,000 to Phipps Center for the Arts, Hudson, WI. For annual support.

$25,000 to Girl Scouts of the U.S.A., Saint Croix Valley Council, Saint Paul, MN. For annual support.

$20,000 to Saint Croix Valley Sexual Assault Response Team, Baldwin, WI.

$15,000 to Community Action, Hudson, WI.

$15,000 to Education Foundation of Hudson, Hudson, WI.

$10,000 to Hope Adoption and Family Services International, Oak Park Heights, MN. For annual support.

$10,000 to Minnesota Orchestral Association, Minneapolis, MN.

$8,000 to Courage Center, Golden Valley, MN. For annual support.

$5,000 to Skits Outreach Services (SOS), Hudson, WI. For annual support.

$1,407 to Saint Croix County Department of Health and Human Services, New Richmond, WI. For Birkmose Fund.

9899
Melitta S. Pick Charitable Trust ◇
c/o Foley & Lardner LLP
777 E. Wisconsin Ave., Ste. 3800
Milwaukee, WI 53202-5306 (414) 297-5748
Contact: Harold J. McComas, Tr.

Established in 1972 in WI.

Donor: Melitta S. Pick†.

Foundation type: Independent foundation.

Financial data (yr. ended 1/31/06): Assets, $25,228,548 (M); expenditures, $1,031,263; qualifying distributions, $919,364; giving activities include $859,000 for 53 grants (high: $100,000; low: $1,000).

Purpose and activities: Giving primarily to a private operating foundation; support also for the arts, including museums, music, and the performing arts, higher education, and human services.

Fields of interest: Museums; Performing arts; Performing arts, music; Arts; Higher education; Human services; YM/YWCAs & YM/YWHAs; Youth, services.

Type of support: General/operating support; Annual campaigns; Capital campaigns; Building/ renovation; Endowments; Emergency funds.

Limitations: Giving primarily in southeastern WI. No grants to individuals.

Application information: Application form not required.

Initial approach: Letter
Deadline(s): None
Board meeting date(s): Usually quarterly

Trustees: Harold J. McComas; Joan M. Pick.

EIN: 237243490

Selected grants: The following grants were reported in 2005.

$336,500 to West Bend Art Museum, West Bend, WI.

$100,000 to Milwaukee Public Museum, Milwaukee, WI.

$100,000 to Milwaukee Symphony Orchestra, Milwaukee, WI.

$100,000 to United Performing Arts Fund, Milwaukee, WI.

$50,000 to Milwaukee Art Museum, Milwaukee, WI.

$30,000 to Neighborhood House of Milwaukee, Milwaukee, WI.

$25,000 to Cedar Community Foundation, West Bend, WI.

$25,000 to College of Wooster, Wooster, OH.

$10,000 to Milwaukee School of Engineering, Milwaukee, WI.

$3,000 to Center for Deaf-Blind Persons, Milwaukee, WI.

9900
Pollybill Foundation, Inc. ✧
111 E. Kilbourn Ave., 19th Fl.
Milwaukee, WI 53202-6622

Incorporated in 1960 in WI.
Donors: William D. Van Dyke; Polly H. Van Dyke.
Foundation type: Independent foundation.
Financial data (yr. ended 12/31/04): Assets, $4,855,041 (M); gifts received, $1,691,875; expenditures, $1,252,329; qualifying distributions, $1,252,329; giving activities include $1,250,250 for 68 grants (high: $350,000; low: $500).
Purpose and activities: Giving primarily for arts and culture, particularly for the symphony, an institute of art and design, resource conservation, particularly a botanical garden and the Audubon Society, hospitals, family planning, social services, and federated giving programs.
Fields of interest: Arts education; Museums (art); Performing arts, orchestra (symphony); Higher education; Environment, natural resources; Botanical gardens; Hospitals (general); Reproductive health, family planning; Human services; Children, services; Federated giving programs.
Limitations: Applications not accepted. Giving primarily in Milwaukee, WI. No grants to individuals.
Application information: Contributes only to pre-selected organizations.
Officers and Directors: * Polly H. Van Dyke,* Pres. and Treas.; William D. Van Dyke III,* V.P.; Paul F. Meissner,* Secy.; Leonard C. Campbell.
EIN: 396078550
Selected grants: The following grants were reported in 2005.
$60,000 to Historic Third Ward Association, Milwaukee, WI.
$25,000 to Greater Milwaukee Foundation, Milwaukee, WI.
$20,000 to Masters School, Dobbs Ferry, NY.
$15,000 to Connecticut College, New London, CT.
$15,000 to Saint Christophers Episcopal Church, Milwaukee, WI.
$12,500 to Milwaukee Institute of Art and Design, Milwaukee, WI.
$10,000 to Columbia Foundation, Milwaukee, WI.
$10,000 to Mequon Nature Preserve, Mequon, WI.
$7,500 to United Performing Arts Fund, Milwaukee, WI.
$7,500 to United Way of Greater Milwaukee, Milwaukee, WI.

9901
Gene & Ruth Posner Foundation, Inc. ✧
c/o Michael Best & Friedrich LLP
100 E. Wisconsin Ave., No. 3300
Milwaukee, WI 53202-4108
Contact: Joshua L. Gimbel, Dir.

Established in 1963 in WI.
Donors: Gene Posner; Ruth Posner.
Foundation type: Independent foundation.
Financial data (yr. ended 12/31/05): Assets, $6,139,824 (M); gifts received, $1,290; expenditures, $439,460; qualifying distributions, $439,460; giving activities include $348,505 for 46 grants (high: $150,000; low: $100).
Purpose and activities: Grants limited to educational, civic, medical and religious fields.
Fields of interest: Arts; Education; Health care; Health organizations, association; Jewish federated giving programs; Jewish agencies & temples.
Limitations: Giving primarily in Milwaukee, WI. No grants to individuals.
Application information: Application form not required.
Initial approach: Letter
Deadline(s): None
Board meeting date(s): May and Nov.
Directors: Joshua L. Gimbel; Frederic G. Posner; Barbara P. Ward.
Number of staff: 1 part-time support.
EIN: 396050150

9902
PPC Foundation
(formerly Pieperpower Foundation, Inc.)
5070 N. 35th St.
Milwaukee, WI 53209-5302 (414) 462-7700
Contact: Donna Ebert, Exec. Asst.

Established in 1968.
Donors: Pieper Electric, Inc.; PPC Partners, Inc.
Foundation type: Company-sponsored foundation.
Financial data (yr. ended 12/31/03): Assets, $0 (M); gifts received, $223,000; expenditures, $330,584; qualifying distributions, $330,437; giving activities include $330,437 for 336 grants (high: $100,000; low: $25).
Purpose and activities: The foundation supports organizations involved with arts and culture, education, health, human services, and government and public administration.
Fields of interest: Arts; Education; Health care; Children/youth, services; Human services; Federated giving programs; Government/public administration.
Type of support: General/operating support; Employee matching gifts.
Limitations: Giving primarily in Milwaukee, WI. No grants to individuals.
Application information: Application form not required.
Initial approach: Proposal
Copies of proposal: 1
Deadline(s): Oct. 15
Board meeting date(s): Nov.
Officers: Ronnie Hinson, Pres.; Richard R. Pieper, Sr., Secy.; Thomas Ohlgart, Treas.
EIN: 396124770

9903
Prescott Family Foundation, Inc. ✧ ☆
c/o Beth Fellenz
2412 W. Washington St., Ste. 200
West Bend, WI 53095

Established in 2002 in WI.
Donors: Prescott's Supermarket, Inc.; George Prescott.
Foundation type: Independent foundation.
Financial data (yr. ended 12/31/05): Assets, $6,223,650 (M); gifts received, $800,629; expenditures, $378,216; qualifying distributions, $347,741; giving activities include $337,000 for 22 grants (high: $99,000; low: $1,000).
Purpose and activities: The foundation supports organizations involved with underprivileged youth and Parkinson's disease research.
Fields of interest: Parkinson's disease research; Youth, services.
Type of support: Program development; Curriculum development; Continuing support; Annual campaigns; Capital campaigns; Building/renovation; Seed money; Matching/challenge support.
Limitations: Applications not accepted. Giving primarily in Washington County, WI. No support for religious or political organizations.
Publications: Annual report; Grants list.
Application information: Contributes only to pre-selected organizations.
Officers and Directors: * Judith A. Prescott,* Pres.; Matthew Prescott,* Secy.; Patrick Prescott,* Treas.; Beth Fellenz; Cheryl Prescott-Miller; George E. Prescott.
EIN: 061667125
Selected grants: The following grants were reported in 2005.
$164,000 to Boys and Girls Club. 3 grants: $15,000, $50,000, $99,000
$26,000 to Big Brothers/Big Sisters. 2 grants: $21,000, $5,000
$12,000 to United Way.
$8,500 to Living Hope International, Clackamas, OR.
$7,500 to YMCA.
$4,000 to American Red Cross.

9904
Puelicher Foundation, Inc. ✧
770 N. Water St.
Milwaukee, WI 53202 (414) 765-7707
Contact: James B. Wigdale, Pres.

Established in 1956.
Donor: John A. Puelicher†.
Foundation type: Independent foundation.
Financial data (yr. ended 12/31/05): Assets, $7,795,839 (M); expenditures, $1,823,761; qualifying distributions, $1,786,500; giving activities include $1,786,500 for 35 grants (high: $500,000; low: $1,000).
Purpose and activities: Funding primarily for a university and for wildlife conservation.
Fields of interest: Arts; Higher education; Environment, natural resources; Animals/wildlife, preservation/protection; Human services.
Type of support: General/operating support; Scholarship funds.
Limitations: Giving primarily in Milwaukee, WI.
Application information: Application form not required.

Initial approach: Letter, including expected community benefits
Copies of proposal: 1
Deadline(s): None
Board meeting date(s): Summer and early Dec.
Officers: James B. Wigdale, Pres.; Diane L. Sebion, Secy.-Treas.
EIN: 396055461
Selected grants: The following grants were reported in 2003.
$500,000 to Milwaukee Public Schools, Milwaukee, WI.
$60,000 to Marquette University, Milwaukee, WI.
$50,000 to Bear Trust International, Missoula, MT.
$50,000 to Childrens Hospital of Wisconsin, Milwaukee, WI.
$50,000 to Messmer High School, Milwaukee, WI.
$50,000 to Ozaukee Ice Association, Mequon, WI.
$50,000 to University of Wisconsin, School of Veterinary Medicine, Madison, WI.
$50,000 to YMCA of Metropolitan Milwaukee, Milwaukee, WI.
$30,000 to United Way of Greater Milwaukee, Milwaukee, WI.
$25,000 to Urban Ecology Center, Milwaukee, WI.

9905

Purple Moon Foundation, Inc. ✧ ☆
715 Dunning St.
Madison, WI 53704

Established in 1999 in WI.
Donor: Dale Leibowitz.
Foundation type: Independent foundation.
Financial data (yr. ended 12/31/05): Assets, $2,001,698 (L); gifts received, $1,390,000; expenditures, $1,366,045; qualifying distributions, $1,366,045; giving activities include $1,366,000 for 9 grants (high: $900,000; low: $1,000).
Fields of interest: Arts; Higher education.
Limitations: Applications not accepted. Giving primarily in WI. No grants to individuals.
Application information: Contributes only to pre-selected organizations.
Officers and Director:* Dale Leibowitz, Pres.; Gillian Blake,* V.P.; Sheri Kole, Secy.-Treas.
EIN: 391975376
Selected grants: The following grants were reported in 2004.
$100,000 to Parental Stress Center, Madison, WI.
$22,500 to OutReach, Inc., Madison, WI.
$10,000 to Progressive, Inc., Madison, WI.
$2,500 to Atwood Community Center, Madison, WI.
$1,000 to Jewish Social Services of Madison, Madison, WI.
$500 to Madison Childrens Museum, Madison, WI.
$500 to Wil-Mar Neighborhood Center, Madison, WI.
$500 to Wisconsin Chamber Orchestra, Madison, WI.
$500 to Wisconsin Youth Symphony Orchestra, Madison, WI.
$250 to In the Life Media, New York, NY.

9906

Racine Community Foundation, Inc.
(formerly Racine County Area Foundation, Inc.)
245 Main St., Garden Level
Racine, WI 53403 (262) 632-8474
Contact: Margaret L. Kozina, Exec. Dir.
FAX: (262) 632-3739; E-mail: info@racinecf.org;
URL: http://www.racinecf.org

Incorporated in 1975 in WI.
Foundation type: Community foundation.
Financial data (yr. ended 12/31/05): Assets, $30,733,148 (M); gifts received, $1,587,904; expenditures, $1,563,416; giving activities include $1,247,177 for grants.
Purpose and activities: The mission of the foundation is to encourage and provide opportunities for charitable giving, to manage and distribute the funds in a responsible manner, and to enhance the quality of life for the people of Racine County, WI.
Fields of interest: Performing arts, music; Arts; Education; Environment; Health care; Human services; Community development; Youth; Aging.
Type of support: Endowments; Equipment; Program development; Conferences/seminars; Seed money; Scholarships—to individuals; Matching/challenge support.
Limitations: Giving limited to Racine County, WI. No support for church or missionary groups unless for entire community benefit, grantmaking foundations, or social, athletic, veterans', labor, or fraternal organizations. No grants to individuals (except for donor directed scholarships), or for capital expenditures, including building funds, endowment funds, research, travel, or publications.
Publications: Application guidelines; Annual report; Informational brochure; Newsletter.
Application information: Visit foundation Web site for application guidelines. Application form required.
Initial approach: Telephone
Copies of proposal: 19
Deadline(s): Jan. 15, Apr. 15, July 15, and Oct. 15
Board meeting date(s): Mar., June, Sept., and Dec.
Final notification: By letter after meeting in which proposal was discussed (2 months after deadline)
Officers and Directors:* Greg A. Ruidl,* Pres.; Jean M. Jacobson, V.P., Mktg.; Elizabeth A. Powell,* V.P., Grants; Hon. Nancy E. Wheeler,* V.P., Donor Rels.; Arthel L. Howell,* Secy.; John P. Crimmings,* Treas. and Finance Chair.; Robert O. Walker,* Investment Chair.; Margaret L. Kozina, Exec. Dir.; Virginia M. Buhler; Randy K. Bush; James A. Eastman; Pamela M. Johnson; Renee S. Kirby; Dorothy A. Metz; Sara E. Naubauer; Dwayne G. Olsen; Jackson V. Parker III; Robert F. Seigert; Michael P. Staeck; Bernice M. Styberg; Robert F. Taylor; Guadalupe G. Villarreal.
Number of staff: 3 full-time professional; 1 part-time professional.
EIN: 510188377

9907

Rath Foundation, Inc. ▼ ✧
P.O. Box 1990
Janesville, WI 53547 (608) 754-9090
Contact: James D. Dodson, Pres.

Established in 1989 in WI.
Donor: V. Duane Rath.
Foundation type: Independent foundation.
Financial data (yr. ended 12/31/05): Assets, $46,625,617 (M); expenditures, $5,113,070; qualifying distributions, $4,915,644; giving activities include $4,875,548 for 34 grants (high: $1,196,248; low: $5,000; average: $5,000–$199,249).
Purpose and activities: Giving primarily for charitable, scientific, literary, and educational purposes.

Fields of interest: Literature; Education; Health care; Philanthropy/voluntarism; Science.
Limitations: Giving on a national basis, with some emphasis on WI. No grants to individuals.
Application information:
Initial approach: Letter
Deadline(s): None
Officers: James D. Dodson, Pres.; James R. Sanger, V.P.; Kate M. Fleming, Secy.
EIN: 391657654
Selected grants: The following grants were reported in 2005.
$1,196,248 to University of Wisconsin Foundation, Madison, WI. For general support.
$593,198 to University of Oklahoma Foundation, Norman, OK. For general support.
$558,352 to Wisconsin Foundation for Independent Colleges and Universities, Milwaukee, WI. For general support.
$518,198 to University of Chicago, Chicago, IL. For general support.
$500,000 to American Red Cross, Janesville, WI. For general support.
$403,876 to Medical College of Wisconsin, Milwaukee, WI. For general support.
$199,249 to University of Wisconsin Foundation, Milwaukee, WI. For general support.
$159,475 to University of Southern California, Marshall School of Business, Los Angeles, CA. For general support.
$159,096 to University of Wisconsin Foundation, Whitewater, WI. For general support.
$79,928 to University of Wisconsin Foundation, Eau Claire, WI. For general support.

9908

Reiman Foundation, Inc. ▼ ✧
(formerly Reiman Charitable Foundation, Inc.)
115 S. 84th St., No. 221
Milwaukee, WI 53214 (414) 456-0600
Contact: Michael J. Hipp, Secy.
FAX: (414) 456-0606;
E-mail: reimanfoundation@hexagoninc.com;
URL: http://www.reimanfoundation.org

Established in 1986 in WI.
Donors: Roy J. Reiman; Roberta M. Reiman; Scott J. Reiman; Joni R. Winston; Cynthia A. Lambert; Julia M. Ellis; Terrin S. Riemer.
Foundation type: Independent foundation.
Financial data (yr. ended 12/31/04): Assets, $157,713,367 (M); gifts received, $10,500,000; expenditures, $12,019,079; qualifying distributions, $10,053,598; giving activities include $10,053,598 for 205+ grants (high: $1,000,000; average: $5,000–$500,000).
Purpose and activities: Giving primarily for education, health care, and children's initiatives.
Fields of interest: Education; Health care; Children, services; Children.
Publications: Application guidelines.
Application information: The foundation will acknowledge receipt of application. See foundation Web site for further details. Application form not required.
Initial approach: Letter
Deadline(s): None
Officers and Directors:* Scott J. Reiman,* Pres.; Brian F. Fleischmann,* V.P.; Roberta M. Reiman,* V.P.; Roy J. Reiman,* V.P.; Michael J. Hipp,* Secy.; Troy G. Hildebrandt.
EIN: 391570264

Selected grants: The following grants were reported in 2004.

$1,000,000 to Atlanta Symphony Orchestra, Atlanta, GA. For general operating support.

$1,000,000 to Denver Art Museum, Denver, CO. For capital campaign.

$1,000,000 to University of Denver, Denver, CO. For hotel, restaurant and tourism management building fund.

$784,441 to Childrens Hospital and Health System Foundation, Milwaukee, WI. For general operating support.

$518,000 to Lees Summit Educational Foundation, Lees Summit, MO. For general operating support.

$250,000 to Denver Dumb Friends League-Humane Society of Denver, Denver, CO. For general operating support.

$50,000 to United Performing Arts Fund, Milwaukee, WI. For general operating support.

$24,440 to Greendale School District, Greendale, WI. For Birdhouse Workshop Project.

$19,965 to West Central Iowa Health Care Foundation, Manning, IA. For general operating support.

$10,000 to Humane Society, Sheboygan County, Sheboygan, WI. For general operating support.

9909
D. B. Reinhart Family Foundation ✧
P.O. Box 2228
La Crosse, WI 54602-2228

Established in 1987 in WI.
Donors: Marjorie A. Reinhart; D.B. Reinhart Enterprises; Reinhart Institutional Foods.
Foundation type: Independent foundation.
Financial data (yr. ended 8/31/05): Assets, $5,326,846 (M); expenditures, $2,390,372; qualifying distributions, $2,389,344; giving activities include $2,389,344 for 30 grants (high: $510,000; low: $100).
Purpose and activities: Giving primarily for education, health, social services, children and youth services, federated giving programs, and Roman Catholic agencies and churches.
Fields of interest: Museums (children's); Higher education; Hospitals (general); Health organizations, association; Medical research, institute; Recreation; Human services; Children/youth, services; Federated giving programs; Roman Catholic agencies & churches.
Limitations: Applications not accepted. Giving primarily in WI, with emphasis on La Crosse. No grants to individuals.
Application information: Contributes only to pre-selected organizations.
Manager: Nancy Hengel.
Trustees: Gerald E. Connolly; Marjorie A. Reinhart.
EIN: 391564353
Selected grants: The following grants were reported in 2004.

$500,000 to Childrens Hospital of Wisconsin, Milwaukee, WI.

$500,000 to Franciscan Skemp Foundation, La Crosse, WI.

$400,000 to Gundersen Lutheran Medical Center, La Crosse, WI. For Cancer Center.

$200,000 to La Crosse Medical Health Science Consortium, La Crosse, WI.

$75,000 to Diocese of La Crosse, La Crosse, WI.

$60,000 to Chileda Institute, La Crosse, WI.

$25,000 to Western Wisconsin Technical College, La Crosse, WI.

$16,000 to La Crosse Symphony Orchestra, La Crosse, WI.

$10,000 to United Fund for the Arts and Humanities, La Crosse, WI.

$1,000 to Philharmonic Center for the Arts, Naples, FL.

9910
The Oscar Rennebohm Foundation, Inc. ✧
P.O. Box 5187
Madison, WI 53705-0187 (608) 274-5991
Contact: Steven F. Skolaski, Pres. and Treas.

Incorporated in 1949 in WI.
Donors: Oscar Rennebohm†; Leona Sondregger.
Foundation type: Independent foundation.
Financial data (yr. ended 12/31/04): Assets, $57,067,200 (M); expenditures, $3,001,992; qualifying distributions, $2,700,783; giving activities include $2,565,543 for 8 grants (high: $1,565,000; low: $25,000; average: $50,000–$200,000).
Purpose and activities: Emphasis on higher education; support also for the arts, conservation, and health and social service agencies.
Fields of interest: Arts, multipurpose centers/programs; Higher education; Environmental education; Medical care, rehabilitation; Foundations (community).
Type of support: Building/renovation; Equipment; Research.
Limitations: Giving primarily in WI.
Application information: Application form not required.
> *Initial approach:* Letter
> *Deadline(s):* None
Officers: Steven F. Skolaski, Pres. and Treas.; Patrick E. Coyle, V.P.; Curtis F. Hastings, Secy.
Directors: Robert B. Rennebohm; Gary L. Schaefer; Lenor B. Zeeh.
EIN: 396039252

9911
Michael T. Riordan Family Foundation ✧
c/o Michael T. Riordan
W3563 Meredith Ln.
Green Lake, WI 54941

Established in 2001 in WI.
Donor: Michael T. Riordan.
Foundation type: Independent foundation.
Financial data (yr. ended 12/31/05): Assets, $11,817,325 (M); expenditures, $675,958; qualifying distributions, $560,670; giving activities include $554,400 for 29 grants (high: $202,500; low: $200).
Fields of interest: Elementary/secondary education; Higher education; Education; Health care; Health organizations, association; Human services; YM/YWCAs & YM/YWHAs; Children/youth, services; Family services; Federated giving programs; Roman Catholic agencies & churches.
Limitations: Applications not accepted. Giving primarily in Green Bay, WI. No grants to individuals.
Application information: Contributes only to pre-selected organizations.
Trustee: Michael T. Riordan.
EIN: 306000348

9912
Rockwell Automation Charitable Corp.
1201 S. 2nd St.
Milwaukee, WI 53204 (414) 382-1548
Contact: Eileen Walter
E-mail: jlpanek@ra.rockwell.com; URL: http://www.rockwellautomation.com/about_us/citizenship.html

Established in 2003 in WI.
Donors: Rockwell International Corporation Trust; Rockwell Automation.
Foundation type: Company-sponsored foundation.
Financial data (yr. ended 9/30/05): Assets, $2,898,076 (M); gifts received, $5,000,000; expenditures, $3,977,559; qualifying distributions, $3,973,494; giving activities include $3,570,869 for 126 grants (high: $425,000; low: $1,000), and $386,648 for employee matching gifts.
Purpose and activities: The foundation supports organizations involved with arts and culture, education, health, human services, and civic affairs. Special emphasis is directed toward programs designed to promote K-12 science, technology, engineering, and math education.
Fields of interest: Arts; Elementary/secondary education; Higher education; Education; Health care; Human services; Federated giving programs; Mathematics; Engineering/technology; Science; Government/public administration.
Type of support: General/operating support; Scholarship funds; Employee matching gifts.
Limitations: Giving on a national basis with some emphasis on SC and WI; giving also to national organizations. No support for religious, fraternal, or social organizations. No grants to individuals.
Publications: Application guidelines.
Application information: Application form required.
> *Initial approach:* Download application form and mail to nearest company facility; download application form and mail to foundation for national organizations
> *Copies of proposal:* 1
> *Deadline(s):* Oct. 15, Jan. 15, Apr. 15, and July 15
> *Board meeting date(s):* Quarterly
Officers and Trustees: Keith D. Nosbusch, Chair.; Mary Jane Hall, Secy.; John D. Cohn; James V. Gelly; Doug M. Hagerman; U.S. Bank, N.A.
EIN: 481307009

9913
Hamilton Roddis Foundation, Inc. ✧
c/o Augusta D. Roddis
1108 E. 4th St.
Marshfield, WI 54449-4539

Incorporated in 1953 in WI.
Donors: Hamilton Roddis†; Augusta D. Roddis; Catherine P. Roddis; Roddis Plywood Corp.
Foundation type: Independent foundation.
Financial data (yr. ended 12/31/03): Assets, $6,717,323 (M); gifts received, $200,000; expenditures, $371,563; qualifying distributions, $347,709; giving activities include $345,730 for 43 grants (high: $150,000; low: $100).
Purpose and activities: Giving primarily to Episcopal churches and for religious education, social services, medical research, education, historic preservation, local associations, and conservative political organizations.
Fields of interest: Historic preservation/historical societies; Education; Medical research, institute; Human services; Federated giving programs;

Religious federated giving programs; Public affairs, single organization support; Protestant agencies & churches.

Limitations: Applications not accepted. Giving on a national basis, with some emphasis on WI, particularly Marshfield. No grants to individuals.

Application information: Contributes only to pre-selected organizations.

Officers: William H. Roddis II, Pres.; Augusta D. Roddis, Secy.-Treas.

EIN: 396077001

Selected grants: The following grants were reported in 2004.

$107,500 to Camp Five Museum Foundation, Laona, WI. 2 grants: $57,500, $50,000

$35,000 to Mayo Foundation, Rochester, MN.

$25,000 to Heritage Foundation, DC.

$12,000 to Living Church Foundation, Milwaukee, WI.

$10,000 to North Wood County Historical Society, Marshfield, WI.

$7,500 to Wisconsin Policy Research Institute, Mequon, WI.

$2,500 to Eagle Forum Education and Legal Defense Fund, Alton, IL.

9914

Robert T. Rolfs Foundation, Inc. ✧ ☆

c/o U.S. Bank, N.A.

P.O. Box 2043, Rm. MKLC4

Milwaukee, WI 53201-9116

Application address: c/o Lisa Sivanich, US Bank, 777 E. Wisconsin Ave., Milwaukee, WI 53202

Established in 1981 in WI.

Donors: Robert T. Rolfs; Amity Leather Products Co.

Foundation type: Independent foundation.

Financial data (yr. ended 9/30/05): Assets, $14,337,952 (M); gifts received, $704; expenditures, $1,444,073; qualifying distributions, $1,246,275; giving activities include $1,230,000 for 70 grants (high: $150,000; low: $1,000).

Purpose and activities: Giving primarily for social services; giving also for the arts and health.

Fields of interest: Arts; Health care; Health organizations, association; Human services.

Limitations: Giving primarily in WI. No grants to individuals.

Application information: Application form not required.

Initial approach: Letter

Deadline(s): None

Officers: Robert T. Rolfs, Pres.; Marilyn Rolfs, V.P.; J. Lewis Perlson, Secy.-Treas.

Directors: Mark T. Rolfs; Robert T. Rolfs, Jr.

EIN: 391390015

Selected grants: The following grants were reported in 2005.

$150,000 to Western Golf Association, Golf, IL.

$75,000 to Operation USA, Los Angeles, CA.

$70,000 to Milwaukee Symphony Orchestra, Milwaukee, WI.

$65,000 to Catholic Relief Services, Baltimore, MD.

$50,000 to Boys and Girls Club.

$43,000 to University of Wisconsin-Washington County, West Bend, WI.

$20,000 to Bruce Guadalupe Community School, Milwaukee, WI.

$20,000 to Salvation Army.

$15,000 to United Negro College Fund, Fairfax, VA.

$12,000 to Channel 10/36 Friends, Milwaukee, WI.

9915

Roundy's Foundation, Inc. ✧ ☆

M.S. 2175

P.O. Box 473

Milwaukee, WI 53201-0473 (414) 231-6159

URL: http://www.roundys.com/modules/content/index.php?id=5&secid=1

Established in 2003 in WI.

Donors: Roundy's, Inc.; Roundy's Supermarkets, Inc.

Foundation type: Company-sponsored foundation.

Financial data (yr. ended 12/31/04): Assets, $55,327 (M); gifts received, $393,720; expenditures, $354,393; qualifying distributions, $354,393; giving activities include $226,400 for 28 grants (high: $75,000; low: $2,500), and $69,993 for 9 in-kind gifts.

Purpose and activities: The foundation supports organizations involved with literacy, hunger, and family services.

Fields of interest: Education, reading; Food services; Family services.

Type of support: General/operating support; Donated products.

Limitations: Giving primarily in areas of company operations in IL, MN, and WI. No support for religious organizations not of direct benefit to the entire community, educational institutions for regular programs, foundations, or athletic teams. No grants to individuals, or for capital campaigns or sporting events.

Application information: An application form is required for requests of over $5,000.

Initial approach: Proposal; download application form and mail to foundation for requests of over $5,000

Deadline(s): None

Directors: Flamont T. Butler; Gerardo Gonzalez; Darren W. Karst; Ed Kitz; Robert A. Mariano; Colleen J. Stenholt; Sarah Jane Voichcik.

EIN: 200299349

9916

Pleasant T. Rowland Foundation, Inc. ▼

3415 Gateway Rd., Ste. 200

Brookfield, WI 53045-5111

Contact: Marti Sebree, Grants Mgr.

Application address: 1 S. Pinckney St., No. 810, Madison, WI 53703

Established in 1997 in WI.

Donor: Pleasant T. Rowland.

Foundation type: Independent foundation.

Financial data (yr. ended 12/31/04): Assets, $111,203,802 (M); expenditures, $16,048,790; qualifying distributions, $14,831,944; giving activities include $14,764,124 for 89 grants (high: $2,352,032; low: $500; average: $1,000–$100,000), $67,820 for 8 grants to individuals (high: $14,000; low: $1,500), and $1,690,728 for 1 foundation-administered program.

Purpose and activities: Giving primarily for arts, education and historic preservation.

Fields of interest: Historic preservation/historical societies; Arts; Education.

Type of support: Program development; Scholarships—to individuals; Matching/challenge support.

Limitations: Giving primarily in WI, with emphasis on Dane County. No support for religious or political organizations.

Publications: Application guidelines.

Application information: Application form required.

Initial approach: Telephone

Copies of proposal: 1

Deadline(s): Mar. 30, June 30, Sept. 30, and Nov. 30

Board meeting date(s): Apr., July, Oct., and Dec.

Final notification: 4 - 6 weeks

Trustees: Barbara Thiele Carr; W. Jerome Frautschi; Valerie Tripp; Rhona E. Vogel.

Number of staff: 1 full-time professional.

EIN: 391868295

Selected grants: The following grants were reported in 2004.

$5,656,770 to Wells College, Aurora, NY. 4 grants: $1,476,012 (For building maintenance. Grant made in form of stock), $187,640 (For buildings), $1,993,931 (For building maintenance. Grant made in form of stock), $1,999,187 (For building maintenance. Grant made in form of stock).

$4,829,011 to Madison Community Foundation, Madison, WI. 5 grants: $2,352,032 (For Great Performance Fund. Grant made in form of stock), $824,994 (For Great Performance Fund. Grant made in form of stock), $151,630 (For Great Performance Fund), $984,284 (For Great Performance Fund. Grant made in form of stock), $516,071 (For Great Performance Fund. Grant made in form of stock).

$400,000 to Madison Symphony Orchestra, Madison, WI. For organ refinements.

9917

Edward and Hannah M. Rutledge Charities, Inc. ✧ ☆

(formerly Edward Rutledge Charity)

P.O. Box 758

Chippewa Falls, WI 54729-0738

Contact: Betty Manning

Incorporated in 1911 in WI.

Donor: Edward Rutledge‡.

Foundation type: Independent foundation.

Financial data (yr. ended 5/31/06): Assets, $20,115,992 (M); gifts received, $2,206; expenditures, $526,824; qualifying distributions, $319,213; giving activities include $319,213 for grants.

Purpose and activities: To furnish relief and charity for worthy poor and to aid charitable associations or institutions; also administers college scholarship program.

Fields of interest: Education; Alcoholism; Human services; Youth, services; Aging, centers/services; Economically disadvantaged.

Type of support: General/operating support; Program development; Grants to individuals; Scholarships—to individuals; Student loans—to individuals.

Limitations: Giving limited to Chippewa County, WI. No grants for endowment funds.

Application information: Application form required for scholarships and other grants to individuals.

Initial approach: Letter

Copies of proposal: 1

Deadline(s): Scholarship applications must be submitted by June 1; no deadline for other grants

Board meeting date(s): Once a week

Final notification: 2 months for scholarships

Officers and Directors:* Gerald J. Naiberg,* Pres.; Richard H. Stafford,* V.P.; David Hancock,* Secy.-Treas.

Number of staff: 1 full-time professional; 1 full-time support.
EIN: 390806178

9918
Sand County Foundation, Inc. ☆
c/o David Allen
5999 Monona Dr.
P.O. Box 6587
Monona, WI 53716 (608) 663-4605
FAX: (608) 663-4617; E-mail: info@sandcounty.net;
URL: http://www.sandcounty.net

Classified as a private operating foundation in 1987.
Donors: Nash Williams†; Wisconsin Dept. of Natural Resources; Norman Basset Foundation; U.S. Fish and Wildlife; Ed Warner; Wisconsin Dept. of Transportation.
Foundation type: Operating foundation.
Financial data (yr. ended 12/31/05): Assets, $7,611,323 (M); gifts received, $2,295,334; expenditures, $1,912,102; qualifying distributions, $1,509,711; giving activities include $383,201 for 19 grants (high: $179,296; low: $1,000), and $1,826,453 for foundation-administered programs.
Purpose and activities: Giving to advance the use of ethical and scientifically sound land management practices and partnerships for the benefit of people and the ecological landscape.
Fields of interest: Education; Environment, water resources; Environment, land resources.
International interests: Southern Africa.
Type of support: General/operating support; Program development; Conferences/seminars; Research.
Limitations: Applications not accepted. No grants to individuals.
Publications: Newsletter.
Application information: Contributes only to pre-selected organizations.
   Board meeting date(s): Feb., June, Sept., and Dec.
Officers and Directors:* Reed Coleman,* Chair.; Brent M. Haglund,* Pres.; David Allen, V.P.; David J. Hanson,* Secy.-Treas.; Indy Burke; Donald Haldeman; George Kennedy; Scott Klug; David Langford; Terry Mulcahy; Weldon Schenck; Chuck Thompson; John Umlauf; Ed Warner; and 7 additional directors.
Number of staff: 6 full-time professional; 1 full-time support.
EIN: 396089450

9919
Oscar C. & Augusta Schlegel Foundation ✧
c/o Marshall & Ilsley Bank
P.O. Box 2980
Milwaukee, WI 53201-2980

Established in 1987 in WI.
Foundation type: Independent foundation.
Financial data (yr. ended 3/31/05): Assets, $8,085,249 (M); expenditures, $398,297; qualifying distributions, $363,000; giving activities include $363,000 for 43 grants (high: $36,000; low: $1,500).
Fields of interest: Arts; Secondary school/education; Hospitals (general); Human services; Youth, services.

Limitations: Applications not accepted. Giving limited to WI. No grants to individuals.
Application information: Contributes only to pre-selected organizations.
   Board meeting date(s): Quarterly
Officers: Marilyn L. Holmquist, Chair.; Roger T. Stephenson, Vice-Chair.; Steven J. Schumacher, Secy.
Director: Tom Lindell.
Trustee: Marshall & Ilsley Bank.
EIN: 391586544
Selected grants: The following grants were reported in 2005.
$20,000 to Washington County Historical Society, West Bend, WI. 2 grants: $10,000 each
$15,000 to Boys and Girls Club, West Bend, West Bend, WI.
$15,000 to United Way of Washington County, West Bend, WI.
$10,000 to West Bend Art Museum, West Bend, WI.
$6,000 to American Red Cross, Milwaukee, WI.
$6,000 to Full Shelf Food Pantry, West Bend, WI.
$6,000 to Lakeland College, Sheboygan, WI.
$6,000 to United Performing Arts Fund, Milwaukee, WI.
$4,000 to Family Center of Washington County, West Bend, WI.

9920
Schneider National Foundation, Inc. ✧
P.O. Box 2545
Green Bay, WI 54306-2545
Contact: Donald J. Schneider, Pres.

Established in 1983.
Donor: Schneider National, Inc.
Foundation type: Company-sponsored foundation.
Financial data (yr. ended 12/31/05): Assets, $78,936 (M); gifts received, $501,000; expenditures, $669,061; qualifying distributions, $669,061; giving activities include $669,061 for grants.
Purpose and activities: The foundation supports organizations involved with education, human services, and health.
Fields of interest: Education; Health organizations, association; Human services; Children/youth, services; Federated giving programs; Christian agencies & churches.
Limitations: Giving primarily in WI.
Application information: Application form not required.
   Initial approach: Proposal
   Deadline(s): None
Officers: Donald J. Schneider, Pres.; Thomas A. Gannon, Secy.-Treas.
EIN: 391457870
Selected grants: The following grants were reported in 2003.
$40,000 to United Way. For general support.
$24,000 to Family Services of Northeast Wisconsin, Green Bay, WI. For general support.
$20,000 to Northwestern University, Evanston, IL. For general support.
$15,000 to Encompass Child Care, Green Bay, WI. For general support.
$2,000 to United Way of the Mid-South, Memphis, TN. For general support.
$1,200 to Muscular Dystrophy Association, Tucson, AZ. For general support.
$1,000 to United Way of Metropolitan Dallas, Dallas, TX. For general support.

$750 to March of Dimes Birth Defects Foundation, Madison, WI. For general support.
$500 to Freedom House, DC. For general support.
$250 to Goodwill Industries. For general support.

9921
Schoenleber Foundation, Inc. ✧
c/o Janet Hoehnen
111 E. Wisconsin Ave., Ste. 1800
Milwaukee, WI 53202-4809 (414) 276-3400
Contact: Peter C. Haensel, Pres.

Established in 1965 in WI.
Donors: Marie Schoenleber†; Louise Schoenleber†; Gretchen Schoenleber†.
Foundation type: Independent foundation.
Financial data (yr. ended 12/31/05): Assets, $8,924,092 (M); expenditures, $550,516; qualifying distributions, $442,508; giving activities include $442,500 for 22 grants (high: $62,500; low: $5,000).
Purpose and activities: Giving primarily to a public library foundation, as well as for arts and culture, education, and human services, particularly to a center for people who are blind and/or deaf, and federated giving programs.
Fields of interest: Arts; Libraries (public); Education; Animals/wildlife, management/technical aid; Animals/wildlife, association; Human services; Federated giving programs; Disabilities, people with.
Type of support: General/operating support; Endowments; Scholarship funds.
Limitations: Giving primarily in WI, with emphasis on Milwaukee. No support for religious purposes, or for primary or secondary education. No grants to individuals.
Publications: Informational brochure (including application guidelines).
Application information: Application form required.
   Initial approach: Letter requesting application form
   Copies of proposal: 1
   Deadline(s): Aug. 30
Officers and Directors:* Peter C. Haensel,* Pres.; Frank W. Bastian,* Secy.; Walter Schorrak.
Number of staff: 1 full-time professional; 1 part-time support.
EIN: 391049364

9922
Sensient Technologies Foundation, Inc. ✧
777 E. Wisconsin Ave.
Milwaukee, WI 53202-5304
Contact: Doug Arnold

Incorporated in 1958 in WI.
Donors: Universal Foods Corp.; Sensient Technologies Corp.
Foundation type: Company-sponsored foundation.
Financial data (yr. ended 12/31/04): Assets, $9,974,463 (M); expenditures, $636,263; qualifying distributions, $619,731; giving activities include $619,731 for 97 grants (high: $100,000; low: $25).
Purpose and activities: The foundation supports organizations involved with arts and culture, education, health, mental health, medical research, hunger, nutrition, human services, community development, minorities, and homeless people.
Fields of interest: Performing arts; Arts; Education, research; Education, fund raising/fund distribution;

Higher education; Education; Hospitals (general); Health care; Mental health/crisis services; Medical research, institute; Food services; Nutrition; Children/youth, services; Family services; Residential/custodial care, hospices; Homeless, human services; Human services; Urban/ community development; Community development; Voluntarism promotion; Federated giving programs; General charitable giving; Minorities; Homeless.
Type of support: General/operating support; Annual campaigns; Capital campaigns; Building/ renovation; Endowments; Emergency funds; Program development; Scholarship funds; Research; Matching/challenge support.
Limitations: Giving primarily in Indianapolis, IN, St. Louis, MO, and Milwaukee, WI. No support for sectarian religious, fraternal, or veterans' organizations. No grants to individuals.
Application information: Application form not required.
  Initial approach: Letter of inquiry
  Copies of proposal: 1
  Deadline(s): 1 month prior to board meetings
  Board meeting date(s): Jan. and June/July, or as needed
  Final notification: Prior to Dec.
Officers: Kenneth P. Manning, Pres.; Richard Carney, V.P.; Richard F. Hobbs, V.P.; Stephen J. Rolfs, Secy.-Treas.
EIN: 396044488

9923
Sentry Insurance Foundation, Inc. ◇
(formerly Sentry Foundation, Inc.)
c/o Sentry Insurance
1800 N. Point Dr.
Stevens Point, WI 54481-1253
Contact: Peggy Sullivan, V.P. and Exec. Dir.

Incorporated in 1963 in WI.
Donor: Sentry Insurance.
Foundation type: Company-sponsored foundation.
Financial data (yr. ended 12/31/05): Assets, $5,759,748 (M); gifts received, $5,185,000; expenditures, $932,786; qualifying distributions, $932,465; giving activities include $548,743 for 43 grants (high: $188,980; low: $149), and $383,722 for 189 employee matching gifts.
Purpose and activities: The foundation supports organizations involved with arts and culture, education, health, and government and public administration.
Fields of interest: Arts; Higher education; Education; Health care; Federated giving programs; Government/public administration.
Type of support: General/operating support; Scholarship funds; Employee matching gifts.
Limitations: Giving primarily in WI. No support for religious organizations.
Publications: Occasional report.
Application information: Application form not required.
  Initial approach: Proposal
  Copies of proposal: 1
  Deadline(s): None
  Board meeting date(s): Dec.
Officers and Directors: * James J. Weishan, Chair. and Pres.; Peggy Sullivan, V.P. and Exec. Dir.; William M. O'Reilly, Secy.; William J. Lohr,* Treas.; Dale R. Schuh; David Schuler.
EIN: 391037370
Selected grants: The following grants were reported in 2004.

$134,930 to United Way of Portage County.
$72,833 to University of Wisconsin Stevens Point Foundation, Stevens Point, WI. 2 grants: $60,833, $12,000
$40,000 to Community Industries, Stevens Point, WI.
$12,000 to University of Wisconsin Oshkosh Foundation, Oshkosh, WI.
$10,000 to Family Crisis Center of Prince Georges County, Brentwood, MD.
$7,500 to Rawhide, New London, WI.
$6,700 to United Way. 2 grants: $4,020, $2,680
$5,000 to Chicago Lights, Chicago, IL.

9924
Seramur Family Foundation, Inc. ◇ ☆
c/o John C. Seramur
P.O. Box 5097
Wausau, WI 54402-5097

Established in 1994 in WI.
Donor: John C. Seramur.
Foundation type: Independent foundation.
Financial data (yr. ended 9/30/05): Assets, $6,219,488 (M); expenditures, $367,168; qualifying distributions, $346,490; giving activities include $346,490 for 24 grants (high: $100,000; low: $200).
Purpose and activities: Giving primarily for educational and community oriented programs.
Fields of interest: Higher education; Education; Recreation; Human services; Children/youth, services.
Limitations: Applications not accepted. Giving primarily in WI. No grants to individuals.
Application information: Contributes only to pre-selected organizations.
Officers: John C. Seramur, Pres.; Gary T. Pucci, V.P.; Joan Seramur, Secy.-Treas.
Director: Brian Seramur.
EIN: 391806609

9925
Herman and Gwen Shapiro Foundation
c/o Foley & Lardner LLP
P.O. Box 1497
Madison, WI 53701-1497
Contact: David W. Reinecke, Secy.

Established in 1996 in WI by the late Herman Gwen Shapiro.
Donors: Gwendolyn H. Shapiro†; Gwen Shapiro Revocable Trust.
Foundation type: Independent foundation.
Financial data (yr. ended 7/31/05): Assets, $12,363,554 (M); expenditures, $707,549; qualifying distributions, $593,103; giving activities include $533,500 for grants.
Purpose and activities: Giving primarily for scholarships for the study of medicine and nursing at the University of Wisconsin.
Fields of interest: Medical school/education; Nursing school/education.
Type of support: Scholarship funds.
Limitations: Applications not accepted. Giving limited to Madison, WI.
Application information: Unsolicited requests for funds not accepted.
  Board meeting date(s): Quarterly
Officer and Trustees: * David W. Reinecke,* Secy.; Dean Philip M. Farrell, M.D., Ph.D.; Henry W. Ipsen;

Dean Katharyn A. May, DNSc., RN; John W. Thompson; David G. Walsh; John B. Walsh.
EIN: 391941051

9926
S. F. Shattuck Charitable Trust ◇ ☆
c/o JPMorgan Chase Bank, N.A.
P.O. Box 1308
Milwaukee, WI 53201
Application address: 111 E. Wisconsin Ave., Neenah, WI 54957, tel.: (920) 735-1379

Established in 1951 in WI.
Foundation type: Independent foundation.
Financial data (yr. ended 10/31/05): Assets, $3,038,982 (M); expenditures, $650,478; qualifying distributions, $621,100; giving activities include $621,100 for grants.
Fields of interest: Museums (art); Higher education; Hospitals (general); Youth development, centers/ clubs; Human services; Children/youth, services; Community development, citizen coalitions; Community development.
Limitations: Giving primarily in Neenah, WI. No grants to individuals.
Trustee: JPMorgan Chase Bank, N.A.
EIN: 396048820
Selected grants: The following grants were reported in 2004.
$58,000 to Yale-New Haven Hospital, New Haven, CT.
$20,000 to Tufts University, Medford, MA.
$20,000 to YMCA Community Center of Neenah-Menasha, Neenah, WI.
$15,000 to University of New Haven, West Haven, CT.
$5,000 to Scripps College, Claremont, CA.
$5,000 to Yale University, New Haven, CT.
$4,000 to Connecticut Food Bank, New Haven, CT.
$2,000 to Amnesty International USA, DC.
$2,000 to New Haven Symphony Orchestra, New Haven, CT.
$1,000 to Community Soup Kitchen, New Haven, CT.

9927
Siebert Lutheran Foundation, Inc. ▼
300 N. Corporate Dr., Ste. 200
Brookfield, WI 53045 (262) 754-9160
Contact: Ronald D. Jones, Pres.
FAX: (262) 754-9162;
E-mail: contactus@siebertfoundation.org;
URL: http://www.siebertfoundation.org

Incorporated in 1952 in WI.
Donors: A.F. Siebert†; Reginald L. Siebert†.
Foundation type: Independent foundation.
Financial data (yr. ended 12/31/05): Assets, $93,047,960 (M); expenditures, $5,827,029; qualifying distributions, $4,921,530; giving activities include $4,708,800 for 310 grants (high: $500,000; low: $1,000; average: $5,000– $50,000).
Purpose and activities: Support for Lutheran institutions, including colleges, schools, churches, and Lutheran religious welfare agencies.
Fields of interest: Elementary/secondary education; Education, early childhood education; Child development, education; Secondary school/ education; Higher education; Education; Human services; Child development, services; Aging,

centers/services; Protestant federated giving programs; Protestant agencies & churches; Religion; Aging; Minorities.

Type of support: Annual campaigns; Capital campaigns; Program development; Seed money; Consulting services; Matching/challenge support.

Limitations: Giving primarily in WI. No grants to individuals, or for endowment funds, scholarships, or fellowships; no loans.

Publications: Application guidelines; Annual report (including application guidelines); Grants list; Informational brochure (including application guidelines); Newsletter; Program policy statement.

Application information: Grantees are required to sign Grant Agreement Form. Application form not required.

> *Initial approach:* Letter or telephone
> *Copies of proposal:* 1
> *Deadline(s):* Mar. 1, June 1, Sept. 1, and Dec. 1
> *Board meeting date(s):* Jan., Apr., July, and Oct.
> *Final notification:* 1 week after board meeting

Officers and Directors:* John Zimdars,* Chair.; David W. Romoser,* Vice-Chair.; Ronald D. Jones, Pres.; Knute Jacobson,* Secy.; Julie Van Cleave,* Treas.; Richard C. Barkow; Chris M. Bauer*; Ned Bechthold*.

Number of staff: 1 full-time professional; 1 full-time support.

EIN: 396050046

Selected grants: The following grants were reported in 2005.

$500,000 to Lutheran High School Association of Greater Milwaukee, Milwaukee, WI. For capital campaign to construct school facility for Lake County Lutheran High School.

$400,000 to Carthage College, Kenosha, WI. For capital campaign.

$217,000 to Evangelical Lutheran Church in America, Northwest Synod of Wisconsin, Rice Lake, WI. For continued support of Bishop's Initiative.

$150,000 to Evangelical Lutheran Church in America, Greater Milwaukee Synod, Milwaukee, WI. 2 grants: $20,000 (For summer youth camps in Racine congregations), $130,000 (For continued support of youth focused ministries).

$125,000 to Lutheran Social Services of Wisconsin and Upper Michigan, Milwaukee, WI. Toward purchase of building to house Waukesha regional center.

$80,000 to Lutheran Church of the Reformation, Milwaukee, WI. For continued support of Outreach Ministry.

$75,000 to Lutheran Services of America, West Hartford, CT. Toward continued development funding for Lutheran Adoption Network.

$50,000 to Mount Calvary Lutheran Church, Milwaukee, WI. To renovate and expand school building.

$43,400 to Christos Family Ministries, Milwaukee, WI. For continued support of Wellness Coaching Program for Clergy.

9928
Frances C. & William P. Smallwood Foundation ◇

(also known as Smallwood Foundation)
c/o JPMorgan Chase Bank, N.A., attn.: Rick S. Piersall, Tr.
P.O. Box 1308
Milwaukee, WI 53201
Application address: c/o JPMorgan Chase Bank, N.A., P.O. Box 2050, Fort Worth, TX 76102, tel.: (817) 884-4442

Established in 1968.

Donor: William P. Smallwood Trust.

Foundation type: Independent foundation.

Financial data (yr. ended 12/31/05): Assets, $8,770,747 (M); expenditures, $476,892; qualifying distributions, $422,775; giving activities include $401,779 for 29 grants (high: $50,000; low: $2,500).

Purpose and activities: Giving primarily for higher and other education, the arts, health care, and children, youth, family, and community services.

Fields of interest: Performing arts; Arts; Elementary/secondary education; Child development, education; Higher education; Libraries (public); Education; Environment, natural resources; Hospitals (general); YM/YWCAs & YM/YWHAs; Children/youth, services; Family services; Community development.

Limitations: Giving primarily in Chapel Hill, NC, NV and Tarrant County, TX. No grants to individuals.

Application information: Requirements vary depending on type of grant requested.

> *Initial approach:* Request guidelines
> *Deadline(s):* None

Trustees: Saul Baker; Harry Bartel; Sally Muller; Rick Piersall; Suzy Stockdale.

Agent: JPMorgan Chase Bank, N.A.

EIN: 237000306

Selected grants: The following grants were reported in 2005.

$35,809 to Family Support Council of Douglas County, Minden, NV.

$25,000 to University of Nevada Reno Foundation, Reno, NV.

$15,000 to Fort Worth Museum of Science and History, Fort Worth, TX.

$12,500 to Fort Worth Symphony Orchestra Association, Fort Worth, TX.

$12,500 to Hill School of Fort Worth, Fort Worth, TX.

$12,500 to Tarrant County College Foundation, Fort Worth, TX.

$10,000 to All Church Home for Children, Fort Worth, TX.

$10,000 to Cassata High School, Fort Worth, TX.

$10,000 to Fort Worth Opera Association, Fort Worth, TX.

$10,000 to YMCA of Metropolitan Fort Worth, Fort Worth, TX.

9929
A. O. Smith Foundation, Inc. ◇

P.O. Box 245001
Milwaukee, WI 53224-9510
Contact: Edward J. O'Connor, Secy.
Application address: P.O. Box 245010, Milwaukee, WI 53224-9510; URL: http://www.aosmith.com/about/aosfoundation/foundationindex.htm

Incorporated in 1955 in WI.

Donor: A.O. Smith Corp.

Foundation type: Company-sponsored foundation.

Financial data (yr. ended 12/31/05): Assets, $4,171,654 (M); expenditures, $1,138,291; qualifying distributions, $1,133,439; giving activities include $1,108,914 for 198 grants (high: $187,000; low: $100), and $24,525 for 48 employee matching gifts.

Purpose and activities: The foundation supports programs designed to strengthen higher education throughout the country; promote the civic, cultural, and social welfare of communities; and advance medical research and improve local health services.

Fields of interest: Arts; Higher education; Health care; Medical research; Human services; Community development; Federated giving programs; Public affairs.

Type of support: General/operating support; Capital campaigns; Sponsorships; Program development; Continuing support; Annual campaigns; Building/renovation; Scholarship funds; Employee matching gifts.

Limitations: Giving primarily in areas of company operations in IL, IN, KS, KY, NC, OH, SC, TN, TX, WA, and WI. No grants to individuals.

Publications: Annual report (including application guidelines).

Application information: Proposals should be submitted using organization letterhead. Application form not required.

> *Initial approach:* Proposal
> *Copies of proposal:* 1
> *Deadline(s):* Oct. 30
> *Board meeting date(s):* June and Dec.
> *Final notification:* 3 months

Officers and Directors:* Bruce M. Smith,* Pres.; Robert J. O'Toole,* V.P.; Edward J. O'Connor,* Secy.; John J. Kita, Treas.; Paul W. Jones.

Number of staff: 1 part-time support.

EIN: 396076924

Selected grants: The following grants were reported in 2004.

$101,978 to Scholarship America, Saint Peter, MN. For program support.

$50,000 to School Choice Wisconsin, Milwaukee, WI. For program support.

$50,000 to United Performing Arts Fund, Milwaukee, WI.

$25,000 to Milwaukee Institute of Art and Design, Milwaukee, WI. For capital campaign.

$20,000 to Bradley Technology and Trade School Foundation, Milwaukee, WI. For construction of high school campus.

$20,000 to Milwaukee Symphony Orchestra, Milwaukee, WI.

$12,000 to Harambee Community School, Milwaukee, WI.

$10,000 to Channel 10/36 Friends, Milwaukee, WI. For instructional television programming.

$10,000 to Urban Day School, Milwaukee, WI. For capital campaign.

$10,000 to Youth Leadership Academy, Milwaukee, WI. For program support.

9930
Daniel M. Soref Charitable Trust ◇

c/o Audrey J. Strnad
P.O. Box 170504
Milwaukee, WI 53217

Established in 2002 in WI.

Donor: Soref Operating Trust.

Foundation type: Independent foundation.

Financial data (yr. ended 6/30/05): Assets, $66,040,521 (M); expenditures, $3,155,104;

qualifying distributions, $2,765,641; giving activities include $2,543,577 for 33 grants (high: $750,000; low: $5,000).
Fields of interest: Museums; Performing arts, theater; Hospitals (general); Boys & girls clubs; Human services; Youth, services; Jewish agencies & temples.
Limitations: Applications not accepted. Giving primarily in Milwaukee, WI. No grants to individuals.
Application information: Contributes only to pre-selected organizations.
Trustee: Audrey Strnad.
EIN: 396758434

9931
Nancy Woodson Spire Foundation, Inc. ✧
602 First American Ctr.
Wausau, WI 54403 (715) 845-9201
Contact: San W. Orr, Jr., Pres.
Application address: P.O. Box 65, Wausau, WI 54402

Foundation type: Independent foundation.
Financial data (yr. ended 6/30/05): Assets, $41,708,854 (M); gifts received, $100,000; expenditures, $1,813,486; qualifying distributions, $1,627,412; giving activities include $1,599,000 for 4 grants (high: $1,000,000; low: $54,000).
Fields of interest: Museums (art); Historic preservation/historical societies.
Limitations: Giving primarily in Wausau, WI.
Application information: Application form not required.
Deadline(s): None
Officers and Directors:* San W. Orr, Jr.,* Pres.; Ann M. Dubore, Secy.-Treas.; Daryl E. Gebhart; Thomas J. Howatt.
EIN: 391367383
Selected grants: The following grants were reported in 2004.
$1,000,000 to YMCA of Wausau Foundation, Wausau, WI. For construction of community health care clinic.
$175,840 to Leigh Yawkey Woodson Art Museum, Wausau, WI. 3 grants: $100,000 (For general operating support), $18,250 (For purchase of artwork for permanent collection), $57,590 (For capital support).
$30,000 to Community Foundation of North Central Wisconsin, Wausau, WI. For general operating support.

9932
Split Rail Foundation, Inc. ✧ ☆
N144 W127 Pioneer Rd
Mequon, WI 53097
Contact: Patricia A. Van Housen, Pres. and Treas.

Established in 1985.
Donors: E.I. Van Housen†; Dorothy P. Van Housen.
Foundation type: Independent foundation.
Financial data (yr. ended 12/31/05): Assets, $1,350,710 (M); expenditures, $586,640; qualifying distributions, $584,983; giving activities include $584,328 for 45 grants (high: $501,828; low: $500).
Purpose and activities: Giving primarily to WI agencies in which the family is active or particularly interested.
Fields of interest: Arts; Higher education; Health sciences school/education; Education;

Environment, natural resources; Human services; Children/youth, services; Foundations (private grantmaking); Federated giving programs.
Type of support: General/operating support; Continuing support; Annual campaigns; Capital campaigns; Building/renovation; Research.
Limitations: Giving primarily in WI, and WY.
Application information: Does not respond to staff-signed or general mail requests. Application form not required.
Initial approach: Proposal signed by a volunteer, not by paid staff
Copies of proposal: 1
Deadline(s): Oct. 1
Board meeting date(s): Nov.
Officers: Patricia A. Van Housen, Pres. and Treas.; Barbara A. Van Housen, V.P.; Daniel R. Van Housen, Secy.
EIN: 391537158

9933
St. Croix Valley Community Foundation
516 2nd St., Ste. 214
P.O. Box 39
Hudson, WI 54016 (715) 386-9490
Contact: David H. Griffith, Pres.; For grants: Jill A. Shannon, Dir., Community Partnerships
FAX: (715) 386-1250; E-mail: info@scvcf.org; Additional E-mail: dgriffith@scvcf.org; Grant inquiry E-mail: jshannon@scvcf.org; URL: http://www.scvcf.org

Established in 1995 in WI and MN.
Foundation type: Community foundation.
Financial data (yr. ended 6/30/05): Assets, $7,461,790 (L); gifts received, $2,026,350; expenditures, $1,285,644; giving activities include $916,311 for 256 grants (high: $125,000; low: $100), $18,320 for 43 grants to individuals (high: $3,380; low: $100), and $184,745 for 4 foundation-administered programs.
Purpose and activities: The foundation's mission is to advance the quality of life in the St. Croix Valley of WI and MN.
Fields of interest: Arts; Education; Environment; Human services; Community development.
Limitations: Giving primarily in Chisago and Washington counties, MN and Pierce, Polk and St. Croix counties, WI.
Publications: Application guidelines; Annual report; Financial statement; Informational brochure; Newsletter.
Application information: Visit foundation Web site for application forms and additional guidelines per grant type. Application form required.
Initial approach: Letter
Copies of proposal: 8
Deadline(s): Varies
Board meeting date(s): 2nd Tues. of each month
Final notification: Within 2 months of submission
Officers and Directors: Gretchen Stein,* Chair.; Karen Hansen,* Vice-Chair.; David H. Griffith, Pres.; Charles Arnason,* Secy.; Michael Johnson,* Treas.; William E. Campbell; Patricia Draxler; Chris Galvin; James Gillespie; Nate Jackson; Peter Kilde; Erv Neff; Mark Vanasse; David Wettergren.
Number of staff: 2 full-time professional; 2 part-time support.
EIN: 411817315

9934
Stackner Family Foundation, Inc. ✧
411 E. Wisconsin Ave.
Milwaukee, WI 53202-4497
Contact: Paul J. Tilleman, Treas.
FAX: (262) 646-5409; E-mail: Stackner@msn.com

Incorporated in 1966 in WI.
Donors: John S. Stackner†; Irene M. Stackner†.
Foundation type: Independent foundation.
Financial data (yr. ended 8/31/05): Assets, $16,499,088 (M); expenditures, $983,234; qualifying distributions, $834,772; giving activities include $695,230 for 158 grants (high: $25,000; low: $250).
Purpose and activities: Support for social service and youth agencies, including family services, the homeless, hunger programs, child welfare, employment, and minorities, health agencies, including those serving the mentally ill and the handicapped, and drug and alcohol abuse programs.
Fields of interest: Health care; Substance abuse, services; Mental health/crisis services; Employment; Food services; Human services; Children/youth, services; Family services; Minorities/immigrants, centers/services; Homeless, human services; Community development; Disabilities, people with; Minorities.
Type of support: General/operating support; Capital campaigns; Building/renovation; Program development.
Limitations: Giving limited to Milwaukee and Waukesha counties, WI. No grants to individuals, or for deficit financing or fellowships; no loans.
Application information: Application form not required.
Initial approach: Letter
Copies of proposal: 1
Deadline(s): Dec. 15, Mar. 15, June 15, and Sept. 15
Board meeting date(s): Jan., Apr., July, and Oct.
Final notification: Within 3 weeks after board meetings
Officers and Directors:* Patricia S. Treiber,* Pres.; John A. Treiber,* V.P., Secy. and Exec. Dir.; Paul J. Tilleman, Treas.; David L. MacGregor.
Number of staff: 1 full-time support.
EIN: 396097597
Selected grants: The following grants were reported in 2003.
$25,000 to Grand Avenue Club, Milwaukee, WI.
$25,000 to Ten Chimneys Foundation, Genesee Depot, WI.
$25,000 to YMCA, Town and Country, Oconomowoc, WI.
$25,000 to YWCA of Waukesha, Waukesha, WI.
$20,000 to Community Memorial Foundation of Menomonee Falls, Menomonee Falls, WI.
$20,000 to Shepherds Home, Union Grove, WI.
$20,000 to Wheaton College, Wheaton, IL.
$15,000 to Womens Center, Waukesha, WI. For program support.
$10,000 to Cardinal Stritch University, Milwaukee, WI.
$10,000 to Carroll College, Waukesha, WI.

9935
Stark Family Foundation, Ltd. ✧ ☆
6836 N. Barnett Ln.
Fox Point, WI 53217

Established in 2000 in WI.

Donor: Brian J. Stark.
Foundation type: Independent foundation.
Financial data (yr. ended 12/31/05): Assets, $1,065,000 (M); expenditures, $796,990; qualifying distributions, $791,167; giving activities include $791,167 for 12 grants (high: $450,000; low: $1,000).
Fields of interest: Museums (children's); Performing arts, theater; Performing arts, orchestra (symphony); Arts; Education; Hospitals (specialty); Human services; Jewish federated giving programs.
Limitations: Applications not accepted. Giving primarily in Milwaukee, WI. No grants to individuals.
Application information: Contributes only to pre-selected organizations.
Directors: Colin Lancaster; Brian J. Stark; Debra Stark.
EIN: 392013796

9936
Bert L. and Patricia S. Steigleder Charitable Trust ✧
c/o Quarles & Brady LLP
411 E. Wisconsin Ave., Ste. 2040
Milwaukee, WI 53202-4497 (414) 277-5000
Contact: Henry J. Loos, Tr.

Established in 1991 in WI.
Donor: Bert L. Steigleder†.
Foundation type: Independent foundation.
Financial data (yr. ended 6/30/05): Assets, $10,176,129 (M); expenditures, $621,513; qualifying distributions, $527,469; giving activities include $509,166 for 34 grants (average: $5,000–$25,000).
Purpose and activities: Giving primarily for education, and to healthcare organizations.
Fields of interest: Museums; Higher education; Business school/education; Hospitals (general); Health care.
Type of support: General/operating support; Building/renovation.
Limitations: Giving primarily in the Milwaukee, WI, area. No grants to individuals.
Application information: Application form not required.
Initial approach: Letter
Deadline(s): None
Trustees: Henry J. Loos; U.S. Bank, N.A.
EIN: 396541246

9937
Jack & Joan Stein Foundation, Inc. ✧
5400 S. 27th St.
Milwaukee, WI 53221

Established in 1994 in WI.
Donors: Jack Stein; Joan Stein.
Foundation type: Independent foundation.
Financial data (yr. ended 12/31/05): Assets, $260,801 (M); expenditures, $658,722; qualifying distributions, $658,722; giving activities include $656,832 for 81 grants (high: $300,000; low: $100).
Purpose and activities: Giving primarily for the arts, education, health associations, and human services.
Fields of interest: Museums; Arts; Higher education; Education; Health organizations, association; Human services; Children/youth, services; Christian agencies & churches.

Limitations: Applications not accepted. Giving on a national basis. No grants to individuals.
Application information: Contributes only to pre-selected organizations.
Managers: Jack Stein; Joan Stein.
EIN: 391805213

9938
Stewardship Trust ✧
P.O. Box 3181
Eau Claire, WI 54702-3181

Established in 1997 in WI.
Donors: NBI, Inc.; Grace Bible Church.
Foundation type: Independent foundation.
Financial data (yr. ended 12/31/05): Assets, $240,385 (M); gifts received, $750,000; expenditures, $865,638; qualifying distributions, $865,000; giving activities include $865,000 for 4 grants (high: $800,000; low: $2,500).
Purpose and activities: Giving primarily for education, including Christian education; funding also for a Christian church.
Fields of interest: Education; Christian agencies & churches.
Limitations: Applications not accepted. Giving primarily in Eau Claire, WI. No grants to individuals.
Application information: Contributes only to pre-selected organizations.
Trustee: Roger Amundson.
EIN: 416429623

9939
K. C. Stock Foundation, Inc.
111 N. Washington St., Ste. 450
Green Bay, WI 54301 (920) 490-8290
Contact: Sheri R. Prosser, Admin.
FAX: (920) 490-8620;
E-mail: cornerstone@cfnew.org

Established in 1990 in WI.
Donors: Kenneth C. Stock; Georgia L. Stock.
Foundation type: Independent foundation.
Financial data (yr. ended 12/31/05): Assets, $11,487,348 (M); gifts received, $1,107,904; expenditures, $593,575; qualifying distributions, $480,307; giving activities include $480,307 for 71 grants (high: $100,000; low: $20).
Purpose and activities: Giving primarily for hospitals, athletics and recreation, human services, and federated giving programs. Also giving must benefit the residents of Brown and Oconto Counties, WI.
Fields of interest: Arts, alliance; Hospitals (general); Athletics/sports, professional leagues; Boys & girls clubs; Youth development; YM/YWCAs & YM/YWHAs; Homeless.
Type of support: General/operating support; Continuing support; Annual campaigns; Capital campaigns; Building/renovation; Equipment; Endowments; Program development; Curriculum development; Technical assistance.
Limitations: Giving primarily in Brown and Oconto Counties, WI. No grants to individuals.
Publications: Application guidelines.
Application information: Application form not required.
Initial approach: Letter
Copies of proposal: 1
Deadline(s): None

Board meeting date(s): Apr., June, Sept., and Dec.
Final notification: Immediately following board meetings
Officers: Kenneth C. Stock, Pres.; Georgia L. Stock, V.P.; Steven Stock, Secy.-Treas.
Number of staff: 1 part-time support.
EIN: 391688221

9940
The Stone Foundation, Inc. ✧
c/o National Exchange Bank, Trust Dept.
130 S. Main St.
Fond du Lac, WI 54935

Donors: Peter E. Stone; NEB Corp.; American Bank.
Foundation type: Independent foundation.
Financial data (yr. ended 12/31/05): Assets, $21,280,494 (M); gifts received, $1,750,000; expenditures, $665,592; qualifying distributions, $641,883; giving activities include $638,750 for 41 grants (high: $250,000; low: $500).
Purpose and activities: Giving primarily for education, and health and community services.
Fields of interest: Arts; Elementary/secondary education; Higher education; Human services; Children/youth, services; Christian agencies & churches; Roman Catholic agencies & churches.
Limitations: Applications not accepted. Giving primarily in Fond du Lac, WI. No grants to individuals.
Application information: Contributes only to pre-selected organizations.
Officers and Directors:* Peter E. Stone,* Pres. and Treas.; Dale G. Brooks,* V.P.; Eric P. Stone,* V.P.; S. Adam Stone,* V.P.; Barbara S. Stone,* Secy.; Michael L. Burch; James R. Chatterton.
EIN: 391597843

9941
Hesta Stuart Christian Charitable Trust ✧
c/o JPMorgan Chase Bank, N.A.
P.O. Box 1308
Milwaukee, WI 53201
Application address: c/o Robert Lansford, JPMorgan Chase Bank, N.A., 420 Throckmorton, Fort Worth, TX 76113, tel.: (817) 884-4151

Established in 1973 in TX.
Foundation type: Independent foundation.
Financial data (yr. ended 6/30/05): Assets, $6,912,386 (M); expenditures, $824,123; qualifying distributions, $710,214; giving activities include $696,000 for grants.
Purpose and activities: Grants to Methodist organizations, including hospitals, educational institutions, and churches.
Fields of interest: Higher education; Human services; Protestant agencies & churches.
Type of support: General/operating support; Matching/challenge support.
Limitations: Giving primarily in TX. No grants to individuals.
Application information: Application form not required.
Initial approach: Proposal
Copies of proposal: 1
Deadline(s): Sept. 30
Board meeting date(s): Nov.
Final notification: Prior to Dec. 31
Trustee: JPMorgan Chase Bank, N.A.
EIN: 756177306

Selected grants: The following grants were reported in 2004.

$125,000 to United Methodist Church, Central Texas Conference, Fort Worth, TX. For general support.

$100,000 to Texas Wesleyan University, Fort Worth, TX. For general support.

$25,000 to Texas Methodist Foundation, Austin, TX. For general support.

$15,000 to Texas Christian University, Fort Worth, TX. For general support.

$15,000 to University of Texas, Arlington, TX. For general support.

$12,000 to Southern Methodist University, Dallas, TX. For general support.

$7,500 to Tarleton State University, Stephenville, TX. For general support.

$5,000 to Baylor University, Waco, TX. For general support.

$5,000 to Hill College, Hillsboro, TX. For general support.

$5,000 to Navarro College, Corsicana, TX. For general support.

9942
Elbridge and Evelyn Stuart Foundation ✧

c/o JPMorgan Chase Bank, N.A.
P.O. Box 1308
Milwaukee, WI 53201
Additional Address: c/o JPMorgan Chase Bank, N.A., 1 Bank Plz., Chicago, IL 60670, tel.: (312) 732-4304

Trust established in 1961 in CA.
Foundation type: Independent foundation.
Financial data (yr. ended 12/31/05): Assets, $10,737,541 (M); expenditures, $575,282; qualifying distributions, $548,592; giving activities include $540,000 for 39 grants (high: $135,000; low: $1,000).
Purpose and activities: Giving primarily for higher and other education; funding also for a museum of wildlife art.
Fields of interest: Museums; Secondary school/education; Higher education; Business school/education; Hospitals (general); Youth, services; Christian agencies & churches.
Limitations: Giving primarily in CA; funding also in Jackson Hole, WY. No grants to individuals.
Application information: Application form not required.
  Initial approach: Letter
  Deadline(s): None
Trustee: JPMorgan Chase Bank, N.A.
EIN: 956014019

9943
W. B. & Ellen Gordon Stuart Trust ✧

c/o JPMorgan Chase Bank, N.A.
P.O. Box 1308
Milwaukee, WI 53201
Application address: c/o JPMorgan Chase Bank, N.A., P.O. Box 2050, Fort Worth, TX 76113

Established in 1970 in TX.
Donor: Helen G. Stuart Trust.
Foundation type: Independent foundation.
Financial data (yr. ended 6/30/05): Assets, $4,681,493 (M); gifts received, $98,690; expenditures, $579,966; qualifying distributions,

$463,280; giving activities include $452,489 for 16 grants (high: $120,000; low: $789).
Purpose and activities: Awards grants for the treatment or study of heart disease, cancer, and infant paralysis.
Fields of interest: Hospitals (general); Cancer; Heart & circulatory diseases; Medical research, institute; Cancer research; Heart & circulatory research.
Type of support: General/operating support; Equipment.
Limitations: Giving primarily in Fort Worth, TX.
Application information:
  Initial approach: Proposal
  Deadline(s): Sept. 30
  Final notification: As needed
Trustee: JPMorgan Chase Bank, N.A.
EIN: 756014224

9944
E.C. Styberg Foundation, Inc. ✧

1600 Goold St.
P.O. Box 788
Racine, WI 53401-0788
Contact: E.C. Styberg, Jr., Pres.

Established in 1981 in WI.
Donors: E.C. Styberg, Jr.; Bernice M. Styberg.
Foundation type: Independent foundation.
Financial data (yr. ended 6/30/05): Assets, $7,098,144 (M); gifts received, $414,605; expenditures, $511,787; qualifying distributions, $458,060; giving activities include $457,650 for 80 grants (high: $100,000; low: $200).
Purpose and activities: Support primarily for a theological seminary, community development, education, and youth and health organizations.
Fields of interest: Arts; Theological school/education; Education; Environment, natural resources; Health organizations, association; Human services; Youth, services; Community development; Federated giving programs; Protestant agencies & churches.
Type of support: General/operating support; Capital campaigns.
Limitations: Giving primarily in southeastern WI; giving also in Evanston, IL. No grants to individuals.
Application information: Application form required.
  Deadline(s): None
  Final notification: Within 90 days
Officers: E.C. Styberg, Jr., Pres.; Bernice M. Styberg, V.P. and Secy.; Paul L. Guenther, Treas.
EIN: 391410323
Selected grants: The following grants were reported in 2005.

$125,000 to Garrett-Evangelical Theological Seminary, Evanston, IL. 2 grants: $100,000, $25,000

$50,000 to United Way of Racine County, Racine, WI.

$26,500 to Prairie School, Racine, WI. 2 grants: $1,500, $25,000

$25,000 to Manor Park Foundation, Milwaukee, WI.

$25,000 to Racine Heritage Museum, Racine, WI.

$10,000 to Milwaukee School of Engineering, Milwaukee, WI.

$5,000 to Center for Deaf-Blind Persons, Milwaukee, WI.

$1,500 to Racine United Arts Fund, Racine, WI.

9945
Sub-Zero Foundation, Inc. ✧ ☆

c/o Sub-Zero Freezer Co., Inc.
4717 Hammersley Rd.
Madison, WI 53711 (608) 270-3202
Contact: Laurie Sullivan

Established in 1998 in WI.
Donor: Sub-Zero Freezer Co., Inc.
Foundation type: Company-sponsored foundation.
Financial data (yr. ended 4/30/06): Assets, $257,192 (M); gifts received, $299,931; expenditures, $332,065; qualifying distributions, $331,995; giving activities include $331,995 for grants.
Purpose and activities: The foundation supports organizations involved with arts and culture, education, health, diabetes, youth development, children, human services, and community development.
Fields of interest: Arts; Education; Hospitals (general); Health care; Diabetes; Youth development; YM/YWCAs & YM/YWHAs; Children, services; Residential/custodial care, hospices; Human services; Community development; Federated giving programs.
Limitations: Giving primarily in Madison, WI.
Application information: Application form not required.
  Initial approach: Letter of inquiry
  Deadline(s): None
Trustees: Helen A. Bakke; James J. Bakke; Deborah A. Schwartz.
EIN: 391918462

9946
T & O Foundation, Inc. ✧ ☆

6101 N. Shore Dr.
Eau Claire, WI 54703

Established in 1987 in WI.
Donor: David B. Westrate.
Foundation type: Independent foundation.
Financial data (yr. ended 12/31/05): Assets, $5,840,127 (M); expenditures, $497,042; qualifying distributions, $465,750; giving activities include $465,750 for grants.
Purpose and activities: Giving support for family values and Christian evangelical causes.
Fields of interest: Family services; Christian agencies & churches.
Type of support: General/operating support; Equipment; Seed money; Scholarship funds.
Limitations: Applications not accepted. Giving on a national basis. No grants to individuals.
Application information: Contributes only to pre-selected organizations.
Officers: David B. Westrate, Pres.; Mike Westrate, V.P.; Brian Westrate, Secy.-Treas.
EIN: 391615711
Selected grants: The following grants were reported in 2005.

$8,400 to Grove City College, Grove City, PA.

$1,950 to Young Life, Colorado Springs, CO.

$300 to Judicial Watch, DC.

$160 to Navigators, The, Colorado Springs, CO.

9947
Jack DeLoss Taylor Charitable Trust

701 Deming Way, No. 100
Madison, WI 53717 (608) 827-6400
Contact: Christopher Bugg, Tr.

Established in 1989 in WI.
Foundation type: Independent foundation.
Financial data (yr. ended 6/30/05): Assets,
$7,160,880 (M); expenditures, $428,034;
qualifying distributions, $392,420; giving activities
include $372,000 for 80 grants (high: $83,000;
low: $1,000).
Purpose and activities: Giving primarily to
organizations which provide financial assistance to
needy people throughout the world, with preference
given to children of underdeveloped countries whose
needs are the most fundamental, such as food and
medical care.
Fields of interest: Food services; Nutrition;
Housing/shelter, development; Human services;
Children/youth, services; Child development,
services; Federated giving programs; Christian
agencies & churches.
International interests: Developing countries.
Type of support: Building/renovation; Equipment;
Emergency funds; Program development; Matching/
challenge support.
Limitations: Giving in the U.S., with some emphasis
on WI, and in underdeveloped and developing
countries. No grants to individuals.
Application information: Application form not
required.
Initial approach: Letter
Copies of proposal: 1
Deadline(s): Jan. 31
Board meeting date(s): As needed
Final notification: June 30
Trustees: Christopher Bugg; Lyle Larson; Catherine
H. Taylor.
EIN: 396510710
Selected grants: The following grants were reported
in 2005.
$83,000 to United Way International, Alexandria,
VA.
$20,000 to Catholic Charities USA, Alexandria, VA.
$20,000 to Nepalese Youth Opportunity
Foundation, Sausalito, CA.
$9,000 to Hope for Haiti, Naples, FL.
$8,000 to International Committee for the Peace
Council, Cambridge, WI.
$7,000 to CARE, Atlanta, GA.
$7,000 to Shelter for Life.
$6,000 to Habitat for Humanity, Madison, WI.
$6,000 to Wheels for Humanity, North Hollywood,
CA.
$5,000 to Global Outreach, Neenah, WI.

9948
Fred and Harriett Taylor Foundation ✧

c/o JPMorgan Chase Bank, N.A.
P.O. Box 1308
Milwaukee, WI 53201
Contact: Dave Devries

Established in 1976 in NY.
Donor: Fred C. Taylor‡.
Foundation type: Independent foundation.
Financial data (yr. ended 12/31/05): Assets,
$9,965,351 (M); expenditures, $502,000;
qualifying distributions, $452,857; giving activities
include $439,400 for grants.

Fields of interest: Libraries (public); Education;
Hospitals (general); Health organizations,
association; Youth development, scouting agencies
(general); Human services; Children/youth,
services; Community development.
Type of support: General/operating support.
Limitations: Applications not accepted. Giving
limited to Steuben County, NY. No grants to
individuals.
Application information: Contributes only to
pre-selected organizations.
Trustee: JPMorgan Chase Bank, N.A.
EIN: 166205365

9949
Thrivent Financial for Lutherans
Foundation ▼

(formerly Lutheran Brotherhood Foundation)
4321 N. Ballard Rd.
Appleton, WI 54919-0001 (800) 236-3736
Contact: Karen Coonen, Exec. Dir.
FAX: (920) 628-5165;
E-mail: foundation@thrivent.com; Additional
application addresses: Lutheran Grant Prog.: Kathy
Larson, Church and Community Engagement,
Thrivent Financial for Lutherans, Lutheran Grant
Prog., 4321 N. Ballard Rd., Appleton, WI
54919-0001, tel.: (920) 628-5099, FAX: (920)
628-5165, Corporate Community Grant Prog., Twin
Cities, MN: David Jones, Community Rels., Thrivent
Financial for Lutherans, 625 4th Ave. S.,
Minneapolis, MN 55415-1624, tel.: (612)
340-8281, Fox Cities, WI: Jenni Eickelberg,
Community Rels., Thrivent Financial for Lutherans,
4321 N. Ballard Rd., Appleton, WI 54919-0001, tel.:
(920) 628-4610; E-mail for Charitable Gifting
Initiative: charitablegifting@thrivent.com;
URL: http://www.thriventfoundation.com

Established in 1982 in MN.
Donors: Lutheran Brotherhood; Lutheran
Brotherhood Research Corp.; Aid Association for
Lutherans; Thrivent Financial for Lutherans.
Foundation type: Company-sponsored foundation.
Financial data (yr. ended 12/31/05): Assets,
$90,483,457 (M); gifts received, $15;
expenditures, $2,518,837; qualifying distributions,
$2,415,253; giving activities include $2,402,725
for 33 grants (high: $330,000; low: $3,375).
Purpose and activities: The foundation supports
organizations involved with arts and culture, K-12
education, health, human services, volunteerism,
the Lutheran community, youth, and economically
disadvantaged people.
Fields of interest: Arts, equal rights; Arts;
Elementary/secondary education; Health care;
Human services, financial counseling; Human
services; Voluntarism promotion; Religion,
management/technical aid; Religion, fund raising/
fund distribution; Protestant agencies & churches;
Youth; Economically disadvantaged.
Type of support: General/operating support; Income
development; Management development/capacity
building; Endowments; Emergency funds; Program
development; Conferences/seminars; Seed money;
Curriculum development; Research; Cause-related
marketing; Consulting services; Program evaluation;
Employee matching gifts; Matching/challenge
support.
Limitations: Giving on a national basis for the
Lutheran Grant Program; giving limited to the Twin
Cities, MN, including Minneapolis and St. Paul, and
the Fox Cities, WI, including Appleton, for Corporate

Community Grants; giving to national organizations
for the Charitable Gifting Initiative. No support for
national or international organizations or churches
or church organizations for expenses normally
regarded as church responsibility for Corporate
Community Grants. No grants to individuals, or for
political activities or causes; no grants for ordinary
and ongoing program or organizational operating
expenses, financial subsidy, lobbying activities,
major capital projects, debt reduction, or missions
related to political, moral, theological, or doctrinal
issues that tend to be divisive within the Lutheran
community for the Lutheran Grant Program; no
grants for services duplicated by other
organizations, religious causes, or endowments for
Corporate Community Grants; no loans or
investments for Corporate Community Grants.
Publications: Application guidelines; Informational
brochure (including application guidelines).
Application information: Extraneous proposal
materials and video submissions are not
encouraged. Proposals should be no longer than 2
pages. Proposals should be submitted using
organization letterhead. The foundation utilizes an
invitation only Request For Proposal (RFP) process
for the Charitable Gifting Initiative; unsolicited
requests are not accepted. The Minnesota Common
Grant Application Form is required for organizations
located in the Twin Cities, MN, area for Corporate
Community Grants. Application form required.
Initial approach: Download application form and
mail or fax proposal and application form to
application address for Lutheran Grant
Program
Copies of proposal: 1
Deadline(s): None; end of the second week in
Dec., Feb., Apr., June, Aug., and Oct. for
requests of over $25,000 for Lutheran Grant
Program
Board meeting date(s): Monthly
Final notification: 30 days for requests of less
than $25,000 for Lutheran Grant Program; up
to 75 days for requests of over $25,000 for
Lutheran Grants Program; 60 to 90 days for
Corporate Community Grants
Officers and Trustees: Bradford Hewitt,* Chair. and
Pres.; Timothy T. Schwan,* V.P.; Randall L.
Boushek,* Treas.; Karen Coonen,* Exec. Dir.; Jenni
Eikelberg; Debbie Fox; Tina Hanson; Jody Jonas;
David Jones; Kathy Larson; Jennifer H. Martin,
Ph.D.; Julie Pritzl; Marie A. Uhrich; Laurie Wilkinson;
John Wollner; Jim Yagow.
EIN: 411449680
Selected grants: The following grants were reported
in 2004.
$1,875,000 to Evangelical Lutheran Church in
America, Chicago, IL. For churchwide grant.
$1,425,000 to Lutheran Church-Missouri Synod,
Saint Louis, MO. For churchwide grant.
$1,000,000 to Concordia University System, Saint
Louis, MO. For The Sake of The Church.
$425,000 to ELCA Foundation, Chicago, IL. For
Raising Up a New Generation of Leaders.
$412,500 to Wisconsin Evangelical Lutheran
Synod, Milwaukee, WI. For churchwide grant.
$353,525 to Lutheran Services in America,
Baltimore, MD. For online auction.
$100,000 to Basket of Hope, Saint Louis, MO. For
national expansion.
$66,000 to Evangelical Lutheran Synod, Mankato,
MN. For churchwide grant.
$61,400 to Lutheran Immigration and Refugee
Service, Baltimore, MD. For financial literacy for
newcomers.

$25,000 to Metropolitan Lutheran Ministry, Kansas City, MO. For senior mobile case management program.

9950
The Timken Company Charitable Trust ◇ ☆
c/o Bank One Trust Co., N.A.
111 E. Wisconsin Ave.
Milwaukee, WI 53202
Application address: c/o The Timken Co., 1835 Dueber Ave. S.W., Canton, OH 44706

Trust established in 1947 in OH.
Donor: The Timken Co.
Foundation type: Company-sponsored foundation.
Financial data (yr. ended 12/31/05): Assets, $1,799,808 (M); gifts received, $1,250,000; expenditures, $1,407,181; qualifying distributions, $1,396,331; giving activities include $1,379,456 for 104 grants (high: $427,706; low: $200).
Purpose and activities: The foundation supports organizations involved with arts and culture, higher education, and housing.
Fields of interest: Arts; Higher education; Housing/shelter; Federated giving programs.
Type of support: General/operating support.
Limitations: Giving primarily in areas of company operations. No grants to individuals.
Application information: Application form not required.
  Initial approach: Proposal
  Deadline(s): None
Trustees: Sallie B. Bailey; James W. Griffith; W.J. Timken.
Number of staff: 3 full-time professional; 3 full-time support.
EIN: 346534265
Selected grants: The following grants were reported in 2004.
$125,000 to Fund for the Arts in Stark, Canton, OH.
$80,000 to Ohio Foundation of Independent Colleges, Columbus, OH.
$70,000 to Junior Achievement of Stark County, Canton, OH.
$48,000 to United Way of Lawrence County, New Castle, PA.
$48,000 to United Way, Bucyrus Area, Bucyrus, OH.
$46,661 to United Way of Connecticut, Rocky Hill, CT.
$40,000 to Malone College, Canton, OH.
$40,000 to Walsh University, North Canton, OH.
$31,000 to United Way of Westmoreland County, Greensburg, PA.
$11,000 to United Way of the Piedmont, Spartanburg, SC.

9951
The Tulsa Foundation ◇
c/o JPMorgan Chase Bank, N.A.
P.O. Box 1308
Milwaukee, WI 53201

Established in 1919 in OK.
Foundation type: Community foundation.
Financial data (yr. ended 12/31/04): Assets, $19,884,291 (M); expenditures, $1,160,172; giving activities include $999,051 for 36+ grants.
Purpose and activities: Support to organizations that provide services that enhance the quality of life for the citizens of Tulsa, OK.

Fields of interest: Human services; Community development.
Limitations: Giving limited to Tulsa, OK, area. No grants to individuals.
Application information: Application form not required.
  Initial approach: Letter
Trustees: JPMorgan Chase Bank, N.A.
EIN: 736090617

9952
U.S. Oil/Schmidt Family Foundation, Inc.
c/o Raymond Schmidt, Secy.
425 S. Washington St.
P.O. Box 25
Combined Locks, WI 54113-1049

Established in 1984 in WI.
Donors: Raymond Schmidt; Arthur J. Schmidt; William Schmidt; Thomas A. Schmidt; U.S. Oil Co., Inc.
Foundation type: Independent foundation.
Financial data (yr. ended 7/31/05): Assets, $3,992,271 (M); gifts received, $1,011,925; expenditures, $719,033; qualifying distributions, $698,655; giving activities include $698,655 for grants.
Purpose and activities: Giving primarily for Roman Catholic organizations and churches; support also for community funds, education, and hospitals.
Fields of interest: Education; Hospitals (general); Federated giving programs; Roman Catholic agencies & churches; Religion.
Type of support: General/operating support; Continuing support; Annual campaigns; Building/renovation; Equipment; Land acquisition; Emergency funds; Publication; Seed money; Employee matching gifts; Matching/challenge support.
Limitations: Applications not accepted. Giving primarily in WI. No grants to individuals.
Application information: Contributes only to pre-selected organizations.
Officers: Arthur J. Schmidt, Pres.; William Schmidt, V.P.; Raymond Schmidt, Secy.
Director: Thomas Schmidt.
Number of staff: 1 part-time professional; 2 part-time support.
EIN: 391540933

9953
David and Julia Uihlein Charitable Foundation, Inc. ◇
735 N. Water St., Ste. 712
Milwaukee, WI 53202-4104

Established in 1995 in WI.
Donor: David V. Uihlein, Jr.
Foundation type: Independent foundation.
Financial data (yr. ended 12/31/04): Assets, $7,666 (M); gifts received, $3,439,620; expenditures, $3,439,226; qualifying distributions, $3,439,226; giving activities include $3,418,075 for 63 grants (high: $1,030,000; low: $50; average: $1,000–$100,000).
Purpose and activities: Giving primarily for the arts and education; funding also for human services.
Fields of interest: Museums; Museums (art); Performing arts; Historic preservation/historical societies; Arts; Higher education; Medical school/

education; Education; Human services; Federated giving programs.
Limitations: Applications not accepted. Giving primarily in Milwaukee, WI. No grants to individuals.
Application information: Contributes only to pre-selected organizations.
Officers and Directors:* David V. Uihlein, Jr.,* Pres. and Treas.; Julia A. Uihlein,* V.P. and Secy.
EIN: 391822364

9954
Henry Uihlein II & Mildred A. Uihlein Foundation ◇
648 N. Plankinton Ave., Ste. 260
Milwaukee, WI 53203

Established around 1979 in WI.
Donor: Henry Uihlein II‡.
Foundation type: Independent foundation.
Financial data (yr. ended 12/31/04): Assets, $20,506,621 (M); gifts received, $1,604; expenditures, $1,305,850; qualifying distributions, $1,167,684; giving activities include $717,337 for 25 grants (high: $250,000; low: $5,000).
Purpose and activities: Giving primarily for education, funding also for the arts, recreation, and human services.
Fields of interest: Arts; Higher education; Education; Hospitals (general); Recreation; Human services; Foundations (community).
Limitations: Applications not accepted. Giving limited to NY, with emphasis on Lake Placid. No grants to individuals.
Application information: Contributes only to pre-selected organizations.
Officer: John D. Leekley, Jr., Chair.
Trustees: James McKenna; John McKenna; Eleonore Wotherspoon; William W. Wotherspoon.
EIN: 391322495
Selected grants: The following grants were reported in 2003.
$250,000 to New York Ski Education Foundation, NY. For general support.
$125,000 to Uihlein Mercy Center, Lake Placid, NY. For general support.
$35,000 to Adirondack Community Trust, Lake Placid, NY. For general support.
$25,000 to Northwood School, Lake Placid, NY. For general support.
$20,000 to Lake Placid Center for the Arts, Lake Placid, NY. For general support.
$15,000 to National Sports Academy, Lake Placid, NY. For general support.
$11,000 to Lake Placid Ambulance Service, Lake Placid, NY. For general support.
$10,000 to Adirondack Medical Center Foundation, Saranac Lake, NY. For general support.
$5,000 to Adirondack Council, Elizabethtown, NY. For general support.
$5,000 to Lake Placid Public Library, Lake Placid, NY. For general support.

9955
Robert A. Uihlein Foundation ◇ ☆
c/o Glenora Co.
735 N. Water St., Ste. 712
Milwaukee, WI 53202-4104

Established in 1942 in WI.
Donors: Robert A. Uihlein III; James J. Uihlein.
Foundation type: Independent foundation.

Financial data (yr. ended 12/31/05): Assets, $3,788,007 (M); gifts received, $25,000; expenditures, $493,335; qualifying distributions, $476,016; giving activities include $475,500 for 28 grants (high: $281,000; low: $500).
Fields of interest: Museums (sports/hobby); Arts; Education; Health care; Health organizations, association; Boys & girls clubs; Human services; Federated giving programs; Christian agencies & churches.
Limitations: Applications not accepted. Giving primarily in Milwaukee, WI. No grants to individuals.
Application information: Contributes only to pre-selected organizations.
Officers and Directors:* Lorraine G. Uihlein,* Pres.; Thomas F. Lechner,* V.P. and Secy.-Treas.
EIN: 396033236
Selected grants: The following grants were reported in 2004.
$50,000 to Medical College of Wisconsin, Milwaukee, WI.
$25,000 to Blood Center of Wisconsin, Milwaukee, WI.
$17,500 to Boys and Girls Clubs of Greater Milwaukee, Milwaukee, WI.
$10,000 to Make-A-Wish Foundation, Milwaukee, WI.
$5,000 to Goodwill Industries of Southeastern Wisconsin, Milwaukee, WI.
$3,000 to Milwaukee Art Museum, Milwaukee, WI.
$2,500 to United Way of Greater Milwaukee, Milwaukee, WI.
$2,000 to Americas Second Harvest of Wisconsin, Milwaukee, WI.
$1,000 to Aurora Family Service, Milwaukee, WI.
$1,000 to Junior Achievement of Wisconsin, Milwaukee, WI.

9956
Vine and Branches Foundation, Inc.

c/o The Legacy Group
125 N. Executive Dr., Ste. 206
Brookfield, WI 53005 (262) 754-2799
Contact: Patricia Woehrer, Philanthropic Advisor
FAX: (262) 364-2639;
E-mail: pwoehrer@legacyatwork.com; URL: http://www.vineandbranchesfoundation.org

Established in 1995 in WI.
Foundation type: Independent foundation.
Financial data (yr. ended 12/31/05): Assets, $38,893,873 (M); expenditures, $1,843,515; qualifying distributions, $1,403,623; giving activities include $1,003,462 for 48 grants (high: $120,000; low: $1,000; average: $10,000–$75,000).
Purpose and activities: The foundation's mission is to promote Christianity and the building of God's Kingdom through partnerships with organizations that have the same beliefs and that overtly express faith in their programs. Funding is targeted primarily to southeastern WI organizations whose primary focus is the spiritual development of Christian pastors, healthy marriages, or evangelism and discipleship of youth.
Fields of interest: Youth development, religion; Religion, formal/general education; Christian agencies & churches.
Type of support: General/operating support; Continuing support; Management development/capacity building; Technical assistance; Matching/challenge support.

Limitations: Giving on with a special emphasis on southeastern WI. No grants to individuals; no loans.
Publications: Informational brochure (including application guidelines).
Application information: E-mailed applications are accepted and preferred. Proposals will be invited. Applicants should submit a detailed description of the project including the amount of funding requested. It is the Board of Directors' philosophy that the foundation's work is in response to a calling to glorify the Lord and not themselves. Therefore, all gifts are to remain anonymous, and the foundation's name may not be used without permission. Application form not required.
Initial approach: Brief letter of inquiry
Copies of proposal: 1
Deadline(s): Call foundation for deadlines
Board meeting date(s): Spring, summer and fall
Final notification: One week following board meeting
Officer: Patricia Woehrer, Philanthropic Advisor.
EIN: 391827808

9957
The Wagner Foundation, Ltd. ◇

(formerly R. H. Wagner Foundation, Ltd.)
P.O. Box 307
Lyons, WI 53148-0307

Established in 1981 in WI.
Donors: Richard H. Wagner; Roberta L. Wagner; Ken Essman; Marcy Essman; Bob O'Neil; Julie O'Neil; Fr. Gould; Burlington Rotary Club.
Foundation type: Independent foundation.
Financial data (yr. ended 6/30/05): Assets, $11,764,571 (M); gifts received, $445,100; expenditures, $961,599; qualifying distributions, $953,399; giving activities include $864,522 for 26 grants (high: $152,242; low: $1,208), and $75,000 for 1 grant to an individual.
Purpose and activities: Giving primarily for humanitarian aid in Central America and Africa; support also for education.
Fields of interest: Education; Human services; Children/youth, services; International relief.
International interests: Belize; Bermuda; Central America; Philippines.
Type of support: Equipment; Scholarship funds.
Limitations: Applications not accepted. Giving in the U.S., primarily in IA and WI, and in Central America, South America, Africa, and the Philippines.
Application information: Contributes only to pre-selected organizations.
Officers: Richard H. Wagner, Pres.; Roberta L. Wagner, V.P.
Directors: Paul B. Edwards; Ken Essman; Marcy Essman; Bob O'Neill; Julie O'Neill.
Trustees: Bob O'Neill; Paul B. Edwards; Marcy Essman; Julie O'Neill.
EIN: 391311452
Selected grants: The following grants were reported in 2004.
$259,007 to Davosan, Santa Cruz, Bolivia. For medicine and supplies.
$101,209 to Mano a Mano, Salem, OR.
$100,055 to Museum of Flight, Seattle, WA.
$40,000 to Sight to the Blind, Grove, OK.
$10,000 to Saint Johns Lutheran School, Lannon, WI. For scholarships.
$10,000 to Saint Marys Catholic School, Random Lake, WI. For scholarships.
$6,000 to Burlington, City of, Burlington, IA.

$3,060 to Shepherd of the Hills, Quezon City, Philippines. For orphanage.
$1,500 to Smiles, Darien, WI.
$1,000 to Right to Life, Wisconsin, Milwaukee, WI.

9958
Melvin F. and Ellen L. Wagner Foundation ◇

(formerly Melvin F. Wagner Foundation)
c/o U.S. Bank, N.A.
P.O. Box 663
Sheboygan, WI 53081
Contact: Dennis Ohl, Secy.

Established in 1965.
Donor: Ellen L. Wagner†.
Foundation type: Independent foundation.
Financial data (yr. ended 12/31/05): Assets, $8,477,113 (M); expenditures, $442,606; qualifying distributions, $430,525; giving activities include $430,000 for 11 grants (high: $39,091; low: $39,090).
Fields of interest: Higher education; Hospitals (general); Muscular dystrophy; Alzheimer's disease; Human services; Federated giving programs; Christian agencies & churches; Protestant agencies & churches.
Type of support: General/operating support.
Limitations: Applications not accepted. Giving limited to Sheboygan, WI. No grants to individuals.
Application information: Contributes only to pre-selected organizations.
Board meeting date(s): Quarterly
Officer: Dennis Ohl, Secy.
Trustees: James Raffel; Dolores Slesrick; Eugene D. Weber; U.S. Bank, N.A.
EIN: 396129125

9959
Byron L. Walter Family Trust ◇

c/o JPMorgan Chase Bank, N.A.
P.O. Box 1308
Milwaukee, WI 53201
Application address: c/o JPMorgan Chase Bank, N.A., 200 S. Adams, Green Bay, WI 54301, tel.: (920) 436-2612

Established in 1981 in WI.
Donor: Arlene B. Walter†.
Foundation type: Independent foundation.
Financial data (yr. ended 4/30/05): Assets, $12,677,482 (M); expenditures, $761,419; qualifying distributions, $673,864; giving activities include $579,620 for 49 grants (high: $50,000; low: $500).
Fields of interest: Museums; Arts; Higher education; Hospitals (general); Health organizations, association; Cerebral palsy research; Human services; YM/YWCAs & YM/YWHAs; Children/youth, services; Philanthropy/voluntarism.
Type of support: Capital campaigns; Building/renovation; Equipment; Program development.
Limitations: Giving limited to Brown County, WI. No grants to individuals, or for matching gifts; no loans.
Publications: Application guidelines.
Application information: Application form not required.
Initial approach: Letter
Copies of proposal: 2
Deadline(s): None

Board meeting date(s): Jan., Apr., June, Sept., and Dec.

Final notification: 6 months

Trustees: Richard J. Blahnik; JPMorgan Chase Bank, N.A.

EIN: 396346563

Selected grants: The following grants were reported in 2004.

$100,000 to YWCA. For capital campaign.

$50,000 to University of Wisconsin, Green Bay, WI.

$40,000 to NEWIST/CESA No. 7, Milwaukee, WI. For production of television documentary.

$30,000 to Saint Vincent Hospital, Green Bay, WI.

$23,000 to National Railroad Museum, Green Bay, WI.

$20,000 to Boy Scouts of America, Bay-Lakes Council, Appleton, WI.

$17,500 to Neighborhood Housing Services of Milwaukee, Milwaukee, WI.

$16,200 to Saint Norbert College, De Pere, WI. For Walter Theater Lighting Project.

$15,000 to Lakeland College, Sheboygan, WI. For classroom furniture project fund.

$10,000 to Green Bay Symphony Orchestra, Green Bay, WI. For concert.

9960
Waukesha County Community Foundation

2727 N. Grandview Blvd., Ste. 122
Waukesha, WI   53188   (262) 513-1861
Contact: David R. Schultz, Pres.
E-mail: wccf@waukeshafoundation.org; URL: http://www.waukeshafoundation.org

Established in 1999 in WI.

Foundation type: Community foundation.

Financial data (yr. ended 12/31/05): Assets, $14,263,880 (M); gifts received, $8,708,197; expenditures, $973,308; giving activities include $752,065 for 157 grants (high: $131,633; low: $100).

Purpose and activities: The foundation is a pool of permanent endowment and project funds created primarily by and for the people of Waukesha County to provide grant support to charitable organizations.

Fields of interest: Historic preservation/historical societies; Arts; Education; Environment; Health care; Human services; Community development.

Type of support: General/operating support; Continuing support; Annual campaigns; Building/renovation; Equipment; Program development; Curriculum development; Technical assistance.

Limitations: Giving primarily in Waukesha County, WI. No support for religious organizations. No grants to individuals.

Publications: Application guidelines; Annual report (including application guidelines); Financial statement; Grants list; Informational brochure; Newsletter.

Application information: Visit foundation Web site for application guidelines. Following receipt of letter of intent, the foundation's Board will determine if a full proposal is of interest. Application form required.

Initial approach: Letter of intent (no longer than 2 pages)

Copies of proposal: 5

Deadline(s): Aug. 1 for letter of intent; Oct. 1 for full proposal

Board meeting date(s): Oct.

Final notification: Nov.-Dec.

Officers and Directors:* Peter J. Lettenberger,* Chair.; David R. Schultz,* Pres.; Betty L. Arndt,* V.P.; Thomas E. Dalum,* V.P.; Jeffrey D. Wiesner,*

Secy.; Keith Rupple,* Treas.; Ronald L. Bertieri; Andrea B. Bryant; Anne Foster; Donald W. Fundingsland; Karin M. Gale; John P. Macy; Rhody J. Megal; E. John Raasch; Dick Richards; James P. Riley; Donald J. Stephens; Bryce P. Styza; Francis J. Wagner.

Number of staff: 1 full-time professional; 1 part-time support.

EIN: 391969122

9961
The Todd Wehr Foundation, Inc. ✧

555 E. Wells St., No. 1900
Milwaukee, WI   53202-3819   (414) 273-2100
Contact: Ralph G. Schulz, Pres.

Incorporated in 1953 in WI.

Donor: C. Frederic Wehr†.

Foundation type: Independent foundation.

Financial data (yr. ended 12/31/05): Assets, $13,640,121 (M); expenditures, $650,542; qualifying distributions, $574,392; giving activities include $533,000 for 11 grants (high: $100,000; low: $10,000).

Purpose and activities: Giving primarily for higher education.

Fields of interest: Museums (science/technology); Higher education; Boys & girls clubs; Community development; Federated giving programs.

Limitations: Giving primarily in WI. No grants to individuals.

Application information: Application form not required.

Initial approach: Letter

Copies of proposal: 1

Deadline(s): None

Officers and Directors:* Allan E. Iding,* Pres.; James A. Feddersen,* V.P. and Secy.; M. James Termondt,* V.P. and Treas.; Richard J. Harland,* V.P.

Number of staff: 1 full-time professional.

EIN: 396043962

9962
Stefanie H. Weill Charitable Fund, Inc. ✧

636 Wisconsin Ave.
P.O. Box 171
Sheboygan, WI   53082-0171
Contact: Jon C. Keckonen, Treas.

Established in 1969.

Donors: Stefanie Weill†; Otto Byk†.

Foundation type: Independent foundation.

Financial data (yr. ended 12/31/05): Assets, $2,229,155 (M); expenditures, $401,638; qualifying distributions, $389,286; giving activities include $387,300 for 7 grants (high: $225,000; low: $300).

Purpose and activities: Giving only to the arts, music, and education fields.

Fields of interest: Performing arts; Performing arts centers; Performing arts, theater; Arts; Libraries (public); Education.

Type of support: Continuing support; Building/renovation; Program development; Seed money.

Limitations: Giving primarily in Sheboygan, WI. No grants to individuals.

Application information: Application form required.

Initial approach: Letter

Copies of proposal: 4

Deadline(s): None

Board meeting date(s): 1st Tues. of Mar., June, Sept., and Dec.

Final notification: Varies

Officers: Eldon Bohrofen, Pres.; K. Allan Voss, Secy.; Jon C. Keckonen, Treas.

Trustee: Wells Fargo Bank Wisconsin, N.A.

EIN: 930757054

9963
West Bend Community Foundation ✧

c/o Greater Milwaukee Foundation
1020 N. Broadway, Ste. 112
Milwaukee, WI   53202-3157

Established in WI.

Foundation type: Community foundation.

Financial data (yr. ended 12/31/05): Assets, $21,305,042 (M); gifts received, $2,058,251; expenditures, $1,514,744; giving activities include $1,377,368 for 140 grants (high: $243,000; low: $400).

Fields of interest: Museums (art); Secondary school/education; Higher education; Boys & girls clubs; YM/YWCAs & YM/YWHAs; Religion.

Type of support: Scholarship funds.

Officers and Directors:* James A. Spella,* Pres.; Maureen Josten,* V.P.; John F. Duwell,* Secy.; Raymond Lipman,* Treas.; Patti Dew; Gaytha Hillman; Douglas M. Jansson; Daniel P. Johnson; James H. Schloemer; Sharon Ziegler.

EIN: 391971548

9964
Ruth St. John & John Dunham West Foundation, Inc. ✧

915 Memorial Dr.
Manitowoc, WI   54220
Contact: Thomas J. Bare, Chair., C.E.O. and Pres.
FAX: (920) 684-7381;
E-mail: info@westfoundation.us

Established in 1957.

Donors: Ruth St. John West†; John Dunham West†.

Foundation type: Independent foundation.

Financial data (yr. ended 12/31/05): Assets, $55,617,572 (M); expenditures, $2,450,545; qualifying distributions, $2,192,174; giving activities include $1,810,666 for 74 grants (high: $200,000; low: $50), and $250,925 for foundation-administered programs.

Purpose and activities: Giving primarily for civic affairs and humanitarian causes; some support for the arts and higher education; also maintains and operates a public garden.

Fields of interest: Arts; Higher education; Botanical gardens; Human services; Public affairs.

Type of support: Annual campaigns; Building/renovation; Equipment; Land acquisition; Endowments; Debt reduction; Program development; Scholarship funds; Matching/challenge support.

Limitations: Giving primarily in Manitowoc County, WI. No support for religious, political, veterans', social or fraternal, or undergraduate organizations, or parochial, public or private schools. No grants to individuals.

Publications: Application guidelines; Annual report (including application guidelines); Financial statement.

Application information: Application form required.

Initial approach: Proposal

Copies of proposal: 6
Deadline(s): 1 week prior to monthly meeting
Board meeting date(s): Monthly (3rd week)
Final notification: 1 month from receipt
Officers and Directors:* Thomas J. Bare,* Chair, C.E.O. and Pres.; August J. Schuette,* Vice-Chair. and V.P.; Evelyn Childs, Secy.; Phyllis Schippers, Treas.; Bernadine Zimmer.
Number of staff: 1 full-time professional; 1 part-time professional.
EIN: 396056375

9965
Wilson Foundation ◇
(formerly Elaine P. and Richard U. Wilson Foundation)
c/o JPMorgan Chase Bank, N.A.
P.O. Box 1308
Milwaukee, WI   53201

Established in 1963 in NY.
Donor: Katherine M. Wilson†.
Foundation type: Independent foundation.
Financial data (yr. ended 12/31/05): Assets, $5,234,855 (M); expenditures, $645,732; qualifying distributions, $589,755; giving activities include $579,500 for 15 grants (high: $130,000; low: $3,000).
Purpose and activities: Emphasis on higher education; support also for performing arts groups and museums.
Fields of interest: Performing arts, theater; Performing arts, music; Higher education; Education.
Type of support: Annual campaigns; Capital campaigns; Building/renovation; Scholarship funds.
Limitations: Applications not accepted. Giving primarily in NY. No grants to individuals.
Application information: Contributes only to pre-selected organizations.
Trustee: JPMorgan Chase Bank, N.A.
EIN: 166042023

9966
Windhover Foundation, Inc.
c/o Quad/Graphics, Inc.
N63 W23075 Main St.
Sussex, WI   53089-2827
Contact: Eileen T. Graves
URL: http://www.qg.com/whoarewe/windhover.html

Established in 1983.
Donor: Quad/Graphics, Inc.
Foundation type: Company-sponsored foundation.
Financial data (yr. ended 12/31/04): Assets, $13,163,098 (M); gifts received, $4,011,373; expenditures, $2,412,671; qualifying distributions, $2,332,773; giving activities include $2,058,000 for 48 grants (high: $450,000; low: $1,000), and $263,000 for 158 grants to individuals (high: $2,500; low: $1,250).
Purpose and activities: The foundation supports organizations involved with arts and culture, education, health, and human services.
Fields of interest: Museums; Arts; Higher education; Education; Health care; Youth, services; Human services.
Type of support: Matching/challenge support; Annual campaigns; General/operating support; Employee-related scholarships.

Limitations: Giving primarily in WI. No support for religious organizations or teams. No grants to individuals (except for employee-related scholarships), or for fundraising events, competitions, or contests.
Application information: Application form not required.
Initial approach: Proposal
Copies of proposal: 1
Deadline(s): None
Officers: Elizabeth E. Quadracci, Pres.; Thomas A. Quadracci, V.P.; John C. Fowler, Treas.
Director: Elizabeth Q. Harned.
EIN: 391482470
Selected grants: The following grants were reported in 2004.
$450,000 to Medical College of Wisconsin, Milwaukee, WI.
$400,000 to Skidmore College, Saratoga Springs, NY.
$200,000 to Divine Savior Holy Angels High School, Milwaukee, WI.
$100,000 to Grand Avenue Club, Milwaukee, WI.
$100,000 to Milwaukee Institute of Art and Design, Milwaukee, WI.
$100,000 to Saratoga Care Foundation, Saratoga Springs, NY.
$50,000 to Next Door Foundation, Milwaukee, WI.
$50,000 to Trinity College, DC.
$46,165 to Family Resource Center, La Crosse, WI.
$10,000 to Journey House, Milwaukee, WI.

9967
Wisconsin Energy Corporation Foundation, Inc. ▼ ◇
(formerly Wisconsin Electric System Foundation, Inc.)
231 W. Michigan St., Rm. P423
Milwaukee, WI   53203-0001   (414) 221-2107
Contact: Patricia L. McNew, Admin.
FAX: (414) 221-2412;
E-mail: patti.mcnew@we-energies.com; URL: http://www.wec-foundation.com/

Incorporated in 1982 in WI.
Donor: Wisconsin Energy Corp.
Foundation type: Company-sponsored foundation.
Financial data (yr. ended 12/31/05): Assets, $25,830,489 (M); gifts received, $5,000,000; expenditures, $6,036,625; qualifying distributions, $6,013,903; giving activities include $5,848,211 for 1,351 grants (high: $435,000).
Purpose and activities: The foundation supports organizations involved with arts and culture, education, the environment, emergency services, and human services.
Fields of interest: Arts; Education; Environment; Disasters, preparedness/services; Human services; Federated giving programs.
Type of support: General/operating support; Capital campaigns; Equipment; Endowments; Scholarship funds; Sponsorships; Employee matching gifts; In-kind gifts.
Limitations: Giving limited to areas of company operations in the Upper Peninsula, MI, area and WI. No support for political action or legislative advocacy organizations or veterans' or fraternal organizations. No grants to individuals, or for trips, tours, pageants, team or extra-curricular school events, or student exchange programs, programs whose primary purpose is the promotion of religious doctrine or tenets, or programs whose purpose is solely athletic in nature.

Application information: Additional information may be requested at a later date. Application form required.
Initial approach: Complete online application form or download application form and mail to foundation
Deadline(s): At least three months before funds are needed
Board meeting date(s): As required
Final notification: 90 days
Directors: Charles R. Cole; Gale E. Klappa; Rick Kuester; Allen Leverett; Kristine A. Rappe; Thelma A. Sias.
EIN: 391433726

9968
John H. Witte, Jr. Foundation ◇
c/o U.S. Bank, N.A.
P.O. Box 2043, Ste. LC4NE
Milwaukee, WI   53201-9116
Application address: c/o Terri Dowell, U.S. Bank, 201 Jefferson St., IA 52601

Established in 1979 in IA.
Donor: John H. Witte, Jr.†.
Foundation type: Independent foundation.
Financial data (yr. ended 8/31/06): Assets, $7,937,391 (M); expenditures, $521,545; qualifying distributions, $450,029; giving activities include $450,029 for grants.
Purpose and activities: Giving primarily for education and social services.
Fields of interest: Arts; Elementary/secondary education; Higher education; Environment, natural resources; Human services; Children/youth, services; Community development; Federated giving programs.
Type of support: Building/renovation; Equipment; Program development.
Limitations: Giving primarily in the Burlington, IA, area. No grants to individuals.
Application information:
Initial approach: Letter
Deadline(s): None
Trustee: U.S. Bank, N.A.
EIN: 426297940
Selected grants: The following grants were reported in 2004.
$100,000 to Burlington Public Library, Burlington, IA.
$35,000 to Girl Scouts of the U.S.A., Burlington, IA.
$21,000 to United Way, Burlington Area, Burlington, IA.
$15,000 to Hope Haven Area Development Center Corporation, Burlington, IA.
$15,000 to YMCA of Burlington, Burlington, IA.
$11,000 to Burlington Civic Music Association, Burlington, IA.
$10,514 to Boy Scouts of America, Mississippi Valley Council, Keokuk, IA.
$10,000 to Southeast Iowa Symphony Association, Mount Pleasant, IA.
$5,000 to Historical Society of Des Moines County, Burlington, IA.
$1,000 to Nest of Des Moines County, Burlington, IA.

9969
The Aytchmonde Woodson Foundation, Inc. ✧

P.O. Box 65
Wausau, WI 54402-0065 (715) 845-9201
Contact: San W. Orr, Jr., Treas.

Incorporated in 1947 in WI.
Donor: Members of the Woodson family.
Foundation type: Independent foundation.
Financial data (yr. ended 6/30/05): Assets, $17,019,705 (M); expenditures, $853,803; qualifying distributions, $709,024; giving activities include $705,000 for 3 grants.
Purpose and activities: Support almost exclusively for an art museum.
Fields of interest: Museums (art).
Limitations: Giving limited to Wausau, WI. No grants to individuals, or for endowment funds.
Application information: Application form not required.
  Initial approach: Letter
  Copies of proposal: 1
  Deadline(s): None
  Board meeting date(s): Sept.
Officers and Directors:* Alice W. Smith,* Pres.; Robert S. Hagge, Jr.,* V.P.; Stephen C. Spire,* V.P.; John E. Forester,* Secy.; San W. Orr, Jr.,* Treas.; Gale W. Fisher; Nancy-Leigh Fisher; A. Woodson Hagge.
EIN: 391017853
Selected grants: The following grants were reported in 2004.
$600,000 to Leigh Yawkey Woodson Art Museum, Wausau, WI. For general operating support.
$1,500 to University of Wisconsin Marathon County Center Foundation, Wausau, WI. For general operating support.
$1,000 to Marathon County Historical Society, Wausau, WI. For general operating support.

9970
WPS Foundation, Inc. ✧

(formerly Wisconsin Public Service Foundation, Inc.)
700 N. Adams St.
Green Bay, WI 54301
Contact: P.J. Reinhard
Application address: P.O. Box 19001, Green Bay, WI 54307-9001; URL: http://www.wpsr.com/community/solarwise.asp
Scholarship application address: c/o Scholarship Prog., Scholarship Assessment Svc., P.O. Box 5189, Appleton, WI 54912-5189

Incorporated in 1964 in WI.
Donor: Wisconsin Public Service Corp.
Foundation type: Company-sponsored foundation.
Financial data (yr. ended 12/31/04): Assets, $19,161,797 (M); gifts received, $500,000; expenditures, $1,034,328; qualifying distributions, $1,021,593; giving activities include $846,026 for grants, and $171,700 for grants to individuals.
Purpose and activities: The foundation supports organizations involved with arts and culture, education, health, and human services and awards college scholarships.
Fields of interest: Museums; Performing arts; Historic preservation/historical societies; Arts;

Higher education; Education; Environment, natural resources; Hospitals (general); Health care; Health organizations, association; Family services; Human services.
Type of support: General/operating support; Continuing support; Annual campaigns; Capital campaigns; Building/renovation; Equipment; Program development; Scholarship funds; Research; Employee matching gifts; Scholarships—to individuals.
Limitations: Giving generally limited to upper MI and northeastern WI. Generally, no grants for endowments.
Publications: Application guidelines; Informational brochure.
Application information: Application form required.
  Initial approach: Download application form
  Copies of proposal: 1
  Deadline(s): Dec. 15 for scholarships
  Board meeting date(s): May and as required
  Final notification: Feb.
Officers: L.L. Weyers, Pres.; T.P. Meinz, V.P.; B.J. Wolf, Secy.; J.P. O'Leary, Treas.
EIN: 396075016

9971
Julie Ann Wrigley Foundation, Inc. ✧ ☆

c/o James L. Mohr & Assocs. LLP
1233 N. Mayfair Rd., No. 304
Wauwatosa, WI 53226

Established in 2001 in WI.
Donor: Julie A. Wrigley.
Foundation type: Independent foundation.
Financial data (yr. ended 12/31/05): Assets, $7,218,109 (M); expenditures, $589,479; qualifying distributions, $536,743; giving activities include $536,743 for 20 grants (high: $260,000; low: $150).
Fields of interest: Higher education; Human services; Federated giving programs.
Limitations: Applications not accepted. Giving primarily in AZ and ID. No grants to individuals.
Application information: Contributes only to pre-selected organizations.
Officers: Julie A. Wrigley, Pres.; James L. Mohr, V.P.; Brian D. Collins, Secy.
EIN: 030395312
Selected grants: The following grants were reported in 2005.
$49,500 to Celebrity Fight Night Foundation, Phoenix, AZ.
$30,000 to Whispering Hope Ranch Foundation, Payson, AZ.
$20,000 to Peregrine Fund, Boise, ID.
$20,000 to Saint Lukes Wood River Foundation, Ketchum, ID.
$20,000 to Sun Valley Writers Conference, Ketchum, ID.
$7,843 to Community Library, Ketchum, ID.
$2,500 to Sun Valley Summer Symphony, Sun Valley, ID.
$1,000 to American Cancer Society, Boise, ID.

9972
Irvin L. Young Foundation, Inc. ✧ ☆

15535 St. Therese Blvd.
Brookfield, WI 53005 (262) 781-6204
Contact: David S. Fisher, Pres.

Incorporated in 1949 in WI.
Donors: Irvin L. Young†; Fern D. Young†; David S. Fisher.
Foundation type: Independent foundation.
Financial data (yr. ended 12/31/05): Assets, $2,006,084 (M); expenditures, $724,830; qualifying distributions, $724,830; giving activities include $724,830 for 10 grants (high: $500,000; low: $550).
Purpose and activities: Grants largely for Protestant medical missionary programs in Africa, including the training of African medical workers; some support also for education.
Fields of interest: Higher education; Education; Hospitals (general); Human services; Protestant agencies & churches.
International interests: Africa.
Type of support: General/operating support; Building/renovation; Equipment; Scholarship funds; Matching/challenge support.
Limitations: Giving primarily in Africa. No grants to individuals.
Application information: Application form not required.
  Initial approach: Letter
  Copies of proposal: 1
  Deadline(s): Nov. 1
  Board meeting date(s): As required
Officers and Directors:* David S. Fisher,* Pres.; David Voetman,* V.P.; Robert W. Reninger,* Secy.; Bonnie E. Fisher,* Treas.; L. Arden Almquist; Mary Longbrake; Mitchell J. Simon.
EIN: 366077858

9973
Joseph J. and Vera Zilber Family Foundation, Inc. ✧

(formerly Joseph J. Zilber Family Foundation, Inc.)
710 N. Plankinton Ave., Ste. 1200
Milwaukee, WI 53203-2404

Established in 1962.
Donors: Joseph J. Zilber; Vera J. Zilber.
Foundation type: Independent foundation.
Financial data (yr. ended 6/30/05): Assets, $17,310,772 (M); gifts received, $3,333,302; expenditures, $684,822; qualifying distributions, $676,292; giving activities include $676,292 for grants.
Purpose and activities: Giving primarily for education, science and Jewish organizations.
Fields of interest: Higher education; Science; Jewish agencies & temples.
Limitations: Applications not accepted. Giving primarily in WI. No grants to individuals.
Application information: Unsolicited requests for funds not accepted.
Officers and Directors:* Joseph J. Zilber,* Pres.; James F. Janz,* Secy.; Stephan J. Chevalier,* Treas.; Marcy Jackson; Melissa S.A. Jackson; Shane M. Jackson; Gerald M. Stein; John K. Tsui; Marilyn Zilber.
EIN: 396077241

WYOMING

9974

The Andrew Allen Charitable Foundation ◇
c/o Thomas N. Long
P.O. Box 87
Cheyenne, WY 82003

Established in 1998 in PA.
Donor: Andrew Allen†.
Foundation type: Independent foundation.
Financial data (yr. ended 10/31/05): Assets, $29,154,026 (M); expenditures, $1,844,596; qualifying distributions, $1,407,500; giving activities include $1,407,500 for 68 grants (high: $255,000; low: $50).
Fields of interest: Higher education; Law school/education; Education; Health care.
Limitations: Applications not accepted. Giving in the U.S., primarily in PA and WY. No grants to individuals.
Application information: Contributes only to pre-selected organizations.
Trustees: Arlin M. Adams; Thomas N. Long; William Ver Brugge.
EIN: 237862257
Selected grants: The following grants were reported in 2005.
$255,000 to Saint Marys School, Cheyenne, WY.
$236,000 to University of Wyoming Foundation, Cheyenne, WY.
$210,000 to Xavier College Preparatory High School, Palm Desert, CA.
$89,317 to University of Pennsylvania, Philadelphia, PA.
$75,000 to Community Bereavement Care, Cheyenne, WY.
$65,000 to Susquehanna University, Selinsgrove, PA.
$50,000 to Cornell University, Ithaca, NY.
$50,000 to Vanderbilt University Childrens Hospital, Nashville, TN.
$50,000 to Wellesley College, Wellesley, MA.
$30,000 to Albert Einstein Medical Center, Philadelphia, PA.

9975

Archie W. and Grace Berry Foundation ◇
1122 Soldier Creek Rd.
Wolf, WY 82844

Established in 1988 in PA.
Donor: Archie W. Berry, Sr.
Foundation type: Independent foundation.
Financial data (yr. ended 6/30/05): Assets, $7,635,184 (M); expenditures, $430,991; qualifying distributions, $380,970; giving activities include $380,000 for 22 grants (high: $50,000; low: $1,000).
Purpose and activities: Giving primarily for the arts, natural resource conservation, and for human services.
Fields of interest: Arts; Higher education, university; Environment, natural resources; Animals/wildlife; bird preserves; Human services; Foundations (private grantmaking).
Limitations: Applications not accepted. Giving primarily in WY; some funding nationally. No grants to individuals.

Application information: Contributes only to pre-selected organizations.
Trustees: Archie Berry, Jr.; Robert B. Berry; Louis F. Rivituso.
EIN: 236951678
Selected grants: The following grants were reported in 2004.
$50,000 to American Bird Conservancy, The Plains, VA. For operating support.
$50,000 to Nature Conservancy, Little Rock, AR. For preservation.
$50,000 to Philadelphia Zoo, Philadelphia, PA. For Building Fund.
$45,000 to Peregrine Fund, Boise, ID. For operating support.
$25,000 to Piedmont Environmental Council, Warrenton, VA. For operating support.
$25,000 to University of Minnesota, Raptor Center, Saint Paul, MN. For operating support.
$20,000 to Cornell University, Laboratory of Ornithology, Ithaca, NY. For operating support.
$20,000 to Philadelphia Senior Center, Philadelphia, PA. For operating support.
$10,000 to Philadelphia Museum of Art, Philadelphia, PA. For operating support.
$10,000 to Wyoming Outdoor Council, Lander, WY. For operating support.

9976

Chapman Family Fund ◇
P.O. Box 431
Moose, WY 83012

Established in 1987 in NY.
Donor: Max C. Chapman, Jr.
Foundation type: Independent foundation.
Financial data (yr. ended 12/31/04): Assets, $4,853,875 (M); expenditures, $788,968; qualifying distributions, $761,450; giving activities include $727,850 for 74 grants (high: $200,000; low: $50).
Purpose and activities: Giving primarily for the arts, including an institute for arts and humanities, education, animal welfare, health associations, including a juvenile diabetes foundation, a national park and human services.
Fields of interest: Museums (specialized); Humanities; Historic preservation/historical societies; Business school/education; Education; Animal welfare; Animals/wildlife; Hospitals (general); Health organizations, association; Medical research, institute; Recreation, parks/playgrounds; Human services.
Limitations: Applications not accepted. Giving primarily in NC, NY and VA. No grants to individuals.
Application information: Contributes only to pre-selected organizations.
Trustees: Katharine M. Chapman; Max C. Chapman, Jr.
EIN: 133388410
Selected grants: The following grants were reported in 2003.
$100,000 to Educational Foundation, Chapel Hill, NC. For general support.
$100,000 to University of North Carolina, Institute for The Arts and Humanities, Chapel Hill, NC. For general support.
$33,650 to Historic Hudson Valley, Tarrytown, NY. For general support.
$25,000 to Physicians for Peace Foundation, Norfolk, VA. For general support.

$10,000 to Childrens Hospital Foundation at Westchester Medical Center, Valhalla, NY. For general support.
$10,000 to National Fish and Wildlife Foundation, DC. For general support.
$5,000 to Buoniconti Fund to Cure Paralysis, Miami, FL. For general support.
$5,000 to Yellowstone Park Foundation, Bozeman, MT. For general support.
$2,500 to Wildlife of the American West, Jackson, WY. For Rungius Society.
$2,000 to Elmsford Animal Shelter, Elmsford, NY. For general support.

9977

Community Foundation of Jackson Hole
255 E. Simpson St.
P.O. Box 574
Jackson, WY 83001 (307) 739-1026
Contact: For grants: Susan Eriksen-Meier, Prog. Off.
FAX: (307) 734-2841;
E-mail: info@cfjacksonhole.org; Grant application
E-mail: semeier@cfjacksonhole.org; URL: http://www.cfjacksonhole.org

Established in 1989 in WY as a component fund of Wyoming Community Foundation; in 1995 became a separate entity.
Foundation type: Community foundation.
Financial data (yr. ended 12/31/04): Assets, $39,263,359 (M); gifts received, $12,911,093; expenditures, $15,779,578; giving activities include $14,265,313 for grants.
Purpose and activities: The foundation seeks to enhance philanthropy and strengthen the sense of community in the Jackson Hole, WY, area, by providing a permanent source of funding and other support for nonprofit organizations and scholarship recipients.
Fields of interest: Arts; Education; Environment; Health care; Human services; Community development, neighborhood development.
Type of support: General/operating support; Continuing support; Capital campaigns; Building/renovation; Equipment; Endowments; Emergency funds; Program development; Conferences/seminars; Publication; Seed money; Curriculum development; Scholarship funds; Research; Technical assistance; Consulting services; Program evaluation; Program-related investments/loans; Grants to individuals; Scholarships—to individuals; In-kind gifts; Matching/challenge support.
Limitations: Giving limited to Teton County, ID and Teton County, WY. No support for religious programs. No grants for debt retirement, tickets for benefits, or telephone solicitations.
Publications: Application guidelines; Annual report (including application guidelines); Grants list; Informational brochure.
Application information: Visit foundation Web site for application and additional guidelines per grant type. Immediate Impact grants are available of up to $1,000; visit Web site for details. Application form required.
Initial approach: Submit organization financial info. form and proposal
Copies of proposal: 20
Deadline(s): Last business day of Mar., June, Sept., and Dec. from $1,000 to $10,000; June 30 for grants from $10,000 to $25,000

Board meeting date(s): 6 times annually
Final notification: Within following quarter for grants from $1,000 to $10,000; Aug. 18 for grants from $10,000 to $25,000
Officers and Directors:* Missy Falcey,* Chair.; Jim Moses,* Vice-Chair.; Bill Weiss,* Vice-Chair.; Katharine Conover, Pres.; Sara Flitner,* Secy.; Karen Coleman, C.F.O.; Liza Hoke,* Treas.; Mike Brennan; Marion Buchenroth; Sophie Craighead; Carol Gonnella; Steve Hancock; Jeff Heilbrum; Alan Hirschfield; Carrie Kirkpatrick; Ted Ladd; Pete Lawton; Manuel Lopez; Rusty Palmer; Veronica Silberberg; Karen Terra; Frances Tessler; Mike Wardell.
Number of staff: 5 full-time professional; 2 full-time support.
EIN: 830308856

9978
Connemara Fund
c/o Polly J. Friess
P.O. Box 11655
Jackson, WY 83002

Established in 1968 in NC.
Donor: Mary R. Jackson†.
Foundation type: Independent foundation.
Financial data (yr. ended 6/30/05): Assets, $7,887,687 (M); expenditures, $521,097; qualifying distributions, $402,700; giving activities include $373,115 for 42 grants (high: $90,000; low: $115).
Purpose and activities: Grants primarily for church support and religious welfare associations; support also for social services, cultural programs, and education.
Fields of interest: Historic preservation/historical societies; Arts; Higher education; Education; Environment; Hospitals (general); Legal services; Human services; Children/youth, services; Federated giving programs; Religious federated giving programs; Religion, equal rights; Religion, formal/general education; Christian agencies & churches; Religion, interfaith issues.
Type of support: General/operating support; Continuing support.
Limitations: Applications not accepted. Giving primarily in New England. No grants to individuals.
Application information: Unsolicited requests for funds not accepted.
Board meeting date(s): As required
Trustees: Polly J. Friess; Herrick Jackson; Alison J. Van Dyk.
EIN: 566096063
Selected grants: The following grants were reported in 2004.
$60,000 to Temple of Understanding, New York, NY.
$50,000 to Westminster School, Simsbury, CT.
$10,000 to Connecticut Association for Children and Adults with Learning Disabilities, East Norwalk, CT.
$10,000 to Fellowship Place, New Haven, CT.
$8,000 to Saint Johns Episcopal Church, Jackson, WY.
$7,000 to Aloha Foundation, Fairlee, VT.
$5,000 to Hopkins School, New Haven, CT.
$5,000 to Marion Institute, Marion, MA.
$3,000 to Jazz Haven, New Haven, CT.
$2,000 to Arts Council of Greater New Haven, New Haven, CT.

9979
Cumming Foundation ▼ ◇
165 Huckleberry Dr.
Jackson, WY 83001
Contact: Elaine C. Emmi, Admin.

Established in 1986 in UT.
Donor: Ian M. Cumming.
Foundation type: Independent foundation.
Financial data (yr. ended 12/31/04): Assets, $35,345,931 (M); gifts received, $6,759,635; expenditures, $8,780,268; qualifying distributions, $8,614,490; giving activities include $8,422,648 for 132 grants (high: $2,485,406; low: $39).
Purpose and activities: General charitable giving with emphasis on education, M.S. associations, and reproductive health care facilities and allied services.
Fields of interest: General charitable giving.
Limitations: Applications not accepted. Giving primarily in UT. No grants to individuals.
Application information: Contributes only to pre-selected organizations. Unsolicited requests for funds not considered.
Board meeting date(s): Varies
Officers and Trustees:* Ian M. Cumming,* Pres.; Annette P. Cumming,* V.P.; Corinne Maki, Secy.-Treas.; David E. Cumming; John Darnaby Cumming; Stephen D. Swindle.
Number of staff: 1 part-time professional; 1 full-time support.
EIN: 870440091
Selected grants: The following grants were reported in 2004.
$5,080,094 to Harvard Business School Fund, Boston, MA. 3 grants: $2,485,406, $2,438,240, $156,448
$857,825 to University of Utah, Salt Lake City, UT. 3 grants: $250,000, $250,000 (For Moran Eye Center), $357,825 (For Roland Christensen Center).
$250,000 to Nature Conservancy, Salt Lake City, UT.
$250,000 to Planned Parenthood Federation of America, New York, NY.
$203,670 to Northwestern University, Evanston, IL. For Feinberg School of Medicine, Division of Immunotherapy.
$202,500 to United States Ski Team Foundation, Park City, UT.

9980
Matthew and Virgie O. Dragicevich Wyoming Foundation Trust No. 1 ◇
P.O. Box 385
Teton Village, WY 83025-0385 (307) 733-4520
Contact: Janis M. Stoner

Established in 1998 in NY.
Donor: Calvin Mathieu.
Foundation type: Independent foundation.
Financial data (yr. ended 9/30/05): Assets, $7,830,740 (M); expenditures, $636,187; qualifying distributions, $553,517; giving activities include $495,541 for 26 grants (high: $93,900; low: $5,000).
Purpose and activities: Giving primarily for education, hospitals, the homeless, childcare, and battered and abused children; some funding also for rescue missions.
Fields of interest: Education; Hospitals (general); Crime/violence prevention, child abuse; Foundations (community).

Limitations: Giving primarily in Jackson, WY.
Application information:
Initial approach: Letter
Deadline(s): Dec. 31
Trustees: Jolene C. Harmes; Lloyd Maryanov; Calvin Mathieu.
EIN: 836046045
Selected grants: The following grants were reported in 2005.
$93,900 to Community Foundation of Jackson Hole, Jackson, WY.
$71,741 to Central Wyoming College, Riverton, WY.
$50,000 to Grand Teton National Park Foundation, Moose, WY.
$23,900 to Teton County Library Foundation, Jackson, WY.
$15,000 to Good Samaritan Mission, Jackson, WY.
$15,000 to Off Square Theater Company, Jackson, WY.
$12,000 to Jackson Hole Community School, Jackson, WY.
$10,000 to Community Childrens Project, Jackson, WY.
$10,000 to Community Safety Network, Jackson, WY.
$10,000 to Curran Seeley Foundation, Jackson, WY.

9981
The John P. Ellbogen Foundation ◇ ☆
P.O. Box 1928
Casper, WY 82602
Contact: Mary L.E. Garland, Pres.

Established in 2003 in WY.
Donor: John P. Ellbogen.
Foundation type: Independent foundation.
Financial data (yr. ended 12/31/05): Assets, $23,621,632 (M); gifts received, $1,000,000; expenditures, $1,038,201; qualifying distributions, $822,617; giving activities include $822,617 for grants.
Purpose and activities: To create or cause change, primarily for the benefit of the people of the state of WY, through the support of science, education, and charity.
Fields of interest: Higher education; Education; Science.
Type of support: Annual campaigns; Capital campaigns; Endowments; Program development; Conferences/seminars; Fellowships; Scholarship funds; Research; Program evaluation.
Limitations: Giving primarily in WY.
Publications: Application guidelines.
Application information: Application form not required.
Initial approach: Letter
Copies of proposal: 1
Deadline(s): None
Board meeting date(s): May and Oct.
Final notification: May and Oct.
Officers: Mary L.E. Garland, Co-Chair./Pres.; Martin H. Ellbogen, Co-Chair.; John P. Ellbogen II, V.P.; Neysa Erickson, Secy.; Steve Ott, Treas.
Directors: Theresa A. Ellbogen; Thomas M. Ellbogen; Rod Moss; Terrance M. Whitaker.
Number of staff: 1 full-time professional.
EIN: 830355691

9982
The Lynn and Foster Friess Family Foundation
(formerly Life Enrichment Foundation)
P.O. Box 9790
Jackson, WY 83002
Contact: Foster Friess, Pres.

Established around 1981 in DE.
Donor: Foster S. Friess.
Foundation type: Independent foundation.
Financial data (yr. ended 4/30/05): Assets, $102,117,641 (M); expenditures, $1,708,623; qualifying distributions, $1,593,687; giving activities include $1,436,079 for 6 grants (high: $1,400,000; low: $500).
Purpose and activities: Giving primarily to faith-based entrepreneurial inner-city programs, especially one-on-one mentoring.
Type of support: General/operating support; Program-related investments/loans; Matching/challenge support.
Limitations: Applications not accepted. Giving primarily in Wilmington, DE, Jackson, WY, and Maryvale (Phoenix), AZ.
Publications: Occasional report.
Application information: Unsolicited requests for funds not accepted.
Officers: Foster S. Friess, Pres.; Herman A. Friess, V.P. and Treas.; Lynnette E. Friess, Secy.; Tim Reis, Admin.
EIN: 510260302
Selected grants: The following grants were reported in 2005.
$1,400,000 to National Christian Charitable Foundation, Atlanta, GA.
$17,600 to March of Dimes Birth Defects Foundation, Phoenix, AZ.
$8,491 to Wildlife of the American West, National Museum of Wildlife Art, Jackson, WY.
$8,488 to Friendship Ministries Foundation, Devon, PA.
$1,000 to Ministry of Caring, Wilmington, DE.
$500 to MentorKids, Phoenix, AZ.

9983
The Robert S. and Grayce B. Kerr Foundation, Inc. ◇
P.O. Box 20000
PMB 25106
Jackson, WY 83001-7000
Contact: William G. Kerr, Chair.

Chartered in 1986 in OK.
Donor: Grayce B. Kerr Flynn†.
Foundation type: Independent foundation.
Financial data (yr. ended 12/31/03): Assets, $37,970,044 (M); expenditures, $1,366,816; qualifying distributions, $1,259,421; giving activities include $941,223 for 63 grants (high: $50,000; low: $500).
Purpose and activities: Giving limited to organizations that benefit the specified fields of interest and geographic affiliations of the foundation.
Fields of interest: Arts education; Environment, natural resources; Animals/wildlife, preservation/protection.
Type of support: General/operating support; Building/renovation; Equipment; Emergency funds; Matching/challenge support.

Limitations: Applications not accepted. Giving primarily in OK and WY. No grants to individuals, or for endowments, annual campaigns, memberships, or medical or scientific research.
Application information: Unsolicited proposals not considered.
Board meeting date(s): June and Dec.
Officers and Trustees:* William G. Kerr,* Chair.; Jo Arthur G. Kerr,* Vice-Chair.; Kavar Kerr,* Pres.; Mara Kerr,* Secy.-Treas.
Number of staff: 1 part-time professional.
EIN: 731256123
Selected grants: The following grants were reported in 2004.
$100,000 to Dean A. McGee Eye Institute, Oklahoma City, OK. For building campaign.
$100,000 to University of Oklahoma Foundation, Norman, OK. 3 grants: $10,000 (For athletic department), $15,000 (For C.M. Russell Catalog Raisonne project), $75,000 (For C.M. Russell Center graduate assistant for study of art of the American West).
$50,000 to Westminster School. For building campaign.
$46,586 to National Museum of Wildlife Art, Jackson, WY. 3 grants: $15,120 (For programs), $11,466 (For marketing), $20,000 (For Audubon acquisition funds).
$28,731 to Wyoming Public Television, Riverton, WY. For News Hour.
$11,466 to Wyoming Public Radio, Laramie, WY. For operating support.

9984
The Martin Family Foundation ◇
c/o Larry G. Bean
P.O. Box 1737
Casper, WY 82602-1737

Established in 2001 in WY.
Donors: John W. Martin; Larry G. Bean.
Foundation type: Independent foundation.
Financial data (yr. ended 12/31/05): Assets, $14,062,766 (M); gifts received, $2,000,000; expenditures, $936,225; qualifying distributions, $927,105; giving activities include $878,900 for 29 grants (high: $100,000; low: $1,500; average: $10,000–$50,000).
Fields of interest: Arts; Higher education; Health care; Human services; Children/youth, services.
Limitations: Applications not accepted. Giving primarily in CO and WY. No grants to individuals.
Application information: Contributes only to pre-selected organizations.
Officers and Directors:* John W. Martin,* Pres.; Cynthia L. Martin Beers,* V.P.; Brian J. Martin,* Secy.; Larry G. Bean,* Treas.; Mari Ann Martin.
Number of staff: 1 full-time professional.
EIN: 830335099
Selected grants: The following grants were reported in 2005.
$100,000 to American Red Cross, Denver, CO. For Katrina disaster relief.
$100,000 to Arrupe Jesuit High School, Denver, CO. For capital campaign.
$75,000 to Our Lady of Perpetual Help, Daly City, CA. For operating support.
$50,000 to Boys and Girls Club of Yellowstone County, Billings, MT. For after-school snack endowment.
$50,000 to CareNet of Billings, Billings, MT.
$50,000 to Sacred Heart House of Denver, Denver, CO. For operating support.

$32,500 to Warren Village, Denver, CO. For campaign.
$29,650 to Saint Patricks Co-Cathedral, Billings, MT. For capital campaign.
$27,500 to Boys and Girls Clubs of Central Wyoming, Casper, WY.
$25,000 to Seeds of Hope Charitable Trust, Denver, CO. For special event.

9985
The McMurry Foundation ◇
P.O. Box 2016
Casper, WY 82602-2016 (307) 261-9953
Contact: Trudi McMurry, Fdn. Dir.
FAX: (307) 234-4631; E-mail: trudie@mcmurry.net; URL: http://www.mcmurryfoundation.org/

Established in 1998 in WY.
Donors: Neil A. McMurry; Mick McMurry; Susie McMurry.
Foundation type: Independent foundation.
Financial data (yr. ended 12/31/04): Assets, $67,140,649 (M); gifts received, $350; expenditures, $3,131,060; qualifying distributions, $2,353,056; giving activities include $2,190,271 for 185 grants (high: $300,000; low: $50; average: $500–$150,000), and $80,330 for 1 foundation-administered program.
Purpose and activities: The foundation places special emphasis on the areas of education, religion, children and advocacy for children, health and human services, the arts and humanities, and a favorable business environment. In carrying out its work, the foundation is guided by the values of excellence and compassion. The foundation invests in innovative ventures as well as established community programs that have the potential to make a lasting difference. It provides seed money to start new programs as well as general funds to expand or improve services offered by established agencies. The foundation also helps organizations within its community become more self-sufficient and efficient through strategic planning, increasing management capacity and board development, in order to better serve community needs.
Fields of interest: Humanities; Arts; Education; Human services; Children/youth, services; Religion.
Type of support: General/operating support; Continuing support; Capital campaigns; Building/renovation; Equipment; Endowments; Emergency funds; Program development; Seed money; Technical assistance.
Limitations: Giving primarily in WY, with special emphasis on Natrona County. No grants to individuals.
Publications: Application guidelines.
Application information: See application guidelines. Application form required.
Initial approach: Letter or telephone
Copies of proposal: 1
Deadline(s): Contact foundation for deadlines
Board meeting date(s): Quarterly
Final notification: Within 2 months
Officers and Directors:* Mick McMurry,* Pres.; Susie McMurry,* Secy.; George Bryce,* Treas.
Number of staff: 2 part-time professional.
EIN: 830323982
Selected grants: The following grants were reported in 2003.
$1,068,026 to Boys and Girls Clubs of Central Wyoming, Casper, WY. 2 grants: $68,026 (For award and recognition match project), $1,000,000 (For Building Campaign Project).

$500,000 to Casper College Foundation, Casper, WY. For Casper College Academic Campus LAN Project.

$500,000 to Saint Anthony Catholic School, Casper, WY. For E.D.G.E Campaign Project.

$227,471 to Rotary Club Foundation, Casper, Casper, WY. For Newport Park Project.

$133,211 to Nicolaysen Art Museum, Casper, WY. For general and unrestricted support.

$100,000 to Mountain States Legal Foundation, Denver, CO. 2 grants: $50,000 (For general and unrestricted support), $50,000 (For operating support).

$93,480 to Meals on Wheels, Casper, WY. For general and unrestricted support.

$50,000 to Community Health Center of Central Wyoming, Casper, WY. For general and unrestricted support.

9986
Corbin & Dorice S. McNeill Foundation ✧ ☆

(formerly McNeill Family Foundation)
c/o Dorice S. McNeill
525 N.W. Ridge Rd., Box 8 Skyline Ranch
Jackson, WY 83001

Established in 2001 in WY.
Donor: Corbin A. McNeill, Jr.
Foundation type: Independent foundation.
Financial data (yr. ended 12/31/05): Assets, $6,152,879 (M); expenditures, $563,622; qualifying distributions, $520,000; giving activities include $520,000 for grants.
Fields of interest: Higher education, college; Federated giving programs.
Limitations: Applications not accepted. No grants to individuals.
Application information: Contributes only to pre-selected organizations.
Officers: Corbin A. McNeill, Jr., V.P.; Dorice S. McNeill, Secy.
Directors: Alicia McNeill; Corbin McNeill IV; Kevin McNeill; Timothy McNeill; Michele Poirer-McNeill.
EIN: 364475641
Selected grants: The following grants were reported in 2004.
$125,000 to United States Naval Academy Foundation, Annapolis, MD.
$100,000 to Clarke College, Dubuque, IA.
$25,000 to Mercy Vocational High School, Philadelphia, PA.

9987
The Richardson Family Foundation ✧

5025 Campstool Rd.
Cheyenne, WY 82007
Contact: Keith W. Richardson, Pres.

Established in 1994 in WY.
Donors: Sierra Trading Post; Keith Richardson; Richardson Family Partnership.
Foundation type: Independent foundation.
Financial data (yr. ended 3/31/05): Assets, $4 (M); gifts received, $545,800; expenditures, $555,986; qualifying distributions, $550,800; giving activities include $550,800 for 23 grants (high: $207,100; low: $900).
Purpose and activities: Funding primarily for social services and Christian organizations.

Fields of interest: Human services; Family services; Civil liberties, right to life; Christian agencies & churches.
Limitations: Giving on a national basis, with emphasis on AZ, CO, NV, and WY. No grants to individuals.
Application information:
Initial approach: Letter
Deadline(s): None
Officers: Keith W. Richardson, Pres.; Roberta Richardson, V.P.; Norman J. Wyman, Secy.-Treas.
EIN: 830310875
Selected grants: The following grants were reported in 2005.
$207,100 to Navigators, The, Colorado Springs, CO.
$52,500 to Alliance Defense Fund, Scottsdale, AZ.
$49,550 to Richardson Support Organization, Cheyenne, WY.
$44,900 to Focus on the Family, Colorado Springs, CO.
$36,300 to Young Life, Colorado Springs, CO.
$31,100 to SIM USA, Charlotte, NC.
$18,500 to Fellowship of Christian Athletes, Lander, WY.
$12,500 to Wycliffe Bible Translators, Orlando, FL.
$12,250 to Pregnancy Counseling Center, Reno, NV.
$12,250 to Pregnancy Resource Center of Northern Colorado, Greeley, CO.

9988
S & G Foundation, Inc. ▼ ✧

P.O. Box 20000, No. 25185
Jackson, WY 83001 (307) 733-7707

Established around 1995 in WY.
Donors: Gale L. Davis; Shelby M.C. Davis.
Foundation type: Independent foundation.
Financial data (yr. ended 6/30/05): Assets, $268,505,531 (M); gifts received, $31,647,400; expenditures, $10,276,907; qualifying distributions, $10,256,646; giving activities include $10,256,646 for 81 grants (high: $7,839,131; low: $50; average: $1,000–$10,000).
Purpose and activities: Giving primarily for arts, educational institutions and organizations, and Christian agencies and churches.
Fields of interest: Arts; Higher education; Education; Environment; Christian agencies & churches.
Type of support: General/operating support.
Limitations: Applications not accepted. Giving primarily on the East Coast, with emphasis on FL, ME, NJ, and NY; some giving also in NM. No grants to individuals.
Application information: Contributes only to pre-selected organizations.
Officers: Shelby M.C. Davis, Pres.; Mary Ann McGrath, V.P.; Gale L. Davis, Secy.-Treas.
EIN: 364193183
Selected grants: The following grants were reported in 2005.
$7,854,931 to United World College of the American West, Montezuma, NM. 2 grants: $15,800 (For general operating support), $7,839,131 (For general operating support).
$1,505,000 to Princeton University, Princeton, NJ. For general operating support.
$200,000 to Maine Coast Heritage Trust, Topsham, ME. For general operating support.
$200,000 to Proctor Academy, Andover, NH. For general operating support.

$63,000 to American Cathedral in Paris, Paris, France. For general operating support.
$51,890 to Washington and Lee University, Lexington, VA. For general operating support.
$46,000 to Middlebury College, Middlebury, VT. For general operating support.
$40,000 to Episcopal Diocese of Southern Ohio, Cincinnati, OH. For general operating support.
$30,000 to Methodist College, Fayetteville, NC. For general operating support.

9989
Newell B. Sargent Foundation ✧

P.O. Box 50581
Casper, WY 82605-0581
Contact: Charles W. Smith, Tr.

Established in 1984 in UT and WY.
Donor: Newell B. Sargent.
Foundation type: Independent foundation.
Financial data (yr. ended 10/31/05): Assets, $28,029,455 (M); gifts received, $8,037,776; expenditures, $1,747,833; qualifying distributions, $1,358,653; giving activities include $1,298,650 for 28 grants (high: $1,000,000; low: $500).
Purpose and activities: Giving primarily to a local museum for building and general support.
Fields of interest: Museums; Education; Animal welfare; Hospitals (general); Human services; Children/youth, services.
Type of support: General/operating support; Building/renovation; Land acquisition.
Limitations: Giving primarily in WY, with emphasis on Worland.
Application information: Application form not required.
Initial approach: Letter of less than 1 page
Copies of proposal: 1
Deadline(s): None
Board meeting date(s): Apr. and Oct. (Other months via teleconference)
Final notification: Oct. meeting
Trustees: Ron Hansen; Douglas W. Morrison; Charles W. Smith.
EIN: 830271536
Selected grants: The following grants were reported in 2005.
$1,000,000 to Schwab Fund for Charitable Giving, San Francisco, CA. For endowment.
$150,000 to Foundation for the Episcopal Diocese of Wyoming, Laramie, WY. For general support.

9990
The Arthur B. Schultz Foundation

620 Table Rock West Rd.
Alta, WY 83414 (307) 413-2273
Contact: Erik B. Schultz, Dir.
FAX: (307) 353-2273;
E-mail: info@absfoundation.org; URL: http://www.absfoundation.org

Established in 1985 in CA.
Donor: Arthur B. Schultz.
Foundation type: Independent foundation.
Financial data (yr. ended 11/30/05): Assets, $6,371,662 (M); gifts received, $117,358; expenditures, $545,937; qualifying distributions, $545,937; giving activities include $377,917 for 41 grants (high: $98,429; low: $168; average: $1,000–$10,000).

Purpose and activities: Giving primarily for international microenterprise, global understanding, wildlands conservation, and disabled recreation and mobility.

Fields of interest: Environment, natural resources; Animals/wildlife, preservation/protection; Physical therapy; International relief; Economic development; Disabilities, people with.

International interests: Honduras; Israel; Vietnam; West Bank/Gaza.

Type of support: General/operating support; Continuing support; Building/renovation; Equipment; Land acquisition; Endowments; Program development; Seed money; Scholarship funds; Research; Program-related investments/loans; Exchange programs; Matching/challenge support.

Limitations: Giving in western North America for disabled recreation, the Yellowstone to Yukon eco-region of the U.S. and Canada for wildlands conservation, and the Third World for disabled mobility. Geographic preference for international microenterprise is currently limited to Honduras and Vietnam. Funding interests also include Israel and Palestine. There is no geographic preference for global understanding. No support for strictly religious organizations. No grants to individuals.

Publications: Financial statement; Grants list; Program policy statement.

Application information: No plastic folders or binders. Application is available on foundation Web site; unsolicited inquiries are accepted but unsolicited proposals are not accepted. Other publications available online include grant history, grant guidelines, program descriptions and founder's statement. The foundation prefers letters of inquiry received by e-mail, with attachments in MS Office (Word, Excel, etc.), and/or Adobe PDF format. Eligible organizations will be invited to submit a full proposal. Application form not required.

Initial approach: Letter of inquiry by e-mail preferred
Copies of proposal: 1
Deadline(s): Varies
Board meeting date(s): Spring and summer
Final notification: After meetings

Trustee and Director:* Erik B. Schultz*.

Number of staff: 1 full-time professional.

EIN: 953980014

9991
Homer A. & Mildred S. Scott Foundation
P.O. Box 2007
Sheridan, WY 82801-2007
Contact: Lynn Mavrakis, Exec. Dir.
FAX: (307) 672-1443; E-mail: lmavrakis@fib.com

Established in 1982 in WY.

Donors: Homer A. Scott†; Mildred S. Scott†.

Foundation type: Independent foundation.

Financial data (yr. ended 2/28/06): Assets, $28,951,151 (M); gifts received, $58,083; expenditures, $1,466,736; qualifying distributions, $1,319,726; giving activities include $1,174,921 for 270 grants (high: $175,000; low: $25; average: $1,000–$5,000).

Purpose and activities: The trustees will look favorably upon grant requests that are designed to intervene in and prevent the problems of young people; build public awareness of early childhood and youth issues particularly in Sheridan County, WY; and promote coordination and communication among programs and agencies serving young people and the larger community. The trustees also encourage grants that support community development and improvement.

Fields of interest: Humanities; Arts; Education; Health care; Human services; Children/youth, services; Community development.

Type of support: Curriculum development; General/operating support; Continuing support; Program development; Scholarship funds; Employee matching gifts; Matching/challenge support.

Limitations: Giving primarily within a 35-mile radius of Sheridan, WY, and in specific areas of MT. No grants to individuals.

Publications: Application guidelines; Program policy statement.

Application information: Application form required.

Initial approach: Telephone for guidelines
Copies of proposal: 1
Deadline(s): Varies, contact office for dates
Board meeting date(s): Quarterly
Final notification: 1 week after board meeting

Officers and Trustees:* Sandra Scott Suzor,* Chair.; Lynn Mavrakis, Exec. Dir.; Jay M. McGinnis; Frank Rotellini; James R. Scott; Julie Scott; Lynette Scott; Michelle Sullivan.

Number of staff: 1 full-time professional; 1 part-time support.

EIN: 742250381

Selected grants: The following grants were reported in 2005.

$150,000 to Sheridan County Library Foundation, Sheridan, WY. For Library Improvement Project.

$80,000 to YMCA of Sheridan County, Sheridan, WY. For YMCA of Tomorrow Capital Building Campaign: YCamp and EC Daycare.

$50,000 to Boys and Girls Club of Billings and Yellowstone County Endowment Foundation, Billings, MT. For Back-a-Kids Gifts.

$50,000 to Sheridan College Foundation, Sheridan, WY. For operating support.

$45,000 to Childrens Center, Sheridan, WY. For immunizations, workshops, operating support and scholarships.

$18,204 to Sheridan Community Education Foundation, Sheridan, WY. For Even Start Early Childhood Preschool.

$15,000 to Alberta Bair Theater, Billings, MT. For Art in Education Programs.

$15,000 to Montana Child Care Resource and Referral Network, Missoula, MT. For Montana Afterschool Network.

$8,000 to Montana State University Foundation, Bozeman, MT. For Building Arts Participation (BAP) Project.

$5,000 to Community Leadership Development, Billings, MT. For Community Development Youth Works.

9992
Paul Stock Foundation ✧
P.O. Box 2020
Cody, WY 82414-2020
Contact: Charles G. Kepler, Pres.

Incorporated in 1958 in WY.

Donors: Paul Stock†; Eloise J. Stock.

Foundation type: Independent foundation.

Financial data (yr. ended 12/31/04): Assets, $1,402,136 (M); expenditures, $693,510; qualifying distributions, $673,861; giving activities include $414,186 for 7 grants (high: $200,000; low: $3,412), and $250,000 for grants to individuals.

Purpose and activities: Awards scholarships to Park County, WY residents for higher education; substantial support for a university. Giving also for recreation and for human services, particularly in the city of Cody, WY.

Fields of interest: Higher education; Athletics/sports, baseball; Human services.

Type of support: Annual campaigns; Building/renovation; Research; Scholarships—to individuals.

Limitations: Giving primarily in Park County, WY; student aid limited to those who have resided in WY for one year or more.

Application information: Application form not required.

Initial approach: Letter
Deadline(s): None
Board meeting date(s): July and Dec.

Officers: Charles G. Kepler, Pres.; Esther C. Brummage, V.P. and Secy.; Donald M. Robirds, V.P. and Treas.

Number of staff: 1 part-time professional.

EIN: 830185157

9993
Nion Robert Thieriot Foundation ✧ ☆
P.O. Box 74
Elk Mountain, WY 82324

Established in 2000 in CA and MA.

Foundation type: Independent foundation.

Financial data (yr. ended 12/31/05): Assets, $8,199,543 (M); expenditures, $430,721; qualifying distributions, $316,100; giving activities include $316,100 for 3 grants (high: $150,000; low: $16,100).

Limitations: Applications not accepted. Giving primarily in MA. No grants to individuals.

Application information: Contributes only to pre-selected organizations.

Trustees: Alice Richmond; Peter E. Thieriot.

EIN: 830332938

9994
Harry T. Thorson Foundation ✧ ☆
26 S. Seneca Ave.
Newcastle, WY 82701

Donor: James D. Thorson.

Foundation type: Independent foundation.

Financial data (yr. ended 12/31/05): Assets, $663,880 (M); gifts received, $494,438; expenditures, $355,847; qualifying distributions, $352,264; giving activities include $352,264 for 57 grants (high: $200,000; low: $100).

Fields of interest: Education; Health care; Health organizations, association; Human services; Community development; Federated giving programs; Christian agencies & churches.

Limitations: Applications not accepted. Giving primarily in CO and WY. No grants to individuals.

Application information: Contributes only to pre-selected organizations.

Directors: Mary T. Gullikson; James D. Thorson; Thomas A. Thorson.

EIN: 830255344

9995
The John R. & Georgene M. Tozzi Foundation ✧
50 King St.
P.O. Box 4741
Jackson, WY 83001
Contact: John Tozzi, Pres.

Established in 1987 in CA.
Foundation type: Independent foundation.
Financial data (yr. ended 12/31/04): Assets, $2,567,657 (M); expenditures, $557,607; qualifying distributions, $520,325; giving activities include $520,325 for 22 grants (high: $310,000; low: $25).
Purpose and activities: Giving primarily for the arts including a center for the arts, and the environment; some giving for health care and human services.
Fields of interest: Museums; Arts; Higher education; Environment, natural resources; Recreation, fairs/festivals; Foundations (community); Christian agencies & churches.
Limitations: Applications not accepted. Giving primarily in CA. No grants to individuals.
Application information: Contributes only to pre-selected organizations.
Officers: John Tozzi, Pres.; Georgene Tozzi, Secy.
EIN: 680119864
Selected grants: The following grants were reported in 2003.
$500,000 to University of Michigan, Ann Arbor, MI. For general operating support.
$100,000 to Center for the Arts. For general operating support.
$21,000 to Juvenile Diabetes Research Foundation International, New York, NY. For general operating support.
$15,000 to San Francisco Museum of Modern Art, San Francisco, CA. For general operating support.
$10,000 to Boys and Girls Club. For general operating support.
$10,000 to Saint Johns Health Center, Santa Monica, CA. For general operating support.

9996
True Foundation ✧
P.O. Drawer 2360
Casper, WY 82602-2360
Contact: Cherie Miller, Exec. Secy.

Established in 1958 in WY.
Donors: True Oil LLC; H.A. True, Jr.†; Jean D. True.
Foundation type: Company-sponsored foundation.
Financial data (yr. ended 11/30/05): Assets, $3,266,781 (M); expenditures, $384,555; qualifying distributions, $379,566; giving activities include $379,566 for 121 grants (high: $60,000; low: $50).
Purpose and activities: The foundation supports organizations involved with arts and culture, education, health, human services, and community development.
Fields of interest: Arts; Higher education; Education; Health care; Health organizations, association; Human services; Community development; Federated giving programs.
Type of support: Employee-related scholarships.
Limitations: Applications not accepted. Giving primarily in WY and the Rocky Mountain area.
Application information: Contributes only to pre-selected organizations.

Trustee: Jean D. True.
EIN: 836004596

9997
William E. Weiss Foundation, Inc.
P.O. Box 14270
Jackson, WY 83002
Contact: Liz D. Hutchinson

Incorporated in 1955 in NY.
Donors: William E. Weiss, Jr.†; Helene K. Brown†.
Foundation type: Independent foundation.
Financial data (yr. ended 3/31/06): Assets, $9,285,964 (M); expenditures, $591,239; qualifying distributions, $509,363; giving activities include $506,000 for 29 grants (high: $69,000; low: $2,500).
Purpose and activities: Giving primarily to museums and for arts and cultural programs.
Fields of interest: Museums; Arts; Education; Environment; Human services; Family services.
Type of support: General/operating support; Continuing support; Capital campaigns; Building/renovation; Program development.
Limitations: Applications not accepted. Giving limited to CA, NY, TN, WY, and MO. No grants to individuals.
Application information: Contributes only to pre-selected organizations. Unsolicited requests for funds not considered.
Board meeting date(s): Mar.
Officers and Directors:* Daryl B. Uber,* Pres.; Monte Brown,* V.P.; Katrina W. Ryan,* Secy.; William U. Weiss,* Treas.; Dwyer Brown; William D. Weiss.
Number of staff: 1 part-time support.
EIN: 556016633
Selected grants: The following grants were reported in 2004.
$59,000 to Miss Porters School, Farmington, CT. For athletic program.
$33,000 to Delta Society, Renton, WA. For capital construction.
$32,500 to Museum of the City of New York, New York, NY. For City Resilient exhibit.
$25,000 to Ganna Walska Lotusland, Santa Barbara, CA. For kitchen renovation.
$25,000 to Hotchkiss School, Lakeville, CT. For music and arts initiative.
$25,000 to Randall Museum Friends, San Francisco, CA. For program support.
$25,000 to Santa Barbara Bowl Foundation, Santa Barbara, CA. To install safety handrails.
$23,000 to Golden Gate National Parks Conservancy, San Francisco, CA. For community outreach.
$20,000 to Memphis Child Advocacy Center, Memphis, TN. For forensic interview program.
$20,000 to Wildlife of the American West, National Museum of Wildlife Art, Jackson, WY. For endowment fund.

9998
Whitney Benefits, Inc. ✧
245 Broadway
P.O. Box 5085
Sheridan, WY 82801 (307) 674-7303
Contact: Patrick Henderson, Exec. Dir.
FAX: (307) 674-4335;
E-mail: info@whitneybenefits.org; URL: http://www.whitneybenefits.org

Incorporated in 1927 in WY.
Donors: Edward A. Whitney†; Scott Foundation; Sheridan County YMCA.
Foundation type: Independent foundation.
Financial data (yr. ended 6/30/05): Assets, $109,351,973 (M); gifts received, $25,000; expenditures, $1,978,303; qualifying distributions, $2,933,385; giving activities include $1,527,220 for 7 grants, and $1,214,092 for loans to individuals.
Purpose and activities: To provide interest-free student loans to graduates of Sheridan County, WY, high schools; loans for baccalaureate degrees only. Support also for a local youth agency.
Fields of interest: Higher education; YM/YWCAs & YM/YWHAs.
Type of support: General/operating support; Program-related investments/loans; Student loans—to individuals.
Limitations: Giving limited to Sheridan County, WY.
Publications: Annual report.
Application information: Applications accepted for loan program only. Application form required.
Initial approach: Request loan application
Board meeting date(s): Monthly
Officers and Trustees:* Tom Kinnison,* Pres.; Roy Garber, V.P.; Tom Belus,* Secy.; Kim Love,* Treas.; Patrick Henderson, Exec. Dir.; Mrs. Val Burgess; John P. Chase; Maureen Humphrys; Mary Ellen McWilliams; Peter Schoonmaker; Sam Scott; John M. Smith; David J. Withrow.
Number of staff: 1 full-time professional; 1 full-time support.
EIN: 830168511
Selected grants: The following grants were reported in 2005.
$675,002 to YMCA of Sheridan County, Sheridan, WY. For maintenance of facilities and purchase of further facilities.
$395,316 to Sheridan, City of, Sheridan, WY. 3 grants: $21,333, $14,426 (For water contribution for city parks), $359,557 (For building for arts community).
$325,902 to Sheridan College, Sheridan, WY. For construction and equipment.
$120,000 to Sheridan Community Education Foundation, Sheridan, WY. For program support.

9999
The Wolf Creek Charitable Foundation ▼ ✧
c/o PNC Bank
1122 Soldier Creek Rd.
Wolf, WY 82844
Contact: Robert Berry, Tr.

Established in 1995 in WY.
Donor: A.W. Berry Charitable Remainder Unitrust.
Foundation type: Independent foundation.
Financial data (yr. ended 12/31/04): Assets, $81,267,274 (M); expenditures, $3,631,719; qualifying distributions, $3,294,185; giving activities include $3,277,000 for 59 grants (high: $1,000,000; low: $500; average: $2,000–$100,000).
Purpose and activities: Giving primarily to conserve ecologically significant land and the biodiversity of life it supports.
Fields of interest: Animals/wildlife, preservation/protection.
Limitations: Applications not accepted. Giving on a national basis. No support for religious or political organizations. No grants to individuals.

Application information: Contributes only to pre-selected organizations.

Agent: PNC Bank, N.A.

Trustee: Robert Berry.

EIN: 830310959

Selected grants: The following grants were reported in 2004.

$1,000,000 to University of Texas M. D. Anderson Cancer Center, Houston, TX. For research on colon cancer.

$600,000 to Peregrine Fund, Boise, ID. For general support.

$600,000 to University of Wyoming, Laramie, WY. For fellowships.

$200,000 to Nature Conservancy, Santa Fe, NM. For Southern Plains Grassland Bird Program.

$100,000 to American Bird Conservancy, The Plains, VA. For general support.

$100,000 to Cornell University, Ithaca, NY. For general support.

$25,000 to Sheridan College Foundation, Sheridan, WY. For general support.

$20,000 to Conservation Fund, Arlington, VA. For general support.

$15,000 to Trout Unlimited, Seattle, WA. For Western Water Alliance.

$1,000 to Research to Prevent Blindness, New York, NY. For general support.

10000
Wyoming Community Foundation

313 S. 2nd St.

Laramie, WY 82070 (307) 721-8300

Contact: George H. Gault, Pres.; For grants: Samin Dadelahi, Sr. Prog. Off.

FAX: (307) 721-8333; E-mail: wcf@wycf.org;

Additional tel.: (866) 708-7878; Grant application E-mail: samin@wycf.org; URL: http://www.wycf.org

Incorporated in 1989 in WY.

Foundation type: Community foundation.

Financial data (yr. ended 12/31/05): Assets, $49,340,813 (M); gifts received, $4,913,112; expenditures, $2,093,788; giving activities include $1,931,866 for grants, and $220,792 for foundation-administered programs.

Purpose and activities: The foundation seeks to foster the community and enhance the quality of life for Wyoming residents through asset building, grantmaking and increased civic engagement, participation and leadership. Current statewide areas of need from the foundation's unrestricted funds are children and youth and civic projects.

Fields of interest: Arts; Education; Environment, natural resources; Health care; Health organizations, association; Children/youth, services; Community development, public/private ventures; Rural development; Community development; Voluntarism promotion.

Type of support: General/operating support; Continuing support; Management development/capacity building; Program development; Conferences/seminars; Seed money; Technical assistance; Program evaluation; Scholarships—to individuals; Matching/challenge support.

Limitations: Giving primarily in WY. No grants to individuals (except for scholarships), or generally for block grants, capital campaigns, annual campaigns, or debt retirement.

Publications: Application guidelines; Annual report; Grants list; Informational brochure (including application guidelines); Newsletter; Program policy statement.

Application information: Visit foundation Web site for application forms and guidelines. Application form required.

Initial approach: Submit cover sheet, narrative, and attachments

Copies of proposal: 11

Deadline(s): Mar. 1, July 1, and Nov. 1

Board meeting date(s): Quarterly

Final notification: Mar. 15, June 15, and Oct. 15

Officers and Directors:* Robert B. "Budd" Betts,* Chair.; Russell Zimmer,* Vice-Chair.; George H. Gault, Pres.; Lynette J. Morris, V.P., Finance; Serena Cobb,* Secy.; William Ankeny, Jr.,* Treas.; Laurie Bateman; Linda Bryce; Tad Daly; Diane Harrop; Arne C. Jorgensen; David Kathka; Rick Lawton; Arden Lindsey; Carol R. McKinley; Maggie Maier Murdock; Lollie Benz Plank; Martha Ptasnik; Kent Richins; Susan Samuelson; Liza Sperling; Sandra Wallop.

Number of staff: 5 full-time professional; 2 part-time professional; 1 full-time support.

EIN: 830287513

Selected grants: The following grants were reported in 2005.

$50,000 to Boy Scouts of America, Longs Peak Council, Brush, CO.

$50,000 to McKenzie Meningitis Foundation, Pinedale, WY.

$34,756 to Rock Springs, City of, Rock Springs, WY. For grant made through Dellas and Dorothy Larsen Endowment Fund.

$30,000 to Kemmerer, City of, Kemmerer, WY. For Recreation Center. Grant made through Kemmerer Foundation Endowment Fund.

$27,000 to University of Wyoming Foundation, Laramie, WY. For Wyoming Collaborative Mentorship Academy.

$25,000 to Crook County Library System, Sundance, WY.

$15,000 to Boys and Girls Clubs of Central Wyoming, Casper, WY. For grant made through Janet S. and Richard C. Schneider Fund.

$15,000 to Community Health Center of Central Wyoming, Casper, WY.

$15,000 to Sheridan County Memorial Hospital Foundation, Sheridan, WY.

$15,000 to Womens Self-Help Center, Casper, WY. For grant made through Janet S. and Richard C. Schneider Fund.

APPENDIX A

The following foundations appeared in the previous edition of *The Foundation Directory* but are not included in this edition for the reasons stated.

1525 Foundation, The
Cleveland, OH
The foundation plans to terminate at the end of 2006.

2 C 9 Foundation, Inc.
Peachtree City, GA
Specified beneficiary.

ABC, Inc. Foundation
(Formerly Capital Cities/ABC Foundation)
New York, NY
Inactive foundation.

Adams Family Foundation, Stephen & Denise
Ventura, CA
Grantmaking suspended.

Alburger Charitable Trust, H. A. & J. W.
(Formerly Alburger Charitable Trust, Harry A. & Jane W.)
Orlando, FL
Specified beneficiaries.

Alburger Charitable Trust, Harry A. & Jane W.
See Alburger Charitable Trust, H. A. & J. W.

Allentown Area Foundation
Winston-Salem, NC
The foundation terminated on June 14, 2005.

ALS Hope-The Chris Hobler and James Maritz Foundation
See Hope Happens

American Center for Civil Justice, Inc.
Brooklyn, NY
Status changed to a Public Charity.

Anderson Living Trust, Clarence E., The
Valencia, CA
Specified beneficiaries.

Andersson Children's Foundation, Hanna
Portland, OR
The foundation terminated in 2006.

AT&T Foundation
New York, NY
Grantmaking suspended.

AT&T National Pro-Am Youth Fund
(Formerly Crosby Youth Fund, Inc., Bing)
Monterey, CA
The grantmaker terminated on Oct. 14, 2005.

Ayoub Foundation Charitable Trust, The
New Canaan, CT
Current information not available.

Azeez Foundation
Palm Beach Gardens, FL
The foundation terminated on Dec. 31, 2004.

Baldwin Family Foundation, Inc.
Boca Raton, FL
The foundation terminated in 2005.

Ballman Foundation, Ed
Fort Smith, AR
The foundation terminated on Dec. 31, 2005.

Bank One Foundation
See Chase Foundation

Banyan Foundation, Inc.
Tampa, FL
The foundation terminated on Mar. 31, 2006.

Beall Foundation, Donald & Joan, The
Newport Beach, CA
The foundation terminated on Oct. 25, 2002.

Behrend Trust Fund, E. R.
Erie, PA
The fund terminated in 2004 and transferred its assets to the Eric Community Foundation.

Belcher, Jr. Foundation, S. E.
Tuscaloosa, AL
The foundation terminated on Dec. 31, 2004.

Bing Fund, Inc.
Reno, NV
The fund terminated on Feb. 28, 2006.

Bloch Foundation, Henry W. and Marion H., The
Kansas City, MO
The foundation terminated in Sept. 2005, and transferred its assets to the Greater Kansas City Community Foundation.

Blount Educational Charitable Foundation, Inc., Roberts & Mildred, The
Montgomery, AL
The foundation terminated in 2004.

Brand-Boeshaar Foundation
Lincoln, NE
The foundation terminated in 2005.

Braun Trust, Carl F.
Los Angeles, CA
Specified beneficiary.

Briarcliff Foundation, Inc., The
Birmingham, AL
The foundation terminated on Jan. 1, 2006.

Broad Foundation, Eli & Edythe L.
Los Angeles, CA
As of Jan 1, 2007, the Eli & Edythe L. Broad Foundation merged into the Broad Foundation.

Brockway Charitable Trust
Scottsdale, AZ
The foundation terminated in 2006.

Burlington Resources Foundation
(Formerly Burlington Resources/Meridian Oil Foundation)
Houston, TX
The company was acquired by ConocoPhillips on Mar. 31, 2006. The foundation has terminated.

Burlington Resources/Meridian Oil Foundation
See Burlington Resources Foundation

Buyse Foundation, The
Anoka, MN
The foundation terminated on Dec. 31, 2005.

Capital Cities/ABC Foundation
See ABC, Inc. Foundation

Carlson Charitable Trust, Chester & Dorris
Rochester, NY
The trust terminated in 2005.

Carper Foundation
Atlanta, GA
Current information not available.

Center for Integrative Health, Medicine and Research
Los Angeles, CA
The foundation terminated in 2005.

CFS Foundation, The
See Shouse Foundation, Catherine Filene

Chase Foundation
(Formerly Bank One Foundation)
Chicago, IL
The foundation merged with the JPMorgan Chase Foundation in 2005.

Cherne Foundation
See Cherne Foundation, Albert W.

Cherne Foundation, Albert W.
(Formerly Cherne Foundation)
Minneapolis, MN
The foundation is in a 60-month termination period beginning in 2006.

Cicala Charitable Trust
Hinsdale, IL
Non-grantmaking operating foundation.

Cinergy Foundation, Inc.
(Formerly PSI Foundation, Inc.)
Cincinnati, OH
Grantmaking suspended.

Coastal Villages Investment Fund
Anchorage, AK
The fund terminated in 2002.

Cobalt Corporation Foundation, Inc.
(Formerly United Wisconsin Services Foundation, Inc.)
Milwaukee, WI
The foundation terminated on Dec. 31, 2003.

Columbia Charitable Foundation
Beverly Hills, CA
The foundation terminated in 2003 due to a merger into the Thomas Spiegel Family Foundation.

Cooper Foundation, Inc., Harriet & Eli
Little Neck, NY
Current information not available.

Crosby Youth Fund, Inc., Bing
See AT&T National Pro-Am Youth Fund

Crown Charitable Fund, Edward A.
Chicago, IL
The fund terminated on March 31, 2003.

CRS Charitable Foundation
Youngstown, OH
The foundation terminated in 2003.

Davis Foundation, Inc., Hugh & Helen
Rome, GA
The foundation terminated on Dec. 31, 2005.

di Rosa Foundation, Rene & Veronica, The
Napa, CA
Specified beneficiary.

Dibner Fund, Inc., The
Wilton, CT
The grantmaker terminated in 2006 as a result of a restructuring into 4 newly created family foundations following the death of David Dibner.

Dick Family Foundation
Knoxville, TN
The foundation terminated in 2005.

Discuren Charitable Foundation
Seattle, WA
The foundation terminated in 2005.

DJN Foundation
See Skywords Family Foundation

Dominion Foundation
See Seven Woods Foundation

Dow Foundation, The
Tuxedo Park, NY
Current information not available.

Dumont Foundation
Los Angeles, CA
Specified beneficiaries.

East West Management Institute, The
New York, NY
The foundation is in a 60 month termination period.

Eaton Foundation, Ralph H. & Frances M.
Phoenix, AZ
The foundation terminated in 2005.

Eckerd Corporation Foundation
(Formerly Eckerd Foundation)
Plano, TX
The foundation has terminated.

Eckerd Foundation
See Eckerd Corporation Foundation

Ely Foundation, Inc., Sylvia S.
Potomac, MD
The foundation has transferred all of its assets of every mature, in equal shares, to Dennis Berman Family Foundaiton, Inc. and Deana and Michael David Epstech Family Foundation, Inc.

Evinrude Foundation, Ole, The
See OMC Foundation, The

Falk Foundation, Dr. Ralph and Marian
(Formerly Falk Medical Research Foundation, Dr. Ralph and Marian)
Irving, TX
The foundation merged into the Kohl Foundation in 2005.

Falk Medical Research Foundation, Dr. Ralph and Marian
See Falk Foundation, Dr. Ralph and Marian

Farber Family Foundation, Jake and Janet
Van Nuys, CA
The foundation terminated on Dec. 31, 2002.

Feldman Foundation, The
Dallas, TX
The foundation terminated on Dec. 31, 2005.

Fieldcrest Cannon Foundation
(Formerly Fieldcrest Foundation)
Richardson, TX
The foundation terminated in 2004 and transferred its assets to the Foundation for the Carolinas.

Fieldcrest Foundation
See Fieldcrest Cannon Foundation

Findley Foundation, Inc., Ralph F. & Gertrude S.
See Foundation of Faith, Inc.

Fisher Landau Foundation, The
New York, NY
The foundation terminated in 2005.

Florik Charitable Trust
Chicago, IL
The trust terminated on Apr. 30, 2006.

Ford Foundation, Inc., Gerald J., The
Dallas, TX
The foundation terminated in 2005.

Foundation of Faith, Inc.
(Formerly Findley Foundation, Inc., Ralph F. & Gertrude S.)
Brookfield, WI
The foundation terminated on Dec. 31, 2005.

Franklin Holding Corporation
Corte Madera, CA
The foundation merged into the Metta Fund on Dec. 16, 2004.

French Family Foundation, Inc., J. L.
Milwaukee, WI
The foundation terminated in 2005.

Frieze Family Foundation, Inc.
Boston, MA
The foundation terminated in 2005.

G & P Charitable Foundation, Inc., The
See G & P Foundation for Cancer Research, Inc., The

G & P Foundation for Cancer Research, Inc., The
(Formerly G & P Charitable Foundation, Inc., The)
New York, NY
Status changed to Public Charity.

Gilbert Foundation
See Gilbert Foundation, Rosalinde & Arthur, The

Gilbert Foundation, Rosalinde & Arthur, The
(Formerly Gilbert Foundation)
Los Angeles, CA
The foundation terminated in 2003 due to a merger with a successor foundation of the same name.

Gimelstob Family Foundation, Inc., Herbert
Boca Raton, FL
The foundation terminated in 2005.

GMO Charities, Inc.
Milwaukee, WI
The foundation terminated on May 31, 2005 and transferred its assets to Milwaukee Golf Charities.

Gold Foundation, Gloria and Peter
Glendale, CA
The foundation terminated on Sept. 30, 2005.

Gray Family Fund, Joseph J.
Chicago, IL
The fund terminated in 2005.

Green, Jr. Charitable Trust, John P.
Clearwater, FL
Specified beneficiaries.

Griffiths Trust, E. S. and M.
Cleveland, OH
Specified beneficiaries.

Gross Family Charitable Trust, Harold K.
Wellesley, MA
The foundation terminated in 2005.

Gruber Foundation, Peter
St. Thomas, VI
The foundation terminated in 2005 and transferred its assets to the Peter Gruber Foundation in Delaware.

Gualala Foundation Trust, The
Winston-Salem, NC
Specified beneficiary.

Guthman Fund, Leo S., The
Chicago, IL
The fund terminated in 2005.

Guttag Foundation, Inc., Irwin & Marjorie
Delray Beach, FL
The foundation terminated in 2005.

Guzzardi/Guzzardi Memorial Foundation, Tina
Winston-Salem, NC
The foundation terminated on Dec. 31, 2004.

Hanson Foundation, Jack and Vivian, The
New York, NY
Specified beneficiaries.

HAR-BER Village Foundation, The
Springdale, AR
Specified beneficiary.

Harcourt Foundation, Inc., Alfred, The
Silver Spring, MD
Specified beneficiaries.

Harrison Foundation, Helen M.
Chicago, IL
The foundation terminated in 2005 and transferred its assets to the Helen M. Harrison Foundation, Inc.

Hasbro Children's Foundation
Pawtucket, RI
The foundation merged with the Hasbro Charitable Trust, Inc. on Apr. 1, 2006.

Hascoe Foundation, The
Greenwich, CT
The foundation terminated on Mar. 31, 2003.

Hazen Foundation, Ann-Eve
Oakland, CA
The foundation terminated on Dec. 7, 2005.

Henningsen Family Foundation, Inc.
Chapel Hill, NC
Specified beneficiary.

Herzog Foundation, Inc., Carl J., The
Greenwich, CT
The foundation terminated in 2006.

Holdcroft Trust, Samuel W.
Richmond, VA
Specified beneficiaries.

Hooker Charitable Trust, Janet A.
Philadelphia, PA
The trust terminated in 2006.

Hope Afghanistan Foundation
Brentwood, TN
The foundation terminated in 2005.

Hope Happens
(Formerly ALS Hope-The Chris Hobler and James Maritz Foundation)
St. Louis, MO
Status changed to a public charity.

Horton Foundation, Polly
Chicago, IL
Specified beneficiaries.

Horwitch Brothers Foundation, The
(Formerly Horwitch Foundation, Albert A., The)
Scottsdale, AZ
The foundation terminated on Dec. 31, 2003.

Horwitch Foundation, Albert A., The
See Horwitch Brothers Foundation, The

Hudgens Family Foundation, Inc.
Duluth, GA
The foundation terminated on Sept. 30, 2005.

Huizenga Foundation, Elizabeth I.
Chicago, IL
The foundation terminated in 2005.

Interbel Foundation
Beverly Hills, CA
The foundation terminated in 2005.

Jones Center for Families, Harvey and Bernice
(Formerly MBM Charitable Foundation)
Springdale, AR
Specified beneficiary.

Jurodin Fund, Inc.
Newark, DE
The fund is in the process of terminating.

Kahn Testamentary Foundation, Robert J., The
Philadelphia, PA
Current information not available.

Kellman Foundation
See Kellman Foundation

Kellman Foundation
(Formerly Kellman Foundation)
Chicago, IL
The Kellman Foundation merged into The Joseph Kellman Family Foundation in 2002.

Khudari Foundation, The
Southborough, MA
The foundation terminated in 2005.

Kimmel Foundation, Helen & Martin, The
New York, NY
The foundation terminated Dec. 31, 2005.

Kirlin Foundation
Bellevue, WA
The foundation terminated on Nov. 30, 2005, and transferred its assets to the Kirlin Charitable Foundation.

Kraft Foundation, Robert and Myra
See MRK Foundation

Kratka Foundation, Inc.
Roseland, NJ
The foundation terminated in 2005.

Krehbiel Family Foundation
Wilmette, IL
The foundation terminated in 2003.

Kuester Foundation, Inc., Dennis J. and Sandra S.
See Thousand Hills Foundation, Inc.

Kushner Charitable Foundation, Charles and Seryl
Florham Park, NJ
Current information not available.

Landers Charitable Trust, Hilda C.
Linthicum, MD
Specified beneficiaries.

Landon Foundation, Inc., Kirk A. & Dorothy P.
Miami, FL
Specified beneficiary.

Langsam Foundation, Jack
San Francisco, CA
Specified beneficiaries.

Lapka Limited Charitable Trust
New York, NY
The foundation terminated in 2005.

Laraja Foundation, Inc., The
Montclair, NJ
The foundation terminated in 2005.

Littler Trust, Stephen
St. Louis, MO
Specified beneficiary.

Lowenstein Foundation, Alan V. and Amy
Roseland, NJ
The foundation terminate on Nov. 30, 2003.

MacDonnell Foundation, The
Menlo Park, CA
The foundation terminated on Dec. 31, 2005.

Martin Foundation, Agnes
Garden City, NY
The foundation terminated in 2004.

MBM Charitable Foundation
See Jones Center for Families, Harvey and Bernice

McKee Charitable Trust, Thomas M.
Loveland, CO
The trust terminated on Aug. 31, 2006.

McNair Foundation
Fort Worth, TX
The foundation terminated in 2005.

Metris Companies Foundation
Prospect Heights, IL
The foundation terminated on Nov. 30, 2005.

MetroWest Community Health Care Foundation, Inc.
Framingham, MA
Status changed to a Public Charity in 2003.

Mintz Scholarship Trust, Jessie
Phoenix, AZ
The foundation terminated in 2006.

Modern Poetry Association, The
See Poetry Foundation, The

Monk Cancer Research Foundation, Donald, The
Austin, TX
Specified beneficiary.

Moore Foundation, Inc., Edward S.
Greenwich, CT
The foundation terminated in 2004.

Morgan Foundation, Todd and Cheri
Los Angeles, CA
The foundation terminated on Dec. 31, 2004.

Morrill Charitable Foundation, Inc.
Chicago, IL
The foundation terminated in 2004.

MRK Foundation
(Formerly Kraft Foundation, Robert and Myra)
Foxboro, MA
The foundation terminated in 2003.

Muehlstein Foundation, Inc., Herman, The
New York, NY
The foundation terminated on Nov. 30, 2005.

Multiple Sclerosis Center of Atlanta, The
(Formerly Multiple Sclerosis Foundation of Atlanta, The)
Atlanta, GA
Grantmaker status changed to Public Charity.

Multiple Sclerosis Foundation of Atlanta, The
See Multiple Sclerosis Center of Atlanta, The

Nadeau Charitable Foundation, Inc., The
Fort Lauderdale, FL
The foundation terminated in 2005.

National Organization for Hearing Research Foundation
Narberth, PA
Status changed to Public Charity.

Needham Trust, Marie D.
Winston-Salem, NC
Specified beneficiaries.

New Haven Savings Bank Foundation, Inc., The
New Haven, CT
The New Haven Savings Bank Foundation, Inc. merged with the NewAlliance Foundation, Inc. in 2004.

New Horizon Foundation
Tacoma, WA
The foundation merged into the Sequoia Foundation in 2005.

Ng Charitable Foundation, Anna F.
Saratoga, CA
The foundation terminated on Apr. 30, 2006.

Nordstrom Charitable Foundation, Ilsley B.
Seattle, WA
The foundation terminated in 2006.

Nuclear Threat Initiative, Inc.
Washington, DC
Status changed to a Public Charity.

Numero-Steinfeldt Foundation
Minneapolis, MN
The foundation terminated in 2005.

O'Brien Foundation, Inc., Cornelius
See O'Brien Foundation, Inc., Cornelius and Anna Cook

O'Brien Foundation, Inc., Cornelius and Anna Cook
(Formerly O'Brien Foundation, Inc., Cornelius)
Milwaukee, WI
The foundation terminated in 2005.

O'Gara Foundation, Thomas M. & Victoria
Aspen, CO
The foundation terminated in 2004.

OMC Foundation, The
(Formerly Evinrude Foundation, Ole, The)
Kenosha, WI
The foundation terminated in 2005.

Omidyar Foundation, The
Redwood City, CA
The foundation terminated in Dec. 2004 and transferred its assets to the Omidyar
    Network Fund, Inc.

Oschin Family Foundation, Mr. & Mrs. Samuel
(Formerly Oschin Foundation, Inc., Samuel)
Los Angeles, CA
The foundation terminated as a result of a merger with a successor foundation of the
    same name in 2004.

Oschin Foundation, Inc., Samuel
See Oschin Family Foundation, Mr. & Mrs. Samuel

Oser Foundation, Margaret E., The
Santa Rosa, CA
The foundation terminated in 2006 and transferred its assets to Orange County
    Community Foundation.

Parsons Foundation, Alison J. & Ella W., The
Norfolk, VA
The foundation became a fund of The Norfolk Foundation.

Pasadena Area Residential Aid, A Corporation
Pasadena, CA
The foundation terminated on Jan. 31, 2006.

Peeler Charitable Trust, R. G. and Claudine Pope
Amarillo, TX
Specified beneficiary.

Petrie Foundation, Carroll and Milton, The
New York, NY
The foundation terminated in 2005, and trasferred its assets to The Carroll and Milton
    Petrie Foundation, Inc.

Poetry Foundation, The
(Formerly Modern Poetry Association, The)
Chicago, IL
Status changed to a Public Charity.

Prensky Family Foundation, Inc., The
New York, NY
The foundation terminated in 2004.

PSI Foundation, Inc.
See Cinergy Foundation, Inc.

Reeves Trust B, George C.
Winston-Salem, NC
The trust terminated on Dec. 31, 2004.

Rice Foundation, Helen Steiner, The
Cincinnati, OH
The foundation became a fund of The Greater Cincinnati Foundation in 2005.

Rotto Family Foundation
The Woodlands, TX
The foundation terminated on June 6, 2005.

Safdeye & Sons Foundation, Inc., Ellis A.
New York, NY
Current information not available.

Sandercock Trust, Marian
Sonoma, CA
The foundation terminated in 2003.

Scott Charitable Trust, Alton N.
Mobile, AL
Status changed to a public charity in 2005.

Seven Woods Foundation
(Formerly Dominion Foundation)
Mill Creek, WA
Current information not available.

Sheridan Foundation, James & Chantal
London, England
Foreign Foundation.

Shouse Foundation, Catherine Filene
(Formerly CFS Foundation, The)
Alexandria, VA
The foundation terminated on Dec. 31, 2003.

Skywords Family Foundation
(Formerly DJN Foundation)
San Francisco, CA
The foundation terminated in 2005.

Smith Foundation, Jody & Layton
(Formerly Smith Fund, Layton F.)
Clifton, VA
Current information not available.

Smith Fund, Layton F.
See Smith Foundation, Jody & Layton

Snook Foundation
Summerdale, AL
Current information not available.

Stabile Foundation, Vincent A.
Naples, FL
The foundation is in the process of being closed.

Stone Foundation, Irving & Jean
Beverly Hills, CA
The foundation terminated in 2004.

Sumasil Foundation, Inc.
Stillwater, MN
The foundation terminated in 2006.

Swalm Foundation
Houston, TX
The foundation terminated in 2006.

Sylvana Trust
Wauwatosa, WI
Current information not available.

Tawil Foundation, Inc., Ralph
New York, NY
Status changed to Public Charity.

Thompson Charitable Trust, B. R., The
Knoxville, TN
The trust terminated in Sept. 1, 2005 and transferred its assets to the Elgin
    Foundation.

Thousand Hills Foundation, Inc.
(Formerly Kuester Foundation, Inc., Dennis J. and Sandra S.)
Milwaukee, WI
The foundation terminated on Dec. 31, 2003.

Times Mirror Foundation, The
Chicago, IL
The foundation terminated in 2005.

U.S. Friends of Shine
Bedford Hills, NY
Specified beneficiary.

United Vision Foundation
Rockleigh, NJ
Status changed to a Public Charity in 2005.

United Wisconsin Services Foundation, Inc.
See Cobalt Corporation Foundation, Inc.

USAA Foundation II, a Charitable Trust
See USAA Foundation, a Charitable Trust, The

USAA Foundation, a Charitable Trust, The
(Formerly USAA Foundation II, a Charitable Trust)
San Antonio, TX
The trust terminated in 2005 and transferred its assets to the USAA Foundation, Inc.

VanVlack Family Charitable Trust
Portage, MI
The trust terminated in 2005.

VH1 Save The Music Foundation
(Formerly Viacom Foundation)
New York, NY
Status changed to public charity.

Viacom Foundation
See VH1 Save The Music Foundation

Virginia Environmental Endowment
Richmond, VA
Status changed to Public Charity.

Warwick Foundation, The
Philadelphia, PA
The foundation terminated on Jan. 1, 2003 and transferred its assets to the Warwick Foundation of Bucks County.

Webster Family Foundation, Dean K.
Andover, MA
The foundation terminated in June 2005 and transferred its assets to the Essex County Community Foundation.

Welborn Baptist Foundation, Inc.
Evansville, IN
The foundation merged into the Welborn Foundation in 2004.

Whitaker Foundation, The
Arlington, VA
The foundation terminated on June 30, 2006.

Whitaker Fund, Helen F., The
Mechanicsburg, PA
The fund terminated on July 31, 2006.

Witkin Charitable Trust of 1982, Bernard E. & Alba
Berkeley, CA
The trust terminated on Oct. 31, 2003.

Womble Charitable Trust, Lelia S.
Apex, NC
The trust terminated on Dec. 31, 2005.

WRG Foundation
New York, NY
Current information not available.

Y-Ma Foundation, The
Grand Junction, CO
The foundation terminated on June 30, 2005.

York Foundation, Marie Denise DeBartolo, The
Youngstown, OH
The foundation terminated on Jan. 31, 2006.

APPENDIX B

The following organizations are classified as private non-operating foundations under the IRS tax code. On the basis of statements from the organizations or an analysis of their most recent fiscal statements, it appears that these foundations contribute only to a few specified beneficiaries or to the support of a single organization or institution. Therefore, they are not included in this volume. Without further information, grantseekers are advised NOT to apply to these foundations for grant support. EIN refers to the Employer Indentification Number assigned to the foundation by the IRS.

STATE	EIN
Alabama	
Beeson Charitable Trust, Dwight M., Birmingham	636150745
Forchheimer Memorial Foundation, Louis & Josie, Mobile	636161119
Marinos Trust, George, Mobile	636018531
Roberts Charitable Trust, E. A., Mobile	636215720
Arizona	
Cosden Trust f/b/o University of Arizona College of Medicine, Curtis C., Phoenix	866174343
Craig Trust, Robert W., Phoenix	866021278
Metz Foundation, Arthur R., Scottsdale	366054389
California	
Anderson Living Trust, Clarence E., The, Valencia	957121299
Beaver Foundation, Oakland	941682883
Bowles Memorial Fund, Ethel Wilson Bowles & Robert, Pasadena	956481575
Braun Trust, Carl F., Los Angeles	956016828
Burgess Trust, Florence E., San Francisco	946713665
Colburn Music Fund, Los Angeles	954804766
Doelger Charitable Trust, Daly City	946468716
Dumont Foundation, Los Angeles	956220370
Elizabeth Foundation, Inc., Long Beach	954302261
Faulkner Foundation, Hobart W. and Lottie C., San Francisco	954446743
Griswold Charitable Trust, Santa Barbara	776135696
Hammer United World College Trust, Armand, The, Los Angeles	954031114
Hansen Foundation, Fred J., San Diego	953247772
Homan Charitable Foundation Trust, Los Angeles	953872427
Langsam Foundation, Jack, San Francisco	942550799
Perenin Foundation, Rose, Fortuna	680004983
Posey Trust, Addison, San Francisco	946612930
Powell Foundation, Charles Lee, The, La Jolla	237064397
Root Foundation, Ednah, Palm Desert	956209188
Seaver Trust f/b/o California Institute of the Arts, Richard C., Pasadena	956964069
Simon Foundation, Norton, The, Pasadena	956035908
Strauch Family Foundation, The, Irvine	330760532
Thomas Family Foundation, Los Angeles	954274964
Van Nuys Charitable Remainder Trust, Emily, San Francisco	956587698
Webb Trust, Harry H., San Francisco	946054898
Zemeckis Charitable Foundation, The, Los Angeles	954678226
Colorado	
Berry Foundation, Walter V. and Idun Y., Estes Park	330284355
Davis 1993 Charitable Trust, Sam and Freda, The, Greenwood Village	846261346

STATE	EIN
Delaware	
Bishop Trust B for the SPCA of Manatee County, Florida, Edward E., Wilmington	237366312
Bohmfalk Charitable Trust, Newark	133501941
Bourne Charitable Trust, William, Newark	516505985
Downs Perpetual Charitable Trust, Ellason, Wilmington	516158138
Fund for European Scouting, Newark	136804976
Homan, Jr. Trust, B. H., Newark	136741112
Huntington Trust f/b/o American Academy and Institute of Arts and Letters and National Institute of Arts, Archer M., Newark	136035643
Hyacinth Foundation, The, Wilmington	516183634
Lesieur Foundation, Henri and Flore, Newark	510378395
Phelps Trust f/b/o Tuttle Fund, Newark	136026698
Rankin and Elizabeth Forbes Trust, William, Newark	136584984
District of Columbia	
Strong Trust, Gordon, Washington	526025980
Florida	
Ashley Foundation, Harold W., The, Orlando	597100646
Genius Foundation, Elizabeth Morse, Winter Park	136115217
Green, Jr. Charitable Trust, John P., Clearwater	316654891
Landon Foundation, Inc., Kirk A. & Dorothy P., Miami	237148133
Moore Endowment and Scholarship Fund, Anna Fowler Moore and Robert Harless, Orlando	546336104
Naselli Trust, Helen W., Orlando	526239477
Titus Foundation, Ray E. & Staseli B., West Palm Beach	592828498
Georgia	
2 C 9 Foundation, Inc., Peachtree City	582646128
MLI, Inc., Augusta	582260185
Rollins Foundation, Gary W. & Ruth M., The, Atlanta	586263946
Southeastern Poultry & Egg/Harold E. Ford Foundation, Tucker	582098298
Hawaii	
Wodehouse Faculty Benefit Trust at Hawaii Preparatory Academy, C. N., Honolulu	990301432
Wodehouse Faculty Benefit Trust at Seabury Hall, C. N., Honolulu	990301434
Wodehouse Salvation Army Trust, C. N., Honolulu	990301431
Idaho	
Kasiska Family Foundation, The, Pocatello	820414752
Illinois	
Allen Charitable Trust, Harry J., Chicago	656386878

STATE	EIN
Buehler Trust, Phoebe B., Peoria	370196790
Coon Foundation, Owen L., Chicago	366066907
Edelstein, Joseph Judson and Martin Horrell Charitable Trust, Sara Horrell, The, Chicago	367280667
Fleming Charitable Trust, Joseph F., Bloomington	376222186
Hancock Charitable Trust, Marian Mullin, Chicago	956947778
Perritt Charitable Trust, Richard A., Chicago	367046562
Pro Archia Foundation, The, Chicago	366784984
Quarrie Charitable Fund, Chicago	366646475
Quarrie Charitable Trust No. 2, Chicago	366646474
Solomon Foundation, Sarah M., Winnetka	366613406
Souers Charitable Trust, Chicago	436079817
Swanson and Cynthia Shevlin Charitable Foundation, Robert, Chicago	367237696
Van Vechten-Lineberry Taos Art Museum Foundation, Chicago	367161322
Volen Charitable Trust, Benjamin, Chicago	656018806
White Memorial Trust, Kelton E. & Alma M., Chicago	436236634
Young Charity Trust, Chicago	366897850

Iowa

Jiruska Family Foundation, Cedar Rapids	421527834

Kentucky

Pennyroyal Area Museum Trust, Hopkinsville	611280844

Louisiana

Burden Foundation, Baton Rouge	726030712

Maryland

Baskerville Trust, Hamilton M., Baltimore	546204609
Harcourt Foundation, Inc., Alfred, The, Silver Spring	136084636
Landers Charitable Trust, Hilda C., Linthicum	526808936
Shuff Foundation, The, Linthicum	526955775
Williams and Sue W. Massie Fund, A. D., Baltimore	546034753

Massachusetts

Elliot Charitable Trust, John S. & Sarah C., Boston	046282546
Ginn Trust, Edwin, Boston	046039187
Luce Charitable Foundation, Stephen C., Boston	237105691
Projects for Asia, Inc., Hingham	043422112
Sears Trust, Clara Endicott, Boston	046025576
Shaw Fund, Miriam, Boston	046497465

Michigan

Akers Trust, Forrest H., Okemos	386066391
Diebolt Foundation, Plymouth	383444677
Foss Family Foundation, Farmington Hills	383326775
Hart Irrevocable Trust, Vera Marie, Detroit	386705201
Wilson, Jr. Medical Research Foundation, Ralph C. Wilson, Sr. and Ralph C., The, Grosse Pointe Park	383505430

Minnesota

Hotchkiss Foundation, W. R., St. Paul	416038562
Whiteside Charitable Trust, Muriel, St. Paul	416370669

Missouri

Blewett Trust, Scott H., St. Louis	436018190
Bohan Foundation, Ruth H., Kansas City	436269867
Burger Scholarship Fund, Adeline and Edna L., Clayton	436189843
Evans Trust, Walter & Frederica, St. Louis	436390422
Littler Trust, Stephen, St. Louis	376023121
Meeker Trust, Corry T., St. Louis	436019664
Parrish Charitable Trust, Elizabeth, St. Louis	436673904

Montana

Haynes Foundation, Helena	816013577

STATE	EIN

Nebraska

Hutzell Foundation, Omaha	356533689

New Hampshire

Friendship Fund, Inc. Trust f/b/o Institute of Current World Affairs, Hanover	136045127
Rowell Intervivos Trust, Annie, Concord	026110470

New Jersey

American Friends of Yeshiva Nachlat Josef, Inc., Lakewood	133683765
Gambino Medical & Science Foundation, Inc., Kearny	133586460
Lang Foundation, Inc., Susan, Millburn	223807990
Leavitt Foundation, N. R., Warren	226034106
Plummer Charitable Foundation, Inc., Hellen I., The, Cresskill	223365605

New Mexico

Oishei Consolidated Trust No. 2, John R., Santa Fe	166521727

New York

Bamberger Foundation, Eileen W., New York	137053837
Beach Charitable Trust, Edward P., The, New York	136971897
Bibi Charitable Trust, Nawab, Gloversville	141797883
Brunner Foundation, Inc., Robert, The, New York	136067212
Dixon-Comstock Scholarship Fund, New York	137117658
Dyson Vision Research Institute Trust, M. M., New York	136974073
Father Flanagan's Boys Home Trust No. 3, New York	900102166
God Bless America Fund, New York	136105770
Grenfell Association of America, The, New York	136083942
Haifa Foundation (North America), Inc., New York	133278992
Heller Foundation, Dr. Bernard, New York	132887370
HLMH, Inc., New York	134072644
JLRJ, Inc., New York	134077806
LMCL, Inc., New York	134077883
Miklat Shelter from Abuse, Inc., New York	134035508
MRHM, Inc., New York	134077880
Murphy Charitable Fund, George E. and Annette Cross, New York	136887044
Museum of Scotland & Heritage Trust Foundation, The, New York	510254205
Nagel Trust, Margaret A., Roslyn	116411431
Paine Foundation, M. S., New York	136074009
Phipps Family Foundation, John S., New York	136861582
Ramerica Foundation, New York	133407012
Rheinstrom Fund B, Irene and Carroll, The, New York	137174711
Smith-John G. Green Trust, Gerardus, Glenville	222507158
Stanton Fund, Ruth and Frank, New York	133598005
Steinhardt Family Foundation, New York	137067570
Stibbe Charitable Trust, Katherine S., The, New York	226715670
Teague Trust f/b/o Christian Family Care Agency, Inc., New York	866309087
Wehle, Sr. Foundation, Inc., John L., Rochester	223041829
Whitehead Trust f/b/o The National Spiritual Assembly of the Baha'i, O. Z., New York	137202416
Yee Foundation, Inc., S. K., New York	133202047

North Carolina

Baird Foundation, Winston-Salem	586307787
Burr Trust, Anna C., Winston-Salem	236972920
Carter Charitable Trust, Wilbur Lee, Charlotte	237420174
Coleman Trust, S. J., Winston-Salem	226335516
Davis Trust, James W., Charlotte	566038479
Dobbins Memorial Trust for Union Association of Children's Home, M., Winston-Salem	236215424
Elkins Fund, Lewis, Winston-Salem	236214962
Friends of the Kenan Foundation Asia, Chapel Hill	562044215
Henningsen Family Foundation, Inc., Chapel Hill	311623193
Hitchner Trust f/b/o Memorial Hospital of Salem, J. E., Winston-Salem	232751711
Kenan, Jr. Fund for Ethics, William R., Chapel Hill	561919423
Magee Trust for Convalescent Hospital, Winston-Salem	236215296
Mannheimer Trust, Hans S., Winston-Salem	226161919
Needham Trust, Marie D., Winston-Salem	586026107
Rose Trust, Lenox S., Winston-Salem	226024267
Schneller Scholarship Trust, Priscilla J., Winston-Salem	656163293

STATE	EIN	STATE	EIN
Vinik Trust, Tolly, Winston-Salem	596994221		

Ohio

Clements Foundation, Vida S., Westerville	316095287
Dunlap Testamentary Trust, Leo W., Zanesville	316325807
Frey f/b/o YMCA, Old Dutch Church, et al., Harry Dubois, Cleveland	166336547
Griffiths Trust, E. S. and M., Cleveland	116577624
Mitchell Foundation, William & Mary, Cleveland	356536740
Newcomb Fund, Helen D. and Adrian G., Cleveland	346754483
Pfeiffer Foundation, Frederick J., Cleveland	356593983
Pierstorf Memorial Scholarship Fund, The, Cleveland	346946124
Price Foundation, Harley C. & Mary Hoover, Cleveland	346510993
Schell Sole Survivor Trust, Charles E., Cincinnati	316019719
Sulsberger Foundation, The, Zanesville	316210487
Third Federal Savings and Loan Association, MHC and Subsidiaries Deferred Asset Accumulation Trust, Cleveland	347093341
Women's Philanthropic Union, Cleveland Heights	340782268

Oklahoma

Grimes Foundation, Otha H., Tulsa	731293858
Weeks and Marie Stuart Smith Memorial Charitable Trust, Margaret Smith, Ardmore	736242611

Oregon

Al-Athel Foundation, Inc., The, Portland	043527638

Pennsylvania

Brennan Foundation, Albert A., Pittsburgh	616094299
Farley Family Foundation, James N. and Nancy J., Philadelphia	363938355
Froelich Charitable Trust, Edward, Lancaster	236711561
Gahagen Charitable Foundation, Zella J., Pittsburgh	256219884
Gumberg Family Foundation, Ira J., Pittsburgh	251842389
Lavino Foundation, Edwin M., Pittsburgh	232032639
Rudy, Jr. Trust, George B., York	236708045
Sullivan Fund, Frances W., Philadelphia	232657930
Tippett Trust f/b/o United Methodist Homes, E., Pittsburgh	236910775

Rhode Island

Belding Fund, Alvah N., Providence	237425259
Hellmann Trust f/b/o American Cancer Society, et al., Rhoda M., Providence	066263343
Hellmann Trust f/b/o Sibella Hellmann Fund, Rhoda M., Providence	066263709
Swebilius Trust, C. G., Providence	066021035

South Dakota

McCrossan Foundation, Sioux Falls	460241590

Tennessee

Potter Trust, Valerie B., Nashville	581309898

Texas

Bass Arts Corporation, Perry and Nancy Lee, Fort Worth	752677599
Bass Endowment Corporation, Perry and Nancy Lee, Fort Worth	752677598
Kahn Dallas Symphony Foundation, Louise W. and Edward J., Dallas	756368880
Longenbaugh Foundation, Gillson, Bellaire	760001952
Loose Trust, Ella C., Dallas	446009265
MBC Foundation, Houston	746108373
McWilliams Memorial Hospital Trust, Dallas	436062691
Newell Charitable Trust, W. P. & Dell Andrews, Abilene	756059309
O'Connor Foundation, Michael O'Connor and Karen L., Corpus Christi	742969840
O'Hanlon Wholly Charitable Trust, Sherman	756429380
Peeler Charitable Trust, R. G. and Claudine Pope, Amarillo	756599973
Stonestreet Trust, Eusebia S., Dallas	756009142

Virginia

Grant Charitable Trust, E. Stuart James, Danville	546315085
Holdcroft Trust, Samuel W., Richmond	546030447
St. Andrew's Association, Richmond	546039947

Washington

Baker Foundation Trust, James A. and Laura L., Seattle	527237499
Egtvedt Charitable Trust, Clairmont L. and Evelyn S., The, Seattle	916062228
Gehr Foundation, Emma C., Seattle	916279262
Irvine Testamentary Trust, Lizzie Brownell & John H., Bellevue	916027040
Kogan Foundation, Inc., Michael and Asya, Freeland	521966485
Rasmuson Endowment Trust for the Boy Scouts of America in Alaska, Elmer E., Seattle	926031574
Trimble Fund, George W., Seattle	916026531
Wells Foundation, A. Z., Seattle	916026580

Wisconsin

Delfing Charitable Trust, Sister Irmgard, Milwaukee	396781271
Kennedy Memorial Fund, Mark H., Milwaukee	550684352
Raynor Charitable Trust, Father John P., Milwaukee	396781273
Rieth Foundation for Environmental Education, Lee A. & Mary Jane, The, Milwaukee	351979838
Ruggiero Memorial Trust, A. J. & M. D., Milwaukee	866240840
Shinnick Trust, William M., Milwaukee	316024875
Surgical Science Foundation for Research & Development, Madison	930846339

Wyoming

Griffith Foundation, Vernon S. & Rowena W., Sheridan	237135835

INDEX TO DONORS, OFFICERS, TRUSTEES

Adams, Jeff, 9488
Adams, Jerry, 156
Adams, Joanna, Rev., 2474
Adams, Joe, 1060
Adams, Joel B., Jr., 267
Adams, John, 7673
Adams, John H., 5551
Adams, John K., 194
Adams, John King, 194
Adams, John W., 7008
Adams, Joseph T., 8167
Adams, K.S., Jr., 9230
Adams, Lee, 5883
Adams, Lewis, 4930
Adams, Lois, 828
Adams, Lynne Butler, 2646
Adams, Madeline R., 2309
Adams, Margaret, 4611
Adams, Marla, 7346
Adams, Marla T., 267
Adams, Marty E., 7859
Adams, Mary Lou, 9184
Adams, Morgan, Jr., 194
Adams, Moss, LLP, 9548
Adams, Nancy N., 9230
Adams, Nell, 3470
Adams, Patrick, 5564
Adams, Peter W., 7679, 7680
Adams, Richard, 3562
Adams, Richard L., Jr., 3562
Adams, Richard M., 4700
Adams, Richard N., 7748
Adams, Rob, 3867
Adams, Robert M., 5338
Adams, Roy M., 5198
Adams, Sam, 3509
Adams, Sara Trillo, 4209
Adams, Susan, 1123
Adams, Susan C., 3867
Adams, Suzanne, 407
Adams, Thomas T., 1481
Adams, Valencia I., 2323
Adams, Vickee, 5184
Adams, Wanda, 8583
Adams, Yvonne B., 3458
Adams-Brooks, Jennifer, 1087
Adams-Phillips, Nazamovia "Naz", 7867
Adamski, Paul, 9778
Adamson, Katharine J., 1647
Adamson, Rebecca, 5606
Adamson, Roland C., 8916
Adaya, Ahmad, 200
Adaya, Amina, 200
Adaya, Salim, 200
ADC Corp., 4496
ADC Telecommunications, Inc., 4496
ADCS, Inc., 1306
Addams, Cynthia G., 8007
Adderley, Terence E., 4359
Addicks, Frank M., 8671
Addington, Whitney Wood, 3016
Addis, Dennis J., 2388
Addison, Josh, 520
Addison, R. Elaine, 7474
Addiss, Susan S., 1519
Adelman, Andrea, 8197
Adelman, Jack, 5857
Adelman, Larry S., 3125
Adelmann, Gerald, 2706
Adelson, Andrew, 5108
Adelson, Ellen G., 7941
Adelson, Ellen Jane, 7941
Adelson, James, 7984
Adelson, Nancy, 5108
Adenekan, Samuel Abiola, 6389
ADEO, LLC, 4877
Ader, Richard M., 5793
Aderhold, John E., 2502
Ades, Alan M., 5516
Ades, Joan, 5516
Adesola, Akin Oludele, 6389
ADG-L5, LLC, 8210
Adik, Stephen, 3213
Adilman, Joree, 6485

Adjmi Dwek Foundation, 5518
Adjmi, Eric, 5518
Adjmi, Harry, 5519
Adjmi, Jack, 5518, 5520
Adjmi, Mark, 5518
Adjmi, Rachel, 5518
Adjmi, Ronald, 5518
Adkerson, Nancy L., 3481
Adkerson, Richard C., 3481
Adkins, James A., 3693
Adkisson, Hermoine Corlew, 8712
Adler, Anne, 9861
Adler, Bette, 9861
Adler, Catherine, 1871
Adler, Diane, 9278
Adler, Donald, 4065
Adler, Doris J., 7875
Adler, E.B., 9861
Adler, Frederick R., 1871
Adler, Helen R., 5521
Adler, Homer, 3470
Adler, James, 607
Adler, Jeff, 1942
Adler, John, 5521
Adler, Karen, 5673
Adler, Leo, 7996
Adler, Madeline Wing, 8141
Adler, Marcia F., 957
Adler, Marie, 553
Adler, Mitchell, 6557
Adler, Morton M., 5521
Adler, Stephen, 7247
Adler, William, 6777
Adleta, Charles Derek, Psy.D., 9012
Adnopoz, Jean, 1519
ADP Rental Co., 2366
Adreani, Raymond J., 2585
Adrian & James, Inc., 6240
Adriano, Kim B., 9826
Adumson, Pete, III, 7988
Advance Magazine Group, 61, 5905
Advance Publications, Inc., 6623
Advance Stores Co., Inc., 9524
Advanced Cardiovascular Systems, Inc., 3159
Advanced Respiratory, Inc., 4708
Advest, Inc., 8188
Advocate and Greenwich Times Holiday Fund, The, 1647
Adwan, Teresa B., 7974
Aeder, Arthur, 6251
Aedo, Charles "Chuck", 342
AEGON USA, Inc., 3259
Aeneas Capital Management, LP, 5523
Aerotek, Inc., 3565
AES Corp., 1852
Aetna, 7040
Aetna Freight Lines, Inc., The, 3629
Aetna Inc., 1479
Afek, Ehud, 5673
Afeyan, Noubar, 3773
Aft, David, 2359
Agabani, Motaz, 1946
AGAO, LLC, 4877
Agarwal, Adhish, 9313
Agather, Ruth K., 8984
Agather, V. Neils, 8801
Agee, Bob, 3587
Agee, Eloise R., 4999
Agee, John, 1782
Agee, Nancy Howell, 9419
Agee, Richard W., 4999
Aggarwal, Braham, 1942
Agger, David, 961
Aghdami, Farhad, 9402
Agilent Technologies, Inc., 3563
AGL Foundation, 2312
AGL Resources Inc., 2312
Agle, George, 6977
Agouron Institute, 1510
Agrawal, Sudhir K., 8661
Aguayo, Constance, 9424
Aguiar, Guma, 2079
Aguiar, Lauren E., 6998

Aguillard, Susan M., 8638
Agus, Bernard, 5956, 6008, 7299
Agus, Bertrand, 5528, 5608, 5765, 5838, 5929, 6228, 6394, 7197, 7284
Agvar Chemicals, Inc., 5315
Ahaba Ve Ahva Congregation, 5740
Ahern, John E., 9800
Ahern, Joseph A., 2654
Ahmadi, Hoshang, 5530
Ahmanson, Howard F., 198
Ahmanson, Howard F., Jr., 197, 198
Ahmanson, Robert H., 198
Ahmanson, Roberta G., 197
Ahmanson, William H., 198
Ahmanson, William Hayden, 198
Ahmanson, William Howard, 198
Ahmed, Mohamed A., 4285
Ahold Financial Services, LLC, 8463
Ahrens, Chad W., 3260
Ahrens, Claude W., 3260
Ahuja, Elias, 1715
Aichenbrenner, John, 3326
Aicher Trust, Paul J., The, 5109
Aicher, Paul J., 5109
Aicher, Peter, 5109
Aid Association for Lutherans, 9949
Aidekman, Gary O., 5228
Aidekman, Rick, 6219
Aidner, Sandye, 5128
AIDS Walk San Diego, Inc., 204
AIDSERVE Indiana, 3164
Aiello, Leslie C., 7244
AIG, 7040
AIG 2001 Trust, 6110
AIG Warranty Guard, 9482
Aiken, J. Kirby, 2976
Aiken, Jeffrey P., 8518
Aiken, Scott, 8408
Aiken, Tim E., 7436
Aiken, William, 4210
Aikenhead, David S., 657
Aikenhead, Kathleen Hannon, 645
Aikens, Ann S., 4215
Aikens, Robert B., 4215
Aikman, Sheryl, 7346
Ailes, Garry, 5005
Ainslie, Laurie, 2545
Ainul, Jamal, 6926
Aiosa, Douglas R., 1956
Air Products and Chemicals, Inc., 8481
Aircast, Inc., 8074
AirTouch Communications, Inc., 1267
Aitcheson, A. Tracy, 9521
Aitchison, Bill, 3165
Aitken, Frances, 8103
Aitken, Randi Ross, 354
Ajax Metal Processing, Inc., 4250
Ajello, James, 9144
Ajmera, Maya, 5905
AK Steel Corp., 7525
Akbar, Raana, 4428
Akcan, Carolyn B., 283
Akel, Ferris G., 5846
Akel, George, 5781
Akel, Ron, 6329
Akers, Betsy, 2447
Akers, Ruth Ruggles, 1945
Akin, Hank, 8996
Akin, Hugh Clark, 9218
Akina, Charman J., 2544
Akins, C.B., Sr., 3407
Akins, Darrell D., 8671
Akins, Martin P., 4811
Akman, Larry, 3622
Akman, Nonie, 3622
Al-Hibri, Azizah, 1791
Al-Qutub, Ishaq Y., 7531
Alabama Oxygen Co., Inc., 41
Alabama Power Co., 1
Alabama-Coushatta Entertainment Center, 1781
Alafi, Chris, 201
Alafi, Margaret, 201

Alafi, Moshe, 201
Alafi, Shireen, 201
Alandt, Lynn F., 4301
Alario, Robert C., 4057
Alatis, James E., 1847
Alban, James C., IV, 3568
Albatros Enterprises Trust, 7030
Alberding, Ellen S., 2820
Alberg, Tom A., 9670, 9680
Albers, C. Hugh, 2673
Albers, Genevieve, 9592
Alberts, Bruce, 563, 913, 5707
Alberts, Thomas P., 3253
Albertson, Donavon, 5089
Albertson, J.A., 2562
Albertson, Kathryn, 2562
Albin, Arthur E., 4470
Albinder, Barbara Zucker, 7303
Albrecht, Bill, 4534
Albrecht, F. Steven, 7526
Albrecht, Ralph W., 1872, 2103
Albrecht, Ralph W., Sr., 1872
Albrecht, Sophie E., 7591
Albrecht, Wendy, 9123
Albrechtsen, B. Dennis, 4252
Albright, Adam, 1840, 2600
Albright, C. David, 3344
Albright, George F., 9486
Albright, Joseph P., 1840
Albright, Liza, 9544
Albright, Nancy, 9885
Albright, Nile I., 9142
Albright, Rachel, 2600
Albright, Susanne D., 7342
Albrittain, Nancy A., 9371
Albritton, O.L., 9089
Albro, Les, 3130
Alcala, Lorna Tchang, 1229
Alcantar, Joe, 8950
Alchu, Kay F., 5049
Alcoa Inc., 8075
Alcorn, Marie F., 8671
Alcorn, W., 9115
Alden, A.F. Drew, 1514
Alden, Elizabeth K., 2731
Alden, George I., 3776
Alden, Ginger, 9777
Alden, Priscilla, 3777
Alderfer, Alan, 3186
Aldredge, Alison, 5775
Aldridge, David P., 2713
Aldridge, Elizabeth, 7397
Aldridge, Elizabeth A., 7963
Aldridge, Fred C., Jr., 8362
Aleppo, Ezio, 1882
Aleppo, Georgia, 1883
Aleppo, Joseph A., 1882, 1883
Alerus Financial, 7514
Alevizon, Sarah, 220
Alex, Josephine, 5559
Alexander & Baldwin, 2530
Alexander, Allan L., 362
Alexander, Andrew M., 8752
Alexander, Anne M., 9741
Alexander, Arthur W., 6926
Alexander, Bruce D., 1514
Alexander, Bruce K., 1394
Alexander, Cleopatra B., 2943
Alexander, Cynthia K., 8776
Alexander, David, 1118, 7244
Alexander, Donald C., 6639
Alexander, Elisabeth H., 7806
Alexander, Emily H., 3024
Alexander, George, 9165
Alexander, Helen C., 8999
Alexander, Henrietta K., 8999
Alexander, James L., 2751, 9879
Alexander, James N., 3016
Alexander, Jeff, 8841
Alexander, Jimmy, 2582
Alexander, Joan, 8752
Alexander, John, 3024
Alexander, John D., Jr., 8999
Alexander, John E., 4480, 9740

Alexander, John H., Jr., 1398
Alexander, Joseph, 5532
Alexander, Juliet, 6484
Alexander, Kathleen H., 4828
Alexander, Martha J., 3024
Alexander, Nanci, 2150
Alexander, Nicholas, 1080
Alexander, Pamela A., 7806
Alexander, Pamela G., Hon., 4623
Alexander, Paule R., 6423
Alexander, Quentin, 7806
Alexander, Scott E., 1943
Alexander, Sheryl J., 405
Alexander, Stanford, 8752
Alexander, Stuart, 4549
Alexander, Sydenham B., 7488
Alexander, Ted J., 4751
Alexander, Thomas S., 2680, 3024
Alexander, Timothy F., 8876
Alexander, W. Robert, 1393, 1394
Alexander, Walter, 3024
Alexander, Wynn, 4745
Alexander-Holt, Sharon, 1377
Alexander-Stewart Lumber Co., 3024
Alexandra Trust, 2916
Alfa Mutual Fire Insurance Co., 2
Alfa Mutual Insurance Co., 2
Alfiero, Charles C., 5534
Alfiero, James J., 5534
Alfiero, Salvatore H., 5534
Alfiero, Victor S., 5534
Alfond, Barbara, 3769
Alfond, Dorothy, 3521
Alfond, Harold, 3521
Alfond, Joan, 3523
Alfond, Justin, 3523
Alfond, Kenden, 3523
Alfond, Peter, 3521
Alfond, Peter G., 3522
Alfond, Reis, 3523
Alfond, Theodore, 3521, 3523, 3769
Alfond, William, 3521, 3522, 3523
Alfonso, Carlene, 4745
Alford, A.L., Jr., 9665
Alford, Bobby R., 8754
Alford, Ericka, 7046
Alford, L.E., 639
Alford, Ronald B., 7714
Alford, Sandra E., 8772
Algiero, Nicholas, 5194
Algra, Diana Rodriguez, 4243
Alhadeff, Victor D., 9675
Ali, Fred J., 1288
Ali, Mohammed, 3775
Alice Manufacturing Co., Inc., 8599
Alito, Noelie, 9269
Alix, Jay, 4216
Alix, Maryanne, 4216
Aljian, James D., 812
Alkek, Albert B., 8754
Alkek, Margaret M., 8753, 8754
All American Collectibles, 7174
All American Products, 4922
Allaire, Dennis, 8419
Allan, Karen C., 8003
Allan, Richard, 8450
Allare, Ellen Steele, 87
Allbritton, Barbara, 8755
Allbritton, Joe L., 8755
Allbritton, Robert L., 8755
Allday, Doris Fondren, 8906
Allday, R. Edwin, 8906
Allegiance Corp., 2611
Allegis Group, Inc., 3565
Allegretti, Antoniette, 2586
Allegretti, Carol, 2586
Allegretti, Elizabeth, 2586
Allegretti, Fred, 2586
Allegretti, James, 2586
Allegretti, Jean, 2586
Allegretti, Joseph, 3135
Allen Foundation for Medical Research, Paul G., The, 9550
Allen Foundation for Music, The, 9550

Allen J. Graham Marital Trust, 7382
Allen Trust, Roscoe B., 8756
Allen Virtual Education Foundation, Paul G., The, 9550
Allen, A.J., 2425
Allen, Alexandra F., 5611, 5894
Allen, Alton C., 8866
Allen, Andrew, 8487, 9974
Allen, Andrew D., 5611, 5894
Allen, Andy, 183
Allen, Anne, 1780
Allen, Arthur Yorke, 7207
Allen, Barbara Powell, 3381
Allen, Bo, 2259
Allen, Brent, 8758
Allen, C. Donald, 264
Allen, Carney, 3415
Allen, Charles C., Jr., 4860
Allen, Christine, 5611, 5894
Allen, Christopher D., 5611, 5894
Allen, Corinne, 8644
Allen, David, 9918
Allen, David F., 7586
Allen, Debbie, 7984
Allen, Dick, 957
Allen, Doris T., 7399
Allen, Douglas E., 5611
Allen, Edith W., 3852
Allen, Elisabeth F., 5611
Allen, Elizabeth P., 6700
Allen, Elizabeth Peale, 5564
Allen, Franklin P. "Pepper", 8638
Allen, Frederick, 3852
Allen, G. Ashley, 6552
Allen, George, 2814
Allen, Gloria, 81
Allen, Heath, 8390
Allen, Helaine B., 3799
Allen, Herbert A., III, 5536
Allen, Herman, Dr., 2170
Allen, Hugh B., 2460
Allen, Ivye, 172
Allen, Ivye L., 4743
Allen, Jack W., 2460
Allen, James C., 1516
Allen, James Floyd, 9161
Allen, James Richard, 8876
Allen, Janice H., 4746
Allen, Jeffrey, 249
Allen, Jessie L., 8866
Allen, Jim, 3387
Allen, Joan E., 9414
Allen, Joelle, 2165
Allen, Johanna, 4256
Allen, John, 9890
Allen, John H., 6150
Allen, Jon, 1949
Allen, Jose R., 6998
Allen, Karen Tanner, 6626
Allen, Laurell, 2460
Allen, Lee Barclay Patterson, Mrs., 2460
Allen, Leigh B., III, 4770
Allen, Lew, Jr., 750
Allen, M.H., 2465
Allen, Martha, 76
Allen, Michael D., 8876
Allen, Milton N., 7254
Allen, Nicholas E., 5611, 5894
Allen, Patrick E., 3328
Allen, Paul G., 9550
Allen, Paul J., 3602
Allen, Philip D., 5611, 5894
Allen, Ralph, 1944
Allen, Renee, 3197
Allen, Richard, 4442
Allen, Rob, 85, 3159
Allen, Robert, 2263, 8153
Allen, Samuel R., 2699
Allen, Sharon, 156
Allen, Sharon L., 1527
Allen, Susan K., 5536
Allen, Suzie, 1942
Allen, Thomas F., 7542, 7549
Allen, Thomas R., 8868

Allen, Thomas W., 1945
Allen, Toloria, 8762
Allen, Tom, 8840
Allen, W. James, 4407
Allen, William D., II, 9527
Allen, William James, 4217
Allen, William L., Jr., 1706
Allen, Yvonne L., 7688
Allen-Bradley Co., 9763
Allen-Meares, Paula, 6092
Allendale Mutual Insurance Co., 8537
Aller, Thomas L., 3343, 9742
Allergan, Inc., 203, 5990
Allesee, Margaret Acheson, 4254
Alley, Mark, 4243
Alley, Steve, 91
Alliance Capital Management Corp., 2789, 7140
Alliance for Affordable Healthcare Association, Inc., 8836
Alliant Energy Corp., 9742
Alliant Techsystems Inc., 4509
Allianz AG, 205
Allied Development, 3301
Alligood, Harvey, 9894, 9895
Allingham, Thomas J., II, 6998
Allison, Ashley, 3897
Allison, Carolyn J., 8757
Allison, Diane M., 1533, 1536, 1630
Allison, Frank, 8967
Allison, Herbert M., Jr., 5537
Allison, Jane S., 8757
Allison, Jim, 8758
Allison, Robert J., 8757
Allison, Robert J., Jr., 8757
Allison, Simin Nazemi, 5537
Allison, Walter W., 7953
Alliss, Charles C., 4498
Alliss, Ellora Martha, 4498
Allocco, Andrew, 1479
Alloo, Richard, 3407
Allred, Jeffery C., 2313
Allred, Jeffrey, 2313
Allred, Jennifer, 2313
Allred, Ron, 1465
Allred, S. Eugene, 2388
Allsbrook, David, 1044
Allstate Corp., The, 2588
Allstate Insurance Co., 2588
AllStyle Coil Co., L.P., 9031
Allton, John D., 7839
Allura Imports, Inc., 6501
Allwin, James M., 5538
Allwin, Maria, 5538
Allyn, Amy, 5539
Allyn, David, 5539
Allyn, Dawn N., 5539
Allyn, Eric R., 5539
Allyn, Janet J., 5539
Allyn, Lew F., 5539
Allyn, Scott, 5539
Allyn, William F., 5539
Allyn, William N., 5539
Alm, John R., 2351
Almand, James W., 3599
Almar Sales Co. Inc., 5572
Almario, J.S., 7464
Almas, Jim, 4737
Almgren, Raymond, 9088
Almo, Eli J., 9675
Almond, Martha, 2489
Almoney, Jeff, 7818
Almquist, L. Arden, 9972
Alna Envelope Co., 248
Alon, Ruth, 206
Alon, Zvi, 206
Alost, Mike, 3469
Alpaugh, Peter A., 7527
Alper, Carolyn, 3735
Alper, Jonathan, 7345
Alperin, Barry, 8516
Alperin, Melvin, 8516
Alpern, Bernard E., 5540
Alpers, Ann, 423

Alpers, Christian, 5073
Alpert & Alpert Iron & Metal, Inc., 207
Alpert, Alan, 207
Alpert, Barbara, 209
Alpert, Charles, 6844
Alpert, Herb, 208
Alpert, Jane, 5541
Alpert, Joseph, 6844
Alpert, Lani Hall, 208
Alpert, Norman W., 5541
Alpert, Raymond, 207, 209
Alpert, Teri, 209
Alpert, Warren, 8517
Alpeter, James A., 2717
Alpha Bancorp, 2726
Alpine Gardens, 1359
ALS Foundation, The, 9324
Alsdorf, James W., 2590
Alsdorf, Jeffrey A., 2590
Alsdorf, Marilynn A., 2966
Alsdorf, Marilynn B., 2590
Alsheimen, Ann, 5902
Alson, Ernest, 5924
Alsop, David, 8495
Alsop, Jane, 3387
Alt, Willis, 3185
Altec Industries, Inc., 4
Altenbaumer, Larry, 2900
Alter Trust, Dennis, 8078
Alter, Dennis, 8078
Alter, Gisela, 8078
Alter, Helen, 8078
Alter, Wayne E., Jr., 3600
Alterman, Mindi, 9166
Alternative Investment Manager, 1093
Althaus, Ruth Ann, 2681
Altheide, Paul D., 9138
Altheimer Foundation, Ben J., The, 155
Altheimer Trust, Ben J., 155
Altheimer, Ben J., Jr., 155
Althoff, Steve, 3697
Alticor Inc., 4279
Altman, Arthur, 3839
Altman, Benjamin, 5542
Altman, Brian D., 6743
Altman, David R., 2494
Altman, Donald B., 6743
Altman, Drew E., 739
Altman, Georgia, 5543
Altman, Jeffrey A., 5543
Altman, Jenifer, 211
Altman, Lawrence, 1338, 5543
Altman, Lawrence B., 5240
Altman, Lawrence K., 6471
Altman, Lisa, 210
Altman, Mary Ilu, 3188
Altman, Michael S., 4625
Altman, Pearl, 5965
Altman, Raymond, 3637
Altman, Richard M., 5544
Altman, Robert C., 5544
Altman, Roger C., 5544, 6536
Altman, Steve, 210
Altmeyer, James E., 9713
Altobello, Daniel J., 1825
Altorfer, Richard, 3275
Altria Group, Inc., 5545
Altschul, Arthur G., 6675
Altschul, Arthur G., Jr., 6675
Altschul, Charles, 6675
Altschul, Frank, 6675
Altschul, Helen G., 6675
Altschul, Jeanette Cohen, 5546
Altschul, Louis, 5546
Altschul, Serena, 6675
Altschul, Stephen F., 6675
Altshuler, David, 4036
Altshuler, Ruth Sharp, 8839, 9180
Altshuler, Sharman, 4035
Aluminum Co. of America, 8075
Alumni Association Foundation, 941
Alvarado, David R., 1093
Alvarado, Gilbert, 1151, 9111
Alvarado, Linda, 1443

Alvarez, Carlos Enrique, 9133
Alvarez, Cesar L., 2097
Alvarez, Maria de Guadalupe, 9133
Alvarez, Rodolfo, 550
Alvarez, Ronald, 1939
Alvarez-Rodriguez, Deborah, 474
Alverio, Marilyn, 1519
Alvernini, John M., 4930
Alverno Health Care Corp., 3143
Alvord, Joel B., 3778
Alvord, Sarah H., 3778
Alvord, Seth W., 3778
Alwang, Walter G., 1603
Alworth, Marshall W., 4499
Alworth, Nick, 4499
Alzheimer's Association, 304
Amacher, Howard R., 8741
Amado, Bernice, 212
Amado, Maurice, 212
Amado, Ralph A., 212
Amado, Ralph D., 212
Amante, Char, 4258
Amarillo National Bank, 8760, 9142
Amas Limited, 3952
Amato, Theresa, 2922
Amaturo, Douglas Q., 1873
Amaturo, Joseph C., 1873
Amaturo, Lawrence V., 1873
Amaturo, Winifred J., 1873
Amaturo, Winifred L., 1873
Ambach, Gordon M., 7209
Ambach, Lucy E., 6907
Ambler, Bruce, 3564
Ambler, Sarah H.C., 4037
Amboy National Bank, 5112
Ambrose, Julika, 1364
Ambrosi, Michael, 220
Ambrus, Mary Lou, 5110
Ambuel, Helen B., 9867
Ambutas, Vytas, 5072
AMCORE Bank, N.A., 2591
AMCORE Financial, Inc., 2591
Ameis, Marie S., 3174
Ameren Corp., 4772
America Online, Inc., 7142
American and Efird Mills, Inc., 7355
American Bag & Paper Corp., 8279
American Bank, 9940
American Biosystems, 4708
American Builders Financial Corp., 2935
American Buildings Co., 8713
American Century Companies, 8853
American Century Cos., Inc., 4773
American Eagle Outfitters, Inc., 8079
American Express Co., 5553
American Family Life Assurance Co. of
    Columbus, 2311, 2314
American Financial Holdings, Inc., 1482
American Funds, 2356
American Future Systems, Inc., 8424
American General Finance, Inc., 3098
American Healthways, 2547, 4521
American Honda Motor Co., Inc., 217
American Hospital Supply Corp., 2611
American Industries, Inc., 8019
American Jewish Joint Distribution
    Committee, Inc., The, 4102
American Livestock Insurance Co., 3024
American Lumber, LP, 5504
American Manufacturers Mutual
    Insurance Co., 2832
American Manufacturing Corp., 8093
American Motorists Insurance Co., 2832
American Mutual Life Insurance Co.,
    3261
American National Bank, 1453, 4671
American National Bank and Trust Co.,
    9386
American Nevada Corp., 5034
American Ocean Campaign, 1060
American Promotional Events, Inc., 7
American Retail Group, Inc., 6212
American Retail Properties, Inc., 6212
American Savings Bank, 3558

American Scandia, 8433
American Service and Product Inc., 2930
American Ship Management, LLC, 894
American Snuff Co., 8663
American Standard Cos., Inc., 5113
American Standard Inc., 5113
American Trading and Production Corp.,
    3575, 3719, 3744
American Trailers, Inc., 4679
American United Life Insurance Co.,
    3220
American Woodmark Corp., 9368
AMERIGROUP Corp., 9369
Amerine, I. Robert, 7791
Amerman, Anne J., 218
Amerman, Garrett J., 218
Amerman, Jerome T., 218
Amerman, John W., 218
AmerUs Group Co., 3261
Ames, Aubin Z., 5230, 5391
Ames, Edward A., 5712
Ames, George J., 6546
Ames, Harriett, 8080
Ames, Kathleen L.F., 6147
Ames, Marshall, 2109, 2140
Ames, Stephen C., 5785
Ames, Steven, 8080
Amestoy, Jay, 1828
AMETEK, Inc., 8081
Amethyst, Inc., 354
Amgen Inc., 219, 3677
Ami, Karen, 2938
Amica Mutual Insurance Co., 8518
Amirsaleh, Fran, 5114
Amirsaleh, Mahyar, 5114
Amirsaleh, Mehrdad, 5114
Amirsaleh, Morad, 5114
Amiss, Jason, 7031
Amity Leather Products Co., 9914
Amlung, Stephanie R., 7824
Ammerman, Ellen, 406
Amoco Corp., 80, 2628
Amoco Production Co., 2628
Amodio, Louis G. "Gerry", 1515
Amodio-DeMartis, Gina, 5388
Amor, Jack, 2270
Amory, Daniel, 3969
Amory, Mary, 3969
Amory, Robert, 3969
Amos Trust, Jean, 2315
Amos Trust, Paul, 2315
Amos, Catherine M., 2458
Amos, Daniel P., 2314, 2315
Amos, Elena Diaz-Verson, 2316
Amos, Jean R., 2314
Amos, John Shelby, II, 2316
Amos, Kathleen V., 2311
Amos, Lauren A., 2314, 2315
Amos, Paul S., 2314, 2315
Amos, Paul S., II, 2314
Amos, Shannon L., 2315
AMP Inc., 8485
AMPCO-Pittsburgh Foundation, 8192
Amper, Linda E., 6670
Amrani, Nora, 655
Amro, Hady, 5668
AmSouth Bancorporation, 5
AmSouth Bank, 5, 12, 24, 40, 46, 52,
    75, 2053, 2170, 3469, 3514,
    8636, 8668
Amstad, Mary, 8026
Amsted Industries Inc., 2593
Amster, Richard L., 5228
Amsterdam, Peggy, 8378
Amundson, Barbara, 4500
Amundson, Jack, 4534
Amundson, L.A., 4500
Amundson, Lloyd, 4500
Amundson, Roger, 9938
Amway Corp., 4467
Amzak Corp., 2827
Anadell, Robert, 3189
Anagnos, Alex, 6543
Anand, Kapila, 5288

Anast-May, Linda, 3143
Anaya, Mike, 5471
Ancel, Guadalupe, 9779
Anchorage Times Publishing Co., 81
Anda, Rick, 9614
Anday, Anton, 9778
Andelin, John P., 9371
Anders, Betty, 3295
Anders, Paul, 3096
Anders, Thomas, 7539
Andersen Corp., 4512
Andersen, Christine E., 4502
Andersen, Frank N., 4219
Andersen, Fred C., 4501, 4589
Andersen, G. Chris, 5558
Andersen, Gracia B., 1875
Andersen, Holly S., 6187
Andersen, Hugh J., 4502
Andersen, Jane K., 4502
Andersen, John A., 2637
Andersen, Judith, 4245
Andersen, Katherine B., 4502, 4589
Andersen, Ralph, 1080
Andersen, Richard G., 3319
Andersen, Sarah J., 4502
Andersen, Sung Han, 5558
Andersen, William, 1949
Anderson Family Administrative Trust,
    222
Anderson Management Svcs., 7
Anderson Merchandisers, 7
Anderson News Co., 7
Anderson, Alan C., 2750, 4673
Anderson, Andrew E., 7639
Anderson, Anne Heller, 666
Anderson, Arthur H., Jr., 3073
Anderson, Audrea, 2240
Anderson, Barb, 4593
Anderson, Barbara, 4330
Anderson, Barbara W., 3064
Anderson, Beth B., 6
Anderson, Bond, III, 7318
Anderson, Bradbury H., 4516
Anderson, Bradley S., 2057
Anderson, Bruce, 4540
Anderson, Calvin, 8732
Anderson, Carl C., Sr., 8759
Anderson, Carol F., 3812
Anderson, Carolyn, 3186
Anderson, Charles C., 6, 7
Anderson, Charles C., Jr., 6, 7
Anderson, Charles M., 9551
Anderson, Charles W., 7529
Anderson, Charlie, 7139
Anderson, Christopher, 1094
Anderson, Clyde B., 7
Anderson, Colleen, 264
Anderson, Craig, 6681
Anderson, Curtis B., 3420
Anderson, Cynthia, 7920
Anderson, D. Kent, 8961
Anderson, D. Reed, 8511
Anderson, Darcy Glen, 9119
Anderson, Darrel, 769
Anderson, Dave, 1426
Anderson, David, 1093
Anderson, David G., 8690
Anderson, David H., 1726
Anderson, David J., 2594
Anderson, Dean, 4534
Anderson, Dean H., 4534
Anderson, Don, 4325, 7653
Anderson, Donald, 1581
Anderson, Dorothy, 6643
Anderson, Dorothy I., 9551
Anderson, Douglas, 1644
Anderson, Dwight P., II, 769
Anderson, Edwin J.S., 5295
Anderson, Edy, 5498
Anderson, Erik Kjell, 222
Anderson, Eugene K., 9188
Anderson, Frohman, 1513
Anderson, Gary, 4737
Anderson, George, 1271, 1272

Anderson, George A., 2200
Anderson, Gerald, 4309
Anderson, Gordon, 9898
Anderson, Grant A., 673
Anderson, Harold M., 7
Anderson, Harold O., 9229
Anderson, Ivan V., Jr., 8603
Anderson, J. Michael, 9164
Anderson, Jack R., 8761
Anderson, James, 691, 4798
Anderson, James D., 3047
Anderson, James M., 7878
Anderson, Jay, 5949
Anderson, Jeffrey R., 2594
Anderson, Jeffrey W., 7529
Anderson, Jennifer A., 4549
Anderson, Joanne M., 4496
Anderson, Joel R., 7
Anderson, John, 7156, 8691
Anderson, John R., 2594
Anderson, John T., 2820
Anderson, John W., 3099
Anderson, Jonathan S., 4673
Anderson, Josephine, 8760
Anderson, Judy M., 2395, 2494
Anderson, K., 1245
Anderson, Katherine E., 1876
Anderson, Katherine M., 1876
Anderson, Kathy Ann, 1139
Anderson, Keith T., 8815
Anderson, Kerri B., 7902
Anderson, Kristin, 2645
Anderson, Kristin L., 2594
Anderson, Larry, 6329
Anderson, Lawrence L., 8876
Anderson, Lee, 3353
Anderson, Lee R. "Andy", Jr., 1876
Anderson, Lee R., Sr., 1876
Anderson, Linda L., 2594
Anderson, Linda Mattson, 4554
Anderson, Lisa, 9643, 9650
Anderson, Lorraine W., 1452
Anderson, Lynn, 8840
Anderson, M.D., 8762
Anderson, Marie Jo, 8759
Anderson, Mary Pat, 7882
Anderson, Matthew C., 7529
Anderson, Melissa M., 8247
Anderson, Melissa Neubauer, 8363
Anderson, Michael, 3276, 9643
Anderson, Michael D., 7969
Anderson, Michael S., 9201
Anderson, Michael Scott, 9079
Anderson, N. Christian, 957
Anderson, Nancy B., 2358
Anderson, Neil R., 8761
Anderson, Pamela R., 2647
Anderson, Pat, 9861
Anderson, Patricia, 7313
Anderson, Patricia A., 7313
Anderson, Peyton Tooke, Jr., 2317
Anderson, Philip, 4574
Anderson, Priscilla M., 3082
Anderson, R.A., 7751
Anderson, Ralph, 2594
Anderson, Raymond E., 1452
Anderson, Richard, 2323, 5786, 9371
Anderson, Richard C., 3343
Anderson, Richard M., 7529
Anderson, Richard P., 7529, 7883
Anderson, Rick, 9548
Anderson, Rob, 4986
Anderson, Robert, 1438
Anderson, Robert C., 5074
Anderson, Robert W., 9825
Anderson, Roger, 860
Anderson, Roger O., 2680
Anderson, Ronald R., 8438
Anderson, Ronene E., 1533
Anderson, Rose-Marie, 8761
Anderson, Ross E., 3064
Anderson, Shannon, 9322
Anderson, Stefan S., 3104
Anderson, Stella, 8692

Armstrong, Alan S., 7989
Armstrong, Allen L., 4734
Armstrong, Ann L.H., 9436
Armstrong, Beverley W., 9402
Armstrong, Elaine, 3276
Armstrong, Eleanor S., 4211
Armstrong, Fred L., 3166
Armstrong, George W., Sr., 4734
Armstrong, Harvey L., 266, 5027
Armstrong, J. Samuel, IV, 5704
Armstrong, Jean Snyder, 8448
Armstrong, Karen M., 8202
Armstrong, Lisa O., 9491
Armstrong, Mike, 1465
Armstrong, Nora, 8294
Armstrong, R. Stephen, 4647
Armstrong, Richard, 3165
Armstrong, Robert E., 6453
Armstrong, Rose Ann, 8294
Armstrong, Sally, 5028
Armstrong, Sarah, 1776
Armstrong, Thomas K., 4734
Armstrong, Thomas K., Jr., 4734
Armstrong, William L., 9763
Arnason, Charles, 9933
Arnason, Sia, 3801, 7176
Arndt, Betty L., 9960
Arndt, Celestine Favrot, 8897
Arnell, Nathan L., 5828
Arnell, Paula, 2902
Arnell, Robyn, 7049
Arnett, Stephen C., 8671
Arney, Susan Scheidt, 8726
Arnhold Ceramics, Inc., 5722
Arnhold Foundation, 5722
Arnhold, Clarisse, 5568
Arnhold, Henry H., 5568, 5722, 6593
Arnhold, John P., 5568, 5722, 6593
Arnhold, Michele, 5568
Arnholt, Dan, 3166
Arnn, Larry, 5524
Arno, Andrew, 7186
Arno, Rebecca, 1364
Arnold, Ann Kies, 1616
Arnold, Anna Bing, 5022
Arnold, Bobbie N., 4450
Arnold, Chris, 4729
Arnold, Craig, 7617
Arnold, Dale, 2678
Arnold, Daniel C., 8754
Arnold, David J., 4450
Arnold, Don, 7582
Arnold, Eldon, 2677
Arnold, Ernest J., 2478
Arnold, Florence, 2319
Arnold, Frances P., 2478
Arnold, Fred E., 4840
Arnold, G. Dewey, III, 3687
Arnold, Isaac, Jr., 8854
Arnold, James C., 8975
Arnold, Jerry L., 9033
Arnold, Julie Keeton, 2356
Arnold, Kathleen, 8206
Arnold, Kay Kelley, 172, 3474
Arnold, Kelly, 1471
Arnold, Kimberlee K., 4450
Arnold, Louise Willson, 8823
Arnold, Mary Ann Ritter, 156
Arnold, Mary Hazen, 6160
Arnold, Nancy, 1271, 1272
Arnold, Norman J., 8566
Arnold, Patricia, 4513
Arnold, Phyllis H., 9710
Arnold, Robert H., 6752
Arnold, Robert O., 2319
Arnold, Steven L., 1289
Arnold, Thomas C., 8584
Arnold, Wallace, Maj. Genl., 8141
Arnold, William A., IV, 1616
Arnstein, Jeff, 4223
Arntson, Peter A., 9478
Arntz, Donald M., 236
Arntz, Eugene S., 236
Arntz, K. Allan, 236

Arntz, Katherine, 236
Arntz, Thomas E., 236
Aron, Adam, 1468
Aron, Peter A., 5569
Aron, Robert, 5569
Arone, Vincent J., 3958
Aronoff, Cynthia, 128
Aronoff, Donald M., 3122
Aronoff, George, 2156
Aronoff, Steven K., 128, 2073
Aronov, Jake F., 9
Aronov, Marjorie, 9
Aronov, Owen W., 9
Aronson, Edgar D., 6721
Aronson, Nancy C., 8208
Aronson, Nancy P., 6721
Aronson, Ray, 6568
Arredondo, Joel, 7582
Arreola, Rafael A., 1087
Arrhenius, Gustaf, 196
Arrien, Angeles, 607, 4297
Arrigo, Joseph F., 5301
Arrillaga, John, 237
Arrillaga, John, Jr., 237
Arrillaga, Laura, 237
Arrillaga, Laura K., 406
Arrington, John R., 1488
Arriola, Dennis, 1087
Arrison, Clement R., 5570
Arrison, Graig, 5570
Arrison, Karen, 5570
Arsenault, Cynda Collins, 1336
Arsenault, John F.C., 1336
Arsenault, Marcel J.C., 1336
Arshad, Alison, 3825
Arthaud, Katherine, 4036
Arthur F. Bell, Jr., 3679
Arthur, Michael, 8005
Arthur, Vicki, 8572
Arthurs, Alberta B., 6604
Artis, Gary A., 1126
Arum, Lovee, 660
Arundel, Morgan, 4531
Arvest Trust Co., N.A., 7978
Arvey Corporation, 2962
Arvin, Charles, 3206
ArvinMeritor, Inc., 4224
Arwade, Florence F., 1824
Arzt, Gainor Wessinger, 8067
As-Sayed, Farouk, 5646
Asam, Claire L., 2545
Asbeck, Katherine A., 5794
Asch, Andrew J., Jr., 9441
Asch, Anthony James, 9441
Asch, George, 1442
Asch, Patricia M., 9441
Asch, Thomas A., 9441
Asche, Fred B., 9246
Aschenbrener, Thomas D., 8048
Ash, Adam, 7106
Ash, C. Neil, 1031
Ash, Sara, 7106
Ashby, Donna S., 3648
Ashby, G.L. Garnett, 2251
Ashcroft, Janet, 3375
Asher, Barbara, 3152
Asher, Bobbi, 2922
Asher, Charles, 3152
Asher, Daniel, 9584
Asher, Daniel M., 9685
Asher, David L., 3030
Asher, Donald, 3030
Asher, Gilbert, 3030
Asher, James M., 6161, 6162
Asher, Jane, 1776
Asher, John D., 284
Asher, Robert, 1776
Asher, Thomas J., 2472
Asher, Thomas R., 3902, 5300, 9544
Asher, Tom, 795
Ashford, Brytain, 346
Ashken, Ian, 5978
Ashkenazie, Harry J., 5572
Ashkenazie, Jack R., 5572

Ashkenazie, Raymond J., 5572
Ashley, Mary Frost, 9833
Ashmun, Candace McKee, 5199
Ashner, Michael, 5573
Ashner, Susan, 5573
Ashton, Alan C., 9303
Ashton, Brigham, 9303
Ashton, Dore, 5847
Ashton, Elizabeth, 9303
Ashton, Erma, 9303
Ashton, George A., 7748
Ashton, Karen, 9303
Ashton, Melissa, 9303
Ashton, Morgan, 9303
Ashton, Robert, 5606
Ashton, Samuel, 9303
Ashton, Spencer, 9303
Ashton, Stephanie, 9303
Ashton, Stephen, 9303
Ashton, Traci, 9303
Ashworth, Frieda, 9087
Ashworth, Kathy, 3468
Askew, Lynda D., 2458
Askew, Rebecca, 4751
Askew, Robert E., 9184
Askin, Christopher, 5028
Askith, Bertram J., 5250
Askwith, Edna, 5250
Aslanian, Sandra Secchia, 4431
Asman, Laura, 2351
Aspe, Pedro, 5707
Aspen Charitable Remainder Unitrust
   No. 3, 1852
Asplundh, Carl H., 8091
Asplundh, Christopher B., 8091
Asplundh, Edward L., 8091
Asplundh, Kurt H., 8091
Asplundh, Lester, 8091
Assa, Isaac, 5554
Assaf, Joshua, 6001
Assemi, Darius, 1282
Assemi, Farid, 1282
Assemi, Farshid, 1282
Associated Banc-Corp, 9844, 9885
Associated Hospital Service of Maine,
   3549
Astaire, Frederic, Jr., 331
Astbury, Paul, 2156
Asten, Erika V., 8495
Aster, Sara E., 9864
Astin, Katherine T., 1466
Astorga, Tony, 87
Asworth Corp., 2810
AT&T Inc., 8765
Atcheson, Elizabeth, 429
Atchinson, Michelle Cooke, 3784
Atchinson, Robert G., 3784
Aten, Jack S., 2579
Aten, Marcia, 4253
Atherton, Flora C., 8811
Atherton, Frank C., 2532, 2533
Atherton, Geary, 5480
Atherton, Holt, 5480
Atherton, Juliette M., 2532
Atherton, Leburta G., 2533
Atherton, Liz, 300
Atherton, Peggy E., 3626
Athletics Investment Group, LLC, 948
Atkeson, Barbara Ann, 1397
Atkins, Chester G., 4014
Atkins, Craig S., 238
Atkins, George W.P., 2444
Atkins, Norman, 5459
Atkins, Sarah Humphreys, 4800, 4833
Atkinson, David R., 5119
Atkinson, Drew, 181
Atkinson, Esther M., 4173
Atkinson, Eugenia, 7896
Atkinson, George H., 239
Atkinson, Graham D., 3044
Atkinson, Harold S., 2338
Atkinson, Herbert J., 4173
Atkinson, Hope, 3783
Atkinson, Jean S., 239

Atkinson, John, 1647
Atkinson, Mildred M., 239
Atkinson, Patricia D., 5119
Atkinson, Paul D., 5119
Atkinson, Ray N., 239
Atkinson, Richard C., 774, 775
Atkinson, Steven R., 5119
Atkiss, Anthony W., 8995
Atlan Management Corp., 5574
Atlantic Foundation, The, 2198
Atlantic Philanthropies, Inc., 359
Atlantic Realty Co., 2364
Atlantic Research & Analysis, 1781
Atlantic Richfield Co., 2628
Atlantic Trust Co., N.A., 2310
Atlas Realty Co., 559
Atlas, Lezlie, 241
Atlas, Richard S., 241
Atlas, Sol G., 5604
Atofina Chemicals, Inc., 8089
Atran, Frank Z., 5575
Attaway, John, 2180
Attebury, Julie, 8758
Atterbury, Kristin McCarthy, 868
Attfield, Gillian, 1708, 3533
Attias, Daniel K., 903
Atticus Capital LLC, 5576
Attiyeh, Robert, 394
Attkisson, Randall, 3448
Attridge, R. Byron, 2509
Attwell, J. Evans, 9273
Atwater, Edward, 6039
Atwater, Edward S., IV, 5435
Atwater, H. Brewster, Jr., 4659
Atwater, Martha Clark, 4659
Atwater, Verne S., 6391
Atwater, William E., 2542
Atwell, William L., 1110
Atwood, Chuck, 8685
Atwood, Marjorie, 5871
Atwood, Robert B., 81
Atwood, Whitney Bourne, 6591
Atz, Joe, 3214
Atzeff, Anne, 2883
Au, Carlton K.C., 2537
Aubrey, Denise, 147
Aubuchon, Gary, 2240
Aubuchon, William E., III, 4057
Auburn, Ann, 1516
Auburn, Sandy, 7526
Auchincloss Foundation, Lily, 5577
Auchincloss, Lily, 5577
Auchincloss, Louis, 5937
Audet, Anne-Marie J., 5779
Audi, Edward J., 5724
Auen, Joan C., 281
Auen, Ronald M., 242, 281
Auerbach, Harold, 2305
Auerbach, Judith, 5578
Auerbach, Neil, 5578
Aufmuth, Lawrence A., 264
Aufzien, Alan, 5337
Augur, Harrison N., 2801
Augur, Marilyn, 165, 8766
August, Bruce A., 6579
Auguste, Byron, 671
Auguste, Macdonald, 2189
Auguste, Rhonda, 5454
Augustine, Avery, 3216
Augustine, Ed, 1947
Auld, Patrice Marden, 2127
Aull, William E., 2537, 2555
Ault, James F., 3197
Ault, John D., 7891
Ault, Marilyn C., 8800
Ault, Wendy L., 3550
Auman, Christine M., 8151
Aupperle, Tammy B., 8240
Auritt, Joycellen, 4115
Aurora Capital Assocs., LLC, 5720
Aurora Foundation, The, 1883
Ausburn, Kevin, 4798
Ausonio, Nancy B., 401
Austad, Dave, 8630

Austen, W. Gerald, 2097
Austin Athletic Scholarship Foundation, 8748
Austin Ethiopian Women Assn., 8747
Austin, Ann W., 8457
Austin, Carlos, 7163
Austin, Donald G., Jr., 7535
Austin, Douglas R., 4214, 4257
Austin, Edward H., Jr., 8936
Austin, Gary, 9705
Austin, George E., 9889
Austin, Gloria, 6067
Austin, James W., 7535
Austin, Leah Meyer, 3196
Austin, Martha Vukelich, 9854
Austin, Mary K., 738
Austin, Maryland L., 3161
Austin, Paul W., 7535
Austin, Rick, 7344
Austin, Samuel H., 7535
Austin, Sharyn, 2922
Austin, Stewart G., Jr., 7535
Austin, Stewart G., Sr., 7535
Austin, Thomas G., 7535
Austin, Tracy L., 6560
Austin, William F., 1545
Austin, Winifred N., 7535
Auston, David, 748
Ausubel, Jesse, 1824
Auto Rental Corp., 4103
Auto Specialties Manufacturing Co., 4460
Automatic Service, 3683
Autry Foundation, 1248
Autry, Gene, 243
Autry, Jacqueline, 243
Autry, Pat, 4767
Autumn Ventures, 3766
Autzen, Thomas J., 7997
Auvil, Walt, 9730
Avampato, Charles M., 9714, 9715
Avanessians, Armen, 5580
Avanessians, Janette, 5580
Avansino, Kristen A., 5077
Avansino, Raymond C., Jr., 5077
Avanzino, Richard, 845
Avedisian, James R., 239
Aventis Pharmaceuticals Inc., 5121
Averett, Joe N., Jr., 3469
Averill, Marybeth, 8658
Averitt, George R., 3143
Avery Dennison Corp., 244
Avery Foundation, R. Stanton, The, 245
Avery, Caroline D., 471
Avery, Dennis S., 245
Avery, Halina, 471
Avery, Judith, 265, 471
Avery, Mark J., 1161
Avery, Sally M., 5581
Aviad, Janet, 5673
Aviation Fuel Terminals, Inc., 7330
Avila, Guillermo, 8881, 8950
Avila, Ramon, 3128
Avis, Anne R., 246
Avis, Greg, 698
Avis, Gregory M., 246, 406
Avlon, John, 6779
Avon Products, Inc., 5583
Avondale Mills, 22
Avram, Ruth, 7573
AW Family Limited Partnership, 9540
Awaya, Alvin, 3759
Awaya, Tsutomu, 6560
AXA Financial, Inc., 5584
AXA Foundation Charitable Gift Fund, 7174
Axel, Blair, 6358
Axelrad, Bertram, 2255
Axelrod, Emily, 3819
Axelrod, Margaret G., 6298
Axelson, Frances R., 8881
Axtell, Roger E., 9820
Axworthy, Lloyd, 2868
Ayau, Manuel F., 3157

Ayaub, John J., 4427
Ayer, David, 4096
Ayer, Everett L., 3536
Ayer, Laura, 6915
Ayers, James W., 8640
Ayers, Janet, 3126
Ayers, John, 8640
Ayers, John S., 7349
Ayers, Jon, 8640
Ayers, Margaret C., 5761
Ayers, Nancy Sharon, 8640
Ayers, William C., 3084
Ayling, Alice S., 3785
Aylsworth, Jon, 4331
Aylward, James F., 9683
Aylward, Rayna, 9476
Ayo, Brenda B., 3518
Ayres, Margaret Bowers, 9183
Ayres, Martha, 3214
Ayres, Nancy, 3216
Ayres, Patricia Shield, 9183
Ayres, Robert Atlee, 9183
Ayres, Robert M., Jr., 9183
Ayres, Warren, 9280
Azark, Dan, 2769
Azeez, Anne, 1885
Azeez, Kathleen, 1885
Azeez, Michael, 1885
Azeez, Michael B., 2221
Azose, David, 9675
Azrak & Sons Foundation, Marvin, 5554
Azrak, Adam, 5585
Azrak, Elliot, 5585
Azrak, Marvin, 5585
Azrak, Victor, 5585
Azus, Al, 248

B&B Lease Co., 4565
B-W Footwear Co., Inc., 4145
B.F.Goodrich Co., The, 7378
B.O.A.T. Fund, 1516
B.P.O.E., 3587
Baader, Marilyn J., 5785
Baalmann, Richard F., Jr., 2582
Baba, Gwen, 300
Babab, Chaim, 7068
Babab, Joseph, 7068
Babaoff, Kambiz, 5554
Babb, Ralph W., Jr., 4438
Babbio, Lawrence T., Jr., 7209
Babbitt, Edward, 5586
Babbitt, Susan, 5586
Babcock, Ann Kelsey, 556
Babcock, Bruce M., 7308
Babcock, C. Patrick, 4357
Babcock, Charles H., 7308
Babcock, Gwendolyn Garland, 556
Babcock, John Carlile, 556
Babcock, Mary, 7537
Babcock, Mary Reynolds, 7308, 7458
Babcock, Sarah Garland, 556
Babcock, Susan Hinman, 556
Babcock, Timothy, 3255
Babe, Gregory S., 8096
Baber, Charles T., 9390
Baber, Wilbur, Jr., 8866
Babick, Gary N., 222
Babicka, Jerry, 1533, 1630
Babicka, Jonathan, 1533
Babicka, Lynn P., 1533, 1536, 1630
Babii, Ana, 1177
Babington, Catherine V., 2579, 2580
Babington, Wallace K., 9536
Babson, James A., 3787
Babson, Katherine L., Jr., 4159
Babson, Paul T., 3787
Baby Boom Consumer, 5627
Babylon, Caroline, 3597
Baca, Patricia, 1356
Baca, Polly B., 1377
Bacak, Sandra, 8754
Bacardi, Facundo, 1886
Bacardi, Hilda, 1886

Bace, Jack, 8773
Bach, Duane R., 2594
Bach, Neil C., 2649
Bach, Norma J., 2019
Bachar, Bonnie, 6777
Bachman, Dale S., 2541
Bachman, Edward A., 7538
Bachman, James B., 7771
Bachman, Lynda A., 7538
Bachman, Nathan D., 7538
Bachman, Robert B., Mrs., 3811
Bachmann, B., 5587
Bachmann, Bruce R., 2946
Bachmann, Louis, 5587
Bachner, Robert, 6992
Bachynski, Marianne, 6577
Bacigalupi, Victor J., 1008
Backberg, Bruce A., 4690
Backer, Betty, 5498
Backhaus, Barry E., 3332
Backstrom, C. Stephen, 8152
Backus, Carol S., 9632
Backus, Edward A., 9632
Backus, Frances A., 9632
Backus, John T., 9632
Backus, Manson, 9632
Backus, Valerie F., 9632
Bacon, Albert S., III, 9693
Bacon, Andrew, 1340
Bacon, Carolyn R., 9096
Bacon, Herbert, 1340
Bacon, Jody, 7526
Bacon, John O., 7612
Bacon, Katherine Weld, 7278
Bacon, Kenneth J., 1793
Bacon, Laura May, 1340
Bacon, Louis M., 6570
Bacon, Robert L., 501
Bacon, Scott, 3558
Bacon, Stephen, 1340
Bacow, Lawrence S., 3871
Bacque, Odon, 3468
Badcock, Philip A., 2416
Bade, Mark J., 2775
Baden, Helen T., 8589
Bader, Daniel J., 9749
Bader, David M., 9749
Bader, Kathryn S., 4896
Bader, Linda C., 9749
Badgeley, Rose, 5588
Badgett, Guy M., III, 73
Baecher-Brown, Dee, 9363
Baechler, Bud, 4729
Baehren, Jim, 7569
Baenziger, Tom, 352
Baer, Helen K., 4778
Baer, Jr. Trust, Sidney R., 4779
Baer, Kathy, 4944
Baer, Marcia, 4944
Baer, Ralph A., 6484
Baer, Steve, 2996
Baer, Theodore, 4944
Baer, Thomas H., 6536
Baer, Tim, 4697
Baety, Jonathan, 1942
Bag One Arts, Inc., 7033
Bagge, R. Bruce P., 2664
Bagley, Nancy R., 1767, 7458
Bagley, Nicole, 1767, 2479
Bagley, Smith W., 1767, 7458
Bagley, Thomas F., III, 4057
Bagnall, Emily T., 1031
Bagneris, Madlyn B., 3503
Bagnola, James, 7787
Baharestani, Martin, 7121
Bahl, Arvind, 3330
Bahl, Rana, 1096
Bahl, William, 7912
Bahle, Melvin C., 4803
Bahner, Max, 8660
Bahnik, Claude, 5589
Bahnik, Lore, 5589
Bahnik, Roger L., 5589
Baier, John F., 5590

Baier, John F., Jr., 5590
Bailes, Lamar, 8588
Bailey Nurseries, Inc., 4510
Bailey Trust, Larkin, 7923
Bailey, Andrew C., 3789, 4069, 4104
Bailey, Ann Haslam, 8687
Bailey, Beverly W., 1887
Bailey, Bobbie, 7309
Bailey, Bobbie, Ms., 7309
Bailey, Brenda, 8771
Bailey, Brenda M., 2039
Bailey, Christopher, 9642
Bailey, Dan, 7895
Bailey, Dean R., 2142
Bailey, Donald, 1444
Bailey, Douglas, 8771
Bailey, Emily F., 8567
Bailey, Gary S., 2039
Bailey, Gordon J., 4510
Bailey, Hoyt Q., 7356
Bailey, James, 9785
Bailey, Joe M., 8754
Bailey, John, 7895
Bailey, John Hill, Jr., 2403
Bailey, John P., 4510
Bailey, Larry, 1785, 9625
Bailey, Lauren L., 3713
Bailey, Lawrence B., 9655, 9664
Bailey, Leon, 1514
Bailey, Lesley, 7895
Bailey, Liza, 5807
Bailey, M D, 8771
Bailey, Malcolm D., 8771
Bailey, Malcolm, Jr., 8771
Bailey, Melanie, 3345
Bailey, Patricia, 8771
Bailey, Patricia B., 3780
Bailey, Ralph, 3096, 3258
Bailey, Rodney P., 4510
Bailey, Ron K., 1887
Bailey, Ronnie Kyle, 1887
Bailey, Ryan Kent, 1887
Bailey, S.B., 7879
Bailey, Sallie B., 9950
Bailey, Sam, 7895
Bailey, William N., 8655
Bailin, Michael, 8371
Bailit, Howard L., 1529
Baillie Lumber, 5504
Baillie Properties, 5504
Bailon, Katherine, 1483
Bain, Connie, 1578
Bain, Mary Anne, 3132
Bain, Peter L., 3672
Bain, William W., Jr., 3788
Bainbridge, Phil, 3123
Bains, Harrison M., Jr., 5143
Bainum, Barbara, 3596
Bainum, Bruce, 3596
Bainum, Kerrie, 87
Bainum, Roberta, 3596
Bainum, Stewart, Sr., 3596
Baiocchi, Christina K., 7191
Baiocchi, Christina Kind, 8289
Bair Ranch Foundation, 4931
Bair, Alberta M., 7998
Baird, Brian D., 5591
Baird, Bridget, 1517
Baird, Bridget B., 5591
Baird, Bruce C., 5591
Baird, Cameron, 5592
Baird, Flora M., 5592
Baird, Frank B., Jr., 5592
Baird, Jane D., 5591
Baird, Laura Trammell, 8906
Baird, Mark, 3243
Baird, Nolan H., Jr., 1189, 2587
Baird, Rob, 4870
Baird, Sally, 4798
Baird, William C., 5592
Bajan, Janet, 6891
Bajek, Gerard B., 2119
Bakalis, Desi, Mrs., 2702
Bakaly, Charles, 711

Barbonchielli Trust, Joseph L., 256
Barbosky, Sherry, 7581
Barbour, Bernice, 5124
Barbour, Cora Buhl, 4934
Barbour, F.E., Mrs., 5565
Barbour, Margaret Sewall, 1648
Barbour, Patricia A., 5089
Barbour, Thomas C., 4934
Barclay, John W., 1510
Barcus, Marian, 4520
Barczykowski, Anthony, Sr., 3489
Bard, C.R., Inc., 5125
Bard, Herbert, 7200
Bard, Holly, 9570
Bard, James R., 7559
Bard, Loretta M., 9786
Bardack, Phillip M., 613
Bardi, Dina H., 9139
Bardige, Betty, 3828
Bardige, Betty S., 6477
Bardige, Myla Kore, 6477
Bardusch, William E., Jr., 4766
Bare, John, 2325
Bare, Thomas J., 9964
Barfield, John W., 8879
Barfield, Mary Louise Frist, 8678
Barfield, Norma C., 4254
Barg, Stanley, 8142
Barger, C. Phillip, 9521
Barger, May C., 7342
Barhoum, Ann Francis, 4816
Barick, William R., 2620
Baright, Hollis I., 4945
Barillaro, Laura, 6264
Barinaga, Marcia, 474
Bark, Dennis L., 4291
Bark, France de Sugny, 448
Barkan, Mel P., 5690, 6053
Barker, Clyde F., 8342
Barker, Donald R., 257
Barker, James M., 5599
Barker, James R., 5599
Barker, John R., 7967
Barker, Judith Liff, 8662
Barker, Margaret R., 5599
Barker, Margaret S., 5599
Barker, Mary L., 138, 9345
Barker, Norman, Jr., 750
Barker, Peter K., 728, 750
Barker, Robert R., 5599
Barker, Robert W., 458
Barker, Suzanne, 5466, 5491
Barker, W.B., 5599
Barker, William P., 8334
Barker, William S., 5599
Barkhouser, Richard, 9401
Barkhurst, William J., 818
Barkley, Carlene, 3403
Barkley, Jan Schmidt, 8055
Barkley, Kirsten Hansen, 2782
Barkow, Richard C., 9927
Barks, Herbert, 8684
Barksdale, Edgar W., Jr., 1537
Barksdale, James L., 4756
Barksdale, Mary F., 3149
Barksdale, Sally M., 4756
Barksdale, William, 674
Barletta, Robert J., 6750, 7026
Barlette, Sheldon W., Jr., 7570
Barlev, Rivka, 546
Barley, Inc., 4043
Barlin, Wayne A., 1954
Barlow, David S., 350
Barlow, Ed, 1465
Barlow, Franklin H., 5295
Barlow, Julia Carleton, 5177
Barmore, Mary, 4986
Barna, Roger, 9476
Barnard, Alice, 2904
Barnard, D. Douglas, Jr., 2357
Barnard, Richard, 5028
Barnard, Ronald L., 1975
Barneby, Kenneth A., 2271
Barnell, Shirley, 4968

Barnes Group Inc., 1488
Barnes, Andrew E., 2245
Barnes, Brenda C., 2982
Barnes, Brett W., 3024
Barnes, Bruce, 1319
Barnes, Chaplin B., 2201
Barnes, Chris, 3024
Barnes, Deborah M., 1085
Barnes, E.L., 8593
Barnes, Frank S., Jr., 8593
Barnes, Gerald D., 1085
Barnes, John M., Jr., 8593
Barnes, Kenneth W., 3024
Barnes, L.A., Jr., 8593
Barnes, Lorna M., 3275
Barnes, Melody Charisse, 1835
Barnes, Paula, 8959
Barnes, Robert A., 7714
Barnes, Ronald R., 940
Barnes, Samuel, 3422
Barnes, Samuel G., 3407
Barnes, Sara, 854
Barnes, Stan, 1945
Barnes, Steve, 620
Barnes, Thomas E., 7771
Barnes, Thomas O., 1488, 1594
Barnes, William F., 7969
Barnes, William T., 7433
Barness, W.E., 4619
Barnet & Son, William, 8568
Barnet, Geoff, 765
Barnet, Howard, Jr., 765
Barnet, Jane, 765
Barnet, Peter, 765
Barnet, Saretta, 765
Barnet, Valerie, 8568
Barnet, Will, 5548
Barnet, William, II, 8568
Barnet, William, III, 5892, 7359, 8568
Barnett Trust, H., 2904
Barnett, Billie, 7924
Barnett, Carol, 2180
Barnett, Cindy, 7866
Barnett, Crawford, 2523
Barnett, Florence L.J., 7924
Barnett, Howard G., 7924
Barnett, Hoyt, 2180
Barnett, Isabel, 5601
Barnett, James Joseph, 5601
Barnett, Janet, 3124
Barnett, Kathleen M., 2960
Barnett, Laurey J., 5601
Barnett, Lawrence R., 5601
Barnett, Lawrence R., Jr., 5601
Barnett, Martha, 1945
Barnett, Robert B., 1826
Barnett, Terry, 6640
Barnette, Joseph D., Jr., 3180
Barney, John, 3135
Barney, Thomas W., 3800
Barneycastle, Melinda, 9208
Barnhar, Douglas E., Inc., 1306
Barnhardt, Zeb E., 7345
Barnhart, Lorraine, 1798, 5244
Barnhill Family Fund, 6232
Barnhill, Joanna R. Schima, 8796
Barnhill, Robert E., Jr., 7438
Barnholt, Edward W., 972
Baron, Charles B., 4903
Baron, Frederick M., 8774
Baron, John F., 1604
Baron, Jules M., 6053
Baron, Lisa A. Blue, 8774
Baron, Richard K., 6053
Baron, William B., 316
Barone, Anna M., 7266
Barone, Janine Mason, 506
Barone, Richard, 7555
Barone, Samuel, 7583
Barontini, Jim, 2195
Barr, C. Hilyard, 731
Barr, Courtland, III, 731
Barr, Donald M., 1493
Barr, Edward F., 9884

Barr, Garland H., III, 3407
Barr, George, 641
Barr, Harry C., 4074
Barr, John F., 3600
Barr, John McFerran, 3453
Barr, L. Graham, Jr., 1875
Barr, Lynn E., 268
Barr, Patricia, 2362
Barr, Wallace R., 8648
Barrak, Marion, 1568
Barranco, Carl, 20
Barre, H. Walter "Wally", 8616
Barre, H. Walter, II, 8569
Barreda, Antonio, 3144
Barreiro, Daniel, 2680
Barrett, Ann Dobson, 982
Barrett, Bill, 4986
Barrett, Brett, 1463
Barrett, C.F. Larry, 531
Barrett, Craig R., 8022
Barrett, David, 1505
Barrett, David C., 7735
Barrett, Diana, 6324
Barrett, Donna, 5282
Barrett, J. Andrew, 7446
Barrett, James A., Jr., 5044, 5074
Barrett, John Adams, 9230
Barrett, John F., 7619, 7903
Barrett, Julie, 9305
Barrett, Mary Ellen, 1943
Barrett, Thomas J., Jr., 1401
Barrett, William L.D., 6917
Barrie, R.H., 2051
Barrios, Domingo, 8960
Barrish, Gloria, 7106
Barrish, Neil, 7106
Barritt, Dan, 9599
Barron, Adele L., 3792
Barron, Douglas S., 3792
Barron, Hal, 562
Barron, John H.C., Jr., 1780
Barron, Norman W., 3792
Barron, Patricia C., 134, 5760
Barron, Scott V., 3792
Barron, Steve, 9117
Barron, Thomas A., 79
Barrow, John D., 8475
Barrow, Justin, 4651
Barrow, Sara Perlman, 4651
Barrows, Dana R., 3855
Barrows, G.M., 4781
Barrows, Mary, 3783
Barrows, Pauline, 1578
Barrueta, Fern, 1778
Barry, Alan H., 4387
Barry, B. John, 4511
Barry, David, 1463
Barry, Dorothy, 6659
Barry, Jessica M., 4511
Barry, John, 5797
Barry, John E., 7994
Barry, Michael B., 4511
Barry, Neil, 2350
Barry, Richard Allen, 3793
Barry, Richard F., III, 9455
Barry, Roy, 3550
Barry, Susan A., 8511
Barry, Thomas J., 4511
Barry, Tina S., 8992
Barsam, Joyce, 5426
Barsanti, John R., Jr., 4791
Barsky, Barbara, 5493
Barsky, Jennifer, 8046
Barson, Sharon, 2586
Barsotti, J., 8150, 8301
Barsotti, Priscilla Ann, 9573
Bartee, Jerry M., 4994
Bartel, Harry, 9928
Bartell, James R., 2923
Bartelmo, Thomas, 2093
Bartels, T.R., 2148
Bartels, Theodore R., 2148
Bartelt, James, 9861
Barter, Davida D., 3556

Barth, Andrew C., 7935
Barth, Deborah, 2091
Barth, John, 9823
Barth, Kevin G., 4797
Barth, Robert, 258
Barth, Suzanne, 258
Barth, Theodore H., 5603
Barthebaug, Richard, 7593
Barthebaug, Richard, Mrs., 7593
Bartholic, Robert L., 1355
Barti, James F., 1740
Bartkowski, Fred J., 9848
Bartl, James F., 1739
Bartle, Elizabeth Dowling, 3828
Bartlett, Edward E., 9753
Bartlett, Gilbert A., 9393, 9541
Bartlett, Kathie, 5028
Bartlett, Norma, 4785
Bartley, Anne, 211
Bartman, Cecile C., 259
Bartman, N., 259
Bartner, Beverly D.N., 9362
Bartner, Robert G., 9362
Barto, Amy, 8381
Bartolomel, Carolyn, 314
Barton Trust, Barbara, The, 9282
Barton, Dick K., 8174
Barton, Gerald, 420
Barton, John W., Sr., 3462
Barton, Katherine M., 6041
Barton, Laura, 1364
Bartos, Adam, 6686
Bartos, John N., 4450
Bartoshuk, David J., 1081
Bartram, Ann, 1941
Bartram, Thomas, 1541
Bartsch, Ruth, 1688
Bartwink, Theodore S., 6145
Bartz, Karen, 4825
Baruch, Jordan J., 7311
Baruch, Lawrence K., 7311
Baruch, Rhoda W., 7311
Barwald, Gay L., 4891
Barwick, Ed, 557
Barwick, Kent L., 5762
Basden, Mildred V., 1237
Basha, Leigh-Alexandra, 9486
Basham, Arthur A., 1256
Bashinsky, Joann, 11
Bashinsky, Sloan Y., Sr., 11
Basile, Susan L., 9723
Baske, Mary Friedman, 2014
Basker, James, 6030
Baskes, Daniel L., 2607
Baskes, Jeremy A., 2607
Baskes, Julie Z., 2607
Baskes, Roger S., 2607
Baskin, Carol, 8788
Baskin, Jack, 403
Baskin, Joan, 8923
Baskin, Richard, 1204
Baskins, Ann O., 672
Basler, Wayne G., 8641
Bass Pro Trademark, LP, 4869
Bass Pro, Inc., 4869
Bass, Doris L., 8777
Bass, Edward P., 8776, 9147
Bass, F.W., 8889
Bass, Harry W., Jr., 8777
Bass, Henry, 7192
Bass, John T., 1361
Bass, Lawrence D., 7192
Bass, Lee M., 8775, 8776, 8778, 9147
Bass, Letty, 1354
Bass, Morton, 5604
Bass, Nancy Lee, 8775, 9147
Bass, Perry R., 8775, 8776
Bass, Perry R., Inc., 8776
Bass, Ramona S., 8778
Bass, Robert, 4540
Bass, Rose, 2040
Bass, Sandra Atlas, 5604
Bass, Sid R., 9147
Basset Foundation, Norman, 9918

Bassett, Betty, 7522, 7523
Bassett, Cynthia, 7813
Bassett, David, 2094
Bassett, J.E., III, 3432
Bassett, Robert, 1629
Bastedo, Eugene J., 8638
Bastedo, Melinda Neal, 7433
Bastian, Bruce W., 9307
Bastian, Edith, 8482
Bastian, Edith J., 8482
Bastian, Frank W., 9921
Bastian, Melanie L., 9306
Bastien, Nellie J., 1892
Batchelder, Earle, 3833
Batchelder, Herbert, 3810
Batcheller, Thomas, 8625
Batchelor Enterprises, 1893
Batchelor, Anne O., 1893
Batchelor, George E., 1893
Batchelor, Michael L., 8188
Bate, Bud, 9321
Bate, David S., 5252, 5390
Bateman, Janey F., 8943
Bateman, Laurie, 10000
Bateman, Mary Michael, 3047
Bateman, Maureen, 4110
Bateman, Sharon A., 4371
Bates, Alben F., Jr., 2608
Bates, Arthur, 5734
Bates, Henry G., 2608
Bates, Hudson K., 7436
Bates, Janet Fleishhacker, 518
Bates, Jeanne, 4824
Bates, Leon, 8395
Bates, Mark, 3135
Bates, Sarah J., 7540
Bates, Vickie J., 1876
Bates, W. Carter, III, 2358
Bates, William F., 7921
Bathina, Radha R., 1096
Batson, R. Neal, 2525
Battaglia, Joseph P., 628
Battaglia, Richard, 628
Batte, Charles R., III, 8759
Batten, Dorothy N., 9373
Batten, Frank, 9374, 9455
Batten, Frank, Jr., 9373, 9375, 9455
Batterman, Christopher T., 9754
Batterman, Eric D., 9754
Batterman, Marilyn H., 9754
Batterman, Theodore W., 9754
Battie, Hank, 1946
Battistoni, Rick, 9141
Battle, A. George, 260
Battle, Daniel K., 260
Battle, Emily T., 260
Battle, G. Thomas, 9723
Battle, Lucius D., Amb., 1796
Battle, T. Westray, III, 8425
Battle-Brown, LaToya, 5454
Battles, Denise, 3039
Batusic, Dave, 3135
Bau-Madsen, Emily, 8219
Bauder, Lillian, 4438
Baudot, Elise, 6233
Bauer, Ann, 8015
Bauer, Brad, 1489
Bauer, Carol, 1489
Bauer, Charles Douglas, 8779
Bauer, Charles T., 8779, 8780
Bauer, Charles W., 1515
Bauer, Chris M., 9927
Bauer, Craig, 2926
Bauer, Deborah A., 8833
Bauer, Evalyn M., 261, 2609
Bauer, Gary W., 3254
Bauer, George P., 1489
Bauer, Janet, 4310
Bauer, Jill, 5691
Bauer, Joan, 4243
Bauer, Jocelyn, 1489
Bauer, M.R., 261
Bauer, Mary F.L., 3436
Bauer, Michael P., 9615

Bauer, Modestus R., 2609
Bauer, Ruth J., 8779
Bauer, Theodore Wingate, 8780
Bauer, Walter, 6033
Bauernfeind, George G., 3428
Bauersfeld, Gay, 3400
Baugh, Barbara, 8781
Baugh, Eula Mae, 8781
Baugh, John F., 8781
Baugh, Richard A., 9400
Baughman Farms Co., John W., The, 3346
Baughman, Corinne, 9548
Baughman, Robert W., 3346
Baughman, Willard, 7593
Bauknight, Russell L., 8577
Baum, Alexio R., 4322
Baum, Dale, 4217
Baum, Jonathan E., 4842
Baum, Steve C., 6686
Baum, Steven, 7184
Baum, Steven C., 8531
Bauman, Elizabeth, 1894
Bauman, Jeffrey, 1771
Bauman, John, 1894
Bauman, Lionel R., 1770
Bauman, Patricia, 1770, 1894, 5614
Bauman, Robert, 1894
Bauman, Steve, 171
Bauman, William H., 7999
Baumann, Joe, 8098
Baumberger, Charles, Jr., 8782
Baumeisters & Samuels, 6356
Baumgaertner, Elise M., 847
Baumgardner, Earl C., 60
Baumgardner, Roberta A., 60
Baumgardt, James A., 3159
Baumstein, Barbara Lieb, 6420
Baumstein, Richard, 6420
Bausch & Lomb Inc., 5605
Bausch, David K., 8137, 8303
Baush Machine Tool Co., 9802
Bauta, Christian, 1617
Bauta, Gretchen A., 1617
Bauta, Humberto P., 1617
Bauta, Nicholas, 1617
Bauta, Pilar, 1617
Bavarian Irrevocable Complex Trust, 3406
Bavarian Trucking Co., Inc., 3406
Bavasi, Margaret, 9583
Bavaso, Johnna, 1423
Bavendick, Frank J., 7516
Bavly, Beverly G., 2016
Bawabeh, Jennifer, 5617
Bawabeh, Solar, 5617
Baxter Allegiance Foundation, The, 7567
Baxter International Inc., 2611
Baxter, C. Kenneth, 1895
Baxter, Delia B., 263
Baxter, Frank E., 262
Baxter, George J., 1948
Baxter, Jim, 9571
Baxter, Joe, 9057
Baxter, Kim, 4991
Baxter, Laura, 1895
Baxter-Heuer, Laura, 7530
Bay Distributors, Inc., 2341
Bay Mgmt., 7068
Bay State Bancorp, Inc., 3794
Bay State Federal Savings Bank, 3794
Bay Street Corp., 4748
Bay, Charles Ulrick, 5606
Bay, Frederick, 5606
Bay, Mogens C., 4984, 5013
Bayard, Jane U., 6503
Bayardelle, Eddy, 6537
Bayer Corp., 8096
Bayern, William T., 9166
Bayette, John G., 7596
Bayless, Betsy, 87
Baylis, Eileen Grace McKenzie, 1601
Baynard, Robert P., 7413
Bayne Trust, Louise Van Beuren, 5607

Baynes, Jerell, 1642
Bayrd, Blanche S., 3795
Bayrd, Frank A., 3795
Bayston, Brett, 3123
Bayyari, Fadil, 169
Bazan-Manson, Andrea, 7496
Bazzell, Darrell, 9854
BB & TW, Inc., 1301
BB&T, 3456, 7332, 7479, 7508, 9366, 9463, 9498, 9716, 9722, 9723, 9730
BB&T Corp., 7312, 9710
BBDO, 7174
Bcownlee, Susan H., 8221
BEA Assocs., Inc., 6215
Beach Terrace Care Center, 6871
Beach, Berdena J., 3278
Beach, Charles S., 1482
Beachlawn Mortgage Co., 4250
Beachley, David, 3600
Beacom, Miles, 8630
Beagles, Ruth H., 9363
Beaird, Harold, 8891
Beal, Barry A., 8783
Beal, Carlton, 8783
Beal, Carlton E., Jr., 8783
Beal, Keleen H., 8783
Beal, Kelly S., 8783
Beal, Mitty, 7490
Beal, Richard M., 547
Beal, Spencer E., 8783
Beale, E. Warren, Jr., 9421
Beall, Diane, 9736
Beall, Dorothy M., 2240
Beall, Kenneth S., Jr., 2297
Beam, Carla, 78
Beam, Jeff, 7770
Beaman, Kelly S., 8642
Beaman, Lee A., 8642
Beaman, Sally M., 8642
Beamer, William E., 979
Bean, Atherton, 4508
Bean, Bruce W., 4508
Bean, Charles, 9371
Bean, David A., 7481
Bean, Elizabeth N., 5080
Bean, George, 5369
Bean, Glen Atherton, 4508
Bean, Jane Riskin, 5369
Bean, Larry G., 9984
Bean, Mary F., 4508
Bean, Mitch, 4991
Bean, Norwin S., 5080
Bean, Ralph J., Jr., 8099
Bean, Robert R., 2545
Bean, Roy H., 7534
Bean, Terrence P., 8020
Bean, Winifred W., 4508
Beane, Agnes R., 7336
Beans, Patrick E., 4987
Beapol, Inc., 1057
Bear Stearns & Co., 5115
Bear Stearns Cos. Inc., The, 5609
Bear, Geraldine, 5902
Bear, Steve, 5666
Bear, Stuart, 1508
Beard, Anson McCook, Jr., 1663, 6150
Beard, Donna, 1357
Beard, Ellanor Allday, 8906
Beard, Jean Jones, 1663
Beard, Joan, 2108
Beard, John E., 4175
Beard, Myron, 1377
Beard, Peter, 1793
Beard, William M., 7969
Beardmore, S.J., 2555
Beardslee, Verlyn, 4481
Beardsley, George, 6643
Beardsley, George B., 1380
Beardsley, James M., 6680
Beardsley, Jerry, 6643
Beardsley, Pamela D., 1344
Bearman, Arlene, 3570
Bearman, Sheldon, 3570

Bearn, Alexander G., 3654
Beasley Trust, Robert P., 9755
Beasley, Charles E., 3461
Beasley, Robert R., 8784
Beasley, Theodore P., 8784
Beason, Jeffrey I., 8882
Beattie, Art P., 1
Beattie, Catherine H., 8589
Beattie, Pat, 1765
Beattie, Richard I., 6354, 6355
Beattie, William H., 267
Beatty, Benjamin M., 7804
Beatty, David, 3983
Beatty, David L., 3797
Beatty, Helen D. Groome, 8097
Beatty, Lloyd L., Sr., 3693
Beatty, Mary Dombrowsky, 7804
Beaty, John T., Jr., 5748
Beauchamp, Charlie, 2040
Beauchamp, E. William, Rev., 3196
Beauchamp, Gary K., 6566, 7196
Beaud, Marie-Claude, 5550
Beaudelte, Edna, 7139
Beaudet, Debra, 4684
Beaudoin, Roseann K., 8294
Beaudoin-Schwartz, Buffy, 3595
Beaulieu, Rita H., 4191
Beaumont Investments, Ltd., 1339
Beaupre, Rosemary Conway, 1515
Beaver Street Fisheries, Inc., 1897
Beaver, Deborah E., 7313
Beaver, Donald C., 7313
Beaver, Ellie, 8136
Beaver, Thomas, 4298
Beaver, Tom, 8509
Beavers, Inc., The, 268
Beavers, John P., 7759
Beavers, Joseph, 2713
Beavers, Susan, 7581
Beaverson, Audrey L., 7541
Beazley, Fred W., 9376
Beazley, Fred W., Jr., 9376
Beazley, Hamilton, 8878
Beazley, Marie C., 9376
Bebee, Leslie A., 4965
Beccali, Ferdinando, 1553
Beccaria, Lorna, 673
Beccaria, Louis J., 8141, 8381
Bechily, Maria C., 2661
Bechinski, Linda, 3143
Bechtel Corp., 269
Bechtel Group, Inc., 269
Bechtel Power Corp., 269
Bechtel Systems of Infrastructure, Inc., 269
Bechtel, Elizabeth H., 270, 1144
Bechtel, Gary Hogan, 526
Bechtel, Harold, 3265
Bechtel, Jacquie L., 526
Bechtel, R.P., 269
Bechtel, S.D., Jr., 270
Bechtel, Stephen D., Jr., 1030
Bechthold, Ned, 9927
Bechthold, Ned W., 9876
Bechtle, Joachim, 7274
Bechtle, Nancy, 1109, 7274
Bechtol, Susan, 8049
Beck, Ann, 4637
Beck, Cheryl Tatano, 1529
Beck, Henry C., III, 8855
Beck, Henry C., Jr., 8843
Beck, John C., 6508
Beck, Judith, 7191, 9670
Beck, Martin, 1505
Beck, Nina M., 4987
Beck, Phyllis W., Hon., 8266
Beck, Robin, 5486
Beck, Scott A., 1348
Beck, Sue, 3333
Beck, Sydney Y., 7512
Beck, Wayne, 3160
Becker, David, 3116
Becker, David E., 271
Becker, Douglas L., 3741

Becker, Howard C., 7785
Becker, Jeanne, 8010, 8059
Becker, Jeffrey, 3564
Becker, John D., 3503
Becker, Katrina H., 5600
Becker, Newton D., 271
Becker, Pauline S., 1898
Becker, Richard C., 2987
Becker, Rochelle, 271
Becker, Scott, 8153
Becker, Stephen, 5147
Becker, Steve, 627
Becker, Steven R., 2260
Beckerdite, Luke, 9447
Beckett Corp., R.W., The, 7647
Beckett, Carolyn, 9291
Beckett, John D., 7647
Beckett, Riley, 5043
Beckford, Neal S., 8638
Beckley, Douglas, 5047
Beckman, Arnold O., 272
Beckman, Arnold W., 272
Beckman, Charles, 2307
Beckman, G. Patricia, 272
Beckman, Joel, 7202
Beckman, Joseph, 3135
Beckman, Mabel M., 272
Beckner, Jay, 6538
Beckort, Paul, 3161
Beckos, Dean, 7272
Beckos-Wood, Georgia, 7272
Beckwith, Dave, 7774
Beckwith, F. William, 3266
Beckwith, G. Nicholas, III, 1689, 8099
Beckwith, James S., III, 1689
Beckwith, Leola I., 3266
Beckwith, Virginia P., 1689
Beckworth, Laura H., 8954
Bed Bath & Beyond, Inc., 5187
Bedard, Kipp A., 2571
Bedell, Peter, Jr., 6643
Bedell, Thomas W., 3267
Bedenbaugh, James R., 9239
Bedient, Patricia M., 9703
Bednarowski, Keith P., 4642
Bedolfe, Herbert M., 855
Bedsole, Ann Smith, 63
Bedsole, J.L., 12
Bedsole, M. Palmer, Jr., 12
Bedsole, T. Massey, 12
Bedsole, Travis M., Jr., 12
Beebe, Frederick S., 1804
Beebe, Larry, 1463
Beebe, Steve, 7931
Beeber, Ronald L., 4271
Beech, Thomas F., 4297, 8801
Beecher, Judy C., 6540
Beecher, Thomas R., Jr., 6540
Beecherl, John T., 8792
Beecherl, Julia T., 8792
Beecherl, Louis, 8878
Beecherl, Louis A., III, 8792
Beecherl, Louis A., Jr., 8792
Beecherl, William C., 8792
Beede, Russell S., 4160
Beeghly, Bruce R., 7585
Beemer, Michael, 2592
Beemer, Michael G., 2592
Beene, Dennis, 8800
Beer Institute, 3564
Beer, Anne, 7533
Beer, Elliot, 5972
Beer, Henri, 5972
Beer, Rachel, 5972
Beer, Robert, 1541
Beer, Robert A., 1491, 1501, 1507
Beer, Ron, 7931
Beer, Willy, 5972
Beere, Polly, 6186
Beering, John G., 8389
Beering, Steven, 3129
Beerman, Abe, 8153
Beerman, Arthur, 7543
Beerman, Jessie, 7543

Beers, Carol A., 9541
Beers, Cynthia L. Martin, 9984
Beery, Robin C., 1396
Beesley, Nancy, 3123
Begemann, Brett D., 4868
Begg, J.W., 7879
Beggs, Gary, 3276
Beggs, Shirley, 3404
Begley, Christopher, 2804
Begley, William Michael, 7346
Begoun, Sherwin, 3000
Beha, James A., 5945
Beha, Macy Ann, 5945
Behle, Hope Eccles, 9327
Behler, Roger, 1468
Behlf, Hope Eccles, 9318
Behmann, Arno W., 8785
Behmann, Herman W., 8785
Behmke, John, 1949
Behn, Richard J., 1584
Behr, Greg, 8221
Behr, Linda Cucchiara, 1346
Behrakis, Drake, 3796
Behrakis, George D., 3796
Behrakis, Margo, 3796
Behrakis-Liakos, Stephanie, 3796
Behrens, Christopher C., 5612
Behrens, Mary Taylor, 5612
Behrens, Roger, 3293
Behring, David E., 1899
Behring, Kenneth E., 1899
Behrman, Linda F., 3166
Beidler, Francis, III, 2613
Beidler, Prudence R., 2661
Beiler, Anne, 8082
Beiler, Jonas, 8082
Beiler, LaVale, 8082
Beim, N.C., 4513
Beim, Raymond N., 4513
Beimfohr, Edward, 5310
Beimfohr, Edward G., 5932
Beinecke, Elizabeth G., 6750
Beinecke, Frances G., 5551
Beinecke, Frederick W., 6357, 6750, 7026
Beinecke, John B., 6750, 7026
Beinecke, William S., 6750, 7026
Beinhorn, Esther, 7283
Beinhorn, Marvin, 7283
Beischer, David D., 7371
Beischer, Susan Fox, 7371
Beiser, Bernard J., 1125
Beiser, Kathy, 6577
Beisler, Ralph, 6820
Bekavac, Nancy, 1118
Beker, Harvey, 1677, 5613, 8268
Beker, Jayne, 5613
Bekins Co., The, 273
Bekins, Jacqueline, 273
Bekins, Michael, 273
Bekins, Milo W., 273
Bekins, Richard, 273
Belanger, Beth, 4257
Belcher, Dennis, 9486
Belcher, Philip B., 8569
Belcourt, Lew, 1944
Belda, Ricardo E., 8075
Beldecos, J. Nicholas, 8178
Belden, Diana Davis, 7787
Belden, Frederick H., Jr., 9723
Belden, Marshall B., Jr., 7787
Belden, Ted, 156
Belding, Annie K., 5971
Belding, Milo M., 5971
Beles, Norman J., 2713
Belew, David L., 7660
Beley, James F., 1457
Belfer Corp., 5616
Belfer, Laurence D., 5615, 5616
Belfer, Norman, 5616
Belfer, Renee E., 5615, 5616
Belfer, Robert A., 5615, 5616
Belic, Ellen Stone, 3025
Belier, Anne, 8082

Belin, Daniel N., 6357
Beling, Betty, 304
Beling, Willard A., 304
Belk Charitable Lead Trusts, Irwin, 7314
Belk Department Stores, The, 7315
Belk Enterprises, 7315
Belk, Bill, 7314
Belk, Carl G., 7314
Belk, Claudia W., 7315
Belk, Inc., 7315
Belk, Irwin, 7314
Belk, John M., 7315
Belk, Matthews, 7315
Belk-Cook, Katherine McKay, 7315
Belk-Simpson Co., 7392
Belknap, Marjorie, 249
Belknap, Robert L., 7253
Bell Atlantic Corp., 5439
Bell Family Trust, 274
Bell, Andrew, 9580
Bell, Andy, 7866
Bell, Barbara, 1090
Bell, Ben H., Jr., 1355
Bell, Bradley P., 2614
Bell, Charles H., 4514
Bell, Cheryl Jefferson, Rev., 3372
Bell, Christy W., 5240
Bell, Daniel M., 1901
Bell, Daniel M., Jr., 1901
Bell, David A., 3453
Bell, Diane Fisher, 1542
Bell, Ford W., 4514
Bell, Frank M., Jr., 7420
Bell, Gene, 3177
Bell, George, 8049
Bell, Howard H., 826
Bell, Ida M., 2145
Bell, J. Bruce, 1737
Bell, J. Spicer, 3599
Bell, James A., 2145
Bell, James Ford, 4514
Bell, James M., 1168
Bell, Jeff, Jr., 8833
Bell, Jeffrey J., 9589
Bell, Jess A., 7544
Bell, Johanna, 9580
Bell, John H., Jr., 6484
Bell, Judith M., 1374
Bell, Julianna, 7544
Bell, Katharine, 8786
Bell, L. Andrew, III, 1940
Bell, Larry, 8783
Bell, Lauralee K., 2614
Bell, Lawrence T., 4557
Bell, Lee Phillip, 2614
Bell, Margaret L., 9756
Bell, Mariana, 1737
Bell, Martha A., 274
Bell, Mary E., 5806
Bell, Mary Lynn, 1217
Bell, Otis, 9580
Bell, Patricia B., 1901
Bell, Paula J., 9756
Bell, R. Terry, 9154
Bell, R.S., 8786
Bell, Ranlet S., 7420
Bell, Richard A., 7974
Bell, Robert T., 5448
Bell, Rodney H., 1901
Bell, Russell L., 9537
Bell, Samuel H., Jr., 4514
Bell, Samuel P., 728
Bell, Sharon J., 7984
Bell, Stacey K., 262
Bell, Steven C., 9756
Bell, Stuart M., 8317
Bell, Susan, 671
Bell, Susan S., 2639
Bell, Vance D., 2359
Bell, Walter A., 25
Bell, Walter W., 2903
Bell, William, 9567
Bell, William C., 9566
Bell, William J., 2614

Bell, William James, 2614
Bell, William Joseph, 2614
Bell-Flynn, Kathleen, 274
Bell-Rose, Stephanie, 6056
Bellairs, Robert J., Jr., 9759
Bellamah, Dale J., 837
Bellamy, Howell Vaught, Jr., 8579
Bellamy, Robert R., 1902
Bellanca, Rose B., 4257
Bellard, Chris, 1949
Bellatti, Barbara, 9154
Belles, Lawrence L., 2658
Bellgrau, Donald, 4899
Bellinger, Barbara P., 1537
Bellinger, Geraldine G., 6009
Bellini, Jenneifer, 4587
Bellmann, Charles H., 2357
Bello, Richard, 6105
Belloff, Mary Gretchen, 1922
Bellor, Mary M., 1804
Bellotti, Francis X., 3780
Bellows, Nancy Johnson, 8833
BellSouth Corp., 2323
Belly, Armando, 7021, 7023, 7024
Belmonte, Kathleen J., 2219
Belmuth, G., 6227
Belo Corp., 8787
Belo Corp., A.H., 8787
Belser, Mary R., 8605
Belsky, Nancy Kaplan, 6288
Belsky, Scott Kaplan, 6288
Belt, John, 7964
Belt, John L., 7952
Belton, Mark, 4570
Belton, Sharon Sayles, 4587
Beltramo, Larry, 1277
Beltran-Del Olmo, Magdalena, 350
Beltz, Susan W., 8385
Beluga, Inc., 5518
Belus, Tom, 9998
Belz Enterprizes, 8853
Belz, Jack A., 8638, 8643
Belz, Martin S., 8643
Belz, Philip, 8643
Belz, Ron, 8638
Belz, Ronald A., 8643
Belzberg, Wendy, 7031
Belzner, Bill, 5496
Bemiller, F. Loyal, 8396
Bemis Co., Inc., 4515
Ben & Jerry's Homemade Inc., 9355
Ben-Haim, Jody, 5617
Ben-Haim, Zvi, 5617
Benaroya, Jack A., 9556
Benaroya, Larry R., 9556
Benaroya, Rebecca B., 9556
Benaroya, Sherry-Lee, 9556
Benbough, Legler, 276
Benckenstein, Eunice R., 9209
Bendall, Joanne, 3215
Bender, Brant R., 868
Bender, Curtis, 8048
Bender, David S., 1772
Bender, George A., 1262
Bender, Howard M., 1772
Bender, Jack I., 1772
Bender, James J., 7989
Bender, Karen, 3333
Bender, Michael, 7567
Bender, Nan, 1772
Bender, Rachel McCarthy, 868
Bender, Richard A., 480
Bender, Sondra D., 1772
Bender, Stanley S., 1772
Bender, Susie, 7344
Bendheim Foundation, Charles & Els, Inc., 5126
Bendheim, Andrew, 6449
Bendheim, Daniel M., 5126
Bendheim, Gail B., 5126
Bendheim, Jack C., 5126
Bendheim, John M., 6449
Bendheim, John M., Jr., 6449
Bendheim, Kim, 6449

Bendheim, Robert, 6449
Bendheim, Shulamit Y., 5126
Bendheim, Thomas L., 6449
Benear, John B., 9314
Beneche, Elizabeth R., 3906
Benedict, Andrew, 8741
Benedict, Anna Savage, 9340
Benedict, Kennette M., 409
Benedict, Matt, 3199
Benedict, Rodman, Mrs., 6932
Beneducci, Joseph, 510
Benedum, Michael Late, 8099
Benedum, Paul G., Jr., 8099
Benedum, Sarah N., 8099
Beneficial Corp., 1703
Beneficial New Jersey, 1703
Benenson, Amy, 5619
Benenson, Blanche, 5619
Benenson, Bruce W., 5620
Benenson, Charles, 6779
Benenson, Charles B., 5620
Benenson, Esther, 5619
Benenson, Frederick C., 5620
Benenson, James, III, 7892
Benenson, James, Jr., 7892
Benenson, Lawrence B., 5620
Benenson, Michael, 5619
Benet, Jay, 4690
Beneto, Darlene, 277
Beneto, Stephen, 277
Benetollo, April Suzanne, 56
Benevento, Anthony, 1911
Bengard, Kim C., 704
Bengard, Thomas P., 704
Bengard, Tyler T., 704
Benglis, Lynda, 6080
Benham, Bruce, 1411
Benham, Helen, 1744
Benidt, Beatrice A., 9758
Benidt, Charles E., 9758
Benis, David, 8387
Benjack, Claire K., 9447
Benjamin (School House), Bob, 5708
Benjamin, Adelaide, 3507
Benjamin, Christopher J., 2530
Benjamin, Clarence, 1099
Benjamin, Elizabeth, 5127
Benjamin, Esther, 5905
Benjamin, John F., 2961
Benjamin, Leah, 5047
Benjamin, Michael, 6926
Benka, Carla, 1622
Benkert, Jerome A., Jr., 3249
Benko, Catherine A., 1527
Bennack, Frank A., Jr., 6161, 6162
Benner, Bruce, 4461
Bennett, Alan M., 1479
Bennett, Bruce, 1490
Bennett, C. Eugene, 1690
Bennett, Carl, 1490
Bennett, Cheryl S., 1450
Bennett, David J., 3125
Bennett, David W., 512
Bennett, Dennis, 279
Bennett, Dorothy, 1490
Bennett, Ed, 4986
Bennett, Eric W., 9237
Bennett, George F., Jr., 3797
Bennett, George F., Sr., 3797
Bennett, Harvey, 8003
Bennett, J. Mac, 8577
Bennett, James A., 8444
Bennett, Jay L., 4712, 4713
Bennett, Joan, 4939
Bennett, John, 2570, 5449, 9549
Bennett, Justin, 3014
Bennett, Karl E., 1690
Bennett, Louis Gaylord, 7966
Bennett, Louise Gaylord, 7937
Bennett, Lynn M., 5021
Bennett, M.K., 996
Bennett, Marc, 1490
Bennett, Marie, 9549
Bennett, Pat, 9388

Bennett, Peter C., 3797
Bennett, Rob, 9321
Bennett, Robert, 7050
Bennett, Robert B., 3797
Bennett, Robert G., 9388
Bennett, Robert M., 5785, 6660
Bennett, Robert Q., 5350
Bennett, Robert W., 2957
Bennett, Roger, 5673
Bennett, Russell E., Jr., 7463
Bennett, S.W., 996
Bennett, Stephen M., 696
Bennett, Steven Alan, 9245
Bennett, Steven E., 2386
Bennett, Susan, 2240
Bennett, Thompson, 4266
Bennett, Tim, 3077
Bennett, Tina, 6118
Bennett, Tony, 6532
Bennett, Twia, 8039
Bennett, Vera, 989
Bennett, William E., 3016
Bennett, William G., 5021
Benning, James, 9113
Bennington, Ronald K., 7675
Bennyhoff, George R., 8500
Benoit, Joe, 1250
Benoliel, Joel, 9556
Bensco, Inc., 8788
Bensen, James, 4520
Bensford, John L., 6713
Bensley, Bruce N., 5368
Bensman, Daniel, 7584
Benson Football, LLC, 8788
Benson, Bruce D., 1341
Benson, Clifton L., Jr., 7443
Benson, David, 1341
Benson, Donald, 4611
Benson, G. Richard, 3210
Benson, Greg, 4703
Benson, Gregory L., 4501
Benson, Larry, 8788
Benson, Margaret P., 7443
Benson, Marguerite, 1341
Benson, Mark A., 9475
Benson, Martha, 9217
Benson, Mary Grace, 6905
Benson, McCray V., 7344
Benson, Nancy, 1364
Benson, P. Bruce, 1341
Benson, Renee, 8788
Benson, Suzanne R., 9193, 9194, 9197
Benson, Tom, 8788
Benson, Vickie, 4595
Benson-Brown, Polly, 1341
Benten, R. Anthony, 6620
Bentinck-Smith, Elizabeth W., 4538
Bentinck-Smith, Peter, 3869
Bentley, Barbara F., 491
Bentley, Charlotte M. F., 7040
Bentley, Kenneth W., 9648
Bentley, Marie C., 559
Bentley, Ralph, 7354
Benton, Charles, 1773
Benton, Daniel C., 1483, 6433
Benton, Dave, 9651
Benton, Janet Inskeep, 5992
Benton, Jeffrey T., 7581
Benton, Lawton, 8579
Benton, William, 1773
Bentzen, Michael P., 1797
Benware, Gary, 5517
Benya, Richard V., 4899
Benz, Bill, 1006
Benz, Doris L., 3798
Benz, Norman E., 2253
Benz, Robert J., 7848
Bepko, Gerald L., 3196
Beran, R.D., 2653
Berardesco, Charles A., 3602
Berbee, James, 4599
Berber, Donna, 8747, 8748
Berber, Philip, 8747, 8748
Berberfam, Ltd., 8747

Berca, Jane J. Hampson, 4336
Bercow, Elizabeth S., 3905
Bercu, Steven, 5321
Bere, Barbara L., 2616
Bere, Barbara Van Dellen, 2616
Bere, David L., 2616
Bere, James F., 2616
Bere, James F., Jr., 2616
Bere, Robert P., 2616
Berelson, Ellen S., 5603
Beren, Adolph, 3348
Beren, David, 1342
Beren, Harry H., 1342
Beren, Israel Henry, 3347
Beren, Robert M., 3347, 3348
Beren, Zev, 1342
Berenbom, Merilyn, 4837
Berenson, Evelyn G., 3799
Berenson, Theodore W., 3799
Berenstein, Craig S., 3332
Berezan, David R., 146
Berg Revocable Trust, Ruth A., 381
Berg Settlor Trust, David, 5621
Berg, Christopher H., 381
Berg, David P., 4516
Berg, Gary N., 4716
Berg, Gilchrist B., 1903
Berg, Nancy M., 381
Berg, Paul, 3677
Berg, Ruth A., 381
Berg, Sally W., 3801
Berg, T.C., 2593
Berg, Thomas K., 4608
Bergdolt, Marian, 7485
Bergeman, Richard P., 5132
Bergen, Charlotte V., 7316
Bergen, Jack, 5400
Bergendahl, Anders, 6165
Bergendahl, Maria Heineman, 6165
Bergenfield, Burt, 2235
Berger Boiler Corp., 7179
Berger Foundation, H.N. and Frances C., 242, 1285
Berger, Barry S., 5660, 6187
Berger, David, 8101
Berger, Gretchen, 983
Berger, John L., 5117, 5118, 5122, 5234, 5259, 5267, 5332, 5340, 5421
Berger, John N., 281
Berger, Michael B., 7271
Berger, Paul S., 1805
Berger, Renee, 5128
Berger, Robert G., 8576
Berger, Sol, 5128
Berger, Sylvia J., 5802
Bergeron, Brant, 9778
Bergeron, Ellen, 3310
Bergeron, Nicole, 1297
Bergert, Nancy W., 8297
Bergeson, Eric, 4637
Bergey, James R., Jr., 3599
Berghoef, Henry, 2920
Berghold, Amy, 6523
Berghold, David, 6523
Berghold, Elisabetta, 6523
Berghold, Joanne M., 6523
Berghold, William D., 6523
Berghold, William Mark, 6523
Bergholtz, Steve, 3897
Bergin, Suzanne M., 1599
Berglund, Mary, 1040
Berglund, Rachel, 8389
Bergman, Alan, 6532
Bergman, Charles C., 6736
Bergman, Dan, 6559
Bergman, David, 4637
Bergman, John, 9117
Bergman, Marilyn, 1204
Bergman, Stanley N., 5571
Bergner, Yoav, 3843
Bergoff, Clara, 4151
Bergquist, Diana S., 7069
Bergreen, Bernard D., 6032

Bergsma, Nancy, 4481
Bergstrand, Margaret F., 6445
Bergstrom, Edith H., 282
Bergstrom, Erik E., 282
Bergstrom, Richard, 9776
Bergsund, Joan, 1178
Bergtold, Susanna, 6918
Berhard, William L., 6439
Berhendt, June, 436
Berick, James H., 7711
Beringer, David P., 982
Berinstein, Henry W., 1485
Berk, Sam, 7779
Berk, Tony B., 6693
Berk, William, 4245
Berke, Jacqueline, 4986
Berkey, Ann, 879
Berkley Corp., W.R., 1492, 1691
Berkley, Forrest, 3548
Berkley, William R., 1492, 1691
Berkley, William R., Jr., 1691
Berkley, William S., 4842
Berklund, Elwood, 8006
Berkman Co., Louis, The, 7545
Berkman, Cynthia Ann, 9019
Berkman, David J., 8102
Berkman, Jack N., 8102
Berkman, Larry, 9019
Berkman, Louis, 7545, 8192
Berkman, Louis, Mrs., 7545
Berkman, Monroe E., 8102
Berkman, Myles P., 8102
Berkman, Stephen L., 8102
Berkman, William H., 8102
Berkman, William Lance, 9019
Berkower, Amy, 5905
Berkowitz, Alan, 3604, 3637, 5321
Berkowitz, Arnold, 5936
Berkowitz, Barney, 5498
Berkowitz, David, 5321
Berkowitz, Ettil, 3751
Berkowitz, Francesca, 754
Berkowitz, Hershel, 3751
Berkowitz, Howard P., 5622
Berkowitz, Israel, 7125
Berkowitz, Judith, 1468
Berkowitz, Judith R., 5622
Berkowitz, Leonard, 5321
Berkowitz, Leopold, 7125
Berkowitz, Linda, 5321
Berkowitz, Morris, 7125
Berkowitz, Rita, 5892
Berkowitz, Roger S., 5622
Berkowitz, Sandra L., 5622
Berkowsky, Pamela B., 9363
Berkshire Hathaway Inc., 283, 302, 926, 1339, 1903, 3522, 3523, 3547, 3769, 4950, 6043, 8523
Berkshire Hills Bancorp, Inc., 3800
Berkson, Daniel, 2847
Berkson, Kay, 2847
Berkson, Rita D., 1557
Berkson, Steven, 6618
Berlamino, Betty Ellen, 7163
Berlanti, Donald V., 5475
Berlanti, Karen L., 5475
Berlanti, Matthew D., 5475
Berlanti, McKenna L., 5475
Berley, Amy, 6710
Berley, Jennifer, 6710
Berley, Madaleine, 6710
Berley, Mark, 6710
Berley, Nancy, 6710
Berliant, Jennie Rosenthal, 7826
Berlik, L.J., 5335
Berlin, Charles, 6434
Berlin, George R., 7816
Berlin, Howard R., 89
Berlin, Howard R., Jr., 89
Berlin, Joy M., 89
Berlin, Madeline, 7546
Berlin, Mark D., 3937
Berlin, Michael D., 554
Berlind, Roger, 5129

Biddle, Robert, 3425
Biderman, Jacob I., Rabbi, 6383
Bidlingmeyer, Larry, 7539
Bidwell, Glenn P., Jr., 9421
Bieber, Charles, 7957
Bieber, Gretta E., 2680
Bieber, Julian M., 747
Bieber, Marcia McGee, 7957
Bieber, William F., 4518
Biedenharn, Catherine Susan, 3463
Biedenharn, R.Z., 3463
Biedenharn, Sydney, 3463
Biefeldt, Carlotta, 2620
Biehl, George C., 5066
Biehl-Owens, Amy, 4986
Bielat, Robert G., 9475
Bieler, Mark, 6083
Bielfeldt, Gary K., 2620
Bieloh, William, 9645
Bielstein, Susan, 2767
Biemer, Linda, 6329
Bieraguel, Nancy, 9743
Bierbaum, John F., 2937
Bierbaum, Rosina, 483, 9480
Bierbower, William J., 1850
Bierman, John F. "Rick", 3325
Bierman, Larry, 8630
Biermann, Janet, 2904
Biernenberg, David, 4540
Biersach, Katherine M., 9803
Biesecker, Frederick N., 8106
Biesecker, Suzanne K., 8106
Bieser, Irven J., Jr., 7875
Bietler, Charles E., 4281
Big Horn Coal Co., 4983
Bigelow, Eileen, 4519
Bigelow, Frederick Russell, 4519
Bigelow, Peggy, 2592
Bigelow, Teresa, 9706
Biggar, Robert M., 7555
Biggins, Edward J., Jr., 5361
Biggs, A.R., 8609
Biggs, Alan, 3115
Biggs, Alison, 1333
Biggs, Barton M., 6815
Biggs, Charles L., 3627
Biggs, Franklin B., 1699
Biggs, John H., 4803
Biggs, Judith L., 1496
Biggs, Sewell C., 1699
Biggs, Sheridan C., 5782
Bigley, Tom, 3227
Biglow, Timothy B., 4204
Bigner, W. Michael, 2041
Bigue, Christa P., 1907
Bikoff, Mary E. "Betsy", 3147
Bilbro, Carol, 7496
Bildirici Hesed Foundation, Gabriel & Sara, 5554
Bildner, Allen, 5133
Bildner, James L., 4367
Bildner, Joan, 5133
Biles, Mary V. "Vicci", 7770
Bilezikian, Charles G., 3805
Bilezikian, Doreen, 3805
Bilezikian, Gregory C., 3805
Bilezikian, Jeffrey D., 3805
Bilger, Arthur, 289
Bilger, Dahlia, 289
Bilheimer, John, 571
Biller, Les, 290
Biller, Sheri, 290
Billings, Alan, 9861
Billings, Clyde A., Jr., 8677
Billings, Eric, 9377, 9425
Billings, Jane, 1943
Billings, Marianne, 9377, 9425
Billings, Tricia, 8315
Billingslea, Albert, 2358
Billingsley, Helen Lee, 5868
Billingsley, James R., 5868
Billingsley, James R., Jr., 5868
Billiton, 7436
Billman, Elizabeth, 3115

Bills, Tom, 4245
Bilodeau, Kenneth D., 4256
Bilski, Berthold, 6434
Bilski, Mark A., 6434
Bilsky, Bert L., 9744
Bilson, Ira E., 1195
Bilter, D. Keith, 502
Bilzin, Brian, 2141, 2149
Bilzin, Brian L., 2140
bin Abdul Aziz, Turkin, HRH Prince, 7531
Binda, Elizabeth H., 4233
Binda, Guido A., 4233
Binda, Robert, 4233
Bindeman, Stuart L., 3607
Binder, Adele, 291
Binder, Gordon M., 291
Binder, Katherine, 9630
Binder, Leslie E., 6532
Bing, Dave, 4389
Bing, Kenneth, 4258
Bing, Leo S., 5022
Bing, Mary A., 5790
Bing, Peter S., 5022
Binger, Anne, 4617
Binger, Benjamen M., 4617
Binger, E.T., 4646
Binger, Erika L., 4617
Binger, James H., 4617
Binger, James M., 4617
Binger, Patricia S., 4616, 4617
Binger, Virginia M., 4617
Bingham, Charlton Reed, 5045
Bingham, Darcy C., 1087
Bingham, Wade, 941, 1099
Bingham, William, II, 1493
Binner, Wes, 4723
Binswanger, Louisa, 553
Binswanger, Suzanne H., 1779
Binyon, Bryan A., 3098
Biogen, Inc., 3806
Biomet, Inc., 3106
Biondi, Cynthia G., 1494
Biondi, Michael J., 1494
Biondi, O. Francis, Jr., 6325
Biotegra, Inc., 3841
Birch, Edward E., 920
Birch, Stephen, 1692
Birchard, Rosemary, 8294
Birck, Michael, 3034
Bird Oil Corp., 1438
Bird, B.A., 2519
Bird, Carolyn G., 4096
Bird, Earl C., 3066
Bird, Hobart M., 8001
Bird, Jennifer J., 8759
Bird, Marian A., 8001
Bird, Peter F., Jr., 8679, 8690
Bird, Walter M., III, 4096
Bird, Walter M., Jr., 4096
Birdsall, Mabel, 6915
Birdshill, Inc., 8002
Birdsong, William M., Jr., 9421
Bireley, Frank, 2240
Bireley, Frank W., 292
Bireley, William Robert, 292
Birembaut, Mylene, 5484
Birk, Peggy J., 4617
Birkbigler, Dale, 1389
Birkelund, John P., 5632
Birkemeier, Ken, 3110
Birkett, Warren O., Jr., 3462
Birkeuhead, Susan, 5883
Birmingham, John P., 3807
Birmingham, Mark, 9405
Birmingham, Martin F., 9424
Birmingham, Paul J., 3807
Birnbach, Richard J., 6612
Birnbaum, Ezra, 6245
Birnhak, J. Robert, 8108
Birnhak, Marilyn J., 8108
Bischoff, Winfried F.W., Sir, 5755
Bisciotti, Stephen J., 3565
Bisesi, James T., 3155
Bisgrove Foundation, 141

Bisgrove, Debra, 141
Bisgrove, Gerald, 141
Bisgrove, Gerald "Jerry", 87
Bisgrove, John J., 5958
Bishop, Amy, 6645
Bishop, Archer W., III, 4457
Bishop, Arthur Giles, 9759
Bishop, Ashley Nicole, 9312
Bishop, Baker O'Neil, 4457
Bishop, Beth, 1477
Bishop, Brad, 3186
Bishop, Brent L., 9304
Bishop, Christiann M., 5584
Bishop, Dan S., 9697
Bishop, David M., 7422
Bishop, Donald F., II, 6645
Bishop, E. Liston, III, 2351
Bishop, E.E. "Top", Jr., 26
Bishop, G. David, 8619
Bishop, Gene H., 8843
Bishop, Gus, 4327
Bishop, John J., 7765
Bishop, John L., 2976
Bishop, Julie E. Denkers, 9317
Bishop, Leslie A., 4887
Bishop, Lillian H., 1693
Bishop, Paul R., 7604
Bishop, Richard S., 8431
Bishop, Robert J., 5990
Bishop, Robert L., II, 6645
Bishop, Sandra K., 4457
Bishop, Thompson A., 4457
Bishop, Timothy R., 8007, 8008, 8009
Bishop, William, 3432
Bismarck, Mona, 5633
Bissell, G. William, 8324
Bissell, Howard C., 7370
Bissell, J. Walton, 1495
Bissell, Robert K., 7813
Bissell, Sara H., 7390
Bissinger, Frederick L., 6299
Bisson, Ellen, 3241
Bissonnette, Michael, 2117
Bistricer, Elsa, 6464
Bistricer, Moric, 6464
Bito, Laszlo, 5634
Bittenbender, Freddie, 8135
Bitterman, Mary G.F., 961, 2535
Bittle, William G., 7536
Bittner, George S., 4842
Bittner, Lawrence, 9885
Bittner, R. Richard, 3263, 3264, 3265
Bitz, Rod, 4509
Bitzan, Mimi, 4534
Bivens, M.L., 4356
Bivins, Julian M., Jr., 9390
Bivins, Mark, 8758
Bixby, R. Philip, 4892
Bixby, Walter Edwin, Sr., 4892
Bizzell, Thomas M., 2217
Bjella, Brian R., 7516
Bjerke, David W., 9768
Bjorklund, Alexandra O., 4614
Bjorklund, Victoria, 5607, 6104
Bjornson, Donald R., 2566
Black Entertainment, Inc., 9444
Black Insurance Agency, Thomas, Inc., 4147
Black, Bonita K., 3414
Black, Carl O., 34
Black, Chris, 3415
Black, Dameron, III, 2373, 2456
Black, Dameron, IV, 2380
Black, Daniel A., 5738
Black, Debra R., 5636
Black, Dennis E., 3598
Black, Esther McEwan, 7718
Black, Gary, Jr., 3559
Black, Gary, Sr., 3559
Black, Harry C., 3559
Black, Heather Bilandic, 2661
Black, Jack, 293
Black, James, 8946
Black, James B., III, 7438

Black, James Floyd, 2380
Black, James I., III, 6037
Black, Jane C., 2380
Black, Janice R., 8208
Black, Jeremy, 3825
Black, John B., 7718
Black, Joyce, 293
Black, Leon D., 5636
Black, Louis E., 5867
Black, Lynne, 4326
Black, Marilyn S., 34
Black, Michael, 3229
Black, Natalie A., 9840
Black, Paula Cooper, 1477
Black, Peter M., 7718
Black, Robert, 5635
Black, Sammy, 7354
Black, Samuel P., III, 8109
Black, Sheila Markley, 7867
Black, Sherry Salway, 1810
Black, Sophie, 3825
Black, Stanley, 293
Black, Susan, 2048
Black, Suzanne, 7175
Black, Thomas B., 2361
Black, Thomas F., III, 8542
Black, Timothy, 6234
Blackburn, Carol, 3597
Blackburn, Deirdre, 8418
Blackburn, Elizabeth L., 2207
Blackburn, John L., 27
Blackburn, Joseph D. "Jody", 27
Blackburn, Lois V. Shakarian, 5310
Blackburn, Marcia Ross, 2207
Blackburn, Mark, 7650
Blackburn, William R., 2207
Blackin, Jack, 5438
Blacklock, Katherine, 7150
Blackman, Linda, 2359
Blackman, Marie, 294
Blackman, Martin, 6999
Blackmar, Alfred O., 2311
Blackstone, Richard, 3505
Blackwell, Angela, 1203
Blackwell, Anna D., 2541
Blackwell, Daisy S., 4748
Blackwell, David R., 8611
Blackwell, Jean, 3136
Blackwell, Jessie L., 7973
Blackwell, Todd, 4697
Blackwood, Michael, 8247
Blackwood, Richard, 8098
Blades, A.T., 3574
Blades, Mary H., 3574
Blades, Terrence F., 3599
Blahnik, Richard J., 9959
Blaikie, David L., 2077
Blaine, Joan S., 1757
Blair & Co., William, L.L.C., 2621
Blair, Bertha Brossman, 8120
Blair, Billie, 5496
Blair, Diane, 4637
Blair, Dorothy, 2622
Blair, Edward McCormick, Jr., 2957
Blair, Edward McCormick, Sr., 2957
Blair, Edward, Jr., 1040
Blair, James B., 182
Blair, Jeffrey, 8926
Blair, Kathy, 8647
Blair, Randall, 329
Blair, Sloan B., 9109
Blais, Earle C., 1126
Blais, Robert H., 9616
Blake, Benjamin L., 9129
Blake, Beverly, 7373
Blake, Gillian, 9905
Blake, Joe, 1364
Blake, Jonathan D., 8530
Blake, Kathryn T., 7952
Blake, Mary Kay, 9424
Blake, Michael, 637
Blake, Patricia, 6286
Blake, Patrick, 879
Blake, Ruth E. Mengle, 8347

Blake, William D., 3485
Blakely, Carolyn, 157
Blakely, David, Rev., 3245
Blakeman, Don, 169
Blakemore, Frances L., 9558
Blakemore, Thomas L., 9558
Blakeslee, Ann G., 1913
Blakeslee, Derek J., 1913
Blakley, Bruce G., 1087
Blalock, Bill, 2094
Blalock, Robert, 1693
Blalock, Robert G., 1738
Blamey, Ann E., 9800
Blanc, Gene, 2902
Blanchard, Anna Neal, 7485
Blanchard, Arthur F., 8111
Blanchard, Billy, 2497
Blanchard, Brenda, 6640
Blanchard, Cayce, 9476
Blanchard, Lawrence, 9442
Blanchard, Lisa G., 4412
Blanchard, Peter P., III, 8211
Blanchard, Peter P., Jr., 8110
Blanchard, Sofia, 1606
Blanchard, Thomas M., Jr., 2357
Blanco, Mary, 851
Blanco, Odilo, 2346
Bland, C. Wayne, 7982
Bland, Calvin, 5265
Bland, Cara, 7970
Bland, Jim, Jr., 8647
Blandford, M. Margaret, 3067
Blandin Foundation, 4574, 4637
Blandin, Charles K., 4520
Blanding, Beatrice W., 7217
Blaney, Carolyn E., 8179
Blaney, Charlotte E., 6022
Blaney, Dana, 8179
Blaney, Thomas F., 6513
Blank, A.H., 3268
Blank, Andrew S., 1909
Blank, Arthur M., 2325
Blank, Danielle, 2325
Blank, Dena, 2325
Blank, Jerome, 1909
Blank, Kenny, 2325
Blank, Mark, 2004
Blank, Martin, Jr., 575
Blank, Michael, 2325
Blank, Myron N., 3268
Blank, Nancy, 2325
Blank, Ruth, 1080
Blank, Stephanie, 2325
Blankenship, Charles, 3137
Blankenship, David, 3259
Blankenship, Elizabeth, 7986
Blankenship, Elizabeth Warren, 7987
Blankenship, Robert P., 870
Blankfein, Laura, 5637
Blankfein, Lloyd C., 5637
Blankfield, Bryan J., 9887
Blankfort, Lowell A., 1779
Blanks, R. Steve, 9419
Blanton, Anne, 2661
Blanton, Ben W., 3119, 3120
Blanton, Darren, 8886
Blanton, Eddy S., 9175
Blanton, Jack S., Jr., 9175
Blanton, Jack S., Mrs., 9175
Blanton, Jack S., Sr., 9175
Blanton, Julie E., 8886
Blanton, Thomas K., 2143
Blasdale, R. William, 3770
Blasdale, R. William, Mrs., 3770
Blaser, Dean B., 7559
Blasi, Tracey Mason, 2356
Blassberg, Franci J., 6794
Blatnick, Gary, 691
Blattmachr, Jonathan, 79
Blau, Lawrence, 6200
Blau, Olivia, 6200
Blau, Sandra, 2957
Blausey, William W., Jr., 7617
Blaustein, Jacob, 3575

Blaustein, Jeanne P., 3576
Blaustein, Mary Jane, 3576
Blaustein, Morton K., 3576
Blaustein, Robert S., 7012
Blaylock, Lou Ann, 9150
Blaylock, Marcia S., 8658
Blazek, George T., 5005
Blazek-White, Doris D., 1787, 1814
Bleck, Eugene E., 639
Bleiberg, Rob, 1471
Bleichroeder, A., 5722
Bleichroeder, S., 5722
Bleier, Edward, 5827
Bleser, Carol A., 9760
Bleser, Clarence P., 9760
Bleser, James F., 9760
Blessing, Buck, 1437
Blessing, Linda J., 98
Blessing, Mary Ann, 8700
Blessing, Melissa, 5508
Bleustein, Jeffrey L., 9812
Blevins, Kerrie, 4525
Blevins, Michael, 891
Blew, Denise, 8303
Blickensderfer, Sharon L., 4844
Blickle, John, 7570
Blickle, Rainer, 5652, 7132
Blinder, Alan S., 6894
Blinkenberg, Linda J., 411, 527, 586,
  824, 889, 1108, 1304, 1323
Blinkilde, Peter, 4331
Bliss, Cheryl, 5281
Bliss, Joyce, 3161
Bliss, Patricia Dillon, 1093
Blissard, Lani, 2002
Blitz, Sylvia, 5190
Bliumis-Dunn, Sarah W., 5694
Blobel, Guenter, 6281
Bloch, Alan, 8104
Bloch, Henry W., 4823
Bloch, Mary, 4876
Bloch, Milton J., 5783
Bloch, Nancy Berman, 8104
Bloch, Thomas M., 4842
Block Family Foundation, 1251
Block, Adele, 5638
Block, Adele G., 5638
Block, Alexandra Skestos, 7683
Block, Amie Willard, 1861
Block, Bernice, 6260
Block, Ellen, 8540
Block, Herbert L., 1776
Block, James A., 5840
Block, Joel A., 4899
Block, Judith S., 2728
Block, Ken, 3897
Block, Leonard N., 5638
Block, Robert, 9761
Block, Thomas, 5638
Block, Valerie, 5840
Blockett, Charles, Jr., 4243
Blodgett, Joth, 4498
Bloem, James H., 3428
Blohm, Jon, 7573
Blohm, R.E., Jr., 9270
Blokker, Joanne W., 889
Blokker-Dalquist, Donja, 889
Blomberg, Jeff, 1333
Blomberg, Justin P., 4459
Blomquist, Ingrid K., 195
Blomquist, Olov A., 195
Blomquist, Willma, 195
Blomseth, Warren, 516
Blondet, Virgil, Jr., 1564
Blondia, Jeanne M., 3602
Blood, Alison, 5639
Blood, David, 5560
Blood, David W., 5639, 7116
Bloodgood, Jack, 3747
Bloodworth, Carolyn A., 4260
Bloody Forland, LP, 5397
Bloom, Aimee Simon, 6987
Bloom, Barry L., 7104, 7144, 7145,
  7146, 7147, 7148, 7149

Bloom, Barry R., 3621
Bloom, Bruce, 4237
Bloom, Edward D., 6823
Bloom, Kemery, 4827
Bloom, Martha L., 4221
Bloom, Martin, 9482
Bloom, Peter, 5905
Bloomberg, 7040, 7174
Bloomberg, Michael R., 5707
Bloomfield, Doug, 7781
Bloomfield, Randall D., 5990
Bloomfield, Rie, 295
Bloomfield, Sam, 295
Bloomquist, Karen, 9702
Bloss, Leigh V., 8881
Bloss, Margaret Varner, 8950
Blossom, C. Bingham, 7549
Blossom, C. Perry, 7549
Blossom, David B., 7549
Blossom, Elizabeth B., 7542, 7549
Blossom, John, 537
Blossom, Jonathan B., 7549
Blossom, Laurel, 7549
Blossom, Robin Dunn, 7549
Blossom, Virginia O., 7549
Blough, Rhoda M., 7867
Blount Foundation, Roberts and Mildred,
  14
Blount, David, 9368
Blount, Inc., 14
Blount, Joseph W., 13
Blount, S. Roberts, 13
Blount, Thomas A., 13
Blount, Tom, 7326, 7397
Blount, W. Houston, 40
Blount, William K., 8045
Blount, Winton M., III, 13, 20
BLTN Holdings, LLC, 5122
BLTN Holdings, LLP, 5122
BLTN, LLC, 5122
Blue Ball National Bank, 8231
Blue Chip Casino, Inc., 3205
Blue Cross and Blue Shield, 3512
Blue Cross and Blue Shield of Alabama,
  Inc., 18
Blue Cross and Blue Shield of Florida,
  Inc., 1911
Blue Cross and Blue Shield of Georgia,
  Inc., 2411
Blue Cross and Blue Shield of Iowa,
  3343
Blue Cross and Blue Shield of
  Minnesota, 4521
Blue Cross and Blue Shield of North
  Carolina, Inc., 7319
Blue Cross and Blue Shield of South
  Carolina, 8570
Blue Cross and Blue Shield of South
  Dakota, 3343
Blue Cross of Idaho Health Service, Inc.,
  2571
Blue Cross of Northeastern
  Pennsylvania, 8112
Blue Moon Fund, Inc., 9488
Blue Moon Fund, The, 483
Blue School, 5518
Blue, Ronald W., 8704
Blue, Suzanne, 4663
BlueCross BlueShield of Tennessee,
  8732
Bluemle, Lewis W., 8157
Bluestein, Ronald, 8491
Bluhdorn, Dominique, 5642
Bluhdorn, Paul, 5642
Bluhdorn, Yvette, 5642
Bluhm, Mark, 2657
Blum Foundation, Edith C., 5643
Blum Revocable Trust, Adi, 1912
Blum Trust, 2961
Blum, Carolyn P., 3577
Blum, Christine L., 7614
Blum, Eva T., 8388
Blum, Felicia H., 5762
Blum, Harry, 2625, 2844

Blum, Howard Z., 8671
Blum, Irving, 3577
Blum, Jeffrey D., 3577
Blum, John R.H., 5886
Blum, Jonathan D., 3457
Blum, Kenneth J., 834
Blum, Lawrence A., 3577
Blum, Mark J., 1594
Blum, Mary J., 7614
Blum, Nathan, 2624
Blum, Richard C., 297
Blum, Tracy A., 7614
Blum, W. Charles, 7614
Blume, Jene S., 298
Blume, John A., 298
Blume, Marshall E., 8342
Blume, Ruth C., 298
Blumenfeld, Jay, 5228
Blumenfrucht, Jonah, 5451
Blumenstein, Harold, 4234
Blumenstein, Penny B., 4234, 4254
Blumenstein, Randall S., 4234
Blumenstein, Richard C., 4234
Blumenthal, Alan, 7320
Blumenthal, Cynthia M., 6480
Blumenthal, Herman, 7320
Blumenthal, I.D., 7320
Blumenthal, Jabe, 9563
Blumenthal, Margo, 3281
Blumenthal, Philip, 7320
Blumenthal, Samuel, 7320
Blumer, Herman, 6915
Blummer, William E., 9246
Blunt-Bradley, Lisa, 1706
Bluntzer, John Lloyd, 8785
Blurton, Jerry H., 8935
Blythe, Curtis L., 3294
Blythe, Mary Ann, 3294
BMC West, 1359
BMG Charitable Foundation, 5965
BMT Corp., 9802
BNG Management, 4578
BNY Capital Corp., 5598
Boardman, Braye C., 2357
Boardman, C.P., II, 2357
Boardman, Thomas A., 4492
Boas, Andrew M., 6490
Boateng, Joseph A., 9566
Boatman, Dennis L., 3290
Boatman, Sandra M., 1357
Bob's Steak & Chop House, 9068
Bobbitt, Robert, 7570
Bober, Mark, 7526
Bober, Stan, 7719
Bobilli Blind School, 4569
Bobilya, David A., 3149
Bobrow, Edythe, 6917
Bobrow, Irving S., 6842, 6843
Bobst, Elmer H., 5646
Bobst, Mamdouha S., 5646
Boccardi, Louis D., 9424
Bochnowski, David, 3189
Bochow, Carl E., Sr., 8876
Bocian, Pete, 7773
Bock, Eric J., 5157
Bock, Fain, 8878
Bocko, Miranda Fuller, 5090
Bodenhamer, Lee, 158
Bodenhausen, Galen R., 4851
Bodenmann, Linda, 3854
Bodensteiner, Clem, 3325
Bodenweber, Holly, 1941
Bodenwein, Theodore, 1497
Bodie, Carroll A., 3711
Bodine, Jack, 4784
Bodine, Jean G., 8340
Bodine, Mary Jane, 4784
Bodman, George M., 5647
Bodman, Louise C., 5647
Bodner, David, 5648, 6206
Bodner, Eric S., 5228
Bodner, Moishe, 5648
Bodner, Naomi, 5648, 6206
Bodney, Stephen, 3130

Bodney, Steven, 3161
Bodzin, Stephen A., 1845
Bodziony, Dennis J., 7555
Boe, David, 8395
Boeckman, Duncan E., 9096
Boeckmann, Alan L., 523
Boeckmann, Herbert F., II, 299
Boeckmann, Jane, 299
Boehl, Kenneth F., 1730
Boehm, Charlotte, 227
Boehm, D.J., Dr., 4221
Boehm, Edward G., 8431
Boehm, Mary, 2323
Boehm, Ron J., 227
Boehne, Dean, 1740
Boehnen, David L., 4695
Boehner, Leonard, 8561
Boehner, Leonard B., 5677
Boehringer Ingelheim Pharmaceuticals, Inc., 1498
Boeing Co., The, 9560
Boensch, Dorothy Frist, 8678
Boentje, J.D., Jr., 4646
Boer, Carrie L., 4261
Boernke, Michelle, 9861
Boes, Gary, 4898
Boeschenstein, Elizabeth M., 7728
Boeschenstein, Harold, 7569
Boeschenstein, Josephine M., 7728
Boeschenstein, William W., 7728
Boesel, Stephen W., 3709
Boesen, James M., 2704
Boesky, Seema S., 6979
Boettcher, C.K., 1344
Boettcher, C.K., Mrs., 1344
Boettcher, Charles, 1344
Boettcher, Charles, II, Mrs., 1344
Boettcher, Fannie, 1344
Boettcher, Mae B., 1344
Boettiger, John R., 6790
Boeyink, Jeffrey R., 3319
Boezaart, Arnold "Arn", 4252
Bogan, Barbara, 1874
Bogan, Ernest, 5555
Bogan, Stanley, 5555
Bogart, Jane Olds, 700
Bogart, Jim, 401
Bogart, Martha, 6231
Bogart, Max, 6231
Bogart, Stacy, 4702
Bogen, Andrew E., 1288
Bogen, Sheryl, 9297
Bogen, Stanley, 5555
Boger, Jennifer B., 7488
Bogert, Jeremiah M., 6263, 6547, 7275
Bogert, Jeremiah M., Jr., 6547, 7275
Bogert, Margot C., 7275
Bogert, Milicient D., 7275
Bogetto, Philip D., 1872
Boggan, Daniel, 346
Boggess, Anna, 8067
Boggs, Paula E., 9690
Boggs, Sue, 7673
Bogguss, J. Scott, 3275
Boggust, Paula Friedland, 4963
Boghetich, Jilene K., 7971
Boghetich, Tony, 7971
Boghosian, Varujan, 5548
Bogner, Stephen B., 7633
Bogo, Alexis G., 8684
Bogoni, Irene, 5134
Bogoni, Paul, 5134
Bogue, Richard, 1942
Bohan, Deirdre L., 4153
Bohart, James, Jr., 1533
Bohen Charitable Trust, Mildred M., 1346
Bohls, John M., 3249
Bohlsen, John, 5649
Bohlsen, Kurt, 5649
Bohlsen, Linda, 5649
Bohlsen, Michael, 5649
Bohman, Susan, 9702
Bohn, Karen, 4521, 4624

Bohn, Robert G., 9887
Bohnen, Michael, 4071
Bohnen, Michael J., 8560
Bohnen, Teresa, 4534
Bohnen, Thomas, 401
Bohnert, Jennifer, 2612
Bohnett, David C., 300
Bohrofen, Eldon, 9962
Boillot, Dominique, 6375
Boillot, Etienne, 5623
Boillot, Nicholas, 5721
Boisi, Geoffrey T., 5650, 5707
Boisi, Norine I., 5650
Boissonnas, Eric, 9170
Boissonnas, Jacques C., 9170, 9277
Boissonnas, Nicolas N., 9170, 9277
Boissonnas, Sylvinia, 1717
Boisvert, Pamela K., 4209
Boitano, Caroline O., 572
Bok, Derek C., 3015
Boklund, Thomas B., 578
Bokor, Peter, 3576
Bokram, Heather, 4257
Bolano, Andres, Jr., 2132
Boldemann-Tatkin, Tracy, 956
Bolden, Emmie C., 15
Bolden, Herman D., 15
Bolden, Stanley C., 15
Boldrick, Suzy, 9117
Boldt, Dana, 1071
Boleky, Ed, 5051
Boles, David R., 1684
Boles, Joseph L., Jr., 2238
Boles, Sarah L., 1684
Bolger, David F., 5136, 5179
Bolger, Heidi A., 4428
Bolger, John G., 5136
Bolger, Susan, 9239
Bolick, Jerome W., 7321
Bolin, D. Phil, 9280
Bolk, David R., Hon., 3250
Bolker, Amelia Taper, 1226
Bolker, Cynthia Taper, 1226
Boll, John A., 4235
Boll, Marlene, 1468
Boll, Marlene L., 4235
Bollero, John, Jr., 3038
Bolles, Larry D., 2701
Bolliger, Ralph, 8007
Bolling, Landrum R., 1796
Bolling, Robert H., III, 1762
Bolling, Robert H., Jr., 1762
Bollinger, Brad, 507
Bollinger, Lee C., 4367
Bollman, Lynda, 2936
Bolser, Benjamin, 4253
Bolthouse Farms, William, Inc., 301
Bolthouse, William J., 301
Bolton, Betty Duane, 9293
Bolton, Carrie, 7496
Bolton, Charles L., 7862
Bolton, Charles P., 7576, 7798
Bolton, Frances P., 7798
Bolton, J. Roger, 1479
Bolton, James L., 9293
Bolton, John B., 7798
Bolton, Kenyon C., III, 7798
Bolton, Pamela, 3029
Bolton, Perry J., 3761
Bolton, Philip P., 7798
Bolton, Thomas C., 7798
Bolton, William B., 7798
Boltz, Gerald E., 678
Bolwell, Harry J., 7806
Bolz Charitable Lead Trust, Eugenie M., 9762
Bolz, Eugenie M., 9762
Bolz, John A., 9762
Bolz, Julia M., 9762
Bolz, Robert M., 9762
Bolz, Sara L., 9762
Boman, Keith G., 5056
Boman, Mary Jo, 3291
Boman, Peter L., 4556

Bomberger, Carolyn L., 2098
Bomberger, Dorothy C., 2098
Bomberger, Matthew A., 2098
Bomberger, Michelle H., 2098
Bomberger, Rachel A., 2098
Bomberger, William A., 2098
Bomet, Priscilla, 8812
Bomfim, Carlos Bertaco, 6893
Bon Appetit Danish, Inc., 757
Bon, Lauren, 8084
Bonacci, Frank, 9732
Bonacci, Kathleen S., 9732
Bonanni, Fabrizio, 219
Bonanno, Anthony, Jr., 5194
Bonanno, Richard, 5194
Bonavia, Patricia, 2591
Bonchack, Robert M., 7591
Bond, A.D., III, 4822
Bond, Bradford, 9314
Bond, Christopher S., 4822
Bond, Duane, 3400
Bond, Enriqueta C., 7333
Bond, Gwendolyn G., 5704
Bond, Ina B., 3409, 3410
Bond, Steven, 6607
Bond, Walter, 1913
Bondurant, William L., 6688
Boney, Sion A., 7398
Boney, Sion A., III, 7398
Bonieskie, Lynda, 1776
Bonieskie, Raymond, 1776
Bonilla, Steve, 417
Bonine, James D., 3199
Bonister, Bessie, 2491
Bonne Bell, Inc., 7544
Bonner, Alexandra L., 2370
Bonner, Bertram F., 5137
Bonner, Bonnie F., 2345
Bonner, Corella A., 5137
Bonner, Lola L., 8833
Bonner, Marsha, 6160
Bonner, Marsha E., 854
Bonner, Mary Claire, 1479
Bonner, Sarah H., 1981
Bonner, Sarah Lane, 374
Bonner, Timothy, 4520
Bonner, William, 8278
Bonney, Flora Macdonald, 6468
Bonney, Weston, 3542
Bonomi, Darby Furth, 543
Bonovitz, Sheldon M., 8172, 8312
Bonsall, Susan, 4725
Bonter, Louise, 3146
Bontrager, Wilbur, 3145
Bonura, Joseph A., Jr., 5564
Bonzani, A., 6221
Boogaard, Marcia, 3750
Boogaard, Tom, 3750
Booke, Keith D., 9247
Booker, Dave, 1090
Booker, Ernest, 5343
Booker, Lewis T., 9506
Booker, Marilyn, 6577
Booker, William W., 9717
Bookout, Carolyn S., 8791
Bookout, John F., III, 8791
Bookout, John F., Jr., 8791
Boomer, Walter E., Gen., 3511
Boon, Carl N., 7427
Boon, Myron P., 3082
Boon, Thierry, 5973
Boone Circuit Court, 3433
Boone, LaBarron, 20
Boone, Larry, 8670
Boone, Robert S., 2993, 9726
Boone, William, 8717
Boos, Mary C., 4701
Booth, Alex, Jr., 1914
Booth, Beth A., 1726
Booth, Betsy L., 1726
Booth, Chancie Ferris, 5651
Booth, David, 303
Booth, Lee, 4721
Booth, Margaret, 6615

Booth, Otis, Jr., 302
Booth, Suzanne Deal, 303
Booth, Vicki, 1248
Booth, Willis H., 5651
Borawski, Robert, 329, 418
Borchardt, Kristi Franklin, 8908
Borchers, Edward, 7584
Borchers, Judith L., 9785
Borchers, Stephen C., 3253
Borczynski, Chester E., 6883
Borda, Richard, 401
Borden, Ann R., 1741
Borden, Bertram H., 5138
Borden, Harold W., Jr., 5435
Borden, John C., Jr., 5138
Borden, Thomas A., 5138
Bordine, Corey, 4256
Borek, Jo Anne, 4072
Borek, John M., Jr., 2394
Borel, James C., 1706
Boren, Ashley, 3557
Boren, David, 7931
Boren, Lael, 3108
Boren, LaRita R., 3108
Boren, Leland E., 3108
Borer, Jeffrey S., 6032
Bores, Jim, 8039
Borgen, Bjorn Erik, 1468
Borgerding, Pam, 4511
Borges, Francisco L., 1564
Borgida, Adam, 1529
Borgos, Seth, 6615
Borick, Louis L., 305
Borick, Robert, 305
Borick, Steven J., 305, 1413
Borin, James L., 4450
Boris, Leslie Baker, 8092
Borislow, Daniel, 5174
Borislow, Michele, 5174
Borja-Villel, Manuel J., 5550
Borkson, Elliot P., 2029
Borlinghaus, Scott, 4812
Borm, Mary, 9233
Borman, Karen T., 4695
Born Trust, Walter W., 7552
Born, Ross J., 8113
Born, Wendy, 8113
Bornblum, Bert, 8645
Bornblum, David, 8645
Bornstein, Lester M., 5228
Bornstein, Ronald E., 1210
Borofsky, Michael C., 6716
Borowsky, Kurt T., 5324
Borrelli, Neil J., 3597
Borrok, Charles, 6779
Borsic, Nick, 8449
Borthwick, Maribeth, 1262
Bortle, Catherine, 1448
Borto, Ron, 3135
Borton, Karl, 7906
Borton, Thomas, 7906
Boruch, Robert F., 6092
Boruff, Joy, 2902
Borwell, Naomi T., 2627
Borwell, Robert C., Jr., 2627
Borwell, Robert C., Sr., 2627
Borwell, Robert C., Sr., Mrs., 2627
Bosack & Bette M. Kruger Foundation, CA, Leonard X., The, 3809
Bosack, Leonard, 3809
Boschwitz, Nancy Zellerbach, 1326
Boscia, Jon A., 3195
Bosco, Gary, 4229
BOSE Corp., 3810
Boseker, Donna Martin, 3141
Boseman, James T., 8588
Boskin, Michael J., 774, 775
Bosl, Ginger, 9208
Bosquez, Roberto, 8833
Boss, LaVerne H., 4233
Boss, W. Andrew, 4595
Bosse, James F., 2075
Bosse, Lois, 2075
Bossenberry, Earl C., 4395

Bossidy, Lawrence A., 1500, 5326
Bossmann, Lori L., 2582
Bosson, Dondi Anne, 2518
Bost, Ruthanna Jolley, 2423
Boston Scientific, 3841
Boston Scientific Corp., 3813
Boston University, 3667
Bostron, Catherine A., 6161, 6162
Boswell Charitable Lead Trust, Lois K., The, 4786
Boswell Foundation, Amie, 4786
Boswell Foundation, Joe, 4786
Boswell Foundation, Johnathon, 4786
Boswell Foundation, Julie, 4786
Boswell, Bennie, Jr., 2356, 7373
Boswell, J.G., II, 2564
Boswell, James G., 308
Boswell, James W., 308, 417
Boswell, John J., 4786
Boswell, Tiffany, 4786
Boswell, W.W., 417
Boswell, W.W., Mrs., 417
Bosworth, Arthur H., II, 1350
Bosworth, Mary Ellen, 5005
Bosworth, Robert E., 8684
Botek, Fred G., 837
Botham, Lydia, 4602
Bothe, Cathryn S., 9833
Bothin, Ellen Chabot, 309
Bothin, Henry E., 309
Botkin, Patricia, 4256
Botsford, Margot, Hon., 3871
Botsford, Nina, 75
Botstein, Leon, 6665
Bott, Thomas, 3047
Bottimore, Elizabeth R., 9507
Bottler, Elisabeth A., 9642
Bottling Group, LLC, 6713
Bottomley, John T., 5090
Bottoms, David N., Jr., 7030
Bottoms, Robert G., 2820
Botts, Patrick, 3210
Botwinick, Andrew, 5653
Botwinick, Benjamin, 5653
Botwinick, Bessie, 5653
Botwinick, Edward, 5653
Bouchard, Laurie L., 4989
Bouchard, Michael J., 4989
Bouchard, Morton S., III, 6404
Bouchard, Ryan M., 4989
Boucher, Miriam M., 8611
Boucher, Peter, 1396
Boucher, Ted A., 6823
Bouchey, Steven B., 5782
Boudreau, Norman, 4057
Boudreau, Thomas M., 4811
Boulanger, Carol, 5347, 5549
Boulanger, Mena, 2922
Boulanger, Richard A., 3887
Boulden, Allyson, 3088
Bouldin, Granville S.R., 8654
Boulier, Charles J., III, 1482
Bouligny, Gene, 8833
Bouligny, James, 8974
Boulpaep, Emile, Sir., 5973
Bouma, Mary, 571
Bouque, Roy L., 1210
Bouras, Nicholas J., 5139
Bourdeau, Paul, 1636
Bourgois, Nicole, 5879
Bourne, JoAnn, 1250
Bourne, Robert B., 3612
Bournstein, Catherine J., 7594
Bouscaren, Helen Hunt, 8261
Boushek, Randall L., 9949
Boutaugh, Joseph W., 9716
Boutault, Delores J., 1186
Boutault, E.C., 1186
Boutell, Arnold, 4236
Boutell, Gertrude, 4236
Bouterse, Mary, 2190
Boutin, Joseph, 9356
Boutin, Stephen F., 1080
Boutwell, Jeffrey H., 3956

Boutwell, Ken, 1945
Boutz, Richard W., 9589
Bouwman, Laurie, 4217
Bovaird, Mabel W., 7927
Bovard, Jeanne A., 8431
Bove, Joyce, 6969
Bove, Joyce M., 6613
Bovender, Jack O., 8690
Bovender, Jack O., Jr., 8662
Bovenizer, Lynn S., 5399
Bovin Family Foundation, 8210
Bovin, Denis A., 5654
Bowden, Henry, Jr., 2399
Bowdich, Julie, 5466
Bowdle, Margaret B., 8797
Bowen, Arthur, 8848
Bowen, Burton A., 2614
Bowen, Ethel N., 9711
Bowen, Gretchen Reuter, 7817
Bowen, Henry, 9711
Bowen, Howard "Blackie", 3600
Bowen, Jimelle, 9735
Bowen, Matthew J., 7817
Bowen, Otis R., 3194
Bowen, Phyllis, 2479
Bowen, Sheryl E., 8880
Bowen, Vera Ayres, 9183
Bowen, William G., 5326, 6525
Bowen, William H., 155
Bower, Alice R., 3693
Bower, Charles W., 1703
Bower, George L., Jr., 7323
Bower, James A., 7867
Bower, Jeffrey M., 8136
Bower, John, 4736
Bowerman, Bryan P., 1549, 1594
Bowerman, Mary, 4259
Bowers, Abigail Phipps, 7255
Bowers, Ann S., 944
Bowers, Debra, 2677
Bowers, Reveta, 345
Bowes, Frances F., 310
Bowes, John, 310
Bowes, John G., 310
Bowes, William K., Jr., 311
Bowie, W. Russell, III, 4975
Bowlby, Janet, 8168
Bowles, Beatrice, 834
Bowles, Crandall Close, 8617
Bowles, Margaret C., 3120
Bowles, Sally, 1109
Bowling, Barbara Williams, 2518
Bowling, Dan, 2351
Bowlus, Brad, 971
Bowman Family Foundation, 7262
Bowman, George A., 4158
Bowman, Jerry L., 572
Bowman, Joane Lappe, 8094
Bowman, John W., 8271
Bowman, Jon, 9599
Bowman, Lawrence, 312
Bowman, Linda, 3188
Bowman, Margaret, 2498
Bowman, Marianne H., 2409
Bowman, Max S., 4749
Bowman, Robert T., 7582
Bowman, Roberta B., 7319, 7360
Bowman, Roberta D., 1640
Bowmer, Jim D., 9033
Bowne & Co., Inc., 5655
Bowne, Garrett D., 3540
Bowser, Nancy S., 5145
Bowser, Shirley D., 4357
Box, Charles E., 2812
Box, Judith C. Kellar, 9449
Box, Nathan, 9449
Boxell, John F., 8692
Boxer, Leonard, 5656
Boxer, Steven E., 5656
Boxwell, Nancy L., 544
Boxx, Dennis, 3682
Boxx, Linda McKenna, 8337
Boxx, T. William, 8337, 8338
Boyar, Anthony, 478

Boyce, Ann Allston, 3709
Boyce, Donna J., 3540
Boyce, Doreen E., 8124
Boyce, James A., 1031
Boyce, Paula, 2551
Boyce, Phillip R., 1256
Boyd, Brian F., 9586, 9681
Boyd, Bruce, 7584
Boyd, Celeste, 1178
Boyd, David E., 2339
Boyd, Dennis W., 7517
Boyd, Fred, 5028
Boyd, John F., 2563
Boyd, John W., 670
Boyd, Louis J., 5610, 6017
Boyd, Mall, 9571
Boyd, Martha Lee, 8462
Boyd, Mary S., 2416
Boyd, Michael, 8462
Boyd, Mike, 9165
Boyd, Morton, 3421
Boyd, Pierce, 27
Boyd, Ralph F., Jr., 9422
Boyd, Sam A., 5023
Boyd, Samuel J., 5023
Boyd, Sara Russell, 4994
Boyd, Sheila, 5454
Boyd, W. Glen, 8000
Boyd, Willard L., 3274
Boyd, William, 349
Boyd, William R., 5023
Boyd, William S., 5023
Boyden, Brian, 3019
Boye, Nancy R., 5140
Boye, Robert B., 5140
Boye, Robert R., 5140
Boye, William D., 5140
Boye, William E., Jr., 5140
Boyer, Daniel B., III, 8103
Boyer, Herbert M., 563
Boyer, Herbert W., 313
Boyer, John Scott, 5378
Boyer, Joyce, 1991
Boyer, Margaret G., 247
Boyer, Marigrace, 313
Boyer, Peter S., 247
Boyer, Phoebe, 7139
Boyer, Ted, 5357
Boyer, Verdi S., 843
Boyes, Tina, 7526
Boyett, Michael, 417
Boyette, Christopher J., 2367
Boyle, B. Snowden, Jr., 2277
Boyle, Beverly, 1542
Boyle, Gertrude, 8034
Boyle, Jim, 4026
Boyle, John, 3737
Boyle, Kevin, 5194
Boyle, Kim M., 3503
Boyle, Robert D., 5146
Boyle, Stephen J., 3558
Boyle, Suzanne R., 3084
Boylen, Elaine, 5155
Boylin, Jane H., 3420
Boymel, Rachel, 7553
Boymel, Samuel, 7553
Boymel, Steven, 7553
Boynton, Adrianne K., 1639
Boynton, Cynthia Binger, 4617
Boynton, Paul G., 2189
Boysen, Thomas C., 898
Boyum, Kelley P., 7514
Bozarth, Glenn, 218
Bozman, Ellen, 3684
Bozman, Ellen M., 9371
Bozorth, Louise M., 6917
Bozym, Michael, 4252
Bozzone, Robert P., 8114, 8386
BP Alaska, 80
BP America Inc., 2628
BP Amoco Corp., 2628
BP Corp., 4657
BP Corp. North America Inc., 2628
Brace, Frederic F., 3044

Brace, Jack E., 7559
Brach, Helen, 2630
Brach, Zigmond, 5657
Brachfeld, Jonas, 8197
Brachfeld, Joseph, 5936
Brachfeld, Rosalind, 8197
Brack, Gabriel, 5843
Brack, Robert B., 3869
Bracken, Frank, 8929
Bracken, Frank A., 3104
Bracken, Richard M., 8690
Bracken, S. Terry, 8939
Bracken, William M., 3103
Brackenridge, George W., 8793
Bradberry, Edwin G., 159
Bradberry, John G., 159
Bradberry, Karlee, 159
Bradberry, Robert W., 159
Bradberry, William B., 159
Bradbury, Elizabeth, 4897
Bradbury, Elizabeth Woods, 4928
Braddock, Brad S., 8581
Brademas, John, 7185
Bradford Exchange, Ltd., 2867
Bradford, Cedric, 20
Bradford, Dana, 4946
Bradford, David T., 2742
Bradford, Elaine, 5349
Bradford, Elisa, 1603
Bradford, Gary W., 7339
Bradford, Pamela, 8050
Bradford, Robert P., 3278
Bradford, Sharon H., 1323
Bradley Foundation, Lynde and Harry, Inc., The, 1841, 6030
Bradley Trust, Mark S., 3814
Bradley, Betsy, 2806
Bradley, Bill, 5029
Bradley, Caroline D., 9763
Bradley, Daniel, 2323
Bradley, David A., 2806
Bradley, David G., 1783
Bradley, Ed, 5821
Bradley, Eddie, 8758
Bradley, Ernestine Schlant, 5199
Bradley, Gini, 1463
Bradley, H. Elizabeth, 8396
Bradley, Harry L., 9763
Bradley, James, 8617
Bradley, Jane C., 3824
Bradley, John F., 1188
Bradley, John J., 3861
Bradley, Joseph S., 5029
Bradley, Katherine B., 1783
Bradley, Kathryn, 3317
Bradley, Margaret B., 9763
Bradley, R. Bruce, 9455
Bradley, Robert, 891
Bradley, W.C., 2326
Bradley, W.R., 315, 891
Bradley, William O., 5029
Bradner, J. Lawrence, 2482
Bradshaw, Betty, 2713
Bradshaw, James H., 4519
Bradshaw, Robert W., Jr., 8576
Bradshaw, Wilson G., 4524, 4671
Bradt, David M., Jr., 1785
Bradt, Samuel E., 9857
Brady, Benjamin F., 2327
Brady, James C., 5141
Brady, Katherine D., 3605
Brady, Larry, 9697
Brady, Louise F., 7343
Brady, Nelvia M., 2957
Brady, Nicholas, 5141
Brady, Nicholas F., 3605
Brady, Terry, 1468
Brady, W. Thomas, 2579
Brady, William P., 8362
Brady, William Thomas, 2579
Braem, Barbara, 4210
Braestrup, Angel, 1837
Braestrup, Angelica, 6634
Braffett, Fid, 1471

Brager, Nancy, 5011
Bragg, Caprice H., 7576
Brailsford, Carolyn E., 8577
Brain, David L., 2328
Brain, Frances H., 2328
Brain, Nancy R., 2328
Brainerd, Judith B., 1502
Brainerd, Lyman B., Jr., 1502
Brainerd, Mary K., 4671
Brainerd, Paul, 9561
Brainerd, Richard P., 1502
Brainerd, Sherry, 9561
Brakens, Vicki, 5724
Braly, Angela, 1292
Braly, Angela F., 3101, 3102
Braman, Bill, 4331
Braman, D.H., Jr., 9095
Braman, Irma, 1915
Braman, Mary O'Connor, 9095
Braman, Norman, 1915
Bramante, Christina, 3823
Bramble, Forrest F., Jr., 3694
Brame, Scott, 3470
Bramlett, Robert, 7962
Bramlett, Robert M., 7932
Bramsen, Elizabeth C., 2780
Branch, Anita, 8794
Branch, C.B., 8794
Branch, George, 2495
Branch, J. Read, 9381
Branch, J. Read, Jr., 9381
Branch, Janet D., 1969
Branch, Jeffrey P., 5496
Branch, Patteson, Jr., 9381
Branch, Stephanie J., 4991
Branches Charitable Annuity Trust, 8623
Brand, John, III, 5784
Brand, Lipot, 5658
Brand, Rachel, 5658
Brand, S. Richard, 8130
Brandeis, E. John, 4944
Branden, Cris V., 2068
Branden, Gary R., 8038
Brandenborg, John, 4522
Brandenborg, Laurie Douglass, 4522
Brandenburg, Diane M., 316
Brandenburg, Eric L., 316
Brandenburg, Julius, 1890
Brandenburg, Karen, 316
Brandenburg, Lee H., 316
Brandenburg, R.N., 9594
Brandenburg, William L., 316
Brandenburger, Stephen A., 1080
Brandes Investment Partners, 7526
Brandes, Charles, 317
Brandes, Linda, 317
Brandes, Roxanne, 4990
Brandford, Napoleon, III, 347
Brandman, Etta, 6145
Brandon, Edward B., 7829
Brandrup, Douglas W., 1487
Brandt, Diane Carol, 6415
Brandt, Don K., 2565
Brandt, E.N., 4322
Brandt, John, 5198
Brandt, John H., 2565
Brandt, Richard B., 9435, 9442
Brandt, Steve, 8583
Brandwein, Milton, 1355
Brandwein, Steve, 4628
Brane, Marcela, 1776
Branfman, Alan R., 5142
Branfman, Alan R., Mrs., 5142
Branfman, Joyce, 5142
Brannon, Bobby C., 3461
Brannon, Greer, 2435
Brannon, Milton W., 2435
Brannon, Timothy H., 2189
Bransfield, John R., Jr., 6859
Bransford, John D., 359
Branson, Tracy, 957
Brant, Karen A., 4347
Brantley, Overtis Hicks, 172
Brantley, Rena, 663

Brantley, Thomas M., 7310
Brants, Harry M., 9172
Brasel, Susan S., 4913
Brass, Lawrence, M.D., 1529
Braswell, Alison Garrott, 8638
Braswell, Flecia, 1924
Braswell, James R., 7323
Brataas, Nancy, 4624
Bratcher, Joe W., III, 9013
Brattle Co. Corp., The, 4128
Bratton, Teresa, 3012
Brauer, Camilla, 4787
Brauer, Keith E., 3159
Brauer, Rhonda L., 6620
Brauer, Stephen F., 4787
Braufman, Jill E., 5660
Braught, Barbara, 7956
Brauman, John I., 5886
Braun, Andrew G., 3993
Braun, Barbara, 6612
Braun, David, 318
Braun, Henry A., 7041
Braun, Hugo E., Jr., 4483
Braun, Janis L., 6777
Braun, Jim, 3127
Braun, Mary C., 1725
Braun, Mary Connolly, 1687
Braun, Mary Lynne, 9573
Brauner, David, 5690
Brauner, David A., 6053
Braunschweig, Ridge A., 9766
Braunstein, Meryl L. Mandell, 1595
Braunstein, Richard, 7596
Braunstein, Richard L., 6023
Braverman, Philip, 5132
Bravmann, Carol, 5661
Bravmann, Lotte, 5661
Bravmann, Ludwig, 5661
Brawley, Wendy C., 8577
Brawner, Kent, 939
Braxton, Deborah, 2922
Braxton, Mildred M., 7349
Bray, Benny, 407
Bray, Richard S., Hon., 9376
Bray, Thomas J., 4291
Brazelton, Lewis E., 8944
Brazley, Carl, 3414
Brean, JoEllen, 495
Brebaugh, Bill, 148
Brechbuhler, Stan, 7533
Brecher, Benjamin, 6914
Brecher, Howard A., 5624
Brecher, Shraga, 7066
Breck, Henry R., 5691
Breckenridge, Nancy Reding, 4890
Breckenridge, Yvette, 3124
Breckinridge, Isabella G., 3684
Brecount, Margaret W., 7561
Brede, Helen, 2215
Brede, J. Daniel, 2215
Bredin, Octavia DuPont, 1737
Bredin-Bell, Alletta DuPont, 1737
Breece, Margaret C., 9731
Breed, William C., III, 7155
Breeden, Annabelle T., 7324
Breeden, Douglas T., 7324
Breeden, Josie C., 7324
Breeden, Russell, III, 7324
Breeden, Steven K., 3595
Breeding, Timothy, 3127
Breedlove, John P., 4695
Breene, William E., Hon., 8380
Bregar, H.H., 2844
Bregar, Hymen, 2625
Bregger, Ray, 4237
Brehm, Lyle, 5417
Breidinger, Dave, 8152
Breier, Robert G., 2121
Breit, Catherine, 2999
Breitenbach, Thomas G., 7603, 7875
Breitmeyer, Julie F., 3493
Breitstone, Stephan M., 5681
Breitweiser, Sheila S., 8569
Breivogel, Donald R., Jr., 3098

Bremekamp, Theodore H., III, 3714
Bremer Bank, N.A., 7514
Bremer Foundation, The, 4637
Bremer, Otto, 4523
Bremer, Paul C., 2197
Bren, Donald L., 320
Brenan, Michael R., 8577
Brenden, Blythe, 4611
Brenden, John, 4611
Brendle, Marie, 7354
Brenengen, Robert, 3730
Brenizer, Bruce, 9476
Brennan, A. Francis, 3414
Brennan, Ann, 7554
Brennan, B. Lawrence, 304
Brennan, David L., 7554
Brennan, David L., Mrs., 7554
Brennan, George G., 5112
Brennan, Hilary K., 2680
Brennan, James C., 8342
Brennan, Janice, 5303
Brennan, John D., 257
Brennan, John J., 8490
Brennan, M. Lynn, 4139
Brennan, Mary B., 6142
Brennan, Michael, 3247
Brennan, Mike, 9977
Brennan, Murray, 9408
Brennan, Nancy, 7554
Brennan, Patrick, 9779
Brennan, Paul F., 8093
Brennan, Sybil Ann, 5974
Brennan, Thomas A., 7574
Brennan, Troyen A., 1479, 6103
Brenneman, Douglas O., Sr., 7583
Brenner, Charles S., 6124
Brenner, Edgar H., 6124
Brenner, James, 9651
Brenner, Mervyn L., 321
Brenner, Newton D., 1682
Brenner, Paul R., 1506, 5363
Brenner, Susan, 6917
Brennock, Erin, 1222, 1223
Brenny, Bonita, 4536
Brensinger, Barry L., 5098
Brent, Robert E., 2680
Breon, Nicki, 8608
Breon, Willard S., 7593
Bresee, Patricia, 989
Breskin, David, 3006
Breskin, Julie, 3006
Breslau, Carol, 1356
Breslauer, Benjamin F., 1179
Breslauer, Gerald, 1050, 1322
Bresler, Shirley B., 7176
Breslin, Cindy, 6746
Breslin, Hugh J., III, 3600
Bresnahan, Ann W., 1761
Bresnahan, William J., 7585
Bressler, Alan S., 3815
Bressler, Daryl, 3815
Bressler, Karen S., 3815
Bressler, Lorraine D., 3815
Bressler-Starn, Nancy, 3815
Brest, Paul, 671
Bresten, Theresa, 3957
Bretelle, Jean Francis, 5623
Brett, Emily Shoemaker, 1349
Brett, Jay, 2240
Brett, Matthew Stephen, 1349
Brett, Stephen M., 1349
Brett, Steve, 1358
Brett, Thomas R., 7954
Brettbard, Robert, 337
Bretzlaff, Hilda E., 4238
Brew, Emily, 8046
Brewbaker, Carol, 76
Brewer, Charles H., 2685
Brewer, Flora P., 9112
Brewer, Janet J., 7773
Brewer, Mark, 1942
Brewer, Michael F., 2820
Brewer, R. Denver, 2632
Brewer, Robert N., 2632

Brewer, Sebert, Jr., 8644
Brewer, Sharon, 402
Brewer, William A., III, 8790
Brewer, William H., 2685
Brewers Association of Canada, 3564
Brewster, Benjamin, 9537
Brewster, Helen, 1648
Breznay, Deborah B., 6967
Brian, Sherry, 8608
Brice, Deborah L., 5662
Bricker, John F., 3464
Bricker, Nina B., 3464
Brickman, John M., 6409
Brickman, Sally, 8116
Brickman, Scott W., 8116
Brickman, Steven G., 8116
Brickman, Theodore, 8116
Brickner, Rebecca Scripps, 7848
Brickson, Richard A., 7738
Bridgeland, James R., Jr., 7851
Bridges, Dorothy, 4636
Bridges, Dorothy J., 4623
Bridges, Kenneth, 7959
Bridges, Ronnie L., 2450
Bridges, Susan A., 8609
Bridges, Wilbur Y., 7382, 7476
Bridges, William A., 7382
Bridgestone/Firestone, Inc., 8646
Bridgeway Capital Management, Inc., 8796
Bridgeway Charitable Foundation, 1426
Bridgforth, Allen, 4739
Bridgman, John, 9130
Bridwell, J.S., 8797
Bridwell, Ralph S., 8797
Bridwell, Tucker S., 9106, 9226
Briedis, Irene Sedgwick, 7849
Brien, Ronald F., 8381
Briere, Betsy L., 4228
Briganti, Stephen, 5874
Briger, Peter L., Jr., 5663
Briggs & Stratton Corp., 9765
Briggs Residuary Trust, Thomas W., 8647
Briggs, David M., 7897
Briggs, Deborah Plutzik, 6066
Briggs, Eleanor, 4577
Briggs, Jason, 1068
Briggs, Jessica, 8098
Briggs, June C., 7040
Briggs, Kathleen, 204
Briggs, Margaret, 8117
Briggs, Robert G., 4666
Briggs, Robert W., 2097, 7643
Briggs, Stephen Michael, 8975
Briggs, Susan S., 521
Brigham, L.G., 624
Brigham, Paul L., 3940
Bright, Ashley S., 3475
Bright, Calvin E., 322
Bright, Christopher R., 8818
Bright, Clay V.N., 8818
Bright, H. Dale, 3269
Bright, James R., 7881
Bright, Lois L., 3269
Bright, Mary, 8842
Brightbill, L.O., III, 8841
Brighton, Cynthia Z., 1683
Brighton, W. Curtis, 3173
Brighton-Best Socket Screw Manufacturing, Inc., 5362
Briglia, Beth Harper, 8141
Brignola, Paul J., 6156
Brill, David, 7803
Brill, Deborah, 1265
Brill, Lisa, 2441
Brill, Lisa S., 2329
Brill, Pamela, Ed.D., 7103
Brill, Ronald M., 2329
Brill, Steve, 7803
Brilliant, Larry, 606
Brin, Sergey, 606
Brinberg, Simeon, 6833

Brind, Ira, 8157
Brine, Kevin R., 5665
Brine, Madeline, 5665
Brining, Linda, 1426
Brining, Robert, 1426
Brink, Melinda, 4325
Brinkman, Robert J., 5833
Brinkman, Sue, 343
Brinkmoeller, George, 3230
Brinks, Dawn, 4280
Brinks, Kurt, 4280
Brinn, Mildred C., 6366
Brinn, Raymond C., 9857
Brinson, Gary P., 2633
Brinson, Monique, 2633
Brinson, Suzann Boaz, 2633
Brinton, Demaris, 407
Brinton, S. Jervis, Jr., 5368
Brisbane, Art, 768
Briscoe, D. Daniel, 7486
Briskin, Andrew, 4429
Briskin, Barry D., 4429
Briskin, Edith S., 4429
Briskin, Susannah M., 4429
Bristol County Savings Bank, 3816
Bristol Door and Lumber Co., Inc., 1932
Bristol West, 930
Bristol, Brian T., 8118
Bristol, Edith W., 8118
Bristol, James D., 8118
Bristol, Michal W., 8118
Bristol, Pamela W., 8118
Bristol, Susannah B., 8118
Bristol-Myers Squibb Co., 5143, 5666
Bristol-Myers Squibb Pharmaceutical
    Research Institute, The, 3677
Bristow, Peter, 8587
British Embassy, 7040
Britt, Deirdre H., 9749
Britt, Stacie, 2356
Brittain, Randolph W., 2717
Britton, Bob, 3107
Britton, Brigham, 7556
Britton, Charles S., II, 7556
Britton, Gertrude H., 7556
Britton, Lynda R., 7556
Britton, Terence B., 7556
Britton, Timothy C., 7556
Broach, James, 3677
Broad, Edythe L., 323, 324
Broad, Eli, 323, 324
Broad, Morris N., 1916
Broad, Ruth K., 1916
Broad, Shepard, 1916
Broadbent, Robert R., 7769
Broaddus, William G., 9435
Broadfoot, John W., 9049
Broadhead, Elaine, 2970
Broadhurst, Anna, 6820
Broadhurst, James, 8386
Broadrick, George H., 7438
Broadway Cares, 3164
Broadway National Bank, 8834, 9011,
    9166, 9281
Brobeck, David, 7831
Broccoli, Albert R., 326
Broccoli, Barbara, 326
Broccoli, Christina, 326
Broccoli, Dana, 326
Brocher, Karen, 1223
Brock, Frank A., 8686, 8704
Brock, G. Porter, Jr., 25
Brock, Harry B., III, 16
Brock, Harry B., Jr., 16
Brock, Jane H., 16
Brock, Jean Ann, 9205
Brock, Kimberly Grady, 1944
Brock, M.H., 8974
Brock, Macon F., 9532
Brock, Nathaniel, 8219
Brock, Paul K., Jr., 8644
Brock, Stanley M., 16
Brock, Steve, 9205
Brockman, Carla D., 7965

Brockman, Jay C., 9453
Brockmann, Shirley, 9693
Brockmeyer, Alison J., 8468
Brockton Wholesale Beverage Co., Inc.,
    4116
Brockway, Jerry, 7534
Brockway, Larry T., 8488
Brode, George, 7890
Broder, Alan J., 1781
Broder, Lois, 5138
Brodersen, Ellen H., 1265, 9400
Brodeur, Susan W., 2299
Brodhead, Richard H., 5707
Brodhead, William M., 4438
Brodie, Barbara, 3074
Brodie, Bertram Z., 2629
Brodie, Brenda B., 1707
Brodie, Bryson B., 1707
Brodie, Cameron K., 1707
Brodie, Donald, 3074
Brodie, Douglas, 6639
Brodie, E.H., 1707
Brodie, H. Keith H., 1707
Brodie, Kent, 3074
Brodie, L.S., 1707
Brodie, Mollyann, 739
Brodie, Tyler H., 1707
Brodnax, Paula, 3509
Brodsky, Barbara, 8310
Brodsky, Bert, 5667
Brodsky, Daniel, 5668, 5669, 6780
Brodsky, David, 5667
Brodsky, Estrellita, 5669
Brodsky, Jeffrey, 5667
Brodsky, Julian, 8152
Brodsky, Katherine, 5668
Brodsky, Lee, 5667
Brodsky, Nathan, 5668
Brodsky, Shirley, 5668
Brodsky, William H., 4941
Brodsley, William, 1121
Brody, Arthur, 5144
Brody, Bernard B., 9424
Brody, Carolyn, 1777
Brody, Christopher, 6379
Brody, Daniel M., 9390
Brody, David S., 7325, 7438
Brody, Donald, 5144
Brody, Hyman J., 7325
Brody, J.S., 7325
Brody, Janice, 5144
Brody, Jay Howard, 4456
Brody, Kenneth D., 1777
Brody, Laura C., 7325
Brody, Leo, 7325
Brody, Sophie, 5144
Brody, Stacy C., 7325
Brody, William R., 3568, 3636, 5779
Broek, Doreen, 1197
Broetje Orchards, 9699
Broetje, Cheryl, 9699
Broetje, Ralph, 9699
Broetje, Sara, 9699
Broetje, Suzanne, 9699
Brogan, Francis B., Jr., 2143
Brogan, Frank, 2181
Brogan, Robert H., 9848
Brogna, Christopher, 6894
Broidy, Steven D., 1288
Broin, Kenneth, 4707
Brokaw, Norman, 6380
Brokaw, Thomas C.T., 1737
Brokaw, Thomas J., 5670
Broker, Gerald, 8119
Broker, William K., 2479
Broman, Susan, 4446
Bromley, John R., 4228
Bromley, S. Stewart, 2480
Bron Family Fund, William, 6609
Bron Industries, 6609
Bronfman Foundation, S., Inc., 4071
Bronfman, Adam R., 5672
Bronfman, Andrea M., 5673
Bronfman, Ann L., 1917

Bronfman, Charles R., 4071, 5671,
    5673
Bronfman, Clare W., 5672
Bronfman, Edgar M., 4071, 5672
Bronfman, Edgar M., Jr., 5672
Bronfman, Jeffrey, 8767
Bronfman, Matthew, 5672
Bronfman, Samuel, II, 5672
Bronfman, Sara R., 5672
Bronner, Jim, 1477
Bronson, Edgerton, 4583
Bronson, Robert, 8060
Bronstein, Jean, 6260
Bronstein, Richard J., 1525
Bronstein, Solomon, 8119
Bronzi, Marilyn, 3539
Bronzi, Marilyn T., 3554
Brooke, Dell S., 65
Brooking, Gladys T., 9240
Brooklawn Gardens, Inc., 5394
Brooklyn Queens Nursing Home, 7125
Brooks Bank Fund, 1516
Brooks, Balbi A., 2533
Brooks, Barbara, 327
Brooks, Bernard E., 8569
Brooks, Cali, 5517
Brooks, Clifford, 9873
Brooks, Conley, 4612
Brooks, Conley, Jr., 4612
Brooks, Dale G., 9800, 9940
Brooks, Donna, 9690
Brooks, Edward, 4612
Brooks, Eric, 8470
Brooks, Esther Cohen, 6367
Brooks, Gillian R., 3533
Brooks, Harold, 8520
Brooks, Harry W., Jr., Genl., 9424
Brooks, Helen M., 2297
Brooks, Henry G., 3546
Brooks, Hilda, 5902
Brooks, John, 327
Brooks, John G., 4038
Brooks, John H., 1516
Brooks, Kathleen Swann, 1986
Brooks, Larry J., 2635
Brooks, Loel P., 4987
Brooks, Markell C., 4612, 4724
Brooks, Nancy, 9248
Brooks, Paula J., 734
Brooks, Robert A., 98
Brooks, Roger K., 3281
Brooks, Stephen B., 4612
Brooks, Suzanne S., 9495
Brooks, Theodore L., Sr., 1514
Brooks, William Mathews, 327
Brooksbank, Kaye D., 8670
Brookshire, Michelle, 8876
Broom, Charles, 1008
Broome, John, 1318
Brophy, J. Ernest, 6482
Brophy, Tom, 9748
Brorsen, Jennifer L., 5851
Brosnahan, Jan, 4729
Brosnan, Joseph S., 6219
Brosnan, Tim, 8747
Brossman Charitable Foundation,
    William and Jemima, 8121
Brosterhous, Patricia, 2084
Brostowitz, James M., 9812
Brotchi, Jacques, Sir., 5973
Brothers, Laura, 4452
Brothers, M. Elizabeth, 7010
Brotherton, Dorothy R., 9503
Brotherton, Fred J., 5145
Brotherton, Glen, 5145
Brotherton, Wayne A., 5145
Brotherton, William P., 5145
Brotman, Jeffrey H., 9562
Brotman, Susan T., 9562
Brotman, Toni, 328
Brott, Steven R., 4554
Brotz, Adam T., 9767
Brotz, Ralph R., 9767
Brotz, Stuart W., 9767

Brougher, Charley, 7866
Brougher, Nancy, 8122
Brougher, W. Dale, 8122
Broughton Charitable Remainder
    Unitrust, William, 5675
Broughton, Carl L., 7735
Broussard, Jerome T., 7557
Brouwer Family Ltd., 1197
Brouwer, Chris, 1197
Brouwer, Garrett, 1197
Brouwer, Jack, 1197
Brouwer, Jacob, 1197
Brouwer, Jeanette, 1197
Brouwer, Richard, 1197
Browder, J. Bond, 9085
Browder, R.J., 74
Brower, Robert D., 4261
Brown & Root, Inc., 8935
Brown & Sons Inc., Alex., 3578
Brown Brothers Harriman Trust Co.,
    5700, 6613, 6622
Brown Charitable Lead Trust, Robert J.,
    4396
Brown Group, Inc., 4789
Brown Shoe Inc., 4789
Brown, Albertine M., 4396
Brown, Alice Cary, 3411
Brown, Alice Pratt, 8799
Brown, Alvin I., 3579
Brown, Andrew, 2811
Brown, Ann Noble, 7963
Brown, Anne Johnson Cole, 3549
Brown, Arthur, 7449
Brown, Barbara, 2811, 7684
Brown, Barbara J., 4213
Brown, Bernard H., Jr., 6639
Brown, Bertram S., 8193
Brown, Beth Goldsmith, Jr., 8682
Brown, Betty M., 8662
Brown, Bill, 7593
Brown, Bob, 183
Brown, Bradley V., 2701
Brown, Brent, 9021
Brown, Brooke Lee, 3408
Brown, Bruce, 3855
Brown, Bruce M., 8444
Brown, C. Foster, III, 2896
Brown, C. Kim, 8511
Brown, C. Roger, 2681
Brown, Carol Anne Smullin, 1169
Brown, Carol R., 8241
Brown, Carolyn Thompson, 4297
Brown, Charles S., Mr., 2579
Brown, Charles S., Mrs., 2579
Brown, Chester H. "Trip", Jr., 7343
Brown, Chris, 4289
Brown, Christina Lee, 3408
Brown, Christine James, 8371
Brown, Christopher, 223
Brown, Chuck, 7160
Brown, Clare M., 1264
Brown, Craig C., 4213
Brown, Crichton W., 3475
Brown, Cynthia Marvell, 6287
Brown, D., 1921
Brown, D. Randolph, Jr., 7963
Brown, D. Warren, 2332
Brown, Dana, 4788
Brown, David, 6028
Brown, David A., 3196
Brown, Deborah M., 4941
Brown, Denise Hall, 3598
Brown, Diane L., 5781
Brown, Diane Solomon, 3594
Brown, Diane Solomon, Dr., 3594
Brown, Donald, 7000
Brown, Donald D., 3677
Brown, Dorothy Dorsett, 3465
Brown, Dorothy S., 4239
Brown, Douglas M., 5466
Brown, Douglas W., 2332
Brown, Drew M., 98
Brown, Dwaine, 9268
Brown, Dwyer, 9997

Brown, Elizabeth, 5888
Brown, Elizabeth A., 1335
Brown, Elizabeth Byron, 3070
Brown, Elizabeth M., Mrs., 8639
Brown, Elizabeth M., Ms., 8639
Brown, Eric, 4270
Brown, Eric A., 4588
Brown, Estelle, 2935
Brown, Faith, 9361
Brown, Forrest C., 2104
Brown, Frances A., 2353
Brown, Frances Carroll, 9464
Brown, Francis K., II, 3795
Brown, Fred L., 3141
Brown, Frederick O., 4396
Brown, Frederick S., 5494
Brown, Gail Feiger, 2811
Brown, George R., 8799
Brown, George W., 1265
Brown, Gloria, 989
Brown, Gregg W., 7280
Brown, H.L., Jr., 9197
Brown, Hank, 1362
Brown, Harmon, 1465, 2922
Brown, Harold, 861
Brown, Harold A., 544
Brown, Helene K., 9997
Brown, Henry, 2811
Brown, Herman, 8799
Brown, Hermione K., 544
Brown, Hillary, 6918
Brown, Himan, 6765
Brown, Howard J., 9833
Brown, Howard S., 3603
Brown, Hugh M., 2077
Brown, J. Graham, 3409
Brown, James, 3333, 9525, 9693
Brown, James E., 2359
Brown, James K., 9714
Brown, James Keith, 7215
Brown, James M., 357
Brown, James W., Jr., 60
Brown, Jane, 3616
Brown, Janet, 3798
Brown, Janice J., 2332
Brown, Jeanette Grasselli, 7688
Brown, Jeffrey N., 3166
Brown, Jeffrey R., 2811
Brown, Jerry, 4986
Brown, Jess, 403
Brown, JoAnn Fitzpatrick, 3950
Brown, JoBeth G., 4776
Brown, Joe W., 3465
Brown, John, 670
Brown, John E., III, 189
Brown, John Seely, 2868
Brown, John W., 4240
Brown, Joi E., 9521
Brown, Joyce, 3130
Brown, Judith, 91
Brown, Julie, 4798
Brown, Julie A., 7559
Brown, Kathleen, 346
Brown, Kathryne L., 7326
Brown, Kay, 8758
Brown, Keith A., 7632, 7761
Brown, Kevin J., 7823
Brown, Kevin P., 2418
Brown, Kevin Smullin, 1169
Brown, Kim, 3387
Brown, Kiyoko O., 5868
Brown, Kristal, 8962
Brown, Laura Lee Lyons, 3451
Brown, Lauren, 2238
Brown, Lawrence R., Jr., 8428
Brown, Leelee D'Olier, 6391
Brown, Leslie, 9559
Brown, Linda, 1244, 1854, 9696
Brown, Linda W., 3677
Brown, Louis M., 2896
Brown, Louis M., Jr., 2896
Brown, Louise Ingalls, 7684
Brown, Lucia R., 6676
Brown, Lynora S., 1238

Brown, Malcolm McDougal, 3070
Brown, Margaret A., 6998
Brown, Margarett Root, 8799
Brown, Margarite, 432
Brown, Marilyn, 3844, 9265
Brown, Marion F., 9797
Brown, Martin S., 3410
Brown, Martin S., Jr., 8639
Brown, Martin S., Sr., 8639
Brown, Mary, 9748
Brown, Mary A., 7310
Brown, Mary B., 91
Brown, Mary M., 8938
Brown, Mary Rose, 9247
Brown, Mason A., 3711
Brown, Meghan Binger, 4617
Brown, Michael Gene, 2569
Brown, Michael L., 4212, 6583
Brown, Michael S., 3677
Brown, Michael W., 6379
Brown, Mickey, 2395
Brown, Minette, 3516
Brown, Monique, 9525
Brown, Monte, 9997
Brown, Montgomery B., 4291
Brown, Myron, 9213
Brown, Nancy Juckett, 6903
Brown, Nancy L., 6384
Brown, Nathaniel T., 9550
Brown, Neil A., 7628
Brown, Neil W., 4699
Brown, Norman, 4218, 4233
Brown, Owen, 2811
Brown, Owsley, II, 3408, 3410
Brown, Owsley, III, 3408
Brown, Patricia A., 286
Brown, Paul, 4057
Brown, Paul D., 2935
Brown, Pauline, 5583
Brown, Peggy S., 3579
Brown, Peter, 4820, 4829
Brown, Peter A., 3907
Brown, Peter D., 4239
Brown, Phyllis, 6423
Brown, Priscilla S., 3195
Brown, Prudence, 6409
Brown, R.D., 7751
Brown, R.K., 8452
Brown, Rachel, 134
Brown, Raymond L., 4745
Brown, Rexford G., 1377
Brown, Richard, 6423
Brown, Richard A., 6056, 9642
Brown, Richard H., 8877
Brown, Robert C., 1257, 7367
Brown, Robert J., 4396, 7397
Brown, Robert M., 4396
Brown, Robert M., Jr., 4396
Brown, Robert S., 1391
Brown, Robert W., 8816, 8841
Brown, Robin D., 5676
Brown, Roger O., 2811
Brown, Roscoe, 7157
Brown, Rosemary K., 4240
Brown, Russell, 3375
Brown, Ryan, 1445
Brown, Sara S., 3410, 8639
Brown, Sara Shallenberger, 3411
Brown, Sharon Shiroma, 2542
Brown, Sheri, 1941
Brown, Sherri, 318
Brown, Simpson "Skip" O., Jr., 7508
Brown, Sis, 2359
Brown, Solange Pezon, 3070
Brown, Stephen L., 7003
Brown, Steven, 6083
Brown, Stuart, 3594
Brown, Stuart R., 3411
Brown, Susan, 7963
Brown, Susanne B., 5466
Brown, Suzi, 220
Brown, T.J., 8798
Brown, Terri Hamilton, 7576
Brown, Theodore L., 272

Brown, Thomas, 9525
Brown, Thomas H., 8937
Brown, Thomas W., Jr., 2509
Brown, Tom Watson, 2509
Brown, Virginia S., 4803
Brown, W. Hill, III, 9513
Brown, W.L. Lyons, 3410
Brown, W.L. Lyons, Jr., 3411
Brown, W.L. Lyons, Mrs., 3408, 3410, 3411
Brown, Walter J., 2509
Brown, Walter R., 5868
Brown, Wendy, 1090
Brown, Willard W., Jr., 7684
Brown, William, 7743
Brown, William Gardner, 3070
Brown, William Hill, III, 9417
Brown, William W., 8573, 8574
Brown, Willie, 3019
Brown-Gort, Albert, 3131
Brown-Springer, Geraldine, 1515
Browne, Bill, 4309
Browne, Caroline Cooley, 8010
Browne, Caroline Muir, 2402
Browne, Christopher H., 6728
Browne, Chuck, 627
Browne, David, 8010
Browne, G. Morgan, 6670
Browne, Matthew T., 7031
Browne, Raymond J., 18
Browne, Rodney M., 2468
Brownell, Bob, 8015
Brownell, Frank R., III, 3270
Brownfield, Edward H., Jr., 9390
Brownfield, Roberta F., 9495
Browning, Barbara K., 4933
Browning, Brent, 26
Browning, Bruce W., 9308
Browning, Dorothy W., 7811
Browning, Jay D., 9247
Browning, John A., 9308
Browning, Jr. Charitable Lead Unitrust, L.L., 7811
Browning, Matt S., 4933
Browning, Nicholas V., 7858
Browning, Suzie, 4753
Browning, Val A., 9308
Brownlee, Robert G., 329
Brownlie, E.C., 1982
Brownson, John, 4534
Brownstein, Christine, 2871
Broyhill Furniture Industries, Inc., 7328
Broyhill, James E., 7328
Broyhill, M. Hunt, 7328
Broyhill, Paul H., 7328
Broyles, Thomas C., 9532
Brozik, Patricia, 7585
Brozowski, Catherine, 1093
Brubaker, Grace M., 653
Brubaker, Nancy, 4668
Bruce Living Trust, Julia, 2634
Bruce, Ailsa Mellon, 6525
Bruce, Betty, 9735
Bruce, Carl, 2634
Bruce, Carole W., 7329, 7337
Bruce, Charles M., 1855
Bruce, Donald, 6032
Bruce, James McDuffie, III, 7407
Bruce, Jean C., 9541
Bruce, John L., 8571
Bruce, Julia H., 2634
Bruce, Julia Harrison, 2790
Bruce, Mamie J., 7407
Bruce, Peter W., 9876
Bruch, Ron, 4919
Brucia, Charles J., 6323
Brucia, Frank, 931
Bruckner, Ben, 8758
Bruckner, Sandra, 725
Bruder-Stiftung, 5568
Brudin, Carole S., 9366
Brueggemann, Bernard, 3406
Brueggemann, James, 3406
Brueggemann, John, 3406

Brueggemann, W. George, 3227
Bruen, Arthur J., Jr., 3073
Bruen, William, Jr., 4766
Bruening, Eva L., 7558
Bruening, Joseph H., 7074
Bruening, Joseph M., 7558
Bruer, John T., 4864
Bruett, William, 5148
Bruhn, Heidi S., 9732
Brumback, D.L., III, 7891
Brumbaum, Ava Jean, 482
Brumfield, Bruce A., 8611
Brumit, Janice W., 7346
Brumley, Amy, 8294
Brumley, George W., Jr., 2529
Brumley, Jean S., 2529
Brumley, Nancy J., 2529
Brumm, James E., 6560
Brummage, Esther C., 9992
Brummett, Paul E., II, 3520
Brummund, Carolyn, 4253
Brunckhorst, Barbara, 5678
Brunckhorst, Frank, III, 5678
Brundage, Barbara, 5087
Brune, A.J., III, 9117
Brunecz, Michael, 6638
Bruner, James D., 130
Bruner, Jennifer A., 8650
Bruner, Joshua E., 3819
Bruner, Martha, 3819
Bruner, R. Simeon, 3819
Bruner, Rudy, 3819
Brunette, Harry E., Rev., 3595
Brunie, Charles H., 5679
Brunie, Jean I., 5679
Bruning, Charles, III, 2635
Bruning, Edwin C., 2635
Bruning, Herbert F., 2635
Bruning, John, 2635
Bruning, Kathleen, 2635
Bruning, Paul J., 2635
Brunken, Teresita L., 7078
Brunner, Alice, 4964
Brunner, George, 9780
Bruno, Barry A., 6743
Bruno, Barry A., 7428
Bruno, Carmela June, 6567
Bruno, Jennifer E., 7428
Bruno, John Paul, 344
Bruno, Marge, 828
Bruno, Mike, 828
Bruno, S. Joseph, 1778
Bruns, Peter J., 3654
Brunson, Jane, 26
Brunst, Robert, 801
Brunswick Corp., 2636
Brunswick, Edward B., 3466
Brunswick, Richard A., 3466
Brunt, Deborah, 5493
Brusati, Peter J., 559
Bruser, Lawrence, 6561
Bruski, Larry, 4253
Bruso, Eleanor, 5091
Brusseau, Carolyn J., 4519
Brutsch, Sheila Johnson, 5680
Bryan, Ann M., 7330
Bryan, C. Russell, 7317
Bryan, David, 3894
Bryan, James S., 8253
Bryan, John D., 2344
Bryan, John M., 311
Bryan, Joseph M., 7329
Bryan, Joseph M., Jr., 7306
Bryan, Marian H., 8931
Bryan, Martha, 2344
Bryan, Mary Lynn M., 7349
Bryan, R.A., III, 7330
Bryan, R.A., Jr., 7330
Bryan, Richard C., Jr., 5813
Bryan, Richard H., 5047
Bryan, Ruby M., 7330
Bryan, Sharon, 4098
Bryan, Sophie, 5894
Bryan, Stephen C., 7330

Bryan, Summer, 8649
Bryant, Andrea B., 9960
Bryant, Arthur H., II, 9380
Bryant, Arthur H., Jr., 9380
Bryant, Barton, 4373
Bryant, Candice C., 1804
Bryant, Diane B., 2328
Bryant, Doris B., 7490
Bryant, Douglas E., 8835
Bryant, Elaine M., 7349
Bryant, Elizabeth A., 1367
Bryant, Ernest A., III, 602
Bryant, J.C. Herbert, 9380
Bryant, John, Jr., 1770
Bryant, Magalen O., 6659
Bryant, N.W., 7987
Bryant, Nancy, 2267
Bryant, Ruth D., 6660
Bryant, Sam, 8768
Bryce, George, 9985
Bryce, Hugh G., 9898
Bryce, Linda, 10000
Bryd, Leverett S., 4037
Bryn Mawr Trust Co., The, 8378
Bryn, Mark J., 2132
Bryson, Jane T., 8064
Bryson, John E., 214, 346, 750
Bryson, Louise H., 570
Bryson, Nancy F., 1918
Bryson, Vaughn D., 1918
Bryson, William D., 1918
Brzezinski, Zbigniew, Hon., 1632
BT Capital Corp., 5854
Bubb, Hillary, 4231
Buccaneer L.P., 2024
Bucci, James, 7582
Bucey, David C., 2352
Buch, Joseph J., 9716
Buchalter, Lawrence R., 5228
Buchan, R.W., 5335
Buchanan, Carol P., 9399
Buchanan, Charlie, 9888
Buchanan, D.W., Jr., 2637
Buchanan, D.W., Sr., 2637
Buchanan, J. Robert, 7301
Buchanan, John, 9888
Buchanan, Julia G., 2760
Buchanan, Kenneth H., 2637
Buchanan, Leslie, 1981
Buchanan, Linda, 9441
Buchanan, Paul D., 9399
Buchanan, Sally Corning, 5496
Buchanan, Valda M., 7962
Buchanan, Vern, 1946
Buchanan, Virginia, 2110
Buchenroth, Marion, 9977
Bucher, Dan, 9736
Bucher, Haidee D., 8858
Bucher, Jeffrey M., 1009
Bucher, Robert L., II, 8858
Buchholzer, Bruce H., 7790
Buchler, Judith, 5202
Buchman, Joel, 6086
Buchmann, Josef, 5681
Bucholtz, Gary A., 2255, 2256
Bucholz, Frederick S., 5008, 5009
Bucholz, Kurt S., 5008, 5009
Bucholz, Laura S., 5008
Bucholz, Lori, 5009
Buck, Alexander K., Jr., 3541
Buck, Alexander K., Sr., 3541
Buck, Anne E., 3541
Buck, Carol Franc, 330, 5025
Buck, Christopher, 5682
Buck, David, 9563
Buck, Eva Benson, 330
Buck, Lyman A., III, 5738
Buck, Michael, 5682
Buck, Michelle A., 716
Buck, N. Harrison, 3541
Buck, Nancy B., 3541
Buck, Paul, 330
Buck, Sara L., 3541
Buck, Walter, 330

Buckhoy, Nikita, 2757
Buckingham, Cynthia B., 7356
Buckingham, William, 7533
Buckler, Robert J., 4289
Buckles, Jack E., 3128
Buckless, Shawn P., 4108
Buckley, Bruce, 8270
Buckley, Constance, 8382
Buckley, David P., Jr., 2871
Buckley, George W., 2636
Buckley, J.S., 5151
Buckley, Jean C., 3037
Buckley, Jerome M., 1356
Buckley, Jerry S., 5151
Buckley, Mark, 4156
Buckley, Michael F., 6823
Buckley, Paul R., 4556
Buckley, Robert, 5037, 7586
Buckley, Stephen, 2245
Buckley, Thomas D., 4947
Buckley, Tim, 8490
Buckley, Walter W., Jr., 8303
Buckley, William, 3968
Buckley, William F., 7756
Buckmaster, Raleigh D., 3313
Buckner, Elizabeth, 1695
Buckner, Helen W., 1695, 7220
Buckner, Jr. Revocable Trust, Charles
  M., 4790
Buckner, Kamala, 6722
Buckner, Linda, 8868
Buckner, Liz, 7220
Buckner, Thomas W., 1695, 6722
Buckner, Walker, 7220
Buckner, Walker G., Jr., 1695, 4176
Buckner, William Gordon, 4790
Bucksbaum, Carolyn, 3272
Bucksbaum, Jacolyn, 3272
Bucksbaum, John, 3272
Bucksbaum, Martin, 3271
Bucksbaum, Mary, 3271
Bucksbaum, Matthew, 3271, 3272
Bucksbaum, Maurice, 3271
Bucksbaum, Melva, 3271, 6054
Buckwalter, John M., 8459
Buda, J.B., 2653
Buder, G.A., IV, 4791
Buder, Kathryn M., 4791
Buder, Marshall O., 4791
Buder, Theodore A., 4791
Budinger, Donald V., 136
Budinger, Jean-Paul, 8951
Budinger, Susan, 87
Budinger, William D., 136
Budnick, Neil G., 6512
Bue, David, 4729
Buechele, Lester J., 4896
Buechner, Judith M., 4036
Buechner, Paul E., 321
Buechner, Thomas S., 5794
Buehler, Albert C., 2638
Buehler, Emil, 5146
Buehler, Patricia, 2638
Buehner, Robert W., Jr., 8135
Buel, Steve F., 111
Buell, Allan D., 9573
Buell, Bruce T., 1373, 1437, 9573
Buell, Jack A., 9665
Buell, Stephanie, 4986
Buell, Temple Hoyne, 1350
Buenger, Ann M., 7560
Buenger, Clement L., 7560
Buergenthal, Randi, 3597
Buerger, Bob, 7653
Buerk, Artie, 9599
Buescher, Rebecca, 93
Buesing, Gregory P., 5282
Buesing, Guy K., 5282
Buesing, Jean, 5282
Buettner, Alfred P., 4899
Buffalo News, Inc., 57
Buffalo, Henry M., Jr., 4671
Buffett Foundation, Susan A., 4948
Buffett, Devon G., 2639

Buffett, Doris B., 7490
Buffett, E., 2639
Buffett, Howard G., 2639
Buffett, Jennifer, 6641
Buffett, Jimmy, 4904
Buffett, Katherine, 3964
Buffett, Pamela, 2640
Buffett, Peter, 4948
Buffett, Peter A., 4950, 6641
Buffett, Sarah, 2640
Buffett, Susan, 4948
Buffett, Susan A., 4949, 4950
Buffett, Susan T., 2639, 4950
Buffett, Thomas M., 3964
Buffett, Warren E., 2639, 4949, 4950,
  6641, 9591
Buffett, Wendy O., 3964
Buffett, William N., 3964
Buffett-Kennedy, Noah E., 3964
Buffington, Peter, 7040
Buffkin, Buron, 2721
Buffmire, Donald K., 98
Buford Foundation, 9177
Buford, Jeff, 8876
Buford, Robert P., 9177
Bugdanowitz, Sheila R., 1445
Bugg, Christopher, 9947
Bugg, J. Bruce, Jr., 9235
Bugge, Mark, 4467
Bugher, Frederick McLean, 5683
Buhl, Henry M., 5684
Buhl, Henry, Jr., 8124
Buhl, Lawrence D., Jr., 4934
Buhler, Shelly, 3372
Buhler, Virginia M., 9906
Buhlman, Karla, 243
Bui, Andy, 373
Buice, Charles U., 7053
Buice, William T., III, 7053
Buie, Herbert, 8876
Builders, 3683
Building Owners & Mgrs. of O.C., 1248
Buisson, Beau T., 2333
Buisson, Elizabeth M., 2333
Buisson, Marion R., 2333
Buisson, Robert T., 2333
Buisson, Robert T., Jr., 2333
Buitrago, Kerrie, 6736
Bujalski, John, 9861
Buker, Robert H., Jr., 2276
Bukrinsky, Marian, 224
Bukstein, Roy, 253
Bulger, Elise Donaldson, 7127
Bull, George, III, 854
Bull, Lauren, 5783
Bull, Luiz Antonio, 6893
Bull, Marcia, 1541
Bull, Maud L., 331
Bull-Humphries, Jonca C., 1786
Bullard Foundation, George Newton,
  8740
Bullard, George, 8701
Bullard, George N., 8662
Bullard, Peter, 3854
Bullard, Robert L., 4624
Bulle, Jason L., 1458
Bulle, Krista J., 1458
Bullen, Lawrence, 4474
Bullens, Stephen J., 7593
Bulletin Co., 8340
Bullis, William, 2290
Bullitt, Dorothy S., 9563
Bullitt, Harriet, 9563
Bullock, Diane, 4224
Bullock, Ellis F., 4579
Bullock, Lisa, 7343
Bullock, Maree G., 2805
Bullock, Mary Brown, 5750
Bullock, Michael, 7770
Bumpus Revocable Trust, Bernice E.,
  3820
Bunch, Charles E., 8394
Bunch, Herb, 3165
Bunch, Patricia D., 3355

Buncher Co., The, 8125
Buncher Rail Car Service Co., 8125
Buncher Trust, Jack G., 8125
Buncher, Bernita, 8125
Buncher, Jack G., 8125
Bundy, Anne S., 332
Bundy, Bruce, 332
Bundy, Charles A., 8617
Bundy, Emory, 9599
Bundy, Richard H., 9130
Bundy, Robert, 79
Bunegar, James, 3090
Bunge North America, Inc., 4792
Bunge, John, 3278
Bunje, Bob, 886
Bunk, Thomas, 488
Bunker, Stephanie A., 3548
Bunkley, Phyllis B., 8611
Bunnen, Lucinda W., 2438
Bunnen, Melissa, 6635
Bunnen, Robert L., Jr., 6635
Bunnen, Robert L., Sr., 2438
Bunning, Barbara K., 2642
Bunning, David G., 2641, 2642
Bunning, Denise A., 2641, 2642
Bunning, James E., 2642
Bunning, Michael, 2641, 2642
Bunning, Steve, 2641
Bunshoft, Barry, 886
Buntin, Louie P., 8716
Bunting, Barbara E., 5417
Bunting, Chris, 3580
Bunting, Dorothy W., 3580
Bunting, George L., 3580
Bunting, George L., Jr., 3559, 3568,
  3580, 6103
Bunting, George L., Sr., 3580
Bunting, Jeff, 3580
Bunting, Joseph O., III, 9378, 9429
Bunting, Josiah, III, 6118
Bunting, June C., 9768
Bunting, Marc, 3580
Bunting, Mary C., 3580
Bunting, Robert, 9548
Bunting, Susan R., 5089
Buntrock, Cecily, 1908
Buntrock, Dana L., 1908
Buntrock, Dean L., 2643
Buntrock, Elizabeth H., 1908
Buntrock, Rosemarie, 2643
Buntz, M.A., 7986, 7987
Bunzl, Frances B., 2334
Bunzl, Richard, 2334
Bunzl, Walter Y., 2334
Burak, H. Paul, 6658
Burch, Catherine C., 5686
Burch, Dale J., 5686
Burch, Michael L., 9940
Burch, R.D., 5790
Burch, Robert D., 334
Burch, Robert L., III, 5686
Burch, Robert L., IV, 5686
Burch, Steve, 8152
Burcham, David W., 645
Burcham, Grant, 4842
Burchenal, Martha L., 7594
Burchett, Charla M., 1946
Burchfield, Albert H., III, 8130
Burd, Janet L., 2469
Burd, Loretta M., 3166
Burd, Nancy, 8378
Burden, Charmaine S., 5687
Burden, Childs Frick, 8211
Burden, Dixon Frick, 8211
Burden, Edward P.H., 5687
Burden, Florence V., 5687
Burden, Frances D., 8211
Burden, Henry S., 8211
Burden, I. Townsend, III, 8211
Burden, Jean E.P., 5687
Burden, Ordway P., 5687
Burden, Susan L., 5687
Burden, Wendy L., 5687
Burdett, Douglas M., 1545

Burdett, Jack, 9060
Burdette, H. Speer, III, 2336, 2337
Burdette, Milo, 8768
Burdick, Christopher, 3993
Burdick, Lalor, 3993
Burdick, Patricia Saucedo, 8881
Burdick, Sheryl J., 2760
Burditt, Deborah J., 2587
Burelli, Cristina, 2282
Buren, Don, 7897
Buresh, E.J., 3290
Burfeind, Henry F., 5165
Burg, Ellen, 7526
Burgan, Anne, 3597
Burgan, Gloria DeGol, 8167
Burger, Edward, 8878
Burger, Edward A., 5481
Burger, Max M., 5652
Burger, Tom, 3897
Burgess, Charlotte G., 1036
Burgess, James E., 9854
Burgess, Malcolm S., Jr., 2358
Burgess, Melanie A., 2143
Burgess, Val, Mrs., 9998
Burgett, Chip, 9777
Burghard, Anne W., 3069
Burgin, Walter, 3533
Burgon, John, 1029, 7705
Burgos, Joe, 3132
Burgoyne, Anne Marie, 466
Burick, Marcia, 3855
Burk Trust, Henrietta Lange, 2848
Burk, Frank W., 8782
Burk, Mary Ann, 3278
Burke & Herbert Bank and Trust Co.,
    9366
Burke, Anthony E., 6800
Burke, Austin J., 8431
Burke, Charles R., Jr., 8221
Burke, Charles R., Sr., 8221
Burke, Coleman P., Jr., 5257
Burke, Colleen D., 2709
Burke, Daniel, 5784
Burke, Daniel, Bro., 8198
Burke, Daniel, II, 5257
Burke, Diane W., 5149
Burke, F. William, 1823
Burke, Frank M., Jr., 9033
Burke, Gretchen, 8126
Burke, Indy, 9918
Burke, James C.E., 5149
Burke, James D., 4817
Burke, James E., 5149
Burke, James M., 5542
Burke, James W., 2299
Burke, John, 4156
Burke, John C., 4975
Burke, Joseph, 1642
Burke, Joseph J., 5341
Burke, Kathleen J., 1211
Burke, Kimberley R., 367
Burke, Lucie, 1606
Burke, Marianne, 5097
Burke, Martha Sodaro, 1174
Burke, Mary Griggs, 4577
Burke, Patricia Grable, 8221
Burke, Philip L., 6823
Burke, Rick, 7709
Burke, Sandra H., 8661
Burke, Sheila, 306, 307
Burke, Sheila P., 739
Burke, Spencer, 4860
Burke, Stephen B., 8126
Burke, Steven E., 8221
Burke, Thomas C., 5542
Burke, Vincent, 1606
Burke, Vincent C., III, 3591
Burke, Vincent C., Jr., 3591
Burke, Walter, 3627
Burke, Walter F., III, 3627
Burke, Ward R., 9227
Burke, Yvonne Brathwaite, 214
Burket, Connie, 3387
Burkett, Norman D., Sr., 2359

Burkey, Brett L., 1318
Burkey, J. Brad, 1318
Burkey, James, 1318
Burkey, Noelle Claeyssens, 1318
Burkhard, Ronald J., 7539
Burkhart, Megan, 4251
Burkholder, Eugene N., 8163
Burkholder, J. Michael, 8163
Burkholder, Kenneth N., 8163
Burkholder, Leon Ray, 8163
Burkland, Miriam, 2922
Burkle, Ron, 1029
Burkle, Ronald W., 8041
Burks, Ellis, 7577
Burks, Lawrence, 4327
Burks, Lawrence E., 4450
Burks, William P., 5357
Burleigh, Anne Catherine, 7561
Burleigh, Catherine Anne Husted, 7561
Burleigh, David W., 7561
Burleigh, William R., 7561, 7848
Burley, Joanne E., 8386
Burley, John, 7749
Burlingame, John H., 7848
Burlington Northern Santa Fe Corp.,
    2644
Burlington Rotary Club, 9957
Burlison, Bud, 430
Burlock, Walter E., Jr., 335
Burma Bibas, Inc., 6328
Burman, J. Dale, 3288
Burmeister, Neil, 6616
Burmeister, Thomas G., 2195
Burn, Harry, III, 1602
Burn, Jean, 1602
Burnand, Audrey Steele, 1189
Burnap, Bartlett, 2290
Burnap, Candida D., 2700
Burnap, Christiane, 2290
Burnap, Ian, 2290
Burnes, Kennett F., 3823
Burnes, Richard, 9408
Burnes, Richard M., 3812
Burnet, Kimberly, 4709
Burnet, Peggy P., 4709
Burnet, Ralph W., 4709
Burnet, Ryan W., 4709
Burnet, Stephanie, 4709
Burnett Co., Leo, Inc., 2645
Burnett, Bruce, 8800
Burnett, Bruce K., 1919
Burnett, Candace, 648
Burnett, Carol, 2570
Burnett, Charles P., III, 9598
Burnett, Charles, III, 9093
Burnett, Gene, 8714
Burnett, Gertrude W., 8738
Burnett, H.L., 2168
Burnett, Helen P., 336
Burnett, J. Albert, 1919
Burnett, James F., 1713
Burnett, Joe G., Bishop, 4946
Burnett, Miriam W., 9093
Burnett, Nancy, 1919
Burnett, Nancy Packard, 972
Burnett, Robert, 3281
Burnett, Shirley, 9598
Burnett, Timothy Brooks, 7430
Burnett, Vivian, 9598
Burnett, William, 9598
Burnett, William, Jr., 9598
Burney, Janet E., 7830
Burnham Real Estate, John, 1295
Burnham Way, 337
Burnham, Alice B., 7679
Burnham, Malin, 337
Burnham, Margaret E., 3527
Burnham, Melissa M., 8926
Burnham, Otis B., 2361
Burnham, Patricia R., 8718
Burnham, Philip C., 8444
Burnham, Roberta, 337
Burno, Katherine, 2791
Burno, Philip M., 2791

Burns, Angie, 9869
Burns, Donald A., 1920
Burns, E.W., 6579
Burns, Fred C., 9292
Burns, Fritz B., 338
Burns, Hilda, 3126
Burns, Jacob, 5689
Burns, Jeffrey, 3141
Burns, John M., 3298
Burns, Kathleen M., 8265
Burns, Kevin J., 3319
Burns, Linda, 6589
Burns, Marvin G., 476
Burns, Mike, 7599
Burns, Patricia, 956
Burns, Red, 6789
Burns, Richard R., Jr., 3795
Burns, Robert A., 9736
Burns, Ruth, 1920
Burns, Ruthelen Griffith, 3158
Burns, Wes, 1006
Burns, William L., Jr., 7491
Burns-Jepson, Kathryn, 805
Burnside, Daylene T., 8317
Burnum, Celeste, 54
Burpee, A. Leland, 2200
Burr, Anne Monteleone, 3502
Burr, Robert B., Jr., 8344, 8346
Burr, Willie O., 1578
Burrage, Darrell, 281
Burrage, Steve, 7955
Burrage, Walter S., Jr., 4079
Burrell, Raymond E. "Gene", 7463
Burress, J.W., Inc., 7331
Burress, John W., III, 7331, 7508
Burress, Mary Louise Walker, 7331
Burrill, W. Gregory, 3958
Burris, Burlean Miller, 2728
Burris, John, 3931
Burroughs Scholarship Trust, 7332
Burroughs Wellcome Co., 7333
Burroughs Wellcome Fund, The, 3677
Burroughs, Michael D., 3199
Burrow, Cherie L., 3160
Burrow, Ray, 7397
Burrows, Jim, 4552
Burrus, John E., 8190
Burslem, William, III, 6909
Burstein, Sanders, 5088
Burston, James, 7444
Burt, Allen, 8876
Burt, Barbara A., 3149
Burt, Mary Jane, 1514
Burt, R.M., 269
Burton Industries, Wm. T., Inc., 3467
Burton, Ann, 4253
Burton, Ann M., 1518
Burton, B. Scott, 2418
Burton, David G., 1706
Burton, Davis S. "Buddy", Jr., 27
Burton, Eve B., 6161, 6162
Burton, Judy, 3243
Burton, Julie, 1836
Burton, Kate Sato, 5384
Burton, Kenneth R., 9351
Burton, Marion, 173
Burton, Robert, 7866
Burton, Robert Harold, 9309
Burton, William T., 3467
Burwell, Keith, 7882, 7883
Burwitz, Jacqueline E., 2721
Bury, David, 5606
Burza, Eileen F., 3705
Burzlaff, Hugo, 4253
Busbee, Howard J., 9541
Busby, Ann, 7326
Buscaglia, Frank, 2218
Buscarino, Carolyn M., 6617
Busch Entertainment Corp., 4900
Busch, August A., III, 4776
Busch, Dean E., 4584
Busch, Georgine L., 2534
Busch, Howard W., 8444
Busch, Lawrence S., 8346

Busch, Virginia M., 4900
Busch-Vishniac, Ilene, 670
Busey, Yuell, 25
Bush, Archibald Granville, 4524
Bush, Barbara, 5989, 8975
Bush, Beth, 1578
Bush, Betsey R., 8671
Bush, Bette, 2124
Bush, Carol, 1439
Bush, Edyth Bassler, 1922, 4524
Bush, Gene, 8789
Bush, Gerald R., 759
Bush, John L., 3311
Bush, Lawrence P., 3311
Bush, Patricia M., 3311
Bush, Randy K., 9906
Bush, Terrence, 1221
Bush, Walter L., Jr., 4607
Bush, William, 1871, 5137
Bush, William H.T., 4896, 5032
Bush, William L., 4321
Bush, William, Mrs., 7039
Bushkin, Kathryn, 7142
Bushman, Patrick, 829
Bushore, Jay, 1017
Bushyeager, Peter, 6617
Business Real Estate, 1295
Busk, Linda, 1406
Busot, Aldo C., 2121
Buss, William D., II, 7742
Busse, Keith, 3125
Bussel, Ann B., 1916
Bussel, Daniel J., 1916
Bussel, Deborah, 1916
Bussel, John M., 1916
Bussell, Mark E., 134
Bussell, Rod, 2678
Bussewitz, Marilyn, 3190, 3191
Bussing, Constance K., 3111
Bussing, Wilfred C., III, 3111
Bussing, Wilfred C., Jr., 3111
Bussing-Burks, Marie A., 3111
Bussman, Courtney, 6369
Bussmann, Claudia, 6369
Bussmann, Margaret, 6369
Bussmann, Martin, 6369
Bussmann, Richard, 6369
Bustad, Leo, 78
Bustamante, Carlos J., 7333
Bustamante, Thomas, 5496
Buster, Robert, 3345
Buster, Sandra, 3345
Bustle, Greg, 2094
Bustle, Mary Beth, 2094
Butcher, James R., 3617
Butcher, Jeanne D., 3617
Butcher, Joseph F., 8317
Butcher, Sue, 7749
Butera, Richard T., 1365
Buthman, Mark A., 8992
Butler Capital Corp., 5691
Butler Charitable Lead Trust, 2646
Butler Foundation, J.E. and Z.B., 1779
Butler Manufacturing Co., 4793
Butler Wick Trust Co., 7572, 7672,
    7816
Butler, Aimee Mott, 4525
Butler, Alice L., 3273
Butler, Andrew J., 3273
Butler, Brigid M., 4525
Butler, Calvin G., 2707
Butler, Carol W., 20
Butler, Carroll, 8842
Butler, Catherine, 4525
Butler, Cecelia M., 4525
Butler, Christa, 7562
Butler, Cliff, 1945
Butler, Cynthia I., 9453
Butler, Debra, 3273
Butler, Edna Loewy, 6444
Butler, Ernest C., 8802
Butler, Ettie, 7173
Butler, Eugene W., 2917
Butler, Flamont T., 9915

Butler, George Lee, Genl., 9490
Butler, Gilbert, 5691
Butler, Gregory B., 1614
Butler, Henry King, 8654
Butler, Ildiko, 5691
Butler, J.T., 9453
Butler, Jack E., 5692
Butler, James E., III, 2335
Butler, James E., Jr., 2335
Butler, Jane, 6937
Butler, John E., 3273
Butler, John K., 4525
Butler, Julia, 882
Butler, Katharine, 1501
Butler, Kelly Ochylski, 3321
Butler, Kevin, 7562
Butler, Kimberly, 8551
Butler, Laurel A., 1517
Butler, Linda E., 8802
Butler, Lynn S., 7873
Butler, Marty, 7562
Butler, Mary Sue, 7562
Butler, Matt, 7514
Butler, Nancy Chasanoff, 5735
Butler, Patricia M., 4525
Butler, Patrick, 4525
Butler, Patrick, Jr., 4525
Butler, Paul S., 4525
Butler, Peter M., 4525
Butler, Rex, 2562
Butler, Rhett W., 2646
Butler, Rob, 7139
Butler, Robert E., 8802
Butler, Robert N., 6232
Butler, Roberta H., 8537
Butler, Samuel, 2263
Butler, Sandra K., 4400, 4525
Butler, Sarah, 8802
Butler, Stephen T., 2326
Butler, Susan C., 2335
Butler, Susan Storz, 5006
Butler, William, 6937
Butler, William P., 7562
Butler, Zella B., 5692
Butner, Ces, 381
Butt Grocery Co., H.E., 8804
Butt, Barbara Dan, 8804
Butt, Charles C., 8803
Butt, Howard E., Jr., 8804
Butt, Howard E., Sr., 8804
Butt, Khalid M.H., 7247
Butt, Tariq H., 3016
Butt, William "Jackson", II, 169
Butte, Amy S., 6619
Buttenwieser, Catherine F., 5693
Buttenwieser, Lawrence B., 6856
Buttenwieser, Paul A., 5693
Butterfield, Andrew, 6917
Butterfield, Bruce, 3895
Butterfield, Frank, 2451
Butterworth, George W., III, 3811
Butterworth, Katherine Deere, 2647
Buttinger, Muriel M., 6621
Buttner, Jean B., 5624
Buttrey, Donald W., 3233
Buttrey, Karen Lake, 3233
Buttrick, Marguerite D.R., 6628
Butts, Calvin O., Rev., 6637
Butts, David R., 4428
Butts, Robert R., 5564
Butz, Barbie, 1090
Butzel, Laura E., 5750
Butzer, Bart, 4697
Buuck, David A., 4526
Buuck, Gail P., 4526
Buuck, John R., 4526
Buuck, Robert E., 4526
Buuck, Robert P., 4526
Buurma, Rachel, 5381
Buyck, Mark, Jr., 8571
Buyher, Sharen, 3122
Buzaglo, Meir, 5582
Buzard, Donald S., 9744
Buzbee, Terry, 3337

Buzza, John, 9778
Buzzard, James A., 7745
Buzzelli, David T., 4412
Buzzet, Billy, 2244
Bye, James E., 1379, 1438, 1439
Bye, Larry, 4628
Bye, Ray, 1945
Byelich, Robert G., 4228
Byer, Allan G., 339
Byer, Marian, 339
Byer, Thomas D., 9402
Byerly, Stacy S., 8730
Byers Choice, Ltd., 8127
Byers, Alison M., 8344, 8346
Byers, Jeffrey D., 8127
Byers, Joyce F., 8127
Byers, Marie G., 8743
Byers, Patricia Burch, 5379
Byers, Robert L., 8127
Byers, Robert Leslie, 8127
Byers, W. Russell G., Jr., 8346
Byington, Bob, 4227
Byk, Kim, 7667
Byk, Otto, 9962
Byker, Gaylen, 5026
Byme, Brendan Thomas, 5199
Bynum, William J. "Bill", 4743
Byrd, A. Dean, 9348
Byrd, Ames, 4037
Byrd, Avalee, Mrs., 8988
Byrd, Chris, 3161
Byrd, D. Harold, Jr., 8952
Byrd, Edward R., 970
Byrd, Emily J., 4037
Byrd, Harry F., 4037
Byrd, Jeanne, 7449
Byrd, Manford, Jr., 2957
Byrd, Phil, 3131
Byrd, Ray A., 9716
Byrd, Richard E., III, 4037
Byrd, Sandra P., 7346
Byrd, Stephanne S., 9400
Byrd, Susan, 786
Byrd-Lewis, Renee, 2356
Byrne, Brendan, 5710
Byrne, Bruce, 5454
Byrne, Dorothy M., 5081
Byrne, John J., 5081
Byrne, John J., III, 5081
Byrne, Joseph, 5502
Byrne, L. Nelle, 5502
Byrne, Mark J., 5081
Byrne, Michael J., 4122
Byrne, Nancy J., 5502
Byrne, Patrick M., 5081
Byrnes, Brian T., 9361
Byrnes, John H., 7158
Byrnes, Mary Elizabeth, 3821
Byrnes, Mollie Tower, 7158
Byrnes, Randall W., 3821
Byrnes, William L., 3821
Byrns, Priscilla Upton, 4466
Byrns, Steven, 4466
Byron, William J., Rev., 1825
Byron-Weston Co., 3864
Byrum, D.M., 2301
Bytof, Jocye, 9776

C & E Enterprises, 7478
C & K Enterprises, Ltd., 1386
Caamano, Ralph F., Rev., 6199
Cabaleiro, Mariela, 7491
Cabaniss, William Nathan, 9025
Cabe, Charles L., Jr., 2648
Cabe, Charles Lee "Sandy", 2648
Cabe, Horace C., 2648
Cabe, Robert D., 157
Cabe, Thomas H., 2648
Cabela, James W., 4960
Cabela, Richard N., 4960
Cabell, Charles L., 9381
Cabell, John B., 9381
Cabell, Maude Morgan, 9381

Cabell, Robert G., III, 9381
Cabell-Mains, Susan, 9495
Cable, Andrew M., 4115
Cable, Dale, 2240
Cable, Howard W., Jr., 9755
Cable, Thomas J., 9701
Cabot 1986 Conduit Trust, Thomas D., 3825
Cabot 1994 Charitable Lead Unitrust, Thomas D., 3825
Cabot 1996 Charitable Lead Unitrust, Virginia W., 3825
Cabot Corp., 3823
Cabot Revocable Trust, Virginia W., 3825
Cabot, Amanda, 3825
Cabot, Betsy, 3825
Cabot, Edmund B., 3822
Cabot, Elizabeth W., 3822
Cabot, Godfrey L., 3824
Cabot, Janet, 3049
Cabot, John G.L., 3824
Cabot, Louis W., 3824
Cabot, Mabel, 3825
Cabot, Mithran, 3825
Cabot, Penny, 3825
Cabot, Thomas D., III, 3825
Cabot, Thomas D., Jr., 3825
Cabot, Virginia, 3825
Caceres, Dora, 6642
Caceres, Melanie G., 5212
Cachine, Michael M., Sr., 1830
Cacique Distributors, U.S., 342
Cacique, Inc., 342
Caddie Homes, Inc., 3604
Caddock, James C., 343
Caddock, John B., 343
Caddock, Richard E., Jr., 343
Cader, Andrew, 5696
Cader, Michael, 5696
Cadieux, Chester, 7984
Cadigan, Elise, 2679
Cadigan, Linda R., 8988
Cadwallader, Glenda M., 7158
Cadwallader-Staub, Julie, 9361
Cady, John, 6520
Cady, John L., 6519
Caesars Entertainment, Inc., 8648
Cafarella, William, 5984
Cafaro Charitable Lead Trust, Alyce, 7563
Cafaro Charitable Lead Trust, William M., 7563
Cafaro, Anthony M., 7563
Cafaro, Flora M., 7563
Cafesjian, Cleo T., 4527
Cafesjian, Gerard L., 4527
Caffray, Gil, 7139
Caffrey, John, 6513
Caffrey, John J., 6384
Caffrey, Thomas F., 8548
Cafritz, Anthony W., 1780
Cafritz, Calvin, 1780
Cafritz, Elliot S., 1780
Cafritz, Gwendolyn D., 1780
Cafritz, Jane Lipton, 1780
Cafritz, Jane R., 9508
Cafritz, Morris, 1780
Cagle, Ronald E., 7959
Cahalan, Joseph M., 1680
Cahalin, Helen J., 1992
Cahill, John T., 6713
Cahill, Patrick, 3250
Cahill, Robert V., 375
Cahillane, Mary J., 3015
Cahn, Becky, 4552
Cahners, Nancy L., 4091
Cahoon, Frank K., 8923
Cahouet, Frank V., 8241
Caiaze, Robert M., 1594
Cailloux, Floyd A., 8807
Cailloux, Kathleen C., 8806, 8807
Cailloux, Kenneth F., 8806, 8807
Cailloux, Sandy, 8807
Caimi, Gina, 5937

Cain, Daniel M., 5697
Cain, Edmund J., 5037
Cain, Effie Marie, 8808
Cain, Gordon A., 8809
Cain, Gordon R., 8809
Cain, James B., 8808
Cain, James E., 5697
Cain, John C., 8808
Cain, Mary H., 8809
Cain, R. Wofford, 8808
Cain, William M., 5697
Cain, William, S.J., Rev., 762
Cain-Pozzo, Diane, 8039
Caine, Antony, 1426
Caine, Marie Eccles, 9310
Caine, Terri, 1426
Caine, Virginia A., 3164
Calabresi, Anne T., 4533
Calamari, John, 8134
Calandra, Joseph J., 7010
Calandro, John, 939
Calawerts, Mike, 9810
Calcott, Monica R., 2679
Calder, Louis, 1506
Calder, Peter D., 1506
Calderon, Eric, 1338
Calderon, Ernest, 87
Calderon, Jorge, 5854
Calderone, Philip D., 5597
Calderwood, Stanford M., 3826
Caldor, Inc., 1490
Caldwell, Barry, 9265
Caldwell, Carlyle G., 134
Caldwell, Charles, 9617
Caldwell, Christa R., 6108
Caldwell, Christopher, 300
Caldwell, David H., 4125
Caldwell, Elizabeth W., 8740
Caldwell, James D., 9160
Caldwell, L.H., Jr., 8649
Caldwell, Lee, 8840
Caldwell, Linda, 9617
Caldwell, Mark A., 8649
Caldwell, Mary, 407
Caldwell, Mike, 3123
Caldwell, R. Craig, 7444
Caldwell, Robert H., 8649
Caldwell, Robert H., Jr., 8649
Caldwell, Robin M., 9115
Caldwell, Theodore C., 8649
Caldwell-Johnson, Teree, 3281, 3317
Calechman, Jack, 4154
Calheno, Agastino J., 4210
Calhoon, Ann, 170
Calhoun, David T., 3468
Calhoun, F. David, 8777
Calhoun, John C., 3482
Calhoun, Julia, 9655, 9664
Calhoun, Julia Larson, 9625
Calhoun, Ken, 8976
Calhoun, Marianne K., 2798
Calhoun, Michael, 8777
Calhoun, Nancy H., 3461
Calhoun, Phillip L., 8199
Calhoun, Susan Hyde, 8693
Calicchio, John, 5698
California Italian-American Cultural Institute, Inc., 419
California Physicians' Service Agency Inc., 296
California Wellness Foundation, The, 661
Caligiuri, Sam S.F., 1518
Calihan, Joseph J., 8386
Calisti, Robyn, 6052
Calkins, Anabeth, 4881
Calkins, Beth, 9702
Calkins, Christopher C., 193
Calkins, Tom, 2458
Calkins, William D., 9877
Call, Bradley C., 1249
Call, Richard, 1118
Callaghan, Lorraine M., 5824
Callahan, Christopher M., 3147

Callahan, Daniel J., III, 1780
Callahan, Edward, 4237
Callahan, Eugene J., 6138, 8718
Callahan, F.J., 7564, 7710
Callahan, Kathy, 4992
Callahan, Patrick S., 9498
Callahan, Rence, 7508
Callahan, Robert, 2813
Callahan, T.H., 3440
Callahan, T.J., 7564
Callam, Pamela, 4349
Callan, John, 268
Callan, Mary Beth, 5255
Callan, Nancy, 9255
Callarman, Denise, 3034
Callas, Koula, 9113
Callaway Institute, Inc., 2337
Callaway Mills, 2337
Callaway, Amy Roach, 9150
Callaway, Fuller E., Sr., 2336
Callaway, J.L., Jr., 8810
Callen, Kathy, 3125
Callen, Margaret D., 7422
Callender, Mary, 549
Callender, Mary S., 895
Calleton, Theodore, 994
Callicott, Bradley L., 8571
Callicutt, Thomas L., Jr., 3461
Callier, James A., 3511
Calliham, J. Robert, 8619
Callihan, William, 3471
Callison, Fred W., 351
Callison, Kay, 4873
Callon, Marian, 3178
Calloway, Robert, 8671
Calloway, W. Harold, 3254
Calmat Co., 73
Calpeter, Lynn A., 933
Calpin, William J., 8117, 8431
Caltrider, Marie E., 9730
Calvert Group, 5905
Calvert, Bruce W., 6613
Calvillo, Alida, 613
Calvin, Peter DeMille, 450
Calvo-Torres, Betty, 5780
Camacho, Marcos, 376
Camarillo, Louis, 1203
Cambell, Catherine, 2750
CAMBR Co., 5699
CAMBR Labs, 5699
Cambridge Trust Co., 3828
Camden, Andrew L., 4254
Camden, Carl T., 4359
Camden, W. Starke, 9463
Cameron, Anthony, 669
Cameron, Cara E., 1873
Cameron, Danielle, 1939
Cameron, David, 8812
Cameron, Isabel C., 8812
Cameron, James, 8983
Cameron, Sam W., 4757
Cameron, Susan S., 8980
Cameron, Sylvia, 8812
Cameron, William H., 7336, 7352
Camilleri, Louis C., 5545
Cammarata, Bernard, 3829, 4183
Cammett, David B., 4055
Cammett, Eileen I., 4055
Cammett, Richard, 4194
Cammett, Richard N., 4055
Cammett, Richard N., Jr., 4055
Cammett, Susan V., 4055
Camp, James L., 9382
Camp, John M., III, 9382
Camp, John M., Jr., 2338, 5700, 9382, 9383
Camp, P.D., 9382
Camp, Paul D., III, 5700, 9383
Camp, Tom, 326
Camp, Tom R., 544
Camp, W.M., Jr., 9382
Campa, Luz, 1905, 2185, 4642, 4682, 8628
Campaniano, Robin, 2547

Campano, Gus, 7344
Campau, Anne E., 4347
Campbell Group, The, 8002
Campbell Soup Co., 5151
Campbell, Alice J., 2611
Campbell, Andrew, 5188
Campbell, Aurelie S., 6637
Campbell, Barbara Smith, 5056
Campbell, Benjamin K., 6345
Campbell, Bert L., 8854
Campbell, Beth, 631
Campbell, Beth Newlands, 3540
Campbell, Billy, 4819
Campbell, Brenda, 8451
Campbell, Bushrod H., 3830
Campbell, C. David, 4389, 9089
Campbell, Carmen D., 4528
Campbell, Carol, 234
Campbell, Charles, 9254
Campbell, Charles Talbot, 8128
Campbell, Cheryl N., 7587
Campbell, Chris, 3512, 7906
Campbell, Christian L., 3457
Campbell, Clara G., 8813
Campbell, Colin G., 6827
Campbell, Cynthia A., 8002
Campbell, D., 9181
Campbell, Dennis M., 7359
Campbell, Duncan, 8049
Campbell, E.M., 9028
Campbell, Edward M., 3663
Campbell, Edward P., 7781
Campbell, Eleanor L., 4037
Campbell, Eleanor S., 4037
Campbell, Elizabeth Turner, 8650
Campbell, Eugenie, 7749
Campbell, Hazard K., 6345
Campbell, J. Bulow, 2339
Campbell, J. Duncan, Jr., 8002
Campbell, Jack A., 4954
Campbell, James R., 4528
Campbell, Jeanne C., 8659
Campbell, John, 8987
Campbell, John D., 5368
Campbell, John M., 4414
Campbell, John O., 8208
Campbell, John P., 1723, 6240
Campbell, John W., 5240
Campbell, Keith, 3582
Campbell, Keith M., 4677
Campbell, Lebrena F., 8564
Campbell, Leonard C., 9900
Campbell, Levin H., Jr., 4037
Campbell, Liz, 7534
Campbell, Malcolm David, 531
Campbell, Marcia, 100
Campbell, Margaret G., 9532
Campbell, Marion D., 2700
Campbell, Marshall J., 4249, 4257
Campbell, Martha S., 698
Campbell, Mary Ann, Hon., 8103
Campbell, Michael H., 3634
Campbell, Morris C., 8584
Campbell, Nancy Harris, 223
Campbell, Nelson D., 8703
Campbell, Patrick, 7906
Campbell, Paul, 6737
Campbell, Paul, III, 8660
Campbell, Peter, 5905
Campbell, Peter I., 4528
Campbell, Phyllis J., 9680
Campbell, R. Bruce, 7769
Campbell, R. Larry, 7463
Campbell, Rhett, 9231
Campbell, Richard O., 1417, 1448
Campbell, Robert E., 5265
Campbell, Robert H., 8377
Campbell, Robert L., 1659, 2664
Campbell, Roberta, 352
Campbell, Ruth Taylor, 1464
Campbell, Samantha, 3582
Campbell, Sarah C., 8813
Campbell, Sarah P., 4414
Campbell, Stephen, 2621

Campbell, Stewart, 9042
Campbell, T.C., 8813
Campbell, Theresa, 1463
Campbell, Thomas H., 5435
Campbell, Thomas R.B., 5564
Campbell, Tom, 9634
Campbell, William Durant, 7275
Campbell, William E., 9933
Campbell, William V., 352
Campini, Frank A., 353
Campion, Ashley C., 1398
Campion, Berit K., 1398
Campion, Lynn H., 1398
Campion, Thomas B., Jr., 1398
Campisi, Anthony P., 8511
Campo, Ric, 8960
Campobasso, Laura, 1303
Campuzano, Mary K., 3372
Canada, Geoffrey, 6665
Canada, Robert, 3425
Canada, Susan H., 7042
Canaday, Mariam C., 5701
Canaday, Ward M., 5701
Canales, James E., 698
Canalis, Ernesto, 1529
Canavan, Gregory H., 670
Cancelli, Dante A., 8431
Canciglia, Joseph R., 5371
Candioty, Linda, 378
Candler, Peter M., 2339
Canepa, Patricia, 1243
Canfora, Phillip H., 7539
Canizares, Gail Anderson, 8761
Cann, Alex N., Sr., 8263
Cann, Samuel A., 8263
Canna, Stephen, 1512
Cannan, Patricia, 1956
Cannedy, Dennis D., 8879, 8890
Cannedy, Mac W., Jr., 8797, 8879, 8890
Cannefax, Amy D., 9245
Canning, Dwight D., 4896
Canning, John A., Jr., 2650, 2661
Canning, Rita, 2650
Cannon Manufacturing Co., 3931
Cannon Mills Co., 7335
Cannon, Bedford, 7307
Cannon, Charles A., 7335
Cannon, Charles G., 1380
Cannon, Jerry, 4327
Cannon, John, 1944
Cannon, John, III, 8143
Cannon, Kathryn Gracey, 8651
Cannon, Mark, 2350
Cannon, Paul, 8840
Cannon, Robert E., 8651
Cannon, Robert Howard, 8651
Cannon, Timothy Hall, 8651
Cannon, W. Stephen, 9392
Cannon, W.C., Jr., 7335
Cannon, Warren F., 2680
Canoles, Leroy T., Jr., 9376
Canon, Joseph E., 8868, 9226
Canonge, Richard, 8098
Cantara, Dan, 5958
Canter, Joel, 5564
Canter, Lisa, 9151
Canterbury Consulting, 1093
Canterbury Trust Company, 24
Cantor Fitzgerald Inc., 354
Cantor Fitzgerald Securities, 7174
Cantor Fitzgerald, LP, 354
Cantor, B. Gerald, 354
Cantor, Iris, 354
Cantor, Richard, 5152
Cantor, Sanford, 2803
Cantori, Gregory, 3666
Cantrell, Barbara B., 1851
Cantrell, Diane, 3110
Canty, Leo C., 1519
Canute, Scott A., 3192
Caouette, Jack, 6512
Caouette, John, 6512
CAP America Trust, 9384

Capanna, Robert, 8395
Capdevilla, Martin J., 356
Capdevilla, Wendy Gillespie, 356
Cape Cod Bank and Trust Co., 3558
Cape Cod Five Cents Savings Bank, 3832
Cape Fear Memorial Health Care Corp., 7336
Cape, Murray E., 25
Capel, Felton J., Sr., 7438
Capel, William, 8487
Capers, Cynthia, 7526
Caperton, Gaston, Gov., 8099
Capezio, Thomas C., 8431
Capita, Emil R., 5154
Capita, Marianna, 5154
Capita, Robert, 5154
Capital Athletic Foundation, LLC, 1781
Capital Bank & Trust Co., 357
Capital City Bank, 1924
Capital City Bankshares, Inc., 3386
Capital City First National Bank, 1924
Capital Gazette Communications, Inc., 3584, 3689, 9455
Capital Group Cos., Inc., The, 357
Capital Guardian Trust Co., 267, 624
Capital International, 357
Capital Management Services, 357
Capital Research & Management Co., 357, 1093
Capital Ventures of NV, 5026
Capito, Charles L., Jr., 9723
Capitol Aggregates, 9296
Capitol Federal Financial, 3350
Caplan, Constance R., 3568
Caplow, Dorothy D., 5611
Caplow, Mildred R., 6860
Caplow, Theodore, 5611
Caplow, Theodore, Jr., 5894
Capobianco, Anthony, 5782
Capone, Eileen M., 2171, 6346
Caporale, Nicholas A., 4125
Capp, Esther, 4529
Capp, Lisa, 4529
Capp, Martin, 4529
Cappella, Inc., 3841
Cappelli, Louis R., 5703
Cappelloni, Robert J., 834
Capps, John, 4926
Cappy, Joe, 7984
Capra, Ellen M., 6255
Capra, James R., 6255
Capranica, Ruth M., 3664, 3665
Capranica, Steven F., 3664, 3665
Caprio, Tony, 7567
Capron, Jeffery P., 1797
Capstone Funding, LLC, 2429
Capute, Charles T., 3693
Caputo, Joseph A., 8427
Carabias, Julia, 6389
Carano, Donald L., 5053
Carapezzi, William R., Jr., 5110
Caratan, Tina, 9548
Caraway, Ann M., 4264
Caraway, Ray, 1357
Caraway, Roberta Gorenstein, 9775
Carbajal, David, 4428
Carbo, Steven M., 6643
Carbone, Don, 5783
Carbone, Paul J., 9750
Carboneau, David K., 8051
Cardaras, Van, 7791
Carden, Lance, 3895
Cardenas, Jose A., 130
Cardiac Dimensions, 3841
Cardillo, Mark J., 5886
Cardimen, Frank, 4256
Cardin, Sanford R., 7975
Cardinal Health, Inc., 7567
Cardinale, Ruth, 4913
Cardinali, Albert J., 6179
Cardiomind, 3841
Cardon, Carol M., 5618
Cardon, Helen Hemingway, 9328

Cardon, Melissa S., 9472
Cardone Foundation, Michael, 8129
Cardone, Jacqueline, 8129
Cardone, Michael, III, 8129
Cardone, Michael, Jr., 8129
Cardone, Ryan D., 8129
Cardullo, Frank, 6428
Cardwell, Bickerton W., Jr., 2339
Cardwell, Samuel P., 9463
Carendi, Jan, 205
Carey, C.M., 8016
Carey, Charles P., 2660
Carey, Dan, 7521
Carey, Elizabeth P., 5704
Carey, Francis J., 5704
Carey, Francis J., III, 5704
Carey, H. Augustus, 5704
Carey, Henry H., 2479
Carey, Jennifer L., 4556
Carey, Joe Tina, 5554
Carey, John M., 7540
Carey, Kathryn A., 217
Carey, Robin, 9702
Carey, William P., 5704
Carfagna, Rita Murphy, 7768
Cargill Charitable Trust, 4530
Cargill, Inc., 4530
Cargill, Shelley, 687
Carillon Importers, Ltd., 6086
Carino, Olivia, 5634
Carl, Charles W., Jr., 6915
Carl, R. Barton, 7969
Carle, Judy, 4649
Carlee, Jane H., 3835
Carleton, Dick, 1463
Carleton, James T., 3836
Carleton, Sharon E., 3836
Carley, Kevin, 3557
Carlile, Rhett, 8060
Carlino, Peter D., 8379
Carlisle, Barbara, 5062
Carlisle, David M., 3525
Carlisle, John, 9068
Carlisle, Lorenzo T., 7688
Carlos, Andrew C., 2340
Carlos, Eula, 2340, 2341
Carlos, Laurie, 4595
Carlos, Maria H., 3015
Carlos, Michael C., 2341, 4630
Carlos, Thalia N., 2341
Carls, William, 4244
Carlsen, Lois, 5902
Carlson 2000 BCG Charitable Annuity
    Trust, Arleen M., 4532
Carlson, Arleen M., 4532
Carlson, Arthur, 1505
Carlson, Barbara, 9161
Carlson, Bruce M., 4297
Carlson, Bud, 1945
Carlson, C. Kent, 9701
Carlson, Cheryl C., 4191
Carlson, Christopher A., 7785
Carlson, Clint D., 8815
Carlson, Cody, 9161
Carlson, Colette L., 4534
Carlson, Curtis L., 4532
Carlson, Dave, 1201
Carlson, Deborah, 4073
Carlson, Dennis, 4540
Carlson, Dick, 4968
Carlson, Herbert E., 7593
Carlson, Herbert E., Jr., 4191
Carlson, Jennie, 4704
Carlson, Jennie P., 7659
Carlson, Karen, 8398
Carlson, Lon, 2804
Carlson, Matt, 9594
Carlson, Nancy Packer, 8815
Carlson, Richard E., 1031
Carlson, Robert E., 982
Carlson, Robert J., Bishop, 4428
Carlson, Steven E., 9598
Carlson, W.W., 1982
Carlson, Wendy, 3269

Carlson, Willard, 9885
Carlstrom, R. William, 9594
Carlton, Andrea Waitt, 5489
Carlton, John M., Jr., 2360
Carlyss, Ann Schein, 3730
Carmack, John M., 292
CarMax Auto Superstores, Inc., 9385
Carmel, Judy, 660
Carmello-Harper, Wayne, 23
Carmen Family Charitable Foundation,
    3915
Carmichael, Arthur, 828
Carmichael, Dan R., 7784
Carmichael, Daniel P., 3194
Carmichael, Jean, 828
Carmichael, John A., 6465
Carmichael, Susan Lehman, 2479
Carmichael, Trent, 7139
Carmody, Jack E., Jr., 8630
Carmola, Jack, 7378
Carnahan, Katharine J., 5706
Carnaroli, Craig R., 8157
Carnation Co., 9648
Carnegie Corporation of New York, 359
Carnegie, Andrew, 359, 5707, 8130
Carneros, Ann, 1307
Carneros, Antonio, 1307
Carnes, Jimmy, 2015
Carney, Cleve E., 2713
Carney, Daniel M., 3404
Carney, Jane, 698
Carney, Patrick, 3837
Carney, Richard, 9922
Carney, Tana N., 7576
Carnival Cruise Lines, Inc., 1881
Caro, Robert A., 6119
Carob Trust, 5702
Carol Electric, Inc., 368
Carolan, Richard C., 5156
Carolan, Richard V., 5156
Carolan, Tina, 5156
Carolan-Faga, Kimberly M., 5156
Carolina First Bank, 8615
Carolina Power & Light Co., 7453
Caroll, Jennifer, 1291
Caroll, John, 1291
Carolla, Margaret, 4798
Carothers, Lucille E., 7720
Carothers, Suzanne C., 5655
Carpel, Andrew, 3598
Carpenter, Alfred S.V., 8003
Carpenter, Carroll M., 1715
Carpenter, D.R., III, 9455
Carpenter, Dale, 7360
Carpenter, Dan, 2721
Carpenter, David R., 1249
Carpenter, E. Rhodes, 8131
Carpenter, Ed N., II, 1715
Carpenter, Edmund M., 1488
Carpenter, Gordon R., 9218
Carpenter, Helen Bundy, 8003
Carpenter, Joan M., 360
Carpenter, Karen H., 4069
Carpenter, Leona B., 8131
Carpenter, Michael A., 5755
Carpenter, Richard, 5471
Carpenter, Stephen, 8556
Carpenter, T. Michael, 360
Carpenter, Todd C., 360
Carpenters Home Church, 8604
CARR Lane Manufacturing, 4922
Carr, Ann K., 2836
Carr, Barbara, 5708
Carr, Barbara Thiele, 9916
Carr, David R., 7496
Carr, Elliott, 3832
Carr, Francie, 9693
Carr, Gregory C., 3838
Carr, Jacqueline, 82
Carr, James H., 1793
Carr, Jim, 2109
Carr, Joseph S., 2770
Carr, Julie B., 8116
Carr, Justine M., 5900

Carr, Kathleen D.H., 1825
Carr, L.J., 82
Carr, Rebecca, 5098
Carr, Richard C., 2836
Carr, Robert F., 2962
Carr, Robert F., III, 2770, 2947
Carr, Robert Venn, 1516
Carr, Sasha, 5708
Carr, Wilma, 82
Carrabine-Dalton, Cara, 4444
Carras, Barbara D., 4288
Carras, Steven, 4288
Carreau, Robert A., 6915
Carreras, Eduardo M., 2400
Carreras, Lisa S., 2857
Carrico, James T., 5077
Carrico, John D., 5252
Carriere, Margaret E., 8935
Carrigan, Chris, 3825
Carrigg, James A., 5846
Carrington, Alexander Berkeley, 9386
Carrington, Lisa A., 3216
Carrington, Ruth Simpson, 9386
Carrion, Gladys, 6615
Carrison, Molly, 7343
Carrol, Paul, 4124
Carroll Trust, Florence V., 3114
Carroll, Cynthia, 386
Carroll, Daniel B., 8328
Carroll, David M., 7502
Carroll, Edward P., 19
Carroll, George, 2940
Carroll, Heather, 1373
Carroll, J. Martin, 1498
Carroll, James D., Jr., 5444
Carroll, Jane, 5353
Carroll, Joe, 906
Carroll, Judith, 1291
Carroll, Lelia, 1351
Carroll, Mary Ann, 3250
Carroll, Mary Beth, 7630
Carroll, Mary Fran, 1946
Carroll, Michael, 2245
Carroll, Michael P., 837
Carroll, Richard J., 2681, 6221
Carroll, Robert S., 3855
Carroll, Russell L., 8037
Carroll, Thomas, 5194
Carroll, Thomas W., Mrs., 7224
Carroll, Timothy G., 2791
Carroll, Walter J., 8328
Carrucci, Richard T., 3457
Carrus, Gerald, 2651
Carrus, Janet, 2651
Carruth, Brady F., 9292
Carruthers, Suzanne, 7533
Carse, Jimmie I., 1925
Carse, Wayne L., 1925
Carsey, John J., 361
Carsey, Marcia L., 361
Carson International, Inc., 19
Carson Pirie Scott & Co., 19
Carson, Allen, 9719
Carson, Benjamin S., Sr., 3568
Carson, Cecily M., 5709
Carson, David, 1563
Carson, Deborah O., 9106
Carson, Douglas, 5047
Carson, Edward S., 5709
Carson, Jill, 8300
Carson, John W., 362
Carson, Judith M., 5709
Carson, Mark H., 1451
Carson, Mary L., 7988
Carson, Philip L., 3156
Carson, Robert L., 3984
Carson, Russell L., 5709, 8366
Carson, Susan, 2892
Carson, Thomas J., 7988
Carstarphen, William P., 7342
Carstens, Bill, 1465
Carstens, Godfrey H., Jr., 6800
Carswell, Bruce, 1582
Carswell, Gale Fisher, 2559

Carswell, Mary, 1839
Carswell, Robert, 6102
Cartales, Helen M., 9565
Cartales, John A., 9565
Carter Foundation Production Co., 8816
Carter, Amon G., 8816, 8817
Carter, Anne Strong, 2555
Carter, Beatrice C., 8261
Carter, Beirne B., 9387
Carter, Bernard E., 9712
Carter, Douglas A., 2458
Carter, Edward F., 7821
Carter, Elliot, 5789
Carter, Elsie P., 9723
Carter, Ernest, 7464
Carter, Georgia, 9712
Carter, Harriet H., 280
Carter, Hazo, Jr., 9723
Carter, Herb, 5400
Carter, Hugh C., 276
Carter, James, 9164
Carter, James A., 9290
Carter, James J., Jr., 69
Carter, Jean Gordon, 7496
Carter, Jennifer, 9598
Carter, John S., Jr., 8522
Carter, Ken, 3497
Carter, Kristen A., 8606
Carter, Larry, 5047
Carter, Larry R., 388
Carter, Lee A., 7619
Carter, Leigh H., 7688
Carter, Leslie R., 9712
Carter, Letitia M., 8522
Carter, Linda B., 1941
Carter, Marjorie Sells, 1507
Carter, Marybeth, 430
Carter, N.B., 8816
Carter, Nicholas S.F., 3850
Carter, Peggy, 7508
Carter, Richard J., Jr., 5954
Carter, Robert S., Jr., 1605
Carter, Ruth Ann, 8179
Carter, Steve, 7770
Carter, Susan M., 2395, 2494
Carter, Terry, 7984
Carter, Theresa, 7789
Carter, Wilson, 9401
Cartier, Kelly, 1947
Cartiglia, Katherine Gilweit, 5068
Cartledge, George B., III, 9388
Cartledge, George B., Jr., 9388
Cartledge, Olive M., 9388
Cartmell, Carvel H., 6917
Cartolano, Lisa Lewis, 6415
Cartwright, Cheri D., 7974
Cartwright, David W., 243
Cartwright, Herbert L., 8749
Cartwright, Phyllis J., 7843
Cartwright, Roy G., 7923
Carty, Penny, 83
Caruso, Anthony F., 3794
Caruso, Christina J., 363
Caruso, Frank A., 4172
Caruso, Gloria G., 363
Caruso, Henry J., 363
Caruso, Marc A., 363
Caruso, Rick J., 363
Caruso, Robert A., 4014
Caruso, Tina P., 363
Caruth, W.W., III, 8952
Caruth, W.W., Sr., Mrs., 8952
Carvajal, Raymond, 9166
Carvalho, Ricardo, 2474
Carvel 1991 Trust, Agnes, The, 5710
Carvel Unitrust Remainderman, Thomas,
    5710
Carvel, Agnes, 5710
Carvel, Thomas, 5710
Carver, Doris, 1426
Carver, Joel, 166
Carver, John A., 3274
Carver, Roy J., Jr., 3274
Carver, Roy J., Sr., 3274

Cetti, Carlo, 705
CFA Properties, Inc., 2520
CFS Bancorp, Inc., 3118
CGS Industries, Inc., 6904
CH2M Hill, 2654
Chace, Arnold B., 8523
Chace, Arnold B., Jr., 8523
Chace, Beatrice O., 8523
Chace, Malcolm G., 8523
Chace, Malcolm G., III, 8523
Chace, Malcolm G., Jr., 8523
Chace, Richard, M.D., 5089
Chace, Scott, 7139
Chada Foundation, 5910
Chadburn, Carl T., 1627
Chadderdon, Doug, 2570
Chaddick, Elaine M., 2655
Chaddick, Harry F., 2655
Chadick, Gary R., 3328
Chadwick, Dorothy J., 5726
Chadwick, John W., 5341
Chadwick, Keith, 5781
Chadwick, Laura Farish, 8894
Chadwick, Patricia W., 8518
Chafetz, Howard, 3842
Chafetz, Irwin, 3842
Chafetz, Laurence, 3842
Chafetz, Roberta, 3842
Chaffee, Paul, 4428
Chaffin, Lawrence, Jr., 1261
Chafuen, Alejandro A., 9391
Chagin, Doris Salomon, 3084
Chaho, Doris C., 1568
Chaho, Michael, 1568
Chai, Ping Yin, 4125
Chaille, Gregory A., 8049
Chain, John T., Jr., Genl., 2832
Chain, Mark M., 1527
Chaintreuil, Rennie, 6135
Chais, Emily, 371
Chais, Mark, 371
Chais, Pamela, 371
Chais, Stanley, 371
Chais, William, 371
Chait, Gerald, 8214
Chakere, Pauline, 7866
Chakko, M., 1239
Chalkley, Michael, 7436
Chalmers, Bruce A., 3940
Chalmers, Don, 5466
Chalsty, John S., 7126
Chamberlain Group, Inc., 2711
Chamberlain, Bryce B., 2750
Chamberlain, Charles C., 6863
Chamberlain, David, 495
Chamberlain, David M., 4172
Chamberlain, Karin, 495
Chamberlain, Kathryn C., 6863
Chamberlain, Michael, 5491
Chamberlin, Dolly, 1594
Chamberlin, John, 156
Chamberlin, Nat, 4035
Chamberlin, Patience, 5098
Chamberlin, Patience M., 4035
Chambers, Anne Cox, 2318, 2367
Chambers, Burke, 76
Chambers, Caroline E., 4251
Chambers, Carolyn R., 8881
Chambers, Carolyn S., 8004
Chambers, Coeta, 828
Chambers, Constance E., 372
Chambers, Elizabeth, 8004
Chambers, Evelyn H., 1354
Chambers, James Cox, 2318
Chambers, Jennifer G., 5324
Chambers, John T., 372, 388
Chambers, Julius L., 7439
Chambers, Karla S., 8013
Chambers, Merle C., 1354
Chambers, Michael J., 5324
Chambers, Patricia A., 5324
Chambers, Raymond G., 5324, 5367
Chambers, T. Edgar, 5207
Chambers, Tina Brown, 5324

Chambers, Virginia, 3243
Chambers, William D., 9723
Chamblee, Angie, 3131
Chameli, Kathy Wahlert, 2284
Chamley, Amy C. Kilgus, 3232
Champagne, Joseph, 4256
Champassak, Thun, 4258
Champion, Nancy Kopper, 1453
Champlin, Brad L., 70
Champlin, George S., 8524
Champlin, James E., 1505
Chan, Amy H. Caplow, 6860
Chan, Andrew, 562
Chan, Annie M.H., 490
Chan, Belinda, 7092
Chan, Deborah, 6457
Chan, Gerald, 4043
Chan, Lo-Yi, 3801
Chan, Ronnie, 4043, 5989
Chancellor, Shane A., 3117
Chancellor, Steven E., 3117
Chand, M. Rizwan, 8284
Chandler, Bridgett, 9694
Chandler, Carol, 3993
Chandler, Charles Q., 3369
Chandler, Charles Q., IV, 3369
Chandler, Edward K., 3016
Chandler, Fay Martin, 7787
Chandler, Heather, 823
Chandler, John, 2379
Chandler, Joy, 8284
Chandler, Kent, Jr., 2637
Chandler, Linda, 3230
Chandler, Lynn F., 8576
Chandler, Martha, 9003
Chandler, Ralph B., 37
Chandler, Richard B., Jr., 2356
Chandler, Roy W., 9796
Chandler, Stephen M., 1257
Chandler, Theodore L., 9454
Chandley, Brian M., 4209
Chane, Lawrence S., 8197
Chaney Enterprises, L.P., 3587
Chaney, Francis H., II, 3587
Chaney, Hulet, 8732
Chaney, Mary M., 3587
Chaney, Mike, 3255
Chaney, Reginald J., 9485
Chaney, Victoria Lea, 2850
Chaney, William R., 7143
Chang, Andrew I.T., 2547
Chang, Deborah J., 1786
Chang, Jae Min, 214
Chang, Kathy, 7599
Chang, Lita W., 7118
Chang, Pancho, 725
Chang, Robert N., 5160
Chang, Samuel, 121
Chang-Barnes, Ann, 5018
Chanin, Leona, 5730
Chann, Shirley J., 91
Channel 4/SD Padres Package, 1306
Channing, Susan Stockard, 2007
Chanticleer Charitable Trust, The, 8140
Chapell, Hugh, 2288
Chapin, Barbara Bishop, 1939
Chapin, Charles M., III, 5440
Chapin, Charles S., 7384
Chapin, Chester F., 7384, 7452
Chapin, Robert D., 2191
Chapin, S.B., 8579
Chapin, Samuel C., 7384, 7452
Chapin, Terry D., 1236
Chapin, William H., 8644
Chapla, Robert, 4252
Chaplin, Charles E., 5360
Chaplin, Christina Stafford, 2247
Chaplin, Harvey R., 2260, 4187
Chaplin, Paul B., 2260
Chaplin, Wayne E., 2260
Chapman High School, 8595
Chapman, Adaline Dinsmore, 374
Chapman, Ben, 5322
Chapman, Daniel H., 9049

Chapman, Dennis, 3160
Chapman, Don, 8014
Chapman, Elizabeth W., 3252
Chapman, George B., Jr., 7688
Chapman, H.A., 7928
Chapman, Howard L., 3125, 3252
Chapman, Hugh M., 2513, 7359
Chapman, Jack, 9111
Chapman, Jack T., 8898
Chapman, Joan, 2656
Chapman, John, 8833
Chapman, John S., 2768
Chapman, Katharine M., 9976
Chapman, Kelly Boles, 4228
Chapman, Linda, 4962
Chapman, Lise P., 5351
Chapman, Mary K., 7928
Chapman, Max C., Jr., 9976
Chapman, Norman, 2656
Chapman, Norman H., 8595
Chapman, Patricia Tynan, 647
Chapman, Richard E., 3434
Chapman, Robert H., III, 8569, 8595, 8612
Chapman, Roxanne B., 842
Chapman, Steve, 3136
Chapman, Thomas W., 1786, 1834
Chapman, Tom, 2379
Chappel, Don R., 7989
Chappell, Charles A., Jr., 6026
Chappell, M.E., 9147
Chappell, Norman, 3177
Charach, Jeffrey, 4381
Charach, Manuel, 4381
Charach, Natalie, 4381
Charaf, Ricardo, 9363
Charbonneau, Stacie, 4166
Charbonnet, John D., 3475
Charbonnet, Michael D., 3475
Charette, Jane, 1578
Charitable Lead Annuity Trust under H. Gershman Survivors Trust, 567
Charitable Lead Trust, The, 4378
Charitable Lead Unitrust, 4047
Charitable Lead Unitrust under Harold Gershman Survivors Trust, 567
Charles Interim Trust, Roy, 9389
Charles River Laboratories, Inc., 3844, 3914
Charles Trust, Roy R., 9389
Charles, Les, 377
Charles, Marion Oates, 5892
Charles, Michael H., 7040
Charles, Nicole, 4392
Charles, Willis, 3218
Charles, Zora, 377
Charlop, Zevulun, 6832
Charlotte Pipe and Foundry Co., 7357
Charlson, Lynn L., 4537
Charlton, Earle P., Jr., 3846
Charlton, Erik Allen, 8827
Charren, Peggy, 6604
Charron, Paul R., 5758
Charter Manufacturing Co., Inc., 9772
Charter One Bank, F.S.B., 8526
Charter One Bank, N.A., 8526
Chartock, Lewis, 4903
Chasanoff, Allan, 5735
Chasanoff, Judith, 5735
Chasanoff, Michael J., 5735
Chasanoff, Nancy, 5735
Chasanoff, Robert, 5735
Chasanoff, Stephen, 5735
Chasco Co., 5735
CHASE, 7867
Chase Charitable Lead Annuity Trust, W. Rowell, 3413
Chase Manhattan Bank, The, 6277
Chase, Alfred E., 3847
Chase, Alison Mason, 3413
Chase, Arnold L., 1508
Chase, Barbara K., 3413
Chase, Beverly F., 7244
Chase, Cheryl A., 1508

Chase, Cheryl O., 9391
Chase, Colton Hoover, 7674
Chase, David T., 1508, 1509
Chase, Derwood S., Jr., 9391
Chase, Edgar L., III, 3503
Chase, Edith, 1518
Chase, Gabriela C., 9391
Chase, Gregory C., 2598
Chase, Jerry, 4026
Chase, Johanna B., 9391
Chase, John M., Jr., 4385
Chase, John P., 9998
Chase, Lavinia B., 4133
Chase, Lee J., III, 8638
Chase, R. Kingsbury, 3413
Chase, Rhoda L., 1509
Chase, Stuart F., 9391
Chase, W. Rowell, 3413
Chase, William J., 3884
Chase-Lansdale, P. Lindsay, 5971
Chasin, Charlie, 6577
Chasin, Richard, 6825
Chasman, Paul, 9704
Chatam, Inc., 5099, 5105
Chatham Ventures, Inc., 6277
Chatham, Lucy Hanes, 7430
Chatlos, Carol J., 1932
Chatlos, Janet, 1932
Chatlos, William F., 1932
Chatlos, William J., 1932
Chatman, Lavern J., 9486
Chatmon, Kathryn L., 5780
Chattem, Inc., 8684
Chatterjee, Purnendu, 5737
Chatterton, James R., 9940
Chavanne, David, 9100
Chavaree, Laura, 561
Chavez, Paul, 376
Chavez, Richard, 376
Chavez, Ryan, 6772
Chavez, Victor, 5466
Chazen, Jerome, 5739
Chazen, Simona, 5739
Cheatham, Elizabeth, 7375
Checchia, Anthony P., 8395
Cheek, Dennis W., 4843
Cheek, Donna, 8636
Cheek, Georgia L., 8598
Cheek, Vance W., Jr., 8671
Cheeley, C. Ron, 5387
Chehebar Family Foundation, Joseph, 5740
Chehebar, Albert, 5740
Chehebar, Isaac, 5740
Chehebar, Jack, 5740
Chehebar, Joseph, 5740, 5741
Cheiftain, 3302
Chellgren, Paul W., 7574
Chelovich, Peter, 1209
Chemerow, Elynor, 9833
Chemical Investments, Inc., 6277
Chen, Arthur, 346
Chen, Chi Yueh, 6177
Chen, Elizabeth McCoy, 871
Chen, Ida K., 8198
Chen, Stanley, 1319
Chen, Star, 8861
Chen, Thomas F., 2579
Chen, Winston H., 977
Chen, Y.C., 7118
Chenault, Kenneth I., 5553
Chencinski, Isaac, 5742
Chencinski, Moses, 5742
Cheney Trust, Elizabeth F., 2658
Cheney, Amy L., 7574
Cheney, Ben B., 9569
Cheney, Bradbury F., 9569
Cheney, Carolyn J., 9569
Cheney, Daniel L., 5177
Cheney, Eleanora L., 5177
Cheney, Jeffrey P., 9840
Cheney, Piper, 9569
Cheney, Stuart F., 4360
Cheng, Linda Y.H., 1000

Cheng-Kingdon, Anla, 6613
Chenoweth, Pamela A., 9736
Chenoweth, Richard A., 7643, 7761, 7762
Cherbo, Joni M., 1638
Cherian, John, 8319
Cherian, Mariamma, 8319
Cherin, Elizabeth, 4315
Chernesky, Richard J., 7737
Cherng, Andrew, 975
Cherniak, Steven, 7020
Cherniak, Steven M., 7019
Chernin, Megan, 5743
Chernin, Peter, 5743
Chernov, Olga, 395
Cherny, Peg, 8096
Cherokee 2000 Investments, 7988
Cherp, Macon, 2421
Cherrier, Steve, 7319
Cherry, Adam Z., 6159
Cherry, Cathy, 7369
Chertavian, Gerald, 3812
Chesebrough, Robert, Jr., Mrs., 936
Cheshier, Gloria, 8098
Chesney, James D., 9141
Chesnoff, Adam, 1079
Chessum, Darrell D., 1252
Chester, G.M., 9771
Chester, Jack, 2659
Chester, John Chapman, 9771
Chester, William M., Jr., 9771
Chetham, Enid, 4858
Chetsanga, C.J., 6389
Cheu, Leslie A., 7166
Chevalier, Stephan J., 9973
Chevrefils, Dick, 5088
Chevron Corp., 380
Chevron U.S.A., Inc., 80
ChevronTexaco Corp., 380
ChevronTexaco Corporation, 5989
Chevy Chase Bank, 1781
Chewning, T.N., 8173
Chez, Edward B., 2807
Chia, Candice, 1933
Chia, Douglas, 1933
Chia, Frances T.C., 1933
Chia, Katherine, 1933
Chia, Kitty S.H., 1933
Chia, Pei-Yuan, 1933
Chiang, Ann, 1319
Chiang, Gloria K., 445
Chiang, Tiffany, 2757
Chiara, Judith L., 5748
Chiaramonte, Cheryle, 7534
Chiarito, Susan, 4769
Chiarotti, John M., 3109
Chicago Board of Trade, 2660
Chicago Community Foundation, 3021
Chicago Mercantile Exchange Inc., 2662
Chicago Tourism Fund, 3046
Chicago Tribune Co., 2663
Chick, Linda L., 1706
Chick-fil-A, Inc., 2520
Chief Industries, Inc., 4961
Chieger, Kathryn J., 2636
Chiesa, Robert L., 5095
Chihak, Michael A., 91
Chikowski, Brian, 1175
Child Foundation, 5114
Child, Jeff, 963
Child, O. Rex, 138
Child, Orville Rex, 9345
Childears, John, 4991
Childears, Linda, 1362
Childers, Beverly, 4836
Childers, Terry, 23
Children's Apparel Network, Ltd., 6479
Children's Investment Fund, LP, The, 5749
Children's Investment Fund, Ltd., The, 5749
Childress, Owens F., 150
Childress, Vincent D., Jr., 7346
Childs, Beatrice I., 5687

Childs, Daniel H., 7039
Childs, Evelyn, 9964
Childs, James E., 1510
Childs, James, Rev., 4231
Childs, Jean A.R., 5687
Childs, John W., 1510
Childs, Kirsten, 5883
Childs, Margaret Burden, 5687
Childs, Richard S., Jr., 1510
Childs, Roberta M., 3848
Childs, Starling W., 1510
Childs, William F., IV, 3587
Chiles, Douglas C., 8781
Chiles, Earle A., 8005
Chiles, Earle M., 8005
Chiles, Virginia H., 8005
Chill, Virgina G., 4741
Chilton, Arthur L., 8826
Chilton, Elizabeth E., 9723
Chilton, Leonore, 8826
Chilton, Maureen K., 1511
Chilton, Nelle Ratrie, 9710, 9723
Chilton, Richard Lockwood, Jr., 1511
Chilton, Richard Lockwood, Jr., Mrs., 1511
Chilutti, Mark, 8348
Chin, Michael, 2787
Chin, Timothy, 1294
Ching, Edric M., 2540
Ching, Elizabeth Lau, 2540
Ching, Gerry, Mrs., 2551
Ching, Han Hsin, 2540
Ching, Han Ping, 2540
Ching, Hung Wo, 2540
Ching, Meredith J., 2530
Ching, Shelli Mei Li, 2540
Chinnery, Carl, 4842
Chinnis, C. Cabell, Jr., 2158
Chiquita Brands International, Inc., 7571
Chirico, Emanuel, 6725
Chirinos, Nancy, 765
Chirls, Andrew A., 8378
Chiron Corp., 383
Chisholm, A.F., 5753
Chisholm, Dolly, 2480
Chisholm, E.G., 5752
Chisholm, Gertrude K., 7809
Chisholm, M.A., 5752
Chisman, James R., 9533
Chisum, Gloria Twine, 8377
Chitjian, Janice, 993
Chitto, Randy, 5496
Chitty, Kay K., 8581
Chitwood, Dewayne E., 8924
Chmelnicki, Cila, 6751
Chmelnicki, Samuel, 6751
Choate, Arthur B., 6591
Choate, Timothy, 6591
Choate, Tom, 8840
Choban, Tony, 9125
Chobanian, Aram, 4206
Chochon, Richard, 4990
Chocola, Sarah, 3145
Choe, Martha, 9680
Chofnas, Eric S., 2327
Choice Hotels International, Inc., 3589
Chokey, James A., 9828
Chollet, Susan R., 5088
Chong, Michael A., 1599
Chong, Tae Y., 3548
Choo, Michael P., 2530
Chopp, Rebecca, 359
Choppin, Purnell, 3677
Choppin, Purnell W., 6379
Chortek, Peter J., 554
Chosky, Philip, 8142
Chosy, James L., 4656
Chouinard, Yvon, 1331
Chow, Alan, 7773
Choy, Octavio G., 1504
Chrisman, Nancy, 160
Chrisman, Sarah L., 1103
Chrisman, Stephen I., 1126
Christ, Chris T., 4233

Christ, Donald, 865
Christ, Manon-Lu, 1515
Christel DeHaan Family Foundation, 3164
Christen, Morgan, 78
Christen, Morgan, Hon., 85
Christen, Paul, 8625
Christensen, Allen D., 384
Christensen, C. Diane, 384
Christensen, Carmen M., 384
Christensen, E.J., 1426
Christensen, Henry, III, 6186, 6369, 6531, 6974, 7076
Christensen, Maren, 933
Christensen, Ross D., 3313
Christenson, James E., 7694
Christian, Carolyn McKnight, 4533
Christian, Fran R., 4669
Christian, Frank P., 9156
Christian, Harley, 126
Christian, Mary W., 2043
Christian, Ronald E., 3249
Christian, William R., 1324
Christiansen, Bernadette, 4617
Christianson, David O., 8623
Christianson, Theresa L., 4539
Christianson, Todd J., 8623
Christianson, Trudy A., 8623
Christianson, Warren G., 4539
Christie, Elizabeth W., 5431
Christie, James D., 8375
Christin, Nicholas E., 6591
Christman Irrevocable Trust, Anne, 7572
Christman, Jolley Bruce, 7407
Christman, Ray, 2355
Christman, Thomas H., 8481
Christmas Charitable Remainder Trust, R.L., 3982
Christopher, Brent E., 8839
Christopher, Doris K., 2665
Christopher, Jay W., 2665
Christopher, Julie A., 2665
Christopher, Mark M., 3976
Christopherson, Mark, 4560
Christopherson, Sue, 9845
Christy, David M., 4819
Christy, Larry, 3275
Christy, Ralph D., 172
Chronister, Mark, 4623
Chronquist, Gladys, 9861
Chronquist, Harry, 9861
Chrysler Corp., 4265
Chrysler Military Sales Corp., 6057
Chrysler, Harold Zeigler, 4424
Chrzan, Janet C., 3195
CHS Inc., 4540
Chu, Benjamin K., 5779
Chu, Charles, 6107
Chu, David, 5754
Chu, Gina Lin, 5754
Chu, Jack W., 423
Chu, Steven, 671
Chubb, Hendon, 5162, 5440
Chubb, Percy, III, 5162, 5440
Chubb, Sally, 5440
Chulick, Micki, 2701
Chumley, Brenda, 4842
Chun, Craig Mar, 6418
Chun, Grant Y.M., 2530
Chun, Marie, 6418
Chun, Michael, 2535
Chun, Michael J., 2547
Chun-Deduonni, Gail, 6418
Chundi, Vijay, 1096
Chupinsky, Kenneth, 5067
Church, Steve A., 3184
Churchill, Brian, 3161
Churchill, Clint, 2536
Churchill, Clinton R., 2535
Churchill, Hugo, 8107
Churchill, Suzanne Smith, 2548
Churchman, Caroline A., 8123
Churchman, J. Alexander, 8123
Churchman, Lee Stirling, 8123

Churchman, Leidy McIlvaine, 8123
Churchman, W. Morgan, 8123
Ciampa, Dominick, 6859
CIBC, 9068
CIBC World Markets Corp., 1642
Ciccolo, Raymond J., 4026
Ciccone, Madonna, 1034
Cicconi, James W., 8765
Cicero, Jill M., 6823
Cicero, Richard J., 1764
Cichy, Evelina J., 2701
Ciciora, Susan, 3367
Cieloha, Julie D., 9644
Ciga, LLP, 1431
Cigarroa, Joaquin Gonzales, Jr., 8927
CIGNA Corp., 8143
Cihak, Val, 5194
Cimbalik, Marian L., 4450
Cimino, Audrey S., 3597
Cina, John, 5564
Cincinnati Foundation, Greater, The, 3137
Cincinnati Milacron Inc., 7751
Cincinnati, New Orleans and Texas Pacific Railway Co., The, 9485
Ciocca, Arthur, 387
Ciocca, Carlyse, 387
Cioffi, Cristine, 5782
Cipollone, Tony, 3585
Ciraulo, Jerry, 6086
Circuit City Stores, Inc., 9392
Ciresi, Michael V., 4667
Ciriello, Nicholas G., 395
Cirillo, A.C., Jr., 4492
Cirillo, Ceil, 403
Cirone, Frank, 8381
Cirone, William J., 1093
Cischke, Susan M., 4307
Cisco Systems, Inc., 388
Cisco, Cliff K., 2547
Cisco, Thomas E., 276
Cisel, Scott, 2677
Cisle, Donald M., 7660
Cisler, Tim, 9810
Cisneros, Angie, 537
Cisneros, Jeanette, 401
Ciszewski, Robert, 6234
Citation Homes Central, 948
Citibank, N.A., 108, 2393, 5755, 5790, 6552, 6613, 6711, 7065, 7471
Citicorp, 5755
Citicorp Trust Co., 1216
Citigroup Inc., 5755
Citigroup Trust, 2201
Citigroup UK, 7040
Citigroup Venture Capital Ltd., 5755
Citizens Bank, 4236, 5093, 8526, 8544, 8553, 8657
Citizens Bank of New Hampshire, 8562
Citizens Bank of NH, 8545
Citizens Bank of Rhode Island, 8527
Citizens Bank of Southern Pennsylvania, 8208
Citizens Bank Wealth Management, N.A., 4248
Citizens Bank, N.A., 4292
Citizens Banking Corp., 4248
Citizens Business Bank, 652
Citizens Financial Group, Inc., 8527
Citizens First Savings Bank, 4249
Citizens Helping Citizens Fund, 3118
Citizens of Southern Oklahoma, 7979
Citron, Jeffrey Adam, 5293
Citron, Suzanne Lyman, 5293
City National Bank of Charleston, 9723
Ciulla, Joseph F., 7861
Ciulla, Patricia, 7861
Civil, Patricia T., 6026
CJS Partnership, 6916
Ckodre, Gary, 9300
Clabaugh, Gavin T., 4399
Clabes, Judith G., 7848
Claeyssens Charitable Trust, 1318
Claeyssens, Ailene B., 1318

Claeyssens, Pierre P., 1318
Claflin, Janis A., 4297
Claiborne, Catherine H., 9531
Claiborne, Liz, Inc., 5758
Clain, Michael F., 6053
Clamme, Rosalie, 3223
Clancy, Maureen K., 6779
Clancy, Michael, 8502
Clancy, Sheila, 1625
Claneil Enterprises, Inc., 8144
Clanin, Robert J., 3585
Clapham, Clarence, 7707
Clapp, Allen N., Mrs., 3811
Clapp, Anne Melby, 7575
Clapp, George H., 8145
Clapp, James N., II, 9640
Clapp, Joseph M., 7643
Clapp, M. Roger, 7575
Clapp, Margaret, 9640
Clapp, Matthew N., Jr., 9640
Clapp, Paula, 9640
Clapp, Tamsin, 9640
Claps, John L., 91
Clapttrap Trust, 6586
Claramunt, Morrall M., 4428
CLARCOR Inc., 8658
Clardy, Harold D., 8579
Clare, C. Nanette, 9166
Clare, David R., 5164
Clare, Margaret C., 5164
Clarie, D'Arcy R., 2006
Clark Charitable Lead Trust, Audrey I.,
    7189
Clark County Nevada, 5048
Clark Dynasty Chartiable Lead Unitrust,
    Reed, 7189
Clark Endowment, The, 3590
Clark Foundation, 6264
Clark Revocable Trust, Gladys & Franklin,
    9393
Clark Trust, Edith Allen, 6264
Clark, A. James, 3590
Clark, Allen O., 8590
Clark, Andrew, 6428
Clark, Ann, 985
Clark, Audrey I., 7189
Clark, Benic M., III, 8703
Clark, Beverly S., 3453
Clark, Bruce E., 7039
Clark, C.A., 4356
Clark, Carol, 5137
Clark, Carole, 8968
Clark, Carolyn Levy, 9029
Clark, Celeste A., 4358
Clark, Celia, 5703
Clark, Charles E., Sr., 2361
Clark, Charles, Rev., 4309
Clark, Dan, 4986
Clark, Dave, 910, 3425
Clark, David W., 7624
Clark, Dennis, 3278
Clark, Diana B., 9537
Clark, Duncan W., 5252
Clark, Edna McConnell, 5760, 6712
Clark, Edwina Blackwell, 7749
Clark, Elizabeth G., 3591
Clark, Emory T., 9773
Clark, Eugene V., Rev. Msgr., 6199
Clark, Florence B., 7971
Clark, Frank E., 5759
Clark, Frank M., 2661
Clark, G. Thomas, 6067
Clark, Gary, 1947
Clark, Gregory F., 9826
Clark, H. Lawrence, 5760, 6125
Clark, Harold, 5207
Clark, Harris W., 6125
Clark, Hays, 5760, 6125, 6712
Clark, Henry B., Jr., 2551
Clark, J. Murray, 3116
Clark, J.H. Cullum, 9043, 9134
Clark, James, 3353, 7964, 9537
Clark, James E., 5027
Clark, James K., 5027

Clark, James M., 6951
Clark, James M., Jr., 6951
Clark, James M., Mrs., 6951
Clark, James McConnell, 5760, 6712
Clark, James McConnell, Jr., 5760
Clark, Jan, 5051
Clark, Jane, 6569
Clark, Jane F., 5952
Clark, Jane Forbes, 5762
Clark, Jane Rogers, 3937
Clark, Jessie Wilcox, 1603
Clark, Joanne, 7772
Clark, John, 3849
Clark, Jon, 869
Clark, Joseph W., 1986
Clark, Julius, 3423
Clark, K., 3965
Clark, Karen K., 8785
Clark, Kate D., 1780
Clark, Kathy, 1248
Clark, Kevin, 5099
Clark, Kim, 3854
Clark, Kristen, 8240
Clark, Kristin K., 4412
Clark, Lawrence S., 1164
Clark, Lucille, 3353
Clark, Marcella S., 7864
Clark, Margaret B., 5599
Clark, Marilyn, 3407, 7622
Clark, Mary, 9007
Clark, Mary Chichester duPont, 1698
Clark, Michael, 3354, 4243, 5807,
    8968
Clark, Nita C., 9134
Clark, Paul, 9131
Clark, Peggy, 174
Clark, Peter B., 4291
Clark, Peter R., 7189
Clark, Richard, 6777
Clark, Richard T., 7537
Clark, Robert E., 5047
Clark, Robert Sterling, 5761
Clark, Rosamond S., 6125
Clark, Rusty, 3448
Clark, Sarah, 3423
Clark, Stephen, 3965
Clark, Stephen B., 1356
Clark, Stuart A., 3749
Clark, Susan Reed, 235, 399
Clark, Sylvia, 6605
Clark, Terrell S., 1986
Clark, Thomas, 3425
Clark, Thomas H., 7588
Clark, Tom, 4751
Clark, Virginia, 7305
Clark, Vivien, 6387
Clark, W. Van Alan, 5760
Clark, W. Van Alan, Jr., 3965
Clark, William C., III, 3703
Clarke, Athalie R., 1160
Clarke, Bonnie A., 3703
Clarke, Charles F., Jr., 3016
Clarke, David, 2195
Clarke, Glenn, 6561
Clarke, Jeff, 85
Clarke, Kathleen M., 2883
Clarke, Kristy, 4990
Clarke, Lindsey B., 3703
Clarke, Lois A., 9530
Clarke, Meredith A., 3703
Clarke, Pamela J., 4498
Clarke, Robert F., 2546
Clarke, Steven W., 3703
Clarke, William C., III, 3703
Clarke, William C., III, Mrs., 3703
Clarke, William V.H., 9292
Clarkson, Andrew M., 8695
Clarkson, Bayard D., 6156
Clarkson, Brian, 6569
Clarkson, Carole G., 8695
Clarkson, Ted, 9532
Clarkson, William M., 8695
Clarkton Estates, Inc., 6879
Clarno, Leona M., 9683

Claro, Cesar J., 6800
Clary, Lee, 6639
Clary, Mark, 8583
Clary, Tom S., 3250
Clasby, Dwight D., 8839
Clasquin, Lorraine, 8997
Classen, Roger F., 7555
Claster, Mark, 6490
Claster, Susan, 6490
Clatpag Trust, 6586
Clatscatt Trust, 6586
Clattaur Trust, 6586
Clattecam Trust, 6586
Clattesad Trust, 6586
Clauder, Mary Frances W., 7907
Claus, Thomas H., 4261
Clausen, Hillary H., 8019
Clauson, Peter C., 5591
Claussen, Rich, 4987
Clavin, Nancy, 809
Claxton, Dave, 3368
Claxton, Gary, 739
Claxton, Robert, 3107
Clay, Adryon H., 9714
Clay, Buckner W., 9714
Clay, Buckner W., Mrs., 9714
Clay, David, 3260
Clay, Garland, 7939
Clay, Hamilton G., 9714
Clay, Laura, 7979
Clay, Lyell B., 9714, 9715
Clay, Richard H.C., 3441
Clay, Robert N., 3407
Claybourn, Colleen, 9240
Claycomb, Murray, 156
Clayton Trust No. 1, Susan Vaughan,
    9250
Clayton, Constance, 1599
Clayton, David A., 3654
Clayton, Elizabeth, 7476
Clayton, James L., 8659
Clayton, Janice K., 8659
Clayton, Lawrence, 6428
Clayton, Melissa Ann, 9340
Clayton, Norma, 4785
Clayton, Ruth B., 8659
Clayton, Susan V., 8830
Clayton, William L., 8830
Clear Channel Communications, Inc.,
    8831
Clear, Ellen, 989
Cleary, Dennis, 1594
Cleary, Gail K., 9774
Cleary, Kristine H., 9774
Cleary, Marilyn, 3128
Cleary, Russell G., 9774
Cleary, Sandra G., 9774
Cleere, Sonny, 9164
Cleland, Bruce, 3702
Cleland, Isobel, 3702
Clem, Linda, 1463
Clemens, Ethel M., 8006
Clemens, Rex, 8006
Clement, Anne A., 1517
Clement, Dale, 8634
Clement, Dianne W., 3420
Clement, J.C., Jr., 9003
Clement, Sally D., 4710
Clemente, C.L., 6742
Clements, B. Gill, 8832, 8919
Clements, Rita, 9096
Clements, Thomas, 1949
Clements, William P., Jr., 8832
Clemm, Horace T., 9330
Clemons, Shelia, 8732
Cless, Bryan C., 2668
Cless, Gerhard, 2668
Cless, Jennifer U., 2668
Cless, Martin, 2668
Cless, Ruth I., 2668
Cless, Stephen G., 2668
Cleveland Clinic Foundation, The, 7629
Cleveland Electric Illuminating Co., The,
    7630

Cleveland Indians Baseball Co., Inc.,
    7577
Cleveland, Alfred, 7425
Cleveland, Barbara, 2500
Cleveland, Charles A., Sr., 4541
Cleveland, Clif, 8660
Cleveland, David, 7984
Cleveland, Harlan, 6538
Cleveland, John L., 4541
Cleveland, Judy A., 9571
Cleveland, Kenneth S., III, 9521
Cleveland, Rose Ann, 1780
Clevenger, Beth, 9736
Clevenger, Jerry, 3186
Cleworth, Kim, 9547
Cliff, Ursula, 6084, 6208
Cliff, Walter C., 6084, 6208
Clifford, Charles H., 788
Clifford, Charles H., Jr., 788
Clifford, Cornelia W., 5460
Clifford, Ed, 169
Clifford, John, 4690
Clifford, Karen, 8431
Clifford, Nancy, 3189
Clifford, Robert C., 4647
Clifford, Stewart B., 5460
CliffStar Corp., 2248
Clifton, Clarence C., 3494
Clifton, Dotsy S., 9419
Clifton, Karen A., 104
Clifton, Paul T., 104
Clifton, Troy, 9475
Cline Co., Inc., The, 8580
Cline, Brenda, 7415
Cline, Bud, 4327
Cline, Dale, 7415
Cline, David, 79
Cline, David M., 8580
Cline, Junior, 4870
Cline, Linda, 4392
Cline, Martha, 8580
Cline, N.Q., Sr., 8580
Clingen, Brian T., 2669
Clingen, Deidre M., 2669
Clingen, Kenneth W., 2669
Clinton Investment Co., 8567
Clinton, Chelsea V., 5763
Clinton, Edward X., 2664
Clinton, Hillary Rodham, 5763
Clinton, J.D., 2151
Clinton, John H., Jr., 989
Clinton, Mary Kay, 3077
Clinton, Mary Susan, 2151
Clinton, William Jefferson, 5763
Clippard, Bernard, Jr., 8640
Clive, Winifred Johnson, 8146
Clodfelter, Daniel G., 7458
Cloninger, Kermit, 7366
Cloonan, Edward T., 5529
Clorox Co., The, 389
Clorox Company Foundation, The, 381
Close, Anne Springs, 8617
Close, Chuck, 5484
Close, Derick S., 8617
Close, Elliott Springs, 8617
Close, Frances A., 8617
Close, H.W., 7370
Close, H.W., Jr., 8617
Close, Jake, 9779
Close, Katherine Anne, 8617
Close, M. Scott, 8617
Clothier, Brad, 3354
Cloud, Amanda, 9189
Cloud, Betty, 9447
Cloud, Ernest, Jr., 9421
Cloud, Sanford, 1519
Cloud, Sanford, Jr., 1563
Clough, Charles I., Jr., 4211
Clough, Leonard G., Rev., 1515
Clough, William P., III, 5631
Clover Capital Mgmt., 7526
Clowe, David C., 1870, 1961, 1962
Clowes, Alexander W., 3120
Clowes, Allen W., 3119, 3120

Clowes, Edith W., 3120
Clowes, George H.A., 3120
Clowes, George H.A., Jr., 3120
Clowes, Jonathan J., 3120
Clowes, Lynn L., 3120
Clowes, Margaret J., 3120
Clowes, Thomas J., 3120
Club & Restaurant Wines, Inc., 5074
Clubb, Megan F., 9559
Cluck, Monte, 8758
Clune, David F., Dr., 1481
Clusen, Charles M., 5551
Cluster, Darryl W., 762
Clyde, Calvin, Jr., 9285
Clymer, John, 9898
Clymer, John H., 3961
Clymer, Ray, 9280
Clyne, Richard A., 5031
CMRCC, Inc., 6277
CNA Financial Corp., 2670
CNL Financial Group, Inc., 2231
Coad, Nettie L., 7343
Coakley, Robert M., 826
Coan, John, 175
Coan, Kathleen, 7984
Coate, Carol, 7748
Coates, Elizabeth Huth, 8834
Coates, John, 391
Coates, Norman, 391
Coates, Philip, 5574
Coates, Stella, 391
Coates, Thomas, 823
Coates, Vincent J., 391
Coats, Nancy L., 7964
Cobb, Barbara R., 8233
Cobb, Bradley, 1936
Cobb, Calvin H., Jr., 1796
Cobb, Charles E., Jr., 1935
Cobb, Christian M., 1935
Cobb, Colleen O., 1935
Cobb, G. Elliott, Jr., 9421
Cobb, Gay Plair, 1088
Cobb, Helene O'Neil, 3701
Cobb, Henry N., 5548
Cobb, John, 2900
Cobb, Luisa S, 1935
Cobb, Rhoda W., 1936
Cobb, Sara B., 3180, 3194
Cobb, Serena, 10000
Cobb, Steve, 345
Cobb, Sue M., 1935
Cobb, Tobin T., 1935
Cobb, Tyrus R., 2349
Cobb, William L., Jr., 7244
Cobb, William R., 1936
Cobell, Elouise, 4636, 4937
Coberly, Mark, 3368
Cobie, Nancy, 7744
Coblence, Alain, 5623
Coblentz, William, 250
Coblentz, William K., 774, 775
Coblin, James M., 7440
Coblitz, Gary, 7764
Coblitz, Rick, 7534
Coborn, Dan, 4534
Cobos, Peter J., 6326
Coburn, Jean Crummer, 432
Coca-Cola Bottlers' Assn., 2350
Coca-Cola Co., The, 2352, 2377, 8082
Coca-Cola Enterprises Inc., 2351
Cocchiarella, Elizabeth B., 4934
Cochran, Jan, 4057
Cochran, John R., III, 1730, 8149
Cochran, Martha, 1338
Cochran, Patricia, 1080
Cochran, Patricia A., 8149
Cochran, Paula, 7618
Cochran, Steven B., 7991
Cochrane, Eugene W., Jr., 7359
Cochrane, Katharine C., 30
Cocke, Dudley, 4524
Cockerham, Sally, 3470
Cockrell, David A., 8835
Cockrell, Dula, 8835

Cockrell, Ernest D., II, 8835
Cockrell, Ernest H., 8835, 8960, 9273
Cockrell, Ernest, Jr., 8835
Cockrell, Janet S., 8835
Cockrell, Virginia H., 8835
Cockren, Robert W., 5379
Cockrum, Brigid Anne, 9013, 9123
Cocumelli, Karen Smythe, 1170
Coddington, Ricci, 607
Code, Andrew W., 2671
Code, Susan K., 2671
Codell, J. Hagan, 3449
Codey, John, 6171
Codispoti, Joyce, 5165
Codispoti, Nicholas, 5165
Codrington, George W., 7578
Cody, Dennis M., 3816
Cody, J. Terrence, 3130
Cody, Mary Ellen, 1668
Cody, Nympha H., 6999
Cody, Thomas G., 7574, 7624
Coe, Charles R., Jr., 7962
Coe, Elizabeth Merrick, 7962
Coe, James, 4790
Coe, Kenneth, 7441
Coe, Ross, 7962
Coe, Ward I., 7962
Coelho, Daniel S., 222
Coen, Beverly J., 7781
Coen, Kent, 4997
Coen, Steve, 3372
Cofer, Susan Seydel, 2525
Coffey Trust, Harold F., 7339
Coffey, Robert L., 9094
Coffey, Robin S., 2787
Coffey, W. Lee, 7932
Coffield, Daniel, 4255
Coffill, William J., 1178
Coffin, Alice S., 1510
Coffin, Anne, 6917
Coffin, Donna S., 889
Coffin, Susan, 3897
Coffman, Dionisia Bejarano, 9422
Coffman, Marcia, 4964
Cofrin, David A., 2310, 9738
Cofrin, David H., 2310
Cofrin, Edith D., 2310
Cofrin, Gladys G., 2310
Cofrin, Mary Ann, 9738
Cofrin, Mary Ann H., 2310
Cofrin, Mary Ann P., 2310
Cofrin, Paige W., 2310
Cogan, Gregory, 3851
Cogan, John F., Jr., 3851
Cogan, Michele M., 5099
Cogen, Ruth P., 7097
Coggin, James A., 61
Coggins, Colleen M., 4045
Coglianese, Marcy, 9885
Cogswell, Karen A., 403
Cogswell, Leander A., 5084
Cogswell, Wilton W., III, 1447
Cogut, Craig, 5766
Cogut, Deborah, 5766
Cohan, Eugene L., 6657
Cohen Family Foundation, Inc., The, 3148
Cohen Trust, Ben, 3592
Cohen Trust, Lori, 5771
Cohen, Abby J., 5767
Cohen, Abraham E., 5769
Cohen, Abraham J., 5771
Cohen, Alan, 3148
Cohen, Alan H., 3183
Cohen, Albert H., 3598
Cohen, Alexandra M., 1512
Cohen, Andrea, 8237
Cohen, Barbara, 8237
Cohen, Barton J., 4820
Cohen, Ben, 3592
Cohen, Betsy Z., 8088
Cohen, Bette D., 3683
Cohen, Betty S., 6367, 6954
Cohen, Bluma D., 6278

Cohen, Bonnie, 4116
Cohen, Bonnie R., 1835
Cohen, Cathy J., 4223
Cohen, Chaim, 5965
Cohen, Charlotte McKee, 9045
Cohen, Daniel H., 5769
Cohen, David, 3931, 5986
Cohen, David J., 5771
Cohen, David L., 8152
Cohen, David M., 5767
Cohen, David S., 1363
Cohen, Debra L., 3675
Cohen, Denise A., 5769
Cohen, Edward E., 8088
Cohen, Edward H., 7056
Cohen, Edward L., 3675
Cohen, Eileen, 1739
Cohen, Eileen Phillips, 1740
Cohen, Elizabeth, 8237
Cohen, Ellen, 8237
Cohen, Ellen M., 5767
Cohen, Emanuel, 3594
Cohen, Erin, 393
Cohen, Gary D., 3148
Cohen, H. Rodgin, 7093
Cohen, Howard K., 3668
Cohen, Israel, 3594
Cohen, Jack D., 5771
Cohen, James E., 1514
Cohen, Jarrod, 5770
Cohen, Jerome O., 9675
Cohen, Jerry, 5337, 6779
Cohen, John, 6952
Cohen, Jonathan L., 5579, 5955, 6405, 7241
Cohen, Jordan J., 5750, 6471
Cohen, Joseph M., 5770
Cohen, Julian, 3968
Cohen, Julie W., 7993
Cohen, K.P., 8889
Cohen, Karen B., 5166
Cohen, Kenneth P., 7126
Cohen, Lauren A., 4234
Cohen, Leon H., 3905
Cohen, Marilyn, 6041
Cohen, Mark L., 3593
Cohen, Martin, 1804, 5768
Cohen, Maryjo R., 1739, 1740
Cohen, Melvin S., 1739, 1740, 3593
Cohen, Michael, 5971
Cohen, Michele, 5768
Cohen, N.M., 3594
Cohen, Nancy, 3668
Cohen, Naomi, 3594
Cohen, Nathalie, 5702
Cohen, Nechama, 5965
Cohen, Neil D., 3593
Cohen, Nina R., 3905
Cohen, Oscar, 6737
Cohen, Paul, 6546, 6646
Cohen, Peter, 3741
Cohen, Philip T., 7690
Cohen, R.S., 1520
Cohen, Rhoda R., 3905
Cohen, Robert, 393
Cohen, Robert E., 6104
Cohen, Russell A., 3905
Cohen, Ryna G., 3593
Cohen, S.Y., Chief Rabbi, 5959
Cohen, Sarle H., 8237
Cohen, Sheldon, 1788
Cohen, Stephanie S., 771
Cohen, Stephen J., 554
Cohen, Stephen M., 3654
Cohen, Steven A., 1512
Cohen, Suzanne F., 3568
Cohen, Suzy, 5986
Cohen, Sylvan, 5206
Cohen, Wendy H., 2027
Cohen, Yetta K., 9426, 9489
Cohen, Zelda G., 3592
Cohen, Zev, 6367
Cohenca, Emy, 5773
Cohenca, Jacques, 5773

Cohenca, Philip, 5773
Cohn, Alan D., 6260
Cohn, Allan L., 3228
Cohn, Bobby Smith, 9194, 9197
Cohn, Gary D., 6719
Cohn, Jeffrey H., 24
Cohn, John D., 9912
Cohn, Mary Louise, 8037
Cohn, Mike, 87
Cohne, Herbert, 4206
Cohrs, Oscar, 7573
Coil, Henry, 405
Coish, Barbara, 5087
Coit, Barbara E., 9317
Coit, David M., 3548
Coit, Susan, 9317
Coit, William E., 9317
Coker, C.W., 8614
Coker, Edna Raine, 2506
Coker, Elizabeth H., 2506
Coker, Frances M., 8922
Coker, Richard G., 2288
Coker, Robert E., 2276
Coker, Roberta, 4919
Coker, Tom, 5492
Colagiuri, Patricia, 6348
Colaianne, Melonie B., 4387
Colame, Barney, 5184
Colatrella, Brenda, 5326
Colavecchio, Alan, 1516
Colbert, Celia A., 5326, 5327, 5329, 8349
Colbourne, Richard K., 1279
Colburn, Betsy P., 2742
Colburn, David, 9395
Colburn, Kathleen, 9395
Colburn, Keith W., 2742
Colburn, Richard D., 394
Colburn, Richard W., 2909
Colburn, Robin Tennant, 2909
Colburn, Tara G., 395
Colby, Benjamin N., 1879
Colby, David C., 1292, 3101, 3102
Colby, F. Jordan, 1879
Cold Heading Co., 4250
Coldwell, Karen, 8381
Cole, Andrea, 4438
Cole, Charles R., 9967
Cole, Christopher A., 6106
Cole, Dan, 1080
Cole, David, 4272
Cole, David C., 9396
Cole, Doug, 764
Cole, Hugh F., Jr., 3595
Cole, Ilene S., 2672
Cole, Jennifer, 8954
Cole, Jennifer R., 2672
Cole, Jerome J., 2672
Cole, John, 5902
Cole, Johnnetta B., 5326
Cole, Joseph L., 869, 1247
Cole, Julie L., 2672
Cole, Kenneth, 5774
Cole, Kimberly A., 8606
Cole, Laura Charlton, 8827
Cole, Lewis, 8081
Cole, Margaret B., 2545, 9396
Cole, Maria Cuomo, 5774
Cole, Nancy, 3124
Cole, Olive B., 3121
Cole, Piper, 1214
Cole, Quincy, 9397
Cole, Richard R., 3121
Cole, Robert A., 3098
Cole, Ronnie, 9191
Cole, Sarah R., 7535
Cole, Sue W., 7493
Cole, Susan P., 7176
Cole, Wallace, 79
Cole-Corona, Gretchen, 7535
Colebank, Laura S., 1570
Colello, Joan, 6728
Coleman, Amy B., 4367
Coleman, B.T., 5498

Coleman, Barbara B., 5324
Coleman, Barbara Bell, 5367
Coleman, Barbara Mary, 5470
Coleman, Baron, 1937
Coleman, Beverly S., 5840
Coleman, Caretha, 989
Coleman, Chase, 7139
Coleman, Claudia, 828
Coleman, Darrell, 9280
Coleman, Deborah L., 3161
Coleman, Dorothy W., 2673
Coleman, Faith P., 3352
Coleman, George, 6746
Coleman, George E., 5470
Coleman, Gregory J., 548
Coleman, H. Richard, 3352
Coleman, Hurley J., Jr., Rev., 4428
Coleman, J. Reed, 2832
Coleman, J. Wilbur, 5207
Coleman, J.D. Stetson, 2673
Coleman, James E., 548
Coleman, Jeffrey E., 5470
Coleman, Joe E., 9041, 9198
Coleman, John, 5207
Coleman, John B., Jr., 8670
Coleman, Karen, 9977
Coleman, Kathleen A., 7579
Coleman, Kenneth J., 7579
Coleman, Larry, 2094
Coleman, Leonard S., Jr., 5391
Coleman, Lester E., 7579
Coleman, Lewis W., 913
Coleman, Louise, 2812
Coleman, M. Graham, 6323
Coleman, Maggie, 4227
Coleman, Marjorie Thalheimer, 3744
Coleman, Mary Sue, 2097
Coleman, Nan L., 9419
Coleman, Paul, 349
Coleman, Reed, 9918
Coleman, Robertha K., 7340
Coleman, Ruth, 1937, 9775
Coleman, Sally C., 2775
Coleman, Thomas Brooks, III, 7340
Coleman, William T., Jr., 7031
Colen, Gerald R., 1938
Colen, Ina A., 1938
Colen, Kenneth D., 1938
Colen, Leslee R., 1938
Colen, Robert, 1938
Colen, Sidney, 1938
Coles, Courtney, 4123
Coles, Isobel, 5775
Coles, Jan, 1463
Coles, Joan C., 5775
Coles, Martin, 9690
Coles, Michael C., 5775
Coles, Michael H., 5775
Coles, Richard, 5775
Coles, T.T., 9181
Coletti, Brynne F., 7623
Coletti, Robert E., 7623
Colgan, Michael, 6708
Colgate Investments, 3662
Colglazier, Boyd, 7573
Colin, Barbara, 5776
Colin, Cynthia Green, 6096
Colin, Fred, 5776
Colin, Jean, 5194
Colin, Rebecca, 5776
Colin, Samuel F., 5776
Colin, Stephen, 5776
Coll, Cynthia Garcia, 8551
Collamore, Thomas J., 5545
Collat, Charles A., 47
Collat, Patsy W., 47
Collaton, Elizabeth, 9522
Collazo, Ernest J., 6613
Colleen Investments, LLC, 5652, 7132
College Gardens, 3683
Collen, Desire, 5973
Collesano, Marguerite, 7050
Collette Travel Service, Inc., 8558
Collette, Gay, 9044

Colley-Lee, Myrna, 6824
Collier, Christina C., 9146
Collier, David, 1139, 3095
Collier, Glenn, 7866
Collier, Martin, 9595
Collier, Miles C., 2160
Collier, Parker J., 2160
Collier, Robert, Hon., 7460
Collingsworth, Connie, 9591
Collins Building Services, 7174
Collins Foundation, Carr P., 9180
Collins, Angelo, 5283
Collins, Anthony L., 2429
Collins, Arthur D., Jr., 4622
Collins, Atwood, III, 1662
Collins, Bob, 9780
Collins, Brian D., 9971
Collins, Calvert K., 8837
Collins, Carol H., 5778
Collins, Carol L., 397
Collins, Carol Ohmer, 1939
Collins, Carr P., 8837
Collins, Charles H., 1510
Collins, David C., 396
Collins, Diane, 2145
Collins, Donald A., 8178
Collins, Douglas, 5894
Collins, Duane E., 7796
Collins, Frances, 5894
Collins, Fred, 8582
Collins, Fulton, 7930
Collins, G. Fulton, III, 7929
Collins, H. Michael, 193
Collins, James A., 397
Collins, James E., 3776, 4209
Collins, James H., 2699
Collins, James M., 8838
Collins, Jerry, 4256
Collins, John P., Jr., 1161, 1166, 1167
Collins, John R., 2917
Collins, Joseph, 5777
Collins, Julia D., 5778
Collins, Kelly L., 397
Collins, Kristine E., 4886
Collins, Linda S., 6912
Collins, Maribeth W., 8007
Collins, Mark M., Jr., 5894
Collins, Mark R., 581
Collins, Mary C., 396
Collins, Mary E., 2429
Collins, Meaghan Jones, 1349
Collins, Michael G., 4758
Collins, Michael J., 8838
Collins, Patrick, 671
Collins, Patrick F., 657
Collins, Paul J., 134, 5778
Collins, Phyllis Dillon, 5894
Collins, Priscilla B., 9659
Collins, Richard H., 8837
Collins, Roger B., 7930
Collins, Roland A., 5778
Collins, Roy T., 4886
Collins, Rudy V., 4255
Collins, Ruth M., 1166
Collins, Susan, 5508
Collins, Susanne, 2441
Collins, Suzanne M., 7929, 7930
Collins, Thomas C., 983
Collins, Timothy C., 6812
Collins, Tom, 9583
Collins, Tom H., Jr., 9255
Collins, Truman W., 8009
Collins, Truman W., Jr., 8007, 8009
Collins, Whitfield J., 8798
Collins, William F., Jr., 3886
Collins, William, Jr., 4521
Collins-Warner, Nancy M., 9589
Collis, Charles A., 1513
Collis, Elfriede A., 1513
Collis, Lisa D., 9398
Collison, Arthur R., 2623
Collister, Richard A., 4251
Collopy, Francis W., 1392
Colman, Carolyn, 4939

Colomb, Marjorie, 3501
Colombel, Andrea, 6237
Colombel, Eric, 6237, 7169
Colombini, Jeffrey, 420
Colombo, Barrett, 4593
Colombo, Elsie T., 398
Colon, Anthony J., 5971
Colon, Nelson I., 8515
Colonial Company, 42
Colonial Oil Industries, Inc., 2353
Colonial Properties, 61
Colson, Charles W., 9464, 9505
Colson, Philip L., 4759
Colt, James D., 4139
Colten, M.L., 1520
Colton, Barnum L., Jr., 3657
Colton, S. David, 129
Coltrane, Michael R., 7370
Colucci, Anthony J., Jr., 5780
Columbia Energy Group, 3213
Columbia Gas of Ohio, Inc., 3213
Columbia Gas System, Inc., The, 3213
Columbia Management Co., 8049
Columbia Ventures Corp., 9662
Columbia/HCA Healthcare Corp., 8690
Columbus Bank and Trust Co., 2497
Columbus Foundation, The, 7791
Columbus Life Insurance Co., 7903
Colvin, Dorcas L., 7158
Colvin, Richard, 2166
Colvis, Linda, 553
Comai, Barbara L., 4394
Comai, William, 4442
Comart, Jack, 3549
Comay, Estelle, 8193
Comb, David, 4052
Combs, Donald G., 4052
Combs, Earle M., III, 2674
Combs, Earle M., IV, 2674
Combs, Eric C., 2674
Combs, James Leon, 4798
Combs, Jennifer Malloy, 1656
Combs, Loula Long, 4858
Combs, Samuel, III, 7967
Combs, Sara Walter, Hon., 3449
Combs, Virginia M., 2674
Combs, W.G., 825
Combs, William G., 826
Comcast CICG, LP, 8152
Comcast QVC, Inc., 8152
Comden, Betty, 5883
Comdisco, Inc., 2835
Comenos, Phillip, 3925
Comer Foundation, The, 2676
Comer, Charles, 3144
Comer, Donald W., Jr., 9498
Comer, Frances, 2675
Comer, G.L., 8741
Comer, Gary, 2676
Comer, Gary C., 2675
Comer, Guy, 2676
Comer, Jane S., 65
Comer, John D., 2317
Comer, Mark, 478
Comer, Mary A., 2358
Comer, Neil, 3229
Comer, Norman, 3245
Comer, Richard J., Jr., 22
Comer, Stephanie, 2675, 2676
Comer-Avondale Mills, Inc., 22
Comerford, Richard, 5243
Comerica Bank, 4251, 4252, 4354, 4387, 4419, 4444, 4457, 4474
Comerica Inc., 4251
Comey, Paul, 9358
Comfort, William T., Jr., 6150
Comis, Robert L., 8180
Comisky, Gus H., Jr., 8960
Comisky, Marvin, 8119
Commerce Bancshares, Inc., 4797
Commerce Bank, N.A., 4849, 4876, 4896, 4909, 4911
Commerce Trust Co., 4821
Commercial Federal Bank, FSB, 4951

Commercial Security Mortgage Credit, Inc., 5917
CommonSense Partners, 8049
Community Foundation for the National Capital Region, The, 1306
Community Hospitals of Indiana, 3164
Community Quest, LLC, 2720
Community TV Corp., 3999
Companion Healthcare Corp., 8570
Companjen, Johan, 954
Compass Bank, 24, 28, 8855
Comprehensive Cleaning Co., Inc., 5302
Compression, 3683
Compton, Clyde D., 3099
Compton, Elizabeth K., 6113
Compton, James R., 409, 4803
Compton, Kelly H., 8956
Compton, Marshal J., 409
Compton, Robert A., 8718
Compton, W. Danforth, 409
Comstock, Robert F., 3713
ConAgra Foods, Inc., 4952, 4953, 7174
ConAgra, Inc., 4952, 4953
Conant, Miriam H., 2407
Conarroe, Joel, 6119
Conaty, William J., 1553
Concino, Frank J., Jr., 8202
Conde Nast Publications, Inc., The, 565, 6623
Condie, Parker, 4896
Condliffe, David C., 6156
Condon, Christine, 410
Condon, Gerald C., Jr., 9870
Condon, Julie H., 410
Condon, Larry E., 6538
Condon, Paul S., 1044
Condon, Robert C., 3186
Condon, Thomas H., 410
Condon, Thomas J., 410
Condon, Vance, 4990
Condos, Barbara S., 9156
Condron, Christopher M., 5584
Cone, Ceasar, II, 7337
Cone, Ceasar, III, 7337
Cone, Dawn M., 8203
Cone, Edward F., 7493
Cone, Edward H., 8159, 8203
Cone, Elizabeth W. "Betty", 7343
Cone, Fred M., Jr., 2200
Cone, Janet G., 7337
Cone, Judith, 4843
Cone, Martha A., 7337
Cone, Philip, 8159
Cone, Robert L., 8159, 8203
Cone, Sally B., 7493
Cone, Stephen E., 8159
Cone, Walter "Butch", 7337
Conese, Anna May, 1950
Conese, Eugene P., Jr., 1950
Conese, Eugene P., Sr., 1950
Conestoga Wood Specialities Corp., 8231
Conexant, 272
Confer, Peter, 3255
Confidence Services, 5302
Congregation Z.Y.C., 5518
Congressional Quarterly, 2245
Coniglio, Peter, 910
Conklin, Charles R., 7536
Conklin, Laura J., 9739
Conklin, Patricia Berry, 284
Conlan, Terry, 2545
Conlee, Cecil D., 2428
Conley, Gloria C., 9539
Conley, Joan C., 3700
Conley, Renae E., 3474
Conley, Sue S., 9780
Conley, Terence P., 5157
Conlin, Jan, 4667
Conlon, Joy, 6773
Conlon, Michael, 9300
Conlon, Peggy, 1505
Conlon, Robyn T., 9234
Conn, Edith F., 1951

Conn, Fred K., 1951
Conn, Harry R., 7831
Conn, James P., 951
Conn, Kathe, 9764
Connecticut Light and Power Co., The, 1614
Connell, Christopher, 412
Connell, Courtenay E., 3856
Connell, George, 8123
Connell, Hope Holding, 7481
Connell, James V., 7688
Connell, Jennifer, 5075
Connell, Michael J., 412, 602
Connell, Susan M., 8208
Connell, Tara, 9428
Connell, Terence A., 3856
Connell, Timothy P., 3856
Connell, William C., 3856
Connell, William F., 3856
Connelly, Arthur R., 8520
Connelly, Christine C., 8157
Connelly, Daniele M., 8157
Connelly, Deirdre, 3192
Connelly, John F., 8157
Connelly, John J., 8488
Connelly, Josephine C., 8157
Connelly, Thomas S., 8157
Conner, Betty A., 3164
Conner, Mike, 1175
Conner, Susan O., 3196
Conners, John, 218
Connery, Bruce L., 8882
Connery, Crispin H., 6146
Connett, Charlene R., 3413
Connolly, Arthur G., III, 1725
Connolly, Arthur G., Jr., 1687, 1725
Connolly, Arthur G., Sr., 1687, 1725
Connolly, Brian, 5583
Connolly, Cynthia Sprague, 924, 1184
Connolly, Elizabeth Atwater, 4659
Connolly, Frank J., Jr., 3940
Connolly, George R., 9833
Connolly, Gerald E., 9773, 9909
Connolly, Joseph G.J., 8170
Connolly, Michael W., 7137
Connolly, Phillip, 7586
Connolly, Richard F., Jr., 3857
Connolly, Robert M., 8328
Connolly, Ronald G., 413
Connolly, Ruth E., 3157
Connolly, Thomas A., 413, 1725
Connolly, William M., 7335
Connolly-Keesler, Eileen, 9885
Connor, C.M., 7855
Connor, James W., 7953
Connor, Michael J., 5724, 7858
Connor, Robert P., 5599
Connor, W. Robert, 7126, 7439
Connors, Adele, 5517
Connors, Gregory, 9403
Connors, John, 9572
Connors, Julia B., 9403
Connors, Kathy, 9572
Connors, Martin F., 4057
Connors, Mary Jean, 768
Connors, Michael M., 9403
Connors, Mick, 9572
Connors, Patrick E., 9403
Connors, Ross, 9572
Connors, Sean, 9572
Connors, Shannon, 9572
Connors, Timothy J., 5089
ConocoPhillips Co., 7933
Conomikes, John G., 6161, 6162
Conor Medsystems, 3841
Conover, Beth, 4513
Conover, Catherine M., 1764
Conover, Charles W., 3099
Conover, Jeffrey, 2172
Conover, John C., III, 2172
Conover, Katharine, 9977
Conover, Margo, 4513
Conover, Robert V., 9836
Conover, Walter, 1874

Conover, Woolsey S., 3869
Conrad, Bruce R., 7436
Conrad, Deborah, 1270
Conrad, Frank P., 3945
Conrad, Heather, 8456
Conrad, William, 8456
Conrado, Susan, 7099
Conrail Inc., 8507
Conroy, Kathryn "Kit", 6613
Conroy, Richard, 2041
Considine, Ray, 3956
Considine, Terry, 9763
Consolidated Childrens Apparel, 5518
Consolidated Commodities Ltd., 2079
Consolidated Electrical Distributors, Inc., 2712, 2742
Consolidated Natural Gas Co., 8173
Consolidated Papers, Inc., 9867
Consolidated Press, Inc., 4112
Constable, Linda, 3404
Constance, Byron, 4842
Constance, Jamie, 586
Constance, Marcia W., 586
Constantin, E., Jr., 8843
Constantin, E., Jr., Mrs., 8843
Constantine, Ruth, 3855
Constanza, Phyllis Kurlander, 5749
Constellation Energy Group, Inc., 3602
Consumers Energy Co., 4260
Consumers Power Co., 4260
Contant, John A., 2407
Conte, John, 414
Conte, Kristen, 1834
Conte, Sirpuhe, 414
ContiGroup Cos., Inc., 5786
Continental Can Co., Inc., 1520
Continental Grain Co., 5786
Continental Ore Corp., 6802
Continental Sales & Enterprises, Inc., 2938
Contos, Sherry, 3197
Contra Costa Waste, Inc., 553
Contractors Register, Inc., 6648
Contran Corp., 9188
Contreras, Faviola, 9571
Contreras, Jaime, 2579
Contreras, Mark, 7848
Convergys Corp., 7587
Converse, Jane B., 2620
Converse, Kyle Merrill, 4282
Conway, Dennis, 9779
Conway, Diana E., 2953
Conway, Diane, 9810
Conway, Gerald A., 7621
Conway, Gerald A., Jr., 7621
Conway, James F., III, 4014
Conway, John H., Jr., 7954
Conway, John K., 2832
Conway, Kevin C., 7621
Conway, Martine V., 7621
Conway, Robert A., Sr., 7588
Conway, Robert M., 5787
Conway, Ruth J., 7588
Conway, Sean P., 7588
Conway, William, 5757
Conway, William G., 5551
Conway, William G., Dr., 6633
Conwill Co., 3683
Conwood Co., 8663
Coogan, J. Jerome, 3816
Cook Charitable Trust, Donald O., 4262
Cook Inlet Region, Inc., 83
Cook Trust, Peter C., 4261
Cook, Averill, 7242
Cook, B.J., 3046
Cook, Bruce L., 4262
Cook, Byron, 4331
Cook, Camberly G., 734
Cook, Carl S., Jr., 8924
Cook, Carlton, Dr., 4376
Cook, Chadwick W., 734
Cook, Charles, 8587
Cook, Charles C., 1683
Cook, Charles W., Jr., 8662

Cook, Claire Chapin, 8579
Cook, Clyyne, 5064
Cook, Daniel W., III, 8839
Cook, Dawn, 9601
Cook, Dexter L., Jr., 8611
Cook, Donald O., 4262
Cook, Edwin M., 7633
Cook, Emajean, 4261
Cook, Florence-Etta, 4262
Cook, Floyd P., Jr., 1137
Cook, G. Henry, 8153
Cook, Gordon, 4373
Cook, Heleny, 7242
Cook, Jacqueline P., 4262
Cook, Jeanne M., 2146
Cook, Jeverley R., 8839
Cook, John, Jr., 7242
Cook, Kathleen, 5080
Cook, Kelly G., 8845
Cook, Laurie Caszatt, 4262
Cook, Lod, 1310
Cook, Lucille T., 2648
Cook, Malcolm W., 9440
Cook, Marsha, 3186
Cook, Mary Beth, 6694
Cook, Mary McDermott, 8855, 9043
Cook, Michael L., 8768
Cook, Paul C., 4262
Cook, Peter C., 4261
Cook, Phyllis, 250, 730, 961, 1065
Cook, Ralph D., 24
Cook, Rebecca, 7242
Cook, Robert E., 734
Cook, Scott, 415
Cook, Scott D., 696
Cook, Susan J., 7617
Cook, Thomas B., 4262
Cook, Thomas D., 6894
Cook, Thomas Hills, 8493
Cook, Thomas M., 4261
Cook, Tom, 5043
Cook, Wallace L., 5826, 5827, 6668
Cook, Warren C., 7242
Cook, Wayne S., 6863
Cook, Willard, 7242
Cooke Investment Group, 3164
Cooke, Anna C., 2541
Cooke, Audrey P., 7271
Cooke, Dean, 3250
Cooke, Jack Kent, 9405
Cooke, John Kent, Jr., 1949
Cooke, John Kent, Sr., 9405
Cooke, Jon, 6638
Cooke, Kevann M., 2598
Cooke, Nancy Hamlin, 8917
Cooke, Samuel A., 2541, 2545, 2555
Cooksey, Ben R., 3420
Cooksey, Byron T., 2228
Cooksey, Terrence, 7931
Cooley, Arthur M., 3599
Cooley, Gordon M., 3598
Cooley, Ronald W., 4249, 4257
Cooley, Sue D., 8010, 8059
Cooley, Toni, 4737
Cooley-Gilliom, Brian Charles, 8059
Cooley-Gilliom, Robert, 8059
Coolidge, E. David, III, 2621
Coolidge, Francis L., 3891
Coolidge, J. Linzee, 3885
Coolidge, Lawrence, 4038, 4083, 4200
Coombs, Juliette W., 4197
Coombs, Nancy, 4253
Coon, Anne, 2787
Coonen, Karen, 9949
Cooney, C. Michael, 966
Cooney, Cathy, 7567
Cooney, J. Michael, 3413, 7912
Cooney, Loretta W., 2682
Cooney, Robert J., 2682
Cooney, Robert J., Jr., 2682
Cooney, Sandra, 3314
Cooney, William J., 2905
Cooper Charitable Lead Annuity Trust, John and Mary, 92

Cooper Charitable Lead Trust, Eric C., 8158
Cooper Industries, Inc., 8846
Cooper Tire & Rubber Co., 7589
Cooper, Anita, 2911
Cooper, Ann, 6080
Cooper, Beckwith Archer, 2363
Cooper, Beverly A., 6416
Cooper, Bonnie, 9401
Cooper, Breta C., 7739
Cooper, Brian S., 3045
Cooper, Carl, 91
Cooper, Cary, 1463
Cooper, Charles A., Jr., 4228
Cooper, Charles W., 3361
Cooper, Charlotte, 8509
Cooper, Christine, 92
Cooper, David, 9736
Cooper, Dennis, 2441
Cooper, Dennis E., 2477
Cooper, Donald R., 7346
Cooper, Eric C., 8158
Cooper, Frank G., 8171
Cooper, Frederick E., 2363, 2514
Cooper, Frederick E., Jr., 2363
Cooper, Gary, 92
Cooper, Gena, 1446
Cooper, Helen D., 2363
Cooper, J. Gary, 25
Cooper, J. Patterson, 6519
Cooper, James C., III, 9736
Cooper, Jeffrey, 5031
Cooper, Jimmy, 7931
Cooper, Joanne, 1197
Cooper, John, 92, 4798
Cooper, John W., 5417
Cooper, Johnson Joseph, 2363
Cooper, Joseph H., 4954
Cooper, Lynn, 9089
Cooper, Marsh A., 750
Cooper, Marvin D., 9703
Cooper, Mary, 92
Cooper, Michelle R., 8193
Cooper, Milton, 5788
Cooper, Nan Rothschild, 5895
Cooper, Pat, 4743
Cooper, Peter T., 8660
Cooper, R. Casey, 7927
Cooper, Richard H., 2683
Cooper, Rose Mary, 8012
Cooper, Russell, 5703
Cooper, Sonya, 5147
Cooper, Stacey, 6637
Cooper, Stanley, 7192
Cooper, Thomas Joshua, 5484
Cooper, Todd, 5788
Cooper, Wendy A., 9447
Cooper, William A., 4699
Cooper, William C., 9126
Cooper-Hohn, Jamie, 5749
Cooper-Siegel Foundation Charitable Lead Trusts, 8158
Cooperfund, Inc., 2683
Cooperman, Leon, 5923, 6303
Cooperman, Leon G., 5168
Cooperman, Michael S., 5168
Cooperman, Toby F., 5168
Cooperman, Wayne M., 5168
Cooperrider, Keith, 1860
Coor, Lattie F., 4804
Coors Foundation, Adolph, 1352
Coors, Adolph, Jr., 1360
Coors, Dallas M., 1787
Coors, Gertrude S., 1360
Coors, Holland H., Amb., 1352, 1360
Coors, Janet, 1360
Coors, Jeffrey H., 1352, 1360
Coors, Peter H., 1352, 1360
Coors, William K., 1352, 1360
Cooskey, Bryon T., 5409
Cope, Andrew G., 8735
Cope, Carol I., 4955
Cope, Marty, 5491
Copeland, A. Gladys, 3859

Covington, Mary, 2362
Covino, Gregory F., 1569
Cowal, Sally Grooms, 7143
Cowan, Barbara, 4933
Cowan, Barbara Browning, 4933
Cowan, G.M., 9181
Cowan, Geoffrey, 347, 4950
Cowan, George A., 5474
Cowan, Helen Dunham, 5474
Cowan, Ivy, 7486
Cowan, James R., 7486
Cowan, Lisa, 4933
Cowan, William, 4933
Cowan, William B., 4933
Cowans, Christopher, 3897
Coward, E. Walter, Jr., 384
Cowden, Barbara, 3019
Cowden, Louetta M., 8848
Cowden, W.H., Jr., 9120
Cowdin, Christi, 4488
Cowell, John, 7474
Cowell, Julia, 3049
Cowell, Phyllis S., 7474
Cowell, S.H., 423
Cowen, Randolph L., 5801
Cowen, Robert J., 8783
Cowherd, Robert, 4836
Cowie, James, 344
Cowikee Mills, 22
Cowin, Daniel, 5802
Cowin, Joyce B., 5802
Cowin, Richard P., 7629
Cowles Media Co., 4691
Cowles Publishing Co., 9574
Cowles, Charles, 5170
Cowles, E.A., 9574, 9575
Cowles, Florence C., 3279
Cowles, Gardner, 5170
Cowles, Gardner, III, 5170
Cowles, Gardner, Sr., 3279
Cowles, Jan, 5170
Cowles, Jay, III, 4671
Cowles, John, III, 4624
Cowles, Michael A., 4556
Cowles, W.S., 9574, 9575
Cowley, James M., 1087
Cownie, James S., 3281
Cowsert, Susan, 4560
Cox Communications, Inc., 1306
Cox Enterprises, Inc., 2367
Cox, Anita, 1471
Cox, Betsy, 2271
Cox, Bill, 1139
Cox, Bridge, 7979
Cox, C. Lee, 401
Cox, Christopher, 4330
Cox, Conrad L., 402
Cox, Courtney Ellen, 8849
Cox, Cynthia, 3250
Cox, David C., 4543
Cox, Donald M., 5803
Cox, Ferber & Associates, LLC, 3758
Cox, Gary, 9164
Cox, Gordon D., 3128
Cox, Gregory A., 7508
Cox, James M., 2531
Cox, James M., Jr., 7596
Cox, Jerry S., 8849
Cox, Joe, 2258
Cox, Joe B., 2226
Cox, John L., 8850
Cox, Joshua Paul, 8849
Cox, Kathryn, 8382
Cox, Kay, 8849
Cox, Kelly, 8850
Cox, Kenneth, 1830
Cox, Kyle W., 7698
Cox, L. Courtney, 9571
Cox, Lois J., 9146
Cox, Maria R., 5803
Cox, Mark A., 7698
Cox, Martha B., 8001
Cox, Martha W., 3863
Cox, Maurine T., 8850

Cox, Michelle, 9166
Cox, Patricia Nixon, 5646
Cox, Ralph, 3483
Cox, Russell N., 5096
Cox, Samuel, 4255
Cox, Stephanie, 6926
Cox, Steve, 7570
Cox, T. Randolph, 9723
Cox, T.A., 4940
Cox, Tricia Nixon, 2190
Cox, Vicki B., 4543
Cox, William C., Jr., 3863
Coxhead, Peter, 6628
Coxhead, Ralph N., 6628
Coy, Oona, 1671, 4035
Coy, Robert E., 1265
Coye, Molly J., 1479
Coyle, Alcuin, Fr., 5134
Coyle, Dennis P., 2010
Coyle, Frank, 9622
Coyle, Kara, 989
Coyle, Katherine G., 8751
Coyle, Martin A., 6009
Coyle, Patrick E., 9910
Coyne, Ava, 1137
Coyne, Eric P., 424
Coyne, Jean A., 424
Coyne, Joseph F., 2945
Coyne, Marshall B., 1788
Coyne, Martha R., 424
Coyne, Patrick S., 424
Coyte, Julia D., 4590
Cozart, Adrienne, 9021
Cozen, Stephen A., 8499
CPL Industries, Inc., 9766
Crabb, Wendy, 2536
Crabill, Casey, 691
Crabill, John C., 5945
Crabtree, Bethanie, 494
Crabtree, David, Hon., 2296
Cracchiolo, Andrea, III, 142
Cracchiolo, Carol A., 4264
Cracchiolo, Constance M., 4263
Cracchiolo, Daniel, 142
Cracchiolo, Peter J., 4263
Cracchiolo, Peter T., 4263
Cracchiolo, Thomas A., 4264
Craddock, Hubert, 8737
Craddock, R. Frank, Jr., 8821
Cradick, Susan J., 3293
Cradle Togs, Inc., 6479
Craft, Brenda, 1944
Craft, Deborah Ann, 4347
Craft, Robin, 7586
Cragg, Bill, 2922
Cragin, Charles L., 3556
Crahan, Michele McGarry, 863
Craig, Anthony L., 8418
Craig, Arlene R., 694
Craig, Bob, 1463
Craig, Debbie F., 8042
Craig, Eleanor D., 1700
Craig, Geri, 5671
Craig, Jane Alice, 2336, 2337
Craig, Jenny, 425
Craig, Jerome H., 1156
Craig, John E., Jr., 5779, 6103
Craig, Kim, 8153
Craig, Rex, 3243
Craig, Sid, 425
Craighead, Sophie, 9977
Craighead, Sophie Engelhard, 5932
Craigie, Walter, 7494
Crain, Alan R., Jr., 8772
Crain, Ann Lacy, 8851
Crain, Ann Lacy, II, 8851
Crain, B. Walter, III, 8851
Crain, Beatrice, 2727
Crain, Cathy T., 7574
Crain, James T., Jr., 3416
Crain, John W., 9217
Crain, Rogers L., 8851
Cram, Catherine Neilson, 4631
Cramer, Daphna, 5804

Cramer, Douglas, 5804
Cramer, Gerald, 5804
Cramer, Gerald B., 5804
Cramer, Harold, 8379
Cramer, Kimberly, 5804
Cramer, Lauren, 5804
Cramer, Mike, 9068
Cramer, Theiline Wyckoff, 9692
Cramer, Thomas, 5804
Crames, Charles F., 6787
Crampton, Stuart B., 134
Cranberg, Alex, 1406
Cranberg, Alexis, 1406
Crandall, Fonda, 3234
Crandall, Nancy L., 4252
Crandall, William W., Jr., 239
Crane & Co., Inc., 3864
Crane Co., 2687
Crane, Carlotta, 7843
Crane, Charles, 3603
Crane, Debra K., 7784
Crane, Douglas A., 3864
Crane, Ellen, 4483
Crane, Ellen E., 4428
Crane, Frank, Jr., 7843
Crane, James R., 8852
Crane, Josephine B., 3865
Crane, Louise, 3866
Crane, Marjorie Knight, 2097
Crane, Price, 3483
Crane, Robert, 483, 6257, 6538
Crane, Stoddard, 1960
Crane, Tanny, 7580
Crane, Timothy T., 3864
Crane, W. Carey, II, 6659
Crane, William S., 5139
Crank, Celia Whitfield, 8906
Cranston, Colette, 828
Cranston, Kim, 828
Crapple, George E., 1677, 5613, 8268
Crary Public Trust, 5806
Crary, Bruce L., 5806
Crary, Evans, Jr., 2102
Crary, Horace I., Jr., 5513, 5647
Crary, JoAnn, 4428
Crary, Miner D., Jr., 5761
Crass, Loni, 9617
Craven, David, 8847
Craven, David L., 1727
Craven, Elizabeth, 7503
Craven, Elizabeth B., 7496
Craven, Julie H., 4588
Craven, Mari Hatzenbuehler, 2655
Craven, Tracy M., 8847
Cravens, Patsy, 7923
Cravens, Tom, 8841
Cravitz, Herschel, 6895
Crawford Investment, 2356
Crawford, Alva Jean, 7574
Crawford, Amy K., 4655
Crawford, Antonio, 1956
Crawford, Dona, 427
Crawford, E.R., 8162
Crawford, Edward, III, 3469
Crawford, Emily, 6917
Crawford, Felix A., 1956
Crawford, Gordon, 427
Crawford, Helen H., 1570
Crawford, Jeffrey G., 427
Crawford, John J., 1514
Crawford, Lucy, 3441
Crawford, Nancy R., 3867
Crawford, Nancy S., 3867
Crawford, Orsi Z., 427
Crawford, Patricia J., 3281
Crawford, Peter T., 3867
Crawford, Thomas, IV, 3867
Crawford, Thomas, Jr., 3867
Crawford, William D., 669
Crawley, Bernice S., 2224
Crawley, James B., 7934
Crawley, Linda S., 7934
Crawley, Mary W., 7934
Crawley, Sara B., 7934

Cray, Cloud L., 4801
Cray, Cloud L., Jr., 4801
Cray, Laura A., 9222
Cray, Richard B., 4801
Creach, Dale, 4866
Creal, Paul, 4237
Creamer & Son, J. Fletcher, Inc., 5171
Creamer, Dale A., 5171
Creamer, J. Fletcher, 5171
Creamer, J. Fletcher, Jr., 5171
Crean, Andrew, 428
Crean, Donna S., 428
Crean, John C., 428
Creason, Karen K., 8027
Creative Artists Agency, LLC, 341
Creative Hairdressers, Inc., 9501
Creative Investors L.P., 8280
Credit Bureau of Nashville, Inc., 8656
Credit Suisse First Boston Corp., 5807
Credit Suisse First Boston LLC, 5807, 7174
Creech, Kathleen Fox, 8577
Creech, Kay Akey, 7597
Creech, Randolph S., 7597
Creecy, Gloria M., 9498
Creed, Greg, 3457
Creed, Victoria, 7308
Creek, Phillip G., 7729
Creel, James P., 8619
Creighton, Albert M., III, 4047
Creighton, Albert M., Jr., 4047
Creighton, Hilary H., 4047
Creighton, Lorenzo, 8648
Creighton, Peter H., 4047
Crenshaw, Carol Y., 2661
Crenshaw, E. Brown, Jr., 8611
Crenshaw, Hal D., 8661
Crenshaw, Lucia, 8653
Cresci, Andrew A., 559
Cressey, Bryan C., 2689
Cressey, Christina I., 2689
Cressman, Paul R., Jr., 9631
Cressman, Paul R., Sr., 9631
Crest Foundation, The, 5623
Crestar Bank, 9523
Creticos, Angelo P., 3058
Creveling, Ginny, 7967
Crews, Barbara K., 8987
Crews, James, 9730
Crha, Tom, 9615
Cribb, T. Kenneth, Jr., 8425
Crichton, John H., 8811
Crim, Gloice Y., 2517
Crimi, William F., 1519
Crimmings, John P., 9906
Crion Trust, Marion O., 2681
Cripe, Jim, 9780
Cripton, Michael J., 531
Crisco, J. Keith, 7438
Criscuoli, Phyllis M., 5867
Criser, Marshall M., 2197
Crislip, Stephen R., 9723
Crisman, C. Benjamin, Jr., 6998
Crisp, Charles R., 2448
Crisp, Don W., 9158
Crisp, Peter O., 5809
Crisp-Ridge, Sherry, 3141
Crispen, Deanna, 3115
Crispin, Robert, 2418
Criss, C.C., 4544
Criss, Mabel L., 4544
Crissman, Penny, 4256
Critchfield, Jack, 7174
Critchfield, Linda, 227
Critchfield, Paul N., 130
Critchlow, Paul W., 6537
Crites, Bill, 9730
Crites, Dale, 3138
Critser, Charlotte, 3446
Crittenden, Gary, 5553
Crittenden-Palacios, Elizabeth, 5498
Critz, Dale C., Jr., 2480
Croak, Francis R., 9897
Croce, Rudy G., 1089

Curtis, Diane, 5600
Curtis, Donald W., 7438
Curtis, Elizabeth A., 586, 889, 1323
Curtis, Elizabeth H., 239
Curtis, Emma Eliza, 9356
Curtis, Gerald, 3656
Curtis, Gerald L., 7185
Curtis, Gregory D., 8386
Curtis, John, 433
Curtis, Patricia A., 1194
Curtis, Rachel, 3743
Curtis, Sarah, 9881
Curtis, Vincent, 1505
Curtis, William, 3743
Curtiss, Charles B., 4229
Curtiss, Isabelle V., 1518
Curves International, Inc., 8945
Cusac, Richard S., 1031
Cusack, Anne M., 8226
Cusenza, Geraldine, 433
Cusenza, John, 433
Cushing, Barbara, 740
Cushing, Ed, 7344
Cushing, Harvey E., 4024
Cushing, Ray, 7779
Cushing, Robert T., 6915
Cushnie, Douglas J., 7698
Cushnie, Karen W., 7698
Cusson, Richard P., 4209
Custard, Linda P., 8955
Custard, Linda Pitts, 8839
Custer, G. Stanley, 9861
Custer, M.D., III, 3535
Custer, Violet, 9861
Custom Putting Green, 1306
Custom Shops, The, 5305
Customer 1 One, Inc., 8681
Cutaia, Anthony J., 3564
Cutchins, William W., 9382
Cuthbert, Neal I., 4617
Cuthell, Catherine S., 1724
Cutler, Joan H., 3872
Cutler, Laura Katz, 2081
Cutler, Linda Beech, 560
Cutler, Richard, 8631
Cutler, Robert, 3872
Cutler, Stephen, 6251
Cutler, Theodore H., 3872
Cutlip, Kimberly E., 7845
Cutlip, R.B., 9048
Cutrell, Pamela S., 4123
Cutshall, Ronny L., 9302
Cutter, Nancy L., 5089
Cutter, Philip D., 1557
Cutting, Helen M., 5141
Cuzo, Carol, 5091
Cuzzocrea, John, 5194
Cuzzola-Kern, Amy, 8188
Cuzzort, Pamela K., 8735
CVS Corp., 8529
CVS Pharmacy, Inc., 8529
Cybelonics, 1995
Cyphers, Judith B., 1851
Czapski, Max, 7130
Czarnecki, Linda M., 96
Czerepowicz, Judy, 4310

D & H Distributing Co., 8430
d'Adolf, Lila Gimprich, 6035
D'Agostino, Max, 5818
D'Alessandro, Albert A., 1778
D'Alessandro, Arlene, 2151
D'Alessandro, Michael, 2151
D'Aloia, G. Peter, 5113
D'Alonzo, William F., 1706
D'Amaro, Rich, 2411
D'Amato & Lynch, 7040
D'Amato, Catherine, 3812
D'Amato, Janice M., 9656
D'Amato, Michael, 1865
D'Ambrosio, A. Daniel, 1612
D'Amelio, Frank A., 5110
D'Amico, Rudy, 5783
D'Angelo, Luella Chavez, 1377

D'Angelo, Margaret A., 5175
D'Angelo, Peter, 4153
D'Angelo, Peter P., 5175, 5287
D'Antignac, Louisa Glenn, 2399
D'Arcangelo, Debra A., 5357
D'Arcy, Charlotte Donaldson, 7127
D'Arcy, Jessica S., 9269
D'Arcy, Stephen R., 4343
d'Aspremont-Lynden, Claude, Count, 5973
D'Augustino, Gianfranco, 2124
D'Autremont, Gene, 8038
D'Elia, Lorraine, 559
d'Harnoncourt, Anne, 6453
D'Oench, Russell G., III, 6156
D'Olier, H. Mitchell, 2537
Da Frota, Robert, 2240
Daaleman, Henry J., 5334
Daaleman, Timothy P., 5334
Dabah, Barbara, 5820
Dabah, Eva, 5819
Dabah, Ezra, 5819
Dabah, Haim, 5820
Dabah, Kim, 5518
Dabah, Morris, Jr., 5820
Dabah, Renee, 5819
Dabah, Solomon, 5518
Daberkow, Don, 4990
Daberko, David A., 7772
Dabney, Hovey S., 9390
Dabney, Thomas N., 3888
Dachs, Alan M., 270, 435, 535
Dachs, Lauren B., 270, 435, 535
Dacra Development Corp., 1915
Dada, Nargis, 200
Dadakis, John D., 5552, 5612, 5743
Dadd, Robert, 5350
Dadisman, Carrol, 1945
Daetz, Alta, 4252
Daft, Delphine H., 2370
Daft, Douglas N., 2370
Daft, Nicholas, 2370
Daggert, Suzanne, 541
Daggett, Christopher J., 5391
Dahan Homes, Inc., 3604
Dahan, Elisabeth, 1958
Dahan, Haron, 3604
Dahan, Nissim, 3604
Dahan, Rene, 1958
Dahl, James H., 1959
Dahl, Jean M., 3753
Dahl, Larry, 1139
Dahl, Marilyn, 3320
Dahl, William, 1959
Dahl, William L., 1959
Dahley Co., 3683
Dahlkemper, Kathleen A., 8188
Dahlquist, Steven N., 1946
Dahlstrom, Larry, 8632
Dahmen-Ray, Patricia A., 9589
Dahod, Ashraf, 4056
Daigle, Bruce, 1594
Dailey, Julia, 1483
Daily News, LP, 7163
Daily, Julia, 1483
Daily, Mary Ann, 4200
DaimlerChrysler Corp., 4265
Dain Rauscher Inc., 4661
Dainelo Foundation, 1010
Daitch, Lillian, 4365
Dajani, Virginia, 5548
Dakin, John, 1468
Dakri, Musa A., 8960
Dalamater, Jim, 3530
Dalby, Michael, 474
Dale, Berteline Baier, 5590, 6281
Dale, Caroline, 6778
Dale, Harvey P., 5574
Dale, Jeanne M., 3048
Daley, Charles J., 3672
Daley, Clayton C., Jr., 7807
Daley, Elizabeth, 1773
Daley, John P., 6453, 6615
Daley, Michael J., 2660, 3038

Daley, Pamela, 1553
Dalio, Matthew, 1522
Dalio, Paul, 1522
Dalio, Raymond T., 1522
Dalis, Joan W., 9406
Dalis, M. Dan, 9406
Dall'Olmo, Gail, 4327
Dallegge, Sue, 4968
Dalton, Ann V., 1981
Dalton, Arthur T., 3066
Dalton, Barbara J., Ph.D., 6232
Dalton, Beverley E., 9414
Dalton, Charles, 8588
Dalton, Daniel, 5415
Dalton, Dillon, 4444
Dalton, Dorothy U., 4266
Dalton, Dusty, 4444
Dalton, James F., 8063
Dalton, Lynn, 4444
Dalton, Mark, 1465
Dalton, Mark F., 6037
Dalton, P. Hunter, Jr., 7397
Dalton, Sharon C., 1479
Dalton, Thomas, 4444
Dalum, Thomas E., 9960
Daly, Aileen H., 2596
Daly, Andrew, 1468
Daly, Beth A., 2133
Daly, Charles U., 2820
Daly, David M., 6922
Daly, Edward J., 436
Daly, James J., 2133, 5674
Daly, Jim, 9597
Daly, Michael P., 3800
Daly, Paul E., 2288
Daly, Robert, 437
Daly, Robert A., 437
Daly, Robert P., 1570
Daly, Tad, 10000
Daly, Walter J., 3228
Daly, William, 6603
Dalzell, David B., Jr., 9716
Damas, Mary, 5105
Damasco, Jude, 1315
Damato, Charles A., 6053
Dameris, Brian, 9259
Damico, Greg, 9628
Damie, Robert, 3725
Damon, John L., Mrs., 4074
Damon, Peter S., 8551
Damonte, Dirk, 239
Damonti, John L., 5143, 5666
Damroth, David, 4001
Damschroder, Jane T., 4412
Dana Corp., 7599
Dana Foundation, The, 5825
Dana, Catherine, 6747
Dana, Charles A., 5827
Dana, Charles A., III, 5827
Dana, Eleanor Naylor, 5826, 5827
Dana, Herman, 3873
Dana, Lowell B., 4252
Dana, Marshall A., 3873
Dana, Nancy Randall, 4579
Dance, Harold W., 9311
Dance, Ruth B., 9311
Dandekar, Swati A., 3275
Dando, B. Gary, 3737
Dandrew, Bob, 6641
Dane, Edward W., 3981
Danelian, Louise, 414, 1003
Daneman, Gerri Grena, 5194
Daney, Lee E., 8444
Danford, Gladys B., 438
Danforth, Douglas D., 8386
Danforth, John C., Hon., 4803
Danforth, William H., 4803
Danforth, William H., Mrs., 4803
Dangremond, Mary, 1517
Daniel Bader Charitable Trust, 9749
Daniel Industries, Inc., 4809
Daniel International Corp., 8585
Daniel, Barbara F., 8902
Daniel, Bill, 8758, 9131

Daniel, Charles E., 8585
Daniel, Charles W., 31
Daniel, Christopher J., 8902
Daniel, Dan, 3166
Daniel, Desmon, 4428
Daniel, Eric, 3093
Daniel, Jamal, 9008
Daniel, James, 7964
Daniel, James H., Jr., 2396
Daniel, James L., Jr., 8902
Daniel, James S., 23
Daniel, Laree, 9748
Daniel, Lyndra P., 31
Daniel, Mary P., 1199
Daniel, Rania, 9008
Daniel, Ronald, 9254
Daniel, Suzanne T., 8383
Daniel, William L. "Bill", 7516
Daniell, Barbara E., 1523
Daniell, Robert F., 1523
Daniels, Aaron, 1505
Daniels, Anthea R., 7555
Daniels, Bill, 1362
Daniels, Charlotte, 8842
Daniels, Daniel L., 1537
Daniels, Edgar Foster, 5473
Daniels, Eleanor G., 8530
Daniels, Emma, 6813
Daniels, Fred H., 8530
Daniels, Fred H., II, 8530
Daniels, Janet B., 8530
Daniels, John W., 9876
Daniels, Lillian I., 6529
Daniels, Matthew D., 8659
Daniels, Noel, 4737
Daniels, R.W., Jr., 1362
Daniels, Sandra Phyllis Segerstrom, 1122
Daniels, Sandra Segerstrom, 1123
Daniels, Sandy, 3178
Daniels, William R., 724
Danielson, Barbara D., 2700
Danielson, Barbara S., 2700
Danielson, Dave, 9566
Danielson, Donald C., 3165
Danielson, Richard E., Jr., 2700
Dankberg, Jeff, 957
Danker-Basham Foundation, 7174
Dankers, Paul, 6562
Dann, Melissa S., 1858
Danneberg, Linda K., 7698
Danneberg, William H., 7698
Danner, Douglas, 4104
Danner, J.L.C., 5460
Danner, Judith B., 8664
Danner, Raymond L., 8664
Dano, Kimberly R., 4131
Danos, Johnny, 3281
Dansby, Stewart, 75
Danser, G.O., 5153
Dantchik, Arthur, 8470, 9394
Dantzig, Anne, 3206
Danz, Alison, 9577
Danz, Frederic A., 9577
Danz, William F., 9577
Danzi, Michael, 957
Danziger, Peggy Block, 5638
Danziger, Richard M., 5587
Danziger, Sidney, 5829
Daoud, Tarik S., 4254
Darbee, Peter A., 1000
Darby, Ed, 4986
Darcy, Randy G., 4570
Darden Restaurants, Inc., 1960
Darden, Joshua P., Jr., 9484
Darden, Mary, 1960
Dardess, Margaret B., 7439
Dargan, John B.H., 8616
Darivoff, Betsy S., 5831
Darivoff, Philip M., 5831
Dark, Barbara W., 7346
Darland, Tye, 3374
Darling Homes, 8818
Darling, Anne Helow, 2055

Darling, Hazel, 440
Darling, Hugh, 440
Darling, Stan, 4962
Darmon, Avital, 5582
Darnell, James E., Jr., 3677
Darnell, Stephen D., 7603
Darnieder, Gregory M., 2943, 3021
Darnold, Jennifer, 3230
Daro, Phil, 944
Darragh, Dorothy, 8348
Darrah Revocable Trust, Maxene D., 7570
Darrell, Norris, Jr., 3196
Darrow, Anita S., 3069
Darrow, Jessica, 3069
Darrow, K.L., 4368
Darrow, Philip, 3069
Dart Foundation, W.A., 4267
Dart, Claire T., 4267
Dart, Kenneth B., 4267
Dart, Robert C., 4267
Dart, William A., 4267
Darter, Charles W., Jr., 9299
Dartis, Carla, 474
Dartley, Karen, 1524
Dartley, Peter, 1524
Darwin, Elaine Bennett, 1939
Das, E.S.P., 5832
Das, Kuntala, 5832
Dasburg, John H., 4545
Dasburg, Mary Lou, 4545
Daschle, Tom, 9424
Dashefsky, Samuel, 8784
DaSilva Charitable Lead Annuity Trust, Christopher E. and Krista Mary, The, 2120
Dassori, F. Davis, 4064
Daste, Stephen, 3489
Daswani, Vivek A., 9363
Datatel, Inc., 9407
Dater, Charles H., 7600
Dates, Michael, 6380
Datnchik, Arthur, 8470
Dattels, Timothy, 7031
Daube, Sam, 7932
Daubert, Madeline, 7344
Dauch Trust, Helen R., 4268
Dauch, Richard E., 4268
Dauch, Sandra J., 4268
Daughdrill, James H., III, 4770
Daugherty, Barbara, 7223
Daugherty, David M., 1818
Daugherty, Dennis, 1267
Daugherty, Douglas, 8705
Daugherty, Gerald H., 7
Daughrity, Patti, 6638
Daughtery, Earl, 9730
Daughtery, Robert M., Jr., 2132
Daughtrey, Shelly K., 9105
Daughtridge, Gif, 7464
Daughtry, Chris, 3132
Dauler, L. Van V., Jr., 8254
Daum, Virginia Bekins, 273
Dauphin, Charline, 8856
Dauphin, Robin, 8856
Daurelle, Larry, 8168
Daus, Barbara, 9780
Dauthat, Neil T., 9196
Davdowitz, Joseph, 6881
Davdowitz, Rosalind, 6881
Dave, Bernard L., 7690
Davee, Ken M., 2696
Davee, Ruth D., 2696
Davelia, Frank, 8528
Davenport, Chester, 3717
Davenport, Duane, 2356
Davenport, Edna Marion, 8434
Davenport, Erwin, 8879
Davenport, George P., 3531
Davenport, Judith, 8241
Davenport, Mariam M., 8874
Davenport, Peter D., 8164
Davenport, Scott D., 8164
Daverio, George, Jr., 7526

Davey, Linda W., 6823
Davich, George, Msgr., 9302
David Bader Charitable Trust, 9749
David, Betty, 6917
David, Carol, 7601
David, Jeffrey, 7601
David, Larry, 442
David, Laurence R., 9209
David, Laurie, 442
David, Leo, 443
David, Mark, Inc., 7437
David, Pamela H., 636
David, Patricia, 6898
David, Paul, 7601
David, Ruth, 443, 670
Davidow, Diana R., 444
Davidow, Robert A., 444
Davidow, Sheryl T., 4837
Davidowitz, Jacob, 5834
Davidowitz, Leah, 5834
Davidowitz, Rosalind, 6585
Davidson Kempner Advisors, Inc., 5835
Davidson, Andrew M., 3438
Davidson, Anita, 445
Davidson, Betsy, 6290
Davidson, Carleton F., 7602
Davidson, Charles W., 445
Davidson, Curtis, 7932
Davidson, Denise S., 8970
Davidson, Donald, 1482
Davidson, Donnie, 8713
Davidson, Ezra C., Jr., 296, 350
Davidson, Frances, 9598
Davidson, Fredricka, 3189
Davidson, G. Bradford, 6290
Davidson, George A., Jr., 8386
Davidson, Gretchen D., 4613
Davidson, Hilary, 7360
Davidson, J. Matthew, 6290
Davidson, Jay, 1404
Davidson, Joan K., 6290
Davidson, Linda B., 8511
Davidson, Linda Borick, 305
Davidson, Luck, 7343
Davidson, Marty, 4763
Davidson, Marvin H., 5835
Davidson, Patricia F., 1493
Davidson, Peter W., 6290
Davidson, Richard K., 5012
Davidson, Sarah, 8713
Davidson, Scott, 5835
Davidson, Sheila K., 6617
Davidson, Stuart, 7273
Davidson, Terrence M., 1040
Davidson, Thomas R., 9407
Davidson, Tom, 2156
Davidson, Wesley, 3549
Davidson, William, 4333
Davies, Ann, 979
Davies, Barbara, 8501
Davies, Charles R., 3634
Davies, David, 7223
Davies, Hugh, 1040
Davies, Jack, 1785
Davies, Jamie, 404
Davies, John G., 3462
Davies, Louise M., 446
Davies, Mary Elinore, 3783
Davies, Michael B., 6117
Davies, Paul C., 8475
Davies, Paul L., Jr., 783
Davies, Paul Lewis, III, 783
Davies, Pilar H., 783
Davies, Richard, 8671
Davies, Richard W., 1569
Davies, Robert N., 7173
Davies, Sandra Frey, 6923
Davies, Taran, 5662
Davies, Trevor C., 2673
Daviglus, George P., 2153
Davignon, Emile, Viscount, 5973
Davis Charitable Lead Trust, Alma F., 1546
Davis Foundation, Elizabeth Lloyd, 1062

Davis Irrevocable Trust, Harriet, 59
Davis Trust, M.G., 5837
Davis, A. Dano, 1961
Davis, A. Darius, 1870
Davis, Adelaide Shull, 8689
Davis, Alan J., 8377
Davis, Alan S., 9368
Davis, Alfred A., 4630
Davis, Alfred M., 2366
Davis, Alfred P., 1363
Davis, Alice K., 1962
Davis, Amy, 1363
Davis, Andrew Adams, 3608
Davis, Ann, 2366
Davis, Anne, 3049
Davis, Anne M., 4050
Davis, Arthur Vining, 1964
Davis, Belva, 296
Davis, Billie, 8842
Davis, Bradley K., 2238
Davis, Brenda S., 5181
Davis, Brigit Ann, 1398
Davis, Carl A., 8857
Davis, Carolyn P., 4738
Davis, Catherine, 1653, 7163
Davis, Champion McDowell, 7352
Davis, Charles, 8926
Davis, Charles A., 6744
Davis, Christopher Cullom, 3608
Davis, Christopher J., 8418
Davis, Clarence, 8577
Davis, Clark, 4926
Davis, Claude E., 3174
Davis, Clive J., 5836
Davis, Cora, 3607
Davis, Courtenay C., 1363
Davis, D. Scott, 2503, 3585
Davis, Dana Michelle, 6615
Davis, Danny, 7397
Davis, Dave, 982
Davis, David, 3834, 9787
Davis, David C., 8654
Davis, Derek, 3853
Davis, Dix F., 4209
Davis, Donald R., 4831
Davis, Dwight E., 9741
Davis, Edie, 2697
Davis, Edward, 2701, 6298
Davis, Edwin W., 4546
Davis, Eleanor L., 8157
Davis, Elissa R., 1253
Davis, Elizabeth K., 8297
Davis, Ellen, 1525
Davis, Elwood B., 1610, 1653
Davis, Erroll B., Jr., 9742
Davis, Eugene L., 8014
Davis, Evelyn Green, 6096
Davis, Flobelle Burden, 5687
Davis, Florence, 7040
Davis, Florence A., 7048
Davis, Florence S., 8689
Davis, Frank, 7335
Davis, Fred L., 8638
Davis, Fred W., II, 4546
Davis, Frederick W., 4546
Davis, G. Franklin T., 7353
Davis, G. Gervaise, III, 973
Davis, G. Murphy, 9130
Davis, Gale L., 9988
Davis, Gale Lansing, 4577
Davis, Gary B., 1253
Davis, Gary S., 1525
Davis, George, 226
Davis, George E., 3195
Davis, George V., 25
Davis, H. Scott, Jr., 3427
Davis, H. Stewart, 2354
Davis, Harrison S., 8689
Davis, Hilda J., 1526
Davis, Holbrook R., 1964
Davis, J. Bradley, 2882
Davis, J. Haywood, 7411, 7412, 7413
Davis, J. Morton, 6585
Davis, J.D., 8957

Davis, J.H. Dow, 1964
Davis, Jack, 87
Davis, Jack E., 86
Davis, Jaclyn L., 3160
Davis, James, 9231
Davis, James C., 3565, 3606
Davis, James S., 4050
Davis, Jay C., 670
Davis, Jay M., 2366
Davis, Jennifer, 4025, 7556
Davis, Joe C., 8665
Davis, Joel P., 1964
Davis, John B., Jr., 4498
Davis, John H., 3607, 3875
Davis, John Martin, 8995
Davis, John P., III, 7688
Davis, Joseph Homer, Jr., Rev., 9071
Davis, Judith M., 8570
Davis, Julianna Beecherl, 8792
Davis, Karen, 3834, 5779
Davis, Karen K., 6346
Davis, Karyll A., 8204
Davis, Kathleen M., 3598
Davis, Kathryn W., 3608
Davis, Kathy, 9776
Davis, Kimberly J., 3606
Davis, Lansing A., 3608
Davis, Laurianne T., 4460
Davis, Lee W., 1870
Davis, Leroy, 1983
Davis, Lois E., 8857
Davis, Lucy, 1363
Davis, M.E., 7219
Davis, M.L., 4769
Davis, Martin C., 8988
Davis, Mary E., 4546
Davis, Michael M., 3769
Davis, Michael W., 3595
Davis, Mike, 5433, 6233
Davis, Milton Austin, 1962
Davis, Moshe, 2697
Davis, Nancy, 91, 9126
Davis, Norm, 17
Davis, Peggy, 5596
Davis, Preston, 1526
Davis, Qudsia, 3161
Davis, R. Scott, 3422
Davis, Rebecca K., 2311
Davis, Richard, 4704
Davis, Richard A., 7944
Davis, Rick, 7593
Davis, Rita M., 3874
Davis, Robert D., 1870, 1961
Davis, Robert G., 9245
Davis, Robert J., 3874
Davis, Robert L., 3712
Davis, Robert S., 4583, 4703, 8547
Davis, Sallie, 8457
Davis, Sam L., 4243
Davis, Samuel B., 2074
Davis, Samuel S., 2074, 4546
Davis, Sandra, 4237
Davis, Sarah Crutchfield, 7348
Davis, Sarah H., 1964
Davis, Scott P., 3446
Davis, Shelby Cullom, 3608
Davis, Shelby M.C., 9988
Davis, Shelby Moore Cullom, 3608
Davis, Sonya Meyers, 4868
Davis, Stanley, 4544
Davis, Stephanie, 3255
Davis, Stephen, 3855
Davis, Stephen A., 3875
Davis, Steve, 1443, 2075, 9680
Davis, Steven, 1051
Davis, T. Wayne, 1961
Davis, Ted C., 4321
Davis, Thomas H., 7353
Davis, Thomas H., Jr., 25, 7353
Davis, Tine W., 1963
Davis, Tine Wayne, Jr., 1963
Davis, Todd F., 933
Davis, Travis, 8957
Davis, Ulla, 639

Deetz, Randall J., 3141
Deevy, Brian, 1362
DeFalco, Lou, 3076
DeFelice, Louise S., 9732
DeFelippo, Olga, 1729
DeFinnis, John E., 8135
deForest Estate, 3612
DeForest, Jeff, 3333
deForest, Lydia Collins, 3612
DeFrancesco, Anne, 3780
DeFrantz, Anita L., 214
DeFreitas, Rosalie, 3876
DeFreitas, V. Eugene, 3876
Degen, Joe I., 2304
DeGeorge, Florence A., 5848
DeGeorge, Lawrence J., 5848
Degheri, Bert, 6654
DeGol, Bruno, 8167
DeGol, Bruno, Jr., 8167
DeGol, David, 8167
DeGol, Dennis, 8167
DeGol, Donald, 8167
DeGol, Lena, 8167
DeGolia, Peter A., 7742
DeGraan, Edward F., 8518
Degraw, Eric, 6220
Degroot, Louise, 4270
DeHaan, Christel, 3140
DeHaan, J. Holden, 1966
DeHaan, Jon Holden, 1966
DeHaan, Keith A., 3140
DeHaan, Kirsten A., 3140
DeHaan, Thomas H., 1966
DeHaan, Timothy E., 3140
DeHart, Michael, 3468
DeHaven, Char, 3320
Dehavenon, Anna Lou, 6662
Dehner, Helen, 4628
DeHoff, Robert, 7867
DeHoff, Sara Jane, 7882
DeHoff, Sara Jane, 7883
Dehoyos, Rick, 9165
Deighan, Jean M., 3548
Deikel, Beverly, 4517
Deikel, Theodore, 4548
Deinema, Caroline, 8630
Deitchman, Martin J., 5401, 5410
Deitrick, Scott R., 643
Deitsch, Gloria S., 6954
Deitz, Diane, 8152
deJongh, John, Jr., 9363
Dekelboum Revocable Trust, Marvin, 3613
Dekelboum, Elsie, 3613
Dekelboum, Marvin, 3613
Dekker, Hans, 5167
Dekko, Chester E., 3142
Dekko, Chester E., Jr., 3142
Dekko, Erica D., 3142
Deknatel, Elizabeth, 4168
Deknatel, Gabriel, 4168
Deknatel, Maria, 4168
DeKruif, Robert M., 198
Del Frisco's New York, 7174
Del Sol, C., 5151
del Sol, Pedro D., 1939
Del Tredici, David, 5789
Del Zotto, Dorna, 2536
Delabretonne, Paula P., 3505
Delacote, Goery, 563
Delafield, JoAnn, 6156
DeLan, Lisa, 569
Deland, Emme L., 6350
Delaney, Andrew, 8862
Delaney, Brenda, 3116
Delaney, Janet L., 8862
Delaney, Mary D., 8204
Delaney, P.B., 7965
Delaney, Pauline M., 8862
Delaney, Philip A., Jr., 1946
Delaney, Quinn, 199
Delaney, Veronica, 7247
Delaney, Wayne E., 9191
deLang, R-Lene, 982

DeLano, Mike, 9476
Delany, Beatrice P., 1705
Delany, Celine C., 8157
Delany, Sean, 5815
Delaplaine, Edward S., 3614
Delaplaine, Elizabeth B., 3614
Delaplaine, George B., III, 3614
Delaplaine, George B., Jr., 3614
Delaplaine, James W., 3614
Delaplaine, John F., 3614
DeLaski, Donald, 9409
DeLaski, Kathleen, 1778
DeLaski, Nancy L., 9409
Delavan Foundation, Nelson B., 1796
Delaware Community Foundation, 6524
Delaware Management Co., 8362
DeLawder, C. Daniel, 7795
Delbridge, Ed, 8654
Delcap, Inc., 7482
Delcor, Inc., 7482
DeLeon, Nelson, 8103
Delevati, Hank, 826
Delgado, Elena, 3174
Delgado, Jane L., 4367
Delgado, Robert M., 87
DelGivdice, Gina, M.D., 5366
Delice, Shelly L., 3360
Dell Computer Corp., 8864
Dell Inc., 8864
Dell USA, 8864
Dell'Amico, Len, 886
Dell, Alexander, 8863
Dell, Michael, 8863
Dell, Peter, 1389, 2701
Dell, Susan, 8863
Della Monica, Joseph, 5345
Dellenbach, Mike, 1357
Deller, Michael, 9583
Dellinger, Donald B., Jr., 8511
Dellinger, Kent, 217
Delmar, Charles, 9410
Delmar, Elizabeth A., 9410
Delmar, Roland H., 9410
Delmas, Gladys V.K., 3990, 5850
Delmas, Jean Paul, 5850
Delmauro, Ellen, 5397
DeLoach, Harris E., Jr., 8572
DeLoache, Bond Davis, 8665
DeLoache, William R., 8665
DeLoache, William R., Jr., 8665
Deloitte & Touche LLP, 1527
Deloitte & Touche USA LLP, 1527
Deloitte Haskins & Sells, 1527
deLone, Madeline, 6160
DeLong, Michele Gurto, 2181
Delori, Rosamond P., 5100
Delp, Judy, 3199
Delperdang, Joseph P., 3332
Delphi Automotive Systems Corp., 4271
Delphi Corp., 4271
Delruelle, Janine, Baroness, 5973
Delsol, Alain, 1368
Delsol, Lucy D., 1368
Delta Air Lines, Inc., 2372
Delta Biotechnology, Ltd., 563
Delta Dental Plan of Kansas, Inc., 3354
Delta Dental Plan of Massachusetts, 4061
DeLuca, Anthony F., 9187
DeLuca, Francis, 1541
DeLuca, Kathleen M., 3877
DeLuca, William P., 3877
Delucia, Marilyn, 9639
DeLuria, Layla, 8199
DeLury, Bernard E., Jr., 8648
Deluxe Corp., 4549
Demakis, Gregory C., 3925
Demakis, John N., 3925
Demakis, Paul C., 3925
Demakis, Thomas C., 3925
Demakis, Thomas L., 3925
DeMarco, Paul, 407
DeMars, Don R., 3180
Demartini, James G.B., III, 1022

DeMartini, James G.B., III, 1158
Demartini, Richard M., 5851
Demas, Raine, 63
DeMatteis, Frederick, 5852
DeMatteis, Nancy, 5852
DeMatteis, Richard F., 5852
DeMatteis, Scott L., 5852
Dembrow, Victor D., 2269
deMeester, Paul, Baron, 5973
Demere, R.H., Jr., 2353
Demers, Diane, 4229
Demetree, Betty A., 1967
Demetree, Christopher C., 1967
Demetree, Elisa A., 1967
Demetree, Jack C., 1967
Demetree, Jack C., Jr., 1967
Demetree, Mark C., 1967
Demetree-Doherty, Leslie A., 1967
Deming, Chris, 2481
Deming, Wendy, 2041
Demirjian, Betsy, 4066
Demmer, Mae E., 9791
Demmy, Frank, Rev., 8135
Demola, Alfred, 4930
DeMoor, Barbara, 4269
Demopoulos, Harry B., 5892
Demorest, John, 1004
Demos, Nicholas, 2702
Demoss, April Williams, 2517
DeMoss, Arthur S., 1968
DeMoss, Charlotte, 1968
DeMoss, Elizabeth J., 1968
DeMoss, Nancy S., 1968
DeMoss, Robert G., 1968
Demoulas Super Markets, Inc., 3878
Demoulas, Arthur T., 3878, 3879
Demoulas, Irene, 3879
Demoulas, Telemachus A., 3879
Dempsey, Mary A., 2684
Dempze, Nancy E., 3817
Demsey, John D., 6466
DeMuth, Christopher, 1632, 2994
Demyan, Kirk C., 8208
Den Herder, Susan, 4258
Dena, Mario, 4496
Denaro, Charles T., 8168
Denault, Leo P., 3474
Denbo, Samuel, 3996
Denekas, Craig N., 3546
Denenberg, Howard M., 2684
Denham, Robert E., 2868, 6894
Denhart, Gun, 9673
Denigan, Susan, 4872
Denious, Robert W., 8395
Denis, Angel R., 5359
Denis, Melisa A., 5288
Denish, Diane Daniels, 1362
Denison, Robert, 2079
Denison, Robert J., 720
Denit, Helen P., 3615
Denius, F. Wofford, 8808
Denius, Franklin W., 8808
Denker, Jeffrey, 7569
Denkers, Kelli Sue, 9312
Denkers, Stephen E., 9312, 9317
Denkers, Stephen G., 9312, 9317
Denkers, Susan E., 9312, 9317
Denkers-Bishop, Julie, 9312
Denlea, Leo E., Jr., 797
Denman, Leroy G., Jr., 8793, 8936, 8998, 9235
Denmark, David, 8704
Denmark, Gerald A., 3800
Dennery, Linda, 5199
Denning, Roberta, 5905
Denning, Steve, 5905
Denning, Steven A., 1431, 1640
Denninger, William C., 1488
Dennings, Carole, 4392
Dennis, Andre, 8266
Dennis, Edward A., 1040
Dennis, Elizabeth O., 1969
Dennis, Jane, 4745

Dennis, Janet Jackson, 1969
Dennis, John R., 4550
Dennis, Kathryn H., 2358
Dennis, Kimberly O., 2994, 4291
Dennis, Mark V., 6924
Dennis, Martha, 1087
Dennis, Maryanne, 4550
Dennis, Minfong Ho, 6418
Dennis, Overton D., Jr., 1969
Dennis, Robert, Jr., 5194
Dennis, Robert, Sr., 5194
Dennison, Allan, 8153
Dennison, Harriet H., 9196
Dennison, Lynn, 7673
Dennison, Phillip, 7920
Dennison-Budak, Jennie, 7898
Denny, Catherine M., 2703
Denny, James M., 2695, 2703
Denny, Norm, 3138
Denomme, Thomas, 4489
DeNooyer, Jeffrey L., 4352
Densch Charitable Trust, Wayne M., 2205
DENSO International America, Inc., 4272
Denson, Charlie, 8046
Denson, William F., III, 73
Dent, Abrahm, 217
Denton, A. Louis, 8095
Denton, Barbara, 3597
Denton, Gus B., 8732
Denton, James N., III, 8741
Denys, Susan N., 168
DePalchi, Alfred, 8216
DePaoli, Edward M., Rev., 2218
DeParle, Nancy-Ann, 5265
Department of Education, 898
DePetris, Michael, 8616
DePhillips Trust, Helene Arlene, 5179
Depiero, Janet, 4172
DePillis, Mark S., 8502
Depillo, David S., 400
Depler, Thomas A., 7819
Depolo, Gary L., 284
Deposit Guaranty National Bank, 4733
DePree, Barbara, 4435
DePree, Esther, 4435
DePree, Kris, 4435
DePree, Max O., 4435
DePrez, John, Jr., 3107
Dept. of Energy, Energy Biosciences Research Division, 3677
Deptula, George S., 5785
DePue, Nancy, 1090
Deramus, William N., IV, 3355
Derby, Julia W., 9674
Derby, Richard A. Longoria, 8920
Derendoff, Shane, 84
Derheimer, Kathryn, 2095
Dering, Jeanne, 6569
Derisley, Arthur B., 4244
Derisley, Brian A., 4244
DeRoo, Curtis J., 4275
Derossi, Daniele, 5853
DeRoy, Helen L., 4273
Derrer, Suzanne, 6790
Derrickson, Lloyd J., 1798
Derry Publishing Co., 4112
Derry, Patrick T., 2679
Derry, William S., 7891
Des Granges, Pauline, 337
Desai, Bharat, 1976
Desai, Rohit M., 6229
DeSanti, Frederick D., 5361
DeSantis, Daniel G., 537
DeSantis, Frank, 3199
DeSantis, Michael J., 3589
Descher, Greg, 4745
Descoteaux, Carol, Sr., 5092
DeSerrano, Aline, 4250
DeShazo, Gil, 8840
Deshe, Ann, 7606, 7610
Deshe, Ari, 7606
Desler, Michael D., 1257
Desmond, William C., 2298

Dimling, John A., Mrs., 7039
Dimmer, Carolyn, 9579
Dimmer, Diane C., 9579
Dimmer, John B., 9579
Dimmer, John C., 9579
Dimmer, Marilyn, 9579
Dimon, James, 5864
Dimon, Judith K., 5864
Dimon, Theodore, 5864
Dimond, Paul R., 4254
Dimopoulas, Linda J., 1960
DiMuccio, Robert A., 8518
Dinapoli, Douglas, 2348
DiNardo, Allison Cryor, 1785
Dindo, Kathryn, 7526
Dindo, Kathryn W., 7643
Dine-Jergens, Peter H., 7689
Dineen, Robert E., Jr., 6792
Dines, Allen, 1368
Dines, Bruce, 1362
Dines, Connie, 1368
Dines, Sidney A., 1368
Dines, Tyson, III, 1363
Dingee, Alexander L.M., 3827
Dingell, Deborah I., 4254, 4319, 4320
Dinges, Brian K., 2628
Dingman, Michael, 5105
Dingman, Duane, 9743
Dingwell, Park T., 495
Dinkin, Jeffrey A., 771
Dinnegan, Kenneth, 1041
Dinnen, Jane, 4245
Dinner, Joan Withers, 639
Dinovitz, Paul I., 6161, 6162
Dinsdale, Jack, 4957
Dinsdale, Roy, 4957
Dinse, Ann G., 5431
Dinsmoor, Dorothy, 5886
Dinsmore, Nancy L., 5177
Dinsmore, Richard D., 5177
Dintersmith, Ted R., 8586
Dinwoodie, Dawn, 84
Dion, Ernest E., 5095
Diorio, Leonard P., 2692
DiPonio, Margaret E., 4281
Diquollo, Robert J., 5354
Dircks, Robert E., 5180
Dircks, Robert J., 5180
Dircks, Thomas C., 5180
Dircks, William C., 5180
Dirkes, George R., 1180
Dirks, Carolyn, 609
Dirks, Martin, 609
Diro, James J., 8051
Dirzo, Rodolfo, 384
DiSepio, Marguerite, 5112
Disher, J.W., 7499
Disley, Henry, 894
Disney Co., Walt, The, 456
Disney Worldwide Services, Inc., 7174
Disney, Abigail E., 5830
Disney, Lillian B., 457
Dispatch Printing Co., The, 7915
Disser, Daniel J., 7884
Distelhorst, Neil B., 7759
Distin, Mildred L., 6418
Ditenhafer, Stephanie R., 4131
Ditmore, Dana, 1222
DiTrolio, Joe, 8152
Dittman Incentive Marketing, 7174
Dittman, Frederic, 8348
Dittman, Ralph E., 8963
Ditto, Dale, 3448
Ditto, Kane, 4737
Dittrich, Amy R., 4112
Dittrich, Norbert, 9273
Dittrick, William G., 4943
Ditz, Nancy J., 1098
Ditzler, Hugh W., III, 495
Ditzler, Hugh W., Jr., 495
Ditzler, Kate, 495
Ditzler, Nancy M., 495
Diver, Karen, 4520
Divers-White, Beverly, 4743, 6160

Diversified Technology, Inc., 4740
Divine, Harold S., 1366
Divine, John, 3387
Divine, Rita L., 1366
Dix, Gary W., 2121
Dix, Nancy, 7714
Dix, Stuart, 7047
Dixie Denning Supply Co., 7393
Dixon, Betsy, 2331
Dixon, David C., 3548
Dixon, David E., 32
Dixon, Diane B., 244
Dixon, Edith Robb, 8502
Dixon, Edwin M., 32
Dixon, F. Eugene, Jr., 8502
Dixon, Frank J., 7585
Dixon, Gertrude S., 9533
Dixon, Michael, 378
Dixon, Michael L., 3732
Dixon, Phyllis S., 8632
Dixon, Richard E., 7931
Dixon, Stewart S., 3016
Dixon, Suzanne S., 3029
Dixon, Thomas F., 6146
Dixon, Wesley M., Jr., 3029
Dixson, Bruce, 1471
Djordjevich, Alex, 1209
Djordjevich, Michael D., 1209
DL Capital, LLC, 2401
DL Trust, 1989
DLD Assocs., 6454
DLM Holdings, Inc., 5504
Doak, Mark, 9736
Doak, Thomas D., 7539
Doane, W. Allen, 2530
Dobbin, Charles E., 7339
Dobbins, Allen L., 663
Dobbins, Z.E., Jr., 7486
Dobbs, R. Howard, Jr., 2373
Dobbs, Stephen Mark, 961
Doberstein, Stephen C., 1702
Dobey, Lisa, 1244
Dobkin, Barbara, 5866
Dobkin, Eric S., 5866
Dobkin, Rachel L., 5866
Dobleske, Cheryl L., 5328
Dobras, Amy, 7870
Dobras, Dawn, 7870
Dobras, Mary Ann, 7870
Dobrof, Rose, 6615
Dobrusin, Charles E., 3033
Dobson, Andrea M., 172
Dobson, Charles C., 4533
Dobson, Christopher, 407
Dobson, Douglas, 8456
Dobson, Tom, 8833
Dockery, J. Lee, 2134
Dockery, Michael L., 2134
Docking, Jill, 4121
Docking, William R., 3372
Dockter, Doug, 3448
Doctors Hospital, 7791
Dodds, Hamish, 2047
Doden, Brenda J., 3201
Doden, Daryle L., 3201
Doden, Eric R., 3201
Doden, Laurie, 3201
Dodge, Anne N., 3781
Dodge, Bayard, 5867
Dodge, Cleveland E., Jr., 5867
Dodge, Cleveland H., 5867
Dodge, David S., 5867
Dodge, Donald S., Jr., 674
Dodge, Geraldine R., 5181
Dodge, Holly, 7209
Dodge, James A., 4636
Dodge, John B., 1939
Dodge, Nettie Orthwein, 4878
Dodge, Philip R., 4860
Dodge, Steven B., 3781
Dodge, Stewart P., 1447
Dods, Walter A., Jr., 2542
Dodson, Barbara, 9415
Dodson, Barry Z., 7444

Dodson, Betty Jo, 9399
Dodson, Charles F., 3948
Dodson, David, 1810, 7485
Dodson, Debra L., 9401
Dodson, James D., 9907
Dodson, Melissa, 3948
Dodson, Stephanie, 4169
Dodson, Thomas L., 7352
Doellefeld-Clancy, Kathy, 4893
Doemel, Nancy, 3206
Doerfler, Ronald J., 6161, 6162
Doerger, Brian, 933
Doerhoff, Neil, 1230
Doerr, Ann Howland, 278
Doerr, L. John, 278
Doerr, L. John, III, 278
Doggett, William B., 7617
Doggrell, Henry Patton, 8651
Doheny Foundation Corp., Carrie Estelle, 460
Doheny, Edward L., Mrs., 460
Doherty, Deborah R., 4112
Doherty, Diana Loukedis, 8209
Doherty, Edmund J., 3780
Doherty, Edward, 6823
Doherty, Harry P., 6972
Doherty, Henry L., Mrs., 5868
Doherty, Janice L., 3371, 3394
Doherty, Peter J., 3118
Doherty, Robert K., 5182
Doherty, Susan O'Connell, 5182
Dohn, Otto W., 7515
Dohn, Robert P., 7247
Dohrer, Kim, 9346
Dohrmann, Bruce, 482
Doiron, Mark, 3540
Dokmo, Cynthia, 5088
Dokos, Diana H., 8000
Dolan, Charles F., 5869
Dolan, Helen A., 5869
Dolan, James F., 8244
Dolan, John F. X., 6619
Dolan, Joseph S., 5513, 5647
Dolan, Katherine C., 5870
Dolan, Matthew J., 9259
Dolan, Mike, 8174, 9385
Dolan, Peter R., 5666, 5870
Dolan, Robert F., 8087
Dolan, Ronald J., 7785
Dolan-Heitlinger, John, 1949
Dolatshahi, Hassan, 757
Dolce, Joan Dell, 8842
Dole, James, 8015
Dolejs, Don, 4962
Dolezal, Tom, 3243
Dolinski, Richard, 4392
Dolinsky, Alan, 6234
Doll, Becky, 3185
Doll, Carol Ann, 461
Doll, Dixon R., 461
Doll, Henry C., Rev., 7742
Doll, Paul W., Jr., 2119
Doll, Thomas, 5415
Dollar Land Syndicate, 6497
Dollar, Joann F., 2371
Dollar, Robert G., 5782
Dolle, Molly W., 1321
Dollens, Ronald W., 462, 3159
Dollens, Stephanie J., 462
Dollens, Susan S., 462
Dollens, Williams G., 462
Dolmatch, Rosalie, 6035
Domaille, Nancy, 4668
Domani Trust, The, 7655, 7799
Domanski, Ken, 1949
Domaschko, Jane V., 7574
Domich, Dain, 1454
Dominguez, Al, 1359
Dominguez, Jorge I., 7899
Dominion Energy, Inc., 8173
Dominion Resources, Inc., 8173
Dominis, Inge, 2940
Domino's Pizza, Inc., 4225
Domke, Doreeta J., 870

Dompier, Sandra Smith, 9193, 9194, 9197
Don, Stephanie, 2106
Donaghue, Ethel F., 1529
Donahey, Dorothy O'Neill, 7783
Donahey, Robert W., 7783
Donahue, Alphonsus J., Jr., 1628
Donahue, Ann C., 8174
Donahue, David W., 3881
Donahue, J. Christopher, 8196
Donahue, Joe, 4014
Donahue, John A., 2987
Donahue, John F., 8174, 8196
Donahue, Mary B., 7742
Donahue, Nancy L., 3881
Donahue, Rhodora J., 8174
Donahue, Richard K., 3881
Donahue, Richard K., Jr., 3881
Donahue, Richard K., Sr., 4014
Donahue, Thomas R., 8196
Donahue, William J., 8174
Donaldson Co., Inc., 4552
Donaldson, David A., 73
Donaldson, Don, 7953
Donaldson, Evelyn, 7127
Donaldson, John K., 8419
Donaldson, Matthew S., Jr., 8342
Donaldson, Oliver S., 5871
Donaldson, Phil, 4512
Donaly, Joyce, 2670
Donati, John, 1078
Donchian, Alma G., 1530
Donchian, Richard D., 1531
Doneghy, Charles J., 7883
Doneghy, Charles J., Hon., 7882
Donerkiel, Linda Leuthold, 4605
Dong, Susan, 349
Donghia, Angelo, 5872
Doniger, Beatrice B., 5692
Doniger, Bruce, 5692
Donithen, Joe D., 2332
Donker, Maureen, 4392
Donkersloot, Norman, 4309
Donley, Edward, 8404
Donley, Edward J., 8175
Donley, Inez C., 8175
Donlon, Marcia, 822
Donnell, Barry, 9280
Donnell, Cathlin, 1367
Donnell, John, 1367
Donnell, John D., 1367
Donnelley & Sons Co., R.R., 2707
Donnelley, Barbara C., 2708
Donnelley, David E., 2708
Donnelley, Dorothy Ranney, 2706
Donnelley, Elliott, 2708
Donnelley, Elliott R., 2706
Donnelley, Gaylord, 2706
Donnelley, Inanna, 2706
Donnelley, James R., 2708, 2773
Donnelley, Laura, 603
Donnelley, Miranda S., 2708
Donnelley, Nina H., 2708
Donnelley, Robert G., 2708
Donnelley, Shawn M., 2706
Donnelley, Strachan, 2706
Donnelley, Thomas E., II, 2708
Donnelley-Morton, Laura, 2706
Donnelly, Anne Cohn, 9238
Donnelly, Caroline J., 3548
Donnelly, Elizabeth A., 8176
Donnelly, John L., 6898
Donnelly, Joseph C., Jr., 4074
Donnelly, Mary J., 8176
Donnelly, Peter F., 9621
Donnelly, Robert W., Sr., 2058
Donnelly, Robert, Jr., 2058
Donnelly, Thomas J., 8176, 8196
Donner, Alexander B., 5873
Donner, Carl, 1373
Donner, Daniel W., 5873
Donner, Deborah, 5873
Donner, Joseph W., III, 5873
Donner, Robert, Jr., 5873

Donner, Timothy E., 5873
Donner, William H., 5873, 8266
Donnici, Peter J., 673
Donohoe, Carol, 2871
Donohoe, Robin R., 466
Donohue, Bernadine Murphy, 928
Donohue, Craig S., 2662
Donohue, Daniel J., 928
Donohue, Elise R., 4726
Donohue, John F., 3780
Donohue, Pat, 8317
Donohue, Rosemary E., 928
Donovan, Bonnie, 6203
Donovan, Carol A., 3871
Donovan, David, 4243
Donovan, David A., 2740
Donovan, James M., 928
Donovan, Kristin, 1362
Donovan, Linda Ramsey, 5874
Donovan, Michael D.S., 5874
Donovan, Mike, 3131
Donovan, Patrick J., 4671
Donovan, Paul, 3813
Donovan, Thomas F., 8157
Donovan, Thomas J., 5080
Donten, David S., 1895
Doodson, Michael E., 5328
Doolan, Carol, 3560
Doolan, Edward E., 7398
Doolin, Thomas L., 8188
Dooling, John E., Jr., 4853
Doordan, Helen R., 1741
Doore, Daniel, 1256
Dora, James E., 3220
Doran, Barbara, 5971
Doran, Evelyn H., 5875
Doran, Robert W., 5875
Dordelman, William E., 8152
Doren, Andre, 6233
Dorf, Alexis, 1622
Dorhauer, Robert, Rev., 4791
Dorhout, Peter K., 134
Doris, Peter E., 2812
Dorko, Carol, 1941
Dorn, Estelle M., 7612
Dorn, Nancy, 1553
Dornbush, Dennis, 4325
Dorneman, Ross, 9454
Dornette, Helen G., 7613
Dornette, Martha, 7746
Dornette, W. Stuart, 7746
Dornsife, David H., 663
Doromus, Mark C., 172
Doroshow, Carol, 5486
Doroshow, Helen, 5486
Doroshow, James, 5486
Dorr, Alix F., 2280
Dorr, John, 5086
Dorrance, Bennett, 87, 95
Dorrance, Bennett, Jr., 95
Dorrance, Charles A., 5461
Dorrance, G. Morris, 8443
Dorrance, Gunda S., 5461
Dorrance, Jacqueline, 272
Dorrance, Jacquelynn W., 95
Dorrance, John T., III, 5461
Dorrance, John T., IV, 5461
Dorris, James F., 4736
Dorris, Jeanette, 8668
Dorris, Thomas B., 2613
Dorsa, Caroline, 5326, 5327, 5329, 8349
Dorsa, Rosemary, 3116
Dorsett, Betty, 7463
Dorsett, Burt N., 134
Dorsett, Stuart B., 7438
Dorsey, Gayle S., 3454
Dorsey, Gregory, 3597
Dorsey, J. Kevin, 2812
Dorsey, Lynne L., 1698
Dorsey, Patrick B., 7137
Dorsey, Susan Ford, 264, 989
Dorsky, Alvin, 8384
Dortch, Sebastian, 2245

Dorwart, Fred, 7984
Dorwart, Frederic, 7947
Doscher, Drew, 7174
Dosh, Linda, 3131
Doshay, Glenn, 1128
Doshay, Karen, 1128
Doss, M.S., 8869
Doss, Meek Lane, 8869
Dossa, Alfred, 1173
Dossey, Dale A., 9137
Dossman, Curley M., Jr., 2397
Dot Foods, Inc., 3037
Dotson, Darlene B., 7540
Dotson, Greg D., 4394
Dotson, Michael, 931
Dotson, Nancy K., 9736
Dotter, Richard G., 7969
Dotterweich, Maria Miceli, 4474
Doty, Barbara E., 1532
Doty, Carol, 2431
Doty, Everett L., 2562
Doty, George E., 1532
Doty, George E., Jr., 1532
Doty, Marie J., 1532
Doty, Virginia M., 1532
Doty, William W., 1532
Dotzel, Cynthia A., 8511
Doub, Dorothy, 3595
Doubleday, Sandy, 87
Doucet-Miller, Kathleen, 5780
Doudera, Ralph J., 9412
Dougherty, David F., 7587
Dougherty, Gregory, 463
Dougherty, M.J., 96
Dougherty, M.J., Mrs., 96
Dougherty, Nancy, 463
Dougherty, Robert J., Jr., 5361
Douglas, Anne, 464
Douglas, Charles, 2166
Douglas, Chester W., DMD, 4061
Douglas, Craig C., 4428
Douglas, David W., 1857
Douglas, Jean W., 1857
Douglas, Kirk, 464
Douglas, Laura M., 3414
Douglas, Laurinda Lowenstein, 7398
Douglas, Michael, 3141
Douglas, Peter, 464
Douglas, Ron, 3215
Douglas, Scott, 7774
Douglas, Sharon H., 2311
Douglas, Walter E., 4438
Douglas-Bailey, Hyacinth, 1495
Douglass, Dean, 8667
Douglass, F. Karl, 2361
Douglass, Lee, 157
Douglass, Leslie, 8667
Douglass, Rosann B., 8667
Douglass, Steven J., 3380
Douglass, Susan, 7648
Douglass, Terry D., 8667
Douglass, W. Birch, III, 9441, 9459, 9494
Douthitt, Jane, 5473
Douzinas, Nancy R., 6774
Dove Givings Foundation, 3765
Dove, Carol L., 7771
Dove, Kent, 9067
Doverspike, Terry, 7938
Dovid, Khal Binyomin, 7125
Dovydenas, Elizabeth D., 4710
Dow 2005 Charitable Annuity Trust, 4286
Dow Charitable Trust, Alden B., 3556
Dow Charitable Unitrust, Vada B., 4288
Dow Chemical Co., The, 4284
Dow Corning Corp., 4285
Dow Jones & Co., Inc., 5879
Dow Jones Foundation, 5184
Dow, Alden, 4288
Dow, Barbara C., 4286
Dow, Christina Seix, 5183
Dow, Grace A., 4287
Dow, Herbert H., 4286

Dow, Melvin, 8752
Dow, Michael Lloyd, 4287, 4288
Dow, Pamela G., 4286
Dow, Peggy Ann, 1154
Dow, Rhea, 4246
Dow, Robert S., 5183
Dow, Steven, 7975
Dow, Vada, 4288
Dow, Willard H., II, 4286
Dowd, Brian, 8073
Dowd, Hector, 6990
Dowd, Homer M., 8841
Dowd, W. Frank, IV, 7357
Dowden, Rick, 1477
Dowding, Andrea Walters, 7770
Dowdle, James C., 2709
Dowdle, James C., Jr., 2709
Dowdle, Sally S., 2709
Dowdy, Antoinette, 2355
Dowdy, Jacqueline, 4826
Dowe, P. James, Jr., 3525
DowElanco, 2388
Dowley, Jennifer, 3801
Dowling, Charles T., 6974, 7076
Dowling, J. Robert, 3780
Down, Ann M., 2569
Down, Gerald C., 495
Downer, Edwin E., 4747, 4763
Downes, Kate, 5618
Downes, Laurence M., 5336
Downey, Harriette R., 7907
Downey, Janis, 6387
Downey, John A., 7198
Downey, Nancy A., 5881
Downey, Robert N., 5881
Downey, Thelma U., 9491
Downing, Barry L., 3358
Downing, Frances V.S., 7082
Downing, Helen, 2480
Downing, Jack G., 7614
Downing, John O., 7082
Downing, Merlyn H., 4376
Downing, Paula M., 3358
Downing, Randy, 2937
Downs, Frederick S., Jr., 3882
Downs, Harry S., 2349
Downs, Jeanne Floyd, 522
Downs, John H., Jr., 2351, 2352
Downs, Patty Salo, 4499
Downs, Richard S., 8381
Downton, Christine V., 5574
Dowty, Dawson, 4987
Dox, Lillian, 3555
Doxey, Bobby L., 70
Doyle, Alice P., 1669
Doyle, Allen, 1669
Doyle, Catherine I., 8843
Doyle, Cynthia Tower, 7158
Doyle, Frank, 6466
Doyle, Jean G., 275
Doyle, Kay, 4014
Doyle, L.F. Boker, 7117
Doyle, Leah F., 5830
Doyle, Louise I., 8532
Doyle, Paul, 4326
Doyle, Robert A., 2591
Doyle, Robert M., 7158
Doyle, Terence, 4524
Doyle, Thomas M., 5900
Doyle, Valentine, 1669
Doyle, William J., 2388
Doyle, William M., Jr., 3092
Doyon Ltd., 84
Drabik, Patricia, 2123
Drabik, Robert F., 2123
Drabing, Darin B., 527
Drackett, Jeanne, 7912
Drackett, Roger, 7912
Draeger, Thomas R., 268
Dragon, Robert E., 4191
Drain, Randall G., 6275
Drain, Scott, 4364
Drake, Daniel, 1749
Drake, Daniel W., 7411, 7412, 7413

Drake, Duane, 1087
Drake, Erin, 6532
Drake, George, 3325
Drake, Randy B., 9382
Drake, Robert W., 7349
Drake, Shelley C., 6465
Dramis, Francis A., Jr., 2323
Drane, Frank N., 9089
Draper Corp., 3958
Draper, Dana, 6117, 6118
Draper, Melissa, 465
Draper, Phyllis, 465
Draper, Polly, 465
Draper, Rebecca, 465
Draper, Stephen E., 2522
Draper, Tim, 465
Draper, Tim C., 465
Draper, William, 465
Draper, William H., III, 466
Drapkin, Donald, 5185
Drapkin, Donald G., 6716
Drapkin, Jonathan, 5610, 6017
Drasheff, Linda M., 5325
Draughon, Elizabeth F., 8668
Drawe, Carol L., 8822
Draxler, Patricia, 9933
Dray, James R., 6928
Drayton, Cynthia W., 8140
Drazich, Mary Lou, 8686
Dreben, Raya, 7030
Drebin, Allan, 2658
Dreby, Edwin C., III, 8428
Dreese, Catherine C., 2343
Dreibelbis, M.D., 3308
Dreiseszun, Irene, 3359
Dreiseszun, Richard, 3359
Dreiseszun, Sherman, 3359
Dreiss, Meredith L., 9064
Dreiss, Meredith Mitchell, 9064
Dreitzer, Albert J., 5884
Dreitzer, Mildred H., 5884
Drell, Martin, 3489
Drennan, A. Don, 3479
Drennan, Dorothea F., 7640
Drennan, James, 7640
Drennan, Rudith A., 3479
Drenth, Kenneth, Dr., 4259
Drescher, Tod, 4693
Dresdale, Richard C., 7174
Dresdner, K. Philip, 6709
Dresher, James T., Jr., 3617
Dresher, James T., Sr., 3617
Dresher, Jeffrey M., 3617
Dresher, Joshua, 3617
Dresher, Patricia K., 3617
Dresher, Patti, 3617
Dresher, Virginia M., 3617
Dresner, Bruce M., 3627
Dress, Norman, 1329
Dresser, Joyce G., 5565
Dresser, Mary, 4452
Drew, David M., 1549
Drew, Dennis M., 683
Drew, Ellen, 467
Drew, Ellen Todd, 467
Drew, Elton F., 3891
Drew, Everett, 2244
Drew, Gail McMichael, 7426
Drew, Gary, 4327
Drew, John, 467
Drew, Lawrence, 504
Drew, Pamela J., 3544
Drewes, Alfred H., 6713
Drexel, Carolyn, 6637
Drexel, Noreen, 865
Drexler, Millard S., 5885
Drexler, Peggy, 5885
Drexler, Peggy F., 5885
Dreyer's Grand Ice Cream, Inc., 468
Dreyer, Alec G., 8874
Dreyer, Michael S., 968
Dreyfus, Alfred, 9413
Dreyfus, Alice L., 2693
Dreyfus, Camille, 5886

Dreyfus, Carolyn S., 2693
Dreyfus, Louis, 5887
Dreyfus, Mark, 9413
Dreyfus, Max, 5888
Dreyfus, Mildred, 9413
Dreyfus, Victoria, 5888
Drezner, Michael H., 4153
Driehaus, Elizabeth, 2710
Driehaus, Richard H., 2710
Dries, Kristen Larsen, 5296
Driggers, John, 9600
Driker, Eugene, 4484
Drinko, Elizabeth G., 7747
Drinko, J. Randall, 7747
Drinko, John D., 7747, 7802, 7829
Drinkwater, Clover M., 5784
Driscoll, Alexandra L., 6375
Driscoll, Dawn-Marie, 2240
Driscoll, Elizabeth S., 4555
Driscoll, George E., 3009
Driscoll, Jane L., 1627
Driscoll, John, 3250
Driscoll, Richard D., 3845
Driscoll, Timothy, 5089
Driscoll, W. John, 4555, 9681
Driskill, Walter S., 1975
Driver, David W., 9400
Drizin, Moshe, 6511
Drizin, Sholom, 6511
Drizin, Shoshana, 6511
Drobac, Jennifer, 739
Droege, Peter, 1362
Drost, Carolyn Jill, 8179
Drost, William T., 3467
Drown, Joseph W., 469
Drowota, Frank F., III, 8679
Druckenmiller, Fiona, 5707, 5889
Druckenmiller, Stanley F., 5889
Drucker, Bertram A., 3883
Drueding, Albert J., Jr., 8177
Drueding, Bernard J., Jr., 8177
Drueding, James, 8177
Druker, Ronald M., 3883
Drukier, Charles, 5890
Drukier, Gale, 5890
Drukier, Ira, 5890
Drukier, Jennifer, 5890
Druliner, Kathryn, 4954
Drum, Frank G., 470
Drumm, David G., 9218
Drumm, Susan Rodgers, 1334
Drummond, Barbara, 25
Drummond, Don, 4227
Drummonds, Joy, 169
Drumwright, Elenita M., 6529
Drumwright, Elizabeth R.M., 6529
Drushel, William H., Jr., 8854
Druskin, Robert, 5755
Druss, Ellen, 9178
Druzak, Jeffrey, 8098
Drymiller, Michael K., 3277
du Pont de Nemours and Co., E.I., 1995
Du Pont, Pierre "Pete" S., 9884
Duan, Yong Ping, 486
Duarte, Concha, 3368
Dubey, Anjani K., M.D., 7247
Dubiago, Nicholas, 1541
Dubin, Adam, 7000
Dubin, Eva Andersson, 5891
Dubin, Glenn R., 5891
Dubin, Melvin, 7000
Dubina, Beth, 76
Dubler, Ariela, 6002
DuBois, Philip, 1749
DuBois, Robert, 7192
Dubore, Ann M., 9931
DuBose Family Charitable Annuity Trust, 2374
Dubose, Aubrey M., 14
DuBose, Beverly M., III, 2374
DuBose, Eileen Erickson, 2374
DuBose, Elizabeth Egleston, 2374
DuBose, Frances W., 2374
Dubose, Sam, 7963

Dubose, Vivian N., 7963
Dubovsky, Elizabeth, 6972
Dubow, Carrie, 5131
DuBow, Helen A., 1977
Dubow, Lawrence, 2071
DuBow, Lawrence J., 1977
DuBow, Linda J., 1977
DuBow, Michael, 1977
DuBow, Susan E., 1977
DuBray, F. Joseph, 3343
Dubrow, David Lewis, 1756
Dubrow, Eli B., 473
Dubuque Packing Co., 2284
Dubuque, Kenneth R., 9228
Duchossois Fortino, Dayle, 2711
Duchossois Industries, Inc., 2711
Duchossois TECnology Partners, LLC, 2711
Duchossois, Craig J., 2711
Duchossois, Kimberly, 2711
Duchossois, R. Bruce, 2711
Duchossois, Richard L., 2711
Ducks Unlimited, 3512
Duckwall, Frank E., 1978
Duckworth, Connie K., 6282
Duckworth, Thomas J., 6282
Duda, Fritz L., 8871
Duda, Fritz L., Jr., 8871
Duda, Fritz L., Mrs., 8871
Duda, James F., 8871
Duda, Mary L., 8871
Dudek, Louis P., 5785
Dudgeon, Clair, 7891
Dudley, Elisabeth C., 5363
Dudley, Eunice, 7343
Dudley, Gatewood, 2448
Dudley, Henry A., Jr., 1842
Dudley, Henry C., 5363
Dudley, Jane C., 5363
Dudley, Joan R., 3409
Dudley, John D., 9792
Dudley, Louise M., 9390
Dudley, Mary C., 9792
Dudley, Richard D., 9741, 9792
Dudley, Robert J., II, 9792
Dudley, Scott, 5194
Dudley, Spottswood P., 1842
Dudley, Tamara Felton, 2170
Dudman, Paul W., 7964
Dudnick, Andrew L., 3621
Duehay, Francis H., 3828
Duello, J. Donald, 4902
Duemling, Louisa C., 1734
Duer, Carmel, 9702
Duerr, Patrick, 4378
Duesenberg, Phyllis B., 4805
Duesenberg, Richard W., 3157, 4805
Duff, Christopher Bruce, 1373
Duff, James C., 9424
Duff, Sean, 1373
Duff, Susan, 3449
Duffell, Carol, 9179
Duffell, David K., 8549
Duffey, Harry J., III, 6896
Duffey, Lois S., 6896
Duffield, Cheryl D., 845
Duffield, David A., 845
Duffield, Michael D., 845
Duffield, Richard, 145
Duffield, Sally, 4782
Duffy Homes, 7618
Duffy, Angela, 3611
Duffy, B. Joseph, III, 4865
Duffy, Bill A., 6219
Duffy, Edmund, 6962
Duffy, Elizabeth A., 5181
Duffy, Joe, 4668
Duffy, Martin P., 3438
Duffy, Michael A., 5750
Duffy, Pamela Brewster, 1648
Duffy, Paul, 6391
Duffy, Robert A., 670
Duffy, Susan G., 9680
Duffy, Terrence A., 2662

Duffy, Vivien Stiles, 6830
Dufour, Edith Libby, 3494
Dufrene, Uric, 3130
Dugan, Bill, 4962
Dugan, Gordon F., 5704
Dugan, Tom, 2296
Dugas, Laura Jo, 8737
Dugas, Laura Jo Turner, 8669
Dugas, Stephen H., 8669
Dugas, Wayne F., Jr., 8669
Dugas, Wayne F., Sr., 8669
Dugas, William B., 8669
Dugas-Thomas, Shelley, 5784
Dugdale, J.W., Jr., 2696
Duggal, Anjuly Chib, 6389
Duggan, Agnes B., 3409
Duggan, Teresa O'Shaugnessy, 4639
Duggan, William R., Jr., 4310
Duggar, Jan, 160
Dugger, Albia, 6634
Duhme, Carol M., 4893
Dukatt, Merv, 2763
Dukatt, Steve, 2763
Duke Energy Corp., 7360
Duke Energy Field Services, LP, 7360
Duke Power Co., 7347, 7360
Duke, Anthony Drexel, 5513, 5647
Duke, Doris, 5892
Duke, Dwight B., 2482
Duke, James Buchanan, 7359
Duke, Jennifer Johnson, 2198
Duke, Lisa, 4629
Duke, Robin Chandler, 7185
Duke, Winslow H., 4014
Duker, Brack, 1303
Duker, Elizabeth, 1303
Dukes, David D., 53
Dukes, Gilbert F., Jr., 30
Dukes, Joan M., 9803
Dukess, A. Carleton, 6615
Dulaney, Robert W., 3441
Dulaney, Tommy E., 4763
Dulin, Eugenia B., 9418
Dulin, R. Kenneth, 308
Dulin, Susan W., 308
Duloc, Andrea, 8278
Duman, Louis J., 1347
Dumas, David, 8646
Dumke, Andrea S., 9316
Dumke, Carol Browning, 9308
Dumke, Ezekiel R., Jr., 9316
Dumke, Katherine W., 9316
Dumont-Smith, Cheryl, 1594
DuMouchel, William H., 3780
Dun & Bradstreet Corp., The, 5893
Dunagan, Robert, 2599
Dunaway, Carol W., Mrs., 8841
Dunbar, Charles D., 9727
Dunbar, Wendell, 4461
Dunbar, Will, 9365
Duncan, Dale, 3258
Duncan, Deana P., 8100
Duncan, Deborah, 435
Duncan, Deborah L., 535
Duncan, F. Jeff, Jr., 8037
Duncan, Gail, 4256
Duncan, George L., 4014
Duncan, James, Jr., 5496
Duncan, Jock, 5243
Duncan, Joe, 7748
Duncan, Linda, 494
Duncan, Louise Head, 9793
Duncan, Mark, 2571
Duncan, Nancy, 9702
Duncan, R. Foster, 3475
Duncan, Richard, 7770
Duncan, Robert D., 8960
Duncan, Sarah, 2881
Duncan, Stan, 7344
Duncan, Susan M., 1450
Duncan, Tommye, 8881
Duncan, William G., Jr., 3421
Dunckel, Jeanette M., 1326
Duncker, C. Steven, 6264

Dunford, Leslie A., 7576
Dunford, Lissa, 2541
Dungan, Neal, 5469
Dungan, Robert, 2063
Dunham, John L., 4861, 7738
Dunham, Linda R., 9100
Dunigan, E. Bryan, 3055
Dunigan, Helen, 3168
Dunigan, Larry, 3168
Dunigan, Sharon, 3168
Dunkelman, Robert A., 3512
Dunker, Robert E., 9407
Dunklau, Paul, 4958
Dunklau, Rupert, 4958
Dunkle, Terry K., 8153
Dunlaevy, J. Williar "Bill", 3801
Dunlap, Benjamin B., 8569
Dunlap, Ellen S., 4209
Dunlap, Larry, 3367
Dunlap, Melodee, 316
Dunlap, Nancy, 40
Dunlap, Susannah B., 4711
Dunlap, William C., 9160
Dunlavey, Michael, 1080
Dunlop, Becky Norton, 1841
Dunlop, Joan B., 3801, 6665
Dunlop, Tim, 2701
Dunmire, C.J., 8632
Dunmire, Cyril C., Jr., 8455
Dunn Charitable Lead Trust, Elizabeth Ordway, 1979
Dunn Trust, William A., 1980
Dunn, Amy, 8306
Dunn, Arlene, 3247
Dunn, Brett, 8306
Dunn, Charles A., 2121
Dunn, Debra, 672
Dunn, Debra L., 1158
Dunn, Dolores McGovern, 3178
Dunn, Eileen, 8529
Dunn, Geoffrey P., 8188
Dunn, Jeanine, 7744
Dunn, Jed, 7343
Dunn, John, 1090
Dunn, John M., 3254
Dunn, John S., Jr., 8872
Dunn, John S., Sr., 8872
Dunn, John W., 9777
Dunn, Keith, 1948
Dunn, Kenneth B., 8306
Dunn, Louise, III, 3884
Dunn, Marcia, 7016
Dunn, Margaret, 3884
Dunn, Martin, 3884
Dunn, Norman S., 3839
Dunn, Pamela R., 8306
Dunn, Peggy, 4842
Dunn, Peggy J., 4816
Dunn, Peter, 3884
Dunn, Raymond J., III, 3884
Dunn, Raymond J., IV, 3884
Dunn, Rebecca M., 2323
Dunn, Rebecca Walter, 1939
Dunn, Terrence P., 4873
Dunn, William A., 1980
Dunnan, D. Stuart, Rev., 1487
Dunnan, Diana B., 1487
Dunning, Richard, 4315
Dunnington, Patricia, 7035
Dunsmore, Lorri A., 9557
Dunstan, Christopher T., 6660
Dunton, Gary C., 6512
Dunwiddie, Alan W., 9820
Dupee, Michael, 9358
Duperreault, Brian, 8073
Dupkin, Carol N., 3618
Dupkin, Manuel, II, 3618, 3723
duPont Trust, Margaret F., 1728
duPont, A. Felix, Jr., 1698
duPont, A.I., 2688
duPont, Allaire, Sr., 1698
DuPont, Augustus I., 2687
Dupont, Brenda K., 9368
Dupont, Christopher T., 1698

Epstein, Marianne, 2985
Epstein, Michael, 3572
Epstein, Michael David, 3623
Epstein, Neil B., DMD, 4061
Epstein, Paul H., 5843
Epstein, Robert, 8747
Epstein, Roger, 2554
Epstein, Samantha, 3623
Epstein, Samuel, 8186
Epstein, Shelley, 2677
Epstein, Sidney, 2946
Epstein, Thomas, 5934
Epstein, Thomas W., 296
Epstein, William A., 5934
EQD Holdings Co., LLC, 8187
Equifax Inc., 2379
Equimax Mortgage, Inc., 379
Equipart Assocs., 5936
Equitable Cos. Inc., The, 5584
Equitable Life Assurance Society of the
　U.S., The, 5584
Equitable Production Co., 8187
Eramet, 7436
Erb, Darrell, Jr., 1148
Erb, Eric, 7735
Erbacher, John N., 6915
Erbaugh, J. Martin, 7761
Erburu, Robert F., 198, 460, 728, 980
Erdahl, Rebecca L., 4533
Erdel, Laura W., 4822
Erdle, Allison, 9534
Erdman, Christian P., 330, 5025
Erdman, Dan, 9854
Erdman, Daniel, 9797
Erdman, Steve, 598
Ergon Asphalt & Emulsions, Inc., 4740
Ergon Exploration, Inc., 4740
Ergon Nonwovens, Inc., 4740
Ergon Refining, Inc., 4740
Ergon, Inc., 4740
Ergon-West Virginia, Inc., 4740
Erica Enterprises, LLC, 5117
Erichsen, Peter C., 570
Erichson, John W., 7404
Erickson, Alan, 4991
Erickson, Andrea C., 3658
Erickson, Andrew M., 8518
Erickson, Bob, 1270
Erickson, Craig A., 3624, 3658
Erickson, David, 6395
Erickson, Don, 1175
Erickson, Erica, 571
Erickson, Greg, 8733
Erickson, Gregory E., 8637
Erickson, Hubbard H., Jr., 2592
Erickson, James, 405
Erickson, Jeffrey R., 1943
Erickson, Jenny, 3325
Erickson, Joan C., 2592
Erickson, John C., 3624, 3658
Erickson, John H., 2592
Erickson, Mark P., 3624
Erickson, Mark R., 3658
Erickson, Nancy A., 3624, 3658
Erickson, Neysa, 9981
Erickson, Norman E.W., 1482
Erickson, Paul L., 3658
Erickson, Peter, 2592
Erickson, Peter E., 2592
Erickson, Peter H., 2592
Erickson, Scott R., 3658
Erickson, Thomas, 4392
Ericson, Dick, 4693
Erker, William H., 4921
Erklens, Brent, 9307
Erlandson, Patrick J., 4705
Erlbaum Foundation, 7497
Erlbaum, Daniel A., 8189
Erlbaum, Gary E., 8189
Erlbaum, Jon L., 8189
Erlbaum, Marc N., 8189
Erlbaum, Steven, 7497
Erlbaum, Vicki, 8189
Erlin, Beatrice, 7007

Erlingsson, Ellen S., 9338
Ernst & Young, LLP, 7174
Ernst & Young, 8747
Ernst, Dorothy A., 2792
Ernst, Kate, 381
Ernst, Katherine R., 1889
Ernst, Lisa, 1350
Ernst, Mark A., 4823, 4842
Ernst, Robert, 1889
Ernstoff, Barry D., 9675
Erpf Charitable Trust, 5937
Erpf, Armand B., 5937
Erpf, Armand G., 5937
Erpf, Cornelia A., 5937
Errico, Joy, 4156
Erskine, David J.M., 8195
Ertel, Barbara, 8387
Erwert, Bill, 9615
Erwin, Harry C., III, 182
Erwin, James, 3199
Erwin, Judy, 2661
Erxleben, Bette, 3255
Esala, Jack, 3135
Esbenshade, Richard D., 302, 926
Esber, Suzanne Huffman, 523
Eschen, Mark T., 264
Eschenburg, Katherine, 4310
Escher, Patricia G., 91
Escobar, F. Patrick, 214
Escobosa, Paul, 1108
Escondido Ready Mix Concrete, Inc.,
　1197
Escondido Serenas Develop, Inc., 1078
Escuro, Maria, 7582
Eshelman, Joyce, 3115
Eshima, Sharon K., 1336
Eskelund, Lance C., 8551
Eskew, Michael L., 2503, 3585
Eskind, Annette, 8674
Eskind, Donna, 8675
Eskind, Irwin, 8674, 8675
Eskind, Jane, 8673
Eskind, Jeffrey, 8674, 8675
Eskind, Richard, 8673
Eskind, Richard J., 8662
Eskind, Steven, 8674
Eskind, William H., 8673
Eskow, Sam, 5438
Eskridge, Tilford H., 7927
Eslami, Judith, 1518
Esmiol, Morris A., Jr., 1447
Esping, Heather H., 8886
Esping, Kathryn R., 8886
Esping, Perry E., 8886
Esping, William P., 8886
Espinoza, Ana, 403
Esplanade Venture Partnership LP, The,
　6316
Esplin, J. Kimo, 9329
Esposito, Anthony G., 7785
Esposito, Kathleen, 2725
Esposito, Louis J., 8282
Esposto, James E., 777
Esquibel, Barbara, 7383
Esrey, William, 1468
ESSA Bank & Trust, 8190
Essad, Georgette, 9679
Esseff, George J., 488
Esseff, George J., Jr, 488
Esseff, George, Sr., 488
Esseff, Rosemary C., 488
Esseff, Rosemary, Inc., 488
Esseff, Sheryl Lynn, 488
Esser, Richard, 6299
Esses, Eda, 9617
Essig, Stuart, 5251
Essman, Ken, 9957
Essman, Marcy, 9957
Esteban, Manuel, 1151
Estee Lauder Charitable Trust, 6232
Estep, David G., Col., 9490
Esterline, Bruce H., 9049
Estes, C.E., 9415
Estes, Jane M., 1964

Estess, Sandra, 8952
Estey Charitable Income Trust, 3989
Estill, Gentry, 8888
Estopinal, B.M., 3465
Estrin, Mary Lloyd, 823, 1381
Estrin, Robert L., 823, 1381
Estrin, Zoe Lloyd, 823, 1381
Etheredge, Jeannette, 2919
Etheridge, Anne, 943
Etheridge, Frank S., III, 2361
Etnier, Oliver L., 1711
Etra, Lionel, 5643
Ettelson, John R., 2621
Etten, Stewart L., 9777
Etters, Bonnie C., 2674
Ettinger, Barbara P., 1533, 1536
Ettinger, Christian P., 1533
Ettinger, Elsie, 1533
Ettinger, Heidi P., 1533, 1536
Ettinger, Leland P., 1533
Ettinger, Matthew, 1533
Ettinger, Richard P., 1533
Ettinger, Richard P., Jr., 1533
Ettinger, Virgil P., 1533
Ettinger, Wendy P., 1536
Ettinger, Wendy W.P., 1533
Eule, Daniel R., 7021, 7023, 7024
Eurich, Juliet A., 3568
Eustis, Janet W., 4200
Euwer, Paul, Jr., 8272
Evans, Ashley Reid, 5940
Evans, Barbara R., 7398
Evans, Barbara Reed, 6752
Evans, Barbara W., 5457
Evans, Bridgitt B., 3898
Evans, Bruce R., 3898
Evans, Carol, 3131
Evans, Caswell, 3016
Evans, Charles D., 7438
Evans, Cynthia Sherwood, 5181
Evans, Dan, 7620
Evans, Debra, 509
Evans, Dwight, 2494
Evans, Edward P., 9416
Evans, Eli, 6604
Evans, Ernest L., 7464
Evans, Gareth, 3538
Evans, Genevieve Wise, 9284
Evans, Geraldine A., 9407
Evans, Heather Richards, 5715
Evans, Jack, 3538
Evans, Jack B., 3290
Evans, Jae, 4331
Evans, Janet, 214
Evans, Jean, 3538
Evans, John C., 6453
Evans, John H., 5457
Evans, John Michael, 5715
Evans, John T., 5880
Evans, Jonathan Perry, 5940
Evans, Karen, 1162
Evans, Laura, 5457
Evans, Linda, 2480
Evans, Linda P., 9049
Evans, Malik, 6823
Evans, Marie, 5880
Evans, Mary Lou, 76
Evans, Megan A., 3370
Evans, Nick W., Jr., 2357
Evans, Peggy, 7620
Evans, R. Bradford, 6752
Evans, Ralph, 9776
Evans, Randall E., 9072
Evans, Ray, 6532
Evans, Robert S., 2687, 5940
Evans, Roy Gene, 8843
Evans, Sian, 3538
Evans, Steve, 1945
Evans, Susan C., 5940
Evans, Thomas H., 3648
Evans, Thomas J., 7620
Evans, Trevor, 3538
Evans, V. Lynn, 8661
Evans-Rael, Maggie, 5498

Evans-Tranum, Shelia, 9566
Evarts, Helen C., 7198
Evarts, William M., 5762
Eveheart, Janet, 9268
Evenhouse, George A., 9777
Evening Post Publishing Co., 8603
Everard, Donald, 9582
Everard, Glenda C., 9582
Everard, Lloyd D., 9582
Everest, Christine Gaylord, 7937, 7944,
　7966
Everest, Christy, 7969
Everest, Tricia, 7944
Everett Mutual Savings Bank, 9583
Everett, Barbara, 26
Everett, Carolyn, 5941
Everett, Chandler, 7680
Everett, David F., 5941
Everett, Edith B., 5941
Everett, Henry, 5941
Everett, Leslie H., 1000
Everett, Margaret P., 6700
Everett, Sally, 4156
Everett, Timothy C., 8992
Everetts, Kelley J., 1377
Evergreen Bank, N.A., 9660
Evergreenbancorp, Inc., 9660
Everhart, Thomas E., 748
Evers, Charles D., Jr., 58
Evers, Henry K., 482
Evers, Leslie, 724
Evers, Melinda Ellis, 995
Evers-Manly, Sandra, 942
Evert, Herbert P., 8395
Evins, Jennifer C., 8616
Evins, T. Alexander, 8569
Evjue, William T., 9797
Evmar Oil Corp., 6116
Evnin, Anthony B., 5506
Evnin, Judith W., 5506
Ewald, Charles H., 9514
Ewasyshyn, Frank J., 4265
Ewbank, Thomas P., 3180
Ewen, Elaine S., 644
Ewend, Peter, 4483
Ewers, Gordon, 7709
Ewig, Thelma, 1559
Ewing, Frank M., 3626
Ewing, Judith J., 3626
Ewing, Lucinda B., 1032
Ewing, Mark, 3122
Ewing, Stephen E., 4289, 4438
Ewry, Robert, 588
Ex, Merri, 2661
Exacta Sweaters, 6061
Excell Mktg., 3331
Executive Focus International, 4202
Exner, Margaret L., 9847
Exotic Metals Forming Co., 9630
Express Scripts, Inc., 4811
Extra Sportswear, 5420
Exxon Corp., 8889
Exxon Mobil Corp., 8889
Eychaner, Fred, 2589
Eychner, Thomas D., 941, 1099
Eyckmans, Luc, 5973
Eye, Ear, Nose and Throat Hospital,
　3475
Eyer, Robert J., 8153
Eyer, Thomas E., 8056
Eykamp, Rita, 3254
Eyman, Amy, 7622
Eyskens, Mark, 5973
Ezell, Dewitt, Jr., 8732
Ezell, F. Miles, Jr., 8676
Ezell, F. Miles, Sr., 8676
Ezell, John W., 8676
Ezell, Miles, Jr., 8741
Ezell, Rhoda Thompson, 8987
Ezell, Roy C., 8676
Ezell, Stanley M., 8676
Ezerski, Ronald, 4647
Ezerski, Ronald E., 4647
Ezersky, Peter, 6758

Feeney, James E., 8438
Feeney, Thomas J., 1092, 3164
Feerers, Jane, 3033
Fegan, Ann B., 8402
Fegan, Howard D., 8402
Fegan, John H., 8402
Fehl, Mark, 3520
Fehlman, Bruce R., 2750
Fehr, Edith, 6165
Fehr, Gloria J., 7522, 7523
Fehsenfeld, Cecile C., 4326
Fei, Barbara, 7216
Feibus, Arthur J., 7056
Feibus, Nancy Rozen, 7056
Feidler, Mark, 2323
Feigenbaum, Harvey, 3228
Feil, Carole, 5949
Feil, Gertrude, 5949
Feil, Jeffrey, 5949
Feil, Louis, 5949
Feil, Ralph L., 9390
Fein, Edward, 497
Feinberg, Abraham, 5950
Feinberg, Andrew, 8898
Feinberg, Betsy, 1765
Feinberg, David C., 8898
Feinberg, Harold, 6166
Feinberg, Helen H., 2066
Feinberg, Janice, 2727
Feinberg, Joseph, 2727
Feinberg, Mark, 2938
Feinberg, Milton D., 8898
Feinberg, Paul, 7813
Feinberg, Reuben, 2727
Feinberg, Stephen L., 8898
Feinberg, William I., 8898
Feinblatt, Lois Blum, 3577
Feinbloom, Joan L., 6823
Feiner, Vicki, 5511
Feinman, Alfred, 6042
Feinman, Frances, 1266
Feinman, Jeffrey S., 6707, 6708
Feinour, Edwin R., 9419
Feinstein, Alan Shawn, 8534, 8535
Feinstein, Amy, 5951
Feinstein, Leonard, 5951
Feinstein, Michael, 6532
Feinstein, Susan, 5951
Feintech Family Foundation, The, 500
Feintech, Evelyn M., 498, 499
Feintech, Irving, 498, 499, 500
Feintech, Lisa A., 500
Feintech, Lynn Diane, 499
Feintech, Norman, 498, 499
Feintech, Vivian A., 499
Feintech, Wendy, 500
Feit, Norman, 5789
Feitelberg, John J., 3854
Feith, Susan A., 9867
Feitler, Joan, 1651
Feitler, Robert, 1651
Fejes, Frank S., 6210
Fekete, Frank L., 5216
Fel-Pro Inc., 2912
Felburn, Phil, 3629
Feld, Alan R., 5582
Feldbaum, Bruce L., 8645
Feldberg Family Foundation, 5412
Feldberg, Elizabeth, 4162
Feldberg, Max, 3901
Feldberg, Morris, 3901
Feldberg, Stanley H., 3901
Feldberg, Sumner, 3901
Feldberger, Chaskel, 1342
Felderstein, Sandra, 1111
Feldman, Beth, 6408
Feldman, Donald, 7522, 7523
Feldman, Earl, 592
Feldman, Lynn A., 5157
Feldman, Marc, 5898
Feldman, Myron, 4630
Feldman, Richard E., 6969
Feldman, Roberta, 2767
Feldman, Wendy F., 8533

Feldmann, Fabio, 6389
Feldmann, Suzanne Mead, 8920
Feldstein, Lewis M., 5098
Feldstein, Martin, 1632
Feldstein, Richard, 808
Felger, Charles, 8768
Felgoise, Judith Abramson, 1868
Feliciano, Juan Gonzalez, 8515
Felix, Peter M, 7040
Fella, Leon, 6928
Fella, Robert H., 6928
Fellahnejad, Manucher, 8226
Fellenz, Beth, 9903
Feller, Nancy P., 5970
Fellman, Kenneth L., 9833
Fellner, Susan, 2128
Fellows, Lauren P., 9497
Fellows, William H., 7762
Felmet, Mark H., 2542
Fels, Samantha, 2109
Fels, Samuel S., 8198
Feltes, Tom, 4986
Felton, J. Louis, 4352
Felts, Anita T., 9421
Felts, Jean C., 3461
Felts, Thomas J., 3149
Felty, Julie Johns, 5482
Feltz, Carl, Jr., 5341
Femino, Dominic, 501
Femino, James J., 501
Femino, Marie, 501
Femino, Sue, 501
Fenchel, Joel H., 2853
Fenich, Randy, 9548
Fennebresque, Quincy, 7139
Fennelly, Christine, 4110
Fennessy, Anne, 9563
Fenno, J. Brooks, 3946
Fenster, Suzanne, 4425
Fenstermaker, Joan, 2701
Fenton, Devon Elizabeth, 5663
Fenton, Geoffrey, 7567
Fentress, Elizabeth C., 7438
Fenway Partners, 7174
Feoli, Ludovico, 3503, 3519
Feoli, Stephanie Stone, 3519
Ferber, Roman, 4296
Ferdinand, Jo Ann, 7216
Ferdowski, Farzin, 8662
Ferejohn, John A., 6894
Ferguson Irrevocable Trust, Mildred F.,
  7625
Ferguson, Bettye Poetz, 502
Ferguson, Bob, 910
Ferguson, Ellen Lee, 9585
Ferguson, Hugh S., 9585
Ferguson, Jane Avery, 9585
Ferguson, Jerry L., 3106
Ferguson, Jerry L., Mrs., 3106
Ferguson, John, 4968
Ferguson, John J., 1637
Ferguson, Judy, 8842
Ferguson, Katherine C., 3903
Ferguson, Randall, 4919
Ferguson, Sanford B., 8178
Ferguson, Stephen L., 3228
Ferguson, Thomas C., Amb., 3511
Fernald Trust, Kylee McVaney, 1430
Fernalld, Kylee A., 1430
Fernandes, Jorge, 406
Fernandez, Claude, 5704
Fernandez, Eugenio, 4243
Fernandez, James N., 7137
Fernandez, Jean-Marie, 1794
Fernandez, Jose, 1483
Fernandez, Manuel J., 5288
Fernandez, Miguel B., 1997
Fernandez, Mike, 4952, 4953
Fernandez, Nancy, 1483
Fernandez, Raul J., 1794
Fernandez, Robert C., 8213
Fernholz, Patricia, 2969
Fernstermacher, Mark, 1468
Ferrales, Sid, 9672

Ferranti, Anthony L., 6721
Ferrara, Al, 7525
Ferraresi, Daniel J., 1893
Ferrari, Andrew U., 5953
Ferrari, Barbara, 5953
Ferrari, Barbara Q., 5953
Ferrari, Clarence J., Jr., 862
Ferraro, James L., 1998
Ferraro, Kris, 4520, 4574
Ferraro, Louis, 1998
Ferraro, Luella S., 1998
Ferrasci, Frank E., 647
Ferree, Robert B., IV, 8457
Ferree, Russell J., Mrs., 3693
Ferrell, Mark C., 9716
Ferrell, Mary Beth, 1054
Ferrell, Paget, 7872
Ferrero, Thomas V., 7867
Ferriby, Robin D., 4254
Ferriday, Carolyn, 5954
Ferrier, Ellen Roberts, 1635
Ferrier, Peg, 8844
Ferrigno, C. James, 8135
Ferrigno, Steve, 3591
Ferrill, Sharon A., 5484
Ferris, Baker Watts, Inc., 3628
Ferris, Carolyn Zecca, 1220
Ferris, George M., Jr., 3628
Ferris, Lisa, 4661
Ferris, Vincent J., 4243
Ferritor, Dan, 166
Ferritor, Daniel E. "Dan", 169
Ferrucci, Richard, 5703
Ferry, Nick, 3132
Ferry, Sherri D., 2522
Fersner, Susan, 2240
Fertel Charitable Lead Unitrust, Ruth U.,
  3477
Fertel, Randy, 3477
Fertitta, Frank J., III, 5033
Fertitta, Frank J., Jr., 5033
Fertitta, Lorenzo J., 5033
Fertitta, Victoria, 5033
Ferullo, Brian D., 4122
Ferwerda, Constance M., 9833
Fery, Sandra, 2570
Fesenmyer, Bob, 7599
Fesko, Donald, 3129
Fesko, Frankie, 3129, 3189
Fesler, C., 1299
Festinger, Trudy, 6315
Festivale Maritime, Inc., 1881
Fetah, David, 4689
Fetner, Harold A., 6779
Fetter, Jane Trevor, 1087
Fetter, Trevor, 9229
Fetterman, Annabelle L., 7438
Fetting, Mark R., 3729
Fetz, Courtney Gaines, 2393
Fetzer Memorial Trust, John E., 4297
Fetzer Revocable Trust, J.E., 4298
Fetzer, Bruce, 4298
Fetzer, Bruce F., 4297
Fetzer, John E., 4297
Feuerman, Anne Pelletier, 1538
Feuerman, Kurt, 1538
Feuerstein, Charles, 6723
Feuerzeig, Henry L., 9363
Feuerzeig, Penny, 9363
Feuille, Richard Harlan "Rickie", 8881
Feuille, Rickie, 8950
Feulner, Edwin J., Jr., 8425, 8607
Feulner, Edwin, Jr., 5524
Fey, Caroline, 9888
Fey, Lynn, 9888
Fialkow, Ira, 2195
Fibers Nemours, 8333
Fibiger, H. Christian, 219
Ficalora, Joseph, 6859
Ficalora, Joseph R., 6800
Fick, Jeffrey D., 3293
Fick, Kathy, 3199
Ficken, Eric B., 8619
Fidel, Arthur C., 8359

Fidelity Charitable Gift Fund, 8535
Fidelity Charitable Gift Trust, 8917
Fidelity Products Co., 4565
Fidelity State Bank and Trust Co., 3389
Fidelity Ventures Ltd., 3818, 3904
Fidgeon, Timothy F., 4070
Fidicuary Trust Co., Int'l., 4895
Fidler, Christopher D., 7776
Fidler, John, 3145
Fidler, Maureen, 4085
Fiduciary Management, Inc., 9830
Fiduciary Trust Co., 1615, 4009, 4017,
  4186
Fiduciary Trust Co. International, 6306,
  6613
Field Private Trust, Frances K., The, 504
Field, Arthur Norman, 6769
Field, Brad, 1358
Field, Claire-Marie, 1570
Field, Eris M., 503
Field, Joseph M., 8200
Field, Ken, 5357
Field, Lawrence N., 503
Field, Lisa S., 503
Field, Marie H., 8200
Field, Marshall, 2728
Field, Marshall, IV, 2728
Field, Marshall, V, 2661, 2962
Field, Robyn L., 503
Fielder, Ann C., 8995
Fielder, Mary C., 4863
Fielding, Donna M., 5535
Fielding, Retha, 5092
Fielding, Ronald, 5535
Fielding, Ronald H., 5535
Fields, Bertram, 6861
Fields, Candice, 1111
Fields, Carmen, 6320
Fields, Curtland E., 5431
Fields, David, 9297
Fields, Gregory F., 1698
Fields, Kenneth H., 6339
Fields, Laura, 7449
Fields, Laura Kemper, 4849, 4850,
  4876
Fields, Leo, 9297
Fields, Michael D., 4797, 4849, 4909
Fields, Sara A., 3044
Fields, William A., 7735
Fieldstone Communities, Inc., 506
Fienberg, Linda, 1771
Fiery, Michael A., 9735
Fife, Amy S., 5955
Fife, Barbara J., 6265
Fife, David, 5955
Fife, Eugene V., 5955
Fife, Francis H., 9495
Fife, Stephen, 6265
Fifth Third Bank, 2170, 4252, 7557,
  7568, 7574, 7594, 7603, 7613,
  7626, 7647, 7666, 7726, 7820,
  7840, 7841, 7869, 7895, 7913
Figge, Thomas K., 3284
Figge, Vivian Otto, 3284
Figlilio, Carmine, 1975
Figueroa, Jennifer, 5388
Figueroa, John G., 879
Figueroa, Juan A., 1537
Figueroa, Laura, 5203
Figureres, Jose Maria, 6389
Fikes, Amy L., 8899
Fikes, Brendan J., 8899
Fikes, Catherine W., 8899
Fikes, Lee, 8899
Fikes, Leland, 8899
Fila, Andrew, 4058
Filan, Marian S., 5290
Filene, Lincoln, 3907
Filer, Wanda D., 8511
Filger, Brian, 1295
Fillion, George, 2551
Fillippo, Thomas, 8141
Fillit, Howard M., 6232
Filo, David, 7282

Fitton, Rebecca P., 7660
Fitts, David W., 4192
Fitts, Harriet W., 4711
Fitts, William S., 4711
Fitzgerald, Ann, 359
Fitzgerald, Anne, 1678
Fitzgerald, Bernard, 7374
FitzGerald, C.M., 8889
Fitzgerald, Caren, 4509
Fitzgerald, Caroline D., 1870
Fitzgerald, Dennis M., 7195
Fitzgerald, Dennis W., 2882
Fitzgerald, Eileen M., 8584
Fitzgerald, Ella, 514
Fitzgerald, Gail M., 3598
Fitzgerald, Gloria, 107
Fitzgerald, J. Daniel, 7586
Fitzgerald, Margaret Boles, 6453
Fitzgerald, Michele C., 7195
Fitzgerald, Stephen B., 7310
Fitzgerald, Tracy E., 2594
Fitzgerald, Vicki Netter, 1607
Fitzgerald, William A., 4951
Fitzgerald-Schultz, Shannon, 3260
Fitzgibbon, Herbert S., 6214, 7114
Fitzgibbon, Susan H., 7444
Fitzgibbons, Don, 8840
Fitzmorris, Ann, 3460
Fitzmorris, Patrick Wadsworth, 3460
Fitzmorris, Scott, 1858
Fitzmyers, Thomas J., 1157
Fitzpatrick Companies, Inc., 3950
Fitzpatrick, Alice F., 1517
Fitzpatrick, Barry C., 454
Fitzpatrick, Christopher, 515
Fitzpatrick, Edward J., 5008, 5009
Fitzpatrick, Elizabeth A., 923
Fitzpatrick, Jack, 559
Fitzpatrick, Jane P., 3950
Fitzpatrick, John H., 3950
Fitzpatrick, Kimberly, 515
FitzPatrick, Laurel, 7139
Fitzpatrick, Michael J., 515, 5341
Fitzpatrick, Michael J., Jr., 515
Fitzpatrick, Nancy J., 3950
Fitzpatrick, Patricia W., 515
Fitzpatrick, Robert, 5550
Fitzpatrick, Susan M., 4864
Fitzsimmons, Hugh A., Jr., 8936
FitzSimmons, John S., 5898
Fitzsimmons, John T., 5846
Fitzsimmons, Kelly, 4025
FitzSimons, Michael, 4412
Fitzwater, John, 1944
Fitzwater, Timothy, 7526
Five Way Partners, LLP, 1584
Fix, Duard, 1405
Fixen, Paul E., 2388
Fizdale, Dee, 3437
Fizer, Don, 6504
Flack, Charles D. "Rusty", Jr., 8317
Flack, David, 9131
Flagg, James R., 517
Flagg, M. Elizabeth, 517
Flagg, Morgan, 517
Flaherty, William T., 1664
Flake, Floyd, Rev., 1793
Flakes, J.H., Jr., 2361
Flam, Jack, 5847
Flamme, Larry, 4962
Flanagan, John L., 3407
Flanagan, Katherine P., 9118
Flanagan, Leo M., Jr., 2717
Flanagan, Patricia J., 8551
Flanagan, Sheila B., 1644
Flander, Doris, 661
Flanders, George W., 8611
Flanders, Graeme L., 3770
Flanigan, Brigid S., 6755
Flanigan, Peter M., 6755
Flanigan, Robert W., 6755
Flanigan, Timothy P., 6755
Flannery, Mary Christine, 2592
Flanzer, Gloria, 5963

Flanzer, Louis, 5963
Flaten, Eric, 9702
Flather, Newell, 4069
Flatley, Thomas J., 3911
Flatto, Olivia, 5926
Flaville, Victoria K., 8157
Flaws, James B., 5784, 5794
Flax, Gordon, 7866
Fleck, Robert E., 8202
Fleckenstein, Andrew J., 9799
Flecter Trust, Emma, 4074
Fleece, William H., 5966
Fleeman, Stewart, 301
Fleenor, William, 9645
Fleer Trading Cards, 7174
FleetBoston Financial Corp., 7174
FleetBoston Financial Foundation, 7310
Fleetguard, Inc., 3136
Flegenheimer, Mark S., 4428
Fleischer, Henry, 4244
Fleischer, Larry, 148
Fleischman, Charles D., 7435
Fleischman, Richard J., 7435
Fleischmann, Brian F., 9908
Fleischmann-Colgan, Ruth H., 7264
Fleishhacker, David, 518
Fleishhacker, Jeffrey, 518
Fleishhacker, Mortimer, 518
Fleishhacker, Mortimer, Jr., 518
Fleishhacker, Mortimer, Sr., 518
Fleishhacker, William, 518
Fleishman, Eleanor W., 7349
Fleishman, Ernest, 1745
Fleishman, Martine, 5522
Fleishman, Stanley, 5522, 6500
Fleming, Allison, 3281
Fleming, Charles L., Mrs., 6932
Fleming, David D., 2890
Fleming, David W., 345
Fleming, Donna, 7313
Fleming, George M., 8903
Fleming, James F., 2356
Fleming, John N., 7346
Fleming, Kate M., 9907
Fleming, Michael, 300
Fleming, Patricia, 9020
Fleming, R.H., 3046
Fleming, Richard, 8206
Fleming, Roberta, 8206
Fleming, Samuel C., 5779
Fleming, Scott, 8903
Fleming, Thomas, 7585
Fleming, Virginia, 2240
Fleming, William, 8904
Flemming-McGrath, Lucy, 6199
Flen, Anderson, 2458
Flesch, William, Rev., 4729
Fletcher, Allen W., 3912, 4165
Fletcher, Betty, Hon., 9599
Fletcher, Burton, 9530
Fletcher, Connie, 9401
Fletcher, David A., 5188
Fletcher, Don C., 4257
Fletcher, Ernest P., Jr., 6820
Fletcher, Gary, 4257
Fletcher, Mary F., 3912
Fletcher, Melvyn, 1911
Fletcher, Oscar, 7494
Fletcher, Paris, 3912
Fletcher, Patricia A., 3912
Fletcher, Rachel G., 3801
Fletcher, Ruth, 1037
Fletcher, Warner S., 3776, 3912, 3954, 4165, 4209
Flexon, Courtney, 2346
Flextronics International U.S.A., Inc., 519
Flick, Don, 8098
Flick, Robert, 1118
Flickinger, Louise M., 6507
Flickner, James H., 3177
Fliehman, Dennis W., 4243
Flieller, James, 8768
Flier, Edith, 1328

Flier, Jonathan, 1328
Flinn, Gail, 142
Flinn, Irene, 98
Flinn, Lawrence, Jr., 1543
Flinn, Polly, 2628
Flinn, Robert S., 98
Flinn, Stephanie, 1543
Flint, David H., 2321
Flipper, Cassandra, 854
Flippin, Doreen, 1964
Flitner, Sara, 9977
Flock, Michael, 8135
Floerchinger, Craig, 83
Flom, Joseph H., 6998
Flood, Stanley R., 2579
Floodman-McAllister, Sheila, 3354
Flora Family Foundation, 5905
Flora, Cornelia Butler, 4636
Flora, Jon, 1029, 7705
Flore, James P., 9434
Florence, Priscilla, 214
Flores, Armando B., 86
Flores, Hope, 3133
Flores, John, 3245
Flores-New, Fernando, 4321
Florian, Sonia, 2915
Florian, William C., 2915
Florida Co., The, 8825
Florida Coastal School of Law, 1887
Florida Hospital Medical Center, 2205
Florida Power & Light Co., 2010
Florida Progress Corp., 7453
Florida Rock Industries, Inc., 2003
Florida Sports Foundation, 2024
Florie, Walter, Jr., 901
Florino, Joanne V., 7162
Florio, Carl, 6207
Florman, Betty E., 2004
Florman, Neil, 2004
Flory, Lee J., 2768
Flournoy, Houston I., 728
Flow, Donald E., 7368
Flow, Robbin B., 7368
Flower, Walter C., III, 3483
Flowers, Bill, 26
Flowers, J. Christopher, 7251
Flowers, Rockne G., 9768
Flowers, Thomas I., 6211
Flowers, Wilford, 9294
Flowers, William H., Jr., 2384
Floyd, C. Edward, 8571
Floyd, Frank A., Jr., 8577
Floyd, Franklin B., 7901
Floyd, Garcia J., 3180
Floyd, James M., Sr., 7424
Floyd, Jim, 2511
Floyd, John B., 2463
Floyd, Marjorie A., 2041
Floyd, Mary Bell, 522
Floyd, Tony, 8572
Floyd, Vikki, 23
Floyd, William S., 522
FLS Properties, 4565
Fludzinski, Marek T., 5964
Flug, Laura, 6121
Fluharty, Marlene J., 4218
Fluor Corp., 523
Fluor, J. Robert, II, 523
Fluor, Peter J., 9273
Fluoroware, Inc., 4712
Fly W/Best, 1306
Flynn*, Steve, 274
Flynn, Edward M., 7050
Flynn, Garrett S., 1598
Flynn, Grayce B. Kerr, 3661, 7949, 9983
Flynn, Jennifer R., 4131
Flynn, John A., 320
Flynn, Kevin, 3148
Flynn, Paul B., 2240
Flynn, Ruth S., 2600, 2923
Flynt, Allen, 4754
Flynt, Katherine McCarty, 4754
Flynt, Wayne, 7308
FMR Corp., 3904, 3970

Fockler, Robert M., 8661
Foderaro, Denise A., 1024
Foege, William, 2489, 7401
Foege, William H., 6826, 9567
Foellinger, Esther A., 3149
Foellinger, Helene R., 3149
Foerderer, Norma, 7167
Fogarty, Michael, 7383
Fogel, Aaron, 5965
Fogel, Esther, 5965
Fogelsong, Roger, 4814
Fogg, Sally, 4246
Fogg, Sandra, 3783
Fogle, James, 4927
Fogle, Jim, 1453
Fogle, John A., 3066
Fohs, Cora B., 8012
Fohs, F. Julius, 8012
Foisie, Caren B., 5082
Foisie, Jeanmarie, 5082
Foisie, Michael R., 1643
Foisie, Robert A., 1643
Folberg, Jay, 711
Folbre, Nancy, 5971
Folcroft, 3683
Folden, Dennis, 3302
Foley, Carol J., 2005
Foley, David A., 1527
Foley, Edward J., III, 5453
Foley, Jane, 898
Foley, Joan, 5453
Foley, John C., 5453
Foley, John W., 5781
Foley, Lawrence G., 1544
Foley, Lindsay E., 2005
Foley, Megan M., 1544
Foley, Michael E., 7721
Foley, Stephen P., 7040
Foley, Susan Behlke, 78
Foley, Susan Reynolds, 6232
Foley, Thomas S., 7185
Foley, Timothy, 5783
Foley, William P., 2005
Foley, William P., II, 2005
Folger, John Dulin, 9418
Folger, Juliet C., 9418
Folger, Kathrine Dulin, 9418
Folger, Lee Merritt, 9418
Folger, Nancy "Bitsey", 1785
Folger, Peter, 866
Folick, Jeff M., 971
Folkestad, Christopher A., 8038
Folkstone Ltd., 2427
Follansbee Steel Corp., 7545
Follett, Bob, 9871
Follett, Brian, 9871
Follett, Mark, 9871
Follett, Nancy, 1463
Follett, Neil, 9645
Follett, Sally S., 9871
Follett, Scott S., 9871
Follis, James G., 525
Follis, R. Gwin, 525
Folsom Ford, 8853
Folsom, Charles Stuart, 1545
Folsom, Margaret D., 8905
Folsom, Robert S., 8905
Folsom, Robert Stephen, 8905
Folts, Kimberly Spire, 8434
Foltz, Sidney A., III, 7819
Folz, Cecilia, 1468
Folz, Joseph S., 4473
Fonda, Jane S., 2385, 2386
Fondation Ventose, 9176
Fondren, Bentley B., 8906
Fondren, Leland T., 8906
Fondren, Robert E., 8906
Fondren, W.W., Sr., Mrs., 8906
Fondren, Walter W., III, 8906
Fondren, Walter W., IV, 8906
Fong, Bernadine Chuck, 359, 989
Fong, Ivan, 7567
Fong, Kevin A., 406
Fong, Lance, 1329

Fox, Michael, 1817
Fox, Norman, 231
Fox, Randolph Dudley, 7371
Fox, Richard J., 8210
Fox, Rick, 9680
Fox, Robert K., 7638
Fox, Robert L., 7638
Fox, Rodman, 1547
Fox, S., 897
Fox, Sam, 4815
Fox, Stacy L., 4472
Fox, Steven, 4815
Fox, Susan M., 898
Fox, Ted, 1203
Fox, William C., 2721
Fox-Claman, Pamela, 4815
Foxworth, Richard, Hon., 4735
Foy, Douglas J., 3103, 3104, 3105
Foy, Joe, 8842
Foy, Michael, 7653
Foyer, Julie Kemper, 4849, 4850
Foyo, George W., 1957
Frable, Frank, 3137
Fracyon, Noelle, 3714
Fracyon, Noelle M., 1741
Fradin, Paul, 4630
Fraenkel, Barnet H., 8292
Fraenkel, Fabian I., 8292
Fraenkel, George, 5575
Frafjord, Teresa, 9617
Frahn, Carl A., 5282
Fraim, Martha B., 7547
Fraim, William L., 7547
Fraint, Eric, 8378
Fraleigh, C.J., 2982
Fraley, George, 2300
Fraley, John L., Jr., 7342
Fralin, W. Heywood, 9420
Framel, James, 7981
Frampton, Harry, III, 1468
Frampton, Joseph H., 3415
Frampton, Stephen, 4669
Franc, Terry L., 4896
France Stone Co., The, 7639
France, Annita, 3632
France, George A., 7639
France, Jacob, 3632
France, Susan H., 1347
France, William M., Jr., 7783
Frances E., The, 9448
Franceschelli, Anthony D., 5927
Francis, David, 3503
Francis, David V., 4816
Francis, Frank, 571
Francis, H.D., 1870, 1961, 1962
Francis, J. Scott, 4816
Francis, John R., 9419
Francis, Mary B., 4816
Francis, Michael, 5228
Francis, Parker B., 4816
Francis, Parker B., III, 4816
Francis, Paul, 7089
Francis, Richard B., 938
Francis, Roger, 1178
Francis, Steve, 7673
Francis, Thomas L., 3250
Franck, C. Duffy, Jr., 8714
Franconia Foundation, 5910
Francqui, Frederic, Count, 5973
Francsis, Michael, 4697
Francy, J.C., 7751
Francy, Patricia L., 6975
Frandsen, Jean, 2683
Frank and Sarah Salizzoni Foundation, 4823
Frank Consolidated Enterprises, 2733
Frank Family Trust, H.R., 1028
Frank Lumber Co., Inc., 8016
Frank Timber Products, Inc., 8016
Frank, A.J., 8016
Frank, Billy, 2259
Frank, D.D., 8016
Frank, David A., 8090
Frank, Diana D., 1028

Frank, Diane Folsom, 8905
Frank, Elizabeth T., 5338
Frank, Ernst H., 5974
Frank, Ernst L., 5974
Frank, Faith, 5584
Frank, George W., 6774
Frank, Harold R., 1028
Frank, J.T., 8016
Frank, James A., 1028
Frank, James S., 2733
Frank, John, 1740
Frank, John V., 7761
Frank, Karen, 2733
Frank, L.D., 8016
Frank, Larry, 8715
Frank, M. Allan, 6028
Frank, Patricia, 6779
Frank, Paul M., 6668
Frank, Roxanne H., 2972
Frank, Seth E., 6458
Frank, Sidney E., 5975
Frank, Stanley J., Jr., 7600
Frank, Susan Regenstein, 2962
Franke, Barbara E., 2734
Franke, Jerold P., 9833
Franke, Richard J., 2734
Franke-Molner, Jane, 2734
Frankel, Bruce, 4313
Frankel, Edward M., 7669
Frankel, Erin R., 4413
Frankel, Ernest, 5976
Frankel, Evan R., 5976
Frankel, Gerald, 2735
Frankel, Gustav, 2735
Frankel, Herman, 4342
Frankel, Jean, 4312, 4313, 4314
Frankel, Judith, 4311, 4314
Frankel, Julius N., 2735
Frankel, Maxine, 4312
Frankel, Samuel, 4312, 4313, 4314
Frankel, Stanley, 4311, 4313, 4314
Frankel, Stuart, 4312, 4313
Frankenberg, Regina Bauer, 5977
Frankino, Connie M., 5196
Frankino, Samuel J., 5196
Franklin Holding Corp., 892
Franklin Holdings, Inc., 1520
Franklin, Alice, 6635
Franklin, Andrew D., 6635
Franklin, Carl M., 5065
Franklin, Charlotte A., 8908
Franklin, Chris, 8398
Franklin, David, 2550
Franklin, G.A., 4356
Franklin, John, 2389
Franklin, John C., 9295
Franklin, Julie, 5978
Franklin, Kathy, 5250
Franklin, Larry, 5065
Franklin, Larry D., 8908, 9182
Franklin, Martin E., 5978
Franklin, Mary O., 2389
Franklin, Nick, 971
Franklin, Oliver St. C., 8378
Franklin, Robert M., 1983
Franklin, Ronald, 8852
Franklin, Sterling C., 5065
Franklin, William E., 9558
Franklin, William P., 8895
Franks, Alta V., 3478
Franks, John, 3478
Franks, Lawrence, 5603
Franson, Richard C., 9435
Franson, Wallace D., 722
Frantz, Phil, 3223
Frantz, Thomas R., 9475
Franz, J. Denise, 4839
Franz, Jean, 8303
Franz, William, 1943
Franzblau, Charles A., 2280
Franzblau, Jo, 2280
Franzblau, Robert M., 2280
Frasch, Elizabeth Blee, 5979

Fraser Foundation, Richard M. & Helen T., 3917
Fraser, Cathy, 9229
Fraser, H.H., 3535
Fraser, H.H., Jr., 3535
Fraser, Helen T., 3917
Fraser, Ian, 7198
Fraser, Joseph B., III, 8584
Fraser, Richard M., 3917
Fraser, Russell, 1078
Fratzke, Katherine E., 4526
Frauenthal, Harold, 4252
Frautschi, Christopher J., 9804
Frautschi, Elizabeth J., 9804
Frautschi, Grant J., 9889
Frautschi, John J., 9804
Frautschi, Lance A., 9889
Frautschi, Peter W., 9804
Frautschi, W. Jerome, 9797, 9889, 9916
Fray, Anne K., 2303
Fray, John C., 4209
Frazee, Alexena, 8509
Frazer, David R., 98
Frazer, John, 2259
Frazer, John B., Jr., 9665
Frazer, Thomas L., 3462
Frazier Charitable Lead Trust, Charles, 5389
Frazier Charitable Lead Trust, Kelly A., 5389
Frazier, Charles O., 8662
Frazier, Clifford, Jr., 7427
Frazier, D. Mell, 3315
Frazier, Ed, III, 2189
Frazier, Elizabeth B., 3687
Frazier, Gary W., 2011
Frazier, J. Walter, 3479
Frazier, James Walter, Jr., 3479
Frazier, Kenneth C., 5327
Frazier, Mell Meredith, 3314
Frazier, Sylvia L., 3479
Frazier, Thomas H., 9239
Frazier, Tracy R., 8678
Frazier, W. Rob, 2224
Frazier, W. Robinson, 2059
Frazier, William H., 9042
Frazier, William R., 2224
Frazza, George S., 5265
Frear, Mary D., 2543
Frear, Walter F., 2543
Freas, Arthur K., 1548
Freas, Margery H., 1548
Frech, Andy, 3145
Frechette, Peter L., 4647
Freckman, Joanie C., 1048
Frederick Trust, C. Lydia, 2664
Frederick, Brian R., 7582
Frederick, E. Kristen, 5782
Frederick, Sherman, 5047
Frederick, William C., 6800
Fredericks, Tracy, 876
Fredericksen, Jay A., 2189
Free, Carole J., 2012
Free, Douglas J., 2012
Free, Harry J., 2012
Free, JoLynn, 8768
Free, Karen P., 1639
Free, Thomas E., 2012
Freeberg, Don, 338
Freeburg, Carol, 4718
Freed, Allen, 5925
Freed, Daniel J., 2736
Freed, Daniel S., 2736
Freed, Dean, 8039
Freed, Elizabeth Ann, 1798
Freed, Evelyn, 1712
Freed, Frances W., 1798
Freed, Frank, 1712
Freed, Gerald A., 1798
Freed, James W., 9338
Freed, Jane M., 1798
Freed, Joseph, 2736
Freed, Laurance, 2736

Freed, Nan, 9401
Freedman, Alisa S., 7030
Freedman, Aliza, 6334
Freedman, Deborah, 1552
Freedman, Edith, 6753
Freedman, Jane, 1552
Freedman, Joel E., 1552
Freedman, Karen, 6985
Freedman, Naomi K., 1552
Freedman, Nina P., 6985
Freedman, Richard, 1552
Freedman, Susan, 8197
Freedman, Susan K., 6985
Freehling, Paul, 2737
Freeland, Wesley, 4352
Freels, Gary W., 9741, 9792
Freeman Charitable Lead Trust, Carl M., 3633
Freeman, Alfred B., 3480
Freeman, Carlton L., 3513
Freeman, Charles, 3629
Freeman, Darrell S., 8662
Freeman, Doreen, 5981
Freeman, Douglas, 720
Freeman, Douglas K., 748, 938
Freeman, Gary, 393
Freeman, Gayle Gorman, 7819
Freeman, Geoffrey T., 8144
Freeman, George C., III, 9531
Freeman, Glenn, 156
Freeman, Graeme, 5981
Freeman, Harry B., 3513
Freeman, Harry B., Mrs., 3513
Freeman, Harry C., 9753
Freeman, Houghton, 5981
Freeman, J.B., 23
Freeman, John, 160
Freeman, Joshua M., 3633
Freeman, Louis M., 3480
Freeman, Louis M., Jr., 3507
Freeman, Mansfield, 5981
Freeman, Marc L., 9528
Freeman, Michelle D., 3633
Freeman, Morgan, 6824
Freeman, Nancy, 3489
Freeman, R. West, III, 3480
Freeman, Richard B., 2375
Freeman, Richard W., 3480
Freeman, Richard W., Jr., 3480, 3503, 3507
Freeman, Robert, 2911
Freeman, Ron, 3223
Freeman, Samuel, 5980
Freeman, Shirley, 1949
Freeman, Terri Lee, 1785
Freeman, Tina, 3507
Freeman, W. Harrell, 3513
Freeman, W. Neal, 2508
Freeman-Woolpert, David, 5092
Freer, Douglas C., 7819
Freer, Lester, 5564
Frees, C. Norman, 8909
Frees, David M., III, 8141
Frees, David M., Jr., 8381
Frees, Shirley B., 8909
Frehse, Robert M., Jr., 6161, 6162
Freiberg, Stephen J., 5755
Freidkin, Norman, 3716
Freidus, Bunny, 1465
Freilicher, Morton, 5909
Freisen, John, 1139
Freiwald, Gregory, 4284
Frekko, Katherine, 2995
Frelinghuysen, George L.K., 6721
Frelinghuysen, Peter, 5513, 5647
Fremming, Michele, 4560
Fremont Bank, 534
Fremont Sequoia Holding, L.P., 535
Fremont, Lisa M., 4546, 4725
French, Douglas D., 7694
French, Ernie, 4986
French, Forrest, 23
French, Gregory, 5359
French, Jameson S., 5098

French, Janel, 4573
French, Jerry L., 4902
French, Kindy, 1799, 9425
French, Marina K., 6308
French, Michael, 3039
Frenkel, Debra, 1781
Frenkel, Jacob, 1781
Frenz, Robert, 4689
Frerichs, Ernest S., 8531
Frese, Penelope, 7762
Freston, Andrew, 5982
Freston, Kathleen L., 5982
Freston, Thomas E., 5982
Freudman, Alex I., 5529
Freund, Conrad R., 214
Freund, Frederick W., 4324
Freundlich, Amy Reisen, 5228
Frevert, Mark, 3929
Frewin, William A., Jr., 5869
Frey, Allan H., 3562
Frey, David G., 4316
Frey, Dorothy L., 1324
Frey, Edward J., Jr., 4316
Frey, Edward J., Sr., 4316
Frey, Eugene U., 4566
Frey, Frances T., 4316
Frey, James R., 4566, 4671
Frey, John J., 4566
Frey, John M., 4316
Frey, Kathryn, 5983
Frey, Kip, 7496
Frey, Mary Caroline "Twink", 4316, 4404
Frey, Mary F., 4566
Frey, Mary W., 4566
Frey, Robert, 5983
Frey, Robert H., 7105
Freyer, Carl J., 5197
Freyer, Sylvia, 5197
Freygang, Antje, 7640
Freygang, Dale G., 7570, 7640
Freygang, David B., 7640
Freygang, Katherine A., 7640
Freygang, Marie A., 7640
Freygang, W. Nicholas F., 7640
Freygang, Walter Henry, 7640
Freyou, Ernest, 3468
Freysinger, David S., 9144
Friauf, Cynthia K., 9763
Fribourg, Charles, 5984
Fribourg, Mary-Ann, 5984, 6802
Fribourg, Michel, 5984
Fribourg, Paul J., 5786
Fribourg, Paul Jules, 5984
Frick, Henry C., 8124
Fricke, Walt, 4587
Fricks, Deanie D., 2013
Fricks, William P., 2013
Friday, Lucille R., 277
Friddell, Guy, 9455
Fridley, Harrison L., Jr., 9367
Fried, Arthur W., 5582, 6317, 7140
Friedberg, Barry S., 5985
Friedberg, Bruce F., 510
Friedberg, Elinor, 6287
Friedberg, Leslie, 6287
Friedeman, William B., 3058
Friedenberg, David, 9675
Frieder, L. Peter, Jr., 8431
Friedlaender, Helmut N., 8081
Friedland & Bros., Ralph, Inc., 5554
Friedland, David L., 4963
Friedland, Edward, 4963
Friedland, Jack, 6033
Friedland, Lauri Levitt, 7267
Friedland, Lawrence N., 8295
Friedland, Melissa R., 4963
Friedland, Nancy B., 4963
Friedlander, Lillian, 2347
Friedlander, Robert, 2770
Friedman French Foundation, 5905
Friedman, Aaron, 441
Friedman, Alan D., 9005
Friedman, Ann, 7161
Friedman, Ann B., 3272

Friedman, Arthur, 5788
Friedman, Barbara, 5986
Friedman, Barry, 6225
Friedman, Benjamin, 5764
Friedman, Billings, Ramsey & Co., Inc., 9425
Friedman, Bob, 6300
Friedman, Brenda, 35
Friedman, Carolyn Fine, 8201
Friedman, Cheri, 6694
Friedman, Darrell D., 3603
Friedman, David, 1088, 5986, 6532
Friedman, David A., 538
Friedman, Dorothy, 5988
Friedman, Edward A., 8136
Friedman, Eleanor, 538
Friedman, Elise D., 540
Friedman, Elliott M., 2600
Friedman, Emanuel, 1799, 9425
Friedman, Eugenie S., 2014
Friedman, Frances M., 5643
Friedman, Frank, 35
Friedman, Fred H., 35
Friedman, Freda, 953
Friedman, Gary, 196
Friedman, Gary M., 6154
Friedman, Gerald J., 5988
Friedman, Glen H., 3169
Friedman, Harold, 6219
Friedman, Harold E., 7637
Friedman, Howard, 538
Friedman, Ira David, 441
Friedman, Jacob, 441, 6673
Friedman, Jane, 5988
Friedman, Jordan, 35
Friedman, Kerry A., 7346
Friedman, Lawrence, 6225
Friedman, Lea, 441
Friedman, Leah, 35
Friedman, Louis F., 3725
Friedman, Marcine, 539
Friedman, Marjorie Northrop, 6147
Friedman, Michael, 1805
Friedman, Morton L., 539
Friedman, Nancy S., 7637
Friedman, Orly D., 3272
Friedman, Phyllis K., 538
Friedman, Richard A., 5987
Friedman, Robert E., 538, 1065
Friedman, Robert G., 2014
Friedman, Stephen, 1468
Friedman, Stephen B., 5986
Friedman, Terry D., 5229
Friedman, Theodor, 196
Friedman, Thomas L., 3272
Friedman, Tully, 1465
Friedman, Tully M., 540
Friedman, Walker C., 9005
Friedman, Wilbur H., 5643, 6011
Friedman, William, Jr., 3281
Friedmann, Albert B., 2738
Friedmann, Debbie, 5402
Friedmann, Peter, 5402
Friedmann, Philip M., 2738
Friedsam, Michael, Col., 5542
Friedt, Theodore, 2108
Friel, Matthew, 5099
Friel, Robert F., 4077
Friend, Edward M., III, 24
Friend, Kathy, 3125
Friend, Robert, 774, 775, 961
Friends of St. Luke, 983
Friends' Fund, Inc., A, 1866
Friendship House, Inc., 1647
Frierson, Charles, 160
Fries, Carrie, 148
Fries, Gary, 1505
Friesen, Robert H., 91
Friess, Foster S., 9982
Friess, Herman A., 9982
Friess, Lynnette E., 9982
Friess, Polly J., 9978
Frimel, Susan, 945
Frink, Clayton, 9797, 9854

Friou, Roger P., 4752
Frisbie, Sharon W., 7907
Frisch, Alfred, 1897
Frisch, Benjamin, 1897
Frisch, Hans, 1897
Frisch, Karl, 1897
Frishman, Gerald, 2736
Frisman, Linda, 1529
Frist, Dorothy Cate, 8678
Frist, Patricia C., 8679
Frist, Robert A., 8678
Frist, Thomas F., III, 8679
Frist, Thomas F., Jr., 8662, 8678, 8679, 8690
Frist, Thomas F., Sr., 8678
Frist, William H., 8678
Frist, William R., 8679
Fritel, Steve, 4540
Frith, Maria Teresa Amos, 2316
Fritsch, C. Stephen, 8794
Fritsche, E. Alan, 8938
Fritts, Edward O., 1505
Fritts, Marilyn, 3215
Fritz, Kathy May, 5046
Fritz, Martin A., 8187
Fritz, Michael, 3855
Fritz, Ronald A., 3220
Frizen, Edwin L., Jr., 1361, 3042
Frizzell, Lockwood, 9390
Froburg, Art, 5088
Froderman, Carl M., 3153
Froderman, Harvey, 3153
Froderman, Harvey, Mrs., 3153
Froelich, Dan, 2388
Froelich, Georgia A., 7671
Frohlich, Phil, 7984
Frohlich, Susan, 1088
Frohman, Blanche P., 7641
Frohman, Daniel C., 7641
Frohman, Sidney, 7641
Frohnmayer, David B., 8013
Frohring, Maxine A., 5993
Frohring, Paul R., 5993
Frol, Deborah D., 9559
Frolich, Julia, 2547
Fromm, Alfred, 541
Fromm, David George, 541
Fromm, Hanna, 541
Fromm, Ronald A., 4789
Frommelt, Jeffrey J., 2681
Fronczkowski, Stanley, 8333
Frontczak, Joan, 2996
Fronterhouse, Gerald W., 8955
Fronterhouse, Jeff, 9068
Frontier Capital Mgmt., 7526
Frosh, Wendy J., 5089
Fross, Roger R., 2820
Frost Family, 8990
Frost National Bank, 8824, 9133, 9136, 9145, 9166, 9178
Frost National Bank, The, 8824
Frost, Andrew, 8470
Frost, Christina, 4376
Frost, Genevieve Tchang, 1229
Frost, Jeanne L., 1044
Frost, Joan M., 5894
Frost, Judy, 1093
Frost, Mike, 3333
Frost, Patricia H., 8910
Frost, Robert D., 6434
Frost, Thomas C., 8910
Frost, Virginia C., 5476
Frost, William Lee, 6434
Fruchthandler Bros. Enterprises, 5995
Fruchthandler, Abraham, 5995
Fruchthandler, Abraham H., 5995
Fruchthandler, Joseph, 5995
Fruchthandler, Solomon, 5995
Fruchthandler, Zachary, 5995
Fruchtman, Jack, Jr., 3668
Fruchtman, Joann C., 3668
Fruchtman, Liana, 3668
Frueauff, Charles A., 161
Frueauff, David A., 161

Frueauff, Sue M., 161
Frueauff-Williams, Anna Kay, 161
Fruehauf, Harvey C., Jr., 5077
Fruge, Don L., Sr., 4756
Frulla, William E., 8638
Frutiger, Robert P., 9239
Frutkin, Harvey L., 1800
Fry, Amy, 1498
Fry, David E., 3556
Fry, Lloyd A., 2740
Fry, Lloyd A., III, 2740
Fryberger, Carol, 4499
Frye, Clayton W., Jr., 6246, 6451
Frye, Henry E., 7343, 7438
Frye, Irene, 2681
Frye, Shirley, 7329
Frye, Shirley T., 7439
Fryer, Larry, 9021
Frymoyer, John W., 6471
Fu, Freddie H., 8074
Fubacher, Stephen A., 8874
Fuccillo, Ralph, 4061
Fuchs Trust, Gottfried, 9590
Fuchs, Bernard, 5996
Fuchs, Gottfried, 9590
Fuchs, Ira H., 6525
Fuchs, Lawrence M., 5464
Fuchs, Mary, 9590
Fuchs, Morris, 5996
Fuchs, Serena, 5996
Fuchsberg & Fuchsberg, 5997, 5998
Fuchsberg Family Foundation, 5998
Fuchsberg, Abraham, 5997, 5998
Fuchsberg, Alan L., 5997
Fuchsberg, Jacob D., 5997
Fuchsberg, Seymour, 5998
Fuchsberg, Shirley, 5997
Fudge, Ann M., 6826
Fudurich, Dana, 1295
Fudurich, Edward, 1295
Fuemmeler, Carl D., 4822
Fuentes, Humberto, 4636
Fuentes, Joe, 1460
Fuentes, Thomas A., 1841
Fuentes-Afflick, Elena, 9348
Fuerst, Jan F., 8901
Fuerst, Martee F., 8901
Fuesler, Don, 9570
Fugate, Jeff, 2075
Fugel, Esther, 5965
Fugett, Anthony S., 6416
Fuhrman, Susan H., 359, 1838, 5199
Fuji Films, Japan, 7033
Fujimoto, Kunio, 7096
Fujimoto, Lisa C., 373
Fujioka, Robert T., 2542
Fujisawa, Tetsufumi, 7005
Fukami, Toshu, 6235
Fukukawa, Shinji, 7185
Fulce, Marion, 3131
Fuld, Florentine M., 5999
Fuld, Kathleen Bailey, 6000
Fuld, Leonhard Felix, 5999
Fuld, Richard S., 6000
Fuld, Richard S., Jr., 6000
Fuldner, Henry E., 9821
Fulk Farms, Inc., 4964
Fulk, Robert W., 4964
Fulk, Wilma B., 4964
Fulkerson, Isobel Wyker, 77
Fuller Co., H.B., 4567
Fuller, Alvan T., Sr., 5090
Fuller, Charles, 4870
Fuller, George Freeman, 3918
Fuller, Howard L., 2820
Fuller, Janice L., 3918
Fuller, Joyce I., 3918
Fuller, Kathryn S., 5970
Fuller, Kenneth, 1900
Fuller, Lincoln E., 3918
Fuller, Mark W., 3918
Fuller, Peter, 5090
Fuller, Peter D., Jr., 5090
Fuller, Richard B., 7642

Fuller, Sybil H., 3918
Fullerton, Alma H., 8589
Fullerton, Baxter, 1378
Fullerton, Jessica, 1378
Fullerton, John B., 1378
Fullwood, Emerson, 1680
Fulmer, Craig, 3145
Fulp, J.R., Jr., 8564
Fulp, John R., III, 8564
Fulstone, Suellen, 5046
Fulton Financial Advisors, N.A., 8208
Fulton, Adna, 3600
Fulton, Annette, 1359
Fulton, Daniel S., 9703
Fulton, Mike, 4251
Fulton, Steven P., 8403
Fulton, V. Neil, 578
Fultz, Daniel G., 8202
Fulweiler, Pamela S., 7287
Funck, W. Michael, 1537
Fund for the Poor, Inc., 1426
Fundingsland, Donald W., 9960
Fung, Bill, 4043
Funger, Keith Parker, 9426
Funger, Morton, 9426
Funger, Norma Lee, 9426
Funger, William Scott, 9426
Funk, Alan, 9324
Funk, Duncan, 2741
Funk, Gary, 4798
Funk, J. Merrill, 147
Funk, John L., 2741
Funk, Mark, 147
Funke, Susan B., 2104
Funston, Joy Crockett, 1939
Fuqua Family Charitable Lead Unitrust,
    J.B., 2391
Fuqua, Dorothy C., 2391
Fuqua, Duvall S., 2470
Fuqua, J. Rex, 2391, 2470
Fuqua, J.B., 2391
Fuqua, John R., 368
Furber, Robert, 616
Furey, E.F., 2168
Furia, Helen M., 2029
Furlong, Andrew T., Jr., 3544
Furlong, Barbara, 2922
Furlong, Mark F., 9860
Furlong, R. Michael, 2673
Furlotti, Nancy Swift, 1233
Furlow, John, Jr., 7622
Furman, Frieda, 6003
Furman, Gail, 6002
Furman, Jason, 6002
Furman, Jay, 6002
Furman, Jeffrey, 9355
Furman, Jesse, 6002
Furman, Joyce, 8049
Furman, Roy L., 6003
Furmansky, Stewart, 8292
Furnas, Leto M., 2782
Furnas, W.C., 2782
Furney, Katharine S., 3906
Furniss, Adrianne Benton, 1773
Furniture Brands International, Inc.,
    4835
Furr, Richard L., 7491
Furst, Darlene J., 2679
Furst, Debra L., 8911
Furst, Jack D., 8911
Furst, John D., 8911
Furst, John S., 8911
Furst, Michael, 2157
Furst, Robert S., 8911
Furth, Donna W., 543
Furth, Frederick P., 543
Furth, Hope L., 6004
Furth, John L., 5971, 6004
Furth, Peggy J., 543
Fuscone, Marjorie M., 1550
Fuscone, Richard M., 1550
Fuson, Esten, 3153
Fuson, Mark J., 3153
Fuson, Scott E., 4285

Fuss, Helen, 6192
Fusscas, Amanda C., 3990
Fusscas, Christopher P., 3990
Fusscas, Frederick B., 3990
Fussell, Stephen R., 2579
Futo, Kyle Monfort, 1429
Future Care, 5302
Fye, Kenny, 3133
Fyler, Carlton D., 1516
Fyler, Jenny R., 1516

G-Bar Ltd. Partnership, 1884
G.C. Investments, 5034
G.P.G. Foundation, 569
Gaalswyk, Kathy, 4521, 4593
Gabbianelli, Rose M., 8345
Gabel, Caroline D., 3727
Gabelli, Marc J., 5200
Gabelli, Mario J., 5200
Gabelli, Matthew R., 5200
Gabelli, Michael, 5200
Gaber, David, 5503
Gaber, Stephen, 5503
Gaber, Stephen G., 5496
Gaberino, John A., Jr., 7987
Gabier, Russell L., 4324
Gabrian, Dennis, 4226
Gabriel, Chris, 8333
Gabriel, Nicholas M., 5970
Gabriele, Stephanie K. Skestos, 7683
Gabrieli Family Foundation, 4025
Gabrieli, Christopher F., 4025
Gabrieli, Christopher F.O., 3919
Gabrieli, Hilary B., 3919
Gabrieli, John D.E., 3919
Gabrieli, Lila, 3919
Gabrielson, Mark J., 1537
Gach, Gregory H., 7395
Gackle, Gregory B., 3277
Gadbois, Richard, III, 577
Gadd, Michael S., 9665
Gaddie, David, 2164
Gaddis, Larry R., 1437
Gaddy, Charles W., 7438
Gaddy, Joe E., 7479
Gaddy, Sandra Herring, 7396
Gadinsky, Elizabeth "Liebe", 1957
Gadsden, William, 5111
Gaffen, Harvey, 3063
Gaffney, Barbara, 8063
Gaffney, Debbie, 1358
Gaffney, Dorothy, 7526
Gaffney, John C., 699
Gaffney, Joseph M., 9647
Gaffney, Michael, 1529
Gaffney, Thomas J., 9583
Gagarin, Andrew, 99
Gagarin, Jamie, 99
Gage, Barbara C., 4532
Gage, Howell N., Jr., 4769
Gage, Kelly K., 4532
Gage, Nancy Brooke, 9797
Gage, Richard C., 4532
Gage, Scott C., 4532
Gagel, Pamela, 1367
Gagen, Tim, 1463
Gagliardi, Joan, 9634
Gagnon, Beth, 7539
Gagnon, Brian, 5201
Gagnon, Christine L., 1992
Gagnon, Lois E., 5201
Gagnon, Neil J., 5201
Gagnon, Sharon, 83
Gaguine, Alexander, 225
Gaguine, Benito, 225
Gaguine, John, 225
Gahagan, Alexis, 1698
Gahagan, Katharine, 1698
Gail, Leonard A., 3021
Gain, Judith K., 244
Gaines, Adrian, 6559
Gaines, Courtney Knight, 2393
Gaines, Ezekiel Baldwin, III, 2393

Gaines, Jacquelyn, 8048
Gaines, Joan, 3407
Gaines, Louisa M., 3427
Gaines, Priscilla P., 4688
Gaines, Thomas W., Jr., 9793
Gaines, Tyler B., 4975
Gains, Nancy, 261
Gainsborough, Jeffrey P., 1157
Gainsley, Gloria, 2549
Gair, Chris, 2240
Gaisman, Catherine V., 1551
Gaisman, Henry J., 1551
Gaitan, Jose, 9680
Gaiter, Donald, 8527
Gaither, James C., 671
Gaither, Jim, Jr., 1244
Galas, David J., 670
Galasso, August J., 6005
Galasso, Emil J., 6005
Galasso, Martin A., 6005
Galbraith, James R., 5037
Galbraith, John W., 9427
Galbraith, Margaret R., 1114
Galbraith, Mary, 4718
Galbraith, Rebecca Louise, 9427
Galbraith, Robert E., 8253
Galbraith, Rosemary Patricia, 9427
Gale, Benjamin, 7542
Gale, Catherine A., 5785
Gale, Edwin, 8913
Gale, G. David, 4842
Gale, Jane T. Greenspun, 5034
Gale, Karin M., 9960
Gale, Mark, 4771
Gale, Mary E., 7542
Gale, Pat, 4991
Gale, Rebecca S., 8913
Gale, Thomas H., 7542
Gales, Kewin, 8073
Galey, Glenn, 4735
Galia, Gary, 4293
Galiano, Paul A., 7027
Galines Foundation, Tony, 2634
Galinson, Murray, 1016
Galinson, Murray L., 1288
Gall, Blake, 8136
Gallagher & Co., Arthur J., 2744
Gallagher, J. Patrick, Jr., 2744
Gallagher, J. Peter, 7398
Gallagher, John F., 1447
Gallagher, John J., 4394
Gallagher, Lindsay R., 3666
Gallagher, Margaret W., 7398
Gallagher, Michael, 9873
Gallagher, Michael E., 2166
Gallagher, Michael L., 4984
Gallagher, Patricia A., 1722
Gallagher, Patrick S., 6679
Gallagher, Paul J., 3828
Gallagher, Robert E., 2743, 2744
Gallagher, Thomas G., 8117
Gallagher, Tim, 7848
Galland, Michael S., 7905
Gallant, Martin, 1909
Gallegos, Deborah, 5491
Gallegos, Gerald, 1468
Gallegos, Merlinda, 2769
Gallegos, Victoria L., 2835
Galli, Linda, 5064
Galli-Zugaro, Emilio, 205
Gallion, William J., 3433
Gallo Survivor's Trust, Aileen, 548
Gallo Winery, E & J., 547
Gallo, Aileen, 548
Gallo, Carlene R., 8431
Gallo, Ernest, 547
Gallo, Greg, 406
Gallo, John, 961
Gallo, John R., 548
Gallo, Joseph E., 547
Gallo, Julio R., 548
Gallo, Maria, 1250
Gallo, Mary I., 547
Gallo, Robert J., 548

Gallo, Ronald V., 8551
Galloway, David A., 7848
Galloway, Jean, 1445
Galloway, Jessica, 309
Galloway, Peter, 9634
Galloway-Tabb, Pamela Y., 9371, 9424
Galluci-Davis, Sheila, 5415
Gallup, George H., Jr., 8475
Gallwas, Gerald E., 272
Galt, Louise, 4931
Galter, Dollie, 2745
Galter, Jack, 2745
Galter, William, 2745
Galtney, William F., Jr., 8960
Galvano, Bill, 2148
Galvez, Fred, 9313
Galvin, Chris, 9933
Galvin, Christopher, 2746
Galvin, Christopher B., 2747
Galvin, Helen M., 2746
Galvin, John, 1468, 8558
Galvin, Mary G., 2747
Galvin, Robert, 2746
Galvin, Robert E., 4082
Galvin, Robert W., 2747
Galyen, Jeff, 3165
Gamb, James D., 982
Gamber, Brice R., 5162
Gambet, Daniel G., 8285, 8481
Gambill, Sandra E., 1912
Gambino, Joseph H., Jr., 3550
Gamble, George F., 549
Gamble, George T., 549
Gamble, James N., 247
Gamble, Jim, 549
Gamble, Joan L., 549
Gamble, Launce E., 549
Gamble, Launce L., 549
Gamble, Linda J., 8513
Gamble, Mark D., 549
Gamble, Mary Caroline, 7474
Gamble, Mary S., 549
Gamble, Pat, 78
Gamble, Sandra, 9699
Gamble, Sean, 933
Gamble-Booth, Gwyneth, 8051
Gambrell, Sarah Belk, 7438
Games, Steve, 192
Gammill, Ted, 156
Gamper, Christopher E., 4936
Gamper, David E., 4936
Gamper, Harriet E., 4936
Gampka, Paul J., 4226
Ganassi, Floyd R., 8107
Gancarz, Alex J., Jr., 5496
Gandal, Larry N., 3579
Gandara, Marilda L., 1479
Ganger, M. Joe, 4237
Gangl, Walter T., 8090
Gann, Herbert M., 2016
Gann, Joseph, 2016
Gann, Peggy P., 3018
Gann, Rae, 2016
Gann, Ronald, 2432
Gannett Co., Inc., 9428
Gannett, John D., 3958
Gannett, William B., 3958
Gannon, Thomas A., 9920
Gannon, Tony, 8747
Gannon, William S., Rev., 5431
Gano, Charles H., 4412
Gansbourg, Hensha, 7871
Ganser, Katherine Gosin, 9869
Gansler, Jill, 3683
Gant, Alison A., 6006
Gant, Christopher T., 6006
Gant, Donald R., 6006
Gant, Gail, 9640
Gant, Jane T., 6006
Ganther, Nathan, 6219
Gantt, Harvey B., 7370
Gantz, George, 4057
Gantz, Linda, 2748
Gantz, Linda T., 2748

Gantz, Matthew J., 2748
Gantz, Norman J., 2779
Gantz, Wilbur H., 2748
Ganulin, Judy, 537
Ganz, Lionel "Aryeh", 5527
Ganz, Simona Abraham, 5527, 5727
Ganzi, Victor F., 6161, 6162
Gap, Inc., The, 551
Gara, James, 5577
Garabedian, John, 552
Garavaglia, James, 4251
Garaventa Enterprises, Inc., 553
Garaventa, Mary, 553
Garaventa, Silvio, 553
Garb, Andrew S., 1225
Garb, Melvin, 554
Garbarino, John R., 5341
Garbe, F. James, 2680
Garber Neidich, Brooke, 6606
Garber, Chris, 3132
Garber, Eugene B., Sr., 3518
Garber, Karlene Beal, 8783
Garber, Ross, 8748
Garber, Roy, 9998
Garcett, Sukey, 1071
Garcetti, Eric, 1071
Garcetti, Gil, 659, 1071
Garcia, Anne M., 1445
Garcia, Carlos A., 6823
Garcia, Frances, 1810
Garcia, Frank, 4258
Garcia, Gary W., 8855
Garcia, Jesus G., 3084
Garcia, Joe, 1437
Garcia, John, 3395
Garcia, John T., Jr., 4932
Garcia, Jorge L., 2153
Garcia, Joseph, 1948
Garcia, Juan C., 3154
Garcia, Juanita, 560
Garcia, Juliet V., 5970
Garcia, Juliet Villarreal, 1844
Garcia, Maria N., 3154
Garcia, Mildred, 6156
Garcia, Pedro, 8005
Garcia, Rafael I., 4842
Garcia, Ralph P., 347
Garcia, Randy, 5047
Garcia, Roberto, 3387
Garcia, Sandy, 3255
Gard, Robert G., Jr., 374
Gardenswartz, Ian D., 1475
Gardiner Savings Institution, F.S.B., 3536
Gardiner, David D., 4352
Gardiner, Thomas E., 8523
Gardner Family 2000 Charitable Trust, 7644
Gardner, Ames, Jr., 7853
Gardner, Brian, Mrs., 7039
Gardner, Cindy, 933
Gardner, Cynthia B., 3164
Gardner, David, 9329
Gardner, David J., 4965
Gardner, Denise E., 7482
Gardner, Dorothy H., 2961
Gardner, Dorsey R., 9416
Gardner, Douglas, 9623
Gardner, Emerson, Lt. Genl., 9490
Gardner, Frederick C., 4428
Gardner, Gary E., 4706
Gardner, George, 7559
Gardner, George J., 4568
Gardner, George W., 4568
Gardner, Howard E., 3015
Gardner, Jacqui, 4568
Gardner, James, 2156
Gardner, James J., 7644
Gardner, Jean, 9640, 9659
Gardner, Jeanne M., 4965
Gardner, Jill, 9623
Gardner, Joan A., 7644
Gardner, Joan L., 4519
Gardner, Kirk N., 4965

Gardner, Patricia, 4232
Gardner, Patricia F., 7644
Gardner, R.M., 1991
Gardner, Roger L., 6274
Gardner, Shelli, 9323
Gardner, Spencer J., 7644
Gardner, Stephen D., 6945
Gardner, Sterling, 9323
Gardner, Susan M., 4568
Gardner, Warren, 1603
Garen, Eric R., 555
Garen, Nancy J., 555
Garey, Patricia M., 1741
Garey, Patrick, 6915
Garfield, Brian, 3921
Garfield, Seth, 3854
Garfinkel, Barry H., 6998
Garfinkle, Gillian, 2017
Garfinkle, Nicholas, 2017
Garfinkle, Norton, 2017
Garfinkle, Paul, 6186
Gargaro, Eugene A., Jr., 4382, 4387
Gargiulo, Andrea, 3780
Gargiulo, Evanne S., 6897
Garibaldi, Marie L., 5216
Garity, Troy, 2385
Garland, Hillary Duque, 556
Garland, Jeffery, 3325
Garland, Mary L.E., 9981
Garland, T.J., 9181
Garland, William M., II, 556
Garlington, Jennie Turner, 2501
Garlington, Sarah Jane Turner, 4464
Garlotte, Helen W., 3157
Garmisa, William J., 2928
Garner, John Michael, 2018
Garner, Katrina, 3275
Garner, Lynne, 1529
Garner, Wes, 9810
Garner, William, 1843
Garnett, Sandra, 1450
Garnsey, Cecily Coors, 1352, 1360
Garnsey, John, 1468
Garofalo, Donald L., 4512, 4671
Garofolo, Nicholas, 5194
Garofolo, Peter, 5194
Garr Tool Co., 4377
Garr, Louis J., Jr., 4853
Garrard, Gardiner W., 2425
Garrard, Gardiner W., Jr., 2361
Garrett Group, LLC, The, 285
Garrett, Diane, 285
Garrett, Horace, Mrs., 9151
Garrett, Jan B., 9419
Garrett, John R. (Bob), 8891
Garrett, Leon, 23
Garrett, Paul, 285
Garrett, Robert, 3559, 5867
Garrett, Robert P., 5288
Garrett, Wendy, 9108
Garrick, Renee E., M.D., 7247
Garris, Garry A., 7336
Garrison, James, 4057
Garrison, L. Alvin, 9393
Garrison, Lynne, 7319
Garrison, Marceda, 7931
Garrison, Natalie, 162
Garrison, Thomas R., 162
Garrity, Sheila, 9845
Garrott, Allison, 8653
Garrott, Thomas M., 8680
Garrou, John L.W., 7474
Garson, Ann, 7530
Garson, John D., 7805
Garson, Palmer P., Mrs., 9493
Garst, Dolores, 3280
Gart, Ken, 1465
Gart, Marjorie, 1445
Garten, Jeffrey E., 1479
Garth, Bryant G., 2903
Garthwaite, Albert A., Jr., 8212
Garthwaite, Diane, 8212
Gartland, Michael G., 6514
Gartlir, Bernard D., 6801

Gartner, Michael G., 9424
Garton, Caitlin, 7264
Garton, Deirdre Wilson, 7264
Garton, Elenore, 7264
Garton, Josie, 7264
Gartrell, Bernice, 7573
Garvey Charitable Trust No. 1, Willard W., 3363
Garvey Charitable Trust No. 11, 3364
Garvey Charitable Trust No. 2, Willard W., 3363
Garvey Foundation, 8914
Garvey Homes, 8818
Garvey Revocable Trust, Jean K., 3363
Garvey, Inc., 3363
Garvey, James S., 8914
Garvey, Jean K., 3363
Garvey, Jeffrey C., 8763
Garvey, Richard F., 8914
Garvey, Shirley F., 8914
Garvey, Willard W., 3363
Garwood, Susan Clayton, 9250
Garwood, William L., Jr., 8830
Gary, Leah S., 7830
Gary, Nancy, 1439
Gary, Samuel, 1379, 1439
Garza, Antony "Tony", 3186
Garza, Sonny, 9021
Gasch, Alice True, 1854
Gasch, Daniel, 134
Gasch, Wendy, 1765
Gaskin, Roy, 331
Gaskins, Cynthia, 3122
Gaskins, Stephen, 7345
Gassaway, James M., 8228
Gassel, James, 4160
Gasser, Peter A., 557
Gasser, Vernice H., 557
Gassert, Timothy B., 3812
Gassman, Paul R., 6124
Gassman, Robert S., 6124
Gast, Aaron E., 5338
Gast, D. Lou, 4317
Gast, Thomas C., 9739
Gast, Warren E., 4317
Gasten, Karen H., 2379
Gaston, Karl, 7749
Gaston, Patrick R., 5439
Gaston, Roger, 1460
Gatchel, Cathy, 3132
Gately, James, 8371
Gates Foundation, 359
Gates Foundation, Bill and Melinda, The, 5707
Gates, Anne O'Neill, 5111
Gates, Carol Ware, 8070, 8141
Gates, Charles C., 1380
Gates, Charles C., Sr., 1380
Gates, Giff, 8015
Gates, Hazel, 1380
Gates, Henry Louis, Jr., 6789
Gates, James, 4225
Gates, John, 1380
Gates, Joseph R., 8070
Gates, June S., 1380
Gates, Kimberly, 4225
Gates, Margaret J., 7438
Gates, Melinda French, 9591
Gates, Moore, Jr., 5111
Gates, Paul W., 8070
Gates, Signe S., 1488
Gates, Valerie, 1380
Gates, William H., III, 9591
Gates, William H., Sr., 9591
Gatewood, James C., 2448
Gathof, W. Lawrence, 3457
Gatins, Martin, 2456
Gatins, Phillip, 2456
Gattis, Anne K., 1157
Gattis, Grace Gaines, 2393
Gatto, Joseph D., 6007
Gatto, Susan, 6007
Gatton, C.M., 8681
Gatzemeier, Paul, 7517

Gaudette, Gerald "Lee", III, 4209
Gaudi, Arthur R., 336
Gaudiani, Claire L., 6453
Gaudoin, Ross C., 9718
Gauerke, James, 7593
Gaughan, John, 4814
Gaughran, Robert J., 5281, 5291
Gaughran, Robert, 5444
Gault, George H., 10000
Gault, Stanley C., 7761
Gauntlett, Barbara, 449
Gauntlett, Suwanna, 449
Gauntt, Miles, 2292
Gauron, Paul R., 4050
Gaus, Norbert, 5400
Gaus, William T., 9813
Gausas, Roberta, 6565
Gauthier, Anne S. Barrios, 3482
Gauthier, Celeste A., 3482
Gauthier, Cherie A., 3482
Gauthier, Michelle A., 3482
Gautier, Agnes, 6165
Gavel, Frank J., Jr., 8578
Gavel, Stephen L., 8578
Gavin, Austin F., 460
Gavin, Carol, 3034
Gavin, James J., Jr., 2749
Gavin, James R., III, 5265
Gavin, Kevin P., 2749
Gavin, Steven J., 2749
Gavin, Zita C., 2749
Gawron, Elizabeth, 3833
Gawryk, Terry, 2797
Gawthrop, Samuel M., 8224
Gay, Brigida C., 5827
Gay, Carol, 3672
Gay, Eleanor J., 1940
Gay, Frank William, 3654
Gay, Rebecca, 1911
Gayar, Hesham E., 4318
Gayden, Cynthia N., 8915
Gayden, William K., 8915
Gayden, William, Mrs., 8915
Gaydosh, Carlene, 5047
Gayheart, Jack, 7653
Gayle Trust, 809
Gayle, Gibson, Jr., 8762
Gayle, Martha, 9530
Gayle, William E., Jr., 9463
Gaylord, Bill, 91
Gaylord, Charles Reid, 1036
Gaylord, Edith Kinney, 7935, 7944
Gaylord, Edward L., 7937
Gaylord, Guilford W., 6403
Gaylord, Thelma F., 7937
Gaynor, George N., 2917
Gaynor, Vere W., 7788
Gaytan, Jorge, Dr., 2362
Gayton, Carver, 9599
Gayton, Rod, 7519
GB 30 Year Char. Trust, 2811
GE Engine Serives, Inc., 1950
Geare, Lori, 111
Gearen, John J., 2987
Gearhardt, Paul, 7748
Gearhart, Tom, 3124
Geary, G. Stanton, 5106
Geary, James E., 3548
Geary, Janet H., 8017
Geary, Jr. Irrevocable Trust, H.H., 7645
Geary, Karen M., 3595
Geary, Richard, 8017
Geballe, Adam, 489
Geballe, Adam P., 489
Geballe, Alison F., 489
Geballe, Frances K., 489
Geballe, Gordon T., 489, 1203
Geballe, Theodore H., 489
Gebbie, Marion B., 6009
Gebel, Riva, 971
Gebhard, Elizabeth, 2702
Gebhard, Gwenn H.S., 1846
Gebhard, Paul R.S., 1846
Gebhardt, Ann, 5860

Gebhart, Daryl E., 9931
Gebhart, Jill, 3597
Gebrian, Eileen P., 6622
Geddes, Robert D., 8067
Geddy, Vernon M., III, 9411
Gee, Bobbie, 8840
Gee, Gordon, 9424
Gee, Heather, 8378
Geer, George R., Jr., 8581
Geers, Jim, 828
Geeslin, Douglas R., 7518
Gefen, Nan, 827
Geffen, David, 558, 746
Gegick, Mary Lourdes, 8187
Gehin-Scott, Gilbert A., 5378
Gehl, Stephanie, 234
Gehner, Timothy C., 7595
Gehrig, Cynthia A., 4595
Gehring, Kurt, 8800
Gehringer, Natalie, Dr., 9776
Gehrke, Charles R., 1876
Gehrke, Harold, 9843
Gehrke, Leone, 9843
Geib, Kathryn, 7961
Geier, Faith, 5204
Geier, Philip H., Jr., 5204
Geiger, Bill, 3241
Geiger, David, 4745
Geiger, Ralph G., 5205
Geiger, William G., 6977
Geil, Peter Gus, 7866
Geilich, Peter N., 7464
Geisel, Jean F., 5605
Geiser, Thomas C., 1112
Geisse, John F., 7646
Geisse, Lawrence J., 7646
Geisse, Mary A., 7646
Geisse, Timothy F., 7646
Geissinger, Frederick W., 3098
Geist Trust, Bradley L., 2544
Geist, Carol Berg, 5631
Geistweidt, Ray, 8957
Gelb, Bruce S., 6011
Gelb, John T., 6011
Gelb, Lawrence M., 6011
Gelb, Lawrence N., 6011
Gelb, Phyllis N., 6011
Gelb, Richard L., 6011
Gelbaugh, Bruce, 4418
Geldin, Sherri, 7215
Gelinas, Andre A., 4195
Gelinas, Charles, 4057
Gell, Carl L., 1823
Gell, Jonathan, 8003
Geller, Michele, 354
Geller, Thomas, 7174
Gellerstedt, Larry L., III, 2515
Gellert, Carl, 559
Gellert, Celia Berta, 559
Gellert, David B. Spohn, 6012
Gellert, Gertrude E., 559
Gellert, Jill S., 3801
Gellert, Michael E., 3428, 6012
Gellert, Robert J., 6012, 7079
Gelley, Heidi, 6933
Gellman Family Trust, Jack E., 6013
Gellman, Arthur M., 6013
Gellman, George I., 6013
Gellman, Jack E., 6013
Gelly, James V., 9912
Gelman Charitable Lead Trust, Susan R., 3695
Gelman, Michael C., 3695
Gelman, Susan, 594
Gelman, Susan R., 3695
Gelvin, Lyle M., 7938
Gelzer, Scott E., 9864
Gemmill, Elizabeth H., 8496
Gemmill, Helen, 8496
Gemmill, Helen J., 8496
Gemple, Nylda, 989
Gemunder, Joel F., 3443, 3444
Genachowski, Julius, 6220
Gename, David L., 2632

Genauer, Eli, 9675
GenCorp Foundation Inc., 560, 7789
Gender, Robert A., 5529
Gendler, Carol, 4994
Genentech, Inc., 561, 562, 563
General Accident Insurance Co. of America, 4060
General Atlantic Corp., 5574
General Atlantic LLC, 5905
General Atlantic Service Corp., 1431, 1634
General Corporation, 9725
General Electric Co., 1553
General Electric Foundation, 6915
General Electric, Inc., 1950, 4202
General Growth Properties, Inc., 3724
General Mills, Inc., 1089, 2563, 4570, 4633
General Motors Corp., 4319, 4320
General Motors Foundation, Inc., 4271, 4319
General Trust Co., 3272
Generous, Eric, 9425
Genesee Valley Group Health Assoc., 5785
Genet, Robert J., 7539
Gengler, Charles J., 5595
Genius, Richard M., Jr., 9879
Genn, Jonathan, 3641
Genova, Kristin M., 1444
Genter, Anne, 8493
Genter, Beth H., 2220
Genter, Edward F., Jr., 6229
Genter, Elizabeth H., 8130
Gentile, James M., 134
Gentis, Kim, 3255
Gentle, William J., 2964
Gentry, Barbara B., 9245
Gentry, Debbie, 8604
Gentry, Gary, 8604
Gentry, John R., 321
Gentry, Kevin, 1820
Gentry, Kevin L., 1819
Gentry, Nolden, 3317
Gentsch, Richard A., 1706
Genuardi, Anthony D., 8213
Genuardi, Charles A., 8213
Genuardi, David T., 8213
Genuardi, Dominic S., Jr., 8213
Genuardi, Francis L., 8213
Genuardi, Gasper A., 8213
Genuardi, James V., 8213
Genuardi, Laurence P., 8213
Genuardi, Michael A., 8213
Genuine Parts Company, 2464
Genzlinger, Lynn, 8219
Genzyme Corp., 3922
Geopedior Assocs., LP, 8278
Georgantas, Aristides, 5111
Georgas, John L., 2735
George Trust, Noel, 7776
George, A.F., 5151
George, A.P., 8916
George, Albert, 2922
George, Alexander S., 9474
George, Anton Hulman, 3173
George, Armond, 6329
George, Bonnie, 1222
George, Boyd, 7372
George, G. Lee, 7372
George, James, 4453
George, James N., 7776
George, Jeffrey Pilgram, 4572
George, Jonathan Roulette, 4572
George, Mamie E., 8916
George, Mari Hulman, 3173
George, Mary, 1943
George, Mildred, 7776
George, Penny Pilgram, 4572
George, Rachel, 4968
George, Richard, 1244
George, Robert P., 9763
George, Russell, 1344
George, Terrence R., 2537

George, Tony, MD, 1529
George, William W., 4572
Georgehead, Chris "Kit", 3414
Georgescu, Andrew, 1554
Georgescu, Barbara, 1554
Georgescu, Peter, 1554
Georgia Financial, LLC, 7794
Georgia Gas Co., 2312
Georgia Institute of Technology, 4622
Georgia Medical Plan, Inc., 2394
Georgia Power Co., 2395
Georgia-Pacific Corp., 2397
Georvievich, Dragoslav, 1209
Geppert, Bill K., 1087
Gerace, Frank, 4322
Geraci, Anita, 1947
Gerald, Michael C., 8619
Geramian, Mohammad, 5530
Geranium, Inc., 4043
Gerard, Anne, 7653
Gerard, Jamie, 1609
Gerard, Karen, 1462
Gerard, Paul J., 7784
Gerard, Sheridah, 1241
Gerard, Wendy W., 8876
Geraty, Lawrence T., 713
Gerbavsits, Karin, 5590
Gerber, Ann Rogers, 5476
Gerber, Deena, 3489
Gerber, Eve, 6002
Gerber, James L., 7897
Gerber, Margaret L., 8703
Gerber, Murry S., 8187
Gerber, Roger M., 6668
Gerber, Terry, 3094
Gerber, William, 4359
Gerberding, Ruth, 9599
Gerberding, William P., 9621
Gerbode, Frank A., 564
Gerdes, Stephanie, 3189
Gerdes, Steven H., 9193
Gerdin, Ann S., 3286
Gerdin, Russell A., 3286
Gere, Richard, 565
Geren, Charles Lupton, 8798
Gergely, Michael, 4298
Gerhard, Kristen, 6015
Gerhard, Peter C., 6015
Gerhart, Jack S., 8459
Gericare Pharmaceuticals, 6956
Gerke, Henry, 7192
Gerke, Tom, 3395
Gerken, Walter B., 750
Gerlach, David P., 7648
Gerlach, John B., 7648
Gerlach, John B., Jr., 7580, 7648
Gerlach, John J., 7648
Gerlach, Pauline, 7648
Gerlinger, Charles D., 3823
Germ, John F., 8732
Germain, Gary R., 5724
Germaine, Steve, 6456
Germanow, Leon, 7271
Gernant, Michael L., 2750
Gerner, Elizabeth W., 9342
Gernon, Andrea S., 9689
Gerome-Acuff, Amy, 1993
Geronime, Karen, 4552
Gerrie, Robert E., 8768
Gerrish, Merrily S., 7310
Gerrity, Dorothy A. "Dottie", 1943
Gerry, Adam, 5610, 6017
Gerry, Alan, 6017
Gerry, Annelise, 6017
Gerry, Elbridge T., Jr., 6146
Gerry, James E., 8085
Gerry, Martha Farish, 8894
Gerry, Peggy N., 6016
Gerry, Robyn, 5610, 6017
Gerry, Roger G., 6016
Gerry, Sandra, 5610, 6017
Gerschel, Alberta, 6018
Gerschel, Laurent, 6018
Gerschel, Marianne, 7036

Gerschel, Patrick A., 6019, 8210
Gershen, William, 1465
Gershman Char. Annuity Trust, Harold, 566
Gershman Char. Lead Unitrust, Harold, 566
Gershman Family Survivors/ Administrative Trust, Harold, 567
Gershman Investment Corp., 4818
Gershman, Bettie, 4818
Gershman, Catherine, 567
Gershman, Cynthia Palmer, 566
Gershman, Elaine, 5206
Gershman, Elaine Levitt, 5206
Gershman, Jeffrey S., 4818
Gershman, Joel, 5206
Gershman, Mortimer, 5188
Gershman, Randy, 9861
Gershman, Ronald A., 567
Gershon Fund, Ben-Ephraim, 1835
Gershon, Steven A., 4837
Gershwind, Erik, 6020, 6248
Gershwind, Marjorie, 6020
Gershwind, Mark, 6020
Gersie, Mike, 3326
Gerson, Barbara N., 6021
Gerson, James, 6021
Gerson, Joe R., 3248
Gerson, Ralph J., 4333
Gerson, Shelley, 4245
Gerstacker, Carl A., 4322
Gerstacker, Eda U., 4322
Gerstacker, Lisa J., 4322, 4407
Gerstein, David, 5337
Gerstein, Lee S., 266
Gerstel, Linda, 5840
Gerstle, Allan, 1465
Gerstle, Michael, 6616
Gerstley, Carol, 8133
Gerstner, Elizabeth R., 2020
Gerstner, Louis V., III, 2020
Gerstner, Louis V., Jr., 2020
Gerstung, Sandra L., 3645
Gerstung, Sandra Levi, 3568
Gerth, Robert L., 9553
Gertler, Anna P., 3937
Gertler, Clark Chessin, 3937
Gertler, Jonathan P., 3937
Gertler, Menard M., 3937
Gertmenian, Dennis, 345
Gertz, H.F., 4368
Gertz, Jami, 1043
Gerzanick, Mary, 4339
Geschke, Charles M., 568
Geschke, John M., 568
Geschke, Kathleen A., 568
Geschke, Nan, 828
Geschke, Nancy A., 568
Geske, Janine P., 9876
Geswein, Greg, 7818
Geter, William F., 7343
Gethers, Dave, 3253
Gething, Thomas W., 9558
Getman, Frank, 5856
Getman, Michael F., 5856
Gettenberg, Gary, 6385
Gettenberg, Lynn, 6385
Gettings, William P., 3188
Gettle, Inc., 8290
Gettler, Benjamin, 7649, 7690, 7824
Gettler, Benjamin R., 7649
Gettler, Delian A., 7649, 7824
Gettler, Thomas D., 7649
Gettleson, Harvey S., 601
Getty, Gordon P., 569
Getty, J. Paul, 570
Getty, William P., 8099
Gettys, Sky, 7622
Getz, Alan, 6561
Getz, Bert A., 87, 101
Getz, Bert A., Jr., 101
Getz, Dennis A., 8458, 8459
Getz, Emma, 2753
Getz, George F., 101

Girgus, Joan S., 7244
Girvin, Gordon J., 5638
Gische, Samuel R., 6150
Gislason, James H., 3122
Gissy, Jim, 2296
Gitchell, Gerald C., 870
Githiora-Updike, Wambui B., 3828
Gitlin, Harvey S., 8217
Gittell, Marilyn, 872
Gittis, Howard, 6716
Gittleman, Sol, 7126
Giuffra, Robert J., Jr., 5301
Giuliani, Lisa Knight, 5281
Giuntini, Margie, 9690
Given, Davis, Rev., 1964
Givins, Tony, 9219
Giviskos, Anne, 6619
GLA Foundation, 234
Glackens, Ira D., 2218
Gladden, Gordon D., 3648
Gladden, William C., 2345
Glade, Carolyn, 4997
Glade, Fred, 4997
Glade, Gordon, 4997
Glade, Sarah, 4997
Glade, Susan, 4997
Gladish, Nina, 834
Gladstein, Gary, 1555, 7024
Gladstein, Jeff, 1555
Gladstone, Henry A., 8464
Glaesel-Hollenback, Helga, 6154
Glaeser, Elizabeth, 4568
Glagola, Mary E., 3595
Glancy, Alfred R., III, 4254, 4343
Glancy, Ruth R., 4389
Glarner, Terrence, 4636
Glaser, Barbara L., 5782
Glaser, Daniel E., 7319
Glaser, Gary, 7608
Glaser, Margery E., 7608
Glaser, Nancy, 5583
Glaser, Paul F., 9594
Glaser, Reuben, 7608
Glaser, Rob, 9672
Glaser, Robert D., 9595
Glaser, Robert J., 973
Glass, David D., 163
Glass, Dennis, 7405
Glass, Jackie, 766
Glass, Lawrence D., 2770
Glass, Mary Beth, 7931
Glass, Michael, 4256
Glass, Robert F., Jr., 7770
Glass, Ruth A., 163
Glasscock, Larry, 1292
Glasscock, Larry C., 3101, 3102
Glasscock-Simpson, Melanie, 3407
Glasser, Emily, 2693
Glasser, James J., 91, 2693
Glasser, Louise R., 2693
Glassman, Howard, 8197
Glassman, Jeffrey, 1135, 1136, 1276
Glassman, Jennifer, 7024
Glassman, M.B., 1383
Glassman, Shana, 1383
Glatfelter, George H., II, 8511
Glaubinger, Jane, 2023
Glaubinger, Lawrence D., 2023
Glaubinger, Lucienne M., 2023
Glave, James M., Mrs., 9474
Glaxo Wellcome Americas Inc., 7439
GlaxoSmithKline, 3677
GlaxoSmithKline Holdings (Americas)
  Inc., 7439
Glazer, Bryan, 2024
Glazer, Edward, 2024
Glazer, Eva, 792
Glazer, Jay M., 9596
Glazer, Jeffrey W., 3307
Glazer, Joel, 2024
Glazer, Lowell R., 3635
Glazer, Malcolm, 2024
Glazer, Marsha Sloan, 9596
Glazer, Michael, 1642

Glazer, Michael F., 3607
Glazer, Noland, 4630
Glazer, Shari Arison, 1881
Gleacher, Anne G., 6038
Gleacher, Eric J., 6038
Gleason, George G., II, 164
Gleason, Hazel, 7891
Gleason, James S., 6039
Gleason, Janis F., 6039
Gleason, Linda D., 164
Gleason, Nancy, 6009
Gleason, Ron, 8896
Gleason, Tracy, 6039
Gleaton, Maroulla, 3549
Gleaves, Vernon, 257
Gleba, Michael W., 8132, 8425
Gleberman, Carson, 6040
Gleberman, Joseph H., 6040
Gleeson, John W., 3332
Gleicher, Warren, 7087
Gleim, Michael L., 8511
Gleixner, Alfred A., 8454
Gleixner, E.H., 8454
Glendale, Inc., 2099
Glendi Publications, Inc., 8278
Glenmede Trust Co., The, 8377, 8378,
  8476, 8495
Glenn Irrevocable Trust, Wilbur, 2399
Glenn, Clydenne R., 9419
Glenn, Gordon H., 3724
Glenn, J. Kirk, Jr., 7376
Glenn, J. Thomas, 2582
Glenn, James K., 7376
Glenn, James K., Jr., 7376
Glenn, James Kirk, Jr., 7315
Glenn, Louise R., 2399
Glenn, Paul F., 581
Glenn, Thomas K., II, 2399
Glenn, W. Raoul, Jr., 8591
Glenn, Wadley R., III, 8591
Glenn-Murray, Bernadette, 1300
Glenner, Lisa, 2759
Glenner, Sidney, 2759
Glennon, Lauren F., 1643, 5082
Glennon, Victoria P., 2649
Glenstone Foundation, 8853
Glenview Trust Co., The, 3439
Glew, William, 1765
Glezer, Maggie, 9775
Glick, Adam P., 6690
Glick, Carrie, 4347
Glick, Eugene B., 3155
Glick, Madeline, 6615
Glick, Marilyn K., 3155
Glickenhaus, James, 6042
Glickenhaus, Sarah, 6042
Glickenhaus, Seth M., 6042
Glickman, Alma, 582
Glickman, Edward M., 8467
Glickman, Marvin S., 582
Glist, Jill, 4093
Global Cornerstone Healthcare Services,
  Inc., 874
Global Rental Co., 4
Global Securities, Inc., 3861
Globe Oil and Refining Companies, 4639
Gloekler, William J., 3816
Glor, Bruce J., 2543
Glossberg, Joseph, 2970
Glosser, Daniel, 8153
Glosser, William L., 8153
Glosson, Buster C., 3564
Glover & MacGregor, Inc., 8260
Glover, Buddy, 8300
Glover, Dominic W., 3166
Glover, Ella, 5203
Glover, Marion B., 2389
Glowiak, Brian G., 4265
Gloyd, Delma M., 2760
Gloyd, Lawrence E., 2760
Gloyd, Steve, M.D., 3229
Gluck, Maxwell H., 584
Gluck, Muriel, 584
Gluck, Suzanne, 6789

Gluckstern, Judith O'Connor, 6456,
  6681
Gluckstern, Steven M., 6456, 6681
Glunt, Joan, 8389
Gluth, Robert, 2590
Glyn, D.R., 8227
Glynn, Gary A., 8488
Glynn, Suzanne E. McMeel, 4774
GM, LLC, 4569
GMO City of London, 8049
Gober, Karen E., 3651
Goble, Gary, 8904, 9261
Goble, Jane, 2240
Gobron, Laura, 3941
Gochnauer, Richard W., 3045
Gocken, Cherry, 4962
Godchaux, Charles R., 3495
Godchaux, Frank A., III, 3495
Godchaux, Frank K., 3495
Godchaux, Frank M., 3495
Godchaux, Leslie K., 3495
Goddard Systems, Inc., 8093
Goddard Trust, Adele H., 2121
Goddard, Bill, 7979
Goddard, Charles B., 7939
Goddard, Colin, 6670
Goddard, Deborah M., 1115
Goddard, Richard P., 7861
Goddard, Robert C., 2464
Goddard, Terry, 1773
Goddard, William R., 7939
Goddard, William R., Jr., 7939, 7963
Gode, Jeanne M., 4649
Godfrey, Brace B., Jr., 3462
Godfrey, David L., 1533, 1536, 1630
Godfrey, Dudley J., Jr., 9785
Godfrey, Flavel McMichael, 7426
Godfrey, Helen, 9778
Godfrey, N.J., 3051
Godfrey, Ronald G., 7583
Godinger Silver Art, Ltd., 6044
Godinger, Arnold, 6044
Godinger, Rita, 6044
Godlasky, Thomas C., 3261
Godward, William W., 507
Godwin, Cindy, 91
Godwin, Laurna, 4896
Godwin, Marcia Williams, 8839
Godwin, Pamela H., 8378
Godwin, Sally Smythe, 1170
Godwin, Stephen, 1170
Goebel, Chris, 3404
Goebel, J. Martin, 1852
Goeddel, David V., 3677
Goedeker, Del, 8098
Goedert, John P., 3066
Goedhart, LaWonna, 8082
Goel, Poonam, 587
Goel, Prabhu, 587
Goeller, David H., 3170
Goergen, Franz Josef, 1498
Goergen, Pamela M., 1556
Goergen, Robert B., 1556
Goergen, Robert B., Jr., 1556
Goergen, Todd A., 1556
Goeringer, Louis F., 8317
Goertzen, Jack E., Hon., 644
Goethals, James, 4452
Goettee, John S., 8577
Goettler, Ralph H., 8076
Goetz, Daniel A., 8107
Goff, James H., 3525
Goff, Phyllis A. Rawls, 4671
Goff, Robert W., Jr., 9039
Gogg, Rich, 3325
Goggins, Jean A., 2283
Goggins, John, 6569
Gogian, John, 588
Gogian, John J., Jr., 588
Gogian, Rosalia, 588
Gogolak, John, 87
Gohmann, Stephen, 3093
Goins, Charlynn, 6613
Goisman, Richard, 9791

Goizueta, Javier C., 2400
Goizueta, Roberto C., 2400
Gojo Industries, Inc., 7719
Golcher, Alberto, 3519
Golcher, Alison Stone, 3519
Gold Kist Inc., 2388
Gold Mine Gin, Inc., 3509
Gold, Barbara, 5195
Gold, Billie, 4071
Gold, Carolyn, 4828
Gold, Dave, 591
Gold, David, 591, 5567
Gold, David B., 590
Gold, Elaine, 590
Gold, Emily, 590
Gold, Howard, 591
Gold, Ilene C., 589
Gold, Jeff, 591
Gold, Judith, 5424
Gold, Julie Breidenthal, 3349
Gold, Norman M., 618
Gold, Paula, 4085
Gold, Phil, 7333
Gold, Richard, 7135
Gold, Rick A., 8329
Gold, Sherrie, 8842
Gold, Sherry, 591
Gold, Stanley P., 589
Gold, Steven A., 590
Gold-Bubier, Diane, 590
Gold-Lurie, Barbara, 590
Goldammer, Vance, 8630
Goldbach Life Trust, Marie S., 9806
Goldbach, Marie S., 9806
Goldbeck, Richard B., 8232
Goldberg Interim Trust, 592
Goldberg, Alan E., 6950
Goldberg, Alan J., 2029
Goldberg, Albert S., 3926
Goldberg, Andrew, 8237
Goldberg, Avram J., 3767, 3927, 4090
Goldberg, Barbara S., 3926
Goldberg, Brian L., 1802
Goldberg, Carol R., 3767, 3927, 4090,
  4091
Goldberg, David, 7576, 7786
Goldberg, David S., 6426
Goldberg, Deborah B., 3927, 4090
Goldberg, Diana, 1802
Goldberg, Diana L., 1802
Goldberg, Donna, 2455
Goldberg, Dorothy, 592
Goldberg, Edward, 593
Goldberg, Elizabeth, 6114
Goldberg, Frank M., 593
Goldberg, Harvey E., 3926
Goldberg, Henry D., 8577
Goldberg, Herbert A., 3926
Goldberg, Israel, 3926
Goldberg, Jane, 9597
Goldberg, Jay L., 8197, 8237
Goldberg, Jerold, 7056
Goldberg, Joel, 2472
Goldberg, Joshua R., 3927, 4090
Goldberg, Lauren B., 1802
Goldberg, Lee, 593
Goldberg, Leo, 5907
Goldberg, Madeline L., 2761
Goldberg, Maureen McKenna, Hon.,
  8551
Goldberg, Maxine, 8237
Goldberg, Michael, 6674, 8237
Goldberg, Miriam P., 6950
Goldberg, Morey, 8147, 8148
Goldberg, Paul, 2727
Goldberg, Rae, 1802
Goldberg, Robert, 7786
Goldberg, Robert M., 6426
Goldberg, Robert S., 592
Goldberg, Robin, 6426
Goldberg, Rosalie A., 5689
Goldberg, Roy A., 3915
Goldberg, Stephen, 1802
Goldberg, Stephen A., 1802

Goldberg, Steven A., 9786
Goldberg, Stuart W., 1802
Goldberg, Veronica, 5209
Goldberg, William, 5541
Goldberger, Laurie, 6772
Goldblatt, Richard A., 8521
Goldblum, Bonnie, 3489
Goldbrenner, Isaac, 5936
Golden Leaf Foundation, 7319
Golden State Foods Corp., 627
Golden, Adolph, 7593
Golden, Alanna, 3014
Golden, Andrew, 5814
Golden, Andrew K., 5357
Golden, Carol, 8551
Golden, Charles E., 3192, 3193
Golden, Connie, 2568
Golden, Elroy E., 2701
Golden, Grace E., 5675
Golden, Jonathan, 2435
Golden, Michael, 2435, 6620
Golden, Morley, 2568
Golden, Pamela P., 6046
Golden, Robert C., 5360
Golden, Samuel, 9430
Golden, Sibyl L., 6046
Golden, Sibyl R., 6046
Golden, Terence C., 1780
Golden, Valerie, 401
Golden, William T., 6046, 6662, 6864
Golden-Icahn, Gail, 6222, 6224
Goldenberg, Agnes, 7297
Goldenberg, Blanche S., 1564
Goldenberg, Chaim, 7297
Goldenberg, Leon, 7297
Goldenberg, Stephen, 2032
Goldenson, Maxine W., 6047
Goldenvoice, LLC, 1060
Golder, David B., 2762
Golder, G.D., 9028
Golder, Joan J., 2762
Golder, Kenneth, 2762
Golder, Stanley C., 2762
Goldfarb, Kathy, 6026
Goldfarb, Robert D., 5705, 6999
Goldfarb, Stanley, 8342
Goldfield, Herschel, 6244
Goldfield, Jacob D., 6244
Goldfield, Priscilla, 6244
Goldfrank, Jack C., 7745
Goldfrank, Lionel, III, 6048
Goldhammer, Gina, 2026
Goldhammer, Richard, 2026
Goldhammer, Robert F., 2026
Goldhirsh, Benjamin, 1557
Goldhirsh, Bernard A., 1557
Goldhirsh, Elizabeth, 1557
Goldin, Claudia Brett, 1349
Goldin, Marc S., 428
Golding, Stacy Rogers, 5214
Goldman 1997 Char. Lead Trust,
    Douglas E., 596
Goldman 1997 Charitable Lead Annuity
    Trust, Richard, 3695
Goldman Charitable Trust, Sol, The,
    6050
Goldman Children Trust, 6052
Goldman Fund, 359
Goldman Grandchildren Trust, 6052
Goldman Sachs, 6597, 7174
Goldman Sachs & Co., 5489, 5580,
    5645, 5715, 5796, 5831, 5987,
    6106, 6296, 6424, 6496, 6539
Goldman Sachs Family Office, 7051
Goldman Sachs Group, Inc., The, 6056
Goldman, A.R., 1905
Goldman, Allan H., 6051
Goldman, Amy, 6050
Goldman, Amy R., 2185
Goldman, Dorian, 6052
Goldman, Douglas E., 594, 596
Goldman, George N., 2763
Goldman, Guido, 5571, 5702, 6483
Goldman, Harold S., 8197

Goldman, Herbert, 3690
Goldman, Herman, 6053
Goldman, Irene, 2892
Goldman, Jane H., 6051
Goldman, Janis, 293
Goldman, John D., 594, 595, 597, 636
Goldman, Judith, 2763
Goldman, Lisa M., 596
Goldman, Marcia L., 595
Goldman, Melvin, 2892
Goldman, Patricia, 5692
Goldman, Peggy, 2892
Goldman, Peter, 9620
Goldman, Philip, 4642
Goldman, Rebecca B., 9723
Goldman, Rhoda H., 594, 597
Goldman, Richard, 1222
Goldman, Richard N., 594, 597
Goldman, Robert, 341, 5485
Goldman, Robert F., 968
Goldman, Robert I., 6054
Goldman, Robert P., 4141
Goldman, Roger A., 817, 1485, 7245
Goldman, Sachs & Co., 6055, 6056
Goldman, Sol, 6050, 6051
Goldman, Stephen, 2763, 2892
Goldman, William S., 636
Goldman-Soriano, Nanci, 2763
Goldner, David, 3698
Goldrich & Kest Industries, 598, 754
Goldrich Family Foundation, The, 455
Goldrich Trust, 598
Goldrich, Andrea, 598
Goldrich, Doretta, 754
Goldrich, Jona, 598, 754
Goldrich, Melinda, 598
Goldrick, James M., 6354, 7090
Goldring Corp., N., 3484
Goldring, Allen A., 6057
Goldring, Gary F., 5210
Goldring, Jeffrey, 3484, 3516
Goldring, Lola A., 6057
Goldring, William, 3484, 3516
Goldsbury Charitable Trust, 8920
Goldsbury, Angela Aboltin, 8920
Goldsbury, Christopher, Jr., 8920
Goldschmid, Harvey J., 6103
Goldschmidt, David M., 235
Goldschmidt, Karla, 2764
Goldschmidt, Pinchas, Rabbi, 6383
Goldschmidt, Susan, 2764
Goldschmidt, Walter, 2764
Goldseker, Ana, 3636
Goldseker, Deborah, 3636
Goldseker, Morris, 3636
Goldseker, Sharna, 3636
Goldseker, Sheldon, 3568, 3636
Goldseker, Simon, 3636
Goldsen, Sue, 4376
Goldsmith Charitable Trust, Barbara
    Lubin, 6059
Goldsmith, Anne S., 2680
Goldsmith, Barbara L., 6059
Goldsmith, Beth, 934, 3637
Goldsmith, Bram, 478, 599
Goldsmith, Bram, Mrs., 599
Goldsmith, Bruce L., 599, 2680
Goldsmith, Clifford H., 6058
Goldsmith, Dara J., 5047
Goldsmith, Elaine, 599
Goldsmith, Elvis G., 8682
Goldsmith, Fred, III, 8682
Goldsmith, Harry L., 8682
Goldsmith, Horace W., 6060
Goldsmith, Karen, 599
Goldsmith, Katherine W., 6058
Goldsmith, Larry J., 8682
Goldsmith, Marcia, 6260
Goldsmith, Melvin, 8682
Goldsmith, Paul, 8583
Goldsmith, Richard E., 9166
Goldsmith, Robert H., 1031
Goldsmith, Russell, 599
Goldsmith, Stephen, 1632, 1793

Goldsmith, Thomas B., 8682
Goldstein, Alan J., 2156
Goldstein, Alfred R., 2027
Goldstein, Ann L., 2027
Goldstein, Arlene, 6062
Goldstein, Arnold, 6062
Goldstein, Charles A., 6261
Goldstein, Cynthia, 2027
Goldstein, Danielle, 6845
Goldstein, Darin, 6845
Goldstein, Dorothy, 6063
Goldstein, Douglas R., 1993
Goldstein, Edward J., 8661
Goldstein, Eliot, 2347
Goldstein, Elizabeth Geer, 1993
Goldstein, Ellen, 2347
Goldstein, Elliott, 2347
Goldstein, Frederic, 5959
Goldstein, Gilbert, 1413
Goldstein, Harriet, 2347
Goldstein, Jan, 5584
Goldstein, Jeffrey, 4212
Goldstein, Jerome, 6063
Goldstein, Jerome E., 1993
Goldstein, Joseph L., 3654, 3677
Goldstein, Joshua, 5211
Goldstein, Kari Wolff, 4486
Goldstein, L. Steven, 4524
Goldstein, Leslie, 6064
Goldstein, Marvin, 6999
Goldstein, Michael L., 6053
Goldstein, Miriam, 6061
Goldstein, Orit, 4212
Goldstein, R.A., 6227
Goldstein, Richard, 2027
Goldstein, Rodney L., 3016
Goldstein, Roslyn, 6064
Goldstein, Sam, 6061
Goldstein, Seth M., 5959
Goldstein, Shepard, DMD, 4061
Goldstein, Simeon H.F., 5959
Goldstein, Steven R., 2027
Goldstein, Stuart D., 6845
Goldstein, Susan R., 6845
Goldstein, Sydney E., 1993
Goldstein, Sylvia, 5789
Goldsten, Janice W., 3757
Goldstine, Robert I., 3156
Goldstone, Elizabeth, 6065
Goldstone, Steven F., 6065
Goldwater, Marge, 6260
Goldwyn, Anthony, 600
Goldwyn, Catherine, 600
Goldwyn, Frances H., 600
Goldwyn, Francis, 600
Goldwyn, John, 600
Goldwyn, Peggy, 600
Goldwyn, Samuel, 600
Goldwyn, Samuel, Jr., 600
Goldy, Marjorie L., 3547
Golgorsky, Michael, M.D., 7247
Golick, Edward A., 4256
Golieb, Abner J., 6298
Golieb, John A., 5876, 6298
Golisano, B. Thomas, 6067
Golkin, Donna, 6068
Golkin, Perry, 6068
Gollihue, Alan E., 9499
Gollin, James D., 223
Gollin, Suzanne D., 223
Gollust, Keith R., 6069
Golston, Allan C., 9591
Goltz, Neill, 3325
Golub Corp., 6746
Golub, David, 6746
Golub, Estelle, 6070
Golub, Jane, 6070, 6746
Golub, Michael K., 8529
Golub, Mona, 6070
Golub, Neil M., 6070, 6746
Golub, William, 6070
Gomach, David G., 2662
Gomer, Adelaide R., 6688
Gomez, Barbara, 417

Gomez, Elizabeth M., 350
Gomez, Iris, 3961
Gomez, Jesse Bethke, 4623
Gomez, Louis M., 359
Gomez, Maria S., 1834
Gomory, Ralph E., 7003
Gompers, Edward "Ted", 9716
Gompf, Thomas E., 5058
Goncz, Edward J., 8178
Gonda, Kelly S., 601
Gonda, Louis L., 601
Gonella, Paul, 828
Gonnella, Carol, 9977
Gonzales, David L., 6714
Gonzales, Felice, 5496
Gonzales, Miriam, 5266
Gonzales, Ramon, 5493
Gonzales, Tanya, 1093
Gonzalez, Armando, 520
Gonzalez, Bethaida C., 6026
Gonzalez, Gerardo, 9915
Gonzalez, Leni, 9371
Gonzalez, Paul M., 6005
Gonzalez, R. Louie, 3245
Gonzalez, Rey B., 2812
Gonzalez, Robert, 9032
Gonzalez, Shirley, 9032
Gonzalez, Steven, 3205
Gonzalez-Falla, Celso M., 6033
Gonzalez-Falla, Sondra Gilman, 6033
Gooch, J.A., 8798
Gooch, James, 8691, 8741
Gooch, Robert D., III, 8661
Goodale, Jennifer, 5545
Goodall, 4694
Goodall, Candace, 7748
Goodall, D. Christian, 8577
Goodall-Komar, Teri, 6203
Goode, David R., 9485
Goode, R. Ray, 2213
Goodell, William R., 6818
Gooden, Andrea, 1214
Goodenow, Stephen J., 4624
Goodes, David R., 5212
Goodes, Melvin R., 5212
Goodes, Michelle R., 5212
Goodfellow, Charles, 5646
Goodfellow, Charles C., 5137
Goodfellow, Charles C., III, 449
Goodfriend, Amy O., 6071
Goodfriend, Sidney E., 6071
Goodhardt, William A., 3683
Goodhue, Wilma Rae, 4082
Goodier, Tonya, 3126
Goodin, Robert R., 3414
Gooding, Lucy B., 2028
Gooding, Nancy A., 1384
Gooding, Richard L., 1384
Gooding, Terence J., 604
Goodish, John H., 8488
Goodlatte, Maryellen F., 9419
Goodling, William F., 8511
Goodman, Albert I., 2599
Goodman, Alvin I., 7247
Goodman, Barbara F., 6072
Goodman, Carol Lanier, 2431
Goodman, Carroll R., 9212
Goodman, Charles, 2691
Goodman, Clare F., 6050
Goodman, Corey S., 4616
Goodman, David, 7657
Goodman, Edward T., 8140
Goodman, Ellis M., 2765
Goodman, Gary, 3552
Goodman, Gillian, 2765
Goodman, Helen, 5098
Goodman, Irwin A., 9807
Goodman, Jerome S., 1868
Goodman, John C., 9391
Goodman, Karen, 2745
Goodman, Lawrence M., Jr., 605
Goodman, Louise, 3652
Goodman, Maria, 2599
Goodman, Michael I., 7582

Goodman, Paul, 2765
Goodman, Robert D., 9807
Goodman, Robert M., 5466
Goodman, Roy M., 6072
Goodman, Scott, 2431
Goodman, Shira G., 4156
Goodner, Gregg, 160
Goodnight, Ann Baggett, 7377
Goodnight, James H., 7377
Goodnight, Leah A., 7377
Goodnow, Charles, 4252
Goodnow, Edward B., 1558
Goodnow, Roberta, 9680
Goodreau, Marilyn L., 3528
Goodrich Corp., 7378
Goodrich, Bernard A., 1830
Goodrich, David W., 3220
Goodrich, Enid, 3157
Goodrich, Gillian C., 22
Goodrich, Gillian White, 24
Goodrich, Harry L., 9401
Goodrich, Lee, 9401
Goodrich, Monette, 1519
Goodrich, Pierre F., 3157
Goodrow, Elizabeth Toole, 131
Goodspeed, Lisa, 5244
Goodstein, Sandra, 8220
Goodwell, William R., 7139
Goodwillie, Eugene W., Jr., 5231
Goodwin, Carl, 2634, 2790
Goodwin, David, 4793, 5084
Goodwin, David A., 7367
Goodwin, Ed, 2634, 2790
Goodwin, Leo, Jr., 2029
Goodwin, Michael, 8853
Goodwin, Morris, Jr., 4623
Goodwin, Neva R., 6825
Goodwin, Peter, 5265
Goodwin, Richard L., 3536
Goodwin, Robert L., 3464
Goodwin, William M., 3194
Goodyear, Clarice Cato, 8576
Goodyear, Kimberly A., 1971
Google Inc., 606
Goolis, Jennifer, 560
Gooss, Henry E., 6092
Goossen, John, 3278
Gootrad, Harold, 1518
Goppert, Clarence H., 4819
Goppert, Richard D., 4819
Goppert, Thomas A., 4819
Gorden, H. Stephen, 933
Gordon Food Service, Inc., 4323
Gordon I. Segal Income Trust, 2995
Gordon, Albert H., 6076, 6077
Gordon, Alvin A., 8645
Gordon, Amy S., 6074
Gordon, Andrew M., 6074
Gordon, Anna Melissa, 8795
Gordon, B. Diane, 7897
Gordon, Bernice W., 8683
Gordon, Bruce P., 7831
Gordon, C. Leonard, 5976
Gordon, Catherine Hutto, 693
Gordon, Cecil C., Jr., 1706
Gordon, Christina M., 3928
Gordon, Courtney Lynn, 8390
Gordon, Donald, 6287
Gordon, Elizabeth, 607
Gordon, Ellen R., 4117
Gordon, Frank E., 8683
Gordon, Gail E., 8683
Gordon, Gwen L., 8683
Gordon, H. Don, 8107
Gordon, Hunter R., 8340
Gordon, James D., 4323
Gordon, Jeffrey M., 7379
Gordon, Joel C., 8662, 8683
Gordon, John M., Jr., 4323
Gordon, John R., 6076
Gordon, Joseph K., 8340
Gordon, Julie S., 8683
Gordon, Kiendl D., 6076
Gordon, Lois, 518

Gordon, Marguerite M., 8795
Gordon, Mark J., 2030
Gordon, Melvin J., 4117
Gordon, Michael, 6075
Gordon, Michael S., 3928
Gordon, Mondana Mashhoon, 757
Gordon, Richard, Mrs., 3811
Gordon, Robert, 5130
Gordon, Robert A., 8683
Gordon, Rudolph, 8583
Gordon, Scott, 1477
Gordon, Stephen H., 400
Gore & Assoc., WL, 3841
Gore Trust, R.H., 2031
Gore, George, 2031
Gore, Peter, 2031
Gore, Ruth T., 8579
Gore, Theodore T., 2031
Goree, Julia, 60
Gorelick, Jamie S., 2868
Gorelick, Jeff, 7380
Gorelick, Pamela, 7380
Gorelick, Patricia, 7381
Gorelick, Scott, 7380
Gorelick, Shelton, 7380
Gorelick, Sylvia, 5425
Gorelick, Todd A., 7381
Gorelick, William, 7381
Goren, Paul D., 3015
Goresh, Michael, Jr., 8135
Gorham, Daniel K., 5478
Gorham, Frank D., III, 5478
Gorham, Frank D., Jr., 5478
Gorham, John, 8524
Gorham, Marie K., 5478
Gorham, Mark, 5466
Gorham, Mark L., 5478
Gorham, Robert H., II, 5478
Gorham, Timothy, 8524
Gorham, Timothy W., 5478
Gorham, William, 1016
Gorin, Howard, 2032
Gorin, Nehemias, 2032
Gorin, Ralph, 2032
Gorin, William, 2032
Goriup, Mary A., 663
Gorkuscha, Mischa, 7952
Gorlin, Robert H., 4333
Gorlin, Steve, 1426
Gorman, Alice M., 6078
Gorman, Christopher, 7700
Gorman, David A., 8922
Gorman, Dennis, 4209
Gorman, James W., Jr., 8922
Gorman, John T., Jr., 3542
Gorman, Marguerite R., 6311
Gorman, Michael R., 700
Gorman, Owen, 6078
Gorman, Rowena C., 8922
Gorman, Stephen P., 1786
Gorman, Timothy W., 2937
Gormley, Pat, 1340
Gorrie, M. Miller, 24
Gorsich, Mary Ann, 4939
Gorski, John, 3129
Gorsline, Ida Mae, 8800
Gorsuch, Charles A., 7743
Gorsuch, Joan, 2962
Gorter, Audrey F., 6079
Gorter, David F., 6079
Gorter, James P., 6079
Gorter, James P., Jr., 6079
Gorzhevskaya, Svetlana, 632
Goschi, P.E., 2873
Gosdin, Linda, 9199
Goslee, Charles G., 3599
Goss, Ann, 9317
Goss, Carol A., 4438
Goss, Hanna, 179
Goss, Janet Reed, 7878
Gosse, Thomas A., 9539
Gosselin, Steve, 2677
Gosselink, Julie, 3260
Gosule, John V., 87

Gother, Ronald E., 345
Gotlieb, Jaquelin, 2394
Goto, Tatsunosuke, 2926
Gotschall, Brittany, 608
Gotschall, Edward F., 608
Gotschall, Susan K., 608
Gottesman Foundation, D.S. and R.H., 8531
Gottesman, Alice R., 1803
Gottesman, David S., 1803
Gottesman, Laurel, 4967
Gottesman, Robert W., 1803
Gottesman, Ruth L., 1803
Gottesman, William L., 1803
Gottlieb, Adolph, 6080
Gottlieb, Art, 631
Gottlieb, Esther, 6080
Gottlieb, Jill, 2206
Gottlieb, Leo, 6081
Gottlieb, Menachem, 9452
Gottlieb, Meyer, 600
Gottlieb, Robert A., 6510
Gottlieb, Robert D., 4231
Gottovi, Dan, 7352
Gottschalk, John, 4995
Gottstein, Robert, 83
Gottwald, Ann, 9431
Gottwald, Bruce C., 9431
Gottwald, Floyd D., Jr., 9431, 9437
Gottwald, Floyd D., Sr., 9431
Gottwald, James T., 9431
Gottwald, James T., Jr., 9437
Gottwald, William, 9437
Gough, John, 5784
Gough, Thomas, 7539
Goughnour, Sam, 9736
Gould 1919 Trust, 6083
Gould 1923 Trust, 6083
Gould Trust (Woodycrest Greer), 6083
Gould, Anthony, 6082
Gould, Edwin, 6083
Gould, Florence J., 6084
Gould, Fr., 9957
Gould, Frederick Beau, 9643
Gould, Fredric H., 6085
Gould, Greg, 8449
Gould, Helaine, 6085
Gould, Jason, 1204
Gould, Jeffrey, 6085
Gould, Jeffrey A., 6085
Gould, Joseph B., 609
Gould, Julie, 9643
Gould, Matthew, 6085
Gould, Matthew J., 6085
Goulder, Larry, 483
Gouldin, David M., 6428
Gouldin, Deborah A., 5781
Goulet, Dan, 5047
Goundar, Nalraj, 250
Gourdeau, Richard, 4125
Gourielli, Helena Rubinstein, 6876
Gourneau, Dwight, 4524
Gouvernet, Suzanne, 6823
Governanti, Michael, 7749
Government Employees Insurance Co., 3634
Govitz, L. Scott, 4392
Gow, Ian F., 432
Gowan, Bill, 1306
Gowen, Herbert, 9598
Gowen, Laura, 9598
Gowen, Louisa, 9598
Gowen, William C., 9598
Goyins, Yvonne, 5454
GPU Service, Inc., 7630
Grabarski, Robert, 4540
Grabe, David, 4900
Grabe, William, 5905
Grabel, Jeffrey N., 6442
Graber, Samuel W., 9034
Grable, Minnie K., 8221
Grabois, Neil, 5707, 6260
Grabow, Raymond J., 7555
Grabowski, Gary G., 9757

Graboys, George, 8551
Grace & Co., W.R., 3638
Grace Baptist Church, 904, 7442
Grace Bible Church, 9938
Grace, Guy, 9082
Grace, J. Peter, 6905
Grace, James S., 4347
Grace, Margaret F., 5900, 6905
Grace, Melinda M., 9082
Grace, Patrick P., 5900, 6905
Graceffa, Al C., 3536
Graceton Estates, Inc., 6879
Gracias, Antonio, 2769
Graco Inc., 4573
Gradient, 3683
Grado, John, Jr., 4195
Gradowski, Ann O'Neil, 3701
Grady, Christina, 7997
Grady, James, 349
Grady, Lesley, 2355
Grady, Stafford R., 881
Grady, T.M., 7335
Grady-White Boats, Inc., 7478
Graeb, Wendy, 5417
Graeber, James P., 4744
Graeber, James P., Jr., 4744
Graeber, John C., 4744
Graeber, Lewis A., Jr., 4744
Graeber, William M., 4744
Graf, Don, 8823
Graf, Robert T., 7725
Graff, George, 1411
Graff, Kathleen, 8431
Graff, Nicole Bartner, 9362
Grafman, Laura R., 130
Grafstein, Bernice, 3931
Grafstein, Mindy A., 1555
Graham Capital Corp., 8222
Graham Engineering Corp., 8222
Graham Packaging Co., L.P., 8222
Graham Packaging Holdings Co., 8222
Graham, Adeline W., 7280
Graham, Allen J., 7382
Graham, Anita Brown, 7458
Graham, Arnold, 3370, 8976
Graham, Croley W., Jr., 8650
Graham, Dale I., 1869
Graham, David R., 2526, 9223
Graham, Donald C., 8222
Graham, Donald E., 1804
Graham, Edmund C., III, 4533
Graham, Ernest R., 2767
Graham, Gene, 9154
Graham, Gordon, 5087
Graham, H. Devon, Jr, 9194
Graham, H. Devon, Jr., 9197
Graham, Ingrid A., 8222
Graham, J. Todd, 3298
Graham, John, 2622
Graham, John J., 3461
Graham, John K., 8294
Graham, Judy N., 4403
Graham, Julie, 6675
Graham, Katharine, 1804
Graham, Kathryn C., 6675
Graham, Kathryn G., 6675
Graham, Kerry, 8662
Graham, Kristiane C., 6659
Graham, Lani F.B., 3549
Graham, Laura, 9125
Graham, Laurel A., 9223
Graham, Laurel A.W., 9223
Graham, Louise T., 4412
Graham, Malcolm C., 7475
Graham, Mary, 2868
Graham, Patricia Albjerg, 6471, 9884
Graham, Richard, 5194
Graham, Robert C., Jr., 6396, 6675
Graham, Robert H., 9223
Graham, Robert M., 9319
Graham, Spencer R., 9223
Graham, Terry, 705, 7931
Graham, Vera A., 1861
Graham, Whitney Laurel, 9223

Grain Processing Corp., 3318
Grainger, David W., 2768
Grainger, Hally W., 2768
Grainger, Joseph C., 647
Grainger, William W., 2768
Gralen, Donald J., 2681
Gram, W. Dunbar, 3657
Gramke, Kathleen, 7749
Gramm, Frank G., 3039
Grammer, Allen Kelsey, 610
Grams, Blake, 4702
Gramshammer, Pepi, 1468
Granadillo, Pedro P., 3193
Grand Circle Corp., 3929
Grand Lodge F & AM of California, 348
Grand Piano and Furniture Co., 9388
Grand Victoria Casino, 2769
Grand, Cindy, 611
Grand, Marcia, 611
Grand, Rena, 611
Grand, Richard, 611
Grandchamps Charitable Remainder
    Trust, G., 3982
Grandinetti, Francis, 8456
Grandis, Harriet, 9432
Grandis, Harry, 9432
Grandmaison, James, 3550
Grandon, Carleen, 3290
Grandy, Edith G., 9458
Granger Associates, Inc., 4328, 4329
Granger Construction Co., 4328
Granger Electric, 4329
Granger Energy, 4329
Granger Energy of Decatur, LLC, 4329
Granger Energy of Honeybrook, LLC,
    4329
Granger Holdings, LLC, 4329
Granger Meadows, LLC, 4329
Granger, Alton L., 4328
Granger, Dawn M., 4329
Granger, Donald L., 9348
Granger, Donna, 4328
Granger, Janice, 4328
Granger, Jerry P., 4328
Granger, Keith L., 4329
Granger, Lynne, 4328
Granger, Renee A., 4100
Granger, Robert C., 6092
Granger, Ronald K., 4328
Granger, Todd J., 4329
Granite Construction Co., 268
Granlund, Cheryl, 4610, 4715
Granoff, Leon L., 612
Granoff, Martin J., 6089
Granoff, Michael, 6089
Granoff, Perry, 6089
Granquist, Deborah W., 9361
Grans, Sue, 2679
Gransden, Bridgette, 4392
Grant, Alison A., 6006
Grant, Carol, 8551
Grant, Cy, Hon., 7464
Grant, David, 5181, 7103
Grant, David A., 9848
Grant, Donald R., 6031
Grant, Emily, 6090
Grant, Eugene, 6779
Grant, Eugene M., 6090
Grant, Frederic, 7743
Grant, Hugh A., 1354
Grant, John, 4247
Grant, Joseph M. "Jody", 8839
Grant, Katherine R., 2479
Grant, Madeleine B., 3696
Grant, Maria O., 928, 1114
Grant, Mary D., 6091
Grant, Mike, 3206
Grant, Patty, 3132
Grant, Richard A., 412
Grant, Richard A., Jr., 928
Grant, Robert N., 2590
Grant, S.J. "Bud", 5990
Grant, Terry E., 6090
Grant, Verlene, 4693

Grant, William T., 6092
Grantham, Jeremy, 3930
Grantham, R. Jeremy, 3930
Granville Homes, Inc., 1282
Granville, Richard C., 3693
Grasberger, F. Nicholas, 8284
Grass Instrument Co., 3931
Grass, Albert M., 3931
Grass, Alex, 8223
Grass, Ellen R., 3931
Grass, Henry J., 3931
Grassey, Ernest J., 3995
Grassi, Robert, 5784
Grassilli, Robert J., 559
Grassmann, Edward J., 5213, 5435
Grasso, Angelo J., 3893
Grasso, Catherine Smythe, 1170
Grasso, Lorraine P., 5552
Grasso, Maria J., 3893
Grasso, Richard, 7040
Grasso, Richard A., 5552
Grata, Mel, 8438
Gratry, Barbara Bolton, 7798
Gratton, Mike, 8967
Graubart, Noel, 8944
Grauer, Laura M., 6094
Grauer, Peter T., 6094
Graunke, James W., 983
Graustein, Archibald R., 1559
Graustein, Hallie H., 1559
Graustein, Jean, 1559
Graustein, Lisa, 1559
Graustein, William C., 1559
Graven, Irene C., 8483
Graver, Barbara, 8621
Graver, Walter J., 8621
Graves, Barbara, 407
Graves, Beverly Garner, 2018
Graves, Cheryl, 2757
Graves, Earl G., Sr., 1479
Graves, Elena W., 8740
Graves, Frances B., 2403
Graves, Kathleen M., 9400
Graves, Milton T., 8835
Graves, Nicholas M., 639
Graves, R. Danner, 9599
Graves, Ronald N., 2574
Graves, Sayre O., 9433
Graves, Susan R., 7931
Graves, William M., 2403
Graves, William M., Jr., 2403
Gravett, Benjamin C., 9534
Gravett, Charlotte Smith, 9534
Gravett, Guy M., 9478
Gravin, Laurence A., 1779
Gravina, Amy, 1919
Gray Fund, Joseph J., 1884
Gray Revocable Trust, Mae K., 1884
Gray, Alan, 9582
Gray, Alexandra T., 6717
Gray, Allison, 995
Gray, Avrum, 1884
Gray, B.A., 1921
Gray, Barry A., 1921
Gray, Barry W., 6240
Gray, Carol M., 8419
Gray, Carolyn B., 5800
Gray, Catherine, 3582
Gray, Charles, 2702
Gray, Charles A., 3823
Gray, Charles C., 1318
Gray, Chris, Rev., 2041
Gray, Christy E., 4926
Gray, Constance F., 7359
Gray, D.A., 1921
Gray, Dan L., 7335
Gray, David, 3171
Gray, Doreen H., 8224
Gray, Edward W.T., III, 5800
Gray, Elizabeth B., 7547
Gray, Frank B., 8671
Gray, Frank T., 3739
Gray, G.S., 1921
Gray, Hanna H., 3654

Gray, Harry B., 272
Gray, J.M., 1921
Gray, Jack, 9184
Gray, James, 1884
Gray, John D., 2966
Gray, John M., 6717
Gray, Joyce, 1884
Gray, Kenneth B., Jr., 8224
Gray, Kimberly H., 8224
Gray, Laman A., 3421
Gray, Lawrence V., 2565
Gray, Lloyd H., Jr., 69
Gray, Lucile J., 1359
Gray, Mary L., 2771
Gray, Mathew, 1884
Gray, Matthew E.P., 6717
Gray, Meredith L., 8224
Gray, Monte, 6423
Gray, Patricia, 8987
Gray, Peter G., 5800
Gray, R.C., 1921
Gray, Richard, 2771
Gray, Robert, 8180
Gray, Saundria Chase, 8960
Gray, Sharon Whitehill, 4798
Gray, Susan J., 3827
Gray, Taylor T., 5800
Gray, W. Todd, 7750
Gray, Wendy, 9693
Gray, Winifred P., 6717
Graybill, Charles S., 7959
Graycor, Inc., 2771
Graye, Mildred, 5396
Grayson, Bruns H., 3932
Grayson, Perrin M., 3932
Graziadio, G. Louis, III, 613
Graziadio, George L., Jr., 613
Graziadio, Reva, Jr., 613
Graziano, Judith O., 8112, 8117, 8431
Graziano, Rick, 1563
Graziano, Robert V., 214
Grden, Nancy L., 9369
Great Chesapeake Bay Swim, Inc., 3699
Great Circle Trust, 6029
Great Lakes, 9885
Great Southern Liquor Co., Inc., 3484,
    3516
Great Western Bank, 4945
Greatbatch, Ami, 5901
Greatbatch, Eleanor, 5899, 5901
Greatbatch, Warren, 5901
Greatbatch, Warren D., 5901
Greatbatch, Wilson, 5899
Greater Bay Bancorp, 264
Greater Talent Network, Inc., 7149
Greathead, R. Scott, 5551, 7026
Greathouse, Marcella, 8924
Greathouse, Micah, 8924
Greaton, Wilson B., Jr., 2288
Greaves, Michael, 3271, 3272
Greaves, Richard F., 8391
Grebe, Francis R., 8350
Grebe, Michael W., 9763, 9839
Greco, Dick A., 1948
Greczyn, Robert J., Jr., 7319
Gredenhag, Juliette C., 1926
Gredy, Mimi, 7503
Greehey, William E., 9247
Green Bay Packaging, Inc., 9844
Green Charitable Trust, Helen Wade,
    4079
Green Fund, Inc., The, 6024, 6095
Green Unitrust, G.M., 102
Green, Alice K., 1385
Green, Allan, M.D., 6232
Green, Allen P., 4822
Green, Bennie, 9154
Green, Calvin, 5215
Green, Catherine, 6095
Green, Cathy Obriotti, 9296
Green, Charles A., 7397
Green, Christopher C., 4319
Green, Daniel B., 8225
Green, David, 2772

Green, Don C., 3317
Green, Donald J., 5215
Green, Edward S., 6026
Green, Eleanor F., 6915
Green, Emese, 614
Green, Ernestine R., 7050
Green, Ernie, 7604
Green, Florence E., 8225
Green, Frances M., 1385
Green, Fred, 301
Green, Friday A., 1464
Green, George Mason, 102
Green, Gerald L., 3368
Green, Holcombe, 2513
Green, Howard, 3160
Green, Howard L., 5215
Green, Jean Bellet, 2008
Green, Jeffery A., 619
Green, Jessica A., 3432
Green, John, 7964
Green, John T., 9295
Green, Josephine B., 4822
Green, Joshua, 9598
Green, Joshua, III, 9598
Green, Joshua, Mrs., 9598
Green, Joyce, 480
Green, Kent, 5053
Green, Kimberly, 2033
Green, Laura, 1519
Green, Leonard I., 614
Green, Les, 4534
Green, Lois B., 3954
Green, Lois C., 102
Green, Louis, 6095
Green, Louis A., 6096
Green, Louis S., 1939
Green, Mary Winton, 2772
Green, Melinda, 5357
Green, Michael, 6444
Green, Nancy, 4821
Green, Patricia, 6095
Green, Patricia F., 6096
Green, Phyllis, 5801
Green, Richard, 3186
Green, Richard C., 4824, 9222
Green, Rocinda J., 3344
Green, Roe, 7652
Green, Stephan A., Jr., 4821
Green, Stephen W., 1252
Green, Steven J., 2033
Green, Suzanne, 614
Green, Sydney, 1942
Green, Tee, 2362
Green, Walter H., 1031
Green, William G., 913
Green-Holley, Reba, 7464
Greenawalt, W. Eileen, 1347
Greenbaum, James R., Jr., 615
Greenbaum, Maurice C., 1596, 6852
Greenberg Charitable Trust No. 1, 6098
Greenberg, Allan M., 2153
Greenberg, Allen, 2640, 4950, 6817
Greenberg, Arthur, 5971
Greenberg, Ben, 617
Greenberg, Beverly P., 1564
Greenberg, Corinne P., 6098
Greenberg, Daniel B., 617
Greenberg, Eileen Bender, 1772
Greenberg, Evan, 8073
Greenberg, Evan G., 6098
Greenberg, Fay, 5906
Greenberg, Filomena M. D'Agostino,
    5818
Greenberg, Gary, 1636
Greenberg, Glen, 1636
Greenberg, Glenn H., 6097
Greenberg, Hermen, 3639
Greenberg, Jack M., 2661
Greenberg, Jeffrey W., 6098
Greenberg, Joel, 8470
Greenberg, Lawrence S., 6098
Greenberg, Lester A., 817
Greenberg, Lise Temple, 9525
Greenberg, Mary Jo, 616

Greenberg, Maurice R., 6098, 7048
Greenberg, Michael, 6624
Greenberg, Monica, 3639
Greenberg, Richard, 1772
Greenberg, Robert M., 8774
Greenberg, Sidney, 1636
Greenberg, Stephen D., 6034
Greenberg, Steven, 9525
Greenberg, Susan, 1647
Greenberg, William, Rabbi, 9675
Greenblatt, Joel, 6947
Greenblatt, Joel N., 6592
Greenblatt, Jonathan, 9690
Greenblatt, Julia, 6592
Greenblatt, Nancy W., 6288
Greenblatt, Richard, 6592
Greenblatt, Sandra P., 1957
Greenburg, Harry, 2034
Greenburg, Jon, 5194
Greene, Alan I., 6099
Greene, Allison Roberts, 2968
Greene, Arthur B., 3545
Greene, Carl F., 4442
Greene, Carole, 472
Greene, Danita, 4620
Greene, David H., 9325
Greene, David J., 6099
Greene, Davis C., 3866
Greene, Davis Crane, 3865
Greene, Dawn M., 6100
Greene, Enid, 9325
Greene, Finley, 5780
Greene, James, 6099
Greene, Jerome L., 6100
Greene, Joe C., 4869
Greene, John Kaul, 40
Greene, John M., 8588
Greene, Joseph D., 2357
Greene, Josephine B., 3865
Greene, Kim, 2121
Greene, Margaret, 2323
Greene, Marion E., 799
Greene, Michael C., 6099
Greene, Mickey, 3558
Greene, Milton, 1565
Greene, Paul F., 4005
Greene, Randi, 9325
Greene, Rose Ellen, 3690
Greene, Roxanne D., 9666
Greene, Roxanne Davis, 1115
Greene, Schaeffer, 4310
Greene, Tammis, 9693
Greene, W.M. Britton, 2244
Greene, Wade, 5614, 7168, 7252
Greene, Warren E., 472
Greene-Sawtell, Alice, 2404
Greenebaum, Mary, 6613
Greener, Charles V. "Chuck", 1793
Greener, Gary, 4836
Greener, Sharon S., 4733
Greenfield, David W., 8284
Greenfield, Jennifer, 565
Greenfield, Jerry, 9355
Greenfield, Julius, 6049
Greengard, Paul, 5652
Greenhalgh, Laurette, 9801
Greenhaven Assocs., 7204
Greenhill, Gayle G., 6101
Greenhill, Robert F., 6101
Greenleaf, Arline Ripley, 7035
Greenleaf, Cynthia, 3015
Greenleaf, Michael, 5262
Greenleaf, Peter W., 3539
Greenlick, Merwyn R., 8048
Greeno, Richard, 3110
Greenough, Julia M., 1733
GreenPoint Bank, 6637
Greensboro News Co., 9455
Greenside, Peggy, 4574
Greenspon, Irving L., 9543
Greenspun, Barbara, 5034
Greenspun, Brian L., 5034

Greenspun, Daniel A., 5034
Greenstein, Ira, 5248
Greenwall, Anna A., 6103
Greenwall, Frank K., 6103
Greenway-Leibowitz, Tara, 6398
Greenwell, F. Gerald, 3414
Greenwich Air Svcs., Inc., 1950
Greenwich Co., Ltd., The, 1950
Greenwood Gardens, Inc., 5394
Greenwood, Greg, 3403
Greenwood, John T., 2750
Greer, Alice D., 3462
Greer, Bruce, 1947
Greer, Gayle, 1362
Greer, George C., 8182
Greer, Jack, 7573
Greer, Margaret Jewett, 718
Greer, Nancy, 618
Greer, Philip, 618
Greer, Philip Lee, 3407
Greer, Stacey, 1275
Greer, William Hershey, Jr., 718
Greer-Stokes, Whitney, 3407
Greevy, Charles F., III, 8387
Grefenstette, C.G., 8249
Greffin, Bill, 2922
Grefig, Max E., 9788
Gregg, Ingrid A., 4291
Gregg, Jason, 2198
Gregg, Kirk P., 5794
Gregg, Simon, 2198
Gregg, Steve, 6977
Gregg, Vicky, 8732
Gregorian, Vartan, 5707
Gregory, Alicia, 2199
Gregory, Beth, 3276
Gregory, Brent, 3415
Gregory, C.E., III, 2435
Gregory, Carlton S., 9390
Gregory, Charles, 2435
Gregory, Charles R., Jr., 2239
Gregory, Dena, 9702
Gregory, Dennis, 4534
Gregory, Edmond B. "Ted", 3598
Gregory, James, 8700
Gregory, Joan P., 8700
Gregory, John M., 8700
Gregory, Joseph A., 8710
Gregory, Joseph M., 6395
Gregory, Joseph R., 8710
Gregory, Julia P., 6232
Gregory, Lloyd J., Jr., 8872
Gregory, Lucinda J., 8710
Gregory, Mary L., 275
Gregory, Peter S., 3823
Gregory, R. Frederick, 9209
Gregory, Wayne A., Jr., 2199
Greifeld, Robert, 3700
Greil, Gail D., 8664
Grein, Joan, 6387
Greiner, Amelia, 6026
Greiner, James, 3189
Greiner, John T., Jr., 7935
Greiner, K. Don, 7940
Greiner, Shellie, 7940
Greisch, John J., 2611
Gresham, Cary "Thomas", 9442
Gresham, Suzanne, 3128
Greswold, Kate M., 1240
Greue, John H., 3300
Greupner, James, 4662
Greve, Larry, 7891
Greve, Mary P., 6104
Greven, Philip J., Jr., 7409
Grewell, Jan, 2657
Greyhavens, Timothy, 9705
Greystone Funding Corp., 6847
Gribetz, Judah, 6776
Gridish, Eli, 6319
Gridish, Rebecca, 6319
Gridish, Rebecca Abraham, 5727
Gridley, William G., Jr., 1510, 6917
Griego, Linda, 972, 5265
Grien, James, 2441

Grier, M.N., 8173
Grier, Rosey, 898
Griesback, George M., 8661
Griesbeck, William G., 8666
Griff, Christine, 6714
Griffen, Gale L., 5132
Griffin Foundation, John A., Inc., 1426
Griffin, Archie M., 7580
Griffin, Dan, 9113
Griffin, Diane Pomeroy, 9376
Griffin, Donald W., 2925
Griffin, F. O'Neil, 8925
Griffin, Jack, 78
Griffin, John A., 5640, 6105, 7139
Griffin, John F., 2036
Griffin, Kenneth C., 2667
Griffin, Leslie A., 7349
Griffin, Martin P., 2036
Griffin, Nancy M., 2036
Griffin, Richard D., 8925
Griffin, Samuel S., III, 9140
Griffin, Sandra L., 7925
Griffin, Thomas C., 8571
Griffin, William E., 5710
Griffin, William M., 6186
Griffin-Cole, Barbara, 6106
Griffis, Buckly, 6107
Griffis, David, 9097
Griffis, Hughes, 6107
Griffis, Jennifer, 6107
Griffis, Mary Helen McCarty, 4754
Griffis, Nickolas, 6107
Griffis, Nixon, 6107
Griffis, Stanton, 6107
Griffith, Bronwyn A.E., 4711
Griffith, Charles P., Jr., 3158
Griffith, Chip, 3304
Griffith, David H., 9933
Griffith, Donald E., 1946
Griffith, Elizabeth B., 8577
Griffith, Frances L., 1412
Griffith, H. Russell, 9407
Griffith, J. Brian, 4866
Griffith, J. Larry, 3274
Griffith, James W., 9950
Griffith, John, 4697
Griffith, John J., 4951
Griffith, Lawrence S.C., 7103
Griffith, Mark, 1913
Griffith, Mary, 3304
Griffith, Ruth Perry, 3158
Griffith, Sima, 4623
Griffith, W. Louis, 8594
Griffith, Walter S., 3158
Griffith, William C., 3158
Griffith, William C., III, 3158
Griffith, William G., 1412
Griffiths, Brian, 7694
Grigal, Dennis, 4552
Griggs, Alfred L., 1907
Griggs, C.E. Bayliss, 4577
Griggs, Carl L., 2359
Griggs, Mary L., 4577
Griglun, Thomas, 1603
Grignon, Peter, 9669
Grillo, Christopher, 5610, 6017
Grillo, Stephan, 6670
Grim, Gregory E., 8303
Grimes, Anne Windfohr, 8801
Grimes, D.R., 2355
Grimes, Doug, 9171
Grimes, Gregg, 7749
Grimes, Mick, 1178
Grimm, Barbara M., 620
Grimm, Faith Sodaro, 1174
Grimm, Kari L., 619
Grimm, Robert A., 619
Grimm, Royden A., 1517
Grimm, Stephen K., 1616
Grimmway Enterprises, Inc., 619, 620
Grimsley, Diane, 7490
Grimsley, John G., 1888
Grimstad, Gary, 9548
Grin, David, 5641

Grin, Eugene, 6109
Gringras, Sally, 1939
Grinspoon Foundation, Harold, 4071
Grinspoon, Harold, 3935, 4071
Grinspoon, Jeffrey, 3935
Grinspoon, Steven, 3935
Grinstein, Gerald, 2372, 9680
Grisanti, Eugene P., 6566, 7196
Griscom, Karin A., 5490
Grise, Cheryl W., 1614
Grisham, Elizabeth Renee, 4760
Grisham, John R., 4760
Grisham, John R., Jr., 4760
Grissom, S.L., 2864
Griswell, J. Barry, 3326
Griswell, Michele, 3281
Griswold Industries, Inc., 766
Griswold, D. Ross, Jr., 2773
Griswold, John C., 2773
Griswold, Mark, 2773
Grobe, Lynn G., 3298
Grobman, Duane, 9481
Groce, Fred F., Jr., 7346
Grocers Supply Co., 9009
Grodin, Jay H., 1291
Groen, Jock W., 9599
Groenendyke, Cheryl F., 4340
Groff, Ellen Arnold, 8300
Groff, Mary E., 8226
Grogan, Paul S., 2097, 3812
Grohman, Martin, 5631
Grohne, David, 2774
Grohne, Jeffrey, 2774
Grohne, Margaret, 2774
Groisser, Suzanne J., 5228
Groll, Matthew A., 8076
Gronauer, Helen Scheidt, 8726
Gronewaldt, Alice Busch, 2037
Gronli, Michael E., 2605
Groopman, Jerome, 6789
Grose, Charles, 4661
Grosfeld, James, 4332
Grosfeld, Nancy, 4332
Grosh, Gregory, 2808
Groisser, Suzanne J., 5228
Gross, Allen I., 6110
Gross, Ben, 6111
Gross, Bernard, 6857
Gross, Bill, 1006
Gross, Brian, 6110
Gross, Chaim, 6112
Gross, Charles H., 4376
Gross, Daniel, 6112
Gross, Edgar, 565
Gross, Edie, 6110
Gross, Elizabeth Cochary, 3936
Gross, Esther, 6112
Gross, Faigie, 6112
Gross, Heddy, 6111
Gross, Inez, 3937
Gross, Jenard M., 9289
Gross, Jerome, 7254
Gross, Jonathan, 6110, 6111
Gross, Malcolm J., 8481
Gross, Meryl, 5195
Gross, Norman, 6426
Gross, Patrick W., 1810
Gross, Phil, 4169
Gross, Phillip T., 3936
Gross, Pinchus, 6112
Gross, Richard, 4083
Gross, Stella B., 621
Gross, Steven E., 5228
Gross, Sue, 622, 3652
Gross, William, 622
Gross, William H., 1006
Gross, William, Mrs., 622
Grossenburg, Barry, 8631
Grosser, Sharon G., 6859
Grossman, Alan R., 6833
Grossman, Beverly, 4578
Grossman, Daniel, 1065
Grossman, Ernie, 1244
Grossman, Gina, 9353
Grossman, Isaac, 1342

Grossman, Jeffrey, 5907
Grossman, Lynn, 5925
Grossman, N. Bud, 4578
Grossman, Nathan, 2910
Grossman, Robert, 7056
Grossman, Robin F., 6876
Grossman, Sanford J., 1560
Grossman, Thomas, 5523
Grossnickle, Jeanne, 3186
Grote, Matt, 2922
Groth, Lynne, 1943
Groth, William A., 7660
Grotjohn, Mo, 7960
Grotnes, Alice D., 32
Grotto, Joseph, 6779
Group Health Assn., Inc., 1786
Grousbeck, E., 623
Grousbeck, H. Irving, 623
Grousbeck, Susanne B., 623
Grousbeck, Wycliffe K., 623
Grout, Elizabeth O., 624
Grove, Andrew S., 625
Grove, Eva K., 625
Grove, Karen, 625
Groveman, Andrew, 8643
Groveman, Jan B., 8643
Grover, Jay, 383
Grover, Martha E., 9415
Groves, Helen K., 8999
Groves, Hope C., 3812
Grow, David C., 7076
Growald, Adam, 6827
Growald, Daniel, 6827
Growald, Eileen, 6827
Growe, Joan Anderson, 4623
Growney, James, 2536
Grt. Grand Charitable Remainder
    Unitrust, 6265
Grubb, David H., Jr., 1221
Grubb, Edgar H., 474
Grubb, John R., 3289
Grubb, John R., Inc., 3289
Grubb, John W., 3289
Grube, Stanley M., 405
Gruber, Jon D., 626
Gruber, Linda W., 626
Gruber, Richard, 9780
Grubman, Eric P., 6113
Gruen, Daniel F., 653
Gruen, Margaret A., 653
Gruenberg, Jennifer, 6497
Gruenes, Dave, 4593
Grumbach, Antonia M., 7253
Grumbacher, M.T., 8227
Grundhauser, John J., 1957
Grundhofer, Beverly J., 4580
Grundhofer, Jerry A., 4704, 7659
Grundhofer, John F., 4580
Grundy, Joseph R., 8228
Gruner, Nancy, 8457
Gruntorad, Dale E., 4987
Gruodis, Victor, 6302
Grupe County Fair, 1089
Grupp, Peggy, 5902
Grusin, Teri A., 9
Gruss Petroleum Corp., 6116
Gruss, Audrey Butay, 2038
Gruss, Brenda, 6114, 6115
Gruss, Emanuel, 6114, 6115
Gruss, Leslie, 6115
Gruss, Martin D., 2038
Gruss, Oscar, 6114
Gruss, Regina, 6114
Gruss, Riane, 6114, 6115
Gryttenholm, Jerry A., 9768
Grzewinski, Philip M., 4057
Grzywinski, Joan A., 4671
GSC, Inc., 8657
GST Charitable Lead Trust, 5587
GTE Federal Credit Union, 2040
Guameri, John D., 2303
Guaranty Trust Co. of Missouri, The,
    4894, 4896
Guard, SuzanneClair, 6917

Guardian Industries Corp., 4333
Guarini, Frank J., 5216
Gubser, Peter, 1796
Gudas, Linda J., 5784
Gudbranson, Robert N., 7757
Gudelsky, John, 3641
Gudelsky, Martha, 3641
Gudelsky, Medda, 3641
Gudim, Melissa Collins, 397
Gudmunson, Daniel, 2701
Gudwin, Barbara, 5496
Guedj, Kate, 3812
Guempel, Scot R., 5167
Guennewig, Victoria B., 8846
Guenther, Jack, 9048, 9244
Guenther, Jack E., Jr., 9244
Guenther, Paul B., 5712
Guenther, Paul L., 9944
Guenther, Pearl H., 628
Guenther, Richard Prosser, 8651
Guenther, Valerie Urschel, 9244
Guerin, Dana, 1135, 1136
Guerin, Lisa, 1135, 1136
Guerin, Michael, 1136
Guerin, Paul, 1135, 1136
Guerin, Vera, 1135, 1136
Guerrero, Anthony R., Jr., 2542, 2545
Guerrero-Anderson, Esperanza, 4524
Guerry, John P., 8684
Guerry, Zan, 8684
Guess ?, Inc., 629
Guess, Francis, 8662
Guess, Mark, 7653
Guest Realty, 6497
Guest, Christopher, 3398
Guest, Jamie Lee Curtis, 3398
Guest, Penny, 9700
Guest, Sandra M., 4756
Guettel, Mary Rogers, 6828
Guez, Hubert, 493
Guez, Roxanne, 493
Gugenheim, Ada Mary, 3016
Guggenheim, Daniel M., 6117
Guggenheim, Florence, 6117
Guggenheim, Harry Frank, 6118
Guggenheim, Simon, 6119
Guggenheim, Simon, Mrs., 6119
Guggenhime, Richard J., 788
Guggino, Kathleen P., 837
Guibao, Renee Clark, 7305
Guice, Ann, 4745
Guice, Reed, 4745
Guidant, 3841
Guidant Corp., 3159
Guided Alliance Healthcare Services,
    874
Guido, Tara, 8191
Guidone, Rosemary L., 1442
Guidotti, Helen B., 4096
Guidugli, John J., 7660
Guigou, Kevin, 4392
Guilarte, Olga, 2190
Guilbert, Rob, 9748
Guild, Daniel L., 8229
Guild, Lloyd V., 8229
Guild, Richard L., 8229
Guilden, Louise B., 5147
Guilden, Paul B., 5147
Guillaume, Alfred, Jr., 3131
Guillermo, Tessie, 346
Guills, Jesse O., Jr., 9719
Guin-Kittner, Harriet, 8279
Guinier, Lani, 6665
Gulf Power Co., 2042
Gulick, Barbara, 2880
Gulick, E. Leeds, 9613
Gulick, George G., 9613
Gulick, Robert S., 3885
Gullen, David J., 98
Gulley, F. Stuart, 2463
Gulley, Joan, 8388
Gulley, Philip G., 8457
Gullikson, Mary T., 9994
Gulmi, James S., 8662

Gulton, Edith, 5217
Gulton, Leslie K., 5217
Gumb, Barry D., 8581
Gumbiner, Alis, 631
Gumbiner, Burke, 631
Gumbiner, Josephine S., 631
Gumbiner, Lee, 631
Gumenick, Sophia, 9432
Gumerson, Jean G., 7969
Gumm, Vicki, 766
Gummer, Donald, 5404
Gummer, Meryl S., 5404
Gummey, Charles F., 1728
Gump, Patricia, 521
Gund Trust, Gordon and Llura Liggett,
    7654
Gund, Agnes, 7655, 7799
Gund, Ann L., 7657
Gund, Catherine, 7657
Gund, Geoffrey, 7656, 7657
Gund, George, 7657
Gund, George, III, 798, 7657
Gund, George, IV, 798
Gund, Gordon, 5218
Gund, Llura A., 5218, 7657
Gund, Louise L., 7916
Gund, Zachary, 7657
Gunden, June, 8246
Gunderson, Warren, Mrs., 6932
Gundlach, Susan Jones, 3491
Gundling, Henry, 557
Gunkelman, Jay, 430
Gunn, Bill, 1386
Gunn, Carol Carlson, 9280
Gunn, Curtis, Jr., 8866
Gunn, Louise Staton, 2420
Gunn, Philip J., 3503
Gunnar, Rolf, 2601
Gunnarson, Anna Karin M., 3773
Gunnell, Peggy, 4315
Gunnin, John M., 577
Gunsteens, Anne, 1827
Gunter, Linda Hays, 9045
Gunther, Craig, 937
Gunther, Jack D., Jr., 5182
Gunzenhauser, Lynn C., 7384, 7452
Gupta, Benjamin, 4967
Gupta, Geeta Rao, 1835
Gupta, Jai, 1716
Gupta, Jai N., 1716
Gupta, Jess, 4967
Gupta, Jyoti, 4221
Gupta, Narenda, 406
Gupta, Rajat, 6826
Gupta, Shashi, 1716
Gupta, Umang, 989
Gupta, Vinod, 4967
Guptill, Patricia A., 4938
Gural, Aaron, 6120, 6779
Gural, Barbara, 6120
Gural, Jeff, 6219
Gural, Jeffrey R., 6779
Gurary, Tema, 7151
Guren, Debra Hershey, 7671
Gurieva, Diana M., 5898
Gurowitz, Viki, 3446
Gursky, Steven R., 6183
Gurwin, Eric, 6121
Gurwin, Joseph, 6121
Gussman, Barbara, 7941
Gussman, Herbert, 7941
Gussman, Roseline, 7941
Gust, Anne, 551
Gustafson, Bob, 4509
Gustafson, Edwin, Jr., 6726
Gustafson, Karl W., 5497
Gustafson, Reno, 9280
Gustafson, Sarah Geary, 8017
Gustafson, Wayne, 8631
Gustin, Marie, 1568
Gustin, Marie S., 1482
Guten, Sharon, 7719
Gutfarb, William B., 4211
Gutfreund, Pauline, 7291

Gutfreund, S., 7291
Guth Charitable Lead Unitrust, P.W.,
    6695
Guth, James Black, 2775
Guth, Jeremy, 7273
Guth, Joel K., 2563
Guth, John H.J., 7273
Guth, Polly, 6695, 7273
Guthman, Sandra P., 2946
Guthridge, Charles M., 9513
Guthrie, Carlton L., 2820
Guthrie, Donald, 9604
Guthrie, J. Marvin, 2170
Gutierrez, Amanda, 3387
Gutierrez, Felix F., 9424
Gutman, Joseph D., 6122
Gutman, Sheila H., 6122
Gutmann, Amy, 5707
Gutmann, Karen, 6123
Gutmann, Linda, 9693
Gutmann, Stephen, 6665
Gutshall, James, 9573
Gutterman, Jordan U., 6379
Guttierez, Angel (Lito), 5785
Guttman, Charles, 6124
Guttman, Joshua, 6368
Guttman, Stella, 6124
Guttormsen, Neil F., 9833
Guy, Ethel, 8467
Guy, Gina, 1333
Guy, Martha, 7438
Guy, R. Kent, 9558
Guy, William, III, 7514
Guyaux, Joseph C., 8388
Guyer, Cricket, 4574
Guyer, Leigh, 990
Guyer, Luisa Adrianzen, 990
Guylas, Joan D., 110
Guynn, Douglas L., 9521
Guynn, Jack, 2355
Guyol, Frank J., III, 4896
Guyon, Cynthia A., 8782
Guyton, Samuel P., 9344
Guziejka, Kelly R., 6417
Guzik, Nahum, 632
Guzman, Mariano, 898
Guzman, Ramiro, 8881, 8950
Gwaltney, Nancy R., 60
Gwathmey, Bette-Ann, 6737
Gwin, Hugh F., 9898
Gwin, James S., Hon., 7536
Gwynne-Timothy, Holly Cluett, 7430

H + H Excavation, 1359
H&R Block, Inc., 4823
Ha, Paul, 4817
Haab, Larry, 2678
Haack, Lois, 4256
Haagenson, Roger, 1886
Haagenson, Sherry, 1886
Haake, Donald J., 263
Haake, H.R., 263
Haake, Kelly, 263
Haake, Martha B., 263
Haar, Nan, 3828
Haarmann, Chris, 3093
Haas Charitable Trusts, Otto Haas &
    Phoebe W., 8371
Haas, Chara L., 8230
Haas, Charles J., 633
Haas, David W., 8371
Haas, Dayee G., 9599
Haas, Deesa, 9599
Haas, Duncan A., 8371
Haas, Elise S., 635, 636
Haas, Ellen Jo, 633
Haas, Evelyn D., 637
Haas, Flora Oppenheimer, 6666
Haas, Frederick R., 8371
Haas, Gene F., 634
Haas, Jean H., 8589
Haas, John C., 8230
Haas, Miriam L., 635

Harris Corp., 2050
Harris Trust and Savings Bank, 2787, 3079
Harris Trust, William, 2686
Harris, A.P., 5042
Harris, Alan, 4438
Harris, Albert W., 2661
Harris, Andrew, 2104
Harris, Benjamin, 2789
Harris, Bernard A., Jr., 8960
Harris, Bette D., 2788
Harris, Bobbye F., 2408
Harris, Brent, 1006
Harris, Cameron M., 7390
Harris, Carey A., 8107
Harris, Carla, 6577
Harris, Charles, 6292
Harris, Clyde P., Jr., 7438
Harris, Consuelo W., 7689
Harris, David, 2789, 3424
Harris, Diane B., 3277
Harris, Don, 3424
Harris, Dorothy May, 602
Harris, Dorothy V., 3595
Harris, Dwight, 1594
Harris, E.S. "Steve", 4265
Harris, Edward, 563
Harris, Elizabeth A., 9204
Harris, Ellen H., 2336, 2337
Harris, Elmer, 1
Harris, Elmer E., 52
Harris, Franco, 8242
Harris, Gary, 3424
Harris, Gayla, 3424
Harris, George, 6434
Harris, George F., 9805
Harris, Gina H., 9499
Harris, Glenda, 1
Harris, Henry U., III, 4201
Harris, Henry U., Jr., 4201
Harris, Irving D., 2686
Harris, Isaiah, Jr., 2323
Harris, J., 240
Harris, J. Ira, 2946, 6148
Harris, Jack S., 9833
Harris, Jacqueline S., 6148
Harris, James J., 7390
Harris, Jane A., 8686
Harris, Jeff, 3124
Harris, Jerrol L., 669
Harris, Joan W., 2789
Harris, Johanna H., 3944
Harris, John W., 7390
Harris, Jonathan, 6148
Harris, Joseph, 6532
Harris, Juliana K., 5704
Harris, Katherine, 1541, 2788
Harris, Kelly L., 3666
Harris, Kimberly L., 2211
Harris, King W., 2661, 2788
Harris, Leo N., 9313
Harris, Linda C., 2840
Harris, Lisa, 5064
Harris, M.W., 240
Harris, Marilyn, 87, 4987
Harris, Martin R., 9124
Harris, Marydel, 9204
Harris, Nancy G., 257
Harris, Nelson, 2788
Harris, Nicki, 6148
Harris, O. Ben, 2395
Harris, Paul, 7700
Harris, Paul W., 8955
Harris, Phillip G., 9605
Harris, R., 240
Harris, Randall, 9042
Harris, Randy, 7383
Harris, Raymond, 9204
Harris, Richard E., Sr., 3166
Harris, Richard M., 2104
Harris, Richard V., 5035
Harris, Robert C., 578
Harris, Roberta, 2686
Harris, Rosalind W., 6315

Harris, Sally S., 9180
Harris, Sanders Morris, 493
Harris, Shane, 5337
Harris, Stephen R., 9204
Harris, T. Britton, IV, 5439
Harris, Thomas, 4793
Harris, Timothy, 3424
Harris, Trina B., 5035
Harris, W. Patrick, 8816
Harris, W.N., 240
Harris, William C., 2649
Harris, William H., 3944
Harris, William W., 2686
Harris, Wilmot L., Jr., 1537
Harris, Zelema, 2769
Harrison Foundation, Helen M., 2791
Harrison, Albert E., 2409
Harrison, Alferdteen, 4737
Harrison, Beth, 2041
Harrison, Caroline Diamond, 6800
Harrison, Dalen, 9669
Harrison, David A., III, 9436
Harrison, David A., IV, 9436
Harrison, Douglas P., 2409
Harrison, Francena T., 6149
Harrison, Fred G., 2790
Harrison, George A., 9436
Harrison, Gregg, 544
Harrison, J. Frank, 2350
Harrison, James I., III, 27
Harrison, James I., Jr., 36
Harrison, Jim, 5469, 5471
Harrison, John M., 2409
Harrison, Laura J., 4734
Harrison, Laurie Sands, 9158
Harrison, Lawrence M., 1243
Harrison, Leslie, 6354
Harrison, Lois Cowles, 5170
Harrison, Lois Eleanor, 5170
Harrison, Louise C., 1333
Harrison, Margaret B., 4104
Harrison, Marian P., 9128
Harrison, Mary A., 9436
Harrison, Mary P.T., 7451
Harrison, Milton, 5454
Harrison, Mortimer J., 5225
Harrison, Nora Eccles Treadwell, 1243
Harrison, Patti S., 9137
Harrison, Peggy T., 36
Harrison, R. Harold, 2410
Harrison, Robert S., 2542, 7134
Harrison, Sally, 4330
Harrison, Sande Vincent, 9165
Harrison, Stephen C., 7254
Harrison, Susan, 4649
Harrison, Verna, 3582
Harrison, William B., Jr., 5326
Harrison, William T., Jr., 2255, 2256
Harrity, Grant E., Rev., 8137
Harrod, Alice J., 7408
Harrop, Diane, 10000
Harsco Corp., 8236
Harsh, Arvin, 9736
Harsh, Donald R., Jr., 3600
Harshman, Deroy, 5005
Harshman, Leta, 5005
Harslem, Eric, 8997
Harslem, Kate, 8997
Hart, Angela S., 2361
Hart, Barbara, 2180
Hart, Bettieanne, 2479
Hart, Bruce W., 669
Hart, Cathy J., 4732
Hart, Dehler, 8617
Hart, Gary, 421
Hart, Ginny Vander, 4277, 4279
Hart, Gladys, 5902
Hart, Helen Douglas, 2828
Hart, Irwin W., Jr., 3073
Hart, James M., 8570
Hart, Karen Schwartz, 6769
Hart, Kenneth, 8135
Hart, Louise, 4921
Hart, Max A., Mrs., 6117

Hart, Michael, 9428
Hart, Nancy E., 1986
Hart, Nini, 8631
Hart, Phil, 8015
Hart, Randy, 7539
Hart, Robert, 8853
Hart, Sam, 1944
Hart, Suzanne Leever, 1583
Hart, William, 1264
Harte, Richard, Jr., 4201
Harte, Sarah, 9166
Hartenstein, James S., 7591
Hartfield, Ronne, 2706
Hartford Courant Co., The, 1563
Hartford, George L., 6150
Hartford, John A., 6150
Hartigan, Grace, 6559
Hartigan, Michael, 5816
Hartin, Susan Fasken, 8895
Hartje, Keith, 8050
Hartke, Selma, 2792
Hartl, Leonard L., 9861
Hartl, Michael J., 1644
Hartlage, Teri A., 3434
Hartle, Clifford G., 557
Hartley, B.G., 8891
Hartley, Fred L., Jr., 653
Hartley, James R., Mrs., 1398
Hartley, Jane, 6925
Hartley, Margaret A., 653
Hartley, Michael, 2041
Hartline, Robert, 4650
Hartloff, Paul W., 1247
Hartman, Alexander, 6151
Hartman, Cherryl L., 7353
Hartman, Claudette L., 8942
Hartman, David A., 8942
Hartman, Debra F., 2793
Hartman, Douglas M., 8942
Hartman, Francis M., 6513
Hartman, Israel, 5936
Hartman, Janet Bauer, 8780
Hartman, John E., 8942
Hartman, Joyce, 7175
Hartman, Larry, 8455
Hartman, Larry A., 8329
Hartman, Robert, 2793, 3366
Hartman, Sid, 854
Hartman, Sima, 6151
Hartman, Tracy, 7514
Hartman, Wayne P., 8942
Hartmann, George, 9810
Hartmarx Corp., 2794
Hartnell, Melissa, 8026
Hartness, Sean, 8583
Hartnett, Edward J., 5265
Hartog, Robbert, 9190
Hartough, Jan, 4227
Hartquist Trust, Mildred, 7391
Hartshorn, Sue, 5564
Hartshorn, Terry, 971
Hartshorne, Harold, Jr., 8579
Hartson, Verne, 2480
Hartstein, Gail, 3613
Hartung, Frederick, 4669
Hartung, Rod, 4745
Hartung, Suzanne R., 4669
Hartwell, David B., 4514
Hartwell, Lucy B., 4687
Hartwell, Ralph M., 2570
Hartwell, Stephen, 1796, 1859
Hartwick, Kevin, 691
Hartwig, Dean, 4990
Hartwig, Rhonda, 9780
Hartwig, Ron, 570
Harty, Linda, 7567
Hartz, Deborah, 5471
Hartz, Greg, 172
Hartzell, Michelle C., 7310
Hartzog, George B., Jr., 1842
Harvest Foundation, 4712
Harvey, Ann, 6621
Harvey, Brian L., 654
Harvey, C. Felix, 7393

Harvey, Cannon Y., 1335
Harvey, Charlene, 1088
Harvey, Constance, 6621
Harvey, David J., 8037
Harvey, David, Sheriff, 1945
Harvey, Felix, 7393
Harvey, Hal, 6621
Harvey, Helen C., 9481
Harvey, Herbert J., Jr., 3460
Harvey, James D., 7822
Harvey, Joan, 6621
Harvey, John C., 7040
Harvey, Kazie M., 7040
Harvey, Kenneth L., 4074
Harvey, Larry, 9021
Harvey, Larry B., 654
Harvey, Margaret B., 7393
Harvey, Marion W., 3460
Harvey, Patricia A., 4623
Harvey, Peter, 9559
Harvey, Philip D., 6234
Harvey, Phyllis M., 654
Harvey, Ralph, 9280
Harvey, Ralph, III, 9131
Harvey, Robert W., 9144
Harvey, Teena W., 1332
Harvey, Thomas B., 5357
Harvey, Tom, 2323
Harvey, W. Brantley, Jr., 9481
Harvey, Warren, 9481
Harvey, William D., 9742
Harward, Donald W., 6268
Harwell, Aubrey B., Jr., 8662
Harwell, Jonathan, 8708
Harwit Trust, Manya, 655
Harwit, Manya, 655
Harwit, Steven, 655
Harwood, Lisa Ivy, 3733
Hasan, Aliya Gull Khan, 1389
Hasan, Malik M., 1389
Hasan, Malika Asma Gull, 1389
Hasan, Seeme Gull Khan, 1389
Hasbro, Inc., 8539, 8540
Hasburg, Charles, 1603
Haseltine, William A., 6152
Haselwood, Lewis, Jr., 8583
Hasenfeld, Alexander, 6153
Hasenfeld, Zissy, 6153
Hasenfeld-Stein Inc., 6153
Hashimoto, Takeshi, 7120
Hashorva, Tanya, 8086
Haskell, David, 191
Haskell, Robert G., 970
Haskell, Robert H., 1844
Haskins, Lillian Escobar, 8494
Haslam, Anne S., 1231
Haslam, Cristen G., 8652
Haslam, Cynthia A., 8688
Haslam, James A., II, 8687
Haslam, James A., III, 8687, 8688
Haslam, Natalie L., 8687
Haslam, Susan B., 8688
Haslam, Susan W., 8688
Haslam, William E., 8652, 8687
Hasler, James A., 389
Haslinger, Benjamin G., 7664
Haslinger, Douglas S., 7664
Haslinger, Jennifer S., 7664
Haslinger, Kimberly M., 7664
Haslinger, Melissa A., 7664
Haslinger, Myriam Eve, 7664
Haslinger, Richard P., 4326
Haslinger, Sandra L., 7664
Hass, Thomas, 9442
Hassan, Parvez, 6389
Hassel, Calvin, 8237
Hassel, Morris, 8237
Hasselmo, Nils, 359
Hassenfeld Charitable Lead Trust, Stephen, 8540
Hassenfeld, Alan G., 8539, 8540
Hassenfeld, Sylvia K., 8540
Hasson, Eddie I., 9675
Hasten, Andrea, 2692

Hasten, Anna Ruth, 3163
Hasten, Bernard, 3162
Hasten, Edward, 3163
Hasten, Hart N., 3162
Hasten, James J., 2692
Hasten, Joseph, 4704
Hasten, Joshua, 3162
Hasten, Judith, 3163
Hasten, Mark, 3163
Hasten, Michael, 3163
Hasten, Simona, 3162
Hastings, Curtis F., 9910
Hastings, David R., II, 3551
Hastings, G. Richard, 3375
Hastings, George C., 1529
Hastings, Gordon H., 1505
Hastings, Joseph V., 6478
Hastings, Marcia, 78
Hastings, Peter G., 3551
Hatayama, Kuniki, 9836
Hatch, Augustus, 5833
Hatch, Bill, 560
Hatch, Francis W., 4036, 4120
Hatch, George, 4120
Hatch, Robert A., 9330
Hatch, Serena M., 4036, 4120
Hatcher, Claud A., 2462
Hatcher, Sally B., 2387
Hatcher, William K., 2462
Hateley, J. Michael, 942
Hatfield, Deborah, 656
Hatfield, J.R., 7965
Hatfield, Kenneth Wahl, 9161
Hatfield, Mark O., 8048
Hatfield, Michael, 656
Hatfield, Sandra, 9161
Hathaway, Catherine Gray, 9417
Hathaway, D.C., 8236
Hathaway, Derek C., 8293
Hathaway, Harry L., 693, 1052
Hathaway, Phillips, 3694
Hathaway, Ronald J., 368
Hattem, Gary S., 5854
Hatten, Steven P., 9731
Hattenhauer, John M., 9777
Hattersley, Scott T., 8141
Hattery, Max, 3215
Hattier, Robert L., 3483
Hattler, Denise M., 1825
Hattler, Hilary A., 1825
Hattler-Bramson, Andrea M., 1825
Hattman, David W., 3780
Hatton, Esther Marie, 7665
Hatton, Jay, 3138
Hatton, Katherine, 5265
Hatton, Kenneth, 7665
Hatton, Nikki C., 1169
Hatzfeldt, Hermann, 6190
Hauber, Charles G., 1427
Hauck, David P., 4828
Hauck, Edward C., 8417
Hauck, Frederick, 7666
Hauck, John C., 4828
Hauck, John M., 4828
Hauck, John W., 7666
Hauck, Oliver, 5400
Hauck, Steven J., 4828
Hauenstein, Karla, 4339
Hauenstein, Ralph, 4339
Hauer, Joe, 7519
Hauersperger, Joe, 3107
Hauge, Jennifer Chandler, 5247
Hauge, Rachel H., 836
Haugen, Richard, 2485
Haugen, Rick, 506, 512
Haught, Melvin, 3323
Haught, William, 156
Haugland, Alexander D., 8018, 9603
Haugland, Richard P., 8018, 9603
Haugland, Rosaria P., 8018, 9603
Hauke, Donald, 3122
Haun, Piaw, 5207
Hauptfuhrer, Robert P., 8095
Hauselt, Denise A., 5794

Hauser, Gustave M., 6155
Hauser, Judy, 3177
Hauser, Pierre, II, 5830
Hauser, Rita E., 6155
Hausler, Lisa M., 556
Hausmann, Carl L., 4792
Hausner, Stanley, 1155
Hauss, C.J., 1578
Hauswirth, Lisa Guggenhime, 788
Havard, Donald, 1813
Havard, Harris W., 1813
Havard, Joyce, 1813
Havard, Mary J., 1813
Havard, Stephanie, 1813
Havelin, Melanie, 823
Haveman, Robert, 4416
Havener, Janet W., 8474
Havens, Philip V., 3533
Haverlin, Robert, 5194
Haverty, J. Rhodes, 2394
Haverty, Michael R., 4842
Haviland Plastic Products Co., 7832
Haviland, Virginia, 3301
Hawaii Community Services Council,
   2547
Hawaii Institute for Integrative
   Healthcare Research, 2547
Hawaiian Commercial and Sugar Co.,
   2530
Hawaiian Electric Industries, Inc., 2546
Hawk, Malcolm, 1477
Hawker, Mary Stake, 4804
Hawkes, David, 3528
Hawkes, Mark S., 9325
Hawkins Construction Co., 4970
Hawkins Trust, Kathryn Ackley, 5036
Hawkins, Ann B., 8719
Hawkins, Barry C., 1537
Hawkins, Bruce E., 7583
Hawkins, Chaille W., 9212
Hawkins, Christopher R., 5674
Hawkins, David M., 3141
Hawkins, Edward L., 7444
Hawkins, Eliot D., 6757
Hawkins, Fred, Jr., 4970
Hawkins, Fred, Sr., 4970
Hawkins, Jeffrey A., 256
Hawkins, John F., 7103
Hawkins, Kim, 4970
Hawkins, Lauren, 3660
Hawkins, O. Mason, 8719
Hawkins, Prince A., 5036
Hawkins, Robert Z., 5036
Hawkins, Wendy, 8022
Hawkins, William, 2352
Hawkins, William H., II, 7587
Hawkins, Winsome, 2474
Hawks, Heather L., 4971
Hawks, Howard L., 4971
Hawks, Neal H., 4971
Hawks, Rhonda A., 4971
Hawks, Tom, 4971
Hawks, Troy T., 4971
Hawley, Anne, 5892
Hawley, James M., 1390
Hawley, MacDonald, 1390
Hawley, Patrick, 9776
Hawley, Philip M., 659
Hawn, Bruce Sams, 9163
Hawn, Gates, 5807
Hawn, Gates Helms, 5226, 5762
Hawn, Joe V., Jr., 8943
Hawn, Margaret, 8943
Hawn, Mary C., 8943
Hawn, Mildred, 8943
Hawn, Nancy E., 9163
Hawn, W.R., 8943
Hawn, William Russell, Jr., 8943
Hawthorn, Neal, 8851
Hawthorne Financial Corp. and Subs.,
   400
Hawthorne, Robert H., 9371
Hawthorne, Samuel, 9021
Haxton, Danielle A., 4100

Hay, Andrew MacKenzie, 7040
Hay, Donald, 2041
Hay, Dub, 9690
Hay, Gary W., 3351
Hay, James I., 2383
Hay, Jay, 3353
Hay, Kay, 3353
Hay, Lewis, III, 2010
Hay, Romona, 3247
Hay, Thomas S., 8386
Hayden, A.R., 2051
Hayden, Carl T., 5784
Hayden, Charles, 6158
Hayden, David S., 657
Hayden, Donald C., 2051
Hayden, George R., Jr., 4794
Hayden, James G., 3887
Hayden, Joanne, 4055
Hayden, John W., 7750
Hayden, Joseph P., III, 7750
Hayden, Lisa, 4055
Hayden, Marcia M., 657
Hayden, Patrick C., 863
Hayden, Richard M., 6157
Hayden, Stanley D., 657
Hayden, Stephen, 4055
Hayden, Susan F., 6157
Hayden, William B., 2768
Hayden, William R., 657
Hayden, William R., II, 657
Hayden, William R., Mrs., 657
Hayden, William T., 7263
Hayes Industrial Brake, Inc., 7554
Hayes Trust, Ella, 8701
Hayes, Arthur H., Jr., 6471
Hayes, Betty F., 3657
Hayes, Charles W., 818
Hayes, Christine P., 2052
Hayes, Denis, 483, 9563
Hayes, Derrick K., 3125
Hayes, Diane K., 1268
Hayes, Ella, 8672
Hayes, James D., 4589
Hayes, Jerome A., 2052
Hayes, Jim, 509
Hayes, Katherine D.R., 4589
Hayes, Linda Snyder, 8448
Hayes, Mariam C., 7335
Hayes, Mary B., 9760
Hayes, Merrick C., 3007
Hayes, Pam, 3160
Hayes, Patricia, 9238
Hayes, R.C., 7335
Hayes, Ralph W., 1700
Hayes, Richard, 205
Hayes, Rob, 3317
Hayes, Robin N., 7040
Hayes, Shaun, 4926
Hayes, Stephen L., 1252
Hayes, Synnova B., 5606
Hayes, Thomas E., 5336
Hayes, Timothy M., 3098
Hayes-Giles, Joyce, 4289
Haygood, Billy, 4746
Haygood, Paul, 3483
Haygood, Paul M., 3503
Hayling, Crystal, 296
Haylor, Jane T., 7877
Haymes, Robin, 7490
Haymond, George, 3185
Haymore, H.F., 9401
Haymore, Todd, 9531
Hayne, Margaret, 8239
Hayne, Richard A., 8239
Hayner, James K., 9559
Haynes, Anna Jo, 1364
Haynes, Harold J., 658
Haynes, John Randolph, 659
Haynes, John Randolph, Mrs., 659
Haynes, Joseph B., 2515
Haynes, Larry N., 8654
Haynes, Lawrence E., 8438
Haynes, Lukas, 6538
Haynes, Michael, 2448

Haynes, Norine, 9029
Haynes, Reta, 658
Haynes, W. Thomas, 2350
Haynesworth, Mason, 9419
Haynsworth, Knox, Jr., 8583
Hays, Carolyn, 9039
Hays, George, 7831
Hays, Mary Ann, 7689
Hays, Michael B., 7689
Hays, Preston, 2375
Hays, Thomas C., 7689
Hays, William H., III, 3835
Hays, William H., III, Mrs., 7224
Hayward, Homer M., 9327
Hayward, John T., 2053
Hayward, Nancy Eccles, 9327
Hayward, Nathan, III, Mrs., 1734
Hayward, Pierre duP., 1699
Hayward, Sophie, 1642
Hayward, Steven F., 2994
Hayward, Wendy A., 9327
Hayward, Winifred M., 2053
Hayworth, Carol Sue, 3115
Hayworth, Christine G., 8140
Hayworth, David, 7397
Hayworth, David R., 7351
Hazan, Morris A., 660
Hazan, Morris A., Jr., 660
Hazard, Elizabeth S., 8586
Hazard, Susan J., 790
Hazel, Joanne, 8047
Hazel, John T., 1823
Hazel, William A., Jr., 9435
Hazelett, Merilee, 8957
Hazelip, Harold, 8741
Hazelrigg, Charles R., 1398
Hazeltine, Carlie W., 1283
Hazen, Edward Warriner, 6160
Hazen, Elizabeth, 134
Hazen, Helen Russell, 6160
Hazen, Lucy Abigail, 6160
Hazlewood, Patsy, 8660
Hazzard, Shirley, 5548
HBI Financial Inc., 234
HCA Inc., 8690
HCA—The Healthcare Co., 8690
HCR Manor Care, Inc., 7667
Head, Beverly P., III, 40
Head, Deidra S., 866
Head, Hillery, 40
Head, Howard, 3644
Head, Marion Daniel, 31
Head, Martha, 1468, 3644
Head, Randy, 3115
Head, Sheila McBean, 866
Headley, Dorothy, 1931
Headley, Harry P., 1931
Heafy, Paul G., 7926
Heafy, Rhonda L., 7926
Heald, Catherine Maclellan, Mrs., 8704
Heald, Daryl, 8704
Heald, Edward S., 8521
Heald, Michael R., 9825
Heald, Otis P., 695
Healey, James P., 4211
Healey, Margaret S., 5227
Healey, Monica C., 3856
Healey, Robert K., 7782
Healey, Robert K., Jr., 7782
Healey, Robert K., Mrs., 7782
Healey, Roberta, 8348
Healey, Thomas J., 5227, 6826
Healey, Thomas Jeremiah, 5227
Health Care Services Corp., 2812
Health Net Corp., 350
Health Options, Inc., 1911
Health Plan Hawaii Foundation, 2547
Healthcare CEO Summit, 1248
Healy Family Foundation, M.A., Inc.,
   5479
Healy, David S., 7627
Healy, Edmund, 5479
Healy, James T., 1246
Healy, John "Mac", 7349

Healy, John R., 5574
Healy, Karen L., 4271
Healy, Kevin, 9068
Healy, Martha, 5468
Healy, Martha A., 5468
Heaney, John J., 1413
Heany, Mimi, 8191
Heard, Drew R., 9046
Heard, J. Garrett, IV, 1946
Hearin, Robert M., Jr., 4748
Hearin, Robert M., Sr., 4748
Hearin, William J., 37
Hearn, Thomas A., 2976
Hearne, Nancy S., 5366
Hearst, George R., Jr., 6161, 6162
Hearst, John R., Jr., 6161, 6162
Hearst, Margaret C., 1091
Hearst, William R., III, 1091, 6161, 6162
Hearst, William Randolph, 6161, 6162
Heart to Heart for Kids, Inc., 1426
Heartland Trust Co., 7514
Heast Corp., 7040
Heath, Charles K., 2587
Heath, Harriet A., 2587
Heath, John E.S., 2587
Heath, Josie, 1358
Heath, Karen, 4227, 6674
Heath, Robert F., 9765
Heath, Ruth, 7393
Heaton, Edward F., 475
Heaton, John R., 3250
Heaton, Mary Alice J., 4482
Heatwole, W. Michael, III, 9400
Heavin, Diane, 8945
Heavin, Gary, 8945
Hebert, Curt L., Jr., 3474, 4743
Hebert, Effie Mae, 8946
Hebert, Elizabeth, 9604
Hebert, Joe, 8946
Hebert, Raymond J., 3468
Hebert, Wilton P., 8946
Hecht, Alexander, 3645
Hecht, Margaret, 9542
Hecht, Michael, 6447, 7002
Hecht, Selma H., 3645
Heck, Gary, 3123
Heck, Julie Perry, 3217
Heck, Margaret Quirt, 9861
Heck, Mike, 9764
Heck, Otto, 628
Heckard, Tom, 3115
Heckert, Linda, 9780
Heckmann, Brock P., 6163
Heckmann, Mary M., 6163
Heckmann, Richard J., 6163
Heckmann, Scott M., 6163
Heckmann, Thomas R., 6163
Heckscher, August, 6164
Hedberg, Paul H., 5738
Heddens, B. Spencer, 4816
Hedges, James R., III, 8734
Hedges, Larry V., 6894
Hedinger, Barkley H., 8019
Hedinger, Blake H., 8019
Hedinger, Howard H., 8019
Hedrick, Janie, 9736
Heenan, David A., 2535
Heenan, Earl I., III, 4291
Heeney, Jason, 2823
Heer, Peg, 1642
Heerema, Bruce, 3292
Heerema, M. Timothy, 3292
Heerema, Sandy, 3292
Heerema, Steven, 3292
Heeschen, Paul, 487
Heeschen, Paul C., 957, 1293
Heeter, David, 3210
Heffelmire, Mike, 3137
Hefferline, Arline, 9650
Heffernan, E. Mary, 6633
Heffernan, William J., 2153
Hefni, Ibrahim, 4180
Hefni, Wensley, 4180

Heft, Sharon M., 2644
Hegarty, Kay L., 3275
Hegel, Garrett R., 28
Hegelund, Barbara, 4500
Hegg, William G., 1080
Heggie, Richard G., 474
Hegman, Kurt T., 9348
Hegwer, Mildred, 664
Hegwer, Raymond, 664
Heher, Garrett M., 5264
Hehir, Sara A., 2451
Hehir, Sara Armour, 2452
Hehl, D.K., 4368
Heide, Elizabeth C., 3945
Heide, Ulf B., 3945
Heidelburg, Joan C., 7886
Heider, Charles F., 4972
Heider, Jon, 7821
Heider, Mark J., 4972
Heider, Mary C., 4972
Heider, Scott C., 4972
Heidman, Richard, 7570
Heidrick, Clarke, 9184
Heidt, John M., 1261
Heidt, Julia Scripps, 7848
Heidtman Steel Products, Inc., 7540
Heikel, Barbara, 5017
Heiland, Donna, 7126
Heilbrum, Jeff, 9977
Heilbrunn Foundation, 6043
Heilbrunn, Robert, 5465, 7119
Heileman, Paula, 8807
Heileman, Paula L., 8806
Heilig, William W., 8444
Heilman, E. Bruce, 9506
Heim, Mark, 1123
Heiman, Gary, 7669, 7690
Heiman, Kim, 7669
Heiman/Fidelity Foundation, 1510
Heimbinder, Isaac, 7670
Heimbinder, Sheila, 7670
Heimbold, Charles A., Jr., 1566
Heimbold, Eric C., 1566
Heimbold, Joanna M., 1566
Heimbold, Leif C., 1566
Heimbold, Monika A., 1566
Heimbold, Peter, 1566
Heimerman, Quentin O., 4583
Hein, Edward H., 6125
Heine, Deborah, 7031
Heine, Lucilee, 2579
Heineman, Dannie N., 6165
Heineman, Greg, 8630
Heineman, Marilyn, 6165
Heineman, William M., 5840
Heineman-Morris, June, 6165
Heineman-Schur, Joan, 6165
Heinrich, Daniel J., 389
Heinrich, Tim, 9742
Heinsheimer, Alfred M., 6615
Heinsheimer, Louis A., 6615
Heintz, Paul C., 8378
Heintz, Stephen B., 6825
Heinz Co., H.J., 8240
Heinz III Charitable and Family Trust, H. John, 8243
Heinz III Charitable Trust, Teresa and H. John, 8243
Heinz, Andre, 8243
Heinz, Andre T., 8242
Heinz, Christopher, 8241
Heinz, Chuck, 9021
Heinz, Drue, 8241, 8244
Heinz, Elizabeth Rust, 8241
Heinz, H. John, IV, 8241
Heinz, Howard, 8241
Heinz, Kenneth G., 665
Heinz, Patricia B., 665
Heinz, Scott K., 665
Heinz, Teresa F., 8241, 8242, 8243
Heinz, Vira I., 8242
Heinze, Mona, 520
Heise, Kay, 4246
Heiskell, Marian S., 7095

Heisler, Clara, 6166
Heisler, Robert B., Jr., 7700
Heisler, Solomon, 6166
Heitmann, Kathryn, 4996
Heitz, Eric, 483
Heitz, Mark V., 3261
Heitzman, Joanna Hill, 7748
Hejna, JoAnn, 4895
Hekhscher, Martin A., 8395
Helber, Richard, 2040
Helbert, Patrick, 8814
Held, Huyler C., 4036, 6016, 6791
Held, Michael, 9185
Helder, Jeff, 4258
Heldman, Lou, 3404
Heldman, Paul, 1029, 7705, 8041
Helen Clay Frick Foundation, The, 8211
Helen, Suzanne L., 2118
Helfaer, Evan P., 9813
Helfgott, Michael, 1586
Helfman, Alan, 5228
Helfman, Helen, 2044
Helfman, Max, 2044
Helfrich, Thomas E., 7700
Helies, Brenda, 6348
Helis, Bettie Conley, 3486
Heller, Alfred, 666
Heller, Anne C., 7301
Heller, Benjamin, 6168
Heller, Carol Joy, 6955
Heller, Clarence E., 666
Heller, David B., 6169
Heller, Desiree, 4623
Heller, Fanny, 6168
Heller, Fanya, 6168
Heller, Francie, 6512
Heller, H. William, 1948
Heller, Jacqueline, 6168
Heller, Jordan, 6010
Heller, Lawrence H., 601
Heller, Lesley, 2080
Heller, Miranda, 666
Heller, Robert M., 6169
Heller, Ruth, 666
Heller, Tobias, 6167
Hellman, Daryl A., 3886
Hellman, Deb, 3230
Hellman, F. Warren, 667, 7274
Hellman, Judith, 667
Hellman, Marco, 667
Hellman, Patricia C., 667, 7274
Hellman, Peter S., 7781
Hellman, Sabrina, 667
Hellman, Warren, 250
Hellwig, John, 225
Helm, Cyrus Vard, 8947
Helm, Glora Bee, 8947
Helm, Harold, 5230
Helm, John C., 8027
Helm, John R., 5230
Helm, Peyton R., 8303
Helm, Robert J., 4879
Helm, Susan, 8947
Helman, Frank G., 7211
Helmer, Michael, 5417
Helmerich, Hans, 7984
Helmerich, Matthew, 1949
Helmerich, W.H., 7942
Helmerich, Walter H., III, 7942
Helmholz, Carl, 9623
Helmholz, Elizabeth, 9623
Helmken, John C., II, 2480
Helmly, Robert L., 8593
Helms, Ann Marie, 8346
Helms, Gates McG, 5343
Helms, Michael, 436
Helms, Michael L., 505
Helmsley Enterprises, Inc., 6170
Helmsley, Harry B., 6171
Helmsley, Leona M., 6170, 6171
Helmuth, Paul J., 7857
Helow, George A., 2055
Helow, Joseph P., 2055
Helow, Margaret O., 2055

Helpenstell, Sus, 2570
Helps, Robert Eugene, 5789
Helsell, Christine, 9677
Helsell, Frank P., 9677
Helsell, Peter F., 9677
Helsell, Virginia S., 9677
Helsell, William A., 9677
Helseth, Nancy L., 8009
Helsom, Frank E., 1941
Helstrom, Brian L., 9605
Helstrom, Carl, 6263, 6547
Helstrom, Carl O., 8607
Helstrom, Norris, 9605
Helstrom, Robert L., 9605
Helstrom, Yvonne E., 9605
Heltner, Don, 3019
Helton, Audwin A., 3414
Heltzer, James R., 4613
Helvie, Todd, 2372
Helzberg, Barnett C., III, 4829
Helzberg, Barnett C., Jr., 4829
Helzberg, Bush C., 4829
Helzberg, Shirley B., 4829
Hembree, R. Michael, 2437
Hemenway, Robert E., 4824
Heminger, G.R., 9028
Heminger, Karl I., 7627
Hemingway, Ann, 9328
Hemingway, Henry S., 9328
Hemingway, Richard Keith, 9328
Hemingway, Shirley Stranquist, 9328
Hemingway, Susan G., 9606
Hemmady, Gokul V., 4496
Hemme, Dennis, 2670
Hemmelstein, J., 2652
Hemmelstein, Julius, 2652
Hemmer, J. Michael, 5012
Hemmerdinger, H. Dale, 6779
Hemmings, Ira L., Jr., 3422
Hemphill, Ronnie L., 5467
Hemphill, Ross F., 1632
Hempstead, David M., 4254, 4300, 4301, 4302, 4303, 4304, 4305, 4306, 4308, 4353, 4434, 4485
Hemrick, Christine F., 524
Hemsley, Barbara K., 4542
Hemsley, Matthew S., 4542
Hemsley, Stephen J., 4542
Hench Family Living Trust A, 668
Hench Family Living Trust B, 668
Hench, John C., 668
Hench, Lowry, 668
Hendee, Brett, 2272
Hendel, Myron, 6172
Hendel, Ruth, 6172
Hendel, Stephen, 6172
Henderson, Allen Douglas, 2056
Henderson, Barbara K., 2056
Henderson, Barclay, 3946
Henderson, Benson G., 1811
Henderson, Darryl K., 7423
Henderson, David, 562
Henderson, Dink, 2015
Henderson, Ernest, 3946
Henderson, Ernest, III, 3946
Henderson, Eugene L., 3109
Henderson, George B., 3946
Henderson, Gordon, 9796
Henderson, Helen Lee, 1811
Henderson, Helen Ruth, 1811
Henderson, Jack D., 1356
Henderson, James D., II, 5090
Henderson, James O., II, 5090
Henderson, Lenneal, 3595
Henderson, Linda E., 9371
Henderson, Lucia, 2056
Henderson, Patrick, 9998
Henderson, Phillip, 7103
Henderson, Rhoe B., III, 6009
Henderson, Robert, 3581
Henderson, Scot, 1029, 8041
Henderson, Scott, 7705
Henderson, Todd, 3581
Henderson, Troy, 3581

Henderson, Virginia, 9797
Hendler, Lee M., 3691, 3692
Hendrick Automotive Group, 7395
Hendrick Motorsports, Inc., 7395
Hendrick, Jenny, 7931
Hendrick, Paul A., 7886
Hendrick, William A., 4483
Hendricks, Ben F., 2468
Hendricks, Diane, 9757
Hendricks, Gaynell, 52
Hendricks, John S., 3647
Hendricks, Maureen D., 3647
Hendricks, Ronald N., 6428
Hendrickson, D. Hunt, 3598
Hendrickson, Douglas, 3425
Hendrickson, John T., 4410
Hendrickson, Kathryn B., 7811
Hendrickson, Stephen J., 3947
Hendrickson, Virginia, 2796
Hendrickson, William G., 134
Hendrie, Gardner C., 3862
Hendrix, Adelia R., 60
Hendrix, Dennis R., 9273
Hendrix, Doug, 7354
Hendrix, Frances, 8691
Hendrix, Harville, 6994
Hendrix, James, 8691
Hendrix, Jim, 7344
Hendrix, Lynn P., 1400
Hendrix, Tanya, 984
Hendry, Barbara, 9020
Hendry, Michelle Smith, 9192
Hendry, Richard, 8581
Henduson, Lauce, 1158
Heneberry, J. Dawn, 9390
Heneghan, Bartly, 5877
Heneghan, Eileen, 5878
Heneghan, John A., 5877
Heneghan, Kevin, 5878
Heneghan, Kevin J., 5877, 5878
Heneke, Thomas L., 3267
Heneveld, Ed, 1244
Hengel, Nancy, 9909
Henigson, David T., 5624
Heningburg, Gustav, 5199
Heninger, George, 1529
Henke, Bradley F., 9666
Henke, Mark, 4912
Henkel, John R., 813
Henkel, Oliver C., Jr., 7917
Henkels & McCoy, Inc., 8245
Henkels, Barbara B., 8245
Henkels, Christopher B., 8245
Henkels, Paul M., 8245
Henkels, Paul M., Jr., 8245
Henley Group, Inc., The, 1194
Henley Manufacturing, Inc., 1194
Henley, A.B., 7397
Henline, Carson S., 7475
Henn, Carol Dean, 8303
Henn, Fritz, 5652
Henn, Mike, 1187
Henneman, Jack, 5251
Hennessee, David C., 8958
Hennessey, Frank M., 4343
Hennessey, Kevin, 1944
Hennessy, Carol, 2921
Hennessy, Marilyn, 2964
Hennessy, Michael W., 2673
Hennessy, S.P., 7855
Henney, Jane E., 5750, 5779
Hennig, Ruth G., 4036
Henning, Don V., 9801
Henning, Peter H., 2680
Henning, Ruth G., 5614
Henning, Tom, 4987
Hennion, Lynn, 8049
Henretty, P.B., 8889
Henrich, Martin, 6640
Henrich, William J., 8308
Henrickson, Ronald J., 311
Henrikson, C. Robert, 6542
Henrotin Hospital, 3058
Henry, Brent L., 1844

Henry, Brian L., 9794
Henry, C. Wolcott, III, 1808, 1837
Henry, Cathe, 2158
Henry, D.F., 2301
Henry, Esther Helis, 3486
Henry, Frederick B., 1346, 5550
Henry, Frederick B., Jr., 1346
Henry, George F., III, 7342
Henry, H. Alexander, 1808, 1837
Henry, Hayden, 7979
Henry, Jack, 4961
Henry, Kim, 7974
Henry, Leland W., 7547
Henry, Mary, 6875
Henry, Merton G., 3553, 3556
Henry, Nancy Cummings, 1808
Henry, Patricia, 9640
Henry, Peter A., Col., 9490
Henry, Ragan, 1505
Henry, Robert, Hon., 7931
Henry, Scott, 8317
Henry, Shirley Gee, 8944
Henry, Susan Hough, 2066
Henry, Susie, 4798, 4869
Henry-Keller, Piper, 9640
Hensel, Nancy, 2696
Henseler, Gerald A., 9776
Hensey, Susan, 3360
Henshaw, G. Tyler, 5082
Henske, Robert B., 696
Hensleigh, Inez M., 2890
Hensler, Bill, 3127
Hensley, Nisa, 3107
Henson, Jackson W., 7459
Henson, Richard A., 3648
Hensyn, Inc., 5394
Hentgen, Steve, 3132
Hentz, Kathryn Iacocca, 3963
Heras-De Leon, M.L. Luli, 1252
Herberger Revocable Trust, G.R., 106
Herberger, G.R., 87, 106
Herberger, G.R., Mrs., 106
Herberger, Gary K., 106
Herberger, Judd R., 106
Herbert, Benjamin, 6124
Herbert, Bruce, 4246
Herbert, Dale M., 5
Herbert, Elizabeth, 9604
Herbert, Gavin, Sr., 272
Herbert, Georgia H., 9480
Herbert, James H., II, 1088
Herbert, Kathleen, 3503
Herbert, Mickey, 1504
Herbert, Mike, 3354
Herbert, Peter A., 6124
Herbst, Ann Colin, 6024
Herbst, Cristie L., 5738
Herbst, David A., 645
Herbst, Herman H., 669
Herbst, Jay A., 9600
Herbst, Linda Vitti, 1442
Herbst, Maurice H., 669
Herbst, Solomon, Rabbi, 5928
Herd, Amy D., 8569
Herd, Bob L., 8948
Herd, Patsy L., 8948
Herd, Tevis, 8749, 8895
Herda, Sarah, 2767
Herder, Charles H., 8916
Herdman, Vernita, 79
Herdrich, Donald J., 6173
Herdrich, Frances I., 6173
Heritage Partners, 5014
Heritage Trust Co., 7922, 7977
Herland, Joyce, 7073
Herlihy, Edward D., 7205
Herlin, Cara P., 9240
Herlin, Jean T., 9240
Herlin, Susan, 9240
Herma, John E., 9814
Herma, Susan M., 9814
Herman Furniture Co., 4393
Herman, Catherine W., 9542
Herman, Charlotte, 6174

Herman, Gloria, 8944
Herman, Irving, 1111
Herman, Mary, 8768
Herman, Ronald D., 3282
Herman, Russ, 3497
Herman, Tom, 663
Hermance, Frank S., 8081
Hermann Charitable Remainder Trust 2000, Francoise, 3948
Hermann, Diana P., 6917
Hermann, Francoise, 3948
Hermann, Grover M., 2798
Hermann, Richard, 3071
Hermann, William M., 4254
Hermanson, Everett J., 3300
Hermocillo, Jose, 1151
Hermundslie, Carol, 107
Hermundslie, Gerold D., 107
Hernandez, Antonia, 345, 6826
Hernandez, Carlos, 5359
Hernandez, Colleen, 1793
Hernandez, Diego E., VADM., 3511
Hernandez, Gladys, 1578
Hernandez, John, 3471
Hernandez, Robert, 8073
Hernandez, Sandra R., 1088
Hernandez, Silvia, 1177
Hernandez, William H., 8394
Herndon, David, 26
Herndon, John E., Jr., 9401
Herndon, Mardie R., Jr., 2358
Herndon, Sue, 1295
Hero, Peter, 406
Heroes Celebrity Baseball, 9068
Herold, H. Robert, II, 5351
Herold, Jill M., 3828
Herold, Matthew G., Jr., 5351
Heron, James H., 4711
Herr Foods, Inc., 8246
Herr, Edwin, 8246
Herr, Gene, 8246
Herr, James M., 8246
Herr, James S., 8246
Herr, Miriam, 8246
Herr, Philip C., II, 7341, 8230
Herrada, Leonardo, 8208
Herrell, John E., 239
Herren, Mark, 3437
Herrera, Sharon Hays, 9045
Herres, Rebecca Gilbreth, 8603
Herrick Corp., 663
Herrick, Anne, 1465
Herrick, Hazel M., 4341
Herrick, Kent B., 4341
Herrick, Ray W., 4341
Herrick, Todd W., 4341
Herrick, William J., 1031
Herrick-Pacific Corp., 663
Herrin, Judy, 1940
Herring, Albert Lee, 7396
Herring, Gordon, 8583
Herring, James, 8758
Herring, Kay, 3333
Herring, Leonard G., 7396
Herring, Paula, 9049
Herring, Rozelia S., 7396
Herrington, Marilyn A., 6207
Hermann, David S., 9298
Hermann, Karen H., 9298
Hermann, Lesley S., 6030
Hermann, Lois, 5603
Hermann, Ronald J., 9298
Herro, David, 2799
Herron, Mary, 979
Herschede, Allison, 7913
Herschede, Holly, 7913
Herschend, Bruce, 4830
Herschend, Dianna, 4830
Herschend, Jack R., 4830
Herschend, James R., 4830
Herschend, Ronald J., 4830
Herschend, Sherry J., 4830
Herscher, Uri D., 6999
Hersh Foundation, 5302

Hersh, Ahron, 6177
Hersh, Christopher K., 9499
Hersh, Dorothy B., 2058
Hersh, Toby, 6177
Hershberg, Elliot M., 5272
Hershey Trust Co., 8208
Hershey, Barry J., 3949
Hershey, Connie, 3949
Hershey, John, Jr., 3600
Hershey, Loren W., 7671
Hershey, Margaret J., 2103
Hershey, Mark, 8265
Hershey, Roy M., 5782
Hershiser, Jamie, 2131
Hershiser, Orel, 2131
Hershmann, Valerie, 2000
Herskovits, David, 886
Herson, Richard J.L., 3819
Herst, Dean W., 138
Hertel, Kristen, 2983
Hertel, Ronald L., Sr., 1264
Herterich, Karyn Kennedy, 2087
Hertneky, Bill, 1359
Hertog, Roger, 7140
Hertz, Debra, 1628
Hertz, Douglas J., 2412
Hertz, Fannie K., 670
Hertz, Jennings M., Jr., 2412
Hertz, John D., 670
Hertz, Richard, 5496
Hertz, Seymour, 5835
Hertzberg, Jill, 1794
Herz, Debra, 1445
Herz, Sandy, 1158
Herzan, Alexandra, 7191
Herzan, Alexandra A., 5577
Herzan, Paul K., 5577
Herzfeld, Ethel D., 9815
Herzfeld, Richard P., 9815
Herzka, Judy, 6885
Herzka, Ralph, 6885
Herzog, Aaron, 5202
Herzog, Arie, 6112
Herzog, David, 5202
Herzog, Eleanor W., 3999
Herzog, Eli, 5202
Herzog, Gary, 5202
Herzog, Herman, 5202
Herzog, James, 3999
Herzog, Joseph, 5202
Herzog, Kim, 4537
Herzog, Kurt, 381
Herzog, Michael, 5202
Herzog, Michael B., 5202
Herzog, Mordechai, 5202
Herzog, Morris, 5202
Herzog, Nathan, 5202
Herzog, Phillip, 5202
Herzog, Robert, 5202
Herzstein, Albert H., 8949
Herzstein, Ethel Avis, 8949
Herzstein, Stanley, 774, 775
Heselden, John E., 9424
Heselton, George W., 3536
Hess, Donald, 38, 61
Hess, Donald T., 9068
Hess, Gail, 9761
Hess, Gregory L., 1942
Hess, Heidi C., 38
Hess, James, 7533
Hess, Jerry, 2565
Hess, John B., 5231
Hess, Judy G., 3161
Hess, Leon, 5231
Hess, Lisa, 6092
Hess, Mandy L., 9763
Hess, Mark, 9761
Hess, Marlene, 5231
Hess, Milton, 9761
Hess, Myrtle E., 9816
Hess, Norma, 5231
Hess, Ronne, 38
Hess, Timothy C., 9521
Hessberg, Sally, 1947

Hesse, Frank, 792
Hessert, Nancy, 9777
Hession, Cathleen Collins, 397
Hesskett, Jimmy, 417
Hessler, David J., 7692
Hessler, Deborah J., 1922
Hessley, Bernard J., 8154
Hesslink, Geoffrey, 9356
Hestand Trust, Magalou W., 9024
Hester, James M., 6397
Hester, Mary Coleman, 76
Hester, Phillip, 2458
Hester, Richard, 779
Heter, Roberta, 1093
Hetherington, Karen, 5484
Hettinger Foundation, 6264
Hettinger, Albert J., Jr., 6178
Hettinger, Betty, 6178
Hettinger, Corina, 6178
Hettinger, John, 6178, 6264
Hettinger, William R., 6178
Hetzel, Katherine, 2279
Hetzler, Robert, 4229
Heubusch, John D., 1275
Heuck-Diekroeger, Angie, 9778
Heuer, Michael A., 7530
Heuer, Russell P., Jr., 1720
Heuermann, B. Keith, 4973
Heuermann, Bernard K., 4973
Heuermann, Norma F., 4973
Heuffner, Peggy, 9219
Heun, Robert, 5638
Heuschele, Richard, 4483
Hewett, Christopher, 1426
Hewit, Betty Ruth, 1391
Hewit, Randi, 5784
Hewit, William D., 1391
Hewitt, Bradford, 9949
Hewitt, Conrad, 741
Hewitt, Gary M., 9884
Hewitt, Louis, 5262
Hewitt, Mark, 4637
Hewitt, Robert J., 9094
Hewitt, Robert J., Jr., 9094
Hewlett Foundation, 1058
Hewlett Foundation, William and Flora,
    The, 359, 483
Hewlett, Bill, 521
Hewlett, Elizabeth, 3548
Hewlett, Flora Lamson, 521, 671
Hewlett, John H., III, 8141
Hewlett, Walter, 521
Hewlett, Walter B., 671, 973
Hewlett, William, 521
Hewlett, William R., 671
Hewlett-Packard Co., 672
Hews, Kenneth H., 3525
Heyano, Nina Miller, 79
Heyde, Lee, 3185
Heydon, Henrietta M., 4398
Heydon, Peter N., 4398
Heyert, Martin, 9536
Heyler, David B., Jr., 864
Heylin, Martha, 2923
Heyman, Annette, 1567
Heyman, Barbara G., 7936, 7941
Heyman, Joseph S., 7639
Heyman, Kenneth, 5228
Heyman, Ronnie F., 1567
Heyman, Samuel J., 1567
Heyman, Stephen, 6615
Heyman, Stephen J., 7936
Heyman, T.J., 1358
Heymann, Andrew W., 5926
Heymann, Jerry, 3487
Heymann, Jimmy, 3487
Heymann, Jimmy, Mrs., 3487
Heymann, Jonas John, 3487
Heymann, Leon, 3487
Heymann, Leon, Mrs., 3487
Heymann, Marjorie, 3487
Heymann, Peter E., 4725
Heyneman, John, 4937
Heyward, Elisabeth C., 3548

Heyward, Jenifer, 6179
Hi-Rollers Sportswear, 5420
Hiam, Alexander W., 4201
Hiam, Robert P., 2547
Hiatt, Amy R., 3766
Hiatt, Arnold, 4036, 4171
Hiatt, Arnold S., 3766
Hiatt, Frances L., 3989
Hiatt, Howard, 4120
Hiatt, Jacob, 3989
Hiatt, Jane, 4737
Hiatt, Matthew T., 3766
Hiatte, P.D., 2644
Hibara, Shoji, 9476
Hibben, Seabury J., 2993
Hibberd, William F., 6882
Hibbitts, Louis L., Jr., 9498
Hibel, Andy, 2922
Hibernia National Bank, 9263
Hickey, Deborah, 9779
Hickey, Francis G., Jr., 108
Hickey, James H., 252
Hickey, John W., 9781
Hickey, Kevin, 8928
Hickey, Mark, 1267
Hickey, Robert A., 9486
Hickman, David S., 4376
Hickman, Dewey, 2411
Hickman, Paula H., 3469
Hickok, Jeffrey, 5091
Hickok, Katharine Pauley, 9494
Hickok, Mary B., 1706
Hickox, Charles V., Mrs., 5600
Hickox, Danielle, 2007
Hickox, Danielle A., 5600
Hickox, John B., 5600
Hicks, Ann C., 2059
Hicks, Carol Siyahi, 7603
Hicks, Daniel, 2075
Hicks, David M., 2059
Hicks, Doris L., 7488
Hicks, Duval Q., Jr., 9423
Hicks, Elise Goldsmith, 8682
Hicks, Frederick L., 1941
Hicks, James N., 10
Hicks, Jennifer I., 3009
Hicks, John E., Jr., 3009
Hicks, Lee S., 8572
Hicks, Linda, 8208
Hicks, Michael E., 7789
Hicks, Ricky, 1426
Hicks, Robert E., 2403
Hicks, Stephen L., 474
Hicks, Thomas O., 9083
Hickson, Janet, 4737
Hidalgo, Diego, 6743
Hidary & Co., M., Inc., 6181
Hidary Co., M., Inc., 6182
Hidary, Abraham B., 6182
Hidary, Abraham J., 6181
Hidary, David J., 6182
Hidary, Isaac, 6182
Hidary, Jack A., 6181
Hidary, Jacob I., 6182
Hidary, Morris, 6181
Hidchenko, Nicolas A., 778
Hieber, Carl O., 8387
Hiedtke, Brian, 6219
Hield, James, 4722
Hieronimus, Jill M., 3691
Hiersteiner, Joseph L., 4837
Hiestand, N. Lynn, 6998
Hietbrink, Larry, 2256
Higbee, Alan, 2147
Higgins, Alexander, 5207
Higgins, Arabella Bartner, 9362
Higgins, Brian J., 6325
Higgins, Gloria J., 1397, 1418
Higgins, John, 8015
Higgins, Julie, 7872
Higgins, Kathy, 7319
Higgins, Pam, 3132
Higgins, Robert F., 1557
Higgins, Sharon, 1373

Higgins-Jacob, Coleen P., 6119
Higginson, Corina, 3649
Higginson, Cornelia W., 5553
Higgs, Elizabeth C., 1926
Higgs, John H., 6562
High Point Safety and Management
    Corp., 4085
Highfield, Luz, 9364
Highland Homes, 8818
Highley, Randall M., 2949
Highmark Inc., 8247
Hightower, Ben W., 2251
Hightower, Dennis, 4795, 9566
Hightower, George H., Jr., 2354
Hightower, H. Wayne, 8884
Hightower, H. Wayne, Jr., 8884
Hightower, Julian T., 2354
Hightower, Neil H., 2354
Hightower, Neil H., Jr., 2354
Hightower, W. Price, 39
Hightower, Walter H., 8950
Hightower, William H., IV, 2354
Higley, Stephen S., 7536
Hiiggins, Brian J., 6325
Hilb, Rogal and Hamilton Co., 9439
Hilbert, Robert J., 1374
Hilbert, Stephen C., 3167
Hilbert, Tomisue S., 3167
Hilbert, William M., 8188
Hilboldt, James S., 1081, 4241, 4415
Hilbrich, Gerald F., 1922
Hildebrand, Dean, 7520
Hildebrand, Georgene, 4253
Hildebrand, Jeffrey D., 8951
Hildebrand, John G., 3931
Hildebrand, Melinda B., 8951
Hildebrandt, A. Thomas, 5833
Hildebrandt, Austin E., 5833
Hildebrandt, Leslie, 4217
Hildebrandt, Mary, 5833
Hildebrandt, Troy G., 9908
Hildestad, Terry D., 7517
Hildner, Katherine K., 5726
Hildreth, Bonnie, 4227
Hildreth, Horace, 3548
Hildt, Dorothy Tremaine, 1662
Hiler, Margaret F., 3247
Hilf, Peter, 842
Hilfiger U.S.A., Tommy, Inc., 6183
Hilfiger, Susan D., 5235
Hilfiger, Thomas J., 5235
Hilfiker, Alan, 2226
Hilgeman, Thomas F., 4831
Hilger, Andy, 4534
Hilger, D. William, 1243
Hilgers, Paul, 9294
Hilibrand, Deborah Z., 6184
Hilibrand, Lawrence E., 6184
Hilkemeyer, Gilbert, 4898
Hilker, Donald G., 2218
Hilker, Georgeanne B., 4624
Hill Trust, A. Copeland, 2067
Hill, Allen E., 2503
Hill, Allen M., 7604
Hill, Amy Bacon, 1340
Hill, Ann Onstead, 9102
Hill, Arthur B., 1809
Hill, Bill, 9132
Hill, Bill J., 8783
Hill, Calynne, 1945
Hill, Cathy, 8881
Hill, Charles E., 9552
Hill, Charlotte Bishop, 6645
Hill, Connie Wilson, 934
Hill, David, 936
Hill, David K., Sr., 7951
Hill, Dennis A., 4347
Hill, Douglas E., 4838
Hill, E. Eldred, 6423
Hill, Elizabeth A., Sr., 6229
Hill, Gene, 2360
Hill, George R., 7725
Hill, Gerald K., 7444
Hill, Grace, 4082

Hill, Harvey, 5088
Hill, J. Edwin, 1477
Hill, J. Jerome, 4595
Hill, James A., Jr., 8048
Hill, John P., 5475
Hill, Jonathan A., Sr., 7446
Hill, Joseph C., 3413
Hill, Julie, 957
Hill, Karra Mays, 9036
Hill, Katherine E., 4579
Hill, Katherine P., 9128
Hill, Kay, 7951
Hill, Lindan, 3126
Hill, Louis F., 4579
Hill, Louis Fors, 4636
Hill, Louis Shea, 4579
Hill, Louis W., Jr., 4579
Hill, Louis W., Sr., 4636
Hill, Luther L., Jr., 3279
Hill, Margaret M., 6185
Hill, Margy, 2701
Hill, Marion, 936
Hill, Mary Jane, 7612
Hill, Mary Jo Gheens, 3421
Hill, Maud, 4636
Hill, Melissa, 8667
Hill, Michael, 8531
Hill, Norris, 8667
Hill, Pamela, 6645
Hill, Peter, 4534
Hill, Ralph, 7989
Hill, Robert W., 8027
Hill, Scott, 4376, 4579
Hill, Shirley, 5236
Hill, Steve, 4257
Hill, Steven K., 2356
Hill, Suzanne, 6645
Hill, Thomas A., 7951
Hill, Thomas J., 4557
Hill, Tom, 7951
Hill, Vernon W., II, 5236
Hill, Virginia W., 1392
Hill, W. Inge, Jr., 20
Hill, William W., 7534
Hill-Scott, Karen, 5971
Hillan, Kathy, 1016
Hillard, Beulah H., 7509
Hillblom, Larry L., 673
Hillblom, Terry C., 673
Hillblom, Walter, 673
Hille, Jo Bob, 7943
Hille, Mary Ann, 7943
Hillegass, George W., 2408
Hillegonds, Paul, 4289
Hillegonds, Paul C., 4367
Hillenbrand, Carol, 2060
Hillenbrand, Gretchen, 8624
Hillenbrand, Heidi, 8624
Hillenbrand, Justin, 2060
Hillenbrand, Margaret, 8624
Hillenbrand, Michael R., 2060
Hillenbrand, Ray, 8624
Hillenbrand, W. August, 7604
Hiller, Anatol, 5237
Hiller, David, 2663
Hiller, Lisa G., 9749
Hiller, Pnina, 5237
Hiller, William T., 7688
Hillgren, Gregory R., 1031
Hillhouse, John M., 4896
Hilliard, Dozier, 2094
Hilliard, Ethele, 8638
Hilliard, Herbert H., 8732
Hilliard, Thomas J., Jr., 8130
Hilliard-Smith, Emlee, 2922
Hilliker, Don, 2589
Hillis, Jennifer Friedman, 2014
Hillis, Robert, 4962
Hillis, W. Daniel, 670
Hillman & Sons Co., J.H., 8249
Hillman Charitable Lead Trust, Henry
    Lea, 8205, 8251, 8252, 8442
Hillman Land Co., 8249
Hillman, Alex L., 6186

Hillman, Anne, 3131
Hillman, David McL., 8130
Hillman, Elsie H., 8249
Hillman, Gaytha, 9963
Hillman, Henry L., 8249, 8250
Hillman, Henry Lea, Jr., 8252
Hillman, John Hartwell, Jr., 8249
Hillman, M. Scott, 2303
Hillman, Maggie, 1463
Hillman, Rita K., 6186
Hillman, William Talbott, 8251
Hills, Dave, 2577
Hills, Edward E., 674
Hills, Ingrid von Mangoldt, 674
Hills, Reuben W., III, 674
Hillyard, Gerald R., Jr., 1398
Hillyard, Steven J., 9703
Hillyer, Blair A., 7890
Hillyer, Kevin, 984
Hilory, Bonnie B., 9599
Hilsheimer, Cindy, 7775
Hilsheimer, Lawrence A., 1527
Hilt, George, 4252
Hilt, Jack, 4252
Hilt, John, 4252
Hilt, Meredith, 3034
Hilton Foundation, Charles and Lela, 2061
Hilton, Barron, 5037
Hilton, Charles, 2061
Hilton, Conrad N., 5037
Hilton, Conrad N., III, 5037
Hilton, Eric M., 5037
Hilton, Lela, 2061
Hilton, R. Robertson, 7742
Hilton, Steven M., 5037
Hilton, William B., Jr., 5037
Hiltz, Francie S., 7658, 7842
Hiltz, L. Thomas, 7658, 7842
Himmelman, Bonnie, 3627
Himmelreich, David, 1540
Himonetos, Stella, 1992
Hinchman, S.B., 9028
Hinck, John, 4724
Hinckley, Alonzo A., 9350
Hinderaker, Irving, 8631
Hindery, Leo J., Jr., 1362
Hindle, David, 4194
Hindley, Donald, 836
Hindlian, Richard, 3877
Hindman, James, 9164
Hinds County Workforce Investment Network, 4757
Hinduja Family Foundation, 3952
Hinduja Trust, 3952
Hinduja, G.P., 3952
Hinduja, P.P., 3952
Hinduja, S.P., 3952
Hines, Glynn A., 3125
Hines, Jenny L., 8671
Hines, Judith Randal, 9480
Hines, Kathleen, 3897
Hines, Leslie D., Jr., 7339
Hines, R. Ken, 9039
Hines, Robert S., 6668
Hines, Susan, 2041
Hing, Gerald, 351
Hingst, Bob, 3126
Hingst, Dave, 4962
Hinitz, Connie M., 7690
Hinkle, Janet, 1945
Hinman, Mark F., 7076
Hinnant, Patrice A., 7343
Hinojosa, Andrea, 2411
Hinojosa, Fausto, 537
Hinrichs, Charles, Mr., 4906
Hinrichs, Jerry, 4968
Hinshaw, Carol, 3253
Hinshaw, Edward, 9815
Hinson, J.A., 2168
Hinson, Ronnie, 9902
Hinson, Wilson, 1945
Hintz, Melvin A., 9861
Hinz, Lila, 675

Hinz, Roland, 675
Hipp, Kevin, 7139
Hipp, Michael J., 9908
Hipp, W. Hayne, 8592, 8597
Hippler, Thomas, 8463
Hipwell, Arthur P., 3428
Hirabayashi, Shinichi, 6561
Hirano, Irene Y., 4367, 5970
Hirose, Masaaki, 9836
Hirrel, Richard J., 247
Hirrel, Tracy G., 247
Hirsch, Bradford, 8953
Hirsch, Bruce A., 666
Hirsch, Daria Lee, 8953
Hirsch, David, 196, 2800, 8516
Hirsch, David M., 8551
Hirsch, Douglas A., 6187
Hirsch, Edward, 6119
Hirsch, Esther, 2800
Hirsch, Hope L., 8516
Hirsch, John B., 1779
Hirsch, Laurence, 8953
Hirsch, Neil S., 6188
Hirsch, Paul, 2800
Hirsch, Richard, 2800
Hirsch, Robert, 2800
Hirsch, Sanford, 6080
Hirsch, Steven R., 1779
Hirsch, Susan, 8953
Hirsch, Wayne, 4931, 4932
Hirschbiel, Paul O., Jr., 9484
Hirschbiel, Susan, 9532
Hirschfeld, Arlene, 1445
Hirschfeld, Benjamin G., 4974
Hirschfeld, Daniel J., 4974
Hirschfeld, Monya A., 4974
Hirschfield, Alan, 9977
Hirschfield, Ira S., 637
Hirschhorn, Barbara B., 3575, 3650
Hirschhorn, Daniel B., 3650
Hirschhorn, David, 3650
Hirschhorn, Gina B., 3575
Hirschhorn, Michael J., 3575, 3650
Hirschi, John, 9280
Hirschl, Irma T., 1721
Hirschman, Esther, 3751
Hirschman, Orin Z., 3751
Hirschtick, Jon K., 3953
Hirschtick, Melissa H., 3953
Hirsh, Alexandra, 1779
Hirsh, Barry, 1204
Hirsh, Georgina, 1779
Hirsh, Jerry, 87
Hirsh, Jill, 3032
Hirt, Arthur J., 5329
Hirth, Ana, 598
Hirth, Emanuel, 598
Hirtzel, Beatrice Dewey, 8253
Hirtzel, Orris C., 8253
His Way Homes, 4770
Hissong, Robert E., 9755
Hitachi, Ltd., 1810
Hitch, Henry H., 5111
Hitchcock Trust, Eleanor H., 2801
Hitchcock, Holly, 1530
Hitchcock, Martha H., 4975
Hite, Ruth Joyce, 9018
Hites, Raymond D., 4831
Hitt, John C., 2303
Hittman, Fred, 3651
Hittman, Judith E., 3651
Hittman, Sandra, 3651
Hittman, Stephen J., 3651
Hittner, Barry G., 8518
Hitz, David, 676
Hitz, Yen, 676
Hix, Steve, 9570
Hixon, Adelaide F., 202
Hixon, Alexander P., 202, 3764
Hixon, Dylan H., 3764
Hixon, Shanti S., 3764
Hixon, Sheila K., 3764
Hixson, Christina M., 5041
HJH Enterprises, 8333

Hliboki, Joann, 9617
Hliboki, Larry James "Jim", 9617
Hlobik, Lawrence, 2575
HNI Corp., 3293
HNW Charitable Trust, 3072
Ho, Betty Chin, 982
Ho, Gregory P., 5637
Ho, Karen S., 8944
Ho, Peter, 2545
Ho, Winson, 1642
Ho, Yvonne Cheung, 4623
Hoag, C. Larry, 679
Hoag, George Grant, 678
Hoag, George Grant, II, 678
Hoag, George Grant, III, 678
Hoag, Grace E., 678
Hoag, Helen, 679
Hoag, Jay, 677
Hoag, Jay C., 677
Hoag, JoAnn, 4643
Hoag, Michael, 679
Hoag, Michaela, 677
Hoag, Rita J. Wolfe, 7915
Hoagland, Annie, 2911
Hoagland, John, 4327
Hoagland, Karl K., Jr., 2904
Hoagland, Laurance, Jr., 671
Hoagland, Sara, 2904
Hoagland, William, 2911
Hobart, Laura W., 481
Hobbie, Lynn K., 9855
Hobbs, Bill, 7989
Hobbs, Debbie, 20
Hobbs, Horton, 7866
Hobbs, Joyce C., 2802
Hobbs, Kathy, 680, 6235
Hobbs, Michael W., 3420
Hobbs, Richard F., 9922
Hobbs, Roger C., 680
Hobbs, Roland L., 9716
Hobbs, Truman M., 2802
Hobbs, Truman M., Jr., 1837, 2802
Hobby, Diana P., 8954
Hobby, Paul W., 8954, 8960
Hobby, W.P., 8954
Hoberman, Robert A., 5189
Hobick, Joy, 4919
Hobkirk, James, 9559
Hoblitzelle, Esther T., 8955
Hoblitzelle, Karl St. John, 8955
Hobson, Mary Ellen, 1594
Hoch, Larry H., 4397
Hochberg Family Foundation, 271
Hochberg, Andrew S., 2803
Hochberg, Joseph, 2803
Hochberg, Larry J., 2803
Hochfelder, Peter, 6191
Hochfelder, Stacy, 6191
Hochman, Kenneth G., 7718
Hochschild, Adam, 5721, 6190, 6375
Hochschild, David, 6190
Hochschild, David R., 6375
Hochschild, Jennifer L., 6894
Hochstein, Bernard, 6192
Hochstein, Michael, 6192
Hochstein, Miriam, 6192
Hochstein, Richard, 6192
Hochstein, Stephen, 6192
Hochwalt, J.R., 7894
Hock, W. Fletcher, Jr., 5256
Hockaday, Irvine O., Jr., 4824
Hockberger, John J., 2572
Hocker, Sam L., 9007
Hockert, Lorance, 7032
Hockfield, Susan, 5707
Hoctor, Susan F., 3544
Hodder, Melville T., 3828
Hodes, Michael C., 3699
Hodes, Robert B., 6944
Hodge, Edwin, Jr., 8254
Hodge, Eleanor D., 8530
Hodge, Gail, 2924
Hodge, Janet A., 2713
Hodge, Kathleen O'Shaugnessy, 4639

Hodge, Kay, 3869
Hodge, Mike, 7139
Hodges, Ashley W., 7504
Hodges, Cheryl D., 3443, 3444
Hodges, Diane L., 7171
Hodges, Edith C., 2429
Hodges, George, 8506
Hodges, L. Allen, III, 8841
Hodges, Liz, 8079
Hodges, William H., Hon., 9376
Hodges, William J., 87
Hodges-Lawton Charities, 8556
Hodgkin, Krista L., 3665
Hodgkins, Methyl A., 3526
Hodgkins, Ralph L., Jr., 3526
Hodgkins, William E., 3505
Hodgson, David, 5905
Hodgson, David C., 5905
Hodgson, Laurie, 5905
Hodgson, Robert M., 25
Hodjat, Mehdi, 5530
Hodnik, David F., 2582
Hodo, Doug, 9161
Hodo, Sadie, 9100
Hodous, Robert P., 9390
Hodsdon, Louise, 7195
Hodson, Andrew, 9521
Hoechst Marion Roussel, Inc., 5120, 5121
Hoefich, June W., 5785
Hoefinghoff, Richard, 7573
Hoefle, Daniel C., 5089
Hoefler, Brenda, 3273
Hoehn, Barbara K., 5782
Hoehn, Catheryn Emily, 681
Hoehn, Dorothy, 681
Hoehn-Saric, R. Christopher, 3741
Hoel, George O., 4501
Hoelz, Hanns Michael, 5854
Hoelzer, Alfred M., 6484
Hoenemeyer, F.J., 5153
Hoenig, Thomas M., 4843
Hoenlein, Malcolm, 6261, 6383
Hoerle, Robert F., 6194, 7122
Hoerle, Sheila A., 6194
Hoernle Foundation, A.W., 2062
Hoerster, Richard, 8957
Hoeschler, Linda L., 4636
Hofer, Annabel, 9346
Hofer, Curtis, 4976
Hofer, Curtis L., 4976
Hofer, Larry J., 8136
Hofer, Linda, 4976
Hofer, Linda M., 4976
Hofer, Steven C., 8783
Hoff, Ann W., 5107
Hoff, Marvin D., Rev., 4309
Hoff, Robert A., 5107
Hoff, Robert A., Mrs., 5107
Hoff, Sheryl A., 8202
Hoff, Susan S., 4516
Hoff, Tina, 739
Hoffberger, Bruce, 3652
Hoffberger, C. Peter, 3652
Hoffberger, David, 3652
Hoffberger, Judith R., 3719
Hoffberger, LeRoy E., 3652
Hoffenberg, Betty S., 1195
Hoffenberg, David A., 1195
Hoffenberg, Marvin, 1195
Hoffenberg, Peter H., 1195
Hoffer, Taffy, 2769
Hoffer, Walter C., 813
Hoffheimer, Jon, 7573
Hoffman, Alfred, Jr., 3529
Hoffman, Ann G., 3275
Hoffman, Arthur S., 6802
Hoffman, Beth, 9778
Hoffman, Blake, 8631
Hoffman, Bob, 3215
Hoffman, Brent W., 2458
Hoffman, Carol, 2444
Hoffman, Carol A., 699
Hoffman, Charlotte, 2507

Hoffman, Charlotte S., 2506
Hoffman, Christopher A., 3319
Hoffman, Deborah, 1087
Hoffman, Effe K.D., 3955
Hoffman, Elaine S., 682
Hoffman, Eli, 5256
Hoffman, Elisabeth, 3529
Hoffman, George I., 1205
Hoffman, Geraldine Schottenstein, 7844
Hoffman, H. Leslie, 682
Hoffman, Harold, 6171
Hoffman, James, 7700
Hoffman, James E., 9742
Hoffman, Jean Marie, Sr., 7573
Hoffman, John E., Jr., 3955
Hoffman, Joseph, 1504
Hoffman, Joyce, 3326
Hoffman, Karen A., 198
Hoffman, Leonard R., 9182
Hoffman, Lynn R., 130
Hoffman, Margueritte, 9139
Hoffman, Marion O., 6195
Hoffman, Maximilian, 6195
Hoffman, Mike, 4702
Hoffman, Nancy E., 5782
Hoffman, Raymond R., 8454
Hoffman, Ross, 3124
Hoffman, Shay Shelton, 9182
Hoffman, Thelma S., 9718
Hoffman, Tyler P., 7224
Hoffman, Walter W., 822
Hoffman-Zehner, Jacquelyn M., 7293
Hoffmann, Richard, 3282
Hoffmeister, Jerry, 1087
Hoffritz, Helen, 6196
Hoffrogge, Dean C., 4511
Hofheimer, James, 3038
Hofman, Thomas D., 4329
Hofmann 1987 Revocable Trust, The, 683
Hofmann Co., The, 683
Hofmann Foundation, 948
Hofmann, Kenneth H., 683, 948
Hofmann, Martha J., 683
Hofmann, Martha Jean, 683
Hogan, Beverly Wade, 4743
Hogan, Bill, 4708
Hogan, Billie M., 9266
Hogan, Clark N., 9492
Hogan, David O., 7935, 7937, 7944, 7966
Hogan, Elise W., 3514
Hogan, Jean, 5750
Hogan, John E., 3121
Hogan, John L., 9665
Hogan, Lee W., 8960
Hogan, Marilyn, 1463
Hogan, Randall J., 4649
Hogan, William N., Jr., 9732
Hogarty, Daniel J., Jr., 7166
Hoge, Franz J., 7603
Hogel, Carol C., 2712
Hogel, Carol Colburn, 394
Hogel, Catherine C., 2712
Hoggs, Robert, 3144
Hoglund, Forrest E., 8956
Hoglund, Sally R., 8956
Hoglund, William E., 7003
Hogue, Cyrus D., Jr., 1902, 7352
Hogue, Kristin M., 1973
Hoguet, Karen, 7624
Hohenberg, Paul M., 5782
Hohenberger, Kathy, 4708
Hohler, Robert, 4034
Hohlstein, Christopher D., 2361
Hoke, Elizabeth S., 9342
Hoke, Karen M., 4401
Hoke, Liza, 9977
Hoke, Michael N., 49
Hoke, S., 1056
Holaday, G. Stephen, 2530
Holbert, Ronald, 1541
Holbrook, Alice Hager, 2037
Holbrooke, Richard, Amb., 1465

Holcomb, Barbara, 7586
Holcomb, Gary, 6329
Holcomb, John, 2083
Holcomb, Robin R., 8023
Holcomb, Victor, 2083
Holcombe, Marie, 5710, 5908
Holcombe, Paul S., Jr., 7439
Holcombe, Robert L., Jr., 8617
Holden, Arlene, 3294
Holden, Arthur S., Jr., 7688
Holden, Brent, 1006
Holden, D. Wayne, 1706
Holden, Don L., 8957
Holden, Joseph M., 7591
Holden, Karol A., 3294
Holden, Nancy, 2063
Holden, Ralph, 2063
Holden, Richard S., 5184
Holden, Ronald W., 3294
Holden, Ruby E., 3294
Holder Construction Co., 2413
Holder, Elizabeth D., 2413
Holder, Eric H., Jr., 1834
Holder, J.R., 7977
Holder, Julie Fasone, 4284
Holder, Lofton, 6083
Holder, Thomas M., 2413
Holderness, Haywood, 7485
Holding, Frank B., 7399, 7481, 8587
Holding, Lewis R., 7399, 7438
Holding, Maggie B., 7399
Holding, Robert, 7399
Holdren, Sheryl, 9730
Holdren, Thomas, 7770
Holek, Charles F., 6617
Holekamp, Kerry L., 4832
Holekamp, William F., 4832
Holiday Home Health Care Corp. of Evansville, 3168
Holiday Leasing Corp., 3168
Holiday Retirement Village, 3168
Holiday, Charles, 2263
Hollabaugh, Beth, 7559
Hollan, Douglas, 530
Holland, Alex, 1665
Holland, Betty G., 2392
Holland, Bruce B., 4896
Holland, Charles M., 2555
Holland, Darrell, 7386
Holland, Dixie, 8800
Holland, Hudson, Jr., 4343
Holland, James T., 9380
Holland, John, 9229
Holland, John J., 4793
Holland, Larry, 1946
Holland, Marilyn M., 4977
Holland, Nancy L., 7778
Holland, Richard D., 4977
Holland, Robert, Jr., 134
Holland, Teresa, 779
Hollander, Alan S., 8112
Hollander, Annette, 2078
Hollander, Jeffry, 6318
Hollander, John, 5548
Hollander, Sidney, 2847
Holleman, Matthew L., III, 4748
Hollenbeck, David W., 2104
Hollenbeck, Douglas W., 2104
Hollenbeck, Drew, 2104
Hollenbeck, Michael, 3137
Hollendonner, Joan, 5357
Holler, William E., 451
Hollern, Michael P., 4576
Hollern, Thomas R., 7896, 7920
Holley, Kimberly L., 4228
Holley, Ronnie, 8572
Holley, Terry, 8671
Holley, Thomas, 2303
Holliday, Susan, 6804
Hollidge, Vernon R., 9407
Hollifield, J.J., 2266
Holliman, Vonda, 1819, 1820, 3374
Holling, H.W., 2653
Hollinger-Petters, Colleen, 4534

Hollingsworth, Susan Hunt, 8261
Hollington, Richard R., Jr., 7662
Hollis, Meredith H., 1596
Hollister, Don, 7653
Hollister, Terry, 7876
Holloway, Alan, 1173
Holloway, Deborah S., 2993
Holloway, J.L., 4749
Holloway, Janet, 4868
Holloway, Jeannette, 8888
Holloway, John, 1477
Holloway, Shirley, 83
Holloway, Ted, 2411
Hollowell Unitrust, Otto, 9719
Hollowell, Margaret F., 9719
Hollowell, Sharon, 3138
Holly, Herta D., 2153
Holly, Julie A.Rodecker, 4273
Holm, Herbert W., 1922
Holm, Renee, 4755
Holman, Henry, 4627
Holman, Janelle, 4627
Holman, John W., III, 5247
Holman, John W., Jr., 5247, 5599
Holman, Kim D.L., 4627
Holman, Thomas H., Jr., 4627
Holmberg, Dennis M., 5487
Holmberg, Ruth S., 7095, 8660
Holmer, Alan F., 7031
Holmes Holmes and Associates, 9321
Holmes Trust, Charles M., 8020
Holmes, A.L. "Judge", 1944
Holmes, Alexandra Skestos, 7683
Holmes, Andrea L., 4242, 4290
Holmes, Ann, 9566
Holmes, Beverly, 1599
Holmes, Bob, 156
Holmes, Carlette F., 8564
Holmes, Christine, 4471
Holmes, Christine M., 4290, 4471
Holmes, Edward A., 5252
Holmes, Howard S., 4290
Holmes, Howard S. "Howdy", 4426
Holmes, Kathryn W., 4290, 4426
Holmes, Keith R., 8648
Holmes, Louise, 7735
Holmes, Mary B., 4290
Holmes, Mary M., 7349
Holmes, Ned S., 8960
Holmes, Richard, 2395
Holmes, Robert W., Jr., 4104
Holmes, Robert, Jr., 1
Holmgren, Janet L., 359
Holmquist, Carl, 9852
Holmquist, Marilyn L., 9919
Holod, Evan, 6347
Holoman, Smallwood, Jr., 4428
Holshouser, James E., Jr., Gov., 7438
Holsinger, James W., Jr., 3422
Holson, Brenda, 2303
Holstein, Kim L., 1049
Holstein, Lester S., 1049
Holt Companies, 8958
Holt, Anne, 8958
Holt, Benjamin D., III, 8958
Holt, Benjamin D., Jr., 8958
Holt, George "Pete", 6638
Holt, Larry G., 8918
Holt, Leon C., Jr., 8404
Holt, Patti, 4798
Holt, Peter M., 8958
Holt, Richard B., 8539
Holt, Ron, 7332
Holt, Ronald G., 3372
Holt, Russel, 8147
Holt, Shirley, 4718
Holt, William Knox, 5480
Holt, Yuille, III, 9463
Holtel, Joseph A., 7791
Holthouse, Colleen, 8959
Holthouse, Lisa, 8959
Holthouse, Michael H., 8959
Holtman, Ron, 7778
Holtman, Ronald E., 7897

Holtmeier, Jeffrey, 7665
Holton, A. Linwood, Jr., 1823
Holton, Earl D., 4446
Holton, John, 735
Holton, Richard, 8691
Holton, Thomas A., 1795
Holtsford, Jeanine, 2940
Holtz, Jean, 9785
Holtz, Larry, 4661
Holtze, Elizabeth, 1333
Holtzman, Jeffrey, 485
Holtzman, Jennifer Maslow, 8327
Holtzmann, Howard M., 6198
Holtzmann, Jacob L., 6198
Holtzmann, Lillian, 6198
Holwerda, Donald J., 8705
Holz, Dorothy, 9817
Holz, Jerome J., 9817
Holzapfel, Alice A., 5188
Holzer, Erich, 5238
Holzer, Robert, 5238
Holzer, Vivian, 5238
Holzhauer, Stan, 4327
Holzman, Katharine, 9869
Holzrichter, John F., 670
Homberger, Rosmarie E., 6103
Home Savings and Loan Co., 7672
Home Towne Suites - Bowling Green LLC, 4922
Home Towne Suites - Clarksville LLC, 4922
Homer, Kristina L., 684
Homer, Michael J., 684
Homer, Paul, 2736
Homestead Co., 3438
Hommer, Katheryn M., 7400
Hommert, Douglas D., 4777
HON INDUSTRIES Inc., 3293
Honan, James P., 2171
Honda of America Mfg., Inc., 7673
Honey, Martha, 1946
Honeycutt, Terri W., 7359
Hong, Beverly, 1228
Hong, Chung Wha, 6615
Hong, Myung K., 713
Honickman, Harold, 5239
Honickman, Jeffrey, 5239
Honickman, Lynne, 8255
Honneycutt, J. Brian, 8590
Honnold, Paul, 3276
Honzel, Andrew J., 8021
Honzel, Beverly J., 8021
Hood, Bob, 9115
Hood, Charles H., 3956, 3957
Hood, Charles H., II, 3956
Hood, Donald C., 6118
Hood, James W., 4733
Hood, Jane Renner, 4954
Hood, Mary Elizabeth, 5689
Hood, Valerie, 9680
Hooff, M. David, 8048
Hoogeboom, Marge, 5026
Hoogendoorn, Case, 2922
Hook, Sanders, 3305
Hooks, Larry, 2392
Hooks, Larry B., 2368
Hooks, Lawrence, 4602
Hoolihan, James, 4520
Hooper, Adrian S., 8256
Hooper, Bruce H., 8256
Hooper, Henry O., 128
Hooper, Jack, 9198
Hooper, Jack H., 9041
Hooper, Jeanne R., 128
Hooper, Mark, 4243
Hooper, Mary Bolton, 7798
Hooper, Ralph W., 8256
Hooper, Ruth R., 2587
Hooper, Thomas, 8256
Hooper-Rasberry, Gloria, 5724
Hoopes, Judith H., 8494
Hoops, Alan, 971
Hooser, C. Wally, 8962
Hooser, John D., 8962

Hooser, Karen R., 7815
Hoosty, Kay, 8135
Hooter, Dwight, 3229
Hootkin, Pamela N., 6725
Hooton, Paula, 8902
Hoover Foundation, The, 7674
Hoover, Ann, 7952
Hoover, Charles H., 7675
Hoover, Cynthia K., 3169
Hoover, David C., 3169
Hoover, Deborah D., 7761
Hoover, Elizabeth Lacey, 7674
Hoover, James E., 3169
Hoover, Katherine C., 3169
Hoover, Lawrence H., Jr., 9400
Hoover, Lawrence R., 7675
Hoover, M.S., 7733
Hoover, Mildred M., 3169
Hoover, Rose, 8192
Hoover, Thomas H., 7675
Hop, Jim, 4392
Hope, Steve, 985
Hopgood, Elaine, 1630
Hopkins, Donald J., 1335, 1354
Hopkins, Donald R., 2868
Hopkins, Edward A., 3663
Hopkins, Flossie, 8572
Hopkins, John, 523
Hopkins, John E. "Jack", 4352
Hopkins, John H., 9695
Hopkins, Judy, 3333
Hopkins, Maureen A., 5599
Hopkins, Michael J., 9891
Hopkins, Robert D., 3761
Hopkins, S.B., 9181
Hopkins, Sarah, 179
Hopkins, T.E., 7855
Hopkins, Vince, 7573
Hopkins, Virginia, 7399
Hopkins, Wendy, 1946
Hopkins-Staten, Theresa, 1614
Hopkinson, Sealy H., 3694
Hoplamazian, Mark, 2952
Hopp, Daniel F., 4480
Hoppe, Wendy G., 980
Hopper, Berenice, 1380
Hopper, Cameron F., 1616
Hopper, John J., 8882
Hopper, Robert, 1380, 3254
Hoppman, Elsa M., 8271
Hopwood, John M., 8257
Hopwood, Mary S., 8257
Hopwood, William T., 8257
Horak, Lucy, 4229
Horak, Thomas J., 4636
Horan, Laurence P., 374
Horan, Peggy A., 1779
Hord, Juanita A., 2596
Hord, Robert E., Jr., 2596
Hord, Robert E., Sr., 2596
Hord, Thomas, 8654
Horejsi, Inc., 3367
Horejsi, John, 3367
Horejsi, Stewart, 3367
Horgan, William S., Jr., 3887
Horger, Robert R., 8577
Horing, Ellen T., 4454
Horiuchi, Minoru, 531
Horizon Casino Resort, 8853
Horizon Healthcare Services, Inc., 5240
Hormel Foods Corp., 4588
Hormel, James C., 1088
Hormel, Rampa R., 583
Hormel, Terrence L., 8511
Hormel, Thomas D., 583
Horn, Alan F., 686
Horn, Albert J., 989
Horn, Cindy, 686
Horn, Craig W., 4483
Horn, Cynthia, 686
Horn, David, 7525
Horn, Jeff, 2657
Horn, Ken, 4428

Horn, Lonnie, 408
Horn, Marianne, 3223
Horn, Michael M., 5167
Horn, Mildred V., 3427
Horn, Robyn, 189
Horn, Thomas E., 1069
Hornburg, Philip T., 360
Horne, Amelia S., 8594
Horne, Eleanor, 5357
Horne, Eleanor V., 8494
Horner, Constance, 3585
Horner, Constance J., 5360
Horner, David, 9255
Horner, Donald G., 2542
Horner, Gary C., 8153
Horner, Matina S., 6103
Horney, Bill, 7397
Horney, Jeff, 7326
Hornig, Steven A., 4553
Horning, Chuck, 1465
Hornung, Arlene, 9797
Horonzy, Joseph G., 4458
Horowitz Charitable Lead Trust, Gedale B., 6202
Horowitz, Barbara, 6202
Horowitz, Ellen Levy, 4378
Horowitz, Faith, 3595
Horowitz, Gedale B., 6202, 6898
Horowitz, Gerald D., 2415
Horowitz, Jeffrey, 1068
Horowitz, Leonard, 4529
Horowitz, Lynn, 1068
Horowitz, Pearlann, 2415
Horowitz, Richard, 6201
Horowitz, Robert H., 6505
Horowitz, Ruth, 6202
Horowitz, Sara, 5814
Horowitz, Scott, 2415
Horowitz, Seth, 6202
Horr, Susan B., 6639
Horrell, Dorothy A., 1347
Horsford, Steven, 5048
Horsley, Waller H., 9402
Horst, Richard, 3284
Horstmann, James D., 3277
Horton, Alan M., 7848
Horton, Alice K., 7496
Horton, Alice Kirby, 5279
Horton, Andy, 2362
Horton, Barbara, 4718
Horton, James A., 1294
Horton, Karen, 7926
Horton, Kathi, 4255
Horton, William R., 8570
Hortsmann, John, 537
Horvitz Foundation, Lois U., 8399, 9657
Horvitz, David, 1941
Horvitz, David W., 1989, 2065, 4367
Horvitz, Francie, 2065
Horvitz, Joan L., 7676
Horvitz, Leonard C., 7676
Horvitz, Lois U., 7677
Horvitz, Marcy R., 7678
Horvitz, Michael J., 7704
Horvitz, Norma, 2199
Horvitz, Peter, 9680
Horvitz, Peter A., 9657
Horvitz, Richard A., 7678
Horvitz, William D., 2199
Horwitz, Joy A., 8377
Horwitz, Paul, 2919
Horwood, Richard M., 2756
HoSang, Daniel, 6160
Hosea, Tom, 9693
Hoser, Albert, 5400
Hosey, Michael, 5784
Hoshaw, Betsy, 3126
Hosking, John, 4233
Hoskins, Wes, 8833
Hospira, Inc., 2804
Hospital Corp. of America, 8679
Hospitality Consulting and Supply, 5302
Hoss, Shelley, 957
Hosser, Ottilie Wagner, 8562

Hostek, Loren D., 9679
Hoster, David, 4737
Hostetter, Amos B., Jr., 3791
Hostetter, Barbara W., 3791
Hostetter, G. Richard, 8686, 8704
Hostetter, Mark D., 3959
Hotaling, Bruce, 8348
Hotchkis, John F., 712
Hotchkis, Preston B., 712
Hotel Americana, 7145
Hottle, Robert Y., 9486
Hottman, David, 8633
Hottman, David G., 8629
Hotzler, Heidi, 6613
Houck, Gayle L., 6660
Houck, Joyce, 9463
Houff Transfer, Inc., 9438
Houff, Charlotte R., 9438
Houff, Cletus E., 9438
Houff, Douglas, 9438
Houff, Dwight E., 9438
Houge, Ritchie, 4637
Hough, Hazel C., 2066
Hough, Jeffrey, 6823
Hough, W. Robb, 2066
Hough, William R., 2066
Houghton, James L., 7954
Houghton, James R., 5794
Houghton, Maisie, 7173
Houghton, Ralph H., Jr., 4281
Houghton, Sherrill M., 3684
Houglan, Don, 7897
Houin, Tammy, 3199
Houlehan, John, 4912
Houlihan, Cathy, 1726
Houlsby, John R., 2805
Hounsell, Susan, 6063
Houpt, Mary H., 2787
Housatonic Curtain Co., 3950
House of Lloyd Inc., 3375
House, David, 687
House, E. James, 70
House, Helen Fasken, 8895
House, Karla, 687
House, Lynn Di Geronimo, 7609
House, Robert, 687
House, Sarah, 3750
House, Susan T., 247
Houser, Kent T., 7997
Houssels, J.K., 5038
Houssels, Nancy C., 5038
Houston, Gary, 8721
Houston, J. Wayne, 73
Houston, Janet L., 7811
Houston-Philpot, Kim R., 4285
Houstoun, Feather O'Connor, 8371
Hovas, Jennifer, 8865
Hoverstock, Rolland W., Rev., 1456
Hoverter, Julia, 8258
Hoverter, Lawrence, 8258
Hovey, P.J. Younglove, 2362
Hovick, Edward, M.D., 8381
Hovnanian, Anna, 5241
Hovnanian, Armen, 5241
Hovnanian, Edele, 5241
Hovnanian, Hirair, 5241
Hovnanian, Kevork S., 5242
Hovnanian, Leela, 5241
Hovnanian, Sirwart K., 5242
Hovnanian, Tanya, 5241
How, Melissa, 4950
Howa, Leslie Peery, 9337
Howab Trust, 3861
Howard Trust, Jack R., 7848
Howard, A.E., 7367
Howard, Dave M., 3042
Howard, Deanna, 5088
Howard, Fernanda, 9371
Howard, J., 9028
Howard, James, 7931
Howard, Janet, 7042
Howard, Jay M., 6240
Howard, Jean, 4802
Howard, Johanna Geier, 5204

Howard, John T., 4774
Howard, Katherine Kelly, 3683
Howard, Kelly D., 8006
Howard, Kenneth, 64
Howard, Marven E., 661
Howard, Pamela, 7848
Howard, Robert G., 7042
Howard, Robert S., 5006, 9609
Howard, Scott P., 3503
Howard, Stephen R., 3895
Howard, Wayne L., 8006
Howard, William, 8632
Howard, Zoe, 3186
Howatt, Thomas J., 9931
Howe, Calvin E., 9464
Howe, Helen H., 3296
Howe, Jack, 5243
Howe, James E., 5186
Howe, John J., 4226
Howe, Jonathan T., 1964
Howe, Linda M., 2530
Howe, Mary Louise, 1765
Howe, Maureen L., 8036
Howe, Michael M., 474
Howe, Stanley M., 3293, 3296
Howe, Suzanne R., 5243
Howe, Tina, 5883
Howe, Wesley J., 5243
Howell, Alfred H., Jr., 5867
Howell, Arthel L., 9906
Howell, Donna, 1477
Howell, Elizabeth Kenan, 7413
Howell, Gary M., 9153
Howell, George B., III, 2219
Howell, James S., 7499
Howell, Jim, 4246
Howell, Joe, 7952
Howell, Lewis, 2244
Howell, Louise L., 8598
Howell, Peggy J., 8961
Howell, Philip B., 5476
Howell, R. Rodney, 2121
Howell, Ronald S., 9701
Howell, Thomas R., 7330
Howell-Beach, Pam, 7872
Howenstein, William K., 4254
Howenstine, James, 3095
Hower, M.J., 2593
Howes, Deborah, 5830
Howes, Katherine Kinder, 8994
Howey, Gregory B., 1482
Howington, Francis L., 2240
Howington, Jerry W., Mrs., 2357
Howitt, Joan S., 5459
Howitt, Robert, 5191, 6158
Howitt, Robert M., 5459
Howland, John, 9008
Howlett, Virginia, 9564
Howson, Robert E., 3461, 3503
Howze, Mark A., 2699
Hoy, Laura Jackson, 8619
Hoy, Ronald, 3931
Hoy, Steve, 8881
Hoya, Margaret Bright Vonder, 8818
Hoyes, Louis W., 1793
Hoyt, Alex Crawford, 8259
Hoyt, Alice P., 3960
Hoyt, F. Sherman, 3960
Hoyt, Franklin K., 3960
Hoyt, Kathy, 9361
Hoyt, May Emma, 8259
Hoyt, Richard M., 1504
Hoyt, Willma C., 6203
Hoyum, Ray A., 2388
Hrabowski, Freeman A., III, 3568, 3632, 9567
Hrabowski, Jacqueline C., 3559, 3709
HRB Management, Inc., 4823
Hroblak, Gerald J., 3619
HS Processing, LP, 7540
HSBC Bank USA, 5588, 5780, 5783, 5999, 6274, 6613, 7040
HSBC Bank USA, Inc., 6204
HSBC Bank USA, N.A., 6204

Hsia, Olivia, 689
Hsu, F. Richard, 7118
Hsu, Ming Chen, 7118
Hsu, T.C., 7048
HT-Hotel Equities, Inc., 2810
HTC Global Svcs., Inc., 4369
Huang, Alice, 6826, 9131
Huang, Paul D.C., 6772
Huard, John R., 3550
Hubbard Broadcasting, Inc., 4590
Hubbard, A.C., Jr., 3709
Hubbard, Anne A., 1708
Hubbard, Anne M., 4978
Hubbard, B.H.B., III, 9539
Hubbard, Claire M., 4978
Hubbard, David J., 1708
Hubbard, Debbie, 3332
Hubbard, Frank M., 1866
Hubbard, G. Morrison, Jr., 5247
Hubbard, Jean, 982
Hubbard, Joan Dale, 5481
Hubbard, John, 107
Hubbard, Karen H., 4590
Hubbard, Katharine M., 8577
Hubbard, Kenneth, 18
Hubbard, L. Evans, 1866, 2168
Hubbard, Margaret "Peggy", 6823
Hubbard, Mark, 3254
Hubbard, Michael E., 1866
Hubbard, R.D., 5481
Hubbard, Robert P., 2680
Hubbard, Robert W., 4590
Hubbard, Ruth, 1866
Hubbard, Stanley E., 4590
Hubbard, Stanley S., 4590
Hubbard, Theodore F., Jr., 4978
Hubbard, Thomas J., 1708, 5887
Hubbard-Sargent, Rick, 4935
Hubbell Inc., 1569
Hubbell, James W., Jr., 3297
Hubbs, Donald H., 5037
Huber, David R., 3653
Huber, Debra, 3653
Huber, Don, 2911
Huber, Gerald A., 8154
Huber, Hans A., 5244
Huber, Joseph F., 8305
Huber, Kevin, 420
Huber, Laurel D., 5244
Huber, Linda, 6569
Huber, Michael W., 5244
Huber, Patricia, 3135
Huber, Robert, 762
Huber, Thomas J., M.D., 3343
Huberfeld, Laura, 6205, 6206
Huberfeld, Murray, 6205, 6206
Huberfeld, Rae, 6205
Huberfeld-Bodner Family Foundation, 6205
Hubert, Hiram, 9117
Hubert, Richard N., 7401
Hubschman, Henry A., 1553
Hubspot Co., 5735
Huck, J. Lloyd, 5181
Huckabee, Donna, 173
Huddleson, Lisa, 8864
Huddleston, Mark W., 7581
Huddleston, William H., III, 8654
Hudetz, Frank C., 2713
Hudgins, Cheryl G., 3711
Hudgins, Cindy L. Sontag, 2239
Hudner, Philip, 470, 505
Hudner, Philip, Jr., 446
Hudock, Barbara B., 8202
Hudson Co., J.L., The, 4343
Hudson River Bank & Trust Co., 6207
Hudson, Carla, 401
Hudson, Charles D., Jr., 2336, 2337
Hudson, Edward R., Jr., 8801
Hudson, Gilbert, 4343
Hudson, Harris W., 2068
Hudson, J. Clifford, 5970
Hudson, J.D., 8828
Hudson, Janice, 23

Hudson, Jerry E., 8007, 8051
Hudson, Joseph L., IV, 4343
Hudson, Joseph L., Jr., 4254, 4343
Hudson, Karl G., 7438
Hudson, Lester A., 8612
Hudson, M.R., 8962
Hudson, Mark, 8840
Hudson, Murdock, 8962
Hudson, Richard, 9730
Hudson, Stanton H., Jr., 5901
Hudson, Stewart J., 1662
Hudson, Suzanne, 2655
Hudson, Vantisa, 8836
Hudspeth, Albert James, 7333
Huebner, Carl, 4253
Huebner, Constance, 4017
Huehne, Peter, 205
Huerta, Dolores, 376
Huetig, Edward, 2268
Huey, Bruce E., 2664, 3118
Huey, John W., 4793
Huey, Ward L., Jr., 8787
Huff, Danny W., Jr., 2397
Huff, Gisele, 692
Huff, J. Stephen, 2732
Huff, Lula, 2361
Huff, Robert M., 9451
Huff, W.C., 822
Huffaker, Lucinda, 3206
Huffard, Evett, 8670
Huffines, Patty, 8768
Huffington, Michael, 8963
Huffington, Roy M., 8963
Huffington, Terry L., 8963
Huffman, Charmel, 1110
Huffman, Daniel B., 3420
Huffman, G.V., 9663
Huffman, Kathleen, 3127, 9329
Huffman, Sherry, 3130
Huffmaster, Lyle, 3011
Huffnagle, Henry, 8300
Hufford, Jamie, 97
Huge, Donald S., 8944
Huger, Eugenie Jones, 3491
Huger, Gregory F., 1252
Huget, Werner, 2922
Huggins, Andrew M., 9400
Huggins, Charles "Chip", 989
Huggins, James S., 1074
Huggins, Norella, 2904
Huggins, Pamela T., 9521
Hughes Corp., The, 3724
Hughes, Alfred E., 2284
Hughes, Art, Jr., 941, 1099
Hughes, Bill M., 4947
Hughes, Bruce W., 8577
Hughes, C.B., 4356
Hughes, Carolyn McKee, 9045
Hughes, Carolyn R., 3149
Hughes, Catherine, 1505
Hughes, Charles, 7464
Hughes, Christopher R., 9610
Hughes, Ed, 8946
Hughes, Geoffrey C., 6208
Hughes, George, 8014
Hughes, Hattie, 534
Hughes, Holly J., 4252
Hughes, Howard R., 3654
Hughes, J.C., 2628
Hughes, Jan, 8768
Hughes, Jay, 2303
Hughes, John C., 9597
Hughes, John E., 2673
Hughes, Joseph T., 1482
Hughes, Karyl Kay, 9610
Hughes, Katherine Nouri, 898
Hughes, Keith, 4534
Hughes, Kenneth M., 7346
Hughes, Kevin, 4534, 9650
Hughes, Linda, 9594
Hughes, Mabel Y., 1393
Hughes, Mareen D., 9410
Hughes, Mark, 3613
Hughes, Mark F., Jr., 5777

Hughes, Mary Ellen, 9650
Hughes, Olga P., 778
Hughes, Page, 6682
Hughes, R. Bruce, 9410
Hughes, Rodney, 7312
Hughes, Shelby, 1318
Hughes, Teresa F., 2548
Hughes, Thomas J., 5854
Hughes, Thomas P., 2356
Hughes, Timothy W., 2367, 7596
Hughes, Tracey, 9522
Hughey, James F., Jr., 31
Hughey, Richard M., Jr., 4324
Hughey, Richard M., Sr., 4324
Hughley, Jan, 2015
Hugin, Kathleen M., 5245
Hugin, Robert J., 5245
Hugley, David, 9088
Huhn, Les M., 710
Huhndorf, Sharon, 83
Huisking, Charles L., III, 1570
Huisking, Frank R., 1570
Huisking, Paul, 1570
Huisking, Richard V., 1570
Huisking, Richard V., Jr., 1570
Huisking, Sarah F., 1570
Huisking, William W., 1570
Huitt, J. Fred, 9240
Huizenga Foundation, E.I., 4350
Huizenga Foundation, Elizabeth I., 4247
Huizenga, H. Wayne, 2068
Huizenga, H. Wayne, Jr., 2068
Huizenga, Heidi A., 2806
Huizenga, John C., 4247
Huizenga, Laura B., 4247
Huizenga, Martha Jean, 2068
Huizenga, P.J., 2806
Huizenga, Peter H., 2806
Huizenga, Tim, 2806
Hulbert, Henry L., 6742, 7217
Hulbert, Maureen P., 6742, 7217
Hulings, Albert D., 4589
Hulings, Mary Andersen, 4589
Hull, Alan, 4736
Hull, Gerry, 2398
Hull, James M., 2357
Hull, John E., 6525
Hull, John P., 3704
Hull, Lisa, 3179
Hull, M. Blair, Jr., 2807
Hull, Orson A., 4644
Hull, Orson A., Mrs., 4644
Hull, Peter, 2148
Hull, Shannon Sadler, 1939
Hull-Parsons, Emily, 374
Hullet, Diane, 4288
Hullet, Diane Dow, 4287
Hulme, Aura R., 8260
Hulme, Charles Scott, 1045
Hulme, Elizabeth R., 1045
Hulst, Titia, 7089
Hultquist, Timothy A., 6894
Human Svcs. Corp., 4014
Humana Inc., 3428
Humann, L. Phillip, 2496, 2524
Humann, L.P., 2378, 2442
Humbarger, Robert, 4442
Humber, Candace A., 1031
Hume, Caroline H., 692
Hume, Cornelia, 6915
Hume, Gene, 277, 1255
Hume, George H., 692
Hume, Jaquelin H., 692
Hume, William J., 692
Huml, Jeffrey P., 2601
Humleker, Jana Johnson, 7344
Hummel, Bobbie J., 7612
Hummel, Harrison, III, 5783
Hummel, Richard J., 8137
Hummel, Rolf E., 2162
Hummel, Waltrude E., 2162
Hummell, Merry, 1345
Hummelstein, Sam, 160

Hummer, Philip Wayne, 2728
Hummers, William, 8615
Humphrey, Bill, 7931
Humphrey, David, 8047
Humphrey, George M., 7679
Humphrey, Jeanne, 6532
Humphrey, Jim E., 4512
Humphrey, Louise, 1945
Humphrey, Mark, 1819, 1820
Humphrey, Pamela S., 7679
Humphrey, Rebecca Barclay, 8238
Humphreys, David C., 4800, 4833
Humphreys, Donald D., 8889
Humphreys, Ethelmae C., 4800, 4833
Humphreys, Ethelmae Craig, 4833
Humphreys, Geraldine Davis, 8965
Humphreys, Henry J., 6513
Humphreys, J.P., 4833
Humphreys, Jack, 7922
Humphreys, Kent, 7922
Humphreys, Kirk, 7922
Humphreys, Ruth Boettcher, 1344
Humphries, Bill, 9171
Humphries, Cary, 4712
Humphrys, Maureen, 9998
Humpton, Charles B., 8443
Huncke, L.W., 7515
Hund, Thomas N., 2644
Hundelt, Claire Vatterott, 4921
Hundley, James D., M.D., 7336
Hung, Betty, 6643
Hungerford, Eric S., 7543
Hunia, Edward M., 4367
Hunnicutt, Anne S., 9720
Hunnicutt, H.P., 9720
Hunsaker, H. Scott, 8939
Hunstman, James H., 9329
Hunt Alternative Fund, Helen, 6994
Hunt, A. James, 8261
Hunt, Alexandria K., 8261
Hunt, Andrew McQ., 8261
Hunt, Brenda L., 4228
Hunt, Caroline H., 8261
Hunt, Cathryn J., 8261
Hunt, Christopher, 2878
Hunt, Christopher M., 8261
Hunt, Craig, Mr., 4906
Hunt, Daniel K., 8261
Hunt, David, 174
Hunt, Dennis, 346
Hunt, Fiona M., 2878
Hunt, Gary H., 272, 699
Hunt, Gayle G., 8966
Hunt, Helen LaKelly, 6994
Hunt, Hunter L., 9084
Hunt, Ian C., 2878
Hunt, James, 832
Hunt, James B., 5707
Hunt, Jean, 2156
Hunt, John B., 8261
Hunt, Nancy Ann, 9084
Hunt, Natasha, 866
Hunt, Neen, 6379
Hunt, Penny A., 4622
Hunt, Ray L., 8877, 9084
Hunt, Richard E., 7748
Hunt, Richard L., 1074
Hunt, Richard M., 8261
Hunt, Roger B., 3982
Hunt, Roy A., 8261
Hunt, Roy A., III, 8261
Hunt, Samuel P., 5093
Hunt, Sarah Anschutz, 1334, 1335
Hunt, Swanee, 4174
Hunt, Timothy J., 4125
Hunt, Torrence M., Jr., 8261
Hunt, Torrence W.B., 8261
Hunt, V. William, 3166
Hunt, William E., 8261
Hunt, Woody L., 8966
Hunt-Badiner, Marion M., 8261
Hunt-Meeks, Lillian, 4174
Hunter, A.V., 1394
Hunter, Brian, 4256

Hunter, Carol Bright, 8818
Hunter, Catrelia, 7466
Hunter, Christine F., 3285
Hunter, Coleman A., 2069
Hunter, Dick, 8864
Hunter, E.K., 3465
Hunter, Emily S., 2069
Hunter, Gary, 3387
Hunter, George Thomas, 8644
Hunter, Gerald L., 3345, 3376
Hunter, Jack, 3121
Hunter, James, Rev., 3144
Hunter, Jeffery, 220
Hunter, JoAnn, 3597
Hunter, Kathryn M., 7821
Hunter, Michael, 1764
Hunter, Shirley H., 7042
Hunter, Susan B., 322
Hunter, Thomas A., 4257
Hunter, Virginia Castagnola, 366
Hunter, William T., 3285
Hunter, William T., Jr., 3693
Hunting, David D., Jr., 4446
Hunting, John R., 5614
Huntington Bancshares Inc., 7577
Huntington Bank, The, 7867
Huntington National Bank, 7675
Huntington National Bank, The, 2207, 4252, 7532, 7574, 7576, 7580, 9723
Huntington, Archer M., 5548
Huntington, Jennifer, 79
Huntington, John, 7680
Huntington, Lawrence S., 6213, 6471
Huntington, Roberta, 401
Huntington, Tom, 990
Huntley, Joanne, 7479
Huntley, Larke, 4574
Huntrods, Ann, 4624
Huntsman, David H., 9329
Huntsman, Jon M., 9329
Huntsman, Karen H., 9329
Huntsman, Kenneth A., 5246
Huntsman, M. Pauline, 5246
Huntsman, Marcia K., 5246
Huntsman, Paul C., 9329
Huntting, Susan J., 8279
Huntzinger, Ernest H., 2859
Hupfer, C.J., 8614
Hupprich, Sharon E.A., 9363
Hurd, Betty, 2578
Hurd, James E., 4607
Hurd, Jennifer Jacoby, 2691
Hurd, Marie, 1553
Hurd, Priscilla Payne, 2934
Hurdus, Syde, 6214, 7114
Huret, Robert, 2535
Hurford, John B., 6215
Hurlbut, Robert S., Jr., 3828
Hurlbut, Sally D., 4074
Hurlbut, Thomas, 9485
Hurley, Cheryl, 6357
Hurley, Geraldine T., 7403
Hurley, Gordon P., 7402, 7403
Hurley, J.F., III, 7402
Hurley, Jack, 9424
Hurley, James F., 7403, 7466
Hurley, John, 2868
Hurley, Joseph G., 980
Hurley, Mark, 312
Hurley, Patricia R., 3818, 3970
Hurley, Rebecca, 9239
Hurley, Shirley Ann, 1093
Hurley, Webster H., 2964
Hurley, Willard L., 39
Huron, 3683
Huron & Orleans Building Corp., 2976
Hurst, Alexander B., 6216
Hurst, Amanda K., 6216
Hurst, Anthony P., 4344
Hurst, Dean W., 9345
Hurst, Elizabeth S., 4344
Hurst, Peter F., 4344
Hurst, Peter F., Jr., 1504

Hurst, Robert J., 5787, 6216
Hurst, Robert W., 9488
Hurst, Robin A., 1
Hurst, Soledad D., 6216
Hurst, Willard R., 525
Hurst-Hyde, Kristen, 9345
Hurt, Kathleen C., 1300
Hurt, Linda J., 2644
Hurt, Richard T. "Rick", 1942
Hurt, Sarah S., 1300
Hurt, William H., 1300
Hurtubise, Mark, 9589
Hurwich, Cecelia, 235
Hurwitz, Kenneth D., 5606
Hurwitz, Roger T., 4876
Hurwitz, Stephen A., 1015
Husain, Kamran, 264
Huse, Mary, 4200
Huseby, Sven, 1533
Huseman, Sue Ann, 3550
Hushion, Joan, 7735
Huskey, Alex, 3124
Huskins, Sandra L., 668
Huss, Alvin J., 4592
Huss, Alvin J., Jr., 4592
Huss, Ruth S., 4592
Hussain, Brian, 8581
Hussey, Buzzy, 8647
Hussey, David L., 7917
Hussey, Herbert E., 2240
Hussey, Jeffrey S., 9611
Hussman, John P., 3655
Hussman, Walter, Jr., 165
Hustad, Bruce, 4571
Huston, Barbara T., 4373
Huston, Charles L., III, 8141, 8263, 8264
Huston, Charles L., IV, 8264
Huston, Charles L., Jr., 8264
Huston, Edwin A., 1941
Huston, Eldon, 3343
Huston, Kathleen, 474
Huston, Robert L., Mrs., 7039
Huston, Ruth, 8264
Huston, Scott G., 8263
Huston, Stewart, 8263
Hutaff, Lucile, 7349
Hutaff, William R., III, 7357
Hutcheson, Dorothea W., 189
Hutcheson, Karen, 189
Hutcheson, Mary E., 189
Hutcheson, Mary Ellen, 1922
Hutcheson, Mary Ross Carter, 9387
Hutcheson, Richard, 189
Hutcheson, Susanne Lilly, 4606
Hutcheson, William L., 189
Hutchings, Jack, 3056
Hutchings, Patricia, 359
Hutchins, Bruce, 1
Hutchins, Daniel, 3365
Hutchins, Deborah O., 6217
Hutchins, Elizabeth E., 6218
Hutchins, Glenn H., 6217
Hutchins, Mary J., 6218
Hutchins, Nancy, 4237
Hutchins, Priscilla, 1
Hutchins, Robert, 1712
Hutchins, Waldo H., Jr., 6218
Hutchins, Waldo, III, 6218
Hutchins, William B., III, 1
Hutchinson, Elaine S., 6409
Hutchinson, Fred D., 7496
Hutchinson, Herman R., 8095
Hutchinson, Murray H., 1031
Hutchinson, Robert E., 7463
Hutchinson, Shirley F., 8944
Hutchison, Laura, 1776
Hutchison, S.L., 426
Hutchison, Susan, 9686
Hutchison, Susan S., 9691
Hutchison, Thomas R., 3279
Hutson, Robert E., 8917
Hutta, Jane, 7005
Hutter, Richard F., 2570

Hutterer, Vincent K., 4648
Hutterly, Jane M., 9826
Huttler, Stephen B., 3633
Hutto, Clare P., 693
Hutto-Powers, Eileen, 693
Hutton Trust, Betty L., 694
Hutton, Edward A., 7681
Hutton, Edward L., 7681
Hutton, John, 3400
Hutton, Kathryn Jane, 7681
Hutton, Patricia E., 933
Hutton, Thomas C., 7681
Hux, Vernon E., 3170
Huyck, E.B., 624
Huzella, Lisa W., 4479
Hvolbeck, Marian V.C., 5515
Hwang, Bill, 7139
Hwang, Mimi, 6823
Hyams, Godfrey M., 3961
Hyams, Sarah A., 3961
Hyatt Corporation, 2810
Hyatt, Linda S., 9455
Hyatt, Steve, 1941
Hyatt, Susan M., 989
Hyatt, William H., Jr., 5349
Hybl, Kathleen H., 1437
Hybl, Kyle H., 1374
Hybl, William, 1468
Hybl, William J., 1374
Hyche, J. Tod, 8583
Hyde Park Nursing Home, Inc., 6330
Hyde, Barbara R., 8693
Hyde, Charles F., Jr., 9818
Hyde, Doug, 9886
Hyde, Douglas W., 9818
Hyde, J.R. III, 8693
Hyde, J.R., Sr., 8693
Hyde, Jeannette, 7438
Hyde, Joseph R., Jr., 6467
Hyde, Joyce W., 9818
Hyde, Lawrence H., Jr., 3962
Hyde, Lillia Babbitt, 5247
Hyde, Thomas R., 9818
Hyder, Ifrah, 9612
Hyder, Jameel, 9612
Hyder, Rizwan, 9612
Hylton Charitable Lead Trust, Irene V., 9440
Hylton, Cecil D., 9440
Hylton, Cecilia M., 9440
Hylton, Conrad C., 9440
Hyman, Alan, 534
Hyman, Howard, 534
Hyman, Steven, 5652
Hyman, Steven E., 5827
Hymon-Parker, Shirley, Dr., 3599
Hyndman, Thomas M., Jr., 8395
Hynek, Jacqueline, 9238
Hynes, James E.S., 7390
Hynes, Mary Ann, 2989
Hynes, Thomas W., 1540, 1654
Hynnek, Eric M., 4589
Hynnek, Julia L., 4589
Hypler, Robert, Ph.D., 5228

I'Anson, Lawrence W., Jr. 9376
I2 Cam UC Davis, 349
IAC/InterActiveCorp, 6220
Iacocca, Lido A., 3963
Iaderosa, Michael, 7735
Iakovos, Metropolitan, 2702
Iams, Joseph, 3131
Iannaccone, Sophia, 3082
Iannaconi, Teresa, 5288
Iannuzzi, Richard, 6594
Iapalucci, Sam, 2654
IAT Syndicate, Inc., 6311
Ibarguen, Alberto, 2097, 9424
Ibarra, Irene M., 346, 1356, 9566
IBM, 7470
Icahn, Carl C., 6222, 6223, 6224
Icahn, Gail Golden, 6223
Ichinaga, Nancy, 421

Ickler, Nancy, 3131
Iddings, Andrew S., 7682
Iddings, Roscoe C., 7682
Ide, Georgiana Roberts, 5783
Ide, Robert D., 9361
Idels, Michele, 1717
Idelson, Charles, 2240
Idema, William, 1369
Idema, William W., 4348
Iding, Allan E., 9961
Idshida, Franklin, 4309
IDT Corp., 5248, 5266, 7178
Ierlan, Terry, 6639
IFG Corp., 5518
Ifland, Rick, 3440
Iger, Robert A., 456
Igler, Sarah, 8462
Igler, Thomas, 8462
Ignat, Eleanor, 7779
Ignat, Erin, 7779
Ignat, Pam, 7779
Ignell, Mary, 2977
Ignell, Rose Ann, 1275
Ihlenfeld, Jay V., 4492
Ihne, Sally J., 9665
Ihnen, Theodore, 550
IIMI, Inc., 6394
Ikeda, Daniel M., 1106
Ikle, Fred C., 1632
Ikoma, Kunio, 254
IKON Office Solutions, Inc., 8265
Ilchman, Alice, 7220
Ilchman, Warren F., 7022
Iler, Donald Carey, 3004
Iler, N. Carey, Jr., 3004
Iler, Robert Gordon, 3004
Iler, Robert Gordon, Jr., 3004
Ilfeld, Fred, Dr., 1244
Iliff, Jennifer L., 7859
Iliff, Warren, 901
Ill, Katherine C., 1519, 1529
Illges, John P., 2416
Illges, John P., III, 2416
Illges, Richard B., 2416
Illick, Virginia B., 7811
Illig, Dale, 8986
Illig, Donald, 7582
Illingworth, Dave, 7160
Illinois Consolidated Telephone Co., 2864
Illinois Tool Works Inc., 2813
Ilten, Hark, 9778
Imboden, Connie E., 3567
IMG, 7174
Imhoff, Kat, 9390
Imhoff, Quincey, 529
Imlay, Gerard G., 2417
Imlay, John P., III, 2417
Imlay, John P., Jr., 2417
Imlay, Lucinda, 2417
Imlay, Mary Ellen, 2417
Imlay, Paula, 2417
Immerwahr, John, 7244
Imorde, Scott, 8707
Imowitz, Mark R., 6581
Imperial Promenade Assocs., LLC, 237
Imsdahl, Bruce T., 7517
Inaba, Yoshumi, 7160
Inaciak, Mary Beth, 4271
Inco, Ltd., 7436
Indeck, Jennifer Bartner, 9362
Indenbaum, Michael A., 4341
Independence Communications, Inc., 8340
Independence Community Bank Corp., 6229
Independent Publications, Inc., 8340
Independent Stave Co., Inc., 4786
Indiana Energy, Inc., 3249
Indiana Gas and Chemical Corp., 3173
Indiana Mills & Manufacturing, Inc., 3172
Indiana State Dept. of Health, 3164
Indiana Thrift for AIDS, 3164

Industrial & Mill Suppliers, Inc., 9430
Industrial Bank of Japan Trust Co., The, 6562
Industrial Bank of Japan, Ltd., The, 6562
Industry Initiatives, 1222
Indy Pride, 3164
Indyke, Darren, 7904
Indyke, Darren K., 5695
Infanti, Irene, 5255
Ingalls, Alicia E., 8474
Ingalls, David S., 7684
Ingalls, David S., Jr., 7684
Ingalls, Louise H., 7684
Ingalls, Nina S., 7684
Ingemanson, Paul, 333
Ingemanson, Susan, 333
Ingerman, Sandra, 5494
Ingersoll, Ellen M., 149
Ingle, Clyde, 7969
Ingle, Ronald R., 9407
Ingle, Sallie, 7866
Inglee, Gale D., 2704
Inglee, Mark, 2704
Inglesby, Thomas, 5417
Inglis Trust, Ramona K., 2121
Inglis, T., 8150, 8301
Inglish, David, 4461
Ingmand, Robert C., 7533
Ingmire, Robert E., 7018
Ingold Family 5 Year Charitable Lead Trust, 695
Ingold, Arlyne A., 695
Ingold, Randall, 695
Ingold, Richard G., 695
Ingold, Robert F., 695
Ingraham, Bonnie, 3132
Ingraham, Patricia, 6329
Ingram Industries Inc., 8694
Ingram, Becky, 9730
Ingram, Ernie, 9597
Ingram, Freeman P., 5359
Ingram, James, 329
Ingram, Joe, 4834
Ingram, John C., 7405
Ingram, John R., 8694
Ingram, Marci, 7775
Ingram, Martha A., 8694
Ingram, Martha R., 8694
Ingram, Milliard, 7932
Ingram, Orrin H., 8694
Ingram, Richard E., 5149
Ingram, Robert A., 7439
Ingrassia, Francis J., 6230
Ingstad, D. Scott, 3274
Ingwersen, James C., 239
Inks, Wayne, 7449
Inland Empire Paper Co., 9574
Inman Mills, 8595
Inman, Arthur N., 424
Inman, Douglas L., 3223
Inman, Frances L., 848
Inman, Gordon, 8662
Innucci, Nunzio, 5194
Insel, Michael S., 5912, 6348, 6460
Inserra, Carol Ann, 5517
Inskeep, Harriett J., 3181
Inskeep, Harriett Jane, 3181
Inskeep, Richard G., 3181
Inskeep, Thomas R., 3181
Inskip, Gregory A., 1714
Institute for Research on Unlimited Love, 4297
Institution Food House, Inc., 7372
Integra LifeSciences Corp., 5251
Intel Capital Corp., 8022
Intel Corp., 8022
Intel Foundation, 7470
InterActiveCorp, 6220
Intercon Overseas, Inc., 1881
Interfaith Council, 1647
Interlake Corp., The, 2758
Intermedics, Inc., 2054, 3159
International Air Leases, Inc., 1893
International Bank of Commerce, 8859

International Bible College, 7442
International Business Machines Corp., 6221
International Cobalt, 7436
International Flavors & Fragrances, Inc., 6227
International Medical and Educational Data LINK, Inc., 3710
International Ore and Fertilizer Corp., 6802
International Paper Co., 1571
International Peace Foundation, 1860
International Shinto Foundation, 6235
International, The, 1395
Internosis, 1794
Interocean Industries, Inc., 5195
Interpacific Holdings, Inc., 5574
Interstate Marine Transport Co., 8256
Interstate Ocean Transport Co., 8256
Interstate Towing Co., 8256
Interviewing Services of America, 7174
Intone, James E., 5785
INTRUST Bank, N.A., 3369
Intuit Inc., 696
Inui, Thomas S., 5750
Ioka Fund, 2802
Iovino Charitable Lead Annuity Trust, The, 6236
Iovino, Judith, 6236
Iovino, Lauren, 6236
Iovino, Michael, 6236
Iovino, Thomas, 6236
Iowa Periodicals, Inc., 3331
Iowa West Racing Assn., 3298
Iozzia, Rachel, 1428
Ipsen, Henry W., 9925
Irada, Ismael, 5459
Irby Co., Stuart C., 4750
Irby Corp., 4750
Irby, Abby C., 2324
Irby, Charles L., 4733, 4750
Irby, Joseph A., 4750
Irby, Stewart C., Jr., 4750
Irby, Stuart M., 4750
Ireland, Catherine, 1291
Ireland, Ellen, 7603
Ireland, George R., 7736
Ireland, Gregg A., 2454
Ireland, James D., III, 7736
Ireland, Kate, 2465
Irick, Larry, 3403
Iridian Asset Mgmt., 8049
Irions, Tom, 3145
Irish, Ann K., 4291
Irish, Carolyn T., 9347
Irmas Charitable Foundation, Audrey & Sidney, The, 938
Irmas, Audrey M., 697
Irmas, Robert J., 697
Irmas, Sydney M., 697
Irmscher, Thomas A., 3203
Irvin, John, 4836
Irvin, Margaret J., 9443
Irvin, Nike, 1054
Irvin, Patricia L., 6525
Irvine Medical Center, Inc., 699
Irvine, Horace H., II, 4018
Irvine, J. Nelson, 8745
Irvine, James, 698
Irvine, Ronald A., 8060
Irving, J. Bruce, 2305
Irving, James M. "Marty", 9365
Irving, Joe D., 2419
Irwin Charitable Remainder Annuity Trust, Richard D., 2814
Irwin Financial Corp., 3174
Irwin Mortgage Corp., 3174
Irwin Trust No. 1, Richard D., 2814
Irwin Union Bank & Trust Co., 3174
Irwin, Bonnie, 1102
Irwin, Fannie M., 700
Irwin, Gregory P., 3309
Irwin, John, 7220
Irwin, John N., 8256

Irwin, John N., II, Mrs., 7220
Irwin, John N., III, 5513, 5647, 7253
Irwin, Michael E., 1102
Irwin, Philip D., 843
Irwin, Robert J.A., 5592, 5813
Irwin, Terry, 9057
Irwin, Tom, 4246
Irwin, Vincent, 5194
Irwin, William B., 5592
Irwine, James, 8746
Isaac I Foundation, The, 8853
Isaac Stauffer Clinic, 3475
Isaac, Lewis J., 7346
Isaacs, Jeremey M., 6395
Isaacson, Irving, 3542
Isaksson, Tomas, 1267
Isaly, Samuel D., 2077
Isaza, Orlando, 3855
Isberg, Margaret, 1006
Iscol, Jill, 6226
Iscol, Kenneth, 6226
Isdaner, Scott Rosen, 8464
Ise, Hikonobu, 3656
Ise, N.H., 3656
Iselin, John Jay, 6471
Isen, Simone, 701
Isen, Stuart, 701
Isenberg, Diane S., 2070
Isenberg, Eugene M., 2070
Isermann, Betty, 5253
Isermann, Carol, 5253
Isermann, Howard, 5253
ISGO Corp., 2761
Isgrig, Thomas R., 3444
Isherwood, Elizabeth, 3854
Ishigami, Kunio, 5415
Ishiyama, George S., 702
Ishiyama, Nelson, 702
Ishiyama, Patsy, 702
Ishiyama, Setsuko, 702
Isinger, William R., 997
Isis Pharmaceuticals, 3841
Iskrant, John D., 1526
Island Gardens, 5736
Isler, William H., 8221
Isles, Philip H., 6397
Isley, Dawn, 8486
Isom, Ralph, 2566
Ispahani, Mahnaz, 6686
Israel, Adrian C., 6240
Israel, Allen D., 9550
Israel, Brian, 3006
Israel, Kilhillet, 1212
Israel, Mike, 9675
Israel, Samuel, 9675
Israel, Thomas C., 6240
Israel, William B., 34
Issa, Darrell E., 703
Issa, Katharine S., 703
Issac, John, 8039
Isselbacher, Eric, 3915
Isselbacher, Kurt J., 3915
Issleib, Lutz, 892
Istock, Judith A., 2815
Istock, Verne G., 2815
Istre, M.J., 2301
Italian Club of Dallas, 9068
Itasca Medical Center Foundation, 4574
Ith, Rich, 9307
Ito, Paul K., 2530
ITT Rayonier Inc., 2189
ITT Sheraton Corp., 7049
Ittigson, Mary, 4255
Ittleson, Blanche F., 6241
Ittleson, H. Anthony, 6241
Ittleson, H. Philip, 6241
Ittleson, Henry, 6241
Ittleson, Henry, Jr., 6241
Ittleson, Lee F., 6241
Ittleson, Nancy S., 6241
Itzinger Irrevocable Trust, Eli, 7151
Iuliano, Susan, 4173
Ivanca, Tere, 4499, 4574
Ivens, Barbara J., 4321

Iversen, Addie Jo, 5492
Iverson, Brent, 134
Ives, Charles, 5548
Ives, Deborah M., 1288
Ives, Diane, 583, 1770
Ives, Lynn C., 7474
Ives, Patricia Salazar, 5496
Ivey, Harriet M., 3225
Ivie, J. Russell, 2458
Ivory, Ellis, 9329
Iwanami, Toshilmitsu, 6605
Iwashita, Kenneth M., 7725
Iwata, Robert, 894
Ix, Robert G., 6513
Izlar, Charles E., 2434
Izzo, Ralph, 5361
Izzo, Scott D., 8344, 8346

J & J Partnership, 2958
J&D Family Foundation, 714
J&S Construction Co., Inc, 8713
J. & S. Investment Co., 7325
J.G.L. Foundation, 1417
Jabara, Andrea, 1537
Jabara, Kirk, 4246
Jacangelo, Nicholas, 5595, 6643
Jack in the Box Inc., 705
Jackel, Margareta, 6195
Jacklin, Duane, 2570
Jacknewitz, Dennis J., 4896
Jackoboice, Maureen McMeel, 4774
Jackson Family Charitable Trust, Ann, The, 706
Jackson Hole Preserve, Inc., 5551
Jackson, Alice Carlson, 3127
Jackson, Ann G., 706
Jackson, Anne O., 3548
Jackson, Basil L., Jr., 9711
Jackson, Betty Hill, 23
Jackson, Brenda, 4228
Jackson, Carmelle, 8627
Jackson, Carol, 3587
Jackson, Carol C., 2458
Jackson, Catherine T., 8662
Jackson, Charles, 121
Jackson, Charles A., 706
Jackson, Courtney, 5466
Jackson, David, 2685, 8807
Jackson, David D., Hon., 9217
Jackson, Deborah C., 3886
Jackson, Dominick, 8739
Jackson, Don, 9081
Jackson, Doug, 8636
Jackson, Douglas J., 5
Jackson, Edgar R., 980
Jackson, Edward D., Jr., 2349
Jackson, Emily Tow, 1660, 1661
Jackson, Eugene W., 8209
Jackson, Gayle P.W., 134
Jackson, Geoffrey W., 8209
Jackson, Helena E., 4556
Jackson, Herrick, 9978
Jackson, James H., 706
Jackson, James W., Rev., 2623
Jackson, Jimmy S., 7446
Jackson, John, 1295
Jackson, John J., 7463
Jackson, Kelvin, 9313
Jackson, Kenneth T., 6453
Jackson, Lawrence V., 184
Jackson, Lisa, 3358, 5698
Jackson, Lloyd G., II, 8099
Jackson, Marcy, 9973
Jackson, Maria C., 8024
Jackson, Marie-Louise, 8209
Jackson, Mark A., 8671
Jackson, Mary R., 9978
Jackson, Melissa S.A., 9973
Jackson, Mike, 9703
Jackson, Monty J., 9107
Jackson, Nancy L., 2705
Jackson, Nate, 9933
Jackson, Orton P., Jr., 8140

Jackson, Palmer G., 706
Jackson, Palmer G., Jr., 706
Jackson, Patricia, 2048
Jackson, Pauline, 9845
Jackson, Peggy, 790
Jackson, Polly C., 7370, 8611
Jackson, Richard E., 3531
Jackson, Rick C., 3350
Jackson, Robert T., 4773
Jackson, Ronald, 3415
Jackson, Sandra, 4237
Jackson, Shane M., 9973
Jackson, Sonya, 3044
Jackson, Stephon A., 3568
Jackson, Teri L., 989
Jackson, Vernell, 3404
Jackson, W. Richard, 3966
Jackson, William L., 706
Jacksonville Housing Authority, 2059
Jacksonville Jaguars, Ltd., 2071
Jacob, John E., 4776
Jacob, Larry, 4842
Jacob, Lynn H., 2778
Jacob, P. Bernard, 2042
Jacob, Tom, 4587
Jacobi, Daniel E., 3324
Jacobi, Judy, 3143
Jacobius, Bina H., 638
Jacobs Engineering Group Inc., 707
Jacobs, Alice, 6743
Jacobs, Barbara, 2634, 2790
Jacobs, Barbara M., 7605
Jacobs, Bill, 2435
Jacobs, Brenda, 2880
Jacobs, Bruce E., 9860
Jacobs, David H., 7605
Jacobs, Debra, 2035
Jacobs, Debra M., 2230
Jacobs, Evelyn, 1139
Jacobs, Frank, 7744
Jacobs, Frank D., 7882, 7883
Jacobs, Fred, 4227
Jacobs, Gail Gordon, 8683
Jacobs, Gary, 2769
Jacobs, Gary E., 1087
Jacobs, Howard S., 2826
Jacobs, Jason, 6607
Jacobs, Jay, 309
Jacobs, Jeffrey M., 8683
Jacobs, Joseph J., 707, 708
Jacobs, Libby, 3326
Jacobs, Margaret E., 708
Jacobs, Mark, 9144
Jacobs, Mark M., 9144
Jacobs, Marvin L., 3511
Jacobs, Milbrey R., 1713
Jacobs, Milton, 294
Jacobs, Nancy, 4693
Jacobs, Phoebe, 5567
Jacobs, Randall, 3145
Jacobs, Roy, 5907
Jacobs, Russell C., III, 2480
Jacobs, Sylvia Ely, 3572
Jacobs, Violet J., 708
Jacobs, Violet Jabara, 708
Jacobson & Sons, Benjamin, 6247
Jacobson, Arthur L., 6247
Jacobson, Arthur, Jr., 6247
Jacobson, Benjamin, Jr., 6247
Jacobson, Bernard H., 9722
Jacobson, Blanche E., 9722
Jacobson, Howard T., 4837
Jacobson, James A., 6247
Jacobson, Jean M., 9906
Jacobson, Jeffrey A., 3624
Jacobson, Joanna, 3967, 4169
Jacobson, Jonathon, 3967
Jacobson, Julie J., 4991
Jacobson, Kathy Howard, 6248
Jacobson, Knute, 9927
Jacobson, Laura A., 9847
Jacobson, Leslie A., 6657
Jacobson, Malcolm B., 8133
Jacobson, Mitchell, 6248

Jacobson, Richard O., 3299
Jacobson, Robert J., Jr., 6247
Jacobson, Robert J., Sr., 6247
Jacobson, Sibyl C., 6542
Jacobson, Tryg, 9840
Jacobson, Yonina B., 5126
Jacobus Co., 9819
Jacobus, Charles D., 9819
Jacobus, Charles D., Jr., 9819
Jacobus, Eugene, 9819
Jacobus, Eugenia, 9819
Jacobus, Eugenia T., 9819
Jacoby, Jennie Hutton, 7681
Jacoby, Lenore, 1266
Jacoby, Peter J., 1518
Jacoff, Daniel, 6249
Jacoff, Helen, 6249
Jacoff, Michael, 6249
Jacoff, Sydney, 6249
Jacques Moret, Inc., 5222
Jacubowitz, Tomasita, 7343
Jade, Hathaway F., 8144
Jaeb, Lorena, 1900
Jaeb, Robert, 1900
Jaeb, Stephen, 1900
Jaech, Jeffery A., 537
Jaeger, Joseph A., Jr., 3490
Jaegers, Sylvia W., 3409
Jaffe, David R., 6250
Jaffe, Eleanor, 2072
Jaffe, Elise P., 6250
Jaffe, Ellen, 4136
Jaffe, Elliot, 6250
Jaffe, Elliot S., 6250
Jaffe, Ira J., 4389
Jaffe, Irving, 2072
Jaffe, Jack, 2072
Jaffe, Kenneth, 5228
Jaffe, Mary H., 671
Jaffe, Richard E., 6250
Jaffe, Robert S., 9671
Jaffe, Roslyn, 6250
Jaffe, Ruth, 4229
Jaffe, Suzanne D., 134
Jaffe, Wendy, 4918
Jaffe, William A., 8136
Jaffee, June, 6975
Jaffrey, Jonathan D., 447, 750
Jaffy, Stanley A., 4515
Jagelski, Janice, 439
Jagoda, Andy, 2732
Jaharis, Kathryn, 2073
Jaharis, Mary, 2073
Jaharis, Michael, 2073
Jaharis, Michael, Jr., 2073
Jaharis, Steven, 2073
Jahn, Carolyn L., 2816
Jahn, Charles L., 2816
Jahn, Reinhardt E., 2816
Jahn, Reinhardt H., 2816
Jahn, Shirley R., 2816
Jaindl, David, 8269
Jaindl, Mark, 8269
Jakoubek, Jane, 3127
Jalkut, Thomas P., 3179, 3980, 4046,
    4109, 4143
Jalonick, I., 9219
Jalonick, K., 9219
Jalonick, Mary M., 8855
Jamail, David G., 8969
Jamail, Joseph D., 8970
Jamail, Joseph D., III, 8970
Jamail, Lee H., 8970
Jamail, Lillie H., 8970
Jamail, Randall Hage, 8970
Jamail, Robert Lee, 8970
Jamail, Sharon, 8969
Jamal, Esther, 7037
Jamerson, Terry Hall, 9463
James Epstein Investment Trust, 2684
James, Amabel B., 5254
James, Ardis, 6252
James, Barbara L., 4352
James, Bradley G., 709

James, C. Ronald, 3415
James, Christopher M., 709
James, Diana L., 8402
James, Don, 40
James, Donald M., 73
James, Gloria, 2443
James, Hamilton E., 5254
James, Holly M., 4031
James, J. Hatcher, III, 4734
James, Jeannette, 4980
James, Jerry J., 1074
James, John, 5005
James, John H., 4734
James, John J., Esq., 4321
James, Keith Alan, 2181
James, Larry, 9203
James, Laura Anne, 709
James, Lawrence, 4980
James, Lawrence R., 4980
James, Lynda, 9129
James, Matt, 739
James, Meg, 1726
James, Paula, 170
James, Ralph M., 6252
James, Robert, 6252
James, Ron, 4690
James, Rose McKinney, 5048
James, Thomas M., 1447, 2874
James, William R., 4733
James, Wilmot G., 5970
James-Brown, Christine, 6092
Jameson, Bill, 8916
Jameson, Ida M., 710
Jamieson, Kathleen Hall, 6894, 8083
Jamieson, Michael L., 1948
Jamison, Alan, 3320
Jamison, Conny, 1087
Jamison, David C., 26
Jamison, Nelle Woods, 5018
Jamison, Zean, Jr., 7418, 7499
Jammal, Eleanor A., 7534
Jamula, M. Melissa, 6681
Janavs, Michelle, 887
Janco, John, 1516
Jander, S., 5151
Janes, Beth A., Ph.D, MD, 1529
Janes, Peter, 1463
Janesky Unitrust, A. & M., 8964
Janeway, Elizabeth Bixby, 712
Janeway, Kate, 9599
Janeway, Katherine A., 9707
Janeway, Katherine Ann, 9680
Janeway, William H., 6756
Jang, G. David, 713, 3813
Jang, G. David, M.D., 713
Janklow, Linda LeRoy, 6254
Janklow, Lucas, 6254
Janklow, Morton L., 6254
Jankus, A. Allan, 9833
Jannarone, Gary, 5145
Janney, Mary D., 1851
Jannotta, Edgar D., 2621
Jannusch, Rey, 2741
Janoch, T., 7710
Janoch, Thomas J., 7724
Janochoski, Jim, 4534
Janovic, Adam, 5905
Jansen, Adalia, 9776
Jansen, Carol Lyn, 3185
Jansen, Heather, 7573
Jansma, Joanne R., 4345
Jansma, Sidney J., III, 4345
Jansma, Sidney J., Jr., 4345
Janson, Robert, 4218
Janssen Pharmaceutica Inc., 5255
Janssen, Daniel, Baron, 5973
Janssen, Dean, 715
Janssen, Kathleen, 715
Jansson, Douglas M., 9876, 9963
Janukowicz, Robert, 6568
Janulis, Theodore P., 6395
Janus Capital Corp., 1396
Janus Capital Management LLC, 1396
Janus, Ernest A., 2592

Januzelli, Eric, 4331
Januzik, Michael J., 346
Janway, Dale, 5469
Janz, Deborah, 9861
Janz, James F., 9973
Japale, Ltd., 9057
Jaqua, George R., 5256
Jaquette-Tosh, Kathy, 8155
Jaramillo, Arturo, 5471
Jarcho, Fredrica, 6103
Jardine, Kimberly H., 25
Jarecki, Henry G., 5943
Jared, Jerry, 4798
Jareske, Michael J., 4993
Jarma, Debra Folsom, 8905
Jarrett, Charles E., 7808
Jarrett, James, 2359
Jarrett, Martha, 2041
Jarrott, Valerie B., 2820
Jarrott, Leonard S., 1074
Jarvis, Charlene Drew, 9424
Jarvis, Charles H., 1241
Jarvis, Michael, Mrs., 9474
Jarvis, Mike, 3178
Jarvis, Ron, Rev., 2075
Jason Industrial, Inc., 5773
Jaspan, Michael, 5959
Jaspan, Ronald, 5959
Jaspan, Steven, 5959
Jasse, Andre C., Jr., 3886
Jastrow, Kenneth M., II, 9228
Jath Oil Co., 7956
Javor, Julie, 408
Jay, Ann F., 4217
Jay, Vicky, 8923
Jaynes, Larry D., 9141
Jayroe, Jayne, 7964
Jazwinski, Robert C., 8438
JB 680 5th Avenue Associates LP, 5681
JBC Investment Co., 7934
Jealous, Benjamin Todd, 1065
Jeannero, Jane M., 4321
Jeans, Michael D., 8518
Jeavons, Thomas, 1983
Jecko, Stephen H., Rt. Rev., 1983
Jed Trust, The, 3973
Jeffe, Elizabeth R., 1572
Jeffe, Robert A., 1572
Jefferis, Judith Donaldson, 7127
Jeffers, John G., 5350
Jefferson Smurfit Corp. (U.S.), 4906
Jefferson State Bank, 9166
Jefferson, Robert, 8073
Jefferson, Tanya, 4255
Jefferson-Pilot Corp., 7405
Jeffery, Clara L.D., 5257
Jeffery, Linda, 3400
Jeffery, Margaret, 4421
Jeffery, Susan, 3206
Jeffords, David G., III, 2433
Jeffress, Elizabeth G., 9435
Jeffress, Robert M., 9442
Jeffrey, Bruce, 3529
Jeffries, M. Hill, Jr., 2525
Jeffris, Thomas M., 9821
Jeg's Automotive, Inc., 7687
Jeld-Wen Co. of Arizona, 8025
Jeld-Wen Fiber Products, Inc. of Iowa,
    8025
Jeld-Wen Holding, Inc., 8025
Jeld-Wen, Inc., 8025
Jelin, Sima K., 5228
Jelinek, Don, 4997
Jelks, Allen, 2076
Jelks, Allen N., Jr., 2076
Jelks, Bobby, 3469
Jelks, Bobby E., 3478
Jelks, Deborah Stephens, 2076
Jelks, Howard L., 2076
Jelks, Lisa Grace, 2076
Jelks, Mary, 2076
Jemison, Samuel R., 7668
Jencks, Anne B., 4160
Jencks, Christopher, 3015

Jendricks, Elizabeth C., 4188
Jendricks, John, 4188
Jenkins Trust, Mervyn W., 4836
Jenkins, Benjamin P., III, 7502
Jenkins, Carolyn S., 1433
Jenkins, Charles E., II, 9458
Jenkins, Charles, Sr., 2360
Jenkins, Christopher S., 1433
Jenkins, David D., 1433
Jenkins, David J., 7629
Jenkins, Donna, 1951
Jenkins, Douglas A., 7998
Jenkins, Forest N., 8638
Jenkins, Franklin Clay, 7463
Jenkins, George W., 2180
Jenkins, James C., 2099
Jenkins, James R., 2699
Jenkins, John E., Jr., 9721
Jenkins, John O., 504
Jenkins, John S., 4770
Jenkins, Laura, 1972
Jenkins, Paul, 3076
Jenkins, Paul R., 8099
Jenkins, Roger, 1251
Jenkins, Samuel, 4785
Jenkins, Sanela, 1251
Jenkins, Scott M., 8157
Jenkins, Tim, 7139
Jenkins, Tony, 1911
Jenkins, Victoria, 7406
Jenkins-Scott, Jackie, 3812
Jenkinson, Michael, 8551
Jenks, John R., 698
Jenks, John T., 2092
Jenks, R. Murray, 2092
Jenness, Jeff, 3197
Jennings, Bruce, 3199
Jennings, Christina, 8272
Jennings, Cynthia B., 8272
Jennings, Drue, 9222
Jennings, Elizabeth Cabell, 9381
Jennings, Evan D., II, 8272
Jennings, Frank G., 6231
Jennings, J. Webb, 8835
Jennings, Joel, 4658
Jennings, Karen E., 8765
Jennings, Keith S., 4030
Jennings, Madelyn P., 9424
Jennings, Martha Holden, 7688
Jennings, Mary Hillman, 8272
Jennings, Mary Lee, 4658
Jennings, Perry G., 7423
Jenrette, Richard H., 7359
Jensen, A.C., 4581, 4582
Jensen, Colin C., 3332
Jensen, James J., 9103
Jensen, Janet, 8836
Jensen, Janet Jarie, 8770
Jensen, Jeff, 8836
Jensen, Joan, 2811
Jensen, Julie, 8971
Jensen, Lou Anne, 8836
Jensen, Melissa S. Smith, 7860
Jensen, Pamela Simon, 1156
Jensen, Patricia A., 4636
Jensen, R.J., 8971
Jensen, Robert W., 1979
Jensen, Ronald L., 8836
Jensen, Verlyn N., 929
Jensen, William, 1468
Jephson, Lucretia Davis, 6258
Jepson, Hans G., 5569
Jepson, Larry, 4955
Jerde, Roxie, 4842
Jeremiah, Barbara S., 8075
Jeresaty, Robert M., 1568
Jergens, Andrew M., Rev., 7689
Jergens, Andrew N., 7689
Jergens, Linda Busken, 7689
Jeris, Darlene, 2020
Jernberg, Gary R., 4644
Jernstedt, Derek, 663
Jernstedt, Dorothy, 663
Jerome, Frank, 717

Jerome, Richard, 717
Jerry, Melissa, 183
Jersey Central Power & Light Co., 7630
Jerue, Richard A., 4275
Jerviss, Shelly, 6231
Jeschke, Thomas, 3317
Jeske, Marc, 3176
Jespersen, Marshall, 4026
Jesperson, Daryl, 1411
Jessell, Thomas M., 4616, 7254
Jesselson, Benjamin, 6259
Jesselson, E., 4071
Jesselson, Erica, 4071, 6259
Jesselson, Ludwig, 6259
Jesselson, M., 4071
Jesselson, Michael, 4071, 5968, 6259
Jessen, Helen, 2959
Jessen, Howard, 2959
Jessen, Paul C., 4994
Jessiman, Andrew G., 4074
Jessor, Richard, 3564
Jessup, Andrew T., Sr., 405
Jessup, Dan, 1454
Jessup, Jim, 3247
Jester, Chad A., 7771
Jeter, Derek S., 7174
Jeter, Dorothy, 7174
Jeter, James M., 2360
Jeter, Lydia, 4919
Jeter, Mark L., 4699
Jeter, Sanderson Charles, 7174
Jeter, Thomas H., 1008
Jett, Richard W., Jr., 8876
Jewell, Mary Louise Morris Brown, 2331
Jewell, Paul, 8098
Jewett, Brenda C., 4725
Jewett, Dunham F., 8866, 9210
Jewett, George Frederick, 718
Jewett, George Frederick, Jr., 718
Jewett, Lucille McIntyre, 718
Jewett, Truda C., 6083
Jezek, George, 1290
JFC Enterprises, 9802
Jian, Song, 6389
Jiganti, John J., 2869
Jimenez, Carlos, 9716
Jines, Michael L., 9144
Jinks, G.C., III, 2422
Jinks, G.C., Jr., 2422
Jinks, Peggy J., 2422
Jischke, Patty, 3188
JJB Land Company, LP, 1197
JJS Partnership, 4443
JLR Management Corp., 2958
JLRJ, Inc., 6394
JM Family Enterprises, Inc., 2143
JM Shoe Group Inc., 649
JME Charitable Lead Trust, 6700
JME II Charitable Lead Trust, 6700
Joan Fabrics Corp., 4029
Jobe, Warren, 2500
Jobin-Leeds, Greg, 4132, 6431
Jobin-Leeds, Maria, 4132
Jochens, William, 4881
Jochum, Anna Marie, 5738
Jochum, Emil, 7692
Jochum, Emma, 7692
Jodar, Carol W., 7907
Joelson, Julius, 6265
Joerres, Jeffrey A., 9858
Joffe, Harvey G., 981
Joffe, Josef, 6056
Joffe, Ruth, 6021
Jogerst, Allen L., 9072
Joh, Erik Edward, 2237
Johannsen, Mark, 9776
Johansen, David G., 9635
Johansen, Karen, 3862
John, Lester M., 8026
John, Lisa Latz, 3123
John, Mildred D., 8273
John, Paul R., 8273
John, Regina M., 8026
Johansen, Laurie, 8814

Johns, Cynthia, 5482
Johns, Gary D., 7644
Johns, Jeffrey, 5482
Johns, John D., 58
Johns, Kenneth E., 5482
Johns, Margaret M., 7644
Johns, Martha V., 7176
Johns, Sheryl L., 8961
Johns, William M., 7939
Johnson & Johnson, 5255, 5261
Johnson & Son, S.C., Inc., 9826
Johnson 1951 and 1961 Charitable Trusts, J. Seward, 2198
Johnson and Johnson, 3677
Johnson Charitable Lead Trust, Charlotte, 6268
Johnson Charitable Lead Trust, Robert, 426
Johnson Controls, Inc., 9823
Johnson Foundation, Robert Wood, The, 5905
Johnson Foundation, William M. and Phyllis B., Inc., The, 2381
Johnson Fund, Edward C., 3818
Johnson Richards Charitable Trust, Mary Lea, 1896
Johnson, Abigail P., 3904, 3970
Johnson, Alan C., 426
Johnson, Alan H., 4501
Johnson, Alvin, 557
Johnson, Andy A., 6395
Johnson, Angie Newman, 9389
Johnson, Ann, 517
Johnson, Ann L., 426, 723
Johnson, Anthony, 7248
Johnson, Arnold L., 4219
Johnson, Arthur, 8508
Johnson, Arthur E., 1398
Johnson, Arthur L., 112
Johnson, Asa B., 9421
Johnson, Asa J., 8274
Johnson, Barbara J., 3311
Johnson, Barbara L., 7444
Johnson, Barbara Piasecka, 5263
Johnson, Ben, Rev., 4534
Johnson, Betty W., 5680, 6266, 6270, 6273
Johnson, Betty Wold, 6267
Johnson, Beverly, 8696
Johnson, Beverly P., 8697
Johnson, Bob, 1471
Johnson, Brad, 3255
Johnson, Brett, 1175
Johnson, Brian C., 7985
Johnson, Brian P., 9800
Johnson, Bridget B., 5738
Johnson, Burdine C., 8830, 8973
Johnson, Calvin M., 2142
Johnson, Carl W., 722
Johnson, Carol R., 3015
Johnson, Carolyn E., 426
Johnson, Catherine Holman, 724
Johnson, Catherine Shea, 1141
Johnson, Charles B., 723, 3351
Johnson, Charles V., Hon., 9599
Johnson, Charles W., 4412
Johnson, Charlotte S., 4523
Johnson, Chris Leevy, 8577
Johnson, Christian A., 6268
Johnson, Christine, 1364
Johnson, Christine D., 4993
Johnson, Christopher, 6272, 9702
Johnson, Christopher W., 6266, 6270
Johnson, Cindy Faye, 4534
Johnson, Claire W., 9857
Johnson, Craig C., 426
Johnson, Cynthia D., 3563
Johnson, D. Kim, 7438
Johnson, Dale D., 4573
Johnson, Dana, 355
Johnson, Daniel, 4521
Johnson, Daniel P., 9963
Johnson, Darrell F., 9578
Johnson, David, 5517

Johnson, David A., 9578
Johnson, David G., 6271
Johnson, David J., 3092
Johnson, David M., 8972
Johnson, David P., 9486
Johnson, Dean, 4637
Johnson, Dennis, 7519, 7882
Johnson, Dennis G., 7883
Johnson, Derrick, 7582
Johnson, Diana, 5109
Johnson, Diane N., 2077
Johnson, Donald, 4355
Johnson, Donald E., Jr., 4482
Johnson, Donald P., 721
Johnson, Dorothy A., 4357
Johnson, Douglas, 693
Johnson, Douglas L., 1052
Johnson, Douglas R., 5846, 6428
Johnson, E. Lynn, 3254
Johnson, Edward C., II, 3970
Johnson, Edward C., III, 3818, 3904, 3970
Johnson, Edward C., IV, 3970
Johnson, Elizabeth Hill, 8027
Johnson, Elizabeth L., 3970
Johnson, Elizabeth Ross, 6267
Johnson, Eric C., 426, 8205, 8249, 8250, 8251, 8252, 8442
Johnson, Felton, 5815
Johnson, Forde, 2566
Johnson, Frances, 1426
Johnson, Frances M., 9825
Johnson, Franklin L., 724
Johnson, Franklin Pitcher, Jr., 724
Johnson, Fred D., 8661
Johnson, G. Elaine, 3164
Johnson, G. Timothy, 3947
Johnson, Gary, 9810
Johnson, Gene, 3124
Johnson, George D., 8602
Johnson, George Dean, Jr., 8602
Johnson, George L., 8570
Johnson, George R., 8696, 8697
Johnson, Gerard G., 8103
Johnson, Glen D., 7955
Johnson, Glenn W., III, 8074
Johnson, Glenn W., Jr., 8074
Johnson, Graham L., 9825
Johnson, Greg A., 3125
Johnson, Gregg, 9690
Johnson, Gregory Ben, 3503
Johnson, Gregory E., 1706
Johnson, Gretchen W., 5153
Johnson, H. Fisk, 9824, 9826
Johnson, Hamlin, 8456
Johnson, Harold B., 6633
Johnson, Harriet, 6946
Johnson, Harry A., III, 8677
Johnson, Harry S., 3568
Johnson, Haynes, 1776
Johnson, Heather Rae, 6974
Johnson, Helen K., 1398
Johnson, Holly, 4325
Johnson, Howard Marshall, 8895
Johnson, Imogene P., 9824
Johnson, Ivan, 3317
Johnson, J., 1056
Johnson, J. Seward, Jr., 5264
Johnson, J. Seward, Sr., 5263
Johnson, J. Thomas, 8577
Johnson, J.L., 8173
Johnson, J.M., 8973
Johnson, J.S., III, 5262
Johnson, J.S., Jr., 5262
Johnson, James, 7891
Johnson, James A., 1812
Johnson, James E., Jr., 7390
Johnson, James J., 7496
Johnson, James L., 101, 5153, 8253
Johnson, James M., 8274
Johnson, Jane T., 8274
Johnson, Janet, 5902
Johnson, Janet L., 7595

Johnson, Jeff, 9776
Johnson, Jennifer, 7248
Johnson, Jerry, 9131
Johnson, Jerry L., 426
Johnson, Jesse D., 8274
Johnson, Jill, 7985
Johnson, Jim, 1178, 4968
Johnson, Joanne, 1356
Johnson, John, 8631
Johnson, John C., 30
Johnson, John W., 8972
Johnson, Joia M., 2355
Johnson, Joseph, 6402, 8840
Johnson, Joseph S., 2664
Johnson, Joyce H., 5264
Johnson, Jr. Charitable Annuity Lead
   Trust, J. Seward, 5264
Johnson, Judith, 520
Johnson, Judy, 421
Johnson, Julie A., 1081
Johnson, June M., 2794
Johnson, Justice, 7756
Johnson, Karen B., Jr., 9389
Johnson, Kate, 8816
Johnson, Kathryn M., 9035
Johnson, Kathryn Shannon, 1133
Johnson, Kathy, 4227
Johnson, Katie Mertz, 9164
Johnson, Keith A., 506, 9188
Johnson, Keith W., 6270
Johnson, Kevin P., 4349
Johnson, Larry K., 7444
Johnson, Lawrence A., 150
Johnson, Lawrence M., 2545
Johnson, Lee E., 4580
Johnson, Leigh, 4668
Johnson, Leonard W., 4096, 4159
Johnson, Lester O., 9825
Johnson, Lillie A., 8974
Johnson, Linda C. Batterman, 9754
Johnson, Lisa, 4349
Johnson, Lloyd P., 100
Johnson, Lynne, 2541
Johnson, M.G., 8974
Johnson, Madeleine Rubin, 6878
Johnson, Madeleine Rudin, 6877, 6879
Johnson, Marcus, III, 725
Johnson, Margaret, 9389
Johnson, Margaret Ann, 6269
Johnson, Margaret P., 8146
Johnson, Margaret Shaw, 4729
Johnson, Margie S., 4764
Johnson, Marianne E. Boyd, 5023
Johnson, Marilyn, 4380
Johnson, Marilyn B., 4349
Johnson, Marjorie, 150
Johnson, Mark E., 3093
Johnson, Mark L., 8816, 8817
Johnson, Mary W., 721
Johnson, Michael, 9933
Johnson, Michael P., 7989
Johnson, Mike, 4520
Johnson, Milton, 8690
Johnson, Nancy, 1789
Johnson, Nancy K., 3189
Johnson, Neal, 2677
Johnson, Neil E., 3619
Johnson, Noreen, 7650
Johnson, Norman E., 8658
Johnson, Otis, 7308
Johnson, Pamela B., 2712
Johnson, Pamela M., 9906
Johnson, Patricia B., 4252
Johnson, Patricia C., 8027
Johnson, Paul C., 100, 4252
Johnson, Paul D., 4962
Johnson, Paul H., 4349
Johnson, Paul T., 7595
Johnson, Paula A., 8500
Johnson, Peter, 196
Johnson, Peter J., 4499
Johnson, Peter James, 6272
Johnson, Peter James, Jr., 6272
Johnson, Philip, 4082

Johnson, Phillip M., 2397
Johnson, Phillip R., 1883
Johnson, Phyllis B., 2381
Johnson, Rafer, 214
Johnson, Raymond L., 2009
Johnson, Reba J., 1273
Johnson, Reuben B., III, 1939
Johnson, Richard S., 2197
Johnson, Rick, 3166
Johnson, Robbin S., 4530
Johnson, Robert, 426, 3247, 4315,
   9444
Johnson, Robert C., 3384
Johnson, Robert H., 150
Johnson, Robert K., 304
Johnson, Robert L., 2345
Johnson, Robert O., 2304
Johnson, Robert W., 721
Johnson, Robert W., IV, 6270, 6273
Johnson, Robert Wood, 5265
Johnson, Robert Wood, IV, 5265, 6616
Johnson, Ron, 7343
Johnson, Ronald P., 7306
Johnson, Ronald S., 1370
Johnson, Roni, 3128
Johnson, Rosalind G., 100
Johnson, Rosemary, 204
Johnson, Royce, 641
Johnson, Rupert H., Jr., 726
Johnson, Russell, 100
Johnson, Ruth, 8972
Johnson, S. Curtis, 9824, 9826
Johnson, Samuel S., 8027
Johnson, Sandra, 1598
Johnson, Saundra E., 98
Johnson, Seth, 3529
Johnson, Sharon, 7537
Johnson, Sheila, 9444
Johnson, Sheila B., 8816
Johnson, Skip, 3368
Johnson, Stanley D., 8611
Johnson, Susan P., 8602
Johnson, Suzanne M. Nora, 6271
Johnson, Suzanne Nora, 6056
Johnson, Ted, 1201
Johnson, Terri L., 3215
Johnson, Theodore R., 2077
Johnson, Thomas, 4698, 8274
Johnson, Thomas G., Jr., 9447
Johnson, Thomas N.P., III, 9389
Johnson, Thomas P., 6269, 8146, 8274
Johnson, Thomas P., Jr., 8146
Johnson, Thomas Phillips, 8274
Johnson, Thomas S., 6269, 7185
Johnson, Timothy D., 3118
Johnson, Timothy E., 7595
Johnson, Tina, 2180
Johnson, Tom, 2890
Johnson, Toni, 3145
Johnson, Truitt K., 14
Johnson, Veronica, 6272
Johnson, Vivian M., 2077
Johnson, Wade L., 9389
Johnson, Walter E., 8960
Johnson, Walter S., 725
Johnson, Walter, Genl., 8581
Johnson, Wendy S., 7308
Johnson, Willard T.C., 6270
Johnson, William, 406, 2058, 7453
Johnson, William A., 973
Johnson, William B., 1
Johnson, William G., 7509
Johnson, William H., 8162
Johnson, William M., 2381
Johnson, William T., 8973
Johnson, Willis J., 1273
Johnson, Wilma, 7472
Johnson, Worthington, 1679
Johnson, Worthington, Jr., 1679
Johnson-Helm, Elizabeth K., 8027
Johnson-Hill, Marlene, 3250
Johnson-Leipold, Helen, 9824
Johnson-Leipold, Helen P., 9826
JohnsonDiversey, Inc., 9826

Johnston, Allan, 78
Johnston, Berkeley, 1457
Johnston, Bill, 8842
Johnston, Coy, 2706
Johnston, D. Chapman, Jr., 8616
Johnston, David, 26
Johnston, David C., 9796
Johnston, David S., 4436
Johnston, Fred, 7593
Johnston, Fred E., 7593
Johnston, Gerald E., 389
Johnston, J.C., III, 7897
Johnston, J.W., 4368
Johnston, James, 1720
Johnston, James M., 3657
Johnston, John C., III, 7541
Johnston, John R., Mrs., 3811
Johnston, Lavinia, 8735
Johnston, Linda A., 3800
Johnston, M. Harlan, 2200
Johnston, Mary E., 3445
Johnston, Mary Kaye, 4436
Johnston, Michael, 4472
Johnston, Michael J., 5390
Johnston, Murray L., Jr., 9296
Johnston, Penelope, 5824
Johnston, Peter E., 7791
Johnston, Rebecca, 3030
Johnston, Regina, 9021
Johnston, Renee S., 4428
Johnston, Robert T., 4451
Johnston, Rose M., 8600
Johnston, S.K., III, 8735
Johnston, S.K., Jr, 8735
Johnston, Seth, 7749
Johnston, Sid G., 8610
Johnston, Steven J., 7650
Johnston, Vivian G., Jr., 25, 46
Johnston, William, 4451
Johnston, William D., 4451
Johnston, William E., 5484
Johnstone, Carol Levy, 4378
Johnstone, Gail E., 5780
Johnstone, John W., 134
Johnstone, R.C., Jr., 1144
Johnstone, Shana B., 1144
Joiner, Clinton Thorpe, 8721
Jokiel, Judith Ann, 2019
Jolley, James E., 7407
Jolley, James F., 7633
Jolley, R.A., Jr., 7407
Jollie, William P., 9857
Jollivette, Cyrus M., 1911
Jolly, Eric J., 4623
Jolson, Joseph A., 727
Jolson, Kathleen, 727
Jonas, Debbie, 5266
Jonas, Donald K., 7370
Jonas, Gary F., 1785
Jonas, Howard, 5266
Jonas, Jody, 9949
Jonassen, Hans A.B., 3461
Jonathan Manufacture Corp., 5686
Jones & Co., Edward D., L.P., 4838
Jones Charitable Lead Trust, Seby B.,
   7408
Jones Charitable Remainder Annuity
   Trust, Joseph E., 1813
Jones Charitable Remainder Annuity
   Trust, Marjorie B., 1813
Jones Foundation, Dodge, 9226
Jones Foundation, W. Alton, 477, 6043
Jones Trust, Walter S. and Evan C., 3370
Jones, Alfred W., III, 2330
Jones, Alfred, Jr., 8136
Jones, Alinda F., 7927
Jones, Alison, 8482
Jones, Alison C., 8482
Jones, Arthur G., 3016
Jones, B. Bryan, III, 4741
Jones, B. Todd, 4667
Jones, B.L., 8895
Jones, B.T., 4733
Jones, Barbara J., 6823

Jones, Bernard B., II, 4741
Jones, Beth B., 7594
Jones, Boisfeuillet, Jr., 1834
Jones, Brenda, 9357
Jones, Caroline, 5457
Jones, Carolyn, 9439
Jones, Charles "C.J.", 1515
Jones, Charles A., 7603
Jones, Charles E., 7630
Jones, Charles H., 2424
Jones, Charles I., Jr., 9725
Jones, Charles W., 7725
Jones, Christina B., 7408
Jones, Christopher W., 5457
Jones, Claiborne S., 2491
Jones, Clara, 183
Jones, Claudia, 7582
Jones, Clayton, 3328
Jones, Cora, 3245
Jones, D. Paul, Jr., 28
Jones, Daisy Marquis, 6274
Jones, Dan B., 8754
Jones, David, 5652, 7622, 9949
Jones, David A., 3412, 3428
Jones, David A., Jr., 3428
Jones, David R., 673, 6918
Jones, Dee Lipka, 5194
Jones, Dennis M., 4839
Jones, Dennis M., Jr., 4839
Jones, Diane, 8853
Jones, Don E., 3469
Jones, Donald, 9827
Jones, Donald F., 134
Jones, Donna B., 8511
Jones, Doug, 1445
Jones, Duane, 4315
Jones, Dwight C., 2424
Jones, E. Lee, 9713
Jones, E. Richard, 989
Jones, Earle, 4737
Jones, Edward L., Jr., 8086
Jones, Elaine F., 3491
Jones, Eleanor Miniger, 7756
Jones, Elizabeth, 9357
Jones, Ellen W., 8482
Jones, Emily J., 9049
Jones, Emma Eccles, 9330, 9331, 9332
Jones, Erlon, 3528
Jones, Ernest E., 8494
Jones, Eugenie P., 3491
Jones, F. Austin, 3325
Jones, Fletcher, 728
Jones, Frank C., 2358
Jones, Geoffrey, 5457
Jones, George M., III, 7756
Jones, George M., Jr., 7756
Jones, Gerard, 7138
Jones, Harry T., III, 2360
Jones, Helayne B., 1445
Jones, Helen DeVitt, 8975
Jones, Helen Jeane, 5055
Jones, Hendrick, 4315
Jones, Herbert B., 9615
Jones, Homer A., Jr., 9448
Jones, Ingrid Saunders, 2352
Jones, Irene, 941
Jones, J. Michael, 172
Jones, J. Stephen, 3370
Jones, James, 739
Jones, James H., 2673
Jones, James R., 7408
Jones, Jan, 8685
Jones, Jan Laverty, 5048
Jones, Janice, 8877
Jones, Janie P., 8698
Jones, Jean C., 1356
Jones, Jeanne C., 513
Jones, Jerry D., 2882
Jones, Jerry G., 5496
Jones, Jesse H., 8961
Jones, Jesse H., Mrs., 8961
Jones, Jo Ann, 8820
Jones, Joan, 2015
Jones, JoAnn, 1947

Jones, John P., III, 8404
Jones, Johnny C., 7977
Jones, Joseph M., 3491
Jones, Joseph W., 2352
Jones, Judith A., 630, 4839
Jones, Judith A., DDS, 4061
Jones, Judith B., 9308
Jones, Karyne, 1786
Jones, Kim, 1214
Jones, Kim B., 2362
Jones, L. Bevel, III, Bishop, 2463
Jones, Larry W., 3420
Jones, Leigh H., 7385
Jones, Lorine, 9071
Jones, Louise G., 4519
Jones, Lucy H., 7349
Jones, Lucy R., 4725, 4726
Jones, Margaret W., 3430
Jones, Marjorie B., 1813
Jones, Mary D.T., 7359
Jones, Mary Eddy, 7946
Jones, Mary T., 7317
Jones, Melissa A., 8961
Jones, Melvin, 9723
Jones, Meredith, 3548
Jones, Michael, 5008, 5009, 8853
Jones, Michael D., 5011
Jones, Michelle, 3039
Jones, Miles E., 4347
Jones, Morgan R., 8256
Jones, Nancy E., 8840
Jones, Nancy S., 7873
Jones, Nathan J., 2647
Jones, Nina M., 4255
Jones, O.D., 825
Jones, Orville, III, 4987
Jones, Otis P., 2382
Jones, Pamela S., 2552
Jones, Pat, 7344
Jones, Patricia M., 474
Jones, Patrick, 7963
Jones, Paul, 1619
Jones, Paul T., II, 1664, 6037
Jones, Paul W., 9929
Jones, Peggy Dutton, 9614
Jones, Phillip, 9801
Jones, R. Scott, 4671
Jones, Raymond E., 4902
Jones, Reginald, 3021
Jones, Reginald H., 9357
Jones, Reginald N., 9506
Jones, Reid, Jr., 9443
Jones, Richard, 8993
Jones, Richard I. G., 8141
Jones, Robert, 8957
Jones, Robert J., 4524
Jones, Robert L., 3630, 7408, 7438
Jones, Robert N., 3430
Jones, Robert S., 3430
Jones, Ron, 9265
Jones, Ronald, 3250
Jones, Ronald D., 9927
Jones, Rosetta E., 1517
Jones, Russell L., 87
Jones, Ruth Leggett, 8868
Jones, Sandra I., 2382
Jones, Sarah Hopper, 2330
Jones, Scott A., 3179
Jones, Seby B., 7408
Jones, Seby B., Jr., 7408
Jones, Seby Russell, 7408
Jones, Seitu, 4595
Jones, Stephen C., 4878, 4896
Jones, Susan Shands, 4737
Jones, Teena, 1914
Jones, Terri, 9827
Jones, Theodore T., 8482
Jones, Thomas E., 7954
Jones, Thomas K., 3393
Jones, Timothy A., 1442
Jones, Timothy J., 4297
Jones, Todd, 3258
Jones, Ves, 2424
Jones, W. Allan, 8698

Jones, W. Alton, 9379
Jones, W.D., III, 3094
Jones, Walter M., 2359
Jones, Warren, 8482
Jones, Warren Tanner, 8482
Jones, William E., 2307
Jones, William H., 6207
Jones-Church, Nyda, 192
Jones-Jemison, Rebecca, 7668
Jones-Kelley, Helen, 7603
Jonesboro Central Planning Assoc., 160
Jonsen, Albert R., 1151
Jonsson Foundation, The, 729, 8977
Jonsson, Christina A., 8977
Jonsson, David Mark, 729
Jonsson, Diane, 729
Jonsson, Kenneth, 729
Jonsson, Kenneth B., 8977
Jonsson, Michael, 729
Jonsson, Philip R., 8977
Jonsson, Robert Erik, 729
Jonsson, Steven W., 8977
Jonsson, Suzanne W., 8977
Joo, Dong Moon, 1860
Joos, David W., 4260
Jope, Alan C., 5434
Jordache Enterprises, Inc., 6600
Jordache Ltd., 6600
Jordan, Arthur, 3180
Jordan, Barbara M., 8144
Jordan, Brian, 8967
Jordan, C. Dexter, Jr., 2361
Jordan, Catherine, 4595
Jordan, D. Raines, 2361
Jordan, Darrell L., 2680
Jordan, Ettie A., 4840
Jordan, Gerald R., Jr., 3971
Jordan, Helen S., 2425
Jordan, Henry A., 8141
Jordan, Jack, 3199
Jordan, Jennifer B., 6388
Jordan, John R., Jr., 7438
Jordan, John W., II, 4843
Jordan, Juanita T., 2317, 2358
Jordan, Kathryn H., 8978
Jordan, Lorna Pauley, 9494
Jordan, Mary Ranken, 4840
Jordan, Michael, 8046
Jordan, Rodney G., 1355
Jordan, Rodney W., 4636
Jordan, Roger, 5808
Jordan, Taylor, 5808
Jordan, Vernon E., 3583
Jordan, Veronica, 7175
Jordan, Virginia, 5417
Jordan, Virginia W., 5808
Jordan, Wayne, 199
Jordan, William Chester, 7126
Jordan, William R., 2273
Jordan, Wilma, 6708
Jordheim, Neil, 7514
Jordon, James E., 2023
Jorge, Bob, 627
Jorgensen, Arne C., 10000
Jorgensen, Grace, 6915
Jorgensen, Kim, 4310
Jorgenson, Erik, 3014
Jorgenson, James A., 4588
Jorgenson, Judy, 9876
Jorgenson, Krystin, 7496
Jorgenson, Megan, 3014
Jorndt, L. Daniel, 3051
Joscelyn, Verla Nesbitt, 3371
Jose, Katharine P., 4688
Joseloff Foundation Trust, Morris, 1575
Joseloff, Lillian L., 1575
Joseloff, Morris, 1575
Joseph F. Miller Foundation, 3164
Joseph, Alice, 6287
Joseph, Amy F., 7623
Joseph, Andrew, 6287
Joseph, Benjamin, 6287
Joseph, Brian E., 9713
Joseph, Carol, 6760

Joseph, Dallas, 8660
Joseph, Edwin, 1426
Joseph, Elaine, 3489
Joseph, George R., 7623
Joseph, James A., 7496
Joseph, Jim, 730, 4071
Joseph, Margaret Elise Elkins, 8883
Joseph, Peggy, 76
Joseph, Peter A., 6760
Joseph, Robert, 2745
Joseph, Sharon, 8842
Joseph, Todd M., 7158
Joseph, William F., 20
Josephson, John, 6438
Josey, Lenior M., 8897
Joshi, Krishan K., 7693
Joshi, Nina, 7693
Joshi, Shashi S., 7693
Joshi, Vicky M., 7693
Joslin, David C., 4321
Jostad, Bob, 8631
Josten, Maureen, 9963
Jostens, Inc., 4596
Joubert, Cassandra, 4254
Joukowsky, Artemis A.W., 6275
Joukowsky, Martha S., 6275
Joul, Steven R., 4534
Journal-Gazette Co., 3181
Jowett, Ted, 3354
Joy Global Inc., 9828
Joy, H. Joan, 6276
Joy, Hayden N., 1399
Joy, Judith N., 2817, 2898, 2899
Joy, Lene, 6276
Joy, Madison C., 1399
Joy, Mary Alice, 6276
Joy, Paul W., 6276
Joy, Sara R., 1399
Joy, Stephen T., 6276
Joy, William N., 1399
Joyce, Bernard F., 5307, 6429
Joyce, Cynthia, 7031
Joyce, Lisa, 6433
Joyce, Severn, 7756
Joyce, Steve, 7307
Joyner, C. Dan, 8583
Joyner, Pamela, 347
JPMorgan Chase & Co., 5845, 8333
JPMorgan Chase Bank, N.A., 1506,
    1688, 1695, 1705, 1708, 1709,
    1718, 1719, 1721, 1722, 1744,
    1745, 1746, 1750, 1752, 1754,
    1761, 1880, 2225, 2661, 2679,
    2833, 3462, 3469, 3533, 4466,
    5514, 5563, 5651, 5759, 5839,
    5841, 5919, 5948, 5966, 5977,
    6091, 6130, 6135, 6196, 6258,
    6277, 6421, 6452, 6470, 6613,
    6666, 6748, 6797, 7014, 7040,
    7053, 7220, 7224, 7264, 7526,
    7574, 7576, 7580, 7603, 7682,
    7699, 7714, 7819, 8537, 8806,
    8830, 8855, 8982, 9005, 9151,
    9166, 9198, 9250, 9251, 9269,
    9279, 9716, 9723, 9746, 9753,
    9755, 9759, 9769, 9782, 9783,
    9787, 9790, 9791, 9793, 9795,
    9796, 9798, 9805, 9809, 9811,
    9816, 9835, 9849, 9853, 9866,
    9876, 9879, 9880, 9885, 9892,
    9893, 9926, 9928, 9941, 9942,
    9943, 9948, 9951, 9959, 9965
JPMorgan Private Client Svcs., 7174
Jrr Mgmt., 7292
Jubilee Group, 740
Jubitz Investments, LP, 8028
Jubitz, Fred, 8029
Jubitz, Gail, 8029
Jubitz, Katherine H., 8028
Jubitz, M. Albin, Jr., 8028
Jubitz, Matthew, 8029
Jubitz, Sarah C., 8028
Juchter, Elia, 5902
Juckett, J. Walter, 6903

Juckett, Rhoda, 1936
Juday, Suzanne, 2701
Judd, Jackie, 739
Judd, Robert, 2108
Judd, Robert B., 1941
Judd, Virginia K., 3428
Judd, Wendell W., 9107
Judge & Dolph, Ltd., 3076
Judge, Natalie Pruitt, 2179
Judkins, Don, 732
Judkins, Donavan, 732
Judkins, Greg, 732
Judkins, Maxine, 732
Judlau Contracting, Inc., 6236
Judson, K. Leonard, 581
Judy, Rhonda F., 4340
Juett, Katherine Crossland, 8703
Juge, Anne S. Wallace, 1674
Julian, Carole, 4981
Julian, Joe, 9132
Julian, Joseph, 7831
Julian, Robert E., 4981
Julian, Robert, Hon., 5783
Julius, David, 4616
Julson, Althea, 5902
Junck, Mary, 3306
Juneman, Lou, 217
Jung, Joel, 383
Jung, Lucy, 713
Jungbauer, Erin, 3185
Junge, Kim, 8219
Jungwirth, Helen, 9779
Juniata Valley Bank, The, 8208
Junker, Edward P., III, 8188
Junker, George, II, 3230
Jurczyk, Nathan, 220
Jurgensen, W.G., 7771
Jurgenson, Paula, 2040
Jurries, James, 4350
Jurries, James L., 4350
Jurries, Jim, 4258
Jurries, Virginia, 4350
Jurries, Virginia L., 4350
Jury, John, 9778
Jurzykowski, Alfred, 6278
Jurzykowski, M. Christine, 6278
Jurzykowski, Yolande L., 6278
Justice, Bridget, 3431
Justice, Frank, 3431
Justice, Frank, II, 3431
Justice, Jason, 3431
Justice, Mattie, 3431
Justice, Melody C., 2352
Justice, Rita F., 9399
Justice-Moore, Kathleen, 913
Justice-Moore, Kathleen E., 912
Justin, Jane C., 8979
Justin, Mary C., 8979
Justin, Robert, 4256
Justis, Jane Leighty, 1437
Justus, Edith C., 8276
Jutte, Larry, 7673

K N Energy, Inc., 1403
K-Swiss Inc., 190
Kabacinski, Mary, 9776
Kabacoff, Gloria S., 3492
Kabacoff, Lester E., 3492
Kabacoff, Maurice P., 3492
Kabbes, David G., 4792
Kabbes, Scott R., 4647
Kabcenell, Charlene C., 737
Kabcenell, Dirk A., 737
Kabelin, Jerry, 3247
Kabler, Elizabeth R., 6852
Kacal, Melinda M., 9210
Kachel, Beth, 3124
Kacic, Edward B., 699
Kacin, A. Richard, 8155
Kade, Fritz, Jr., 6281
Kade, Max, 6281
Kaden, Lewis B., 5755
Kadesh Investments Ltd., 4043

Kadifa, Sally Rathmann, 3715
Kadish, Alice B., 9829
Kaelin, Bruno A., III, 3613
Kaemmer, Arthur W., 4589
Kaemmer, Frederick C., 4589
Kaemmer, Martha H., 4589
Kaempfer, Christopher L., 5074
Kaeo, Mervina Cash, 2545
Kaesemeyer, C. Thomas, 1380
Kagan, Cheryl C., 3633
Kagan, Elena, 6998
Kahane, Batya, 5277
Kahane, Claire, 5277
Kahane, David, 5277
Kahle, Brewster L., 738
Kahle, Charles, 9367
Kahle, John H., 3182
Kahle, Rita D., 2582
Kahler, Camille T., 5783
Kahler, Debra, 3339
Kahler, Ellen, 9361
Kahn, Alan R., 6260
Kahn, Claude, 2581
Kahn, Claudia J., 6537
Kahn, David D., 4351
Kahn, Irving, 6260
Kahn, Joseph, 3973
Kahn, Julius "Sandy", III, 941, 1099
Kahn, Karen M., 235
Kahn, Mady, 828
Kahn, Mel, 828
Kahn, Michael, 6790
Kahn, Richard D., 5599
Kahn, Robert C., 7464
Kahn, Roger, 1244
Kahn, Stephen B., 235
Kahn, Stephen S., 8980
Kahn, Terence P., 3164
Kahn, Virginia, 6790
Kahne, Daniel, 7254
Kahrer, Mark G., 5361
Kahrs, Kenneth L., 933
Kahului Trucking and Storage, 2530
Kailbourne, Erland E., 6660
Kain, Herbert, 1256
Kainz, John, 2822
Kainz, Joseph A., 2822
Kainz, Michael J., 2822
Kainz, Patrick J., 2822
Kainz, Susan J., 2822
Kaiser Foundation Health Plan of the
   Northwest, 8048
Kaiser, Bess F., 739
Kaiser, C.J., Jr., 9716
Kaiser, Christina, 6283
Kaiser, Ferdinand C., 5565
Kaiser, George B., 7984
Kaiser, Gerald, 6283
Kaiser, Henry J., 739
Kaiser, Henry J., Jr., 739
Kaiser, Herman, 7948
Kaiser, Michael, 739
Kaiser, Miranda, 6827
Kaiserman Enterprises, LP, 8277
Kaiserman Marital Trust, Kevy K., 8277
Kaiserman, Hortense M., 8277
Kaiserman, Kenneth S., 8277
Kaiserman, Ronald L., 8277
Kaizer, Pam, 212
Kajiwara, Gary, 2547
Kakabadse, Yolanda, 5970
Kalama, Corbett A K., 2542
Kalat, Peter A., 6659
Kalb, Marianne Bernstein, 1775
Kalb, Robert, 1775
Kalberer, Jean C., 7695
Kalberer, Lori, 7695
Kalberer, Walter E., 7695
Kaldis, Catherine Daniel, 8902
Kaleak, George T., Sr., 80
Kaliakin, Nikolai A., 778
Kalick, Dennis, 6201
Kalikow, Peter, 6779
Kalin, Richard L., 8136

Kalinske, Thomas J., 898
Kalish, Katherine M., 2468
Kaliszewski, John, 4593
Kalkbrenner, David L., 264
Kall, Sheldon G., 6739
Kallaus, Kurt J., 4913
Kalleward, Howard, 4266
Kallgren, Charles, 516
Kallgren, Edward E., 516
Kallman, Ellen B., 6260
Kallstrom, Robert E., 3598
Kalmanovitz, Lydia, 741
Kalnow, Andrew H., 7809
Kalnow, Carl F., 7809
Kalnow, Loretta K., 7809
Kalogerakis, Michael G., 6315
Kalsi, Sarla, 3166, 3175
Kalter, Albert, 6141
Kalter, Aryeh L., 6284
Kalter, Dahlia, 6141
Kalter, Frady, 5965, 6284
Kalter, Moshe, 5965, 6284
Kaltman, Ira J., 5134
Kam, Thomas, 1785
Kamahele, Wanda J., 9592
Kamara, Melissa, 4258
Kamath, Geetha, 1096
Kamath, Ravishankar, 1096
Kamen, Barbara, 5968
Kamen, Steven R., 5228
Kamensky, Marvin, 2664
Kameo, Victor, 5554
Kami, Nancy S., 596
Kamin, Samuel P., 8505
Kaminer, Ariel, 6285
Kaminer, Henry, 6285
Kaminer, Martin, 6285
Kaminer, Phyllis, 6285
Kaminow, Linda R., 6849
Kaminsky, Marcia S., 3046
Kamm, Solomon M., 6757
Kammer, Randy M., 1911
Kammerer, Harry, 8148
Kamp, Kenneth R., 8958
Kamper, Carol, 4668
Kampfer, Merlin W., 98
Kamphorst, Jaap, 954
Kampmann, Abigail G., 9244
Kamras, Marvin, 1111
Kanai, Toshiharu, 7436
Kananck, Arnold F., 5609
Kanarek, Robin B., 1490
Kanas, Elaine, 6286
Kanas, John, 6286
Kanas, John A., 6286
Kanas, John Adam, 6637
Kanas, Mary, 1373
Kandasamy, Diana, 7126
Kandel, Eric R., 3621
Kandel, Richard, 7226
Kandell, Alice, 6287
Kandell, Florence, 6287
Kandell, Leonard, 6287
Kandell, Leslie, 6287
Kandravy, John, 5179
Kane, Chad D., 9756
Kane, David Paul, 1225
Kane, Dennis O., 8596
Kane, Eileen, 5894
Kane, Eileen B., 5611
Kane, Eric, 6408
Kane, Eugene I., 8596
Kane, Jacqueline P., 389
Kane, Jami S., 284
Kane, John C., 2579
Kane, John F., 7953
Kane, Marion, 3791
Kane, Maureen, 1603
Kane, Michael E., 8153
Kane, Robert J., 7558
Kane, Robin Berlin, 7546
Kane, Russell, 6408
Kane, Susan, 6408
Kaneda, Thomas, 8212

Kaneko, Hisashi, 6605
Kaney, Thomas K., 8218
Kanfer, Joseph, 7719
Kanfer, Mamie, 7719
Kang, Matt, 7667
Kang, Ted, 7139
Kangas, Paul, 4183
Kangisser, Dianne, 5655
Kanik, James R., 6639
Kann, Peter, 5184
Kann, Peter R., 5879
Kanno, Marie, 2540
Kanofsky, Gordon R., 934
Kanoy, "Chuck", 7653
Kantardjieff, Stefan A., 1164
Kanter, Burton W., 9445
Kanter, Janis, 9445
Kanter, Joel S., 9445
Kanter, Joshua S., 9445
Kanter, Robert, 7690
Kanter, Stephanie, 2757
Kantor, Aaron B., Lt., 4347
Kantor, Warren, 5184
Kantrowitz, Arthur R., 670
Kanubaddi, Venkateswara Reddy, 1096
Kao, Frances, 6998
Kaohi, Aletha, 2559
Kaoitsky, Chuck, 510
Kapadia, Kelly L., 7755
Kaplan Charitable Lead Annuity Trust,
   Rita J. and Stanley H., The, 6288
Kaplan, Alan, 2824
Kaplan, Amelia H., 2078
Kaplan, Ann F., 5531
Kaplan, Anne, 2823
Kaplan, Annie Garcia, 1514
Kaplan, Barbara S., 7696
Kaplan, Bruce M., 5684
Kaplan, Burton B., 2823, 2943
Kaplan, Carol K., 2824
Kaplan, Charlie, 2823
Kaplan, Curt, 2823
Kaplan, David, 2823
Kaplan, Diane S., 85
Kaplan, Edward, 2824
Kaplan, Edward H., 3659
Kaplan, Eve F., 2078
Kaplan, Gary S., 9680
Kaplan, Helene L., 5707, 6046
Kaplan, Herbert, 8517
Kaplan, Hilary, 2823
Kaplan, Inc., 5708
Kaplan, Irene, 3659
Kaplan, Irving, 6954
Kaplan, J.L., 1093
Kaplan, Jean, 2823
Kaplan, Jerome A., 3659
Kaplan, Joel, 3003
Kaplan, Laurence S., 2852
Kaplan, Leonard J., 7495
Kaplan, Lynne, 2967
Kaplan, Martin, 2824
Kaplan, Martin S., 3924, 4094
Kaplan, Mary E., 6290
Kaplan, Michael D., 1338
Kaplan, Mike, 2823
Kaplan, Morris, 2823
Kaplan, Morris A., 2823
Kaplan, Myran, 7696
Kaplan, Myron J., 7686
Kaplan, Myron M., 2078
Kaplan, Neil S., 3613
Kaplan, Randall, 7343
Kaplan, Renee, 9566
Kaplan, Richard D., 6290
Kaplan, Richard M., 7696
Kaplan, Rita J., 6288
Kaplan, Robert, 2823
Kaplan, Robert S., 6289, 7229
Kaplan, Roberta, 2184
Kaplan, Sarah, 2823
Kaplan, Stanley H., 6288
Kaplan, Stanley M., 7686, 7696
Kaplan, Steven J., 7696

Kaplan, Susan Beth, 6288
Kaplan, Thomas, 2079
Kaplan, Tobee W., 7495
Kaplen, Alexander, 5268
Kaplen, Lawrence, 5268
Kaplen, Margaret R., 5268
Kaplen, Wilson R., 5268
Kapnick, Jim, 4376
Kapoor, Editha Sue, 2825
Kapoor, John N., 2825
Kapor, Mitchell, 743
Kapp, Constance Elizabeth Mellon, 8346
Kapp, John M., 8181
Kappa Graphics, LP, 8278
Kappa Media Group, Inc., 8278
Kappner, Augusta Souza, 7209
Kappos, George, Jr., 7555
Kapur, Ramon, 5357
Kapusta, Susan M., 8488
Karabots, Athena, 8278
Karabots, Nicholas, 8278
Karakul, Kenn, 1939
Karamanoukian, Alber K., 7171
Karamchandani, Mahesh, 4228
Karamitis, Linda, 2755
Karan, Donna, 6291
Karas, Joe, 9548
Karatsu, Jeanne, 901
Karbowiak, Christine, 8646
Karches, Peter, 6292
Karches, Susan, 6292
Kardashian, Joan, 690
Kardon, Emanuel S., 8279
Karel, Betsy, 1853
Karel, Frank, III, 1853
Karesh, Randy, 2320
Karesh, Randy M., 2444
Karet, Laura M., 8437
Karfiol, Max, 5965
Karfiol, Wolf, 5965
Karfunkel Family Foundation, 5747,
   6193
Karfunkel, Ann, 5747
Karfunkel, George, 5747
Karfunkel, Leah, 6193
Karfunkel, Michael, 5747, 6193
Karfunkel, Rene, 5747
Karges, James M., 4621, 4710, 4731
Karges, Tom, 4574
Karkut, Kevin, 523
Karl Hoblitzelle Trust, 8955
Karlin, Trish Devine, 823
Karlstrom, Paul, 1114
Karlweis, Georges C., 5843
Karmazin Char. Lead Annuity Trust, 6293
Karmazin Char. Lead Annuity Trust II,
   6293
Karmazin Charitable Lead Annuity Trust,
   Sharon, 5269
Karmazin, Bruce, 2864
Karmazin, Craig, 5269
Karmazin, Melvin, 6293
Karmazin, Sharon, 5269
Karmin, Beth, 2823
Karnes, Mark, 174
Karnig, Albert K., 405
Karno, Marvin, 530
Karoff, Peter, 2185
Karp, Donald M., 6229
Karp, Jill E., 3974
Karp, Mark E., 1482
Karp, Stephen R., 3974
Karpinski, Gene, 5614
Karpowich, Paul, 5194
Karr, Howard H., 2542
Karr, Robert A., 6197
Karr, Susanne, 6197
Karras, Nolan, 9341
Karsch, Sol, 6753
Karsh, Bruce A., 744
Karsh, Martha L., 744
Karst, Darren W., 9915
Karst, Jan F., 5704
Karsten Manufacturing Co., 139

Karter, Trish, 1810
Kartsotis, Bill, 6694
Kartsotis, Sofia, 6694
Karun, Harold, 1490
Karwick, Michael, 8141
Kasai, Takashi, 2926
Kasarda, Jayne, 8349
Kasch, Louise, 1031
Kasdorf, Gail B., 4396
Kaser, Roy, 3206
Kash, Gary, 2666
Kasl, Stanislav V., 1529
Kasperski, Michael, 4229
Kass, Jonathan, 7775
Kass, Matthew, 2805
Kass, Roberta E., 1252
Kassin, Jackob, 5554
Kastanis, Laure W., 1304
Kastelic, John, 7819
Kasten, G. Frederick, Jr., 9750
Kastenholz, James P., 3021
Kaster, Ann, 1139
Kastner, Rich, 4567
Kasuga, Theresa, 1509
Kaswick, Jon A., 584
Kasza, Carol, 79
Katch, Robert J., 1264
Katcher, Gerald, 2080
Katcher, Jane, 2080
Katcher, Richard D., 7205
Katen, Karen L., 4319
Katerman, Joanne M., 8320
Kates, Dana, 662
Kates, Jennifer, 739
Kathe, John H., 2153
Kathka, David, 10000
Kathman, Daniel E., 6009
Katkov, David, 1008
Katnik, Michelle A., 370
Kato, Hiroyuki, 6561
Kator, Irving, 1813
Katrana, Carol L., 8779
Katsuragi, Akio, 6395
Kattan, David, 5554
Kattan, Elliott, 5554
Kattan, Steve, 5554
Katten Muchin Rosenman LLP, 2826
Katten Muchin Zavis, 2826
Katten Muchin Zavis Rosenman, 2826
Katterjohn, Eugene, Jr., 3415
Katz Charitable Income Trust, 3692
Katz Charitable Income Trust II, 3692
Katz, A.V., Jr., 7522, 7523
Katz, Ben, 9778
Katz, Daniel, 2081
Katz, Daniel F., 1817
Katz, Daniel R., 5300
Katz, David, 8280
Katz, David M., 509, 6295
Katz, Dean Laurence M., 3603
Katz, Diane, 6281
Katz, Eleanor M., 2081, 3692
Katz, Ellen, 6294, 6297
Katz, Ellen Philips Schwarzman, 6294
Katz, Esther, 7130
Katz, Ezra, 2109
Katz, Gerald M., 3635
Katz, Harold, 8280
Katz, Herbert D., 2081
Katz, Howard, 6294
Katz, Howard C., 6297
Katz, Iris J., 6295
Katz, Jane L., 6296
Katz, Joel A., 4904
Katz, Karen Peck, 9894, 9895
Katz, Lewis, 5270, 5337
Katz, Linda Marks, 6489
Katz, Madelyn, 745
Katz, Marlene, 8280
Katz, Michael S., 6260
Katz, Monique C., 5271
Katz, Mordecai D., 5271
Katz, Peggy, 8280
Katz, Phillipe, 7130

Katz, Randy, 745
Katz, Richard, 4483
Katz, Robert J., 6055, 6296
Katz, Roberta R., 9694
Katz, Ronald, 745
Katz, Sally, 2081
Katz, Saul B., 6295
Katz, Thomas O., 2081
Katz, Todd, 745
Katz, Tova, 6881
Katz, Walter, 2081
Katzen, Cyrus, 9446
Katzen, Jay, 9446
Katzen, Lynn, 9446
Katzenbach, Shirley S., 6508
Katzenberg Family Trust, 746
Katzenberg, Jeffrey, 746
Katzenberg, Marilyn, 746
Katzenberg, Susan B., 3568, 3636
Katzenberger, Helen Katherine, 6298
Katzenberger, Walter B., 6298
Katzin, Jerome, 1087
Katzman, Ronald M., 8258
Katzowitz, Lauren Shenfield, 6209
Katzu, Dan, 324
Kauai Coffee Co., 2530
Kauai Commerical Co., Inc., 2530
Kaudisch, Gerda, 8846
Kauffman, Adelaide, 5272
Kauffman, Ewing M., 4843
Kauffman, Fritz, 5272
Kauffman, Julia Irene, 4844
Kauffman, Katherine A., 3232
Kauffman, Muriel McBrien, 4844
Kaufman Charitable Lead Trust, Henry, 2082
Kaufman, Alon, 4296
Kaufman, Ann P., 8944, 8981
Kaufman, Arlene G., 1805
Kaufman, Craig S., 2082
Kaufman, Daniel S., 2082
Kaufman, Edward G., 9447
Kaufman, Elaine, 2082
Kaufman, George M., 9447
Kaufman, Glenn D., 2082
Kaufman, Glorya, 747
Kaufman, Henry, 2082
Kaufman, Howard, 4904
Kaufman, James, 7057
Kaufman, Jean, 8981
Kaufman, Linda H., 9447
Kaufman, Marvin A., 6901
Kaufman, Robert M., 6011, 6613
Kaufman, Rosalind F., 5997
Kaufman, Sharon, 6219
Kaufman, Stephen M., 8960, 8981
Kaufman, Victor, 6220
Kaufmann, Barbara W., 4492
Kaufmann, Marion Esser, 6299
Kaufthal, Ilan, 5130
Kaufthal, Judith E., 5661
Kaul, Hugh, 40
Kaul, Ralph, 2083
Kaup, Sarah, 7749
Kautz, Caroline M., 6300
Kautz, Daniel B., 6300
Kautz, James C., 6300, 7304
Kautz, John T., 3318
Kautz, Leslie B., 6300
Kautz, Rob, 1244
Kauzlarich, Susan M., 134
Kavadas, Kathryn B., 1400
Kavanagh, Mike, 4661
Kavanagh, T. James, 8282
Kavanagh, Thomas E., 8282
Kavanau, Earl W., 1137
Kavanau, Flavia J., 1137
Kavanaugh, Edward A., 8154
Kavanaugh, Peter T., 3854
Kavich, Daphne, 755
Kavli, Fred, 748
Kawai, Saburo, 6389
Kawamura, Yoshinori, 7005

Kawasaki Heavy Industries (USA), Inc., 4982
Kawasaki Motors Corp., U.S.A., 4982
Kawasaki Motors Manufacturing Corp., U.S.A., 4982
Kawasaki Rail Car, Inc., 4982
Kawasaki Steel Investments, Inc., 7525
Kawashima, Yoshiyuki, 6561
Kay, David R., 6053
Kay, Deborah S., 4147
Kay, Elizabeth D., 1368
Kay, F. Stevon, 8588
Kay, Gerri, 8386
Kay, Herma Hill, 1065
Kay, Ina, 3660
Kay, Jack, 3660
Kay, Jami, 3375, 3391
Kay, Jean S., 1192
Kay, Linda, 3291
Kay, Michael, 2355
Kay, Richard, 1794, 6765
Kay, Sarah, 9442
Kay, Terry, 1192
Kay, Timothy J., 957
Kayden, David S., 5258
Kayden, Gabrielle Reem, 5258
Kayden, Herbert, 5258
Kayden-Killian, Joelle, 5258
Kaye, Danny, 1815
Kaye, Dena, 1815
Kaye, Donna, 2240
Kaye, Howard, 6219
Kaye, Sylvia Fine, 1815
Kaye, Wendy Lewis, 6415
Kayes, Henry M., 3420
Kaylie, Gloria, 6301
Kaylie, Harvey, 6301
Kaylie, Roberta, 6301
Kaylor, Howard S., 3600
Kayne, Jerry D., 749
Kayne, Richard A., 749
Kayne, Suzanne L., 749
Kazickas, Alexandra, 6302
Kazickas, John A., 6302
Kazickas, Joseph M., 6302
Kazickas, Joseph P., 6302
Kazickas, Jurate, 5544, 6302
Kazickas, Michael, 6302
Kazimour, Korlin, 3275
Kazma, Gerald, 2827
Kazma, Leigh-Anne, 2827
Kazma, Margaret, 2827
Kazma, Michael, 2827
Kealy, Ellen M., 6303
Kealy, William F., 6303
Kealy, William J., 6303, 7438
Kean, Anne Marie, 7391
Kean, Beatrice Joyce, 2820
Kean, Janet H., 7391
Kean, Stewart B., 5106
Kean, Susan, 405
Kean, Teresa Anne, 7391
Kean, Thomas H., 5707
Kean, Thomas H., Hon., 5265
Kean, Thomas J., Jr., 7391
Keane, John, 3975
Keane, John J., 7781
Keane, Karl N., 9836
Keane, Marilyn, 3975
Keane, Michael E., 9697
Kearney, Christopher J., 7484
Kearney, Daniel P., 2820
Kearney, Eric H., 7689
Kearney, James, Bro., 6384
Kearney, John E., Sr., 2101
Kearney, Kevin R., 4209
Kearney, Lee, 9570
Kearney, Terrence, 2804
Kearney, Terrence C., 2579
Kearns, Bill, 4939
Kearns, Carol R., 1892
Kearns, Joseph P., 8013
Kearns, Laurel, 6643
Keat, Simona, 691

Keatara Investments, 8853
Keating, Arthur E., 2084
Keating, Dwight M., 8099
Keating, Edward, 2084
Keating, Elaine, 2084
Keating, James J., III, 3544
Keating, Lee B., 2084
Keating, Lucie S., 2084
Keating, Mary Jo, 1614
Keating, Michael, 3812
Keating, Michael K., 7560
Keating, William J., 7560, 7588
Keck, Brian L., 7738
Keck, Donald B., 5784
Keck, Howard B., Jr., 750
Keck, Katherine Cone, 881
Keck, Stephen M., 750
Keck, Theodore J., 750
Keck, W.M., II, 750
Keck, W.M., III, 750
Keck, William M., 750
Keck, William M., II, 751
Keck, William M., Jr., 751
Keckonen, Jon C., 9962
Kedash, David B., 1730
Keddy Trust, Lawrence J., 3528
Keddy, James, 346
Kee, John L., Jr., Mrs., 1964
Kee, William G., 1964
Keefe, Anita L., 6305
Keefe, Catherine G., 8334
Keefe, Harry V., III, 6305
Keefe, Harry V., Jr., 6305
Keefe, Pamela B., 7679
Keefe, Patrick E., 3443, 3444
Keefe, Peter, 9449
Keefe, Stephen T., 7679
Keegan, Dennis J., 5273
Keegan, John P., 5186
Keegan, Karen S., 5273
Keegan, Lucille, 1927
Keegan, Peter W., 6443
Keeler Fund, The, 4355
Keeler, Dennis C., Jr., 3534
Keeler, Isaac S., 4355
Keeler, John M., 6203
Keeler, Margaret P., 7697
Keeler, Mary Ann, 4355
Keeler, Miner S., II, 4355
Keeler, Robert T., 7697
Keeler, Ruth, 6306
Keeley, Clay M., 3438
Keeling, J. Wayne, 7444
Keeling, Rudolph W., 3417
Keen, Allan E., 2303
Keen, G. Comforted, 3894
Keen, Gordon L., Jr., 8123
Keenan, Charles M., 3123
Keenan, Clarmarie, 2922
Keenan, Frances Murray, 3559
Keenan, James F., 3190, 3191, 4414
Keenan, Jim, 3131
Keenan, John C., Mrs., 7039
Keenan, Julie, 5417
Keenan, Katherine G., 8915
Keenan, Nancy, 1533
Keene, Donald, 3656
Keene, Margaret, 1118
Keene, Richard, 2535
Keeneland Association Inc., 3432
Keener, Kathleen A., 2257
Keeney, Anne Herold, 5351
Keeney, Gioia, 9089
Keeney, Matthew Mayro, 5351
Keery, Thomas R., II, 4026
Keesee, Christian K., 7952, 7964
Keeshin, Joyce J., 7689
Keeth, M.F., 9181
Keeton, Carole, 9294
Keeve, E. Beth, 2662
Keever, Graham, 7346
Keever, William, 1267
Keevil, Julian, 9531
Keevil, Mary T.H., 9436

Keffer, E. Brooks, Jr., 8428
Kegerreis, Robert J., 7875
Kegley Trust, J. Henry, The, 9448
Kegley, J. Henry, 9448
Keidan, Sarah W., 4273
Keifer, Robert B., 3141
Keil, Susan, 9570
Keilty, Nancy B., 3103
Keily, Sandra L., 7888
Keinath, Pauline M., 4553
Keinath, Warren G., Jr., 4553
Keiser, Michael, 9763
Keiser, Michael L., 2828
Keiser, Michael, Mrs., 9763
Keiser, Nanette, Dr., 4231
Keiser, Rosalind C., 2828
Keith, Brian, 8658
Keith, Charles L., 6551
Keith, Daniel, 7174
Keith, Garnett L., 3654
Keith, Graeme M., Jr., 7410
Keith, Greg, 7410
Keith, India E., 7410
Keith, Jayne, 7126
Keith, John M., Jr., 3407
Keith, Stephen L., 3207
Keith, Susan S., 8935
Keithley Charitable Lead Trust, Nancy, 8983
Keithley, Cynthia O., 8983
Keithley, Joseph P., 7576
Keithley, Roy F., 8983
Keler, Marianne M., 1778
Kellam, John, 3165
Kellar, Arthur, 9449
Kellar, Elizabeth, 9449
Kellar, Leslie Livingston, 2435
Kellar, Mary K., 9449
Kellar, Rick, 7762
Kelleher, Carol A., 6307
Kelleher, David, 3164
Kelleher, David N., 8984
Kelleher, Denis P., 6307
Kelleher, Denis P., Jr., 6307
Kelleher, Dennis P., 6972
Kelleher, Harry B., Jr., 3494
Kelleher, Herbert D., 8984
Kelleher, J. Michael, 6005, 8984
Kelleher, Joan N., 8984
Kelleher, Robert S., 1331
Kelleher, Sean M., 6307
Kellen Foundation, A.M. & S.M., 5722
Kellen, Anna-Maria, 6308
Kellen, Michael, 5722, 6308
Kellen, Stephen M., 5722, 6308
Keller & Associates, J.J., Inc., 9831
Keller Group Investment, The, 223
Keller, Adelaide M., 752
Keller, Betsy Holden, 834
Keller, Brian, 9831
Keller, Charles, Jr., 3493
Keller, Constance T., 2829
Keller, Dan, 2570
Keller, David M., 2829
Keller, Dennis J., 2829
Keller, Fred P., 4357
Keller, George M., 752
Keller, James J., 9831
Keller, James R., 9703
Keller, Jeffrey B., 2829
Keller, John J., 9831
Keller, John T., 2829
Keller, Parry, 7555
Keller, Rayford L., 9079, 9201
Keller, Rick, 4708
Keller, Robert, 9776
Keller, Robert G., 6320
Keller, Robert L., 9831
Keller, Roberta, 8052
Keller, Rosa F., 3493
Keller, Stephen F., 492
Keller, Sue, 4253
Keller, Susan K., 3845
Keller, Thomas A., III, 4559

Keller, Thomas L., 9079
Keller-Krikava, Marne, 9831
Kellerman, Christopher A., 4249
Kellerman, Faye, 753
Kellerman, Jonathan, 753
Kellerman, Norman, 2779
Kellett, Martine, 4052
Kelley, Barbara M., 5605
Kelley, Brady, 4842
Kelley, Brian S., 3850
Kelley, Bruce G., 3282
Kelley, Bruce R., 8030
Kelley, Bryana, 3368
Kelley, Craig C., 8030
Kelley, Darcy, 7244
Kelley, David K., 5157
Kelley, E. Dennis, Jr., 3816
Kelley, Ed, 4921
Kelley, Edward B., 9166
Kelley, James L., 6800
Kelley, Joan, 8985
Kelley, John, 4638
Kelley, Karen D., 8030
Kelley, Kent R., 8030
Kelley, Lora L., 8030
Kelley, Marilyn Golden, 2568
Kelley, Mark, 8030
Kelley, Martin N., 8030
Kelley, Marty S., 9195
Kelley, Michelle, 7522, 7523
Kelley, Phil O., 8892
Kelley, Richard W., 4994
Kelley, Robin, 1786
Kelley, Stephen S., 8030
Kelley, Thomas J., 1246
Kelley, William H., 5326
Kelley-Ariwoola, Karen, 4623
Kelling, G.V., Jr., 3535
Kelling, Robert S., Jr., 639
Kellman, Raymond, 134
Kellner, Catherine, 6309
Kellner, George, 6309
Kellner, Jack F., 9830
Kellner, Jack W., 9830
Kellner, Martha, 6309
Kellner, Mary, 9830
Kellner, Mary T., 9864
Kellner, Peter, 6309
Kellner, Ted D., 9830
Kellogg Co., 4358, 7174
Kellogg Foundation Trust, W.K., 4357
Kellogg LLC, 268
Kellogg Trust, Carrie Staines, 4357
Kellogg, Carolyn, 4819
Kellogg, Charles K., 6311
Kellogg, Cynthia K., 6311
Kellogg, Elizabeth I., 6310
Kellogg, Fernanda M., 7137
Kellogg, James C., IV, 6310
Kellogg, Jennifer, 6523
Kellogg, Lee I., 6311
Kellogg, M. Charles, 4819
Kellogg, Madelaine, 9832
Kellogg, Morris W., 6310
Kellogg, Peter N., 3806
Kellogg, Peter R., 6310, 6311
Kellogg, Richard I., 6310
Kellogg, Terry, 18
Kellogg, W.K., 4356, 4357
Kellogg, William S., 9832
Kellwood Co., 4845
Kelly Foundation, Dee, 8801
Kelly Services, Inc., 4359
Kelly Tractor Co., 2086
Kelly Trust, Eugene, 6231
Kelly, A. William, 8450
Kelly, Barry, 6428
Kelly, Beth, 4643
Kelly, Bronwen, 5125
Kelly, Byrd M., 2830
Kelly, Carolyn, 9680
Kelly, Charles G., 4257
Kelly, Charles W., 3693
Kelly, D. Michael, 8577

Kelly, Daniel M., 3269
Kelly, Daniel P., 5980
Kelly, Dee J., 8979
Kelly, Don, 3497
Kelly, Donald P., 2830
Kelly, Douglas L., 4885
Kelly, Eamon M., 7899
Kelly, Edmund F., 4006
Kelly, Edward J., 2964
Kelly, Eileen I., 2086
Kelly, Ellsworth, 6312
Kelly, Eugene, 6231
Kelly, Flaminia Odescalchi, 1347
Kelly, Greg, 939
Kelly, James E., 2517
Kelly, James M., 1978, 2219
Kelly, James P., 3585
Kelly, James P., III, 2406
Kelly, Jeffrey D., 7808
Kelly, John M., 8890
Kelly, Joseph, 1404, 3384
Kelly, Kathleen, Sr., 644
Kelly, Linda J., 1564
Kelly, Louisa, 2086
Kelly, Loyd G., 2086
Kelly, Loyd Patrick, 2086
Kelly, Marjorie H., 2086
Kelly, Matthew D., 8141
Kelly, Michael, 7139
Kelly, Michael E., 87, 3065
Kelly, Michael W., 1795
Kelly, Mike, 4229
Kelly, Molly, 5092
Kelly, Nancy, 6264
Kelly, Nicholas D., 2086
Kelly, Patrick J., 2830
Kelly, Paul, 7112
Kelly, Paul E., Jr., 8283
Kelly, Raymond B., III, 9174
Kelly, Rex E., 4758
Kelly, Richard C., 4732
Kelly, Robert A., 1087
Kelly, Robert W., 2086
Kelly, Robert W., Jr., 2086
Kelly, Sheila, 9634
Kelly, Stanhope A., 7502
Kelly, Thomas E., 8895
Kelly, Thomas F., 6428
Kelly, Thomas N., 2830
Kelly, Timothy M., 3407
Kelly, Timothy P., 3759
Kelly, V., 2085
Kelly, William, 6615
Kelly, William M., 6662
Kelsay, William, 403
Kelsey, Elizabeth S., 4008
Kelsey, Forest, 9617
Kelsey, G. Lea Dobbs, 4008
Kelsey, Margen, 4008
Kelsey, Ruth, 9617
Kelsey, Suzanne V.A., 4008
Kelsey, Thomas V.A., 4008
Kelsey, William, 4008
Kelso, Anne, 1793
Kelso, John G., 7346
Keltner, Donald H., 1457
Keltner, Kathleen, 1457
Kemmerer, John L., 5275
Kemmis, Daniel, 4636
Kemp, Jack, 1468
Kemp, Lou Thelen, 4798
Kemp, Michael F., 2411, 2480
Kemp, Michael W., 8769
Kemper Revocable Trust, William T., 4849
Kemper, Alexander C., 4848
Kemper, David W., 4797, 4849, 4850
Kemper, Enid J., 4848
Kemper, James M., Jr., 4849, 4850
Kemper, James Scott, 2831, 2832
Kemper, John Mariner, 4846
Kemper, Jonathan M., 4797, 4849, 4850, 4909
Kemper, Mary S., 4848

Kemper, R. Crosby, 4847
Kemper, R. Crosby, Jr., 4846, 4848
Kemper, R. Crosby, Sr., 4846, 4848
Kemper, Rufus Crosby, III, 4846
Kemper, Talfourd H., 9387
Kemper, William T., 4849
Kemph, Patricia A., 7858
Kempner, Hetta Towler, 8987
Kempner, Thomas L., Jr., 6313
Kenagy, Robert T., 4480
Kenahan, Michael P., 2601
Kenan, Anne, 1626
Kenan, Anne R., 2495
Kenan, Annice H., 7456
Kenan, Brutus C., 2495
Kenan, Elizabeth, 7413
Kenan, Elizabeth Price, 7411, 7412
Kenan, Frank H., 7413
Kenan, James G., 2495
Kenan, James G., III, 2495, 5930, 6150, 7456
Kenan, Jr. Charitable Trust, William R., 7412, 7413
Kenan, Thomas S., III, 7317, 7359, 7411, 7412, 7413, 7456
Kenan, William R., Jr., 7456
Kendall Trust, Henry Way, 3977
Kendall, Andrew W., 3977
Kendall, Becky, 1175
Kendall, Chuck, 1031
Kendall, Debra, 6257
Kendall, Donald M., 6714
Kendall, Edward C., 134
Kendall, George R., Sr., 2833
Kendall, George, Jr., 2833
Kendall, Helen, 2833
Kendall, Henry, 3977
Kendall, James A., 4407
Kendall, John P., 3977
Kendall, Larry, 1357
Kendall, Nannie, 7886
Kendall, Richard C., 3864
Kendall, Ted, III, 4743
Kendall, Thomas, 2833
Kendrick, Douglas, 1319
Kendrick, E.G., Jr., 9407
Kendrick, James M., 5789
Kendzior, Tony, 2015
Kennametal Inc., 8284
Kennard, Lydia H., 1249
Kenneally, Beverly T., 3780
Kennebec Savings Bank, 3543
Kennebunk Savings Bank, 3544
Kennedy, Barbara C., 2421
Kennedy, Brian, 5028
Kennedy, Bruce C., 7891
Kennedy, C. Ray, 7370
Kennedy, Caroline, 1816
Kennedy, Cheryl, 3004
Kennedy, Christopher, 1816, 8768
Kennedy, Clay K., 2421
Kennedy, Coleman W., 6314
Kennedy, Craig, 1795, 6377
Kennedy, David B., 4291
Kennedy, David E., 8511
Kennedy, Dick, 4327
Kennedy, Donald, 972
Kennedy, Donald P., 511, 661, 957
Kennedy, Edward A., 1975
Kennedy, Edward M., Jr., 1816
Kennedy, Edward M., Sen., 1816
Kennedy, Elizabeth C., 2089
Kennedy, Gene, 3833
Kennedy, George, 9918
Kennedy, George D., 2834
Kennedy, Holly, 1768
Kennedy, Howard, 3305
Kennedy, Hugh A., 8898
Kennedy, Jack E., 1391
Kennedy, James C., 2367, 2421
Kennedy, James C., Jr., 2421
Kennedy, James Cox, 2531, 7596
Kennedy, James W., 2089
Kennedy, Jim, 7653

Kennedy, John C., 4360
Kennedy, John R., 2089
Kennedy, John R., III, 2089
Kennedy, John R., Sr., 2089
Kennedy, Joseph P., 1816
Kennedy, Joseph P., Mrs., 1816
Kennedy, Jr. Foundation, Joseph P., 6689
Kennedy, Karen A., 6314
Kennedy, Kendel, 2087
Kennedy, Kevin W., 6314, 7209
Kennedy, Kimberly, 2087
Kennedy, Leo, 4921
Kennedy, Lesley, 2757
Kennedy, Margaret T., 8988
Kennedy, Maria, 31
Kennedy, Mary E., 5276
Kennedy, Michael D., 2654
Kennedy, Nancy G., 4360
Kennedy, Neil, 25
Kennedy, Parker S., 511, 728
Kennedy, Paula, 2089
Kennedy, Quentin J., 5276
Kennedy, Quentin J., Jr., 5276
Kennedy, Rory E., 1816
Kennedy, Ruth, 7244
Kennedy, Sarah K., 2495
Kennedy, Susan, 3964
Kennedy, Thomas, 8451
Kennedy, Thomas J., 3394
Kennedy, Thomas L., 8317
Kennedy, Valerie P., 2834
Kennedy, W. George, 2087
Kennedy, William F., 6314
Kennedy, William T., 3854
Kennedy-Olsen, Kathleen, 2087
Kenner, Patricia, 5250
Kenney Trust, William C., 1401
Kenney, Barbara W., 2294
Kenney, Brigid, 3049
Kenney, Edward F., 4211
Kenney, Horace S., 1401
Kenney, Jay P., 1401
Kenney, John, 3655
Kenney, Robert T., 1482
Kennickell, Al, Jr., 2480
Kennon, A. William, 7371
Kenny, Gerard M., 268
Kenny, John J., 6443
Kenny, Kevin, 7139
Kenrick, Ilona, 2268
Kent, Connie, 3333
Kent, E. Robert, Jr., 3568
Kent, Fred I., III, 5551
Kent, Fred, Jr., 1982
Kent, J.H., 3318
Kent, Mark B., 8612
Kent, Patricia, 8523
Kentfield, Katherine, 7452
Kentz, Frederick C., III, 5372
Kenworthy, Marion E., 6315
Keny-Guyer, Alissa, 990
Kenyon, Dione D., 8524
Kenyon, John W., III, 105
Kenyon, Robert W., 8524
Kenyon, Suzanne Escobar, 105
Kenyon, Varnum "Chip", 1911
Keohane, Nannerl O., 5892
Keon, Margaret L., 2864
Keough, Donald R., 2426
Keough, Marilyn M., 2426
Kepco, Inc., 6363
Kepler, Charles G., 9992
Keppy Memorial Trust, Walter & Carol, 2750
Kerbow, Jessie, 8820
Kerin, Joe, 8079
Kerker, Michael A., 6532
Kerkorian, Kirk, 812
Kerlagon, Raymond L., 4831
Kerley, Marsha L., 9896
Kerlin, Kay, 9748
Kerlin, William H., Jr., 8222, 8511
Kerman, Michael G., 2464

Kern, Anita, 2464
Kern, Carol H., 7400
Kern, Diana, 5028
Kern, Herbert A., 2837
Kern, Janine, Hon., 8632
Kern, Jerome, 1402
Kern, John C., 2837
Kern, Marie-France, 5905
Kern, Mary, 1402
Kern, Patricia E., 9834
Kern, Peter L., 7400
Kern, Rene, 5905
Kern, Robert D., 9834
Kernen, A. William, 4995
Kerns, Judy L., 7370
Kerr, Anne, 1944
Kerr, Breene M., 3661
Kerr, Catherine, 5867
Kerr, Cody T., 7949
Kerr, Dave, 3368
Kerr, Ellen Stern, 7720
Kerr, Jennie, 4253
Kerr, Jo Arthur G., 9983
Kerr, John J., 8576
Kerr, Kavar, 9983
Kerr, Lou C., 7949
Kerr, Mara, 9983
Kerr, Marge, 3135
Kerr, Michael, 6614
Kerr, Robert S., Mrs., 7949
Kerr, Sheryl V., 3661
Kerr, Steven. S., 7949
Kerr, William G., 9983
Kerr, William T., 3314
Kerr-McGee Corp., 7950
Kerridge, Isaac C., 8772
Kerrigan, Joseph, 4956
Kerrigan, Joseph M., 5094
Kerrigan, Patrick J., 4956
Kersch-Schultz, Sheri, 9679
Kerst, Dan, 9287
Kerstein, David A., 3486
Kersten, Katherine, 4530
Kersten, Priscilla, 2838
Kersten, Samuel, Jr., 2838
Kersten, Steven, 2838
Kersten, Steven A., 2838
Keslar, Peter, 7876
Kesler, Charles R., 8338
Kesler, Delores, 1940, 2090
Kesler, Robert, 3047
Kessel, Gerry R., 6716
Kesselly, Binyah, 5255
Kesselman, Donna R., 5926
Kesselring, Charlotte, 5883
Kessinger, John R., 2170
Kessinger, Tom G., 5750
Kessinger, William B., 4790
Kessler, Barbara, 2963
Kessler, David, 739
Kessler, Dennis L., 2963
Kessler, Emily R., 6275
Kessler, Gary, 217
Kessler, Howard J., 3978
Kessler, Ira, 5998
Kessler, Michael, 4705
Kessler, Patricia M., 3978
Kessler, Richard, 5620
Kessler, Ronnie, 5998
Kessler, Steve, 4229
Kessler, Warren, 3549
Kest, Benjamin, 754
Kest, Clara, 754
Kest, Ezra, 754
Kest, Matthew, 733
Kest, Michael, 733, 754
Kest, Sol, 733, 754
Kest, Susanne, 733
Kestner, R. Steven, 7808
Ketcham, Eleanor, 5230
Ketcham, John, 5230
Ketcham, Luree, 3137
Ketcham, Richard, 6638
Ketcham, Susan, 671

Ketchum, Stuart M., 1262
Ketelsen, James L., 8960
Keter Torah Synagogue Sephardic Community, 6472
Kett, Mary E., 4209
Kettenbach, Frances Demoulas, 3879
Ketterer, Sarah H., 712
Kettering, Charles F., 7699
Kettering, Charles F., III, 7698
Kettering, E.W., 7698
Kettering, Jean S., 7698
Kettering, Lisa S., 7698
Kettering, Susan S., 7698, 7699
Kettering, Virginia W., 7698, 9835
Kettering, Mike, 1359
Kettle, J. Michael, 2204
Keuhner, Jennie Akerlund, 4968
Keusch, Suzanne H., 6260
Kewlich, Stephanie J., 8146
Key, Adelaide Daniels, 7346
Key, Amy B., 8530
Key, Emily M., 3
Key, James W., 2462
KeyBank N.A., 3154, 5780, 7550, 7558, 7574, 7576, 7578, 7580, 7603, 7617, 7633, 7645, 7651, 7656, 7674, 7691, 7700, 7701, 7715, 7819, 7822, 7847, 7849, 7858, 7867, 7870, 7873, 7882, 7885, 7905, 7916, 8646, 9689
KeyCorp, 7700
Keyes, Barbara, 9274
Keyes, James H., 9823
Keyes, Steve, 4473
Keys, Brian S., 7142
Keys, Patricia M., 5112
Keyse-Walker, John, 7582
Keyser, Richard L., 2768
Keysor, Rhonda, 3010
KeySpan Corp., 6320
Keyston, David, 5524
Keystone Foods Corp., 8314
Keystone Foundation, The, 9730
Keystone Nazareth Bank & Trust Co., 8285, 8286
Keystone Savings Bank, 8286
Kezer, C. Henry, 3795
KG Investments, 3302
Khachaturian, Henry, 755
Khachaturian, Natasha, 755
Khachaturian, Rita M., 755
Khan, Jamal H., Dr., 9723
Khanna, Shyam, 5154
Kharizak Foundation, 5114
Khaury, Susan M., 4568
Khayat, Robert, 9424
Kheel, Ann S., 7124
Kheel, Robert, 7124
Kheel, Theodore W., 7124
Khinduda, Shanti K., 4791
Khosla, Neeru, 213
Khosla, Vinod, 213
Khouri, Naif A., 4289
Khoury, Coreen B., 8611
Khoury, David, 8237
Khoury, Kenneth F., 2397
Khoury, Lisa, 8237
Khoury, Marilyn, 8237
Khurana, Sunil, 5564
Kia, Shirin, 9341
Kiang, Heng-Pin "Ping", 9558
Kibbe, Sharon, 3155
Kibbey, Josephine, 4096
Kibble, Robert F., 756
Kibble, Vanessa M., 756
Kiburis, Doris, 3217
Kick, Frank J., 5694
Kidd, Christen L., 6268
Kidd, Julie J., 6268
Kidd, Molly N., 9128
Kidd, Sharon Smith, 8881
Kidder, Dorothy R., 5726
Kidder, Fred, 7725
Kidder, Michael R., 3979

Kidder, Rushworth M., 4399
Kieckhefer, John I., 113
Kieckhefer, John W., 113
Kieckhefer, R., 87
Kiefer, Markell, 4612
Kieffer, William H., III, 3548
Kieling, Nancy W., 5357
Kieman, Christine K., 8283
Kiemle, George, 7793
Kienholz, Corey, 8396
Kierlin, Laura, 4585
Kierlin, Monique, 4585
Kierlin, Robert A., 4585
Kiernan, Eaddo H., 6321
Kiernan, Mary Lee, 1537
Kiernan, Peter D., 6321
Kiernat, Elizabeth M., 4519
Kies, Mabel B., 1616
Kies, W.S., 1616
Kies, William S., III, 1616
Kieu, Quynh, 661
Kiewit & Sons Co., Peter, 4983
Kiewit Construction Group Inc., 4983
Kiewit Diversified Group Inc., 4983
Kiewit Sons', Peter, Inc., 4983
Kiewit, Eva-Alta D., 4984
Kiewit, Peter, 4984
Kight, Bennett, 2334
Kight, Dan, 7667
Kight, Peter J., 3746
Kight, Teresa J., 3746
Kihi Foundation, 1137
Kihn, Cecily, 1764
Kijima, Tsunao, 6560
Kikkoman Foods, Inc., 9836
Kilborn, Vincent F., 68
Kilbourne, Edgar, 4985
Kilde, Peter, 9933
Kildebeck, Margaretta, 1315
Kile, James, 4540
Kiley, Thomas R., 3780
Kilgore, Don, 4991
Kilgore, Keith, 7570
Kilgore, Ronald N., 4266, 4408
Kilgus, Joann A., 3232
Kill, Robert, 3131
Killam, Constance, 3980
Killeen, Michael F., 7555
Killen, John V., 8451
Killin, Jennifer Clarkson, 8695
Killinger, Clayton E., 9247
Killinger, Kerry, 9618
Killinger, Linda, 9618
Killins, Sherri, 3585
Killion, Benjamin C., 7973
Killory, Joseph E., Jr., 9514
Kilmer, Joseph R., 3197
Kilpatrick, Marjorie K., 1723
Kilroy, Lillian S., 3712
Kilroy, Lora Jean, 8991
Kilroy, Mari Angela, 8991
Kilroy, William S., 8991
Kilroy, William S., Jr., 8991
Kilts, James M., 2603
Kilts, James M., Jr., 2603
Kilts, Sandra M., 2603
Kim, Agnes C., 8287
Kim, Ho-il, 3823
Kim, James J., 8287
Kim, Mickey, 3166
Kim, Robin H.J., 758
Kim, Steve Y., 758
Kim, Susan Y., 8287
Kimak, Nancy C., 4919
Kimball International, Inc., 3182
Kimball, Anne, 759
Kimball, David, 7491
Kimball, Elizabeth, 1168
Kimball, Gretchen, 759
Kimball, H. Brown, 7354
Kimball, H. Earle, 8542
Kimball, Jeffrey, 759
Kimball, Mary Ellen, 3333
Kimball, Sara H., 759

Kimball, Sherry Partridge, 314
Kimball, Stephen, 759
Kimball, William R., 759
Kimber, Nancy, 901
Kimberly, James H., 7888
Kimberly, Newton S., Jr., 7888
Kimberly, Susan, 4671
Kimberly-Clark Corp., 8992
Kimble, Deborah G., 4428
Kimble, Doris, 7636
Kimble, Floyd E., 7636
Kimble, Greg, 7636
Kimble, S.J., 2111
Kimbrell, W. Duke, 7342
Kimbrough, Thomas M., 3125
Kime, Jack E., 8241, 8242, 8243
Kimelman, Charlotte, 9363
Kimelman, Henry L., 9363
Kimerling & Sons, M., Inc., 41
Kimerling, David, 41
Kimerling, Hyman, 41
Kimerling, Jonathan, 41
Kimerling, Joseph, 41
Kimerling, Max L., 41
Kimmel, David, 2091
Kimmel, Edward A., 2091
Kimmel, Gregory A., 2895
Kimmel, Helen, 1853
Kimmel, Lucille, 2091
Kimmel, Martin S., 5788
Kimmel, Sidney, 8288
Kimmell, Garman O., 7951
Kimmelman Foundation, Helen and
  Milton, The, 1853
Kimmelman, Carol, 6322
Kimmelman, Douglas W., 6322
Kimmelman, Milton A., 6400
Kimmelman, Peter, 5860
Kimmet, Gary, 6039
Kimoto, Paul, 673
Kimpara, Shunichiro, 6560
Kimpton, Graham Lawrence, 886
Kimpton, Isabelle, 886
Kimpton, Laura, 886
Kimpton, William D., 886
Kimsey, C. Windom, 8692
Kimsey, James V., 1817
Kimsey, Mark J., 1817
Kimsey, Michael P., 1817
Kimsey, Ray, 1817
Kimura, Ron, 1031
Kincaid, Keith, Pastor, 3177
Kincaid, Thomas R., 8993
Kinch, Elizabeth, 3354
Kind World Foundation, 5489
Kind, Donald G., 2814
Kind, Ken, 8289
Kind, Kenneth A., 7191
Kind, Patricia, 7191, 8289
Kind-Rubin, Valerie, 7191, 8289
Kindel, Maureen, 214
Kinder Morgan, Inc., 1403
Kinder, Nancy G., 8994
Kinder, Richard D., 8994
Kindfuller, Andrew, 7191, 8289
Kindle, Jo Ann, 4916
Kindle, Jo Ann Taylor, 4810
Kindler, Jeffrey, 6720
Kindred Healthcare Operating, Inc.,
  3434
Kindred Healthcare, Inc., 3434
Kindred Hospice Charities, Inc., 3434
Kindred, John J., III, 6130
Kinen, Norbert, 8055
King Trust, Charlene, The, 5039
King, A.B., 9531
King, Abby D., 8354
King, Alan, 8219
King, Benjamin A., 2076
King, Bruce, 341
King, Bruce E., 341
King, Bryan, 2076
King, Carl B., 8995
King, Charles, 8758

King, Charles A., 3981
King, Charlie, 2545
King, Charlotte G., 8695
King, Chris, 3107
King, Christopher B., 2076
King, David W., 3548
King, Diana, 6323
King, Dorothy E., 8995
King, Dorothy Warren, 7987
King, E.H., 3051
King, Edna R., 9421
King, Edward H., 3052
King, Edward M., 459
King, Emily H., 2731
King, Florence E., 8995
King, Gayle, 3077
King, Gioconda, 6324
King, Grace, 9117
King, Helen J., 2076
King, James A., III, 24
King, James N., 5466
King, James P., 474, 7112
King, Jamie, 7603
King, Jena Fassett, 760
King, John P., Jr., 998
King, John Thomas, 9507
King, Judith S., 4165
King, Kathy A., 8816
King, Kenneth Kendal, 1404
King, L. Govan, 9455
King, Leigh, 8840
King, Linda J., 9405
King, Louise Straus, 7085
King, Margaret, 3131
King, Marjorie W., 7240
King, Mary E., 1767
King, Mary Jane, 4886
King, Maxwell, 8241, 8242
King, Michael, 760
King, Michael J., 559
King, Nancy, 3131
King, Patricia, 739
King, Raymond B., 2378, 2442, 2496,
  2524
King, Reatha Clark, 4567
King, Rick, 2922
King, Robert E., 2731
King, Robert E., Jr., 2731
King, Robert L., 87
King, Roberta F., 4326
King, Roderick E., MD, 4061
King, Saking, 1517
King, Sandy, 4723
King, Sharon, 2629
King, Sharon B., 5542, 6176
King, Sibyl Fine, 8201
King, Stephen E., 3545
King, Susan Robinson, 5707
King, Tabitha, 3545
King, Thomas, 7085
King, Thomas A., 3180, 3193
King, Victor E.D., 5192
King, W. Winburne, III, 1632
King, William A., 4151
King, William B., 8662
King, William Toben, 4851
King, Winburne, 7461
King, Yale, 1476
King-O'Neal, Renate, 890
Kingdon, Mark, 6326
Kingfisher, Pamela, 6643
Kingma, Todd W., 4410
Kingman, Elise, 4591
Kingman, Joseph R., III, 4624
Kings Point Industries, Inc., 6121
Kingsbury, Brigitte L., 4062
Kingsbury, Sherilyn, 1830
Kingsland, Richard M., 1257
Kingsley Fund, Sidney S., 5883
Kingsley, F.G., 1724
Kingston, Thomas W., 4624
Kington, Ann A., 9450
Kington, Helen J., 9450
Kington, Mark J., 9450

Kinisky, Thomas G., 8419
Kinko's Corporation, 958
Kinlaw, Dennis, 3448
Kinley, Bill, 4221
Kinn, Zona, 4574
Kinnamon, Susan, 7526
Kinnebrew, Jack M., 8839
Kinneen, Simon, 9651
Kinney, Catherine R., 6619
Kinney, H. Lee, 7810
Kinney, Jonathan C., 9371
Kinney, Laura, 1008
Kinney, Martha Hodsdon, 7195
Kinnison, Tom, 9998
Kinray, Inc., 7167
Kinsel, Rick A., 7199
Kinsell, Stephen J., 3177
Kinsley Construction, Inc., 8290
Kinsley, Anne W., 8290, 8511
Kinsley, Christopher A., 8290
Kinsley, Robert A., 8290
Kinsley, Timothy J., 8290
Kinsman, Elizabeth T., 8031
Kinsman, John W., 8031
Kinsman, Keith, 8031
Kinsman, Paige, 8031
Kintner, Edwina, 3131
Kintz, James P., 2181
Kintzel, Lee, Mrs., 4108
Kiplinger, Austin H., 1818
Kiplinger, Knight A., 1818
Kiplinger, Todd L., 1818
Kiplinger, Willard M., 1818
Kipp, Robert A., 4824
Kippen, Christina McKnight, 3688
Kipper, Barbara Levy, 2840
Kipper, David, 2840
Kipper, Lisa, 3140
Kipper, Richard E., 304
Kiralla, Gail, 848
Kirbo, Bruce W., 2092
Kirbo, Charles H., Jr., 2092
Kirbo, Irene B., 2092
Kirbo, Thomas M., 2092
Kirby, Alexandra Louise, 9434
Kirby, Allan P., Jr., 5280
Kirby, Allan P., Sr., 5279
Kirby, Ann K., 9434
Kirby, Annette S., 9434
Kirby, Arlene, 8630
Kirby, Coray S., 5280
Kirby, Dan, 8631
Kirby, F.M., 5279
Kirby, James W., Jr., 9434
Kirby, Jefferson W., 5279
Kirby, Linda T., 9434
Kirby, Milan S., 5280
Kirby, Phyllis, 1925
Kirby, Renee S., 9906
Kirby, Roger H.W., 9434
Kirby, S. Dillard, 5279
Kirby, Slater B., 5280
Kirby, Steve, 1942
Kirby, Wade H.O., 9434
Kirby, Walker D., 5279
Kirchen, Evan, 8621
Kirchen, Helen, 8621
Kirchen, Robert, 8621
Kirchenbauer, Ronald W., 3328
Kirchgasler, Barbara, 3019
Kirchheimer Trust, 2961
Kirchner, Bob, 9570
Kirchner, Leon, 5548
Kirgan, Mary Anne, 3706
Kirgan, Robert S., 3706
Kirincic, Paul, 879
Kirk, Alex, 6395
Kirk, Anne, 9706
Kirk, Clay Kenan, 2495
Kirk, Garrett, Jr., 7456
Kirk, Thomas H., 9460
Kirkbride, Vicki, 1785
Kirkham, Kate B., 7548
Kirkham, W. Gates, 7548

Kirkland 2004 Charitable Foundation,
  8699
Kirkland Foundation, Robert E. & Jenny
  D., 8721
Kirkland, Bedford F., 8699
Kirkland, Christopher, 8699
Kirkland, David "Mit", 26
Kirkland, Derek, 6209
Kirkland, Fletcher, 8583
Kirkland, Jenny D., 8699
Kirkland, Milton, 7397
Kirkland, Robert E., 8699, 8721
Kirkland, William G., 6209
Kirkman, Don, 4569
Kirkpatrick Oil Co., 7952
Kirkpatrick, Carrie, 9977
Kirkpatrick, Eleanor B., 7952
Kirkpatrick, Elizabeth, 2777
Kirkpatrick, Isabel, 2240
Kirkpatrick, Joan E., 7952
Kirkpatrick, John, 2015
Kirkpatrick, John E., 7952
Kirkpatrick, Melanie, 5184
Kirkpatrick, Shaun A., 93
Kirkwood, Allan, 9570
Kirkwood, Amanda H., 1196
Kirkwood, James, 5883
Kirkwood, John, 8180
Kirkwood, John H., 275, 1196
Kirkwood, Robert C., 275
Kirsch, Dorothy Orgill, 8661
Kirsch, Martin J., 1802
Kirsch, Rodney P., 8136
Kirschenbaum, Malcolm R., 9424
Kirschner, Rachelle, 6500
Kirschner, Richard, 5522, 6500
Kirscht, Ron, 4723
Kirsh, Michael A., 2157
Kirshenbaum, Kenneth, 384
Kirshner, Charles, 8142
Kirtland, Jennifer E., 8886
Kirtland, John E., 8886
Kirtley, Donald R., 1706
Kirtley, Olivia F., 3414
Kischel, Deane, 4499
Kisco Management Corp., 2171
Kiser, Anthony C.M., 6104
Kiser, Arthur G., 9390
Kiser, John W., III, 6104
Kishner, Judith Z., 7993
Kishner, Judy Z., 7991
Kislak Family Fund, Inc., 2093
Kislak, J.I., Inc., 2093
Kislak, Jay I., 2093
Kislak, Jean H., 2093
Kislak, Jonathan I., 2093
Kisler, Susan Gray, 8881, 8950
Kissane, Barbara, 3186
Kissick, John H., 763
Kissick, M. Kathleen, 763
Kissin, Cindy S., 1504
Kissinger, Henry A., 6679
Kissinger, Jim, 3395
Kissinger, Thomas F., 9859
Kissman, Nadra, 4231
Kissner, Ronald, 6944
Kistenbroker, David H., 2826
Kistler Instruments Inc., 6729
Kita, John J., 9929
Kitch, Patti, 3199
Kitchen, Michael B., 9786
Kitchings, Chester W., Jr., 1574
Kitchings, Chester W., Sr., 1574
Kitchings, Margaret Howe, 1574
Kitrick, Judith, 5362
Kitt, Tyler, 3209
Kittner, David, 8279
Kittredge, Francine S., 6395
Kittredge, Lisa, 3983
Kittredge, Michael, 3983
Kittredge, Robert P., 4293
Kittsmiller, Katherine, 2268
Kitz, Ed, 9915
Kitzi, Jerry, 4816

Kitzmiller, Edna B., 1405
Kitzmiller, Howard L., 1859
Kivell, Rochelle, 6868, 6869
Kiwanis Club of Bradenton, Inc., 2094
Kizziah, Barbara H. Malott, 2872
Kjets, LLC, 1794
Klaasse, Sandra, 7789
Klabzuba, Doris, 8996
Klabzuba, John, 8996
Klabzuba, Melinda, 8996
Klabzuba, Robert, 8996
Klagsbrun, Edward, 7250
Klahn, Roswitha, 5203
Klahr, Suzanne Mckechnie, 6998
Klappa, Gale E., 9967
Klapper, David, 3148
Klapper, David I., 3183
Klapper, Mary Elizabeth, 3183
Klapperich, Frank L., Jr., 1943
Klarfeld, Simon, 5673
Klarman, Beth S., 3985
Klarman, Seth A., 3985
KLAS-TV, 9455
Klatskin Assocs., 5518
Klatskin, Charles, 5396
Klatsky, Bruce J., 6725
Klatzky, Howard T., 4556
Klau Foundation, David W. and Sadie, 5942
Klau, James D., 8514
Klau, Susan L., 8514
Klaus, Arthur, 6328
Klaus, Lester, 6328
Klaus, Mortimer, 6328
Klausmeyer, David L., 3801
Klavan, Ruchel Friedman, 441
Klavans, Nancy G., 3924
Klebe, Terry A., 8846
Kleberg, Caesar, 8998
Kleberg, Helen C., 8999
Kleberg, Robert J., Jr., 8999
Kleberg, Stephen J., 8998
Klecha, Roy W., 4257
Klecka, Kevin O., 918
Klee, Conrad C., 6329
Klee, Virginia, 6329
Kleehamer, Robert E., 3130
Kleffner, Gregory W., 4845
Kleger, Lisa, 740
Klegon, Frank O., 4265
Kleiman, Gary D., 8197
Klein Diamonds Inc., Julius, 7102
Klein's Super Markets, Inc., 3662
Klein, Abraham, 6330, 6331, 6871, 7102
Klein, Adele, 6332
Klein, Barbara G., 6333
Klein, Bertram W., 3435
Klein, Beth Paxton, 3435
Klein, Brad, 1525
Klein, Bruce A., 8658
Klein, Chaim, 5865
Klein, Charles D., 6543
Klein, Christopher E., 2393
Klein, Conrad Lee, 690
Klein, David, 3435
Klein, David L., 765
Klein, Elaine B., 3435
Klein, Elisabeth, 764
Klein, Elisabeth H., 764
Klein, Gabrielle, 3321
Klein, George, 6332
Klein, Gershon, 5865
Klein, Hank, 1957
Klein, Howard S., 3662
Klein, Jacqueline, 5290
Klein, James L., 764
Klein, Jane P., 6543
Klein, Jason A., 6333
Klein, Jeffrey, 6419
Klein, John A., 1504
Klein, Julia H., 8103
Klein, Kathryn, 8990
Klein, Kenneth, 764, 5684

Klein, Laura Colin, 6024
Klein, Lawrence R., 5704
Klein, Linda, 1644
Klein, Linda Dorn, 823
Klein, Lloyd E., 764
Klein, Mark, 8990
Klein, Marshall, 3662
Klein, Michael, 4690
Klein, Michael J., 3662
Klein, Michelle, 6419
Klein, Miriam, 765, 5865
Klein, Miriam K., 8291
Klein, Raizi, 5658
Klein, Ralph L., 3662
Klein, Raymond, 8291
Klein, Richard, 3435
Klein, Richard L., 7891
Klein, Rosemary, 4907
Klein, Ruth L., 6333
Klein, Sarah Dinah, 6330, 6331
Klein, Seymour M., 6333
Klein, Shirley S., 3662
Klein, Stephen, 3435
Klein, Stephen B., 8291
Klein, Tibor, 5865
Klein, Timothy, 8990
Klein, Zoe S., 6333
Klein-Shoemaker, Patricia, 4237
Kleine, Richard G., 3277
Kleiner, Charlene C., 866
Kleinert, Christoper W., 9084
Kleinfeld, Klaus, 5400
Kleinhenz, Larry, 3166
Kleinman, Beth, 6334
Kleinman, Josph S., 6334
Kleinman, Martin, 6334
Kleinschmidt, Amy, 4560
Kleinsmith, Vickey, 4988
Kleissner, Karl, 736
Kleissner, Lisa, 736
Kleist, Peter D., 2095
Klem, Shirley, 2922
Klemens, Thomas A., 511
Klempner, Jay L., 3414
Klenck, Marilyn, 3254
Klenck, Marilyn J., 3122
Klenk, Laverne, 8989
Klepfer, Kathleen L., 4868
Kleptz, Melissa A., 7886
Klessig, Christine, 9778
Kleven, Cynthia F., 4492
Klien, James M., 4837
Klimis, Carol, 7700
Kline, Bessie H., 8293
Kline, Charles, 8292
Kline, Cheryl, 7599
Kline, Daniel L., 2623
Kline, Darrell, 7977
Kline, Debra, 8367
Kline, Edward C., 7301
Kline, Figa Cohen, 8292
Kline, Gary H., 2728, 4899
Kline, Josiah W., 8293
Kline, Karlys, 3598
Kline, LeRoy D., 8208
Kline, Lowell L., 1361
Kline, Lowry F., 2351
Kline, Nancy W., 8067
Kline, Ray, 7949
Kline, Sid, 8509
Kline, Sidney D., Jr., 8103
Kling, Allen, 766
Kling, Breckenridge, 7264
Kling, Christian G., 7264
Kling, Daryl, 766
Kling, Donalyn, 766
Kling, Donalyn G., 766
Kling, Fritz, 9492
Kling, Josh, 7264
Kling, William H., 720
Klingen, Andrew D., 6128
Klingensmith, James M., 8247
Klingensmith, Robert L., 9573

Klingenstein Charitable Lead Trust, Andrew, 6335
Klingenstein Fund, Esther A. and Joseph, 6340
Klingenstein, Alan, 6336
Klingenstein, Andrew, 6335, 6340
Klingenstein, Esther A., 6338
Klingenstein, Frederick A., 6337, 6338, 7059
Klingenstein, John, 6128, 6335, 6338, 6339, 7059
Klingenstein, Joseph, 6338
Klingenstein, Julie, 6335
Klingenstein, Kathy, 6340
Klingenstein, Lee Paul, 6336
Klingenstein, Patricia, 6335, 6339
Klingenstein, Patricia D., 6338, 7059
Klingenstein, Paul H., 6336
Klingenstein, Sharon, 6337
Klingenstein, Sharon L., 6338, 7059
Klingenstein, Susan, 6340
Klingenstein, Thomas, 6340
Klingenstein, Thomas D., 6128, 6335
Klinger, Linda L., 3313
Klinghoffer, Lori K., 5289
Klinghoffer, Steven, 5289
Klingner, Linda L., 2572
Klingzel-Carlin, Stephanie, 3387
Klinkham, Judy, 9615
Klintworth, William C., 9314
Kloenhamer, Janet S., 510
Klooster, Henry, 4252
Klopcic, Rick, 9801
Klopp, Marjorie K.C., 6345
Klopping, George, 941, 1099
Klorfine, Leonard, 9619
Klorfine, Norma E., 9619
Klosk, Lawrence, 6167
Kloska, Ronald F., 3139
Kloza, Brian T., 7056
Kluber, William, 4194
Klug, Jon, 8765
Klug, Patricia, 9842
Klug, Scott, 9918
Kluge, John W., 3663, 6970
Kluge, John, Jr., 9451
Kluge, Maria T., 3663
Kluge, Patricia M., 9451
Kluger, Joseph E., 8317
Klumpp, H. William, 8417
Klumpyan, David M., 9800
Klunk, Stephen H., 8511
Klusman, James E., 3188
Klusmann, Scott G., 8069
Kluth, Paula, 3655
Kluttz, Margaret, 7370
Kluttz, Margaret H., 7466
KMP Charitable Trust II, 6584
KMP Charitable Trust VI, 6584
KMP Trust I, 5935
KMP Trust V, 5935
Knabusch Marital Trust, Edward M., 4363
Knabusch, E.M., 4368
Knabusch, Edward M., 4362
Knafel, Andrew G., 6341
Knafel, Douglas R., 6341
Knafel, Sidney R., 6341
Knakal, Joseph C., Jr., 9463
Knapp Foundation, Inc., The, 3664
Knapp Realty Co., 3301
Knapp, Carol, 6342
Knapp, David E., 6342
Knapp, George R., 8477
Knapp, Gwen, 2841
Knapp, Jane, 6342
Knapp, John, 402
Knapp, Joseph Palmer, 3665
Knapp, Judy, 1359
Knapp, Jules, 2841
Knapp, Priscilla S., 6342
Knapp, Roger, 3301
Knapp, W.A., 3312
Knapp, William C., 3301

Knapp, Wlliam C., II, 3301
Knapp, William L., 6342
Knaup, Marianne, 4810
Kneale, James C., 7967
Knebel, John A., 1505
Knecht, David, 1529
Knecht, Randy, 4540
Knecht, Timothy H., 4255
Knedlik, Ron, 7372
Kneeland, Chris, 1357
Kneeley, Anita M., 5341
Kneezel, Ronald D., 9752
Kneisly, Kevin R., 7542
Knell, Theresa N., 3694
Kneppler, Robert, Jr., 8845
Knestout, Mark, Rev., 2257
Knez, Brian J., 3986, 4150
Knez, Debra S., 4150
Knez, Debra Smith, 3986
Knierim, Lou, 939
Knife & Son, L., Inc., 4140
Knife River Corp., 7517
Kniffen, Jan R., 4861, 7738
Knight Trust, James A., 4364
Knight, Athelia, 1776
Knight, Bernice D., 9364
Knight, Colleen, 4237
Knight, Dale A., 9726
Knight, David, 4364
Knight, Herbert T., 2627
Knight, J.A., 5281
Knight, Jack, 1250
Knight, James A., 9764
Knight, James A., Sr., 9764
Knight, James E., 8457
Knight, James L., 2097
Knight, Jeffrey A., 4333
Knight, John S., 2097
Knight, Kathy, 7872
Knight, Laura, 9734
Knight, Lawson F., 9559
Knight, Leo E., Jr., 7603
Knight, Lyle, 4937
Knight, M. Scott, 1505
Knight, Melanie Ann, 7356
Knight, Norman, 3987
Knight, Penelope P., 8032
Knight, Philip, 8046
Knight, Philip H., 8032
Knight, Randolph H., 9363
Knight, Renee Miller, 9764
Knight, Robert M., Jr., 5012
Knight, Roger D., Jr., 1398
Knight, Thomas E., 8797
Knight, Timothy, 7163
Knight, Travis A., 8032
Knight, W.H., Jr., 3019
Knight, Warren, 711
Knight, Will A., 8891, 9285
Knight-Drain, Carol, 4364
Knight-Ridder, Inc., 768
Knip, John J., Jr., 4721
Knisley, F.W., 8368
Knispel, Lester, 1204
Knistrom, Fanny, 5282
Knistrom, Svante, 5282
Knitzele, Jim, 3205
Knoblach, Janet, 4534
Knoble, William T., 5833
Knoepfle, Clarence, 7999
Knoll International Holdings, Inc., 1137
Knoll, Ruth, 4220
Knoll, Thomas, 4220
Knoll, Tom, 7601
Knopf, Max, 6343
Knopf, Rika, 6343
Knopp, Abby, 5840
Knopp, Dave, 3214
Knoth, Donald, 7653
Knott, C.F., 5335
Knott, Eric C., 3666
Knott, Henry J., Sr., 3666
Knott, Jan M., 4607
Knott, Kerry, 8152

Knott, Marion, 769
Knott, Marion I., 3666
Knott, Martin G., Jr., 3666
Knott, Martin G., Sr., 3666
Knott, Owen M., 3666
Knous, Kristi, 3281
Knowles, Amy Elizabeth, 56
Knowles, C. Harry, 5283
Knowles, Harold, 1945
Knowles, Janet H., 5283
Knowles, Jeremy R., 3654
Knowles, Merry L., 7971
Knowles, Rachel Hunt, 8261
Knowlton, Christopher, 5971
Knowlton, Nancy V., 4598
Knowlton, Richard L., 4598
Knowlton, Timothy S., 4356, 4358
Knox Gelatine, Inc., 8294
Knox, Boone A., 2427
Knox, Eleanor E., 8294
Knox, Jefferson B.A., 2427
Knox, John O., Jr., 2383
Knox, John T., Hon., 232
Knox, Julia P. R., 2427
Knox, Kimberly, 8294
Knox, Ltd., 2427
Knox, M.S., 269
Knox, Norman L., 126
Knox, Northrup R., Jr., 6345
Knox, Randy, 9801
Knox, Robert E., Jr., 2357
Knox, Seymour H., 6345
Knox, Seymour H., IV, 6345
Knox, W. Graham, 5777
Knox, Wendell J., 3886
Knox, Wyck A., Jr., Mrs., 2357
Knudsen, Calvert, 9701
Knudsen, Derek T., 596
Knudsen, Earl, 7702
Knudsen, Leon, 8556
Knudsen, Mogen, 4986
Knudsen, Nancy, 7880
Knudsen, Richard, 4954
Knudson, Dave, 828
Knudson, Julie K., 2942
Knueven, Ron, 3230
Knutsen, Harry L., 3319
Knutson, Craig, 7931
Knutson, Robert B., 7276
Kobak, Bernard S., 7868
Kobara, John, 345
Kobayashi, Hidetoshi, 5415
Kobayashi, Naomi, 357
Kobayashi, Yotaro, 7185
Kobel, Cynthia, 2903
Kobernick, Todd, 592
Koblenzer, Dale, 7526
Kobren, Catherine S., 3988
Kobren, Eric M., 3988
Kobusch, Margaret W., 4806
Koch Enterprises, Inc., 3184
Koch Foundation, Fred C., 1819
Koch Foundation, Fred C. and Mary R., 1820
Koch Industries, Inc., 3374
Koch Sons, George, Inc., 3184
Koch Sons, George, LLC, 3184
Koch Trusts for Charity, Fred C., 1819
Koch, Barbara G., 4575
Koch, Carl E., 2098
Koch, Charles Chase, 1819, 1820
Koch, Charles G., 1819, 1820, 3374
Koch, Curtis J., 7839
Koch, David A., 4575
Koch, David H., 3374
Koch, David M., 3184
Koch, Donald G., 7641
Koch, Elizabeth B., 1819, 1820, 3374
Koch, Elizabeth Robinson, 1819, 1820
Koch, Fred C., 3374
Koch, James S., 6638
Koch, Kevin A., 8810
Koch, Kevin R., 3184
Koch, Loretta M., 3111

Koch, Mary R., 3374
Koch, Nancy N., 6067
Koch, Paula, 2098
Koch, Robert L., II, 3184
Koch, William C., Jr., Hon., 8662
Koch-Schumaker, Robyn, 7866
Kochheiser, George W., 3282
Kochmann, Richard A., 4647
Kociba, Richard J., 4407
Kock, E. James, Jr., 3494
Kocol, Camilla, 584
Kocol, Robert, 1460
Kodosky Foundation, 8878
Kodosky, Gail T., 9000
Kodosky, Jeff, 8768
Kodosky, Jeffrey L., 9000
Koe, Susan K., 275
Koeberle, Maurice, 628
Koegel, Albert J., 4409
Koegel, Barbara L., 4409
Koegel, Jane, 4409
Koegel, John, 4409
Koegel, John C., 4409
Koegel, Kathryn, 4409
Koegel, Lisa A., 4409
Koehler, Fred, 3127
Koehler, Marcia, 9001
Koehler, Reginald S., III, 9587
Koehn, Christine, 2181
Koehn, Linda, 3281
Koella, Carl, 8659
Koella, Maribel W., 8671
Koelle, Lisa, 8524
Koenes, Larry, 3178
Koenig, Bradford, 770
Koenig, Brian C., 2482
Koenig, Harold G., 8475
Koenig, Lauren, 770
Koenig, Lori, 4489
Koepsel, Ronald, 1946
Koerber, Cyndy, 4962
Koffman, Sharon, 7344
Kofol, Milan, 3813
Kogan, Jay, 4365
Koglin-Fideldy, Louise, 4574
Kogod, Arlene R., 9452, 9517
Kogod, Robert P., 9452, 9517
Kogovsek, C.J., III, 8454
Koguan, Leo, 5284
Koh, John T., 134
Kohl Charitable Trust, Max, 2099
Kohl Charitable Trust, No. AK2, Max, 771
Kohl Charities, Herbert H., Inc., 9838
Kohl, Allen D., 771, 9837, 9838
Kohl, Dolores, 9838
Kohl, Dolores K., 9837
Kohl, Dorothy, 2099
Kohl, Herbert H., 9837, 9838
Kohl, John E., 7783
Kohl, Mary, 9837
Kohl, Sidney, 2099
Kohl, Sidney A., 9837, 9838
Kohlberg Foundation, The, 6346
Kohlberg, Andrew, 6346
Kohlberg, James A., 2171
Kohlberg, Jerome, 6346
Kohlberg, Karen B., 6346
Kohlberg, Nancy S., 2171
Kohlberg, Pamela, 6346
Kohlberg, Suzanne, 2171
Kohler, Charlotte M., 9839
Kohler, Evangeline, 9840
Kohler, Herbert V., 9840
Kohler, Lillie B., 9840
Kohler, Marie C., 9840
Kohler, R. Hagan, 2196
Kohler, Ruth DeYoung, II, 9840
Kohn, Al, 6532
Kohn, Bernhard L., Jr., 1575
Kohn, Bernhard L., Sr., 1575
Kohn, Christine, 4331
Kohn, Henry, 4807
Kohn, Immanuel, 5632
Kohn, Joan J., 1575

Kohn, Laura, 9599
Kohn, Mike, 5566
Kohnstamm, Abby F., 6221
Kohs, LaVerne R., 9861
Kojima, Ahira, 7185
Kokjer, Ralph L., Jr., 647
Kokomoor, Karl, 2041
Kokot, Eugene V., 6323
Kokot, Nadyne, 3144
Kola, Lenora A., 7917
Kolatch, Jonathan L., 5285
Kolatch, Mindy S., 5285
Kolb, John E., 750
Kolb, Sandra Kiely, 7830
Kolbe, K. William, 5685
Kole, Sheri, 9905
Kolhmeir, J. Bleich, 5902
Kolisch, H. Vira, 1760
Kolkka, Constance, 8278
Kolkman, DiAnn, 4991
Kollar, Robert Jeffs, 3038
Koller, Stanley, 7613
Kolquist, LeRoy T., 4556
Kolschowsky, Gerald A., 2843
Kolschowsky, Karen A., 2843
Kolschowsky, Michael J., 2843
Kolschowsky, Timothy J., 2843
Koly, David M., 7709
Komansky, David H., 6347
Komansky, Elyssa M., 6347
Komansky, Jennifer R., 6347
Komansky, Phyllis J., 6347
Komaroff, Stanley, 5843
Komisar, William, 9895
Komisar, William L., 9894
Kommerstad, Lila M., 772
Kommerstad, Robert M., 772
Komp, George, III, 4735
Komstadius, Lori, 2670
Konahia, Jerry, 8660
Kong, Diana, 1213
Kongsgaard, Lorrain, 404
Kongsgaard, Martha, 9620
Konidaris, Jason, 5523
Konig, Esther, 6238
Konig, Michael, 6238
Konigsberg, Julie, 2126
Konigsberg, Julie E., 2126
Konkel, Katherine, 9178
Konkol, Alexis J., 8132
Konner, Joan, 5390
Konner, Melvin, 6894
Kononowitz, Thomas J., 5336
Konrad, Peter, 1333
Konstam, Robert L., 7819
Konstant, William, 6495
Kontos, Arthur, 5286
Kontos, James, 5286
Kontos, Michael, 5286
Koo, Carlos Chang, 6418
Koo, Grace, 5807
Kool, Tim, 4228
Kool, Tom, 4452
Koon, Janette, 3178
Koons, Wendy, 177
Koontz, Dean R., 773
Koontz, Frederick Singley, 3754, 3755
Koontz, Gerda A., 773
Koop, Deb, 4280
Koop, Dick, 8974
Koop, J.P., 4280
Koop, Mitchell, 8989
Koos, John, 6559
Kooyker, Willem, 6567
Kopczick, E.M., 2687, 2688
Kopel, Shelly Bauerly, 4534
Kopf, R.C., 4280
Kopf, Richard S., 535
Kopin, Melinda, 876
Kopkin, Lisa R., 1845
Kopko, Peter, 7536
Koplan, Jeffrey, 2441
Koplow, Meyer, 8220
Kopp, Barbara, 4599

Kopp, Bradford, 8527
Kopp, Charles G., 8467
Kopp, Kristin, 4599
Kopp, LeRoy, 4599
Kopp, Robert F., 5782
Koppel, Edward J., 3667
Koppel, Grace Anne Dorney, 3667
Koppelman, Janet, 6349
Koppelman, Lisa, 6349
Koppelman, Murray, 6349
Koppelman, Suzanne, 6349
Kopper, Carolyn, 1453
Kopper, W. Bruce, 1453
Kopperl, Joan Hudson, 4106
Kopps-Wagner, Jennifer, 9748
Koprulu, Nina J., 6275
Kora, Vidya, 3247
Koran, Ida, 4600
Korbel, Sandy, 7514
Korber, Mark F., 1564
Koreeda, Shusuke, 1828
Korein, Beth, 8295
Korein, James, 8295
Korein, Jonathan, 8295
Korein, Julius, 8295
Korein, Sarah, 8295
Korell, Brad, 4954
Koren, Beverly, 3595
Koret Foundation, 775
Koret, Joseph, 774
Koret, Stephanie, 774
Koret, Susan, 774, 775
Korf, Gene R., 5297
Korf, Scott, 5297
Korff, Phyllis, 6260
Korgenski, Marcy, 9346
Korman, Bernard J., 8379
Korman, Berton E., 8296
Korman, Hyman, Inc., 8296
Korman, Jane, 8996
Korman, Josh, 8996
Korman, Leonard I., 8296
Korman, Scott, 6831
Korman, Steven H., 8296
Korman, Timothy J., 9439
Korn, Alissa, 3935
Kornfeld, Emily Davie, 6350
Kornfeld, Stuart A., 4860
Korniczky, Anna T., 6146, 6147, 6882
Kornitzer, John C., 3398
Kornwasser, Jacob, 776
Kornwasser, Mila, 776
Korologos, Ann McLaughlin, 5827
Korstange, Jason E., 4699
Korszen, Dorothy, 2041
Kort, William B., 531
Kortepeter, Wendy Griffith, 3158
Kortun, Vasif, 5550
Kortz, Donald L., 1445
Korybut, Sharron Lannan, 5484
Kosar, Bernie J., 7703
Kosar, Bernie J., Sr., 7703
Kosarek, Charles L., Jr., 8785
Kosarek, Frances R., 8785
Kosarek, Joshua, 8785
Kosarek, Willie J., 8785
Kosasa, Minnie, 2549
Kosasa, Paul J., 2549
Kosasa, Sidney S., 2549
Kosasa, Susan M., 2549
Kosasa, Thomas S., 2549
Kosaso, Paul, 2545
Kosch, Philip C., 3871
Kosche, Peter C., Jr., 2925
Kosh, Mitch, 6737
Kosheba, Kelly, 8079
Koshland, Daniel E., Jr., 777, 6379
Koshland, Douglas, 3559
Koshland, Douglas E., 777, 3677
Koshland, James M., 777
Koshland, Marian E., 777
Koshland, Yvonne, 777
Kosin, Stanley E., 3651
Koske, Doug, 8583

Kuester, Rick, 9967
Kuffner, Charles P., 1221
Kuffner, Helene, 5904
Kuflik, Karen, 6360
Kuflik, Mitchell, 6191, 6360
Kugielsky, Daniel, 5556
Kuhar, Gary, 9615
Kuhn, J.A., 7392
Kuhn, John A., 7392
Kuhn, Kurt, 4990
Kuhn, Lori, 7760
Kuhn, Lucy S., 7392
Kuhn, Peter A., 7677, 9657
Kuhn, Stacy M., 9220
Kuhn, Thomas E., 4867
Kuhne, J.A., 7472
Kuhne, Lucy, 7472
Kuhnley, Marc, 4560
Kuhre, Carol, 6643
Kuioka, Alton, 2535
Kuiper, Elizabeth E., 2287
Kukovich, Allen, 8457
Kukovich, Nancy, 8155
Kula, Irwin, Rabbi, 6947
Kulak, Sharon J., 2650
Kulas, Brian, 9743
Kulas, E.J., 7706
Kulas, Fynette H., 7706
Kulas, Julian E., 2797
Kullman, Mary C., 4852
Kullman, Mary Ellen, 232
Kullman, Ruth, 3489
Kulynych, Petro, 7415, 7416
Kum & Go LC, 3302
Kumble, Peggy, 6361
Kumble, Roger, 6361
Kumble, Steven J., 6361
Kumble, Todd, 6361
Kumler, Barbara, 7622
Kumm, David W., 9756
Kumm, Lillian H., 9774
Kummer, Robert W., Jr., 728
Kump, Marsha A., 4482
Kundtz, Mary Ann, 3041
Kung, Edward Y., 8378
Kunin, Constance B., 4519
Kunin, David B., 4664
Kunin, Myron, 4664
Kunka, Stan, 5400
Kunkel, Bernard, 3406
Kunkel, John C., II, 8297
Kunkel, Joseph, 9385
Kunkel, Paul A., 8297
Kunkel, Russell, 8379
Kunstadter, Christopher T.W., 6362
Kunstadter, Geraldine S., 6362
Kunstadter, Lisa, 6362
Kuntz, Frank J., 9571
Kuntz, John F., 5359
Kuntz, Lee A., 1480
Kuntzman, David L., 7867
Kunz, Dan, 9745
Kunz, Heidi, 296
Kunz, Kenneth D., 2388
Kunz, Kenneth O., 5194
Kunz, Vicki, 9745
Kunze, Mel, 9236
Kunzman, Kenneth F., 5137
Kuper, David H., 3298
Kupferberg, Jesse, 6363
Kupferberg, Lloyd S., 2927
Kupferberg, Martin, 6363
Kupferberg, Max, 6363
Kupferberg, Saul, 6363
Kupiec, Suzanne, 9144
Kuppler, Karl, 2677
Kupsky, Dan, 1139
Kurack, Sandra, 9660
Kurczewski, W.W., 3018
Kuretich, Stephen, 4743
Kurgan-Van Hentenryk, Regine, 5973
Kuritz, Lindi, 9810
Kurland, Stanford L., 422
Kurn, Neal, 87

Kurth, Ernest L., 9003
Kurth, Sandra G., 9003
Kurtz, Carol, 6364
Kurtz, Daniel, 6921
Kurtz, Daniel L., 5546, 7032
Kurtz, David, 8302
Kurtz, Glenn R., 3537
Kurtz, Gregory P., 7555
Kurtz, Kelli, 7660
Kurtz, Lawrence W., 879
Kurtz, Nancy, 3783
Kurtz, Richard, 3537
Kurtz, Ronald, 6364
Kurtz, Virginia H., 3537
Kurtz, Virginia Hoyt, 3537
Kurtzman, Amy, 7497
Kurtzman, Ellen B., 8194
Kurz, Ellen, 6365
Kurz, Herbert, 6365
Kurz, Leonard, 6365
Kurz, Theodore, 5099
Kurzig, Carol, 5583
Kurzman, H. Michael, 832
Kurzman, Jayne M., 6215
Kushlan, Paula Frohring, 5993
Kushner, Charles, 5740
Kushner, Jack, 8104
Kushner, Samuel A., 9401
Kusman, Shelley Trager, 3452
Kusmer, James, 7808
Kusnetzky, Leon G., 4819
Kuster, Ann McLane, 5098
Kutak Rock LLP, 6512
Kutch, David B., 8345
Kuth, Byron, 799
Kuth, Lyda, 799
Kutliroff, Susan, 5395
Kutteroff, Frederick, 8303
Kutzin, Michael, 5578
Kuykendall, John, Rev. Dr., 5137
Kuykendall, Verna, 811
Kuyper, E. Lucille Gaass, 3304
Kuyper, Peter H., 3304
Kvamme, Damon, 781
Kvamme, E. Floyd, 781
Kvamme, Jean, 781
Kvamme, Todd, 781
Kwast, Terry, 417
Kwiecinski, Henry, 8105
Kwoh, Stewart, 350, 1793
Kwong, Peter, 6615
KWWH Trust, 2788
KXAS-TV, 8817
Kydd, Michelle, 341
Kyle, David, 7984
Kyle, David L., 7967
Kyle, Donald, 3131
Kyle, James Lewis, II, 346
Kyle, Louis B., 2579
Kyte, Lawrence, 7777
Kyte, Lawrence H., Jr., 7907

L&D Foundation, 4439
L-K Marketing, 9057
La Badie, Helen Ruth, 9773
La Belle, John D., Jr., 1644
La Brea Property, LLC, 379
La Camera, Paul, 3812
La Fetra, Anthony W., 782
La Fetra, Michael W., 782
La Fetra, Suzanne, 782
La Vea, James Annenberg, 8298
La Veque, Edgar G., 1256
La-Z-Boy Chair Co., 4368
La-Z-Boy Inc., 4368
Labadie, Gary, 4229
LaBahn, Charles P., 9766
LaBahn, Mary Ann, 9766
Labalme, George, Jr., 5850, 6375
Labalme, Lisa, 5721
Labaree, Aaron, 6675
Labaree, Frances, 6675
Labatt, Gloria, 8811

Labcoat Limited, 3841
Labeck, Timothy P., 1148
Labkowski Irrevocable Trust, Chmvel, 7151
Laborde, Alden, 3459
Laborde, James, 3459
Laborde, John, 3459
Laborde, Margaret, 3459
Labounty, Gordon, 2882
Labovitz, Joel, 4601
Labovitz, Sharon, 4601
LaBranche, George M.L., IV, 6619
Labrato, Ronnie R., 2042
Labutka, Carolyn E., 2598
Lacasse, Robert P., 3536
Lacayo, Henry L. "Hank", 1264
Lacchia, Patrick, 4156
Lacey, Dee, 1090
Lacinak, Charles, Jr., 3502
Laclede Gas Co., 4852
Lacy 20, Inc., 379
Lacy, Benjamin H., 3850
Lacy, F. Dwight, 8804
Lacy, Lois D., 3383
Lacy, Stephen, 3314
Lacy, Terri, 7899
Ladd, David J., Rev., 3907
Ladd, George E., III, 3992
Ladd, J. Scott, 3907
Ladd, Jennifer, 4076
Ladd, John D., 3907
Ladd, Jr. Charitable Trust, George E., 3992
Ladd, Kate Macy, 6471
Ladd, Lincoln F., 3907, 3992
Ladd, Robert M., 3907, 3992
Ladd, Ted, 9977
Ladenburger, Robert, 1446
Ladensohn, Claudia, 9166
Laderman, Ezra, 5548
Ladish Co., Inc., 9846
Ladish, Herman W., 9847
Ladish, William J., 9847
Ladislaw, Robert A., 5926
Ladner, Ann Marie, 3436
Ladner, Frank S., 3436
Ladner, Gerald, 3093
Ladner, Julia M., 3436
Ladner, Margaret M., 3436
Ladner, Thomas M., 3436
Ladner, William P., 3436
Ladt, Vicki, 3415
LaDuke, Winona, 384
Lady, David, 4844
Ladzinski, Casimir H., Msgr., 5341
Lafer, Fred S., 5298, 5424, 5425
Lafever, D.G., 2301
Laff, Amy, 5884
Laffall, LaSalle D., Jr., 4319
Laffey-Mchugh Foundation, The, 413
Laffitte, Helen, 9481
Laffont, Ingrid C., 3464
Laffoon, Polk, 768
LaFleche, Paul E., 8537
LaFleur, Richard B., 4108
Lafond, James F., 1785
LaFortune, Bill, 7984
Lafromboise, Jean K., 9622
LaFurgey, Allen J., 4361
Lagasse, Ronald L., 5675
Lagenthal, Judith, 3698
Lageschulte, Roger, 9646
Lagorio, Evelyn, 715
LaGrange Memorial Health System, 2681
Lahey, John H., 3746
Lahn, John L., 1164
Lahner, Kenneth J., 2781
Lahr, Sherry A., 7791
LaHurd, Ryan, 2832
Laidig, Jon, 3131
Laidlaw, Andrew R., 3003
Laikin, Robert J., 3116
Laimbeer, William, Sr., 1943

Laing, Mercedes A., 2661
Lainovic, Rebecca, 6598
Lainovic, Sacha, 6598
Laird Norton Co. LLC, 9623
Laird Norton Trust Co., 9623
Laird, E. Cody, Jr., 2373
Laird, E.E., Jr., 4748
Laird, Fiona C., 5434
Laird, Helen, 8395
Lairson, Earl C., 8878
Laitman, Nanette L., 6378
Laizure, Lisa S., 114
Laizure, Robert S., 114
LaKamp, Larry, 1454
LaKamp, Martha, 1454
Lake, Antonia, 8509
Lake, Jeffrey, 6329
Lake, Mary Anne Douglas, 8588
Lake, Natalie, 1473
Lake, Robert, 3247
Lake, William W., 4259
Lakeshore International Corporation, 565
Lakey, Ronald L., 685
Lakin, Charles, 836
Lakin, Phil, 7984
Lakireddy, Hanimireddy, 784
Lakireddy, Sidhardha, 784
Lakireddy, Vijaya, 784
Lalin, Matt, 7174
Lallathin, Mark, 3148
Lally, Margaret, 8624
LaLonde, Gerald, 3325
Lalor, Willard A., 3993
Lam, Cynthia, 466
Lam, Joseph, 1319
LaManna, Kimberly F., 3608
Lamar, Charles C., 2786
LaMarche, Gara, 5574, 6665
Lamastra, Joseph M., 5235
Lamb Trust, Walter E., 8299
Lamb, Beverly, 9379
Lamb, Catherine L., 4711
Lamb, James R., 1611, 1612
Lamb, Julia M., 4711
Lamb, Marguerite B., 4931
Lamb, Nash, 9034
Lamb, Peter, 5098
Lamb, Richard C., 3801
Lamb, Robert E., 8299
Lamb, Stephen P., 1706
Lambe, Claude R., 1820
Lamberson, Barbara Nelson, 8712
Lamberson, Nelson, 8712
Lamberson, Thomas, 8712
Lambert Brake Corp., 4460
Lambert, Bill, 6370
Lambert, Cynthia A., 9908
Lambert, Greg, 5064
Lambert, Harold M., 9453
Lambert, Henry M., 3503
Lambert, J. Hamilton, 9478
Lambert, Joseph, 1078
Lambert, LaDoyce, 9117
Lambert, Linda, 7952
Lambert, Melanie A., 9217
Lambert, Oleta, 1080
Lambert, Samuel W., III, 1863, 5148, 5323
Lambert, Sheila, 6370
Lambert, Stephen J., 7382
Lambert, Susan R., 7382
Lambertus, Christine L., 1941
Lambie, James T., 7508
Lamboley, Cathy A., 9181
Lamere, David F., 8345
Lamesa National Bank, 9268
Laminated Products, Inc., 9761
Lamkin, Martha D., 3196
Lamm, Peter, 3994
Lammers, Bruce, 2591
Lammers, James D., 4267
Lammert, Richard A., 6465
Lamond, Christine, 785

Lamond, Pierre, 785
Lamontagne, Raymond A., 5898
LaMothe, Alexis, 4370
LaMothe, Patricia A., 4370
LaMothe, William E., 4370
LaMotte, Beryl E., 8584
Lamoureux, Lionel, 4026
Lamp, Vernett, 8568
Lampert, Alan G., 5095
Lampert, Mark, 786
Lamping, Robert F., 2871
Lampros, Jack D., 138, 9345
Lampton, Dorothy Lee, 4740
Lampton, Lee C., 4740
Lampton, Leslie B., 4740
Lampton, Leslie B., III, 4740
Lampton, Robert H., 4740
Lampton, William W., 4740
Lamson, Fred I., 3795
Lamson, Steve Zumbach-Belin, 3316
Lamy, Judy, 1357
Lancaster Newspapers, Inc., 8458, 8459
Lancaster, Colin, 9935
Lancaster, George, 9049
Lancaster, H. Martin, 7438
Lancaster, James B., Jr., 1943
Lancaster, Rose C., 9240
Lancaster, Sally R., 9049
Lance, David, 2359
Lance, Howard L., 2050
Lance, Inc., 7418
Lanci, Marc, 860
Lanctot, Francis J., 4005
Land and Gravel Pit, 8892
Land O'Lakes, Inc., 4602
Land, Edwin H., 1749
Land, Helen M., 1749
Landaker, James, 7616
Landau Trust, A., 6687
Landau, Barbara, 7232
Landau, Chaim, 6687
Landau, David, 6687
Landau, Efraim, 6687
Landau, Howard M., 2847
Landau, Kenneth, 2847
Landau, W. Loeber, 7232
Landefeld, Stewart M., 9680
Landegger, Carl, 6371
Landegger, George F., 6371
Landers, Anne Sheehan, 4140
Landers, Elizabeth, 294
Landers, William D., 7897
Landes, Phyllis M., 1943
Landes, Stephanie, 1003
Landesman, Nash, 1533
Landesman, North, 1533
Landess, C. Barton, 7370
Landess, John, 7889
Landess, Sara, 7889
Landewich, Joseph L., 3434
Landgraf, John C., 2579
Landino, Frank, 5087
Landis, Edwin C., Jr., 5423
Landis, Gregory P., 9550
Landis, Sharon, 87
Landis-Seid, Barbara, 2996
Landman, Bette E., Dr., 8086
Landman, Carole S., 6164
Landman, William, 8147
Landmark Communications, Inc., 9455
Landmark Developers of Macon, 2424
Landon, Allan R., 2535
Landreth, Jeanne, 401
Landrigan, James R., 9434
Landro, Laura A., 6897
Landrum, Brian, 9144
Landrum, Martha McDermott, 3503
Landry, C. Kevin, 3995
Landry, Edward A., 692, 790, 928, 1235
Landsberg, Gloria, 9297
Landsberg, Jeff, 9297
Landsman, Emanuel E., 3996
Landsman, Sheila E., 3996

Landstar Homes, 8818
Landy, Laura K., 5368
Lane, Andrew D., 6731, 6772
Lane, Bernard B., 9456
Lane, Bland, 2002
Lane, Deborah Anne, 2677
Lane, Dennis J., 3595
Lane, Eric, 3122
Lane, Helen M., 1940
Lane, Jackie, 8671
Lane, James N., 6372
Lane, Janice, 4055
Lane, Jean M., 4520
Lane, Jeffrey B., 1735, 6373, 6395
Lane, Joan, 787
Lane, Minnie B., 9456
Lane, Nancy Wolfe, 7915
Lane, Nancy Z., 6373
Lane, Ralph, 787
Lane, Richard D., 4428
Lane, Robert W., 2699
Lane, Susan W., 6372
Lane, Terry Saunders, 3812
Lane, Thomas H., 4285
Lane, Thomas M., 2513
Lane, Timothy E., 5194
Lane, William, 7581
Lane, William A., Jr., 1981
Laney, James T., 6453
Laney, Sandra E., 7681
Lang, Belinda, 6374
Lang, Bruce W., 7754
Lang, Corlene, 3387
Lang, Eugene M., 6219, 6374
Lang, Helen, 6675
Lang, Jane, 1848, 6374
Lang, Joseph, 9861
Lang, Keith H., 8524
Lang, Kristina, 6374
Lang, Linda, 705
Lang, Margaret A., 6675
Lang, Nancy, 5496
Lang, Ralph, 4723
Lang, Robert Todd, 1721, 7225
Lang, Stephen, 6374
Lang, Theresa, 6374
Lang-Miers, Elizabeth A., 8855
Langbauer, Del, 9546, 9600
Langbauer, Robert, 9600
Langbauer, William H., 9600
Langbo, Arnold G., 4371
Langbo, Martha M., 4371
Langbo, Maureen, 4371
Langdon, Larry R., 284
Lange, Alexander C., 3097
Lange, Alexander T., 3097
Lange, Anna, 2550
Lange, Cathy, 9486
Lange, Cynthia M., 3097
Lange, Laurence E., 1313
Lange, Nora E., 2550
Langeloth, Jacob, 6375
Langenberg, Mary B., 4880
Langenberg, Oliver M., 4860, 4880
Langendorf, Stanley S., 788
Langenkamp, Albert H., 3112
Langenthal, Herschel L., 3698
Langenthal, Judith, 3698
Langer, Christelle, 4623
Langer, Irving, 6376
Langer, Linda, 5852
Langer, Richard J., 9667
Langford, David, 9918
Langford, Donovan A., III, 2643
Langham, S.C., 2111
Langloh, John A. "Drew", 1706
Langlois, David R., 506
Langlois, Marie J., 8524
Langmead, Paula, 3597
Langner, Jay B., 6477
Langone, Ken, 2441
Langstaff, Carol, 6118
Langwell, Dennis, 4006
Laniado, Hagai, 5554

Lanier Foundation, Helen S., Inc., 2431
Lanier, Bruce N., Jr., 2511
Lanier, Campbell B., III, 2429
Lanier, David Gaines, 2429
Lanier, Elizabeth W., 2429
Lanier, George H., 2428
Lanier, George H., II, 2511
Lanier, J. Hicks, 2428
Lanier, J. Reese, 2430
Lanier, J. Smith, II, 2429
Lanier, Jane Z., 2429
Lanier, Julie W., 2428
Lanier, Linda L., 239
Lanier, Richard S., 7168
Lanier, Sartain, 2428
Lanier, Susan I., 2416
Lanigan, Bernard, Jr., 2363, 2514
Lankfer, Marilyn A., 4326
Lankowsky, Zenon P., 8529
Lannan, J. Patrick, 5484
Lannan, J. Patrick, Jr., 5484
Lannan, John J., 5484
Lannan, John R., 5484
Lannan, Lawrence P., Jr., 5484
Lanni, Deborah M., 789
Lanni, J. Terrence, 789
Lanning, Mark R., 4708
Lanoga Corp., 9623
Lanphear, Gail E., 4217, 4322, 4407
Lansbury, Susan S., 283
Lansdell, Lyle T., 906
Lansenhorst, Dian, 3049
Lansing, John, 5517
Lansky, Gregg I., 8677
Lantum, Hoffman Moka, 6823
Lantz, David, 8715
Lantz, Grace T., 790
Lantz, Joanne B., 3149
Lantz, John, 9693
Lantz, Walter, 790
Lanum, Robert W., 3218
Lanza Family Foundation, The, 5294
Lanza, Frank, 5294
Lanza, Patricia, 5294
Lanzillotta, A. Paul, 9486
Lanznar, Howard S., 2826
Lapadula, Kimberly A., 5342
Lapatin, J., 7279
Lapera, Martin S., 3598
Lapham, Lewis H., 6118
Lapham, Thomas H., 6041
Laphen, James A., 5010
Lapides, Allene, 5485
Lapides, Jerome, 5485
Lapides, Leola, 403
Lapidow, Seth J., 5696
Lapine, Mark, 1541
LaPlace, William B., 7862
LaPlant, Gary, 4259
LaPonsie, Margaret, 4259
LaPook, Jonathan, 5300
LaPorte, Christopher, 8657
LaPorte, Joseph, 8657
LaPorte, Joseph, III, 8657
LaPorte, Roberta, 2763
LaPorte, Sam, 8657
LaPorte, Stephen, 8657
Lappan, Steve, 4253
Lappin, Robert I., 3997
Lapriore, Cheryl M., 3941
Lapuma, Edward V., 5704
Laraway, Steve, 4534
Lard, Mary P., 9005
Laredo National Bank, The, 8927
Larenas, Monica, 542
Largay, Dorothy F., 1224
Large, George K., 5295
Largey, Marjorie L., 3816
Larich, Jeffrey, 5993
Lario Oil and Gas Co., 4639
Larison, Ralph G., 268
Lariviere, Stephanae D., 6031
Lark, Andy, 1214
Lark, J. Andrew, 5145, 5815

Larkin, June Noble, 6633
Larkin, June Noble, Mrs., 6633
Larkin, Richard, 1594, 3931
Larkin, Thomas E., Jr., 214
Larochelle, Carolyn L. Parmer, 2932
LaRosa, Alfred, 5925
LaRosa, William R., 2053
Larrabee Fund, 1578
Larsand Corp., 1011
Larsen, Caitlin, 9229
Larsen, Chad M., 1579
Larsen, Christopher, 1579
Larsen, David P., 4485
Larsen, Dorothy M., 5296
Larsen, Edward L., 4178
Larsen, Garret W., 5296
Larsen, Jeff, 3370
Larsen, John C., 3278
Larsen, John S., 9693
Larsen, Jonathan Z., 1579
Larsen, Ken, 9810
Larsen, Lauren, 4643
Larsen, Leonard, 4540
Larsen, Libby, 4595
Larsen, Ralph S., 5265, 5296
Larsen, Roy E., 1579
Larsen, Sara E., 9739
Larsen, Wayne E., 9846
Larson Manufacturing Co. of SD, Inc., 8627
Larson, Amanda A., 6078
Larson, Barbara J., 4603
Larson, Carol S., 972
Larson, Chris, 9655, 9664
Larson, Christopher, 9625
Larson, Dale, 9624
Larson, David, 6638
Larson, Donald V., 4646
Larson, Janet B., 3998
Larson, Jeffrey B., 3998
Larson, Jesse, 8962
Larson, Joanne G., 6078
Larson, Kathy, 9949
Larson, Kenneth R., 4603
Larson, Larry R., 4958
Larson, Lyle, 9947
Larson, Maree, 8627
Larson, Marshall K., 8962
Larson, Miriam, 8014
Larson, Nancy S., 222
Larson, O. Dale, 8627
Larson, Patricia, 8627
Larson, Patricia M., 8627
Larson, Peter N., 2636
Larson, Phyllis, 9624
Larson, Robert, 2911
Larson, Robert C., 4367
Larson, Robert F., 5538
LaRussa, Anne B., 17
LaRussa, Benny M., Jr., 17
LaRusso, Sophia, 1946
LaSalle Bank, N.A., 2661
Lasater, Donald E., 4835
Lascalles, Mark, 1139
Lasch, Frank M., 5782
Lascher, Wendy Cole, 1264
Lascor, Michael, 1470
Lasdon, Jacob S., 6378
Lasdon, Mildred D., 6378
Lasdon, William S., 6378
Laserson, Fran, 6569
Lash, Abigail S., 6396
Lash, Jonathan, 1858
Lash, Wendy Lehman, 6396
Lasher, Allan, 472
Lasher, Darlene, 472
Lasher, Donna C., 1515
Lashinsky, Arthur E., 5225
Lashley, Elinor Huston, 8264
Laska, Robert H., 1504
Laske, Arthur C., Jr., 6579
Lasker, Mary W., 6379
Laskin, John A., 7430
Lasko, Gary, 4373

Lasko, John C., 4373
Laskow, Barbara Bender, 1772
Laskow, Mark, 8130
Lasky, Floria V., 6441, 6817
Lasky, Mark, 9885
LaSota, John A., Jr., 96
Laspa, J.P., 269
Lass, Meg, 1463
Lassalle, Honor, 6635
Lassalle, Philip E., 6635
Lassen, Helen Lee, 5868
Lasser, Mary R., 5127
Lasser, Miles L., 6964
Lasser, Peter, 5127
Lasseter, John A., 791
Lasseter, Nancy T., 791
Lassiter, James, 1162
Lassiter, Rosemary E., 1986
Lastavica, Catherine C., 4192
Lastavica, John, 4192
Lastfogel, Abe, 6380
Lastfogel, Frances, 6380
Lastinger, Erin Jette, 222
LaSurdo, I.J., 5559
Lataif, Louis E., 3963
Latham, John Brace, 1501
Lathbury, Norman K., 8136
Lathem, J. Ernest, 8583
Lathrop, John C., 7427
Latimer, William H., III, 8732
Latona Associates Inc., 5099
Latta, James, 7383
Latterell, Larry, 4574
Lattes, Conrad, 1358
Lattner, Forrest C., 2104
Lattner, Forrest C., Mrs., 2104
Lattner, Frances H., 2104
Lattore, Patrick, 6532
Latz, Gordon W., 6482
Lau, Constance H., 2546
Lau, Grace Y., 87
Laub, Carol N., 4264
Laub, Philippe, 6164
Laucke, Michael, 6466
Lauda, Thomas C., 5159
Lauder 2002 Trust, Estee, The, 6383
Lauder Foundation, The, 6382
Lauder, Aerin, 6381
Lauder, Estee, 5549, 6381, 6383
Lauder, Estee, Inc., 6381, 6383
Lauder, Estee, Mrs., 6382
Lauder, Evelyn, 6381
Lauder, Evelyn H., 6382
Lauder, Jo Carole, 6383
Lauder, Joseph H., 6381
Lauder, Laura, 961
Lauder, Leonard A., 5549, 6232, 6381,
    6382
Lauder, Ronald S., 6232, 6261, 6381,
    6383
Lauder, William, 5549, 6381
Lauderbach, William, 4217
Lauer, Jay, 3894
Lauer, Rhonda H., 5393
Lauer, Robert, 337
Laufer, Doris, 5533
Laufer, Mayer, 5533
Laughlin, David W., 4464
Laughlin, Wilbur P., 1081
Laughon, Kenneth, 9387
Laughter, Kristy, 8608
Launius, Leigh Ann, 7596
Laura J. Niles Revocable Trust, 1612
Laureate Education, Inc., 3741
Lauren, David, 6737
Lauren, Ralph, 6737
Laurenti, Yuki Moore, 5357
Laurie, Irving, 5297
Lauritzen, Andrew R., 9754
Lauritzen, Bruce R., 4946
Lauro, Shirley, 5883
Lautenberg Charitable Trusts, Frank R.,
    5298
Lautenberg, Frank R., 5298

Lautenberg, Lois, 5298
Lautenschleger, Candace, 7536
Lauter, Nancy A., 2881
Lautz, Terrill E., 6453
Laux, Giles, 3223
LaValley, Daniel J., 7708
LaValley, Frederick J.M., 8228, 8378
LaValley, Jimmy, 9265
LaValley, Richard G., 7708
LaValley, Richard G., Jr., 7708
Lavalley, Richard G., Jr., 7882
LaValley, Richard G., Jr., 7883
Lavander, John M., 4623
Lave, Penny, 828
Lave, Roy, 828
Lavecchia, Dan, 7174
Lavelle, John H., 5782
Lavelle, Larna, 4866
Lavender, Kevin P., 8662
Laver, Rhonda, 1642
Laverack, Cordelia, 1580
Laverack, William, 1580
Laverty, Chris, 4243
Lavery, Kevin T., 4347
Lavey, Richard, 3941
Lavezzorio, Joan F., 2877
Lavezzorio, Leonard M., 2877
Lavezzorio, Nicholas J., 2877
Lavie, Catherine F., 8899
Lavietes, Estelle, 1581
Lavietes, Raymond P., 1581
Lavin, Bernice E., 2849
Lavin, Jerold, 3005
Lavin, Leonard H., 2849
Lavin, Sheldon, 3005
Lavin, Steven, 3005
Lavin, Sylvia, 3005
Lavina, Richard, 1957
Lavinder, Joyce King, 2351
Lavine, Richard A., 793
Lavine, Ruth J., 793
Lavine, Steve, 421
Lavis, Victor, 212
Lavizzo-Mourey, Risa, 5265
Law, Caroline Wiess, 9006
Law, Fred, 7725
Law, Grant, 8660
Law, Julia, 1947
Law, Naomi, 2922
Lawford Co., 3683
Lawford, Patricia K., 6689
Lawhorne, Susan C., 2361
Lawien, John P., 4556
Lawler, Cynthia, 1578
Lawler, Dell R., 8635
Lawler, F. Rodney, 8635
Lawler, Frank C., 5484
Lawler, John J., 3823
Lawler, Jon R., 8635
Lawler, Kathleen A., 9812
Lawler, Linda Guild, 8229
Lawler, Paul J., 4357
Lawless, Bob, 8878
Lawless, Kathy, 3372
Lawless, Robert J., 3671
Lawner, Edward, 7038
Lawrence, Andrew, 5861
Lawrence, Anne I., 7684
Lawrence, Barbara, 8371
Lawrence, Barbara A., 9551
Lawrence, Belinda Turner, 2097
Lawrence, Brad, 3215
Lawrence, Charles M., 836
Lawrence, Christopher, 5807
Lawrence, Cynthia Cross, 1604
Lawrence, David, 5971
Lawrence, Edward P., 3771, 3808
Lawrence, Gary M., 9243
Lawrence, Inger, 2609
Lawrence, James A., 4570
Lawrence, Jeff, 794
Lawrence, John T., III, 7684, 7851
Lawrence, John T., Jr., 7619
Lawrence, John T., Jr., Mrs., 7851

Lawrence, Kathleen A., 2609
Lawrence, Keith, 1005
Lawrence, Kent, 2609
Lawrence, Lind, 9457
Lawrence, Linda, 2610
Lawrence, Mark A., 5871
Lawrence, Myra S., 5780
Lawrence, Paula S., 7048
Lawrence, Priscilla A., 5871
Lawrence, Robert A., 4126
Lawrence, Robert J., 2610
Lawrence, Robert P., 5871
Lawrence, Robert P., Rev., 3854
Lawrence, Ryan, 5049
Lawrence, Sandra A.J., 4824, 4842,
    9222
Lawrence, Starling R., 1510
Lawrence, Steve, 3038
Lawrence-Lightfoot, Sara, 2868, 5574
Lawrie, Henry DeVos, Jr., 1072
Lawson, A. Peter, 2906
Lawson, Barbara K., 3595
Lawson, Frederick Q., 9330, 9331,
    9332, 9338
Lawson, Janet Q., 9332, 9338
Lawson, Jeff, 8583
Lawson, Jill T., 1892
Lawson, Latham, 3199
Lawson, Peter Q., 9332, 9338
Lawson, Phillip O., 8635
Lawson, Robert C., Jr., 9419
Lawson-Johnston, Peter O., 6118
Lawson-Johnston, Peter, II, 6118
Lawton, Abbey Francis, 8556
Lawton, Jack E., Jr., 3467
Lawton, Jack E., Sr., 3467
Lawton, Patrick S., 9750
Lawton, Pete, 9977
Lawton, Rick, 10000
Lawton, Robert B., 645
Lawton, William B., 3467
Lawyers Title Insurance Corp., 9454
Lay, Henry A., 4853
Layden, Barbara, 7419
Layden, Charles Max, 3202
Layden, Donald W., 7419
Layer, Davida, 4855
Layman, Dan, 3115
Layman, Sandy, 4520
Layne, Brenda, 4231
Layton, Elizabeth, 1637
Layton, Howard R., 1706
Layton, Thomas C., 564
Lazar, Bill, 79
Lazar, Ellen, 1793
Lazar, Helen B., 8035
Lazar, Jack, 8035
Lazar, Shelley, 5708
Lazar, William B., 8035
Lazard Freres & Co., 36
Lazarof, Janice Taper, 1226
Lazarus Charitable Fund, 2961
Lazarus, Charles, 5299
Lazarus, David, 9677
Lazarus, Katherine, 9677
Lazarus, Leonard, 7019
Lazarus, Rochelle B., 5326
Lazenby, F.W., 8662
Lazor, Cynthia M., 7867
Lazzara, Gasper, 2105
Lazzara, Irene, 2105
LB Foundation, 6395
LCR-M Corp., 2712
Le Bonheur Health Systems Foundation,
    8653
Le Grand, Roger, 9845
Le Moal-Gray, Michele J., 5800
Lea, Charles L., Jr., 3693
Lea, Christopher G., 2850
Lea, Hurdle H. "Trip", III, 9363
Lea, L. Bates, 2850
Lea, Marcia W., 2850
Leabo, J. Philip, 2490
Leabo, J. Philip, Jr., 2490

Leabo, Karen S., 2360, 2490
Leach, Brock, 6714
Leach, Charles Henry, II, 6388
Leach, Charles, Jr., 1515
Leach, Duane M., 8998
Leach, Frances V., 7516
Leach, Gary, 9071
Leach, Paul, 910
Leach, Phillip M., 9227
Leach, Sheryl S., 1649
Leach, Thomas Royce, 2785
Leach, Thomas W., 7516
Leach, Willis R., 1186
Leadbetter, Bonnie T., 2498
Leaders, Rance L., 4394
Leaf, Frederick P., 1514
League, David W., 2582
Leahey, William J., 5349
Leahy, Hugh D., Jr., 1706
Leahy, Jeffrie B., 6823
Leahy, Mary Jo, 4014
Leahy, Mary Lee, 2957
Leake, Earl D., 7418
Leake, Ellen, 4737
Leake, Louise Briley, 9849
Leaman, Dean, 8916
Lean, Geoffrey, 6389
Lear Corp., 4374
Lear, Ginny, 828
Lear, Kate Breckir, 5300
Lear, Lyn, 795
Lear, Maggie, 5300
Lear, Norman, 795
Learning Annex of New York, The, 5836
Leary, Carol, 3855
Leary, Carol A., 1907
Leary, Hugh K., 9493, 9513
Leary, J.J., Jr., 9668
Lease and Rental Mgmt. Corp., Inc.,
    3877
Leath, Berneice, 9280
Leath, Berneice R., 9130, 9131
Leatherbury, Ann, 628
Leatherby, Eleanor, 796
Leatherby, Joann, 796
Leatherby, Kathryn, 796
Leatherby, Ralph, 796
Leatherby, Russell, 796
Leatherman, J. Martin, 1517
Leavenworth, Elaine R., 2579
Leaver, Walter C., III, 8729
Leavey Charitable Lead Annuity Trust,
    767
Leavey, Dorothy E., 797
Leavey, J.J., 797
Leavey, Thomas E., 797
Leavitt, John, 3145
Lebanon Citizens National Bank, The,
    7574, 7721
LeBaron, Kathy, 4987
Lebens, Susan S., 4993
Lebensfeld Revocable Trust, Harry, 5301
LeBlond, Mary C., 8350
LeBow, Bennett S., 2106
LeBow, Geraldine C., 2106
Lebow, Jane, 5861
LeBreton, Pierre, 2623
LeBuhn, Robert, 5181
Lebworth, Caral G., 6034, 6390
Lebworth, Marion J., 6390
Lechleiter, John C., 3192, 3193
Lechner, B.J., 8188
Lechner, Thomas F., 9955
Leck, Jeffrey, 1426
Leclair, Michelle R., 5935
LeClerc, Paul, 6525
Leclerc, Raymond, 4000
Leder, Phillip, 6789
Lederberg, Joshua, 3621, 5886
Lederer, Adrienne, 2851
Lederer, Anne P., 2852
Lederer, Mitchell, 2851
Lederer, Sharon, 2851
Lederman, Laurie, 6498

Ledger, Mark T., 8444
Ledin, Richard L., 4681
Ledley, James, 1673
Ledoux, Judy, 9278
Ledsinger, Charles A., Jr., 3589
Lee Enterprises, Inc., 3306
Lee, Amy Roberts, 6731
Lee, Andreas, 4503
Lee, Andrew, 5814
Lee, Andrew W., 1783
Lee, Anna Mae, 7667
Lee, B.C., 7973
Lee, Barbara, 4001
Lee, Barbara Fish, 4001
Lee, Benson P., 7576
Lee, Bill Lann, 1065
Lee, Charles, 1157, 8661
Lee, Charles R., 1582
Lee, Chung H., Hon., 2356
Lee, Daniel, 1364
Lee, Daniel R., 2853
Lee, Danner & Bass, Inc., 8679
Lee, Diana, 1364
Lee, Duncan, 5047
Lee, Eugene, 9558
Lee, F. Graham, 3693
Lee, Frank, 655, 747
Lee, Frank B., Sr., 8571
Lee, Gerald, 8302
Lee, Herbert, 2107
Lee, Holden, 1211
Lee, Iara, 798
Lee, Ilda G., 1582
Lee, Jack T., 2170
Lee, James, 7139
Lee, James P., 8862
Lee, James T., 6391
Lee, Janine E., 2325
Lee, Jerry, 1505, 8302
Lee, Joe R., 1960
Lee, John, 2156
Lee, John W., 2357
Lee, Karen, 4257
Lee, Karen K., 2853
Lee, Kathleen, 4795
Lee, Mary Elizabeth, 2432
Lee, Mildred S., 2107
Lee, Nancy, 1151
Lee, Patricia, 1857
Lee, Ray M., 2432
Lee, Richard H., 1797
Lee, Robert S., 4001
Lee, Robert W., 7906
Lee, S. Zachary, 4001
Lee, Sherri E., 9369
Lee, Sherri P., 8671
Lee, Stephen, 1947
Lee, Suzanne, 5784
Lee, Tatwina Chinn, 1088
Lee, Thay Q., 8074
Lee, William, Hon., 7910
Leeburg, Louis, 607, 4298
Leeder, Patricia, 1271, 1272
Leedom-Ackerman, Joanne, 1769
Leeds, Andrea, 6392
Leeds, Andrea R., 6392
Leeds, Daniel H., 1792
Leeds, Gerald G., 4132
Leeds, Gerard, 9616
Leeds, Gerard G., 4132, 6392, 6431
Leeds, Jennifer, 6023
Leeds, Lilo J., 6023
Leeds, Liselotte, 9616
Leeds, Liselotte J., 4132, 6392, 6431
Leeds, Michael S., 6392
Leeds, Richard, 9616
Leeds, Sunita G., 1792
Leedy, Thomas, 3142
Leek, Beverly A., 6680
Leekley, John D., Jr., 9954
Leemhuis, Andrew J., 4716
Lees, Albert E., III, 3854
Leeson, Cathy, 8954
Leeth, Melanie Bialko, 2417

Leever, Andrew, 1583
Leever, Daniel, 1583
Leever, Harold, 1583
Leever, Ruth Ann, 1583
Leever, Thomas, 1583
Lefcourt, I., 6890
LeFeber, Marilyn S., 4399
Lefere, Carlene Walz, 4347
Leferer, John, 3258
LeFevour, Suzanne A., 4525
LeFevre, Howard E., 7714
Leff, Deborah, 1844
Leffall, LaSalle D., 5827
Leffall, Lasalle D., Jr., 5825
Leffell, Lisa, 6393
Leffell, Michael, 6393
Lefko, Allen, 4919
Lefkowitz, Burton, 5231
Lefkowitz, Stanley, 5943
Lefkowitz, William, 6044
Lefuel, Olivier, 6460
Legacy Heritage Fund Limited, 7284
Legallet, L., 1239
Legatski, S. Lynn, 7349
Legendre, Bokara, 4179
Leger, Diane, 2041
Legg Mason, 8303, 9885
Legg Mason, Inc., 3672
Legg, Dexter R., 4006
Leggat, Sarah, 3845
Leggat, Thomas E., 4069
Leggett, Martha E., 9192
Leggio, Anthony L., 301
Leghorn, Ken, 79
LeGrand, Patrice, 9861
Leh, John, II, 8137
Lehan, Joseph D., 3298
Lehew, Mary Louis, 9484
Lehigh Cement Company, 8481
Lehigh Consumer Products Corp., 8093
Lehigh Valley Hospital, 8481
Lehman Brothers Holdings Inc., 6395
Lehman Brothers Trust Co., 5810
Lehman Brothers Trust Co. of Delaware,
    1735
Lehman Brothers Trust Co., N.A., 6613
Lehman, E. Dennis, 7577
Lehman, Edith A., 6396
Lehman, Ellen E., 8662, 8673
Lehman, Elliot, 2912
Lehman, Elton D., 7536
Lehman, Frances, 2912
Lehman, Frederick A., 3095
Lehman, Herbert H., 6396
Lehman, Marie, 6397
Lehman, Melanie A., 8511
Lehman, Paul, 2912
Lehman, Peter, 2912
Lehman, Robert, 4298, 6397
Lehman, Robert F., 4297
Lehman, Robert Owen, 6397
Lehmann, Libby Friedman, 441
Lehmann, M.R., 935
Lehner, Carl P., 4062
Lehner, Charles, 7709
Lehner, Heidi, 4062
Lehner, Jane, 7709
Lehner, Lisa DeHart, 3137
Lehner, Marie, 7709
Lehr, Ronald L., 1398
Lehr, William, Jr., 8208
Lehrer, Joseph D., 4881
Lehrer, Karen, 800
Lehrer, Seymour, 800
Lehrer, Shirley, 800
Lehrman, Charlotte F., 1821
Lehrman, D. Gilbert, 1584
Lehrman, Jacob J., 1821
Lehrman, Lewis E., 1584, 6030
Lehrman, Louise, 1584
Lehrman, Robert, 1821
Lehrman, Samuel, 1821
Lehto, Emily, 9888
Leibold, John A., 7618

Leibold, William J., 7566
Leibowitz, Dale, 2854, 9905
Leibowitz, Eileen W., 8136
Leibowitz, Jane, 6399
Leibowitz, Lawrence, 6398
Leibowitz, Lew, 2854
Leibowitz, Martin L., 5707
Leibowitz, Pearl R., 2854
Leibowitz, Reuben S., 6399
Leibowitz, Sheldon L., 2854
Leibowitz, Todd, 2854
Leibrock, Robert C., 8749
Leichtag, Andre, 801
Leichtag, Max, 801
Leichtle, Robert A., 8570
Leichtman, Karl, 5315
Leichtman, Lauren B., 802
Leiden, Jeffrey, 3677
Leidy, John J., 3673
Leidy, Thomas D., 8103
Leif, Carol A., 1281
Leifeste, Kathleen, 5188
Leigh Fibers Holdings, Inc., 4062
Leigh Fibers, Inc., 4062
Leigh, Abby, 6400
Leigh, Mitch, 6400
Leightman, Raymond, 1941
Leighton, Judd, 3190
Leighton, Judd C., 3191
Leighton, Katherine, 4724
Leighton, Katherine M., 4576, 4612
Leighton, Mary Morris, 3191
Leighton, Michael E., 4994
Leinart, Brad, 3512
Leinart, Wyatt, 9003
Leinbach, Tracy A., 2213
Leininger, Brian C., 8847
Leininger, Cecelia A., 8847
Leininger, James R., 8847
Leinster, Carter, 7343
Leinwand, Shari, 712
Leir, Erna D., 6802
Leir, Henry J., 6802
Leisen, John, 4534
Leiser, Alfred E., 8878
Leiser, Josephine S., 2108
Leith, Shirley, 4270
Leithauser, Mark, 9447
Leitman, Nanetta L., 6378
Leitner, Allegra, 5303
Leitner, James, 5303
Leitner, Sandra, 5303
Leizirowitz, Abraham, 6330
Lelaurin, Christine, 1252
LeLaurin, Elaine H., 1615
Lelong, C.A., Jr., 9531
Lemaistre, Charles E., 9184
Lemann, Thomas B., 3460, 3519
Lematta, Bart, 9628
Lematta, Betsy, 9628
Lematta, Nancy, 9628
Lematta, Wes, 9628
Lematta-Abel, Marci Ann, 9628
Lemberg, Samuel, 6401
Lemeilleur, Lynn, 9120
Lemelson, Dorothy, 5040
Lemelson, Eric, 5040
Lemelson, Jennifer Bruml, 5040
Lemelson, Robert, 530, 5040
Lemelson, Robert B., 5040
Lemelson, Susan Morse, 530
Lemieux, John, 8537
Lemieux, Linda J., 4482
LeMire, William, III, 4259
Lemke, Nancy, 9615
Lemler, James B., 3119
Lemmel, David, 2251
Lemmon, Patricia, 3368
Lemoine, Leonard K., 3468
Lemon, James H., Jr., 1859
Lemon, Jo, 3185
Lemons, Thomas, 797
Lempke, R. Michael, 9763
Lenahan, Joan O., 3428

Lenci, Thomas D., 1504
Lende, Robert, 9156
Lender, Heidi, 1585
Lender, Helaine, 1585
Lender, Keith, 1585
Lender, Marvin, 1585
Lender, Sondra, 1585
Lendt, David W., 8235
Lenfest, Brook J., 8304
Lenfest, Dawn, 8304
Lenfest, H.F., 8305
Lenfest, H.F., Mrs., 8305
Lenfest, Marguerite, 8077, 8305
Lenfest, Marguerite B., 8304
Lenfestey, Susan, 9888
Lenhart, Brenda, 9400
Lenhart, Carole S., 1906, 1907
Lenkoski, L. Douglas, 7917
Lenkowsky, Leslie, 5513, 5647
Lenna, Elizabeth S., 6402
Lenna, Reginald A., 6402
Lennar Corp., 2109
Lennar Foundation, 3021
Lennartz, Ann F., 3304
Lenner, Marc J., 5189
Lennon, Fred A., 7710
Lennon, George, 4470
Lennon, John, 7033
Lennon, Yoko Ono, 7033
Lennox Industries, Inc., 1726
Lennox, Bagby, 9007
Lennox, David, 9007
Lennox, Martha, 9007
Lentell, J.V., 3369
Lents, James, 483
Lentz, Carole, 2566
Lentz, Edward, 8303
Lentz, Jay A., 3380
Lentz, Mervyn D., 4630
Lenz, Donald, 419, 7258
Lenz, Donald G., 420
Lenz, Frederick P., Jr., 803
Lenz, Janis C., 9788
Lenzen, David, 4565
Lenzmeier, Allen U., 4516
Leocadio, Joe, 8608
Leon, Mercedes M., 6613
Leonard, Angeline Brown, 2896
Leonard, Anna B., 2946
Leonard, Candace H., 804
Leonard, Douglas, 3166
Leonard, Harry J., 3704
Leonard, Herman B. "Dutch", 1810
Leonard, J. Wayne, 3474
Leonard, J.P., 9861
Leonard, Jennifer, 6823
Leonard, Jim, 804
Leonard, Joan S., 3654
Leonard, Jon, 804
Leonard, Judith S., 5611
Leonard, Margaret A., 403
Leonard, Mark G., 804
Leonard, Marty V., 8841
Leonard, Scot A., 2940
Leonard, Stephanie, 3545
Leonard, William, 804
Leonard, Wilma F., 804
Leone, Donna, 6175
Leone, Philip E., 6388
Leong, Maxine W., 2560
Leong, Robert H.Y., 2560
Leong, Robin L., 2560
Leong, Toni L., 2560
Leonhardt, Anne S., 1537
Leonhardt, Barbara, 1537
Leonhardt, Frederick H., 6403
Leonsis, Lynn M., 1822
Leonsis, Theodore J., 1822
Leopold, Estella, 9563
Lepage, Betty G., 9432
Lepard, Matthew, 4258
Lephart, Susan Pressly, 8074
Leplante, Michael, 7743
Leppanen, Karen L., 4254

Leppert, Thomas C., 9242
Leppien, Cleo M., 4377
Leppien, John C., 4377
Leprino Foods Company, 1417
Leprino, James G., 1417
Leprino, Laura, 1408
Leprino, Mary, 1408
Leprino, Mike, 1408
Leprino, Nancy, 1408
Lequerica, Sheila Hille, 7943
Lerandeau, Michelle, 561
Lerer, Ken, 7142
Lerman, Isodoro, 2659
Lerman, Jorge, 2659
Lerner, Alfred, 7711
Lerner, Annette M., 3675
Lerner, Arnold S., 4014
Lerner, Helaine, 6043, 7119
Lerner, Leslie, 3913
Lerner, Mark, 3674
Lerner, Mark D., 3675
Lerner, Michael, 211, 409, 1165
Lerner, Norma, 7711
Lerner, Ralph, 1587
Lerner, Randolph, 7711
Lerner, Sandy, 3809
Lerner, Theodore N., 3675
Lerner, Traci, 3674
Leroux, Judith, 2198
LeRoy, Gary L., 7603
Lesar, David J., 8935
Lesenne, Denis, 453
Lesesne, Joab, 2509
Lesesne, Joe, 8590
Lesher Communications, Inc., 805
Lesher, Cynthia, 4671
Lesher, Cynthia A., 805
Lesher, Cynthia L., 4732
Lesher, Dean S., 805
Lesher, Joseph, 805
Lesher, Margaret L., 805
Lesher, Steve, 805
Lesher, Tim, 805
Lesk, Ann B., 6459
Lesko, Megan Lewis, 2114
Leslie Lead Annuity Trust, 806
Leslie, Debra A., 806
Leslie, Jim, Jr., 4591
Leslie, Joshua M., 806
Leslie, Mark, 806
Leslie, Seth P., 806
Leslie, Steven W., 3564
Lesner, Julius, 898
Lessard, Paul, 7397
Lesser, Clare E., 4002
Lesser, Edward A., 6083
Lesser, Lawrence, 898
Lesser, Richard G., 4002
Lessersohn, James C., 6620
Lessig, Donald, 7449
Lessing, Sandra M., 6404
Lessing, Stephen M., 6395, 6404
Lester, Charles R., 9740
Lester, Daryl, 7503
Lester, Harry, 9484
Lester, Jack, 1267
Lester, Kirk, 807
Lester, Margaret E., 9414
Lester, Mary, 807
Lester, Terry, 8878
Lester, W. Howard, 807
Letcher, Edith Gilmore, 8380
Letizia, John, 1594
Letourneau, Jane E., 4566
Lett, Sam, 9101
Lettenberger, Peter J., 9960
Letterman, David, 215
Lettis, James F., 5856
Letwin, James, 9705
Letwin, Rosanna W., 9705
Leung, Sandra, 5143, 5666
Leuschen, David M., 6405
Leuthold, Kurt, 4605
Leuthold, Michael, 4605

Leuthold, Russell, 4605
Leuthold, Steven C., 4605
Lev, Holly Bronfman, 5672
Levan, Alan, 1891
Levan, David M., 8307
Levan, Jennifer S., 8307
LeVan, John A., 5476
Levan, Todd M., 8307
Levanovich, Kimberly Aikens, 4215
Levas, Dimitri, 6485
Levee Charitable Trust, James
    Annenberg, 8298
Levee, Polly Annenberg, 8308
Leveille, Raymond G., Jr., 4005
Leven, Ann R., 7215
Leven, Michael, 2441
Leven, Steve, 9232
Levendis, George P., 3695, 9453, 9486
Levenhagen, Donald, Rev., 4958
Levenick, S.L., 2653
Levenson, Michelle Riley, 1789
Leventhal Foundation, Ira and Beth,
    3765
Leventhal, Bennett L., 2812
Leventhal, Beth, 6406
Leventhal, Ira, 6406
Leventhal, Norman B., 2169
Leventhal, Walter, 2250
Lever Bros. Co., 5434
Leveraging Investment in Creativity,
    2710
Leverett, Allen, 9967
Leverett, Margaret A., 2566
Leverich, Rick, 8758
Levering, Doug, 8300
Levering, L. Bruce, 7583
Levey, Lionel M., 5228
Levi, Agnes E., 2855
Levi, Alexander H., 3645
Levi, Claudia Dreyfus, 9413
Levi, Ray & Shoup, Inc., 2855
Levi, Richard H., 2855, 3645
Levi, Robert H., 3645
Levi, Robin, 542
Levi, Ryan M., 2855
Levi, Ryda H., 3645
Levin, Adam, 5304
Levin, Alan, 6720
Levin, Alan A., 3116
Levin, Allen, 7712
Levin, Barbara, 7712
Levin, Elisabeth L., 6407
Levin, Frederic G., 2110
Levin, H. Debra, 2753
Levin, Ilene F., 4556
Levin, Irving J., 8053
Levin, Janice H., 5304
Levin, Jeffrey S., 6499
Levin, John, 6407
Levin, John A., 5662, 6407
Levin, John P., 1066, 4655
Levin, Karen, 7712
Levin, Louis, 7712
Levin, Martin H., 2110
Levin, Philip J., 5304
Levin, Richard C., 671
Levin, Ryan, 7712
Levin, Scott, 1445
Levin, Shira, 7001
Levin, Stephen A., 2181
Levin, Suzan, 4655
Levin, Suzie, 616
Levin, Terri, 2110
Levin, Terryl A., 4655
Levine Foundation, Laurence W., Inc.,
    2111
Levine, A.L., 2113
Levine, Abner, 2112
Levine, Adam, 2666
Levine, Arnold J., 3621
Levine, Arthur E., 802
Levine, Arthur L., 2113
Levine, Caroline C., 5094
Levine, Diane L., 4818

Levine, Hirschell E., 5527, 5727, 5991,
    6609, 6952
Levine, Howard, 7421
Levine, James, 6408
Levine, James M., 86
Levine, Janet, 5997
Levine, Jay, 6408
Levine, Jay David, 115
Levine, Jeffrey, 2216
Levine, Jerome L., 6631
Levine, Jerry, 9510
Levine, Jill, 8660
Levine, Joel A., 655
Levine, Jonathan L., 115
Levine, Kenneth R., 4003
Levine, Laurence W., 6408
Levine, Lawrence I., 2112
Levine, Leon, 7421
Levine, Linda, 582
Levine, Meldon, 809
Levine, Michael, 6408
Levine, Michael F., 2112
Levine, Mildred, 2112
Levine, Peter, 5997
Levine, Peter H., 4209
Levine, Peter L., 2113
Levine, Richard E., 3718
Levine, Robert, 4004
Levine, S. Robert, 4004
Levine, Sandra, 7421
Levine, Sidney, 5856
LeVine, Victoria M., 8095
Levine, William S., 115
Levings, Willard S., Mrs., 3811
Levinson, Carl A., 5486
Levinson, Douglas, 5486
Levinson, Edward, 2306
Levinson, Ellen, 1483
Levinson, John, 1483
Levinson, Julian, 5486
Levinson, Marshall J., 5609
Levinson, Max, 5486
Levis Trust, Adolph, 8310
Levis, Adolph, 8309
Levis, William E., 7569
Levisay, Betsy, 2912
Levison, S. Jarvin, 2394
Levit, Leah S., 9009
Levit, Max S., 9009
Levit, Milton H., 9009
Levit, Rochelle, 9009
Levitan, Matthew, 5433
Levitas, Catherine O., 3704
Levitas, Catherine Otenasek, 3704
Levithan, Allen, 5117, 5118, 5122,
    5234, 5259, 5267, 5332, 5340,
    5421
Levithan, Beth, 5228
Levitt and Sons, Inc., 6409
Levitt, Abraham, 6409
Levitt, Alfred, 6409
Levitt, Alvin T., 730
Levitt, AnneMarie, 5305
Levitt, J. David, 5206
Levitt, Jeanne, 3676
Levitt, Larry, 739
Levitt, Madelyn M., 3281, 3307
Levitt, Mark, 3676
Levitt, Matthew L., 4647
Levitt, Mortimer, 5305
Levitt, Randall, 3676
Levitt, Richard S., 3307, 3676
Levitt, Steven, 6364
Levitt, William, 6409
Levitt, William J., III, 5206
Levoff, Janet, 5577
Levsky, Virginia, 4121
Levy Charitable Trust, 810
Levy Co., Edward C., 4378
Levy Venture Mgmt., Inc, 2856
Levy, Andrew H., 6624
Levy, Austin T., 4005
Levy, Berthold W., 8165
Levy, Bertram, 2355

Levy, Brooke, 3359
Levy, Carol, 4378
Levy, Carole, 2856
Levy, Caroline, 5986
Levy, David B., 6877, 6879
Levy, Edward C., Jr., 4378
Levy, Ellen, 4378
Levy, Ellen White, 6529
Levy, Frances, 6411
Levy, Francis N., 6412
Levy, H.G., 4368
Levy, Jack, 6411
Levy, Jill S., 6499
Levy, Joseph W., 6499
Levy, Joseph, Jr., 2856
Levy, Jr. Trust, Joseph, 2856
Levy, Julie, 5554
Levy, Kara, 5306
Levy, Kenneth, 5306
Levy, Laurie, 5306
Levy, Leo, 6602
Levy, Leon, 6413, 6414
Levy, Lester, 711
Levy, Louis, II, 3498
Levy, Mary, 2446
Levy, Milton P., Jr., 8839
Levy, Norman F., 6412
Levy, Paul, 6410
Levy, Peter, 6300
Levy, Richard D., 1294
Levy, Robert, 2920
Levy, Robert A., 4518
Levy, Robert N., 8136
Levy, Roberta Morse, 4095
Levy, Robin V., 5357
Levy, S. Jay, 6413
Levy, S.J., 6413
Levy, Saul D., 5195
Levy, Shuki, 810
Levy, Tamara, 810
Levy-Church, Jeanne, 6257
Levy-Hinte, Jeffrey, 6257
Lew, Denise, 1087
Lewent, Judy C., 5327, 8349
Lewin, John, 6878, 6879
Lewin, Stephen, 6878, 6879
Lewin, William N., 7346
Lewinter, David J., 5893
Lewis and Early, 8818
Lewis Broadcasting Corp., 2434
Lewis Motor Co., J.C., 2434
Lewis, A. Bart, 4239
Lewis, A.D., 4563
Lewis, Adam J., 7713
Lewis, Adam L., 7805
Lewis, Alan, 3929
Lewis, Alan E., 3929
Lewis, Alfred Allan, 2119
Lewis, Amy, 9693
Lewis, Andre, 4661
Lewis, Andrew L., IV, 8311
Lewis, Art, 9476
Lewis, Barbara G., 7574
Lewis, Bill, 9680
Lewis, Bradford H., 1410
Lewis, Brian E., 513
Lewis, Carol A., 1410
Lewis, Cathy M., 7657
Lewis, Charles A., 2857
Lewis, Christie, 1946
Lewis, Christina S.N., 6416
Lewis, Craig, 3694
Lewis, Daniel E., Jr., 3247
Lewis, Daniel R., 2025
Lewis, Danita, 3425
Lewis, David Baker, 4438
Lewis, David D., 9635
Lewis, DeLancey B., 9666
Lewis, Diana, 2114, 4743
Lewis, Diana D., 4557
Lewis, Diane, 1786
Lewis, Dorothy V., 2433
Lewis, Drew, 8311
Lewis, Edward, 2114

Logan, Kent, 1468
Logan, Lyle, 2728, 3015
Logan, Margaret, 3387
Logan, Marguerite, 5386
Logan, Richard, 2860
Logan, Thomas, 3108
Logan, Victor, 2505
Loggins, D.G., 2519
Logser Charitable Lead Trust, John and Mary, 92
Logue, Lesley, 6408
Lohman, Mark E., 2750
Lohmuller, Deborah, 4828
Lohr, David H., 8488
Lohr, William J., 9923
Lohse, Florence, 102
Lohse, Linda, 102
Lohse, Robert, 102
Lohse, Thomas, 102
Loiacono, Nicholas A., 879
Loke, Kenneth, 8989
Lokhammer, Christine, 5357
Lomas La Jolla Financial, Inc., 1078
Lomax, Manning N. "Nick", 8588
Lombard, Jane K., 7698, 7699
Lombard, Nathalie R., 7698
Lombard, Richard D., 7698
Lombard, Richard J., 7698
Lombardi, Richard, 7581
Lombardo, Philip J., 1505
Lomonaco, L. Dianne, 8084
Loncki, Susan B., 136
London, Jack, 4206
London-Wilson, Roberta, 8388
Londra, Kathryn E., 8081
Lone Pine Capital, LLC, 1589
Long Beach Grandell Co., Inc., 6871
Long, Ann H., 7662
Long, Clay, 2526
Long, David B., 9218
Long, George A., 1590
Long, George P., III, 8388
Long, Gordon, 7662
Long, Grace L., 1590
Long, Hugh C., 8494
Long, Jacob F., 118
Long, James E., 531
Long, John F., 118
Long, John K., 7342
Long, Joseph M., 825
Long, Lucinda E., 4930
Long, M. Chrysa, 3845
Long, Marianne C., 2648
Long, Maud-Alison, 1185
Long, Maud-Alison C., 1185
Long, Mick, 3096
Long, Milton, 825
Long, Monica, 9068
Long, Robert A., 4865
Long, Robert E. "Bobby", 7343
Long, Robert F., 4357
Long, Robert M., 825, 827
Long, Russell, 2479
Long, Sidne J., 826
Long, Stephen H., 5755
Long, T. Dixon, 1185
Long, Thomas J., 826
Long, Thomas N., 9974
Long, Valerie, 5092
Long, Vera M., 825, 827
Long, Will, 3245
Long, William A., 7354
Longaberger Co., The, 7722
Longaberger, Richard, 7722
Longaberger, Tamala, 7722
Longacre, Leslie, 1947
Longbine, Jeff, 3370
Longbrake, Mary, 9972
Longenecker, Janet E. Rhoden, 3383
Longo, Kathleen, 4678
Longstreth, George B., III, 1504
Longyear, Mary Beecher, 3895
Lont, John, 5155
Loo, Katherine H., 1437

Loock Trust, Margaret, 9763
Look, Peter, 4472
Loomis, Carol, 4950
Loomis, Laura, 6823
Looney, Martha W., 2436
Looney, Wilton D., 2266, 2428, 2436, 2521
Looper, Doris, 9016
Looper, Terry, 9016
Loos, Henry, 9868
Loos, Henry J., 9772, 9936
Loose, Carrie J., 9017
Loose, Harry Wilson, 9017
Lopata Charitable Lead Trust No. 4, 4859
Lopata, James R., 4859
Lopata, Lucy, 4859
Lopata, Stanley, 4859
Lopatin, Jonathan M., 6446
Loper, Graham B., 3409
Lopez, Al "Papa Rap", 172
Lopez, Christina, 3082
Lopez, Estela, 1563
Lopez, Jorge Luis, 1957
Lopez, Manuel, 9977
Lopez, Manuel Mariano, 4671
Lopez, Mary K., 256
Lopez, Michael B., 319
Lopez, Owen M., 5488
Lopez, Rich, 1364
Lopiccolo, Mary E., 8177
LoPresti, Louis, 5194
LoPrete, James H., 4478
LoPrete, Kent G., 4478
LoPrete, Ruth, 4478
Loraas, Richard, 4556
Lorber, Robert L., 1080
Lorberbaum, Alan S., 2118
Lorberbaum, Jeffrey, 2118
Lorberbaum, Mark, 2118
Lord Baltimore Capital Corp., 3576, 3744
Lord, Bette Bao, 9424
Lord, Charles, 4420
Lord, David, 4420
Lord, G.S., 5151
Lord, Gay P., 1851
Lord, Grogan, 9018
Lord, Henry C., 8545
Lord, John S., 1922
Lord, Kay, 7508
Lord, R. Griffin, 9018
Lord, Richard, 4420
Lord-Wolff, Edith, 4420
Lordan, Tim, 3595
Lore, John, 4229
Lorenz, Anton, 7211
Lorenz, Donald, 853
Lorenz, Donald A., 852
Lorenz, Sheridan Mitchell, 9064
Lorenz, Tina, 9780
Lorge, Yolanda, 4798
Lorimer, Lisa, 9361
Loring, Caleb, III, 4072
Loring, Donna M., 3548
Loring, Jonathan B., 4005
Loring, Patricia H., 3835
Loring, Peter B., 4038, 4203
Loring, Robert W., 4123
Loring, Valerie S., 4165
Lorne, Bill, 4246
Lorraine, Richard, 9794
Lorton, George, 2054
Lorton, George H., 2054
Los Angeles Chamber of Commerce, 1060
Los Angeles Olympic Organizing Comm., 214
LoSchiavo, John, Rev., 741
Losinger, Sarah McCune, 5488
Losness, Jon, 4668
Lotano, Amy W., 5341
Lothian, Charlotte, 4331
Lotman, Herbert, 8314

Lotman, Jeffrey, 8314
Lotman, Karen, 8314
Lou, Donna, 9680
Loud, Karen A.G., 6209
Louden, G. Malcolm, 8904, 9261
Louden, Nancy M., 6466
Louden, Thomas, 7581
Louder, Gary, 531
Loughlin, Caroline, 3507
Loughlin, Caroline K., 3493
Loughlin, Peter, 5089
Loughlin, Thomas K., 3493
Loughran, John, 1823
Loughran, Marcia B., 3750
Loughrey, F. Joseph, 3136
Loughridge, Mark, 6221
Loughry, Ed C., Jr., 8654
Louis Foundation, John J., 2862
Louis, Herbert J., 2861
Louis, J. Jeffry, III, 2862
Louis, John J., Jr., 2862
Louis, Josephine P., 2862
Louis, Michael W., 2861
Louisiana-Pacific Corp., 8037
Louisville Timber Co., 3438
Lounsbery Foundation Trust, Richard, Inc., 1824
Lounsbery, Richard, 1824
Lourenco, Vera, 5682
Loux, Lloyd F., Jr., 7747
Lovaas, Helen, 585
Lovaas, Leeland M., 585
Lovato-Farmer, Cindy, 5496
Love Family Charitable Lead Trust, 2437
Love Trust, Audrey B., 2119
Love, Andrew Sproule, Jr., 2863
Love, Ann Burnside, 3598
Love, Ayanna, 7723
Love, C. Phillip, 3164
Love, Cheryl, 7723
Love, Daniel Spoule, 2863
Love, David, 1203
Love, Davis, III, 2330
Love, Dennis M., 2437
Love, Doug, 562
Love, Gay M., 2437
Love, Howard M., 8241
Love, Hugh, Jr., 4739
Love, Janet R., 4958
Love, Jerry, 7957
Love, Judith, 7964
Love, Kim, 9998
Love, L. Ross, Jr., 7723
Love, W. Stephen, 9239
Lovelace, Charles E., Jr., 7430
Lovelace, James B., 357, 720
Lovelace, Jeffrey K., 720
Lovelace, Jon B., 720
Lovelace, Lillian P., 720
Lovelace, Robert W., 720
Lovelady, Mel, 8891
Lovelady, Melvin B., 8876, 9149
Lovelady, Sam, 8758
Lovell, David C., 119
Lovell, Lura M., 119
Lovell, Richard H., 3981
Lovell, Royal, 1359
Lovell, Stephen J., 119
Loventhal, Leonard J., 2953
Lovett, Anne B., 4013
Lovett, Anne R., 4013
Lovett, D. Clay, 2036
Lovett, Richard, 341
Lovett, Robert G., 8504
Lovett, Tiffany W., 4346, 4399
Loving Co., T.A., 7330
Loving, Rush, 1982
Lovrien, Phyllis, 9854
Low, Harry W., 347
Low, Lisa, 7101
Low, Nathan, 7101
Lowder, Catherine, 42, 43, 44
Lowder, Charlotte G., 43
Lowder, James K., 42

Lowder, Jarman F., 44
Lowder, Margaret B., 20, 42
Lowder, Robert E., 43
Lowder, Thomas H., 24, 42, 44
Lowdnes, Rita, 1942
Lowe Foundation, 5883
Lowe's Cos., Inc., 7423
Lowe's Food Stores, Inc., 7372
Lowe, Catherine M., 7734
Lowe, Elizabeth, 980
Lowe, Erma, 9020
Lowe, Heather, 2579
Lowe, Jane K., 45
Lowe, John F., 348
Lowe, Kenneth W., 7848
Lowe, Leslie, 6643
Lowe, Linda, 2411
Lowe, Margaret, 3138
Lowe, Margaret L., 4531
Lowe, Mary Ralph, 9020
Lowe, Richard, 2306
Lowe, Rick, 7215
Lowe, Sandra, 2306
Lowe, Terry D., 220
Lowe, Thomas P., 4531, 4607
Lowe, Thomas P., III, 4531
Lowe, Walter M., 6541
Lowe, William, 690
Lowell Museum Corp., 4014
Lowell, Charlotte, 390
Lowell, James H., II, 3771
Lowell, John, 4015
Lowell, William A., 3826, 4072
Lowenfels, Fred M., 5849, 6802, 7045
Lowenstein, Leon, 6449
Lowenstein, Steven S., 2666
Lowenthal, Constance, 6123
Lower, James P., 750
Lower, Judith A., 750
Lowery, Clinton R., 8389
Lowery, R. Brinckerhoff, 3764
Lowery, Thomas A., 8876
Lowett, Henry A., 6434
Lowinger, Andrew, 6450
Lowinger, Edith, 6450
Lowinger, Ronald, 6450
Lowman, Josephine B., 5618, 7103
Lowney, Jeremiah J., Jr., 1655
Lowrey, E. James, 8781
Lowrey, Pedrick, 8583
Lowry, John, 7567
Lowry, Lolita L., 826
Lowry, Michael H., 7039
Lowry, Robert L., 3225
Lowry, Scott T., 5125
Lowry, William E., 2868
Lowther, David, 8006
Lowther, Fred, 8006
Lowther, John R., 7650
Lowther, Steven, 8006
Loy, Steve, 3206
Loynd, Richard B., 4835
Lozano, Joe, 9166
Lozano, Jose, 6998
Lozano, Monica, 1288
Lozano, Monica C., 347
Lozick, Catherine, 7724
Lozick, Catherine L., 7724
Lozick, E.A., 7710
Lozick, Edward, 7724
Lozick, Edward A., 7724
Lozier, Allan, 4988
Lozier, Dianne, 4988
LPL Finanacial, 8188
LRC Love LP, 7723
LRL Investments, 7723
LSM Management Co., 7066
Lu, Weiming, 4623
Lubar, David J., 9851, 9876
Lubar, Marianne S., 9851
Lubar, Sheldon B., 9851
Lubben, David J., 4705
Lubberstedt, W. Wes, 4986

Lubcher, Frederick, 6442, 6459, 6657, 6897
Luber, Howard J., 127
Lubert, Ira M., 8315
Lubert, Jonathan, 8315
Lubert, Kristine, 8315
Lubin, Arline J., 6578
Lubin, Dennis E., 7752, 7753
Lubin, Donald, 2840
Lubin, Joseph I., 2027, 6059
Lubin, Kate E., 4016
Lubin, Kenneth A., 6578
Lubin, Marvin, 6578
Lubin, Nancy K., 4016
Lubin, Richard K., 4016
Lubrizol Corp., The, 7725
Lubs, Jane Mason, 9863
Lucas Petroleum Group, 8878
Lucas, Ann S., 1208
Lucas, Benjamin F., II, 3694
Lucas, Bill, 3404
Lucas, Brian, 5310
Lucas, Carol, 8878
Lucas, Charles C., III, 7359
Lucas, Colin, 6525
Lucas, David, 2240, 5310
Lucas, David P., 4228
Lucas, Eugene B., 880
Lucas, Harry, Jr., 8878
Lucas, Kelly, 9779
Lucas, Linda, 5310
Lucas, Linda S., 5310
Lucas, Melinda, 5310
Lucas, Stuart E., 1206
Lucas, Timothy, 5194
Lucas, William L., 295
Lucchese, John J., 3434
Lucchesi, Carlotta, 2922
Lucchetti, David, 1080
Lucckese, Deborah, 9534
Luce, Clare Boothe, 6453
Luce, Henry R., 6453
Luce, Tom, 9096
Lucent Technologies Inc., 5110
Lucente, Tony, 939
Luchsinger, Amelia D., 9022
Luchsinger, John W., 9022
Lucido, William, 537
Luck Stone Corp., 9461
Luck, Charles S., III, 9461
Luckes, David R., 4896
Luckey, Tom, 4259
Luckow Corp., Robert W., The, 6455
Luckow, Audrey, 6455
Luckow, Robert, 6455
Luckow, Robert W., 6455
Lucore, Rebecca, 8096
Ludcke, Eleanor R., 4017
Ludcke, Gipp L., 4017
Ludemann, Roger R., 5010
Ludington, John S., 4450
Ludington, Thomas L., 4322
Ludlam, Charles Stewart, 1527
Ludwick, Andrew, 830
Ludwick, Arthur J., 829
Ludwick, Christopher, 830
Ludwick, Eileen, 829
Ludwick, Erik Arthur, 829
Ludwick, Jocelyn, 830
Ludwick, Sarah Lynne, 829
Ludwick, Theodore, 830
Ludwick, Worth Z., 830
Ludwig, Allan, 3145
Ludwig, Carol, 1826
Ludwig, Eugene A., 1826
Ludwig, Jim, 3403
Ludwig, Robert A., 5785
Ludwig, Roger W., 3833, 5450
Luedeke, J. Barton, 5338
Luedeking, Otto, 7573
Lueders, Todd, 401
Lueders, Wayne R., 9744
Luedtke, Cindy, 828
Luedtke, Dave, 828

Luers, William H., 6825, 7168
Luetkemeyer, John A., Jr., 3718
Luff, Robin, 1358
Luffman, Judith E., 9498
Lufkin, Dan, 6962
Luftglass, R., 6720
Lugar, Carol, 1516
Lugar, Frederick D., 1946
Luger, Ellen, 4570
Lui, Francis C., 6457
Lui, Lawrence, 6457
Lui, Livia Wan, 6457
Lui, Meizhu, 3961
Lui, Yvonne, 6457
Lujan, Joseph A., 9056
Lujan, Larry, 5466
Lukas, John, 6032
Lukas, Suzanne R., 2679
Luke, Cathy, 2545
Luke, Monica, 8733
Lukowski, Stanley J., 3886
Lumarda, Joe, 345
Lumber Yard, The, 8506
Lumbermens Mutual Casualty Co., 2832
Lumia, Melanie M., 8317
Lumia, Melanie Maslow, 8327
Lumina Foundation for Education, 359
Lummis, David, 8944
Lummis, William R., 3654
Lummus, Donna McKinney, 1979
Lumpkin, Besse Adamson, 2864
Lumpkin, John H., Jr., 8577
Lumpkin, John R., 5265
Lumpkin, Mary G., 2864
Lumpkin, Richard Adamson, 2864
Lumpkin, Richard Anthony, 2864
Lund, Arthur K., 369, 621
Lund, Bradford D., 831
Lund, Cynthia D., 1091
Lund, Jay, 4512
Lund, Margaret T., 9897
Lund, Mark, 3276
Lund, Michelle A., 831
Lund, Sharon D., 831
Lund, Steven J., 9322
Lunda, Larry, 9852
Lunda, Lydia, 9852
Lunda, Milton, 9852
Lundback, Lee C., 8457
Lundberg, Minnie P., 1404
Lundcpen, Ken, 4520
Lundeen, Cathy, 8608
Lunder, Alan, 3547
Lunder, Marc, 3547
Lunder, Paula, 3547
Lunder, Peter, 3547
Lunder, Steven, 3547
Lundevall, Jessica, 2823
Lundgren, Carl G., 531
Lundgren, Lee Anne, 4499
Lundin, Craig, 474
Lundin, Gloria, 2679
Lundquist, Hollis K., 1476
Lundquist, Ingrid, 7816
Lundregan, William J., III, 4125
Lundstrom, Gilbert G., 5010
Lundy, Randall, 9388
Lunger, Caroline M., 1706
Lungren, Daniel E., 728
Lunney, J. Robert, 6384
Lunsford, Carleen F., 4413
Lunsford, David H., 9735
Lunsford, Margaret, 7665
Lunsford, Walter, 7665
Lunskis, Marilyn, 2173
Lunt, Martha W., 4204
Lunt, Thomas D., 7243
Luoma, Matthew R., 1396
Luongo, Frank J., 4480
Luongo, Lucille F., 1505
Lupfer, Sally, 7866
Lupica, John, 8073
Lupin, Arnold M., 3498
Lupin, Jay S., 3498

Lupin, Lisa, 3498
Lupin, Louis, 3498
Lupin, Ralph, 3498
Lupin, Samuel, 3498
Lupin, Timothy, 3498
Lupton, Bob, 2474
Lupton, C.A., 8798
Lupton, T. Cartter, 8703
Lupton, T. Cartter, II, 8703
Lurcy, Georges, 6458
Luria, J.A., Rabbi, 6509
Lurie, Alison, 5548
Lurie, Andrew, 2865
Lurie, Ann, 2865
Lurie, Benjamin, 2865
Lurie, Brian L., Rabbi, 541
Lurie, Cathy J., 4024
Lurie, Christina, 4024
Lurie, George S., 832
Lurie, Helen, 6459
Lurie, Jeffrey R., 4024
Lurie, Judith A., 9571
Lurie, Lori Christina, 3760
Lurie, Louis R., 832
Lurie, Robert, 2865
Lurie, Robert A., 832
Lusardi, Henry, 3948
Luscomb, Brian, 705
Luskey, Randolph K., 5726
Luskin, Meyer, 605
Luskus, William T., 8232
Lussier, James D., 9797
Lussier, John H., 9797
Lussier-Lee, Laura J., 9797
Lust, Angela, 8758
Lustberg, Lawrence S., 5199
Luster, Elizabeth, 953
Lustgarten, Susan B., 1915
Lustig, Gerald I., 6774
Lustig, Lois, 6849
Lute, Jane Holl, 4174
Luter, Joseph W., III, 9519
Luter, Joseph W., IV, 9519
Lutes, Joe, 8148
Lutes, Joseph, 8147
Lutey, Katherine A., 4367
Lutgert, Scott, 2151
Lutgert, Simone, 2151
Luther Trust, Frances R., 7726
Lutheran Brotherhood, 9949
Lutheran Brotherhood Research Corp., 9949
Lutnick, Howard, 7174
Lutrin, Ralph, 2119
Lutron Electronics Co., Inc., 8316
Luttgens, Leslie L., 1065
Luttrell, Claudia Skaggs, 9302
Luttrell, Donna, 7653
Luttrell, Laura, 2117
Luttrell, Scott, 2117
Lutz, Elizabeth G., 833
Lutz, Ellen, 4052
Lutz, Gregory P., 833
Lutz, Nathan, 1458
Lutz, Theodore M., 1804
Lux, Michael, 1767
Lux, Miranda W., 834
Luxembourg, Robert, 5894
Luy, Peg, 2678
Luzius, Kate B., 7548
Luzzi, Richard D., 8500
LVB Funding, Inc., 5332
LWG Family Partners, 6381
Lyall, Thomas M., 7770
Lyash, Jeff, 7453
Lybarger, Stan, 7984
Lykouretzos, John, 7139
Lyle Pacific Corp., 7938
Lyle, James, 7139
Lyle, James R., 6461
Lyle, William "Buck", 3368
Lyles, Thomas W., Jr., 8847
Lyles, W.M., IV, 286
Lyman Lumber Co., 4607

Lyman, Carol L., 4639
Lyman, Gregory A., 4357
Lyman, Lincoln P., 7219
Lyman, Rachel, 9023
Lyman, Robert W., Mrs., 7039
Lyman, Steve, 8079
Lynagh, John J., 5618, 7103
Lynch, Annette, 7508
Lynch, Charles E., 3161
Lynch, Charles R., 1591
Lynch, Debra, 8259
Lynch, Dennis L., 7902
Lynch, Harry H., 5487
Lynch, James E., 8008
Lynch, James M., 1599
Lynch, Judith, 8218
Lynch, Lee, 1773
Lynch, Luba H., 6477
Lynch, Michael J., 2813
Lynch, Michael R., 6462
Lynch, Paul D., 8542
Lynch, Paul M., 8581
Lynch, Richard, 9854
Lynch, Robert W., 2814
Lynch, Ronald P., 1591
Lynch, Scott, 2132
Lynch, Stephanie S., 7359
Lynch, Stephen A., III, 1983
Lynch, Susan E., 1591
Lynch, Thomas, 8209
Lynch, Thomas P., 1186
Lynch, Wayne K., 8087
Lynch, William O.J., 7352
Lynd, Lee, 6428
Lynett, George V., 8431, 8494
Lyneus, Mary M., 4478
Lynham, John M., Jr., 1789, 1851
Lynn, C.E., 2120
Lynn, Darlene, 835
Lynn, David, 835
Lynn, Don, 835
Lynn, E.M., 2120
Lynn, E.M., Mrs., 2120
Lynn, Edward R., 3343
Lynn, Elizabeth A., 9633
Lynn, Elizabeth R., 5162
Lynn, Gregory E., 3116
Lynn, Jeff, 9633
Lynn, Karen, 3309
Lynn, Richard, 6729
Lynn, Theodore S., 7133
Lynn, Traci, 9633
Lynton, Carol, 6463
Lynton, Marion, 6463
Lynton, Michael, 6463
Lyon, Donna M., 2866
Lyon, E.H., 7953
Lyon, James M., 2056
Lyon, Marina Munoz, 4657
Lyon, Melody, 7953
Lyon, Robert H., 2866
Lyon, Wilford C., Jr., 1940, 2028
Lyons Magnus, Inc., 1168
Lyons, Amy, 597
Lyons, Barbara, 739
Lyons, Claire, 3798
Lyons, John W., Jr., 9042
Lyons, Judith, 5782
Lyons, Leo M., 6274
Lyons, Louis, 2649
Lyons, Mark A., 9042
Lyons, Maureen, 3337
Lyons, Patti, 2550
Lyons, Richard T., 9024
Lyons, Sammie, 9024
Lyons, Scott A., Jr., 7526
Lyons, Thomas F., 3854
Lyons, Timothy L., 7982
Lyons, Volina V., 8589
Lyons, William M., 4773
Lyons-Gardner, Melissa, 9042
Lyons-Spier, Michelle, 9042
Lysne, Lee, 5483
Lytel, Bertha Russ, 836

M & T Bank, 3756
M&R Management, 6614
M&T Bank, 3706, 5780, 6274, 6465, 8208, 8275, 8330, 8390, 8414, 8468, 8483
M&T Investment Group, 8485
M.D.C. Holdings, Inc., 1413
M/I Schottenstein Homes, Inc., 7729
Ma'a, Stacie, 564
Maag Trust, Hazel F., 838
Maag, Jim, 3400
Maas, Benard L., 4379
Maas, George E., 4608
Maas, J. David, 3196
Maas, Patricia A., 4608
Mabe, Emily A., 3227
Mabee, J.E., 7954
Mabee, Joe, Sr., 7954
Mabee, Joseph Guy, Jr., 7954
Mabee, L.E., 7954
Mabie Trust, Inez, 839
Mabie, Inez, 839
Mabie, William J., 839
Mac Kinnon, George, 9861
Mac, Lara, 840
MacAdams, Michael J., 1395
MacAffer, John, 5782
MacAleer, R. James, 6816
MacAlister, Patricia A., 2623
MacAllaster, Archie F., 5762
MacArthur Foundation, 3021
MacArthur Foundation, John D. and Catherine T., 483, 2710, 2949, 6604
MacArthur, Catherine T., 2868
MacArthur, J. Roderick, 2867
MacArthur, John D., 2868, 2964
MacArthur, John R., 2867
MacArthur, Jon, 1883
MacArthur, Kelly Jo, 9672
MacArthur, Solange D., 2867
Macartney, Linda, 5783
MacAskill, Bridget, 6092
Macauley, Alma Jane, 1592
Macauley, Melinda Rice, 1592
Macauley, Robert C., 1592
Macauley, Robert C., Jr., 1592
Macauley, Victoria J., 8468
Macaya, Claudia Cisneros, 1934
Macaya, Javier, 1934
MacCallum, Lisa, 8046
MacClarence, Margaret P., 5935
MacClure, Laurens M., Jr., 3616
MacConnell, Jocelyn H., 8260
MacCormick, A. Malcolm, 7280
MacCrellish, William H., Jr., 4143
MacDermott, Kristin B., 4457
Macdonald, Agnes, 6915
MacDonald, Brian, 8864
MacDonald, Bruce, 3730
MacDonald, Corey Fuller, 5090
MacDonald, Donna Marie, 841
MacDonald, Harold C., 9070
MacDonald, John A., 4824, 4825
MacDonald, Mark, 841
Macdonald, Maybelle Clark, 8038
MacDonald, Michael R., 19
MacDonald, Nicole de Sugny, 448
MacDonald, Rhonda J., 9543
MacDonald, Robert D., 4492
MacDonald, Scott, 3550
MacDonnell, Mellissa, 4006
MacDougald Family Limited Partnership, 2122
MacDougald, James E., 2122
MacDougald, Joseph J., 2122
MacDougald, Suzanne M., 2122
MacDougall, David, 9780
MacDougall, Joseph W., Jr., 3941
Macedo, Rosemary, 7220
MacElree, Jane, 5879
MacFadden, William S., 4933
MacFarlane, Annesley R., 1045
MacFarlane, John, III, 4259

MacFarlane, Ron, 1947
MacFarquhar, Roderick, 1632
MacGlashan, Catherine D., 6896
MacGregor, David L., 9934
MacGregor, Paul, 9651
Mach Foundation, The, 5623
Machetti, Terry, 2677
Machold, Roland M., 7126
Macht, Amy, 3603, 3683
Macht, Philip, 3683
Macht, Sophia, 3683
Machtinger, Sidney, 1287
Machtinger, Sidney J., 1289
Machtley, Ronald K., 8518
Machuga, John Victor, 5311
Macias-Harrison, Gloria, 405
MacIlwinen, Frances G., 7382
Maciunas, Algirdas, 947
Maciunas, Genevieve, 947
Maciunas, Robert, 947
Maciunas-Mockus, Dana, 947
Mack Oil Co., 7956
Mack, Carol, 5087
Mack, Charlotte S., 1065
Mack, Christy K., 6469
Mack, David, 5312
Mack, Deborah K., 2458
Mack, Dianne, 6156
Mack, Earle I., 5314
Mack, James, 7369
Mack, Jenna A., 6469
Mack, John J., 5892, 6469
Mack, John W., 1288
Mack, Judith A., 1667
Mack, Michael J., Jr., 2699
Mack, Richard, 7806
Mack, Rosell, III, 6083
Mack, Thomas M., 3356
Mack, William, 5313
Mackall, John, 1268
Mackall, John R., 1247
MacKay, Barrett B., 16
Mackay, Calder M., 881
Mackay, Colin B., 134
MacKay, Malcolm, 6229
Mackay, Richard N., 881
Mackay, Robert B., 6016
MacKay, Robert B., 6199, 7041
MacKay, Timothy M., 4428
Mackay-Smith, Alexander, Jr., 3649
Mackay-Smith, Virginia L., 3649
Macke, Betsy, 3337
Macke, Nancy, 4991
Mackell, John, 5053
Mackell, Thomas J., Jr., 6615
MacKenzie, Charles E., 8154
Mackenzie, Doug, 910
MacKenzie, George, 5350
MacKenzie, John L., 9599
MacKenzie, Robert K., 8518
MacKenzie, Sophia, 843
MacKenzie, Tod J., 6714
MacKenzie, Wendy, 8242
Mackenzie, Wendy, 8243
Mackey, Bruce B., 4380
Mackey, Dayton, 4879
Mackey, Eddina F., 4879
Mackey, Robert B., 4380
Mackey, Stanley D., 4380
Mackey, Wendy, 8123
Mackey, William K., 3865, 3866, 4199
Mackey, William R., 578
Mackey, Winnie C., 3866
Mackey, Winnie Crane, 3865
Mackie, Matthew D., Jr., 8117
Mackintosh, Rocky, 3598
Mackler, Harvey, 5532
Mackler, Helen, 5532
Macklin, B.G., 8889
Macklosky, Diane L., 1594
MacLachlan, Jim, 4325
MacLaury, Bruce, 1810
Maclellan, Christopher, 8704
Maclellan, Daniel, 8704

Maclellan, Hugh O., Jr., 8704
MacLellan, Kathrina H., 8705
Maclellan, R.L., Mrs., 8704
Maclellan, Robert H., 8704
MacLellan, Robert H., 8705
Maclellan, Robert J., 8704
MacLeod, Barbara B., 7566
MacLeod, Gary, 9640
MacLeod, Missy, 9819
Macleod, R. Malcolm, 2077
MacLeod, Thomas B., 7566
MacMichael, H. Ross, 991
MacMillan, Albert, 8705
Macmillan, Courtney D., 1300
MacMillan, Elizabeth S., 4722
MacMillan, Pat, 8704
Macmillan, Terrance A., 1300
MacMillan, Whitney, 4722
MacMillan, Whitney, Jr., 4722
MacNaughton, Angus A., 844
MacNaughton, Cathy C., 844
MacNeil, Robert, 9424
MacNutt, Francis, 3894
Macomb, Richard, 9060
Macomber, George, 3845
Macomber, Robert D., 1265
Macon, Jane H., 6975
MacPhee, Chester R., Jr., 1092
MacPhee, Chester, Jr., 516
MacPherson, Rob, 3116
Macrini, John A., 9026
Macrini, Nancy J., 9026
Macrini, Thomas G., 9026
Macropoulous, George J., 3925
Macvest Group, Inc., 8138
Macy, John P., 9960
Madaj, Kim, 4272
Madden, Frank, 5252
Madden, Robert V., 760
Madden, Susan C., 5386
Madden, William, 4935
Madding, Bruce W., 739
Maddock, Todd, 2570
Maddox Trust, Margaret, 4753
Maddox, Benjamin W., 5487
Maddox, Catherine M., 5487
Maddox, Dan, 4753
Maddox, Don, 5487
Maddox, J.F, 5487
Maddox, James M., 5487
Maddox, Jennifer S., 3199
Maddox, John L., 5487
Maddox, Mabel S., 5487
Maddox, Margaret H., 4753
Maddox, Patricia, 2303
Maddox, R. Scott, 7466
Maddox, Thomas M., 5487
Maddux, W.E., 7973
Maddy, Chris, 4571
Madec, Andre, 8889
Maden, John J., 2681
Madeo, Linda W., 6688
Madich, Gary, 7581
Madigan, Holly W., 2869
Madigan, John W., 2869
Madison Gas and Electric Co., 9855
Madison, Joseph W., 4428
Madison, William E., 3474
Madlock, Yvonne S., 8661
Madonia, Peter, 6826
Madori, Nick, 2859
Madorsky, Marsha G., 1957
Madrigal, Mary Ann, 8888
Madrigal, Tony, 3404
Madsen, Max, 2856
Madsen, Tom, 9559
Madson, Deborah B., 4521
Madzel, Malynda H., 3595
Maebius, Clayton, 9020
Maechtlen, Rodger, 3354
Maffitt, James S., 3661
Magaram, Philip S., 469
Magasinn, Vicki, 478

Magasinn, Vicki Fisher, 872
Magayern, James L., 5785
Magden, Josh, 1359
Magdiel LLC, 379
Magee Industrial Enterprises, 8320
Magee, Audrey R., 8320
Magee, Drue A., 8320
Magee, James A., 8320
Magen Israel Society, 5740
Magennis, Rachael Carr, 8870
Mager, Ezra P., 5840
Mager, Reeva S., 6260
Mager, Scott, 2079
Maggs, Thomas O., 6915
Magid, Lawrence, 5371
Magill, Alice H., 2124
Magill, Arthur F., 2124
Magill, Hugh, 2702
Magill, Sherry B., 1983
Magill, William H., 6777
Maginn, John, 4992, 4994
Magistro, Charles M., 847
Magistro, Mary N., 847
Magliocco, Robert R., 9848
Maglione, Louis A., 7591
Magness, Debby Smith, 5056
Magnetics, Inc., 8452
Magnolia Liquor Co., Inc., 3484, 3516
Magnolia Marine Transport Co., 4740
Magnus Asset Management Trust, The, 2870
Magnus, Alexander B., Jr., 2870
Magnus, Maria, 2870
Magnuson, Brenda E., 1294
Mago, Marianne Cracchiolo, 142
Magoon, Nancy, 1338
Magowan, Doris A., 6473
Magowan, Mark, 6164, 6473
Magowan, Mark E., 6473
Magowan, Merrill L., 6473
Magowan, Peter A., 6473
Magowan, Robert A., Jr., 6473
Magowan, Robert A., Sr., 6473
Magowan, Robin, 6473
Magri, Patrick, 5329
Magruder Trust, Chesley G., 2125
Magruder, Elaine, 8749
Maguire, Frances M., 8321
Maguire, James G., 4211
Maguire, James J., 8321
Maguire, Jennifer, 84
Maguire, John D., 720
Maguire, Lynne M., 3175
Maguire, Pamela Mitchell, 9064
Maguire, Perry, 514
Mahadevan, Kumar, 2148
Mahan, J.T., 4492
Mahana, Elliott, 5518
Mahana, Joy, 5518
Mahavier, William, 8878
Maher, Angela B., 8204
Maher, John, 1468
Maher, Nathaniel J.W., 4725
Maheras, Leslie L., 6475
Maheras, Thomas G., 6475
Mahle, Steve, 4622
Mahler, Nancy, 7449
Mahler, William W., 9750
Mahn, Thomas E., 3599, 3705
Mahne, Sherri A., 4147
Mahnken, Richard, 3198
Mahnken, sally, 3198
Mahnken, Sally M., 3198
Mahon, Arthur J., 1593, 7227
Mahon, Arthur J., 5563
Mahon, Deborah P., 4609
Mahon, Myra, 1593
Mahon, Peter M., Jr., 4609
Mahone, Andrea Torres, 8457
Mahoney, Brooke W., 6774
Mahoney, Chris, 6569
Mahoney, Cornelius D., 4210
Mahoney, Elaine, 469
Mahoney, Hildegarde E., 5827

Marshall, Siri S., 4570
Marshall, Stephanie P., 3034
Marshall, Stephanie Pace, 2740
Marshall, Steve, 3110
Marshall, Sue Ellen, 3438
Marshall, Theresa, 8326
Marshall, Thomas, 8326
Marshall, Thomas C., 469
Marshall, Thurgood, Jr., 5970
Marshall, Virginia, 8326
Marshall, William H., 3119, 3120, 3795
Marshall-Chapman, Paula, 7984
Marshalls of MA, Inc., 4183
Marshfield Assocs., 3628
Marsho, Tim, 3325
Marshon, Karen, 6819
Marsicano, Michael, 7370
Marsico, Christopher, 1416
Marsico, Cydney, 1416
Marsico, Tom, 1416
Marston, Ed, 9764
Marston, Richard, 3549
Marston, Wes, 2015
Martahus, Craig R., 7578
Martahus, Craig T., 7578
Martell Foundation, T.J., 5708
Martell, Sally Klingenstein, 6340
Martell, Sarah, 6340
Marti, George W., 9030
Marti, Jo C., 9030
Marti, Michelle, 9030
Martin Charitable Fund, Bert, 2874
Martin Foundation, 9584
Martin Foundation, Inc., 3916
Martin Investment Trust G, 3271
Martin Marietta Corp., 3682
Martin, Ada La May, 2874
Martin, Albert Jay, 8706
Martin, Alice A., 3200
Martin, Aubert, 5400
Martin, Bert W., 2874
Martin, Betty B., 9400
Martin, Brian J., 19, 61, 9984
Martin, C. Alan, 1
Martin, Carol E., 1992
Martin, Casper, 2130, 3916
Martin, Charles C., 8656
Martin, Charles N., Jr., 8708
Martin, Charlotte Y., 9634
Martin, Christopher, 5359
Martin, Christopher P., 93
Martin, Conrad, 1836
Martin, Cynthia S., 3170
Martin, Daniel P., 4993
Martin, David, 5255
Martin, Deidre W., 7310
Martin, Del, 5063
Martin, Donna S., 7449
Martin, E.B., Jr., 4762
Martin, Eff W., 6496
Martin, Elizabeth, 9584
Martin, Esther, 2130
Martin, F. William, 8876
Martin, Frank, 9580
Martin, G., 5097
Martin, Geneva, 7593
Martin, George M., 3621
Martin, Geraldine, 9584
Martin, Geraldine F., 2130
Martin, Gilbert J., 860
Martin, Glenn, 7444
Martin, Glenn R., Mrs., 9503
Martin, H. Lee, 8671
Martin, Harold L., Dr., 7508
Martin, J. Landis, 1347
Martin, J.C., III, 9253
Martin, Jack, 4254
Martin, Jack, Rev., 5334
Martin, Jacob H., Mrs., 3811
Martin, James R., 940, 9644
Martin, James S., 1537
Martin, James W., 8603
Martin, Jamie Planck, 4762
Martin, Janet Dowler, 9862

Martin, Jennifer H., 9949
Martin, Jennifer L., 2130
Martin, Jessa, 7264
Martin, Joanne, 9683
Martin, John, 4221
Martin, John G., 1598
Martin, John H., 4282
Martin, John H., III, 63
Martin, John W., 9984
Martin, John, Fr., 9695
Martin, Joshua W., III, 1700
Martin, Judith W., 7264
Martin, K., 5097
Martin, Keith, 9203
Martin, Kenneth J., 9571
Martin, Larry B., 8671
Martin, Lawanna S., 9031
Martin, Lawrence J., 9390
Martin, Lee, 2130
Martin, Lee P., Jr., 9457
Martin, Lendell, 9031
Martin, Leslee, 2566
Martin, Lisa, 2130, 7343
Martin, Malcolm, 1490
Martin, Malcolm E., 6130
Martin, Mari Ann, 9984
Martin, Marina E. Haugland, 8018
Martin, Mary K., 8844
Martin, Mitzi, 3178
Martin, Nancy E., 3404
Martin, Nate, 2679
Martin, Patricia F., 389
Martin, Patricia J., 3309
Martin, Patricia M., 6496
Martin, Patrick, 1460
Martin, Paul, 1992
Martin, R. Brad, 61, 8707
Martin, R. Eden, 2598
Martin, Rex, 3094, 3145, 3200
Martin, Rob, 512
Martin, Robert, 954, 7843
Martin, Rodney E., 7438
Martin, Roger D., 9031
Martin, Roger L., 1158
Martin, Ross, 2130
Martin, Shannon, 7653
Martin, Shannon Presley, 8708
Martin, Stephen D., 7581
Martin, Stephen G., 859
Martin, Teresa H., 5295
Martin, Theodore E., 5760
Martin, Thomas B., 8844
Martin, Thomas B., Jr., 8844
Martin, Tracie, 3125
Martin, Valerie K., 8475
Martin, Vincent L., 9862
Martin, Webb F., 4399
Martin, William H., 8136
Martindale, Elizabeth F., 492
Martindale, Harry T., 492
Martinelli, A.W., 8318
Martinelli, Alfred W., 8318
Martinelli, Aline, 8318
Martinelli, Christine, 8318
Martinelli, David, 8318
Martinelli, Gary E., 6968
Martinenza, Stephen A., 1701
Martines, Monica, 7868
Martinez, Barbara, 5184
Martinez, Carolina, 542
Martinez, George, 8960
Martinez, Guadalupe, 9032
Martinez, Juan J., 2097
Martinez, Lilia, 9032
Martinez, Manuel, 1364
Martinez, Maricarmen, 1957
Martinez, Michael, 1364
Martinez, Virginia, 2922, 8881, 8950
Martini, Nicholas, 5319
Martini, William J., 5319
Martinique Hotel, Inc., 4299
Martino, Marilyn, 4173
Martino, Mary S., 6660
Martino, Roxanne, 2601

Martinson, John H., 5320
Martinson, Margaret M., 5320
Martinson, Ross T., 5320
Martodam, Don, 4723
Marton-Lefevre, Julia, 6389
Martore, Gracia C., 9428
Martz, Dayna A., 163
Marvald, Kenneth A., 7099
Marvec Corp., The, 8138
Marvel Group, The, 8139
Marvin, Carol Young, 9295
Marvin, L. Edward, 9295
Marx Co., Joseph E., Inc., 6497
Marx Foundation, Virginia and Leonard, 851
Marx Realty & Improvement Co., Inc., 5620
Marx, Helen Schulman, 6498
Marx, Leonard, 6497
Marx, Magda, 7130
Marx, Moses, 7015, 7130
Marx, Otto, Jr., 6499
Marx, Page M., 6499
Marx, Paul Frederic, 957
Marx, Robert, 6901
Marx, Virginia, 6497
Marx, William, 6498
Mary Louise and Marjori Lord Trust Fund, 7667
Mary, Inc., 4694
Maryanov, Lloyd, 9980
Maryland Investments, Inc., 132
Maryland, LLC, 132
Maryles, Matthew, 5661
Marziali, Eric A., 1644
Marzio, Peter C., 7209, 9006
Mascarenas, Jose Manuel, 8950
Mascio, Gina, 1946
Masco Corp., 4383, 4387
Mascott, Mary McDonald, 6639
Mascotte, Jake, 1338
Maseeh, Fariborz, 4027
Masey, James E., 2900
Mashhoon, Mahasti, 757
Mashhoon, Zia, 757
Masi, Wendy S., 6477
Masin, Michael T., 750, 7227
Masiyiwa, Strive, 6826
Maslow, Allison, 8327
Maslow, Douglas, 8327
Maslow, Richard, 8327
Mason Shoe Manufacturing Co., 9863
Mason, Carol K., 2859
Mason, Christina M., 5912
Mason, David E., 2805
Mason, Don E., 4758
Mason, Frances E., 8136
Mason, Howard K., Jr., 459
Mason, J. Thomas, 7729
Mason, James W., 7464
Mason, Jane Hemingway, 9328
Mason, Jeannine, 8756
Mason, Joyce, 5248
Mason, Kathleen, 3185
Mason, Kathleen B., 4291
Mason, Louise, 3199
Mason, Marguerite F., 2444
Mason, Otis, 2238
Mason, Raymond, 3672
Mason, Rockie, 3448
Mason, Shelly R., 8438
Mason, Stephen, 7964
Mason, Steve, 3132
Mason, Susan, 696
Mason, Terri, 4918
Mason, Wayne H., 2356
Mason, William Clarke, 8340
Masowitz Trust, Aaron, 617
Massachusetts Mutual Life Insurance Co., 1599
Massachusetts State Automobile Dealers Association, Inc., 4026
Massaro, George E., 3886
Masselink, Carla, 4258

Massengil, R. Scott, 5113
Massey, Alyne, 8709
Massey, Betty, 9092
Massey, Craig L., 9467
Massey, Don, 1471
Massey, Doris J., 8328
Massey, E. Morgan, 9467
Massey, Gregory L., 7955
Massey, H.B., 8328
Massey, Henry H., Jr., 7342
Massey, Joe B., 8328
Massey, John L., 7955
Massey, Kayanne S., 2458
Massey, Michael J., 3380
Massey, Walter E., 5779, 6525
Massey, William Blair, Jr., 9467
Massey, William E., Jr., 9467
Massey, William P., 7306
Massie, Timmian C., 5898
Massinga, Ruth, 4795
Massingale, Cheryl, 8671
Massmutual Financial Group, 3935
Masson, Richard, 8456
Masson, Rick C., 8718
Massry, Esther, 6502
Massry, Morris, 6502
Massry, Norman, 6502
Massry, Sam, 5630
Mast, Allen, 2463, 2507
Master Equities Corp., 6849
Master, Carol, 6889
Master, Elroy P., 8271
Masterplan, 3683
Masters, Seth J., 7244
Masterson, Velma, 277
Mastria, Richard, 4026
Mastrogiorgio, Maryellen, 6047
Mastronardi, Charles A., 1729
Mastronardi, Margaret, 1729
Mastronardi, Nicholas D., 1729
Mastropieri, Robert W., 3683
Masuda, Mel, 1324
Masumoto, David Mas, 698
Matarazzo, Hadley, 8457
Matarazzo, James M., 7263
Matchett, Gerald T., 3275
Mateer, Rodney W., 9486
Mateo, Laura D., 783
Mateo, Segundo, 783
Matheny, Edward T., Jr., 4823
Matheny, N. Dale, 1166, 1167
Matheny, N.D., 1161
Mather, Elizabeth Ring, 7736
Mathern, Tim, 4524
Mathers, G. Harold, 6504
Mathers, Leila Y., 6504
Mathers, William L., 3756
Mathes, Stephen J., 6409
Matheson, Alline, 5600
Matheson, Bonnie B., 4287
Matheson, Esther Quintana, 1358
Mathews, Jessica T., 6826
Mathews, Margaret, 7046
Mathews, Mary, 4534
Mathews, Sylvia M., 9591
Mathewson, Ann, 5045
Mathewson, Charles N., 5045
Mathewson, Curtis N., 5045
Mathey, Dean, 5148
Mathias, Lee, 4930
Mathiasen, Karl, 1835
Mathieson, Ann, 854
Mathieson, Peter F., 8124, 8130, 8386
Mathieu, Calvin, 9980
Mathile, Clayton Lee, 7737
Mathile, MaryAnn, 7737
Mathis, Allen W., III, 21
Mathis, Allen W., Jr., 21
Mathis, David B., 2832
Mathis, James E., Jr., 2458
Mathis, William N., 8799
Mathison, Betsy, 3036
Matis, Nina B., 2826

McCance, Henry F., 4030
McCandless, June, 6208
McCandliss, Len, 1151
McCann Foundation, 5564
McCann, James J., 6514
McCann, Nancy W., 7706, 7769
McCann, Thomas, 670
McCanna, Katherine, 4462
McCannel, Dana D., 4711
McCargo, William F., 2482
McCarrick, Theodore E., Cardinal, 1825
McCarroll, Andrew R., 8719
McCart, Joe, 2356
McCartan, Patrick F., 7706
McCarter, Fred, 3137
McCarter, Jerry, 4534
McCarthy Bush Corp., 3311
McCarthy Group, Inc., 4971
McCarthy Improvement Co., 3311
McCarthy, A. Gregory, IV, 1825
McCarthy, Albert G., III, 1825
McCarthy, Amelia, 1788
McCarthy, Ann F., 7248
McCarthy, Brian A., 6516
McCarthy, Dan, 7187
McCarthy, Deborah Berg, 5579
McCarthy, Denis, 6515
McCarthy, Edward J., 2299
McCarthy, Edwin J., 4614
McCarthy, Gerald, 9451
McCarthy, James T., 868
McCarthy, Jane D., 868
McCarthy, John, 797
McCarthy, John J., 3067, 8548
McCarthy, Kathleen L., 767, 797
McCarthy, Kathleen M., 4009
McCarthy, Kevin B., 3112
McCarthy, Louise Roblee, 4893
McCarthy, Lucy, 6515
McCarthy, Lucy A., 6515
McCarthy, Margaret E., 6516
McCarthy, Margaret M., 9141
McCarthy, Michael, 4994
McCarthy, Michael D., 5579
McCarthy, Michael J., 3761
McCarthy, Michael W., 6516
McCarthy, Neil M., 3801
McCarthy, Pamela, 6515
McCarthy, Patrick, 3585
McCarthy, Patrick C., 6516
McCarthy, Patrick M., 6516
McCarthy, Peter F., 6515
McCarthy, Robert H., 6515
McCarthy, Robert P., 6515
McCarthy, Roger, 1463
McCarthy, Terri, 4476
McCarthy, Thomas A., 7586
McCarthy, Thomas F., 3648
McCarthy, Thomas O., 4614
McCarthy, Winifred, 6515
McCartney, James E., 4403
McCartney, John F., 2914
McCartor, Alice, 8045
McCarty, H.F., Jr., 4754
McCarty, John R., 4754
McCarty, Marilu H., 2389
McCarty, Mary Ann, 4754
McCarty, Michael A., 4754
McCarty, Shellye S., 4754
McCarty, Stuart, 6428
McCarvel, Cynthia, 3403
McCasland, Monica, 7931
McCasland, T.H., Jr., 7956
McCasland, Tom, Jr., 7931
McCaslin, Teresa E., 5786, 5984
McCaul, Elizabeth, 6230
McCaul, Linda M., 9035
McCaul, Mack E., Jr., 8661
McCauley, Donald L., 3127
McCauley, Tamme K. "Descouteau", 3239
McCausland, Thomas N., 5400
McCaw Foundation, The, 9552
McCaw, Bruce R., 9552, 9694

McCaw, Craig O., 869, 9637
McCaw, Jolene M., 9552, 9694
McCaw, Keith, 9636
McCaw, Mary Kay, 9636
McCaw, Susan R., 9637
McCaw, Wendy P., 869
McCaw, William J., 3202
McCelland, Vincent, 5517
McClain Smith, Mariwyn, 9736
McClain, Barrie, 3115
McClain, Lydia Joy, 9426
McClain, Michael, 7555
McClain, Terry J., 5013
McClamroch, Michael T., 8671
McClanahan, Marjorie, 87
McClanathan, Jeffrey P., 2067
McClaskey, Jim, 9570
McClatchy Co., The, 4691
McClaughry, Richard, 3129
McClave, Christin C., 8129
McClay, Paul F., 3536
McClean, Mary Gaylord, 7937, 7966
McCleary, Monique M., 8038
McCleery, Tania L.J., 6118
McClellan, James G., 9109
McClellan, Margaret, 5088
McClellan, Rowland J., 9820
McClelland, Stephanie P., 6517
McClelland, W. Carter, 6517
McClendon Revocable Trust, Katie Rose, 4894
McClendon, Katie Rose W., 4894
McClerkin, Hayes C., 157
McClimon, Timothy, 5553
McClintock, Emily, 7779
McClintock, John R.D., 3848, 3920, 4075
McClintock, Virginia, 9109
McCloskey, Bonnie P., 1419
McCloskey, Shaun, 7673
McCloskey, Thomas D., Jr., 1419
McCloud Investments, 57
McClough, Brad, 7395
McClughen, Ron, 3126
McClung, James F., Jr., 941
McClure, Caterine, 4245
McClure, Elise, 9690
McClure, Gail D., 4357
McClure, Teri, 2503, 3585
McClurg, Lori, 4987
McCluski, Stephen C., 5605
McClymont, Mary E., 5970
McCole, Kevin, 2922
McCollum, Yancey L., 2430
McComas, Harrold, 9791
McComas, Harrold J., 9899
McComas, Murray K., 8154
McComb, Tiney, 7775
McCombo, Lynda G., 9037
McCombs Family Charitable Lead Trust, 9037
McConahey, Greg, 5088
McCone, Theiline M., 9650
McConkey, Cindy, 7848
McConn, Christiana R., 9212
McConn, Margaret E., 9154
McConnell, Beverly, 8123
McConnell, Carl R., 870
McConnell, Diane E., 7539
McConnell, Doug, 79
McConnell, Doug C., 3042
McConnell, Jane, 1358
McConnell, Jo Ellen, 3096
McConnell, Kathryn, 7344
McConnell, Leah F., 870
McConnell, LeeAnn, 4452
McConnell, Matthew, 1407
McConnell, Paul R., 1586
McConnell, September, 3258
McConnell, Trudy, 2181
McCooey, Robert H., Jr., 6619
McCord, David, 3165
McCord, Larry, 7543
McCord, Margot R., 5281

McCord, Shawn, 9702
McCorkindale, Douglas H., 9428
McCorkle, Leon, 7902
McCorkle, Mae L., 7741
McCorkle, Nanci L., 7741
McCorkle, William R., III, 7741
McCorkle, William R., Jr., 7741
McCormack, Duncan, III, 1180
McCormack, Elizabeth, 134, 6861
McCormack, Elizabeth J., 5574, 7168
McCormack, Kristen J., 4133, 6158
McCormack, Pat, 7139
McCormack, William, 5252
McCormack, William J., 1733
McCormick Trust, Brooks, 2878
McCormick Trust, Charles Deering, 2878
McCormick Trust, Roger, 2878
McCormick, Ann, 5397
McCormick, Anne, 8330
McCormick, Brian, 1516
McCormick, Brooks, 2878
McCormick, Charlotte Deering, 2878
McCormick, Dick, 9599
McCormick, Fray, 2497
McCormick, Judy D., 7603
McCormick, Mary Patricia, 1420
McCormick, Nancy B., 3597
McCormick, Nancy V.T., 2878
McCormick, Richard D., 1420
McCormick, Robin, 3142
McCormick, Stephanie Kaskel, 3156
McCormick, Thomas J., 9740
McCormick, Thomas P., 5600
McCourtney, Flora, 2879
McCourtney, Plato, 2879
McCoy, Alan H., 7525
McCoy, Anne, 871
McCoy, Bowen H., 871
McCoy, Charles W. "Chuck", 3462
McCoy, David, 3129
McCoy, Emmett F., 9038
McCoy, Fred, 3159
McCoy, James N., 9039
McCoy, Jim, 9280
McCoy, Joan, 78
McCoy, John B., 871
McCoy, Kevin, 9843
McCoy, Louise Boney, 7398
McCoy, Mark, 9039
McCoy, Michael J., 4588
McCoy, Miriam M., 9038
McCoy, Nelson, Jr., 7743
McCoy, Richard, 8333
McCoy, Richard T., 1263
McCoy, Robert C., 1762
McCoy, Virginia B., 4412
McCracken, Gail, 125
McCracken, Paul W., 4291
McCrady, Christopher R., 8130
McCrady, Priscilla J., 8130
McCrae, Angela H., 8617
McCrane, Grace, 9464
McCrary, Charles D., 1
McCrary, Giles C., 8907
McCrary, Guy, 9117
McCrary, Margaret, 1570
McCraw, Roy J., Jr., 1948
McCray, Robert B., 204
McCray, Ronald D., 8992
McCrea, Colin, 5574
McCrea, Mary Corling, 9040
McCready, Mathilda Staunton Craig, 8457
McCreary, Robert G., III, 7680
McCree-Lewis, Kathleen, 4254
McCreight, Paul W., 9731
McCreight, Wendy, 1477
McCrimlisk, George H., 614, 1187
McCrimon, Mary Catherine, 1956
McCrodden, Bruce, 7772
McCrory, Jenks E., 8670
McCrory, Kenneth, 8107
McCrury, Phillip W., 8841
McCuaig, Victor C., 6859

McCubbin, Don A., 4902
McCubbin, Donald J., 759
McCue, Howard M., III, 2740, 3058
McCue, Howard, III, 2658
McCulley, Michael, 8487
McCulley, Michael B., 5255
McCulley, Paul, 1006
McCulloch, Deb, 7831
McCulloch, Dorothy R., 8547
McCulloch, Norman Estes, Jr., 8547
McCulloch, Rob, III, 7831
McCullogh, Thomas E., 374
McCullouch, John M., 2323
McCullough, Hubert L., Jr., 8654
McCullough, James T., 9041
McCullough, P. Mike, 8766, 9049
McCullough, Ralph H., 9041
McCullough, Ruth J., 9041
McCullough, Samuel A., 8103
McCully, A.C., 161
McCune, Charles L., 8332
McCune, David F., 872
McCune, Florence M., 3376
McCune, John R., IV, 8331
McCune, John R., VI, 5488, 8332
McCune, Marshall L., 5488
McCune, Perrine Dixon, 5488
McCune, Sara Miller, 872
McCurchie, Jack, 8023
McCurry, David, 3294
McCurry, David G., 3294
McCurry, Susan, 3294
McCurry, Susan H., 3294
McCusker, F.C., 9726
McCutchen, Brunson S., 5322
McCutchen, Charles W., 5322
McCutchen, Margaret W., 5322
McCutcheon, Hilary H., 2878
McCutcheon, Vincent, Rev., 3144
McDade, Robert E., 4760
McDade, Sandy D., 9703
McDaniel, A. Stephen, 8661
McDaniel, Brenda, 3387
McDaniel, Glen P., 1235
McDaniel, John P., 1823
McDaniel, Mark, 4330
McDaniel, Ronald, 2880
McDaniel, Ronald L., 2880
McDaniel-Lowe, Sharon L., 9566
McDavid, G.N., 4862
McDavid, Stephan L., 4766
McDede, David, 5372
McDemmond, Marie V., 3196
McDermott, Eugene, 9043
McDermott, Eugene, Mrs., 9043
McDermott, Gregory, 7526
McDermott, Kathleen E., 4633
McDermott, Peter, 5749
McDermott, Renee, 7449
McDermott, Thomas M., 1377
McDevitt, Amy, 743
McDevitt, Sheila, 2270
McDevitt, Thomas, 1860
McDonald Industries, A.Y., Inc., 3312
McDonald Investments, Inc., 7577
McDonald's Corp., 8333
McDonald, Alonzo L., 4388
McDonald, Alonzo L., Jr., 4388
McDonald, B.D., 3437
McDonald, Barbara Anderson, 8761
McDonald, Charles R., 4417
McDonald, David, 1563
McDonald, Deanna, 1911
McDonald, Deborah V., 5076
McDonald, Denis H., 3494
McDonald, Douglas B., 5068
McDonald, Ellice, Jr., 1714
McDonald, Gregory C., 5076
McDonald, Holly, 2629
McDonald, Hugh, 3509
McDonald, Hugh T., 3474
McDonald, J.M., III, 3312
McDonald, J.M., Sr., 4989
McDonald, James M., IV, 4989

McDonald, James M., Sr., 1421
McDonald, James P., 8345
McDonald, Janet Strain, 66
McDonald, Johanne, 5673
McDonald, Judith C., 5076
McDonald, Judy, 979
McDonald, Kenton, 8912
McDonald, Kevin, 4221
McDonald, M.B., 3312
McDonald, Mackey J., 7498
McDonald, Malcolm, 4610
McDonald, Malcolm W., 4579
McDonald, Meg, 8075
McDonald, Peter, 4388
McDonald, Peter D., 3044
McDonald, R.D., 3312
McDonald, Rosa H., 1714
McDonald, S. Bruce, 1939
McDonald, Sam E., Jr., 5076
Mcdonald, Sharon, 8924
McDonald, Suzanne M., 4388
McDonald, Walter J., 8009
McDonald, William E., 7772
McDonnell Charitable Trust A, James S., 4031
McDonnell Charitable Trust B, James S., 4031
McDonnell Douglas Corp., 4785
McDonnell Foundation, James S., 4841
McDonnell Group Employee Relief Fund, 3490
McDonnell, Alicia S., 4031
McDonnell, Archie R., 4747
McDonnell, James S., III, 4031, 4841, 4864
McDonnell, Jean, 4863
McDonnell, Jeffrey M., 4841, 4864
McDonnell, John F., 1422, 4031, 4841, 4864
McDonnell, John J., Jr., 9468
McDonnell, Marian J., 9468
McDonnell, Matthew J., 1422
McDonnell, Patricia L., 1422
McDonnell, Thomas A., 4843
McDonnell, Tom, 4863
McDonough, Allison, 9865
McDonough, Bernard P., 9726
McDonough, Bill, 4745
McDonough, David, 3039
McDonough, Joanne, 5417
McDonough, John J., 9865
McDonough, Kathleen F., 1706
McDonough, Kevin M., Rev., 4636
McDonough, Lindsay Y., 8637
McDonough, Marie, 797
McDonough, Marilyn N., 9865
McDonough, Maureen E., 4512
McDonough, Robert E., 873
McDougal, Alfred L., 2881
McDougal, Jan, 2881
McDougal, Stephen, 2881
McDougal, Thomas, 2881
McDougall, Ruth Camp, 5700
McDowell Manufacturing, 7661
McDowell, Boyd, 2922
McDowell, Boyd, III, 2993
McDowell, Elsa F., 8581
McDowell, Jay H., 5857
McDuffee, Thomas P., 8419
McDuffie, Anthony D., 8685
McEachern, D.V., 9638
McEachern, Ida J., 9638
McElrath, Karen K., 4537
McElroy, Joe, 9003
McElroy, Mark, 5049
McElroy, R.J., 3313
McElveen, Darnell, 4552
McElvy, Gerald W., 8889
McElwain, Floyd H., 8259
McElwain, William W., 7810
McElwee, Charles R., 9723
McEnaney, Theresa, 4510
McEncroe, Jack, 1306
McEvoy, George H., 4032

McEvoy, Mildred H., 4032
McEvoy, Patrick, Jr., 8843
McEwen, Beatrice G., 1517
McEwen, Dorothy Roberts, 4745
McFadden Trust, 2384
McFadden, Bruce, 920
McFadden, Dave, 3132
McFadden, Harriet, 8653
McFadden, Mary, 874
McFadden, Melsetta H., 5738
McFadden, Samuel, 3854
McFadden, Timothy, 874
McFaddin, Eugene H.B., 9263
McFaddin, James L.C., Jr., 9263
McFadyden, Barbara, 6629
McFadyen, Barbara Nicholson, 8221
McFall, Clara B., 9780
McFall, William R., 9399
McFarland, Charlie, 7889
McFarland, David, 8572
McFarland, Dolly, 2657
McFarland, Duncan, 8144
McFarland, Duncan M., 3817
McFarland, Elizabeth K., 8987
McFarland, Elizabeth M., 3817
McFarland, Ellen B., 3817
McFarland, John, 183
McFarland, Linda Brack, 8839
McFarland, Richard D., 4617
McFarland, Steve, 5058
McFarland, William J., 5813
McFarlane, Brian, 954
McFarlane, Clare P., 4061
McFarlane, Rodger, 1382
McFarlane, Shawn, 9144
McFarlin, Diane, 1946
McFate, Patricia A., 5496
McFate, William J., 8380
McFawn, Lois Sisler, 7858
McFayden, Shannon W., 7502, 8494
McFee, Jane W., 4725
McFeely, Nancy K., 8334
McFerran, Billie Love, 9089
McGaffey, Jere D., 9749
McGalla, Susan, 8079
McGarey, Jennifer, 9471
McGarr, Frank J., 3066
McGarry, James, 7173
McGarvey, Ray L., 8188
McGaughey, David, 3188
McGaughey, Frank, 2451
McGee and Sons, Thomas, 4865
McGee, David, 4865
McGee, Dean A., 7957
McGee, Flo, 9024
McGee, Frank, 4865
McGee, Frank, Mrs., 4865
Mcgee, Gary C., 9495
McGee, Henry, 7142
McGee, John R., 4865
McGee, Joseph J., 1537, 4865
McGee, Joseph J., Jr., 4865
McGee, Joseph J., Mrs., 4865
McGee, Julie, 4865
McGee, Louis B., 4865
McGee, Simon, 4865
McGee, Simon P., 4865
McGee, Suzanne P., 9118
McGee, Thomas F., 4865
McGee, Thomas R., Jr., 4865
McGee, Vincent, 99, 5596, 5934, 6675, 6994
McGeehan, Tim D., 4516
McGehee, Hobson C., III, 4741
McGehee, Hobson C., Jr., 4741
McGehee, Kirk Payne, 4741
McGehee, Robert B., 7453
McGeorge Contracting Co., 181
McGeorge, Harvey W., 181
McGeorge, Scott, 181
McGeorge, Wallace P., III, 181
McGeough, Robert S., 7629
McGettigan, Kristen, 1829
McGettigan, Michael P., 1829
McGettigan, Patrick H., 1829

McGill, Charmaine D., 8808
McGill, Joe K., 8869
McGill, Peter R., 3666
McGill, Thomas, 156
McGillis, Joanne S., 9334
McGillis, Richard L., 9334
McGillis, Roger, 9334
McGinnes, Larry D., 2143
McGinnis, Gerald E., 8335, 8403
McGinnis, Jay M., 9991
McGinnis, John W., 8571
McGinnis, Kermit E., 9721
McGinnity, Dan, 9856
McGivern, Arthur J., 2905
McGivern, John, Rev., 2969
McGlinn, Barbara T., 8151
McGlinn, John F., II, 8151
McGlinn, Terrence J., Jr., 8151
McGlinn, Terrence J., Sr., 8151
McGlothlin, Ann, 3165
McGlothlin, Frances, 9530
McGlothlin, James W., 9469, 9530
McGlothlin, Michael D., 9469
McGlothlin, Nancy D., 7353
McGlothlin, Thomas D., 9469
McGlothlin, Woodrow W., 9469
McGlynn, William C., 5162
McGoldrick, John, 5666
McGoldrick, Kathleen R., 4725
McGonagle, Dextra Baldwin, 6518
McGonigle, John W., 8196
McGorrian, Clare D., 4061
McGougan, Joseph, 2591
McGovern, John E., Jr., 2722
McGovern, John P., 9044
McGovern, Kathrine G., 9044
McGovern, Kevin, 6537
McGovern, Margaret, 836
McGowan, Andrew J., Msgr., 1830, 8317
McGowan, Bill, 1214
McGowan, Brenda, 1996
McGowan, Clarence "Bud", 3230
McGowan, David M., 2713
McGowan, Gertrude, 1830
McGowan, Gertrude C., 8317
McGowan, J. Joseph, 5564
McGowan, Leo, 1830
McGowan, Sue Gin, 1830
McGowan, Thomas, 1830
McGowan, W. Brian, 3638
McGowan, William G., 1830
McGrath, Christopher R., 3951
McGrath, David J., III, 3951
McGrath, David J., Jr., 3951
McGrath, Dennis, 7969
McGrath, Dorn, Jr., 1847
McGrath, Holly L., 3951
McGrath, J., 967
McGrath, J. Paul, 5113
McGrath, JoAnn, 3951
McGrath, Laura K., 2830
McGrath, Mary, 2812
McGrath, Mary Ann, 9988
McGrath, R., 967
McGrath, Robert P., 967
McGrath, Scott J., 3951
McGrath, Sean P., 3951
McGrath, Susan B., 8116
McGraw Charitable Trust, D., 6519
McGraw Foundation, Donald C., Inc., 6520
McGraw Hill Companies, 7040
McGraw, A. William, 7762
McGraw, Christy Hamilton, 1387
McGraw, David W., 6519
McGraw, Donald C., 6519
McGraw, Donald C., III, 6519
McGraw, John, 6520
McGraw, John L., Jr., 6520
McGraw, Karleen, 3137
McGraw, Lee, Ms., 6520
McGraw, Max, 2882
McGraw, Regina, 3069
McGraw, Richard F., 2882

McGraw-Edison Co., 2882
McGregor, A. Bruce, 4194
McGregor, Katherine W., 4389
McGregor, Mark D., 1460
McGregor, Tracy W., 4389
McGriff, Perry, 2015
McGrogan, Daniel, 8174
McGrory, Jack, 1016
McGrory, Patrick, 3714
McGrory, Patrick W., 1741
McGruder, John, 2481
McGruder, Mary Helen, 2481
McGuigan, Chris Ann, 4252
McGuigan, E. Gayle, Jr., 6682
McGuigan, Phillip P., 6682
McGuiness, Luke, 2601
McGuinn, Ann M., 8130
McGuinn, Bill, 7397
McGuire, C. Kent, 8494
McGuire, Christopher M., 281
McGuire, Ellen H., 1517
McGuire, G.J., 4284
McGuire, Grant, 9735
McGuire, J.N., Jr., 8671
McGuire, James C., 1655
McGuire, Janet, 4392
McGuire, Marty, 4392
McGuire, Mary Jo, 2921
McGuire, Nadine M., 4615
McGuire, Patricia A., 1834
McGuire, Raymond J., 6186
McGuire, Rick, 3174
McGuire, Thomas H., 7485
McGuire, Vanessa J.B., 2811
McGuire, William W., 4615, 4705
McGuirl, Thomas, 5879
McGuirl, Thomas W., 5184
McHale, David R., 1614
McHale, James E., 4357
McHale, Patrick J., 4573
McHargue, Mary, 4990
McHenry, Hugh, 8670
McHenry, Richard J., 1824
McHenry, W. Barnabas, 5551
McHugh, Alice L., 1725
McHugh, Frank A., Jr., 1725
McHugh, Katherine, 3869
McHugh, Marie Louise, 1725
McHugh, Robert C., 1437
MCI Communications Corp., 9471
MCI WORLDCOM, Inc., 9471
MCI, Inc., 9471
McIlhenny, John S., 3471
McIlvenny, J., 4284
McInerney, Christina, 6100
McInerney, Elaine, 4225
McInerney, Martin, 4225
McInerney, Thomas J., 2418
McInerny, Elizabeth DeCamp, 5845
McInerny, Ella, 2551
McInerny, James D., 2551
McInerny, William H., 2551
McIninch, Douglas A., 5093
McInnes, Beverly W., 8728
McInnes, D. Joseph, 14
McInnes, Harold, 8208
McInnes, William V., 8728
McInnes, William W., 8728
McInnis, James J., 4058
McInnis, Marybeth, 4058
McInnis, Wade, 7397
McIntee, David, 5371
McIntire, John, 7743
McIntosh, C.B., 1940
McIntosh, Colin H., 1831
McIntosh, David, 2883
McIntosh, Hunter H., 1831
McIntosh, J.B., 910
McIntosh, James C., 2537, 2538
McIntosh, Joan H., 1831
McIntosh, Josephine H., 1831
McIntosh, Judith, 5784
McIntosh, Karen, 1831
McIntosh, Marie Joy, 1831

McIntosh, Michael, 2883
McIntosh, Michael A., 1831
McIntosh, Michael A., Jr., 1831
McIntosh, Peter, 1831
McIntosh, Robert E., 4822
McIntosh, William A., 2883
McIntosh, Winsome D., 1831
McIntrye, John Scott, Jr., 3338
McIntyre, Amanda, 876
McIntyre, David I., 4108
McIntyre, Diane, 468
McIntyre, Ernestine, 3138
McIntyre, James A., 876
McIntyre, Jim, 3126
McIntyre, John, 2500
McIntyre, Larry, 4702
McIntyre, Susan, 5984
McIntyre, William, 4225
MCJ Foundation, 5337
McJunkin, Donald R., 1421
McJunkin, Judith N., 9723
McJunkin, Reed L., 1421
McJunkin, Thomas N., 9723
McKane, Laura Gregory, 27
McKasy, Bert J., 4519
McKay, Alan L., 295
McKay, Barbara S., 3213
McKay, Elaine, 877, 1084
McKay, Emily B., 9867
McKay, James C., 3687
McKay, James E., 4404
McKay, Janet, 6891
McKay, Jeanne, 1247
McKay, John, 1084
McKay, John P., 877
McKay, Marcella, 4757
McKay, Patricia G., 9640
McKay, Patrick, 4256
McKay, Robert, 877
McKay, Robert L., 1084
McKay, Robert L., Jr., 1084
McKay, Robert L., Sr., 877
McKay, Sally T., 8577
McKay, Verlon L., 295
McKean, Linda B., 5138
McKean, Quincy A.S., III, 5138
McKean, Robert, 5758
McKearly, Georgia, 3556
McKee, C. Steven, 9045
McKee, Clyde V., III, 9209
McKee, David C., 9045
McKee, Diana, 471
McKee, E. Marie, 5794
McKee, Evelyn, 9045
McKee, F. James, 9045
McKee, Ginney, 8039
McKee, James T., 9045
McKee, Joan H., 3104
McKee, John S., Jr., 9045
McKee, Louis B., 9045
McKee, Marla J., 3368
McKee, Michael, 320
McKee, Michael D., 728
McKee, Philip Russell, 9045
McKee, R. Brian, 9045
McKee, Robert E., 9045
McKee, Robert E., Inc., 9045
McKee, Robert E., IV, 9045
McKee, Roger J., 3143
McKee, Rose A., 8099
McKee, Susan J., 9045
McKee, Timothy E., 3372
McKeehan, David, 4057
McKeen, Mark A., 9716
McKeithan, Daniel F., Jr., 9884
McKeithan, Patricia, 9876
McKellar, Marie T., 3048
McKelvy, Nancy H., 1808
McKelvy, Sydney, 1816
McKenna, Andrew J., 2598
McKenna, Cheryl, 7582
McKenna, Deborah J., 8443
McKenna, Dianne, 878
McKenna, James, 9954

McKenna, John, 9954
McKenna, Katherine M., 8337
McKenna, Laura K., 7191
McKenna, Laura Kind, 8289
McKenna, Margaret, 9407
McKenna, Marion, 2346
McKenna, Philip M., 8338
McKenna, Regis, 878
McKenna, Rosemary Weaver, 5732
McKenna, Thomas M., 8371
McKenna, Wilma F., 8337
McKenney, Phil, 1244
McKenzie, Charles K., 6820
McKenzie, D. Ray, Jr., 2336, 2337
McKenzie, Duncan, 4745
McKenzie, Floretta Dukes, 3649
McKenzie, James Richard, 1601
McKenzie, Jennifer Kathleen, 1601
McKenzie, Margaret Byrne, 1601
McKenzie, Richard C., Jr., 1601
McKeone, Tod, 4986
McKeough, Mike, 4325
McKeown, Deb, 4227
McKeown, Edward C., 3207
McKeown, Ellen, 9089
McKernan, John P., 8419
McKesson Corp., 879
McKesson HBOC, Inc., 879
McKey, Carol, 3253
McKibben, William, 5390
McKibbon, Ed, 4256
McKiernan, Holiday Hart, 3196
McKim, Karen P., 7590
McKinley, Brent, 9324
McKinley, Carol R., 10000
McKinnell, Henry A., Jr., 6720
McKinney, Anne M., 8671
McKinney, Catherine A., 8339
McKinney, Charlie, 9068
McKinney, David, 7220
McKinney, David B., 7927
McKinney, Fred, 1504
McKinney, Robert F., 2396
McKinney, Tom, 3243
McKinney-James, Rose, 483
McKinney/Pearl Restaurant Partners,
    L.P., 8853
McKinnon, Michele A.W., 9402
McKinnon, Paul, 8864
McKinzie, Carl W., 1054
McKirdie, Suzanna, 8045
McKissick, Caroline, 8599
McKissick, E. Smyth, III, 8612
McKissick, Ellison Smyth, III, 8599
McKleroy, John P., Jr., 11
McKlung, James F., Jr., 1099
McKnight Foundation, The, 483, 4616,
    4637
McKnight, Evelyn Franks, 2134
McKnight, H. Turney, 3688
McKnight, Laura, 4842
McKnight, Maude L., 4617
McKnight, Robert, Jr., 9117
McKnight, Steven L., 3677
McKnight, Sumner T., 3688
McKnight, V. Gregory, 2680
McKnight, William L., 4617
McKonly, G. Steven, 8511
McLachlan, Cyndie, 2757
McLachlan, Kate, 2757
McLachlan, Neil A., 7745
McLain, Tim, 7770
McLanahan, Duer, 6423
McLanahan, Sara, 6092
McLane, David, 8390
McLane, Derek, 1533
McLane, Greg, 9219
McLane, John P., 6541
McLane, Linda Harper, 4033
McLane, P. Andrews, 4033
McLaughlin, Barbara, 3215
McLaughlin, Donald E., 5341
McLaughlin, Edward, 1505
McLaughlin, Gladys, 9660

McLaughlin, Jill A., 2049
McLaughlin, John J., 6536
McLaughlin, Justin, 2741
McLaughlin, Mark R., 2647
McLaughlin, Mary, 3250
McLaughlin, Mary Lou, 8386
McLaughlin, Michael J., 970
McLaughlin, Philip, 5098
McLaughlin, Russell, 7582
McLaughlin, Stephen M., 2049
McLaughlin, Virginia, 9541
McLean, Christopher, 9390
McLean, Elizabeth P., 8340
McLean, Elizabeth R., 8340
McLean, Linda, 9730
McLean, Lisa, 8340
McLean, Mary Louise, 5087
McLean, Melvin F., 880
McLean, Michael H., 1198
McLean, Robert, 8340
McLean, Sandra, 8340
McLean, Sandra L., 8340
McLean, Susan Johnson, 6209
McLean, Tom, 7425
McLean, Wendy, 8340
McLean, William L., III, 8340
McLean, William L., IV, 8340
McLean, William L., Jr., 8340
McLendon, Barbara, 6917
McLendon, William E., 2356
McLeod, James A.W., 7248
McLeod, Mac, 20
McLeod-Bryant, Stephen, 8581
Mclone, Tally Sue, 2633
McLoraine, Helen M., 1438
McLoughlin, Hugh, 6012
McLoughlin, Patrick, 9888
McMacken, Ellen, 1806
McMahan, Daniel W., 3414
McMahan, Ginger Bragg, 9737
McMahan, Kent H., 6417
McMahon, Ashley R., 57
McMahon, Betty T., 57
McMahon, Bill, 6577
McMahon, Caroline D., 8172
McMahon, Carrie C., 57
McMahon, David A., 57
McMahon, Eugene D., 7959
McMahon, Joel D., III, 9224
McMahon, Joel W., 57
McMahon, John, 50
McMahon, John J., III, 57
McMahon, John J., Jr., 57
McMahon, John, Jr., 40
McMahon, Julie T., 4454
McMahon, Kevin G., 8823
McMahon, Laurie K., 2713
McMahon, Leslie W., 9259
McMahon, Louise D., 7959
McMahon, Mary M., 8172
McMahon, Patrick J., 8431
McMahon, Paul, 5434
McMahon, Robert A., 5329
McMahon, Ron, 356
McManaman, Sharon M., 2929
McManigle, Rick, 8842
McManus, Brian E., 8995
McManus, Gregg M., 3249
McManus, Joseph, 9490
McManus, Sydney, 4327, 4370
McManus, Timothy K., 6197
McMaster, Alan, 7744
McMaster, Harold A., 7744
McMaster, Helen E., 7744
McMaster, Ronald A., 7744
McMeel, Bridget J., 4774
McMeel, John P., 4774
McMeel, Susan S., 4774
McMerty, Sarah Bellamy, 1902
McMichael, Barbara L., 7444
McMichael, Dalton L., Jr., 7426
McMichael, Dalton L., Sr., 7426
McMichael, R. Daniel, 8132, 8425
McMichael, Warren, 2443

McMillan Trust, D.W., 49
McMillan, Barbara, 5086
McMillan, Charles, Sr., 2480
McMillan, Douglas D., 4519
McMillan, Ed Leigh, II, 49
McMillan, Mary Moore, 9046
McMillan, Peter, 5086
McMillan, Richard, 9117
McMillan, Thomas G., 9719
McMillan, Toney, 174
McMillan, V. Bruce, 9046
McMillen, Dale W., 3203
McMillen, Dale W., III, 3203
McMillen, Erin, 9639
McMillen, Greg, 3116
McMillen, John F., 3203
McMillen, Mike, 9639
McMillen, Robert B., 9639
McMillian, Helen W., 3
McMillian, Lonnie S., 3
McMillion, Donald C., 7427
McMinn, Wendi, 8608
McMinn, William A., 8809
McMorris, Clare T., 5677
McMullan, Carlette, 2884
McMullan, James M., 2884
McMullan, Madeleine, 2884
McMullan, Margaret, 2884
McMullan, Milton, 2884
McMullen, Arthur, 8155
McMullen, Brian, 837
McMullen, Catherine, 5325
McMullen, Jacqueline, 5325
McMullen, John J., Jr., 5325
McMullen, John J., Sr., 5325
McMullen, Karen, 5359
McMullen, Peter, 5325
McMullin, Keith B., 9348
McMurdy Fund, Robert & Janet, 2664
McMurray, McCain, 5618
McMurray, Sharon, 4251
McMurrey, Charles D., 8937
McMurry, Mick, 9985
McMurry, Neil A., 9985
McMurry, Susie, 9985
McMurtrie, Sandra, 4504
McNab, Connie M., 9037
McNabb, F. William, 8490
McNabb, Jane, 2244
McNabb, Larry, 572
McNair, Fred, 9486
McNair, Janice, 9047
McNair, John F., III, 6688
McNair, Leon, 3050
McNair, Robert, 9047
McNairy, Jack H., 8303
McNairy, John O., 7458
McNairy, Leigh H., 7393
McNally III Trust, A., 2885
McNally, Andrew, IV, 2885
McNally, Danny, 7445
McNally, Jeanine S., 2885
McNally, John J., 6384
McNally, William, 4219
McNamara, Christine, 2135
McNamara, Elizabeth, 1370, 2135
McNamara, Gerald C., 2169
McNamara, J. Daniel, 1862
McNamara, James M., 2135
McNamara, Lana, 2023
McNamara, Lisa T., 3856
McNamara, Patricia B., 3550
McNamara, Paula, 4045
McNamara, Richard F., 4618
McNamara-Corley, Kelly, 6577
McNamee, Brian M., 219
McNaughton, Brian, 9660
McNaughton, Stan W., 9660
McNay, Colin, 4053
McNay, Joseph C., 4053
McNea, Melvin, 4939
McNeal, Edward, 7883
McNeal, Jean, 2296
McNealy, Scott, 333

McNealy, Susan, 333
McNeely, Ash, 989
McNeely, Donald G., 4610, 4715
McNeely, Gregory, 4610, 4619, 4715
McNeely, Harry G., III, 4619
McNeely, Kevin, 4610, 4619, 4715
McNeely, Nora, 4610, 4715
McNeely, Robert A., 1250
McNeely, Valerie C., 6125
McNeer, J. Frederick, 7987
McNeil Pharmaceuticals, 1995
McNeil, Collin F., 8095
McNeil, Henry S., 8144
McNeil, Jennifer, 8144
McNeil, John R., 25
McNeil, Michael, 4668
McNeil, Robert D., 8144
McNeil, Robert L., III, 8095
McNeil, Robert L., Jr., 8095
McNeil, Stanley, 2887
McNeil, William, 4729
McNeil-Miller, Karen, 7457
McNeill, Alicia, 9986
McNeill, Corbin A., Jr., 9986
McNeill, Corbin, IV, 9986
McNeill, Dorice S., 9986
McNeill, Kevin, 9986
McNeill, Timothy, 9986
McNeill, William, 3425
McNeilus, Brandon, 4569
McNeilus, Denzil, 4569
McNeilus, Garwin, 4569
McNeilus, Marilee, 4569
McNicholas, Anthony J., III, 2181
McNichols, George, 3133
McNichols, Gerald R., 9472
McNichols, Gerald R., Jr., 9472
McNichols, Paula A., 9472
McNulty, Anne Welsh, 6521
McNulty, Despina, 8278
McNulty, Donna, 1776
McNulty, John P., 6521
McNutt, Amy Shelton, 9048
McNutt, Laura, 9166
McParland, Nathaniel P., 2964
McPeek, Nancy, 7674
McPhail, Elizabeth, 204
McPhail, Gary R., 3261
McPhail, Ian D., 403
McPhee, Penelope "Penny", 2325
McPhee, Sharon, 2543
McPherson, Charles, 1944
McPherson, Mary Patterson, 6471,
    6525, 7126
McPherson, Michael S., 3015
McPhillips, James, 3597
McQuade, Kathryn B., 9485
McQuaide, Scott, 7539
McQuain Trust, Hazel Ruby, 9727
McQuain, Hazel Ruby, 9727
McQueen, Jerald E., 9051
McQueen, Robert D., 7280
McQueeney, Chris, 3160
McQuirk, John, Rt. Rev., 6513
McRae, Carolyn, 1426
McRae, Richard D., Jr., 4733, 4755
McRae, Richard D., Sr., 4755
McRae, Richard, Sr., 4755
McRae, Selby W., 4755
McRae, Vaughan W., 4755
McRae, Willard, 1586
McRee, Laurie, 4748
McRee, Mike, 4737
McReynolds, J. Scott, 7574
McShane, Michael P., 824, 1304
McSherry, William, 6075
McShine, Kynaston, 5550
McStay, Ellen, 9075
McStay, John, 9075
McStay, John D., 9075
McStay, John D., Mrs., 9075
McStay, Judge, 9075
McSwain, Jason, 7592
McSwain, Phyllis, 7592

McSwain, Ronald H., 7592
McTeer, Charles Victor, 4743
McTier, John, 2360
McVaney Family Foundation, 1454
McVaney, Colleen K., 1409
McVaney, Kevin E., 1409
McVann, Dorothy, 983
McVay, M.D., 4620
McVay, Mary, 4620
McVay, Scott, 5283
McVeigh, Owen, 5194
McVey, John, 1894
McVey, Patricia, 1894
McVicker, Henry J., 8074
McVie, Alexander M., III, 3204
McVie, Douglas S., 3204
McVie, Sue Anne, 3204
McWane, C. Phillip, 50
McWane, Inc., 50
McWard, M. Kathleen, 970
McWaters, Jeffrey L., 9369
McWha, Todd R., 4991
McWhinney Holding Comp., 1423
McWhinney, Lori, 1423
McWhinney, Robin, 1423
McWilliams, Anne G., 572
McWilliams, Jim, 4444
McWilliams, Mary Ellen, 9998
McWilliams, Suzanne, 3049
MDSC, 4694
MDU Resources Group, Inc., 7517
Meachum, Bruce, 3047
Mead, B. Kathlyn, 204
Mead, Betsy, 1832
Mead, Betsy A., 1832
Mead, Brenda O., 9435
Mead, D. Richard, Jr., 2888
Mead, D.R., Sr., 2888
Mead, E. Scott, 6522
Mead, Elise G., 881
Mead, George W., 9867
Mead, Gilbert, 9779
Mead, Gilbert D., 1832
Mead, James, 8208
Mead, James M., 6522
Mead, Jane W., 881
Mead, Jaylee M., 1832
Mead, Marilyn K., 1832
Mead, Parry W., 881
Mead, Stanley Budge, 2888
Mead, Suling C., 6522
Mead-Siohan, Diana, 1832
Mead-Siohan, Diana C., 1832
Meade, Andrew, 1515
Meade, Caroline O., 969
Meade, Gary J., 969
Meade, N. Mitchell, Hon., 3449
Meade, Thomas, 969
Meaden, Laura A., 8204
Meader, Edwin, 4465
Meader, Mary, 4465
Meader, Mary U., 4465
Meador, S.M., 9473
Meadowbrook Investment Advisors,
    4417
Meadowcroft, W. Howarth, 9642
Meadowlea Foods, 1609
Meadows, Algur Hurtle, 9049
Meadows, Amy M., 8787
Meadows, Curtis W., Jr., 9049
Meadows, Eric R., 9049
Meadows, John M., 9049
Meadows, Karen, 9049
Meadows, Robert A., 9049
Meadows, Virginia, 9049
Meadows, William W., 9218
Meadows, Willis L., 3517
Meadows-Efram, Corinne, 340
Meagher, Bonnie, 5564
Meagher, Bruce J., 9842
Meaher, Augustine, III, 53
Meaher, Joseph L., 53
Meakem, Diane B., 8341
Meakem, Glen T., 8341

Meakin, Charles J., III, Dr., 7342
Meaney, Lisa Collins, 2878
Meaney, Dennis E., 4347
Means, Jim, 8631
Means, Melissa, 9089
Means, Rick L., 4902
Meany, D.M., 6227
Meares, Samuel H., 7349
Mears, A.W. Downing, Jr., 9077
Mears, Lisa M., 9077
Measey, William Maul, 8342
Mebane, G. Allen, IV, 7427
Mebane, G. Allen, V, 7427
Mebane, John G., 7317
Mebane, Marianne, 7427
Mebane, W. Carter, III, 7336, 7352
Mechem, Charles S., Jr., 7560
Meckel, Amy M., 9194, 9197
Meckley, David G., 8511
Medcalf, Joseph A., 4326
Medellin, Joe, 3189
Medellin, Joseph, 3176
Medgyesy, Laszlo Steven, 3730
Medi, Michael, 3617
Medich, Martha, 8155
Medina, Marcela C., 1088
Medina, Velma, 9021
Medina-Mora, Manuel, 5755
Medinol, 3841
Medleycott, Alice E., 8343
Medleycott, Mary E., 8343
Medlin, Galen, 939
Medlin, John G., Jr., 7359
Medline Industries, Inc., 2889
Medlock Trust, Mary L., 2664
Medplans 2000, Inc., 3361
Medrud, Mariagnes, 1358
Medsker, Malinda, 3250
Medtronic Danvers, 3841
Medtronic Vascular, Inc., 3841
Medtronic, Inc., 2054, 4622
Medure, Pat, 4574
Medusa Corp., 8821
Meduski, Richard P., 1644
Medvedenko, Stanislav, 882
Medvin, Harvey N., 2598
Medwid, Robert P., 3780
Meehan, Avice A., 3654
Meehan, Daniel E., 9868
Meehan, Dorothy, 1151
Meehan, Eileen, 9868
Meehan, Emily Souvaine, 6523
Meehan, F. Thomas, 1457
Meehan, Miriam F., 6523
Meehan, Peter J., 7496
Meehan, Richard, 2645
Meehan, Terence S., 6523
Meehan, William M., 6523
Meehan-Felknor, Theresa, 9868
Meek, Sue Ann, 9460
Meeker, Carol, 4694
Meeker, Cindy, 7886
Meeker, Robert D.C., Jr., 6508
Meeks, Elsie, 4636
Meeks, Max, 7397
Meenan, Julie, 631
Meers, Elizabeth B., 7549
Meese, Cheryl, 4499
Meeus, Juliette, 6708
Megal, Rhody J., 9960
Megrue, John F., Jr., 6524
Megrue, Lizanne G., 6524
Mehall, J. Robert, 9166
Mehallis, Stephen G., 6482
Mehl Family Trust, George and Deborah,
    7746
Mehl, Bonnie, 7746
Mehl, David, 7746
Mehler, Philip, 1383
Mehta, Bhupat J., 9052
Mehta, Dinesh, 7470
Mehta, Isah B., 9052
Mehta, Jainesh, 9052
Mehta, Rahul, 9052

Mehta, Rahul B., 9052
Meiberger, Herbert, 294
Meider, Teri, 7581
Meien, Aileen, 3258
Meier, Anne E., 1889
Meier, Deborah, 359
Meier, Linda R., 264, 989
Meier, Steve, 997
Meier, Walter, 381
Meier, Walter C., 1889
Meier, Walter, Mrs., 381
Meijer, Frederik G.H., 4390
Meijer, Inc., 4390
Meijer, Lena, 4390
Meijer, Mark, 4326
Meiling, Dean, 1006, 5051
Meinders, Herman, 7960
Meinders, LaDonna, 7960
Meinders, Robert, 7960
Meiners, Diane, 3259
Meiners, Gerard, 4814
Meinhardt, Edward, 5402
Meinhardt, Evi, 5402
Meinig, Nancy E., 7961
Meinig, Peter C., 7961
Meinz, T.P., 9970
Meisel, Wayne, 5137
Meisels, Maurice, 5928
Meisler, Herbert A., 25
Meisner, Don "Skip", 3332
Meisner, Mary Jo, 3812
Meisner, Richard S., 5157
Meissner, Edwin B., Jr., 4783
Meissner, Paul F., 9829, 9900
Meissner, Rose, 3131
Meister, Mark W., 7579, 7725
Meister, Paul, 5099
Meister, Paul M., 5105
Mekras, George D., 2121
Mekrut, William A., 8537
Melanson, Haley Davis, 1964
Melarkey, Michael J., 5024
Melarkey, Mike, 5039
Melbostad, Paul H., 1069
Melby, Karen, 4349
Melby, Margie, 8881, 8950
Melby, Scott A., 4349
Melchick, Annelise, 5610
Melching, Rick, 9570
Melchner, Susan, 7056
Mele, Charles A., 5373
Mele, Patrick J., Jr., 3801
Melgary, Bruce, 8077, 8304, 8305
Melhus, Mark, 4643
Melillo, Samuel T., 5341
Melis, T.W., 973
Melkus Partners, Ltd., 8711
Melkus, Barbara L., 8711
Melkus, Kenneth J., 8711
Melkus, Lauren E., 8711
Mellam, Laural D., 883
Melle, Gary, 9191
Mellen, Edward J., 7747
Mellert, Donald R., 1164
Mellette, Kerry C., 9541
Melley, Maura L., 1627
Mellin, Dorothy, 2710
Mellon Bank Corp., 8345
Mellon Bank, N.A., 1964, 8071, 8094,
    8097, 8110, 8111, 8145, 8158,
    8166, 8173, 8175, 8185, 8188,
    8208, 8216, 8238, 8244, 8248,
    8253, 8309, 8310, 8313, 8337,
    8338, 8350, 8386, 8429, 8440,
    8461, 8468, 8492, 8498
Mellon Financial Corp., 7793, 8075,
    8345, 8504
Mellon Financial Group, 8378
Mellon, Armour N., 8346
Mellon, Constance B., 8344
Mellon, Margaret, 4804
Mellon, Paul, 6525
Mellon, Richard A., 8344, 8346
Mellon, Richard K., 8346

Meyer, A.C., Jr., 2895
Meyer, Adolph H., 4218
Meyer, Agnes E., 1834
Meyer, Alex A., 3290
Meyer, Alice Jane, 9057
Meyer, Alice K., 9145
Meyer, Anthony, 6544
Meyer, Arthur I., 2137
Meyer, August C.F., 2895
Meyer, Averil Payson, 7254
Meyer, Barbara, 2446
Meyer, Barbara C., 2446
Meyer, Barbara J., 7254
Meyer, Barry, 893
Meyer, Carla E., 4131
Meyer, Carroll, 7778
Meyer, Daniel, 2789, 2972
Meyer, Daniel, M.D., 8371
Meyer, David L., 4361
Meyer, Donald E., 3453
Meyer, Donald L., 5504
Meyer, Doris C., 5504
Meyer, Edward C., Genl., 1632
Meyer, Edward H., 6544
Meyer, Eugene, 1834
Meyer, Eva Chiles, 8005
Meyer, Fred G., 8042
Meyer, Harriet, 2789
Meyer, Henry L., III, 7548
Meyer, Ida M., 4218
Meyer, Jack R., 3812
Meyer, Jane, 9057
Meyer, Jane K., 7742
Meyer, Jerome, 6545
Meyer, John E., 52
Meyer, Karen, 4702
Meyer, Karen H., 2895
Meyer, Larry, 2097
Meyer, Laura L., 7370
Meyer, Margaret, 6544
Meyer, Mary C., 2446, 5724
Meyer, Michael G., 4649
Meyer, Michelle, 4534
Meyer, Nancy, 2789, 2972
Meyer, Paul, 1087
Meyer, Paul D., 2480
Meyer, Paul J., Sr., 9057
Meyer, Phillipe, 6546
Meyer, R., 8301
Meyer, Randall, 8960
Meyer, Reynold, 187
Meyer, Robert R., 52
Meyer, Ron, 933
Meyer, Roslyn, 6545
Meyer, Roslyn M., 6556
Meyer, Russell W., Jr., 3351
Meyer, Sandra, 6544
Meyer, Sheryl, 4315
Meyer, Sydelle F., 2137
Meyer, Thomas, 2972
Meyer, Vincent, 6546
Meyer, Virginia A.W., 1622
Meyer, Wendell, 4361
Meyer, Wendy, 893
Meyer, William, 7573
Meyer, William A., 2181
Meyerhoff Charitable Income Trust,
    3692
Meyerhoff Charitable Income Trust II,
    3692
Meyerhoff, Harvey M., 3691, 3692
Meyerhoff, Jane B., 3690
Meyerhoff, Joseph, 3692
Meyerhoff, Joseph, II, 3691
Meyerhoff, Joseph, Mrs., 3692
Meyerhoff, Neil A., 3690
Meyerhoff, Robert E., 3690
Meyers, Beverly, 3698
Meyers, David, 404
Meyers, David H., 933
Meyers, Evan, 3372
Meyers, Gail, 6164
Meyers, Geoffrey G., 7883
Meyers, Hannes, Jr., 4258

Meyers, Ishmael A., 9363
Meyers, James, 9294
Meyers, Lori L., 3108
Meyerson, Ivan D., 879
Meyerson, Marvin, 2964
Meyerson, Morton H., 9058
Meza, Carolyn W., 2943
MFA Inc., 4866
MFA Oil Co., 4866
Mi Zel, Larry A., 1427
Miami Corp., 2700
Miami Jewish Federation, The, 2093
Miani, Philip, 1949
Micallef, Joseph S., 4538, 4629, 4726
Michaan, Joseph, 2138
Michaan, Nevine, 5773
Michaan, Suzanne, 2138
Michael, Dacia D., 3151
Michael, Gary, 2562
Michael, Marcie, 3617
Michael, Mary Ann, 9723
Michael, Mary Lou, 3554
Michael, Ralph, 4704
Michaelis, Elias K., 6232
Michaelis, Mary F., 7956
Michaelis, Mary Frances, 7956
Michaels, Gilbert N., 408
Michaels, Howard, 7712
Michaels, Jack D., 3293
Michaels, JoAnn, 1255
Michaels, Laurie, 1338
Michaels, Ronald F., 4226
Michaels, William, 2252
Michalak, Steven R., 7430
Michalka, Rodney J., 9242
Michalski, Jo, 78
Michel, Betsy S., 5181, 5260
Michel, Robert T., 9752
Michel, Sally J., 3559
Michelotti, Carla R., 2645
Michels Corp., 9874
Michels, Kevin P., 9874
Michels, Patrick D., 9874
Michels, Ruth L., 9874
Michels, Steven R., 9874
Michels, Timothy J., 9874
Michelson, Ellen A., 895
Michelson, Gary Karlin, 896
Michelson, Gertrude G., 6876
Michelson, Jere G., 3546
Michelson, Joseph, 4135
Michelson, Michael W., 895
Michener, Elizabeth, 8177
Michigan, Alan, 6053
Michl, Gerry, 3127
Michler, John F., 9741
Michno, Rose, 2156
Michot, Michael J., 3468
Miciotto, Donna, 3512
Mick, Will, 2054
Mickel, Buck A., 8585
Mickel, Charles, 8585
Mickelson, Mark, 8631
Mickelton, Mike, 3587
Mickiewicz, Ellen, 7244
Microelectronics Advanced Research
    Corp., 7470
Microfibres, Inc., 8547
Micron Semiconductor Products, Inc.,
    2571
Micron Technology, Inc., 2571
Middaugh, Amy, 3199
Middendorf, Alice C., 3694
Middendorf, J. William, Jr., 3694
Middendorf, Patricia A., 1450
Middlebrook, Stephen B., 1564
Middlebrooks, Sidney E., 2358
Middleditch, Leigh B., Jr., 9478
Middlegate Insurance Agency, Ltd.,
    7106
Middlegate Securities, Ltd., 5740,
    5741, 7106
Middlesworth, Maxine, 7354
Middleton, Carol J., 7921

Middleton, Mary, 3281
Middleton, Payne, 7254
Middleton, Ralph "Sonny", 68
Middleton, Richard A., 359
Middleton, Scott, 9089
Midgley, C. Edward, Mrs., 7039
Midkiff, Robert R., 2532
Midkiff, Robin S., 2542
Midland Co., The, 7750
Midland Investment Co., 202
Midwest Dental Products Corp., 9865
Midyette, Thomas, 7445
Mielock, Douglas A., 4243
Miers, Gina, 27
Mifal Ezra Zichron Yehida, 5302
Mifflin, Robert B., 8654
Mignone, Roberto, 7139
Migord-Rivera, Lori, 9641
Miho, Mariko, 2545
Mijares, Bert, 9111
Mikaeloff, Herve, 5550
Mikell, JoAnn, 8845
Mikelonis, Joseph, 7793
Mikles, Donalyn, 766
Miklinski, James, 5958
Milacron Inc., 7751
Milam, Elizabeth Irby, 4750
Milanese, W., 5151
Milano, Bernard J., 5288
Milas, Lawrence W., 7009
Milbank, Albert G., 6529
Milbank, Jeremiah, 6263
Milbank, Jeremiah, III, 6263, 6547
Milbank, Jeremiah, Jr., 6263, 6547
Milbank, Katharine S., 6263
Milbank, Michelle, 6529
Milbank, Samuel L., 6529
Milbank, Thomas L., 6529
Milbourn, George B., 7688
Milbury, Cassandra M., 8344
Milburz, E. Van R., 8425
Milby, Charles D., Jr., 8938
Milby, Katharine M., 3437
Milder, Daniel C., 5158
Milder, Donald B., 5158
Milder, Terri L., 5158
Mildren, William, Sr., 7735
Mildren, William, Sr., Mrs., 7735
Miles Production, Co., Inc., 9060
Miles, Art, 9570
Miles, Arthur, 9548
Miles, Connie, 3141
Miles, David P., 4823
Miles, Edward, 1020
Miles, Ellison, 9060
Miles, Francie Gomez, 5496
Miles, J. Michael, 4610, 4715
Miles, Katherine B., 13
Miles, Lee L., 9313
Miles, Lydia, 1817
Miles, Richard, 670
Milewicz, Richard K., 5899
Miley, Stephen R., 8821
Milfs, Audrey L., 970
Milgard, Carol B., 9641
Milgard, Mark, 9641
Milgard-De Goede, Cari, 9641
Milias, Mary Ann, 1326
Military Car Sales, Inc., 6057
Miljanich, Ralph, 403
Milken Family Foundation, 938
Milken, D., 897
Milken, Ferne, 898
Milken, Gregory A., 898
Milken, J., 897
Milken, L., 897
Milken, Lori A., 898
Milken, Lowell, 898
Milken, Michael, 898
Milken, R., 897
Milken, S., 897
Milken, Sandra, 898
Milken-Noah, Joni, 898
Milkes, Joe W., 9286

Milkes, Marjorie, 9286
Millan, Jacqueline R., 6714
Millar, G. Don, 4856
Millar, Kenneth, 1247
Millar, Margaret, 1247
Millard, Adah K., 2897
Millard, Elizabeth, 5807
Millard, Katrina Gilbert, 1604, 6572
Millard, Michael B., 6823
Millard, Philip H., 4412
Millard, Robert B., 6548
Millbank, J.M., III, 6118
Millbrook Partners LLC, 7233
Miller and Smith, Inc., 3736
Miller Charitable Fund LLLP, 2141
Miller Charitable Lead Annuity Trust,
    Sydell L., 7752, 7753
Miller Charitable Trust, Jack, 2817,
    2899
Miller Clock Co., Howard, 4393
Miller Family Charitable Foundation,
    Audrey & Jack, 2817
Miller Family Charitable Fund, Audrey and
    Jack, 2899
Miller Foundation, I.L. and Bertha
    Gordon, 9061
Miller Irrevocable Trust, Dora, 2001
Miller Irrevocable Trust, Sadye, 2001
Miller, Abraham, 5566, 7754
Miller, Adrienne E., 7362
Miller, Alan B., 8354
Miller, Alice, 8333
Miller, Alice A., 8137
Miller, Allen B., 4394
Miller, Alon, 900
Miller, Amos, 8258
Miller, Andrew, 8821
Miller, Arnold M., 9061
Miller, Arnold M., Jr., 9061
Miller, Arthur H., 4198
Miller, Ashley, 9062
Miller, Barbara, 899
Miller, Barbara H., 2957
Miller, Barry L., 3719
Miller, Ben R., Jr., 3515
Miller, Bertha Gordon, 9061
Miller, Bette, 9286
Miller, Betty, 9164
Miller, Betty Lou, 7339
Miller, Bonnie K., 4326
Miller, Brenda, 4327
Miller, Burkett, 8734
Miller, C. Richard, Jr., 3598
Miller, Carey K., 9642
Miller, Carl E. "Eddie", III, 24
Miller, Carol, 9408
Miller, Catherine B., 3800
Miller, Catherine G., 3175
Miller, Charles D., 214, 2359
Miller, Christopher D., 457
Miller, Clara, 5761
Miller, Constance Marks, 6489
Miller, D. Byrd, III, 8568
Miller, D.J., 4654
Miller, D.L., 7879
Miller, Dane A., 3106
Miller, Dane A., Mrs., 3106
Miller, Daniel P., 9836
Miller, Danyel, 3108
Miller, Darryl, 3135
Miller, David J., 1364
Miller, David O., 7771
Miller, David S., 7397
Miller, Dawn E., 220
Miller, Dean, 1090
Miller, Dean M., 4752
Miller, Deborah, 1642
Miller, Dee, 8758
Miller, Diane, 6436
Miller, Diane Disney, 457
Miller, Diane Edgerton, 9379
Miller, Don, 5482
Miller, Doreen D., 5882
Miller, Doris, 4735

Miller, Douglas, 8355
Miller, E. Tyler, III, 1031
Miller, Ed, 3276
Miller, Edward J., 4254
Miller, Edward M., 9538
Miller, Edward S., 7105
Miller, Elisabeth, 9642
Miller, Elizabeth G., 3175
Miller, Ella Warren, 8323
Miller, Ellen K., 2112
Miller, Eric, 401, 8355
Miller, Ethan A., 9379
Miller, Eugene A., 4254, 4389
Miller, Forrest E., 8765
Miller, Frances Cameron, 8812
Miller, Frank, 7586
Miller, Frank R., 2680
Miller, Fred, 899
Miller, Fred D., 8051
Miller, George D., Jr., 4354
Miller, Gerald W., 7873
Miller, Gilbert B., 2324
Miller, Glen, 2810, 2952
Miller, Glenn, 3096
Miller, Goldie Wolf, 2817
Miller, Goldie Wolfe, 2899
Miller, Gordon, 9815
Miller, Gordon E, 309
Miller, Greg, 3199
Miller, Gregory N., 4708
Miller, Gregory S., 9335
Miller, H. Fred, 3143
Miller, Harvey R., 7225
Miller, Harvey S., 5581
Miller, Harvey S. Shipley, 6866
Miller, Harvey S.S., 8086
Miller, Helen, 3288, 4941
Miller, Herbert, 3126
Miller, Herman, 4039
Millam, Herman, Inc., 7694
Miller, Holly D., 1523
Miller, Howard, 9748
Miller, Howard J., 4393
Miller, Hugh Thomas, 3175
Miller, I. George, 7333
Miller, Ian W., 6550
Miller, Irene D., 6550
Miller, Irv, 7160
Miller, Jack, 2898
Miller, Jack H., 4393
Miller, Jack K., 7897
Miller, James C., 8417
Miller, James E., 1599, 8043
Miller, James F., 8045
Miller, James H., 7346, 8355
Miller, James O., 7839
Miller, Janet H., 9538
Miller, Janice McCoy, 871
Miller, Jeffrey, 2141
Miller, Jennifer, 7985
Miller, Jerold L., 9498
Miller, Jerome, 2372
Miller, Jessica, 5667
Miller, Jill S., 8354
Miller, Jim, 3160, 4534
Miller, Joann Schoenbaum, 2227
Miller, Joel, 2262
Miller, John, 1731, 4174
Millian, John A., Jr., 8588
Miller, John F., 505
Miller, John R., III, 8136
Miller, Joseph A., 5794
Miller, Joseph, Jr., Mr., 2579
Miller, Joseph, Jr., Mrs., 2579
Miller, Josephine, 8833
Miller, Judith R., 6550
Miller, Judy M., 5037
Miller, Julia A., 5431
Miller, Karen G., 9335
Miller, Karen Halverstadt, 2819
Miller, Kate, 1563
Miller, Kate W., 7806
Miller, Katharine P., 4408
Miller, Katharine S., 8323

Miller, Katherine H., 3049
Miller, Kathleen, 9702
Miller, Ken, 3387
Miller, Kenneth, 9401
Miller, Kenneth D., 7480
Miller, Kevin, 4057
Miller, Kim, 2101
Miller, Kimberley, 8353
Miller, Kristie, 145
Miller, L. James, 5732
Miller, Larry, 4327
Miller, Larry H., 9335
Miller, Laura Isabelle, 9771
Miller, Lawrence H., 9335
Miller, Lawrence J., 8298
Miller, Lawrence R., 8210
Miller, Lee, 9599
Miller, Leonard, 2141
Miller, Leslie A., 8356
Miller, Lila G., 8043
Miller, Linda, 4986, 5472
Miller, Lisa, 3549
Milne, Lorraine, 2795
Miller, Louise B., 4394
Miller, Lucy, 1669
Miller, Luther L., 7806
Milone, M.D., 4654
Miller, M.J., 4654
Miller, Marc D., 8354
Miller, Margaret I., 3175
Miller, Maria, 7754
Miller, Mark, 8353
Miller, Mark F., 6161, 6162
Miller, Mark McCormick, 145
Miller, Marlene, 884
Miller, Marlin, Jr., 8355, 8509
Miller, Martha Barnes, 6300
Miller, Mary Frances, 2890
Miller, Mary J., 3709
Miller, Maurice Lim, 346
Miller, Mavis S., 2177
Miller, Melanie E.R., 4515
Miller, Michael, 4690
Miller, Myron, 4039
Miller, Myron "Micky", 1445
Miller, Nellie E., 8352
Miller, Norman, 3122
Milton, Norman C., 9875
Miller, Norman F., 7434
Miller, Patricia A., 7867
Miller, Patricia H., 8179
Minar, Paul F., III, 8323
Miller, Paul F., Jr., 8323, 8377
Miller, Paulina, 9875
Miller, Peter, 8147, 8148
Miller, Philip D., 4393
Miller, Phillip Lowden, 2957
Miller, Phillip S., 8044
Miller, Polly C., 2324
Miller, R.M., 4492
Miller, R.N. "Bo", 4284
Miller, Randolph L., 8051
Miller, Randy W., 479
Miller, Regina, 8355
Miller, Rich, 2156
Miller, Rita L., 4355
Miller, Robert B., 4394
Miller, Robert B., Jr., 4394
Miller, Robert C., 2174, 6215
Miller, Robert J., 1582, 1610
Miller, Robert, Jr., 6638
Miller, Rodney, 5807
Miller, Roger L., 9335
Miller, Rosana, 900
Miller, Roy D., 867
Miller, Rozella, 7581
Miniaci, Ruth, 5566
Miller, Ruth C.H., 1866
Miller, S.D., 4654
Miller, S.L., 4654
Miller, Sally Cheney, 9049
Miller, Samuel H., 7634, 7754
Miller, Scott, 1338
Miller, Sharon, 2180

Miller, Sharon A., 2817, 2898, 2899
Miller, Sheila M., 9062
Miller, Shelley, 3253
Miller, Shelly, 4228
Miller, Stanley T., 5829
Miller, Stephen B., 7488
Miller, Steve, 3140, 3367
Miller, Steve J., 9875
Miller, Steven L., 8960, 9062
Miller, Steven L., Jr., 9062
Miller, Stuart, 2141
Miller, Stuart A., 2109, 2140
Miller, Susan, 2141
Miller, Susan L., 3062
Milligan, Suzanne S., 9061
Miller, T. Wainwright, Jr., 2177
Miller, Tammy Lee, 1731
Miller, Ted, 8043
Miller, Theodore W., 9875
Miller, Timothy S., 9475
Miller, Trina Dahl, 1959
Miller, Vance, 2573
Miller, Vicki, 9249
Miller, Virginia, 2101
Miller, Wade, 2360
Miller, Walter E.D., 457
Miller, Warren, 1996
Miller, Warren Pullman, 2957
Miller, Wayne J., Jr., 7339
Miller, Will, 2868
Miller, William I., 3136, 3166, 3174, 3175
Miller, William R., 6550, 7040
Miller, William T., 8937, 9025
Miller, Winlock W., 9642
Miller, Xenia S., 3175
Miller-Armbrister, Julane W., 5167
Miller-Rosenstein, Gladys, 5362
Millerick, Gail E., 1515
Millham, Alida, 5092
Millhiser, Mary McGue, 9470
Millhiser, Ross R., 9470
Millhiser, Ross R., Jr., 9470
Millhiser, Thomas McNally, 9470
Millhiser, Timothy McGue, 9470
Millhone, Jim, 3276
Millhouse, Barbara B., 7308
Milligan, Cynthia H., 4357
Milligan, Douglas, 3095
Milligan, James H., 7971
Milligan, Lois Darlene, 7971
Milligan, Michael J., 7971
Milligan, Patrick, 7584
Milligan, Suanne, 3206
Milliken and Co., 6552
Milliken, Christine T., 9371
Milliken, Gerrish H., 1747, 6552
Milliken, Gerrish H., III, 1763
Milliken, Gerrish H., Jr., 1732
Milliken, Gerrish H., Sr., 1747
Milliken, Justine V., 1747
Milliken, Nancy, 1747
Milliken, Peter, 1732
Milliken, Phoebe, 1732
Milliken, Roger, 1732, 1747, 6552
Milliken, Stephen G., 1763
Milliken, W.D., 628
Millikin, James, 2900
Milliman, Alison Wyckoff, 9692
Millipore Corp., 4040
Millner, H. Victor, Jr., 9401
Millner, Virginia Wright, 2447
Mills, Alice duPont, 1698
Mills, Andrew, 2889
Mills, Andrew J., 2901
Mills, Catherine L., 9363
Mills, Charlie, 2889
Mills, Chris, 4288
Mills, Frank F., 7479
Mills, Isobel P., 2390
Mills, J. Timothy, 1446
Mills, J.T., 9028
Mills, James, 2889
Mills, Janet M., 3556

Mills, Jon, 2889
Mills, Jonathan M., 2901
Mills, Kelly L., 3216
Mills, Lloyd, 4288
Mills, Melbourne, Jr., 3433
Mills, Phyllis J., 5712
Mills, Rick J., 3136
Mills, Robert A., 2028
Mills, Sophie, 1698
Mills, Suzanne B., 4243
Mills, Tony G., 2419
Mills, W. Richard, 999
Mills, William P., 3510
Millspaugh, Gordon A., Jr., 5440
Millsport, 7174
Millstein, Diane G., 6553
Millstein, Ira, 6553
Millstein, Ira M., 6553, 7225
Millstone, Colleen, 4867
Millstone, Goldie G., 4867
Millstone, I.E., 4867
Millstone, Robert, 4867
Milne, Douglas J., 2251
Milner, George M., 8581
Milner, John C., 1714
Milnor, George S., II, 2904
Milone, James P., 4128
Milstein Family Foundation, 6545, 6554, 6555, 7288
Milstein, Cheryl, 6732
Milstein, Constance, 5756
Milstein, Constance J., 7110
Milstein, Edward, 6556
Milstein, Edward L., 6554
Milstein, Howard, 6556
Milstein, Howard P., 6555
Milstein, Irma, 6545, 6554, 6555, 6556, 7288
Milstein, Joanna, 5756
Milstein, Paul, 6545, 6554, 6555, 6556, 7288
Milstein, Philip L., 6732, 7110
Milstein, Seymour, 5756, 7110
Milstein, Vivian, 5756, 7110
Milston, Martin J., 6786
Miltenberger, Carolyn Snyder, 8448
Miltimore, Irene Belk, 7314
Milton, John D., Jr., 2003
Milwaukee Golf Development Corp., 2692
Mimberg, Rainer H., 5132
Minar, Clyde T., 941, 1099
Minard, Sally, 2017
Minczewski, Sherian, 8980
Mindala, James, 7755
Mindala, James J., 7755
Mindala, Joanne N., 7755
Mindich, Bernard, 5960
Mindich, Eric M., 6558
Mindich, Stacey B., 6558
Mindnich, David, 5194
Mine Safety Appliances Co., 8357
Minehan, Cathy E., 5796
Minehan, John H., 7427
Mineman, Julie Owens, 2929
Miner, Josh, 4163
Miner, Joshua L., IV, 4164
Miner, Justine, 253
Miner, Mary M., 253
Miner, Nicola, 253
Miner, Nina, 6984
Miner, Paula, 3894
Miner, Phebe S., 4163, 4164
Mines, Raymond C., 2713
Mingst, Caryll S., 924
Mingst, Caryll Sprague, 1184
Miniaci, Albert, 1941
Minich, Sophie, 83
Miniotos, Kristin Susan Lawless, 3671
Mink, Earl G., 350
Minkoff, Irene, 5998
Minkoff, Jonathan, 5998
Minnesota Life Insurance Co., 4677

Minnesota Mining and Manufacturing Co., 4492
Minnesota Organization for Fetal Alcohol Syndrome, 4571
Minnich, Margaret W., 350
Minnick, Darlene, 7859
Minnick, Mary E., 2352
Minnicks, Edith, 5367
Minno, Alexander M., 8504
Minnowburn Liquidating Trust, 1406
Minow, Martha, 6789
Minow, Newton N., 6148
Minter, Michele, 5357
Minter-Dowd, Christine, 3684
Minton, Frank D., 9642
Mintz, Joshua J., 2868
Mintzer, Laura Becker, 271
Minyard, Lisbeth F., 8855
Mirabella, Richard J., 6218
Mirabello, Francis J., 8233
Miracle, Louise McMichael, 7426
Mirak Building Trust, 4041
Mirak, Artemis, 4041
Mirak, John, 4041
Mirak, Robert, 4041
Mirakhor, Abbas, 5530
Mirelman, Victor, 2922
Mirgon, Thomas, 3589
Mirhady, Mary Bauman, 7999
Mirkovitch, Michel, 778
Miro, Jeffrey H., 4455
Miron, Gerald T., 91
Mirota, Jeff, 1364
Mirsky, Burton M., 5825, 5827
Mirsky, Robert, 1911
Mirvis, Theodore N., 5272
Mischer, Mary A., 9063
Mischer, Paula, 9063
Mischer, Walter M., 9063
Mischer, Walter M., Jr., 9063
Mishan, Ahrin, 6186
Misner, J.W., 4356
Mississippi Band of Choctaw Indians, 1781
Mississippi Board of Nursing, 4757
Mississippi Development Authority, 4757
Mississippi Power Co., 4758
Mississippi State Dept. of Health, 4757
Missry Foundation, Herbert and Yvonne, 7106
Mister, Melvin A., 7117
Mistlin, Anthony, 902
Mistlin, Joan, 902
Mitau, Lee R., 4623, 4704
Mitcham, Carla, 9144
Mitchell, A.S., 53
Mitchell, A.S., Mrs., 53
Mitchell, Anna, 903
Mitchell, Arlene, Mrs., 25
Mitchell, Brian Gregory, 9064
Mitchell, Callie J., 7989
Mitchell, Carleton Grant, 9064
Mitchell, Carolyn, 7586
Mitchell, Chuck, 1945
Mitchell, Cynthia W., 9064
Mitchell, D.L., 4368
Mitchell, Daisy, 4632
Mitchell, David, 406
Mitchell, Debbie, 8381
Mitchell, Don, 7819
Mitchell, Don Q., 4737
Mitchell, Duncan, 388
Mitchell, Edward D., 903
Mitchell, Garfield, 9093
Mitchell, George K., 157
Mitchell, George P., 9064
Mitchell, George Scott, 9064
Mitchell, J. Daniel, 8100
Mitchell, James, 2577
Mitchell, James J., 3083
Mitchell, James J., III, 3083
Mitchell, Janice P., 2173
Mitchell, Jeffrey Todd, 9064

Mitchell, Joan, 6559
Mitchell, John A., 5780
Mitchell, John Kirk, 9064
Mitchell, John P., Rev., 5431
Mitchell, Jonathan E., 903
Mitchell, Joseph C., 5850, 6265, 6901
Mitchell, Joseph N., 903
Mitchell, Karen H., 8569
Mitchell, Kayla, 903
Mitchell, Lee Roy, 9065
Mitchell, Lesa, 4843
Mitchell, Linda Kay, 3083
Mitchell, Lois, 958
Mitchell, Lori Read, 794
Mitchell, Louis A., 2156
Mitchell, Lucy C., 4688
Mitchell, Mack C., Jr., 3564
Mitchell, Margaret, 4625
Mitchell, Mark Douglas, 9064
Mitchell, Mary S., 8031
Mitchell, Melissa, 234
Mitchell, Michael Kent, 9064
Mitchell, Mike, 3206
Mitchell, Miriam P., 8100
Mitchell, Orlan, 3325
Mitchell, Richard, 8147
Mitchell, Richard A., 7791
Mitchell, Steve, 4496
Mitchell, Sydney L., 8036
Mitchell, Tandy, 9065
Mitchell, Thomas E., 25
Mitchell, Thomas N., 5574
Mitchell, Wildey H., 4625
Mitchelson, Peter L., 4684
Mitchelson, William H., 4125
Mitchon, Ross, 8785
Mitgang, Herbert, 5883
Mithoefer, Peter P., 7697
Mithoff, Caroline, 9066
Mithoff, Michael, 9066
Mithoff, Richard Warren, 9066
Mithoff, Richard Warren, Jr., 9066
Mithoff, Virginia, 9066
Mithun Enterprises, Inc., 4626
Mithun Trust, Doris, 4626
Mithun, Doris B., 4626
Mithun, John C., 4626
Mithun, Lewis M., 4626
Mithun, Raymond O., Jr., 4626
Mithun, Robert O., Sr., 4626
Mitralign, 3841
Mitsubishi Corp., 6560
Mitsubishi Electric Corp., 9476
Mitsubishi International Corp., 6560
Mitsui & Co. (U.S.A.), Inc., 6561
Mitsui, Mary Elizabeth, 8350
Mittack, Ollie, 8842
Mitte, Joann Cole, 9067
Mitte, M. Scott, 9067
Mitte, Roy F., 9067
Mittendorf, George, 3085
Mittermeier, Russell, 6495
Mittra, Sid, 4256
Mituen, Scott, 2050
Mitus, Steve, 4026
Mitzel, David P., 7770
Mitzelfeld, Pamela, 4256
Mix, Jeannette C., 2448
Mix, Kendall A., 4505
Mixer, John L., Dr., 4252
Mixner, A.R., 4500
Mixner, David, 8020
Mixon, A. Malachi, III, 7757
Mixon, Barbara W., 7757
Mixtacki, Steve, 9797
Mize, Ann, 3379
Mize, David C., 3379
Mize, Gary, 8912
Mize, John, 3387
Mizel, Carol, 1427
Mizel, Larry A., 1413, 1427
Mizrahi, Lisya, 1182
Mizuho Corporate Bank (USA), 6562
Mizuho Securities USA Inc., 6562

Mnuchin Foundation, The, 9429
Mnuchin, Heather Crosby, 6564
Mnuchin, Robert E., 6534, 6564
Mnuchin, Steven T., 6564
Moberg, Glen, 9777
Moberg, John A. "Jack", 7735
Mobley, Ernestine L. Finch, 7366
Mobley, Margreta D., 4319
Moceri, Gregory, 4269
Moceri, Gregory C., 4269
Moceri, Margaret, 4269
Moceri, Margaret E., 4269
Mock, Kathy, 4521
Mock, Louis, 1948
Mockenhaupt, Connie, 8204
Mockus, Vytautas, 947
Modano, Michael T., 9068
Model Charitable Lead Trust, 6565
Model Foundation, Jane and Leo, 6565
Model, Alan L., 6468
Model, Alice H., 6468
Model, Allen, 6565
Model, Leo, 6565
Model, Pamela, 6565
Model, Paul, 6565
Model, Peter H., 6565
Moderow, Joseph R., 3585
Modetz, John, 4256
Modglin, Donald L., 904
Modglin, Grace M., 904
Modglin, Steven, 904
Modine Manufacturing Co., 9878
Modisette, Dorothy, 8856
Modjeski, Maggie, 4729
Modlin, Mark A., 3433
Modrall, Jim, 4327
Modugno, Patrick J., 5037
Modugno, Thomas A., Rev. Msgr., 6513
Modzelewski, Kate, 3259
Modzelewski, Stephen, 9477
Moe, Palmer, 9002
Moe, Richard, 5970
Moe, Thomas O., 4530
Moeckel, Bruce, 5087
Moellenbrock, George, Jr., 8136
Moeller, Joseph W., 2449
Moeller, Mary F., 2449
Moenius, Chandler, 3400
Moffat, Abby Spencer, 3608
Moffat, William, 8003
Moffatt, Joyce A., 2919
Moffett, Gary E., 7831
Moffett, George M., 2297
Moffett, George M., II, 2297
Moffitt, Allen W., 368
Moffitt, F. Brower, 1491
Moffitt, George W., Jr., 8087
Moffitt, Larry, 1860
Mogan, Karen M., 4759
Moger, Stanley M., 1505
Mogharebi, Hamed, 905
Mogharebi, Kerry, 905
Mogi, Yuzaburo, 9836
Mogy, Joel, 2084
Moh, Celia, 906
Moh, Michael, 906
Mohamed, Aneezal, 7567
Mohammed, Ruksana, 200
Mohan, Pat, 2678
Mohl, Jarl, 907
Mohler, Lowell, 2863
Mohn, Jarl, 907, 7848
Mohn, Pamela, 907
Mohr, Dean C., 3324
Mohr, James L., 9971
Mohr, Kathryn, 4376
Mohr, Michael, 952
Mohr, Rita D., 3107
Mohr, Robert H., 1948
Mohraz, Judy Jolley, 130
Mohre, J. Craig, 7775
Mohrgeld, Cherie, 533
Moini, Ingrid A., 9528
Moirao, Dave, 468

Moise, Beth, 5466
Molchan, Janet, 2085
Moldow, Susan Jane, 327
Mole, Sally Dodge, 5867
Molella, Salvador, 5710
Moley, Elizabeth, 908
Moley, Richard, 908
Molina, Mario J., 2868
Molinaro, Samuel L., Jr., 5609
Molinaro, Vincent, 5110
Moline, Kenneth A., 1228
Molinello Revocable Trust, John, 4395
Molinello Revocable Trust, Richard, 4395
Moll, Curtis E., 7578, 7692
Moll, Darrell, 7692
Moll, Jon H., 3104
Moll, Robin Wright, 9708
Moll, Theodore S., 7692
Mollenberg, Trudy A., 7248
Moller, Dorothy D., 122
Moller, Joseph A., 122
Molnar, Attila, 8096
Molnar, Bruce J., 757
Moloney, Jaqueline F., 4014
Moloney, Margaret, 1760
Moloney, Patrick, 1760
Molpus, Dick, 4737
Molstad, Coleith, 9146
Moltz, James E., 5760, 6825
Molumby, Lawrence E., 1849
Molyneux, Cynthia M., 3481
Moman, Anne, 27
Momjian, Albert, 1003
Monaco Partners, LP, 5027
Monagan, Michael, 3144
Monaghan, John R., 4257
Monaghan, Thomas S., 4225
Monahan, Michael J., 4557
Monahan, Michael T., 4254
Monardo, Gregory, 533
Monardo, Gregory G., 892
Monastiere, Pamela, 4229
Monbruk Abstract Co., 5771
Moncrief, C.B., 9069
Moncrief, Elizabeth B., 9069
Moncrief, Kit Tennison, 8798
Moncrief, R.W., 9069
Moncrief, W.A., 9069
Moncrief, W.A., Jr., 9069
Mondale, Walter F., 4705
Monder, Steven, 7913
Mondowney, Jo Anne G., 4255
Monell, Ambrose K., 6566, 7196
Monetti, Catherine R., 8577
Money, Peter, 4711
Monez, Jared, 1255
Monfort, Charlie, 1429
Monfort, Dick, 1429
Monfort, Kenneth, 1428
Monfort, Kenneth W., 1429
Monfort, Myra, 1428, 1429
Monheimer, Marc H., 321
Monk, Albert, 2156
Monk, Ellis E., 3269
Monkarsh, Jerry, 909
Monkarsh, Joy, 909
Monkhouse, Christopher, 8536
Monnier, Kenneth, 7584
Monroe Bank & Trust, 4362
Monroe, Ann F., 5785
Monroe, J. Edgar, 3501
Monroe, Joseph P., 3501
Monroe, Rachel Garbow, 3759
Monroe, Ray, 8690
Monroe, Robert, 4229
Monroe, Robert J., 3501
Monsanto Co., 4868
Monse, Michelle D., 8995
Monsma, Durham J., 1537
Monson, Peggy O., 3116
Monsted, Charles N., III, 3475
Monsted, Charles, III, 3483
Montagu, Jean, 3775

Montagu, Kyra, 3775
Montagu, Sasha, 3775
Montague, Carlton C., 3197
Montague, Kristina, 8660
Montague, Lasley Thomas, 8703
Montalbano, Richard M., Sr., 3066
Montan, Christopher D., 722
Montana Dakota Utilities Co., 7517
Montana Rail Link, Inc., 4941
Montana Resources, Inc., 4941
Monte, Constance, 7205
Montebello Trust, 6769
Monteca, Dawn, 2151
Monteiro-Tribble, Velma, 8075
Monteith, Ray, 3185
Monteleone, David G., 3502
Monteleone, Joseph A., 9076
Monteleone, William A., Jr., 3502
Monterey Fund, The, 7123
Montero, Hilda C., 1930
Montez, Steve, 2677
Montgomery Trust A, Rose C., 8600
Montgomery, Ann M., 8796
Montgomery, Bruce, 8395
Montgomery, C.E., 5335
Montgomery, Christine, 2704
Montgomery, Edward E., 7593, 7758
Montgomery, Frances B., 7758
Montgomery, Geraldine, 3415
Montgomery, Harle G., 2903
Montgomery, John N.R., 8796
Montgomery, Joseph S., 7758
Montgomery, Joseph W., 9393
Montgomery, Kenneth F., 4398
Montgomery, Linda, 4737
Montgomery, Paul, 9794
Montgomery, Philip O'Bryan, III, 8839
Montgomery, Philip, Jr., 9096
Montgomery, Scott, 7758
Montgomery, Thatcher O., 8724
Montgomery, Virginia, 6695, 7273
Montgomery, Walter S., 8600
Montgomery, Walter S., Jr., 8565, 8600
Montgomery-Talley, La June, 4357
Montle, Jeff, 4358
Montoya, Nancy T., 4743
Montoya, Ronald E., 1445
Montrone, Angelo, 5099
Montrone, Jerome, 5099
Montrone, Paul M., 5099, 5105
Montrone, Sandra G., 5099
Montross, Christopher A., 1479
Moo-Battue, Inc., 9894
Moody's Corp., 6512
Moody's Investors Service, Inc., 6569
Moody, Amy Willis, 2839
Moody, Frank M., Sr., 54
Moody, Gloria N., 54
Moody, Kevin, 3468
Moody, Libbie Shearn, 9070
Moody, Nancy B., 9407
Moody, Natalie P., 6032
Moody, Rebecca Ann, 159
Moody, Robert L., 9092
Moody, Robert L., Sr., 9070
Moody, Ross R., 9070
Moody, William Lewis, Jr., 9070
Moody, Yvonne R., 9231
Moody-Dahlberg, Frances A., 9070
Moog, Donna L., 4918
Moog, Dorothy, 4918
Moog, James R., 4918
Moog, Mary, 4918
Moog, Thomas H., 4918
Moon, Frederick F., III, 5618, 7103
Moon, Holly, 4315
Moon, Ja, 561
Moon, Lawrence E., 4255
Moon, Meg, 3595
Moone, Robert H., 7650
Mooney and Moses of Ohio, Inc., 7618
Mooney, Beth, 8636
Mooney, Dee M.K., 2563
Mooney, Gregory, 2676

Mooney, Maureen, 5304
Mooney, Michael E., 3907
Mooney, Tracy Hagen, 9422
Moor, M. Eugene, Jr., 18
Moor, Walter, 3696
Moore Capital Mgmt., LLC, 6570
Moore, Albert, 6039
Moore, Andre, 7979
Moore, Ann S., 7209
Moore, Anne, 6613
Moore, Ardon E., 8776
Moore, Betty I., 912, 913
Moore, Bill, 3403
Moore, Billy S., 7909
Moore, Blanche Davis, 9071
Moore, Bob, 9151
Moore, Bruce A., 3599
Moore, Bruce, Jr., 8690
Moore, C.R., 1036
Moore, Calvert Sanders, 6242
Moore, Carla, Hon., 7526
Moore, Carolyn, 3730
Moore, Catherine B., 9539
Moore, Catherine Bryson, 1918
Moore, Charles L., 9218
Moore, Cheryl Jerome, 9286
Moore, Christopher, 6423
Moore, Claude, 9478
Moore, Conrad L., 8038
Moore, D.C., 9531
Moore, David E., 6571
Moore, David E., Sr., 6571
Moore, David W., 6563
Moore, Diana MacDonald, 9025
Moore, Douglas, 6573
Moore, E. Kevin, 5387
Moore, Edward, 4358
Moore, Elaine, 55
Moore, Ernestine L., 520
Moore, Frank M., 3207
Moore, Franklin H., 4257
Moore, Frederick S., 4257
Moore, G. Michael, 9525
Moore, George W., 8472
Moore, Gerald W., 2018
Moore, Gordon E., 912, 913
Moore, Grace Danley, 8358
Moore, Hannah, 3965
Moore, Harry C., Jr., 9757
Moore, Harry S., 9723
Moore, Harvin C., 9128
Moore, Irene, 7533
Moore, Jack, 8926
Moore, Jackson W., 70
Moore, Jacqueline G., 2773
Moore, James, 3110
Moore, James C., 55
Moore, James D., 3404
Moore, James H., 2458
Moore, James L., 4733
Moore, James W., 2018
Moore, Janet Wilson, 4209
Moore, Jaqueline Morrison, 8781
Moore, John, 3038
Moore, John A., 7345
Moore, John E., 3351
Moore, John H., 4291
Moore, Jonathan B., 2259
Moore, Judy A., 2478
Moore, Katherine C., 6571
Moore, Kathleen Beecher, 6540
Moore, Kathy, 8747
Moore, Kenneth G., 912, 913
Moore, Kevin S., 5762, 5952
Moore, Kristen L., 912, 913
Moore, Lauren, 9690
Moore, Leslie, 8747
Moore, Linda, 8049
Moore, Lisa, 6476
Moore, Lois Merriweather, 854
Moore, Malcolm, 9642
Moore, Malcolm A., 6705
Moore, Margaret D., 6714
Moore, Martha G., 2142

Moore, Martin J., 3207
Moore, Mary J.P., 6563
Moore, Mary N., 8655
Moore, Michael, 3965
Moore, Michael W., 9205
Moore, Nancy Powell, 9128
Moore, Nicholas J., 6563
Moore, P. William, Jr., 9521
Moore, Patrick C., 4743
Moore, Patrick, Mr., 4906
Moore, Randolph, 2538
Moore, Randolph G., 2537
Moore, Renee A., 359
Moore, Richard L., 7504
Moore, Rob, 2922
Moore, Robert B., 3038
Moore, Rosemary, 3044
Moore, Sandra C., 7189
Moore, Sanford E., 5325
Moore, Sara Giles, 2451, 2452
Moore, Starr, 2451, 2452
Moore, Stephen, 2994
Moore, Stephen A., 3955
Moore, Stephen C., 2181
Moore, Stephen O., 4747
Moore, Steve, 1944
Moore, Steven E., 912, 913, 7965
Moore, Steven G. W., 9644
Moore, Susan J., 3207
Moore, T.R., 2111
Moore, Taylor Frost, 5476
Moore, Terence F., 4287
Moore, Theresa Jean Harris, 3424
Moore, Thomas, 9003
Moore, Thomas A., 6574
Moore, Thurston R., 9493
Moore, Virginia L., 2657
Moore, Virginia Reid, 1036
Moore, W. Theodore, 8655
Moore, W.R., 1036
Moore, Walter, 562
Moore, Walter M., IV, 9458
Moore, Wenda Weekes, 4357
Moore, William S., 7714
Moore-Morris, Rocharda, 3118
Moorehead, Jim, 402
Moorehead, Myron E., 3503
Moores, Harry C., 7759
Moorhead, Douglas P., 8253
Moorhead, Rod, 1757
Moorhead, Tracy, 7514
Moorman, Bette D., 4546
Moorman, Carol E., 2882
Moose Mountain Trust, 4062
Moose, Sandra O., 7003
Moosman, George L., 9302
Moot, John R., 7248
Moot, Richard E., 7248
Moot, Welles V., 7248
Moot, Welles V., Jr., 7248
Morain, Tom, 3333
Morales, Christian, 8022
Morales, David, 3185
Morales, Estella, Sr., 639
Morales, Hugo, 346, 1065, 1088
Moran, Asha Morgan, 4534, 7760
Moran, Audrey McKibbin, 1983
Moran, Beverly S. "Cheri", 9521
Moran, Colleen, 3123
Moran, Elizabeth R., 8141
Moran, James M., 2143
Moran, Janet, 4593
Moran, Janice M., 2143
Moran, John R., 1392
Moran, Karen, 3554
Moran, Marty, 7760
Moran, Melvin, 7931
Moran, Thomas, 3078
Moran, Tim, 3071
Moran, W.T., Mrs., 9072
Morasch, Linda F., 914
Moravitz, Edward, 3124
Morby, Carolyn R., 4321
Morcom, Brad A., 2144

Morcom, Eugenia M., 2144
Morcom, Russell, 2144
Morcom, Todd R., 2144
Morcom, W. Russell, 2144
Mordecai, Janet, 6575
Mordell, Jayne S., 284
Mordo, Barbara, 828
Mordo, Jean, 828
More, Peter K., 550
More, Robert, 8202
Morean, Kelly D., 1985
Morean, William D., 1985
Moreau, D. William, Jr., 3116
Morehead, Ellen, 1289
Morehead, John Motley, III, 7430
Morehead, Rhonda, 1359
Morehead, Richard H., 2579
Morehouse, Bob, 1358
Morehouse, C. Schuyler, 7007
Morehouse, Elizabeth S., 7007
Morehouse, Gordon C., 2359
Moreland, Darell, 4325
Moreland, Jeffrey, 2644
Moreland, Larry, 6092
Morella, Constance A., Hon., 1780
Morelli, Rita, 4395
Morelli, William P., 8694
Morello, Maurizio J., 6566, 7196
Morelock, Gregg, 3160
Morency, Jeanne L., 8035
Morency, Michael, 8035
Moreno, Albert F., 1065
Moreno, Arturo, 123
Moreno, Carole, 123
Moreno, Tirso, 2446
Moret, H.J., 4563
Moreton, Frederick A., Jr., 9309
Moreton, Mike, 9309
Moretta, Daniel N., 7536
Moretti, Frank, 5194
Moretti, Richard, 627
Moretti, Wayne, 2655
Moretz, R. Dale, 4347
Morey, Krista, 4397
Morey, Lon, 4397
Morey, Norval, 4397
Morey, Terra, 4397
Morf, Darrel A., 3290
Morff, Robert, 1954
Morford, Bill, 4253
Morgan Charitable Lead Annuity Trust,
   Frank, 3377
Morgan Charitable Lead Unitrust, Frank,
   3377
Morgan Co. of Laurel Hill, Inc., The, 7431
Morgan Farms, Inc., 7431
Morgan Guaranty Trust Co. of New York,
   6780
Morgan Mills, Inc., 7431
Morgan Stanley, 6577
Morgan Stanley & Co. Inc., 6577
Morgan Stanley Dean Witter & Co., 6577
Morgan Stanley Group Inc., 6577
Morgan Stanley, Dean Witter, Discover &
   Co., 6577
Morgan Trust, Frank, 3377
Morgan Trust, Jacqueline Spencer, 5467
Morgan Trust, Russell Guy and Ruth
   Louise, 661
Morgan, Amy L., 4490
Morgan, Anne Hodges, 4843, 7952
Morgan, Bartow, Jr., 2356
Morgan, Bill, 9654
Morgan, Burton D., 7761, 7762
Morgan, Bushe, 9224
Morgan, Carol Varga, 9559
Morgan, Catherine A., 9074
Morgan, Charles A., Jr., 7607
Morgan, Charles O., 1932
Morgan, Charles P., 3208
Morgan, Christine R., 9074
Morgan, Denny, 2156
Morgan, Dorothy, 1517
Morgan, Doug, 1949

Morgan, Edwin, 7431
Morgan, Edwin E., 4759
Morgan, Elise, 7431
Morgan, Elizabeth E., 7431
Morgan, Frank, 3377
Morgan, G.E., 4759
Morgan, Gia, 3463
Morgan, Gina A., 9056
Morgan, Glen W., 9073
Morgan, Glenn R., 2794
Morgan, Hugh, 4221
Morgan, Jack C., 9514
Morgan, James C., 226, 915
Morgan, James F., 7397
Morgan, James L., Jr., 7431
Morgan, James S., Jr., 7431
Morgan, Jess S., 722
Morgan, Jim, 7397
Morgan, Judy B., 1870, 1961, 1962
Morgan, Judy L., 914
Morgan, K. Barry, 7432
Morgan, Kile, Jr., 914
Morgan, Lee M., 7760
Morgan, LeRoy, 4650
Morgan, Lillian A., 7466
Morgan, Margaret Clark, 7762
Morgan, Marian, 3960
Morgan, Marietta McNeill, 9479
Morgan, Marilyn J., 3377
Morgan, Mark A., 3377
Morgan, Matthew, 7760
Morgan, Melvin, 2240
Morgan, Michael, 1403, 3374
Morgan, Michael B., 3377
Morgan, Michael C., 8960, 9074
Morgan, Pat, 9280
Morgan, Paul F., 2532
Morgan, Pauline, 3245
Morgan, Rebecca, 7776
Morgan, Rebecca Q., 915
Morgan, Rick, 9723
Morgan, Ronnie, 8747
Morgan, Roxanna L., 3208
Morgan, Ruby C., 4759
Morgan, Samuel T., Jr., 9479
Morgan, Sara, 9654
Morgan, Sara S., 9074
Morgan, Sarah, 3446
Morgan, Susan, 7882
Morgan, Susan E., 7883
Morgan, Suzanne, 7762
Morgan, Thomas S., 3377
Morgan, Todd D., 3377
Morgan, Victoria A., 7760
Morgan, William, 4255
Morgan, William V., 9074
Morgan, Yvonne, 8202
Morgens West Charitable Lead Annuity
    Trust, 2453
Morgens, E.H., 2453
Morgens, Edwin H., 7259
Morgens, Howard J., 7259
Morgens, J.H., 2453
Morgens, Lauren, 7259
Morgens, Linda M., 7259
Morgens, S.F., 2453
Morgenstern, Frank N., 916
Morgenstern, Morris, 916
Morgenthau, Jenny, 5840
Morgin, Barb, 3177
Morgridge, John D., 1240
Morgridge, John P., 388, 1240
Morgridge, Tashia F., 1240
Mori, Yasuhiro, 4982
Moriarty, Brunilda, 5247
Moriguchi-Matsuno, Tomoko, 9563
Morimoto, Gary S., 2544
Morimoto, Tokiwa, 7120
Morino Institute, 5905
Morita, Joe Hideo, 1465
Mork, John F., 1372
Mork, Julie M., 1372
Morley, John C., 7763
Morley, Michael P., 6823

Morley, Sally S., 7763
Morning Star Family Limited Partnership,
    The, 9075
Morning, John, 4399, 6825
Moroney, James M., Jr., 8787
Morong, Caroline W., 1761
Morooka, Reiji, 7096
Morrell, Michael, 5439
Morretti, Frank, III, 5194
Morrice, Susan, 1406
Morrill, Amy, 7910
Morrill, Christopher, 1563
Morrill, Kay, 2904
Morrill, Richard L., 7126
Morrin, Patrick J., 439
Morris Agency, William, Inc., 6380
Morris Bell, Ida, 2145
Morris Co., Allen, The, 2145
Morris Communications Co., LLC, 2454
Morris Communications Corp., 2454
Morris Cos. Inc., Philip, 5545, 6459
Morris Family Business, 2145
Morris Investments, 2145
Morris, Arthur M., 3065
Morris, Belinda, 2455
Morris, Ben T., 9167
Morris, Bette M., 3378
Morris, Calvin S., Rev., 3069
Morris, Carl W., 917
Morris, Carloss, Jr., 9100
Morris, Charles M., 8359
Morris, Chester H., 2153
Morris, Christopher, 605
Morris, Diane Y., 1869, 2145
Morris, Donna T., 4450
Morris, E.A., 7432
Morris, E.A., Mrs., 7432
Morris, Eleanor W., 8160
Morris, Gabriella, 3585
Morris, Gabriella E., 5360
Morris, Gary L., 3250
Morris, Gary V., 8935
Morris, Glen, 6165
Morris, Granville R., 1517
Morris, I. Wistar, III, 8160
Morris, Ida Akers, 2145
Morris, J.R., 7933
Morris, Jack B., 9076
Morris, James F., 3599
Morris, James T., 3220
Morris, Jason Z., 3871
Morris, Johanna K. Simon, 6987
Morris, John R., 6972
Morris, Johnny L., 4869
Morris, Joseph W., 7974
Morris, Katherine Belk, 7315
Morris, Kelli R., 9464
Morris, Kenneth M., 5062
Morris, Kenneth R., 917
Morris, Lee West, 8742
Morris, Leland M., 6578
Morris, Linda A., 917
Morris, Linda C., 9076
Morris, Louise F., 2993
Morris, Lydia P., 8160
Morris, Lynette J., 10000
Morris, Margaret T., 124
Morris, Marilyn C., 3871
Morris, Mark L., Jr., 3378
Morris, Martha, 8160
Morris, Martha H., 8160
Morris, Max K., Dr., 1964
Morris, Melissa H., 8160
Morris, Michael, 2441, 2455
Morris, Michael G., 1614
Morris, Norman E., 6578
Morris, Patrick J., Hon., 405
Morris, Paul, 8923
Morris, Paul T., 4753
Morris, R. Larry, 2110
Morris, Robert E., 6578
Morris, Robert W., 8583
Morris, Ronald D., Jr., 2505
Morris, Rosemary, 2927

Morris, Sally, 3230
Morris, Scott J., 9884
Morris, Stacey B., 330
Morris, Stephen A., 3544
Morris, Stewart, Jr., 9100
Morris, Stewart, Sr., 9100
Morris, Susan, 6580
Morris, Thomas Q., 5674, 5762
Morris, Virginia H., 4590
Morris, W. Allen, 1869, 2145
Morris, William, 6580
Morris, William E., 2573
Morris, William P., 1377
Morris, William S., III, 2357
Morris, William S., IV, 2357, 2454
Morris, William T., 6579, 8647
Morris-Tyndall, Lucille, 1221
Morrisette, Karl S., 9499
Morrish, Brenda, 2050
Morrison Family, Harold M. & Adeline,
    3021
Morrison Knudsen Corp., 2578
Morrison, Al, III, 8300
Morrison, Alan, 9522
Morrison, Alan B., 1779
Morrison, Anne S., 1779
Morrison, Betty D., 67
Morrison, Branden, 8653
Morrison, Christina, 4930
Morrison, David, 9845
Morrison, Diane, 6707
Morrison, Douglas W., 9301, 9989
Morrison, Edward W., 9731
Morrison, G. Lowe, 1978
Morrison, Harry W., 2572
Morrison, Howard J., Jr., 2480
Morrison, Ian, 347
Morrison, J. Holmes, 9710, 9725
Morrison, Jack R., 8974
Morrison, James K., 836
Morrison, Jerri L., 5138
Morrison, John M., 2146
Morrison, John M., Jr., 2146
Morrison, Julia M., 4280
Morrison, Julie, 2146
Morrison, June, 125
Morrison, Kenneth, 4998
Morrison, Lucian L., 9179
Morrison, Mary Sue, 2146
Morrison, Michael A., 134
Morrison, N. Jane, 4964
Morrison, Nathaniel A., 709
Morrison, Ralph, 2463
Morrison, Rebecca, 1779
Morrison, Richard, 409
Morrison, Richard N., 125
Morrison, Robert S., 7764
Morrison, Susan M., 2146
Morrison, Velma V., 2572
Morrisroe, Sylvia, 3245
Morrissey, Colleen Shea, 1142
Morrissey, Francis X., 6708
Morrissey, John C., 685
Morrissey, Karen, 3823
Morrissey, Mike, 5047
Morrissey, Robert J., 3814, 4021, 4167
Morrow, Allan, 6581
Morrow, Christopher, 3189
Morrow, D. Stephen, 8661
Morrow, Dillard, 7486
Morrow, Joseph, 3129
Morrow, Peter C., 1727, 1762
Morrow, Terry, 9003
Morsani, Carol D., 2147
Morsani, Frank L., 2147
Morse, Alan R., Jr., 4095
Morse, Carole, 8051
Morse, Claire W., 4044
Morse, David J., 5265
Morse, Dorothea, 1743
Morse, Douglas A., 6582
Morse, Enid W., 6582
Morse, Eric, 9365
Morse, Eric Robert, 4095

Morse, Herbert E., 3812
Morse, John, Jr., 4095
Morse, Katherine S., 6583
Morse, Lester S., Jr., 6582
Morse, Lindsey A., 6583
Morse, Mark, 8534
Morse, Mary F., 5783
Morse, Peter C., 6263
Morse, Phillip H., 6583
Morse, Richard P., 4044
Morse, Ruth, 4044
Morse, Sarah D., 8530
Morse, Shelley H., 6583
Morse, Stephan A., 5148
Morse, Susan, 5040
Morse, Susan K., 6583
Morse, Suzanne E., 9414
Morse, Timothy, 4095
Morss, Everett, 4123
Mortensen, William, 1605
Mortenson, Trice, 1605
Mortimer, David H., 6147
Mortimer, Kathleen H., 6147
Mortin, Malinda J., 2423
Morton, Brian T., 918
Morton, Don E., 8686
Morton, Dorothea L., 3097
Morton, Helen K., 918
Morton, James T., 8611
Morton, Jeff, 9132
Morton, Jim, 939
Morton, John, 603
Morton, Margaret H., 3904
Morton, Paul F., 918
Morton, Peter, 919
Morton, S. Sidney, 941
Morton, Steve, 9776
Morton, Steven D., 9363
Morton, Teresa, 9699
Morton, Thomas A., 918
Morvant, Camille A., III, 3496
Mosbacher Jr. Charitable Annuity Trust,
    Emil, The, 1098
Mosbacher, Barbara, 9077
Mosbacher, Diane, 9077
Mosbacher, Emil, 9077
Mosbacher, Emil, Jr., 1098, 9077
Mosbacher, Gertrude, 9077
Mosbacher, Kathryn, 9077
Mosbacher, Patricia R., 1098
Mosbacher, R. Bruce, 1098
Mosbacher, Robert A., 9077
Mosbacher, Robert A., Jr., 9077
Mosbo, E. Paul, 8878
Moscovitz, Bernard C., 8584
Moseley, Alexander, 520
Moseley, Carlos, 5826
Moseley, Carlos D., 6901
Moseley, Cassandra, 520
Moseley, David, 520
Moseley, Don, 7567
Moseley, Francis Loring, 520
Moseley, Joe L., 4902
Moseley, Kathleen C., 6628
Moseley, Louisa, 520
Moseley, Sarah Sockit, 520
Moser, Eyvonne, 9212
Moser, John R., 7660
Moser, Margaret, 8773
Moses, Ansley, 8660
Moses, Billy, 3467
Moses, Henry L., 6587
Moses, Janet, 6255
Moses, Jim, 9977
Moses, John P., 8112
Moses, Larry S., 7904
Moses, Lucy G., 6587
Moses, William, 9451
Moses, Yolanda T., 5970
Mosher, Margaret C., 920
Mosher, Paul, 979
Mosher, Samuel B., 920
Mosich, A.N., 644
Mosier, Lynn, 5056

Moskalski, E.A. "Buck", 1359
Moskowitz, Harvey W., 2321
Moskowitz, Henry, 6588
Moskowitz, Mark, 6588
Moskowitz, Rose, 6588
Mosler, Warren, 2281
Mosley, Charles, 5489
Mosley, Daniel L., 5904, 6633, 6679, 6728, 6987, 7220
Mosley, Glenn R., 8475
Mosley, I. Sigmund, Jr., 2417
Mosley, Ralph W., 8662
Mosner, Lawrence J., 4549
Moss Trust for Euluos Moss, Jack, 2579
Moss, Andree K., 3503
Moss, Ann Holbrook, 921
Moss, Arnold, 5510
Moss, Charlotte A., 5985
Moss, Diane, 6876
Moss, Florence M., 9078
Moss, Harry S., 9078
Moss, I. Barney, 8296
Moss, Jerome S., 921
Moss, Jody, 9633
Moss, Leann O., 3503
Moss, Mary, 8422
Moss, Nancy, 4271
Moss, Nicole, 6589
Moss, Otis, Jr., Rev., 7576
Moss, Robert, 6589, 6876
Moss, Rod, 9981
Moss, Stephen, 6589
Moss, Steven, 6589
Moss, Susan E., 3434
Mossavar-Rahmani, Bijan, 6718
Mossavar-Rahmani, Sharmin, 6718
Mossier, Kevin J., 4628
Mossman, Douglas, 4365
Mostue, A. Brian, 8003
Mostue, Emily C., 8003
Mosty, John, 9120
Motch, Patricia P., 9361
Mote, Doris, 2345
Mote, William R., 2148
Motes, Holly, 2570
Motherwell, Robert, 5847
Motley, George B., 4123
Motley, Herbert J., Jr., 4711
Motley, Teri M., 4711
Motorists Mutual Insurance Co., 7765
Motorola, Inc., 2906
Motsavage, Maria, 6203
Mott Trust, C.S. Harding, 4338
Mott, C.S. Harding, 4337
Mott, C.S. Harding, II, 4337
Mott, Charles Stewart, 4399
Mott, Hanno D., 6430
Mott, Kerry K., 750
Mott, Maryanne, 340, 1280, 4399
Mott, Maryanne T., 4400
Mott, Michael R., 8874
Mott, Milo I., 4338
Mott, Ruth R., 1836, 4400
Mott, Stewart R., 1836
Mottier, Bradley D., 2239
Mottola, Maria, 6615
Mottola, Michele, 939
Moulder, Bill, 9257
Moulder, Electra, 9257
Moulton, Franklin F., 1261
Mounger, Callie Brandon, 4768
Mounger, William M., II, 4768
Mount, Marguerite, 5357
Mount, Robert C., 3598
Mountain, Janet, 8863
Mountaineer Gas Co., 1372
Mountcastle, Katharine B., 7308, 7458
Mountcastle, Katherine R., 7308
Mountcastle, Kenneth F., III, 7308
Mountcastle, Laura L., 7308
Mountcastle, Mary, 7308, 7458
Mountcastle, Mary B., 7496
Mountjoy, Michael B., 3414, 3421
Mountsier, Silas R., III, 6630

Mourier Construction, John, Inc., 922
Mourier, John, III, 922
Mourier, Laura, 922
Moushey, Ann, 119
Moutray, Vicki, 5469
Movic, Mark, 3326
Mow, Shirley, 1587
Mowat, Donald W., 9691
Mowdy, Mike, 1947
Mower, Judith, 6026
Moxon, Kathleen, 691
Moyer, Charles I., 3366
Moyer, D. Scott, 7770
Moyer, Keith, 4691
Moyer, Robert W., 6742
Moyer, Sara Jane, 3253
Moyer, Scott W., 6375
Moyer, Sherill T., 8455
Moyers, Bill D., 5390
Moyle, Judith Burton, 9309
Moyle, O.W., III, 304
Moyle, Rebecca, 9309
Moyle, Wood, 9309
Moyler, J. Edward, Jr., 9382
Moyniham, Timothy J., 1644
Moynihan, Elizabeth, 6414
Moynihan, George P., 9599
Mozel Development Corp., 9446
Mozer, Eric, 4401
Mozer, Rudolf W., 4401
Mozilo, Angelo R., 422, 923
Mozilo, Phyllis G., 923
Mr. White LLC, 7167
Mrad, Rachel, 9534
MRHM, Inc., 6394
Mroz, Gregory S., 7310
Mrozkowski, Phyllis, 5675
Mrvan, Anthony, 3144
MSG Charitable Trust, 549
MSP Distribution Services LLC, 5329
MTD Products, Inc., 7692
MTGLQ Investors, L.P., 6055
MTS Assocs. LLC, 6908
Muccia, Carrol A., Jr., 6513
Muchemore, Agnes B., 4992
Muchin, Allan, 2818
Muchmore, Iris E., 3290
Muchnic, Daphne Nan, 3379
Muchnic, H.E., 3379
Muchnic, Helen Q., 3379
Mucklow, C.J., 1477
Mudd, Daniel H., 1793
Mudd, Jane W., 8588
Mudd, John O., 4934
Mudgett, Dorothy, 7586
Muegge, Linda, 3107
Muehlbauer, Brad, 3184
Muehlbauer, James H., 3184
Muehlhauser, Regina L., 698
Muehrcke, Allan O., 3065
Mueller, Aimee, 1483
Mueller, Amy Luster, 953
Mueller, Dan, 588
Mueller, Douglas, 1483
Mueller, Julie, 3292
Mueller, Kathleen C., 9403
Mueller, Linda G., 7644
Mueller, Nancy Sue, 6348
Mueller, Thomas J., 7644
Muench, Margaret, 204
Mugar, Carolyn G., 3786
Muha, Joseph, 4327
Muhammad, Mark D., 6026
Muhart, Monica Ross, 354
Muhlbach, John L., Jr., 7536
Muhlfeld, Lucy, 6302
Muir, Andy, 4245
Muir, Cameron K., 4478
Muir, Douglas Gordon, III, 2402
Muir, Gordon J., 4478
Muir, Martha M., 4478
Muir, Nigel D., 1629
Mukkamala, Bobby, 4255
Mulcahy, Anne M., 1680

Mulcahy, Betty Jane, 7658
Mulcahy, Forrest, 2087
Mulcahy, James, 5934
Mulcahy, Katie M., 2929
Mulcahy, Terry, 9918
Mulder, G. Arnold, 982
Mulderrig, Steve, 7163
Muldoon, Bob, 4156
Muldoon, Joseph W., 6652
Muldowney, John J., 9527
Mulford, Clarence E., 3551
Mulford, Donald, 3696
Mulford, Edith, 3696
Mulford, Nancy P., 9118
Mulford, Vincent S., 3696
Mulford, Vincent S., Jr., 3696
Mulhall, Lisa N., 1939
Mulheren, Alexander, 6251
Mulheren, John, 6251
Mulheren, John, Jr., 6251
Mulheren, Nancy, 6251
Mulhern, Kymberly, 4404
Mulholland, Donna, 9003
Mulholland, Richard G., 6218
Mulitz, Laura Bryna Gudelsky, 1805
Mulitz, Shelley G., 1805
Mullan, Ellen H., 3559
Mullan, John, 942
Mullan, Mary Jo, 6176
Mullane, D.A., 572
Mullaney, John J., 7779
Mullany, Jane M., 8378
Mullen, Alicia, 2907
Mullen, Donald R., 6595
Mullen, J.T., 7576
Mullen, James C., 3806
Mullen, Judith, 4158
Mullen, Lynda, 6826
Mullen, Peter P., 6998
Mullen, Richard G., 2907
Mullen, Scott M., 9059
Mullen, Timothy, 2907
Muller, Frank, 925
Muller, Henry H., 6590
Muller, James, 925
Muller, John, 925
Muller, Joyce Ann, 9811
Muller, Karen P., 4567
Muller, Leonard J., 3066
Muller, Peter, 5828
Muller, Robert, 5708
Muller, Sally, 9928
Muller, Shiela, 925
Muller, Timothy, 925
Mullet, John, 7963
Mullett, William E., 9723
Mulligan, Ed, 7593
Mulligan, Frederic H., 4209
Mulligan, John, 5028
Mulligan, Luke A., 2089
Mulligan, Terence, 404
Mulliken, Elizabeth, 4962
Mullikin, John E., 8351
Mullin, Patrick S., 7605
Mullin, Shan J., 9553
Mullinax, Theron "Tim", 7344
Mullins, Joe, 7653
Mullins, John, 3509
Mullins, R. Robert, 9072
Mullins, Rick, 9399
Mullins, Shelley Dru, 7963
Mullins, Terrell, 8974
Mullins, Timothy P., 661
Mullins, Vurn, 7866
Mullins, Walter, 6859
Mullins, William R., 2701
Mullis, James, Jr., 23
Mulroney, Brian, 9424
Mulrooney, M.M., 215
Mulroy, Thomas M., 8352
Multicon Builders, Inc., 7618
Multivest, 4332
Mulvoy, James E., 4375
Muma, Brian, 562

Munana, Clare M., 2914
Munch, Debbie, 8648
Munck, Paul, 9778
Munday, Heidi B., 2960
Mundell, William, 3176
Mundy, George E., 69
Mundy, Joe S., 9080
Mundy, John T., 9080
Mundy, Marion E., 9080
Mundy, Rodney O., 1
Mundy, Sue E., 9080
Munford, John D., 9382
Munger, Charles T., 302, 390, 926
Munger, Charles T., Jr., 390
Munger, Molly, 698
Munger, Nancy B., 926
Munger, Wendy, 982
Mungo, Robert, 8075
Munitz, Barry, 421
Munk, Stephen, 4245
Munn, James, 4245
Munn, Suzanne, 7575
Munro, Christopher R., 8038
Munro, Clark C., Jr., 8038
Munro, Clark C., Sr., 8038
Munro, Don, 4743
Munro, Julie Simon, 6987
Munro, Maurie M., 8038
Munro, Warner R., 8038
Muns, Betty Bell, 8786
Muns, James N., 8786
Muns, John B., 8786
Munsinger, Gary, 93
Munson, Jon, 141
Muntz, Myrtle, 7917
Munyan, Winthrop R., 5761
Munz, Georgie I., 9227
Munzer, Anne Bourne, 927
Munzer, Daniel W., 927
Munzer, Daphne A., 927
Munzer, Rudolph J., 927
Munzer, William J., 927
Murabito, John M., 8143
Muraski, Edward K., 8944
Murata, Tets, 230
Muravchik, Emanuel, 5575
Murch, Creighton B., 7766
Murch, Maynard H., 7766
Murch, Maynard H., V, 7766
Murch, Robert B., 7766
Murchinson, John R., III, 7352
Murchison, Virginia L., 9081
Murdock, Kent H., 9347
Murdock, Maggie Maier, 10000
Murdock, Melvin Jack, 9644
Murdough, Jody P., 7767
Murdough, Joy P., 7767
Murdough, Marshall C., 7767
Murdough, Peter R., 7767
Murdough, Thomas G., 7767
Murdough, Thomas G., Jr., 7767
Murfey, William W., 7528
Murfree, Matt B., III, 8654
Murguia, Ramon, 4816
Murillo, Mary, 819
Murphy, Allan, 4931
Murphy, Barbara M., 5564
Murphy, Bart T., 2964
Murphy, Becky, 1944
Murphy, Brian F., 7768
Murphy, Bruce D., 7700, 7742
Murphy, Carmen C., 3113
Murphy, Carol, 1446
Murphy, Charles H., Jr., 167
Murphy, Charles H., Rev., 8567
Murphy, Chris J., 4969
Murphy, Christopher J., III, 3094, 3113
Murphy, Daniel L., 6859
Murphy, Daniel P., Jr., 3415
Murphy, Darrell, 7712
Murphy, David, 8878
Murphy, Debra L., 4210
Murphy, E. Ray, 9521
Murphy, Eugene W., Jr., 1912

Murphy, Frank B., 7714
Murphy, George H., 9463
Murphy, Gerald B., 4931
Murphy, Henry L., Jr., 3805
Murphy, Hope Ford, 7524
Murphy, James, 2716
Murphy, James R., 329
Murphy, John F., 3794
Murphy, John P., 7769
Murphy, John W., 98
Murphy, Judith, 1173
Murphy, Kathleen, 2418
Murphy, Kelly, 4452
Murphy, Kevin K., 8103
Murphy, Larry S., 2388
Murphy, Lillian, Sr., 1356
Murphy, Lucy, 2678
Murphy, Margaret S., 7768
Murphy, Marguerite M., 1164
Murphy, Mark, 4530
Murphy, Mark M., 5199
Murphy, Mary, 1424, 1425
Murphy, Mary C., 9571
Murphy, Michael P., 5898
Murphy, Mitchell, 9475
Murphy, Murlan J., Jr., 7768
Murphy, Murlan J., Sr., 7768
Murphy, Pat, 3589
Murphy, Paul B., Jr., 8960, 8961
Murphy, Paul J., 7768
Murphy, Philip D., 6597
Murphy, Phillip D., 7031
Murphy, R. Madison, 167
Murphy, Raymond M., 7768
Murphy, Raymond R., Jr., 8686
Murphy, Richard, Amb., 1796
Murphy, Robert J., 3940
Murphy, Sandra, 9723
Murphy, Susan, 1586
Murphy, Tammy S., 6597
Murphy, Tom, 3395
Murphy, Walter Y., 2349
Murphy, William K., 8303
Murr, Eva, 9645
Murr, Michael, 9645
Murrah, Alfred Paul, Jr., 9218
Murrah, Jack E., 8703
Murray Family Annuity, 4045
Murray Irrevocable Trust, Grace Healy,
    3697
Murray, Barbara B., 5343
Murray, Bruce R., 9500
Murray, Catherine Underwood, 8906
Murray, Chester, 6569
Murray, Dennis J., 6514
Murray, Douglas R., 7748
Murray, Eileen, 6577
Murray, Elizabeth Simpson, 1157
Murray, Eulene H., 2457
Murray, Gene, 202
Murray, Geraldine M., 8360
Murray, Grace H., 3697
Murray, Haydn H., 5213, 5435
Murray, Hilda, 8660
Murray, J. Manson, 59
Murray, James, 3254
Murray, James B., Jr., 9390, 9500
Murray, James D., 6067
Murray, Jane E., 8360
Murray, Jason, 7819
Murray, Jerome S., 3697
Murray, Joan D., 1857
Murray, John, 1088
Murray, Joyce B., 9576
Murray, Katherine A., 8882
Murray, Katherine C., 9551
Murray, Linda T., 7195
Murray, Marcia E., 4671
Murray, Megan, 4045
Murray, Michael R., 9576
Murray, Mick, 1214
Murray, Patricia L., 8360
Murray, Patrick J., Jr., 3816
Murray, Patty, 8022

Murray, Philip W., 7790
Murray, Reilly, 3697
Murray, Richard, 6428
Murray, Robert, 634
Murray, Robert C., 5361
Murray, Robert E., 5186
Murray, Robert, II, 5469
Murray, Stanley, 4309
Murray, Terrence, 4045
Murray, Thomas J., 1800
Murray, Troy Y., 5599
Murray, Verne, 2485
Murray, William E., 5871, 5980
Murrell, J. Campbell, 9082
Murtlow, Ann D., 3116
Murvine, Marion, 9831
Muscari, Joseph C., 8075
Muse, John R., 9083
Muse, Lyn R., 9083
Muse, Martha T., 7143
Muselman, Arthur K., 3209
Muselman, Gloria E., 3209
Musen, Ken, 5571
Musen, Kenneth M., 6483
Musgrave, Jeannette, 4870
Mushett Estate, The, 5334
Mushett, Charles, 5334
Musilli, Brenda, 8022
Musolino, Michelle S., 2621
Muss, Stephen, 2149
Mussarra, Arthur F. DuCouet, 7050
Musselman, Scott, 4252
Musser, Clifton R., 1381
Musser, Laura J., 4629
Musser, Marcie, 1338
Musser, Marcie J., 1381
Musser, Margaret K., 1381
Musser, Marshall, 9719
Musser, Robert W., 1381
Musser, Warren V., 8361
Mustoe, Linda M., 4877
Mutch, Ruth O'Donnell, 9096
Muth, Maria G., 7528
Muth, Mary, 929
Muth, Peter, 929
Muth, Richard J., 929
Muth, Robert H., 6204
Mutschler, Cathryn, 9776
Mutterperl, William C., 8388
Mutual Federal Savings Bank, 3210
Mutual of Omaha Insurance Co., 4993
Mutz, John M., 3196
Muyskens, Chris, 4280
Muyskens, Kathy, 4280
Muzzy, Jim, 1006
Muzzy, Phoebe W., 9040
Mybeck, John W., 3129
Myer, Diane Lenfest, 8077
Myerberg, Neal P., 449
Myers Hewlett, Kimberly Leilani, 521
Myers, Alan C., 6998
Myers, Alex, 828
Myers, Beverly, 3698
Myers, Calvin R., 2680
Myers, Carol P., 4402
Myers, David G., 4402, 8475
Myers, Dick, 3165
Myers, Gary L., 4902
Myers, Israel, 3698
Myers, James J., 2327
Myers, John Peterson, 211
Myers, Jon, 3115
Myers, Jonathan P., 3698
Myers, Leon S., 8103
Myers, Malcolm J., 9492
Myers, Margery, 4178
Myers, Melvin, 3047
Myers, Michele, 3627
Myers, Robert C., 7039
Myers, S.L., 2286
Myers, Sally, 3126
Myers, Susan H., 2405
Myers, Susan Hanley, 2405
Myers, Susanne, 9400

Myers, Wyckoff, 2161
Myhers, Richard, 1740
Mylan Laboratories Inc., 9728
Myott, Shirley, 7272
Myrdahl, Rosemarie, 7519
Myres, Brian, 4534
Myrick, Gordon H., 4745
Myrin, Karin, 8495
Myrin, Mabel Pew, 8377
Myszka, Michele, 970

N.E.W. Customer Service Cos., Inc.,
    9482
Nabers, Hugh Comers, Jr., 22
Nabholz, David J., 168
Nabholz, John P., 168
Nabholz, Nancy A., 168
Nabholz, R. Dan, 168
Nabholz, Robert D., 168
Nabholz, Timothy A., 168
Nabisco Brands, Inc., 7459
Nabisco Holdings Corp., 6351
Nabit, Charles J., 3699
Nabit, Merwin J., 3699
Nabors, James D., 60
Nabors, Phillip, 7719
Naccarato, Vincent A., 2713
Nacey, Mike, 4061
Nacken, L.J.G., 7436
Nadeau, Louise, 3564
Nadel, Susanne, 7211
Nader, Anthony, 9482
Nadler, Andrea M., 847
Nadler, Charles, 1111
Nadler, Rita, 5172
Nadolski, Lesli D., 4460
Nadosy, Peter A., 1852
Nadzikewycz, Paul, 2797
Naegelin, Urs, 6640
Naffah, Paul, 2681
Nagahama, Mitsuhiro, 6562
Nagarajan, Kamesh, 6823
Nagata, Brian Kensho, Rev., 5685
Nagel Beverage Co., Inc., 2573
Nagel Trust, Edward M., 931
Nagel, David, 1477
Nagel, David B., 3693
Nagel, Edward M., 931
Nagel, Frederick E., 9898
Nagel, Mildred E., 2573
Nagel, Ralph J., 1431
Nagel, Rob D., 7209
Nager, Charles, 495
Nager, Elizabeth, 7449
Nager, Karen, 495
Nagle, Arthur J., 6599
Nagle, James, 2767
Nagle, Juliet, 3897
Nagle, Paige L., 6599
Nagle, Patricia, 962
Nagle, Patricia Herold, 5351
Nagle, Patricia T., 961
Nagler, Barry, 8539
Nagler, Tracy S., 6754
Nagy, Holly Davidson, 7273
Nagy, Julia Ann, 5244
Nahai Insurance Services, 216
Nahigian, Patricia, 3012
Naiberg, Gerald J., 9917
Naidoff, Stephanie W., 8494
Nail, Dawson, 1505
Naiman, David M., 1355
Nakada, David, 2545
Nakahara, Asuka, 8378
Nakajima, Takaaki A., 1250
Nakajima, Toshio, 6605
Nakamura, Alyson J., 2530
Nakamura, Ken, 691
Nakanishi, Greg, 8772
Nakash, Avi, 6600
Nakash, Joseph, 6600
Nakash, Ralph, 6600
Nakatani, Nobuyuki, 2926

Nakazono, Sami, 1364
Nakutis, Joan F., 2515
Nalbach, Kay C., 2794
Nalbor, Sally, 3135
Nalibotsky, Philip, 8499
Nalle, Eleanor G., 8294
Nally, Joseph, 460
Nalty, Elizabeth S., 3508
Nalty, Jill K., 3508
Nalty, Morgan S., 3475
Namco Capital Grp., Inc., 379
Namco Insurance, 379
Namee, Eric S., 3362
Namvar, Ezri, 379
Namvar, Homayoun, 379
Namvar, Hooshang, 379
Namvar, Mousa, 379
Namvar, Ramin, 379
Nance, Frederick R., 7576
Nanda, Y.C., 3330
Nanni, Christopher, 3131
Nanon, Patricia, 6624
Nanula, Richard D., 219
Naon, Inc., 6655, 6698
Napoli, Patricia A., 6405
Napolitano, Barbara T., 9536
Napolitano, Steven V., 2826
Naquin, David J., 9529
Naquin-Borger, Elizabeth, 3145
Naragon, Ralph, 3132
Narahari, Renu, 8153
Nardi, Nicholas J., 1521
Narducci, Lucille Reed, 7555
Narenkivicius, MaryAnn, 7113
Narodick, Sally, 9701
Narron, James W., 7438
Narten, Janet E., 7558
Narum, Larry, 2717
Nary, Gilbert R., 2782
NASA Ames Research Center, 349
NASA Dryden Flight Research Center,
    349
NASA Langley Research Center, 349
Nasdaq Stock Market, Inc., The, 3700
Nash Finch Co., 4633
Nash, Beth, 6045
Nash, Beth Goldberg, 6602
Nash, Bob J., 172
Nash, Helen, 6602
Nash, Jack, 5661, 6602, 6962
Nash, John A., 3174
Nash, Joshua, 6045, 6602
Nash, Lucia S., 7862
Nash, Martin, 2087
Nash, Phil, 1445
Nash, Theodore E., 9085
Nash, William A., 9419
Nasher, Raymond D., 9086
Nasicmento, Renata de Camargo, 8075
Nason Foundation, The, 1606, 7727
Nason, Alexander G., 1606
Nass, Connie K., 3254
Nassau, Richard, 8197
Natalicio, Diana, 6826
Natbony, William, 2826
Nathan, David G., 5898
Nathan, Edward A., 1260
Nathan, James R., 2240
Nathan, Pat, 8864
Nathan, Scott, 79
Nathan, Walter R., 2961
Nathanson, Ruth Leventhal, 2250
Nation, James, 9087
Nation, James H., 9087
Nation, Merle, 9087
Nation, Oslin, 9087
Nation, Robert F., 8293
Nation, Sally, 9087
National AIDS Fund, 204
National Bank of Commerce, 24, 2259
National Bank of Indianapolis, The, 3164
National Bank of Lancaster, 3448
National Center for Public Policy
    Research, 1781

National City Bank, 3146, 3164, 4252, 4352, 4372, 7526, 7551, 7565, 7576, 7603, 7631, 7637, 7643, 7663, 7685, 7714, 7772, 7797, 7806, 7850, 7867, 7896, 7900, 7911, 8128, 8154, 8186, 8188, 8215, 8276, 8331, 8332, 8339, 8359, 8386
National City Bank of Indiana, 7910
National City Bank of Kentucky, 7772
National City Bank of Pennsylvania, 7615
National City Bank, Columbus, 7580, 7819
National City Bank, Northeast, 7920
National City Corp., 7772
National Council of Negro Women, 2205
National Distributing Co., Inc., 2341, 2366, 2476, 4187
National Electronics Warranty Corp., 9482
National Endowment for the Humanities, 6604
National Football League Players Association, The, 1843
National Football League, The, 1843
National Health Mgmt. Svcs., 5667
National Hockey League, 6603
National Indemnity Co., 4829
National Instruments Corp., 9088
National Oceanic & Atmospheric Administration, 349, 9651
National Parks Service, 870
National Presto Industries, Inc., 1740
National Science Foundation, 6604
National Starch and Chemical Co., 5335
Nationwide Corp., 7771
Nationwide Life Insurance Co. of America, 7771
Nationwide Mutual Insurance Co., 7771
Nattkemper, C. Don, 3250
Nature's Therapy, Inc., 7174
Nau, Thomas R., Fr., 3420
Naubauer, Sara E., 9906
Naud, Hillary Maslow, 8327
Naughton, Gail K., 193
Naughton, John P., 5813
Naugle, Joni S., 8103
Nauman, Paul, Rev., 4968
Naumburg, George W., Jr., 5840
Naumes, Sue, 8003
Navarrette, Steve, 4962
Navarro, Patricia Lewis, 2114
Navratil, Gerald A., 5162
Navyosky, Wilma, 7831
Nayak, P. Ranganath, 1559
Naylor, Blair, 5472
Naylor, Charles, 4631
Naylor, Douglas C., Sr., 7810
Naylor, Jeffrey, 4183
Nazarian Family Foundation, Y&S, 5554
Nazarian, Parviz, 216
Nazarian, Soraya J., 932
Nazarian, Younes, 932
Nazel Family Trust, 5910
Nazemetz, Patricia M., 1680
NBC Universal, Inc., 933
NBI, Inc., 9938
NCR Corp., 7773
NDC Distributors, Inc., 2341
Neafsey, Patricia, RD, Ph.D., 1529
Neal, Brenda, 6365
Neal, Darla M., 3368
Neal, David L., 7458
Neal, Edward W., 2387
Neal, Homer A., 1824
Neal, Howard, 9088
Neal, John P., III, 2359
Neal, Peter C., 7433
Neal, Rachelle, 4243
Neal, Robert F., 4745
Neal, Shannon, 3014
Neal, Stephen C., 671
Neal, Stephen L., 7458

Neal, Thomas C., 7433
Neal, Tobianne M., 7433
Neal, Tracy L., 1415
Neale, Gail L., 720
Neale, Gary L., 3213
Neale, William R., 3196
Nealey, Terry, 9559
Neary, Megan K., 8620
Neaves, Hope C., 8524
NEB Corp., 9940
Nebbe, Douglas E., 3288
Nebben, Dean A., 8739
Nebeker, Stephen B., 9338
Nebel, Janet, 9742
Neben, Michael D., 220
NEC Corp., 6605
NEC USA, Inc., 6605
Nedele, Chuck, 3241
Nedelman, Phyllis, 7866
Nedley, R.E., 1982
Nee, David M., 1559
Needham, Judith, 3580
Needler, Michael S., 7627
Neeleman, Stanley D., 1398
Neels, Guido, 3159
Neely Administrative Trust, C.W., 125
Neely, Christine E., 764
Neely, Mary M., 4407
Neely, Suzanne S., 4741
Neely, Walter, 4736
Nees, Kenneth L., 6658
Neese, Alonzo A., Jr., 9757
Neese, Elbert H., Sr., 9757
Neese, Gordon C., 9757
Neese, Walter K., 9757
Neeser, Craig D., 9703
Nef, Evelyn S., 1839
Neff, Daniel A., 7205
Neff, Erv, 9933
Neff, Kathy A., 2485
Neff, Mark, 3437
Neff, Paul A., 2485
Neff, Peter Gibbons, 2297
Neff, Phillip R., 3404
Neff, Richard B., 5209
Neff, Sue W., 7742
Nefsky, Robert, 4954
Negley, Leslie, 8799
Negley, Nancy Brown, 8799
Nehrbas, Andrew R., 8115
Neidich, Daniel M., 6606
Neidorff, Michael F., 4796
Neier, Aryeh, 6665, 7023
Neier, Yvette, 5860
Neihouse, John, 169
Neill, Robert H., 126
Neill, Rolfe, 2097
Neilsen, Craig H., 934
Neilsen, Ray H., 934
Neilson, Benjamin R., 8140
Neilson, Emily, 9455
Neilson, George W., 4631
Neiman, Janet, 6607
Neiman, Leroy, 6607
Neiman, Steven H., 8208
Neimann, Diane B., 4514, 4572
Neis, Arnold Hayward, 7040
Neiss, Charles, 7179
Neiss, Fay, 7179
Neiss, Jacob, 7179
Neisser, Edward, 2910
Neisser, Judith E., 2910
Neisser, Katherine M., 2910
Neithercut, Edward J., 4409
Neithercut, Elizabeth M., 4409
Nejes, Peter F., 5275
Nekoshima, Akio, 6562
Nelkin, Amy, 6608
Nelkin, Harold, 6608
Nelkin, Leslie Andrew, 6608
Nelkin, Ruth, 6608
Nellie Mae Foundation, 4025
Nellis, Jenny, 4723
Nelson, Anna Spangler, 7482

Nelson, Anne, 121
Nelson, Arthur H., 3869
Nelson, Arvid R., 1632
Nelson, Aune, 2911
Nelson, Barbara I., 2679
Nelson, Barclay, 4871
Nelson, Betty, 3188
Nelson, Brian S., 9571
Nelson, C.M., 1056
Nelson, Carol J., 9881
Nelson, Cathryn B., 2882
Nelson, Cherie, 7775
Nelson, Chupa, 1468
Nelson, Clarence J., 8163
Nelson, Clark, 866
Nelson, Curtis C., 4632
Nelson, Cynthia, 3765
Nelson, David L., 8949
Nelson, Diana L., 4532, 4632
Nelson, Don, 550
Nelson, Donald, 5539
Nelson, Douglas R., 2570
Nelson, Douglas W., 3568, 3585, 4795
Nelson, Edward, Jr., 9101
Nelson, Frederick O., 9809
Nelson, Fredric C., 423
Nelson, Gary, 588
Nelson, Gary D., 2411
Nelson, Gene, 7931
Nelson, George, 9854
Nelson, Glen D., 4532, 4632
Nelson, Grant E., 9881
Nelson, Greg, 402
Nelson, Jane S., 8549
Nelson, Jonathan M., 8549
Nelson, Karen Kriendler, 5427
Nelson, Kathleen, 722
Nelson, Kathryn L., 4480
Nelson, Kent C., 3585, 4795
Nelson, L.L., 2654
Nelson, Lance, 3215
Nelson, Larry W., 2164
Nelson, Laura L. Peaster, 4761
Nelson, Leonard M., 5571, 5702
Nelson, Lynn, 7519
Nelson, Marilyn C., 4532, 4632
Nelson, Marjorie A., 4532, 4632
Nelson, Mark, 355
Nelson, Mary D., 9882
Nelson, Mary Goodwillie, 4446, 4476
Nelson, Marybeth, 9881
Nelson, Marylyn C., 4532
Nelson, Merlin, 6561
Nelson, Merlin E., 6562
Nelson, Michael M., 1215
Nelson, Michael S., 7948
Nelson, Mitchell, 7153
Nelson, Nancy, 4521
Nelson, Pamela B., 7948
Nelson, Paul, 1361
Nelson, Randolph, 3765
Nelson, Randolph M., 7948
Nelson, Rod, 4729
Nelson, Rodney G., 9881
Nelson, Russell C., 4623
Nelson, Sally A., 7583
Nelson, Steve, 7593
Nelson, Susan, 3278, 4871
Nelson, Thomas C., 7370
Nelson, Timothy B., 7948
Nelson, Todd, 148, 3325
Nelson, V.C., 1056
Nelson, W. Linton, 8362
Nelson, Wendy M., 4532, 4632
Nelson, William C., 2535, 9222
Nelson, William J., 4540
Nemanich, Scott E., 2931
Nemec, Fred J., 8833
Nemecek, Karen, 3275
Nemy, Enid, 7088
Neppl, Walter J., 5181
Neptune, Lionel W., 1804
Neri, Janis G., 1594
Nerland, Rick, 78

Nerren, Evonne, 9228
Nesbeda, Peter, 3965
Nesbitt, Anne B., 8740
Nesbitt, David C., 3356
Nesbitt, William A., 9049, 9141
Neschis, Janet C., 6014
Neshek, Milton E., 9836
Nesholm, Elmer J., 9647
Nesholm, Erika J., 9647
Nesholm, John F., 9647
Nesholm, Kirsten, 9647
Nesholm, Laurel, 9647
Ness, Ian, 6466
Ness, James, 2307
Ness, Judy, 4919
Ness, Mary K., 4730
Nessel, Melvin B., 2152
Nesser, Noel, 9101
Nessier, Stephen, 1314
Nestegard, Susan K., 4557
Nestle Purina PetCare Co., 4872
Nestle USA, Inc., 935, 9648
Nestler, Eric, 4616
Nestor, Karen R., 7558, 7680, 7688
Netanya Endeavors, LLC, 5526
Neth, Robert H., Jr., 5145
Nethery, Jack, 1874
NetJets Aviation, Inc., 7174
Nett, Roy W., 3218
Netter, Barbara, 1607
Netter, Donald, 1607
Netter, Edward, 1607
Netter, Richard, 1607, 6990
Netting, Conrad J., IV, 9166
Nettles, Thomas A., IV, 27
Netzer, Dick, 6080
Netzky, Theodore, 701, 2745
Neu, Cheryl, 7598
Neu, John L., 6610
Neu, Richard, 7598
Neu, Robert T., 6610
Neu, Wendy K., 6610
Neubauer, Joseph, 8363
Neubauer, Lawrence, 8363
Neubauer, Nickolas, 2660
Neuberger Berman Inc., 1735
Neuberger, James A., 6611
Neuberger, Marie S., 6611
Neuberger, Roy R., 6611
Neuberger, Roy S., 6611
Neugent, Gerard D., 3301
Neuharth, Allen H., 9424
Neuharth, Jan, 9424
Neuhoff, Joseph Boyd, 8843
Neuhoff, Pauline A. Seay, 8919
Neukom, Gillian, 9649
Neukom, John McMakin, 9649
Neukom, Josselyn, 9649
Neukom, Samantha, 9649
Neukom, William H., 9649
Neuman, Celeste, 3407
Neuman, Dawn, 9779
Neuman, Tricia, 739
Neumann, Charlotte G., 9348
Neumann, Doug, 3275
Neumann, James W., 9800
Neumann, Jean, 3017
Neumann, Jean L., 3017
Neumann, Joseph, 6509
Neumann, Kenneth, 3017
Neumann, Kenneth P., 3017
Neumann, Rachel, 6509
Neumann, Roland M., 9767
Neumann, Roland M., Jr., 9839
Neumann, Sharlene, 7819
Neumann, Susan M., 2563
Neumeyer, Greg, 3275
Neumiller, Rayna, 83
Neuner, Frank X., Jr., 3468
Neureuther, Don, 2185, 4642, 4682, 8628
Neurochem, Inc., 6232
Neuroth, Loras, 3337
Neustadt, Dolores K., 9260

Nissan North America, Inc., 939
Nisselson, Alan, 6053
Nissim, Matook, 294
Nitschke, John A., 2989
Nitta, Jeffrey W., 9703
Nitz, Owen, 5031
Niven, Linda, 1347
Nivet, Marc A., 6471
Nix, Craig L., 8587
Nix, Jerry W., 2389
Nix, John M., 2458
Nixon, Carolyn Davison, 8789
Nixon, Gerald, 3137
NL Industries, Inc., 9188
Noack, David, 4534
Noah, Ian, 898
Nobile, Richard W., 4057
Noble Smith, E. J., Mr., 6633
Noble, Alice M., 7778
Noble, David D., 7778
Noble, Donald E., 7778
Noble, Donald, II, 7778
Noble, Edward John, 6633
Noble, Ethel G., 6632
Noble, John H., 6632
Noble, Lloyd, 7963
Noble, Maria, 7963
Noble, Matthew, 7778
Noble, Rusty, 7963
Noble, Sally, 7962
Noble, Ted, 3042
Nobles, Gerald C., Jr., 8895
Noce, Walter W. "Bill", Jr., 347
Nochumson, Howard, 3058
Nocito, Lori A., 8317
Nocon, Nannette, 6823
Noe, Lawrence M., 6570
Noel, Clyde, 828
Noel, John M., 9856
Noel, Patricia D., 9856
Nofer, George, 8105
Nofer, George H., J.D., 8365
Nogales, Luis G., 570
Nogi, Yoshiyuki, 9836
Nogimori, Masafumo, 2602
Nohra, Joseph S., 7563, 7920
Noia, Alan J., 3600
Nojaim, Paul, 5724
Nolan, Cori, 2966
Nolan, Daniel P., 5734
Nolan, Eleanor, 4508
Nolan, Ellin J., 3687
Nolan, James P., 5785
Nolan, Jeff, 183
Nolan, Jim, 2982
Nolan, Justin, 3038
Nolan, Maureen, 3320
Nolan, Michael J., 5288
Nolan, Peter G., 2966
Nolan, Robin G., 2966
Nolan-Boye, Melinda L., 5140
Noland, Mariam C., 2097, 4254
Noland, N. Douglas, Jr., 9521
Noland, Rick, 2143
Nolen, George, 5400
Nolfi, Joseph, 2586
Noll, Martin, 2922
Noll, Martin J., 3065
Nolt, Edwin B., 8163
Nolt, Sheryl Robins, 9506
Nolting, Cheryl, 9067
Nonneman, Elaine M., 9568
Nonte, Anthony, 3133
Noon, Nicholas, 5490
Noon, Prudence J., 936
Noonan, D. Michael, 4534
Noonan, Frank M., 8550
Noonan, John F., 5391
Noonan, Patrick F., 5551
Noonan, Peter, 7866
Noonan, T.M., 2687
Noone, Laura Palmer, 148
Noorda, Lewena "Tye", 9336
Nootens, Raymond, 2601

Nooyi, Indra K., 6714
Nopper, Marie, 4939
Noranda, 7436
Norblom, Harold A., 9573
Norcross, Arthur D., 6634
Norcross, Arthur D., Jr., 6634
Norcross, Mark A., 7437
Norcross, Rena R., 7437
Nord, Cindy, 7779
Nord, Eric T., 7780
Nord, Ethan, 7779
Nord, Ethan W., 8577
Nord, Jane B., 7780
Nord, Walter G., 7779
Nord, Walter G., Mrs., 7779
Nordby, Earl, 8631
Nordell, Ellen, 8482
Nordeman, Anne, 5815
Nordick, Brett A., 7518
Nordick, Ralph B., 7518
Nordick, Yvonne, 7518
Nordlof, Richard D., 2591
Nordlund, D. Craig, 3563
Nordson Corp., 7779, 7781
Nordstrom, Mike, 417
Nordt, John C., III, 2121
Nored, Anita M., 3536
Noreen, Roger F., 4635
Noren, Ron, 1504
Noretto, Michael, 7890
Norfleet, Edward A., 7488
Norfleet, Robert F., Jr., 9513
Norfolk Southern Corp., 9485
Norgaard, Corine T., 1519
Norgard, Susanne, 402
Norgren, Harriet S., 4722
Norick, Ronald J., 7964
Noriega, Miguel, 5854
Noriega, Mona, 2757
Nork, A. Edward, 8317
Norling, Dennis A., 3277
Norman Foundation, The, 6180
Norman Fund, Aaron E., Inc., The, 6636
Norman, Aaron E., 6635
Norman, Abigail, 6635, 6636
Norman, Andrew E., 6636
Norman, Anne, 1765
Norman, Caresse, 1034
Norman, Elisabeth W., 2712
Norman, Harold, 3258
Norman, Margaret, 6635, 6636
Norman, Marilyn, 4280
Norman, Patricia, 7441
Norman, Rebecca, 6635
Norman, Rebecca D., 6636
Norman, Roger W., 5051
Norman, Sarah, 6635, 6636
Norman, Thomas, 4280
Norment, Matthew R., 9406
Norment, Michael H., 9406
Normile, Robert John, 861
Norquist, S. Griffin, Jr., 4752
Norrington, Margaret, 982
Norrington, Ralph, 982
Norris, Bradley K., 940
Norris, David E., 1648
Norris, Dellora A., 2917
Norris, Diana, 8496
Norris, Edward, 9869
Norris, Eileen L., 940
Norris, Elizabeth, 3305
Norris, Harlyne J., 940
Norris, J. Carl, 9054
Norris, Jerry, 7139
Norris, Jon L., 1644
Norris, Kenneth T., 940
Norris, Kim, 4227
Norris, Lester J., 2917
Norris, P.C., 7745
Norris, Pamela, 2917
Norris, Robert C., 2917
Norris, Stefan, 1726
North American Rescue Products, Inc., 8601

North Central Trust Co., 9745, 9808, 9845
North Community Bank, 2726
North Side Bank & Trust Co., 7574
North Star Ventures, 1905, 4642
North, Gary J., 2530
North, Robert L., 3164
North, Susan D., 3599
North, Walter, 4259
Northcutt, Gordon L., 8876
Northeast Nuclear Energy Co., 1614
Northeast Utilities, 1614
Northen, Mary Moody, 9092
Northenor, Jean, 3186
Northern Life Insurance Co., 2418
Northern Trust Bank of Florida, N.A., 1983, 2170, 2212
Northern Trust Bank, N.A., 2622, 2908, 4783
Northern Trust Co., The, 2084, 2606, 2626, 2661, 2739, 2837, 2888, 2897, 2913, 2918, 2971, 2993, 3059, 3078, 4809, 4882, 9040, 9302, 9876
Northey, Lyle W., 4556
Northrail, 3683
Northridge, Mark, 5084
Northrip, Nancy, 2762
Northrop Grumman Corp., 942
Northrop, Amanda, 4158
Northrop, Wilhelm E., 6146
Northrup, Sharon C., 6026
Northumberland National Bank, 8432
Northwest Savings Bank, 8154
Northwestern Mutual Life Insurance Co., The, 9884
Northwood, Edward C., 6276
Norton Co., 8419
Norton, Alice, 2904
Norton, Allison, 9303
Norton, Benjamin P., 7870
Norton, Brent, 7870
Norton, Daniel, 145
Norton, David, 7049
Norton, Eileen, 943
Norton, Elizabeth B., 1775
Norton, George W., Mrs., 3441
Norton, Grace Geraldi, 2752
Norton, H. Wilbert, Jr., 9424
Norton, Helen A., 8471
Norton, James M., 5155
Norton, Jane, 7582, 7870
Norton, John A., 5155
Norton, Jon, 4496
Norton, Kelly, 1944
Norton, Lauren, 2355
Norton, Lenore "Trilby", 5155
Norton, Lenore C., 5155
Norton, Mary T., 5155
Norton, Michael A., 5155
Norton, P.H., 4368
Norton, Paul S., 5155
Norton, Peter, 943
Norton, Phoebe, 1456
Norton, Richard M., 2770
Norton, Robert, 1775, 6720
Norton, Thomas A., 5155
Norton, Toby, 9303
Norton, Vincent C., 2717
Norwest Corp., 1294
Norwest Ltd., 1294
Norwood, Felicia, 1479
Norwood, Heather, 8572
Nosbusch, Keith D., 9912
Nostitz, Drewry H., 7387
Nosworthy, Douglas, 332
Notebaert, Richard, 1443
Notis, Tippy Friedman, 441
Notopoulos, Philip J., 3845
Notter, John L., 5037
Nottingham, Ben G., 7367
Nottingham, C.D., II, 7367
Nottingham, Michael, 3253
Nova-Hildesley, Julia, 5040

Novack, Deborah S., 8057
Novack, Ken, 7142
Novack, Kenneth M., 8057
Novak, Caroline B., 20
Novak, David C., 3442, 3457
Novak, Joe, 3333
Novak, Mary, 7749
Novak, Robert D., 1841
Novak, Susan B., 3442
Novak, Wendy L., 3442
Novakov, Lydia H., 8931
Novakov, Lydia Haggar, 8839
Novartis Corp., 3677
Novartis Corp., Inc., 1995
Novartis Inc., 6640
Novelly, Paul A., 4777
Novick, Azriel, 5582
Novik, Steven, 4838
Noville, Deborah, 1505
Novo Foundation, 4948
Novogratz, Jacqueline, 6642
Novogratz, Michael, 6642
Novotny, Yetta Deitch, 8364
Nowak, Betty, 9326
Nowak, Carole M., 7628
Nowak, Henry, 9326
Nowell, Lionel L., III, 6714
Nowers Fund, Lola E., 2303
Nowicki, Douglas R., 8334
Nowicki, Sandra G., 286
Nowinski, Frank L., 3277
Nowland, Rod, 7793
Nowlin, Wade T., 8841
Nowling, Michael D., 9589
Noxell Corp., 3711
Noyce Residual Trust, Robert N., 944
Noyce, Elizabeth B., 3546
Noyce, Pendred, 944
Noyce, Pendred E., 3546
Noyes, Charles F., 6643
Noyes, Elizabeth H., 3216
Noyes, Evan L., Jr., 3216
Noyes, Henry S., 3216
Noyes, Marguerite Lilly, 3216
Noyes, Nicholas H., 3216
Noyes, Nicholas S., 3216
Noyes, William, 3038
NS Associates, Inc., 3000
NSPB Corp., 3168
Nu Skin Enterprises, Inc., 9322
Nuce, Michael, 9735
Nuckles, Pat, 7586
Nucor Corp., 7440
Nugen, J. Bryan, 3141
Nugent, Christopher W., 2957
Nugent, Conn, 6290
Nuhn, Adriaan, 2982
Nulsen, Carol, 4513
Numanville, Brian, 4633
Nunan, Caroline S., 8458
Nunes, Geoffrey, 4040
Nunes, Mary Louise, 3854
Nunez, Joann, 8658
Nunez-Deguits, Anna Delia, 3245
Nunley, K. David, 3941
Nunley, Kim, 5466
Nunley, Wallace C., 9367
Nunn, Larry E., 3227
Nunn, Mary Ann, 3227
Nunn, Warne, 8042
Nunns, Barbara, 3368
Nureyev, Rudolf, 2919
Nurmi, Marguerite Elaine Abell, 3560
Nurmi, Thomas D., 3560
Nurse, Paul, Sir, 3654
Nusbaum, Jack H., 1492, 5777
Nussbaum, Jeremy, 6035
Nussbaum, Max, 6035
Nussbickel, Wayne L., 5564
Nussdorf, Lawrence C., 3590
Nutt, Ollie, 910
Nutter, Mary, 7653
Nutter, McClennen & Fish, LLP, 3992
Nutter, W. Lee, 2189

Nutting, Robert M., 9729
Nutting, William O., 9716, 9729
Nyberg, Bruce E., 4254
Nye, David E., 1615
Nye, Elizabeth, 6107
Nye, Grace S., 1615
Nye, Homer E., 4244
Nye, Timothy U., 6503
Nygren, Sara, 2920
Nygren, William C., 2920
Nylander, Inga Olsson, 9491
Nyman, Joelyn, 4313
NYNEX Corp., 5439
Nypl, Milan, 9736
Nyquist, Laura K., 7773
NYRA Charities, 6264
Nystedt, Bradley Jon, 91
Nystrom, Bud, 4729
Nystrom, Hazel, 2495
Nystrom, William B., 870

O'Bannion, Chris, 939
O'Brian, Timothy, 4307
O'Brian, William, 894
O'Brien, Alice, 8758
O'Brien, Chris, 945
O'Brien, Connie, 4525
O'Brien, Dennis C., 945
O'Brien, Donal C., Jr., 173, 6451, 7168
O'Brien, Francis X., 5436
O'Brien, Gloria A., 945
O'Brien, Ida, 673
O'Brien, James A., 8438
O'Brien, James E., 4674
O'Brien, Jeanine, 1483
O'Brien, Kevin, 1483
O'Brien, Kevin E., 6433
O'Brien, Kevin J., 3663
O'Brien, Mary Lynn, 8047
O'Brien, Michael G., 241
O'Brien, Michael J., 3047
O'Brien, Michelle Atlas, 241
O'Brien, Pat, 4496
O'Brien, Patricia, 7870
O'Brien, Paul, 8438
O'Brien, Paul E., 8438
O'Brien, Robert, 5807
O'Brien, Robert S., 7674
O'Brien, Rosanne, 942
O'Brien, Thomas E., 2716
O'Brien, Tina, 8438
O'Bryan, Frank E., 222
O'Bryan, Sean, 4310
O'Bryon, Margaret K., 1786
O'Connell, Barbara, 6146, 6147
O'Connell, Betsy Paull, 1765
O'Connell, Brian, 3833
O'Connell, D., 8209
O'Connell, Jane B., 5542, 6384
O'Connell, Kathleen, 6026
O'Connell, Mary Adams, 194
O'Connell, Mary Ann, 9334
O'Connell, Mary Kathleen, 4197
O'Connell, Meg, 5539
O'Connell, Paul V., 2499
O'Connell, Richard T., Jr., 4178
O'Connell, Robert, 3343
O'Connell, S. Colman, 4534
O'Connor & Hewitt Foundation, The, 9095
O'Connor, Barrett J., 2717
O'Connor, Carroll, 946
O'Connor, David P., 4257
O'Connor, Dennis, 9094, 9095
O'Connor, Dorothy Hanna, 9094
O'Connor, Edward J., 9929
O'Connor, Elizabeth F., 2014
O'Connor, J.A., Jr., 8131
O'Connor, James J., 2630
O'Connor, John H., 8799
O'Connor, Julie, 4552
O'Connor, Kathleen G., 4518
O'Connor, Kathryn S., 9095

O'Connor, Kerry, 4259
O'Connor, Kristen K., 198
O'Connor, Louise, 9095
O'Connor, Maconda Brown, 8799
O'Connor, Mary Jane, 2921
O'Connor, Maureen, 7319
O'Connor, Michael, 5517
O'Connor, Michael E., 5724
O'Connor, Michael F., 8511
O'Connor, Nancy F., 946
O'Connor, Olive B., 6645
O'Connor, Robert, 483
O'Connor, Robert D., 3871
O'Connor, Sandra Day, 6826
O'Connor, Sarane R., 5600
O'Connor, Susan, 5932
O'Connor, Tom, Jr., 9095
O'Connor, William F., 2921
O'Data, Charles N., 8098
O'Day, Terry, 487
O'Dell, D.R., 3051
O'Dell, Robert R., 685
O'dell, Wynne, 1357
O'Donald, John, 4331
O'Donnell Foundation, The, 3677
O'Donnell, David R., 3160
O'Donnell, Doris, 8076
O'Donnell, Edith Jones, 9096
O'Donnell, Harry J., 9652
O'Donnell, Harry J., Jr., 9652
O'Donnell, Joseph, 4059
O'Donnell, Katherine, 4059
O'Donnell, Kerry J., 8193
O'Donnell, Laurence J., 5184
O'Donnell, Mackey, 238
O'Donnell, Mariette E., 9652
O'Donnell, Mark, 5571, 6483
O'Donnell, Michael, 3189
O'Donnell, Michael W., 3213
O'Donnell, Patrick, 8141
O'Donnell, Paul J., 5181
O'Donnell, Peter, Jr., 9096
O'Donnell, Sally, 7890
O'Donoghue, J. Kevin, 3065
O'Dwyer, Brian, 6551
O'Dwyer, Deborah, 1470
O'Farrell, Michael K., 226
O'Flynn, Margaret, 2812
O'Flynn, Thomas M., 5361
O'Gara, John, 5017
O'Gara, Nellie, 8928
O'Gara, Susanne Wellman, 7901
O'Gorman, Scott, Jr., 9371
O'Grady, Gerald B., 3785
O'Grady, Judith, 5251
O'Hanlon, Helen J., 5025
O'Hara, James, 7656
O'Hara, Kevin, 7447
O'Hara, Peter, 351
O'Hara, Robert L., 8571
O'Hara, S., 1245
O'Hare, Susan, 8660
O'Herron, Edward M., Jr., 7441
O'Herron, Jonathan, 6646
O'Herron, Kennedy, 7441
O'Herron, Shirley, 6646
O'Herron, William, 7441
O'Keefe, Andrew, 5194
O'Keefe, Andrew J., 5194
O'Keefe, Mary, 3281, 3326
O'Keefe, Raymond T., Jr., 6391
O'Keefe, Regis J., 8074
O'Keeffe, Arthur, 2154
O'Keeffe, Brian, 2154
O'Keeffe, Clare, 2154
O'Keeffe, Daniel, 2154
O'Keeffe, Esther B., 2154
O'Keeffe, Kathryn, 6041
O'Keeffe, Ruth, 2154
O'Keere, Raymond T., Jr., 6779
O'Leary Gill, Daniela, 2787
O'Leary, Brian J., Jr., 933
O'Leary, J.P., 9970
O'Leary, James, 1516

O'Leary, John D., 6523
O'Leary, Kevin, 5372
O'Leary, Kevin J., Rev., 3828
O'Leary, Maureen M., 6523
O'Leary, Maureen Meehan, 6523
O'Leary, Patrick J., 7484
O'Leary, Thomas M., 2936
O'Loughlin, James L., 4877
O'Loughlin, Johanna G., 8187
O'Maley, David B., 7785
O'Malley, Courtney, 7048
O'Malley, Donald J., 2142
O'Malley, Edward V., Jr., 98
O'Malley, James J., 6648
O'Malley, Kevin, 4689
O'Malley, Mary, 6648
O'Malley, Mary Alice, 6647
O'Malley, Michael, 8142
O'Malley, Peter, 214
O'Malley, Sheila, 6648
O'Malley, Thomas D., 6647
O'Malley, Timothy, 6647
O'Mary, Mark, 26
O'Meara, Alice, 936
O'Meara, Margaret A., 9657
O'Meara, Steve, 691
O'Meara, Vicki A., 2213
O'Neal, Candace Cheri, 2518
O'Neal, Cynthia, 7819
O'Neal, E. Stanley, 6537
O'Neal, Fred, 2362
O'Neal, Larry W., 54
O'Neal, Louis, 369, 621
O'Neal, Solon F., Jr., 2219
O'Neil, Abby McCormick, 2878
O'Neil, Albert T., 4638
O'Neil, Bob, 9957
O'Neil, Brian S., 5265
O'Neil, Casey Albert, 4638
O'Neil, Grace, 3701
O'Neil, Helene Connellan, 3701
O'Neil, Jean, 2155
O'Neil, John, 944, 9673
O'Neil, John J., 3701, 6918, 7002
O'Neil, John J., Jr., 3701
O'Neil, Julie, 9957
O'Neil, M.G., 2155
O'Neil, Priscilla, 6649
O'Neil, Ralph M., 6649
O'Neil, William, 3701
O'Neill, Abby M., 6825
O'Neill, Bob, 9957
O'Neill, Charrise, 2732
O'Neill, Dorothy K., 7783
O'Neill, F.J., III, 7782
O'Neill, Francis J., 7782
O'Neill, George D., Jr., 286
O'Neill, Grover, Jr., 6668
O'Neill, H.M., 7782
O'Neill, Hampton K., Mrs., 4597
O'Neill, Hugh, 7782
O'Neill, Jack, 7749
O'Neill, James C., 4597
O'Neill, James W., 4597
O'Neill, James W., Mrs., 4597
O'Neill, John, 1765
O'Neill, Julie, 9957
O'Neill, June E., 1632
O'Neill, Kelley, 4597
O'Neill, Kelley, Mrs., 4597
O'Neill, Linda D., 6650
O'Neill, Michael E., 2535
O'Neill, P.J., 7782
O'Neill, Peter J., 5785
O'Neill, Steven, 4802
O'Neill, Thomas J., Jr., 3833
O'Neill, Timothy J., 6650
O'Neill, Timothy M., 7783
O'Neill, William D., 1644
O'Neill, William J., 7782
O'Neill, William J., Jr., 7783
O'Quinn, John M., 9097
O'Reilly, Nancy, Dr., 4798
O'Reilly, William M., 9923

O'Rourke, Dara, 3557
O'Rourke, Eileen M., 3559
O'Rourke, J. Tracy, 8629, 8633
O'Rourke, Joan C., 1246
O'Rourke, L.D., 836
O'Rourke, Terry, 4224
O'Shaughnessy, Eileen A., 4639
O'Shaughnessy, I.A., 4639
O'Shaughnessy, John F., 4639
O'Shaughnessy, John F., Jr., 4639
O'Shaughnessy, Mary Hurst, 9487
O'Shaughnessy, Michael W., 4639
O'Shaughnessy, Terence P., 4639
O'Shaughnessy, Timothy J., 4639
O'Shaughnessy, Timothy P., 4639
O'Shaughnessy, W.J., Jr., 2358
O'Shaughnessy, William, 1505
O'Shaugnessy, Barbara J., 4639
O'Shaugnessy, Lawrence M., 4639
O'Shea, Erin K., 7254
O'Shea, Michele K., 6651
O'Shea, Peggy, 5783
O'Shea, Robert J., 6651
O'Shea, W.J., 5151
O'Sullivan, Anne S., 9098
O'Sullivan, Carole, 6652
O'Sullivan, Daragh M., 970
O'Sullivan, James J., 1828
O'Sullivan, Kevin P., 6652
O'Sullivan, Marie T., 9098
O'Sullivan, Patricia, 1598
O'Sullivan, Patrick, 157
O'Sullivan, Sean M., 9098
O'Toole, Dennis A., 3337
O'Toole, Judith H., 8155
O'Toole, Paula M., 6653
O'Toole, Robert J., 9860, 9929
O'Toole, Terence M., 6653
O'Toole, Theresa, 6654
O'Toole, Thomas, 3337
O-Z Gedney Co., LLC, 7484
Oak Assocs., 7526
Oak Foundation, 5905
Oak Trust, The, 3552
Oakes, Sybil Ridings, 5724
Oakland Mall Ltd., 4365
Oakley Family Trust, 949
Oakley, Hollie N., 3217
Oakley, Tracy, 2259
Oakwood Homes, Inc., 5394
Oates, James F., 2965
Oates, Marian E., 8671
Oates, William A., Jr., 3817
Obama, Michelle R., 3016
Obata, Gyo, 4817
Ober, Agnes E., 4613
Ober, Gayle M., 4613
Ober, Richard B., 4613
Ober, Theodore E., 4139
Ober, Timothy M., 4613
Oberfeld, Neil, 1445
Oberfest, Bruce D., 2056
Oberg, Paul W., 4594
Oberkotter, Mildred L., 8365
Oberkotter, Paul, 8365
Oberlander, Eileen, 5892
Oberlie, Stephanie, 3205
Oberlin, Wendy, 3141
Oberman, Alicia, 2899
Obermanns, H. Richard, 7847
Obermeier, Chess, 3038
Oberndorf, Susan C., 950
Oberndorf, William E., 950
Oberstein, Norman S., 803
Obetz, Richard, 6221
Obrock, John A., 8293
Obrow, Norman C., 469
Obser, Fred, 6164
Ocasio, Raymond, 6229
Ocean Federal Savings Bank, 5341
Ocean Financial Corp., 5341
OceanFirst Bank, 5341
OceanFirst Financial Corp., 5341
Oceanside Care Center Inc., Inc., 6871

Ochs, Gail J., 512
Ochs, Peter M., 506, 512
Ochs, Ronald K., 9820
Ochsman, Bruce David, 9489
Ochsman, Jeffrey Wayne, 9489
Ochsman, Meurice C., 9489
Ochsman, Michael Paul, 9489
Ochsman, Ralph, 9489
Ochylski, Daniel, 3321
Ochylski, Edward, 3321
Ochylski, Edward, III, 3321
Ochylski, Edward, Mrs., 3321
Ochylski, Eleanor, 3321
Ochylski, Juliana, 3321
Ochylski-Wertsch, Mary C., 3321
Ockerbloom, Richard C., 3871
Ocmulgee Fields, Inc., 2424
Oda, Jim, 7748
Odahowski, David A., 1922
Oddleifson, Eric, 4101
Oddleifson, Janna, 4101
Oddo, Nancy E., 5888
Odean, Tana S., 3277
Odell, Helen Pfeiffer, 951
Odell, Mary, 1249
Odell, Robert Stewart, 951
Oden, Thomas H., 7677, 8399, 9657
Odgers, Richard, 1260
Odle, Samuel L., 3180
ODM, Ltd., 1869
Odne, Kathleen L., 805
Odom, Charles L., 7397, 7494
Odom, Dan, 7397
Odom, Paul B., Jr., 7964
Odom, Roderick D., 2323
Oegerle, Robin O., 3628
Oehmig, Gordon D., 9099
Oehmig, Margaret W., 8809, 9099
Oehmig, Randolph D., 9099
Oehmig, William B., 9099
Oehmig, William V., 8809, 9099
Oesterle, Richard, 3189
Oesterle, Stephen, 4622
Oestreich, Dean C., 3324
Oestreicher, Ann, 6656
Oestreicher, Sylvan, 6656
Oetinger, Judith F., 3103
Ofat, Theodore M., 7791
Offen, Rebecca, 6886
Officer, Lisa, 4798
Offield, Chase, 2924
Offield, Dorothy Wrigley, 2924
Offield, James S., 2924
Offield, Meighan, 2924
Offield, Paxson H., 2924
Offutt, Harry C., III, 2228
Offutt, James A., 4902
Ofstedal, Donald S., 4628
Oftedal, Gunnhild, 954
Ogata, Nancy, 570
Ogawa, Diane Harrison, 5466
Ogaz, Brian, 919
Ogburn, Shirley, 22
Ogden, Douglas, 483
Ogden, Henry M., 5417
Ogden, Margaret G. "Peggy", 5724
Ogden, Margaret H., 6657
Ogden, Ralph E., 6657
Ogg, Thomas C., 7765
Ogie, Elizabeth C., 2324, 2361, 2463
Ogihara, Yoshimitsu "Yoshi", 3166
Ogilvie, Dian, 7160
Ogilvie, Donna Brace, 1501
Ogle, Laura K., 7949
Ogle, Paul W., 3218
Ogletree, Charles J., Jr., 739
Ogorzaly, Mary, 5932
Ogstrup-Pedersen, Anne-Margrete, 4094
Oh, Sang W., 3595
Ohel, Izhak, 546
Ohga, Midori, 6658
Ohga, Norio, 6658
Ohio Casualty Corp., 7784
Ohio Co., The, 7915

Ohio Edison Co., 7630
Ohio National Financial Svcs., 7785
Ohio National Life Insurance Co., The, 7785
Ohio Savings Bank, 7786
Ohl, Dennis, 9958
Ohlander, Jan H., 3036
Ohlendorf, Patricia C. "Patti", 8768
Ohlgart, Thomas, 9902
Ohlmann, Bill, 4986
Ohlmansiek, Jane, 3137
Ohlsen, Ronald, 2923
Ohm, Paul R., 4394
Ohman, Clifton W., 256
Ohnmacht, Susan, 9163
Ohotnicky, Roberta, 1516
Ohrstrom, Clarke, 6659
Ohrstrom, George F., 6659
Ohrstrom, George L., II, 6659
Ohrstrom, George L., Jr., 6659
Ohrstrom, Richard R., 6659
Ohta, Kazuo, 4982
Oifer, David, 5426
Oishei Consolidated Trust No. 1, 6660
Oishei Consolidated Trust No. 2, 6660
Oishei, John R., 6660
Ojakli, Ziad, 4307
Okada, Alan, 5755
Okada, Kiyoshi, 7120
Okenica, Kathleen, 6512
Okeson, Ken, 7830
Oki, Laurie, 9653
Oki, Scott, 9653
Oklahoma Gas and Electric Co., 7965
Oklahoma Publishing Co., The, 7966
Okonak, James R., 8334
Okray, Heidi, 9778
Okubo, Naoki, 7005
Okuda, Roy, 1222
Okun, Andrew M., 5380
Okun, Laurie R., 5380
Okuyama, Hirofumi, 6605
Olander, Chris, 6263, 6547
Olavarrieta-Coker, Trudie, 2506
Olayan, Hutham S., 6661
Olbricht, Joel C., 5087
Olcomendy, Patricia, 256
Olcott, Emery G., 2156
Old American Insurance Co., 4865
Old Dominican Trust Co./AMG Guaranty Trust, 9498
Old Hospital Corp., 9421
Old National Trust Co., 3158, 3173
Oldenburg, Barbara S., 7742
Oldershaw, Peter W., 6717
Oldfather, Alan, 4955
Oldford, Will, 4257
Oldham, Morris Calvin, 9100
Oldham, William M., 7767
Olds, William L., III, 700
Olds, William Lee, Jr., 700
Oldt, Patricia, 4404
Olem Shoe Corp., 2157
Olemberg, Isaac, 2157
Olemberg, Nieves, 2157
Olemberg, Roberto, 2157
Olen Foundation, John M., 6030
Oleson, Donald W., 4405
Oleson, Frances M., 4405
Oleson, Gerald E., 4405
Oleson, Gerald W., 4405
Olfers, Sarah H., 9240
Olin Corp., 2925
Olin Foundation, Spencer T. and Ann W., 2904
Olin, Jack, 7520
Oliphant, Don W., 1031
Oliva, George, III, 7800
Oliva, Jan, 9570
Olivarez, Juan R., 4326
Olive, J. Terry, 8656
Oliveira, Ana, 6615
Oliveira, Ron, 9294
Oliver, Andrew, Jr., 1784

Oliver, Bartley P., 1246
Oliver, Chris, 3124
Oliver, Christine Bireley, 292
Oliver, Daniel, 1784
Oliver, David F., 9222
Oliver, Gertrude M., 7788
Oliver, Harry M., Jr., 2957
Oliver, John C., 7788
Oliver, Julia, 4243
Oliver, Louise, 1784
Oliver, Richard D., 7788
Oliver, Richey, 9164
Oliver, Starr, 9499
Oliver, Steve, 3983
Oliver, T. Richey, 9165
Oliver, William, 4757, 5207
Olivera, Armando J., 2010
Olivier, Jeanne, 7220
Olivier, Jeanne C., 6792
Olivio, Adolfo "Rudy", 3166
Olivo, Susan, 6778
Ollinger, Joseph R., 3599
Olmstead, Tommy, 2468
Olmsted, George, 9490
Olmsted, Robert M., 5148
Olnich, Helen J., 2425
Oloffson, Richard, 3056
Olofson, Christopher E., 4875
Olofson, Elizabeth, 6124, 7032
Olofson, Jeanne H., 4875
Olofson, Scott W., 4875
Olofson, Tom H., 4875
Olofson, Tom W., 4875
Olrogg, Elgin E., 9569
Olrogg, Marian Cheney, 9569
Olsen, Barbara Jean, 9184
Olsen, David M., 9690
Olsen, Dwayne G., 9906
Olsen, Eeva-Liisa Aulikki, 4170
Olsen, Gregory H., 5342
Olsen, Kenneth H., 3976, 4170
Olsen, Michael J., 101
Olsen, Robert, 687
Olsen, Stephen G., 4252
Olsen, Thad, 4723
Olsen, Tom, 8631
Olshan, Carole, 6663
Olshan, Morton, 6663
Olshin, Jennifer, 7199
Olson, Alan, 4327
Olson, Barb, 4665
Olson, Beverly Knight, 2097
Olson, Brian, 7139
Olson, Brian T., 1618
Olson, Bruce A., 4896
Olson, Catherine Grier, 863
Olson, Charles, 1627
Olson, Cindy K., 8051
Olson, Clarine, 4327
Olson, Dale, 4962
Olson, David W., 2579
Olson, Earl B., 4640
Olson, Eric A., 9651
Olson, Gary S., 8190
Olson, Gilbert N., 7516
Olson, James, 7160
Olson, Jill, 7139
Olson, Jill J., 1618
Olson, Keith D., 4512
Olson, Kerry A., 509
Olson, Lisa, 1377
Olson, Lyle, 2927
Olson, Lyndon, 9141
Olson, Lynn, 894
Olson, M. Richard, 4447
Olson, Mary, 9779
Olson, Neil D., 5439
Olson, R. Thomas, 9594
Olson, Rex A., 970
Olson, Ron, 3275
Olson, Ronald O., 2639
Olson, Steven C., 7139
Olson, Theodore A., 2579
Olson, Thomas L., 9781

Olsson, C. Elis, 9491
Olsson, Shirley C., 9491
Olsson, Signe Maria, 9491
Olsson, Sture G., 9491
Olsson, Walter, 5026
Olvanny, George, 5194
Olwell, Carol, 9305
Olympia & York Financial Co., 5995
Olympia Industries, Inc., 4868
Omaha World Herald Branching Out, 4995
Omaha World-Herald Co., 4995
Oman, Darcy S., 9402
Oman, Mark, 3281
Oman, Richard H., 7815
Omann, Pamela E., 4657
Omdusa, Inc., 7174
Omidyar Network, LLC, 952
Omidyar, Elah'e Mir-Djalali, 1847
Omidyar, Pamela, 952
Omidyar, Pierre, 1847
Omidyar, Pierre M., 952
Omnibus Charitable Trust, 6676
Omnicare Foundation, 3443
Omnicare, Inc., 3443, 3444
Omnien, Kaye, 9743
Omron Electronics Inc., 2926
Omron Electronics LLC, 2926
Omron Healthcare, Inc., 2926
Ondersma, James R., 4410
One Heart, Inc., 6456
One Step Up, 5519
One to One Charitable Foundation, 6570
One Valley Bank, N.A., 9710
ONeill, Hampton K., 4597
ONEOK, Inc., 7967
Ono, Raymond S., 2542
Ono, Yoko, 7033
Onstead, Charles M., 9102
Onstead, Kay M., 9102
Onstead, Mary, 9102
Onstead, R. Randall, Jr., 9102
Onstead, Robert R., 9102
Onyx Holdings, Inc., 4043
Opack, Colleen M., 2257
Opatow, Lorna, 5853
Opatrny, Donald C., Jr., 6664
Opatrny, Judith T., 6664
Open Society Institute, 6237
Operation Days Work, 8747
Opferman, Thomas G., 2962
Opheim, Barb, 3278
Opi Products, Inc., 1100
Opler, Edmond, 2927
Opler, Scott, 2158
Oppenheim, Jane, 8431
Oppenheim, Paula K., 6699, 7720
Oppenheim, William J., 6699
Oppenheimer, Catherine, 5501
Oppenheimer, Edward H., 2928
Oppenheimer, Eric, 955
Oppenheimer, Gail, 956
Oppenheimer, Gerald H., 956
Oppenheimer, Hal, 955
Oppenheimer, Hamilton G., 955
Oppenheimer, Harold, 956
Oppenheimer, Harry D., 2928
Oppenheimer, Harry J., 2928
Oppenheimer, James, 2928
Oppenheimer, James K., 2928
Oppenheimer, Mark, 956
Oppenheimer, Reed, 955
Oppenheimer, Seymour, 2928
Oppens, Ursula, 5789
Oppenstein, Michael, 4876
Opperman, Dwight D., 2151, 4641
Opperman, Fane W., 4641
Opperman, John R., 3558
Opperman, Vance K., 4641
Oppitz, Richard J., 3712
Oppolo, Kathy, 3245
Opus Corp., 4642
Opus U.S. Corp., 4682

Opus, LLC, 4642
Oram, Steven H., 3613
Orband, William J., Jr., 6329
Orbanek, George, 1446
Orchard, Roland, 5400
Orchard, Stanwich & Pierce Trusts, 5547
Orco Block Co., Inc., 929
Orcutt, Pamela S., 7860
Ordean, Albert L., 4643
Ordean, Louise, 4643
Ordines, Randy, 6402
Orduna, Ruben, 3812
Ordway, Alan, 3940
Oreffice, Paul F., 4322
Oregon Ethiopian Community
    Organization, 8747
Oremus, Frederick L., 7791
Orenstein, Brian A., 1644
Orenstein, Carolyn Sue, 5344
Orenstein, Frederick, 5344
Orenstein, Henry, 5344
Orentreich Medical Group, 6667
Orentreich, David, 6667
Orentreich, Norman, 6667
Oretzky, Perry, 224
Orfalea, Natalie A., 958
Orfalea, Paul J., 958
Orgain, John B., 7372
Oriel, Pat, 4217
Oriel, Patrick J., 4407
Orion Corp., 9766
Oristaglio, Jeryl, 4063
Oristaglio, Stephen, 4063
Orlando, Ellen Lehrer, 800
Orlick, Joan F., 5178
Orme, H.J., 9313
Orme, Hence, 7139
Ormiston, Donna, 3110
Ormond, Neal, III, 2680
Ormsby, Michael C., 9589
Ormseth, Milo E., 8024, 8065
Ornest, Cindy, 959
Ornest, Laura, 959
Ornest, Maury, 959
Ornest, Michael, 959
Ornest, Ruth, 959
Orosz, Florence Upjohn, 4465
Orosz, Joel, 4233
Orosz, Joel J., 4404
Orozco, Isaiah, 6675
Orpilla, Mel, 1175
Orr, Arthur, 6329
Orr, Charles W., 3294
Orr, Douglas M., Jr., 4766
Orr, Franklin M., Jr., 972
Orr, J. Steven, 8839
Orr, James F., 7587
Orr, James F., III, 1939, 6826
Orr, Mary Lu, 3227
Orr, Robert, 7790
Orr, San W., Jr., 9763, 9931, 9969
Orr, Susan Packard, 972, 973
Orr, Tilda R., 1751
Orr, Yvonne T., 8581
Orradre, Mary, 401
Orris, Christine Bieber, 4518
Orrock, Nan Grogan, 2479
Orscheln Co., 4877
Orscheln, D.W., 4877
Orscheln, Phillip A., 4877
Orscheln, W.C., 4877
Orscheln, W.L., 4877
Orsi, Bernard, 741
Orsino, Jeannette M., 3780
Orswell, Lois, 8519
Ortega, Orlando, 342
Ortega, Ruth, 5496
Oregren, Marla, 4990
Ortenberg, Arthur, 5757
Ortenberg, Elisabeth Claiborne, 5757
Ortenstone, Susan B., 8882
Ortenzio, John M., 8366
Ortenzio, Martin J., 8366
Ortenzio, Robert A., 8366

Ortenzio, Rocco A., 8366
Orth, Karen A., 8377
Orthman, Bill, 4986
Ortho Biotech Inc., 5255
Ortho-McNeil Pharmaceutical, Inc.,
    1995, 5255
Orthwein, Laura R., 4878
Orthwein, William R., 4878
Ortiz, Augustine, 5194
Ortiz, Edward, 1723
Ortiz, Emmanuel, 8198
Ortiz, Julia Morrison, 8781
Ortiz, Pat, 5493
Ortiz, Roger, 8881, 8950
Ortwein, Linda, 4095
Orvis, Mae Zenke, 6668
Osberg, Eric, 1795
Osberg, Sally, 1158
Osbom, Melissa Coors, 1360
Osbon, Julian W., 2357
Osborn, Charles J., 9848
Osborn, Chris, 1357
Osborn, David W., 9111
Osborn, Donald R., 7076
Osborn, Edward B., 6669
Osborn, John, 1434
Osborn, John E., 1434
Osborn, Joseph F., 3250
Osborn, June E., 6471
Osborn, Mark M., 1434
Osborn, Mary, 1434
Osborn, Mary E., 1434
Osborn, Matthew P., 1434
Osborn, Melissa Coors, 1352
Osborn, Robin, 5779
Osborn, S. Bartley, 4600
Osborne Building Corp., 8714
Osborne Enterprises, Inc., 8714
Osborne, Burl, 8787
Osborne, Dee S., 9041, 9193
Osborne, Dori, 6342
Osborne, Duncan E., 8767, 9250
Osborne, Elizabeth B., 9250
Osborne, Hamish S., 3693
Osborne, Karen, 7735
Osborne, Kathleen, 8523
Osborne, Michael, 249
Osborne, Richard de J., 7143
Osborne, Richard J., 7360
Osborne, T. Travis, 6729
Osburn, Carroll, 8814
Osburn, Debra Pozega, 4243
Oschin, Daniel, 960
Oschin, Lynda, 960
Oschin, Michael, 960
Osgood, Edward H., 4005
Osgood, Hamilton, 3982
Oshei, Jean R., 6660
Oshei, R. John, 6660
Osheowitz, Michael W., 6083
Osher, Barbro, 961, 962
Osher, Bernard, 962
Osher, Bernard A., 961, 962
Oshkosh B'Gosh, Inc., 9886
Oshkosh Truck Corp., 9887
Oshman's Sporting Goods, Inc., 9104
Oshman, Barbara, 963
Oshman, David R., 963
Oshman, Jeanette, 9104
Oshman, M. Kenneth, 963
Oshman, Marilyn, 9104
Oshman, Peter L., 963
OSI Pharmaceuticals, Inc., 6670
Oski, Jessica A., 7727
Osman, Ibrahim, 6233
Osmer, Patrick S., 134
Osmun, Doreen E., 7688
Osprey Investment Partners, 7526
Ostahowski, Mark, 4217
Ostaszewski, John S., 1484
Ostby, Signe, 415
Osteen, H.M., Jr., 2357
Oster, Paul, 4479
Osterman, Sandra L., 5477

Ostin, Joyce, 964
Ostin, Michael, 964
Ostin, Morris, 964
Ostin, Rachel, 964
Ostreicher, Harry, 6671
Ostreicher, Helen, 6671
Ostreicher, Marvin, 6672
Ostreicher, Susan, 6672
Ostrem, John, 4637
Ostrofsky, Steve, 7106
Ostrosky, Ann, 5388
Ostrovsky, Rose, 6673
Ostrovsky, Vivian S., 6673
Ostrow, John B., 2002
Ostrow, Richard D., 3003
Oswald, Charles W., 4645
Oswald, David C., 4645
Oswald, Ellen Smart, 1651
Oswald, Julie, 4645
Oswald, Kathleen, 4645
Oswald, Robin Turner, 7429
Oswald, Sara, 4645
Oswald, Thomas, 4645
Oswald, William, 1651
Oswalt, James, 3133
Otenasek, Francis H., 3704
Otenasek, John H., 3704
Otenasek, Margaret B., 3704
Otenasek, Richard J., III, 3704
Otero, Ray, 4986
Otih, Otis O., 9466
Otis, Clarence, Jr., 1960
Otis, Jeffrey, 1603
Ott, Alan W., 4322, 4407
Ott, David, 7139
Ott, David J., 3558
Ott, Joseph L., 8719
Ott, Steve, 9981
Ottaway, James H., Jr., 5879
Otte, Sarah Wilson, 3116
Otten, Irene, 561
Ottens, John, 128
Ottens, Sophie, 128
Ottenstroer, Duane L., 1940
Otterlei, John, 6176
Otterstetter, Debbie, 8039
Otting, Joseph M., 4704
Ottinger, Betty Ann, 1863
Ottinger, Jennifer, 6674
Ottinger, June Godfrey, 6674
Ottinger, Lawrence, 6674
Ottinger, Lea Anne, 6674
Ottinger, Randy, 6674
Ottinger, Richard L., 6674
Ottinger, Ronald, 6674
Ottino, Madeline R., 5464
Ottley, Judy Fowler, 2356
Ottley, Marian W., 1678, 2523
Ottmar, Joanne H., 7519
Otto, C.R., 7807
Otto, Douglas G., 3166
Otto, Gene P., 8300
Ottum, Jeff, 9810
Otunnu, Olara A., 5707
Ouchi, William G., 5037
Ouellette, Louise, 5116
Ould, Susan, 6551
Oussani, James J., 2062
Oustalet, Richard C., 3520
Outcalt, David B., 7792
Outcalt, Jane Q., 7792
Outcalt, Jon H., 7688, 7792
Outcalt, Jon H., Jr., 7792
Outcalt, Robin M., 7792
Outerstuff, Ltd., 5451
Outhwaite Revocable Trust, 1994 June
    G., The, 966
Outlaw, Karen, 6634
Outpost, 3683
OVB Charitable Trust, 9710
Ovel, John A., 4909
Overby, Amy T., 9854
Overby, Charles L., 9424
Overby, Jeff, 1949

Overend, Carol C., 2377
Overend, G. David, 2377
Overend, George D., 2377
Overend, William M., 2377
Overlock, Emily Phelps, 5930
Overlock, Katharine, 5930
Overlock, Willard J., 5930
Overlock, Willard J., Jr., 5930
Overlock, William J., III, 5930
Overly, Edith H., 4064
Overseas Adventure Travel, 3929
Overseas Military Sales Corp., 6057
Overstreet Charitable Trust, M., 2159
Overstreet Investment Co., 2159
Overstreet, Jane, 1361
Overton, Carter, 9231
Overton, David, 378
Overton, Sheila, 378
Overton, Suellen, 3298
Oviatt, Kim A., 1126
Ovitz, Jane, 2701
Ovitz, Michael S., 968
Owades, Lorri S., 4147
Owen Foundation, Dian Graves, 9226
Owen, B.B., 9107
Owen, Eleanor M., 7346
Owen, Jay L., 9890
Owen, Laura N., 4496
Owen, Linda, 4392
Owen, Mary M., 4484
Owen, Norman, 941, 1099
Owen, Richard, 4540
Owens Corning, 7793
Owens, Anna E., 4262
Owens, Brig, 1843
Owens, Christine M., 2503
Owens, Denise, 4737
Owens, Dimple, 2980
Owens, Edward T., 2980
Owens, Frederick W., 2489
Owens, J.W., 2653
Owens, Jack B., 548
Owens, Jeannine, 2980
Owens, Kenneth R., 2462
Owens, Mary M., 2929
Owens, Michael, 2929
Owens, Mitchell S., 7559
Owens, Nancy C., 3488
Owens, Paul D., Jr., 33
Owens, Reginald, 5184
Owens, Robert T., 2211
Owens, Terri, 3133
Owens, Thomas M., 2929
Owens, Thomas M., Jr., 2929
Owens, William A., 5707
Owens-Illinois, Inc., 7569
Owings Family Foundation, 8608
Owsley, Alvin M., 9108
Owsley, Alvin M., Jr., 9108
Owsley, David T., 9108
Owsley, Lucy B., 9108
Oxendine, Mary C., 7431
Oxford League, Inc., The, 5099
Oxley, John C., 7968, 7984
Oxley, John T., 7968
Oxley, Timothy J., 3375
Oxman, David C., 1559
Oxman, Phyllis S., 6731
Oxnam, Robert B., 5937, 6825
Oxnard, Ben, III, 2346
Oxnard, Ben, Jr., 2346
Oxnard, Thomas Thornton, 969
Oxner, Glenn, 8583
Oxner, Louis, 8583
Oyler, Gregory, 3591
Oyler, John, 8208
Ozinga Bros., Inc., 2930
Ozinga, Beverly, 2930
Ozinga, Charles J., 9822
Ozinga, James A., 2930
Ozinga, Judith A., 9822
Ozinga, Kenneth J., 9822
Ozinga, Martin, III, 2930
Ozinga, Martin, Jr., 2930

Ozinga, Richard K., 2930
Ozmun, Beverly L., 5030

P & L Charity Foundation, 5527
Pabalan, Steven S., 2121
Pabst, Jerry, 4554
PACCAR Inc, 9656
Pace, C. Nick, 9085
Pace, David A., 9690
Pace, Dorothy, 4065
Pace, George W., 9400
Pace, James C., Jr., 8595
Pacenta, Patricia, 7526
Pacesetter Corp., The, 5001
Pacesetter Fabrics, 379
Pacesetter Systems, Inc., 2054
Pacheco, Emilio J., 3157
Pacheco, Fernando, 123
Pacheco, Rod, 405
Pachon, Harry P., 659
Pachtner, John, 474
Pacific Century Trust, 2545, 2547
Pacific Coast Construction Co., 559
Pacific Cold Storage, Inc., 588
Pacific Life Insurance Co., 970
Pacific Mutual Holding Co., 970
Pacific Tube Co., 8283
PacifiCare Health Plan Administrators,
    Inc., 971
PacifiCare Health Systems, Inc., 971
PacifiCare of California, Inc., 971
PacifiCorp, 8050
Pacilio, Robert C., 2944
Pack, Gary, 8690
Pack, Zachary J., 5704
Packaging Tape, Inc., 9806
Packaging, Inc., 4568
Packard Foundation, David and Lucile,
    The, 483, 973
Packard, David, 972
Packard, David W., 973
Packard, George R., 7185
Packard, Julie, 4513
Packard, Julie E., 972
Packard, Lucile, 972
Packard, Pamela M., 973
Packard, Ralph K., 8490
Packer Family Foundation, The, 5126,
    7174
Packer, Augusta L., 5777
Packer, Barbara, 6931
Packer, Barbara Bell, 8786
Packer, Barry D., 8786
Packman, Jeffrey N., 4007
Packman, Karen Linde, 4007
Pactor, Mort, 351
Padar, Ed, 8960
Paddack, Susan, 7931
Paddison, David, 2480
Paddock, James W., 3384
Paddock, Karen Schwartz, 6944
Paddock, Robert W., 8960
Paden, Leona, 4962
Padgett, Melissa Rodgers, 1334
Padgett, Nancy B., 9543
Padilla, Edward, Jr., 5493
Padnos Foundation, Louis & Helen,
    4406
Padnos Iron and Metal Co., Louis, 4406
Padnos, Cynthia B., 4406
Padnos, Daniel P., 4406
Padnos, Douglas B., 4406
Padnos, Jeffrey S., 4406
Padnos, Mitchell W., 4406
Padnos, Shelley E., 4406
Padnos, William R., 4406
Padron, Eduardo J., 359
Paduano, Daniel P., 6677
Paduano, James A., 6677
Paduano, Nancy C., 6677
Paen, Mariana S., 5323
Paez, Sergio, 4057
Pagano, Janet, 355, 404

Page, Amy Hattler, 1825
Page, Anthony, 8789
Page, Arthur, 4123
Page, Arthur B., 3830, 4091
Page, Beatrice H., 1683
Page, Clarence, 1776
Page, David K., 4254
Page, Frank C., 9434
Page, Henry, 7569
Page, John J., 7890
Page, Johnny, 2270
Page, Kenneth R., 7079, 7176
Page, Larry, 606
Page, Lincoln, 5604
Page, Louis, 2554
Page, Max, 9424
Page, Richard M., 3833, 8048
Page, Suzie, 2110
Pagen, Barbara Pauley, 984
Paglia, Catherine James, 6252
Pagliuca, Stephen, 3972
Pagliuca, Stephen G., 3972
Pagoaga, Jim, 7667
Pahl, J.C., 4648
Pahl, J.M., 4648
Paige, Joy E., 7438
Paige, Michele A., 6917
Paige, Rod, 1795
Paight, Audrey S., 1616
Paight, Joseph, 1616
Pail, Norbert J., 8338
Pailthorp, C. James, 1823
Paine Foundation, Martin S., 7176
Paine, Anne Marie, 1532
Paine, Annette, 9793
Paine, Brent, 9651
Paine, Cary, 9691
Paine, Louis B., 8965
Paine, Peter, 5517
Paine, Robert H., 4738
Paine, Stephen D., Mrs., 4074
Paine, W.K., 4738
PaineWebber Inc., 5433
Painter, Dean E., Jr., 7438
Painter, Jean W., 7255
Pakis, William R., 9255
Pakula, Annette, 3640
Pakula, Lawrence, 3640
Pakula, Sheila S., 3640
Palacio, Ana, 5707
Palacios, Mario, 3245
Palash, Carl, 6570
Palenchar, David J., 1374
Palermo, James P., 8345
Palestroni, Alfiero, 5345
Palestroni, Lucia, 5345
Paley, Robert A., 4868
Paley, William C., 6679
Paley, William S., 6679
Palfney, John, 4025
Palisano, Harriet A., 6680
Palisano, Vincent H., 6680
Paller, Carolyn, 2440
Pallotta, James J., 1664
Palm, Ashley G., 7280
Palm, Gregory K., 6055
Palm, Michael, 6681
Palmer, Alphonse, 1541
Palmer, Barbara R., 6683
Palmer, Charles, 6683
Palmer, Charles L., 1941
Palmer, Daniel A., 9085
Palmer, David, 6683
Palmer, David A., 2463
Palmer, Francis Asbury, 6682
Palmer, Gerald, 2680
Palmer, H. William, 7342
Palmer, Ian C., 1907
Palmer, James R., 6683
Palmer, Johnnye K., 8564
Palmer, Joseph Beveridge, 1907
Palmer, Kaye, 3220
Palmer, L. Guy, II, 5827
Palmer, Lesley, 6562

Palmer, Malcolm M., 2360
Palmer, Mary, 9890
Palmer, Mary Jane, 7749
Palmer, Nancy J., 1421
Palmer, Ralph W., 4945
Palmer, Rebekah Thompson, 8723
Palmer, Richard, 5194
Palmer, Richard N., 1563
Palmer, Rogers, 9890
Palmer, Rusty, 9977
Palmer, Sheryl Rogers, 9155
Palmer, Vicki R., 2351
Palmer, Virginia, 1621
Palmerian, Sidonio, 417
Palmert, Mark R., 9348
Palmisano, Samuel J., 6221
Palmore, Roderick A., 2982
Palmrose, Kirsten, 3392
Palo, John, 7764
Paloheimo Trust, Leonora Curtin, 974
Paloheimo, George, 974
Palotay, Marc, 933
Palumbo, A.J., 8368
Palumbo, Michael J., 2372
Palumbo, P.J., 8368
Paluszek, Stephen J., 6912
Pamida, Inc., 9891
Pampusch, Anita, 4498
Pampusch, Anita M., 4524
Panaggio, Peter, 4166
Panarites, Chris, 5255
Panaritis, Andrea, 6790
Panazzi, D., 8150, 8301
Pancoast, Terrence R., 8064, 8065
Pancoast, Terry, 8032
Panda Management Co., Inc., 975
Panda Restaurant Group, Inc., 975
Pandoli, Barbara S., 7269
Pane, Norma R., 5291
Paneth, Morton, 6685
Paneth, Samuel, 6685
Paneth, Thomas, 6685
Pang, Sarah, 2670
Panic, Dawn, 976
Panic, Milan, 976
Panico, Al, 1275
Pannell, William C., 9218
Pannu, Rajender K., 3503
Panoringan, Mario, 989
Pansing, Thomas R., 4977
Pansing, Thomas R., Jr., 4994
Panter, Scott, 1382
Pantola, Paul, 3038
Pantozzi, Paul M., 5359
Panzier, Ira, 6849
Paoli, Francis E., 4259
Paolozzi, Anthony, 5783
Papa, Anthony T., 4742
Papa, Barzella, 2015
Papa, J.A., 5261
Papachristou, Mark, 2259
Papadakis, Eliana, 8378
Papantonio, J. Michael, 2110
Papantonio, Michael, 2110
Papantonio, Terri, 2110
Paparelli, Ellen, 2660
Paperin, Stewart J., 6665, 7023
Papouras, Christopher, 2070
Papp, Rosellen C., 98
Pappajohn, John, 3322
Pappajohn, Mary, 3322
Pappas, Arthur M., 4067
Pappas, Helen K., 4066
Pappas, John, 4066
Pappas, Martha R., 4067, 4209
Pappas, Theodore J., 1957
Pappas, Thomas Anthony, 4066
Pappas, Thomas C., 4066
Pappas, Thomas E., Jr., 7854
Pappas, Tom, 6594
Pappous, Perry, 9476
Papson, Costa L., 7164
Paradis, Bruce, 4587
Paradis, Daisy, 5607

Paradis, J.A., 3409
Paragon Capital Mgmt., 3373
Paragon Ranch, Inc., 1384
Parcych, Charyl A., 7905
Pardee, Elsa U., 4407
Pardee, J. Douglas, 978
Pardee, Marian R., 978
Pardes, Herbert, 6471
Pardo, Damian J., 1957
Pardoe Trust, Helen P., 4068
Pardoe, Charles E., 4068
Pardoe, Charles H., II, 4068
Pardoe, Edward D., III, 7176
Pardoe, P. Bruce, 4068
Pardoe, Samuel P., 4068
Pardue, Mary Lou, 7333
Parent, Tom, 3188
Parente, Maggie, 474
Parenti, Renato R., 229
Parham, Helen, 9454
Parigi Group, Ltd., 7037
Paris, Nancy M., 2394
Paris, Peter, 2176
Pariseau, Edward P., 3816
Parish, Ivy, 4629
Parish, Preston L., 4408
Parish, Suzanne D., 4266
Parish, Suzanne U.D., 4408
Parisi, Camille, 5804
Parisi, Joseph, 1256
Pariso, Tony, 1359
Parizeau, William M., 4195
Park Corp., 7794
Park Foundation, Inc., 7162
Park Grove Realty Co., 3683
Park Mgmt., 7068
Park National Bank, The, 2661, 7714,
    7795
Park National Corp., 7795
Park Place Entertainment Corp., 8648
Park Terrace Care Center, 6871
Park, Alice, 8996
Park, Christine, 5110
Park, Dale, Jr., 2638, 2831
Park, Dan K., 7794
Park, Dorothy D., 6688
Park, James, 7582
Park, James C., 4232
Park, Janice, 1504
Park, Judy, 8996
Park, Kelly C., 7794
Park, Ki Suh, 345
Park, Patrick M., 7794
Park, Piper A., 7794
Park, Raymond P., 7794
Park, Richard A., 8745
Park, Roy H., 6688
Park, Roy H., III, 7162
Park, Roy Hampton, Jr., 7162
Park, Sunny K., 2355
Parke, David W., II, 7969
Parke, Davis & Co., 1995
Parke, Jennifer Hudson, 4343
Parke, Kevin, 9259
Parker Foundation, Theodore Edson,
    The, 4014
Parker Pen Co., The, 9820
Parker Trust, 2384
Parker Trust, Ruth F., 7642
Parker, Adelaide, 6915
Parker, Alan M., 3552
Parker, Alan S., 1590
Parker, Andrea, 2677
Parker, Ann L., 472
Parker, Arthur, 3934
Parker, Arthur H., 4133
Parker, Bertram B., 6009
Parker, Beverly A., 1957
Parker, Bill, 26
Parker, Bradley, 9704
Parker, Byron A., 9086
Parker, Daniel, 3214
Parker, David, 7667
Parker, Deana A., 9492

Parker, Diane Helow, 2055
Parker, Diane W., 2514
Parker, Elizabeth Rindskopf, 1080
Parker, Ellen K., 7349
Parker, Faith K.P., 5346
Parker, Franklin E., IV, 5440
Parker, Gerald T., 979
Parker, Glen P., 5346
Parker, Gray S., 3464
Parker, Henry E., 1519
Parker, Hilary Joyce Barr, 731
Parker, Inez Grant, 979
Parker, J.H., III, 9461
Parker, Jack, 6690
Parker, Jackson V., III, 9906
Parker, Jette, 3552
Parker, John F., 5440
Parker, John O., 3956
Parker, Josh, 6083
Parker, Judith W., 9704
Parker, Julia Ryan, 8416
Parker, Kate, 1163
Parker, Katherine, 6884
Parker, Kathys S., 7576
Parker, Kenneth W., 3598
Parker, Latanae R., Jr., 2121
Parker, Leroy, 9408
Parker, Leroy M., 6884
Parker, Maclyn T., 3121
Parker, Margaret H., 5440
Parker, Mark, 8046
Parker, Mary, 1693
Parker, Mary E., 1738
Parker, Mary Kay, 3464
Parker, Mary Webber, 4343
Parker, Michael, 472
Parker, Molly, 1518
Parker, Nancy F., 2390
Parker, Patrick, 5524
Parker, Peggy S., 8584
Parker, R. Jerry, Jr., 9492
Parker, Raymond P., 8341
Parker, Renee, 8634
Parker, Richard, 3199
Parker, Richard Carlyle, 2390
Parker, Ron, 6714
Parker, Ronald C., 8013
Parker, Rosalie L., 6884
Parker, Ruth F., 7642
Parker, Sally L., 4711
Parker, Sandra, 4994
Parker, Scott, 9120
Parker, Stephen T., 2514
Parker, Steven, 3707
Parker, Susan, 694
Parker, Theodore Edson, 4069
Parker, Thomas, 694, 1093
Parker, Thomas C., 694
Parker, Thomas W., 2514
Parker, Westbrook, 9382
Parker, William A., III, 2390
Parker, William A., Jr., 2364, 2390
Parker-Hannifin Corp., 7796
Parkey, Glen, 8758
Parkhill, Don, 7593
Parkhill, Sheila, 7593
Parkhurst, Patricia D., 6896
Parkin, Jennifer H., 9329
Parkin, John, 6258
Parkinson, Geoffrey M., 1526, 1530,
    1531, 1611, 1612
Parkinson, Molly O., 7176
Parkinson, Susan, 9325
Parkison, Kathy, 3177
Parks, Blanche C., 3400
Parks, Carol S., 4128
Parks, Diane, 562
Parks, Dorothy C., 2931
Parks, Edward M., 4458
Parks, Floyd L., 4324, 4465
Parks, Fred, 9109
Parks, Gary, 5052
Parks, Joseph A., Jr., 4128
Parks, Loren E., 5052

Parks, Martin A., 6820
Parks, Mary Alice, 9623
Parks, Michael M., 7603
Parks, Ray, 5052
Parkton, Frances R., 5059
Parkview Realty Co., 6691
Parkway Corp., 8147
Parlee, Donald E., 8181
Parmer, Barbara J., 8369
Parmer, Carolyn Noonan, 2932
Parmer, George A., 8369
Parmer, James W., 2932
Parmer, John F., 2932
Parmer, Raymond C., 2932
Parnassus, George J., 286
Parnell, Marc, 183
Parnell, Todd, 4798
Parnes, Emanuel, 5348
Parnes, Herschel, 5348
Paroo, Iqbal, 952
Paroski, Margaret W., 5785
Parr, Cheri S., 6692
Parr, Gary W., 6692
Parr, Helen Frye, 5440
Parr, Martha Sue, 9893
Parran, Theodore V., Jr., 7917
Parravano, Carlo, 5327
Parravano, Teresa Haggerty, 8932
Parrino, Emily, 9462
Parrish, Bill, 8747
Parrish, Carol, 5692
Parrish, Charlotte, 3437
Parrish, Cynthia V., 7660
Parrish, Daniel I., 1080
Parrish, John M., 3624
Parrish, Lee H., 7660
Parrish, Margaret, 8747
Parrish, Steven C., 5545
Parrish, Susan, 2015
Parrott, John C., II, 9419
Parrott, Peter, Jr., 8584
Parrotte, Dianne, 4142
Parrs, Marianne, 1571
Parry, Gwyn P., 678
Parry, Suzanne V., 194
Parshelsky, Moses L., 6693
Parsky, Gerald, 320
Parsley, Georganna S., 9215
Parsons, Andrew, 5671, 5673
Parsons, James D., 2633
Parsons, Kathryn M., 4614
Parsons, Laura, 6437
Parsons, Marvin, 9736
Parsons, Mary Morton, 9493
Parsons, Michael J., 9239
Parsons, Ralph M., 980
Parsons, Richard D., 6383, 6825, 7142
Parsons, Robert W., Jr., 5247
Parsons, Roger, 6694
Parsons, Roger B., 5247
Parsons, Stuart, 7537
Parsons, Stuart N., 7795
Parsons, Susan E., 3184
Parsons, Vera Davis, 1961
Parsons, William, Jr., 1697, 7224
Partee, Sue Garrett, 9151
Partners Trust Bank, 6645
Partners, Abel, 3970
Partnership for a Drug-Free America,
    7174
Partridge, Charles Kent, 314
Partridge, Charles W., 314
Partridge, George F., 9726
Partridge, Herbert Scott, 314
Partridge, Judith, 930
Partridge, Kathryn B., 314
Partridge, Lamar J., 8732
Partridge, Mary B., 5257
Parvin, Albert B., 981
Parvin, Phyllis, 981
Parvin, Stanley, 981
Pascal, Clara, 1929, 2163
Pascal, Robin, 2163
Pascoe, Samuel J., 4725

Pascoualle, Marie, 1156
Pascualy, Ralph, 1040
Pascucci, Christopher S., 6696
Pascucci, Michael C., 6696
Pascucci, Ralph P., 6696
Pasek, Jeffrey I., 5333
Paskach, David M., 4676
Pasky, Cynthia J., 4254
Pasquale, Caren Demoulas, 3879
Pasqualoni, Sheri C., 1482
Pasquerilla, Mark E., 8153
Pasquinelli, Anthony R., 2933
Pasquinelli, Bruno A., 2933
Pass, Deborah, 2090
Pass, Mark, 2090
Passafaro, Jeffrey G., 6638
Passaro, Tim, 4231
Passen, Richard B., 5399
Passios, Tom, 1671
Passman, Donald S., 544
Pastin, Max, 2623
Pastorello, Thomas J., 1586
Pastrick, Courtney Clark, 3590
Pastula, Joanne, 193
Patch, Thomas N., 3175
Pate, J.M., 2519
Pate, Mike, 1945
Pate, William C., 2323
Patek, Christopher, 1692
Patek, Patrick J., 1692
Patek, Rose B., 1692
Patel, Harshadray, 1082
Patel, Kiran P., 8208
Patel, Nilesh, 1082
Patel, Raj, 7856
Patel, Ramila, 1082
Patenaude, Wayne F., 3800
Paterna Enterprises, LLP, 127
Paterson, Allan G., Jr., 9156
Paterson, Basil A., 6320
Paterson, Jill, 510
Paterson, Sheila M., 5496
Patience, 3683
Patino, Douglas X., 350, 4399, 9567
Patkotak, Crawford, 80
Patricelli, Alison J., 1623
Patricelli, Margaret S., 1623
Patricelli, Robert E., 1623
Patricelli, Thomas R., 1623
Patrick, Carl L., 2459
Patrick, Carl L., Jr., 2459
Patrick, Charles F., 416
Patrick, Deval L., 2352
Patrick, Donna, 9736
Patrick, Frances E., 2459
Patrick, Howard W., 2015
Patrick, John J., Jr., 1482
Patrick, Katherine, 4347
Patrick, Michael D., 6634
Patrick, Michael E., 9049, 9146
Patrick, Michael W., 2459
Patriot Contract Services, LCC, 894
Patry, Kenneth, 5017
Patt, Ruth Marcus, 5297
Pattee, Russell S., 8037
Patterson Trust No. 2, Robert, 1624
Patterson Trust, Cissy, The, 1840
Patterson Trust, Proctor, 7797
Patterson, Ana Maria, 3893
Patterson, Andy, 8630
Patterson, Aubrey Abbott, 3368
Patterson, Bill, 4591
Patterson, Carolyn L., 56
Patterson, Clara Guthrie, 1624
Patterson, Cynthia B., 3993
Patterson, David, 7244
Patterson, David T., 7906
Patterson, Deborah J., 4868
Patterson, Donald H., Jr., 9455
Patterson, Frederick W., 2460
Patterson, H. Donald, 7814
Patterson, J. Michael, 406
Patterson, James F., 7771
Patterson, Jane S., 7458

Patterson, Katheryn C., 6313
Patterson, Lauren H., 4746
Patterson, Liz, 4315
Patterson, Marvin Breckinridge, 3684
Patterson, Rich, 3275
Patterson, Richard B., 2989, 3058
Patterson, Robert Leet, 1624
Patterson, Robert P., Jr., Hon., 6156
Patterson, Sally D., 4519
Patterson, Sam G., 4746
Patterson, Samuel R., 8388
Patterson, Solon, 2500
Patterson, Stella, 2424
Patterson, Susan W., 7355
Patterson, Thomas L., 56
Patterson, Wes, 5498
Patterson, William, 1446
Pattillo Properties, Robert, Inc., 2474
Pattillo Split Interest Trust, 2464
Pattillo, Kathleen Barksdale, 2474
Pattillo, Robert A., 2474, 2515
Pattillo-Cohen, Lynn L., 2464
Patton Boggs, LLP, 6356
Patton, Bob, 3361
Patton, Brenda, 3214
Patton, Henry, 2468
Patton, Jo Allen, 9550
Patton, Kristin, 3084
Patton, Michael B., 34
Patton, Robert W., III, 7997
Patton, Samuel, 3121
Patton, Sharyle, 1165
Patton, Thomas J., 7814
Pattullo, Matt S., 7078
Patty, Frank, Jr., 4739
Patyrak, Robert S., 9165
Patzer, Shane A., 4213
Patzer, Tiffany L., 4213
Pau, Peter, 1149
Pau, Susanna, 1149
Paul, Andrew M., 6697
Paul, Andrew S., 1664
Paul, Dana F., 7817
Paul, Donna Berkman, 7545
Paul, Douglas L., 5807
Paul, Gregory M., 1198
Paul, Heidi Reuter, 7817
Paul, Josephine Bay, 5606
Paul, Judith, 1435
Paul, Kathryn A., 1356
Paul, Margaret B., 6697
Paul, Mia, 1435
Paul, Robert A., 7545, 8192
Paul, Steven M., 3192, 3193
Paul, Terrance, 1435
Paul, Toni H., 2788
Paul, Weiss, Rifkind, Wharton & Garrison
    LLP, 5905
Paule, Barbara, 8320
Pauley, Ann, 6087
Pauley, Dorothy A., 9494
Pauley, Matthew V., 984
Pauley, Rachael, 8870
Pauley, Stanley F., 9494
Pauley, Stephen M., 984
Pauli, Ann G., 9111
Pauli, Diane, 402
Paulin, Kit, 2678
Pauling, Delayne H., Rev., 4244
Paulk, Kathryn Anne, 2018
Paull, Lee C., III, 9716
Paulos, Angela D., 9112
Paulos, James J., 9112
Paulos, John J., 9112
Paulos, Kristen, 5343
Paulos, Sam G., 9112
Paulson, Amanda Clark, 5645
Paulson, Henry M., Jr., 5645
Paulson, Henry Merritt, III, 5645
Paulson, Jean Ellen, 3426
Paulson, Kenneth A., 9424
Paulson, L. Edwin, Jr., 3426
Paulson, Wendy J., 5645
Paulucci, Jeno F., 2164

Pfeiffer, Robert H., 5351
Pfeil, Robin Atwood, 7866
Pfenninger, Steve, 3165
PFI, Inc., 8516
Pfirman, Frank, 7660
Pfister, A.J., 98
Pfizer Inc., 3677, 5990, 6232, 6720, 7174
Pfizer Pharamaceutical Co., Inc., 1995
Pfizer/Warner Lambert, 2732
Pflaum, Jeffrey D., 4496
Pfleger, George T., 998
Pfleger, Sandra B., 998
Pfleger, Thomas G., 998
Pfluger, Bob, 9164
Pfluger, Karen, 9165
Pforzheimer, Carl A., 6721
Pforzheimer, Carl H., III, 6721
Pforzheimer, Carol K., 6721
Pforzheimer, Elizabeth S., 6721
Pfrommer, James L., 5058
PG&E Gas Transmission, Texas Corp., 1000
PGA, 3512
PGA Tour, 1395
PGH Conf. on Analytical Chemistry and Applied Spectroscopy, 8449
Phan-Gruber, Mary, 8107
Phanstiel, Howard, 971
Phares, Edward W., 4725
Phares, Margene, 4991
Pharma, 7436
Pharmacia & Upjohn, Inc., 5990, 7174
Pharmacy Network National Corp., 7446
Pharmacy Network National Corporation Trust, 7446
Phayer, Alberta, 7449
Phelan, Daniel J., Dr., 4347
Phelan, Frank, 6723
Phelan, Joseph, 6207
Phelan, Kevin C., 3812
Phelan, Mary, 6723
Phelizon, Jean-Francois, 8419
Phelps Dodge Corp., 129
Phelps Foundation, Mary, 7176
Phelps, Carol B., 1002
Phelps, Irene S., 3009
Phelps, James S., 1002
Phelps, Jennifer, 4533
Phelps, John W., 1002
Phelps, Michael E., 1001
Phelps, Michael F., 3806
Phelps, Patricia E., 1001
Phelps, Suzanne Dansby, 75
Phelps, W.H., 7956
Phelps, William H., 404
Phibro Animal Health Corp., 5126
Philadelphia Gear Corp., 8093
Philanthropic Collaborative, 583
Philbin, Ann, 5550, 7215
Philipp, Alicia, 2355, 2489
Philippakos, Laurel G., 5964
Philips Foundation, Jesse & Caryl, The, 1642
Philips, Blaine T., Jr., 1713
Philips, Caryl, 7804
Philips, Gerald R., Mrs., 6932
Philips, Jesse, 7804
Philips, Joann, 844
Philips, John F., 7443
Phillip Brothers Chemicals, Inc., 5126
Phillips Charitable Trust, Waite and Genevieve, 5492
Phillips International, Inc., 1841
Phillips Petroleum Co., 7933
Phillips Plastics Corp., 9743
Phillips Publishing International, Inc., 1841
Phillips, Alexandria C., 927, 994
Phillips, Ann D., 7039
Phillips, Arthur William, 8380
Phillips, Bessie Wright, 4083
Phillips, Betsy, 169
Phillips, Betty M., 8716

Phillips, Blaine T., 1713, 1734
Phillips, Britt Hansen, 2782
Phillips, C. Deborah, 4057
Phillips, Candace, 6724
Phillips, Carmen R., 8013
Phillips, Charles G., 6724
Phillips, D. Martin, 9122
Phillips, Daniel A., 3828, 4200
Phillips, David, 3682
Phillips, Dean, 4655
Phillips, Deborah R., 5574
Phillips, Della, 2168
Phillips, Dennis, 7653
Phillips, Donald, 3457
Phillips, Ed, 7653
Phillips, Edith, 1739
Phillips, Edward J., 4655
Phillips, Edward Jay, 4630
Phillips, Edwin, 4082
Phillips, Elizabeth K., 2587
Phillips, Elliott W., 5492
Phillips, Genevieve, 5492
Phillips, George, 414, 1003
Phillips, Howard, 2168
Phillips, Hoyt, 7405
Phillips, Inc., Dr., 2168
Phillips, Jay, 4655
Phillips, Jeanne, 4655
Phillips, Joel, 2345
Phillips, Liane M., 9122
Phillips, Lisa, 7215
Phillips, Louie M., 8716
Phillips, Marian, 17
Phillips, Mary K., 1983
Phillips, Merry Lee, 169
Phillips, Michael, 8995
Phillips, Michael, Jr., 5194
Phillips, Morton B., 4655
Phillips, Nathaniel P., Jr., 3464
Phillips, Pat, 4968
Phillips, Pauline, 4655
Phillips, Ronald, 9831
Phillips, Susan M., 3019
Phillips, T. Ward, 3317
Phillips, Thomas, 3324
Phillips, Thomas L., 1841
Phillips, Virginia, 5492
Phillips, William, 3145
Phillips, William S., 7207
Phillips-Van Heusen Corp., 6725
Philp, Lisa L., 7014
Philpot, Buddy D., 186
Philpott, Susan, 4817
Philpotts, Douglas, 2555
Phinney, Allison, 1018
Phinney, David G., 1132
Phinney, Jan, 1018
Phinny, Peter, 4327
Phipps, Amy Dameron, 9296
Phipps, Beulah G., 9399
Phipps, Harriet, 5352
Phipps, Helen Clark, 9898
Phipps, Howard, Jr., 5352, 6633
Phipps, Mary S., 5513, 5647
Phipps, Stephen C., 9898
Phoebus, Richard W., Sr., 3600
Phoenix Charitable Trust, Anne & Julius, 5193
Phoenix Cos., Inc., The, 1627
Phoenix Home Life Mutual Insurance Co., 1627
Phoenix National Trust Co., 1627
Phoenix, Anne, 5193
Phoenix, Frank, 7496
Phoenix, Frank J., 5193
Phoenix, J. Staurt, 5193
Phoenix, James E., 5193
Piana, Beth Panesh, 6482
Pianalto, Sandra, 7576
Piano, Phyllis, 219
Pianowski, Mike, 3145
Piasecka, Beata P., 5263
Piasecki, Christopher, 5263
Piasecki, Gregory, 5263

Piasecki, Wojciech, 5263
Piassick, Joel B., 2408
Picariello, Richard, 8463
Piccone, Debbie, 6529
Picek, John, 4509
Picerne, Kenneth A., 1004
Pichel, Christy, 1206
Picheny, Stanley, 6219
Pichon, Emily, 3226
Pichon, Emily E., 3121
Pichon, John N., 3226
Pichon, John N., Jr., 3121
Pick, Albert, III, 2943
Pick, Albert, Jr., 2943
Pick, Joan M., 9899
Pick, Melitta S., 9899
Pickard, Frank C., 7498
Pickard, Mary, 4690
Pickard, Max R., 5738
Pickard, William F., 4254
Pickens, William B., 8588
Picker, Harvey, 5659
Pickering, Jeffrey R., 1942
Pickering, Kenneth E., 3461
Pickering, Thomas R., Amb., 5707
Pickett, Cecil, 3677
Pickle, James W., 8717
Pickler, Irv, 220
Pico 26, LLC, 379
Picotte, Brooke A., 5935
Picotte, John D., 5935
Picotte, John D., Jr., 5935
Picotte, Kathleen M., 6584
Picotte, Margaret L., 6584
Picotte, Michael B., 6584
Picower, Barbara, 2169
Picower, Jeffry M., 2169
Piediscalzi, Nick, 825
Piedmont Natural Gas Co., Inc., 7447
Piepel, John D., 4501
Pieper Electric, Inc., 9902
Pieper, Richard R., Sr., 9902
Pier, Nancy G., 6042
Pierce, Barbara P., 2904
Pierce, Charles E., 3627
Pierce, Charles F., 2303
Pierce, David Hyde, 648
Pierce, Ed, 300
Pierce, Edna B., 1690
Pierce, Elsie, 4269
Pierce, Eve, 8382
Pierce, Fenner & Smith, 6537
Pierce, Gretchen, 8382
Pierce, Harold Whitworth, 4084
Pierce, J. Peter, 8382
Pierce, Joseph E., 3316
Pierce, Karen, 8382
Pierce, Kathleen F., 8382
Pierce, Larry S., 1403
Pierce, Leo W., Jr., 8270, 8382
Pierce, Leo W., Sr., 8382
Pierce, Marjorie L., 8382
Pierce, Mary Elizabeth, 8382
Pierce, Michael, 8382
Pierce, Nancy L., 3634
Pierce, Richard B., 3149
Pierce, Sandra E., 4254
Pierce, Sarah Rob Colby, 1879
Pierce, Thomas M., 3527
Pierce, Todd, 562
Pierce, Vicki, 4758
Pierce, Watson, 4269
Pierce, Winifred Davis, 7353
Piercy, Ralph, 5047
Piereson, James, 6987
Pierne, James, 3600
Pierpont, Robert Joe, 8443
Pierre, Ron, 1883
Pierre, Scott, 2766
Pierre-Oetker, Leigh, 880
Pierremont Anesthesia Consultants, 3512
Piersall, Rick, 9928
Pierskalla, William P., 4524

Piersol, Catherine V., 4524
Pierson, Catherine, 3489
Pierson, Robert, 3673
Pierson, W. Michel, 3673
Pierson, Wayne G., 8042
Pietrafitta, Clifford E., 8195
Pietrini, Andrew G., 5301
Pietroforte, Gerald, 1527
Pietzner, Clemens, 8495
Pifer, Janeth K., 8449
Pigott, Charles M., 9650, 9656
Pigott, Dana, 9650
Pigott, Gaye T., 9643
Pigott, James C., 9643, 9650
Pigott, Kenneth G., 3040
Pigott, M.C., 9663
Pigott, Mark C., 9656
Pigott, Mary, 9650, 9677
Pigott, Maureen, 9643
Pigott, Maureen "Dina", 9643
Pigott, Michael J., 9677
Pigott, Paul, 9643
Piha, Morris, 9675
Pike, Carleton "Davis", 3548
Pike, Charles L., 1644
Pike, Drummond, 583
Pike, James, 1883
Pike, Robert W., 2588
Piland, Deborah Dech, 9487
Piland, Richard, 9487
Pilchard, A. Franklin, 2944
Pilcher, Gregory F., 7950
Pilcher, Ronald M., 2327
Pildner, Henry, Jr., 8459
Pilegge, Robert J., 9051
Pilenko, Thierry, 6926
Piletic, William, Rev., 460
Pilger, Henry, 1013
Pilgrim, Gary L., 8383
Pillar, John, 8352
Pillari, Ross J., 2628
Pillsbury Co., 4536
Pillsbury, Donaldson C., 3028, 6613
Pillsbury, George S., Jr., 4688
Pillsbury, John, 4883, 4884
Pillsbury, John S., 4688
Pillsbury, John S., III, 4688
Pillsbury, Joyce S., Mr., 4883, 4884
Pillsbury, Marian S., 3028
Pillsbury, Marnie S., 6827
Pillsbury, Marnie, Ms., 6633
Pillsbury, Ruth, 4884
Pillsbury, William E., 4883
Pilnick, Gary, 4358
Pilon, Mary Claudia Belk, 7315
PIM Holding Co., 6556
Pina, Bonnie, 1594
Pinck, Laurie, 6609
Pinck, Laurie A., 5727
Pinck, Laurie Abraham, 5727, 5991
Pinck, Menachem, 5991, 6609
Pinckney, C. Cotesworth, 9513
Pinckney, Cotesworth, Mrs., 9474
Pinco, Susan, 6219
Pincus Brothers, Inc., 8384
Pincus, David, 8384
Pincus, Gerry, 8384
Pincus, Henry, 6726
Pincus, Lionel I., 6241, 6726
Pincus, Matthew, 6726
Pincus, Nathan, 8384
Pincus, Ronald, 3502
Pincus, Suzanne, 6726
Pincus, Wendy, 8384
Pinder, Martha, 3325
Pine Bluff Sand & Gravel Co., 181
Pine, Mark J., 4008
Pineda, Patricia Salas, 698
Pines, Heather K., 2731
Pines, Joan, 3001
Pinewood Foundation, 211
Pingeon, Hendon C., 1510
Pingle, Dean, Rev., 9861
Pingree, Charles W., 4203

Polzin, Mark F., 7676, 7678
Pomer, Frank, 1498
Pomerantz, Carrie Schwab, 1110
Pomerantz, Marvin A., 3316
Pomerantz, Stephanie, 5277
Pomerantz, Yvette C., 5769
Pomerleau, Ernest A., 9361
Pomeroy, Ellen R.C., 6246, 6451
Pomeroy, Katherine, 1518
Pomeroy, Richard, 4210
Pompadur, Martin, 6047
Ponchick, E.T., 255
Ponchick, Elliot, 255
Pond, Alethea Marder, 8391
Pond, Charles N., Jr., 8391
Pond, Dale C., 7423
Pond, Donna S., 8391
Ponder, Herbert M., Jr., 2358
Ponitz, David H., 1795
Pontarelli, Tom, 2670
Ponte, Rose, 1516
Pontikes, Nicholas K., 2835
Pontius, Gil R., 3143
Pontius, John, 8693
Pontius, John M., 5856
Pontius, Stanley N., 7784
Pontius, Teresa, 9280
Pontzer, Deborah, 8456
Ponzio, Craig, 1440
Ponzio, June, 1440
Pool, Peggy Cook, 8845
Pool, Philip B., Jr., 7126
Pool, Robert M., 4388
Pool, Susan S., 4400
Poole, Ann H., 5721
Poole, Charles, Rev., 4252
Poole, Diana, 1367
Poole, Donald C., 1080
Poole, Dorothy Gay, 2466
Poole, J. Gregory, Jr., 2156
Poole, James P., 2466
Poole, Michael W., 2303
Poole, R.W., 7933
Poole, Rebecca A., 187
Poole, Steven W., 4321
Poon, Audrey Sheldon, 6536
Poorbaugh, Kathleen, 9487
Poore, Christina Bezos, 9557
Poore, Stephen S., 9557
Poorman, Kevin, 2955
Poorvu, Lia G., 4086
Poorvu, William J., 4086
Poos, Thomas W., 3371
Pope, Amanda Joyce, 7450
Pope, David, 326, 6740
Pope, Ellen, 3548
Pope, G. Phillip, 18
Pope, Generoso, 6740
Pope, James Arthur, 7450
Pope, Janet DeVlieg, 4275
Pope, John Rodgers, 9046
Pope, Joyce W., 7450
Pope, Lois B., 2174
Pope, M.A., 320
Pope, Mark C., III, 2467
Pope, Tony E., 8617
Popeck, Raymond J., 8422
Popenhagen, Nancy K., 1268
Poplawski, Anthony, 894
Popovich, J. Kristoffer, 682
Popovich, Jane H., 682
Popp, Tim, 9743
Poppen, Donald, 5489
Poppick, Libbie Naman, 5992
Popsicle Playwear, Ltd., 5518
Porath, Arnold, 1338
Porges, David L., 8187
Porges, Leigh Simon, 6987
Porras, Amparo, 3245
Porrata, Carlos, 854
Portaro, Sam A., Jr., Rev., 2957
Portcullis Partners, L.P., 9074
Porte, Thierry G., 5989
Portell, Barbara, 3123

Portenoy, Norman S., 5888
Portenoy, Winifred Riggs, 5888
Porteous, William D., 5427
Porter Revocable Trust, The, 5905
Porter, A. Alex, 6119
Porter, Andrew, 1838
Porter, Barbara, 9702
Porter, Betty Robins, 9506
Porter, Catherine, 211
Porter, Charles, 8214
Porter, Clif, 7667
Porter, David L., 3666
Porter, Donald L., 7349
Porter, Frances G., 7376
Porter, Frank B., Jr., 3828
Porter, Haigh, 8571
Porter, J. Kenneth, 8671
Porter, J. Stanton, 147
Porter, James Hyde, 2468
Porter, Jim, 1244
Porter, Joanna O., 3666
Porter, John E., 2832
Porter, John W., 4399
Porter, Kathryn A., 1385
Porter, Margaret M., 24
Porter, Martin F., 3666
Porter, Mary L., 9169
Porter, Michael C., 4289
Porter, Pamela, 5477
Porter, Patricia A., 8995
Porter, R. Gordon, 147
Porter, Ralph, 939
Porter, Reed, 147
Porter, Robert C., Jr., 7573
Porter, Robert, III, 7573
Porter, Russell M., 5633
Porter, Scott, 147
Porter, Shawn, 147
Porter, Stan, 147
Porter, Susan, 6484
Porter, Susan J., 7848
Porter, Tom, 8881
Porter, Warren, 9764
Porter, Wayne, 147, 3095
Porter, William, 344
Portera, Malcolm, 4763
Porterfield, Charlotte K., 9419
Porterfield, Mark J., 1006
Porth, Richard, 1564
Porth, Thomas, 3278
Portland General Electric Co., 8051
Portman, William C., III, 7574
Portnoi, Lee, 8747
Portnoy, Fern, 4174
Portnoy, Robert A., 8141
Portrait Homes-North Carolina, LLC, 2933
Porzig, Ullrich E., 3380
Posada, Alex, 1093
Poses, Frederic, 5354
Poses, Nancy, 5354
Posewitz, James, 4935
Posey, Bill, 7748
Posey, Samuel F., Jr., 6563
Posner, Frederic G., 9901
Posner, Gene, 9901
Posner, Ruth, 9901
Posoff, Mindy M., 8198
Poss, Ellen M., 4087
Possis Medical, Inc., 3841
Post, Carolyn, 1765
Post, Herschel, 7273
Post, John A., 5355
Post, Lawrence, 1011
Post, Lawrence A., 1011
Post, Margaret, 5355
Post, Marjorie Merriweather, 1842
Post, Martin R., 2169, 6484
Post, Richard G., 7448
Post, Sandra, 1011
Post, Thomas R., 2165
Post, William J., 86
Post-Newsweek Stations, 1804
Posten, Kathryn R., 1902

Poster, Dennis B., 1485
Poston, Met R., 7404
Potamkin, Alan, 2176
Potamkin, Robert, 2176
Poteat-Flores, Jennifer R., 4461
Potenziani, A.F., 837
Potenziani, Cyrena K., 837
Potenziani, Frank A., 837
Potenziani, Frederich A., 837
Potenziani, Martha M., 837
Potenziani, William, 837
Poteshman, Michael, 2275
Potesta, Ron L., 9723
Potiker, Jori, 1012
Potiker, Lowell, 1012
Potiker, Sheila, 1012
Potlach Foundation II, 9665
Potlatch Corp., 9665
Pottash, Carter, 6438
Potter, Bruce W., 4625
Potter, Camilla Jillson, 1578
Potter, Clare P., 1697
Potter, Delcour S., 6391
Potter, Elizabeth Stone, 6917
Potter, Helen A., 5521
Potter, Lillian W., 6742
Potter, Myrtle, 1941
Potter, Myrtle S., 562
Potter, Peter, 331
Potter, Philip E., 6742
Potter, Philip E., Mrs., 6742
Potter, R. Michael, 8661
Potter, Robert W., 8136
Pottorff, Gary W., 3213
Pottruck, David S., 1013
Pottruck, Emily Scott, 1013
Potts, Al, 4327
Potts, J. Brian, 4009
Potts, Robert, 2166
Potvin, Shelly, 828
Poucher, John S., 966
Poulos, James A., 3685
Poulson, Richard J.M., 1823, 9519
Poulton, Shirley, 4325
Pounion, Steve, 6356
Pourchot, Bob, 1454
Povich, Maurice R., 7167
Powell, Andrew L., 2725
Powell, Ben H., Jr., 9128
Powell, Ben H., V, 9128
Powell, Diane Linen, 1505
Powell, E. Bryson, 9402, 9513
Powell, Earl A., III, 1780
Powell, Earl W., 2097
Powell, Elizabeth A., 9906
Powell, George E., III, 3381
Powell, George E., Jr., 3381
Powell, George E., Sr., 3381
Powell, Gregory, 3521, 3522, 3523
Powell, Hugh R., Jr., 2460
Powell, Ivy Lewis, 5249
Powell, Jacklen E., 1743
Powell, James B., II, 7346
Powell, Jerry W., 28
Powell, John B., Jr., 3566, 3681
Powell, Kendall, 4570
Powell, Kitty King, 9128
Powell, Larry, 7749
Powell, Laurence, 8704
Powell, Lee Etta, 409
Powell, M. Cleland, III, 3494, 3503
Powell, Marc, 5249
Powell, Mary, 25
Powell, Mike, 3124
Powell, Myrtis H., 1844, 7574
Powell, Nicholas K., 3381
Powell, Paul W., 9155
Powell, Robert L., 7343
Powell, Ron, 3137
Powell, Scott, 3415
Powell, W.H., 5335
Powell, Weldon, 1527
Powell, William, 7920
Power, Eugene B., 4415

Power, J. Edward, 3281
Power, Jeffery, 4397
Power, Jeffrey B., 4283
Power, Jill W., 3794
Power, Kathleen K., 4415
Power, Philip H., 4415
Power, Sadye H., 4415
Powers, Bill, 1006
Powers, Cynthia, 3189
Powers, Donald S., 3129
Powers, James A., 2679
Powers, Joe, 4668
Powers, John, 1533
Powers, John J., 6744
Powers, John L., 2534
Powers, John P., 1536, 1630
Powers, Linda E., 6744
Powers, Noah, 7749
Powers, Roy, 5036
Powers, Stefanie, 720
Powers, Timothy H., 1569
Powers, William T., 7173
Powlick, George, 190
Poynter, Henrietta M., 2245
Poynter, Nelson, 2245
Poythress, Anthony I., 8584
Pozen, Robert C., 5779, 8197
Poznanski, Dorothy, 8052
Poznanski, Robert, 8052
PPC Partners, Inc, 9902
PPG Industries, Inc., 8394
PPL Corp., 8481
Prager, David W., 6681
Prager, William W., Jr., 7097
Prager, Yossi, 5582
Praiss, Thomas F., 8228
Pralle Family Foundation, Robert R. and Helga, 1014
Pralle, Helga, 1014
Pralle, Robert, 929
Pralle, Robert R., 1014
Prasco, Tory, 3189
Prater, Tom, Dr., 4798
Prather, John E., 7865
Prather, Lisa L., 7865
Prather, Sammie, 9021
Prather, Will, 2240
Pratt, Abby, 5861
Pratt, Adrian, 8136
Pratt, Andy, 7748
Pratt, Brent K., 3631
Pratt, Christine, 3677
Pratt, David C., 4771
Pratt, Gerry, 8042
Pratt, Harold I., 4084
Pratt, Helen, 2148
Pratt, Joel P., 3106
Pratt, Larry C., 7442
Pratt, Lawrence, 5861
Pratt, Mike, 4496, 6615
Pratt, Mitchell C., 6918
Pratt, Richard, 1693
Pratt, Richard W., 1738
Prawdzik, Maria, 1601
Praxair, Inc., 1629
Pray, Donald E., 5056, 7925
Pray, Natalie Thomas, 7040
Prazak, James, 5143
Preate, Carlon E., 8431
Preato, Edward, 5194
Preble, Bob, 9597
Prechter Charitable Lead Trust, Heinz C., 4489
Prechter, Heinz C., 4489
Prechter, Paul, 4489
Prechter, Stephanie, 4489
Prechter, Waltraud, Mrs., 4489
Precision Strip, Inc., 8011
Precourt, Jay A., 1441
Predhomme, Michael J., 4385
Preece, William H., Jr., 2579
Preede, Linda, 4256
Prehn, Linda E., 9777
Preller, Cindy, 3039

Premier Bank, 9801
Premier Christian Crusies, 8604
Premier Productions, Inc., 8604
Prempas Trust, Helen, 2681
Prendergast, S. Lawrence, 5431
Prendy, Bonnie, 820
Prentice, James S., 9024
Prentice, Katherine C., 5515
Prentice, Linda, 8768
Prentiss, Elisabeth Severance, 7806
Prentiss, John K., 3533
Prepouses, Nicholas T., 1243
Presbyterian/St. Luke's Healthcare
    Corp., 1356
Prescott's Supermarket, Inc., 9903
Prescott, George, 9903
Prescott, George E., 9903
Prescott, Heidi, 7266
Prescott, Judith A., 9903
Prescott, Matthew, 9903
Prescott, Patrick, 9903
Prescott-Miller, Cheryl, 9903
Preslar, Clyde, 7418
Presley, Cecilia DeMille, 450
Presley, Kimberley, 940
Press, Donald, 6509
Press, James, 7160
Press, Thomas E., 3281
Pressberg, Gail, 1796
Presser Foundation, Theodore, 8395
Presser, Theodore, 8395
Pressler, Paul, 551
Pressler, Sheryl, 347
Pressley, J. Daniel, 8671
Pressley, Monica, 1088
Pressman, Ronald R., 4842
Pressutti, Joseph, 514
Prest, Carole, 3596
Prestolite Wire Corp., 5099
Preston Ctr., 8747
Preston, Frances, 1505
Preston, Hattie L., 3446
Preston, James E., 5760
Preston, Jennifer, 3446
Preston, Leigh Anne, 3446
Preston, Margaret, 3578
Preston, Percy, Jr., 6117
Preston, Raymond B., 3446
Preston, Seymour S., III, 8095
Prestrud, Stuart H., 9553
Preuss, Peggy, 1015
Preuss, Peter G., 1015
Preuss, Peter J., 1015
Previn, Andre, 6532
Prevratil, Joseph F., 232
Preyer, Jane B., 1632
Preyer, Sarah F., 7318
Pribnow, Steve, 4962
Price Associates, T. Rowe, Inc., 3709
Price Family Foundation, Julian, 7414
Price Family Foundation, The, 5905
Price Group, T. Rowe, Inc., 3709
Price Trust, Mary Grant, 1018
Price, Aimee Gamble, 549
Price, Aliese, 2177
Price, Allen, 9164
Price, Allison, 1016
Price, Anne Sage, 4427
Price, Calvin, 1586
Price, Carol Swanson, 4888
Price, Charles H., 6211
Price, Clement A., 5181, 5199
Price, Crystal B., 7848
Price, Dallas P., 1017
Price, David G., 1017
Price, David Glyn, 1017
Price, Donald L., 3931
Price, Ed, 7397
Price, Ella C., 982
Price, Forest W., 2679
Price, Harold, 1442
Price, Harry T., 404
Price, Helen Smith, 2352
Price, James R., 3254

Price, Jamie B., 1017
Price, Jo-Ann, 1608
Price, John D., 7463
Price, John E., 2177
Price, John E., Jr., 2177
Price, Jordan M., 5356
Price, Kim, 7808
Price, Kim S., 7342
Price, Louis, 1442
Price, Margaret, 78, 8773
Price, Maxie, Jr., 2356
Price, Michael F., 5356
Price, Phil, 9021
Price, Richard C., 1017
Price, Robert, 1016, 6747
Price, Sheri L., 1017
Price, Sol, 1016
Price, Steve, 711
Price, Steven, 6745
Price, Thomas, 6402
Price, Tina, 6745
Price, Vann, 4987
Price, W. James, IV, 3586
Price, W.L., 1019
Price, William, 8918
Pricer, Robert, 9807
PricewaterhouseCoopers, LLC, 7174
PricewaterhouseCoopers, LLP, 5905
Prichard, Peter S., 9424
Prickett Fund, Lynne R. and Karl E., 7384
Prickett, Caroline, 1698
Prickett, Lynn R., 7452
Priddy, Ashley H., 9131
Priddy, Betsy, 9130
Priddy, Robert T., 9130, 9131, 9280
Priddy, Robert T., Mrs., 9130
Priddy, Russell, 2177
Priddy, Swannanoa H., 9131
Priddy, Walter M., 9131
Pridham, Herbert H., 7572
Priebe, Daniel, 4589
Priem, Curtis, 1020
Priem, Veronica, 1020
Prien, Mary S., 7888
Priest, William W., Jr., 6215
Priestap, Terry L., 7793
Priester, Susan, 8583
Prillaman, L.I., Jr., 9485
Prim Ventures, Inc., 5054
Prim, Wayne L., 5054
Prim, Wayne L., Jr., 5054
Prime, Meredith, 5517, 5806, 7234
Primes, David M., 605
Primich, Jack, 3189
Primo, Quintin E., III, 2661
Prina, Dean, 1364
Prince & Co., F.H., Inc., 2949
Prince Corp., 4416
Prince Foundation, 4277
Prince Holding Corp., 4443
Prince, Carol K., 309
Prince, Edgar D., 4416
Prince, Elsa D., 4416
Prince, Erik D., 4416
Prince, Frederick Henry, 2948, 2949
Prince, Frederick Henry, IV, 2948
Prince, Joan Marie, 9876
Prince, Larry, 2500
Prince, Larry L., 2339
Prince, Mary Martha, 96
Prince, Stephen, 7139
Prince, William Norman Wood, 2948,
    2949
Princess Diana Trust, 1041
Princeton in Chicago, 3021
Principal Life Insurance Co., 3326
Principato, Jerold, 3710
Principato, Marjorie, 3710
Principi, Amy Wahlert, 2284
Pringle, Bruce A., 3405
Pringle, Douglas S., 3405
Pringle, Mary, 9570
Prinster, Joseph, 1471
Printpack Inc., 2437

Printz, Jean, 9390
Prinz, Leslie, 4156
Prior, Dan A., 5098
Prior, Michael, 3897
Prior, Trudie J., 9363
Priour, Kyle, 9120
Prisby, Thomas F., 3118
Prisyon, Maxine D., 6304
Pritchard, Barbara, 4246
Pritchard, Mary E., 2701
Pritchard, Mary Helow, 2055
Pritchard, Robert O., 7447
Pritt, Julia L., 9702
Pritzker Cousins Foundation, 1021,
    1645, 3033
Pritzker Foundation, 1021, 1645, 2810,
    2858, 3033
Pritzker's Cousin Foundation, 9114
Pritzker's Foundation, 9114
Pritzker, Anthony N., 1021, 2950
Pritzker, Daniel F., 2953
Pritzker, Jacob, 2858
Pritzker, James N., 3033
Pritzker, Jay Robert, 1021, 2950
Pritzker, Jeanne, 2950
Pritzker, John, 961
Pritzker, John A., 1022
Pritzker, Joseph, 2858
Pritzker, Karen, 1645
Pritzker, Karen M., 2953
Pritzker, Linda, 1645, 9114
Pritzker, Lisa, 1022
Pritzker, Margot, 2951
Pritzker, Marian, 2810
Pritzker, Marian F., 2954
Pritzker, Mary Kathryn, 1021
Pritzker, Nicholas J., 2769, 2810, 2858,
    2952
Pritzker, Penny, 2955
Pritzker, Penny S., 2952
Pritzker, Regan, 2858
Pritzker, Robert A., 2952
Pritzker, Roland B., 9114
Pritzker, Rosemary, 9114
Pritzker, Susan S., 2858
Pritzker, Thomas J., 2810, 2951, 2952
Pritzker-Vlock, Karen, 1645
Pritzl, John, 9949
Pritzlaff, Mary Dell, 2904
Privat, Kenneth O., 3499
Private One of NY, LLC, 6491
Pro Performance Sports, LLC, 7174
Probasco, Lloyd, 4958
Probert, Edward W., 5368
Probst, Marian, 7266
Probst, Robert, 3214
Prochnow, Lisa, 7384
Prochnow, Lisa V., 7452
Prochnow, Mary, 828
Procter & Gamble Co., The, 2205, 7807
Proctor, Joy, 1944
Proctor, Nancy, 3528
Proctor, Palmer, 1945
Proctor, Venable B., 9095
Proctor-Shaw, Billye, 8840
Proczko, Taras R., 2794
Proffitt, Gary E., 3369
Proffitt, Larry, 488
Progress Energy, Inc., 7453
Progressive Casualty Insurance Co.,
    7808
Prohofsky, Dennis, 4677
Prominski, Susan S., 9371
Promotion, Inc., 7
Promotions Network, The, 7174
Prophet Corp., The, 4658
Propolanis, Patricia J., 445
Propp, Ephraim, 6749
Propp, M.J., 6749
Propp, Morris S., 6749
Prosperi, David P., 2662
Prosser, Adrian, 9364
Prosser, Dawn E., 9364
Prosser, Eric, 612

Prosser, John W., Jr., 707
Prosser, Sheri, 9781
Prosser, Thomas J., 9869
Protection Svc., Inc., 8455
Protective Life Insurance Co., 58
Prothro, Caren H., 8955, 9134
Prothro, Charles B., 9280
Prothro, Charles N., 9116
Prothro, David H., 9116
Prothro, Elizabeth P., 9116
Prothro, Joe N., 9116
Prothro, Mark H., 9116
Prothro, Vincent H., 9134
Prothrow-Stith, Deborah, 6375
Protsch, Eliot, 9742
Protz, Edward L., 9092
Prout, Curtis, 3830
Prout, Elissa R., 6821
Prout, James E., 5782
Providence Development Partners, LLC,
    7442
Providence Journal Co., The, 9135
Provident Bank of Maryland, 3712
Provident Bank, The, 3712, 7574
Provident Financial Group, Inc., 7717
Provident Financial Services, Inc., 5359
Prudential Financial, 7174
Prudential Insurance Co. of America,
    The, 5360
Prudhomme, Florence, 1717
Pruet, Chesley, 170
Pruet, Elizabeth J., 170
Pruett, Herbert E., 402
Pruett, J. Curtis, 2410
Pruett, Thelma Fordham, 1795
Pruett, Virginia S., 2410
Pruis, John J., 3103, 3104
Pruitt, Frances M., 2179
Pruitt, Gary B., 698
Pruitt, J. Crayton, 2179
Pruitt, Regina D., 9034
Prunaret Trust, Henri, 3920
Prunaret, Mildred Gardinor, 3920
Prusoff Charitable Lead Annuity Trust,
    William H., 1631
Prusoff, Alvin, 1631
Prusoff, Laura, 1631
Prussian, Gordon S., 2946
Pruzan, Lucy, 9675
Pruzan, Robert A., 6764
Pruzan, Tracey, 6764
Pryde, James, 4919
Pryor, Daniel A., 8396
Pryor, Esther A., 8396
Pryor, Frederic L., 8396
Pryor, John, 1465
Pryor, Kevin, 5194
Pryor, Marcus, 5782
Pryor, Mary S., 8396
Pryor, Millard H., 8396
Przybyl, Kimberly T., 9527
PSCU, 2040
Psiol, Alex D., 778
Ptacek, Louis, 3931
Ptasnik, Martha, 10000
Ptaszek, Edward G., Jr., 7877
PTI Investments Inc., 7482
Public Service Co. of New Hampshire,
    1614
Public Service Co. of New Mexico, 5493
Public Service Electric and Gas Co.,
    5361
Public Service Enterprise Group, Inc.,
    5361
Pucci, Gary T., 9924
Pucci, Nina, 277
Puccio, M. Shawn, 8419
Pucillo, Deborah Dale, 1939
Puck, Robert J., 2004, 2065
Pucker, GiGi Pritzker, 2954
Pucker, Michael, 2954
Puckett, Julie Phillips, 5492
Puckett, Kate, 1337
Puckett, Katherine M., 1337

Puckett, Marlene M., 2578
Puelicher, John A., 9904
Puentes, George J., 8042
Puerzer, Paul, 4610, 4715
Puff, Randy A., 4321
Puffer, Richard A., 8572
Pugh, Cindy, 156
Pugh, George B., 7816
Pugh, Mary, 9680
Pugliese, Charles M., 7810
Pugliese, Thelma M., 7810
Puhala, James, 1599
Pujana, Maria Jose, 7576
Pula, Mary Ann, 5899
Pulatie, David, 129
Puleio, Annmarie, 5379
Pulido, Mark, 1031
Pulitzer, Ceil, 4889
Pulitzer, Emily, 6312
Pulitzer, Michael E., 4889
Pulles, Gregory S., 4699
Pulles, Joanne, 8690
Pulliam, Jane B., 3224, 3242
Pulliam, Larry A., 7932, 7979
Pulliam, Myrta J., 3116, 3224
Pulliam, Rose, 9361
Pulliam, Russell B., 3242
Pullin, Randolph L., 9276
Pulling, Thomas L., 6453
Pullman, George Mortimer, 2957
Pullman, Harriet Sanger, 2957
Pullo, Robert W., 8511
Pulsifer, Thomas R., 1699, 1706
Pumford, Susan A., 4428
Puntureri, Albert R., 8438
Punzeit, Kenneth, 5086
Punzeit, Shirley M., 5086
Puorro, Michael P., 6859
Purath, Gary, 4637
Purcell, Anne McNamara, 2886
Purcell, Cindy, 9346
Purcell, David P., 2886
Purcell, Michael J., 2886
Purcell, Nancy, 1292
Purcell, Nancy L., 3101, 3102
Purcell, Paul, 9750
Purcell, Paul M., 2886
Purcell, Philip J., 2886
Purcell, Terri L., 2351
Purcell, Thomas, 2132
Purdue, Starr H., 2358
Pures, Robert J., 5240
Purinton, Richard, 3897
Purkey, Sheila L., 3636
Purks, Robert K., 4769
Purmort, F.W., III, 7891
Purmort, Paul W., Jr., 7891
Purnell, Katharine J., 1300
Purnell, Kelley A., 1300
Purnell, Mark L., 1300
Purnell, Russell A., 3599
Purvis, Debbie, 4733, 4750
Purvis, E. Gail, 9240
Pusateri, Lawrence X., 3031
Puskar, Milan, 9728
Puterbaugh, Jay Garfield, 7970
Puterbaugh, Leela Oliver, 7970
Putman, Gerald E., 5846
Putnam Investments, Inc., 4088
Putnam Trust Co., 1486
Putnam, David F., 5100
Putnam, George, 4089
Putnam, George, III, 4089
Putnam, James A., 5098, 5100
Putnam, Rosamond P., 5100
Putnam, Theodore I., 5813
Putnam, Thomas P., 5100
Putney, Charles H., 5433, 8045
Putterman, Lawrence, 6123
Putze, Robert L., 9421
Puzo, Michael J., 3863
Pydo, Donald G., 3076
Pyle, Ida M., 9263
Pyle, James, 4858

Pyron, R. Scott, 93
Pytte, Agnar, 3627

Quaas, Mary K., 3275
Quad/Graphics, Inc., 9966
Quaden, Guy, 5973
Quadracci, Elizabeth E., 9966
Quadracci, Thomas A., 9966
Quain, Barbara, 4310
Quaker Oates Co., 7174
Qualsett, Bart, 4962
Quam, Jess, 4622
Quambusch, Sue, 4987
Quan, Phyllis, 204
Quandt, William B., 1796
Quant, Ted, 3489
Quarles, Orage, III, 9424
Quartet Manufacturing Co., 2772
Quatrini, Vincent J., Jr., 8155
Quattrone, Frank P., 1024
Quay, Mary, 4496
Quaye, Brenda Radichel, 4660
Quayle, Marilyn, 1465
Qubein, Nido, 7397
Queen, Yvonne, 2628
Queens Nassau Nursing Home, 6871
Queensgate, 3683
Queller, Robert L., 4291
Quencer, Catherine B., 6639
Quenon, Robert H., 4835
Quernemoen, Dan, 4712
Quesada, Joaquin, 220
Quesada, Kate Davis P., 3534
Quesada, Peter W., 3534
Quesada, Strand O., 3534
Quesada, T. Ricardo, 3534
Quesenberry, Irvin W., 3414
Quick, Alan, 3123
Quick, David, 9778
Quick, Elizabeth L., 7335
Quick, Gail A., 8584
Quick, John, 3166
Quick, Leslie C., Jr., 6762
Quick, Patricia, 6761
Quick, Patricia C., 7867
Quick, Regina A., 6762
Quick, Thomas C., 2182
Quiet Harbor Trust, The, 9623
Quigg, Rob, 3253
Quigley Family Partners, LP, 5163
Quigley, Dan C., 1000
Quigley, Eileen, 9672
Quigley, Eliza K., 8987
Quigley, John G., 5163
Quigley, Kathryn, 5163
Quill, Thomas H., Jr., 4005
Quillian, William F., Jr., 9463
Quilter, James F., 2882
Quimby, Renee, 2183
Quimby, Roxanne, 2183
Quinan, Deborah Pechet, 3897
Quinby, Bill, 1778
Quine, Michael, 2677
Quinlan, Frank, 320
Quinlan, Michael J., 3556
Quinlan, Thomas J., 2707
Quinn, Amy, 214
Quinn, Barbara, 8382
Quinn, Cydney P., 6763
Quinn, Donald, 5203
Quinn, Eileen S., 3713
Quinn, George J., Jr., 3713
Quinn, J.A., 5042
Quinn, James E., 7137
Quinn, Jane, 5655
Quinn, John, 1745
Quinn, John C., 9424
Quinn, John J., 3116
Quinn, Joseph I., 3816
Quinn, Kathleen M., 3713
Quinn, Kathleen Sr., 3129
Quinn, Mary, 5583
Quinn, Mary S., 4128

Quinn, Matthew J., 9405
Quinn, R. Patrick, 6859
Quinn, Stephen D., 6763
Quinn, Thomas D., 6138
Quinney, David E., Jr., 9338
Quinney, S.J., 9338
Quinson, Bruno A., 6917
Quintana, Kimberley M., 3519
Quintas, Paul Z., 3027
Quintero, Ana Helvia, 8515
Quintos, Karen, 8864
Quirk, Kathleen L., 3481
Quirk, Thomas V., 3936
Quirk, Tom, 7910
Quiroz, Lisa, 7142
Quisenberry, Cynthia, 2538
Quisenberry, Kevin, 9258
Quisenberry, Liz, 9258
Quismorio, James P., 6395
Quistad, Janice E., 673
Qwest Communications International
    Inc., 1443

R G I Group Incorporated, 6716
R&R Investors Inc., 3327
R. & R. Realty Co., 4111
R. Stanton Avery Foundation, 265
R. Tarica, Samuel, 212
Raab, Karen, 3135
Raasch, E. John, 9960
Rabaut, David, 8303
Rabb, Esther V., 4091
Rabb, James M., 3767
Rabb, Jane M., 3767
Rabb, Sidney R., 4090
Rabbi of Temple B'Nai Israel, 9178
Rabe, Karen, 6323
Raber, Phillip, 7636
Rabinowitch, Victor, 483
Rabinowitz, Alan, 4076
Rabinowitz, Andrea, 4076
Rabinowitz, Dov, 5736
Rabinowitz, Goldy, 5736
Rabinowitz, Hannah, 6781
Racette, Karen, 4352
Rachal, Ed, 9138
Racher, Susan, 1954, 1955
Rachford, Jon, 417
Rachofsky, Howard Earl, 9139
Rachosfsky, Cindy, 9139
Racine, Peter M., 2071
Rackoff, Nancy L., 8130, 8386
Radcliffe, R. Stephen, 3220
Radcliffe, Sandra J., 9135
Radder, Janice Peterson, 8376
Radder, Timothy W., 8376
Raddey, James C., 8425
Radecki, Eugene, 4520
Rader, Donna, 7508
Radfar, India T., 3464
Radford, Martha, 1529
Radia, Suku V., 3314
Radiator Specialty Co., 7320
Radichel Family Intervivos Charitable
    Lead Trust, 4660
Radichel, Bradley P., 4660
Radil, Gary, 5017
Radil, Gary W., 4554
Radin, Edward C., 6863
Radin, Leta H., 1025
RadiOhio, Inc., 7915
Radley, Gail C., 4092
Radley, James A., 4092
Radloff, Louise, 2356
Rado, Annette, 521
Rado, Patricia A., 5361
Radoff, Leonard, 8858
Radoff, Lisel, 8858
Rados, Alexander, 1164
Radosevich, Carol, 5493
Radov, Joseph, 2963
Radov, Sylvia M., 2963
Radsch, Robert W., 7287

Radtke, Duane, 8173
Radtke, Gerald W., 4238
Radtke, Janelle M., 4238
Rady, Ernest S., 1026
Rady, Evelyn, 1026
Rae, Clifford A., 6974
Rae, Nancy A., 4265
Raether, Paul E., 6766
Raether, Wendy S., 6766
RAF Foundation, 4049
Rafal, Alex, 7139
Rafal, Dyanne, 1517
Raff, Mary Ellen, 3251
Raffa, Louise, 7764
Raffel, James, 9958
Raffel, Kathleen Keefe, 6305
Rafferty, Emily, 5691
Rafferty, Gary J., 1221
Raffiani, Laura, 6767
Raffiani, Philip, 6767
Raffin, Margaret, 702
Raftery, Betsy K., 1616
Ragaini, Paul, 2308
Ragan, Carolyn King, 7455
Ragans, Robert H., Jr., 1925
Rager, R. Russell, 8759
Rager, R. Scott, 3332
Raggio, William J., Esq., 5077
Ragin, Luther M., Jr., 6176
Ragin, Shirley, 5493
Ragland, John, 3218
Ragland, W. Trent, III, 7438
Ragland, W. Trent, Jr., 7438
Ragone, Daniel J., 8410
Ragone, David V., 6453
Ragsdale, Anne E., 8722
Ragsdale, Eric, 3123
Ragsdale, Kevin G., 8722
Ragsdale, Richard E., 8722
Ragsdale, Richard E., II, 8722
Rahal, William, 5145
Rahimian, Ali, 1027
Rahimian, Javad, 1027
Rahimian, Ladan, 1027
Rahimian, Majid, 1027
Rahimian, Maryam, 1027
Rahimian, Mehry, 1027
Rahjas, Doyle D., 3366
Rahn, William F., 172
Raiff, Robert M., 6768
Raikes, Jeffrey S., 9668
Raikes, Patricia M., 9668
Rail Investment Co., 9485
Railsback, R. Sherman, 308
Raim, Nina Ellenbogen, 2134
Rainbolt, David, 7969
Rainbolt, H.E. Gene, 7931
Rainbolt, Hal, 8765
Rainbolt, Jeannine, 7931
Rainbow Apparel Companies, 5740
Rainbow Store, Inc., 5740
Rainer Arnhold Trust, 6593
Raines, Carl, 7770
Raines, Marjorie D., 5162
Rainey, Daniel V., 172
Rainey, Esther S., 2336, 2337
Rainey, John S., 8566, 8605
Rainey, Rebeca Romero, 5491
Rainey, Robert M., 8588, 8605
Rainier Pacific Financial Group, Inc.,
    9669
Rainsford, Bettis, 2357
Raintree, 3683
Rainwater, Gary L., 4772
Raiser, Jennifer M., 989
Raizes, Deborah, 6946
Rajakulendran, Jerry, 2554
Rajan, T.V., 1529
Rajchel, James, 3245
Rajchenbach, Jack, 2958
Rajchenbach, Judith, 2958
Rakatansky, Carol R., 1778
Raker, M.E., 3226
Rakolta, John, Jr., 4254

Raleigh Linen Svc., Inc., 2366
Rales, Debra, 3716
Rales, Debra L., 3716
Rales, Joshua B., 3716
Rales, Mitchell P., 9429
Rales, Norman R., 2184
Rales, Steven M., 9378
Raley, J. Gary, 9826
Ralmondi, Josephine, 1691
Ralphs Grocery Co., 1029
Ralphs, Anthony W., 280
Ralphs, Bernadatte M., 280
Ralphs, Maria De Pillar, 280
Ralston Purina Co., 4872
Ralston Purina Trust Fund, 2721
Ralston, Craig, 1437
Ralston, Hugh J., 1264
Ramadan, Mujahid, 5047
Ramar, Suanne, 8052
Ramasamy, Kala Kuru, 4428
Rambo, Barbara, 5357
Rambo, Cindy, 1326
Ramer, Bruce, 1050, 1322
Ramer, Bruce M., 544
Ramer, James T., 4412
Ramirez, M. Carmen, 1264
Ramirez, Maria Fiorini, 6229
Ramnath, Marna, 7756
Ramo, Barry, 5466
Ramo, Simon, 750
Ramone, Phil, 6532
Ramos, Carlos, 401
Ramphela, Mamphela, 6826
Ramsay, Nonie B., 270, 1030
Ramsay, Patricia, 6538
Ramsay, Sheldon C., 1030
Ramsay, Stephen A., 1030
Ramsay, Susie, 1373
Ramsdel, Joe, 204
Ramsden, Richard J., 3196
Ramser, Forrest L., 2469
Ramser, Helen M., 2469
Ramser, Mark R., 7583
Ramsey, Chris, 8660
Ramsey, Rich, 7775
Ramsey, Robert, 3253
Ramsey, Robert David, 1246
Ramseyer, Roger, 3374
Ramsland, Jane B., 8783
Ramunno, Charles A., 1400
Ranalli, Walt, 9736
Ranch Mart, Inc., 3402
Rancho Santa Fe Thrift, 8225
Rand Realty and Development Co., 2946
Rand-Whitney Packaging Corp., 3989
Randaccio, Sharon, 5958
Randall, Beverly, 9140
Randall, Carole L., 7864
Randall, Craig, 5517
Randall, Jack P., 9140
Randel, Don Michael, 6525
Randell, Barbara, 3750
Randell, David, 3750
Randle, Bev, 3177
Randle, Kathryn A., 1932
Randles, Steven G., 7770
Randolph, C. Carl, 1957
Randolph, Carter, 7777
Randolph, Jeff, 4225
Randolph, Peter B., Dr., 3828
Randolph, Robert M., 4083
Random, Cindee L., 1932
Rands, Robert D., 3869
Randt, Virginia, 6161, 6162
Raneri, Stephanie A., 7176
Raney, William A., Jr., 7345
Ranger Investments, L.P., 5863
Ranger, Michael W., 6770
Ranger, Thomas F., 4218
Ranger, Virginia Ray, 6770
Rangos, Alexander, 8400
Rangos, Jenica, 8400
Rangos, Jill, 8400
Rangos, John G., Jr., 8400

Rangos, John G., Sr., 8400
Ranier, Drew, 3497
Rankin, Elizabeth V., 7402, 7403
Rankin, Evelyn Gordy, 2402
Rankin, R. Alex, 3409
Rankin, Susan B., 3753
Rankin, Thomas S., 4766
Ranney, Ann P., 7680
Ranney, George A., Jr., 2728
Ranney, Peter K., 7813
Ransing Trust, Ruben and Elizabeth, 223
Ransom Irrevocable Trust, Christiana, 3082
Ransom, Christiana L., 3082
Ransom, Earl, 3082
Ransom, Gail, 9659
Ransom, Mark, 3123
Ransom, Nancy Buck, 1032
Rantzow, Richard C., 8647
Rapaport, Marvin, 363
Raphaelson, Susan C., 5997
Rapier, Jill M., 826
Rapoport, Abby, 9141
Rapoport, Arnold C., 8375
Rapoport, Audre, 9141
Rapoport, Bernard, 9141
Rapoport, Bernard R., 6449
Rapoport, Emily, 9141
Rapoport, Judith, 5652
Rapoport, Patricia, 9141
Rapoport, Paul, 6772
Rapoport, Ronald B., 9141
Rapp, David, 2245
Rapp, Derek K., 4896
Rapp, Donna, 4392
Rapp, Joanne S., 336
Rapp, Marcia, 4326
Rapp, Steven M., 6713
Rappaport, Alan H., 1640, 6701
Rappaport, James W., 4093
Rappaport, Jerome Lyle, 4093
Rappaport, Jill P., 6701
Rappaport, Phyllis E., 4093
Rappaport, Steven N., 6188
Rappe, Kristine A., 9967
Rappleyea, Holly, 6207
Rapport, Carmi, 3801
Raps Industries, LLP, 1137
Rapson, Richard "Rip", 4367
Rapson, Rip, 4616
Rardin, Hugh Barr, 5868
Rardin, Jacob C., IV, 5868
Rardon, Ronald D., 7759
Rasberry, Sharol, 3404
Raskin, Cynthia, 3025
Raskin, Roy, 5804
Raskin, Shelley, 5804
Raskob, Anthony W., Jr., 1741
Raskob, Helena, 1741
Raskob, John J., 1741, 3714
Raskob, Richard G., 1741
Raskob, Russell, 1741
Raskob, Timothy T., 1741, 3714
Raskob, William F., III, 1741
Rasmuson, Cathryn, 85
Rasmuson, Ed, 81
Rasmuson, Edward B., 85
Rasmuson, Elmer E., 85
Rasmuson, Jenny, 85
Rasmuson, Judy, 85
Rasmuson, Mary Louise, 85
Rasmussen, Aino Kann, 4094
Rasmussen, Astrid Kann, 4094
Rasmussen, Charles W., 4725
Rasmussen, Hans Kann, 4094
Rasmussen, Jay, 9350
Rasmussen, Judy, 2577
Rasmussen, Kurt, 3281
Rasmussen, Paul A., 4684
Rasmussen, Ralph, 9303
Rasmussen, Steven, 5489
Rasmussen, Thomas F., 4725
Rassas, George, Bishop, 2692
Rassas, Theresa, 3012

Ratcliff, Roberta, 1647
Rath Trust, F.E., 8452
Rath, D.F., 8452
Rath, Frank E., Jr., 8452
Rath, Robert A., Jr., 8452
Rath, Robert H., Sr., 2555
Rath, V. Duane, 9907
Rathbun, Jan, 1516
Rathbun, William J., 9558
Rathjen, Carolyn P., 9118
Rathmann, Frances Joy, 3715
Rathmann, George, 3715
Rathmann, George B., 3715
Rathmann, James Louis, 3715
Rathmann, Joy, 3715
Rathmann, Laura Jean, 3715
Rathmann, Margaret Crosby, 3715
Rathmann, Richard G., 3715
Ratliff, Eugene F., 3194
Ratnavale, John R., 3598
Ratner, Audrey, 1645
Ratner, Audrey G., 2852
Ratner, Charles, 7634
Ratner, Dennis F., 9501
Ratner, James A., 7576
Ratner, Mikhail, 5840
Ratner, Milton M., 4417
Ratner, Roger, 6002
Ratner, Warren A., 9501
Ratray, Peter, 5883
Ratshesky, A.C., 4095
Rattner 2000 LT Trust, Steven, The, 6773
Rattner, Andrew, 1726
Rattner, Steven, 6758
Rattner, Steven L., 6773
Ratzan, Susan, 1529
Rau, John, 2700, 2878
Raucci, Mary Lou, 395
Rauch, Louis J., 6774
Rauch, Philip, 6774
Rauch, Philip J., 6774
Rauch, Ruth T., 6774
Rauch-Becker, Delinda, 1843
Rauenhorst Family Foundation, Gerald, 2185
Rauenhorst, Gerald, 2185
Rauenhorst, Gia, 1905
Rauenhorst, Jeffrey M., 8628
Rauenhorst, Joseph J., 2185, 8628
Rauenhorst, Karen, 4682
Rauenhorst, Loretta, 4682
Rauenhorst, Margaret, 1905
Rauenhorst, Mark, 2185, 4642
Rauenhorst, Matthew G., 1905
Rauenhorst, Michael, 4682
Rauenhorst, Rebecca Elizabeth, 1905
Rauh, John M., 7950
Rauhut, Anthony, 5816
Rauhut, Meredith, 5816
Rauner, Bruce V., 2969
Rauner, Diana, 2969
Rausch, James, 5087
Rausman, Norman, 6775
Rauzi, Robert L., 7583
Rav-Noy, Varda, 1033
Rav-Noy, Zeev, 1033
Rava, Susan R., 4817
Ravenscroft, Gretchen F., 111
Ravenscroft, Robert B., 111
Ravenscroft, Robert C., 111
Raver, Bill, 1090
Raver, Mark, 3243
Ravitch, Diane, 1795
Ravitch, Joseph, 6776
Ravitch, Michael, 6776
Ravitch, Richard, 6776
Ravitz Revocable Living Trust, Edward, The, 4418
Ravitz, Robert, 6099
Rawert, Norbert, 3161
Rawl, Gail W., 6417
Rawl, Lawrence G., 6417
Rawl, Lawrence V., 6417

Rawley, Joe, 7397
Rawlings Co., LLC, The, 2186
Rawlings, Beverly S., 2186
Rawlings, George R., 2186
Rawlings, Herbert M., 2186
Rawlinson, Joseph E., 338
Rawlinson, Rex J., 338
Rawls, Olga Goizueta, 2400
Rawls, S. Waite, Jr., 9382
Rawls, Sol W., Jr., 9382, 9421
Ray Plastic, Inc., 4000
Ray, Adele Richardson, 1632
Ray, Amy, 9463
Ray, C. Niles, 8583
Ray, David, 3131
Ray, Gilbert T., 659
Ray, Gloria, 8732
Ray, James, 3165
Ray, John L., 9722
Ray, Richard E., 9382
Ray, Robert J., 9382
Ray, Robin D., Mrs., 9532
Ray, Van, 4739
Ray, William K., 4735
Rayback, James M., 8136
Raybin, Linda, 1939
Rayburn, David B., 9878
Raye, John L., 1545
Raygar Realty Group, 2187
Rayl, Eric, 9580
Rayl, Kristie, 9580
Raymond Charitable Lead Trust, Mary R., 9339
Raymond Foundation, Robert, Inc., 9339
Raymond James Trust Co., 2170
Raymond, Carolyn M., 8340
Raymond, Frank, 7586
Raymond, John C., 1087
Raymund, Sonia V., 2188
Raymund, Steven A., 2188
Raynolds, Robert, 5106, 5274
Raynor, Geoffrey P., 9101
Rayonier Inc., 2189
Rayport, Jeffrey F., 4774
Rayzor Ranch, 9004
Razo, Gregory, 83
Razor, Jim, 417
RBC Dain Rauscher Corp., 4661
RBC Dain Rauscher Inc., 1099
RBM Shopping Centers, Inc., 8707
RBS Foundation, 4439
RCK Properties, 2742
RCS II, LLC, 9518
Re, Michael, 1221
Rea, Bayard D., 5867
Rea, Jay F., 9167
Read, Alexander R., 9872
Read, Alice E., 9872
Read, Charlie H., 8937
Read, Deborah Z., 7688
Read, Gilan M., 965
Read, James P., Jr., 965
Read, Marion C., 9771, 9872
Read, Marion Merrill Chester, 9872
Read, Michael O., 3503
Read, Roger T., 7591
Read, Thomas Merrill, 9872
Read, V. Ross, III, 9872
Read, Verne R., 9771, 9872
Read, William A., 98
Reader's Digest Association, Inc., The, 6777
Reading, James G., 8381
Ready Charitable Fund, 5367
Ready, George W., Jr., 2508
Reagan, Nelwyn, 9255
Reagan, Richard S., 6634
Real Estate Board of New York, Inc., The, 6780
Real, Bill, 5493
RealNetworks, Inc., 9672
Realsearch, 3683
Reamer, Karen, 4718
Reams, Fred W., 8606

Reams, Karen A., 8606
Reams, Matthew D., 8606
Reardon, Daniel C., 4523
Reardon, Edward J., II, 4797
Reardon, Elizabeth, 2967
Reardon, Mark, 2967
Reaser, Sue, 5806
Reaud, Jon A., 9143
Reaud, Wayne A., 9143
Reaves, Donald J., 8518
Reaves, Jeanne, 1080
Reavis, Peggy Flynt, 524
Reay, Harry, 9051
Reay, Katherine Blackburn, 2207
Rebelo, John G., 193
Rebelo, John G., Jr., 276
Rebenwurzel, Debby, 6174
Rebhorn, Rebecca Linn, 5343
Rebmann, David, 9476
Rebozo, Charles F., 2190
Rebozo, Charles G., 2190
Rebrovick, Linda, 8662
Rebsamen Insurance, Inc., 171
Recasner, Anthony, 3489, 3503
Receveur, Sharon A., 3414
Rechelbacher, Horst, 4662
Rechelbacher, Peter, 4662
Rechler, Bennett, 6781
Rechler, Beverley, 6781
Rechler, Deborah, 6010
Rechler, Morton, 6781
Rechler, Scott, 6010
Rechler-Newman, Yvetta, 6781
Rechnitz, Joan, 5465
Rechnitz, Robert, 5465
Recht, Arthur, 9713
Rechter, Ben R., 8662
Reckling, Isla C., 9212
Reckling, James S., 9212
Reckling, John B., 9212
Reckling, Stephen M., 9212
Reckling, T.R. "Cliff", IV, 9212
Reckling, T.R., III, 9212
Reckling, Thomas K., 9212
Records, George, 7952
Records, George J., 7972
Rector, S.R., 9574, 9575
Recycled Paper Greetings, Inc., 2738, 2828
Red Lion Inn, 3950
Red Wing Shoe Co., Inc., 4663
Reddick, John, 6423
Redding, John P., 1508, 1509
Reddington, Ginger, 1426
Reddy, Lata N., 5360
Reddy, Madhava, 4369
Reddy, Madhava G., 4369
Reddy, Narendranath A., 1096
Reddy, Pratibha B., 5364
Reddy, Ravi B., 5364
Reddy, Sobha, 4369
Redell, Helene E., 6453
Reder, Jeff, 1412
Reder, Robert F., 6917
Redfearn, J. Michael, 8839
Redfern, Jerry L., 4870
Redfield Trust, Nell J., 5055
Redfield, Nell J., 5055
Redick, John R., 9390
Reding, Nicholas L., 4890
Reding, Patricia J., 4890
Reding, S. Nicholas, 4890
Redman, Manville, 7959
Redmond, John, 2769
Redmond, LaDonna, 6643
Redmond, Mary R., 9339
Redmond, Velma A., 8208
Redpoint Management LLP, 1248
Redstone, Edward, 4097
Redstone, Sumner M., 4097
Redtman, Gail E., 3620
Redwine, Emily, 2452
Reeber, Larke, 1222

Reebok International Ltd., 3148, 4098, 9068
Reece, Ken G., 7438
Reece, Matt, 2578
Reece, Paris G., III, 1413
Reed, Ann L., 8140
Reed, Arthea "Charlie", 7346
Reed, Bruce, 9623
Reed, C. Lawson, 7878
Reed, C.L., III, 7878
Reed, Charles C., 1249
Reed, Cynthia, 6783
Reed, David W., 3447
Reed, Diana L., 6682
Reed, Donald K., 8487
Reed, Dorothy Foster, 7878
Reed, Dorothy W., 7878
Reed, Elizabeth S., 1724
Reed, Emily B., 7660
Reed, Foster A., 7878
Reed, Gene, 8916
Reed, Glenn, 9651
Reed, Ingrid W., 5167
Reed, J. Brad, 8709
Reed, Jasper P., 7345
Reed, Joel, 2457
Reed, John S., 6783
Reed, John W., 4221
Reed, Juanita, 2263
Reed, K.E., 4492
Reed, Karen, 5092
Reed, Lawrence, 4422
Reed, Linda E., 4939
Reed, Linda F., 2730
Reed, Marsha L., 456
Reed, Mary Lou, 9589
Reed, Michael E., 2664
Reed, Michele, 3475
Reed, Nancy, 468
Reed, Randall R., 9736
Reed, Reginald C., 5288
Reed, Rhoda Newberry, 4420
Reed, Richard, 8386
Reed, Richard W., Jr., 8457
Reed, Ronald, 3832
Reed, Royce, 4156
Reed, Sheila, 2110
Reed, Susan, 1471
Reed, Susan K., 6682
Reed, Thomas, 8098
Reed, William G., Jr., 9656
Reeder, Breinne, 4376
Reeder, David, 828
Reeder, Deborah J., 7583
Reeder, Paul A., 4099
Reeder, Paul A., III, 4099
Reeder, Robert M., 8387
Reeder, Vicki, 828
Reedy, Thomas, 9385
Reeg, Gloria, 9566
Reekie, Robert B., 3042
Reen, Mary, 6625
Rees, John Nesbit, 8401
Rees, Nigel, 879
Rees, Sarah Henne, 8401
Reese, Caleb F., 133
Reese, Crystal, 7344
Reese, David E., 133
Reese, Donald J., 2129
Reese, Eleanor Steele, 7053
Reese, Emmet P., 7053
Reese, Everett, 133
Reese, Everett D., 133
Reese, Everett D., II, 133
Reese, Gary W., 8775
Reese, J. Gilbert, 7620, 7714
Reese, Louella H., 7620
Reese, Louise R., 133
Reese, T. Terrance, 8155
Reetz, Harold R., Jr., 2388
Reeve, Dennis, 3185
Reeves, Allen, 7537
Reeves, Betty Lou, 4737
Reeves, Carlton, 4737

Reeves, Elizabeth W., 1045
Reeves, Gayle, 7582
Reeves, Helen F., 7814
Reeves, J.E., Jr., 5365
Reeves, John A., 3081
Reeves, Laura H., 4900
Reeves, Margaret J., 7814
Reeves, Robert N., 81
Reeves, Samuel J., 7814
Reeves, Samuel T., 1045
Reeves-Darby, Vonda, 4737
Reffner, Robert, 7526
Regal Home Collections, 5554
Regalado, Cristina M., 350
Regan, Amy H., 5223
Regan, Andrew W., 2037
Regan, Ann, 3701
Regan, Barbara, 5570
Regan, Grace O'Neil, 3701
Regan, James S., 5223
Regan, John M., III, 2191
Regan, John M., Jr., 2191
Regan, Julie W., 4348
Regan, Mary, 3701
Regan, Michael J., 1132
Regan, Peter M., 2191
Regan, Prudence S., 2191
Regan, R. Christopher, 2191
Regan, Timothy D., 4249
Regan, William, 2161
Regelbrugge, Laurie, 1252
Regenstein, Helen, 2962
Regenstein, Joseph, 2962
Regenstein, Joseph, III, 2962
Regino, Rita, 3641
Regions Bank, 24, 30, 59, 168, 176, 8663
Regis Corp., 4664
Regis, Inc., 4664
Regnery, Alfred S., 1841
Regnier, Catherine M., 3402
Regnier, Helen, 3402
Regnier, Robert B., 3402
Regnier, Robert D., 4842
Regnier, Victor A., 3402
Rehak, Linda, 9454
Rehder, Mark, 1946
Reherman, Ronald G., 3254
Rehm, Cynthia, 2192
Rehm, Jack, 2192
Rehr, David K., 3564
Rehrig, Brian H., 3905
Rehtmeyer, Clint, 2741
Reich & Tang, 7122
Reich 1983 Charitable Lead Trust No. 1, Anne S., 1845
Reich 1983 Charitable Lead Trust No. 2, Anne S., 1845
Reich, Anne S., 1845
Reich, Carol F., 6754
Reich, David, 2610
Reich, Deborah, 6754
Reich, Harvey, 5907
Reich, Hilary, 1845
Reich, Joseph H., 6754
Reich, Lawrence A., 2610
Reich, Raymond, 6784
Reich, Sue, 6784
Reich, Victoria J., 2636
Reichard, William E., 7670
Reichardt, Doug, 3281
Reiche, Nancy, 3855
Reichel, Aaron, Rabbi, 5959
Reichel, Hillel, Rabbi, 5959
Reichel, O. Asher, Rabbi, 5959
Reichelderfer, Ann, 5357
Reichert, Albert P., Jr., 2358
Reichert, James A., 9274
Reichheld, James H., 4014
Reichling, Jerald L., 3335
Reichman, Chaya, 6001
Reichman, Harry, 6001
Reichman, John H., 5228
Reichsman, Ann, 7917

Reid, Barbara, 5092
Reid, Bruce, 1837
Reid, Charles M., 7493
Reid, Dan, 9559
Reid, David F., 7612
Reid, E. Lewis, 346, 673
Reid, Ella Hancock, 1036
Reid, J. Marshall, 3567
Reid, J. Russell, 8841
Reid, J.S., Jr., 7829
Reid, James W., 8431
Reid, Jennifer, 8551
Reid, Lew, 407
Reid, Linda Bacon, 1340, 1471
Reid, Miller David, 4759
Reid, Patricia H., 2412
Reid, R. Miller, 4759
Reid, Ralph, 3395
Reid, Robert J., 5487
Reid, Suzanne, 7837
Reid, Will J., 1036
Reid-Radford, Malia, 9702
Reiden, Tony Inder, 5921
Reidinger, Mary Ann, 4256
Reidler, Carl J., 8402
Reidler, John W., 8402
Reidler, Paul G., 8402
Reidler, Verna C., 8402
Reighley, H. Ward, 3533
Reigle, Thomas J., 9826
Reiher, John, 3335
Reiley, Joseph, 1505
Reilly, Edward A., 5886
Reilly, Edward T., 1505
Reilly, Jennifer Eplett, 3462, 4743
Reilly, William K., 972
Reily Foods Co., 3506
Reily, Robert D., 3503, 3506
Reily, William B., III, 3506
Reiman, Eric M., 98
Reiman, Roberta M., 9908
Reiman, Roy J., 9908
Reiman, Scott J., 9908
Reimer, Dolores, 4665
Reimer, Lynn, 4665
Reimer, Mary, 7660
Reimer, William, 4665
Reimers, Arthur J., III, 6425
Reimers, Lindsay, 6425
Reimers, Lindsay J.H., 1537
Rein, Catherine A., 6542
Rein, Gary David, 6203
Reinalt-Thomas Corporation, 103
Reinberger, Clarence T., 7815
Reinberger, Louise F., 7815
Reinberger, Robert N., 7815
Reinberger, William C., 7815
Reinecke, Dave, 9854
Reinecke, David W., 9925
Reineke, Susanne, 7533
Reinemund, Steven S., 6714
Reiner, Jennifer Pollack, 6734
Reiner, John P., 6444
Reiner, Robert M., 3730
Reiners, Linda, 3177
Reingold, Stephen C., 3931
Reinhard, Ian, 1037
Reinhard, Myra, 1037
Reinhard, Neil, 1037
Reinhardt, J. Alec, 7627
Reinhardt, Reginald, 7210
Reinhardt, Richard, 495
Reinhart Enterprises, D.B., 9909
Reinhart Institutional Foods, 9909
Reinhart, Dietrich, Br., 4534
Reinhart, Leon H., 1038
Reinhart, M.H., 8131
Reinhart, Marjorie A., 9909
Reinhart, Myron H., 9502
Reinhart, Peter S., 5167
Reinhart, Randyn D., 1038
Reinhart, William L., 9502
Reinhart-Mahony, 9885
Reinheimer, Letha, 8431

Reinhold, B. Terry, 1039
Reinhold, Baldwin, Jr., 1039
Reinhold, Carol A., 1039
Reinhold, Henry, 6193
Reinhold, John, 6276
Reinhold, Mary E., 1039
Reinhold, Paula Joy, 6276
Reininga, Daniel, 6638
Reinis, Richard G., 584
Reinke, Kathy, 9810
Reinsch, Lola C., 9371
Reinsdorf, Jerry, 2818
Reintzel, Warren A., 8493
Reis, David, 2193
Reis, Jerry D., 9218
Reis, Tim, 9982
Reische, J. Gordon, 3461
Reiser, Margaret C., 2355, 2407
Reiser, Robert E., Jr., 2407
Reisin, Richard, 3006
Reisler, Raymond F., 1226
Reisman, Barbara, 5391
Reisner, Wayne, 6683
Reison, Gretchen Haury, 5992
Reiss Charity Account, 5527
Reiss, Abraham, 5507, 6279
Reiss, Helene, 6785
Reiss, Mahir A., 6785
Reiss, Marie, 5507
Reiss, Richard, 7084
Reiss, Vicki, 6970
Reissner, James L., 4618
Reister, Raymond, 4707
Reitan, Bernt, 8075
Reiten, Richard, 8049
Reiten, Richard G., 8049
Reiter, Elizabeth Bower, 7574
Reiter-Faragalli, Robin, 2165
Reitman, Alayne L., 7576
Reitz, Carl E., 4232
Reitz, Sid, 3387
Reitz, Sidney A., 3376
Reitz, Susan N., 3376
Rekab Properties, 251
Reliable Health Systems, 6609
Reliable Health Systems, Inc., 5991
Reliance Standard Life Insurance Co., 8168
Reliant Energy Ventures, Inc., 9144
Reliant Energy, Inc., 9144
ReliaStar Bankers Security Life Insurance Co., 2418
ReliaStar Financial Corp., 2418
ReliaStar Life Insurance Co., 2418
ReliaStar United Services Life Insurance Co., 2418
Rembe, Toni, 1260
Remillard, Arthur J., III, 4100
Remillard, Arthur J., Jr., 4100
Remillard, Regan P., 4100
Remillard, Robert P., 4100
Remington, C. Wesley, 4891
Remington, Patricia, 4891
Remington, Scott, 4891
Remington, Stephanie, 4891
Remme, Brenda M., 9038
Remmel, Raymond R., 171
Remmel, Ruth, 171
Remmel, Ruth R., 171
Remvac Group, Inc., The, 8138, 8139
Remy, Claude A., 9693
Renaghan, Denise M., 3794
Renard, Henry P., 1723
Renard, James S., 8790
Renfield, Beatrice, 6786
Renfield, Joseph W., 6786
Renfield-Miller, Jean, 6786
Renfro, George D., 5346
Renfro, John F., Jr., 8569, 8595
Renfro, Robert, 2577
Reninger, Robert W., 9972
Renken, Keith, 527
Renken, Keith W., 1249
Rennebohm, Oscar, 9910

Rennebohm, Robert B., 9910
Renner, Beth, 7514
Renner, Christopher, 1533
Renner, Tom, 836
Renner, Trevor, 1533
Rennert, Irwin L., 4904
Rennie, Renate, 7143
Renninger, Carolyn, 8098
Renov, Kalman M., 6881
Renov, Nathan, 6881
Renov, Ruki, 6585
Renschler, Scott, 3596
Renterghem, Lemont, 4331
Rentrop, Gary, 4218
Renwick, Glenn M., 7808
Renz, Sharon, 8172
Repass, Randy, 1742
Repine, John E., 1347
Replogle, David, 1846
Reppa, Jerome J., 3118
Repplier, Banning, 6917
Repplinger, William M., 1381
Republic Die and Tool Co., 4373
Resch, Marion G., 7816
Research Corporation Technologies, Inc., 93
Residential Funding Corp., 4587
Residential Warranty Corp., 8369
Resio, Ricardo, 4428
Resler, John B., 2194
ResMed Inc., 1040
Resnick & Sons, Jack, Inc., 5615
Resnick Family Foundation, Inc., 1041
Resnick, Alan H., 6823
Resnick, B., 6780
Resnick, Burton, 6779
Resnick, Ira M., 6787
Resnick, Jeffrey P., 5935
Resnick, Lynda, 898
Resnick, Lynda R., 1041
Resnick, Michael, 2584, 2686, 2972
Resnick, Stewart A., 570, 1041
Resnik, Denise, 87
Resnik, Jeffrey P., 3970
Resor, Story Clark, 5551
Respironics, Inc., 8403
Resseguier, Olga, 1622
Ressler, Alison, 1042
Ressler, Antony, 1043
Ressler, Richard, 1042
Restivo, Christina, 7140
Restucci, R.M., 9181
Retail Credit Co., 2379
Retemeyer, Deon, 6605
Rett Syndrome Research Foundation, 3677
Retter, Betty, 6848
Retter, Marcus, 6848
Retter, Maria Elena, 2400
Reuben, Don H., 2947
Reum, W.R., 2593
Reusch, Belinda, 2438
Reusch, Belinda Bunnen, 6635
Reusche, Robert F., 2702
Reuscher, Benedict R., 8454
Reuscher, R.B., 8454
Reuscher, Richard J., 8454
Reuscher, William E., 8454
Reuss, Henry, 6788
Reusswig, Michael A., 3309
Reuter, Christopher R., 7817
Reuter, Irving J., 7404
Reuter, Jeannett M., 7404
Reuter, Robert, 7817
Reuter, Robert A., 7817
Reuterfors, Robert E., 3085
Reutter, Randall C., 3288
Reveley, W. Taylor, III, 6525
Revelle, Charles L., III, 7464
Revelle, Charles L., Jr., 7481
Revelle, Geoffrey G., 9642
Revels, Carey, 4735
Revenaugh, Elsie B., 2627
Revere, Elspeth A., 2868

Revesz, Michael, 5359
Revesz, Tomas, 7524
Revocable Living Trust of Elmer J. Trulaske, 2094
Revolution Studios, 7040
Revson, Charles H., 6789
Revson, Charles H., Jr., 6789
Rex Veneer Co., 8006
Rex, Gloria Ortega, 1939
Rexford, Jean L., 1519
Rexon, Robert, 5207
Rey, Lilli J., 1046
Rey-Murphy, Ramona, 637
Reyelts, Paul C., 4706
Reyes, Angel, 5498
Reyes, Carlos J., Jr., 1941
Reyes, Carmen, 5551
Reyes, Carolina, 345
Reyes, Greg, 1047
Reyes, Juan J., 8515
Reyes, Lori W., 3080
Reyes, M. Jude, 3080
Reyes, Maria, 9571
Reyes, Penny, 1047
Reynders, John C., 3332
Reynolds and Reynolds Co., The, 7818
Reynolds Irrevocable Trust, David P., 9503
Reynolds Tobacco Co., R.J., 7459
Reynolds, A. Sheffield, 8556
Reynolds, Andrea L., 5564, 8661
Reynolds, Annemarie, 2479
Reynolds, Bobbie Ann, 2410
Reynolds, Craig B., 8403
Reynolds, David P., 9503
Reynolds, Donald W., 5056
Reynolds, Edgar, 4997
Reynolds, Eric, 3223
Reynolds, Frances, 4997
Reynolds, Golda, 3229
Reynolds, H. Rand, 9083
Reynolds, H.H., 8828
Reynolds, Heather D., 8100
Reynolds, Irene, 2479
Reynolds, Jack, 690
Reynolds, Jeffrey, 6982
Reynolds, Jock, 7215
Reynolds, Joe, 1411
Reynolds, Joe S., 126
Reynolds, Julia L., 9503
Reynolds, Kate B., 7457
Reynolds, Kent, 8828
Reynolds, Kent, Mrs., 8828
Reynolds, Libby Holman, 6790
Reynolds, Mary B., 4183
Reynolds, Nancy S., 1767, 7458
Reynolds, Pamela, 8031
Reynolds, Pearl G., 4892
Reynolds, Philip, 1495
Reynolds, Randolph N., 9503
Reynolds, Richard J., III, 7460
Reynolds, Richard J., Jr., 2479, 7458
Reynolds, Richard M., 4450
Reynolds, Richard S., III, 9503
Reynolds, Robert H., 3116, 3216
Reynolds, Rose Cellino, 7984
Reynolds, Sigrid S., 1851
Reynolds, Stan J., 3281
Reynolds, Timothy T., 7983
Reynolds, W. Calvin, 7326
Reynolds, William A., 4934
Reynolds, William N., 7458
Rhea, Katherine, 4962
Rhea, S. Herbert, 8647
Rhea, Stephen H., Jr., 8647, 8661
Rhind, James T., 1200
Rhine, David S., 6441
Rhine, Diane F., 5341
Rhinehart, Brenda S., 8511
Rhines, Steven, 7963
Rhoades, Alice, 3095
Rhoades, Ann, 5466
Rhoades, Hazel T., 2965
Rhoades, Otto L., 2965

Rhoads, Katheryn V., 2798
Rhoads, Paul K., 2798
Rhoads, Ross H., 3600
Rhodebeck, Mildred T., 6791
Rhoden, Marilyn A., 3383
Rhodenbaugh, Laura, 3367
Rhodes, Allan R., 8681
Rhodes, Aubrey C., Jr., 2357
Rhodes, Bryce W., 1323
Rhodes, Carleen K., 4519, 4671
Rhodes, Charlotte, 8758
Rhodes, Elaine, 7370
Rhodes, Frank H.T., 5574, 6056
Rhodes, Harry C., Dr., 3693
Rhodes, Harry S., 9419
Rhodes, J. Thomas, Jr., 3693
Rhodes, J.W., 380
Rhodes, Maureen, 1696
Rhodes, Paul, 4644
Rhodes, Robert, 7742
Rhodes, Robert C., 174
Rhodes, Thomas L., 9763
Rhodes, William R., 6792
Rhodes, Winifred W., 1323
Rhodus, G. Tomas, 9049
Rhonda Management, LLC, 5267
Rhone, Sylvia, 7142
Rhone, Thomas J., 4843
RHP, Inc., 6688
Rhyne, Clyde J., 7438
Ribakoff, Charles K., 4103
Ribakoff, Charles K., II, 4102
Ribakoff, Eugene J., 4102, 4103
Ribakoff, Patricia F., 4102
Ribeiro, Carl, 3770
Ribeiro, Carl, Mrs., 3770
Ricca, Mark, 1665
Ricci, A. Leo, 1603
Ricciardi, Lawrence R., 6525
Ricciardi, Louis M., 3816
Riccobene, Mary, 9726
Rice, Ada, 2966
Rice, Bruce C., 4252
Rice, C. Daniel, 1940
Rice, Catherine B., 2471
Rice, Charles B., Sr., 2471
Rice, Charles M., 2566
Rice, Cherie, 9265
Rice, Constance W., 9680
Rice, Daniel F., 2966
Rice, Derica, 3192
Rice, Ed, 7602
Rice, Edward H., 6793
Rice, Eve H., 6793
Rice, Gina, 9504
Rice, Gwendolyn M., 2943
Rice, Henry F., 2555
Rice, Henry Hart, 6793
Rice, J. Elisabeth, 4072
Rice, Jeffery, 1947
Rice, Joanne, 9165
Rice, John W., 5434
Rice, Joseph A., 6119
Rice, Joseph L., 6794
Rice, Joseph L., III, 6794
Rice, Katherine B., 4589
Rice, Kathryn, 6915
Rice, Lela G., 4788
Rice, Linda, 7960
Rice, Lois Dixon, 6118
Rice, Margaret S., 6793
Rice, Martin, 6915
Rice, Mary E., 4589
Rice, Mary H., 4589
Rice, Molly E., 4589
Rice, Neil W., 3903
Rice, Nell M., 7392, 7472
Rice, Paul, 9504
Rice, Rick, 3131
Rice, Terrie L., 7683
Rice, Timothy S., 3855
Rice, Ulysses, 1765
Ricedorf, Charles W., 8427
Rich & Co., D.W., Inc., 1559

Rich Products Corp., 6795
Rich's, Inc., 2472
Rich, Barbara, 5827
Rich, David A., 6795
Rich, David M., 8070
Rich, Evelyn Jones, 6873
Rich, Harvey S., 5297
Rich, Ivor, 5215
Rich, Lisa, 8070
Rich, Randy, 1001
Rich, Robert E., 6795
Rich, Robert E., Jr., 6795
Rich, Robert S., 1334
Rich, Ron, 3250
Rich, Zan M., 8338
Rich, Zan McKenna, 8337
Richard, Alison, 5757
Richard, D. Eugene, 459
Richard, Nancy, 1199
Richard, Robert, 3343
Richard, Ronald B., 7576
Richard-Davis, Gloria, 3503
Richards, Artie, 2362
Richards, Carol A., 325
Richards, Cynthia R., 9502
Richards, David K., 325
Richards, Dick, 9960
Richards, Edgar G., 1651
Richards, Elizabeth Brady, 5141
Richards, Florence, 1651
Richards, Frederic M., 1510
Richards, Gail, 3178, 7992
Richards, Gail Z., 7991
Richards, Grahame, 8077, 8305
Richards, James, 3129
Richards, Jeffrey C., 5564
Richards, Jennifer, 4227
Richards, Jim, 257
Richards, John F., 9463
Richards, John M., 9665
Richards, Mabel Wilson, 1048
Richards, Maragret T., 4701
Richards, Rebecca, 7992
Richards, Robert Charles, 6466
Richards, Robert J., 5096
Richards, Sharon, 78
Richards, Steven, 4521
Richards, Tim, 2139
Richards, Timothy W., 4057
Richards, Tom, 2362
Richards, Vincent William, Jr., 1688
Richardson, Danforth K., 8257
Richardson Carbon and Gasoline Co.,
  Sid, 8776
Richardson Family Partnership, 9987
Richardson Pontiac, 1295
Richardson, Anne S., 6797
Richardson, Barbara, 2589
Richardson, Barbara B., 7349
Richardson, Beatrix W., 7398
Richardson, Blair, 1444
Richardson, Brent, 2720
Richardson, Chris, 3018
Richardson, Christopher, 2720
Richardson, Clyde B., 1849
Richardson, Connie, 3276
Richardson, Douglas J., 8968
Richardson, Earl S., 3636
Richardson, Eudora L., 7398
Richardson, Evans, 4785
Richardson, Faye, 4404
Richardson, Frank E., 6796
Richardson, Frank E., III, 6796
Richardson, Gail, 2720
Richardson, Grace Jones, 1632, 7462
Richardson, H. Smith, 7461
Richardson, H.S., Sr., 1632
Richardson, Harry, 407
Richardson, Helen, 8729
Richardson, James, 3942
Richardson, James Lunsford, 7398
Richardson, Jannie, 1437
Richardson, Keith, 9987
Richardson, Keith W., 9987

Richardson, Lunsford, Jr., 1632, 7398
Richardson, M. Catherine, 6026
Richardson, Marge, 8257
Richardson, Mary, 3276
Richardson, P.L., 7462
Richardson, Peter L., 1632, 7461
Richardson, Roberta, 9987
Richardson, Rockette "Rocky", 7859
Richardson, S.S., 7462
Richardson, Sarah A., 2949
Richardson, Sarah Beinecke, 6750,
  7026
Richardson, Sid W., 9147
Richardson, Stuart S., 1632, 7461
Richardson, Sue, 9735
Richardson, Susan H., 6198
Richardson, Suzanne F., 8968
Richel, Victor, 5188
Richel, Victor M., 6229
Richenthal, Arthur, 5994, 6798
Richenthal, Donald, 6798
Richey, Van L., 24
Richie, Beth E., 3084
Richie, Sheldon E., 8892
Richins, Kent, 10000
Richland Bank, Mansfield, 7819
Richland Trust Co., The, 7795
Richloom Fabrics Group, Inc., 6799
Richloom Sales Corp., 6799
Richman, Arnold I., 3568
Richman, Fred, 6799
Richman, Frederick A., 361
Richman, James, 6799
Richman, Lawrence, 2779
Richman, Martin F., 6721
Richman, Rita, 6799
Richman, Terry M., 6823
Richmond County Financial Corp., 6800
Richmond Memorial Hospital
  Foundation, 7463
Richmond, Alice, 9993
Richmond, Frank, 6801
Richmond, Henry R., 8064
Richmond, Howard S., 6801
Richmond, Julius B., 5971
Richmond, Katherine K., 7337
Richmond, Lawrence, 6801
Richmond, Matthew D., 7337
Richmond, Merritt, 7337
Richmond, Phillip, 6801
Richmond, Robert, 6801
Richmond, Ruth B., 8064
Richmond, William L., 2277
Richmond-Schulman, Elizabeth, 6801
Richter, Jack, 4729
Richter, Janice L., 8379
Richter, Lyle H., 9888
Richwine, Marilyn, 3351
Rickard, Barbara A., 2165
Rickard, David B., 8529
Rickard, Jean J., 1776
Rickard, Polly Piper, 8805
Ricker, Jay B., 3197
Ricker, Michell, 3333
Rickman, Ronald L., 3305
Ricks, Charles V., 7395
Ricks, Ecleamus, 2411
Ricks, Mary, 5350
Ricordati, Timothy R., 2681
Ridall, John, 8152
Ridder, P. Anthony, 768
Riddick, Cheryl, 1940
Riddle, Don R., 9148
Riddle, Jenny L., 9148
Riddle, Judy, 2447
Riddle, Nancy L., 1049
Riddle, Pamela Cogan, 3851
Riddle, Richard A., 1049
Riddle, Scott A., 1049
Riddle, Todd Arlis, 9148
Riddle-Baumgartner, Stacy, 9148
Ridell, Joan Eldridge, 2770
Ridenour, Karen L., 3267
Ridenour, Mark E., 7540

Rideout, Vicky, 739
Rideoutte, James T., 1943
Rider, G. William, 9092
Rider, Grace F., 8936
Rider-Pool, Dorothy, 8404
Ridge Mgmt., 7068
Ridgewood, Inc., 7330
Ridihalgh, James R., 3320
Riding, Amy, 147
Ridley, A. Alexander, 8212
Ridley, Clarence H., 2377
Ridley, Knox, Jr., 3512
Ridout, Kyle, 3130
Riecker, John E., 4461
Riecker, Margaret Ann, 4287, 4461
Riecker, Steven Towsley, 4461
Riede, Richard, 249
Riedel, Ruth Lyn, 204
Riedel, Vicki J., 2355
Riedel, W.G., III, 9209
Rieder, Corrine H., 6150
Rieder, Leslie, 6803
Rieder, Miriam, 6803
Riedman Corp., 6804
Riedman, John R., 6804
Rief, Frank J., III, 1948, 1978
Riegel, Amanda J.T., 1658
Riegel, Leila E., 6907
Rieger, Abraham, 6805
Rieger, Abraham Jacob, 6805
Rieger, John A., 7935
Rieger, Kathryn K., 1575
Rieger, Rachel, 6805
Riehl, Margie, 3666
Riehl, Margie M., 3666
Rieke, Blaine, 9823
Rieke, Jack, 8967
Rieke, Terry, 4968
Rieker Charitable Remainder Trust,
  Rieker, 2579
Rieman, Robert, 2622
Riemer, Louise C., 3903
Riemer, Terrin S., 9908
Riendeau, Brian J., 3457
Rier Realty Co., Inc., 6497
Riesen, Albert, Jr., 7932
Rieveschl, Ellen, 7820
Rieveschl, Gary T., 7820
Rieveschl, George, Jr., 7820
Rieveschl, Jan L., 7820
Rife, John Arthur, 3338
Rifkin, Betty, 6832
Rifkind, Arleen, 6806
Rifkind, Richard A., 6119, 7267
Rifkind, Robert S., 6789, 6806
Rigas, John N., 8090
Rigdon, Lisa M., 970
Rigg, Remus, 4237
Riggio, Leonard, 6807
Riggio, Louise, 6807
Riggs, C. Dennis, 3414
Riggs, Earl, 2240
Riggs, Earl, Mrs., 2240
Riggs, Gail, 4449
Riggs, Greg L., 2372
Riggs, Judson T., 1231
Riggs, Marie, 1168
Riggs, William R., 3220
Right, Elizabeth B. Schwarzman, 6294
Rigler, James, 1051
Rigler, Lloyd E., 1051
Rigopoulos, Sandy, 7567
Riguardi, Edward, 6780
Rikimoto, Chere, 4723
Riklis, Meeshulam, 6808
Rikoon, Robert Allen, 5494
Riley, Anne Marie, 7599
Riley, Barbara W., 8157
Riley, Brigid A., 6809
Riley, Charles, 4921
Riley, Charles E., 9598
Riley, Daniel G., 4419
Riley, Daniel P., 572
Riley, Dolores, 4419

Riley, Ellen C., 6809
Riley, Emily C., 8157, 8378
Riley, Gail W., 4763
Riley, George, 4419
Riley, George K., 4419
Riley, H. John, Jr., 8846
Riley, James P., 9960
Riley, James P., Jr., 6809
Riley, James S., 9100
Riley, James, Jr., 6719
Riley, Katherine Murphy, 2456
Riley, Kerrylyn, 6809
Riley, Mabel Louise, 4104
Riley, Margaret M., 1963
Riley, Mark B., 2428
Riley, Mary Ann, 4763
Riley, Michael, 3855
Riley, Michael J., 4419
Riley, Pamela A., 262
Riley, Richard F., Jr., 4763
Riley, Richard W., 5707
Riley, Shannon C., 6809
Riley, Sheila, 4452
Riley, Susan, 1052
Riley, Thomas A., 8157
Riley, Thomas A., 3894
Riley, W.P. "Pat", 4512
Riley, William D., 4419
Riley, William G., 4763
Rimdo Properties Inc., 8423
Rimel, Rebecca W., 8377
Rimsky, Robert, 6454
Rincker, William H., 6203
Rindal, Edie, 518
Rinella, Bernard B., 2882
Ring, Duane, Jr., 9845
Ring, Timothy M., 5125
Ringel, Betsy, 3576
Ringel, Betsy F., 3575, 3650, 3719,
  3744
Ringel, Deborah Taper, 1226
Ringness, Edward, 9602
Ringness, Marjorie, 9602
Ringsmuth, Dennis, 4534
Ringwelski, Mark, 4439
Ringwelski, Susan, 4439
Ringwood, David J., 5564
Rinkenberger, James, 2677
Rinker Materials Inc., 2195
Rinker, David B., 2077, 2197
Rinker, Diane J., 1053
Rinker, Harry S., 1053
Rinker, John J., 2196
Rinker, Leighan R., 2197
Rinker, M.E., Sr., 2197
Rinker, Marilyn Powell, 4887
Rinker, Sheila A., 2196
Rintelmann, Richard F., 4600
Rion, Michael, 1529
Riordan Fund, The, 5705
Riordan, Jill, 1054
Riordan, Kathy, 1054
Riordan, Michael T., 9911
Riordan, Nancy Daly, 750, 1054
Riordan, Richard J., 1054
Rios, Dan, 3245
Ripley, Richard L., 9295
Ripley, S. Dillon, 134
Rippel, Julius S., 5368
Rippeto, Doug, 1468
Rippey Commercial LLC, 8853
Rippey, James F., 8023
Rippey, Jeffrey L., 8023
Rippey, Sally W., 1352, 1360
Rippey, Shirley K., 8023
Rippey, Timothy M., 8023
Ripplewood Holdings LLC, 6812
Rippy, Mary L., 4537
Riser, Mary Martin, 63
Rishagen, Nancy, 6532
Rishel, Jane, 2706
Rising Sun Regional Foundation, 3137
Rising, Nelson C., 1055
Rising, Sharon L., 1055

Riskin, Philip W., 5369
Risley, David M., 4368
Risner, Ollie J., 7639
Risor, Bob, 183
Rist, Judith, 8621
Ristine, Thomas H., 3147
Ritchey, Lori, 3210
Ritchie, Allen W., 58
Ritchie, Bill, 2148
Ritchie, Dan, 1362
Ritchie, Daniel L., 1350
Ritchie, Mabel M., 7821
Ritenour, Susan D., 2042
Riter, A.W., III, 9149
Riter, A.W., Jr., 9149
Riter, Betty Jo B., 9149
Riter, Charles, 8631
Riter, Cynthia S., 9149
Riter, George, 8348
Riter, Whit, 8876
Ritten, Jon E., 4745
Rittenberry, Jeanie, 2259
Ritter Foundation, May Ellen & Gerald, 5708
Ritter, Alan I., 6814
Ritter, Bruce, 1633
Ritter, C. Dowd, 5
Ritter, David, 6814
Ritter, Diane, 1633
Ritter, George W., 7822
Ritter, Gerald, 6813
Ritter, Irene, 6814
Ritter, Kathryn, 1633
Ritter, Lena, 6814
Ritter, Louis, 6814
Ritter, May Ellen, 6813
Ritter, Phil, 9232
Ritter, Philip J., 8855
Ritter, Russell J., 4941
Ritter, Sidney, 6814
Ritter, Toby G., 6814
Ritz, David, 2156
Ritz, Gordon H., 1579
Ritz, Susan Z., 1579
Ritz-Barr, Beate, 530
Rivard, Laurie, 4528
Rivas, Scott, 9385
Rivera, Efrain, 5605
Rivera, Henry, 1773
Rivera, James S., 1093
Rivera, Jose, 6577
Rivera, Miriam, 606
Rivera, Susan, 8073
Rivera-Fathallah, Sheila, 2579
Rivero, Jose, 5925
Rivers, Edna, Mrs., 25
Rives, Browder, 2053
Rives, Howard P., 2053
Rives, S. Bradford, 3417
Rivich, Joseph, 3144
Riviera Mgmt., 7068
Rivituso, Louis F., 9975
Rivitz, Jan, 3738
Rivkin, Arthur L., 1057
Rivkin, Bob, 1057
Rivkin, Jeannie P., 1057
Rivkin, Linda, 1057
Rivkin, Luciene, 1057
Rivkin, Michael, 1057
Rivkin, Mike, 1057
Rivkin, Robert, 1057
Rivlin, Alice M., 1780
Rix, Lynn M., 9803
Rizer, Michael P., 7502
Rizley, Robert S., 7974
Rizzi, Gary, 6618
Rizzo, Guy, 2087
Rizzo, John G., 3536
Rizzo, Stephen, 5983
RJH Investment Partners, L.P., 6216
RJR Acquisition Corp., 7459
RJR Nabisco Holdings Corp., 7459
RJR Tobacco Intl., 7459
RL Assocs., 5736

RLTS II, 6319
Roach, Dennis A., 1227
Roach, James, 8988
Roach, Jean W., 9150
Roach, John V., 9150
Roach, Kevin L., 531
Roach, Lori Anne, 9150
Roach, Michele C., 1932
Roach, Morgan, 641
Roan, Caroline, 6720
Roane, Gay A., 9189
Roane, George Grant, IV, 9189
Roark, AnnMarie, 4014
Roarty, Susan, 3617
Robak, Kim M., 4987
Robb, Anne, 4105
Robb, Brady, 3400
Robb, J.Y., III, 9118, 9119
Robb, James B., 9144
Robb, Kim, 4105
Robb, Lindsey, 4105
Robb, Marge, 4105
Robb, Richard, 4105
Robb, Richard G., 6688
Robb, Steve, 4105
Robb, Walter, 4105
Robb, Walter L., Dr., 6915
Robbins & Myers, Inc., 7823
Robbins, Amy, 6533
Robbins, Barry, 3934
Robbins, Beverly, 1634
Robbins, Bob, 4327
Robbins, Cathy, 7944
Robbins, Clifton S., 1634
Robbins, Diane H., 3918
Robbins, Edwin, 1634
Robbins, Felicia C., 8582
Robbins, Gregory A., 9514
Robbins, Jerome, 6817
Robbins, Joseph C., 4106
Robbins, Kris A., 3390
Robbins, Larry, 6533
Robbins, Lois O., 6955
Robbins, Mary, 4969
Robbins, Michael D., 6955
Robbins, N. Clay, 3194
Robbins, Patricia H., 8595
Robbins, Patty, 5487
Robbins, Peter J., 5750
Robbins, Valerie C., 9486
Robbins, William D., 6860
Robers, Frank, 7789
Roberson, Bill, 8333
Roberson, Delores N., 3437
Roberson, Ed, 8663
Robert H. & Ann Lurie Trust, 2865
Robert W. Baird and Co., 9750
Roberts Foundation, Flora, 5883
Roberts Trust, Jessie Castle, 1044
Roberts, Aileen K., 8406
Roberts, Alfred M., Jr., 2201
Roberts, Annie Lee, 9217
Roberts, Austin L., 9442
Roberts, Belle G., 59
Roberts, Benita, 405
Roberts, Bernard, 7055
Roberts, Bettina, 5371
Roberts, Betty, 3119
Roberts, Bill, 1358
Roberts, Bradley A., 5536
Roberts, Brian L., 8406
Roberts, Cate M., 8559
Roberts, Christopher L., 3601
Roberts, Claude C., 8965
Roberts, Cokie, 739
Roberts, David, 4923, 5562
Roberts, Denton, 3395
Roberts, Dolly Bodick, 1943
Roberts, Donald D., 423
Roberts, Dora, 9151
Roberts, Dorothy H., 2201
Roberts, Elaine Stein, 7055
Roberts, Elizabeth M., 8303
Roberts, Elyse Meredith, 2968

Roberts, Eugene L., Jr., 4774
Roberts, Gareth, 5370
Roberts, George H., Jr., 6242
Roberts, George R., 1058
Roberts, Gilroy, 8405
Roberts, Gretchen, 4998
Roberts, Gwenna, 5370
Roberts, Henry, 7979
Roberts, James E., 2215
Roberts, Jennifer S.D., 3833
Roberts, Jill A., 5562
Roberts, John B., 7198
Roberts, John J., 3601, 7048
Roberts, John T., 8405
Roberts, Judith V., 2572
Roberts, Kenneth L., 8679
Roberts, Kevin J., 1017
Roberts, Larry, 7931
Roberts, Leanne B., 1058
Roberts, Leonard, 1635
Roberts, Lillian, 8405
Roberts, Lisa S., 8392
Roberts, Lucy, 7653
Roberts, Mary Gordon, 6077
Roberts, Mary Jane, 5370
Roberts, Morris S., 6350
Roberts, Nancy Elizabeth, 8766
Roberts, Nancy L., 3601
Roberts, Norman, 5371
Roberts, R. Donn, 3210
Roberts, Ralph J., 8152, 8407
Roberts, Raymond J., 2968
Roberts, Rebecca B., 3601
Roberts, Ronald N., 9730
Roberts, Stu, 1477
Roberts, Sue Marshall, 8326
Roberts, Susan M. Morrison, 4998
Roberts, Suzanne F., 8407
Roberts, Terry A., 1017
Roberts, Terry L., 2388
Roberts, Tom, 3171
Roberts, Valerie, 6028
Roberts, William J., 5614
Roberts, William L., Jr., 9506
Robertson, Alan T., 9635
Robertson, Alex T., 7466
Robertson, Carolyn F., 16
Robertson, Charles S., 1889
Robertson, David A., Jr., 3907
Robertson, Gloria J., 4394
Robertson, I.R., 7985
Robertson, Jeanne, 1059
Robertson, Jodee, 119
Robertson, Josephine T., 6818
Robertson, Julian H., Jr., 6818, 7139, 7466
Robertson, Leslie, 3130
Robertson, Lindsay B., 2458
Robertson, Marie H., 1889
Robertson, Mark, 7952
Robertson, Sanford R., 1059
Robertson, Sara, 9706
Robertson, Scott, 5007
Robertson, Spencer R., 7466
Robertson, Stuart, 8869
Robertson, W. Scott, 98
Robertson, Walter S., III, 9402
Robertson, Wilhelmina E., 8854, 9273
Robertson, Wilhelmina E. "Beth", 8960
Robertson, William R., 7806, 7888
Robertson, William S., 1889
Robertson, Wyndham, 7466, 7485
Robeson, Mark D., 7761
Robideau, Gladys E., 4421
Robideau, James J., 4421
Robideau, Jeffrey T., 4421
Robie, Deborah S., 6117
Robie, Richard S., III, 4088
Robinett, P. Ward, Jr., 9376
Robins, Charles, 204
Robins, E. Claiborne, 9506
Robins, E. Claiborne, Jr., 9506
Robins, Gregory C., 9506

Robins, Kaplan, Miller & Ciresi L.L.P., 4667
Robins, Kate, 1517
Robins, Lora M., 9506
Robins, Marylou, 8944
Robinsin, Roger W., Jr., 8425
Robinson & Lawing, LLP, 7460
Robinson, Anthony L., 3714
Robinson, Barbara Paul, 5971, 6103, 6150, 6684, 7126, 7187
Robinson, Bernie, 6219
Robinson, Betty D., 3548
Robinson, Bill, 4257
Robinson, Bob, 9716
Robinson, Bonnie Lynne, 9820
Robinson, Brandi, 6640
Robinson, Brenda, 4991
Robinson, Brent, 9710
Robinson, Bruce, 9089
Robinson, Byron, 4107
Robinson, Byron C., 4107
Robinson, Constance, 8277
Robinson, Constance K., 8277
Robinson, Cynthia R., 3557
Robinson, David, 9152
Robinson, Deborah, 8667
Robinson, Donald H., 3434
Robinson, Dorothea, 4107
Robinson, Dorothy J., 3203
Robinson, Dwight P., 9422
Robinson, E.B., Jr., 4733
Robinson, Eddie, 3714
Robinson, Edward H., 3714
Robinson, Edward O., 3449
Robinson, Elmer D., 8135
Robinson, Emilie W., 4207
Robinson, Flavia, 5853
Robinson, Flavia D., 5853
Robinson, Florence L., 1745
Robinson, Frank Brooks, 8130
Robinson, G.W., 2202
Robinson, Gary, 1222
Robinson, Guy N., 7287
Robinson, J. Mack, 2473
Robinson, Jack A., 4254
Robinson, James D., III, 6819
Robinson, Janet L., 5707, 6620
Robinson, Jean, 8209
Robinson, Jean A., 8124
Robinson, Jennifer Lea, 2850
Robinson, Jesse, 3115
Robinson, Jill, 2473
Robinson, John F., 1361
Robinson, John G., 384
Robinson, John H., 8816, 8817
Robinson, John R., 7255
Robinson, Joseph R., 4400
Robinson, Kate, 2202
Robinson, Kenneth S., 8647
Robinson, Kristin, 8608
Robinson, Kristy H., 8956
Robinson, Lance, 8667
Robinson, Leroy, 7315, 8572
Robinson, Lewis J., Jr., 1564
Robinson, Linda G., 6819
Robinson, Linda Gosden, 6819
Robinson, Lori E., 5927
Robinson, Lucia, 3714
Robinson, Lucia I., 1741
Robinson, Lynne, 4315
Robinson, M. Bruce, 5224
Robinson, M. Trish, 3855
Robinson, Malcom Ari, 5224
Robinson, Margaret, 7985
Robinson, Margaret Y., 1741
Robinson, Maria Rosa, 3714
Robinson, Mark A., 4107
Robinson, Martha T., 8644
Robinson, Marty, 8660
Robinson, Maurice R., 1745
Robinson, Melanie, 3617
Robinson, Michael, 5940
Robinson, Peter, 3714
Robinson, Phil K., 9313

Romanotto, Salvatore, 6214, 7114
Romanow, Julia Narvarte, 8869
Rombauer Vineyards, Inc., 5074
Rome, Dan, 1105
Rome, Martin, 6978
Romeril, Robert D., 8303
Romero, Eleanor, 5498
Romero, Gail, 3468
Romero, Jesus, 2701
Romero, Louis, 8842
Romero, Marie C., 3520
Romero-Wirth, Carol, 5496
Rominski, Kathryn Hubbard, 4590
Romita, Camille, 5716
Romita, Mauro C., 5716
Romita, Michael, 5716
Romoser, David W., 9927
Rompala, Richard M., 4706
Ronald Trust, 809
Ronan, Martin W., Jr., 6513
Rondeau, Jacques-Antoine, 7436
Roney, Blake M., 9322
Roney, Brooke, 9322
Roney, Paul, 4225
Ronk, Alan E., 9419
Ronquist, Kyle, 4412
Roob, Nancy, 5760
Roof, Don, 9828
Rooke, Andrew K., 5458
Rooke, Charles C., 5458
Rooke, Natalie D., 5161
Rooke, Robert C., 5161
Rooke, Robert C., Jr., 5161
Rooke, Robert L., 5161, 5458
Rooke, William W., 5458
Roome, Anne, 1570
Rooms To Go, Inc., 2204
Rooney, Marianne, 7963
Rooney, Mary Ann, 4033
Rooney, Pat Garrett, 3116
Rooney, Patrick T., 7935, 7944
Rooney, Paul H., Jr., 8112
Roos, Geraldine, 4110
Roos, John T., 7319
Roos, Linda, 4883, 4884
Roosa, David E., 8552
Roosth, Sam, 8876
Root, Carol Jean, 2882
Root, Daniel R., 3135
Root, Dorothy L., 813
Roozen, Marion W., 9666
Roper, Lynn, 5018
Roper, William L., 5265
Roraback, Margaret, 1516
Rorem, Ned, 5548
Rorer, Edward C., 8411
Rorer, Gerald B., 8411
Rorer, Herbert T., 8411
Rorick, Marvin H., 7574
Roriston, Robert, 7278
Ros, Frank, 2355
Rosa, Bruce N., 7707
Rosa, Karen L., 5542
Rosa, Margarita, 5971
Rosado, Jose Luis, 8515
Rosand, David, 5847
Rosanksy Trust, B., 6832
Rosario, Carlos Vazquez, 8515
Roscoe, James P., 4931
Roscoe, Stacy A., 1264
Rose Charitable Foundation, Samuel and
    David, 6836, 6837, 6839
Rose Trust, 983
Rose, Adam, 6834
Rose, Adam M., 6834
Rose, Adam R., 6837
Rose, Ann C., 1734
Rose, Barbara, 4718, 9723
Rose, Billy, 6838
Rose, Christy, 7825
Rose, Daniel, 6779, 6839
Rose, David, 1327
Rose, David Heineman, 6165
Rose, Deborah, 6835, 6837

Rose, Diana C., 6448
Rose, Elihu, 6836
Rose, Eugene S., 7825
Rose, Frank, 9164
Rose, Frederick P., 6837
Rose, Gary D., 5199
Rose, Glenn E., 552
Rose, James A., 6165
Rose, Jaqueline T., 7825
Rose, Jean H., 9211
Rose, Jean Weinberg, 7230
Rose, Jonathan F.P., 6448, 6837
Rose, Judy, 3449
Rose, Lawrence D., 544
Rose, Marian Heineman, 6165
Rose, Marshall, 6833
Rose, Matt, 2644
Rose, Sandra, 6448
Rose, Sandra Priest, 6837
Rose, Simon, 6165
Rose, Stuart A., 7825
Rose, Susan, 6836
Rose, Victoria M., 9301
Rose, William, 7882
Rose, William E., 7883
Rosebrock, Charles A., 3992
Rosemore, Inc., 3719
Rosen Family Charitable Trust, 2263
Rosen Foundation, Harris, Inc., The,
    2263
Rosen, Andrew, 6874
Rosen, Andrew M., 4789
Rosen, Benjamin M., 6841
Rosen, Bruce A., 6753
Rosen, Burt, 6640
Rosen, Donna, 6841
Rosen, Elaine D., 4367
Rosen, Gordon, 27
Rosen, Harris, 2205, 2263
Rosen, Jack, 6751
Rosen, Jeanette D., 6842
Rosen, Jeannette, 6843
Rosen, Jonathan P., 6842, 6843
Rosen, Leizor, 1467
Rosen, Lois, 191
Rosen, Martin M., 4903
Rosen, Miriam N., 6842
Rosen, Sarah, 5417, 5815
Rosen, Selma, 5228
Rosen, Seth D., 2269
Rosenbach, Kurt M., 9484
Rosenbaum, David, 5374
Rosenbaum, Dovid, 5374
Rosenbaum, Gary, 3595
Rosenbaum, Howard, 6164
Rosenbaum, I.A., 4763
Rosenbaum, Joseph, 5374
Rosenbaum, Moshe, 5374
Rosenberg, Abraham, 6845
Rosenberg, Ann, 2206, 9157
Rosenberg, Cheryl, 6847
Rosenberg, Claude N., Jr., 1066
Rosenberg, Daniel L., 2938
Rosenberg, David, 2938, 6260
Rosenberg, David M., 8412
Rosenberg, Deborah, 3005
Rosenberg, Donald, 2206
Rosenberg, Dorothy L., 3720
Rosenberg, Dulcy D., 2476
Rosenberg, Frank B., 3720
Rosenberg, Gail, 6846
Rosenberg, H. Jerome, III, 2476
Rosenberg, Henry, 6846
Rosenberg, Henry A., Jr., 3719, 3720
Rosenberg, James, 2206
Rosenberg, Jennifer, 2206
Rosenberg, John, 2206
Rosenberg, Linda, 2206
Rosenberg, Louise J., 1066
Rosenberg, Marcus, 9157
Rosenberg, Marjorie D., 8412
Rosenberg, Max L., 1065
Rosenberg, Michael, 2938
Rosenberg, Michael L., 6845

Rosenberg, Norman, 1835, 6057
Rosenberg, Richard, 7247
Rosenberg, Robert, 2206
Rosenberg, Ruth Blaustein, 3719
Rosenberg, Scott, 1821
Rosenberg, Sheli Z., 2865
Rosenberg, Sheryl, 455
Rosenberg, Sonia, 6845
Rosenberg, Stanley, 8788
Rosenberg, Steve, 9157
Rosenberg, William, 2206
Rosenberg, William F., 7435
Rosenberger, David M., 4462
Rosenberry, Charles W., II, 4726
Rosenblatt Trust, E.G., 6849
Rosenblatt, Arthur S., 3801
Rosenblatt, C., 6848
Rosenblatt, Cynthia, 4529
Rosenblatt, Lief D., 5582
Rosenblatt, Roger, 6103
Rosenblatt, Ruth, 7032
Rosenblatt, Stanley, 2002
Rosenblatt, Stuart A., 5205
Rosenblatt, Susan, 2002
Rosenblatt, Toby, 698
Rosenbloom, Alan, 2149
Rosenbloom, Ben, 3721
Rosenbloom, Esther, 3721
Rosenbloom, Howard, 3721
Rosenbloom, Keith, 3721
Rosenbloom, Michelle G., 3721
Rosenbloom, Robert, 3721
Rosenblum, Daniel, 6850
Rosenblum, Jay, 5491
Rosenblum, Leonard, 6850
Rosenbower, William, 3135
Rosenburg, Stephen, 6847
Rosenfeld, Eugene S., 1067
Rosenfeld, Gerald, 7290
Rosenfeld, Howard, 1649
Rosenfeld, Lester, 8413
Rosenfeld, Maxine, 1067
Rosenfeld, Monica Hasten, 3163
Rosenfeld, Rachel, 6112
Rosenfeld, Robert, 8413
Rosenfeld, Shea, 6112
Rosenfield, Allan, 739, 972
Rosenfield, Bruce A., 8123, 8365
Rosenfield, Herbert, 6396
Rosenfield, Patricia, 6118
Rosenhouse Family Trust, 1111
Rosenkranz Foundation, The, 6185
Rosenkranz, Nicholas, 6851
Rosenkranz, Robert, 6851
Rosenkranz, Stephanie, 6851
Rosenson, Whitney, 393
Rosenstein, Anita May, 464, 5046
Rosenstein, Brian, 5046
Rosenstein, Carl, 5362
Rosenstein, Morton G., 537
Rosenstein, Neal, 5362
Rosenstein, Perry, 5362
Rosenstiel, Blanka A., 6852
Rosenstiel, Lewis S., 6852
Rosensweig, David, 1660, 1661
Rosenthal & Rosenthal, Inc., 6853
Rosenthal, Babette H., 2693
Rosenthal, Benjamin J., 2970
Rosenthal, Betty M., 3450
Rosenthal, Charles, 6854
Rosenthal, Eric, 6853
Rosenthal, Harry, 5521
Rosenthal, Hinda Gould, 1638
Rosenthal, Jack, 6620
Rosenthal, Jonathan, 6542
Rosenthal, Lois, 7826
Rosenthal, Lois R., 7826
Rosenthal, Lynne, 2776
Rosenthal, Marie-Louise, 2693
Rosenthal, Marion, 9508
Rosenthal, Morris H., 6602
Rosenthal, Nancy, 9508
Rosenthal, Nancy Stephens, 1638
Rosenthal, Noah, 1638

Rosenthal, Phyllis, 6854
Rosenthal, Richard, 7826
Rosenthal, Richard H., 7826
Rosenthal, Rick, 1638
Rosenthal, Robert M., 9508
Rosenthal, Samuel L., 2693
Rosenthal, Samuel R., 2693
Rosenthal, Sandi, 6028
Rosenthal, Stephen, 6853
Rosenthal, Warren W., 3450
Rosenwald Family Fund, W.H., 1796
Rosenwald, Bradley C., 73
Rosenwald, Edward John, Jr., 6856
Rosenwald, Lindsay, 6857
Rosenwald, Nina, 6855
Rosenwald, Patricia, 6856
Rosenwald, William, 6855
Rosenzweig, Dora, 4425
Rosenzweig, Harry, 4425
Rosenzweig, Herschel, 4425
Rosenzweig, Joseph, 4425
Rosenzweig, Leonard, 4425
Rosenzweig, Newton, 87
Roser, Eleanor, 9305
Rosetti Handbags, Ltd., 6177
Rosewood Corp., The, 9158
Rosholt, John, 2570
Rosholt, Robert A., 7771
Rosica, A. Joseph, 1830
Rosica, Daniel, 1830
Rosica, Kathryn, 1830
Rosica, Lenore, 1830
Rosica, Mark, 1830
Rosin, Axel G., 6918
Rosin, Katharine S., 6918
Rosing, Wayne, 1224
Rosing, Wayne E., 1224
Roskam, Don, 4424
Roskam, Donald O., 4424
Roskam, Robert O., 4424
Roskens, Ron, 3350
Roskos, Joseph W., 8466
Rosloniec, James, 4467
Roslyn Bancorp, Inc., 6859
Rosman, Fran E. Morris, 514
Rosman, Richard D., 514
Rosmarin, Jefry, 6219
Rosner, Bernat, 6473
Rosner, Carol, 6846
Rosner, June, 6860
Rosner, Myron, 5130
Rosoff, William A., 8078
Rosovsky, Henry, 7899
Ross Group, Fischer, 2386
Ross Revocable Trust, Robert A., 1069
Ross Willoughby Co., 7618
Ross, Alexander B., 5600
Ross, Alfred S., 4010
Ross, Alison G., 2207
Ross, Amory, 5376
Ross, Arthur, 6243, 6864
Ross, Barbara, 1241
Ross, Benson T., 5376
Ross, Carson, 4919
Ross, Cheryl L., 1952
Ross, Courtney S., 6861
Ross, David, 3189
Ross, David J., 9159
Ross, Dean John, 8715
Ross, Deborah H., 9159
Ross, Dennis L., Dr., 3404
Ross, Dickinson C., 728
Ross, Dorothea Haus, 6863
Ross, E. Burke, Jr., 5376
Ross, Elizabeth M., 2207
Ross, Elizabeth Manbeck, 2207
Ross, Elmer, 941, 1099
Ross, Eric F., 5375
Ross, Esther C., 174
Ross, F., 1952
Ross, Frances R., 8589
Ross, George A., 2207
Ross, George M., 6862
Ross, J. David, 7371

Ross, James A., 8431
Ross, James J., 6447
Ross, Jane, 174
Ross, Janet C., 6243, 6864
Ross, Jim, 156
Ross, Kristin, 8371
Ross, Larry, 156
Ross, Libby, 9371
Ross, Lore, 5375
Ross, Lyn M., 6862
Ross, M. Charles, 7247
Ross, Margaret M., 2207
Ross, Mary Caslin, 6263
Ross, Merry, 6862
Ross, Michael A., 9159
Ross, N. Barry, 6850
Ross, R., 1952
Ross, R. Dale, 9159
Ross, R. J., Rev., 1356
Ross, Rachael E., 2207
Ross, Ralph, 1256
Ross, Richard M., Jr., 2207
Ross, Robert J., 7935, 7944
Ross, Robert K., 346
Ross, Robin S., 1952
Ross, Samuel D., Jr., 8293
Ross, Sarane H., 5600
Ross, Sharryn, 3786
Ross, Stacey, 5255
Ross, Stan, 320
Ross, Stephen, 6779
Ross, Steven J., 6861
Ross, Susan M., 1537
Ross, Suzan, 3425
Ross, Thomas, 217
Ross, Thomas W., 7458
Ross, Troy K., 3274
Ross, Vidia, 9736
Ross, W. Thomas, 7633
Ross, William J., 7935, 7944
Rosse, Florence M., 4113
Rosse, Thomas A., 4113
Rossen, Mary Jo, 4417
Rosser, Harold O., II, 2208
Rosser, James M., 345
Rosser, Rita Elaine, 2208
Rosser, Shannon, 1782
Rossettie, Richard, 5784
Rossi, Anthony T., 1882, 1883
Rossi, E. Jeffrey, 7585
Rossi, E.J., 7629
Rossi, Moira, 5800
Rossi, Nick S., 948
Rossi, Sanna, 1883
Rossi, Sanna B., 1882
Rossi, Steven B., 768
Rossi-Landi, Beatrice, 8870
Rossiter, Bill, 7793
Rossley, Paul R., 4032, 4209
Rost, Rynthia M., 3634
Rosta, Fannie, 5319
Rostad, Lee B., 7998
Rostami, Ardeshir, 5361
Rostan, James H., 7467
Rostan, John P., III, 7467
Rostan, John P., Jr., 7467
Rostan, John P., Jr., Mrs., 7467
Rostan, Naomi B., 7467
Roswell, Arthur E., 3575, 3722
Roswell, Barbara, 3722
Roswell, Barbara S., 3575
Roswell, Elizabeth B., 3575, 3722
Roswell, Marjorie B., 3722
Roswell, Robert A., 3722
Roswick, John T., 7516
Roszell, Stephen, 4623
Rotan, Caroline P., 8894
Rotary Foundation of Washington, 1426
Rotella, Steve, 9680
Rotellini, Frank, 9991
Rotenstreich, Glenda Susan, 6865
Rotenstreich, James I., 6865
Rotenstreich, Jon W., 6865
Rotgin, Charles M., Jr., 9390

Roth and Co., Louis, 1071
Roth, David M., 1989
Roth, Eugene, 8327
Roth, Eugene A., 2741
Roth, Fannie, 1071
Roth, Harold J., 9718
Roth, Harry, 1071
Roth, Linda H., 1989
Roth, Louis, 1071
Roth, Michael, 5190
Roth, Michael P., 1071
Roth, Rachel, 1071
Roth, Robert, 1332
Roth, Sarah, 1071
Roth, Steven, 5377
Roth, Susan, 5190
Roth, Theodore D., 1306
Roth, Walter, 2838, 2970, 3004
Roth, William F., 4339
Roth-Fedida, Andrea, 1071
Roth-Medina, Dianne, 5190
Rothberg, Heidi B., 2960
Rothberg, Henry M., 2209
Rothberg, Jean C., 2960
Rothberg, Jonathan M., 2209
Rothberg, Lee Patrick, 2960
Rothberg, Lilliam R., 2209
Rothberg, Michael, 2960
Rothberg, Michael J., 2209
Rothberg, Richard S., 6054
Rothberg, Samuel, 2960
Rothblatt, Ben, 2860
Rothchild, Emily, 5895
Rothenberg, Allen W., 3968
Rothenberg, Ann, 3968
Rothenberg, Daniel E., 3968
Rothenberg, Edward, 3968
Rothenberg, Lawrence, 2100
Rothenberg, Lloyd, 6235
Rothenberg, Marvin, 476
Rothenberg, Stuart, 6056
Rothenberg, Susan, 3968
Rothenberger, Patricia A., 2485
Rothermel, Elizabeth B., 8271
Rothman, David, 6665
Rothman, Howard, 6029, 6030
Rothman, Margaret, 2210
Rothman, Mark D., 1785
Rothman, Robert, 2210
Rothschadl, Terri Anderson, 4637
Rothschild, A. Frank, Jr., 1072
Rothschild, Alan F., Jr., 2361, 2387
Rothschild, Bruce I., 3595
Rothschild, Cory, 3723
Rothschild, David, 3723
Rothschild, David N., 1072
Rothschild, Dorothy B., 1072
Rothschild, Holly B., 1072
Rothschild, Hulda B., 2971
Rothschild, Jonathan, 91
Rothschild, Judith, 6866
Rothschild, Nathaniel, 5576
Rothschild, Peter, 3548
Rothschild, Stanford Z., Jr., 3618, 3723
Rothstein, Joel, 354
Rothstein, Robin S., 1777
Rothstein, William, 5546
Rothstein-Schwimmer, Susan, 5546
Rothwell, David, 183
Rothwell, Sharon, 4387
Rothwell, Timothy, 5120
Rotsch, Jeff, 4570
Rottenberg, Alan, 4168
Rottenberg, Alan W., 3799, 4141
Rotter, Jeff, 8147
Rottman, Burton, 2783
Rottman, Howard, 2783
Rottman, Michael, 2783
Rotty, Sharon, 8039
Rounds, Charles, 4628
Roundy's Supermarkets, Inc., 9915
Roundy's, Inc., 9915
Rounsavall, Robert W., III, 3409
Rountree, Paul, 1947

Rountree, Stephen D., 198
Rourk, Sheba A., 2372
Rourke, Floyd H., 6041, 6903
Rourke, Michael, 4574
Rouse Co., The, 3724
Rouse Company Incentive
Compensation Statutory Trust, The,
3724
Rouse, Charles F., III, 5120, 5121
Rouse, Christopher, 5789
Rouse, Eloise Meadows, 9049
Rouse, Joseph P., 7913
Roush, David, 3597
Roush, G. James, 9546
Roush, Galen, 7643
Roush, Roy Michael, 3199
Roush, Ruth C., 7643
Roush, William Morgan, 9546
Rousselot, Doris, 9164
Routhier, Edward J., 8553
Roux, Christina, 7223
Roux, Henry, 828
Roux, Michel, 6086
Roven, Rose Webb, 1070, 1284
Rover, Edward F., 5825, 5827
Rovezzi, Guy, 1516
Rovinsky, Paul, 5130
Rovira, Luis D., Hon., 1350
Rowan, Henry M., 5378
Rowan, Paul G., 2563
Rowan, Virginia, 3480
Rowe, Abigail M., 1748
Rowe, Bradley M., 9725
Rowe, Christine, 3141
Rowe, Daphne C., 8070
Rowe, George, Jr., 6566, 7191, 7196
Rowe, J.S., 9531
Rowe, John, 1748
Rowe, John W., 1479, 1748
Rowe, Meredith L., 1748
Rowe, R. Roger, 1031
Rowe, Rebecca J., 1748
Rowe, Sara M., 9725
Rowe, Thomas W., 9725
Rowe, Valeria, 1748
Rowe, Valerie A., 1748
Rowe, William L.S., 9402
Rower, Judy M., 7627
Rowland, Charles G., III, 8581
Rowland, Diane, 739
Rowland, Marilyn, 2457
Rowland, Pleasant T., 9916
Rowland, Sandra, 8698
Rowlett, Kay, 2094
Rowley, Claude, 4376
Rowley, Lynn, 3197
Rowley, Richard, 7764
Rowling, Robert B., 9160
Rowling, Robert B., Jr., 9160
Rowling, Terry H., 9160
Rowling, Travis Blake, 9160
Roxe, Joseph D., 6867
Roxe, Maureen L., 6867
Roxy 15 LLC, 379
Roy, Adelard A., 4114
Roy, Wendy, 4574
Royal Brand Roofing, Inc., 4800
Royal Wine Corp., 5202
Royal, Anita, 91
Royal, Gloria Z., 4352
Royal, Nina, 223
Royal, Susan B., 8092
Royal, Willie, 7499
Royalty, David L., 2989
Royce, Charles M., 1639
Royce, Janet, 4403
Royce, Joseph W., 9041, 9198
Royer, Kevin, 5400
Royes, Lawrence E., 6568
Royfe, Ephrain, 8237
Roylance, David, 9144
Royster, R. Randall, 5466
Royston, Colette Carson, 1087
Rozell, Denise, 1765

Rozen, Toby Stein, 7056
Rozett, Martha Tuck, 7170
RSSJ Associates, LLC, 1716
RTM Restaurant Group, 2477
RTM, Inc., 2477
RUAN Transport Management Systems,
3329
Ruan, Elizabeth, 3329
Ruan, Janis, 3281
Ruan, John, 3329
Ruane, Joy M., 6810
Ruane, William J., 1873, 5705, 6810
Ruark, Davis R., 3648
Rubacka, Kristen E., 5927
Rubadeau, Mary, 1465
Rubbermaid Inc., 2913
Ruben, Dennis, 2973
Ruben, Joyce, 2973
Ruben, Lawrence, 5616, 6868
Ruben, Lenore, 6868, 6869
Ruben, Richard, 5616, 6868, 6869
Ruben, Selma, 6868, 6869
Rubenstein, Amy, 1845
Rubenstein, Amy Sara, 1845
Rubenstein, Anne C., 4115
Rubenstein, Barry, 6870
Rubenstein, Barton, 1845
Rubenstein, Barton S., 1845
Rubenstein, Beth Dana, 1845
Rubenstein, Brian, 6870
Rubenstein, Ernest, 6124
Rubenstein, Estelle, 5305
Rubenstein, Harold, 4116
Rubenstein, Jeffrey M., 5724
Rubenstein, Jerry, 9162
Rubenstein, Joshua S., 2826, 6828
Rubenstein, Lawrence J., 4115
Rubenstein, Marilyn, 6870
Rubenstein, Maury, 9162
Rubenstein, Rebecca, 6870
Rubenstein, Terry, 3692
Rubenstein, Terry M., 3691
Rubenstein, William H., 4502
Rubenstein, William S., 6124
Rubin and Sons, Joseph, Inc., 4117
Rubin Foundation, Samuel, Inc., 6872
Rubin, Alvan D., Rabbi, 4903
Rubin, Burton, 145
Rubin, Charles, 5367
Rubin, Dina, 6871
Rubin, Donald, 6873
Rubin, Dorothy, 6871
Rubin, Eugene, 6871
Rubin, Gerald M., 3654
Rubin, Howard, 6875
Rubin, Howard S., Jr., 7867
Rubin, Jacob M., 2211
Rubin, Jane Gregory, 6782
Rubin, Judith O., 2974
Rubin, L., 6330
Rubin, Lara R., 6782
Rubin, Liebel, 6871
Rubin, Maia A., 6782
Rubin, Michael, 220
Rubin, Miles, 6874
Rubin, Nancy, 6874
Rubin, Pearl W., 6274
Rubin, Peter J., 4804
Rubin, Peter L., 6782
Rubin, Reed, 6782
Rubin, Richard, 5847
Rubin, Robert E., 2974
Rubin, Robert M., 5082
Rubin, Rochelle A., 5540
Rubin, Ronald, 8415
Rubin, Samuel, 6782
Rubin, Shelley, 2109, 6873
Rubin, Solomon, 6871
Rubin, Steven I., 5540
Rubin, Steven M., 9710
Rubin, Tova, 5834
Rubin, Wendy H., 4671
Rubin, William S., 1358
Rubinelli, Joseph O., Jr., 2877

Rubinelli, Mary Jane, 2877
Rubinow, Laurence P., 1644
Rubinstein, Frederic A., 6841
Ruble, Blair, 7168
Ruble, Cindy S., 4233
Rubschlager, Joan S., 2975
Rubschlager, Paul A., 2975
Ruby, Burton B., 3143, 3247
Ruby, Paul J., 353, 1205
Rudd, Alexandria A., 1073
Rudd, Andrew T., 1073
Rudd, Christopher A., 1073
Rudd, Jeffrey, 9680
Rudd, Jim, 26
Rudd, Leslie G., 3385
Rudd, Natalie A., 1073
Rudd, Nicholas S., 1073
Rudd, Virginia A., 1073
Ruddy Charitable Trust, Raymond & Marilyn, 3923
Ruddy, Ginger A., 3923
Ruddy, James J., 5611, 5894
Ruddy, Marilyn A., 4118
Ruddy, Raymond B., 3923, 4118
Ruddy, Thomas P., 3904
Rude, Janice R., 5058
Rude, N. Jean, 4581, 4582
Rudel, Doris, 8632
Rudell, Michael, 6678
Rudenstine, Neil L., 6056
Ruderman, Debra F., 2736
Rudin Estates Co., LP, 6879
Rudin, Eric C., 6877, 6878, 6879
Rudin, Jack, 6877, 6878, 6879
Rudin, Jeffrey, 4040
Rudin, Katherine L., 6877, 6878
Rudin, Mark P.H., 6877
Rudin, Mary C., 981
Rudin, Samantha Mia, 6877
Rudin, Stephen, 5727
Rudin, William, 6780
Rudin, William C., 6877, 6878, 6879
Rudisill, Ben R., 7342
Rudisill, Phillip M., 9498
Rudman, Edward I., 3973
Rudner, Diane R., 8718
Rudner, Jocelyn P., 8718
Rudner, William, 8718
Rudnick, Andrew J., 5780
Rudo, Saul E., 2826
Rudolph, Alexander S., 3024
Rudolph, Franci Golman, 1948
Rudolph, Frank W., 9752
Rudolph, Geoffrey E., 3024
Rudy, Ike, 5740
Rudy, John, 3189
Ruebel, Richard J., 7574
Rueckert, William Dodge, 5867
Ruegsegger, Brian D., 3141
Ruehle, Judi A., 716
Ruehle, William J., 716
Ruemenapp, Harold A., 4232
Rues, David, 9407
Ruesga, Albert, 1834
Ruettgers, Abagail, 4119
Ruettgers, Christopher, 4119
Ruettgers, Maureen, 4119
Ruettgers, Michael, 4119
Ruettgers, Polly, 4119
Ruffier, Joan, 1922, 2303
Ruffner, Jay S., 98
Rufty, Archibald C., 5059
Rufty, Archibald C., Jr., 5059
Rufty, Diane B., 5059
Rufty, Frances F., 5059
Rugeley, Virginia, 9723
Ruggiero, Chatka, 2922
Rugland, Walter S., 9776
Ruhl, Donald, 4194
Ruhlman, Barbara P., 7802
Ruhlman, Randall M., 7802
Ruidl, Greg A., 9906
Ruiz, Cecilia, 376
Ruiz, Lisa Garcia, 319

Rumbough, J. Wright, Jr., 2297
Rumbough, Nina Craig, 1842
Rumelhart, Judith D., 4461
Rummel, Mason B., 3409
Rump, Rick, 7667
Rumpke, Linda, Rev., 3422
Rumsey, Charles Cary, 6882
Rumsey, David, 6357
Rumsey, Julie, 4552
Rumsey, Mary A.H., 6882
Rumsey, Mary M., 6882
Rumsfeld, Donald H., 2695
Rumsfeld, Joyce P., 2695
Runes, Gary, 249
Runestad, Mary, 1620
Runestad, Rodney, 1620
Runion, Christopher S., 9400
Runkel, J., 8240
Runnebohm, Nick, 3107
Runnells, Clive, III, 8926
Runningwater, N. Bird, 6604
Runser, C. Allan, 7891
Runstad, Judy, 9680
Runte, Rosann O., 9475
Rupe, Arthur N., 1074
Rupe, Beverly M., 1074
Rupel, Brad, 3137
Rupkey-Cohrt, Lois, 3278
Rupp, Christina D., 6883
Rupp, Frances O., 6883
Rupp, Gary L., 2145
Rupp, Gerald E., 7198
Rupp, Joan C., 5597
Rupp, Kathryn M., 2145
Rupp, Richard W., 6883
Rupp, Sheron A., 4669
Rupp, Susan S., 6883
Rupp, Warren, 4669
Rupp, William R., 6883
Ruppert, Elizabeth, 7882
Ruppert, Elizabeth S., 7883
Rupple, Keith, 9960
Rupprecht, Daniel P., 3327
Rupprecht, Phyllis M., 3327
Rurik, Dion, 9673
Ruscitto, Kathryn H., 5785
Rusek, Leslie, 9778
Rush, Leonard M., 9750
Rush, Richard, Dr., 1264
Rushing, Don, 9021
Rushing, Ted, 9021
Rushton, J. Philippe, 6729
Rushton, Stephen, 6729
Rusk, Dick, 3115
Ruskin, Florita, 1312
Ruskin, Glenn S., 4907
Ruskin, Maura, 5197
Russ, Jack, 836
Russ, Mike, 9060
Russ, Randy J., 4329
Russ, Susan F., 6777
Russack, Richard A., 2644
Russel, Marjorie, 6565
Russell Trust f/b/o Mary J. Dickie, F.D., 2976
Russell, Angus M., 7409
Russell, Benjamin, 60
Russell, Charles P., 399
Russell, Christine, 1853, 5779
Russell, Christine H., 399, 545
Russell, Dan C., 9310
Russell, Deborah L., 1943
Russell, Dee, 20
Russell, Donna, 7828
Russell, Eric, 9673
Russell, Frank E., 3225
Russell, G. Richard, 4984
Russell, George F., Jr., 9673
Russell, George, Jr., 9673
Russell, Gordon, 359
Russell, Grover B., 3591, 3619
Russell, H.M., 2478
Russell, Ida H., 2336, 2337
Russell, James, 263

Russell, Jane H., 263
Russell, Jane T., 9673
Russell, Jenny, 4035
Russell, Jileen, 9673
Russell, John, 5045
Russell, John A., 8293
Russell, John F., 5781
Russell, John G., 4260, 4347
Russell, Josephine Schell, 7827
Russell, Justine V.R., 1747
Russell, Letty, 4309
Russell, Madeleine H., 399
Russell, Manon C., 9310
Russell, Nancy M., 3225
Russell, Richard, 9673
Russell, Richard W., Mrs., 3811
Russell, Robby, 7346
Russell, Rogene, 9254
Russell, Ron, 7653
Russell, Ruth L., 1622
Russell, T. Alan, 3157
Russell, Thomas C., 2976
Russell, Vale Asche, Mrs., 9246
Russell, Wayland J., 7828
Russell, William "Bill", 2356
Russell-Shapiro, Alice C., 399
Russert, Timothy J., 9424
Russett, Jack, 7770
Russo, Daniel, 234, 9593
Russo, Marcy, 6260
Russo, Patricia F., 5110
Russo, Ralph D., 7627
Russo, Thomas A., 3732, 5943, 6395
Rust, Carole D., 3122
Rust, Cheryl, 3549
Rust, Edward B., Jr., 3019
Rust, James O., 8724
Rust, John M., 8724
Rust, Laura, 2365
Rust, Mary L., 7697
Rust, R. Mark, 8724
Rust, Randy, 9597
Rust, Robert B., 8724
Rust, S.M., Jr., 8724
Rustad, Dale, 2166
Rutan, Letitia, 9247
Ruth, Alice, 913
Ruth, David, 5326
Ruth, Jim, 220
Rutherfurd, Winthrop, Jr., 7275
Rutkowski, Walter F., 8130
Rutledge, Amanda D., 6896
Rutledge, Edward, 9917
Rutledge, Joyce, 183
Rutledge, Peter L., 6896
Rutledge, Ronald E., 4793
Rutledge, Stephen G., 2
Rutledge, Tom, 7142
Rutman, Michael, 1050, 1322
Rutt, Celia W., 5495
Rutt, James P., 5495
Rutt, Sheila, 7611
Ruttenburg, Ruth, 1786
Rutter, William, 3677
Ruvo, Camille, 5060
Ruvo, Larry, 5060
Ruwe, Richard C., 2785
Ruyle, David, 356
Ruyle, Mary, 356
Ryals, Hilegard, 8509
Ryals, Mike, 2015
Ryan Enterprises Corp. of Illinois, 2977
Ryan Holding Corp. of Illinois, 2977
Ryan Trust, Gladys B., 1075
Ryan, Ann, 4574
Ryan, Anne E., 1075
Ryan, Arthur F., 5360
Ryan, Carl, 8950
Ryan, Carl E., 8881
Ryan, Carol, 5000
Ryan, Carolyn, 2206
Ryan, Constance, 5000
Ryan, Cynthia A., 4131
Ryan, Daniel H., 8416

Ryan, Daniel M., 2239
Ryan, David, 1076
Ryan, David J., 7775
Ryan, David M., 1075
Ryan, Dennis, 2694
Ryan, Eileen, 5000
Ryan, Elaine, 9407
Ryan, Gladys B., 1075
Ryan, James, 4872
Ryan, James D., 6928
Ryan, Jerome D., 1075
Ryan, Jill, 805
Ryan, Jim, 2812
Ryan, JoAnn, 1516
Ryan, John R., Jr., 4624
Ryan, John T., III, 8416
Ryan, Katrina W., 9997
Ryan, Kevin J., 2944
Ryan, Lawrence M., 3164
Ryan, Mark, 8096, 9135
Ryan, Mary, 3853
Ryan, Mary A., 2978
Ryan, Mary Irene, 8416
Ryan, Michael, 2206
Ryan, Michael Denis, 8416
Ryan, Michael F., 1075, 3174
Ryan, Michael G., 9378, 9429
Ryan, Mike, 1411, 3038
Ryan, Pamela M., 9186
Ryan, Patrick G., 2598, 2977
Ryan, Patrick G., Jr., 2977
Ryan, Robert J.W., 2977
Ryan, Robin, 1076
Ryan, Scott, 1244
Ryan, Sheila, 1778
Ryan, Shirley W., 2977
Ryan, Stacy, 5000
Ryan, Stephen J., 750
Ryan, Steve, 3387, 5000
Ryan, T. Timothy, Jr., 7185
Ryan, Terry, 1795
Ryan, Teya, 6389
Ryan, Theresa Helow, 2055
Ryan, Thomas M., 8529
Ryan, Tim, 5000
Ryan, Vincent J., 4131
Ryan, Wayne L., 5000
Ryan, William F., 8416
Ryan, William G., 2978
Ryan, William J., 3546
Ryans, Jerome, 1948
Rybak, David, 7296
Ryberg, Claire Dumke, 9315
Ryburn, W. Scott, 9117
Ryckman, Tom, 1234
Ryco Assocs., 1075
Rydberg, Charles R., 9821
Rydell, Gerry L., 3269
Ryden, Rex J., 3337
Ryder System, Inc., 2213
Ryder, James E., Jr., 3477
Ryder, Thomas O., 6777
Ryerson, Richard, 7931
Ryhanych, Margaret, 6584
Ryker, Debra B., 529
Ryker, Robert, 9548
Rynd, Mary Jane, 130
Rynda, Scott, 4690
Ryscamp, Charles, 5499
Ryskamp, Charles Andrew, 6119
Ryzman, Betty, 1077
Ryzman, Zvi, 1077

S 2 Yachts, 4439
S&T Bancorp, Inc., 8417
S&T Bank, 8417
S.P.I. Spirits (Cyprus) Limited, 1781
Saak, Silva, 942
Saal, Betsy, 7842
Saal, William D., 7658, 7842
Saalfield, John, 8456
Saathoff, Steve, 2842
Saavedra, Carlos, 1852

Saavedra-Keber, Sylvia, 3828
Sabaa, Morris, 5554
Sabal Co., 2170
Saban, Cheryl, 1079
Saban, Haim, 1079
Sabas, Jennifer, 2545
Sabatini Cos., Frank C., Inc., 3386
Sabatini, Alice C., 3386
Sabatini, David D., 1824
Sabatini, Frank C., 3386
Sabatino, Thomas, 5387
Sabella, Gianna, 5251
Sabes, Amy, 4670
Sabes, Esther, 4670
Sabes, Janet, 4670
Sabes, Moe, 4670
Sabes, Robert, 4670
Sabes, Steven, 4670
Sabia, Arthur V., 7050
Sabin, Andrew E., 5976
Sabiron, Claudette, 1268
Sablosky Family Foundation, Inc., The, 3148
Sablosky, Larry, 3148
Sabo, Richard W., 5560, 7116
Saboe, Karen E., 8606
Saboor, John, 1942
Sabourin, Francis, 4114
Sac Capital Advisors, LLC, 1512
Saccomanno, Geno, 1446
Saccomanno, Virginia, 1446
Sacconaghi, Michael C., 7142
Saccone, Nicholas D., 531
Sacerdote Charitable Lead Trust, P.M., 6887
Sacerdote, Grace, 1940
Sacerdote, Peter M., 6157, 6887
Sachatello-Sawyer, Bonnie, 9634
Sacher, Sophia, 4066
Sacherman, Jim, 519
Sachs, & Co., Goldman, 7052
Sachs, Allison, 6888
Sachs, David, 6888
Sachs, Diane G., 8661
Sachs, Eleanor B., 7098
Sachs, Hal, 705
Sachs, Henry, 1447
Sachs, Howard J., 7098
Sachs, Katharine C., 7098
Sachs, Keith, 5555
Sachs, Michael T., 7098
Sachs, Ned R., 1943
Sachs, Peter G., 7098
Sachs, Samuel, II, 6736
Sachs, William L., Rev., 1481
Sachtjen, Vic, 2565
Sack, Michael, 1276
Sack, Nathaniel, 3003
Sackett, Deanna, 83
Sackett, John I., 2566
Sackler Charitable Remainder Trust, Else, The, 6889
Sackler, Beverly, 6892
Sackler, Elizabeth A., 6889, 6891
Sackler, Jonathan D., 6892
Sackler, K.A., 6890
Sackler, M.D.A., 6890
Sackler, Mortimer D., 6890
Sackler, Raymond R., 6892
Sackler, Richard S., 6892
Sackler, S.S., 6890
Sackler, T.E., 6890
Sackley, Margaret, 3012
Sackley, Patrick, 3012
Sacks, A. Lee, 2979
Sacks, Cari A., 2979
Sacks, Kenneth, 2979
Sacks, Lawrence J., 8717
Sacks, Michael, 2979
Saddlebrooke Development Co., 135
Sadeghian, Christopher K., 1223
Sadler, Brenner, 3472
Sadler, Dorothy C., 2486
Sadler, Gale, 7959

Sadler, Phillip E., 2486
Sadler, Robert E., Jr., 6465
Sadlier, R. Daniel, 7886
Sadlo, Kristine I., 7783
Sadow, Jenny, 2904
Sadowsky, James, 4121
Sadowsky, Ronald, 4121
Saelzler Unitrust, Pamela S., 7065
Saeman, Carolyn, 1448
Saeman, Carolyn Ann, 1448
Saeman, John V., 1448
Saeman, John V., II, 1362
Saeman, John V., III, 1448
Saemann, Franklin I., 3232
Saemann, Irene L., 3232
Safchik, Jeffrey A., 2033
Safco Products Co., 4565
Saffell, Paul K., 1963
Saffer, Sheindy E., 6284
Safford, John E.A., 4074
Safir, Alan, 7226
Safire, William L., 5825, 5827
Safra National Bank of New York, 6893
Safra, Jacob, 6893
Safra, Joseph Yacoub, 6893
Safran, Marc R., 8074
Safrit, Lynne Scott, 7370
Saft, Stephen J., 5925
Saft, Stephen M., 2178
Sagansky, Jeff, 7848
Sage, Charles F., 4427
Sage, Effa L., 4427
Sage, Russell, Mrs., 6894
Sager, Elaine H., 4122
Sager, Julie, 711
Sager, Mimi, 9800
Sager, Robert C., 4122
Sager, Shane E., 4122
Sager, Tess, 4122
Saginaw Chippewa Indian Tribe, 1781
Sagner, Alan, 5381
Sagner, Deborah, 5381
Sagner, Ruth Levin, 5381
Sahakian, Siran, 5241
Sahara Coal Co., Inc., 5018
Sahl, Ellen, 4171
Sahlaney, Michael, 8153
Sahni, S., AVM, 3330
Saia, John S., 3586
Saich, Anthony J., 5750
Saigh, Fred M., 4895
Saigh, Josephine, 4453
Saika, Peggy, 350, 6538
Sailor, Rod, 7989
Sailstad, Thomas, 4571
Saines, Shelly, 4347
Saint James, Susan, 1465
Saint Laurent, Yves, 5623
Saint, John, 25
Saint-Amand, Alexander, 5753
Saint-Amand, Cynthia C., 5753
Saint-Amand, Emilia A., 6359
Saint-Amand, Nathan E., 5753
Saiontz, James, 2141
Saiontz, Steven, 2141
Saito, Kazumasa, 2602
Saito, Kazuo, 2926
Saizan, Courtney, 3462
Sajak, Lesly, 1083
Sajak, Pat, 1083
Sajdak, Robert, 4444
Sajdak, Robert A., 4244
Sakacs, Linda, 6317
Sakmar, Thomas, 7254
Saks Inc., 61
Saks, Betty, 9363
Saks, Howard J., 1162
Sala, Rex, 4574
Saladino, Craig, 494
Salah, Beatrice, 4124
Salah, James M., 4124
Salamone, Michael, 4811
Salanitri, Marie, 5319

Salas, Joseph, 4310
Salazar, John P., 5466
Salazar, Kathleen H., 1249
Salazar, Mac, 2680
Salazar, Marguerite, 1350
Saldanha, Anne, 5780
Sale, Josh, 1465
Saleh, Amy, 410
Saleh, Sam, 9268
Salem Five Cents Savings Bank, 4125
Salem, Paul J., 8554
Salerno, Joseph D., 5407
Salerno, Judith, 3869
Salgado, Sebastio, 5484
Salganicoff, Alina, 739
Sali, Ron, 2570
Saligman, Alice, 6895
Saligman, Carolyn, 6895
Saligman, Ira, 6895
Saligman, Robert, 6895
Salin Bank and Trust Co., 3211
Salinas, Mario, 5469
Salinger, Joyce J., 7590
Salisbury Development L.C., 9321
Salisbury, Alicia, 3400
Salit, P.A., 5335
Salizzoni, Frank L., 4823
Salkind, Louis, 5664
Sall, John Phillip, 7471
Sall, Virginia B., 7471
Sallee, Jacklyn, 83
Salmon Atlas, LP, 2070
Salmon, Marla E., 5265
Salmon, Michael, 3247
Salmon, Walter, 3915
Salogga, Michael, 1471
Salois, R. Joseph, 4209
Salome, Tom, 9255
Salomon Brothers Inc, 6898
Salomon, Arthur, 3407
Salomon, Christina, 6897
Salomon, David, 6897
Salomon, Jennifer, 6897
Salomon, Lionel J., 6615
Salomon, Mary F., 7725
Salomon, Richard B., 6897
Salomon, Richard E., 6827, 6897, 7003
Salomon, Susan H., 6117
Saloom, Doris J., 7908
Salsberg, Eric, 9190
Salsbery, Lorene Dekko, 3142
Salsman, Gloria, 3333
Salter, Lee W., 870
Salter, Michael, 2047
Saltman Charitable Lead Trust, Eric, 6900
Saltonstall, Alice W., 4037
Saltonstall, G. West, 4037, 4123
Saltonstall, Mary "Polly", 3548
Saltonstall, Patrick G., 4037
Saltonstall, Richard, 4126
Saltonstall, Timothy, 4037
Saltonstall, William, 4123
Saltonstall, William L., 4037
Saltonstall, William L., Jr., 4037
Saltonstall-Isace, Amy E., 4123
Saltsgiver, Joann, 8420
Saltsgiver, Thomas M., 8420
Saltz Charitable Lead Annuity Trust, Leonard, 6899
Saltz Charitable Lead Annuity Trust, Ronald, 6899
Saltz Charitable Lead Annuity Trust, Susan, 6899
Saltz, Anita, 6899
Saltz, Jack, 5616, 6899
Saltz, Leonard, 5616, 6899
Saltz, Linda, 8499
Saltz, Ronald, 6899
Saltz, Susan, 6899
Saltzgaber, Gaylord, 7891
Saltzman, Arnold, 6900
Saltzman, Arnold A., 6900
Saltzman, Joan R., 6900

Saltzman, Paul S., 8581
Saltzman, Rob, 300
Salvadore, Tammy E., 8168
Salvaggio, Anthony, 8421
Salvaggio, Christy A., 8421
Salvaggio, Norene L., 8421
Salvaggio, Suzie A., 8421
Salvaggio, Thomas A., 8421
Salvio, Lisa B., 1643
Salvitti, Constance A., 8422
Salvitti, Constance S., 8422
Salvitti, E. Ronald, 8422
Salyer, Meg, 7952
Salyer, Richard D., 1186
Salzer, Richard L., Jr., 6103
Salzman, Lois, 3498
Salzman, Martin J., 6075
Salzmann, Benjamin M., 9739
Samaritan Asset Management, Inc., 2980
Samator, Hussein, 4623
Samberg, Arthur, 9510
Samberg, Arthur J., 1625
Samberg, Laura J., 9510
Samberg, Rebecca, 9510
Sambol, Bob, 9068
Samborsky, Ron, 560
Samet, Jan, 7397
Samet, Jerold J., 3732
Samet, Norman, 7343
Samet, Theodore S., 3968
Samford, John S.P., 71
Samloff, Harold, 7271
Sample, David F., 4940
Sample, Helen S., 4940
Sample, John Glen, 4940
Sample, Joseph S., 4940
Sample, Kristina Lloyd, 5124
Sample, Michael S., 4940
Sample, Miriam T., 4940
Sample, Patrick G., 4940
Sampson Foundation, Twila, 8423
Sampson, Allison, 394
Sampson, Cynthia, 3529
Sampson, David S., 5551
Sampson, Holly C., 4556
Sampson, J. Faye, 8423
Sampson, Morris E., 2184
Sampson, Myles S., 8155, 8423
Sams, Ashlund, 4569
Sams, Claire V., 8361
Sams, Earl C., 9163
Sams, Hansford, Jr., 2483
Samsky, Scott B., 1264
Samson, Laura, 2589
Samstag, Gordon, 2214
Samuel Oschin Trust, 960
Samueli 1995 Family Trust, The, 1086
Samueli Charitable Trust No. 00-1, 1086
Samueli, Henry, 1086
Samueli, Susan, 1086
Samuels, Barbara, 1200
Samuels, Fan Fox, 6901
Samuels, Joseph T., 9390
Samuels, Leslie R., 6901
Samuels, Peter, 294
Samuels, Rhoda, 2306
Samuels, Robert, 3915
Samuels, Sandor E., 422
Samuels, Theodore R., 357
Samuels, Victoria Woolner, 6624
Samuelson, Carole W., 24
Samuelson, Herman, 3725
Samuelson, John L., 1356
Samuelson, Shannon, 3199
Samuelson, Susan, 10000
San Diego Union Shoe Fund, 416
Sanborn, J. Gregg, 5089
Sanbrano, Angela, 6160
Sanchez, Frank M., 214, 1249
Sanchez, Gilbert, 5491
Sanchez, Margaret A., 6823
Sanchez, Mary, 172
Sanchez, Miren duPont, 1728

Sanchez, Richard A., 400
Sanchez, Tony F., 5048
Sanchez, Victor R., 4228
Sand, Anne, 4637
Sand, Carolyn, 1857
Sandak, Jay, 6990
Sandberg, Rebecca L., 2231
Sandberg, Sheryl, 606
Sandbo, Judith, 7618
Sande, Ervin, 1946
Sandeen, Cheryl, 4511
Sandeen, Rod, 9424
Sandefur, Charles C., 1265
Sandercock, Tara McKenzie, 7343
Sandercott, Mark, 4693
Sanders, 8818
Sanders CRUT, Lawrence A., 2215
Sanders Enterprises, Lawrence, 2215
Sanders Rev. Trust, Lawrence A., 2215
Sanders, Arthur D., 7029
Sanders, Blackwell, 4794
Sanders, Charlene, 8717
Sanders, Charles A., 2371, 7439
Sanders, David, 7866, 9566
Sanders, Deen Day, 2371
Sanders, Derek A., 813
Sanders, Derial H., 8159, 8203
Sanders, Don A., 9167
Sanders, Elina, 5333
Sanders, Elizabeth, 3750
Sanders, H. Walker, 7343
Sanders, Henry M., 3956
Sanders, John G., 9367
Sanders, Judith A., 3246
Sanders, Kevin R., 813
Sanders, Marc, 5333
Sanders, Mark A., 3144
Sanders, Michael, 2238
Sanders, Michael J., 7749
Sanders, Mike, 9780
Sanders, Morton, 6436
Sanders, Nancy, 8853
Sanders, Robert W., 813
Sanders, Rod, 8853
Sanders, Rodger M., 9205
Sanders, Scott E., 3438
Sanders, Susan, 8603
Sanders, Thomas J., 6525
Sanders, W.F., Jr., 45
Sanderson, Edward J., Jr., 1031
Sanderson, John, 5400
Sandhill Properties, 1149
Sandhop, Edwin, Jr., 8918
Sandia National Laboratories, 349
Sandler Foundation, Arthur & Annie,
    9512
Sandler, Annie L., 9511
Sandler, Arthur B., 9511, 9512
Sandler, Barbara, 1048
Sandler, David P., 8086
Sandler, Ellen, 898
Sandler, Harvey, 2216
Sandler, Mara, 6902
Sandler, Phyllis, 2216
Sandler, Raymond C., 978
Sandler, Richard, 898
Sandler, Ricky, 6902
Sandler, Steven B., 9511, 9512
Sandler, Toni, 9512
Sandlin, Larry, 9032
Sandlin, Maria Louisa, 9032
Sandman, Dan D., 8130, 8488
Sandman, Paul, 3813
Sandness, Paul K., 7517
Sando, Geoffrey, 319
Sandoz Corp., 6640
Sandquist, Peter, 3038
Sandrich, Jay, 1338
Sands, David K., 9158
Sands, Donald, 3129
Sands, Estelle M., 5382
Sands, George H., 5382
Sands, Jeffrey H., 5382
Sands, Jon F., 1333

Sands, Patrick B., 9158
Sands, Rodney J., 8920
Sands, Stephen H., 9158
Sands, Steve, 3185
Sandvold, Deanne, 9582
Sandy, George H., 1092
Sanfilippo, Anthony, 8685
Sanford, Jill, 1443
Sanford, Kay, 8823
Sanford, Laura, 8765
Sanford, Louis H., 4327
Sanford, T. Paul, 10
Sanger, Abbie W., 5912
Sanger, James R., 9907
Sanger, Karen O., 4672
Sanger, Linda M., 5912
Sanger, Michael, 6547
Sanger, Stephen W., 4570, 4672
Sanger, Terence D., 5912
Sanger, Victoria, 5912
Sani, Ashok, 6904
Sani, Lal C., 6904
Sani, Sham G., 6904
Sani, Sunil, 6904
Sani, Suresh, 6904
Saniuk, Melissa, 8841
Sanjenis, Julie, 6853
Sankey, Beth H., 7833
Sankey, James K., 7833
Sankey, Richard W., 7833
Sanna, Polly Weintz, 6144
Sannes, Tom, 8631
Sansing, Peggy L., 2217
Sansing, Robert C., 2217
Sansone, Daniel F., 73
Sansone, James W., 2761
Sansone, Jeffery T., 2116
Sansone, Laura A., 2116
Sansone, Thomas A., 2116
Sant, Alexis, 1852
Sant, Caroline M., 4856
Sant, Leo M., 7985
Sant, Maralynn V., 7985
Sant, Michael, 1852
Sant, Roger, 1852
Sant, Roger W., 1852
Sant, Steven, 8259
Sant, Victoria P., 1785, 1852
Santa Barbara Bank & Trust, 331
Santa Fe Pacific Corp., 2644
Santangelo, Joseph A., 5565
Santiago, Nestor V., 3654
Santigati, Richard, 4058
Santini, Delise F., 5033
Santini, Gino, 3192, 3193
Santini, Leonard, 2240
Santis, Jorge H., 2218
Santisi, Maria, 5357
Santo, Anthony F., 5048
Santomero, Anthony M., 8198
Santori, Jim, 3126
Santori, Mary Beth, 4643
Santos, Frank, 2205
Santos, John F., 2964
Santos, Peta Smit, 8621
Sanyal, Subir K., 5737
Sanyour, Michael, 8147
Saperstein, Marc, 933, 1553
Saperstein, Shira, 1835, 1852
Sapirstein, Jacob, 7834
Sapoch, Jamie Kyte, 5148
Sapp, Hubert, 2446
Sapp, Nancy Ware, 8367
Sapp, Richard A., 6906
Sapp, Shari M., 6906
Sapper, Jon, 691
Sara Lee Corp., 2982
Saracino, David, 8135
Saraga, John, 7653
Saravia, Nancy, 2031
Saraya, Yusuke, 7185
Sardar, Frida Jack, 5554
Sargent, Arthur, 5498
Sargent, Barbara, 740

Sargent, Leonard, 4935
Sargent, Newell B., 9989
Sargent, Ronald L., 4156
Sargent, Sara Ann, 8153
Sargent, William, 4052
Sarin, Arun, 1267
Sarkeys, S.J., 7974
Sarkis, George, 7526
Sarkowsky, Cathy, 9676
Sarkowsky, Faye, 9676
Sarkowsky, Herman, 9676
Sarkowsky, Steve, 9676
Sarlo, Arnold L., 2240
Sarmiento, Gil M., 2820
Sarofim, Allison, 9169
Sarofim, Christopher, 9169
Sarofim, Christopher B., 8799, 9168
Sarofim, Fayez, 9168
Sarofim, Louisa S., 9169
Sarofim, Louisa Stude, 8799, 9168
Sarosdy, Emma, 8254
Sarosiek, James J., 9869
Sarpy, Maxine, 3469
Sarram, Shiva, 7139
Sarratt, Mark, 4986
Sarrica, Lewis, 1891
Sarro, Eileen, 7491
Sartin, Betty, 9401
Sartin, Robert V., 3440
Sartor, C. Lane, 3517
Sarver, James H., 9720
Sarver, James H., II, 9720
Sarver, Penny, 1095
Sarver, Robert, 1095
Sarvey, John H., 3961
Sasakawa, Yohei, 7185
Sasaki, Robert K., 2530
Sassano, James F., 7164
Sasser, Barbara Weston, 8987
Sasser, Leslie Keith Elkins, 8883
Sasser, Rhone, 7319
Sassetti, Robert, 2922
Sasso, Greg, 3186
Sasson, Albert, 5437
Sasson, Sam N., 5437
Sasson, Samantha, 5437
Sassouni, Eli, 216
Sassounian, Harut, 812
Sastre, Cesar J., 2153
Satchell, Harold, 1991
Satcher, David, 739, 2355
Satell, Edward M., 8424
Sather, Annwin B., 1437
Sather, Paul T., 7514
Sato Lead Trust 80C-74C03, 5384
Sato Lead Trust 80C-7C04, 5384
Sato, Kozo, 5384
Sato, Nieves, 5384
Sato, Sonia, 5384
Sato, Suzanne M., 6604
Satre, Jennifer A., 5028
Satre, Philip G., 8685
Satre, Tami, 9743
Satter, Muneer, 2166, 7031
Satter, Muneer A., 2983
Satterfield, B.K., 9711, 9733
Satterfield, William, 9717
Satterlee, Ellen, 4476
Satterthwaite, Kevin, 8147
Saturno, Joseph, 1097
Saturno, Victor, 1097
Satz, Joseph, 1290
Satz, Joseph R., 1016
Sauer, Bradford B., 9417
Sauer, Janet Lewis, 9417
Sauer, Richard A., 5727, 6319, 6609
Sauer, Sheri, 2274
Sauer, William, 1078
Sauerland, Paul C., Jr., 5295
Sauers, Kathy, 942
Saugatuck Capital, 1647
Saul, Dianne P., 2904
Saunders, A. Brent, 4749
Saunders, C. Stephen, 8768

Saunders, Carole M., 6909
Saunders, Carolyn, 3470
Saunders, Dave, 7139
Saunders, Nancy A., 4104
Saunders, R.R., 3470
Saunders, Ruby Lee, 2219
Saunders, Ruth, 1517
Saunders, Shirley R., 2016
Saunders, Thomas A., III, 6242
Saunders, Thomas A., IV, 6242
Saunders, Whitney G., 9376
Saunders, William N., 2219
Saur, Dwight E., Jr., 9254
Saurage, Donna, 3515
Saurage, H. Norman, III, 3462
Sauvayre, Sarah Chubb, 5440
Sauve, Brad E., 4285
Savage Industries, Inc., 9340
Savage Services Corp., 9340
Savage, Ann T., 5677
Savage, Arthur V., 5806, 6156, 7207
Savage, C. Jack, 9713
Savage, Emilee Jayne, 9340
Savage, Gregory James, 9340
Savage, Harlow D., Jr., 1641
Savage, Nathan Neal, 9340
Savage, Philip M., III, 405
Savage, Seddon R., 1641
Savage, Steve, 6604
Savage, Toy D., Jr., 9382, 9484
Savane, Marie Angelique, 6389
Savedoff, Stuart H., 2121
Savereide, John, 4693
Savesky, Kathleen, 3809
Savin, Robert, 5555
Savings Bank of Manchester Foundation,
    Inc., 1644
Savino, Frank, 5597
Sawch, William B., 1484
Sawers, Kit, 9068
Sawtell, Sarah, 5496
Sawyer, Bo, 7773
Sawyer, Edward, 3445
Sawyer, Frank, 4128
Sawyer, Gail L., 5061
Sawyer, John, 3445
Sawyer, John C., 2319
Sawyer, John S., 3440
Sawyer, Kathy, 20
Sawyer, L. Diane, 5821
Sawyer, L. Gordon, 2458
Sawyer, Mildred E., 4128
Sawyer, Raymond T., 7578
Sawyer, Robin Gibson, 5184
Sawyer, Sandy, 3215
Sawyer, William, 4128
Saxon, Ken, 1093
Saxton, Martha, 8303
Saxton, Pamela L., 9573
Saybrook Charitable Trust, 5082
Saybrook, Inc., 8028
Sayers, Donald D., 7509
Sayler, Elizabeth Jubitz, 8028
Saylor, Clifford W., 126
Saylor, Michael J., 9404
Sayrafe, Kristine, 5345
Sayre, Richard H., 3845
Sayre, Scott E., 149
Sazerac Co., Inc., 3484, 3516
SBC Communications Inc., 8765
SBH Intimates Inc., 5222
Scagliotti, Nackey E., 7848
Scahill, Lawrence, 1529
Scaife, C., 8301
Scaife, David N., 8178
Scaife, Frances G., 8178
Scaife, Jennie K., 2220
Scaife, Margaret R., 8076
Scaife, Richard M., 8076, 8132, 8425
Scaife, Sara D., 8178
Scaife, Sarah Mellon, 2220, 8425
Scaife, Walter B., 941
Scaldara, John A., Jr., 3595
Scaler Foundation, Inc., 1717

Scales, Julie, 2170
Scalise, Robert A., Jr., 1515
Scalvino, Pauline C., 8490
Scaminace, J.M., 7855
Scammell, Charles J., 5295
Scangas, Christopher, 3925
Scanlan, John M., 4519
Scanlan, Mary, 1338
Scanlan, Sallie A., 8980
Scanlon, Joseph P., 5559
Scanlon, Melissa S., 2835
Scanlon, Thomas J., 1844
Scanlon, Thomas M., Jr., 6665
Scanlon, William, Jr., 8920
ScanSource, Inc., 8608
Scarafile, Judy Walden, 4211
Scarborough, Collin W., 3661
Scardaci, Rita, 346
Scardina, Julie, 4900
Scardino, Frank P., 6532
Scardino, Marjorie M., 2868
Scarfone, Anthony C., 4549
Scarince, William, 4593
Scarlati, Frank S., Jr., 2976
Scarlett, Mark, 7113
Scarpa, John F., 2221
Scarpa, Michael, 5758
Scarpello, Fred, 5053
Scaruffi, Amelia, 557
Scattergood, Donna, 9810
Scavo, Alton J., 3724
Schaack, R. Bard, 6638
Schaaf, Steve, 3324
Schaal, Kevin, 2075
Schack, Paul, 2058
Schadler, Holly, 5614
Schadt, Charles F., Jr., 8725
Schadt, Charles F., Sr., 8725
Schadt, Harry E., 8725
Schadt, Harry E., Jr., 8725
Schadt, Harry E., Sr., 8725
Schadt, Reid, 8725
Schadt, Stephen C., Sr., 8725
Schaefer, Alan R., 9833
Schaefer, Barbara, 7562
Schaefer, Barbara W., 5012
Schaefer, Charles V., III, 5399
Schaefer, Charles V., Jr., 5399
Schaefer, David R., 1514
Schaefer, Eileen Bonnie, 2222
Schaefer, Gary L., 9910
Schaefer, John, 93
Schaefer, John P., 134
Schaefer, Mary B., 1104
Schaefer, Robert, 3247
Schaefer, Robert E., 2750
Schaefer, Robert W., 3632
Schaefer, Roberta R., 4209
Schaefer, Rowland, 2222
Schaefer, Sylvia, 2222
Schaefer, William, 7749
Schaeffer, Adele K., 8267
Schaeffer, Anthony L., 8267
Schaeffer, Donald M., 5852
Schaeffer, Forrest R., 8427
Schaeffer, George, 1100
Schaeffer, Harold G., 8267
Schaeffer, James R., 8267
Schaeffer, Jayne R., 8103
Schaeffer, Jerry, 3165
Schaeffer, Leonard, 1292
Schaeffer, Miriam, 1100
Schaeffer, Richard, 6618
Schaeffer, Robert D., 8267
Schaeffer, Stanley, 8758
Schaenen, Douglas K., 5795
Schaenen, Nancy, 5795
Schaenen, Nelson, 5795
Schafale, Mark A., 2721
Schafer, Alan, 4668
Schafer, Betty R., 3767
Schafer, Don, 537
Schafer, Mary J., 4243
Schafer, Oscar S., 6117, 6910

Schafer, Sigrid U., 6910
Schaffer, Henry, 6911
Schaffer, Mark, 7756
Schaffer, Marvin, 6716
Schaffer, Robert, 6102
Schaffer, Thomas, 7514
Schaffler, Charles D., 8638
Schaffner, Mary E., 1294
Schaller, Albert, 4225
Schaller, Ben, 3199
Schaller, Marilyn, 4225
Schaller, Sandra J., 3157
Schamp, Niceas, 5973
Schankweiler, David A., 8208
Schantz, Dan, 3230
Schaper, David H., 8455
Schaperkotter, John D., 4783
Schapiro, Daniel E., 6912
Schapiro, Morris A., 6912
Schapiro, Seth, 5546
Schapman, Laura, 4310
Scharbauer, Clarence, III, 8749
Schardien, J. David, 5106, 5274
Scharf, Alexander, 6316
Scharf, Cheryl, 5527
Scharf, Daniel L., 4837
Scharf, David, 6316
Scharf, Dvora, 6913
Scharf, Irene, 5910
Scharf, Leon, 5910
Scharf, Lipa, 6913
Scharf, Manuel, 5928
Scharf, Michael M., 4792
Scharf, Morris, 6913
Scharf, Scharf, & Beer, 5910
Scharf, Solomon T., 6316
Scharf, Yehuda, 5527
Scharff, Joseph T., 5415
Scharff, Matthew D., 7254
Scharfstein, Howard F., 6965
Scharlin, David Michael, 2223
Scharlin, Gloria, 2223
Scharlin, Gloria G., 2223
Scharlin, Howard R., 2223
Scharlin, Kerri Sue, 2223
Scharlin, Peggy Ann, 2223
Scharlin, Sheldon, 801
Scharpf, George E., 5112
Scharsu, Alan, 337
Schattgen, Deborah B., 8300
Schatz, Bruce, 3548
Schatz, Myrna, 6033
Schatz, Susan, 6260
Schatzle, Billy, 9476
Schauder, Kenneth, 8219
Schaufeld, Frederick, 9482
Schaufeld, Karen, 9482
Schaughency, Betty Sue, 8098
Schaul, Mark H., 9723
Schautz, Walter L., 8431
Schavone, Philip T. "Terry", 7580
Schawk, Clarence A., 2984
Schawk, Marilyn G., 2984
Schechtel, Andrew J., 5401
Schechter, Dena, 809
Schechter, Dov, 6914
Schechter, Irv, 809
Schechter, Mordechai, 6914
Schechter, Richard, 6914
Schechter, Saul, 6914
Schechter, Shelly, 6914
Scheck, John W., 1944
Schecter, Leroy, 5385
Schecter, Shoshana, 5385
Scheeler, C. Ronald, 7438
Scheets, Patrick S., 3106
Schefer, Norman A., 6426
Scheff, Robert, 6306
Scheffel, William N., 4796
Scheffield, Linda C., 7745
Scheflen, John W., 1730
Scheibel, Elizabeth D., 3855
Scheid, Karen, 1501
Scheid, Peter, 7695

Scheidt, E. Elkan, 8726
Scheidt, Helen H., 8726
Scheidt, Rudi E., 8726
Scheidt, Rudi E., Jr., 8726
Scheinfeld, Elizabeth, 3032
Scheirman, Scott T., 1377
Schell, Braxton, 7411, 7412, 7413
Schellenger, James P., II, 8362
Scheller, Ernest, Jr., 8426
Scheller, Roberta, 8426
Schenck, Lillian Pitkin, 5386
Schenck, Todd, 9313
Schenck, Weldon, 9918
Schenck, William, 3129
Schendel, Richard, 9138
Schendler, Auden, 1381
Schenectady International, Inc., 7280
Schenk, Deborah M., 7633, 7819
Schenk, Julie, 7985
Schenk, Lynn, Hon., 3806
Schenk, Nora, 2969
Schenkel, Donald F., 3156
Schenker Family Foundation, 7174
Schenker, Andrew, 7112
Schenker, Curtis, 6916
Schenker, Leo, 6916
Schenker, Livia, 6916
Schepp, Florence L., 6917
Schepp, Leopold, 6917
Scherek, Kathleen, 4693
Scherer, Ned S., 9377
Scherf, Willie, 8096
Schering-Plough Corp., 5387
Schermer, Betty A., 1449
Schermer, Greg, 3306
Schermer, Lloyd G., 1449
Schermerhorn, Sarah J., 6915
Schervish, Thomas W., 7867
Scherzer, Alfred I., 5928
Scherzinger, Steve, 7665
Scheu, William E., 1940
Scheuer Family Foundation, S.H. and
    Helen R., The, 6921
Scheuer, Alida Brill, 6921
Scheuer, Elizabeth H., 6760, 6920
Scheuer, Joan G., 6919
Scheuer, Laura, 5840
Scheuer, Laura L., 6920
Scheuer, Richard J., 6919, 6920
Scheuer, Steven H., 6921
Scheuermann, Edward, 6737
Scheumann, John B., 3235
Scheumann, John B., II, 3235
Scheumann, Sylvia, 3095
Scheumann, Theiline P., 9650
Schewel, Elliot S., 9463
Schiavone, Marianne, 3065
Schibanoff, Harry A., 5092
Schick, Thomas, 5553
Schickel, Peter J., 3161
Schiedegger, Charles, 4310
Schieffelin, Sarah I., 6922
Schiel, George R., 1333
Schield, Charlotte H., 2985
Schield, Michael A., 2985
Schield, William H., Jr., 2985
Schierbeek, Robert H., 4277, 4279,
    4469
Schierl, Bill, 9778
Schierl, Carol A., 9781
Schierl, Michael J., 2983, 9781
Schierl, Paul J., 9781
Schiewetz, Richard F., 7835
Schiff Food Products Co., 5358
Schiff, Adele K., 7838
Schiff, Andrew N., 6923
Schiff, David T., 6923
Schiff, Dorothy, 1750
Schiff, Edith B., 6923
Schiff, Hardin & Waite, 6700
Schiff, James A., 7836
Schiff, John J., 7837
Schiff, John J., Jr., 7837
Schiff, John M., 6923

Schiff, Mary R., 7837
Schiff, Peter G., 6923
Schiff, Robert C., 7836, 7838
Schiff, Robert C., Jr., 7836
Schiff, Tamara W., 898
Schiff, Thomas R., 7837
Schiffer, David Paul, 3937
Schiffer, Karen, 591
Schiffman, Michael, 896
Schiffman, Theodore, 5557
Schifter, Jennifer, 3726
Schifter, Richard P., 3726
Schiller, Elmyra F., 3629
Schiller, J.R., 2565
Schiller, Paul, 8630
Schiller, Richard A., 1116
Schiller, William A., 9826
Schilling, Carol P., 3225
Schilling, Chip, 9845
Schilling, Jack, 4571
Schilling, Richard, 9521
Schillinger, Erwin, 6640
Schilt, Tim, 7139
Schimburg, Alice, 2961
Schimmel, Rosalba, 1101
Schimmel, Stephen Harold, 1101
Schindler, David L., 3634
Schingledecker, Connie, 2094
Schipper, David J., 7876
Schipper, Jean Anne, 7876
Schippers, Phyllis, 9964
Schirmer, Ginger, 5784
Schirmers, Nancy A., 8037
Schlack, Marilyn J., 4352
Schlacter, Doris, 106
Schlafer Trust, Shirley K., 4429
Schlafer, Shirley K., 4429
Schlafly Charitable Lead Trust, Thomas
    F., 4915
Schlafly, Adelaide, 4915
Schlafly, Daniel, 4915
Schlafly, Daniel, Mrs., 4915
Schlafly, Maria Bryne, 4915
Schlafly, Theresa Bryne, 4915
Schlafly, Thomas, 4915
Schlafly, Thomas, Mrs., 4915
Schlagel, John, 4593
Schlapbach, David, 1377
Schlater, Kenneth, 7584
Schlauch, W.F., 5335
Schlecht, Rebecca, 3047
Schlegal, Theodore F., 1344
Schleicher, William T., 2676
Schleider, Rick, 9131
Schleifer, Cristina, 8583
Schlein, Michael, 5755
Schlemmer, Robert M., 7886
Schlener, Denise, 6634
Schlensky, Steven A., 2991
Schlereth, John V., 5056
Schlesinger, Clifford, 8197
Schlesinger, Edward S., 5810
Schlesinger, Harvey E., Hon., 1940
Schlesinger, Leonard A., 7580
Schlesinger, Mark L., 545
Schlesinger, Robert A., 6441
Schlesinger, William A., 221
Schlessman, Dolores J., 1450
Schlessman, Florence M., 1450
Schlessman, Gary L., 1450
Schlessman, Gerald L., 1450
Schlessman, Lee E., 1450
Schley, Mary W., M.D., 2361
Schlice, Paula, 9778
Schlichting, Nancy M., 4367
Schlicker, Elise M., 6778
Schlieder, Edward G., 3508
Schliesman, Paul, 4581, 4582
Schliesman, Paul D., 7516
Schlimgen, Leesa D., 9789
Schlindwein, Paul C., II, 9792
Schlinger Trust, William and E.G., The,
    1102
Schlinger, Michael S., 1103

Schlinger, Norman W., 1103
Schlinger, Warren G., 1103
Schlink, Albert G., 7839
Schlink, Olive H., 7839
Schlitt, Albert, 3132
Schlitz, Timothy D., 7675
Schloemer, James H., 9963
Schloenbach, Steven, 7526
Schloesser, Jack, 9885
Schloss, Barry I., 3759
Schlosser, C. William, 1104
Schlosser, Charles W., 1104
Schlosser, Elizabeth, 1104
Schlosser, Nancy B., 1104
Schlosstein, Ralph L., 6925
Schlough, Tom, 4534
Schlozman, Daniel, 2912
Schlozman, Kay, 2912
Schluchter, Wayne, 4534
Schlue, Larry, 3308
Schlukebier, Bill, 4596
Schlumberger N.V., 6926
Schmalz, Doug, 2678
Schmalz, Robert L., 233
Schmalz, Robert N., 1510
Schmank, James, 3400
Schmeelk, Priscilla M., 6927
Schmeelk, Richard J., 6927
Schmelzer, Henry L.P., 3548
Schmerling, Michael D., 8662
Schmid, Chris, 7778
Schmid, David W., 1277
Schmid, Don W., 1277
Schmid, Richard R., 1277
Schmid, Walter R., 1277
Schmid, Walter, Jr., 1874
Schmider, Ernie, 1006
Schmidhauser, Eric, 8747
Schmidhauser, Lucie, 8747
Schmidlapp, Jacob G., 7840, 7841
Schmidt, Arthur J., 9952
Schmidt, Barbara M., 2225
Schmidt, Buzz, 6176
Schmidt, Carl, 3306, 4673
Schmidt, Catherine B., 2225
Schmidt, Charles E., 2225
Schmidt, Chris, 9548
Schmidt, Daniel P., 9763
Schmidt, Diane, 9379
Schmidt, Edward R., 3196
Schmidt, Evelyn, 8055
Schmidt, Fred, 9810
Schmidt, George, 7660
Schmidt, George W., 3098
Schmidt, Gina, 4507
Schmidt, Gina M., 4507
Schmidt, Gladys, 223
Schmidt, J. Frank, III, 8055
Schmidt, J. Frank, Jr., 8055
Schmidt, J.C., 2224
Schmidt, Jareen E., 8880
Schmidt, Jennifer L., 7835
Schmidt, John, 2986, 7192
Schmidt, John F., 2986
Schmidt, Lynne D., 8394
Schmidt, Margaret C., 2986
Schmidt, Michael, 6035
Schmidt, Michele R., 5901
Schmidt, Paul W., 4320
Schmidt, Peter, 5988
Schmidt, Peter W., 1492
Schmidt, Raymond, 9952
Schmidt, Richard L., 2225
Schmidt, Richard W., 1355
Schmidt, Rick, 7378
Schmidt, Ronald, 8782
Schmidt, Stanley H., 8782
Schmidt, T., 8301
Schmidt, Thomas, 2986, 9952
Schmidt, Thomas A., 4507, 9952
Schmidt, Tom, 4507
Schmidt, Tschudy G., 1412
Schmidt, Verna, 4673
Schmidt, William, 9952

Schmidt, William E., 2986
Schmidt, William H., 3820
Schmidt, William L., 1412
Schmieding, H.C., 175
Schmieding, L.H., 175
Schmink, Kelly, 3197
Schmissrauter, Lynn, 8660
Schmitt, Alan, 2969
Schmitt, Alfons J., 7167
Schmitt, Arthur J., 2987
Schmitt, Carl, 6199
Schmitt, Caroline, 7392
Schmitt, Caroline F., 6928
Schmitt, Jerome B., 9716
Schmitt, Kilian J., 6928
Schmitt, Thomas L., 4994
Schmoke, Kurt, 6998
Schmolka, Leo, 1721
Schnabel, Truman G., 8342
Schnack, Thomas W., 4557
Schneider National, Inc., 9920
Schneider, Alan J., 3088
Schneider, Arnold, Jr., 8161
Schneider, Bernard, 220
Schneider, Carolyn E., 1892
Schneider, Donald J., 9920
Schneider, Dorothy H., 8161
Schneider, Helen, 6929
Schneider, Hilary A., 768
Schneider, Irving, 6779, 6929
Schneider, Jacqueline, 6587
Schneider, Jan, 1847
Schneider, Katie, 5780
Schneider, Keith, Jr., 1395
Schneider, Kirk, 7856
Schneider, Kris, 3230
Schneider, Lynn C., 6929
Schneider, Lynn V., 8625
Schneider, Mahlon C., 4588
Schneider, Margaret, 5703
Schneider, Martin H., 5540
Schneider, Melvyn H., 3009
Schneider, Milton S., 8399
Schneider, Mindy, 6929
Schneider, Nanka A., 4793
Schneider, Pam H., 8399
Schneider, Pamela C., 5794
Schneider, Scott, 1661
Schneider, Scott N., 1660
Schneider, Stanley, 243
Schneider, Steven G., 7214
Schneider, Thomas G., 1943
Schneider, Vivian L., 911
Schneider, William, 7517
Schneidman, Richard, 6029
Schnitzer, Arlene, 8056
Schnitzer, Gilbert, 8057
Schnitzer, Harold J., 8056
Schnitzer, Jordan D., 8056
Schnitzer, Thelma, 8057
Schnuck, Mark J., 4896
Schnuck, Scott, 2863
Schnurmacher, Adolph, 6930
Schnurmacher, Charles M., 6931
Schnurmacher, Ruth, 6930
Schnurr, Andrew V., Jr., 5268
Schobert, Rita, 3186
Schoch, Arch K., IV, 7494
Schock, Alvin A., 8625
Schock, Clarence, 8427
Schocken, Dora, 1105
Schocken, Dora S., 1105
Schocken, Miriam, 1105
Schocken, Shimon, 1105
Schocken, Solomon, 1105
Schoeb, Melissa, 1081
Schoedler, Scott G., 7333
Schoel, Lynn C., 7784
Schoen, Cathy, 5779
Schoen, Julie, 115
Schoen, Kathryn L., 2226
Schoen, Laurie G., 4130
Schoen, Nancy Bernstein, 1775
Schoen, Robert, 1775

Schoen, Scott A., 4130
Schoen, Sharon A., 2226
Schoen, William J., 2226
Schoenbaum, Alex, 2227
Schoenbaum, Betty Frank, 2227
Schoenbaum, Emily, 2227
Schoenbaum, Jeffry F., 2227
Schoenbaum, Raymond D., 2227
Schoenbaum, Stephen C., 5779
Schoenborn, Brian, 4534
Schoenecker, Barbara, 4674
Schoenecker, Guy, 4674
Schoenecker, Larry, 4674
Schoeneckers, Inc., 4674
Schoenfeld, Gerald, 6970
Schoenleber, Gretchen, 9921
Schoenleber, Louise, 9921
Schoenleber, Marie, 9921
Schoenthaler, Sue, 1058
Schoenthaler, Susan P., 895
Schoenwetter, L. Jim, 4671
Schoettler, Gail S., 1356
Schoewe, Thomas M., 184
Schofer, Paul, 4843
Schoferig, S., 5910
Schofield, John J., 3630
Schokking, Ronald, 9190
Scholar, 3683
Scholastic Inc., 1745
Scholl, Daniel, 2989
Scholl, Jack E., 2989
Scholl, Jeanne M., 2989
Scholl, Pamela, 2989
Scholl, Susan, 2989
Scholl, William M., 2989
Scholler, F.C., 8428
Schollmaier, Edgar H., 8841, 9172
Schollmaier, Rama L., 9172
Scholten, Betsy, 3387
Scholten, Maarten, 6926
Scholz, Denise, 4942
Scholz, Douglas C., 7603
Schomer, Gary W., 3250
Schon, Anna, 6166, 6933
Schon, Baron, 6933
Schon, Henry A., 6933
Schonwald, Joseph, 5057
Schooler Family Foundation, 4764
Schooler, Edith, 7593
Schooler, Seward, 7593
Schooley, Susan, 4389
Schools, Bob, 3540
Schools, Burton R., 8581
Schoonmaker, Peter, 9998
Schoonover, Nan, 169
Schoonover, Paul A., 7616
Schoppa, Paul, Jr., 8797
Schor, Edward L., 5779
Schorrak, Walter, 9921
Schoshinski, James J., 9781
Schott, Harold C., 7658
Schott, Joseph J., 7842
Schott, Lewis M., 6934
Schott, Margaret U., 7843
Schott, Michael A., 8922
Schott, Milton B., Jr., 7658
Schott, Nash W., 6934
Schott, Patricia A., 1106
Schott, Stephen, 948
Schott, Stephen C., 1106
Schott, Steven G., 6934
Schottenstein Stores Corp., 7610
Schottenstein, Gary, 7729
Schottenstein, Geraldine, 7610
Schottenstein, Jay, 7844
Schottenstein, Jeffrey, 7844
Schottenstein, Jonathan, 7844
Schottenstein, Joseph, 7844
Schottenstein, Robert H., 7729
Schottenstein, Saul, 7844
Schottenstein, Steven, 7729
Schotz, Edward M., 5172
Schow, Howard, 1107
Schow, Melanie J., 1107

Schow, Nan, 1107
Schow, Roger L., 1107
Schow, Steven, 1107
Schowalter, J.A., 3388
Schrack, Dion, 3325
Schrafft, Bertha E., 4133
Schrafft, William E., 4133
Schrage, Lawrence B., 2458
Schrager, Harley, 5001
Schrager, Leonard, 1773
Schrager, Phillip G., 5001
Schrager, Richard A., 5001
Schrager, Terri L., 5001
Schrager, Timothy, 5001
Schramm, Carl J., 4843
Schrank, Douglas R., 4410
Schreck, Charles, 5508
Schreck, Charles R., 5508
Schreder, Carleen, 3090
Schreffler, John P., 8151
Schreiber, Mary, 6848
Schreier, Bradley, 4698
Schreier, Warren, 3039
Schreiner, Linda V., 7745
Schreyer, Joan L., 5389
Schreyer, John Y., 5231
Schreyer, William A., 5389
Schrirfer, Barbara, 1835
Schrock, Bonnie, 3415
Schroeder, Charles E., 2700, 2878
Schroeder, Gratia, 2041
Schroeder, Michael J., 1943, 9750
Schroeder, Patricia, 9567
Schroeder, Robert A., 580
Schroeder, Steven A., 698
Schroff, Christie Schwartzkopf, 4987
Schroffel, Judy, 1021, 2950
Schroth, Virginia Cowles, 5170
Schrum, David F., 3177
Schubert, Arthur H., 4497
Schubert, Gage A., 4497
Schubert, Helen D., 4497
Schubert, John Dwan, 4497
Schubert, Leland, 4497
Schubert, Leland W., 4497
Schuberth, Kenneth, 3761
Schuchardt, Bob, 160
Schuchinski, Luis, 5132
Schuck, Steve, 1362
Schueler, Jane T., 321
Schuering, Maureen, 3037
Schuerlein, Kristen M., 9702
Schuerman, Janice, 4866
Schuessler, John T., 7902
Schuette, August J., 9964
Schuette, William D., 4322, 4407
Schuetz, Stephanie J., 6494
Schuffler, Loraine, 9817
Schuh, Dale R., 9923
Schuh, Jim, 9778
Schuh, Kevin, 9869
Schuh, Mark, 494
Schuldt, Brad, 3199
Schuler 1999 CRUT, 1108
Schuler, Ari B., 1108
Schuler, Barry, 1108
Schuler, Christopher T., 2552
Schuler, Dana D., 4286
Schuler, David, 9923
Schuler, Jack W., 2990
Schuler, James A., 2552
Schuler, Jean A., 9678
Schuler, Mark J., 2552
Schuler, Patricia T., 2552
Schuler, Renate R., 2990
Schuler, Tanya E., 2990
Schuler, Therese H., 2990
Schuler, Tino H., 2990
Schuler, Tracy, 1108
Schuler, Wendy R., 9739
Schulhof, Michael P., 6935
Schulhof, Paola, 6935
Schullinger, John N., 5186
Schulman, Joanna, 6449

Scruggs, Richard, 3497
Scruggs, T.M., 9125
Scrushy, Christa E., 62
Scrushy, Richard M., 62
SCS Development, 1106
Scudder Charitable Foundation, 7221
Scudder, Caroline, 5775
Sculco, Cynthia D., 6949
Sculco, Thomas P., 6949
Scull, Christine E., 9571
Scully 1994 Family Trust No. 2, 1171
Scully, Arthur M., Jr., 8130
Scully, Diana C., 3549
Scully, Irene S., 1116, 1171
Scully, James S., 61
Scully, John C., 3220
Scully, John H., 1171
Scully, Joseph C., 2992
Scully, Judith A., 2992
Scully, Mary Ann, 3595
Scurlock Oil Co., 9175
Scurlock, E.C., 9175
Scurlock, E.C., Mrs., 9175
Sczygelski, Sidney C., 9777
SDI Industries, Inc., 1137
Seabrook, Cordes G., Jr., 8588
Seabury, Charles Ward, 2993
Seabury, Louise Lovett, 2993
Seacay Corporation, 6974
Seacrest, Eric, 4991
Seafam Corporation, 6974
Seago, David M., 2356
Seagraves, Charles, Jr., 8015
SEAKR Engineering, Inc., 1452
Seal, Leo W., III, 4764
Seal, Leo W., Jr., 4745, 4764
Seal, W. Lee, 4764
Seale, R.A., Jr., 9024, 9193
Seale, Robert A., Jr., 8883
Seals, Molly S., 7585
Seaman, Elizabeth, 9479
Seaman, Jeffrey, 2204, 2229
Seaman, Jordan, 6093
Seaman, Julie, 2229
Seaman, Nancy M., 6939
Seaman, Richard N., 7761
Seaman, Scott B., 8754
Sean & Tucker, 1306
Searcy, Byron, 8996
Searfoss, David W., 1627
Searle, D. Gideon, 2994
Searle, D.C., 2994
Searle, Gabrielle, 954
Searle, Michael D., 2994
Sears, Fred C., II, 1706
Sears, Lester D., 2513
Sears, Marvin, 425
Sears, Marvin L., 1683
Sears, Theresa G., 5900, 6905
Searson, Christine K., 4624, 4671
Seashore, Eugene H., Jr., 4515
Seaton, Kristin Maxwell, 3387
Seats, Michael, 4587
Seaver, Beatrice, 6952
Seaver, Carlton, 1118
Seaver, Christopher, 1118
Seaver, Martha, 1118
Seaver, Oakley, 1947
Seaver, Patrick, 1118
Seaver, Richard, 1118
Seavitte, Samuel, 9833
Seay, Nancy Clements, 8832, 8919
Sebade, Jane, 8625
Sebastian, Audrey M., 4430
Sebastian, David S., 4430
Sebastian, James R., 4430
Sebastian, John O., 4430
Sebastian, Rona, 208
Sebastiani Vineyards, Inc., 1119
Sebastiani, Don, 1119
Sebastiani, Nancy, 1119
Sebastiani, Sylvia, 1119
Sebesta, Carol, 2580
Sebesta, Gerald J., 2601

Sebion, Diane L., 9904
Sebree, Betty L., 3127
Sebring, Penny Bender, 2857
Secchia, Peter F., 4431
Seckel, Douglas, 8852
Second Childrens Charitable Trust, The,
9440
Second Grandchildren's Charitable
Trust, The, 9440
Secory, Lynne M., 4257
Secosky, Phyllis, 205, 510
Securian Holding Co., 4677
Security Benefit Life Insurance Co.,
3390
Security Finance Corp., 8609
Security National Bank, 3287, 7889
Security National Trust Co., 9716
Sedgwick Claims Mgt. Services, Inc.,
3512
Sedgwick, Elizabeth W., 7849
Sedgwick, Ellery, III, 7849
Sedgwick, Ellery, Jr., 7849
Sedgwick, Jane, 7575
Sedgwick, Theodore, 7849
Sedgwick, Walter Cabot, 7849
Sedillo, Margaret Anne, 729
Sedrowski, Robert J., 4488
Sedwick, Debby, 78
Sedwick, Helen, 253
Sedzmak, Joe, 7831
See, Edgar T., 1537
Seed, Harris W., 1247
Seegull, Fran, 4001
Seehausen, Verne, 3189
Seelbach, William R., 7578
Seeley, Lynne, 7625
Seeley, Nancy, 7625
Seelig, Charles B., Jr., 5676
Seely, Christopher W., 5244
Seeno Construction Co., 1120
Seeno, Albert D., III, 1120
Seeno, David T., 1120
Seeno, Jacqueline M., 1120
Seeno, Jr. Living Trust, Albert D., 1120
Seeno, Lisa Hofmann, 683
Seeno, Sandra L., 1120
Seese, Jerry L., 4428
Seetaram, Kassie, 6083
Seevak, Elinor A., 1752
Seevak, Sheldon, 1752
Seevers, Gary L., 6953
Seevers, Gary L., Jr., 6953
Seevers, Sharon, 6953
Sefton, Claudia, 4493
Sefton, Stephen R., 4493
SEG Trucking, 553
Segal, Amy, 3931
Segal, Carole B., 2995
Segal, George, 5395
Segal, Helen, 5395
Segal, Marilyn M., 6477
Segal, Odile, 99
Segal, Rena, 5395
Segal, Richard D., 6477
Segal, Robert, 345, 2995
Segal, Susan L., 7143
Segarra, Ann, 5958
Segel Foundation, 8405
Segerstrom & Sons, C. J., 1123
Segerstrom Residuary Trust, Harold T.,
1123
Segerstrom Trust, Nellie R., 1123
Segerstrom, Anton, 1123
Segerstrom, Clark, 1178
Segerstrom, Henry T., 1123
Segerstrom, Jeanette, 1123
Segerstrom, Jeanette E., 1122
Segerstrom, Sally Eileen, 1122
Segerstrom, Ted, 1123
Segerstrom, Theodore Walter, 1122
Seget, Alan D., 5884
Seggio, Kim, 6800
Seguin, Kathryn A., 4528
Segura, William, 9407

Sehgal, Edda G., 3330
Sehgal, Jay, 3330
Sehgal, Rajat M., 3330
Sehgal, Surinder M., 3330
Sehlin, Sidney R., 4575
Sehn, Francis J., 4432
Sehn, James T., 4432
Sehnert, Greg, 7586
Seibel, Abe, 9178
Seibel, Annie, 9178
Seibel, Barb, 79
Seiber, John M., 454, 1031
Seiberlich, William C., 8419
Seibert, Henry E., 7548
Seid, Barre, 2996
Seidel, Garth B., 8377
Seiden, Barbara, 5396
Seiden, Mark, 5396
Seiden, Norman, 5396
Seiden, Pearl, 5396
Seiden, Stephen, 5396
Seidenberg, Douglas, 1646
Seidenberg, Ivan, 1646
Seidenberg, Ivan G., 5439
Seidenberg, Lisa, 1646
Seidenberg, Phyllis, 1646
Seidler, Lee J., 6970
Seidler, Stanley B., 3331
Seidler, Susan, 3331
Seidler, Terry, Mrs., 460
Seidman, Edward, 6092
Seidman, Jonathan G., 1529
Seifert, Carolyn, 8387
Seifert, Darlene, 3160
Seifert, George, 4256
Seiferth, Irma, 9463
Seigel, Lisa, 1996
Seigenthaler, John, 9424
Seigert, Robert F., 9906
Seigle, David C., 957
Seigle, Harold T., 2997
Seigle, Harry J., 2997
Seigle, Lora, 2997
Seigle, Mark S., 2997
Seigles Inc., 2997
Seiler, Donald H., 264, 597
Seiler, Lena, 6954
Seiler, Nathan, 6954
Seinfeld, Jerome, 1124
Seiple, Penn, 8432
Seiple, Rachel D., 8432
Seiple, Stan, 8432
Seitchik, Adam D., 3961
Seitler, Harriet, 3077
Seitz, Charles E., 2700
Seitz, Collins J., Jr., 1725
Seitz, Frederick, 134, 1824
Seitz, Howard G., 6586
Seitz, Steve, 160
Seiwert, Robert C., 7897
Sejima, Ryuzo, 3656
Sekera, Helen Mary, 8450
Selander, Mary L., 9847
Selber, Sara Speer, 8874
Selby, Charles W., 7953
Selby, Doug W., 3598
Selby, Leland C., 1530, 1531, 1611,
1612
Selby, Marie, 2230
Selby, Sandra R., Rev., 7526
Selby, William G., 2230
Selden, Jo Hershey, 7671
Seldin, Donald W., 3677
Selen, Mats A., 134
Self, Evelyn, 5120, 5121
Self, J.C., III, 8610
Self, James C., 8610
Self, Sally E., 8610
Self, Virginia Preston, 8610
Self, W. Matthew, 8612
Self, W.M., 8610
Selfe, Jane B., 22
Selfon, Merle, 8433
Selig Enterprises, Inc., 2484

Selig, Cathy, 2484
Selig, Charles, Jr., 7056
Selig, Charles, Jr., Mrs., 7056
Selig, John S., 155
Selig, Linda, 2320
Selig, Martin, 9675
Selig, Michael J., 155
Selig, S. Stephen, III, 2484
Seligman, Cathy, 6378
Seligman, Irving, 4433
Seligman, Mary K., 4433
Seligman, Thomas K., 384
Selim, Francine, 402
Selinger, Maurice A., Jr., 5542
Selis Article Fourth Trust, Sara, 6955
Selis, Sara, 6955
Seljeskog, Peg, 8631
Sell, Bradley N., 3600
Sell, E.S., Jr., 2317
Sell, Ed S., III, 2317
Sell, Ed, III, 2468
Sellars, W.E., 8587
Sellers, Alanna G., 1375
Sellers, M. Edward, 8570
Sellers, M.A., 2301
Sellers, R. Scot, 1375
Sellers-Walker, Margaret, 4326
Sellner, Patricia A., 4700
Sells, Carol B., 5025
Sells, T.D., Jr., 8833
Sellstrom, John L., 8275
Selock, Thomas, 7770
Selover, R. Edwin, 5361
Seltzer, David, 8392
Semancik, Joseph, 3144
Semancik, Joseph, Msgr., 3129
Semans, James D.B.T., 7317
Semans, Mary D.B.T., 7359
Semegen, Susan F., 2729
Semel, Beth, 5385
Semel, Carleton, 5385
Semel, Jane, 1125
Semel, Terry, 1125
Semelsberger, Ken D., 7617
Semiconductor Research Corp., 7470
Seminara, Joseph F., 6073
Seminole Hard Rock Hotel & Casino,
7174
Semler, Bernard, 2579
Semler, Jerry D., 3220
Semler, Matthew D., 1398
Semling, Linda F., 9777
Semlitz/Glaser Foundation, 6056
Semmes, Douglas R., 9179
Semmes, Douglas R., Jr., 9179
Semmes, Julia Yates, 9179
Semmes, Patricia A., 9179
Semmes, Thomas R., 9090, 9179
Semnani, Ghazelah, 9341
Semnani, Khosrow B., 9341
Sempier, Carl, 8361
Sempier, Philip J., 5162
Semple, Louise Taft, 7851
Sempowski-Ward, A.R., 7807
Sena, Eric P., 5471
Sendak, Timothy R., 3135
Sender, Milton, 3915
Senders, Jane Gural, 6120
Sendzimir, Arri B., 1518
Senecal, H. Jess, 1188
Seneff, Dayle L., 2231
Seneff, James M., 2231, 9177
Seneff, James M., Jr., 2231
Seneff, Timothy J., 2231
Senekjian, Harry, 9313
Senese, Christine, 8164
Seng, Orris, 3011
Seng, Tom, 3160
Senhauser, Rebecca, 1793
Senior Home Care, Inc., 6316
Senkler, Robert L., 4677
Senkowski, Steven J., 8090
Sennott, Tad, 6523
Sensenbrenner, Nancy B., 9869

Sensient Technologies Corp., 9922
Senske, Michael, 9834
Sentous, Marge, 828
Sentry Insurance, 9923
Sentry Trust Co., 8208
Senturia, Brenda Baird, 5591
Senyei, Andrew E., 1127
Senyei, Jo Ann C., 1127
Senzel, Bruce, 6083
Seow, Choon-Leong, 4309
Sepulveda, Eugene, 8768
Seramur, Brian, 9924
Seramur, Joan, 9924
Seramur, John C., 9924
Sergi, Vincent A.F., 2826
Serna, Sandy, 1054
Serodino, Pete, 8660
Serota, Joseph H., 1957
Serota, Susan P., 6889
Serotta, Abram, 2357
Serpe, Ralph, 5357
Serr, Erik H., 4426
Serra, Amanda, 1686
Serra, Benjamin, 1686
Serra, Deanna, 1686
Serra, Deanna L., 1686
Serra, Jeffrey R., 1686
Serraino, Beth, 9113
Sertori, Catherine A., 496
Seruya, Eli, 5518
ServiceMaster Co., The, 2723
ServiceMaster L.P., 2723
ServiceMaster Venture Fund L.L.C, 2723
Servitex, Inc., 2366
Session, Oscar B., 3250
Sessions, Kathy, 1165
Sessler, Gina, 5086
Sessoms, William D., Jr., 9532
Sestak, Elizabeth, 4898
Sethi, Neerja, 1976
Setser, Steven M., 9636
Settle, Ernest, 4252
Setton International Foods of Brooklyn, 6957
Setton, Joshua, 6957
Setton, Morris, 6957
Setzer, Fred C., Jr., 7603
Setzer, G. Cal, 1130
Setzer, Hardie C., 1130
Setzer, Mark, 1130
Setzer, Scott, 1130
Seubert, Patrick, 9885
Severance, William, 6220
Severns, David W., 1131
Severns, Helen A., 1131
Severns, Jerry, 3415
Severns, Nancy E., 1131
Severns, Robert L., 1131
Severns, Sharon L., 1131
Severson, Gary, 9566
Severson, Gary R., 9567
Severson, Gregory D., 2931
Severson, Lawrence, 4666
Sevier, Wayne, 7555
Sevilla, Michael J., 7831
Sevillian, Clarence, II, 4255
Sevrin, Alexander, 5973
Sewall, Elmina B., 1648
Seward, Byron, 4739
Seward, R. Lee, 1359
Sewell, Alvin D., Dr., 2358
Sewell, Elizabeth, 3425
Sewell, Frederick, 4678
Sewell, Gloria, 4678
Sewell, Mark, 229
Sewell, Phyllis S., 7690
Sewell, Stace, 8880
Sexter, Allan S., 5933, 7033
Sexton, Gwendolyn W., 1132
Sexton, James, 4679

Sexton, M. Yvonne, 4679
Sexton, Thomas P., 4679
Sexton, Tim, 3131
Seybold, Dorothea M., 3940
Seydel, J. Rutherford, II, 2501
Seydel, John R., 2525
Seydel, Laura Turner, 2501, 4464
Seydel, Paul V., 2525
Seydlitz, Orval, 7691
Seyfarth Shaw LLP, 3003
Seymour, Charlena, 3855
Seymour, James D., 9833
Seymour, Jenene H., 7370
Seymour, Robert, 4756
Seymour, S. Mark, 1629
Seymour, Thaddeus, 2303
Seymoure, Cathy, 3214
Sfara, David L., 1583
SFX-American Century, 8853
Shabeeb, Nabil, 3129
Shabel, Fred A., 8447
Shabshelowitz, Andrew, 3934
Shack, Ruth, 1957, 2288
Shackelton, Scott, 725
Shacknai, Jonah, 127
Shadley, Robert, 4509
Shadyside Assocs. Limited Partnership, 1802
Shafer, George A., 8955
Shafer, Julie, 1154
Shaffer Administration Trust, Ula G., 4450
Shaffer Worrell Charitable Lead Trust, The, 1971
Shaffer, Bonnie, 3131
Shaffer, Cecile, 8436
Shaffer, David, 8436
Shaffer, Jack M., 8436
Shaffer, John, 7570
Shaffer, Julie, 1469
Shaffer, Michael, 7559
Shaffer, Rebecca, 6769
Shaffer, Rose, 8436
Shaffer, Susan, 8436
Shaffir, Melvyn L., 7026
Shafir, Eldar, 5920
Shafter, Beverly, 1647
Shafton, Marjorie P., 2938
Shah, Mansukh J., 5724
Shah, Roopal, 930
Shaheen, David M., 5063
Shaheen, Linda F., 5063
Shaheen, Sam, 4428
Shaheen, Susan M., 2085
Shailor, Barbara A., 6357
Shainberg, Raymond, 8643
Shaker Advertising Agency, Inc., 2999
Shaker, Anthony, 1867
Shaker, Anthony R., 2999
Shaker, Elizabeth, 2999
Shaker, John E., 2999
Shaker, Joseph G., 2999
Shaker, Joseph R., 2999
Shalala, Donna E., 739
Shalam, Eli, 5554
Shallat, Barton A., Rabbi, 6771
Shallenberger, Anne M., 9041
Shallow, Nancy, 509
Shalom, Max, 6501
Shalom, Raymond, 6501
Shamblen, Louise, 1002
Shamis, Jeffrey B., 2892
Shamley, Mark W., 2275
Shamrock Industries, Inc., 4565
Shamy, Mustafa D., 7531
Shanahan, Rebecca M., 2178
Shands, Alfred, III, Rev., 179
Shands, H.J., III, 9227
Shane, W. John, 3047
Shane, William H., Jr., 3503
Shank, Walter T., 9234
Shankman, Abraham, 6739
Shanks, Earl, 7587
Shanley, Kevin, 5440

Shannon, Ann Dudley, 9792
Shannon, Bruce L., 1133
Shannon, David J., 3392
Shannon, E.L., Jr., 1133
Shannon, Harry L., 9730
Shannon, James, 4014
Shannon, Janet A., 3392
Shannon, Julie E., 3392
Shannon, Kathleen, 983
Shannon, Kathleen E., 5529
Shannon, Ken, 3392
Shannon, Lynn, 1222
Shannon, Michael, 1468
Shannon, Michael L., 1133
Shannon, Paul B., 8329, 8455
Shannon, Ruth B., 1133
Shanor, Susan M., 4755
Shapell Industries, 499, 500, 1135
Shapell Lead Unitrust, David and Fela, The, 1147
Shapell Lead Unitrust, Nathan, The, 1136
Shapell, David, 1134
Shapell, Fela, 1134
Shapell, Nathan, 1135
Shapell, Rochelle, 1147
Shapira, Anne L., 8058
Shapira, David, 8214
Shapira, David S., 8437
Shapira, Deborah B., 8437
Shapira, Edith L., 8386
Shapira, Elijahu, 8058
Shapira, Jeremy M., 8437
Shapira, Karen A., 8437
Shapiro Revocable Trust, Gwen, 9925
Shapiro, Abraham, 4135
Shapiro, Alison, 1137
Shapiro, Alison D., 1137
Shapiro, Barbara J., 1138
Shapiro, Bruce, 1490
Shapiro, Carl, 4136
Shapiro, Charles, 3001
Shapiro, Daniel, 3000, 7027, 7655, 7799
Shapiro, Edward L., 1138
Shapiro, Gwendolyn H., 9925
Shapiro, Harold D., 2776
Shapiro, Harold T., 7003
Shapiro, Henry M., 5195
Shapiro, Isaac, 3656, 7168
Shapiro, Jane K., 3668
Shapiro, John M., 6960
Shapiro, Joseph, 6959
Shapiro, Leonard, 6959
Shapiro, Lester, 3000
Shapiro, Libby, 6959
Shapiro, Linda Grass, 8223
Shapiro, Marc J., 9289
Shapiro, Mark, 7577
Shapiro, Mary, 3001
Shapiro, Molly, 3001
Shapiro, Morris R., 3001
Shapiro, Nathan, 3000
Shapiro, Norman, 2357
Shapiro, Norman, Mrs., 2357
Shapiro, Norton, 3000
Shapiro, Peter W., 1137
Shapiro, Ralph J., 1137
Shapiro, Robert, 3000, 4135, 6779, 7138
Shapiro, Robert B., 4827
Shapiro, Robert N., 4175
Shapiro, Ruth, 4136
Shapiro, Sarah H., 3575, 3650
Shapiro, Shirley, 1137
Shapiro, Stephen R., 1326
Shapiro, Vivian, 6581
Shapleigh, Anne T., 4896
Shapley, Laurie, 6876
Shar, Albert O., 5265
Sharber, Virginia Anne, 8660
Share, Charles Morton, 7977
Share, Hugh, 4900
Sharf, Frederic A., 4137

Sharf, Jean S., 4137
Sharkey, Edward D., 5397
Sharkey, Ruth, 5397
Sharkey, Thomas J., Jr., 5397
Sharkey, Thomas J., Sr., 5397
Sharko, Matthew, 3014
Sharko, Michelle, 3014
Sharma, Brahma, 1096
Sharp, Bill, 7526
Sharp, Charles S., 9180
Sharp, Doug, 8089
Sharp, Evelyn, 6961
Sharp, H. Rodney, III, 1727
Sharp, J. Baxter, III, 156
Sharp, Karen, 1949
Sharp, Larry, 405
Sharp, Marilyn, 4442
Sharp, Peggy, 2566
Sharp, Peter J., 6962
Sharp, Phil, 483
Sharp, Phillip A., 3677, 4319
Sharp, Richard L., 9515
Sharp, Ruth Collins, 9180
Sharp, Stacy Mays, 9036
Sharp, Terry, 4315
Sharp, Tracie, 8607
Sharp, Walter M., 812
Sharp, William M.W., Mrs., 1734
Sharp, Winifred J., 8146
Sharpe, Helen, 175
Sharpe, Henry D., Jr., 3002, 9135
Sharpe, Larry, 6537
Sharpe, Lynn A., 1992
Sharpe, Mary Elizabeth, 3002
Sharpe, Peggy B., 3002
Sharra, Sue, 4221
Shashaty, Yolanda, 6559
Shaskan, George, 6447
Shatteen, Westina L. Matthews, 6537
Shattuck, Mayo A., III, 3578, 3602, 3728
Shattuck, Mayo A., IV, 3728
Shattuck, Molly Ann George, 3728
Shatz, Carla J., 4616
Shaughnessy, Kimberly B., 3713
Shauk, Gazala, 200
Shaulson, Abraham, 6933
Shavelson, Richard J., 3015
Shavoley, Kathy, 713
Shaw Trust, Evelyn, 3556
Shaw's Supermarkets, Inc., 8555
Shaw, Arch W., 4901
Shaw, Arch W., II, 4901
Shaw, Bill, 7163
Shaw, Bob, 169
Shaw, Bruce P., 4901
Shaw, Daniel, 1338
Shaw, Deborah Lynn, 7852
Shaw, Dorothy S., 7432
Shaw, Eric W., 3647
Shaw, Frederick W., 3792
Shaw, Gardiner Howland, 4139
Shaw, George B., 3415
Shaw, Gerald, 7852
Shaw, Harold, 7853
Shaw, Harry, 7425
Shaw, Irene R., 8416
Shaw, Jack, 8583
Shaw, Jack R., 3228
Shaw, Jean Young, 3004
Shaw, Jeffrey W., 5066
Shaw, Judy, 1210
Shaw, Lani A., 1381
Shaw, Louise, 7853
Shaw, Marie Russell, 9310
Shaw, Mary Ann, 5724
Shaw, Mary Elizabeth Dee, 138
Shaw, Mary Louise, 7853
Shaw, Maurice K., 6800
Shaw, Minor M., 7359, 8585
Shaw, Norman, 1912
Shaw, Patsy L., 7852
Shaw, Richard L., 8098
Shaw, Roger D., Jr., 4901

Shaw, Run Run, Sir, 2554
Shaw, Ruth G., 7360, 7370
Shaw, Walden W., 3004
Shaw, William W., 4901
Shay, Andrea B., 6911
Shay, Robert P., Jr., 7509
Shaye, Eva, 532
Shaye, Katja, 532
Shaye, Robert, 532
Shayne Charitable Lead Trust, Herbert M., 1140
Shayne Charitable Lead Trust, May W., 1140
Shayne, David, 1140
Shayne, Elizabeth, 1140
Shayne, Herbert M., 1140
Shayne, Joan Blum, 1140
Shayne, May W., 1140
Shdeed, William, 7964
Shea Co., J.F., Inc., 1142
Shea Trust, Alison Brannen, 1143
Shea Trust, James William, 1143
Shea Trust, Matthew Gilbert, 1143
Shea, Andrew B., 5942
Shea, Bill, 8318
Shea, Carolyn H., 1141
Shea, Christina L., 4570
Shea, Dorothy, 983
Shea, Dorothy B., 1143
Shea, Edmund H., Jr., 685, 1142
Shea, Felice K., 5942
Shea, James W., 6058
Shea, John F., 685, 1143
Shea, John F., Jr., 1143
Shea, Jr. Trust, John F., 1143
Shea, Judith, 8283
Shea, Julia V., 5542
Shea, Lindsay Davidson, 7273
Shea, Mary B., 1695
Shea, Mary S., 1142
Shea, Peter O., 685, 1141
Shea, Steven J.C., 5942
Shea, Susan, 8318
Sheahan, E. Thomas, 9848
Sheahan, Margaret M. "Peg", 1504
Sheakley Group, Inc., The, 7854
Sheakley, Larry A., 7854
Sheakley, Rhonda L., 7854
Shear, Jack, 6312
Shearer, Charles L., 3423
Shechtel, Andrew J., 5401, 5410, 5421
Shechtel, Raquel, 5401, 5410
Shedivy, James, 1946
Sheehan, Bill, 4596
Sheehan, Elizabeth, 4140
Sheehan, Leo, 9622
Sheehan, Margaret, 4140
Sheehan, Robert C., 6998
Sheehan, William, 7917
Sheenan, Thomas E., 5359
Sheer, Joel M., 7496
Sheerr, Betsey R., 4103
Sheesley, DeVere L., 8347
Sheets, Mary Ellen, 4243
Sheets, Thomas R., 5066
Sheetz, Darryl, 766
Sheffer, Ann E., 1537
Sheffield, Edwin, 6218
Sheffield, Frank, 2488
Shefter, Jan, 7344
Shehan, Susan, 5702
Shehebar, Isaac, 5740
Shehi, Betty, 438
Sheiffer, Arnold, 6765
Sheinberg, Eric P., 6963
Shelby, Jim R., 8687
Shelby, Kerry, 1949
Shelden, Allan, III, 4434
Shelden, Elizabeth Warren, 4434
Shelden, Virginia Durand, 7420
Shelden, W. Warren, 4434
Shelden, William W., Jr., 4389, 4434
Shelden, William Warren, 7420
Sheldon Trust, Ralph C., 6964

Sheldon, Brooke, 9236
Sheldon, Danley, 4842
Sheldon, Isabell M., 6964
Sheldon, James, 9546
Sheldon, Jane E., 6964
Sheldon, Michael J., 9875
Sheldon, Robin O., 2159
Shelhamer, Betty S., 584
Shell Oil Co., 80, 9181
Shell, Frederick E., 4289
Shellabarger, Tracy L., 3125
Shellenbarger, Dave, 4256
Shellenbarger, David, 2240
Shelley, Steve, 4593
Shellito, David, 4480
Shelnitz, Mark A., 3638
Shelter Mutual Insurance Co., 4902
Shelton, Andrew B., 9182
Shelton, Joe, 252
Shelton, Ruby W., 9182
Shelton, Russ, 4256
Shelton, Ruth, 8895
Shelton, W. Brett, 4376
Shemanski, Alfred, 9682
Shemanski, Tillie, 9682
Shemo, Michael A., 7914
Shen Family 2003 Charitable Lead Trust, The, 5398
Shen, Carla, 5398
Shen, Theodore P., 5398
Shenandoah Valley Products, Inc., 3573
Shenefelt, Jamie, 9345
Shenfeld, Steven, 6085
Shenfeld, Wendy, 6085
Shenk, Janet, 1767
Shenk, Thomas E., 5326
Shenk, Willis W., 8458, 8459
Shenker, Joseph, 7209
Shenkman, Barry A., 5689
Shenkman, Jamie, 5689
Shepard, Charles E., 9869
Shepard, Donald J., 3259
Shepard, J. Michael, 5598
Shepard, James D., 867
Shepard, Judy, 4729
Shepard, Julia Sparkman, 1780
Shepard, Larry, 4958
Shepard, Lorrie A., 1838
Shepard, Mikki, 6229, 6538
Shepard, Ray B., 5157
Shepard, Sandy, 8876
Shepard, Stanley W., 1482
Shephard, Thomas, Sr., 1089
Shepherd, Anne H., 8938
Shepherd, Curtis E., 7859
Shepherd, E.M., 8741
Shepherd, F. John, III, 8833
Shepherd, Georgiana F., 1032
Shepherd, Katherine B., 2332
Shepherd, Nancy, 3906
Shepherd, Nathanael, 4096
Shepherd, Nina S., 460
Shepherd, Robin, 3132
Shepherd, Ruth H., 3906
Shepherd, Steve, 828
Shepherd, T. Nathanial, 3906
Shepherd, Thomas R., 3906
Sheppard, John W., 2240
Sheppard, Judy, 9730
Sheppe, Jack E. "Ted", 3254
Sheraton Corp., The, 7049
Sherbrooke, Ross E., 3904
Sherburne, Philip S., 4543
Sheridan County YMCA, 9998
Sheridan, Brian, 4941
Sheridan, Chris R., 2433
Sheridan, Chris R., Jr., 2358
Sheridan, Deborah, 6396
Sheridan, Don, 3333
Sheridan, Elizabeth M., 3729
Sheridan, Hope, 6965
Sheridan, John J., 2630
Sheridan, Thomas B., 3729
Sheriff, Edd, 8564

Sherin, Keith S., 1553
Sherman & Sterling, 7040
Sherman Management, 7067
Sherman Mgmt., 7292
Sherman, Alison A., 6721
Sherman, Beatrice B., 4141
Sherman, Cindy, 7215
Sherman, Claire B., 4141
Sherman, Ernest, 9675
Sherman, George, 4141
Sherman, George M., 2233
Sherman, Harris D., 1344
Sherman, Jane Ellen, 4299
Sherman, Jeff, 9229
Sherman, John, Jr., 9402
Sherman, L.J., 3312
Sherman, Max, 8768
Sherman, Michael B., 328, 3886
Sherman, Norton L., 4141
Sherman, Otey, 6824
Sherman, Peter, 7216
Sherman, Richard, 558
Sherman, Sandy, 3161
Sherman, Susan E., 8266
Sherman, Susan McCune, 872
Sherogan, Diana Wege, 4476
Sherr, Daniel, 1518
Sherratt, Peter R., 6395
Sherrerd, John J.F., 8439
Sherrerd, Kathleen C., 8439
Sherril, Henry F., 8587
Sherrill, Edmund K., II, Rev., 1715
Sherrill, F. Anderson, Jr., 7354
Sherrill, H. Sinclair, 1715
Sherrill, H. Virgil, 8999
Sherrill, Joe, 9280
Sherrill, Joseph N., Jr., 9130, 9275
Sherrill, Stephen C., 7254
Sherry, Christine, 1217
Sherry, Judith, 8457
Sherry, Maria M., 847
Sherry, Peter, Jr., 4307
Sherry, Sarah, 84
Sherwell, Jon P., 3648
Sherwin, Douglas, 3305
Sherwin-Williams Co., The, 7855
Sherwood, Dolly, 9723
Sherwood, Donald, 9683
Sherwood, Virginia, 9683
Sheskey, Susan, 8864
Shetter, Allison M., 2876
Shevick, Steven K., 1223
Shevlin, Patricia A., 2987
Shey, Stephen, 2015
Shi, Susan, 8583
Shiebler, Christina, 4680
Shiebler, Jason, 4680
Shiebler, Joanne, 4680
Shiebler, William, 4680
Shield, Fred W., 9183
Shield, Robin R., 9506
Shield-Taylor, Juliet E., 9506
Shields, David D., 1734
Shields, Elaine H., 8589
Shields, George L., 3730
Shields, Harold, 1642
Shields, Herm, 4871
Shields, Jane, 9390
Shields, Margaret M., 8151
Shields, Marsha M., 9037
Shields, Maury Flowers, 2384
Shields, Rosemary, 5825
Shiely, John S., 9765
Shier, John W., 4257
Shifler, Eve H., 8182
Shiflett, Laura, 9240
Shifman, Burton R., 4418
Shifran, Kenneth, 6618
Shigaragi, Takamaro, Rev., 5685
Shiley, Darlene V., 1145
Shiley, Donald P., 1145
Shillito, Charles, 1168
Shillman, Robert J., 4142
Shimek, Dan, 4681

Shimek, Daniel C., 4681
Shimek, Kay, 4681
Shimek, Kay N., 4681
Shimer, John C., 9587
Shimomura, Setsuhiro, 9476
Shindeldecker, David, 9189
Shindler, Eli, 6956
Shine, Frederick J., III, 2542
Shineman, Edward W., Jr., 5565
Shingle, James, 2536
Shingleton, Barbara, 4340
Shining, Stewart, 6485
Shinkle, Debra A., 7540
Shinn, George L., 134
Shinn, Gloria, 3255
Shinners, James J., 4428
Shinnyo-En Foundation, 4297
Shipley, Allison P., 7269
Shipley, Charles R., Jr., 4143
Shipley, Dorothy B., 7269
Shipley, Frederick H., 9730
Shipley, Grant M., 8435
Shipley, John P., 7269
Shipley, Judith L., 7269
Shipley, Lucia H., 4143
Shipley, Pamela J., 7269
Shipley, Shirley, 2156
Shipley, Walter V., 7209, 7269
Shipp, Pam, 1437
Shippee, Patricia M., 6107
Shir, Philip, 4135
Shireman, Mark, 3161
Shires, Dana, 4736
Shirey, Chuck, 3278
Shirk, Betty, 3007
Shirk, Betty J., 3007
Shirk, James A., 3007
Shirk, Richard D., 2411
Shirk, Russell O., 3007
Shirk, Tana M., 8179
Shirley, Carl, 5260
Shirley, Carl, Mrs., 5260
Shirley, E. Mary, 9684
Shirley, Jon A., 9684
Shirley, Nancy Pillsbury, 4883
Shisler, Arden L., 7771
Shiva, Alexandra, 6966
Shiva, Andrew, 6966
Shively, Peggy, 3185
Shives, Paula J., 1960
Shklar, Daymel G., 1146
Shklar, Eugene, 1146
Shleifer, Scott, 7139
Shlenker, Simon, III, 4630
Shmavonian, Nadya K., 6826, 7103
Shmelev, Anatol, 778
Shoaff, Thomas, 7910
Shoaff, Thomas M., 3203
Shobe, William, 3133
Shock, Ellen, 5043
Shockley-Mall, Dianne A., 8661
Shockney, Brian, 3115
Shoemaker, Dale, 4436
Shoemaker, Dale A., 4436
Shoemaker, Don C., 4996
Shoemaker, Edwin J., 4368, 4436
Shoemaker, Erich C., 4436
Shoemaker, George Franklin, 4996
Shoemaker, J. Richard, 4996
Shoemaker, Linda J., 1349
Shoemaker, Marcy Abramson, 1868
Shoemaker, Ray S., 8440
Shoemaker, Robert L., 4436
Shoemaker, Sandra, 7584
Shoemaker, William, 4996
Shoffner, Gary E., 1005
Shogan, Stephen H., 1445
Sholl, James K., 4228
Shontere, James G., 685
Shoolman, Edith Glick, 6967
Shopa, Thomas J., 1706
Shoptaw, Robert L., 157
Shore, Billy, 5905
Shore, Brian, 7989

Simmons, Therese, 4617
Simmons, Virginia W., 9187
Simmons, William T., Hon., 8107
Simms, Joshua, 849
Simms, Julie, 849
Simms, Nancy Gordy, 2402
Simms, Rhea P., 8317
Simms, Ronald A., 849, 1155
Simms, Victoria Mann, 849, 1155
Simo, Rita, 3069
Simon and Associates, Melvin, Inc., 3236
Simon Foundation, Sidney, Milton & Leoma, 2235
Simon Foundation, William E., 9152
Simon Foundation, William E., Inc., 5405
Simon, Allison S., 9211
Simon, Arnold, 6986
Simon, Bren, 3236, 3239
Simon, Cynthia, 5405
Simon, Daniel L., 2998
Simon, David E., 3237, 3239
Simon, Deborah, 3164, 3239
Simon, Deborah J., 3239
Simon, Deborah Joy, 3238
Simon, Donald, 1156
Simon, Donald Ellis, 1156
Simon, Douglas, 1156
Simon, Eric, 1156
Simon, Eve B., 5002
Simon, Frederick J., 5002
Simon, Heinz K., 9211
Simon, Herbert, 3240, 4903
Simon, Howard L., 6053
Simon, J. Peter, 5233, 6987
Simon, Jacqueline S., 3237
Simon, Jennifer K., 3240
Simon, John G., 6665, 7117
Simon, Joseph, 2998
Simon, Julian, 4903
Simon, Kelly, 2998
Simon, Leonard, 329
Simon, Lucille Ellis, 1156
Simon, Melvin, 196, 3236, 3239
Simon, Mildred, 4903
Simon, Mitchell J., 9972
Simon, Neal, 1785
Simon, Paul, 1202
Simon, Paul G., 2998
Simon, Philip B., 3621
Simon, R. Matthew, 2630
Simon, Ralph, 1202
Simon, Raymond F., 2630, 2946
Simon, Renee B., Hon., 232
Simon, Sandra, 2998
Simon, Stephen H., 3240
Simon, Todd, 5001
Simon, Todd D., 4994
Simon, William, 1202
Simon, William A., 7173
Simon, William E., 6987
Simon, William E., Jr., 5405, 6987
Simonds, Carter, 7139
Simonds, Juliet Lea Hillman, 8442
Simone, Christine M., 4383
Simone, David, 4383
Simone, Louise M., 4383
Simone, Mark, 4383
Simonet, J. Thomas, 4703
Simonetti, Carol, 78
Simons, Angela, 7313
Simons, Carl, 6988
Simons, Fay, 6988
Simons, James H., 6989
Simons, Marilyn, 6989
Simons, Rob, 7313
Simons, Susan W., 8662
Simons, Tom, 3241
Simonsen, Scott, 4968
Simonson, Ann Larsen, 1579
Simonson, Eric A., 2588
Simonson, Loreen, 7533
Simonyi, Charles, 9686
Simpkins, Jacqueline D., 7035

Simpkins, Nancy, 6340
Simpkins, Nancy K., 6128
Simplot Co., J.R., 2574
Simplot, Don J., 2574
Simplot, Gay C., 2574
Simplot, John Edward, 2574
Simplot, Scott R., 2574
Simpson Charitable Remainder Trust, L., 2489
Simpson Manufacturing Co., Inc., 1157
Simpson, Amy C., 1157
Simpson, Barclay, 1157
Simpson, Dazelle D., 2121
Simpson, James A., 1031
Simpson, Jean D., 1157
Simpson, John B., 1157
Simpson, Jon, 4227
Simpson, Julie Inskeep, 3181
Simpson, Julie M., 1157
Simpson, K. Russell, 2480
Simpson, Kate, 7472
Simpson, Kate M., 7392
Simpson, LeTrell, 2458
Simpson, Paul, 8164
Simpson, Paulelle M., 847
Simpson, Rhoda Mims, 2418
Simpson, Rita Price, 3186
Simpson, Robert, 7758, 9265
Simpson, Roderic, 3389
Simpson, Russell, 7405
Simpson, Sharon, 1157
Simpson, Stanley D., 3389
Simpson, Steve, 3189
Simpson, W. Hunter, 9701
Simpson, W.H.B., 7472
Simpson, W.H.B., Mrs., 7472
Simpson, William H., 8471
Sims, Cheryle M., 4742
Sims, Frank L., 4530
Sims, Howard F., 4254
Sims, Janie, 2156
Sims, Joanne, 4231
Sims, Linda L., 4428
Sims, Mac, 7343
Sims, Robert L., 5029
Sims, Sally, 983
Sims, Sid, 4733
Simses, Robert G., 1628
Simshauser, Peter, 6998
Simwood Co., 4342
Sinapi, Michael J., 4930
Sinclair, Gloria J., 2768
Sinclair, James L., 3729
Sinclair, Janice C., 3798
Sinclair, John B., 3729
Sinclair, John P., 1714
Sinclair, K. Richard, 9710
Sinclair, K. Richard C., 9723
Sinclair, Michael R., 739
Sinclair, Norman W., 6108
Sinclair, R.T., Jr., 7336, 7352
Sinclair, Ronald, 7336
Sinclair, Scott, 7139
Sinclair, Sylvia F., 2200
Sindelar, Nancy E., 2713
Singer Trust, Peter, The, 6990
Singer Trust, Steven, The, 6990
Singer, Andrew, 1753, 7749
Singer, Gordon, 1753
Singer, Herbert M., 6990
Singer, James R., 3539, 3554
Singer, Jeanne, 3600
Singer, Joanne, 582
Singer, Joseph, 5211
Singer, Linda, 1753
Singer, Maxine F., 3677
Singer, Nell, 6990
Singer, Paul E., 1753
Singer, Rick, 3255
Singer, Roger M., 4060
Singer, Sidney, 670
Singer, Susan, 5236
Singer, Terry L., 3414
Singh, Dinakar, 6991, 7031

Singh, Florence Ann, 6991
Singh, Lekha, 9185
Singh, Ravi Mo, 6991
Singh, Vishwa, 7031
Singletary, Julia, 2490
Singletary, Karen L., 2490
Singletary, Lewis Hall, 2490
Singletary, Lewis Hall, II, 2490
Singletary, Rebecca, 2490
Singletary, Richard L., 2490
Singletary, Richard L., Jr., 2490
Singletary, Tim, 2490
Singleton, Olivia R., 9723
Singleton, Palmer, Jr., 3129
Sinnett, Clifford H., 3527
Sinrod, Allison R., 49
Sinsheimer, Alexander L., 1754
Sinsheimer, Alexandrine, 1754
Sinsheimer, Warren, 1090
Sinton, Jane, 1090
Sinykin, Gerald B., 699
Sioukas, Lillian, 1080
Siperstein, Gary S., 8557
Siperstein, Mynde S., 8557
Siragusa, Alexander C., 3009
Siragusa, John R., 3009
Siragusa, Richard D., 3009
Siragusa, Ross D., 3009
Siragusa, Ross D., III, 3009
Siragusa, Ross D., Jr., 3009
Siragusa, Sinclair C., 3009
Siriani, Andrew, 2101
Sirinakis, Harry, 3597
Sirinsky, Marc, 8003
Siriporn, Chaiyasuta, 1252
Sirkin, Sidney, 5590
Sirko, Diano, 1338
Sirot, Margaret, 872
Sirota, Wilbert H., 3584, 3645, 3689
Sirote, Stanley, 5852
Sirovy, Loel, 1386
Sisco, Gary, 9424
Sisco, Robbie D., 3823
Sisco, William Martin, 8721
Sisek, James H., 7816
Sisenwein, Branna, 6993
Sisenwein, Irving, 6993
Sisk, John, 79
Sisley, Christine, 728
Sissel, Mary, 1364
Sisson, Douglas L., 8346
Sisson, William W., 3250
Sister Sister, Inc., 5520
Sit Investment Associates, Inc., 4684
Sit Investments, 4519
Sit, Debra A., 4684
Sit, Eugene C., 4683, 4684
Sit, Ronald D., 4684
Sitarik, Denise, 5255
Sites, Cindy, 1650
Sites, John C., Jr., 1650
Sitnick, Irving, 6587
Sitt 1992 Charitable Trust, Jack, The, 7108
Sitt Foundation, Joseph Jack, 5554
Sitt, David, 6995, 6996
Sitt, Isaac J., 6997
Sitt, Jeffrey, 6996
Sitt, Marjorie, 6995
Sitt, Morris, 6996
Sittko, Steven G., 1454
Sivertsen Trusts, Sarah-Maud W., 4726
Sivertsen, Robert J., 4726
Sizemore, Jeff, Rev., 2075
Sjoberg, Virginia L., 1108
Sjolund, Dawn, 4685
Sjolund, Paul, 4685
Sjoquist, Gregg D., 4716
Sjostedt, Judy, 9730
Skaalrud, Nancy, 4573
Skadden, Arps, Slate, Meagher & Flom, 6998
Skaden Arps, 7040
Skaggs, Don L., 9302

Skaggs, L.S., 9302
Skaggs, Mark S., 9302
Skaggs, Robert C., Jr., 3213
Skahan, Paul L., 4929
Skakel, Megan F., 6755
Skalicky, Norman C., 4534
Skarbek, Cynthia J., 3736
Skatz Realty Corp., 5865
SKC Inc., 8229
Skeehan, Joseph, 983
Skelly, Gertrude E., 2237
Skelly, Richard, 2156
Skelton, Brenda F., 9884
Skelton, Catherine M., 4765
Skelton, H.J., 1870, 1961, 1962
Skelton, Homer D., 4765
Skelton, W.E., 9443
Skestos, George A., 7683
Skestos, George Anthony, 7683
Skestos, George Arthur, 7683
Skestos, Jason, 7683
Skestos, Jason J., 7683
Skestos, Justine, 7683
Skestos, Justine A., 7683
Skestos, Stephanie K., 7683
Skidmore, Brenda L., 9523
Skilling Trust, Hugh H., 4437
Skilling, Hazel D., 4437
Skillman, Rose P., 4438
Skilton, Carmen, 9797
Skinner, Frank H., 7459
Skinner, Franklin, 2500
Skinner, Joe, 1471
Skinner, Marilyn, 3126
Skinner, Ray, 2259
Skinner, Richard G., Jr., 1940
Skinner, Richard H., 9197
Skinner, Robert, 1241
Skinner, Susan, 3437
Skinner, W.K., 338
Skinner, William L., 3103
Skipper, J. Ronald, 1946
Skipping, William, 9067
Skirball Investment Co., 6999
Skiva International, 5740
Skjodt, Cynthia A. Simon, 3239
Skjodt, Cynthia Simon, 3116, 3234, 3239
Skjodt, Paul, 3234
Sklar, Eric, 1767
Sklar, Linda, 2034
Sklar, Mark, 9775
Skloot, Edward, 7103
Sklut, Eric R., 7473
Sklut, Lori L., 7473
Sklut, Lori Levine, 7421, 7473
Skodol, Andrew, 5652
Skoglund, Adelaide, 2156
Skoglund, William B., 2680
Skogman, Gary, 3275
Skolaski, Steven F., 9910
Skoll, Jeff, 406
Skoll, Jeffrey S., 1158
Skolnick, Allen, 5699
Skolnick, Connie, 5699
Skomorowski, Christopher, 1563
Skopil, Trace, 9548
Skora, Susan S., 3277
Skoug, John L., 9806
Skuse, Terry M., 6482
Skwiersky, Paul, 5304
Sky Bank, 7625, 7810, 7867, 7898, 9716
Sky Financial Group, Inc., 7859
Sky Holdings, Inc., 7859
Skypech, Don, 3093
Slade, Jennifer K., 3184
Slaggie, Barbara J., 4686
Slaggie, Michael J., 4686
Slaggie, Stephen, 4686
Slaggie, Steve, 4686
Slagle, Frederick, 2441, 2455
Slagle, Frederick S., 2440
Slagle, Richard, 3050

Smith, James C., 7860
Smith, James Christopher, 3054
Smith, Jan, 4442
Smith, Janet, 7007
Smith, Janice R., 9197
Smith, Jean Bixby, 1249
Smith, Jean K., 6689, 9195
Smith, Jean Kennedy, 1816
Smith, Jeanne Hoffman, 7944
Smith, Jeanne R., 1163
Smith, Jeff, 9113
Smith, Jefferson V., III, 7476
Smith, Jeffrey, 9541
Smith, Jeffrey A., 7008
Smith, Jennifer L., 3840
Smith, Jeremy T., 6633
Smith, Jeremy T., Mr., 6633
Smith, Jerome A., 2701
Smith, Jerry, 9854
Smith, Jerry M., 2462
Smith, Jill W., 6260
Smith, Jim, 1517, 1949
Smith, Jo, 3437
Smith, Jo A., 7478
Smith, Joan Irvine, 1160
Smith, Joan M., 3840
Smith, Joanne E., 2592
Smith, John Cash, 9209
Smith, John E., 1594
Smith, John E., II, 2491
Smith, John F., Jr., 4319
Smith, John I., 7476
Smith, John M., 9998
Smith, John R., 5361
Smith, Jon D., Jr., 6161, 6162
Smith, Jonathan, 5056
Smith, Jordan P., 2570
Smith, Joseph A., 3282
Smith, Joyce, 2596
Smith, Julia A., 2883
Smith, Julia T., 2491
Smith, Julie, 4512
Smith, June A., 3854
Smith, Karen L., 4440
Smith, Kathleen D., 1741, 3714
Smith, Kathryn "Kathy", 1849
Smith, Kathryn H., 1601
Smith, Kelvin, 7862
Smith, Kendall A., 4441
Smith, Kenneth L., 3393
Smith, Kenneth W., 9245
Smith, Keren P., 2173
Smith, Kerri, 5219
Smith, Kevin, 9688
Smith, Kevin P., 1793
Smith, Kim, 9869
Smith, Kimberleigh, 6772
Smith, L.R., 7398
Smith, Langhorne B., 8144
Smith, Lanty L., 7359
Smith, Larry, 2441
Smith, Leo A., 3021
Smith, Lesly, 1628
Smith, Lesly Stockard, 2007
Smith, Lester H., 9192
Smith, Lillian Strecker, 7735
Smith, Linda, 1832, 5028, 9265
Smith, Linda H., 7819
Smith, Linda S., 109
Smith, Lois E. H., 4094
Smith, Lura, 4014
Smith, Lydia B., 9869
Smith, Manning J., III, 5378
Smith, Margaret, 5407
Smith, Margaret Chase, 3556
Smith, Margaret D., 5408
Smith, Margaret J., 1724
Smith, Marian, 4024, 4150
Smith, Maribeth, 6633
Smith, Marjorie L., 5162
Smith, Mark Douglas, 232, 347
Smith, Marschall I., 2636
Smith, Martha B., 2361
Smith, Martin, 4751

Smith, Mary Ann Chelius, 8103
Smith, Mary Jane C., 7007
Smith, Mary L., 8443
Smith, Mary Rose, 6574
Smith, Matt, Jr., 4259
Smith, Matthew J., 5409
Smith, May, 1166, 1167
Smith, Melinda Hoag, 678
Smith, Michael, 1773, 9303
Smith, Michael J., 4399
Smith, Michael L., 3116
Smith, Michelle, 9518
Smith, Miriam D., 5101
Smith, Molly R., 7398
Smith, Monroe, 2345
Smith, Morris, 7140
Smith, Munson, 8974
Smith, Nana G.H., 4987
Smith, Nancey E., 7860
Smith, Nancy, 4176
Smith, Nancy B., 4005
Smith, Nancy M., 4782
Smith, Nancy S., 4114
Smith, Neil T., 9196
Smith, Nick, 4636
Smith, Norma, 7326
Smith, Norman J., 8013
Smith, Norton, 1165
Smith, Oliver C., 9869
Smith, Ora K., 1724
Smith, Orin, 9690
Smith, Orin C., 9688
Smith, Orville D., 7959
Smith, P.R., Jr., 1902
Smith, Pamela C., 5871
Smith, Pamela J., 191
Smith, Park B., 7006
Smith, Pat, 7346
Smith, Patricia, 1370
Smith, Patricia G., 4752
Smith, Patricia M., 1386, 4441
Smith, Patrick J., 3037
Smith, Patti, 8661
Smith, Patty A., 9195
Smith, Peggy, 7933
Smith, Peter, 3245, 6674
Smith, Philip E., 349
Smith, Philip J., 6970
Smith, Phillips, 3533
Smith, R. Gordon, 9435
Smith, R. Lee, Jr., 2357
Smith, R.E., 9194
Smith, Rachel A., 3840
Smith, Ralph, 26, 3585, 8494
Smith, Ralph L., 9196
Smith, Randall, 7008
Smith, Randall D., 7008
Smith, Rankin M., Sr., 2383
Smith, Raymond, 6826
Smith, Raymond W., 5707
Smith, Richard, 3253, 3415
Smith, Richard A., 4148, 4150
Smith, Richard G., III, 7398
Smith, Richard J., 3474
Smith, Richard M., 6728
Smith, Rick, 3126
Smith, Robert, 23, 4149, 4168
Smith, Robert A., 4149, 4150
Smith, Robert A., III, 460
Smith, Robert B., 4782
Smith, Robert B., II, 4782
Smith, Robert B., III, 4782
Smith, Robert F., 5101
Smith, Robert F., Jr., 5101
Smith, Robert H., 1924, 9517, 9518
Smith, Robert L., 3192
Smith, Robert L., Jr., 1791, 3278
Smith, Robin, 5477
Smith, Roger B., 4319
Smith, Roger K., 1724
Smith, Rosa A., 4132
Smith, Roy C., 5775
Smith, Russell, 3925
Smith, Ruth Anne, 2508

Smith, S. Kinnie, Jr., 4260
Smith, S.W., 4274
Smith, Sadie Herzstein, 8949
Smith, Sally, 9195
Smith, Samuel H., 9694
Smith, Sarah, 3199
Smith, Sarah A., 7009
Smith, Scott D., 4441
Smith, Scott R., 9195
Smith, Sheila, 5783
Smith, Sherry M., 4695
Smith, Sherwood H., 7438
Smith, Sidney W., Jr., 4274
Smith, Stanley, 3250
Smith, Stella B., 176
Smith, Stephen B., 2615
Smith, Stephen D., 109
Smith, Stephen E., Jr., 1816
Smith, Stephen R., 2758
Smith, Steve, 3122, 8877
Smith, Steven J., 9864
Smith, Steven R., 1087
Smith, Stewart R., 1163
Smith, Stuart M., 9192
Smith, Sue Ashcraft, 9192
Smith, Sunshine, 4904
Smith, Susan Adams, 9230
Smith, Susan F., 4148, 4150
Smith, Susan N., 109
Smith, Sybil H., 63
Smith, Taylor W., 2383
Smith, Ted, 79
Smith, Terry, 9615
Smith, Theodore M., 3977
Smith, Thomas A., 2115
Smith, Thomas G., 7634
Smith, Thomas W., 1666
Smith, Timothy R., 34
Smith, Tony, 3241
Smith, Verlin W., 9478
Smith, Verne, 1471
Smith, Virgil L., 7458
Smith, Virginia N., 9534
Smith, Virginia Rowan, 5378
Smith, Virginia Stanton, 3801
Smith, Vivian L., 9193, 9194, 9197
Smith, W. Fred, 8876
Smith, W. Hinckle, 8444
Smith, W.R., 9077
Smith, Wallace H., 4782
Smith, Walter, 9594
Smith, Walter L., 9439
Smith, Wes, 5056
Smith, Wesley, 23
Smith, Willard, II, 1162
Smith, William A., 9198
Smith, William A., Genl., 7479
Smith, William E., Jr., 24
Smith, William G., Jr., 1924
Smith, William H., 4441
Smith, William Wikoff, 8443
Smith, Winthrop H., 5408
Smith, Winthrop H., Jr., 5408
Smith, Zachary T., 7458
Smith-Hams, Denise, 562
Smith-Rosario, Toni, 1563
Smitham, Peter, 5574
Smithers Foundation, Christopher D., 7174
Smithers Foundation, Christopher D., 7174
Smithers, Christopher B., 7010
Smithers, Christopher D., 7010
Smithers, Mabel B., 7010
Smithers, O. Lester, 7866
Smithers, R. Brinkley, 7010
Smithers-Fornaci, Adele, 7174
Smithers-Fornaci, Adele C., 7010
SmithKline Beecham Corp., 8218
Smithwick, Jack A., 3512
Smithwick, Robert, III, 8661
Smits, Catherine, 9625
Smits, James, 4280
Smits, Kerri Sue, 4280

Smitson, Robert M., 3104
Smittcamp, Earl, 1168
Smittcamp, Muriel, 1168
Smittcamp, Robert, 1168
Smittcamp, William, 1168
Smock, Laura L., 5004
Smokler Trust, Toba, 2096
Smokler, Carol S., 2096
Smokler, Irving A., 2096
Smolen-Rosenberger, Rebecca, 8197
Smolens, H. Marcia, 533
Smoot, J. Thomas, Jr., 2240
Smoot, Raymond D., Jr., 9443
Smoot, Thomas, 6617
Smorag, Douglas J., 7783
Smotrich, Steven, 5223
Smoyer, Don, 454
Smoyer, Elizabeth D., 454
Smucker Co., J.M., The, 7864
Smucker, Jenny, 7897
Smucker, Merrill, 8082
Smucker, Richard K., 7864
Smucker, Timothy P., 7864
Smulian, Rob, 2355
Smullin, Patricia D., 1169
Smullin, Patsy, 1169
Smullin, William B., 1169
Smurfit-Stone Container Enterprises, Inc., 4906
Smyjunas, Mary Ruth, 7588
Smyre, Calvin, 2497
Smysor, Catherine H., 3011
Smysor, John L., 3011
Smyth, D. Edward I., 8240
Smyth, Geralynn D., 3666
Smyth, John C., 3666
Smyth, Maureen H., 4399
Smyth, Patrick J., 3666
Smyth, Peggy, 3666
Smyth, Richard, 8082
Smythe, James J., 1170
Smythe, Linda, 1170
Smythe, Michael D., 1170
Smythe, Nevill, 5564
Smythe, Thomas M., 3254
Smythe, William D., 1170
Smythe, William D., Jr., 1170
Snappy Materials LLC, 488
Snead, Benji, 9021
Snead, Cheryl W., 8518
Snead, Christen E., 9520
Snead, Thomas G., Jr., 9520
Snead, Vickie M., 9520
Sneden Foundation, Robert W. and Margaret D., 4269
Sneden, Kathleen, 4269
Sneden, Kathleen M., 4269
Sneden, Marcia A., 4269
Snee, Katherine E., 8446
Sneed, Darial, 1571
Sneed, Norris, 9794
Snell, George B., 5981
Snell, Jeffrey T., 9747
Snell, Richard, 87
Snider Holdings, LLC, 5366
Snider, Arnold H., 5366
Snider, Charles W., 8937
Snider, Don P., 98
Snider, Edward M., 8447
Snider, Eliot I., 1939
Snider, Gordon, 7622
Snider, Jody Binswager, 1779
Snider, Karen, 8208
Snider, Katherine M., 5366
Snider, Richard C., 6879
Snider, Rick, 7622
Snidow, W. Todd, 1381
Sniffen, Barbara, 8015
Snipes, James C., 1783
Snite, Fred B., 3012
Snodgrass, John D., 2492
Snodgrass, John F., 7979
Snooks, Jan, 1456
Snow, Cheryl, 795

Snow, Cheryl M., 544
Snow, Cubbedge, Jr., 2433
Snow, Gene, 7749
Snow, Gerald T., 9337
Snow, Jeanne, 4327
Snow, John Ben, 7011
Snow, Jonathan L., 7011
Snow, Sally, 3177
Snow, Thomas G., 5784
Snow-Jackson, Thelma, 78
Snow-Johnson, S.G., 5153
Snowden, Gail, 3812
Snowden, James M., 4896
Snowdon, Andrew, 1809
Snowdon, Ashley, 1809
Snowdon, Edward W., Jr., 1809, 7012
Snowdon, Elizabeth, 1809
Snowdon, Marguerite H., 1809
Snowdon, Richard W., 1785, 7012
Snowdon, Richard, III, 1809
Snowdon, Roger S., 3147
Snowline Partners, LP, 8341
Snyder, Abram M., 8387
Snyder, Ann Marie, 5169
Snyder, Beryl L., 7013
Snyder, Brian S., 7013
Snyder, Charles, 5169
Snyder, Cheryl L., 7795
Snyder, Dennis L., 7583
Snyder, Donna D., 4532, 4632
Snyder, Dudley R., 9199
Snyder, Frost, 9689
Snyder, G. Whitney, Jr., 8448
Snyder, Harold, 7013
Snyder, Harry D., 7018
Snyder, James D., 9367
Snyder, James M., 3058
Snyder, James T., 5341
Snyder, Jay, 7013
Snyder, Jay T., 7013
Snyder, John, 7593
Snyder, John C., 9199
Snyder, Leonard N., 8228
Snyder, Marcus M., 9199
Snyder, Margaret, 9689
Snyder, Mary Beth, 4256
Snyder, Michele, 5905
Snyder, Nancy T., 9199
Snyder, Ralph, 8197
Snyder, Richard, 3145
Snyder, Robert E., 5081
Snyder, Rolf D., 3349
Snyder, Ruth B., 3349
Snyder, Sheba Torbert, 7014
Snyder, Solomon H., 3677
Snyder, Stephen R., 3198
Snyder, Sue, 5169
Snyder, Susan, 5169
Snyder, T.J., 3349
Snyder, Wesley V., 9199
Snyder, Willard B., 3349
Snyder, William P., III, 8130
Snyder, William W., 4810
Snyderman, Perry, 2763
So, Anthony, 5905
Sobel, Denise Renee, 820
Sobel, Jonathan, 7016
Sober, Daniel, 931
Sobol, Judith, 354
Soboroff, Steven L., 1288
Sobotka, Arlene, 3333
Sobrato Charitable Capital Trust, 1172
Sobrato Charitable Lead Trust I, 1172
Sobrato Charitable Lead Trust II, 1172
Sobrato Charitable Lead Trust III, 1172
Sobrato Charitable Lead Trust IV, 1172
Sobrato Trust Estate, Ann, 1172
Sobrato, Abby J., 1172
Sobrato, John A., 1172
Sobrato, John M., 1172
Sobrato, John Michael, 406
Sobrato, Lisa, 1172
Sobrato, Sheri J., 1172
Sobrato, Susan, 1172

Soby, Dayton, 4719
Society Capital Corp., 7700
Society Corp., 7700
Soda Trust, Y. Charles, 1173
Soda, Helen C., 1173
Soda, Hiroshi, 217
Soda, Rosemary, 1173
Soda, Y. Charles, 1173
Sodaro, Donald E., 1174
Sodaro, Felicity A., 1174
Soden, Glenn W., 7771
Soderberg, Elsa A., 5539
Soderberg, Jon, 5539
Soderberg, Libby, 5539
Soderberg, Peer, 5539
Soderberg, Peter, 5539
Soderberg, Robert, 5539
Soderberg, Sydney, 3387
Soderquist Char. Lead Annuity Tr., 177
Soderquist, Donald G., 177
Soderquist, Jeffrey, 177
Soderquist, Joann, 177
Soderquist, Mark, 177
Soderstrom, Carl, 4224
Soens, Gene F., 9833
Sofaer, Abraham D., 774, 775
Sofka, Richard F., 7817
Soful, Michael G., 7570
Sogohomrian, Sam, 983
Sohn Charitable Lead Trust, Fred & Frances, 8012
Sohn, Donald R., 4151
Sohn, Edward F., 8012
Sohn, Frances F., 8012
Sohn, Fred, 8012
Sohn, Gerard F., 8012
Sohn, Howard F., 8012
Sohn, Mark F., 8012
Sohn, Richard F., 8012
Sohn, Ruth, 8012
Soiefer, Ronald M., 5434
Soifer, Douglas S., 4479
Sojourner, David C., Jr., 8577
Sokol, Hilton, 7038
Sokol, Leo N., 6832
Solana, John D., 8855
Solana, Nancy J., 8899
Solangi, Karim B., M.D., 7247
Solano, Patrick J., 8450
Solano, R., 5097
Solari, Bruce, 220
Solari, Mary C., 1176
Solari, Richard C., 1176
Solberg, John, 4642
Solberg, Larry D., 8529
Solberg, Liz, 3188
Soldivieri, Susan I., 5167
Solek, Ellen Coote, 1605
Soler, Esta, 296
Solheim, Allan D., 139
Solheim, David, 139
Solheim, Joy, 139
Solheim, Karsten, 139
Solheim, Karsten Louis, 139
Solheim, Louise C., 139
Soling, Cevin, 140
Soling, Chester P., 140
Solinger, Hope G., 6034
Sollazzo, Jack, 5925
Sollender, Elyse Knapp, 2841
Sollins, Karen R., 6918
Solmon, Lewis C., 898
Solomon Trust, Lillian Cohen, 9544
Solomon, Alfred L., 7018
Solomon, Daniel, 3594, 9544
Solomon, David, 3594
Solomon, David L., 9189
Solomon, Esther, 6609
Solomon, Gary N., 3503
Solomon, Gene, 2240
Solomon, J. Eugene, 544
Solomon, Jane, 3594, 9544
Solomon, Jeffrey, 5671, 5673
Solomon, Jerry, 6609

Solomon, Lillian Cohen, 3594
Solomon, Mark, 8147
Solomon, Mark I., 8148
Solomon, Martin B., 1948
Solomon, Michael, 8060
Solomon, Peter J., 6434, 7017
Solomon, Ron, 294
Solomon, Sherry, 4243
Solomon, T.J., II, 7342
Solomon, Thomas J., 251
Solomon, Tom, 3127
Solomon, William T., 8955
Solomon, William T., Jr., 8855
Solomont, Alan D., 4152
Solot, Claire, 851
Solot, Edwin, Jr., 851, 6497
Solot, Jerald A., 8130
Solow, Roger M., 7003
Solow, Sheldon, 6779
Solow, Sheldon H., 7019, 7020
Soloway, Howard B., 9405
Solso, Theodore M., 3136
Solso, Tim, 3166
Solt, Dana D., 3319
Solt, Genie, 4990
Solt, Robert H., 3319
Soltz, Judith E., 8143
Solutia Inc., 4907
Soman, Roger, 1957
Somerhalder, John W., II, 8882
Somers, Bonnie, 898
Somers, Carolyn, 6559
Somerset Trust Co., 8501
Somerville, Kurt F., 4070
Somerville, Ron, 4596
Someya, Mitsuo, 9836
Somma, Robert, 3003
Sommer, Alfred, 6379
Sommer, Kurt, 5473
Sommer, Lorraine G., 7644
Sommerhauser, Peter M., 9751, 9814, 9832, 9884
Sommers, John G., 1644
Sommers, Sharon, 3186
Sommi, John B., 1589
Sondheim, Walter, Jr., 3559, 3567
Sondregger, Leona, 9910
Sonenstein, Burton, 3585
Sones, Randall D., 3565
Sonet, Jerrold M., 5872
Sonet, Steven G., 5872
Song, Unmi, 2740
Songer, Thomas F., II, 8136
Sonne, Christian R., 3696
Sonneborn, Dirk E., 5724
Sonoco Products Co., 8614
Sonsini, Lisa Sobrato, 1172
Sontag, Frederick B., 2239
Sontag, Frederick T., 2239
Sontag, Howard, 6735, 6773
Sontag, Susan T., 2239
Sonterre, Lynn, 4649
Sontheimer, Stephen L., 3503
Sony Corp., 7040
Sony Corp. of America, 6658
Sony Music Entertainment, 5708
Soo Hoo, Frank, 2661
Sooch, Navdeep S., 9200
Sopakco Inc., 8739
Sopher, Raeman P., 9359
Sordoni, Andrew J., III, 8450
Sordoni, Andrew J., III, Mrs., 8450
Sordoni, Andrew J., Jr., 8450
Sordoni, Andrew J., Jr., Mrs., 8450
Sordoni, Andrew J., Sr., 8450
Sordoni, Andrew J., Sr., Mrs., 8450
Sordoni, Margaret F., 8450
Sordoni, Matthew R., 8450
Sordoni, Susan F., 8450
Sordoni, William B., 8450
Sordoni, William E., 8450
Soref Operating Trust, 9930
Soref, Ida, 9775
Soref, Jeffrey, 6581

Sorensen, Arlo G., 411, 889
Sorensen, Catherine H., 764
Sorensen, Chris, 7175
Sorensen, Harvey L., 1180
Sorensen, J. William, 1344
Sorensen, Maud C., 1180
Sorensen, Ruth Cummings, 5814
Sorenson Devel., Inc., 9343
Sorenson, Beverly T., 9343
Sorenson, Damone, 4253
Sorenson, Daniel, 4644
Sorenson, Howard E., 2679
Sorenson, James LeVoy, 9343
Sorgente No. 3 Trust, 906
Soriano, Mark, 2763
Sorkin, Ira Lee, 5555
Soros 1982 Charitable Lead Trust, George, 6237
Soros Charitable Foundation, 7024
Soros Charitable Lead Trust, George, 7023
Soros Foundation, 6237
Soros Foundation-Hungary, 7024
Soros, Daisy, 7022
Soros, George, 6237, 6665, 7021, 7023, 7024
Soros, Jonathan, 6665, 7023
Soros, Jonathan Allan, 7021, 7024
Soros, Paul, 7022
Soros, Susan Weber, 6237, 7021, 7024
Sorrentino, Colleen P., 6307
Sorrentino, Tony, 8608
Sorrick, Marcia A., 3352
Sortino, Peter G., 4803
Sosland, Charles, 4908
Sosland, Estelle, 4876
Sosland, L. Joshua, 4908
Sosland, Morton I., 4823, 4824, 4908
Sosland, Neil, 4908
Sosland-Edelman, Debbie, 4908
Sosna, Fay, 7553
Sosnoff, Martin T., 7025
Sosnoff, Toni, 7025
Soter, Sarah Ross, 2207
Soterion Corp., 3430
Sotiros, Diane, 2740
Soto, Jose J., 4987, 5018
Sotzing, Jeffrey, 362
Soublet, Richard C., 879
Souder, Jr. Charitable Lead Trust, William F., 3013
Souder, Susanna J., 3013
Souder, William F., Jr., 3013
Souede, Rachel, 6957
Soukup, Mark, 1357
Soulliere, Anne-Marie, 3904, 3970
Soumah, Morgan Ware, 2287
Sound Around, Corp., 5657
Sound Capital, 9885
Sound Capital Vanguard, 9885
Soupata, Lea, 3585
South, Donna M., 2493
South, John T., III, 2493
South, Sharon, 3333
Southampton Memorial Hospital Endowment Fund, 9421
Southeastern Asset Management, Inc., 8719
Southeastern Investment Trust, Inc., 3419
Southeastern Mutual Insurance Co., 3102
Southern Area of The Links, Inc., 2205
Southern Bancshares, Inc., 7481
Southern Bank and Trust Co., 7481
Southern Co., The, 2494
Southern Coach Manufacturing Co., Inc., 15
Southern Community Bank and Trust, 7388
Southern Crushed Concrete, Inc., 4475
Southern Furniture Co. of Conover, Inc., 7321

Steendam, Jan, 3666
Steer, Dee, 9147
Steere, Lynda, 1653
Steere, William C., Jr., 6720
Steere, William, Jr., 1653
Steers, Lauren J., 6088
Steers, Robert H., 6088
Stefan, Amanda May, 5046
Stefanics, Liz, 5496
Stefanik, Paul, 7868
Stefano, Ralph, 5760
Stefanov, Kenneth E., 7577
Stefanski, Marc A., 7868
Stefanski, Rhonda, 7868
Steffens, John L., 7054
Steffens, Marian, 1745
Steffens, Roger S., 2494
Steffensen, Britt, 9184
Steffl, Robin, 9736
Stefka, Rob, 4991
Stegall, Lael, 5614
Stegemann, Klaus, 5400
Steger, J.A., 7751
Steger, Kim, 4991
Steger, Mindy L., 6284
Stehling, James, 9120
Stehly, R. Charles, 8286
Stehr, Gary M., 5779
Stehy, R. Charles, 8285
Steider, Norman D., 3143
Steiger, Adam J., 2113
Steiger, Andrew R., 2113
Steiger, Carole Ann, 2113
Steiger, David L., 2113
Steiger, Debra R., 9532
Steiger, Joel J., 2113
Steiger, Paul, 2097
Steigleder, Bert L., 9936
Steiglitz, Charles W., 5914
Stein Charitable Lead Trust No. 2, Doris Jones, 956
Stein Charitable Lead Trust No. 4, Doris Jones, 956
Stein Charitable Lead Trust, Doris Jones, 6262
Stein Charitable Trust, Doris Jones, 955
Stein Revocable Trust, Elaine S., 7056
Stein, Allen A., 7055
Stein, Amy B., 2666
Stein, Arlyne, 7058
Stein, Avy, 3022
Stein, Bessie, 2250
Stein, Carol, 6377
Stein, Carolyn Stafford, 2247
Stein, Daniel, 7130
Stein, Elaine S., 7056
Stein, Elliot D., 1899
Stein, Eric, 4168, 7055
Stein, Eugene P., 1190
Stein, Fred, 7057
Stein, Gerald M., 9973
Stein, Gerda, 4168
Stein, Gregory L., 3599
Stein, Gretchen, 9933
Stein, Henry, 5220
Stein, Howard, 5596
Stein, Isaac, 698
Stein, Jack, 9937
Stein, Jane, 4168, 5392
Stein, Janet, 5596
Stein, Jay, 2249
Stein, Jean, 6262
Stein, Jennifer Shilling, 466
Stein, Jill Levine, 809
Stein, Joan, 9937
Stein, John S., 11
Stein, Joshua, 4168
Stein, Joyce, 414, 1003
Stein, Kenneth L., 6049
Stein, Lewis, 2204, 2229
Stein, Louis, 2250
Stein, Marcie, 3022
Stein, Margot, 7055
Stein, Marilyn L., 1190

Stein, Martin, 7058
Stein, Martin A., 2535
Stein, Mary Ann, 1835
Stein, Michael, 6910
Stein, Myron, 7152
Stein, Nikki Will, 2946
Stein, Noah, 1835
Stein, Richard H., 8959
Stein, Rita E., 8413
Stein, Roger, 7056
Stein, Ron, 1917
Stein, Ronald, 5569
Stein, Ronald J., 6155
Stein, Sharon, 7055
Stein, Sharon Haugh, 7057
Stein, Stein & Engel, 2250
Stein, Steven N., 7058
Stein, Stuart M., 7056
Stein, Susan Haugh, 7057
Stein, Sydney, Jr., 6377
Stein, Tara Diann, 384
Steinau, Brooke, 3655
Steinau, Leslie, 6979
Steinbach, Milton, 7059
Steinberg, Diane H., 7060
Steinberg, Harold, 7061
Steinberg, James D., 7061
Steinberg, Jean, 7062
Steinberg, Joan E., 6577
Steinberg, Joseph S., 7060
Steinberg, Julian M., 7725
Steinberg, Meyer, 7062
Steinberg, Michael A., 7061
Steinberg, Paul, 2001
Steinberg, Richard A., 7158
Steinberg, Robert, 6568, 6663, 7063
Steinberg, Suzanne, 7063
Steinberg, Thomas M., 5823, 7104, 7144, 7145, 7147, 7148, 7149
Steinbock, R. Ted, 3409
Steinbright, Edith C., 8086
Steinbright, Marilyn Lee, 8086
Steinbrook, William J., Jr., 2344
Steiner Sports Memorabilia, 7174
Steiner, Daniel L., 6662
Steiner, David, 9265
Steiner, David S., 5411
Steiner, Deron, 3122
Steiner, Elizabeth, 6662
Steiner, George A., 2482
Steiner, Gerald A., 4868
Steiner, Jennifer, 7667
Steiner, Joshua, 6662, 6758
Steiner, Lisa A., 7254
Steiner, Lou, 8155
Steiner, Melissa Friedland, 4963
Steiner, Prudence L., 6662
Steiner, Rosemary, 3258
Steiner, Ruth, 6593
Steiner, Sylvia, 5411
Steiner, William K., 495
Steiner, Yaromir, 7775
Steinfield, Rebecca Morse, 4095
Steinhafel, Greg, 4697
Steinhardt, John, 5555
Steinhardt, Judith, 7064
Steinhardt, Michael, 4071, 6963, 7064
Steinhart Charitable Remainder Unitrust, Ella, 5005
Steinhart, Ella S., 5005
Steinhart, Morton, 5005
Steinhauer, Bruce W., 4389
Steinhause, Mitchell, 6618
Steinkraus, Eric M., 1683
Steinkraus, Helen Z., 1683
Steinkraus, Philip, 1683
Steinman, Beverly R., 8458
Steinman, James Hale, 8458
Steinman, Jeffrey, 6878, 6879
Steinman, John Frederick, 8459
Steinman, Peter D., 6878
Steinman, Robert, 6879
Steinman, Shirley W., 8459
Steinmann, David P., 6543, 6855

Steinmann, Frederick, 3723
Steinmetz Bros., Inc., 7292
Steinmetz Trust, Emanuel & Clara, 7067
Steinmetz, Bernat, 5772, 7066
Steinmetz, Charles William, 1192
Steinmetz, Clara, 7292
Steinmetz, David, 7067
Steinmetz, Emanuel, 7292
Steinmetz, Esther, 7067, 7068
Steinmetz, Mary L., 1192
Steinmetz, Michael, 5772, 7066
Steinmetz, Solomon, 7068, 7292
Steinmetz, William, 1192
Steinmetz, William A., 1192
Steinmetz, Yitzchak, 7292
Steinour, Stephen, 8527
Steinschneider, Jean M., 1570
Steinward, Todd, 7516
Stella, Frank, 1736
Stemberg, Dola H., 4161
Stemberg, Thomas G., 4161
Stemler, J. Robert, 8155
Stempel, Calvin P., 7069
Stempel, Ernest E., 7048, 7069
Stempel, Neil F., 7069
Stempinski, Loretta L., 2988
Stender, Bruce, 4520
Stender, Oswald K., 2546
Stenerson, James, 7514
Stengel, William R., Jr., 2698
Stenger, Allen, 8878
Stenhaug, David, 4668
Stenholt, Colleen J., 9915
Stenner, Richard A., Jr., 3166
Stenson, Gerald, 4623
Stenson, Robert T., 313
Stenzel, Duane, 4540
Step, Eugene L., 1087
Stepanian, Tania W., 429
Stepansky Co., LLC, 5340
Stepelman, Jay, 5959
Stepelton, Brett, 2246
Stepelton, Douglas A., 2246
Stepelton, Sean, 2246
Stepelton, Virlee Stacy, 2246
Stephan, Stephanie, 7653
Stephanoff, Kathryn, 8481
Stephany, Elizabeth G., 2288
Stephen and Ruth Hendel Foundation, 6056
Stephen, Tegan, 3538
Stephenitch, Mark, 2777
Stephens, Ann C., 409
Stephens, Austin, 2385
Stephens, Bess, 672
Stephens, C. Austin, 2386
Stephens, Charles P., 1961, 1962
Stephens, Craig, 5469
Stephens, David B., 4485
Stephens, Donald J., 9960
Stephens, Donna, 7848
Stephens, Elton B., Jr., 65
Stephens, F.L., 9165
Stephens, F.L. "Steve", 9164
Stephens, Gene, 8646
Stephens, James T., 65
Stephens, John T., 3118
Stephens, Joseph, 3137
Stephens, Juanita W., 8729
Stephens, K.F., 1245
Stephens, Mel, 4374
Stephens, Michael D., 678
Stephens, Mike, 3230
Stephens, Neika, 8729
Stephens, Ray, 9268
Stephens, Robert, 972
Stephens, Robert W., Jr., 9726
Stephens, Sandra D., 1962
Stephens, Sherri E., 4255
Stephens, Sylvia L., 4074
Stephens, Thomas J., 9633
Stephens, W.E., Jr., 8729
Stephenson, Barbara, 1193
Stephenson, Betty L., 7982

Stephenson, Craig, 187
Stephenson, Elizabeth W., 7890
Stephenson, John W., 2339, 2364
Stephenson, Randall L., 8765
Stephenson, Roger T., 9919
Stephenson, Rollie, 9776
Stephenson, Sarah Taylor, 1861
Stephenson, Thomas F., 1193
Stepp, Janet, 8326
Stepworth Holdings, Inc., 5671
Sterba, Jeffry E., 5466
Sterkx, Mamie, 3472
Sterling Financial Trust Co., 8433
Sterling, Eileen, 9597
Sterling, Eric, 5096
Sterling, Mary K., 129
Sterling, Rick, 1358
Sterling, Thomas W., 8488
Stermer, Jerome, 2812
Stern, A. Joseph, 5412
Stern, Barbara, 3901
Stern, Barbara F., 4162
Stern, Beatrice, 6657
Stern, Bernice, 7072
Stern, Burton S., 4162
Stern, Charles A., 2696
Stern, Daniel, 6817
Stern, David M., 9522
Stern, Denise R., 7071
Stern, Edgar B., Jr., 9344
Stern, Edward A., 7521
Stern, Edwin H., III, 5840
Stern, Eli, 5412
Stern, Elisabeth Ellen, 6657
Stern, Ellen L., 7070
Stern, Eva, 1194
Stern, Eva S., 1194
Stern, Frieda, 5412
Stern, Geoffrey S., 7070
Stern, H. Peter, 6657
Stern, Irene, 7073
Stern, Irvin, 3023
Stern, Jean L., 7074
Stern, Jerome L., 7070
Stern, Jim, 9799
Stern, John M., Jr., 3599
Stern, John Peter, 6657
Stern, Joseph A., 6459
Stern, Julian N., 557
Stern, Karen G., 4818
Stern, Lawrence J., 946
Stern, Lynn S., 6034
Stern, Marc I., 1194
Stern, Max, 5302
Stern, Nicholas S.G., 6034
Stern, Pauline S., 9344
Stern, Philip M., 9522
Stern, Robert A., 7074
Stern, Robert J., 7074
Stern, Ronald A., 7070
Stern, Roy, 7073
Stern, S. Sidney, 1195
Stern, Sam, 5302, 7521
Stern, Steven, 7073
Stern, Thomas D., 6097, 7071
Stern, Tzirel, 5302
Stern, William, 7521
Sternberg, Lisa Kampfmann, 7075
Sternberg, Stuart L., 7075
Sternberg, Sy, 6617
Sternberger, Sigmund, 7493
Sterne, Charles S., 143
Sterne, Dorothy, 143
Sterne, Eleanor M., 6573
Sterner, Bill, 1358
Sternlicht, Barry, 1756
Sternlicht, Barry F., 7049
Sternlicht, Miriam Klein, 1756
Sternlicht, Russell, 1756
Sternlieb, David, 5574
Sterns, B. Kevin, 6772
Stetler, Gary, 4275
Stetler, Gerald, 4275
Stetson, Anne, 4036, 4120

Stetson, E. William, III, 1632, 7461
Stetson, Jane W., 1761
Stettheimer, Joe, 9021
Steuart, Guy T., II, 1780
Steuerle, Eugene, 1785
Steuert, Mike, 523
Steuri, John, 156
Steury, David, 7533
Steven's Baby Boom, Ltd., 5627
Stevens Richardson Trust, 6083
Stevens, Abbot, 4163
Stevens, Barbara, 3166
Stevens, Connie, 3387
Stevens, Derek, 4250
Stevens, Dorothy W., 5192
Stevens, Elizabeth, 4250, 4754
Stevens, G.W., 129
Stevens, George C., 8581
Stevens, Georgiana G., 1196
Stevens, Gregory, 4250
Stevens, H. Allen, 3795
Stevens, J. Whitney, 5192
Stevens, Jackie, 8996
Stevens, James, 7510
Stevens, James J., 2873
Stevens, James W., 5181
Stevens, Janet, 8996
Stevens, Joel W., 3544
Stevens, John V., Jr., 144
Stevens, John V., Sr., 144
Stevens, Joseph B., Jr., 3693
Stevens, Marcella M., 4864
Stevens, Mark, 523
Stevens, Michael J., 2196
Stevens, Nathaniel, 4164
Stevens, Patti, 4754
Stevens, Richard, 7510
Stevens, Rick, 1944
Stevens, Robert T., Jr., 5192
Stevens, Tamara T., 3950
Stevens, Thomas L., 4326
Stevens, Virgil A., 2251
Stevens, Whitney, 5192
Stevens, William A., 4754
Stevens, William J., 18
Stevens, William R., 5783
Stevenson, Adair, 8791
Stevenson, John M., 8841
Stevenson, Karen, 474
Stevenson, Mike, 4941
Stevenson, Robert F., 970
Stevenson, Robert, III, 2677
Stevenson, Ruth Carter, 8816
Stevenson-Colley, Ann, 6570
Steward, Al, 8135
Steward, Kathy B., 3414
Steward, Larry E., 4289
Steward, Robert E., Jr., 8136
Stewart & March, Inc., 8460
Stewart & Tate, Inc., 8460
Stewart III Trust, William P., 5931
Stewart Living Trust, 1198
Stewart Trust, Gregory, 5931
Stewart Trust, Jeffrey, 5931
Stewart Trust, Lisa, 5931
Stewart, Alan M., 8854
Stewart, Barbara, 5931
Stewart, Chester L., 3065
Stewart, Christina, 363
Stewart, Craig W., 9552, 9694
Stewart, Darlene, 4991
Stewart, Diana D., 8177
Stewart, Dorothy I., 982
Stewart, Doug, 2922
Stewart, Douglas, 4299
Stewart, Douglas G., 2620
Stewart, Eliot Brady, 5141
Stewart, Elizabeth D.S., 9345
Stewart, Faye H., 8060
Stewart, Gary A., 8460
Stewart, Harvey, 4939
Stewart, Havilah, 6357
Stewart, James O., III, 9213
Stewart, James O., Jr., 9213

Stewart, Jan C., 3634
Stewart, Jerry L., 1
Stewart, Joseph M., 4357
Stewart, Kimberly Louis, 2862
Stewart, Kirk, 8046
Stewart, Leanne M., 4633
Stewart, Lindsay D., 8046
Stewart, Lisa, 8882
Stewart, Malcolm H., 552
Stewart, Marcia, 8046
Stewart, Margaret, 3137
Stewart, Marise M.M., 4399
Stewart, Marise Meynet, 340, 1280
Stewart, Marlene, 9213
Stewart, Mary E., 1850
Stewart, Maureen, 3650
Stewart, Maureen L., 3575, 3722
Stewart, Max, Jr., 3370, 8976
Stewart, Michele, 5931
Stewart, Ralph W., 8136
Stewart, Randy, 4990
Stewart, Richard, 8581
Stewart, Robert G., 3827
Stewart, Robert H., Jr., 8460
Stewart, Stacey Davis, 1793
Stewart, Sylvia, 4737
Stewart, Terrence S., 8460
Stewart, Tim, 519
Stewart, Victor E., 7040
Stewart, William, 7743
Stewart, William P., 5931
Steyer, Helen, 7077
Steyer, Hume, 5885
Steyer, Stanley, 7077
Steyer, Thomas M., 7077
Stibbe, John, 7514
Stichman, Bennett, 1788
Stickley, Mimi, 2447
Stickney, Lara J., 2405
Stiefel Laboratories, 7078
Stiefel, Charles W., 7078
Stiefel, Ernst C., 7079
Stiefel, Werner K., 7078
Stiefel-Francis, Cheryl, 7748
Stieg, Edward C., 4244
Stieg, Elizabeth A., 4244
Stieg, Harold E., 4244
Stieglitz, Charles M., 6546, 6646
Stiehl, Cynthia F. Moeller, 9877
Stiener, Gil, 3135
Stifle, Bill, 3126
Stiggers, Michael, 2345
Stigman, Jim, 4534
Stiles, Leslie H., 4537
Stiles, Robert, 5605
Stiller, David G., 7704
Stiller, Robert, 9358
Stiller, Robert J., 9358
Stiller, Shale D., 3603, 3651, 3739, 3759
Stilley, R. James, Jr., 4919
Stillman, Chauncey, 6199
Stillman, Katherine, 5894
Stillman, Waddell W., 6119
Stillwell, Logan W., 126
Stilson, Valerie, 249
Stimpel, Richard J., 870
Stimson, Catherine R., 359
Stine, Curtis L., 2808
Stine, David J., 8462
Stine, Harry H., 3335
Stine, Helen A., 8427
Stine, James M., 8462
Stine, Lindsay, 8462
Stine, Lynn B., 2616
Stine, Margaret V., 8462
Stine, Molly S., 3335
Stinehart, William, Jr., 228, 924, 1815, 5022, 5790
Stingley, Mark, 1882
Stinnett, J. Daniel, 4797
Stinnett, Maggie Davis, 9255
Stinson Morrison Hecker, LLP, 9173
Stinson, Marien, 9034

Stiny, Pier, 1480
Stipe, Beth A., 9571
Stirn, Cara S., 7862
Stites, James R., 8713
Stites, John D., II, 8713
Stites, Mary, 8713
Stites, Rosemary T., 8713
Stith, Melvin T., 2143
Stitt, Kirk G., 405
Stivelman, William, 949
Stobbe, April, 7931
Stobbs, Larry, 4991
Stocco, Kathleen, 9021
Stock, Eloise J., 9992
Stock, Georgia L., 9939
Stock, John P., 1257
Stock, Kenneth C., 9939
Stock, Paul, 9992
Stock, Steven, 9939
Stock, Todd, 3241
Stockdale, Judith M., 2706
Stockdale, Susan, 1370
Stockdale, Suzy, 9928
Stocker, Beth K., 7870
Stockholm, Charles M., 564
Stockholm, Maryanna G., 564
Stocking, Charles, 7882, 7883
Stocking, Charles A., 3895
Stockman, Hervey S., 5497
Stockman, Hervey S., Jr., 5497
Stockman, Sally, 5497
Stockman, Sarah A., 5497
Stocks, Bryant, 142
Stockwell, Lance, 7927
Stoddard, George E., 5704
Stoddard, Harry G., 4165
Stoddard, James A., 5481
Stoddard, Jenny B., 3074
Stoddard, Stanford C., 4447
Stoddard-Freeman, Annette, 9785
Stoddart, Cassandra O., 9392
Stodghill, Curtis W., 8601
Stoel, Thomas B., 8067
Stoelting, Scott, 9113
Stoffel, Gayle, 9021
Stoffel, James L., 4695
Stoffel, Marco, 5652, 7132
Stoffel, Paul, 9214
Stoga, Alan, 7143
Stogdill, Thomas, 3255
Stogner, Frank, 9021
Stoick, Catherine Emison, 4586
Stoico, Robert F., 4166
Stokar, Suzanne, 3498
Stokely, Clayton F., 8730
Stokely, Kay H., 8730
Stokely, Shelley K., 8730
Stokely, William B., III, 8730
Stokely, William B., IV, 8730
Stokely, William B., Jr., 8730
Stokes, Hannah L., 7080
Stokes, Jerome W.D., 1844
Stokes, Mary S., 7422
Stokes, Patricia D., 8177
Stokes, Paul M., 2273
Stokes, Samuel N., 3684
Stokes, Thomas C., 1380
Stolaruk, Marc J., 4448
Stolaruk, Steve, 4448
Stolle, Carl, 8864
Stollenwerk, Robert T., 9847
Stoller, Craig, 7832
Stoller, Philip, 9632
Stoller, Russell, 7832
Stoller, Susan B., 9632
Stoller, Todd, 7832
Stollings, Juanita, 3449
Stolper, Michael, 8078
Stone Holdings LLC, 5421
Stone Mountain Industrial Park, Inc., 2464
Stone, Albert, 4057
Stone, Amy, 1200
Stone, Anne, 5343

Stone, Anne L., 3718
Stone, Barbara S., 9940
Stone, Barbara West, 1200
Stone, Carol Gordon, 4178
Stone, Cathleen Douglas, 5551
Stone, Cecilia V., 4020
Stone, Charles Lynn, 1654
Stone, Charles Lynn, Jr., 1654
Stone, Cynthia, 3025
Stone, David, 1200, 1651, 7140
Stone, David C., 4445
Stone, David L., 3873
Stone, Deborah, 1200
Stone, Deryck, 954
Stone, Donald, 7081
Stone, Edward C., Jr., 750
Stone, Edward E., 1654
Stone, Eric P., 9940
Stone, Erica, 297
Stone, Gregory P., 1187
Stone, Haydee T., 3519
Stone, Helen, 7871
Stone, Holly, 3641
Stone, Howard L., 3063
Stone, Hugh Lamar, III, 9165
Stone, Irving I., 7871
Stone, James, 7081
Stone, James H., 3025
Stone, Jean, 7081
Stone, Jeffrey, 2631
Stone, Jennifer, 1200
Stone, Jerome H., 3025
Stone, Jessie V., 1200
Stone, Kathryn W., 4740
Stone, Kent, 4704
Stone, Larry D., 7423
Stone, Leslie B., 1587
Stone, Loren R., 3063
Stone, Marion H., 1654
Stone, Marjorie, 2631
Stone, Maximilian Dana, 4020
Stone, Michael A., 1200
Stone, Nan, 3828
Stone, Norah Sharpe, 1200
Stone, Norman C., 1200
Stone, Peter E., 9940
Stone, Regina, 405
Stone, Roger, 3026
Stone, Roger D., 5937
Stone, S. Adam, 9940
Stone, Samuel Z., 3519
Stone, Sandra, 1200
Stone, Sara, 1200
Stone, Sharon Jean, 3004
Stone, Sheldon M., 345
Stone, Sherwin J., 2631
Stone, Steve L., 4057
Stone, Steven, 1200
Stone, Susan, 3026
Stone, Susan A., 2631
Stone, Terry, 9693
Stone, Todd A., 8721
Stone, W. Clement, 1200
Stone, Walter R., 8551
Stonecorner Corp., 4043
Stonecutter Mills Corp., 7486
Stoneman, James M., 4167
Stoneman, Miriam, 4168
Stoneman, Miriam H., 4168
Stoneman, Sidney, 4168
Stoner, Alden, 3747
Stoner, Chelle, 3747
Stoner, John P., 7570
Stoner, Katharine E., 3747
Stoner, Max, 6909
Stoner, Michael, 4229
Stoner, Thomas H., 3747
Stonesifer, Patricia Q., 9591
Stonesifer, Patty, 9680
Stonestreet, James D., 2045
Stonington, Anne, 1463
Stonisch, Helen, 4449
Stonisch, Mary Sue, 4449
Stonisch, Rudy, 4449

Stookey, John Hoyt, 5761, 5762
Stookey, Katherine Emory, 6907
Stoops, Reed, 78
Stop & Shop Cos., Inc., The, 3767
Stop & Shop Supermarket Co. LLC, The, 8463
Stop & Shop Supermarket Co., The, 3767, 8463
Stopak, Carolyn, 3757
Stopfel, Virginia B., 3895
Stophel, Glenn C., 8714
Storage Technology Corp., 1460
Storch, Jerry, 4697
Storer, James P., 2252
Storer, Peter, 2252
Storey, Barry L., 2357
Storey, Charles, 27
Storey, Charles P., 8952
Storey, Lynn B., 1726
Storey, Robert D., 4367
Stork, Stephen E., 5496
Storms, John W., 9024, 9063, 9231
Story, Janice, 7416
Story, Orville L., 9044
Story, Richard W., 3595
Story, Thomas E., 7416
Storz, Robert Herman, 5006
Stotsenberg, Henry, 1005
Stott, Frances, 1533
Stott, Joan Johnson, 1679
Stouder, A.G., 7886
Stoughton, Daphne, 1528
Stout, Charles L., 3761
Stout, Charlotte, 7729
Stout, David M., 7439
Stout, Helen, 156
Stout, Jean C., 6210
Stout, Joan K., 6210
Stout, Joan M., 6210
Stout, John K., 6210
Stout, Karen A., 9407
Stout, Mark, 939
Stout, Michael Ward, 6485
Stout, Nan, 4156
Stout, Ray E., 6210
Stout, Richard M., 5068
Stout, Ross B., 5068
Stovall, Guy F., III, 8926
Stover, Joan C., 1201
Stover, John, 2263
Stover, Susan J., 1201
Stover, W. Robert, 1201
Stover, Wilbur G., 2571
Stowe Mills, R.L., Inc., 7487
Stowe, Brenda M., 5101
Stowe, Daniel Harding, 7487
Stowe, Harold C., 8619
Stowe, Richmond H., 7487
Stowe, Robert Lee, III, 7487
Stowe, Robert Lee, Jr., 7487
Strachan, Camille, 3483
Strachan, Richard, 2700
Strachan, Stephen M., 2700
Strader, Deeta, 3360
Strader, Timothy L., 699
Strain, John T., 66
Strain, Juanelle D., 66
Strain, Julia, 66
Straitor, George A., 4300, 4301, 4302, 4303, 4304, 4305, 4306
Strake, George W., Jr., 8949, 9215
Strake, George W., Sr., 9215
Strake, Susan K., 9215
Stranahan, Abbot, 7774
Stranahan, Ann, 7882
Stranahan, Bob, IV, 7872
Stranahan, Daniel, 7774
Stranahan, Duane, Jr., 1943, 7882
Stranahan, Frank D., 7872
Stranahan, George, 7882
Stranahan, George S., 7774
Stranahan, Mary C., 7774
Stranahan, Mary Celeste, 7882
Stranahan, Michael, 7882

Stranahan, Molly, 7774
Stranahan, Pat, 7872
Stranahan, Robert A., 7872
Stranahan, Robert A., Jr., 7873
Stranahan, Sarah S., 7774
Stranahan, Stephen, 7872, 7882
Strand Hill, 5736
Strand, Allan E., 4766
Stranden, 3683
Strange, Peter S., 7574
Strangfeld, John R., Jr., 5360
Stransky, Inc., 2253
Stransky, Robert J., 2253
Strasburg, Robert, 4629
Strasfeld, Janice E., 7585
Strassburger, John, 8305
Strasser, Jonathan, 7083
Strassler, Abbie, 5602
Strassler, Alan, 5602
Strassler, David, 5602
Strassler, David H., 5602
Strassler, Gary, 5602
Strassler, Karen, 5602
Strassler, Lorna, 5602
Strassler, Matthew, 5602
Strassler, Robert, 5602
Strassler, Robert B., 5602
Strassler, Samuel A., 5602
Stratton, Frederick P., Jr., 8629, 8633, 9765, 9876
Straub Lincoln Mercury, 7174
Straub, Gertrude S., 2553
Straub, John C., 1800
Straub, John W., 3069
Strauch, Hans, 6590
Strauch, Ommy, 9166
Strauch, Roger, 6590
Straughn, Sue, 2110
Straus Family Trust, 508
Straus, Bethia G., 3027
Straus, Daniel E., 5413, 5414
Straus, David, 7085
Straus, David A., 6117
Straus, Donald Roy, 7086
Straus, Faye, 508
Straus, Harry H., Sr., 7085
Straus, Joyce G., 5413
Straus, Katherine Bea, 7086
Straus, Laura, 6117
Straus, Lynn G., 7086
Straus, Melville, 7084
Straus, Michael, 7215
Straus, Moshael J., 5413, 5414
Straus, Oscar S., II, 6117
Straus, Oscar S., III, 7176
Straus, Philip A., 7086
Straus, Sandor, 508
Straus, Zahava, 5414
Strausburg, Ginny, 7604
Strauss & Co., Levi, 1203
Strauss, Barbara Bachmann, 5587
Strauss, Benjamin, 8464
Strauss, Diana, 9020
Strauss, Ernst, 7087
Strauss, Jerome F., III, 7333
Strauss, Lee J., Jr., 1072
Strauss, Leon, 1202
Strauss, Maurice L., 8464
Strauss, Mildred B., 5548
Strauss, Peter, 670
Strauss, Renato, 7087
Strauss, Richard C., 9004
Strauss, Robert Perry, 8464
Strauss, Thomas W., 5587, 7185
Strausser, Nancy, 671
Stravitz, Richard Todd, 5678
Stravolemos, Jill, 1358
Straw, Nancy, 4723
Strawbridge Foundation, Margaret Dorrance, 8465, 8466
Strawbridge, George, Jr., 8465
Strawbridge, Marie S., 7769
Strawbridge, Nina S., 8465
Strawbridge, Robin, 518

Strawn, Kathryn A., 7745
Strawsburg, Jon, 7818
Strawsburg, Stephen R., 7459
Strayer University Educational Foundation, 1887
Strayer, Laurie, 1776
Strayer, Stephen, 7637
Straz, Catherine Lowry, 1948
Straz, David A., Jr., 2254
Strear Farms Co., Inc., 1461
Strear, Irma, 1461
Strear, Leonard, 1461
Stredde, Sharon, 2680
Streep, Mary B. Simon, 6987
Street, David, 9530
Street, Fay, 9530
Street, James E., 1403
Street, Jerry O., 8934
Street, Joe, 8758
Street, Nicholas, 9530
Street, Stephanie H., 8934
Streeter, Bill, 4866
Streeter, Mary Alice, 7897
Streeter, Stephanie A., 9752
Streiff, David, 761
Streim, Edward, 5745
Streim, Lynn, 5744, 5745
Streinger, Peter, 1483
Streisand, Barbra, 1204
Strelsin, Dorothy, 7088
Stremlau, Carolyn, 1769
Stremler, Barbara, 4310
Streng, William P., 9007
Strey, Keith, 9861
Stribling, Elizabeth, 6780
Stribling, Jera G., 17
Stricker, Ruth Ann, 4731
Strickland, Carol A., 7180
Strickland, James T., 7486
Strickland, Neil, 26
Strickland, R. Michael, 2196
Stricof, Richard J., 6978
Stride Rite Charitable Foundation, Inc., The, 4172
Stride Rite Corp., The, 4171, 4172
Stride Rite Philanthropic Foundation, The, 4171
Stried, Amy W., 4725
Striegel, L. Eugene, 2632
Strietmann, William H., 7573
Strimbu, William J., 8438
Stringer, Edward, 4498
Stringer, Howard L., 8662
Stringer, Howard, Sir, 7040
Stringer, Sherry, 160
Striplin, Albert, 20
Stripling, T. Wyatt, 9247
Strmecki, Marin J., 1632
Strmiska, Kenneth D., 9810
Strnad, Audrey, 9930
Strobl, Amy, 9730
Stroble, Jim, 7570
Strode, Mark, 8508
Strode, Scott, 8508
Stroh, Debra Tawney, 9636
Stroh, Sharon E., 3241
Stroh, Vivian Day, 4254
Stroker, Kathy S., 2261
Strom, Lee D., 432
Strom, Ronald A., 7496
Stromberg, Burle U., 9499
Stromberg, C.W., 138, 9345
Stromberg, Jean G., 671
Stromberg, Richard, 9345
Strong, Bente, 1851
Strong, Caroline, 5365
Strong, Greg, 4677
Strong, Hattie M., 1851
Strong, Henry, 1851
Strong, Henry L., 1851
Strong, John D., Jr., 7925
Strong, John O., 661
Strong, Jonathan, 4017
Strong, L. Corrin, 1851

Strong, Laurel Durst, 5895
Strong, Maurice, 6389
Strong, Robert A., 3525
Strong, Ted, 4636
Strong, Wendi E., 9245
Strosacker, Charles J., 4450
Strote, Bert, 7891
Strother, Haas, 74
Strother, Jack W., Jr., 3420
Stroucken, Al, 4567
Stroud, Joan M., 1757
Stroud, John B., 9089
Stroud, Morris W., 1757
Stroud, Stephen, 1757
Stroud, W.B. Dixon, 1757
Stroup, Keegan, 9371
Stroup, Paul A., 7499
Stroup, Paul A., III, 7418
Strouse, Evelyn P., 4137
Strouse, Robert H., 8093
Strouss Trust, Mildred V., 1205
Strowd, Irene H., 7488
Struble, Mary Catherine L., 43
Strudwick, Phoebe Shelby, 179
Strueber, M., 8150
Struif, L. James, 2911
Strumpf, Linda B., 5970
Strunk, Albert L., 5368
Strunk, Amy Adams, 9230
Struthers, Harvey J., Jr., 7039
Struthers, Richard K., 1758
Struthers, Sharon M., 1758
Struve, Roger, 3333
Struyk, Robert J., 4617
Strycker, Dean, Dr., 3131
Stryer, Lubert, 4616
Stryker, Jon L., 4223, 4465
Stryker, Linda, 6204
Stryker, Mark, 8747
Stryker, Pat, 1345
Stryker, Ronda E., 4352, 4451
Stuart Trust, Helen G., 9943
Stuart, Alexander D., 3028
Stuart, Brett Fullerton, 1207
Stuart, Bruce F., 1208
Stuart, Connie Bond, 1700
Stuart, Douglas F., 1208
Stuart, Dwight L., 1208
Stuart, Dwight L., Jr., 1206, 1208
Stuart, E. Hadley, Jr., 1206
Stuart, Elbridge A., 1206
Stuart, Elbridge H., 1206
Stuart, Elbridge H., III, 1206
Stuart, Frances Langford, 2102
Stuart, George B., 8468
Stuart, John, 5074
Stuart, Lisa G., 7090
Stuart, Marion Butler, 1207
Stuart, Mary H., 1206
Stuart, Nan M., 1207
Stuart, Paula, 5343
Stuart, Racheal, 5098
Stuart, Robert D., Jr., 3028
Stuart, Scott M., 7090
Stuart, William W., 1208
Stubbing, Holly K. Welch, 7370
Stubbins, Brent A, 7743
Stubbs, Amber, 8020
Stubing, William C., 6103
Stuchell, Harry, 9583
Stuckeman, H. Campbell, 8408
Stucky, Cathy, 3095
Stucky, Wes, 7931
Stude, Herman L., 8799
Stude, M.S., 8799
Studebaker, Stacy, 79
Studley, Julien J., 7091
Stuenkel, Art, 7344
Stuermer, Amanda, 5472
Stuewer, S.K., 8889
Stuit, Thomas, 5026
Stukey, Rachel L., 7722
Stull, Ann, 1129
Stull, Ann R., 1129

Stull, Roger C., 1129
Stuller, Catharine O., 3510
Stuller, Matthew G., 3510
Stulman, Leonard, 3739
Stulsaft Testamentary Trust, Morris, The, 1210
Stumne, Deb, 4560
Stump, MaryAnn, 4521
Stumpp, Charles F., Jr., 7627
Stupp Bridge Co., 4910
Stupp Bros. Bridge & Iron Co., 4910
Stupp, John P., Jr., 4910
Stupp, Norman J., 4911
Stupp, Robert P., 4910
Stupski, Joyce L., 1211
Stupski, Lawrence J., 1211
Sturgeon, Barry M., 3531
Sturges, Caren V., 7684
Sturges, Carrie Trammell, 8906
Sturges, Jennifer, 3138
Sturgis, Christine, 178, 9216
Sturgis, Ellen D., 4710
Sturgis, Roy, 178
Sturm, Brad, 9845
Sturm, Carren, 3269
Sturm, David, 4834
Sturm, Donald L., 1462
Sturm, Roland, 5069
Sturm, Susan M., 1462
Sturm, Terri, 5069
Sturz, Herbert, 6665
Stutt, Carolyn, 5711
Stutt, David S., 5711
Stutt, William C., 5711
Stutts, Mary, 561, 562
Styberg, Bernice M., 9906, 9944
Styberg, E.C., Jr., 9944
Styslinger, Lee J., III, 4
Styslinger, Lee J., Jr., 4
Styza, Bryce P., 9960
Stzurma, Paula, 6570
Su'a, Kelly M., 468
Suares, Rahamin "Rocky", 232
Suarez, Rocio, 5594
Sub-Zero Freezer Co., Inc., 9945
Subaru of America, Inc., 5415
Subotnick, Stuart, 3663, 6970
Subramaniam, Shivan S., 8537
Suburban Communities, LLC, 4342
Suchomel, Frank, Jr., 1760
Sudakoff Trust, Harry and Ruth, The, 2255
Sudakoff, Harry, 2255
Sudakoff, Roberta L., 2256
Sudakoff, Ruth, 2255
Suddath, Michael O., 1851
Sudders, Marylou, 4061
Sudderth, Leisa, 2002
Sudderth, Robert J., Jr., 8644
Sudikoff, Jeffrey, 1212
Sudikoff, Joan, 1212
Sudikoff, Joyce, 1212
Sudler, Claire, 5416
Sudler, Claire E., 5416
Sudler, Peter, 5416
Sudler, Samuel, 5416
Suetens-Bourgeois, Greta, Baroness, 5973
Sugar Creek Baptist Church, 9161
Sugarman, Jay, 7092
Sugarman, Kelly, 7092
Sugg, Joy, 183
Suggs, Carol Wilson, 3511
Suggs, David Gray, 8588
Suggs, Thomas E., 8577
Sugiura, Yasuyuki, 6560
Suglia, John, 5523
Suhowatsky, Stephen J., 5785
Suits, Brenda L., 7310
Sukke, Paul, 4723
Sukup, Charles, 3336
Sukup, Eugene, 3336
Sukup, Mary, 3336
Sukup, Steven, 3336

Sullick, Richard M., 6721
Sullivan & Cromwell LLP, 7093
Sullivan Properties, Inc, 4967
Sullivan Voss, Sheila, 4900
Sullivan, Algernon Sydney, Mrs., 4766
Sullivan, Barry M., 8090
Sullivan, Brian, 8470
Sullivan, Brian C., 2718
Sullivan, Carrie E., 2718
Sullivan, Charlene, 3188
Sullivan, Charles, 3396
Sullivan, Chris, 7174
Sullivan, D. Harold, 3878, 3879
Sullivan, Daniel, 1087
Sullivan, Daniel J., Jr., 7094, 8558
Sullivan, David, III, 1504
Sullivan, Dennis G., 5360
Sullivan, Dorothy G., 198
Sullivan, Edward, 4124
Sullivan, Elizabeth C., 4367
Sullivan, Frank C., 7576
Sullivan, George Hammond, 4766
Sullivan, Glory L., 2257
Sullivan, Jack, 9885
Sullivan, Jacqueline, 3396
Sullivan, James, 711, 2677, 7445
Sullivan, James F., Sr., 6078
Sullivan, Jane C., 7345
Sullivan, Jay, 3037
Sullivan, Jeremiah M., 7793
Sullivan, John, 4534
Sullivan, John J., Jr., 4912
Sullivan, John, Mrs., 3915
Sullivan, Joseph, 8570
Sullivan, Joseph M., Bishop, 6637
Sullivan, Judy, 4968
Sullivan, Kathleen, 5091
Sullivan, Kathryn, 9623
Sullivan, Lawrence E., 4297
Sullivan, Louis W., 4319
Sullivan, Marjorie O., 7094
Sullivan, Mark, 1571
Sullivan, Mark E., 3810
Sullivan, Marsha Joy, 6276
Sullivan, Martin, 7040
Sullivan, Martin J., 5529
Sullivan, Mary P., 4269
Sullivan, Mary Sneden, 4269
Sullivan, Michael, 6276, 6448
Sullivan, Michael D., 6834
Sullivan, Michael F., 4611, 4639
Sullivan, Michael L., 4943
Sullivan, Michelle, 9991
Sullivan, Monica F., 3118
Sullivan, Patti M., 4754
Sullivan, Paul, 1945
Sullivan, Pauline Allen Gill, 8919
Sullivan, Peggy, 9923
Sullivan, Peter B., 6964
Sullivan, Ray H., 1655
Sullivan, Richard J., 5199
Sullivan, Sallie, 7800
Sullivan, Sallie P., 7800
Sullivan, Silva, 8004
Sullivan, Susan, 3369
Sullivan, T. Dennis, 6103
Sullivan, Terence C., 8885
Sullivan, Thomas F., Jr., 2257
Sullivan, Thomas F.P., 2257
Sullivan, Timothy, 3396
Sullivan, Virginia M., 4400
Sullivan, W.T., 3218
Sullivan, William P., 3563
Sulpizio, Maria G., 846
Sulpizio, Richard, 846
Sulsona, Judy, 401
Sultzbach, Don A., 7536
Sulzberger, Arthur Hays, 7095
Sulzberger, Arthur Ochs, 7095
Sulzberger, Cathy J., 6620
Sulzberger, Iphigene Ochs, 7095
Sulzberger, Judith P., 7095
Sulzer, Deborah M., 3482
Sumansky, Walt, 8449

Sumida, Sheila M., 2542
Sumitomo, 7436
Sumitomo Bank Capital Markets, Inc., 7005
Sumitomo Corporation of America "SCOA", 7096
Summe, Gregory L., 4077
Summer Assocs., 7015
Summer Prize Fruit Co., 1168
Summerell, Lucy P., 9507
Summerfield, Esthel M., 3559
Summerfield, Solon E., 7097
Summerlin, James T., 47
Summers, Douglas J., 7099
Summers, Jayne C., 7099
Summers, John M., 7099
Summers, Kelly B., 7874
Summers, Mark H., 7874
Summers, Pamela A., 7874
Summers, William B., 7874
Summersett, Melodie Zamora, 9088
Summey, M.L., 7486
Summit Fund, LLC, The, 9530
Sumner, Elizabeth N., 7342
Sumner, Ernest W., 7342
Sumney, Larry W., 7470
Sumter, Geraldine, 7370
Sun Lakes Marketing LP, 135
Sun Microsystems, Inc., 1214
Sun Valley Center, 1060
Sun, David, 1213
Sun, Diana, 1213
Sun, Vincent, 1010
Sunbeam Development Corp., 1877
Sunbeam Properties, Inc., 1877
Sunbeam Television Corp., 1877
Sunday, C.W., 9072
Sundberg, Susanne, 628
Sundean, Edith P., 1215
Sundean, Harold A., 1215
Sunderland, Charles, 3397
Sunderland, James P., 3397
Sunderland, Kent, 3397
Sunderland, L.D., 3397
Sunderland, Lester T., 3397
Sunderland, Pamela S., 7603
Sunderland, Paul, 3397
Sunderland, W.J., 3397
Sundet, Lee, 4694
Sundet, Leland N., 4694
Sundet, Louise C., 4694
Sundet, Sam, 9885
Sundgren, Donald E., 1221
Sundheim, Jeffrey J., 6023
Sundlass, Satinder, 9810
Sundquist, David, 9646
Sundquist, Diane Y., 9646
Sundquist, Kristi, 9646
Sundquist, Kristina M., 9646
Sundquist, Larry J., 9646
Sundquist, Nathan, 9646
Sundram, Clarence J., 7191
Suniville, Thomas, 798
Sunnen Products Company, 4913
Sunnen, Joseph, 4913
Sunrise Apartments LLC, 5736
Sunrise Venture LLC, 7102
Sunset Hills Assn., 4409
SunTrust Bank, 1847, 1879, 1910, 1964, 1969, 2031, 2046, 2069, 2125, 2134, 2170, 2232, 2237, 2259, 2261, 2266, 2277
Suntrust Bank, 2279
SunTrust Bank, 2331, 2338, 2339, 2349, 2356, 2378, 2404, 2420, 2431, 2442, 2456, 2463, 2468, 2496, 2500, 2506, 2507, 2524, 7491, 7508, 8680, 8691, 8702, 8718, 9463, 9498, 9523, 9526
SunTrust Bank of Augusta, N.A., 2369
SunTrust Bank, Atlanta, 2496
SunTrust Banks, Inc., 2496, 4789
Superior Ready Mix Concrete, LP, 1197
Superior Tube Co., 8283

Superpac, Inc., 8343
SUPERVALU INC., 4695
Supple, Cathy, 9067
Supplee, Henderson, III, 8395
Supra Alloys, 488
Surbaugh, William L., 3197
Surgala, M.J., 8469
Surma, John P., 8488
Surrey, Mary P., 5888
Surrey, Sara R., 5888
Suryanarayanan, C.S., 1203
Susik, W. Daniel, 2213
Suski, Richard, 1644
Susman, Ellen, 9220
Susman, Harry P., 9220
Susman, Louis, 3030
Susman, Louisa, 5197
Susman, Stephen D., 9220
Susquehanna Bank, 8208
Susquehanna Cable Co., 8471
Susquehanna Motel Corp., 6005
Susquehanna Pfaltzgraff Co., 8471
Susquehanna Radio Corp., 8471
Suss, Bernard, 6857
Sussman Family Foundation, The, 7104
Sussman, Arthur M., 2868
Sussman, Laurie Tisch, 7145
Sussman, Richard, 2181
Sussman, S. Donald, 7104
Susswein, Philip M., 5843
Suter, Albert E., 4896
Sutherland, J. Mark, 7725
Sutland, Frank, 3640
Sutro, Marina Johnson, 1679
Sutter, Fred A., 4573
Sutter, Marion, 7593
Suttle, Jay Linton, 7356
Sutton Family Foundation, Jane & Sam, 5554
Sutton Fund, Joseph and Eileen, Inc., 7107
Sutton Sales Corp., E.S., 5420
Sutton Warehousing, Inc., 5420
Sutton, Albert, 7106
Sutton, Albert J., 5420, 7107
Sutton, Bob, 8631
Sutton, Celia, 7108
Sutton, Dianna, 1949
Sutton, Donald C., 7891
Sutton, Donald R., 7638
Sutton, E.S., Inc., 5420
Sutton, Eileen, 5420, 7107
Sutton, Elliot, 7106
Sutton, Howard G., 9135
Sutton, Isaac, 7106, 7108
Sutton, Jack, 7109
Sutton, Jack A., 7109
Sutton, Joseph, 5420, 7107
Sutton, Karen A., 2226
Sutton, Marion Mulligan, 7593
Sutton, Mark, 5433
Sutton, Morris, 7106
Sutton, Percy, 7157
Sutton, Rusty, 4986
Sutton, Solomon A., 7109
Sutton, Thomas C., 970
Sutton, Zook, Hon., 941, 1099
Suzman, Ruth, 9297
Suzor, Sandra Scott, 9991
Suzor, Sandy, 4937
Sveen, David E., 2705
Sveen, Donald E., 2705
Sveen, Marjorie L., 2705
Svendsen, John, 4452
Svensson, Karin, 1093
Svizeny, Susanne, 8494
Svoboda, John A., 3016
Swager, Duane, II, 8107
Swaim, Doris, 8082
Swain, Judith L., 7333
Swain, Kristin A., 5794
Swain, Laura Taylor, Hon., 6156
Swain, Malcolm T., 7884
Swain, Phil, 3255

Swalling, J.C. "Chris", 78
Swallow, John D. "Jack", 9117
Swalm, Beth, 9299
Swalm, D. Clark, Jr., 2258
Swalm, D. Clarke, 2258
Swalm, Dave, 9299
Swalm, Nicole B., 2258
Swamp, Karl, 4593
Swan Manufacturing Co., 7618
Swan, Ann, 5958
Swan, Barbara, 9742
Swan, E. James, 4233
Swan, Edward M., Jr., 3961
Swan, Philip V., 527, 991
Swan, William C., 4200
Swaney, Chuck, 7866
Swaney, Nancy C., 5751
Swaney, Richard G., 5751
Swaney, William C., 5751
Swanke, Patricia, 7653
Swann, James T., 1986
Swann, Melvin C., Jr., 7343
Swanson Charitable Remainder Unitrust, 1217
Swanson, Alexis, 4914
Swanson, Dean C., 2458
Swanson, Dennis, 1505
Swanson, E. William, 639
Swanson, Earl, 6298
Swanson, Eleanor K., 4554
Swanson, Elizabeth, 4914
Swanson, Frances L., 3252
Swanson, Jill, 9745
Swanson, John W., II, 4252
Swanson, Judy C., 1217
Swanson, Leoda, 4696
Swanson, Linda V., III, 6009
Swanson, Lynwood W., 9644
Swanson, Marti, 3247
Swanson, Mat, 3215
Swanson, Nancy K., 7574
Swanson, Robert, Rev., 8153
Swanson, Susan E., 1216
Swanson, Tami, 9346
Swanson, Vernon H., 9848
Swanson, W. Charles, 9346
Swanson, W. Clarke, Jr., 4914
Swanson, W.C., 9346
Swantek, Sandra, 2623
Swantz, Richard, 9845
Swart, Nancy, 1937
Swartz, James R., 7111
Swartz, Jerome, 7112
Swartz, Joan, 4649
Swartz, Judith W., 4175
Swartz, Lee A., 4891
Swartz, Lonnie, 4643
Swartz, MaryPat, 1830
Swartz, Sidney W., 4175
Swarzman, Howard, 6614
Swearer, John B., 3368
Sweasy, William J., 4663
Sweat, Carol G., 8914
Sweatt, Blaine, III, 1960
Sweeney, Aileen, 854
Sweeney, Eileen, 2906
Sweeney, G.T., 5807
Sweeney, John J., III, 8419
Sweeney, Kevin M., 1599
Sweeney, Lois Irene, 941
Sweeney, Michelle, 7866
Sweeney, Paul, 8098
Sweeney, Randall J., 5738
Sweeney, Robert F., 1404
Sweeney, Thomas J., 5887, 6728, 7411, 7412, 7413
Sweeney, Thomas R., 826
Sweeney, Tom, 6937
Sweeny, Jack C., 9228
Sweet, Adele Hall, 1750
Sweet, Ann, 5087
Sweet, Frederic H., 9884
Sweet, George P., 3116
Sweet, Howard A., 9807

Sweet, Jane, 5899
Sweet, John H.K., 5278
Sweet, John W., 8013
Sweet, Kimberly Noel, 4737
Sweet, Patricia, 7898
Sweet, Robert D., 8153
Sweet, Stedman G., 1518
Sweet, William R., 5278
Sweetbriar Syndicate, 4980
Sweetman, Mary Pat, 8630
Sweetnam, James E., 7617
Sweets Co. of America, Inc., The, 4117
Swegler, Jeffrey F., 4177
Sweig, Michael, 5070
Sweigart Irrevocable Trust, Anne B., 8120
Sweitzer, Susan, 1537
Swennen, Bert, 7436
Swenson, Erik, 2128
Swenson, James I., 1218
Swenson, James R., 5245
Swenson, Judy P., 9677
Swenson, Susan G., 1218
Swensrud, Anthony S., 4177
Swensrud, Leslie R., 4177
Swensrud, S. Blake, II, 4177
Swensrud, Stephen B., 4177
Swensson, Macy D., 8699
Swetman, Chevis, 4745
Swett, Daniel R., 478
Swett, Eileen, 9221
Swett, Jeffrey, 9221
Swett, Michael, 9221
Swett, Ralph, 9221
Swett, Timothy, 9221
Swewczul, Krzysztof, 2870
Swezey, Carroll M., Jr., 6342
Swezey, John, 6342
Swezey, Nancy, 6342
Swidler, Alisa Feinstein, 5147
Swieczkowski, Julie Case, 4428
Swienton, Gregory T., 2213
Swier, Richard, 1946
Swift, Carl, 3241
Swift, James L., 1233
Swift, John, 1219
Swift, John F., 1233
Swift, Kirsten, 1219
Swift, Peter D., 1233
Swift, Sara Taylor, 1464
Swig, Benjamin H., 1220
Swig, Kent, 1220, 6779
Swigert, Ernest C., 8061
Swigert, Henry T., 8061
Swiggett, James E., 6859
Swim, Katherine, 9301, 9324
Swim, Lauralyn B., 9301, 9324
Swim, Roger C., 9301
Swindells, Ann, 8062
Swindells, Charles, 8062
Swindells, William, 8062
Swindells, William R., 8062
Swinden, James I., 1160
Swindle, Jack E., 9232
Swindle, P.W., 7987
Swindle, Patricia Warren, 7987
Swindle, Stephen D., 9979
Swinehart, Dane, 7622
Swinerton Inc., 1221
Swinford, Troy, 2678
Swink, Henry, 8571
Swink, Mark, 1911
Swinney, Edward F., 9222
Swinney, Jim, 3122
Swinney, R. Andrew, 8378
Swisher, Charles, 1843
Swistock, James, 8136
Switz, Robert E., 4496
Switzer, Mark, 3557
Switzer, Patricia, 3557
Switzer, Patricia D., 3557
Switzer, Paula M., 4338
Switzer, Peter, 3557
Switzer, Robert, 3557

Swoboda, Frank, 1776
Swope, Marie, 3259
Swope, Philip S., 7897
Swope, W. Chandler, 9733
Sword, Leslie Lewis, 6416
SYB, Inc., 11
Sydney, Kristen J., 7759
Sydney, Sharon Benenson, 5619
Sykes, Donald M., 5349
Sykes, Frances P., 5349
Sykes, Gene T., 7115
Sykes, James W., Jr., 6104
Sykes, John H., 2261
Sykes, Ron, 7775
Sykes, Stella Gray Bryant, 4737
Sykes, Susan, 2261
Sykes, Susan W., 2261
Sykes, Tiernan E., 5349
Sylia, Casey J., 2588
Sylvan Learning Systems, Inc., 3741
Sylvan, Barbara, 7981
Sylvan, Dave R., 7981
Sylvester, Dan, 7770
Sylvia, Michelle, 1990
Symington, Ann H., 1761
Symington, Stuart, Jr., 4783
Symmes, F.W., 7492
Symonik, Beverly, 1022
Syms, Sy, 5422
Symson, Adam, 7848
Synder, Mary Grace, 8177
Synopsys Technology Education Opportunity Foundation, 1222
Synopsys, Inc., 1223
Synovec, Mark, 3400
Synovus Financial Corp., 2497
Sypher, Eleanor K., 7191
Syrmis, Pamela Lee, 6241
Syrmis, Victor, 6241
Syron, Richard F., 9422
Syrvalin, Kristine C., 7789
Sytek, Donna, 5098
Sytman, Alex, 9675
Syvertsen, John, 2767
Szapary, Gladys, 865
Szatko, Kim, 4990
Szekely-Goode, Lynn, 828
Szemetylo, Kristy, 7770
Szews, Charles L., 9887
Szoka, Elizbieta, 9013
Szold, Myron, 2612
Szostak, M. Anne, 8551
Sztukowski, John A., 4861, 7738
Szucs, Liane M., 7574
Szwarc, Bernardo Pedro, 2659
Szymoniak, Elaine E., 3343

Tabah, Marie D., 7264
Tabak, Ronald J., 6998
Tabankin, Margery, 1050, 1204
Tabankin, Margery A., 1767
Taber, Richard E., 1541
Tablada, Marco, 7139
Tabler, Michael Rex, 9626, 9627
Tabor, Albert S., 9128
Tabor, Ann Irish, 4325
Tacha, Deanell Reece, Hon., 3372
Tada, Hiroshi, 6561
Tada, Joni Erickson, 9505
Tada, Jun, 6605
Tada, Pierre Y., 1264
Tadmor, David E., 5582
Tadros, Niveen, 1079
Taff, Reuvin, Rabbi, 1111
Taft, Dudley S., 7851
Taft, Ed, 3682
Taft, John, 4661
Taft, John E., 4173
Taft, Robert A., II, Mrs., 7851
Taggart, Richard J., 9703
Taguchi, Toshiaki, 7160
Tai & Co., J.T., 7118
Tai, Jun Tsei, Inc., 7118

Tair, Ltd., 8947
Taisey, Robert D., 6258
Taishoff, Lawrence B., 2262
Taishoff, Randall P., 2262
Taishoff, Robert P., 2262
Taishoff, Ruth S., 6900
Tait, Frank M., 7875
Tait, Frank M., Mrs., 7875
Tajima, Yoshihiro, 7120
Tajiri, Rea, 6604
Takahaski, Masahiro, Rev., 5685
Takaki, Donald M., 2535
Takanishi, Ruby, 5971
Takatsuji, Norio, 5685
Take 2 Interactive, 7174
Takenaka, Touichi, 2602
Taketa, Kelvin H., 2545
Takian, John, Jr., 8556
Takiff, Bobette, 3032
Takiff, Sanford, 3032
Takton, Marjorie J., 9773
Takuma, Takeo, 7185
Tal, Jacob, 546
Talamantes, Pat, 4691
Talberth, Charlotte, 5486
Talbot, C.G., 7807
Talbot, Melanie, 7449
Talbot, Nancy F., 2706
Talbot, Tommy, 3512
Talbots, Inc., The, 4178
Taleff, Lynne, 4747
Tallant, Larry, 8608
Tallarigo, Lorenzo, 3192, 3193
Tallent, Charles, 5565
Tallent, Michael, 8152
Talley, Chris L., 3157
Talley, Wilson K., 670
Tallon, James R., Jr., 5779
Talltimber, 3683
Tally, Richard, 1471
Tamaki, Meriko, 9695
Tamarind Foundation, The, 6043
Tamayo, Abe, 4962
Tamba, Shoichi, 4982
Tambakeras, Markos I., 8284
Tambellini, Robert G., 4246
Tamer Restated Living Trust, James, 4453
Tamer, James, 4453
Tamko Asphalt Products, Inc., 4800
Tamsberg, Joseph L., Jr., 8581
Tamura, Toshinari, 2602
Tanabe, Barbara J., 2535
Tanaka Ikubikai Educational Corp., 7120
Tanaka, Kenji, 7120
Tanaka, Kimiko, 7120
Tanaka, Makiko, 7120
Tanaka, Taeko, 7120
Tanakeyowma, Lilia M., 661
Tanchum, Letty, 3077
Tancredi, Robert, 2166
Tandon, Chandrika, 7121
Tandon, Ranjan, 7121
Tandy, Anne Burnett, 8801
Tandy, Daniel W., 6619
Tanenbaum, Charles J., 6260
Tanenbaum, Marla L., 3675
Tanenbaum, Robert K., 3675
Tang Industries, Inc., 5072
Tang, Cyrus, 5072
Tang, Donald, 5071
Tang, Jane Y., 5423
Tang, Michael, 5072
Tang, Oscar, 1468
Tang, Oscar L., 7122
Tang, Patricia, 5500
Tang, Tom Y.C., 5423
Tang, Tracy L., 7122
Tang, Zhen Jean, 5071
Tangeman, Carolyn S., 3175
Tangeman, John T., 3175
Taniguchi, Barry K., 2545
Tank, David, 4616
Tank, William M., 3337

Tankenoff, Gary L., 4696
Tankenoff, Marsha J., 4696
Tankenoff, Scott M., 4696
Tankersley, Billy, 9171
Tankersley, Joan N., 4403
Tankersley, Rayburn H., 8739
Tannenbaum, Allison Atlas, 241
Tannenbaum, David, 241
Tannenbaum, Jeanne L., 7493
Tannenbaum, Leah Louise B., 7493
Tannenbaum, Nancy B., 7493
Tannenbaum, Sigmund I., 7493
Tannenbaum, Susan M., 7493
Tanner, David, 6758
Tanner, David A., 6626
Tanner, Estelle, 6626
Tanner, Estelle "Nicki" Newman, 6613
Tanner, Estelle Newman, 6626
Tanner, Harold, 6626, 6789
Tanner, James M., 6626
Tanner, K.S., Jr., 7486
Tanner, Kim, 8971
Tanner, L. Gene, 3216
Tanner, Laurence A., 1482
Tanner, Mary, 8660
Tanner, Michael S., 7346
Tanner, Obert C., 9347
Tanner, Robin C., 1851
Tannir, Tehmina, 200
Tanoue, Donna A., 2535
Tanribilir, Kevin, 8135
Tanselle, G. Thomas, 6119
Tansey, Andrew, 5631
Tansey, Elsa, 8944
Tansey, Linda, 421
Tansik, Linda, 93
Tantlinger, Irvin, 8155
Taper, S. Mark, 1226
Taplin, Jack G., 2264
Taplin, Martin W., 2264
Taplin, Sheila Elias, 2264
Tapp, Frances Carr, 8870
Tapp-Sanders, Marcia, 3125
Taradash, Bernard A.G., 3934
Tarbel, Swannie Zink, 7994
Tarbet, G. Stephen, 9335
Target Corp., 4697
Tarica, Mark, 212
Taricani, Dolores A., 8136
Tarnoff, Jerome, 6419
Tarnopol, Lynne, 7123
Tarnopol, Michael, 7123
Tarola, Jeffrey, 616
Tarola, Robert M., 3638
Taroni, John C., 5584
Tarr, Jeff C., 6256
Tarr, Jeff, Jr., 6256
Tarr, Jennifer, 6256
Tarr, Patricia G., 6256
Tarrant, Amy E., 2265
Tarrant, Brian, 2265
Tarrant, Jeremiah, 2265
Tarrant, Richard E., Jr., 2265
Tarta, Joy, 8305
Tartan Partners, LP, 1370
Tartar, Joy, 8077, 8304
Tartikoff, Lilly, 1251
Tartt, Hope Pierce, 9224
Tarumi, Hiroyuki, 6560
Tarver, Sarah Thompson, 8723
Tarwater, Janet L., 7662
Tasaki, Akira, 9476
Tash, Paul, 2245
Tashjian, Adrienne V., 7171
Tashman, Hal, 87
Task, Robert, 5646
Tassot, Beatrice, 5110
Tatar, Jerome F., 7603
Tatar, Myrna, 7871
Tatar, Steven, 7834
Tate, Bryan K., 8511
Tate, Charles W., 9225
Tate, Gail, 1456
Tate, Harry B., 7969

Tate, J. Kenneth, 1941
Tate, Judy Spence, 9225
Tate, Kerry, 8768
Tate, Linda Crowe, 2690
Tate, Lloyd P., Jr., 7458
Tate, Penfield, 1364
Tate, William A., 27
Tate, Zachary Reynolds, 3583
Tatel, David S., 359
Tatlock, Anne M., 3654, 5326, 6525, 7126
Tattersall, Fred T., 9402
Tatum, Alan J.W., 2266
Tatum, Linda L., 805
Tatum, Nenetta Carter, 8817
Taub, Arlene, 5425
Taub, Henry, 4071, 5424, 5582
Taub, Henry J.N., 9289
Taub, Henry J.N., II, 9289
Taub, Ira, 5424
Taub, Joseph, 5425
Taub, Marilyn, 5424
Taub, Steven, 5424
Taube, Dianne M., 1228
Taube, Richard A., 970
Taube, Tad, 774, 775
Taube, Thaddeus N., 1228
Tauber, Alfred I., 3742
Tauber, Benjamin Brian, 4454
Tauber, Channa, 5302
Tauber, Chaya Shaindy, 6958
Tauber, Ingrid D., 3742
Tauber, Joel D., 4454
Tauber, Laszlo N., 3742
Tauber, Ron, 6300
Tauber, Ronald S., 6297
Tauber, Shelley J., 4454
Tauber, Stuart, 5126
Taubman, A. Alfred, 4455
Taubman, Eugenia L., 9524
Taubman, Nicholas F., 9524
Taubman, Robert S., 4438
Tauck, Arthur C., 1657
Tauck, Arthur C., Jr., 1657
Tauke, Thomas J., 5439
Taunton, Michael J., 6320
Taunton, Peggy, 2345
Taurel, Sidney, 3192, 3193
Tauscher, Shehla, 4525
Tausig, Eva-Maria, 5974
Tavares, Jose, 6156, 7096
Taves, Kurt W., 9498
Tavitian, Assadour, 5426
Tavlin, Michael J., 5018
Tawil Foundation, Ralph, 5554
Tawney, Robin, 4935
Tayloe, Edward D., II, 9495
Taylor Char. Trust, Elizabeth, 3042
Taylor Charitable Lead Trust, Galen D., 2267
Taylor Corp., 4698
Taylor Development Corp., 2269
Taylor Energy Co., 3511
Taylor Estates, Inc., 6879
Taylor Group, Inc., The, 4767
Taylor Irrevocable Trust, Charles M., 179
Taylor, Albert, 4251
Taylor, Albert J., 9498
Taylor, Alexander S., 8474
Taylor, Alexander S., II, 7548
Taylor, Andrew C., 4810, 4916
Taylor, Angela, 3108
Taylor, Anna Diggs, Hon., 4254
Taylor, Anne Coolidge, 5704
Taylor, Barbara Olin, 2722
Taylor, Benjamin, 4691
Taylor, Betsy, 3749, 6674
Taylor, Bruce C., 8661
Taylor, C. Fred, 5401
Taylor, Carl D., 7464
Taylor, Caroline E., 8473
Taylor, Catherine H., 9947
Taylor, Charles, 7533
Taylor, Cheryl K., 3149

Taylor, Christine, 6716
Taylor, Clifford A., Jr., 8841
Taylor, Connie, 5419
Taylor, D., 5048
Taylor, Daniel J., 3399
Taylor, Daniel J., Jr., 3399
Taylor, Danny, 9280
Taylor, David, 4144
Taylor, David H., 5833
Taylor, Dawn, 3281
Taylor, Douglas F., 5833
Taylor, Edward C., 5419
Taylor, Edward N., 5419
Taylor, Elizabeth, 2269
Taylor, Emma Scott, 9513
Taylor, Eric, 1023
Taylor, F. Morgan, Jr., 2722
Taylor, Fran, 3432
Taylor, Fred, 1364
Taylor, Fred C., 9948
Taylor, Frederick B., 7798
Taylor, Frederick M., III, 2722
Taylor, Galen D., 2267
Taylor, Gary, 3474
Taylor, George, 7345
Taylor, Gerald, 2267
Taylor, Glen, 4698
Taylor, Glenn, 27
Taylor, Gregory, 2482
Taylor, Gwendolyn, 4737
Taylor, Harold, 8786
Taylor, Humphrey, 6379
Taylor, J.M. Bryan, 7414
Taylor, J.P., 9151
Taylor, Jack, 2269
Taylor, Jack C., 4810, 4916
Taylor, Jacqueline M., 6901
Taylor, James, 1946, 3188
Taylor, James B., 2372
Taylor, James C., 1464
Taylor, James W., 2722
Taylor, Janet C., 3771
Taylor, Jean, 4698
Taylor, Jeff, 954
Taylor, Jerry, 4866
Taylor, Joe E., Jr., 8577
Taylor, John, 7414
Taylor, John N., Jr., 2156
Taylor, John R., 5327, 8243
Taylor, Julia Joan, 179
Taylor, Julie Johns, 5482
Taylor, Justin, 4551
Taylor, Karen, 2261
Taylor, Karen D., 9144
Taylor, Kathleen Baer, 3399
Taylor, Kenneth H., Jr., 8473
Taylor, Kenneth N., 3042
Taylor, Kenneth, Hon., 6117
Taylor, Kris, 9571
Taylor, Kris J., 4557
Taylor, L. Graig, 9321
Taylor, L.F., Maj. Gen., 3511
Taylor, Lance, 175
Taylor, Larry, 4698
Taylor, Laurie H., 7345
Taylor, Lois, 3833
Taylor, Louis H., 3599
Taylor, Lyn, 1023
Taylor, Margaret, 4745
Taylor, Margaret L., 845
Taylor, Margaret W., 3042
Taylor, Mark D., 3042
Taylor, Mary F., 7593
Taylor, Maura, 4798
Taylor, Maxine, 717
Taylor, Melody, Co-, 8653
Taylor, Milt, Jr., 7622
Taylor, Mitchell, 2269
Taylor, Nick R., 4945
Taylor, Penelope J., 1730
Taylor, Peter J., 570, 698
Taylor, Peter W., 3042
Taylor, Phillipa P., 1844
Taylor, Phyllis M., 3503, 3511

Taylor, Portia, 2015
Taylor, R. Bruce, 3845
Taylor, Rick B., 7819
Taylor, Rise, 3125
Taylor, Ritchey Nelson, 2268
Taylor, Robert, 9778
Taylor, Robert C., 9126
Taylor, Robert F., 9906
Taylor, Robert K., 321, 669
Taylor, Ronald R., 1040
Taylor, Ruthie, 8653
Taylor, Sandra, 9690
Taylor, Sharon C., 5360
Taylor, Shawn, 7414
Taylor, Sherril, 1505
Taylor, Sheryl, 9063
Taylor, Spencer O., 2722
Taylor, Steven W., 7970
Taylor, Stuart A., 7343
Taylor, Sue Ann, 8088
Taylor, Susan H., 1369
Taylor, Susanne, 3213
Taylor, Teresa Jane, 5858
Taylor, Terri, 4698
Taylor, Thomas A., 8518
Taylor, Tiffany, 2041
Taylor, Vernon F., Jr., 1464
Taylor, Virginia C., 5419
Taylor, W. Earl, 3145
Taylor, W.A., Jr., 4767
Taylor, W.L., 9531
Taylor, William, 8618
Taylor, William G., 8617
TBMC, Inc, 5773
TCF National Bank, 4699
TCF National Bank Minnesota, 4699
Tchang, Paul K., 1229
Tchang, Rose, 1229
Tchang, Theodore, 1229
Tchen, Christine M., 2728
TCIF Fund, 5749
TD Banknorth Inc., 3558
TD Banknorth Wealth Management Group, 6041
Teachers Foundation, 9660
Teaff, Bob, 8820
Teagle, Rowena Lee, 7126
Teagle, Walter C., 7126
Teagle, Walter C., III, 7126
Teagle, Walter C., Jr., 7126
Teague, L. Barry, 2339
Teal, Shawn, 4534
Teamer, Cheryl R., 3503
Teammates for Kids Foundation, 948
Tebbe, Elizabeth, 5867
Tebbe, Glenn, 3138
Techbilt Homes, Inc., 1229
TECO Energy, Inc., 2270
Tedesco, Francis J., 2349
Tee-Teas, LLC, 493
Teegardin, Tricia, 8863
Teel, Jim, 1230
Teel, Joyce, 1230
Teeter, Fred K., Jr., 3597
Teeuws, Leen, 1843
Tegman, Deyonne, 9622
Tehan, Jean C., 9777
Teich, Jerome, 6342
Teich, Priscilla S. Knapp, 6342
Teich, Tegin, 3850
Teicher, Florence E., 5934
Teicher, Milton S., 5934
Teichert & Son, A., Inc., 1231
Teichert, Fred, 1080
Teichert, Frederick A., 1231
Teichert, Inc., 1231
Teichert, Melita M., 1231
Teitel, Martin, 3840
Teitelbaum, Helene, 5527
Teitelbaum, Joshua, 5527
Tekippe, Ronald N., 3298
Tektronix, Inc., 8063
Tekulve, Cheryl A., 3112
Tekulve, Daniel R., 3112

Telfer, William, 7910
Tell, Anne P., 7876
Tell, Michael, 7876
Tellabs, Inc., 3034
Tellado, Marta L., 5970
Teller, Joseph, 2787
Telles, Cynthia, 345
Telles, Cynthia Ann, 346
Tellez, Cora M., 423
Tellez, Trinidad, 5088
Telliez, Jean-Luc, 5484
Tembreull, M.A., 9663
Tempero, Stephen, 3400
Temple, Arthur, III, 9227, 9228
Temple, Cassie L., 7982
Temple, Charlotte, 9227
Temple, David E., 7982
Temple, Diana Hastings, 7282
Temple, Diane E., 9525
Temple, Katherine S., 9227
Temple, L. Peter, 8141
Temple, Nancy L., 9525
Temple, Pamela Y., 8611
Temple, Paul N., 9525
Temple, Robin R., 9525
Temple, Thomas D., 9525
Temple-Inland Forest Products Corp., 9228
Temple-Inland Inc., 9228
Templeton Religious Trust, 8475
Templeton World Charity Foundation, 8475
Templeton, Coulter, 9054
Templeton, D. Jeffrey, 4210
Templeton, Esther, 3718
Templeton, Handly, 8475
Templeton, Herbert A., 8064
Templeton, Jennifer A., 8475
Templeton, John M., Jr., 8397
Templeton, John Marks, 8475
Templeton, John Marks, Jr., 8475
Templeton, John Marks, Sir, 8475
Templeton, Josephine J., 8397
Templeton, Mary, 7128
Templeton, Richard, 7128
Templin, Robert G., Jr., 1834
TEMTCO, 4767
Ten Pas, Paul H., 9840
Tenenbaum Co., A., Inc., 180
Tenenbaum Trust, Michael and Pola, 7129
Tenenbaum, Bert M., 2480
Tenenbaum, Bonnie, 1232
Tenenbaum, Harold, 180
Tenenbaum, J.M., 180
Tenenbaum, Jay M., 1232
Tenenbaum, Samuel J., 8577
Tenet Healthcare Corp., 9229
Teng, Fred, 5284, 6437
Tennant Co., 4700
Tennant, Russ, 9570
Tennant, T. Michael, 2356
Tennell, Lori, 3107
Tennen, Howard, 1529
Tennenbaum, Morris, 7129
Tennery, Frances E., 3626
Tennessee Football, Inc., 9230
Tennille, Jocelyn D., 2700
Tennison, Lee Lupton, 8798
Tennity Charitable Trust, Marilyn Smith Swift, 1233
Tennity, Marilyn Swift, 1233
Tenny, Barron M., 5970
Tensiltech Corp., 3683
Tenuta, Ralph J., 9833
Tenzer, David, 9430
Tepha, 3841
Tepner, Ronald, 8646
Tepper, Michael S., 2666
Tercek, Mark R., 770
Termeer, Henri A., 3922
Termondt, M. James, 2638, 2740, 9961
Ternan, Lawrence, 4256
Terni, Diane D., 8578

Terpstra, Lori J., 2582
Terra, Karen, 9977
Terracciano, Anthony, 8508
Terracina, Christopher, 3496
Terrazas, Alfredo, 474
Terre Haute Gas Corp., 3173
Terrell, Alan, 3215
Terrell, J.H., Jr., 2519
Terrell, Jacquelyn, 220
Terrell, Mona, 5255
Terrill, Marc B., 3568, 3636
Terrill, Thomas, 7174
Terry, Anne, 5322
Terry, C. Herman, 2271
Terry, Charles P., 3816
Terry, Charles R., Sr., 39
Terry, Evan R., 9334
Terry, Frederick A., 7232
Terry, Frederick A., Jr., 1831, 6190
Terry, Glen, 404
Terry, H.L., 9231
Terry, Howard L., 9231
Terry, James, 8583
Terry, Lisa, 3110
Terry, Mary Virginia, 2271
Terry, Nancy M., 9231
Terry, Scott, 8876
Terry, Wade, 217
Teruzzi, Lilliana, 7232
Terwilliger, J. Ronald, 2498
Terwilliger, Patricia B., 2498
Tesher, Robert, 2306
Tessler, Frances, 9977
Tetlak, Joseph F., 7877
Tetzner, Hermann, 1498
Teufel, Dawn, 9623
Tevlin, Beth A.A., 3250
Texaco Inc., 380
Texas Instruments Inc., 9232
Texas Pipe & Supply Co, Inc., 9162
Textile Benefit Assn., 2337
Textile From Europe, 5554
Textor, Donald F., 7131
Textor, Elaine R., 7131
Textron Inc., 8559
TFS Key Trust Donations, 7868
Thabit, Robert W., 7531
Thacher, Carter P., 233, 1305
Thacher, Gladys, 1088
Thacher, Mary Wilbur, 233
Thackson, Carroll, 9401
Thain, John A., 5560, 6619, 7116
Thaler, F. Roger, 9541
Thalheimer, Louis B., 3744
Thames, Judith G., 2303
Thanhouser, Sally P., 3618
Thanvi, Om, 3330
Thao, Yang Pao, 9778
Tharp, Linda, 8661
Tharpe, Lisa, 6028
Thatcher Irrevocable Trust, Mary, 2273
Thatcher, Gerald, 7891
Thatcher, John W., 2273
Thatcher, K. Blake, 2926
Thatcher, Mary W., 2273
Thaw, Clare E., 5499
Thaw, Clare Eddy, 5500
Thaw, Eugene V., 5499, 6505
Thaw, Eugene Victor, 5500
Thaw, Nicholas, 5500
Thaw, Nicholas E., 5499
Thawerbhoy, Nazim G., 707
Thayer, Brooks S., 3833
Thayer, Douglas, 3229
Thayer, Gladys Brooks, 5674
THC Business SVC, 904
The Indianapolis Foundation, 3164
The MONY Group, Inc., 5584
Theiler, Robert J., 4553, 4722
Theis, Joe, 873
Theobald, Jon A., 4519, 4583, 4671, 4703
Theobald, Patty, 1463
Theobold, Thomas C., 2868

Theofilactidis, Alexis, 6964
Theosophical Book Gift Institute, The, 2837
Theosophical Order of Service, 2837
Theosophical Society in America, 2837
Theriot, Julie, 7254
Thesman, Michael, 8853
Thewes Charitable Annuity Lead Trust, The, 4375
Thiel, Judith, 1941
Thiel, Larry O., 1395
Thielen, Richard N., 1557
Thielman, Jeffrey D., 364
Thieman, Frederick W., 8124, 8241
Thiemann, Frank H., III, 3438
Thier, Samuel O., 5326, 5779
Thieriot, Peter E., 9993
Thiesfield, Yvette Melendez, 1564
Thietje, Joanne, 4962
Thille, Nick, 1090
Third Federal Savings and Loan Assn., 7868
Thivierge, Ann D., 6815
Thivierge, Arthur, 6815
Thoburn, Tina, 8155
Thoele, Blake, 2671
Thoeni, Ruedi, 2550
Thoma, Carl D., 3035
Thoma, Marilynn J., 3035
Thoman, Lynn B., 6449
Thomas J. Petters Inc., 4653
Thomas Revocable Trust, Harriet Kay, 4456
Thomas, Allen S., 1527
Thomas, Anne M., 5295
Thomas, Bart, 9232
Thomas, Bill, 3161
Thomas, Billie D., 9234
Thomas, Bruce, 8615
Thomas, C.M., 9473
Thomas, Carl M., 3421
Thomas, Carol, 9669
Thomas, Catherine M., 2297
Thomas, Corolyn W., 9542
Thomas, Darrell, 3160
Thomas, David, 8676
Thomas, David A., Hon., 750
Thomas, David W., 2535
Thomas, Doreen, 1517
Thomas, Douglas D., 5427
Thomas, Edward E., 9363
Thomas, F. Lee, 7344
Thomas, Franklin A., 6102
Thomas, G.L. "Tom", 4919
Thomas, George, 2458
Thomas, George I., 9701
Thomas, Gerald V., II, 2525
Thomas, Gillis, 9234
Thomas, Gladys R., 7048
Thomas, Glenn E., 3429
Thomas, H. Gillis, 9234
Thomas, Harold, 2577
Thomas, Harold E., 2577
Thomas, Howard, 5051
Thomas, Hugh Rowe, 54
Thomas, Ida, 1874
Thomas, J. Grover, Jr., 3039
Thomas, Jacki, 9571
Thomas, James A., 980
Thomas, Jane, 9635
Thomas, Jane R., 4438
Thomas, Joan E., 3429
Thomas, John S., 7432
Thomas, Jonathan, 4218
Thomas, Joseph, 4453
Thomas, Katharine, 7432
Thomas, Keith, 6423
Thomas, Kris, 8839
Thomas, L. Newton, 8099
Thomas, L. Newton, Jr., 9717, 9723
Thomas, Lee, 1006
Thomas, Lee B., 3429
Thomas, Linda Ryan, 8876
Thomas, Lisa B., 1216

Thomas, Lowell S., Jr., 8095
Thomas, Lyda Ann, 8987
Thomas, Lynelle, 1519
Thomas, Lynn Schadt, 8725
Thomas, M. Antoinette, 7215
Thomas, Marcia, 2579
Thomas, Marcia A., 2579
Thomas, Margot K., 3492
Thomas, Martha, 8246
Thomas, Mary C., 7537
Thomas, Mary Hager, 2037
Thomas, Mary L., 8616
Thomas, Mary P.R., 7200
Thomas, Maureen, 8572
Thomas, Michael E., 2572
Thomas, Michael M., 6397
Thomas, Nicole, 4662
Thomas, Oliver S., 8671
Thomas, Olivette, 1578
Thomas, Pamela, 4751
Thomas, Pat, 1359
Thomas, Paul D., 8075
Thomas, Phyllis, 2577
Thomas, Phyllis S., 2577
Thomas, Raymond V., 1087
Thomas, Rick, 2577
Thomas, Robert, 7984
Thomas, Robert L., 4209
Thomas, Robert M., 7593
Thomas, Roger M., 3955
Thomas, Russell, Jr., 2448
Thomas, Sandra D., 9725
Thomas, Steven, 4422
Thomas, Thomas D., 8976
Thomas, Thomas L., 9713
Thomas, Tom, 3370
Thomas, W. Dennis, 1571
Thomas, William, 7984
Thomas, William E., 1943
Thomas, Wilmer J., Jr., 5427
ThomasGriffith, Marie E., 9363
Thomason, John M., 8571
Thomasson, Charles W., 9010
Thomasson, Jeff, 9177
Thomasson, Jeffrey, 1918
Thomasson, Jeffrey H., 3222
Thomaston Cotton Mills, 2354
Thome, Dennis W., 512
Thome, Jim, 7577
Thompson Charitable Trust, B. Ray, 8723
Thompson Charitable Trust, Juanne, 8723
Thompson Tractor Co., 67
Thompson USA, J. Walter, Inc., 8831
Thompson, Adella Sands, 8723
Thompson, Al J., 9680
Thompson, Alvin W., Hon., 1529
Thompson, Ana A., 1109
Thompson, Angela E., 1658
Thompson, Ann J., 4858
Thompson, Ann K., 8890
Thompson, Anne H., 218
Thompson, Anthony T., 2579
Thompson, Arthur, 3548
Thompson, Astrid I., 9660
Thompson, B. Ray, III, 8723
Thompson, B. Ray, Jr., 8723
Thompson, B.R., Sr., 8733
Thompson, Barbara M., 4745
Thompson, Barry, 1594
Thompson, Betty E., 6231
Thompson, Bill, 1006
Thompson, Bill M., 7463
Thompson, Billie, 8869
Thompson, Brian J., 6428
Thompson, Catherine Vance, 8723
Thompson, Charles A.Y., 1658
Thompson, Charlie, 8631
Thompson, Cherie F., 3503
Thompson, Christy, 9218
Thompson, Chuck, 9918
Thompson, Cynthia Jones, 4741
Thompson, D. Alan, 1032

Tredway, Philip M., 8188
Treeger, Thomas C., 7097
Trees Trust, Edith L., 8480
Trees, George S., Jr., 2664
Trees, Peter E., 8581
Treff, Douglas J., 4549
Trefler, Alan N., 4185
Trefler, Pamela L., 4185
Treiber, John A., 9934
Treiber, Patricia S., 9934
Treiger, Irwin L., 9593, 9621, 9675, 9680
Treiger, Louis, 9676
Tremaine, Barbara S., 1662
Tremaine, Burton G., III, 1662
Tremaine, Burton G., Jr., 1662
Tremaine, Burton G., Sr., 1662
Tremaine, Emily Hall, 1662
Tremaine, John M., 1662
Tremaine, Sarah C., 1662
Tremaine, Susan, 1662
Tremblay, Wade, 9495
Tremble, Helen R., 4444
Trenary, Bob, 1465
Trenner, Robert F., 9555
Tressider, Susan Jackson, 8209
Treusan, Maurizio, 5785
Treutel, David, Jr., 4745
Trevino, Fernando, 3245
Trevino, J.M., 9028
Trexler, Harry C., 8481
Trexler, Laurie, 7438
Trexler, Mary M., 8481
Tri State Quality Ford Dealers, 7174
Triad Hospitals, Inc., 9239
Triangle Trust, 6687, 6805
Triantafillopoulos, Nick, 7789
Tribble, Bernice W., 8594
Tribble, J. Lee, 2521
Tribune-Star Publishing Co., 3173
Trice, Robert, 3682
Trice, Thomas L., IV, 3648
Trick, Bill, 7749
Tricon Global Restaurants, Inc., 3457
Tridan Industries, 9802
Trifish LLC, 379
Trimble Revocable Living Trust, The, 9505
Trimble, Arch, III, 8714
Trimble, Charles R., 2556
Trimble, Francis H., 3761
Trimble, Gordon M., 2556
Trimble, Joan W., 1487
Trimble, Margaret Brown, 9464
Trimble, Robert A., 2556
Trimble, Sonia U., 2556
Trimboli, Michael C., 2253
Trimpe, Terry, 3275
Trinh, Denise, 345
Trinkle, Robert S., 1948
Triplet Investment Company, LLC, 5234
Triplett, R. Faser, 4756
Triplett-Brady, Sheila, 7328
Tripp, Amos, 691
Tripp, Maria, 346
Tripp, Valerie, 9916
Tripp, William V., III, 4074
Trippe, Blair Landau, 7232
Trismen, Richard F., 1875
Tristani, Gloria, 1773
Tritsch, Mary Jane, 7968
Tritt, John E. "Jack", 3598
Trochinski, Eugene, 2263
Troderman, Diane, 3935
Troisi, Frank X., 7164
Trolz, Jerry, 3145
Tropin, Kenneth G., 1619
Trosky, Ben, 1006
Trost, Charles A., 8662
Trost, Marci, 3273
Troth, Diane, 794
Trotman, John, Sr., 20
Trott, Byron D., 7165
Trott, James C., 8749

Trott, Tina L., 7165
Trotta, F.P., 1584
Trotter, Jack, 8762
Trotter, Jack T., 9197
Trotter, Lloyd G., 1553
Trotter, Mark C., 979
Trout, David M., 1548
Trout, Rebecca F., 1548
Troutman, Donald, Bishop, 8454
Trowbridge, Zara, 711
Trower, Jim, 3387
Trower, Thomas H., 7927
Troxel, Douglas D., 2539
Troxel, G.D., 9015
Troxel, Michael Douglas, 2539
Troxel, Sergei George, 2539
Troy Financial Corp., 7166
Troy Savings Bank, The, 7166
Troy, Ed, 8073
Troy, Elizabeth Thornton, 1235
TRT Holdings, Inc., 9160
Truchard, James, 9088
Truck Rental Co., 2366
Trucklease Corp., 4103
Trudeau, Garry B., 6087
Trudeau, Jane P., 6087
True Oil LLC, 9996
True, Bill, 9708
True, Calvin E., 3525, 3548
True, H.A., Jr., 9996
True, Jean D., 9996
True, Lawrence, 9696
Trueb, Martin R., 8539
Trueblood, Harry A., Jr., 1466
Trueblood, John B., 1466
Trueblood, Lucile B., 1466
Trueheart, William E., 8386
Trueman, Barbara, 7580
Truemper, Mark E., 2680
Truex, Mindy, 3186
Truhlsen, Barbara, 5011
Truhlsen, Dorothy D., 5011
Truhlsen, Stanley M., 5011
Truhlsen, Stanley M., Jr., 5011
Truhlsen, William C., 5011
Truitt, Carla, 8874
Trujillo-Penman, Marcia, 5037
Truland Systems Corp., 9528
Truland, Mary W., 9528
Truland, Robert W., 9528
Trull, Florence M., 9240
Trull, R. Scott, 9240
Trull, R.B., 9240
Truman, Mildred Faulkner, 8483
Trumbull, Margaret, 4466
Trump Park Ave., LLC, 7167
Trump, Donald J., 7167
Trump, Marie, 3185
Trundle, Sarah, 1346
Truslow, William A., 3788
Trust Co. of Oklahoma, The, 7958
Trust Co. of Sterne, Agee and Leach, The, 24
Trust Co. of the West, 1093
Trust, David, 5103
Trust, Diane, 5103
Trust, Laura, 5103
Trust, Martin, 5103
Trustco Capital Mgmt., 2125
Trustey, Joseph, 3897
Trustmark Insurance Co., 3039
Trustmark National Bank, 8716
Trusty, David, 7447
Truszkowski, Andrew, 3743
Truszkowski, Madeline, 3743
Trythall, Barbara H., 5466
Trzcinski, Cheryl, 7887
Trzcinski, Ronald, 7887
TSI Holding Co., 4828
Tsimbinos, John M., 6859
Tsoumas, Richard, 4233
Tsui, John K., 9973
Tsuji, Masaaki, 254
Tsutsumi, Seiji, 3656

TT Charitable Annuity Lead Trust, The, 4375
Tubb, Marilyn, 2015
Tuber, Craig, 1468
Tubergen, Jerry L., 4276, 4277, 4278, 4279, 4463, 4469
Tubergen, Kim, 3241
Tubergen, Marcia D., 4463
Tubito, Vincent, 2139
Tuch, Michael, 7170
Tuchman, Debra Mautner, 1467
Tuchman, Herbert, 5429
Tuchman, Kenneth D., 1467
Tuchman, Margaret, 5429
Tuchman, Martin, 5429
Tuchman, Morris, 6557
Tuchman, Nelson, 6557
Tuck, Alan, III, 1712
Tuck, Barry, 1712
Tuck, Brett, 1712
Tuck, Daniel H., 7170
Tuck, David A., 7170
Tuck, Jonathan S., 7170
Tuck, Kenneth D., 9419
Tucker Foundation, Max and Rose, 8065
Tucker, Cara, 3186
Tucker, Carll, III, 3750
Tucker, Elmer D., 9320
Tucker, Geraldine J., 8768
Tucker, Howard W., Jr., 8572
Tucker, Kristen, 3122
Tucker, Luther, Jr., 3750
Tucker, Marcia Brady, 3750
Tucker, Patrick, 5017
Tucker, Richard G., 7418
Tucker, Richard L., 2356
Tucker, Robert A., 1703
Tucker, Rose E., 8065
Tucker, Toinette, 3750
Tucker, William E., 8798
Tucker, William H., 2357
Tucker-Duncan, Gary, 3750
Tuckson, Reed V., 4705
Tudor Arbitrage Partners, 1664
Tudor Group Holdings, LLC, 1664
Tudor Investment Corp., 1664
Tudor Proprietary Trading, LLC, 1664
Tudor, Brenda E., 9589
Tudor, Fiona, 496, 1040
Tudor, Katherine J., 8735
Tuel, Leslie, 1180
Tufenkian, David F., 7171
Tufenkian, James, 7171
Tuft, Diane H., 7172
Tuft, Thomas E., 7172
Tuggle, Clyde C., 2352
Tuke, John P., 3801
Tulin, Stanley B., 5584
Tulin, Stephen Wise, 6315
Tull Metal and Supply Co., J.M., Inc., 2500
Tull, J.M., 2500
Tull, Toby, 4327
Tulley, Michael, 2591
Tullis, Michael J., 3141
Tullius, Raymond L., Jr., 7954
Tullius, Thomas D., 134
Tully, Alice, 7173
Tully, Daniel G., 1665
Tully, Daniel P., 1665
Tully, Ellen Danaher, 3040
Tully, Grace, 1490
Tully, Grace I., 1665
Tully, Herbert B., 233, 1305
Tully, Mac, 4842
Tully, Sally Gipson, 7136
Tully, Thomas M., 3040
Tulsky, James A., 6103
Tunberg, Jon, 2902
Tune, James F., 9621
Tuner, Jack C., 9401
Tung, Zhoe Yu "Frank", 5160
Tunheim, Kathryn H., 4524
Tunquist, Eric, 705

Tuohy, Alice Tweed, 1247
Tuohy, John L., 3041
Tuohy, Mary Frances, 3041
Tuohy, Patricia J., 3041
Tuohy, Walter J., Jr., 3041
Tuohy, Walter Joseph, 3041
Tupancy, Oswald A., 4186
Tupper, Christopher, 3965
Tupper, Cricket, 3965
Tupper, Margaret C., 1516
Tupperware U.S., Inc., 2275
Turben, David C., 7888
Turben, John F., 7888
Turben, Nicholas A., 7888
Turben, Susan H., 7888
Turbett, Keith, 2259
Turcik, John, 8344
Turcik, John J., 8346
Turcotte, Jean Claire, 8833
Turer, Clarice, 9744
Turgeon, Robert E., 4814
Turille, Stuart J., 9463
Turino, James G., 6917
Turino, Mary, 1729
Turissini, Christina H., 1380
Turletes, Vincent N., 6549
Turley, Henry M., Jr., 8706
Turley, Stewart, 1468
Turley, Thomas A., 6513
Turmon, Henry, 5124
Turn 2 Enterprises, Inc., 7174
Turn 2, Inc., 7174
Turnage, Frances V., 4758
Turnage, Roxanne, 340, 1280
Turnbow, Walter, 169
Turnbull, Paula E., 4043
Turner 97 Trust, Harry M., 7889
Turner Construction Co., 9242
Turner, Allen, 2810
Turner, Allen M., 2810
Turner, Bernard, 5272
Turner, Betty M., 8731
Turner, Bobby, 938
Turner, Brian Mills, 7429
Turner, C.F.C., 7751
Turner, Cal, Jr., 8738
Turner, Cal, Sr., 8737, 8738
Turner, Carolyn, 8484
Turner, Cere, 9780
Turner, Clay H., Rev. Dr., 8616
Turner, Courtney S., 9241
Turner, Cyril, 2351
Turner, D.A., 2326, 2511
Turner, Deborah, 9455
Turner, Deborah F., 8662
Turner, Diana Lassalle, 6635
Turner, Donna, 4544
Turner, Donnetta H., 8738
Turner, Donny, 2345
Turner, Elizabeth B., 2326
Turner, Elizabeth T. Jones, 8766
Turner, Ernest J., 4935
Turner, Frank B., 2319
Turner, George C., 7475, 7489
Turner, H. Calister, 8738
Turner, Hurley C., III, 8738
Turner, Isla Carroll, 9212
Turner, Jack B., 8662
Turner, Jackie, 7347
Turner, James, 2108
Turner, James Stephen, 8736
Turner, James Stephen, Jr., 8736
Turner, James Stephen, Sr., 8736
Turner, James W., 7429
Turner, Jane Smith, 4464
Turner, Jeffrey F., 3599
Turner, Jeffrey S., 4682
Turner, John B., 2102
Turner, Judith Payne, 8736
Turner, Karen, 5282
Turner, Kent, 5781
Turner, Laura, 8736, 8737
Turner, Laura Jennings, 8835
Turner, Laurey Stackpole, 8456

Vatterott, Daniel, 4921
Vatterott, Frank J., 4921
Vatterott, Glennon R., Jr., 4921
Vatterott, John C., 4921
Vatterott, John Harvey, 4921
Vatterott, Joseph A., 4921
Vatterott, Mary Patricia, 4921
Vatterott, Paul B., Jr., 4921
Vaughan, Ben F., III, 8870
Vaughan, Curtis T., III, 8866
Vaughan, Frances, 607
Vaughan, Frances E., 4297
Vaughan, Genevieve, 8870
Vaughan, Jesse, 1080
Vaughan, Kay, 3333
Vaughan, Martin L., III, 9439
Vaughan, Mary Lynn, 9249
Vaughan, Peter, 4558
Vaughan, Richard C., 3195
Vaughan, Rosemary, 9249
Vaughn Nelson Investment Mgmt., 8944
Vaughn, C. Roland, III, 2279
Vaughn, Clarence, Jr., 2279
Vaughn, Edgar H., 9251
Vaughn, Gregory G., 4231
Vaughn, James A., Jr., 2279
Vaughn, James M., Jr., 9251
Vaughn, James P., 2279
Vaughn, Jim M., 9251
Vaughn, John, 1982
Vaughn, Lillie Mae, 9251
Vaught, Audrey, 4968
Vawter, Paul E., 1669
Vazquez, Carlos J., 8515
Vazquez, Francisco H., 407
Vazquez, George, 939
Vazquez, John, 5496
Vazquez, Maria, 4994
Veal, Mary Alice, 26
Veasey, Zoe, 4194
Veazey, Samuel J., 7932
Vecchiarelli, Daniel A., 1417
Vech, Beth, 4962
Vectren Corp., 3249
Vedak, Madhu, 3166
Veden Trust, Frank, 4707
Veeder, Sybil P., 8130
Veerman, Ralph, 9505
Vega, Carlos, 280
Vega-Marquis, Luz, 350, 9567
Vega-Perez, Elsa, 4671
Vegesna, Anatoki Raju, 1263
Vegesna, Bala, 1263
Vegh, Mark, 1139
Veillon, E. Warner, 3468
Veitch, Christopher O., 969
Veitch, Julie, 969
Veitch, Robert D., 7853
Veitch, Sally Louise, 7853
Veitenhans, Karen L., 9703
Veith, Paul G., 9486
Vela-Wagner, Anne, 3088
Velasco, Caridad, 1893
Velasquez, Carmen, 2601
Velasquez, Chris, 4392
Velasquez, Jenee, 4287
Velay, Christopher J., 6684
Velay, Frances A., 6684, 7187
Veld Kamp, Theresa, 1197
Velde, Gretchen Swanson, 5008, 5009
Veldkamp, Arnold, 1197
Veliotes, Nicholas A., 1796
Velis, Marion B., 2333
Vella, James G., 4307, 4308
Velocity Vending, 8604
Velsicol Corporation, 2962
Velto, Alex C., 6639
Velux Trust, The, 4094
Venable, J. Mike, 2361
Venable, Robert J., 9750
Vencor, Inc., 3434
Veninga, James F., 9777
VenJohn, Marilynne, 3389
Venne, Anne C., 8491

Venne, Clarence J., 8491
Venne, Richard A., 8491
Ventas, Inc., 3434
Ventura, Vincent, 5157
Venture Strategy Group, 1248
Ventures Group, Allard, LLC, 4102
Venus, Choy, 2554
Veon, Greg, 3306
Ver Brugge, William, 9974
Vera, George, 972
Verbel, Fay Hiller, 5237
Verbitsky, Nick, 1505
Verblaauw, Karen Larsen, 5296
Verble, Kay W., 2239
Verdecchia, Anthony, 6157
Verdone, Elizabeth, 3859
Verdone, Martha, 3859
Verduzco, Joseph, 3245
Vereb, Karen A., 7730, 7731, 7732
Veres, Andrew F., 9252
Veres, Barbara, 9252
Vergara Trust, Lamar Bruni, 8927
Vergara, Lamar Bruni, 9253
Vergas, Sophia G., 8597
Vergon, Jan Wright, 2677
Verhaeghe, Leon, 3199
Verity, C. William, Jr., 750
Verity, C.William, 7749
Verity, Jonathan G., 8584
Verizon Communications Inc., 5439
Verlinde, Al, 4310
Vermeer Farms, Inc., 3341
Vermeer Manufacturing Co., 3341
Vermeer, Christina, 3341
Vermeer, Daniel, 3341
Vermeer, Gary J., 3341
Vermeer, Lois J., 3341
Vermeer, Matilda, 3341
Vermeer, Robert L., 3341
Vermie, Craig, 3259
Vermillion, William, 7999
Vermilye, W. Moorhead, 3693
Verner, Elizabeth H., 4766
Vernof, Ruben R., 2617
Vernon, Joe, 8946
Vernon, Keith R., 9678
Vernon, Miles Hodsdon, 7195
Vernon, Molly, 2060
Veron, Heidi, 4895
Veronis, Sophie Marr, 5937
Verplanck, Eva L., 8141
Verplank, L.J., 4325
Verrecchia, Alfred J., 8539
Verrette, Charles B., 3422
Verruno, Eduardo, 493
Verslues, Ernie, 4866
Vertetis, Jennifer, 5293
Vesledahl, Dale, 4719
Vesper Corp., 7892
Vespoli, Leila, 7630
Vest, Charles, 748
Vest, Lee Diane Collins, 8007
Vestal, Ellen M., 9573
Vester, Linda J., 6097
Vetlesen, George Unger, 7196
Vetlesen, Maude Monell, 6566
Vetrovec, Pauline, 710
Vetter Holding, Inc, 5014
Vetter, Dennith D., 5014
Vetter, Eldora D., 5014
Vetter, Jack D., 5014
Vetter, Todd, 5014
Veysey, Michael C., 2482
Vezzosi, Greg, 4690
VHIV, Inc., 6394
Via, Edward, 8633
Via, Edward Becher, 8629
Viacor, 3841
Viad Corp, 149
Viall, William A., 8544
Viccellio, Henry, Jr., Genl., 9490
Vich, Josef M., 3278
Vick, Michael D., 3001
Vickers, Gregory A., 1395

Vickers, H. Eugene, 8087
Vickers, Jack A., 1395
Vickers, R. Guy, 6183
Vickery, Andrew C., 3801
Vickter, David, 1266
Victor, Royall, III, 1939
Victory Memorial Park Foundation, 5138
Vidalakis, George N., 9698
Vidalakis, John N., 9698
Vidalakis, Nancy G., 9698
Vidalakis, Nick S., 9698
Vidalakis, Nicole N., 9698
Vidalakis, Perry N., 9698
Video Indiana, Inc., 7915
Vidinha, Antone, 2557
Vidinha, Edene, 2557
Vidra, Leslie, 3130
Viebig, V. Richard, Jr., 8773, 9066
Viederman, Steve, 7774
Viehbacher, Christopher A., 7439
Viele, Charles W., 9553
Vierk, Richard J., 4954
Viersen, Sam K., Jr., 7985
Vierthaler, Dave, 9885
Vietor, Lynn A., 691
Vietor, Vera P., 691
Vigeland, Julie, 8024, 8067
Vignes, Vera, 983
Vignos, Edith Ingalls, 7684
Vik, Alaxander M., 1672
Vik, G.M., 1672
Vilcek, Jan, 7199
Vilcek, Marica, 7199
Vill, Robert, 5758
Villalon, Daniel M., 1741
Villalta, Monica, 1786
Villani, Allison, 4513
Villani, Edmond D., 6825
Villarosa, Lori, 172
Villarreal, Guadalupe G., 9906
Villarreal, Luis, 7779
Villarreal, Lydia M., 698
Villasenor, Al, 588
Villasuso, Raul, 3066
Villere, Frances G., 3503
Villere, St. Denis J., 3475
Villers, Jerry L., 9730
Vilmure, Richard, 925
Vinardi, John J., 4544
Vincent, Anna M., 8492
Vincent, Anne B., 1637
Vincent, David, 9730
Vincent, Harry L., 2914
Vincent, Leonard, 1102
Vincent, Patricia K., 4732
Vincent, Richard A., 7791
Vincent, Valerie, 1637
Vincent, William, 1637
Vincer, Julia, 2880
Vinciguerra, Maggie, 5782
Viner, Clifford, 2281
Viner, Clifford A., 2281
Viner, Jill, 2281
Vines, Jacqueline D., 3462
Vines, Jason H., 4265
Vines, Lanny S., 72
Viniar, David, 6055
Vinik, Jeffrey N., 4193
Vinik, Mary Penny, 4193
Vinitsky, Elyse, 3573
Vinolus, Peter A., 7050
Vinovich, Bonnie, 3135
Vinovich, Jennifer, 3189
Vinovich, William N., 3099
Vinson, Frank B., Jr., 53
Vinson, Kenneth G., 53
Violett, Ellen M., 7200
Violich, Deanne Gillette, 1314
Vipond, J.R., 2687
Vipond, Jonathan, 8208
Viragh, Albert P., 3753
Viragh, Katherine, 3753
Viragh, Katherine A., 3753
Viragh, Mark S., 3753

Viragh, Robert J., 3753
Virch, Claus, 6961
Virden, Mary Lee J., 9211
Virgil Eihusen Estate, 4961
Virginia Capital Bancshares, Inc., 9423
Virginia Hill Trust, 7667
Virginia Scrap Iron & Metal Co., Inc.,
  9430
Virginian-Pilot, The, 9455
Virgo Ventures, Inc., 2938
Virkler, Laura H., 5279
Visages RPS, Inc., 565
Visbal, J. Malcolm, 559
Visceglia, Peter C., 5441
Visick, Vern, 9764
Vista Metals Corp., 207
Visteon Corp., 4472
Visual Architectural Designs, 7174
Vit, Paul, 958
Vita, John, 2094
Vitale, David, 1759
Vitale, Jean E., 2679
Vitale, Marilyn, 1759
Vitalis, Rita, 9888
Vitense, Mark, 9807
Vito, Joseph A., 4257
Vitti, Bonnie, 1442
Vittitow, Helen, 3419
Vituccio, Mary, 7735
Vivar, Jorge, 8967
Vivendi Universal Entertainment, LLP,
  1251
Vivinetto, Jack, 7152
Vizza, Robert F., 5852
Vladeck, David M., 1786
Vliet, Marni, 3372
Vlock, Michael, 1645
Vochko, Louise, 8098
Vock, Michelle, 4665
Vodafone Americas Inc., 1267
Voegtle, Carrie, 4245
Voelkel, Alice K., 3666
Voelker, David R., 3503
Voetman, David, 9972
Vogel, Judith, 3317
Vogel, Judith M., 2504
Vogel, Kate, 7346
Vogel, Rhona E., 9889, 9916
Vogel, Robert J., 5167
Vogel, William A., 2504
Vogelsang, Peter J., 657
Vogelstein, Andrew A., 7201
Vogelstein, Barbara Manfrey, 7201
Vogelstein, Deborah H., 3650
Vogelstein, Hans A., 7201
Vogelstein, John L., 7201
Vogen, Kristin Carlson, 2796
Vogt, Mary, 2904
Vogt, Shirley M., 5675
Vogt, Susan J., 4238
Voichcik, Sarah Jane, 9915
Voilleque, Anne, 2576
Voilleque, Anne S., 2566
Vojvoda, Antoinette P., 3664, 3665
Vokoun, Cori Sampson, 4987
Volanakis, Peter F., 5794
Volentine, Mary G., 1268
Volentine, Myatt W., 1268
Voleti, Choudary D., 1096
Volger, Suzy Brodie, 3074
Voliva, Ann, 3254
Volk, Edward, 3247
Volk, Norman H., 6150
Volkema, Michael A., 7694
Volkerts, Linda L., 1255
Volkman, Matt, 3122
Volland, Patricia J., 5542
Vollmer Foundation, Inc., 2282
Vollmer, Alberto F., 5443
Vollmer, Alberto J., 2282
Vollmer, Gustavo A., 5443
Vollmer, Gustavo J., 5443
Vollrath, David, 7586

Walker, Martha L., 2104
Walker, Mary Jo Sanders, 2177
Walker, Meg, 4629
Walker, Michael, 6928
Walker, Myrtle E., 4922
Walker, Nancy F., 7590
Walker, Patricia L., 1395
Walker, Paul, 4786
Walker, Randy, 3463
Walker, Reina, 3463
Walker, Rett, 2358
Walker, Robert L., 9138
Walker, Robert O., 9906
Walker, S. Benton, III, 2505
Walker, S. Michael, 5466
Walker, Sandra D., 2160
Walker, Scott, 5343
Walker, Sidney H., 8590
Walker, Stanley D., 2505
Walker, Stanley D., Jr., 2505
Walker, Sue, 9639
Walker, Susan, 8788
Walker, Terri, 3278
Walker, Terry L., 3103, 3128
Walker, Terry M., 8797
Walker, Thomas B., III, 7208
Walker, Thomas P., 7486
Walker, Thomas Slater, 9218
Walker, Tyra, 3215
Walker, W.E., III, 4770
Walker, W.E., Jr., 4770
Walker, William W., 39
Walker, William W., Jr., 27
Walkey, Catherine E., 3890
Walkup, Betsy, 8662
Wall, Carol C., 409
Wall, Carol Vance, 5445
Wall, Carolyn, 7818
Wall, Douglas V., 5445
Wall, E.D., 1921
Wall, John, 3136
Wall, John W., 9135
Wall, Sue Burress, 7331
Wall, Terence D., 5445
Wallace, Alice Dodge, 1339
Wallace, Ann D., 9533
Wallace, Ann Fowler, 5614
Wallace, Barbara, 2564
Wallace, Bonita, 6823
Wallace, Brian M., 8969
Wallace, Bruce, 7593
Wallace, C. Harold, 8872
Wallace, Candy, 7867
Wallace, Charles F., 5199
Wallace, Christine, 7773
Wallace, Christy A., 1858
Wallace, David W., 1674, 1681
Wallace, Denise, 1947
Wallace, DeWitt, 7209
Wallace, Diane, 560
Wallace, George R., 4195
Wallace, Gordon G., 1858
Wallace, H. Scott, 1858
Wallace, H.B., 3342
Wallace, Helen G. Pruitt, 2179
Wallace, Henry A., 1857, 1858
Wallace, Henry D., 3342
Wallace, Herbert M., 8226
Wallace, Ilo B., 1858
Wallace, J. Bransford, Jr., 8740
Wallace, Jackie, 1858
Wallace, Jean M., 1674
Wallace, Jean W., 1681
Wallace, Jocelyn M., 3342
Wallace, John D., 5357
Wallace, Lila Acheson, 7209
Wallace, Margaret Boynton, 1339
Wallace, Mark A., 8960
Wallace, Michael, 534
Wallace, Nancy Sue, 2570
Wallace, Nora Ann, 5777
Wallace, Peter C., 7823
Wallace, R. Bruce, 1858
Wallace, R. Douglas, 9272

Wallace, Randall C., 1858
Wallace, Rebecca, 8215
Wallace, Robert B., 1858
Wallace, Robert C., 9680
Wallace, Ron, 4309
Wallace, Sarah, 7620, 7714
Wallace, Scott, 4959
Wallace, Susan, 1858
Wallace, William Dodge, 1339
Wallace, William H., 5036
Wallace-Gray, Linda, 3342
Wallach, Diane Gates, 1380
Wallach, Ira D., 5723, 7204, 7210
Wallach, Judith, 5884
Wallach, Kenneth L., 5723, 7204, 7210
Wallach, Mary K., 7210
Wallach, Miriam G., 7210
Wallach, Susan S., 7210
Wallach, Sylvan, 5884
Waller, Bret, 3119
Waller, Jeffrey M., 9826
Waller, June I., 3232
Waller, Roberta Schaefer, 2222
Waller, William, 383
Wallerstein, Bernard, 5447
Wallerstein, Jane, 5447
Wallerstein, Julian, 5447
Wallerstein, Julian W., 5446
Wallerstein, Melvin J., 5446
Wallerstein, Mitchel B., 5446
Wallerstein, Rita, 5446
Wallestad, Phadoris, 4712
Wallgren, Donald L., 4556
Wallick, Margaret, 8491
Wallin, Franklin W., 6538
Wallin, G. George, Ph.D., 4593
Wallin, Maxine H., 4714
Wallin, Rebecca L., 4714
Wallin, Winston R., 4714
Walling Halbert Trust, JoAnn, 8814
Wallingford, Debra, 3425
Wallis, Ana Luisa, 5443
Wallis, Beth, 1276
Wallis, Brent, 1276
Wallis, Del, 941, 1099
Wallis, Franklin F., 464, 4895
Wallis, Hal B., 1276
Wallis, Marilyn Belk, 7314
Wallman, Joyce, 7514
Wallop, Sandra, 10000
Walsh Construction Co. of Illinois, The, 3055
Walsh, Ann Eliza McCaddin, 6513
Walsh, Christopher, 7254
Walsh, Dale, 5075
Walsh, Daniel J., 3055
Walsh, Darin, 5075
Walsh, David G., 9925
Walsh, Edna, 5075
Walsh, Edward J., Jr., 6838, 7266
Walsh, F. Howard, Jr., 8904
Walsh, F. Howard, Sr., 9261
Walsh, Frank E., III, 5383
Walsh, Frank E., Jr., 5383
Walsh, G.M., 2637, 7920
Walsh, Gary W., 8488
Walsh, Gerald, 7585
Walsh, James, 3278
Walsh, James P., 96
Walsh, Jeffrey R., 5383
Walsh, Joan D., 5180
Walsh, John B., 9925
Walsh, John E., 5341
Walsh, John N., III, 7248
Walsh, John N., Jr., 5813
Walsh, Joseph, 5324, 5383
Walsh, Joyce S., 3055
Walsh, Lorna J., 1873
Walsh, Lynne, 249
Walsh, Mark, 5075
Walsh, Mary, 3311
Walsh, Mary D., 5383, 8904, 9261
Walsh, Matthew M., 3055
Walsh, Meghan, 5383

Walsh, Patricia, 5075
Walsh, Patricia R., 3055
Walsh, Richard F., 4077
Walsh, Richard J., 1960
Walsh, Semmes G., 3567
Walshok, Mary, 580
Walske, Jennifer C., 4196
Walske, Steven, 4196
Walske, Steven C., 4196
Walstrom, Michele, 3309
Waltemath, Glen, 4991
Walter Industries, Inc., 2286
Walter, Arlene B., 9959
Walter, Beverly Railey, 8099
Walter, Brian, 3595
Walter, Brian S., 3595
Walter, Donald F., 4414
Walter, Fran D., 7211
Walter, Henry C., 5886
Walter, Henry G., Jr., 7212
Walter, J. Thomas, 9118
Walter, J.C. "Rusty", III, 8960
Walter, Keith A., 5177
Walter, Michael D., 2639
Walter, Otto L., 7211
Walter, Patricia E., 5177
Walter, R.A., 2286
Walter, Ronald A., 8661
Walter, Rosalind P., 7212
Walter, William R., 8732
Walterman, Laura L., 9000
Walters, Barbara, 5092
Walters, Carole Hershey, 7671
Walters, G. King, 93, 134
Walters, John R., 822
Walters, Richard, 7819
Walters, Robin K., 5289
Walters, Stephen B., 7076
Walters, William G., 7213
Waltersdorf, John M., 3600
Walther, B.W., 7823
Walton & Co., Inc., 8290
Walton Enterprises, LLC, 186
Walton, Aaron A., 8247, 8386
Walton, Alice A., 186
Walton, Alice L., 186
Walton, Benjamin S., 186
Walton, D.T., Jr., 2358
Walton, Edward, 8535
Walton, Helen R., 186
Walton, James D., 2579
Walton, James L., 9693
Walton, James M., 8130, 8242, 8425
Walton, Jason, 9019
Walton, Jim C., 186
Walton, John M., 4745
Walton, John T., 186
Walton, Joseph C., 8178
Walton, Mark L., 8841
Walton, Mary T., 2220
Walton, Ric, 4347
Walton, Richard E., 404
Walton, S. Robson, 186
Walton, Sally, 3425
Walton, Sam M., 186
Walton, Samuel R., 186
Walton, Steuart L., 186
Walton, Thomas L., 186
Walton, William, III, 2200
Waltrip, Karen, 2296
Waltrip, Mark, 2296
Wampler, Kevin, 3148
Wampner, Steve, 3124
Wamsley, Gary, 1357
Wan, Sze-Kar, 4309
Wanamaker, John, 85
Wander, Herbert S., 2826, 2961
Wang, Alice, 768
Wang, An, 4197
Wang, Anthony W., 6968
Wang, Charles B., 5448
Wang, Courtney S., 4197
Wang, David S., 842
Wang, Frederick A., 4197

Wang, Gilbert A., 6787
Wang, Kenneth, 7015
Wang, Kimberly, 5448
Wang, Lorraine C., 4197
Wang, Lulu C., 6968
Wang, Michael, 483
Wang, Nancy Li, 5448
Wang, T. Chester, 689
Wang, Ta-Cheng, 689
Wang-Becker, Vera, 7015
Wanger, Eric David, 2583
Wanger, Leah Zell, 2583
Wanger, Leonard Ralph, 2583
Wanger, Ralph, 2583
Wanlass, George Ralph, 9310
Wanlass, Kathryn C., 9310
Wanlass, Ralph, 9310
Wanner, Eric, 6894
Warble, Roxanne M., 2664
Warburg Pincus Partners LLC, 7214
Warburg, James P., 5694
Warburg, James P., Jr., 5694
Warburg, Jennifer, 5694
Warburg, Joan M., 5694
Warburg, Philip N., 5694
Ward, Adelaide C., 4924
Ward, Alexandra, 5477
Ward, Barbara P., 9901
Ward, Benjamin F., Jr., 7745
Ward, Brenna, 1278
Ward, Carol J., 8143
Ward, Catherine, 1278
Ward, Catherine M., 720
Ward, Cynthia R., 9262
Ward, David A., 7005
Ward, Edwin R., 6882
Ward, Gayllis, 5683
Ward, George, 1278
Ward, Harold A., III, 2043
Ward, Heather M., 7280
Ward, Janice P., 2458
Ward, Janie Victoria, 3828
Ward, Joanne, 3012
Ward, John, 8943
Ward, Judy G., 9573
Ward, Katherine J., 9262
Ward, Kaye C., 1429
Ward, Keith T., 1957
Ward, Kevin J., 5359
Ward, Laysha, 4697
Ward, Mabel B., 12, 30
Ward, Mamie McFaddin, 9263
Ward, Martha, 5569
Ward, Mary Ann, 9430
Ward, Nancy, 1201
Ward, Patricia L., 9022
Ward, Philip, 4452
Ward, Ralph, Jr., 9046
Ward, Regina, 5409
Ward, Robert, 3854
Ward, Robert F., 4747
Ward, Robert, II, 7533
Ward, Scott H., 4924
Ward, Scott R., 4622
Ward, Suzanne, 169
Ward, T. Bestor, III, 12
Ward, Teresa Ann, 9137
Ward, Terry W., 8894
Ward, William C., 9262
Ward, William R., 1374
Ward, William T., 6979
Ward, William T., Jr., 6979
Wardeberg, George E., 9860
Wardell, Mike, 9977
Warden, Chandler D., 2874
Warden, F. Andrew, 2874
Warden, Winifred M., 2874
Wardlaw, Edna, 2506
Wardlaw, Gertrude, 2507
Wardlaw, Julia Milner, 2506
Wardlaw, William C., III, 2506, 2507
Wardlaw, William C., Jr., 2507
Wardle, Corinne G., 8620
Wardle, Douglas G., 8620

Wardle, Robert B., 8620
Wardle, Robert V., 8620
Wardle, William G., 8620
Wards Co., Inc., 9392
Wardwell, Ann, 9736
Ware 2003 Charitable Lead Annuity, Marian S., 8508
Ware III Charitable Lead Annuity, John H., 8508
Ware, B.T., II, 9264
Ware, III Charitable Lead Annuity, John H., 8367
Ware, John Charles, 8367
Ware, John H., IV, 8367
Ware, John H., Jr., 2287
Ware, John L., 8855
Ware, Julia A., 8199
Ware, Karen, 8367
Ware, Marilyn, 8508
Ware, Martha, 2287
Ware, Mary S., 9264
Ware, Paul W., 8199
Ware, Richard A., 4291
Ware, Richard C., II, 9264
Ware, Richard, II, 8758
Ware, T. Kirkland, III, 3947
Ware, W.R., 9264
Wareham, C.L.C., 5460
Wareing, Elizabeth B., 9175
Warfield, Ranelle Q., 7447
Wargo, Bruce W., 3099
Warhol, Andy, 7215
Warhola, John, 7215
Warick, Charles H., III, 2019
Waring, Bayard D., 4073, 4182
Waring, Philip B., 4073, 4182
Waring, Tom, 4962
Wark, David M., 3057
Wark, Mary Ann Barrows, 3057
Warlow, T. Picton, IV, 1875
Warlow, Thomas P., III, 1875
Warman, Michele S., 6525
Warmath, John T., Jr., 7493
Warmflash, David, 7033
Warmuth, Michael J., 2579
Warn, Elizabeth K., 3558
Warne, Thomas, 91
Warner Brothers, 565
Warner Foundation, Lee and Rose, 4619
Warner, C. Elizabeth, 1844
Warner, D. Michael, 7503
Warner, Ed, 9918
Warner, Elizabeth Henry, 8581
Warner, Glen W., 7534
Warner, Joseph, 2235
Warner, Ken, 4534
Warner, M. Richard, 9228
Warner, Mark R., 9398
Warner, Meryll, 2235
Warner, Norton E., 4954
Warner, Rose, 4715
Warner, Sabrina, 8140
Warner, Sharon L., 829
Warner, Steven C., 8259
Warner, Theodore H., 3553
Warner, Tom, 829
Warner-Lambert Co., 1995
Warner-Powell, Christine, 7714
Warnick, Bob, Rev., 2075
Warnock, Carolyn P., 3420
Warnock, Laurie, 5087
Warren Equities, Inc., 8517
Warren, Barbara, 7593
Warren, Benjamin, 8752
Warren, Cheryl, 1483
Warren, Dick, 9597
Warren, Dorian T., 3069
Warren, Elizabeth, 9700
Warren, Elizabeth K., 8061
Warren, Frank J., 8800
Warren, Frank R., 1279
Warren, George M., Jr., 9448
Warren, Ingrid R., 5867
Warren, Jean, 7986

Warren, Joanne C., 1279
Warren, Joe, 9081
Warren, John, 8525
Warren, John-Kelly C., 7987
Warren, Judith, 528
Warren, Katherine Cannon, 8651
Warren, Kirk, 9300
Warren, Nani S., 9700
Warren, Peter F., Jr., 3682
Warren, Robert, 3455
Warren, Ron, 3243
Warren, Shirley, 5833
Warren, Stephen K., 7987
Warren, Sydney, 7415, 7416
Warren, Vivian, 8800
Warren, W.B., 2111
Warren, W.K., Jr., 7986, 7987
Warren, Wendy, 8061
Warren, William B., 7305
Warren, William K., 7986, 7987
Warren, William K., Mrs., 7987
Warrick, Meghan, 1942
Warriner, Jane Cunningham, 3219
Warriner, Laura, 7952
Warrington, Elsie H., 7895
Warsh, Herman, 340
Warsh, Herman E., 1280, 4400
Warsh, Michael, 340, 1280
Warshaw, Milton, 6304
Warshaw, Robert S., 1722
Warwick Founation, The, 8496
Warwick, Robert F., 7336
Warwin, Jason, 6615
Wasco, Wilma, 1529
Wascoe, Thomas M., 2579, 2580
Wasdin, Gelon, 2362
Washburn, Earl, 1151
Washburn, Thomas D., 3174
Washington Corporations, 4941
Washington Group International, Inc., 2578
Washington Magazine, Inc., 3584, 3689
Washington Post Co., The, 1804
Washington School Employees Credit Union, 9660
Washington Speakers Bureau, 1248
Washington Trust Co., The, 1850, 8563
Washington, A. Eugene, Jr., 347
Washington, Dennis, 4941
Washington, Fred S., Jr., 8581
Washington, Laura S., 3084
Washington, Nancy D., 8386
Washington, Phyllis, 4941
Washington, Phyllis J., 4941
Washington, Reginald L., 1356
Washington, Reginald L., M.D., 1350
Washingtonian, The, 3584
Washkewicz, D.E., 7796
Wasie, Donald A., 4716
Wasie, Marie F., 4716
Wasie, Stanley L., 4716
Wasily, Anne V., 1760
Wassenberg, Charles F., 7891
Wasserman, Bert W., 7218
Wasserman, Casey, 1281
Wasserman, Debra, 7218
Wasserman, Edith B., 1281
Wasserman, Ellen W.P., 3758
Wasserman, George, 3757
Wasserman, Harry H., 5886
Wasserman, Lew R., 1281
Wasserman, Lynne, 1281
Wasserman, Sandra, 7218
Wassmann, Mariam, 2701
Wassner, Mala, 6131
Wassong, Larry, 7449
Wasta, John L., 3275
Wasta, V. Prem, 9190
Waste Management, Inc., 9265
Waste, Laura, 495
Waste, William, 495
Watanabe, August M., 3251
Watanabe, Hirofumi, Bishop, 5685
Watanabe, Jeffrey N., 2545, 2546

Watanabe, Joy, 5015
Watanabe, Margaret R., 3251
Watanabe, Terry K., 5015
Waterbury, James B., 3313
Watercress, Inc., 4043
Waterfall, Clark, 3258
Waterfield, Anne K., 3252
Waterfield, Randolph H., Jr., 3196
Waterfield, Richard D., 3252
Waterhouse Family Foundation, The, 6583
Waterman Broadcasting Corp., 4198
Waterman, Bernard E., 4198
Waterman, Edith B., 4198
Waterman, Mary, 4979
Waterman, Robert E., 134
Waterman, William M., 1733
Waters Fund, James L., 8449
Waters, Barbara, 7988
Waters, Ernest J., 8511
Waters, Feron, 7988
Waters, Jane Allen, 3801
Waters, John, 4527, 7215
Waters, Judy, 2356
Waters, Judy Gayle, 7988
Waters, Mary C., 6894
Waters, Nina M., 1940
Waters, Richard C., 9476
Waters, Robert S., 8498
Waters, Ronald V., 3088
Waters, Sandra, 1675
Waters, Stephen M., 1675
Waters, Tom, 1946
Watkins Associated Industries, Inc., 2508
Watkins, Amy A., 8757
Watkins, Bill, 2508
Watkins, Carol, 7567
Watkins, Don, 4534
Watkins, Gary, 9350
Watkins, George C., 2508
Watkins, Gregg D., 4273
Watkins, H. Craig, 8258
Watkins, Jane G., 9402
Watkins, Jerry, 183
Watkins, Jerry W., 167
Watkins, John F., 2508
Watkins, Joseph A., 1642
Watkins, Joy, 1945
Watkins, Julia S., 9342
Watkins, Kimberly, 2508
Watkins, Michael L., 2508
Watkins, Orlando C., 3503
Watkins, Ruth Ann, 2964
Watkins, Susan, 1220
Watkins, Tony, 3415
Watkins, W.B., IV, 2508
Watrous, Helen, 1436
Watson 1995 Trust, Douglas, 911
Watson Clinic Foundation, 2054
Watson Foundation, Thomas J., 1761
Watson Trust, William J., 2664
Watson, Alonzo W., Jr., 1243, 9319, 9320, 9338
Watson, Anne, 9320
Watson, Arthur K., 7220
Watson, Arthur K., Jr., 1761
Watson, B.L., 4630
Watson, Carlton A., 4209
Watson, Charles, 4766
Watson, Charles L., 9266
Watson, Dale E., 3161
Watson, Daniel E., 1403
Watson, David J., 1761
Watson, Douglas, 3965
Watson, Douglas F., 4717
Watson, Eliza Jane, 5247
Watson, Frederick O., 4717
Watson, Gerald G., Maj. Genl., 23
Watson, Geraldine F., 6825
Watson, Gordon R., 1943
Watson, James, 3677
Watson, Jared, 9680
Watson, Jeannette K., 7220

Watson, Jennie Lehua, 637
Watson, Jo-Ann, 3965, 4123
Watson, Johnnie B., 8661
Watson, Karen, 2446
Watson, Kim R., 9266
Watson, Lenna, 1446, 1471
Watson, Matthew S., 1786
Watson, Michael, 8344, 8346
Watson, Noel G., 707
Watson, P.K., 4769
Watson, Rachel Leah Galbraith, 9427
Watson, Ray L., 320
Watson, Richard T., 4428, 6586, 6695, 7273, 7654, 7763
Watson, Roslyn M., 3961
Watson, Solomon B., IV, 6620
Watson, Solomon, IV, 6998
Watson, Stanley W., 4199
Watson, Stephen M., 4717, 6241
Watson, Steven L., 9188
Watson, Stuart, 7220
Watson, Stuart H., 1761
Watson, Susan, 5388
Watson, Thomas J., III, 7220
Watson, Thomas J., Jr., 7220
Watson, Trinkie, 1244
Watson, Walter E., 7896
Watson, Wendy K., 4506
Watson, William R., 1720
Watson-Comissiong, Thelma Ruth, 9363
Watt, Alston P., 2514
Watt, Debra S., 7370
Watt, James L., 2279
Watt, Joan, 9693
Watt, Katherine, 1278
Watt, Robert, 8979
Watt, Robert A., 9680
Watt, Robert L., 7444
Watterson, Barbara N., 3849
Wattis Trust, Phyllis C., 1283
Wattis, Paul L., III, 1283
Wattis, Paul L., Jr., 1283
Wattles, Alexander B., 5607
Wattles, Charles D., 4324
Wattles, Gurdon B., 5607
Wattles, Gurdon S., 5607
Wattles, John C., 4396
Wattlesworth, Roberta, 3343
Watts, Beverly, 7221
Watts, C. Gregory, 5295
Watts, David, 609
Watts, David B., 7221
Watts, David D., 722
Watts, John A., Jr., 9463
Watts, Judith, 3489
Watts, Mitchell W., 7446
Watts, Richard, 1712
Watts, Russell E., 3795
Watts, T. Ashby, III, 9463
Watts, Vinson A., 3449
Watts, William R., Sr., 2288
Watumull Bros., Ltd., 2558
Watumull, Gulab, 2558
Watumull, Jaidev, 2558
Watumull, Jhamandas, 2558
Watumull, Jyoti, 2558
Watumull, Khubchand, 2558
Watumull, Vik, 2558
Waugh, Richard, 942
Waughtal, Bill, 9852
Wavering, Emer H., 3059
Wawona Frozen Foods, 1168
Waxman, Harvey L., 5229
Way, Eric Leong, 6418
Way, Griffith, 9558
Way, John, 6977
Wayburn, Cynthia, 9546
Wayland, F. Warren, 401
Wayland, Fred G., Jr., 9460
Wayman, Robert P., 672
Waymire, Robert, 8014
Wayne, Valerie Rockefeller, 6825
Waz, Joseph W., Jr., 8152
WBAP Radio, 8817

WBH Evansville, Inc., 3254
WBI Holdings, Inc., 7517
WBNS-TV, Inc., 7915
WCN Bancorp, 9756
WEA Enterprises Co., Inc., 7281
Weadock, Roger, 3095
Weaklend, Dave, 4723
Weakley, Joan, 5550
Wean, Gordon B., 7898
Wean, Raymond John, Sr., 7898
Wear, James, 1465
Wearing, Betsy, 3387
Weary, Daniel C., 9241
Weathead Charitable Trust, 7899
Weatherhead, Albert J., III, 7899
Weatherhead, Albert J., Jr., 7899
Weatherhead, Celia J., 7899
Weatherhead, David Parmely, 3850
Weathers, James A., 7438
Weatherspoon, Van L., 7374
Weatherstone, Dennis, 7003
Weatherup, Constance K., 7222
Weatherup, Craig E., 7222
Weatherwax Trust I, K.A., 4474
Weatherwax, Scott, 9597
Weaver Charitable Trust, William M., 9268
Weaver, Dale M., 8486
Weaver, Delores B., 2289
Weaver, Delores Barr, 2071
Weaver, Dorothy Collins, 8838
Weaver, E.H., 7504
Weaver, Edith M., 8486
Weaver, Elizabeth Eudora, 9267
Weaver, Francine Lavin, 1469
Weaver, Galbraith McF., 9267
Weaver, George, 5146
Weaver, H. Michael, 7329, 7504
Weaver, Irene M., 8486
Weaver, J. Wayne, 2071, 2289
Weaver, James D., 8809
Weaver, John F., 4363
Weaver, Katherine, 7504
Weaver, Lance L., 1730
Weaver, Linda Alexander, 7403
Weaver, Lindsey A., Jr., 1469
Weaver, Merrylyn, 1517
Weaver, Philip G., 7589
Weaver, R.H., 9151
Weaver, Sharyn A., 8809
Weaver, Thomas A., 670
Weaver, Victor F., 8486
Weaver, W.H., 7504
Weaver, Warren W., 4876
Weaver, William R., 9267
Webb, Charles B., Jr., 75, 4400
Webb, Del E., 150
Webb, Grace S., 1495
Webb, J. David, 3202
Webb, Jack H., 6026
Webb, Laura A., 7346
Webb, Lee, 3549
Webb, Lewis, Jr., 281, 1285
Webb, Linda G., 8578
Webb, Louis A., 982
Webb, Lyman, 4607
Webb, Marion L., 982
Webb, Marjorie H., 9436
Webb, Max, 1070, 1284
Webb, Randy, 9499
Webb, Raymond, 2225
Webb, Robert B., 8386
Webb, Susan Mott, 75
Webb, Thomas T., 4260
Webb, Wilbur, 3124
Webb-Petett, Freddye, 4743
Webber, Adrian, 9269
Webber, Arthur L., 9269
Webber, Eloise, 4343
Webber, Joan, 4475
Webber, Neil, 8747, 9269
Webber, Richard, 4343
Webber, Sue, 520
Webber, W. Temple, III, 9227

Webber, W. Temple, Jr., 9227
Webber, Wayne, 4475
Webel, Richard C., 6859
Weber, Arnold, 2691
Weber, Deborah, 3425
Weber, Doug, 4221
Weber, Edward, 7756
Weber, Eugene D., 9958
Weber, Felicia P., 2510
Weber, Fred E., 7603
Weber, Frederick E., 4200
Weber, Gene, 7573
Weber, Jacqueline, 151
Weber, Jill, 4604
Weber, Joseph F., 2510
Weber, Joseph R., 7554
Weber, Lisa M., 6542
Weber, Marianne E., 5869
Weber, Mark, 4994
Weber, Murray, 6237
Weber, Robert W., 3394
Weber, Russ, 8613
Weber, Sue, 4723
Weber, Thomas R., 2701
Weber, Wayne E., 3100, 3202
Weberg, Jacqueline, 151
Weberg, John P., 151
Webster Trust Co., N.A., 1514, 1573, 1603
Webster, Alec J., 1286
Webster, Ann S., 4042
Webster, Curtis M., 5323
Webster, Cynthia F., 7628
Webster, Edwin S., 4201
Webster, Elizabeth McGraw, 5323
Webster, Elroy, 4540
Webster, Helen, 1286
Webster, James, III, 5028
Webster, Jean Schmidt, 8055
Webster, Jeffrey H., 4647
Webster, John A., Jr., 4042
Webster, John W., 4975
Webster, June Norcross, 6634
Webster, Martin H., 762
Webster, Norma, 5028
Webster, Richard B., 1286
Webster, Robert, Jr., 7628
Webster, Ronald S., 9274
Webster, Theo M., 5323
Webster, Wade J., 8584
Webster, Wendell C., 2059
Webster, Wilton, Jr., 1286
Wechsler, Caryn Wolf, 7914
Wechsler, Debra B., 1915
Wechsler, Irving A., 8272
Wechsler, Joseph, 6908
Wechsler, Lewis, 6365
Wechsler, Samuel, 6908
Weckbaugh, Eleanore Mullen, 1470
Wedeen, Rachel, 403
Wedeking, Ila, 4968
Wedel, Kermit, 3372
Wedum, John A., 4719
Wedum, Mary Beth, 4719
Wedum, Maynard C., 4719
Weed, Paula J., 2517
Weeden Fund, Frank, 7223
Weeden, Alan N., 7223
Weeden, Donald A., 7223
Weeden, Donald E., 7223
Weeden, Frank, 7223
Weeden, John D., 7223
Weeden, Leslie, 7223
Weeden, Norman, 7223
Weeden, Robert, 7223
Weeden, William F., 7223
Weekes, Elizabeth B., 8190
Weekley Homes, L.P., 8818
Weekley, Anne S., 4254
Weekley, Bonnie S., 9271
Weekley, David M., 8960, 9271
Weekley, M. Jane, 4994
Weekley, Weldon T., 9271
Weekly, Michael C., 4993

Weeks, Janis C., 3931
Weeks, R. Thomas, 6108
Weeks, Wendell P., 5326, 5794
Weems, George, 3144
Weems, Katharine Lane, 5548
Weems, Lew E., 8671
Weese, Ben, 2767
Weese, Elizabeth Grass, 8223
Weese-Mayer, Debra, 5814
Wege, Christopher, 4476
Wege, Jonathan C., 4476
Wege, Peter M., 4476
Wege, Peter M., II, 4446, 4476
Wegener, Stuart, 2015
Wegner, Carol, 4990
Wehco Video, Inc., 165
Wehmhoff, James C., 4653
Wehr, C. Frederic, 9961
Wehrle, Joseph H., Jr., 9245
Weiant, William S., 7616
Weidenfeld, Edward L., 1815
Weidenhammer, John P., 8509
Weider, Eric, 1287
Weider, Joe, 1287
Weidman, John N., 8427
Weidman, Steven C., 5933
Weidmann, Richard G., 3818
Weiffenbach, B., 7698
Weigand, K.R., 3051
Weight Watchers of Philadelphia, Inc., 8108
Weiksner, Sandra, 3627
Weil, Amanda, 6635
Weil, Andrew L., 8272
Weil, Audrey, 7142
Weil, Audrey York, 9535
Weil, David M., 7031
Weil, Denie S., 6180
Weil, Frank A., 6180
Weil, Gotshal & Manges LLP, 7225
Weil, John D., 4881
Weil, Kenneth M., 9535
Weil, Richard L., 6512
Weil, Robert J., 4691
Weil, Sandison E., 6635
Weil, Susan F., 7080
Weil, William B., Jr., 4321
Weil, William S., 6180, 6635
Weiland, John H., 5125
Weiler, Alan, 6779
Weiler, Alan G., 6727
Weiler, Anna, 2923
Weiler, Elaine, 6727
Weiler, Ralph J., 2290
Weiler, Siegfried, 2923
Weiler, Theodore R., 7226
Weiler, Victor N., 9833
Weiler-Arnow Investment Co., The, 6727
Weill, Joan H., 7227
Weill, Richard I., 6512
Weill, Sanford I., 7227
Weill, Stefanie, 9962
Weiller, Edwin A., III, 2291
Weiller, Jean A., 2291
Weiller, Margaret S., 2472
Wein, Irving L., 3060
Wein, Joseph, 3060
Wein, Zahava, 3060
Wein-Bernhardt, Susan, 3060
Wein-Reis, Dina, 2193
Weinbach, Joanne, 5228
Weinberg, A.J., 2347
Weinberg, Amy S., 7229
Weinberg, Charlotte Cohen, 3592
Weinberg, David A., 2963
Weinberg, David B., 3061
Weinberg, Deborah L., 7228
Weinberg, Donn, 3568, 3759
Weinberg, Eli, 7126
Weinberg, Harry, 3759
Weinberg, Jack A., 3061
Weinberg, Jeffrey, 6280
Weinberg, John L., 7230
Weinberg, John S., 7229

Weinberg, Judd A., 3061
Weinberg, Lewis C., 2963
Weinberg, Marjorie G., 3061
Weinberg, Penni, 7732
Weinberg, Peter A., 7228, 7231
Weinberg, Richard G., 3061
Weinberg, Sharon L., 6260
Weinberg, Sharona, 6280
Weinberg, Sidney J., Jr., 7231
Weinberg, Sue Ann, 7230
Weinberg, Sydney H., 7231
Weinberger, Stanley, 4534
Weiner, April A., 2512
Weiner, Brian, 216
Weiner, Bruce, 8156
Weiner, Edward G., 5849, 7045
Weiner, Faith, 8463
Weiner, Jerold G., 2512
Weiner, Leigh, 5557
Weiner, Leonard, 2184
Weiner, Lillian, 1156
Weiner, Patrick A., 7343
Weiner, Sharyn, 5557
Weiner, Stanley P., 3391
Weiner, Susan, 8156
Weiner, Walter H., 6054
Weinfeld, Sonya, 5539
Weingart, Ben, 1288
Weingart, Stella, 1288
Weingarten, Abraham, 5772
Weingarten, Carol, 7505
Weingarten, Charles Annenberg, 8084
Weingarten, Fay, 5772
Weingarten, Gregory Annenberg, 8084
Weingarten, Mr., 6751
Weingarten, Richard, 7505
Weingarten, Rosemarie, 6166
Weingarten, Seth, 7061
Weingrod, Louise, 5255
Weinlander, Walt, 2101
Weinreb Management, 5910
Weinreb, Deborah, 6279
Weinreb, Jacob, 5507, 6279
Weinreb, Sabina, 6279
Weinschenk, Fritz, 7211
Weinsheimer, William C., 3310
Weinstein, Alan, 6083
Weinstein, Barry L., 2919
Weinstein, Daniel, 711
Weinstein, Elaine, 6320
Weinstein, Harvey, 6375
Weinstein, Hilary, 2919
Weinstein, Ira J., 6931
Weinstein, Irving, 7233
Weinstein, Joseph D., 9636
Weinstein, Judith E., 3722
Weinstein, Judith R., 3575
Weinstein, Kenneth C., 3722
Weinstein, Peter, 6931
Weinstein, Stuart, 294
Weinstock, Albert, 7298
Weinstock, Mendel, 7298
Weinstock, Regina, 5195
Weintraub, Barbara A., 2292
Weintraub, Irving J., 6380
Weintraub, Joseph, 2292
Weintraub, Michael, 2292
Weintraub, Robert, 5532
Weintraub, Teresa Valdes-Fauli, 1957
Weintz, Elisabeth B., 6144
Weintz, Eric Cortelyou, 6144
Weintz, J. Fred, Jr., 6144
Weintz, Karl Fredrick, 6144
Weir, Amelia F., 7234
Weir, Ann L., 3588
Weir, Candace K., 7234
Weir, Matthew T., 3588
Weirether, Anne Marie, 1592
Weis, Barbara Holz, 9817
Weis, J.J., 9817
Weis, Konrad M., 8242
Weis, Traci, 9817
Weisberg, Arthur, 5449
Weisberg, Jack, 5449

Weisberger, Gerald L., 1321
Weisbrod Unitrust, Mary, 7900
Weisbrod, Carl B., 5970
Weisbrod, Mary E., 7900
Weise, Alisa, 9564
Weise, Daniel, 670
Weise, Daniel W., 670
Weise, David, 9564
Weise, David N., 670
Weisenburger, Randall R., 5547
Weiser, Carolyn, 6110
Weiser, Esther, 6112
Weiser, Howard, 7235
Weiser, Irving, 4661
Weiser, John M., 9272
Weiser, Marc, 4221
Weiser, Naftali, 6112
Weiser, Terri L., 9272
Weishaar, Henry, 2804
Weishan, James J., 9923
Weishoff, Marla Schaefer, 2222
Weiskner, Sandra S., 5942
Weisl, Edwin L., Jr., 6397
Weisman Trust of 1991, Frederick R., 1289
Weisman, Billie Milam, 1289
Weisman, Carol, 7062
Weisman, Jim, 7160
Weisman, Walter L., 6357
Weismann, Dietrich, 1735
Weiss Irrevocable Trust, Idy, 5746
Weiss Trust, Michael, 5746
Weiss, Abraham, 6318
Weiss, Alison B., 1642
Weiss, Anthony, 3760
Weiss, Arthur, 4311, 4313
Weiss, Barry, 6318
Weiss, Bill, 9977
Weiss, Carolyn M., 5228
Weiss, Catherine, 5244
Weiss, Cathy M., 8144
Weiss, Christa, 1914
Weiss, Cora, 6872
Weiss, D.D., 4706
Weiss, Daniel, 5905, 6872
Weiss, David E., 92
Weiss, David W., 3062
Weiss, Edna, 480
Weiss, Elie, 7834, 7871
Weiss, Gary, 7834, 7871
Weiss, George A., 1642
Weiss, Howard M., 1823, 3636
Weiss, Jeffrey, 7834, 7871
Weiss, Joseph H., 7235
Weiss, Josephine B., 3062
Weiss, Judith, 7834
Weiss, Judith Stone, 7871
Weiss, Judy, 6872
Weiss, Lisa, 3760
Weiss, Louis P., 6380
Weiss, Margie, Ph.D., 9869
Weiss, Marion W., 3469
Weiss, Martin E., 4257
Weiss, Michael, 5746
Weiss, Miriam F., 7235
Weiss, Morry, 7834, 7871
Weiss, Peter, 6872
Weiss, Robert E., 8995, 9049
Weiss, Robert L., 7635
Weiss, Roger J., 7236
Weiss, Solomon M., 7015
Weiss, Stanley, 3760
Weiss, Stephan, 6291
Weiss, Stephen, 618, 7236
Weiss, Stephen H., 7126
Weiss, Steven P., 3062
Weiss, Suzanne, 7236
Weiss, Tamara, 6872
Weiss, Warren, 1878
Weiss, William D., 9997
Weiss, William E., Jr., 9997
Weiss, William L., 3062
Weiss, William U., 9997
Weiss, Zev, 7834, 7871

Weiss-Fischmann, Susan, 1100
Weissberg, Marvin F., 9536
Weissberg, Nina V., 9536
Weissberg, Norbert, 5950
Weissberg, Weslie M., 9536
Weissblum, Cynthia Rivera, 6083
Weisse, Robin L., 3597
Weisselberg, Allen, 7167
Weisser, Jim, 7519
Weissfeld, Joachim A., 8519, 8544
Weissglass, Allan, 6972
Weissman, Daniel, 7237
Weissman, Ellen, 7237
Weissman, George, 7237
Weissman, Harriet L., 7238
Weissman, Janelle, 1358, 1366
Weissman, Michael A., 7238
Weissman, Mildred, 7237
Weissman, Paul, 7237
Weissman, Paul M., 7238
Weissman, Peter A., 7238
Weissman, Stephanie T., 7238
Weissmann, Gerald, 3621
Weisz, David, 6840
Weisz, Rachelle, 6840
Weisz, Sylvia, 1291
Weitz, Andrew S., 5016
Weitz, Barbara V., 5016
Weitz, Roger, 5016
Weitz, Roger T., 5016
Weitz, Roy, 1226
Weitz, Wallace, 4949
Weitz, Wallace R., 4977, 5016
Weitzel, John, 4534
Weitzel, Stephen E., 3117
Weitzenhoffer, Max, 7952
Weitzul, Jim, 9067
Weizenbaum, Norman, 8214
Welch & Forbes, 4139
Welch Allyn, Inc., 5539
Welch, Becky, 454
Welch, Deborah D., 8758
Welch, Edwin H., 9407, 9710
Welch, George, 5784
Welch, Ingrid, 8147
Welch, J. Russell, 2477
Welch, Jack, 4516
Welch, James C., 4446
Welch, John F., Jr., 4202
Welch, Kelly C., 8847
Welch, Mary K., 4348
Welch, P. Craig, III, 4348
Welch, P. Craig, Jr., 4348
Welch, Pamela, 8636
Welch, Richard H., 8847
Welch, Robert, 8847
Welch, Robert A., 9273
Welch, Scott M., 531
Welch, Steve, 8015
Welch, Thomas J., 4348
Welch, W. Perry, 7254
Weld, Edward W., 3982
Weld, Julia Power, 4844
Weldon, Nancy, 5005
Weldon, William, 3038
Welhorsky, Lynn C., 5390
Welke, Thomas, 4480
Welker, T.E. "Tim", 1404
Welland, David R., 9200
Wellcome Trust, The, 7333
Wellde, George W., Jr., 7239
Wellde, Patricia A., 7239
Welle, Paul, 4631
Weller, Diana B., 310
Weller, J.M., 935
Weller, James T., Sr., 8438
Weller, Lucy I., 7736
Welles, Christopher S., 5808
Welles, David E., 5808
Welles, David K., 5808
Welles, David K., Jr., 5808, 7882
Welles, David K., Sr., 7882
Welles, Georgia, 7882
Welles, Georgia E., 5808

Welles, Hope J., 7882
Welles, Hope V., 5808
Welles, Hope, IV, 5808
Welles, Jeffrey F., 5808
Welles, Kathrene, 5808
Welles, Maud, 5808
Welles, Peter C., 5808
Wellford, Adele, 8653
Wellin, Keith S., 7240
Wellin, Peter J., 7240
Welling, Eleanor, 7492
Wellington Management, 7497, 8049
Wellington, Herbert J., Jr., 6748
Welliver, Thomas, 3597
Wellman, Barclay O., 6964
Wellman, Brent Alan, 2293
Wellman, Brian Ashley, 2293
Wellman, Donna Bias, 2293
Wellman, F. Selby, Jr., 2293
Wellman, S.K., 7901
Wellman, W.F., 3189
Wellmark, Inc., 3343
Wellons, Elmer J., Jr., 7438
WellPoint Health Networks Inc., 1292
WellPoint, Inc., 3101
Wells Capital Management, 8049
Wells Fargo & Co., 1294
Wells Fargo Bank, 8748
Wells Fargo Bank Indiana, N.A., 3219, 3248, 4985, 5004, 5020
Wells Fargo Bank Minnesota, N.A., 4495, 4623, 4671
Wells Fargo Bank Nebraska, N.A., 4955, 4979, 4995
Wells Fargo Bank Northwest, N.A., 138, 9308, 9309, 9310, 9317, 9327, 9330, 9339, 9345
Wells Fargo Bank South Dakota, N.A., 8634
Wells Fargo Bank West, N.A., 1392
Wells Fargo Bank Wisconsin, N.A., 9962
Wells Fargo Bank, N.A., 85, 94, 143, 385, 536, 537, 571, 691, 742, 863, 951, 974, 1093, 1097, 1191, 1242, 1393, 3114, 3187, 4937, 7514, 8764, 8923, 9166, 9318, 9320, 9553, 9839
Wells, Albert, 211
Wells, Ann E., 5
Wells, Ashley, 4754
Wells, Barry L., 5724
Wells, Betty, 7819
Wells, Carrie, 1338
Wells, Christine, 9424
Wells, Craig, 3178
Wells, David, 4840
Wells, Ethel R., 5897
Wells, Francis, 1578
Wells, Frank G., 487, 1293
Wells, Frederick B., 4721
Wells, G. Greeley, 2294
Wells, George B., II, 5508
Wells, Gregory, 5074
Wells, James M., 2378, 2496
Wells, Jim, 2524
Wells, John O., 3254
Wells, Joseph L., 2170
Wells, Kappy J., 1836
Wells, Kevin, 487
Wells, Leslie, 4754
Wells, Lloyd D., 1295
Wells, Luanne C., 487, 1293
Wells, Lyndon, 3369
Wells, Lynn D., 1295
Wells, Marsha McCarty, 4754
Wells, Mike, 8916
Wells, Owen W., 3546
Wells, Preston A., Jr., 2294
Wells, Robert A., 3800
Wells, Robert G., 487
Wells, Samuel A., Jr., 4319
Wells, Steve, 7622
Wells, Thomas, 5136
Wells, Thomas A., 3634

Wells, Thomas M., 5179
Welsh Construction, 3683
Welsh, Bill, 7139
Welsh, Carol A., 2295
Welsh, David D., 9040
Welsh, Edward C., 9040
Welsh, Eric A., 2295
Welsh, Jay, 711
Welsh, John L., III, 9040
Welsh, John L., Mrs., 9040
Welsh, John W., 7633
Welsh, Patrick J., 2295
Welsh, Robert, 3129
Welsh, Robert H., Mrs., 3811
Welstead, Marvin G., 4962
Welte, Wendy B., 4773
Welters, Anthony, 9540
Welters, Beatrice W., 9540
Welty, Joseph S., 3598
Wenco, Inc. of North Carolina, 8025
Wenco, Inc. of Ohio, 8025
Wendel, Clyde F., 4865
Wendel, Kristin, 4552
Wendel, Larry L., 7891
Wendell, Nancy, 5976
Wendell, Peter C., 5326
Wender, Ann Colgin, 7241
Wender, Joseph H., 7241
Wender, Nancy L., 5505
Wendland, Craig, 4668
Wendler, Paul, 4219
Wendler, William F., II, 3709
Wendling, Cheryl J., 3140
Wendt, Charles, 8989
Wendt, Gary C., 1561
Wendt, Greg, 423
Wendt, Margaret L., 7243
Wendt, Nancy, 8025
Wendt, Nancy J., 8066
Wendt, R.C., 8025
Wendt, R.L., 8025
Wendt, Richard, 8066
Wendt, Roderick, 8066
Wendt, Rosemarie, 1561
Wendy's International, Inc., 7902
Wendy's of Montana, Inc., 5076
Wenger, Brian D., 2937
Wenger, Consuelo S., 4477
Wenger, Phil, 8300
Wenglikowski, Linda M., 370
Wenh-in Ng, Greer Anne, 4309
Wenick-Kutz, Bonnie, 4259
Wenner-Gren, Axel L., 7244
Wennesland, Kathleen W., 9542
Wennesland, Kim S., 9542
Wenngatz, Halbert, 4969
Wenngatz, Kathleen S., 4969
Wenrich, Rose, 3132
Wenske Enterprises, Inc., 3063
Wenske, Florence, 3063
Wenske, Herbert C., 3063
Wentling, Thomas J., Jr., 8457
Wentling, Thomas L., Jr., 8130
Wentworth, Elizabeth B., 9759
Wentworth, Lynn, 2355
Wentzell, Willett E., 1693, 1738
Weny, Frank X., 5450
Wenzel, Anne, 1471
Wenzel, Jean, 6841
Wenzel, John, 6774
Weprin, Barbara B., 7543
Weprin, William S., 7543
Werber, Suzanne E., 6741
Werblow, Nina W., 7245
Werderman, D.V., 628
Werderman, Del V., 150
Werdiger, Esther, 5451
Werdiger, Solomon, 5451
Werking, Helen, 2200
Werlinich, Lucille, 5509
Werly, Charles M., 2115, 4127
Werly, Jane E., 2115
Werly, John, 4127
Werner, Carolyn, 1296

Werner, Edward, 1296
Werner, Gloria, 5007
Werner, Jackie, 1940
Werner, Jill, 1296
Werner, John B., 9381
Werner, Leah, 6685
Werner, Rick S., 9613
Werner, S.R., 7643
Werner, Sarah R., 9613
Werner, Susan K., 4806
Werner, Thomas, 1296
Werner, William N., 3058
Werner-Robertson, Gail, 5007
Wernig, Raymond R., 7591
Werren, John R., 7867
Werthan, Bernard, 8636
Wertheimer, Barbara, 4272
Wertlieb, Barry, 1821
Wertz, Ronald W., 8205, 8249, 8250, 8251, 8252, 8442
Wes-Tex Drilling Co., 8924
WesBanco Bank, Inc., 9723, 9724, 9730
WesBanco Trust & Investment Services, Inc., 9716
Wesby, Meridith D., 8530
Weschler, R. Ted, 906
Wescombe, Gary T., 272
Wesley, Gregory, 9864
Wesley, James A., 2067
Wesner, Stephen J., 3156
Wessels, Pete M., 3277
Wessely, Boris A., 6825
Wessies, Rosemarie, 2969
Wessinger Trust, Paul, 8067
Wessinger, E. Charles, 8067
Wessinger, Henry W., 8067
Wessinger, Joseph M., 8067
Wessinger, William W., 8067
Wessley, Robert, 5957
Wessner, David K., 3064
Wessner, Norma C., 3064
Wessner, Patricia A., 3064
Wesson, Mark D., 8597
Wesson, Oliver, 7117
West Baking Co., 8743
West Co., Inc., The, 8500
West Pharmaceutical Services, Inc., 8500
West Point-Pepperell, Inc., 2513
West Trusts, E. & J., 941
West, Adele, 1854
West, Arline, 6581
West, Carole Wilson, 8742
West, Christopher R., 3761
West, Darlene, 2443
West, Douglas M., 7160
West, Ellen B., 9275
West, Emily A., 3256
West, Etta M., 1432
West, Florence G., 8743
West, Gordon T., 9275
West, Gordon T., Jr., 9275
West, John Dunham, 9964
West, John L., 7354
West, Juliana D., 7353
West, Laura, 9326
West, Margaret Hoath, 8742
West, Mary, 1704
West, Nancy, 1123
West, Neva Watkins, 9276
West, Paul S., 3462
West, Phyllis M., 3256
West, Reece A., 9275
West, Richard A., 8743
West, Robert, 9195
West, Ronald D., 5927, 6541
West, Ruth St. John, 9964
West, Sherece, 4743
West, Stephen R., 3256
West, Terri, 9232
West, Terry W., 7974
West, Thomas, 8535
West, Thomas H., 3958

West, Thomas H., Jr., 3958
West, Togo D., Jr., 1851
West, Tom, 3324
West, W. Richard, 5970
West, Wesley, 9276
West, Wesley, Mrs., 9276
Westar Energy, Inc., 3403
Westbrook, E.M., 1036
Westbrook, Elizabeth Moore, 1036
Westbrook, Tracey, 1940
Westcott, Bruce J., 6499
Westcott, Carl, 9278
Westcott, Court, 9278
Westcott, David, 8049
Westcott, Helen, 6499
Westcott, Jimmy, 9278
Wester, Nelson G., 8537
Westerfelt, Paul T., 3473
Westergaard, Steadman H., 5577
Westergom, Andrea P., 1896
Westerheide, Judy, 7584
Westerman, Samuel L., 4478
Western & Southern Life Insurance Co., The, 7903
Western Birch Co., LLC, 5118
Western Environmental Solutions, LLC, 5302
Western Massachusetts Electric Co., 1614
Western Pacific Mutual Insurance Co., 8369
Western Resources, Inc., 3403
Western, David, 5757
Westfall, Heath, 9303
Westfall, Leslie M., 880
Westfall, Rebekah, 9303
Westfeldt, Thomas D., 3508
Westgate, David F., 3854
Westhafer, Sandi, 3138
Westhues, Barbara A., 4877
Westin, Curt, 1389
Westlake, James L., 4925
Westlake, Nellie M., 4925
Westland Gardens Co., 3683
Westly, Anita, 1297
Westly, Steve, 1297
Westmaas, Allan J., 4231
Westman, Steve, 2670
Westmeyer, David E., 3246
Weston, Cori, 2535
Weston, Eric, 5452
Weston, Graham, 9093
Weston, Heather, 5452
Weston, Josh S., 5452
Weston, Judy, 5452
Weston, Mary Webber, 8208
Weston, Peter, 4034
Weston, Sharon R., 5089
Westover, Katherine, 9776
Westphal, Robert, 2645
WestPoint Stevens Inc., 2513
Westrate, Brian, 9946
Westrate, David B., 9946
Westrate, Mike, 9946
Westrum, John T., 3688
Westwater, Angela, 7138
Wetherington, Lee, 1946
Wetmore, D.J., 6227
Wetmore, Jessica, 6628
Wetterau, Mark, 627
Wetterau, Mark S., 627
Wettergren, David, 4703, 9933
Wettstein, John, 9845
Wetz, P.A., 8889
Wetzel, Mark R., 3892
Wetzel, Todd H., 3892
Wexler, Ann, 1785
Wexner Charitable Fund, Leslie H., The, 5695, 7904
Wexner Charitable Remainder Unitrust, Bella, 5528, 5608, 5765, 5838, 5929

Wexner Revocable Trust, Susan, 5528, 5608, 5765, 5838, 5929, 6228, 6394, 7299
Wexner, Abigail, 7904
Wexner, Abigail S., 7249
Wexner, Bella, 7197
Wexner, Leslie H., 4071, 7249, 7904
Wexner, Susan, 5956, 6008, 6228, 6394, 7299
Wexner, Susan R., 5528, 5608, 5765, 5838, 5929, 6601, 6655, 6698, 6757, 7197, 7284
Weyer, Thomas, 9730
Weyerhaeuser Co., 9703
Weyerhaeuser Corporation, 301
Weyerhaeuser Irrevocable Trust, C. Davis, 9691
Weyerhaeuser Trusts, Carl A., 4726
Weyerhaeuser, Annette B., 9586, 9681, 9691
Weyerhaeuser, C. Davis, 9586, 9681
Weyerhaeuser, Charles A., 4538
Weyerhaeuser, F.T., 9681
Weyerhaeuser, Frederick T., 4498
Weyerhaeuser, Gail T., 9586, 9681
Weyerhaeuser, George H., Jr., 9703
Weyerhaeuser, Henry G., 4538
Weyerhaeuser, Justin H., 4725
Weyerhaeuser, Robert M., 4538
Weyerhaeuser, William T., 9586, 9681, 9691
Weyers, L.L., 9970
Weyher, Michelle, 6729
Weyhing, R.L., III, 4293
Weyland, Ronald P., 3798
Weyland, Wendell P., 3798
Weymar, Caroline, 5432
Weymar, F. Helmut, 5432
Weymar, Mathew, 5432
Weymouth, George, 8076
Weymouth, Theodore S., 2946
Weynand, Jerome F., 8782
Weyrich, David, 1298
Weyrich, Mary, 1298
WFI Government Services, Inc., 1306
WGI Holdings England, 2578
Whalen, Daniel A., 1299
Whalen, Daniel C., 1299
Whalen, George T., Jr., 6549
Whalen, Gus, 2458
Whalen, Katharine C., 1299
Whalen, Katherine C., 1299
Whalen, Michael S., 1004, 1188
Whalen, Robert W., 6549
Whalen, Ryann, 5503
Whalen, Wayne, 3087
Whaley, Darlene K., 3106
Whaley, J. Patrick, 602
Whaley, Rickey, 2448
Wham, S. Smith, 8588
Wharton, Clifton R., 5762
Wharton, Daniel B., 9730
Wharton, John G., 8596
Whatley, Melba Davis, 9029
WHDH-TV, Inc., 1877
Wheatland Trust, David P., 4204
Wheatland, Barbara, 4204
Wheatland, Rebecca, 4204
Wheatland, Richard, 4204
Wheatley, Charles N., 3084
Wheatley, Henry U., 9363
Wheelabrator Technologies Inc., 9265
Wheeler Bros., Inc., 8501
Wheeler, Anita, 4952, 4953
Wheeler, Charles B., 8068
Wheeler, Charles E., 3693
Wheeler, Christopher, 3241
Wheeler, Coleman H., 8068
Wheeler, Coleman H., Jr., 8068
Wheeler, Cornelia T., 8068
Wheeler, Daniel, 2767
Wheeler, David A., 848
Wheeler, David L., 8501
Wheeler, Edward T., 8068

Wheeler, George, 1471
Wheeler, Harold W., 8501
Wheeler, Harold W., III, 8501
Wheeler, Joan M., 8501
Wheeler, John C., 8068
Wheeler, Kathryn, 344
Wheeler, Kathryn A., 4159
Wheeler, Ken, 3415
Wheeler, Max E., 2706
Wheeler, Nancy E., Hon., 9906
Wheeler, Paul J., 8501
Wheeler, Robert, 4798
Wheeler, Ruth B., 4287
Wheeler, Samuel C., 8068
Wheeler, Steven M., 98
Wheeler, Thomas B., 4556
Wheeler, Thomas K., 8068
Wheeler, Thomas M., 4479
Wheeler, Thomas R., 4479
Wheeler, Wayne, 7845
Wheeless, Richard W., 6391
Whelan, Karen M.L., 9531
Whelan, Sidney S., Jr., 6218
Wheless, N. Hobson, 3514
Wheless, Nicholas Hobson, Jr., 3514, 3517
Whelihan, J. Bruce, 1862
Whelpley, Kathy A., 1785
Whelton, Joan M., 3825
Whetstone, Susan, 1514
Whicker, John, 3255
While, Larry J., 3629
Whinfrey, Peter K., 2680
Whipple, Ken, 4254
Whipple, Kenneth, 4260, 8878
Whipple, Mary, 174
Whipple, William P., 3290
Whirlpool Corp., 4480
Whitaker, Harold H., Sr., 4757
Whitaker, Janice M., 7439
Whitaker, Mae M., 4926
Whitaker, Shannon McNeely, 4619
Whitaker, Terrance M., 9981
White Hat Management, 7554
White Mountains Foundation, 3539
White Party Benefit, 8853
White Plains Hotel Limited Partnership, 6316
White, A. Scott, 2240
White, Andrew J., 9527
White, Andrew S., 9186
White, Ann, 3231
White, Ann B., 5418
White, Anna Seim, 3119
White, Annette F., 3476
White, B. Briscoe, III, 9417
White, Barbara, 3999
White, Barbara E., 3257
White, Barrie M., 6529
White, Benjamin T., 2355, 2487
White, Betty Lou, 4363
White, C. Edward, Jr., 4337
White, Carol L., 4481
White, Charles E., 4481
White, Claire M., 4399
White, Claire Mott, 4337, 4346
White, Clarence, 4534
White, Clifford A., 9482
White, Collette Mary, O.P., Sr., 2969
White, Craig, 3257
White, Daniel A., 1332
White, David B., 4481
White, David K., 1221
White, David, Rabbi, 404
White, Dean V., 3257
White, Dela W., 8829
White, E.B., 7589
White, Edward D., III, 1344
White, Edward L., Jr., 2371
White, Eric S., 1332
White, Frances H., 642
White, G.R., 9279
White, George C., 6532
White, Glenn, 3963

Wilmers, Elisabeth Roche, 6822
Wilmers, Robert G., 6465, 6822, 7215, 7246
Wilmington Trust Co., 1693, 1694, 1704, 1707, 1711, 1720, 1724, 1738, 1763, 5479
Wilmington Trust of Pennsylvania, 8378
Wilmott, Tim, 8685
Wilms, Dirk, 7344
Wilner, Myron, 4110
Wilner, Suzanne B., 2334
Wilpon, Fred, 6779, 7261
Wilpon, Jeffrey, 7261
Wilpon, Judith, 7261
Wils, Madelyn, 6391
Wilshire 19, LLC, 379
Wilsnack, Sharon C., 3564
Wilson Co., H.W., Inc., The, 7263
Wilson, Alfred G., 4485
Wilson, Alisa M., 5074
Wilson, Andrea, 1234, 6344
Wilson, Angelina M., 3515
Wilson, Ann, 183
Wilson, Anthony S., 3344
Wilson, Becky, 8638
Wilson, Betty H., 3164
Wilson, Blair J., 3075
Wilson, Bruce, 1560
Wilson, C. Ivan, 8833
Wilson, Charles, 2698
Wilson, Charles K., Jr., 8744
Wilson, Charles N., 9227
Wilson, Christina P., 1031
Wilson, Dale, 8833
Wilson, Dan L., 6108
Wilson, David, 1234, 6344, 7506
Wilson, David K., 3075
Wilson, Denver, 3515
Wilson, Diane Wenger, 4477
Wilson, Dianne, 3515
Wilson, Donna D., 8664
Wilson, Dorothy Cheney, 9049
Wilson, Douglas A., 7643
Wilson, Dwayne, 523
Wilson, Elisa Gabelli, 5200
Wilson, Faye, 578
Wilson, Frances Fondren, 8906
Wilson, Frances W., Mrs., 2519
Wilson, Frank, 2487
Wilson, Fred B., 2519
Wilson, Fred W., 1234, 6344
Wilson, Garnet A., 7909
Wilson, Gary L., 1308
Wilson, Gayle, 980
Wilson, Gloria, 831
Wilson, Grant M., 8521
Wilson, H., 3018
Wilson, H.W., 7263
Wilson, H.W., Mrs., 7263
Wilson, Harold S., 8714
Wilson, Helene T., 8521
Wilson, Henry, 7506
Wilson, Henry, III, 7506
Wilson, Howard O., 991, 1195
Wilson, Huey J., 3515
Wilson, Hugh H., 2300
Wilson, Isabel Brown, 8799
Wilson, J. Bradley, 7319
Wilson, J. Christine, 7264
Wilson, J. Richard, 4232, 7264
Wilson, James B., 3009
Wilson, James C., Jr., 8613
Wilson, James E., 7593
Wilson, James M., 4205
Wilson, Jane, 5548
Wilson, Janet, 7506
Wilson, Janet D., 3789
Wilson, Janice J., 8696, 8697
Wilson, Jean D., 7333
Wilson, Jean H., 152
Wilson, Jesse B., III, 9478
Wilson, Jill G., 403
Wilson, John, 3515, 4464
Wilson, John H., 68

Wilson, John H., II, 9124
Wilson, John H.T., 1503, 5892
Wilson, John K., 4959
Wilson, John M., Jr., 7901
Wilson, Joseph C., 7264
Wilson, Joseph R., 7264
Wilson, Julie Kann, 4094
Wilson, Justin P., 3075
Wilson, Katherine M., 7264, 9965
Wilson, Kathleen H., 7356
Wilson, Keith, Jr., 3349
Wilson, Kemmons, 8742
Wilson, Kenneth, 384
Wilson, Kent R., 1239
Wilson, Kim, 4637
Wilson, Kirsten, 8521
Wilson, Lana L., 1239
Wilson, Leland, 9233
Wilson, Linda, 6344
Wilson, Lisa, 6512
Wilson, M., 1239
Wilson, M. Jane, 4205
Wilson, Marie C., 7264
Wilson, Mark, 4624, 7504
Wilson, Mary, 8386
Wilson, Mary M., 4484
Wilson, Mary P., 2300
Wilson, Matilda R., 4485
Wilson, Michael, 4743
Wilson, Michael G., 326
Wilson, Michael J., 5098
Wilson, Myrtle, 3131
Wilson, Nancy J., 3344
Wilson, Norman L., 1339
Wilson, Otis, 7343
Wilson, Pamela, 1234
Wilson, Pat L., 9166
Wilson, Paula, 5883
Wilson, Pete, Hon., 320
Wilson, Peter, 2670
Wilson, Peter A., 3976, 4170
Wilson, Ralph C., Jr., 4484
Wilson, Randon W., 7207
Wilson, Richard A., 412
Wilson, Richard F., 152
Wilson, Robert A., 8744
Wilson, Robert C., 9097
Wilson, Robert L., 831
Wilson, Robert W., 7262
Wilson, Rod, 2244
Wilson, Rosine M., 9263
Wilson, Roxanne, 1118
Wilson, Russ, 9548
Wilson, Sandra W., 1503
Wilson, Shannon T., 148
Wilson, Sherry, 9060
Wilson, Spence, 8647
Wilson, Spence L., 8744
Wilson, Stanley P., 9182
Wilson, Susan N., 5357
Wilson, Suzanne C., 152
Wilson, T., 1239
Wilson, Thomas, 3761
Wilson, Thomas J., 2588
Wilson, Tom, 4254
Wilson, Ursula, 2717
Wilson, Vera, 8395
Wilson, Victoria, 8842
Wilson, Wayne, 214
Wilson, William M., 3075
Wilson-Moore, Elizabeth, 8744
Wilson-Taylor, Martella, 3961
Wilson-West, Carol, 8744
Wilson-Young, Lauren, 8744
Wilt, Toby, 8636
Wilton, Jane L., 6613
Wiltsek, Nancy, 99, 1013
Wiltz, James W., 4647
Wimberley, Ruby J., 9209
Wimmer, Betty L., 8505
Wimpenny, Jonathan B., 7040
Wimsatt, William, 4320
Winchcole, Dorothy C., 3591
Winchell, Jean Rogers, 9156

Winchester, David J., 2966
Winchester, Dawn, 3528
Winckler, Haddon O., 8905
Winder, Phoebe, 3977
Winders, Mary Ann, 7762
Windham, Donald, 5793
Windheim, Randi, 5532
Windle, Janice W., 8881
Windmueller, Steven, 6035
Windsor, 3683
Windsor, Barbara, 3598
Windsor, Robert G., 1360
Windsor, Robert G., Rev., 1352
Wine & Spirits Distributors of Illinois, 3076
Wine, C. Douglas, 9400
Wineka, Mark, 7403
Winer, Elizabeth Star, 2248
Winfree, Rupert, Mrs., 9474
Winfrey, Oprah G., 3077
Wing Enterprises, Inc., 9352
Wing, Harold R., 9352
Wingard, Raymond R., 25
Wingate, Carole, 1913
Wingate, Don, 1913
Wingate, Roy S., 9209
Wingens, Gary, 5228
Winger, Dennis L., 1484
Wingerter, Dorothy, 7882
Wingerter, Robert, 7882
Wingfield, W.T., 2519
Wingo, Nancy, 8233
Winikates, James, 3065
Winikates, Jim, 2922
Winkelman, Dorinda P., 7028
Winkelman, Marius O., 7028
Winkelman, Mark O., 7028
Winkelried, Abby, 7265
Winkelried, Jon, 7265
Winkenwerder, John G., 7346
Winkhaus, Gwenn S., 7122, 7695
Winkleman, Dennis, 9828
Winkler, Catherine, 9542
Winkler, David J., 554
Winkler, Mark, 9542
Winkley, Tanya, 1185
Winn, William R., 3963
Winn-Dixie Stores, Inc., 2301
Winnard, Diane, 2579
Winnell, Todd, 4412
Winner, James E., Jr., 8438
Winner, Michael A., 7784
Winnick, Adam, 1310
Winnick, Alex, 1310
Winnick, Gary, 1310
Winnick, Karen, 1310
Winoker, Laurence, 6716
Winsett, Byron B., Jr., 8732
Winship, William, 5631
Winslow, Julia D., 1863
Winsor, Cristina, 5873
Winsor, Curtin, III, 5873
Winsor, Curtin, Jr., Hon., 5873
Winsor, Frank, 2572
Winsor, Monica, 5873
Winsor, Rebecca, 5873
Winspear, William, 531
Winston Foundation, N.K., Inc., The, 7267
Winston, Annette E., 8671
Winston, Bert F., III, 9212
Winston, Bert F., Jr., 9212
Winston, Blake W., 9212
Winston, Charles M., 7507
Winston, Charles M., Jr., 7507
Winston, Eleanor C., 4688
Winston, Florence B., 7507
Winston, Frank, 8681
Winston, Hathily, 725
Winston, James H., 2271, 2302
Winston, James H., Jr., 2302
Winston, Joni R., 9908
Winston, Kenneth, 8381
Winston, L. David, 9212

Winston, Marion T., 7507
Winston, Melinda, 983
Winston, Norman K., 7267
Winston, Patrick H., Jr., 9367
Winston, Robert W., III, 7507
Winston, Samuel G., 2623
Winston-Mason, Mary, 2302
Wint, Stan, 3354
Winter, David, 920
Winter, Fred, 5498
Winter, Ilona B., 3620
Winter, Larry, 2359
Winter, Laura, 8049
Winter, Nancy C.H., 2780
Winter, Peter, 2464
Winter, Phillip R., 9521
Winter, William L., Ph.D., 5056
Winter, William, Hon., 4743
Winters, Melanie, 1827
Winters, Peter, 2464
Winthrop Trust Co., 6770
Winthrop, Inc., 5099
Winthrop, Marilyn, 842
Winton, Alexa Griffith, 4711
Winton, Christopher J., 9722
Wintriss, Lynn, 3575, 3576, 3650, 3722
Wintrob, Jay S., 570
Wintrode, David C., 5341
Wintzer, William, 1971
Wipple, Ross M., 174
Wire, Bill, 8636
Wirginis, Terrence L., 8107
Wirshup, David, 1147
Wirshup, Rochelle Shapell, 1147
Wirth, Christopher, 1863
Wirth, Kelsey, 1863
Wirth, Kimberly, 1571
Wirth, Peter, 3922
Wirth, Wren Winslow, 1863
Wirthlin, David B., 9337
Wirtz, Arthur M., Jr., Mrs., 3058
Wirtz, Mary, 9779
Wisbey, Ron, 1265
Wischer, Jerry, 3446
Wisconsin Dept. of Natural Resources, 9918
Wisconsin Dept. of Transportation, 9918
Wisconsin Energy Corp., 9967
Wisconsin Power and Light Co., 9742
Wisconsin Public Service Corp., 9970
Wisdom, Andrew, 3507
Wisdom, Betty, 3507
Wise, Anderson, 6639
Wise, Bradford A., 3540
Wise, Catherine J., 6396
Wise, Charles W., 8394
Wise, Daniel P., 4200
Wise, Emma F., 9285
Wise, Janelle, 2567
Wise, Jessie Kenan, 9417
Wise, Katherine, 2752
Wise, Marie Figge, 9284
Wise, Michael, 7852
Wise, Patricia, 7882
Wise, Phillip C., 2900
Wise, Robert E., 5826
Wise, Tami F., 8490
Wise, Terri L., 4845
Wise, Watson W., 9285
Wise, William A., 9284
Wiseman, Frances, 220
Wiseman, Linda, 5418
Wiseman, Mary Whitten, 3420
Wiseman, Michael L., 7765
Wiseman, William F., 5418
Wisen, Kristen, 2766
Wisenburg, Ralph, 7593
Wiser, Bob, 9543
Wiser, Wanda G., 9405
Wishart, Alfred W., Jr., 8130
Wishcamper, Carol, 3554
Wishna, Jeanette, 4837
Wishnia, Steve, 8718

Woodling, Sue, 7870
Woodman Partners, LLC, 379
Woodman, George B., 7816
Woodner Family Collection, Ian, Inc., 7277
Woodner, Andrea, 7277
Woodruff, Chevin, 2522
Woodruff, Ethel I., 2522
Woodruff, J. Barnett, 2522
Woodruff, James W., 2522
Woodruff, James W., III, 2522
Woodruff, Judy C., 9424
Woodruff, Robert W., 2521
Woodruff, Steve B., 2522
Woods Charitable Fund, Inc., 3084
Woods, Alexandra, 7278
Woods, Alfred, 5454
Woods, Bob, 8265
Woods, David, 3160
Woods, Donna W., 4987, 5018
Woods, Edwin Newhall, 936
Woods, Emily L., 4016
Woods, Eugene A., 3407
Woods, Frank H., 5018
Woods, Frank H., Jr., 5018
Woods, Gary D., 3298
Woods, Gary V., 9037
Woods, H.A., 9045
Woods, Hank, 5018
Woods, Henry C., 5018
Woods, Henry Clay, 8721
Woods, Jacqueline F., 7576
Woods, James H., 4928
Woods, James H., Jr., 4928
Woods, Janet, 9615
Woods, John R., 4897, 4928
Woods, John R., Jr., 4897
Woods, Joseph Patrick, 5293
Woods, Laura-Lee Whittier, 824, 1304
Woods, Margaret, 3855
Woods, Nelle C., 5018
Woods, Patrick, 854
Woods, Priscilla B., 7278
Woods, Thomas C., III, 5010
Woods, Thomas C., Jr., 5018
Woods, Ward W., Jr., 7278
Woods, Willie G., 3693
Woodshick, Herbert, 8135
Woodson, Margaret C., 7509
Woodson, Marvin C., Jr., 8569
Woodson, Mary Anne, 7509
Woodson, Mary H., 7509
Woodson, Nathaniel, 1668
Woodson, Paul B., Jr., 7509
Woodson, Sam P., III, 8798
Woodson, William, 2124
Woodsum, Harold E., Jr., 1648
Woodsum, Stephen G., 4013
Woodward Charitable Lead Trust, Helen, 1323
Woodward Governor Co., 3085
Woodward, Ann Eden, 7279
Woodward, Charles G., 1578
Woodward, Helen, 7582
Woodward, Helen W., 1323
Woodward, Joanne, 1609
Woodward, O. James, III, 537
Woodward, Robert B., 134
Woodworth, Robin, 1264
Woodworth, Roger D., 9589
Woody, Kerry, 9846
Woodyard Trust, Dorothy M., 2657
Woodyard, Rose Marie, 8511
Wooley, David, 483
Wooley, Joe H., 2345
Woolf, Geraldine H., 3517
Woolf, William C., 3517
Woolfolf, William C., III, 2387
Woolfolk, Odessa, 24
Woolford, Linda, 3916
Woolford, T. Guy, 2524
Woollam Co., John A., Inc., 5019
Woollam, John A., 5019
Woollam, Philip, 3480

Woollam, Tina F., 3480
Woollcott, James W.G., 7404
Woollen, Phyllis B., 7310
Woolley, Fergus W., 4594
Woolley, R.B., Jr., 580
Woolley, Scott, 580
Woolley, Vasser, 2525
Woolmington, Robert, 9361
Woolsey, R. James, 1632
Woolson, John, 3276
Wooten, David, 7347
Wooten, James, 2813
Wooten, Robin Swett, 9221
Wootton, Sharon, 9219
Worcester, Frederick L., 3845
Word, Carol A., 8130
Wordsworth, James M., 9486
Worek, Bob, 3205
Work Area Protection Corp., 8455
Workman Publishing Co., 7250
Workman, Carolan, 7250
Workman, Carolyn, 4645
Workman, John, 4252
Workman, M. James, Rev., 8520
Workman, Mickey, 7897
Workman, Mildred C., 7897
Workman, Peter, 7250
Workman, Rusty, 9081
Works, Ann, 1540
World Events, LLC, 1060
World-Wide Volkswagen Corp., 5924
WorldCom, Inc., 9471
Worley, Geneva B., 3086
Worley, Gordon R., 3086
Worley, Peyton, 8618
Worley, Richard B., 5265, 8356
Worls, G. Randolph, 8099
Wornall, Kearney, 4929
Worner, Jacob, 7894
Wornick, Anita L., 1320
Wornick, Jonathan, 1320
Wornick, Kenneth, 1320
Wornick, Michael, 1320
Wornick, Ronald C., 1320
Woroniecki, James, 4272
Woronoco Savings Bank, 4210
Worrell, Bobby B., 9382
Worrell, Odette A., 1971
Worrell, Thomas E., 1971
Worrell, Thomas E., Jr., 1971
Worsham, Margit S., 8671
Wortel, Gary, 8619
Worth, David, 7343
Worth, Robert, 1294
Worth, Robert R., 6190
Wortham, Gus S., 9292
Wortham, Lyndall F., 9292
Wortham, R.W., III, 9292
Worthington, Terry, 1944
Worthley, Christopher, 510
Worthley, Christopher, Rev., 205
Wortley, Neil, 4870
Woschitz, Frank, 1843
Wosepka, John, 4719
Wotherspoon, Eleonore, 9954
Wotherspoon, William W., 9954
Wou, Humphrey, 1401
Wozniak, Ed, 1517
WPIX, Inc., 7163
Wraith, Ellen Jacob, 5135
Wrap-On Co., Inc., 2976
Wrather, Christopher C., 1321
Wray, Donald "Buddy", 169
Wray, Gay F., 2729
Wray, Tim F., 2729
Wren, Elizabeth G., 7342
Wren, John, 5547
Wren, Nancy G., 9498, 9499
Wren, Thomas D., 1706
Wrenn, Peter J., 2987
Wright, Anne L., 9367
Wright, Arnold W., Jr., 8143
Wright, Barbara P., 972, 973
Wright, Bernard H., Jr., 7721

Wright, Betty J., 9293
Wright, Bill, 6577
Wright, Bob, 3497
Wright, Bradley, 8608
Wright, C. Bagley, 9708
Wright, Candance E., 3462
Wright, Charles B., III, 9708
Wright, Charles K., 2487
Wright, Dave, 4237
Wright, Donna B., 8745
Wright, Earl L., 1388
Wright, Eldon S., 7816
Wright, Elizabeth, 3124
Wright, Erin, 4479
Wright, Eugene E., Jr., 7349
Wright, Howard S., 9707
Wright, Jack F., Jr., 9419
Wright, James, 3627
Wright, Jean, 5537
Wright, Jim, 3333
Wright, John G., 2470
Wright, Johnie E., 9294
Wright, Kay, 7749
Wright, Kernan, 7891
Wright, Korynne H., 9707
Wright, Lucy Babb, 3762
Wright, Martha C., 7337
Wright, Mary Garner, 2018
Wright, Mary R., 401
Wright, Merrill, 9708
Wright, Michaleon A., 4479
Wright, Minturn T., III, 1743
Wright, Morgan, 4479
Wright, Nancy, 4246
Wright, O'Neal O., 4226
Wright, Orville, 1830
Wright, Pamela M., 6494
Wright, Patricia D., 2628
Wright, Patricia L., 9293
Wright, Peggy, 156
Wright, Phillip D., 7989
Wright, Prentice B., 9708
Wright, Randy L., 8975
Wright, Richard L., 5199
Wright, Robert, 3110
Wright, Ron D., 7574
Wright, Sally S., 9707
Wright, Soraya M., 389
Wright, Spencer H., 8745
Wright, Thomas, 4497
Wright, Thomas H., 6449
Wright, Tim, 9740
Wright, Vaden, 9401
Wright, Vernon H.C., 1730, 3762
Wright, Virginia B., 9708
Wright, W.R., 1964
Wright, Wayne, 9571
Wright, Wilhelmina M., 4613
Wright, William D., 9293
Wright, William Dan, 9293
Wright, William E., 9293
Wright, William H., II, 6471
Wright, William L., 6211
Wright, William T., II, 8297
Wrightson, Lois I., 3807
Wrigley Jr. Co., Wm., 3088
Wrigley, Julie A., 7848, 9971
Wrigley, William, Jr., 3088
Wriston, Kathryn D., 6150
Wrobleski, Paul, 5858
Wroclawski, John, 6918
WTVF-News Channel 5 Network, 9455
Wu, Whiting, 6437
Wuerl, Donald W., Bishop, 8174
Wulf, Gene C., 4515
Wulf, Jerold W., 4501
Wuliger, E. Jeffrey, 7918
Wuliger, Ernest M., 7918
Wuliger, Gregory, 7918
Wuliger, Timothy F., 7918
Wulliger, Hirsch, 6509
Wunderman, Severin, 5079
Wunsch, Eric M., 7281
Wunsch, Ethel, 7281

Wunsch, Joseph W., 7281
Wunsch, Peter, 7281
Wunsch, Samuel, 7281
Wurmb, Robert O., 4866
Wurtele, V., 4558
Wurtz, Rebecca M., 3016
Wurtz, Thomas J., 7502
Wurzer, Marvin A., 9170, 9176, 9277
Wuthrich, Alan, 3186
WV Culture and Arts Grant, 9735
WWF, Ltd., 9538
WWP/Young & Rubicam, 7040
Wyant, Clair F., 154
Wyant, Dom H., 2320
Wyant, James C., 154
Wyant, Louise A., 154
Wyatt, Audrey, 9371
Wyatt, Dot, 7349
Wyatt, J.D., 935
Wyatt, Jane C., 69
Wyatt, Kim, 9089
Wyatt, Mary F., 3747
Wyche, Paul B., Jr., 7315
Wyckoff, Ann Pigott, 9650, 9692
Wyckoff, Christy, 9650
Wyckoff, E. Lisk, Jr., 6199
Wyckoff, Paul L., 9692
Wyckoff, T. Evans, 9692
Wyckoff-Byrne, Martha, 9692
Wyckoff-Dickey, Sheila, 9692
Wycliff, Don, 2663
Wyers, Kirk, 4315
Wyeth, 3677, 4930
Wyeth, Phyllis Mills, 1698
Wyett, Pamela Applebaum, 4222
Wygod, Martin J., 5373
Wygod, Pamela, 5373
Wyker, J.W., III, 77
Wyker, J.W., Jr., 77
Wyland, James H., 2332
Wyld, Deborah H., 9485
Wylie, Ann C., 1385
Wylie, J. Michael, 8777
Wylie, John, 1087
Wylie, Rick, 9559
Wyly, Charles J., Jr., 8839
Wyman, David E., 9709
Wyman, Francis S., 4000
Wyman, Hal, 9709
Wyman, Henry W., 1622
Wyman, Marguerite A., 1622
Wyman, Maria, 1622
Wyman, Norman J., 9987
Wyman, Ralph M., 1622
Wyman, Thomas, 2677
Wyman, Virginia, 9709
Wyman, William, 9885, 9886
Wymbs, Harriet S., 2307
Wymbs, Norman E., 2307
Wyndsor Custom Homes, 8818
Wyner, Joshua S., 9405
Wynia, Ann, 4567
Wynn, Bee, 1324
Wynn, Carl, 1324
Wynn, Deryl W., 4842
Wynn, John R., 3, 45
Wynn, Leila Clark, 4743
Wynn, Mark, 3127
Wynn, Phail, Jr., Dr., 7496
Wynn, Ronnie J., 20
Wynne, James J., Rev., 1246
Wynne, John O., 9484
Wynne, Richard B., 7404
Wyse, Alden M., 2086
Wysong, Kathryn Lyman, 4639
Wysong, Mary, 3214
Wyss, Hansjoerg, 1864, 8510
Wyss, Loren L., 8064
Wytana, Inc., 4983
Wythes, Carol Krause, 9841
Wyzga, Michael S., 3922

Xcel Energy Inc., 4732

GEOGRAPHIC INDEX

Foundations in boldface type make grants on a national, regional, or international basis; the others generally limit giving to the city or state in which they are located. For local funders with a history of giving in another state, consult the "see also" references at the end of each state section.

ALABAMA

Alexander City: Russell 60
Anniston: Community 23
Atmore: **Corman 29**
Birmingham: Alabama 1, **Altec 4**, AmSouth 5, Anderson 7, Ard 8, Barber 10, **Bashinsky 11**, Blount 13, Bolden 15, Brock 16, Bruno 17, Caring 18, Carson 19, Comer 22, Community 24, Compass 28, Daniel 31, Dixon 32, Founders 34, Friedman 35, Hess 38, Kaul 40, Kimerling 41, Lowder 44, Mayer 47, McWane 50, Meyer 52, Patterson 56, Pleiad 57, Protective 58, Saks 61, Scrushy 62, Stephens 65, Strain 66, Thompson 67, **Union 70**, Upchurch 71, Vines 72, **Vulcan 73**, Webb 75
Brewton: Finlay 33, McMillan 49
Camden: Wallace 74
Childersburg: **Christian 21**
Decatur: Wyker 77
Dothan: Community 26, McLendon 48
Florence: Anderson 6
Huntsville: Lowe 45
Madison: Alpha 3
Mobile: Bedsole 12, Community 25, Crampton 30, Hearin 37, May 46, Mitchell 53, Roberts 59, Smith 63, Treadwell 68, Trippe 69
Monroeville: Stallworth 64
Montgomery: Alfa 2, Aronov 9, Blount 14, Central 20, Lowder 42, Lowder 43, Methvin 51, Working 76
Mountain Brook: Hill 39
Tuscaloosa: Community 27, Harrison 36, Moody 54, Moore 55

see also 560, 1837, 2180, 2314, 2323, 2339, 2345, 2361, 2429, 2494, 2513, 2802, 2925, 3142, 3705, 4446, 5758, 5919, 7781, 9472, 9765, 9812

ALASKA

Anchorage: Alaska 78, Alaska 79, Arctic 80, Atwood 81, Carr 82, CIRI 83, Rasmuson 85
Fairbanks: Doyon 84

see also 847, 881, 1245, 1831, 3853, 8041, 9550, 9563, 9585, 9588, 9600, 9602, 9634, 9639, 9644, 9651, 9681, 9705

ARIZONA

Carefree: Berlin 89
Chandler: Neely 126
Flagstaff: Wilson 152
Gilbert: **Johnson 112**, Neely 125, Trend 147
Oro Valley: Hansen 104
Paradise Valley: Farrington 97, Linde 117, Reese 133
Phoenix: A.P.S. 86, Arizona 87, Aurora 88, Cooper 92, Dee 94, Dougherty 96, Flinn 98, Gesner 100, Help 105, Levine 115, Long 118, Marley 120, Moreno 123, Phelps 129, Schwartz 137, Shaw 138, **Solheim 139**, Steele 142, Sterne 143, University 148, Viad 149
Prescott: **Kieckhefer 113**, Morris 124
Rio Verde: **Gagarin 99**
Scottsdale: Dorrance 95, **Globe 101**, Halle 103, Herberger 106, Hickey 108, **IFS 109**, Jazzbird 111, **Moller 122**, Noah's 127, Piper 130, **Rae 132**, **Rodel 136**, Stardust 141, **Torhjelm 146**, **Weberg 151**
Sedona: Ottens 128
Sun Lakes: Robson 135
Surprise: Laizure 114, Stevens 144
Tempe: Lewis 116, WWJD 153
Tucson: Cacioppo 90, Community 91, Cottrell 93, Green 102, Hermundslie 107, Jasam 110, Lovell 119, Marshall 121, Pocono 131, **Research 134**, Soling 140, **Tankersley 145**, Wyant 154
Wickenburg: Webb 150

see also 28, 55, 497, 611, 696, 831, 971, 1095, 1351, 1458, 1499, 1864, 2128, 2253, 2325, 2478, 2629, 2729, 2746, 2825, 2861, 2924, 2940, 2986, 3225, 3326, 3367, 3589, 4096, 4286, 4403, 4526, 4628, 5049, 5066, 5077, 5360, 5919, 6060, 6297, 6298, 6394, 7222, 7662, 7746, 7801, 7870, 8022, 8025, 8140, 8500, 9023, 9290, 9368, 9578, 9705, 9971, 9982, 9987

ARKANSAS

Arkadelphia: Ross 174
Bentonville: Glass 163, Wal-Mart 184, Walton 186
Conway: Nabholz 168
El Dorado: Murphy 167, Pruet 170, Union 183
Eudora: White 187
Fayetteville: Bradberry 159, Garrison 162, Walker 185
Fort Smith: Whitt 188
Jonesboro: East 160
Little Rock: Altheimer 155, Arkansas 156, Blue 157, Bodenhamer 158, **Frueauff 161**, Gleason 164, Hussman 165, Rebsamen 171, Rockefeller 172, Rockefeller 173, Smith 176, Sturgis 178, Taylor 179, Tenenbaum 180
Pine Bluff: Trinity 181
Rogers: **Soderquist 177**
Siloam Springs: **Windgate 189**
Springdale: Jones 166, Northwest 169, Schmieding 175, **Tyson 182**

see also 560, 2648, 3309, 3397, 3474, 4368, 4480, 4743, 5056, 5068, 5763, 7949, 7954, 8661, 8977, 8995, 9015, 9216, 9665

CALIFORNIA

Alameda: Chintu 382, **Maddie's 845**
Aliso Viejo: Eaton 475, Fluor 523, McDonough 873, Nicholas 937
Altadena: Webster 1286
Anaheim: Anaheim 220, Anderson 222, Sambar 1085, Servants' 1129
Anaheim Hills: My 930
Aptos: Borina 306, Borina 307, Solari 1176
Arcadia: BayTree 265, Cobb 392, Sathya 1096
Atherton: Gill 576, Goel 587, Lamond 785
Bakersfield: **Bolthouse 301**, Grimm 619, Grimm 620, Judkins 732
Bayside: Humboldt 691
Belmont: Taube 1228
Belvedere: Silberstein 1153
Berkeley: Alafi 201, Battle 260, Baxter 262, La Fetra 782, Lutz 833, **Rosengarten 1068**, Smullin 1169, Swanson 1216, Witkin 1313
Beverly Hills: Ahmanson 198, **American 216**, Barth 258, Black 293, Bohnett 300, Burch 334, CAA 341, Carson 362, Cheeryble 377, Daly 437, **DJ & T 458**, Douglas 464, Edgerton 477, Eisner 481, Factor 491, Feintech 498, Feintech 499, Feintech 500, Field 503, **Four 532**, G.T.R. 544, Gershman 566, Goldsmith 599, Gonda 601, Greenberg 616, JG 719, Karsh 744, Kellerman 753, King 760, **Kohl 771**, **Lear 795**, Leichtman 802, Levine 809, Lincy 812, Mann 849, Marciano 850, Meyer 893, **Mohn 907**, Moss 921, **Nimoy 938**, O'Connor 946, Oppenheimer 955, Oppenheimer 956, Ornest 959, Post 1011, Schaeffer 1100, Seinfeld 1124, Semel 1125, Shapell 1134, Shapell 1135, Shapell 1136, Shapiro 1137, Smith 1164, Spiegel 1182, Stewart 1198, Stuart 1208, **Tchang 1229**, Webb 1284, Winnick 1310
Bradbury: Kommerstad 772, Riddle 1049
Brea: Femino 501
Brentwood: Goldman 595
Buellton: **S.G. 1078**
Burbank: Burns 338, DeMille 450, Disney 456, Gold 589, Lantz 790, Rigler 1051
Burlingame: Fitzpatrick 515, Lane 787, Swanson 1217
Calabasas: Countrywide 422, Shapiro 1138
Calabasas Hills: Cheesecake 378
Camarillo: Rogers 1062, Smidt 1159, Ventura 1264
Carmel: Berkshire 283, Bunker 333, Chapman 374, Moley 908, Otter 965, Segal 1121
Carpinteria: **Glenn 581**
Chula Vista: **Oak 947**
City of Industry: Cacique 342, Majestic 848
Claremont: Magistro 847, Stewart 1199
Clovis: Radin 1025, Smittcamp 1168
Commerce: Family 493
Concord: Garaventa 553, Hofmann 683, Seeno 1120
Corcoran: Corcoran 417
Corona: **Versacare 1265**
Corona del Mar: Croul 431, Sprague 1183
Coronado: **Benson 280**, Lipp 818
Corte Madera: BP 314, Franklin 533, Metta 892, Springcreek 1185

COLORADO

Englewood: **First 1377**, **Hansen 1388**, Lewis 1410, **Malone 1415**, Merage 1424, Merage 1425, Osborn 1434, Tuchman 1467, Wilhite 1473

Evergreen: **Hawley 1390**, McDonald 1421, Ponzio 1440

Fort Collins: Bohemian 1345, Community 1357

Fort Morgan: Williams 1474

Glendale: Hunter 1394

Golden: McDonnell 1422

Grand Junction: Bacon 1340, Saccomanno 1446, Western 1471

Greeley: Community 1359, Monfort 1429

Greenwood Village: Esther 1375, Gooding 1384, International 1395, Liniger 1411, Marisco 1416, Servant 1454

Lakewood: Kinder 1403

Littleton: Leptas 1409, Morgan 1430

Longmont: Mallon 1414

Louisville: Price 1442, **StorageTek 1460**

Loveland: Hach 1386, McWhinney 1423, **Working 1476**

Manitou Springs: Norwood 1433

Pueblo: Hasan 1389, White 1472

Rye: Stealth 1458

Steamboat Springs: Yampa 1477

Telluride: Telluride 1465

Vail: Precourt 1441

Westminster: Green 1385

Wheat Ridge: **Avenir 1339**

Woody Creek: Dornick 1369

Wray: Kitzmiller 1405

see also 28, 103, 128, 143, 219, 319, 333, 439, 609, 685, 695, 696, 752, 813, 848, 891, 914, 971, 999, 1129, 1148, 1201, 1268, 1764, 1815, 1864, 2080, 2223, 2310, 2369, 2614, 2629, 2753, 2777, 2796, 2801, 2864, 2892, 2940, 3044, 3085, 3208, 3283, 3346, 3353, 3378, 3395, 3589, 3750, 3822, 4096, 4413, 4479, 4513, 4522, 4699, 4773, 5009, 5052, 5323, 5415, 6107, 6147, 6382, 6392, 6539, 6575, 6628, 6896, 7256, 7628, 7644, 7746, 7779, 7878, 7944, 7949, 7961, 7995, 8022, 8044, 8235, 8392, 8900, 8930, 9016, 9284, 9573, 9600, 9671, 9746, 9747, 9764, 9984, 9987, 9994

CONNECTICUT

Bloomfield: **Brainerd 1502**, Daniell 1523, Rogow 1636

Branford: Freas 1548, Goldhirsh 1557, **Seedlings 1645**

Bridgeport: Bridgeport 1504

Bristol: Barnes 1488, Main 1594, Roberts 1635

Chester: Nevas 1608

Cos Cob: Vervane 1671

Danbury: **Praxair 1629**

Darien: Fippinger 1540, Goodnow 1558, **Heimbold 1566**, Seidenberg 1646, Stone 1654, Tully 1665, **Ziegler 1683**

East Windsor: Nirenberg 1613

Enfield: MassMutual 1599

Fairfield: **Doty 1532**, **GE 1553**, Prusoff 1631

Falls Village: Hartwell 1565

Farmington: FSB 1549, Martin 1598

Greens Farms: Worthington 1679

Greenwich: **ALFA 1480**, Baldwin 1487, Bennett 1490, Berkley 1492, Biondi 1494, Bluebell 1496, Bondi 1499, Bridgemill 1503, Broadcasters 1505, Collis 1513, Davis 1525, **Davis 1526**, Donchian 1530, Donchian 1531, Flinn 1543, **Folsom 1545**, Foster 1546, Fuscone 1550, Gaisman 1551, Gladstein 1555, Goergen 1556, Grossman 1560, GW 1561, Jeffe 1572, Lehrman 1584, Lone 1589, Lynch 1591, **McKenzie 1601**, Melville 1602, Moore 1604, **Niles 1611**, **Niles 1612**, Oaklawn 1616, Olson 1618, Panwy 1622, Robbins 1634, Rose 1637, Royce 1639, Sage 1640, Sites 1650, Tsunami 1663, **Tudor 1664**, TWS 1666, **Vasey 1670**, Vik 1672, Wallace 1674, **Waters 1675**,

Wiener 1677, Young 1681, Zimmel 1684, ZOOM 1685

Guilford: **Huisking 1570**

Hamden: Graustein 1559

Hartford: **Aetna 1479**, Bodenwein 1497, Chase 1508, Chase 1509, Ensworth 1535, Hartford 1563, Hartford 1564, Larrabee 1578, Long 1590, Matthies 1600, Northeast 1614, Owenoke 1620, Palmer 1621, **Patterson 1624**, Phoenix 1627, Savage 1641, Say 1642, Sullivan 1655, Zachs 1682

Killingworth: **Bingham 1493**

Madison: Mahon 1593

Manchester: SBM 1644

Meriden: **Tremaine 1662**

Middletown: Liberty 1586

New Britain: American 1482, Community 1515, Connecticut 1519

New Canaan: Bauer 1489, Calder 1506, Fox 1547, LittleJohn 1588, **Tombros 1659**

New Haven: Childs 1510, Community 1514, Ellis 1534, Jones 1573, **Lingnan 1587**, Sewall 1648, United 1668

New London: Community 1517, Kitchings 1574

Newington: Mandell 1595

Newtown: Brace 1501, **October 1617**

Niantic: Thompson 1658

Norwalk: **Applera 1484**, Culpeper 1521, **Fink 1539**, **Orchard 1619**, **Stanley 1652**, Tauck 1657

Old Greenwich: **Vranos 1673**

Orange: Hubbell 1569

Ridgefield: Boehringer 1498, Bossidy 1500, Perrin 1626, Ritter 1633

Rowayton: Feuerman 1538

Roxbury: Diebold 1528

Shelton: Lavietes 1581

Sherman: Mandeville 1596

Simsbury: Patricelli 1623

Southport: Abramowitz 1478, Foley 1544, **Tyrrell 1667**

Stamford: Andor 1483, Baker 1486, Berbecker 1491, Carter 1507, Chilton 1511, Cohen 1512, **Conway 1520**, First 1541, Garden 1552, International 1571, Kramer 1577, Laverack 1580, Lee 1582, **Macauley 1592**, Manger 1597, Nason 1606, Netter 1607, Niblack 1610, Pitt 1628, Rosenthal 1638, Senior 1647, **Sun 1656**, Tow 1660, Whittingham 1676, **Xerox 1680**

Torrington: Community 1516

Warren: Shei'rah 1649

Waterbury: Connecticut 1518, Leever 1583, Meriden 1603

Watertown: Woodward 1678

West Hartford: Bissell 1495, Donaghue 1529, Fisher 1542, **Hampshire 1562**, **Hoffman 1568**, Kohn 1575, Larsen 1579, Mortensen 1605, Nye 1615, Saybrook 1643, **Valentine 1669**

Westport: Aronson 1485, Dalio 1522, Dartley 1524, **Educational 1533**, **Ettinger 1536**, Georgescu 1554, Heyman 1567, **Kossak 1576**, **Newman's 1609**, Pequot 1625, **Prentice 1630**, **Richardson 1632**, Steere 1653

Wilton: Ambler 1481, **Deloitte 1527**, Fairfield 1537, **Smart 1651**, Tow 1661

Woodbridge: Lender 1585

see also 7, 224, 313, 391, 435, 618, 696, 927, 1098, 1225, 1688, 1689, 1701, 1710, 1724, 1755, 1756, 1761, 1975, 2020, 2057, 2206, 2209, 2371, 2708, 2734, 2864, 2925, 2947, 3326, 3523, 3557, 3558, 3570, 3740, 3767, 3776, 3801, 3820, 3824, 3885, 3905, 3907, 3955, 3956, 3971, 3976, 4034, 4046, 4053, 4054, 4062, 4075, 4096, 4128, 4184, 4191, 4202, 4533, 4825, 5082, 5109, 5273, 5309, 5339, 5363, 5404, 5408, 5505, 5538, 5569, 5607, 5624, 5632, 5649, 5682, 5687, 5726, 5733, 5790, 5796, 5812, 5824, 5841, 5851, 5855, 5870, 5881, 5923, 5925, 5930, 5954, 6000,

6004, 6012, 6021, 6027, 6048, 6050, 6064, 6077, 6082, 6101, 6107, 6117, 6134, 6144, 6147, 6171, 6172, 6184, 6226, 6240, 6253, 6269, 6270, 6315, 6321, 6336, 6425, 6480, 6524, 6526, 6545, 6563, 6572, 6578, 6579, 6632, 6646, 6647, 6650, 6664, 6676, 6699, 6704, 6709, 6717, 6746, 6752, 6766, 6767, 6797, 6829, 6867, 6880, 6892, 6896, 6907, 6930, 6941, 6963, 7024, 7028, 7063, 7090, 7098, 7134, 7154, 7159, 7163, 7193, 7230, 7239, 7242, 7255, 7260, 7285, 7293, 7501, 8143, 8164, 8355, 8376, 8396, 8403, 8411, 8451, 8463, 8528, 8552, 8563, 8695, 9362, 9575, 9978

DELAWARE

Greenville: **Glencoe 1714**, Struthers 1758

Montchanin: Crystal 1702

Newark: Bartsch 1688, Beckwith 1689, Buckner 1695, **Cedar 1697**, Delany 1705, Dickenson 1708, Eisenberg 1709, Hall 1718, Hamel 1719, Hirschl 1721, Hofmann 1722, Morania 1733, Newman 1736, Robinson 1744, **Robinson 1745**, Roby 1746, Rowland 1749, Schiff 1750, Seevak 1752, Sinsheimer 1754, Wasily 1760, Watson 1761

Wilmington: ABE 1686, Arguild 1687, Bennett 1690, Berkley 1691, **Birch 1692**, Bishop 1693, Bishop 1694, Cawley 1696, Chichester 1698, Choptank 1699, Common 1700, Crestlea 1701, **CTW 1703**, Day 1704, Delaware 1706, Devonwood 1707, Esperance 1710, Etnier 1711, Evelyn 1712, **Fair 1713**, **Good 1715**, Gupta 1716, **Gynesis 1717**, Heuer 1720, Kent 1723, Kingsley 1724, Laffey 1725, Lennox 1726, Longwood 1727, Marmot 1728, Mastronardi 1729, MBNA 1730, Miller 1731, **Milliken 1732**, Mt. 1734, **Neuberger 1735**, Orange 1737, Parker 1738, Phillips 1739, Presto 1740, **Raskob 1741**, Repass 1742, Reynolds 1743, Romill 1747, Rowe 1748, **Schwartz 1751**, Singer 1753, Spilka 1755, Sternlicht 1756, **Stroud 1757**, Vitale F 1759, Welfare 1762, **Winky 1763**

see also 1983, 3326, 3633, 3705, 5177, 5715, 5937, 6123, 6465, 8077, 8304, 8305, 8333, 8371, 8388, 8393, 8494, 9982

DISTRICT OF COLUMBIA

Washington: Agua 1764, Aid 1765, **Antonovych 1766**, **Arca 1767**, Arcana 1768, **Banyan 1769**, **Bauman 1770**, Beech 1771, Bender 1772, Benton 1773, **Berman 1774**, Bernstein 1775, Block 1776, Brody 1777, Building 1778, **Butler 1779**, Cafritz 1780, **Capital 1781**, **Case 1782**, **CityBridge 1783**, **Coleman 1784**, Community 1785, Consumer 1786, Coors 1787, **Coyne 1788**, Dimick 1789, Dweck 1790, **El-Hibri 1791**, Enfranchisement 1792, **Fannie 1793**, Fernandez 1794, Fordham 1795, **Foundation 1796**, Fowler 1797, Freed 1798, Friedman 1799, **Future 1800**, Gewirz 1801, **Goldberg 1802**, Gottesman 1803, Graham 1804, Gudelsky 1805, Hanley 1806, Harman 1807, Henry 1808, **Hill 1809**, **Hitachi 1810**, HRH 1811, Johnson 1812, Jones 1813, Jovid 1814, Kaye 1815, **Kennedy 1816**, Kimsey 1817, Kiplinger 1818, **Koch 1819**, **Lambe 1820**, Lehrman 1821, Leonsis 1822, Loughran 1823, **Lounsbery 1824**, **Loyola 1825**, Ludwig 1826, Marriott 1827, Mazda 1828, McGettigan 1829, McGowan 1830, McIntosh 1831, Mead 1832, Merriman 1833, Meyer 1834, **Moriah 1835**, **Mott 1836**, Munson 1837, **National 1838**, Nef 1839, Patterson 1840, **Phillips 1841**, Post 1842, **Professional 1843**, **Public 1844**, Reich 1845, Replogle 1846, Roshan 1847, Sprenger 1848, Spring 1849, Stewart 1850, Strong 1851, **Summit 1852**, Trellis 1853, True 1854, Vaterstetten 1855, Vradenburg 1856, **Wallace 1857**, **Wallace 1858**, Washington 1859, Washington 1860, Willard 1861, Willoughby 1862, **Winslow 1863**, Wyss 1864, Zients 1865 see also 291, 334, 371, 413, 477, 617, 798, 815, 933, 935, 1010, 1041, 1081, 1165, 1492, 1560, 1696, 1724, 1899, 1917, 1996, 2036, 2184, 2203, 2262, 2267, 2294, 2305, 2614, 2622, 2662, 2686, 2695, 2729, 2806, 2828, 2948, 2970, 3044, 3080, 3295, 3395, 3560, 3561, 3573, 3576, 3584, 3586, 3588, 3589, 3590, 3591, 3593, 3596, 3605, 3607, 3613, 3619, 3622, 3623, 3625, 3628, 3630, 3633, 3634, 3639, 3649, 3657, 3660, 3667, 3675, 3676, 3684, 3685, 3687, 3689, 3701, 3708, 3710, 3712, 3716, 3717, 3726, 3733, 3734, 3735, 3740, 3747, 3748, 3757, 3760, 3942, 3946, 4116, 4274, 4341, 4378, 4459, 4489, 4491, 4605, 4628, 4800, 5052, 5077, 5163, 5218, 5227, 5380, 5394, 5411, 5421, 5485, 5495, 5687, 5714, 5726, 5870, 5874, 5937, 6008, 6082, 6089, 6148, 6228, 6300, 6324, 6394, 6398, 6415, 6424, 6431, 6465, 6546, 6650, 6688, 6689, 6880, 7085, 7094, 7095, 7239, 7242, 7266, 7311, 7685, 7783, 7801, 7949, 8256, 8388, 8596, 8624, 8685, 8908, 8915, 8980, 9125, 9269, 9365, 9369, 9377, 9378, 9396, 9403, 9404, 9410, 9418, 9422, 9425, 9426, 9445, 9446, 9489, 9501, 9508, 9517, 9518, 9536, 9540, 9544, 9696, 9811

FLORIDA

Altamonte Springs: **Foundation 2009**
Aventura: Dahan 1958, Gordon 2030, Silverman 2234
Bal Harbour: Gann 2016, Sragowicz 2243
Bay Harbor Islands: Taylor 2269
Boca Raton: Albrecht 1872, Bay 1896, Bernstein 1904, **Cobb 1936**, **Coleman 1937**, Deaver 1965, Garfinkle 2017, GSB 2039, Hahn 2044, Hoernle 2062, Jaffe 2072, Kaufman 2082, **KMD 2096**, Lanie 2103, Lynn 2120, Maroone 2129, **Nanci's 2150**, Rales 2184, Rosenberg 2206, Sanders 2215, Schmidt 2225, Simon 2235, Stein 2250, Toppel 2274, Viner 2281
Boynton Beach: Plangere 2172, **Skelly 2237**
Bradenton: **Aurora 1882**, **Aurora 1883**, Kiwanis 2094, Taylor 2268
Cape Coral: **Hardison 2048**
Captiva: **Stafford 2247**
Clearwater: Eckerd 1986, Free 2012, **Hayward 2053**, Pinellas 2170, Raymund 2188
Clermont: Community 1947
Clewiston: Kelly 2086, United 2276
Coconut Grove: Global 2025, Green 2033
Coral Gables: **Adam 1869**, Bell 1901, Bellamy 1902, Cobb 1935, Dunspaugh 1981, Fernandez 1997, Ferraro 1998, Kennedy 2087, MacDonald 2121, **Morris 2145**, Potamkin 2176, Raygar 2187, Reis 2193, Ware 2287
Deerfield Beach: Moran 2143
Delray Beach: Dharma 1971, Driskill 1975, Lattner 2104, **Levine 2112**, Libra 2115, **Pope 2174**, **Regan 2191**, Rothberg 2209, Waldbaum 2285, Wymbs 2307
Fernandina Beach: Burton 1921
Fisher Island: Ds 1976
Fort Lauderdale: Amaturo 1873, Bacardi 1886, BankAtlantic 1891, BJ's 1908, **Campbell 1923**, Community 1941, Edgemer 1989, Florman 2004, Friedman 2014, Goodwin 2029, Gore 2031, Henderson 2056, Horvitz 2065, Huizenga 2068, Kaplan 2079, Katz 2081, Kelco 2085, Leiser 2108, Moore 2142, River 2199, Sansom 2218, **Stacy 2246**, Taylor 2267, Watts 2288, Wells 2294
Fort Myers: Kleist 2095, Price 2177, Southwest 2240, Wahlert 2284
Gainesville: Epilepsy 1995, Gainesville 2015, **Koch 2098**, Maren 2128, Pamphalon 2162, Robinson 2202
Hillsboro Beach: **Holden 2063**
Hobe Sound: Caspersen 1927, **Rehm 2192**

Hollywood: Behring 1899, **Edelstein 1988**, **Kaplan 2078**, MIDA 2139
Homestead: DiMare 1974
Indialantic: Morcom 2144
Islamorada: Einstein 1991
Jacksonville: ADFAM 1870, Baldwin 1888, Beaver 1897, **Berg 1903**, Blue 1911, Cascone 1926, Community 1940, Crawford 1956, Dahl 1959, Davis 1961, **Davis 1962**, **Davis 1963**, **Davis 1964**, Demetree 1967, DuBow 1977, duPont 1982, duPont 1983, Edelman 1987, Florida 2003, Foley 2005, Gooding 2028, Helow 2055, Henriksen 2057, Hicks 2059, Jacksonville 2071, Kesler 2090, Kirbo 2092, Petway 2167, Posnack 2175, Rayonier 2189, River 2198, Riverside 2200, **Samstag 2214**, Schippmann 2224, Stein 2249, Stevens 2251, Terry 2271, Weaver 2289, **Winn 2301**, Winston 2302, Wolfson 2304
Jacksonville Beach: Hayes 2052
Jensen Beach: **Hayden 2051**, Langford 2102
Juno Beach: FPL 2010
Jupiter: **Abramson 1868**, Beveridge 1906, Beveridge 1907, **Goldhammer 2026**, Maltz 2126
Key Biscayne: Love 2119, **McNamara 2135**
Key Largo: Harrington 2049, Ocean 2156
Key West: Community 1949
Lake Mary: **Priority 2178**
Lakeland: Community 1944, Publix 2180
Longboat Key: Castellani 1928
Longwood: **Chatlos 1932**
Lutz: Morsani 2147
Maitland: Ginsburg 2022
Mango: **Believers 1900**
Melbourne: Harris 2050, Six 2236, Stransky 2253
Melbourne Beach: Glaubinger 2023
Miami: Abraham 1867, Ansin 1877, **Arison 1880**, Arison 1881, Batchelor 1893, Blank 1909, **Braman 1915**, Broad 1916, Catlin 1929, Cejas 1930, Cisneros 1934, Conese 1950, Coulter 1954, **Coulter 1955**, Dade 1957, Dickinson 1973, Dunn 1979, **Flight 2002**, Garner 2018, Greenburg 2034, Katcher 2080, **Knight 2097**, LeBow 2106, Lennar 2109, Lorberbaum 2118, Miller 2140, Miller 2141, Olemberg 2157, Pascal 2163, Peacock 2165, **Pearce 2166**, Rebozo 2190, Resler 2194, Russell 2212, Ryder 2213, Sandler 2216, Schaefer 2222, Scharlin 2223, **SWS 2260**, Taplin 2264, Thatcher 2273, **Vollmer 2282**, Weintraub 2292, Wolfson 2305, Wollowick 2306
Miami Beach: Five 2001, Muss 2149, Sherman 2233
Miami Lakes: **Kislak 2093**
Naples: **Anderson 1876**, Banbury 1889, Better 1905, Community 1943, **Consolidated 1952**, DeHaan 1966, **Fricks 2013**, Gorin 2032, Griffin 2036, Hillenbrand 2060, Jasam 2074, Martin 2130, Morrison 2146, Naples 2151, P & M 2160, **Rauenhorst 2185**, **Rosser 2208**, Schoen 2226, Star 2248, Taishoff 2262, Wellman 2293
North Miami: Applebaum 1878, North 2153
Ocala: Colen 1938, Tarrant 2265
Odessa: Speer 2241
Oneco: **Jehovah 2075**
Orlando: A Friends' 1866, Andersen 1875, Blount 1910, Carse 1925, Community 1942, Darden 1960, Dennis 1969, Densch 1970, Hamilton-Forbes 2046, Hard 2047, Hunter 2069, Magruder 2125, Masters 2131, McKnight 2134, Overstreet 2159, Phillips 2168, Rosen 2205, Seneff 2231, Shackelford 2232, SunTrust 2259, Tangelo 2263, Tatum 2266, **Tupperware 2275**, Van Vleet 2277, Vaughn 2279, **von Liebig 2283**, Westgate 2296
Osprey: Wilson 2300
Palm Beach: Adler 1871, Blum 1912, Burns 1920, Engelberg 1994, Faigen 1996, **Fiterman 2000**, Fortin 2007, **Foundation 2008**, Gemcon 2019, Gerstner 2020, Gronewaldt 2037, Gruss 2038, Kohl 2099, Lee 2107, Marden 2127, McKeen 2133, Michaan 2138, Nessel 2152, Palm Beach

2161, **Picower 2169**, Quick 2182, Quimby 2183, Rollnick 2203, Scarpa 2221, **Vanneck 2278**, Weiler 2290, **Whitehall 2297**
Palm Beach Gardens: Avrum 1884, **Azeez 1885**, Magill 2124, O'Neil 2155
Panama City: Hilton 2061, Jelks 2076
Panama City Beach: St. Joe 2244
Pensacola: Gulf 2042, Hollinger 2064, Levin 2110, Sansing 2217
Pompano Beach: Bastien 1892
Ponte Vedra Beach: Lazzara 2105, Roberts 2201, **Sontag 2239**, **Sullivan 2257**
Port St. Lucie: Bronfman 1917
Punta Gorda: Charitable 1931
Redington Beach: Life's 2116
Riviera Beach: **Lewis 2114**
Saint Petersburg: Eagle's 1985
Sanford: Paulucci 2164
Sarasota: Schmid 1874, Appleby 1879, Bank 1890, Becker 1898, Community 1946, Elster 1993, **Gibney 2021**, Goldstein 2027, **Greenfield 2035**, Hersh 2058, Keating 2084, Kramer 2100, Madigan 2123, Mote 2148, Schoenbaum 2227, Selby 2230, Sudakoff 2255, Sudakoff 2256, Sunshine 2258, Weiller 2291
Seffner: Rooms 2204, Seaman 2229
South Pasadena: Forbes 2006
St. Augustine: Smith 2238
St. Petersburg: Dickins 1972, Dyer 1984, Edwards 1990, HTR 2067, MacDougald 2122, Opler 2158, Pruitt 2179, St. Petersburg 2245
Stuart: **Bauman 1894**, Booth 1914, Dunn's 1980
Switzerland: Williams 2299
Tallahassee: Capital 1924, Community 1945
Tamarac: Merrill 2136
Tampa: Bailey 1887, Community 1948, Conn 1951, Couch 1953, Duckwall 1978, Glazer 2024, GTE 2040, Heartbeat 2054, Hough 2066, **Kaul 2083**, Krauss 2101, Light 2117, McCann 2132, **Plan 2171**, Poe 2173, Rothman 2210, Saunders 2219, Spurlino 2242, Straz 2254, Sykes 2261, TECO 2270, Thanksgiving 2272, Victory 2280, Walter 2286, Zwan 2308
Tarpon Springs: Ellis 1992
Tavernier: Storer 2252
Venice: Gulf 2041
Vero Beach: **Bryson 1918**, Frazier 2011, Kennedy 2088, Kennedy 2089, **Ross 2207**, Schumann 2228, Welsh 2295
Wellington: Levine 2113, **Rawlings 2186**
West Palm Beach: Baxter 1895, Chia 1933, Community 1939, **DeMoss 1968**, Fisher 1999, **Isenberg 2070**, **Johnson 2077**, Kimmel 2091, **Levine 2111**, Meyer 2137, O'Keeffe 2154, Quantum 2181, Rinker 2195, Rinker 2196, Rinker 2197, Rubin 2211, **Scaife 2220**, Wilkes 2298
Weston: **Jaharis 2073**
Williston: Hall 2045
Winter Garden: Bond 1913
Winter Park: Burnett 1919, Bush 1922, Gurtler 2043, Winter 2303

see also 5, 28, 48, 49, 61, 292, 456, 807, 815, 897, 933, 1368, 1424, 1428, 1430, 1491, 1521, 1543, 1606, 1628, 1636, 1688, 1689, 1693, 1694, 1718, 1719, 1728, 1738, 1764, 1794, 1808, 1833, 1837, 2310, 2312, 2314, 2323, 2339, 2431, 2447, 2451, 2465, 2489, 2494, 2508, 2513, 2517, 2605, 2606, 2622, 2638, 2659, 2672, 2690, 2783, 2841, 2850, 2874, 2888, 2935, 2956, 2964, 2991, 3013, 3034, 3062, 3070, 3072, 3086, 3089, 3236, 3445, 3521, 3522, 3561, 3569, 3613, 3629, 3634, 3734, 3769, 3792, 3863, 3910, 3917, 3926, 3978, 4080, 4103, 4130, 4136, 4175, 4239, 4267, 4279, 4354, 4420, 4469, 4477, 4479, 4545, 4566, 4584, 4615, 4716, 4724, 4768, 4786, 4893, 4940, 5102, 5146, 5170, 5253, 5264, 5310, 5360, 5376, 5385, 5409, 5489,

2996, SF 2998, Shapiro 3001, Sharpe 3002, **Shaw 3003**, Shaw 3004, **Shifting 3006**, Siragusa 3009, Sirius 3010, Souder 3013, **Spencer 3015**, Sprague 3016, Steadley 3020, Steans 3021, Stein 3022, Stern 3023, Stone 3025, Susman 3030, Swanson 3031, Tawani 3033, Traders 3038, Tully 3040, **Tuohy 3041**, United 3044, USG 3046, Vibern 3048, VNA 3049, Walk 3053, Walsh 3055, Ward 3056, Wark 3057, Washington 3058, Wavering 3059, Wein 3060, Weinberg 3061, Weiss 3062, Wenske 3063, **Wessner 3064**, Whitwam 3068, Wieboldt 3069, Willett 3073, Wilson 3075, Wine 3076, Winfrey 3077, Wohlers 3078, Wolf 3079, **Wood 3081, Woodbury 3082**, Woods 3084, WPW 3087, **Wrigley 3088**, Yulman 3089, Zell 3090, **Zimmerman 3092**

Cicero: **Burlington 2644**
Columbia: Schmidt 2986
Crest Hill: Parks 2931
Danville: Vermilion 3047
Decatur: Buffett 2639, Community 2678, Meriweather 2893, Millikin 2900, Ullrich 3043
Deerfield: **Astellas 2602, Baxter 2611**, Cole 2672, **Walgreen 3051**, Walgreen 3052
Des Plaines: Bruning 2635, Frank 2733, Schawk 2984, **United 3045**, Wilkie 3071
East Alton: Olin 2925
Elgin: Elgin 2717, Seigle 2997
Elmhurst: Bates 2608, Hammersmith 2781
Evanston: Jahn 2816, Lewis 2857, New 2912, Pritzker 2950, Straus 3027
Frankfort: Woods 3083
Franklin Grove: Knox 2842
Geneseo: Geneseo 2750
Glen Ellyn: Ball 2604
Glencoe: Goldschmidt 2764, **Goodman 2765**, Knapp 2841, Lavin 2849, Takiff 3032
Glenview: Illinois 2813, Lea 2850
Godfrey: **Monticello 2904**, Nelson 2911
Gurnee: Petersen 2941
Herrin: Bruce 2634, Harrison 2790
Highland Park: Braeside 2631, Buffett 2640, Kaplan 2823, Kaplan 2824, Mesirow 2894, Mills 2901, Sacks 2979, Shapiro 3000
Hillside: Clingen 2669
Hinsdale: Bere 2616, Christopher 2665, Community 2681, **Harper 2786**, Illinois 2812, Little 2859, **Ryan 2978**
Homewood: **ARIA 2600**
Huntley: Meyer 2896
Inverness: Canning 2650
Itasca: Gallagher 2743, **Gallagher 2744**
Jacksonville: Hobbs 2802
Kenilworth: McIntosh 2883
Lake Forest: **Brunswick 2636**, Buchanan 2637, Bunning 2641, Bunning 2642, Farrell 2725, Grainger 2768, Grant 2770, Hospira 2804, Kapoor 2825, McMullan 2884, Red 2959, Schuler 2990, Stuart 3028, Trustmark 3039, Wilemal 3070
Libertyville: D.A.S. 2694
Lincolnwood: Hartman 2793, Rajchenbach 2958, Ruben 2973
Lisle: GKN 2758, Kazma 2827
Mattoon: Lumpkin 2864, Smysor 3011
Melrose Park: Kipper 2840
Moline: Butterworth 2647, Deere 2699, Moline 2902, Sangre 2981
Monmouth: Mellinger 2890
Mount Carroll: **Willow 3074**
Mount Sterling: Tracy 3037
Mundelein: **Keller 2829**, Medline 2889
Naperville: Tellabs 3034
Niles: Cuneo 2692, **MacArthur 2867**
North Aurora: Melrene 2892
Northbrook: **Allstate 2588**, Barancik 2605, Cless 2668, Cressey 2689, Dunard 2712, **Galashiels 2742**, Green 2772, Hochberg 2803, JYN 2821, Lee

2853, McGraw 2882, Negaunee 2909, **Scholl 2989**, Schwartz 2991, **Searle 2994**, Segal 2995, Sudix 3029
Northfield: Snite 3012, Stone 3026, White 3067, Worley 3086
Oak Brook: **Ace 2582**, Cooper 2683, Houlsby 2805, Huizenga 2806, Kelly 2830
Oak Park: Eddema 2714, Master 2875, Oak Park 2922, Shaker 2999, West 3065
Oakbrook Terrace: **Buntrock 2643**, Russell 2976, Westlake 3066
Orland Park: **Andrew 2595**, Andrew 2596, Ozinga 2930
Palatine: Freed 2736, Pilchard 2944, **Square 3018**
Palos Heights: Owens 2929
Park Ridge: Butler 2646
Peoria: Caterpillar 2653, Community 2677, Fites 2730, Gloyd 2760, Redhill 2960
Peoria Heights: Bielfeldt 2620
Plainfield: **Wadsworth 3050**
Pontiac: Camp 2649
Rock Island: Day 2698
Rockford: AMCORE 2591, Anderson 2594, Community 2679, Torstenson 3036, Woodward 3085
Rolling Meadows: PepsiAmericas 2937
Rosemont: Rich 2967, Speh 3014, Wonderful 3080
Schaumburg: Blowitz 2623, Cornell 2685, Galvin 2747, Goldberg 2761, Kainz 2822, **Motorola 2906**, Omron 2926, Zurich 3093
Skokie: **Glenner 2759**, Levy 2856, Rice 2966
South Barrington: **Samaritan 2980**
Springfield: Endless 2720, Hartke 2792, Levi 2855, Walnut 3054
St. Charles: Helen's 2795, **Norris 2917**
Sterling: Dillon 2704
Sycamore: DeKalb 2701
Teutopolis: Zerrusen 3091
Vernon Hills: Circle 2666, Edwardson 2715
Warrenville: **BP 2628, Spreading 3017**
Waukegan: **Abbott 2579**
Wayne: Hamill 2780
Westchester: **Irwin 2814**
Western Springs: Grohne 2774, Hermann 2798
Westmont: Amicus 2592
Wheaton: Crane 2687, **Crane 2688**, Domanada 2705, DuPage 2713, **Fairwyn 2723**, Grace 2766
Wilmette: Kendall 2833, Krehbiel 2845, Schield 2985, Schmitt 2987, Thoma 3035
Winfield: McNamara 2886
Winnetka: Appleton 2599, Chapman 2656, Gantz 2748, **Gavin 2749**, Golder 2762, Kemper 2831, Kennedy 2834, Nichols 2916, Parmer 2932

see also 19, 303, 371, 416, 640, 832, 1072, 1200, 1464, 1688, 1705, 1759, 1830, 1846, 1884, 1905, 2084, 2123, 2294, 2307, 3118, 3254, 3265, 3277, 3295, 3309, 3395, 3415, 3427, 3443, 3676, 3717, 3823, 3947, 4117, 4160, 4274, 4477, 4522, 4630, 4665, 4699, 4772, 4797, 4825, 4849, 4893, 4896, 4899, 4901, 4906, 4964, 5016, 5026, 5070, 5071, 5142, 5335, 5415, 5503, 5600, 5808, 6079, 6122, 6148, 6269, 6282, 6298, 6549, 6561, 6562, 6656, 7165, 7505, 7529, 7625, 7694, 7772, 8115, 8175, 8333, 8363, 8486, 8526, 8541, 8658, 8874, 9238, 9242, 9369, 9445, 9596, 9742, 9757, 9764, 9782, 9785, 9802, 9822, 9865, 9879, 9915, 9944

INDIANA

Anderson: Madison 3197
Angola: Steuben 3241
Auburn: DeKalb 3141
Batesville: **BVM 3112**, Ripley 3230
Bedford: Community 3133
Berne: Muselman 3209
Bluffton: Wells 3255

Carmel: Jones 3179, Noyes 3216, Samerian 3234, Simon 3237, Simon C 3238, Watanabe 3251
Columbia City: Whitley 3258
Columbus: **Cummins 3136**, Heritage 3166, Irwin 3174, Irwin 3175, Reeves 3227
Corydon: Harrison 3161
Crawfordsville: Montgomery 3206
Crown Point: Crown Point 3135
Decatur: Adams 3095
East Chicago: East Chicago 3144, Ispat 3176, Twin 3245
Elkhart: Decio 3139, Elkhart 3145, Martin 3200
Evansville: American 3098, Bussing 3111, Chancellor 3117, Community 3122, Holiday 3168, Koch 3184, Vectren 3249, Welborn 3254
Fort Wayne: Cole 3121, Community 3125, English 3146, Foellinger 3149, Four 3151, Goldstine 3156, Journal 3181, Kuhne 3187, Lincoln 3195, **Master 3201**, McMillen 3203, Newman 3211, Niblick 3212, Peabody 3221, Raker 3226, Rolland 3231, Valiant 3248, Waterfield 3252
Franklin: Johnson 3178
Greenfield: Hancock 3160
Greensburg: Decatur 3138
Indianapolis: ADL 3097, Annis 3100, **Anthem 3101**, Anthem 3102, Branigin 3109, Central 3116, Clowes 3119, Clowes 3120, Cornelius 3134, DeHaan 3140, Fairbanks 3147, Finish 3148, Freedom 3152, Glick 3155, **Goodrich 3157**, **Guidant 3159**, Hasten 3162, **Hasten 3163**, Health 3164, Hilbert 3167, Hoover 3169, **IFSA 3171**, Jordan 3180, Klapper 3183, **Lilly 3192, Lilly 3193**, Lilly 3194, **Lumina 3196**, Met 3204, Moore 3207, Morgan 3208, OneAmerica 3220, Perelman 3222, Pulliam 3224, Pulliam 3225, Regenstrief 3228, Saltsburg 3233, Simon 3236, Simon 3239, Simon 3240, Storehouse 3242, Tobias 3244, West 3256
Jasper: Kimball 3182
Jeffersonville: Ogle 3218
Kendallville: Dekko 3142
Kokomo: Community 3126
Lafayette: Lafayette 3188, McAllister 3202, Scheumann 3235
Lawrenceburg: Dearborn 3137
Ligonier: Noble 3214
Logansport: Cass 3115
Madison: Community 3127
Marion: Adams 3096, Community 3124
Merrillville: Legacy 3189, NiSource 3213, White 3257
Michigan City: Duneland 3143, Michigan 3205, Unity 3247
Muncie: Ball 3103, Ball 3104, Ball 3105, Community 3128, Griffith 3158, Mutual 3210
Munster: Citizens 3118, Community 3129
Nashville: Brown 3110
New Albany: Community 3130
New Castle: Henry 3165
North Manchester: Community 3132
Osgood: Reynolds 3229
Plymouth: Marshall 3199
Portland: Portland 3223
Rensselaer: Jasper 3177
Richmond: Wayne 3253
Riley: Hux 3170
Rochester: Northern 3215
Shelbyville: Blue 3107
South Bend: 1st 3094, Carmichael 3113, Carroll 3114, Community 3131, Garcia 3154, Leighton 3190, Leighton 3191, Oliver 3219
Syracuse: Mahnken 3198
Terre Haute: Froderman 3153, Indiana 3173, Oakley 3217, Wabash 3250
Tipton: Tipton 3243
Upland: Boren 3108
Valparaiso: Anderson 3099
Versailles: Tyson 3246

Wabash: Ford 3150
Warsaw: Biomet 3106, Kosciusko 3185, Kosciusko 3186, Saemann 3232
Westfield: **IMMI 3172**
Zionsville: Community 3123

see also 215, 462, 1129, 1271, 1716, 1874, 2023, 2130, 2589, 2715, 2794, 2831, 2880, 2925, 2964, 2981, 3069, 3261, 3326, 3427, 3705, 4341, 4480, 4586, 4699, 4805, 4985, 5020, 5058, 5335, 5442, 5600, 6185, 7324, 7529, 7540, 7557, 7574, 7681, 7772, 7859, 7877, 7910, 8388, 8432, 8486, 8526, 8606, 9368, 9853, 9922

IOWA

Adel: Stine 3335
Ames: Good 3288
Ankeny: Bucksbaum 3271, Bucksbaum 3272
Belle Plaine: Mansfield 3308
Boone: Beckwith 3266
Cedar Rapids: **AEGON 3259**, Cedar Rapids 3275, Hall 3290, **Rockwell 3328**, United 3338, Wallace 3342
Clarinda: Clarinda 3276
Coralville: Gerdin 3286, Holden 3294
Council Bluffs: Iowa 3298
Davenport: Bechtel 3263, Bechtel 3264, Bechtel 3265, Community 3277, Figge 3284, **Lee 3306**, McCarthy 3311
Des Moines: AmerUs 3261, Blank 3268, Cowles 3279, Des Moines 3281, Employers 3282, Hubbell 3297, Jacobson 3299, Kruidenier 3303, Meredith 3314, Meredith 3315, Mid-Iowa 3317, **Ochylski 3321**, Pappajohn 3322, Principal 3326, Ruan 3329, **Sehgal 3330**, Seidler 3331, Stark 3334, Wellmark 3343
Dubuque: Butler 3273, McDonald 3312
Elgin: Valley 3339
Forest City: Hanson 3291
Fort Dodge: Deardorf 3280
Grinnell: Ahrens 3260, Poweshiek 3325
Hampton: Sukup 3336
Johnston: **Pioneer 3324**
Leon: South 3333
Marshalltown: Fisher 3285, Tye 3337
Mason City: Kinney 3300, Lee 3305
Mitchellville: **Andringa 3262**
Montezuma: Brownell 3270
Muscatine: Carver 3274, HNI 3293, Holthues 3295, Howe 3296, Muscatine 3318, **New 3319**
Newton: Maytag 3309, Maytag 3310
Oelwein: Northeast 3320
Pella: Farver 3283, Heerema 3292, Kuyper 3304, Pella 3323, Vermeer 3341
Sheldon: **Van Wyk 3340**
Sioux City: Gilchrist 3287, Siouxland 3332
Spirit Lake: Bedell 3267
Urbandale: Levitt 3307
Waterloo: Community 3278, McElroy 3313
West Des Moines: Bright 3269, Grubb 3289, Knapp 3301, Krause 3302, Mid 3316, R & R 3327, Winterhaven 3344

see also 1275, 1386, 1726, 2284, 2539, 2698, 2699, 2782, 2831, 2890, 2902, 2964, 2981, 3059, 3142, 3232, 3676, 4248, 4362, 4393, 4604, 4636, 4975, 4979, 4984, 4992, 4993, 4994, 4995, 5136, 5483, 5489, 6974, 7515, 7787, 8025, 8627, 8641, 9697, 9742, 9764, 9786, 9968

KANSAS

Atchison: **Muchnic 3379**
Dodge City: Scroggins 3389
Emporia: Jones 3370

Fairway: Powell 3381
Fort Scott: Ellis 3361
Hutchinson: Hutchinson 3368
Lawrence: Rice 3384
Liberal: Baughman 3346, Cooper 3353
Logan: Hansen 3366
Newton: **Schowalter 3388**
Overland Park: Delta 3354, Deramus 3355, Dreiseszun 3359, Haglage 3365, Kaplan 3373, Lloyd 3375, Smith 3393, Sprint 3395, Sullivan 3396, Sunderland 3397, V & H 3402
Pittsburg: Coleman 3352, Pritchett 3382
Prairie Village: Rhoden 3383
Salina: Bane 3345, Horejsi 3367, Joscelyn 3371, McCune 3376, Salina 3387, Smoot 3394
Shawnee Mission: Breidenthal 3349, Morgan 3377, Servant 3391, SYZYGY 3398
Topeka: Capitol 3350, Morris 3378, Payless 3380, Sabatini 3386, Security 3390, Topeka 3400, Westar 3403
Wellington: DSSR 3360
Wichita: Beren 3347, **Beren 3348**, Cessna 3351, Devlin 3356, DeVore 3357, Downing 3358, Farah 3362, Garvey 3363, Garvey 3364, INTRUST 3369, Kansas 3372, Koch 3374, Rudd 3385, Shannon 3392, Taylor 3399, Wichita 3404, Wiedemann 3405
Winfield: Tyler 3401

see also 295, 955, 1830, 2104, 2804, 3261, 3335, 4773, 4774, 4794, 4797, 4801, 4819, 4823, 4825, 4837, 4842, 4848, 4849, 4863, 4865, 4908, 4912, 4924, 5481, 7949, 7954, 7967, 8079, 8976, 9173, 9207, 9241, 9605

KENTUCKY

Anchorage: Novak 3442
Ashland: Foundation 3420
Covington: Omnicare 3443, **Omnicare 3444**
Edgewood: **Chase 3413**, Kentucky 3433
Fort Mitchell: Fischer 3418
Gilbertsville: Reed 3447
Henderson: Preston 3446
La Grange: Horn 3427
Lexington: Blue 3407, Good 3422, Hagan Ch 3423, Hep 3426, Keeneland 3432, Little 3437, Mustard 3440, Robinson 3449, Rosenthal 3450, Young 3455
Louisville: Brown 3408, Brown 3409, Brown 3410, **Brown 3411**, C.E. 3412, Community 3414, Cralle 3416, E.ON 3417, Ford 3419, Gheens 3421, Harris 3424, **Humana 3428**, J & L 3429, **Jones 3430**, Kindred 3434, Klein 3435, Ladner 3436, Marshall 3438, McKellar 3439, Norton 3441, Sutherland 3451, Trager 3452, Woosley 3453, **Yum! 3457**
Maysville: Hayswood 3425
Newport: Orleton 3445
Owensboro: Young 3454, Young 3456
Paducah: Community 3415
Pikeville: Justice 3431
Stanford: River 3448
Walton: Bavarian 3406

see also 263, 2323, 2328, 2382, 2964, 3102, 3184, 3254, 3705, 4663, 5794, 6132, 6550, 6631, 7053, 7362, 7456, 7522, 7523, 7562, 7573, 7574, 7588, 7619, 7659, 7665, 7772, 7803, 7811, 7863, 8025, 8187, 8388, 8650, 8656, 8658, 8681, 8723, 8733, 8737, 9099, 9368, 9469, 9765, 9793

LOUISIANA

Abbeville: **Live 3495**
Alexandria: Coughlin 3470, Deming 3472, Huie 3488
Baton Rouge: Baton Rouge 3462, Pennington 3505, Wilson 3515

Benton: **Biedenharn 3463**
Broussard: Stuller 3510
Crowley: Mauboules 3499
Jefferson: Goldring 3484, **Woldenberg 3516**
Jennings: Zigler 3520
Lafayette: Community 3468
Lake Charles: Burton 3467, Hardtner 3485, Louisiana 3497
Mandeville: German 3483
Metairie: Brown 3465, Eye 3475, Gauthier 3482, Jaeger 3490, Lupin 3498
Minden: Frazier 3479
Monroe: Scott 3509
Morgan City: Young 3518
New Iberia: Factor 3476
New Orleans: Adams 3458, Almar 3459, Azby 3460, Baptist 3461, Booth 3464, Brunswick 3466, Coypu 3471, Diboll 3473, Entergy 3474, Fertel 3477, Freeman 3480, Freeport 3481, Helis 3486, Heymann 3487, Institute 3489, Jones 3491, Kabacoff 3492, Keller 3493, Libby 3494, Monroe 3501, Monteleone 3502, New Orleans 3503, Reily 3506, RosaMary 3507, Schlieder 3508, Taylor 3511, **TWL 3513**, Zemurray 3519
Shreveport: Community 3469, Franks 3478, **Merkle 3500**, Toms 3512, Wheless 3514, Woolf 3517
Thibodaux: Lorio 3496, Peltier 3504

see also 1828, 2040, 2323, 2333, 2905, 3421, 3823, 4743, 5472, 5476, 5569, 8669, 8788, 8845, 9209, 9267, 9344, 9849

MAINE

Augusta: Kennebec 3543, Maine 3549, Melmac 3550
Bangor: Bangor 3525, King 3545
Bath: Davenport 3531
Belfast: **Golden 3538**, Switzer 3557
Brunswick: Gallagher 3535
Cape Elizabeth: Gateway 3537
Damariscotta: Baker 3524, Falcon 3532
Ellsworth: Maine 3548
Falmouth: Catalyst 3529
Farmington: **Sandy 3555**
Fryeburg: Mulford 3551
Gardiner: Gardiner 3536
Gray: Crockett 3530
Kennebunk: Kennebunk 3544
Lewiston: JTG 3542
Portland: Alfond 3521, Alfond 3522, Alfond 3523, Burnham 3527, **Ford 3533**, Fore 3534, Great 3539, Hannaford 3540, Horizon 3541, Libra 3546, Lunder 3547, **Oak 3552**, Peters 3553, Smith 3556, TD 3558
South Freeport: **River 3554**
South Windham: Butnam 3528
Westport Island: Berry 3526

see also 93, 224, 335, 1225, 1487, 1507, 1648, 1657, 1678, 1696, 1707, 1724, 1726, 1730, 1761, 2128, 2183, 2206, 2328, 2371, 2478, 2513, 3466, 3702, 3769, 3771, 3776, 3785, 3822, 3824, 3853, 3885, 3905, 3907, 3940, 3956, 3960, 3964, 3965, 3971, 3992, 4032, 4035, 4046, 4047, 4050, 4053, 4054, 4062, 4075, 4096, 4106, 4128, 4184, 4303, 4513, 5089, 5095, 5109, 5260, 5335, 5611, 5631, 5687, 5691, 5794, 5894, 6827, 6907, 7242, 7625, 8261, 8403, 8555, 9339, 9978, 9988

MARYLAND

Accokeek: Higginson 3649
Annapolis: Berlitz 3571, Campbell 3582, Capital 3584, TKF 3747
Arnold: Rathmann 3715

Baltimore: Abell 3559, **Alcoholic 3564**, Baker 3566, Baker 3567, Baltimore 3568, Bank 3569, **Blaustein 3575**, Blaustein 3576, Blum 3577, Brown 3578, **Casey 3585**, Cohen 3592, Concordia 3601, Constellation 3602, Crane 3603, Davison 3609, deForest 3612, Denit 3615, Dresher 3617, Eliasberg 3620, France 3631, Goldseker 3636, Goldsmith 3637, Hackerman 3642, Hahn 3643, **Head 3644**, Hirschhorn 3650, Hittman 3651, Hoffberger 3652, Jonan 3658, Knott 3666, Krieger 3668, Krongard 3669, Langenfelder 3670, Lawless 3671, Legg 3672, Lerner 3674, **Life 3677**, Lockhart 3681, Macht 3683, McKnight 3688, Merrill 3689, Meyerhoff 3691, Meyerhoff 3692, Middendorf 3694, Myers 3698, Nabit 3699, Osprey 3703, Otenasek 3704, Plitt 3706, Price 3709, Provident 3712, Rollins 3718, Rosenberg 3719, Rosenberg 3720, Rosenbloom 3721, Roswell 3722, Rothschild 3723, Shattuck 3728, Straus 3738, Stulman 3739, Sylvan 3741, Ten 3743, Thalheimer 3744, Thunder 3746, Tzedakah 3751, Waidner 3754, Wallis 3755, Wareheim 3756, Wilson 3761

Bel Air: **Dahan 3604**

Beltsville: Cohen 3593

Bethesda: **Brown 3579**, Clark 3590, Clark 3591, **Cohen 3594**, **Davis 3608**, **Dean 3610**, **Ellison 3621**, England 3622, Greenberg 3639, Lockheed 3682, Marriott 3685, **Marriott 3686**, Marshall 3687, **Morningstar 3695**, Principato 3710, RFI 3716, Rock 3717, Small 3734, Small 3735, Sunrise 3740, Tauber 3742, Torray 3748, Wasserman 3757, Weiss 3760, **Zickler 3763**

Brooklandville: Deutsch 3616

Catonsville: Erickson 3624

Chestertown: **Shared 3727**

Chevy Chase: Abell 3560, Dekelboum 3613, Eaton 3619, Evergreen 3625, **Ewing 3626**, **Fairchild 3627**, GEICO 3634, **Hughes 3654**, Johnston 3657, Locke 3680, O'Neil 3701, Polinger 3708, Silverman 3733

Cockeysville: Meyerhoff 3690

College Park: Smith 3737

Columbia: Columbia 3595, Grace 3638, HRLD 3653, Rouse 3724, Van Lunen 3752, Viragh 3753

Crownsville: Helena 3646, **Raskob 3714**

Davidsonville: Decesaris 3611

Easton: Kerr 3661, Mid 3693, **Town 3749**, Tucker 3750

Elkton: Thorn 3745

Ellicott City: Hussman 3655

Forest Hill: Klein 3662

Frederick: Community 3598, Delaplaine 3614

Gaithersburg: Casey 3586

Galena: ISE 3656

Germantown: **Agilent 3563**

Hagerstown: Community 3600

Hanover: Allegis 3565

Hunt Valley: **Little 3679**, Procter 3711, Sheridan 3729

Jarrettsville: **Calvin 3581**

Kensington: Abramson 3561, Lerner 3675, Quinn 3713

Lineboro CPO: Wright 3762

Linthicum: Cannon 3583, Hecht 3645, Mulford 3696

Lutherville: Davis 3606

Marlow Heights: Pohanka 3707

North Bethesda: Fisher 3630

Olney: Freeman 3633

Owings: **Murray 3697**

Owings Mills: **Weinberg 3759**

Pikesville: Wasserman 3758

Potomac: **Adams 3562**, Koppel 3667, Shrensky 3731, **Smith 3736**

Preston: Blades 3574

Riderwood: Gross 3640

Rockville: **Berman 3572**, Berman 3573, Davis 3607, Epstein 3623, Foulger 3631, Kaplan 3659, **Kluge 3663**, Levitt 3676, **Nasdaq 3700**, **Shields 3730**

Salisbury: Community 3599, Henson 3648, Perdue 3705

Silver Spring: Charlotte's 3588, Choice 3589, Commonweal 3596, FBW 3628, Felburn 3629, Gudelsky 3641, **Hendricks 3647**, Kay 3660, MARPAT 3684, Schifter 3726, Shultz 3732

St. Michaels: **Knapp 3664**, **Knapp 3665**

Timonium: **Bearman 3570**, Bunting 3580, Glazer 3635

Towson: Dupkin 3618, Leidy 3673, Linehan 3678, Orokawa 3702, Samuelson 3725

Trappe: Darby 3605

Waldorf: Chaney 3587

Westminster: Community 3597

---

see also 93, 344, 1083, 1162, 1215, 1696, 1698, 1764, 1772, 1776, 1777, 1780, 1785, 1786, 1787, 1789, 1790, 1797, 1799, 1805, 1806, 1807, 1822, 1823, 1832, 1834, 1837, 1845, 1848, 1905, 1931, 1996, 2036, 2184, 2233, 2262, 3080, 3810, 3893, 3932, 3946, 3952, 4491, 4960, 5159, 5177, 5209, 5218, 5332, 5389, 5485, 5535, 5686, 5711, 5714, 5880, 5993, 6018, 6113, 6379, 6398, 6415, 6465, 6631, 6774, 6896, 7011, 7085, 7311, 7362, 7685, 7694, 7783, 8149, 8223, 8256, 8336, 8371, 8388, 8397, 8430, 8446, 8451, 8462, 8486, 8493, 8525, 9099, 9269, 9281, 9365, 9368, 9369, 9377, 9396, 9422, 9425, 9426, 9482, 9489, 9497, 9501, 9508, 9517, 9540

MASSACHUSETTS

Amherst: Colombe 3852, Felix 3902

Andover: Berthiaume 3803, DeLuca 3877, Foundation 3916, SDSC 4134

Arlington: **Mirak 4041**

Avon: Fireman 3910

Belmont: Pappas 4066

Beverly: **New England 4052**

Billerica: Millipore 4040

Boston: **A & A 3764**, A.M. 3766, Aaron 3767, Adams 3771, Adams 3772, **Agostine 3774**, Alden 3777, Alvord 3778, Arbella 3780, Ashton 3782, Ayling 3785, Babson 3787, Bain 3788, Baldwin 3789, Balfour 3790, Barr 3791, Barron 3792, Barry 3793, Berenson 3799, Bertolon 3804, Bilezikian 3805, Birmingham 3807, Black 3808, Boston 3811, Boston 3812, Bradley 3814, Brookfield 3818, Bumpus 3820, Byrnes 3821, Cabot 3822, Cabot 3823, Cabot 3824, Cabot 3825, Calderwood 3826, Campbell 3830, Canaday 3831, Carlee 3835, Cedar 3840, Charlton 3846, Chase 3847, Clarke 3849, Clipper 3850, Cogan 3851, Common 3853, Connell 3856, **Conservation 3858**, Cox 3863, Croll 3868, DiMaura 3880, Downs 3882, Druker 3883, Dusky 3885, Eaton 3888, Edgerly 3889, Elqui 3893, Farnsworth 3899, Fessenden 3903, **Fidelity 3904**, Filene 3907, Fireman 3909, Fraser 3917, Germeshausen 3924, Goldberg 3927, Gordon 3928, Grand 3929, Grantham 3930, Greene 3933, Gross 3936, Hagerty 3938, Harmsworth 3942, **Hershey 3949**, Hinduja 3952, Hoche 3954, Hoffman 3955, Hood 3956, **Hostetter 3959**, Hoyt 3960, Hyams 3961, **Iacocca 3963**, Iavarone 3964, **Jebediah 3969**, Johnson 3970, Jordan 3971, JSJN 3972, Kahn 3973, Keel 3976, **Kendall 3977**, Kidder 3979, Killam 3980, King 3981, Knight 3987, Kobren 3988, Krupp 3991, Ladd 3992, **Lalor 3993**, Lamm 3994, Levy 4005, Liberty 4006, Linde 4007, Linden 4008, Lindsay 4009, Loebs 4011, Lovett 4013, Lowell 4015, Ludcke 4017, Manitou 4018, Mannion 4019, Massachusetts 4025, Massachusetts 4026, **Massiah 4027**, Mazar 4028, McDonnell 4031, McLane 4033, Melville 4034, **Merck 4036**, **Middlecott 4037**, Mifflin 4038, Miller 4039, Murray 4045, MWC 4046, Narada 4047, NBT 4048, New 4050, New 4053, O'Donnell 4059, **OneBeacon 4060**, Oral 4061, Orchard 4062, Oristaglio 4063, Overly 4064, Pace 4065, Pardoe 4068, Parker 4069, Parlin 4070, **Partnership 4071**, Peabody 4072, Peabody 4074, **Peppercorn 4076**, Perpetual 4078, Perry 4079, Peters 4081, Pierce 4084, Plymouth 4085, Putnam 4088,

Putnam 4089, Rabb 4090, Rabb 4091, Rappaport 4093, Rasmussen 4094, Ratshesky 4095, Reeder 4099, Reynolds 4101, Ribakoff 4102, Riley 4104, Robbins 4106, Roddy 4108, **Rodgers 4109**, Rubenstein 4115, Rubenstein 4116, **Ruettgers 4119**, Rx 4120, **Sager 4122**, Sailors' 4123, Saltonstall 4126, **Saquish 4127**, Sawyer 4128, Schaffer 4129, Schoen 4130, **Schooner 4131**, Schrafft 4133, Shapiro 4136, **Shattuck 4138**, Sherman 4141, Shipley 4143, Silverman 4146, Simches 4147, Solomont 4152, Stamps 4155, Stare 4157, **State 4158**, Stearns 4159, Stemberg 4161, Stoneman 4167, Stoneman 4168, **Stratford 4170**, Stride 4171, Swartz 4175, **Sweet 4176**, **Swensrud 4177**, Thompson 4181, Travelli 4184, Tupancy 4186, Vance 4191, Vingo 4192, Wallace 4195, **Wang 4197**, Weber 4200, Webster 4201, Welch 4202, Weld 4203, Wheatland 4204

Boxford: Benz 3798, Gabrieli 3919

Braintree: Corcoran 3860, Flatley 3911, **Grass 3931**, **Harris 3944**, Tye 4187

Bridgewater: Carney 3837

Brookline: Abrams 3768, **Alchemy 3775**, Center 3841, Ford 3913, Morse 4044, Poss 4087

Cambridge: **Azadoutioun 3786**, Bay 3794, Biogen 3806, **Bruner 3819**, Cambridge 3828, Carr 3838, Ellison 3891, Lee 4001, Neighborhood 4049, Poorvu 4086, Schott 4132, Sohn 4151, Swanee 4174, Wood 4207, **Wood 4208**

Canton: **Reebok 4098**, Salah 4124

Charlestown: Foundation 3915

Chelmsford: Demoulas 3878, Demoulas 3879

Chelsea: Hood 3957

Chestnut Hill: Casty 3839, Janey 3968, Klarman 3985, Marcus 4022, Marks 4024, Sharf 4137, Smith 4148, Smith 4150, Walske 4196

Cohasset: Finnegan 3908

Concord: Cammarata 3829, Connolly 3857, Crawford 3867, Monsweag 4042, Stearns 4160

Cummaquid: Valerio 4189

Dalton: Crane 3864

Danvers: Essex 3897

Dedham: Marino 4023, Radley 4092, Redstone 4097, Yawkey 4211

Dorchester: Chahara 3843

Dover: Haley 3939, Many 4020

Easthampton: Easthampton 3887

Fall River: Grimshaw 3934, Rodgers 4110

Falmouth: Crane 3865, Crane 3866, Watson 4199

Fitchburg: North 4057

Foxboro: Kraft 3989, New 4054, Rodman 4111, Shaw 4139

Framingham: BOSE 3810, Feldberg 3901, Genzyme 3922, Highland 3951, Rosse 4113, Roy 4114, **Staples 4156**, **Stern 4162**, TJX 4183

Franklin: Bernon 3802

Gloucester: Caldwell 3827, Tilson 4182

Great Barrington: Berkshire 3801

Groveland: Nichols 4055, Wadleigh 4194

Harvard: EOS 3896

Harwich Port: Hyde 3962

Hingham: New 4051, Talbots 4178

Hopedale: Hopedale 3958

Hudson: Corkin 3861

Kingston: Sheehan 4140

Leominster: Ansin 3779, Leclerc 4000

Lexington: **Afeyan 3773**, Atchinson 3784, Behrakis 3796, Hirschtick 3953, Stride 4172

Lincoln: Leaves 3999

Littleton: Dunn 3884

Longmeadow: Sadowsky 4121

Lowell: Donahue 3881, Lowell 4014

Lynn: Eastern 3886, Gerondelis 3925

Manchester: ASD 3781, Jackson 3966

Mansfield: Kingsbury 3982

Marblehead: Robb 4105

Marion: Garfield 3921, Island 3965, Tara 4179

Taylor: Manoogian 4382, Manoogian 4383, Masco 4387

Tecumseh: Lenawee 4376

Traverse City: Grand 4327, **H.I.S. 4334**, Oleson 4405

Trenton: World 4489

Troy: **ArvinMeritor 4224**, **Delphi 4271**, Frankel 4311, Frankel 4312, Frankel 4314, Kelly 4359, **Kresge 4367**, Lachimi 4369, Stange 4445, Thomas 4456

Vicksburg: Fetzer 4298

Walled Lake: Baker 4226

Warren: Cold 4250, Kahn 4351

West Bloomfield: HFF 4342

White Lake: Wenger 4477

Whitmore Lake: **Skilling 4437**

Winn: Morey 4397

Zeeland: Miller 4393

see also 110, 133, 333, 687, 742, 906, 939, 1072, 1688, 1710, 2014, 2213, 2627, 2714, 2806, 2865, 2924, 2940, 2993, 3013, 3068, 3105, 3134, 3941, 4699, 4727, 4730, 5019, 5026, 5330, 5335, 5922, 6953, 7174, 7341, 7529, 7540, 7691, 7694, 7751, 7772, 7801, 7859, 8396, 8485, 8526, 9697, 9759, 9764, 9816, 9822, 9967, 9970

MINNESOTA

Austin: Hormel 4588, Knowlton 4598

Bayport: **Andersen 4501**, Andersen 4502, Bayport 4512

Bemidji: Neilson 4631, Northwest 4637

Bloomington: Adams 4495, Capp 4529, Reimer 4665, **Toro 4702**

Burnsville: Shiebler 4680

Chanhassen: Aslan 4507, People 4650

Clear Lake: Charity 4536

Dodge Center: Garmar 4569

Duluth: Alworth 4499, Duluth 4556, Generations 4571, Labovitz 4601, Mitchell 4625, Ordean 4643

Eagan: Blue 4521

Eden Prairie: Acorn 4494, Hillswood 4586, Sundet 4694

Edina: ATK 4509, Charlson 4537, Dennis 4550, Edina 4560, **Emmerich 4562**, Hallett 4581, Kopp 4599, Maas 4608, Mossier 4628, Vintage 4709

Excelsior: Caridad 4531, Lyman 4607

Fergus Falls: West 4723

Golden Valley: **Pentair 4649**

Grand Rapids: Blandin 4520, Grand Rapids 4574

Hibbing: Pacific 4646

Inver Grove Heights: **CHS 4540**

Lakeville: Christianson 4539

Little Canada: **Larson 4603**

Little Falls: Initiative 4593

Mankato: Andreas 4503, **Andreas 4504**, Radichel 4660

Marshall: Schwan's 4676

Minneapolis: **A Better 4493**, **ADC 4496**, AHS 4497, Ankeny 4505, Arcee 4506, Athwin 4508, Beim 4513, Bell 4514, Bemis 4515, Beverly 4517, Buuck 4526, **Cafesjian 4527**, Campbell 4528, Cargill 4530, Carlson 4532, Carolyn 4533, Chadwick-Loher 4535, Cleveland 4541, Cloverfields 4542, Cox 4543, Dayton 4547, Desiring 4551, **Donaldson 4552**, Dorea 4553, **Ecotrust 4558**, Edelstein 4559, Fiterman 4565, Frey 4566, General 4570, George 4572, Graco 4573, Greystone 4576, Grossman 4578, Grotto 4579, Grundhofer 4580, **Homeownership 4587**, Hudson 4591, Jostens 4596, Leonard 4604, Leuthold 4605, Mahon 4609, Marbrook 4612, McGuire 4615, **McKnight 4616**, McKnight 4617, McNamara 4618, Meadowood 4621, **Medtronic 4622**, Minneapolis 4623, Mithun 4626, National 4630, **Nelson 4632**, NFC 4633, Opperman 4641, Pax 4648, Perlman 4651, Peterson 4652, Phileona 4654, Phillips 4655, Piper 4656, Pohlad 4657, Prospect 4659, RBC 4661, **Rechelbacher 4662**,

Regis 4664, **Robins 4667**, Rupp 4669, Sabes 4670, Schoenecker 4674, Schulze 4675, Sewell 4678, Shimek 4681, Sit 4683, **Slt 4684**, Sjolund 4685, Southways 4688, Star 4691, Stone 4692, Sundance 4693, **SUPERVALU 4695**, Tankenoff 4696, Target 4697, Tennant 4700, **U.S. 4704**, Valspar 4706, W.M. 4710, Walker 4711, **Wallestad 4712**, Wallestad 4713, Wallin 4714, Wasie 4716, Watson 4717, Wedum 4719, WEM 4722, Westcliff 4724, Whitney 4728, **Wood 4731**, Xcel 4732

Minnetonka: Deikel 4548, Gardner 4568, McVay 4620, Opus 4642, Oswald 4645, **Petters 4653**, Sieben 4682, United 4705, WCA 4718

Newport: Bailey 4510, Barry 4511

North Mankato: Taylor 4698

Owatonna: Federated 4563, Prophet 4658

Plymouth: Bieber 4518, Greycoach 4575

Red Wing: Red Wing 4663

Richfield: **Best 4516**

Rochester: Rochester 4668, Schmidt 4673

Sleepy Eye: Amundson 4500

St. Cloud: Central 4534, Sexton 4679

St. Louis Park: Smikis 4687

St. Paul: 1988 4491, **3M 4492**, Alliss 4498, Bigelow 4519, Bremer 4523, Bush 4524, Butler 4525, Cherbec 4538, Criss 4544, Davis 4546, Deluxe 4549, Drew 4554, Driscoll 4555, **Ecolab 4557**, Edwards 4561, Fischman 4564, **Fuller 4567**, Griggs 4577, Hallett 4582, Hardenbergh 4583, Hersey 4584, HRK 4589, Hubbard 4590, Huss 4592, Jerome 4595, Kelley 4597, Koran 4600, **Land 4602**, Lilly 4606, Manitou 4610, Mardag 4613, McCarthy 4614, McNeely 4619, Minnesota 4624, Morning 4627, Musser 4629, Nicholson 4634, Noreen 4635, Northwest 4636, O'Neil 4638, **O'Shaughnessy 4639**, Hull 4644, **Patterson 4647**, Saint Paul 4671, Securian 4677, **St. Jude 4689**, St. Paul 4690, Tozer 4703, Veden 4707, Vest 4708, Warner 4715, Weesner 4720, Wells 4721, **Weyerhaeuser 4725**, Weyerhaeuser 4726, Weyerhaeuser 4727

Stillwater: Rivers 4666

Wayzata: Brandenborg 4522, Jeffers 4594, Mann 4611, Sanger 4672, TCF 4699, Thorpe 4701, Wolohan 4730

Willmar: Olson 4640

Winona: Hiawatha 4585, Slaggie 4686, Winona 4729

Woodland: Dasburg 4545

see also 106, 119, 590, 620, 720, 804, 1218, 1370, 1579, 1812, 1846, 1905, 1965, 2146, 2164, 2716, 2763, 2811, 2998, 3057, 3071, 3295, 3676, 3715, 3813, 4018, 4805, 5016, 5335, 5360, 6200, 6669, 7051, 7100, 7514, 7521, 7760, 8000, 8623, 8628, 9368, 9665, 9742, 9745, 9881, 9915, 9933

MISSISSIPPI

Gulfport: Gulf 4745, Mississippi 4758, **Seal 4764**

Hattiesburg: Asbury 4735

Hernando: Maddox 4753

Jackson: AmSouth 4733, Community 4737, Community 4738, Ergon 4740, Feild 4741, Ford 4742, Foundation 4743, Hearin 4748, Holloway 4749, Irby 4750, Luckyday 4752, McCarty 4754, McRae 4755, Morgan 4759, Providence 4762, Telos 4768, Walker 4770

Louisville: Taylor 4767

Madison: Mississippi 4757

Marks: Graeber 4744

Meridian: Hardin 4747, Riley 4763

Natchez: **Armstrong 4734**

Olive Branch: Skelton 4765

Oxford: **Sullivan 4766**

Picayune: Lower 4751

Ridgeland: Bower 4736

Tupelo: Hancock 4746, Oakwood 4760

University: Mississippi 4756

Vicksburg: Vicksburg 4769

Yazoo City: Day 4739, Peaster 4761

see also 186, 939, 2232, 2323, 2494, 2884, 3465, 3474, 3629, 4341, 4368, 4480, 4894, 5753, 6160, 6824, 8648, 8661, 8727, 8845, 9099

MISSOURI

Birch Tree: Shaw 4901

Branson: Herschend 4830

Chesterfield: Brauer 4787, Cornelsen 4799, Nelson 4871, Smith 4905

Chillicothe: Jenkins 4836

Clayton: Apex 4777, Brown 4789, Green 4821, Rosewood 4894, Seaworld 4900, Taylor 4916

Columbia: MFA 4866, Shelter 4902

Creve Coeur: Pettus 4882

Fenton: Fabick 4812

Independence: Truman 4919

Jefferson City: Schwartze 4898

Joplin: Craig 4800, **Humphreys 4833**

Kansas City: American 4773, Andrews 4774, Barrows 4781, Butler 4793, Carter 4794, Commerce 4797, Cray 4801, Curry 4802, Forster 4814, **Francis 4816**, Goppert 4819, Gottlieb 4820, H & R 4823, Hall 4824, Hallmark 4825, Helzberg 4829, Jewish 4837, Kansas 4842, **Kauffman 4843**, Kauffman 4844, Kemper 4846, Kemper 4847, Kemper 4848, Kemper 4849, Kemper 4850, **Lockton 4857**, Long 4858, McDonnell 4863, McGee 4865, Nichols 4873, **Olofson 4875**, Oppenstein 4876, Powell 4887, Price 4888, Reynolds 4892, **Singing 4904**, Sosland 4908, Stern 4909, Sullivan 4912, Swanson 4914, Uhlmann 4920, Ward 4924, Wornall 4929

Ladue: Bodine 4784, Holekamp 4832

Lebanon: Boswell 4786

Marshall: Buckner 4790

Maryland Heights: Express 4811

Mexico: Green 4822

Moberly: Orscheln 4877

Salisbury: Ingram 4834

Springfield: Community 4798, Hammons 4826, **Morris 4869**, Musgrave 4870, Pearl 4879

St. Ann: Vatterott 4921

St. Joseph: King 4851, Remington 4891

St. Louis: AJP 4771, Ameren 4772, Anheuser 4775, **Anheuser 4776**, Baer 4778, Baer 4779, Ballman 4780, Bellwether 4782, Bernoudy 4783, Boeing 4785, Brown 4788, Buder 4791, **Bunge 4792**, Casey 4795, Centene 4796, Danforth 4803, **Deer 4804**, Duesenberg 4805, Dula 4806, Edison 4807, Edison 4808, Emerson 4809, **Enterprise 4810**, Feraldo 4813, **Fox 4815**, Gateway 4817, Gershman 4818, **Hana 4827**, Hauck 4828, Hites 4831, Interco 4835, Jones 4838, Jones 4839, Jordan 4840, JSM 4841, Kellwood 4845, Laclede 4852, Lay 4853, Lemons 4854, Lichtenstein 4855, Litzsinger 4856, Lopata 4859, **Mallinckrodt 4860**, **May 4861**, McDavid 4862, **McDonnell 4864**, Millstone 4867, Monsanto 4868, Nestle 4872, **Oceanic 4874**, Orthwein 4878, Pershing 4880, Pershing 4881, **Pillsbury 4883**, Pillsbury 4884, PMJ 4885, Pott 4886, **Pulitzer 4889**, Reding 4890, Roblee 4893, Saigh 4895, Saint Louis 4896, **Sayler 4897**, Schweppe 4899, Simon 4903, Smurfit-Stone 4906, Solutia 4907, Stupp 4910, Stupp 4911, Sunnen 4913, Sycamore 4915, Tilles 4917, Trio 4918, Walker 4922, Wampus 4923, Westlake 4925, Whitaker 4926, Wolff 4927, Woods 4928, **Wyeth 4930**

see also 163, 955, 1473, 1833, 1984, 2123, 2213, 2604, 2719, 2721, 2775, 2863, 2964, 2972, 3008, 3020, 3184, 3355, 3359, 3365, 3377, 3378, 3381, 3383, 3391, 3393, 3395, 3396, 3397, 3402, 3427, 3753, 4031, 4362, 4368,

4553, 4663, 5120, 5278, 5335, 6188, 6200, 6974, 7811, 7949, 7954, 7983, 8848, 9017, 9173, 9196, 9206, 9207, 9222, 9241, 9605, 9765, 9812, 9922, 9997

MONTANA

Billings: Bair 4931, Bair 4932, First 4937, Sample 4940
Bozeman: Gilhousen 4938
Great Falls: Browning 4933
Helena: Cinnabar 4935, Montana 4939
Missoula: Chutney 4934, Washington 4941
Red Lodge: **Edwards 4936**

see also 1464, 1864, 2007, 2690, 2708, 2822, 3036, 4513, 4523, 4636, 5076, 6405, 7053, 7475, 7517, 7594, 7614, 7998, 8030, 9315, 9550, 9563, 9588, 9600, 9602, 9634, 9644, 9666, 9705, 9991

NEBRASKA

Aurora: Hamilton 4968, Heuermann 4973
Bellevue: Baer 4944
Cambridge: Perkins 4996
Central City: Dinsdale 4957, Merrick 4990
Chappell: Buckley 4947
Fort Calhoun: Hofer 4976
Fremont: Dunklau 4958, Fremont 4962
Grand Island: Cope 4955, Eihusen 4961, Reynolds 4997
Hastings: Roberts 4998
Kearney: Hirschfeld 4974
Lexington: Lexington 4986
Lincoln: Abbott 4942, Cooper 4954, Dillon 4956, Fulk 4964, Hubbell 4979, Kawasaki 4982, Lincoln 4987, **McDonald 4989**, Rogers 4999, TierOne 5010, Woods 5018, Woollam 5019
Nebraska City: Steinhart 5005
North Platte: Mid-Nebraska 4991
Omaha: Arkoosh 4943, Baright 4945, Bishop 4946, Buffett 4948, Buffett 4949, **Buffett 4950**, Commercial 4951, **ConAgra 4952**, **ConAgra 4953**, Durham 4959, Eagle 4960, Friedland 4963, GFH 4966, **Global 4967**, Harper 4969, Hawkins 4970, Hawks 4971, Heider 4972, Hitchcock 4975, Holland 4977, Hubbard 4978, James 4980, Julian 4981, Kiewit 4983, Kiewit 4984, Kilbourne 4985, Lozier 4988, Muchemore 4992, Mutual 4993, Omaha 4994, Omaha 4995, Ryan 5000, Schrager 5001, Simon 5002, **Slosburg 5003**, Smock 5004, Storz 5006, Sunshine 5007, Swanson 5008, Swanson 5009, Truhlsen 5011, **Union 5012**, Valmont 5013, Vetter 5014, Watanabe 5015, Weitz 5016, Wiebe 5017, Zollner 5020
Wakefield: Gardner 4965

see also 362, 488, 970, 1268, 1275, 2897, 3298, 3308, 3326, 3332, 3397, 4544, 4554, 5041, 8500, 8658, 9709

NEVADA

Carson City: Mallory 5043
Crystal Bay: Shaheen 5063
Henderson: Greenspun 5034, Parks 5052, Sawyer 5061, Wendy's 5076
Incline Village: **Buck 5025**, Harris 5035, **Lemelson 5040**, **Omega 5050**, Parasol 5051, Trans 5073, **Walsh 5075**
Las Vegas: Bennett 5021, Boyd 5023, Christian 5026, Crescere 5030, Engelstad 5031, Fertitta 5033, Houssels 5038, Lied 5041, Marnell 5044, Nevada 5047, O'Bannon 5049, Reynolds 5056, Rufty 5059, Ruvo 5060, Southwest 5066, Spector 5067, Sturm 5069, Tang 5071, **Tang 5072**, Tuscany 5074, Williams 5078, Wunderman 5079

Minden: Fairweather 5032
North Las Vegas: Nevada 5048
Reno: **Bing 5022**, Bretzlaff 5024, Clark 5027, Community 5028, Cord 5029, Hawkins 5036, **Hilton 5037**, Keyser 5039, Lifestyle 5042, Mathewson 5045, May 5046, Pennington 5053, Redfield 5055, Rochlin 5057, Sierra 5064, Smith 5065, Stout 5068, Wiegand 5077
Sparks: Rude 5058
Stateline: **SFO 5062**
Zephyr Cove: Prim 5054, Sweig 5070

see also 150, 497, 609, 676, 696, 725, 848, 867, 934, 971, 1270, 1864, 2296, 3184, 5200, 5726, 6668, 7011, 8648, 8685, 9040, 9455, 9535, 9600, 9928, 9987

NEW HAMPSHIRE

Chesterfield: Chesterfield 5082
Concord: Bean 5080, Eastman 5087, Endowment 5088, HNHfoundation 5092, New Hampshire 5098
Etna: Byrne 5081
Hampton: **Penates 5099**, **Winthrop 5105**
Hanover: Couch 5085
Keene: Putnam 5100
Manchester: Cogswell 5084, Gale 5091, Hunt 5093, Lindsay 5095, Smith 5101, von Weber 5104
Nashua: Levine 5094
New Castle: **Linnell 5096**
Portsmouth: **Dorr 5086**, Foundation 5089
Rye Beach: Fuller 5090, Martin 5097
Salem: Trust 5103
Stratham: Treat 5102
Wolfeboro Falls: **Christian 5083**

see also 224, 770, 1494, 1495, 1507, 1523, 1648, 1657, 1678, 1719, 1761, 1828, 2206, 2371, 3474, 3523, 3539, 3540, 3557, 3558, 3588, 3619, 3776, 3785, 3798, 3824, 3870, 3885, 3905, 3907, 3934, 3940, 3946, 3955, 3956, 3971, 3999, 4008, 4013, 4033, 4035, 4046, 4053, 4054, 4062, 4068, 4075, 4096, 4112, 4128, 4159, 4184, 4477, 5161, 5282, 5538, 5557, 5687, 5870, 5881, 5930, 6524, 6746, 6896, 7242, 8105, 8175, 8205, 8261, 8323, 8340, 8403, 8451, 8463, 8545, 8555, 8562, 9357, 9978

NEW JERSEY

Allendale: **Carlson 5155**
Alpine: Drapkin 5185
Basking Ridge: Gibson 5208, **Rippel 5368**, **Verizon 5439**
Bayonne: Galanta 5202
Berkeley Heights: Mazer 5321, Thomas 5427
Bernardsville: **Anderson 5115**, Doherty 5182, Gagnon 5201, Jockey 5260
Bridgewater: Aventis 5120, **Aventis 5121**, McCutchen 5322, National 5335
Brielle: **Lafitte 5293**
Butler: **Vollmer 5443**
Caldwell: Orenstein 5344
Camden: Campbell 5151
Cedar Grove: Krieger 5290, Turock 5430
Cedar Knolls: Weisberg 5449
Chatham: Kemmerer 5275, Knistrom 5282, Nicolais 5339, Orange 5343
Cherry Hill: Branfman 5142, **GHH 5207**, Green 5215, Heart 5229, Hill 5236, Katz 5270, **Scholarship 5388**, Subaru 5415
Clark: Riskin 5369
Cliffside Park: **Lautenberg 5298**
Clifton: Berger 5128, Cooperman 5168, Dagish 5176, Entin 5189, Martini 5319
Cranbury: Stern 5412

Cranford: Gabelli 5200, Sharkey 5397
Cresskill: Kauffmann 5272, Smith 5408
Deal: Harary 5222, V'Emunah 5437
Denville: Family 5191, **Pfeiffer 5351**, **WKBJ 5459**
East Rutherford: New Jersey 5337, Smilowitz 5406
Edison: Keren 5277, Mamiye 5316, Parnes 5348, Visceglia 5441
Elizabeth: 1772 5106, Elizabethtown 5188, Harrison 5225, Kean 5274
Elmwood Park: Rose 5373
Englewood: C 5150, **Freyer 5197**, Holzer 5238, Katz 5271, Woolley 5460
Englewood Cliffs: D & K 5174, Kolatch 5285, Merkin 5331, Palestroni 5345, Unilever 5434
Fairfield: **International 5252**
Far Hills: Marianthi 5318
Flemington: Large 5295
Florham Park: **Jaqua 5256**, KDK 5273, Long 5310
Fort Lee: Mack 5312, **Mack 5313**, Straus 5413, Straus 5414, **Tang 5423**
Franklin Lakes: Boye 5140, Garcia 5203
Freehold: Dealessandro 5178
Gladstone: Brady 5141, Mushett 5334
Glen Ridge: Victoria 5440
Hackensack: **Barbour 5124**, Buehler 5146, Creamer 5171, Isermann 5253, Lear 5300
Hamburg: Levitt 5305
Hamilton: Johnson 5262
Hasbrouck Heights: Cantor 5152
Hopewell: Bunbury 5148, Johnson 5264
Iselin: **Siemens 5400**
Jamesburg: Seiden 5396
Jersey City: First 5194, Guarini 5216, Lebensfeld 5301, Leib 5302, Provident 5359
Kearny: Schecter 5385
Kenilworth: Schering 5387
Kinnelon: Roberts 5371
Lakewood: Cyh 5173, Goldstein 5211, Rosenbaum 5374
Lambertville: Hickory 5232
Lawrenceville: Dow 5183, Martinson 5320, Princeton 5357, Sunup 5419
Lebanon: Baker 5123
Little Falls: Makk 5315
Livingston: Bildner 5133, Geiger 5205, Hawn 5226, Healthcare 5228, **James 5254**, Sagner 5381, Shen 5398, Silbermann 5403, Taub 5424, Taub 5425
Lodi: Fishoff 5195
Madison: Graymer 5214
Maple Shade: Gershman 5206
Marlboro: Tolchin 5428
Marlton: Danellie 5177
Mendham: **Carolan 5156**, **Goodes 5212**, Kirby 5280
Middletown: Knight 5281, Kurr 5291, Vopicka 5444
Midland Park: **Bogoni 5134**
Millburn: Schenck 5386
Milltown: Link 5307
Monmouth Beach: **Kontos 5286**
Montclair: Bershad 5131, McMullen 5325, **Schumann 5390**, Schumann 5391, Turrell 5431, **Wall 5445**, Weston 5452
Montvale: **KPMG 5288**
Montville: Capita 5154
Moorestown: Knowles 5283
Morristown: Charles 5161, Community 5167, Dodge 5181, Healey 5227, Hidden 5233, Hilfiger 5235, Kirby 5279, Lissak 5309, MCJ 5324, Poses 5354, Rigorous 5367, Ross 5376, Sandy 5383, Silver 5404, Simon 5405, Withington 5458
Mount Laurel: Schwartz 5393
Mountain Lakes: **Bestfoods 5132**, Dircks 5180, Levy 5306
Mountainside: Halpern 5220, Halpern 5221, L.A.W. 5292, Schwarz 5394, Wilf 5456
Murray Hill: Alcatel 5110

New Brunswick: Burke 5149, **Clare 5164**, Fund 5199, **Janssen 5255**, **Johnson 5261**, Larsen 5296
New Providence: Bard 5125, Willits 5457
New Vernon: Bohnert 5135, Cesatam 5159
Newark: Armour 5116, **Edison 5186**, Horizon 5240, **IDT 5248**, Jonas 5266, Prudential 5360, PSEG 5361, Upton 5436, Wight 5454
North Bergen: Providence 5358
North Brunswick: Segal 5395
North Plainfield: Levin 5304
Nutley: Roche 5372
Old Bridge: Amboy 5112
Oldwick: Cape 5153
Paramus: Indian 5250, Point 5353, Roth 5377
Parsippany: Cendant 5157, Reddy 5364, Sudler 5416
Pennington: Abar 5107, **Ceres 5158**, Chang 5160, Civitas 5163, Fenwick 5193, **Huntsman 5246**, Kerr 5278, Lanza 5294, Merillat 5330, Parker 5346, **Roberts 5370**, Sato 5384, Smith 5407, Smith 5409, Vision 5442
Pennsauken: Honickman 5239
Piscataway: American 5113, Wicks 5453
Pittstown: Hackett 5219
Plainfield: **Fanwood 5192**
Plainsboro: **Bristol 5143**, Integra 5251
Pottersville: Benjamin 5127
Princeton: Aicher 5109, **Allen 5111**, Atkinson 5119, **Bonner 5137**, Cohen 5166, D'Angelo 5175, **Dow 5184**, Geier 5204, Gund 5218, Harbourton 5223, Imada 5249, **Johnson 5263**, **Johnson 5265**, Karma 5269, Kovner 5287, McGraw 5323, Monius 5333, **Newcombe 5338**, Olsen 5342, Rheuminations 5366, RuthMarc 5380, Sands 5382, Schreyer 5389, Sierra 5401, ST2 5410, Tuchman 5429, Twin 5432
Princeton Junction: **YPI 5461**
Rahway: Werdiger 5451
Rancocas: **Rowan 5378**
Red Bank: Codispoti 5165, Hovnanian 5242, Quercus 5363, Sunfield 5418, Zobel 5464, Zodiac 5465
Ridgefield Park: Bendheim 5126, **Jeffery 5257**
Ridgewood: Bolger 5136, Copper 5169, Dephillips 5179, Howe 5243, **Marcon 5317**, **Parnassus 5347**
Ringwood: Brotherton 5145
River Edge: Shepherd 5399
Roseland: Arnold 5117, **Aspen 5118**, B'Seter 5122, Berlind 5129, Brody 5144, **Hess 5231**, **High 5234**, Jensam 5258, JHJ 5259, JSY 5267, Laurie 5297, Mack 5314, Milstein 5332, NSN 5340, Schwartz 5392, Silberman 5402, Steiner 5411, Sweetfeet 5421
Rumson: Borden 5138, Cowles 5170, **Huber 5244**
Saddle Brook: Wang 5448
Saddle River: Zimmer 5463
Sayreville: Sutton 5420
Sea Bright: Pascale 5349
Secaucus: Amirsaleh 5114, **Syms 5422**
Sergeantsville: Goldberg 5209
Short Hills: Goldring 5210, Price 5356, **Wilf 5455**
Somerset: Koguan 5284
South Orange: Harris 5224, Kreitchman 5289
Summit: Bouras 5139, Hugin 5245, Lipper 5308, **Reeves 5365**, Summit 5417
Teaneck: Berrie 5130, **Puffin 5362**, Zayat 5462
Tenafly: Adelson 5108, Kaplen 5268, Kennedy 5276
Tinton Falls: **Hovnanian 5241**
Toms River: OceanFirst 5341
Totowa: Machuga 5311
Tranquility: Post 5355
Union: Eisenberg 5187, **Eshet 5190**
Upper Montclair: Helm 5230
Vineland: **Frankino 5196**
Wall: New Jersey 5336
Warren: **Chubb 5162**, Grassmann 5213, **Gulton 5217**, Hiller 5237, Hyde 5247, Union 5435
Wayne: Lazarus 5299, Valley 5438, Weny 5450

Weehawken: UBS 5433
West Orange: Croman 5172, Ross 5375, Wallerstein 5446, Wallerstein 5447
West Windsor: Bulova 5147
Westfield: Perrin 5350, Rummel 5379
Whitehouse Station: **Merck 5326**, Merck 5327, **Merck 5328**, Merck 5329
Woodbridge: Phipps 5352
Woodcliff Lake: Fund 5198, **Tavitian 5426**
Wyckoff: Leitner 5303

see also 421, 999, 1194, 1464, 1552, 1589, 1660, 1672, 1696, 1707, 1711, 1752, 1927, 2058, 2060, 2082, 2118, 2172, 2221, 2295, 2312, 2461, 3541, 3601, 3605, 3612, 3722, 3751, 3776, 4008, 4383, 4497, 5515, 5585, 5595, 5607, 5611, 5613, 5617, 5626, 5632, 5638, 5646, 5647, 5654, 5663, 5684, 5687, 5725, 5758, 5795, 5797, 5798, 5815, 5831, 5841, 5849, 5894, 5896, 5914, 5917, 5925, 5937, 6006, 6015, 6069, 6089, 6106, 6113, 6117, 6126, 6158, 6192, 6223, 6224, 6227, 6229, 6238, 6251, 6269, 6270, 6310, 6311, 6314, 6315, 6322, 6429, 6435, 6445, 6479, 6539, 6567, 6597, 6610, 6618, 6629, 6651, 6653, 6654, 6709, 6767, 6796, 6816, 6847, 6880, 6982, 7024, 7037, 7044, 7111, 7163, 7164, 7182, 7186, 7192, 7265, 7269, 7298, 7311, 7316, 7500, 7630, 8077, 8110, 8139, 8147, 8281, 8282, 8304, 8305, 8312, 8371, 8388, 8391, 8410, 8451, 8463, 8494, 8648, 9369, 9517, 9988

NEW MEXICO

Albuquerque: Albuquerque 5466, **Gorham 5478**, **Johns 5482**, PNM 5493, Stockman 5497
Carlsbad: Carlsbad 5469
Farmington: Coleman 5470
Gallup: Holt 5480
Hobbs: Maddox 5487
Las Vegas: Domanica 5475
Los Alamos: Delle 5474
Ruidoso: Bancroft 5467, Hubbard 5481
Santa Fe: Brindle 5468, Con 5471, Cudd 5472, **Daniels 5473**, Frost 5476, Garfield 5477, Kind 5483, **Lannan 5484**, Lapides 5485, **Levinson 5486**, McCune 5488, Messengers 5489, New 5490, New Mexico 5491, Phillips 5492, **Pond 5494**, Proteus 5495, Santa Fe 5496, Thaw 5499, **Thaw 5500**, Thornburg 5501, Tipton 5502, Walbridge 5503
Taos: Healy 5479, Taos 5498

see also 28, 128, 129, 560, 955, 974, 1073, 1855, 1864, 1971, 2322, 2695, 2864, 3571, 4513, 5862, 6197, 6580, 7199, 7870, 7949, 7954, 8022, 8759, 8869, 8898, 8950, 9111, 9117, 9169, 9171, 9290, 9315, 9705, 9988

NEW YORK

Albany: Community 5782, Dolan 5870, Equinox 5935, Fuld 6000, Gifford 6027, Gutman 6122, Lipp 6432, Massry 6502, Morse 6584, O'Toole 6653, **Pearson 6701**, Templeton 7128, Weatherup 7222, Weill 7227, Weir 7234
Amawalk: O'Malley 6648
Amherst: Gellman 6013, Tower 7158
Ardsley-on-Hudson: St. Faith's 7039
Armonk: **IBM 6221**, Klein 6333, **Magowan 6473**, **MBIA 6512**, Zankel 7289
Atlantic Beach: Hammerman 6139
Auburn: Emerson 5927, Metcalf 6541
Ballston Spa: Lane 6373
Barneveld: **Bugher 5683**
Bayside: **East 5900**
Bedford: Morris 6578, Pollack 6734, Rice 6793
Bedford Corners: **Cader 5696**, Sachs 6888

Bellmore: **Levy 6410**
Binghamton: Community 5781, Decker 5846, Hoyt 6203, Klee 6329, Link 6428, O'Connor 6645
Bridgehampton: Mallah 6481
Bronx: **Dodge 5867**, Equipart 5936, **Wilson 7263**
Bronxville: Behrens 5612, **Brunie 5679**, Demartini 5851, Edelweiss 5908, Nagle 6599, Paul 6697
Brooklyn: Alff 5533, Ben-Haim 5617, Blue 5640, Brach 5657, Brand 5658, Brunckhorst 5678, Chaim 5728, Chasdei 5736, Chehebar 5740, Chehebar 5741, Chencinski 5742, Chesed 5746, Davidowitz 5834, Eisenreich 5917, Elbogen 5918, Emes 5928, Fuchs 5996, Fund 6001, Gindi 6036, Gross 6111, Gross 6112, Hager 6131, Harary 6143, Hartman 6151, Heisler 6166, Herman 6174, IDF 6225, Independence 6229, Kalter 6284, **Klein 6330**, Kleinman 6334, **Knopf 6343**, Kornfeld 6350, Langer 6376, Leibowitz 6398, M & E 6464, Marmurstein 6491, Mashala 6501, Mayore 6511, **Monterey 6568**, Moore 6572, Paneth 6685, Park 6687, Parkview 6691, Parshelsky 6693, Providence 6751, Reich 6784, Rieder 6803, Rieger 6805, Ritter 6813, Rosedorf 6840, Rubin 6871, S.O. 6886, Scharf 6913, Schechter 6914, Schon 6933, SES 6956, **Sicherman 6973**, Sitt 6995, Sitt 6996, Sitt 6997, Steinmetz 7067, Steinmetz 7068, Sutton 7108, TBF 7125, Tennenbaum 7129, TNG 7151, Traditional 7161, Tzedaka 7177, **Tzur 7179**, Weiler 7226, Wilson 7262, Yitzchok 7283, Zichron 7297, Zichron 7298
Buffalo: 1101 5504, Alfiero 5534, Arrison 5570, Baird 5591, Baird 5592, Community 5780, Community 5785, **Cummings 5813**, Fatta 5947, Knox 6345, M & T 6465, Messer 6540, Oishei 6660, Palisano 6680, Rich 6795, Rupp 6883, Statler 7050, Wendt 7243, Western 7248, Zemsky 7294
Canajoharie: Arkell 5565
Canandaigua: Schwartz 6941
Chappaqua: Clinton 5763, Frog 5992, Goldie 6049, Herdrich 6173, Hettinger 6178, James 6252, Leventhal 6406
Clarence: E & WG 5899
Clifton Park: Charitable 5732, Charitable 5734
Clinton Corners: Winley 7266
Cold Spring: Ryan 6884
Cold Spring Harbor: Lessing 6404
College Point: Iovino 6236
Commack: Setton 6957
Copake: Ungar 7183
Corning: Corning 5794
Corona: Klein 6331
Dunkirk: Northern 6638
East Durham: **Stiefel 7078**
East Hampton: **Frankel 5976**, **Waterfowl 7219**
East Norwich: Hoffman 6195
East Rochester: Schmitt 6928
Eastchester: Raffiani 6767
Elizabethtown: Crary 5806
Elmira: **Aequus 5524**, Community 5784
Elmsford: Westchester 7247
Fairport: Polisseni 6733
Far Rockaway: Zedakah 7291
Farmingdale: Feinstein 5951, Jacobson 6247
Flushing: Benenson 5619, Kupferberg 6363, Masada 6500, Ueltschi 7181
Forest Hills: Farkas 5945, **Frank 5974**
Garden City: Downs 5882, Rauch 6774
Glen Cove: De La Cour 5842, **Li 6418**
Glen Head: Banfi 5597, Barker 5600, DeMatteis 5852, Rubenstein 6870
Glens Falls: Glens Falls 6041, Morse 6583, Wood 7272
Glenville: Broughton 5675
Granite Springs: Schwartz 6940
Great Neck: Armstrong 5567, Bass 5604, Elmezzi 5925, Gould 6085, **International 6234**, Katz 6295, Kaylie 6301, Nelkin 6608, Wilpon 7261, Zitrin 7302
Greenvale: Slant 7000

Hammond: Sweetgrass 7113

Harrison: Adnim 5522, Castle 5716, Jandon 6253, Jarx 6255, Pulier 6753

Hauppauge: Casey 5714, McCarthy 6516

Hempstead: New York 6616

Hicksville: KeySpan 6320, Seventeen 6958

Hudson: Hudson 6207

Hudson Falls: Sandy 6903

Huntington: Rapaport 6771

Islandia: **NEC 6605**

Ithaca: Park 6688, Sigma 6977, Triad 7162

Jamestown: Carnahan 5706, Chautauqua 5738, Gebbie 6009, Hultquist 6211, Lenna 6402, Sheldon 6964

Jericho: Alpern 5540, Ashner 5573, Boxer 5656, Chasanoff 5735, MRM 6592, Rechler 6781

Katonah: Lisabeth 6433, Lostand 6448, Peckham 6702

Lake Placid: Adirondack 5517

Lake Success: **Friends 5990**, Trump 7167, Widgeon 7255

Lancaster: Galasso 6005

Larchmont: Chernow 5744, Chernow 5745, Fischer 5960, Hendel 6172, **Staley 7042**, Strypemonde 7089

Latham: Muldoon 6594

Lawrence: Edelman 5906, Jaaaa 6245, L. & L. 6368, Lawrence 6385, Ostreicher 6672, Rosenblatt 6849, **Rosenwald 6857**, **Rukal 6881**, Tziterman 7178, Zichron 7296

Liberty: Beaverkill 5610, Gerry 6017

Lindenhurst: **Dynamic 5897**, **Gilbert 6028**

Lockport: First 5958, Grigg 6108

Locust Valley: Karches 6292

Long Island City: Klaus 6328, **MetLife 6542**

Mamaroneck: Millstein 6553, **Ritter 6814**, Siegel 6976, Silberstein 6978, Straus 7086

Manhasset: Colin 5776

Massapequa Park: Schmeelk 6927

Melville: Bohlsen 5649, Geds 6010, Horowitz 6201, Kanas 6286, Kraus 6337, North 6637, **OSI 6670**, Pascucci 6696, Phelan 6723, Tormondsen 7154

Merrick: Hurdus 6214, **Syde 7114**

Middle Village: Strasser 7083

Mill Neck: **Smithers 7010**

Millbrook: Dyson 5898, MAH 6474, Millbrook 6549

Mineola: Buchmann 5681

Monsey: **American 5556**, Arm 5566, Auerbach 5578, Diamond 5859, Menche 6530, Rausman 6775, Sunrise 7102

Mount Kisco: Aeneas 5523, **Kohlberg 6346**, **Mathers 6504**, Silberstein 6979

Mountainville: Ogden 6657

New City: **Whitney 7254**

New Hyde Park: Cooper 5788, Litwin 6436, Marx 6499, New York 6614

New Rochelle: Bernstein 5625, Frank 5975, **Kaufmann 6299**

New York: 291 5505, A.E. 5506, A.R. 5507, **Abelard 5508**, Abraham 5510, Abrons 5511, Abrons 5512, Achelis 5513, Achilles 5514, Acorn 5515, Ades 5516, Adjmi 5518, Adjmi 5519, **Adjmi 5520**, Afognak 5525, Ahava 5526, Ahavas 5527, AHBA 5528, **AIG 5529**, **Alavi 5530**, Alexander 5531, Alexander 5532, Allen 5536, Allwin 5538, Altman 5542, Altman 5543, **Altman 5544**, **Altria 5545**, Altschul 5546, Altus 5547, **American 5548**, American 5549, **American 5550**, **American 5551**, American 5552, **American 5553**, **American 5554**, American 5555, Amicus 5557, Andersen 5558, Antz 5560, Apfelbaum 5561, Appleman 5562, **Archbold 5563**, Arnhold 5568, Aron 5569, ASDA 5571, Ashkenazie 5572, **Atlantic 5574**, **Atran 5575**, Atticus 5576, Auchincloss 5577, Avalon 5579, Avanessians 5580, Avery 5581, **AVI 5582**, **Avon 5583**, **AXA 5584**, Azrak 5585, Babbitt 5586, Badgeley 5588, Baier 5590, **Baker 5594**, Baldwin 5595, Bank 5598, Barker 5599, **Barth 5603**, **Bay 5606**, Bayne 5607, BCHB 5608, Bear 5609,

Bedminster 5611, Beker 5613, **Beldon 5614**, Belfer 5615, Belfer 5616, Benedict 5618, **Benenson 5620**, Berg 5621, **Berlys 5623**, Bernhard 5624, Berry 5626, Betesh 5627, Betesh 5628, Bialkin 5629, Bildirici 5630, Bingham 5631, Birkelund 5632, **Bismarck 5633**, **Bito 5634**, **Black 5635**, Black 5636, Blankfein 5637, Block 5638, **Blood 5639**, Blue 5641, Bluhdorn 5642, Blum 5643, Blythmour 5644, **Bobolink 5645**, Bobst 5646, Bodman 5647, Bodner 5648, Boisi 5650, Booth 5651, **Borderline 5652**, Botwinick 5653, Bovin 5654, Bowne 5655, **Branta 5659**, Braufman 5660, **Brice 5662**, Briger 5663, Bright 5664, Brine 5665, **Bristol 5666**, Brodsky 5668, Brodsky 5669, **Brokaw 5670**, **Bronfman 5671**, **Bronfman 5672**, **Bronfman 5673**, **Brooks 5674**, Brown 5676, Brownington 5677, Brutsch 5680, Buck 5682, Buhl 5684, Bukkyo 5685, Burch 5686, Burden 5687, **Burke 5688**, **Burpee 5690**, Butler 5691, Butler 5692, Buttenwieser 5693, **Bydale 5694**, **C.O.U.Q. 5695**, Cain 5697, Calicchio 5698, Cambr 5699, Campbell 5700, Canaday 5701, Canary 5702, **Carey 5704**, Carmel 5705, **Carnegie 5707**, Carr 5708, Carson 5709, Carwill 5711, Cary 5712, Case 5713, Castelnau 5715, Cayne 5717, Cayre 5718, **Cayre 5719**, Cayre 5720, Cedar 5721, Centennial 5722, Century 5725, Chadwick 5726, Chai 5727, Chana 5729, Chanin 5730, Charina 5731, **Chatterjee 5737**, **Chazen 5739**, Charitable 5733, Chesed 5747, Chiara 5748, **Chernin 5743**, Chesed 5747, Chiara 5748, **Children's 5749**, **China 5750**, Chisholm 5752, Chisholm 5753, Chu 5754, **Citigroup 5755**, CJM 5756, **Claiborne 5757**, Claiborne 5758, Clark 5759, **Clark 5760**, Clark 5761, Clark 5762, Cloud 5764, **CLRC 5765**, **Cogut 5766**, Cohen 5767, Cohen 5768, Cohen 5769, Cohen 5770, Cohen 5771, Cohen 5772, Cohenca 5773, Cole 5774, Coles 5775, **Collins 5777**, Collins 5778, **Commonwealth 5779**, ContiGroup 5786, **Conway 5787**, **Copland 5789**, Cordelia 5790, Corey 5791, Cornell 5792, **Cornell 5793**, Cornpaw 5795, Corrigan 5796, Corzine 5798, Coulson 5799, Countess 5800, Cowen 5801, Cowin 5802, Cox 5803, **Cranaleith 5805**, Credit 5807, Cricket 5808, Crisp 5809, Croll 5810, Cullman 5811, Cullman 5812, **Cummings 5814**, Cummings 5815, Curran 5816, Curry 5817, D'Agostino 5818, **Dabah 5819**, Dabah 5820, **Daedalus 5821**, **Damaris 5822**, Damial 5823, Dammann 5824, Dana 5825, **Dana 5826**, **Dana 5827**, Dancing 5828, Danziger 5829, Daphne 5830, Darivoff 5831, **Das 5832**, Davidson 5835, Davis 5836, Davis 5837, DBID 5838, de Coizart 5839, **de Hirsch 5840**, de Kay 5841, **de Rothschild 5843**, Debs 5844, DeCamp 5845, **Dedalus 5847**, DeGeorge 5848, Delancey 5849, **Delmas 5850**, **Derossi 5853**, **Deutsche 5854**, Devlin 5855, Diamond 5857, Diamond 5860, Dickler 5861, Diker 5862, Diller 5863, Dimon 5864, Ditmars 5865, Dobkin 5866, **Doherty 5868**, Donaldson 5871, **Donghia 5872**, **Donner 5873**, Donovan 5874, Doran 5875, Double 5876, Dow 5879, Dowling 5880, Downey 5881, **Dramatists 5883**, Dreitzer 5884, Drexler 5885, **Dreyfus 5886**, Dreyfus 5887, Druckenmiller 5889, Drukier 5890, Dubin 5891, **Duke 5892**, **Dun 5893**, Dunwalke 5894, Durst 5895, Dweck 5896, Ebb 5903, Eberstadt 5904, **Echoing 5905**, Edelstein 5907, **Edouard 5909**, Educational 5910, Effron 5911, **EHA 5912**, Ehrenkranz 5913, Eig 5914, Einhorn 5915, Einhorn 5916, Elebash 5919, Elias 5920, Elishis 5921, Ellis 5923, Elmaleh 5924, Emerald 5926, EMLE 5929, Emwiga 5930, **Endowment 5931**, **Engelhard 5932**, Englander 5933, Epstein 5934, Erpf 5937, Eunice 5939, Evans 5940, Everett 5941, **Falconwood 5943**, Falk 5944, Fascitelli 5946, Faulkner 5948, Feil 5949, **Feinberg 5950**, **Fernleigh 5952**, Ferrari 5953, Ferriday 5954, Fife 5955, FIMF 5956, Finlay 5957, **Fischel 5959**, Fisher 5961, Fisher 5962, Flanzer 5963, Fludzinski 5964, Forbes 5966, **Forbes 5967**, Forchheimer 5968, Ford 5969, **Ford 5970**, **Foundation 5971**, Franconia 5972, **Francqui 5973**, **Frankenberg 5977**, Frasch 5979, Freeman

5980, Freeman 5981, Freston 5982, Fribourg 5984, Friedberg 5985, Friedman 5986, Friedman 5987, **Friedman 5988**, Friends 5989, **Friends 5991**, Frohring 5993, Fromkes 5994, **Fruchthandler 5995**, Fuchsberg 5997, Fuchsberg 5998, **Fuld 5999**, Furman 6002, Furman 6003, Furth 6004, Gant 6006, Gatto 6007, GBRG 6008, **Gelb 6011**, Gellert 6012, Gelman 6014, Gerhard 6015, Gerry 6016, Gerschel 6018, Gerschel 6019, Gershwind 6020, Gerson 6021, Giant 6023, Gibbs 6024, Gibson 6025, Gilder 6029, **Gilder 6030**, Gilliam 6031, Gilman 6032, **Gilman 6033**, Gimbel 6034, **Gimprich 6035**, **Glades 6037**, Gleacher 6038, Gleberman 6040, **Global 6043**, Goldberg 6045, Golden 6046, Goldfrank 6048, Goldman 6050, Goldman 6051, **Goldman 6052**, Goldman 6053, **Goldman 6054**, Goldman 6055, **Goldman 6056**, Goldschmidt 6058, Goldsmith 6059, Goldsmith 6060, Goldstein 6063, Goldstein 6064, Goldstone 6065, Goldwasser 6066, Golkin 6068, Gollust 6069, Goodfriend 6071, Goodman 6072, Goodman 6073, Gordon 6074, Gordon 6075, Gordon 6076, Gordon 6077, Gorter 6079, **Gottlieb 6080**, Gottlieb 6081, Gould 6082, Gould 6083, **Gould 6084**, Grand 6086, Granoff 6089, **Grant 6090**, **Grant 6091**, **Grant 6092**, Grateful 6093, **Grauer 6094**, Green 6095, Green 6096, **Greenberg 6097**, Greenberg 6098, Greene 6099, Greene 6100, Greenhill 6101, Greentree 6102, **Greenwall 6103**, Greve 6104, Griffin 6105, Griffin 6106, Griffis 6107, Grin 6109, Gross 6110, Grubman 6113, Gruss 6114, Gruss 6115, **Gruss 6116**, Guggenheim 6117, **Guggenheim 6118**, **Guggenheim 6119**, Gural 6120, Gutmann 6123, Guttman 6124, **H.R.C. 6125**, Haas 6126, Haas 6127, Habe 6128, Haber 6129, Hagedorn 6130, Haggin 6132, **Haje 6133**, Hajim 6134, Halis 6136, Hall 6137, **Halloran 6138**, **Handler 6141**, Hansen 6142, Harbor 6144, Harkness 6145, **Harriman 6146**, Harriman 6147, Harris 6148, Harrison 6149, **Hartford 6150**, Haseltine 6152, **Hasenfeld 6153**, Hau'Oli 6154, **Hauser 6155**, Havens 6156, **Hayden 6157**, Hayden 6158, Hazen 6159, Hazen 6160, **Hearst 6161**, **Hearst 6162**, Heckmann 6163, Hecksher 6164, **Heineman 6165**, **Heller 6167**, Heller 6168, Heller 6169, Helmsley 6170, Helmsley 6171, Hermione 6175, **Heron 6176**, Hersh 6177, Heyward 6179, **Hickrill 6180**, Hidary 6181, Hidary 6182, Hilfiger 6183, Hilibrand 6184, Hill 6185, Hillman 6186, Hirsch 6187, Hirsch 6188, **His 6189**, **HKH 6190**, Hochstein 6192, Hod 6193, Hoerle 6194, Hoffritz 6196, Hollyhock 6197, Holtzmann 6198, **Homeland 6199**, Horowitz 6202, HSBC 6204, Huberfeld 6205, Huberfeld 6206, **Hughes 6208**, Hughes 6209, Hugoton 6210, **Humanitas 6212**, Huntington 6213, Hurford 6215, Hurst 6216, **Hutchins 6217**, Hutchins 6218, I Have 6219, **IAC 6220**, Icahn 6222, Icahn 6223, Icahn 6224, IFF 6227, IIMI 6228, Ingrassia 6230, **Institute 6232**, **International 6233**, International 6235, Iris 6237, Isaac 6238, **Isdell 6239**, **Ittleson 6241**, Ivor 6242, J & AR 6243, J G 6244, Jackson Hole 6246, Jacobson 6248, Jacoff 6249, JAM 6251, Janklow 6254, JCT 6256, **JEHT 6257**, Jephson 6258, Jesselson 6259, Jewish 6260, Jewish 6261, JKW 6262, **JM 6263**, **Jockey 6264**, Joelson 6265, Johnson 6266, Johnson 6267, **Johnson 6268**, Johnson 6269, Johnson 6270, Johnson 6271, Johnson 6272, **Johnson 6273**, **Joukowsky 6275**, **JPMorgan 6277**, Jurzykowski 6278, JW 6279, **Kade 6281**, Kadrovach 6282, Kaminer 6285, Kandell 6287, Kaplan 6288, Kaplan 6289, Kaplan 6290, Karan 6291, Karmazin 6293, Katz 6294, Katz 6296, Katz 6297, Katzenberger 6298, Kautz 6300, Kazickas 6302, Kealy 6303, Kearns 6304, **Keefe 6305**, Keeler 6306, Kelleher 6307, Kellen 6308, Kellner 6309, Kellogg 6310, Kellogg 6311, Kempner 6313, Kennedy 6314, Kenworthy 6315, Keren 6316, **Keren 6317**, Keren 6318, Keshet 6319, Kiernan 6321, Kimmelman 6322, **King 6323**, King 6324, King 6325, Kingdon 6326, **Kitov 6327**, Klein 6332, **Klingenstein 6335**, Klingenstein 6337, **Klingenstein 6338**,

Klingenstein 6339, **Klingenstein 6340**, Knafel 6341, Knossos 6344, Komansky 6347, **Kopf 6348**, Koppelman 6349, **Kraft 6351**, Kravis 6353, Kravis 6354, Kravis 6355, **Kreindler 6356**, **Kress 6357**, Kriendler 6358, Krimendahl 6359, Kumble 6361, **Kunstadter 6362**, Kurtz 6364, L and L 6366, Ladenburg 6369, Lambert 6370, **Lane 6372**, Lang 6374, Langeloth 6375, **LaSalle 6377**, Lasdon 6378, Lasker 6379, Lastfogel 6380, Lauder 6381, Lauder 6382, **Lauder 6383**, Lavelle 6384, LBC 6386, LCU 6387, Leach 6388, **Lead 6389**, Lebworth 6390, Lee 6391, Leffell 6393, Legacy 6394, Lehman 6395, Lehman 6396, Lehman 6397, Leibowitz 6399, Leigh 6400, Lemberg 6401, Leonhardt 6403, Leuschen 6405, Levin 6407, Levine 6408, Levitt 6409, Levy 6411, Levy 6412, Levy 6413, Levy 6414, Lewis 6415, **Lewis 6416**, LGR 6417, Liberman 6419, Lieb 6420, **Liebmann 6421**, Liman 6422, Lincoln 6423, Linden 6424, Lindmor 6425, Lindsay 6427, Link 6429, **Lipchitz 6430**, Lipmanson 6431, Littauer 6434, Litterman 6435, Liu 6437, Loeb 6438, Loeb 6439, Loeb 6440, Loewe 6441, Loewenberg 6442, Loews 6443, **Loewy 6444**, Lopatin 6446, Lortel 6447, Lowenstein 6449, Lowinger 6450, **LSR 6451**, Luce 6452, **Luce 6453**, Lucerne 6454, **Luckow 6455**, **Lucky 6456**, Lui 6457, **Lurcy 6458**, Lurie 6459, Lutece 6460, Lyle 6461, Lynch 6462, Lynton 6463, M.A.C. 6466, M.U.S. 6467, MacKall 6470, **Macy 6471**, Magen 6472, Maheras 6475, Mai 6476, **Mailman 6478**, Maleh 6479, Malkin 6480, Manitoba 6483, Manning 6484, **Mapplethorpe 6485**, Marcus 6486, Mariposa 6487, Mark 6488, Marks 6489, Marks 6490, Marron 6492, Marron 6493, Mars 6494, **Marsh 6495**, Martin 6496, Marx 6497, Marx 6498, MAT 6503, Matisse 6505, Matlin 6506, **Matthews 6507**, **Mayday 6508**, **Mayer 6509**, **Mayer 6510**, **McCaddin 6513**, McClelland 6517, McGraw 6519, McGraw 6520, McNulty 6521, **Mead 6522**, Meehan 6523, Megrue 6524, **Mellon 6525**, Melly 6526, Melohn 6527, Melohn 6528, **Memton 6529**, **Menschel 6531**, **Mercer 6532**, Mercury 6533, Mercy 6534, **Meriwether 6535**, **Merlin 6536**, **Merrill 6537**, **Mertz 6538**, Mesdag 6539, Metropolitan 6543, Meyer 6544, Meyer 6545, Meyer 6546, **Milbank 6547**, Millard 6548, Miller 6550, Miller 6551, **Milliken 6552**, Milstein 6554, Milstein 6555, Milstein 6556, Mindel 6557, Mindich 6558, **Mitchell 6559**, **Mitsubishi 6560**, Mitsui 6561, Mizuho 6562, MJPM 6563, Mnuchin 6564, Model 6565, **Monell 6566**, Monteforte 6567, Moody's 6569, **Moore 6570**, Moore 6573, Moore 6574, Mordecai 6575, Morgan 6576, **Morgan 6577**, Morris 6579, Morris 6580, Morrow 6581, Morse 6582, Morton 6585, Mosaic 6586, Moses 6587, Moskowitz 6588, Moss 6589, Mosse 6590, Mostyn 6591, **Mulago 6593**, **Mullen 6595**, Mullen 6596, Murphy 6597, Naddisy 6598, Nakash 6600, NAON 6601, **Nash 6602**, **National 6603**, **National 6604**, Neidich 6606, Neiman 6607, Netzach 6609, Neu 6610, Neuberger 6611, New York 6613, New York 6615, New York 6617, New York 6618, New York 6619, New York 6620, **New 6621**, Newcastle 6622, **Newhouse 6623**, Newman 6625, Newman 6626, Nicholas 6627, Nichols 6628, Nicholson 6629, **Nicolitch 6630**, Noble 6632, **Noble 6633**, **Norcross 6634**, **Norman 6635**, Normandie 6636, **Novartis 6640**, **NoVo 6641**, Novogratz 6642, **Noyes 6643**, O'Herron 6646, O'Malley 6647, O'Neil 6649, O'Neill 6650, O'Shea 6651, O'Toole 6654, OCLO 6655, Oestreicher 6656, **Ohga 6658**, Ohrstrom 6659, **Olayan 6661**, Olive 6662, Olshan 6663, Opatrny 6664, **Open 6665**, Oppenheimer 6666, Orentreich 6667, Orvis 6668, Osborn 6669, Ostreicher 6671, **Ostrovsky 6673**, **Ottinger 6674**, **Overbrook 6675**, Overhills 6676, Paduano 6677, Paestum 6678, Palm 6681, **Palmer 6682**, Palmer 6683, **Panaphil 6684**, Pannonia 6686, Park 6689, Parker 6690, **Parsons 6694**, Partridge 6695, PBHP 6698, PBO 6699, Peco 6703, Pedersen 6704, **Peierls 6705**, Pels 6706, Pels 6707, Pels 6708, Penick 6709, Penner 6710, Penson 6711,

Penzance 6712, Perella 6715, **Perelman 6716**, Perkin 6717, Persepolis 6718, Pevaroff 6719, Pfizer 6720, **Pforzheimer 6721**, Phaedrus 6722, Phillips 6724, **Phillips 6725**, Pincus 6726, Pines 6727, Pinkerton 6728, **Pioneer 6729**, Pittman 6730, Plant 6731, PLM 6732, Pollack 6735, **Pollock 6736**, Polo 6737, Polsky 6738, **Popplestone 6741**, Potter's 6743, Powers 6744, Price 6745, Price 6747, Pritchard 6748, Propp 6749, **Prospect 6750**, PTM 6752, Pumpkin 6754, Purchase 6755, Pyewacket 6756, QIBQ 6757, Quadrangle 6758, Quarry 6759, Queensgate 6760, **Quick 6761**, Quick 6762, Quinn 6763, R & TP 6764, Radio 6765, Raether 6766, Raiff 6768, **Ramapo 6769**, Ranger 6770, Rapoport 6772, Rattner 6773, Ravitch 6776, Realty 6779, REBNY 6780, Reed 6782, **Reed 6783**, Reiss 6785, Renfield 6786, Resnick 6787, Reuss 6788, Revson 6789, **Reynolds 6790**, Rhodebeck 6791, Rhodes 6792, Rice 6794, Richardson 6796, Richardson 6797, Richenthal 6798, **Richman 6799**, **Richmond 6801**, Ridgefield 6802, Rifkind 6806, Riggio 6807, Riklis 6808, Riley 6809, Riordan 6810, Ripple 6811, **Ripplewood 6812**, Riversville 6815, RJM 6816, Robbins 6817, **Robertson 6818**, Roche 6822, Rock 6824, **Rockefeller 6825**, **Rockefeller 6826**, Rockefeller 6827, Rodgers 6828, Rogers 6829, Rohatyn 6830, Rohr 6831, Rosansky 6832, Rose 6833, Rose 6834, Rose 6835, Rose 6836, Rose 6837, Rose 6838, Rose 6839, Rosen 6841, Rosen 6842, **Rosen 6843**, Rosen 6844, Rosenberg 6845, Rosenberg 6846, Rosenblatt 6848, Rosenblum 6850, Rosenkranz 6851, Rosenstiel 6852, Rosenthal 6853, Rosenthal 6854, Rosenwald 6855, Rosenwald 6856, Rosh 6858, Ross 6861, Ross 6862, Ross 6864, Rotenstreich 6865, **Rothschild 6866**, Roxe 6867, Ruben 6868, Ruben 6869, **Rubin 6872**, **Rubin 6873**, **Rubin 6874**, Rubin 6875, Rubinstein 6876, Rudin 6877, Rudin 6878, Rudin 6879, Ruffin 6880, Rumsey 6882, RZH 6885, Sacerdote 6887, Sackler 6889, Sackler 6890, Sackler 6891, Sackler 6892, Safra 6893, **Sage 6894**, Saligman 6895, Salmon 6896, Salomon 6897, Salomon 6898, Saltz 6899, **Saltzman 6900**, Samuels 6901, Sandler 6902, Sani 6904, **Sapp 6906**, Sasco 6907, **Sato 6908**, Schafer 6910, Schapiro 6912, Schenker 6916, **Schepp 6917**, Scherman 6918, Scheuer 6919, Scheuer 6920, **Scheuer 6921**, Schieffelin 6922, Schiff 6923, Schlosstein 6925, **Schlumberger 6926**, Schneider 6929, Schnurmacher 6930, Schnurmacher 6931, Scholarships 6932, Schott 6934, Schulhof 6935, Schulweis 6936, Schurgot 6937, Schwartz 6938, Schwartz 6939, Schwartz 6942, Schwartz 6943, Schwartz 6944, Schwartz 6945, Schwarz 6947, Sculco 6949, SDA 6950, Sealark 6951, Seaver 6952, Seevers 6953, Selis 6955, Shapiro 6960, Sharp 6961, Sharp 6962, Sheinberg 6963, Sheridan 6965, Shiva 6966, Shoolman 6967, SHS 6969, **Shubert 6970**, **Shulamit 6971**, Siebens 6974, Siebert 6975, **Silfen 6980**, Silver 6981, Silverman 6982, Silverman 6983, Silverstein 6984, Silverweed 6985, Simon 6986, Simon 6987, Simons 6988, Simons 6989, Singer 6990, Singh 6991, Sirus 6992, Sisenwein 6993, Sister 6994, **Skadden 6998**, Skirball 6999, Slifka 7001, Slifka 7002, **Sloan 7003**, Slovin 7004, **SMBC 7005**, Smith 7006, Smith 7008, Smith 7009, Snowdon 7012, Snyder 7013, Snyder 7014, SO 7015, Sobel 7016, **Solomon 7017**, Solow 7019, **Solow 7020**, Soros 7021, **Soros 7022**, Soros 7023, Soros 7024, Sperry 7026, Speyer 7027, SPIA 7028, Spiegel 7029, **Spiegel 7030**, **Spinal 7031**, Spingold 7032, **Spirit 7033**, Spitzer 7034, Sprague 7035, Spunk 7036, Srour 7037, SSM 7038, St. George's 7040, **St. Giles 7041**, Stanton 7043, Stanton 7044, Stanton 7045, Starfish 7046, Starker 7047, **Starr 7048**, Stecher 7051, **Steel 7052**, Steele 7053, Steffens 7054, Stein 7055, Stein 7057, Stein 7058, **Steinbach 7059**, Steinberg 7060, Steinberg 7061, Steinberg 7062, Steinberg 7063, **Steinhardt 7064**, Steiniger 7065, **Stempel 7069**, Stern 7070,

Stern 7071, Stern 7072, Stern 7073, Stevens 7076, Steyer 7077, Stiefel 7079, Stokes 7080, Stone 7081, **Stony 7082**, Straus 7084, Strauss 7087, Strelsin 7088, Stuart 7090, Studley 7091, Sugarman 7092, Sullivan 7093, Sullivan 7094, Sulzberger 7095, **Sumitomo 7096**, **Summerfield 7097**, Summerhill 7098, Summit 7100, Sunrise 7101, **Surdna 7103**, Sussman 7104, Sutton 7106, Sutton 7107, Sutton 7109, **SVM 7110**, Swartz 7111, **Sykes 7115**, T-4 7116, Taconic 7117, **Tai 7118**, Tamarind 7119, **Tanaka 7120**, Tandon 7121, **Tang 7122**, Tarnopol 7123, **Teagle 7126**, **Teddy 7127**, Terumah 7130, Textor 7131, **Third 7132**, **Thorne 7133**, Thornton 7134, Three 7135, **Tiffany 7137**, **Tiffany 7138**, Tiger 7139, **Tikvah 7140**, **Time 7142**, **Tinker 7143**, Tisch 7144, Tisch 7145, Tisch 7146, Tisch 7147, Tisch 7148, Tisch 7149, Tishman 7150, Tober 7152, Tomorrow 7153, **Tortuga 7155**, **Toshiba 7156**, Touch 7157, Townsend 7159, **Toyota 7160**, Tribune 7163, Troisi 7164, Trott 7165, **Trust 7168**, **Tsadra 7169**, Tuch 7170, Tufenkian 7171, Tuft 7172, Tully 7173, Turn 7174, Turner 7175, Tuttle 7176, **U.S. 7180**, Unanue 7182, Union 7184, **United 7185**, Unterberg 7186, Uphill 7187, Ushkow 7188, Valentine 7189, van Ameringen 7190, van Ameringen 7191, Van Pelt 7192, Vance 7193, Varadhan 7194, **Vetlesen 7196**, VHIV 7197, Vidda 7198, Vilcek 7199, Violett 7200, Vogelstein 7201, **Volpert 7202**, von der Heyden 7203, Wachtell 7205, Wagner 7206, Walker 7208, **Wallace 7209**, **Walter 7211**, Walter 7212, Walters 7213, **Warburg 7214**, **Warhol 7215**, Warner 7216, Wasserman 7218, **Watson 7220**, Watts 7221, **Weeden 7223**, Weezie 7224, Weil 7225, **Weinberg 7228**, Weinberg 7229, Weinberg 7230, Weinberg 7231, Weinman 7232, **Weinstein 7233**, Weiss 7235, Weiss 7236, Wellde 7239, Wender 7241, Wendling 7242, **Wenner 7244**, Werblow 7245, West 7246, **Wexner 7249**, Whispering 7250, White 7251, Whitehead 7252, Whiting 7253, Wiegers 7256, Wiener 7257, **Wigmore 7258**, Wildwood 7259, Williams 7260, Winkelried 7265, Winston 7267, Witmer 7268, WJS 7269, **Wolfensohn 7270**, Woodcock 7273, Woodheath 7274, Woodland 7275, Woodner 7277, **Woods 7278**, Woodward 7279, Wunsch 7281, **YLRY 7284**, Young 7285, Young 7286, **Youth 7287**, Zalaznick 7288, Zarin 7290, Zehner 7293, **Zenkel 7295**, ZIIZ 7299, **Zilkha 7300**, **Zimmermann 7301**, Zucker 7303, Zuckerberg 7304

North Merrick: Lindner 6426

Nyack: Kurz 6365

Old Westbury: Kaiser 6283, O'Sullivan 6652

Oneonta: Dewar 5856, Potter 6742, Warren 7217

Orchard Park: Smith 7007

Oriskany: Eastern 5902

Ossining: Horncrest 6200

Oyster Bay: Bahnik 5589

Patchogue: Knapp 6342

Pawling: Peale 6700

Penfield: Davenport 5833

Pittsford: Golisano 6067

Plainview: Shapiro 6959

Pleasantville: Abeles 5509, Burns 5689, Reader's 6777, **Reader's 6778**

Pomona: Walbridge 7207

Port Chester: L'Maan 6367, Seiler 6954, Straus 7085

Port Jefferson: Frey 5983

Port Washington: Brodsky 5667, Task 7124

Poughkeepsie: Area 5564, McCann 6514, Nuhn 6644, Schlobach 6924

Pound Ridge: IF 6226

Purchase: Alpert 5541, **Baker 5593**, Central 5723, **Essel 5938**, Hochfelder 6191, Kuflik 6360, Lookout 6445, **Moore 6571**, **PepsiCo 6714**, Wachenheim 7204, Wallach 7210

Rego Park: Goldstein 6062

Rhinebeck: Sosnoff 7025

Ridgewood: Godinger 6044

Riverdale: Bravmann 5661
Rochester: Alison 5535, Bausch 5605, Gleason 6039, Jones 6274, Mangurian, 6482, Riedman 6804, Rochester 6823, **Ross 6863**, Saunders 6909, Summers 7099, Wilson 7264, Wolk 7271
Rockville Centre: Gurwin 6121
Ronkonkoma: Shoreland 6968
Roslyn: Roslyn 6859, **Sussman 7105**
Roslyn Heights: **Initial 6231**
Rye: Dove 5877, Dove 5878, Elkes 5922, Franklin 5978, Grandview 6088, **Mack 6469**, Niehaus 6631, Schwartz 6946, Sternberg 7075, Weissman 7237
Rye Brook: **Landegger 6371**
Saratoga Springs: Bachmann 5587, Berkowitz 5622, **Chinnick 5751**, Corzine 5797, **Robinson 6819**, Solomon 7018, Woodmere 7276, Yellow 7282
Scarsdale: **Adler 5521**, Allison 5537, Glickenhaus 6042, Klingenstein 6336
Schenectady: Golub 6070, Price 6746, Schaffer 6911, Schenectady 6915, Wright 7280
Seaford: F. & J.S. 5942
Setauket: Swartz 7112
Sherrill: Gorman 6078
Skaneateles: Allyn 5539
Sleepy Hollow: Vernon 7195
Somers: **Pepsi 6713**
South Salem: Handler 6140, McGonagle 6518
Southampton: Balm 5596
Spencertown: **Kelly 6312**
Spring Valley: Goldstein 6061, Steinmetz 7066, Zedukah 7292
Stamford: Robinson 6820
Staten Island: Richmond 6800, SI 6972
Suffern: **Jaffe 6250**, Rosenberg 6847
Syosset: Leeds 6392, Neuwirth 6612
Syracuse: Central 5724, Gifford 6026, Pomeranz 6739, Snow 7011
Tarrytown: **Diamond 5858**
Troy: McCarthy 6515, Robison 6821, Troy 7166
Tuckahoe: Goldenson 6047, Pope 6740, Santa 6905
Tuxedo Park: Parr 6692
Unadilla: Tianaderrah 7136
Uniondale: Wellin 7240
Utica: Community 5783
Valhalla: Cappelli 5703, **Paley 6679**
Watertown: Northern 6639
Webster: Halcyon 6135
White Plains: **Barnett 5601**, Barrington 5602, Cramer 5804, **Dreyfus 5888**, Grandison 6087, Israel 6240, Macdonald 6468, **Mailman 6477**, Newman 6624, Rosner 6860, Schwebel 6948, Starwood 7049, Stein 7056, Stern 7074, Weissman 7238
Whitestone: Fogel 5965
Williamsville: East 5901, **Geyer 6022**, Joy 6276
Woodbury: Antun 5559, Dolan 5869, Goldring 6057, Tilles 7141
Woodmere: JW 6280
Yonkers: Carvel 5710

see also 61, 140, 215, 231, 245, 254, 291, 303, 323, 335, 371, 372, 375, 393, 413, 422, 437, 441, 444, 455, 456, 493, 546, 551, 558, 567, 582, 589, 611, 617, 618, 632, 650, 714, 733, 765, 798, 806, 811, 817, 819, 859, 883, 885, 886, 893, 897, 899, 908, 916, 933, 935, 939, 968, 969, 1000, 1006, 1018, 1019, 1072, 1073, 1094, 1098, 1100, 1124, 1125, 1134, 1135, 1144, 1194, 1200, 1212, 1232, 1253, 1274, 1284, 1287, 1297, 1298, 1309, 1310, 1315, 1322, 1336, 1346, 1421, 1424, 1442, 1464, 1467, 1478, 1483, 1485, 1492, 1494, 1496, 1499, 1501, 1503, 1506, 1510, 1511, 1512, 1524, 1528, 1531, 1540, 1543, 1546, 1551, 1552, 1554, 1555, 1556, 1560, 1561, 1567, 1572, 1577, 1579, 1584, 1589, 1591, 1595, 1596, 1604, 1606, 1607, 1608, 1618, 1625, 1627, 1631, 1634, 1636, 1637, 1638, 1639, 1640, 1646, 1649, 1650, 1653, 1657, 1658, 1660, 1661, 1663, 1665, 1666, 1671, 1672, 1674, 1678, 1681, 1684, 1695, 1707, 1708, 1711, 1718, 1721, 1722, 1723, 1724, 1729, 1733, 1744, 1746, 1748, 1750, 1752, 1753, 1754, 1755, 1756, 1760, 1761, 1777, 1790, 1792, 1799, 1803, 1807, 1812, 1815, 1830, 1839, 1871, 1878, 1881, 1889, 1896, 1905, 1917, 1928, 1933, 1934, 1950, 1971, 1975, 1987, 1993, 1994, 1999, 2001, 2017, 2020, 2023, 2025, 2027, 2034, 2037, 2038, 2060, 2072, 2079, 2080, 2081, 2082, 2088, 2089, 2091, 2099, 2100, 2123, 2127, 2133, 2136, 2137, 2138, 2157, 2175, 2182, 2184, 2193, 2203, 2216, 2222, 2235, 2249, 2250, 2253, 2285, 2290, 2298, 2318, 2324, 2461, 2465, 2584, 2603, 2607, 2651, 2659, 2662, 2667, 2672, 2686, 2695, 2712, 2734, 2739, 2762, 2783, 2794, 2804, 2825, 2841, 2845, 2864, 2883, 2885, 2896, 2925, 2973, 2974, 2985, 3001, 3023, 3024, 3027, 3089, 3162, 3261, 3271, 3285, 3295, 3347, 3395, 3474, 3486, 3487, 3532, 3540, 3558, 3561, 3576, 3601, 3605, 3612, 3623, 3634, 3640, 3656, 3659, 3660, 3667, 3692, 3696, 3701, 3702, 3706, 3711, 3716, 3726, 3748, 3750, 3751, 3760, 3768, 3776, 3801, 3840, 3851, 3873, 3898, 3937, 3942, 3946, 3952, 3957, 3968, 3988, 3994, 4001, 4008, 4035, 4062, 4106, 4117, 4129, 4132, 4152, 4179, 4181, 4202, 4222, 4299, 4314, 4341, 4351, 4355, 4381, 4383, 4413, 4418, 4429, 4477, 4484, 4564, 4577, 4584, 4595, 4628, 4773, 4779, 4844, 4901, 4982, 5045, 5057, 5068, 5077, 5081, 5108, 5109, 5116, 5119, 5123, 5126, 5127, 5128, 5129, 5130, 5131, 5133, 5139, 5145, 5147, 5149, 5152, 5154, 5157, 5163, 5166, 5168, 5170, 5172, 5174, 5175, 5183, 5185, 5187, 5189, 5195, 5200, 5201, 5202, 5204, 5210, 5218, 5219, 5220, 5221, 5222, 5225, 5227, 5232, 5235, 5237, 5243, 5247, 5250, 5253, 5260, 5262, 5264, 5268, 5270, 5271, 5272, 5276, 5284, 5285, 5287, 5289, 5292, 5294, 5299, 5300, 5301, 5302, 5304, 5305, 5306, 5307, 5309, 5312, 5315, 5316, 5318, 5322, 5331, 5334, 5339, 5344, 5345, 5348, 5349, 5352, 5353, 5354, 5358, 5366, 5369, 5371, 5373, 5374, 5375, 5377, 5381, 5383, 5385, 5389, 5392, 5394, 5396, 5398, 5401, 5402, 5404, 5407, 5408, 5410, 5411, 5414, 5416, 5420, 5421, 5425, 5427, 5428, 5432, 5433, 5446, 5448, 5449, 5452, 5456, 5460, 5499, 7311, 7317, 7417, 7435, 7501, 7505, 7550, 7566, 7610, 7655, 7656, 7677, 7719, 7730, 7732, 7783, 7799, 7844, 7871, 7878, 7916, 7961, 7976, 8079, 8080, 8092, 8102, 8110, 8115, 8119, 8126, 8133, 8147, 8148, 8158, 8164, 8170, 8216, 8220, 8223, 8244, 8251, 8253, 8275, 8298, 8316, 8355, 8363, 8364, 8376, 8415, 8430, 8463, 8469, 8478, 8483, 8513, 8516, 8523, 8536, 8713, 8726, 8913, 9091, 9157, 9168, 9169, 9220, 9297, 9333, 9339, 9340, 9362, 9369, 9396, 9489, 9502, 9510, 9517, 9537, 9540, 9544, 9557, 9645, 9738, 9790, 9805, 9811, 9818, 9865, 9948, 9954, 9965, 9976, 9988, 9997

NORTH CAROLINA

Ahoskie: Roanoke 7464
Asheville: Community 7346, Janirve 7404, Mills 7429
Belmont: Stowe 7487
Burlington: Hayden 7394
Carthage: Nias 7435
Cary: Curran 7350, Goodnight 7377, **Sall 7471**
Chapel Hill: Breeden 7324, Kenan 7411, Kenan 7412, Kenan 7413, Morehead 7430, Randleigh 7456, Strowd 7488, SunTrust 7491
Charlotte: Bailey 7309, **Bank 7310**, Belk 7314, Belk 7315, Blumenthal 7320, Crutchfield 7348, Dickson 7355, Dowd 7357, Duke 7359, Duke 7360, Easley

7361, Everett 7364, Family 7365, Foundation 7370, Goodrich 7378, Gorelick 7380, Gorelick 7381, Graham 7382, Halton 7386, Harris 7390, Hartquist 7391, Hendrick 7395, Hubert 7401, Jenkins 7406, Keith 7410, KPB 7414, Lance 7418, Levine 7421, Martin 7424, **Neal 7433**, NFM 7434, Nucor 7440, O'Herron 7441, **P & B 7442**, Richmond 7463, Sklut 7473, Smith 7476, Spangler 7482, SPX 7484, Tzedakah 7497, Van Every 7499
Concord: Cannon 7335
Conover: Bolick 7321
Durham: Biddle 7317, BIN 7318, Blue 7319, Fox 7371, **Morris 7432**, **Nickel 7436**, Warner 7503
Fayetteville: Cumberland 7349, McLean 7425
Garner: Yeargan 7511
Gastonia: Community 7342
Goldsboro: Bryan 7330
Greensboro: Anonymous 7306, Armfield 7307, Bryan 7329, Cemala 7337, Community 7343, Greensboro 7383, Gunzenhauser-Chapin 7384, Haley 7385, Hillsdale 7398, **Jefferson 7405**, **Prickett 7452**, **Richardson 7461**, **Richardson 7462**, Smith 7477, SOL 7480, Tannenbaum 7493, Toleo 7495, V.F. 7498, Weaver 7504, Zelnak 7513
Greenville: Smith 7478
Harrisburg: Gordon 7379
Hendersonville: Baruch 7311, Community 7344
Hickory: Beaver 7313, George 7372
High Point: Brown 7326, High Point 7397, Norcross 7437, Terry 7494
Huntersville: Merancas 7428
Kinston: Brody 7325, Harvey 7393
Laurel Hill: Morgan 7431
Lenoir: Broyhill 7328, Coffey 7339, Wilson 7506
Lexington: Young 7512
Madison: McMichael 7426
Marion: Corpening 7347
Mocksville: Mebane 7427
Mooresville: Ebert 7362, Giles 7374, Livingstone 7422, **Lowe's 7423**
Morehead City: **Sunshine 7490**
Mount Olive: Southern 7481
New Bern: Coleman 7340
North Wilkesboro: Herring 7396
Raleigh: Finley 7367, Gipson 7375, Jones 7408, North Carolina 7438, Palin 7443, Perkins 7445, Pharmacy 7446, **Pope 7450**, Progress 7453, Sloan 7475, Stewards 7485, Summer 7489, Winston 7507
Reidsville: Penn 7444
Research Triangle Park: **Burroughs 7333**, North Carolina 7439, **S.R.C. 7470**, Triangle 7496
Salisbury: **Food 7369**, Hurley 7402, Hurley 7403, Robertson 7466, Woodson 7509
Shallotte: Ladane 7417
Shelby: Dover 7356
Smithfield: Holding 7399
Spindale: Stonecutter 7486
Statesville: Davis 7354
Tryon: Polk 7449, Weingarten 7505
Valdese: Rostan 7467
Wadesboro: Braswell 7323
Wilkesboro: Kulynych 7415, **Kulynych 7416**
Wilmington: Cape Fear 7336, Community 7345, Davis 7352
Wilson: Burroughs 7332, Smith 7479
Winston Salem: Comloquoy 7341
Winston-Salem: Adams 7305, **Babcock 7308**, BB&T 7312, Bergen 7316, Branan 7322, Brown 7327, Burress 7331, Butler 7334, Charlotte 7338, Daveler 7351, Davis 7353, Drue 7358, Edgar 7363, Finch 7366, Flow 7368, Gilbert 7373, Glenn 7376, Hanes 7387, Hanes 7388, Haney 7389, Harvest 7392, Hommer 7400, Jolley 7407, Keasbey 7409, Layden 7419, Legatus 7420, Piedmont 7447, **Pianseon 7448**, Price 7451, Provident 7454, Ragan 7455, Reynolds 7457,

Reynolds 7458, Reynolds 7459, Reynolds 7460, Roberts 7465, Rumbaugh 7468, Ryan 7469, Simpson 7472, Slick 7474, Spring 7483, Symmes 7492, Van Houten 7500, Vanderbilt 7501, **Wachovia 7502**, Winston-Salem 7508, Woodward 7510

see also 55, 267, 676, 906, 1201, 1308, 1369, 1491, 1707, 1828, 1902, 1961, 1970, 1981, 2018, 2323, 2339, 2382, 2391, 2478, 2513, 2529, 2622, 2699, 2804, 2896, 2976, 3062, 3070, 3583, 3657, 3705, 3806, 3964, 3972, 4363, 4368, 4436, 4445, 5059, 5193, 5279, 5335, 5514, 5794, 6079, 6688, 6692, 6939, 7008, 7053, 7159, 7162, 7203, 7222, 7787, 8025, 8385, 8485, 8486, 8500, 8574, 8589, 8602, 8613, 8615, 8618, 8658, 8864, 9133, 9281, 9401, 9455, 9489, 9527, 9535, 9928, 9976

NORTH DAKOTA

Bismarck: Huncke 7515, Leach 7516, MDU 7517, North Dakota 7519, North Dakota 7520
Fargo: Fargo 7514, Stern 7521
West Fargo: Nordick 7518

see also 3589, 4523, 4524, 4604, 4636, 5489

OHIO

Akron: Akron 7526, Berlin 7546, Born 7552, Brennan 7554, Children's 7570, Corbin 7591, Ferguson 7625, FirstEnergy 7630, **Freygang 7640**, GAR 7643, Hamlin 7661, Haslinger 7664, Lehner 7709, Lippman 7719, Orr 7790, Ritchie 7821, **Sankey 7833**, Shaw 7852, Sisler 7858, **Tell 7876**
Alliance: Mangano 7733
Amelia: Midland 7750
Amherst: Nord 7779
Ashland: Ashland 7533
Ashtabula: Ashtabula 7534, Morrison 7764
Aurora: **Austin 7535**
Barberton: Barberton 7539
Beachwood: Lozick 7724, Murphy 7768, Outcalt 7792, Turben 7888, Wolf 7914
Bowling Green: Sky 7859
Brecksville: **Vesper 7892**
Bryan: Bryan 7559
Canfield: Russell 7828, Williamson 7908
Canton: Austin 7536, David 7601, Hoover 7675, Olive 7787, Stark 7867, Timken 7879, **Timken 7880**, Yoder 7919
Chagrin Falls: **Geisse 7646**, Mindala 7755
Cincinnati: A Good 7522, A Good 7523, **Alpaugh 7527**, Bachman 7538, Broussard 7557, Buenger 7560, **Burleigh 7561**, Butler 7562, Castellini 7568, **Chiquita 7571**, Cincinnati 7573, Cincinnati 7574, **Convergys 7587**, Conway 7589, Corbett 7590, Cornerstone 7592, Cotswold 7594, **Covenant 7595**, Dater 7600, **Dewald 7608**, Dornette 7613, Downing 7614, Emery 7619, Farmer 7623, **Federated 7624**, Fifth 7626, Gardner 7644, Gettler 7649, Haile 7659, Hatton 7665, Hauck 7666, Heiman 7669, Hutton 7681, Jarson 7686, Jergens 7689, Jewish 7690, Kaplan 7696, Keeler 7697, Kroger 7705, Lindner 7716, Lindner 7717, LKC 7720, Love 7723, Luther 7726, May 7738, Mayerson 7739, Mehl 7746, Milacron 7751, Nippert 7777, Ohio 7785, Oliver 7788, Peters 7801, Pfau 7803, **Procter 7807**, Pulley 7811, Rieveschl 7820, Rockwern 7824, Rosenthal 7826, Russell 7827, Schiff 7836, Schiff 7837, Schiff 7838, Schmidlapp 7840, Schmidlapp 7841, Schott 7843, **Scripps 7848**, Semple 7851, Sheakley 7854, Slemp 7860, Smith 7863, Spaulding 7865, Stillson 7869, Thendara 7878, **Warrington 7895**, Western 7903, Wodecroft 7912, Wohlgemuth 7913
Cleveland: Abington 7524, American 7528, Andrews 7530, **Armington 7532**, Bicknell 7548, Black 7551, Brentwood 7555, Britton 7556, Bruening 7558, Campbell 7565, Cleveland 7576, Cleveland 7577, Codrington 7578, CRN 7598, DBJ 7605, Duff 7615, **Eaton 7617**, Firman 7628, Fleming 7631, Forest 7634, Fox 7637, Geary 7645, **Goatie 7651**, Green 7652, **Gund 7654**, Gund 7656, Gund 7657, H.C.S. 7658, Hankins 7662, Harding 7663, Heavenly 7668, Hoover 7674, Horvitz 7677, Humphrey 7679, Huntington 7680, Jackson 7685, Jennings 7688, Jochum 7692, Jubilee 7694, **Key 7700**, **Knowles 7701**, Knudsen 7702, Kramer 7704, Kulas 7706, Lennon 7710, Lewis 7713, Lincoln 7715, Lippitt 7718, Mandel 7730, Mandel 7731, Mandel 7732, Mather 7736, McBride 7740, Mellen 7747, Miller 7754, Mixon 7757, Morley 7763, Murch 7766, Murphy 7769, NCC 7772, O'Neill 7783, **Ohio 7786**, Park 7794, Parker 7796, Patterson 7797, Payne 7798, **Perkins 7800**, Peterson 7802, Prentiss 7806, **Pruina 7809**, Reinberger 7815, Reuter 7817, Sage 7829, Saint 7830, **Sapirstein 7834**, Schott 7842, Scott 7847, Sedgwick 7849, Seifert 7850, Sherwin 7855, Smith 7862, Stefanski 7868, Stone 7871, Stranahan 7873, Tetlak 7877, Tippit 7881, Watson 7896, Weisbrod 7900, White 7905, Williams 7907, Wilson 7910, Wilson 7911, Women's 7916, Woodruff 7917
Cleveland Heights: Sloat 7861
Columbus: Columbus 7580, Deshe 7606, Diamond 7610, Edwards 7618, Fox 7638, Gerlach 7648, Gingher 7650, IHS 7683, Lancaster 7707, M/I 7729, McCorkle 7741, Moores 7759, Motorists 7765, Nationwide 7771, NFG 7776, Osteopathic 7791, Schottenstein 7844, Wildermuth 7906, Wolfe 7915
Concord Township: Hershey 7671
Coshocton: Coshocton 7593, Montgomery 7758
Dayton: Beerman 7543, Berry 7547, Cardinal 7566, **Cox 7596**, Creech 7597, Dayton 7603, Dayton 7604, Iddings 7682, Joshi 7693, **Kettering 7698**, Kettering 7699, Levin 7712, Mathile 7737, MeadWestvaco 7745, NCR 7773, Philips 7804, Reynolds 7818, Robbins 7823, Rose 7825, Schiewetz 7835, Shaw 7853, Tait 7875, **Tomkins 7884**, Toulmin 7885, Wallace 7894
Delaware: Community 7581, Jegs 7687
Dover: Reeves 7814
Dublin: **Arab 7531**, **Cardinal 7567**, Wendy's 7902
East Cleveland: McGregor 7742
East Liverpool: Gund 7655, Peninsula 7799
Euclid: Wellman 7901
Fairfield: Ohio 7784
Fairlawn: **OMNOVA 7789**
Findlay: **Cooper 7589**, Findlay 7627
Freeport: Foundation 7636
Gates Mills: Kalberer 7695
Hamilton: Boymel 7553, Hamilton 7660, Marcum 7734
Haviland: Samaritan 7832
Highland Heights: **Lerner 7711**
Hudson: Morgan 7761, Morgan 7762, Murdough 7767
Kirtland: Clapp 7575
Lakewood: Bell 7544, Ranney 7813
Lancaster: Fairfield 7622
Lebanon: Loeb 7721
Lorain: Community 7582, Stocker 7870
Louisville: Silk 7857
Mansfield: Richland 7819
Marietta: Marietta 7735
Marysville: Community 7586, Honda 7673
Maumee: Anderson 7529
Mayfield Heights: Horvitz 7676, Horvitz 7678, R.T. 7812
Mayfield Village: **PLACE 7805**, Progressive 7808
Middletown: AK 7525, Middletown 7749
Moreland Hills: Di Geronimo 7609, Wuliger 7918
Mount Vernon: Community 7583
New Albany: New 7775, **Wexner 7904**
New Philadelphia: Tuscarawas 7890

Newark: Evans 7620, Licking 7714, **Longaberger 7722**, Park 7795
North Canton: **Deuble 7607**, Diebold 7611
North Royalton: Trzcinski 7887
Norwalk: Schlink 7839
Novelty: Coleman 7579
Oberlin: Nord 7780
Orrville: Smucker 7864
Pataskala: Babcock 7537
Pepper Pike: Fairfax 7621, **Kosar 7703**, LZ 7727
Perrysburg: M/B 7728
Piqua: Miami 7748
Poland: Scotford 7846
Portsmouth: Scioto 7845
Rocky River: Bee 7542, **Bingham 7549**, Summer 7874
Salem: Salem 7831
Sandusky: Dorn 7612, Frohman 7641, Frost 7642
Shaker Heights: Ingalls 7684, **Weatherhead 7899**
Sidney: Community 7584
Solon: Miller 7752, Miller 7753, O'Neill 7782
Springfield: Davidson 7602, Springfield 7866, Turner 7889
Steubenville: Berkman 7545, Pugliese 7810
Sylvania: LaValley 7708, McMaster 7744
Toledo: Bates 7540, Binzer 7550, Charities 7569, Dana 7599, Ford 7633, France 7639, **Generation 7647**, **HCR 7667**, Jobst 7691, Miniger 7756, **Needmor 7774**, Owens 7793, Ritter 7822, Stranahan 7872, Toledo 7882, Toledo 7883, Zenith 7921
Troy: Troy 7886
Uniontown: Wagler 7893
Van Wert: Van Wert 7891
Warren: First 7629, Wean 7898
Warrensville Heights: Callahan 7564
Waverly: Wilson 7909
Westerville: **Durell 7616**
Westlake: Focus 7632, Heimbinder 7670, Nordson 7781
Wickliffe: Lubrizol 7725
Woodmere: Siegal 7856
Wooster: Beaverson 7541, Foss 7635, Noble 7778, Wayne 7897
Xenia: Greene 7653
Yellow Springs: Morgan 7760
Youngstown: Cafaro 7563, Christman 7572, Community 7585, Home 7672, Resch 7816, Youngstown 7920
Zanesville: McIntire 7743, Muskingum 7770

see also 119, 416, 523, 568, 714, 1422, 1700, 1730, 1795, 2014, 2074, 2095, 2123, 2126, 2155, 2194, 2213, 2332, 2804, 3040, 3309, 3396, 3406, 3418, 3420, 3425, 3427, 3445, 3535, 3750, 4099, 4245, 4268, 4286, 4299, 4322, 4341, 4480, 4484, 4497, 4645, 4669, 5464, 5993, 6300, 6821, 6919, 7362, 8011, 8115, 8139, 8261, 8388, 8396, 8399, 8438, 8476, 8482, 8500, 8526, 8658, 8742, 8864, 9252, 9535, 9697, 9716, 9730, 9755, 9787, 9835

OKLAHOMA

Ardmore: Community 7932, Goddard 7939, Noble 7963, Southern 7979
Bartlesville: **ConocoPhillips 7933**, Lyon 7953, Silas 7978
Duncan: McCasland 7956
Durant: Massey 7955
Edmond: Grace 7940
Eufaula: Gelvin 7938
Fort Gibson: Young 7990
Lawton: McMahon 7959
McAlester: Puterbaugh 7970
Norman: Sarkeys 7974
Nowata: Richardson 7973
Oklahoma City: **8:32 7922**, Better 7926, Communities 7931, Crawley 7934, **Ethics 7935**, Gaylord 7937,

Somerset: Wheeler 8501
Southampton: Katz 8280, Medleycott 8343
St. Davids: Hooper 8256
St. Marys: St. Mary's 8454, Stackpole 8456
St. Thomas: Edwards 8183
State College: Centre 8136
Strasburg: **Woods 8508**
Stroudsburg: ESSA 8190
Swarthmore: Pryor 8396
Titusville: Rees 8401
Trevose: Korman 8296
Uniontown: Eberly 8179
Unionville: **Forney 8207**
Upper Darby: Archer 8087
Valley Forge: IKON 8265, Saint 8419
Venetia: Miller 8353
Villanova: Dibona 8169, Rorer 8411, Rosenberg 8412
Warren: Community 8154
Warrendale: American 8079
Washington Crossing: Huplits 8262
Wayne: Cavitolo 8134, Chanticleer 8140, Eden 8181, Haas 8230, Hamilton 8233, Jake 8270, Musser 8361, Nelson 8362, Safeguard 8418, SVF 8472, Zisman 8513
West Chester: **AO 8085**, Chester 8141, Smith 8445, **Wyss 8510**
West Conshohocken: Allerton 8077, Connelly 8157, Fox 8210, Innisfree 8267, Lenfest 8304, Lenfest 8305, Lotman 8314, McDonald's 8333, Sherrerd 8439, Smith 8443, **Templeton 8475**, Weiss 8499
West Point: **Merck 8349**
Wilkes Barre: Blue 8112, Luzerne 8317
Williamsport: First 8202, Plankenhorn 8387, **Saltsgiver 8420**
Willow Grove: Asplundh 8091, Fourjay 8209
Winfield: John 8273
Wormleysburg: Grass 8223
Wyalusing: Taylor 8473
Wyndmoor: Barra 8095, Maguire 8321
Wyomissing: Colonial 8151, Janssen 8271, Sovereign 8451, Wyomissing 8509
York: Brougher 8122, Graham 8222, Grumbacher 8227, Johnson 8275, McCormick 8329, McCormick 8330, Pollock 8390, Stewart 8460, Susquehanna 8471, Truman 8483, Wolf 8506, York 8511
Zionsville: Fleming 8206

see also 716, 772, 847, 1162, 1201, 1325, 1464, 1548, 1556, 1588, 1642, 1663, 1672, 1689, 1696, 1701, 1711, 1720, 1727, 1736, 1743, 1758, 1762, 1811, 1830, 1933, 2081, 2104, 2106, 2229, 2250, 2806, 2864, 2934, 3062, 3466, 3535, 3606, 3715, 3722, 3754, 3776, 3823, 3966, 4105, 4115, 4207, 4293, 4354, 5116, 5119, 5122, 5174, 5206, 5219, 5236, 5250, 5259, 5279, 5280, 5291, 5301, 5318, 5327, 5335, 5360, 5383, 5389, 5393, 5421, 5432, 5528, 5608, 5687, 5726, 5758, 5799, 5831, 5838, 5889, 5929, 5969, 6188, 6248, 6300, 6374, 6379, 6398, 6465, 6470, 6506, 6521, 6524, 6546, 6565, 6576, 6584, 6597, 6683, 6698, 6746, 6757, 6829, 6862, 6880, 6895, 7123, 7131, 7191, 7276, 7299, 7341, 7389, 7465, 7468, 7483, 7545, 7551, 7565, 7588, 7630, 7702, 7772, 7859, 7879, 7900, 7911, 8658, 9339, 9394, 9619, 9728, 9812, 9974

PUERTO RICO

Carolina: **FNZ 8514**
San Juan: Puerto Rico 8515

see also 219, 523, 3522, 5387, 7459

RHODE ISLAND

Cranston: Feinstein 8534, **Feinstein 8535**, Shriners 8556
Hope Valley: Kimball 8542
Johnston: **FM 8537**
Lincoln: **Amica 8518**
Middletown: Kings 8543, van Beuren 8561
Pawtucket: Alperin 8516, Fain 8533, Hasbro 8539, **Hassenfeld 8540**, Sullivan 8558
Providence: **Alpert 8517**, **Bafflin 8519**, Brooks 8520, Carter 8522, Chace 8523, Charlesmead 8525, Charter 8526, Citizens 8527, Cuno 8528, Daniels 8530, **Dorot 8531**, Doyle 8532, Felicia 8536, Grinnell 8538, Jackson 8541, Littlefield 8544, Lord 8545, Mann 8546, McAdams 8547, McCarthy 8548, Nelson 8549, Noonan 8550, Rhode Island 8551, Roosa 8552, Routhier 8553, Salem 8554, Shaw's 8555, **Textron 8559**, Usen 8560, Wagner 8562
Wakefield: CARLISLE 8521
Warwick: Champlin 8524, Siperstein 8557
Westerly: Washington 8563
Woonsocket: CVS 8529

see also 219, 224, 523, 567, 865, 1507, 1513, 1648, 1657, 1666, 1674, 1678, 1681, 1689, 1695, 1950, 2104, 2206, 2371, 2948, 3002, 3523, 3557, 3767, 3769, 3776, 3824, 3849, 3885, 3905, 3907, 3934, 3956, 3965, 3971, 3991, 4005, 4011, 4035, 4045, 4046, 4053, 4054, 4062, 4075, 4096, 4108, 4110, 4128, 4160, 4166, 4184, 4477, 5200, 5353, 5541, 5626, 5632, 5687, 6579, 6768, 6792, 6854, 6858, 6940, 7242, 7781, 8313, 8403, 8451, 8463, 9135, 9978

SOUTH CAROLINA

Anderson: Abney 8564, Foothills 8588, Rainey 8605
Charleston: Cato 8576, Ceres 8578, Coastal 8581, Dintersmith 8586, Post 8603, Reams 8606
Clinton: Bailey 8567
Columbia: Arnold 8566, Blue 8570, Cassels 8575, Central 8577, First 8587, Lipscomb 8598
Easley: McKissick 8599
Florence: Bruce 8571
Fort Mill: Springs 8617
Fripp Island: **Wardle 8620**
Gaffney: Fullerton 8589
Greenville: Campbell 8573, Campbell 8574, Collins 8582, Community 8583, Daniel 8585, Glenn 8591, Hipp 8592, Liberty 8597, North 8601, **Roe 8607**, ScanSource 8608
Greenwood: Self 8610
Greer: Sirrine 8612
Hartsville: Byerly 8572, Sonoco 8614
Hilton Head Island: Community 8584, Kane 8596, **Youths' 8621**
Inman: Inman 8595
Lancaster: Sims 8611, TSC 8618
Lexington: South 8615
Myrtle Beach: Chapin 8579, Waccamaw 8619
N Charleston: Zucker 8622
Orangeburg: Horne 8594
Rock Hill: Hopewell 8593
Salem: **Premier 8604**
Simpsonville: Cline 8580
Spartanburg: Arkwright 8565, Barnet 8568, Black 8569, Gibbs 8590, Montgomery 8600, Phifer 8602, **Security's 8609**, Smith 8613, Spartanburg 8616

see also 267, 523, 1747, 2124, 2180, 2250, 2323, 2325, 2339, 2357, 2478, 2509, 2513, 2706, 3309, 3705, 4035, 4293, 4464, 4466, 5282, 5335, 7359, 7360, 7370, 7382, 7392, 7407,

7441, 7447, 7453, 7472, 7476, 7492, 7499, 7542, 7779, 8092, 8485, 8739, 9414

SOUTH DAKOTA

Brookings: Larson 8627
Huron: Griffith 8625
Mitchell: Hofer 8626
Pierre: South Dakota 8631
Rapid City: Dakota 8624, Stearns 8632, Vucurevich 8634
Sioux Falls: Branches 8623, Opus 8628, Peters 8629, Sioux Falls 8630, Via-Bradley 8633

see also 1275, 3332, 3343, 4495, 4524, 4573, 4604, 4636, 5489, 7517, 8025

TENNESSEE

Brentwood: Beaman 8642, EBS 8672, Massey 8709
Bristol: Gatton 8681, Lazarus 8700, Master's 8710
Chattanooga: Benwood 8644, Caldwell 8649, Chrysalis 8655, Community 8660, Hamico 8684, Harris 8686, Hurlbut 8692, Johnson 8697, Lyndhurst 8703, **Maclellan 8704**, MacLellan 8705, Osborne 8714, Tennessee 8732, Tonya 8734, Tucker 8735, **Westwood 8743**, Wright 8745
Cleveland: Johnson 8696, Jones 8698
Collierville: Martin 8706
Cookeville: No 8713
Elizabethton: Citizens 8657
Franklin: CLARCOR 8658
Greeneville: Unaka 8739
Kingsport: Basler 8641
Knoxville: 1939 8635, Aslan 8637, Charis 8652, Clayton 8659, Douglass 8667, East 8671, Haslam 8687, Haslam 8688, Pettway 8715, Redbird 8723, Stokely 8730, Thompson 8733
Memphis: Assisi 8638, Belz 8643, Bornblum 8645, Briggs 8647, Caesars 8648, Cannon 8651, Children's 8653, Community 8661, Conwood 8663, Day 8666, Durham 8670, First 8677, **Garrott 8680**, Goldsmith 8682, Harrah's 8685, Hyde 8693, Jeniam 8695, Martin 8707, Plough 8718, Longleaf 8719, Schadt 8725, Scheidt 8726, Sparks 8727, West 8742, Wilson 8744
Murfreesboro: Christy 8654
Nashville: AmSouth 8636, Atticus 8639, **Bridgestone 8646**, Campbell 8650, CIC 8656, Community 8662, Danner 8664, Davis 8665, Draughon 8668, Dugas 8669, Eskind 8673, Eskind 8674, Eskind 8675, Ezell 8676, Frist 8678, Frist 8679, Gordon 8683, Hawthorn 8689, HCA 8690, Hendrix 8691, Ingram 8694, LifeWorks 8701, Lindahl 8702, Martin 8708, Melkus 8711, Nelson 8712, Phillips 8716, Pickle 8717, Potter 8720, Ragsdale 8722, Starfish 8728, Stephens 8729, T & T 8731, Turner 8736, Turner 8737, Turner 8738, Wallace 8740, Washington 8741
Parsons: Ayers 8640
Readyville: **Rust 8724**
Union City: Kirkland 8699, Promethean 8721

see also 5, 6, 560, 939, 1140, 1565, 2118, 2180, 2259, 2277, 2296, 2309, 2312, 2323, 2339, 2382, 2408, 2774, 2925, 3075, 3309, 3427, 3699, 3705, 4341, 4368, 4457, 4480, 4753, 4765, 5335, 5387, 6467, 7053, 7095, 7280, 7305, 7362, 7447, 7454, 7990, 8600, 8864, 9023, 9099, 9230, 9368, 9448, 9450, 9455, 9469, 9530, 9997

TEXAS

Abilene: Campbell 8813, Community 8840, Dodge 8868, Greathouse 8924, Owen 9106, Shelton 9182, Taylor 9226
Addison: **Anderson 8761**, Folsom 8905, Haggar 8931

Amarillo: Amarillo 8758, Anderson 8760, Brumley 8800, Mays 9036, Read 9142, Ware 9264

Argyle: Miles 9060

Austin: **A Glimmer 8747**, **A Glimmer 8748**, Aragona 8763, Austin 8768, Butler 8802, Cailloux 8806, Cain 8808, Convergence 8844, Delaney 8862, **Dell 8863**, Educational 8878, Fasken 8895, Greathouse 8923, **Hartman 8942**, Jamail 8969, Keithley 8983, **KLE 8997**, Kodosky 9000, **Link 9013**, Lowe 9020, **MFI 9059**, Mitte 9067, Murrell 9082, National 9088, **O'Sullivan 9098**, Pine 9123, Plus 9125, Reynolds 9145, **RGK 9146**, Shivers 9184, **Silverton 9186**, Sooch 9200, **Swett 9221**, Temple 9228, Tocker 9236, Topfer 9238, Webber 9269, Works 9291

Beaumont: Dauphin 8856, Essar 8887, Gale 8913, Mechia 9050, Morgan 9073, Reaud 9143, Ward 9263

Beeville: Dougherty, 8870

Boerne: Branch 8794

Bryan: Astin 8764, Gibson 8918, Keown 8989

Buda: Johnson 8973

Cameron: Williams 9283

Carrollton: Halliburton 8935

Cleburne: Marti 9030

Colleyville: **Mevatek 9056**

Corpus Christi: Behmann 8785, Coastal 8833, Durrill 8873, Estill 8888, Futureus 8912, Kennedy 8988, Lichtenstein 9010, Moore 9071, Rachal 9138, Sams 9163

Corsicana: Eady 8875, Navarro 9089

Cypress: **Randall 9140**

Dallas: Ackerman 8750, Anderson 8759, Augur 8766, Bailey 8771, Baron 8774, Bass 8777, Beasley 8784, **Bell 8786**, Belo 8790, Bickel 8790, Bosque 8792, Carlson 8815, Castle 8818, Chatham 8825, Chilton 8826, Chinquapin 8827, Clements 8832, Collins 8838, Communities 8839, Constantin 8843, Cowden 8848, Cuban 8853, Dallas 8855, Deason 8861, Diener 8867, Duda 8871, Enrico 8885, Esping 8886, Fikes 8899, Furst 8911, Gayden 8915, Gill 8919, Haggar 8929, Haggar 8930, Haggerty 8932, Halbert 8933, Hanley 8940, Hawn 8943, Hillcrest 8952, Hirsch 8953, Hoblitzelle 8955, Hoglund 8956, **Hull 8964**, Jones 8976, Jonsson 8977, Jordan 8978, Kahn 8980, King 8995, Kurth 9003, Lantana 9004, Lightner 9012, Littauer 9014, Lockheed 9015, Loose 9017, Lyman 9023, Mankoff 9027, Marcus 9029, McDermott 9043, Meadows 9049, Merrick 9055, Meyerson 9058, Modano 9068, Morning 9075, Moss 9078, Murchison 9081, Muse 9083, NAH 9084, Nasher 9086, Nation 9087, O'Donnell 9096, Partnership 9110, **Pearle 9113**, Penney 9115, Pogue 9126, Pollock 9127, Proctor 9132, Prothro 9134, Providence 9135, Rachofsky 9139, Rogers 9156, Rosenberg 9157, Rosewood 9158, Schutte 9173, **Sei 9177**, Simmons 9188, Smith 9191, Smith 9195, Smith 9196, Sowell 9202, Sowell 9203, Sparrow 9204, Sparrow 9205, Speas 9206, Speas 9207, Stoffel 9214, Sturgis 9216, Summerlee 9217, Sumners 9218, Sunnyside 9219, Swinney 9222, **Tenet 9229**, Texas 9232, Thomas 9234, Tolleson 9237, Turner 9241, Turner 9242, Unkefer 9243, Vanberg 9248, Vaughan 9249, Waggoner 9256, Wagner 9259, Wal 9260, Ward 9262, Weaver 9267, Westcott 9278, Williams 9282, Wolens 9286, Young 9295, Zale 9297

DeSoto: Collins 8837

El Paso: El Paso 8881, Feinberg 8898, Hightower 8950, Hunt 8966, McKee 9045, Paso 9111, Stewart 9213

Fair Oaks Ranch: **Interdenominational 8968**

Fairview: Martinez 9032

Fort Worth: B & B 8769, Bass 8775, Bass 8776, Bass 8778, **Bridge 8795**, Brown 8798, Burnett 8801, Carter 8816, Carter 8817, Community 8841, Deakins 8860, Edwards 8880, Fleming 8904, Garvey 8914, **Imaca 8967**, Justin 8979, Keith 8982, Klabzuba 8996, Lard 9005, Moncrief 9069, Morris 9076, Once 9101, Paulos 9112, Richardson

9147, Roach 9150, Roberts 9151, Schollmaier 9172, Scott 9174, Snyder 9199, Walsh 9261, Weiser 9272, White 9279

Fredericksburg: **Adams 8751**, Holden 8957, Wolf 9287

Galveston: Kempner 8987, Moody 9070, Northen 9092, Seibel 9178

Garland: Allen 8756

Georgetown: Kelley 8986, Lord 9018, Wright 9294

Grapevine: Kincaid 8993

Hallettsville: Dickson 8866

Houston: Alexander 8752, Alkek 8753, Alkek 8754, **Allbritton 8755**, Anderson 8762, Baker 8772, Barnhart 8773, Bauer 8779, **Bauer 8780**, Baugh 8781, Bookout 8791, Bridgeway 8796, Brown 8799, Cain 8809, Cameron 8812, **CEMEX 8821**, CFP 8822, Clayton 8830, Cockrell 8835, Cook 8845, **Cooper 8846**, Cox 8849, Crane 8852, Cullen 8854, **Davis 8857**, Dawley 8858, di Portanova 8865, Dunn 8872, Dynegy 8874, El Paso 8882, Elkins 8883, Ellwood 8884, Fant 8892, Farb 8893, Farish 8894, Favrot 8897, Finger 8900, Fish 8902, Fleming 8903, Fondren 8906, Frees 8909, GHS Foun 8917, Goodman 8921, Hackett 8928, Hamill 8937, Hamman 8938, Hankamer 8939, Healthcare 8944, Helm 8947, Herzstein 8949, Hildebrand 8951, Hobby 8954, Holthouse 8959, Houston 8960, Houston 8961, Huffington 8963, Jamail 8970, Johnson 8972, Kaufman 8981, KFFH 8990, Kilroy 8991, Kinder 8994, Law 9006, **Levant 9008**, Levit 9009, Looper 9016, Luchsinger 9022, Lyons 9024, MacDonald 9025, Macrini 9026, Marathon 9028, Martin 9031, McCrea 9040, McCullough 9041, McGovern 9044, McNair 9047, Medallion 9051, Mehta 9052, Mendenhall 9053, Miller 9061, Miller 9062, Mischer 9063, Mithoff 9066, Moran 9072, Morgan 9074, Mosbacher 9077, Mundy 9080, Nightingale 9091, **Notsew 9093**, O'Quinn 9097, Oehmig 9099, **Oldham 9100**, Onstead 9102, Oshman 9104, Otter 9105, Owsley 9108, Pema 9114, Petrello 9121, Powell 9128, Reliant 9144, Riddle 9148, Rockwell 9154, RSMIS 9161, Rubenstein 9162, Sanders 9167, Sarofim 9168, Sarofim 9169, **Scaler 9170**, Scurlock 9175, **Search 9176**, **Shell 9181**, Simmons 9187, Simmons 9189, Smith 9192, Smith 9193, **Smith 9194**, Smith 9197, Smith 9198, **Starling 9210**, Sterling 9212, Strake 9215, Susman 9220, Tapeats 9223, Tate 9225, Tennessee 9230, Terry 9231, Vale 9246, Vaughan 9250, Vaughn 9251, **Waste 9265**, Watson 9266, Wedge 9270, Weekley 9271, Welch 9273, West 9274, West 9276, **Westbury 9277**, Wolff 9288, Wolff 9289, Wortham 9292, Zimmer 9300

Hurst: **Jenesis 8971**

Irving: B.E.L.I.E.F. 8770, Caris 8814, **College 8836**, **ExxonMobil 8889**, Harmon 8941, Kimberly 8992, **Onward 9103**, Rowling 9160, Sixty 9190, Stemmons 9211, Von Seggern 9254

Keller: Hudson 8962

Kerrville: Butt 8804, Cailloux 8807, Community 8842, Griffin 8925, Peterson 9120

Lamesa: Weaver 9268

Laredo: De Llano 8859, Hachar 8927, Vergara 9253

Liberty: Humphreys 8965

Livingston: Bergman 8789

Longview: Crain 8851

Lubbock: Beal 8783, CH 8823, Jones 8975, Lubbock 9021

Lufkin: Temple 9227

Marshall: Tartt 9224

Midland: Abell 8749, Cox 8850, Permian 9117, Prairie 9129, Scarborough 9171

Mineola: Meredith 9054

Orange: Stark 9209

Overton: McMillan 9046

Palacios: Trull 9240

Paris: Lennox 9007

Pearland: Wise 9284

Plano: **EDS 8877**, Mitchell 9065, Perot 9118, Perot 9119, Triad 9239

Port Neches: Hebert 8946

Post: Franklin 8907

Richardson: Owen 9107, Sidhu 9185

Richmond: George 8916

Round Rock: Dell 8864

San Angelo: San Angelo 9164, San Angelo 9165, Wolslager 9290

San Antonio: 80/20 8746, **AT&T 8765**, Baumberger 8782, Benson 8788, Brackenridge 8793, **Butt 8803**, Cameron 8811, **Catto 8819**, Charitable 8824, Circle 8829, Clear 8831, Coates 8834, Covenant 8847, Franklin 8908, Frost 8910, Goldsbury 8920, Gorman 8922, Halff 8934, Halsell 8936, Holt 8958, Kelleher 8984, **Kleberg 8998**, **Kleberg 8999**, Koehler 9001, Kronkosky 9002, Light 9011, Lord's 9019, Mays 9035, McCombs 9037, McNutt 9048, Newman 9090, Piper 9124, Progress 9133, Pryor 9136, Robinson 9152, San Antonio 9166, Semmes 9179, Shield 9183, Tobin 9235, Urschel 9244, USAA 9245, Valero 9247, Willard 9281, Zachry 9296, Zeller 9298

San Marcos: McCoy 9038, Texas 9233

Schulenburg: Stanzel 9208

Seminole: Doss 8869

Sherman: Mayor 9034

Sonora: Cauthorn 8820

Spring: Waggoners 9258

Sugar Land: Parks 9109, Phillips 9122, Ross 9159

Temple: Callaway 8810, Mayborn 9033

Texas City: McDaniel 9042

The Colony: Sharp 9180

The Woodlands: Allison 8757, Mitchell 9064, Rockjensen 9153

Tyler: East 8876, Fair 8891, Faulconer 8896, Fisch 8901, Herd 8948, Riter 9149, Rogers 9155, Wise 9285

Vernon: Waggoner 9257

Victoria: Johnson 8974, Mott 9079, O'Connor 9094, O'Connor 9095, South 9201

Waco: **C.I.O.S. 8805**, Christian 8828, Heavin 8945, Meyer 9057, Nash 9085, Rapoport 9141, Waco 9255

Wellington: Zephyr 9299

West University Place: Veres 9252

Wharton: Gulf 8926

Wichita Falls: Bridwell 8797, Edwards 8879, Fain 8890, Kelley 8985, McCoy 9039, Perkins 9116, Priddy 9130, Priddy 9131, West 9275, Wichita 9280, Wright 9293

Wimberley: **Aurora 8767**, PSH 9137

see also 28, 88, 93, 163, 393, 523, 696, 807, 939, 971, 1263, 1372, 1441, 1464, 1466, 1473, 1666, 1686, 1828, 1984, 2104, 2213, 2312, 2369, 2382, 2513, 2648, 2804, 2905, 3072, 3184, 3309, 3337, 3395, 3474, 3479, 3502, 3634, 3753, 3823, 4286, 4436, 4825, 5009, 5360, 5480, 5481, 5492, 5580, 6417, 6442, 6561, 7128, 7157, 7280, 7598, 7670, 7725, 7783, 7817, 7919, 7934, 7939, 7949, 7954, 7961, 7967, 8022, 8092, 8474, 8485, 8713, 8739, 9369, 9769, 9783, 9866, 9880, 9892, 9893, 9928, 9941, 9943

UTAH

Alpine: Gardner 9323

Farmington: B. Attitudes 9304, Simmons 9342

Kaysville: Dumke 9315, Dumke 9316

Logan: Dance 9311

North Ogden: Wideman 9351

Ogden: Denkers 9312, Dialysis 9313, Hall 9326, Swanson 9346

Orem: ALS 9301, Bastian 9306, Bastian 9307, Esther 9321, GFC 9324, Noorda 9336

Park City: Lockwood 9333, Stern 9344, **Wishnick 9353**

Pleasant View: Wadman 9349

Provo: Ashton 9303, **Force 9322**

Salt Lake City: **ALSAM 9302**, Bamberger 9305, Browning 9308, Burton 9309, Caine 9310, Dreamweaver 9314, Eccles 9317, Eccles 9318, Eccles 9319, Eccles 9320, Greene 9325, **Hayward 9327**, Hemingway 9328, **Huntsman 9329**, Jones 9330, Lawson 9331, Lawson 9332, McGillis 9334, Peery 9337, Quinney 9338, Raymond 9339, Savage 9340, Semnani 9341, Sorenson 9343, Stewart 9345, Tanner 9347, **Thrasher 9348**, Watkins 9350, Zions 9354

Sandy: Miller 9335

Springville: Wing 9352

see also 94, 128, 138, 304, 506, 560, 615, 814, 1243, 1446, 1864, 1909, 2296, 3631, 3653, 4368, 4680, 4933, 5077, 5546, 6763, 7009, 7111, 7207, 7739, 8022, 8050, 9600, 9666, 9705, 9979

VERMONT

Burlington: General 9356

Middlebury: Vermont 9361

Milton: Mergens 9360

Shelburne: Lintilhac 9359

South Burlington: **Ben 9355**

Waterbury: **Green 9358**

White River Junction: Gilman 9357

see also 224, 720, 1495, 1507, 1530, 1648, 1657, 1678, 1761, 2056, 2206, 2265, 2371, 2708, 3474, 3523, 3540, 3557, 3558, 3776, 3785, 3824, 3885, 3905, 3906, 3907, 3956, 3971, 4035, 4046, 4053, 4054, 4062, 4075, 4096, 4128, 4181, 4184, 5081, 5082, 5095, 5419, 5431, 5687, 5701, 5870, 5881, 5948, 5981, 6147, 6646, 6746, 6896, 7154, 7242, 7625, 7727, 8175, 8403, 9747, 9978

VIRGIN ISLANDS

Christiansted: Prosser 9364

St. Croix: Bartner 9362

St. Thomas: Community 9363

see also 7221

VIRGINIA

Alexandria: Adams 9366, Collis 9398, Connors 9403, Kellar 9449, Kington 9450, **Nirman 9483**, **Winkler 9542**

Altavista: Lane 9456

Arlington: Arlington 9371, Billings 9377, **Freedom 9424**, Friedman 9425, Kogod 9452, **Mitsubishi 9476**, **Mustard 9481**, Rosenthal 9508, Samberg 9510, Smith 9517, Smith 9518, **Stern 9522**, Washington 9534, Weissberg 9536

Ashburn: **MCI 9471**, Woodbury 9544

Baileys Crossroads: Katzen 9446

Blacksburg: Joco 9443

Bremo Bluff: Graves 9433

Bristol: Kegley 9448, McGlothlin 9469, United 9530

Casanova: Evans 9416

Charlottesville: **Blue 9379**, **CAP 9384**, Charlottesville 9390, **Chase 9391**, Galbraith 9427, Kluge-Moses 9451, **Oak 9488**, Perry 9495, Praxis 9500, **Scripps 9514**, Wellspring 9537, **WestWind 9538**

Clifton: **Three 9525**

Covington: Alleghany 9367

Dale City: Hylton 9440

Danville: Carrington 9386, Community 9401

Fairfax: **Datatel 9407**, Moore 9478, Peterson 9497, Weil 9535, Wiser 9543

Falls Church: Delmar 9410, **Lambert 9453**, **Olmsted 9490**

Franklin: Camp 9382, Franklin 9421

Fredericksburg: Fredericksburg 9423, Silver 9516

Glen Allen: Grandis 9432, HRH 9439, Lawrence 9457

Goochland: Gottwald 9431, Herndon 9437

Great Falls: **DeLaski 9409**

Harrisonburg: Community 9400

Hopewell: Harrison 9436

Irvington: Wiley 9539

Keswick: Batten 9373

Lansdowne: **Cooke 9405**, **M.E. 9464**

Leesburg: **Riverside 9505**

Lynchburg: English 9414, Lynchburg 9463

McLean: 118 9365, **Bansal 9372**, Blue 9378, Constitution 9404, **de Beaumont 9408**, Folger 9418, Freddie 9422, Funger 9426, **Gannett 9428**, **Glenstone 9429**, **Malek 9465**, Mars 9466, McDonnell 9468, Northern 9486, Ochsman 9489

Middleburg: **Johnson 9444**, McNichols 9472

Norfolk: Batten 9374, Batten 9375, Dalis 9406, **Kaufman 9447**, Landmark 9455, Lincoln 9458, Norfolk 9484, **Norfolk 9485**, Smithfield 9519, VuBay 9533

Portsmouth: Beazley 9376, Portsmouth 9498, Portsmouth 9499

Reston: **Ames 9370**, Claws 9394, Colburn 9395, **Modzelewski 9477**, **Mousetrap 9480**, Truland 9528

Richmond: Cabell 9381, Campbell 9383, CarMax 9385, Carter 9387, Charles 9389, Circuit 9392, Cole 9397, Columbus 9399, Community 9402, Estes 9415, Flagler 9417, Guilford 9434, Gwathmey 9435, Jackson 9441, Jeffress 9442, LandAmerica 9454, Lipman 9459, Luck 9461, Massey 9467, McGue 9470, Memorial 9474, Morgan 9479, Olsson 9491, **Parker 9492**, Parsons 9493, Pauley 9494, Reinhart 9502, Reynolds 9503, Robins 9506, Roller 9507, Scott 9513, Sharp 9515, Snead 9520, SunTrust 9523, Thurman 9526, Ukrop 9529, Universal 9531

Roanoke: Cartledge 9388, Foundation 9419, Fralin 9420, Golden 9430, Ludington 9462, Taubman 9524

Salem: Meador 9473

Stephens City: Bryant 9380

Sterling: N.E.W. 9482

Sutherland: Titmus 9527

The Plains: Sacharuna 9509, Wrinkle 9545

Vienna: Kanter 9445, Ratner 9501, Wilkinson 9540

Virginia Beach: AMERIGROUP 9369, **Doudera 9412**, Dreyfus 9413, Miller 9475, Perry 9496, Sandler 9511, Sandler 9512, Virginia Beach 9532

Warrenton: Loeb 9460, O'Shaughnessy 9487, Rice 9504

Washington: Cole 9396

Waynesboro: Staunton 9521

Weyers Cave: Houff 9438

Williamsburg: Clark 9393, **Dorothy 9411**, Williamsburg 9541

Winchester: American 9368

see also 334, 387, 488, 560, 696, 726, 1602, 1716, 1737, 1764, 1776, 1780, 1785, 1786, 1787, 1789, 1794, 1797, 1811, 1822, 1823, 1830, 1834, 1837, 1845, 1887, 1910, 1928, 1931, 1969, 1983, 1993, 2069, 2184, 2262, 2312, 2338, 2363, 2374, 2391, 2642, 2777, 2822, 2828, 3034, 3080, 3427, 3596, 3607, 3619, 3630, 3633, 3634, 3649, 3653, 3687, 3704, 3705, 3710, 3716, 3717, 3740, 3756, 3882, 4274, 4368, 4800, 5335, 5495, 5700, 5714, 5794, 5824, 5874, 5955, 6242, 6278, 6379, 6415, 6457, 6659, 6676, 6880, 7159, 7239, 7332, 7357, 7361, 7368, 7494, 7685, 7733, 7783, 7860, 8192, 8388, 8485, 8592, 8629, 8633, 8733, 8811, 9092, 9245, 9269, 9549, 9711, 9731, 9733, 9976

WASHINGTON

Arlington: **Sage 9674**

Beaux Arts: Quest 9666

Bellevue: **444S 9546**, Akibene 9549, Anderson 9551, Apex 9552, Aven 9554, Bas 9555, Danz 9577, Ellison 9581, Glaser 9594, Kaleidoscope 9616, Lochland 9630, Oki 9653, PACCAR 9656, **Pendleton 9661**, **Pigott 9663**, Simonyi 9686, Washington 9702

Bow: Paulus 9658

Bremerton: Coulter 9573

Eastsound: Jones 9614

Edmonds: Geneva 9592, Lie 9629

Ephrata: Lauzier 9626, Lauzier 9627

Everett: Evertrust 9583, UNOVA 9697

Federal Way: **Weyerhaeuser 9703**

Gig Harbor: De Falco 9578, Russell 9673

Greenbank: Hebert 9604

Hoquiam: Grays 9597

Issaquah: Brotman 9562, McMillen 9639

Kent: Everard 9582, **PAH 9657**

Kirkland: Lafromboise 9622, McCaw 9637, Razore 9671

Lacey: Helstrom 9605

Medina: Connors 9572

Mercer Island: Glazer 9596, Lockwood 9631

Mill Creek: Fortune 9587, Lynn 9633

Montesano: Kelsey 9617

Mount Vernon: Heritage 9607

Olympia: Haugland 9603

Prescott: **Vista 9699**

Sammamish: **Hyder 9612**

Seattle: Ackerley 9547, Adams 9548, Allen 9550, Archibald 9553, Benaroya 9556, Bezos 9557, **Blakemore 9558**, **Boeing 9560**, **Brainerd 9561**, Bullitt 9563, Burning 9564, Casey 9566, **Casey 9567**, Channel 9568, Crystal 9576, **Edwards 9580**, **Fabert 9584**, Ferguson 9585, Foster 9588, **Gates 9591**, GLA 9593, **Glaser 9595**, Green 9598, Haas 9599, Harvest 9602, **Hemingway 9606**, Horizons 9608, Howard 9609, Hughes 9610, Hussey 9611, Islands 9613, Jones 9615, Killinger 9618, Klorfine 9619, **Kongsgaard 9620**, Kreielsheimer 9621, **Laird 9623**, Laurel 9625, Lucky 9632, Martin 9634, Maxwell 9635, McCaw 9636, McEachern 9638, Medina 9640, Miller 9642, Moccasin 9643, **Natan 9646**, Nesholm 9647, Nestle 9648, Neukom 9649, Norcliffe 9650, North 9651, O'Donnell 9652, OneFamily 9654, Opportunities 9655, Peach 9659, PEMCO 9660, Positive 9664, Quixote 9667, Raikes 9668, Raven 9670, RealNetworks 9672, **Samis 9675**, Sarkowsky 9676, Satterberg 9677, Schuler 9678, Schultz 9679, Seattle 9680, Shemanski 9682, Shirley 9684, Shulman 9685, Sloan 9687, Smith 9688, **Starbucks 9690**, T.E.W. 9692, Talaris 9694, Tamaki 9695, True 9696, Vidalakis 9698, Washington 9701, Wilburforce 9705, Williams 9706, Wright 9707, Wright 9708, Wyman 9709

Spokane: Cowles 9574, Cowles 9575, Foundation 9589, Potlatch 9665

Tacoma: Cheney 9569, Dimmer 9579, Forest 9586, Fuchs 9590, Harder 9600, Milgard 9641, Rainier 9669, Sequoia 9681, Snyder 9689, **Stewardship 9691**, Tacoma 9693

Vancouver: Cartales 9565, Community 9570, Lematta 9628, Murdock 9644, Peterson 9662

Vashon Island: **Wiancko 9704**

Walla Walla: Blue 9559, Murr 9645, Sherwood 9683

Washougal: Warren 9700

Wenatchee: Community 9571

Woodinville: Larson 9624

Yakima: Harman 9601

see also 100, 219, 520, 523, 560, 718, 819, 881, 965, 971, 990, 1094, 1206, 1317, 1657, 2130, 2189, 2556, 2577, 3120, 3326, 3715, 4275, 4546, 4636, 4799, 5077, 5419, 6561, 7498,

7870, 8010, 8011, 8022, 8025, 8027, 8031, 8041, 8042, 8043, 8048, 8050, 8056, 8313, 8539, 8898, 9312, 9344, 9822

WEST VIRGINIA

Beckley: Carter 9712
Bluefield: Bowen 9711, Shott 9733
Charleston: BB&T 9710, Clay 9714, Clay 9715, Daywood 9717, Jacobson 9722, Kanawha 9723, Maier 9725
Huntington: Huntington 9721, Prichard 9731, Teubert 9735
Lewisburg: Hollowell 9719
Morgantown: McQuain 9727, Mylan 9728
Parkersburg: McDonough 9726, Parkersburg 9730, Stout 9734
Parsons: Tucker 9736
Princeton: Hunnicutt 9720
St. Albans: Whittaker 9737
Wheeling: Chambers 9713, Community 9716, Hoffmann 9718, Laughlin 9724, Nutting 9729, Schenk 9732

see also 1372, 2045, 2227, 3184, 3420, 3427, 3823, 5955, 6465, 7733, 7735, 7859, 8099, 8187, 8336, 8446, 9368

WISCONSIN

Appleton: Community 9776, **Outagamie 9888, Thrivent 9949**
Beloit: Beloit 9757
Black River Falls: Lunda 9852
Brookfield: Benidt 9758, Fleck 9799, Fotsch 9802, Ladish 9847, Mercy 9871, Rowland 9916, Siebert 9927, Vine 9956, **Young 9972**
Brownsville: Michels 9874
Chippewa Falls: Mason 9863, Rutledge 9917
Combined Locks: U.S. 9952
Cudahy: Ladish 9846
De Pere: Meng 9870
Eau Claire: Stewardship 9938, **T & O 9946**
Elm Grove: Helfaer 9813, Herma 9814, Managed 9857
Fond du Lac: Fond du Lac 9800, Jones 9827, Stone 9940
Fort Atkinson: Fort 9801
Fox Point: **Meehan 9868**, Stark 9935
Grafton: Brookbank 9766
Green Bay: Cornerstone 9781, Green Bay 9810, Kress 9844, Pamida 9891, Schneider 9920, Stock 9939, WPS 9970
Green Lake: Riordan 9911
Hudson: Nelson 9881, Phipps 9898, St. Croix 9933
Iola: Krause 9842

Janesville: Community 9780, Janesville 9820, Jeffris 9821, **Rath 9907**
Kenosha: **Bless 9761**, Kenosha 9833, **Palmer 9890**
Kimberly: MMG 9877
Kohler: Kohler 9840
La Crosse: Antioch 9745, Cleary 9774, Gordon 9808, La Crosse 9845, Reinhart 9909
Lyons: **Wagner 9957**
Madison: Alliant 9742, Bolz 9762, Bradshaw 9764, CUNA 9786, Evjue 9797, Frautschi 9804, Goodman's 9807, **Johnson 9825**, Madison 9854, Madison 9855, Overture 9889, Purple 9905, Rennebohm 9910, Shapiro 9925, Sub 9945, **Taylor 9947**
Manitowoc: West 9964
Marathon: Goldbach 9806
Marshfield: Marshfield 9861, **Roddis 9913**
Menasha: Banta 9752
Mequon: Batterman 9754, Nicholas 9883, Split 9932
Milwaukee: 1923 9738, Anon 9744, Archer 9746, Argosy 9747, Assurant 9748, Bader 9749, Baird 9750, Bartlett 9753, Beasley 9755, Bishop 9759, **Bradley 9763**, Bryce 9769, Casper 9770, Chapman 9771, Charter 9772, Clark 9773, Coleman 9775, Cox 9782, Crump 9783, Cudahy 9784, Cudahy 9785, Davis 9787, Delavan 9790, Demmer 9791, Duncan 9793, **Eastman 9794**, Eastman 9795, Evans 9796, **Firestone 9798**, Glover 9805, Gould 9809, Handleman 9811, Harley 9812, Herzfeld 9815, Hess 9816, Holz 9817, Jacobus 9819, Johnson 9823, Joy 9828, Kadish 9829, Kelben 9830, Kellogg 9832, Kettering 9835, Kohl 9837, Kohl 9838, Krause 9841, Leake 9849, **Lewis 9850**, Lubar 9851, Lynn 9853, Manpower 9858, Marcus 9859, Marshall 9860, Martin 9862, McBeath 9864, McDonough 9865, McQueen 9866, Merrill 9872, Miller 9875, Milwaukee 9876, Morse 9879, Munson 9880, Nelson 9882, Northwestern 9884, Pangburn 9892, Parr 9893, Peck 9894, Peck 9895, Pettit 9897, Pick 9899, Pollybill 9900, Posner 9901, PPC 9902, Puelicher 9904, **Reiman 9908, Rockwell 9912**, Rolfs 9914, Roundy's 9915, Schlegel 9919, Schoenleber 9921, Sensient 9922, Shattuck 9926, Smallwood 9928, **Smith 9929**, Soref 9930, Stackner 9934, Steigleder 9936, **Stein 9937**, Stuart 9941, Stuart 9942, Stuart 9943, Taylor 9948, Timken 9950, Tulsa 9951, Uihlein 9953, Uihlein 9954, Uihlein 9955, Walter 9959, Wehr 9961, West 9963, Wilson 9965, Wisconsin 9967, Witte 9968, Zilber 9973
Minocqua: JKO 9822
Monona: Sand 9918
Mount Horeb: **DeAtley 9789**
Neenah: Keller 9831, Menasha 9869
Oconomowoc: Merten 9873
Oshkosh: Hyde 9818, Oshkosh 9885, Oshkosh 9886, Oshkosh 9887

Pewaukee: Four 9803
Port Edwards: Alexander 9740
Prescott: AnnMarie 9743
Racine: Johnson 9824, Johnson 9826, Modine 9878, Racine 9906, Styberg 9944
Shawano: Bleser 9760
Sheboygan: Acuity 9739, Brotz 9767, **Kohler 9839**, Wagner 9958, Weill 9962
Stevens Point: Community 9778, **Make 9856**, Sentry 9923
Stoughton: Bryant 9768
Sturgeon Bay: Peterson 9896
Sussex: Windhover 9966
Thiensville: Lakeview 9848
Tomah: Krejci 9843
Walworth: Kikkoman 9836
Waukesha: Dawes 9788, **Kern 9834**, Waukesha 9960
Wausau: Alexander 9741, Community 9777, Dudley 9792, Seramur 9924, Spire 9931, Woodson 9969
Wauwatosa: Briggs 9765, Wrigley 9971
West Bend: Prescott 9903
Whitefish Bay: Baker 9751
Wisconsin Rapids: Bell 9756, Community 9779, Mead 9867

see also 620, 681, 1218, 1435, 1739, 1740, 1965, 2014, 2101, 2254, 2310, 2674, 2699, 2804, 2831, 2940, 2964, 2985, 3013, 3085, 3232, 3326, 3629, 4248, 4341, 4502, 4512, 4523, 4556, 4589, 4604, 4607, 4650, 4699, 4901, 5269, 5503, 5880, 6142, 6200, 8180, 8988

WYOMING

Alta: **Schultz 9990**
Casper: Ellbogen 9981, Martin 9984, McMurry 9985, Sargent 9989, True 9996
Cheyenne: Allen 9974, Richardson 9987
Cody: Stock 9992
Elk Mountain: Thieriot 9993
Jackson: Community 9977, Connemara 9978, Cumming 9979, Friess 9982, Kerr 9983, McNeill 9986, S & G 9988, Tozzi 9995, Weiss 9997
Laramie: Wyoming 10000
Moose: Chapman 9976
Newcastle: Thorson 9994
Sheridan: Scott 9991, Whitney 9998
Teton Village: Dragicevich 9980
Wolf: Berry 9975, **Wolf 9999**

see also 709, 1370, 1392, 1464, 1640, 1864, 2158, 3053, 3184, 4541, 4935, 4937, 4984, 5275, 6246, 6405, 6494, 7517, 8050, 8473, 8735, 8984, 9315, 9600, 9705, 9932, 9942

INTERNATIONAL GIVING INDEX

List of terms: Names of countries, continents, or regions used in this index are drawn from the complete list below. Terms may appear on the list but not be present in the index.

Index: In the index itself, foundations are listed under the countries, continents, or regions in which they have demonstrated giving interests. Within these country or regional groupings, foundations are arranged by state location, abbreviated name, and sequence number.

Afghanistan	Congo	Indonesia	Myanmar (Burma)
Africa	Costa Rica	Iran	Namibia
Albania	Croatia	Iraq	Nauru
Algeria	Cuba	Ireland	Nepal
Andorra	Curacao	Isle of Man	Netherlands
Angola	Cyprus	Israel	Netherlands Antilles
Anguilla	Czech Republic	Italy	New Caledonia
Antarctica	Denmark	Ivory Coast	New Zealand
Antigua & Barbuda	Developing countries	Jamaica	Nicaragua
Arctic Region	Djibouti	Japan	Niger
Argentina	Dominica	Jersey	Nigeria
Armenia	Dominican Republic	Jordan	North Korea
Aruba	East Timor	Kazakhstan	Northeast Africa
Asia	Eastern Europe	Kenya	Northern Ireland
Australia	Ecuador	Kiribati	Norway
Austria	Egypt	Korea	Oceania
Azerbaijan	El Salvador	Kuwait	Oman
Bahamas	England	Kyrgyzstan	Pakistan
Bahrain	Equatorial Guinea	Laos	Palau
Bangladesh	Eritrea	Latin America	Panama
Barbados	Estonia	Latvia	Papua New Guinea
Belarus	Ethiopia	Lebanon	Paraguay
Belgium	Europe	Leeward Islands	Peoples Dem. Rep. of Yemen
Belize	Fiji	Lesotho	Peru
Benin	Finland	Liberia	Philippines
Bermuda	France	Libya	Poland
Bhutan	French Guiana	Liechtenstein	Portugal
Bolivia	Gabon	Lithuania	Qatar
Bonaire	Gambia	Luxembourg	Romania
Bosnia-Herzegovina	Georgia (Republic of)	Macau	Russia
Botswana	Germany	Macedonia	Rwanda
Brazil	Ghana	Madagascar	Saint Kitts-Nevis
Brunei	Gibraltar	Malawi	Saint Lucia
Bulgaria	Gilbert Islands	Malaysia	Saint Vincent & the Grenadines
Burkina Faso	Global programs	Maldives	Samoa
Burundi	Greece	Mali	Saudi Arabia
Cambodia	Greenland	Malta	Scandinavia
Cameroon	Grenada	Marianas	Scotland
Canada	Guadeloupe	Marshall Islands	Senegal
Cape Verde	Guam	Martinique	Serbia
Caribbean	Guatemala	Mauritania	Seychelles
Caroline Islands	Guernsey	Mauritius	Sierra Leone
Cayman Islands	Guinea	Mexico	Singapore
Central Africa	Guinea-Bissau	Micronesia	Slovakia
Central African Republic	Guyana	Middle East	Slovenia
Central America	Haiti	Moldova	Solomon Islands
Chad	Honduras	Monaco	Somalia
Chile	Hong Kong	Mongolia	South Africa
China	Hungary	Montenegro	South America
China & Mongolia	Iceland	Montserrat	South Korea
Colombia	India	Morocco	Southeast Asia
Comoros	Indian Subcontinent & Afghanistan	Mozambique	Southern Africa

Soviet Union (Former)
Spain
Sri Lanka
Sub-Saharan Africa
Sudan
Suriname
Swaziland
Sweden
Switzerland
Syria
Tahiti

Taiwan
Tajikistan
Tanzania
Thailand
Togo
Tonga
Trinidad & Tobago
Tunisia
Turkey
Turkmenistan
Turks & Caicos Islands

Tuvalu
Uganda
Ukraine
United Arab Emirates
United Kingdom
Uruguay
Uzbekistan
Vanuatu
Vatican City
Venda
Venezuela

Vietnam
Wales
West Bank/Gaza
Western Africa
Western Samoa
Yemen Arab Republic
Yugoslavia (Federal Republic of)
Yugoslavia (Former)
Zaire
Zambia
Zimbabwe

Africa

California: Battle 260, Delano 449, Lee 798, Open 954
Colorado: Working 1476
District of Columbia: Banyan 1769, Loyola 1825
Florida: Stacy 2246
Illinois: MacArthur 2868
Indiana: West 3256
Iowa: Pioneer 3324
Kansas: Lloyd 3375
Maine: Oak 3552
Massachusetts: Alchemy 3775, Grand 3929, Grass 3931, Hyde 3962, Schooner 4131
Michigan: Gayar 4318
Mississippi: Telos 4768
Missouri: Monsanto 4868
Nevada: Hilton 5037
New York: American 5553, Bristol 5666, Carnegie 5707, Claiborne 5757, Ford 5970, McCaddin 6513, Rockefeller 6826, Saltzman 6900
Pennsylvania: Annenberg 8084, Archer 8087, Huston 8264
Tennessee: Maclellan 8704, Westwood 8743
Texas: Kempner 8987
Virginia: Dorothy 9411
Washington: Gates 9591
Wisconsin: Cudahy 9785, Young 9972

Albania

New York: Trust 7168

Antarctica

New York: Tinker 7143

Argentina

California: Foundation 529
Maryland: Hughes 3654
New York: Rosenberg 6847

Armenia

Massachusetts: Afeyan 3773
Michigan: Manoogian 4383
Minnesota: Cafesjian 4527
New Jersey: Hovnanian 5241

Asia

California: Christensen 384, Delano 449, Gere 565, Open 954, Spencer 1181, Strauss 1203
Connecticut: Richardson 1632
District of Columbia: Loyola 1825
Florida: Stacy 2246

Illinois: Baxter 2611, Fairwyn 2723, Omron 2926
Maine: Oak 3552
Maryland: Agilent 3563
Massachusetts: Grand 3929, Hyde 3962
Michigan: Whirlpool 4480
Minnesota: Medtronic 4622
Missouri: Monsanto 4868
Nevada: Hilton 5037
New York: American 5553, China 5750, Claiborne 5757, Ford 5970, Freeman 5981, Luce 6453, McCaddin 6513, Miller 6550, United 7185
Ohio: Convergys 7587
Pennsylvania: Annenberg 8084
Tennessee: Maclellan 8704, Westwood 8743
Washington: Gates 9591

Australia

California: Christensen 384, Smith 1161
Connecticut: Tudor 1664
Florida: Samstag 2214
Maryland: Hughes 3654
Massachusetts: Grand 3929
Minnesota: ADC 4496, Toro 4702
New York: American 5553, Commonwealth 5779
Pennsylvania: Alcoa 8075, Archer 8087

Austria

Colorado: Avenir 1339
New York: Lauder 6383

Bahamas

California: Mac 840, Smith 1161
District of Columbia: Merriman 1833
Florida: Taylor 2267
Illinois: Little 2859
New Jersey: YPI 5461

Bangladesh

Maryland: Hughes 3654
Oregon: NIKE 8046

Belarus

New York: Lauder 6383, Trust 7168

Belgium

Michigan: Dow 4285
New York: Francqui 5973

Belize

Wisconsin: Wagner 9957

Bermuda

New York: Stempel 7069
Virginia: Datatel 9407
Wisconsin: Wagner 9957

Bolivia

Maryland: Shared 3727
Minnesota: Oswald 4645

Bosnia-Herzegovina

California: Whalen 1299
New York: Trust 7168

Botswana

Michigan: Kellogg 4357

Brazil

California: K.L. 736
Indiana: Cummins 3136
Maryland: Hughes 3654
Michigan: Dow 4285
Missouri: Monsanto 4868
New York: Jurzykowski 6278
Ohio: Timken 7880
Oregon: NIKE 8046
Pennsylvania: Alcoa 8075

Bulgaria

Maryland: Hughes 3654
New York: Lauder 6383, Trust 7168

Cambodia

Minnesota: McKnight 4617

Cameroon

Massachusetts: New England 4052

Canada

California: Gap 551, Good 603, Intuit 696, Smith 1161, Smith 1167, Weider 1287
Florida: Glaubinger 2023
Georgia: Chesed 2348, Foundation 2388, Scientific 2482, UPS 2503, Worwin 2526
Illinois: Baxter 2611, Crane 2687, Graham 2767, State 3019

Indiana: Hasten 3163
Maryland: Alcoholic 3564, Hughes 3654, Shared 3727
Massachusetts: Fidelity 3904, Hershey 3949, Kendall 3977, Krieble 3990
Michigan: DENSO 4272, Kellogg 4356, Steelcase 4446
Minnesota: Medtronic 4622
Missouri: Enterprise 4810, Monsanto 4868
New Jersey: Goodes 5212, Parnassus 5347
New York: American 5553, Commonwealth 5779, Cummings 5813, Deutsche 5854, Frank 5974, Guggenheim 6119, Homeland 6199, LaSalle 6377, McCaddin 6513, Mitsubishi 6560, National 6603, Wigmore 7258
North Carolina: Burroughs 7333, Nickel 7436
Ohio: Convergys 7587, OMNOVA 7789, Timken 7880
Oregon: Lazar 8035
Pennsylvania: Carnegie 8130, Pew 8377
Rhode Island: FM 8537
Texas: Sidhu 9185, Summerlee 9217, Waste 9265
Virginia: Datatel 9407
Washington: 444S 9546, Bullitt 9563, Hyder 9612, Kongsgaard 9620, Starbucks 9690, Wilburforce 9705

Caribbean

Colorado: General 1381
District of Columbia: Henry 1808, Summit 1852
Massachusetts: New England 4052, Robinson 4107
Michigan: Kellogg 4357
New Jersey: International 5252
New York: American 5553, Guggenheim 6119, Reed 6782
Pennsylvania: Alcoa 8075, Archer 8087
Virginia: WestWind 9538

Central America

California: Arntz 236, Atkinson 239, Compton 409, Living 821, Peterson 996
Colorado: General 1381
District of Columbia: Kennedy 1816
Maine: Oak 3552
Massachusetts: Grand 3929, New England 4052
New York: Claiborne 5757, Saltzman 6900
Ohio: Fairfax 7621, Geisse 7646
Texas: Aurora 8767, Interdenominational 8968
Wisconsin: Wagner 9957

Chile
California: Foundation 529, Good 603
Maryland: Hughes 3654
New York: Weeden 7223

China
California: Energy 483, Panda 975
Colorado: First 1377
Connecticut: GE 1553, Lingnan 1587
Hawaii: Shaw 2554
Indiana: Cummins 3136
Kansas: Lloyd 3375, Servant 3391
Michigan: Dow 4285, Foundation 4309, H.I.S. 4334
Minnesota: Medtronic 4622
Nevada: Tang 5072
New Jersey: Tang 5423
New York: Goldman 6056, Kunstadter 6362, Li 6418, Luce 6453, National 6603, SMBC 7005, Tang 7122
Ohio: OMNOVA 7789, Timken 7880
Oregon: NIKE 8046
Pennsylvania: Alcoa 8075
Washington: Edwards 9580

China & Mongolia
New York: China 5750, Soros 7024

Congo
California: White 1302

Costa Rica
Texas: Interdenominational 8968

Croatia
New York: Trust 7168

Cuba
Georgia: Rockdale 2474
New York: Reynolds 6790

Czech Republic
Maryland: Hughes 3654
New York: Lauder 6383, Trust 7168
Ohio: Timken 7880
Washington: RealNetworks 9672

Developing countries
California: Delano 449, First 512, Rivendell 1056, Saje 1084
District of Columbia: Loyola 1825
Indiana: Lilly 3193
Massachusetts: Conservation 3858
Montana: Edwards 4936
New Jersey: Hackett 5219
New York: Children's 5749, Claiborne 5757, International 6234
Ohio: Geisse 7646
Oregon: NIKE 8046
Tennessee: Lazarus 8700
Texas: ExxonMobil 8889
Wisconsin: Taylor 9947

Dominican Republic
New Jersey: Verizon 5439

Eastern Europe
Alabama: Corman 29
Michigan: Mott 4399
New York: Lauder 6383, Saltzman 6900, Whitehead 7252
Tennessee: Maclellan 8704

Ecuador
California: Kvamme 781
Maryland: Shared 3727
Washington: Edwards 9580

El Salvador
District of Columbia: Public 1844

England
California: Columbia 399
Connecticut: Tudor 1664
Massachusetts: Sager 4122
Michigan: Kellogg 4356
Minnesota: ADC 4496
New Jersey: Parnassus 5347, YPI 5461
New York: Berg 5621, Conway 5787, Hayden 6157, New 6621, Spiegel 7030, Spirit 7033, Weinberg 7228, Winkelried 7265
Pennsylvania: Annenberg 8084, Fine 8201
Texas: A Glimmer 8747
Virginia: Guilford 9434
Washington: RealNetworks 9672

Estonia
Maryland: Hughes 3654
New York: Lauder 6383

Ethiopia
California: Christensen 384
Oregon: NIKE 8046
Texas: A Glimmer 8747, A Glimmer 8748

Europe
California: Living 821, Strauss 1203
Connecticut: Richardson 1632
District of Columbia: Wallace 1858
Florida: Stacy 2246
Illinois: Baxter 2611
Indiana: West 3256
Iowa: Pioneer 3324
Maine: Oak 3552
Maryland: Agilent 3563
Massachusetts: Grand 3929
Minnesota: Medtronic 4622
Missouri: Monsanto 4868
New York: American 5553, Dana 5825, Goldman 6056, Johnson 6268, Kade 6281, Kress 6357, Lauder 6383
North Carolina: Nickel 7436
Ohio: Convergys 7587
Pennsylvania: Archer 8087
Washington: Gates 9591

Fiji
Massachusetts: Grand 3929

Finland
Ohio: OMNOVA 7789

France
Maryland: Hughes 3654
New York: Berlys 5623, Bismarck 5633, de Rothschild 5843, Gould 6084, Lurcy 6458
Ohio: Timken 7880
Pennsylvania: Annenberg 8084
Texas: Scaler 9170, Search 9176, Westbury 9277
Washington: RealNetworks 9672

Georgia (Republic of)
New York: Trust 7168

Germany
California: Preuss 1015
Delaware: Hofmann 1722
Maryland: Hughes 3654
Michigan: Dow 4285
New York: Baier 5590, Buchmann 5681, Kade 6281, Lauder 6383, Walter 7211
Ohio: Timken 7880
Pennsylvania: Wyss 8510

Ghana
Massachusetts: New England 4052

Global programs
California: Delano 449
Colorado: Working 1476
Texas: Aurora 8767

Greece
Illinois: Demos 2702
Maryland: Hughes 3654
Massachusetts: Gerondelis 3925
Pennsylvania: Institute 8268

Guatemala
District of Columbia: Moriah 1835
Maryland: Shared 3727
Massachusetts: New England 4052
New York: Derossi 5853
Tennessee: Ezell 8676
Wisconsin: Palmer 9890

Guinea
Maryland: Hughes 3654

Haiti
Colorado: Mercy 1426
District of Columbia: Public 1844
Washington: Vista 9699

Honduras
Florida: Wahlert 2284
Tennessee: Ezell 8676
Texas: Interdenominational 8968
Wyoming: Schultz 9990

Hong Kong
Connecticut: Lingnan 1587
New York: China 5750

Hungary
Maryland: Hughes 3654
New York: Bito 5634, Lauder 6383, Spirit 7033, Trust 7168
Pennsylvania: Alcoa 8075

India
Alabama: Corman 29
California: Amar 213, K.L. 736, Living 821, Sai 1082
Colorado: First 1377
Connecticut: GE 1553
Hawaii: Watumull 2558
Illinois: MacArthur 2868
Indiana: Cummins 3136
Iowa: Sehgal 3330
Kansas: Lloyd 3375
Maryland: Hughes 3654, Shared 3727
Massachusetts: Hinduja 3952
Michigan: Dow 4285
Minnesota: ADC 4496, Medtronic 4622
Nebraska: Global 4967
New York: Chatterjee 5737
Ohio: Convergys 7587, OMNOVA 7789, Timken 7880
Oregon: Foreign 8014
Tennessee: Westwood 8743
Washington: Hyder 9612, Vista 9699

Indian Subcontinent & Afghanistan
California: Gap 551

Indonesia
Maryland: Shared 3727
New York: China 5750, SMBC 7005
Washington: Edwards 9580

Ireland
Delaware: Struthers 1758
New Jersey: McMullen 5325, Schering 5387, YPI 5461
New York: Curran 5816
Texas: A Glimmer 8747

Israel
California: American 216, Blackman 294, Chais 371, David 443, Eichenbaum 478, Eisenberg 480, Fein 497, Fromm 541, Goldman 597, Goldrich 598, Goldsmith 599, Harkham 649, Koret 774, Reinhard 1037, Saban 1079, Shapell 1134, Swig 1220, Winnick 1310
Colorado: Divine 1366, Weaver 1469
District of Columbia: Bernstein 1775, Capital 1781, Foundation 1796, Gudelsky 1805, Moriah 1835
Florida: Abramson 1868, Braman 1915, Edelstein 1988, Engelberg 1994, Gorin 2032, Greenburg 2034, Katz 2081, Posnack 2175, Russell 2212, Wollowick 2306
Illinois: Crown 2691, Gidwitz 2756, Landau 2847, Relations 2963, Stern 3023, Wein 3060
Indiana: Hasten 3163
Louisiana: Woldenberg 3516
Maryland: Berman 3572, Blaustein 3575, Cohen 3594, Dahan 3604, England 3622, Hoffberger 3652, Hughes 3654, Meyerhoff 3691, Meyerhoff 3692, Morningstar 3695, Polinger 3708
Massachusetts: Goldberg 3927, Grinspoon 3935

Michigan: Berman 4230
Missouri: Fox 4815, Millstone 4867, Simon 4903
New Jersey: Bendheim 5126, Eshet 5190, Lautenberg 5298, Sweetfeet 5421, Syms 5422
New Mexico: Levinson 5486
New York: American 5554, AVI 5582, Berg 5621, Botwinick 5653, Bronfman 5673, Chazen 5739, Cummings 5814, de Hirsch 5840, de Rothschild 5843, Dobkin 5866, Englander 5933, Everett 5941, Fischel 5959, Forchheimer 5968, Friends 5991, GBRG 6008, Gimprich 6035, Goldie 6049, Goldsmith 6060, Grant 6090, Gruss 6116, Gurwin 6121, Guttman 6124, Hauser 6155, Heller 6167, Herman 6174, Jesselson 6259, Kitov 6327, Klein 6330, Littauer 6434, Model 6565, Nash 6602, Ostrovsky 6673, Phillips 6725, Revson 6789, Ridgefield 6802, Ritter 6814, Rosenberg 6847, Rosenblatt 6848, Schulweis 6936, Slifka 7001, Stein 7055, Steinhardt 7064, Steyer 7077, Tikvah 7140, Tisch 7145, Tzur 7179
Ohio: Jewish 7690, Mandel 7730
Oklahoma: Schusterman 7975
Oregon: Fohs 8012
Pennsylvania: Berman 8104, Epstein 8186, Federation 8197, Grass 8223, Kaiserman 8277, Strauss 8464
Puerto Rico: FNZ 8514
Rhode Island: Dorot 8531
Tennessee: Belz 8643
Texas: Wolens 9286
Washington: Samis 9675
Wisconsin: Bader 9749
Wyoming: Schultz 9990

Italy
California: Saturno 1097
Delaware: Good 1715
Florida: Opler 2158
Idaho: Micron 2571
Michigan: Secchia 4431
New York: Delmas 5850
Ohio: OMNOVA 7789, Timken 7880
Pennsylvania: Alcoa 8075, Huston 8264

Jamaica
Pennsylvania: Alcoa 8075
South Dakota: Opus 8628
Washington: Vista 9699

Japan
California: Ishiyama 702
Idaho: Micron 2571
Illinois: Omron 2926
Maryland: ISE 3656
Michigan: Dow 4285
New York: American 5553, Luce 6453, United 7185
North Carolina: Nickel 7436
Tennessee: Community 8660

Kenya
Florida: DeMoss 1968
Minnesota: Oswald 4645
Washington: Vista 9699

Korea
New York: China 5750, Luce 6453

Laos
Minnesota: McKnight 4617

Latin America
Alabama: Corman 29
California: Angelica 223, Delano 449, Fund 542, Hewlett 671, Open 954, Strauss 1203
District of Columbia: Loyola 1825, Moriah 1835, Summit 1852, Wallace 1857
Georgia: Exposition 2380, Murphy 2456
Illinois: Baxter 2611
Kansas: Lloyd 3375
Maine: Oak 3552
Massachusetts: Grass 3931, Merck 4036
Michigan: Kellogg 4357, Mott 4399
Missouri: Monsanto 4868
New Jersey: International 5252
New York: American 5553, Deutsche 5854, Ford 5970, Guggenheim 6119, Mitsubishi 6560, Overbrook 6675, Prospect 6750, Tinker 7143
Ohio: Convergys 7587
Tennessee: Maclellan 8704
Virginia: Delmar 9410, Dorothy 9411, WestWind 9538

Latvia
New York: Lauder 6383

Lebanon
Florida: Abraham 1867

Lesotho
California: Firelight 509
Michigan: Kellogg 4357

Lithuania
Maryland: Hughes 3654
New York: Lauder 6383

Macedonia
New York: Trust 7168

Madagascar
Massachusetts: New England 4052

Malawi
California: Firelight 509
Michigan: Kellogg 4357

Malaysia
Maryland: Shared 3727
New York: China 5750, SMBC 7005

Mexico
Arizona: Community 91
California: Angelica 223, Arntz 236, Atkinson 239, Christensen 384, Compton 409, Marisla 855, San Diego 1087

Colorado: First 1377, General 1381, StorageTek 1460
Connecticut: GE 1553
District of Columbia: Public 1844
Georgia: Scientific 2482, UPS 2503
Illinois: Baxter 2611, MacArthur 2868
Indiana: Cummins 3136
Iowa: Pioneer 3324
Maine: Golden 3538
Maryland: Hughes 3654, Shared 3727
Massachusetts: Grand 3929
Michigan: DENSO 4272, H.I.S. 4334, Kellogg 4356
Minnesota: ADC 4496, Medtronic 4622, Oswald 4645, Toro 4702
Missouri: Monsanto 4868
New Jersey: Knistrom 5282
New York: Derossi 5853, Kohlberg 6346, LaSalle 6377, Tinker 7143
Pennsylvania: Alcoa 8075
South Dakota: Opus 8628
Texas: El Paso 8881, Kempner 8987, Summerlee 9217
Washington: Vista 9699
Wisconsin: Palmer 9890

Middle East
California: Firedoll 508, Living 821, Open 954, Philibosian 1003
Colorado: Working 1476
Connecticut: Richardson 1632
Florida: Catlin 1929
Georgia: Rockdale 2474
Illinois: Landau 2847
Kansas: Lloyd 3375
Massachusetts: Technical 4180
Missouri: Simon 4903
New Jersey: International 5252, Sweetfeet 5421
New York: American 5553, Dodge 5867, Ford 5970, Hauser 6155, Olayan 6661, Slifka 7001
Ohio: Arab 7531
Tennessee: Maclellan 8704

Moldova
New York: Lauder 6383, Trust 7168

Monaco
New Jersey: Johnson 5263

Mongolia
New York: Luce 6453, Trust 7168
Utah: Swanson 9346

Morocco
New York: Berlys 5623

Mozambique
Michigan: Kellogg 4357

Nepal
California: McConnell 870
Massachusetts: Sager 4122
Nevada: Omega 5050

Netherlands
Pennsylvania: Alcoa 8075

New Zealand
Massachusetts: Grand 3929
New York: Commonwealth 5779, Luckow 6455

Nicaragua
District of Columbia: Kennedy 1816
Texas: Interdenominational 8968

Nigeria
Illinois: MacArthur 2868
Tennessee: Ezell 8676

Oceania
California: Living 821
Illinois: Baxter 2611
Missouri: Monsanto 4868
New Jersey: International 5252
New York: Claiborne 5757
Ohio: Convergys 7587

Pakistan
California: Al-Ameen 200
Maryland: Shared 3727
Washington: Hyder 9612

Papua New Guinea
Massachusetts: New England 4052

Peru
Connecticut: Hampshire 1562
Maryland: Shared 3727
New Jersey: Carlson 5155
New York: Homeland 6199
Texas: Interdenominational 8968

Philippines
California: Jerome 717
District of Columbia: CityBridge 1783
New Jersey: International 5252
New York: China 5750
Wisconsin: Wagner 9957

Poland
Maryland: Hughes 3654
New Jersey: Johnson 5263
New York: Jurzykowski 6278, Lauder 6383, Rosenstiel 6852, Trust 7168
Ohio: Timken 7879, Timken 7880

Portugal
New York: Tinker 7143

Romania
Kentucky: Humana 3428
New York: Lauder 6383, Trust 7168
Ohio: Timken 7879, Timken 7880

Russia
California: Delano 449
District of Columbia: Moriah 1835
Illinois: MacArthur 2868
Maryland: Hughes 3654
Michigan: Mott 4399
New Mexico: Thaw 5500

New York: Carnegie 5707, Ford 5970, Trust 7168, Weeden 7223

Rwanda
California: Firelight 509, White 1302
Massachusetts: Ruettgers 4119

Scotland
California: Sun 1214
Delaware: Glencoe 1714
Illinois: Driehaus 2710

Serbia
New York: Rockefeller 6825

Singapore
Idaho: Micron 2571
New York: China 5750, SMBC 7005

Slovakia
Maryland: Hughes 3654
New York: Lauder 6383, Trust 7168

Slovenia
New York: Trust 7168

South Africa
California: Firelight 509, Kaiser 739, Smith 1161, Strauss 1203
District of Columbia: CityBridge 1783, Public 1844
Maryland: Hughes 3654
Massachusetts: Sager 4122
Michigan: Kellogg 4356, Kellogg 4357, Mott 4399
New York: Baird 5592, Overbrook 6675, Rockefeller 6825
Ohio: Timken 7880

South America
California: Foundation 529, Living 821
Indiana: West 3256
Iowa: Pioneer 3324
Maine: Oak 3552
Massachusetts: Garfield 3921, Grand 3929, Hyde 3962, New England 4052, Stare 4157
Nevada: Hilton 5037
New York: Claiborne 5757, Frank 5974, McCaddin 6513, Saltzman 6900
Pennsylvania: Archer 8087
Texas: Aurora 8767, Interdenominational 8968, Kempner 8987

Washington: Gates 9591

South Korea
Michigan: Dow 4285

Southeast Asia
California: Gap 551, Open 954
Colorado: Working 1476
District of Columbia: Banyan 1769
New York: China 5750, Ford 5970, Kunstadter 6362, Luce 6453, Rockefeller 6826

Southern Africa
New Jersey: International 5252
Wisconsin: Sand 9918

Soviet Union (Former)
Alabama: Corman 29
Connecticut: Richardson 1632
District of Columbia: Wallace 1857
New York: Rosenberg 6847
Puerto Rico: FNZ 8514

Spain
New Jersey: Carlson 5155
New York: Tinker 7143
Pennsylvania: Alcoa 8075

Sri Lanka
California: K.L. 736

Sub-Saharan Africa
California: Compton 409, Firelight 509, Gap 551
Massachusetts: Sager 4122
New York: Carnegie 5707

Sudan
California: White 1302

Suriname
Pennsylvania: Alcoa 8075

Swaziland
Michigan: Kellogg 4357

Sweden
California: Four 532
Ohio: OMNOVA 7789

Switzerland
Maryland: Hughes 3654
Pennsylvania: Wyss 8510

Taiwan
Maryland: Hughes 3654
New York: China 5750

Tanzania
California: Firelight 509
Florida: DeMoss 1968
Massachusetts: New England 4052
Minnesota: McKnight 4617, Oswald 4645

Thailand
New York: China 5750, SMBC 7005

Turkey
California: Christensen 384

Turks & Caicos Islands
Massachusetts: Krieble 3990

Uganda
Florida: DeMoss 1968
Maryland: Hughes 3654
Minnesota: McKnight 4617

Ukraine
District of Columbia: Antonovych 1766, Moriah 1835
Illinois: Heritage 2797
Maryland: Hughes 3654
New York: Lauder 6383, Trust 7168
Oklahoma: Schusterman 7975
Texas: Search 9176

United Kingdom
California: Gap 551, Smith 1161
District of Columbia: Butler 1779
Illinois: Louis 2862
Indiana: Lincoln 3195
Maryland: Hughes 3654
Missouri: Enterprise 4810

New Mexico: Stockman 5497, Thaw 5500
New York: Commonwealth 5779, Lehman 6396, Miller 6550, Moody's 6569, OSI 6670, St. George's 7040, Tanaka 7120
Ohio: OMNOVA 7789, Timken 7880
Virginia: Gannett 9428

Uruguay
Maryland: Hughes 3654

Vatican City
Iowa: Ochylski 3321
New York: Homeland 6199

Venezuela
Florida: Vollmer 2282
Maryland: Hughes 3654
New Jersey: Verizon 5439, Vollmer 5443

Vietnam
Massachusetts: Alchemy 3775
Minnesota: McKnight 4617
New York: Endowment 5931, SMBC 7005
Wyoming: Schultz 9990

Wales
Michigan: Dow 4285
Pennsylvania: Alcoa 8075

West Bank/Gaza
Wyoming: Schultz 9990

Western Africa
Alabama: Corman 29

Yugoslavia
California: Studenica 1209

Zambia
California: Firelight 509
Oregon: NIKE 8046

Zimbabwe
California: Firelight 509
Maine: Oak 3552
Michigan: Kellogg 4357

TYPE OF SUPPORT INDEX

List of terms: Terms for the major types of support used in this index are listed below with definitions.

Index: In the index itself, foundation entries are arranged under each term by state location, abbreviated name, and sequence number. Foundations in boldface type make grants on a national, regional, or international basis. The others generally limit giving to the state or city in which they are located.

Annual campaigns: any organized effort by a nonprofit to secure gifts on an annual basis; also called annual appeals.

Building/renovation: money raised for construction, renovation, remodeling, or rehabilitation of buildings; may be part of an organization's capital campaign.

Capital campaigns: a campaign, usually extending over a period of years, to raise substantial funds for enduring purposes, such as building or endowment funds.

Cause-related marketing: linking gifts to charity with marketing promotions. This may involve donating products which will then be auctioned or given away in a drawing with the proceeds benefiting a charity. The advertising campaign for the product will be combined with the promotion for the charity. In other cases it will be advertised that when a customer buys the product a certain amount of the proceeds will be donated to charity. Often gifts made to charities stemming from cause-related marketing are not called charitable donations and may be assigned as expenses to the department in charge of the program. Public affairs and marketing are the departments usually involved.

Conferences/seminars: a grant to cover the expenses of holding a conference or seminar.

Consulting services: professional staff support provided by the foundation to a nonprofit to consult on a project of mutual interest or to evaluate services (not a cash grant).

Continuing support: a grant that is renewed on a regular basis.

Curriculum development: grants to schools, colleges, universities, and educational support organizations to develop general or discipline-specific curricula.

Debt reduction: also known as deficit financing. A grant to reduce the recipient organization's indebtedness; frequently refers to mortgage payments.

Donated equipment: surplus furniture, office machines, paper, appliances, laboratory apparatus, or other items that may be given to charities, schools, or hospitals.

Donated land: land or developed property. Institutions of higher education often receive gifts of real estate; land has also been given to community groups for housing development or for parks or recreational facilities.

Donated products: companies giving away what they make or produce. Product donations can include periodic clothing donations to a shelter for the homeless or regular donations of pharmaceuticals to a health clinic resulting in a reliable supply.

Emergency funds: a one-time grant to cover immediate short-term funding needs on an emergency basis.

Employee matching gifts: a contribution to a charitable organization by a corporate employee which is matched by a similar contribution from the employer. Many corporations support employee matching gift programs in higher education to stimulate their employees to give to the college or university of their choice. In addition, many foundations support matching gift programs for their officers and directors.

Employee volunteer services: an ongoing coordinated effort through which the company promotes involvement with nonprofits on the part of employees. The involvement may be during work time or after hours. (Employees may also volunteer on their own initiative; however, that is not described as corporate volunteerism). Many companies honor their employees with awards for outstanding volunteer efforts. In making cash donations, many favor the organizations with which their employees have worked as volunteers. Employee volunteerism runs the gamut from school tutoring programs to sales on work premises of employee-made crafts or baked goods to benefit nonprofits. Management of the programs can range from fully-staffed offices of corporate volunteerism to a part-time coordinating responsibility on the part of one employee.

Employee-related scholarships: a scholarship program funded by a company-sponsored foundation usually for children of employees; programs are frequently administered by the National Merit Scholarship Corporation which is responsible for selection of scholars.

Endowments: a bequest or gift intended to be kept permanently and invested to provide income for continued support of an organization.

Equipment: a grant to purchase equipment, furnishings, or other materials.

Exchange programs: usually refers to funds for educational exchange programs for foreign students.

Fellowships: usually indicates funds awarded to educational institutions to support fellowship programs. A few foundations award fellowships directly to individuals.

Film/video/radio: grants to fund a specific film, video, or radio production.

General/operating support: a grant made to further the general purpose or work of an organization, rather than for a specific purpose or project; also called unrestricted grants.

Grants to individuals: awards made directly by the foundation to individuals rather than to nonprofit organizations; includes aid to the needy. (See also "Fellowships," "Scholarships—to individuals," and "Student loans—to individuals.")

In-kind gifts: a contribution of equipment, supplies, or other property as distinct from a monetary grant. Some organizations may also donate space or staff time as an in-kind contribution.

Income development: grants for fundraising, marketing, and to expand audience base.

Internship funds: usually indicates funds awarded to an institution or organization to support an internship program rather than a grant to an individual.

Land acquisition: a grant to purchase real estate property.

Lectureships: see "Curriculum development."

Loaned talent: an aspect of employee volunteerism. It differs from the usual definition of such in that it usually involves loaned professionals and executive staff who are helping a nonprofit in an area involving their particular skills. Loaned talents can assist a nonprofit in strategic planning, dispute resolution or negotiation services, office administration, real estate technical assistance, personnel policies, lobbying, consulting, fundraising, and legal and tax advice.

Loans: see "Program-related investments/ loans" and "Student loans—to individuals.")

Loans—to individuals: assistance distributed directly to individuals in the form of loans.

Management development/capacity building: grants for salaries, staff support, staff training, strategic and long-term planning, capacity building, budgeting and accounting.

Matching/challenge support: a grant which is made to match funds provided by another donor. (See also "Employee matching gifts.")

Operating budgets: see "General/operating support."

Professorships: a grant to an educational institution to endow a professorship or chair.

Program development: grants to support specific projects or programs as opposed to general purpose grants.

Program evaluation: grants to evaluate a specific project or program; includes awards both to agencies to pay for evaluation costs and to research institutes and other program evaluators.

Program-related investments/loans: a loan is any temporary award of funds that must be repaid. A program-related investment is a loan or other investment (as distinguished from a grant) made by a foundation to another organization for a project related to the foundation's stated charitable purpose and interests.

Public relations services: may include printing and duplicating, audio-visual and graphic arts services, helping to plan special events such as festivals, piggyback advertising (advertisements that mention a company while also promoting a nonprofit), and public service advertising.

Publication: a grant to fund reports or other publications issued by a nonprofit resulting from research or projects of interest to the foundation.

Renovation projects: see "Building/renovation."

Research: usually indicates funds awarded to institutions to cover costs of investigations and clinical trials. Research grants for individuals are usually referred to as fellowships.

Scholarship funds: a grant to an educational institution or organization to support a scholarship program, mainly for students at the undergraduate level. (See also "Employee-related scholarships.")

Scholarships—to individuals: assistance awarded directly to individuals in the form of

educational grants or scholarships. (See also "Employee-related scholarships.")

Seed money: a grant or contribution used to start a new project or organization. Seed grants may cover salaries and other operating expenses of a new project. Also known as "start-up funds."

Special projects: see "Program development."

Sponsorships: endorsements of charities by corporations; or corporate contributions to all or part of a charitable event.

Student aid: see "Fellowships," "Scholarships— to individuals," and "Student loans—to individuals."

Student loans—to individuals: assistance awarded directly to individuals in the form of educational loans.

Technical assistance: operational or management assistance given to nonprofit organizations; may include fundraising assistance, budgeting and financial planning, program planning, legal advice, marketing, and other aids to management. Assistance may be offered directly by a foundation staff member or in the form of a grant to pay for the services of an outside consultant.

Use of facilities: this may include rent free office space for temporary periods, dining and meeting facilities, telecommunications services, mailing services, transportation services, or computer services.

Annual campaigns

Alabama: Brock 16, Bruno 17, Community 25, Compass 28, Friedman 35, Hess 38, Kaul 40, Protective 58, Saks 61, Smith 63, **Vulcan 73**, Webb 75

Arizona: Dee 94, **Globe 101**, Green 102, Hansen 104, **Kleckhefer 113**, Phelps 129, Sterne 143

Arkansas: **Frueauff 161**, Murphy 167, Northwest 169

California: **Angelica 223**, Aratani 230, Atlas 241, Baker 251, **Baker 252**, Bannerman 255, Bechtel 270, Bireley 292, Boswell 308, Brenner 321, Buck 330, **Bull 331**, Burch 334, **Cantor 354**, Center 369, Davidson 445, Disney 456, Doheny 460, Drum 470, Eisenberg 480, Eucalyptus 489, Flora 521, Fluor 523, Follis 525, Foothills 526, Garb 554, Garland 556, Geffen 558, Gellert 559, Getty 569, Gill 576, Gilmore 578, Goldman 595, Goldsmith 599, Goldwyn 600, Gruber 626, Haas 635, Hutton 694, JL 720, **K.L. 736**, Keller 752, Knight 768, Koret 774, Leichtag 801, Levine 809, Moore 912, Morgan 915, Mosher 920, Norris 940, Oppenheimer 955, Outhwaite 966, Parker 979, Pauley 984, Philibosian 1003, Price 1016, Rancho 1031, Reid 1036, **Saban 1079**, Serenity 1128, Shenandoah 1144, Sorensen 1180, Stern 1195, Strauss 1202, Synopsys 1223, Taper 1226, Thornton 1236, Ueberroth 1248, Union 1250, **Unocal 1252, Wells 1294**, Wilbur 1305, Wood 1318, Wornick 1320

Colorado: Bohen 1346, Community 1358, **Gill 1382**, Hughes 1393, Johnson 1398, McDonald 1421, Price 1442, Schlessman 1450, Schramm 1451, **StorageTek 1460**, Summit 1463, Telluride 1465, Wilhite 1473, Yampa 1477

Connecticut: Baldwin 1487, Barnes 1488, Chilton 1511, Collis 1513, Culpeper 1521, Freas 1548, Garden 1552, Hartford 1564, Heyman 1567, Hubbell 1569, Larsen 1579, Leever 1583, Meriden 1603, Patricelli 1623, Rogow 1636, Senior 1647, Sewall 1648, Thompson 1658, Zachs 1682, **Ziegler 1683**

Delaware: Bennett 1690, Cawley 1696, Crestlea 1701, **CTW 1703**, Laffey 1725, Lennox 1726

District of Columbia: Aid 1765, Bender 1772, Bernstein 1775, Dimick 1789, Freed 1798, Kiplinger 1818, Loughran 1823

Florida: A Friends' 1866, Banbury 1889, Beveridge 1907, Burns 1920, Caspersen 1927, Cisneros 1934, Community 1949, Elster 1993, Engelberg 1994, **Goldhammer 2026**, Gooding 2028, Greenburg 2034, Gulf 2042, Katz 2081, Kaufman 2082, Keating 2084, Lee 2107, Maltz 2126, **Morris 2145**, Rayonier 2189, **Rehm 2192**, Russell 2212, Ryder 2213, Silverman 2234, Straz 2254, Taishoff 2262, Toppel 2274, Wahlert 2284, Watts 2288, Weaver 2289, **Winn 2301**, Wollowick 2306

Georgia: Aflac 2311, AGL 2312, Azalea 2322, Brown 2332, Butler 2335, Callaway 2337, Chatham 2346, Chatham 2347, Community 2357, Cousins 2365, Cox 2368, DuBose 2374, Dunn 2375, Exposition 2380, Franklin 2389, **Gage 2392**, Georgia 2395, **Georgia 2397**, Harrison 2410, Horowitz 2415, Illges 2416, Imlay 2417, Jinks 2422, Knox 2427, Lee 2432, Livingston 2435, Lubo 2438, Moore 2451, Moore 2452, Patterson 2460, Rich 2472, Sapelo 2479, Savannah 2480, **Scientific 2482**, Southern 2494, Synovus 2497, Wilson 2519, Zeist 2529

Hawaii: Alexander 2530, Atherton 2532, Bank 2535, First 2542

Illinois: Alsdorf 2590, **Andrew 2595**, Bere 2616, Blair 2621, **Brach 2630, Burlington 2644**, Butler 2646, Caterpillar 2653, Charleston 2657, Chicago 2660, Circle 2666, Crane 2687, **Crane 2688**, Crown 2691, Deere 2699, Dillon 2704, Donnelley 2708, Duchossois 2711, Emerson 2719, Firestone 2729, Flagg 2731, Franke 2734, Freehling 2737, Geraldi 2752, Gray 2771, Griswold 2773, Halligan 2779, Hansen 2782, Harris 2787, Harris 2788, Hermann 2798, Illinois 2813, Kenny's 2835, Logan 2860, Louis 2862, Lumpkin 2864, McGraw 2882, Northern 2918, Olin 2925, PepsiAmericas 2937, Sara 2982, Shaker 2999, Siragusa 3009, Souder 3013, Speh 3014, **Square 3018**, Stuart 3028, Takiff 3032, **Tuohy 3041**, United 3044, USG 3046, White 3067, Woodward 3085

Indiana: American 3098, Anderson 3099, Ball 3103, Biomet 3106, Bussing 3111, Central 3116,

Community 3124, Crown Point 3135, **Cummins 3136**, DeHaan 3140, Fairbanks 3147, Irwin 3175, Jordan 3180, Koch 3184, Kuhne 3187, **Lilly 3192**, Lilly 3194, Lincoln 3195, Montgomery 3206, NiSource 3213, Noyes 3216, Oliver 3219, Pulliam 3225, Rolland 3231, Samerian 3234, Tipton 3243, Waterfield 3252, West 3256

Iowa: Blank 3268, Farver 3283, Hubbell 3297, Kuyper 3304, Maytag 3309, Maytag 3310, Meredith 3315, Principal 3326

Kansas: Bane 3345, **Beren 3348**, Capitol 3350, Cessna 3351, DeVore 3357, Hutchinson 3368, Payless 3380, Powell 3381, Security 3390, Servant 3391, Sprint 3395, Sunderland 3397, Topeka 3400

Kentucky: Brown 3410, Community 3414, Community 3415, Ford 3419, **Humana 3428**, Klein 3435, Sutherland 3451

Louisiana: **Biedenharn 3463**, Freeman 3480, Goldring 3484, Huie 3488, Jones 3491, Monroe 3501, RosaMary 3507, Wheless 3514

Maine: Alfond 3521, Alfond 3523, Burnham 3527, **Ford 3533**, Lunder 3547

Maryland: **Agilent 3563**, Blades 3574, Brown 3578, **Cohen 3594**, Darby 3605, Davis 3607, Delaplaine 3614, Eliasberg 3620, England 3622, **Ewing 3626**, Freeman 3633, Gudelsky 3641, **Head 3644**, Henson 3648, Hirschhorn 3650, Klein 3662, Levitt 3676, Linehan 3678, Macht 3683, Meyerhoff 3691, Meyerhoff 3692, **Morningstar 3695**, Mulford 3696, Principato 3710, Procter 3711, Provident 3712, Rollins 3718, Rosenberg 3719, Roswell 3722, Rouse 3724, Sheridan 3729, Small 3735, Straus 3738, Tucker 3750, Wasserman 3757, **Zickler 3763**

Massachusetts: Acushnet 3770, Barr 3791, Bayrd 3795, Bertolon 3804, Biogen 3806, Cabot 3823, Cabot 3824, Cabot 3825, Cape Cod 3833, Carney 3837, Chase 3847, Cox 3863, Crane 3864, Davis 3875, Donahue 3881, Eastern 3886, Easthampton 3887, Ellsworth 3892, Evans 3898, Fuller 3918, Goldberg 3927, Grayson 3932, Grinspoon 3935, Ham 3940, High 3950, Highland 3951, Hoffman 3955, Hopedale 3958, Linde 4007, Marcus 4022, Miller 4039, Morse 4044, Pappas 4066, Poss 4087, Rodgers 4110, Rosse 4113, Shapiro 4136, Sharf 4137, Smith 4150, **State 4158**, Stearns 4160, Stoddard 4165, Stoico 4166, Stride 4171, Tupancy 4186, Vance 4191, Wallace 4195, **Wood 4208**

Michigan: **Arcus 4223**, Barry 4227, Burdick 4241, Community 4256, Cook 4262, **DaimlerChrysler 4265**, DeVos 4276, DeVos 4277, DeVos 4278, DeVos 4279, Dow 4288, Farver 4295, Ford 4307, General 4320, Gerstacker 4322, Gilmore 4324, Granger 4328, **H.I.S. 4334**, Harding 4337, Herrick 4341, Hudson 4343, **Isabel 4346**, Kelly 4359, Lansing 4372, Masco 4387, Miller 4394, Monroe 4396, Oleson 4405, Power 4415, **Sage 4427**, Shelden 4434, Towsley 4461, **Tubergen 4463**, Upton 4466, Vanderende 4469, Weatherwax 4474, Wege 4476, Wickes 4483

Minnesota: **ADC 4496**, Andersen 4502, Ankeny 4505, ATK 4509, Bemis 4515, Butler 4525, Buuck 4526, **Cafesjian 4527**, Capp 4529, Charlson 4537, Dasburg 4545, Davis 4546, Deikel 4548, Deluxe 4549, **Donaldson 4552**, Frey 4566, **Fuller 4567**, Greycoach 4575, Greystone 4576, Griggs 4577, Grossman 4578, Hardenbergh 4583, HRK 4589, Huss 4592, Kelley 4597, Kopp 4599, Leonard 4604, Lilly 4606, Maas 4608, Marbrook 4612, **Medtronic 4622**, **Nelson 4632**, O'Neil 4638, **O'Shaughnessy 4639**, Pacific 4646, **Patterson 4647**, RBC 4661, Regis 4664, Securian 4677, Southways 4688, Target 4697, TCF 4699, **Toro 4702**, Tozer 4703, Walker 4711, Wells 4721, Weyerhaeuser 4726, Whitney 4728, Winona 4729

Mississippi: AmSouth 4733, Community 4737, Ford 4742, Irby 4750, McRae 4755, Mississippi 4758, Walker 4770

Missouri: Ameren 4772, Boeing 4785, Brown 4788, Brown 4789, Butler 4793, Commerce 4797,

Community 4798, Cray 4801, Edison 4807, **Enterprise 4810**, H & R 4823, Helzberg 4829, JSM 4841, Kemper 4849, Laclede 4852, Lichtenstein 4855, Lopata 4859, **Mallinckrodt 4860**, Millstone 4867, Musgrave 4870, **Nestle 4872**, Orscheln 4877, Pershing 4880, Pott 4886, Reding 4890, Reynolds 4892, Shaw 4901, Sosland 4908, Sycamore 4915, Ward 4924

Nebraska: Commercial 4951, **ConAgra 4953**, Dunklau 4958, **Global 4967**, Hawkins 4970, Heuermann 4973, Kiewit 4983, Kilbourne 4985, Lozier 4988, Perkins 4996, Storz 5006, Zollner 5020

Nevada: Parasol 5051, Smith 5065, Southwest 5066

New Hampshire: Hunt 5093, **Penates 5099**

New Jersey: Cowles 5170, **Fanwood 5192**, Goldberg 5209, Hidden 5233, Holzer 5238, **Huber 5244**, **Johnson 5261**, Karma 5269, Kirby 5279, Krieger 5290, **Lautenberg 5298**, McGraw 5323, OceanFirst 5341, PSEG 5361, Schering 5387, Sudler 5416, Wallerstein 5447, **Wilf 5455**

New Mexico: Hubbard 5481, Kind 5483, McCune 5488, Messengers 5489, New Mexico 5491, Santa Fe 5496, Taos 5498

New York: A.E. 5506, Abeles 5509, Abrons 5511, Abrons 5512, Adirondack 5517, Alexander 5532, **American 5553**, Aron 5569, **Atran 5575**, **AXA 5584**, Bahnik 5589, Barker 5599, Barker 5600, Barrington 5602, **Barth 5603**, Bayne 5607, Bedminster 5611, Berg 5621, Bernhard 5624, Booth 5651, Botwinick 5653, Buhl 5684, Burns 5689, Carwill 5711, Charina 5714, Claiborne 5758, Credit 5807, Cullman 5812, Curran 5816, Dewar 5856, **Diamond 5858**, Dickler 5861, Dow 5879, **Dun 5893**, Dunwalke 5894, Dyson 5898, Emerson 5927, **Engelhard 5932**, Englander 5933, Equinox 5935, **Frankel 5976**, **Freeman 5980**, Galasso 6005, Gebbie 6009, Gilder 6029, Gilliam 6031, Gleason 6039, Golden 6046, Goldman 6053, Goldstein 6064, **Grant 6090**, **Gruss 6116**, Harriman 6147, **Hauser 6155**, Hoerle 6194, Hughes 6209, Hultquist 6211, Icahn 6224, IF 6226, Joy 6276, Kaplan 6288, Katzenberger 6298, Kautz 6300, Kealy 6303, Kennedy 6314, Klein 6333, Knapp 6342, **Kohlberg 6346**, Lang 6374, Lastfogel 6380, Lauder 6381, Lee 6391, Lehman 6396, M & T 6465, Macdonald 6468, McCann 6514, McCarthy 6515, McGonagle 6518, Meehan 6523, **Memton 6529**, Metcalf 6541, Miller 6551, **Monell 6566**, Monteforte 6567, **Moore 6571**, Moses 6587, Neuberger 6611, New York 6618, New York 6619, New York 6620, **New 6621**, Nichols 6628, Normandie 6636, Northern 6639, O'Connor 6645, O'Toole 6654, Ohrstrom 6659, **Paley 6679**, Park 6689, **Peierls 6705**, Penick 6709, Perkin 6717, **Phillips 6725**, Price 6746, Raffiani 6767, Raiff 6768, **Reed 6783**, Richmond 6800, Rockefeller 6827, Rose 6833, Rose 6836, Rubenstein 6870, Schaffer 6911, Scherman 6918, Schiff 6923, Schmeelk 6927, Schmitt 6928, Sheldon 6964, Simons 6988, Slifka 7001, **SMBC 7005**, Smith 7008, **Solomon 7017**, Spingold 7032, **Steel 7052**, Stein 7055, Straus 7086, Strypemonde 7089, Sulzberger 7095, **U.S. 7180**, Ungar 7183, **Vetlesen 7196**, Vidda 7198, Wachenheim 7204, Wachtell 7205, Weinberg 7230, Weissman 7237, White 7251, Whitehead 7252, **Wolfensohn 7270**, Woodland 7275, **Zenkel 7295**

North Carolina: **Bank 7310**, BB&T 7312, Belk 7315, BIN 7318, Blumenthal 7320, Bryan 7330, Community 7345, Dover 7356, Finch 7366, Finley 7367, Fox 7371, Goodrich 7378, Gorelick 7380, Gorelick 7381, Halton 7386, Hanes 7387, Hanes 7388, Harris 7390, Mebane 7427, Merancas 7428, Mills 7429, Morgan 7431, Progress 7453, Reynolds 7457, Smith 7479, Southern 7481, Triangle 7496, Weaver 7504

North Dakota: MDU 7517, North Dakota 7519, Stern 7521

Ohio: American 7528, Anderson 7529, Andrews 7530, **Armington 7532**, Ashtabula 7534, Bicknell 7548, Brennan 7554, Britton 7556, Cleveland 7577,

Codrington 7578, Dana 7599, Dater 7600, Diamond 7610, Diebold 7611, Edwards 7618, Fairfax 7621, **Federated 7624**, Ferguson 7625, Fifth 7626, Firman 7628, First 7629, FirstEnergy 7630, Forest 7634, Fox 7637, Fox 7638, France 7639, GAR 7643, **Geisse 7646**, Gund 7656, Home 7672, Hoover 7675, Humphrey 7679, **Kettering 7698**, **Key 7700**, Knudsen 7702, Kramer 7704, Kulas 7706, Lippitt 7718, LKC 7720, Lubrizol 7725, Luther 7726, M/I 7729, Mather 7736, Mayerson 7739, McMaster 7744, Milacron 7751, Miller 7753, Montgomery 7758, Moores 7759, Morley 7763, Motorists 7765, Murch 7766, Murdough 7767, Murphy 7768, Murphy 7769, Nationwide 7771, NCC 7772, Nippert 7777, Nordson 7781, Ohio 7784, Ohio 7785, **OMNOVA 7789**, Pulley 7811, Reinberger 7815, Reynolds 7818, Ritchie 7821, Robbins 7823, Rosenthal 7826, Salem 7831, Scotford 7846, Sedgwick 7849, Smith 7862, Stranahan 7872, Tait 7875, Tuscarawas 7890, Watson 7896, Wodecroft 7912, Wolfe 7915, Wuliger 7918

Oklahoma: Better 7926, Bovaird 7927, Chapman 7928, Collins 7930, Goddard 7939, Hille 7943, Kaiser 7948, Kerr 7950, McGee 7957, McMahon 7959, Meinders 7960, Meinig 7961, Merrick 7962, Oklahoma 7965, Oxley 7968, Puterbaugh 7970, Records 7972, **Schusterman 7975**, Southern 7979, Tulsa 7984, Zarrow 7993, Zink 7994

Oregon: Ackerman 7995, Carpenter 8003, Kinsman 8031, Macdonald 8038, PacifiCorp 8050, **Schmidt 8055**, Schnitzer 8056, Schnitzer 8057, Swigert 8061, Tektronix 8063

Pennsylvania: 1675 8070, **Alcoa 8075**, Allerton 8077, Ames 8080, AMETEK 8081, Arcadia 8086, Arete 8088, Arkema 8089, **Armstrong 8090**, Baker 8092, Born 8113, Cassett 8133, Centre 8136, Century 8137, CIGNA 8143, Clapp 8145, **Colcom 8150**, Colonial 8151, Community 8156, DeGol 8167, **Dominion 8173**, Donnelly 8176, Ferree 8199, Fine 8201, Fisher 8205, Graham 8222, Hamilton 8233, Hankin 8234, Heinz 8240, Hillman 8250, Hillman 8251, Hillman 8252, Hopwood 8257, Hoyt 8259, Hunt 8261, Huston 8264, Jennings 8272, Justus 8276, Kavanagh 8282, Kelly 8283, Keystone 8286, Kline 8293, Lenfest 8305, Levee 8308, Lindback 8312, Little 8313, Mandell 8322, Marshall 8326, McFeely 8334, McKenna 8337, Mellon 8344, Mine 8357, Plankenhorn 8387, **PPG 8394**, Pryor 8396, Rangos 8400, Rees 8401, Roberts 8405, Rockwell 8408, Safeguard 8418, Saint 8419, Snyder 8448, Sordoni 8450, Sovereign 8451, Stabler 8455, Stackpole 8456, Steinman 8458, Steinman 8459, Strawbridge 8466, Tippins 8477, West 8500, Wheeler 8501, Wyomissing 8509

Rhode Island: **Amica 8518**, Carter 8522, Charlesmead 8525, Daniels 8530

South Carolina: Abney 8564, First 8587, Kane 8596, **Roe 8607**, Springs 8617

South Dakota: Larson 8627

Tennessee: Beaman 8642, **Bridgestone 8646**, Caldwell 8649, CLARCOR 8658, EBS 8672, Frist 8678, HCA 8690, Martin 8708, Phillips 8716, **Rust 8724**, Stokely 8730, T & T 8731, Tucker 8735, Wilson 8744

Texas: Abell 8749, **Adams 8751**, Augur 8766, Austin 8768, Bauer 8779, Brown 8799, Cailloux 8807, Cain 8809, Carter 8816, CFP 8822, CH 8823, Coates 8834, Cockrell 8835, **Cooper 8846**, Cullen 8854, Dougherty 8870, Eady 8875, El Paso 8882, Fikes 8899, Finger 8900, Fisch 8901, Fish 8902, Fleming 8904, Halliburton 8935, Halsell 8936, Hamill 8937, Hamman 8938, Herzstein 8949, Hoglund 8956, Houston 8960, Houston 8961, Huffington 8963, Jonsson 8977, Kahn 8980, Keith 8982, Kempner 8987, Kilroy 8991, Kinder 8994, Kodosky 9000, Light 9011, Lightner 9012, Lockheed 9015, Lyons 9024, Mankoff 9027, Marathon 9028, Martinez 9032, Mays 9036, McDermott 9043, McKee 9045, Mitte 9067, Moss 9078, Navarro 9089, O'Connor 9094, O'Connor

9095, Owsley 9108, Penney 9115, Rachofsky 9139, Rosewood 9158, Sams 9163, San Antonio 9166, Scott 9174, Scurlock 9175, **Shell 9181**, Shield 9183, Simmons 9188, **Smith 9194**, Smith 9195, Smith 9197, Sterling 9212, Strake 9215, Tapeats 9223, **Tenet 9229**, Tennessee 9230, Texas 9232, Trull 9240, Vaughan 9250, Waggoner 9256, Wal 9260, Walsh 9261, **Waste 9265**, Weaver 9267, Weekley 9271, Willard 9281, Works 9291, Wortham 9292, Young 9295, Zachry 9296.

Utah: Browning 9308, Burton 9309, Eccles 9319, Stewart 9345, **Wishnick 9353**

Vermont: Mergens 9360

Virginia: American 9368, Camp 9382, Campbell 9383, Circuit 9392, Delmar 9410, Kanter 9445, Kington 9450, LandAmerica 9454, Landmark 9455, Mars 9466, Massey 9467, **Norfolk 9485**, Perry 9495, Portsmouth 9498, Reynolds 9503, **Scripps 9514**, SunTrust 9523, Titmus 9527, Ukrop 9529, United 9530, Universal 9531, Washington 9534, **Winkler 9542**

Washington: De Falco 9578, Dimmer 9579, Fuchs 9590, **Gates 9591**, Glazer 9596, Harder 9600, **Hemingway 9606**, Klorfine 9619, **Kongsgaard 9620**, Lucky 9632, Milgard 9641, Norcliffe 9650, Oki 9653, PACCAR 9656, Rainier 9669, Shirley 9684, Wright 9707

West Virginia: Daywood 9717, Maier 9725, McDonough 9726, Shott 9733

Wisconsin: Alliant 9742, Bader 9749, Banta 9752, Bishop 9759, **Bradley 9763**, Briggs 9765, Chapman 9771, Charter 9772, Cleary 9774, Cornerstone 9781, Cudahy 9785, Four 9803, Hess 9816, Jacobus 9819, Johnson 9823, Johnson 9826, Joy 9828, Kelben 9830, Kikkoman 9836, Krause 9841, Krause 9842, Kress 9844, Ladish 9846, Managed 9857, Marshfield 9861, Mead 9867, Menasha 9869, Miller 9875, Northwestern 9884, Oshkosh 9887, Peck 9895, Peterson 9896, Pettit 9897, Pick 9899, Prescott 9903, Sensient 9922, Siebert 9927, **Smith 9929**, Split 9932, Stock 9939, U.S. 9952, Waukesha 9960, West 9964, Wilson 9965, Windhover 9966, WPS 9970

Wyoming: Ellbogen 9981, Stock 9992

Building/renovation

Alabama: Bedsole 12, Blount 14, Bruno 17, Carson 19, Community 23, Community 24, Community 25, Crampton 30, Friedman 35, Hearin 37, Hess 38, Hill 39, Kaul 40, Meyer 52, Moody 54, Smith 63, Webb 75

Arizona: Arizona 87, Dee 94, Gesner 100, **Globe 101**, Green 102, **Johnson 112, Kieckhefer 113**, Linde 117, Marshall 121, Morris 124, Piper 130, Steele 142

Arkansas: **Frueauff 161**, Northwest 169, Ross 174, Schmieding 175, Walker 185, White 187

California: Ahmanson 198, Amateur 214, Aratani 230, **Atkinson 240**, Avery 244, Ayrshire 247, Baker 251, **Baker 252**, Bannerman 255, Barker 257, Baxter 263, Bechtel 270, Bireley 292, Bothin 309, Bowes 311, Boyer 313, Bright 322, Buck 330, **Bull 331**, California 346, **Cantor 354**, Carsey 361, Carson 362, Caruso 363, Collins 397, Columbia 399, Community 401, Confidence 411, Copley 416, Cowell 423, Crockett 430, Dachs 435, Darling 440, **DJ & T 458**, Doheny 460, Drum 470, Eisner 481, Eucalyptus 489, Factor 491, Finley 507, Firedoll 508, **Firelight 509, First 512**, Fleishhacker 518, Flora 521, Fluor 523, Follis 525, French 536, Garb 554, Garland 556, Gasser 557, Gellert 559, Gilmore 578, Godric 586, Gogian 588, Gold 590, Goldman 595, Goldman 596, Goldsmith 599, Gonda 601, Grammer 610, Gruber 626, Haas 635, Haas 636, Hale 639, Hannon 644, Hannon 645, Hayden 657, Hedco 663, Herbst 669, Hoag 678, Humboldt 691, Hutton 694, Irwin 700, Jackson 706, Jewett 718, JL 720, Jones 728, **K.L. 736, Keck 750, Kim 758**, Koret 774, Kvamme 781, Leatherby 796, Leichtag 801, Lesher 805, Levine 809, Los Altos 828, Ludwick 829, Lund 831, Lytel

836, Mabie 839, Marin 854, McBean 865, McLean 880, Mericos 889, Milken 897, Milken 898, Miller 901, Monterey 910, Moore 912, Morgan 915, Mosher 920, Norris 940, Outhwaite 966, Parker 979, Parsons 980, Pasadena 982, Patron 983, Pauley 984, Peters 993, Rancho 1031, Rivkin 1057, **Saban 1079**, Sacramento 1080, San Diego 1087, San Luis 1090, Santa Barbara 1093, Segal 1121, Serenity 1128, Severns 1131, Shasta 1139, Sobrato 1172, Sonora 1178, Sorensen 1180, Stauffer 1188, Steele 1189, Stern 1195, Stulsaft 1210, Sudikoff 1212, Taper 1226, Taube 1228, Thornton 1236, Tuohy 1247, Ueberroth 1248, Union 1250, Valley 1257, Van Nuys 1261, Ventura 1264, Von der Ahe 1269, Vons 1270, Waltmar 1277, Warren 1279, Weingart 1288, Wilbur 1305, Wood 1318, WWW 1323

Colorado: Animal 1333, Aspen 1338, Boettcher 1344, Bohemian 1345, Bohen 1346, Bonfils 1347, Brett 1349, Buell 1350, Community 1358, Coors 1360, **Daniels 1362**, Denver 1364, Edmondson 1373, El Pomar 1374, Gates 1380, Johnson 1398, King 1404, Kitzmiller 1405, M.D.C. 1413, McDonald 1421, **Mercy 1426**, Pikes 1437, Rose 1445, Schramm 1451, **Seay 1453**, Summit 1463, Taylor 1464, Yampa 1477

Connecticut: Baldwin 1487, Calder 1506, Collis 1513, Community 1514, Community 1515, Community 1517, Connecticut 1518, Culpeper 1521, Garden 1552, Hartford 1563, Hartford 1564, Hubbell 1569, **Huisking 1570**, Liberty 1586, **Lingnan 1587**, Main 1594, Martin 1598, Matthies 1600, Stone 1654, Tauck 1657, Thompson 1658, Wallace 1674, Woodward 1678, Worthington 1679, Zachs 1682

Delaware: Cawley 1696, Chichester 1698, Crestlea 1701, Crystal 1702, **CTW 1703**, Delaware 1706, **Fair 1713, Glencoe 1714**, Hamel 1719, Laffey 1725, Lennox 1726, Longwood 1727, Marmot 1728, Phillips 1739, **Raskob 1741, Schwartz 1751**, Welfare 1762

District of Columbia: Aid 1765, Bender 1772, Fowler 1797, Graham 1804, Gudelsky 1805, Kaye 1815, Kiplinger 1818, **Loyola 1825**, Meyer 1834, Willard 1861, Willoughby 1862

Florida: A Friends' 1866, Amaturo 1873, Banbury 1889, Bank 1890, Beveridge 1907, Bush 1922, Caspersen 1927, **Chatlos 1932**, Community 1943, Community 1947, Community 1949, Conn 1951, Dade 1957, **Davis 1964**, Duckwall 1978, Elster 1993, Engelberg 1994, **Goldhammer 2026**, Gooding 2028, Gulf 2041, Gulf 2042, Hersh 2058, Hough 2066, Jacksonville 2071, **Jaharis 2073**, Keating 2084, Kennedy 2087, **Knight 2097, Koch 2098**, Lattner 2104, Maltz 2126, Opler 2158, Phillips 2168, Pinellas 2170, Publix 2180, Rayonier 2189, **Rehm 2192**, Rinker 2196, Rosenberg 2206, Russell 2212, Saunders 2219, Selby 2230, Silverman 2234, Southwest 2240, St. Joe 2244, Storer 2252, Straz 2254, **Sullivan 2257**, Wahlert 2284, Waldbaum 2285, Watts 2288, Weaver 2289, Wilson 2300, **Winn 2301**, Wolfson 2304

Georgia: AEC 2310, AGL 2312, Amos 2315, Atlanta 2320, Brown 2331, Brown 2332, Callaway 2336, Callaway 2337, Campbell 2339, Cawood 2342, Chatham 2346, Chatham 2347, Community 2356, Community 2362, Courts 2364, Cousins 2365, Cox 2367, Cox 2368, Day 2371, **Dobbs 2373**, DuBose 2374, English 2378, Equifax 2379, Exposition 2380, Franklin 2389, **Gage 2392**, Georgia 2394, **Georgia 2397**, Greene 2404, Harland 2407, Harrison 2410, Horowitz 2415, Illges 2416, Imlay 2417, Jinks 2422, Knox 2427, Lanier 2428, Lee 2432, Livingston 2435, Marshall 2442, Moore 2451, Moore 2452, Morris 2454, Murphy 2456, Patterson 2460, Pitts 2463, Porter 2468, Rich 2472, Rollins 2475, Savannah 2481, **Scientific 2482**, Southern 2494, SunTrust 2496, Synovus 2497, Tull 2500, University 2502, Watson 2509, Williams 2514, Wilson 2519, Woodruff 2521, Woodward 2523, Woolford 2524, Woolley 2525, Zeist 2529

Hawaii: Alexander 2530, Atherton 2532, Bank 2535, Campbell 2536, Castle 2538, Cooke 2541, First 2542, Frear 2543, McInerny 2551, Vidinha 2557, Watumull 2558, Wilcox 2559

Idaho: CHC 2566, Cunningham 2567, Idaho 2570, Morrison 2572, Simplot 2575

Illinois: **Amsted 2593, Andrew 2595**, Arthur 2601, Bersted 2619, Blair 2621, **Brach 2630, Brunswick 2636, Burlington 2644**, Butler 2646, Camp 2649, Chaddick 2655, Charleston 2657, Chicago 2661, Circle 2666, Coleman 2673, Community 2679, Community 2680, Crown 2691, Cuneo 2692, Day 2698, Deere 2699, DeKalb 2701, Dillon 2704, Donnelley 2708, Dunard 2712, DuPage 2713, Field 2728, Flagg 2731, Geraldi 2752, Grainger 2768, Grant 2770, Griswold 2773, Hansen 2782, Harris 2787, Harris 2788, Hermann 2798, Hobbs 2802, Illinois 2812, Kemper 2831, Levi 2855, Logan 2860, Louis 2862, McGraw 2882, McNeil 2887, Meyer 2896, Millard 2897, Northern 2918, Olin 2925, Omron 2926, Payne 2927, Petersen 2941, Prentice 2947, Regenstein 2962, Shaker 2999, Souder 3013, Speh 3014, **Square 3018**, Steans 3021, Stern 3023, Takiff 3032, Tawani 3033, Tellabs 3034, **Tuohy 3041**, USG 3046, **Woodbury 3082**

Indiana: American 3098, Ball 3103, Ball 3104, Blue 3107, Brown 3110, Bussing 3111, Central 3116, Clowes 3119, Clowes 3120, Cole 3121, Community 3124, Community 3125, Community 3126, Community 3127, Community 3128, Community 3130, Community 3132, **Cummins 3136**, Dearborn 3137, Decatur 3138, DeKalb 3141, Dekko 3142, Fairbanks 3147, Foellinger 3149, Ford 3150, Froderman 3153, Griffith 3158, Harrison 3161, Henry 3165, Heritage 3166, Irwin 3175, Johnson 3178, Jordan 3180, Koch 3184, Kosciusko 3186, Kuhne 3187, Legacy 3189, Leighton 3191, Lilly 3194, Lincoln 3195, Madison 3197, McMillen 3203, Montgomery 3206, NiSource 3213, Noble 3214, Northern 3215, Ogle 3218, Oliver 3219, Peabody 3221, Portland 3223, Pulliam 3225, Raker 3226, Rolland 3231, Steuben 3241, Tipton 3243, Tyson 3246, Unity 3247, Waterfield 3252, Welborn 3254, Wells 3255

Iowa: Ahrens 3260, Bechtel 3264, Blank 3268, Carver 3274, Cedar Rapids 3275, Community 3277, Community 3278, Cowles 3279, Farver 3283, Hall 3290, HNI 3293, Iowa 3298, Kinney 3300, Kuyper 3304, **Lee 3306**, Mansfield 3308, Maytag 3309, Maytag 3310, McElroy 3313, Meredith 3315, Pella 3323, Principal 3326, Siouxland 3332, Tye 3337, Vermeer 3341

Kansas: Bane 3345, Baughman 3346, **Beren 3348**, Capitol 3350, Cessna 3351, Cooper 3353, DeVore 3357, Farah 3362, Garvey 3363, Hansen 3366, INTRUST 3369, Payless 3380, Rhoden 3383, Rice 3384, Sabatini 3386, Sunderland 3397, Topeka 3400

Kentucky: Bavarian 3406, Blue 3407, Brown 3409, Brown 3410, Community 3414, Cralle 3416, E.ON 3417, Foundation 3420, Gheens 3421, Hayswood 3425, Horn 3427, **Humana 3428**, Justice 3431, Keeneland 3432, Klein 3435, Little 3437, **Omnicare 3444**, Orleton 3445, Preston 3446, Reed 3447, Robinson 3449, Sutherland 3451

Louisiana: Baton Rouge 3462, Booth 3464, Community 3469, Coughlin 3470, Diboll 3473, Freeman 3480, Goldring 3484, Huie 3488, Jones 3491, Monroe 3501, Pennington 3505, Reily 3506, RosaMary 3507, Wheless 3514, Wilson 3515, **Woldenberg 3516**, Woolf 3517, Zigler 3520

Maine: Alfond 3521, Burnham 3527, Davenport 3531, **Ford 3533**, Hannaford 3540, King 3545, Libra 3546, **Oak 3552, Sandy 3555**

Maryland: Abell 3559, Baker 3566, Blades 3574, **Blaustein 3575**, Brown 3578, Clark 3591, **Cohen 3594**, Columbia 3595, Community 3598, Constellation 3602, Davis 3607, Dresher 3617, Eaton 3619, England 3622, France 3632, Gudelsky 3641, Hahn 3643, Henson 3648, Hoffberger 3652, **Hughes 3654**, Kerr 3661, Knott 3666, Leidy

3673, Linehan 3678, MARPAT 3684, Marshall 3687, Meyerhoff 3691, Meyerhoff 3692, Mid 3693, Middendorf 3694, Mulford 3696, Otenasek 3704, Procter 3711, Provident 3712, Rollins 3718, Rosenberg 3719, Rouse 3724, Sheridan 3729, **Smith 3736**, Straus 3738, Thalheimer 3744, Tucker 3750, Wasserman 3757, **Weinberg 3759**, Wright 3762, **Zickler 3763**

Massachusetts: Acushnet 3770, Adams 3772, Alden 3776, Barr 3791, Bayrd 3795, Behrakis 3796, **Bosack 3809**, Cabot 3823, Cabot 3824, Cabot 3825, Campbell 3830, Cape Cod 3832, Cape Cod 3833, Charlesbank 3845, Clipper 3850, Community 3854, Community 3855, Crossroads 3869, Davis 3875, Dusky 3885, Eastern 3886, Easthampton 3887, Ellsworth 3892, Farnsworth 3899, **Fidelity 3904**, Fletcher 3912, Fuller 3918, Goldberg 3927, Ham 3940, High 3950, Highland 3951, Hoffman 3955, **Jebediah 3969**, Johnson 3970, Levy 4005, Linde 4007, Melville 4034, Mifflin 4038, Miller 4039, Morse 4044, Oral 4061, Pappas 4066, Pardoe 4068, Parker 4069, Peabody 4072, Peabody 4073, Pierce 4084, Rabb 4091, Riley 4104, Rodgers 4110, Roy 4114, Shapiro 4136, Smith 4148, Smith 4150, **State 4158**, Stearns 4160, Stevens 4163, Stevens 4164, Stoddard 4165, Stoico 4166, Thompson 4181, Tupancy 4186, Vance 4191, Wadleigh 4194, Wallace 4195, Webster 4201

Michigan: Americana 4218, Andersen 4219, **Arcus 4223**, Barry 4227, Battle Creek 4228, Bay 4229, Besser 4232, Burdick 4241, Capital 4243, Community 4252, Community 4253, Community 4256, Community 4257, Community 4258, Consumers 4260, Cook 4262, Dalton 4266, Dart 4267, Davenport 4269, **DENSO 4272**, DeVos 4276, DeVos 4278, DeVos 4279, DiPonio 4281, **Dow 4285**, Dow 4286, Dow 4287, Fabri 4293, Farver 4295, Ford 4302, Fremont 4315, Gerstacker 4322, Gilmore 4324, Grand Rapids 4326, Grand 4327, Greenville 4331, **H.I.S. 4334**, Herrick 4341, Hudson 4343, Hurst 4344, Jackson 4347, Kahn 4351, Kalamazoo 4352, Kennedy 4360, Knight 4364, **Kresge 4367**, La-Z-Boy 4368, Lansing 4372, Lenawee 4376, Masco 4387, McGregor 4389, Merillat 4391, Midland 4392, Miller 4394, Monroe 4396, Oleson 4405, Perrigo 4410, Petoskey 4412, Plym 4414, Power 4415, Ratner 4417, **Sage 4427**, Saginaw 4428, **Secchia 4431**, Shelden 4434, Spoelhof 4443, Steelcase 4446, Stolaruk 4448, Strosacker 4450, Sturgis 4452, Tauber 4454, Tiscornia 4460, Towsley 4461, Upton 4466, Vanderweide 4469, Weatherwax 4474, Wege 4476, Wickes 4483, Wilson 4485, Young 4490

Minnesota: **3M 4492**, Adams 4495, AHS 4497, Andersen 4502, Bemis 4515, Beverly 4517, Bigelow 4519, Bremer 4523, Bush 4524, Capp 4529, Central 4534, Christianson 4539, Deikel 4548, **Deluxe 4549**, **Donaldson 4552**, Edina 4560, Frey 4566, Graco 4573, Greycoach 4575, Greystone 4576, Griggs 4577, Hardenbergh 4583, **Land 4602**, Lilly 4606, Maas 4608, Marbrook 4612, Mardag 4613, McKnight 4617, Meadowood 4621, Neilson 4631, **O'Shaughnessy 4639**, **Petters 4653**, Phillips 4655, RBC 4661, Regis 4664, Rochester 4668, Rupp 4669, Saint Paul 4671, Southways 4688, Target 4697, Tozer 4703, Valspar 4706, Walker 4711, Wasie 4716, WCA 4718

Mississippi: Community 4737, Hardin 4747, Irby 4750, Lower 4751, Maddox 4753, Riley 4763

Missouri: Ameren 4772, **Anheuser 4776**, Baer 4778, Brown 4788, Brown 4789, Commerce 4797, Community 4798, Curry 4802, Edison 4807, **Enterprise 4810**, Forster 4814, Gateway 4817, Goppert 4819, Green 4821, Green 4822, H & R 4823, Hall 4824, Hallmark 4825, Helzberg 4829, Jenkins 4836, Jewish 4837, Jordan 4840, JSM 4841, Kemper 4849, Laclede 4852, Long 4858, Musgrave 4870, **Nestle 4872**, Oppenstein 4876, Orscheln 4877, Pillsbury 4884, Reynolds 4892, Shaw 4901, Sosland 4908, Stern 4909, Stupp 4911, Walker 4922, Whitaker 4926, Woods 4928

Nebraska: Baright 4945, Buckley 4947, Commercial 4951, **ConAgra 4953**, Cope 4955, Dunklau 4958, Fremont 4962, Friedland 4965, Gardner 4965, **Global 4967**, Hawkins 4970, Heuermann 4973, Hirschfeld 4974, Hitchcock 4975, Kiewit 4983, Kiewit 4984, Lexington 4986, Lincoln 4987, Lozier 4988, **McDonald 4989**, Mid-Nebraska 4991, Omaha 4994, Omaha 4995, Perkins 4996, Reynolds 4997, Storz 5006, **Union 5012**, Zollner 5020

Nevada: Bretzlaff 5024, Cord 5029, Fairweather 5032, Hawkins 5036, **Hilton 5037**, Pennington 5053, Redfield 5055, Reynolds 5056, Southwest 5066, **Tang 5072**, **Walsh 5075**

New Hampshire: Bean 5080, Eastman 5087, Hunt 5093, Lindsay 5095, **Penates 5099**

New Jersey: 1772 5106, **Barbour 5124**, Borden 5138, Buehler 5146, Cape 5153, Charles 5161, **Clare 5164**, Cowles 5170, Danellie 5177, **Frankino 5196**, Gabelli 5200, **Goodes 5212**, Grassmann 5213, Healthcare 5228, Hyde 5247, **International 5252**, Johnson 5262, Karma 5269, Kirby 5279, Laurie 5297, **Lautenberg 5298**, OceanFirst 5341, Provident 5359, **Rippel 5368**, Ross 5375, Schenck 5386, Schering 5387, Sudler 5416, Summit 5417, Sunfield 5418, Turrell 5431, Union 5435, Victoria 5440, Wallerstein 5447, **Wilf 5455**

New Mexico: Carlsbad 5469, Hubbard 5481, Kind 5483, **Lannan 5484**, Maddox 5487, McCune 5488, Messengers 5489, PNM 5493, Taos 5498

New York: Abrons 5511, Adirondack 5517, **Alavi 5530**, Alexander 5532, Allyn 5539, Arkell 5565, Aron 5569, Barker 5599, Barker 5600, Bedminster 5611, Bernhard 5624, Booth 5651, Botwinick 5653, Bravmann 5661, Brooks 5674, Carnahan 5706, Carvel 5710, Central 5724, Chadwick 5726, Charina 5731, Chautauqua 5738, **Chazen 5739**, Clark 5759, Clark 5762, Community 5780, Community 5781, Community 5783, Community 5784, Community 5785, Corning 5794, **Cummings 5813**, Curran 5816, Davenport 5833, DeCamp 5845, Decker 5846, Delancey 5849, DeMatteis 5852, Dewar 5856, **Diamond 5858**, **Dodge 5867**, Dolan 5869, Dunwalke 5894, Dyson 5898, East 5901, **EHA 5912**, Emerson 5927, **Engelhard 5932**, Englander 5933, Faulkner 5948, First 5958, **Forbes 5967**, **Frankel 5976**, **Frankenberg 5977**, Frohring 5993, Galasso 6005, Gebbie 6009, Gifford 6026, Gilman 6032, Gleason 6039, Glens Falls 6041, Golden 6046, Goldman 6053, Goldsmith 6060, Goldstein 6064, Golisano 6067, Grigg 6108, Hagedorn 6130, Hayden 6158, Heckscher 6164, Hoyt 6203, Hudson 6207, Hultquist 6211, Icahn 6224, Independence 6229, Jones 6274, Joy 6276, Kaplan 6288, Kennedy 6314, Knapp 6342, **Kraft 6351**, Kunstadter 6362, **Lauder 6383**, Lehman 6396, Lemberg 6401, Lenna 6402, Leonhardt 6403, Liberman 6419, Lindner 6426, Link 6429, M & T 6465, Macdonald 6468, **Matthews 6507**, McCann 6514, **Memton 6529**, Metcalf 6541, **Monell 6566**, New York 6618, Nichols 6628, **Norcross 6634**, Northern 6638, Northern 6639, Nuhn 6644, O'Connor 6645, O'Toole 6654, Ohrstrom 6659, Penick 6709, Perkin 6717, Raffiani 6767, Rapoport 6772, **Reed 6783**, Rhodebeck 6791, Richmond 6800, **Ritter 6814**, Robinson 6820, Robison 6821, Rochester 6823, Rose 6836, **Ross 6863**, Rubenstein 6870, Schaffer 6911, Schenectady 6915, Sheldon 6964, SI 6972, Siebens 6974, Simons 6988, Smith 7007, Snow 7011, Snyder 7014, **Solomon 7017**, Sosnoff 7025, Statler 7050, Stein 7055, Stevens 7076, Straus 7086, Sulzberger 7099, Sweetgrass 7113, Tisch 7145, Tuttle 7176, **U.S. 7180**, Ungar 7183, Van Pelt 7192, **Vetlesen 7196**, Vidda 7198, Wachenheim 7204, Warner 7216, Weinberg 7230, Western 7248, Widgeon 7255, Woodland 7275, Wright 7280, **Zenkel 7295**, Zichron 7298

North Carolina: **Bank 7310**, BB&T 7312, Belk 7315, BIN 7318, Blumenthal 7320, Bryan 7330, Cannon 7335, Cape Fear 7336, Cemala 7337, Coleman 7340, Community 7342, Community 7345, Davis 7352, Dover 7356, Duke 7359, Easley 7361, Ebert 7362, Finch 7366, Finley 7367, Fox 7371, Glenn 7376, Goodrich 7378, Gorelick 7380, Gorelick 7381, Hanes 7387, Hanes 7388, Harris 7390, Hendrick 7395, Hurley 7402, Hurley 7403, Janirve 7404, Jones 7408, Mebane 7427, Mills 7429, Morgan 7431, Palin 7443, Pharmacy 7446, Polk 7449, Reynolds 7457, Reynolds 7460, Robertson 7466, Smith 7479, Southern 7481, Tannenbaum 7493, Van Houten 7500, Vanderbilt 7501, Weaver 7504, Winston-Salem 7508

North Dakota: Fargo 7514, Leach 7516, MDU 7517, North Dakota 7519, Stern 7521

Ohio: Anderson 7529, Ashland 7533, Ashtabula 7534, **Austin 7535**, Babcock 7537, Barberton 7539, Bee 7542, Beerman 7543, Bicknell 7548, **Bingham 7549**, Brennan 7554, Bruening 7558, Byrn 7559, Cincinnati 7574, Columbus 7580, Community 7583, Community 7585, **Convergys 7587**, Corbin 7591, Coshocton 7593, **Covenant 7595**, **Cox 7596**, Dana 7599, Dater 7600, David 7601, Dayton 7603, Diamond 7610, **Eaton 7617**, Edwards 7618, Emery 7619, Evans 7620, Fairfield 7622, Farmer 7623, Ferguson 7625, Fifth 7626, Findlay 7627, Firman 7628, First 7629, FirstEnergy 7630, Ford 7633, Foundation 7636, Fox 7637, GAR 7643, Greene 7653, H.C.S. 7658, Haslinger 7664, Hauck 7666, Hershey 7671, Humphrey 7679, Iddings 7682, Ingalls 7684, Jergens 7686, Jewish 7690, Kettering 7699, **Kosar 7703**, Kulas 7706, Lehner 7709, Levin 7712, Licking 7714, Lippitt 7718, LKC 7720, Lubrizol 7725, M/I 7729, Mangano 7733, Marietta 7735, Mather 7736, Mathile 7737, Mayerson 7739, McMaster 7744, Mellen 7747, Miami 7748, Middletown 7749, Milacron 7751, Montgomery 7758, Morgan 7760, Morgan 7761, Morgan 7762, Morley 7763, Motorists 7765, Murch 7766, Murdough 7767, Murphy 7768, Murphy 7769, Muskingum 7770, Nippert 7777, Nord 7779, Nordson 7781, Ohio 7784, Ohio 7785, **OMNOVA 7789**, Osteopathic 7791, Payne 7798, Prentiss 7806, Reeves 7814, Reinberger 7815, Richland 7819, Ritchie 7821, Russell 7827, Salem 7831, Schlink 7839, Scotford 7846, Sedgwick 7849, Semple 7851, Sherwin 7855, Silk 7857, Sisler 7858, Slemp 7860, Sloat 7861, Smith 7862, Smith 7863, Spaulding 7865, Stark 7867, Stocker 7870, Stranahan 7872, Tait 7875, **Timken 7880**, Troy 7886, Turner 7889, Tuscarawas 7890, Van Wert 7891, Wallace 7894, Watson 7896, Wayne 7897, White 7905, Wodecroft 7912, Wolfe 7915, Wuliger 7918, Youngstown 7920

Oklahoma: Bailey 7923, Bernsen 7925, Bovaird 7927, Chapman 7928, Collins 7930, Community 7932, Gaylord 7937, Gelvin 7938, Goddard 7939, Helmerich 7942, Hille 7943, Kaiser 7948, Kerr 7949, Kerr 7950, Mabee 7954, McCasland 7956, McGee 7957, McMahon 7959, Meinig 7961, Merrick 7962, Noble 7963, Oklahoma 7965, Oklahoman 7966, ONEOK 7967, Puterbaugh 7970, Rapp 7971, Sarkeys 7974, **Schusterman 7975**, Share 7977, Southern 7979, Stevens 7980, Titus 7983, Tulsa 7984, Viersen 7985, Warren 7987, Williams 7989, Zink 7994

Oregon: Ackerman 7995, Adler 7996, Autzen 7997, Braemar 8001, Carpenter 8003, Chambers 8004, Collins 8007, Collins 8008, Ford 8013, Four 8015, Haugland 8018, Jeld 8025, Kinsman 8031, Macdonald 8038, Meyer 8042, Miller 8043, Oregon 8049, Schnitzer 8056, Schnitzer 8057, Swigert 8061, Swindells 8062, Tucker 8065, Wessinger 8067, Young 8069

Pennsylvania: 1675 8070, **Alcoa 8075**, Allerton 8077, AMETEK 8081, Arcadia 8086, Arkema 8089, **Armstrong 8090**, Beatty 8097, Blanchard 8111, Brossman 8120, Cassett 8133, Central 8135, Centre 8136, Century 8137, **Cestone 8138**, Cestone 8139, Chester 8141, Claneil 8144, Clapp 8145, Colonial 8151, Community 8154, Community 8155, Community 8156, Connelly 8157, Crels 8163, DeGol 8167, Dietrich 8171, **Dominion 8173**, Donley 8175, Donnelly 8176, DSF

8178, Eden 8182, Erie 8188, Fels 8198, Ferree 8199, Fine 8201, First 8202, FISA 8204, Fisher 8205, Fourjay 8209, Glencairn 8219, Graham 8222, Grundy 8228, Hankin 8234, Hassel 8237, Heinz 8240, Heinz 8241, Heinz 8242, **Heinz 8243**, Hillman 8249, Hillman 8250, Hillman 8251, Hillman 8252, Hirtzel 8253, Hodge 8254, Hooper 8256, Hopwood 8257, Hoyt 8259, Hunt 8261, Huston 8263, Huston 8264, Jennings 8272, John 8273, Justus 8276, Kelly 8283, **Kennametal 8284**, Keystone 8285, Keystone 8286, Kline 8292, Kline 8293, Laurel 8301, Lehigh Valley 8303, Lilliput 8311, Little 8313, Mandell 8322, Maslow 8327, McCune 8331, McCune 8332, McFeely 8334, McKenna 8337, McLean 8340, Mellon 8344, Mellon 8345, Mellon 8346, Miller 8352, Mine 8357, Moore 8358, Morris 8359, Penn 8371, Phillips 8380, Phoenixville 8381, Pierce 8382, Plankenhorn 8387, PNC 8388, **Presser 8395**, Rees 8401, Reidler 8402, Rockwell 8408, S & T 8417, Safeguard 8418, Saint 8419, **Seraph 8434**, Shaffer 8436, Shenango 8438, Simonds 8442, Smith 8443, Smith 8444, Smith 8445, Snee 8446, Sordoni 8450, Sovereign 8451, Stabler 8455, Stackpole 8456, Steinman 8458, Steinman 8459, Tippins 8477, Trexler 8481, Truman 8483, United 8486, **Waldorf 8495**, West 8500, Widener 8502, Willis 8504, Wyomissing 8509

Rhode Island: **Amica 8518**, Brooks 8520, Carter 8522, Champlin 8524, Daniels 8530, Hasbro 8539, Jackson 8541, Kimball 8542, McCarthy 8548, Rhode Island 8551, Shaw's 8555, **Textron 8559**, van Beuren 8561, Washington 8563

South Carolina: Abney 8564, Bruce 8571, Byerly 8572, Chapin 8579, Coastal 8581, Community 8584, Daniel 8585, First 8587, Kane 8596, Post 8603, **Roe 8607**, Sims 8611, South 8615, Spartanburg 8616, Springs 8617

South Dakota: Larson 8627, Sioux Falls 8630, South Dakota 8631

Tennessee: Beaman 8642, Benwood 8644, **Bridgestone 8646**, Briggs 8647, Caesars 8648, Christy 8654, Community 8660, East 8671, Frist 8678, Frist 8679, HCA 8690, Hyde 8693, Jeniam 8695, Johnson 8697, Lindahl 8702, Lyndhurst 8703, Martin 8708, Osborne 8714, Phillips 8716, Plough 8718, **Rust 8724**, Stephens 8729, Tonya 8734, Tucker 8735, Wilson 8744

Texas: Abell 8749, **Adams 8751**, Alkek 8754, Amarillo 8758, Anderson 8760, Anderson 8762, Austin 8768, Bass 8776, Bass 8777, Bass 8778, Bauer 8779, Beasley 8784, Bosque 8792, Bridwell 8797, Brown 8799, Cailloux 8807, Cain 8809, Cameron 8812, Carter 8816, Carter 8817, CFP 8822, CH 8823, Clayton 8830, Coates 8834, Cockrell 8835, Collins 8837, Communities 8840, Community 8840, Community 8842, Constantin 8843, **Cooper 8846**, Cowden 8848, Cullen 8854, Dallas 8855, Dickson 8866, Doss 8869, Dougherty, 8870, Eady 8875, El Paso 8882, Elkins 8883, Fair 8891, Favrot 8897, Fikes 8899, Finger 8900, Fisch 8901, Fish 8902, Fondren 8906, Gill 8919, Griffin 8925, Gulf 8926, Haggerty 8932, Halsell 8936, Hamman 8938, Hebert 8946, Herzstein 8949, Hightower 8950, Hillcrest 8952, Hoblitzelle 8955, Hoglund 8956, Houston 8960, Houston 8961, Huffington 8963, Hunt 8966, Johnson 8974, Jonsson 8977, Keith 8982, Kelleher 8984, Kempner 8987, Kinder 8994, King 8995, Klabzuba 8996, **Kleberg 8999**, Kodosky 9000, Koehler 9001, Kronkosky 9002, Law 9006, Light 9011, Lightner 9012, Lowe 9020, Lubbock 9021, Lyons 9024, Mankoff 9027, Martinez 9032, Mayborn 9033, Mayor 9034, McDermott 9043, McGovern 9044, McKee 9045, McNutt 9048, Meadows 9049, Mitte 9067, Moody 9070, Moss 9078, Navarro 9089, Northen 9092, O'Connor 9094, O'Connor 9095, **Oldham 9100**, Once 9101, Owen 9107, Owsley 9108, Perkins 9116, Perot 9119, Peterson 9120, Priddy 9131, Pryor 9136, Rachal 9138, Rachofsky 9139, Reynolds 9145, Richardson 9147, Rockwell 9154, Rogers 9155, Rosewood 9158, Sams 9163, San Angelo 9165, San Antonio 9166, Sarofim 9168,

Schutte 9173, Scott 9174, Scurlock 9175, Shield 9183, Simmons 9188, Simmons 9189, Smith 9191, Smith 9195, Smith 9197, Speas 9206, Stark 9209, Stemmons 9211, Sterling 9212, Strake 9215, Sturgis 9216, Summerlee 9217, Tapeats 9223, Tate 9225, Temple 9227, **Tenet 9229**, Tennessee 9230, Texas 9232, Topfer 9238, Trull 9240, Urschel 9244, Vanberg 9248, Vaughan 9250, Waco 9255, Waggoner 9256, Waggoner 9257, Ward 9263, West 9276, White 9279, Wichita 9280, Willard 9281, Wolslager 9290, Works 9291, Wright 9294, Young 9295, Zephyr 9299

Utah: ALS 9301, **ALSAM 9302**, Browning 9308, Burton 9309, Eccles 9317, Eccles 9319, Esther 9321, **Hayward 9327**, Hemingway 9328, Jones 9330, Stewart 9345

Vermont: Lintilhac 9359, Mergens 9360, Vermont 9361

Virginia: Alleghany 9367, American 9368, Beazley 9376, Cabell 9381, Camp 9382, Campbell 9383, Carter 9387, Columbus 9399, Flagler 9417, Folger 9418, Fralin 9420, **Gannett 9428**, Gwathmey 9435, Jackson 9441, Kanter 9445, Kington 9450, Landmark 9455, Lawrence 9457, Lynchburg 9463, Mars 9466, McGlothlin 9469, Moore 9478, Morgan 9479, Norfolk 9484, **Norfolk 9485**, Parsons 9493, Perry 9495, Portsmouth 9498, Reynolds 9503, Robins 9506, Roller 9507, Scott 9513, SunTrust 9523, Titmus 9527, United 9530, Washington 9534, **Winkler 9542**

Washington: Ackerley 9547, Allen 9550, Anderson 9551, Archibald 9553, Benaroya 9556, **Boeing 9560**, Cheney 9569, Community 9571, Dimmer 9579, Evertrust 9583, Forest 9586, Fortune 9587, Foster 9588, Foundation 9589, Fuchs 9590, **Gates 9591**, Glazer 9596, Grays 9597, Green 9598, Harvest 9602, **Hemingway 9606**, Klorfine 9619, Lucky 9632, Lynn 9633, Martin 9634, McEachern 9638, Medina 9640, Milgard 9641, Murdock 9644, Nesholm 9647, Norcliffe 9650, PACCAR 9656, Rainier 9669, **Samis 9675**, Seattle 9680, Sherwood 9683, Tacoma 9693, **Weyerhaeuser 9703**, Wright 9707

West Virginia: Chambers 9713, Clay 9714, Community 9716, Daywood 9717, Hollowell 9719, Kanawha 9723, Maier 9725, McDonough 9726, Parkersburg 9730, Schenk 9732, Shott 9733

Wisconsin: Alexander 9741, Alliant 9742, Bader 9749, Banta 9752, Beloit 9757, Bishop 9759, **Bless 9761**, **Bradley 9763**, Briggs 9765, Brotz 9767, Chapman 9771, Clark 9773, Community 9777, Community 9778, Community 9779, Community 9780, Cornerstone 9781, Cudahy 9785, Dudley 9792, Fleck 9799, Four 9803, Goldbach 9806, Helfaer 9813, Herzfeld 9815, Hess 9816, Holz 9817, Jacobus 9819, Jeffris 9821, Johnson 9823, Johnson 9826, Kelben 9830, Kohler 9840, Krause 9841, Krause 9842, Kress 9844, Lakeview 9848, **Lewis 9850**, Lunda 9852, Madison 9854, Managed 9857, Mead 9867, Menasha 9869, Miller 9875, Milwaukee 9876, Modine 9878, Munson 9880, Northwestern 9884, Oshkosh 9885, Oshkosh 9887, Peck 9894, Peterson 9896, Pettit 9897, Phipps 9898, Pick 9899, Prescott 9903, Rennebohm 9910, Sensient 9922, **Smith 9929**, Split 9932, Stackner 9934, Steigleder 9936, Stock 9939, **Taylor 9947**, U.S. 9952, Walter 9959, Waukesha 9960, Weill 9962, West 9964, Wilson 9965, Witte 9968, WPS 9970, **Young 9972**

Wyoming: Community 9977, Kerr 9983, McMurry 9985, Sargent 9989, **Schultz 9990**, Stock 9992, Weiss 9997

Capital campaigns

Alabama: Alabama 1, Bedsole 12, Brock 16, Bruno 17, Community 24, Crampton 30, Friedman 35, Hearin 37, Hess 38, Hill 39, Kaul 40, Moody 54, Protective 58, Saks 61, Smith 63, **Vulcan 73**, Webb 75

Alaska: Alaska 78

Arizona: A.P.S. 86, **Globe 101**, Green 102, **Johnson 112**, Linde 117, Marshall 121, Morris 124, Piper 130, Steele 142, Sterne 143

Arkansas: Altheimer 155, **Frueauff 161**, Northwest 169, **Tyson 182**, Walker 185

California: Ahmanson 198, Amateur 214, Amgen 219, Aratani 230, **Atkinson 240**, Avery 244, Ayrshire 247, **Baker 252**, Bannerman 255, Bechtel 270, Bettingen 286, Bothin 309, Buck 330, **Bull 331**, California 345, **Cantor 354**, Collins 397, Community 401, Copley 416, Cowell 423, Crail 426, Crockett 430, Dachs 435, Daly 437, Darling 440, Davies 446, Disney 456, **DJ & T 458**, Doheny 460, Eisner 481, Eucalyptus 489, Femino 501, Firedoll 508, Flora 521, Fluor 523, Follis 525, Foothills 526, Garb 554, Garland 556, Gasser 557, Geffen 558, Gellert 559, Geschke 568, Gill 576, Gilmore 578, Gold 590, Goldman 595, Goldman 596, Goldman 597, Goldsmith 599, Gonda 601, Greer 618, Gruber 626, Haas 635, Haas 636, Hale 639, Hannon 644, Hannon 645, Harden 647, Hayden 657, Hoag 678, Humboldt 691, Hutton 694, Irwin 700, Jackson 706, JL 720, Jones 728, **K.L. 736**, Keck 750, Keller 752, Koret 774, Leichtag 801, Lesher 805, Levine 809, Los Altos 828, **Ludwick 830**, Lund 831, **M & T 837**, Mabie 839, Majestic 848, Marin 854, McBean 865, McBean 866, McCarthy 868, **McConnell 870**, Miller 901, Monterey 910, Moore 912, Morgan 915, Mosher 920, Newhall 936, Osher 961, Outhwaite 966, Outrageous 967, Pacific 970, **Packard 972**, Parsons 980, Pasadena 982, Patron 983, Rancho 1031, Rivkin 1057, Roth 1071, Santa Barbara 1093, Schlinger 1103, Schwab 1109, Serenity 1128, Smullin 1169, Sobrato 1172, Soda 1173, Sonora 1178, Stulsaft 1210, Taper 1226, Tesuque 1234, Towbes 1241, Tuohy 1247, Ueberroth 1248, Valley 1256, Valley 1257, Van Nuys 1261, Von der Ahe 1269, Waltmar 1277, Wasserman 1281, Weingart 1288, Wilbur 1305, Wood 1318, Wornick 1320

Colorado: Aspen 1338, Boettcher 1344, Bohemian 1345, Bonfils 1347, Brett 1349, Buell 1350, Chambers 1354, Community 1358, Coors 1360, **Daniels 1362**, Denver 1364, Donnell 1368, Edmondson 1373, El Pomar 1374, Gates 1380, **Gill 1382**, Johnson 1398, Kitzmiller 1405, McDonald 1421, Pikes 1437, Piton 1439, Rose 1445, Saeman 1448, Schlessman 1450, Summit 1463, Wilhite 1473, Yampa 1477

Connecticut: American 1482, Baldwin 1487, Bodenwein 1497, Calder 1506, Chilton 1511, Collis 1513, Community 1514, Community 1515, Connecticut 1518, Culpeper 1521, Freas 1548, Garden 1552, Hartford 1563, Hartford 1564, Heyman 1567, Hubbell 1569, Larsen 1579, Leever 1583, Liberty 1586, Martin 1598, MassMutual 1599, Matthies 1600, Phoenix 1627, Rogow 1636, Stone 1654, Tauck 1657, Vik 1672, Wallace 1674, Woodward 1678, Worthington 1679, Zachs 1682

Delaware: Crestlea 1701, Crystal 1702, Delaware 1706, Lennox 1726, Longwood 1727, Marmot 1728, Mastronardi 1729, Welfare 1762

District of Columbia: Aid 1765, Bender 1772, Bernstein 1775, Fowler 1797, Graham 1804, Gudelsky 1805, Kiplinger 1818, Meyer 1834, Reich 1845, Willoughby 1862

Florida: A Friends' 1866, Banbury 1889, Beveridge 1907, Bush 1922, Caspersen 1927, Community 1944, Community 1949, Conn 1951, Darden 1960, **Davis 1964**, Duckwall 1978, Dunspaugh 1981, Elster 1993, Engelberg 1994, FPL 2010, Gooding 2028, Gulf 2041, Gulf 2042, Hersh 2058, Hough 2066, Jacksonville 2071, Katz 2081, Keating 2084, Kennedy 2087, Kleist 2095, **Knight 2097**, Lattner 2104, Lee 2107, Opler 2158, Phillips 2168, Publix 2180, Rayonier 2189, **Rehm 2192**, Rinker 2196, Rinker 2197, Roberts 2201, Rosenberg 2206, Russell 2212, Selby 2230, Silverman 2234, Southwest 2240, St. Joe 2244, Straz 2254, TECO 2270, Vaughn 2279, Wahlert 2284, Waldbaum 2285, Watts 2288, Weaver 2289, Wilson 2300

Georgia: AEC 2310, Aflac 2311, AGL 2312, Atlanta 2320, Azalea 2322, Beloco 2324, Brain 2328,

Brown 2331, Brown 2332, Callaway 2336, Callaway 2337, Campbell 2339, Chatham 2347, Community 2356, Community 2357, Courts 2364, Cousins 2365, Cox 2367, Cox 2368, Day 2371, **Dobbs 2373**, DuBose 2374, English 2378, Equifax 2379, Exposition 2380, Franklin 2389, Fraser 2390, Georgia 2395, **Georgia 2397**, Glenn 2399, Greene 2404, **Hanley 2405**, Harland 2407, Harrison 2410, Horowitz 2415, Illges 2416, Imlay 2417, Knox 2427, Lanier 2428, Lee 2432, Livingston 2435, Marshall 2442, Moore 2451, Moore 2452, Morris 2454, Murphy 2456, Patterson 2460, Rich 2472, Russell 2478, **Scientific 2482**, Singletary 2490, Smith 2491, Southern 2494, SunTrust 2496, Synovus 2497, Tull 2500, **Turner 2501**, Watson 2509, Wilson 2519, Woodruff 2521, Woodward 2523, Woolford 2524, Zeist 2529

Hawaii: Alexander 2530, Atherton 2532, Bank 2535, Castle 2538, Cooke 2541, First 2542, Hawaiian 2546, McInerny 2551, Watumull 2558

Idaho: CHC 2566, Simplot 2575

Illinois: Alsdorf 2590, **Andrew 2595**, Bere 2616, Blair 2621, Blowitz 2623, **Brunswick 2636**, Butler 2646, Caterpillar 2653, **CH2M 2654**, Chicago 2660, Chicago 2661, Circle 2666, Coleman 2673, Community 2677, Community 2680, Crown 2691, Deere 2699, Dillon 2704, Donnelley 2708, Driehaus 2710, Duchossois 2711, Dunard 2712, Eisenberg 2716, Field 2728, Firestone 2729, Flagg 2731, Franke 2734, Freehling 2737, Geraldi 2752, GKN 2758, Grainger 2768, Gray 2771, Hamill 2780, Hansen 2782, Harris 2787, Harris 2788, Hobbs 2802, **Irwin 2814**, Louis 2862, McGraw 2882, Meyer 2896, Northern 2918, Olin 2925, Prince 2948, Regenstein 2962, **Shifting 3006**, Speh 3014, **Square 3018**, Stuart 3028, Takiff 3032, Tawani 3033, **Tuohy 3041**, United 3044, USG 3046, VNA 3049, Ward 3056, Woodward 3085

Indiana: Ball 3103, Ball 3104, Blue 3107, Boren 3108, Brown 3110, Bussing 3111, Central 3116, Clowes 3120, Community 3125, Community 3126, Community 3127, Community 3128, Community 3130, Crown Point 3135, **Cummins 3136**, DeHaan 3140, DeKalb 3141, Dekko 3142, Fairbanks 3147, Foellinger 3149, Ford 3150, Glick 3155, Griffith 3158, Harrison 3161, Henry 3165, Heritage 3166, Jordan 3180, Journal 3181, Koch 3184, Kosciusko 3186, Kuhne 3187, Lafayette 3188, **Lilly 3192**, Lilly 3194, Lincoln 3195, Madison 3197, Montgomery 3206, Noble 3214, Noyes 3216, Oliver 3219, OneAmerica 3220, Portland 3223, Pulliam 3225, Rolland 3231, Samerian 3234, Steuben 3241, Tipton 3243, Vectren 3249, Wabash 3250, Waterfield 3252, Welborn 3254, West 3256, Whitley 3258

Iowa: Ahrens 3260, Carver 3274, Cedar Rapids 3275, Community 3277, Community 3278, Farver 3283, Hall 3290, HNI 3293, Hubbell 3297, Iowa 3298, Kuyper 3304, **Lee 3306**, Maytag 3309, Maytag 3310, McElroy 3313, Meredith 3315, Pella 3323, Principal 3326, **Rockwell 3328**, Tye 3337

Kansas: Capitol 3350, Cessna 3351, DeVore 3357, Farah 3362, Hutchinson 3368, Payless 3380, Powell 3381, Rice 3384, Salina 3387, Security 3390, Sullivan 3396, Sunderland 3397, Topeka 3400, Wiedemann 3405

Kentucky: Brown 3409, Brown 3410, C.E. 3412, Community 3415, Cralle 3416, Ford 3419, Gheens 3421, Hayswood 3425, **Humana 3428**, Keeneland 3432, Klein 3435, **Omnicare 3444**, Sutherland 3451

Louisiana: Baton Rouge 3462, Booth 3464, Community 3469, Coughlin 3470, Diboll 3473, Freeman 3480, Goldring 3484, Huie 3488, Jones 3491, Keller 3493, Monroe 3501, Pennington 3505, Reily 3506, RosaMary 3507, Schlieder 3508, Wheless 3514, Wilson 3515, **Woldenberg 3516**, Woolf 3517

Maine: Alfond 3521, Alfond 3523, Burnham 3527, **Ford 3533**, Gallagher 3535, Hannaford 3540, King 3545, Libra 3546, Lunder 3547, TD 3558

Maryland: Abell 3559, Blades 3574, **Blaustein 3575**, Brown 3578, Choice 3589, **Cohen 3594**, Community 3598, Concordia 3601, Constellation 3602, Darby 3605, Davis 3607, Delaplaine 3614, Dresher 3617, England 3622, **Ewing 3626**, France 3632, Gudelsky 3641, Hahn 3643, Helena 3646, Henson 3648, Hirschhorn 3650, Kerr 3661, Klein 3662, Knott 3666, Lerner 3674, Linehan 3678, Lockhart 3681, Macht 3683, Marshall 3687, Meyerhoff 3691, Meyerhoff 3692, Mid 3693, Middendorf 3694, **Morningstar 3695**, Mulford 3696, Polinger 3708, Price 3709, Principato 3710, Procter 3711, Provident 3712, Rathmann 3715, Rosenberg 3719, Rouse 3724, Sheridan 3729, Small 3735, Straus 3738, Thalheimer 3744, Tucker 3750, **Weinberg 3759**, Zickler 3763

Massachusetts: Acushnet 3770, Adams 3772, Alden 3776, Barr 3791, Bayrd 3795, Behrakis 3796, Bertolon 3804, Cabot 3823, Cabot 3824, Cabot 3825, Cape Cod 3832, Cape Cod 3833, Carlee 3835, Carney 3837, Clipper 3850, Community 3855, Cox 3863, Crane 3864, Crane 3865, Crane 3866, Crossroads 3869, Davis 3875, Donahue 3881, Dusky 3885, Eastern 3886, Easthampton 3887, Farnsworth 3899, Fields 3905, Fletcher 3912, Fuller 3918, Goldberg 3927, Ham 3940, Harrington 3943, High 3950, Highland 3951, Hoche 3954, Hoffman 3955, Hopedale 3958, Island 3965, Johnson 3970, Lee 4001, Levy 4005, Liberty 4006, Linde 4007, Marcus 4022, Mifflin 4038, Miller 4039, Morse 4044, Pardoe 4068, Parker 4069, Peabody 4072, Peabody 4073, Pierce 4084, Poss 4087, Riley 4104, Rogers 4112, Roy 4114, **Schooner 4131**, Shapiro 4136, Sharf 4137, Smith 4148, Smith 4150, Stearns 4160, Stevens 4163, Stevens 4164, Stoddard 4165, Stoico 4166, Swartz 4175, Thompson 4181, Tupancy 4186, Vance 4191, Wallace 4195, Webster 4201

Michigan: Andersen 4219, **Arcus 4223**, Barry 4227, Besser 4232, Burdick 4241, Capital 4243, Carls 4244, Comerica 4251, Community 4258, Community 4259, Consumers 4260, Cook 4262, Dalton 4266, Davenport 4269, DeVos 4276, DeVos 4277, DeVos 4278, DeVos 4279, Doornink 4283, **Dow 4285**, Dow 4286, Dow 4288, DTE 4289, Fabri 4293, Farver 4295, Ford 4307, Fremont 4315, Frey 4316, Gerstacker 4322, Gilmore 4324, Grand Haven 4325, Grand Rapids 4326, Granger 4328, Greenville 4331, **H.I.S. 4334**, Herrick 4341, Hudson 4343, Jackson 4347, Jurries 4350, Kalamazoo 4352, Knight 4364, **Kresge 4367**, Lansing 4372, Lear 4374, Lenawee 4376, Masco 4387, McGregor 4389, Miller 4394, Monroe 4396, Oleson 4405, Power 4415, **Sage 4427**, Shelden 4434, Shepherd 4435, Steelcase 4446, Sturgis 4452, Tiscornia 4460, Towsley 4461, **Tubergen 4463**, Upton 4466, Vanderweide 4469, Weatherwax 4474, Webber 4475, Wege 4476, Wolters 4487, World 4489

Minnesota: **3M 4492**, AHS 4497, **Andersen 4501**, Andersen 4502, Ankeny 4505, Athwin 4508, Bayport 4512, Bemis 4515, **Best 4516**, Beverly 4517, Bigelow 4519, Bremer 4523, Bush 4524, **Cafesjian 4527**, Capp 4529, Cargill 4530, Charlson 4537, Dasburg 4545, Deikel 4548, Deluxe 4549, **Donaldson 4552**, Driscoll 4555, Edina 4560, Edwards 4561, Frey 4566, General 4570, Graco 4573, Greycoach 4575, Griggs 4577, Hardenbergh 4583, Hubbard 4590, Huss 4592, Kelley 4597, Kopp 4599, **Land 4602**, Marbrook 4612, Mardag 4613, McKnight 4617, McVay 4620, Minneapolis 4623, **Nelson 4632**, O'Shaughnessy 4639, **Petters 4653**, Phillips 4655, Pohlad 4657, Red Wing 4663, Regis 4664, Rupp 4669, Saint Paul 4671, Schoenecker 4674, Securian 4677, Slaggie 4686, Smikis 4687, Southways 4688, St. Paul 4690, Target 4697, TCF 4699, Tennant 4700, Thorpe 4701, Tozer 4703, **U.S. 4704**, Wasie 4716, WCA 4718, Wells 4721

Mississippi: AmSouth 4733, Community 4737, Irby 4750, Maddox 4753, McRae 4755, Mississippi 4758, Walker 4770

Missouri: AJP 4771, Ameren 4772, **Anheuser 4776**, Bernoudy 4783, Boeing 4785, Brown 4788, Brown 4789, Butler 4793, Commerce 4797, Curry 4802, Danforth 4803, Edison 4807, **Enterprise 4810**, Goppert 4819, H & R 4823, Hall 4824, Hallmark 4825, Helzberg 4829, Jenkins 4836, Jordan 4840, JSM 4841, Kansas 4842, Kellwood 4845, Kemper 4849, Lichtenstein 4855, Long 4858, Lopata 4859, **Mallinckrodt 4860**, McGee 4865, Musgrave 4870, **Nestle 4872**, Oppenstein 4876, Pershing 4880, Pillsbury 4884, Reynolds 4892, Shaw 4901, Sosland 4908, Stern 4909, Stupp 4911, Sunnen 4913, Trio 4918, Vatterott 4921, Ward 4924, Whitaker 4926

Montana: Sample 4940

Nebraska: Buckley 4947, Commercial 4951, **ConAgra 4953**, Cope 4955, Dunklau 4958, Eihusen 4961, Fremont 4962, Friedland 4963, Gardner 4965, **Global 4967**, Heuermann 4973, Hirschfeld 4974, Hitchcock 4975, Kiewit 4983, Kiewit 4984, Lexington 4986, Lincoln 4987, Lozier 4998, Mid-Nebraska 4991, Perkins 4996, Storz 5006, **Union 5012**, Zollner 5020

Nevada: Fairweather 5032, **Hilton 5037**, Nevada 5047, Sierra 5064, Southwest 5066, **Walsh 5075**

New Hampshire: Bean 5080, Eastman 5087, Hunt 5093, Lindsay 5095, **Penates 5099**, Putnam 5100

New Jersey: Borden 5138, Bunbury 5148, **Carlson 5155**, Charles 5161, Cowles 5170, Danellie 5177, Grassmann 5213, Harbourton 5223, Healthcare 5228, Helm 5230, Horizon 5240, Hyde 5247, Isermann 5253, Karma 5269, Kirby 5279, Knistrom 5282, Krieger 5290, Laurie 5297, **Lautenberg 5298**, Machuga 5311, McMullen 5325, OceanFirst 5341, Orange 5343, Provident 5359, PSEG 5361, **Reeves 5365**, Schering 5387, Turrell 5431, Union 5435, Victoria 5440, **Wilf 5455**, Withington 5458, **WKBJ 5459**

New Mexico: Frost 5476, Kind 5483, Maddox 5487, Messengers 5489, Taos 5498

New York: A.E. 5506, Adirondack 5517, Alexander 5532, Allyn 5539, Aron 5569, Auchincloss 5577, Bahnik 5589, Baird 5592, Barker 5599, Barker 5600, Barrington 5602, Bayne 5607, Bedminster 5611, Bernhard 5624, Bingham 5631, Booth 5651, Botwinick 5653, Bravmann 5661, Buhl 5684, Burns 5689, Butler 5691, Carnahan 5706, Carson 5709, Carwill 5711, Central 5724, Chadwick 5726, Charina 5731, **Chazen 5739**, Clark 5762, Community 5781, Community 5783, Corning 5794, Cullman 5812, **Cummings 5813**, Curran 5816, Davenport 5833, Decker 5846, **Diamond 5858**, Dickler 5861, Dreyfus 5887, Dunwalke 5894, Dyson 5898, Emerson 5927, **Engelhard 5932**, Englander 5933, First 5958, Fischer 5960, **Frankel 5976, Frankenberg 5977**, Galasso 6005, Gebbie 6009, Gifford 6026, Gilder 6029, Gilliam 6031, Gleason 6039, Glens Falls 6041, Golden 6046, Goldman 6053, Goldsmith 6060, Goldstein 6064, Golisano 6067, Grigg 6108, Harriman 6147, **Hauser 6155**, Hayden 6158, **Hearst 6161, Hearst 6162**, Hoyt 6203, Hultquist 6211, Independence 6229, **JEHT 6257**, Joy 6276, Kaplan 6288, Kautz 6300, Kealy 6303, **Keefe 6305**, Kennedy 6314, Klein 6333, Lauder 6381, Lehman 6396, Lenna 6402, Liberman 6419, M & T 6465, **Matthews 6507**, McCarthy 6515, Meehan 6523, **Memton 6529, Merrill 6537**, Metcalf 6541, Millbrook 6549, **Monell 6566, Moore 6571**, New York 6619, Nicholas 6627, Nichols 6628, Northern 6639, O'Connor 6645, O'Sullivan 6652, O'Toole 6654, **Ohga 6658**, Penick 6709, Perkin 6717, Pollack 6735, **Prospect 6750**, Raffiani 6767, **Reed 6783**, Rhodebeck 6791, Richardson 6797, Richmond 6800, Riggio 6807, **Ritter 6814**, Rose 6836, Ross 6864, Rubenstein 6870, Ruffin 6880, Schaffer 6911, Schenectady 6915, Schiff 6923, Schmitt 6928, Schnurmacher 6931, Sheldon 6964, SI 6972, Simons 6988, Simons 6989, **Smithers 7010, Solomon 7017, Steel 7052**, Stein 7055, Straus 7086, **Summerfield 7097**, Sweetgrass 7113, **Tanaka 7120**, Troy 7166, **U.S. 7180**,

Vetlesen 7196, Wachenheim 7204, Weinberg 7230, Weissman 7237, Western 7248, White 7251, Whitehead 7252, Widgeon 7255, **Wolfensohn 7270**, Woodland 7275, Wright 7280, **Zenkel 7295**

North Carolina: BB&T 7312, Belk 7315, Blumenthal 7320, Bryan 7330, Cannon 7335, Cape Fear 7336, Cemala 7337, Community 7342, Community 7345, Davis 7352, Dover 7356, Duke 7359, Easley 7361, Fox 7371, Goodrich 7378, Gorelick 7380, Gorelick 7381, Graham 7382, Halton 7386, Hanes 7387, Hanes 7388, Harris 7390, Harvest 7392, Janirve 7404, Jolley 7407, Mebane 7427, Merancas 7428, Mills 7429, Morgan 7431, Polk 7449, Reynolds 7457, Robertson 7466, Simpson 7472, Sloan 7475, Smith 7476, Smith 7479, Southern 7481, SPX 7484, Strowd 7488, Tannenbaum 7493, Triangle 7496, V.F. 7498, Van Houten 7500, Weaver 7504, Winston-Salem 7508

North Dakota: Fargo 7514, Leach 7516, MDU 7517, Stern 7521

Ohio: Abington 7524, Anderson 7529, Andrews 7530, Ashland 7533, **Austin 7535**, Barberton 7539, Bates 7540, Beaverson 7541, Bee 7542, Bicknell 7548, **Bingham 7549**, Brennan 7554, Bruening 7558, Bryan 7559, Cincinnati 7574, Cleveland 7576, Codrington 7578, Columbus 7580, Community 7583, Community 7584, Community 7585, Community 7586, **Convergys 7587, Cooper 7589**, Corbett 7590, Coshocton 7593, **Covenant 7595, Cox 7596**, Dana 7599, David 7601, Dayton 7603, Diamond 7610, Diebold 7611, **Eaton 7617**, Edwards 7618, Emery 7619, Fairfax 7621, Fairfield 7622, Farmer 7623, **Federated 7624**, Ferguson 7625, Fifth 7626, Findlay 7627, Firman 7628, First 7629, FirstEnergy 7630, Fox 7637, Fox 7638, Frohman 7641, GAR 7643, H.C.S. 7658, Hauck 7666, Hershey 7671, Home 7672, Hoover 7674, Hoover 7675, Iddings 7682, Ingalls 7684, Jergens 7689, Jewish 7690, Jochum 7692, **Kettering 7698**, Kettering 7699, Knudsen 7702, Kroger 7705, Kulas 7706, Lehner 7709, Levin 7712, Licking 7714, Lippitt 7718, LKC 7720, Lubrizol 7725, M/I 7729, Mangano 7733, Mathile 7737, Mayerson 7739, McMaster 7744, Miami 7748, Middletown 7749, Milacron 7751, Miniger 7756, Moores 7759, Morgan 7760, Morgan 7761, Morgan 7762, Murch 7766, Murphy 7768, Murphy 7769, Muskingum 7770, Nationwide 7771, NCC 7772, Nippert 7777, Noble 7778, Nord 7779, Nordson 7781, Ohio 7785, **OMNOVA 7789**, Osteopathic 7791, Owens 7792, Payne 7798, Reinberger 7815, Richland 7819, Ritchie 7821, Rosenthal 7826, Russell 7827, Sage 7829, Schlink 7839, Scotford 7846, **Scripps 7848**, Sedgwick 7849, Semple 7851, Sherwin 7855, Silk 7857, Sisler 7858, Smith 7862, Smith 7863, Spaulding 7865, Stark 7867, Stillson 7869, Stranahan 7872, **Timken 7880**, Troy 7886, Tuscarawas 7890, Van Wert 7891, Wallace 7894, Watson 7896, Wayne 7897, Wean 7898, White 7905, Wodecroft 7912, Wuliger 7918, Youngstown 7920, Zenith 7921

Oklahoma: Bernsen 7925, Bovaird 7927, Chapman 7928, Collins 7930, Community 7932, Gelvin 7938, Helmerich 7942, Hille 7943, Inasmuch 7944, Kaiser 7948, Kerr 7950, Lyon 7953, Mabee 7954, McGee 7957, McMahon 7959, Meinig 7961, Merrick 7962, Noble 7963, Oklahoma 7965, ONEOK 7967, Oxley 7968, Puterbaugh 7970, Rapp 7971, Records 7972, Sarkeys 7974, **Schusterman 7975**, Southern 7979, Stevens 7980, Tulsa 7984, Viersen 7985, Williams 7989, Zink 7994

Oregon: Carpenter 8003, Collins 8007, Ford 8013, Four 8015, Haugland 8018, Jackson 8024, John 8026, Kinsman 8031, Macdonald 8038, Meyer 8042, Oregon 8049, Schnitzer 8056, Schnitzer 8057, Swigert 8061, Swindells 8062, Tucker 8065, Wessinger 8067, Young 8069

Pennsylvania: 1675 8070, Allerton 8077, Arcadia 8086, Baker 8092, Bayer 8096, Beatty 8097, Berks 8103, Birmingham 8107, Blanchard 8111, Born 8113, Brossman 8120, Centre 8136, Century

8137, **Cestone 8138**, Cestone 8139, Chester 8141, Claneil 8144, Clapp 8145, Colonial 8151, Community 8154, Community 8155, Connelly 8157, Crels 8163, Dietrich 8171, **Dominion 8173**, Donley 8175, Donnelly 8176, Eden 8182, Equitable 8187, Erie 8188, Ferree 8199, Fine 8201, First 8202, FISA 8204, Fisher 8205, Genuardi 8213, Graham 8222, Hankin 8234, Heinz 8240, Heinz 8241, Heinz 8242, **Heinz 8243**, Hillman 8249, Hillman 8250, Hillman 8251, Hillman 8252, Hirtzel 8253, Hopwood 8257, Hoyt 8259, Hulme 8260, Hunt 8261, Huston 8263, Jennings 8272, Justus 8276, Katz 8281, Kelly 8283, Keystone 8285, Keystone 8286, Kline 8292, Kline 8293, Laurel 8301, Lehigh Valley 8303, Lenfest 8304, Lenfest 8305, Lindback 8312, Mandell 8322, Marshall 8326, Maslow 8327, McCune 8331, McCune 8332, McFeely 8334, McKenna 8337, McKinney 8339, McLean 8340, Mellon 8344, Mellon 8346, Mengle 8347, Mine 8357, Moore 8358, Morris 8359, Penn 8371, Phillips 8380, Phoenixville 8381, Pierce 8382, PNC 8388, **PPG 8394**, Pryor 8396, Rees 8401, Reidler 8402, Roberts 8405, Rockwell 8408, S & T 8417, Safeguard 8418, Saint 8419, **Seraph 8434**, Shaffer 8436, Simmons 8441, Simonds 8442, Smith 8444, Smith 8445, Sordoni 8450, Sovereign 8451, Stackpole 8456, Steinman 8458, Steinman 8459, Tippins 8477, Trexler 8481, Truman 8483, United 8486, **United 8488**, West 8500, Wheeler 8501, Willis 8504, Wyomissing 8509

Rhode Island: **Amica 8518**, Brooks 8520, Carter 8522, Champlin 8524, Charlesmead 8525, Daniels 8530, Doyle 8532, Hasbro 8539, Kimball 8542, Littlefield 8544, McAdams 8547, McCarthy 8548, Rhode Island 8551, Shaw's 8555, **Textron 8559**, van Beuren 8561, Washington 8563

South Carolina: Bruce 8571, Byerly 8572, Chapin 8579, Coastal 8581, Daniel 8585, First 8587, Foothills 8588, Kane 8596, Post 8603, **Roe 8607**, Sims 8611, Sonoco 8614, South 8615, Springs 8617

South Dakota: South Dakota 8631, Vucurevich 8634

Tennessee: Assisi 8638, Beaman 8642, Benwood 8644, **Bridgestone 8646**, Briggs 8647, Caldwell 8649, CLARCOR 8658, Community 8660, Ezell 8676, Frist 8678, Frist 8679, HCA 8690, Hyde 8693, Jeniam 8695, Lyndhurst 8703, Martin 8708, Osborne 8714, Phillips 8716, Plough 8718, **Rust 8724**, Stephens 8729, Stokely 8730, Thompson 8733, Tucker 8735, Wilson 8744

Texas: Abell 8749, **Adams 8751**, Alkek 8754, Anderson 8759, Augur 8766, Austin 8768, Bass 8776, Beasley 8784, Belo 8787, Bosque 8792, Brown 8799, Brumley 8800, Burnett 8801, Cailloux 8807, Cain 8809, Carter 8816, CFP 8822, CH 8823, Coates 8834, Cockrell 8835, Communities 8839, Community 8842, Constantin 8843, **Cooper 8846**, Cowden 8848, Cullen 8854, Dallas 8855, Dougherty, 8870, Eady 8875, Edwards 8880, Elkins 8883, Fain 8890, Fikes 8899, Fisch 8901, Fish 8902, Fondren 8906, Frost 8910, Garvey 8914, George 8916, Gill 8919, Gulf 8926, Haggerty 8932, Hamill 8937, Hamman 8938, Herzstein 8949, Hightower 8950, Hillcrest 8952, Hoblitzelle 8955, Hoglund 8956, Houston 8960, Houston 8961, Hunt 8966, Jamail 8970, Johnson 8974, Jonsson 8977, Keith 8982, Kelleher 8984, Kempner 8987, Kilroy 8991, Kinder 8994, King 8995, Klabzuba 8996, Kodosky 9000, Koehler 9001, Kronkosky 9002, Light 9011, Lightner 9012, Lowe 9020, Lubbock 9021, Lyons 9024, Mankoff 9027, Marathon 9028, Martinez 9032, Mayborn 9033, Mays 9036, McDermott 9043, McKee 9045, McNutt 9048, Meadows 9049, Mitte 9067, Moody 9070, Moss 9078, Navarro 9089, Northen 9092, Once 9101, Owen 9107, Perot 9119, Priddy 9131, Progress 9133, Providence 9135, Pryor 9136, Rachal 9138, Rachofsky 9139, Reynolds 9145, Rockwell 9154, Rosewood 9158, San Angelo 9165, Schutte 9173, Scott 9174, Scurlock 9175, **Shell 9181**, Shield 9183, Simmons 9188, Simmons 9189, Smith 9191, **Smith 9194**, Smith 9195, Smith 9197, Smith 9198, Speas 9206, Stark

9209, Stemmons 9211, Sterling 9212, Strake 9215, Sturgis 9216, Summerlee 9217, Tapeats 9223, Tate 9225, Temple 9227, **Tenet 9229**, Tennessee 9230, Texas 9232, Topfer 9238, Turner 9241, Vanberg 9248, Vaughan 9250, Waggoner 9256, Wal 9260, Ward 9262, Ward 9263, Weekley 9271, West 9276, Wichita 9280, Willard 9281, Wolslager 9290, Works 9291, Wortham 9292, Young 9295, Zachry 9296, Zeller 9298, Zephyr 9299

Utah: Browning 9308, Eccles 9317, Eccles 9319, Stewart 9345, **Wishnick 9353**

Virginia: Alleghany 9367, American 9368, Beazley 9376, Cabell 9381, Campbell 9383, Carter 9387, Delmar 9410, Flagler 9417, Freddie 9422, **Gannett 9428**, Gottwald 9431, Gwathmey 9435, Hylton 9440, Kanter 9445, LandAmerica 9454, Landmark 9455, Lawrence 9457, Lynchburg 9463, Norfolk 9484, **Norfolk 9485**, Parsons 9493, Portsmouth 9498, Reynolds 9503, Robins 9506, Scott 9513, SunTrust 9523, Titmus 9527, Ukrop 9529, United 9530, Universal 9531, Washington 9534, **Winkler 9542**, Wrinkle 9545

Washington: Ackerley 9547, Allen 9550, Archibald 9553, **Boeing 9560**, Cheney 9569, Community 9571, Cowles 9574, Dimmer 9579, Ferguson 9585, Forest 9586, Fortune 9587, Foundation 9589, Fuchs 9590, **Gates 9591**, Glazer 9596, Grays 9597, Green 9598, Harvest 9602, Horizons 9608, Klorfine 9619, **Laird 9623**, Laurel 9625, Lucky 9632, Lynn 9633, McEachern 9638, Medina 9640, Milgard 9641, Nesholm 9647, Norcliffe 9650, Oki 9653, PACCAR 9656, Rainier 9669, Seattle 9680, Sherwood 9683, Tacoma 9693, **Weyerhaeuser 9703**, Wilburforce 9705, Wright 9707, Wright 9708

West Virginia: Chambers 9713, Daywood 9717, Hollowell 9719, Kanawha 9723, Maier 9725, McDonough 9726, Parkersburg 9730, Schenk 9732, Shott 9733

Wisconsin: Alexander 9741, Alliant 9742, Bader 9749, Baird 9750, Beloit 9757, Briggs 9765, Brookbank 9766, Chapman 9771, Charter 9772, Clark 9773, Cleary 9774, Community 9777, Cornerstone 9781, CUNA 9786, Dudley 9792, Fleck 9799, Four 9803, Herzfeld 9815, Holz 9817, Jacobus 9819, Janesville 9820, Johnson 9823, Johnson 9826, Kelben 9830, **Kohler 9839**, Kohler 9840, Krause 9841, Krause 9842, Kress 9844, La Crosse 9845, Ladish 9846, Lakeview 9848, Lubar 9851, Lunda 9852, Madison 9855, Managed 9857, Marshall 9860, Mead 9867, Menasha 9869, Miller 9875, Milwaukee 9876, Modine 9878, Northwestern 9884, Oshkosh 9885, Oshkosh 9886, Peck 9895, Peterson 9896, Pettit 9897, Pick 9899, Prescott 9903, Sensient 9922, Siebert 9927, **Smith 9929**, Split 9932, Stackner 9934, Stock 9939, Styberg 9944, Walter 9959, Wilson 9965, Wisconsin 9967, WPS 9970

Wyoming: Community 9977, Ellbogen 9981, McMurry 9985, Weiss 9997

Cause-related marketing

Georgia: Aflac 2311

Wisconsin: **Thrivent 9949**

Conferences/seminars

Alabama: Community 23, **Corman 29**

Alaska: Alaska 79

Arizona: **Johnson 112, Kieckhefer 113**

Arkansas: Arkansas 156, Northwest 169

California: Alafi 201, Aratani 230, Archstone 232, Atlas 241, Ayrshire 247, Bay 264, Berry 284, Brotman 328, Buck 330, **C.S. 340**, California 346, California 350, **Castagnola 366, Christensen 384**, Community 403, Drum 470, **First 512**, Flintridge 520, Flora 521, Follis 525, **Foundation 529**, French 536, **Fund 542**, Gaia 545, Girard 580, **Glenn 581**, Hannon 644, Jacobs 708, **Kalliopela 740**, Levine

809, **Lloyd 823**, Los Altos 828, Mabie 839, Marin 854, Mental 886, Milken 897, Milken 898, Modglin 904, Orange 957, Peninsula 989, **Saban 1079**, Sierra 1151, Sonora 1178, Taper 1226, Thornton 1235, Towbes 1241, True 1245, Trust 1246, Ueberroth 1248, Ventura 1264, **Warsh 1280**

Colorado: Animal 1333, Community 1358, Donnell 1368, **General 1381, Gill 1382**, Piton 1439, Summit 1463, **Weaver 1469**, Yampa 1477

Connecticut: **Aetna 1479**, Bridgeport 1504, Community 1514, Community 1515, Connecticut 1518, Connecticut 1519, **Deloitte 1527**, Graustein 1559, **Lingnan 1587**, Main 1594, Palmer 1621, **Richardson 1632**, Rosenthal 1638, Tauck 1657, **Tremaine 1662**

Delaware: **Good 1715, Raskob 1741**

District of Columbia: **Arca 1767, Bauman 1770**, Benton 1773, Consumer 1786, **Coyne 1788, Foundation 1796**, Gudelsky 1805, Henry 1808, **Koch 1819, Moriah 1835**, Munson 1837, Roshan 1847, **Winslow 1863**

Florida: **Believers 1900**, Community 1939, Community 1947, Community 1949, Conn 1951, duPont 1983, Engelberg 1994, **Koch 2098, Morris 2145**, North 2153, Opler 2158, Stevens 2251, **Winn 2301**

Georgia: AEC 2310, **Challenge 2344**, DuBose 2374, Georgia 2394, Georgia 2395, **Georgia 2397**, Healthcare 2411, Lee 2432, Livingston 2435, Pitts 2463, **Rockdale 2474**, Savannah 2480, **Scientific 2482**, Watson 2509, Zeist 2529

Hawaii: Hawaii 2545

Idaho: Albertson 2562, Morrison 2572

Illinois: Bauer 2609, **Brach 2630**, Chaddick 2655, Coleman 2673, Community 2677, Community 2681, **Foundation 2732**, Girl's 2757, **Graham 2767**, Harris 2788, Heritage 2797, **Joyce 2820, Kemper 2832**, Little 2859, McDougal 2881, Olin 2925, **Searle 2994**, Tellabs 3034, **Tyndale 3042**

Indiana: Ball 3103, Bussing 3111, Central 3116, Community 3124, Community 3127, Community 3128, Community 3130, Dekko 3142, **Goodrich 3157, Guidant 3159**, Hancock 3160, Harrison 3161, Health 3164, Henry 3165, Heritage 3166, Irwin 3175, Lilly 3194, Lincoln 3195, Montgomery 3206, Noble 3214, Steuben 3241, Tipton 3243, Unity 3247, Wayne 3253, Welborn 3254

Iowa: Ahrens 3260, Carver 3274, Cedar Rapids 3275, Community 3277, Community 3278, Maytag 3310, Siouxland 3332

Kansas: Capitol 3350, Cooper 3353, Hutchinson 3368, Payless 3380, Rhoden 3383, Salina 3387

Kentucky: **Humana 3428**

Louisiana: Community 3469, Coypu 3471, Institute 3489

Maine: **Ford 3533**, Horizon 3541, Maine 3549, **River 3554**, Smith 3556

Maryland: Abell 3559, **Casey 3585**, Columbia 3595, Community 3599, **Ellison 3621**, Higginson 3649, Macht 3683, Meyerhoff 3691, Rathmann 3715, Thalheimer 3744

Massachusetts: Barr 3791, Behrakis 3796, Berkshire 3801, **Bosack 3809, Bruner 3819**, Cape Cod 3832, Cape Cod 3833, Chahara 3843, Community 3855, Crossroads 3869, **Fidelity 3904, Iacocca 3963**, Lee 4001, Lowell 4015, Melville 4034, Merck 4035, **Partnership 4071**, Schott 4132, Shapiro 4136, Sheehan 4140, Stevens 4164

Michigan: Americana 4218, Ann Arbor 4221, **Arcus 4223**, Barry 4227, Battle Creek 4228, Branch 4237, Community 4252, Community 4253, Dart 4267, Dow 4288, **Earhart 4291, Fetzer 4297**, Ford 4307, Four 4310, Fremont 4315, Gilmore 4324, Lansing 4372, **Mott 4399**, Weatherwax 4474

Minnesota: Bremer 4523, Central 4534, Dasburg 4545, Grand Rapids 4574, Greystone 4576, Northwest 4637, Walker 4711, Winona 4729

Mississippi: **Armstrong 4734**, Community 4737, Foundation 4743, Hardin 4747, Maddox 4753

Missouri: Commerce 4797, Community 4798, Green 4822, **Kauffman 4843**, Kemper 4849, **Mallinckrodt 4860, Monsanto 4868**

Montana: Cinnabar 4935

Nebraska: Dunklau 4958, Mid-Nebraska 4991, Omaha 4994

Nevada: Nevada 5047, **Walsh 5075**

New Hampshire: Bean 5080, Eastman 5087, Endowment 5088, Hunt 5093

New Jersey: **Clare 5164**, Dodge 5181, **Eshet 5190**, Fund 5199, Kirby 5279, Knowles 5283, Summit 5417, **WKBJ 5459**

New Mexico: Carlsbad 5469, Con 5471, Frost 5476, **Levinson 5486**, McCune 5488, New Mexico 5491, **Thaw 5500**

New York: Achelis 5513, **Adler 5521**, Alexander 5532, **American 5551, Atran 5575, AVI 5582, Bay 5606**, Bedminster 5611, **Beldon 5614**, Berg 5621, Bodman 5647, Bowne 5655, **Bronfman 5673**, Burns 5689, **Bydale 5694, Carnegie 5707**, Chautauqua 5738, **China 5750**, Community 5780, Community 5781, Community 5783, Community 5784, Community 5785, Cricket 5808, **Dedalus 5847**, Dyson 5898, **Engelhard 5932, Ford 5970, Foundation 5971**, Gifford 6026, Glens Falls 6041, **Goldman 6052**, Gould 6083, **Grant 6092**, Grigg 6108, **Hartford 6150, Hauser 6155**, Hermione 6175, **Humanitas 6212**, IF 6226, **Initial 6231, Institute 6232**, Joy 6276, **Klingenstein 6338, Kress 6357, Kunstadter 6362**, Lang 6374, Littauer 6434, **Macy 6471**, McCann 6514, **Milbank 6547**, Miller 6551, Mitsui 6561, **NEC 6605**, Northern 6639, O'Connor 6645, Perkin 6717, **Ramapo 6769**, Rapoport 6772, Rauch 6774, **Reynolds 6790**, Richmond 6800, Rochester 6823, **Rockefeller 6825, Rockefeller 6826**, Rosner 6860, Ross 6864, **Sage 6894**, Schaffer 6911, Schnurmacher 6930, Schnurmacher 6931, Slifka 7001, **Smithers 7010**, Sweetgrass 7113, **Tinker 7143**, Triad 7162, Vilcek 7199, **Wallace 7209, Warhol 7215**, Wendling 7242, **Wenner 7244**, Western 7248, Widgeon 7255, Wilson 7264

North Carolina: Biddle 7317, Blumenthal 7320, Cemala 7337, Community 7343, Community 7345, Cumberland 7349, Duke 7359, Hanes 7388, North Carolina 7438, Polk 7449, Progress 7453, Robertson 7466, Strowd 7488

North Dakota: Fargo 7514, North Dakota 7519

Ohio: Anderson 7529, Austin 7536, Barberton 7539, **Bingham 7549**, Brentwood 7555, Bryan 7559, Community 7583, Coshocton 7593, **Durell 7616**, Gund 7657, Hamilton 7660, **Kettering 7698**, Kulas 7706, Levin 7712, Marietta 7735, Miami 7748, Muskingum 7770, Nord 7779, O'Neill 7783, Osteopathic 7791, Saint 7830, Scioto 7845, **Scripps 7848**, Wallace 7894

Oklahoma: Bernsen 7925, Bovaird 7927, **Ethics 7935**, Inasmuch 7944, Oklahoma City 7964, **Schusterman 7975**, Zarrow 7991

Oregon: Carpenter 8003, Kinsman 8031

Pennsylvania: **Alcoa 8075**, Annenberg 8083, Arete 8088, Baker 8092, Barra 8095, Berks 8103, **Carthage 8132**, Centre 8136, Chester 8141, CIGNA 8143, Claneil 8144, Dolfinger 8172, **Dominion 8173**, Falk 8193, First 8202, FISA 8204, Genuardi 8213, Grable 8221, Hopwood 8257, McLean 8340, **Merck 8349**, Morris 8359, **Scaife 8425**, Scranton 8431, Society 8449, **Templeton 8475, Waldorf 8495**, York 8511

Puerto Rico: Puerto Rico 8515

Rhode Island: Rhode Island 8551

South Carolina: Community 8583, **Roe 8607**, Spartanburg 8616

South Dakota: Sioux Falls 8630, Vucurevich 8634

Tennessee: Assisi 8638, Benwood 8644, Durham 8670, East 8671

Texas: Austin 8768, Community 8840, Favrot 8897, Halliburton 8935, Houston 8960, Houston 8961, Kempner 8987, **Kleberg 8999**, Kodosky 9000, McGovern 9044, McKee 9045, Moody 9070, **RGK**

9146, Richardson 9147, San Angelo 9165, Simmons 9188, Sterling 9212, Summerlee 9217, Sumners 9218, Tocker 9236, Trull 9240, Vanberg 9248

Utah: Esther 9321, Hemingway 9328, Swanson 9346

Vermont: Lintilhac 9359, Vermont 9361

Virginia: Delmar 9410, Freddie 9422, **Gannett 9428**, Moore 9478, Samberg 9510, **WestWind 9538**, Williamsburg 9541, **Winkler 9542**

Washington: **Blakemore 9558, Brainerd 9561**, Fortune 9587, Harvest 9602, **Kongsgaard 9620**, Miller 9642, Quixote 9667, **Weyerhaeuser 9703**

West Virginia: Community 9716

Wisconsin: Bader 9749, **Bradley 9763**, Bradshaw 9764, Community 9776, Community 9778, Community 9780, Janesville 9820, **Kohler 9839**, Kohler 9840, Marshfield 9861, Miller 9875, Oshkosh 9885, Racine 9906, Sand 9918, **Thrivent 9949**

Wyoming: Community 9977, Ellbogen 9981, Wyoming 10000

Consulting services

Alabama: **Corman 29**, Smith 63

Alaska: Alaska 79

Arizona: **Johnson 112**

Arkansas: Ross 174

California: California 345, Community 401, Community 406, Community 407, **Compton 409**, Cowell 423, Crockett 430, Flintridge 520, Flora 521, Gerbode 564, Haas 637, Heller 666, Humboldt 691, Jacobs 708, **K.L. 736**, Marin 854, Miller 901, Modglin 904, Mosher 920, Peninsula 989, San Luis 1090, Sonora 1178, Truckee 1244, True 1245, Vons 1270

Colorado: Bohemian 1345, Community 1358, Community 1359, **Gill 1382**, Kenney 1401, Telluride 1465, **Weaver 1469**

Connecticut: Bridgeport 1504, Community 1514, Community 1515, Community 1517, Connecticut 1518, Connecticut 1519, Graustein 1559, Hartford 1564, Palmer 1621

Delaware: **Raskob 1741**

District of Columbia: Fowler 1797, **Kennedy 1816**, Meyer 1834

Florida: Bush 1922, Community 1939, Community 1940, Community 1948, Conn 1951, Dade 1957, **Davis 1964**, duPont 1983, Greenburg 2034, Southwest 2240

Georgia: **Challenge 2344**, Lee 2432, Zeist 2529

Hawaii: Cooke 2541, Geist 2544, Hawaii 2545

Illinois: **Abbott 2579**, Chicago 2661, Community 2681, Oak Park 2922, Speh 3014

Indiana: Blue 3107, Central 3116, Community 3125, Community 3127, Community 3128, Dekko 3142, Foellinger 3149, Hancock 3160, Harrison 3161, Henry 3165, Heritage 3166, Irwin 3175, Johnson 3178, Lilly 3194, Lincoln 3195, Marshall 3199, Noble 3214, Northern 3215, Tipton 3243

Iowa: Cedar Rapids 3275, Community 3277

Kentucky: Foundation 3420

Maine: **River 3554**

Maryland: Baker 3567, Baltimore 3568, **Casey 3585**, Columbia 3595, Community 3599, Deutsch 3616, Goldseker 3636, Straus 3738

Massachusetts: Barr 3791, Berkshire 3801, Boston 3812, Cape Cod 3833, Clipper 3850, Crossroads 3869, Davis 3875, **Fidelity 3904**, Melville 4034, Oral 4061, Parker 4069, **Schooner 4131**, Stevens 4164

Michigan: **Arcus 4223**, Barry 4227, Charlevoix 4246, Community 4252, Fremont 4315, Gilmore 4324, Hudson 4343, Jackson 4347, Lansing 4372, Midland 4392, Miller 4394, Sturgis 4452, Weatherwax 4474

Minnesota: Beverly 4517, Butler 4525, Deikel 4548, Duluth 4556, Northwest 4637, Rochester 4668

Mississippi: Foundation 4743, Lower 4751, Riley 4763

Missouri: Brown 4788, Community 4798, H & R 4823, Jewish 4837, **Kauffman 4843**, Long 4858, Saint Louis 4896

Nebraska: Lincoln 4987, Woods 5018

Nevada: **Walsh 5075**

New Hampshire: Bean 5080, Eastman 5087, New Hampshire 5098

New Jersey: **Clare 5164**, Pascale 5349, Victoria 5440

New Mexico: Carlsbad 5469, Kind 5483

New York: Abrons 5511, **American 5551, Beldon 5614, Bronfman 5673, Clark 5760**, Clark 5761, Community 5781, Community 5783, Community 5784, Community 5785, Cricket 5808, Cummings 5815, Dyson 5898, **Ford 5970, Friends 5990**, Hoyt 6203, **Humanitas 6212, Initial 6231**, Jackson Hole 6246, Muldoon 6594, New York 6613, Rauch 6774, Rochester 6823, **Rockefeller 6825, Teagle 7126**

North Carolina: Community 7343, Community 7345, Community 7346, Duke 7359, North Carolina 7438, Weaver 7504, Winston-Salem 7508

Ohio: **Armington 7532**, Brentwood 7555, Cleveland 7576, Dater 7600, Dayton 7603, Findlay 7627, First 7629, Kulas 7706, Murphy 7769, Muskingum 7770, O'Neill 7783, Reuter 7817, Saint 7830, Scioto 7845, Stark 7867

Oklahoma: Communities 7931, Oklahoma City 7964, **Schusterman 7975**, Tulsa 7984

Oregon: Carpenter 8003, Kinsman 8031

Pennsylvania: Berks 8103, Central 8135, Chester 8141, Claneil 8144, Falk 8193, Grable 8221, Lancaster 8300, Luzerne 8317, Pryor 8396, Scranton 8431, York 8511

Puerto Rico: Puerto Rico 8515

Rhode Island: Rhode Island 8551

South Carolina: Bruce 8571, Byerly 8572, Coastal 8581, Community 8584, Self 8610, Spartanburg 8616

Tennessee: Assisi 8638, East 8671, Frist 8679, Hyde 8693, **Maclellan 8704**

Texas: Austin 8768, Community 8840, Houston 8960, Kronkosky 9002, Meadows 9049, Northen 9092, **Shell 9181**, Simmons 9188

Utah: Hemingway 9328

Vermont: Vermont 9361

Virginia: Alleghany 9367, Arlington 9371, Freddie 9422, Norfolk 9484, Robins 9506, Weissberg 9536

Washington: Fortune 9587, Fuchs 9590, Quixote 9667, Tacoma 9693, Wilburforce 9705

Wisconsin: Assurant 9748, Miller 9875, Siebert 9927, **Thrivent 9949**

Wyoming: Community 9977

Continuing support

Alabama: Carson 19, **Corman 29**, Dixon 32, McMillan 49, Meyer 52, Moody 54, Moore 55, Saks 61, **Vulcan 73**, Webb 75

Alaska: Alaska 79, CIRI 83

Arizona: Arizona 87, **Globe 101, Kieckhefer 113**, Lovell 119, Ottens 128, Phelps 129, Piper 130, Sterne 143

Arkansas: Arkansas 156, **Frueauff 161**, Schmieding 175, Taylor 179, Walker 185

California: **Altman 211, Amado 212, American 217**, Anderson 221, Aratani 230, Arrillaga 237, Atkinson 239, Atlas 241, **Baker 252**, Barker 257, Bechtel 270, Benbough 276, Berry 284, Boswell 308, Brotman 328, Brownlee 329, **Bull 331**, Burch 334, **C.S. 340, Caddock 343**, California 345, California 350, **Cantor 354**, Caruso 363, **Castagnola 366, Christensen 384**, Cisco 388, Collins 397, Columbia 399, Community 401, Community 403, Community 407, **Compton 409**, Danford 438, Disney 456, **DJ & T 458**, Doheny 460, Drum 470, Eisenberg 480, Eisner 481, Eldorado 482, Eucalyptus 489, Factor 491, Firedoll 508, **Firelight 509**, Fitzgerald 514, Flintridge 520, Flora 521, Follis 525, Forest 527, **Foundation 529**, Fresno 537, **Fund 542**, Gaia 545,

Garb 554, Garland 556, Gellert 559, Getty 569, Gilmore 578, Girard 580, Global 583, Gold 590, Goldman 596, Goldman 597, Goldsmith 599, Gross 621, Gruber 626, Gumbiner 631, Haas 635, Haas 636, Hannon 645, Hayden 657, Heller 666, Hewlett 671, James 709, Keller 752, **Kim 758**, Kirchgessner 762, Koret 774, Kvamme 781, Lesher 805, Levine 809, Livingston 822, **Lloyd 823**, Lutz 833, Lux 834, Lytel 836, Majestic 848, Marin 854, McBean 866, McKesson 879, Mental 886, Miller 901, Morgan 915, Murphy 928, Norris 940, Northrop 942, Noyce 944, Orange 957, Pacific 970, **Packard 972**, Paloheimo 974, Parker 979, Patron 983, Pauley 984, Peery 986, Peninsula 989, Peppers 991, Philibosian 1003, Pottruck 1013, Rancho 1031, Reid 1036, **Reinhard 1037, Righteous 1050**, Roberts 1058, Ryan 1075, **S.G. 1078, Saban 1079**, San Diego 1087, San Luis 1090, Sandy 1092, **Schlinger 1102**, Schwab 1109, Schwab 1110, Serenity 1128, **Smith 1161**, Smith 1165, Sobrato 1172, Sonora 1178, Steele 1189, Stevens 1196, Strauss 1202, **Strauss 1203, Streisand 1204**, Stuart 1206, Stulsaft 1210, **Stupski 1211**, Taube 1228, Thornton 1235, Thornton 1236, Truckee 1244, Union 1250, **Unocal 1252**, Valley 1256, Van Nuys 1261, Vodafone 1267, **Warsh 1280, Wells 1294**, Whitecap 1303, Wilbur 1305, Wood 1318, Zellerbach 1326

Colorado: Aspen 1338, Bohemian 1345, Brett 1349, Buell 1350, Chambers 1354, Colorado 1356, Community 1358, Donnell 1368, Edmondson 1373, El Pomar 1374, **First 1377, Gill 1382**, Hughes 1394, **Janus 1396**, Johnson 1398, KBK 1400, Kitzmiller 1405, McDonald 1421, Pikes 1437, Price 1442, Qwest 1443, Schlessman 1450, Schramm 1451, **StorageTek 1460**, Summit 1463, **Weaver 1469**, Yampa 1477

Connecticut: **Aetna 1479**, Bridgeport 1504, Collis 1513, Community 1514, Community 1515, Community 1516, **GE 1553**, Hartford 1564, **Huisking 1570**, International 1571, **Lingnan 1587**, Long 1590, Perrin 1626, Rosenthal 1638, Sewall 1648, Stone 1654, Tauck 1657, **Tremaine 1662, Valentine 1669, Xerox 1680, Ziegler 1683**

Delaware: Cawley 1696, **CTW 1703**, Day 1704, Delaware 1706, **Glencoe 1714**, Lennox 1726, Mastronardi 1729, MBNA 1730, **Schwartz 1751**

District of Columbia: **Arca 1767, Banyan 1769, Bauman 1770**, Bernstein 1775, Cafritz 1780, Consumer 1786, Coors 1787, Dimick 1789, Freed 1798, Gudelsky 1805, Jovid 1814, Kiplinger 1818, Leonsis 1822, Loughran 1823, McGowan 1830, Mead 1832, **Moriah 1835, Public 1844**, Reich 1845, Replogle 1846, Spring 1849, Stewart 1850, **Summit 1852**, Trellis 1853, **Wallace 1857, Wallace 1858, Winslow 1863**

Florida: A Friends' 1866, Amaturo 1873, **Aurora 1882**, Banbury 1889, **Believers 1900**, Caspersen 1927, Community 1949, Conn 1951, **Davis 1964**, Dunspaugh 1981, Elster 1993, Engelberg 1994, Gooding 2028, Greenburg 2034, Gulf 2042, Henderson 2056, Jacksonville 2071, Katz 2081, Keating 2084, Kramer 2100, Lee 2107, MacDonald 2121, **Morris 2145**, North 2153, Peacock 2165, **Picower 2169**, Pinellas 2170, Price 2177, Rayonier 2189, **Rehm 2192**, Rinker 2195, Roberts 2201, Rosenberg 2206, Russell 2212, Silverman 2234, Smith 2238, Taishoff 2262, **Vanneck 2278**, Watts 2288, **Winn 2301**

Georgia: Beloco 2324, Brain 2328, Brown 2332, Callaway 2337, Cox 2368, Day 2371, Delta 2372, Franklin 2389, Fraser 2390, Georgia 2395, **Georgia 2397**, Glenn 2399, Harris 2408, **Keough 2426**, Knox 2427, Lee 2432, Livingston 2435, Lubo 2438, **Meyer 2446**, Patterson 2460, Pitts 2463, Sapelo 2479, **Scientific 2482**, Southern 2494, **Turner 2501**, Wilson 2519, WinShape 2520

Hawaii: Bank 2535, Campbell 2536, McInerny 2551, Wong 2560

Idaho: Idaho 2570, Simplot 2575

Illinois: **Abbott 2579**, Abbott 2580, **Amsted 2593**, Arthur 2601, Bauer 2609, Bere 2616, Bersted

2619, Blair 2621, Blowitz 2623, Brinson 2633, **Brunswick 2636, Burlington 2644**, Butler 2646, Chaddick 2655, Chicago 2660, Chicago 2661, Circle 2666, CNA 2670, Comer 2675, Community 2681, Crane 2687, **Crane 2688**, Crown 2691, Cuneo 2692, Deere 2699, Dillon 2704, Donnelley 2708, Dunard 2712, Emerson 2719, Firestone 2729, Flagg 2731, Fry 2740, **Galashiels 2742**, Girl's 2757, GKN 2758, Grainger 2768, Griswold 2773, Halligan 2779, Hamill 2780, Harris 2787, Harris 2788, Hospira 2804, Houlsby 2805, Illinois 2813, **Joyce 2820**, Kaplan 2823, Kelly 2830, Kemper 2831, Landau 2847, Little 2859, Louis 2862, McDougal 2881, McGraw 2882, Meyer 2896, Millard 2897, **Motorola 2906**, Negaunee 2909, New 2912, Northern 2918, Olin 2925, Omron 2926, PepsiAmericas 2937, Pick 2943, Polk 2946, Prince 2948, **Relations 2963**, Schmitt 2987, **Scholl 2989, Shifting 3006**, Speh 3014, **Square 3018**, Steans 3021, Stuart 3028, Takiff 3032, USG 3046, White 3067, Wieboldt 3069, Woods 3084, Woodward 3085, Worley 3086

Indiana: American 3098, Anderson 3099, Brown 3110, Bussing 3111, Cole 3121, Community 3132, Crown Point 3135, **Cummins 3136**, DeHaan 3140, Dekko 3142, Elkhart 3145, Fairbanks 3147, Foellinger 3149, Griffith 3158, Harrison 3161, Health 3164, Henry 3165, Irwin 3175, Leighton 3191, **Lilly 3192**, Lilly 3194, Moore 3207, NiSource 3213, Noyes 3216, Oliver 3219, Samerian 3234, Waterfield 3252

Iowa: Community 3277, Community 3278, Cowles 3279, Farver 3283, Hubbell 3297, Maytag 3309, Maytag 3310, Principal 3326, **Rockwell 3328**

Kansas: Capitol 3350, Cooper 3353, DeVore 3357, Hansen 3366, Hutchinson 3368, Koch 3374, Payless 3380, Powell 3381, Security 3390, Smith 3393, Sprint 3395, Sunderland 3397, Topeka 3400

Kentucky: Community 3414, Cralle 3416, **Humana 3428**, Norton 3441, Robinson 3449, Sutherland 3451

Louisiana: Baptist 3461, Brown 3465, Community 3469, Coughlin 3470, Goldring 3484, Huie 3488, Institute 3489, Jones 3491, Reily 3506, RosaMary 3507, Wheless 3514, Wilson 3515, **Woldenberg 3516**, Woolf 3517

Maine: Burnham 3527, Libra 3546, **Oak 3552, Sandy 3555**

Maryland: Blades 3574, Blaustein 3576, Brown 3578, Columbia 3595, Commonweal 3596, Constellation 3602, Davis 3607, Delaplaine 3614, Deutsch 3616, Dresher 3617, England 3622, **Ewing 3626**, Freeman 3633, **Head 3644**, Henson 3648, Higginson 3649, Hoffberger 3652, Klein 3662, Macht 3683, MARPAT 3684, Meyerhoff 3691, Meyerhoff 3692, Mulford 3706, Polinger 3708, Price 3709, Provident 3712, Rathmann 3715, **Shared 3727**, Sheridan 3729, TKF 3747, **Town 3749**, Wasserman 3757, Weiss 3760, **Zickler 3763**

Massachusetts: Acushnet 3770, Behrakis 3796, Bertolon 3804, Cabot 3824, Campbell 3830, Cape Cod 3832, Cape Cod 3833, Chahara 3843, Childs 3848, Clipper 3850, Cox 3863, Crane 3865, Crane 3866, Crawford 3867, Davis 3875, Donahue 3881, Dusky 3885, Ellsworth 3892, Fireman 3909, Fuller 3918, Goldberg 3927, Henderson 3946, High 3950, Highland 3951, Hoche 3954, Hoffman 3955, Hyams 3961, Hyde 3962, Lee 4001, Levy 4005, Liberty 4006, Lowell 4015, Merck 4035, Morse 4044, New 4050, New 4054, Orchard 4062, Pappas 4066, Poss 4087, Ratshesky 4095, Schott 4132, Schrafft 4133, Shaw 4139, Sheehan 4140, **State 4158**, Stearns 4159, Stearns 4160, Stevens 4163, Stevens 4164, Stoddard 4165, Stoico 4166, Stride 4171, **TJX 4183**

Michigan: **Arcus 4223**, Besser 4232, Burdick 4241, Community 4252, **DaimlerChrysler 4265**, Dalton 4266, Dart 4267, DeVos 4276, DeVos 4277, DeVos 4278, DeVos 4279, Dow 4286, Dow 4288, Farver 4295, Ford 4307, Four 4310, Fremont 4315,

General 4320, Gerstacker 4322, Gilmore 4324, **H.I.S. 4334**, Harding 4337, Herrick 4341, Hudson 4343, **Isabel 4346**, Kelly 4359, McGregor 4389, **Mott 4399**, Mott 4400, Oleson 4405, Power 4415, Ratner 4417, **Sage 4427**, Shelden 4434, Strosacker 4450, Tiscornia 4460, Towsley 4461, Vanderweide 4469, Westerman 4478, Whirlpool 4480

Minnesota: Adams 4495, Andersen 4502, Bell 4514, Bemis 4515, Blandin 4520, Blue 4521, Bremer 4523, Butler 4525, Buuck 4526, Cargill 4530, Davis 4546, Deikel 4548, **Donaldson 4552**, George 4572, Graco 4573, Greystone 4576, Griggs 4577, Hardenbergh 4583, HRK 4589, Jerome 4595, Kelley 4597, Lilly 4606, Marbrook 4612, Minneapolis 4623, Minnesota 4624, O'Neil 4638, **O'Shaughnessy 4639**, Ordean 4643, Oswald 4645, **Patterson 4647**, RBC 4661, Red Wing 4663, Schoenecker 4674, Star 4691, Target 4697, TCF 4699, Tennant 4700, Tozer 4703, Wells 4721, Weyerhaeuser 4726, Weyerhaeuser 4727, Whitney 4728, Winona 4729

Mississippi: **Armstrong 4734**, Community 4737, Foundation 4743, Gulf 4745, Irby 4750, McRae 4755, Riley 4763

Missouri: Ameren 4772, **Anheuser 4776**, Boeing 4785, Brown 4789, Butler 4793, Commerce 4797, Community 4798, Cray 4801, Curry 4802, **Francis 4816**, H & R 4823, Hallmark 4825, Jordan 4840, Kemper 4849, Millstone 4867, Musgrave 4870, **Nestle 4872**, Orscheln 4877, Pettus 4882, **Pillsbury 4883**, Pillsbury 4884, Pott 4886, Reynolds 4892, Shaw 4901, **Singing 4904**, Sosland 4908, Stern 4909, Sycamore 4915, Truman 4919, Vatterott 4921

Montana: **Edwards 4936**

Nebraska: Buckley 4947, **ConAgra 4953**, Kilbourne 4985, Lozier 4988, **McDonald 4989**, Omaha 4994, Perkins 4996, Weitz 5016, Woods 5018, Zollner 5020

Nevada: **Buck 5025**, Fairweather 5032, **Hilton 5037**, Sierra 5064, Southwest 5066, **Walsh 5075**

New Hampshire: Eastman 5087, Fuller 5090, Hunt 5093, **Linnell 5096**, **Penates 5099**

New Jersey: Alcatel 5110, **Barbour 5124**, Bildner 5133, **Bonner 5137**, Borden 5138, Copper 5169, Cowles 5170, Danellie 5177, Dodge 5181, **Edison 5186**, **Eshet 5190**, Fund 5199, Hidden 5233, Holzer 5238, Horizon 5240, **Huber 5244**, **Johnson 5261**, Kirby 5279, Knowles 5283, **KPMG 5288**, Krieger 5290, McGraw 5323, McMullen 5325, Merkin 5331, National 5335, OceanFirst 5341, Pascale 5349, Princeton 5357, PSEG 5361, Roberts 5371, **Schumann 5390**, Schumann 5391, Silbermann 5403, Sudler 5416, Turrell 5431, Victoria 5440, **Vollmer 5443**, Withington 5458, Zobel 5464

New Mexico: Albuquerque 5466, Bancroft 5467, Carlsbad 5469, Cudd 5472, Frost 5476, Kind 5483, McCune 5488, New Mexico 5491, Santa Fe 5496, Taos 5498, Thornburg 5501

New York: Abrons 5511, Abrons 5512, Adirondack 5517, **Alavi 5530**, Altschul 5546, **American 5551**, American 5555, **Archbold 5563**, **Atran 5575**, **Avon 5583**, Badgeley 5588, Bahnik 5589, Barker 5599, Barker 5600, **Barth 5603**, **Bay 5606**, Bedminster 5611, **Benenson 5620**, Berg 5621, Botwinick 5653, Bowne 5655, Buhl 5684, **Bydale 5694**, Carnahan 5706, **Carnegie 5707**, Cary 5712, Chadwick 5726, Charina 5731, Chautauqua 5738, Chernow 5745, **Citigroup 5755**, **Claiborne 5757**, Claiborne 5758, **Clark 5760**, Clark 5761, Clark 5762, Credit 5807, Cricket 5808, **Cummings 5814**, Curran 5816, Dammann 5824, Daphne 5830, **de Hirsch 5840**, **Deutsche 5854**, Dewar 5856, **Diamond 5858**, Dickler 5861, Dow 5879, **Dun 5893**, Dunwalke 5894, Dyson 5898, **East 5900**, **EHA 5912**, **Engelhard 5932**, Englander 5933, **Ford 5970**, **Foundation 5971**, **Frankel 5976**, **Freeman 5980**, Galasso 6005, Gebbie 6009, Gilder 6029, Gilman 6032, **Gilman 6033**, Gimbel 6034, Goldman 6053, **Goldman**

6056, Goldsmith 6060, Gould 6083, Greve 6104, Griffis 6107, Grigg 6108, Guttman 6124, **Hartford 6150**, Hayden 6158, Hermione 6175, **Heron 6176**, Hughes 6209, Hultquist 6211, I Have 6219, IF 6226, **JEHT 6257**, Johnson 6272, **Joukowsky 6275**, Joy 6276, Kaplan 6288, Kaplan 6290, Katzenberger 6298, Kautz 6300, Kennedy 6314, Kenworthy 6315, **Klingenstein 6338**, Knapp 6342, **Kopf 6348**, **Kunstadter 6362**, Lang 6374, Lauder 6381, **Lauder 6383**, Lee 6391, Lehman 6396, Leonhardt 6403, Lincoln 6423, Link 6428, Lortel 6447, Macdonald 6468, **Mayer 6510**, McCann 6514, McCarthy 6515, Meehan 6523, **Mellon 6525**, **Memton 6529**, **Merrill 6537**, **Mertz 6538**, Metcalf 6541, **MetLife 6542**, Miller 6551, **Mitsubishi 6560**, Mizuho 6562, **Monell 6566**, Moody's 6569, **Moore 6571**, Moses 6587, Neuberger 6611, New York 6615, New York 6617, New York 6620, **New 6621**, Nichols 6628, **Noble 6633**, **Norman 6635**, Normandie 6636, **Noyes 6643**, O'Connor 6645, O'Toole 6654, Ohrstrom 6659, **Ostrovsky 6673**, **Paley 6679**, Penick 6709, Perkin 6717, **Phillips 6725**, Price 6746, Raffiani 6767, Rapoport 6772, **Reader's 6778**, Reed 6782, **Reed 6783**, Revson 6789, **Reynolds 6790**, Robison 6821, Rock 6824, **Rockefeller 6825**, **Rockefeller 6826**, Rockefeller 6827, Rosenberg 6845, Rosenstiel 6852, Roslyn 6859, Ross 6864, Rubenstein 6870, Rubinstein 6876, Santa 6905, Sasco 6907, Schaffer 6911, Scherman 6918, Schieffelin 6922, Schmeelk 6927, Schnurmacher 6930, Schnurmacher 6931, Sirus 6992, Slifka 7001, Solow 7019, **Solow 7020**, Spingold 7032, St. Faith's 7039, Stein 7055, Stern 7072, Stiefel 7079, Straus 7086, Strypemonde 7089, Sulzberger 7095, **Surdna 7103**, Taconic 7117, **Teagle 7126**, **Thorne 7133**, Tiger 7139, Tisch 7145, Troy 7166, Tuch 7170, Turner 7175, Tuttle 7176, **U.S. 7180**, Ungar 7183, Van Pelt 7192, **Vetlesen 7196**, Vidda 7198, Warner 7216, **Watson 7220**, **Weeden 7223**, Weissman 7237, Wendling 7242, White 7251, Wilson 7264, **Wolfensohn 7270**, Woodcock 7273

North Carolina: **Bank 7310**, Belk 7315, Bryan 7330, Cape Fear 7336, Community 7345, Dover 7356, Duke 7359, Easley 7361, Finch 7366, Finley 7367, Fox 7371, Goodrich 7378, Hurley 7402, Hurley 7403, Kenan 7411, Kenan 7412, Kenan 7413, Mebane 7427, Mills 7429, Morgan 7431, Nias 7435, Polk 7449, Progress 7453, Randleigh 7456, Reynolds 7457, Reynolds 7458, Reynolds 7459, Robertson 7466, Smith 7479, Strowd 7488, Triangle 7496, Warner 7503, Weaver 7504

North Dakota: Leach 7516, MDU 7517, Stern 7521

Ohio: American 7528, **Armington 7532**, **Austin 7535**, Austin 7536, **Bingham 7549**, Brennan 7554, Brentwood 7555, Britton 7556, Cleveland 7577, Codrington 7578, Columbus 7580, Community 7585, Coshocton 7593, **Covenant 7595**, Dana 7599, Dater 7600, Diamond 7610, Fairfield 7622, **Federated 7624**, Fifth 7626, First 7629, Fox 7637, France 7639, GAR 7643, **Geisse 7646**, Gund 7657, **HCR 7667**, Hoover 7674, Humphrey 7679, Jennings 7688, Kulas 7706, Lippitt 7718, Lippman 7719, Lubrizol 7725, McMaster 7744, Milacron 7751, Morgan 7762, Murphy 7768, Murphy 7769, Nationwide 7771, NCC 7772, Nippert 7777, Nord 7779, Nordson 7781, Ohio 7784, **OMNOVA 7789**, Prentiss 7806, Reeves 7814, Reuter 7817, Reynolds 7818, Ritchie 7821, Salem 7831, Sisler 7858, Smith 7862, Spaulding 7865, Stranahan 7872, **Tell 7876**, Tuscarawas 7890, Wallace 7894, Watson 7896, Wayne 7897, Weisbrod 7900, Wolfe 7915, Youngstown 7920

Oklahoma: **8:32 7922**, Bailey 7923, Better 7926, Bovaird 7927, Community 7932, Goddard 7939, Hille 7943, Kaiser 7948, Kerr 7950, Kirkpatrick 7952, Meinig 7961, Oklahoma City 7964, Oklahoma 7965, Puterbaugh 7970, **Schusterman 7975**, Southern 7979, Stevens 7980, Viersen 7985, Zink 7994

Oregon: Autzen 7997, Carpenter 8003, Chambers 8004, Jackson 8024, Johnson 8027, Kinsman 8031, PacifiCorp 8050, **Schmidt 8055**, Schnitzer 8056, Swigert 8061, Tektronix 8063, Templeton 8064

Pennsylvania: **Alcoa 8075**, Allerton 8077, Arcadia 8086, Arete 8088, Arkema 8089, Baker 8092, Bayer 8096, Born 8113, Buhl 8124, Campbell 8128, **Carnegie 8130**, Central 8135, Century 8137, **Cestone 8138**, Claneil 8144, Clapp 8145, Colonial 8151, Community 8153, Community 8154, Connelly 8157, Dietrich 8170, **Dominion 8173**, Fels 8198, First 8202, FISA 8204, Fisher 8205, Fourjay 8209, Grable 8221, Hankin 8234, Harsco 8236, Heinz 8240, Heinz 8241, Heinz 8242, Hillman 8249, Hillman 8250, Hillman 8251, Hillman 8252, Hopwood 8257, Hoyt 8259, Justus 8276, Kavanagh 8282, Kelly 8283, **Kennametal 8284**, Kline 8293, Lenfest 8304, Lenfest 8305, Little 8313, Mandell 8322, Maslow 8327, McCune 8331, McFeely 8334, Mellon 8344, Mellon 8346, Mine 8357, Morris 8359, **Pew 8377**, Philadelphia 8378, Phoenixville 8381, **Pincus 8384**, PNC 8388, **PPG 8394**, Rees 8401, Rider 8404, Roberts 8405, Rockwell 8408, Safeguard 8418, Saint 8419, **Scaife 8425**, Scholler 8428, Scranton 8431, Smith 8443, Smith 8444, Sordoni 8450, Stabler 8455, Strawbridge 8466, Trexler 8481, Weiss 8499, West 8500, Wheeler 8501, Wyomissing 8509

Puerto Rico: Puerto Rico 8515

Rhode Island: **Amica 8518**, Carter 8522, Daniels 8530, **Dorot 8531**, Littlefield 8544

South Carolina: Abney 8564, Black 8569, Bruce 8571, Byerly 8572, Chapin 8579, Daniel 8585, Foothills 8588, Post 8603, **Roe 8607**, Sims 8611, Spartanburg 8616

South Dakota: Vucurevich 8634

Tennessee: Beaman 8642, Benwood 8644, **Bridgestone 8646**, EBS 8672, Ezell 8676, Hamico 8684, Lyndhurst 8703, Martin 8708, Phillips 8716, **Rust 8724**, Stokely 8730, Wilson 8744

Texas: Abell 8749, Augur 8766, Austin 8768, Bass 8777, Bauer 8779, Belo 8787, Brown 8799, Cailloux 8807, Cain 8809, Campbell 8813, Carter 8816, CFP 8822, Clayton 8830, Coates 8834, **Cooper 8846**, Covenant 8847, Dougherty, 8870, Eady 8875, **EDS 8877**, El Paso 8881, El Paso 8882, Esping 8886, Fikes 8899, Fisch 8901, Fish 8902, Fleming 8904, Fondren 8906, Frees 8909, Greathouse 8924, Halff 8934, Halliburton 8935, Hamman 8938, Healthcare 8944, Herzstein 8949, Hightower 8950, Houston 8960, Houston 8961, **Jenesis 8971**, Jonsson 8977, Keith 8982, Kempner 8987, Kimberly 8992, Kinder 8994, Kodosky 9000, Kronkosky 9002, Light 9011, Lockheed 9015, Lubbock 9021, Lyons 9024, Marathon 9028, Mays 9036, McDermott 9043, McGovern 9044, McKee 9045, Meadows 9049, Mitte 9067, Northen 9092, O'Connor 9094, O'Connor 9095, Owsley 9108, Parks 9116, Rachofsky 9139, Richardson 9147, Rockwell 9154, Rosewood 9158, Sams 9163, San Antonio 9166, **Scaler 9170**, Scott 9174, Scurlock 9175, **Shell 9181**, Simmons 9188, Simmons 9189, **Smith 9194**, Smith 9195, Smith 9197, Stark 9209, Strake 9215, Sumners 9218, Swinney 9222, Tapeats 9223, Tate 9225, Texas 9232, Topfer 9238, Trull 9240, Waggoner 9256, Wal 9260, Walsh 9261, Weaver 9267, Willard 9281, Works 9291, Wortham 9292, Wright 9294, Young 9295, Zephyr 9299

Utah: Bamberger 9305, Browning 9308, Burton 9309, Caine 9310, Eccles 9320, **Hayward 9327**, Hemingway 9328, Jones 9330, Swanson 9346

Vermont: Lintilhac 9359, Mergens 9360, Vermont 9361

Virginia: Alleghany 9367, American 9368, Arlington 9371, Community 9402, Delmar 9410, Flagler 9417, Freddie 9422, Mars 9466, Moore 9478, **Norfolk 9485**, Northern 9486, Portsmouth 9498, Samberg 9510, Truland 9528, Washington 9534,

Weissberg 9536, **WestWind 9538**, Williamsburg 9541

Washington: Blue 9559, **Brainerd 9561**, Bullitt 9563, Casey 9566, De Falco 9578, Dimmer 9579, **Edwards 9580**, Evertrust 9583, Ferguson 9585, Fuchs 9590, **Gates 9591**, Harder 9600, Harvest 9602, **Hemingway 9606**, Klorfine 9619, **Kongsgaard 9620, Laird 9623**, Laurel 9625, Lockwood 9631, Martin 9634, Miller 9642, Oki 9653, Quixote 9667, **Samis 9675, Stewardship 9691**, Tacoma 9693

West Virginia: Daywood 9717, Kanawha 9723, Tucker 9736

Wisconsin: Alliant 9742, Assurant 9748, Banta 9752, Bishop 9759, **Bradley 9763**, Community 9778, Cornerstone 9781, Cudahy 9785, CUNA 9786, Eastman 9795, Evjue 9797, Four 9803, Green Bay 9810, Herzfeld 9815, Holz 9817, Jacobus 9819, Johnson 9823, Joy 9828, Kelben 9830, Krause 9841, Kress 9844, La Crosse 9845, Managed 9857, Marshfield 9861, McBeath 9864, Mead 9867, Menasha 9869, Miller 9875, Modine 9878, Morse 9879, Northwestern 9884, Oshkosh 9885, Oshkosh 9887, Peterson 9896, Prescott 9903, **Smith 9929**, Split 9932, Stock 9939, U.S. 9952, Vine 9956, Waukesha 9960, Weill 9962, WPS 9970

Wyoming: Community 9977, Connemara 9978, McMurry 9985, **Schultz 9990**, Scott 9991, Weiss 9997, Wyoming 10000

Curriculum development

Alabama: Community 24, Friedman 35, Kaul 40, Meyer 52, Webb 75

Alaska: Rasmuson 85

Arizona: **Globe 101**, Hansen 104, Ottens 128

Arkansas: Northwest 169

California: Ackerman 193, **Amado 212, American 217**, Aratani 230, Archstone 232, Baxter 262, Bay 264, Bechtel 270, Buck 330, Caruso 363, **ChevronTexaco 380**, Collins 397, Columbia 399, Crail 426, Eucalyptus 489, **First 512**, Fleishhacker 518, Flora 521, Garland 556, Gasser 557, GenCorp 560, Genentech 563, Girard 580, Godric 586, Haas 635, Heller 666, Hughes 690, **K.L. 736, Keck 750, Lloyd 823**, Marin 854, Miller 901, Peninsula 989, Rancho 1031, **Reinhard 1037, Righteous 1050, Rivendell 1056, Saban 1079**, San Diego 1087, **Schuler 1108**, Severns 1131, Sierra 1151, Sonora 1178, Stevens 1196, Stone 1200, Stuart 1206, **Stupski 1211**, Taper 1226, Trust 1246, Ueberroth 1248, UniHealth 1249, Van Nuys 1261, Ventura 1264, **Versacare 1265**

Colorado: Animal 1333, Community 1359, **Crowell 1361**, ECA 1372, **Janus 1396**, Pikes 1437, Piton 1439, Schlessman 1450, Summit 1463, **Weaver 1469**, Yampa 1477

Connecticut: **Bingham 1493**, Calder 1506, Community 1515, Connecticut 1518, **Deloitte 1527, GE 1553**, Graustein 1559, Hartford 1564, International 1571, Larsen 1579, **Lingnan 1587**, Main 1594, **Tremaine 1662**, Tully 1665

Delaware: MBNA 1730, **Raskob 1741, Robinson 1745**

District of Columbia: **Bauman 1770**, Bender 1772, Block 1776, Mazda 1828, Mead 1832, Reich 1845, Roshan 1847, Spring 1849, Strong 1851, Willoughby 1862

Florida: **Believers 1900**, Burns 1920, **Chatlos 1932**, Community 1948, Community 1949, **Davis 1964**, duPont 1983, Engelberg 1994, Gulf 2041, Henderson 2056, **Johnson 2077, Knight 2097, Koch 2098**, Lattner 2104, St. Joe 2244, Toppel 2274

Georgia: **Challenge 2344, Coca-Cola 2352**, Cox 2368, Creel 2369, Harrison 2410, Imlay 2417, Lee 2432, Livingston 2435, **Scientific 2482**, Zeist 2529

Hawaii: Atherton 2532, Campbell 2536, Castle 2538, Wong 2560

Idaho: Albertson 2562, Idaho 2570, **Micron 2571**

Illinois: Arthur 2601, Chaddick 2655, Chicago 2661, Coleman 2673, Field 2728, Flagg 2731, Fry 2740, **Graham 2767**, Illinois 2812, Kemper 2831, **Kemper 2832**, Kendall 2833, Logan 2860, McDougal 2881, McNeil 2887, Olin 2925, Polk 2946, Retirement 2964, Speh 3014, Sprague 3016, **State 3019**, Steans 3021, Takiff 3032, Tellabs 3034, **Tuohy 3041**

Indiana: Ball 3103, Blue 3107, Bussing 3111, Central 3116, Community 3132, Dekko 3142, **Guidant 3159**, Hancock 3160, Harrison 3161, Lilly 3194, Madison 3197, Pulliam 3225, Steuben 3241, Tipton 3243, Welborn 3254

Iowa: Carver 3274, Cedar Rapids 3275, Farver 3283, Maytag 3310, Principal 3326, Tye 3337

Kansas: Hutchinson 3368

Kentucky: Good 3422, **Humana 3428**

Louisiana: Baptist 3461, Community 3469

Maine: **Ford 3533**, Horizon 3541, Libra 3546, Maine 3549

Maryland: Abell 3559, Columbia 3595, Deutsch 3616, Higginson 3649, **Hughes 3654**, Kerr 3661, Klein 3662, Meyerhoff 3691, Mid 3693, **Nasdaq 3700**, Polinger 3708, Provident 3712, Rathmann 3715, Thalheimer 3744, Wright 3762, **Zickler 3763**

Massachusetts: Berkshire 3801, Cambridge 3828, Clarke 3849, Crawford 3867, Crossroads 3869, Donahue 3881, **Fidelity 3904**, Island 3965, Lee 4001, Linde 4007, Lowell 4015, Millipore 4040, Morse 4044, **New England 4052**, New 4054, **Partnership 4071**, Poss 4087, Riley 4104, Rodgers 4110, Rubenstein 4115, Sheehan 4140, Smith 4150

Michigan: **Arcus 4223**, Barry 4227, Battle Creek 4228, Bay 4229, Berrien 4231, Binda 4233, Community 4258, **DaimlerChrysler 4265**, Dart 4267, Davenport 4269, **Dow 4285, Earhart 4291**, Ford 4307, **Foundation 4309**, Fremont 4315, Grand 4327, Herrick 4341, Oleson 4405, Weatherwax 4474, Wege 4476

Minnesota: **3M 4492, ADC 4496, Best 4516**, Duluth 4556, Edina 4560, Grand Rapids 4574, Greycoach 4575, McNeely 4619, Walker 4711, West 4723

Mississippi: Community 4737, Foundation 4743, Hardin 4747

Missouri: Commerce 4797, Community 4798, Green 4822, H & R 4823, **Kauffman 4843**, Kemper 4849, **Monsanto 4868**, Oppenstein 4876, Pershing 4880, Sosland 4908

Nebraska: **ConAgra 4953, Global 4967**, Hirschfeld 4974, Mid-Nebraska 4991

Nevada: **Hilton 5037, Walsh 5075**

New Hampshire: **Dorr 5086**

New Jersey: Dircks 5180, Dodge 5181, Elizabethtown 5188, Hidden 5233, Princeton 5357, Prudential 5360, Schenck 5386, Victoria 5440, **WKBJ 5459**

New Mexico: Cudd 5472, Domanica 5475, Frost 5476, Maddox 5487, Taos 5498

New York: Achelis 5513, Adirondack 5517, Alexander 5532, **American 5553, AVI 5582**, Berg 5621, Bodman 5647, Booth 5651, Bowne 5655, **Bristol 5666, Bronfman 5673**, Burden 5687, Burns 5689, Carnahan 5706, **Carnegie 5707**, Charina 5731, **Citigroup 5755**, Community 5781, Community 5783, Community 5784, Corning 5794, Curran 5816, **Ford 5970**, Freeman 5981, **Friends 5990**, Frog 5992, **Fuld 5999**, Gifford 6026, Gilman 6032, Gleason 6039, **Goldman 6056, Grant 6090, Gruss 6116**, Harkness 6145, **Hartford 6150**, Heckscher 6164, **Homeland 6199**, Hoyt 6203, **Humanitas 6212**, IF 6226, **Johnson 6268**, Joy 6276, Kornfeld 6350, Lehman 6396, M & T 6465, **Macy 6471, Mailman 6477**, Mars 6494, **Memton 6529**, Miller 6551, **Mitsubishi 6560, Monell 6566**, Oishei 6660, Pfizer 6720, Raffiani 6767, **Rockefeller 6826**, Rose 6833, Rosenberg 6845, Schaffer 6911, Schnurmacher 6930, Schnurmacher 6931, Slifka 7001, Snow 7011, **Staley 7042**, Straus 7086, **Teagle 7126, Time 7142, Toyota 7160**, Troy 7166, Tuch 7170, **United 7185**

North Carolina: BB&T 7312, BIN 7318, Blue 7319, Cape Fear 7336, Community 7342, Community 7344, Community 7345, Community 7346, Duke 7359, Easley 7361, Finley 7367, Fox 7371, Mebane 7427, Polk 7449, Progress 7453, Robertson 7466

North Dakota: Leach 7516

Ohio: Ashtabula 7534, Austin 7536, Barberton 7539, **Bingham 7549**, Brentwood 7555, Bryan 7559, Coshocton 7593, Diamond 7610, Fairfield 7622, First 7629, FirstEnergy 7630, GAR 7643, **HCR 7667**, Hershey 7671, Hoover 7675, Jennings 7688, **Kettering 7698**, McMaster 7744, Miami 7748, Middletown 7749, Morgan 7761, Murphy 7769, Nippert 7777, O'Neill 7783, Ohio 7784, Osteopathic 7791, Saint 7830, Scioto 7845, Sisler 7858, Slemp 7860, Sloat 7861, Springfield 7866, Stocker 7870, Troy 7886, Wallace 7894, Wean 7898

Oklahoma: Bovaird 7927, **Ethics 7935**, Hille 7943, Inasmuch 7944, Kerr 7949, Kirkpatrick 7952, Meinig 7961, **Schusterman 7975**, Tulsa 7984, Zink 7994

Oregon: Braemar 8001, Carpenter 8003, Chambers 8004, Intel 8022, Kinsman 8031, PacifiCorp 8050, Swigert 8061

Pennsylvania: Baker 8092, Bayer 8096, **Cestone 8138**, Cestone 8139, Claneil 8144, Community 8155, **Dominion 8173**, Erie 8188, Fels 8198, Fine 8201, Grable 8221, Jennings 8272, Kind 8289, Kline 8293, Laurel 8301, PNC 8388, Rees 8401, **Scaife 8425**, Scranton 8431, Shenango 8438, **Templeton 8475**

Puerto Rico: Puerto Rico 8515

South Carolina: Byerly 8572, Community 8584, Daniel 8585, Spartanburg 8616

South Dakota: Sioux Falls 8630, South Dakota 8631

Tennessee: Assisi 8638, Frist 8679, Plough 8718, Wilson 8744

Texas: Bass 8778, Brown 8799, CH 8823, Coates 8834, Cullen 8854, Dougherty, 8870, El Paso 8882, Esping 8886, Houston 8960, Houston 8961, Jonsson 8977, Kempner 8987, Kimberly 8992, Kodosky 9000, Koehler 9001, Light 9011, Marcus 9029, McDermott 9043, McGovern 9044, McNair 9047, Meadows 9049, Mitte 9067, Northen 9092, Powell 9128, Reynolds 9145, Rockwell 9154, San Antonio 9166, **Shell 9181**, Simmons 9188, Stark 9209, Stemmons 9211, Sterling 9212, Summerlee 9217, Sumners 9218, Trull 9240, Waggoner 9256, Willard 9281, Works 9291, Young 9295

Utah: Caine 9310, Esther 9321, Hemingway 9328

Vermont: Lintilhac 9359, Vermont 9361

Virginia: Alleghany 9367, American 9368, Arlington 9371, Flagler 9417, Landmark 9455, **MCI 9471**, Memorial 9474, **Mitsubishi 9476**, Norfolk 9484, Samberg 9510, Staunton 9521, Weissberg 9536

Washington: Ackerley 9547, Blue 9559, **Boeing 9560**, Grays 9597, Harvest 9602, **Hemingway 9606**, Lucky 9632, Martin 9634, Norcliffe 9650, Quixote 9667, True 9696, **Weyerhaeuser 9703**

West Virginia: Tucker 9736

Wisconsin: **Bradley 9763**, Bradshaw 9764, Community 9777, Community 9778, Community 9780, Crump 9783, Green Bay 9810, Helfaer 9813, Kelben 9830, La Crosse 9845, Lakeview 9848, **Lewis 9850**, Menasha 9869, Miller 9875, Phipps 9898, Prescott 9903, Stock 9939, **Thrivent 9949**, Waukesha 9960

Wyoming: Community 9977, Scott 9991

Debt reduction

Arizona: Morris 124

California: Drum 470, Flora 521, Garland 556, Gasser 557, Marin 854

Colorado: Schramm 1451

Delaware: Cawley 1696

Florida: Banbury 1889, **Chatlos 1932**, Rayonier 2189, Watts 2288

Georgia: AEC 2310, Glenn 2399, Lee 2432, **Scientific 2482**, Zeist 2529
Illinois: Hamill 2780
Indiana: Bussing 3111
Kansas: Hutchinson 3368
Kentucky: Community 3415
Louisiana: Booth 3464
Maryland: Blades 3574, Meyerhoff 3692
Massachusetts: Donahue 3881, Ellsworth 3892, Ham 3940, High 3950
Michigan: Dalton 4266, Gilmore 4324, Knight 4364
Minnesota: Slaggie 4686
Missouri: McGee 4865
Montana: **Edwards 4936**
New Jersey: Hyde 5247
New York: Griffis 6107, Lee 6391
North Carolina: Cannon 7335, Cape Fear 7336, Mebane 7427, Morgan 7431, Southern 7481, Strowd 7488, Weaver 7504
Ohio: Ashtabula 7534, **Covenant 7595**, GAR 7643, McMaster 7744
Oregon: Kinsman 8031
Pennsylvania: Century 8137, Crels 8163, Graham 8222, Justus 8276, McFeely 8334, Trees 8480
South Carolina: Bruce 8571
Tennessee: Martin 8708, Phillips 8716
Texas: Cullen 8854, Herzstein 8949, Houston 8960, Keith 8982, Koehler 9001, Kronkosky 9002, Lightner 9012, Meadows 9049, Sterling 9212
Washington: Lucky 9632
West Virginia: Daywood 9717
Wisconsin: Bader 9749, Banta 9752, Bishop 9759, Cornerstone 9781, Kelben 9830, Managed 9857, Miller 9875, Peterson 9896, West 9964

Donated equipment

California: Gap 551
District of Columbia: **Fannie 1793**
Georgia: Georgia 2395
Missouri: **Monsanto 4868**
Tennessee: **Bridgestone 8646**
Texas: El Paso 8882

Donated land

Georgia: Georgia 2395

Donated products

California: Clorox 389, Gap 551, Genentech 561, **Mattel 861, Sun 1214**
Connecticut: Boehringer 1498
Illinois: Hospira 2804, Sara 2982
Indiana: **Lilly 3192, Lilly 3193**
Kansas: Delta 3354
Massachusetts: Genzyme 3922
Minnesota: Vest 4708
Missouri: **Wyeth 4930**
New Jersey: **Aventis 5121, Bristol 5143, Janssen 5255, Merck 5328**, Merck 5329, Roche 5372
Wisconsin: Roundy's 9915

Emergency funds

Alabama: Community 23, Community 25, McMillan 49, Saks 61, Webb 75
Alaska: Alaska 78, Alaska 79
Arizona: Arizona 87, Green 102, **Kieckhefer 113**, Neely 125, Wilson 152
Arkansas: **Frueauff 161**, Ross 174
California: Anaheim 220, **Baker 252**, Change 373, Clorox 389, Community 401, Community 402, Community 403, Community 405, Community 406, Community 407, Crail 426, **Delano 449**, Doheny 460, Drum 470, Firedoll 508, Flora 521, Forest

527, Garb 554, Garland 556, Gilmore 578, Gumbiner 631, Hewlett 671, Hughes 690, Humboldt 691, Irmas 697, Keller 752, Knight 768, Levine 809, **Lloyd 823**, Lutz 833, Marin 854, McKesson 879, McLean 880, **Packard 972**, Parker 979, Peninsula 989, **Peterson 996**, Rancho 1031, Rivkin 1057, Sacramento 1080, Santa Barbara 1093, Serenity 1128, Sobrato 1172, Sonora 1178, Stern 1195, Taper 1226, Trust 1246, Union 1250, vanLobenSels 1260, Van Nuys 1261, Ventura 1264, Von der Ahe 1269, Vons 1270
Colorado: Animal 1333, Aspen 1338, Brett 1349, Community 1358, Community 1359, Edmondson 1373, El Pomar 1374, **First 1377, General 1381, Gill 1382**, Hughes 1393, Kenney 1401, King 1404, Pikes 1437, Price 1442, Yampa 1477
Connecticut: **Aetna 1479**, Baldwin 1487, Chilton 1511, Collis 1513, Community 1514, Community 1515, Community 1516, Community 1517, Hartford 1564, Main 1594
Delaware: **Glencoe 1714**, Laffey 1725, **Raskob 1741**
District of Columbia: Aid 1765, Block 1776, Gudelsky 1805, **Moriah 1835**, Reich 1845, Spring 1849
Florida: A Friends' 1866, Banbury 1889, Beveridge 1907, Bush 1922, Caspersen 1927, Community 1940, Community 1943, Community 1946, Community 1948, Community 1949, Conn 1951, Dade 1957, Engelberg 1994, Greenburg 2034, Gulf 2042, Hayes 2052, **Knight 2097**, Levin 2110, Opler 2158, Quantum 2181, Rayonier 2189, Silverman 2234, **Skelly 2237**, Southwest 2240, **SWS 2260**, Taylor 2267, Wahlert 2284, Wollowick 2306
Georgia: Brain 2328, Brown 2332, Community 2356, Cox 2367, Day 2371, Georgia 2395, Glenn 2399, Horowitz 2415, Lee 2432, Lubo 2438, Savannah 2480, **Scientific 2482**, Southern 2494, Woolley 2525
Hawaii: Bank 2535
Illinois: **Abbott 2579, BP 2628**, Chicago 2661, Community 2679, Day 2698, Deere 2699, Dillon 2704, Driehaus 2710, Field 2728, Flagg 2731, Houlsby 2805, Illinois 2812, Landau 2847, Meyer 2896, Olin 2925, Owens 2929, Speh 3014, **Square 3018**, Stern 3023, Woodward 3085
Indiana: Brown 3110, Bussing 3111, Central 3116, Clowes 3120, Community 3123, Community 3124, Community 3125, Community 3127, Community 3128, Community 3130, Crown Point 3135, **Cummins 3136**, Decatur 3138, Harrison 3161, Henry 3165, Heritage 3166, Irwin 3175, Johnson 3178, Lafayette 3188, Lilly 3194, Lincoln 3195, Madison 3197, Noble 3214, Northern 3215, Rolland 3231, Tipton 3243, Wabash 3250, Waterfield 3252, Wells 3255, Whitley 3258
Iowa: Cedar Rapids 3275, Community 3277, Community 3278, Farver 3283, Maytag 3310, McElroy 3313
Kansas: **Beren 3348**, Capitol 3350, Cessna 3351, Cooper 3353, Salina 3387, Sunderland 3397, Topeka 3400, Westar 3403, Wiedemann 3405
Kentucky: C.E. 3412, Community 3414, Community 3415, Foundation 3420
Louisiana: Baton Rouge 3462, **Biedenharn 3463**, Community 3469, Coughlin 3470, Goldring 3484, Monroe 3501, New Orleans 3503, Wilson 3515, **Woldenberg 3516**
Maine: Davenport 3531, Libra 3546
Maryland: Blades 3574, Blaustein 3576, Columbia 3595, Community 3598, Davis 3607, Knott 3666, Meyerhoff 3691, Meyerhoff 3692, Mid 3693, Mulford 3696, Procter 3711, Provident 3712
Massachusetts: Acushnet 3770, Barr 3791, Bayrd 3795, Berkshire 3801, **Bosack 3809**, Cambridge 3828, Cape Cod 3833, Chahara 3843, Clipper 3850, Community 3854, Davis 3875, Ellsworth 3892, Essex 3897, Fields 3905, Fuller 3918, High 3950, Morse 4044, Rubenstein 4115, **State 4158**, Stevens 4164, Stoddard 4165, Thompson 4181, Weber 4200

Michigan: Ann Arbor 4221, Battle Creek 4228, Charlevoix 4246, Community 4252, Community 4256, **DaimlerChrysler 4265**, Dalton 4266, Farver 4295, Ford 4307, Fremont 4315, General 4320, Gerstacker 4322, Gilmore 4324, Herrick 4341, Kalamazoo 4352, Kelly 4359, Lansing 4372, Miller 4394, Saginaw 4428, Tiscornia 4460, Weatherwax 4474
Minnesota: Beverly 4517, Bremer 4523, Deikel 4548, Deluxe 4549, Duluth 4556, Edina 4560, Grand Rapids 4574, Greystone 4576, Kopp 4599, Northwest 4637, O'Neil 4638, Rochester 4668, Target 4697, WCA 4718
Mississippi: Irby 4750
Missouri: Ameren 4772, Brown 4789, Commerce 4797, Community 4798, **Enterprise 4810**, Goppert 4819, Green 4822, H & R 4823, Hall 4824, Jewish 4837, **Kauffman 4843**, Laclede 4852, Lopata 4859, Millstone 4867, **Nestle 4872**, Oppenstein 4876, Pershing 4880, **Pillsbury 4883**, Reynolds 4892, Shaw 4901, Stern 4909
Montana: **Edwards 4936**
Nebraska: Buckley 4947, Heuermann 4973, Hirschfeld 4974, Lincoln 4987, Omaha 4994
Nevada: Cord 5029, Fairweather 5032, Nevada 5047, Southwest 5066, **Walsh 5075**
New Hampshire: **Dorr 5086**, Endowment 5088, Fuller 5090, Hunt 5093, **Penates 5099**
New Jersey: **Carolan 5156**, Cowles 5170, Hidden 5233, Hyde 5247, **International 5252**, Karma 5269, Kirby 5279, **Lautenberg 5298**, Pascale 5349, Princeton 5357, Roberts 5371, Sudler 5416, Summit 5417, Victoria 5440, Weston 5452
New Mexico: Carlsbad 5469, Cudd 5472, Domanica 5475, McCune 5488, Santa Fe 5496, Taos 5498
New York: Abeles 5509, **American 5553**, Bravmann 5661, Chautauqua 5738, **Citigroup 5755**, Community 5780, Community 5781, Community 5783, **Dramatists 5883, Edouard 5909**, Emerson 5927, Gifford 6026, Glens Falls 6041, Glickenhaus 6042, **Gottlieb 6080**, Gould 6083, Grigg 6108, Hermione 6175, Hoyt 6203, Independence 6229, Katzenberger 6298, Kennedy 6314, **Kraft 6351**, Lee 6391, Lehman 6396, Macdonald 6468, Metcalf 6541, **National 6603**, New York 6618, O'Connor 6645, O'Toole 6654, Ohrstrom 6659, Perkin 6717, **Phillips 6725**, Raffiani 6767, Raiff 6768, Richmond 6800, **Ritter 6814, Ross 6863**, Schnurmacher 6930, Schnurmacher 6931, Sheldon 6964, Siebens 6974, Simons 6988, Slifka 7001, St. George's 7040, Straus 7086, Sulzberger 7095, **Thorne 7133**, Warner 7216, Weissman 7237, Western 7248, White 7251, Wilson 7264
North Carolina: **Bank 7310**, BB&T 7312, Belk 7315, Blumenthal 7320, Cemala 7337, Community 7343, Community 7344, Community 7345, Community 7346, Dover 7356, Duke 7359, Easley 7361, Goodrich 7378, Hanes 7387, Hanes 7388, Mills 7429, Robertson 7466, Smith 7476, Smith 7479, Tannenbaum 7493, Triangle 7496, Weaver 7504, Winston-Salem 7508
North Dakota: Fargo 7514, Leach 7516, Stern 7521
Ohio: Abington 7524, Anderson 7529, **Armington 7532**, Ashtabula 7534, Austin 7536, Britton 7556, Bruening 7558, Butler 7562, Cincinnati 7574, **Covenant 7595**, Dana 7599, Diamond 7610, Diebold 7611, **Generation 7647**, Gund 7657, Hamilton 7660, Humphrey 7679, Jewish 7690, Levin 7712, Mayerson 7739, Middletown 7749, Miniger 7756, Murphy 7768, Nationwide 7771, Nordson 7781, Reuter 7817, Richland 7819, Saint 7830, Slemp 7860, Stark 7867, Stocker 7870, Stranahan 7873, Troy 7886, Wallace 7894, Wayne 7897, White 7905, Wolfe 7915, Woodruff 7917, Wuliger 7918
Oklahoma: Bernsen 7925, Community 7932, Goddard 7939, McMahon 7959, Sarkeys 7974, **Schusterman 7975**, Tulsa 7984, Viersen 7985
Oregon: Boyd 8000, Chambers 8004, Johnson 8027, Kinsman 8031, PacifiCorp 8050, Schnitzer 8056, Swigert 8061, Templeton 8064

Pennsylvania: **Alcoa 8075**, Arkema 8089, Blanchard 8111, Born 8113, Centre 8136, **Cestone 8138**, Cestone 8139, Colonial 8151, Community 8155, Dolfinger 8172, Erie 8188, Fourjay 8209, Hankin 8234, Heinz 8240, Hooper 8256, Hopwood 8257, Huston 8263, Huston 8264, Justus 8276, Kline 8293, Lehigh Valley 8303, Little 8313, McFeely 8334, Mine 8357, Philadelphia 8378, **PPG 8394**, Pryor 8396, Saint 8419, Shenango 8438, Smith 8443, Smith 8445, Sovereign 8451, Steinman 8459, Truman 8483, West 8500, Wheeler 8501, Wyomissing 8509

Puerto Rico: Puerto Rico 8515

Rhode Island: Carter 8522, Daniels 8530, Kimball 8542, Rhode Island 8551, Shaw's 8555

South Carolina: Abney 8564, Bruce 8571, Chapin 8579, Coastal 8581, Community 8583, Self 8610, Spartanburg 8616

South Dakota: Vucurevich 8634

Tennessee: Assisi 8638, **Bridgestone 8646**, Danner 8664, Frist 8679, **Rust 8724**, Wilson 8744

Texas: Amarillo 8758, Augur 8766, Bridgeway 8796, Cailloux 8807, Carter 8816, Communities 8839, **Cooper 8846**, Cowden 8848, Edwards 8880, Elkins 8883, Fikes 8899, Fleming 8904, Greathouse 8924, Hamill 8937, Houston 8960, Keith 8982, Kempner 8987, Koehler 9001, Kronkosky 9002, Light 9011, Lockheed 9015, Lubbock 9021, Lyons 9024, McGovern 9044, McKee 9045, Meadows 9049, Owsley 9108, Permian 9117, Rachal 9138, Rachofsky 9139, San Angelo 9165, San Antonio 9166, Scurlock 9175, Shield 9183, Simmons 9188, Speas 9206, Sterling 9212, Sunnyside 9219, Temple 9227, Waco 9255, Waggoner 9256, Wal 9260, **Waste 9265**, Willard 9281, Wortham 9292

Utah: Burton 9309, Hemingway 9328, Simmons 9342, Swanson 9346

Vermont: Vermont 9361

Virginia: Arlington 9371, Camp 9382, Community 9402, Flagler 9417, Foundation 9419, HRH 9439, Landmark 9455, Lynchburg 9463, Norfolk 9484, **Norfolk 9485**, Northern 9486, Titmus 9527, Universal 9531, Virginia Beach 9532, Washington 9534, **Winkler 9542**

Washington: **Brainerd 9561**, Bullitt 9563, Cheney 9569, Fuchs 9590, Grays 9597, Green 9598, Haas 9599, **Hemingway 9606**, Horizons 9608, Klorfine 9619, **Kongsgaard 9620**, Lockwood 9631, Medina 9640, Quixote 9667, **Samis 9675**, Seattle 9680, Tacoma 9693, **Weyerhaeuser 9703**

West Virginia: Daywood 9717, Kanawha 9723, McDonough 9726, Parkersburg 9730

Wisconsin: Alexander 9741, Alliant 9742, Banta 9752, Bishop 9759, Bradshaw 9764, Community 9776, Community 9779, Community 9780, Cornerstone 9781, CUNA 9786, Dudley 9792, Evjue 9797, Fond du Lac 9800, Green Bay 9810, Johnson 9823, Kelben 9830, Krause 9842, Managed 9857, Mead 9867, Menasha 9869, Miller 9875, Northwestern 9884, Oshkosh 9887, Pick 9899, Sensient 9922, **Taylor 9947**, **Thrivent 9949**, U.S. 9952

Wyoming: Community 9977, Kerr 9983, McMurry 9985

Employee matching gifts

Alabama: AmSouth 5, Blount 14, Protective 58

Arizona: **Globe 101**, Phelps 129, Piper 130

Arkansas: Union 183, Wal-Mart 184

California: Amgen 219, Bay 264, **Bechtel 269**, **Beckman 272**, California 345, California 346, California 350, Cisco 388, Clorox 389, Community 406, Copley 416, Cowell 423, Crail 426, Disney 456, East 474, Fieldstone 506, Fireman's 510, Flora 521, Fluor 523, Gap 551, GenCorp 560, **Getty 570**, Haas 636, Haas 637, Hewlett 671, Intuit 696, Irvine 698, Jacobs 708, **Kaiser 739**, **Keck 750**, Knight 768, Majestic 848, Marin 854, **Mattel 861**, **McConnell 870**, McKesson 879, **Moore 913**, Northrop 942, **Omidyar 952**, Orfalea 958, **Packard 972**, Peninsula 989, PG&E 1000, San Diego 1087,

San Francisco 1088, Schwab 1109, **Schwab 1110**, Sierra 1151, Solano 1175, **Strauss 1203**, Stuart 1206, **Sun 1214**, Synopsys 1223, UniHealth 1249, Union 1250, **Unocal 1252**, Waitt 1275, Weingart 1288, **WellPoint 1292**, **Wells 1294**

Colorado: Chambers 1354, Colorado 1356, Community 1358, **Daniels 1362**, ECA 1372, El Pomar 1374, **First 1377**, Gill 1382, **Janus 1396**, Kinder 1403, Piton 1439, Qwest 1443, **StorageTek 1460**

Connecticut: **Aetna 1479**, **Applera 1484**, **Deloitte 1527**, **Educational 1533**, GE 1553, Hubbell 1569, International 1571, Phoenix 1627, **Praxair 1629**, Vik 1672, **Xerox 1680**

District of Columbia: Cafritz 1780, **Coyne 1788**, **Fannie 1793**, Kiplinger 1818, Trellis 1853

Florida: Bush 1922, Darden 1960, **Davis 1964**, FPL 2010, Gulf 2042, Harris 2050, Johnson 2077, **Knight 2097**, Publix 2180, Quantum 2181, Rayonier 2189, Ryder 2213, **SWS 2260**, **von Liebig 2283**, **Winn 2301**

Georgia: Blank 2325, Delta 2372, Georgia 2395, **Georgia 2397**, Goizueta 2400, ING 2418, **Rockdale 2474**, SunTrust 2496, Tull 2500, **UPS 2503**, WestPoint 2513

Hawaii: Alexander 2530, Hawaiian 2546

Idaho: **Washington 2578**

Illinois: Abbott 2580, **Allstate 2588**, **Amsted 2593**, **Aon 2598**, **Baxter 2611**, **BP 2628**, **Brunswick 2636**, **Burlington 2644**, Caterpillar 2653, Chicago 2661, Chicago 2663, CNA 2670, Community 2677, Crane 2687, Crown 2691, Donnelley 2706, Energizer 2721, Field 2728, **Gallagher 2744**, GKN 2758, Grand 2769, Harris 2787, Harris 2789, Hartmarx 2794, Hospira 2804, Illinois 2813, **Joyce 2820**, Lumpkin 2864, **MacArthur 2868**, McGraw 2882, **Motorola 2906**, Northern 2918, Olin 2925, Omron 2926, PepsiAmericas 2937, Polk 2946, Prince 2948, Prince 2949, **Samaritan 2980**, Sara 2982, **Spencer 3015**, **Square 3018**, **State 3019**, USG 3046, **Wrigley 3088**, Zurich 3093

Indiana: American 3098, Anthem 3102, Citizens 3118, Clowes 3120, **Cummins 3136**, **Guidant 3159**, Koch 3184, **Lilly 3192**, Lilly 3194, Lincoln 3195, **Lumina 3196**, Unity 3247, Vectren 3249

Iowa: **AEGON 3259**, HNI 3293, Maytag 3309, Meredith 3314, Pella 3323, **Pioneer 3324**, Principal 3326, **Rockwell 3328**

Kansas: Capitol 3350, Cessna 3351, Security 3390, Sprint 3395, Topeka 3400, Westar 3403

Kentucky: Community 3414, E.ON 3417, Keeneland 3432, **Yum! 3457**

Louisiana: Booth 3464

Maine: TD 3558

Maryland: Abell 3559, **Agilent 3563**, **Blaustein 3575**, Chaney 3587, Choice 3589, Constellation 3602, France 3632, Freeman 3633, GEICO 3634, Grace 3638, Kerr 3661, Knott 3666, Lockheed 3682, Mid 3693, Price 3709, Procter 3711

Massachusetts: Biogen 3806, Boston 3812, Cabot 3823, Eastern 3886, **Fidelity 3904**, Liberty 4006, Millipore 4040, **OneBeacon 4060**, **Reebok 4098**, **State 4158**, Stride 4171

Michigan: **Arcus 4223**, Consumers 4260, **DaimlerChrysler 4265**, Dow 4284, **Dow 4285**, DTE 4289, Ford 4307, Fremont 4315, Frey 4316, General 4320, Gilmore 4324, Grand Rapids 4326, Hudson 4343, Kalamazoo 4352, **Kellogg 4357**, Kellogg's 4358, **Kresge 4367**, McGregor 4389, **Mott 4399**, Skillman 4438, Steelcase 4446, Towsley 4461, Whirlpool 4480, Wolverine 4488

Minnesota: **3M 4492**, **ADC 4496**, ATK 4509, Bayport 4512, Bemis 4515, Blandin 4520, Deluxe 4549, **Donaldson 4552**, **Ecolab 4557**, **Fuller 4567**, General 4570, Graco 4573, Hormel 4588, Jostens 4596, **Land 4602**, McKnight 4617, McNeely 4619, **Medtronic 4622**, **Pentair 4649**, Piper 4656, Pohlad 4657, RBC 4661, Red Wing 4663, Securian 4677, Southways 4688, St. Paul 4690, Star 4691, TCF 4699, Tennant 4700, **Toro 4702**, **U.S. 4704**, **Wallestad 4712**, Xcel 4732

Mississippi: AmSouth 4733, Mississippi 4758

Missouri: Ameren 4772, Andrews 4774, **Anheuser 4776**, Brown 4789, Butler 4793, Danforth 4803, Emerson 4809, **Enterprise 4810**, H & R 4823, Hallmark 4825, Kansas 4842, **Kauffman 4843**, Kauffman 4844, Kellwood 4845, Laclede 4852, **May 4861**, **Monsanto 4868**, **Nestle 4872**, Sosland 4908

Nebraska: **ConAgra 4953**, Lincoln 4987, Lozier 4988

Nevada: **Hilton 5037**, Reynolds 5056, Sierra 5064, Southwest 5066, **Walsh 5075**

New Hampshire: **Winthrop 5105**

New Jersey: American 5113, Bard 5125, Campbell 5151, **Clare 5164**, Dodge 5181, Horizon 5240, **Johnson 5261**, Johnson 5265, **KPMG 5288**, **Merck 5326**, National 5335, Prudential 5360, PSEG 5361, Schering 5387, **Scholarship 5388**, Subaru 5415, Summit 5417, UBS 5433, Unilever 5434, **Verizon 5439**

New Mexico: **Lannan 5484**, PNM 5493

New York: Altman 5542, **American 5553**, **Avon 5583**, **AXA 5584**, Bank 5598, **Beldon 5614**, **Bristol 5666**, **Bronfman 5673**, **Carnegie 5707**, **Citigroup 5755**, Claiborne 5758, Clark 5761, **Commonwealth 5779**, Corning 5794, **Dana 5827**, **Deutsche 5854**, **Dodge 5867**, **Duke 5892**, **Dun 5893**, **Ford 5970**, Galasso 6005, **Guggenheim 6118**, **Harriman 6146**, **Hartford 6150**, Hazen 6160, **Heron 6176**, **IBM 6221**, IFF 6227, Independence 6229, **JM 6263**, **JPMorgan 6277**, **Kraft 6351**, **Kress 6357**, Littauer 6434, Loews 6443, **Luce 6453**, **MBIA 6512**, **Merrill 6537**, **MetLife 6542**, **Milbank 6547**, Mitsui 6561, Mizuho 6562, Moody's 6569, New York 6613, New York 6617, New York 6619, New York 6620, North 6637, **Novartis 6640**, **Open 6665**, Park 6688, **Pepsi 6713**, **PepsiCo 6714**, Pfizer 6720, Pinkerton 6728, Price 6746, **Prospect 6750**, Reader's 6777, **Rockefeller 6825**, **Rockefeller 6826**, **Sage 6894**, Simon 6987, **Teagle 7126**, Triad 7162, Tribune 7163, **Wallace 7209**

North Carolina: **Bank 7310**, Duke 7360, Goodrich 7378, Reynolds 7458, Reynolds 7459, Spangler 7482, SPX 7484, SunTrust 7491, Triangle 7496, **Wachovia 7502**, Weaver 7504, Winston-Salem 7508

Ohio: AK 7525, Austin 7536, **Cardinal 7567**, Charities 7569, **Convergys 7587**, **Cooper 7589**, Coshocton 7593, Dana 7599, Diebold 7611, Dorn 7612, **Eaton 7617**, **Federated 7624**, Fifth 7626, First 7629, FirstEnergy 7630, **HCR 7667**, Hoover 7675, **Key 7700**, Lubrizol 7725, MeadWestvaco 7745, Middletown 7749, Nationwide 7771, NCC 7772, NCR 7773, Nord 7779, Ohio 7785, **OMNOVA 7789**, Parker 7796, **Procter 7807**, Progressive 7808, Robbins 7823, **Scripps 7848**, Sherwin 7855, **Tomkins 7884**

Oklahoma: Kerr 7950, McCasland 7956, Noble 7963, Oklahoma 7965, ONEOK 7967, Williams 7989

Oregon: Ford 8013, Intel 8022, Mentor 8039, Meyer 8042, PacifiCorp 8050, Tektronix 8063

Pennsylvania: **Alcoa 8075**, Arkema 8089, **Armstrong 8090**, Buhl 8124, CIGNA 8143, Connelly 8157, **Dominion 8173**, GlaxoSmithKline 8218, Hankin 8234, Harsco 8236, Heinz 8240, IKON 8265, **Kennametal 8284**, McCune 8332, Mellon 8345, Penn 8371, **Pew 8377**, PNC 8388, **PPG 8394**, Rees 8401, Safeguard 8418, Saint 8419, Sovereign 8451, **United 8488**, Vanguard 8490, West 8500

Rhode Island: **Amica 8518**, **FM 8537**, Hasbro 8539, **Textron 8559**

South Carolina: Cline 8580, Sonoco 8614

South Dakota: Larson 8627

Tennessee: **Bridgestone 8646**, CLARCOR 8658, Frist 8679, HCA 8690, Hyde 8693, Lyndhurst 8703

Texas: Abell 8749, **AT&T 8765**, Baker 8772, Brown 8799, Community 8842, **Cooper 8846**, El Paso 8882, **ExxonMobil 8889**, Halliburton 8935, Houston 8960, Houston 8961, Kempner 8987, Kimberly 8992, Marathon 9028, Meadows 9049,

Once 9101, Rosewood 9158, **Shell 9181**, Temple 9227, Temple 9228, **Tenet 9229**, Texas 9232, Valero 9247

Virginia: Bryant 9380, CarMax 9385, Circuit 9392, Freddie 9422, **Freedom 9424, Gannett 9428**, LandAmerica 9454, **Mitsubishi 9476, Mustard 9481, Norfolk 9485, Parker 9492**, SunTrust 9523, Ukrop 9529

Washington: Apex 9552, Bullitt 9563, **Casey 9567**, Cheney 9569, **Gates 9591**, Murdock 9644, PACCAR 9656, Rainier 9669, **RealNetworks 9672**, Russell 9673, UNOVA 9697, **Weyerhaeuser 9703**

West Virginia: McDonough 9726

Wisconsin: Alliant 9742, Assurant 9748, Banta 9752, CUNA 9786, Johnson 9823, Johnson 9826, Mead 9867, Menasha 9869, Munson 9880, Northwestern 9884, PPC 9902, **Rockwell 9912**, Sentry 9923, **Smith 9929, Thrivent 9949**, U.S. 9952, Wisconsin 9967, WPS 9970

Wyoming: Scott 9991

Employee volunteer services

Alabama: Vulcan 73
Arkansas: Wal-Mart 184
California: **Bechtel 269**, Clorox 389, Gap 551, **GSF 627**, Intuit 696, **Mattel 861**, McKesson 879, **Schwab 1110, Strauss 1203, Sun 1214, WellPoint 1292**
Connecticut: **Aetna 1479**, Boehringer 1498, International 1571, **Praxair 1629, Xerox 1680**
Delaware: MBNA 1730
District of Columbia: **Fannie 1793, Hitachi 1810**
Florida: Darden 1960
Georgia: Aflac 2311, BellSouth 2323, Georgia 2395, **Georgia 2397**, ING 2418
Hawaii: Alexander 2530
Illinois: **Allstate 2588, Baxter 2611, BP 2628, Brunswick 2636, Donnelley 2707**, Harris 2787, **Motorola 2906**, Northern 2918, Sara 2982, **State 3019**, Zurich 3093
Indiana: **Guidant 3159**, Koch 3184, **Lilly 3192**, Vectren 3249
Iowa: Meredith 3314, Pella 3323
Maine: TD 3558
Maryland: Choice 3589, Price 3709
Massachusetts: Cabot 3823, Millipore 4040
Michigan: DTE 4289
Minnesota: **Best 4516**, Deluxe 4549, Jostens 4596, **Land 4602, Medtronic 4622**, RBC 4661, St. Paul 4690, Star 4691, TCF 4699, Tennant 4700, Xcel 4732
Missouri: H & R 4823, Hallmark 4825
New Jersey: Alcatel 5110, **Merck 5326**, Prudential 5360, **Verizon 5439**
New York: **Bristol 5666, Citigroup 5755**, First 5958, **MBIA 6512**, Moody's 6569, **Morgan 6577**, New York 6617, **Pepsi 6713, PepsiCo 6714**, Pfizer 6720, Reader's 6777
North Carolina: **Bank 7310, Lowe's 7423, Wachovia 7502**
Ohio: **Cardinal 7567, Eaton 7617, Federated 7624, Key 7700**, MeadWestvaco 7745, Nationwide 7771, **OMNOVA 7789, Scripps 7848**
Oklahoma: ONEOK 7967
Oregon: Intel 8022
Pennsylvania: ACE 8073, American 8079, CIGNA 8143, **PPG 8394**, Tyco 8485
Rhode Island: CVS 8529, Hasbro 8539
Texas: **Cooper 8846**, Dell 8864, El Paso 8882, **ExxonMobil 8889**, Kimberly 8992, Marathon 9028, Penney 9115, **Tenet 9229**, Triad 9239
Virginia: CarMax 9385, Freddie 9422, **Mitsubishi 9476**
Washington: Rainier 9669, **Weyerhaeuser 9703**
Wisconsin: Modine 9878, Northwestern 9884

Employee-related scholarships

Alabama: Alabama 1, **Bashinsky 11**, Compass 28, Saks 61, **Vulcan 73**
Arkansas: Wal-Mart 184, Walton 186
California: **Bechtel 269**, Blue 296, Disney 456, Fluor 523, GenCorp 560, Knight 768, **Mattel 861**, McKesson 879, Mosher 920, Sacramento 1080, Sierra 1152, **Unocal 1252**
Connecticut: Barnes 1488, **Conway 1520**, Garden 1552, **GE 1553**
Delaware: **CTW 1703**, MBNA 1730, Presto 1740
Florida: Community 1939, Rayonier 2189
Georgia: Amos 2314, BellSouth 2323, Coca-Cola 2351, **Georgia 2397, Scientific 2482**
Hawaii: Alexander 2530, Hawaiian 2546
Illinois: **Abbott 2579, Allstate 2588**, Andrew 2596, **Baxter 2611, Brunswick 2636, Burlington 2644, Donnelley 2707**, Harris 2787, Illinois 2813, Medline 2889, **Motorola 2906**, Newell 2913, Olin 2925, Omron 2926, Speh 3014, **State 3019**, Zurich 3093
Indiana: American 3098, Biomet 3106, Harrison 3161, Kimball 3182, Koch 3184
Iowa: Maytag 3309, Pella 3323, Siouxland 3332
Kansas: Koch 3374
Kentucky: Blue 3407, **Humana 3428**
Maine: Hannaford 3540
Maryland: Choice 3589, **Knapp 3664**, Lockheed 3682
Massachusetts: Berkshire 3801, High 3950, Hood 3957, Millipore 4040
Michigan: **ArvinMeritor 4224**, Community 4258, **DaimlerChrysler 4265**, Fabri 4293, Ford 4307, Grand Rapids 4326, Guardian 4333, Steelcase 4446, Whirlpool 4480
Minnesota: **ADC 4496**, ATK 4509, Bemis 4515, **Donaldson 4552**, General 4570, Graco 4573, Jostens 4596, **Patterson 4647**, TCF 4699, Tennant 4700, Valspar 4706
Missouri: Boeing 4785, Butler 4793, Emerson 4809, H & R 4823, Hall 4824, Orscheln 4877
Nebraska: **ConAgra 4953**
New Jersey: American 5113, Campbell 5151, **Chubb 5162**, National 5335, Prudential 5360, Subaru 5415, Unilever 5434
New York: **American 5553, Avon 5583, AXA 5584, Bristol 5666**, Central 5723, Community 5782, Community 5784, Goldman 6055, Loews 6443, **Merrill 6537, MetLife 6542**, New York 6617, **Novartis 6640, PepsiCo 6714**, Reader's 6777, Salomon 6898
North Carolina: **Bank 7310**, Community 7343, Duke 7360, Giles 7374, Nucor 7440, Reynolds 7459, Triangle 7496
North Dakota: MDU 7517
Ohio: AK 7525, May 7738, **OMNOVA 7789, Procter 7807**, Scripps 7848, Timken 7879
Oklahoma: **ConocoPhillips 7933**, Kerr 7950, Noble 7963, Tulsa 7984, Williams 7989
Pennsylvania: **Alcoa 8075**, Arkema 8089, Berks 8103, Community 8154, Farber 8195, Giant 8214, Harsco 8236, **PPG 8394**, Shenango 8438, Sovereign 8451, Steinman 8458, **United 8488**, West 8500, Women's 8507
Rhode Island: CVS 8529, **Textron 8559**
South Carolina: Inman 8595, Post 8603, ScanSource 8608, Spartanburg 8616
South Dakota: Sioux Falls 8630
Tennessee: **Bridgestone 8646**, Tucker 8735, Unaka 8739
Texas: **AT&T 8765**, Carter 8817, **Cooper 8846**, Dallas 8855, Halliburton 8935, Houston 8960, Kimberly 8992, **Shell 9181**, Temple 9228, **Tenet 9229**
Virginia: Circuit 9392, **Gannett 9428**, Lynchburg 9463, **Norfolk 9485**, Northern 9486
Washington: Foundation 9589, Nestle 9648, **Pigott 9663**, Weyerhaeuser 9703
West Virginia: Tucker 9736

Wisconsin: Alliant 9742, Assurant 9748, Banta 9752, Briggs 9765, Community 9776, Johnson 9823, Johnson 9826, Krause 9842, Madison 9855, Manpower 9858, Marshall 9860, **Meehan 9868**, Menasha 9869, Modine 9878, Oshkosh 9887, Windhover 9966
Wyoming: True 9996

Endowments

Alabama: Alabama 1, Blount 14, Brock 16, Bruno 17, Crampton 30, Hearin 37, Hill 39, Moody 54, Moore 55, **Vulcan 73**, Webb 75
Arizona: Dee 94, **Globe 101**, Green 102, **Kieckhefer 113**, Linde 117, Lovell 119, Morris 124, Piper 130, Steele 142, Sterne 143
Arkansas: Arkansas 156, **Frueauff 161**, Murphy 167, Northwest 169, Ross 174, Taylor 179, Walker 185, White 187
California: Amgen 219, Aratani 230, **Atkinson 240**, Ayrshire 247, Barker 257, Bay 264, **Beavers 268**, Bren 320, Burch 334, **Cantor 354, Castagnola 366**, Community 407, Copley 416, Dachs 435, Darling 440, Davies 446, Finley 507, Flora 521, Fluor 523, Garland 556, Gellert 559, Goldsmith 599, Haas 635, Hutton 694, Jacobs 708, Jones 728, **K.L. 736**, Kirchgessner 762, Koshland 777, Levine 809, Lipman 817, **Ludwick 830**, Lutz 833, Mabie 839, McBean 865, Mosher 920, Norris 940, Northrop 942, Oppenheimer 955, Peppers 991, Philibosian 1003, Pickford 1005, Rudd 1073, **Schlinger 1102**, Smith 1160, Smullin 1169, Stauffer 1188, Stern 1195, Tesuque 1234, Thornton 1235, Thornton 1236, Tuohy 1247, Ueberroth 1248, Wasserman 1281, Wilbur 1305, Wollenberg 1317
Colorado: Chambers 1354, Community 1357, Community 1358, Community 1359, Hughes 1393, **Malone 1415**, Pioneer 1438, Schlessman 1450, Taylor 1464
Connecticut: Barnes 1488, Collis 1513, Community 1516, Garden 1552, Heyman 1567, **Huisking 1570**, Oaklawn 1616, Senior 1647, Stone 1654, Woodward 1678, Zachs 1682
Delaware: Devonwood 1707, **Good 1715**, Parker 1738, Phillips 1739, **Schwartz 1751**
District of Columbia: Bender 1772, Kaye 1815, Kiplinger 1818, **Moriah 1835**, Willard 1861
Florida: Banbury 1889, Community 1940, Community 1947, Dade 1957, **Davis 1964**, Duckwall 1978, Dunspaugh 1981, FPL 2010, **Goldhammer 2026**, Gooding 2028, Greenburg 2034, Keating 2084, Kennedy 2087, **Knight 2097**, Lattner 2104, North 2153, Opler 2158, Rayonier 2189, Rinker 2197, Rosenberg 2206, Southwest 2240, St. Joe 2244, Storer 2252, Sunshine 2258, Toppel 2274, Van Vleet 2277, Waldbaum 2285, Watts 2288, Weaver 2289, Wells 2294
Georgia: Aflac 2311, AGL 2312, Brown 2332, Campbell 2339, Chatham 2346, Chatham 2347, Courts 2364, Cousins 2365, Cox 2367, DuBose 2374, Exposition 2380, Glenn 2399, Harris 2408, Knox 2427, Lanier 2428, Livingston 2435, Moore 2451, Moore 2452, Patterson 2460, Rich 2472, Russell 2478, Savannah 2480, **Scientific 2482**, Smith 2491, Southern 2494, Synovus 2497, Tull 2500
Hawaii: Bank 2535, Watumull 2558
Idaho: Cunningham 2567, Simplot 2575
Illinois: Alsdorf 2590, **Aon 2598**, Bauer 2609, Blair 2621, Butler 2646, Chicago 2660, Crown 2691, Dillon 2704, Donnelley 2708, Dunard 2712, Emerson 2719, Flagg 2731, Freehling 2737, Grainger 2768, Gray 2771, Hamill 2780, Hermann 2798, Kelly 2830, Logan 2860, Louis 2862, Lurie 2865, Meyer 2896, **Monticello 2904**, Negaunee 2909, Northern 2918, **Woodbury 3082**, Worley 3086
Indiana: Ball 3103, Blue 3107, Branigin 3109, Bussing 3111, Clowes 3120, Community 3127, Community 3132, **Cummins 3136**, DeHaan 3140, Dekko 3142, Elkhart 3145, Fairbanks 3147, Leighton

3191, Lilly 3194, Northern 3215, Ogle 3218, Oliver 3219, OneAmerica 3220, Pulliam 3225, Rolland 3231, Steuben 3241, Unity 3247, Waterfield 3252, Whitley 3258

Iowa: Blank 3268, Community 3278, Cowles 3279, Farver 3283, Hubbell 3297, Kuyper 3304, **Lee 3306**, Maytag 3310, Meredith 3315, Pella 3323, Poweshiek 3325

Kansas: Bane 3345, Baughman 3346, DeVore 3357, Garvey 3363, Hutchinson 3368, Sabatini 3386, Salina 3387, Sullivan 3396, Sunderland 3397

Kentucky: Brown 3409, Community 3415, Cralle 3416, Keeneland 3432, Norton 3441, Reed 3447, Rosenthal 3450, Sutherland 3451

Louisiana: Almar 3459, Baton Rouge 3462, **Biedenharn 3463**, Booth 3464, Diboll 3473, Freeman 3480, Huie 3488, Jones 3491, **Merkle 3500**, RosaMary 3507

Maine: Alfond 3521, Alfond 3523, **Ford 3533**, King 3545, Libra 3546, Maine 3548, **River 3554**

Maryland: Abell 3559, Baltimore 3568, **Blaustein 3575**, Brown 3578, Delaplaine 3614, Eliasberg 3620, France 3632, Helena 3646, Henson 3648, Hirschhorn 3650, Hoffberger 3652, Kerr 3661, Knott 3666, Meyerhoff 3691, Meyerhoff 3692, Middendorf 3694, Polinger 3708, Procter 3711, Rathmann 3715, Sheridan 3729, Small 3735, Tucker 3750, Wasserman 3757, **Weinberg 3759**, Weiss 3760, **Zickler 3763**

Massachusetts: Alden 3776, Barr 3791, Berkshire 3801, Cabot 3824, Cabot 3825, Crossroads 3869, DeFreitas 3876, Donahue 3881, **Fidelity 3904**, Fields 3905, Goldberg 3927, Grinspoon 3935, Ham 3940, Highland 3951, Johnson 3970, Linde 4007, Morse 4044, North 4057, Pappas 4066, Pierce 4084, Sadowsky 4121, **Schooner 4131**, Stevens 4163, Stevens 4164, Wallace 4195, Webster 4201

Michigan: **Arcus 4223**, Barry 4227, Branch 4237, Charlevoix 4246, Community 4256, Dow 4286, Dow 4287, Dow 4288, Frankel 4314, Fremont 4315, Gerstacker 4322, Grand 4327, Herrick 4341, Jurries 4350, Ratner 4417, **Sage 4427**, Shelden 4434, Strosacker 4450, Towsley 4461, Wege 4476, Westerman 4478, Wilson 4485

Minnesota: AHS 4497, Ankeny 4505, Bell 4514, **Cafesjian 4527**, Capp 4529, Grand Rapids 4574, Greycoach 4575, Griggs 4577, Huss 4592, Lilly 4606, Marbrook 4612, McNeely 4619, Minnesota 4624, **O'Shaughnessy 4639**, Rupp 4669, Southways 4688, Target 4697, Wells 4721, Winona 4729

Mississippi: Community 4737, Hardin 4747, Irby 4750, Maddox 4753, Riley 4763, **Sullivan 4766**, Vicksburg 4769

Missouri: Community 4798, Curry 4802, Goppert 4819, Green 4822, Helzberg 4829, Jordan 4840, JSM 4841, Lay 4853, Lopata 4859, Reding 4890, Reynolds 4892, Shaw 4901, Sosland 4908, Walker 4922, Ward 4924, Woods 4928

Nebraska: Friedland 4963, Gardner 4965, **Global 4967**, Heuermann 4973, Hitchcock 4975, Merrick 4990

Nevada: Bretzlaff 5024, **Buck 5025, Hilton 5037**, Parasol 5051, Redfield 5055, Smith 5065

New Hampshire: Putnam 5100

New Jersey: Bunbury 5148, Charles 5161, Cowles 5170, **Fanwood 5192**, Grassmann 5213, Holzer 5238, Horizon 5240, Kirby 5279, Krieger 5290, **Lautenberg 5298**, McMullen 5325, **Newcombe 5338**, Schering 5387, Taub 5425, Union 5435, **Wilf 5455**

New Mexico: Cudd 5472, Hubbard 5481, Kind 5483, **Lannan 5484**, Messengers 5489, New Mexico 5491, Taos 5498

New York: A.E. 5506, Adirondack 5517, Alexander 5532, **Atran 5575**, Barker 5599, Barrington 5602, **Barth 5603, Benenson 5620, Brooks 5674**, Carwill 5711, Charina 5731, **China 5750**, Chisholm 5753, Coles 5775, Community 5783, Community 5784, Cummings 5815, Dewar 5856, Dickler 5861, **Dodge 5867**, Dunwalke 5894, Eastern 5902,

Elmezzi 5925, Emerson 5927, **Engelhard 5932**, Fife 5955, **Forbes 5967, Ford 5970, Foundation 5971, Frankel 5976**, Gebbie 6009, Gilder 6029, Gilliam 6031, **Gilman 6033**, Glickenhaus 6042, Goldman 6053, Goldsmith 6060, Greve 6104, **Hauser 6155, Hearst 6161, Hearst 6162, Heineman 6165**, Hermione 6175, IF 6226, Independence 6229, **Joukowsky 6275**, Kaplan 6288, Kautz 6300, Kennedy 6314, Klein 6333, Lastfogel 6380, Lehman 6396, Lemberg 6401, Leonhardt 6403, Link 6429, Littauer 6434, Macdonald 6468, McGonagle 6518, **Mellon 6525, Memton 6529**, Metcalf 6541, **Moore 6571**, Moses 6587, Mostyn 6591, **Noble 6633**, Northern 6638, Nuhn 6644, O'Connor 6645, O'Sullivan 6652, Ohrstrom 6659, **Peierls 6705, Pforzheimer 6721**, Reed 6782, Rhodebeck 6791, **Ritter 6814**, Rose 6833, Rose 6836, Ross 6864, Rubinstein 6876, Ruffin 6880, Schaffer 6911, Schmeelk 6927, Schmitt 6928, Schnurmacher 6931, Shoreland 6968, Siebens 6974, Simons 6988, Simons 6989, **Solomon 7017, Solow 7020, Steel 7052**, Steele 7053, Straus 7086, Sulzberger 7095, **Summerfield 7097**, Sweetgrass 7113, **Tanaka 7120, Vetlesen 7196**, Vidda 7198, Wachtell 7205, **Wallace 7209**, Weinberg 7230, Weissman 7237, White 7251, Widgeon 7255, Woodland 7275

North Carolina: BB&T 7312, Belk 7315, Blumenthal 7320, Bryan 7330, Community 7345, Dover 7356, Duke 7359, Easley 7361, Finley 7367, Fox 7371, Gorelick 7380, Gorelick 7381, Graham 7382, Hanes 7387, Hanes 7388, Mebane 7427, Mills 7429, Morgan 7431, North Carolina 7438, Smith 7476, Smith 7479, Vanderbilt 7501, Weaver 7504, Winston-Salem 7508

Ohio: Andrews 7530, Bee 7542, **Bingham 7549**, Brennan 7554, Britton 7556, Community 7582, Community 7585, Community 7586, **Convergys 7587**, Diamond 7610, Dorn 7612, GAR 7643, Gund 7656, H.C.S. 7658, Haslinger 7664, Hershey 7671, Humphrey 7679, **Kettering 7698**, Kettering 7699, Kramer 7704, M/I 7729, Marietta 7735, Mather 7736, McMaster 7744, Morgan 7760, Morgan 7761, Morgan 7762, Morley 7763, Murch 7766, Murphy 7768, Muskingum 7770, **OMNOVA 7789**, Osteopathic 7791, **Pruina 7809**, Richland 7819, Ritchie 7821, Robbins 7823, Rosenthal 7826, Schlink 7839, Schmidlapp 7841, Scotford 7846, **Scripps 7848**, Semple 7851, Silk 7857, Sisler 7858, Slemp 7860, Stocker 7870, Wayne 7897, **Weatherhead 7899**

Oklahoma: Bovaird 7927, Communities 7931, Hille 7943, McGee 7957, Meinig 7961, Noble 7963, Oxley 7968, Presbyterian 7969, Puterbaugh 7970, Rapp 7971, Records 7972, Sarkeys 7974, Stevens 7980, Tulsa 7984, Viersen 7985, Warren 7987

Oregon: Ackerman 7995, Fohs 8012, Jackson 8024, John 8026, Kinsman 8031, Macdonald 8038, **Schmidt 8055**

Pennsylvania: 1675 8070, AMETEK 8081, Arcadia 8086, **Berman 8104**, Chester 8141, Claneil 8144, Clapp 8145, Deaver 8165, DeGol 8167, Eden 8182, **Federation 8197**, Ferree 8199, Fisher 8205, Fourjay 8209, Graham 8222, Hansen 8235, Heinz 8240, Heinz 8241, Heinz 8242, **Heinz 8243**, Hillman 8249, Hillman 8250, Honickman 8255, Hopwood 8257, Hunt 8261, Independence 8266, Jennings 8272, Kelly 8283, Luzerne 8317, Maslow 8327, McCune 8331, McCune 8332, McFeely 8334, McKenna 8337, McKinney 8339, McLean 8340, Phoenixville 8381, Pierce 8382, Rees 8401, Reidler 8402, Rockwell 8408, **Seraph 8434**, Shaffer 8436, Simmons 8441, Simonds 8442, Stabler 8455, Trees 8480, Wyomissing 8509

Rhode Island: **Amica 8518**, Carter 8522, Daniels 8530, McCarthy 8548, van Beuren 8561

South Carolina: Abney 8564, Bruce 8571, Cline 8580, Daniel 8585, First 8587, Springs 8617

South Dakota: South Dakota 8631

Tennessee: Assisi 8638, **Bridgestone 8646**, Hamico 8684, Johnson 8697, Phillips 8716, Plough 8718,

Rust 8724, Stokely 8730, Tucker 8735, Wilson 8744

Texas: Abell 8749, Alkek 8754, Bass 8778, Belo 8787, Brackenridge 8793, Cain 8808, Carter 8816, Cockrell 8835, Community 8842, Cook 8845, Cullen 8854, Doss 8869, Dougherty, 8870, Dunn 8872, East 8876, Educational 8878, Elkins 8883, Fair 8891, Fikes 8899, Finger 8900, Fish 8902, Franklin 8907, Gulf 8926, Herzstein 8949, Hoglund 8956, Houston 8960, Houston 8961, Huffington 8963, Jamail 8970, Kahn 8980, Keith 8982, Kinder 8994, Klabzuba 8996, Kokosky 9000, Kronkosky 9002, Light 9011, Lyons 9024, Mayborn 9033, McCullough 9041, McDermott 9043, McGovern 9044, Mitte 9067, Moss 9078, Perkins 9116, Rachofsky 9139, Reynolds 9145, Richardson 9147, Rockwell 9154, Schutte 9173, Scurlock 9175, Simmons 9189, Smith 9195, **Starling 9210**, Sterling 9212, Sturgis 9216, Summerlee 9217, Sumners 9218, Waggoner 9256, Wolens 9286, Wortham 9292, Young 9295, Zeller 9298

Utah: Browning 9308, Stewart 9345, **Wishnick 9353**

Virginia: Beazley 9376, Cabell 9381, Flagler 9417, Folger 9418, Herndon 9437, Kanter 9445, Mars 9466, Moore 9478, Northern 9486, Reynolds 9503, Robins 9506, Titmus 9527, Universal 9531, Washington 9534, **Winkler 9542**

Washington: Ackerley 9547, Blue 9559, Cowles 9574, Cowles 9575, Dimmer 9579, Harder 9600, **Hemingway 9606**, Klorfine 9619, Milgard 9641, Miller 9642, Norcliffe 9650, Wright 9707

West Virginia: Maier 9725, Tucker 9736

Wisconsin: Cleary 9774, Community 9780, Cornerstone 9781, Four 9803, Hess 9816, **Kohler 9839**, Kohler 9840, Krause 9841, Ladish 9846, Lubar 9851, Marshfield 9861, Mead 9867, Miller 9875, Munson 9880, Oshkosh 9885, Peterson 9896, Pick 9899, Racine 9906, Schoenleber 9921, Sensient 9922, Stock 9939, **Thrivent 9949**, West 9964, Wisconsin 9967

Wyoming: Community 9977, Ellbogen 9981, McMurry 9985, **Schultz 9990**

Equipment

Alabama: Blount 14, Bruno 17, Community 23, Community 24, Crampton 30, Hearin 37, Hill 39, Kaul 40, Meyer 52, Smith 63, Webb 75

Alaska: Alaska 79, Rasmuson 85

Arizona: Arizona 87, Dee 94, Gesner 100, **Globe 101, Johnson 112, Kieckhefer 113**, Ottens 128, Piper 130

Arkansas: **Frueauff 161**, Northwest 169, Ross 174, **Tyson 182**, Walker 185

California: Ackerman 193, Ahmanson 198, Alafi 201, Amateur 214, Auen 242, Ayrshire 247, **Baker 252**, Bannerman 255, Barker 257, Baxter 262, Bireley 292, Bothin 309, Brownlee 329, Buck 330, **Bull 331**, Center 369, Change 373, **Christensen 384**, Collins 397, Community 401, Community 403, Community 405, Connell 412, Copley 416, Cowell 423, Crail 426, Crockett 430, Danford 438, Darling 440, **Delano 449, DJ & T 458**, Doheny 460, Drum 470, Eisner 481, Firedoll 508, **First 512**, Fleishhacker 518, Flora 521, French 536, Fresno 537, Gamble 549, Garland 556, Gasser 557, Gellert 559, GenCorp 560, Ghidotti 571, Gilmore 578, Gogian 588, Goldman 595, Good 602, Gumbiner 631, Haas 635, Haas 636, Hannon 644, Hedco 663, Heller 666, Hoag 678, Hughes 690, Humboldt 691, Hutton 694, Irwin 700, Jewett 718, Jones 728, **Keck 750**, Kirchgessner 762, Kvamme 781, Leichtag 801, Lesher 805, Ludwick 829, Lund 831, Lurie 832, Lux 834, Lytel 836, **M & T 837**, Marin 854, **McConnell 870**, McKesson 879, McLean 880, Mead 881, Mental 886, Mericos 889, Michelson 895, Miller 901, Monterey 910, Moore 912, Mosher 920, Norris 940, Norton 943, Orange 957, Outhwaite 966, Pacific 970, **Packard 972**, Parker 979, Parsons 980, Pasadena 982, Patron 983, **Peterson 996**, Rancho 1031, Rudd 1073, San

Finch 7366, Finley 7367, Goodrich 7378, Hanes 7387, Hanes 7388, Janirve 7404, Mills 7429, Polk 7449, Reynolds 7457, Robertson 7466, Smith 7479, Southern 7481, Van Houten 7500, Weaver 7504

North Dakota: Fargo 7514, Leach 7516, North Dakota 7519, North Dakota 7520, Stern 7521

Ohio: Abington 7524, Ashland 7533, Ashtabula 7534, Austin 7536, Barberton 7539, Bee 7542, **Bingham 7549,** Brentwood 7555, Bruening 7558, Bryan 7559, **Cardinal 7567,** Cincinnati 7574, Codrington 7578, Community 7581, Community 7583, Community 7584, Community 7585, Corbett 7590, Corbin 7591, Coshocton 7593, **Covenant 7595,** Dana 7599, Dater 7600, David 7601, Dayton 7603, Diebold 7611, Dorn 7612, Fairfield 7622, Fifth 7626, First 7629, Fox 7637, Frohman 7641, GAR 7643, **Geisse 7646,** Greene 7653, Haslinger 7664, Hershey 7671, Hoover 7674, Hoover 7675, Humphrey 7679, Iddings 7682, Jergens 7689, Jewish 7690, **Kettering 7698,** Kettering 7699, Kulas 7706, Lehner 7709, Levin 7712, Licking 7714, Loeb 7721, Lubrizol 7725, Marietta 7735, Mathile 7737, Miami 7748, Middletown 7749, Miniger 7756, Morgan 7760, Morgan 7762, Murphy 7768, Murphy 7769, Muskingum 7770, Nordson 7781, Ohio 7784, Osteopathic 7791, Prentiss 7806, Reeves 7814, Reinberger 7815, Richland 7819, Ritchie 7821, Russell 7827, Saint 7830, Salem 7831, Schlink 7839, Schmidlapp 7841, Schott 7842, Scioto 7845, **Scripps 7848,** Semple 7851, Sisler 7858, Slemp 7860, Smith 7863, Spaulding 7865, Springfield 7866, Stark 7867, Stocker 7870, Stranahan 7872, Stranahan 7873, Tait 7875, **Timken 7880,** Troy 7886, Tuscarawas 7890, Van Wert 7891, Wallace 7894, Watson 7896, Wayne 7897, White 7905, Wodecroft 7912, Wolfe 7915, Youngstown 7920

Oklahoma: Bernsen 7925, Bovaird 7927, Community 7932, **Ethics 7935,** Gelvin 7938, Goddard 7939, Helmerich 7942, Hille 7943, Inasmuch 7944, Kaiser 7948, Kerr 7949, Mabee 7954, McGee 7957, McMahon 7959, Noble 7963, Oklahoma 7964, Oklahoma 7965, Presbyterian 7969, Puterbaugh 7970, Rapp 7971, Sarkeys 7974, Share 7977, Southern 7979, Tulsa 7984, Viersen 7985

Oregon: Adler 7996, Braemar 8001, Carpenter 8003, Chambers 8004, Collins 8007, Collins 8008, Collins 8009, Ford 8013, Four 8015, Jeld 8025, Johnson 8027, Kinsman 8031, Meyer 8042, Oregon 8049, Schnitzer 8056, Swigert 8061, Swindells 8062, Tektronix 8063, Tucker 8065, Wessinger 8067, Young 8069

Pennsylvania: **Alcoa 8075,** AMETEK 8081, Arcadia 8086, Arkema 8089, Baker 8092, Blanchard 8111, Born 8113, Bradley 8115, Central 8135, Centre 8136, Century 8137, **Cestone 8138,** Cestone 8139, Claneil 8144, **Colcom 8150,** Community 8153, Community 8154, Community 8155, Connelly 8157, Crels 8163, **Dominion 8173,** DSF 8178, Eden 8182, Erie 8188, Fels 8198, First 8202, FISA 8204, Fisher 8205, Foundation 8208, Fourjay 8209, Genuardi 8213, Grundy 8228, Heinz 8241, Heinz 8242, **Heinz 8243,** Hillman 8249, Hillman 8250, Hirtzel 8253, Huston 8263, Huston 8264, Jennings 8272, Justus 8276, Katz 8281, Kavanagh 8282, **Kennametal 8284,** Keystone 8285, Keystone 8286, Kline 8293, Laurel 8301, Lehigh Valley 8303, Little 8313, McCune 8332, McFeely 8334, McKenna 8337, McLean 8340, Mellon 8344, Mellon 8346, Miller 8352, Moore 8358, Morris 8359, Nelson 8362, Penn 8371, Phillips 8380, Phoenixville 8381, **PPG 8394, Presser 8395,** Rees 8401, Rockwell 8408, **Seraph 8434,** Shenango 8438, Simonds 8442, Smith 8443, Smith 8444, Smith 8445, Snee 8446, Sordoni 8450, Stabler 8455, Stackpole 8456, Trees 8480, Trexler 8481, Truman 8483, Wachovia 8494, Widener 8502, Wyomissing 8509, York 8511

Puerto Rico: Puerto Rico 8515

Rhode Island: Brooks 8520, Daniels 8530, McCarthy 8548, Rhode Island 8551, **Textron 8559**

South Carolina: Abney 8564, Bruce 8571, Byerly 8572, Central 8577, Chapin 8579, Coastal 8581, Community 8583, Community 8584, Daniel 8585, **Roe 8607,** Self 8610, Sims 8611, Spartanburg 8616, Springs 8617

South Dakota: Sioux Falls 8630, Vucurevich 8634

Tennessee: Assisi 8638, Benwood 8644, Christy 8654, Community 8660, East 8671, Ezell 8676, Frist 8679, HCA 8690, Jeniam 8695, Johnson 8697, **Maclellan 8704,** Martin 8708, Phillips 8716, Plough 8718, Tonya 8734

Texas: Abell 8749, Amarillo 8758, Anderson 8762, Austin 8768, Bass 8777, Bridwell 8797, Brumley 8800, Cailloux 8807, Cameron 8812, Carter 8816, CH 8823, Coastal 8833, Communities 8839, Community 8840, Community 8841, Community 8842, Constantin 8843, Cowden 8848, Cullen 8854, Dallas 8855, Doss 8869, Dougherty, 8870, Eady 8875, Edwards 8880, Elkins 8883, Esping 8886, Fair 8891, Farish 8894, Fikes 8899, Fisch 8901, Gulf 8926, Haggerty 8932, Halsell 8936, Hamman 8938, Herzstein 8949, Hightower 8950, Hillcrest 8952, Hoblitzelle 8955, Hoglund 8956, Houston 8960, Houston 8961, Johnson 8974, Jones 8975, Jonsson 8977, Keith 8982, Kempner 8987, King 8995, Klabzuba 8996, **Kleberg 8999,** Koehler 9001, Kronkosky 9002, Light 9011, Lightner 9012, Lubbock 9021, Lyons 9024, McDermott 9043, McKee 9045, Meadows 9049, Meredith 9054, Mitte 9067, Moody 9070, Moss 9078, Newman 9090, **Oldham 9100,** Once 9101, Owen 9107, Peterson 9120, Priddy 9137, Pryor 9136, PSH 9137, Rachal 9138, Rachofsky 9139, Reynolds 9145, Richardson 9147, Rockwell 9154, Sams 9163, San Angelo 9165, San Antonio 9166, Scott 9174, Simmons 9188, Smith 9191, Smith 9195, Smith 9197, Speas 9206, Speas 9207, Stark 9209, Stemmons 9211, Sterling 9212, Strake 9215, Sturgis 9216, Summerlee 9217, Swinney 9222, Tapeats 9223, Temple 9227, **Tenet 9229,** Tennessee 9230, Tocker 9236, Triad 9239, Trull 9240, Vale 9246, Waco 9255, Waggoner 9256, Walsh 9261, Ward 9263, White 9279, Wolslager 9290, Wright 9294, Zachry 9296, Zephyr 9299

Utah: ALS 9301, Ashton 9303, Bamberger 9305, Burton 9309, Dumke 9315, Dumke 9316, Eccles 9317, Eccles 9319, Esther 9321, Hemingway 9328, Stewart 9345, Swanson 9346

Vermont: Lintilhac 9359, Mergens 9360

Virginia: Alleghany 9367, American 9368, Beazley 9376, Cabell 9381, Camp 9382, Carter 9387, Community 9402, Foundation 9419, Fralin 9420, **Gannett 9428,** Graves 9433, Gwathmey 9435, Landmark 9455, Lynchburg 9463, Mars 9466, McGlothlin 9469, Memorial 9474, Morgan 9479, Norfolk 9484, **Norfolk 9485,** Northern 9486, Parsons 9493, Perry 9495, Portsmouth 9498, Robins 9506, Scott 9513, Staunton 9521, SunTrust 9523, Titmus 9527, Washington 9534, Weissberg 9536, **Winkler 9542**

Washington: Anderson 9551, Archibald 9553, Blue 9559, **Boeing 9560,** Bullitt 9563, Cheney 9569, Community 9571, Dimmer 9579, **Edwards 9580,** Foster 9588, Foundation 9589, Fuchs 9590, Grays 9597, **Hemingway 9606, Kongsgaard 9620,** Lockwood 9631, Lucky 9632, Lynn 9633, Martin 9634, McEachern 9638, Medina 9640, Milgard 9641, Miller 9642, Murdock 9644, Nesholm 9647, Norcliffe 9650, Quixote 9667, Seattle 9680, Tacoma 9693, **Weyerhaeuser 9703,** Wilburforce 9705

West Virginia: Chambers 9713, Community 9716, Daywood 9717, Huntington 9721, Kanawha 9723, Maier 9725, McDonough 9726, Parkersburg 9730, Schenk 9732

Wisconsin: Alexander 9741, Alliant 9742, Banta 9752, Beloit 9757, Bishop 9759, **Bless 9761, Bradley 9763,** Bradshaw 9764, Clark 9773, Community 9777, Community 9778, Community 9779,

Community 9780, Cornerstone 9781, Cudahy 9785, Dudley 9792, Green Bay 9810, Holz 9817, Johnson 9826, **Kohler 9839,** Kohler 9840, Lakeview 9848, Lunda 9852, Madison 9854, Marshfield 9861, Mead 9867, Menasha 9869, Miller 9875, Milwaukee 9876, Munson 9880, Oshkosh 9885, Oshkosh 9887, Peterson 9896, Racine 9906, Rennebohm 9910, Stock 9939, Stuart 9943, **T & O 9946, Taylor 9947,** U.S. 9952, **Wagner 9957,** Walter 9959, Waukesha 9960, West 9964, Wisconsin 9967, Witte 9968, WPS 9970, **Young 9972**

Wyoming: Community 9977, Kerr 9983, McMurry 9985, **Schultz 9990**

Exchange programs

California: Aratani 230, Drum 470, Flora 521, **Strauss 1203**

Colorado: Summit 1463, Yampa 1477

Connecticut: **Lingnan 1587**

District of Columbia: Mazda 1828

Georgia: Lee 2432

Illinois: Charleston 2657

Indiana: Henry 3165, Waterfield 3252

Iowa: Community 3278

Maryland: Higginson 3649, Wasserman 3757

Massachusetts: Island 3965

Michigan: Community 4252

Minnesota: Oswald 4645

New Jersey: McMullen 5325

New York: Alexander 5532, **Atran 5575,** Berg 5621, Freeman 5981, Gould 6083, **Kade 6281, Kunstadter 6362, Lauder 6383,** Mitsui 6561, Reed 6782, **Reynolds 6790, Trust 7168**

Ohio: Fox 7638, Murphy 7769

Oklahoma: Puterbaugh 7970

Pennsylvania: AMETEK 8081, Smith 8445

Tennessee: **Bridgestone 8646,** Community 8660

Texas: Houston 8960, Lyons 9024

Washington: **Samis 9675**

Wyoming: **Schultz 9990**

Fellowships

Alabama: Dixon 32, Moody 54

Alaska: CIRI 83

Arizona: Dougherty 96, Piper 130

California: Aratani 230, Avery 244, Baxter 263, Bay 264, Bright 322, California 349, **Cantor 354, Capote 358, ChevronTexaco 380, Christensen 384, Compton 409,** Connell 412, **Draper 466,** Drum 470, Fitzgerald 514, Fleishhacker 518, Flora 521, GenCorp 560, Genentech 563, **Getty 570,** Giannini 572, **Glenn 581,** Haynes 659, **Hertz 670,** Jones 728, **Joseph 730,** Koret 774, Lux 834, Mericos 889, Morgan 915, Northrop 942, **Packard 972,** Parsons 980, Parvin 981, Price 1016, **Righteous 1050,** Roth 1071, San Francisco 1088, **Schlinger 1102,** Schlinger 1103, **Smith 1161,** Stauffer 1188, Synopsys 1223, Taube 1228, Towbes 1241, **Unocal 1252,** Wattis 1283

Colorado: Colorado 1356, Trueblood 1466, **Weaver 1469**

Connecticut: Childs 1510, **Deloitte 1527,** Donaghue 1529, Fippinger 1540, **GE 1553,** Larsen 1579, Lehrman 1584, Rosenthal 1638

Delaware: **Schwartz 1751**

District of Columbia: Aid 1765, Cafritz 1780, **Fannie 1793,** Gudelsky 1805, **Kennedy 1816, National 1838, Phillips 1841,** Replogle 1846, Roshan 1847

Florida: **Davis 1964,** Engelberg 1994, Opler 2158, **Picower 2169,** Russell 2212, **Skelly 2237,** St. Joe 2244, St. Petersburg 2245, Van Vleet 2277, **von Liebig 2283**

Georgia: Aflac 2311, **Coca-Cola 2352,** Lee 2432, Smith 2491, Watson 2509

Hawaii: Watumull 2558

Illinois: Arthur 2601, Blair 2621, Brinson 2633, Butler 2646, Chicago 2661, Crown 2691, Deere 2699, **Graham 2767**, Grainger 2768, **Irwin 2814, MacArthur 2868, Monticello 2904, Mundi 2908**, Olin 2925, Schmitt 2987, **Scholl 2989, Searle 2994**, Siragusa 3009, **Spencer 3015, State 3019**, Steans 3021, Tellabs 3034, Washington 3058

Indiana: Bussing 3111, Clowes 3120, **Guidant 3159, Lilly 3192**, Lilly 3194

Iowa: Maytag 3310, McElroy 3313

Kansas: **Beren 3348**, Capitol 3350

Kentucky: Good 3422

Louisiana: Jones 3491

Maine: Smith 3556, Switzer 3557

Maryland: **Casey 3585**, Deutsch 3616, **Hughes 3654**, ISE 3656, **Life 3677**, Meyerhoff 3692, **Nasdaq 3700**, Rathmann 3715

Massachusetts: Barr 3791, Berkshire 3801, Cabot 3825, **Grass 3931, Iacocca 3963**, King 3981, Morse 4044, Pappas 4066, Rappaport 4093, **Schooner 4131**, Shapiro 4136

Michigan: **Earhart 4291, H.I.S. 4334**

Minnesota: Bush 4524, Buuck 4526, Jerome 4595, **Larson 4603**, McKnight 4617

Mississippi: Hardin 4747

Missouri: **Francis 4816, Kauffman 4843**, Schweppe 4899, Sosland 4908

Nebraska: Heuermann 4973

New Hampshire: New Hampshire 5098

New Jersey: Alcatel 5110, **Allen 5111, Barbour 5124**, Bard 5125, **Dow 5184, Johnson 5261**, Knowles 5283, McMullen 5325, **Newcombe 5338, Pfeiffer 5351, Puffin 5362, Rippel 5368**, Schering 5387, Upton 5436, Zobel 5464

New Mexico: Frost 5476, Holt 5480, **Lannan 5484**

New York: Achelis 5513, Avery 5581, Berg 5621, Bodman 5647, Carr 5708, **China 5750, Commonwealth 5779**, Community 5783, Community 5785, Corning 5794, **Dedalus 5847, Diamond 5858, Dreyfus 5886**, Dunwalke 5894, Dyson 5898, **Echoing 5905, EHA 5912, Ford 5970, Foundation 5971, Frankel 5976**, Freeman 5981, **Friends 5990**, Gilder 6029, Gilliam 6031, Gilman 6032, **Goldman 6052**, Goldman 6053, Grand 6086, **Grant 6090, Grant 6092**, Griffis 6107, **Guggenheim 6118, Guggenheim 6119**, Haas 6126, **Hartford 6150, Hearst 6161, Hearst 6162**, Heckscher 6164, **Heineman 6165**, Hughes 6209, **IBM 6221**, Jewish 6260, **JM 6263**, Kaplan 6288, Kautz 6300, Kennedy 6314, Klee 6329, **Klingenstein 6338, Klingenstein 6340, Kopf 6348**, Kornfeld 6350, **Kress 6357**, Lang 6374, Lemberg 6401, **Li 6418, Liebmann 6421**, Lindner 6426, Link 6428, Link 6429, Lortel 6447, **Luce 6453, Lurcy 6458**, Macdonald 6468, McCann 6514, **Mellon 6525, Mercer 6532, Merrill 6537**, Milbank 6547, Mitsui 6561, Moody's 6569, **Morgan 6577, National 6604**, New York 6613, New York 6620, **Open 6665, Overbrook 6675**, Perkin 6717, **Pforzheimer 6721**, Reed 6782, Revson 6789, **Rockefeller 6825, Rockefeller 6826**, Rubinstein 6876, **Schepp 6917, Schlumberger 6926, Skadden 6998**, Snow 7011, Solow 7019, **Solow 7020**, Soros 7024, **Starr 7048**, Triad 7162, **Tsadra 7169, Watson 7220, Wenner 7244, Whiting 7253, Whitney 7254**, Wilson 7264

North Carolina: Biddle 7317, Cemala 7337, Dover 7356, Duke 7359, Finley 7367, **Nickel 7436**, North Carolina 7439

Ohio: Lubrizol 7725, Muskingum 7770, **Scripps 7848, Wexner 7904**

Oklahoma: Hille 7943, Kerr 7949, **Schusterman 7975**, Tulsa 7984

Oregon: Haugland 8018, Intel 8022, Oregon 8049

Pennsylvania: **Aircast 8074, Alcoa 8075**, Hirtzel 8253, Independence 8266, Lilliput 8311, Lindback 8312, Measey 8342, **Presser 8395, Scaife 8425**, Steinman 8459, **Templeton 8475**

Rhode Island: **Dorot 8531**, Rhode Island 8551

South Carolina: Abney 8564, Kane 8596

Tennessee: **Bridgestone 8646**, Durham 8670

Texas: Coastal 8833, Cockrell 8835, Cullen 8854, Hankamer 8939, Houston 8960, Houston 8961, Kempner 8987, Mitte 9067, Reynolds 9145, Rockwell 9154, **Shell 9181**, Simmons 9188, **Starling 9210**, Sterling 9212, Summerlee 9217, Sumners 9218, Wichita 9280

Utah: Burton 9309, Eccles 9317

Vermont: Lintilhac 9359

Virginia: **Blue 9379, de Beaumont 9408, Mustard 9481**, Olsson 9491, Weissberg 9536, **Winkler 9542**

Washington: **Blakemore 9558**, Blue 9559, Norcliffe 9650, Quixote 9667, Russell 9673

Wisconsin: **Bradley 9763**, Eastman 9795, Johnson 9826, Menasha 9869, Miller 9875

Wyoming: Ellbogen 9981

Film/video/radio

California: Ayrshire 247

Georgia: Glenn 2399

New York: **Ford 5970, Rubin 6872**

Pennsylvania: Baker 8092

Rhode Island: Rhode Island 8551

Texas: Summerlee 9217

General/operating support

Alabama: Alabama 1, Alfa 2, AmSouth 5, **Bashinsky 11**, Bedsole 12, Blount 14, Brock 16, Caring 18, Community 23, Community 25, Compass 28, **Corman 29**, Crampton 30, Finlay 33, Hearin 37, Kaul 40, Lowe 45, Meyer 52, Moody 54, Protective 58, Russell 60, Stephens 65, **Vulcan 73**, Webb 75, Wyker 77

Alaska: Alaska 79, Doyon 84

Arizona: A.P.S. 86, Arizona 87, Aurora 88, Dee 94, **Gagarin 99, Globe 101**, Green 102, **Kleckhefer 113**, Linde 117, Lovell 119, Marley 120, Morris 124, Neely 125, Ottens 128, Phelps 129, Piper 130, Steele 142, Sterne 143

Arkansas: Altheimer 155, Arkansas 156, Blue 157, Bradberry 159, **Frueauff 161**, Murphy 167, Northwest 169, Rockefeller 173, Ross 174, Schmieding 175, Trinity 181, White 187

California: 324 190, Ackerman 193, Adams 194, Alliance 204, Alpert 207, Alpert 208, **Altman 211, Amado 212, American 217**, Amgen 219, Anaheim 220, Anderson 221, **Appleton 225**, Arata 229, Aratani 230, **Arkay 235**, Arntz 236, Atkinson 239, Atlas 241, Auen 242, **Baker 252**, Bannerman 255, Barker 257, Bauer 261, Baxter 262, Bay 264, **Bechtel 269**, Bechtel 270, Bella 275, Benbough 276, Berry 284, Bettingen 286, Bickerton 288, Bireley 292, Blue 296, Bohnett 300, Boswell 308, Bowes 311, Bradley 315, Brenner 321, Bright 322, Broad 323, Broccoli 326, Brooks 327, Brotman 328, Brownlee 329, Buck 330, **Bull 331**, Burch 334, Burlock 335, **C.S. 340, Caddock 343**, California 345, California 346, California 348, California 350, Callison 351, **Cantor 354**, Capdevilla 356, Carsey 361, Carson 362, Caruso 363, Chapman 374, Cheeryble 377, Cheesecake 378, **Chiron 383**, Cisco 388, Clorox 389, Colburn 394, Collins 397, Columbia 399, Community 404, Community 406, Community 407, **Compassion 408, Compton 409, Cortopassi 420**, Crail 426, Crean 428, Crockett 430, Daly 437, Davies 446, **Day 447**, de Dampierre 448, Disney 456, **Disney 457, DJ & T 458**, Doheny 460, Douglas 464, **Draper 466**, Drown 469, Drum 470, Durfee 471, East 474, Eisner 481, **Environment 487**, Eucalyptus 489, Factor 491, Field 503, Fieldstone 506, Finley 507, Firedoll 509, **Firelight 509**, First 511, **First 512**, Fleishhacker 518, Flintridge 520, Flora 521, Fluor 523, Follis 525, Foothills 526, Forest 527, **Foundation 529**, Friedman 538, Friedman 539, **Fund 542**, Gaia 545, Gap 551, Garland 556, Geffen

558, Gellert 559, Geschke 568, Getty 569, Gill 576, Gilmore 578, Glickman 582, Global 583, Godric 586, Gold 590, Goldman 597, Gonda 601, Good 602, **Good 603, Google 606**, Grammer 610, Greer 618, Gross 621, Grout 624, Gruber 626, **GSF 627**, Gumbiner 631, Haas 635, Haas 636, Haas 637, Hager 638, Hale 639, Hannon 645, Harden 647, **Harkham 649**, Heller 666, Hellman 667, Hewlett 671, Hoag 678, Hoffman 682, Hughes 690, **Hume 692**, Hutton 694, Irvine 698, Irvine 699, Irwin 700, **Jack 705**, Jackson 706, Jacobs 708, Jameson 710, Jewett 718, JL 720, Johnson 725, **Joseph 730, K.L. 736, Kalliopeia 740**, Keller 752, King 760, Kingsley 761, Kirchgessner 762, Knight 768, Knott 769, Koret 774, Kvamme 781, Lane 787, Langendorf 788, **Lear 795**, Leatherby 796, Leichtman 802, Lesher 805, Lidow 811, Livingston 822, Los Altos 828, Lund 831, Lurie 832, Lutz 833, Lux 834, Lytel 836, **M & T 837**, Maag 838, Majestic 848, Marin 854, **Marisla 855, Mattel 861**, McBean 866, McCarthy 868, McCoy 871, McCune 872, McKay 877, McKesson 879, McLean 880, Mental 886, Mericos 889, Metabolife 891, Milken 897, Milken 898, Miller 901, Monterey 910, Moore 912, Morgan 915, Morgenstern 916, Mosher 920, Mudd 924, Murphy 928, Nestle 935, Newhall 936, Nissan 939, Norris 940, Norton 943, Noyce 944, **Omidyar 952, On 953**, Oppenheimer 955, Orange 957, Orfalea 958, Osher 961, Outhwaite 966, Pacific 970, **Packard 972**, Parker 979, Parsons 980, Parvin 981, Pauley 984, Pell 987, Penney 990, Peppers 991, Peters 993, **Peterson 996**, Pfaffinger 997, Pickford 1005, **PMI 1008**, Post 1011, Pottruck 1013, Preuss 1015, Ralphs 1029, Rancho 1031, Ransom 1032, Reid 1036, **Righteous 1050**, Riley 1052, Riordan 1054, **Rivendell 1056**, Rivkin 1057, Roberts 1058, Roennberg 1066, Roth 1071, Rudd 1073, Ryan 1075, **S.G. 1078, Saban 1079**, Sacramento 1080, Saga 1081, San Diego 1087, San Francisco 1088, San Luis 1090, Sandy 1092, **Schuler 1108**, Schwab 1109, **Schwab 1110**, Scott 1114, Segal 1121, Serenity 1128, Shapell 1135, Shapiro 1137, Shasta 1139, Shenandoah 1144, Sierra 1152, Silberstein 1153, Simpson 1157, **Smith 1161**, Smith 1164, Smith 1165, **Smith 1166, Smith 1167**, Smullin 1169, Sobrato 1172, Soda 1173, Solano 1175, Sonora 1178, **Soref 1179**, Springcreek 1185, Stamps 1186, Steele 1189, Stern 1195, Stone 1200, Strauss 1202, **Strauss 1203, Streisand 1204**, Stuart 1206, Stuart 1208, Stulsaft 1210, Taper 1226, Taube 1228, Teichert 1231, Tesuque 1234, Thornton 1235, Thornton 1236, Towbes 1241, Treadwell 1243, Truckee 1244, True 1245, Trust 1246, Ueberroth 1248, Valley 1256, Valley 1257, vanLobenSels 1260, Ventura 1264, Vodafone 1267, Waitt 1275, Warren 1279, **Warsh 1280, WellPoint 1292, Wells 1294**, Werner 1296, Wollenberg 1317, Wood 1318, WWW 1323, Zellerbach 1326

Colorado: Animal 1333, Anschutz 1334, **Anschutz 1335**, Aspen 1338, Bernstein 1343, Bohemian 1345, Bohen 1346, Brett 1349, Buell 1350, **Castle 1352**, Chambers 1354, Colorado 1356, Community 1357, Community 1358, Community 1359, Coors 1360, **Crowell 1361, Daniels 1362**, Denver 1364, Distinguished 1365, Donnell 1368, Edmondson 1373, El Pomar 1374, Falkenberg 1376, **General 1381, Gill 1382**, Hughes 1393, Hunter 1394, Johnson 1398, KBK 1400, Kenney 1401, Lewis 1410, McDonald 1421, **Mercy 1426**, Monfort 1429, Norwood 1433, Pikes 1437, Piton 1439, Price 1442, Rose 1445, Saeman 1448, Schlessman 1450, Schramm 1451, **Seay 1453**, St. John's 1456, **StorageTek 1460**, Taylor 1464, Telluride 1465, **Weaver 1469**, Weckbaugh 1470, Western 1471, Wilhite 1473, Wolf 1475, Yampa 1477

Connecticut: **Aetna 1479**, Baldwin 1487, Barnes 1488, Bissell 1495, Boehringer 1498, Bossidy 1500, Bridgeport 1504, Chilton 1511, Collis 1513, Community 1514, Community 1515, Community 1516, Community 1517, Connecticut 1519,

Conway 1520, Culpeper 1521, **Ettinger 1536**, Fairfield 1537, Fisher 1542, Freas 1548, Goergen 1556, Graustein 1559, Hartford 1563, **Hoffman 1568, Huisking 1570**, International 1571, Lehrman 1584, Liberty 1586, **Lingnan 1587**, Lone 1589, Long 1590, Main 1594, Matthies 1600, **McKenzie 1601**, Meriden 1603, Nevas 1608, **October 1617**, Patricelli 1623, Pequot 1625, Perrin 1626, Pitt 1628, **Praxair 1629**, Rogow 1636, Rosenthal 1638, Saybrook 1643, **Seedlings 1645**, Stone 1654, Tauck 1657, Thompson 1658, Tow 1661, **Tremaine 1662**, Tully 1665, TWS 1666, United 1668, **Valentine 1669**, Vervane 1671, Vik 1672, Whittingham 1676, **Xerox 1680**, Young 1681, **Ziegler 1683**

Delaware: Bishop 1693, Cawley 1696, Chichester 1698, Common 1700, Day 1704, Delany 1705, Devonwood 1707, **Glencoe 1714, Good 1715**, Hall 1718, Hamel 1719, Heuer 1720, Kingsley 1724, Lennox 1726, Mastronardi 1729, MBNA 1730, **Milliken 1732, Neuberger 1735**, Parker 1738, Phillips 1739, Presto 1740, **Raskob 1741**, Romill 1747, Rowland 1749, Struthers 1758, Wasily 1760

District of Columbia: Aid 1765, **Arca 1767**, Arcana 1768, **Banyan 1769, Bauman 1771**, Bender 1772, Bernstein 1775, Block 1776, **Butler 1779**, Cafritz 1780, Community 1785, Coors 1787, **Coyne 1788**, Dimick 1789, **Fannie 1793**, Fernandez 1794, **Foundation 1796**, Fowler 1797, Freed 1798, **Goldberg 1802**, Gottesman 1803, Gudelsky 1805, Harman 1807, **Hill 1809**, Jovid 1814, Kaye 1815, Kimsey 1817, Kiplinger 1818, **Koch 1819, Lambe 1820**, Lehrman 1821, Leonsis 1822, Loughran 1823, Mazda 1828, McGowan 1830, McIntosh 1831, Meyer 1834, **Moriah 1835, Mott 1836**, Munson 1837, **Public 1844**, Reich 1845, Replogle 1846, Sprenger 1848, Spring 1849, Stewart 1850, Strong 1851, **Summit 1852**, Trellis 1853, Vradenburg 1856, **Wallace 1857, Wallace 1858, Winslow 1863**, Wyss 1864

Florida: A Friends' 1866, Ansin 1877, Appleby 1879, **Aurora 1882**, Banbury 1889, Bastien 1892, Batchelor 1893, **Believers 1900**, Bellamy 1902, Blank 1909, Bronfman 1917, **Bryson 1918**, Capital 1924, Caspersen 1927, Castellani 1928, **Chatlos 1932**, Cobb 1935, Community 1947, Community 1949, Conn 1951, Dade 1957, Darden 1960, **Davis 1962, Davis 1964**, Dunspaugh 1981, duPont 1982, duPont 1983, Engelberg 1994, Faigen 1996, **Foundation 2008**, Friedman 2014, Garfinkle 2017, **Goldhammer 2026**, Gooding 2028, Goodwin 2029, Gore 2031, Greenburg 2034, Gronewaldt 2037, Gulf 2042, Jacksonville 2071, Kaufman 2082, Kelly 2086, Kennedy 2087, **Knight 2097**, Kramer 2100, Krauss, 2101, Lattner 2104, Lee 2107, Leiser 2108, Lennar 2109, **Lewis 2114**, Lynn 2120, MacDonald 2121, Madigan 2123, Magill 2124, Maltz 2126, Masters 2131, **Morris 2145**, Mote 2148, North 2153, O'Neil 2155, Opler 2158, Peacock 2165, **Picower 2169**, Pinellas 2170, Publix 2180, Quantum 2181, Rayonier 2189, Rinker 2195, Rooms 2204, Rosenberg 2206, Russell 2212, Ryder 2213, **Scaife 2220**, Schmidt 2225, Sherman 2233, **Sontag 2239**, Stevens 2251, Storer 2252, Stransky 2253, **SWS 2260**, Taishoff 2262, Tangelo 2263, Taylor 2267, Victory 2280, **Vollmer 2282**, Wahlert 2284, Walter 2286, Watts 2288, Wells 2294, Westgate 2296, Wilson 2300, Wolfson 2305, Wollowick 2306

Georgia: AEC 2310, Aflac 2311, Atlanta 2320, Azalea 2322, Beloco 2324, Bradley 2326, Brain 2328, Brown 2331, Brown 2332, Buisson 2333, Callaway 2337, Cawood 2342, Chatham 2346, Chatham 2347, **Coca-Cola 2352**, Community 2355, Community 2358, Community 2362, Cousins 2365, Cox 2368, Day 2371, Delta 2372, Dunn 2375, Endover 2377, Exposition 2380, Flowers 2384, Franklin 2389, Fraser 2390, **Gage 2392**, Georgia 2394, Georgia 2395, **Georgia 2397**, Harland 2407, Harris 2408, Healthcare 2411, Imlay 2417, ING 2418, Jinks 2422, **Keough 2426**, Knox 2427, Lanier 2428, Lee 2432, Lewis 2433,

Livingston 2435, Love 2437, Lubo 2438, **Meyer 2446**, Moore 2451, Moore 2452, North 2458, Patterson 2460, Pitts 2463, Pittulloch 2464, Pope 2467, Rich 2472, RTM 2477, Russell 2478, Sapelo 2479, Savannah 2480, **Scientific 2482**, Southern 2494, Synovus 2497, **Turner 2501**, Wardlaw 2507, Watson 2509, WestPoint 2513, Williams 2514, Wilson 2519, Zeist 2529

Hawaii: Alexander 2530, Anthony 2531, Bank 2535, Hawaiian 2546, HMSA 2547, Hughes 2548, McInerny 2551, Schuler 2552, Vidinha 2557, Watumull 2558, Wilcox 2559, Wong 2560

Idaho: Cunningham 2567, Idaho 2570, **Micron 2571**, Morrison 2572, Nagel 2573, Simplot 2575

Illinois: Abbott 2580, **Allen 2587, Allstate 2588**, Alphawood 2589, AMCORE 2591, **Amsted 2593**, Andrew 2595, Andrew 2596, **Aon 2598**, Arthur 2601, Bauer 2609, Bere 2616, Berner 2617, Bersted 2619, Blair 2621, Blowitz 2623, Blum 2625, **BP 2628, Brach 2630**, Brinson 2633, Bruning 2635, **Brunswick 2636, Burlington 2644**, Butler 2646, Butterworth 2647, Camp 2649, **CH2M 2654**, Charleston 2657, Chicago 2660, Chicago 2661, Chicago 2663, Circle 2666, Coleman 2673, Combs 2674, Comer 2675, Community 2677, Community 2681, Cooper 2683, Crane 2687, Cressey 2689, Crown 2691, Cuneo 2692, Davee 2696, Day 2698, Deere 2699, Deering 2700, **Demos 2702**, Dillon 2704, Donnelley 2706, **Donnelley 2707**, Donnelley 2708, Driehaus 2710, Duchossois 2711, Dunard 2712, DuPage 2713, Eisenberg 2716, Energizer 2721, Fasseas 2726, Field 2728, Firestone 2729, Flagg 2731, Fry 2740, **Galashiels 2742**, Geneseo 2750, Geraldi 2752, Girl's 2757, GKN 2758, **Glenner 2759**, Grainger 2768, Grand 2769, Grant 2770, Gray 2771, Griswold 2773, Halligan 2779, Hamill 2780, Harris 2787, Harris 2788, Harris 2789, Harrison 2790, Hartmarx 2794, Hermann 2798, **Joyce 2820**, Kaplan 2823, Kelly 2830, Kemper 2831, Kendall 2833, Kenny's 2835, Kipper 2840, Kolschowsky 2843, Kovler 2844, Landau 2847, Levi 2855, Little 2859, Logan 2860, Louis 2862, Lumpkin 2864, **MacArthur 2867, MacArthur 2868**, Mander 2873, McCormick 2878, McDougal 2881, McGraw 2882, McMullan 2884, McNeil 2887, Meyer 2896, Millard 2897, Millikin 2900, **Motorola 2906**, Mullen 2907, **Mundi 2908**, Negaunee 2909, Nelson 2911, New 2912, Northern 2918, Olin 2925, Omron 2926, Owens 2929, Payne 2934, Pepper 2936, PepsiAmericas 2937, Perlman 2938, Petersen 2941, **Peterson 2942**, Pick 2943, **Ploughshares 2945**, Polk 2946, Prentice 2947, Prince 2948, **Pritzker 2951**, Redhill 2960, Reese 2961, **Relations 2963**, Rice 2966, Sara 2982, Schmitt 2987, **Scholl 2989**, Seabury 2993, Shaker 2999, **Shifting 3006**, Shirk 3007, Siragusa 3009, Souder 3013, Speh 3014, Sprague 3016, **Square 3018, State 3019**, Steans 3021, Stern 3023, Stuart 3028, Susman 3030, Tawani 3033, Tracy 3037, Trustmark 3039, **Tyndale 3042**, Ullrich 3043, United 3044, **United 3045**, USG 3046, VNA 3049, Ward 3056, White 3067, Wieboldt 3069, **Willow 3074, Woodbury 3082**, Woods 3084, Woodward 3085, Worley 3086, **Wrigley 3088**

Indiana: American 3098, Anderson 3099, Anthem 3102, Ball 3103, Boren 3108, Branigin 3109, Bussing 3111, Central 3116, Clowes 3119, Clowes 3120, Cole 3121, Community 3125, Community 3128, Community 3132, Crown Point 3135, **Cummins 3136**, DeHaan 3140, DeKalb 3141, Dekko 3142, Elkhart 3145, Fairbanks 3147, Foellinger 3149, Ford 3150, Glick 3155, **Goodrich 3157, Guidant 3159**, Harrison 3161, Health 3164, Indiana 3173, Irwin 3174, Irwin 3175, Johnson 3178, Jordan 3180, Journal 3181, Kimball 3182, Kuhne 3187, Leighton 3191, **Lilly 3192**, Lilly 3194, Madison 3197, Mutual 3210, Noble 3214, Northern 3215, Noyes 3216, Oakley 3217, Raker 3226, Ripley 3230, Rolland 3231, Samerian 3234, Simon 3239, Tyson 3246, Vectren 3249, Wabash 3250, Waterfield 3252, West 3256

Iowa: **AEGON 3259**, AmerUs 3261, **Andringa 3262**, Bright 3269, Community 3278, Cowles 3279, Gilchrist 3287, HNI 3293, Hubbell 3297, Kruidenier 3303, Lee 3305, Mansfield 3308, Maytag 3309, Maytag 3310, McElroy 3313, Meredith 3314, Mid-Iowa 3317, Principal 3326, R & R 3327, Seidler 3331, Stine 3335

Kansas: Baughman 3346, **Beren 3348**, Capitol 3350, Cooper 3353, Delta 3354, DeVore 3357, Ellis 3361, Garvey 3363, Garvey 3364, Hansen 3366, Hutchinson 3368, INTRUST 3369, Kansas 3372, Koch 3374, Payless 3380, Powell 3381, Rhoden 3383, Rice 3384, Salina 3387, Sprint 3395, Sullivan 3396, Sunderland 3397, Topeka 3400, Wiedemann 3405

Kentucky: Brown 3410, C.E. 3412, Community 3414, Community 3415, Cralle 3416, E.ON 3417, Gheens 3421, Good 3422, Haywood 3425, Horn 3427, **Humana 3428**, Justice 3431, Keeneland 3432, Klein 3435, Norton 3441, Omnicare 3443, Orleton 3445, Preston 3446, Reed 3447, River 3448, Robinson 3449, Rosenthal 3450, Sutherland 3451, Trager 3452, **Yum! 3457**

Louisiana: Almar 3459, Baptist 3461, **Biedenharn 3463**, Brown 3465, Burton 3467, Coughlin 3470, Diboll 3473, German 3483, Goldring 3484, Huie 3488, Institute 3489, Jones 3491, Keller 3493, **Merkle 3500**, Pennington 3505, Reily 3506, RosaMary 3507, Taylor 3511, Wheless 3514, Wilson 3515, **Woldenberg 3516**, Woolf 3517, Young 3518, Zigler 3520

Maine: Berry 3526, Butnam 3528, Davenport 3531, Fore 3534, Gateway 3537, **Golden 3538**, Great 3539, JTG 3542, King 3545, Libra 3546, **Oak 3552, River 3554, Sandy 3555**, Smith 3556

Maryland: Abell 3559, Abell 3560, Abramson 3561, Allegis 3565, Baker 3566, Blades 3574, **Blaustein 3575**, Blaustein 3576, Blum 3577, Brown 3578, Campbell 3582, Capital 3584, **Casey 3585**, Casey 3586, Chaney 3587, Choice 3589, Clark 3590, Clark 3591, **Cohen 3594**, Columbia 3595, Commonweal 3596, Concordia 3601, Constellation 3602, Davis 3607, **Dean 3610**, Delaplaine 3614, Deutsch 3616, Dresher 3617, Eaton 3619, Eliasberg 3620, England 3622, Freeman 3633, GEICO 3634, Goldsmith 3637, Grace 3638, Helena 3646, **Hendricks 3647**, Higginson 3649, Hirschhorn 3650, Hoffberger 3652, ISE 3656, **Kluge 3663**, Knott 3666, Leidy 3673, Lerner 3674, Lerner 3675, Lockhart 3681, Lockheed 3682, Macht 3683, MARPAT 3684, Marshall 3687, Meyerhoff 3691, Meyerhoff 3692, Mid 3693, Middendorf 3694, **Morningstar 3695**, Mulford 3696, O'Neil 3701, Osprey 3703, Polinger 3708, Price 3709, Provident 3712, Rathmann 3715, Rollins 3718, Rosenberg 3719, Roswell 3722, **Shared 3727**, Small 3734, **Smith 3736**, Straus 3738, Stulman 3739, Sunrise 3740, **Town 3749**, Tucker 3750, Wasserman 3757, **Zickler 3763**

Massachusetts: Abrams 3768, Adams 3771, Adams 3772, **Agostine 3774**, Atchinson 3784, **Azadoutioun 3786**, Babson 3787, Balfour 3790, Barr 3791, Benz 3798, Berkshire 3801, Bertolon 3804, Biogen 3806, BOSE 3810, Boston 3811, Bradley 3814, Bristol 3816, Cabot 3823, Cabot 3824, Cabot 3825, Cambridge 3828, Campbell 3830, Canaday 3831, Cape Cod 3833, Carney 3837, Chahara 3843, Charles 3844, Chase 3847, Childs 3848, Clarke 3849, Clipper 3850, Community 3854, Cox 3862, Cox 3863, Crane 3864, Crane 3865, Crane 3866, Crawford 3867, Crossroads 3869, Davis 3875, DeLuca 3877, Donahue 3881, Dusky 3885, Eastern 3886, Easthampton 3887, Eaton 3888, Ellsworth 3892, Evans 3898, Farnsworth 3899, Fletcher 3912, Foster 3914, Gardinor 3920, Germeshausen 3924, Goldberg 3927, Gordon 3928, Grayson 3932, Greene 3933, Grinspoon 3935, Gross 3937, Harrington 3943, Henderson 3946, Highland 3951, Hinduja 3952, Hoffman 3955, Hopedale 3958, Hyams 3961, Island 3965, Janey 3968, **Jebediah 3969, Kendall 3977**, Kingsbury 3982, Leclerc

4000, Lee 4001, Levy 4005, Liberty 4006, Linde 4007, Linden 4008, Marcus 4022, Massachusetts 4026, Melville 4034, Merck 4035, Mifflin 4038, Miller 4039, Millipore 4040, Morse 4044, New 4050, North 4057, Oral 4061, Peabody 4073, **PerkinElmer 4077**, Perpetual 4078, Pierce 4084, Poss 4087, Putnam 4088, Rasmussen 4094, Ratshesky 4095, **Reebok 4098**, Ribakoff 4102, Rodgers 4110, Rogers 4112, Roy 4114, Rubenstein 4115, Rubenstein 4116, **Schooner 4131**, Schott 4132, Shapiro 4136, Shaw 4139, Sheehan 4140, Siff 4145, Smith 4150, Stearns 4159, Stearns 4160, Stevens 4163, Stevens 4164, Stoddard 4165, Stoico 4166, Stoneman 4168, Stride 4171, Swartz 4175, Talbots 4178, Wallace 4195, **Waterman 4198**, Webster 4201, Wheatland 4204

Michigan: Americana 4218, **Arcus 4223**, Baker 4226, Barry 4227, Besser 4232, Boll 4235, Branch 4237, Burdick 4241, Capital 4243, Christian 4247, Citizens 4249, Cold 4250, Comerica 4251, Community 4255, Community 4256, Consumers 4260, Cook 4261, Cook 4262, Cracchiolo 4263, Cracchiolo 4264, **DaimlerChrysler 4265**, Dalton 4266, Dart 4267, Devereaux 4274, DeVlieg 4275, DeVos 4276, DeVos 4277, DeVos 4278, DeVos 4279, Doornink 4283, Dow 4284, Dow 4286, Dow 4287, Dow 4288, DTE 4289, Farver 4295, **Fetzer 4297**, Fetzer 4298, Ford 4302, Fremont 4315, General 4320, Gerstacker 4322, Gilmore 4324, Hampson 4336, Harding 4337, Herrick 4341, Hudson 4343, Hurst 4344, **Isabel 4346**, Jurries 4350, Kahn 4351, Kalamazoo 4352, **Kellogg 4356**, Kellogg's 4358, Kelly 4359, Kennedy 4360, Knabusch 4362, Knight 4364, **Krauss 4366**, La-Z-Boy 4368, **Legion 4375**, Manoogian 4382, **Manthei 4384**, Marcks 4385, Masco 4387, McGregor 4389, Merillat 4391, Miller 4393, Miller 4394, **Mott 4399**, Mott 4400, Nokomis 4404, Oleson 4405, Parish 4408, Power 4415, Prince 4416, Ratner 4417, **Sage 4427**, Sehn 4432, Shelden 4434, Shepherd 4435, Skillman 4438, Slikkers 4439, Spoelhof 4443, St. Deny's 4444, Steelcase 4446, **Stoddard 4447**, Stolaruk 4448, Sturgis 4452, Tamer 4453, Tauber 4454, Thompson 4457, Timmis 4459, Towsley 4461, **Tubergen 4463**, Upton 4466, **Van Curler 4468**, Vanderweide 4469, **Visteon 4472**, Volkswagen 4473, Weatherwax 4474, Westerman 4478, Whirlpool 4480, Whiting 4482, Wilson 4484, Wilson 4485, Wolters 4487, Wolverine 4488, World 4489, Young 4490

Minnesota: 1988 4491, **3M 4492**, Adams 4495, AHS 4497, **Andersen 4501**, Andersen 4502, Andreas 4503, Ankeny 4505, Arcee 4506, Aslan 4507, Athwin 4508, Bayport 4512, Bell 4514, Bemis 4515, Beverly 4517, Blandin 4520, Bremer 4523, Butler 4525, Buuck 4526, **Cafesjian 4527**, Capp 4529, Cargill 4530, Carolyn 4533, Charlson 4537, Christianson 4539, **CHS 4540**, Davis 4546, Deikel 4548, Deluxe 4549, Driscoll 4555, Duluth 4556, **Ecolab 4557**, Edina 4560, Edwards 4561, Federated 4563, Frey 4566, **Fuller 4567**, General 4570, George 4572, Graco 4573, Greycoach 4575, Greystone 4576, Griggs 4577, Grossman 4578, Grotto 4579, Hardenbergh 4583, Hiawatha 4585, **Homeownership 4587**, HRK 4589, Hubbard 4590, Hudson 4591, Huss 4592, Initiative 4593, Jerome 4595, Kelley 4597, Knowlton 4598, Kopp 4599, Koran 4600, **Land 4602, Larson 4603**, Leonard 4604, Lilly 4606, Marbrook 4612, McCarthy 4614, McKnight 4617, McVay 4620, Meadowood 4621, Minneapolis 4623, Minnesota 4624, National 4630, **Nelson 4632**, O'Neil 4638, **O'Shaughnessy 4639**, Ordean 4643, Oswald 4645, Pacific 4646, **Patterson 4647, Pentair 4649**, Pohlad 4657, Prophet 4658, RBC 4661, Red Wing 4663, Regis 4664, Rivers 4666, Rupp 4669, Securian 4677, Smikis 4687, St. Paul 4690, Star 4691, Sundet 4694, Target 4697, TCF 4699, Tennant 4700, Thorpe 4701, Tozer 4703, **U.S. 4704**, Valspar 4706, Vest 4708, Vintage 4709, Walker 4711,

Wasie 4716, WCA 4718, Wells 4721, Whitney 4728, Winona 4729, **Wood 4731**, Xcel 4732

Mississippi: AmSouth 4733, **Armstrong 4734**, Community 4737, Ergon 4740, Feild 4741, Foundation 4743, Gulf 4745, Irby 4750, Maddox 4753, Mississippi 4758, Riley 4763, **Sullivan 4766**, Walker 4770

Missouri: AJP 4771, Ameren 4772, Andrews 4774, Bernoudy 4783, Boeing 4785, Brown 4788, Brown 4789, Butler 4793, Commerce 4797, Community 4798, Cray 4801, Curry 4802, Danforth 4803, Dula 4806, Emerson 4809, **Enterprise 4810**, Forster 4814, **Francis 4816**, Goppert 4819, H & R 4823, Hall 4824, Hallmark 4825, **Hana 4827**, Helzberg 4829, Ingram 4834, Jenkins 4836, Jewish 4837, Jones 4838, Jordan 4840, Kansas 4842, **Kauffman 4843**, Kauffman 4844, Kellwood 4845, Kemper 4846, Kemper 4848, Kemper 4849, Laclede 4852, Lay 4853, Litzsinger 4856, Long 4858, Lopata 4859, **May 4861**, MFA 4866, Millstone 4867, Musgrave 4870, **Nestle 4872**, Oppenstein 4876, Orscheln 4877, Pershing 4880, Pettus 4882, **Pillsbury 4883**, Pillsbury 4884, PMJ 4885, Pott 4886, Powell 4887, Reding 4890, Reynolds 4892, Saint Louis 4896, Schwartze 4898, Seaworld 4900, Shaw 4901, Shelter 4902, **Singing 4904**, Smurfit-Stone 4906, Sosland 4908, Stern 4909, Trio 4918, Truman 4919, Vatterott 4921, Walker 4922, Woods 4928, Wornall 4929

Montana: Bair 4931, Cinnabar 4935, **Edwards 4936**

Nebraska: Arkoosh 4943, Baer 4944, Buckley 4947, **Buffett 4950**, Commercial 4951, **ConAgra 4953**, Cooper 4954, Durham 4959, Eagle 4960, Friedland 4963, **Global 4967**, Heuermann 4973, Hirschfeld 4974, Hitchcock 4975, James 4980, Kiewit 4983, Kiewit 4984, Kilbourne 4985, Lincoln 4987, Lozier 4988, **McDonald 4989**, Perkins 4996, Swanson 5009, **Union 5012**, Weitz 5016, Wiebe 5017, Woods 5018, Zollner 5020

Nevada: Bretzlaff 5024, **Buck 5025**, Community 5028, Cord 5029, Fairweather 5032, **Hilton 5037**, Nevada 5047, **Omega 5050**, Parasol 5051, Pennington 5053, Sierra 5064, Southwest 5066, **Walsh 5075**, Wendy's 5076

New Hampshire: Bean 5080, Eastman 5087, Foundation 5089, Fuller 5090, Hunt 5093, New Hampshire 5098, Putnam 5100, **Winthrop 5105**

New Jersey: Alcatel 5110, Amirsaleh 5114, Arnold 5117, Baker 5123, **Barbour 5124**, Bard 5125, Bolger 5136, Borden 5138, Brady 5141, Bulova 5147, Bunbury 5148, Cape 5153, **Carlson 5155**, Cooperman 5168, Cowles 5170, Dagish 5176, Danellie 5177, Dodge 5181, **Edison 5186, Eshet 5190, Fanwood 5192, Frankino 5196**, Fund 5199, Gabelli 5200, Goldberg 5209, Halpern 5221, Harbourton 5223, Helm 5230, Hidden 5233, Horizon 5240, **Huber 5244**, Isermann 5253, **Johnson 5261**, Karma 5269, KDK 5273, Kerr 5278, Kirby 5279, Knistrom 5282, Krieger 5290, Leib 5302, Martini 5319, McGraw 5323, MCJ 5324, McMullen 5325, **Merck 5326**, National 5335, Orange 5343, Perrin 5350, Princeton 5357, Provident 5359, Prudential 5360, Rigorous 5367, Roberts 5371, Schenck 5386, Schering 5387, **Schumann 5390**, Schumann 5391, Smilowitz 5406, Smith 5409, Subaru 5415, Sunup 5419, **Syms 5422**, Taub 5425, Thomas 5427, Tuchman 5429, Turrell 5431, Unilever 5434, Upton 5436, Valley 5438, Victoria 5440, **Vollmer 5443**, Willits 5457, **WKBJ 5459**, Zobel 5464

New Mexico: Bancroft 5467, Carlsbad 5469, Domanica 5475, **Gorham 5478**, Kind 5483, **Lannan 5484, Levinson 5486**, Maddox 5487, McCune 5488, New Mexico 5491, Santa Fe 5496, Taos 5498, Thornburg 5501

New York: **Abelard 5508**, Abeles 5509, Abrons 5512, Achelis 5513, Adirondack 5517, Aeneas 5523, Ahavas 5527, Alexander 5532, Alfiero 5534, Allen 5536, Allison 5537, Altman 5543, Altschul 5546, **American 5551, American 5553**, Antz 5560, **Archbold 5563**, Aron 5569, ASDA 5571, **Atran 5575**, Atticus 5576, Auchincloss 5577, **Avon**

5583, Badgeley 5588, Baird 5592, **Baker 5594**, Barker 5599, Barker 5600, **Barth 5603, Bay 5606**, Beaverkill 5610, Bedminster 5611, **Beldon 5614**, Berg 5621, Bernhard 5624, Bingham 5631, **Bismarck 5633**, Block 5638, Bluhdorn 5642, Bodman 5647, Botwinick 5653, Bowne 5655, Boxer 5656, Brach 5657, **Branta 5659**, Briger 5663, Bright 5664, **Bristol 5666**, Brodsky 5668, **Bronfman 5672, Bronfman 5673**, Brown 5676, Buck 5682, Buhl 5684, **Burke 5688**, Butler 5691, **Bydale 5694, C.O.U.Q. 5695**, Carnahan 5706, **Carnegie 5707**, Carson 5709, Cary 5712, Central 5723, Chadwick 5726, Chai 5727, Chanin 5730, Charitable 5733, Chautauqua 5738, **Chazen 5739**, Chernow 5745, Chisholm 5753, **Citigroup 5755**, Claiborne 5758, Clark 5759, **Clark 5760**, Clark 5761, Clark 5762, Cohen 5769, Coles 5775, Community 5782, Community 5784, **Copland 5789**, Corning 5794, Corrigan 5796, Countess 5800, Cowen 5801, Credit 5807, Cricket 5808, **Cummings 5814**, Curran 5816, Dammann 5824, **Dana 5827**, Daphne 5830, **de Hirsch 5840, Delmas 5850, Derossi 5853, Deutsche 5854**, Devlin 5855, Dickler 5861, Dobkin 5866, **Donner 5873**, Dow 5879, **Dramatists 5883**, Dreitzer 5884, Dreyfus 5887, **Dun 5893**, Dunwalke 5894, Dyson 5898, **East 5900, Edouard 5909, EHA 5912**, Elias 5920, Ellis 5923, Elmezzi 5925, **Endowment 5931, Engelhard 5932**, Englander 5933, Equipart 5936, **Essel 5938**, Faulkner 5948, Fife 5955, **Fischel 5959**, Fischer 5960, **Forbes 5967, Ford 5970, Foundation 5971, Frankel 5976, Freeman 5980**, Freeman 5981, **Friends 5990**, Frohring 5993, Galasso 6005, GBRG 6008, Gebbie 6009, Gibson 6025, Gifford 6026, Gilder 6029, Gilman 6032, **Gilman 6033**, Gimbel 6034, Gleason 6039, **Global 6043**, Golden 6046, Goldfrank 6048, **Goldman 6052**, Goldman 6053, **Goldman 6056**, Goldsmith 6060, Goldstein 6061, Golisano 6067, Golub 6070, Gorter 6079, Gottlieb 6081, Gould 6083, **Grant 6091**, Greenberg 6098, Greene 6099, Greve 6104, Griffin 6106, Griffis 6107, Grigg 6108, Gross 6110, Guttman 6124, Haas 6126, Hagedorn 6130, **Halloran 6138**, Harkness 6145, **Harriman 6146**, Harriman 6147, Harris 6148, Harrison 6149, **Hearst 6161, Hearst 6162, Heineman 6165**, Hermione 6175, **Heron 6176**, Hettinger 6178, Heyward 6179, Hilibrand 6184, Hillman 6186, **HKH 6190**, Hochstein 6192, Hoerle 6194, **Homeland 6199**, Horncrest 6200, Horowitz 6202, Hudson 6207, Hultquist 6211, **Humanitas 6212**, Hurford 6215, Hutchins 6218, **IBM 6221**, Icahn 6224, IF 6226, Independence 6229, Iris 6237, Israel 6240, Jackson Hole 6246, Jacoff 6249, JAM 6251, **JEHT 6257, Jockey 6264, Johnson 6268**, Johnson 6272, Jones 6274, **Joukowsky 6275**, Joy 6276, **JPMorgan 6277**, Kaplan 6288, Kaplan 6290, Katzenberger 6298, Kaylie 6301, Kealy 6303, **Keefe 6305**, Kennedy 6314, Kenworthy 6315, Klein 6333, **Klingenstein 6338**, Knox 6345, **Kopf 6348**, Kraus 6352, Kravis 6354, **Kunstadter 6362**, Lane 6373, Lang 6374, Lauder 6381, **Lauder 6383**, Lehman 6396, Lenna 6402, Leonhardt 6403, Levy 6412, Liberman 6419, Lindmor 6425, Litterman 6435, Litwin 6436, Liu 6437, Lortel 6447, Lowenstein 6449, Lui 6457, Lurie 6459, Macdonald 6468, Marks 6489, Marks 6490, Mars 6494, MAT 6503, **Mathers 6504, Matthews 6507, Mayer 6509**, McCarthy 6515, McCarthy 6516, Meehan 6523, **Memton 6529, Mercer 6532, Mertz 6538**, Mesdag 6539, Metcalf 6541, **MetLife 6542**, Metropolitan 6543, Meyer 6546, Millbrook 6549, **Monell 6566, Monterey 6568**, Moody's 6569, **Moore 6571, Morgan 6577**, Moses 6587, Mostyn 6591, MRM 6592, Nakash 6600, **NEC 6605**, Neuberger 6611, New York 6615, New York 6617, New York 6618, New York 6619, New York 6620, **New 6621**, Newcastle 6622, Nicholas 6627, **Noble 6633, Norman 6635**, Normandie 6636, North 6637, **Noyes 6643**, Nuhn 6644, O'Herron 6646, O'Malley 6648, O'Toole 6654, **Ohga 6658**, Ohrstrom 6659, Olive 6662, **Open 6665**, Oppenheimer 6666, Ostreicher 6671,

Ottinger 6674, **Overbrook 6675, Paley 6679**, Palisano 6680, Palm 6681, Palmer 6683, Park 6687, Park 6688, Park 6689, Peco 6703, Pels 6706, **Penzance 6712, Pepsi 6713, PepsiCo 6714**, Perkin 6717, Phelan 6723, **Phillips 6725**, Pinkerton 6728, Pollack 6735, Pope 6740, **Popplestone 6741**, Price 6746, Pritchard 6748, **Prospect 6750**, Raether 6766, Raffiani 6767, Rapoport 6772, **Reader's 6778**, Reed 6782, **Reed 6783, Reynolds 6790**, Rhodebeck 6791, Richardson 6796, Richardson 6797, Richmond 6800, Riedman 6804, Riggio 6807, Riley 6809, **Ripplewood 6812, Ritter 6814**, Robison 6821, Rochester 6823, **Rockefeller 6825, Rockefeller 6826**, Rohatyn 6830, Rose 6833, Rosenberg 6845, Rosenstiel 6852, Rosenthal 6854, Rosenwald 6855, Roslyn 6859, **Rubin 6872**, Rubinstein 6876, Rudin 6877, Ruffin 6880, Rupp 6883, Sackler 6890, Sackler 6891, Salomon 6897, Salomon 6898, Sandy 6903, Santa 6905, Schaffer 6911, Schenker 6916, Scherman 6918, Schiff 6923, **Schlumberger 6926**, Schmitt 6928, Schnurmacher 6930, Schnurmacher 6931, Schwartz 6945, Sheinberg 6963, Sheldon 6964, Shoolman 6967, Shoreland 6968, **Shubert 6970**, SI 6972, Siebens 6974, Silver 6981, Simon 6987, Simons 6988, Simons 6989, Sirus 6992, Sister 6994, Sitt 6995, Slifka 7001, **SMBC 7005**, Smith 7008, **Smithers 7010**, Snyder 7014, Solow 7019, **Solow 7020**, Soros 7024, Sosnoff 7025, Spiegel 7029, Spingold 7032, **Spirit 7033**, Spitzer 7034, Sprague 7035, Spunk 7036, **St. Giles 7041, Starr 7048**, Starwood 7049, **Steel 7052**, Steele 7053, Stein 7055, Stein 7056, Steyer 7077, **Stiefel 7078**, Stiefel 7079, Strypemonde 7089, Sulzberger 7095, **Sumitomo 7096, Summerfield 7097**, Sunrise 7102, **Surdna 7103**, Sweetgrass 7113, **Sykes 7115**, Taconic 7117, **Tai 7118, Tanaka 7120**, Tennenbaum 7129, Thornton 7134, Tiger 7139, Triad 7162, Tribune 7163, **Tsadra 7169**, Tuch 7170, Turner 7175, Tuttle 7176, **U.S. 7180**, Valentine 7189, van Ameringen 7190, van Ameringen 7191, Van Pelt 7192, **Vetlesen 7196**, Vidda 7198, Wachtell 7205, **Wallace 7209**, Warner 7216, **Watson 7220, Weeden 7223**, Weinberg 7230, Weinberg 7231, Weissman 7237, Wendling 7242, White 7251, Widgeon 7255, Wilpon 7261, Wilson 7264, Winston 7267, **Wolfensohn 7270**, Wood 7272, Woodcock 7273, Yitzchok 7283, **Youth 7287**, Zehner 7293, **Zenkel 7295**, Zichron 7297

North Carolina: **Bank 7310**, BB&T 7312, Belk 7314, Belk 7315, Blue 7319, Blumenthal 7320, Bryan 7330, Cape Fear 7336, Cemala 7337, Coffey 7339, Comloquoy 7341, Community 7345, Community 7346, Cumberland 7349, Dickson 7355, Dover 7356, Duke 7359, Duke 7360, Easley 7361, Ebert 7362, Finch 7366, Finley 7367, Fox 7371, Glenn 7376, Goodrich 7378, Graham 7382, Halton 7386, Hanes 7388, Harvest 7392, Hendrick 7395, Holding 7399, Hurley 7402, Hurley 7403, Jones 7408, Kenan 7411, Kenan 7412, Lance 7418, **Lowe's 7423**, Mebane 7427, Mills 7429, Palin 7443, Polk 7449, **Prickett 7452**, Progress 7453, Provident 7454, Randleigh 7456, Reynolds 7457, Reynolds 7458, **Richardson 7462**, Roanoke 7464, Robertson 7466, Rumbaugh 7468, Smith 7476, Smith 7479, SOL 7480, Southern 7481, SPX 7484, Stonecutter 7486, Strowd 7488, Summer 7489, SunTrust 7491, Tannenbaum 7493, Terry 7494, V.F. 7498, Vanderbilt 7501, **Wachovia 7502**, Warner 7503, Weaver 7504, Woodson 7509, Woodward 7510, Zelnak 7513

North Dakota: Leach 7516, MDU 7517, North Dakota 7519, Stern 7521

Ohio: A Good 7522, A Good 7523, AK 7525, American 7528, Anderson 7529, Andrews 7530, **Armington 7532, Austin 7535**, Austin 7536, Bee 7542, Beerman 7543, **Bingham 7549**, Black 7551, Brennan 7554, Brentwood 7555, Britton 7556, **Burleigh 7561**, Butler 7562, Cafaro 7563, Callahan 7564, **Cardinal 7567**, Charities 7569, Cleveland 7577, Codrington 7578, Community 7582,

Community 7586, **Cooper 7589**, Corbett 7590, Corbin 7591, Cotswold 7594, **Covenant 7595**, Dana 7599, Dater 7600, Dayton 7604, DBJ 7605, Diamond 7610, Diebold 7611, Dorn 7612, Downing 7614, **Durell 7616, Eaton 7617**, Edwards 7618, Evans 7620, Farmer 7623, **Federated 7624**, Firman 7628, First 7629, Foss 7635, Foundation 7636, Fox 7637, France 7639, Frohman 7641, GAR 7643, **Geisse 7646**, Gerlach 7648, Gettler 7649, Gund 7655, Gund 7656, Gund 7657, H.C.S. 7658, Hamlin 7661, Hankins 7662, Haslinger 7664, **HCR 7667**, Heavenly 7668, Hoover 7674, Hoover 7675, Horvitz 7677, Humphrey 7679, Jegs 7687, Jochum 7692, Jubilee 7694, Kaplan 7696, **Kettering 7698, Key 7700, Knowles 7701**, Knudsen 7702, **Kosar 7703**, Kramer 7704, Kulas 7706, LaValley 7708, Lincoln 7715, Lindner 7717, Lippitt 7718, Lippman 7719, LKC 7720, Lubrizol 7725, M/I 7729, Mandel 7730, Mandel 7732, Mangano 7733, Marietta 7735, Mather 7736, Mathile 7737, Mayerson 7739, McBride 7740, McMaster 7744, MeadWestvaco 7745, Mellen 7747, Miller 7752, Miller 7753, Miller 7754, Moores 7759, Morgan 7760, Morgan 7761, Morgan 7762, Morley 7763, Morrison 7764, Motorists 7765, Murch 7766, Murdough 7767, Murphy 7768, Murphy 7769, Muskingum 7770, Nationwide 7771, NCR 7773, **Needmor 7774**, Nippert 7777, Noble 7778, Nord 7779, Nord 7780, Nordson 7781, O'Neill 7782, **Ohio 7786, OMNOVA 7789**, Orr 7790, Osteopathic 7791, Owens 7793, Park 7795, Parker 7796, Payne 7798, Peninsula 7799, Peterson 7802, Prentiss 7806, Progressive 7808, Reinberger 7815, Reuter 7817, Reynolds 7818, Richland 7819, Ritchie 7821, Ritter 7822, Rosenthal 7826, Sage 7829, Saint 7830, **Sankey 7833, Sapirstein 7834**, Schott 7842, Schottenstein 7844, Scotford 7846, **Scripps 7848**, Seifert 7850, Sherwin 7855, Siegal 7856, Silk 7857, Sisler 7858, Smith 7862, Smucker 7864, Spaulding 7865, Springfield 7866, Stark 7867, Stillson 7869, Stocker 7870, Stranahan 7872, Stranahan 7873, **Tomkins 7884**, Trzcinski 7887, Turben 7888, Turner 7889, Van Wert 7891, **Vesper 7892**, Wagler 7893, Watson 7896, Wayne 7897, **Weatherhead 7899**, Weisbrod 7900, Wendy's 7902, Williamson 7908, Wilson 7910, Wolfe 7915, Wuliger 7918

Oklahoma: **8:32 7922**, Bailey 7923, Better 7926, Bovaird 7927, Chapman 7928, Collins 7929, Collins 7930, Communities 7931, Community 7932, Goddard 7939, Hille 7943, Kerr 7950, Kirkpatrick 7952, McCasland 7956, McGee 7957, McMahon 7959, Meinders 7960, Meinig 7961, Merrick 7962, Noble 7963, Oklahoma City 7964, Oklahoma 7965, Oklahoman 7966, ONEOK 7967, Oxley 7968, Records 7972, **Schusterman 7975**, Southern 7979, Stevens 7980, Titus 7983, Tulsa 7984, Viersen 7985, Warren 7986, Warren 7987, Williams 7989, Zarrow 7991, Zarrow 7992, Zarrow 7993, Zink 7994

Oregon: Ackerman 7995, Bair 7998, Boyd 8000, Braemar 8001, Carpenter 8003, Chambers 8004, Intel 8022, Jeld 8025, Johnson 8027, Kinsman 8031, Lamfrom 8034, **Lazar 8035**, Louisiana 8037, Macdonald 8038, Mentor 8039, Meyer 8041, Meyer 8042, Miller 8043, **NIKE 8046**, Oregon 8049, PacifiCorp 8050, PGE 8051, Schnitzer 8056, Swigert 8061, Tektronix 8063, Templeton 8064, Tucker 8065, Wheeler 8068

Pennsylvania: 1675 8070, ACE 8073, **Alcoa 8075**, Allegheny 8076, Allerton 8077, American 8079, Ames 8080, AMETEK 8081, Angela 8082, Arcadia 8086, Arkema 8089, Baker 8092, Beatty 8097, Beaver 8098, Benedum 8099, Berger 8101, Birmingham 8107, Birnhak 8108, Blanchard 8111, Born 8113, Bozzone 8114, Bristol 8118, Brossman 8120, Campbell 8128, **Carthage 8132**, Central 8135, Centre 8136, Century 8137, **Cestone 8138**, Cestone 8139, Chanticleer 8140, Chester 8141, CIGNA 8143, Claneil 8144, Clapp 8145, **Clive 8146, Colcom 8150**, Colonial 8151, Community 8156, Connelly 8157, **Cornerstone 8159**, Cotswold 8160, Crawford 8162, Crels 8163,

Dietrich 8171, **Dominion 8173**, Donley 8175, Donnelly 8176, DSF 8178, Eden 8181, Eden 8182, Epstein 8186, Equitable 8187, Farber 8194, Farber 8195, Fels 8198, Ferree 8199, Fine 8201, First 8202, FISA 8204, Fisher 8205, Foundation 8208, Fourjay 8209, Garthwaite 8212, Genuardi 8213, Giant 8214, Glencairn 8219, Grable 8221, Graham 8222, Grundy 8228, Hamilton 8233, Hankin 8234, Hansen 8235, Harsco 8236, Hassel 8237, Heinz 8240, Heinz 8241, Heinz 8242, Hill 8248, Hillman 8250, Hillman 8251, Hillman 8252, Hirtzel 8253, Hooper 8256, Hopwood 8257, Hoverter 8258, Hulme 8260, Hunt 8261, Huston 8263, Huston 8264, IKON 8265, Independence 8266, Jennings 8272, Justus 8276, Karabots 8278, Katz 8281, Kavanagh 8282, Kelly 8283, **Kennametal 8284**, Keystone 8285, Keystone 8286, Kind 8289, Klein 8291, Kunkel 8297, Laurel 8301, Lenfest 8304, Lenfest 8305, Levee 8308, Lilliput 8311, Lindback 8312, Little 8313, Mandell 8322, Marshall 8326, McCune 8331, McFeely 8334, McKenna 8337, McKinney 8339, Mellon 8344, Mellon 8345, Mellon 8346, Mengle 8347, Miller 8352, Mine 8357, Morris 8359, Nelson 8362, **Oberkotter 8365**, Parmer 8369, Penn 8371, Perkin 8375, Philadelphia 8378, Phoenixville 8381, Pierce 8382, **Pincus 8384**, Pine 8385, Plankenhorn 8387, PNC 8388, **PPG 8394**, Rees 8401, Reidler 8402, Rider 8404, Roberts 8405, Rockwell 8408, S & T 8417, Safeguard 8418, Saint 8419, **Scaife 8425**, Scholler 8428, Scranton 8431, Seiple 8432, Shaffer 8436, Shenango 8438, Simmons 8441, Simonds 8442, Smith 8444, Smith 8445, Snyder 8448, Society 8449, Sovereign 8451, Spang 8452, St. Mary's 8454, Stabler 8455, Steinman 8459, Stewart 8461, Strawbridge 8466, Toll 8479, Trees 8480, Trexler 8481, Tyco 8485, United 8486, **United 8488**, Vanguard 8490, Weiss 8499, West 8500, Wolf 8506, Wyomissing 8509

Puerto Rico: Puerto Rico 8515

Rhode Island: **Amica 8518**, Brooks 8520, Carter 8522, Chace 8523, Charlesmead 8525, Charter 8526, CVS 8529, Daniels 8530, **Dorot 8531**, Doyle 8532, **FM 8537**, Hasbro 8539, Kimball 8542, McAdams 8547, Rhode Island 8551, Shriners 8556, **Textron 8559**, van Beuren 8561, Washington 8563

South Carolina: Abney 8564, Black 8569, Byerly 8572, Cassels 8575, Chapin 8579, Coastal 8581, Horne 8594, Inman 8595, Liberty 8597, McKissick 8599, **Roe 8607**, Sims 8611, Sonoco 8614, Springs 8617, **Youths' 8621**

South Dakota: Sioux Falls 8630, Vucurevich 8634

Tennessee: 1939 8635, Assisi 8638, Beaman 8642, **Bridgestone 8646**, Briggs 8647, Caesars 8648, Caldwell 8649, Chrysalis 8655, CIC 8656, CLARCOR 8658, Draughon 8668, East 8671, Ezell 8676, Frist 8679, Harris 8686, HCA 8690, Hyde 8693, Johnson 8697, Lindahl 8702, Lyndhurst 8703, **Maclellan 8704**, MacLellan 8705, Martin 8708, No 8713, Phillips 8716, Stokely 8730, Thompson 8733, Tucker 8735, Unaka 8739, Washington 8741, **Westwood 8743**, Wilson 8744

Texas: Abell 8749, **Adams 8751**, Alexander 8752, Alkek 8754, Anderson 8759, Anderson 8760, Aragona 8763, Astin 8764, Augur 8766, B & B 8769, Bass 8775, Bass 8776, Bass 8777, Bass 8778, Bauer 8779, Beal 8783, Beasley 8784, **Bell 8786**, Belo 8787, Bickel 8790, Bridgeway 8796, Bridwell 8797, Brown 8799, Brumley 8800, Burnett 8801, **Butt 8803**, Butt 8804, Cailloux 8807, Cain 8809, Cameron 8811, Cameron 8812, Caris 8814, Carter 8816, Carter 8817, Cauthorn 8820, **CEMEX 8821**, CFP 8822, CH 8823, Clayton 8826, Clements 8832, Coastal 8833, Coates 8834, Cockrell 8835, Collins 8837, Community 8840, Community 8841, Community 8842, **Cooper 8846**, Covenant 8847, Cullen 8854, Dallas 8855, Deakins 8860, Delaney 8862, Dell 8864, di Portanova 8865, Dickson 8866, Dodge 8868, Doss 8869, Dougherty, 8870, Eady 8875, **EDS 8877**, Edwards 8880, El Paso 8881, El Paso 8882,

Ellwood 8884, Enrico 8885, **ExxonMobil 8889**, Fain 8890, Fasken 8895, Favrot 8897, Fikes 8899, Finger 8900, Fisch 8901, Fish 8902, Fleming 8904, Fondren 8906, Frees 8909, George 8916, Gill 8919, Goldsbury 8920, Greathouse 8923, Greathouse 8924, Gulf 8926, Hachar 8927, Haggerty 8932, Halliburton 8935, Hamill 8937, Hamman 8938, Hankamer 8939, **Hartman 8942**, Heavin 8945, Hebert 8946, Herzstein 8949, Hightower 8950, Hoglund 8956, Houston 8960, Houston 8961, Huffington 8963, Hunt 8966, Jamail 8970, **Jenesis 8971**, Jones 8975, Jonsson 8977, Kahn 8980, Keith 8982, Kelleher 8984, Kelley 8985, Kempner 8987, Kilroy 8991, Kimberly 8992, Kinder 8994, Kodosky 9000, Kronkosky 9002, Law 9006, Lichtenstein 9010, Lightner 9012, Lockheed 9015, Lord's 9019, Lowe 9020, Lubbock 9021, Lyons 9024, Marathon 9028, Mayborn 9033, Mayor 9034, McCrea 9040, McCullough 9041, McDermott 9043, McGovern 9044, McKee 9045, McMillan 9046, McNutt 9048, Meadows 9049, Meredith 9054, Miller 9062, Mithoff 9066, Mitte 9067, Moncrief 9069, Morgan 9074, Navarro 9089, Newman 9090, Northen 9092, O'Connor 9094, O'Connor 9095, Oehmig 9099, Once 9101, Owen 9107, Owsley 9108, Parks 9109, Penney 9115, Perkins 9116, Perot 9119, Peterson 9120, Powell 9128, Priddy 9131, Progress 9133, Providence 9135, PSH 9137, Rachal 9138, Rachofsky 9139, Reliant 9144, Reynolds 9145, Richardson 9147, Riddle 9148, Riter 9149, Roberts 9151, Rockwell 9154, Rogers 9155, Rosewood 9158, Sams 9163, San Angelo 9165, San Antonio 9166, **Scaler 9170**, Scarborough 9171, Scurlock 9175, **Search 9176**, Sharp 9180, **Shell 9181**, Shield 9183, Simmons 9188, Simmons 9189, Smith 9194, Smith 9195, Smith 9197, Smith 9198, Snyder 9199, Sowell 9203, Speas 9206, Speas 9207, **Starling 9210**, Sterling 9212, Stoffel 9214, Strake 9215, Sturgis 9216, Sumners 9218, Tapeats 9223, Tate 9225, Temple 9227, Temple 9228, **Tenet 9229**, Texas 9232, Topfer 9238, Triad 9239, Trull 9240, Turner 9242, Unkefer 9243, Urschel 9244, USAA 9245, Valero 9247, Vanberg 9248, Vaughan 9250, Waggoner 9256, Walsh 9261, **Waste 9265**, Weaver 9267, Weekley 9271, West 9276, Westcott 9278, White 9279, Willard 9281, Wise 9284, Wolslager 9290, Works 9291, Wortham 9292, Young 9295, Zale 9297, Zeller 9298, Zephyr 9299, Zimmer 9300.

Utah: ALS 9301, Ashton 9303, Bamberger 9305, Caine 9310, Eccles 9317, Eccles 9319, Eccles 9320, Esther 9321, **Hayward 9327**, Hemingway 9328, Jones 9330, Lawson 9331, Lockwood 9333, Quinney 9338, Simmons 9342, Stern 9344, Swanson 9346, Wing 9352, **Wishnick 9353**, Zions 9354.

Vermont: **Ben 9355**, Lintilhac 9359, Mergens 9360, Vermont 9361.

Virginia: American 9368, AMERIGROUP 9369, Arlington 9371, Beazley 9376, **Blue 9379**, CarMax 9385, Cartledge 9388, Charlottesville 9390, **Chase 9391**, Circuit 9392, Collis 9398, Columbus 9399, Community 9402, **Cooke 9405, de Beaumont 9408, Dorothy 9411**, Estes 9415, Evans 9416, Flagler 9417, Folger 9418, Foundation 9419, Freddie 9422, Friedman 9425, **Gannett 9428**, Golden 9430, Gottwald 9431, Graves 9433, Herndon 9437, Hylton 9440, **Kaufman 9447**, Lawrence 9457, Luck 9461, Massey 9467, **MCI 9471**, Memorial 9474, **Mitsubishi 9476**, N.E.W. 9482, **Norfolk 9485**, Northern 9486, **Olmsted 9490**, Portsmouth 9498, Reynolds 9503, Rosenthal 9508, Sacharuna 9509, Samberg 9510, **Stern 9522**, Titmus 9527, Ukrop 9529, United 9530, Universal 9533, VuBay 9533, Washington 9534, Weil 9535, Weissberg 9536, **WestWind 9538**, Wilkinson 9540, Williamsburg 9541, **Winkler 9542**, Wrinkle 9545.

Washington: **444S 9546**, Adams 9548, Aven 9554, Benaroya 9556, Blue 9559, **Brainerd 9561**, Bullitt 9563, Burning 9564, Casey 9566, **Casey 9567**, Cheney 9569, Coulter 9573, De Falco 9578,

Dimmer 9579, **Edwards 9580**, Evertrust 9583, Ferguson 9585, Forest 9586, Foundation 9589, Fuchs 9590, **Gates 9591**, Geneva 9592, **Glaser 9595**, Grays 9597, Harder 9600, Harvest 9602, Haugland 9603, **Hemingway 9606**, Horizons 9608, Klorfine 9619, **Kongsgaard 9620, Laird 9623**, Laurel 9625, Lucky 9632, Lynn 9633, Martin 9634, Medina 9640, Milgard 9641, Norcliffe 9650, PEMCO 9660, Positive 9664, Quixote 9667, Rainier 9669, **RealNetworks 9672**, Russell 9673, **Samis 9675**, Seattle 9680, Sherwood 9683, Shirley 9684, **Stewardship 9691**, Tacoma 9693, **Weyerhaeuser 9703**, Wilburforce 9705.

West Virginia: BB&T 9710, Bowen 9711, Daywood 9717, Hollowell 9719, Huntington 9721, Maier 9725, McDonough 9726, Prichard 9731, Tucker 9736.

Wisconsin: Acuity 9739, Alliant 9742, AnnMarie 9743, Antioch 9745, Argosy 9747, Assurant 9748, Bader 9749, Baird 9750, Banta 9752, Bishop 9759, Bolz 9762, **Bradley 9763**, Bradshaw 9764, Briggs 9765, Brookbank 9766, Casper 9770, Chapman 9771, Charter 9772, Cornerstone 9781, Cudahy 9785, Delavan 9790, Dudley 9792, Duncan 9793, Eastman 9795, Evjue 9797, **Firestone 9798**, Fleck 9799, Fort 9801, Frautschi 9804, Goldbach 9806, Herzfeld 9815, Hess 9816, Holz 9817, JKO 9822, Johnson 9823, Johnson 9826, Jones 9827, Joy 9828, Kelben 9830, Keller 9831, Kenosha 9833, Kikkoman 9836, Kohl 9838, Krause 9841, Krause 9842, Krejci 9843, La Crosse 9845, Ladish 9846, Madison 9855, Managed 9857, Manpower 9858, Marshfield 9861, McBeath 9864, Mead 9867, Menasha 9869, Miller 9875, Morse 9879, Munson 9880, Northwestern 9884, Oshkosh 9885, Oshkosh 9886, Oshkosh 9887, Pamida 9891, Peck 9894, Peck 9895, Peterson 9896, Pettit 9897, Pick 9899, PPC 9902, Puelicher 9904, **Rockwell 9912**, Roundy's 9915, Rutledge 9917, Sand 9918, Schoenleber 9921, Sensient 9922, Sentry 9923, **Smith 9929**, Split 9932, Stackner 9934, Steigleder 9936, Stock 9939, Stuart 9941, Stuart 9943, Styberg 9944, **T & O 9946**, Taylor 9948, **Thrivent 9949**, Timken 9950, U.S. 9952, Vine 9956, Wagner 9958, Waukesha 9960, Windhover 9966, Wisconsin 9967, WPS 9970, **Young 9972**.

Wyoming: Community 9977, Connemara 9978, Friess 9982, Kerr 9983, McMurry 9985, S & G 9988, Sargent 9989, **Schultz 9990**, Scott 9991, Weiss 9997, Whitney 9998, Wyoming 10000.

Grants to individuals

Alabama: Dixon 32, Moody 54, Protective 58

Alaska: Alaska 79, CIRI 83

Arizona: Help 105

California: Alafi 201, Babcock 249, **Beckman 272**, Bradley 315, Buck 330, California 350, **Cantor 354**, Change 373, Community 406, Durfee 471, **Foundation 529**, Genentech 561, **Getty 570, Harkham 649, Hertz 670, Jack 705, Koulaieff 778**, Lund 831, Oakland 948, Oakley 949, Rest 1044, Sonora 1178, Synopsys 1222

Colorado: Colorado 1355, Sachs 1447, SEAKR 1452

Connecticut: Boehringer 1498, Broadcasters 1505, Donaghue 1529, Larrabee 1578, Lehrman 1584, Main 1594, SBM 1644, Senior 1647

Delaware: Common 1700, MBNA 1730

District of Columbia: **Professional 1843**

Florida: Community 1940, duPont 1982, Friedman 2014, Gainesville 2015, Gore 2031, GTE 2040, **Kaul 2083**, Levin 2110, Ryder 2213, **SWS 2260, von Liebig 2283**

Georgia: Amos 2316, Cawood 2342, Southern 2494

Hawaii: Ching 2540, Hughes 2548

Idaho: **Washington 2578**

Illinois: Abbott 2579, CNA 2670, Driehaus 2710, **Graham 2767**, Little 2859, Morton 2905, **Walgreen 3051**

Indiana: Blue 3107, Community 3123, **Lilly 3193**, Samerian 3234

Kansas: Jones 3370, Salina 3387, Sprint 3395

Kentucky: Bavarian 3406, Mustard 3440

Louisiana: Young 3518

Maine: Maine 3548

Maryland: **Casey 3585, Ellison 3621**, GEICO 3634, **Hughes 3654, Kluge 3663**

Massachusetts: **A Child 3765**, Association 3783, Boston 3811, Cape Cod 3833, Charles 3844, Genzyme 3922, **New England 4052**, Putnam 4089, Rappaport 4093, Weber 4200

Michigan: **Earhart 4291, Fetzer 4297, General 4319, Kellogg 4356**, Volkswagen 4473

Minnesota: **Ecolab 4557**, Jerome 4595, Koran 4600, McKnight 4617, Vest 4708

Mississippi: Skelton 4765

Missouri: Butler 4793, Ingram 4834, **Kauffman 4843**, Seaworld 4900, **Wyeth 4930**

Montana: Montana 4939

Nebraska: **ConAgra 4953**, Dinsdale 4957, Smock 5004

New Jersey: Alcatel 5110, **Aventis 5121**, Berrie 5130, Dodge 5181, First 5194, **Janssen 5255**, Knowles 5283, Leib 5302, **Merck 5328**, Merck 5329, Monius 5333, Orenstein 5344, **Puffin 5362**, Roche 5372, Segal 5395, Silbermann 5403, Thomas 5427

New Mexico: **Lannan 5484, Levinson 5486**

New York: Brand 5658, **Bristol 5666**, Campbell 5700, **Chazen 5739, Collins 5777**, de Kay 5841, **Dedalus 5847, Delmas 5850**, Dove 5877, Ebb 5903, **Ford 5970, Gottlieb 6080, Grant 6090, Guggenheim 6118**, Havens 6156, Heyward 6179, Hutchins 6218, **Jockey 6264, Keren 6317, Klingenstein 6338, Lauder 6383, Luce 6453, Mayer 6509, MetLife 6542, Mitchell 6559**, Muldoon 6594, Netzach 6609, **Open 6665**, Palmer 6683, **Pollock 6736**, Realty 6779, **Rockefeller 6825**, Rosenberg 6847, **Rothschild 6866, Schepp 6917, Soros 7022**, St. George's 7040, **SVM 7110, Tiffany 7138**, Tuttle 7176, **Wenner 7244, Whiting 7253**

North Carolina: Corpening 7347, Davis 7354, Foundation 7370, Strowd 7488, Winston-Salem 7508

Ohio: A Good 7522, A Good 7523, Bryan 7559, Creech 7597, Diamond 7610, Ford 7633, Foss 7635, Lewis 7713, Loeb 7721, Marietta 7735, Patterson 7797, **Procter 7807, Scripps 7848**, Tuscarawas 7890, Wendy's 7902, **Wexner 7904**

Oklahoma: Bailey 7923

Oregon: Lightfoot 8036

Pennsylvania: Berks 8103, **Carnegie 8130**, Crawford 8162, England 8185, **Heinz 8243**, Honickman 8255, **Institute 8268**, Merchants 8348, **Presser 8395**, Shenango 8438, **Templeton 8475**

Rhode Island: **Alpert 8517**, Rhode Island 8551

South Dakota: Sioux Falls 8630

Tennessee: Hurlbut 8692, Lazarus 8700

Texas: Carter 8817, Educational 8878, Lockheed 9015, Moody 9070, Perot 9118, Snyder 9199, Stark 9209, Sunnyside 9219, **Tenet 9229**, West 9275

Utah: Esther 9321

Vermont: Vermont 9361

Virgin Islands: Community 9363

Virginia: Arlington 9371, CarMax 9385, Community 9402, **Cooke 9405, Freedom 9424**

Washington: Russell 9673, Washington 9702

Wisconsin: Fond du Lac 9800, Goldbach 9806, Kohl 9838, Marshfield 9861, Rutledge 9917

Wyoming: Community 9977

In-kind gifts

Alabama: Community 25, **Vulcan 73**

Arkansas: Rockefeller 172, Union 183

California: Bright 322, Gap 551, **Mattel 861, McConnell 870**, Metabolife 891, Orfalea 958,

Schwab **1110**, **Strauss 1203**, Vons 1270, Waitt 1275, **World 1319**

Colorado: Community 1358, El Pomar 1374, Saeman 1448

Connecticut: International 1571, SBM 1644

District of Columbia: **Moriah 1835**

Florida: **Aurora 1883**, Beveridge 1907, Darden 1960, Jacksonville 2071, Rayonier 2189, Ryder 2213, **Stacy 2246**, Toppel 2274

Georgia: Callaway 2337, Georgia 2395, Savannah 2480, **Scientific 2482**

Idaho: Simplot 2575

Illinois: Community 2677, Dillon 2704, Harris 2787, Omron 2926, **Square 3018**

Indiana: Ball 3103, Blue 3107, Community 3128, Elkhart 3145

Iowa: Maytag 3309

Kansas: Topeka 3400, Westar 3403

Maryland: Henson 3648, Mid 3693, Provident 3712

Massachusetts: Cabot 3823, Cape Cod 3833, Ham 3940, Highland 3951, Millipore 4040, New 4054

Michigan: Branch 4237, Community 4258, Dow 4284, Ford 4307

Minnesota: **3M 4492**, Jostens 4596, Target 4697, **Toro 4702**, **U.S. 4704**, Valspar 4706

Missouri: Ameren 4772, **Monsanto 4868**, Truman 4919

Nebraska: Fremont 4962

Nevada: Parasol 5051

New Jersey: **Clare 5164**, Unilever 5434

New Mexico: **Lannan 5484**, New Mexico 5491, Taos 5498

New York: **Bristol 5666**, **Cummings 5814**, **Dedalus 5847**, Kaplan 6288, M & T 6465, **MetLife 6542**, **National 6603**, **Open 6665**, Schaffer 6911

North Carolina: Community 7345, Corpening 7347, Cumberland 7349, Duke 7360, Mebane 7427, Triangle 7496

North Dakota: Fargo 7514

Ohio: **Chiquita 7571**, Cleveland 7577, Community 7586, **Eaton 7617**, Muskingum 7770, **OMNOVA 7789**, Owens 7793, **PLACE 7805**

Oklahoma: Kerr 7949, **Schusterman 7975**, Zink 7994

Pennsylvania: Buck 8123, Community 8156, **Dominion 8173**, Falk 8193, Hankin 8234

Puerto Rico: Puerto Rico 8515

South Carolina: Community 8583, Spartanburg 8616

Texas: **Cooper 8846**, East 8876, Houston 8960, Hudson 8962, McKee 9045, Sams 9163, Stark 9209

Utah: Hemingway 9328, Swanson 9346

Virginia: Landmark 9455, **MCI 9471**, **Norfolk 9485**, Northern 9486, Peterson 9497, Virginia Beach 9532

Washington: **Gates 9591**, Quixote 9667

Wisconsin: Assurant 9748, Charter 9772, Community 9780, Krause 9842, Marshfield 9861, Wisconsin 9967

Wyoming: Community 9977

Income development

California: Aratani 230, Atkinson 239, Flora 521, **K.L. 736**, McCune 872, McKay 877, Truckee 1244, Union 1250

Colorado: Pikes 1437, Rose 1445

District of Columbia: **Moriah 1835**, Vradenburg 1856

Florida: Beveridge 1907, North 2153

Georgia: Glenn 2399, Healthcare 2411

Illinois: Arthur 2601, Chicago 2661, Coleman 2673, Oak Park 2922

Indiana: Clowes 3120, Tipton 3243

Kansas: Capitol 3350

Kentucky: C.E. 3412

Louisiana: Reily 3506

Maine: JTG 3542, **Sandy 3555**

Maryland: Baker 3567, Baltimore 3568, Straus 3738

Massachusetts: Adams 3771, Lowell 4014, **Schooner 4131**

Michigan: Ann Arbor 4221, **H.I.S. 4334**

Minnesota: West 4723

Nevada: **Walsh 5075**

New Hampshire: New Hampshire 5098

New Jersey: **Bestfoods 5132**

New York: **Citigroup 5755**, Clark 5761, Community 5782, Dyson 5898, **Ford 5970**, Luce 6452, New York 6613, **Ross 6863**, Sister 6994, Woodcock 7273

North Carolina: Cape Fear 7336, Community 7346, Cumberland 7349, Warner 7503

Ohio: O'Neill 7783

Oregon: Kinsman 8031, Meyer 8042

Pennsylvania: Centre 8136, **Colcom 8150**, Erie 8188, McCune 8332

South Dakota: South Dakota 8631

Texas: Dougherty, 8870, Houston 8960, Meadows 9049, Simmons 9188, Works 9291

Vermont: Mergens 9360, Vermont 9361

Virginia: Robins 9506

Washington: **Brainerd 9561**, Bullitt 9563, **Casey 9567**, Fortune 9587, Grays 9597, Medina 9640, Quixote 9667, Satterberg 9677

Wisconsin: **Kohler 9839**, Miller 9875, **Thrivent 9949**

Internship funds

Alabama: **Corman 29**, Webb 75

Alaska: Alaska 79, Doyon 84

Arizona: Ottens 128

California: Alafi 201, Buck 330, Connell 412, Drum 470, Flora 521, **Getty 570**, Goldman 595, Koret 774, Lux 834, Parsons 980, Peninsula 989, Union 1250, Van Nuys 1261, Wattis 1283

Connecticut: American 1482, Larsen 1579, **Lingnan 1587**

Delaware: **Robinson 1745**, **Schwartz 1751**

District of Columbia: Aid 1765, Benton 1773

Florida: Community 1940, Community 1943, **Davis 1964**, Greenburg 2034, **Picower 2169**, **Skelly 2237**

Georgia: DuBose 2374, Lee 2432, **Scientific 2482**, Zeist 2529

Illinois: Arthur 2601, Blair 2621, Butler 2646, Comer 2675, Harris 2788, **Kemper 2832**, Lumpkin 2864, **Monticello 2904**, Oberweiler 2923, Olin 2925, **Scholl 2989**, Speh 3014, **State 3019**

Indiana: Clowes 3120, Lilly 3194

Iowa: Hubbell 3297, Maytag 3310, McElroy 3313

Kansas: Capitol 3350

Kentucky: **Humana 3428**

Maine: Horizon 3541

Maryland: Deutsch 3616, Higginson 3649, Procter 3711, Rathmann 3715

Massachusetts: Island 3965, **Kendall 3977**, Morse 4044

Michigan: Americana 4218, Bay 4229, Community 4252, Cook 4262

Minnesota: Bremer 4523, Thorpe 4701

Nebraska: Omaha 4995

New Jersey: Buehler 5146, **Dow 5184**, **Eshet 5190**, **Newcombe 5338**, Schering 5387

New Mexico: New Mexico 5491

New York: Achelis 5513, Avery 5581, Bodman 5647, **Dedalus 5847**, **Deutsche 5854**, Dow 5879, Emerson 5927, Gilman 6032, Goldman 6053, Gould 6083, Guggenheim 6117, Heckscher 6164, Independence 6229, Jewish 6260, **JM 6263**, Kaplan 6288, **Kress 6357**, Lang 6374, Levitt 6409, **Luce 6453**, Memton 6529, **National 6603**, New York 6620, **Noble 6633**, **Open 6665**, **Pforzheimer 6721**, Revson 6789, Rubinstein 6876, Schnurmacher 6931, Sulzberger 7095, **Sussman 7105**, Triad 7162, Tuch 7170, Ungar 7183

North Carolina: **Bank 7310**, Cemala 7337, Duke 7359, Fox 7371, Morehead 7430, Polk 7449, Strowd 7488

Ohio: **Convergys 7587**, Gund 7657, Humphrey 7679, Levin 7712, Muskingum 7770, Nippert 7777, **Scripps 7848**, Wallace 7894

Oklahoma: Kerr 7949, **Schusterman 7975**

Oregon: Kinsman 8031, Macdonald 8038

Pennsylvania: Centre 8136, Fels 8198, **Institute 8268**, Laurel 8301, McLean 8340, **Seraph 8434**, Society 8449, Weiss 8499

Rhode Island: **Dorot 8531**

South Carolina: Abney 8564, Chapin 8579, Community 8583

Tennessee: Tucker 8735

Texas: Covenant 8847, Houston 8960, Lyons 9024, Mays 9036, Simmons 9188, Summerlee 9217, Sumners 9218

Utah: Eccles 9320

Virginia: Delmar 9410

Washington: Blue 9559, **Hemingway 9606**, Miller 9642

Wisconsin: **Bradley 9763**, Evjue 9797

Land acquisition

Alabama: Kaul 40, Meyer 52

Alaska: Rasmuson 85

Arizona: Johnson 112, **Kieckhefer 113**, Morris 124

Arkansas: Taylor 179

California: Ahmanson 198, Ayrshire 247, Bechtel 270, **Castagnola 366**, Community 405, **Compton 409**, Copley 416, Cowell 423, Crockett 430, **Delano 449**, Drum 470, Firedoll 508, Flora 521, **Foundation 529**, Gasser 557, Gold 590, Goldman 597, Hedco 663, Hewlett 671, Irwin 700, Jewett 718, Marin 854, McBean 865, McLean 880, Mead 881, **Moore 913**, Morgan 915, **Packard 972**, Parker 979, **Peterson 996**, Rancho 1031, Reid 1036, San Diego 1087, Santa Barbara 1093, **Schlinger 1102**, Serenity 1128, Stern 1195, Tuohy 1247

Colorado: Boettcher 1344, Edmondson 1373, El Pomar 1374, Gates 1380, Johnson 1398, Summit 1463

Connecticut: Baldwin 1487, **Bingham 1493**, Hartford 1563, Hartford 1564, Larsen 1579, Sewall 1648, Tauck 1657, Thompson 1658, Vervane 1671

Delaware: Crystal 1702, **Fair 1713**, Laffey 1725, Lennox 1726, Longwood 1727, Marmot 1728

District of Columbia: **Wallace 1857**

Florida: A Friends' 1866, Beveridge 1907, Bush 1922, **Chatlos 1932**, Dade 1957, Gooding 2028, Gulf 2041, Hersh 2058, Opler 2158, Rayonier 2189, Rinker 2196, Selby 2230, Stevens 2251

Georgia: AEC 2310, Callaway 2337, Campbell 2339, Courts 2364, Cox 2367, DuBose 2374, Equifax 2379, Lee 2432, Savannah 2480, **Scientific 2482**, Wilson 2519, Woodruff 2521, Woolley 2525, Zeist 2529

Hawaii: Hawaiian 2546

Illinois: Chicago 2661, Dillon 2704, Field 2728, Grand 2769, Nelson 2911, Oberweiler 2923, Olin 2925, Tellabs 3034

Indiana: Brown 3110, Bussing 3111, Central 3116, Cole 3121, Community 3125, Dekko 3142, Foellinger 3149, Harrison 3161, Heritage 3166, Lilly 3194, Lincoln 3195, Noble 3214, Pulliam 3225, Steuben 3241, Unity 3247, Waterfield 3252

Iowa: Maytag 3310

Kansas: Capitol 3350, Cooper 3353, Sunderland 3397

Kentucky: Brown 3409, Brown 3410, C.E. 3412, Rosenthal 3450, Sutherland 3451

Louisiana: Community 3469

Maine: Burnham 3527, King 3545, Libra 3546, Maine 3548

Maryland: Abell 3559, Blades 3574, Concordia 3601, Knott 3666, MARPAT 3684, Marshall 3687, Meyerhoff 3692, Mid 3693, Procter 3711

Massachusetts: Barr 3791, Cape Cod 3832, Cape Cod 3833, Carlee 3835, Community 3855, Cox 3863, Davis 3875, Ellsworth 3892, **Fidelity 3904**, Fields 3905, Fletcher 3912, Fuller 3918, Ham 3940, Island 3965, Melville 4034, Merck 4035, Mifflin 4038, Parker 4069, Peabody 4072, Sheehan 4140, **State 4158**, Stearns 4160, Stevens 4164, Stoddard 4165, **Sweet 4176**

Michigan: Battle Creek 4228, Dalton 4266, Frey 4316, Gerstacker 4322, Gilmore 4324, Grand Haven 4325, Grand Rapids 4326, **H.I.S. 4334**, Herrick 4341, Jackson 4347, **Kresge 4367**, Oleson 4405, Steelcase 4446

Minnesota: Buuck 4526, Greystone 4576, Lilly 4606, Marbrook 4612, Rupp 4669, Southways 4688, Walker 4711

Mississippi: Maddox 4753

Missouri: Brown 4789, Gateway 4817, Green 4822, H & R 4823, Hall 4824, Jenkins 4836, Reynolds 4892

Montana: Cinnabar 4935, Sample 4940

Nebraska: Heuermann 4973, Hirschfeld 4974, Kiewit 4984, Lincoln 4987, Mid-Nebraska 4991

Nevada: **Walsh 5075**

New Hampshire: Fuller 5090, Hunt 5093, **Penates 5099**

New Jersey: Cape 5153, Charles 5161, **Fanwood 5192**, Grassmann 5213, Hyde 5247, Union 5435, Victoria 5440

New Mexico: Kind 5483, **Lannan 5484**, Messengers 5489, Taos 5498

New York: Adirondack 5517, Buck 5682, Cary 5712, Community 5783, **Cummings 5813, Frankel 5976**, Freeman 5981, Gifford 6026, Glens Falls 6041, Hayden 6158, Hultquist 6211, Independence 6229, Jackson Hole 6246, Kealy 6303, **Kohlberg 6346, LaSalle 6377**, Macdonald 6468, Mars 6494, McCann 6514, **Mitsubishi 6560**, Nichols 6628, **Norcross 6634**, Northern 6639, O'Connor 6645, Ohrstrom 6659, **Prospect 6750, Reed 6783, Ross 6863**, Schenectady 6915, Steele 7053, **Waterfowl 7219, Weeden 7223**, Western 7248

North Carolina: Cape Fear 7336, Cemala 7337, Community 7343, Easley 7361, Hanes 7387, Hanes 7388, Robertson 7466, Weaver 7504

North Dakota: North Dakota 7520

Ohio: Ashtabula 7534, Barberton 7539, Columbus 7580, **Covenant 7595**, Dana 7599, Dayton 7603, Ferguson 7625, First 7629, GAR 7643, Gund 7657, Iddings 7682, Kulas 7706, Lippitt 7718, Muskingum 7770, Salem 7831, Schmidlapp 7841, Scotford 7846, Semple 7851, Stark 7867, **Timken 7880**

Oklahoma: Bailey 7923, Community 7932, Gelvin 7938, Helmerich 7942, Inasmuch 7944, McGee 7957, McMahon 7959, Viersen 7985

Oregon: Carpenter 8003, Jeld 8025, Kinsman 8031, Oregon 8049, Swigert 8061, Swindells 8062, Tucker 8065

Pennsylvania: Blanchard 8111, Claneil 8144, **Colcom 8150**, Erie 8188, First 8202, Fisher 8205, Grundy 8228, Hillman 8249, Justus 8276, Kline 8293, Laurel 8301, McKenna 8337, McLean 8340, Mellon 8346, Penn 8371, **Seraph 8434**, Sovereign 8451, Steinman 8459, Trexler 8481

Rhode Island: Champlin 8524, Daniels 8530, Rhode Island 8551, van Beuren 8561

South Carolina: Abney 8564, Coastal 8581, **Roe 8607**

Tennessee: Community 8660, Lyndhurst 8703, Plough 8718, **Rust 8724**, Tonya 8734, Tucker 8735

Texas: Amarillo 8758, Austin 8768, Brown 8799, Cailloux 8807, Carter 8816, Cockrell 8835, Communities 8839, Constantin 8843, Cowden 8848, Cullen 8854, Halsell 8936, Herzstein 8949, Hillcrest 8952, Hoblitzelle 8955, Houston 8960, Houston 8961, Johnson 8974, Keith 8982, King 8995, Kronkosky 9002, McDermott 9043, Meadows 9049, Moody 9070, Richardson 9147, Rockwell 9154, San Angelo 9165, San Antonio 9166, Scurlock 9175, Shield 9183, Simmons

9188, Sterling 9212, Summerlee 9217, Tennessee 9230, Vanberg 9248

Utah: Dumke 9315, Eccles 9317

Vermont: Lintilhac 9359

Virginia: Alleghany 9367, Camp 9382, Fralin 9420, Hylton 9440, McGlothlin 9469, Norfolk 9484, Robins 9506, Titmus 9527, **WestWind 9538**

Washington: Archibald 9553, Community 9571, **Edwards 9580**, Ferguson 9585, Grays 9597, Green 9598, Horizons 9608, **Kongsgaard 9620**, Martin 9634, Quixote 9667, Sherwood 9683, Tacoma 9693, **Weyerhaeuser 9703**

West Virginia: Community 9716, Huntington 9721

Wisconsin: Alexander 9741, Banta 9752, Bishop 9759, Community 9778, Dudley 9792, Janesville 9820, Lunda 9852, Madison 9854, Milwaukee 9876, U.S. 9952, West 9964

Wyoming: Sargent 9989, **Schultz 9990**

Loaned talent

Illinois: Deere 2699

Kentucky: **Yum! 3457**

Minnesota: TCF 4699

Loans—to individuals

Minnesota: Northwest 4637

Management development/capacity building

Alabama: Kaul 40, Meyer 52

Alaska: Rasmuson 85

Arizona: **Johnson 112**

Arkansas: Rockefeller 172

California: Ackerman 193, Aratani 230, Atlas 241, Blue 296, Buck 330, California 345, California 346, Community 403, **Draper 466**, East 474, **Firelight 509**, Flintridge 520, Flora 521, Fresno 537, **Fund 542**, Girard 580, Humboldt 691, **Lloyd 823**, Mabie 839, McCune 872, McKay 877, Orange 957, **Peterson 996, Rivendell 1056**, Sacramento 1080, San Luis 1090, Schwab 1109, Solano 1175, Sonora 1178, Stone 1200, **Strauss 1203**, Truckee 1244, UniHealth 1249, vanLobenSels 1260, Ventura 1304, Weingart 1288

Colorado: Aspen 1338, **Crowell 1361**, ECA 1372, Pikes 1437, Rose 1445

Connecticut: Bridgeport 1504, Community 1517, Connecticut 1518, Connecticut 1519, Fairfield 1537, Hartford 1564, **Lingnan 1587**

Delaware: **Raskob 1741**

District of Columbia: Cafritz 1780, Meyer 1834, **Moriah 1835**, Spring 1849, Vradenburg 1856

Florida: Beveridge 1907, Bush 1922, Community 1939, Community 1941, Community 1942, Community 1949, Conn 1951, duPont 1983, **Gibney 2021**, Gulf 2041, Henderson 2056, North 2153, Quantum 2181, Southwest 2240

Georgia: Glenn 2399, Healthcare 2411, North 2458, **UPS 2503**

Hawaii: Atherton 2532, Castle 2537, Cooke 2541, Hawaii 2545

Idaho: Idaho 2570

Illinois: Arthur 2601, Chicago 2661, Grand 2769, Lumpkin 2864, Retirement 2964, Speh 3014, Steans 3021

Indiana: Clowes 3120, Community 3122, Community 3125, Community 3127, Community 3130, Dekko 3142, Harrison 3161, Heritage 3166, Johnson 3178, Kosciusko 3186, Lilly 3194, Tipton 3243

Iowa: Community 3277, Community 3278

Kansas: Farah 3362, Salina 3387

Kentucky: Blue 3407, C.E. 3412

Louisiana: Community 3469, New Orleans 3503

Maine: Maine 3548, **Sandy 3555**

Maryland: Baker 3567, Baltimore 3568, **Casey 3585**, Community 3599, Knott 3666, Mid 3693, **Zickler 3763**

Massachusetts: Adams 3771, Cabot 3824, Cape Cod 3833, Community 3854, Crossroads 3869, **Kendall 3977**, Lowell 4014, Melville 4034, Oral 4061

Michigan: Ann Arbor 4221, Capital 4243, Community 4255, Community 4257, Fremont 4315, Mott 4400, Nokomis 4404, Upton 4466

Minnesota: Beverly 4517, Bush 4524, Rochester 4668

Missouri: Saint Louis 4896

Nebraska: Lincoln 4987

Nevada: Community 5028, **Walsh 5075**

New Hampshire: New Hampshire 5098

New Jersey: Dircks 5180, Dodge 5181, **Rippel 5368**, Victoria 5440

New Mexico: Santa Fe 5496, Taos 5498

New York: Area 5564, Blue 5640, **Bristol 5666**, Central 5724, **Citigroup 5755**, Clark 5761, Community 5782, Community 5784, Corning 5794, Cricket 5808, Dyson 5898, Elias 5920, **Ford 5970, Goldman 6056, Humanitas 6212, JEHT 6257, JM 6263, Kunstadter 6362**, Luce 6452, Moody's 6569, New York 6613, Richmond 6800, Rochester 6823, Schnurmacher 6931, Sister 6994, Steele 7053, **Tiffany 7137**, Tiger 7139, Tower 7158, Triad 7162, **Wallace 7209**

North Carolina: Cape Fear 7336, Community 7346, Cumberland 7349, Warner 7503, Weaver 7504

Ohio: **Bingham 7549**, Findlay 7627, Jegs 7687, Mayerson 7739, Miami 7748, O'Neill 7783, Scioto 7845, Tuscarawas 7890

Oklahoma: Community 7932, Oklahoma City 7964, Viersen 7985

Oregon: Chambers 8004, Kinsman 8031, Meyer 8042

Pennsylvania: Baker 8092, Birmingham 8107, Chester 8141, Claneil 8144, **Colcom 8150**, Community 8155, Eden 8182, Erie 8188, Heinz 8241, Heinz 8242, Lancaster 8300, McCune 8332, Phoenixville 8381, Pittsburgh 8386

Puerto Rico: Puerto Rico 8515

Rhode Island: Rhode Island 8551

South Carolina: Central 8577, Community 8584, Daniel 8585

Tennessee: Assisi 8638, Community 8660, Community 8661, Frist 8679

Texas: Amarillo 8758, **AT&T 8765**, Dougherty, 8870, Favrot 8897, Houston 8960, Kronkosky 9002, Marathon 9028, Meadows 9049, Powell 9128, Priddy 9131, Rockwell 9154, Simmons 9188, Stark 9209, Tocker 9236

Vermont: Vermont 9361

Virginia: 118 9365, Arlington 9371, Norfolk 9484, Samberg 9510, Weissberg 9536

Washington: Blue 9559, **Brainerd 9561**, Bullitt 9563, **Casey 9567, Edwards 9580**, Fortune 9587, Foundation 9589, Grays 9597, Quixote 9667, Satterberg 9677, Seattle 9680, Sherwood 9683, Tacoma 9693

West Virginia: Parkersburg 9730

Wisconsin: Community 9776, Madison 9854, **Thrivent 9949**, Vine 9956

Wyoming: Wyoming 10000

Matching/challenge support

Alabama: Alabama 1, Blount 14, Bruno 17, Central 20, Community 23, Community 24, Community 25, Compass 28, **Corman 29**, Friedman 35, Hearin 37, Hill 39, Kaul 40, Meyer 52, Smith 63, **Vulcan 73**

Alaska: Alaska 78, Alaska 79, Rasmuson 85

Arizona: A.P.S. 86, Arizona 87, Community 91, Dee 94, **Globe 101, Johnson 112, Kieckhefer 113**, Linde 117, Morris 124, Phelps 129, Piper 130, Sterne 143, Wilson 152

Arkansas: **Frueauff 161**, Rockefeller 172, Ross 174, Wal-Mart 184, **Windgate 189**

California: Ackerman 193, Alafi 201, Amateur 214, **American 217**, Atlas 241, Ayrshire 247,

Bannerman 255, **Beavers 268**, Bechtel 270, Benbough 276, Bireley 292, Buck 330, **Bull 331, C.S. 340**, California 345, **Cantor 354**, Center 369, **Christensen 384**, Collins 397, Community 401, Community 403, Community 405, Community 406, Community 407, **Compton 409**, Confidence 411, Cowell 423, Crail 426, Crocker 429, Darling 440, **Delano 449, DJ & T 458**, Doheny 460, Drown 469, East 474, Eisner 481, **Environment 487**, Fieldstone 506, Firedoll 508, **First 512**, Flora 521, Forest 527, French 536, Garland 556, Gasser 557, Getty 569, **Getty 570**, Girard 580, Global 583, Gogian 588, Goldsmith 599, **Good 603**, Gruber 626, Gumbiner 631, Haas 634, Haas 635, Haas 636, Haas 637, Hale 639, Harden 647, Hedco 663, Hewlett 671, Humboldt 691, Irvine 698, Irvine 699, **Jack 705**, Jacobs 708, Jewett 718, JL 720, Jones 728, **Keck 750**, Kirchgessner 762, Koret 774, Kvamme 781, Lesher 805, Lipman 817, **Living 821**, Livingston 822, Los Altos 828, **Ludwick 830**, Lund 831, Lux 834, Lytel 836, Mabie 839, Majestic 848, Marin 854, McBean 865, McCarthy 868, **McConnell 870**, Mead 881, Mericos 889, Miller 901, Modglin 904, Monterey 910, Morgan 915, Newhall 936, Norris 940, Northrop 942, Noyce 944, Oppenheimer 955, Orfalea 958, Oxnard 969, **Packard 972**, Paloheimo 974, Parker 979, Parsons 980, Peninsula 989, **Righteous 1050**, Riordan 1054, **Rivendell 1056**, Rivkin 1057, Roth 1071, **S.G. 1078, Saban 1079**, Sacramento 1080, San Diego 1087, San Luis 1090, Santa Barbara 1093, Severns 1131, Sierra 1151, Smith 1160, Sobrato 1172, Soda 1173, Sonora 1178, Sorensen 1180, **Spencer 1181**, Stamps 1186, Stauffer 1188, Stern 1195, Stulsaft 1210, Taper 1226, Thornton 1235, Towbes 1241, True 1245, Tuohy 1247, Valley 1256, Valley 1257, Ventura 1264, **Versacare 1265, Warsh 1280**, Weingart 1288, Whittier 1304, WWW 1323
Colorado: Aspen 1338, Boettcher 1344, Bohemian 1345, Chambers 1354, Colorado 1355, Colorado 1356, Community 1357, Community 1359, **Crowell 1361, Daniels 1362**, Denver 1364, ECA 1372, Edmondson 1373, **First 1377**, Gates 1380, **Gill 1382**, Hill 1392, JFM 1397, Johnson 1398, KBK 1400, Kenney 1401, King 1404, Kitzmiller 1405, Pikes 1437, Price 1442, Qwest 1443, Rose 1445, Schlessman 1450, Schramm 1451, **StorageTek 1460**, Summit 1463, Telluride 1465, **Weaver 1469**, Western 1471, Wilhite 1473
Connecticut: **Aetna 1479**, Baldwin 1487, Bodenwein 1497, Calder 1506, Chilton 1511, Collis 1513, Community 1514, Community 1515, Community 1516, Connecticut 1518, Culpeper 1521, **Educational 1533**, Ensworth 1535, **Ettinger 1536**, Fairfield 1537, Freas 1548, Hartford 1563, Hartford 1564, Liberty 1586, Main 1594, Martin 1598, Matthies 1600, Palmer 1621, **Prentice 1630**, Rosenthal 1638, Tauck 1657, **Tremaine 1662**
Delaware: Laffey 1725, Lennox 1726, Marmot 1728, **Raskob 1741**, Welfare 1762
District of Columbia: **Arca 1767, Banyan 1769, Bauman 1770**, Bender 1772, Block 1776, Cafritz 1780, **Foundation 1796**, Fowler 1797, Graham 1804, Henry 1808, **Hitachi 1810**, Kimsey 1817, Loughran 1823, **Lounsbery 1824, Loyola 1825**, McGowan 1830, Meyer 1834, **Moriah 1835**, Munson 1837, **Public 1844**, Reich 1845, Replogle 1846, Spring 1849, **Summit 1852**, Trellis 1853, **Wallace 1857, Wallace 1858, Winslow 1863**
Florida: A Friends' 1866, Amaturo 1873, Bank 1890, Beveridge 1907, Bush 1922, **Chatlos 1932**, Community 1939, Community 1940, Community 1941, Community 1943, Community 1944, Community 1947, Community 1948, Community 1949, Conn 1951, Dade 1957, Darden 1960, **Davis 1964**, Duckwall 1978, Dunn 1979, Dunspaugh 1981, duPont 1983, **Gibney 2021, Goldhammer 2026**, Hayes 2052, Heartbeat 2054, Henderson 2056, Hersh 2058, Jacksonville 2071, **Johnson 2077**, Keating 2084, Kennedy 2087,

Kleist 2095, **Koch 2098**, Lattner 2104, **Morris 2145**, North 2153, Opler 2158, Peacock 2165, Phillips 2168, Price 2177, Quantum 2181, Rayonier 2189, Russell 2212, Saunders 2219, Schmidt 2225, Silverman 2234, **Skelly 2237**, Southwest 2240, **Stacy 2246**, Storer 2252, Sykes 2261, Toppel 2274, **Winn 2301**, Wollowick 2306
Georgia: AEC 2310, Anderson 2317, Brain 2328, Callaway 2336, Callaway 2337, Campbell 2339, **Challenge 2344, Coca-Cola 2352**, Community 2357, Community 2358, Community 2359, Community 2362, Creel 2369, Day 2371, Georgia 2394, Glenn 2399, **Hanley 2405**, Harland 2407, Harris 2408, Jinks 2422, Knox 2427, Lee 2432, Livingston 2435, Lubo 2438, North 2458, Porter 2468, **Rockdale 2474**, Sapelo 2479, **Scientific 2482**, Singletary 2490, Smith 2491, **Turner 2501**, Watson 2509, Williams 2514, Woolley 2525, Zeist 2529
Hawaii: Atherton 2532, Bank 2535, Castle 2538, Cooke 2541, Frear 2543, McInerny 2551, Wilcox 2559
Idaho: CHC 2566, Idaho 2570, Simplot 2575
Illinois: Arthur 2601, Butler 2646, Chicago 2661, Children's 2664, Circle 2666, Coleman 2673, Community 2677, Community 2679, Community 2680, Community 2681, Crown 2691, Cuneo 2692, DeKalb 2701, Dillon 2704, Donnelley 2708, Driehaus 2710, DuPage 2713, Girl's 2757, GKN 2758, Grand 2769, Hamill 2780, Hansen 2782, Harris 2787, Logan 2860, Lumpkin 2864, **MacArthur 2868**, McGraw 2882, McNeil 2887, Meyer 2896, Northern 2918, Oak Park 2922, Oberweiler 2923, Olin 2925, PepsiAmericas 2937, **Relations 2963**, Retirement 2964, Rothschild 2971, **Samaritan 2980**, Seabury 2993, Siragusa 3009, Speh 3014, **Square 3018**, Tawani 3033, **Tyndale 3042**, VNA 3049, Washington 3058
Indiana: Ball 3103, Ball 3104, Blue 3107, Boren 3108, Brown 3110, Central 3116, Clowes 3119, Clowes 3120, Cole 3121, Community 3123, Community 3124, Community 3125, Community 3126, Community 3127, Community 3128, Community 3130, Community 3131, Community 3132, Community 3133, Dearborn 3137, Decatur 3138, DeHaan 3140, Dekko 3142, Elkhart 3145, Fairbanks 3147, Foellinger 3149, Glick 3155, **Guidant 3159**, Hancock 3161, Harrison 3161, Henry 3165, Heritage 3166, Irwin 3175, Jasper 3177, Johnson 3178, Jordan 3180, Koch 3184, Kosciusko 3186, Kuhne 3187, Legacy 3189, **Lilly 3192**, Lilly 3194, Lincoln 3195, **Lumina 3196**, Madison 3197, Montgomery 3206, Noble 3214, Northern 3215, Ogle 3218, Oliver 3219, Portland 3223, Raker 3226, Ripley 3230, Steuben 3241, Tipton 3243, Wayne 3253, Welborn 3254, Wells 3255, West 3256, Whitley 3258
Iowa: Ahrens 3260, Cedar Rapids 3275, Community 3277, Community 3278, Cowles 3279, Des Moines 3281, Hall 3290, Hanson 3291, Hubbell 3297, Iowa 3298, Maytag 3309, Maytag 3310, McElroy 3313, **Pioneer 3324**, Tye 3337
Kansas: Capitol 3350, Hutchinson 3368, Servant 3391, Topeka 3400, Wichita 3404
Kentucky: Blue 3407, Brown 3409, Community 3414, E.ON 3417, Foundation 3420, Hayswood 3425, Robinson 3449
Louisiana: Baptist 3461, Baton Rouge 3462, Booth 3464, Brown 3465, Community 3469, German 3483, Goldring 3484, Huie 3488, Institute 3489, Jones 3491, Monroe 3501, New Orleans 3503, Wilson 3515, Zigler 3520
Maine: Alfond 3521, Davenport 3531, **Ford 3533**, Horizon 3541, King 3545, Lunder 3547, Maine 3548, **Oak 3552, River 3554, Sandy 3555**
Maryland: Abell 3559, Abell 3560, Baltimore 3568, Blades 3574, **Blaustein 3575**, Capital 3584, Columbia 3595, Commonweal 3596, Community 3599, Constellation 3602, England 3622, France 3632, Freeman 3633, Goldseker 3636, Henson 3648, Higginson 3649, Hoffberger 3652, Kerr 3661, **Knapp 3665**, Knott 3666, MARPAT 3684, Marshall 3687, Meyerhoff 3691, Meyerhoff 3692,

Mid 3693, Middendorf 3694, Mulford 3696, Plitt 3706, Polinger 3708, Procter 3711, Rathmann 3715, Rosenberg 3719, **Shared 3727**, Sheridan 3729, TKF 3747, **Town 3749**, Tucker 3750, **Weinberg 3759, Zickler 3763**
Massachusetts: Barr 3791, Behrakis 3796, Berkshire 3801, Boston 3812, Cabot 3823, Cabot 3824, Cabot 3825, Cape Cod 3833, Clarke 3849, Clipper 3850, Community 3855, Davis 3875, **Fidelity 3904**, Fields 3905, Fuller 3918, Ham 3940, High 3950, Highland 3951, Hyams 3961, **Iacocca 3963**, Island 3965, Lee 4001, Linden 4008, Lowell 4015, Melville 4034, Merck 4035, Mifflin 4038, Miller 4039, Millipore 4040, New 4050, **New England 4052**, Parker 4069, Peabody 4072, Peabody 4073, Poss 4087, Riley 4104, **Schooner 4131**, Shapiro 4136, Sheehan 4140, **State 4158**, Stearns 4159, Stevens 4163, Stevens 4164, Stoddard 4165, Sudbury 4173, **Sweet 4176**, Thompson 4181, Wallace 4195
Michigan: Americana 4218, Ann Arbor 4221, **Arcus 4223**, Barry 4227, Battle Creek 4228, Bay 4229, Berrien 4231, Besser 4232, Branch 4237, Capital 4243, Community 4252, Community 4255, Community 4256, Community 4257, Dalton 4266, Dart 4267, DeVos 4276, DeVos 4278, DeVos 4279, Dow 4287, **Fetzer 4297**, Ford 4307, Four 4310, Fremont 4315, General 4320, **Gerber 4321**, Gerstacker 4322, Gilmore 4324, Grand Haven 4325, Grand Rapids 4326, Grand 4327, Greenville 4331, **H.I.S. 4334**, Herrick 4341, Hudson 4343, Jackson 4347, Kalamazoo 4352, **Kellogg 4357, Kresge 4367**, Lansing 4372, Masco 4387, Midland 4392, Miller 4394, Monroe 4396, **Mott 4399**, Mott 4400, Oleson 4405, Petoskey 4412, Plym 4414, Ratner 4417, **Sage 4427**, Saginaw 4428, Steelcase 4446, Sturgis 4452, Towsley 4461, Vanderweide 4469, Weatherwax 4474, Wege 4476, Whirlpool 4480, Wilson 4485
Minnesota: Bigelow 4519, Blandin 4520, Bremer 4523, Bush 4524, **Cafesjian 4527**, Carolyn 4533, Charlson 4537, Deikel 4548, Frey 4566, Graco 4573, Griggs 4577, Hardenbergh 4583, HRK 4589, Initiative 4593, Kopp 4599, **Land 4602**, Lilly 4606, Marbrook 4612, Mardag 4613, McKnight 4617, Neilson 4631, Northwest 4637, **O'Shaughnessy 4639**, Ordean 4643, Oswald 4645, Phillips 4655, Red Wing 4663, Rochester 4668, Rupp 4669, Saint Paul 4671, Slaggie 4686, Southways 4688, **Toro 4702**, Wasie 4716, Wedum 4719, Winona 4729
Mississippi: Community 4737, Foundation 4743, Gulf 4745, Hardin 4747, Irby 4750, Lower 4751, Maddox 4753, Riley 4763
Missouri: Ameren 4772, **Anheuser 4776**, Brown 4788, Community 4798, Curry 4802, Danforth 4803, **Fox 4815**, Gateway 4817, Goppert 4819, Green 4822, H & R 4823, Jenkins 4836, Jewish 4837, JSM 4841, Kansas 4842, **Kauffman 4843**, Lichtenstein 4855, **Monsanto 4868**, Musgrave 4870, **Pillsbury 4883**, Saigh 4895, Saint Louis 4896, Stupp 4911, Sunnen 4913, Truman 4919
Montana: Cinnabar 4935, **Edwards 4936**
Nebraska: **ConAgra 4953**, Cooper 4954, Dunklau 4958, Fremont 4962, Heuermann 4973, Hirschfeld 4974, Hitchcock 4975, Kiewit 4984, Kilbourne 4985, Lexington 4986, Lincoln 4987, Lozier 4988, Omaha 4994, Omaha 4995, Reynolds 4997, Storz 5006, Woods 5018
Nevada: **Buck 5025**, Cord 5029, Fairweather 5032, Hawkins 5036, **Hilton 5037**, Nevada 5047, **Tang 5072, Walsh 5075**
New Hampshire: Bean 5080, **Dorr 5086**, Foundation 5089, Fuller 5090, HNHfoundation 5092, Hunt 5093, Lindsay 5095
New Jersey: **Barbour 5124**, Borden 5138, Buehler 5146, Bunbury 5148, Campbell 5151, **Carlson 5155, Carolan 5156, Clare 5164**, Cowles 5170, Dodge 5181, Fund 5199, Hyde 5247, **International 5252, Johnson 5265**, Knistrom 5282, Machuga 5311, Martini 5319, MCJ 5324, **Newcombe 5338**, OceanFirst 5341, Pascale 5349, **Rippel 5368**, Roberts 5371, **Schumann 5390**, Summit 5417,

Professorships

Colorado: Community 1359
Connecticut: **Deloitte 1527**, Heyman 1567, Larsen 1579, **Lingnan 1587**, Stone 1654, Wallace 1674
Delaware: Bennett 1690, **Good 1715**, Rowland 1749
District of Columbia: Gudelsky 1805, Roshan 1847
Florida: **Davis 1964**, Duckwall 1978, Dunspaugh 1981, duPont 1983, Engelberg 1994, Opler 2158, Rosenberg 2206, St. Joe 2244
Georgia: AEC 2310, Brown 2332, Courts 2364, Harrison 2410, Lee 2432, Mason 2444, Pitts 2463, Woolley 2525
Illinois: Arthur 2601, Coleman 2673, Crown 2691, Davee 2696, Freehling 2737, Geraldi 2752, Grainger 2768, Harris 2788, McGraw 2882, **Square 3018**, Tawani 3033, Tellabs 3034
Indiana: Ball 3103, Ball 3104, Bussing 3111, Clowes 3120, Lilly 3194, Rolland 3231
Iowa: Blank 3268, Carver 3274, Maytag 3310, McElroy 3313, Principal 3326
Kansas: Capitol 3350
Kentucky: Brown 3409, **Humana 3428**
Louisiana: Booth 3464, Coughlin 3470, Coypu 3471, Huie 3488, Jones 3491
Maryland: **Hughes 3654**, Kerr 3661, Meyerhoff 3691, Meyerhoff 3692, Middendorf 3694
Massachusetts: Alden 3776, **Iacocca 3963**, Pappas 4066, Poss 4087, **Schooner 4131**
Michigan: Community 4252, DeVlieg 4275, **Foundation 4309**, Herrick 4341, Towsley 4461
Minnesota: Kelley 4597, Marbrook 4612
Mississippi: Community 4737, Hardin 4747
Missouri: Commerce 4797, Cray 4801, Edison 4807, JSM 4841, Sosland 4908, Sycamore 4915
Nebraska: Hirschfeld 4974, Perkins 4996, Weitz 5016
New Jersey: Cowles 5170, McMullen 5325
New Mexico: Hubbard 5481
New York: **Atran 5575**, Avery 5581, Berg 5621, Bernhard 5624, Carwill 5711, Charina 5731, **Chazen 5739**, Cullman 5812, Dyson 5898, **Frankel 5976**, Freeman 5981, Gilliam 6031, Gleason 6039, Griffis 6107, Kaplan 6288, Kennedy 6314, **Kress 6357**, Lang 6374, Lehman 6396, Leonhardt 6403, **Luce 6453**, Moses 6587, Oishei 6660, **Open 6665**, Penick 6709, **Pforzheimer 6721**, Ruffin 6880, Schaffer 6911, Simons 6989, Solow 7019, **Solow 7020**, **Starr 7048**, Statler 7050, Steele 7053, Ungar 7183, **Vetlesen 7196**, **Walter 7211**, Weinberg 7230, **Zenkel 7295**
North Carolina: BB&T 7312, Belk 7315, Blumenthal 7320, Dover 7356, Duke 7359, Duke 7360, Glenn 7376, Smith 7479, Weaver 7504
Ohio: Fox 7638, Humphrey 7679, Kulas 7706, Morley 7763, Osteopathic 7791, Sage 7829, **Scripps 7848**, Wolfe 7915
Oklahoma: Kerr 7949, McGee 7957, Meinders 7960, Noble 7963, Oklahoma 7965, Presbyterian 7969, Puterbaugh 7970, Sarkeys 7974, **Schusterman 7975**
Oregon: Haugland 8018, Schnitzer 8057, Swigert 8061, Swindells 8062
Pennsylvania: Eberly 8179, Hillman 8249, Independence 8266, Mandell 8322, Roberts 8405, **Seraph 8434**, Simmons 8441, Stabler 8455
Puerto Rico: Puerto Rico 8515
South Carolina: Abney 8564, Bruce 8571
Tennessee: Plough 8718
Texas: Austin 8768, Belo 8787, Brown 8799, Cain 8808, Cain 8809, Carter 8816, Cockrell 8835, Cook 8845, Cullen 8854, Dunn 8872, Fisch 8901, Fish 8902, Fleming 8904, Houston 8960, Houston 8961, Kempner 8987, Kinder 8994, Klabzuba 8996, Lowe 9020, Lyons 9024, McDermott 9043, McGovern 9044, Mitte 9067, Rockwell 9154, San Antonio 9166, **Shell 9181**, Simmons 9188, **Starling 9210**, Sterling 9212, Strake 9215, Summerlee 9217, Temple 9227, Waggoner 9256, Wal 9260, West 9276, White 9279
Utah: Eccles 9319, Stewart 9345
Vermont: Lintilhac 9359

Virginia: de Beaumont 9408, Flagler 9417, Landmark 9455, Olsson 9491, Reynolds 9503, SunTrust 9523, Titmus 9527, **Winkler 9542**
Washington: Anderson 9551, **Boeing 9560**, Lockwood 9631, Norcliffe 9650, Quixote 9667
West Virginia: Maier 9725
Wisconsin: Assurant 9748, **Bradley 9763**, Evjue 9797, Four 9803, Helfaer 9813, **Kohler 9839**, Kress 9844, **Lewis 9850**, Mead 9867

Program development

Alabama: Brock 16, Bruno 17, Caring 18, Central 20, Community 23, Community 24, Community 25, Compass 28, **Corman 29**, Dixon 32, Hearin 37, Hill 39, Kaul 40, Lowe 45, Meyer 52, Moody 54, Protective 58, **Vulcan 73**, Webb 75
Alaska: Alaska 78, Alaska 79, CIRI 83, Rasmuson 85
Arizona: Arizona 87, Community 91, Dee 94, Flinn 98, **Globe 101**, Hansen 104, **Johnson 112**, **Kieckhefer 113**, Lovell 119, Morris 124, Neely 125, Ottens 128, Piper 130, **Research 134**, Wilson 152
Arkansas: Arkansas 156, Blue 157, **Frueauff 161**, Northwest 169, Rockefeller 172, Ross 174, Schmieding 175, Taylor 179, Wingate 189
California: Ackerman 193, Alliance 204, **Allianz 205**, Alpert 208, **Amado 212**, Amateur 214, **American 217**, Amgen 219, Anaheim 220, Anderson 221, Aratani 230, Archstone 232, Argyros 234, **Arkay 235**, Arntz 236, Arrillaga 237, Atkinson 239, Atlas 241, Avery 244, Ayrshire 247, **Baker 252**, Bannerman 255, Barker 257, Baxter 262, Bay 264, **Bechtel 269**, Bechtel 270, Bella 275, Benbough 276, Berry 284, Blue 296, Bohnett 300, Buck 330, **Bull 331**, Burch 334, California 345, California 347, California 350, **Castagnola 366**, Center 369, **ChevronTexaco 380**, Chiron 383, **Christensen 384**, Clorox 389, Collins 397, Columbia 399, Community 401, Community 402, Community 403, Community 404, Community 405, Community 406, Community 407, **Compton 409**, Confidence 411, Connell 412, Cowell 423, Crail 426, Crocker 429, Crockett 430, **Delano 449**, Disney 456, Doheny 460, **Draper 466**, Drown 469, Drum 470, East 474, Eisner 481, Eldorado 482, **Energy 483**, **Environment 487**, Fieldstone 506, Firedoll 508, **Firelight 509**, **First 512**, Fleishhacker 518, Flintridge 520, Flora 521, Fluor 523, Forest 527, **Foundation 529**, French 536, Friedman 538, **Fund 542**, Gaia 545, Gamble 549, Gap 551, Gasser 557, Geffen 558, Gellert 559, GenCorp 560, Genentech 563, Gerbode 564, Geschke 568, **Getty 570**, Gill 576, Girard 580, Global 583, Godric 586, Gogian 588, Gold 590, Goldman 595, Goldman 596, Goldman 597, Goldwyn 600, **Google 606**, Gross 621, Gruber 626, **GSF 627**, Gumbiner 631, Haas 635, Haas 636, Haas 637, Hale 639, Hannon 644, Hannon 645, Heller 666, Hewlett 671, **Hewlett 672**, Hoag 678, Hughes 690, Humboldt 691, **Hume 692**, Intuit 696, Irvine 698, Irvine 699, **Jack 705**, Jacobs 708, Jewett 718, JL 720, Johnson 725, **Joseph 730**, **K.L. 736**, **Kaiser 739**, **Kalliopeia 740**, **Keck 750**, Keller 752, Kimball 759, Kirchgessner 762, Koret 774, Langendorf 788, Leatherby 796, **LEF 799**, Lesher 805, **Lloyd 823**, LLWW 824, Los Altos 828, Lurie 832, Lutz 833, Lux 834, **M & T 837**, Majestic 848, Marin 854, **Marisla 855**, **Mattel 861**, McCarthy 868, McCune 872, McKesson 879, McLean 880, Mead 881, Mental 886, Mericos 889, Michelson 895, Miller 901, Modglin 904, Moore 912, **Moore 913**, Morgan 915, Mosher 920, Murphy 928, NBC 933, Nissan 939, Norris 940, Norton 943, Noyce 944, Oppenheimer 955, Orange 957, Orfalea 958, Osher 961, Pacific 970, **Packard 972**, Paloheimo 974, Parker 979, Parsons 980, Peery 986, Peninsula 989, Penney 990, Peppers 991, **Peterson 996**, PG&E 1000, **PMI 1008**, Pottruck 1013, Ralphs 1029, Rancho 1031, **Reinhard 1037**, **Righteous 1050**, Riordan 1054, **Rivendell 1056**, Roberts 1058, Rosenberg 1065, Rosenberg 1066, **S.G. 1078**, **Saban 1079**, Sacramento 1080, Saga 1081,

San Diego 1087, San Francisco 1088, San Luis 1090, Santa Barbara 1093, **Schuler 1108**, Schwab 1109, Serenity 1128, Severns 1131, Sierra 1151, Sierra 1152, **Smith 1161**, **Smith 1166**, **Smith 1167**, Smullin 1169, Sobrato 1172, Soda 1173, Sonora 1178, Sorensen 1180, **Spencer 1181**, Stamps 1186, Steele 1189, Stern 1195, Stone 1200, **Strauss 1203**, **Streisand 1204**, Stuart 1206, Stuart 1208, Stulsaft 1210, **Stupski 1211**, Sudikoff 1212, **Sun 1214**, Synopsys 1222, Synopsys 1223, Taper 1226, Tesuque 1234, Towbes 1241, Truckee 1244, True 1245, Trust 1246, Ueberroth 1248, UniHealth 1249, Union 1250, Valley 1256, Valley 1257, vanLobenSels 1260, Van Nuys 1261, Ventura 1264, **Versacare 1265**, Vodafone 1267, Vons 1270, Waltmar 1277, Wattis 1283, Weingart 1288, **WellPoint 1292**, **Wells 1294**, Whitecap 1303, Whittier 1304, Witter 1314, Wollenberg 1317, WWW 1323, Zellerbach 1326
Colorado: Animal 1333, Anschutz 1334, Aspen 1338, Bohemian 1345, Bohen 1346, Bonfils 1347, Brett 1349, Chambers 1354, Colorado 1356, Community 1357, Community 1358, Community 1359, Coors 1360, **Crowell 1361**, **Daniels 1362**, Denver 1364, Donnell 1368, ECA 1372, Edmondson 1373, El Pomar 1374, **First 1377**, **General 1381**, **Gill 1382**, Hill 1392, Hughes 1393, **Janus 1396**, JFM 1397, Johnson 1398, Kenney 1401, Kinder 1403, King 1404, Kitzmiller 1405, M.D.C. 1413, **Mercy 1426**, Piton 1439, Price 1442, Qwest 1443, Rose 1445, Saeman 1448, Schlessman 1450, Schramm 1451, Summit 1463, Telluride 1465, **Weaver 1469**, Wolf 1475, Yampa 1477
Connecticut: **Aetna 1479**, American 1482, **Applera 1484**, **Bingham 1493**, Bissell 1495, Bodenwein 1497, Boehringer 1498, Bridgeport 1504, Calder 1506, Collis 1513, Community 1514, Community 1515, Community 1516, Community 1517, Connecticut 1518, Culpeper 1521, **Educational 1533**, Ensworth 1535, **Ettinger 1536**, Fairfield 1537, Fisher 1542, Freas 1548, **GE 1553**, Graustein 1559, Hartford 1563, Hartford 1564, **Hoffman 1568**, **Huisking 1570**, International 1571, Larsen 1579, Liberty 1586, **Lingnan 1587**, Lone 1589, Long 1590, Main 1594, MassMutual 1599, Matthies 1600, **McKenzie 1601**, Mortensen 1605, Palmer 1621, Panwy 1622, Patricelli 1623, Perrin 1626, **Praxair 1629**, **Prentice 1630**, Rosenthal 1638, Stone 1654, Tauck 1657, Tow 1661, **Tremaine 1662**, Tully 1665, **Valentine 1669**, **Xerox 1680**
Delaware: Cawley 1696, **CTW 1703**, Delaware 1706, **Glencoe 1714**, **Good 1715**, Lennox 1726, MBNA 1730, Phillips 1739, **Raskob 1741**, **Robinson 1745**
District of Columbia: Aid 1765, **Arca 1767**, **Banyan 1769**, **Bauman 1770**, Bender 1772, Bernstein 1775, Block 1776, **Butler 1779**, Cafritz 1780, Community 1785, Consumer 1786, **Fannie 1793**, Freed 1798, Graham 1804, Gudelsky 1805, Henry 1808, **Hitachi 1810**, Jones 1813, Jovid 1814, **Kennedy 1816**, Kimsey 1817, **Koch 1819**, Leonsis 1822, McGowan 1830, Mead 1832, Meyer 1834, **Moriah 1835**, Munson 1837, **Public 1844**, Reich 1845, Replogle 1846, Roshan 1847, Spring 1849, Stewart 1850, Strong 1851, **Summit 1852**, Trellis 1853, True 1854, Vradenburg 1856, **Wallace 1857**, **Wallace 1858**, Willoughby 1862, **Winslow 1863**, Wyss 1864
Florida: A Friends' 1866, Bank 1890, **Believers 1900**, Beveridge 1907, Burns 1920, Bush 1922, **Chatlos 1932**, Cisneros 1934, Community 1939, Community 1940, Community 1941, Community 1942, Community 1943, Community 1946, Community 1947, Community 1948, Community 1949, Conn 1951, Dade 1957, Darden 1960, **Davis 1964**, **DeMoss 1968**, Dunn 1979, Dunspaugh 1981, duPont 1983, Engelberg 1994, **Gibney 2021**, **Goldhammer 2026**, Gooding 2028, Greenburg 2034, Gulf 2041, Gulf 2042, Henderson 2056, Jacksonville 2071, Jasam 2074, Katz 2081, Kennedy 2087, **Koch 2098**, Lattner 2104,

MacDonald 2121, **Morris 2145**, Peacock 2165, Phillips 2168, **Picower 2169**, Publix 2180, Quantum 2181, Rayonier 2189, Rosenberg 2206, Russell 2212, Saunders 2219, **Scaife 2220**, Schoenbaum 2227, Southwest 2240, Taylor 2267, TECO 2270, Toppel 2274, Vaughn 2279, Wahlert 2284, **Whitehall 2297**, **Winn 2301**

Georgia: Aflac 2311, AGL 2312, Amos 2314, Anderson 2317, Atlanta 2320, BellSouth 2323, Cawood 2342, **Challenge 2344**, Chatham 2347, **Coca-Cola 2352**, Community 2355, Community 2356, Community 2359, Community 2362, Courts 2364, Cousins 2365, Cox 2367, Cox 2368, Creel 2369, Delta 2372, Exposition 2380, Georgia 2394, Georgia 2395, **Georgia 2397**, Glenn 2399, Goizueta 2400, **Hanley 2405**, Harris 2408, Harrison 2410, Healthcare 2411, Horowitz 2415, Illges 2416, Imlay 2417, ING 2418, Jinks 2422, Knox 2427, Lanier 2428, Lee 2432, Lubo 2438, Mason 2444, **Meyer 2446**, North 2458, **Rockdale 2474**, Sapelo 2479, Savannah 2480, **Scientific 2482**, Southern 2494, Watson 2509, Williams 2514, Woodruff 2521, Woodward 2523

Hawaii: Alexander 2530, Atherton 2532, Bank 2535, Campbell 2536, Castle 2537, Castle 2538, Cooke 2541, First 2542, Frear 2543, Geist 2544, Hawaii 2545, Hawaiian 2546, Lange 2550, McInerny 2551, Vidinha 2557, Watumull 2558, Wilcox 2559

Idaho: Albertson 2562, Cunningham 2567, **Micron 2571**

Illinois: **Allen 2587**, **Allstate 2588**, **Aon 2598**, Arthur 2601, **Baxter 2611**, Blowitz 2623, **Brach 2630**, Brinson 2633, **Brunswick 2636**, **Burlington 2644**, Butler 2646, Caterpillar 2653, Chaddick 2655, Cheney 2658, Chicago 2661, Chicago 2663, CNA 2670, Coleman 2673, Comer 2675, Community 2677, Community 2681, Crown 2691, Deere 2699, Dillon 2704, Donnelley 2706, Driehaus 2710, DuPage 2713, Energizer 2721, Field 2728, Flagg 2731, Fry 2740, Girl's 2757, **Graham 2767**, Grainger 2768, Grand 2769, Grant 2770, Harris 2787, Harris 2789, Hartmarx 2794, Hermann 2798, Hospira 2804, Houlsby 2805, Illinois 2812, **Irwin 2814**, **Joyce 2820**, Kaplan 2823, Kemper 2831, **Kemper 2832**, Kendall 2833, Kenny's 2835, Landau 2847, Little 2859, Lumpkin 2864, **MacArthur 2867**, **MacArthur 2868**, Mayer 2876, McDougal 2881, McNeil 2887, Meyer 2896, Millard 2897, **Mundi 2908**, Nelson 2911, New 2912, Northern 2918, Oak Park 2922, Olin 2925, Pick 2943, Polk 2946, Prince 2948, Pullman 2957, Reese 2961, Regenstein 2962, **Relations 2963**, Retirement 2964, Rothschild 2971, Sara 2982, **Scholl 2989**, Seabury 2993, **Shifting 3006**, Siragusa 3009, Speh 3014, Sprague 3016, **State 3019**, Steans 3021, Stern 3023, Takiff 3032, Tawani 3033, Tellabs 3034, **Tyndale 3042**, USG 3046, VNA 3049, **Wadsworth 3050**, Washington 3058, White 3067, Woods 3084

Indiana: Anderson 3099, Ball 3103, Ball 3104, Blue 3107, Brown 3110, Bussing 3111, Central 3116, Clowes 3119, Clowes 3120, Community 3123, Community 3124, Community 3125, Community 3126, Community 3127, Community 3128, Community 3130, Community 3132, **Cummins 3136**, Dearborn 3137, Decatur 3138, DeHaan 3140, DeKalb 3141, Dekko 3142, Elkhart 3145, Fairbanks 3147, Finish 3148, Foellinger 3149, Glick 3155, **Goodrich 3157**, **Guidant 3159**, Harrison 3161, Health 3164, Henry 3165, Heritage 3166, Irwin 3175, Johnson 3178, Koch 3184, Kosciusko 3186, Kuhne 3187, Legacy 3189, Lilly 3194, Lincoln 3195, **Lumina 3196**, Madison 3197, McMillen 3203, Montgomery 3206, Moore 3207, Noble 3214, Northern 3215, Noyes 3216, Oliver 3219, Portland 3223, Pulliam 3224, Raker 3226, Rolland 3231, Steuben 3241, Tipton 3243, Unity 3247, Vectren 3249, Waterfield 3252, Wayne 3253, Welborn 3254, Wells 3255

Iowa: Ahrens 3260, Carver 3274, Cedar Rapids 3275, Community 3278, Des Moines 3281, Hubbell 3297, Iowa 3298, Maytag 3310, McElroy 3313,

Meredith 3314, Mid-Iowa 3317, Pella 3323, **Pioneer 3324**, Poweshiek 3325, Principal 3326, **Rockwell 3328**, Siouxland 3332, Tye 3337, Wellmark 3343

Kansas: Bane 3345, Baughman 3346, Capitol 3350, Cessna 3351, Delta 3354, DeVore 3357, Farah 3362, Hutchinson 3368, Kansas 3372, Koch 3374, Lloyd 3375, Payless 3380, Rhoden 3383, Sabatini 3386, Salina 3387, Servant 3391, Sprint 3395, Topeka 3400, Wiedemann 3405

Kentucky: Bavarian 3406, C.E. 3412, Community 3414, Community 3415, Cralle 3416, E.ON 3417, Foundation 3420, Gheens 3421, Hayswood 3425, Keeneland 3432, Norton 3441, **Omnicare 3444**, Sutherland 3451

Louisiana: Baptist 3461, Baton Rouge 3462, Community 3469, Coughlin 3470, Coypu 3471, Entergy 3474, Freeman 3480, German 3483, Goldring 3484, Huie 3488, Institute 3489, Jones 3491, New Orleans 3503, Pennington 3505, RosaMary 3507, Wheless 3514, Wilson 3515, **Woldenberg 3516**, Woolf 3517, Zigler 3520

Maine: Burnham 3527, **Ford 3533**, **Golden 3538**, Horizon 3541, JTG 3542, King 3545, Libra 3546, Maine 3548, Maine 3549, **Oak 3552**, **River 3554**, TD 3558

Maryland: Abell 3559, Abell 3560, Baker 3566, Baker 3567, Baltimore 3568, Blades 3574, **Blaustein 3575**, Blaustein 3576, **Casey 3585**, Choice 3589, Columbia 3595, Commonweal 3596, Community 3598, Community 3599, Community 3600, Concordia 3601, Constellation 3602, Delaplaine 3614, Deutsch 3616, England 3622, France 3632, Freeman 3633, Goldseker 3636, Grace 3638, **Head 3644**, Higginson 3649, Hoffberger 3652, **Hughes 3654**, Kerr 3661, Knott 3666, Leidy 3673, Lockhart 3681, Lockheed 3682, Macht 3683, MARPAT 3684, Meyerhoff 3691, Meyerhoff 3692, Mid 3693, **Nasdaq 3700**, O'Neil 3701, Polinger 3708, Price 3709, Provident 3712, Rathmann 3715, Rouse 3724, **Shared 3727**, Sheridan 3729, Straus 3738, Thalheimer 3744, TKF 3747, **Town 3749**, Tucker 3750, Wasserman 3757, Weiss 3760, Wilson 3761

Massachusetts: Adams 3771, **Alchemy 3775**, Alden 3777, **Azadoutioun 3786**, Babson 3787, Balfour 3790, Barr 3791, Bayrd 3795, Behrakis 3796, Berkshire 3801, Birmingham 3807, **Bosack 3809**, Boston 3812, **Bruner 3819**, Cabot 3823, Cabot 3824, Cabot 3825, Cambridge 3828, Campbell 3830, Cape Cod 3832, Chase 3847, Clarke 3849, Clipper 3850, Community 3854, Community 3855, **Conservation 3858**, Cox 3863, Crossroads 3869, Davis 3875, Eastern 3886, Easthampton 3887, Eaton 3888, Essex 3897, Farnsworth 3899, **Fidelity 3904**, Filene 3907, Grand 3929, Grinspoon 3935, Ham 3940, Harrington 3943, High 3950, Highland 3951, Hoche 3954, Hyams 3961, Island 3965, Johnson 3970, **Kendall 3977**, **Lalor 3993**, Lee 4001, Liberty 4006, Linde 4007, Linden 4008, Melville 4034, Merck 4035, **Merck 4036**, Millipore 4040, Morse 4044, **New England 4052**, New 4054, Oral 4061, Orchard 4062, Pardoe 4068, Parker 4069, Peabody 4073, Perpetual 4078, Rasmussen 4094, Ratshesky 4095, **Reebok 4098**, Riley 4104, Rubenstein 4115, Salem 4125, **Schooner 4131**, Schott 4132, Shapiro 4136, Sharf 4137, Shaw 4139, Smith 4150, **State 4158**, Stearns 4159, Stearns 4160, Stevens 4163, Stevens 4164, Stoneman 4168, Swartz 4175, Talbots 4178, Thompson 4181, Webster 4201, Worcester 4209

Michigan: Abrams 4213, Americana 4218, Ann Arbor 4221, **Arcus 4223**, **ArvinMeritor 4224**, Ave 4225, Barry 4227, Battle Creek 4228, Bay 4229, Berrien 4231, Binda 4233, Boutell 4236, Capital 4243, Charlevoix 4246, Community 4252, Community 4253, Community 4254, Community 4255, Community 4257, Community 4258, Cook 4262, **DaimlerChrysler 4265**, Dalton 4266, Dart 4267, Davenport 4269, **DENSO 4272**, DeRoy 4273, DeVos 4276, DeVos 4278, DeVos 4279, Doornink

4283, Dow 4284, **Dow 4285**, Dow 4286, Dow 4287, Eddy 4292, **Fetzer 4297**, Ford 4307, Four 4310, Frankel 4314, Fremont 4315, Frey 4316, General 4320, Gilmore 4324, Grand Haven 4325, Grand Rapids 4326, Grand 4327, Greenville 4331, Herrick 4341, Hudson 4343, Hurst 4344, Jackson 4347, Kalamazoo 4352, Kellogg 4357, Kennedy 4360, Knight 4364, Lansing 4372, Marcks 4385, McGregor 4389, Miller 4394, Monroe 4396, **Mott 4399**, Mott 4400, Nokomis 4404, Perrigo 4410, Petoskey 4412, Plym 4414, Ratner 4417, **Sage 4427**, Saginaw 4428, Skillman 4438, St. Deny's 4444, Steelcase 4446, **Stoddard 4447**, Strosacker 4450, Sturgis 4452, Thompson 4458, Towsley 4461, Upjohn 4465, Upton 4466, Vanderweide 4469, Wege 4476, Westerman 4478, Whirlpool 4480, Whiting 4482, Wilson 4485, Wolters 4487, World 4489

Minnesota: **3M 4492**, Adams 4495, AHS 4497, **Andersen 4501**, Andersen 4502, Ankeny 4505, Athwin 4508, Bayport 4512, Beim 4513, Bell 4514, **Best 4516**, Beverly 4517, Bigelow 4519, Blandin 4520, Blue 4521, Bremer 4523, Bush 4524, Butler 4525, Cargill 4530, Central 4534, **CHS 4540**, Deikel 4548, Duluth 4556, **Ecolab 4557**, Edina 4560, Edwards 4561, Frey 4566, General 4570, George 4572, Graco 4573, Greycoach 4575, Greystone 4576, Grossman 4578, Grotto 4579, Hardenbergh 4583, **Homeownership 4587**, HRK 4589, Initiative 4593, Jerome 4595, Jostens 4596, Kelley 4597, Lilly 4606, Marbrook 4612, Mardag 4613, McKnight 4617, McNeely 4619, **Medtronic 4622**, Minneapolis 4623, Musser 4629, Neilson 4631, Northwest 4637, **O'Shaughnessy 4639**, Ordean 4643, Oswald 4645, **Pentair 4649**, **Petters 4653**, Phillips 4655, RBC 4661, Red Wing 4663, Saint Paul 4671, Schwan's 4676, Securian 4677, Smikis 4687, St. Paul 4690, Star 4691, **SUPERVALU 4695**, Target 4697, TCF 4699, Thorpe 4701, **U.S. 4704**, Walker 4711, Wasie 4716, WCA 4718, West 4723, **Weyerhaeuser 4725**, Winona 4729, Xcel 4732

Mississippi: **Armstrong 4734**, Community 4737, Foundation 4743, Hardin 4747, Irby 4750, Maddox 4753

Missouri: Ameren 4772, **Anheuser 4776**, Baer 4778, Baer 4779, Bellwether 4782, Boeing 4785, Commerce 4797, Community 4798, Cray 4801, Curry 4802, Danforth 4803, **Deer 4804**, **Enterprise 4810**, Fox 4815, **Francis 4816**, Goppert 4819, Green 4822, H & R 4823, Hall 4824, Hallmark 4825, JSM 4841, Kansas 4842, **Kauffman 4843**, Kauffman 4844, Kellwood 4845, Kemper 4849, Laclede 4852, Long 4858, Lopata 4859, **Monsanto 4868**, Musgrave 4870, Nestle 4872, Oppenstein 4876, Pershing 4880, Pillsbury 4884, Saigh 4895, Saint Louis 4896, Seaworld 4900, Shaw 4901, Simon 4903, Sosland 4908, Stern 4909, Stupp 4911, Sunnen 4913, Trio 4918, Truman 4919, Whitaker 4926

Montana: **Edwards 4936**, Washington 4941

Nebraska: **ConAgra 4953**, Cooper 4954, Fremont 4962, Heuermann 4973, Hirschfeld 4974, Kiewit 4984, Lexington 4986, Lincoln 4987, **McDonald 4989**, Mid-Nebraska 4991, Omaha 4994, Omaha 4995, Perkins 4996, **Union 5012**, Woods 5018

Nevada: **Buck 5025**, Community 5028, Cord 5029, Hawkins 5036, **Hilton 5037**, Nevada 5047, Reynolds 5056, Sierra 5064, Southwest 5066, **Walsh 5075**, Wendy's 5076, Wiegand 5077

New Hampshire: Bean 5080, **Dorr 5086**, Eastman 5087, Endowment 5088, Foundation 5089, Fuller 5090, HNHfoundation 5092, Hunt 5093, Lindsay 5095, New Hampshire 5098, Trust 5103

New Jersey: Alcatel 5110, Aventis 5120, **Barbour 5124**, Bard 5125, Borden 5138, Bunbury 5148, Campbell 5151, **Carolan 5156**, Community 5167, Cowles 5170, Danellie 5177, Dircks 5180, Dodge 5181, **Edison 5186**, Elizabethtown 5188, Fund 5199, Harbourton 5223, Healthcare 5228, Hidden 5233, **Huber 5244**, **International 5252**, Johnson

5261, **Johnson 5265**, Karma 5269, Kirby 5279, Laurie 5297, **Lautenberg 5298**, Machuga 5311, **Merck 5326**, OceanFirst 5341, Orange 5343, Pascale 5349, Princeton 5357, Provident 5359, Prudential 5360, PSEG 5361, **Rippel 5368**, Schenck 5386, Schering 5387, **Schumann 5390**, Schumann 5391, Subaru 5415, Summit 5417, Sunfield 5418, **Tang 5423**, **Tavitian 5426**, Turrell 5431, Victoria 5440, Wallerstein 5446, Weston 5452, Zobel 5464

New Mexico: Albuquerque 5466, Carlsbad 5469, Con 5471, Cudd 5472, Domanica 5475, Frost 5476, Holt 5480, **Johns 5482**, Kind 5483, **Levinson 5486**, Maddox 5487, McCune 5488, Messengers 5489, New 5490, New Mexico 5491, PNM 5493, Santa Fe 5496, Taos 5498, **Thaw 5500**, Thornburg 5501

New York: **Abelard 5508**, Abeles 5509, Abrons 5511, Abrons 5512, Achelis 5513, Adirondack 5517, Alexander 5532, Altman 5542, **American 5551**, **American 5553**, **Archbold 5563**, Area 5564, Aron 5569, **Atran 5575**, Auchincloss 5577, **AVI 5582**, **Avon 5583**, **AXA 5584**, Badgeley 5588, Barker 5599, **Barth 5603**, Bausch 5605, **Bay 5606**, **Beldon 5614**, Berg 5621, Bluhdorn 5642, Bodman 5647, Booth 5651, Botwinick 5653, Bowne 5655, **Bristol 5666**, **Bronfman 5673**, Buck 5682, Burden 5687, Burns 5689, **Bydale 5694**, Carnahan 5706, **Carnegie 5707**, Carvel 5710, Cary 5712, Central 5724, Chadwick 5726, Charitable 5732, Charitable 5734, Chautauqua 5738, **China 5750**, Chisholm 5753, **Citigroup 5755**, Claiborne 5758, Clark 5759, **Clark 5760**, Clark 5761, Clark 5762, **Commonwealth 5779**, Community 5780, Community 5781, Community 5782, Community 5783, Community 5784, Community 5785, **Copland 5789**, **Cornell 5793**, Corning 5794, Cricket 5808, **Cummings 5814**, Cummings 5815, Curran 5816, Dammann 5824, **Dana 5826**, de Coizart 5839, **de Hirsch 5840**, DeCamp 5845, Decker 5846, DeMatteis 5852, **Deutsche 5854**, Dewar 5856, Dolan 5869, **Donner 5873**, **Dreyfus 5886**, Dreyfus 5887, Dyson 5898, East 5901, **Edouard 5909**, **EHA 5912**, Elmezzi 5925, Emerson 5927, **Engelhard 5932**, Faulkner 5948, First 5958, **Ford 5970**, **Foundation 5971**, **Frankenberg 5977**, Freeman 5981, Frog 5992, **Fuld 5999**, Gifford 6026, Gilman 6032, **Gilman 6033**, Gimbel 6034, Glens Falls 6041, **Global 6043**, **Goldman 6052**, Goldman 6053, **Goldman 6056**, Goldsmith 6060, Gould 6083, **Grant 6091**, **Grant 6092**, Greentree 6102, **Greenwall 6103**, Grigg 6108, **Gruss 6116**, Guttman 6124, Hagedorn 6130, Harkness 6145, **Hartford 6150**, **Hauser 6155**, Hayden 6158, Hazen 6160, **Hearst 6161**, **Hearst 6162**, Heckscher 6164, **Heineman 6165**, Hermione 6175, **Heron 6176**, **HKH 6190**, Hoyt 6203, HSBC 6204, Hudson 6207, Hugoton 6210, **Humanitas 6212**, Hutchins 6218, **IBM 6221**, Independence 6229, **Initial 6231**, **Ittleson 6241**, Jackson Hole 6246, **JEHT 6257**, **JM 6263**, Johnson 6268, Jones 6274, Joy 6276, **JPMorgan 6277**, **Kade 6281**, Kaplan 6288, Kaplan 6290, **Kaufmann 6299**, **Keefe 6305**, Kenworthy 6315, Klee 6329, **Klingenstein 6338**, **Kohlberg 6346**, Kornfeld 6350, **Kunstadter 6362**, Lang 6374, Langeloth 6375, **LaSalle 6377**, Lastfogel 6380, **Lauder 6383**, Lavelle 6384, Lee 6391, Lemberg 6401, Levitt 6409, Levy 6412, Liberman 6419, Lincoln 6423, Lindner 6426, Littauer 6434, Lowenstein 6449, Luce 6452, **Luce 6453**, M & T 6465, Macdonald 6468, **Macy 6471**, **Mailman 6477**, Mapplethorpe 6485, **Marsh 6495**, Matthews 6507, **Mayer 6510**, **MBIA 6512**, McCarthy 6515, **Mellon 6525**, **Memton 6529**, **Merrill 6537**, **Mertz 6538**, **MetLife 6542**, **Milbank 6547**, Miller 6550, **Mitsubishi 6560**, Mizuho 6562, Moody's 6569, **Morgan 6577**, **National 6603**, **NEC 6605**, New York 6613, New York 6615, New York 6617, New York 6618, New York 6619, New York 6620, **New 6621**, Nichols 6628, **Noble 6633**, **Norman 6635**, Northern 6638, Northern 6639, **Novartis 6640**, **Noyes 6643**, O'Connor 6645, O'Toole 6654,

Ohrstrom 6659, Oishei 6660, **Open 6665**, **Ottinger 6674**, **Overbrook 6675**, Palm 6681, Park 6688, Perkin 6717, Pfizer 6720, **Pforzheimer 6721**, **Phillips 6725**, Pincus 6726, Pinkerton 6728, Price 6746, Raffiani 6767, **Ramapo 6769**, Rapoport 6772, Rauch 6774, **Reader's 6778**, Reed 6782, **Reed 6783**, Revson 6789, Rhodebeck 6791, Richardson 6797, Richmond 6800, **Ripplewood 6812**, Rochester 6823, **Rockefeller 6825**, **Rockefeller 6826**, Rohatyn 6830, Rose 6838, Rosenberg 6845, Rosner 6860, **Ross 6863**, Rubinstein 6876, **Sage 6894**, Samuels 6901, Schaffer 6911, Schiff 6923, **Schlumberger 6926**, Schnurmacher 6931, Siebens 6974, Simons 6988, Sirus 6992, Sister 6994, Slifka 7001, **Sloan 7003**, **SMBC 7005**, Smith 7007, **Smithers 7010**, Snow 7011, Snyder 7014, Sperry 7026, Spingold 7032, Sprague 7035, St. Faith's 7039, **Starr 7048**, Stein 7055, Strypemonde 7089, Sulzberger 7095, **Surdna 7103**, Sweetgrass 7113, Taconic 7117, **Teagle 7126**, **Tiffany 7137**, Tiger 7139, **Tinker 7143**, **Toshiba 7156**, Tower 7158, **Toyota 7160**, Triad 7162, Troy 7166, **Tsadra 7169**, Tuch 7170, Turner 7175, Tuttle 7176, **U.S. 7180**, Ungar 7183, **United 7185**, van Ameringen 7190, van Ameringen 7191, Van Pelt 7192, **Vetlesen 7196**, Vidda 7198, **Wallace 7209**, **Warhol 7215**, **Weeden 7223**, Weill 7227, Wendling 7242, Western 7248, Wilson 7264, **Wolfensohn 7270**, Woodcock 7273

North Carolina: **Babcock 7308**, **Bank 7310**, BB&T 7312, Belk 7315, Bergen 7316, Biddle 7317, Blue 7319, Blumenthal 7320, Broyhill 7328, Bryan 7330, **Burroughs 7333**, Cape Fear 7336, Cemala 7337, Community 7342, Community 7343, Community 7344, Community 7345, Community 7346, Cumberland 7349, Duke 7359, Easley 7361, Finch 7366, Finley 7367, Hanes 7387, Hanes 7388, Harris 7390, Hurley 7402, Mebane 7427, North Carolina 7438, North Carolina 7439, Polk 7449, Progress 7453, Reynolds 7457, Reynolds 7458, Reynolds 7459, Roanoke 7464, Robertson 7466, Smith 7479, Southern 7481, Strowd 7488, Tannenbaum 7493, Triangle 7496, Van Houten 7500, Vanderbilt 7501, Warner 7503, Weaver 7504, Winston-Salem 7508

North Dakota: Fargo 7514, Leach 7516, North Dakota 7519, North Dakota 7520, Stern 7521

Ohio: Abington 7524, Akron 7526, Anderson 7529, **Armington 7532**, Ashland 7533, Ashtabula 7534, Austin 7536, Barberton 7539, Bates 7540, Bicknell 7548, **Bingham 7549**, Brentwood 7555, Bruening 7558, Bryan 7559, **Cardinal 7567**, **Chiquita 7571**, Cincinnati 7574, Cleveland 7576, Cleveland 7577, Codrington 7578, Columbus 7580, Community 7581, Community 7582, Community 7583, Community 7584, Conway 7588, Corbett 7590, Coshocton 7593, **Covenant 7595**, Dater 7600, Dayton 7603, Dorn 7612, **Durell 7616**, **Eaton 7617**, Emery 7619, Fairfield 7622, Farmer 7623, **Federated 7624**, Ferguson 7625, Fifth 7626, Findlay 7627, First 7629, FirstEnergy 7630, Fox 7637, GAR 7643, **Generation 7647**, Gund 7657, H.C.S. 7658, Hamilton 7660, Haslinger 7664, Hauck 7666, **HCR 7667**, Hershey 7671, Hoover 7674, Iddings 7682, Ingalls 7684, Jennings 7688, Jergens 7689, Jochum 7692, **Kettering 7698**, Kettering 7699, **Key 7700**, Kramer 7704, Kulas 7706, Levin 7712, Luther 7726, Marietta 7735, Mathile 7737, Mayerson 7739, McMaster 7744, Miami 7748, Middletown 7749, Milacron 7751, Miller 7753, Morgan 7760, Morgan 7761, Morgan 7762, Murphy 7768, Murphy 7769, Muskingum 7770, Nationwide 7771, NCC 7772, Nippert 7777, Noble 7778, Nord 7779, O'Neill 7783, Ohio 7784, **OMNOVA 7789**, Osteopathic 7791, Owens 7793, Pfau 7803, **PLACE 7805**, Prentiss 7806, Reeves 7814, Resch 7816, Reuter 7817, Reynolds 7818, Richland 7819, Ritchie 7821, Russell 7827, **Sankey 7833**, Schlink 7839, Schmidlapp 7840, Schmidlapp 7841, Schott 7842, Scioto 7845, **Scripps 7848**, Semple 7851, Sisler 7858, Sloat 7861, Smith 7863, Spaulding 7865, Springfield 7866, Stark 7867, Stillson 7869,

Stocker 7870, Stranahan 7872, Stranahan 7873, Tait 7875, Toledo 7883, Troy 7886, Wallace 7894, Watson 7896, Wayne 7897, Wean 7898, **Weatherhead 7899**, White 7905, Women's 7916, Woodruff 7917

Oklahoma: Bailey 7923, Bernsen 7925, Bovaird 7927, Chapman 7928, Community 7932, **Ethics 7935**, Gelvin 7938, Hille 7943, Inasmuch 7944, Kerr 7949, Kirkpatrick 7952, Meinig 7961, Merrick 7962, Oklahoma City 7964, Oklahoman 7966, Presbyterian 7969, Sarkeys 7974, **Schusterman 7975**, Southern 7979, Tulsa 7984, Viersen 7985, Warren 7987, Zarrow 7992, Zink 7994

Oregon: Adler 7996, Autzen 7997, Boyd 8000, Braemar 8001, Carpenter 8003, Chambers 8004, Collins 8009, Ford 8013, Intel 8022, Jeld 8025, Johnson 8027, Kinsman 8031, **Lazar 8035**, Louisiana 8037, Mentor 8039, Meyer 8041, Meyer 8042, **NIKE 8046**, Oregon 8049, PacifiCorp 8050, **Schmidt 8055**, Schnitzer 8057, Swigert 8061, Swindells 8062, Tektronix 8063, Templeton 8064, Tucker 8065, Wessinger 8067, Young 8069

Pennsylvania: 1675 8070, ACE 8073, **Alcoa 8075**, Allegheny 8076, American 8079, **Annenberg 8084**, Arcadia 8086, Baker 8092, Barra 8095, Bayer 8096, Beaver 8098, Benedum 8099, Berks 8103, Birmingham 8107, Blanchard 8111, Blue 8112, Born 8113, Bristol 8118, Buhl 8124, Byers' 8127, Central 8135, Centre 8136, Century 8137, **Cestone 8138**, Chester 8141, CIGNA 8143, Claneil 8144, **Colcom 8150**, Colonial 8151, Comcast 8152, Community 8153, Community 8154, Community 8155, Connelly 8157, Dietrich 8170, Dietrich 8171, Dolfinger 8172, **Dominion 8173**, Donley 8175, Donnelly 8176, DSF 8178, Eberly 8179, Eden 8182, Equitable 8187, Erie 8188, Fair 8192, Falk 8193, Fels 8198, Ferree 8199, Fine 8201, First 8202, FISA 8204, Fisher 8205, Foundation 8208, Fourjay 8209, Genuardi 8213, Grable 8221, Graham 8222, Grundy 8228, Hamilton 8233, Heinz 8240, Heinz 8241, Heinz 8242, Heinz 8244, Hillman 8249, Hillman 8250, Hillman 8251, Hillman 8252, Honickman 8255, Hooper 8256, Hopwood 8257, Huston 8263, Huston 8264, Jennings 8272, Justus 8276, Katz 8281, Kavanagh 8282, Keystone 8285, Keystone 8286, Kind 8289, Lancaster 8300, Laurel 8301, Lehigh Valley 8303, Luzerne 8317, Mandell 8322, Maslow 8327, McCune 8332, McDonald's 8333, McFeely 8334, McKenna 8337, McKinney 8339, McLean 8340, Mellon 8344, Mellon 8346, Miller 8352, Moore 8358, Nelson 8362, Neubauer 8363, Penn 8371, **Pew 8377**, Philadelphia 8378, Phillips 8380, Phoenixville 8381, Pittsburgh 8386, PNC 8388, **PPG 8394**, **Presser 8395**, PTS 8399, Rangos 8400, Rees 8401, Rider 8404, Saint 8419, **Scaife 8425**, Scranton 8431, Shaffer 8436, Shenango 8438, Simmons 8441, Simonds 8442, Smith 8444, Smith 8445, Snee 8446, Sordoni 8450, Sovereign 8451, Stackpole 8456, Staunton 8457, **Templeton 8475**, Trexler 8481, Truman 8483, Tyco 8485, United 8486, Wachovia 8494, **Waldorf 8495**, Widener 8502, Willary 8503, York 8511

Puerto Rico: Puerto Rico 8515

Rhode Island: CARLISLE 8521, Charter 8526, CVS 8529, Daniels 8530, **Dorot 8531**, Hasbro 8539, Littlefield 8544, McCarthy 8548, Noonan 8550, Rhode Island 8551, **Textron 8559**, van Beuren 8561

South Carolina: Black 8569, Byerly 8572, Central 8577, Chapin 8579, Coastal 8581, Community 8583, Community 8584, Daniel 8585, First 8587, Fullerton 8589, Kane 8596, **Roe 8607**, ScanSource 8608, Self 8610, Sims 8611, South 8615, Springs 8617

South Dakota: Larson 8627, Sioux Falls 8630, Vucurevich 8634

Tennessee: Assisi 8638, Benwood 8644, **Bridgestone 8646**, Caesars 8648, Caldwell 8649, CIC 8656, Community 8660, Community 8661, Community 8662, Davis 8665, Durham 8670, East 8671, Frist

8679, HCA 8690, Hyde 8693, Lyndhurst 8703, **Maclellan 8704**, Plough 8718, Thompson 8733, Tucker 8735, Unaka 8739, Wilson 8744

Texas: Abell 8749, **Adams 8751**, Amarillo 8758, Astin 8764, **AT&T 8765**, Augur 8766, Austin 8768, Bass 8777, Behmann 8785, Brackenridge 8793, Bridgeway 8796, Bridwell 8797, Brown 8799, Burnett 8801, Cailloux 8807, Carter 8816, Clayton 8830, Coastal 8833, Coates 8834, Cockrell 8835, Communities 8839, Community 8841, Community 8842, Constantin 8843, **Cooper 8846**, Cowden 8848, Cullen 8854, Dougherty, 8870, Eady 8875, **EDS 8877**, El Paso 8881, El Paso 8882, Elkins 8883, Esping 8886, **ExxonMobil 8889**, Fain 8890, Fair 8891, Farish 8894, Favrot 8897, Fikes 8899, Fisch 8901, Fish 8902, Fleming 8904, Fondren 8906, Frees 8909, George 8916, Gill 8919, Goldsbury 8920, Greathouse 8924, Gulf 8926, Halliburton 8935, Healthcare 8944, Hillcrest 8952, Hoblitzelle 8955, Hoglund 8956, Houston 8960, Houston 8961, **Jenesis 8971**, Kahn 8980, Kempner 8987, Kimberly 8992, Kinder 8994, King 8995, Klabzuba 8996, Kodosky 9000, Koehler 9001, Kronkosky 9002, Light 9011, Lightner 9012, Lubbock 9021, Lyons 9024, Marathon 9028, Marcus 9029, McDermott 9043, McKee 9045, McMillan 9046, McNair 9047, Meadows 9049, Mitte 9067, Moody 9070, Northen 9092, **Oldham 9100**, Once 9101, Owen 9107, **Pearle 9113**, Penney 9115, Permian 9117, Powell 9128, Priddy 9131, Rachofsky 9139, Rapoport 9141, Reynolds 9145, **RGK 9146**, Richardson 9147, Rockwell 9154, Rosewood 9158, Sams 9163, San Angelo 9165, San Antonio 9166, **Scaler 9170**, Scott 9174, **Search 9176**, **Shell 9181**, Shield 9183, Simmons 9188, Simmons 9189, Smith 9191, Smith 9195, Speas 9206, Speas 9207, Stark 9209, Stemmons 9211, Sterling 9212, Strake 9215, Sturgis 9216, Summerlee 9217, Sumners 9218, Swinney 9222, Tate 9225, Temple 9227, **Tenet 9229**, Tennessee 9230, Texas 9232, Tocker 9236, Topfer 9238, Trull 9240, Turner 9241, Vale 9246, Valero 9247, Waco 9255, Waggoner 9256, Walsh 9261, **Waste 9265**, Wichita 9280, Wolens 9286, Wolslager 9290, Works 9291, Wright 9294, Young 9295, Zachry 9296

Utah: Ashton 9303, Browning 9308, Burton 9309, Caine 9310, Dumke 9316, Eccles 9319, Eccles 9320, Esther 9321, Hemingway 9328, Simmons 9342, Swanson 9346

Vermont: **Ben 9355**, Lintilhac 9359, Mergens 9360, Vermont 9361

Virginia: Alleghany 9367, Arlington 9371, Beazley 9376, **Blue 9379**, CarMax 9385, Community 9402, **de Beaumont 9408, Dorothy 9411**, Foundation 9419, Freddie 9422, **Gannett 9428**, Graves 9433, Gwathmey 9435, Kanter 9445, Landmark 9455, Luck 9461, Lynchburg 9463, McGlothlin 9469, **MCI 9471**, Memorial 9474, **Mitsubishi 9476**, Moore 9478, Norfolk 9484, **Norfolk 9485**, Northern 9486, Portsmouth 9499, Robins 9506, Roller 9507, Rosenthal 9508, Samberg 9510, Scott 9513, Staunton 9521, **Stern 9522**, Ukrop 9529, United 9530, Universal 9531, Virginia Beach 9532, Washington 9534, Weissberg 9536, **WestWind 9538**, Williamsburg 9541, **Winkler 9542**, Wrinkle 9545

Washington: **444S 9546**, Ackerley 9547, Allen 9550, **Blakemore 9558**, Blue 9559, **Boeing 9560, Brainerd 9561**, Bullitt 9563, Burning 9564, Casey 9566, **Casey 9567**, Cheney 9569, Community 9571, Dimmer 9579, **Edwards 9580**, Evertrust 9583, Ferguson 9585, Foster 9588, Foundation 9589, Fuchs 9590, **Gates 9591**, Glaser 9594, **Glaser 9595**, Grays 9597, Harvest 9602, **Hemingway 9606**, Horizons 9608, **Kongsgaard 9620**, Laurel 9625, Lucky 9632, Lynn 9633, Martin 9634, Milgard 9641, Miller 9642, Murdock 9644, Nesholm 9647, Norcliffe 9650, Quixote 9667, Rainier 9669, Russell 9673, **Samis 9675**, Seattle 9680, **Starbucks 9690, Stewardship 9691**,

Tacoma 9693, True 9696, **Vista 9699, Weyerhaeuser 9703**, Wilburforce 9705

West Virginia: Carter 9712, Chambers 9713, Clay 9714, Clay 9715, Community 9716, Kanawha 9723, Maier 9725, McDonough 9726, Parkersburg 9730, Schenk 9732, Tucker 9736

Wisconsin: Acuity 9739, Alexander 9741, Alliant 9742, Assurant 9748, Bader 9749, Banta 9752, Beloit 9757, **Bradley 9763**, Bradshaw 9764, Briggs 9765, Community 9776, Community 9777, Community 9778, Community 9779, Cornerstone 9781, Cudahy 9785, CUNA 9786, Dudley 9792, Evjue 9797, Fond du Lac 9800, Green Bay 9810, Herzfeld 9815, Hess 9816, Jacobus 9819, Janesville 9820, Johnson 9826, Joy 9828, Kelben 9830, **Kern 9834, Kohler 9839**, Kohler 9840, Kress 9844, La Crosse 9845, Madison 9854, Managed 9857, Marcus 9859, Marshall 9860, Marshfield 9861, McBeath 9864, Menasha 9869, Miller 9875, Milwaukee 9876, Modine 9878, Morse 9879, **Palmer 9890**, Peterson 9896, Pettit 9897, Prescott 9903, Racine 9906, Rowland 9916, Rutledge 9917, Sand 9918, Sensient 9922, Siebert 9927, **Smith 9929**, Stackner 9934, Stock 9939, **Taylor 9947, Thrivent 9949**, Walter 9959, Waukesha 9960, Weill 9962, West 9964, Witte 9968, WPS 9970

Wyoming: Community 9977, Ellbogen 9981, McMurry 9985, **Schultz 9990**, Scott 9991, Weiss 9997, Wyoming 10000

Program evaluation

Alabama: Bruno 17, Kaul 40, Meyer 52

Alaska: Alaska 79

Arizona: **Johnson 112**

Arkansas: Blue 157, Northwest 169, Rockefeller 172

California: Ackerman 193, Alliance 204, Amgen 219, Anderson 221, Archstone 232, Atlas 241, Baxter 262, Bechtel 270, **Caddock 343**, California 345, California 346, California 347, California 350, **Christensen 384**, Community 403, Community 405, Community 407, East 474, Firedoll 508, **First 512**, Flora 521, **Fund 542**, Geffen 558, Girard 580, Goldman 595, Haas 636, Haas 637, Heller 666, **Hume 692**, Irvine 698, Irvine 699, Koret 774, Los Altos 828, Marin 854, McCune 872, Miller 901, Morgan 915, Mosher 920, Noyce 944, Orange 957, **Packard 972**, Price 1016, Reid 1036, **Righteous 1050**, Sacramento 1080, San Diego 1087, Sierra 1151, Sobrato 1172, Sonora 1178, Stone 1200, **Strauss 1203**, Stuart 1206, Stuart 1208, UniHealth 1249, Ventura 1264, Zellerbach 1326

Colorado: Aspen 1338, Bohemian 1345, Buell 1350, Chambers 1354, Colorado 1356, **Daniels 1362**, Piton 1439, Summit 1463

Connecticut: Bridgeport 1504, Community 1514, Connecticut 1519, Graustein 1559, Hartford 1564, Tow 1661

Delaware: **Raskob 1741**

District of Columbia: Block 1776, Community 1785, Consumer 1786, Fordham 1795, Jovid 1814, **Koch 1819, Moriah 1835**, Roshan 1847, **Summit 1852**

Florida: Community 1943, Conn 1951, **Davis 1964**, duPont 1983, Engelberg 1994, Gulf 2041, Jacksonville 2071, MacDonald 2121, North 2153, Quantum 2181, Toppel 2274

Georgia: **Challenge 2344**, Community 2361, Cousins 2365, Healthcare 2411, North 2458, **Rockdale 2474**, Zeist 2529

Hawaii: Atherton 2532, Castle 2537, Castle 2538, Cooke 2541, Geist 2544

Illinois: Arthur 2601, Bauer 2609, Chicago 2661, Community 2679, Community 2681, Fry 2740, Girl's 2757, Illinois 2812, **Joyce 2820**, Little 2859, Lumpkin 2864, Polk 2946, Reese 2961, Retirement 2964, VNA 3049

Indiana: Bussing 3111, Central 3116, Clowes 3119, Clowes 3120, Community 3125, Community 3132, Fairbanks 3147, Foellinger 3149, Harrison 3161,

Johnson 3178, Lilly 3194, Lincoln 3195, **Lumina 3196**

Iowa: Community 3278, Principal 3326

Louisiana: Baptist 3461, Institute 3489, New Orleans 3503

Maine: Horizon 3541, Maine 3549, **Oak 3552, River 3554, Sandy 3555**

Maryland: Baker 3567, **Blaustein 3575, Casey 3585, Cohen 3594**, England 3622, **Hughes 3654**, Knott 3666, Meyerhoff 3691, Polinger 3708, Rathmann 3715, Straus 3738

Massachusetts: Barr 3791, Berkshire 3801, Davis 3875, Essex 3897, Melville 4034, Morse 4044, Schott 4132, Sheehan 4140, Smith 4150, Worcester 4209

Michigan: **Arcus 4223**, Barry 4227, Battle Creek 4228, Community 4255, Community 4258, **Fetzer 4297**, Fremont 4315, Gilmore 4324, Hudson 4343, Jackson 4347, **Kellogg 4357, Mott 4399**, Mott 4400, Nokomis 4404, Weatherwax 4474

Minnesota: Beim 4513, Beverly 4517, Bremer 4523, **CHS 4540**, Duluth 4556, McKnight 4617, McNeely 4619, Northwest 4637, Phillips 4655, Target 4697, WCA 4718

Mississippi: Riley 4763

Missouri: Community 4798, H & R 4823, Hall 4824, Hallmark 4825, **Monsanto 4868**, Sosland 4908

Nebraska: Lincoln 4987

Nevada: **Hilton 5037, Walsh 5075**

New Hampshire: Bean 5080, Eastman 5087

New Jersey: Alcatel 5110, Dircks 5180, Dodge 5181, **Johnson 5265**, Karma 5269, Pascale 5349, **Rippel 5368**, Wallerstein 5447

New Mexico: Con 5471, Taos 5498

New York: Achelis 5513, Bausch 5605, Bodman 5647, Bowne 5655, **Bristol 5666, Carnegie 5707, Clark 5760, Commonwealth 5779**, Community 5780, Community 5783, Community 5784, Community 5785, Corning 5794, Cricket 5808, **Cummings 5814**, Dyson 5898, **Ford 5970**, Frog 5992, Gifford 6026, **Goldman 6056**, Goldsmith 6060, Golisano 6067, **Grant 6092, Hartford 6150**, Heckscher 6164, **Heron 6176, JEHT 6257**, Kenworthy 6315, **Kohlberg 6346**, Kornfeld 6350, Langeloth 6375, **LaSalle 6377**, Luce 6452, **Macy 6471**, McCarthy 6515, New York 6613, Oishei 6660, Pfizer 6720, Rauch 6774, Richmond 6800, Rochester 6823, **Rockefeller 6825**, Rosenberg 6845, Samuels 6901, Slifka 7001, Tiger 7139, Tower 7158, **Toyota 7160, U.S. 7180, Wallace 7209**, Wilson 7264

North Carolina: Blue 7319, Community 7343, Community 7346, Mebane 7427, Robertson 7466, Strowd 7488, Weaver 7504

Ohio: Community 7583, Findlay 7627, Jennings 7688, Kettering 7699, Kramer 7704, Levin 7712, Miami 7748, O'Neill 7783, Osteopathic 7791, Saint 7830, Scioto 7845, Springfield 7866, Stranahan 7872, Wean 7898

Oklahoma: Chapman 7928, Community 7932, Inasmuch 7944, Kerr 7949, Merrick 7962, Sarkeys 7974, Tulsa 7984

Oregon: Carpenter 8003, Kinsman 8031

Pennsylvania: Chester 8141, Claneil 8144, **Colcom 8150**, DSF 8178, Eden 8182, Erie 8188, Falk 8193, Fine 8201, FISA 8204, Genuardi 8213, Grable 8221, Heinz 8241, Heinz 8242, Keystone 8286, Laurel 8301, Mellon 8346, Phoenixville 8381, Staunton 8457, Wachovia 8494

Rhode Island: **Dorot 8531**, Rhode Island 8551

South Carolina: Black 8569, Byerly 8572, Community 8584, Daniel 8585

South Dakota: Sioux Falls 8630

Tennessee: Assisi 8638, Community 8660, East 8671, Hyde 8693, **Maclellan 8704**, Plough 8718, Wilson 8744

Texas: Cailloux 8807, Dougherty, 8870, Favrot 8897, Fikes 8899, Houston 8960, King 8995, Kronkosky 9002, Marathon 9028, Meadows 9049, Rockwell 9154, Rosewood 9158, San Angelo 9165,

Simmons 9188, Stark 9209, Swinney 9222, Works 9291

Utah: **Hayward 9327**

Vermont: Vermont 9361

Virginia: Freddie 9422, **MCI 9471**, Robins 9506, Samberg 9510, Scott 9513, Staunton 9521, Weissberg 9536, Williamsburg 9541

Washington: **Boeing 9560**, Casey 9566, **Casey 9567**, Foundation 9589, Lucky 9632, Medina 9640, Miller 9642, Quixote 9667

West Virginia: Kanawha 9723

Wisconsin: Dudley 9792, Green Bay 9810, Jacobus 9819, Milwaukee 9876, Morse 9879, **Thrivent 9949**

Wyoming: Community 9977, Ellbogen 9981, Wyoming 10000

Program-related investments/loans

Alabama: Crampton 30

Alaska: Rasmuson 85

Arkansas: Rockefeller 172, Walton 186

California: Auen 242, Benbough 276, Burns 338, California 345, California 346, Community 406, Community 407, **Compton 409**, Cowell 423, Firedoll 508, Fresno 537, Friedman 538, **Fund 542**, Gerbode 564, Hewlett 671, Hutton 694, Irmas 697, Johnson 725, **K.L. 736**, **Koulaieff 778**, Lincy 812, Los Altos 828, Marin 854, Miller 901, **Moore 913**, Mosher 920, **Packard 972**, Peninsula 989, **S.G. 1078**, San Diego 1087, San Francisco 1088, Scripps 1115, **Strauss 1203**, Taper 1226, Wasserman 1281

Colorado: Colorado 1356, Community 1358, Denver 1364, **Weaver 1469**

Connecticut: Community 1514, Graustein 1559, Hartford 1564, Liberty 1586, **Smart 1651**

Delaware: Bennett 1690, **Raskob 1741, Robinson 1745**

District of Columbia: **Butler 1779, Fannie 1793**, Meyer 1834, **Moriah 1835**, Reich 1845

Florida: Bush 1922, Community 1940, Dade 1957, duPont 1983, Engelberg 1994, **Knight 2097**, Phillips 2168, Stevens 2251

Georgia: Callaway 2337, Lanier 2428, Lee 2432, Marcus 2441

Illinois: **Abbott 2579**, Blowitz 2623, Butler 2646, Chicago 2661, Children's 2664, Coleman 2673, Community 2679, Community 2681, Grand 2769, Harris 2787, Landau 2847, **MacArthur 2868**, Prince 2948, Retirement 2964, **Samaritan 2980**, Speh 3014, Steans 3021, VNA 3049, Washington 3058, Wieboldt 3069

Indiana: Community 3123, Decatur 3138

Kansas: Bane 3345, Security 3390

Kentucky: C.E. 3412

Louisiana: Baton Rouge 3462, Brown 3465

Maine: Libra 3546, **Sandy 3555**

Maryland: Abell 3559, **Blaustein 3575, Casey 3585, Cohen 3594**, Columbia 3595, England 3622, Knott 3666, Plitt 3706, Rathmann 3715

Massachusetts: Behrakis 3796, Fireman 3909, Grinspoon 3935, High 3950, Highland 3951, Hyams 3961, Island 3965, Melville 4034, Parker 4069, Schott 4132, Sharf 4137, **State 4158**, Stevens 4163

Michigan: **Arcus 4223**, Battle Creek 4228, Community 4252, Community 4257, Fremont 4315, Grand Rapids 4326, Jackson 4347, Kalamazoo 4352, Miller 4394

Minnesota: Blandin 4520, Bremer 4523, **Cafesjian 4527**, Central 4534, Greycoach 4575, Initiative 4593, Jerome 4595, Kelley 4597, Leonard 4604, McKnight 4617, Minneapolis 4623, Northwest 4636, Northwest 4637, Ordean 4643, Oswald 4645, Sieben 4682, Slaggie 4686, **Wallestad 4712**, Wedum 4719, West 4723, Winona 4729

Mississippi: AmSouth 4733, Foundation 4743, Hardin 4747

Missouri: Baer 4778, Community 4798, Danforth 4803, Hall 4824, Kansas 4842, **Kauffman 4843**, Saint Louis 4896

Montana: **Edwards 4936**

Nebraska: Cooper 4954, Kiewit 4984, Woods 5018

Nevada: **Hilton 5037, Lemelson 5040**

New Hampshire: New Hampshire 5098

New Jersey: Borden 5138, Community 5167, Dodge 5181, **Johnson 5265**, Jonas 5266, Pascale 5349, Prudential 5360, Sudler 5416, Victoria 5440

New Mexico: Carlsbad 5469, **Lannan 5484**, Maddox 5487, McCune 5488, Taos 5498

New York: **American 5551, Atlantic 5574, AVI 5582**, Charitable 5732, Clark 5762, Community 5781, Community 5783, Cricket 5808, **Deutsche 5854**, Dyson 5898, **Ford 5970**, Gerry 6017, Golden 6046, **Goldman 6056**, Goldstein 6064, Hermione 6175, **Heron 6176, HKH 6190**, Hoyt 6203, Independence 6229, **Institute 6232**, Joukowsky 6275, Joy 6276, **JPMorgan 6277**, Kaplan 6290, Lenna 6402, Lindner 6426, **Mertz 6538, MetLife 6542**, O'Connor 6645, Oishei 6660, **Open 6665**, Raffiani 6767, Revson 6789, Richmond 6800, Rochester 6823, **Rockefeller 6825, Rockefeller 6826**, Samuels 6901, **Schlumberger 6926**, Schnurmacher 6931, Silverman 6983, Soros 7021, Tiger 7139, **Tikvah 7140**, Triad 7162, Weinberg 7230, Wendt 7243, Western 7248, Whitehead 7252, Wilson 7262

North Carolina: **Babcock 7308**, Bryan 7329, Community 7343, Community 7345, **Sunshine 7490**, Triangle 7496, Winston-Salem 7508

Ohio: Barberton 7539, Bee 7542, Cleveland 7576, **Covenant 7595**, Dater 7600, Diamond 7610, Findlay 7627, **Geisse 7646**, Gund 7657, Hamilton 7660, Heimbinder 7670, Marietta 7735, Mathile 7737, Murphy 7769, Muskingum 7770, Nord 7779, Richland 7819, Stranahan 7872

Oklahoma: Noble 7963, Presbyterian 7969, Tulsa 7984

Oregon: Meyer 8042, Schnitzer 8056

Pennsylvania: **Alcoa 8075**, Benedum 8099, Berks 8103, Buhl 8124, Central 8135, Community 8153, First 8202, Grable 8221, Heinz 8241, Heinz 8242, Hopwood 8257, Lancaster 8300, McCune 8332, Mellon 8346, Penn 8371, **Pew 8377**, Pittsburgh 8386, PNC 8388, Roberts 8405, **Susquehanna 8470**

Puerto Rico: Puerto Rico 8515

Rhode Island: Charlesmead 8525

South Carolina: Post 8603

Tennessee: Durham 8670, East 8671, Jeniam 8695, Phillips 8716, Plough 8718

Texas: Burnett 8801, **C.I.O.S. 8805**, Christian 8828, Garvey 8914, Houston 8960, Mankoff 9027, Meadows 9049, Pema 9114, Rockwell 9154, San Antonio 9166, Simmons 9188, Temple 9227, Wagner 9259

Utah: Eccles 9319, Esther 9321, **Huntsman 9329**

Vermont: Mergens 9360, Vermont 9361

Virginia: **Blue 9379**, Landmark 9455

Washington: Bullitt 9563, **Gates 9591**, Glazer 9596, Lucky 9632, Miller 9642, Quixote 9667, Tacoma 9693, Washington 9701

West Virginia: Laughlin 9724

Wisconsin: Alexander 9741, Bader 9749, **Bradley 9763**, Crump 9783, Kellogg 9832, Mercy 9871

Wyoming: Community 9977, Friess 9982, **Schultz 9990**, Whitney 9998

Publication

Alabama: Bedsole 12, Blount 14, Community 23, Community 24, Hill 39, Kaul 40, Meyer 52, Webb 75

Alaska: Alaska 79

Arizona: Arizona 87, **Kieckhefer 113**, Linde 117, Lovell 119

Arkansas: Arkansas 156, Ross 174

California: Adams 194, **Amado 212**, Archstone 232, Baxter 262, **C.S. 340**, California 350, **Cantor 354, Castagnola 366**, Columbia 399, Drum 470, Flora 521, **Foundation 529**, Gellert 559, **Getty 570**, Heller 666, Koret 774, **Koulaieff 778, LEF 799, Lloyd 823**, McCarthy 868, Mental 886, Noyce 944, Paloheimo 974, Parker 979, Sacramento 1080, San Diego 1087, **Smith 1166**, Sonora 1178, **Strauss 1203**, Taper 1226, Truckee 1244, Trust 1246, **Warsh 1280**, Witter 1314

Colorado: Bohemian 1345, Colorado 1356, **Crowell 1361**, Donnell 1368

Connecticut: Bodenwein 1497, Community 1516, Connecticut 1518, **GE 1553**, Hartford 1564, **Lingnan 1587**, Matthies 1600, Palmer 1621, **Richardson 1632**, Tremaine 1662

Delaware: **Raskob 1741**

District of Columbia: Aid 1765, **Bauman 1770**, Consumer 1786, **Foundation 1796**, Freed 1798, Henry 1808, Spring 1849

Florida: **Believers 1900, Chatlos 1932**, Dade 1957, **Davis 1964**, duPont 1983, **Gibney 2021**, Gulf 2041, **Koch 2098**, Opler 2158, St. Joe 2244

Georgia: AEC 2310, Georgia 2394, Lee 2432, Lubo 2438, Savannah 2480, Watson 2509

Illinois: **Brach 2630**, Driehaus 2710, **Graham 2767**, Heritage 2797, Logan 2860, **MacArthur 2867**, Rothschild 2971, **Searle 2994**, Sprague 3016, Tawani 3033, **Tyndale 3042**

Indiana: Ball 3103, Bussing 3111, Central 3116, Clowes 3119, **Cummins 3136**, Froderman 3153, Harrison 3161, Henry 3165, Heritage 3166, Lilly 3194, **Lumina 3196**, Marshall 3199, Wayne 3253

Iowa: Cedar Rapids 3275, Community 3277, Community 3278, Maytag 3310

Kansas: Farah 3362, Hansen 3366, Salina 3387

Kentucky: Community 3414

Louisiana: Booth 3464

Maine: Burnham 3527, Smith 3556

Maryland: **Casey 3585**, Community 3598, England 3622, Higginson 3649, Kerr 3661, Macht 3683, MARPAT 3684, Marshall 3687, Meyerhoff 3692

Massachusetts: Berkshire 3855, Community 3855, Crossroads 3869, **Fidelity 3904**, Melville 4034, **Partnership 4071**, Schott 4132, Sharf 4137

Michigan: Americana 4218, Ann Arbor 4221, **Arcus 4223**, Battle Creek 4228, Community 4252, Community 4257, Dart 4267, **Earhart 4291**, General 4320, Gilmore 4324, Greenville 4331, Lansing 4372, Saginaw 4428

Minnesota: Duluth 4556, Greystone 4576, Jerome 4595, Lilly 4606, Rupp 4669, Walker 4711

Mississippi: **Armstrong 4734**, Hardin 4747

Missouri: Jewish 4837, Kemper 4849, Reynolds 4892

Nebraska: Omaha 4994

Nevada: **Hilton 5037**, Nevada 5047, **Walsh 5075**

New Hampshire: Hunt 5093

New Jersey: Dircks 5180, Dodge 5181, Fund 5199, **Huber 5244, Puffin 5362**, Wallerstein 5447

New Mexico: Albuquerque 5466, Carlsbad 5469, Frost 5476, **Lannan 5484, Levinson 5486**, New Mexico 5491, PNM 5493, Santa Fe 5496, Taos 5498, **Thaw 5500**

New York: **Abelard 5508**, Achelis 5513, Adirondack 5517, **American 5551, Atran 5575**, Berg 5621, Bodman 5647, Buhl 5684, Burden 5687, **Bydale 5694, Carnegie 5707**, Central 5724, Chautauqua 5738, **China 5750**, Clark 5761, Community 5784, Cricket 5808, **Dedalus 5847, Engelhard 5932, Ford 5970, Foundation 5971**, Grant 6092, Griffis 6107, **Hartford 6150, Heineman 6165**, Independence 6229, **Initial 6231, Ittleson 6241**, Jackson Hole 6246, **JM 6263**, Kaplan 6290, Kenworthy 6315, **Klingenstein 6338, Kress 6357, Liebmann 6421**, Littauer 6434, **Macy 6471, Mailman 6477, Mapplethorpe 6485**, McCann 6514, **MetLife 6542**, Milbank 6547, **NEC 6605**, New York 6613, **Norcross 6634**, Northern 6639, O'Connor 6645, **Pforzheimer 6721**, Rapoport 6772, Richmond 6800, Rochester 6823,

Rockefeller 6826, **Ross 6863**, **Sage 6894**, Schnurmacher 6931, Snow 7011, Sweetgrass 7113, **United 7185**, **Wallace 7209**, **Warhol 7215**, Weissman 7237, **Wenner 7244**, Western 7248, Widgeon 7255

North Carolina: Blumenthal 7320, Cape Fear 7336, Community 7344, Community 7345, Cumberland 7349, Duke 7359, Hanes 7388, Polk 7449, Reynolds 7458, **Richardson 7461**

North Dakota: Fargo 7514, North Dakota 7519

Ohio: Anderson 7529, **Armington 7532**, Columbus 7580, Dayton 7603, Fairfield 7622, Fifth 7626, Gund 7657, **Kettering 7698**, Levin 7712, Mather 7736, Miami 7748, Murphy 7769, Muskingum 7770, Nord 7779, Saint 7830, Scioto 7845, Springfield 7866

Oklahoma: **Ethics 7935**, **Schusterman 7975**

Oregon: Carpenter 8003, Johnson 8027, Kinsman 8031

Pennsylvania: Arete 8088, Centre 8136, Claneil 8144, **Colcom 8150**, Dietrich 8170, Dolfinger 8172, Erie 8188, Falk 8193, Foundation 8208, Fourjay 8209, Honickman 8255, Lancaster 8300, Laurel 8301, Lehigh Valley 8303, McLean 8340, **Scaife 8425**, Scranton 8431, **Templeton 8475**

Puerto Rico: Puerto Rico 8515

Rhode Island: **Dorot 8531**, Rhode Island 8551

South Carolina: Coastal 8581, **Roe 8607**

South Dakota: South Dakota 8631, Vucurevich 8634

Tennessee: Assisi 8638, Durham 8670, East 8671

Texas: Austin 8768, CH 8823, Community 8840, Community 8842, Covenant 8847, Halsell 8936, Houston 8960, Houston 8961, Kempner 8987, McGovern 9044, Meadows 9049, Moody 9070, Richardson 9147, San Antonio 9166, **Shell 9181**, Simmons 9188, Stark 9209, Sterling 9212, Summerlee 9217, Trull 9240, Vale 9246, Waggoner 9256

Utah: Esther 9321

Vermont: Vermont 9361

Virginia: Alleghany 9367, Freddie 9422, Graves 9433, **Mitsubishi 9476**, Truland 9528, Weissberg 9536

Washington: **Blakemore 9558**, **Gates 9591**, Miller 9642, Quest 9666, Quixote 9667, **Samis 9675**, **Weyerhaeuser 9703**

West Virginia: Kanawha 9723

Wisconsin: **Bradley 9763**, Evjue 9797, Jacobus 9819, Kohler 9840, Marshfield 9861, U.S. 9952

Wyoming: Community 9977

Research

Alabama: Blount 14, Brock 16, Community 23, Dixon 32, Hill 39, Meyer 52, Protective 58, Saks 61

Alaska: CIRI 83

Arizona: Arizona 87, Community 91, Dee 94, Flinn 98, **Globe 101**, Hansen 104, Hermundslie 107, **Johnson 112**, **Kieckhefer 113**, Linde 117, **Research 134**, Steele 142

Arkansas: Arkansas 156, Blue 157, Rockefeller 172, Ross 174

California: **A-T 191**, Alafi 201, **Amado 212**, Amgen 219, **Arkay 235**, **Atkinson 240**, **Baker 252**, Bauer 261, Baxter 262, Baxter 263, Bechtel 270, **Beckman 272**, Benbough 276, Bireley 292, Blue 296, Brotman 328, **Bull 331**, Bundy 332, **C.S. 340**, California 345, California 347, California 350, **Cantor 354**, **Carnegie 359**, **Castagnola 366**, **ChevronTexaco 380**, **Chiron 383**, **Christensen 384**, Cohen 393, Columbia 399, **Compton 409**, Danford 438, Davidson 445, Drum 470, Early 473, Eisenberg 480, Eucalyptus 489, Factor 491, Femino 501, **First 512**, Flora 521, Fluor 523, French 536, Garland 556, Gellert 559, Genentech 563, **Getty 570**, Giannini 572, Girard 580, **Glenn 581**, Goldman 595, Goldsmith 599, Goldwyn 600, Grammer 610, **Harvey 654**, Haynes 659, Heart 662, Heller 666, Hillblom 673, Hoag 678, **Hume 692**, Irvine 696, Irwin 700, Jameson 710, Jewett 718, **K.L. 736**, **Kaiser 739**, **Kalliopeia 740**, Kavli

748, **Keck 750**, Kirchgessner 762, Koret 774, Kvamme 781, **Living 821**, **M & T 837**, Mabie 839, Marin 854, **Maxfield 862**, McBean 866, McCarthy 868, Mead 881, Mental 886, Milken 897, Milken 898, **Moore 913**, Morgan 915, My 930, Norris 940, Noyce 944, Oppenheimer 955, Oxnard 969, **Packard 972**, Parker 979, Parsons 980, Patron 983, Preuss 1015, Rudd 1073, **Saban 1079**, Saw 1098, **Schlinger 1102**, Scripps 1115, **Seaver 1118**, Severns 1131, Smith 1160, **Smith 1161**, **Smith 1166**, Stern 1195, **Strauss 1203**, Stuart 1206, Taper 1226, Thornton 1236, Torrey 1239, Towbes 1241, Treadwell 1243, Ueberroth 1248, Union 1250, **Unocal 1252**, Valley 1256, Valley 1257, Waltmar 1277, Warren 1279, **Warsh 1280**, Wasserman 1281, Webb 1285, **WellPoint 1292**, Whittier 1304, Witter 1314, WWW 1323

Colorado: Bohemian 1345, Bonfils 1347, Chambers 1354, Colorado 1356, Donnell 1368, Hughes 1393, King 1404, M.D.C. 1413, **Malone 1415**, Saccomanno 1446, Taylor 1464, Williams 1474

Connecticut: **Aetna 1479**, **Bingham 1493**, Boehringer 1498, Childs 1510, Connecticut 1518, Connecticut 1519, **Deloitte 1527**, Donaghue 1529, Fippinger 1540, **GE 1553**, Graustein 1559, Heyman 1567, **Huisking 1570**, Larsen 1579, Lehrman 1584, **Lingnan 1587**, Mortensen 1605, Palmer 1621, Patricelli 1623, **Patterson 1624**, **Richardson 1632**, Ritter 1633, Rosenthal 1638, **Smart 1651**, Stone 1654, Tully 1665, **Xerox 1680**, Young 1681, **Ziegler 1683**

Delaware: **CTW 1703**, Hirschl 1721, Marmot 1728, Mastronardi 1729, Phillips 1739, Rowland 1749, **Schwartz 1751**, Sinsheimer 1754, **Stroud 1757**, Wasily 1760

District of Columbia: Aid 1765, **Bauman 1770**, Bender 1772, Benton 1773, **Coyne 1788**, **Fannie 1793**, Fordham 1795, **Foundation 1796**, Jones 1813, Jovid 1814, **Koch 1819**, **Lambe 1820**, Lehrman 1821, Mazda 1828, McGowan 1830, Reich 1845, Roshan 1847, Spring 1849, Stewart 1850, True 1854, **Wallace 1857**, Willard 1861, **Winslow 1863**, Wyss 1864

Florida: Amaturo 1873, Bailey 1887, Banbury 1889, Beveridge 1907, **Campbell 1923**, Caspersen 1927, Community 1941, Coulter 1954, Dade 1957, **Davis 1964**, Duckwall 1978, duPont 1983, Eckerd 1986, **Foundation 2008**, **Goldhammer 2026**, Greenburg 2034, **Hayward 2053**, Keating 2084, Lattner 2104, Maltz 2126, Mote 2148, Peacock 2165, **Picower 2169**, Price 2177, Rayonier 2189, Rosenberg 2206, Rothberg 2209, Silverman 2234, **Skelly 2237**, St. Joe 2244, Storer 2252, Taishoff 2262, **Vanneck 2278**, Vaughn 2279, **von Liebig 2283**, Wells 2294, **Whitehall 2297**, **Winn 2301**, Wollowick 2306

Georgia: AEC 2310, Aflac 2311, Blank 2325, Brown 2332, Delta 2372, DuBose 2374, Equifax 2379, **Foundation 2388**, Franklin 2389, Georgia 2394, Glenn 2399, Healthcare 2411, Imlay 2417, Lee 2432, Mason 2444, Rich 2472, **Turner 2501**, **UPS 2503**, Watson 2509, Zeist 2529

Hawaii: Atherton 2532, Geist 2544, Hawaii 2545, Schuler 2552

Idaho: **Micron 2571**

Illinois: Abbott 2580, Arthur 2601, Bauer 2609, Blowitz 2623, Brinson 2633, Buehler 2638, Butler 2646, Chaddick 2655, Chicago 2661, Coleman 2673, Davee 2696, Deere 2699, Duchossois 2711, **Foundation 2732**, Geraldi 2752, Girl's 2757, GKN 2758, Goldman 2763, **Graham 2767**, Grainger 2768, Grant 2770, Illinois 2812, **Joyce 2820**, Kemper 2831, Kovler 2844, Logan 2860, **MacArthur 2868**, McGraw 2882, McNeil 2887, Meyer 2896, Oberweiler 2923, Olin 2925, Petersen 2941, Redhill 2960, Reese 2961, Regenstein 2962, Retirement 2964, Rothschild 2971, **Scholl 2989**, **Searle 2994**, Siragusa 3009, **Spencer 3015**, Sprague 3016, Tawani 3033, Tellabs 3034, **Tuohy 3041**, United 3044, USG 3046, Washington 3058, Woods 3084, Worley 3086

Indiana: Anderson 3099, Ball 3103, Bussing 3111, Clowes 3119, Fairbanks 3147, Foellinger 3149, **Goodrich 3157**, Harrison 3161, Henry 3165, Heritage 3166, Koch 3184, Lilly 3194, **Lumina 3196**, Oliver 3219, Regenstrief 3228, Rolland 3231

Iowa: Carver 3274, Community 3278, Maytag 3310, McElroy 3313, **Pioneer 3324**, Siouxland 3332, Wallace 3342

Kansas: Cooper 3353, Koch 3374, Rice 3384, Rudd 3385, Sabatini 3386, Westar 3403

Kentucky: Brown 3409, Community 3414, Gheens 3421, Good 3422, Keeneland 3432

Louisiana: Baptist 3461, Baton Rouge 3462, **Biedenharn 3463**, Booth 3464, Brown 3465, Coypu 3471, Goldring 3484, Huie 3488, Institute 3489, Monroe 3501, Schlieder 3508, Wheless 3514, **Woldenberg 3516**, Woolf 3517, Zigler 3520

Maine: Alfond 3521, Burnham 3527, **Ford 3533**, King 3545, Libra 3546, Maine 3549, **Oak 3552**, **River 3554**

Maryland: **Alcoholic 3564**, Blades 3574, **Casey 3585**, Chaney 3587, Choice 3589, Davis 3607, Deutsch 3616, **Ellison 3621**, **Ewing 3626**, Gudelsky 3641, Higginson 3649, **Hughes 3654**, Kerr 3661, **Kluge 3663**, **Life 3677**, Macht 3683, Meyerhoff 3691, Meyerhoff 3692, **Nasdaq 3700**, Procter 3711, Provident 3712, Rathmann 3715, **Shared 3727**, Sunrise 3740, Wasserman 3757, Weiss 3760, Wilson 3761, Wright 3762, **Zickler 3763**

Massachusetts: Alden 3777, Barr 3791, Behrakis 3796, **Bosack 3809**, BOSE 3810, **Bruner 3819**, Cabot 3823, Campbell 3830, Chahara 3843, Charles 3844, **Conservation 3858**, Cox 3863, Endowment 3895, **Fidelity 3904**, Fuller 3918, **Grass 3931**, **Harris 3944**, Henderson 3946, Hinduja 3952, Hood 3956, **Iacocca 3963**, Island 3965, Johnson 3970, **Kendall 3977**, King 3981, Lee 4001, Levy 4005, Marcus 4022, Melville 4034, **New England 4052**, Pappas 4066, Parker 4069, Peabody 4072, Peabody 4074, Pierce 4084, Rosse 4113, Schott 4132, Shapiro 4136, Smith 4150, Talbots 4178, Webster 4201

Michigan: Abrams 4213, Ann Arbor 4221, Barry 4227, Bay 4229, Community 4252, Dalton 4266, Dart 4267, Dow 4286, Dow 4287, **Earhart 4291**, **Fetzer 4297**, Fetzer 4298, Ford 4307, Frey 4316, **General 4319**, General 4320, **Gerber 4321**, Gerstacker 4322, Herrick 4341, Loutit 4372, **Pardee 4407**, Power 4415, Ratner 4417, **Sage 4427**, Shelden 4434, Stonisch 4449, Strosacker 4450, Towsley 4461, Upjohn 4465, Upton 4466, Westerman 4478, Whirlpool 4480, Wilson 4485

Minnesota: Buuck 4526, Deikel 4548, Duluth 4556, Edina 4560, Graco 4573, Greystone 4576, Huss 4592, Jerome 4595, Lilly 4606, Marbrook 4612, **McKnight 4616**, Northwest 4637, **O'Shaughnessy 4639**, **Patterson 4647**, Phillips 4655, Vest 4708, Walker 4711, Wasie 4716, West 4723

Mississippi: **Armstrong 4734**, Hardin 4747, Irby 4750

Missouri: Baer 4779, Bellwether 4782, Community 4798, Edison 4807, **Enterprise 4810**, JSM 4841, Kansas 4843, **Kauffman 4843**, Kemper 4849, **Mallinckrodt 4860**, **McDonnell 4864**, Millstone 4867, **Monsanto 4868**, Pershing 4880, Reynolds 4892, Saigh 4895, Seaworld 4900, Shaw 4901, Sosland 4908, Stupp 4911

Montana: Cinnabar 4935

Nebraska: Heuermann 4973, Lincoln 4987, **McDonald 4989**, Perkins 4996, Weitz 5016

Nevada: Cord 5029, Fairweather 5032, **Hilton 5037**, Lifestyle 5042, Reynolds 5056, Southwest 5066, Tuscany 5074, **Walsh 5075**

New Hampshire: **Dorr 5086**, Endowment 5088, Hunt 5093, Martin 5097

New Jersey: **Allen 5111**, **Barbour 5124**, Bard 5125, Buehler 5146, Cape 5153, Capita 5154, **Carolan 5156**, Dircks 5180, Dodge 5181, **Edison 5186**, **Frankino 5196**, Fund 5199, Gershman 5206, Goldberg 5209, Healthcare 5228, Horizon 5240, Hyde 5247, **Johnson 5265**, Karma 5269, Kirby

Scholarship funds

Oppenheimer 955, Orange 957, Orfalea 958, Parsons 980, Peninsula 989, Peppers 991, Peters 993, **Peterson 996**, PG&E 1000, Philibosian 1003, Pickford 1005, **PMI 1008**, Preuss 1015, Price 1016, Ralphs 1029, Rancho 1031, Richards 1048, **Rivendell 1056**, Roth 1071, **Saban 1079**, Sacramento 1080, San Diego 1087, Sandy 1092, Santa Barbara 1093, Saw 1098, **Schlinger 1102**, Schlinger 1103, **Schuler 1108**, Scripps 1115, Shasta 1139, **Smith 1161**, **Smith 1167**, Smullin 1169, Soda 1173, Sonora 1178, Stauffer 1188, Steele 1189, Stern 1195, Stone 1200, Strauss 1202, **Strauss 1203**, Stulsaft 1210, Swenson 1218, Synopsys 1223, Taper 1226, Thornton 1235, Towbes 1241, Trust 1246, Tuohy 1247, UniHealth 1249, Union 1250, **Unocal 1252**, Valley 1257, Van Nuys 1261, Ventura 1264, **Versacare 1265**, Waltmar 1277, Wasserman 1281, Weingart 1288, **WellPoint 1292**

Colorado: Boettcher 1344, Community 1357, Community 1358, Community 1359, **Crowell 1361**, ECA 1372, El Pomar 1374, **Gill 1382**, Hill 1392, **Janus 1396**, Johnson 1398, King 1404, M.D.C. 1413, Petteys 1436, Saccomanno 1446, Saeman 1448, Schlessman 1450, Summit 1463, Telluride 1465, Trueblood 1466, Weckbaugh 1470, Wilhite 1473, Williams 1474

Connecticut: American 1482, Bodenwein 1497, **Brainerd 1502**, Chilton 1511, Collis 1513, Community 1514, Community 1516, Community 1517, Connecticut 1518, Connecticut 1519, Culpeper 1521, Fairfield 1537, Fippinger 1540, Freas 1548, **GE 1553**, Hartford 1564, **Hulsking 1570**, Jones 1573, Larsen 1579, Leever 1583, Main 1594, **McKenzie 1601**, Oaklawn 1616, Palmer 1621, Pitt 1628, **Praxair 1629**, Rogow 1636, Say 1642, Sewall 1648, Sullivan 1655, Tauck 1657, TWS 1666, Wallace 1674, Woodward 1678, **Xerox 1680**, Zachs 1682

Delaware: Bennett 1690, Cawley 1696, Etnier 1711, Hirschl 1721, Phillips 1739, **Robinson 1745**

District of Columbia: Bender 1772, Cafritz 1780, Gudelsky 1805, Lehrman 1821, Leonsis 1822, Loughran 1823, Mazda 1828, McGowan 1830, Reich 1845, Replogle 1846, Roshan 1847, Sprenger 1848, Spring 1849, Willard 1861

Florida: Amaturo 1873, Ansin 1877, Appleby 1879, Bastien 1892, **Chatlos 1932**, Cisneros 1934, Community 1939, Community 1940, Community 1942, Community 1943, Community 1946, Community 1947, Community 1948, Community 1949, Conn 1951, Dade 1957, **Davis 1964**, Dennis 1969, Duckwall 1978, Florida 2003, **Gibney 2021**, Glaubinger 2023, **Goldhammer 2026**, Goodwin 2029, Greenburg 2034, Gulf 2041, Gulf 2042, Hayes 2052, Jaffe 2072, **Johnson 2077**, Kennedy 2087, Kleist 2095, Lattner 2104, MacDonald 2121, Madigan 2123, North 2153, Opler 2158, Pinellas 2170, Rayonier 2189, Rosen 2205, Rubin 2211, Russell 2212, **Samstag 2214**, Saunders 2219, Schmidt 2225, Schoenbaum 2227, **Skelly 2237**, Smith 2238, Southwest 2240, St. Joe 2244, St. Petersburg 2245, Star 2248, Taishoff 2262, Van Vleet 2277, Vaughn 2279, Wahlert 2284, Watts 2289, Weaver 2289, Wells 2294, Westgate 2296, **Winn 2301**

Georgia: AGL 2312, Amos 2314, Atlanta 2321, Brown 2331, Brown 2332, Cawood 2342, **Challenge 2344**, **Coca-Cola 2352**, Community 2355, Community 2357, Community 2358, Dunn 2375, Exposition 2380, Franklin 2389, Georgia 2395, **Georgia 2397**, Goizueta 2400, Harland 2407, Harrison 2410, Imlay 2417, Lee 2432, Love 2437, Murphy 2456, Patterson 2460, Pitts 2463, Rollins 2475, Savannah 2480, **Scientific 2482**, Smith 2491, Watson 2509, Wilson 2519, Woolley 2525

Hawaii: Anthony 2531, Bank 2535, Campbell 2536, Castle 2538, Hawaii 2545, HMSA 2547, McInerny 2551, Vidinha 2557, Watumull 2558, Wilcox 2559, Wong 2560

Idaho: Cunningham 2567, Idaho 2570, **Micron 2571**, Morrison 2572, Nagel 2573, Simplot 2575

Illinois: Abbott 2580, **Andrew 2595**, Arthur 2601, **Brach 2630**, Brinson 2633, Bruce 2634, **Brunswick 2636**, **Burlington 2644**, Butler 2646, **CH2M 2654**, Chaddick 2655, Charleston 2657, Chicago 2660, Coleman 2673, Comer 2675, Community 2677, Community 2679, Community 2680, Crane 2687, **Crane 2688**, Crown 2691, Cuneo 2692, Day 2698, Deere 2699, **Demos 2702**, Dillon 2704, Dunard 2712, DuPage 2713, Energizer 2721, Flagg 2731, GKN 2758, Grainger 2768, Grand 2769, Harris 2788, Hartmarx 2794, Hermann 2798, Houlsby 2805, **Irwin 2814**, Kelly 2830, Kemper 2831, Lederer 2852, McCourtney 2879, McGraw 2882, McNeil 2887, Meyer 2896, Moline 2902, **Monticello 2904**, **Nureyev 2919**, Oberweiler 2923, Olin 2925, Omron 2926, Owens 2929, Pepper 2936, **Peterson 2942**, Pilchard 2944, Polk 2946, Pullman 2957, Redhill 2960, Schmitt 2987, **Scholl 2989**, Seabury 2993, Shaker 2999, Shirk 3007, Siragusa 3009, Speh 3014, **Square 3018**, **State 3019**, Susman 3030, Takiff 3032, USG 3046, Ward 3056, Washington 3058, White 3067

Indiana: Adams 3095, Adams 3096, Anderson 3099, Ball 3104, Blue 3107, Branigin 3109, Brown 3110, Bussing 3111, Central 3116, Community 3123, Community 3124, Community 3125, Community 3126, Community 3127, Community 3128, Community 3130, Community 3132, Community 3133, Crown Point 3135, Decatur 3138, Elkhart 3145, Froderman 3153, Hancock 3160, Henry 3165, Heritage 3166, Jasper 3177, Johnson 3178, Lafayette 3188, Legacy 3189, Lilly 3194, Lincoln 3195, Madison 3197, Montgomery 3206, Noble 3214, Northern 3215, Noyes 3216, Oakley 3217, Ogle 3218, OneAmerica 3220, Portland 3223, Pulliam 3224, Rolland 3231, Steuben 3241, Tipton 3243, Unity 3247, Wabash 3250, Waterfield 3252, Wayne 3253

Iowa: Carver 3274, Cedar Rapids 3275, Community 3278, Des Moines 3281, Kuyper 3304, Mansfield 3308, Maytag 3309, Maytag 3310, McElroy 3313, Northeast 3320, Pella 3323, Poweshiek 3325, Principal 3326, **Rockwell 3328**, Seidler 3331, Siouxland 3332

Kansas: Bane 3345, Baughman 3346, Capitol 3350, Cessna 3351, Garvey 3363, Garvey 3364, Hansen 3366, Hutchinson 3368, Koch 3374, Payless 3380, Rice 3384, Rudd 3385, Salina 3387, Scroggins 3389, Sprint 3395, Sullivan 3396, Topeka 3400, Westar 3403

Kentucky: Brown 3409, Community 3414, Community 3415, Cralle 3416, E.ON 3417, Ford 3419, Foundation 3420, Gheens 3421, Good 3422, Hayswood 3425, **Humana 3428**, Keeneland 3432, Norton 3441, **Omnicare 3444**, Orleton 3445, Robinson 3449, Young 3454

Louisiana: Almar 3459, Booth 3464, Brown 3465, Community 3469, Coughlin 3470, Huie 3488, Jones 3491, Monroe 3501, Scott 3509, Taylor 3511

Maine: Alfond 3521, Alfond 3523, Berry 3526, Davenport 3531, **Ford 3533**, Gallagher 3535, Lunder 3547, Peters 3553, Switzer 3557

Maryland: Abell 3559, Allegis 3565, Baltimore 3568, Blades 3574, Brown 3578, Choice 3589, Columbia 3595, Commonweal 3596, Community 3598, Community 3599, Community 3600, Concordia 3601, Constellation 3602, Davis 3607, **Dean 3610**, Dresher 3617, Eaton 3619, Goldsmith 3637, Gudelsky 3641, Henson 3648, Hoffberger 3652, Johnston 3657, Kerr 3661, Klein 3662, **Kluge 3663**, Leidy 3673, Linehan 3678, Macht 3683, Marshall 3687, Meyerhoff 3691, Meyerhoff 3692, Mid 3693, Osprey 3703, Price 3709, Procter 3711, Provident 3712, Rathmann 3715, **Smith 3736**, Straus 3738, Sunrise 3740, Wasserman 3757

Massachusetts: Acushnet 3770, Alden 3776, Ayling 3785, Babson 3787, Bayrd 3795, Behrakis 3796, Benz 3798, Berkshire 3801, Birmingham 3807, Black 3808, Cabot 3823, Cabot 3825, Cambridge 3828, Cape Cod 3832, Cape Cod 3833, Clarke 3849, Community 3854, Community 3855, Croll 3868, Cummings 3871, Eastern 3886, Essex 3897, Fuller 3918, Gabrieli 3919, Gerondelis 3925, Gordon 3928, Grinspoon 3935, Hanover 3941, Highland 3951, Jordan 3971, Levy 4005, Liberty 4006, Lowell 4015, Massachusetts 4026, McCallum 4029, Mifflin 4038, Millipore 4040, New 4050, New 4054, North 4057, Pappas 4066, Pierce 4084, **Robinson 4107**, Rosse 4113, Rubenstein 4115, Salah 4124, **Schooner 4131**, Schrafft 4133, Shapiro 4136, Sheehan 4140, Stoico 4166, **Technical 4180**, Travelli 4184, **Waterman 4198**, Worcester 4209, Yawkey 4211

Michigan: Abrams 4213, Andersen 4219, Ann Arbor 4221, Baker 4226, Barry 4227, Battle Creek 4228, Bay 4229, Berrien 4231, Binda 4233, Branch 4237, **Bretzlaff 4238**, Charlevoix 4246, Comerica 4251, Community 4252, Community 4253, Community 4254, Community 4255, Community 4256, Community 4257, Community 4258, Community 4259, Cook 4262, DeVlieg 4275, Dow 4286, Ford 4302, Ford 4307, **Ford 4308**, Four 4310, Fremont 4315, Gilmore 4324, Grand Haven 4325, Grand Rapids 4326, Grand 4327, Greenville 4331, **H.I.S. 4334**, Harding 4337, Herrick 4341, Kahn 4351, Kalamazoo 4352, Lansing 4372, Midland 4392, Morey 4397, Mott 4400, Petoskey 4412, Ratner 4417, **Sage 4427**, Saginaw 4428, **Secchia 4431**, Skillman 4438, St. Deny's 4444, Steelcase 4446, Sturgis 4452, Tamer 4453, Tauber 4454, Thompson 4458, Tiscornia 4460, Upjohn 4465, Weatherwax 4474, Westerman 4478, Whirlpool 4480, Wilson 4485, Young 4490

Minnesota: Adams 4495, **ADC 4496**, Alliss 4498, **Best 4516**, Blandin 4520, Buuck 4526, Central 4534, Christianson 4539, **CHS 4540**, Dasburg 4545, Davis 4546, Deluxe 4549, Donaldson 4552, Duluth 4556, Fischman 4564, Griggs 4577, Kelley 4597, Kopp 4599, Koran 4600, Maas 4608, Mann 4611, Marbrook 4612, McVay 4620, **Medtronic 4622**, National 4630, **Nelson 4632**, Northwest 4637, **O'Shaughnessy 4639**, Ordean 4643, **Pentair 4649**, **Petters 4653**, Pohlad 4657, Red Wing 4663, Regis 4664, Schwan's 4676, Slaggie 4686, Smikis 4687, TCF 4699, Thorpe 4701, **U.S. 4704**, Wasie 4716, WCA 4718, West 4723

Mississippi: AmSouth 4733, Community 4737, Gulf 4745, Irby 4750, Maddox 4753, McRae 4755, Mississippi 4757, Mississippi 4758, **Sullivan 4766**, Vicksburg 4769

Missouri: Ameren 4772, **Anheuser 4776**, Baer 4778, Boswell 4786, Buder 4791, Community 4798, Edison 4807, **Enterprise 4810**, Forster 4814, Goppert 4819, Green 4822, H & R 4823, Hites 4831, Jones 4839, Kansas 4842, **Kauffman 4843**, Lay 4853, **Mallinckrodt 4860**, Millstone 4867, Musgrave 4870, Pershing 4880, Pettus 4882, Pott 4886, Saigh 4895, Saint Louis 4896, Shaw 4901, Shelter 4902, Simon 4903, Sosland 4908, Tilles 4917, Truman 4919, Woods 4928

Montana: **Edwards 4936**, Washington 4941

Nebraska: Buckley 4947, Commercial 4951, **ConAgra 4953**, Dunklau 4958, Eihusen 4961, Hamilton 4968, Hawkins 4970, Hirschfeld 4974, Hitchcock 4975, Kiewit 4983, Kilbourne 4985, Lincoln 4987, Mid-Nebraska 4991, Muchemore 4992, Omaha 4994, Omaha 4995, Reynolds 4997, Wiebe 5017

Nevada: Bretzlaff 5024, Christian 5026, Community 5028, Cord 5029, Hawkins 5036, **Hilton 5037**, Nevada 5047, Redfield 5055, Smith 5065, **Tang 5072**, Wendy's 5076

New Hampshire: **Dorr 5086**, Eastman 5087, Fuller 5090, Lindsay 5095, New Hampshire 5098, **Penates 5099**

New Jersey: **Allen 5111**, Amirsaleh 5114, Bard 5125, Berger 5128, **Bonner 5137**, Cape 5153, Charles 5161, Community 5167, Danellie 5177, Dircks 5180, Geiger 5205, Isermann 5253, **Johnson 5261**, Karma 5269, Krieger 5290, Lanza 5294, **Lautenberg 5298**, McMullen 5325, New Jersey 5337, **Newcombe 5338**, **Pfeiffer 5351**, Princeton 5357, Provident 5359, **Puffin 5362**, Rigorous

5367, Schering 5387, Summit 5417, **Syms 5422, Tang 5423, Tavitian 5426,** Turrell 5431, **Verizon 5439,** Victoria 5440, **Wilf 5455, WKBJ 5459,** Zobel 5464

New Mexico: Albuquerque 5466, Carlsbad 5469, Cudd 5472, Domanica 5475, Holt 5480, Hubbard 5481, Kind 5483, McCune 5488, New Mexico 5491, Santa Fe 5496, Taos 5498

New York: Abrons 5511, Achelis 5513, Adirondack 5517, Alexander 5531, Alexander 5532, Allyn 5539, Area 5564, Arkell 5565, **Atran 5575,** Avery 5581, **AXA 5584,** Bahnik 5589, Barrington 5602, Berg 5621, Bernhard 5624, Bingham 5631, Bluhdorn 5642, Bodman 5647, Botwinick 5653, Bravmann 5661, **Brooks 5674, C.O.U.Q. 5695,** Cain 5697, Carnahan 5706, Carvel 5710, Carwill 5711, Central 5724, Charina 5731, **Chazen 5739, China 5750, Citigroup 5755,** Community 5780, Community 5783, Community 5784, Community 5785, Curran 5786, Davenport 5833, **de Hirsch 5840, Dedalus 5847,** Derossi 5853, Devlin 5855, Dewar 5856, **Diamond 5858, Donghia 5872,** Dow 5879, Dyson 5898, **EHA 5912,** Emerson 5927, First 5958, **Frankel 5976,** Freeman 5981, Frohring 5993, **Fuld 5999,** Galasso 6005, Gebbie 6009, Gilder 6029, Gleason 6039, Goldman 6053, Goldsmith 6060, Gould 6083, **Grant 6090,** Gutman 6122, Gutmann 6123, Harkness 6145, **Hearst 6161, Hearst 6162,** Heckscher 6164, Hermione 6175, Hettinger 6178, **Homeland 6199,** Horncrest 6200, Hughes 6209, I Have 6219, IF 6226, Independence 6229, Jephson 6258, **Johnson 6268,** Joy 6276, Kaplan 6288, **Kaufmann 6299,** Kennedy 6314, Klein 6333, Knapp 6342, **Kopf 6348, Kraft 6351,** Lang 6374, Lee 6391, Lemberg 6401, Lenna 6402, Lincoln 6423, Link 6429, **Luce 6453,** Lurie 6459, M & T 6465, M.U.S. 6467, Macdonald 6468, **Matthews 6507, McCaddin 6513,** McCann 6514, McCarthy 6515, **Memton 6529, Merrill 6537,** Mesdag 6539, Metcalf 6541, Millbrook 6549, **Mitsubishi 6560, Monell 6566,** Moody's 6569, **Moore 6571,** Moore 6573, **Morgan 6577,** Morris 6579, Moses 6587, New York 6613, New York 6618, New York 6619, New York 6620, Nichols 6628, Northern 6638, Northern 6639, **Novartis 6640,** O'Connor 6645, O'Herron 6646, **Ohga 6658,** Oishei 6660, **Open 6665,** Palisano 6680, Park 6688, **Peierls 6705,** Penick 6709, **Pepsi 6713, Pforzheimer 6721,** Pollack 6735, Raffiani 6767, Reader's 6777, Reed 6782, **Ripplewood 6812, Ritter 6814,** Robinson 6820, Rochester 6823, Rock 6824, Rosh 6858, Rosner 6860, **Ross 6863,** Ross 6864, Rubinstein 6876, Rudin 6878, Ruffin 6880, Schenectady 6915, **Schlumberger 6926,** Schmeelk 6927, Schnurmacher 6930, Schnurmacher 6931, Siebens 6974, Simon 6987, **SMBC 7005,** Snow 7011, **Solomon 7017,** Soros 7024, Spiegel 7029, **Starr 7048,** Starwood 7049, Steele 7053, Stone 7081, Straus 7086, Sulzberger 7095, **Summerfield 7097, Tanaka 7120,** Ungar 7183, Vernon 7195, **Vetlesen 7196,** Wachenheim 7204, Wachtell 7205, **Wilson 7263,** Wilson 7264, **Zenkel 7295,** Zichron 7298, Zitrin 7302

North Carolina: **Bank 7310,** Bergen 7316, Biddle 7317, Broyhill 7328, Bryan 7330, Community 7344, Community 7345, Community 7346, Cumberland 7349, Dickson 7355, Dover 7356, Duke 7359, Duke 7360, Easley 7361, Finch 7366, Finley 7367, Foundation 7370, Goodrich 7378, Halton 7386, Harris 7390, Hendrick 7395, Holding 7399, Lance 7418, Martin 7424, Mebane 7427, Mills 7429, North Carolina 7438, North Carolina 7439, Polk 7449, Progress 7453, Reynolds 7459, Smith 7476, Smith 7479, Southern 7481, Tannenbaum 7493, Triangle 7494, Van Houten 7500, Weaver 7504, Winston-Salem 7508

North Dakota: Fargo 7514, Leach 7516, MDU 7517, North Dakota 7519, Stern 7521

Ohio: Akron 7526, Anderson 7529, **Arab 7531,** Ashland 7533, Austin 7536, Bachman 7538, Barberton 7539, Bates 7540, Bicknell 7548, Brennan 7554,

Britton 7556, Butler 7562, **Cardinal 7567,** Cleveland 7576, Cleveland 7577, Columbus 7580, Community 7582, Community 7583, Community 7584, Coshocton 7593, Dater 7600, Diamond 7610, Evans 7620, Fairfield 7622, Farmer 7623, Ferguson 7625, Fifth 7626, Findlay 7627, Firman 7628, First 7629, Fox 7637, France 7639, GAR 7643, **Geisse 7646,** Greene 7653, Gund 7656, Gund 7657, H.C.S. 7658, Hamilton 7660, Haslinger 7664, Hoover 7674, Hoover 7675, Huntington 7680, Hutton 7681, Jewish 7690, Jubilee 7694, Kettering 7699, **Knowles 7701, Kosar 7703,** Kramer 7704, LaValley 7708, Licking 7714, Lubrizol 7725, M/I 7729, Marietta 7735, Miami 7748, Middletown 7749, Milacron 7751, Moores 7759, Morgan 7761, Morgan 7762, Morley 7763, Murch 7766, Murphy 7768, Muskingum 7770, Nippert 7777, Nordson 7781, **Ohio 7786, OMNOVA 7789,** Owens 7793, Park 7795, Peterson 7802, Resch 7816, Richland 7819, Ritchie 7821, Robbins 7823, Saint 7830, Salem 7831, Schlink 7839, Schott 7842, Scioto 7845, Sedgwick 7849, Silk 7857, Sisler 7858, Slemp 7860, Sloat 7861, Stark 7867, **Tomkins 7884,** Troy 7886, Tuscarawas 7890, Van Wert 7891, **Vesper 7892,** Wayne 7897, Wolfe 7915

Oklahoma: Bovaird 7927, Collins 7930, Communities 7931, Community 7932, Hille 7943, Kerr 7950, McGee 7957, McMahon 7959, Meinig 7961, Oklahoma City 7964, Oklahoma 7965, Oxley 7968, Puterbaugh 7970, Rapp 7971, Records 7972, Sarkeys 7974, **Schusterman 7975,** Share 7977, Southern 7979, Stevens 7980, Tulsa 7984, Williams 7989, Zink 7994

Oregon: Boyd 8000, Carpenter 8003, **Chiles 8005,** Clemens 8006, Collins 8009, Fohs 8012, Haugland 8018, Intel 8022, Jeld 8025, John 8026, Johnson 8027, Macdonald 8038, Merrill 8040, Miller 8043, Oregon 8049, PacifiCorp 8050, **Schmidt 8055,** Schnitzer 8056, Swindells 8062, Tucker 8065, Wessinger 8067

Pennsylvania: 1675 8070, ACE 8073, **Alcoa 8075,** AMETEK 8081, Arcadia 8086, Arete 8088, **Armstrong 8090,** Baker 8092, Beaver 8098, Berks 8103, Bristol 8118, Brossman 8120, Centre 8136, Century 8137, **Cestone 8138,** Cestone 8139, Chester 8141, Claneil 8144, Community 8155, Connelly 8157, Crawford 8162, Eberly 8179, Eden 8182, Ellis 8184, Equitable 8187, First 8202, Foundation 8208, Fourjay 8209, Genuardi 8213, Hamilton 8233, Heinz 8240, Hooper 8256, Hopwood 8257, Independence 8266, Kavanagh 8282, **Kennametal 8284,** Keystone 8285, Keystone 8286, Kline 8293, Lancaster 8300, Lehigh Valley 8303, Lenfest 8304, Lilliput 8311, Little 8313, Luzerne 8317, Maronda 8325, Maslow 8327, McFeely 8334, McLean 8340, Measey 8342, Moore 8358, Ortenzio 8366, Perkin 8375, Philadelphia 8380, Phillips 8380, **Pincus 8384,** Pittsburgh 8386, **PPG 8394, Presser 8395,** PTS 8399, Rees 8401, Roberts 8405, Rockwell 8408, Schock 8427, Scranton 8431, **Seraph 8434,** Shenango 8441, Simmons 8441, Smith 8443, Smith 8444, Society 8449, Stabler 8455, Truman 8483, **United 8488, Waldorf 8495,** York 8511

Rhode Island: Charter 8526, Cuno 8528, Daniels 8530, **FM 8537,** Littlefield 8544, Lord 8545, McCarthy 8548, Rhode Island 8551

South Carolina: Abney 8564, Bruce 8571, Central 8577, Chapin 8579, Coastal 8581, Collins 8582, Community 8583, First 8587, Foothills 8588, Kane 8596, McKissick 8599, Spartanburg 8616, Waccamaw 8619, **Youths' 8621**

South Dakota: Larson 8627, Sioux Falls 8630, Vucurevich 8634

Tennessee: Benwood 8644, **Bridgestone 8646,** Caesars 8648, Christy 8654, CIC 8656, Community 8660, Community 8661, Danner 8664, Davis 8665, Durham 8670, East 8671, Frist 8678, HCA 8690, Johnson 8697, Kirkland 8699, Osborne 8714, Phillips 8716, Promethean 8721, Stokely 8730, Tucker 8735, Wilson 8744

Texas: Abell 8749, Alkek 8754, Amarillo 8758, **AT&T 8765,** Augur 8766, B & B 8769, Baker 8772, Bauer 8779, Belo 8787, Brackenridge 8793, Bridgeway 8796, Brown 8799, Brumley 8800, Cailloux 8807, Cain 8808, Cain 8809, Carter 8816, Cauthorn 8820, CH 8823, Clayton 8830, Coastal 8833, Cockrell 8835, Communities 8839, Community 8840, Community 8841, Community 8842, Cook 8845, **Cooper 8846,** Cullen 8854, Dallas 8855, Dickson 8866, Doss 8869, Dougherty, 8870, East 8876, El Paso 8881, Ellwood 8884, Esping 8886, Finger 8900, Fisch 8901, Fish 8902, Franklin 8907, George 8916, Haggerty 8932, Hamill 8937, Hamman 8938, Herzstein 8949, Hoglund 8956, Houston 8960, Houston 8961, Hudson 8962, Huffington 8963, Jamail 8970, Johnson 8974, Jones 8975, Jonsson 8977, Kahn 8980, Kempner 8987, Klabzuba 8996, Kodosky 9000, Lubbock 9021, Marathon 9028, Marti 9030, Martinez 9032, Mayborn 9033, McCrea 9040, McCullough 9041, McDermott 9043, McGovern 9044, McKee 9045, McMillan 9046, McNair 9047, Meredith 9054, Mitte 9067, Moody 9070, Navarro 9089, Newman 9090, **Onward 9103,** Owsley 9108, Permian 9117, Powell 9128, Priddy 9130, Priddy 9131, PSH 9137, Riddle 9148, Rockwell 9154, Rogers 9155, San Antonio 9166, **Shell 9181,** Simmons 9188, Smith 9195, Smith 9198, **Starling 9210,** Sterling 9212, Strake 9215, Sturgis 9216, Sumners 9218, Tartt 9224, Temple 9227, **Tenet 9229,** Terry 9231, Texas 9232, Triad 9239, Trull 9240, Turner 9242, Waco 9255, Waggoner 9256, Waggoner 9257, Waggoners 9258, Wal 9260, Weaver 9267, West 9275, White 9279, Wolens 9286, Wolslager 9290, Works 9291, Young 9295, Zephyr 9299

Utah: ALS 9301, **ALSAM 9302,** Bamberger 9305, Burton 9309, Caine 9310, Eccles 9317, Eccles 9319, Eccles 9320, Esther 9321, Simmons 9342, Stewart 9345, Swanson 9346, Wing 9352

Vermont: Lintilhac 9359, Mergens 9360, Vermont 9361

Virginia: Arlington 9371, Beazley 9376, Camp 9382, Campbell 9383, Charlottesville 9390, Community 9401, **Cooke 9405,** Delmar 9410, Flagler 9417, Folger 9418, Foundation 9419, Gottwald 9431, Herndon 9437, Kanter 9445, Kogod 9452, Landmark 9455, Lynchburg 9463, Memorial 9474, Moore 9478, **Mustard 9481,** Norfolk 9484, **Norfolk 9485,** Northern 9486, Portsmouth 9498, Reynolds 9503, Rosenthal 9508, Titmus 9527, United 9530, Virginia Beach 9532, Washington 9534, Weissberg 9536, Wiley 9539, Williamsburg 9541

Washington: Ackerley 9547, Anderson 9551, Casey 9566, Cheney 9569, De Falco 9578, Dimmer 9579, Evertrust 9583, Foster 9588, Foundation 9589, **Gates 9591, Hemingway 9606,** Lafromboise 9622, Lockwood 9631, Lynn 9633, McMillen 9639, Milgard 9641, Norcliffe 9650, PEMCO 9660, Rainier 9669, **Samis 9675,** Seattle 9680

West Virginia: Bowen 9711, Carter 9712, Community 9716, Kanawha 9723, Maier 9725, Parkersburg 9730, Prichard 9731, Schenk 9732, Tucker 9736

Wisconsin: Alliant 9742, Argosy 9747, Bader 9749, **Bradley 9763,** Clark 9773, Cleary 9774, Community 9776, Community 9778, Community 9779, Crump 9783, CUNA 9786, Eastman 9795, Fleck 9799, Fond du Lac 9800, Green Bay 9810, Hess 9816, Holz 9817, Johnson 9826, Kelben 9830, Kenosha 9833, **Kern 9834,** Kikkoman 9836, Kohler 9840, Kress 9844, La Crosse 9845, Ladish 9846, Lunda 9852, Madison 9855, Managed 9857, Marshall 9860, Marshfield 9861, Mead 9867, **Meehan 9868,** Menasha 9869, Miller 9875, Modine 9878, Northwestern 9884, Oshkosh 9885, Peck 9894, Peterson 9896, Phipps 9898, Puelicher 9904, **Rockwell 9912,** Schoenleber 9921, Sensient 9922, Sentry 9923, Shapiro 9925, **Smith 9929, T & O 9946, Wagner 9957,** West 9963, West 9964, Wilson 9965, Wisconsin 9967, WPS 9970, **Young 9972**

Wyoming: Community 9977, Ellbogen 9981, **Schultz 9990,** Scott 9991

Scholarships—to individuals

Alabama: Bedsole 12, Central 20, Finlay 33, Wallace 74

Alaska: Alaska 79, Arctic 80, CIRI 83, Doyon 84

Arizona: Community 91, University 148

Arkansas: Altheimer 155, Murphy 167, Northwest 169, Trinity 181, **Tyson 182**, Wal-Mart 184, Walton 186

California: Alafi 201, Anaheim 220, BP 314, Buck 330, California 348, **Cantor 354**, Change 373, Children's 381, Community 403, Community 407, Fluor 523, **Foundation 531**, GenCorp 560, Ghidotti 571, Granoff 612, Harbison 646, Humboldt 691, James 709, **Koulaieff 778**, Leavey 797, Los Altos 828, Marin 854, McIntyre 876, McKesson 879, Morgan 914, Northern 941, Orange 957, PacifiCare 971, Peninsula 989, Richards 1048, Sacramento 1080, San Diego 1087, San Francisco 1088, San Luis 1090, Santa Barbara 1093, Scaife 1099, Schwab 1111, Shasta 1139, Solano 1175, Sonora 1178, Strauss 1202, **Studenica 1209**, Ventura 1264, Waitt 1275, **WellPoint 1292**

Colorado: Colorado 1355, Community 1358, **Daniels 1362, First 1377**, Norwood 1433, Saccomanno 1446, Sachs 1447, **Seay 1453**, Telluride 1465, Western 1471, Yampa 1477

Connecticut: Ambler 1481, American 1482, Bridgeport 1504, Broadcasters 1505, Community 1515, Community 1516, Community 1517, Connecticut 1518, Fairfield 1537, **Folsom 1545**, Main 1594, Meriden 1603, Nye 1615, Rogow 1636, Sullivan 1655, **Xerox 1680**

Delaware: Etnier 1711, MBNA 1730

District of Columbia: **Phillips 1841**

Florida: **Abramson 1868**, Bailey 1887, Blount 1910, Booth 1914, Community 1939, Community 1941, Community 1942, Community 1946, Community 1947, Community 1949, Dade 1957, Gore 2031, Gulf 2041, Kelly 2086, Pinellas 2170, Selby 2230, Southwest 2240, St. Petersburg 2245

Georgia: Amos 2316, Callaway 2336, Cobb 2349, Community 2360, **Georgia 2397**, Watson 2509, WinShape 2520

Hawaii: Anthony 2531, Atherton 2532, Geist 2544, Hawaii 2545, Scott 2553, Watumull 2558, Zimmerman 2561

Idaho: **Micron 2571**

Illinois: **Abbott 2579**, AMCORE 2591, Berner 2617, Brewer 2632, **Burlington 2644**, Butterworth 2647, Community 2679, Community 2680, Geneseo 2750, Hansen 2782, Harrison 2790, Hartke 2792, Little 2859, Master 2875, McMullan 2884, Medline 2889, Mellinger 2890, Oak Park 2922, Oberweiler 2923, Peters 2940, **Peterson 2942**, Rochetta 2969, Smysor 3011, **State 3019, Wood 3081, Woodbury 3082**, Zurich 3093

Indiana: Adams 3095, Adams 3096, Blue 3107, Brown 3110, Cass 3115, Central 3116, Cole 3121, Community 3123, Community 3124, Community 3125, Community 3126, Community 3127, Community 3128, Community 3130, Community 3131, Community 3132, Crown Point 3135, Dearborn 3137, Decatur 3138, DeKalb 3141, Elkhart 3145, Harrison 3161, Henry 3165, Johnson 3178, Kosciusko 3186, Lafayette 3188, Legacy 3189, Madison 3197, Mahnken 3198, Marshall 3199, Montgomery 3206, Noble 3214, Portland 3223, Samerian 3234, Steuben 3241, Tipton 3243, Wabash 3250, Wayne 3253, Wells 3255, Whitley 3258

Iowa: Des Moines 3281, Iowa 3298, Lee 3305, Northeast 3320, Poweshiek 3325, Siouxland 3332

Kansas: Bane 3345, Cessna 3351, Hansen 3366, Hutchinson 3368, Jones 3370, Sabatini 3386, Salina 3387, Topeka 3400, Wichita 3404

Kentucky: Blue 3407, Community 3414, Hayswood 3425, Young 3456

Louisiana: Baton Rouge 3462, Zigler 3520

Maine: Maine 3548, Melmac 3550

Maryland: Baltimore 3568, Community 3598, Community 3599, Foulger 3631

Massachusetts: Berkshire 3801, Cape Cod 3833, Charles 3844, Community 3855, Ham 3940, **Phillips 4083**, Salah 4124, Sudbury 4173, Talbots 4178, **Technical 4180**, Trefler 4185, Worcester 4209

Michigan: Battle Creek 4228, Charlevoix 4246, Community 4252, Community 4254, Community 4256, Community 4257, Community 4259, **Earhart 4291**, Fremont 4315, **Gerber 4321**, Grand Haven 4325, Grand Rapids 4326, Grand 4327, Jackson 4347, Kalamazoo 4352, **Legion 4375**, Miller 4393, Petoskey 4412, Saginaw 4428, Sturgis 4452, Tamer 4453, Tiscornia 4460, **Van Curler 4468**

Minnesota: Alworth 4499, Arcee 4506, **Best 4516**, Blandin 4520, Central 4534, **CHS 4540**, Duluth 4556, General 4570, Grand Rapids 4574, Hiawatha 4585, Initiative 4593, **Land 4602**, Minnesota 4624, Northwest 4637, Hull 4644, Wedum 4719, Winona 4729

Mississippi: Community 4737, Skelton 4765

Missouri: Ballman 4780, Feraldo 4813, Kansas 4842, King 4851, McDavid 4862, MFA 4866, Pershing 4880, Shelter 4902, Walker 4922, Westlake 4925

Montana: Bair 4931, Cinnabar 4935, Washington 4941

Nebraska: Baright 4945, **Buffett 4950**, Fremont 4962, Hamilton 4968, Hawks 4971, Kiewit 4984, Lexington 4986, Merrick 4990, Ryan 5000, Steinhart 5005

Nevada: Community 5028, Pennington 5053

New Hampshire: Chesterfield 5082, Eastman 5087, Foundation 5089, New Hampshire 5098

New Jersey: Alcatel 5110, Baker 5123, Knowles 5283, **KPMG 5288**, New Jersey 5337, **Scholarship 5388, Tavitian 5426, Verizon 5439**, Wight 5454, Willits 5457

New Mexico: Albuquerque 5466, Carlsbad 5469, Hubbard 5481, Maddox 5487, Taos 5498

New York: Adirondack 5517, **AXA 5584**, Central 5724, Chautauqua 5738, **Chazen 5739**, Clark 5762, Community 5780, Community 5783, Community 5784, Crary 5806, Druckenmiller 5889, Glens Falls 6041, **Grant 6090**, Jewish 6260, **King 6323, Li 6418, Mayer 6509, Mitchell 6559, Morgan 6577**, Netzach 6609, New York 6620, North 6637, Northern 6638, Northern 6639, O'Sullivan 6652, **Open 6665, PepsiCo 6714**, Potter 6742, Price 6746, Realty 6779, **Rockefeller 6826, Schepp 6917**, Scholarships 6932, **SMBC 7005**, Sperry 7026, **Youth 7287**, Zemsky 7294

North Carolina: Butler 7334, Coffey 7339, Community 7344, Community 7346, Cumberland 7349, Keasbey 7409, Martin 7424, Morehead 7430, Nucor 7440, Pharmacy 7446, Polk 7449, Sloan 7475, **Sunshine 7490**, Tannenbaum 7493, Triangle 7496, Winston-Salem 7508

North Dakota: North Dakota 7519

Ohio: AK 7525, Ashland 7533, Ashtabula 7534, Bryan 7559, Cafaro 7563, Community 7581, Community 7582, Community 7583, Community 7584, Community 7586, Coshocton 7593, Dana 7599, David 7601, Diamond 7610, Duff 7615, Fairfield 7622, Ford 7633, Horvitz 7677, Hutton 7681, **Knowles 7701**, Marietta 7735, McIntire 7743, Middletown 7749, Muskingum 7770, Patterson 7797, Richland 7819, Ritter 7822, Samaritan 7832, **Scripps 7848**, Slemp 7860, Springfield 7866, Stark 7867, Tuscarawas 7890, Van Wert 7891, **Wexner 7904**, Wilson 7909

Oklahoma: Stevens 7980, Tulsa 7984, Zarrow 7993

Oregon: Adler 7996, Clemens 8006, Collins 8008, Ford 8013, Four 8015, Merrill 8040, Oregon 8049

Pennsylvania: Beaver 8098, Berks 8103, Blanchard 8111, Brossman 8121, **Carnegie 8130**, Central 8135, **Cestone 8138**, Cestone 8139, Chester 8141, Comcast 8152, Community 8153, Community 8154, Ellis 8184, England 8185, Epstein 8186, Erie 8188, Foundation 8208, Hassel 8237, Hill 8248, Hirtzel 8253, Hoyt 8259, Innisfree 8267, Kimmel 8288, Lancaster 8300, Lenfest 8305, Luzerne 8317, McKaig 8336, Phoenixville 8381, Postles 8393, **PPG 8394**, Schock 8427,

Shenango 8438, Shoemaker 8440, Society 8449, Steinman 8458, Vincent 8492, West 8500

Puerto Rico: Puerto Rico 8515

Rhode Island: Cuno 8528, Lord 8545, Rhode Island 8551, Shriners 8556, Wagner 8562

South Carolina: Community 8584, Horne 8594, Spartanburg 8616

South Dakota: South Dakota 8631

Tennessee: CIC 8656, Community 8660

Texas: Astin 8764, Baumberger 8782, Bergman 8789, **College 8836**, Communities 8839, Cook 8845, Eady 8875, El Paso 8882, Fant 8892, Fasken 8895, Faulconer 8896, Griffin 8925, Hachar 8927, Hamman 8938, Healthcare 8944, Heavin 8945, Klabzuba 8996, Marti 9030, McMillan 9046, Nation 9087, Piper 9124, San Angelo 9164, San Antonio 9166, **Shell 9181**, Stanzel 9208, Sunnyside 9219, Temple 9228, **Tenet 9229**, Wichita 9280, Zimmer 9300

Utah: Bamberger 9305, Miller 9335

Vermont: General 9356, Vermont 9361

Virginia: Camp 9382, **CAP 9384**, Columbus 9399, Community 9400, Community 9401, Community 9402, **Cooke 9405, Datatel 9407**, HRH 9439, Lincoln 9458, Lynchburg 9463, Meador 9473, **Mustard 9481**, Northern 9486, **Olmsted 9490**, Perry 9496, Wiley 9539

Washington: **Blakemore 9558**, Blue 9559, Community 9571, Grays 9597, Kelsey 9617, Lauzier 9627, Maxwell 9635, McMillen 9639, **PAH 9657**, PEMCO 9660, Potlatch 9665, Tacoma 9693, **Vista 9699**

West Virginia: Bowen 9711, Carter 9712, Chambers 9713, Community 9716, Kanawha 9723, Parkersburg 9730, Stout 9734, Tucker 9736

Wisconsin: AnnMarie 9743, Casper 9770, Community 9776, Community 9779, Community 9780, Fort 9801, Green Bay 9810, Jacobus 9819, Janesville 9820, Johnson 9826, Kelben 9830, Kohl 9838, Kohler 9840, Krause 9842, Krejci 9843, La Crosse 9845, Marshfield 9861, Modine 9878, Munson 9880, Nelson 9882, Oshkosh 9885, Oshkosh 9886, Racine 9906, Rowland 9916, Rutledge 9917, WPS 9970

Wyoming: Community 9977, Stock 9992, Wyoming 10000

Seed money

Alabama: Alabama 1, Bruno 17, Central 20, Community 24, Community 25, Hill 39, Kaul 40, **Vulcan 73**

Alaska: Alaska 78, Rasmuson 85

Arizona: Arizona 87, Flinn 98, **Johnson 112**, Neely 125, Wilson 152

Arkansas: Arkansas 156, Northwest 169, Rockefeller 172, Ross 174

California: **A-T 191**, Ackerman 193, Alliance 204, Alpert 208, **American 217**, Aratani 230, **Arkay 235**, Atkinson 239, Ayrshire 247, Bannerman 255, Bireley 292, California 350, **Castagnola 366, ChevronTexaco 380, Christensen 384**, Columbia 399, Community 402, Community 403, Community 404, Community 405, Community 406, Community 407, Confidence 411, Cowell 423, Crail 426, Crocker 429, Crockett 430, **Draper 466**, Drown 469, Drum 470, East 474, **Environment 487**, Firedoll 508, **First 512**, Flora 521, **Foundation 529**, Fresno 537, **Fund 542**, Gasser 557, Girard 580, Goldman 597, Goldwyn 600, **Good 603**, Gross 621, Haas 636, Haas 637, Harden 647, Heller 666, Hewlett 671, Humboldt 691, Irvine 698, Irvine 699, Jacobs 708, Jewett 718, Johnson 725, **K.L. 736**, Keller 752, Kirchgessner 762, Koret 774, Leatherby 796, **LEF 799**, Lipman 817, **Living 821, Lloyd 823**, Los Altos 828, Lund 831, Lurie 832, Lux 834, Lytel 836, Marin 854, **Mattel 861, Maxfield 862**, McCarthy 868, McKesson 879, McLean 880, Mead 881, Mental 886, Miller 901, Morgan 915, Newhall 936, Nissan 939, Norton 943, Paloheimo 974, Parker 979, Parsons 980, Peninsula 989, **Peterson 996**, Rancho 1031, **Righteous 1050, Rivendell 1056, S.G. 1078, Saban 1079**,

Sacramento 1080, San Diego 1087, Schlinger 1103, **Seaver 1118**, Sobrato 1172, Sonora 1178, **Spencer 1181**, **Strauss 1203**, Stuart 1206, Taper 1226, Truckee 1244, True 1245, Trust 1246, Valley 1256, vanLobenSels 1260, Ventura 1264, Weingart 1288, Whittier 1304

Colorado: Animal 1333, Aspen 1338, Bohemian 1345, Brett 1349, Colorado 1356, Community 1357, Community 1358, Community 1359, Denver 1364, **General 1381**, Hughes 1393, JFM 1397, Pikes 1437, Piton 1439, Price 1442, Qwest 1443, Rose 1445, **StorageTek 1460**, Summit 1463, Telluride 1465, Western 1471, Yampa 1477

Connecticut: Bissell 1495, Bodenwein 1497, Bridgeport 1504, Community 1514, Community 1515, Community 1516, Community 1517, Connecticut 1518, **Educational 1533**, Ensworth 1535, **Ettinger 1536**, Fippinger 1540, Graustein 1559, Hartford 1563, Hartford 1564, International 1571, Leever 1583, **Lingnan 1587**, Main 1594, Matthies 1600, Mortensen 1605, Palmer 1621, Panwy 1622, **Prentice 1630**, **Smart 1651**, Stone 1654, Thompson 1658, Tow 1661, **Tremaine 1662**, **Valentine 1669**, **Xerox 1680**

Delaware: **CTW 1703**, Delaware 1706, Laffey 1725, Mastronardi 1729, **Raskob 1741**, **Robinson 1745**

District of Columbia: Aid 1765, **Arca 1767**, **Bauman 1770**, Bender 1772, **Butler 1779**, Cafritz 1780, Consumer 1786, Fordham 1795, Graham 1804, Henry 1808, Jovid 1814, **Kennedy 1816**, **Koch 1819**, **Lounsbery 1824**, Meyer 1834, **Moriah 1835**, Munson 1837, **Public 1844**, Reich 1845, Spring 1849, **Summit 1852**, Trellis 1853, **Wallace 1857**, Willoughby 1862, **Winslow 1863**, Wyss 1864

Florida: Banbury 1889, Beveridge 1907, Community 1939, Community 1940, Community 1941, Community 1942, Community 1943, Community 1944, Community 1946, Community 1948, Conn 1951, Dade 1957, Dunn 1979, duPont 1983, Engelberg 1994, Henderson 2056, Jasam 2074, Kennedy 2087, **Knight 2097**, **Koch 2098**, MacDonald 2121, **Morris 2145**, Opler 2158, Rayonier 2189, Roberts 2201, St. Joe 2244, **Stacy 2246**, Waldbaum 2285

Georgia: AGL 2312, Anderson 2317, BellSouth 2323, **Challenge 2344**, Community 2356, Community 2357, Community 2359, Community 2362, Day 2371, DuBose 2374, Equifax 2379, Georgia 2394, **Georgia 2397**, **Hanley 2405**, Horowitz 2415, Livingston 2435, Lubo 2438, **Meyer 2446**, North 2458, Porter 2468, Russell 2478, Savannah 2480, Singletary 2490, Woolley 2525

Hawaii: Alexander 2530, Atherton 2532, Campbell 2536, Castle 2537, Castle 2538, Cooke 2541, Frear 2543, Geist 2544, Hawaii 2545, McInerny 2551, Wilcox 2559

Idaho: Cunningham 2567, Idaho 2570

Illinois: Chicago 2661, Community 2677, Community 2679, Community 2680, Community 2681, Day 2698, Deere 2699, DeKalb 2701, Dillon 2704, Donnelley 2708, Driehaus 2710, DuPage 2713, Field 2728, **Foundation 2732**, Grant 2770, Harris 2787, Hermann 2798, Kaplan 2823, **Kemper 2832**, Landau 2847, Lumpkin 2864, **MacArthur 2867**, McGraw 2882, Mellinger 2890, Millard 2897, New 2912, Oak Park 2922, Olin 2925, Prince 2948, **Relations 2963**, Retirement 2964, Rothschild 2971, Seabury 2993, Speh 3014, Sprague 3016, Steans 3021, Stern 3023, Tellabs 3034, VNA 3049, Washington 3058, Woodward 3085

Indiana: Adams 3095, Blue 3107, Brown 3110, Bussing 3111, Central 3116, Clowes 3120, Cole 3121, Community 3123, Community 3124, Community 3125, Community 3126, Community 3127, Community 3128, Community 3130, Community 3132, Dearborn 3137, Decatur 3138, Dekko 3142, Elkhart 3145, Fairbanks 3147, Hancock 3160, Harrison 3161, Health 3164, Henry 3165, Heritage 3166, Irwin 3174, Irwin 3175, Jasper 3177, Johnson 3178, Kosciusko 3186,

Lafayette 3188, Legacy 3189, Lilly 3194, Lincoln 3195, **Lumina 3196**, Marshall 3199, Montgomery 3206, Noble 3214, Northern 3215, Oliver 3219, Portland 3223, Ripley 3230, Steuben 3241, Tipton 3243, Unity 3247, Wabash 3250, Waterfield 3252, Wayne 3253, Wells 3255, Whitley 3258

Iowa: Ahrens 3260, Carver 3274, Cedar Rapids 3275, Community 3277, Community 3278, Cowles 3279, Des Moines 3281, Hubbell 3297, Iowa 3298, Maytag 3309, Maytag 3310, McElroy 3313, Poweshiek 3325, Principal 3326, Siouxland 3332, Vermeer 3341, Wellmark 3343

Kansas: Capitol 3350, Cooper 3353, DeVore 3357, Farah 3362, Hutchinson 3368, Lloyd 3375, Salina 3387, Servant 3391, Topeka 3400, Westar 3403

Kentucky: Blue 3407, Community 3414, Cralle 3416, Foundation 3420, Good 3422, Norton 3441

Louisiana: Almar 3459, Baptist 3461, Baton Rouge 3462, Community 3469, Freeman 3480, German 3483, Institute 3489, Jones 3491, New Orleans 3503, RosaMary 3507

Maine: Davenport 3531, **Ford 3533**, **Golden 3538**, Horizon 3541, JTG 3542, King 3545, Libra 3546, Maine 3548, **River 3554**

Maryland: Abell 3559, Baker 3567, Baltimore 3568, Columbia 3595, Commonweal 3596, Community 3598, Community 3599, Community 3600, Deutsch 3616, England 3622, France 3632, Goldseker 3636, Higginson 3649, Hoffberger 3652, Macht 3683, Marshall 3687, Meyerhoff 3692, Mid 3693, Mulford 3696, Procter 3711, Rathmann 3715, Straus 3738, TKF 3747, **Town 3749**, Tucker 3750, Wasserman 3757, Wilson 3761, **Zickler 3763**

Massachusetts: Acushnet 3770, Adams 3772, Alden 3777, Berkshire 3801, Birmingham 3807, Boston 3812, Cabot 3823, Cabot 3824, Cambridge 3828, Campbell 3830, Cape Cod 3833, Carlee 3835, Community 3854, Community 3855, **Conservation 3858**, Crossroads 3869, Davis 3875, Eaton 3888, Ellsworth 3892, Essex 3897, Farnsworth 3899, Fields 3905, Fletcher 3912, Fuller 3918, Ham 3940, Hoche 3954, **Kendall 3977**, Levy 4005, Melville 4034, Merck 4035, Morse 4044, **New England 4052**, Orchard 4062, Parker 4069, Peabody 4073, Pierce 4084, Ratshesky 4095, **Reebok 4098**, Riley 4104, Robbins 4106, **Schooner 4131**, Shaw 4139, Simches 4147, Smith 4150, Stevens 4163, Stevens 4164, Stoddard 4165, Sudbury 4173, Wadleigh 4194, Wallace 4195, Worcester 4209

Michigan: Ann Arbor 4221, Barry 4227, Battle Creek 4228, Bay 4229, Berrien 4231, Binda 4233, Capital 4243, Carls 4244, Charlevoix 4246, Community 4252, Community 4253, Community 4254, Community 4255, Community 4256, Community 4257, Community 4258, Dalton 4266, Davenport 4269, DeVos 4276, DeVos 4279, **Dow 4285**, Dow 4287, Fremont 4315, Frey 4316, General 4320, **Gerber 4321**, Gerstacker 4322, Gilmore 4324, Grand Haven 4325, Grand Rapids 4326, Grand 4327, Greenville 4331, **H.I.S. 4334**, Hudson 4343, Hurst 4344, Jackson 4347, Kalamazoo 4352, **Kellogg 4357**, Lansing 4372, McGregor 4389, Midland 4392, Miller 4394, **Mott 4399**, Nokomis 4404, Petoskey 4412, Saginaw 4428, Skillman 4438, Steelcase 4446, Strosacker 4450, Tiscornia 4460, Towsley 4461, Upjohn 4465, Upton 4466, Wickes 4483

Minnesota: Bell 4514, Bigelow 4519, Blandin 4520, Bremer 4523, Central 4534, Deikel 4548, Duluth 4556, Greystone 4576, Initiative 4593, Jerome 4595, **Land 4602**, Lilly 4606, Mardag 4613, **Medtronic 4622**, Minneapolis 4623, Musser 4629, Northwest 4637, O'Neil 4638, Oswald 4645, Rochester 4668, Saint Paul 4671, Smikis 4687, Southways 4688, Target 4697, Walker 4711, Wedum 4719, West 4723, **Weyerhaeuser 4725**

Mississippi: Lower 4751, Maddox 4753, Riley 4763

Missouri: Butler 4793, Commerce 4797, Community 4798, **Deer 4804**, **Fox 4815**, Green 4822, H & R 4823, Kansas 4842, **Kauffman 4843**, Kemper

4849, Long 4858, Oppenstein 4876, Pershing 4880, Saint Louis 4896, Shaw 4901, Simon 4903, Trio 4918, Truman 4919, Vatterott 4921, Woods 4928

Montana: **Edwards 4936**

Nebraska: Buckley 4947, Cooper 4954, Fremont 4962, Gardner 4965, Hirschfeld 4974, Kiewit 4984, Lexington 4986, Lincoln 4987, Mid-Nebraska 4991, Omaha 4994, Omaha 4995, Weitz 5016, Woods 5018

Nevada: **Hilton 5037**, Nevada 5047, **Walsh 5075**

New Hampshire: Bean 5080, **Dorr 5086**, Fuller 5090, Hunt 5093, New Hampshire 5098

New Jersey: Alcatel 5110, Borden 5138, Campbell 5151, Cowles 5170, Dodge 5181, **Edison 5186**, Elizabethtown 5188, **Eshet 5190**, Fund 5199, Healthcare 5228, **Huber 5244**, **International 5252**, **Johnson 5265**, Karma 5269, Kirby 5279, Knistrom 5282, **Knowles 5283**, **KPMG 5288**, MCJ 5324, **Merck 5326**, OceanFirst 5341, Pascale 5349, **Pfeiffer 5351**, Princeton 5357, Prudential 5360, **Puffin 5362**, **Rippel 5368**, Schumann 5391, Summit 5417, Turrell 5431, Victoria 5440, Wallerstein 5446, Wallerstein 5447, **WKBJ 5459**

New Mexico: Albuquerque 5466, Carlsbad 5469, Con 5471, Frost 5476, **Levinson 5486**, McCune 5488, New Mexico 5491, PNM 5493, Santa Fe 5496, Taos 5498, **Thaw 5500**

New York: **Abelard 5508**, Achelis 5513, Adirondack 5517, **Adler 5521**, Allyn 5539, **American 5553**, Area 5564, Barker 5599, **Barth 5603**, **Bay 5606**, Bodman 5647, Botwinick 5653, Bowne 5655, Brodsky 5668, **Bronfman 5673**, Burden 5687, **Bydale 5694**, Carnahan 5706, Central 5724, Chadwick 5726, Charina 5731, Charitable 5734, Chautauqua 5738, **Citigroup 5755**, **Claiborne 5757**, Clark 5762, Community 5780, Community 5781, Community 5782, Community 5783, Community 5784, Corning 5794, Cricket 5808, **Cummings 5813**, **Cummings 5814**, Cummings 5815, Dammann 5824, Davenport 5833, **de Hirsch 5840**, DeCamp 5845, **Dedalus 5847**, **Doherty 5868**, **Dreyfus 5886**, Dreyfus 5887, Dyson 5898, **East 5900**, **Echoing 5905**, **EHA 5912**, **Ford 5970**, **Foundation 5971**, **Freeman 5980**, Frog 5992, Gebbie 6009, Gifford 6026, Gilman 6032, **Gimprich 6035**, Glens Falls 6041, **Goldman 6052**, Goldman 6053, **Goldman 6056**, Golisano 6067, Gould 6083, **Grant 6091**, Griffis 6107, Guggenheim 6117, Heckscher 6164, **Heineman 6165**, Horncrest 6200, Hoyt 6203, **Humanitas 6212**, Independence 6229, Institute 6232, Ittleson 6241, JM 6263, Johnson 6268, Kaplan 6288, Kaplan 6290, Kenworthy 6315, **Klingenstein 6338**, **Kohlberg 6346**, **Kopf 6348**, Kornfeld 6350, Lang 6374, **LaSalle 6377**, Lehman 6396, Lincoln 6423, Lindner 6426, Littauer 6434, Lowenstein 6449, M & T 6465, Macdonald 6468, Mars 6494, McCann 6514, McCarthy 6515, McGonagle 6518, **Mertz 6538**, **MetLife 6542**, Mizuho 6562, **NEC 6605**, New York 6613, New York 6615, New York 6618, New York 6620, **New 6621**, **Norman 6635**, Normandie 6636, Northern 6638, Northern 6639, **Noyes 6643**, O'Connor 6645, O'Toole 6654, Ohrstrom 6659, Oishei 6660, **Ottinger 6674**, Park 6688, **Pforzheimer 6721**, Pinkerton 6728, **Ramapo 6769**, Rapoport 6772, Rauch 6774, **Reader's 6778**, Rhodebeck 6791, Rochester 6823, **Rockefeller 6825**, **Rockefeller 6826**, Rosenberg 6845, Rosenstiel 6852, **Ross 6863**, **Rubin 6872**, Rubinstein 6876, Samuels 6901, Santa 6905, Schaffer 6911, Schenectady 6915, Schnurmacher 6931, Sister 6994, Slifka 7001, **Smithers 7010**, Snow 7011, Snyder 7014, Spingold 7032, Spunk 7036, St. Faith's 7039, Stevens 7076, Sweetgrass 7113, **Time 7142**, **Tinker 7143**, Tower 7158, **Toyota 7160**, Triad 7162, Turner 7175, van Ameringen 7190, van Ameringen 7191, Van Pelt 7192, Vidda 7198, **Walter 7211**, **Warhol 7215**, **Weeden 7223**, Weissman 7237, Wendling 7242, **Wenner 7244**, Western 7248, Wilson 7264, **Wolfensohn 7270**

North Carolina: **Babcock 7308**, Biddle 7317, Blumenthal 7320, Cape Fear 7336, Cemala 7337, Community 7342, Community 7343, Community 7344, Community 7345, Cumberland 7349, Duke 7359, Finley 7367, Foundation 7370, Hanes 7387, Hanes 7388, Harris 7390, Kenan 7413, Mebane 7427, Mills 7429, Morgan 7431, North Carolina 7439, Polk 7449, Reynolds 7457, Reynolds 7458, Strowd 7488, Tannenbaum 7493, Triangle 7496, Van Houten 7500, Warner 7503, Weaver 7504, Winston-Salem 7508

North Dakota: Fargo 7514, North Dakota 7519

Ohio: Abington 7524, Akron 7526, Anderson 7529, Ashland 7533, **Austin 7535**, Austin 7536, Bruening 7558, Cincinnati 7574, Cleveland 7576, Columbus 7580, Community 7581, Community 7582, Community 7583, Community 7584, **Convergys 7587**, Corbin 7591, Coshocton 7593, Dater 7600, Dayton 7603, Evans 7620, Fairfield 7622, **Federated 7624**, Ferguson 7625, Fifth 7626, Findlay 7627, Fox 7637, GAR 7643, **Generation 7647**, Gund 7657, Hamilton 7660, **HCR 7667**, Hershey 7671, Hoover 7675, Iddings 7682, Jennings 7688, Kettering 7699, Kroger 7705, Lennon 7710, Levin 7712, Licking 7714, Marietta 7735, Mayerson 7739, Miami 7748, Middletown 7749, Milacron 7751, Montgomery 7758, Moores 7759, Morgan 7761, Muskingum 7770, Nationwide 7771, Nord 7779, Nordson 7781, **PLACE 7805**, Prentiss 7806, Richland 7819, Russell 7827, Saint 7830, Schmidlapp 7840, Schmidlapp 7841, Scioto 7845, **Scripps 7848**, Sisler 7858, Slemp 7860, Smith 7863, Springfield 7866, Stark 7867, Stocker 7870, Tait 7875, Toledo 7883, Troy 7886, Wallace 7894, Wayne 7897, White 7905, Woodruff 7917

Oklahoma: **8:32 7922**, Communities 7931, Goddard 7939, Inasmuch 7944, Kirkpatrick 7952, Merrick 7962, Noble 7963, Oklahoma City 7964, Rapp 7971, **Schusterman 7975**

Oregon: Autzen 7997, Carpenter 8003, Chambers 8004, Collins 8009, Jeld 8025, Johnson 8027, Kinsman 8031, **Lazar 8035**, Meyer 8042, Oregon 8049, Templeton 8064

Pennsylvania: **Alcoa 8075**, Allegheny 8076, Allerton 8077, Barra 8095, Beaver 8098, Benedum 8099, Berks 8103, Blanchard 8111, Born 8113, Buhl 8124, Central 8135, Centre 8136, Century 8137, **Cestone 8138**, Claneil 8144, **Colcom 8150**, Community 8155, Dolfinger 8172, Donley 8175, DSF 8178, Falk 8193, Fels 8198, Fine 8201, First 8202, FISA 8204, Fisher 8205, Foundation 8208, Fourjay 8209, Grable 8221, Heinz 8240, Heinz 8241, Heinz 8242, Hillman 8249, Hillman 8250, Hillman 8251, Hillman 8252, Honickman 8255, Hopwood 8257, Hoyt 8259, Huston 8263, Huston 8264, Justus 8276, Lancaster 8300, Laurel 8301, Lehigh Valley 8303, Lenfest 8304, Lindback 8312, Maslow 8327, McCune 8331, McCune 8332, McFeely 8334, McKenna 8337, McLean 8340, Mellon 8344, Mellon 8346, Miller 8352, Moore 8358, Nelson 8362, Penn 8371, Philadelphia 8378, Phoenixville 8381, Pittsburgh 8386, **Presser 8395**, Rockwell 8408, Saint 8419, **Scaife 8425**, Scholler 8428, Scranton 8431, Shaffer 8436, Smith 8443, Smith 8445, Sordoni 8450, Sovereign 8451, Stackpole 8456, Staunton 8457, Truman 8483, United 8486, Widener 8502, Wyomissing 8509, York 8511

Rhode Island: CARLISLE 8521, **Dorot 8531**, Kimball 8542, McCarthy 8548, Rhode Island 8551

South Carolina: Abney 8564, Black 8569, Bruce 8571, Byerly 8572, Chapin 8579, Coastal 8581, Community 8583, Community 8584, Daniel 8585, Fullerton 8589, **Roe 8607**, Self 8610, Sims 8611, Spartanburg 8616, Springs 8617, **Youths' 8621**

South Dakota: Sioux Falls 8630, South Dakota 8631

Tennessee: Benwood 8644, Community 8660, Community 8661, Davis 8665, Day 8666, Durham 8670, East 8671, Hyde 8693, Jeniam 8695, Lyndhurst 8703, **Maclellan 8704**, Martin 8708, Osborne 8714, Phillips 8716, Plough 8718, **Rust 8724**, Stephens 8729, Wilson 8744

Texas: Abell 8749, Alkek 8754, Amarillo 8758, Anderson 8762, **AT&T 8765**, Austin 8768, Burnett 8801, Cailloux 8807, Carter 8816, Coastal 8833, Communities 8839, Community 8840, Community 8841, Community 8842, Covenant 8847, Cowden 8848, Dougherty, 8870, Educational 8878, El Paso 8881, Fair 8891, Fikes 8899, Fish 8902, George 8916, Halsell 8936, Healthcare 8944, Herzstein 8949, Hoblitzelle 8955, Houston 8960, **Jenesis 8971**, Keith 8982, Kempner 8987, Kodosky 9000, Kronkosky 9002, Lubbock 9021, Marcus 9029, McDermott 9043, McKee 9045, Meadows 9049, Moody 9070, Navarro 9089, Owsley 9108, Permian 9117, Peterson 9120, Rapoport 9141, Richardson 9147, Rockwell 9154, San Angelo 9165, San Antonio 9166, **Scaler 9170**, Simmons 9188, Simmons 9189, Speas 9206, Speas 9207, Sterling 9212, Summerlee 9217, Swinney 9222, Trull 9240, Turner 9241, Waco 9255, Waggoner 9256, Ward 9263, **Waste 9265**, Wichita 9280, Wortham 9292, Zale 9297

Utah: Esther 9321

Vermont: **Ben 9355**, Lintilhac 9359, Vermont 9361

Virginia: Arlington 9371, Camp 9382, Charlottesville 9390, Community 9402, **de Beaumont 9408**, Delmar 9410, **Dorothy 9411**, Flagler 9417, Foundation 9419, Freddie 9422, Jackson 9441, Landmark 9455, Lane 9456, Lynchburg 9463, Memorial 9474, **Mitsubishi 9476, Mustard 9481**, Norfolk 9484, **Norfolk 9485**, Portsmouth 9499, Samberg 9510, Scott 9513, **Stern 9522**, Washington 9534, Weissberg 9536, Williamsburg 9541, **Winkler 9542**, Wrinkle 9545

Washington: Archibald 9553, **Boeing 9560, Brainerd 9561**, Bullitt 9563, Cheney 9569, Community 9571, Ferguson 9585, Foster 9588, Foundation 9589, Glaser 9594, Grays 9597, Harder 9600, Harvest 9602, **Kongsgaard 9620**, Lucky 9632, Martin 9634, Medina 9640, Miller 9642, Murdock 9644, Quixote 9667, **Samis 9675**, Tacoma 9693, **Vista 9699**, Washington 9701, **Weyerhaeuser 9703**, Wilburforce 9705

West Virginia: Chambers 9713, Clay 9714, Clay 9715, Community 9716, Daywood 9717, Kanawha 9723, Parkersburg 9730, Schenk 9732, Tucker 9736

Wisconsin: Alexander 9741, Alliant 9742, Assurant 9748, Bader 9749, Banta 9752, Beloit 9757, Bishop 9759, Bradshaw 9764, Community 9776, Community 9778, Community 9779, Community 9780, Cudahy 9785, Dudley 9792, Evjue 9797, Fleck 9799, Fond du Lac 9800, Green Bay 9810, Janesville 9820, Johnson 9823, Johnson 9826, Kelben 9830, Kenosha 9833, Kohler 9840, La Crosse 9845, Lunda 9852, Madison 9854, Managed 9857, McBeath 9864, Mead 9867, Milwaukee 9876, Morse 9879, Oshkosh 9885, Prescott 9903, Racine 9906, Siebert 9927, **T & O 9946, Thrivent 9949**, U.S. 9952, Weill 9962

Wyoming: Community 9977, McMurry 9985, **Schultz 9990**, Wyoming 10000

Sponsorships

Alabama: Compass 28, Protective 58

California: Fireman's 510, Gap 551, **Jack 705, Mattel 861**, Ralphs 1029, **Schwab 1110**, Synopsys 1222, Synopsys 1223, **WellPoint 1292**

Connecticut: **Aetna 1479, Deloitte 1527, Xerox 1680**

Georgia: AGL 2312, Georgia 2395, **Georgia 2397**

Illinois: **Donnelley 2707**, Sara 2982

Indiana: Koch 3184

Kansas: Payless 3380

Kentucky: **Omnicare 3444, Yum! 3457**

Maine: TD 3558

Massachusetts: Eastern 3886, Easthampton 3887, Salem 4125

Minnesota: **U.S. 4704**

Mississippi: Mississippi 4758

New Jersey: Danellie 5177, **Johnson 5261**, OceanFirst 5341, Provident 5359, Schering 5387

New York: **AXA 5584**, Independence 6229, New York 6618, Price 6746, SI 6972

North Carolina: Belk 7315

Ohio: **Convergys 7587**

Oklahoma: Inasmuch 7944, Oklahoma 7965

Pennsylvania: Equitable 8187, Graham 8222, Keystone 8285

South Carolina: First 8587

Tennessee: **Bridgestone 8646**, Caesars 8648

Texas: Kimberly 8992, **Tenet 9229**, Valero 9247

Virginia: United 9530

Washington: **Boeing 9560**, Evertrust 9583, Rainier 9669

Wisconsin: Acuity 9739, Kikkoman 9836, **Smith 9929**, Wisconsin 9967

Student loans—to individuals

Arizona: Dougherty 96

California: Santa Barbara 1093

Colorado: Colorado 1355, Community 1358

Connecticut: Sullivan 1655

District of Columbia: Strong 1851

Georgia: **Pickett 2462**

Illinois: Community 2680, Mellinger 2890

Indiana: Community 3123, Whitley 3258

Maryland: Plitt 3706, **Raskob 3714**, Thorn 3745

Massachusetts: Berkshire 3801, Cape Cod 3833, Community 3855, Hopedale 3958

Michigan: Eddy 4292, Sturgis 4452

Mississippi: Day 4739, Feild 4741

Missouri: Ingram 4834, McDavid 4862

Nevada: **Walsh 5075**

New Hampshire: New Hampshire 5098

New Mexico: Carlsbad 5469, Taos 5498

New York: **Alavi 5530**

North Carolina: Burroughs 7332, Stonecutter 7486, Winston-Salem 7508

Ohio: **Arab 7531**, Ashland 7533, Findlay 7627, Stark 7867

Oregon: Johnson 8027

Pennsylvania: **Cestone 8138**, Gibson 8215, Heinz 8241, Ross 8414, Shenango 8438

Rhode Island: Cuno 8528

South Carolina: Springs 8617

Texas: Hachar 8927, Marti 9030, Piper 9124, Seibel 9178, Speas 9206

Virginia: **Cooke 9405**

West Virginia: Carter 9712, Laughlin 9724, Stout 9734

Wisconsin: Rutledge 9917

Wyoming: Whitney 9998

Technical assistance

Alabama: Central 20, Community 23, **Corman 29**, Hill 39, Meyer 52, Webb 75

Alaska: Alaska 79, Rasmuson 85

Arizona: Arizona 87, Ottens 128, Piper 130

Arkansas: Arkansas 156, **Frueauff 161**

California: Ahmanson 198, Alliance 204, Archstone 232, **Arkay 235**, Atkinson 239, Atlas 241, Buck 330, **C.S. 340**, California 345, California 346, California 350, Community 401, Community 402, Community 403, Community 406, Community 407, **Draper 466**, East 474, Firedoll 508, **Firelight 509**, Fleishhacker 518, Flintridge 520, **Fund 542**, Gellert 559, Gerbode 564, Girard 580, **Goldman 595**, Goldman 596, Gumbiner 631, Haas 636, Haas 637, Heller 666, Humboldt 691, Irvine 698, Jacobs 708, Jewett 718, Johnson 725, **K.L. 736**, Kirchgessner 762, Lesher 805, **Lloyd 823**, Los Altos 828, Marin 854, **Mattel 861, McConnell 870**, McKay 877, Miller 901, Monterey 910, Morgan 915, Norton 943, Noyce 957, Orange 957, **Packard 972**, Parsons 980, Peninsula 989, Rancho 1031, **Righteous 1050**, Sacramento 1080, San Diego 1087, San Francisco 1088, San Luis 1090,

Sierra 1151, Sobrato 1172, Sonora 1178, **Strauss 1203**, Stuart 1206, Stuart 1208, Stulsaft 1210, **Stupski 1211**, **Sun 1214**, Truckee 1244, True 1245, Union 1250, Valley 1256, Van Nuys 1261, Ventura 1264, **Warsh 1280**, Zellerbach 1326

Colorado: Animal 1333, Anschutz 1334, Aspen 1338, Bohemian 1345, Bonfils 1347, Brett 1349, Buell 1350, Chambers 1354, Colorado 1356, Community 1358, **Crowell 1361**, Denver 1364, Edmondson 1373, **General 1381**, Kenney 1401, Piton 1439, Qwest 1443, Rose 1445, Summit 1463, Telluride 1465

Connecticut: Bridgeport 1504, Community 1514, Community 1515, Community 1516, Community 1517, Connecticut 1518, Connecticut 1519, Ensworth 1535, Fairfield 1537, Graustein 1559, Hartford 1564, Liberty 1586, Long 1590, Main 1594, Mortensen 1605, Tauck 1657, **Tremaine 1662, Valentine 1669, Xerox 1680**

Delaware: Delaware 1706, **Raskob 1741**

District of Columbia: **Bauman 1770**, Benton 1773, Cafritz 1780, Community 1785, Consumer 1786, Fordham 1795, **Kennedy 1816**, Kimsey 1817, McGowan 1830, Meyer 1834, **Moriah 1835, Summit 1852**

Florida: **Believers 1900**, Beveridge 1907, Burns 1920, Bush 1922, **Chatlos 1932**, Community 1939, Community 1940, Community 1941, Community 1943, Community 1948, Conn 1951, Dade 1957, **Davis 1964**, duPont 1983, **Gibney 2021**, Gulf 2041, Henderson 2056, Jacksonville 2071, Kennedy 2087, MacDonald 2121, North 2153, Quantum 2181, Stevens 2251, Weaver 2289

Georgia: AEC 2310, **Challenge 2344**, Community 2355, Community 2362, Healthcare 2411, Lee 2432, **Meyer 2446**, North 2458, Rich 2472, **Rockdale 2474, Scientific 2482, Turner 2501, UPS 2503**, Zeist 2529

Hawaii: Atherton 2532, Bank 2535, Castle 2537, Castle 2538, Cooke 2541, Hawaii 2545

Illinois: Bersted 2619, Chicago 2661, Community 2679, Community 2681, Field 2728, Flagg 2731, Fry 2740, Girl's 2757, Grand 2769, Harris 2787, Lumpkin 2864, Pick 2943, Polk 2946, Prince 2948, Reese 2961, Retirement 2964, Seabury 2993, Speh 3014, Sprague 3016, Steans 3021, USG 3046

Indiana: Ball 3103, Blue 3107, Brown 3110, Bussing 3111, Central 3116, Community 3123, Community 3124, Community 3125, Community 3127, Community 3128, Community 3132, **Cummins 3136**, Decatur 3138, Dekko 3142, Elkhart 3145, Fairbanks 3147, Foellinger 3149, Hancock 3160, Health 3164, Heritage 3166, Irwin 3175, Johnson 3178, Legacy 3189, Lilly 3194, Lincoln 3195, Noble 3214, Steuben 3241, Unity 3247, Wells 3255

Iowa: Ahrens 3260, Cedar Rapids 3275, Community 3277, Des Moines 3281, Maytag 3310, Mid-Iowa 3317

Kansas: Cooper 3353, Hutchinson 3368, Kansas 3372

Kentucky: C.E. 3412, Community 3414, Foundation 3420

Louisiana: Baptist 3461, Community 3469, Institute 3489, New Orleans 3503

Maine: Libra 3546, Maine 3548, Maine 3549

Maryland: Baker 3567, Baltimore 3568, **Blaustein 3575, Casey 3585**, Columbia 3595, Community 3599, France 3632, Freeman 3633, Goldseker 3636, Knott 3666, **Shared 3727**, Straus 3738, TKF 3747, Wasserman 3757

Massachusetts: Barr 3791, Berkshire 3801, Boston 3812, Cabot 3823, Cambridge 3828, Cape Cod 3833, Chahara 3843, Chase 3847, Clipper 3850, Community 3854, Community 3855, **Conservation 3858**, Crossroads 3869, Davis 3875, Essex 3897,

Farnsworth 3899, **Fidelity 3904**, Hyams 3961, Island 3965, Melville 4034, New 4054, **Partnership 4071**, **Reebok 4098**, Riley 4104, Schott 4132, Shapiro 4136, Shaw 4139, Sheehan 4140, **State 4158**, Stearns 4159, Stevens 4163, Stevens 4164, **Sweet 4176**, Worcester 4209

Michigan: Americana 4218, **Arcus 4223**, Barry 4227, Battle Creek 4228, Bay 4229, Branch 4237, Capital 4243, Charlevoix 4246, Community 4253, Community 4254, Community 4255, Community 4257, Community 4258, Community 4259, Fremont 4315, Frey 4316, General 4320, Gilmore 4324, Grand Rapids 4326, Grand 4327, Jackson 4347, Kalamazoo 4352, Midland 4392, **Mott 4399**, Mott 4400, Nokomis 4404, Petoskey 4412, Saginaw 4428, Weatherwax 4474

Minnesota: Blandin 4520, Blue 4521, Bremer 4523, **Cafesjian 4527**, Central 4534, Duluth 4556, Grand Rapids 4574, Initiative 4593, Jerome 4595, McKnight 4617, Minneapolis 4623, Northwest 4636, Northwest 4637, Phillips 4655, Rochester 4668, Saint Paul 4671, Target 4697, West 4723

Mississippi: Gulf 4745, Lower 4751, Maddox 4753, Riley 4763

Missouri: Community 4798, Gateway 4817, H & R 4823, Hall 4824, Hallmark 4825, Jewish 4837, Kansas 4842, **Kauffman 4843**, Kemper 4849, Oppenstein 4876, Roblee 4893, Saint Louis 4896, Stupp 4911

Nebraska: Cooper 4954, Lexington 4986, Lincoln 4987, Omaha 4994, Woods 5018

Nevada: **Hilton 5037**, Nevada 5047, **Walsh 5075**

New Hampshire: Eastman 5087, Endowment 5088, Foundation 5089, New Hampshire 5098

New Jersey: **Barbour 5124**, Dircks 5180, Dodge 5181, Harbourton 5223, Horizon 5240, **Johnson 5265**, Karma 5269, MCJ 5324, **Merck 5326**, Princeton 5357, Prudential 5360, Summit 5417, **Verizon 5439**, Victoria 5440, **WKBJ 5459**

New Mexico: Albuquerque 5466, Carlsbad 5469, Frost 5476, **Lannan 5484**, McCune 5488, New Mexico 5491, Santa Fe 5496, **Thaw 5500**

New York: **Abelard 5508**, Abrons 5511, Achelis 5513, Adirondack 5517, **American 5551**, Badgeley 5588, **Bay 5606, Beldon 5614**, Bodman 5647, Bowne 5655, **Bronfman 5673**, Burden 5687, **Carnegie 5707**, Central 5724, Charitable 5732, **China 5750, Citigroup 5755, Clark 5760**, Clark 5761, Clark 5762, Community 5780, Community 5781, Community 5782, Community 5783, Community 5784, Community 5785, Corning 5794, Cricket 5808, Cummings 5815, **Deutsche 5854**, Dyson 5898, **Echoing 5905, Ford 5970, Foundation 5971**, Gifford 6026, Gleason 6039, Gould 6083, **Grant 6091, Hearst 6161, Hearst 6162, Heineman 6165, Heron 6176**, Hoyt 6203, I Have 6219, Independence 6229, **Initial 6231, Ittleson 6241, JM 6263**, Jones 6274, Joy 6276, **JPMorgan 6277**, Kaplan 6290, **Mailman 6477, Mertz 6538, National 6604**, New York 6613, New York 6615, Northern 6639, O'Connor 6645, Pfizer 6720, Pinkerton 6728, Rapoport 6772, Rauch 6774, **Reynolds 6790**, Richmond 6800, Rochester 6823, **Rockefeller 6825, Rockefeller 6826, Ross 6863**, Scherman 6918, Schnurmacher 6931, SI 6972, Sister 6994, **Surdna 7103**, Tiger 7139, **Time 7142**, Tower 7158, Triad 7162, Tuttle 7176, **Wallace 7209**, Wendling 7242, Western 7248, Wilson 7264, **Wolfensohn 7270**

North Carolina: **Babcock 7308**, Blue 7319, Cape Fear 7336, Community 7343, Community 7344, Community 7345, Community 7346, Cumberland 7349, Duke 7359, Easley 7361, North Carolina 7438, Reynolds 7458, Robertson 7466, Triangle 7496, Warner 7503, Weaver 7504, Winston-Salem 7508

North Dakota: Fargo 7514, Leach 7516, Stern 7521

Ohio: Barberton 7539, **Bingham 7549**, Bryan 7559, Cincinnati 7574, Cleveland 7576, Columbus 7580, Community 7582, Community 7585, Dayton 7603, Fairfield 7622, Findlay 7627, **Generation 7647**, Gund 7657, Humphrey 7679, **Kettering 7698**, Kettering 7699, Marietta 7735, Mayerson 7739, McMaster 7744, Muskingum 7770, Nord 7779, Nordson 7781, O'Neill 7783, Richland 7819, Saint 7830, Schmidlapp 7841, Scioto 7845, **Scripps 7848**, Sloat 7861, Springfield 7866, Stark 7867, Stocker 7870

Oklahoma: Communities 7931, **Ethics 7935**, Merrick 7962, Oklahoma City 7964, **Schusterman 7975**, Tulsa 7984

Oregon: Boyd 8000, Carpenter 8003, Ford 8013, Kinsman 8031, Meyer 8042, Oregon 8049

Pennsylvania: AMETEK 8081, Baker 8092, Benedum 8099, Birmingham 8107, Central 8135, Centre 8136, **Cestone 8138**, Cestone 8139, Claneil 8144, **Colcom 8150**, Community 8155, Erie 8188, Falk 8193, Fels 8198, Ferree 8199, FISA 8204, Foundation 8208, Genuardi 8213, Grable 8221, Heinz 8240, Heinz 8241, Heinz 8242, Hopwood 8257, Huston 8263, Huston 8264, Laurel 8301, Luzerne 8317, McCune 8332, Penn 8371, **Pew 8377**, Philadelphia 8378, Phoenixville 8381, Pittsburgh 8386, Scranton 8431, Smith 8445, Wachovia 8494, York 8511

Puerto Rico: Puerto Rico 8515

Rhode Island: **Dorot 8531**, Rhode Island 8551, **Textron 8559**

South Carolina: Black 8569, Byerly 8572, Central 8577, Chapin 8579, Coastal 8581, Community 8583, Community 8584, Self 8610

South Dakota: Sioux Falls 8630, South Dakota 8631

Tennessee: Assisi 8638, Benwood 8644, Community 8661, Durham 8670, East 8671, Frist 8679, Hyde 8693, Lyndhurst 8703

Texas: **AT&T 8765**, Austin 8768, Burnett 8801, Cailloux 8807, Communities 8839, Community 8840, Community 8841, Community 8842, Dougherty, 8870, El Paso 8881, Halsell 8936, Houston 8960, **Jenesis 8971**, Koehler 9001, Kronkosky 9002, Meadows 9049, Moody 9070, Rockwell 9154, San Angelo 9165, Simmons 9188, Stemmons 9211, Summerlee 9217, Swinney 9222, Trull 9240, Vale 9246, Wichita 9280, Zale 9297

Utah: Dumke 9315, Dumke 9316

Vermont: Vermont 9361

Virginia: Arlington 9371, Community 9402, Freddie 9422, Landmark 9455, Lynchburg 9463, **MCI 9471**, Norfolk 9484, Portsmouth 9499, Samberg 9510, Virginia Beach 9532, Weissberg 9536, Williamsburg 9541

Washington: Blue 9559, **Brainerd 9561**, Bullitt 9563, Casey 9566, **Casey 9567**, Community 9571, **Edwards 9580**, Ferguson 9585, Foundation 9589, Fuchs 9590, **Gates 9591**, Glaser 9595, **Hemingway 9606, Kongsgaard 9620**, Medina 9640, Miller 9642, Quixote 9667, **Samis 9675**, Seattle 9680, Sherwood 9683, Tacoma 9693, **Weyerhaeuser 9703**, Wilburforce 9705

West Virginia: Chambers 9713, Clay 9715, Community 9716, Kanawha 9723, Tucker 9736

Wisconsin: Alexander 9741, Bader 9749, Community 9776, Community 9779, Cudahy 9785, Dudley 9792, Green Bay 9810, Jacobus 9819, Madison 9854, Marshfield 9861, McBeath 9864, Milwaukee 9876, Morse 9879, Stock 9939, Vine 9956, Waukesha 9960

Wyoming: Community 9977, McMurry 9985, Wyoming 10000

SUBJECT INDEX

List of terms: Terms used in this index conform to the Foundation Center's Grants Classification System's comprehensive subject area coding scheme. The alphabetical list below represents the complete list of subject terms found in this edition. "See also" references to related subject areas are also provided as an additional aid in accessing the giving interests of foundations in this volume.

Index: In the index itself, foundation entries are arranged under each term by state location, abbreviated name, and sequence number. Foundations in boldface type make grants on a national, regional, or international basis. The others generally limit giving to the state or city in which they are located.

Adult education—literacy, basic skills & GED
Adult/continuing education
Adults
Adults, women
African Americans/Blacks
Aging
Aging, centers/services
Agriculture
Agriculture, farm bureaus/granges
Agriculture, farm cooperatives
Agriculture, farmlands
Agriculture, soil/water issues
Agriculture/food
Agriculture/food, ethics
Agriculture/food, formal/general education
Agriculture/food, management/technical aid
Agriculture/food, public education
Agriculture/food, public policy
Agriculture/food, research
AIDS
see also AIDS, people with (PWAs)
AIDS research
AIDS, people with
Alcoholism
Alcoholism research
Allergies
Allergies research
ALS
Alzheimer's disease
Alzheimer's disease research
American Red Cross
American studies
Anatomy (animal)
Anatomy (human)
Animal population control
Animal welfare
Animals/wildlife
Animals/wildlife, alliance
Animals/wildlife, association
Animals/wildlife, bird preserves
Animals/wildlife, clubs
Animals/wildlife, endangered species
Animals/wildlife, equal rights
Animals/wildlife, fisheries
Animals/wildlife, formal/general education
Animals/wildlife, management/technical aid
Animals/wildlife, preservation/protection

Animals/wildlife, public education
Animals/wildlife, research
Animals/wildlife, sanctuaries
Animals/wildlife, single organization support
Animals/wildlife, special services
Animals/wildlife, training
Anthropology/sociology
Aquariums
Art & music therapy
Art history
Arthritis
Arthritis research
Arts
see also dance; film/video; museums; music; performing arts; theater; visual arts
Arts councils
Arts education
Arts, administration/regulation
Arts, alliance
Arts, artist's services
Arts, association
Arts, cultural/ethnic awareness
Arts, equal rights
Arts, folk arts
Arts, formal/general education
Arts, fund raising/fund distribution
Arts, government agencies
Arts, management/technical aid
Arts, multipurpose centers/programs
Arts, public education
Arts, research
Arts, services
Arts, single organization support
Asians/Pacific Islanders
Asthma
Asthma research
Astronomy
Athletics/sports, academies
Athletics/sports, amateur competition
Athletics/sports, amateur leagues
Athletics/sports, baseball
Athletics/sports, equestrianism
Athletics/sports, fishing/hunting
Athletics/sports, football
Athletics/sports, golf
Athletics/sports, Olympics
Athletics/sports, professional leagues

Athletics/sports, racquet sports
Athletics/sports, school programs
Athletics/sports, soccer
Athletics/sports, Special Olympics
Athletics/sports, training
Athletics/sports, water sports
Athletics/sports, winter sports
Autism
Autism research
Big Brothers/Big Sisters
Biological sciences
Biomedicine
Biomedicine research
Blind/visually impaired
Botanical gardens
Botanical/horticulture/landscape services
Botany
Boy scouts
Boys & girls clubs
Boys clubs
Brain disorders
Brain research
Breast cancer
Breast cancer research
Buddhism
Business school/education
Business/industry
Camp Fire
Campaign finance reform
Cancer
Cancer research
Cancer, leukemia
Cancer, leukemia research
Cemeteries/burial services
Cerebral palsy
Cerebral palsy research
Chemistry
Child development, education
Child development, services
Children
Children, adoption
Children, day care
Children, foster care
Children, services
Children/youth
Children/youth, services
Christian agencies & churches

Civil liberties, advocacy
Civil liberties, death penalty issues
Civil liberties, due process
Civil liberties, first amendment
Civil liberties, reproductive rights
Civil liberties, right to die
Civil liberties, right to life
Civil rights
Civil rights, advocacy
Civil rights, aging
Civil rights, alliance
Civil rights, association
Civil rights, disabled
Civil rights, equal rights
Civil rights, formal/general education
Civil rights, gays/lesbians
Civil rights, immigrants
Civil rights, minorities
Civil rights, public education
Civil rights, public policy
Civil rights, race/intergroup relations
  see also civil rights
Civil rights, voter education
Civil rights, women
Community development
Community development, association
Community development, business promotion
Community development, citizen coalitions
Community development, civic centers
Community development, equal rights
Community development, government agencies
Community development, management/
  technical aid
Community development, neighborhood
  associations
Community development, neighborhood
  development
Community development, public education
Community development, public policy
Community development, public/private
  ventures
Community development, real estate
Community development, service clubs
Community development, small businesses
Community development, volunteer services
Community development, women's clubs
Computer science
Consumer protection
Courts/judicial administration
Crime/abuse victims
Crime/law enforcement
Crime/law enforcement, association
Crime/law enforcement, correctional facilities
Crime/law enforcement, counterterrorism
Crime/law enforcement, government agencies
Crime/law enforcement, police agencies
Crime/law enforcement, reform
Crime/law enforcement, research
Crime/law enforcement, single organization
  support
Crime/violence prevention
  see also domestic violence; gun control
Crime/violence prevention, abuse prevention
  see also child abuse; domestic violence
Crime/violence prevention, child abuse
Crime/violence prevention, domestic violence
Crime/violence prevention, gun control
Crime/violence prevention, sexual abuse
Crime/violence prevention, youth
Cystic fibrosis
Cystic fibrosis research
Deaf/hearing impaired
Dental care
Dental school/education

Developmentally disabled, centers & services
Diabetes
Diabetes research
Digestive diseases
Digestive disorders research
Disabilities, people with
Disasters, 9/11/01
Disasters, domestic resettlement
Disasters, fire prevention/control
Disasters, floods
Disasters, Hurricane Katrina
Disasters, preparedness/services
Disasters, search/rescue
Dispute resolution
Down syndrome
Down syndrome research
Ear & throat diseases
Ear & throat research
Economic development
Economic development, visitors/convention
  bureau/tourism promotion
Economically disadvantaged
Economics
Education
Education, administration/regulation
Education, alliance
Education, association
Education, community/cooperative
Education, continuing education
Education, drop-out prevention
Education, early childhood education
Education, equal rights
Education, ESL programs
Education, ethics
Education, formal/general education
Education, fund raising/fund distribution
Education, gifted students
Education, information services
Education, management/technical aid
Education, PTA groups
Education, public education
Education, public policy
Education, reading
Education, reform
Education, research
Education, services
Education, single organization support
Education, special
Elementary school/education
Elementary/secondary education
Elementary/secondary school reform
Employment
Employment, equal rights
Employment, formal/general education
Employment, job counseling
Employment, labor unions/organizations
Employment, public education
Employment, public policy
Employment, research
Employment, retraining
Employment, services
Employment, sheltered workshops
Employment, training
Employment, vocational rehabilitation
End of life care
Engineering
Engineering school/education
Engineering/technology
Environment
  see also energy; natural resources
Environment, air pollution
Environment, alliance
Environment, association
Environment, beautification programs

Environment, energy
Environment, ethics
Environment, forests
Environment, formal/general education
Environment, global warming
Environment, land resources
Environment, legal rights
Environment, management/technical aid
Environment, natural resources
Environment, noise pollution
Environment, plant conservation
Environment, pollution control
Environment, public education
Environment, public policy
Environment, radiation control
Environment, recycling
Environment, reform
Environment, research
Environment, toxics
Environment, volunteer services
Environment, waste management
Environment, water pollution
Environment, water resources
Environmental education
Epilepsy research
Eye diseases
Eye research
Family services
Family services, adolescent parents
Family services, counseling
Family services, domestic violence
Family services, parent education
Family services, single parents
Federated giving programs
Financial services
Food banks
Food distribution, groceries on wheels
Food distribution, meals on wheels
Food services
Food services, agency eatery
Food services, commodity distribution
Food services, congregate meals
Foundations (community)
Foundations (private grantmaking)
Foundations (private independent)
Foundations (private operating)
Foundations (public)
Genetics/birth defects
Genetics/birth defects research
Geriatrics
Geriatrics research
Gerontology
Girl scouts
Girls
Girls clubs
Goodwill Industries
Government/public administration
Graduate/professional education
Health care
Health care, alliance
Health care, association
Health care, blood supply
Health care, burn centers
Health care, clinics/centers
Health care, cost containment
Health care, emergency transport services
Health care, EMS
Health care, equal rights
Health care, ethics
Health care, financing
Health care, formal/general education
Health care, fund raising/fund distribution
Health care, HMOs
Health care, home services

Health care, infants
Health care, information services
Health care, insurance
Health care, organ/tissue banks
Health care, patient services
Health care, public policy
Health care, reform
Health care, research
Health care, rural areas
Health care, single organization support
Health care, support services
Health care, volunteer services
Health organizations
Health organizations, alliance
Health organizations, association
Health organizations, equal rights
Health organizations, formal/general education
Health organizations, public education
Health organizations, public policy
Health organizations, research
Health sciences school/education
Heart & circulatory diseases
Heart & circulatory research
Hematology
Hematology research
Hemophilia
Hemophilia research
Higher education
Higher education reform
Higher education, college
see also higher education
Higher education, college (community/junior)
see also higher education
Higher education, university
see also higher education
Hinduism
Hispanics/Latinos
Historic preservation/historical societies
Historical activities
Historical activities, war memorials
History/archaeology
Homeless
Homeless, human services
see also economically disadvantaged; food services; housing/shelter, homeless
Horticulture/garden clubs
Hospitals (general)
Hospitals (psychiatric)
Hospitals (specialty)
Housing/shelter
Housing/shelter, aging
Housing/shelter, alliance
Housing/shelter, development
Housing/shelter, equal rights
Housing/shelter, expense aid
Housing/shelter, home owners
Housing/shelter, homeless
Housing/shelter, information services
Housing/shelter, owner/renter issues
Housing/shelter, public education
Housing/shelter, public housing
Housing/shelter, public policy
Housing/shelter, rehabilitation
Housing/shelter, repairs
Housing/shelter, research
Housing/shelter, search services
Housing/shelter, services
Housing/shelter, temporary shelter
Housing/shelter, volunteer services
Human services
Human services, alliance
Human services, emergency aid
Human services, financial counseling
Human services, mind/body enrichment
Human services, personal services

Human services, public education
Human services, public policy
Human services, reform
Human services, research
Human services, travelers' aid
Human services, victim aid
Humanities
see also history/archaeology; language/linguistics; literature; museums
Immigrants/refugees
Immunology
Immunology research
Indigenous people
Infants/toddlers
International affairs
see also arms control; international peace/security
International affairs, arms control
see also international affairs; international peace/security
International affairs, equal rights
International affairs, foreign policy
International affairs, formal/general education
International affairs, goodwill promotion
International affairs, information services
International affairs, national security
International affairs, public education
International affairs, public policy
International affairs, research
International affairs, U.N.
International agricultural development
International conflict resolution
International development
International economic development
International economics/trade policy
International exchange
International exchange, students
International human rights
International migration/refugee issues
International peace/security
International relief
International relief, 2004 tsunami
International studies
International terrorism
Islam
Jewish agencies & temples
Jewish federated giving programs
Journalism school/education
Kidney diseases
Kidney research
Language (foreign)
Language/linguistics
Law school/education
Law/international law
Leadership development
see also youth development, services
Learning disorders
Learning disorders research
Legal services
Legal services, public interest law
LGBTQ
see also civil rights, gays/lesbians
Libraries (academic/research)
Libraries (law)
Libraries (public)
Libraries (school)
Libraries (special)
Libraries, archives
Libraries/library science
Literature
Liver disorders
Liver research
Lung diseases
Lung research
Lupus
Lupus research

Marine science
Mathematics
Media, film/video
Media, journalism/publishing
Media, radio
Media, television
Media/communications
Medical care, bioethics
Medical care, community health systems
Medical care, in-patient care
Medical care, outpatient care
Medical care, rehabilitation
Medical research
Medical research, association
Medical research, ethics
Medical research, formal/general education
Medical research, information services
Medical research, institute
Medical research, public education
Medical research, public policy
Medical research, single organization support
Medical school/education
see also dental school/education; nursing school/education
Medical specialty research
Medicine/medical care, public education
Men
Mental health, addictions
Mental health, association
Mental health, clinics
Mental health, counseling/support groups
Mental health, depression
Mental health, disorders
Mental health, eating disorders
Mental health, gambling addiction
Mental health, residential care
Mental health, schizophrenia
Mental health, smoking
Mental health, transitional care
Mental health, treatment
Mental health/crisis services
Mental health/crisis services, formal/general education
Mental health/crisis services, hot-lines
Mental health/crisis services, public education
Mental health/crisis services, public policy
Mental health/crisis services, rape victim services
Mental health/crisis services, research
Mental health/crisis services, single organization support
Mental health/crisis services, suicide
Mental health/crisis services, volunteer services
Mentally disabled
Migrant workers
Military/veterans
Military/veterans' organizations
Minorities
see also African Americans/Blacks; Asians/Pacific Islanders; civil rights, minorities; Hispanics/Latinos; Native Americans/American Indians
Minorities/immigrants, centers/services
Mormon agencies & churches
Multiple sclerosis
Multiple sclerosis research
Muscular dystrophy
Museums
Museums (art)
Museums (children's)
Museums (ethnic/folk arts)
Museums (history)
Museums (marine/maritime)
Museums (natural history)
Museums (science/technology)
Museums (specialized)

Museums (sports/hobby)
Native Americans/American Indians
Neighborhood centers
Nerve, muscle & bone diseases
Nerve, muscle & bone research
Neuroscience
Neuroscience research
Nonprofit management
Nursing care
Nursing home/convalescent facility
Nursing school/education
Nutrition
Obstetrics/gynecology
Obstetrics/gynecology research
Offenders/ex-offenders
Offenders/ex-offenders, prison alternatives
Offenders/ex-offenders, rehabilitation
Offenders/ex-offenders, services
Optometry/vision screening
Organ diseases
Organ research
Orthodox Catholic agencies & churches
Orthopedics
Orthopedics research
Parkinson's disease
Parkinson's disease research
Pathology research
Pediatrics
Pediatrics research
Performing arts
Performing arts (multimedia)
Performing arts centers
Performing arts, ballet
Performing arts, choreography
Performing arts, circus arts
Performing arts, dance
Performing arts, education
Performing arts, music
Performing arts, music (choral)
Performing arts, music ensembles/groups
Performing arts, opera
Performing arts, orchestra (symphony)
Performing arts, theater
Performing arts, theater (musical)
Performing arts, theater (playwriting)
Pharmacy/prescriptions
Philanthropy/voluntarism
Philanthropy/voluntarism, administration/
    regulation
Philanthropy/voluntarism, association
Philanthropy/voluntarism, fund raising/fund
    distribution
Philanthropy/voluntarism, information services
Philanthropy/voluntarism, management/
    technical aid
Philanthropy/voluntarism, research
Philanthropy/voluntarism, single organization
    support
Philosophy/ethics
Physical therapy
Physical/earth sciences
Physically disabled
Physics
Planetarium
Political science
Population studies
Poverty studies
Pregnancy centers
Prostate cancer
Prostate cancer research
Protestant agencies & churches
Protestant federated giving programs
Psychology/behavioral science
Public affairs

Public affairs, alliance
Public affairs, association
Public affairs, citizen participation
Public affairs, election regulation
Public affairs, equal rights
Public affairs, ethics
Public affairs, finance
Public affairs, formal/general education
Public affairs, government agencies
Public affairs, information services
Public affairs, political organizations
Public affairs, public education
Public affairs, reform
Public affairs, research
Public affairs, single organization support
Public health
Public health school/education
Public health, bioterrorism
Public health, communicable diseases
Public health, epidemiology
Public health, occupational health
Public health, STDs
Public policy, research
Recreation
Recreation, association
Recreation, camps
Recreation, centers
Recreation, community facilities
Recreation, equal rights
Recreation, fairs/festivals
Recreation, formal/general education
Recreation, fund raising/fund distribution
Recreation, government agencies
Recreation, parks/playgrounds
Recreation, public education
Recreation, single organization support
Recreation, social clubs
Religion
see also Jewish agencies & temples; Protestant agencies
    & churches; Roman Catholic agencies & churches
Religion, association
Religion, equal rights
Religion, formal/general education
Religion, fund raising/fund distribution
Religion, interfaith issues
Religion, management/technical aid
Religion, public policy
Religion, research
Religious federated giving programs
Reproductive health
Reproductive health, abortion clinics/services
Reproductive health, family planning
Reproductive health, fertility
Reproductive health, OBGYN/Birthing centers
Reproductive health, prenatal care
Reproductive health, sexuality education
Residential/custodial care
Residential/custodial care, group home
Residential/custodial care, half-way house
Residential/custodial care, hospices
Residential/custodial care, senior continuing
    care
Residential/custodial care, special day care
Roman Catholic agencies & churches
Roman Catholic federated giving programs
Rural development
Rural studies
Safety, automotive safety
Safety, education
Safety/disasters
Safety/disasters, government agencies
Safety/disasters, public education
Safety/disasters, public policy
Safety/disasters, volunteer services

Salvation Army
Scholarships/financial aid
Science
see also biological sciences; chemistry; computer
    science; engineering/technology; marine science;
    physical/earth sciences
Science, association
Science, equal rights
Science, formal/general education
Science, public education
Science, public policy
Science, research
Science, single organization support
Secondary school/education
see also elementary/secondary education
Sickle cell disease
Skin disorders
Skin disorders research
Social entrepreneurship
Social sciences
see also anthropology/sociology; economics; political
    science; psychology/behavioral science
Social sciences, equal rights
Social sciences, ethics
Social sciences, formal/general education
Social sciences, government agencies
Social sciences, interdisciplinary studies
Social sciences, public education
Social sciences, public policy
Social sciences, research
Social work school/education
Space/aviation
Speech/hearing centers
Spine disorders
Spine disorders research
Spirituality
Student services/organizations
Students, sororities/fraternities
Substance abuse, prevention
Substance abuse, services
Substance abuse, treatment
Substance abusers
Surgery
Surgery research
Teacher school/education
Telecommunications
Telecommunications, electronic messaging
    services
Theological school/education
Theology
Transportation
Urban League
Urban/community development
Venture philanthropy
Veterinary medicine
Veterinary medicine, hospital
Visual arts
Visual arts, architecture
Visual arts, art conservation
Visual arts, design
Visual arts, drawing
Visual arts, painting
Visual arts, photography
Visual arts, sculpture
Vocational education
Vocational education, post-secondary
Voluntarism promotion
Welfare policy/reform
Women
see also civil rights, women; reproductive rights
Women's studies
Women, centers/services
YM/YWCAs & YM/YWHAs
Young adults
Young adults, female

Youth
Youth development
Youth development, adult & child programs
Youth development, agriculture
Youth development, business
Youth development, centers/clubs

Youth development, citizenship
Youth development, community service clubs
Youth development, formal/general education
Youth development, intergenerational programs
Youth development, public education
Youth development, religion

Youth development, scouting agencies (general)
Youth development, services
Youth development, volunteer services
Youth, pregnancy prevention
Youth, services
Zoos/zoological societies

Adult education—literacy, basic skills & GED

Arizona: Arizona 87
Arkansas: Wal-Mart 184
California: Ahmanson 198, Atkinson 239, **Atkinson 240**, Community 406, Copley 416, Lux 834, Marin 854, Sacramento 1080, San Diego 1087, San Francisco 1088, Weingart 1288, Whitecap 1303, Winnick 1310
Colorado: Anschutz 1334, El Pomar 1374
Connecticut: Bodenwein 1497, Fisher 1542, **Xerox 1680**
Delaware: Marmot 1728
District of Columbia: Block 1776, Cafritz 1780, Fowler 1797, Meyer 1834, Strong 1851
Florida: Bank 1890, Community 1939, Community 1943, Gemcon 2019, Price 2177, Wilson 2300
Georgia: Anderson 2317, Atlanta 2320, Harland 2407, Pittulloch 2464
Hawaii: Wilcox 2559
Illinois: Community 2677, Field 2728, Polk 2946, Woodward 3085
Indiana: Ball 3103, Community 3125, Harrison 3161, Wayne 3253
Iowa: Siouxland 3332
Kentucky: Hagan Ch 3423, J & L 3429
Louisiana: Booth 3464, Community 3469, Entergy 3474
Maryland: Rosenberg 3719
Massachusetts: Adams 3772, **Azadoutioun 3786**, Boston 3812, Community 3855, Ratshesky 4095, Yawkey 4211
Michigan: Abrams 4213, Battle Creek 4228, Binda 4233, Comerica 4251, Greenville 4331, Jackson 4347, Knight 4364, Whirlpool 4480
Minnesota: Bell 4514, Bigelow 4519, Mardag 4613, Saint Paul 4671
Missouri: **Fox 4815**, Green 4822
Nevada: Nevada 5047
New Jersey: Cowles 5170, Zobel 5464
New Mexico: McCune 5488, Santa Fe 5496
New York: Achelis 5513, Allyn 5539, Arkell 5565, Booth 5651, Community 5782, Cummings 5815, Dreyfus 5887, **Grant 6091**, **Hearst 6161**, **Hearst 6162**, **Heineman 6165**, **Memton 6529**, Northern 6638, **Pforzheimer 6721**, Rochester 6823, Violett 7200
North Carolina: Cemala 7337, North Carolina 7438, Triangle 7496
Ohio: Columbus 7580, Dayton 7604, Fifth 7626, Findlay 7627, **OMNOVA 7789**, Reinberger 7815, Richland 7819, Stocker 7870, **Timken 7880**
Oregon: Carpenter 8003, Johnson 8027, Oregon 8049
Pennsylvania: Dolfinger 8172, Fourjay 8209, McCune 8332, Stackpole 8456
Rhode Island: Daniels 8530
South Carolina: Central 8577
Tennessee: Aslan 8637, Community 8660
Texas: Bass 8777, Cain 8809, Coastal 8833, Fikes 8899, Fisch 8901, George 8916, Hoblitzelle 8955, Kempner 8987, King 8995, Lubbock 9021, Meadows 9049, Rockwell 9154, San Antonio 9166, Sterling 9212, Trull 9240, Wright 9294
Virginia: Arlington 9371, Delmar 9410, **Gannett 9428**, Moore 9478, Norfolk 9484
Washington: Blue 9559, Community 9571, **Kongsgaard 9620**, Norcliffe 9650
West Virginia: Parkersburg 9730
Wisconsin: Cornerstone 9781, Cudahy 9785

Adult/continuing education

Alabama: Dixon 32
California: Cisco 388, Community 406, Fromm 541, Union 1250
Colorado: El Pomar 1374, Weckbaugh 1470
Connecticut: Bodenwein 1497, Connecticut 1518, Long 1590, Palmer 1621
District of Columbia: Cafritz 1780
Florida: Beveridge 1907, Martin 2130
Hawaii: Hawaii 2545
Illinois: Brinson 2633, Coleman 2673, Community 2677, Kelly 2830, Polk 2946, White 3067
Kentucky: Robinson 3449
Maryland: Thorn 3745
Massachusetts: Bayrd 3795, Boston 3812, Cabot 3823, Community 3855, Hyams 3961, Lowell 4015
Michigan: **Kellogg 4357**, Midland 4392, Miller 4394, Whirlpool 4480
Minnesota: Bell 4514
Missouri: Green 4822, Truman 4919
Nevada: Nevada 5047
New Jersey: Cowles 5170, **Johnson 5263**, **Newcombe 5338**
New Mexico: McCune 5488
New York: **Heineman 6165**, HSBC 6204, **Initial 6231**, Northern 6639, **Walter 7211**
North Carolina: Cumberland 7349, Goodrich 7378, Harris 7390, Triangle 7496
Ohio: Richland 7819, Women's 7916
Oregon: Carpenter 8003
Pennsylvania: Arcadia 8086, Buhl 8124, Connelly 8157, Dolfinger 8172, Stackpole 8456
South Carolina: Spartanburg 8616
Tennessee: **Bridgestone 8646**
Texas: Bass 8777, Constantin 8843, Edwards 8880, Hillcrest 8952, Hoblitzelle 8955, Meadows 9049, San Antonio 9166, Temple 9227, Wright 9294
Vermont: Vermont 9361
Virginia: Norfolk 9484, Portsmouth 9498
Washington: Community 9571, Seattle 9680, Tacoma 9693
Wisconsin: Alexander 9741, Clark 9773, Cudahy 9785, Johnson 9823, Milwaukee 9876

Adults

California: **Chiron 383**

Adults, women

New York: **Carnegie 5707**, NoVo 6641, PepsiCo 6714

African Americans/Blacks

California: California 345, Stern 1195
Colorado: Sachs 1447
Connecticut: Community 1515
District of Columbia: Cafritz 1780, Fowler 1797
Florida: Dade 1957, FPL 2010, Smith 2238
Illinois: Olin 2925, **State 3019**
Indiana: Health 3164
Iowa: Siouxland 3332
Maryland: **Hughes 3654**, Rock 3717
Massachusetts: Hyams 3961, Stevens 4163, Stevens 4164, Worcester 4209
Michigan: Grand Rapids 4326, **Kellogg 4357**
Minnesota: Bell 4514, Bremer 4523, Minneapolis 4623, Phillips 4655, **Robins 4667**

New Jersey: Alcatel 5110, Harris 5224, Healthcare 5228, **KPMG 5288**, **Newcombe 5338**, Victoria 5440
New Mexico: Santa Fe 5496
New York: Abrons 5511, **Bristol 5666**, **Bydale 5694**, Horncrest 6200, **Macy 6471**, New York 6615, Revson 6789
North Carolina: Foundation 7370, Reynolds 7458
Ohio: AK 7525, Akron 7526, Cincinnati 7574, Community 7582
Oregon: Intel 8022
Pennsylvania: **PPG 8394**
Rhode Island: Charter 8526
Texas: Dallas 8855, Sterling 9212
Virginia: **Gannett 9428**
Washington: **RealNetworks 9672**

Aging

Arizona: Arizona 87, **Globe 101**
Arkansas: Wal-Mart 184
California: Anaheim 220, Archstone 232, Ayrshire 247, Barbonchielli 256, Bay 264, Brenner 321, California 345, California 350, Community 401, Copley 416, Doheny 460, Fein 497, Fireman's 510, French 536, Garland 556, Gilmore 578, Gross 621, Grove 625, Lidow 811, Lincy 812, Lytel 836, Marin 854, Mericos 889, Oakland 948, Orange 957, PacifiCare 971, Parsons 980, Parvin 981, Pasadena 982, Peninsula 989, Pickford 1005, Sacramento 1080, San Diego 1087, San Francisco 1088, Sierra 1151, **Smith 1167**, Soda 1173, Sonora 1178, Taper 1226, Teichert 1231, True 1245, Valente 1255, Valley 1256, Van Nuys 1261, Wood 1318
Colorado: Anschutz 1334, Aspen 1338, Colorado 1356, **Daniels 1362**, El Pomar 1374, Hunter 1394, Johnson 1398, KBK 1400, McDonald 1421, Rose 1445
Connecticut: Bodenwein 1497, Bondi 1499, Community 1515, Community 1517, Connecticut 1518, Culpeper 1521, Fisher 1542, Hartford 1564, Long 1590, Martin 1598, Palmer 1621, Senior 1647
Delaware: Crystal 1702, Delaware 1706
District of Columbia: Cafritz 1780, Community 1785, Fowler 1797, Lehrman 1821
Florida: Bank 1890, Bastien 1892, Beveridge 1907, Bush 1922, Community 1939, Community 1940, Community 1942, Community 1946, Community 1948, Dade 1957, duPont 1982, FPL 2010, Gainesville 2015, Gorin 2032, Greenburg 2034, Hall 2045, Ocean 2156, Peacock 2165, Phillips 2168, Quantum 2181, Selby 2230, Stevens 2251, Wilson 2300
Georgia: AGL 2312, Callaway 2337, Community 2356, Irving 2419, Pitts 2463, Rich 2472, Shallenberger 2487, **UPS 2503**, Woodruff 2521
Hawaii: Hawaii 2545, Hughes 2548
Illinois: **Abbott 2579**, **Burlington 2644**, Chicago 2661, Community 2677, Community 2681, Field 2728, **Friedmann 2738**, Oak Park 2922, Reese 2961, Retirement 2964, **Square 3018**, Washington 3058
Indiana: Community 3123, Harrison 3161, Heritage 3166, Wayne 3253
Iowa: Principal 3326, Siouxland 3332, Vermeer 3341
Kansas: Cooper 3353, Hutchinson 3368
Kentucky: **Humana 3428**, Omnicare 3443, **Omnicare 3444**
Louisiana: Baton Rouge 3462, Booth 3464, Community 3469
Maine: JTG 3542

Maryland: Baltimore 3568, Columbia 3595, **Ellison 3621**, **Weinberg 3759**
Massachusetts: Ashton 3782, Association 3783, Bay 3794, Bayrd 3795, Boston 3811, Boston 3812, Campbell 3830, Clipper 3850, Community 3855, DeLuca 3877, Farnsworth 3899, Ford 3913, Grand 3929, Hyams 3961, Marino 4023, Millipore 4040, Nichols 4055, Oral 4061, Sailors' 4123, Salem 4125, Spencer 4154, Stevens 4163, Stevens 4164, Wadleigh 4194, Worcester 4209
Michigan: Ann Arbor 4221, Berrien 4231, Community 4257, Community 4258, Duffy 4290, Fremont 4315, Gerstacker 4322, Grand Rapids 4326, Prince 4416, Saginaw 4428, Steelcase 4446
Minnesota: **Andersen 4501**, Bremer 4523, Deluxe 4549, Kopp 4599, Mardag 4613, **Medtronic 4622**, Minneapolis 4623, Northwest 4637, Ordean 4643, Phillips 4655, Rivers 4666, Rochester 4668, Xcel 4732
Missouri: Ameren 4772, American 4773, Community 4798, Green 4822, Jewish 4837, Simon 4903, Truman 4919
Montana: Chutney 4934
Nebraska: Hamilton 4968, Lincoln 4987
Nevada: Fairweather 5032, Nevada 5047, Pennington 5053, Redfield 5055, Sierra 5064
New Jersey: Aventis 5120, Cowles 5170, **GHH 5207**, Hyde 5247, **Johnson 5261**, **Johnson 5265**, Laurie 5297, **Rippel 5368**, Wallerstein 5446
New Mexico: Frost 5476, Maddox 5487, McCune 5488, New Mexico 5491, Santa Fe 5496
New York: Abrons 5511, Altman 5542, **Atlantic 5574**, Burden 5687, Clark 5761, Community 5781, Community 5783, Community 5785, Corey 5791, **Cummings 5813**, Dreyfus 5887, Glickenhaus 6042, Goldsmith 6060, Gorman 6078, Green 6096, Greene 6099, Guttman 6124, Hagedorn 6130, **Hartford 6150**, **Kaufmann 6299**, Lindner 6426, Litwin 6436, McGonagle 6518, Metcalf 6541, **MetLife 6542**, **Monell 6566**, New York 6615, New York 6618, New York 6619, Noble 6632, Northern 6638, Northern 6639, Parshelsky 6693, **Ramapo 6769**, Rhodebeck 6791, Rochester 6823, Ross 6864, Samuels 6901, Silverman 6983, St. George's 7040, Steffens 7054, **Walter 7211**, Wendt 7243, Western 7248
North Carolina: Community 7344, Davis 7352, Janirve 7404, Nias 7435, North Carolina 7438, Reynolds 7457, Reynolds 7460, Strowd 7488, Triangle 7496, Van Houten 7500
North Dakota: North Dakota 7519, Stern 7521
Ohio: Abington 7524, Akron 7526, **Bingham 7549**, Bruening 7558, Cincinnati 7573, Cincinnati 7574, Clapp 7575, Cleveland 7576, Community 7586, Fairfield 7622, Ford 7633, **HCR 7667**, Loeb 7721, McGregor 7742, Middletown 7749, Muskingum 7770, Nationwide 7771, Richland 7819, Schlink 7839, Schmidlapp 7841, Sisler 7858, Stark 7867, Toledo 7883, Wuliger 7918
Oregon: Fohs 8012, Jackson 8024, Meyer 8042, Oregon 8049
Pennsylvania: 1957 8071, Arcadia 8086, Beatty 8097, Berks 8103, Blue 8112, Clapp 8145, Connelly 8157, Crels 8163, Dolfinger 8172, Equitable 8187, Hassel 8237, Hillman 8249, Hillman 8250, Jaindl 8269, Levis 8309, McCune 8331, McKinney 8339, Morris 8359, Scranton 8431, Shenango 8438, Simonds 8442, Smith 8443, Snee 8446, Trexler 8481, York 8511
Rhode Island: Kimball 8542, Rhode Island 8551
South Carolina: Central 8577, Self 8610
South Dakota: Sioux Falls 8630
Tennessee: Community 8662, Durham 8670
Texas: Abell 8749, Bass 8777, Brumley 8800, Cameron 8812, Carter 8816, CH 8823, Cockrell 8835, Community 8841, Community 8842, Dallas 8855, Finger 8900, Hankamer 8939, Hillcrest 8952, Hoblitzelle 8955, Koehler 9001, Kronkosky 9002, Lightner 9012, Meadows 9049, Moody 9070, Reliant 9144, Rockwell 9154, Speas 9206, Sterling 9212, Weaver 9267, Wright 9294, Zephyr 9299
Utah: Dance 9311, Eccles 9320
Vermont: Vermont 9361

Virginia: Arlington 9371, Beazley 9376, Camp 9382, Community 9400, Delmar 9410, **Gannett 9428**, Lynchburg 9463, Norfolk 9484, Virginia Beach 9532, Williamsburg 9541
Washington: Cheney 9569, Community 9571, Foundation 9589, Glaser 9594, Norcliffe 9650, Tacoma 9693
West Virginia: McDonough 9726
Wisconsin: Cudahy 9785, Evjue 9797, Green Bay 9810, Madison 9854, McBeath 9864, Milwaukee 9876, Oshkosh 9885, Racine 9906, Siebert 9927

Aging, centers/services

Alabama: Community 24, Community 27
Alaska: Rasmuson 85
Arizona: Piper 130
Arkansas: Murphy 167
California: Anaheim 220, Atkinson 239, Auen 242, Autry 243, Bay 264, Blackman 294, Borchard 304, Bothin 309, Bravo 319, Byer 339, California 345, Copley 416, Crockett 430, Doheny 460, French 536, Garaventa 553, Garland 556, Gellert 559, Gilmore 578, **Goldberg 592**, Gross 621, Hale 639, Harden 647, Irvine 699, **Kayne 749**, Laurel 792, Lidow 811, Lincy 812, Lytel 836, **McConnell 870**, Mericos 889, Parker 979, Parsons 980, Peninsula 989, Pickford 1005, Sacramento 1080, San Diego 1087, San Francisco 1088, Santa Barbara 1093, **Smith 1167**, Soda 1173, Sonora 1178, Vadasz 1254, Valley 1256, Van Nuys 1261, Vons 1270
Colorado: El Pomar 1374, Gates 1380, McDonald 1421, Rose 1445, Summit 1463, Wolf 1475
Connecticut: Bodenwein 1497, Community 1515, Community 1516, Community 1517, Connecticut 1518, Fisher 1542, Hartford 1564, Long 1590, Martin 1598, Palmer 1621, Senior 1647
Delaware: Crystal 1702, Reynolds 1743
District of Columbia: Cafritz 1780, Fowler 1797, Lehrman 1821
Florida: Bank 1890, Bastien 1892, Beveridge 1907, Bush 1922, **Coleman 1937**, Community 1940, Community 1944, Community 1948, duPont 1982, Free 2012, Gorin 2032, Greenburg 2034, Gulf 2041, Maltz 2126, Phillips 2168, Pinellas 2170, Selby 2230, Stevens 2251, Tarrant 2265, Wahlert 2284, Wilson 2300, Winter 2303
Georgia: Callaway 2337, Community 2357, Irving 2419, Patterson 2460, Pitts 2463, Shallenberger 2487, Snodgrass 2492, Woodruff 2521
Hawaii: Hawaii 2545, Hughes 2548, Wilcox 2559
Idaho: CHC 2566
Illinois: Borden 2626, Brach 2629, Buehler 2638, Chicago 2661, Community 2677, Eisenberg 2716, Field 2728, Goldberg 2761, Logan 2860, Retirement 2964, Rothschild 2971, Siragusa 3009
Indiana: Adams 3095, Central 3116, Community 3124
Iowa: Siouxland 3332
Kansas: Cooper 3353, Hutchinson 3368, Wiedemann 3405
Kentucky: Omnicare 3443
Louisiana: Baton Rouge 3462, Booth 3464, Community 3469
Maine: Maine 3548
Maryland: Columbia 3595, Quinn 3713, **Weinberg 3759**
Massachusetts: Ashton 3782, Bayrd 3795, Berenson 3799, Boston 3812, Campbell 3830, Clipper 3850, Community 3855, Farnsworth 3899, Sailors' 4123, Wadleigh 4194, Worcester 4209
Michigan: Ann Arbor 4221, Burt 4242, Fremont 4315, Gerstacker 4322, Grand Rapids 4326, Herrick 4341, Prince 4416, Upjohn 4465
Minnesota: **Andersen 4501**, Huss 4592, Mardag 4613, Mitchell 4625, Rivers 4666, Rochester 4668, Thorpe 4701, WCA 4718, Wedum 4719
Mississippi: Maddox 4753
Missouri: Green 4822, Truman 4919
Nebraska: Gardner 4965, Heuermann 4973, Hirschfeld 4974, Lincoln 4987, Smock 5004
Nevada: Fairweather 5032, Nevada 5047, Redfield 5055
New Hampshire: Gale 5091

New Jersey: Cowles 5170, **GHH 5207**, Healthcare 5228, Hyde 5247, **Johnson 5265**, Laurie 5297, OceanFirst 5341, Wallerstein 5446
New Mexico: Frost 5476, Maddox 5487, McCune 5488, Santa Fe 5496
New York: Abrons 5511, Altman 5542, **Atlantic 5574**, Atticus 5576, Auchincloss 5577, Benedict 5618, Berry 5626, Community 5782, Community 5783, **Cummings 5813**, Dreyfus 5887, Faulkner 5948, Gifford 6026, Glickenhaus 6042, Goldsmith 6060, Green 6096, Greene 6099, Grigg 6108, Guttman 6124, **Hartford 6150**, Hilibrand 6184, Hoyt 6203, **IBM 6221**, Lincoln 6423, Lindner 6426, Milstein 6555, Moses 6587, New York 6613, New York 6615, Noble 6632, Northern 6638, Northern 6639, Parker 6690, Parshelsky 6693, Pyewacket 6756, **Ramapo 6769**, Rhodebeck 6791, Schaffer 6911, Schmitt 6928, Silverman 6983, Spingold 7032, Tuch 7170, Tuttle 7176, Vidda 7198, **Walter 7211**, Weill 7227, Wendt 7243, Western 7248
North Carolina: Coffey 7339, Community 7344, Cumberland 7349, Davis 7352, Foundation 7370, Nias 7435, North Carolina 7438, Reynolds 7457, Triangle 7496, Van Houten 7500
North Dakota: MDU 7517, North Dakota 7519, Stern 7521
Ohio: Akron 7526, Bruening 7558, Bryan 7559, Campbell 7565, Cincinnati 7573, Cleveland 7576, Community 7585, Fairfield 7622, Greene 7653, **HCR 7667**, Marietta 7735, McGregor 7742, Pugliese 7810, Richland 7819, Schlink 7839, Schmidlapp 7841, Stark 7867, Stefanski 7868, Stocker 7870, Toledo 7883, Wuliger 7918
Oklahoma: Lyon 7953, Zarrow 7993
Oregon: Fohs 8012, Jackson 8024, Johnson 8027, Macdonald 8038, Meyer 8042, Oregon 8049
Pennsylvania: Arcadia 8086, Cassett 8133, Cavitolo 8134, Century 8137, Connelly 8157, Crels 8163, Dietrich 8171, Dolfinger 8172, Hahn 8231, Huston 8263, Jaindl 8269, Levis 8309, McKinney 8339, McLean 8340, Morris 8359, **Pew 8377**, Shaffer 8436, Smith 8443, Smith 8444, Snee 8446, Trexler 8481
Rhode Island: Kimball 8542
South Carolina: Central 8577, Self 8610, Springs 8617
Tennessee: Community 8662, Durham 8670, Massey 8709, Nelson 8712, Washington 8741
Texas: Abell 8749, Amarillo 8758, Anderson 8759, Anderson 8762, Bass 8777, Cameron 8812, Carter 8816, El Paso 8882, Finger 8900, Greathouse 8924, Hillcrest 8952, Hoblitzelle 8955, Johnson 8974, King 8995, Levit 9009, Meadows 9049, Mitte 9067, Proctor 9132, Rapoport 9141, Reaud 9143, San Antonio 9166, Smith 9191, South 9201, Speas 9206, Weaver 9267, Wright 9294, Young 9295
Utah: Eccles 9320
Virginia: Arlington 9371, Beazley 9376, Camp 9382, Delmar 9410, Lynchburg 9463, Norfolk 9484, Perry 9495, Weil 9535
Washington: Blue 9559, Cheney 9569, Community 9571, Crystal 9576, Foundation 9589, Glaser 9594, Lauzier 9626, Tacoma 9693
Wisconsin: Community 9779, Evjue 9797, Madison 9854, McBeath 9864, Milwaukee 9876, Pettit 9897, Rutledge 9917, Siebert 9927

Agriculture

Arkansas: Rockefeller 172, Rockefeller 173
California: Boswell 308, Crocker 429, **Foundation 529**, Gamble 549, Heller 666, **Peterson 996**, Van Daele 1258
Colorado: Monfort 1429
District of Columbia: **Wallace 1857**
Georgia: **Foundation 2388**, Watson 2509
Iowa: **Pioneer 3324**
Massachusetts: Cedar 3840, **Conservation 3858**
Michigan: Americana 4218, **Kellogg 4357**
Minnesota: **CHS 4540**
Missouri: Barrows 4781, Carter 4794, Kemper 4846, **Monsanto 4868**
Nebraska: Hawkins 4970

New Jersey: **International 5252**
New Mexico: McCune 5488
New York: **de Hirsch 5840**, **Ford 5970**, **Frasch 5979**, **Noyes 6643**, O'Connor 6645
Ohio: Anderson 7529, Bryan 7559, **Chiquita 7571**, Greene 7653, Van Wert 7891
Oregon: **Schmidt 8055**
Tennessee: LifeWorks 8701
Texas: McMillan 9046, Meadows 9049, Robinson 9152
Vermont: **Ben 9355**
Washington: Lauzier 9626

Agriculture, farm bureaus/granges

California: Chavez 376

Agriculture, farm cooperatives

Minnesota: **CHS 4540**

Agriculture, farmlands

Connecticut: **Fink 1539**
Nebraska: Swanson 5009
Texas: Behmann 8785

Agriculture, soil/water issues

Connecticut: **Valentine 1669**
Massachusetts: **New England 4052**
Minnesota: **Land 4602**
Washington: Bullitt 9563

Agriculture/food

Arizona: Aurora 88
California: Columbia 399, **Schlinger 1102**
Connecticut: **Valentine 1669**, Vervane 1671
Illinois: Hartke 2792
Massachusetts: **Conservation 3858**
Michigan: **Kellogg 4357**
Nebraska: **ConAgra 4953**
New York: Durst 5895, **Global 6043**, Independence 6229, Vernon 7195
Pennsylvania: Eden 8182
Washington: **Vista 9699**

Agriculture/food, ethics

Nebraska: **ConAgra 4953**

Agriculture/food, formal/general education

California: Harden 647

Agriculture/food, management/technical aid

Washington: Bullitt 9563

Agriculture/food, public education

Missouri: **Monsanto 4868**
New York: **Rockefeller 6826**

Agriculture/food, public policy

California: Mabie 839

Agriculture/food, research

Missouri: **Monsanto 4868**
New Jersey: Indian 5250

AIDS

Alabama: Blount 13
Arizona: Arizona 87, Community 91

California: Alliance 204, Atkinson 239, Brotman 328, California 345, Campini 353, Community 406, Copley 416, **Firelight 509**, Five 516, Gap 551, Geffen 558, **Gere 565**, Gillespie 577, Gilmore 578, Gonda 601, Irvine 699, **Kaiser 739**, King 760, **Lloyd 823**, Marin 854, McCarthy 868, Moonwalk 911, Norris 940, Norton 943, Parsons 980, Rigler 1051, Sacramento 1080, **Saje 1084**, San Diego 1087, San Francisco 1088, Sierra 1151, **Strauss 1203**, vanLobenSels 1260, Weingart 1288
Colorado: **Gill 1382**
Connecticut: Ambler 1481, Connecticut 1518, Hartford 1564, Long 1590, Palmer 1621
District of Columbia: Bernstein 1775, Cafritz 1780, **Public 1844**
Florida: Bank 1890, Bastien 1892, Community 1939, Community 1941, Dade 1957, Opler 2158, Price 2177
Georgia: Community 2355, Exposition 2380, Moore 2452
Hawaii: McInerny 2551, Wilcox 2559
Illinois: Abbott 2580, Chicago 2661, Comer 2675, Community 2677, Duchossois 2711, Field 2728, Fry 2740, Hirsch 2800, Kapoor 2825, Payne 2934, **Ploughshares 2945**, Polk 2946, Rotonda 2972, Washington 3058
Indiana: Health 3164
Iowa: Cedar Rapids 3275
Massachusetts: Ansin 3779, Babson 3787, Barry 3793, Boston 3812, Community 3855, Hyams 3961
Michigan: Grand Rapids 4326
Minnesota: HRK 4589, Pax 4648, Whitney 4728
Missouri: H & R 4823
Nebraska: Baer 4944, Watanabe 5015
Nevada: Fairweather 5032, May 5046, Nevada 5047
New Hampshire: Martin 5097
New Jersey: Cowles 5170, Danellie 5177, Fund 5199, **International 5252**, **Johnson 5261**, McGraw 5323, Prudential 5360
New Mexico: Frost 5476, McCune 5488, New Mexico 5491, Santa Fe 5496
New York: Brown 5676, Claiborne 5758, Community 5780, Community 5782, Cummings 5815, Daphne 5830, Diller 5863, Ebb 5903, **Ford 5970**, Glickenhaus 6042, Goldsmith 6060, Hagedorn 6130, Herdrich 6173, **International 6234**, **Ittleson 6241**, Johnson 6270, M.A.C. 6466, **Mapplethorpe 6485**, **Memton 6529**, **MetLife 6542**, New York 6613, Northern 6639, **Overbrook 6675**, Palm 6681, **Parsons 6694**, Pfizer 6720, Rapoport 6772, Robbins 6817, Snowdon 7012, Tisch 7145, van Ameringen 7190, Violett 7200, Wallach 7210, Wendt 7243
North Carolina: Community 7343, Cumberland 7349, Reynolds 7457, Triangle 7496
Ohio: Cleveland 7576, Columbus 7580, **Federated 7624**, Gund 7657, Ohio 7785, Stark 7867
Oregon: Holmes 8020
Pennsylvania: 1957 8071, Dietrich 8171, Dolfinger 8172, Philadelphia 8378, **Pincus 8384**, Smith 8443, Sovereign 8451
Rhode Island: Rhode Island 8551
South Carolina: Central 8577
Texas: Burnett 8801, Cain 8809, Cameron 8812, Community 8841, George 8916, Hoblitzelle 8955, Meadows 9049, Moody 9070, Rockwell 9154, San Antonio 9166, Speas 9206, Sterling 9212, Wright 9294
Utah: Eccles 9320
Vermont: **Ben 9355**, Vermont 9361
Virginia: Community 9402
Washington: Community 9571, Foster 9588, **Gates 9591**, **Glaser 9595**, **Kongsgaard 9620**, Norcliffe 9650, O'Donnell 9652, OneFamily 9654, Tacoma 9693
Wisconsin: Community 9776, Kettering 9835, McBeath 9864, Milwaukee 9876, Northwestern 9884

AIDS research

Alabama: Saks 61
Arizona: Arizona 87

California: Aaroe 192, Auen 242, **Beckman 272**, Brotman 328, California 345, Campini 353, Community 406, Daly 437, DeVito 452, McCarthy 868, Norris 940, Rigler 1051, San Diego 1087, **Strauss 1203**
Connecticut: Bodenwein 1497, Ensworth 1535, Long 1590, Palmer 1621
District of Columbia: Bernstein 1775, Cafritz 1780
Florida: Bastien 1892, **Campbell 1923**, Price 2177
Georgia: Moore 2452
Illinois: Community 2677, Duchossois 2711, Kapoor 2825, Payne 2934, Washington 3058
Kansas: Security 3390
Massachusetts: Harmsworth 3942
Nevada: Fairweather 5032, Nevada 5047
New Jersey: Cowles 5170, Hyde 5247, **International 5252**, Kirby 5279, McGraw 5323
New Mexico: Frost 5476
New York: Cole 5774, Community 5780, **Donghia 5872**, Gilman 6032, Glickenhaus 6042, Goldsmith 6060, Johnson 6270, Leibowitz 6398, **Mapplethorpe 6485**, **Monell 6566**, Union 7184, Wendt 7243
Ohio: Cleveland 7576, Columbus 7580, Gund 7657, Ohio 7785, Stark 7867
Oregon: Holmes 8020
Pennsylvania: Dietrich 8171, Dolfinger 8172, Philadelphia 8378, Smith 8443, Sovereign 8451
Texas: Cain 8809, Cameron 8812, Community 8841, Meadows 9049, Moody 9070, San Antonio 9166, Speas 9206, Sterling 9212, Wright 9294
Utah: Bastian 9306
Washington: Norcliffe 9650, **Pendleton 9661**, Tacoma 9693

AIDS, people with

California: California 345, Gilmore 578, Moonwalk 911, Taper 1226
Connecticut: Community 1515
District of Columbia: Cafritz 1780
Florida: Dade 1957, duPont 1983
Georgia: AEC 2310, Community 2355, Rich 2472
Illinois: Washington 3058
Indiana: Health 3164
Massachusetts: Hyams 3961, Worcester 4209
Minnesota: Bremer 4523, HRK 4589, Phillips 4655
New Jersey: MCJ 5324
New Mexico: Santa Fe 5496
New York: New York 6615
Ohio: Akron 7526, Bruening 7558, White 7905
Pennsylvania: Hillman 8250, Simonds 8442
Texas: Sterling 9212
Utah: Bastian 9307
Virginia: **Gannett 9428**

Alcoholism

Arkansas: Wal-Mart 184
California: Atkinson 239, Irvine 699, Norris 940, Sacramento 1080, San Diego 1087, San Francisco 1088, Sierra 1151, Sonora 1178, Von der Ahe 1269
Colorado: **Daniels 1362**
Connecticut: Bodenwein 1497, Palmer 1621
Florida: Banbury 1889, Bastien 1892, Rayonier 2189
Georgia: **Hanley 2405**
Illinois: Community 2677
Indiana: West 3256
Iowa: Siouxland 3332
Maryland: **Alcoholic 3564**
Massachusetts: Stearns 4160
Michigan: Grand Rapids 4326
Minnesota: Huss 4592, Ordean 4643, Walker 4711, Wedum 4719, Whitney 4728
Nevada: Fairweather 5032
New Jersey: Borden 5138
New Mexico: McCune 5488, Santa Fe 5496
New York: Achelis 5513, **Monell 6566**, O'Connor 6645, Ohrstrom 6659, **Smithers 7010**, Wendt 7243, Western 7248
North Carolina: Reynolds 7457, Triangle 7496

American studies

Anatomy (animal)

Anatomy (human)

Animal population control

Animal welfare

Pennsylvania: Allerton 8077, **Annenberg 8084**, Arcadia 8086, Brougher 8122, Century 8137, **Cestone 8138**, **Clive 8146**, Dolfinger 8172, Fleming 8206, Giop 8216, Lamb 8299, **Metcalf 8351**, Scranton 8431, Tippins 8477, Warwick 8496
Rhode Island: Champlin 8524, Doyle 8532, Kimball 8542, Rhode Island 8551
South Carolina: Waccamaw 8619
Tennessee: Aslan 8637, Community 8662
Texas: Austin 8768, **Bridge 8795**, Cailloux 8806, **Catto 8819**, Coastal 8833, Dallas 8855, Delaney 8862, El Paso 8881, Estill 8888, Griffin 8925, Kronkosky 9002, Lubbock 9021, McCrea 9040, McNutt 9048, **Notsew 9093**, Once 9101, Owsley 9108, San Antonio 9166, Summerlee 9217, Temple 9227, Zeller 9298
Utah: Stern 9344, Swanson 9346, **Wishnick 9353**
Virgin Islands: Prosser 9364
Virginia: Graves 9433, Norfolk 9484, Ochsman 9489, Pauley 9494
Washington: Blue 9559, Community 9571, Dimmer 9579, **Glaser 9595**, Paulus 9658, Tacoma 9693
West Virginia: Parkersburg 9730
Wisconsin: Archer 9746, Dawes 9788, Delavan 9790, Evjue 9797, Gordon 9808, Handleman 9811, Peck 9894
Wyoming: Chapman 9976, Sargent 9989

Animals/wildlife

Alabama: **Altec 4**, Mitchell 53, Webb 75
Arizona: **Johnson 112**
California: Aaroe 192, Bakar 250, **Brandes 317**, Giannini 573, Greenberg 616, Jackson 706, JL 720, Mericos 889, Michelson 896, **Schlinger 1102**, Scripps 1115, Severns 1131, **Taub 1227**, Winnick 1310
Connecticut: Bridgemill 1503, Goergen 1556, Matthies 1600, **Niles 1612**
Delaware: **Cedar 1697**, Delaware 1706
District of Columbia: Freed 1798
Florida: Batchelor 1893, Behring 1899, Community 1946, Community 1948, Love 2119, Quimby 2183, Southwest 2240
Georgia: Russell 2478, **Turner 2501**
Illinois: Blair 2622, Bruning 2635, Buffett 2639, Cressey 2689, Halligan 2779, Hobbs 2802, **Keller 2829**, McNally 2885, Stewart 3024, Wilkie 3071
Louisiana: Coypu 3471
Maryland: Columbia 3595, Felburn 3629
Massachusetts: Canaday 3831, Carlee 3835, **Harris 3944**, **Hershey 3949**, Ludcke 4017, Tara 4179, Yawkey 4211
Michigan: Mosaic 4398, Young 4490
Minnesota: Griggs 4577, Schmidt 4673
Missouri: Seaworld 4900
Montana: Browning 4933
Nebraska: Swanson 5009
Nevada: Parks 5052
New Jersey: **Barbour 5124**, Fanwood 5192, **Jeffery 5257**, Twin 5432, **YPI 5461**
New Mexico: Healy 5479
New York: Abraham 5510, Butler 5691, Corrigan 5796, Coulson 5799, **Donner 5873**, Fludzinski 5964, Harriman 6147, Huntington 6213, Lehman 6396, **Memton 6529**, **Rosen 6843**, Rosenthal 6854, Schenker 6916, Sulzberger 7095, Walter 7212, Weatherup 7222
Ohio: American 7528, **Goatie 7651**, Miller 7753, Wellman 7901
Oklahoma: Chapman 7928
Oregon: Kinsman 8031
Pennsylvania: Allerton 8077, **Beneficia 8100**, Berks 8103, **Korein 8295**, Miller 8356
Puerto Rico: **FNZ 8514**
Rhode Island: **FM 8537**, Routhier 8553
South Carolina: Arkwright 8565, TSC 8618
Tennessee: Atticus 8639, Community 8662, LifeWorks 8701
Texas: Bass 8777, Community 8840, Favrot 8897, Hanley 8940, McCoy 9038, Tapeats 9223
Utah: Peery 9337, Raymond 9339, **Wishnick 9353**

Virginia: Virginia Beach 9532
Washington: Bullitt 9563, Crystal 9576, **Fabert 9584**, Ferguson 9585, Kaleidoscope 9616, **Sage 9674**, Seattle 9680
Wyoming: Chapman 9976

Animals/wildlife, alliance

Minnesota: Xcel 4732
Pennsylvania: Huplits 8262

Animals/wildlife, association

California: Cheeryble 377, Greenberg 616
Connecticut: **Tyrrell 1667**
Massachusetts: Foundation 3916
New York: Novogratz 6642
Wisconsin: Schoenleber 9921

Animals/wildlife, bird preserves

California: Garaventa 553
Illinois: Grohne 2774
New York: **Burpee 5690**, **Kelly 6312**, **LaSalle 6377**
Ohio: Philips 7804
Pennsylvania: **Beneficia 8100**, Hodge 8254, SVF 8472
Wyoming: Berry 9975

Animals/wildlife, clubs

New York: Williams 7260

Animals/wildlife, endangered species

California: **Delano 449**
Maryland: **Shared 3727**
Michigan: **Arcus 4223**
Nebraska: **McDonald 4989**
Texas: **ExxonMobil 8889**

Animals/wildlife, equal rights

Florida: **Nanci's 2150**
Washington: **Glaser 9595**

Animals/wildlife, fisheries

California: Firedoll 508, Mead 881, **Packard 972**
Connecticut: Goodnow 1558
District of Columbia: Munson 1837
Michigan: Frey 4316
Montana: Cinnabar 4935
New York: F. & J.S. 5942, **Ripplewood 6812**
North Carolina: Smith 7478
Oregon: Jubitz 8028
Washington: Burning 9564, Martin 9634, Paulus 9658

Animals/wildlife, formal/general education

Massachusetts: Overly 4064
New York: Wildwood 7259

Animals/wildlife, management/technical aid

Illinois: Perritt 2939
Massachusetts: Lindsay 4009
Montana: Cinnabar 4935
Wisconsin: Schoenleber 9921

Animals/wildlife, preservation/protection

Alabama: Barber 10
Alaska: Alaska 79
Arizona: Stevens 144
Arkansas: Rebsamen 171
California: Bechtel 270, Columbia 399, Connell 412, **Delano 449**, **Flynt 524**, **Foundation 529**, Hofmann 683, Littleford 820, Long 825, McBean 866, McCaw 869, Mental 886, **On 953**, Petersen 994,

Roberts 1058, Rothschild 1072, Sorensen 1180, Truckee 1244, Witherbee 1312, ZZYZX 1331
Colorado: **Hawley 1390**
Connecticut: Baker 1486, Baldwin 1487, **Ettinger 1536**, Foster 1546, Larsen 1579, **Orchard 1619**, Sewall 1648
Delaware: **Fair 1713**
District of Columbia: Henry 1808
Florida: **Anderson 1876**, Burton 1921, Martin 2130, Opler 2158, Quimby 2183, Shackelford 2232, Spurlino 2242, Weiler 2290
Georgia: Anncox 2318, Broadfield 2330, Cooper 2363, Gaines 2393, **Georgia 2397**, Ma-Ran 2439, Patterson 2460, Sapelo 2479, **Thoresen 2499**, **Turner 2501**, Williams 2514
Hawaii: Anthony 2531
Illinois: Beidler 2613, Community 2677, Donnelley 2708, DuPage 2713, Fites 2730, Grohne 2774, Huizenga 2806, Huntington 2809, JYN 2821, Love 2863, Madigan 2869, Olin 2925, Rosenthal 2970, **Shifting 3006**, Torstenson 3036
Indiana: Community 3122, Indiana 3173, Marshall 3199, Met 3204
Maine: Fore 3534
Maryland: Felburn 3629, **Knapp 3665**, **Shared 3727**
Massachusetts: Community 3855, **Conservation 3858**, Island 3965, Killam 3980, McEvoy 4032, Red 4096, **Sweet 4176**
Michigan: Burt 4242, Devereaux 4274, Frey 4316, Kellogg's 4358, Saddle 4426, Turner 4464
Minnesota: Bell 4514, Federated 4563, McVay 4620, W.M. 4710, Wedum 4719, Xcel 4732
Missouri: **Monsanto 4868**, **Morris 4869**, Seaworld 4900
Montana: Cinnabar 4935
Nebraska: Rogers 4999
Nevada: Crescere 5030, Tuscany 5074
New Hampshire: Fuller 5090
New Jersey: Dodge 5181, **James 5254**, Kerr 5278, **Lautenberg 5298**, Mushett 5334, Phipps 5352
New Mexico: Lapides 5485, McCune 5488, Messengers 5489, **Pond 5494**, Santa Fe 5496
New York: **American 5551**, Black 5636, **Bobolink 5645**, Brunckhorst 5678, Brutsch 5680, Chadwick 5726, **Claiborne 5757**, Cullman 5812, Demartini 5851, Donaldson 5871, Ellis 5923, **Engelhard 5932**, Erpf 5937, Fludzinski 5964, **Frankenberg 5977**, Gilman 6032, **Heineman 6165**, **Homeland 6199**, Linden 6424, Marcus 6486, **Marsh 6495**, Nichols 6628, **Norcross 6634**, O'Connor 6645, **Reed 6783**, **Ripplewood 6812**, **Rosen 6843**, Rumsey 6882, Schenectady 6915, Schieffelin 6922, **Solow 7020**, **Trust 7168**, Vidda 7198, **Waterfowl 7219**, Wiegers 7256, **Woods 7278**, Woodward 7279, Zucker 7303
North Carolina: Bryan 7330, Cumberland 7349, Triangle 7496
Ohio: Cotswold 7594, Muskingum 7770, **Perkins 7800**, Sedgwick 7849
Oklahoma: Kirkpatrick 7952
Pennsylvania: Ames 8080, Arcadia 8086, Hawksglen 8238, Maple 8323, **Metcalf 8351**, **Pew 8377**
Rhode Island: **Bafflin 8519**
South Carolina: Cline 8580, Montgomery 8600
South Dakota: Sioux Falls 8630
Tennessee: Jeniam 8695
Texas: Aragona 8763, Bass 8775, Keithley 8983, **Kleberg 8998**, **Kleberg 8999**, Meadows 9049, Northen 9092, San Antonio 9166, **Shell 9181**, Summerlee 9217
Utah: **ALSAM 9302**
Virginia: Mars 9466, Sacharuna 9509, Wrinkle 9545
Washington: **444S 9546**, Community 9571, Moccasin 9643, Murr 9645, Norcliffe 9650, **Samis 9675**, **Wiancko 9704**
Wisconsin: Puelicher 9904
Wyoming: Kerr 9983, **Schultz 9990**, **Wolf 9999**

Animals/wildlife, public education

Minnesota: Xcel 4732
Missouri: Seaworld 4900

1708, **Fair 1713**, Hall 1718, Hamel 1719, Kingsley 1724, Lennox 1726, Longwood 1727, Marmot 1728, MBNA 1730, **Neuberger 1735**, Orange 1737, Parker 1738, Phillips 1739, Presto 1740, Reynolds 1743, **Robinson 1745**, Roby 1746, Romill 1747, Rowland 1749, **Schwartz 1751**, Seevak 1752, Singer 1753, Vitale F 1759, Wasily 1760, Welfare 1762
District of Columbia: **Bauman 1770**, **Berman 1774**, Bernstein 1775, Brody 1777, Cafritz 1780, **Coleman 1784**, Community 1785, Dimick 1789, Fernandez 1794, Friedman 1799, Gewirz 1801, Gottesman 1803, Graham 1804, Gudelsky 1805, Harman 1807, Johnson 1812, Kaye 1815, Kimsey 1817, Kiplinger 1818, Loughran 1823, Marriott 1827, Merriman 1833, Meyer 1834, Nef 1839, **Patterson 1840**, Post 1842, Reich 1845, Replogle 1846, Roshan 1847, Vaterstetten 1855, Vradenburg 1856
Florida: A Friends' 1866, **Abramson 1868**, ADFAM 1870, Adler 1871, Ansin 1877, Appleby 1879, **Arison 1880**, Arison 1881, Bank 1890, BankAtlantic 1891, Bay 1896, Becker 1898, **Berg 1903**, BJ's 1908, Blank 1909, Blum 1912, Bronfman 1917, **Bryson 1918**, Bush 1922, Capital 1924, Caspersen 1927, Community 1939, Community 1940, Community 1941, Community 1942, Community 1943, Community 1944, Community 1945, Community 1946, Community 1947, Community 1948, Community 1949, Dade 1957, Darden 1960, Dickins 1972, DuBow 1977, Dunspaugh 1981, duPont 1983, Edelman 1987, Einstein 1991, Elster 1993, Fisher 1999, **Fiterman 2000**, Florida 2003, FPL 2010, Friedman 2014, Gainesville 2015, Garfinkle 2017, Gerstner 2020, Ginsburg 2022, Global 2025, **Goldhammer 2026**, Goldstein 2027, Goodwin 2029, Gorin 2032, Green 2033, **Greenfield 2035**, Gronewaldt 2037, Gruss 2038, Gulf 2041, Hard 2047, Harris 2050, Horvitz 2065, Hunter 2069, **Isenberg 2070**, Jacksonville 2071, Jaharis 2073, Jelks 2076, Katcher 2080, Kaufman 2082, Keating 2084, Kennedy 2088, Kennedy 2089, Kesler 2090, Kimmel 2091, **Knight 2097**, Lattner 2104, Lee 2107, Leiser 2108, Levine 2113, Life's 2116, Love 2119, Lynn 2120, Magill 2124, Magruder 2125, Maltz 2126, Marden 2127, Martin 2130, McCann 2132, Miller 2140, Moran 2143, Nessel 2152, Ocean 2156, **Pearce 2166**, Phillips 2168, Pinellas 2170, Potamkin 2176, **Rehm 2192**, Rinker 2195, Rinker 2196, River 2198, River 2199, Rollnick 2203, Ryder 2213, Sanders 2215, Sandler 2216, Saunders 2219, Schaefer 2222, Scharlin 2223, Schoen 2226, Selby 2230, Sherman 2233, Simon 2235, Southwest 2240, St. Joe 2244, **Stafford 2247**, Stein 2249, Storer 2252, Stransky 2253, Straz 2254, SunTrust 2259, **SWS 2260**, Taylor 2269, TECO 2270, Toppel 2274, United 2276, Walter 2286, Weiller 2291, Williams 2299, Winter 2303, Wolfson 2305
Georgia: Adams 2309, AEC 2310, AGL 2312, Anderson 2317, Atlanta 2320, Bradley 2326, Brill 2329, Brown 2332, Campbell 2339, Charter 2345, Chatham 2346, Chatham 2347, Colonial 2353, Community 2355, Community 2356, Community 2357, Community 2358, Community 2359, Community 2361, Community 2362, Courts 2364, Cousins 2365, Covenant 2366, Cox 2367, Cox 2368, Daft 2370, Delta 2372, English 2378, Equifax 2379, Exposition 2380, Flowers 2384, Fort 2387, Franklin 2389, **Gage 2392**, Gaines 2393, **Georgia 2397**, Graves 2403, Hanna 2406, Harland 2407, Harris 2408, Hertz 2412, Holder 2413, Horowitz 2415, Imlay 2417, ING 2418, JBS 2420, Jinks 2422, Jones 2424, Knox 2427, Lanier 2428, Lanier 2430, Lanier 2431, Lee 2432, Livingston 2435, Love 2437, Lubo 2438, Marshall 2442, Moore 2452, Morris 2454, Murphy 2456, North 2458, Patrick 2459, Patterson 2460, Pechter 2461, Poe 2465, Porter 2468, Rich 2472, Robinson 2473, Rollins 2475, Rosenberg 2476, RTM 2477, Savannah 2480, **Scientific 2482**, Selig 2484, Sheffield 2488, Spray 2495, SunTrust 2496,

Synovus 2497, Tull 2500, WestPoint 2513, Williams 2514, Williams 2516, Woodruff 2521, Woodruff 2522, Woodward 2523, Woolford 2524, Woolley 2525, Young 2527, Zeist 2529
Hawaii: Alexander 2530, Anthony 2531, Atherton 2532, Bank 2535, Castle 2538, First 2542, Frear 2543, Hawaii 2545, Kosasa 2549, McInerny 2551, Watumull 2558, Wilcox 2559
Idaho: CHC 2566, Cunningham 2567, Golden 2568, Good 2569, Idaho 2570, Morrison 2572, Simplot 2574, Simplot 2575
Illinois: Abbott 2580, Abelson 2581, Acorn 2583, **Allen 2587**, Alphawood 2589, Alsdorf 2590, AMCORE 2591, **Amsted 2593**, **Andrew 2595**, Andrew 2596, Anixter 2597, Appleton 2599, Barancik 2605, Bates 2608, BCS 2612, Bell 2614, Bere 2616, Blair 2621, Blum 2625, Borwell 2627, **Brach 2630**, Braeside 2631, **Brunswick 2636**, Buchanan 2637, **Buntrock 2643**, **Burlington 2644**, **Burnett 2645**, Butler 2646, Cabe 2648, **Carylon 2652**, Caterpillar 2653, Chapman 2656, Charleston 2657, Chicago 2661, Chicago 2663, Comer 2675, Community 2677, Community 2678, Community 2679, Community 2680, Cooney 2682, Corboy 2684, Coydog 2686, Crown 2691, D and R 2693, D.H.R. 2695, Davee 2696, Deere 2699, Deering 2700, DeKalb 2701, Donnelley 2706, Driehaus 2710, Duchossois 2711, DuPage 2713, Edwardson 2715, Elgin 2717, Ellis 2718, Emerson 2719, Energizer 2721, Field 2728, Firestone 2729, Flagg 2731, Frank 2733, Franke 2734, Frankel 2735, Freed 2736, Freehling 2737, Fry 2740, **Galashiels 2742**, **Gallagher 2744**, Galvin 2747, Geneseo 2750, Geraldi 2752, Getz 2753, GKN 2758, Gloyd 2760, Goldschmidt 2764, **Goodman 2765**, Grainger 2768, Gray 2771, H.B.B. 2777, Hales 2778, Halligan 2779, Hamill 2780, **Harper 2786**, Harris 2788, Harris 2789, Harrison 2791, Hartmarx 2794, Hitchcock 2801, Houlsby 2805, Huizenga 2806, **Hull 2807**, Huntington 2809, I and G 2811, Illinois 2815, Istock 2815, Jahn 2816, **JMR 2818**, **Joyce 2820**, Kaplan 2823, Katten 2826, **Keller 2829**, Kemper 2831, **Kemper 2832**, Kennedy 2834, Kensington 2836, Kersten 2838, Kipper 2840, Knapp 2841, Krueck 2846, Lange 2848, Lea 2850, Lederer 2851, Leibowitz 2854, Levi 2855, Lewis 2857, Logan 2860, Louis 2862, Madigan 2869, Malott 2872, Mazza 2877, McCormick 2878, McGraw 2882, McNally 2885, Melrene 2892, Meyer 2895, Meyer 2896, Millard 2897, Miller 2898, Miller 2899, Mills 2901, Moline 2902, Montgomery 2903, **Motorola 2906**, Negaunee 2909, Neisser 2910, New 2912, **Niamogue 2914**, NIB 2915, Nichols 2916, Northern 2918, Oak Park 2922, Offield 2924, Omron 2926, Opler 2927, Oppenheimer 2928, Payne 2934, Pepper 2936, PepsiAmericas 2937, Petersen 2941, Pick 2943, Prince 2948, **Pritzker 2951**, **Pritzker 2952**, Pritzker 2954, Red 2959, Rhoades 2965, Roberts 2968, Rosenthal 2970, Rothschild 2971, Rubin 2974, Ryan 2977, Sacks 2979, Sara 2982, **Satter 2983**, Schield 2985, Schmidt 2986, Schuler 2990, Seabury 2993, Segal 2995, Seid 2996, Shaker 2999, Shapiro 3001, Sharpe 3002, **Shaw 3003**, **Shifting 3006**, Siragusa 3009, Sirius 3010, **Square 3018**, Stein 3022, Stone 3025, Stone 3026, Stuart 3028, Sudix 3029, Takiff 3032, Trustmark 3039, **Tuohy 3041**, United 3044, USG 3046, Walgreen 3052, Walsh 3055, Ward 3056, Wein 3060, Weinberg 3061, Wilemal 3070, Wilkie 3071, Willett 3073, **Willow 3074**, Winfrey 3077, Woods 3084, Woodward 3085, Yulman 3089, Zell 3090
Indiana: Adams 3095, ADL 3097, American 3098, Anderson 3099, Annis 3100, Ball 3103, Ball 3104, Ball 3105, Biomet 3106, Blue 3107, Brown 3110, Bussing 3111, Carroll 3114, Central 3116, Citizens 3118, Clowes 3119, Clowes 3120, Cole 3121, Community 3122, Community 3123, Community 3124, Community 3125, Community 3126, Community 3127, Community 3128, Community 3129, Community 3130, Community 3131, Community 3132, Community 3133, Cornelius

3134, Crown Point 3135, **Cummins 3136**, Dearborn 3137, Decatur 3138, Decio 3139, DeHaan 3140, DeKalb 3141, Elkhart 3145, English 3146, Ford 3150, Glick 3155, Griffith 3158, **Guidant 3159**, Hancock 3160, Harrison 3161, Henry 3165, Heritage 3166, Hilbert 3167, Irwin 3174, Irwin 3175, Jasper 3177, Johnson 3178, Journal 3181, Kimball 3182, Klapper 3183, Koch 3184, Kosciusko 3186, Kuhne 3187, Lafayette 3188, Legacy 3189, **Lilly 3192**, Lilly 3194, Lincoln 3195, Madison 3197, Marshall 3199, Martin 3200, Montgomery 3206, Newman 3211, Niblick 3212, Noble 3214, Northern 3215, Noyes 3216, Oakley 3217, Ogle 3218, Portland 3223, Pulliam 3225, Ripley 3230, Rolland 3231, Saemann 3232, Saltsburg 3233, Simon 3239, Steuben 3241, Tipton 3243, Unity 3247, Vectren 3249, Wabash 3250, Watanabe 3251, Wayne 3253, Wells 3255, Whitley 3258
Iowa: **AEGON 3259**, Ahrens 3260, AmerUs 3261, Bechtel 3265, Blank 3268, Bright 3269, Brownell 3270, Bucksbaum 3271, Bucksbaum 3272, Butler 3273, Cedar Rapids 3275, Community 3277, Community 3278, Cowles 3279, Des Moines 3281, Employers 3282, Farver 3283, Figge 3284, Gilchrist 3287, Hall 3290, Hanson 3291, Kinney 3300, Knapp 3301, Kruidenier 3303, Kuyper 3304, Lee 3305, **Lee 3306**, Levitt 3307, Maytag 3309, Maytag 3310, McCarthy 3311, McElroy 3313, Meredith 3314, Meredith 3315, Mid 3316, Pella 3323, Principal 3326, R & R 3327, **Rockwell 3328**, Ruan 3329, Seidler 3331, Siouxland 3332, United 3338
Kansas: Baughman 3346, Cessna 3351, Cooper 3353, DeVore 3357, Dreiseszun 3359, Garvey 3363, Hutchinson 3368, INTRUST 3369, Joscelyn 3371, Kaplan 3373, Koch 3374, McCune 3376, **Muchnic 3379**, Payless 3380, Pritchett 3382, Rice 3384, Salina 3387, Security 3390, Smoot 3394, Sprint 3395, Topeka 3400, Wichita 3404
Kentucky: Blue 3407, Brown 3408, Brown 3410, **Chase 3413**, Community 3414, Community 3415, E.ON 3417, Fischer 3418, Foundation 3420, Gheens 3421, Kindred 3434, Klein 3435, Little 3437, Novak 3442, Preston 3446, Rosenthal 3450, Sutherland 3451, Young 3454, Young 3455, **Yum! 3457**
Louisiana: Azby 3460, Baton Rouge 3462, Booth 3464, Community 3469, Coughlin 3470, Deming 3472, Freeman 3480, Goldring 3484, Heymann 3487, Jones 3491, Kabacoff 3492, Keller 3493, Lupin 3498, Monroe 3501, New Orleans 3503, Reily 3506, RosaMary 3507, Taylor 3511, **Woldenberg 3516**, Young 3518, Zemurray 3519
Maine: Alfond 3521, Bangor 3525, Burnham 3527, Falcon 3532, Fore 3534, Gardiner 3536, **Golden 3538**, Hannaford 3540, Kennebec 3543, Kennebunk 3544, King 3545, Libra 3546, Lunder 3547, Maine 3548, TD 3558
Maryland: Abell 3559, **Adams 3562**, Baker 3567, Baltimore 3568, Bank 3569, **Blaustein 3575**, Blum 3577, Brown 3578, Bunting 3580, Capital 3584, Chaney 3587, Choice 3589, Clark 3590, Clark 3591, Cohen 3593, Columbia 3595, Community 3597, Community 3598, Community 3599, Community 3600, Concordia 3601, **Davis 3608**, Davison 3609, **Dean 3610**, Denit 3615, Eaton 3619, Eliasberg 3620, England 3622, **Fairchild 3627**, FBW 3628, Fisher 3630, Freeman 3633, Goldsmith 3637, Grace 3638, Greenberg 3639, Hahn 3643, **Head 3644**, Hecht 3645, Helena 3646, Henson 3648, Higginson 3649, ISE 3656, Klein 3662, Knott 3666, Legg 3672, Lerner 3675, Levitt 3676, Linehan 3678, Lockheed 3682, Macht 3683, MARPAT 3684, Marriott 3685, Meyerhoff 3692, **Morningstar 3695**, Nabit 3699, Osprey 3703, Pohanka 3707, Polinger 3708, Price 3709, Principato 3710, Procter 3711, Provident 3712, Rathmann 3715, Rosenberg 3719, Rosenberg 3720, Rouse 3724, Sheridan 3729, **Shields 3730**, Small 3734, Small 3735, Sylvan 3741, Thalheimer 3744, TKF 3747, Tucker 3750, Wallis 3755, Wright 3762, **Zickler 3763**

7934, Gaylord 7937, Gussman 7941, Helmerich 7942, Inasmuch 7944, Kerr 7949, Kerr 7950, Kirkpatrick 7952, Lyon 7953, McCasland 7956, McMahon 7959, Meinders 7960, Meinig 7961, Oklahoma City 7964, Oklahoma 7965, Oklahoman 7966, ONEOK 7967, Oxley 7968, Records 7972, Sarkeys 7974, **Schusterman 7975**, Share 7977, Sylvan 7981, Titus 7983, Viersen 7985, Williams 7989, Zarrow 7991, Zarrow 7993, Zink 7994

Oregon: Autzen 7997, Bair 7998, Braemar 8001, Carpenter 8003, Chambers 8004, **Chiles 8005**, Collins 8007, Crabby 8010, Fohs 8012, Geary 8017, Hedinger 8019, Holmes 8020, J.F.R. 8023, Jackson 8024, Jeld 8025, Kelley 8030, Kinsman 8031, Macdonald 8038, Mentor 8039, Meyer 8042, Miller 8045, Oregon 8049, PacifiCorp 8050, PGE 8051, Schnitzer 8057, Swindells 8062, Tektronix 8063, Templeton 8064, Tucker 8065, Wendt 8066, Wheeler 8068

Pennsylvania: 1957 8071, Aaron 8072, ACE 8073, Ames 8080, AMETEK 8081, **Annenberg 8084**, Arkema 8089, Asplundh 8091, Barra 8095, Bayer 8096, **Beneficia 8100**, Berger 8101, Berkman 8102, Berks 8103, Black 8109, Brickman 8116, Brossman 8120, Brougher 8122, Buck 8123, Burke 8126, Byers' 8127, **Cardone 8129**, **Carpenter 8131**, Cassett 8133, Cavitolo 8134, Centre 8136, Century 8137, Chester 8141, Chosky 8142, CIGNA 8143, Claneil 8144, Clapp 8145, **Clive 8146**, CMS 8147, Community 8153, Community 8155, Connelly 8157, Crawford 8162, Davenport 8164, Degenstein 8166, Dietrich 8170, Dolfinger 8172, **Dominion 8173**, Donley 8175, Eberly 8179, Eden 8181, Eden 8182, Equitable 8187, Erie 8188, Fair 8192, Federated 8196, Fels 8198, Fine 8201, First 8202, Foundation 8208, **Frick 8211**, Garthwaite 8212, Genuardi 8213, Giop 8216, Graham 8222, Grass 8223, Gray 8224, Grumbacher 8227, Grundy 8228, Haas 8230, Hamilton 8233, Harsco 8236, Hassel 8237, Heinz 8240, Heinz 8241, Heinz 8242, **Heinz 8243**, Heinz 8244, Hillman 8249, Hillman 8250, Hillman 8252, Hopwood 8257, Hoyt 8259, Hulme 8260, Hunt 8261, Huston 8263, Huston 8264, Independence 8266, Janssen 8271, **Johnson 8274**, Justus 8276, Kavanagh 8282, Kelly 8283, **Kennametal 8284**, Kinsley 8290, Klein 8291, Kline 8293, Kunkel 8297, La 8298, Lancaster 8300, Laurel 8301, Lehigh Valley 8303, Lenfest 8304, Lenfest 8305, Les 8306, Levan 8307, Lilliput 8311, Lindback 8312, Little 8313, Lotman 8314, Lutron 8316, Luzerne 8317, Magee 8320, Maguire 8321, Mandell 8322, Maple 8323, Maslow 8327, Massey 8328, McCune 8332, McFeely 8334, McKenna 8337, Meakem 8341, Mellon 8345, **Metcalf 8351**, Miller 8354, Miller 8356, Mine 8357, Murray 8360, Penn 8371, Perelman 8372, Perelman 8373, Perkin 8375, **Pew 8377**, Philadelphia 8378, Phillips 8380, Pine 8385, Pittsburgh 8386, PNC 8388, Poor 8392, **PPG 8394**, Pryor 8396, PSC 8398, Rees 8401, Rider 8404, Roberts 8405, Roberts 8406, Rockwell 8408, Rosenfeld 8413, S & T 8417, Safeguard 8418, Saint 8419, Sampson 8423, Schoonmaker 8429, Scranton 8431, **Seraph 8434**, Shapira 8437, Sherrerd 8439, Simmons 8441, Simonds 8442, Smith 8445, Snee 8446, Snider 8447, Sordoni 8450, Sovereign 8451, Spang 8452, Speyer 8453, Steinman 8458, Steinman 8459, Stewart 8460, Strauss 8464, **Strawbridge 8465**, Strawbridge 8467, Susquehanna 8471, Tippins 8477, Toll 8478, Trexler 8481, **United 8488**, Vanguard 8490, von Hess 8493, Warwick 8496, Waters 8498, West 8500, Willary 8503, Willis 8504, Wimmer 8505, Wolf 8506, Wyomissing 8509, York 8511

Puerto Rico: **FNZ 8514**, Puerto Rico 8515

Rhode Island: Alperin 8516, **Amica 8518**, Carter 8522, Chace 8523, Champlin 8524, Charter 8526, Citizens 8527, Daniels 8530, **FM 8537**, **Hassenfeld 8540**, Kimball 8542, McCarthy 8548, Nelson 8549, Rhode Island 8551, Shaw's 8555, **Textron 8559**, Usen 8560, Washington 8563

South Carolina: Barnet 8568, Bruce 8571, Cato 8576, Central 8577, Coastal 8581, Community 8583, Community 8584, Dintersmith 8586, First 8587, Hipp 8592, Horne 8594, Liberty 8597, Montgomery 8600, Phifer 8602, Post 8603, Rainey 8605, Self 8610, Sonoco 8614, South 8615, Spartanburg 8616, TSC 8618, Waccamaw 8619, **Wardle 8620**, **Youths' 8621**

South Dakota: Dakota 8624, Larson 8627, Sioux Falls 8630, South Dakota 8631

Tennessee: Atticus 8639, Ayers 8640, Belz 8643, Benwood 8644, **Bridgestone 8646**, Briggs 8647, Caldwell 8649, CLARCOR 8658, Clayton 8659, Community 8660, Community 8661, Community 8662, Conwood 8663, Danner 8664, Day 8666, Dugas 8669, East 8671, EBS 8672, Eskind 8673, Eskind 8674, Eskind 8675, First 8677, Frist 8679, Goldsmith 8682, Gordon 8683, Hamico 8684, Haslam 8687, Haslam 8688, Hawthorn 8689, Hyde 8693, Ingram 8694, Jeniam 8695, Lyndhurst 8703, Martin 8708, Massey 8709, Melkus 8711, Phillips 8716, Plough 8718, Longleaf 8719, Ragsdale 8722, Schadt 8725, Scheidt 8726, Starfish 8728, Stokely 8730, T & T 8731, Thompson 8733, Turner 8737, Turner 8738, Unaka 8739, Wallace 8740

Texas: Abell 8749, Alkek 8753, **Allbritton 8755**, Amarillo 8758, Anderson 8759, Anderson 8760, Astin 8764, **AT&T 8765**, Austin 8768, Baker 8772, Barnhart 8773, Bass 8776, Bass 8777, Bass 8778, Beal 8783, Behmann 8785, Bergman 8789, Bookout 8791, Brackenridge 8793, Bridwell 8797, Brown 8798, Brown 8799, Burnett 8801, Cain 8809, Carter 8816, Carter 8817, **Catto 8819**, **CEMEX 8821**, Charitable 8824, Clear 8831, Clements 8832, Coastal 8833, Coates 8834, Cockrell 8835, Collins 8837, Collins 8838, Communities 8839, Community 8840, Community 8841, Community 8842, Constantin 8843, **Cooper 8846**, Crane 8852, Cullen 8854, Dallas 8855, Deakins 8860, Dickson 8866, Dodge 8868, Duda 8871, Durrill 8873, Eady 8875, East 8876, **EDS 8877**, Edwards 8879, El Paso 8881, Essar 8887, Fain 8890, Fair 8891, Farb 8893, Favrot 8897, Feinberg 8898, Fikes 8899, Finger 8900, Fish 8902, Folsom 8905, Fondren 8906, Gale 8913, Garvey 8914, Gayden 8915, Goldsbury 8920, Goodman 8921, Greathouse 8923, Haggar 8931, Haggerty 8932, Halff 8934, Halsell 8936, Hamman 8938, Hanley 8940, **Hartman 8942**, Hawn 8943, Herd 8948, Herzstein 8949, Hirsch 8953, Hoblitzelle 8955, Houston 8961, Hudson 8962, Huffington 8963, Jamail 8970, Jones 8975, Jonsson 8977, Jordan 8978, Kaufman 8981, Keith 8982, Kelleher 8984, Kempner 8987, Kimberly 8992, Kinder 8994, **Kleberg 8999**, Koehler 9001, Lard 9005, Levit 9009, **Link 9013**, Littauer 9014, Lowe 9020, Lubbock 9021, Mankoff 9027, Marathon 9028, Marcus 9029, McCombs 9037, McDermott 9043, McNair 9047, McNutt 9048, Meadows 9049, Mechia 9050, Mendenhall 9053, Meredith 9054, Miller 9061, Miller 9062, Mitchell 9064, Mithoff 9066, Mitte 9067, Moncrief 9069, Moody 9070, Mosbacher 9077, Mundy 9080, Navarro 9089, Newman 9090, Nightingale 9091, O'Connor 9094, O'Donnell 9096, Oshman 9104, Otter 9105, Owen 9106, Owsley 9108, Paulos 9112, Permian 9117, Perot 9119, Petrello 9121, Pine 9123, Pollock 9127, Powell 9128, Prairie 9129, Priddy 9131, Prothro 9134, Providence 9135, Pryor 9136, PSH 9137, Rachofsky 9139, Reynolds 9145, Richardson 9147, Roach 9150, Roberts 9151, Rockwell 9154, Rogers 9155, Rogers 9156, Rosewood 9158, San Angelo 9164, San Antonio 9166, Sanders 9167, Sarofim 9169, **Scaler 9170**, Schollmaier 9172, Schutte 9173, Scott 9174, Scurlock 9175, Sharp 9180, **Shell 9181**, Shelton 9182, Simmons 9187, Simmons 9188, Smith 9191, Smith 9195, Smith 9196, Smith 9197, Smith 9198, South 9201, Stemmons 9211, Sterling 9212, Stewart 9213, Stoffel 9214, Sturgis 9216, Susman 9220, Swinney 9222, Temple 9227, Temple 9228, **Tenet 9229**, Tennessee 9230, Texas 9232, Tobin 9235, Tolleson 9237, Turner 9241, Turner 9242, USAA 9245, Valero 9247, Vaughan 9249, Vaughan 9250, Vaughn 9251, Waco 9255, Waggoner 9256, Ward 9263, **Waste 9265**, Watson 9266, West 9276, Westcott 9278, Wichita 9280, Wise 9285, Works 9291, Wortham 9292, Wright 9294, Zachry 9296

Utah: Ashton 9303, Bastian 9307, Denkers 9312, Dumke 9315, Eccles 9319, Eccles 9320, Esther 9321, Hemingway 9328, Jones 9330, Lawson 9332, Quinney 9338, Raymond 9339, Swanson 9346, Tanner 9347, **Wishnick 9353**, Zions 9354

Vermont: Mergens 9360, Vermont 9361

Virgin Islands: Bartner 9362, Prosser 9364

Virginia: Arlington 9371, Batten 9373, Batten 9375, Cabell 9381, Camp 9382, Campbell 9383, Carrington 9386, Carter 9387, Cartledge 9388, Charles 9389, Charlottesville 9390, Cole 9396, Cole 9397, Community 9400, Community 9402, Constitution 9404, Flagler 9417, Foundation 9419, Fralin 9420, Friedman 9425, **Gannett 9428**, Golden 9430, Grandis 9432, Graves 9433, Gwathmey 9435, Herndon 9437, Houff 9438, HRH 9439, **Johnson 9444**, Kanter 9445, **Kaufman 9447**, Kegley 9448, Kellar 9449, LandAmerica 9454, Landmark 9455, Lynchburg 9463, **Malek 9465**, Mars 9466, Massey 9467, McDonnell 9468, McGlothlin 9469, McGue 9470, McNichols 9472, Memorial 9474, Morgan 9479, N.E.W. 9482, Norfolk 9484, **Norfolk 9485**, Northern 9486, **Oak 9488**, Olsson 9491, Parsons 9493, Perry 9495, Perry 9496, Portsmouth 9498, Robins 9506, **Scripps 9514**, Smith 9518, Snead 9520, Staunton 9521, SunTrust 9523, Titmus 9527, Truland 9528, Ukrop 9529, United 9530, Universal 9531, Virginia Beach 9532, VuBay 9533, Washington 9534

Washington: Archibald 9553, Blakemore 9558, Blue 9559, **Boeing 9560**, Cheney 9569, Community 9570, Community 9571, De Falco 9578, Dimmer 9579, Evertrust 9583, **Fabert 9584**, Forest 9586, Foster 9588, Foundation 9589, Fuchs 9590, Glazer 9596, Grays 9597, Green 9598, Haugland 9603, Klorfine 9619, **Kongsgaard 9620**, **Laird 9623**, Moccasin 9643, Murdock 9644, Norcliffe 9650, O'Donnell 9652, PACCAR 9656, **PAH 9657**, Raikes 9668, Raven 9670, **RealNetworks 9672**, Sarkowsky 9676, Seattle 9680, Shirley 9684, Shulman 9685, Simonyi 9686, **Starbucks 9690**, Tacoma 9693, True 9696, Warren 9700, Wright 9707, Wright 9708, Wyman 9709

West Virginia: BB&T 9710, Clay 9714, Community 9716, Daywood 9717, Hollowell 9719, Huntington 9721, Jacobson 9722, Kanawha 9723, McDonough 9726, Nutting 9729, Parkersburg 9730, Prichard 9731, Schenk 9732, Shott 9733

Wisconsin: Acuity 9739, Alexander 9741, Alliant 9742, AnnMarie 9743, Argosy 9747, Baird 9750, Banta 9752, Beloit 9757, Bishop 9759, Bolz 9762, **Bradley 9763**, Briggs 9765, Brookbank 9766, Brotz 9767, Bryce 9769, Chapman 9771, Clark 9773, Cleary 9774, Community 9776, Community 9777, Community 9778, Community 9779, Community 9780, Cudahy 9785, Dawes 9788, Delavan 9790, Demmer 9791, Dudley 9792, **Eastman 9794**, Eastman 9795, Evjue 9797, **Firestone 9798**, Fond du Lac 9800, Fort 9801, Fotsch 9802, Four 9803, Frautschi 9804, Green Bay 9810, Harley 9812, Helfaer 9813, Herzfeld 9815, Holz 9817, Jacobus 9819, Johnson 9823, Johnson 9826, Joy 9828, Kadish 9829, Keller 9831, Kenosha 9833, Kettering 9835, Kikkoman 9836, Kohl 9837, Kohler 9840, Krause 9841, Krause 9842, Kress 9844, La Crosse 9845, Ladish 9846, Ladish 9847, Lubar 9851, Lunda 9852, Madison 9854, Madison 9855, **Make 9856**, Managed 9857, Manpower 9858, Marcus 9859, Marshall 9860, Marshfield 9861, Martin 9862, Mason 9863, McDonough 9865, McQueen 9866, Mead 9867, Menasha 9869, Merrill 9872, MGue 9874, Miller 9875, Milwaukee 9876, MMG 9877, Modine 9878, Morse 9879, Munson 9880, Nicholas 9883, Northwestern 9884, Oshkosh 9885, Oshkosh 9887, **Outagamie 9888**, Overture 9889, **Palmer 9890**, Peck 9894, Peck 9895,

Peterson 9896, Pick 9899, Posner 9901, PPC 9902, Puelicher 9904, Purple 9905, Racine 9906, **Rockwell 9912**, Rolfs 9914, Rowland 9916, Schlegel 9919, Schoenleber 9921, Sensient 9922, Sentry 9923, Smallwood 9928, **Smith 9929**, Split 9932, St. Croix 9933, Stark 9935, **Stein 9937**, Stone 9940, Styberg 9944, Sub 9945, **Thrivent 9949**, Timken 9950, Uihlein 9953, Uihlein 9954, Uihlein 9955, Walter 9959, Waukesha 9960, Weill 9962, West 9964, Windhover 9966, Wisconsin 9967, Witte 9968, WPS 9970
Wyoming: Berry 9975, Community 9977, Connemara 9978, Martin 9984, McMurry 9985, S & G 9988, Scott 9991, Tozzi 9995, True 9996, Weiss 9997, Wyoming 10000

Arts councils

Arizona: Cooper 92
California: Fluor 523, Irvine 698
Delaware: Romill 1747
Georgia: Harris 2408
Michigan: Burdick 4241
Missouri: Boeing 4785
New York: Cappelli 5703
North Carolina: Hillsdale 7398
North Dakota: MDU 7517
Oklahoma: McCasland 7956
Tennessee: Cannon 8651, Schadt 8725

Arts education

Arkansas: **Windgate 189**
California: Alpert 208, Broccoli 326, Chapman 374, Cisco 388, Connell 412, **Coyne 424**, Eisner 481, Fluor 523, Greenberg 617, Haas 636, Hale 639, Hench 668, Hutto 693, JL 720, McBean 866, Mericos 889, Stuart 1208, Webb 1285
Connecticut: Bridgeport 1504
Delaware: **Birch 1692**, Wasily 1760
District of Columbia: Sprenger 1848
Florida: Bush 1922, Engelberg 1994, **Kaplan 2078**, Meyer 2137, Opler 2158, Peacock 2165, **Picower 2169**, Sherman 2233
Georgia: Community 2355
Illinois: Alphawood 2589, BCS 2612, Borwell 2627, **Buntrock 2643**, Cressey 2689, Deering 2700, Edwardson 2715, Fites 2730, Franke 2734, Gantz 2748, Lea 2850, Madigan 2869, Melrene 2892, Nichols 2916, Stewart 3024, Walk 3053, Wilemal 3070
Iowa: **Rockwell 3328**
Kentucky: Norton 3441
Maine: Horizon 3541
Maryland: **Blaustein 3575**, Cannon 3583
Massachusetts: Alden 3777, NBT 4048, Ratshesky 4095
Michigan: Community 4252, DeRoy 4273, Frey 4316, General 4320
Minnesota: **3M 4492**, Grossman 4578, McNeely 4619, McVay 4620, St. Paul 4690, **SUPERVALU 4695**, Xcel 4732
Missouri: American 4773, Lay 4853, **Monsanto 4868**
Nebraska: Fulk 4964
New Hampshire: Fuller 5090
New Jersey: **Lafitte 5293**, Victoria 5440
New Mexico: Santa Fe 5496
New York: Avery 5581, **Bay 5606**, **Citigroup 5755**, **Dana 5827**, **Dedalus 5847**, **Deutsche 5854**, Gelman 6014, Gibbs 6024, Gollust 6069, **Hearst 6161**, **Hearst 6162**, Heckscher 6164, Knox 6345, L and L 6366, Lauder 6382, Loewe 6441, Mai 6476, **MetLife 6542**, Pumpkin 6754, Rosenblum 6850, Rubinstein 6876, Sharp 6961, **Summerfield 7097**, **Surdna 7103**, Sussman 7104, **Teagle 7126**, Tully 7173
North Carolina: Kenan 7412, Perkins 7445, Woodward 7510
Ohio: Callahan 7564, Cleveland 7576, Corbett 7590, Dorn 7612, Hershey 7671, Stocker 7870
Pennsylvania: **Annenberg 8084**, Baker 8092, Bayer 8096, Buck 8123, **Carpenter 8131**, Cassett 8133,

Delphi 8168, Dietrich 8170, Eden 8182, England 8185, Grable 8221, Peterson 8376, PNC 8388, **Presser 8395**, von Hess 8493
South Carolina: Arkwright 8565, Montgomery 8600
Texas: Bass 8777, Brackenridge 8793, **EDS 8877**, Haggar 8931, Marcus 9029, Wal 9260
Utah: **ALSAM 9302**
Virginia: Rice 9504
Washington: Harvest 9602, Tacoma 9693
Wisconsin: Demmer 9791, Pollybill 9900
Wyoming: Kerr 9983

Arts, administration/regulation

New York: Sussman 7104
Tennessee: Jeniam 8695

Arts, alliance

Arizona: Neely 126
California: Sudikoff 1212
Delaware: **Robinson 1745**
Maryland: Baker 3567
New York: Brine 5665, Diller 5863, Rudin 6879, Schwartz 6945, Sussman 7104
Ohio: **Dewald 7608**
Washington: Murr 9645
West Virginia: Parkersburg 9730
Wisconsin: Stock 9939

Arts, artist's services

Alabama: Community 24
California: Community 407, Peninsula 989, San Francisco 1088
New York: **Tiffany 7137**, Violett 7200, **Warhol 7215**

Arts, association

Arizona: Herberger 106
Arkansas: Ross 174
California: Binder 291
Delaware: Hofmann 1722
District of Columbia: **Goldberg 1802**
Georgia: Harrison 2409
Illinois: Cooper 2683
Indiana: Tobias 3244
Iowa: Gilchrist 3287
Massachusetts: Greene 3933
Michigan: Hahn 4335
New York: Goldberg 6045, Loewe 6441, **Ohga 6658**
North Carolina: Reynolds 7459, Woodson 7509
Ohio: Bee 7542, Corbett 7590, Gund 7656, Nord 7780, Payne 7798
Oklahoma: McCasland 7956
Pennsylvania: Heinz 8240
Tennessee: Jeniam 8695
Texas: Garvey 8914
Wisconsin: McQueen 9866

Arts, cultural/ethnic awareness

Alaska: CIRI 83, Doyon 84
California: Avery-Tsui 245, **Chiron 383**, **Christensen 384**, Gere 565, **Getty 570**, Irvine 698, Nissan 939, Paloheimo 974, San Francisco 1088, Shenandoah 1144
Connecticut: Community 1514
Florida: Community 1943, Darden 1960
Georgia: **Scientific 2482**
Hawaii: Lange 2550
Illinois: Heritage 2797
Indiana: Central 3116, **Lilly 3192**, Noble 3214, Waterfield 3252
Iowa: HNI 3293, Principal 3326
Kentucky: Community 3415, E.ON 3417
Maryland: France 3632
Massachusetts: Morningside 4043
Michigan: **DaimlerChrysler 4265**, Frey 4316, General 4320, Mott 4400, Whirlpool 4480
Minnesota: HRK 4589, **Pentair 4649**, RBC 4661

Nebraska: Lincoln 4987
New Jersey: Alcatel 5110, **Carolan 5156**, Koguan 5284, Reddy 5364
New York: Altus 5547, **American 5553**, **Atran 5575**, **Hearst 6161**, **Hearst 6162**, **MetLife 6542**, Milstein 6554, New York 6617, Partridge 6695, **Rockefeller 6825**, **Rubin 6873**, Steinberg 7060
North Carolina: Foundation 7370
Pennsylvania: Berks 8103, **Berman 8104**, Comcast 8152, Pittsburgh 8386
Rhode Island: **Dorot 8531**
Texas: **Adams 8751**, Watson 9266
Utah: **Force 9322**, Semnani 9341
Virginia: AMERIGROUP 9369
Wisconsin: Green Bay 9810

Arts, equal rights

Illinois: Sara 2982
Iowa: Principal 3326
Kansas: Sprint 3395
Michigan: Comerica 4251
Minnesota: St. Paul 4690, Xcel 4732
North Carolina: **Wachovia 7502**
Pennsylvania: **PPG 8394**
Wisconsin: Alliant 9742, **Thrivent 9949**

Arts, folk arts

California: Irvine 698
Michigan: Frey 4316

Arts, formal/general education

California: **Field 504**
District of Columbia: **Patterson 1840**
Florida: Burns 1920, Engelberg 1994
Illinois: Bellebyron 2615
Indiana: Tobias 3244
Minnesota: HRK 4589
New Jersey: Johnson 5262
New York: Brine 5665, Moore 6572
Texas: Wedge 9270
Wisconsin: **Lewis 9850**

Arts, fund raising/fund distribution

Ohio: Oliver 7788

Arts, government agencies

Alabama: Finlay 33

Arts, management/technical aid

New Jersey: Johnson 5262

Arts, multipurpose centers/programs

California: **Coyne 424**, Irvine 698, La Fetra 782, Lurie 832
Colorado: Gates 1380, Schermer 1449
Connecticut: Community 1514, **Seedlings 1645**
Florida: Dade 1957, Hough 2066, Kaufman 2082, O'Keeffe 2154
Georgia: Jinks 2422, Lee 2432, Poe 2465
Illinois: Bielfeldt 2620, **Brunswick 2636**, Goldschmidt 2764
Indiana: Leighton 3191
Iowa: Deardorf 3280
Kansas: Downing 3358
Minnesota: Sewell 4678, Stone 4692, Vintage 4709, Winona 4744
New York: Castelnau 5715, Cedar 5721, Chu 5754, East 5901, Elmaleh 5924, Griffis 6107, Jacobson 6247, Levy 6411, Palm 6681, Richenthal 6798, Richmond 6803, Riggio 6807, Wender 7241
Ohio: Dorn 7612, Haile 7659
Oregon: Schnitzer 8056

Pennsylvania: Hodge 8254, Penn 8371, Susquehanna 8471
Tennessee: Clayton 8659, Tucker 8735
Texas: Kronkosky 9002, Once 9101
Virginia: Columbus 9399
Wisconsin: Phipps 9898, Rennebohm 9910

Arts, public education

California: Ransom 1032
Florida: Weiler 2290
Michigan: General 4320
New York: Tiffany 7137
Ohio: OMNOVA 7789

Arts, research

New York: American 5550, Brine 5665, Rose 6838

Arts, services

California: Peninsula 989
New York: Gelman 6014

Arts, single organization support

Minnesota: HRK 4589
New Jersey: Weisberg 5449
New York: 291 5505

Asians/Pacific Islanders

California: California 345, Stern 1195, Sun 1213
District of Columbia: Cafritz 1780
Florida: Chia 1933
Iowa: Siouxland 3332
Maryland: Hughes 3654
Massachusetts: Hyams 3961
Michigan: Grand Rapids 4326
Minnesota: Bell 4514, Blue 4521, Bremer 4523, Minneapolis 4623, Phillips 4655
New Mexico: Santa Fe 5496
New York: SMBC 7005
Ohio: Community 7582
Virginia: Gannett 9428

Asthma

California: Fansler 494, HealthCare 661
Connecticut: Newman's 1609
New Jersey: Aventis 5120

Asthma research

North Carolina: Davis 7353

Astronomy

Arizona: Research 134
California: Tabasgo 1224
Delaware: Bishop 1693
Montana: Edwards 4936
Texas: Meyer 9057

Athletics/sports, academies

California: Sambar 1085

Athletics/sports, amateur competition

California: Mac 840
Colorado: Aspen 1337
Nevada: Trans 5073

Athletics/sports, amateur leagues

California: Amateur 214
Colorado: Daniels 1362
Connecticut: Brainerd 1502

Florida: Dahl 1959
Massachusetts: Easthampton 3887
Nevada: Trans 5073
New York: Woods 7278
Pennsylvania: Roberts 8406
Virgin Islands: Prosser 9364
Virginia: Bryant 9380
Washington: Evertrust 9583

Athletics/sports, baseball

California: Gifford 574
Georgia: RTM 2477
Illinois: Aon 2598
Massachusetts: Davis 3874
Michigan: Dow 4288, Farver 4295
Wyoming: Stock 9992

Athletics/sports, equestrianism

California: Pfleger 999
Maryland: Greenberg 3639
Nebraska: Swanson 5009
New York: Fernleigh 5952, Hettinger 6178, Neuwirth 6612, **Silfen 6980**
Ohio: Broussard 7557, Stillson 7869
Oklahoma: Oxley 7968
Pennsylvania: Beaver 8098, Goodstein 8220, Triple 8482

Athletics/sports, fishing/hunting

Missouri: Sayler 4897
New York: Handler 6140

Athletics/sports, football

California: Reveas 1045
Georgia: Simpson 2489
Louisiana: Lorio 3496

Athletics/sports, golf

Arizona: Farrington 97
California: Lester 807
Colorado: International 1395
Georgia: Creel 2369, Marcus 2440
Illinois: Wadsworth 3050
Massachusetts: Easthampton 3887
Missouri: Emerson 4809
New York: Altman 5543, **Levy 6410**, **Silfen 6980**, Trump 7167
Texas: Westcott 9278
Virgin Islands: Prosser 9364

Athletics/sports, Olympics

California: M & T 837
New Jersey: IDT 5248
New York: Altus 5547, **Luckow 6455**

Athletics/sports, professional leagues

Wisconsin: Stock 9939

Athletics/sports, racquet sports

California: Gifford 574
Georgia: Jones 2424
Massachusetts: Stoneman 4167
Minnesota: Wells 4721
New York: Schott 6934, Walter 7212
Pennsylvania: Alter 8078, Goodstein 8220, Musser 8361, Roberts 8406
Tennessee: Hamico 8684

Athletics/sports, school programs

Alabama: Anderson 6

California: Eisner 481, Gifford 574, It 704, Rudd 1073
District of Columbia: Capital 1781
Florida: Anderson 1876
Illinois: Shirk 3007, Simmons 3008
New York: Altus 5547, Heckscher 6164, Martin 6496
Texas: McCombs 9037
Virginia: O'Shaughnessy 9487
Washington: Martin 9634
Wisconsin: Munson 9880

Athletics/sports, soccer

New York: Brown 5676
North Carolina: Kulynych 7416

Athletics/sports, Special Olympics

Alaska: Atwood 81
California: Anaheim 220, Segerstrom 1123
Florida: Overstreet 2159
Minnesota: Bieber 4518
Missouri: Smurfit-Stone 4906
Nevada: Omega 5050
New York: Ladenburg 6369
Oklahoma: Kerr 7950
Texas: O'Quinn 9097

Athletics/sports, training

California: Amateur 214, **M & T 837**
Colorado: McWhinney 1423
Indiana: Waterfield 3252
Nevada: Nevada 5048
Ohio: Creech 7597, **Kosar 7703**
Texas: Moore 9071
Wisconsin: Mason 9863

Athletics/sports, water sports

California: Volentine 1268
Florida: Gainesville 2015
Hawaii: Bakken 2534
Nevada: Rude 5058
New York: Mesdag 6539
Ohio: Coshocton 7593, **Vesper 7892**
Virginia: Dalis 9406
Wisconsin: Goldbach 9806

Athletics/sports, winter sports

Colorado: Vail 1468
New Jersey: Abar 5107, **Kontos 5286**
New York: Cader 5696
Rhode Island: Salem 8554
Utah: Wishnick 9353

Autism

California: Bireley 292, Gogian 588, HealthCare 661, Krach 779
Connecticut: Cohen 1512
Florida: Gemcon 2019
Massachusetts: Barry 3793, Tilson 4182
New York: Luckow 6455
Pennsylvania: FISA 8204

Autism research

Arizona: Noah's 127
California: JL 720
New Jersey: Geier 5204
New York: Hilibrand 6184, Simons 6989
Oregon: Holmes 8020, Northwest 8047
Tennessee: Thompson 8733

Big Brothers/Big Sisters

California: Carsey 361, Greenbaum 615, **Jack 705**, Kommerstad 772, **M & T 837**
Colorado: Fullerton 1378

Illinois: **Friedmann 2738**, Gloyd 2760, Martin 2874, Russell 2976, **Willow 3074**
Kansas: Capitol 3350
Massachusetts: Jacobson 3967
Nevada: Williams 5078
New York: Aeneas 5523, Dimon 5864, Gerhard 6015, Handler 6140, Liu 6437, Penson 6711, **Reed 6783**, Siegel 6976, Weinberg 7229
Ohio: Campbell 7565, **Deuble 7607**, Dorn 7612
Pennsylvania: S & T 8417
Texas: Haggar 8929, Sumners 9218
West Virginia: Prichard 9731
Wisconsin: AnnMarie 9743, Brotz 9767, Kettering 9835, McQueen 9866

Biological sciences

Arizona: Flinn 98
California: **Agouron 196**, **American 217**, **Beckman 272**, Bundy 332, **Christensen 384**, Genentech 562, Genentech 563, **Glenn 581**, **Hertz 670**, **Keck 750**, **Schlinger 1102**, Stauffer 1188
Connecticut: **Applera 1484**, Foster 1546
District of Columbia: Bernstein 1775
Florida: Banbury 1889, Keating 2084, **Whitehall 2297**
Maryland: **Hughes 3654**, **Life 3677**
Massachusetts: Cabot 3823, **Grass 3931**, Island 3965, Millipore 4040, **Sweet 4176**
Minnesota: Alworth 4499, Bell 4514, **Medtronic 4622**
Missouri: Kansas 4842, Schweppe 4899
Nevada: Fairweather 5032, Wiegand 5077
New Hampshire: **Dorr 5086**
New Jersey: **Allen 5111**, Capita 5154, **Carolan 5156**, Johnson 5263
New York: **Archbold 5563**, Chernow 5745, **Dana 5826**, **Guggenheim 6118**, **Heineman 6165**, **Institute 6232**, **Kade 6281**, **Mathers 6504**, McGonagle 6518, Miller 6550, O'Connor 6645, Pritchard 6748, Revson 6789, **Vetlesen 7196**
North Carolina: **Burroughs 7333**
Ohio: Schlink 7839
Oklahoma: Bernsen 7925, Puterbaugh 7970
Pennsylvania: ACE 8073, **Merck 8349**, **Pew 8377**, Rockwell 8408, Rosenfeld 8413
Texas: Dunn 8872, Elkins 8883, **Kleberg 8999**, Phillips 9122
Washington: **Hemingway 9606**

Biomedicine

California: Ahmanson 198, **Beckman 272**, Genentech 563, Irvine 699, Sierra 1151
Connecticut: Rosenthal 1638
Florida: Bastien 1892, Coulter 1954, Price 2177, **Vollmer 2282**
Georgia: Arnold 2319, Chatham 2347
Iowa: Carver 3274
Louisiana: Booth 3464
Maryland: **Hughes 3654**
Massachusetts: Foundation 3915, **Grass 3931**
Minnesota: Alworth 4499, **Wood 4731**
Missouri: Schweppe 4899
Nevada: Fairweather 5032
New Jersey: Healthcare 5228, **International 5252**, Kirby 5279
New York: **Archbold 5563**, **Chatterjee 5737**, **Cummings 5813**, **de Rothschild 5843**, **Engelhard 5932**, Glickenhaus 6042, Hazen 6159, **Heineman 6165**, **Kade 6281**, **Macy 6471**, McGonagle 6518, Nichols 6628, Perkin 6717, Smith 7009, Wendt 7243
North Carolina: Ryan 7469, Van Houten 7500
Oklahoma: Bernsen 7925
Oregon: Collins 8009
Pennsylvania: DSF 8178, **Pew 8377**, Smith 8443
Rhode Island: Daniels 8530
Texas: Ellwood 8884, Franklin 8907, Kempner 8987, Medallion 9051, Owsley 9108, Smith 9193
Utah: Eccles 9317, Eccles 9320
Virginia: Jeffress 9442
Washington: Glaser 9594, Norcliffe 9650
Wisconsin: McBeath 9864

Biomedicine research

California: Coates 391, Genentech 562
District of Columbia: **Lounsbery 1824**, True 1854
Florida: Fisher 1999, **Picower 2169**
Louisiana: Coypu 3471
Maryland: **Ellison 3621**
Massachusetts: Charles 3844, Pearce 4075
Missouri: **Lockton 4857**
New York: Hazen 6159, New York 6613, Orentreich 6667
Texas: Cameron 8811, Dickson 8866

Blind/visually impaired

California: Aaroe 192, Arata 229, Bundy 332, Jackson 706, Kirchgessner 762, Mericos 889, Ornest 959, Red 1035, Witherbee 1312
District of Columbia: Aid 1765, Hanley 1806
Florida: Driskill 1975
Illinois: **Buntrock 2643**, Cuneo 2692, Master 2875
Maryland: deForest 3612
Massachusetts: Lindsay 4009, Sawyer 4128
Michigan: Molinello 4395, Ratner 4417
New Jersey: Atkinson 5119
New York: Community 5782, D'Agostino 5818, Levine 6408, Oestreicher 6656, **Reader's 6778**, **Syde 7114**
Ohio: Fleming 7631, **Freygang 7640**, Frohman 7641
Pennsylvania: **Bannerot 8094**, Beatty 8097, Hodge 8254
Wisconsin: Helfaer 9813

Botanical gardens

Alabama: Hearin 37
Arizona: Farrington 97, Soling 140
California: Johnson 723, Lantz 790, Rogers 1062, **Schimmel 1101**
Connecticut: Lehrman 1584, Steere 1653, Tow 1660
Delaware: Beckwith 1689, Dickenson 1708
Georgia: Imlay 2417, JBS 2420
Illinois: Bellebyron 2615, Buehler 2638, Froehlich 2739, Harris 2788, Jahn 2816, Kemper 2831, Malott 2872, **Satter 2983**, Sirius 3010, Stone 3026, Sudix 3029, Wilson 3075
Iowa: Beckwith 3266
Louisiana: Azby 3460
Massachusetts: Fessenden 3903, Stamps 4155
Michigan: Frey 4316, Meijer 4390
Minnesota: Drew 4554
Missouri: Bellwether 4782, Boeing 4785, Holekamp 4832, Jordan 4840, Lichtenstein 4855, Litzsinger 4856, Lopata 4859, Pershing 4880, Reding 4890
Nebraska: Abbott 4942
New Jersey: Quercus 5363
New York: Acorn 5515, Butler 5691, Cole 5774, Davidson 5835, Doran 5875, Gerry 6016, Gerschel 6019, Goldfrank 6048, Green 6095, Hagedorn 6130, Kupferberg 6363, LBC 6386, Orentreich 6667, Pumpkin 6754, Rose 6834, Schnurmacher 6931
North Carolina: Adams 7305, Stowe 7487
Ohio: DBJ 7605, Dornette 7613, Mixon 7757, Nord 7780, Outcalt 7792, Schott 7842, **Vesper 7892**
Oregon: Salem 8054
Pennsylvania: **Beneficia 8100**, Chanticleer 8140
Texas: Bass 8777
Utah: **Hayward 9327**
Virginia: Herndon 9437
Wisconsin: Merrill 9872, Pollybill 9900, West 9964

Botanical/horticulture/landscape services

California: La Fetra 782
Georgia: Community 2362
Indiana: Community 3122
Minnesota: Bailey 4510
Missouri: Stupp 4911
New York: Peco 6703, Richardson 6797
Oregon: **Schmidt 8055**
Pennsylvania: Hawksglen 8238

South Carolina: Rainey 8605
Washington: Miller 9642

Botany

Florida: Vaughn 2279
New York: Gerry 6016

Boy scouts

Alabama: Wyker 77
Arkansas: Murphy 167
California: Deutsch 451, First 511, Fremont 535, MacNaughton 844, Martin 860, Munzer 927, Pardee 978, Tomlinson 1238, Waltmar 1277
Colorado: **Hansen 1388**
Delaware: Romill 1747
District of Columbia: Merriman 1833
Florida: Baxter 1895, **Cobb 1936**, Einstein 1991, Hilton 2061
Georgia: Colonial 2353, Love 2437, Williams 2516
Hawaii: Kosasa 2549
Illinois: Cabe 2648, Emerson 2719, Meyer 2895
Indiana: ADL 3097, Met 3204, Oakley 3217
Iowa: Krause 3302
Maryland: Osprey 3703, Rosenberg 3720
Massachusetts: Connell 3856, Levy 4005
Minnesota: Radichel 4660, Sit 4683, **Toro 4702**
Mississippi: AmSouth 4733, Taylor 4767
Missouri: **Humphreys 4833**, Musgrave 4870, Remington 4891
Nevada: Harris 5035
New Jersey: **James 5254**, **Reeves 5365**
New Mexico: **Gorham 5478**
New York: Black 5636, Buck 5682, Dimon 5864, Lee 6391, Weil 7225, Zehner 7293
North Carolina: Jolley 7407, **Morris 7432**, Rostan 7467
Ohio: Coleman 7579, **Cooper 7589**, Frost 7642, Schiewetz 7835
Pennsylvania: Bozzone 8114, McDonald's 8333, Mengle 8347, S & T 8417
South Carolina: Cline 8580, TSC 8618
Tennessee: Caldwell 8649, Haslam 8687, Hawthorn 8689
Texas: Cox 8850, Estill 8888, Fleming 8903, Furst 8911, **Mevatek 9056**, Owen 9107, Prairie 9129, Simmons 9187, Sumners 9218, West 9274, Williams 9283
Vermont: Mergens 9360
Virgin Islands: Prosser 9364
Virginia: Moore 9478
Washington: UNOVA 9697
West Virginia: McQuain 9727
Wisconsin: Bartlett 9753, Bryant 9768, Charter 9772, Keller 9831

Boys & girls clubs

Alabama: Anderson 6, Lowder 42, Lowe 45
Arizona: Arizona 87, Moreno 123, Robson 135
Arkansas: Murphy 167, Tenenbaum 180, Trinity 181, **Tyson 182**, Whitt 188
California: Blume 298, Brenner 321, Broccoli 326, Chambers 372, Cheeryble 377, Doelger 459, First 511, Fitzpatrick 515, Hartley 653, House 687, Ingold 695, **Issa 703**, Jackson 706, Janeway 712, Johnson 723, Koenig 770, MacDonald 841, Magali 846, Markkula 856, Morgan 914, Munzer 927, Neilsen 934, Pardee 978, Phelps 1002, Pralle 1014, Reinhold 1039, **Schlinger 1102**, Short 1148, Teichert 1231, Tomlinson 1238, Waltmar 1277, **Whalen 1299**, WWW 1323
Colorado: Caulkins 1353, International 1395, Monfort 1428
Connecticut: GW 1561, Kohn 1575, Lavietes 1581, Mandell 1595, Meriden 1603, Pitt 1628
Delaware: Sternlicht 1756
District of Columbia: Harman 1807, Merriman 1833
Florida: Baxter 1895, Cascone 1926, Dunspaugh 1981, Eckerd 1986, GTE 2040, Huizenga 2068, Libra 2115, Martin 2130, Rebozo 2190, Six 2236, **Tupperware 2275**, Watts 2288, Weiller 2291

Georgia: Coca 2350, Daft 2370, Williams 2516, Woodruff 2522
Illinois: **Aon 2598**, Camp 2649, Farrell 2725, Gantz 2748, Gidwitz 2755, Hobbs 2802, Istock 2815, Jahn 2816, Russell 2976, Stone 3026, Winfrey 3077
Indiana: Citizens 3118, Michigan 3205
Iowa: Levitt 3307
Kansas: Capitol 3350
Kentucky: Young 3454
Maine: Gardiner 3536, Hannaford 3540
Maryland: Community 3600, Davis 3606, Davis 3607, Thunder 3746
Massachusetts: Acushnet 3770, Bain 3788, Bertolon 3804, Birmingham 3807, Boston 3813, Bristol 3816, Byrnes 3821, Crane 3866, Cummings 3871, DeLuca 3877, Foundation 3916, Gabrieli 3919, Haley 3939, Jordan 3971, Kessler 3978, Klarman 3985, Knez 3986, Knight 3987, Lubin 4016, Narada 4047, **Remillard 4100**, Rubenstein 4116, Smith 4149, Wilson 4205, Woronoco 4210
Michigan: Dart 4267, Dauch 4268, Eddy 4292, Ford 4304, Jurries 4350, Mackey 4380, Padnos 4406, Ravitz 4418, Thomas 4456
Minnesota: **Best 4516**, Dennis 4550, O'Neil 4638, Radichel 4660
Mississippi: AmSouth 4733, Skelton 4765
Missouri: Hammons 4826, Musgrave 4870, Orscheln 4877, Smith 4905
Nebraska: Arkoosh 4943, Muchemore 4992, Wiebe 5017
Nevada: May 5046
New Jersey: Hill 5236, Ross 5376, Union 5435, Valley 5438, Weny 5450
New York: Bachmann 5587, Baird 5592, Charitable 5733, DeGeorge 5848, Dunwalke 5894, Equinox 5935, Fatta 5947, Goldschmidt 6058, Hirsch 6188, Kellogg 6310, Leventhal 6406, Lisabeth 6433, Loeb 6439, McGraw 6519, Mordecai 6575, Perella 6715, Raether 6766, Silberstein 6979, Turn 7174, Walter 7212
North Carolina: High Point 7397, Jolley 7407
Ohio: Campbell 7565, **Deuble 7607**, Dorn 7612, Miniger 7756, R.T. 7812, Williams 7907
Oregon: Ackerman 7995, Bair 7998, Schnitzer 8056
Pennsylvania: McDonald's 8333
Rhode Island: Roosa 8552
South Carolina: Lipscomb 8598, **Security's 8609**
Tennessee: EBS 8672, Goldsmith 8682, Haslam 8687, Potter 8720, T & T 8731
Texas: Baker 8772, Estill 8888, Holthouse 8959, Meyer 9057, Owen 9106, Sooch 9200, Unkefer 9243, Vergara 9253, Waggoner 9256, Waggoner 9257, Westcott 9278, Wolslager 9290, Wright 9293
Vermont: Mergens 9360
Virginia: Billings 9377, Houff 9438, Reinhart 9502, Reynolds 9503
Washington: Evertrust 9583, O'Donnell 9652, PEMCO 9660
West Virginia: McDonough 9726
Wisconsin: Anon 9744, Brotz 9767, Community 9779, Gordon 9808, Hyde 9818, Kadish 9829, Kohl 9837, Krejci 9843, Kress 9844, Lakeview 9848, McQueen 9866, Oshkosh 9887, Soref 9930, Stock 9939, Uihlein 9955, Wehr 9961, West 9963

Boys clubs

Arkansas: Tenenbaum 180
California: Garaventa 553
Florida: Sanders 2215
Georgia: Creel 2369, Franklin 2389
New Jersey: **James 5254**
New York: Dimon 5864, Gordon 6076, Osborn 6669
North Carolina: Jenkins 7406
West Virginia: Prichard 9731

Brain disorders

California: Hillblom 673
New York: Dana 5825

Brain research

California: Preuss 1015
Florida: McKnight 2134, **Sontag 2239**
Illinois: Siragusa 3009
Missouri: **McDonnell 4864**
New Jersey: Branfman 5142
New York: Dana 5825
North Carolina: Reynolds 7460
Ohio: Fairfax 7621
Washington: Talaris 9694

Breast cancer

California: HealthCare 661
Florida: Cejas 1930, Gordon 2030, Hard 2047
Illinois: Siragusa 3009
New Jersey: **Wall 5445**
New York: **Avon 5583**, Herdrich 6173, Karan 6291
Ohio: Kroger 7705
Pennsylvania: CIGNA 8143
Texas: Dauphin 8856, Keithley 8983
Virginia: N.E.W. 9482

Breast cancer research

California: Cusenza 433
Connecticut: Nirenberg 1613
Florida: Hard 2047
Nevada: **Omega 5050**
New York: **Avon 5583**, Chernow 5745, D'Agostino 5818, Hurdus 6214, Klingenstein 6337, Lauder 6382, McGraw 6519, **Quick 6761**, Richardson 6796
Pennsylvania: Cooper 8158
Texas: Smith 9192

Buddhism

California: Guzik 632, **Lenz 803**, Paramitas 977
Massachusetts: **A & A 3764**, **Hershey 3949**, Tara 4179
Michigan: Ford 4300
Missouri: **Hana 4827**
New York: Bukkyo 5685, **Tsadra 7169**
Pennsylvania: Dietrich 8170

Business school/education

California: Avery 244, **Bechtel 269**, Binder 291, Dollens 462, Kanitz 742, Lester 807, Long 825, Mayr 863, Pickford 1005, Schow 1107, Stephenson 1193, Union 1250
Colorado: Monfort 1429, Trueblood 1466
Connecticut: Barnes 1488, Berkley 1492, **Deloitte 1527**, Feuerman 1538, **GE 1553**, Rosenthal 1638, Royce 1639
District of Columbia: Brody 1777, Loughran 1823
Florida: Chia 1933, Kaufman 2082, Rosenberg 2206
Georgia: Harris 2408, Holder 2413
Illinois: **Allstate 2588**, Atlas 2603, Coleman 2673, Cressey 2689, Hartmarx 2794, **Irwin 2814**, Madigan 2869, Mead 2888, **Niamogue 2914**, Olin 2925, **State 3019**
Indiana: Community 3125, Moore 3207
Iowa: Maytag 3309, Principal 3326
Kansas: Sprint 3395
Maryland: Merrill 3689
Massachusetts: Cabot 3823, Connell 3856, Evans 3898, Keane 3975, Rubenstein 4116
Michigan: Comerica 4251, **DaimlerChrysler 4265**, **DENSO 4272**, Ford 4307, General 4320, Grand Haven 4325, World 4489
Minnesota: **3M 4492**, McNeely 4619, Morning 4627, **Patterson 4647**, Wedum 4719, Xcel 4732
Missouri: Boeing 4785, Shaw 4901
Nebraska: Eihusen 4961
Nevada: Wiegand 5077
New Jersey: Amirsaleh 5114, **KPMG 5288**
New Mexico: Frost 5476, Hubbard 5481
New York: American 5552, **Bobolink 5645**, Cain 5697, Charina 5731, **Chazen 5739**, **Citigroup 5755**, Eig 5914, Emwiga 5930, Evans 5940, Everett 5941,

Goldsmith 6060, Gordon 6076, Handler 6140, Harbor 6144, Kadrovach 6282, Kempner 6313, **Kopf 6348**, Kurtz 6364, Lindsay 6427, Martin 6496, Moody's 6569, New York 6619, O'Connor 6645, O'Herron 6646, Paul 6697, Perella 6715, PTM 6752, R & TP 6764, **Ripplewood 6812**, Schwartz 6938, Stanton 7044, Statler 7050, Stein 7056, T-4 7116, Tormondsen 7154, Wiegers 7256, Wildwood 7259, Winkelried 7265
North Carolina: Halton 7386, Kenan 7413, V.F. 7498
North Dakota: MDU 7517
Ohio: Broussard 7557, Charities 7569, Morgan 7761, Nationwide 7771, Stark 7867, Troy 7886, Williamson 7908
Oklahoma: Crawley 7934
Oregon: Knight 8032
Pennsylvania: CIGNA 8143, Little 8313, **PPG 8394**, **United 8488**, Zisman 8513
South Carolina: South 8615
Texas: **A Glimmer 8747**, Abell 8749, **Anderson 8761**, El Paso 8882, Franklin 8907, Hillcrest 8952, Marathon 9028, Penney 9115, **Shell 9181**
Utah: Caine 9310
Virginia: Batten 9374, Universal 9531
Washington: **Boeing 9560**, Jones 9615
Wisconsin: Johnson 9826, Menasha 9869, Northwestern 9884, Steigleder 9936, Stuart 9942
Wyoming: Chapman 9976

Business/industry

Alabama: **Vulcan 73**
California: Moss 921, Short 1148, Union 1250
Connecticut: Community 1514, **Xerox 1680**
Illinois: **Burlington 2644**, Grand 2769
Indiana: East Chicago 3144
Iowa: **AEGON 3259**
Maryland: GEICO 3634
Michigan: **DaimlerChrysler 4265**, **H.I.S. 4334**
Minnesota: Graco 4573
Mississippi: **Armstrong 4734**
Missouri: American 4773
Nevada: **Lemelson 5040**
New York: **American 5553**, **Citigroup 5755**, **Merrill 6537**, Zankel 7289
Ohio: **Longaberger 7722**, Stranahan 7872
Pennsylvania: Comcast 8152
Texas: Marathon 9028, **Shell 9181**, Texas 9232
Virginia: SunTrust 9523, Universal 9531
Washington: **Weyerhaeuser 9703**

Camp Fire

Texas: Perkins 9116

Campaign finance reform

Massachusetts: Orchard 4062
New York: **Carnegie 5707**

Cancer

Alabama: Blount 13, Bolden 15, Brock 16
Arizona: Neely 125
Arkansas: Pruet 170
California: Barth 258, **Beckman 272**, Bireley 292, Bowes 310, Campini 353, **Chiron 383**, Cohen 393, Davidow 444, Early 473, Gershman 567, Goldberg 593, Gross 621, Hench 668, Leatherby 796, Lester 807, Lipinsky 816, **Mac 840**, McGrath 875, Milken 897, Milken 898, Miller 899, Mogharebi 905, Mozilo 923, Norris 940, O'Connor 946, Outhwaite 966, Rey 1046, San Francisco 1088, Sarver 1095, Sebastiani 1119, Setzer 1130, Shapiro 1138, Sprague 1183, Tallen 1225, Wolfen 1316, Wrather 1321, Zyskind 1330
Colorado: Leprino 1408, Monfort 1429, Schramm 1451, Wolf 1475
Connecticut: Barnes 1488, Dartley 1524, Fippinger 1540, Flinn 1543, Hubbell 1569, Lee 1582,

Cancer research

Cancer, leukemia

Cancer, leukemia research

Cemeteries/burial services

Cerebral palsy

Cerebral palsy research

New York: Alpern 5540, Goldenson 6047
Pennsylvania: Cassett 8133
Wisconsin: Walter 9959

Chemistry

Arizona: **Research 134**
California: **American 217, Beckman 272, Hertz 670, Keck 750,** Stauffer 1188
Colorado: Hach 1386
Idaho: **Micron 2571**
Massachusetts: Cabot 3823
Michigan: Dow 4284
Minnesota: Alworth 4499
Nevada: Wiegand 5077
New Hampshire: **Dorr 5086**
New York: **Dreyfus 5886, Frasch 5979, Heineman 6165, Kade 6281**
Texas: Cain 8809, **Shell 9181,** Welch 9273
Virginia: Jeffress 9442

Child development, education

Alabama: Community 23
Arizona: Arizona 87, Dee 94
Arkansas: Walton 186
California: Atkinson 239, Atlas 241, Copley 416, Crail 426, **Field 504,** Fieldstone 506, Fireman's 510, Gilmore 578, Gross 621, Lurie 832, Mericos 889, Milken 898, **Panda 975,** Peninsula 989, Rosenberg 1066, Sacramento 1080, San Diego 1087, San Francisco 1088, Sierra 1151, Soda 1173, Sonora 1178, Weingart 1288
Colorado: Chambers 1354, El Pomar 1374, Weckbaugh 1470
Connecticut: Bodenwein 1497, Community 1515, Connecticut 1518, FSB 1549, Hartford 1563, Long 1590, Rosenthal 1638
District of Columbia: Cafritz 1780, Fowler 1797, Meyer 1834
Florida: Bank 1890, Bastien 1892, Beveridge 1907, Community 1946, Henderson 2056, Phillips 2168, Rosenberg 2206, Selby 2230, Waldbaum 2285
Georgia: Cox 2367, Patterson 2460, Spray 2495, WinShape 2520
Illinois: Chicago 2661, Community 2677, Harris 2789, Kendall 2833, Polk 2946, Siragusa 3009
Indiana: Portland 3223
Iowa: Community 3278, McElroy 3313, Principal 3326, Siouxland 3332
Kansas: Westar 3403
Louisiana: Baton Rouge 3462, Booth 3464
Maryland: Abell 3559, Commonweal 3596
Massachusetts: Alden 3777, Boston 3812, Community 3854, Ellsworth 3892, New 4050, Peabody 4073, Schott 4132
Michigan: Battle Creek 4228, Frey 4316, Skillman 4438, Whirlpool 4480
Minnesota: Bell 4514, Bigelow 4519, Blue 4521, Bremer 4523, Duluth 4556, HRK 4589, Mardag 4613, Minneapolis 4623, Rochester 4668
Missouri: Green 4822, H & R 4823, Hall 4824, Hallmark 4825, Herschend 4830, Pettus 4882, Sunnen 4913
Nebraska: Lincoln 4987
New Jersey: Borden 5138, Cowles 5170, Hyde 5247, **Johnson 5265,** MCJ 5324
New Mexico: McCune 5488, Santa Fe 5496
New York: Central 5724, Drexler 5885, Glickenhaus 6042, Heckscher 6164, **Heineman 6165,** Hoyt 6203, **Kaufmann 6299,** Leach 6388, Mosse 6590, New York 6613, New York 6617, **New 6621,** Northern 6639, O'Connor 6645, Rochester 6823, **Ross 6863,** Shoolman 6967, Spunk 7036, Western 7248
North Carolina: Broyhill 7328, Cemala 7337, Community 7344, Cumberland 7349, Reynolds 7457, Reynolds 7458, Reynolds 7459, Triangle 7496, Van Houten 7500
North Dakota: Leach 7516, Stern 7521

Ohio: Columbus 7580, Coshocton 7593, Dater 7600, Hershey 7671, Jergens 7689, Nord 7779, Richland 7819, Schmidlapp 7841, Stark 7867, **Timken 7880,** Toledo 7883, Troy 7886, Watson 7896, Youngstown 7920
Oregon: Carpenter 8003, Meyer 8042
Pennsylvania: Arcadia 8086, Blue 8112, Buhl 8124, Connelly 8157, Dolfinger 8172, Grable 8221, Nelson 8362, Penn 8371, **Pew 8377,** PNC 8388, Scranton 8431, Smith 8445
South Carolina: Central 8577, Coastal 8581
Tennessee: Community 8660, HCA 8690
Texas: Austin 8768, Bass 8777, Edwards 8880, Elkins 8883, George 8916, **Jenesis 8971,** Kempner 8987, Meadows 9049, Morris 9076, Rockwell 9154, San Antonio 9166, Scott 9174, Simmons 9188, Sterling 9212, Trull 9240, Wright 9294
Vermont: **Ben 9355,** Vermont 9361
Virginia: Estes 9415, Memorial 9474, Norfolk 9484
Washington: Community 9571, **Hemingway 9606, Kongsgaard 9620,** Raikes 9668, Tacoma 9693
West Virginia: Parkersburg 9730
Wisconsin: Bryce 9769, Hess 9816, Madison 9854, Milwaukee 9876, Siebert 9927, Smallwood 9928

Child development, services

Arizona: Arizona 87, Dee 94
California: Atkinson 239, Atlas 241, Bella 275, Bothin 309, Copley 416, Crail 426, Fieldstone 506, Fireman's 510, Gilmore 578, Gross 621, Mericos 889, Milken 898, Ornest 959, **Packard 972,** Peninsula 989, Rosenberg 1066, Sacramento 1080, San Diego 1087, San Francisco 1088, Sierra 1151, Sonora 1178, Weingart 1288
Colorado: El Pomar 1374, Norwood 1433, Rose 1445, Telluride 1465, Weckbaugh 1470
Connecticut: Bodenwein 1497, Community 1515, Connecticut 1518, Hartford 1563, Long 1590, Rosenthal 1638
Delaware: Mastronardi 1729
District of Columbia: Bernstein 1775, Cafritz 1780, Fowler 1797, Meyer 1834
Florida: Bank 1890, Bastien 1892, Beveridge 1907, Engelberg 1994, Gemcon 2019, Henderson 2056, Kennedy 2087, Phillips 2168, Rosenberg 2206, Selby 2230, Waldbaum 2285
Georgia: Cox 2367, Dunn 2375, Harland 2407, Patterson 2460, WinShape 2520
Hawaii: Castle 2538
Illinois: Chicago 2661, Community 2677, Community 2679, Crane 2687, Harris 2789, Kendall 2833, Polk 2946, Siragusa 3009
Iowa: Community 3278, McElroy 3313, Siouxland 3332
Kansas: Hutchinson 3368
Louisiana: Baton Rouge 3462, Booth 3464
Maryland: Commonweal 3596, Freeman 3633
Massachusetts: Alden 3777, Boston 3812, Community 3854, Crawford 3867, Ellsworth 3892, New 4050, Peabody 4073, Rubenstein 4115
Michigan: Battle Creek 4228, Frey 4316, **Mott 4399,** Skillman 4438
Minnesota: Bell 4514, Bigelow 4519, Bremer 4523, Duluth 4556, Mardag 4613, McKnight 4617, Minneapolis 4623, Rochester 4668
Missouri: Green 4822, H & R 4823, Hall 4824, Herschend 4830, Pettus 4882, Sunnen 4913
Nebraska: Lincoln 4987
New Jersey: Borden 5138, Cowles 5170, Hyde 5247, **Johnson 5265,** MCJ 5324
New Mexico: McCune 5488, New Mexico 5491, Santa Fe 5496, Thornburg 5501
New York: Central 5724, Cummings 5815, Eberstadt 5904, Glickenhaus 6042, **Guggenheim 6118, Heineman 6165, Kaufmann 6299,** Kenworthy 6315, **Klingenstein 6340,** Leach 6388, Mosse 6590, Northern 6639, **NoVo 6641,** O'Connor 6645, Pincus 6726, Rochester 6823, **Ross 6863,** Schenectady 6915, Shoolman 6967, Sirus 6992, Spunk 7036
North Carolina: Broyhill 7328, Community 7344, Cumberland 7349, Reynolds 7457, Triangle 7496, Van Houten 7500

North Dakota: Leach 7516, Stern 7521
Ohio: Bicknell 7548, Columbus 7580, Coshocton 7593, Dater 7600, Hershey 7671, Nord 7779, Richland 7819, Schmidlapp 7841, Stark 7867, **Timken 7880,** Toledo 7883, Troy 7886, Watson 7896, Wean 7898, Youngstown 7920
Oregon: Carpenter 8003, Meyer 8042
Pennsylvania: Arcadia 8086, Buhl 8124, Connelly 8157, Dolfinger 8172, Haas 8230, Nelson 8362, Penn 8371, **Pew 8377,** Scranton 8431, Smith 8445, York 8511
South Carolina: Central 8577
Tennessee: **Bridgestone 8646,** Community 8660, HCA 8690
Texas: Austin 8768, Bass 8777, Edwards 8880, Elkins 8883, George 8916, Hoglund 8956, **Jenesis 8971,** Kempner 8987, King 8995, Meadows 9049, Morris 9076, Rockwell 9154, San Antonio 9166, Scott 9174, Sterling 9212, Trull 9240, Weaver 9267, Wright 9294
Vermont: Vermont 9361
Virgin Islands: Community 9363
Virginia: Freddie 9422, Memorial 9474, Norfolk 9484
Washington: Blue 9559, Community 9571, **Hemingway 9606, Kongsgaard 9620,** Norcliffe 9650, Schuler 9678, Tacoma 9693
West Virginia: Parkersburg 9730
Wisconsin: Bryce 9769, Hess 9816, McBeath 9864, Milwaukee 9876, Siebert 9927, **Taylor 9947**

Children

California: **Chiron 383, Jack 705,** McKesson 879, Oakland 948, Peninsula 989, SHP 1149, Teichert 1231
Connecticut: **Aetna 1479,** Mortensen 1605
Florida: Batchelor 1893, Gooding 2028
Georgia: Aflac 2311, Community 2358, Williams 2515
Illinois: Abbott 2580, CNA 2670, Illinois 2812, Logan 2860, Northern 2918
Louisiana: Toms 3512
Michigan: Community 4252
Minnesota: Blue 4521, Cargill 4530, **Fuller 4567**
Missouri: **Monsanto 4868, Nestle 4872**
Nebraska: ConAgra 4952
New Jersey: OceanFirst 5341, PSEG 5361
New Mexico: Taos 5498
New York: Community 5785, Countess 5800, **Foundation 5971, Morgan 6577,** Rochester 6823, Schenectady 6915, Shoolman 6967
Ohio: A Good 7522, Hoover 7674
Pennsylvania: Blue 8112, Philadelphia 8378, Rangos 8400, Seiple 8432, Stop 8463
Rhode Island: CVS 8529, Hasbro 8539
South Carolina: Waccamaw 8619
Tennessee: **Bridgestone 8646**
Texas: Sterling 9212
Vermont: Vermont 9361
Virginia: CarMax 9385, Community 9400
Washington: PACCAR 9656, **Weyerhaeuser 9703**
Wisconsin: **Reiman 9908**

Children, adoption

Georgia: Singletary 2490
Maine: **Sandy 3555**
Massachusetts: **A Child 3765**
New York: Achelis 5513, Bodman 5647
Texas: Bailey 8771, Benson 8788, **Swett 9221**
Wisconsin: **Make 9856**

Children, day care

Alabama: Community 24
California: Baxter 262, Orfalea 958, PacifiCare 971, Santa Barbara 1093, Stuart 1208, Stulsaft 1210
Colorado: Buell 1350, Rose 1445, Telluride 1465
Florida: duPont 1983, Fortin 2007, Moran 2143
Illinois: Grand 2769, Weiss 3062
Indiana: Lafayette 3188
Michigan: Berrien 4231, Frey 4316, Whirlpool 4480
Minnesota: **SUPERVALU 4695**

Mississippi: Skelton 4765
New Jersey: PSEG 5361
New York: **Citigroup 5755**, Eastern 5902, Gimbel 6034, Gorman 6078, Herdrich 6173, **Heron 6176**, Lenna 6402, Mallah 6481, New York 6618, Roslyn 6859, St. Faith's 7039
Ohio: Akron 7526
Tennessee: CLARCOR 8658, Promethean 8721
Texas: **Dell 8863**, **EDS 8877**, Penney 9115, Waco 9255
Wisconsin: Madison 9854

Children, foster care

California: McGrath 875, Solano 1175, Stuart 1206, Stulsaft 1210, vanLobenSels 1260
Florida: Community 1941, Moran 2143
Missouri: Casey 4795
New York: DeCamp 5845, Heckscher 6164, Rosenberg 6845, Schaffer 6911, Taconic 7117, Warner 7216
Texas: Bailey 8771
Virginia: Freddie 9422
Washington: Casey 9566

Children, services

Alabama: Alpha 3, Anderson 6, May 46, Treadwell 68
Arizona: Lewis 116
Arkansas: Hussman 165, Jones 166
California: Amar 213, American 215, Bannerman 255, Bella 275, **Benson 280**, Cantus 355, **Capital 357**, Craig 425, DeVito 452, **Draper 465**, Family 493, Five 516, **Flextronics 519**, Flora 521, Gallo 548, Gershman 566, Geschke 568, Gross 622, **GSF 627**, Guest 630, Hofmann 683, Leichtman 802, Lund 831, Maag 838, Markkula 856, **Mattel 861**, Morton 919, My 930, Penney 990, Reinhold 1039, **Reveas 1045**, **Saban 1079**, Semel 1125, Serenity 1128, Shea 1142, Siebel 1150, Simms 1155, Stephenson 1193, Waltmar 1277, Wells 1295
Colorado: Kern 1402, Lazarus 1406, Liniger 1411, **Mercy 1426**, Richardson 1444, Rose 1445
Connecticut: Bondi 1499, Bridgemill 1503, Dartley 1524, **Davis 1526**, **Macauley 1592**, Perrin 1626, Tow 1660, **Vranos 1673**
Delaware: Beckwith 1689, Hamel 1719, Mastronardi 1729
District of Columbia: **Coyne 1788**, Friedman 1799, Leonsis 1822, Reich 1845, True 1854
Florida: **Anderson 1876**, Bernstein 1904, Darden 1960, Dennis 1969, Dickins 1972, Hard 2047, **Hardison 2048**, Jasam 2074, **Knight 2097**, Leiser 2108, Libra 2115, Plangere 2172, Publix 2180, Sykes 2261, Taylor 2267, **Tupperware 2275**, Weiler 2290
Georgia: Brown 2331, Community 2357, Imlay 2417, Lanier 2431, Spray 2495, **UPS 2503**
Hawaii: HMSA 2547
Illinois: **Allen 2587**, Endless 2720, Herro 2799, Houlsby 2805, Kainz 2822, Kazma 2827, Kenny's 2835, Lumpkin 2864, McDaniel 2880, **Mundi 2908**, Opler 2927, Pasquinelli 2933, Schmidt 2986, Tully 3040, Walsh 3055, Winfrey 3077, Wonderful 3080, **Woodbury 3082**, Zurich 3093
Indiana: Samerian 3234
Iowa: Bright 3269, Maytag 3309
Kentucky: **Humana 3428**, Woosley 3453
Louisiana: Helis 3486, Institute 3489
Maine: JTG 3542
Maryland: Allegis 3565, Baker 3566, Community 3600, Rosenberg 3720, Straus 3738, Ten 3743
Massachusetts: Adams 3771, Association 3783, Chafetz 3842, Charles 3844, Community 3854, Davis 3874, Eastern 3886, Foundation 3915, Jacobson 3967, Kraft 3989, Lindsay 4009, Roddy 4108, Schott 4132, Stamps 4155, **TJX 4183**
Michigan: Christian 4247, Ford 4300, Frey 4316, **McDonald 4388**, **Mott 4399**
Minnesota: **Cafesjian 4527**, **Patterson 4647**, People 4650, Prophet 4658, **Robins 4667**, Schmidt 4673, **Weyerhaeuser 4725**
Mississippi: **Seal 4764**
Missouri: Brown 4788, Carter 4794, Community 4798, Jewish 4837, Lay 4853, Price 4888, Simon 4903

Nebraska: Heuermann 4973
Nevada: Bennett 5021, **Walsh 5075**
New Hampshire: von Weber 5104
New Jersey: Aventis 5120, Geier 5204, Hickory 5232, Summit 5417, Wang 5448
New York: Altus 5547, Amicus 5557, **Atlantic 5574**, Atticus 5576, **Avon 5583**, Bachmann 5587, **Barnett 5601**, Black 5636, **Bobolink 5645**, Brine 5665, **Brunie 5679**, **Cranaleith 5805**, Danziger 5829, Freston 5982, Gerhard 6015, Goldstein 6062, Grandison 6087, Haas 6127, Haseltine 6152, Heckscher 6164, Heller 6169, Hilibrand 6184, Ingrassia 6230, Jarx 6255, Jones 6274, **JPMorgan 6277**, Kaplan 6289, Kaylie 6301, Kingdon 6326, Lehman 6396, Leibowitz 6398, Leonhardt 6403, Leventhal 6406, Lincoln 6423, Magen 6472, **MetLife 6542**, Neuwirth 6612, Niehaus 6631, Peco 6703, Pincus 6726, **Richmond 6801**, Riggio 6807, **Ripplewood 6812**, Saligman 6895, Scheuer 6920, Schwartz 6938, Silver 6981, Sitt 6996, SO 7015, Textor 7131, Tisch 7146, Warner 7216, Weiler 7226, **Weinberg 7228**, Weinman 7232, Wender 7241
North Carolina: Anonymous 7306, Gipson 7375, Hendrick 7395, Holding 7399, Livingstone 7422
Ohio: A Good 7522, Cotswold 7594, Lennon 7710, Levin 7712, **Sankey 7833**, Silk 7857, Thendara 7878
Oklahoma: Hille 7943
Oregon: Eiting 8011, Kelley 8030, Wendt 8066
Pennsylvania: Cavitolo 8134, Cooper 8158, Davenport 8164, Degenstein 8166, ESSA 8190, Garthwaite 8212, Hulme 8260, Katz 8280, Lehigh Valley 8303, Levan 8307, Marshall 8326, Maslow 8327, Mengle 8347, Phoenixville 8381, **Pincus 8384**, Poor 8392, **Susquehanna 8470**
Rhode Island: Chace 8523, Hasbro 8539
South Carolina: Ceres 8578, ScanSource 8608, **Security's 8609**, TSC 8618
Tennessee: Beaman 8642, **Bridgestone 8646**, Children's 8653, Draughon 8668, Dugas 8669, Unaka 8739
Texas: Bass 8777, Benson 8788, Dell 8864, Gorman 8922, Huffington 8963, Kinder 8994, Lyman 9023, MacDonald 9025, Mithoff 9066, Pogue 9126, **Scaler 9170**, South 9201, Vale 9246, Westcott 9278, Zephyr 9299
Utah: Bastian 9306
Virginia: Adams 9366, Clark 9393, Constitution 9404, **Glenstone 9429**, Miller 9475
Washington: Community 9570, Oki 9653
Wisconsin: Dudley 9792, Glover 9805, Madison 9854, Managed 9857, Parr 9893, Peck 9894, Pettit 9897, Pollybill 9900, **Reiman 9908**, Sub 9945

Children/youth

Alabama: Community 27
California: Community 407, Los Altos 828, **Unocal 1252**
Florida: Community 1939, Community 1940, Gainesville 2015
Georgia: Community 2356
Illinois: Chicago 2662, Oak Park 2922
Indiana: Dearborn 3137
Iowa: **Van Wyk 3340**
Maryland: Shultz 3732
Massachusetts: Yawkey 4211
Michigan: Community 4255
Minnesota: Bush 4524, General 4570
New Mexico: Albuquerque 5466
New York: Komansky 6347
Ohio: Morgan 7760
Pennsylvania: Community 8153, La 8298
Washington: Bezos 9557, Martin 9634

Children/youth, services

Alabama: **Altec 4**, Barber 10, Brock 16, Caring 18, Crampton 30, Dixon 32, Founders 34, Hill 39, Kaul 40, Lowder 43, Lowder 44, Lowe 45, McMillan 49, McWane 50, Methvin 51, Mitchell 53, Patterson 56, Russell 60, Thompson 67

Alaska: Rasmuson 85
Arizona: A.P.S. 86, Arizona 87, Community 91, Cooper 92, Dee 94, Farrington 97, **Globe 101**, Green 102, Halle 103, Herberger 106, **IFS 109**, Jasam 110, **Kieckhefer 113**, Long 118, Moreno 123, Morris 124, Neely 126, Pocono 131, **Rae 132**, Robson 135, Stardust 141, Viad 149
Arkansas: **Frueauff 161**, Garrison 162, Murphy 167, Ross 174, Schmieding 175, Trinity 181, Wal-Mart 184, Walker 185, **Windgate 189**
California: Aaroe 192, **Allianz 205**, **American 217**, Amerman 218, Arata 229, Argyros 234, Atkinson 239, Autry 243, Ayrshire 247, **Azus 248**, Baker 251, **Baker 252**, Bandai 254, Barker 257, Bartman 259, Bauer 261, Bekins 273, Bell 274, Benbough 276, Beneto 277, **Benson 280**, Berry 284, Bettingen 286, Bickerstaff 287, **Bilger 289**, Boeckmann 299, Booth 303, Borchard 304, Borick 305, Boswell 308, Bothin 309, Bradley 315, Bravo 319, Brenner 321, Bright 322, Brotman 328, Burnett 336, Burnham 337, California 345, California 350, Campbell 352, Carsey 361, Carson 362, Caruso 363, Cassin 365, Caufield 367, Chartwell 375, Commercial 400, Community 402, Community 405, Community 407, Connolly 413, Cortopassi 419, Crail 426, Cusenza 433, Daly 436, Daly 437, Danford 438, David 442, DeMille 450, Dickinson 454, Doelger 459, Doheny 460, Doll 461, Dougherty 463, **Drew 467**, Dwyer 472, Eaton 475, Edelstein 476, Eucalyptus 489, Factor 491, Fairchild 492, Fansler 494, Fieldstone 506, Finley 507, **Firelight 509**, Fireman's 510, Fitzgerald 514, Five 516, Foothills 526, Forest 527, French 536, Gasser 557, Gershman 567, Ghidotti 571, Giannini 573, Gifford 574, Gilmore 578, Gogian 588, Goldman 595, Goldman 596, Goldwyn 600, Gonda 601, Gooding 604, Grand 611, Greer 618, Gross 621, Guess? 629, Gumbiner 631, Haas 634, Hale 639, Halsell 641, Harden 647, Harman 650, Harrington 652, Harwit 655, HealthCare 661, Hoag 678, Homes 685, Horn 686, House 687, Hughes 690, Humboldt 691, Hutto 693, Hutton 694, Ingold 695, Intuit 696, It 704, Jackson 706, **Jacobs 707**, Jacobs 708, Jay 716, Johnson 725, Jonsson 729, **Kalliopela 740**, **Keck 750**, Keller 752, Kids 757, Kimball 759, King 760, Krach 779, Lampert 786, Langendorf 788, Lantz 790, Lasseter 791, Lehrer 800, Lesher 805, Listwin 819, Littlefield 820, LLWW 824, Long 825, Ludwick 829, Lurie 832, Lux 834, Lynn 835, **M & T 837**, Magali 846, Marciano 850, **Mattel 861**, McAlister 864, McBean 866, McIntyre 876, Menard 884, Mericos 889, Metabolife 891, Meyer 893, Michelson 895, Milken 898, Miller 901, **Mohn 907**, Morton 918, Moss 921, Muller 925, Newhall 936, Norris 940, Norton 943, **Oak 947**, Oberndorf 950, Odell 951, Oppenheimer 955, Orange 957, Ornest 959, Oshman 963, Outrageous 967, PacifiCare 971, Parker 979, Parsons 980, Pasadena 982, Peery 986, Peninsula 989, Philibosian 1003, Price 1017, Price 1019, Radin 1025, Rady Fam 1026, Raintree 1028, **Reinhard 1037**, Ressler 1043, Reyes 1047, **Righteous 1050**, Riordan 1054, Rivkin 1057, Roberts 1058, Robinson 1060, Rogers 1063, Rosenfeld 1067, Ryan 1075, Sacramento 1080, San Diego 1087, San Francisco 1088, Santa Barbara 1093, **Saturno 1097**, Sebastiani 1119, Seeno 1120, Segal 1121, Segerstrom 1123, Seinfeld 1124, Sence 1126, Setzer 1130, Sexton 1132, Shapiro 1137, Shapiro 1138, Short 1148, Sierra 1151, Smith 1164, **Smith 1167**, Smittcamp 1168, Smythe 1170, Soda 1173, Sonora 1178, **Soref 1179**, Springcreek 1185, Steele 1189, Stein 1190, Steiner 1191, Steinmetz 1192, Stern 1195, Strauss 1202, **Streisand 1204**, Stuart 1206, Stulsaft 1210, Taper 1226, **Taub 1227**, Taube 1228, Teichert 1231, Truckee 1244, Tuohy 1247, Ueberroth 1248, Valley 1257, vanLobenSels 1260, Van Nuys 1261, Van Nuys 1262, Vickter 1266, Vodafone 1267, Wallis 1276, Waltmar 1277, Warren 1279, Weingart 1288, Weiss 1290, Westly 1297, Weyrich 1298, WHH 1300, Whitecap 1303, Wilkes 1306, Wilson 1308, Windfall 1309,

Witherbee 1312, Wohlford 1315, Wood 1318, **World 1319**, Wrather 1321, Wunderkinder 1322, WWW 1323, Wynn 1324, Zyskind 1330

Colorado: Anschutz 1334, Bacon 1340, Boettcher 1344, Bohemian 1345, Buell 1350, ECA 1372, Edmondson 1373, El Pomar 1374, Gooding 1384, Hamilton 1387, Hewit 1391, Hughes 1393, Hunter 1394, JFM 1397, Johnson 1398, Leprino 1408, Ludlow 1412, M.D.C. 1413, Marisco 1416, McCormick 1420, McDonald 1421, McDonnell 1422, Pikes 1437, Pioneer 1438, Saeman 1448, Schlessman 1450, Schramm 1451, Sie 1455, St. John's 1456, Sturm 1462, Summit 1463, Telluride 1465, Weckbaugh 1470, White 1472, Wolf 1475

Connecticut: Andor 1483, Biondi 1494, Bissell 1495, Bluebell 1496, Bodenwein 1497, Brace 1501, **Brainerd 1502**, Community 1515, Community 1516, Community 1517, Connecticut 1518, Connecticut 1519, Culpeper 1521, Daniell 1523, **Ettinger 1536**, Fairfield 1537, First 1541, Fisher 1542, Freas 1548, Goodnow 1558, Hartford 1563, Hartford 1564, **Heimbold 1566**, Kitchings 1574, Kramer 1577, Larsen 1579, Lavietes 1581, Lone 1589, Long 1590, Mandeville 1596, Martin 1598, Melville 1602, Netter 1607, **Newman's 1609**, **Niles 1612**, **Orchard 1619**, Palmer 1621, Ritter 1633, Robbins 1634, Rogow 1636, Rose 1637, Say 1642, SBM 1644, Sewall 1648, Tow 1661, **Tudor 1664**, United 1668, **Waters 1675**, Worthington 1679, **Xerox 1680**

Delaware: Arguild 1687, Bishop 1693, Chichester 1698, Crystal 1702, Delaware 1706, Hall 1718, Laffey 1725, Marmot 1728, Parker 1738, **Raskob 1741**, Repass 1742, Robinson 1744, **Robinson 1745**, Schiff 1750, Sternlicht 1756, Vitale F 1759, Wasily 1760

District of Columbia: Arcana 1768, Beech 1771, Cafritz 1780, **CityBridge 1783**, Community 1785, Dimick 1789, Dweck 1790, Fernandez 1794, Fowler 1797, **Goldberg 1802**, Harman 1807, **Hill 1809**, Jones 1813, Kimsey 1817, Loughran 1823, Meyer 1834, Nef 1839, **Public 1844**, Replogle 1846, Stewart 1850, Vaterstetten 1855, Willoughby 1862

Florida: A Friends' 1866, Abraham 1867, ADFAM 1870, Amaturo 1879, Appleby 1879, Baldwin 1888, Bank 1890, BankAtlantic 1891, Batchelor 1893, Baxter 1895, Blum 1912, Bronfman 1917, Burns 1920, Bush 1922, **Chatlos 1932**, **Coleman 1937**, Community 1939, Community 1940, Community 1941, Community 1942, Community 1943, Community 1946, Community 1948, Conese 1950, Conn 1951, Crawford 1956, Dade 1957, Davis 1961, **Davis 1962**, **Davis 1963**, Demetree 1967, Driskill 1975, DuBow 1977, Dunspaugh 1981, Eckerd 1986, Einstein 1991, Ellis 1992, Engelberg 1994, Ferraro 1998, Florida 2003, Fortin 2007, Friedman 2014, Gooding 2028, Goodwin 2029, Harris 2050, Henderson 2056, Hersh 2058, Hunter 2069, Jelks 2076, Katcher 2080, Keating 2084, Kennedy 2087, Kesler 2090, Kiwanis 2094, Langford 2102, Light 2117, Lorberbaum 2118, Maroone 2129, Miller 2141, Naples 2151, Nessel 2152, Palm Beach 2161, Pascal 2163, Petway 2167, Phillips 2168, Pinellas 2170, **Plan 2171**, Potamkin 2176, Publix 2180, Rales 2184, Raymund 2188, Rayonier 2189, River 2198, Rollnick 2203, Rooms 2204, **Ross 2207**, Sansing 2217, Scarpa 2221, Schumann 2228, Smith 2238, Southwest 2240, Spurlino 2242, Storer 2252, Taylor 2268, TECO 2270, Terry 2271, Toppel 2274, United 2276, Ware 2287, Weintraub 2292, Westgate 2296, Wilson 2300, Winter 2303

Georgia: Aflac 2311, Anderson 2317, Azalea 2322, Broadfield 2330, Brown 2332, Campbell 2339, Charter 2345, Chatham 2346, Coca 2350, Colonial 2353, Community 2359, Community 2361, Courts 2364, Cousins 2365, Dunn 2375, Farris 2382, Five 2383, Flowers 2384, Franklin 2389, **Gage 2392**, Gordy 2402, Harland 2407, Harris 2408, Harrison 2409, Hertz 2412, **Hooters 2414**, Illges 2416, ING 2418, Lanier 2430, Lee 2432, Love 2437, Ma-Ran 2439, **Money 2450**, Morris 2454, Murphy 2456, Patterson 2460, Realan 2470, Rich 2472, Rollins

2475, Rosenberg 2476, Shallenberger 2487, Synovus 2497, Terwilliger 2498, Tull 2500, **Wardlaw 2506**, Wilson 2519, WinShape 2520, Woodruff 2521, Woodruff 2522, Woodward 2523, Zeist 2529

Hawaii: Bakken 2534, Campbell 2536, Ching 2540, First 2542, Frear 2543, Geist 2544, Hughes 2548, Kosasa 2549, Lange 2550, Schuler 2552, Wilcox 2559

Idaho: Boswell 2564, CHC 2566, Cunningham 2567, Good 2569, Morrison 2572, Nagel 2573

Illinois: Acorn 2583, Allegretti 2586, **Andrew 2595**, Andrew 2596, **Aon 2598**, **ARIA 2600**, Barnett 2606, Baskes 2607, Bates 2608, Beidler 2613, Bell 2614, Berner 2617, Bersted 2619, Bielfeldt 2620, Blair 2621, Blair 2622, Blowitz 2623, Blum 2625, **Brach 2630**, Braeside 2631, **Buntrock 2643**, Cabe 2648, Camp 2649, Chaddick 2655, Charleston 2657, Chicago 2660, Chicago 2661, Children's 2664, Circle 2666, Cless 2668, Clingen 2669, Code 2671, Comer 2675, Community 2677, Community 2680, Corboy 2684, Crane 2687, Crowe 2690, Cuneo 2692, D.H.R. 2695, Day 2698, **Demos 2702**, Dillon 2704, Donnelley 2708, DuPage 2713, Edwardson 2715, Eisenberg 2716, Emerson 2719, Energizer 2721, Fasseas 2726, Field 2728, Frankel 2735, Galvin 2746, Galvin 2747, Geneseo 2750, Geraldi 2752, Girl's 2757, GKN 2758, Gloyd 2760, Golder 2762, Guth 2775, Guthman 2776, H.B.B. 2777, Hark 2785, **Harper 2786**, Harris 2788, Harris 2789, Harrison 2791, Hirsch 2800, **Hull 2807**, Hunter 2808, **JMR 2818**, Kaplan 2823, Katten 2826, Kemper 2831, Kendall 2833, Kenny's 2835, Kolschowsky 2843, Lange 2848, Lewis 2857, Lurie 2865, Madigan 2869, Mayer 2876, Mazza 2877, McCormick 2878, McDaniel 2880, McMullan 2884, McNeil 2887, Mead 2888, Melman 2891, Mesirow 2894, Meyer 2895, Millard 2897, Millikin 2900, Nygren 2920, Oberweiler 2923, Oppenheimer 2928, Payne 2934, Perritt 2939, Petersen 2941, Polk 2946, Prince 2948, Red 2959, Reese 2961, Rhoades 2965, Rice 2966, Rich 2967, Roberts 2968, Rosenthal 2970, Russell 2976, Sangre 2981, Schuler 2990, Seabury 2993, SF 2998, Shaw 3004, **Shifting 3006**, Shirk 3007, Simmons 3008, Sirius 3010, Souder 3013, Speh 3014, Steans 3021, Stein 3022, Takiff 3032, Tracy 3037, Traders 3038, Trustmark 3039, United 3044, USG 3046, Vermilion 3047, Walgreen 3052, Ward 3056, Wark 3057, Wein 3060, Wenske 3063, White 3067, **Willow 3074**, Woodward 3085

Indiana: Adams 3095, Anderson 3099, Ball 3103, Ball 3105, Biomet 3106, Central 3116, Chancellor 3117, Citizens 3118, Community 3123, Community 3124, English 3146, Finish 3148, Foellinger 3149, Glick 3155, Griffith 3158, Hancock 3160, Health 3164, Heritage 3166, Hux 3170, Indiana 3173, Irwin 3175, Jones 3179, Kimball 3182, Kuhne 3187, Martin 3200, McAllister 3202, McMillen 3203, Moore 3207, Noyes 3216, Portland 3223, Pulliam 3225, Raker 3226, Simon C 3238, Unity 3247, Valiant 3248, Watanabe 3251, Wayne 3253, White 3257

Iowa: Bechtel 3264, Bechtel 3265, Community 3278, Deardorf 3280, Des Moines 3281, Employers 3282, Grubb 3289, Hanson 3291, Hubbell 3297, Kinney 3300, McCarthy 3311, McDonald 3312, McElroy 3313, Meredith 3315, **Ochylski 3321**, Ruan 3329, Siouxland 3332, Stark 3334, **Van Wyk 3340**

Kansas: Coleman 3352, DeVore 3357, Downing 3358, Hutchinson 3368, INTRUST 3369, Jones 3370, Joscelyn 3371, Kansas 3372, Morris 3378, Pritchett 3382, Rhoden 3383, Rice 3384, Rudd 3385, Sabatini 3386, Scroggins 3389, Security 3390, Smoot 3394, Sunderland 3397, Topeka 3400, V & H 3402, Wiedemann 3405

Kentucky: Bavarian 3406, Cralle 3416, Fischer 3418, Harris 3424, Kindred 3434, Norton 3441, Reed 3447, Rosenthal 3450

Louisiana: Azby 3460, Baton Rouge 3462, Coughlin 3470, Frazier 3479, German 3483, Huie 3488,

Reily 3506, Stuller 3510, Wheless 3514, Wilson 3515, Woolf 3517, Zigler 3520

Maine: Alfond 3521, Great 3539, Hannaford 3540, Kennebunk 3544, Lunder 3547, Maine 3548

Maryland: Abell 3559, Baker 3567, **Casey 3585**, Chaney 3587, Clark 3590, Columbia 3595, Commonweal 3596, Darby 3605, Davis 3606, Eaton 3619, FBW 3628, Goldsmith 3637, Grace 3638, Gross 3640, Henson 3648, Hoffberger 3652, Jonan 3658, Klein 3662, Leidy 3673, Lockhart 3681, Marshall 3687, Osprey 3703, Procter 3711, Rathmann 3715, Rouse 3724, **Shields 3730**, Shultz 3732, Sylvan 3741, Viragh 3753, Wareheim 3756, Weiss 3760, Wilson 3761

Massachusetts: **A Child 3765**, Acushnet 3770, Alden 3777, Alvord 3778, Ashton 3782, Bain 3788, Bay 3794, Bayrd 3795, Benfamil 3797, Bilezikian 3805, Birmingham 3807, Boston 3812, Boston 3813, Caldwell 3827, Cambridge 3828, Cape Cod 3832, Chase 3847, Childs 3848, Clipper 3850, Cogan 3851, Community 3854, Community 3855, Copeland 3859, Crotty 3870, Cummings 3871, Davis 3875, Dunn 3884, Dusky 3885, Egan 3890, Ellsworth 3892, Fassino 3900, Fletcher 3912, Gabrieli 3919, Gardinor 3920, Gerard 3923, Goldberg 3927, Hanover 3941, High 3950, Hoche 3954, Hopedale 3958, JSJN 3972, Keane 3975, Kittredge 3983, Klarman 3985, Larson 3998, Levy 4005, Linde 4007, Lovett 4013, Marino 4023, Massachusetts 4025, Mazar 4028, McEvoy 4032, Merck 4035, **Middlecott 4037**, New 4054, **OneBeacon 4060**, Pappas 4066, Parker 4069, Peabody 4073, Peabody 4074, **Peppercorn 4076**, Perpetual 4078, Peters 4081, Phillips 4082, Plymouth 4085, Putnam 4088, Ratshesky 4095, Riley 4104, Rodman 4111, Rubenstein 4115, Rubenstein 4116, **Saquish 4127**, Sawyer 4128, Schrafft 4133, **Shattuck 4138**, Smith 4150, Stare 4157, Stearns 4159, Stevens 4163, Stoneman 4167, Stoneman 4168, Strategic 4169, Stride 4171, Stride 4172, Tupancy 4186, Weber 4200, Webster 4201, Welch 4202, Wilson 4205, Worcester 4209, Yawkey 4211

Michigan: Ann Arbor 4221, Barry 4227, Battle Creek 4228, Besser 4232, Boutell 4236, Brown 4240, Capital 4243, Carls 4244, Charlevoix 4246, Community 4253, Community 4255, Community 4258, Cook 4262, Cracchiolo 4264, Dart 4267, **Degroot 4270**, DeRoy 4273, DeVos 4276, DeVos 4277, Doornink 4283, Dow 4286, Dow 4288, Duffy 4290, Eddy 4292, **Fetzer 4297**, Ford 4301, Ford 4303, Ford 4305, Four 4310, Frankel 4312, Fremont 4315, Frey 4316, Gerstacker 4322, Grand Rapids 4326, Greenville 4331, Hahn 4335, Herrick 4341, Jackson 4347, Kahn 4351, Kelly 4359, Kiwanis 4361, Knabusch 4362, Lear 4374, Leppien 4377, Maas 4379, Manat 4381, Manoogian 4382, Mardigian 4386, Miller 4394, Mott 4400, Rogers 4423, **Sage 4427**, **Secchia 4431**, Shelden 4434, Skillman 4438, Spoelhof 4443, Stonisch 4449, Thomas 4456, Thompson 4457, Timmis 4459, Turner 4464, Vandomelen 4470, **Visteon 4472**, Wege 4476, Westerman 4478, Whiting 4482, Wickes 4483, Wilson 4484, Wolff 4486, Wolters 4487, Wolverine 4488

Minnesota: Andersen 4502, Ankeny 4505, Athwin 4508, Bell 4514, **Best 4516**, Beverly 4517, Bremer 4523, Caridad 4531, Carlson 4532, Charity 4536, Charlson 4537, Christianson 4539, **CHS 4540**, Cloverfields 4542, Criss 4544, Davis 4546, Deluxe 4549, Dennis 4550, Duluth 4556, Federated 4563, Fiterman 4565, Graco 4573, Greycoach 4575, Grotto 4579, Hersey 4584, HRK 4589, Hubbard 4590, Initiative 4593, Kelley 4597, Kopp 4599, Leuthold 4605, Lilly 4606, Marbrook 4612, Mardag 4613, McCarthy 4614, McKnight 4617, McNeely 4619, McVay 4620, Minneapolis 4623, Mitchell 4625, Morning 4627, Neilson 4631, NFC 4633, O'Neil 4638, Opus 4642, Ordean 4643, Oswald 4645, **Pentair 4649**, Perlman 4651, Prophet 4658, Sabes 4670, Saint Paul 4671, Sanger 4672, Schulze 4675, **Slt 4684**, Southways 4688, Star 4691, Stone 4692, Sundet 4694, Thorpe 4701,

Toro 4702, **Wallestad 4712**, Wallestad 4713, Wallin 4714, Wasie 4716, WCA 4718, Wells 4721, West 4723, Whitney 4728

Mississippi: AmSouth 4733, Community 4737, Ergon 4740, Feild 4741, Ford 4742, Foundation 4743, Maddox 4753, McCarty 4754, Mississippi 4758, Taylor 4767, Telos 4768, Walker 4770

Missouri: Baer 4778, Ballman 4780, Barrows 4781, Bernoudy 4783, Boeing 4785, Brauer 4787, Brown 4788, Cornelsen 4799, **Enterprise 4810**, Green 4822, H & R 4823, Hallmark 4825, **Hana 4827**, Herschend 4830, Jordan 4840, Kansas 4842, Kellwood 4845, Laclede 4852, Lemons 4854, Long 4858, Lopata 4859, Musgrave 4870, Orscheln 4877, Pearl 4879, Pershing 4880, Pettus 4882, Pott 4886, **Pulitzer 4889**, Reynolds 4892, Roblee 4893, Saigh 4895, Shelter 4902, **Singing 4904**, Stupp 4911, Sunnen 4913, Tilles 4917, Truman 4919, Walker 4922, Woods 4928

Montana: Browning 4933, **Edwards 4936**, Gilhousen 4938

Nebraska: Baer 4944, Bishop 4946, Buckley 4947, Buffett 4949, Commercial 4951, **ConAgra 4953**, Hawks 4971, Holland 4977, James 4980, Julian 4981, Kilbourne 4985, Lexington 4986, **McDonald 4989**, Omaha 4994, Rogers 4999, Steinhart 5005, TierOne 5010, Truhlsen 5011, Valmont 5013, Wiebe 5017, Woods 5018, Zollner 5020

Nevada: Fairweather 5032, Fertitta 5033, Hawkins 5036, **Hilton 5037**, Lied 5041, May 5046, Nevada 5047, O'Bannon 5049, Pennington 5053, Sawyer 5061, Southwest 5066

New Hampshire: **Christian 5083**, Cogswell 5084, Gale 5091, HNHfoundation 5092, Hunt 5093, Levine 5094, Lindsay 5095, Putnam 5100

New Jersey: Abar 5107, Atkinson 5119, B'Seter 5122, Berger 5128, Bildner 5133, Borden 5138, Brady 5141, Brody 5144, Brotherton 5145, Bunbury 5148, Burke 5149, Campbell 5151, **Carlson 5155**, **Carolan 5156**, Cendant 5157, Cowles 5170, D'Angelo 5175, Danellie 5177, Dircks 5180, Fenwick 5193, **Frankino 5196**, Garcia 5203, Goldberg 5209, Goldring 5210, Grassmann 5213, Harbourton 5223, Hyde 5247, **IDT 5248**, Jockey 5260, **Johnson 5265**, Kauffmann 5272, Kennedy 5276, Keren 5277, Knistrom 5282, **Lafitte 5293**, Large 5295, Laurie 5297, Lear 5300, Levitt 5305, Link 5307, Mamiye 5316, Martini 5319, MCJ 5324, Orange 5343, Palestroni 5345, Poses 5354, Price 5356, Prudential 5360, **Reeves 5365**, Rigorous 5367, Ross 5376, Schenck 5386, Schreyer 5389, Schumann 5391, Simon 5405, Taub 5424, Turrell 5431, Unilever 5434, Union 5435, Upton 5436, Victoria 5440, Vision 5442, **Vollmer 5443**, Vopicka 5444

New Mexico: Albuquerque 5466, Frost 5476, Kind 5483, Maddox 5487, McCune 5488, Phillips 5492, Santa Fe 5496, Taos 5498

New York: Abrons 5511, Achelis 5513, Acorn 5515, Adirondack 5517, Adjmi 5519, Alfiero 5534, Allwin 5538, Allyn 5539, Alpern 5540, Altman 5543, **Altman 5544**, Antun 5559, Antz 5560, **Archbold 5563**, Arkell 5565, **AXA 5584**, Babbitt 5586, Bahnik 5589, Baird 5592, **Baker 5593**, Barker 5600, Bass 5604, Beker 5613, Berkowitz 5622, Berry 5626, Blankfein 5637, Blue 5640, Bluhdorn 5642, Bobst 5646, Bodman 5647, Bohlsen 5649, Booth 5651, **Bristol 5666**, Buhl 5684, Burden 5687, Butler 5692, Campbell 5700, Canaday 5701, Cappelli 5703, Carnahan 5706, Carvel 5710, Carwill 5711, Centennial 5722, Charitable 5733, **Chatterjee 5737**, Chautauqua 5738, **Chernin 5743**, Chiara 5748, Claiborne 5758, Clark 5762, Coles 5775, Community 5780, Community 5782, Community 5783, Cricket 5808, Crisp 5809, **Cummings 5813**, Cummings 5815, D'Agostino 5818, **Dabah 5819**, Dabah 5820, **Daedalus 5821**, Dammann 5824, Daphne 5830, **Das 5832**, Davenport 5833, De La Cour 5842, DeGeorge 5848, Dewar 5856, Diker 5862, Diller 5863, **Dodge 5867**, Dolan 5869, Donaldson 5871, Dove 5878, Dreitzer 5884, Dreyfus 5887, Dunwalke 5894, Dyson 5898, **Echoing 5905**, **Edouard 5909**, EHA

5912, Elmaleh 5924, Elmezzi 5925, Emerson 5927, Emwiga 5930, Fatta 5947, Ferrari 5953, First 5958, Fribourg 5984, Friedberg 5985, Friedman 5987, Frog 5992, Furman 6002, Gebbie 6009, Gerson 6021, Gibbs 6024, Gifford 6026, Gifford 6027, **Gimprich 6035**, **Glades 6037**, Gleacher 6038, Gleason 6039, Glickenhaus 6042, Goldschmidt 6058, Goldsmith 6059, Golub 6070, Gordon 6076, Gorter 6079, Gottlieb 6081, Gould 6083, Gould 6085, **Grant 6091**, Grateful 6093, Greenberg 6098, Greene 6099, Greentree 6102, **Gruss 6116**, Guttman 6124, **Haje 6133**, Hajim 6134, Halcyon 6135, Halis 6136, Harbor 6144, **Harriman 6146**, Harriman 6147, Hayden 6158, **Hearst 6161**, **Hearst 6162**, **Heineman 6165**, Herdrich 6173, Hettinger 6178, Hoyt 6203, Hudson 6207, Hurford 6215, **IAC 6220**, Icahn 6222, Icahn 6224, IF 6226, IFF 6227, Ivor 6242, Jacobson 6247, **Jaffe 6250**, **JM 6263**, Joelson 6265, Johnson 6267, Johnson 6271, Joy 6276, Kadrovach 6282, Kaiser 6283, Kanas 6286, Karmazin 6293, Katz 6296, Katz 6297, Katzenberger 6298, Kautz 6300, Kazickas 6302, Kealy 6303, Keefe 6305, Kellogg 6310, Kellogg 6311, Kempner 6313, Kenworthy 6315, Klee 6329, Klingenstein 6337, Knossos 6344, **Kohlberg 6346**, Kriendler 6358, Krimendahl 6359, Kupferberg 6363, Kurz 6365, L and L 6366, **Lane 6372**, Lastfogel 6380, Leach 6388, Lee 6391, Lemberg 6401, Levitt 6409, Lincoln 6423, Lindner 6426, Lipp 6432, Litwin 6436, Loeb 6438, M & T 6465, Macdonald 6468, **Magowan 6473**, Maheras 6475, Mai 6476, Marcus 6486, Mariposa 6487, Martin 6496, MAT 6503, Matlin 6506, **Mead 6522**, Meehan 6523, **Memton 6529**, Mercury 6533, Mercy 6534, **Merrill 6537**, Millbrook 6549, Miller 6550, **Milliken 6552**, Milstein 6555, **Monterey 6568**, Moore 6572, Morris 6579, Moses 6587, **Mulago 6593**, Neidich 6606, New York 6613, New York 6615, New York 6618, **Newhouse 6623**, Nichols 6628, North 6637, Northern 6639, O'Connor 6645, O'Malley 6647, O'Sullivan 6652, O'Toole 6653, Oestreicher 6656, Oppenheimer 6666, Osborn 6669, Overhills 6676, Park 6689, Parshelsky 6693, Pascucci 6696, Pedersen 6704, **Peierls 6705**, Pevaroff 6719, Phaedrus 6722, Phillips 6724, **Phillips 6725**, Pinkerton 6728, Plant 6731, Pollack 6735, Pumpkin 6754, R & TP 6764, Resnick 6787, Rhodebeck 6791, Rich 6795, Riley 6809, Ripple 6811, **Robinson 6819**, Rochester 6823, Rosenblum 6850, Ross 6862, **Ross 6863**, Rubenstein 6870, Rubin 6875, Rubinstein 6876, Rumsey 6882, Sachs 6888, Salmon 6896, Saltz 6899, **Saltzman 6900**, Sandler 6902, Sandy 6903, Schafer 6910, Schenker 6916, Schieffelin 6922, Schiff 6923, Schlobach 6924, Schmeelk 6927, Schmitt 6928, Schneider 6929, Schulhof 6935, Schurgot 6937, Shapiro 6960, Shoreland 6968, Siebens 6974, **Silfen 6980**, Silverweed 6985, Simon 6986, Simon 6987, Snow 7011, Snyder 7014, Soros 7024, Sosnoff 7025, SPIA 7028, **Spiegel 7030**, **Spirit 7033**, Sprague 7035, Spunk 7036, St. Faith's 7039, **St. Giles 7041**, Starker 7047, Starwood 7049, **Steele 7053**, Stein 7056, **Stempel 7069**, Stern 7072, Strypemonde 7089, Stuart 7090, Sulzberger 7095, **Summerfield 7097**, Summers 7099, Taconic 7117, **Tanaka 7120**, **Teagle 7126**, Tiger 7139, Tilles 7141, **Time 7142**, Tisch 7144, Tisch 7147, Tisch 7148, Tisch 7149, Tomorrow 7153, Tormondsen 7154, Townsend 7159, Triad 7162, Trott 7165, Tuch 7170, Tufenkian 7171, Tuft 7172, Turn 7174, Turner 7175, Unterberg 7186, Van Pelt 7192, Varadhan 7194, Vernon 7195, Vidda 7198, Vogelstein 7201, Warren 7217, Weinberg 7231, Weissman 7238, Wellde 7239, Wendt 7243, Werblow 7245, Western 7248, Whitehead 7252, Wiener 7257, Witmer 7268, Yellow 7282, Zalaznick 7288, Zemsky 7294

North Carolina: Belk 7315, BIN 7318, Blue 7319, Bolick 7321, Branan 7322, Broyhill 7328, Cannon 7335, Cemala 7337, Charlotte 7338, Coffey 7339, Community 7343, Community 7346, Crutchfield 7348, Cumberland 7349, Duke 7359, Ebert 7362,

Family 7365, Foundation 7370, Goodnight 7377, Gordon 7379, Greensboro 7383, Gunzenhauser-Chapin 7384, Haley 7385, Halton 7386, Hanes 7387, Harris 7390, Harvest 7392, Herring 7396, High Point 7397, Hillsdale 7398, Hurley 7402, Janirve 7404, Kulynych 7415, **Kulynych 7416**, Lance 7418, Mebane 7427, Merancas 7428, Nias 7435, North Carolina 7438, O'Herron 7441, Provident 7454, Reynolds 7457, Reynolds 7460, Ryan 7469, Sklut 7473, Smith 7476, Smith 7478, Smith 7479, Stewards 7485, Stonecutter 7486, Strowd 7488, Triangle 7496, Van Houten 7500, Weaver 7504, Woodson 7509

North Dakota: Fargo 7514, Leach 7516, North Dakota 7519, Stern 7521

Ohio: A Good 7523, Akron 7526, American 7528, Anderson 7529, **Armington 7532**, Beaverson 7541, Bell 7544, Bicknell 7548, Born 7552, Brennan 7554, Britton 7556, Bruening 7558, Cafaro 7563, Castellini 7568, Charities 7569, Children's 7570, Cincinnati 7574, Cleveland 7577, Codrington 7578, Community 7583, Community 7585, **Convergys 7587**, Corbin 7591, Coshocton 7593, Dana 7599, Dater 7600, David 7601, Dayton 7603, Diebold 7611, **Eaton 7617**, Fairfield 7622, Fifth 7626, Fleming 7631, Fox 7637, France 7639, **Freygang 7640**, Gardner 7644, Gerlach 7648, Gund 7657, Haile 7659, Hamilton 7660, Hankins 7662, Hauck 7666, Hershey 7671, Hoover 7675, Iddings 7682, IHS 7683, Jackson 7685, Jergens 7689, Jubilee 7694, Knudsen 7702, **Kosar 7703**, Kramer 7704, Lancaster 7707, LaValley 7708, Licking 7714, LKC 7720, **Longaberger 7722**, Luther 7726, M/I 7729, Mangano 7733, Marietta 7735, Mathile 7737, Mayerson 7739, McCorkle 7741, Mehl 7746, Milacron 7751, Miller 7753, Mindala 7755, Miniger 7756, Moores 7759, Murphy 7768, Murphy 7769, Muskingum 7770, Nord 7779, Nordson 7781, O'Neill 7782, Ohio 7785, Olive 7787, Parker 7796, **Perkins 7800**, Pfau 7803, Pulley 7811, Reeves 7814, Reinberger 7815, Richland 7819, Rieveschl 7820, Ritchie 7821, Russell 7827, Salem 7831, Schiff 7838, Schmidlapp 7841, Schott 7842, Schott 7843, Shaw 7853, Sisler 7858, Sloat 7861, Smith 7863, Smucker 7864, Spaulding 7865, Stark 7867, Stocker 7870, Stranahan 7873, Toledo 7883, **Tomkins 7884**, Toulmin 7885, Troy 7886, Turben 7888, Turner 7889, Van Wert 7891, **Warrington 7895**, Watson 7896, Weisbrod 7900, Wellman 7901, Wendy's 7902, Western 7903, White 7905, Williams 7907, Wilson 7910, Wodecroft 7912, Wolfe 7915, Women's 7916, Wuliger 7918, Youngstown 7920

Oklahoma: Bailey 7923, Bernsen 7925, Better 7926, Goddard 7939, Kimmell 7951, Lyon 7953, McGee 7957, McGill 7958, ONEOK 7967, Oxley 7968, Puterbaugh 7970, **Schusterman 7975**, Titus 7983, Viersen 7985, Warren 7986

Oregon: Ackerman 7995, Autzen 7997, Bauman 7999, Boyd 8000, Braemar 8001, Campbell 8002, Carpenter 8003, Collins 8007, Fohs 8012, Hedinger 8019, Jackson 8024, Jeld 8025, Johnson 8027, Jubitz 8028, Lamfrom 8034, Meyer 8042, Miller 8045, Oregon 8049, PacifiCorp 8050, PGE 8051, **Schmidt 8055**, Templeton 8064, Tucker 8065, Wheeler 8068, Young 8069

Pennsylvania: 1957 8071, Aaron 8072, ACE 8073, Alter 8078, Annenberg 8083, Arcadia 8086, **Armstrong 8090**, Beatty 8097, Berger 8101, Berkman 8102, Born 8113, Bozzone 8114, Buck 8123, Buhl 8124, Burke 8126, Cassett 8133, Century 8137, CMS 8147, CMS 8148, Community 8153, Community 8154, Community 8156, Connelly 8157, Crawford 8162, Dietrich 8171, Dolfinger 8172, Drueding 8177, DSF 8178, Eustace 8191, Farber 8195, Ferree 8199, Fisher 8205, Fleming 8206, Fourjay 8209, Goodstein 8220, Grundy 8228, Haas 8230, Hankin 8234, Heinz 8241, Heinz 8242, Heinz 8244, Hillman 8250, Hodge 8254, Hoyt 8259, Huston 8263, Jennings 8272, John 8273, Kavanagh 8282, Keystone 8285, Kline 8293, Lancaster 8300, Lilliput 8311, Magee 8320,

Maguire 8321, Massey 8328, McDonald's 8333, McKinney 8339, McLean 8340, Meakem 8341, Mellon 8346, Miller 8352, Nelson 8362, Penn 8371, Peterson 8376, **Pew 8377**, Phillips 8380, Pine 8385, Plankenhorn 8387, Rangos 8400, Rockwell 8408, Rosenberg 8412, Scranton 8431, Shaffer 8436, Shenango 8438, Simmons 8441, Smith 8443, Smith 8444, Smith 8445, Snee 8446, Snyder 8448, Stackpole 8456, Staunton 8457, Steinman 8458, Steinman 8459, Stewart 8460, Strauss 8464, Strawbridge 8467, Trees 8480, Trexler 8481, **United 8487**, Wheeler 8501, Widener 8502, Wolf 8506, Wyomissing 8509

Rhode Island: Alperin 8516, CARLISLE 8521, Citizens 8527, Daniels 8530, Grinnell 8538, Kimball 8542, McCarthy 8548, Rhode Island 8551, Roosa 8552, Shaw's 8555, Shriners 8556, Sullivan 8558

South Carolina: Abney 8564, Arkwright 8565, Central 8577, Coastal 8581, Community 8583, First 8587, Glenn 8591, Inman 8595, **Security's 8609**, Self 8610, Smith 8613, Sonoco 8614, South 8615, Spartanburg 8616, **Wardle 8620**, **Youths' 8621**

South Dakota: Larson 8627, Stearns 8632, Vucurevich 8634

Tennessee: 1939 8635, Aslan 8637, Atticus 8639, Briggs 8647, Caldwell 8649, Charis 8652, Clayton 8659, Community 8660, Conwood 8663, Day 8666, East 8671, Goldsmith 8682, Haslam 8687, Jones 8698, Kirkland 8699, Martin 8708, Massey 8709, Nelson 8712, Osborne 8714, Longleaf 8719, Ragsdale 8722, Schadt 8725, Stephens 8729, Stokely 8730, T & T 8731, Thompson 8733, Turner 8737, Washington 8741, Wilson 8744

Texas: **A Glimmer 8747**, Abell 8749, Amarillo 8758, Anderson 8760, **Anderson 8761**, Aragona 8763, Augur 8766, Bailey 8771, Baker 8772, Bass 8777, Beal 8783, Beasley 8784, Behmann 8785, Branch 8794, Bridwell 8797, Brumley 8800, Cailloux 8807, Cain 8809, Carter 8817, **Catto 8819**, Chilton 8826, Circle 8829, Clayton 8830, Clements 8832, Coastal 8833, Cockrell 8835, Collins 8837, Community 8840, Community 8841, Community 8842, Constantin 8843, Cowden 8848, De Llano 8859, **Dell 8863**, Dell 8864, di Portanova 8865, Dickson 8866, Doss 8869, Duda 8871, El Paso 8882, Elkins 8883, Ellwood 8884, Esping 8886, Essar 8887, Fasken 8895, Fikes 8899, Fisch 8901, Fish 8902, Folsom 8905, Frees 8909, Furst 8911, Futureus 8912, Garvey 8914, George 8916, Gill 8919, Goldsbury 8920, Goodman 8921, Greathouse 8924, Gulf 8926, Hachar 8927, Hackett 8928, Haggar 8931, Halff 8934, Hamill 8937, Hamman 8938, Hanley 8940, Harmon 8941, Hebert 8946, Herd 8948, Hillcrest 8952, Hirsch 8953, Hobby 8954, Hoblitzelle 8955, Hudson 8962, Jamail 8969, Jamail 8970, **Jenesis 8971**, Johnson 8972, Jonsson 8977, Keith 8982, Keithley 8983, Kelley 8986, KFFH 8990, Kimberly 8992, King 8995, Lantana 9004, Lard 9005, Lennox 9007, Levit 9009, Lightner 9012, **Link 9013**, Littauer 9014, Loose 9017, Lord 9018, Lowe 9020, Lubbock 9021, Lyons 9024, Mays 9035, McCrea 9040, McDermott 9043, McGovern 9044, McKee 9045, McMillan 9046, Meadows 9049, Mechia 9050, Meredith 9054, Modano 9068, Moore 9071, Morgan 9073, Morning 9075, Morris 9076, Mott 9079, O'Connor 9094, O'Quinn 9097, Oshman 9104, Owen 9106, Owen 9107, Owsley 9108, Paulos 9112, Phillips 9122, Pine 9123, Prairie 9129, Proctor 9132, Rachofsky 9139, Rapoport 9141, Riter 9149, Roach 9150, Rockwell 9154, Rosewood 9158, Rubenstein 9162, Sams 9163, San Antonio 9166, Sanders 9167, Schollmaier 9172, Schutte 9173, Scott 9174, Scurlock 9175, Sharp 9180, **Shell 9181**, Shelton 9182, Shield 9183, Sidhu 9185, Simmons 9187, Simmons 9188, Simmons 9189, Smith 9191, Smith 9196, Speas 9206, Stemmons 9211, Sterling 9212, Strake 9215, Swinney 9222, Tapeats 9223, Temple 9228, Tolleson 9237, Topfer 9238, Trull 9240, Turner 9241, Turner 9242, Valero 9247, Vaughan 9249, Vaughn 9251, Vergara 9253, Waco 9255, Waggoner 9256,

Wagner 9259, Wal 9260, Walsh 9261, Ward 9262, Ward 9263, **Waste 9265**, Watson 9266, Weaver 9267, West 9274, Wichita 9280, Willard 9281, Williams 9283, Wise 9285, Wolens 9286, Wolf 9287, Works 9291, Wright 9294, Young 9295, Zale 9297

Utah: ALS 9301, Bamberger 9305, Dumke 9315, Dumke 9316, Eccles 9319, Eccles 9320, Gardner 9323, Hemingway 9328, Peery 9337, Semnani 9341, Simmons 9342, Sorenson 9343, Swanson 9346, Wing 9352, **Wishnick 9353**

Vermont: **Green 9358**, Vermont 9361

Virgin Islands: Bartner 9362, Community 9363

Virginia: Arlington 9371, Billings 9377, Camp 9382, Carter 9387, Cartledge 9388, Charles 9389, Collis 9398, Community 9402, Connors 9403, Dalis 9406, Delmar 9410, Foundation 9419, Fralin 9420, Franklin 9421, Freddie 9422, Herndon 9437, HRH 9439, Jackson 9441, Kellar 9449, LandAmerica 9454, Lynchburg 9463, **Malek 9465**, Mars 9466, Memorial 9474, N.E.W. 9482, Norfolk 9484, Northern 9486, Olsson 9491, Reinhart 9502, Robins 9506, Samberg 9510, Thurman 9526, Titmus 9527, Truland 9528, Ukrop 9529, Universal 9531, Virginia Beach 9532, Washington 9534, **Winkler 9542**

Washington: Anderson 9551, Archibald 9553, Aven 9554, Bezos 9557, Blue 9559, **Casey 9567**, Community 9571, Crystal 9576, De Falco 9578, Foster 9588, Geneva 9592, Glaser 9594, Haugland 9603, **Hemingway 9606**, Heritage 9607, Islands 9613, Kaleidoscope 9616, **Laird 9623**, Lauzier 9626, Lie 9629, Lucky 9632, McEachern 9638, Medina 9640, Milgard 9641, Norcliffe 9650, O'Donnell 9652, PEMCO 9660, Positive 9664, Raven 9670, Sarkowsky 9676, Satterberg 9677, Seattle 9680, Shemanski 9682, Tacoma 9693, Wyman 9709

West Virginia: BB&T 9710, Carter 9712, Daywood 9717, Jacobson 9722, Kanawha 9723, McDonough 9726, Parkersburg 9730, Prichard 9731, Schenk 9732, Shott 9733, Whittaker 9737

Wisconsin: Alexander 9741, Anon 9744, Assurant 9748, Bader 9749, Baird 9750, Bartlett 9753, Beloit 9757, Bishop 9759, Bolz 9762, Bryce 9769, Casper 9770, Chapman 9771, Clark 9773, Cleary 9774, Community 9776, Community 9779, Cox 9782, Cudahy 9784, **DeAtley 9789**, Delavan 9790, Demmer 9791, Duncan 9793, **Eastman 9794**, Evans 9796, Evjue 9797, Handleman 9811, Helfaer 9813, Holz 9817, Jacobus 9819, Kellogg 9832, Kohl 9837, Krause 9842, Kress 9844, La Crosse 9845, Ladish 9846, Leake 9849, **Make 9856**, Marcus 9859, Marshall 9860, McBeath 9864, McQueen 9866, Michels 9874, Miller 9875, Milwaukee 9876, Morse 9879, Munson 9880, Nicholas 9883, Northwestern 9884, Oshkosh 9885, Oshkosh 9886, Pamida 9891, Peterson 9896, Pettit 9897, Phipps 9898, PPC 9902, Reinhart 9909, Riordan 9911, Schneider 9920, Sensient 9922, Seramur 9924, Shattuck 9926, Smallwood 9928, Split 9932, Stackner 9934, **Stein 9937**, Stone 9940, **Taylor 9947**, Taylor 9948, **Wagner 9957**, Walter 9959, Witte 9968

Wyoming: Connemara 9978, Martin 9984, McMurry 9985, Sargent 9989, Scott 9991, Wyoming 10000

Christian agencies & churches

Alabama: Anderson 6, Ard 8, **Christian 21**, **Corman 29**, Founders 34, Hearin 37, Lowder 42, Lowder 44, May 46, Methvin 51, Moore 55, Thompson 67, Upchurch 71, Webb 75, Working 76, Wyker 77

Arizona: Cooper 92, Help 105, Hermundslie 107, Jasam 110, Jazzbird 111, Laizure 114, Long 118, Moreno 123, Neely 125, **Rae 132**, **Solheim 139**, **Torhjelm 146**

Arkansas: Bradberry 159, Garrison 162, Glass 163, Gleason 164, Jones 166, Schmieding 175, **Soderquist 177**, Sturgis 178

California: Adventist 195, Allequash 202, Aquila 227, Arata 229, **Atkinson 240**, Baker 251, Bennett 279, Berry 284, **Bolthouse 301**, Bowman 312, Bradley

315, Bright 322, **Bull 331**, **Caddock 343**, CEC 368, CNC 390, Colombo 398, Crawford 427, **Day 447**, Doll 461, Eaton 475, Eldorado 482, Everlasting 490, **Farallon 495**, Fieldstone 506, **First 512**, Five 516, Furth 543, Goldwyn 600, Gooding 604, Grimm 619, Grimm 620, Guest 630, Haas 634, **Hammer 643**, Harman 650, Harrington 652, Hegwer 664, **Heinz 665**, Hinz 675, Hsin 689, **Issa 703**, It 704, Jackson 706, Janssen 715, Johnson 726, Judkins 732, Keck 751, Khachaturian 755, **Kim 758**, Kvamme 781, Let 808, Linden 813, Lindsey 815, **Living 821**, Lynn 835, Maag 838, Martin 860, McDonough 873, Modglin 904, Mourier 922, Odell 951, **Open 954**, Peery 986, Petersen 994, Philibosian 1003, Price 1018, Promise 1023, **Reveas 1045**, Riddle 1049, Rogers 1063, **Rosengarten 1068**, Ryan 1075, **S.G. 1078**, **Saje 1084**, Samueli 1086, **Schimmel 1101**, Scully 1116, Seaver 1117, Servants' 1129, Setzer 1130, Shannon 1133, Shea 1141, SHP 1149, Smith 1162, Smittcamp 1168, Stamps 1186, **Stewardship 1197**, Stewart 1199, Stover 1201, Sundean 1215, Swenson 1218, Van Daele 1258, Van Daele 1259, **Versacare 1265**, Vose 1272, W.J. 1273, Waterford 1282, Wohlford 1315

Colorado: **Agur 1332**, **Crowell 1361**, Dwan 1370, Esther 1375, King 1404, Leptas 1409, Lewis 1410, Ludlow 1412, McDonnell 1422, Morgan 1430, Newman 1432, Ponzio 1440, Richardson 1444, **Seay 1453**, Stealth 1458

Connecticut: Ambler 1481, Bissell 1495, Bluebell 1496, Bossidy 1500, Daniell 1523, **Doty 1532**, Ellis 1534, **Ettinger 1536**, Feuerman 1538, Foley 1544, Laverack 1580, Lee 1582, Lehrman 1584, Melville 1602, Meriden 1603, Oaklawn 1616, Owenoke 1620, Pitt 1628, Sites 1650, Woodward 1678

Delaware: Bennett 1690, **Birch 1692**, Evelyn 1712, Struthers 1758

District of Columbia: **Coleman 1784**, Washington 1859

Florida: **Adam 1869**, ADFAM 1870, Albrecht 1872, **Aurora 1882**, **Aurora 1883**, Baxter 1895, **Believers 1900**, Beveridge 1907, BJ's 1908, Bond 1913, Burton 1921, Carse 1925, Castellani 1928, Catlin 1929, **Cobb 1936**, Crawford 1956, **Davis 1963**, Demetree 1967, **DeMoss 1968**, duPont 1982, Einstein 1991, Ellis 1992, Florida 2003, **Foundation 2009**, **Fricks 2013**, **Goldhammer 2026**, GSB 2039, Hall 2045, Harrington 2049, Henriksen 2057, **Holden 2063**, Kirbo 2092, Kleist 2095, Levin 2110, Light 2117, Madigan 2123, Magill 2124, Magruder 2125, Masters 2131, Moore 2142, **Morris 2145**, Overstreet 2159, Pamphalon 2162, Pascal 2163, Paulucci 2164, Price 2177, Quick 2182, **Rawlings 2186**, Raygar 2187, Rinker 2196, Robinson 2202, **Ross 2207**, **Rosser 2208**, Sansing 2217, Schoen 2226, Seneff 2231, Smith 2238, **Stacy 2246**, Stransky 2253, SunTrust 2259, Taylor 2268, Thanksgiving 2272, Thatcher 2273, Walter 2286, Williams 2299, Winston 2302

Georgia: Adams 2309, Amos 2315, Beloco 2324, Brady 2327, Callaway 2337, Campbell 2339, Cawood 2342, Courts 2364, Cousins 2365, Day 2371, Ellis 2376, Faith 2381, Farris 2382, Flowers 2384, Good 2401, Gordy 2402, Harrison 2409, **Hooters 2414**, Jinks 2422, Jolley 2423, Jordan 2425, Lanier 2429, Lee 2432, Lewis 2434, Love 2437, Millner 2447, **Morris 2455**, Murray 2457, Patrick 2459, Patterson 2460, Ramser 2469, Robinson 2473, Servant's 2485, Sheffield 2488, Smith 2491, Walker 2505, Watkins 2508, Williams 2517, WinShape 2520, Woodruff 2522

Hawaii: Ching 2540

Idaho: Simplot 2574, Thomas 2577

Illinois: Adreani 2585, **Andrew 2595**, Andrew 2596, Bere 2616, Bersted 2619, **Buntrock 2643**, Cabe 2648, Canning 2650, Chaddick 2655, Chicago 2660, Code 2671, Combs 2674, Corboy 2684, Cornell 2685, Cressey 2689, Domanada 2705, Edwardson 2715, Emerson 2719, **Excelsior! 2722**, **Fairwyn 2723**, **Gallagher 2744**, Grace 2766, Hamill 2780, **Harper 2786**, Harrison 2791, Hartke

2792, Hendrickson 2796, Huizenga 2806, Hunter 2808, **Johnson 2819**, Kemper 2831, Khesed 2839, Lyon 2866, Madigan 2869, Magnus 2870, Makray 2871, McDaniel 2880, Meyer 2896, Millard 2897, **Niamogue 2914**, Ozinga 2930, PDB 2935, Peters 2940, Red 2959, Rhoades 2965, **Samaritan 2980**, Schmidt 2986, Segal 2995, Shaker 2999, Sharpe 3002, Swanson 3031, Traders 3038, **Tyndale 3042**, Vibern 3048, Walnut 3054, Weiss 3062, **Wessner 3064**, Whitwam 3068, Wilemal 3070, Wilkins 3072, Wolf 3079, Zerrusen 3091

Indiana: ADL 3097, Boren 3108, Branigin 3109, Decio 3139, English 3146, Ford 3150, Freedom 3152, Froderman 3153, Glick 3155, Griffith 3158, Holiday 3168, Hux 3170, **IMMI 3172**, Irwin 3175, Journal 3181, **Master 3201**, Moore 3207, Muselman 3209, Niblick 3212, Tyson 3246

Iowa: Bechtel 3265, Beckwith 3266, Bright 3269, Brownell 3270, Farver 3283, Heerema 3292, Kuyper 3304, **New 3319**, Ruan 3329, Vermeer 3341

Kansas: Devlin 3356, DSSR 3360, Haglage 3365, Lloyd 3375, Sabatini 3386, **Schowalter 3388**, Servant 3391, Shannon 3392

Kentucky: Brown 3408, **Chase 3413**, Ford 3419, Hagan Ch 3423, **Jones 3430**, Novak 3442, Preston 3446, River 3448, Robinson 3449, Sutherland 3451

Louisiana: Coughlin 3470, Factor 3476, Franks 3478, Frazier 3479, Huie 3488, Libby 3494, Mauboules 3499, **TWL 3513**, Wheless 3514, Woolf 3517

Maine: Gallagher 3535, Gateway 3537, Mulford 3551

Maryland: Blades 3574, **Calvin 3581**, **Ewing 3626**, Jonan 3658, Legg 3672, **Little 3679**, Osprey 3703, Principato 3710, **Smith 3736**, Ten 3743, Tucker 3750, Van Lunen 3752

Massachusetts: **A & A 3764**, Bay 3794, Behrakis 3796, Bristol 3816, Copeland 3859, Davis 3874, DeFreitas 3876, DeLuca 3877, Demoulas 3878, Demoulas 3879, Encourage 3894, Evans 3898, Flatley 3911, Grayson 3932, Hoffman 3955, Jackson 3966, Leclerc 4000, Loebs 4011, Morningside 4043, Pappas 4067, Perpetual 4078, Rogers 4112, Roy 4114, SDSC 4134, Sicari 4144, **Waterman 4198**

Michigan: **Aikens 4215**, Boll 4235, Brown 4240, Christian 4247, Cook 4261, DeVos 4276, DeVos 4277, DeVos 4278, **DeWitt 4280**, DiPonio 4281, Dow 4286, Fabri 4293, **GII 4323**, Granger 4328, Granger 4329, **H.I.S. 4334**, Harding 4338, **Heritage 4340**, ICN 4345, **Isabel 4346**, **Johnson 4349**, Jurries 4350, Keeler 4355, **Krauss 4366**, Lasko 4373, **Legion 4375**, Leppien 4377, Mackey 4380, **Manthei 4384**, Mardigian 4386, **McDonald 4388**, Miller 4393, Molinello 4395, Oleson 4405, Paulina 4409, Prince 4416, Robideau 4421, Rordor 4424, **Secchia 4431**, Shepherd 4435, Shoemaker 4436, Spoelhof 4443, Stange 4445, Stonisch 4449, Tamer 4453, **Tubergen 4463**, Upjohn 4465, Van Andel 4467, **Van Curler 4468**, Vanderweide 4469, Wege 4476, Wenger 4477, White 4481, Wilson 4484, Wolters 4487

Minnesota: AHS 4497, Ankeny 4505, Aslan 4507, Bieber 4518, Campbell 4528, Carlson 4532, Christianson 4539, Desiring 4551, Dorea 4553, **Emmerich 4562**, Hersey 4584, Hubbard 4590, Knowlton 4595, Labovitz 4601, **Larson 4603**, McVay 4620, Morning 4627, Nicholson 4634, Opperman 4641, People 4650, Prophet 4658, Radichel 4660, Reimer 4665, Rivers 4666, Sjolund 4685, Southways 4688, Sundet 4694, Veden 4707, **Wallestad 4712**, Wallestad 4713

Mississippi: AmSouth 4733, Ergon 4740, Ford 4742, Graeber 4744, Hancock 4746, Irby 4750, McCarty 4754, McRae 4755, Oakwood 4760, **Seal 4764**, Skelton 4765, Telos 4768, Walker 4770

Missouri: Anheuser 4775, Buder 4791, Fabick 4812, Herschend 4830, Jenkins 4836, Lay 4853, Musgrave 4870, Nelson 4871, Pearl 4879, **Pillsbury 4883**, Pillsbury 4884, PMJ 4885, Powell 4887, Sycamore 4915, Vatterott 4921

Montana: Browning 4933, Gilhousen 4938

Nebraska: Eihusen 4961, Hamilton 4968, Hawks 4971, Heider 4972, Heuermann 4973, Hofer 4976,

James 4980, Ryan 5000, **Slosburg 5003**, Steinhart 5005, Wiebe 5017

Nevada: Christian 5026, Crescere 5030, Harris 5035, Redfield 5055, **SFO 5062**, Trans 5073

New Hampshire: **Christian 5083**, Hunt 5093

New Jersey: **Anderson 5115**, **Bonner 5137**, **Carolan 5156**, Danellie 5177, Garcia 5203, Green 5215, **Huntsman 5246**, **James 5254**, Jockey 5260, Kemmerer 5275, Lanza 5294, Larsen 5296, Leitner 5303, Long 5310, Merillat 5330, Palestroni 5345, Perrin 5350, Phipps 5352, Schreyer 5389, Simon 5405, Turock 5430, Upton 5436, Visceglia 5441, Vision 5442, Weny 5450, Zobel 5464

New Mexico: **Johns 5482**

New York: Ades 5516, Arrison 5570, Burch 5686, Campbell 5700, **Carey 5704**, Carnahan 5706, Case 5713, Casey 5714, Chisholm 5752, Coles 5775, Corzine 5798, **Damaris 5822**, Davenport 5833, Dove 5877, Dove 5878, Edelweiss 5908, Farkas 5945, **Fernleigh 5952**, Ford 5969, Galasso 6005, Gibson 6025, Golkin 6068, Goodman 6073, Gorter 6079, **His 6189**, Jacobson 6247, JAM 6251, Johnson 6271, Joy 6276, Kadrovach 6282, Kaiser 6283, Kanas 6286, Kealy 6303, **Lane 6372**, Leuschen 6405, Lindmor 6425, Link 6429, **Luckow 6455**, **Magowan 6473**, **MBIA 6512**, McCann 6514, Millbrook 6549, Miller 6550, Morse 6584, **Mullen 6595**, O'Connor 6645, O'Malley 6648, **Palmer 6682**, Paul 6697, **Pearson 6701**, Pritchard 6748, Ranger 6770, Rich 6795, Robison 6821, **Rosen 6843**, Roxe 6867, Rumsey 6882, Schafer 6910, Schieffelin 6922, Schmitt 6928, Soros 7024, **Staley 7042**, Stuart 7090, Swartz 7111, Touch 7157, Tuft 7172, Valentine 7189, Vernon 7195, Weinberg 7231, Wellin 7240, White 7251, Woodland 7275, Zehner 7293

North Carolina: Beaver 7313, Belk 7315, Bolick 7321, Braswell 7323, Brown 7326, Bryan 7330, Burress 7331, Coleman 7340, Crutchfield 7348, Curran 7350, Ebert 7362, Everett 7364, Finley 7367, Gipson 7375, Harvey 7393, Hillsdale 7398, Hommer 7400, Hurley 7403, Jones 7408, Keith 7410, **Kulynych 7416**, **Morris 7432**, **Neal 7433**, NFM 7434, North Carolina 7438, O'Herron 7441, Palin 7443, Perkins 7445, **Planseon 7448**, Price 7451, Randleigh 7456, **Richardson 7462**, Rostan 7467, Sloan 7475, Smith 7476, Smith 7477, Wilson 7506, Yeargan 7511

North Dakota: Nordick 7518

Ohio: Bates 7540, Berkman 7545, Children's 7570, Christman 7572, **Covenant 7595**, Creech 7597, Dater 7600, Davidson 7602, Dorn 7612, **Durell 7616**, Ferguson 7625, Forest 7634, Frost 7642, Gardner 7644, **Generation 7647**, IHS 7683, Jackson 7685, Jochum 7692, Knudsen 7702, Lindner 7716, Lindner 7717, Marcum 7734, Mehl 7746, Miller 7754, Mindala 7755, Mixon 7757, Orr 7790, **Perkins 7800**, Pulley 7811, Russell 7828, Samaritan 7832, **Sankey 7833**, Smucker 7864, Stranahan 7873, **Tell 7876**, Turben 7888, **Vesper 7892**, Wagler 7893, Weisbrod 7900, Western 7903, Wilson 7911, Wodecroft 7912, Yoder 7919, Zenith 7921

Oklahoma: **8:32 7922**, Barnett 7924, Crawley 7934, Jackson 7945, Jones 7946, Kimmell 7951, McGill 7958, Oklahoman 7966, Oxley 7968, Richardson 7973, Waters 7988, Young 7990

Oregon: **Foreign 8014**, **Honzel 8021**, John 8026, Merrill 8040, Miller 8043, Poznanski 8052, Stewart 8060

Pennsylvania: Arcadia 8086, Asplundh 8091, **Beneficia 8100**, Black 8109, Brickman 8116, Brossman 8120, Buck 8123, Byers' 8127, **Cardone 8129**, CMS 8147, **Cornerstone 8159**, Covenant 8161, Crawford 8162, Eden 8181, England 8185, Eustace 8191, Glencairn 8219, **Guild 8229**, Hahn 8231, **Henkels 8245**, Herr 8246, Hulme 8260, Huston 8263, Huston 8264, John 8273, Kline 8293, Lilliput 8311, M & S 8318, Mach 8319, Meakem 8341, Medleycott 8343, **Metcalf 8351**, Murray 8360, Palumbo 8368, Parmer 8369, Pilgrim 8383, Psalm 8397, Salvaggio 8421, Salvitti 8422, Snee 8446, Tippins 8477, Turner 8484, Usher 8489, Venne 8491

Rhode Island: Kings 8543, McAdams 8547

South Carolina: Abney 8564, Bailey 8567, Chapin 8579, Community 8583, Hopewell 8593, Liberty 8597, North 8601, Phifer 8602, **Premier 8604**, **Security's 8609**, Smith 8613, Springs 8617

South Dakota: Branches 8623

Tennessee: 1939 8635, Atticus 8639, Caldwell 8649, Campbell 8650, Charis 8652, Clayton 8659, Danner 8664, Draughon 8668, EBS 8672, Ezell 8676, Jones 8698, Lazarus 8700, **Maclellan 8704**, MacLellan 8705, Martin 8706, Master's 8710, Melkus 8711, No 8713, Osborne 8714, Pettway 8715, Longleaf 8719, Redbird 8723, Schadt 8725, Sparks 8727, Stephens 8729, Thompson 8733

Texas: Anderson 8759, Anderson 8760, Augur 8766, Bass 8777, Baugh 8781, Beasley 8784, Behmann 8785, **Bell 8786**, Bickel 8790, Bosque 8792, Brown 8798, Butt 8804, **C.I.O.S. 8805**, Caris 8814, Castle 8818, **CEMEX 8821**, Cockrell 8835, Convergence 8844, Covenant 8847, Cox 8849, Crain 8851, **Davis 8857**, Eady 8875, Edwards 8880, Elkins 8883, Esping 8886, Fleming 8903, Franklin 8908, Furst 8911, Gayden 8915, Gorman 8922, Greathouse 8924, Hackett 8928, Halbert 8933, Hamill 8937, Harmon 8941, Heavin 8945, Holt 8958, **Hull 8964**, **Interdenominational 8968**, Jamail 8969, Jamail 8970, Keithley 8983, KFFH 8990, Littauer 9014, Lord 9018, Lord's 9019, Luchsinger 9022, Macrini 9026, Martin 9031, Mays 9035, McNutt 9048, Mendenhall 9053, Merrick 9055, Meyer 9057, Miller 9062, Moore 9071, Morgan 9073, Morning 9075, NAH 9084, Navarro 9089, O'Connor 9095, Oehmig 9099, **Onward 9103**, Owen 9106, Owen 9107, Perot 9119, Rachal 9138, Reaud 9143, Roach 9150, Rockjensen 9153, Rowling 9160, RSMIS 9161, Sanders 9167, Sarofim 9169, **Sei 9177**, Shelton 9182, Smith 9197, Snyder 9199, Sparrow 9204, Stewart 9213, Tate 9225, Temple 9228, Unkefer 9243, Vanberg 9248, Vaughan 9249, Vaughn 9251, Vergara 9253, Weekley 9271, Weiser 9272, White 9279, Williams 9282, Wise 9285, Wright 9293, Zeller 9298

Utah: **Huntsman 9329**, Lawson 9331, Quinney 9338, Wideman 9351

Vermont: Mergens 9360

Virginia: Batten 9375, Blue 9378, Carrington 9386, English 9414, Houff 9438, Hylton 9440, Kluge-Moses 9451, **Lambert 9453**, Lane 9456, **M.E. 9464**, Meador 9473, **Mustard 9481**, **Parker 9492**, Scott 9513, Sharp 9515, **Three 9525**, Thurman 9526, Titmus 9527

Washington: Everard 9582, Green 9598, Heritage 9607, Hughes 9610, Hussey 9611, Larson 9624, Lauzier 9626, Lie 9629, **Natan 9646**, Norcliffe 9650, **Stewardship 9691**, Wright 9707

West Virginia: Carter 9712, Hunnicutt 9720, McQuain 9727, Whittaker 9737

Wisconsin: Archer 9746, **Bless 9761**, Brotz 9767, Bryant 9768, Davis 9787, Duncan 9793, **Firestone 9798**, Glover 9805, JKO 9822, Johnson 9824, **Johnson 9825**, Kohl 9837, Kress 9844, Managed 9857, Marshall 9860, Mercy 9871, Merrill 9872, Nelson 9881, Schneider 9920, **Stein 9937**, Stewardship 9938, Stone 9940, Stuart 9942, **T & O 9946**, **Taylor 9947**, Uihlein 9955, Vine 9956, Wagner 9958

Wyoming: Connemara 9978, Richardson 9987, S & G 9988, Thorson 9994, Tozzi 9995

Civil liberties, advocacy

Alaska: Alaska 79

California: Columbia 399, **Fund 542**, **Streisand 1204**

District of Columbia: Block 1776, **Wallace 1858**

Florida: Zwan 2308

Georgia: Lubo 2438

Indiana: Irwin 3174

Maine: Falcon 3532

Massachusetts: Barry 3793

Minnesota: Kelley 4597

Missouri: **Deer 4804**, **Sayler 4897**

New Mexico: Proteus 5495
New York: **Abelard 5508**, Gimprich 6035, HKH 6190, IF 6226, Normandie 6636, **Overbrook 6675**
Virginia: **Modzelewski 9477**

Civil liberties, death penalty issues

California: **Fund 542**
District of Columbia: **Butler 1779**, **Wallace 1858**
Georgia: Sapelo 2479

Civil liberties, due process

California: vanLobenSels 1260
District of Columbia: **Wallace 1858**
Georgia: Sapelo 2479

Civil liberties, first amendment

District of Columbia: Block 1776
Georgia: Weber 2510
Illinois: Chicago 2663
New York: **Klingenstein 6338**
Ohio: Scripps 7848
Washington: RealNetworks 9672

Civil liberties, reproductive rights

California: Berkshire 283, Feintech 499, Gerbode 564, Grammer 610, Grove 625, Gruber 626, Gumbiner 631, **Packard 972**, Taper 1226
Colorado: **General 1381**
Connecticut: **Educational 1533**, **Ettinger 1536**
District of Columbia: Cafritz 1780, Kaye 1815, **Wallace 1858**
Illinois: Kaplan 2823, New 2912, **Relations 2963**
Massachusetts: **Merck 4036**
Michigan: Grand Rapids 4326
Minnesota: Bell 4514, Phillips 4655
Missouri: **Deer 4804**, Roblee 4893, Sunnen 4913
Nebraska: **Buffett 4950**
New Jersey: **Huber 5244**
New York: **Bydale 5694**, Clark 5761, Gimbel 6034, Lynton 6463, **Macy 6471**, New York 6613, New York 6615, **Noyes 6643**, **Overbrook 6675**, Scherman 6918
North Carolina: Reynolds 7458
Ohio: Stocker 7870
Oregon: Johnson 8027
Pennsylvania: Claneil 8144, Lamb 8299
Texas: Fikes 8899, Owsley 9108
Washington: Quixote 9667

Civil liberties, right to die

California: Columbia 399

Civil liberties, right to life

California: Weyrich 1298
Delaware: Mastronardi 1729
Kansas: Sullivan 3396
Massachusetts: Ruddy 4118
Michigan: **H.I.S. 4334**, Shoemaker 4436
Minnesota: Christianson 4539
New Jersey: **Anderson 5115**, Hidden 5233
Texas: **Davis 8857**
Wyoming: Richardson 9987

Civil rights

Arkansas: Hussman 165, Rockefeller 172
California: **Arkay 235**, **Castagnola 366**, **Draper 466**, Geffen 558, Gerbode 564, Goldman 596, Lutz 833, **Mohn 907**, Morton 919, **Omidyar 952**, Roth 1071, San Francisco 1088, Silberstein 1153, Stern 1195, **Streisand 1204**, vanLobenSels 1260, Wohlford 1315
Colorado: Divine 1366, Rose 1445
Delaware: Singer 1753

District of Columbia: Block 1776, Cafritz 1780, **Goldberg 1802**, Meyer 1834, **Moriah 1835**, **Mott 1836**, **Public 1844**
Florida: Dade 1957, **Isenberg 2070**, Merrill 2136, **Picower 2169**
Georgia: **Fonda 2385**, **Morris 2455**, Sapelo 2479
Illinois: Community 2677, D and R 2693, Davee 2696, DuPage 2713, Goldberg 2761, **Goodman 2765**, Kaplan 2823, Katten 2826, Keiser 2828, Libra 2858, **MacArthur 2867**, New 2912, Olin 2925, Omron 2926, **Shifting 3006**
Indiana: Community 3122, **Cummins 3136**
Iowa: Holthues 3295
Kansas: Hutchinson 3368
Maryland: **Cohen 3594**
Massachusetts: Ansin 3779, Boston 3812, Community 3855, Gerard 3923, **Krieble 3990**, **Reebok 4098**, **Schooner 4131**
Michigan: **Arcus 4223**, Dauch 4268, Pitt 4413
Minnesota: **Andreas 4504**, Bremer 4523, Grotto 4579, Minneapolis 4623, Rochester 4668
Missouri: Community 4798, **Deer 4804**, **Humphreys 4833**, JSM 4841, Uhlmann 4920
New Jersey: Cowles 5170, **Johnson 5263**, Levy 5306
New Mexico: **Pond 5494**, Proteus 5495
New York: Baird 5591, **Bydale 5694**, **Cogut 5766**, **Echoing 5905**, Elias 5920, **Ford 5970**, Fuchsberg 5998, Gellert 6012, Glickenhaus 6042, Gural 6120, **Haje 6133**, Haseltine 6152, **Heineman 6165**, **HKH 6190**, Hochfelder 6191, Hughes 6209, **JEHT 6257**, LBC 6386, Levy 6413, Mai 6476, Marx 6498, Miller 6551, **Mitsubishi 6560**, Mullen 6596, New York 6619, **New 6621**, **Norman 6635**, **Overbrook 6675**, Reed 6782, Revson 6789, **Rosen 6843**, **Rubin 6872**, **Rubin 6874**, Scherman 6918, Spingold 7032, Straus 7086, Turner 7175
North Carolina: Cumberland 7349, Reynolds 7458
Ohio: **Armington 7532**, **PLACE 7805**
Oregon: **NIKE 8046**
Pennsylvania: Falk 8193, FISA 8204, **Pew 8377**, Philadelphia 8378
Rhode Island: Charter 8526
South Carolina: Coastal 8581
Tennessee: **Bridgestone 8646**
Texas: Alexander 8752
Utah: Bastian 9307
Vermont: **Ben 9355**, Vermont 9361
Washington: **Glaser 9595**, **Kongsgaard 9620**, Quixote 9667
Wisconsin: Johnson 9823

Civil rights, advocacy

California: Angell 224, Columbia 399, **Fund 542**, Grove 625, **PMI 1008**, **Righteous 1050**, Simon 1156
Colorado: Chambers 1354
Connecticut: **Valentine 1669**
District of Columbia: Community 1785, **Hill 1809**
Georgia: Snodgrass 2492
Illinois: Takiff 3032
Michigan: Nokomis 4404
Missouri: Bernoudy 4783
New Jersey: **Lafitte 5293**
New York: **Abelard 5508**, Elias 5920, Kaplan 6288, Lipmanson 6431, **Overbrook 6675**, van Ameringen 7190, Violett 7200
Ohio: Akron 7526, Horvitz 7677

Civil rights, aging

District of Columbia: Cafritz 1780
Maryland: Stulman 3739
Michigan: Grand Rapids 4326
Minnesota: Bremer 4523, Minneapolis 4623, Phillips 4655
New Mexico: Santa Fe 5496
New York: New York 6613, New York 6615
Virginia: **Gannett 9428**

Civil rights, alliance

New York: New York 6615
Oregon: **NIKE 8046**

Civil rights, association

New York: Wilson 7262

Civil rights, disabled

California: Stern 1195
Illinois: Reese 2961
Michigan: Grand Rapids 4326
Minnesota: Bremer 4523, Minneapolis 4623, Phillips 4655
New Mexico: Santa Fe 5496
New York: New York 6613, New York 6615
Pennsylvania: FISA 8204

Civil rights, equal rights

California: Fireman's 510, Roth 1071
Connecticut: **GE 1553**
Florida: Darden 1960
Illinois: Chicago 2663, Sara 2982
Michigan: DTE 4289
Minnesota: St. Paul 4690, Xcel 4732
New York: **Morgan 6577**, New York 6619, Taconic 7117
North Carolina: Foundation 7370
Pennsylvania: American 8079, Heinz 8240
Tennessee: **Bridgestone 8646**
Texas: **AT&T 8765**
Wisconsin: Johnson 9823

Civil rights, formal/general education

North Carolina: Reynolds 7458

Civil rights, gays/lesbians

California: Bohnett 300, Haas 637, vanLobenSels 1260
Colorado: **Gill 1382**
Florida: Dade 1957
Massachusetts: Harmsworth 3942
Michigan: **Arcus 4223**, Grand Rapids 4326
Minnesota: Bremer 4523, Phillips 4655
New Mexico: Santa Fe 5496
New York: Kraus 6352, New York 6613, New York 6615, Palm 6681, Rapoport 6772, Snowdon 7012
Oregon: Holmes 8020
Pennsylvania: **Johnson 8274**

Civil rights, immigrants

California: Caufield 367, Firedoll 508, Haas 637, Rosenberg 1065, vanLobenSels 1260
District of Columbia: Cafritz 1780
Michigan: Grand Rapids 4326
Minnesota: Bremer 4523, Minneapolis 4623, Phillips 4655
New Mexico: Santa Fe 5496
New York: **Carnegie 5707**, New York 6613, New York 6615, Speyer 7027

Civil rights, minorities

Arizona: A.P.S. 86
California: vanLobenSels 1260
District of Columbia: Cafritz 1780
Florida: Dade 1957
Illinois: Anixter 2597
Maryland: Rock 3717
Michigan: Grand Rapids 4326
Minnesota: Bremer 4523, Minneapolis 4623, Phillips 4655
New Jersey: New York 5336, Victoria 5440
New Mexico: Santa Fe 5496
New York: Elias 5920, New York 6613, New York 6615, Revson 6789, Scherman 6918
North Carolina: Foundation 7370, Reynolds 7458

Civil rights, public education

California: ChevronTexaco 380
Florida: Picower 2169
Massachusetts: Reebok 4098
Michigan: Ford 4307

Civil rights, public policy

California: vanLobenSels 1260

Civil rights, race/intergroup relations

California: Akonadi 199, California 345, Irvine 698, Orange 957
Colorado: Rose 1445
Connecticut: Larsen 1579
District of Columbia: Mazda 1828, Meyer 1834, **Public 1844**
Florida: Community 1939, FPL 2010, **Knight 2097**
Georgia: **Georgia 2397, Keough 2426**
Illinois: **Allstate 2588**, Field 2728, **Ploughshares 2945**, Polk 2946, **Shifting 3006**, Stuart 3028
Indiana: **Lilly 3192**
Maryland: Hirschhorn 3650
Massachusetts: Boston 3812, Hyams 3961, Poss 4087
Michigan: Community 4254, Grand Rapids 4326, **Mott 4399**, Whirlpool 4480
Minnesota: Bremer 4523, Duluth 4556, Initiative 4593, Minneapolis 4623, Musser 4629, Saint Paul 4671, Walker 4711
Missouri: **Deer 4804**, Kansas 4842, Roblee 4893
New Jersey: Cowles 5170
New Mexico: Santa Fe 5496
New York: Banfi 5597, **Bismarck 5633, Ford 5970**, Gould 6083, Gould 6085, **Guggenheim 6118, Heineman 6165**, Kealy 6303, New York 6615, **Peierls 6705**, Soros 7024, **Walter 7211, Zenkel 7295, Zilkha 7300**
North Carolina: **Babcock 7308**, Cumberland 7349, Reynolds 7458, Triangle 7496
Ohio: Columbus 7580, Dayton 7604, Gund 7657, Richland 7819
Pennsylvania: Dolfinger 8172, Falk 8193
Tennessee: Community 8660
Texas: Kempner 8987, Kinder 8994, Meadows 9049
Vermont: **Ben 9355**
Virginia: Delmar 9410
Washington: **Kongsgaard 9620**
Wisconsin: Fleck 9799, Kikkoman 9836, Milwaukee 9876

Civil rights, voter education

California: Bohnett 300, Koshland 777, **Streisand 1204**
New York: **Carnegie 5707**
Tennessee: **Bridgestone 8646**

Civil rights, women

California: Feintech 499, vanLobenSels 1260
District of Columbia: Beech 1771, Cafritz 1780, **Patterson 1840, Wallace 1858**
Michigan: Grand Rapids 4326
Minnesota: Bremer 4523, Minneapolis 4623, Phillips 4655
New Mexico: Santa Fe 5496
New York: **Bydale 5694**, New York 6613, New York 6615, Revson 6789, Vance 7193, Wendling 7242
North Carolina: Reynolds 7458
Washington: Channel 9568

Community development

Alabama: Alabama 1, AmSouth 5, Brock 16, Bruno 17, Carson 19, Central 20, Community 24, Community 27, Hearin 37, Hill 39, Kaul 40, McWane 50, Protective 58, Smith 63, Trippe 69, **Union 70**
Alaska: Alaska 78, Alaska 79, Rasmuson 85
Arizona: A.P.S. 86, Arizona 87, Community 91, **Globe 101**, Stardust 141

Arkansas: Altheimer 155, Arkansas 156, East 160, Northwest 169, Rockefeller 172, Ross 174, Union 183, Wal-Mart 184, White 187
California: Ackerman 193, Allergan 203, Amgen 219, **Appleton 225**, Ayrshire 247, Baker 251, Barker 257, Bartman 259, Benbough 276, Borina 306, Borina 307, CAA 341, California 345, Callison 351, Cantus 355, Community 401, Community 402, Community 403, Community 406, Community 407, Copley 416, Corcoran 417, Crockett 430, **Draper 466**, Dreyer's 468, East 474, Farrell 496, Fieldstone 506, Fluor 523, Follis 525, Friedman 538, Gellert 559, Genentech 562, Gerbode 564, Gilmore 578, Goldrich 598, Harrington 652, Hewlett 671, Humboldt 691, Hutton 694, Intuit 696, Jackson 706, **Jacobs 707**, Jacobs 708, **Juniata 734, K.L. 736, Kalliopeia 740**, Kapor 743, Keller 752, **KLM 767**, Koret 774, Koret 775, Lampert 786, Lane 787, Leavey 797, Lester 807, Los Altos 828, Marin 854, **McConnell 870**, McCune 872, McKay 877, Milken 898, Mistlin 902, Nestle 935, Nicholas 937, Pacific 970, PacifiCare 971, Parker 979, Parsons 980, Pasadena 982, Peninsula 989, Petersen 994, Pickford 1005, **PMI 1008**, Rancho 1031, Red 1035, **S.G. 1078**, Sacramento 1080, San Diego 1087, San Francisco 1088, San Joaquin 1089, San Luis 1090, Santa Barbara 1093, Sence 1126, Shasta 1139, Short 1148, Sierra 1151, Sierra 1152, Smith 1162, Sobrato 1172, Soda 1173, Solano 1175, Sonora 1178, Springcreek 1185, **Strauss 1203**, Stuart 1206, Swift 1219, Swinerton 1221, Teichert 1231, Truckee 1244, Union 1250, **Unocal 1252**, Waitt 1275, Weingart 1288, WHH 1300, Williams 1307, Zellerbach 1326
Colorado: Anschutz 1334, Aspen 1338, Boettcher 1344, Brett 1349, Community 1357, Community 1359, Denver 1364, Donnell 1367, El Pomar 1374, Gooding 1384, JFM 1397, Johnson 1398, Kitzmiller 1405, Lewis 1410, Pikes 1437, Piton 1439, Price 1442, Qwest 1443, Rose 1445, Western 1471
Connecticut: **Aetna 1479**, Bissell 1495, Bodenwein 1497, Bridgeport 1504, Community 1514, Community 1515, Community 1516, Community 1517, Connecticut 1518, Ensworth 1535, **Ettinger 1536**, Fisher 1542, Flinn 1543, Foley 1544, Hartford 1563, Hartford 1564, Hubbell 1569, Larsen 1579, Liberty 1586, Long 1590, Main 1594, Martin 1598, Matthies 1600, Northeast 1614, Palmer 1621, **Praxair 1629**, Stone 1654, TWS 1666, United 1668, **Xerox 1680**
Delaware: Common 1700, Crestlea 1701, Delaware 1706, Hall 1718, Schiff 1750
District of Columbia: Cafritz 1780, **Case 1782**, Community 1785, **Hill 1809**, Kimsey 1817, Lehrman 1821, Meyer 1834, **Moriah 1835, Public 1844**, Vaterstetten 1855, Vradenburg 1856, Washington 1860
Florida: Adler 1871, Bank 1890, BankAtlantic 1891, Blum 1912, Capital 1924, Carse 1925, Cobb 1935, Community 1939, Community 1942, Community 1944, Community 1945, Community 1946, Community 1947, Community 1948, Dade 1957, duPont 1983, Eckerd 1986, FPL 2010, Garner 2018, Glazer 2024, Gulf 2042, Hicks 2059, Lazzara 2105, Martin 2130, Moran 2143, Nessel 2152, Ocean 2156, Phillips 2168, Quantum 2181, Rales 2184, Raymund 2188, Rayonier 2189, Rinker 2197, Ryder 2213, Selby 2230, Southwest 2240, St. Joe 2244, Sudakoff 2256, TECO 2270, United 2276, **Vanneck 2278, Winn 2301**
Georgia: Atlanta 2320, Callaway 2337, Charter 2345, Community 2355, Community 2356, Community 2357, Community 2358, Community 2359, Community 2361, Community 2362, Cousins 2365, Delta 2372, **Dobbs 2373**, English 2378, **Gage 2392, Georgia 2397**, Harland 2407, Jinks 2422, Lanier 2428, Livingston 2435, Ma-Ran 2439, Marshall 2442, Morris 2454, North 2458, Patterson 2460, Poole 2466, Rollins 2475, Russell 2478, SunTrust 2496, Synovus 2497, **UPS 2503**, Williams 2514, Woolford 2524, Zeist 2529

Hawaii: Alexander 2530, Bank 2535, Castle 2537, Change 2539, Hawaii 2545, Hawaiian 2546, HMSA 2547
Idaho: CHC 2566
Illinois: Abbott 2580, Adreani 2585, Alsdorf 2590, AMCORE 2591, Blair 2622, Bruce 2634, Camp 2649, Charleston 2657, Chicago 2661, Coleman 2673, Community 2677, Community 2678, Community 2679, Community 2681, Cooper 2683, D and R 2693, Deere 2699, DeKalb 2701, Dillon 2704, Elgin 2717, Field 2728, Funk 2741, Geneseo 2750, GKN 2758, Harris 2787, Harrison 2791, Hermann 2798, Houlsby 2805, I and G 2811, JYN 2821, Katten 2826, Libra 2858, **Motorola 2906**, New 2912, Oak Park 2922, Omron 2926, Petersen 2941, Pick 2943, Polk 2946, Russell 2976, Schwartz 2991, Seabury 2993, **Shifting 3006, Square 3018**, Steadley 3020, Steans 3021, Stern 3023, USG 3046, Weiss 3062, Wieboldt 3069, Wilemal 3070, Winfrey 3077, Woodward 3085
Indiana: Adams 3095, Ball 3103, Blue 3107, Brown 3110, Cass 3115, Central 3116, Citizens 3118, Community 3122, Community 3124, Community 3125, Community 3126, Community 3127, Community 3128, Community 3129, Community 3132, Community 3133, Crown Point 3135, **Cummins 3136**, Dearborn 3137, Decatur 3138, DeKalb 3141, Duneland 3143, East Chicago 3144, Elkhart 3145, English 3146, Fairbanks 3147, Ford 3150, Four 3151, Griffith 3158, Hancock 3160, Harrison 3161, Heritage 3166, Irwin 3175, Jasper 3177, Johnson 3178, Kimball 3182, Kuhne 3187, Legacy 3189, **Lilly 3192**, Lilly 3194, Marshall 3199, McAllister 3202, McMillen 3203, Michigan 3205, Moore 3207, NiSource 3213, Noble 3214, Northern 3215, Noyes 3216, Oakley 3217, Ogle 3218, Portland 3223, Pulliam 3225, Ripley 3230, Steuben 3241, Storehouse 3242, Tipton 3243, Tyson 3246, Unity 3247, Vectren 3249, Wabash 3250, Wayne 3253, Welborn 3254, Wells 3255, White 3257, Whitley 3258
Iowa: AmerUs 3261, Bechtel 3263, Bechtel 3264, Bechtel 3265, Cedar Rapids 3275, Community 3277, Community 3278, Des Moines 3281, HNI 3293, Holden 3294, Holthues 3295, Howe 3296, Iowa 3298, Knapp 3301, Krause 3302, Lee 3305, Mansfield 3308, Maytag 3309, Maytag 3310, McDonald 3312, Muscatine 3318, Principal 3326
Kansas: Baughman 3346, Capitol 3350, Cessna 3351, Cooper 3353, Hutchinson 3368, Shannon 3392, Topeka 3400
Kentucky: Blue 3407, Community 3414, Community 3415, Cralle 3416, E.ON 3417, Robinson 3449, Sutherland 3451, Young 3454
Louisiana: Baton Rouge 3462, Brown 3465, Community 3469, Jones 3491, Keller 3493, Lorio 3496, New Orleans 3503, RosaMary 3507, Scott 3509, Wheless 3514, Young 3518
Maine: Alfond 3523, Davenport 3531, Gardiner 3536, **Golden 3538**, JTG 3542, Kennebec 3543, Maine 3548, Mulford 3551, TD 3558
Maryland: Abell 3559, Baker 3566, Baker 3567, Casey 3586, Chaney 3587, Choice 3589, **Cohen 3594**, Columbia 3595, Community 3598, Community 3599, Decesaris 3611, Delaplaine 3614, Felburn 3629, Grace 3638, Kerr 3661, Lockhart 3681, Lockheed 3682, Mid 3693, Perdue 3705, Price 3709, Rouse 3724, TKF 3747
Massachusetts: Adams 3771, Ansin 3779, Barr 3791, Bayrd 3795, Berkshire 3800, Boston 3812, **Bromley 3817, Bruner 3819**, Cabot 3823, Cape Cod 3833, Chase 3847, Clarke 3849, Clipper 3850, Community 3854, Community 3855, Copeland 3859, Crane 3866, Davis 3875, Demoulas 3879, Dunn 3884, Eastern 3886, Edgerly 3889, Ellsworth 3892, **Fidelity 3904**, Fletcher 3912, Garfield 3921, Harrington 3943, High 3950, Highland 3951, Hoche 3954, Hyams 3961, Island 3965, Janey 3968, Knight 3987, Ladd 3992, Liberty 4006, Lowell 4014, McEvoy 4032, Miller 4039, MWC 4046, Neighborhood 4049, North 4057, O'Brien 4058, **OneBeacon 4060**, Parker 4069, **PerkinElmer 4077**, Peters 4081,

Wyoming: Scott 9991, Thorson 9994, True 9996, Wyoming 10000

Community development, association

California: Hoag 679
Florida: Community 1947
New York: **Spirit 7033**

Community development, business promotion

Illinois: Beidler 2613
Indiana: Central 3116, Vectren 3249
Maine: Alfond 3521
Michigan: **Stoddard 4447**
Minnesota: Northwest 4637
Ohio: Nationwide 7771
Texas: Sterling 9212
Wisconsin: Madison 9854

Community development, citizen coalitions

Alabama: Community 25
Florida: Gulf 2041
Illinois: Woods 3084
New Mexico: Santa Fe 5496
New York: **Heron 6176**, Loeb 6439, **Mertz 6538**
Ohio: **Needmor 7774**
Wisconsin: Shattuck 9926

Community development, civic centers

Illinois: Harrison 2790
Michigan: Frey 4316
Texas: Herzstein 8949, Meredith 9054

Community development, equal rights

Georgia: **Georgia 2397**
New York: **Mertz 6538**

Community development, government agencies

California: Vons 1270

Community development, management/ technical aid

California: Irvine 698
New York: **Citigroup 5755**

Community development, neighborhood associations

Alabama: Community 25
Indiana: Community 3124
Massachusetts: Stoneman 4168
New York: Loeb 6439
Pennsylvania: Penn 8371

Community development, neighborhood development

Alabama: Finlay 33
California: Eucalyptus 489, First 511, Haas 637, Herbst 669, Irvine 698, Ludwick 829, McIntyre 876, Peninsula 989
Colorado: Pikes 1437
Connecticut: Community 1514, Roberts 1635
Delaware: Reynolds 1743
Florida: Community 1948, Dade 1957, Gulf 2041, **Knight 2097**
Georgia: Community 2355, Community 2357, Illges 2416, Jones 2424
Idaho: Idaho 2570, Simplot 2575
Illinois: **Allstate 2588**, Geraldi 2752, **MacArthur 2868**, McNally 2885, Moline 2902, Oak Park 2922, Seigle 2997, Sirius 3010

Indiana: Anderson 3099, Ball 3104, Central 3116, Community 3131, Irwin 3174, Lafayette 3188, Legacy 3189, Whitley 3258
Iowa: Cedar Rapids 3275, Poweshiek 3325
Kansas: Garvey 3363, Powell 3381
Louisiana: Jones 3491
Maryland: Baltimore 3568, England 3622, Goldseker 3636, Hoffberger 3652
Massachusetts: Manzi 4021, Melville 4034, Merck 4035
Michigan: Barry 4227, Frey 4316, Grand Rapids 4326, **Kellogg 4357**, Miller 4394, Prince 4416, Upjohn 4465
Minnesota: Manitou 4610, Saint Paul 4671, Smikis 4687
Mississippi: Community 4737, Lower 4751
Missouri: Kemper 4846
Nebraska: Lexington 4986
New Jersey: Jockey 5260, Pascale 5349
New York: Boisi 5650, Community 5780, Community 5784, Gimbel 6034, **Heron 6176**, **Jaffe 6250**, Kearns 6304, Levitt 6409, Paestum 6678, Richmond 6800, **Saltzman 6900**, Schwartz 6938, Wallach 7210, **Wolfensohn 7270**
North Carolina: Community 7343
Ohio: Community 7582, Dorn 7612, Greene 7653, Saint 7830
Pennsylvania: 1957 8071, Allegheny 8076, Beaver 8098, Berks 8103, Chester 8141, Hirtzel 8253, Penn 8371, Truman 8483
South Carolina: Community 8584, Self 8610
Tennessee: Community 8661, Community 8662, Hyde 8693, Thompson 8733
Texas: Burnett 8801, Dallas 8855, El Paso 8882, Fikes 8899, McGovern 9044, Meyer 9057, Smith 9196, Wichita 9280
Virginia: **Oak 9488**, Staunton 9521
Washington: Community 9571, Lauzier 9626
Wisconsin: Assurant 9748, Beloit 9757, Green Bay 9810, Joy 9828, Madison 9854, Marshfield 9861
Wyoming: Community 9977

Community development, public education

California: Jams 711
Michigan: General 4320
New York: Revson 6789

Community development, public policy

California: Jams 711
Illinois: Woods 3084
Pennsylvania: CIGNA 8143

Community development, public/private ventures

Michigan: Frey 4316
Minnesota: Initiative 4593
New York: Butler 5692
Pennsylvania: Pittsburgh 8386
Texas: Jones 8976
Wyoming: Wyoming 10000

Community development, real estate

Texas: Pema 9114

Community development, service clubs

Delaware: Bishop 1694
Georgia: Snodgrass 2492
Indiana: Kimball 3182

Community development, small businesses

California: Firedoll 508, **Google 606**, Intuit 696
Illinois: Coleman 2673
Massachusetts: Babson 3787
Michigan: Comerica 4251
Minnesota: TCF 4699

New York: **Goldman 6056**, **Merrill 6537**, **PepsiCo 6714**
Oregon: **NIKE 8046**
Pennsylvania: Tippins 8477
Washington: Seattle 9680

Community development, volunteer services

Louisiana: Lorio 3496

Community development, women's clubs

Michigan: Nokomis 4404
Texas: Simmons 9187

Computer science

California: **Hertz 670**, **Keck 750**, Northrop 942
Connecticut: Larsen 1579
Idaho: **Micron 2571**
Iowa: Principal 3326
Maryland: **Adams 3562**, Wasserman 3758
Massachusetts: Cabot 3823
New York: **Time 7142**
Ohio: **Timken 7880**
Texas: Dell 8864, **EDS 8877**, San Antonio 9166, **Shell 9181**, Wagner 9259
Virginia: Collis 9398
Washington: Norcliffe 9650

Consumer protection

New York: **Global 6043**
Ohio: Akron 7526, Progressive 7808

Courts/judicial administration

California: Jams 711
Connecticut: Tow 1661
Illinois: Bauer 2609
Maryland: Wareheim 3756
Minnesota: Opperman 4641
New York: Fuchsberg 5998, Gimbel 6034, **Prospect 6750**

Crime/abuse victims

Florida: Langford 2102
New Jersey: OceanFirst 5341
Pennsylvania: Blue 8112
Texas: di Portanova 8865

Crime/law enforcement

Arkansas: Whitt 188
California: Caruso 363, **Draper 466**, Norris 940
Colorado: McDonald 1421
District of Columbia: Cafritz 1780, Meyer 1834
Florida: Banbury 1889
Georgia: Chatham 2347, **Georgia 2397**, Woolley 2525
Hawaii: Wilcox 2559
Illinois: Keiser 2828
Indiana: Community 3128, East Chicago 3144, NiSource 3213, Reeves 3227
Louisiana: Booth 3464, Louisiana 3497
Massachusetts: Community 3855
Michigan: Grand Haven 4325
Minnesota: Athwin 4508, Leonard 4604, Rupp 4669
New Hampshire: **Linnell 5096**
New Mexico: Carlsbad 5469, McCune 5488
New York: **Abelard 5508**, **Bydale 5694**, Goldman 6053, Goldsmith 6060, **Guggenheim 6118**, **Robinson 6819**, Wendt 7243, Western 7248
North Carolina: Cumberland 7349, Triangle 7496
Ohio: Coshocton 7593, FirstEnergy 7630, Gund 7657, Lozick 7724, Stark 7867
Oklahoma: Bernsen 7925
Pennsylvania: Community 8154, Dolfinger 8172, Mandell 8322
South Carolina: Central 8577, Collins 8582, Post 8603

North Carolina: Reynolds 7457
Ohio: Austin 7536
Texas: Hillcrest 8952, Meadows 9049, Speas 9206
Virginia: Sandler 9512
Washington: Norcliffe 9650
West Virginia: Kanawha 9723
Wisconsin: McBeath 9864

Dental school/education

California: **Foundation 531**
Kansas: Delta 3354
Massachusetts: Corkin 3861, Oral 4061
Michigan: Ravitz 4418
New York: Johnson 6272, Werblow 7245
Oregon: Johnson 8027

Developmentally disabled, centers & services

Alabama: Mitchell 53
Arizona: Lovell 119
California: Gogian 588, Lund 831, Orfalea 958, Wells 1295
Colorado: **Daniels 1362**
District of Columbia: **Kennedy 1816**
Florida: Colen 1938, Pinellas 2170
Georgia: Goizueta 2400, Harris 2408, Horowitz 2415, Porter 2468
Illinois: Hartke 2792, Woods 3083
Indiana: Anderson 3099
Kentucky: Fischer 3418, Young 3454
Minnesota: Bieber 4518
Nebraska: Heuermann 4973
New Jersey: Hackett 5219
New York: **Cranaleith 5805**, Lindner 6426, McCarthy 6516, **Quick 6761**
Ohio: DBJ 7605, Haile 7659, Wohlgemuth 7913
Rhode Island: Jackson 8541
Texas: Anderson 8759, Lyons 9024, Ward 9262
Virginia: Adams 9366
Washington: Aven 9554

Diabetes

Arizona: Hermundslie 107
California: Colombo 398, Fitzgerald 514, Hench 668, Hillblom 673, King 760, Mead 881, Ornest 959, Preuss 1015, Rotasa 1070
Colorado: Davis 1363
Connecticut: **Aetna 1479**
Illinois: Harrison 2791
Indiana: **Lilly 3192**
Iowa: R & R 3327
Massachusetts: **Iacocca 3963**
Michigan: Ford 4305
New Jersey: Aventis 5120
New York: Elishis 5921, Gordon 6074, **OSI 6670**, **Parsons 6694**, Rosansky 6832, **Sapp 6906**, Starwood 7049
North Carolina: Reynolds 7457
Ohio: Brennan 7554
Pennsylvania: M & S 8318, McDonald's 8333, **Oberkotter 8365**, Peterson 8376
Texas: Bass 8777, Bickel 8790, Franklin 8908, Holthouse 8959, McCoy 9038, **Pearle 9113**, San Antonio 9166
Washington: Benaroya 9556
Wisconsin: Community 9776, Green Bay 9810, McDonough 9865, Sub 9945

Diabetes research

California: Daly 437, DeVito 452, Mudd 924, Peterson 995, Semel 1125, Solari 1176, Treadwell 1243
Connecticut: **Vasey 1670**
Florida: Schaefer 2222
Georgia: Graves 2403
Illinois: Katten 2826, Lewis 2857
Massachusetts: Fireman 3910, Hagerty 3938, **Iacocca 3963**
Michigan: Dauch 4268, Thomas 4456

Mississippi: Telos 4768
New Jersey: **James 5254**
New York: Emwiga 5930, Hall 6137, Kaplan 6289, Matlin 6506, Spitzer 7034
Ohio: Lennon 7710, **Warrington 7895**
Oklahoma: Hille 7943
Pennsylvania: Cooper 8158, **Oberkotter 8365**
South Carolina: TSC 8618
Tennessee: **Garrott 8680**
Texas: Holthouse 8959, **Pearle 9113**, Vaughan 9249
Utah: Bastian 9306
Wisconsin: Kellogg 9832

Digestive diseases

Georgia: Pope 2467
New York: **Mullen 6595**, New York 6614

Digestive disorders research

California: Burch 334
New York: **Black 5635**, **Mullen 6595**

Disabilities, people with

Alabama: McMillan 49
Arizona: Arizona 87, Morris 124, Noah's 127
California: Atkinson 239, **Baker 252**, Barker 257, Bell 274, Bothin 309, **Bull 331**, California 345, **Chiron 383**, Doheny 460, Eaton 475, Fansler 494, Fireman's 510, Five 516, Forest 527, Gilmore 578, Gross 621, Humboldt 691, Jackson 706, Johnson 722, Ludwick 829, Lytel 836, Marin 854, Norris 940, Oakland 948, Odell 951, Pasadena 982, Peninsula 989, Rosenfeld 1067, Sacramento 1080, San Diego 1087, San Francisco 1088, Sandy 1092, **Smith 1167**, Soda 1173, Sonora 1178, Steiner 1191, Stern 1195, Taper 1226, True 1245, Van Nuys 1261, Vons 1270, Weingart 1288, Wood 1318, Wynn 1324
Colorado: Anschutz 1334, **Daniels 1362**, El Pomar 1374, Hunter 1394, King 1404, McDonald 1421, Schlessman 1450, Summit 1463
Connecticut: Bissell 1495, Community 1515, Community 1517, Connecticut 1518, Culpeper 1521, Long 1590, **Newman's 1609**, **Niles 1612**, **Ziegler 1683**
Delaware: Laffey 1725
District of Columbia: Aid 1765, Cafritz 1780, Loughran 1823, Willard 1861
Florida: Bank 1890, Beveridge 1907, Bush 1922, Community 1943, Community 1946, FPL 2010, Gooding 2028, Gore 2031, Gorin 2032, Pinellas 2170, Rayonier 2189, Storer 2252, Wolfson 2304
Georgia: Goizueta 2400, Harland 2407, Rich 2472, Russell 2478, **UPS 2503**, Woolley 2525
Illinois: Blowitz 2623, **Brach 2630**, Chicago 2661, Coleman 2673, Community 2677, **Gallagher 2744**, Galter 2745, McNally 2885, Northern 2918, Oak Park 2922, Polk 2946, Reese 2961, Rhoades 2965, Siragusa 3009, Snite 3012, **Square 3018**, Thoma 3035, Washington 3058, Woodward 3085
Indiana: Anderson 3099, Central 3116, Community 3123, Community 3125, Montgomery 3206, Noyes 3216, Pulliam 3225, Raker 3226, Wayne 3253
Iowa: Maytag 3310, Siouxland 3332, **Van Wyk 3340**
Kansas: Hansen 3366, Hutchinson 3368
Kentucky: Brown 3409, Gheens 3421, Woosley 3453
Louisiana: Baton Rouge 3462, Community 3469, Lupin 3498, Wilson 3515
Maine: Great 3539
Maryland: Clark 3591, Columbia 3595, Gross 3640, Leidy 3673, **Weinberg 3759**
Massachusetts: Alden 3777, Boston 3812, Cabot 3823, Clipper 3850, Community 3855, Easthampton 3887, Fassino 3900, Hyams 3961, Leclerc 4000, Levy 4005, Peabody 4074, Phillips 4082, **Schooner 4131**, Shapiro 4136, Stevens 4163, Stevens 4164, **TJX 4183**, Worcester 4209
Michigan: **Berman 4230**, Community 4256, Grand Rapids 4326, Lansing 4372, **Sage 4427**, Southwest 4442, Steelcase 4446

Minnesota: Bell 4514, Bieber 4518, Bremer 4523, Deluxe 4549, Duluth 4556, Edwards 4561, Kelley 4597, Kopp 4599, Minneapolis 4623, Ordean 4643, Pacific 4646, **Patterson 4647**, Phillips 4655, Rivers 4666, Rochester 4668, TCF 4699, Thorpe 4701, Tozer 4703
Missouri: American 4773, Butler 4793, **Enterprise 4810**, Green 4822, **Hana 4827**, Lopata 4859, Pettus 4882, Pott 4886
Nebraska: **McDonald 4989**
Nevada: Fairweather 5032, Greenspun 5034, Nevada 5047, Pennington 5053, Redfield 5055, Sierra 5064
New Hampshire: Lindsay 5095
New Jersey: Berger 5128, Brotherton 5145, Cowles 5170, Hackett 5219, Hyde 5247, **Johnson 5261**, **Johnson 5265**, Knistrom 5282, MCJ 5324, **Newcombe 5338**, OceanFirst 5341, Summit 5417
New Mexico: McCune 5488, Santa Fe 5496
New York: Achelis 5513, Arkell 5565, Baird 5592, Barker 5600, **Barth 5603**, Bodman 5647, Butler 5692, Cohen 5768, Community 5781, Community 5782, Community 5783, **Edouard 5909**, Glickenhaus 6042, Goldman 6053, Goldsmith 6060, Hirsch 6188, Hoyt 6203, **Keefe 6305**, Kiernan 6321, Lavelle 6384, Lindner 6426, Litwin 6436, Marx 6498, Metcalf 6541, **Milbank 6547**, **Monell 6566**, Moses 6587, **National 6603**, NEC 6605, New York 6615, New York 6618, Nichols 6628, Noble 6632, Northern 6639, Park 6689, Parshelsky 6693, **Pepsi 6713**, Ross 6864, Snow 7011, St. George's 7040, **St. Giles 7041**, Troisi 7164, Turner 7175, Wendt 7243, Western 7248
North Carolina: Biddle 7317, Cumberland 7349, Janirve 7404, Nias 7435, Reynolds 7457, Reynolds 7460, Triangle 7496
North Dakota: Leach 7516, Stern 7521
Ohio: Akron 7526, Britton 7556, Bruening 7558, Cincinnati 7574, Columbus 7580, Dater 7600, Fairfield 7622, **Freygang 7640**, Kramer 7704, Mayerson 7739, Murphy 7769, Nationwide 7771, Richland 7819, Schiff 7836, Schlink 7839, Schott 7842, Sisler 7858, Stark 7867, Stocker 7870, White 7905, Youngstown 7920
Oklahoma: Zarrow 7993
Oregon: Jackson 8024, Johnson 8027, Tucker 8065
Pennsylvania: **Alcoa 8075**, Arcadia 8086, Blue 8112, Buck 8123, Campbell 8128, Connelly 8157, Dolfinger 8172, Donnelly 8176, Fourjay 8209, Hillman 8249, Hillman 8250, Huston 8263, Jaindl 8269, Kardon 8279, Kline 8293, Lancaster 8300, Mandell 8322, McKinney 8339, Philadelphia 8378, Rockwell 8408, Shenango 8438, Simonds 8442, Smith 8444, Smith 8445, Stackpole 8456, Steinman 8459, Trees 8480, Trexler 8481, Triple 8482, Widener 8502
Rhode Island: CVS 8529, Kimball 8542, Noonan 8550
South Dakota: Sioux Falls 8630
Texas: Abell 8749, Cain 8809, CH 8823, Circle 8829, Cockrell 8835, Community 8841, Constantin 8843, Dallas 8855, Hillcrest 8952, Kempner 8987, Koehler 9001, Kronkosky 9002, McKee 9045, Moody 9070, Reliant 9144, Rockwell 9154, **Shell 9181**, Speas 9206, Strake 9215, Weaver 9267, Wright 9294
Utah: Eccles 9320, Wing 9352
Vermont: Vermont 9361
Virginia: AMERIGROUP 9369, Delmar 9410, **Gannett 9428**, Lynchburg 9463, Memorial 9474, **Mitsubishi 9476**, Norfolk 9484, Perry 9495, Virginia Beach 9532
Washington: Cheney 9569, Community 9571, Glaser 9594, Medina 9640, Norcliffe 9650, Tacoma 9693
West Virginia: Kanawha 9723, McDonough 9726, Parkersburg 9730, Teubert 9735
Wisconsin: Cornerstone 9781, Crump 9783, Cudahy 9785, Milwaukee 9876, Northwestern 9884, Schoenleber 9921, Stackner 9934
Wyoming: **Schultz 9990**

Disasters, 9/11/01

California: Craig 425, PG&E 1000, Resnick 1041, Short 1148
Connecticut: **Niles 1611**
Delaware: **Neuberger 1735**, Singer 1753
Florida: Dade 1957, Hard 2047, Rooms 2204
Illinois: Chicago 2662
Massachusetts: Casty 3839
New York: Babbitt 5586, Bear 5609, Canary 5702, **LI 6418**, **MBIA 6512**, **Mitchell 6559**, New York 6615, Potter's 6743, Riggio 6807, Saligman 6895, **Scheuer 6921**, Silberstein 6979, Sullivan 7093, **Surdna 7103**
Oregon: Wessinger 8067
Texas: Clear 8831, Turner 9242

Disasters, domestic resettlement

New York: AIG 5529

Disasters, fire prevention/control

Alabama: Thompson 67
California: MFU 894
Connecticut: Hubbell 1569
Delaware: **Neuberger 1735**
Indiana: Reynolds 3229, Simon 3236
Minnesota: Schmidt 4673
Missouri: **Monsanto 4868**, Schwartze 4898
New Jersey: Visceglia 5441
New York: American 5552, Campbell 5700, CJM 5756, Tarnopol 7123
North Carolina: Perkins 7445
Ohio: Akron 7526, **Alpaugh 7527**, Beaverson 7541, Loeb 7721, Mangano 7733, Pugliese 7810
Pennsylvania: Degenstein 8166, Hoverter 8258
Rhode Island: **FM 8537**
Tennessee: Thompson 8733
Texas: Bridwell 8797, White 9279
Virginia: **Lambert 9453**, Luck 9461, Meador 9473, Olsson 9491
Washington: Klorfine 9619
Wisconsin: Duncan 9793

Disasters, floods

Florida: Gemcon 2019
New York: AIG 5529

Disasters, Hurricane Katrina

Alabama: Community 25, Community 27
Arizona: Arizona 87
California: **Altman 211**, Community 406, Los Altos 828, Peninsula 989, Ventura 1264
Colorado: Community 1357, Community 1358, Ebrahimi 1371
Connecticut: Community 1514
Illinois: Schneider 2988
Indiana: Johnson 3178
Iowa: Community 3278
Kentucky: Blue 3407
Louisiana: Almar 3459, Baton Rouge 3462, New Orleans 3503
Maryland: Columbia 3595
Michigan: Ann Arbor 4221
Minnesota: Minneapolis 4623
Mississippi: Community 4737, Foundation 4743, Gulf 4745
New Hampshire: New Hampshire 5098
New York: **AIG 5529**, Central 5724, Community 5780, Grateful 6093, **H.R.C. 6125**, Heller 6169
North Carolina: Community 7344, Foundation 7370
Ohio: Akron 7526, Cincinnati 7574, Cleveland 7576, Columbus 7580
Pennsylvania: Centre 8136, Community 8153, Pittsburgh 8386
Texas: Austin 8768, Communities 8839, Dallas 8855, San Antonio 9166
Virginia: Arlington 9371
Washington: Community 9570

Wisconsin: Community 9780

Disasters, preparedness/services

California: Borchard 304, Clorox 389, Flora 521, Knight 768, Steinmetz 1192, Vons 1270
Colorado: **First 1377**
Connecticut: Boehringer 1498
Florida: A Friends' 1866, Fortin 2007, Gulf 2041
Georgia: Southern 2494
Illinois: **BP 2628**
Indiana: Kosciusko 3185
Maine: **Sandy 3555**
Maryland: **Agilent 3563**
Massachusetts: Clipper 3850, Community 3854
Minnesota: General 4570
New York: **AIG 5529**, **American 5553**, **Citigroup 5755**, Mangurian, 6482, **Pepsi 6713**
North Carolina: Merancas 7428
Ohio: **OMNOVA 7789**
Oregon: Collins 8008, Hedinger 8019, Mentor 8039
Tennessee: Ayers 8640, Washington 8741
Texas: Amarillo 8758, Bass 8777, Bridgeway 8796, Penney 9115
Virginia: American 9368, Campbell 9383, CarMax 9385, **de Beaumont 9408**
Wisconsin: Community 9779, Kikkoman 9836, Wisconsin 9967

Disasters, search/rescue

Nevada: **Omega 5050**
New York: Fludzinski 5964
Texas: **Notsew 9093**

Dispute resolution

California: Jams 711, Los Altos 828
New York: **Surdna 7103**

Down syndrome

California: Gogian 588
Florida: Quick 2182
Missouri: **Hana 4827**

Down syndrome research

Colorado: Sie 1455

Ear & throat diseases

California: Pfleger 999
Louisiana: Eye 3475
Massachusetts: Monsweag 4042
Pennsylvania: Fourjay 8209
Texas: Vale 9246

Ear & throat research

California: Caruso 363, Martin 859, Robinson 1060
Nevada: Fertitta 5033
Pennsylvania: **Oberkotter 8365**

Economic development

Alabama: Bedsole 12, Community 26
Alaska: Alaska 79
Arkansas: Wal-Mart 184
California: Community 402, **Draper 466**, Fluor 523, Fresno 537, Friedman 538, Haas 636, Intuit 696, Irvine 698, **Juniata 734**, **PMI 1008**, Roberts 1058, Roth 1071, Sobrato 1172, **Strauss 1203**, Union 1250, **Wells 1294**
Colorado: Anschutz 1334, Pikes 1437
Connecticut: Bridgeport 1504, Community 1514, Community 1515, Connecticut 1518, Fairfield 1537, Hartford 1564, Liberty 1586, Northeast 1614, Phoenix 1627
District of Columbia: **Bauman 1770**, **Hill 1809**

Florida: Community 1939, Community 1945, Dade 1957, duPont 1983, **Knight 2097**, SunTrust 2259
Georgia: Community 2357, Community 2358, Community 2362, Delta 2372, **Georgia 2397**, ING 2418, North 2458, **Scientific 2482**, Woodruff 2521
Illinois: **Aon 2598**, Chicago 2661, Community 2679, Driehaus 2710, Grand 2769
Indiana: Anthem 3102, Central 3116, Community 3124, Community 3128, East Chicago 3144, Madison 3197, Mutual 3210, Wells 3255
Iowa: Community 3277, Maytag 3309, Poweshiek 3325
Kansas: Hutchinson 3368
Kentucky: Blue 3407
Louisiana: New Orleans 3503
Maryland: Constellation 3602, Hoffberger 3652, Provident 3712, Rouse 3724, Thalheimer 3744
Massachusetts: Babson 3787, Cape Cod 3833, Community 3854, Garfield 3921, Island 3965, Lowell 4014, Melville 4034, **New England 4052**, North 4057
Michigan: Ann Arbor 4221, Brown 4240, Charlevoix 4246, Community 4252, Community 4254, Community 4256, Community 4257, Community 4258, Community 4259, **DaimlerChrysler 4265**, Jackson 4347, Kalamazoo 4352, Midland 4392, Miller 4394, **Mott 4399**, Petoskey 4412, Steelcase 4446, Strosacker 4450, World 4489
Minnesota: Bigelow 4519, Blandin 4520, Duluth 4556, Initiative 4593, Minneapolis 4623, Northwest 4637, Saint Paul 4671, St. Paul 4690, TCF 4699, West 4723, Xcel 4732
Mississippi: Foundation 4743, Riley 4763
Missouri: American 4773, Danforth 4803
Montana: Montana 4939
Nebraska: Lincoln 4987
Nevada: **Lemelson 5040**, Nevada 5047
New Jersey: Prudential 5360
New Mexico: Maddox 5487, PNM 5493, Santa Fe 5496, Taos 5498
New York: **Citigroup 5755**, Claiborne 5758, **Echoing 5905**, Gilder 6029, Gimbel 6034, **Grant 6091**, **Heron 6176**, Horncrest 6200, **JPMorgan 6277**, **MetLife 6542**, Mizuho 6562, **Norman 6635**, Richmond 6800, Roslyn 6859, **Surdna 7103**, Vidda 7198
North Carolina: BB&T 7312, Cumberland 7349, Foundation 7370, Goodrich 7378, Piedmont 7447, Progress 7453, **Wachovia 7502**
Ohio: Cleveland 7576, Columbus 7580, Community 7582, Community 7585, Findlay 7627, FirstEnergy 7630, Greene 7653, Haile 7659, MeadWestvaco 7745, Richland 7819, Scioto 7845
Oklahoma: Jones 7946, Williams 7989
Oregon: Boyd 8000, Jeld 8025
Pennsylvania: Beaver 8098, Benedum 8099, Berks 8103, Chester 8141, **Dominion 8173**, First 8202, Heinz 8241, Heinz 8242, McCune 8332, Mellon 8345, Pittsburgh 8386, PNC 8388, **PPG 8394**, Sordoni 8450, **Templeton 8475**, Vanguard 8490, York 8511
Rhode Island: CARLISLE 8521, Charter 8526, Roosa 8552
South Carolina: Byerly 8572
South Dakota: Sioux Falls 8630, South Dakota 8631
Tennessee: Benwood 8644, Plough 8718
Texas: **AT&T 8765**, Collins 8838, **ExxonMobil 8889**, **Silverton 9186**, USAA 9245
Vermont: Vermont 9361
Virginia: **Oak 9488**, Portsmouth 9498
Washington: **Casey 9567**, Crystal 9576, Foundation 9589, Seattle 9680
West Virginia: Kanawha 9723, Parkersburg 9730
Wisconsin: Alexander 9741, Alliant 9742, Bader 9749, Dudley 9792, Madison 9854
Wyoming: **Schultz 9990**

Economic development, visitors/convention bureau/tourism promotion

Indiana: Central 3116
Maryland: Choice 3589

Economically disadvantaged

Alabama: Community 24, McMillan 49

Arizona: A.P.S. 86, Arizona 87, Morris 124

California: Ahmanson 198, **American 217**, Atkinson 239, Barbonchielli 256, Blue 296, California 345, California 346, **Chiron 383**, Community 402, Confidence 411, Cowell 423, Craig 425, Croul 431, Danford 438, Dwyer 472, Eucalyptus 489, Fireman's 510, Friedman 538, Genentech 563, Gilmore 578, Grove 625, Gruber 626, Gumbiner 631, Haas 637, Humboldt 691, Intuit 696, **Jack 705**, Jacobs 708, **Kaiser 739**, Listwin 819, McKesson 879, Milken 898, Norris 940, Orange 957, Parsons 980, Peninsula 989, Pfaffinger 997, Pickford 1005, Price 1016, Rest 1044, Roberts 1058, Rosenberg 1065, Sacramento 1080, San Diego 1087, San Francisco 1088, Sandy 1092, Segal 1121, Sierra 1151, **Smith 1167**, Soda 1173, Sonora 1178, **Strauss 1203**, **Sun 1214**, Taper 1226, Union 1250, Valley 1256, Van Nuys 1261, Ventura 1264, Weingart 1288, Wynn 1324

Colorado: Anschutz 1334, **Anschutz 1335**, Boettcher 1344, Bonfils 1347, Colorado 1355, Coors 1360, **Daniels 1362**, El Pomar 1374, **First 1377**, Hunter 1394, King 1404, Qwest 1443, **StorageTek 1460**

Connecticut: **Bingham 1493**, Boehringer 1498, Bondi 1499, Cohen 1512, Community 1515, Community 1517, Connecticut 1518, Culpeper 1521, Fairfield 1537, Fisher 1542, **GE 1553**, Gladstein 1555, Hartford 1563, Larrabee 1578, Martin 1598, **Newman's 1609**, **Niles 1612**, **Orchard 1619**, Pequot 1625, **Xerox 1680**

Delaware: Crystal 1702, **Good 1715**, MBNA 1730, **Raskob 1741**, Reynolds 1743

District of Columbia: Agua 1764, Arcana 1768, Block 1776, Cafritz 1780, Fowler 1797, **Hill 1809**, **Hitachi 1810**, Meyer 1834, **Public 1844**, Stewart 1850

Florida: Schmid 1874, Banbury 1889, Bank 1890, Bastien 1892, Blue 1911, Bush 1922, Community 1946, Dade 1957, Ds 1976, duPont 1982, duPont 1983, Engelberg 1994, FPL 2010, Frazier 2011, Gainesville 2015, Gooding 2028, Gore 2031, Hall 2045, Kennedy 2087, Martin 2130, Pinellas 2170, Rayonier 2189, Ryder 2213, Southwest 2240, Wilson 2300

Georgia: AGL 2312, BellSouth 2323, Chatham 2347, Cooper 2363, ING 2418, Moore 2452, Patterson 2460, Rich 2472, **UPS 2503**

Hawaii: Hawaii 2545, Hughes 2548

Idaho: **Washington 2578**

Illinois: **Abbott 2579**, **Brach 2630**, **Burlington 2644**, **Burnett 2645**, CNA 2670, Coleman 2673, Community 2677, **Crane 2688**, Energizer 2721, Field 2728, Fry 2740, Kaplan 2823, Libra 2858, New 2912, Northern 2918, Owens 2929, Petersen 2941, Polk 2946, Prince 2948, SF 2998, **Shifting 3006**, Siragusa 3009, **Square 3018**, **Tuohy 3041**, White 3067, Woodward 3085

Indiana: Community 3123, Community 3125, Foellinger 3149, Health 3164, Irwin 3175, Lilly 3194, **Lumina 3196**, Moore 3207, Noyes 3216

Iowa: McElroy 3313, Siouxland 3332

Kansas: Hutchinson 3368, Jones 3370, Rudd 3385, Security 3390

Kentucky: Cralle 3416, Norton 3441, River 3448

Louisiana: Baton Rouge 3462, Booth 3464, Community 3469, Entergy 3474, Eye 3475

Maine: JTG 3542, Maine 3548, TD 3558

Maryland: Abell 3559, Allegis 3565, **Casey 3585**, Community 3600, Constellation 3602, Dresher 3617, Rathmann 3715, Rock 3717, **Weinberg 3759**

Massachusetts: Association 3783, Boston 3811, Boston 3812, Cape Cod 3833, Community 3855, Crawford 3867, Davis 3875, Ellsworth 3892, Goldberg 3927, Hoche 3954, Hyams 3961, Linsey 4010, Merck 4035, Mifflin 4038, Millipore 4040, Parker 4069, Ratshesky 4095, Sailors' 4123, Schrafft 4133, Smith 4150, **Staples 4156**, Stevens 4163, Stevens 4164, **Technical 4180**, **TJX 4183**, Weber 4200, Worcester 4209, Yawkey 4211

Michigan: Binda 4233, Comerica 4251, Community 4254, Community 4255, Fremont 4315, Grand Rapids 4326, Great 4330, Lansing 4372, Mackey 4380, Molinello 4395, **Mott 4399**, Shelden 4434, Skillman 4438, Steelcase 4446

Minnesota: Andersen 4502, Bell 4514, Bigelow 4519, Blue 4521, Cargill 4530, Carolyn 4533, Deluxe 4549, **Donaldson 4552**, Duluth 4556, **Ecolab 4557**, **Fuller 4567**, Grotto 4579, **Medtronic 4622**, Minneapolis 4623, Northwest 4637, Ordean 4643, Phillips 4655, Prophet 4658, RBC 4661, Sexton 4679, St. Paul 4690, **SUPERVALU 4695**, TCF 4699, Thorpe 4701, Xcel 4732

Missouri: American 4773, Boeing 4785, Butler 4793, **Fox 4815**, Goppert 4819, Green 4822, Herschend 4830, Jewish 4837, **Monsanto 4868**, Musgrave 4870, **Nestle 4872**, Roblee 4893, Vatterott 4921, **Wyeth 4930**

Montana: **Edwards 4936**, Washington 4941

Nebraska: Lozier 4988, Weitz 5016

Nevada: Fairweather 5032, Nevada 5047, Pennington 5053

New Hampshire: **Penates 5099**

New Jersey: **Aventis 5121**, Borden 5138, **Bristol 5143**, Brotherton 5145, Community 5167, Danellie 5177, Family 5191, First 5194, Hyde 5247, **Johnson 5263**, MCJ 5324, **Merck 5328**, **Newcombe 5338**, Pascale 5349, Princeton 5357, Reddy 5364, Roche 5372, Turrell 5431, Victoria 5440

New Mexico: McCune 5488, Santa Fe 5496

New York: **Abelard 5508**, Abrons 5511, Altman 5542, **Atlantic 5574**, Babbitt 5586, Baird 5592, Belfer 5615, Burden 5687, **Bydale 5694**, Centennial 5722, Chernow 5745, **Citigroup 5755**, Claiborne 5758, Clark 5759, Clark 5761, Clark 5762, Community 5785, **Cummings 5813**, Cummings 5815, **Daedalus 5821**, Dancing 5828, Daphne 5830, **Deutsche 5854**, **Dramatists 5883**, Dyson 5898, **East 5900**, Elias 5920, Everett 5941, **Ford 5970**, Goldie 6049, Goldman 6053, Gould 6083, Guttman 6124, **Heineman 6165**, Hollyhock 6197, Horncrest 6200, HSBC 6204, Hutchins 6218, I Have 6219, **Jockey 6264**, Johnson 6271, Jones 6274, **Keefe 6305**, Kiernan 6321, Knapp 6342, Lawrence 6385, Leach 6388, Lee 6391, **Macy 6471**, Marron 6493, **MetLife 6542**, **Mitsubishi 6560**, New York 6615, New York 6619, Nichols 6628, **Norman 6635**, Northern 6639, O'Connor 6645, Pedersen 6704, Pinkerton 6728, **PepsiCo 6714**, **Polo 6737**, Rhodebeck 6791, Ritter 6813, Rosenberg 6847, **Ross 6863**, Rubinstein 6876, Scherman 6918, Simon 6987, Sister 6994, Spunk 7036, St. George's 7040, Tiger 7139, Tuch 7170, **U.S. 7180**, Vernon 7195, **Walter 7211**, Wendt 7243

North Carolina: **Babcock 7308**, Community 7346, Corpening 7347, Cumberland 7349, Duke 7360, Foundation 7370, Janirve 7404, Piedmont 7447, Reynolds 7457, Reynolds 7459, Reynolds 7460, Triangle 7496, **Wachovia 7502**, Warner 7503, Weaver 7504

North Dakota: North Dakota 7519, Stern 7521

Ohio: Akron 7526, Beerman 7543, Bruening 7558, Cincinnati 7574, Columbus 7580, Cornerstone 7592, Dater 7600, Fairfield 7622, Ford 7633, GAR 7643, Gund 7657, IHS 7683, **Key 7700**, Levin 7712, Murphy 7768, Nationwide 7771, Nord 7779, Nordson 7781, Patterson 7797, Reuter 7817, Richland 7819, Russell 7827, Schlink 7839, Sisler 7858, Stocker 7870, **Timken 7880**, Watson 7896, White 7905, Wuliger 7918

Oregon: Carpenter 8003, Johnson 8027, Oregon 8049, Tucker 8065

Pennsylvania: 1957 8071, Arcadia 8086, **Armstrong 8090**, Claneil 8124, Clapp 8145, Connelly 8157, Cooper 8158, Dolfinger 8172, Eden 8182, Fourjay 8209, Garthwaite 8212, Hillman 8249, Hillman 8250, Hillman 8252, Hoyt 8259, Huston 8263, Maronda 8325, Merchants 8438, Penn 8371, **Pew 8377**, Philadelphia 8378, PNC 8388, Shenango 8438, Simonds 8442, Smith 8443, Trexler 8481

Puerto Rico: Puerto Rico 8515

Rhode Island: Kimball 8542, Rhode Island 8551

South Carolina: Central 8577, Springs 8617

South Dakota: Opus 8628, South Dakota 8631

Tennessee: Hurlbut 8692, Lazarus 8700

Texas: **A Glimmer 8747**, Abell 8749, Amarillo 8758, Brumley 8800, Cain 8809, CH 8823, Coastal 8833, Community 8841, Constantin 8843, Dallas 8855, di Portanova 8865, Edwards 8880, Fant 8892, George 8916, Hoblitzelle 8955, Kempner 8987, Koehler 9001, Looper 9016, Meadows 9049, Moody 9070, Powell 9128, Proctor 9132, Reliant 9144, **Shell 9181**, Smith 9191, Sturgis 9216, Temple 9227, Topfer 9238, Trull 9240, Waco 9255, Weaver 9267, Zale 9297

Utah: **ALSAM 9302**, Eccles 9320

Vermont: **Ben 9355**, Vermont 9361

Virginia: AMERIGROUP 9369, Arlington 9371, Delmar 9410, **Gannett 9428**, Jackson 9441, Lynchburg 9463, Memorial 9474, Norfolk 9484, Olsson 9491, Silver 9516, Thurman 9526, Virginia Beach 9532

Washington: Ackerley 9547, Community 9571, Crystal 9576, Glaser 9594, Haas 9599, **Hemingway 9606**, Medina 9640, Norcliffe 9650, **RealNetworks 9672**, Sherwood 9683, Tacoma 9693, True 9696, Washington 9702

West Virginia: Chambers 9713, Laughlin 9724, McDonough 9726, Schenk 9732

Wisconsin: Cornerstone 9781, Cudahy 9785, CUNA 9786, Meng 9870, Milwaukee 9876, Northwestern 9884, Rutledge 9917, **Thrivent 9949**

Economics

Arkansas: Rockefeller 172

California: Columbia 399, **Issa 703**, Keck 751, McCune 872, Rosenberg 1065, Towbes 1241, Witter 1314

Colorado: Donnell 1368, Gates 1380, Left 1407, **Staley 1457**

Connecticut: **Richardson 1632**, Rosenthal 1638

District of Columbia: **Coleman 1784**, **Koch 1819**

Indiana: Community 3128, **Goodrich 3157**, Moore 3207

Kentucky: J & L 3429

Maryland: **Davis 3608**

Massachusetts: Merck 4035, Shapiro 4136

Michigan: **Earhart 4291**, **Heritage 4340**

Mississippi: **Armstrong 4734**

Missouri: Cray 4801, **Humphreys 4833**

New Hampshire: **Winthrop 5105**

New Jersey: Kirby 5279

New York: **Aequus 5524**, **Bydale 5694**, Corrigan 5796, **Ford 5970**, O'Connor 6645, Sackler 6890, **Tinker 7143**, **United 7185**

Ohio: Cleveland 7576, GAR 7643, Morgan 7761, Murphy 7769

Pennsylvania: **McKenna 8338**, **Scaife 8425**

Texas: Cain 8809, **Hartman 8942**, Kempner 8987, Plus 9125, Rapoport 9141, **Shell 9181**

Utah: Eccles 9319, GFC 9324

Washington: Crystal 9576, **Kongsgaard 9620**, Quest 9666

Wisconsin: **Bradley 9763**, Menasha 9869

Education

Alabama: Alabama 1, **Altec 4**, AmSouth 5, Anderson 6, Anderson 7, Aronov 9, Barber 10, Blount 14, Bolden 15, Brock 16, Bruno 17, Caring 18, Carson 19, Central 20, Comer 22, Community 23, Community 24, Community 25, Community 26, Community 27, Crampton 30, Daniel 31, Finlay 33, Friedman 35, Hill 39, Kaul 40, Lowder 42, Lowder 44, Lowe 45, May 46, McWane 50, Meyer 52, Mitchell 53, Moore 55, Pleiad 57, Protective 58, Russell 60, Saks 61, Scrushy 62, Smith 63, Stallworth 64, Stephens 65, Thompson 67, **Union 70**, Vines 72, Webb 75, Working 76

Alaska: Carr 82, CIRI 83, Rasmuson 85

Arizona: A.P.S. 86, Arizona 87, Berlin 89, Community 91, Cooper 92, Dee 94, Gesner 100, Halle 103, Hansen 104, Herberger 106, Hermundslie 107, **Kieckhefer 113**, Levine 115, Lewis 116, **Moller**

Kauffmann 5272, KDK 5273, Kemmerer 5275, Kirby 5280, Knight 5281, Knistrom 5282, Knowles 5283, Kolatch 5285, Kovner 5287, L.A.W. 5292, **Lafitte 5293**, Lanza 5294, Large 5295, **Lautenberg 5298**, Lazarus 5299, Lebensfeld 5301, Levy 5306, Lissak 5309, Long 5310, Mack 5312, Martinson 5320, Mazer 5321, McCutchen 5322, McGraw 5323, MCJ 5324, New Jersey 5336, OceanFirst 5341, Orange 5343, Palestroni 5345, Parker 5346, **Parnassus 5347**, Phipps 5352, Poses 5354, Post 5355, Princeton 5357, Providence 5358, Provident 5359, Prudential 5360, Rigorous 5367, Roberts 5371, Rose 5373, Ross 5375, Ross 5376, Roth 5377, **Rowan 5378**, Rummel 5379, Sands 5382, Sandy 5383, Sato 5384, Schecter 5385, Schering 5387, **Scholarship 5388**, Schumann 5391, Schwartz 5393, Seiden 5396, Sharkey 5397, Shen 5398, Sierra 5401, Silver 5404, Smilowitz 5406, Straus 5413, Summit 5417, Sunfield 5418, Sweetfeet 5421, **Syms 5422**, Taub 5423, Taub 5425, Turock 5430, Turrell 5431, UBS 5433, Unilever 5434, Union 5435, Upton 5436, Victoria 5440, Vision 5442, **Vollmer 5443**, **Wall 5445**, Wang 5448, Weston 5452, Wight 5454, **Wilf 5455**, Wilf 5456, Withington 5458, **WKBJ 5459**, **YPI 5461**, Zayat 5462

New Mexico: Albuquerque 5466, Carlsbad 5469, Cudd 5472, Domanica 5475, Frost 5476, **Gorham 5478**, Hubbard 5481, Kind 5483, Maddox 5487, McCune 5488, New 5490, New Mexico 5491, Phillips 5492, PNM 5493, Santa Fe 5496, Stockman 5497, Taos 5498

New York: A.E. 5506, Abrons 5511, Achelis 5513, Acorn 5515, Adirondack 5517, Adjmi 5519, Aeneas 5523, **Alavi 5530**, Allen 5536, Allwin 5538, Allyn 5539, Alpert 5541, Altman 5542, **Altman 5544**, **Altria 5545**, Altschul 5546, American 5552, American 5555, Amicus 5557, Antz 5560, **Archbold 5563**, Area 5564, Arkell 5565, Armstrong 5567, Arnhold 5568, Aron 5569, Atticus 5576, Avalon 5579, **AVI 5582**, **AXA 5584**, Babbitt 5586, Bachmann 5587, Baird 5592, **Baker 5593**, Barker 5599, **Barnett 5601**, Bausch 5605, **Bay 5606**, Bayne 5607, Beaverkill 5610, Bedminster 5611, Behrens 5612, Beker 5613, Ben-Haim 5617, Benenson 5619, **Benenson 5620**, Berkowitz 5622, **Berlys 5623**, Bernstein 5625, Betesh 5628, Bingham 5631, Birkelund 5632, **Bismarck 5633**, Black 5636, **Blood 5639**, Blue 5640, Blythmour 5644, Boisi 5650, Booth 5651, Botwinick 5653, Boxer 5656, Brand 5658, **Branta 5659**, Braufman 5660, Bravmann 5661, **Brice 5662**, Briger 5663, **Bristol 5666**, Brodsky 5667, **Brokaw 5670**, **Bronfman 5671**, Bronfman 5673, Broughton 5675, Brunckhorst 5678, **Brunie 5679**, Bukkyo 5685, Burch 5686, Burden 5687, Butler 5691, Buttenwieser 5693, **Cader 5696**, Campbell 5700, Cappelli 5703, **Carey 5704**, Carmel 5705, Carnahan 5706, Casey 5714, Castle 5716, Cayne 5717, Cayre 5718, **Cayre 5719**, Central 5724, Century 5725, Chadwick 5726, Chaim 5728, Chanin 5730, Charina 5731, Charitable 5732, Charitable 5733, Charitable 5734, Chasanoff 5735, Chautauqua 5738, **Chernin 5743**, Chiara 5748, **Children's 5749**, **Chinnick 5751**, Chisholm 5753, **Citigroup 5755**, CJM 5756, Clark 5761, Clark 5762, Clinton 5763, Cohen 5768, Cole 5774, Coles 5775, Collins 5778, Community 5780, Community 5781, Community 5783, Community 5784, ContiGroup 5786, Cooper 5788, Cordelia 5790, Corey 5791, Corning 5794, Cornpanue 5795, Corzine 5797, Corzine 5798, Coulson 5799, Countess 5800, Credit 5807, Crisp 5809, Cullman 5812, Curran 5816, Curry 5817, Dabah 5820, **Dana 5823**, Danziger 5829, **Das 5832**, Davenport 5833, Davis 5836, De La Cour 5842, **de Rothschild 5843**, Decker 5846, Delancey 5849, Demartini 5851, DeMatteis 5852, **Derossi 5853**, **Deutsche 5854**, Devlin 5855, **Diamond 5858**, Dickler 5861, Diller 5863, Dolan 5869, **Donner 5873**, Donovan 5874, Doran 5875, Dove 5878, Drexler 5885, Dreyfus 5887, **Dreyfus 5888**, Dubin 5891, Dunwalke 5894, Durst 5895, Dweck

5896, Dyson 5898, East 5901, **Echoing 5905**, Effron 5911, Ehrenkranz 5913, Eig 5914, Elkes 5922, Ellis 5923, Elmaleh 5924, Elmezzi 5925, Emwiga 5930, Epstein 5934, Equinox 5935, Erpf 5937, Evans 5940, Everett 5941, **Falconwood 5943**, Farkas 5945, Fatta 5947, Faulkner 5948, **Fernleigh 5952**, Ferrari 5953, Ferriday 5954, Fife 5955, **Fischel 5959**, **Forbes 5967**, Ford 5969, **Ford 5970**, **Frank 5974**, Frank 5975, Frey 5983, Friedberg 5985, Friedman 5987, **Friedman 5988**, Fuchsberg 5997, **Fuld 5999**, Fuld 6000, Fund 6001, Furman 6002, Furman 6003, Furth 6004, Galasso 6005, Gant 6006, Gatto 6007, Gebbie 6009, Gellert 6012, Gerry 6017, Gibbs 6024, Gibson 6025, Gilder 6029, Gilliam 6031, **Gilman 6033**, Gleason 6039, Gleberman 6040, Glickenhaus 6042, Godinger 6044, Goldberg 6045, Goldenson 6047, Goldman 6051, Goldman 6053, **Goldman 6056**, Goldring 6057, Goldsmith 6060, Goldstein 6063, Goldstone 6065, Gollust 6069, Golub 6070, Goodfriend 6071, Goodman 6072, Goodman 6073, Gordon 6075, Gordon 6076, Gorman 6078, Gould 6083, Gould 6085, Grandison 6087, Grandview 6088, **Grant 6091**, **Grauer 6094**, Green 6095, **Greenberg 6097**, Greene 6099, Greenhill 6101, Greentree 6102, Greve 6104, Griffin 6105, Griffin 6106, Griffis 6107, Grigg 6108, Gross 6111, Gross 6112, Gruss 6114, Gruss 6115, Guttman 6124, **H.R.C. 6125**, Haas 6126, Haas 6127, Haber 6129, Hagedorn 6130, **Haje 6133**, Hajim 6134, Halcyon 6135, Halis 6136, **Halloran 6138**, Hammerman 6139, Handler 6140, **Harriman 6146**, Harriman 6147, Harris 6148, **Hayden 6157**, Hayden 6158, **Heineman 6165**, Heisler 6166, Heller 6168, Hettinger 6178, Hilfiger 6183, Hirsch 6187, Hoerle 6194, Hollyhock 6197, **Homeland 6199**, Hoyt 6203, Huberfeld 6206, Hudson 6207, Hughes 6209, Huntington 6213, Hurst 6216, I Have 6219, **IAC 6220**, **IBM 6221**, Icahn 6222, IFF 6227, Independence 6229, **Initial 6231**, Iovino 6236, Isaac 6238, Ivor 6242, Jacobson 6247, **Jaffe 6250**, JAM 6251, Jandon 6253, Janklow 6254, Jesselson 6259, Joelson 6265, Johnson 6266, Johnson 6267, **Johnson 6268**, Johnson 6271, **Johnson 6273**, **Joukowsky 6275**, Joy 6276, **JPMorgan 6277**, JW 6279, Kaiser 6283, Kanas 6286, Kaplan 6288, Karches 6292, Katz 6296, Katz 6297, Kautz 6300, Kaylie 6301, Kealy 6303, Kearns 6304, **Keefe 6305**, Kellner 6309, Kellogg 6310, Kellogg 6311, Kempner 6313, Keren 6317, Keren 6318, KeySpan 6320, Kiernan 6321, Kimmelman 6322, King 6325, Klein 6332, Klein 6333, **Klingenstein 6335**, Klingenstein 6336, Klingenstein 6337, Klingenstein 6339, Knafel 6341, Knapp 6342, Knossos 6344, Knox 6345, **Kopf 6348**, **Kraft 6351**, Kraus 6352, Kravis 6355, Krimendahl 6359, Kuflik 6360, Kupferberg 6363, Kurtz 6364, L. & L. 6368, **Landegger 6371**, **Lane 6372**, Lane 6373, Lang 6374, Lauder 6381, **Lauder 6383**, LBC 6386, Lebworth 6390, Lee 6391, Leeds 6392, Leffell 6393, Legacy 6394, Lehman 6396, Leibowitz 6399, Leonhardt 6403, Lessing 6404, Leuschen 6405, **Levy 6410**, Levy 6411, Liberman 6419, Lincoln 6423, Lindmor 6425, Lindsay 6427, Lipmanson 6431, Litterman 6435, Litwin 6436, Liu 6437, Loeb 6438, Loeb 6440, Lopatin 6446, Lostand 6448, Lowenstein 6449, **Luckow 6455**, **Lucky 6456**, Lyle 6461, M & E 6464, M & T 6465, **Mack 6469**, **Magowan 6473**, MAH 6474, Maheras 6475, **Mailman 6478**, Malkin 6480, Mallah 6481, Mariposa 6487, Mark 6488, Marks 6489, Marron 6492, Marron 6493, Marx 6497, Marx 6499, Massry 6502, MAT 6503, **Matthews 6507**, **Mayer 6509**, **MBIA 6512**, McCarthy 6515, McGraw 6519, McNulty 6521, **Mead 6522**, Meehan 6523, Melly 6526, **Memton 6529**, **Mercer 6532**, **Merrill 6537**, Messer 6540, Metcalf 6541, **MetLife 6542**, Meyer 6544, Meyer 6545, Millard 6548, Mille 6550, **Milliken 6552**, Mindel 6557, **Mitsubishi 6560**, Mitsui 6561, Mnuchin 6564, Model 6565, **Monell 6566**, Monteforte 6567, **Monterey 6568**, Moody's 6569, **Moore 6571**, Moore 6572, Mordecai 6575, Morse

6582, Morse 6584, **Mulago 6593**, **Mullen 6595**, Mullen 6596, Murphy 6597, Naddisy 6598, Nagle 6599, NAON 6601, **National 6603**, Neidich 6606, Neu 6610, New York 6613, New York 6616, New York 6618, New York 6619, Newcastle 6622, Newman 6625, Nicholas 6627, Nichols 6628, Niehaus 6631, **Noble 6633**, Northern 6638, Northern 6639, **Novartis 6640**, Novogratz 6642, O'Herron 6646, O'Malley 6647, O'Sullivan 6652, O'Toole 6653, O'Toole 6654, Oestreicher 6656, Olive 6662, Olshan 6663, Opatrny 6664, **Open 6665**, Orentreich 6667, Ostreicher 6671, Paduano 6677, **Paley 6679**, Pannonia 6686, Park 6688, Parker 6690, Parkview 6691, Parr 6692, Pascucci 6696, PBO 6699, Peale 6700, **Pearson 6701**, Peco 6703, Pedersen 6704, Penick 6709, **PepsiCo 6714**, Perella 6715, Pevaroff 6719, Pfizer 6720, **Pforzheimer 6721**, Phillips 6724, Pincus 6726, Pines 6727, Pittman 6730, Plant 6731, PLM 6732, Pollack 6734, Pollack 6735, Polsky 6738, Pope 6740, **Popplestone 6741**, Powers 6744, Price 6746, **Prospect 6750**, Providence 6751, Pumpkin 6754, Purchase 6755, Quarry 6759, Queensgate 6760, R & TP 6764, Raffiani 6767, Rapaport 6771, Rattner 6773, Ravitch 6776, REBNY 6780, Rechler 6781, Reed 6782, Renfield 6786, Revson 6789, Richardson 6796, Richenthal 6798, Richmond 6800, **Richmond 6801**, Ridgefield 6802, Rieder 6803, Riedman 6804, Riklis 6808, Riordan 6810, Ripple 6811, **Ripplewood 6812**, Ritter 6813, Riversville 6815, **Robertson 6818**, **Robinson 6819**, Robison 6821, Rochester 6823, **Rockefeller 6826**, Rockefeller 6827, Rodgers 6828, Rohatyn 6830, Rose 6833, Rose 6834, Rosen 6841, Rosenberg 6845, Rosenberg 6846, Rosenberg 6847, Rosenblatt 6848, Rosenkranz 6851, Rosenstiel 6852, Rosenthal 6853, Rosenwald 6855, Roslyn 6859, Rosner 6860, Ross 6861, Ross 6862, Rotenstreich 6865, Roxe 6867, Rubinstein 6876, Rudin 6877, Ruffin 6880, **Rukal 6881**, Sacerdote 6887, Sachs 6888, Sackler 6892, Safra 6893, Saligman 6895, Salmon 6896, Saltz 6899, **Saltzman 6900**, Sani 6904, **Sato 6908**, Schafer 6910, Schapiro 6912, Schenectady 6915, Schenker 6916, Schieffelin 6922, Schiff 6923, Schlosstein 6925, **Schlumberger 6926**, Schmeelk 6927, Schnurmacher 6930, Schnurmacher 6931, Schon 6933, Schott 6934, Schulhof 6935, Schulweis 6936, Schwartz 6938, Schwartz 6944, Schwarz 6947, Schwebel 6948, SDA 6950, Seevers 6953, Seiler 6954, Shapiro 6959, Sharp 6962, Sheinberg 6963, Sheldon 6964, SHS 6969, SI 6972, Siebert 6975, Siegel 6976, Sigma 6977, Silver 6981, Silverman 6982, Silverstein 6984, Simon 6987, Skirball 6999, Slant 7000, Slifka 7002, Slovin 7004, **SMBC 7005**, Smith 7006, Smith 7007, Snow 7011, Snyder 7013, SO 7015, **Solomon 7017**, Solomon 7018, Solow 7019, **Soros 7022**, Soros 7024, Sperry 7026, Speyer 7027, SPIA 7028, **Spiegel 7030**, Spingold 7032, Spitzer 7034, Sprague 7035, Spunk 7036, **Staley 7042**, Stanton 7044, Starfish 7046, Starker 7047, **Starr 7048**, Starwood 7049, Steele 7053, Steffens 7054, Stein 7056, Steinberg 7062, **Steinhardt 7064**, Steiniger 7065, **Stempel 7069**, Stern 7071, Stern 7073, Stevens 7076, Straus 7086, Stuart 7090, Sugarman 7092, Sullivan 7093, Sulzberger 7095, Sussman 7104, Sutton 7106, Sutton 7109, Sweetgrass 7113, Tandon 7121, TBF 7125, **Teddy 7127**, Templeton 7128, Textor 7131, Thornton 7134, Three 7135, Tianaderrah 7136, Tiger 7139, **Time 7142**, Tisch 7144, Tisch 7146, Tisch 7148, Tisch 7149, Tishman 7150, **Tortuga 7155**, Tower 7158, Townsend 7159, Triad 7162, Tribune 7163, Trott 7165, Troy 7166, Trump 7167, **Tsadra 7169**, Tuch 7170, Tufenkian 7171, Tully 7173, Ungar 7183, **United 7185**, Ushkow 7188, Van Pelt 7192, Vance 7193, Vernon 7195, Vidda 7198, Vogelstein 7201, von der Heyden 7203, Wachenheim 7204, Walker 7208, **Wallace 7209**, **Walter 7211**, Watson 7220, Weezie 7224, Weill 7227, **Weinberg 7228**, Weinberg 7229, Weinberg 7231, Weinman 7232,

Weiss 7235, Weissman 7237, Wellde 7239, Wellin 7240, Wendt 7243, Werblow 7245, West 7246, **Wexner 7249**, Whispering 7250, White 7251, Williams 7260, Witmer 7268, WJS 7269, **Wolfensohn 7270**, Woodcock 7273, Woodland 7275, Woodmere 7276, Woodner 7277, Wunsch 7281, Yitzchok 7283, **Youth 7287**, Zarin 7290, Zemsky 7294, Zichron 7296, Zichron 7297, Zitrin 7302, Zucker 7303

North Carolina: Armfield 7307, Bailey 7309, **Bank 7310**, Baruch 7311, BB&T 7312, Belk 7315, Bergen 7316, Biddle 7317, Blumenthal 7320, Branan 7322, Braswell 7323, Brody 7325, Brown 7326, Burress 7331, Cape Fear 7336, Charlotte 7338, Coffey 7339, Coleman 7340, Community 7343, Community 7344, Community 7346, Cumberland 7349, Dover 7356, Dowd 7357, Drue 7358, Duke 7360, Everett 7364, Finley 7367, Foundation 7370, Fox 7371, Gilbert 7373, Giles 7374, Gipson 7375, Goodnight 7377, Goodrich 7378, Gordon 7379, Gorelick 7381, Graham 7382, Halton 7386, Hanes 7387, Harris 7390, Harvest 7392, Hayden 7394, High Point 7397, Holding 7399, Hommer 7400, Hurley 7402, **Jefferson 7405**, Keith 7410, Kulynych 7415, **Kulynych 7416**, Lance 7418, Martin 7424, McMichael 7426, Mills 7429, Nias 7435, North Carolina 7438, North Carolina 7439, O'Herron 7441, Perkins 7445, Pharmacy 7446, Polk 7449, **Pope 7450**, Price 7451, **Prickett 7452**, Progress 7453, Provident 7454, Randleigh 7456, Reynolds 7457, Reynolds 7458, Reynolds 7459, Reynolds 7460, Richmond 7463, Robertson 7466, Ryan 7469, **Sall 7471**, Simpson 7472, Sklut 7473, Slick 7474, Smith 7476, Smith 7477, Smith 7478, Smith 7479, Southern 7481, SPX 7484, Summer 7489, **Sunshine 7490**, SunTrust 7491, Terry 7494, Toleo 7495, Triangle 7496, Tzedakah 7497, V.F. 7498, Van Every 7499, Van Houten 7500, Vanderbilt 7501, **Wachovia 7502**, Warner 7503, Weaver 7504, Wilson 7506, Winston 7507, Winston-Salem 7508

North Dakota: Fargo 7514, MDU 7517, North Dakota 7519

Ohio: A Good 7523, Abington 7524, Akron 7526, **Alpaugh 7527**, American 7528, Anderson 7529, **Armington 7532**, Ashland 7533, Ashtabula 7534, Babcock 7537, Barberton 7539, Bates 7540, Bell 7544, Berry 7547, **Bingham 7549**, Boymel 7553, Bruening 7558, Bryan 7559, Buenger 7560, **Burleigh 7561**, Butler 7562, Campbell 7565, Cardinal 7566, **Cardinal 7567**, Castellini 7568, Charities 7569, Christman 7572, Cincinnati 7574, Cleveland 7576, Cleveland 7577, Codrington 7578, Columbus 7580, Community 7581, Community 7582, Community 7583, Community 7584, Community 7585, Community 7586, **Convergys 7587**, **Cooper 7589**, Corbett 7590, Cornerstone 7592, Coshocton 7593, Cotswold 7594, Creech 7597, Dana 7599, Dater 7600, Dayton 7603, Dayton 7604, DBJ 7605, **Deuble 7607**, Diebold 7611, Dorn 7612, Downing 7614, **Durell 7616**, **Eaton 7617**, Edwards 7618, Fairfax 7621, Fairfield 7622, Farmer 7623, **Federated 7624**, Ferguson 7625, Findlay 7627, First 7629, FirstEnergy 7630, Focus 7632, Ford 7633, Forest 7634, Foss 7635, Foundation 7636, Fox 7637, Fox 7638, France 7639, Frohman 7641, Frost 7642, Geary 7645, Gerlach 7648, Gettler 7649, Gingher 7650, Gund 7656, Gund 7657, H.C.S. 7658, Haile 7659, Hamilton 7660, Hankins 7662, Haslinger 7664, Hauck 7666, Heiman 7669, Hershey 7671, Home 7672, Honda 7673, Hoover 7674, Horvitz 7677, Horvitz 7678, Hutton 7681, Iddings 7682, IHS 7683, Jarson 7686, Jubilee 7694, Kaplan 7696, Keeler 7697, **Kettering 7698**, Kettering 7699, **Kosar 7703**, Kramer 7704, Kroger 7705, Kulas 7706, Levin 7712, Licking 7714, Lincoln 7715, Lindner 7716, Lippitt 7718, Lippman 7719, Lozick 7724, Lubrizol 7725, LZ 7727, M/B 7728, M/I 7729, Mangano 7733, Marietta 7735, Mather 7736, Mathile 7737, Mayerson 7739, McBride 7740, McMaster 7744, MeadWestvaco 7745, Mehl

7746, Miami 7748, Middletown 7749, Midland 7750, Milacron 7751, Miller 7753, Miller 7754, Mindala 7755, Miniger 7756, Mixon 7757, Montgomery 7758, Moores 7759, Morgan 7761, Morgan 7762, Morley 7763, Morrison 7764, Murch 7766, Murphy 7768, Murphy 7769, Muskingum 7770, NCC 7772, NCR 7773, New 7775, Nord 7779, Ohio 7784, Ohio 7785, **Ohio 7786**, Olive 7787, **OMNOVA 7789**, Park 7795, Parker 7796, Patterson 7797, Payne 7798, **Perkins 7800**, Peters 7801, **PLACE 7805**, **Procter 7807**, Pugliese 7810, Reeves 7814, Reinberger 7815, Richland 7819, Ritchie 7821, Robbins 7823, Rose 7825, Sage 7829, Salem 7831, Schiff 7838, Schlink 7839, Schmidlapp 7841, Schott 7842, Scioto 7845, **Scripps 7848**, Sedgwick 7849, Semple 7851, Shaw 7852, Sherwin 7855, Sisler 7858, Sky 7859, Slemp 7860, Sloat 7861, Smith 7862, Smucker 7864, Spaulding 7865, Springfield 7866, Stark 7867, Stefanski 7868, Stranahan 7872, Stranahan 7873, Tetlak 7877, Thendara 7878, **Timken 7880**, Toledo 7882, Toledo 7883, **Tomkins 7884**, Troy 7886, Turben 7888, Tuscarawas 7890, **Vesper 7892**, Wallace 7894, **Warrington 7895**, Watson 7896, Wayne 7897, Weisbrod 7900, Wendy's 7902, Western 7903, White 7905, Williams 7907, Williamson 7908, Wilson 7910, Wohlgemuth 7913, Wolfe 7915, Women's 7916, Wuliger 7918, Zenith 7921

Oklahoma: Bailey 7923, Bernsen 7925, Better 7926, Bovaird 7927, Chapman 7928, Collins 7929, Communities 7931, Community 7932, Crawley 7934, Evergreen 7936, Gaylord 7937, Gelvin 7938, Goddard 7939, Grace 7940, Gussman 7941, Helmerich 7942, Hille 7943, Inasmuch 7944, Jackson 7945, Kaiser 7948, Kerr 7949, Kerr 7950, Kimmell 7951, Kirkpatrick 7952, Lyon 7953, McGee 7957, McGill 7958, McMahon 7959, Meinders 7960, Oklahoma City 7964, Oklahoman 7966, ONEOK 7967, Oxley 7968, Puterbaugh 7970, Rapp 7971, Records 7972, Sarkeys 7974, **Schusterman 7975**, Share 7977, Southern 7979, Temple 7982, Titus 7983, Tulsa 7984, Viersen 7985, Warren 7986, Warren 7987, Williams 7989, Zarrow 7993

Oregon: Boyd 8000, Braemar 8001, Carpenter 8003, Crabby 8010, Fohs 8012, Ford 8013, Frank 8016, Hedinger 8019, Holmes 8020, **Honzel 8021**, Intel 8022, Jackson 8024, Jeld 8025, John 8026, Jubitz 8028, Kelley 8030, Knight 8032, Krueger 8033, Lamfrom 8034, Lightfoot 8036, Louisiana 8037, Mentor 8039, Meyer 8042, Miller 8044, Miller 8045, Oregon 8049, PacifiCorp 8050, **Renaissance 8053**, Salem 8054, **Schmidt 8055**, Schnitzer 8056, Schnitzer 8057, Stewart 8060, Tektronix 8063, Tucker 8065, Wendt 8066, Wessinger 8067, Young 8069

Pennsylvania: 1675 8070, 1957 8071, Aaron 8072, ACE 8073, **Alcoa 8075**, Allegheny 8076, Ames 8080, **Annenberg 8084**, Arcadia 8086, Arete 8088, Arkema 8089, Asplundh 8091, Ball 8093, Barra 8095, Bayer 8096, Beatty 8097, Benedum 8099, Berkman 8102, Berks 8103, **Berman 8104**, Black 8109, Born 8113, Briggs 8117, Bristol 8118, Bronstein 8119, Brossman 8120, Brougher 8122, Buck 8123, Buhl 8124, Buncher 8125, Burke 8126, **Cardone 8129**, **Carpenter 8131**, Cavitolo 8134, Central 8135, Centre 8136, Century 8137, Cestone 8139, Chester 8141, Clapp 8145, **Clive 8146**, CMS 8147, Cochran 8149, Colonial 8151, Comcast 8152, Community 8153, Community 8155, Connelly 8157, Cooper 8158, Cotswold 8160, Crels 8163, Davenport 8164, Degenstein 8166, DeGol 8167, Dibona 8169, Dietrich 8171, Dolfinger 8172, **Dominion 8173**, Donahue 8174, Donley 8175, Donnelly 8176, DSF 8178, Eberly 8179, Eden 8181, Eden 8182, Ellis 8184, Equitable 8187, Erie 8188, ESSA 8190, Fair 8192, Falk 8193, Federated 8196, Fels 8198, Ferree 8199, First 8202, **Firstfruits 8203**, Forney 8207, Foundation 8208, **Frick 8211**, Garthwaite 8212, Genuardi 8213, Grable 8221, Graham 8222, Grass 8223, Gray 8224, Grumbacher 8227, Haas 8230,

Hamilton 8233, Harsco 8236, Hassel 8237, Heinz 8240, Heinz 8241, Heinz 8242, **Heinz 8243**, Herr 8246, Hillman 8249, Hillman 8250, Hillman 8251, Hodge 8254, Hooper 8256, Hopwood 8257, Hulme 8260, Huston 8263, Huston 8264, Innisfree 8267, Jaindl 8269, Jake 8270, Jennings 8272, **Johnson 8274**, Justus 8276, Kardon 8279, Katz 8281, Kavanagh 8282, Keystone 8285, Keystone 8286, Kim 8287, Kind 8289, Kinsley 8290, Kline 8292, Kline 8293, Lamb 8299, Lancaster 8300, Lehigh Valley 8303, Lenfest 8304, Lenfest 8305, Les 8306, Lindback 8312, Little 8313, Luzerne 8317, M & S 8318, Maguire 8321, Mandell 8322, Maple 8323, Maslow 8327, McCormick 8329, McFeely 8334, McLean 8340, Mellon 8344, Mellon 8345, Mellon 8346, Mengle 8347, **Metcalf 8351**, Miller 8355, Miller 8356, Moore 8358, Musser 8361, Neubauer 8363, Novotny 8364, Oxford 8367, **Pew 8377**, Philadelphia 8378, Phillips 8380, Pierce 8382, Pilgrim 8383, **Pincus 8384**, Pittsburgh 8386, Pollock 8390, Pond 8391, **PPG 8394**, PSC 8398, Rider 8404, Rockwell 8408, Roemer 8409, Rorer 8411, Rosenberg 8412, Safeguard 8418, Saint 8419, Salvaggio 8421, Satell 8424, **Scaife 8425**, Scranton 8431, **Seraph 8434**, Simmons 8441, Smith 8443, Smith 8444, Smith 8445, Snee 8446, Snider 8447, Society 8449, Sordoni 8450, Sovereign 8451, Stabler 8455, Stackpole 8456, Steinman 8458, Steinman 8459, Strauss 8464, **Susquehanna 8470**, Susquehanna 8471, Tippins 8477, Trexler 8481, Truman 8483, Tyco 8485, **United 8487**, Usher 8489, Vanguard 8490, Warwick 8496, West 8500, Wimmer 8505, **Woods 8508**, Wyomissing 8509, **Wyss 8510**, York 8511

Puerto Rico: **FNZ 8514**, Puerto Rico 8515

Rhode Island: Alperin 8516, **Amica 8518**, Carter 8522, Chace 8523, Champlin 8524, Charter 8526, Citizens 8527, Daniels 8530, **Dorot 8531**, Doyle 8532, **Feinstein 8535**, **FM 8537**, Kimball 8542, Mann 8546, Nelson 8549, Rhode Island 8551, Roosa 8552, Salem 8554, Siperstein 8557, **Textron 8559**, Usen 8560, Washington 8563

South Carolina: Arkwright 8565, Barnet 8568, Bruce 8571, Byerly 8572, Central 8577, Ceres 8578, Coastal 8581, Community 8583, Community 8584, Dintersmith 8586, First 8587, Foothills 8588, Hipp 8592, Hopewell 8593, Liberty 8597, Montgomery 8600, Phifer 8602, Rainey 8605, **Roe 8607**, ScanSource 8608, Self 8610, Sims 8611, Smith 8613, Sonoco 8614, Spartanburg 8616, Waccamaw 8619, Zucker 8622

South Dakota: Opus 8628, Peters 8629, Sioux Falls 8630, South Dakota 8631

Tennessee: AmSouth 8636, Assisi 8638, Atticus 8639, Ayers 8640, Belz 8643, Bornblum 8645, **Bridgestone 8646**, Briggs 8647, Caesars 8648, Community 8660, Community 8661, Community 8662, Davis 8665, Day 8666, Draughon 8668, East 8671, EBS 8672, Eskind 8675, Ezell 8676, Frist 8678, Frist 8679, **Garrott 8680**, Goldsmith 8682, Haslam 8687, Haslam 8688, Hendrix 8691, Jones 8698, Lindahl 8702, MacLellan 8705, Martin 8707, Martin 8708, Massey 8709, Melkus 8711, Osborne 8714, Phillips 8716, Longleaf 8719, Schadt 8725, Scheidt 8726, Starfish 8728, T & T 8731, Thompson 8733, Unaka 8739, Wallace 8740, Washington 8741

Texas: Ackerman 8750, **Adams 8751**, **Allbritton 8755**, Amarillo 8758, Anderson 8760, **Anderson 8761**, Anderson 8762, Aragona 8763, Astin 8764, **AT&T 8765**, **Aurora 8767**, Austin 8768, B.E.L.I.E.F. 8770, Baker 8772, Barnhart 8773, Baron 8774, Bass 8777, Bauer 8779, **Bauer 8780**, Baugh 8781, Beal 8783, Behmann 8785, Benson 8788, Bergman 8789, Bookout 8791, Bosque 8792, Brackenridge 8793, Branch 8794, Bridgeway 8796, Brown 8799, Burnett 8801, Cailloux 8806, Cailloux 8807, Cain 8809, Caris 8814, Carter 8816, Carter 8817, Castle 8818, **Catto 8819**, **CEMEX 8821**, CFP 8822, Charitable 8824, Chinquapin 8827, Clayton 8830, Coastal 8833, Collins 8837, Collins 8838, Communities 8839, Community 8840, Community 8841, Community 8842, Constantin

8843, Convergence 8844, **Cooper 8846**, Cox 8849, Crain 8851, Cullen 8854, Dallas 8855, Deakins 8860, Deason 8861, **Dell 8863**, Dell 8864, Dickson 8866, Diener 8867, Dodge 8868, Duda 8871, Dynegy 8874, Eady 8875, East 8876, **EDS 8877**, Educational 8878, Edwards 8879, El Paso 8881, El Paso 8882, Elkins 8883, Esping 8886, Estill 8888, **ExxonMobil 8889**, Fair 8891, Farb 8893, Farish 8894, Fasken 8895, Favrot 8897, Fikes 8899, Finger 8900, Fisch 8901, Fish 8902, Franklin 8907, Frees 8909, Futureus 8912, Gale 8913, Gayden 8915, George 8916, Gill 8919, Goldsbury 8920, Goodman 8921, Gorman 8922, Greathouse 8923, Haggar 8930, Haggar 8931, Haggerty 8932, Halliburton 8935, Halsell 8936, Hamill 8937, Hamman 8938, Hanley 8940, **Hartman 8942**, Hawn 8943, Hebert 8946, Helm 8947, Herd 8948, Herzstein 8949, Hillcrest 8952, Hirsch 8953, Hoblitzelle 8955, Hoglund 8956, Holthouse 8959, Houston 8961, Hudson 8962, Huffington 8963, Jamail 8970, Johnson 8972, Johnson 8973, Johnson 8974, Jonsson 8977, Keith 8982, Keithley 8983, Kelley 8986, Kempner 8987, Keown 8989, KFFH 8990, Kilroy 8991, Kimberly 8992, King 8995, **KLE 8997**, Lantana 9004, Lard 9005, Lennox 9007, **Levant 9008**, Levit 9009, Lightner 9012, Littauer 9014, Lowe 9020, Lubbock 9021, Luchsinger 9022, Macrini 9026, Mayor 9034, Mays 9035, McCoy 9039, McCrea 9040, McDermott 9043, McGovern 9044, McKee 9045, McNair 9047, McNutt 9048, Meadows 9049, Medallion 9051, Mehta 9052, Meredith 9054, Merrick 9055, Meyer 9057, Miller 9061, Miller 9062, Mischer 9063, Mitte 9067, Moncrief 9069, Moody 9070, Morning 9075, Morris 9076, Mosbacher 9077, Mott 9079, Mundy 9080, Murrell 9082, Muse 9083, NAH 9084, Nation 9087, Navarro 9089, Newman 9090, Nightingale 9091, Northen 9092, O'Connor 9094, O'Donnell 9096, **Oldham 9100**, Once 9101, Onstead 9102, **Onward 9103**, Otter 9105, Owen 9106, Owen 9107, Owsley 9108, Parks 9109, Paulos 9112, Permian 9117, Perot 9119, Pine 9123, Piper 9124, Powell 9128, Prairie 9129, Priddy 9131, Proctor 9132, Prothro 9134, Providence 9135, Pryor 9136, PSH 9137, **Randall 9140**, Rapoport 9141, Read 9142, Reynolds 9145, Richardson 9147, Riddle 9148, Roach 9150, Roberts 9151, Rockwell 9154, Rosewood 9158, Ross 9159, San Antonio 9166, Sarofim 9168, Sarofim 9169, Schollmaier 9172, Schutte 9173, Scurlock 9175, Semmes 9179, **Shell 9181**, Shelton 9182, Sidhu 9185, **Silverton 9186**, Simmons 9187, Simmons 9189, Smith 9191, Smith 9195, Smith 9196, Smith 9197, Smith 9198, Sooch 9200, South 9201, Sowell 9203, Sparrow 9204, Speas 9207, Stark 9209, Stemmons 9211, Sterling 9212, Sturgis 9216, Tapeats 9223, Tate 9225, Temple 9227, Temple 9228, **Tenet 9229**, Tennessee 9230, Texas 9232, Texas 9233, Thomas 9234, Trull 9240, Turner 9241, USAA 9245, Vale 9246, Valero 9247, Vanberg 9248, Vaughan 9249, Vaughan 9250, Vergara 9253, Waco 9255, Waggoner 9256, Wagner 9259, Wal 9260, Ward 9262, Ward 9263, Ware 9264, **Waste 9265**, Webber 9269, West 9274, West 9275, West 9276, Westcott 9278, Wichita 9280, Willard 9281, Williams 9283, Wise 9284, Wise 9285, Wolens 9286, Wolff 9288, Works 9291, Wright 9294, Young 9295, Zale 9297, Zephyr 9299, Zimmer 9300
Utah: ALS 9301, **ALSAM 9302**, Ashton 9303, B. Attitudes 9304, Bastian 9306, Denkers 9312, Esther 9321, GFC 9324, Greene 9325, **Huntsman 9329**, Jones 9330, Lockwood 9333, Noorda 9336, Raymond 9339, Savage 9340, Stewart 9345, Swanson 9346, **Wishnick 9353**, Zions 9354
Vermont: Gilman 9357, Lintilhac 9359, Mergens 9360, Vermont 9361
Virgin Islands: Bartner 9362, Community 9363
Virginia: 118 9365, American 9368, AMERIGROUP 9369, Arlington 9371, Batten 9373, Batten 9374, Beazley 9376, Billings 9377, Bryant 9380, Camp 9382, CarMax 9385, Carter 9387, Cartledge 9388,

Charles 9389, Charlottesville 9390, Circuit 9392, Cole 9396, Cole 9397, Collis 9398, Community 9400, Community 9402, **Cooke 9405**, Dalis 9406, Dreyfus 9413, English 9414, Folger 9418, Foundation 9419, Fralin 9420, Franklin 9421, Friedman 9425, **Gannett 9428**, **Glenstone 9429**, Golden 9430, Gottwald 9431, Grandis 9432, Graves 9433, Gwathmey 9435, Harrison 9436, Jackson 9441, Joco 9443, Kanter 9445, Katzen 9446, Kegley 9448, Kington 9450, Kluge-Moses 9451, LandAmerica 9454, Landmark 9455, Lipman 9459, Loeb 9460, Luck 9461, Lynchburg 9463, Mars 9466, McGue 9470, **MCI 9471**, McNichols 9472, Memorial 9474, Moore 9478, Norfolk 9484, Northern 9486, Ochsman 9489, **Olmsted 9490**, Olsson 9491, Parsons 9493, Perry 9495, Peterson 9497, Portsmouth 9498, Praxis 9500, Reynolds 9503, Rice 9504, Samberg 9510, Scott 9513, Smith 9518, Staunton 9521, Taubman 9524, **Three 9525**, Titmus 9527, Truland 9528, Ukrop 9529, United 9530, Universal 9531, Virginia Beach 9532, Washington 9534, Weil 9535, Weissberg 9536, Wellspring 9537, **WestWind 9538**, Wiley 9539, Wrinkle 9545
Washington: Ackerley 9547, Allen 9550, Anderson 9551, Apex 9552, Archibald 9553, **Blakemore 9558**, Blue 9559, **Boeing 9560**, Cartales 9565, Cheney 9569, Community 9570, Community 9571, Connors 9572, Cowles 9575, Crystal 9576, Dimmer 9579, Ellison 9581, Evertrust 9583, Ferguson 9585, Foster 9588, Foundation 9589, Fuchs 9590, **Gates 9591**, Geneva 9592, Grays 9597, Haas 9599, Haugland 9603, Hebert 9604, **Hemingway 9606**, Howard 9609, Islands 9613, Jones 9615, Kaleidoscope 9616, Kelsey 9617, **Kongsgaard 9620**, **Laird 9623**, Lauzier 9626, Lochland 9630, Lockwood 9631, Lucky 9632, McEachern 9638, Medina 9640, Milgard 9641, Moccasin 9643, Murdock 9644, **Natan 9646**, Nesholm 9647, Norcliffe 9650, Oki 9653, OneFamily 9654, Opportunities 9655, **PAH 9657**, Paulus 9658, PEMCO 9660, Raikes 9668, Rainier 9669, Raven 9670, Russell 9673, **Sage 9674**, Sarkowsky 9676, Satterberg 9677, Schultz 9679, Seattle 9680, Sequoia 9681, Shirley 9684, Shulman 9685, Simonyi 9686, Sloan 9687, Snyder 9689, **Starbucks 9690**, Tacoma 9693, True 9696, UNOVA 9697, **Vista 9699**, Warren 9700, Wright 9707, Wyman 9709
West Virginia: BB&T 9710, Bowen 9711, Chambers 9713, Clay 9714, Community 9716, Daywood 9717, Hoffmann 9718, Hunnicutt 9720, Jacobson 9722, Kanawha 9723, Maier 9725, McDonough 9726, Mylan 9728, Nutting 9729, Parkersburg 9730, Schenk 9732, Shott 9733, Tucker 9736
Wisconsin: Alexander 9741, Alliant 9742, AnnMarie 9743, Antioch 9745, Archer 9746, Argosy 9747, Assurant 9748, Baird 9750, Bartlett 9753, Batterman 9754, Beasley 9755, Bleser 9760, Bolz 9762, **Bradley 9763**, Briggs 9765, Brotz 9767, Bryant 9768, Chapman 9771, Clark 9773, Coleman 9775, Community 9776, Community 9777, Community 9778, Community 9779, Community 9780, Cudahy 9784, Cudahy 9785, CUNA 9786, Dudley 9792, Duncan 9793, Eastman 9795, Evans 9796, Evjue 9797, **Firestone 9798**, Fleck 9799, Fond du Lac 9800, Fort 9801, Four 9803, Goldbach 9806, Gordon 9808, Green Bay 9810, Handleman 9811, Harley 9812, Helfaer 9813, Herzfeld 9815, Hess 9816, Hyde 9818, Janesville 9820, Johnson 9823, Johnson 9824, Johnson 9826, Joy 9828, Kelben 9830, Keller 9831, Kenosha 9833, Kikkoman 9836, Kohl 9837, Kohler 9840, Krause 9841, Krejci 9843, Kress 9844, Ladish 9846, Ladish 9847, Lakeview 9848, Lunda 9852, Madison 9854, Madison 9855, Marcus 9859, Marshall 9860, Marshfield 9861, Martin 9862, McDonough 9865, McQueen 9866, Mead 9867, Menasha 9869, Meng 9870, Mercy 9871, Michels 9874, Miller 9875, Milwaukee 9876, Modine 9878, Munson 9880, Nelson 9881, Nelson 9882, Northwestern 9884, Oshkosh 9885, Oshkosh 9886, Oshkosh 9887, Overture 9889, **Palmer**

9890, Pamida 9891, Pangburn 9892, Peck 9895, Phipps 9898, Posner 9901, PPC 9902, Racine 9906, **Rath 9907**, **Reiman 9908**, Riordan 9911, **Rockwell 9912**, **Roddis 9913**, Rowland 9916, Rutledge 9917, Sand 9918, Schneider 9920, Schoenleber 9921, Sensient 9922, Sentry 9923, Seramur 9924, Siebert 9927, Smallwood 9928, Split 9932, St. Croix 9933, **Stein 9937**, Stewardship 9938, Styberg 9944, Sub 9945, Taylor 9948, U.S. 9952, Uihlein 9953, Uihlein 9954, Uihlein 9955, **Wagner 9957**, Waukesha 9960, Weill 9962, Wilson 9965, Windhover 9966, Wisconsin 9967, WPS 9970, **Young 9972**
Wyoming: Allen 9974, Chapman 9976, Community 9977, Connemara 9978, Dragicevich 9980, Ellbogen 9981, McMurry 9985, S & G 9988, Sargent 9989, Scott 9991, Thorson 9994, True 9996, Weiss 9997, Wyoming 10000

Education, administration/regulation

Florida: Wellman 2293
Illinois: **Excelsior! 2722**
New York: Steiniger 7065, Sulzberger 7095
Ohio: Frost 7642
West Virginia: Hunnicutt 9720

Education, alliance

New Jersey: Indian 5250
New York: Weinman 7232
Ohio: Peters 7801

Education, association

California: **American 217**, **Baker 252**, Hinz 675, **Juniata 734**, Milken 898
District of Columbia: Cafritz 1780
Florida: Price 2177, Rosenberg 2206
Georgia: **Challenge 2344**, Patterson 2460
Illinois: Kelly 2830
Indiana: Community 3128
Massachusetts: Hopedale 3958, McEvoy 4032
Minnesota: Carlson 4532
Mississippi: Hardin 4747
New Jersey: Harbourton 5223
New York: Booth 5651, Everett 5941, Glickenhaus 6042, Kautz 6300, New York 6620, Pumpkin 6754, Scheuer 6919, Silverman 6983, Tisch 7144
North Carolina: Cemala 7337, Dickson 7355, Giles 7374, Halton 7386
Ohio: Anderson 7529, Columbus 7580, Jennings 7688, Kulas 7706, Youngstown 7920
Pennsylvania: **Waldorf 8495**
South Carolina: Post 8603
Texas: Cain 8809, **Shell 9181**, Sterling 9212, Wright 9294
Washington: Norcliffe 9650, PACCAR 9656
Wisconsin: Cornerstone 9781

Education, community/cooperative

New York: Bowne 5655, **Wallace 7209**
Texas: Herzstein 8949

Education, continuing education

Mississippi: Maddox 4753
Ohio: Fairfield 7622

Education, drop-out prevention

Alabama: Community 24
Connecticut: Tauck 1657
Massachusetts: **State 4158**
New Jersey: PSEG 5361
New Mexico: Santa Fe 5496
Pennsylvania: Chester 8141
Texas: Topfer 9238

Education, early childhood education

Education, equal rights

Education, ESL programs

Education, ethics

Education, formal/general education

Education, fund raising/fund distribution

Education, gifted students

Education, information services

Education, management/technical aid

Education, PTA groups

Education, public education

Education, public policy

Education, reading

Kentucky: J & L 3429, Norton 3441
Louisiana: Booth 3464, Community 3469
Massachusetts: **Azadoutloun 3786**, Boston 3812, Community 3855, Orchard 4062, **State 4158**
Michigan: Abrams 4213, Battle Creek 4228, Binda 4233, Comerica 4251, Grand Rapids 4326, Jackson 4347, Skillman 4438
Minnesota: Bell 4514, Bigelow 4519, Deluxe 4549, **Ecolab 4557, Fuller 4567**, General 4570, Mardag 4613, Saint Paul 4671, Star 4691
Missouri: Green 4822
Nevada: Nevada 5047
New Jersey: Cowles 5170, Prudential 5360, PSEG 5361, **Verizon 5439**
New Mexico: McCune 5488
New York: Allyn 5539, Arkell 5565, Booth 5651, Bowne 5655, **Carnegie 5707, Citigroup 5755**, Daphne 5830, Dreyfus 5887, **Heineman 6165**, Kornfeld 6350, Lynton 6463, **Mitsubishi 6560**, New York 6617, Nichols 6628, Northern 6638, **Pforzhelmer 6721**, Reader's 6777
North Carolina: Cemala 7337, North Carolina 7438, Piedmont 7447, Triangle 7496
Ohio: Columbus 7580, Dayton 7604, Fifth 7626, **OMNOVA 7789**, Richland 7819, **Scripps 7848, Timken 7880**
Oregon: Carpenter 8003, Johnson 8027, Oregon 8049, PacifiCorp 8050
Pennsylvania: Blue 8112, Comcast 8152, Cooper 8158, Dolfinger 8172, Stackpole 8456
Rhode Island: Daniels 8530
South Carolina: Central 8577
Tennessee: Community 8660
Texas: Cain 8809, Coastal 8833, Dell 8864, **ExxonMobil 8889**, Fikes 8899, George 8916, Hoblitzelle 8955, Kempner 8987, Lubbock 9021, Meadows 9049, Rapoport 9141, Rockwell 9154, San Antonio 9166, Simmons 9188, Sterling 9212, Wright 9294
Virginia: Arlington 9371, Delmar 9410, **Gannett 9428**, Norfolk 9484
Washington: Community 9571, Norcliffe 9650, **Starbucks 9690**
West Virginia: Parkersburg 9730
Wisconsin: Cudahy 9785, Roundy's 9915

Education, reform

Alabama: **Vulcan 73**
California: Avery 244, Johnson 725
Colorado: **Daniels 1362**
District of Columbia: **Fannie 1793**
Florida: **Plan 2171**
Georgia: BellSouth 2323
Hawaii: Castle 2537
Illinois: New 2912
Indiana: **Lilly 3192**
Maryland: **Blaustein 3575**
Massachusetts: Schott 4132
Michigan: Frey 4316
Missouri: Roblee 4893
New Jersey: Prudential 5360
New York: Achelis 5513, Bodman 5647, **Carnegie 5707, Foundation 5971, Goldman 6056, IBM 6221, MetLife 6542**, Wendling 7242
North Carolina: Zelnak 7513
Ohio: Peters 7801
Pennsylvania: **Annenberg 8084**
Tennessee: Hyde 8693
Virginia: Circuit 9392

Education, research

California: Baxter 262, **Carnegie 359**, Samueli 1086, **Seaver 1118, Stupski 1211**
Connecticut: Larsen 1579
District of Columbia: **National 1838**
Florida: Dahl 1959
Georgia: Moore 2452, **UPS 2503**
Idaho: **Micron 2571**
Illinois: Kelly 2830, **Spencer 3015**, United 3044
Indiana: Lilly 3194

Iowa: Holden 3294
Maryland: Abell 3559
Massachusetts: Cabot 3823
Michigan: **Heritage 4340, Rodney 4422**
Mississippi: **Armstrong 4734**, Hardin 4747
Missouri: Schweppe 4899
New Jersey: Cowles 5170
New York: **Bay 5606**, Everett 5941, **Ford 5970**, Gleason 6039, Goldsmith 6060, **Grant 6092, Heineman 6165, Initial 6231**
Ohio: Britton 7556, Gund 7657, Payne 7798
Oklahoma: Rapp 7971
Oregon: **Schmidt 8055**
Pennsylvania: **Lee 8302, Pew 8377**
Texas: Franklin 8907, Northen 9092, San Antonio 9212
Utah: Caine 9310
Wisconsin: **Bradley 9763**, Sensient 9922

Education, services

California: Dollens 462, Girard 580, Mericos 889, Peninsula 989, **Stupski 1211**, Synopsys 1223
District of Columbia: Spring 1849
Florida: Community 1943
Massachusetts: Easthampton 3887, Ratshesky 4095, Yawkey 4211
Minnesota: Wedum 4719
New York: Bowne 5655, Lynton 6463, Rochester 6823, Valentine 7189, **Wallace 7209**
Ohio: Black 7551
Washington: Sherwood 9683

Education, single organization support

Alabama: Stallworth 64
California: Baxter 262, Dwyer 472, Siebel 1150
Illinois: D.H.R. 2695
Oregon: Wessinger 8067
Pennsylvania: Shadyside 8435

Education, special

California: Roberts 1058
Colorado: Ponzio 1440
Delaware: MBNA 1730
Georgia: Love 2437, Spray 2495
Illinois: Hammersmith 2781, McGraw 2882
Indiana: Adams 3095, Community 3126
Kentucky: Kindred 3434
Maryland: **Murray 3697**
Massachusetts: Harmsworth 3942, Pace 4065
Missouri: **Hana 4827**, Pershing 4881
New York: Butler 5692, Keeler 6306, McCarthy 6516, Schmitt 6928, Warner 7216
Ohio: Bicknell 7548, **Knowles 7701**, Spaulding 7865
Oregon: Shapira 8058
Pennsylvania: **Oberkotter 8365**
Texas: Ellwood 8884
Wisconsin: Handleman 9811

Elementary school/education

Alabama: Alpha 3, Lowder 42
California: Ahmanson 198, **American 217**, California 345, **ChevronTexaco 380**, Community 406, Copley 416, Crail 426, Crocker 429, Drown 469, Family 493, Fitzpatrick 515, Fleishhacker 518, Gellert 559, Gooding 604, Gross 621, Herbst 669, Homer 684, **Keck 750**, Koret 774, Lytel 836, Martin 860, Milken 898, Norton 943, Sacramento 1080, San Diego 1087, San Francisco 1088, Scully 1116, Soda 1173, Sonora 1178, Stuart 1206, Synopsys 1222, Thornton 1235, Van Nuys 1262, Weingart 1288
Colorado: Summit 1463
Connecticut: Fisher 1542, Graustein 1559, Martin 1598, Palmer 1621, **Smart 1651**, Woodward 1678
District of Columbia: Cafritz 1780, Meyer 1834, Post 1842

Florida: Bank 1890, Colen 1938, Community 1939, Community 1948, Ds 1976, Foley 2005, Ryder 2213, Selby 2230
Georgia: Anderson 2317, Callaway 2337, **Challenge 2344**, Goizueta 2400, Pittulloch 2464, Rollins 2475, Snodgrass 2492
Hawaii: Castle 2537, Castle 2538
Illinois: Chicago 2661, Coleman 2673, Community 2677, Field 2728, Fry 2740, Gidwitz 2754, Kaplan 2823, Kelly 2830, Prince 2948, Pritzker 2953
Indiana: Ball 3103, Boren 3108, **Cummins 3136**, Dekko 3142, Moore 3207, Noyes 3216, Samerian 3234
Iowa: McElroy 3313
Kentucky: Norton 3441, **Omnicare 3444**
Louisiana: Baton Rouge 3462, Heymann 3487
Maryland: Abell 3559, Commonweal 3596, Goldsmith 3637, Knott 3666, Krongard 3669, Rollins 3718
Massachusetts: Barr 3791, Boston 3812, High 3950, Lowell 4015, **New England 4052**, Schrafft 4133, Smith 4150, Sudbury 4173
Michigan: Binda 4233, Community 4256, **Kellogg 4357**
Minnesota: Bigelow 4519, Deluxe 4549, Dennis 4550, Greycoach 4575, Huss 4592, Marbrook 4612, Mardag 4613, Morning 4627, Sieben 4682
Missouri: Green 4822, Hall 4824, Rosewood 4894, Stupp 4910
Nebraska: Woods 5018
Nevada: Keyser 5039, Wiegand 5077
New Hampshire: Martin 5097
New Jersey: Bolger 5136, Dodge 5181, Hyde 5247, Lear 5300, McGraw 5323, MCJ 5324, Schreyer 5389, Smith 5408, Unilever 5434, Victoria 5440
New Mexico: Hubbard 5481, McCune 5488, Santa Fe 5496
New York: Altman 5542, Area 5564, **Bay 5606**, Diker 5862, Donaldson 5871, Everett 5941, **Ford 5970**, Gordon 6077, Harrison 6149, Hayden 6158, **Heineman 6165, Initial 6231, Kaufmann 6299**, Lowenstein 6449, Mars 6494, Ohrstrom 6659, Rohatyn 6830, Spunk 7036, **Time 7142, United 7185**, Warner 7216
North Carolina: Reynolds 7458, Reynolds 7459, Triangle 7496
Ohio: Beaverson 7541, Cleveland 7576, Forest 7634, Gund 7657, Hamilton 7660, Hershey 7671, Hoover 7675, Jennings 7688, Middletown 7749, Nordson 7781, Richland 7819, Stark 7867, Stocker 7870, **Timken 7880**, Troy 7886, Van Wert 7891, Wallace 7894, White 7905
Oklahoma: Better 7926
Pennsylvania: AMETEK 8081, Arkema 8089, Buck 8123, Buhl 8124, Connelly 8157, Dolfinger 8172, Kelly 8283, Ortenzio 8366, Penn 8371
Rhode Island: **Feinstein 8535**
South Carolina: Central 8577, Ceres 8578, TSC 8618
Tennessee: Community 8660, Davis 8665, Lyndhurst 8703, Plough 8718
Texas: Alexander 8752, Bailey 8771, Cain 8809, Cameron 8812, Edwards 8879, Elkins 8883, Fikes 8899, Garvey 8914, George 8916, Hachar 8927, Hobby 8954, Kempner 8987, King 8995, McDermott 9043, Peterson 9120, Rockwell 9154, Rogers 9155, Scott 9174, **Shell 9181**, South 9201, Temple 9227, Trull 9240, Vaughn 9251, Vergara 9253, Walsh 9261
Utah: Sorenson 9343
Vermont: Vermont 9361
Virginia: Bryant 9380, Delmar 9410, **Modzelewski 9477**
Washington: Community 9571, O'Donnell 9652
West Virginia: Kanawha 9723
Wisconsin: Alexander 9741, Coleman 9775, Fleck 9799, Frautschi 9804, Kohl 9838, McBeath 9864, Milwaukee 9876

Elementary/secondary education

Alabama: Bedsole 12, Blount 13, Comer 22, Harrison 36, Mitchell 53, Trippe 69, **Vulcan 73**
Arizona: Dorrance 95, Halle 103, Help 105, Long 118, Neely 126, Noah's 127, Pocono 131, Soling 140, WWJD 153

Schottenstein 7844, Scotford 7846, Sky 7859, Stefanski 7868, Stillson 7869, Troy 7886, Turner 7889, **Vesper 7892**, Wellman 7901
Oklahoma: Gaylord 7937, Kerr 7950, McMahon 7959, Oxley 7968, Zarrow 7991
Oregon: Crabby 8010, **Foreign 8014**, Frank 8016, Intel 8022, Jubitz 8028, Macdonald 8038, Mentor 8039, **NIKE 8046**, Salem 8054, Tektronix 8063
Pennsylvania: 1957 8071, Ball 8093, Byers' 8127, Connelly 8157, Crels 8163, Dolfinger 8172, **Dominion 8173**, Equitable 8187, Eustace 8191, Grable 8221, Graham 8222, Hunt 8261, Janssen 8271, Kavanagh 8282, Kim 8287, Korman 8296, Levan 8307, Little 8313, Lotman 8314, Maronda 8325, Meakem 8341, Parmer 8369, PNC 8388, Poor 8392, **PPG 8394**, Psalm 8397, PTS 8399, Roberts 8406, Salvitti 8422, Speyer 8453, St. Mary's 8454, Stewart 8460, Stop 8463, **Strawbridge 8465**, Triple 8482, Tyco 8485, United 8486, Vanguard 8490, **Waldorf 8495**, Weiss 8499, Willis 8504, Young 8512
Rhode Island: Alperin 8516, Charlesmead 8525, CVS 8529, Hasbro 8539, Routhier 8553
South Carolina: Collins 8582, First 8587, Gibbs 8590, Horne 8594, North 8601
South Dakota: Dakota 8624
Tennessee: Basler 8641, Belz 8643, **Bridgestone 8646**, **Garrott 8680**, Hamico 8684, Hendrix 8691, Ingram 8694, Jones 8698, Kirkland 8699, MacLellan 8705, Massey 8709, Nelson 8712, Ragsdale 8722, Stephens 8729, Washington 8741, Wilson 8744
Texas: Alkek 8753, Alkek 8754, Beal 8783, Cain 8808, CFP 8822, CH 8823, Clayton 8830, Clements 8832, Covenant 8847, **Dell 8863**, Dickson 8866, Duda 8871, Educational 8878, Fleming 8904, Goldsbury 8920, Goodman 8921, Hackett 8928, Hirsch 8953, Hudson 8962, Johnson 8973, Kahn 8980, Kurth 9003, Levit 9009, Martinez 9032, Mays 9035, Mays 9036, **Mevatek 9056**, **MFI 9059**, Miles 9060, Mosbacher 9077, O'Connor 9095, Penney 9115, Petrello 9121, Pine 9123, Rachofsky 9139, Reaud 9143, Riter 9149, Rogers 9155, Rosenberg 9157, Ross 9159, San Angelo 9164, Sanders 9167, Scurlock 9175, Sterling 9212, Temple 9228, Texas 9232, Trull 9240, Valero 9247, Vaughan 9249, Wal 9260, Ward 9262, Zachry 9296
Utah: Bamberger 9305, Quinney 9338, Wadman 9349, **Wishnick 9353**
Vermont: Mergens 9360
Virginia: Campbell 9383, CarMax 9385, Colburn 9395, Columbus 9399, English 9414, Flagler 9417, Freddie 9422, **Glenstone 9429**, Graves 9433, **Johnson 9444**, Kogod 9452, **MCI 9471**, Olsson 9491, Perry 9496, Rice 9504, Rosenthal 9508, Sandler 9511, Sandler 9512, Universal 9531, VuBay 9533, Wilkinson 9540
Washington: Anderson 9551, Aven 9554, **Boeing 9560**, Crystal 9576, Green 9598, Lynn 9633, Martin 9634, Norcliffe 9650, Opportunities 9655, PEMCO 9660, Raven 9670, **Samis 9675**, **Starbucks 9690**, T.E.W. 9692, UNOVA 9697
West Virginia: Prichard 9731
Wisconsin: Bell 9756, Brotz 9767, Community 9779, Demmer 9791, **Eastman 9794**, Goldbach 9806, Hess 9816, Janesville 9820, JKO 9822, Ladish 9847, Marshall 9860, Mason 9863, Northwestern 9884, Riordan 9911, **Rockwell 9912**, Siebert 9927, Smallwood 9928, Stone 9940, **Thrivent 9949**, Witte 9968

Elementary/secondary school reform

California: **Broad 324**, **Cortopassi 420**, **Hume 692**
Colorado: Rose 1445
District of Columbia: Fordham 1795
Georgia: **Rockdale 2474**
Hawaii: Castle 2537
New Mexico: Maddox 5487
New York: Achelis 5513, Bodman 5647, Cummings 5815
Ohio: Fairfield 7622

Pennsylvania: **Annenberg 8084**, Penn 8371
Texas: **Dell 8863**

Employment

Arizona: Arizona 87
Arkansas: East 160
California: **American 217**, California 345, Coates 391, Community 401, Community 406, **Draper 466**, Majestic 848, Marin 854, Roberts 1058, San Francisco 1088, **Strauss 1203**, Stuart 1208, Taper 1226, Union 1250, Whitecap 1303
Colorado: El Pomar 1374, Piton 1439, Weckbaugh 1470
Connecticut: Bridgeport 1504, Connecticut 1518, Fairfield 1537, Fisher 1542, **Niles 1612**, **Xerox 1680**
District of Columbia: **CityBridge 1783**, **Hitachi 1810**, Meyer 1834
Georgia: **Georgia 2397**
Illinois: **Burlington 2644**, CNA 2670, Dillon 2704, Field 2728, Fry 2740, Grand 2769, Harris 2787, **Joyce 2820**, Polk 2946, Retirement 2964, Sara 2982
Indiana: Adams 3095, Community 3126, East Chicago 3144, Heritage 3166, Twin 3245, Vectren 3249
Iowa: Maytag 3309
Louisiana: New Orleans 3503
Maryland: Abell 3559, Thalheimer 3744
Massachusetts: Boston 3812, Eaton 3888, Melville 4034, Parker 4069, Riley 4104, Robbins 4106, **State 4158**
Michigan: Comerica 4251, Grand Rapids 4326, Kelly 4359
Minnesota: **3M 4492**, Duluth 4556, **Ecolab 4557**, Marbrook 4612, Securian 4677, Star 4691, **SUPERVALU 4695**, Tennant 4700, **U.S. 4704**, West 4723, Xcel 4732
Missouri: Butler 4793, Craig 4800, Pettus 4882
New Jersey: Prudential 5360, **Verizon 5439**
New Mexico: McCune 5488
New York: Abrons 5511, Achelis 5513, Altman 5542, Butler 5692, **Citigroup 5755**, Clark 5762, Community 5782, DeCamp 5845, **Deutsche 5854**, Everett 5941, **Ford 5970**, HSBC 6204, **JPMorgan 6277**, Mizuho 6562, New York 6613, **Norman 6635**, O'Connor 6645, **PepsiCo 6714**, **Rockefeller 6826**, Roslyn 6859, **Sloan 7003**, Tuch 7170, **U.S. 7180**, Wendling 7242
North Carolina: Cumberland 7349, Duke 7360, **Wachovia 7502**
Ohio: Akron 7526, Fairfield 7622, Gund 7657, **Key 7700**, White 7905
Oregon: **NIKE 8046**
Pennsylvania: **Alcoa 8075**, Bayer 8096, Comcast 8152, Dolfinger 8172, Falk 8193, McCune 8332, **Pew 8377**, Vanguard 8490
South Dakota: Sioux Falls 8630
Tennessee: Caesars 8648, Community 8662
Texas: Anderson 8762, Meadows 9049
Vermont: **Ben 9355**
Washington: Glaser 9594, Lynn 9633, Norcliffe 9650
Wisconsin: Alliant 9742, Madison 9854, Milwaukee 9876, Northwestern 9884, Stackner 9934

Employment, equal rights

Pennsylvania: **Alcoa 8075**

Employment, formal/general education

Illinois: Steans 3021
Ohio: Nordson 7781

Employment, job counseling

Colorado: Rose 1445
Connecticut: Panwy 1622
District of Columbia: Jovid 1814
Maryland: Middendorf 3694
New York: **Merrill 6537**, Sullivan 7094
Ohio: Nordson 7781
Texas: Topfer 9238

Employment, labor unions/organizations

Massachusetts: Adams 3772, Edgerly 3889
New York: **Abelard 5508**, **Atran 5575**
Vermont: **Ben 9355**

Employment, public education

New York: **American 5553**

Employment, public policy

Michigan: **Rodney 4422**

Employment, research

Ohio: Jackson 7685

Employment, retraining

Minnesota: WCA 4718
Texas: **Imaca 8967**

Employment, services

California: **American 217**, Lux 834, Nissan 939, **Wells 1294**
District of Columbia: Block 1776, **Hill 1809**, Spring 1849
Georgia: Goizueta 2400, ING 2418
Illinois: Day 2698, Steans 3021
Indiana: East Chicago 3144, Twin 3245
Maine: TD 3558
Maryland: Abell 3559, deForest 3612, Rosenberg 3719
Massachusetts: **Merck 4036**, Ratshesky 4095
Michigan: Grosfeld 4332, Whirlpool 4480
Missouri: Simon 4903, Truman 4919
New Jersey: Prudential 5360
New York: Achelis 5513, Bodman 5647, Cummings 5815, Gimbel 6034, **Hearst 6161**, **Hearst 6162**, Lincoln 6423, **MetLife 6542**, Overhills 6676, Tiger 7139
Texas: Topfer 9238

Employment, sheltered workshops

Pennsylvania: FISA 8204

Employment, training

California: **Chiron 383**, Irvine 698, Lux 834, **Sun 1214**, Union 1250
Colorado: Rose 1445
Connecticut: International 1571, Northeast 1614, Tauck 1657
Florida: Darden 1960
Georgia: **Georgia 2397**
Illinois: **Burlington 2644**, Chicago 2661, CNA 2670, Day 2698, Sara 2982, Seabury 2993
Iowa: Maytag 3309, Principal 3326
Kansas: Salina 3387
Massachusetts: Melville 4034, **Staples 4156**, **State 4158**, Stoico 4166
Michigan: Comerica 4251, **DaimlerChrysler 4265**, Davenport 4269
Minnesota: **3M 4492**, **SUPERVALU 4695**, WCA 4718, West 4723
Missouri: Butler 4793, **Fox 4815**, Truman 4919
Nevada: Nevada 5048
New Jersey: Alcatel 5110, Danellie 5177, OceanFirst 5341
New York: **American 5553**, Dreyfus 5887, **JPMorgan 6277**, Snyder 7014
North Carolina: Goodrich 7378, Merancas 7428
Ohio: Columbus 7580, **Key 7700**
Oregon: **NIKE 8046**
Pennsylvania: **Alcoa 8075**, Comcast 8152, Grable 8221
South Dakota: Sioux Falls 8630
Tennessee: **Bridgestone 8646**
Texas: **Imaca 8967**, Topfer 9238

Wisconsin: Alliant 9742, Milwaukee 9876

Employment, vocational rehabilitation
North Carolina: Merancas 7428
Ohio: Reinberger 7815
Pennsylvania: FISA 8204

End of life care
California: Hofmann 683, Magistro 847
Colorado: Rose 1445
Connecticut: **Aetna 1479**
Georgia: Spray 2495
Massachusetts: **Hostetter 3959**
Pennsylvania: Blue 8112

Engineering
California: **Bechtel 269**, Bechtel 270, Gellert 559,
   GenCorp 560, **Hertz 670**, **Hewlett 672**, **Keck 750**,
   Parsons 980
Colorado: Hach 1386
Florida: Price 2177
Illinois: **CH2M 2654**, Grainger 2768
Michigan: DeVlieg 4275, DTE 4289
Minnesota: **3M 4492**, Alworth 4499
New Hampshire: **Dorr 5086**
New York: **Kade 6281**, **Schlumberger 6926**
Ohio: Dayton 7604
Texas: O'Donnell 9096, **Shell 9181**
Washington: Coulter 9573

Engineering school/education
Alabama: **Vulcan 73**
California: **Beavers 268**, **Bechtel 269**, Bechtel 270,
   Davidson 445, Fluor 523, Garen 555, Gellert 559,
   GenCorp 560, **Hewlett 672**, **Keck 750**, Kvamme
   781, Parsons 980, Schlinger 1103
Colorado: Hach 1386, Trueblood 1466
Connecticut: **GE 1553**, **Praxair 1629**
Florida: **Hardison 2048**, Price 2177
Idaho: **Micron 2571**
Illinois: Gantz 2748, Olin 2925, Pepper 2936, Tellabs
   3034
Iowa: Maytag 3309, **Rockwell 3328**
Maryland: Gudelsky 3641
Massachusetts: Adams 3772
Michigan: **ArvinMeritor 4224**, **DaimlerChrysler 4265**,
   DENSO 4272, DeVlieg 4275, DTE 4289, Ford 4307,
   General 4320, World 4489
Minnesota: Alworth 4499
New Jersey: Armour 5116
New York: **Dreyfus 5886**, **Schlumberger 6926**
North Carolina: Baruch 7311, Goodrich 7378, Kenan
   7411, Progress 7453
Ohio: Dayton 7604, **Freygang 7640**
Oregon: Intel 8022
Pennsylvania: **United 8488**
South Carolina: Hopewell 8593
South Dakota: Dakota 8624
Texas: **ExxonMobil 8889**, Marathon 9028, National
   9088, **Shell 9181**
Washington: Coulter 9573
Wisconsin: Charter 9772, Holz 9817, Mead 9867

Engineering/technology
Arizona: Arizona 87
California: **American 217**, Bechtel 270, **Beckman 272**,
   Community 406, Femino 501, Fluor 523, **Hertz
   670**, **Hewlett 672**, **Keck 750**, Moore 912, Norris
   940, Northrop 942, **Packard 972**, Schlinger 1103
Colorado: **StorageTek 1460**, Trueblood 1466
Connecticut: Bodenwein 1497, Palmer 1621, **Xerox
   1680**
District of Columbia: **Case 1782**
Florida: Banbury 1889, Community 1941, **Picower
   2169**, Rayonier 2189
Georgia: BellSouth 2323, Cox 2367

Idaho: **Micron 2571**
Illinois: **Motorola 2906**
Massachusetts: **Bosack 3809**, Cabot 3823, Ellsworth
   3892, Hirschtick 3953, Lowell 4015, McEvoy 4032,
   Technical 4180
Michigan: Dart 4267, DeVlieg 4275, Dow 4287, Ford
   4307, Strosacker 4450
Minnesota: **ADC 4496**, Alworth 4499
Missouri: Boeing 4785
Nevada: **Lemelson 5040**
New Jersey: Buehler 5146, **Edison 5186**, **International
   5252**, **Johnson 5263**, PSEG 5361
New Mexico: Holt 5480
New York: Golden 6046, **Heineman 6165**, Link 6428,
   Luce 6453, Schenectady 6915, **Sloan 7003**,
   Vetlesen 7196
North Carolina: **Nickel 7436**
Ohio: Huntington 7680
Oklahoma: Presbyterian 7969
Oregon: **Mentor 8039**
Pennsylvania: Buhl 8124, Rockwell 8408, West 8500
Rhode Island: Champlin 8524, Daniels 8530
Texas: East 8876, Elkins 8883, Moody 9070, **Shell
   9181**, Sturgis 9216, Zachry 9296
Washington: **Boeing 9560**
Wisconsin: **Rockwell 9912**

Environment
Alabama: Alabama 1, **Altec 4**, AmSouth 5, Barber 10,
   Brock 16, Community 24, Community 25,
   Community 26, Community 27, Founders 34,
   Thompson 67, **Vulcan 73**
Alaska: Alaska 79
Arizona: A.P.S. 86, Arizona 87, Community 91, **Globe
   101**, **Johnson 112**, **Kieckhefer 113**, Morris 124,
   Reese 133, **Rodel 136**
Arkansas: Arkansas 156, Trinity 181, Wal-Mart 184
California: Altman 211, **American 217**, Anaheim 220,
   Angelica 223, **Appleton 225**, Arntz 236, Atkins
   238, Ayrshire 247, Baker 251, Bannerman 255,
   Barker 257, Bay 264, **Beagle 266**, Boswell 308,
   Bothin 309, Brotman 328, Burnett 336, **Castagnola
   366**, Caufield 367, **ChevronTexaco 380**,
   Christensen 384, Columbia 399, Community 401,
   Community 402, Community 403, Community 404,
   Community 406, Community 407, **Compton 409**,
   Crocker 429, Crockett 430, Daly 437, David 442,
   Disney 456, **Draper 465**, **Draper 466**, East 474,
   Edgerton 477, Eucalyptus 489, Flora 521, Follis
   525, **Foundation 529**, Fresno 537, G.T.R. 544,
   Gaia 545, Garen 555, Gerbode 564, Global 583,
   Godric 586, **Goldman 594**, Goldman 596, Goldman
   597, **Good 603**, Grand 611, Greenberg 617, Gruber
   626, Harden 647, Hewlett 671, Horn 686, Ishiyama
   702, Jewett 718, **K.L. 736**, Kapor 743, **Lawrence
   794**, Lee 798, Lehrer 800, LLWW 824, Ludwick
   829, **Ludwick 830**, Marin 854, **McConnell 870**,
   McKay 877, Mead 881, Mental 886, Mericos 889,
   Merrill 890, Moore 912, Morgan 915, Morton 919,
   On 953, Orange 957, Osher 961, Pacific 970,
   Packard 972, Pasadena 982, Peninsula 989, PG&E
   1000, Reid 1036, Rigler 1051, Rivkin 1057, Roth
   1071, Rothschild 1072, Sacramento 1080, San
   Diego 1087, San Francisco 1088, San Luis 1090,
   San 1091, Santa Barbara 1093, Segerstrom 1123,
   Shasta 1139, Shenandoah 1144, Sierra 1152,
   Simon 1156, Smith 1160, Sonora 1178,
   Springcreek 1185, Steele 1189, Stephenson 1193,
   Stern 1195, **Streisand 1204**, Swift 1219, Taper
   1226, Teichert 1231, **Tennity 1233**, **Tosa 1240**,
   Truckee 1244, True 1245, Vadasz 1254, Ventura
   1264, Wallis 1276, Wohlford 1315
Colorado: Aspen 1337, Community 1358, Donnell
   1367, Edmondson 1373, El Pomar 1374, Fullerton
   1378, KBK 1400, Kenney 1401, Ludlow 1412,
   Pikes 1437, Summit 1463, Taylor 1464, Telluride
   1465, Vail 1468, **Weaver 1469**, Western 1471,
   Yampa 1477
Connecticut: **Bingham 1493**, Bodenwein 1497,
   Bridgeport 1504, Community 1514, Community
   1515, Community 1516, Community 1517,

Donchian 1530, **Educational 1533**, Ensworth
   1535, **Ettinger 1536**, Fairfield 1537, **Fink 1539**,
   FSB 1549, Goergen 1556, Larsen 1579, Long
   1590, Main 1594, **McKenzie 1601**, Melville 1602,
   Northeast 1614, Palmer 1621, **Praxair 1629**,
   Prentice 1630, Sewall 1648, Tauck 1657,
   Thompson 1658, Tow 1660, **Tremaine 1662**,
   Tyrrell 1667, Vervane 1671, Woodward 1678
Delaware: Delaware 1706, Kingsley 1724, Marmot
   1728, **Milliken 1732**, Orange 1737, Presto 1740,
   Welfare 1762
District of Columbia: **Bauman 1770**, Cafritz 1780,
   Community 1785, **Koch 1819**, Mazda 1828,
   Munson 1837, **Patterson 1840**, **Public 1844**,
   Summit 1852
Florida: Banbury 1889, Bank 1890, Bastien 1892,
   Batchelor 1893, Community 1939, Community
   1941, Community 1943, Community 1944,
   Community 1945, Community 1946, Community
   1948, Community 1949, Dade 1957, Darden 1960,
   Dennis 1969, Duckwall 1978, Dunn 1979, FPL
   2010, Free 2012, Gainesville 2015, Gulf 2041,
   Kennedy 2088, Kesler 2090, Lattner 2104, Martin
   2130, Mote 2148, Ocean 2156, Pinellas 2170,
   River 2198, Southwest 2240, St. Joe 2244, Taylor
   2267
Georgia: AEC 2310, Blank 2325, Community 2357,
   Community 2358, Community 2359, Community
   2362, Cooper 2363, **Dobbs 2373**, Fort 2387, **Gage
   2392**, Georgia 2395, **Georgia 2397**, **JCK 2421**,
   Lubo 2438, Murphy 2456, North 2458, Patterson
   2460, Rice 2471, Rich 2472, Sawnee 2481,
   Southern 2494, Spray 2495, **Thoresen 2499**, Tull
   2500, **Turner 2501**, Williams 2514, Woodruff 2521
Hawaii: Alexander 2530, Atherton 2532, Atherton
   2533, Castle 2537, Change 2539, Cooke 2541,
   Hawaii 2545, Hawaiian 2546, Strong 2555
Idaho: Golden 2568
Illinois: Abbott 2580, Abelson 2581, **ARIA 2600**, Bell
   2614, **Brach 2630**, **Brunswick 2636**, Buchanan
   2637, **Buffett 2639**, **Buntrock 2643**, Butler 2646,
   Caterpillar 2653, Community 2677, Community
   2678, Donnelley 2706, DuPage 2713, Field 2728,
   Gallagher 2744, Grand 2769, H.B.B. 2777, Hamill
   2780, Hitchcock 2801, Huizenga 2806, Istock
   2815, Jahn 2816, **Joyce 2820**, Kainz 2822, **Keller
   2829**, Krehbiel 2845, Louis 2862, Madigan 2869,
   Malott 2872, McGraw 2882, Oak Park 2922,
   Oberweiler 2923, Olin 2925, Omron 2926,
   Ploughshares 2945, Prince 2948, **Relations
   2963**, Seabury 2993, **Shifting 3006**, Siragusa
   3009, Tellabs 3034
Indiana: Ball 3103, Ball 3104, Brown 3110, Community
   3123, Community 3127, Community 3128,
   Community 3130, Community 3132, Crown Point
   3135, Dearborn 3137, DeKalb 3141, Griffith 3158,
   Harrison 3161, Johnson 3178, Kosciusko 3186,
   Lafayette 3188, Legacy 3189, Montgomery 3206,
   NiSource 3213, Northern 3215, Ripley 3230,
   Samerian 3234, Steuben 3241, Unity 3247, Wayne
   3253
Iowa: Bucksbaum 3271, Cedar Rapids 3275,
   Community 3277, Community 3278, McElroy 3313,
   Poweshiek 3325, **Rockwell 3328**, **Sehgal 3330**
Kansas: Salina 3387, Topeka 3400, Wichita 3404
Kentucky: Blue 3407, Community 3414, Community
   3415, E.ON 3417, Sutherland 3451
Louisiana: Baton Rouge 3462, **Biedenharn 3463**, Booth
   3464, Community 3469, Freeport 3481, **Live
   3495**, New Orleans 3503
Maine: Baker 3524, Burnham 3527, Catalyst 3529,
   Kennebunk 3544, Maine 3548, **Oak 3552**, **Sandy
   3555**, Switzer 3557
Maryland: Abell 3559, Baltimore 3568, Brown 3578,
   Bunting 3580, Campbell 3582, Chaney 3587,
   Cohen 3594, Columbia 3595, Community 3599,
   Constellation 3602, France 3632, Higginson 3649,
   Macht 3683, McKnight 3688, Merrill 3689,
   Morningstar 3695, Principato 3710, Rathmann
   3715, **Shared 3727**, **Town 3749**, Tucker 3750
Massachusetts: Adams 3771, **Azadoutioun 3786**, Barr
   3791, Bay 3794, Berkshire 3801, Cabot 3822,
   Cabot 3823, Cabot 3825, Caldwell 3827, Canaday

3831, Cape Cod 3832, Cape Cod 3833, Cedar 3840, Common 3853, Community 3854, Community 3855, **Conservation 3858**, Cox 3863, Essex 3897, Fields 3905, Fieldstone 3906, Foundation 3916, Grantham 3930, Hoyt 3960, Island 3965, Johnson 3970, Kidder 3979, Lowell 4014, Merck 4035, **Merck 4036**, Miller 4039, MWC 4046, North 4057, Orchard 4062, Pappas 4067, Parker 4069, Peabody 4072, Pierce 4084, Rasmussen 4094, **Sager 4122**, **Saquish 4127**, Sawyer 4128, Stearns 4159, Stearns 4160, Stoddard 4165, Sudbury 4173, Tara 4179, Vingo 4192, **Waterman 4198**, Worcester 4209, Yawkey 4211

Michigan: Acheson 4214, **Aikens 4215**, Americana 4218, Ann Arbor 4221, Bay 4229, Binda 4233, Branch 4237, Burt 4242, Capital 4243, Charlevoix 4246, Community 4252, Community 4253, Community 4254, Community 4255, Community 4256, Community 4258, Community 4259, Consumers 4260, **DaimlerChrysler 4265**, Dalton 4266, DeVlieg 4275, Dow 4284, Dow 4288, DTE 4289, Ford 4307, Four 4310, Fremont 4315, Frey 4316, General 4320, Grand Haven 4325, Grand Rapids 4326, Grand 4327, Greenville 4331, Jackson 4347, Kalamazoo 4352, Keeler 4355, **Kresge 4367**, Midland 4392, Mosaic 4398, Oleson 4405, Petoskey 4412, Saginaw 4428, St. Deny's 4444, Steelcase 4446, Upjohn 4465, **Visteon 4472**, Wenger 4477

Minnesota: **3M 4492**, Beim 4513, Bell 4514, Beverly 4517, Bush 4524, Butler 4525, Buuck 4526, Capp 4529, Carolyn 4533, Central 4534, Cox 4543, Duluth 4556, **Ecolab 4557**, **Ecotrust 4558**, Federated 4563, **Fuller 4567**, Grand Rapids 4574, Huss 4592, Lilly 4606, Marbrook 4612, McKnight 4617, McNeely 4619, McVay 4620, Minnesota 4624, Musser 4629, Northwest 4637, Rochester 4668, Rupp 4669, Sexton 4679, Smikis 4687, Thorpe 4701, **Toro 4702**, Warner 4715, Watson 4717, **Weyerhaeuser 4725**, Winona 4729, Xcel 4732

Mississippi: Community 4737, Maddox 4753
Missouri: Ameren 4772, **Anheuser 4776**, Boeing 4785, Brauer 4787, Community 4798, **Deer 4804**, Dula 4806, Green 4822, **Monsanto 4868**, Saint Louis 4896, Trio 4918
Montana: Browning 4933, Chutney 4934, Cinnabar 4935
Nebraska: Cooper 4954, James 4980, Lincoln 4987, Merrick 4990, Mid-Nebraska 4991, **Union 5012**
Nevada: Bretzlaff 5024, Community 5028, Fairweather 5032, Nevada 5047, Parasol 5051, Sierra 5064, Southwest 5066, **Walsh 5075**
New Hampshire: New Hampshire 5098, **Penates 5099**, Putnam 5100
New Jersey: Borden 5138, Bunbury 5148, Community 5167, Cowles 5170, Dodge 5181, Dow 5183, Eisenberg 5187, **Fanwood 5192**, Fund 5199, Grassmann 5213, Hickory 5232, Hyde 5247, **IDT 5248**, **International 5252**, **Johnson 5263**, JSY 5267, **Lautenberg 5298**, Mazer 5321, McGraw 5323, **Merck 5326**, Mushett 5334, OceanFirst 5341, Schering 5387, Schumann 5391, Sunup 5419, Tolchin 5428, Unilever 5434, Union 5435, Victoria 5440, Wallerstein 5447
New Mexico: Albuquerque 5466, Carlsbad 5469, Frost 5476, **Levinson 5486**, McCune 5488, New 5490, PNM 5493, **Pond 5494**, Proteus 5495, Santa Fe 5496, Taos 5498, **Thaw 5500**
New York: Abrons 5511, Adirondack 5517, Alpern 5540, **American 5553**, Andersen 5558, Babbitt 5586, Baird 5592, Baldwin 5595, Barker 5600, **Barth 5603**, **Bay 5606**, Bedminster 5611, Bingham 5631, Butler 5691, **Bydale 5694**, Cary 5712, Castelnau 5715, Central 5724, Chadwick 5726, **Chernin 5743**, Clark 5761, Cloud 5764, Community 5780, Community 5782, Community 5783, Community 5784, Corrigan 5796, **Cummings 5814**, Dolan 5870, Doran 5875, Dubin 5891, **Echoing 5905**, Ellis 5923, Evans 5940, Faulkner 5948, **Ford 5970**, **Frankel 5976**, Gerschel 6018, Giant 6023, Gimbel 6034, Gleacher 6038,

Glickenhaus 6042, Goldstein 6063, Gordon 6077, Gould 6082, Greene 6099, Greentree 6102, Greve 6104, Hajim 6134, Handler 6140, **Heineman 6165**, **HKH 6190**, Hoffman 6195, HSBC 6204, Hughes 6209, **IBM 6221**, **Ittleson 6241**, Jackson Hole 6246, JCT 6256, Kadrovach 6282, Kaplan 6290, KeySpan 6320, Klingenstein 6336, Knafel 6341, **Kohlberg 6346**, Kurtz 6364, Lauder 6382, Lee 6391, Lenna 6402, Levitt 6409, Littauer 6434, Litterman 6435, Loeb 6440, Lookout 6445, **LSR 6451**, **Luce 6453**, Mariposa 6487, Mars 6494, Meehan 6523, **Mellon 6525**, **Memton 6529**, Model 6565, **Moore 6570**, Mosaic 6586, Moses 6587, **Mulago 6593**, Mullen 6596, Neu 6610, New York 6613, New York 6620, **New 6621**, Nicholas 6627, Nichols 6628, **Noble 6633**, **Norcross 6634**, Normandie 6636, Northern 6638, Northern 6639, **Noyes 6643**, O'Connor 6645, Ohrstrom 6659, Osborn 6669, **Ottinger 6674**, Overhills 6676, PBO 6699, Plant 6731, Quadrangle 6758, R & TP 6764, Rauch 6774, Richmond 6800, Rochester 6823, **Rockefeller 6825**, Rockefeller 6827, **Rosen 6843**, Rosenwald 6856, Ross 6864, Sacerdote 6887, Scherman 6918, Sheinberg 6963, Sheldon 6964, Snow 7011, **Solomon 7017**, Starfish 7046, **Starr 7048**, Steele 7053, Straus 7084, **Surdna 7103**, **Sussman 7105**, Sweetgrass 7113, **Sykes 7115**, Tamarind 7119, Task 7124, **Tiffany 7137**, **Tinker 7143**, Tishman 7150, Tober 7152, **Tortuga 7155**, **Trust 7168**, **United 7185**, **Vetlesen 7196**, Vidda 7198, Walbridge 7207, Wallach 7210, **Weeden 7223**, Weinberg 7231, Weissman 7237, Wendling 7242, Wiegers 7256, Wilson 7262, **Wolfensohn 7270**, Wright 7280, **Zenkel 7295**, Zitrin 7302

North Carolina: BB&T 7312, Blumenthal 7320, Coleman 7340, Community 7343, Community 7344, Community 7346, Cumberland 7349, Dover 7356, Duke 7360, Easley 7361, Foundation 7370, Hanes 7387, Hillsdale 7398, Janirve 7404, Legatus 7420, **Nickel 7436**, North Carolina 7438, Piedmont 7447, Price 7451, Progress 7453, Reynolds 7458, Robertson 7466, Slick 7474, Strowd 7488, SunTrust 7491, Triangle 7496, Weaver 7504
North Dakota: MDU 7517, North Dakota 7519
Ohio: Akron 7526, **Alpaugh 7527**, American 7528, **Armington 7532**, Ashland 7533, **Austin 7535**, **Bingham 7549**, Castellini 7568, Cincinnati 7574, Cleveland 7576, Columbus 7580, Community 7581, Community 7582, Community 7584, Community 7585, Community 7586, **Cox 7596**, Dayton 7603, Dayton 7604, Fairfield 7622, **Goatie 7651**, Gund 7657, Honda 7673, Hoover 7674, **Kettering 7698**, Lubrizol 7725, MeadWestvaco 7745, Miller 7753, Morgan 7760, Nationwide 7771, New 7775, Nippert 7777, Nord 7779, Olive 7787, Richland 7819, Smith 7862, Springfield 7866, Stark 7867, Tippit 7881, Troy 7886, Tuscarawas 7890, **Vesper 7892**, **Warrington 7895**, Wayne 7897, Wellman 7901, Wolfe 7915
Oklahoma: Bovaird 7927, Chapman 7928, Hille 7943, Inasmuch 7944
Oregon: Autzen 7997, Carpenter 8003, Crabby 8010, Jackson 8024, Jubitz 8028, Kelley 8030, **Lazar 8035**, Louisiana 8037, Meyer 8042, Tucker 8065
Pennsylvania: 1675 8070, ACE 8073, **Alcoa 8075**, **Annenberg 8084**, Arcadia 8086, Asplundh 8091, Berks 8103, Brickman 8116, Centre 8136, Chester 8141, Claneil 8144, Community 8155, Cooper 8158, Dolfinger 8172, **Dominion 8173**, Fine 8201, First 8202, Fisher 8205, **Forney 8207**, Foundation 8208, Heinz 8241, Heinz 8242, **Heinz 8243**, Hillman 8252, Hopwood 8257, Hunt 8261, Huston 8263, **Korein 8295**, Lancaster 8300, Lehigh Valley 8303, Lenfest 8305, Little 8313, Luzerne 8317, Mandell 8322, Maslow 8327, Mellon 8346, Penn 8371, **Pew 8377**, Pond 8391, Reidler 8402, Scranton 8431, **Seraph 8434**, Snee 8446, Sordoni 8450, Strawbridge 8466, **United 8488**, Vanguard 8490, Willary 8503, Wyomissing 8509, York 8511
Rhode Island: **Amica 8518**, Champlin 8524, Kimball 8542, Rhode Island 8551

South Carolina: Bruce 8571, Central 8577, Ceres 8578, Coastal 8581, Community 8583, Community 8584, Montgomery 8600, Waccamaw 8619
South Dakota: Sioux Falls 8630
Tennessee: Atticus 8639, Benwood 8644, **Bridgestone 8646**, Community 8660, Community 8661, Community 8662, Jones 8698, Lyndhurst 8703, Massey 8709, Tucker 8735
Texas: **Aurora 8767**, Austin 8768, Bass 8778, Cain 8809, **Catto 8819**, **CEMEX 8821**, Coastal 8833, **Cooper 8846**, El Paso 8881, **ExxonMobil 8889**, Fikes 8899, Haggar 8931, Hanley 8940, Herzstein 8949, Kelleher 8984, Kempner 8987, Kimberly 8992, Kinder 8994, **KLE 8997**, Lubbock 9021, Marathon 9028, McCoy 9038, Meadows 9049, Moody 9070, Newman 9090, Northen 9092, Otter 9105, Partnership 9110, Powell 9128, Rockwell 9154, Rosewood 9158, Sams 9163, San Antonio 9166, **Shell 9181**, Simmons 9187, Tapeats 9223, Trull 9240, Waco 9255, **Waste 9265**, White 9279, Wichita 9280, Wright 9294
Utah: Eccles 9317, Eccles 9319, Gardner 9323, Quinney 9338, **Wishnick 9353**
Vermont: **Ben 9355**, **Green 9358**, Lintilhac 9359, Vermont 9361
Virginia: Arlington 9371, Batten 9373, Camp 9382, Carter 9387, Charlottesville 9390, Community 9400, Evans 9416, **Gannett 9428**, Jackson 9441, Kington 9450, Luck 9461, Norfolk 9484, Sacharuna 9509, Smith 9518, Staunton 9521, SunTrust 9523, Virginia Beach 9532, Wellspring 9537, **WestWind 9538**, Wrinkle 9545
Washington: **Boeing 9560**, Bullitt 9563, Community 9570, Community 9571, **Fabert 9584**, Green 9598, Harder 9600, Horizons 9608, Kaleidoscope 9616, Klorfine 9619, **Kongsgaard 9620**, Neukom 9649, Norcliffe 9650, Peach 9659, Quixote 9667, Raven 9670, Russell 9673, **Sage 9674**, Seattle 9680, Tacoma 9693, **Wiancko 9704**, Wilburforce 9705, Wright 9707
West Virginia: Kanawha 9723
Wisconsin: Alliant 9742, Argosy 9747, Bleser 9760, Bradshaw 9764, Community 9776, Community 9778, Community 9780, Cudahy 9785, Demmer 9791, Dudley 9792, Eastman 9795, Fond du Lac 9800, Green Bay 9810, Johnson 9823, Johnson 9826, Kenosha 9833, Krejci 9843, Madison 9854, Marshfield 9861, Menasha 9869, Milwaukee 9876, Oshkosh 9885, Racine 9906, St. Croix 9933, Waukesha 9960, Wisconsin 9967
Wyoming: Community 9977, Connemara 9978, S & G 9988, Weiss 9997

Environment, air pollution

Georgia: AGL 2312, Sapelo 2479
Illinois: Tellabs 3034
Michigan: Community 4252, DTE 4289, Ford 4307
Minnesota: Westcliff 4724
New York: Smith 7008
Washington: **Edwards 9580**, Seattle 9680

Environment, alliance

California: **Arkay 235**
Maine: **Golden 3538**
Michigan: General 4320
Minnesota: Xcel 4732

Environment, association

North Carolina: Progress 7453

Environment, beautification programs

Alabama: Community 24, Hearin 37
California: Jewett 718
Connecticut: Community 1514
Florida: Paulucci 2164
Georgia: AGL 2312

Indiana: Community 3122, Community 3124, Lafayette 3188
Massachusetts: Babson 3787
Michigan: Frey 4316
Minnesota: Xcel 4732
New Mexico: Maddox 5487
New York: Antz 5560, HSBC 6204, Independence 6229, KeySpan 6320, New York 6619, Vidda 7198
North Carolina: **Lowe's 7423**
Ohio: Community 7584, Fairfield 7622, Hamilton 7660
Oklahoma: Oklahoma City 7964
Pennsylvania: Claneil 8144, Eden 8182, Penn 8371
South Carolina: Montgomery 8600
Tennessee: Caldwell 8649
Texas: Wortham 9292
Wisconsin: Fort 9801

Environment, energy

California: **Energy 483, Packard 972**
Connecticut: **Educational 1533**
District of Columbia: **Wallace 1858**
Florida: FPL 2010
Georgia: **Turner 2501**
Illinois: Grand 2769
Maryland: Constellation 3602
Michigan: Bay 4229, **DaimlerChrysler 4265**, DTE 4289, General 4320, Midland 4392
Minnesota: McKnight 4617, Xcel 4732
New Jersey: PSEG 5361
New York: **Heineman 6165**, HSBC 6204, Link 6428, **Mertz 6538, Surdna 7103, United 7185**
North Carolina: Piedmont 7447, Triangle 7496
Ohio: Columbus 7580, Dayton 7604
Pennsylvania: Dolfinger 8172, Hopwood 8257, **Pew 8377**, York 8511
South Dakota: Sioux Falls 8630
Texas: **Shell 9181**
Virginia: **Blue 9379**
Washington: Bullitt 9563, **Edwards 9580**
Wisconsin: Alliant 9742

Environment, ethics

Wisconsin: Bradshaw 9764

Environment, forests

California: **Angelica 223, Delano 449**, Firedoll 508, Flintridge 520, Mead 881
Connecticut: **Tyrrell 1667**
District of Columbia: Post 1842, **Wallace 1858**
Georgia: Sapelo 2479
Massachusetts: Cardinal 3834, DiMaura 3880, Hoffman 3955
New Jersey: Lear 5300
New York: Alfiero 5534, Overhills 6676
Ohio: Fairfax 7621
Pennsylvania: **Alcoa 8075**
Virginia: **WestWind 9538**
Washington: Burning 9564, **Edwards 9580**, **Weyerhaeuser 9703**

Environment, formal/general education

Massachusetts: Cedar 3840
New Mexico: Brindle 5468
Washington: Peach 9659

Environment, global warming

California: Mental 886
District of Columbia: **Butler 1779, Wallace 1858**
Maine: **Oak 3552**
Massachusetts: **Merck 4036**
New York: **Rockefeller 6825**
Washington: Bullitt 9563, **Edwards 9580**

Environment, land resources

Arizona: Reese 133
California: **Foundation 529**, Grout 624, James 709, Jewett 718, McBean 865, Priem 1020, San Diego 1087, Segal 1121, Siebel 1150, Springcreek 1185
Colorado: Gary 1379, Joy 1399, Telluride 1465
Delaware: Lennox 1726
Georgia: Morgens 2453, Poe 2465
Illinois: Borwell 2627, Eddema 2714, Froehlich 2739, Getz 2753, Grand 2769
Indiana: Met 3204, Simon 3240
Kentucky: **Chase 3413**
Maryland: Helena 3646, **Shared 3727**
Massachusetts: Cammarata 3829, Narada 4047, Pardoe 4068, Radley 4092, **Sweet 4176**
Michigan: Community 4252, Ford 4300, Frey 4316
Minnesota: Xcel 4732
Missouri: **Monsanto 4868**
Nebraska: Swanson 5009
New Jersey: Fund 5199, Goldring 5210
New York: Buck 5682, **Burke 5688, Frankel 5976**, Handler 6140, Kealy 6303, Levy 6413, MJPM 6563, Overhills 6676, Partridge 6695, **Penzance 6712**, Scheuer 6919, **Stony 7082, Tiffany 7137**
Oregon: Sky 8059
Pennsylvania: Allerton 8077, Taylor 8473, Thompson 8476, York 8511
Rhode Island: Doyle 8532, van Beuren 8561
Utah: Peery 9337
Virginia: **WestWind 9538**
Washington: Bullitt 9563, Burning 9564, **Edwards 9580**, Murr 9645
Wisconsin: Sand 9918

Environment, legal rights

California: Edgerton 477
Colorado: Kenney 1401
Connecticut: **Valentine 1669**
Massachusetts: Cedar 3840
New Mexico: Brindle 5468
New York: **Norman 6635**
Pennsylvania: **PPG 8394**
Tennessee: Atticus 8639

Environment, management/technical aid

New York: **Beldon 5614**

Environment, natural resources

Alabama: Barber 10, Brock 16, Mitchell 53
Alaska: Alaska 79
Arizona: Arizona 87, **Kieckhefer 113**
California: Aaroe 192, American 215, **American 217**, Barker 257, **Beagle 266**, Beattie 267, Bella 275, Brenner 321, Chais 371, Chintu 382, **Christensen 384**, Columbia 399, **Compton 409**, Cortopassi 419, Crawford 427, Crocker 429, **Delano 449**, Edgerton 477, Eldorado 482, **Environment 487**, Firedoll 508, Flintridge 520, **Foundation 529**, Garen 555, Gill 576, Gilmore 578, Gold 590, Haynes 658, Heller 666, Hewlett 671, JWS 735, King 760, Klein 765, Lipman 817, McCaw 869, Mead 881, Mellam 883, **Mohn 907**, Moore 912, Morton 919, **On 953**, Oppenheimer 955, Pacific 970, **Packard 972**, Peninsula 989, **Peterson 996**, Pfleger 998, Priem 1020, Raintree 1028, Reid 1036, Resnick 1041, Rotasa 1070, Sacramento 1080, San Francisco 1088, Sapling 1094, **Schlinger 1102**, Segal 1121, Shapiro 1137, Smith 1160, Sorensen 1180, Sprague 1184, **Stuart 1207**, True 1245, **Unocal 1252**, Ventura 1264, Vons 1270, Wallis 1276, Webster 1286, Wilbur 1305, Windfall 1309, Witter 1314, Wohlford 1315, Wunderkinder 1322, ZZYZX 1331
Colorado: Aspen 1337, **Avenir 1339, Benson 1341**, Caulkins 1353, El Pomar 1374, Gates 1380, Green 1385, **Hawley 1390**, Joy 1399, Kenney 1401, Norwood 1433, Summit 1463, Taylor 1464

Environment, land resources

Connecticut: Baldwin 1487, Community 1517, **Educational 1533, Ettinger 1536**, Flinn 1543, Garden 1552, **Huisking 1570**, Larsen 1579, **October 1617**, Palmer 1621, Patricelli 1623, **Sun 1656**, Tsunami 1663, Worthington 1679
Delaware: Buckner 1695, Cawley 1696, Chichester 1698, Crestlea 1701, Crystal 1702, Day 1704, Hall 1718, Marmot 1728, Reynolds 1743, Rowland 1749, Singer 1753, **Stroud 1757**
District of Columbia: Agua 1764, Cafritz 1780, Friedman 1799, McIntosh 1831, Munson 1837, **Patterson 1840**, Post 1842, Spring 1849, **Summit 1852, Wallace 1857, Winslow 1863**, Wyss 1864
Florida: Bank 1890, Batchelor 1893, Blank 1909, Burton 1921, Community 1939, Community 1943, Darden 1960, Dunn 1979, GSB 2039, Jelks 2076, Lattner 2104, Maltz 2126, Marden 2127, Martin 2130, Opler 2158, Rayonier 2189, **Regan 2191**, Shackelford 2232, Storer 2252, **Vanneck 2278**
Georgia: AGL 2312, Broadfield 2330, Community 2355, Community 2361, Gaines 2393, **Georgia 2397, Money 2450**, Morgens 2453, Morris 2454, Patterson 2460, Spray 2495, **Turner 2501, Wardlaw 2506**, Williams 2514, Williams 2516, Woodruff 2521, Woodruff 2522, Zeist 2529
Hawaii: Anthony 2531, Hawaii 2545
Idaho: CHC 2566
Illinois: Anderson 2594, **ARIA 2600**, Bersted 2618, Blair 2622, Camp 2649, Comer 2675, Community 2677, Deering 2700, Donnelley 2706, **Excelsior! 2722**, Froehlich 2739, Grand 2769, **Harper 2786**, Huntington 2809, Kainz 2822, Love 2863, Lumpkin 2864, Lurie 2865, **MacArthur 2868**, Madigan 2869, Makray 2871, McCormick 2878, Morton 2905, Nelson 2911, Olin 2925, Prince 2948, Rosenthal 2970, **Satter 2983**, Sharpe 3002, Sirius 3010
Indiana: Ball 3104, Dearborn 3137, Met 3204, Pulliam 3225, Raker 3226, Vectren 3249
Iowa: Community 3278, Gilchrist 3287, Maytag 3310, Meredith 3315, **Sehgal 3330**, Wallace 3342
Kansas: Cessna 3351, Topeka 3400, Wichita 3404
Kentucky: Brown 3410, **Chase 3413**
Louisiana: Brown 3465, Community 3469, Coypu 3471
Maine: Alfond 3522, Baker 3524, Falcon 3532, Fore 3534, **Golden 3538**, Maine 3548, **Oak 3552**
Maryland: Abell 3559, Capital 3584, Concordia 3601, Felburn 3629, France 3632, Grace 3638, **Hendricks 3647**, Kerr 3661, MARPAT 3684, McKnight 3688, Roswell 3722, Schifter 3726, **Shared 3727**, TKF 3747, **Town 3749**
Massachusetts: Barr 3791, **Bromley 3817**, Cabot 3823, Cardinal 3834, Carlee 3835, Childs 3848, Community 3855, **Conservation 3858**, Cox 3863, Crane 3864, Crawford 3867, Dusky 3885, Egan 3890, Fessenden 3903, Fields 3905, Garfield 3921, Grantham 3930, **Harris 3944**, Hoffman 3955, Hoyt 3960, Island 3965, Kahn 3973, **Kendall 3977**, Killam 3980, Loebs 4011, Many 4020, Mazar 4028, Mifflin 4038, Miller 4039, Narada 4047, Rappaport 4093, Rasmussen 4094, Red 4096, Robbins 4106, Saltonstall 4126, Sheehan 4140, Stevens 4163, Stevens 4164, **Sweet 4176**, Tupancy 4186, Van Sloun 4190, Wallace 4195, Weld 4203
Michigan: Ann Arbor 4221, Barry 4227, Burdick 4241, Carls 4244, Community 4255, Community 4256, DeVlieg 4275, Dow 4286, Dow 4287, Duffy 4290, Frey 4316, Knight 4364, LaMothe 4370, Marcks 4385, **Mott 4399**, Saddle 4426, **Skilling 4437**, Turner 4464, **Visteon 4472**, Wege 4476, Young 4490
Minnesota: **3M 4492**, Beim 4513, Bell 4514, Davis 4546, Dayton 4547, **Ecolab 4557, Ecotrust 4558**, Hudson 4591, Leuthold 4605, Lilly 4606, Marbrook 4612, Meadowood 4621, Nicholson 4634, Northwest 4637, **Rechelbacher 4662**, Rivers 4666, Rupp 4669, Schmidt 4673, Stone 4692, W.M. 4710, Watson 4717, Weesner 4720, Westcliff 4724, **Weyerhaeuser 4725**, Weyerhaeuser 4726, Weyerhaeuser 4727
Mississippi: Maddox 4753

Missouri: Bellwether 4782, Boeing 4785, Green 4822, **Monsanto 4868**, Pershing 4881, Woods 4928
Montana: Cinnabar 4935, Montana 4939
Nebraska: Hubbell 4979, Omaha 4995, **Union 5012**, Woollam 5019
Nevada: Fairweather 5032
New Hampshire: Fuller 5090, New Hampshire 5098, **Penates 5099**
New Jersey: Borden 5138, Cape 5153, **Carlson 5155**, Cowles 5170, Dodge 5181, **Fanwood 5192**, Gibson 5208, Grassmann 5213, Harbourton 5223, Hilfiger 5235, Hyde 5247, **International 5252**, **Jeffery 5257**, Jockey 5260, **Johnson 5263**, Johnson 5264, Kemmerer 5275, Kerr 5278, Kirby 5279, McGraw 5323, **Merck 5326**, Nicolais 5339, Phipps 5352, PSEG 5361, Silver 5404, Thomas 5427, **YPI 5461**
New Mexico: Albuquerque 5466, Frost 5476, Healy 5479, Kind 5483, Lapides 5485, McCune 5488, Messengers 5489, Santa Fe 5496, Taos 5498
New York: **Abelard 5508**, Acorn 5515, Afognak 5525, Allen 5536, **American 5551**, Arnhold 5568, Baird 5591, **Baker 5594**, Barker 5599, Bayne 5607, Belfer 5615, **Bobolink 5645**, Bright 5664, **Brokaw 5670**, Brunckhorst 5678, Brutsch 5680, **Burke 5688**, Butler 5691, **Bydale 5694**, Canaday 5701, Carson 5709, Cary 5712, **Claiborne 5757**, Coles 5775, Collins 5778, **Cranaleith 5805**, de Coizart 5839, Drexler 5885, **Duke 5892**, Dunwalke 5894, Emwiga 5930, **Engelhard 5932**, Erpf 5937, **Falconwood 5943**, **Ford 5970**, Freeman 5981, Gerschel 6019, Gleberman 6040, Glickenhaus 6042, **Global 6043**, Goldfrank 6048, Goldsmith 6060, **Grant 6090**, Haas 6127, **Heineman 6165**, **HKH 6190**, Hoffman 6195, HSBC 6204, **Hughes 6208**, **IAC 6220**, IF 6226, Ivor 6242, Jackson Hole 6246, **Jaffe 6250**, Joelson 6265, Kandell 6287, Kaplan 6290, Kealy 6303, **Kelly 6312**, Kennedy 6314, KeySpan 6320, Kriendler 6358, Kurz 6365, **LaSalle 6377**, Leach 6388, Levy 6414, Linden 6424, Litwin 6436, Lostand 6448, Mai 6476, Marcus 6486, **Marsh 6495**, **Mellon 6525**, **Memton 6529**, Metropolitan 6543, MJPM 6563, **Moore 6570**, Mosaic 6586, Mostyn 6591, Neidich 6606, Neuwirth 6612, Nicholas 6627, Nichols 6628, **Noble 6633**, **Norcross 6634**, O'Connor 6645, Ohrstrom 6659, Orentreich 6667, **Overbrook 6675**, Palmer 6683, **Panaphil 6684**, Pels 6706, Penick 6709, Pevaroff 6719, **Prospect 6750**, Ripple 6811, Rochester 6823, **Rockefeller 6825**, **Rosen 6843**, Rumsey 6882, Sasco 6907, Scherman 6918, Schieffelin 6922, Schwartz 6943, Seevers 6953, Silberstein 6979, SPIA 7028, Steele 7053, **Steinhardt 7064**, **Stony 7082**, Sulzberger 7095, **Surdna 7103**, **Sykes 7115**, Task 7124, **Thorne 7133**, Three 7135, **Tiffany 7137**, **Tinker 7143**, **Tortuga 7155**, **Trust 7168**, Walbridge 7207, Weatherup 7222, **Weeden 7223**, Wendt 7243, West 7246, Whitehead 7252, Widgeon 7255, Wilson 7262, WJS 7269, Woodcock 7273, Woodheath 7274, Woodmere 7276, **Woods 7278**, Woodward 7279
North Carolina: Anonymous 7306, Cumberland 7349, Hanes 7387, Hanes 7388, Herring 7396, Janirve 7404, Mills 7429, North Carolina 7438, Piedmont 7447, Polk 7449, Price 7451, Provident 7454, Reynolds 7458, **Richardson 7462**, **Sall 7471**, Smith 7478, Triangle 7496, Vanderbilt 7501, Weaver 7504
North Dakota: MDU 7517, North Dakota 7520
Ohio: **Armington 7532**, Bee 7542, Charities 7569, **Chiquita 7571**, Columbus 7580, Community 7583, Community 7584, Cotswold 7594, **Cox 7596**, Ferguson 7625, Firman 7628, Gettler 7649, Gund 7657, Ingalls 7684, **Kettering 7698**, LZ 7727, Miniger 7756, Mixon 7757, Nippert 7777, O'Neill 7782, Payne 7798, **Perkins 7800**, Scioto 7845, Stark 7867, Toledo 7883, Troy 7886, **Vesper 7892**, **Warrington 7895**, Wellman 7901, Wodecroft 7912
Oklahoma: Kerr 7950, McGee 7957, Oxley 7968
Oregon: Carpenter 8003, Jubitz 8028, Lightfoot 8036, Meyer 8042

Pennsylvania: AMETEK 8081, Arcadia 8086, Bayer 8096, **Beneficia 8100**, Blanchard 8110, Century 8137, Claneil 8144, **Clive 8146**, Community 8153, Dolfinger 8172, Federated 8196, First 8202, Hamilton 8233, Hawksglen 8238, Hillman 8250, Hillman 8252, Hopwood 8257, Huplits 8262, Johnson 8275, Laurel 8301, Little 8313, Maple 8323, McKenna 8337, McLean 8340, Mellon 8344, Mellon 8346, **Metcalf 8351**, Penn 8371, Peterson 8376, **Pew 8377**, Roberts 8407, Rockwell 8408, Roemer 8409, Scranton 8431, **Seraph 8434**, Stewart 8461, Stine 8462, **Strawbridge 8465**, Thompson 8476, Vanguard 8490, Waters 8498, Wyomissing 8509
Rhode Island: **Bafflin 8519**, Chace 8523, Champlin 8524, Kimball 8542, Rhode Island 8551, Roosa 8552
South Carolina: Post 8603
Tennessee: Atticus 8639, **Bridgestone 8646**, Community 8660, Community 8662, EBS 8672
Texas: Bass 8776, **Butt 8803**, Cain 8809, **Catto 8819**, Clayton 8830, Communities 8839, Delaney 8862, **ExxonMobil 8889**, Hobby 8954, Huffington 8963, Kempner 8987, Kimberly 8992, Lennox 9007, McNutt 9048, Meadows 9049, **MFI 9059**, Northen 9092, Partnership 9110, Paulos 9112, San Antonio 9166, **Shell 9181**, Smith 9196, Sterling 9212, Vaughan 9220
Utah: Dumke 9315, **Force 9322**, Tanner 9347, **Wishnick 9353**
Vermont: **Ben 9355**, Vermont 9361
Virginia: **Blue 9379**, Carter 9387, Cole 9396, Collis 9398, Connors 9403, Delmar 9410, **Dorothy 9411**, Fralin 9420, **Gannett 9428**, Hylton 9440, Ludington 9462, Mars 9466, **Mousetrap 9480**, Norfolk 9484, **Norfolk 9485**, **Oak 9488**, Olsson 9491, Truland 9528, **Winkler 9542**, Wrinkle 9545
Washington: **444S 9546**, **Brainerd 9561**, Bullitt 9563, Burning 9564, Community 9571, Connors 9572, **Edwards 9580**, Ferguson 9585, Forest 9586, Harder 9600, Horizons 9608, Islands 9613, Martin 9634, Moccasin 9643, Norcliffe 9650, **Sage 9674**, T.E.W. 9692, Tacoma 9693, **Weyerhaeuser 9703**, **Wiancko 9704**, Wilburforce 9705
West Virginia: Kanawha 9723
Wisconsin: Alliant 9742, Bolz 9762, Bradshaw 9764, Community 9777, **DeAtley 9789**, Duncan 9793, Four 9803, Frautschi 9804, Handleman 9811, Helfaer 9813, Krause 9841, Mason 9863, Menasha 9869, Merrill 9872, Milwaukee 9876, **Outagamie 9888**, Pollybill 9900, Puelicher 9904, Smallwood 9928, Split 9932, Styberg 9944, Witte 9968, WPS 9970
Wyoming: Berry 9975, Kerr 9983, **Schultz 9990**, Tozzi 9995, Wyoming 10000

Environment, noise pollution
Washington: **Edwards 9580**

Environment, plant conservation
Connecticut: Sewall 1648
Florida: Roberts 2201
Georgia: **Foundation 2388**
Mississippi: Maddox 4753
New York: Ellis 5923
North Carolina: Janirve 7404
Pennsylvania: Chanticleer 8140
Washington: **Edwards 9580**

Environment, pollution control
California: Kapor 743, **Lawrence 794**, McCaw 869, San Diego 1087
Georgia: **Turner 2501**
Illinois: DuPage 2713, Grand 2769
Maryland: Community 3598
Michigan: **Mott 4399**
New Jersey: PSEG 5361
New York: **Global 6043**
South Dakota: Sioux Falls 8630

Washington: **Edwards 9580**

Environment, public education
California: Heller 666
Connecticut: Bridgeport 1504
Florida: Batchelor 1893, Darden 1960
Illinois: Grand 2769
Minnesota: Xcel 4732
Missouri: **Monsanto 4868**
New York: **American 5553**, HSBC 6204, Northern 6638
Texas: Bass 8777
Washington: **Edwards 9580**, Seattle 9680
Wisconsin: Argosy 9747

Environment, public policy
California: Heller 666, San Diego 1087
Colorado: Kenney 1401
Georgia: Sapelo 2479
Hawaii: Castle 2537
Massachusetts: Merck 4036
North Carolina: Piedmont 7447
Pennsylvania: **Alcoa 8075**
Washington: **Weyerhaeuser 9703**

Environment, radiation control
Texas: Bridgeway 8796
Washington: Bullitt 9563

Environment, recycling
Florida: Tarrant 2265
Georgia: **Georgia 2397**
Washington: **Edwards 9580**

Environment, reform
New York: Cary 5712
Washington: **Edwards 9580**

Environment, research
Alaska: Alaska 79
California: **Christensen 384**, Heller 666, San Diego 1087, **Smith 1166**
District of Columbia: **Summit 1852**
Florida: Batchelor 1893, Katcher 2080
Georgia: **Money 2450**
Illinois: Lurie 2865
Maryland: Gudelsky 3641
Massachusetts: Colombe 3852, **New England 4052**
New York: HSBC 6204, **Tiffany 7137**
North Carolina: Piedmont 7447
Tennessee: Jeniam 8695
Washington: **Weyerhaeuser 9703**

Environment, toxics
Alabama: Community 24
California: Kapor 743, **Marisla 855**
Georgia: Sapelo 2479, **Turner 2501**
Maine: **Golden 3538**
Massachusetts: Garfield 3921, **Merck 4036**
Minnesota: Blue 4521
New York: **Beldon 5614**, Noyes 6643
Washington: Bullitt 9563, **Edwards 9580**

Environment, volunteer services
California: San Diego 1087

Environment, waste management
California: Kapor 743
Illinois: Tellabs 3034
New York: HSBC 6204
South Dakota: Sioux Falls 8630

Michigan: Ann Arbor 4221, Berrien 4231, Christian 4247, Community 4256, Community 4257, Consumers 4260, DeVos 4277, DeVos 4278, **DeWitt 4280**, DiPonio 4281, Dow 4286, Dow 4288, Frankel 4312, Fremont 4315, Frey 4316, Grand Rapids 4326, Hahn 4335, Kalamazoo 4352, Knight 4364, Prince 4416, Saginaw 4428, Skillman 4438, Spoelhof 4443, Upjohn 4465, Vandomelen 4470, **Visteon 4472**, Whirlpool 4480

Minnesota: **3M 4492**, Andersen 4502, Bell 4514, Butler 4525, Central 4534, Charlson 4537, Duluth 4556, **Ecotrust 4558**, Graco 4573, Grand Rapids 4574, Grotto 4579, Initiative 4593, McKnight 4617, Minneapolis 4623, O'Neil 4638, Ordean 4643, Pax 4648, Phillips 4655, Prophet 4658, RBC 4661, Rochester 4668, Sjolund 4685, Slaggie 4686, Southways 4688, Sundance 4693, Thorpe 4701, **Wallestad 4712**, Wallestad 4713, WCA 4718, West 4723

Mississippi: Community 4737, Community 4738, Foundation 4743, Skelton 4765

Missouri: Cornelsen 4799, Curry 4802, Hall 4824, Herschend 4830, Jewish 4837, Jordan 4840, Kansas 4842, Laclede 4852, McDonnell 4863, Pott 4886, Roblee 4893, Smith 4905, Sunnen 4913

Montana: **Edwards 4936**

Nebraska: Dunklau 4958, Hawks 4971, Lincoln 4987, Mutual 4993, Steinhart 5005, TierOne 5010, Valmont 5013, Wiebe 5017, Woods 5018

Nevada: Nevada 5047, O'Bannon 5049, **Walsh 5075**

New Hampshire: Eastman 5087, Gale 5091, von Weber 5104

New Jersey: **Anderson 5115**, Borden 5138, Bunbury 5148, **Carlson 5155**, **Ceres 5158**, Community 5167, Cowles 5170, **Frankino 5196**, Hyde 5247, Jockey 5260, **Johnson 5265**, KDK 5273, Merillat 5330, Orange 5343, Pascale 5349, Prudential 5360, Ross 5376, Sagner 5381, Schwarz 5394

New Mexico: Brindle 5468, Coleman 5470, Frost 5476, Kind 5483, McCune 5488, New Mexico 5491, Taos 5498, Thornburg 5501

New York: Abrons 5511, Achelis 5513, Acorn 5515, Altman 5542, Arkell 5565, Bahnik 5589, Bayne 5607, Bodman 5647, Bohlsen 5649, Burden 5687, Butler 5692, Campbell 5700, Canaday 5701, Cappelli 5703, Clark 5761, Community 5780, Community 5783, Dammann 5824, Daphne 5830, Dove 5878, Ferrari 5953, Freston 5982, Galasso 6005, Geds 6010, Gibbs 6024, Gilman 6032, Glickenhaus 6042, Gould 6083, Grateful 6093, **Grauer 6094**, Halis 6136, Haseltine 6152, **Hearst 6161**, **Hearst 6162**, Heckscher 6164, IFF 6227, Iovino 6236, **Jaffe 6250**, Kanas 6286, Kealy 6303, **Keefe 6305**, Kenworthy 6315, Knossos 6344, Lowinger 6450, Massry 6502, **Matthews 6507**, Melly 6526, **Memton 6529**, Moore 6572, Morse 6583, **Mulago 6593**, New York 6613, Nichols 6628, Northern 6638, Northern 6639, O'Sullivan 6652, Paduano 6677, PBO 6699, Pincus 6726, Plant 6731, Pumpkin 6754, R & TP 6764, Rauch 6774, Rhodebeck 6791, Riley 6809, Rochester 6823, Saligman 6895, Sasco 6907, Schwartz 6940, Siebens 6974, Silverweed 6985, Sirus 6992, **Sloan 7003**, Spunk 7036, St. Faith's 7039, Steele 7053, Tiger 7139, Union 7184, Van Pelt 7192, Werblow 7245, Western 7248

North Carolina: Blue 7319, Cumberland 7349, Easley 7361, Gordon 7379, Halton 7386, Harris 7390, Hurley 7403, Janirve 7404, NFM 7434, Reynolds 7457, Reynolds 7460, Robertson 7466, Sklut 7473, Smith 7478, Stewards 7485, Triangle 7496, Woodson 7509

North Dakota: Stern 7521

Ohio: Akron 7526, American 7528, Austin 7536, Bates 7540, Bicknell 7548, Children's 7570, Cleveland 7576, Community 7584, CRN 7598, Dater 7600, **Eaton 7617**, Fleming 7631, Greene 7653, Jackson 7685, Knudsen 7702, Lancaster 7707, **Longaberger 7722**, Mayerson 7739, Mehl 7746, Middletown 7749, Miller 7753, Nordson 7781, O'Neill 7783, Olive 7787, Park 7795, **Scripps**

7848, Stark 7867, Stocker 7870, Watson 7896, Weisbrod 7900, White 7905, Youngstown 7920

Oklahoma: ONEOK 7967, Share 7977, Williams 7989

Oregon: Ackerman 7995, Carpenter 8003, Johnson 8027, Jubitz 8028, Meyer 8042, Oregon 8049, Salem 8054

Pennsylvania: 1957 8071, Arcadia 8086, **Armstrong 8090**, Blue 8112, Bozzone 8114, Brougher 8122, Claneil 8144, Colonial 8151, Dolfinger 8172, ESSA 8190, First 8202, Fourjay 8209, Garthwaite 8212, Grumbacher 8227, Haas 8230, Heinz 8240, Heinz 8241, Hulme 8260, Huston 8263, Justus 8276, Katz 8281, Lehigh Valley 8303, Meakem 8341, Mellon 8346, Morris 8359, Penn 8371, **Pew 8377**, Philadelphia 8378, Pilgrim 8383, Pittsburgh 8386, Rockwell 8408, Staunton 8457, Usher 8489, Wyomissing 8509

Rhode Island: Brooks 8520, **CARLISLE 8521**, Daniels 8530, Jackson 8541, Littlefield 8544, Rhode Island 8551, Sullivan 8558

South Carolina: Central 8577, Coastal 8581, Springs 8617

South Dakota: Sioux Falls 8630

Tennessee: Aslan 8637, Atticus 8639, Beaman 8642, Caesars 8648, Community 8660, Eskind 8674, Massey 8709, Plough 8718, Ragsdale 8722, Schadt 8725, Washington 8741

Texas: Abell 8749, Anderson 8759, Anderson 8760, Baron 8774, Bass 8777, Brumley 8800, Cailloux 8807, Cain 8809, Clayton 8830, Community 8842, Cowden 8848, Doss 8869, El Paso 8882, Esping 8886, Fikes 8899, Frees 8909, Gale 8913, George 8916, Haggar 8929, Heavin 8945, Holthouse 8959, Kelley 8986, Kurth 9003, Lennox 9007, Levit 9009, Lowe 9020, Lubbock 9021, Lyons 9024, McGovern 9044, McMillan 9046, Meadows 9049, Mosbacher 9077, Owen 9106, Rapoport 9141, Reliant 9144, Rubenstein 9162, San Antonio 9166, Simmons 9187, Smith 9191, Speas 9207, Sterling 9212, Trull 9240, Waco 9255, Wal 9260, Works 9291, Wright 9294, Young 9295, Zephyr 9299

Utah: Eccles 9320, Lockwood 9333

Vermont: Lintilhac 9359, Vermont 9361

Virgin Islands: Community 9363

Virginia: Collis 9398, Delmar 9410, **Doudera 9412**, Foundation 9419, Freddie 9422, Friedman 9425, Kellar 9449, Lawrence 9457, Lynchburg 9463, Miller 9475, Norfolk 9484, Samberg 9510, Staunton 9521

Washington: Allen 9550, Archibald 9553, Blue 9559, **Casey 9567**, Community 9571, Crystal 9576, Glaser 9594, Green 9598, Laurel 9625, Lematta 9628, Lucky 9632, Murdock 9644, Norcliffe 9650, **RealNetworks 9672**, Satterberg 9677, Schuler 9678, Tacoma 9693

West Virginia: Daywood 9717, Kanawha 9723, Parkersburg 9730

Wisconsin: Alexander 9740, Bell 9756, Beloit 9757, Community 9779, Cudahy 9785, **DeAtley 9789**, Demmer 9791, Evjue 9797, Helfaer 9813, Jacobus 9819, Kress 9844, La Crosse 9845, Lubar 9851, Madison 9854, McBeath 9864, Milwaukee 9876, Northwestern 9884, Phipps 9898, Riordan 9911, Roundy's 9915, Sensient 9922, Smallwood 9928, Stackner 9934, **T & O 9946**, WPS 9970

Wyoming: Richardson 9987, Weiss 9997

Family services, adolescent parents

Alabama: Community 24
Florida: Hayes 2052
Massachusetts: **State 4158**
New Mexico: Santa Fe 5496
New York: Bodman 5647, Butler 5692
Pennsylvania: FISA 8204
Tennessee: Thompson 8733
Texas: Topfer 9238
Washington: Horizons 9608

Family services, counseling

California: Lurie 832

Connecticut: Bondi 1499, Panwy 1622
New York: Butler 5692, Geds 6010
North Carolina: Woodson 7509
Pennsylvania: Staunton 8457
Washington: Horizons 9608

Family services, domestic violence

California: Blue 296, Bradley 315, Fireman's 510, Knott 769, McKenna 878, Peninsula 989, Waltmar 1277
Colorado: Tuchman 1467
Florida: Community 1943, Smith 2238
Georgia: Harris 2408
Illinois: **Allstate 2588**, **Burlington 2644**, Little 2859, Wenske 3063
Michigan: DiPonio 4281
Minnesota: Charity 4536
Missouri: Truman 4919
New Jersey: Healthcare 5228, **Verizon 5439**
New Mexico: Santa Fe 5496
New York: **Avon 5583**, Claiborne 5758, Lostand 6448, Wolk 7271
North Carolina: **Sunshine 7490**
Ohio: Reinberger 7815
Pennsylvania: FISA 8204
Rhode Island: Brooks 8520
Texas: Community 8840, **Link 9013**, Modano 9068, **RGK 9146**
Washington: Grays 9597, Horizons 9608, OneFamily 9654, Schuler 9678

Family services, parent education

Alabama: Community 24
California: Bella 275, Samueli 1086, Whitecap 1303
Colorado: Rose 1445
Connecticut: Panwy 1622
Georgia: Community 2355, Goizueta 2400
Indiana: Noble 3214
Michigan: Frey 4316, **Mott 4399**
Minnesota: **3M 4492**, McKnight 4617
New York: Bowne 5655, Cummings 5815, **MetLife 6542**
Ohio: Nordson 7781
Texas: Kronkosky 9002, Topfer 9238
Virginia: Freddie 9422

Family services, single parents

District of Columbia: **Moriah 1835**
Illinois: Crowe 2690
New York: Dove 5877
Texas: Robinson 9152

Federated giving programs

Alabama: Alabama 1, **Altec 4**, Bolden 15, Brock 16, Caring 18, Carson 19, Community 27, Compass 28, Finlay 33, Lowder 42, Lowder 43, Lowder 44, Mayer 47, Pleiad 57, Saks 61, Thompson 67, **Union 70**, Upchurch 71
Arizona: Cooper 92, Farrington 97, Hermundslie 107, **Kleckhefer 113**, Moreno 123, Robson 135
Arkansas: Murphy 167, Rebsamen 171, Ross 174, Wal-Mart 184, Whitt 188
California: 324 190, Allequash 202, Allergan 203, Avery 244, Avis 246, Bakar 250, Bartman 259, **Bechtel 269**, Bekins 273, Bireley 292, Booth 302, Borick 305, Burnham 337, Carsey 361, Carson 362, Caruso 363, Caufield 367, Cheeryble 377, Ciocca 387, Community 406, Copley 416, Cortopassi 419, Davidson 445, Dollens 462, **Draper 465**, Drum 470, Feintech 500, Flora 521, Gallo 547, Gallo 548, Gross 622, Guess? 629, Harman 651, Harrington 652, Hellman 667, Horn 686, Ingold 695, **Jack 705**, **Jacobs 707**, Janssen 715, Johnson 726, Kling 766, Knight 768, Kvamme 781, Lavine 793, Leichtag 801, Lester 807, Levy 810, **Mattel 861**, Merage 887, Miller 899, Mitchell 903, Moss 921, **Muth 929**, Nestle 935, Northrop 942, Oshman 963, **Panda 975**, Paramitas 977, **Reveas**

1045, Robertson 1059, Robinson 1060, **Rosengarten 1068**, **Schuler 1108**, Semel 1125, Shapiro 1137, Short 1148, Smith 1164, Taube 1228, Teichert 1231, Tenenbaum 1232, Ueberroth 1248, **Unocal 1252**, Vickter 1266, Wagner 1274, Warren 1279, **WellPoint 1292**, **Wells 1294**, Wilkes 1306, Williams 1307, Wolfen 1316, Wrather 1321, Zecca 1325

Colorado: Bacon 1340, Carson 1351, Dornick 1369, Falkenberg 1376, Fullerton 1378, Green 1385, Joy 1399, Lewis 1410, Monfort 1429, Precourt 1441, White 1472

Connecticut: Barnes 1488, Bauer 1489, Bossidy 1500, Brace 1501, Bridgemill 1503, Chase 1508, Dartley 1524, Flinn 1543, Goodnow 1558, **Heimbold 1566**, Hubbell 1569, **Hulsking 1570**, Kitchings 1574, Kohn 1575, Lee 1582, Leever 1583, MassMutual 1599, Meriden 1603, Patricelli 1623, **Praxair 1629**, Rogow 1636, SBM 1644, Tow 1660, United 1668, **Vasey 1670**, Vik 1672, Zachs 1682

Delaware: Arguild 1687, Bishop 1693, Crestlea 1701, Hirschl 1721, Laffey 1725, **Neuberger 1735**, Parker 1738, Presto 1740, Romill 1747, Seevak 1752, Struthers 1758, Wasily 1760

District of Columbia: Fernandez 1794, Merriman 1833

Florida: Ansin 1877, Applebaum 1878, Baldwin 1888, **Bauman 1894**, Better 1905, **Braman 1915**, Burnett 1919, Capital 1924, Cascone 1926, Colen 1938, Coulter 1954, Crawford 1956, **Davis 1963**, Demetree 1967, Dennis 1969, Edelman 1987, Elster 1993, Five 2001, Florida 2003, Fortin 2007, Friedman 2014, Garfinkle 2017, Gorin 2032, Green 2033, GTE 2040, **Hardison 2048**, Harris 2050, Jelks 2076, Keating 2084, Kiwanis 2094, Lee 2107, Lennar 2109, Life's 2116, Martin 2130, Michaan 2138, Miller 2141, **Morris 2145**, O'Neil 2155, Overstreet 2159, Pamphalon 2162, **Pearce 2166**, Petway 2167, Poe 2173, **Pope 2174**, Potamkin 2176, Publix 2180, Rales 2184, Rayonier 2189, Rinker 2195, Rooms 2204, Ryder 2213, Sanders 2215, Sansing 2217, Scarpa 2221, Sherman 2233, Spurlino 2242, Sudakoff 2255, SunTrust 2259, Taplin 2264, TECO 2270, United 2276, Watts 2288, **Winn 2301**, Winter 2303, Wolfson 2305

Georgia: Aflac 2311, Anncox 2318, Arnold 2319, Atlanta 2320, Azalea 2322, Broadfield 2330, Brown 2332, Coca 2350, Covenant 2366, Daft 2370, Equifax 2379, Franklin 2382, Georgia 2395, **Georgia 2397**, Graves 2403, Hertz 2412, Holder 2413, Imlay 2417, JBS 2420, Jones 2424, Lanier 2430, Lanier 2431, Lewis 2434, Love 2437, Moore 2452, Morgens 2453, Morris 2454, **Morris 2455**, Patrick 2459, Poe 2465, Ramser 2469, SF 2486, Synovus 2497, WestPoint 2513, Williams 2516, Woolley 2525, Zaban 2528, Zeist 2529

Hawaii: Alexander 2530, Anthony 2531, Schuler 2552, Strong 2555

Idaho: Simplot 2574

Illinois: **Amsted 2593**, **Aon 2598**, Beidler 2613, Blum 2624, Buchanan 2637, Canning 2650, Caterpillar 2653, Charleston 2657, Community 2677, **Crane 2688**, D.H.R. 2695, Deering 2700, Emerson 2719, Energizer 2721, **Excelsior! 2722**, Farrell 2725, Frank 2733, Franke 2734, Galvin 2747, GKN 2758, Hales 2778, Harris 2788, Hartmarx 2794, Hobbs 2802, **Irwin 2814**, Istock 2815, Katten 2826, Kennedy 2834, Kipper 2840, Lea 2850, Levi 2855, Lewis 2857, Madigan 2869, Malott 2872, Martin 2874, Medline 2889, Meyer 2895, Millard 2897, **Motorola 2906**, Olin 2925, Omron 2926, Oppenheimer 2928, Rothschild 2971, Russell 2976, Ryan 2977, **Ryan 2978**, Sangre 2981, Schawk 2984, Stone 3026, Trustmark 3039, United 3044, USG 3046, Weiss 3062, Whitwam 3068, Woodward 3085, **Wrigley 3088**

Indiana: 1st 3094, American 3098, Anderson 3099, **Anthem 3101**, Anthem 3102, Biomet 3106, Carmichael 3113, Citizens 3118, Cornelius 3134, **Cummins 3136**, Garcia 3154, Glick 3155, Goldstine 3156, Griffith 3158, Journal 3181, Niblick 3212, NiSource 3213, Oliver 3219,

Perelman 3222, Saemann 3232, Simon 3236, Simon 3240, Vectren 3249

Iowa: **AEGON 3259**, Blank 3268, Bucksbaum 3271, Bucksbaum 3272, Employers 3282, Grubb 3289, HNI 3293, Hubbell 3297, Kinney 3300, Knapp 3301, Krause 3302, Levitt 3307, Maytag 3309, McCarthy 3311, McDonald 3312, Meredith 3314, Mid 3316, Muscatine 3318, **New 3319**, R & R 3327, United 3338

Kansas: Capitol 3350, DeVore 3357, Hutchinson 3368, INTRUST 3369, Joscelyn 3371, Morris 3378, Payless 3380

Kentucky: Brown 3408, **Brown 3411**, **Chase 3413**, Ford 3419, Novak 3442, Orleton 3445, Preston 3446, Reed 3447

Louisiana: Hardtner 3485, Helis 3486, Heymann 3487, Keller 3493, **Live 3495**, Monteleone 3502, Reily 3506, Wheless 3514

Maine: Alfond 3522, Alfond 3523, Burnham 3527, Gallagher 3535, Gardiner 3536, Hannaford 3540, King 3545, TD 3558

Maryland: Blum 3577, Bunting 3580, Capital 3584, Community 3600, FBW 3628, Goldsmith 3637, Grace 3638, Hahn 3643, **Head 3644**, Henson 3648, HRLD 3653, Jonan 3658, Klein 3662, Legg 3672, Leidy 3673, Linehan 3678, Price 3709, Procter 3711, Rothschild 3723, Rouse 3724, Shattuck 3728, Straus 3738, Sylvan 3741

Massachusetts: Aaron 3767, Acushnet 3770, Alvord 3778, ASD 3781, BOSE 3810, Bristol 3816, Cabot 3823, Casty 3839, Charlton 3846, Chase 3847, Cogan 3851, Connell 3856, Connolly 3857, Corkin 3861, Crane 3864, Crane 3866, Dunn 3884, Eastern 3886, Edgerly 3889, Finnegan 3908, Fraser 3917, Goldberg 3927, Grayson 3932, Greene 3933, Hanover 3941, Hoche 3954, Hoffman 3955, Hopedale 3958, Jacobson 3967, Jordan 3971, Keane 3975, Kessler 3978, Knez 3986, Knight 3987, Kraft 3989, Liberty 4006, Lovett 4013, Lubin 4016, Massachusetts 4025, Mazar 4028, Murray 4045, New 4050, New 4054, **OneBeacon 4060**, Oristaglio 4063, Persky 4080, Peters 4081, Plymouth 4085, Putnam 4088, Rodgers 4110, Rubin 4117, Saltonstall 4126, **Saquish 4127**, Silverman 4146, Sohn 4151, Stamps 4155, **State 4158**, Stearns 4160, Stemberg 4161, Stride 4172, Talbots 4178, Vance 4191, Weber 4200, Welch 4202, **Wood 4208**

Michigan: Abrams 4213, Acheson 4214, Brown 4240, Citizens 4248, Citizens 4249, Dart 4267, Doornink 4283, Eddy 4292, Fabri 4293, Fisher 4299, Ford 4300, Ford 4301, Ford 4303, Ford 4304, Ford 4305, Ford 4306, Frankel 4313, General 4320, Hahn 4335, Kellogg's 4358, Kelly 4359, La-Z-Boy 4368, Langbo 4371, Lear 4374, Manoogian 4382, Mott 4400, Oleson 4405, Paulina 4409, Perrigo 4410, Petitpren 4411, Pitt 4413, **Rodney 4422**, Tauber 4454, Timmis 4459, **Tracy 4462**, Vanderweide 4469, Weatherwax 4474, Whiting 4482, Wilson 4484, Wolverine 4488

Minnesota: AHS 4497, Ankeny 4505, ATK 4509, Bemis 4515, Bieber 4518, Brandenborg 4522, Carlson 4532, Cloverfields 4542, Dayton 4547, Federated 4563, Fiterman 4565, Gardner 4568, Greystone 4576, Griggs 4577, Grossman 4578, Grundhofer 4580, Kelley 4597, Knowlton 4598, Labovitz 4601, Leuthold 4605, McCarthy 4614, McNamara 4618, McVay 4620, Minnesota 4624, Mitchell 4625, NFC 4633, O'Neil 4638, Olson 4640, Opperman 4641, Prospect 4659, Red Wing 4663, Regis 4664, **Robins 4667**, Sanger 4672, Securian 4677, **Sit 4684**, Southways 4688, Stone 4692, Sundet 4694, **SUPERVALU 4695**, Tennant 4700, **Toro 4702**, **U.S. 4704**, Valspar 4706, Veden 4707, Wallin 4714, Weesner 4720, Xcel 4732

Mississippi: Mississippi 4758

Missouri: Boeing 4785, Boswell 4786, Brauer 4787, **Bunge 4792**, Craig 4800, Curry 4802, Edison 4808, Emerson 4809, **Enterprise 4810**, Fabick 4812, Forster 4814, Hammons 4826, Hauck 4828, Helzberg 4829, Holekamp 4832, Interco 4835, Laclede 4852, Lopata 4859, **May 4861**, Nichols 4873, Orscheln 4877, Pearl 4879, Pershing 4881,

PMJ 4885, Pott 4886, Remington 4891, Rosewood 4894, Smurfit-Stone 4906, Stupp 4910, Woods 4928, Wornall 4929

Nebraska: Abbott 4942, Buffett 4949, **ConAgra 4953**, Dillon 4956, Eihusen 4961, Fulk 4964, **Global 4967**, Harper 4969, Hawkins 4970, James 4980, Kawasaki 4982, Schrager 5001, TierOne 5010, Zollner 5020

Nevada: Community 5028, Marnell 5044, Nevada 5047, Sierra 5064

New Hampshire: Cogswell 5084

New Jersey: American 5113, Bard 5125, Berlind 5129, Brady 5141, Cendant 5157, **Clare 5164**, Cowles 5170, Gershman 5206, **Gulton 5217**, Gund 5218, Hickory 5232, Hilfiger 5235, Indian 5250, **Johnson 5261**, Krieger 5290, Larsen 5296, Lebensfeld 5301, MCJ 5324, National 5335, New Jersey 5336, Post 5355, Reddy 5364, Ross 5376, Schecter 5385, Silberman 5402, Smith 5409, Valley 5438

New Mexico: McCune 5488, Phillips 5492

New York: Alpern 5540, **Altman 5544**, Amicus 5557, Arm 5566, Arrison 5570, **AXA 5584**, Babbitt 5586, **Barnett 5601**, Bayne 5607, Beaverkill 5610, Black 5636, **Blood 5639**, Blum 5643, **Brunie 5679**, Butler 5691, Buttenwieser 5693, Cappelli 5703, Centennial 5722, Century 5725, **Chatterjee 5737**, Corning 5794, Credit 5807, Danziger 5829, Davidson 5835, De La Cour 5842, Diker 5862, Dimon 5864, Donovan 5874, Dow 5879, Dunwalke 5894, Edelweiss 5908, **Edouard 5909**, Emerson 5927, Fatta 5947, Fisher 5961, Freston 5982, Friedman 5987, Gant 6006, Gellman 6013, Gerhard 6015, Gilliam 6031, Goldstein 6064, Golub 6070, Goodman 6072, Gorter 6079, Grandison 6087, Greenhill 6101, Grubman 6113, Gutman 6122, Haas 6127, Hammerman 6139, Harris 6148, Hendel 6172, Hirsch 6187, Hochfelder 6191, Hudson 6207, Hutchins 6218, IDF 6225, IFF 6227, Ivor 6242, Jaaaa 6245, Kaplan 6289, Katz 6295, Kellogg 6310, KeySpan 6320, Klee 6329, Knox 6345, Kraus 6352, **Lane 6372**, Leibowitz 6398, Lewis 6415, Lindmor 6425, Lindsay 6427, Lipp 6432, Litterman 6435, Macdonald 6468, Massry 6502, McCarthy 6516, McNulty 6521, Metcalf 6541, Meyer 6545, **Milliken 6552**, Milstein 6555, Mitsui 6561, Mnuchin 6564, **Monterey 6568**, Morse 6583, Mosse 6590, Neiman 6607, Neuwirth 6612, **Newhouse 6623**, North 6637, Northern 6639, Nuhn 6644, O'Connor 6645, OCLO 6655, Osborn 6669, Park 6689, **Pepsi 6713**, **Perelman 6716**, **Phillips 6725**, Pittman 6730, Plant 6731, Pollack 6735, Price 6746, Pumpkin 6754, Rhodebeck 6791, Rich 6795, **Richmond 6801**, Ripple 6811, Ross 6862, Sandy 6903, Saunders 6909, Schott 6934, Schulweis 6936, Sheinberg 6963, Siegel 6976, Silverweed 6985, Smith 7007, Sobel 7016, **Solomon 7017**, **Spiegel 7030**, Starwood 7049, Stony 7075, Summerhill 7098, Templeton 7128, Tormondsen 7154, Trott 7165, Trump 7167, Tully 7173, Vernon 7195, **Volpert 7202**, von der Heyden 7203, Walter 7212, Watts 7221, Weil 7225, **Weinberg 7228**, Weinberg 7231, Wellde 7239, Wender 7241, Wendt 7243, Werblow 7245, **Wexner 7249**, **Wigmore 7258**

North Carolina: Anonymous 7306, Belk 7315, Branan 7322, Broyhill 7328, Burress 7331, Coffey 7339, Dickson 7355, Finch 7366, Flow 7368, Gilbert 7373, Glenn 7376, Goodrich 7378, Haley 7385, Harvest 7392, Herring 7396, Holding 7399, **Jefferson 7405**, Lance 7418, Layden 7419, Martin 7424, Mills 7429, North Carolina 7438, O'Herron 7441, Perkins 7445, Piedmont 7447, **Planseon 7448**, Reynolds 7459, **Richardson 7462**, Ryan 7469, Simpson 7472, Sloan 7475, Smith 7476, Smith 7478, SunTrust 7491, Tzedakah 7497, Van Every 7499, Winston 7507

North Dakota: MDU 7517

Ohio: AK 7525, **Alpaugh 7527**, Anderson 7529, Broussard 7557, Castellini 7568, Charities 7569, Community 7583, **Convergys 7587**, Conway 7588, **Cooper 7589**, Dana 7599, Dayton 7604, **Deuble 7607**, Diebold 7611, Edwards 7618, FirstEnergy

7630, Forest 7634, Foss 7635, Foundation 7636, France 7639, Frohman 7641, Geary 7645, Gerlach 7648, Gingher 7650, H.C.S. 7658, Haile 7659, Hamlin 7661, Hankins 7662, Home 7672, Hoover 7675, Horvitz 7678, Humphrey 7679, Jochum 7692, Kroger 7705, LaValley 7708, Lincoln 7715, Lippitt 7718, LKC 7720, Love 7723, LZ 7727, M/B 7728, M/I 7729, Mandel 7732, Marcum 7734, Mather 7736, Midland 7750, Milacron 7751, Mixon 7757, Motorists 7765, Murphy 7769, NCC 7772, NCR 7773, Nord 7780, Ohio 7785, **Ohio 7786**, Oliver 7788, Outcalt 7792, Owens 7793, Park 7795, Parker 7796, **Perkins 7800**, Peterson 7802, **PLACE 7805**, Robbins 7823, Sage 7829, **Sankey 7833**, Sedgwick 7849, Sheakley 7854, Sherwin 7855, Stranahan 7872, Stranahan 7873, Toledo 7882, **Tomkins 7884**, Weisbrod 7900, Wendy's 7902, Western 7903, Williamson 7908, Wodecroft 7912, Wolfe 7915

Oklahoma: Goddard 7939, Gussman 7941, Jones 7946, Kerr 7950, McMahon 7959, Oklahoman 7966, ONEOK 7967, Oxley 7968, Puterbaugh 7970, Williams 7989, Zarrow 7991, Zarrow 7993

Oregon: Ackerman 7995, Jeld 8025, Kelley 8030, PacifiCorp 8050, PGE 8051

Pennsylvania: AMETEK 8081, Arkema 8089, **Armstrong 8090**, Ball 8093, Berkman 8102, Berks 8103, Black 8109, Born 8113, Brickman 8116, Brossman 8120, Brougher 8122, Cassett 8133, CMS 8147, Community 8154, Degenstein 8166, Dibona 8169, Equitable 8187, Fair 8192, Farber 8194, Farber 8195, Federated 8196, Fine 8201, Fox 8210, Graham 8222, Grass 8223, Grumbacher 8227, Haas 8230, Hankin 8234, Hansen 8235, Harsco 8236, Hirtzel 8253, Jaindl 8269, Justus 8276, Keystone 8285, Kinsley 8290, Kline 8292, Levan 8307, Levee 8308, Lilliput 8311, Lubert 8315, Lutron 8316, Magee 8320, Meakem 8341, Mengle 8347, Mine 8357, Morris 8359, Murray 8360, Peterson 8376, Pollock 8390, Pryor 8396, PSC 8398, Roberts 8406, Ryan 8416, Safeguard 8418, Salvaggio 8421, Sampson 8423, Satell 8424, Scheller 8426, Schoonmaker 8429, Sherrerd 8439, Simmons 8441, Spang 8452, Speyer 8453, Steinman 8458, Steinman 8459, Stewart 8460, Stine 8462, Strawbridge 8467, Susquehanna 8471, Turner 8484, Tyco 8485, Vanguard 8490, Weiss 8499, West 8500, Wolf 8506, Wyomissing 8509

Rhode Island: **Amica 8518**, Chace 8523, Charter 8526, Citizens 8527, Cuno 8528, Daniels 8530, **FM 8537**, Jackson 8541, Mann 8546, McAdams 8547, McCarthy 8548, Shaw's 8555, **Textron 8559**, Washington 8563

South Carolina: Cato 8576, Community 8583, First 8587, Foothills 8588, Inman 8595, Liberty 8597, Montgomery 8600, Rainey 8605, **Security's 8609**, Smith 8613, South 8615

South Dakota: Dakota 8624, Griffith 8625, Larson 8627, South Dakota 8631, Vucurevich 8634

Tennessee: AmSouth 8636, Atticus 8639, Basler 8641, Caldwell 8649, Chrysalis 8655, Citizens 8657, CLARCOR 8658, Clayton 8659, Eskind 8674, First 8677, Frist 8679, **Garrott 8680**, Goldsmith 8682, Gordon 8683, Hamico 8684, Haslam 8687, Haslam 8688, HCA 8690, Ingram 8694, Johnson 8697, Jones 8698, Martin 8706, Martin 8707, Melkus 8711, Osborne 8714, Schadt 8725, Starfish 8728, T & T 8731, Turner 8737, Washington 8741, Wilson 8744

Texas: Allison 8757, **Anderson 8761**, Baker 8772, Beal 8783, Bridwell 8797, Cauthorn 8820, Charitable 8824, Clear 8831, Collins 8837, **Cooper 8846**, Cox 8850, Dodge 8868, El Paso 8888, Estill 8888, Fain 8890, Garvey 8914, Gayden 8915, Gill 8919, Goodman 8921, Hackett 8928, Halff 8934, Hanley 8940, Herd 8948, Hirsch 8953, Holden 8957, Holthouse 8959, Hunt 8966, Keith 8982, Kempner 8987, Kinder 8994, **Link 9013**, MacDonald 9025, Mankoff 9027, Mays 9035, McDermott 9043, McKee 9045, Mendenhall 9053, Miller 9062, Moncrief 9069, Moran 9072, Owen 9106, Pogue 9126, Prairie 9129, Providence 9135, Reliant

9144, **Scaler 9170**, Sharp 9180, **Shell 9181**, Simmons 9187, Smith 9191, Smith 9198, Snyder 9199, Sowell 9202, Tapeats 9223, Texas 9232, Tobin 9235, Tolleson 9237, Valero 9247, Vaughn 9251, Waggoner 9256, Watson 9266, West 9274, Westcott 9278, Wichita 9280, Wise 9284, Wise 9285, Wolff 9288, Wright 9294

Utah: Bastian 9306, Denkers 9312, Hall 9326, Raymond 9339, Savage 9340, Tanner 9347, Zions 9354

Virginia: AMERIGROUP 9369, Batten 9374, Gottwald 9431, Herndon 9437, Houff 9438, Kellar 9449, LandAmerica 9454, Meador 9473, **Modzelewski 9477**, N.E.W. 9482, **Norfolk 9485**, Perry 9495, Perry 9496, Peterson 9497, Portsmouth 9498, Sharp 9515, Silver 9516, SunTrust 9523, Taubman 9524, **Three 9525**, Ukrop 9529, Universal 9531, Weil 9535

Washington: Archibald 9553, **Boeing 9560**, Ellison 9581, Evertrust 9583, Ferguson 9585, Foster 9588, Glazer 9596, Green 9598, Hughes 9610, Killinger 9618, Lematta 9628, McCaw 9636, Norcliffe 9650, PACCAR 9656, **PAH 9657**, PEMCO 9660, Sarkowsky 9676, Schultz 9679, Shirley 9684, UNOVA 9697

West Virginia: BB&T 9710, Huntington 9721, Jacobson 9722, McDonough 9726, McQuain 9727

Wisconsin: Assurant 9748, Baird 9750, Baker 9751, Bishop 9759, Briggs 9765, Chapman 9771, Charter 9772, Cleary 9774, Demmer 9791, Duncan 9793, **Eastman 9794**, Eastman 9795, Fotsch 9802, Frautschi 9804, Goodman's 9807, Gordon 9808, Harley 9812, Helfaer 9813, Jacobus 9819, Johnson 9823, Kellogg 9832, Kohl 9837, Kress 9844, Ladish 9846, **Lewis 9850**, Madison 9855, Manpower 9858, Marcus 9859, Martin 9862, Menasha 9869, Modine 9878, Northwestern 9884, Oshkosh 9886, Oshkosh 9887, **Outagamie 9888**, Pamida 9891, Pollybill 9900, PPC 9902, Reinhart 9909, Riordan 9911, **Rockwell 9912**, **Roddis 9913**, Schneider 9920, Schoenleber 9921, Sensient 9922, Sentry 9923, **Smith 9929**, Split 9932, Styberg 9944, Sub 9945, **Taylor 9947**, Timken 9950, U.S. 9952, Uihlein 9953, Uihlein 9955, Wagner 9958, Wehr 9961, Wisconsin 9967, Witte 9968, Wrigley 9971

Wyoming: Connemara 9978, McNeill 9986, Thorson 9994, True 9996

Financial services

California: Haas 637
Minnesota: TCF 4699
Pennsylvania: CIGNA 8143
Texas: Pema 9114

Food banks

Alabama: Crampton 30
Arizona: Cooper 92, Farrington 97, Halle 103, Help 105
California: Five 516, Grand 611, Jackson 706, PG&E 1000, Solari 1176, Synopsys 1223
Connecticut: **Orchard 1619**, Pequot 1625
Florida: **Hardison 2048**, Moore 2142, Resler 2194
Georgia: Harrison 2409, Shallenberger 2487
Idaho: Albertson's 2563
Illinois: **Johnson 2819**, Kapoor 2825, Millard 2897, **Niamogue 2914**
Indiana: Journal 3181, Kuhne 3187, McAllister 3202, Pulliam 3225
Kentucky: Harris 3424, **Yum! 3457**
Louisiana: Helis 3486
Massachusetts: Clipper 3850, Cogan 3851, Davis 3874
Michigan: Wilson 4484
Minnesota: Bemis 4515, NFC 4633, **Sit 4684**
Missouri: Shelter 4902, Smith 4905
Nebraska: Steinhart 5005
New Jersey: OceanFirst 5341, Tolchin 5428
New York: **Altria 5545**, Farkas 5945, Schnurmacher 6931
North Carolina: Branan 7322, **Food 7369**, Gipson 7375, Hillsdale 7398

Ohio: Luther 7726, Moores 7759, Reinberger 7815
Oklahoma: Meinders 7960
Oregon: Jubitz 8029
Pennsylvania: Hulme 8260, Wheeler 8501
Rhode Island: **Feinstein 8535**
South Carolina: **Security's 8609**, TSC 8618
Tennessee: Beaman 8642, Citizens 8657
Texas: Aragona 8763, Bass 8777, Fisch 8901, **Link 9013**, Lockheed 9015, Partnership 9110, Vale 9246, Ward 9262, Williams 9282
Utah: Savage 9340
Washington: Geneva 9592, **Laird 9623**
Wisconsin: Brotz 9767

Food distribution, groceries on wheels

New Jersey: Large 5295
North Carolina: Graham 7382
Pennsylvania: Beatty 8097

Food distribution, meals on wheels

California: Edelstein 476, Witkin 1313
Missouri: Ballman 4780
New York: Block 5638, Braufman 5660, Cohen 5770, Grateful 6093, Icahn 6222, Loeb 6439, SPIA 7028
North Carolina: **Food 7369**, Woodson 7509
Pennsylvania: Keystone 8286, Wheeler 8501
South Carolina: **Security's 8609**
Texas: Anderson 8760, Bass 8777, Hankamer 8939, Waggoner 9256
Washington: De Falco 9578

Food services

Arizona: **Kieckhefer 113**
Arkansas: Wal-Mart 184
California: Atkinson 239, **Atkinson 240**, **Baker 252**, Chavez 376, **Chiron 383**, Cisco 388, Community 406, Fluor 523, Forest 527, Haas 633, Laurel 792, Littlefield 820, Norris 940, PacifiCare 971, Ralphs 1029, Sacramento 1080, Smidt 1159, Soda 1173, Sonora 1178
Colorado: Anschutz 1334, Caulkins 1353, El Pomar 1374, **First 1377**, St. John's 1456
Connecticut: Collis 1513, Culpeper 1521, Dartley 1524, **Macauley 1592**, Sites 1650
Delaware: Crystal 1702, Miller 1731
District of Columbia: **Coyne 1788**, Fowler 1797
Florida: Community 1943, Hall 2045, Libra 2115, Sanders 2215, Tarrant 2265
Georgia: **UPS 2503**, Watkins 2508
Idaho: Albertson's 2563
Illinois: **Allen 2587**, Brach 2629, **Burlington 2644**, Community 2677, Edwardson 2715, Field 2728, GKN 2758, Sara 2982, Stern 3023, Woodward 3085
Indiana: Community 3122, Community 3125, Lafayette 3188
Iowa: Krause 3302, **Pioneer 3324**
Kansas: Security 3390
Kentucky: Robinson 3449, **Yum! 3457**
Louisiana: Booth 3464, Brown 3465, New Orleans 3503
Maine: **Sandy 3555**
Maryland: Abell 3559, Abell 3560, Choice 3589, Leidy 3673, **Weinberg 3759**
Massachusetts: Clipper 3850, Copeland 3859, EOS 3896, **Hershey 3949**, Weber 4200
Michigan: Andersen 4219, Duffy 4290, Skillman 4438, Tamer 4453, **Visteon 4472**
Minnesota: Bieber 4518, Duluth 4556, **Ecolab 4557**, General 4570, **Land 4602**, Mitchell 4625, Opus 4642, Ordean 4643, Sexton 4679, **SUPERVALU 4695**
Missouri: Boeing 4785
Nebraska: **ConAgra 4952**, **ConAgra 4953**
Nevada: Nevada 5047
New Jersey: **Bonner 5137**, Cowles 5170, D'Angelo 5175, **International 5252**
New Mexico: Carlsbad 5469, Frost 5476, McCune 5488, **Pond 5494**, Santa Fe 5496

New York: Banfi 5597, Central 5723, Dove 5877, **Edouard 5909**, Ellis 5923, Hau'Oli 6154, **Heineman 6165**, **Jaffe 6250**, **Kraft 6351**, Maheras 6475, Miller 6551, MJPM 6563, New York 6613, Northern 6639, Pascucci 6696, Rhodebeck 6791, Tuch 7170, **Walter 7211**
North Carolina: Coffey 7339, **Food 7369**, George 7372, Layden 7419, Reynolds 7457, Triangle 7496
Ohio: Britton 7556, Forest 7634, Hoover 7675, IHS 7683, Kramer 7704, Kroger 7705, LKC 7720, LZ 7727, Mathile 7737, Murphy 7768, Schmidlapp 7841, Stark 7867, Wagler 7893
Oklahoma: Better 7926
Oregon: Meyer 8041
Pennsylvania: Arcadia 8086, Dolfinger 8172, Fourjay 8209, Huston 8263, Mengle 8347, Musser 8361, Rosenfeld 8413, Shenango 8438, Smith 8443, Sovereign 8451
Rhode Island: Sullivan 8558
South Carolina: Collins 8582
Tennessee: Lazarus 8700, LifeWorks 8701, Thompson 8733
Texas: Baker 8772, Cameron 8812, Coastal 8833, Edwards 8880, Fikes 8899, Hillcrest 8952, Kempner 8987, South 9201, Sterling 9212, Sturgis 9216, Trull 9240, Williams 9283
Utah: **ALSAM 9302**, Bastian 9306, Eccles 9320, Watkins 9350
Vermont: Vermont 9361
Virginia: Arlington 9371, Lane 9456, Lynchburg 9463, Olsson 9491
Washington: Community 9571, Lauzier 9626, Norcliffe 9650, Tacoma 9693
Wisconsin: Bolz 9762, Cudahy 9785, CUNA 9786, Demmer 9791, Evjue 9797, Glover 9805, Milwaukee 9876, Northwestern 9884, Roundy's 9915, Sensient 9922, Stackner 9934, **Taylor 9947**

Food services, agency eatery

New York: Stiefel 7079

Food services, commodity distribution

Maryland: Torray 3748

Food services, congregate meals

Michigan: Dow 4288
Texas: Wolslager 9290

Foundations (community)

Alabama: Alfa 2, Lowder 42, Lowder 44, May 46, Trippe 69
Arizona: Aurora 88, Halle 103, Reese 133
Arkansas: Ross 174, Smith 176
California: Alpert 207, Betterworld 285, Borina 307, Cacique 342, Cantus 355, Dickinson 454, Farrell 496, Friedman 539, G.T.R. 544, Gallo 548, **Goldberg 592**, Graziadio 613, Haas 634, Hamilton-White 642, Hobbs 680, Irvine 698, Janeway 712, JL 720, Johnson 726, JWS 735, Katz 745, Markkula 856, Morgan 915, **Omidyar 952**, Peery 986, Red 1035, Shapiro 1137, Solari 1176, Stein 1190, Synopsys 1223, Zecca 1325
Colorado: Left 1407, M.D.C. 1413, Sturm 1462
Connecticut: Bridgemill 1503, Chase 1509, Kitchings 1574
District of Columbia: **Patterson 1840**, Vaterstetten 1855
Florida: Batchelor 1893, Blum 1912, Burton 1921, Eckerd 1986, Jasam 2074, MIDA 2139, Riverside 2200, Sanders 2215, Scarpa 2221, Taylor 2267, Thanksgiving 2272, Victory 2208, Weiller 2291
Georgia: Aflac 2311, Azalea 2322, GKW 2398, Jordan 2425, Rollins 2475, RTM 2477, Sheffield 2488, **Worwin 2526**
Illinois: Adreani 2585, Ball 2604, Getz 2753, Harrison 2791, Lea 2850, McNally 2885, Schield 2985

Indiana: 1st 3094, Branigin 3109, Carmichael 3113, Glick 3155, Journal 3181, Leighton 3190, Peabody 3221, Pulliam 3224, Storehouse 3242
Iowa: Bucksbaum 3271, Grubb 3289, Kruidenier 3303, Levitt 3307, **Sehgal 3330**
Kansas: Joscelyn 3371, Morgan 3377, Pritchett 3382
Kentucky: **Brown 3411**, Orleton 3445
Maine: **Sandy 3555**
Maryland: Rosenberg 3720
Massachusetts: Acushnet 3770, Adams 3772, Benz 3798, Donahue 3881, Hagerty 3938, Hoffman 3955, Inavale 3964, McCallum 4029, Wheatland 4204
Michigan: Boutell 4236, Citizens 4249, **Dogwood 4282**, Ford 4304, Frey 4316, **Isabel 4346**, Manoogian 4382, Meijer 4390, Monroe 4396, Mott 4400, Perrigo 4410, RNR 4420, Stryker 4451
Minnesota: Amundson 4500, WEM 4722, Westcliff 4724, Wolohan 4730
Mississippi: Maddox 4753
Missouri: Anheuser 4775, Edison 4808
Nebraska: Abbott 4942, Heuermann 4973, Hubbell 4979, Roberts 4998, Steinhart 5005
Nevada: **Walsh 5075**
New Jersey: Abar 5107, Arnold 5117, Bildner 5133, Goldring 5210, Guarini 5216, Gund 5218, Kemmerer 5275, Kurr 5291, Levitt 5305, Olsen 5342, Union 5435, Weny 5450
New Mexico: Walbridge 5503
New York: Bright 5664, Charitable 5732, Community 5785, Corning 5794, Harbor 6144, Kimmelman 6322, Lauder 6382, LGR 6417, MJPM 6563, Ryan 6884, Turn 7174, Ungar 7183
North Carolina: Gipson 7375, Holding 7399, Legatus 7420, Levine 7421, McLean 7425, Reynolds 7460, Smith 7478
Ohio: Bates 7540, Evans 7620, Frohman 7641, Frost 7642, Gerlach 7648, Haile 7659, Lewis 7713, M/I 7729, Marcum 7734, Miller 7752, Morgan 7760, Noble 7778, Pugliese 7810, Toledo 7882
Oklahoma: ONEOK 7967
Oregon: Ackerman 7995, Stewart 8060
Pennsylvania: Brickman 8116, **Johnson 8274**, S & T 8417, Selfon 8433
Rhode Island: Routhier 8553
South Carolina: Barnet 8568, Foothills 8588, Hipp 8592, TSC 8618
Tennessee: Clayton 8659, Ingram 8694, Jeniam 8695, T & T 8731
Texas: Ackerman 8750, Bridwell 8797, Clayton 8830, Fain 8890, Kaufman 8981, **Levant 9008**, Loose 9017, Mayborn 9033, McCoy 9039, Mehta 9052, Morgan 9074, Newman 9090, Oehmig 9099, Owen 9106, Pema 9114, Rapoport 9141, Shelton 9182, Sumners 9218, Swinney 9222
Utah: ALS 9301
Virginia: **Bansal 9372**, Kellar 9449, Olsson 9491, Praxis 9500, Reinhart 9502
Washington: Murr 9645
West Virginia: Hunnicutt 9720, McDonough 9726
Wisconsin: Bolz 9762, Goldbach 9806, Gordon 9808, Nicholas 9883, Oshkosh 9887, Rennebohm 9910, Uihlein 9954
Wyoming: Dragicevich 9980, Tozzi 9995

Foundations (private grantmaking)

Alabama: Wyker 77
Arizona: **Gagarin 99**, Reese 133
California: Benificus 278, Blum 297, Bowman 312, Dwyer 472, Field 503, Foothills 526, Gordon 607, Hamilton-White 642, Hazan 660, Ishiyama 702, Jerome 717, Kabcenell 737, Quattrone 1024, Ray 1034, Red 1035, Rock 1061, Rogers 1064, Scully 1116, Smith 1162, Vadasz 1254, Werner 1296
Colorado: Mallon 1414
District of Columbia: **Patterson 1840**
Florida: Cejas 1930, Conese 1950, DeHaan 1966, Kennedy 2089, P & M 2160, Rales 2184, Sanders 2215, Taylor 2269
Hawaii: Change 2539
Illinois: Freehling 2737, **Galashiels 2742**, **Hull 2807**
Iowa: Hubbell 3297, Mansfield 3308

Massachusetts: Bain 3788, Manzi 4021, Monsweag 4042, Stride 4172
Michigan: Cold 4250, Hauenstein 4339, Manoogian 4382
Minnesota: Carlson 4532, Koran 4600, Mithun 4626
Mississippi: Oakwood 4760
Nebraska: Dunklau 4958
New Jersey: Abar 5107, **Frankino 5196**, Hugin 5245, McMullen 5325, Twin 5432, **YPI 5461**
New York: Alfiero 5534, Castelnau 5715, Cayne 5717, **Das 5832**, Davis 5837, Devlin 5855, Diller 5863, Gellman 6013, **Glades 6037**, Gordon 6076, Heckscher 6164, Hoffman 6195, Icahn 6222, Johnson 6267, Kadrovach 6282, Megrue 6524, Pedersen 6704, Riley 6809, Watts 7221
Ohio: CRN 7598, Jackson 7685, Lancaster 7707, Rose 7825, Silk 7857
Oklahoma: Collins 7930
Oregon: Campbell 8002
Pennsylvania: Hooper 8256, **Woods 8508**
Tennessee: 1939 8635
Texas: Bookout 8791, **Davis 8857**, Jones 8976, McNutt 9048, Riddle 9148, Simmons 9187
Utah: Sorenson 9343
Virginia: **Glenstone 9429**, Grandis 9432, Joco 9443, Morgan 9479, Reinhart 9502, Reynolds 9503
Washington: Jones 9614, Raven 9670
Wisconsin: Split 9932
Wyoming: Berry 9975

Foundations (private independent)

Georgia: Harris 2408
Illinois: Bersted 2618
Minnesota: Slaggie 4686
New York: Bernstein 5625, Sackler 6889
Ohio: Women's 7916
Texas: Morgan 9074
Washington: GLA 9593

Foundations (private operating)

Colorado: Gary 1379
Florida: BJ's 1908, Wymbs 2307
Massachusetts: Parlin 4070
New Jersey: Aicher 5109, Jensam 5258, Wang 5448
New York: Avalon 5579, Milstein 6555
Pennsylvania: Magee 8320
Texas: Tobin 9235

Foundations (public)

Alabama: Pleiad 57
California: **Beagle 266**, Blume 298, Cadence 344, Galil 546, Irvine 698, La Fetra 782, Lanni 789, Laurel 792, Wolfen 1316
Connecticut: **Macauley 1592**
Delaware: Buckner 1695
Florida: Hoernle 2062
Georgia: Brill 2329
Illinois: Citadel 2667
Iowa: Bedell 3267
Maryland: **Berman 3572**
Massachusetts: Gordon 3928
Minnesota: Barry 4511
Mississippi: McCarty 4754
New Jersey: Guarini 5216
New York: Icahn 6223, IIMI 6228, Karmazin 6293, Mnuchin 6564, Paul 6697, Pevaroff 6719, ZIIZ 7299
Pennsylvania: Lamb 8299, McCormick 8330
South Carolina: Collins 8582, Reams 8606, TSC 8618
Texas: **Anderson 8761**, **CEMEX 8821**, Reliant 9144, Sharp 9180, Wright 9293
Virginia: **Bansal 9372**, VuBay 9533
Wisconsin: Demmer 9791, Gordon 9808

Genetics/birth defects

California: Fremont 535
Florida: Rothberg 2209

New York: **National 6603**, Rosenblum 6850
Ohio: Schott 7842

Genetics/birth defects research

Massachusetts: **Waterman 4198**
Missouri: **Lockton 4857**
New York: Diamond 5857, Grateful 6093, Singh 6991
Texas: Wright 9293

Geriatrics

California: Archstone 232, Hillblom 673
Colorado: **Daniels 1362**
Florida: **Foundation 2008**
Illinois: Retirement 2964
Iowa: Principal 3326
Kentucky: Omnicare 3443, **Omnicare 3444**
New Jersey: Healthcare 5228, **Rippel 5368**
New York: Elmezzi 5925, **Hartford 6150**, **MetLife 6542**
Ohio: **HCR 7667**, McGregor 7742
Texas: Wolslager 9290

Geriatrics research

California: **Glenn 581**
Maryland: **Ellison 3621**
New Jersey: **Rippel 5368**
Ohio: **HCR 7667**

Gerontology

California: Archstone 232
Maryland: Erickson 3624, Stulman 3739
New Jersey: **Rippel 5368**

Girl scouts

California: McKenna 878
Colorado: Gooding 1384
Delaware: Struthers 1758
Florida: **Cobb 1936**
Indiana: Annis 3100, Bussing 3111, Simon 3236
Iowa: Krause 3302
Minnesota: Greycoach 4575
New Jersey: Phipps 5352, **Reeves 5365**
New York: Buck 5682
North Carolina: Jolley 7407, Rostan 7467
Pennsylvania: Bozzone 8114, FISA 8204, Hoverter 8258, S & T 8417
Tennessee: Atticus 8639
Texas: Halsell 8936, Williams 9283

Girls

California: Amateur 214
Indiana: Noble 3214
Massachusetts: Perpetual 4078, Stearns 4159
New York: New York 6613
Oregon: **NIKE 8046**
Pennsylvania: Ellis 8184
Wisconsin: Milwaukee 9876, Oshkosh 9885

Girls clubs

Arkansas: Tenenbaum 180
California: Volentine 1268
Delaware: Bishop 1694
Massachusetts: Schott 4132
Nebraska: Buffett 4949
New Jersey: Lear 5300
Pennsylvania: Stabler 8455
Virginia: **Oak 9488**

Goodwill Industries

Florida: Blank 1909
Michigan: Kay 4354
Ohio: Fleming 7631
Texas: Beasley 8784

Wisconsin: Beasley 9755

Government/public administration

Alabama: Carson 19, **Union 70**
Arizona: Arizona 87
California: Eisenberg 480, Finley 507, Fresno 537, Gross 621, Lytel 836, Peery 986, Peninsula 989, Sacramento 1080, San Francisco 1088, Taper 1226, Von der Ahe 1269, Wohlford 1315
Colorado: Gates 1380, Kitzmiller 1405, Petteys 1436, Williams 1474
Connecticut: Bodenwein 1497, Palmer 1621, **Prentice 1630**, **Richardson 1632**
Delaware: **Birch 1692**, **Milliken 1732**, Welfare 1762
District of Columbia: **Fannie 1793**, **Mott 1836**
Florida: Community 1948, Ryder 2213
Georgia: Community 2354, Community 2357, WestPoint 2513, Williams 2514, Woodruff 2521
Illinois: AMCORE 2591, **Amsted 2593**, Andrew 2596, Blair 2621, Blum 2625, Caterpillar 2653, Charleston 2657, Chicago 2661, Community 2677, Dillon 2704, Geneseo 2750, Harrison 2790, Keiser 2828, Louis 2862, Rice 2966
Indiana: American 3098, Central 3116, Cole 3121, Henry 3165, Marshall 3199, NiSource 3213, Noble 3214
Iowa: **AEGON 3259**, Kinney 3300, Mansfield 3308, Siouxland 3332
Kansas: Baughman 3346, Hansen 3366, Topeka 3400
Louisiana: Freeman 3480, Peltier 3504, RosaMary 3507, Young 3518, Zemurray 3519
Maryland: Grace 3638
Massachusetts: Crane 3864, Goldberg 3927, **Krieble 3990**, **OneBeacon 4060**, Sudbury 4173, Worcester 4209
Michigan: Charlevoix 4246, Community 4253, Community 4254, Fremont 4315, General 4320, Gerstacker 4322, Greenville 4331, La-Z-Boy 4368
Minnesota: Bemis 4515, Duluth 4556, Hallett 4581, Rochester 4668, **Wood 4731**
Mississippi: **Armstrong 4734**
Missouri: Boeing 4785, Ingram 4834, Reynolds 4892, Saint Louis 4896, Schwartze 4898, Sosland 4908
Montana: First 4937
Nebraska: Fremont 4962, Kiewit 4984, Omaha 4994, Steinhart 5005
Nevada: Nevada 5047, Sierra 5064
New Hampshire: Putnam 5100
New Jersey: Fund 5199, Hidden 5233, Kirby 5279, New Jersey 5336
New York: **Aequus 5524**, **Baker 5594**, Booth 5651, Chautauqua 5738, Clark 5761, Everett 5941, **Ford 5970**, **Guggenheim 6118**, **Hauser 6155**, McCann 6514, Millbrook 6549, New York 6613, Northern 6639, O'Connor 6645, Ohrstrom 6659, **Pforzheimer 6721**, Revson 6789, Robinson 6820, Sprague 7035, Sweetgrass 7113, **Tinker 7143**, **United 7185**, Weiss 7236, Wendt 7243, Williams 7260
North Carolina: Broyhill 7328, Community 7343, Finch 7366, Smith 7479, Triangle 7496, Winston-Salem 7508
North Dakota: Fargo 7514
Ohio: Anderson 7529, Babcock 7537, Charities 7569, Cleveland 7576, Columbus 7580, Coshocton 7593, Dana 7599, Dayton 7604, Firman 7628, Gund 7657, Mandel 7730, Murphy 7769, Nationwide 7771, Parker 7796, Reeves 7814, Richland 7819, Ritchie 7821, Salem 7831, Stark 7867, Wellman 7901, Western 7903
Oklahoma: Bailey 7923, Kerr 7949, Lyon 7953, Puterbaugh 7970
Oregon: Carpenter 8003, Oregon 8049
Pennsylvania: Arkema 8089, **Armstrong 8090**, Buncher 8125, **Carthage 8132**, CIGNA 8143, Connelly 8157, Dolfinger 8172, Grundy 8228, Hillman 8250, Mandell 8322, **Pew 8377**, Wyomissing 8509
Rhode Island: Rhode Island 8551
South Carolina: Central 8577, Horne 8594
Texas: Abell 8749, Alexander 8762, Anderson 8762, Belo 8787, Carter 8816, **CEMEX 8821**, Franklin 8907, Kurth 9003, Mays 9036, McDermott 9043,

Meadows 9049, Meredith 9054, **Shell 9181**, Sumners 9218, Temple 9227, Valero 9247
Utah: Hemingway 9328
Vermont: Lintilhac 9359
Virginia: Arlington 9371, Bryant 9380, Camp 9382, Campbell 9383, Portsmouth 9498
Washington: Foundation 9589, Tacoma 9693, Wyman 9709
West Virginia: Bowen 9711, Shott 9733
Wisconsin: Bryce 9769, Johnson 9826, Joy 9828, La Crosse 9845, McBeath 9864, Milwaukee 9876, Phipps 9898, PPC 9902, **Rockwell 9912**, Sentry 9923

Graduate/professional education

California: **Carnegie 359**, Johnson 725, Rosenfeld 1067
Georgia: **Coca-Cola 2352**
Illinois: Braeside 2631, Malott 2872
Maryland: Abramson 3561, **Life 3677**
Massachusetts: Lubin 4016
Michigan: **Earhart 4291**
Minnesota: Alliss 4498
Missouri: Jones 4834
New Jersey: Goldberg 5209, Goldring 5210
New Mexico: Proteus 5495
New York: **Citigroup 5755**, Gutman 6122, **Hearst 6161**, **Hearst 6162**, Linden 6424
Ohio: **Arab 7531**, Horvitz 7678
Oregon: Knight 8032
Tennessee: Thompson 8733

Health care

Alabama: AmSouth 5, Anderson 7, Barber 10, Blount 14, Bruno 17, Caring 18, Carson 19, Central 20, Comer 22, Community 23, Community 24, Community 25, Community 26, Community 27, Crampton 30, Daniel 31, Friedman 35, Hill 39, Lowe 45, McMillan 49, McWane 50, Meyer 52, Patterson 56, Protective 58, Roberts 59, Saks 61, Treadwell 68, **Union 70**, Webb 75
Alaska: Rasmuson 85
Arizona: Arizona 87, Community 91, Dee 94, Gesner 100, **Globe 101**, Herberger 106, Hermundslie 107, **Kleckhefer 113**, Levine 115, Phelps 129, Steele 142, Viad 149, Webb 150
Arkansas: Arkansas 156, Blue 157, Bodenhamer 158, **Frueauff 161**, Jones 166, Northwest 169, Rebsamen 171, Smith 176, Wal-Mart 184
California: Aaroe 192, Ackerman 193, Ahmanson 198, Allergan 203, Alliance 204, Amgen 219, **Appleton 225**, Arata 229, Aratani 230, Auen 242, Ayrshire 247, **Azus 248**, Babcock 249, Baker 251, **Baker 252**, Baker 253, Barker 257, Bartman 259, Bay 264, **Beagle 266**, Bell 274, Benbough 276, Berger 281, **Bergstrom 282**, Bireley 292, Blue 296, Boswell 308, **Brandes 317**, Brotman 328, **Bull 331**, Burnett 336, California 345, California 346, California 347, **Cantor 354**, Center 369, **ChevronTexaco 380**, **Chiron 383**, Cisco 388, Colombo 398, Community 401, Community 402, Community 403, Community 404, Community 405, Community 406, Community 407, Confidence 411, Conte 414, Copley 416, Crail 426, Crummer 432, Daly 436, Daly 437, de Dampierre 448, Dougherty 463, Douglas 464, **Draper 466**, Dwyer 472, East 474, Eisenberg 480, Eisner 481, Fairchild 492, Feintech 499, Five 516, Flora 521, Fluor 523, Franklin 533, Fremont 534, Fresno 537, Friedman 539, Garabedian 552, Garland 556, Geffen 558, Genentech 562, **Gere 565**, Ghidotti 571, Gilmore 578, Gold 589, Gold 591, Goldman 595, Goldman 596, Goldwyn 600, Goodman 605, Gould 609, Gross 621, Grout 624, Guess? 629, Haas 633, Hamilton-White 642, Hannon 644, Harden 647, HealthCare 661, Heart 662, Hench 668, Herbst 669, Hillblom 673, Hofmann 683, Humboldt 691, Hutton 694, Intuit 696, Irvine 699, Jackson 706, Jameson 710, Jay 716, Jewett 718, **Kaiser 739**, **Keck 750**, Keck 751, King 760, Kirchgessner 762,

Park 7795, Parker 7796, **Perkins 7800**, Prentiss 7806, Reeves 7814, Reinberger 7815, Richland 7819, Rieveschl 7820, Russell 7827, Saint 7830, Schlink 7839, Schmidlapp 7841, Schott 7842, Scioto 7845, Sisler 7858, Sky 7859, Smith 7862, Smucker 7864, Spaulding 7865, Springfield 7866, Stark 7867, Summer 7874, Thendara 7878, **Timken 7880**, Tippit 7881, Toledo 7882, Toledo 7883, **Tomkins 7884**, Toulmin 7885, Troy 7886, Tuscarawas 7890, Watson 7896, Wayne 7897, Wellman 7901, Williams 7907, Wolfe 7915, Wuliger 7918, Youngstown 7920, Zenith 7921

Oklahoma: Bernsen 7925, Bovaird 7927, Chapman 7928, Communities 7931, Community 7932, Goddard 7939, Helmerich 7942, Inasmuch 7944, Kaiser 7947, Kerr 7949, Kerr 7950, Meinders 7960, Noble 7963, Oklahoma City 7964, ONEOK 7967, Records 7972, Sarkeys 7974, Titus 7983, Warren 7987, Waters 7988, Williams 7989, Zarrow 7991, Zarrow 7992, Zarrow 7993

Oregon: Autzen 7997, Bair 7998, Carpenter 8003, Collins 8007, Hedinger 8019, **Honzel 8021**, Jackson 8024, Jeld 8025, John 8026, Macdonald 8038, Mentor 8039, Meyer 8042, **NIKE 8046**, Northwest 8048, Oregon 8049, PacifiCorp 8050, PGE 8051, Poznanski 8052, Salem 8054, **Schmidt 8055**, Schnitzer 8057, Tucker 8065, Wendt 8066, Wessinger 8067, Wheeler 8068, Young 8069

Pennsylvania: 1675 8070, 1957 8071, **Alcoa 8075**, **Annenberg 8084**, Arcadia 8086, **Armstrong 8090**, Ball 8093, Barra 8095, Bayer 8096, Benedum 8099, Berks 8103, **Berman 8104**, Biesecker 8106, Birmingham 8107, Blue 8112, Born 8113, Buck 8123, **Cardone 8129**, Central 8135, Centre 8136, Chester 8141, CIGNA 8143, Claneil 8144, CMS 8147, Cochran 8149, Community 8155, Connelly 8157, Degenstein 8166, Dolfinger 8172, **Dominion 8173**, Drueding 8177, DSF 8178, Eden 8182, Equitable 8187, Erie 8188, Fair 8192, Falk 8193, Farber 8195, Ferree 8199, Fine 8201, First 8202, FISA 8204, Fisher 8205, Foundation 8208, Fourjay 8209, Genuardi 8213, Giant 8214, Gibson 8215, Gitlin 8217, Graham 8222, Hamilton 8233, Hankin 8234, Harsco 8236, Heinz 8240, Highmark 8247, Hillman 8249, Hillman 8251, Hillman 8252, Hirtzel 8253, Hulme 8260, Hunt 8261, Huston 8263, Huston 8264, Independence 8266, Innisfree 8267, Jennings 8272, Keystone 8286, Kind 8289, Kinsley 8290, Klein 8291, La 8298, Lancaster 8300, Laurel 8301, Lehigh Valley 8303, Luzerne 8317, Mandell 8322, Massey 8328, McCune 8331, McCune 8332, Medleycott 8343, Mellon 8344, Mine 8357, Perelman 8372, **Pew 8377**, Philadelphia 8378, Philadelphia 8379, Phoenixville 8381, Pierce 8382, **Pincus 8384**, Pittsburgh 8386, **Podiatry 8389**, Pond 8391, Psalm 8397, Rees 8401, Respironics 8403, Rider 8404, Rockwell 8408, Rohrer 8410, Ryan 8416, Saint 8419, Scranton 8431, Smith 8443, Snee 8446, Snyder 8448, Sordoni 8450, Sovereign 8451, Stabler 8455, Steinman 8458, Strawbridge 8467, Taylor 8473, **Templeton 8475**, Tippins 8477, Triple 8482, **United 8487**, **United 8488**, Vanguard 8490, Washington 8497, West 8500, Wimmer 8505, Wyomissing 8509, York 8511

Puerto Rico: **FNZ 8514**, Puerto Rico 8515

Rhode Island: Alperin 8516, **Amica 8518**, Brooks 8520, Champlin 8524, Charter 8526, Cuno 8528, CVS 8529, Daniels 8530, **FM 8537**, Hasbro 8539, Kimball 8542, Littlefield 8544, McCarthy 8548, Rhode Island 8551, Sullivan 8558, **Textron 8559**

South Carolina: Abney 8564, Black 8569, Blue 8570, Central 8577, Coastal 8581, Community 8583, Community 8584, Dintersmith 8586, First 8587, Foothills 8588, Fullerton 8589, Glenn 8591, Inman 8595, Liberty 8597, Montgomery 8600, Phifer 8602, Post 8603, Self 8610, Sims 8611, Smith 8613, Sonoco 8614, South 8615, Spartanburg 8616, Springs 8617, **Youths' 8621**, Zucker 8622

South Dakota: Sioux Falls 8630, South Dakota 8631

Tennessee: Aslan 8637, Assisi 8638, Belz 8643, **Bridgestone 8646**, Charis 8652, Christy 8654, CIC

8656, CLARCOR 8658, Clayton 8659, Community 8661, Community 8662, Conwood 8663, Davis 8665, Eskind 8675, Frist 8679, **Garrott 8680**, Goldsmith 8682, Gordon 8683, Hamico 8684, Haslam 8687, Hawthorn 8689, HCA 8690, Martin 8706, Massey 8709, Phillips 8716, Plough 8718, Longleaf 8719, Schadt 8725, Stokely 8730, Tennessee 8732, Thompson 8733, Washington 8741

Texas: Abell 8749, Alexander 8752, Amarillo 8758, **Anderson 8761**, Anderson 8762, Astin 8764, **AT&T 8765**, Austin 8768, Baker 8772, Bass 8777, Beasley 8784, Behmann 8785, Bridwell 8797, **Butt 8803**, Cailloux 8807, Cain 8808, Cameron 8812, Carter 8816, Carter 8817, Cauthorn 8820, **CEMEX 8821**, Chilton 8826, Clements 8832, Coastal 8833, Communities 8839, Community 8840, Community 8841, Community 8842, Constantin 8843, Convergence 8844, **Cooper 8846**, Cullen 8854, Dallas 8855, Deakins 8860, **Dell 8863**, Dell 8864, di Portanova 8865, Dodge 8868, Dunn 8872, East 8876, **EDS 8877**, Edwards 8880, El Paso 8881, Ellwood 8884, Enrico 8885, Esping 8886, Estill 8888, **ExxonMobil 8889**, Fasken 8895, Fikes 8899, Folsom 8905, Fondren 8906, Frees 8909, Garvey 8914, George 8916, Gill 8919, Gorman 8922, Gulf 8926, Haggar 8929, Haggar 8930, Haggar 8931, Haggerty 8932, Hamman 8938, Hawn 8943, Heavin 8945, Herzstein 8949, Hillcrest 8952, Hoblitzelle 8955, Hoglund 8956, Houston 8961, Hunt 8966, Johnson 8974, Keith 8982, Kelley 8986, Kempner 8987, Kennedy 8988, Kimberly 8992, King 8995, **Kleberg 8999**, Lard 9005, Lowe 9020, Lubbock 9021, Lyman 9023, Lyons 9024, Marathon 9028, Mayor 9034, Mays 9035, McCullough 9041, McDermott 9043, McGovern 9044, McMillan 9046, Meadows 9049, Mischer 9063, Mitchell 9065, Moody 9070, Nash 9085, Once 9101, Owen 9106, Parks 9109, Paso 9111, Permian 9117, Powell 9128, Priddy 9131, PSH 9137, Read 9142, Richardson 9147, Roach 9150, Roberts 9151, Rockwell 9154, Rogers 9155, Sams 9163, San Antonio 9166, Scott 9174, Scurlock 9175, Semmes 9179, **Shell 9181**, Sidhu 9185, **Silverton 9186**, Simmons 9188, Simmons 9189, Sixty 9190, Smith 9191, Smith 9195, Smith 9196, South 9201, Sowell 9202, Speas 9206, Speas 9207, Stark 9209, Sterling 9212, Strake 9215, Sturgis 9216, **Swett 9221**, Tapeats 9223, Temple 9227, Temple 9228, **Tenet 9229**, Tennessee 9230, Texas 9232, Triad 9239, Turner 9242, USAA 9245, Vaughan 9249, Waggoner 9256, Ward 9263, Ware 9264, West 9276, Williams 9282, Williams 9283, Wise 9285, Wolslager 9290, Wright 9294, Young 9295, Zachry 9296, Zeller 9298

Utah: Bamberger 9305, Bastian 9306, Burton 9309, Dreamweaver 9314, Dumke 9315, Dumke 9316, Eccles 9317, Eccles 9319, Eccles 9320, Esther 9321, Greene 9325, **Huntsman 9329**

Vermont: **Green 9358**, Lintilhac 9359, Vermont 9361

Virgin Islands: Community 9363

Virginia: 118 9365, AMERIGROUP 9369, Arlington 9371, Beazley 9376, Billings 9377, Bryant 9380, Camp 9382, Carrington 9386, Carter 9387, Charles 9389, Charlottesville 9390, Collis 9398, Community 9400, Connors 9403, **de Beaumont 9408**, **Dorothy 9411**, Evans 9416, Foundation 9419, Friedman 9425, **Gannett 9428**, Golden 9430, Grandis 9432, Guilford 9434, Houff 9438, LandAmerica 9454, Luck 9461, Lynchburg 9463, Mars 9466, Massey 9467, McGlothlin 9469, Morgan 9479, N.E.W. 9482, Norfolk 9484, Northern 9486, **Oak 9488**, Pauley 9496, Portsmouth 9498, Portsmouth 9499, Samberg 9510, Sharp 9515, Staunton 9521, SunTrust 9523, Titmus 9527, Ukrop 9529, United 9530, Universal 9531, Virginia Beach 9532, Weissberg 9536, Williamsburg 9541, **Winkler 9542**

Washington: Allen 9550, Blue 9559, **Boeing 9560**, Cheney 9569, Community 9570, Community 9571, De Falco 9578, Dimmer 9579, **Edwards 9580**, Evertrust 9583, Foster 9588, Foundation 9589,

Gates 9591, Glaser 9594, Grays 9597, Howard 9609, **Laird 9623**, Lauzier 9626, Lematta 9628, Lynn 9633, McCaw 9637, Milgard 9641, Nesholm 9647, Norcliffe 9650, PEMCO 9660, Rainier 9669, Razore 9671, **RealNetworks 9672**, Satterberg 9677, Seattle 9680, Tacoma 9693, Williams 9706, Wright 9707, Wyman 9709

West Virginia: BB&T 9710, Community 9716, Jacobson 9722, Kanawha 9723, McDonough 9726, Mylan 9728, Parkersburg 9730, Schenk 9732, Shott 9733, Tucker 9736

Wisconsin: Acuity 9739, Alexander 9741, AnnMarie 9743, Assurant 9748, Baird 9750, Beasley 9755, Bell 9756, Bryce 9769, Chapman 9771, Community 9776, Community 9777, Community 9778, Community 9779, Community 9780, Cornerstone 9781, Cox 9782, Cudahy 9784, CUNA 9786, Delavan 9790, **Eastman 9794**, Fond du Lac 9800, Green Bay 9810, Johnson 9823, Johnson 9826, Joy 9828, Kelben 9830, Kenosha 9833, Ladish 9846, Ladish 9847, Lubar 9851, Lunda 9852, Lynn 9853, Madison 9855, Marcus 9859, McBeath 9864, Menasha 9869, Miller 9875, Milwaukee 9876, Modine 9878, Nicholas 9883, Northwestern 9884, Oshkosh 9887, **Palmer 9890**, Pettit 9897, Posner 9901, PPC 9902, Racine 9906, **Rath 9907**, **Reiman 9908**, Riordan 9911, **Rockwell 9912**, Rolfs 9914, Sensient 9922, Sentry 9923, **Smith 9929**, Stackner 9934, Steigleder 9936, Sub 9945, **Thrivent 9949**, Uihlein 9955, Waukesha 9960, Windhover 9966, WPS 9970

Wyoming: Allen 9974, Community 9977, Martin 9984, Scott 9991, Thorson 9994, True 9996, Wyoming 10000

Health care, alliance

California: Blue 296
Minnesota: **Medtronic 4622**
New York: Chu 5754
Pennsylvania: Brossman 8120

Health care, association

California: Beneto 277, **Marshall 858**, **Versacare 1265**
Iowa: Gilchrist 3287
Minnesota: Dasburg 4545
Missouri: Taylor 4916
Wisconsin: Parr 9893

Health care, blood supply

California: **Chiron 383**

Health care, burn centers

California: Peters 993

Health care, clinics/centers

California: Weisman 1289
Colorado: Paul 1435
Florida: Marden 2127, Martin 2130, Morsani 2147
Georgia: Smith 2491
Illinois: Krueck 2846, Weiss 3062
Indiana: Duneland 3143, Leighton 3191
Iowa: Mid-Iowa 3317
Kentucky: Harris 3424
Massachusetts: Bristol 3816, Clarke 3849
Minnesota: Generations 4571
New York: Johnson 6272
North Carolina: Graham 7382
Ohio: Harding 7663, Miller 7754, Mixon 7757, Nord 7780, R.T. 7812
Rhode Island: Charter 8526
South Carolina: Blue 8570, Ceres 8578
Tennessee: Scheidt 8726, Tennessee 8732
Texas: **Dell 8863**, Hobby 8954, Lord 9018, Turner 9241, Wolff 9288
Virginia: Golden 9430, **Mousetrap 9480**, Praxis 9500, Taubman 9524, Wiley 9539

Wisconsin: Assurant 9748

Health care, cost containment
California: **WellPoint 1292**
Colorado: Rose 1445
Michigan: **ArvinMeritor 4224**
New Jersey: **Johnson 5265**
New York: Achelis 5513, Bodman 5647
Pennsylvania: CIGNA 8143

Health care, emergency transport services
Oklahoma: Richardson 7973

Health care, EMS
Michigan: RNR 4420
New York: Helmsley 6171

Health care, equal rights
California: Amgen 219, Blue 296, California 346, **Chiron 383**, McKesson 879, PacifiCare 971, **WellPoint 1292**
Connecticut: Boehringer 1498, Connecticut 1519
Hawaii: First 2542
Iowa: Principal 3326
Massachusetts: Oral 4061
Minnesota: Blue 4521
New Jersey: **Merck 5326**, OceanFirst 5341
New York: Pfizer 6720
North Carolina: **Wachovia 7502**
Pennsylvania: **Alcoa 8075**, Blue 8112, CIGNA 8143
Rhode Island: CVS 8529
Texas: **EDS 8877**, **RGK 9146**
Virginia: AMERIGROUP 9369

Health care, ethics
Florida: Henriksen 2057
New Jersey: **Rippel 5368**
New York: **Greenwall 6103**, Kornfeld 6350

Health care, financing
Colorado: Hill 1392
Florida: Blue 1911

Health care, formal/general education
California: Smullin 1169
Illinois: Goldberg 2761
Ohio: Osteopathic 7791
Pennsylvania: Rees 8401
Texas: West 9274
Virginia: Moore 9478
Washington: Klorfine 9619

Health care, fund raising/fund distribution
Florida: Couch 1953
Indiana: Leighton 3191

Health care, HMOs
California: California 347
Texas: **Dell 8863**

Health care, home services
California: Barbonchielli 256
Connecticut: **Aetna 1479**, Senior 1647
Illinois: VNA 3049
New Hampshire: Gale 5091
New York: Keeler 6306
Ohio: Corbin 7591, Nippert 7777, Reinberger 7815
Pennsylvania: McLean 8340, Surgala 8469
Texas: Healthcare 8944

Wisconsin: Dudley 9792

Health care, infants
Arizona: Halle 103
California: Five 516
District of Columbia: Stewart 1850
Florida: Picower 2169
Illinois: Sheba 3005
Michigan: **Gerber 4321**
New York: **Kaufmann 6299**
Texas: Anderson 8759, **Dell 8863**, Topfer 9238
Virginia: Portsmouth 9499
Washington: Anderson 9551, Talaris 9694

Health care, information services
Maryland: Gudelsky 3641
Ohio: Osteopathic 7791

Health care, insurance
Alabama: Community 24
California: California 347, **Packard 972**, WellPoint **1292**
New Hampshire: HNHfoundation 5092
New Jersey: **Johnson 5265**
New York: **Commonwealth 5779**
Ohio: Austin 7536

Health care, organ/tissue banks
Georgia: Mason 2444

Health care, patient services
California: Bowes 311
Illinois: Sheba 3005
Minnesota: HRK 4589, **Medtronic 4622**
Nevada: Bennett 5021
New York: **OSI 6670**, Renfield 6786
Ohio: Kaplan 7696, Miller 7753
Texas: **Dell 8863**
Virginia: Portsmouth 9498
Wisconsin: Assurant 9748

Health care, public policy
California: **Kaiser 739**, Kapor 743, **WellPoint 1292**
Colorado: Rose 1445
Kansas: Kansas 3372
Maine: Maine 3549
New Jersey: **Merck 5326**
New York: **Greenwall 6103**, Milbank 6547
Oregon: Kinsman 8031
Virginia: AMERIGROUP 9369

Health care, reform
Arkansas: Blue 157
Illinois: Sprague 3016
Michigan: **Kellogg 4357**

Health care, research
California: Johnson 722, Mead 881, **Schocken 1105**
Illinois: Reese 2961
Louisiana: **Biedenharn 3463**
Massachusetts: Bressler 3815
Missouri: Hammons 4826
Oregon: Geary 8017
Pennsylvania: ESSA 8190
Texas: Delaney 8862, Franklin 8908
Virginia: AMERIGROUP 9369

Health care, rural areas
New Jersey: **Rippel 5368**
New York: **Friends 5990**

Health care, single organization support
Michigan: **Heritage 4340**
Ohio: **Lerner 7711**
Texas: Holden 8957

Health care, support services
Colorado: Aspen 1337
Connecticut: Donchian 1531
Massachusetts: Peabody 4072
New York: Samuels 6901
Tennessee: West 8742
Texas: Hudson 8962, Paso 9111

Health care, volunteer services
New York: Buck 5682

Health organizations
Alabama: Carson 19, Dixon 32
Arkansas: Walker 185
California: Caufield 367, Cortopassi 419, Danford 438, DeVito 452, Dreyer's 468, Dwyer 472, Fairchild 492, Flora 521, Gallo 548, Gillespie 577, Isen 701, Johnson 726, Pelosi 988, Potiker 1012, **ResMed 1040**, Rigler 1051, Robertson 1059, Rosenberg 1066, Shapiro 1137, Snow 1171, **Strauss 1203**, Werner 1296
Colorado: Dwan 1370, McWhinney 1423
Connecticut: Daniell 1523, **Newman's 1609**, Rogow 1636, Saybrook 1643, Tow 1660
Delaware: Singer 1753, Wasily 1760
District of Columbia: Cafritz 1780, **Coyne 1788**, Meyer 1834
Florida: Batchelor 1893, Becker 1898, Beveridge 1907, **Coleman 1937**, Fortin 2007, Harmel 2091, Quick 2182, Schippmann 2224, Simon 2235, Stein 2250, Taylor 2269
Georgia: Aflac 2311, Beloco 2324
Hawaii: Schuler 2552, Vidinha 2557
Illinois: Bruning 2635, Freed 2736, Getz 2753, Guth 2775, Harrison 2791, Meyer 2895, Opler 2927, Stein 3022, Stone 3026, **Wadsworth 3050**, Winfrey 3077, Wohlers 3078, Wonderful 3080
Indiana: Chancellor 3117, Klapper 3183, **Lilly 3192**, Simon 3236
Iowa: Grubb 3289
Maryland: Langenfelder 3670, Shattuck 3728
Massachusetts: Bay 3794, Crotty 3870, Cummings 3871, Cutler 3872, DiMaura 3880, Dunn 3884, Haley 3939, Hoffman 3955, Jacobson 3967, Kessler 3978, Manzi 4021, **Saquish 4127**, Stoneman 4167
Michigan: Devereaux 4274, Fisher 4299, Frankel 4313, Padnos 4406, Pitt 4413, Rordor 4424, Thomas 4456, Tiscornia 4460, Wilson 4484
Minnesota: Morning 4627, **Robins 4667**
Mississippi: Feild 4741, Ford 4742, **Seal 4764**
New Jersey: **Frankino 5196**, Healthcare 5228, KDK 5273, Union 5435
New York: A.E. 5506, Alexander 5532, Altman 5542, **Altman 5544**, **Barnett 5601**, Bass 5604, Belfer 5615, Brodsky 5668, Buttenwieser 5693, **Chinnick 5751**, Clinton 5763, Danziger 5829, Goldstein 6062, Grateful 6093, Haas 6126, Heckscher 6164, Hermione 6175, Horowitz 6202, **Johnson 6273**, Karmazin 6293, Kelleher 6307, **Kopf 6348**, Lastfogel 6380, Lewis 6415, Miller 6550, Morse 6583, O'Neill 6650, O'Sullivan 6652, Parker 6690, Pedersen 6704, Pevaroff 6719, Raether 6766, Saligman 6895, Schott 6934, Shapiro 6959, Sharp 6962, Sheinberg 6963, **Silfen 6980**, Speyer 7027, Spiegel 7029, Starwood 7049, **Summerfield 7097**, Tisch 7148, Wolk 7271
North Carolina: Comloquoy 7341, Curran 7350, Hanes 7388
Ohio: Beerman 7543, Miller 7752, Miller 7753, Turben 7888
Oklahoma: Oxley 7968
Oregon: Holmes 8020

Pennsylvania: Barra 8095, Berkman 8102, Cassett 8133, Haas 8230, Janssen 8271, Johnson 8275, Levee 8308
Tennessee: Ayers 8640
Texas: **Adams 8751**, Anderson 8762, Cailloux 8807, Gale 8913, Herd 8948, Jonsson 8977, Lantana 9004, MacDonald 9025, Mankoff 9027, Morris 9076, Rapoport 9141, Sharp 9180, Westcott 9278
Utah: Dumke 9316
Vermont: Vermont 9361
Virginia: Ochsman 9489
Washington: Lauzier 9626, Shirley 9684
Wisconsin: Community 9779, Fotsch 9802, Peck 9894

Health organizations, alliance
California: **Chiron 383**

Health organizations, association
Alabama: **Altec 4**, Ard 8, Aronov 9, Barber 10, Bolden 15, Crampton 30, Founders 34, Harrison 36, Hill 39, Lowder 43, McMillan 49, Meyer 52, Scrushy 62, Thompson 67, Treadwell 68, Vines 72
Arizona: A.P.S. 86, Arizona 87, Berlin 89, Cooper 92, Farrington 97, Halle 103, Hermundslie 107, **IFS 109**, **Kieckhefer 113**, Levine 115, Noah's 127, Robson 135, **Solheim 139**, Webb 150
Arkansas: Jones 166, Murphy 167, Smith 176, Tenenbaum 180
California: 324 190, Aaroe 192, Ahmanson 198, Alpert 209, Arata 229, Arbus 231, Arrillaga 237, Auen 242, **Azus 248**, Bakar 250, Barker 257, Barth 258, Bartman 259, Benificus 278, Berger 281, **Bilger 289**, Bireley 292, Blume 298, Borick 305, Boswell 308, **Brandes 317**, Bravo 319, Brenner 321, Brotman 328, **Bull 331**, Bunker 333, Burnham 337, Byer 339, Cacique 342, Cantus 355, Carson 362, Christopher 385, CNC 390, Community 406, Copley 416, Crawford 427, Crummer 432, D & DF 434, Daly 437, Danford 438, Davidow 444, Davidson 445, **Day 447**, Doll 461, Dougherty 463, **Draper 465**, Dreyer's 468, Eichenbaum 478, Eisenberg 480, Factor 491, Fansler 494, Femino 501, Fishback 513, Five 516, Flora 521, Follis 525, French 536, G.T.R. 544, Garen 555, Gershman 566, Gershman 567, Gifford 574, Glickman 582, Gold 589, Goldwyn 600, Goodman 605, Grand 611, Green 614, Greenberg 617, Greer 618, Gross 621, Haas 633, Haas 634, Hazan 660, Hedco 663, Hoag 677, Horn 686, HRH 688, Irvine 699, It 704, Jackson 706, **Jacobs 707**, Johnson 723, **Kayne 749**, Kids 757, King 760, Kissick 763, Klein 765, **KLM 767**, Kvamme 781, Lanni 789, Lantz 790, Leatherby 796, Lester 807, Lipinsky 816, Littlefield 820, Livingston 822, Long 825, Lytel 836, **M & T 837**, Marcus 852, Marcus 853, **Marshall 858**, McAlister 864, Menard 884, Milken 897, Monterey 910, Morton 918, Morton 919, Munger 926, Munzer 927, Oberndorf 950, Odell 951, Ornest 959, Ostin 964, Pardee 978, Patron 983, **Payne 985**, Peninsula 989, Pickford 1005, Price 1019, Ray 1034, **Reinhard 1037**, Ressler 1043, Rothschild 1072, Sacramento 1080, San Diego 1087, San Francisco 1088, Saw 1098, **Schlinger 1102**, Schlinger 1103, Schott 1106, Seeno 1120, Seinfeld 1124, Semel 1125, Setzer 1130, Sexton 1132, Shapell 1134, Shapiro 1138, Shea 1141, Shea 1142, Shea 1143, Shiley 1145, Sierra 1151, Simon 1156, Smith 1164, Sonora 1178, Stern 1195, Swanson 1217, Swig 1220, Swinerton 1221, Tallen 1225, Tenenbaum 1232, Thornton 1235, Tomlinson 1238, Treadwell 1243, Ueberroth 1248, Vadasz 1254, Valente 1255, Van Nuys 1261, Ventura 1264, Vons 1270, Wagner 1274, Webb 1284, Wells 1293, Westly 1297, Weyrich 1298, Winnick 1310, Wohlford 1315, Wood 1318, Wunderkinder 1322
Colorado: Bacon 1340, Boettcher 1344, Colorado 1356, El Pomar 1374, Glassman 1383, Hewit 1391, Hill 1392, Joy 1399, Kern 1402, Liniger 1411, Ludlow 1412, Mallon 1414, McCormick

1420, Schermer 1449, St. John's 1456, **Staley 1457**, Strear 1461, Summit 1463, Weckbaugh 1470, White 1472, Wolf 1475, Yampa 1477
Connecticut: Aronson 1485, Bodenwein 1497, Bossidy 1500, Bridgemill 1503, Chase 1509, Community 1515, Connecticut 1518, Culpeper 1521, Dalio 1522, Dartley 1524, Davis 1525, Ensworth 1535, **Ettinger 1536**, Flinn 1543, Foster 1546, Grossman 1560, Heyman 1567, **Huisking 1570**, Kitchings 1574, Kohn 1575, **Kossak 1576**, Lavietes 1581, Long 1590, Mandell 1595, Mandeville 1596, Martin 1598, Meriden 1603, **Orchard 1619**, Palmer 1621, Prusoff 1631, Robbins 1634, Roberts 1635, Rose 1637, **Tombros 1659**, Tully 1665, TWS 1666, Woodward 1678
Delaware: Bartsch 1688, Berkley 1691, Cawley 1696, Crystal 1702, Delany 1705, Delaware 1706, Marmot 1728, Mastronardi 1729, Phillips 1739, **Raskob 1741**, Roby 1746, Rowland 1749, Schiff 1750, **Schwartz 1751**
District of Columbia: Beech 1771, Bender 1772, Bernstein 1775, Brody 1777, **CityBridge 1783**, Community 1785, Dweck 1790, Friedman 1799, **Goldberg 1802**, Lehrman 1821, **Public 1844**, Reich 1845
Florida: A Friends' 1866, Abraham 1867, Adler 1871, **Anderson 1876**, Banbury 1889, Bank 1890, Bastien 1892, Baxter 1895, Bay 1896, Bellamy 1902, **Berg 1903**, Better 1905, Blum 1912, Bond 1913, Capital 1924, Caspersen 1927, **Chatlos 1932**, Community 1939, Community 1946, Conese 1950, Dade 1957, Davis 1961, DeHaan 1966, Dickins 1972, DuBow 1977, Dunspaugh 1981, Ferraro 1998, **Fiterman 2000**, Five 2001, **Foundation 2008**, Garfinkle 2017, Garner 2018, Goldstein 2027, Gorin 2032, Hersh 2058, Hunter 2069, **Isenberg 2070**, Jelks 2076, Katz 2081, Keating 2084, Kennedy 2088, Kennedy 2089, Kesler 2090, Lattner 2104, Levin 2110, **Levine 2111**, Maroone 2129, Merrill 2136, Muchadin 2138, Morrison 2146, Nessel 2152, O'Keeffe 2154, Overstreet 2159, P & M 2160, Palm Beach 2161, Peacock 2165, Poe 2173, **Pope 2174**, Potamkin 2176, Rales 2184, **Rehm 2192**, Reis 2193, Riverside 2200, Rooms 2204, Rosenberg 2206, Rubin 2211, Sansing 2217, Saunders 2219, Scarpa 2221, Schaefer 2222, Sherman 2233, Spurlino 2242, Stevens 2251, United 2276, Victory 2280, Weintraub 2292, Williams 2299, Winter 2303, Wolfson 2304
Georgia: Adams 2309, Amos 2315, Amos 2316, Anncox 2318, Bradley 2326, Brill 2329, Callaway 2336, Callaway 2337, Camp 2340, Chatham 2346, Chatham 2347, Coca 2350, Exposition 2380, Franklin 2389, **Gage 2392**, Gaines 2393, Georgia 2394, Gordy 2402, Harrison 2410, Hertz 2412, Horowitz 2415, Imlay 2417, Irving 2419, Lanier 2430, Lanier 2431, Lee 2432, Lewis 2434, Looney 2436, Lubo 2438, Ma-Ran 2439, MARTA 2443, Pechter 2461, Poe 2465, Pope 2467, Rich 2472, Rosenberg 2476, Savannah 2480, Selig 2484, Terwilliger 2498, **Thoresen 2499**, Tull 2500, Wardlaw 2507, WestPoint 2513, Williams 2515, Williams 2516, Wilson 2519, Woodruff 2521, Woodruff 2522, Zeist 2529
Hawaii: Anthony 2531, Atherton 2532, Ching 2540, Cooke 2541, HMSA 2547, McInerny 2551, Wilcox 2559, Wong 2560, Zimmerman 2561
Illinois: Acorn 2583, Adreani 2585, Allegretti 2586, **Amsted 2593**, Andrew 2596, Bauer 2610, Bell 2614, Bere 2616, Berner 2617, Borwell 2627, Brach 2629, Braeside 2631, Bruning 2635, **Brunswick 2636**, Buchanan 2637, **Buntrock 2643**, Canning 2650, **Carylon 2652**, Chaddick 2655, Chapman 2656, Circle 2666, Code 2671, Cole 2672, Community 2677, Community 2680, Cooper 2683, Corboy 2684, Cornell 2685, Cressey 2689, Cuneo 2692, Day 2698, Dowdle 2709, Edwardson 2715, Ellis 2718, Emerson 2719, Funk 2741, Galter 2745, Galvin 2746, Geraldi 2752, GKN 2758, Goldberg 2761, Goldschmidt 2764, **Goodman 2765**, H.B.B. 2777, Harris 2788, Hendrickson 2796, Hermann 2798, Huntington

2809, **Irwin 2814**, **JMR 2818**, Kaplan 2824, Kemper 2831, Kersten 2838, Knapp 2841, Kolschowsky 2843, Lederer 2851, Lee 2853, Leibowitz 2854, Levy 2856, Lurie 2865, Madigan 2869, Mazza 2877, Meyer 2896, Miller 2898, Neisser 2910, **Niamogue 2914**, Oberweiler 2923, Polk 2946, Pritzker 2950, Retirement 2964, Rubschlager 2975, Russell 2976, Schield 2985, Segal 2995, Shapiro 3001, Sharpe 3002, **Shaw 3003**, Shirk 3007, Simmons 3008, Siragusa 3009, Sirius 3010, Stone 3025, Susman 3030, Takiff 3032, Trustmark 3039, Tully 3040, Ward 3056, Wenske 3063, Willett 3073, Worley 3086
Indiana: Ball 3103, Central 3116, Community 3125, Community 3127, Community 3128, English 3146, Glick 3155, Griffith 3158, Heritage 3166, Holiday 3168, Hux 3170, McMillen 3203, Northern 3215, Noyes 3216, Oakley 3217, Saemann 3232, Valiant 3248, Watanabe 3251, Wayne 3253, White 3257
Iowa: Bechtel 3264, Kinney 3300, Knapp 3301, Maytag 3310, McCarthy 3311, Mid 3316, **New 3319**, Siouxland 3332
Kansas: Capitol 3350, Deramus 3355, DeVore 3357, Hutchinson 3368, Morgan 3377, **Muchnic 3379**, Rhoden 3383, Scroggins 3389, SYZYGY 3398, V & H 3402, Wiedemann 3405
Kentucky: Blue 3407, E.ON 3417, Gheens 3421, Novak 3442, Rosenthal 3450
Louisiana: Baton Rouge 3462, Booth 3464, Community 3469, Diboll 3473, Helis 3486, Lupin 3498, New Orleans 3503, Wheless 3514
Maine: Alfond 3521, King 3545, Lunder 3547, Maine 3548
Maryland: Bank 3569, Blades 3574, Blum 3577, **Brown 3579**, Chaney 3587, Davis 3607, Decesaris 3611, Eliasberg 3620, Goldsmith 3637, Greenberg 3639, Hahn 3643, Jonan 3658, Legg 3672, Lockheed 3682, Meyerhoff 3691, Osprey 3703, Provident 3712, Rathmann 3715, Rollins 3718, Rothschild 3723, Samuelson 3725, Small 3734
Massachusetts: ASD 3781, Baldwin 3789, Bay 3794, Bayrd 3795, Berenson 3799, Birmingham 3807, Boston 3812, Bradley 3814, Bressler 3815, **Bromley 3817**, Cambridge 3828, Campbell 3830, Carney 3837, Casty 3839, Chafetz 3842, Community 3855, Connolly 3857, Copeland 3859, Corkin 3861, Crane 3866, Donahue 3881, Egan 3890, Ellsworth 3892, Evans 3898, Finnegan 3908, Fireman 3910, Foster 3914, Fraser 3917, Goldberg 3927, Grimshaw 3934, Hanover 3941, **Hershey 3949**, High 3950, Hoche 3954, Knight 3987, Ladd 3992, Lamm 3994, Landsman 3996, Leclerc 4000, McEvoy 4032, **Middlecott 4037**, **OneBeacon 4060**, Oristaglio 4063, Pappas 4066, Pappas 4067, Plymouth 4085, Radley 4092, Ribakoff 4102, Roddy 4108, Rubin 4117, Sailors' 4123, Sawyer 4128, Shapiro 4135, Sherman 4141, Shipley 4143, Siff 4145, Silverman 4146, Solomont 4152, Stare 4157, **Stern 4162**, Stevens 4163, Stevens 4164, Stoddard 4165, Worcester 4209
Michigan: Ann Arbor 4221, Battle Creek 4228, Blumenstein 4234, Brown 4240, Cold 4250, Community 4252, Community 4253, Community 4254, Cook 4261, Cracchiolo 4263, Cracchiolo 4264, Dart 4267, Ford 4303, Four 4310, Frankel 4312, Fremont 4315, **Gerber 4321**, Gerstacker 4322, Grand Rapids 4326, Hampson 4336, Keeler 4355, **Kellogg 4357**, LaMothe 4370, Lansing 4372, Lenawee 4376, Levy 4378, Maas 4379, Manat 4381, Manoogian 4382, Mardigian 4386, McGregor 4389, Nickless 4403, Prince 4416, Ratner 4417, Rogers 4423, **Secchia 4431**, Seligman 4433, Strosacker 4450, Tamer 4453, Thompson 4457, Turner 4464, Westerman 4478, Wolff 4486
Minnesota: Amundson 4500, Aslan 4507, Barry 4511, Brandenborg 4522, Bremer 4523, Christianson 4539, Dennis 4550, Federated 4563, Gardner 4568, Generations 4571, George 4572, Grundhofer 4580, Hardenbergh 4583, Hormel 4588, Marbrook 4612, Nicholson 4634, O'Neil 4638, Pacific 4646, Pax 4648, Phillips 4655,

Prospect 4659, Saint Paul 4671, Sanger 4672, Schmidt 4673, Shiebler 4680, Tankenoff 4696, Wedum 4719, WEM 4722
Mississippi: Community 4737, Graeber 4744, Irby 4750, McCarty 4754
Missouri: Barrows 4781, Boswell 4786, Brauer 4787, Buder 4791, Dula 4806, Edison 4808, Express 4811, Green 4822, Jewish 4837, Kemper 4848, Lopata 4859, Pearl 4879, Reynolds 4892, Rosewood 4894, Sosland 4908
Nebraska: Abbott 4942, Baer 4944, GFH 4966, Hawks 4971, James 4980, **McDonald 4989**, Omaha 4994, Wiebe 5017
Nevada: Bennett 5021, Fairweather 5032, Fertitta 5033, Mathewson 5045, May 5046, Nevada 5047, Redfield 5055, Rufty 5059, Smith 5065, **Walsh 5075**, Wiegand 5077
New Hampshire: Bean 5080, Gale 5091, Levine 5094, New Hampshire 5098
New Jersey: Atkinson 5119, Benjamin 5127, Berger 5128, Berrie 5130, Bildner 5133, Borden 5138, Brody 5144, Cohen 5166, Cooperman 5168, Cowles 5170, D & K 5174, Entin 5189, Gershman 5206, Grassmann 5213, Gund 5218, Healey 5227, Healthcare 5228, Hyde 5247, Indian 5250, **International 5252**, Isermann 5253, Jockey 5260, **Johnson 5265**, Kaplen 5268, Kauffmann 5272, **Kontos 5286**, Kreitchman 5289, Large 5295, Lazarus 5299, Lebensfeld 5301, Levin 5304, Levitt 5305, Link 5307, Lipper 5308, Lissak 5309, Machuga 5311, Mack 5314, Mazer 5321, McCutchen 5322, MCJ 5324, Mushett 5334, New Jersey 5336, Poses 5354, Price 5356, Providence 5358, Riskin 5369, Rose 5373, Ross 5376, Rummel 5379, Sandy 5383, Seiden 5396, Taub 5425, Tuchman 5429, Twin 5432, Visceglia 5441, Wallerstein 5446, Wilf 5456, **YPI 5461**
New Mexico: Carlsbad 5469, Frost 5476, McCune 5488, New Mexico 5491, Phillips 5492, Santa Fe 5496
New York: Acorn 5515, Alpert 5541, Altman 5543, **Altria 5545**, Altus 5547, American 5552, Antun 5559, Antz 5560, Apfelbaum 5561, **Archbold 5563**, Arkell 5565, Aron 5569, Atticus 5576, Azrak 5585, Babbitt 5586, Bachmann 5587, **Baker 5593**, Baldwin 5595, Beaverkill 5610, Belfer 5616, Benenson 5619, **Benenson 5620**, Berkowitz 5622, Berry 5626, Blankfein 5637, Bluhdorn 5642, Bobst 5646, Boxer 5656, Braufman 5660, Brodsky 5667, Brodsky 5669, Brown 5676, Brownington 5677, **Brunie 5679**, Campbell 5700, Canary 5702, Cappelli 5703, Carwill 5711, Cayne 5717, Centennial 5722, Chanin 5730, Chasanoff 5735, Chernow 5744, Chiara 5748, **China 5750**, Cohen 5768, Cohenca 5773, Cole 5774, Colin 5776, Cooper 5788, Corrigan 5796, Cox 5803, Croll 5810, **Cummings 5814**, D'Agostino 5818, **Dabah 5819**, **Daedalus 5821**, Damial 5823, **Dana 5826**, Darivoff 5831, Davenport 5833, Davidson 5835, DeGeorge 5848, Dewar 5856, Diller 5863, Dobkin 5866, Downey 5881, Dreitzer 5884, Drexler 5885, Dreyfus 5887, Eberstadt 5904, **Edouard 5909**, Elishis 5921, Emwiga 5930, Epstein 5934, Erpf 5937, Fascitelli 5946, Fatta 5947, Feil 5949, Feinstein 5951, Forchheimer 5968, Ford 5969, **Frank 5974**, Friedberg 5985, Friedman 5987, Fuld 6000, Furth 6004, Gellert 6012, Gerhard 6015, Gifford 6027, **Gilbert 6028**, **Gilman 6033**, Gleberman 6040, Goldberg 6045, Goldman 6050, Goldman 6051, Goldman 6053, Goldschmidt 6058, Golub 6070, Goodman 6072, Goodman 6073, Gordon 6077, Gorter 6079, Gottlieb 6081, Gould 6085, Granoff 6089, **Grant 6090**, Grateful 6093, **Grauer 6094**, Gruss 6114, Gural 6120, Gurwin 6121, Gutman 6122, Hammerman 6139, Handler 6140, Harbor 6144, **Harriman 6146**, Harriman 6147, **Hayden 6157**, **Heineman 6165**, Hendel 6172, Herdrich 6173, Hilibrand 6184, Hochfelder 6191, Hurdus 6214, **IAC 6220**, Icahn 6222, Icahn 6224, IF 6226, IFF 6227, Israel 6240, Ivor 6242, **Jaffe 6250**, JCT 6256, Jesselson 6259, Johnson 6270, Johnson 6271, Johnson 6272, Joy 6276, Kaminer 6285, Kanas 6286, Katz 6295,

Katz 6296, Katz 6297, Kautz 6300, Kellogg 6310, Kingdon 6326, **Klingenstein 6335**, Knafel 6341, Knapp 6342, **Kohlberg 6346**, **Kopf 6348**, Kriendler 6358, Krimendahl 6359, Kurtz 6364, **Landegger 6371**, Lang 6374, Lasker 6379, Lauder 6382, Lee 6391, Leeds 6392, Leigh 6400, Leonhardt 6403, Levy 6412, Lindmor 6425, Lindner 6426, Lisabeth 6433, Litterman 6435, Litwin 6436, Loeb 6439, Loeb 6440, Lucerne 6454, **Luckow 6455**, **Mack 6469**, **Magowan 6473**, **Mailman 6478**, Malkin 6480, Mallah 6481, Mark 6488, Martin 6496, Marx 6499, McCarthy 6516, McGraw 6519, McNulty 6521, **Mead 6522**, Mercy 6534, **Merlin 6536**, Metropolitan 6543, Millstein 6553, Milstein 6555, **Monell 6566**, Moss 6589, Murphy 6597, **National 6603**, New York 6613, Newcastle 6622, Northern 6639, Novogratz 6642, O'Herron 6646, O'Shea 6651, O'Toole 6653, Oestreicher 6656, Olive 6662, Opatrny 6664, Oppenheimer 6666, Orentreich 6667, Paduano 6677, Pascucci 6696, PBO 6699, **Pearson 6701**, Peco 6703, **Peleris 6705**, **Perelman 6716**, **Pforzheimer 6721**, Pittman 6730, Plant 6731, Pollack 6734, Pollack 6735, Price 6747, Pulier 6753, Purchase 6755, Quick 6762, Raffiani 6767, **Ramapo 6769**, Renfield 6786, Resnick 6787, Rich 6795, Richmond 6800, **Richmond 6801**, Riedman 6804, Riggio 6807, Riley 6809, Robison 6821, Rose 6836, Rosen 6841, **Rosen 6843**, Rosenberg 6846, Rosenblum 6850, Rosenstiel 6852, Rosenthal 6853, Ross 6862, **Ross 6863**, Rubenstein 6870, Rumsey 6882, Ryan 6884, Saltz 6899, Sandler 6902, Sandy 6903, Sani 6904, Schenker 6916, Scheuer 6920, **Scheuer 6921**, Schieffelin 6922, Schnurmacher 6930, Schulhof 6935, Schulweis 6936, Schurgot 6937, Schwartz 6938, Schwartz 6942, Schwartz 6943, Seiler 6954, Silberstein 6979, Silverman 6982, Silverman 6983, Simon 6986, Simons 6988, Sisenwein 6993, Sitt 6996, Smith 7008, Snow 7011, SO 7015, Soros 7024, Sosnoff 7025, SPIA 7028, Stanton 7043, Starker 7047, **Starr 7048**, **Steel 7052**, Steele 7053, Stein 7056, Steinberg 7060, **Stempel 7069**, Sternberg 7075, Straus 7085, Sulzberger 7095, Summerhill 7098, Summers 7099, Sussman 7104, **Syde 7114**, Tarnopol 7123, Task 7124, **Teddy 7127**, Tianaderrah 7136, Tilles 7141, Tisch 7144, Tisch 7146, Tisch 7149, Tormondsen 7154, **Tortuga 7155**, Townsend 7159, Trump 7167, Tuft 7172, Ueltschi 7181, Ungar 7183, Unterberg 7186, Vogelstein 7201, Walker 7208, Weiler 7226, Weinberg 7229, Weinberg 7231, Weinman 7232, Wendt 7243, Werblow 7245, **YLRY 7284**, **Zenkel 7295**, Zuckerberg 7304
North Carolina: Baruch 7311, Broyhill 7328, Bryan 7330, Cemala 7337, Community 7343, Dowd 7357, Foundation 7370, Fox 7371, Greensboro 7383, Gunzenhauser-Chapin 7384, Haley 7385, Herring 7396, Hurley 7402, Janirve 7404, **Jefferson 7405**, Kulynych 7415, Legatus 7420, Mills 7429, **Nickel 7436**, North Carolina 7438, O'Herron 7441, Reynolds 7457, Smith 7478, Triangle 7496, Tzedakah 7497, Van Every 7499, Van Houten 7500, Winston-Salem 7508
North Dakota: Fargo 7514
Ohio: Akron 7526, **Alpaugh 7527**, American 7528, Barberton 7539, Bell 7544, Berkman 7545, Berlin 7546, Berry 7547, Butler 7562, Cafaro 7563, Cardinal 7566, Castellini 7568, Cleveland 7576, Columbus 7580, Community 7582, Community 7583, Community 7584, DBJ 7605, Deshe 7606, Di Geronimo 7609, Dorn 7612, Dornette 7613, Fairfield 7622, Forest 7634, Fox 7638, France 7639, Frohman 7641, Frost 7642, Green 7652, Gund 7655, Hamilton 7660, Hankins 7662, Home 7672, Hutton 7681, IHS 7683, **Knowles 7701**, Kosar 7703, Lennon 7710, Lippitt 7718, McMaster 7744, Midland 7750, Miller 7754, Moores 7759, Murch 7766, Murphy 7769, Nord 7779, O'Neill 7782, Olive 7787, Prentiss 7806, Pulley 7811, R.T. 7812, Reeves 7814, Richland 7819, Schiff 7838, Schmidlapp 7841, Seifert 7850, Sheakley 7854, Stranahan 7872, Stranahan 7873, **Timken 7880**,

Toledo 7883, Wallace 7894, Watson 7896, Weisbrod 7900, Wodecroft 7912, Wuliger 7918
Oklahoma: Bernsen 7925, Better 7926, Bovaird 7927, Chapman 7928, Gussman 7941, Inasmuch 7944, Jones 7946, Kaiser 7948, Kerr 7949, McCasland 7956, Oklahoma City 7964, Oxley 7968, Puterbaugh 7970, **Schusterman 7975**, Titus 7983, Zarrow 7991, Zarrow 7992
Oregon: Ackerman 7995, Crabby 8010, Jackson 8024, Oregon 8049, **Schmidt 8055**, Schnitzer 8056, Wessinger 8067
Pennsylvania: Aaron 8072, Ames 8080, Arcadia 8086, Berger 8101, Black 8109, Briggs 8117, Brossman 8120, Buck 8123, CMS 8147, CMS 8148, Community 8153, Dolfinger 8172, Drueding 8177, ECOG 8180, Eden 8181, Erlbaum 8189, Fleming 8206, Foundation 8208, Fourjay 8209, Garthwaite 8212, Hillman 8249, Hooper 8256, Hopwood 8257, Hulme 8260, Huston 8263, Innisfree 8267, Jaindl 8269, Jennings 8272, John 8273, Katz 8280, Klein 8291, Kline 8293, Kunkel 8297, La 8298, Levis 8309, Lotman 8314, Luzerne 8317, Magee 8320, Maguire 8321, Mandell 8322, Massey 8328, Meakem 8341, Musser 8361, Phillips 8380, Pierce 8382, Pollock 8390, Psalm 8397, PSC 8398, Rees 8401, Rockwell 8408, Rohrer 8410, Rosenberg 8412, Rosenfeld 8413, Safeguard 8418, Salvitti 8422, Sampson 8423, Schwab 8430, Scranton 8431, Smith 8443, Smith 8445, Snee 8446, Snider 8447, Snyder 8448, Sovereign 8451, Steinman 8458, Stine 8462, **Strawbridge 8465**, Strawbridge 8467, Wolf 8506, Wyomissing 8509
Rhode Island: Alperin 8516, Champlin 8524, Daniels 8530, Kimball 8542, Littlefield 8544, Rhode Island 8551, Roosa 8552, Usen 8560
South Carolina: Arkwright 8565, Barnet 8568, Central 8577, Gibbs 8590, Hipp 8592, Reams 8606, Spartanburg 8616, TSC 8618, **Youths' 8621**
South Dakota: South Dakota 8631
Tennessee: Belz 8643, Benwood 8644, Christy 8654, Clayton 8659, Community 8662, Davis 8665, Goldsmith 8682, Gordon 8683, Haslam 8687, Martin 8707, Martin 8708, Massey 8709, Melkus 8711, Potter 8720, Ragsdale 8722, Scheidt 8726, Starfish 8728, T & T 8731, Tennessee 8732, Turner 8738
Texas: Alexander 8752, Anderson 8759, Anderson 8760, **Anderson 8761**, Astin 8764, Beal 8783, Behmann 8785, Bridwell 8797, Brown 8798, Cailloux 8806, Cain 8809, Cameron 8812, **Catto 8819**, Clayton 8830, Clear 8831, Collins 8838, Communities 8839, Community 8841, Constantin 8843, Cullen 8854, Dallas 8855, Dauphin 8856, Deakins 8860, Delaney 8862, Dodge 8868, Duda 8871, Dunn 8872, Dynegy 8874, Elkins 8883, Essar 8887, Farb 8893, Feinberg 8898, Fikes 8899, Garvey 8914, Gayden 8915, GHS Foun 8917, Gill 8919, Hackett 8928, Haggar 8929, Haggar 8930, Haggar 8931, Halsell 8936, Hamill 8937, Hebert 8946, Hillcrest 8952, Hoglund 8956, Huffington 8963, Jamail 8969, Johnson 8974, Jordan 8978, Kaufman 8981, Kempner 8987, Kinder 8994, **Kleberg 8999**, **Levant 9008**, Levit 9009, Lightner 9012, **Link 9013**, Littauer 9014, Lubbock 9021, Luchsinger 9022, Lyman 9023, Mays 9035, McDermott 9043, Mechia 9050, Medallion 9051, Meyer 9057, Miller 9061, Moran 9072, Mosbacher 9077, Mott 9079, Murchison 9081, Nightingale 9091, O'Quinn 9097, Once 9101, Otter 9105, Owen 9106, Owen 9107, Paulos 9112, Prairie 9129, Proctor 9132, Rachal 9138, Richardson 9147, Rockwell 9154, San Antonio 9166, Scarborough 9171, Schutte 9173, Scott 9174, Scurlock 9175, Shelton 9182, Simmons 9187, Stewart 9213, Sturgis 9216, Swinney 9222, Tolleson 9237, Vale 9246, Vaughan 9249, Vaughn 9251, Waggoner 9256, Waggoners 9258, Ware 9264, Watson 9266, Weekley 9271, West 9274, West 9276, **Westbury 9277**, Wichita 9280, Wise 9284, Wise 9285, Wright 9294
Utah: Ashton 9303, Bastian 9306, Burton 9309, Dreamweaver 9314, Eccles 9317, Eccles 9320,

Quinney 9338, Semnani 9341, Sorenson 9343, Stewart 9345, Tanner 9347, **Wishnick 9353**
Virginia: Beazley 9376, Carter 9387, Cartledge 9388, **DeLaski 9409**, Delmar 9410, Evans 9416, Folger 9418, Foundation 9419, Franklin 9421, Funger 9426, **Glenstone 9429**, Gottwald 9431, Grandis 9432, Herndon 9437, Kellar 9449, **Malek 9465**, Meador 9473, **Modzelewski 9477**, Norfolk 9484, Ochsman 9489, Olsson 9491, Peterson 9497, Reynolds 9503, Sharp 9515, Taubman 9524, **Three 9525**, Titmus 9527, Truland 9528, Washington 9534
Washington: Anderson 9551, Cheney 9569, Connors 9572, Crystal 9576, Foster 9588, Geneva 9592, Glaser 9594, **Hemingway 9606**, Larson 9624, Lematta 9628, Lockwood 9631, McEachern 9638, Nesholm 9647, Norcliffe 9650, **PAH 9657**, Raven 9670, Sarkowsky 9676, Schultz 9679, Seattle 9680, Shemanski 9682, Tacoma 9693, True 9696, Warren 9700, Wright 9707
West Virginia: Carter 9712, McDonough 9726, Parkersburg 9730
Wisconsin: Bartlett 9753, Bleser 9760, Bryce 9769, Chapman 9771, Community 9777, Cox 9782, Dawes 9788, Delavan 9790, Frautschi 9804, Helfaer 9813, **Johnson 9825**, Kellogg 9832, Kohl 9837, Krause 9842, Kress 9844, Ladish 9847, Manpower 9858, McBeath 9864, McDonough 9865, McQueen 9866, Menasha 9869, Milwaukee 9876, Morse 9879, Peck 9895, Pettit 9897, Posner 9901, Reinhart 9909, Riordan 9911, Rolfs 9914, Schneider 9920, **Stein 9937**, Styberg 9944, Taylor 9948, Uihlein 9955, Walter 9959, WPS 9970
Wyoming: Chapman 9976, Thorson 9994, True 9996, Wyoming 10000

Health organizations, equal rights
California: vanLobenSels 1260

Health organizations, formal/general education
Alabama: Treadwell 68

Health organizations, public education
California: California 347, **Chiron 383**
Connecticut: **Aetna 1479**
Iowa: Principal 3326
Pennsylvania: Blue 8112
South Carolina: Black 8569

Health organizations, public policy
California: California 347

Health organizations, research
Arizona: Moreno 123
Illinois: **Niamogue 2914**
Massachusetts: Gardinor 3920
New Jersey: **Roberts 5370**
New York: **Friedman 5988**, Pines 6727, Schwartz 6940
Washington: McMillen 9639

Health sciences school/education
Illinois: **Astellas 2602**
Massachusetts: McEvoy 4032
New York: **Macy 6471**
Wisconsin: Split 9932

Heart & circulatory diseases
California: Barker 257, **Beckman 272**, Brandenburg 316, Fitzgerald 514, Gross 621, Heart 662, McAlister 864, Ornest 959, Treadwell 1243
Connecticut: Connecticut 1518
District of Columbia: Vradenburg 1856

Florida: Bastien 1892, Dade 1957, **Foundation 2008**, Greenburg 2034, Heartbeat 2054
Illinois: Community 2677, Siragusa 3009, Swanson 3031
Indiana: **Guidant 3159**, **Lilly 3192**
Maryland: Denit 3615
Massachusetts: Community 3855
Michigan: Citizens 4249
Minnesota: **Medtronic 4622**
Nevada: Fairweather 5032, Nevada 5047, Wiegand 5077
New Jersey: **Johnson 5263**, Kurr 5291, **Rippel 5368**
New Mexico: McCune 5488
New York: **Heineman 6165**, Kravis 6355, Palmer 6683
North Carolina: Halton 7386
Ohio: Ohio 7785
Oregon: Johnson 8027
Pennsylvania: Blue 8112, Roberts 8406, Smith 8443, Washington 8497
Texas: Benson 8788, Cain 8809, Fair 8891, Kempner 8987, Moss 9078, San Antonio 9166, Speas 9206, Sterling 9212, Wright 9294
Washington: McMillen 9639
Wisconsin: Northwestern 9884, Stuart 9943

Heart & circulatory research
Arkansas: Jones 166
California: Barker 257, **Beckman 272**, Gooding 604, Gross 621, Heart 662, McAlister 864, Treadwell 1243
Delaware: Seevak 1752
Florida: Bastien 1892, O'Keeffe 2154, Weintraub 2292
Georgia: Rich 2472
Illinois: Community 2677, Siragusa 3009
Iowa: Bechtel 3264
Massachusetts: Rodgers 4110
Michigan: Ratner 4417
Nevada: Fairweather 5032, Nevada 5047, Wiegand 5077
New Jersey: Heart 5229, **Johnson 5263**, **Rippel 5368**
New York: **Altman 5544**, **Bristol 5666**, **Bugher 5683**, Chasanoff 5735, **Heineman 6165**
North Carolina: Halton 7386
Ohio: Ohio 7785
Pennsylvania: Smith 8443
Texas: Cain 8809, Fair 8891, Kempner 8987, Moss 9078, San Antonio 9166, Speas 9206, Sterling 9212, Wright 9294
Washington: Danz 9577
Wisconsin: Coleman 9775, Northwestern 9884, Stuart 9943

Hematology
Louisiana: Brunswick 3466

Hematology research
California: Solari 1176
New York: Shapiro 6959

Hemophilia
Louisiana: Wilson 3515
Michigan: Cascade 4245

Hemophilia research
Michigan: Cascade 4245
Wisconsin: Charter 9772

Higher education
Alabama: Alfa 2, Alpha 3, **Altec 4**, Anderson 6, Anderson 7, **Bashinsky 11**, Bedsole 12, Blount 14, Brock 16, Comer 22, Community 24, Compass 28, Daniel 31, Finlay 33, Harrison 36, Hearin 37, Hess 38, Hill 39, Lowder 43, Lowder 44, Lowe 45, May 46, Mayer 47, McWane 50, Mitchell 53, Moody 54, Patterson 56, Pleiad 57, Roberts 59, Russell 60,

Strain 66, Thompson 67, Treadwell 68, Upchurch 71, **Vulcan 73**
Alaska: Atwood 81, Carr 82
Arizona: Arizona 87, Cottrell 93, Dee 94, Farrington 97, Flinn 98, Halle 103, Herberger 106, Hickey 108, **IFS 109**, Jazzbird 111, **Kieckhefer 113**, Linde 117, Lovell 119, Marley 120, Marshall 121, **Moller 122**, Morris 124, Neely 126, Noah's 127, Phelps 129, Reese 133, Robson 135, **Solheim 139**, Webb 150, Wilson 152, Wyant 154
Arkansas: Altheimer 155, Arkansas 156, Bodenhamer 158, Bradberry 159, **Frueauff 161**, Garrison 162, Jones 166, Murphy 167, Nabholz 168, Northwest 169, Rebsamen 171, Rockefeller 172, Ross 174, Smith 176, **Soderquist 177**, Sturgis 178, Taylor 179, Trinity 181, **Tyson 182**, Wal-Mart 184, Walker 185
California: **Agouron 196**, Ahmanson 198, Allequash 202, Alpert 207, American 215, **American 217**, Amerman 218, Anderson 222, **Aramont 228**, Arbus 231, Argosy 233, Arrillaga 237, Atkinson 239, Auen 242, Avery-Tsui 245, Bakar 250, Baker 251, **Baker 252**, Baker 253, Barker 257, Bartman 259, Battle 260, Bauer 261, **Beagle 266**, Beattie 267, **Beavers 268**, **Bechtel 269**, Bekins 273, Beneto 277, Bennett 279, Berger 281, Binder 291, Bireley 292, Bloomfield 295, Booth 303, Borchard 304, Borick 305, Boswell 308, Bowes 311, Boyer 313, Brandenburg 316, Bren 320, Brenner 321, Bright 322, Broccoli 326, Burch 334, Burnham 337, Burns 338, Byer 339, Cacique 342, Campbell 352, **Capital 357**, **Capote 358**, **Carnegie 359**, Carsey 361, Caruso 363, Cassin 365, **Castagnola 366**, Center 369, Chais 371, Chambers 372, Cheeryble 377, **ChevronTexaco 380**, Chrysopolae 386, CNC 390, Coates 391, Collins 396, Community 406, Condon 410, Connell 412, Connolly 413, Copley 416, Cotsen 421, **Coyne 424**, Crean 428, Crummer 432, D & DF 434, Daly 437, Danford 438, Danvera 439, Davidow 444, Davidson 445, Davies 446, **Day 447**, de Dampierre 448, DeMille 450, Deutsch 451, DeVito 452, Dhont 453, Doelger 459, Doheny 460, **Draper 465**, **Drew 467**, Drum 470, Eichenbaum 478, Eisenberg 480, Enlight 486, Esseff 488, Fairchild 492, Fein 497, Feintech 499, Feintech 500, Femino 501, Ferguson 502, Field 503, **Field 504**, First 511, Flagg 517, Flora 521, Fluor 523, Foster 528, **Four 532**, Friedman 539, Fromm 541, G.T.R. 544, Gallo 548, Garabedian 552, Garaventa 553, Garen 555, Gellert 559, GenCorp 560, Geschke 568, Gilbert 575, Gill 576, Gluck 584, Gold 589, Goldwyn 600, Goodman 605, Gould 609, Grand 611, Graziadio 613, Greenberg 617, Greer 618, Grimm 619, Grimm 620, Gross 621, **Grousbeck 623**, Grove 625, Guzik 632, Haas 634, Halperin 640, Hamilton-White 642, Hannon 645, **Harkham 649**, Harman 650, Harman 651, Harrington 652, Hazan 660, Hench 668, Hewlett 671, **Hewlett 672**, Hillblom 673, Hills 674, Hofmann 683, Horn 686, Hutto 693, Irmas 697, Irvine 698, Irwin 700, Isen 701, Ishiyama 702, **Issa 703**, Jackson 706, **Jacobs 707**, Jameson 710, Janeway 712, Jang 713, JANS 714, JG 719, JL 720, Johnson 723, Johnson 726, Jones 728, Joyard 731, Kalmanovitz 741, Kanitz 742, Katz 745, Katzenberg 746, Kaufman 747, **Keck 750**, Keck 751, Keller 752, Kellerman 753, **Kim 758**, Kingsley 761, Kissick 763, Knight 768, Koenig 770, Koret 774, Koret 775, Koshland 777, Krach 779, Krause 780, Lakiredday 784, Lamond 785, Lane 787, Lanni 789, Lantz 790, Leatherby 796, Leichtman 802, Levine 809, Linden 813, Lipman 817, Lipp 818, Littlefield 820, Long 825, Los Altos 828, Lytel 836, **M & T 837**, Magali 846, Magistro 847, Mann 849, Marcus 852, Martin 860, **Mattel 861**, Mayr 863, McAlister 864, McCoy 871, McKenna 878, Mericos 889, Meyer 893, Milken 897, Milken 898, Miller 899, Mitchell 903, Moh 906, Moore 912, Morgan 914, Morgenstern 916, Morris 917, Mosher 920, Moss 921, Mozilo 923, Muller 925, Munger 926, Munzer 927, Murphy 928, Nagel 931, Nestle 935, Nicholas 937, Norris 940, Northrop 942, **Oak 947**, Oberndorf 950, Odell 951, **Omidyar**

952, Oppenheimer 955, Oppenheimer 956, Ornest 959, Osher 961, **Osher 962**, Oshman 963, Ostin 964, Ovitz 968, Paloheimo 974, Paramitas 977, Pardee 978, Parsons 980, Parvin 981, Pauley 984, **Payne 985**, Pell 987, Pelosi 988, Peters 993, Peterson 995, Phelps 1001, Philibosian 1003, Pickford 1005, **PMI 1008**, Pralle 1014, Quattrone 1024, Radin 1025, Rady Fam 1026, Reinhold 1039, Ressler 1042, **Reveas 1045**, Riddle 1049, Rinker 1053, Rising 1055, Robertson 1059, Robinson 1060, Rogers 1063, Rosenberg 1066, **Rosengarten 1068**, Rudd 1073, Rupe 1074, Ryan 1075, Sacramento 1080, Saga 1081, San Diego 1087, San Francisco 1088, Saw 1098, **Schlinger 1102**, Schlosser 1104, Schott 1106, Schwees 1112, Seaver 1117, Semel 1125, Sence 1126, Senyei 1127, Shannon 1133, Shapell 1134, Shapell 1135, Shapell 1136, Shapiro 1137, Shasta 1139, Shayne 1140, Shea 1141, Shea 1142, Shea 1143, Shiley 1145, Shklar 1146, Silberstein 1153, Simpson 1157, Smith 1162, Smith 1163, Smittcamp 1168, Smullin 1169, Snow 1171, Soda 1173, Solano 1175, **Soref 1179**, Sprague 1183, Springcreek 1185, Stamps 1186, Stauffer 1188, Steele 1189, Stein 1190, Steinmetz 1192, Stephenson 1193, Stern 1194, Stern 1195, Stevens 1196, Stuart 1206, Sudikoff 1212, Swanson 1217, Swig 1220, Synopsys 1222, Tabasgo 1224, **Taub 1227**, Taube 1228, **Tchang 1229**, Tenenbaum 1232, **Tennity 1233**, Thornton 1235, Thornton 1236, Tomlinson 1238, Torrey 1239, **Tosa 1240**, Towbes 1241, Towne 1242, Vadasz 1254, Valente 1255, Valley 1257, Van Nuys 1262, Ventura 1264, Volentine 1268, Von der Ahe 1269, Wagner 1274, Waltmar 1277, Warren 1279, Wasserman 1281, Webb 1284, Webb 1285, Weingart 1288, Weisman 1289, **WellPoint 1292**, Wells 1293, Werner 1296, Westly 1297, Weyrich 1298, **Whalen 1299**, White 1301, Whittier 1304, Wilbur 1305, Wilson 1308, Winnick 1310, Wiskemann 1311, Witherbee 1312, Witter 1314, Wohlford 1315, Wollenberg 1317, Wrather 1321, Wynn 1324, Zimmer 1328

Colorado: Aspen 1337, **Benson 1341**, Boettcher 1344, Bowana 1348, Donnell 1368, Dornick 1369, El Pomar 1374, Green 1385, Hamilton 1387, Hill 1392, Hughes 1393, Joy 1399, KBK 1400, King 1404, Lewis 1410, Ludlow 1412, M.D.C. 1413, Mallon 1414, McCloskey 1419, McCormick 1420, McDonald 1421, **Mizel 1427**, Monfort 1428, Nagel 1431, Paul 1435, Petteys 1436, Saccomanno 1446, Schermer 1449, Schramm 1451, **Seay 1453**, Sie 1455, **Staley 1457**, Steel 1459, **StorageTek 1460**, Sturm 1462, Taylor 1464, Telluride 1465, Trueblood 1466, Weckbaugh 1470, Wolf 1475

Connecticut: Barnes 1488, Berbecker 1491, Berkley 1492, Bissell 1495, Bluebell 1496, Bridgemill 1503, Bridgeport 1504, Community 1516, Connecticut 1518, **Conway 1520**, Culpeper 1521, Daniell 1523, Davis 1525, **Deloitte 1527**, **Ettinger 1536**, Fairfield 1537, Fippinger 1540, Foster 1546, Fox 1547, Freas 1548, Gaisman 1551, **GE 1553**, Gladstein 1555, Goergen 1556, Grossman 1560, Hartwell 1565, **Heimbold 1566**, Herman 1567, Hubbell 1569, **Huisking 1570**, Jeffe 1572, Jones 1573, **Kossak 1576**, Kramer 1577, Larsen 1579, Laverack 1580, Lavietes 1581, Lee 1582, Lehrman 1584, Lender 1585, **Lingnan 1587**, LittleJohn 1588, Lynch 1591, Mahon 1593, Main 1594, Mandeville 1596, Martin 1598, Melville 1602, Meriden 1603, Mortensen 1605, Nason 1606, Niblack 1610, **Niles 1611**, Nirenberg 1613, Northeast 1614, Oaklawn 1616, Palmer 1621, Patricelli 1623, Phoenix 1627, Pitt 1628, **Praxair 1629**, Prusoff 1631, Ritter 1633, Rogow 1636, Rose 1637, Rosenthal 1638, Sage 1640, Say 1642, Seidenberg 1646, Sewall 1648, Sites 1650, **Tombros 1659**, Tow 1660, Tully 1665, United 1668, **Vasey 1670**, Vervane 1671, Vik 1672, Wallace 1674, **Wiener 1677**, **Xerox 1680**, Young 1681, Zachs 1682, ZOOM 1685

Delaware: Arguild 1687, Berkley 1691, Buckner 1695, Cawley 1696, Crestlea 1701, Crystal 1702, **CTW 1703**, Day 1704, Delany 1705, Devonwood 1707, Etnier 1711, **Fair 1713**, **Good 1715**, Gupta 1716, Hall 1718, Hamel 1719, Hirschl 1721, Kent 1723, Laffey 1725, Marmot 1728, Mastronardi 1729, **Milliken 1732**, **Neuberger 1735**, Parker 1738, Phillips 1739, Presto 1740, Repass 1742, Reynolds 1743, Robinson 1744, **Robinson 1745**, Romill 1747, Rowe 1748, Rowland 1749, Schiff 1750, **Schwartz 1751**, Seevak 1752, Singer 1753, **Stroud 1757**, Struthers 1758, Vitale F 1759, **Winky 1763**

District of Columbia: Bender 1772, Brody 1777, Cafritz 1780, **Coleman 1784**, **Coyne 1788**, Dweck 1790, Enfranchisement 1792, Gottesman 1803, Harman 1807, Henry 1808, Jones 1813, Loughran 1823, Ludwig 1826, Post 1842, Reich 1845, Washington 1859

Florida: A Friends' 1866, **Abramson 1868**, ADFAM 1870, Adler 1871, Applebaum 1878, Appleby 1879, Banbury 1889, Bank 1890, BankAtlantic 1891, Bastien 1892, Batchelor 1893, **Bauman 1894**, Baxter 1895, Bellamy 1902, **Berg 1903**, Better 1905, Blank 1909, Bond 1913, **Braman 1915**, Broad 1916, Bronfman 1917, **Bryson 1918**, Burnett 1919, Burton 1921, Capital 1924, Carse 1925, Cascone 1926, Caspersen 1927, Catlin 1929, Cejas 1930, **Chatlos 1932**, Chia 1933, Cisneros 1934, Cobb 1935, **Cobb 1936**, Colen 1938, Community 1942, Community 1946, Community 1947, Community 1948, Conese 1950, Couch 1953, **Coulter 1955**, Dahl 1959, Davis 1962, **Davis 1963**, **Davis 1964**, Deaver 1965, Dennis 1969, DiMare 1974, Ds 1976, DuBow 1977, Duckwall 1978, Dunspaugh 1981, duPont 1982, duPont 1983, Edelman 1987, Edgemer 1989, Ellis 1992, Elster 1993, Fisher 1999, **Fiterman 2000**, Florida 2003, Florman 2004, Foley 2005, Forbes 2006, Fortin 2007, **Foundation 2008**, FPL 2010, **Fricks 2013**, Friedman 2014, Gainesville 2015, Garfinkle 2017, Gerstner 2020, **Goldhammer 2026**, Gore 2031, Gorin 2032, Green 2033, Gulf 2041, Gulf 2042, Gurtler 2043, **Hardison 2048**, Harris 2050, Henriksen 2057, Hicks 2059, **Holden 2063**, Horvitz 2065, Hough 2066, **Isenberg 2070**, Jacksonville 2071, **Jaharis 2073**, Jasam 2074, **Johnson 2077**, **Kaplan 2078**, Katcher 2080, Katz 2081, Kaufman 2082, Keating 2084, Kennedy 2088, Kennedy 2089, Kesler 2090, Kirbo 2092, Kiwanis 2094, Kleist 2095, **KMD 2096**, Krauss, 2101, LeBow 2106, Lennar 2109, **Levine 2114**, **Lewis 2114**, Life's 2116, Lorberbaum 2118, Lynn 2120, Madigan 2123, Magruder 2125, Maren 2128, Martin 2130, McCann 2132, McKeen 2133, Meyer 2137, Miller 2140, Morcom 2144, Morrison 2146, Morsani 2147, Overstreet 2159, P & M 2160, Palm Beach 2161, **Pearce 2166**, Petway 2167, **Plan 2171**, Plangere 2172, Poe 2173, **Pope 2174**, Pruitt 2179, Quick 2182, Rales 2184, **Rauenhorst 2185**, Raymund 2188, **Regan 2191**, **Rehm 2192**, Rinker 2195, Rinker 2196, River 2199, Rosen 2205, Rubin 2211, Ryder 2213, Sansing 2217, Saunders 2219, Scarpa 2221, Selby 2230, Sherman 2233, Silverman 2234, Southwest 2240, **Stafford 2247**, Star 2248, Stein 2250, Storer 2252, Straz 2254, Sudakoff 2255, Sudakoff 2256, SunTrust 2259, Taylor 2269, Thatcher 2273, Van Vleet 2277, **Vanneck 2278**, Vaughn 2279, Victory 2280, Viner 2281, **Vollmer 2282**, Wahlert 2284, Walter 2286, Ware 2287, Weiler 2290, Weintraub 2292, Wellman 2293, Wells 2294, Wilkes 2298, Williams 2299

Georgia: Adams 2309, AGL 2312, Amos 2314, Amos 2315, Anderson 2317, Arnold 2319, Atlanta 2321, Azalea 2322, BellSouth 2323, Bradley 2326, Broadfield 2330, Buisson 2333, Butler 2335, Callaway 2337, Camp 2338, Campbell 2339, Carlos 2341, Cay 2343, Chatham 2347, **Chesed 2348**, Cobb 2349, Coca 2350, **Coca-Cola 2352**, Colonial 2353, Community 2354, Community 2357, Cooper 2363, Courts 2364, Cox 2368, Daft 2370, DuBose 2374, English 2378, Equifax 2379, Exposition 2380, Fonda 2386, Franklin 2389, Fuqua 2391, **Georgia 2396**, GKW 2398, Goizueta 2400, Graves 2403, Greene 2404, Hertz 2412, Holder 2413, **Hooters 2414**, Imlay 2417, Jones 2424, **Keough 2426**, Knox 2427, Lanier 2430, Lee 2432, Love 2437, Ma-Ran 2439, Marshall 2442, McAfee 2445, Mix 2448, **Money 2450**, Moore 2452, Morgens 2453, Morris 2454, **Morris 2455**, Murphy 2456, Patterson 2460, Pechter 2461, Pitts 2463, Pittulloch 2464, Poe 2465, Poole 2466, Porter 2468, Rice 2471, Rich 2472, Robinson 2473, Rollins 2475, Rosenberg 2476, RTM 2477, Russell 2478, Selig 2484, Servant's 2485, Sheffield 2488, Smith 2491, Spray 2495, SunTrust 2496, Synovus 2497, **Thoresen 2499**, Tull 2500, University 2502, Vogel 2504, Wardlaw 2507, Watson 2509, Weber 2510, Wehadkee 2511, WestPoint 2513, Williams 2514, Williams 2517, Wilson 2519, Woodruff 2521, Woodruff 2522, Woolford 2524, Woolley 2525

Hawaii: Anthony 2531, Geist 2544, HMSA 2547, **Shaw 2554**, Strong 2555, Watumull 2558, Wong 2560

Idaho: Cunningham 2567, Golden 2568, **Micron 2571**, Morrison 2572, Nagel 2573, Simplot 2574, Staton 2576

Illinois: Adjuvant 2584, **Allen 2587**, Alsdorf 2590, **Andrew 2595**, Andrew 2596, **Aon 2598**, **ARIA 2600**, Atlas 2603, Baskes 2607, Bates 2608, BCS 2612, Beidler 2613, Bell 2614, Bere 2616, Berner 2617, Bersted 2618, Bielfeldt 2620, Blair 2621, Blum 2625, Brach 2629, **Brach 2630**, Braeside 2631, Bruning 2635, **Brunswick 2636**, Buchanan 2637, Buehler 2638, Bunning 2641, **Buntrock 2643**, **Burlington 2644**, **Burnett 2645**, Cabe 2648, Carrus 2651, Caterpillar 2653, **CH2M 2654**, Chaddick 2655, Charleston 2657, Chester 2659, Chicago 2661, Christopher 2665, Cless 2668, Clingen 2669, Coleman 2673, Combs 2674, Comer 2676, Community 2677, Community 2680, Coydog 2686, Crane 2687, **Crane 2688**, Cressey 2689, Crowe 2690, Cuneo 2692, D.H.R. 2695, Davee 2696, Deering 2700, Domanada 2705, Edwardson 2715, Eisenberg 2716, Ellis 2718, Emerson 2719, Energizer 2721, **Excelsior! 2722**, **Fairwyn 2723**, Fasseas 2726, Fites 2730, Frank 2733, Franke 2734, Frankel 2735, Freed 2736, Freehling 2737, Funk 2741, **Galashiels 2742**, Galvin 2746, Gantz 2748, Genius 2751, Geraldi 2752, Getz 2753, Gidwitz 2755, GKN 2758, Goldberg 2761, **Goodman 2765**, Grainger 2768, Gray 2771, Green 2772, Hales 2778, Hamill 2780, Hammersmith 2781, Hansen 2782, Hanus 2784, Hark 2785, **Harper 2786**, Harris 2788, Harrison 2791, Hartmarx 2794, Hendrickson 2796, Hermann 2798, Hitchcock 2801, Hobbs 2802, Huizenga 2806, Hunter 2808, Huntington 2809, I and G 2811, **Irwin 2814**, Istock 2815, Kazma 2827, Kelly 2830, Kemper 2831, Kendall 2833, Kennedy 2834, Kensington 2836, Kersten 2838, Kipper 2840, Knapp 2841, Kolschowsky 2843, Kovler 2844, Krehbiel 2845, Krueck 2846, Lavin 2849, Levi 2855, Lewis 2857, Love 2863, Lurie 2865, **MacArthur 2868**, Malott 2872, Martin 2874, Mazza 2877, McCormick 2878, McCourtney 2879, McGraw 2882, McIntosh 2883, McMullan 2884, McNally 2885, Mead 2888, Meyer 2895, Millard 2897, Miller 2898, **Monticello 2904**, **Motorola 2906**, **Mundi 2908**, Negaunee 2909, Neisser 2910, **Niamogue 2914**, **Norris 2917**, O'Connor 2921, Olin 2925, Omron 2926, Pepper 2936, Perlman 2938, Perritt 2939, Peters 2940, **Peterson 2942**, Polk 2946, **Pritzker 2952**, Pritzker 2953, Red 2959, Rhoades 2965, Rice 2966, Rothschild 2971, Rubin 2974, Sacks 2979, Sangre 2981, **Satter 2983**, Schield 2985, Schmidt 2986, Schneider 2988, Schuler 2990, Schwartz 2991, Seabury 2993, Seid 2996, SF 2998, Shapiro 3001, Sharpe 3002, Shirk 3007, Simmons 3008, Siragusa 3009, Sirius 3010, Snite 3012, Souder 3013, **State 3019**, Steans 3021, Stein 3022, Stone 3025, Sudix 3029, Susman 3030, Swanson 3031, **Tuohy 3041**, United 3044, USG 3046,

New Hampshire: Byrne 5081, Chesterfield 5082, Couch 5085, Lindsay 5095, **Penates 5099, Winthrop 5105**
New Jersey: **Allen 5111,** American 5113, **Anderson 5115,** Armour 5116, Baker 5123, Bard 5125, Berger 5128, Berlind 5129, Berrie 5130, **Bonner 5137,** Bouras 5139, Brody 5144, Cesatam 5159, Chang 5160, Charles 5161, Civitas 5163, **Clare 5164,** Cooperman 5168, Cowles 5170, Creamer 5171, Croman 5172, D'Angelo 5175, Doherty 5182, Drapkin 5185, **Frankino 5196,** Gabelli 5200, Gershman 5206, Gibson 5208, Goldberg 5209, Goldring 5210, **Goodes 5212,** Grassmann 5213, Guarini 5216, **Gulton 5217,** Halpern 5221, Hawn 5226, **Hess 5231, High 5234,** Hiller 5237, Holzer 5238, Honickman 5239, Hovnanian 5242, Howe 5243, Hugin 5245, Imada 5249, Indian 5250, Isermann 5253, **Jaqua 5256,** Jockey 5260, **Johnson 5263,** Johnson 5264, Kaplen 5268, Katz 5270, Katz 5271, KDK 5273, Kemmerer 5275, Kennedy 5276, Kerr 5278, Knowles 5283, **Kontos 5286,** Kovner 5287, **KPMG 5288,** Kreitchman 5289, Krieger 5290, Kurr 5291, Larsen 5296, **Lautenberg 5298,** Lebensfeld 5301, Levin 5304, Levitt 5305, Link 5307, Lipper 5308, Machuga 5311, **Mack 5313,** Marianthi 5318, Martini 5319, Martinson 5320, McCutchen 5322, McMullen 5325, Merck 5327, Merillat 5330, Merkin 5331, Mushett 5334, National 5335, **Newcombe 5338,** Nicolais 5339, Olsen 5342, **Parnassus 5347,** Point 5353, Poses 5354, Price 5356, Prudential 5360, **Reeves 5365, Roberts 5370,** Roth 5377, RuthMarc 5380, Sandy 5383, Schering 5387, Schreyer 5389, Sharkey 5397, Shen 5398, Shepherd 5399, Smith 5408, Steiner 5411, Straus 5413, Sudler 5416, **Syms 5422, Tang 5423,** Taub 5424, **Tavitian 5426,** Twin 5432, Union 5435, Visceglia 5441, **Vollmer 5443,** Weston 5452, Wicks 5453, **Wilf 5455,** Willits 5457, Woolley 5460, Zodiac 5465
New Mexico: **Daniels 5473,** Frost 5476, Holt 5480, Hubbard 5481, Maddox 5487, McCune 5488, New 5490, Tipton 5502, Walbridge 5503
New York: Abeles 5509, Achilles 5514, Acorn 5515, Alexander 5531, Alexander 5532, Alfiero 5534, Allwin 5538, Altus 5547, American 5552, Andersen 5558, Antz 5560, Appleman 5562, Arkell 5565, Armstrong 5567, Arrison 5570, ASDA 5571, Avanessians 5580, Avery 5581, **AXA 5584,** Bahnik 5589, Baier 5590, Baird 5591, **Baker 5593, Baker 5594,** Baldwin 5595, Balm 5596, Banfi 5597, Barker 5599, **Barnett 5601,** Barrington 5602, **Barth 5603,** Bass 5604, Bayne 5607, Belfer 5615, Belfer 5616, **Benenson 5620,** Bernhard 5624, Berry 5626, Birkelund 5632, **Bito 5634,** Blankfein 5637, Block 5638, **Blood 5639,** Bluhdorn 5642, **Bobolink 5645,** Bobst 5646, Booth 5651, **Borderline 5652,** Boxer 5656, **Branta 5659, Brice 5662,** Briger 5663, Brine 5665, **Bristol 5666,** Brodsky 5669, **Bronfman 5672, Brooks 5674,** Brown 5676, Brownington 5677, Brutsch 5680, Buchmann 5681, **Burke 5688,** Burns 5689, Butler 5691, **Bydale 5694, C.O.U.Q. 5695,** Calicchio 5698, Campbell 5700, **Carey 5704,** Carnahan 5706, **Carnegie 5707,** Carson 5709, Carvel 5710, Carwill 5711, Casey 5714, Castelnau 5715, Centennial 5722, Central 5723, Chanin 5730, Charina 5731, Charitable 5733, Chasanoff 5735, **Chatterjee 5737, Chazen 5739,** Chernow 5744, Chisholm 5752, Chisholm 5753, **Citigroup 5755,** Clinton 5763, **Cogut 5766,** Cohen 5767, Cohen 5769, Cohen 5770, Cole 5774, Coles 5775, Colin 5776, Community 5781, Community 5783, **Conway 5787,** Cooper 5788, Cordelia 5790, Cornell 5792, **Cornell 5793,** Corning 5794, Cornpauw 5795, Corrigan 5796, Coulson 5799, Cowen 5801, Cramer 5804, **Cranaleith 5805,** Crary 5806, Credit 5807, Croll 5810, Cullman 5812, Cummings 5815, D'Agostino 5818, **Dana 5826,** Darivoff 5831, Davenport 5833, Davis 5836, Debs 5844, Dewar 5856, Diamond 5857, Diker 5862, Diller 5863, Dimon 5864, Dobkin 5866, **Dodge 5867, Doherty 5868,** Dolan 5870, Donaldson 5871, Donovan 5874, Doran 5875, Double 5876,

Dow 5879, Dowling 5880, Downey 5881, Downs 5882, Drukier 5890, Dunwalke 5894, Eberstadt 5904, Edelstein 5907, **EHA 5912,** Ehrenkranz 5913, Einhorn 5915, Einhorn 5916, Elkes 5922, Ellis 5923, Emerald 5926, Emerson 5927, Emwiga 5930, **Engelhard 5932,** Erpf 5937, **Essel 5938,** Evans 5940, Everett 5941, F. & J.S. 5942, **Falconwood 5943,** Fascitelli 5946, Fatta 5947, Feil 5949, **Feinberg 5950,** Ferrari 5953, Ferriday 5954, Fife 5955, Finlay 5957, Flanzer 5963, **Forbes 5967,** Forchheimer 5968, **Ford 5970, Francqui 5973,** Frank 5975, **Frankel 5976, Freeman 5980,** Friedman 5986, Friedman 5987, Frohring 5993, Furman 6003, Furth 6004, Gant 6006, Gatto 6007, Geds 6010, **Gelb 6011,** Gellert 6012, Gerhard 6015, Gerry 6016, Gerschel 6019, Gifford 6026, **Gilbert 6028, Gilder 6030,** Gleacher 6038, Gleason 6039, Goldberg 6045, Golden 6046, Goldfrank 6048, Goldie 6049, Goldschmidt 6058, Goldsmith 6059, Goldsmith 6060, Goldstein 6063, Golkin 6068, Golub 6070, Goodfriend 6071, Goodman 6072, Gordon 6076, Gordon 6077, Gorman 6078, Gorter 6079, Gottlieb 6081, Gould 6082, Gould 6083, Grand 6086, Granoff 6089, **Grauer 6094,** Green 6095, Green 6096, **Greenberg 6097,** Greenberg 6098, Greene 6099, Greenhill 6101, Greentree 6102, Grubman 6113, Gurwin 6121, Gutmann 6123, Haas 6127, Haggin 6132, **Haje 6133,** Hajim 6134, Halis 6136, Harbor 6144, Harriman 6147, Harris 6148, **Hayden 6157, Hearst 6161, Hearst 6162,** Heckmann 6163, Heckscher 6164, **Heineman 6165,** Heller 6168, Heller 6169, Hendel 6172, Hermione 6175, Hilfiger 6183, Hilibrand 6184, Hill 6185, Hillman 6186, Hirsch 6188, **His 6189,** Hoerle 6194, Holtzmann 6198, **Homeland 6199,** Horowitz 6202, Hoyt 6203, HSBC 6204, Hugoton 6210, Hultquist 6211, Huntington 6213, Hurford 6215, **IAC 6220, IBM 6221,** Icahn 6223, Icahn 6224, IF 6226, IFF 6227, Ingrassia 6230, **Institute 6232,** International 6235, Iovino 6236, Iris 6237, Israel 6240, Ivor 6242, Jacoff 6249, **Jaffe 6250,** James 6252, Jandon 6253, JCT 6256, Jephson 6258, Jesselson 6259, JKW 6262, Joelson 6265, **Johnson 6268,** Johnson 6269, Johnson 6271, **Johnson 6273, Kade 6281,** Kadrovach 6282, Kaplan 6289, Karmazin 6293, Katz 6294, Katz 6295, Katz 6296, Katz 6297, Katzenberger 6298, **Kaufmann 6299,** Kautz 6300, Kazickas 6302, Kealy 6303, **Keefe 6305,** Kelleher 6307, Kellen 6308, Kellner 6309, Kellogg 6310, **Kelly 6312,** Kempner 6313, Kennedy 6314, KeySpan 6320, Kimmelman 6322, Kingdon 6326, **Klingenstein 6335,** Knafel 6341, Knossos 6344, **Kopf 6348,** Koppelman 6349, **Kraft 6351,** Kravis 6353, Kravis 6355, **Kreindler 6356,** Kriendler 6358, Kumble 6361, Kurtz 6364, Kurz 6365, Ladenburg 6369, Lambert 6370, **Landegger 6371,** Lane 6373, Lang 6374, Lasker 6379, Lauder 6382, Leeds 6392, Lehman 6396, Lehman 6397, Leigh 6400, Lemberg 6401, Levin 6407, **Levy 6410,** Levy 6412, Levy 6413, Levy 6414, Lewis 6415, **Li 6418,** Lieb 6420, **Liebmann 6421,** Linden 6424, Lindmor 6425, Lindsay 6427, Link 6429, Lipmanson 6431, Lipp 6432, Lisabeth 6433, Littauer 6434, Liu 6437, Loeb 6439, Loewe 6441, Loewenberg 6442, Loews 6443, **Loewy 6444,** Lostand 6448, **Luce 6453,** Lui 6457, **Lurcy 6458,** Lynch 6462, Lynton 6463, M.U.S. 6467, **Magowan 6473,** Mai 6476, **Mailman 6478,** Marcus 6486, Marks 6490, Mars 6494, Martin 6496, Marx 6497, MAT 6503, **Matthews 6507, MBIA 6512,** McCann 6514, McCarthy 6516, McClelland 6517, McGonagle 6518, McGraw 6520, Megrue 6524, **Mellon 6525,** Melly 6526, **Menschel 6531,** Mercy 6534, **Meriwether 6535, Merlin 6536,** Mesdag 6539, **MetLife 6542,** Metropolitan 6543, Meyer 6546, Millard 6548, Miller 6550, **Milliken 6552,** Milstein 6555, Milstein 6556, Mitsui 6561, Model 6565, **Monterey 6568,** Moody's 6569, Moore 6572, Mordecai 6575, Morgan 6576, **Morgan 6577,** Morris 6578, Morris 6579, Morris 6580, Morse 6582, Morse 6583, Morse 6584, Morton 6585, Moses 6587, Mosse 6590, Mostyn 6591,

MRM 6592, Murphy 6597, Nagle 6599, Neidich 6606, Neiman 6607, Neuberger 6611, New York 6620, **Newhouse 6623,** Newman 6624, Newman 6625, Newman 6626, Nicholas 6627, Nichols 6628, Northern 6638, O'Connor 6645, O'Herron 6646, O'Malley 6647, O'Neil 6649, O'Neill 6650, O'Toole 6653, Oestreicher 6656, Ohrstrom 6659, Oishei 6660, **Olayan 6661,** Olive 6662, Orvis 6668, Osborn 6669, Paduano 6677, Palisano 6680, **Palmer 6682,** Palmer 6683, Park 6688, Parr 6692, Parshelsky 6693, Pascucci 6696, Paul 6697, PBO 6699, **Peierls 6705,** Pels 6706, Penick 6709, **Penzance 6712, Pepsi 6713,** Perkin 6717, Persepolis 6718, **Pforzheimer 6721,** Phaedrus 6722, Phelan 6723, Pines 6727, **Pioneer 6729,** Plant 6731, PLM 6732, Polisseni 6733, Polsky 6738, Pope 6740, Price 6746, Propp 6749, PTM 6752, Pulier 6753, Pumpkin 6754, Quadrangle 6758, Quarry 6759, Queensgate 6760, Quick 6762, R & TP 6764, Raiff 6768, **Ramapo 6769,** Rattner 6773, Reader's 6777, Rechler 6781, Reed 6782, **Reed 6783,** Renfield 6786, Reuss 6788, Revson 6789, Rhodes 6792, Rice 6793, Rich 6795, Richardson 6796, **Richmond 6801,** Rifkind 6806, Riggio 6807, Riley 6809, Ripple 6811, **Ripplewood 6812, Ritter 6814,** Riversville 6815, RJM 6816, **Robinson 6819,** Roche 6822, Rodgers 6828, Rose 6833, Rose 6835, Rose 6836, Rose 6837, Rose 6838, Rose 6839, **Rosen 6843,** Rosenkranz 6851, Rosenstiel 6852, Rosenthal 6854, Rosenwald 6856, Rosh 6858, Rosner 6860, Ross 6862, Ross 6864, Roxe 6867, Ruben 6868, Ruben 6869, **Rubin 6872, Rubin 6874,** Rubinstein 6876, Rudin 6879, Ruffin 6880, Rumsey 6882, Sacerdote 6887, Sackler 6892, Saligman 6895, Salomon 6898, Saltz 6899, Sandy 6903, Sani 6904, **Sapp 6906,** Schaffer 6911, Schapiro 6912, Scheuer 6919, Scheuer 6920, **Schlumberger 6926,** Schmitt 6928, Schott 6934, Schulweis 6936, Schwartz 6938, Schwartz 6939, Schwartz 6941, Schwartz 6942, Schwartz 6943, Schwartz 6944, Schwartz 6945, Schwartz 6946, Sculco 6949, Seaver 6952, Seevers 6953, Sharp 6961, Shiva 6966, Siebens 6974, Siegel 6976, **Silfen 6980,** Silverman 6982, **Sloan 7003,** Smith 7006, Smith 7007, Smith 7008, Smith 7009, **Smithers 7010,** Snow 7011, Snyder 7013, SO 7015, **Solomon 7017,** Solow 7019, Sosnoff 7025, Speyer 7027, SPIA 7028, Spitzer 7034, Sprague 7035, Stanton 7043, Stanton 7045, **Starr 7048,** Stecher 7051, **Steel 7052,** Stein 7056, **Steinbach 7059,** Steinberg 7060, Steinberg 7061, **Steinhardt 7064, Stempel 7069,** Stern 7070, Stern 7073, Steyer 7082, **Stony 7082,** Straus 7084, Straus 7085, Studley 7091, Sullivan 7094, Sulzberger 7095, **Summerfield 7097,** Summerhill 7098, Summers 7099, Summit 7100, **Sussman 7105, SVM 7110,** Swartz 7111, Swartz 7112, **Sykes 7115, Tai 7118, Tanaka 7120, Tang 7122,** Tarnopol 7123, Task 7124, **Teagle 7126,** Textor 7131, Three 7135, Tilles 7141, Tisch 7144, Tisch 7145, Tisch 7146, Tisch 7147, Tisch 7149, Tishman 7150, Tomorrow 7153, Tormondsen 7154, Townsend 7159, **Toyota 7160,** Unterberg 7186, Ushkow 7188, Vance 7193, Varadhan 7194, Vernon 7195, Vilcek 7199, Vogelstein 7201, **Volpert 7202,** von der Heyden 7203, Wachenheim 7204, Wachtell 7205, Wagner 7206, Walbridge 7207, Wallach 7210, **Walter 7211,** Walters 7213, **Warburg 7214,** Warren 7217, Wasserman 7218, **Watson 7220,** Watts 7221, **Weinberg 7228,** Weinberg 7230, Weinberg 7231, Weinman 7232, **Weinstein 7233,** Weir 7234, Weiss 7236, Weissman 7238, Wellde 7239, Wellin 7240, Wender 7241, Wendt 7243, Werblow 7245, West 7246, White 7251, Whitehead 7252, **Whiting 7253,** Widgeon 7255, Wiegers 7256, **Wigmore 7258, Wilson 7263,** Winkelried 7265, Winston 7267, Witmer 7268, Woodheath 7274, Woodland 7275, Wright 7280, Yellow 7282, Young 7285, Young 7286, Zankel 7289, **Zenkel 7295, Zilkha 7300, Zimmermann 7301,** Zitrin 7302, Zucker 7303

North Carolina: Adams 7305, Anonymous 7306, Armfield 7307, Bailey 7309, Belk 7315, Biddle 7317, Blumenthal 7320, Bolick 7321, Brody 7325, Brown 7326, Brown 7327, Broyhill 7328, Bryan 7329, Bryan 7330, Cannon 7335, Cemala 7337, Coffey 7339, Comlouquoy 7341, Community 7344, Crutchfield 7348, Cumberland 7349, Daveler 7351, Dickson 7355, Dover 7356, Dowd 7357, Drue 7358, Duke 7359, Duke 7360, Easley 7361, Ebert 7362, Finley 7367, Flow 7368, George 7372, Giles 7374, Glenn 7376, Goodnight 7377, Goodrich 7378, Gunzenhauser-Chapin 7384, Haley 7385, Haney 7389, Harris 7390, Hartquist 7391, Harvest 7392, Harvey 7393, Herring 7396, Hillsdale 7398, Holding 7399, Hurley 7402, Janirve 7404, **Jefferson 7405**, Jolley 7407, Jones 7408, Kenan 7411, Kenan 7412, KPB 7414, Ladane 7417, Lance 7418, Legatus 7420, McLean 7425, McMichael 7426, Morehead 7430, Morgan 7431, **Morris 7432**, **Nickel 7436**, Norcross 7437, North Carolina 7438, O'Herron 7441, Palin 7443, Progress 7453, Ragan 7455, Reynolds 7459, Reynolds 7460, **Richardson 7462**, Rumbaugh 7468, Ryan 7469, Sloan 7475, Smith 7476, Smith 7478, Smith 7479, SOL 7480, Spangler 7482, Stonecutter 7486, Stowe 7487, **Sunshine 7490**, SunTrust 7491, Symmes 7492, Tannenbaum 7493, Triangle 7496, V.F. 7498, Van Every 7499, Weaver 7504, Winston 7507, Woodson 7509, Woodward 7510, Yeargan 7511, Young 7512
North Dakota: Huncke 7515, Leach 7516, MDU 7517, North Dakota 7519, Stern 7521
Ohio: AK 7525, Anderson 7529, Andrews 7530, Bachman 7538, Bates 7540, Beaverson 7541, Beerman 7543, Berkman 7545, Berry 7547, Bicknell 7548, Brennan 7554, Britton 7556, Bruening 7558, Bryan 7559, Buenger 7560, Cafaro 7563, Callahan 7564, Castellini 7568, Charities 7569, Cleveland 7576, Codrington 7578, Coleman 7579, Community 7586, **Convergys 7587**, **Cooper 7589**, Coshocton 7593, **Cox 7596**, Creech 7597, CRN 7598, Dana 7599, Dater 7600, Davidson 7602, DBJ 7605, Di Geronimo 7609, Diebold 7611, Dorn 7612, **Durell 7616**, **Eaton 7617**, Edwards 7618, Emery 7619, Fifth 7626, Firman 7628, Forest 7634, Foundation 7636, France 7639, **Freygang 7640**, Frohman 7641, Frost 7642, GAR 7643, Gerlach 7648, Gingher 7650, Gund 7655, Gund 7657, Haile 7659, Hamlin 7661, Hauck 7666, Home 7672, Hoover 7675, Horvitz 7678, Humphrey 7679, Huntington 7680, Hutton 7681, Ingalls 7684, Jackson 7685, Jobst 7691, Joshi 7693, Jubilee 7694, **Kettering 7698**, Kettering 7699, **Knowles 7701**, Kramer 7704, Kulas 7706, LaValley 7708, Lennon 7710, **Lerner 7711**, Lewis 7713, Lindner 7716, LKC 7720, Lubrizol 7725, M/ I 7729, Mandel 7732, Marcum 7734, Mather 7736, McBride 7740, McMaster 7744, Mellen 7747, Middletown 7749, Milacron 7751, Miller 7752, Miller 7754, Mindala 7755, Miniger 7756, Mixon 7757, Moores 7759, Morgan 7760, Morgan 7761, Morley 7763, Motorists 7765, Murch 7766, Murphy 7769, Nationwide 7771, NCR 7773, Nord 7779, Nord 7780, Nordson 7781, O'Neill 7782, Ohio 7785, Olive 7787, Park 7795, Parker 7796, Payne 7798, Peninsula 7799, **Perkins 7800**, Peters 7801, Peterson 7802, **PLACE 7805**, **Procter 7807**, Pulley 7811, R.T. 7812, Reinberger 7815, Resch 7816, Richland 7819, Rieveschl 7820, Ritchie 7821, Ritter 7822, Robbins 7823, Sage 7829, Schiff 7836, Schiff 7837, Schiff 7838, Schmidlapp 7840, Scotford 7846, Seifert 7850, Shaw 7853, Sherwin 7855, Silk 7857, Sky 7859, Smucker 7864, Stark 7867, Stillson 7869, Stranahan 7872, Summer 7874, **Timken 7880**, Tippit 7881, **Tomkins 7884**, Turben 7888, Turner 7889, Van Wert 7891, **Vesper 7892**, **Warrington 7895**, **Weatherhead 7899**, Wellman 7901, Wendy's 7902, Western 7903, Wildermuth 7906, Williams 7907, Williamson 7908, Wilson 7910, Wodecroft 7912, Wolfe 7915
Oklahoma: **8:32 7922**, Barnett 7924, Chapman 7928, Collins 7929, Collins 7930, **Ethics 7935**, Gaylord

7937, Gussman 7941, Helmerich 7942, Kaiser 7947, Kerr 7950, Mabee 7954, McCasland 7956, McMahon 7959, Meinders 7960, Meinig 7961, Merrick 7962, Noble 7963, Oklahoma 7965, Oklahoman 7966, ONEOK 7967, Oxley 7968, Puterbaugh 7970, Rapp 7971, **Schusterman 7975**, Stevens 7980, Warren 7986, Zarrow 7992, Zink 7994
Oregon: Ackerman 7995, Autzen 7997, Bair 7998, Bauman 7999, Boyd 8000, Campbell 8002, Carpenter 8003, Chambers 8004, **Chiles 8005**, Collins 8007, Collins 8009, Fohs 8012, Frank 8016, Geary 8017, Haugland 8018, Intel 8022, J.F.R. 8023, Jeld 8025, Johnson 8027, Jubitz 8028, Jubitz 8029, Merrill 8040, Meyer 8042, Miller 8043, **Schmidt 8055**, Swindells 8062, Tektronix 8063, Tucker 8065, Wheeler 8068
Pennsylvania: Alter 8078, AMETEK 8081, Annenberg 8083, **Annenberg 8084**, **AO 8085**, Arcadia 8086, Arete 8088, Arkema 8089, **Armstrong 8090**, Ball 8093, Berger 8101, Berkman 8102, Berks 8103, Betz 8105, Bozzone 8114, Bristol 8118, Brossman 8120, Brossman 8121, Buhl 8124, Byers' 8127, Cassett 8133, Chosky 8142, CIGNA 8143, CMS 8147, CMS 8148, Cochran 8149, Connelly 8157, Cooper 8158, Davenport 8164, Deaver 8165, Dietrich 8170, Dietrich 8171, Dolfinger 8172, Donnelly 8176, Eberly 8179, Eden 8182, Eustace 8191, Fair 8192, Farber 8194, Farber 8195, **Federation 8197**, Ferree 8199, Field 8200, Fine 8201, First 8202, **Firstfruits 8203**, Fisher 8205, **Forney 8207**, Fourjay 8209, Fox 8210, **Frick 8211**, Giant 8214, Gibson 8215, Giop 8216, Graham 8222, Groff 8226, Grumbacher 8227, Grundy 8228, Hamilton 8233, Hansen 8235, Harsco 8236, Hassel 8237, Hayne 8239, Heinz 8240, Heinz 8244, **Henkels 8245**, Hill 8248, Hillman 8249, Hillman 8250, Hillman 8252, Hirtzel 8253, Hodge 8254, Hopwood 8257, Hoverter 8258, Hoyt 8259, Hunt 8261, IKON 8265, Janssen 8271, John 8273, **Johnson 8274**, Kardon 8279, Katz 8280, Kavanagh 8282, Kelly 8283, **Kennametal 8284**, Keystone 8285, Keystone 8286, Kim 8287, Kline 8292, **Knox 8294**, Korman 8296, Kunkel 8297, Lamb 8299, Levee 8308, Lilliput 8311, Lutron 8316, Mandell 8322, Maple 8323, Maplewood 8324, Maronda 8325, Massey 8328, McCune 8331, McCune 8332, McGinnis 8335, McKaig 8336, McKenna 8337, **McKenna 8338**, Meakem 8341, **Merck 8349**, Miller 8353, Miller 8354, Miller 8355, Musser 8361, Neubauer 8363, Ortenzio 8366, Palumbo 8368, Parmer 8369, Peirce 8370, Perelman 8374, Perkin 8375, Peterson 8376, Philadelphia 8379, Phillips 8380, Pine 8385, **Podiatry 8389**, **Presser 8395**, Pryor 8396, Psalm 8397, PTS 8399, Rees 8401, Reidler 8402, Respironics 8403, Roberts 8405, Roberts 8406, Roberts 8407, Rockwell 8408, Rohrer 8410, Rosenfeld 8413, Ryan 8416, S & T 8417, **Saltsgiver 8420**, Salvitti 8422, Sampson 8423, **Scaife 8425**, Scheller 8426, Schock 8427, Schoonmaker 8429, Scranton 8431, Shapira 8437, Shenango 8438, Sherrerd 8439, Simmons 8441, Simonds 8442, Smith 8443, Smith 8445, Snyder 8448, Speyer 8453, St. Mary's 8454, Stabler 8455, Stackpole 8456, Steinman 8458, Steinman 8459, Stewart 8460, Strauss 8464, **Strawbridge 8465**, Strawbridge 8466, Strawbridge 8467, Susquehanna 8471, Taylor 8473, Tippins 8477, Toll 8478, Toll 8479, Trexler 8481, Triple 8482, Truman 8483, Turner 8484, **United 8487**, **United 8488**, Vanguard 8490, Vincent 8492, **Waldorf 8495**, Weiss 8499, West 8500, Willary 8503, Willis 8504, Wyomissing 8509
Rhode Island: Alperin 8516, **Alpert 8517**, Champlin 8524, Charlesmead 8525, Charter 8526, Citizens 8527, Cuno 8528, Daniels 8530, Fain 8533, **FM 8537**, Grinnell 8538, **Hassenfeld 8540**, Jackson 8541, Littlefield 8544, Lord 8545, Mann 8546, McAdams 8547, McCarthy 8548, Roosa 8552, Sullivan 8558, **Textron 8559**, Usen 8560, Washington 8563

South Carolina: Abney 8564, Arkwright 8565, Arnold 8566, Barnet 8568, Campbell 8573, Campbell 8574, Cato 8576, Ceres 8578, Collins 8582, Community 8583, Daniel 8585, First 8587, Fullerton 8589, Gibbs 8590, Glenn 8591, Hipp 8592, Hopewell 8593, Inman 8595, Kane 8596, McKissick 8599, Montgomery 8600, North 8601, Phifer 8602, Smith 8613, Sonoco 8614, South 8615, Spartanburg 8616, TSC 8618, **Wardle 8620**, **Youths' 8621**
South Dakota: Dakota 8624, Griffith 8625, Larson 8627, Opus 8628
Tennessee: 1939 8635, Atticus 8639, Basler 8641, Belz 8643, **Bridgestone 8646**, Caldwell 8649, Citizens 8657, CLARCOR 8658, Clayton 8659, Community 8660, Conwood 8663, Danner 8664, Draughon 8668, Dugas 8669, Eskind 8673, Eskind 8674, First 8677, **Garrott 8680**, Gatton 8681, Goldsmith 8682, Gordon 8683, Hamico 8684, Harris 8686, Hawthorn 8689, Ingram 8694, Jeniam 8695, Johnson 8697, Jones 8698, Massey 8709, Master's 8710, Nelson 8712, No 8713, Ragsdale 8722, Starfish 8728, Stephens 8729, Stokely 8730, Tennessee 8732, Turner 8738, Washington 8741, Wilson 8744, Wright 8745
Texas: Abell 8749, Alexander 8752, Alkek 8753, Alkek 8754, **Allbritton 8755**, **Anderson 8761**, B & B 8769, B.E.L.I.E.F. 8770, Baker 8772, Bass 8778, **Bauer 8780**, Baugh 8781, Baumberger 8782, Beasley 8784, Behmann 8785, Belo 8787, Benson 8788, Brackenridge 8793, Brown 8798, Butler 8802, **Butt 8803**, Cain 8808, Cain 8809, Callaway 8810, Cameron 8812, Campbell 8813, Caris 8814, Carter 8816, **Catto 8819**, CFP 8822, CH 8823, Chinquapin 8827, Clayton 8830, Clements 8832, Coastal 8833, Coates 8834, Cockrell 8835, Collins 8837, Collins 8838, Communities 8839, Constantin 8843, Cook 8845, **Cooper 8846**, Crain 8851, Dawley 8858, De Llano 8859, Delaney 8862, Dickson 8866, Doss 8869, Duda 8871, Durrill 8873, Dynegy 8874, Educational 8878, Edwards 8879, El Paso 8882, Elkins 8883, Ellwood 8884, Essar 8887, Estill 8888, **ExxonMobil 8889**, Fain 8890, Fair 8891, Fasken 8895, Faulconer 8896, Feinberg 8898, Fikes 8899, Finger 8900, Fish 8902, Fleming 8903, Fleming 8904, Folsom 8905, Fondren 8906, Franklin 8907, Frost 8910, Garvey 8914, Goodman 8921, Greathouse 8924, Griffin 8925, Gulf 8926, Hachar 8927, Hackett 8928, Haggar 8929, Haggar 8930, Haggar 8931, Halsell 8936, Hamill 8937, Hamman 8938, Hanley 8940, Harmon 8941, **Hartman 8942**, Healthcare 8944, Hillcrest 8952, Hirsch 8953, Hobby 8954, Hoblitzelle 8955, Holt 8958, Hudson 8962, Huffington 8963, **Hull 8964**, Humphreys 8965, Hunt 8966, Jamail 8970, Johnson 8972, Johnson 8973, Johnson 8974, Jones 8975, Jones 8976, Jonsson 8977, Justin 8979, Kahn 8980, Keith 8982, Kempner 8987, Kennedy 8988, Keown 8989, Kilroy 8991, Kinder 8994, King 8995, **Kleberg 8999**, Kodosky 9000, Koehler 9001, Lennox 9007, Levit 9009, Loose 9017, Lord 9018, Luchsinger 9022, Lyman 9023, Lyons 9024, MacDonald 9025, Marathon 9028, Martinez 9032, Mayborn 9033, Mays 9036, McCombs 9037, McCullough 9041, McDaniel 9042, McDermott 9043, McKee 9045, McMillan 9046, McNair 9047, McNutt 9048, Mechia 9050, Mendenhall 9053, **Mevatek 9056**, Meyer 9057, **MFI 9059**, Miles 9060, Mitchell 9064, Moncrief 9069, Moore 9071, Morris 9076, Mosbacher 9077, Murchison 9081, National 9088, Northen 9092, O'Connor 9095, O'Donnell 9096, O'Quinn 9097, Oehmig 9099, Oshman 9104, Owen 9106, Parks 9109, Perkins 9116, Perot 9118, Peterson 9120, Piper 9124, Powell 9128, Priddy 9130, Progress 9133, Providence 9135, Rachal 9138, Rachofsky 9139, Rapoport 9141, Reliant 9144, **RGK 9146**, Richardson 9147, Riddle 9148, Riter 9149, Roach 9150, Roberts 9151, Rogers 9155, Rosenberg 9157, Ross 9159, Rowling 9160, RSMIS 9161, San Angelo 9164, San Antonio 9166, Sanders 9167, **Scaler 9170**, Schollmaier 9172, Scurlock

9175, Sharp 9180, **Shell 9181**, Shelton 9182, Smith 9191, **Smith 9194**, Smith 9196, Smith 9198, Sparrow 9204, Sterling 9212, Strake 9215, Sumners 9218, Tartt 9224, Tate 9225, Temple 9227, Temple 9228, Terry 9231, Texas 9233, Tolleson 9237, Trull 9240, Turner 9241, Vale 9246, Valero 9247, Vaughan 9250, Vaughn 9251, Veres 9252, Waggoner 9256, Waggoner 9257, Waggoners 9258, Wal 9260, Walsh 9261, West 9274, West 9275, West 9276, Westcott 9278, White 9279, Wichita 9280, Willard 9281, Wise 9284, Wise 9285, Wright 9294, Zachry 9296

Utah: Bamberger 9305, Bastian 9306, Browning 9308, Burton 9309, Dance 9311, Dumke 9315, Dumke 9316, Eccles 9318, Eccles 9319, Eccles 9320, Hemingway 9328, McGillis 9334, Quinney 9338, Raymond 9339, Simmons 9342, Tanner 9347, Wadman 9349, Watkins 9350, **Wishnick 9353**

Vermont: Vermont 9361

Virginia: **Ames 9370**, Batten 9374, Beazley 9376, Billings 9377, Bryant 9380, Cabell 9381, Camp 9382, Campbell 9383, Carrington 9386, Cartledge 9388, Clark 9393, Columbus 9399, Delmar 9410, English 9414, Estes 9415, Flagler 9417, Folger 9418, Fralin 9420, Funger 9426, Galbraith 9427, Graves 9433, Guilford 9434, Herndon 9437, Hylton 9440, Jeffress 9442, Kanter 9445, Katzen 9446, Kellar 9449, Kogod 9452, **Lambert 9453**, LandAmerica 9454, Massey 9467, McDonnell 9468, McGlothlin 9469, **Modzelewski 9477**, Moore 9478, Morgan 9479, Norfolk 9484, **Norfolk 9485**, O'Shaughnessy 9487, Olsson 9491, Pauley 9494, Perry 9495, Portsmouth 9498, Ratner 9501, Reinhart 9502, Reynolds 9503, Rosenthal 9508, Sandler 9511, Sandler 9512, **Scripps 9514**, Sharp 9515, Smith 9518, Smithfield 9519, Snead 9520, SunTrust 9523, Truland 9528, Ukrop 9529, United 9530, Universal 9531, VuBay 9533, Weil 9535, **Winkler 9542**

Washington: Adams 9548, Anderson 9551, Aven 9554, Bas 9555, **Blakemore 9558**, Blue 9559, **Boeing 9560**, Brotman 9562, Cheney 9569, Community 9571, Connors 9572, Coulter 9573, Cowles 9574, Cowles 9575, Crystal 9576, Danz 9577, Dimmer 9579, Ellison 9585, Ferguson 9585, Foster 9588, Fuchs 9590, GLA 9593, Glazer 9596, Green 9598, Helstrom 9605, **Hemingway 9606**, Jones 9615, Kaleidoscope 9616, Lafromboise 9622, **Laird 9623**, Lauzier 9626, Lauzier 9627, Lematta 9628, Lockwood 9631, Lucky 9632, Martin 9634, McCaw 9637, Miller 9642, Murdock 9644, Murr 9645, Neukom 9649, Norcliffe 9650, North 9651, Opportunities 9655, **PAH 9657**, PEMCO 9660, Peterson 9662, Raikes 9668, Raven 9670, Sarkowsky 9676, Schuler 9678, Schultz 9679, Sequoia 9681, Shemanski 9682, Shirley 9684, Smith 9688, Snyder 9689, Tacoma 9693, Tamaki 9695, UNOVA 9697, Warren 9700, Wright 9707

West Virginia: BB&T 9710, Bowen 9711, Carter 9712, Clay 9715, Daywood 9717, Hollowell 9719, Huntington 9721, Kanawha 9723, Maier 9725, McDonough 9726, Parkersburg 9730, Prichard 9731, Schenk 9732, Shott 9733

Wisconsin: 1923 9738, Acuity 9739, Alexander 9741, Alliant 9742, Baird 9750, Banta 9752, Bartlett 9753, Bell 9756, Beloit 9757, Bishop 9759, Bleser 9760, Bolz 9762, **Bradley 9763**, Brookbank 9766, Brotz 9767, Bryce 9769, Casper 9770, Chapman 9771, Charter 9772, Clark 9773, Cleary 9774, Coleman 9775, Community 9779, Cox 9782, Davis 9787, Demmer 9791, **Eastman 9794**, Eastman 9795, Evjue 9797, Fotsch 9802, Frautschi 9804, Glover 9805, Gould 9809, Helfaer 9813, Holz 9817, Johnson 9823, Johnson 9824, Johnson 9826, Jones 9827, Kelben 9830, Kikkoman 9836, Kohl 9837, Kohler 9840, Krause 9841, Kress 9844, La Crosse 9845, Ladish 9846, Ladish 9847, **Lewis 9850**, Lubar 9851, Lynn 9853, Manpower 9858, Marshall 9860, Martin 9862, McQueen 9866, Mead 9867, **Meehan 9868**, Menasha 9869, Michels 9874, Milwaukee 9876, MMG 9877, Modine 9878, Munson 9880, Nelson 9882,

Nicholas 9883, Northwestern 9884, Oshkosh 9885, Oshkosh 9886, **Outagamie 9888**, Pamida 9891, Peck 9894, Peterson 9896, Pettit 9897, Pick 9899, Pollybill 9900, Pueliecher 9904, Purple 9905, Reinhart 9909, Rennebohm 9910, Riordan 9911, **Rockwell 9912**, Sensient 9922, Sentry 9923, Seramur 9924, Shattuck 9926, Siebert 9927, Smallwood 9928, **Smith 9929**, Split 9932, Steigleder 9936, **Stein 9937**, Stone 9940, Stuart 9941, Stuart 9942, Timken 9950, Uihlein 9953, Uihlein 9954, Wagner 9958, Walter 9959, Wehr 9961, West 9963, West 9964, Wilson 9965, Windhover 9966, Witte 9968, WPS 9970, Wrigley 9971, **Young 9972**, Zilber 9973

Wyoming: Allen 9974, Connemara 9978, Ellbogen 9981, Martin 9984, S & G 9988, Stock 9992, Tozzi 9995, True 9996, Whitney 9998

Higher education reform

California: Irvine 698
New York: Achelis 5513

Higher education, college

Alabama: Stallworth 64
Arizona: Dorrance 95, Ottens 128, University 148
California: Deutsch 451, Irvine 698, Jay 716, Kanitz 742, Leonard 804, Long 827, Pitzer 1007, Saw 1098
Connecticut: Kramer 1577, Robbins 1634
Delaware: Heuer 1720
Florida: DiMare 1974, Dyer 1984, **Goldhammer 2026**
Georgia: Beloco 2324, Cawood 2342, Endover 2377, Lanier 2429, Patrick 2459, Ramser 2469
Hawaii: Wong 2560
Idaho: Brandt 2565
Illinois: **Friedmann 2738**, **Kemper 2832**, McDaniel 2880, Thoma 3035, Wolf 3079
Indiana: Leighton 3191
Massachusetts: Cardinal 3834, Druker 3883, Karp 3974, Massachusetts 4026, McLane 4033, Walske 4196
Michigan: **Krauss 4366**
Minnesota: Alliss 4498
Missouri: Hites 4831, Pershing 4881, Pillsbury 4884
Nebraska: Buffett 4949
New Hampshire: Martin 5097, Smith 5101
New Jersey: Green 5215
New York: Alison 5535, Curry 5817, Devlin 5855, Gural 6120, King 6324, LCU 6387, Powers 6744, Pyewacket 6756, Raether 6766, Rogers 6829, Rosansky 6832, Saunders 6909, Schlobach 6924, Stanton 7044, Summit 7100
North Carolina: Gipson 7375, Hurley 7403, Richmond 7463
Ohio: LZ 7727
Pennsylvania: Glencairn 8219, Levan 8307, Murray 8360, Rorer 8411
Rhode Island: Kings 8543
South Carolina: Cassels 8575, Foothills 8588, Lipscomb 8598
Tennessee: Hendrix 8691, Tucker 8735
Utah: Stewart 9345
Virginia: Kogod 9452
Washington: Sherwood 9683, Vidalakis 9698
Wisconsin: **Lewis 9850**
Wyoming: McNeill 9986

Higher education, college (community/junior)

Alabama: McLendon 48
California: **Hatfield 656**, Hewlett 671, Kanitz 742
Colorado: Leprino 1408
Idaho: Albertson 2562
Illinois: Ullrich 3043
Maryland: Klein 3662
New York: Gerry 6016
Pennsylvania: Pollock 8390
Tennessee: Ayers 8640
Washington: **Boeing 9560**

Higher education, university

Arkansas: Whitt 188
California: **Angelica 223**, Blume 298, Centofante 370, Christopher 385, Cohen 393, Dachs 435, Hedco 663, Hoag 679, Hoehn 681, House 687, Irvine 698, **Issa 703**, **Juniata 734**, Kanitz 742, Koenig 770, Linden 813, Markkula 856, McDonough 873, Merage 887, Moley 908, Pelosi 988, Rinker 1053, Saw 1098, Sodaro 1174, **Versacare 1265**, Wolfen 1316
Colorado: Mayer 1418
Delaware: Common 1700, **CTW 1703**, Heuer 1720
District of Columbia: HRH 1811
Florida: **Coleman 1937**, Glaubinger 2023, GSB 2039, Hamilton-Forbes 2046, Jelks 2076, LeBow 2106, **Rosser 2208**, Rothman 2210, Sansom 2218, Seaman 2229, Spurlino 2242, Watts 2288
Georgia: Allred 2313, Beloco 2324, Patrick 2459, SF 2486
Idaho: Brandt 2565
Illinois: Adjuvant 2584, **Astellas 2602**, Goldschmidt 2764, Hanson 2783, Madigan 2869, McNamara 2886, Millikin 2900, **Pritzker 2951**, Pritzker 2953, Stewart 3024, Tully 3040
Indiana: Niblick 3212
Iowa: Levitt 3307
Kentucky: Fischer 3418
Louisiana: Lorio 3496
Maryland: Erickson 3624, Fisher 3630, Lerner 3675
Massachusetts: Abrams 3768, Cox 3862, Crotty 3870, DiMaura 3880, Fuller 3918, Hinduja 3952, Kahn 3973, Lee 4001, Levine 4004
Michigan: Baker 4226, Rogers 4423
Minnesota: Alliss 4498, Fischman 4564, Knowlton 4598, McGuire 4615, Peterson 4652
Missouri: Lay 4853, **Olofson 4875**, Walker 4922
Nevada: Harris 5035
New Jersey: Berlind 5129, Capita 5154, **Ceres 5158**, Geiger 5205, Healey 5227, Kemmerer 5275, Koguan 5284, Milstein 5332, Straus 5414
New Mexico: Delle 5474
New York: Atticus 5576, Behrens 5612, Berkowitz 5622, Bovin 5654, Cain 5697, **Carnegie 5707**, Case 5713, **Diamond 5858**, Dove 5877, Druckenmiller 5889, Ford 5969, Fribourg 5984, **Glades 6037**, Grandview 6088, **Grant 6090**, **Handler 6141**, Hudson 6207, **Initial 6231**, JAM 6251, LCU 6387, Lebworth 6390, Levy 6411, MAH 6474, Manning 6484, Mnuchin 6564, Penner 6710, Ranger 6770, **Reed 6783**, Rosansky 6832, Schwartz 6940, Sealark 6951, Shoreland 6968, Sobel 7016, Stanton 7044, Strypemonde 7089, Unanue 7182, **Volpert 7202**, **Weinberg 7228**, Zalaznick 7288, Zehner 7293
North Carolina: Rostan 7467, Terry 7494, Yeargan 7511
Ohio: Focus 7632, Jegs 7687, Lancaster 7707, NFG 7776, Outcalt 7792, Rockwern 7824, Stone 7871, Tetlak 8177
Oklahoma: Barnett 7924, Crawley 7934, Jones 7946
Pennsylvania: Dibona 8169, Jake 8270, Lubert 8315, M & S 8318, McKaig 8336, Pierce 8382, Roberts 8406, SVF 8472, Zisman 8513
Rhode Island: Nelson 8549
South Carolina: Lipscomb 8598, Sirrine 8612
South Dakota: Via-Bradley 8633
Tennessee: Hendrix 8691, Sparks 8727, Starfish 8728
Texas: Bickel 8790, Bosque 8792, Gale 8913, GHS Foun 8917, Gibson 8918, Miller 9062, Mithoff 9066, Mitte 9067, Sarofim 9168, Susman 9220, Wedge 9270, Wright 9293
Utah: Hall 9326, Wing 9352, Zions 9354
Virginia: Blue 9378, McGue 9470, **Nirman 9483**, Perry 9496, Sandler 9511
Washington: Bas 9555, Miller 9642, T.E.W. 9692, Vidalakis 9698
West Virginia: McQuain 9727
Wisconsin: Baker 9751, **Lewis 9850**, Merrill 9872
Wyoming: Berry 9975

Hinduism

California: Lakireddy 784, Vegesna 1263
Delaware: Gupta 1716
New York: Sani 6904

Hispanics/Latinos

Arizona: Aurora 88
California: Cacique 342, California 345, PacifiCare 971, **PMI 1008**, Stern 1195, Ventura 1264, Whitecap 1303
Connecticut: Community 1515
District of Columbia: Cafritz 1780, Fowler 1797
Florida: FPL 2010
Idaho: Simplot 2574
Illinois: **State 3019**
Indiana: Health 3164
Iowa: Siouxland 3332
Maryland: **Hughes 3654**
Massachusetts: Hyams 3961, Stevens 4163, Stevens 4164
Minnesota: Bell 4514, Bremer 4523, Minneapolis 4623, Pax 4648, Phillips 4655
New Jersey: Alcatel 5110, **KPMG 5288**, Victoria 5440
New Mexico: Santa Fe 5496
New York: **Bristol 5666**, **Macy 6471**, New York 6615
North Carolina: Reynolds 7458, Strowd 7488
Ohio: Community 7582
Oregon: Intel 8022
Texas: Sterling 9212, Trull 9240
Virginia: **Gannett 9428**

Historic preservation/historical societies

Alabama: Alpha 3, Anderson 6, Mitchell 53
Arizona: Marley 120
Arkansas: Rebsamen 171, Rockefeller 173, Union 183
California: American 215, Borina 307, Brenner 321, Chambers 372, Community 401, Community 402, Community 403, Cortopassi 419, Garland 556, **Getty 570**, Harman 651, Jackson 706, Johnson 723, Kimball 759, Klein 765, McBean 865, Paloheimo 974, Pelosi 988, Sacramento 1080, San Luis 1090, Seinfeld 1124, Teichert 1231, Windfall 1309
Colorado: Boettcher 1344, El Pomar 1374, Gates 1380, Summit 1463
Connecticut: Chilton 1511, Community 1516, Connecticut 1518, **Ettinger 1536**, **Huisking 1570**, Mortensen 1605, Royce 1639, Sewall 1648, **Sun 1656**, Tauck 1657, Thompson 1658, Vervane 1671, Worthington 1679
Delaware: Common 1700, Hall 1718, Hamel 1719, **Milliken 1732**, Romill 1747
District of Columbia: Brody 1777, **Coleman 1784**, **Coyne 1788**, HRH 1811, **Patterson 1840**
Florida: Bank 1890, Bellamy 1902, Beveridge 1907, Community 1939, Community 1944, Community 1948, Community 1949, Conese 1950, duPont 1983, Garfinkle 2017, HTR 2067, **Kislak 2093**, Ocean 2156, Paulucci 2164, **Pearce 2166**, Roberts 2201, Selby 2230, Southwest 2240
Georgia: Broadfield 2330, Callaway 2337, Charter 2345, Community 2358, Community 2359, Cooper 2363, Creel 2369, DuBose 2374, Exposition 2380, **Georgia 2397**, Imlay 2417, Livingston 2435, Moore 2452, Pope 2467, Porter 2468, Rice 2471, Sheffield 2488, Synovus 2497, Watson 2509, Williams 2514, Woodruff 2522
Hawaii: Hawaii 2545
Illinois: Alphawood 2589, **Buntrock 2643**, Chicago 2661, Community 2677, D.H.R. 2695, Dillon 2704, Donnelley 2708, Driehaus 2710, DuPage 2713, Galvin 2747, Grainger 2768, Gray 2771, Halligan 2779, Huizenga 2806, Kemper 2831, Kennedy 2834, Kipper 2840, Souder 3013, Wilson 3075, **Woodbury 3082**
Indiana: Adams 3096, Community 3122, Community 3126, Crown Point 3135, Decatur 3138, Harrison 3161, Jasper 3177, Leighton 3191, Lilly 3194, Montgomery 3206, Raker 3226, Wayne 3253

Iowa: Cedar Rapids 3275, Community 3278, Mansfield 3308, Ruan 3329, Tye 3337
Kentucky: Brown 3409, **Brown 3411**, Community 3414, Horn 3427, Rosenthal 3450
Louisiana: Azby 3460, Booth 3464, Diboll 3473, Huie 3488, Kabacoff 3492
Maine: Fore 3534
Maryland: Baker 3567, Columbia 3595, Community 3597, Community 3598, Community 3599, Darby 3605, Delaplaine 3614, France 3632, MARPAT 3684, Middendorf 3694, Pohanka 3707, Rollins 3718, Small 3734, Small 3735, Wallis 3755
Massachusetts: Acushnet 3770, Adams 3771, Bristol 3816, Community 3854, Community 3855, Fessenden 3903, Ham 3940, Johnson 3970, Jordan 3971, **Krieble 3990**, Lindsay 4009, McEvoy 4032, **Middlecott 4037**, Rubenstein 4116, Stemberg 4161, Stevens 4163, Stevens 4164, **Swensrud 4177**, Tupancy 4186, Vingo 4192, Walske 4196
Michigan: Americana 4218, Andersen 4219, Berrien 4231, Carls 4244, Community 4258, Community 4259, Cook 4262, **Dogwood 4282**, Frey 4316, Jackson 4347, Knabusch 4362, Manoogian 4382, Oleson 4405, Petoskey 4412, Thompson 4457, Whiting 4482
Minnesota: Greycoach 4575, Hersey 4584, Leuthold 4605, Marbrook 4612, Opperman 4641, Schmidt 4673, Southways 4688, Veden 4707
Mississippi: Gulf 4745
Missouri: Bernoudy 4783, Dula 4806, Green 4822, Truman 4919
Nebraska: Eihusen 4961, Hubbell 4979, Omaha 4995, Steinhart 5005, **Union 5012**
Nevada: Keyser 5039
New Hampshire: Putnam 5100
New Jersey: 1772 5106, Brotherton 5145, Cowles 5170, **Edison 5186**, Grassmann 5213, Hickory 5232, Jockey 5260, Kirby 5279, Levitt 5305, Reddy 5364, Schecter 5385, Sunfield 5418
New Mexico: Albuquerque 5466, **Lannan 5484**, McCune 5488, Stockman 5497, Taos 5498, Thaw 5499
New York: Adirondack 5517, **American 5551**, **American 5553**, Aron 5569, Auchincloss 5577, Baird 5592, Bayne 5607, Berry 5626, Brine 5665, Butler 5691, Campbell 5700, Central 5724, Charitable 5733, Corrigan 5796, Debs 5844, Everett 5941, Fatta 5947, Ferriday 5954, **Freeman 5980**, Friedberg 5985, Gerry 6016, Gerschel 6019, **Gilder 6030**, Gordon 6077, Gorman 6078, Hajim 6134, **Homeland 6199**, Hudson 6207, Kaplan 6290, Kellogg 6311, Kimmelman 6322, Kriendler 6358, **Lauder 6383**, Lebworth 6390, Leigh 6400, Lenna 6402, **LSR 6451**, Lynch 6462, Macdonald 6468, McGraw 6520, **Memton 6529**, MJPM 6563, New York 6613, Northern 6639, O'Connor 6645, Rich 6795, Roche 6822, Rochester 6823, Rockefeller 6827, Rose 6836, Rose 6839, Ross 6864, Schafer 6910, Schieffelin 6922, Schwartz 6945, Sealark 6951, Snow 7011, Stevens 7076, Tianaderrah 7136, **Trust 7168**, Unterberg 7186, Weinberg 7231, Wendt 7243, Wilson 7262
North Carolina: Anonymous 7306, Branan 7322, Coleman 7340, Foundation 7370, Graham 7382, Halton 7386, Hanes 7387, Harvest 7392, North Carolina 7438, Robertson 7466, Simpson 7472, Triangle 7496, Vanderbilt 7501, Winston 7507, Woodson 7509
North Dakota: Stern 7521
Ohio: Akron 7526, Bryan 7559, Campbell 7565, Columbus 7580, Community 7585, Dater 7600, **Dewald 7608**, Ferguson 7625, Hauck 7666, Ingalls 7684, Jackson 7685, Lehner 7709, M/B 7728, Mather 7736, Miniger 7756, Montgomery 7758, Murphy 7769, Nippert 7777, Richland 7819, Schiff 7837, Seifert 7850, Stark 7867, **Timken 7880**, Troy 7886, Van Wert 7891, Watson 7896, Williamson 7908, Youngstown 7920
Oklahoma: Bailey 7923, Communities 7931, Kirkpatrick 7952, McGee 7957
Oregon: Johnson 8027, Kinsman 8031, Merrill 8040, Meyer 8042, Wessinger 8067

Pennsylvania: 1957 8071, Allegheny 8076, Arcadia 8086, Berks 8103, Byers' 8127, Century 8137, Claneil 8144, Dietrich 8170, Dietrich 8171, First 8202, Hamilton 8233, Hooper 8256, Huston 8263, Keystone 8285, Kinsley 8290, Kline 8293, Lehigh Valley 8303, McCune 8332, McLean 8340, Meakem 8341, **Metcalf 8351**, Century 8371, **Pew 8377**, Rockwell 8408, S & T 8417, Scranton 8431, Smith 8445, Steinman 8458, Stewart 8461, Truman 8483, von Hess 8493, Warwick 8496, Waters 8498
Rhode Island: Chace 8523, Champlin 8524, Daniels 8530, Felicia 8536, Jackson 8541, Rhode Island 8551
South Carolina: Phifer 8602, Post 8603
South Dakota: Sioux Falls 8630
Tennessee: Atticus 8639, Community 8662, Haslam 8687, Ingram 8694, Thompson 8733
Texas: Bass 8777, Cain 8809, Clements 8832, Collins 8837, East 8876, Garvey 8914, George 8916, Hoblitzelle 8955, Kelleher 8984, Kempner 8987, Lennox 9007, Lubbock 9021, McCombs 9037, McDermott 9043, Meadows 9049, Northen 9092, Owen 9106, Rockwell 9154, San Antonio 9166, Smith 9191, Sterling 9212, Summerlee 9217, Tennessee 9230, Ward 9263, Wichita 9280, Wortham 9292
Utah: Caine 9310, GFC 9324
Vermont: Vermont 9361
Virginia: Bryant 9380, Cabell 9381, Camp 9382, Community 9400, Delmar 9410, English 9414, Folger 9418, Gottwald 9431, Graves 9433, Gwathmey 9435, Herndon 9437, Jackson 9441, Kington 9450, Mars 9466, Morgan 9479, Norfolk 9484, Olsson 9491, Parsons 9493, Reynolds 9503, Roller 9507, Smith 9518, Taubman 9524, Universal 9531
Washington: Blue 9559, Community 9571, Foundation 9589, Norcliffe 9650, Seattle 9680, Tacoma 9693
West Virginia: Kanawha 9723, Parkersburg 9730
Wisconsin: Community 9777, Community 9779, Community 9780, Duncan 9793, Green Bay 9810, Jeffris 9821, Kenosha 9833, Krejci 9843, Kress 9844, Mead 9867, Milwaukee 9876, **Roddis 9913**, Rowland 9916, Spire 9931, Uihlein 9953, Waukesha 9960, WPS 9970
Wyoming: Chapman 9976, Connemara 9978

Historical activities

California: **Getty 570**, **McConnell 870**
Colorado: Falkenberg 1376
Connecticut: Lehrman 1584
Delaware: Seevak 1752
District of Columbia: Post 1842
Florida: Lattner 2104, Schumann 2228
Georgia: Franklin 2389, Mix 2448, Snodgrass 2492
Hawaii: Castle 2538
Illinois: Hartmarx 2794, Hobbs 2802
Indiana: Community 3133, Decatur 3138, Newman 3211, Vectren 3249
Iowa: Hanson 3291, Howe 3296
Massachusetts: Wheatland 4204
Minnesota: O'Neil 4638
Mississippi: **Armstrong 4734**
Missouri: Emerson 4809
Nevada: Rufty 5059
New Jersey: Kirby 5280
New Mexico: Proteus 5495
New York: Balm 5596, Black 5636, Clinton 5763, Israel 6240, Morse 6583, Newcastle 6622, Wallach 7210, Weir 7234
Ohio: Foundation 7636, Semple 7851
Oregon: Kinsman 8031, Swindells 8062
Pennsylvania: 1675 8070, Asplundh 8091, Ferree 8199
Rhode Island: Alperin 8516
South Carolina: Rainey 8605
Texas: Rosenberg 9157
Utah: Esther 9321
Virginia: Clark 9393
Wisconsin: Bell 9756

Historical activities, war memorials

California: Wunderkinder 1322
Illinois: Fites 2730
Pennsylvania: Smith 8444

History/archaeology

California: **Getty 570**
Delaware: Rowland 1749
District of Columbia: **Coleman 1784**
Florida: Opler 2158
Georgia: Watson 2509
Maine: Horizon 3541
Massachusetts: Krupp 3991, Marcus 4022
Michigan: **Earhart 4291**
Missouri: Green 4822
New Mexico: McCune 5488
New York: **Atran 5575, Grant 6090, Guggenheim 6118, Kress 6357,** Littauer 6434, New York 6619, O'Connor 6645, Scheuer 6919, **Solow 7020,** Wendt 7243, **Wenner 7244,** Young 7286
North Carolina: Cumberland 7349
Ohio: Murphy 7769
Pennsylvania: AMETEK 8081, **Institute 8268,** Lilliput 8311
Rhode Island: van Beuren 8561
Texas: Austin 8768, Clements 8832, Coastal 8833, Kempner 8987, Meadows 9049, Northen 9092, **Search 9176,** Summerlee 9217, Trull 9240
Virginia: Carter 9387, Parsons 9493
Washington: Community 9571, Quest 9666, **Samis 9675**
Wisconsin: **Bradley 9763**

Homeless

Alabama: McMillan 49, Webb 75
Arizona: Arizona 87, Morris 124
California: Ahmanson 198, Alafi 201, Bickerstaff 287, California 345, Cheesecake 378, Community 406, Croul 431, Fireman's 510, Forest 527, Friedman 538, Garland 556, Gilmore 578, Grove 625, Gruber 626, Gumbiner 631, Irvine 699, Marin 854, McCarthy 868, Parsons 980, Peninsula 989, Roberts 1058, Sacramento 1080, San Diego 1087, San Francisco 1088, Snow 1171, Soda 1173, Taper 1226, Van Nuys 1261, Weingart 1288, Witkin 1313, Wynn 1324
Colorado: Boettcher 1344, **Daniels 1362,** El Pomar 1374, Hill 1392, Hunter 1394, King 1404, Pikes 1437, St. John's 1456
Connecticut: Community 1515, Connecticut 1518, Culpeper 1521, Hartford 1563, Martin 1598
Delaware: Crystal 1702, Marmot 1728
District of Columbia: Beech 1771, **Butler 1779,** Cafritz 1780, Fowler 1797, **Hill 1809,** Meyer 1834, **Public 1844**
Florida: Bank 1890, Bush 1922, **Chatlos 1932,** Community 1948, Dade 1957, duPont 1983, FPL 2010, Frazier 2011, Gainesville 2015, Gooding 2028, Lennar 2109, Overstreet 2159, Pinellas 2170, Resler 2194, Wolfson 2305
Georgia: Brown 2331, Chatham 2347, Community 2355, Rich 2472, Tull 2500, **UPS 2503,** Wardlaw 2507
Hawaii: McInerny 2551
Illinois: **Burlington 2644, Burnett 2645,** Chicago 2661, Community 2677, Day 2698, Field 2728, Kapoor 2825, Owens 2929, **Ploughshares 2945,** Polk 2946, Prince 2948, Retirement 2964, **Shifting 3006,** Siragusa 3009, **Tuohy 3041,** Washington 3058, Woodward 3085
Indiana: Community 3125, Griffith 3158, Harrison 3161
Iowa: Siouxland 3332
Kansas: Security 3390, Topeka 3400
Kentucky: Brown 3409, Cralle 3416, Horn 3427
Louisiana: Booth 3464, Brown 3465, Community 3469, Wilson 3515
Maryland: Abell 3559, Abell 3560, Dresher 3617, O'Neil 3701
Massachusetts: Boston 3812, Clipper 3850, Crawford 3867, Fassino 3900, High 3950, Oral 4061,

Perpetual 4078, Smith 4150, **TJX 4183,** Weber 4200, Worcester 4209
Michigan: Ann Arbor 4221, Grand Rapids 4326, McGregor 4389, Skillman 4438
Minnesota: Andersen 4502, Duluth 4556, Edina 4560, Minneapolis 4623, Phillips 4655
Missouri: **Fox 4815,** H & R 4823, Hall 4824, Pott 4886, Roblee 4893
Nebraska: Lozier 4988
Nevada: Nevada 5047
New Jersey: Borden 5138, Cowles 5170, Danellie 5177, Hyde 5247, **Johnson 5265,** MCJ 5324, Orange 5343, UBS 5433, Unilever 5434, Victoria 5440
New Mexico: Frost 5476, McCune 5488, Santa Fe 5496
New York: Abrons 5511, Achelis 5513, Buhl 5684, Central 5724, Clark 5759, Clark 5761, Cummings 5815, **Deutsche 5854,** Dreitzer 5884, Gimbel 6034, Goldsmith 6060, Litwin 6436, Marron 6493, New York 6615, New York 6619, Northern 6639, REBNY 6780, Revson 6789, Rhodebeck 6791, Ross 6864, Schnurmacher 6931, Turner 7175, Union 7184, Van Pelt 7192
North Carolina: Community 7344, Cumberland 7349, Halton 7386, North Carolina 7438, Reynolds 7457, Stewards 7485, Triangle 7496
North Dakota: Stern 7521
Ohio: Akron 7526, Bruening 7558, Cincinnati 7574, Columbus 7580, Fairfield 7622, GAR 7643, Murphy 7768, Nordson 7781, Osteopathic 7791, Schmidlapp 7841, Stark 7867, Toledo 7883, White 7905
Oregon: Collins 8007, John 8026
Pennsylvania: 1957 8071, Barra 8095, Byers' 8127, Connelly 8157, Dolfinger 8172, Fourjay 8209, Hillman 8249, Hillman 8250, Huston 8263, Morris 8359, **Pew 8377,** Saint 8419, Simonds 8442, Smith 8443, Staunton 8457, Surgala 8469
Rhode Island: Kimball 8542
South Carolina: Central 8577, Coastal 8581
Texas: Cain 8809, Cameron 8812, Coastal 8833, Community 8841, Cullen 8854, Frees 8909, Kempner 8987, Kennedy 8988, King 8995, Meadows 9049, Rockwell 9154, Sterling 9212, Sturgis 9216, Trull 9240, Williams 9282, Wright 9294, Zale 9297
Utah: **ALSAM 9302,** Eccles 9320
Vermont: **Ben 9355**
Virginia: Beazley 9376, Delmar 9410, **Gannett 9428,** Lynchburg 9463, Norfolk 9484, Virginia Beach 9532
Washington: Community 9571, De Falco 9578, Fortune 9587, Glaser 9594, Norcliffe 9650, Tacoma 9693
West Virginia: Kanawha 9723
Wisconsin: Cudahy 9785, Northwestern 9884, Sensient 9922, Stock 9939

Homeless, human services

Alabama: McMillan 49
Arizona: Arizona 87, Morris 124
California: Ahmanson 198, Atkinson 239, Baker 251, Borchard 304, Bothin 309, Burch 334, Cobb 392, Community 406, Community 407, Copley 416, Danford 438, Fieldstone 506, Forest 527, Gamble 549, Garland 556, Gilmore 578, Grove 625, Gruber 626, Jackson 706, Keck 751, McBean 866, McCarthy 868, McKay 877, Norris 940, Parsons 980, Peninsula 989, Roberts 1058, Sacramento 1080, San Diego 1087, San Francisco 1088, Siebel 1150, Soda 1173, Weingart 1288
Colorado: Anschutz 1334, Boettcher 1344, **Daniels 1362,** Edmonson 1373, El Pomar 1374, St. John's 1456
Connecticut: Community 1515, Connecticut 1518, Ensworth 1535, Fisher 1542, Hartford 1563, Martin 1598, **Newman's 1609,** Orchard 1619
Delaware: Crystal 1702
District of Columbia: Cafritz 1780, **Fannie 1793,** Fowler 1797, Hanley 1806, Meyer 1834, **Public 1844**
Florida: Bank 1890, Dade 1957, DiMare 1974, Eckerd 1986, Lennar 2109, Taplin 2264

Georgia: Chatham 2347, Community 2355, Love 2437, Patterson 2460, Rich 2472, Tull 2500, **Wardlaw 2506**
Illinois: **Brach 2630, Buntrock 2643, Burnett 2645,** Chicago 2661, Community 2677, Day 2698, Field 2728, Hartmarx 2794, Polk 2946, Retirement 2964, **Shifting 3006,** Siragusa 3009, Stern 3023, **Tuohy 3041,** Woodward 3085
Indiana: Community 3125, Griffith 3158, Leighton 3190
Kansas: Topeka 3400
Kentucky: Brown 3409
Louisiana: Booth 3464, Brown 3465, Community 3469
Maryland: Abell 3560, Mulford 3696, O'Neil 3701, **Shields 3730**
Massachusetts: Boston 3812, Clipper 3850, Cogan 3851, Eaton 3888, High 3950, Hyams 3961, Linden 4008, Melville 4034, Rubenstein 4115, Smith 4150, Weber 4200, Worcester 4209
Michigan: Ann Arbor 4221, Mackey 4380, Skillman 4438
Minnesota: Bremer 4523, Duluth 4556, Ordean 4643, Thorpe 4701
Missouri: Boeing 4785, Hall 4824, Pott 4886
Nebraska: Baright 4945, Lozier 4988
Nevada: Nevada 5047
New Jersey: Borden 5138, Cowles 5170, Danellie 5177, Hyde 5247, **Johnson 5265,** OceanFirst 5341
New Mexico: Domanica 5475, Frost 5476, McCune 5488, Santa Fe 5496
New York: Bodman 5647, Central 5724, Community 5782, Dreitzer 5884, Goldsmith 6060, **Hearst 6161, Hearst 6162,** Lincoln 6423, New York 6613, New York 6615, Northern 6639, REBNY 6780, Rhodebeck 6791, St. Faith's 7039, Turner 7175, Van Pelt 7192, Vernon 7195
North Carolina: Community 7344, Cumberland 7349, Halton 7386, North Carolina 7438, Reynolds 7457, Stewards 7485, Triangle 7496, Weaver 7504
North Dakota: Stern 7521
Ohio: Columbus 7580, Mathile 7737, Murphy 7768, Nordson 7781, Osteopathic 7791, Schmidlapp 7841, Stark 7867, Stocker 7870, Toledo 7883, White 7905
Pennsylvania: 1957 8071, Byers' 8127, Connelly 8157, Dolfinger 8172, Fourjay 8209, Garthwaite 8212, Huston 8263, Morris 8359, **Pew 8377,** Pierce 8382, Shenango 8438, Smith 8443
Rhode Island: CARLISLE 8521, Kimball 8542, Rhode Island 8551
South Carolina: Central 8577, Coastal 8581
Texas: Anderson 8759, Bailey 8771, Cain 8809, Cameron 8812, Coastal 8833, Fikes 8899, Goldsbury 8920, Kempner 8987, Meadows 9049, Rockwell 9154, San Antonio 9166, Sterling 9212, Sturgis 9216, Tolleson 9237, Trull 9240, Wright 9294, Zale 9297
Utah: **ALSAM 9302,** Eccles 9320, Swanson 9346
Vermont: Vermont 9361
Virginia: Beazley 9376, Delmar 9410, **Doudera 9412,** Golden 9430, Lynchburg 9463, Norfolk 9484
Washington: Blue 9559, Community 9571, De Falco 9578, Foster 9588, Glaser 9594, Seattle 9680, Tacoma 9693
West Virginia: Kanawha 9723
Wisconsin: Cudahy 9785, Milwaukee 9876, Northwestern 9884, Sensient 9922, Stackner 9934

Horticulture/garden clubs

Florida: Colen 1938
Massachusetts: Fessenden 3903
Michigan: Meijer 4390
New York: **Burpee 5690,** Shoreland 6968
Ohio: **Vesper 7892**

Hospitals (general)

Alabama: Bedsole 12, Caring 18, Carson 19, Hill 39, Kimerling 41, McMillan 49, Meyer 52, Russell 60

Speas 9207, Sterling 9212, Strake 9215, Sturgis 9216, Temple 9227, Turner 9241, Vaughan 9249, Vaughn 9251, Waggoner 9256, Wolff 9289, Zale 9297, Zimmer 9300
Utah: Dumke 9315, Eccles 9318, Eccles 9319, Eccles 9320, Raymond 9339, Stewart 9345, Watkins 9350, **Wishnick 9353**
Virgin Islands: Bartner 9362
Virginia: Beazley 9376, Camp 9382, Claws 9394, Delmar 9410, Evans 9416, Folger 9418, Funger 9426, Harrison 9436, Hylton 9440, Kellar 9449, LandAmerica 9454, Massey 9467, **Modzelewski 9477**, O'Shaughnessy 9487, Ochsman 9489, Olsson 9491, Perry 9495, Portsmouth 9498, Praxis 9500, Smith 9518, Snead 9520, Truland 9528
Washington: Anderson 9551, Cheney 9569, Community 9571, Cowles 9574, Crystal 9576, Danz 9577, Dimmer 9579, Ellison 9581, Green 9598, Lauzier 9626, Lockwood 9631, Moccasin 9643, Norcliffe 9650, OneFamily 9654, **PAH 9657**, Raven 9670, **Sage 9674**, Sarkowsky 9676, Schuler 9678, Shemanski 9682, Tacoma 9693
West Virginia: BB&T 9710, McDonough 9726
Wisconsin: 1923 9738, Alexander 9740, Baird 9750, Brotz 9767, Bryant 9768, Clark 9773, Community 9779, Cox 9782, Demmer 9791, Evans 9796, Evjue 9797, **Firestone 9798**, Gordon 9808, Harley 9812, Helfaer 9813, Hess 9816, Johnson 9823, Kelben 9830, Kress 9844, Ladish 9846, Ladish 9847, Marshall 9860, Mead 9867, Menasha 9869, Munson 9880, Pettit 9897, Phipps 9898, Pollybill 9900, Reinhart 9909, Schlegel 9919, Sensient 9922, Shattuck 9926, Smallwood 9928, Soref 9930, Steigleder 9936, Stock 9939, Stuart 9942, Stuart 9943, Sub 9945, Taylor 9948, U.S. 9952, Uihlein 9954, Wagner 9958, Walter 9959, WPS 9970, **Young 9972**
Wyoming: Chapman 9976, Connemara 9978, Dragicevich 9980, Sargent 9989

Hospitals (psychiatric)

New York: Bernhard 5624

Hospitals (specialty)

Arizona: Halle 103, Neely 125
Arkansas: Altheimer 155, Schmieding 175
California: Amerman 218, Bekins 273, Connell 412, DeVito 452, Dougherty 463, Edelstein 476, Edgerton 477, Hartley 653, HealthCare 661, Kellerman 753, Mericos 889, Mudd 924, Radin 1025, Rosenfeld 1067, **Saban 1079**, Saw 1098, Seeno 1120, Shapiro 1138, Smith 1163, Smittcamp 1168, Stewart 1198, UniHealth 1249, Van Nuys 1262, Warren 1279
Colorado: Hewit 1391, Leprino 1408, Osborn 1434, Ponzio 1440, Richardson 1444, Wolf 1475
Connecticut: Diebold 1528, Hartwell 1565, Meriden 1603, Steere 1653, Tow 1660
Delaware: Arguild 1687
District of Columbia: **Coyne 1788**, Friedman 1799, **Goldberg 1802**
Florida: Bronfman 1917, **Coleman 1937**, Crawford 1956, Driskill 1975, Five 2001, **Hardison 2048**, Life's 2116, River 2199, Terry 2271, Weaver 2289
Georgia: Creel 2369, Imlay 2417, Spray 2495
Hawaii: Ching 2540
Illinois: Allegretti 2586, **Andrew 2595**, Louis 2861, Mazza 2877, Miller 2898, O'Connor 2921, Ward 3056, Winfrey 3077, Wonderful 3080
Louisiana: Helis 3486
Maryland: Dekelboum 3613, FBW 3628, Kaplan 3659, Kay 3660, Lerner 3674, Marriott 3685
Massachusetts: Bain 3788, Berthiaume 3803, Carney 3837, Hagerty 3938, **Hostetter 3959**, Mannion 4019, Monsweag 4042, Morningside 4043, Radley 4092, **Swensrud 4177**
Michigan: Dow 4286, Frankel 4312, Kay 4354, Kelly 4359, Maas 4379, Webber 4475
Minnesota: Kelley 4597, Schmidt 4673
Mississippi: Ford 4742

Missouri: Brown 4788, Buder 4791, **Lockton 4857**, Rosewood 4894, Smith 4905
Nebraska: Wiebe 5017
New Hampshire: Levine 5094
New Jersey: Burke 5149, **Frankino 5196**, Harrison 5225, Healthcare 5228, Kauffmann 5272, Mushett 5334, Rheumations 5366, **Rippel 5368**, Taub 5425, Upton 5436
New York: Black 5636, Cappelli 5703, Carvel 5710, CJM 5756, Curry 5817, **Das 5832**, Eunice 5939, Furth 6004, Kautz 6300, Kempner 6313, Lee 6391, Loeb 6439, Riley 6809, **Robinson 6819**, Rosen 6841, **Rosen 6843**, Rosenblatt 6849, Schwartz 6849, Snyder 7013, **St. Giles 7041**, Stern 7071, **Syde 7114**, Werblow 7245
North Carolina: Gordon 7379, Gunzenhauser-Chapin 7384, Hillsdale 7398, Roberts 7465, Spring 7483
Ohio: Born 7552, Haslinger 7664, Hauck 7666, IHS 7683, Jegs 7687, Schiff 7838, Stranahan 7873, Wildermuth 7906, Wolfe 7915
Oklahoma: Oxley 7968
Pennsylvania: Bozzone 8114, Cavitolo 8134, Haas 8230, Levee 8308, Ryan 8416
Rhode Island: Roosa 8552, Usen 8560
South Carolina: **Security's 8609**
Tennessee: Children's 8653, Turner 8736
Texas: Anderson 8759, Duda 8871, **Hull 8964**, Justin 8979, Kaufman 8981, McCrea 9040, Owen 9106, Owen 9107, Sanders 9167, South 9201, Urschel 9244, Vaughan 9249
Utah: Semnani 9341
Virginia: Adams 9366, **Glenstone 9429**, N.E.W. 9482
Washington: Anderson 9551, Cartales 9565, Glazer 9596, Lematta 9628, Oki 9653, PACCAR 9656
West Virginia: Carter 9712, McDonough 9726
Wisconsin: Evans 9796, Stark 9935

Housing/shelter

Arizona: Arizona 87
California: Bireley 292, CAA 341, **Chiron 383**, Cisco 388, Community 401, Community 407, Cowell 423, **Draper 466**, Dwyer 472, Esseff 488, Fluor 523, Oakland 948, PacifiCare 971, Rotasa 1070, Santa Barbara 1093, Union 1250, **Wells 1294**
Colorado: Anschutz 1334, Community 1359, McDonnell 1422, Pikes 1437
Connecticut: Bridgeport 1504, Community 1514, Community 1516, Fairfield 1537, Liberty 1586, Northeast 1614, SBM 1644
District of Columbia: **Butler 1779**, **CityBridge 1783**, Community 1785, **Fannie 1793**
Florida: Batchelor 1893, Community 1944, Community 1945, Dade 1957, Eckerd 1986, Gainesville 2015, **Knight 2097**, Pinellas 2170
Georgia: Amos 2314, Buisson 2333, Community 2355, **Georgia 2397**, ING 2418
Illinois: Brach 2629, **Brach 2630**, Community 2679, D and R 2693, Elgin 2717, Grand 2769, Oak Park 2922, Pasquinelli 2933, Steans 3021, Woodward 3085
Indiana: Central 3116, Community 3122, Crown Point 3135, Irwin 3174, Lafayette 3188, Lilly 3194, Unity 3247, White 3257
Iowa: Principal 3326, Winterhaven 3344
Kansas: Capitol 3350
Kentucky: Blue 3407
Louisiana: Lorio 3496, New Orleans 3503, Peltier 3504
Maine: TD 3558
Maryland: Choice 3589, Mulford 3696, Rouse 3724
Massachusetts: Bay 3794, Berkshire 3800, Charlesbank 3845, Community 3854, Eastern 3886, Eaton 3888, Ham 3940, Salem 4125, **State 4158**, Yawkey 4211
Michigan: Bay 4229, Berrien 4231, Comerica 4251, Community 4258, Great 4330, Masco 4387
Minnesota: Blue 4521, **Cafesjian 4527**, Charlson 4537, **Ecolab 4557**, Lyman 4607, Marbrook 4612, Minneapolis 4623, Northwest 4637, Ordean 4643, **Pentair 4649**, Pohlad 4657, Sexton 4679, **Sit 4684**, St. Paul 4690, TCF 4699, **U.S. 4704**, Valspar 4706, Xcel 4732

Missouri: Butler 4793, **Fox 4815**, H & R 4823, Roblee 4893, Stupp 4911
Nebraska: Commercial 4951, TierOne 5010, Weitz 5016
New Hampshire: Cogswell 5084, von Weber 5104
New Jersey: Amboy 5112, OceanFirst 5341, Prudential 5360, PSEG 5361, Reddy 5364, Unilever 5434, Valley 5438
New Mexico: Santa Fe 5496
New York: **Citigroup 5755**, Cohen 5768, De La Cour 5842, **Deutsche 5854**, **Echoing 5905**, Gimbel 6034, Hagedorn 6130, **Hearst 6161**, **Hearst 6162**, Hill 6185, **JPMorgan 6277**, **MetLife 6542**, Mizuho 6562, North 6637, Richmond 6800, **Rockefeller 6826**, Roslyn 6859, Rosner 6860, SI 6972, Troy 7166, **U.S. 7180**, Wilson 7264, Zitrin 7302
North Carolina: Braswell 7323, Gipson 7375, **Wachovia 7502**
Ohio: Columbus 7580, Corbin 7591, Fairfield 7622, Frost 7642, M/I 7729, Nordson 7781, Stocker 7870
Oklahoma: Meinders 7960
Oregon: Holmes 8020, Lightfoot 8036, Louisiana 8037
Pennsylvania: Claneil 8144, Falk 8193, Keystone 8286, Saint 8419, Scranton 8431
Rhode Island: Rhode Island 8551, Washington 8563
Tennessee: East 8671, Harrah's 8685, Hyde 8693, T & T 8731, Thompson 8733
Texas: Baron 8774, Bass 8777, Fisch 8901, Mitte 9067, Morning 9075, Partnership 9110, Permian 9117, Proctor 9132, Simmons 9188, Tennessee 9230
Utah: **ALSAM 9302**, Noorda 9336
Vermont: **Ben 9355**, Vermont 9361
Virginia: 118 9365, American 9368, Arlington 9371, Fredericksburg 9423, **Gannett 9428**, N.E.W. 9482
Washington: Channel 9568, Fortune 9587, **Laird 9623**, Lockwood 9631, Lynn 9633, O'Donnell 9652, Positive 9664, Seattle 9680, **Weyerhaeuser 9703**
West Virginia: Laughlin 9724
Wisconsin: Alliant 9742, CUNA 9786, Dudley 9792, Duncan 9793, Northwestern 9884, Timken 9950

Housing/shelter, aging

California: JWS 735, Mericos 889
Missouri: Shelter 4902
New Hampshire: Gale 5091
New York: Samuels 6901
Tennessee: Washington 8741
Texas: Topfer 9238

Housing/shelter, alliance

District of Columbia: **Fannie 1793**

Housing/shelter, development

Arizona: Arizona 87
California: Beattie 267, California 345, Community 406, Foster 528, Haas 633, **Hatfield 656**, Irmas 697, Knight 768, Marin 854, Morris 917, Norris 940, Parsons 980, Peninsula 989, **PMI 1008**, Sacramento 1080, San Diego 1087, San Francisco 1088, Taper 1226
Colorado: El Pomar 1374, **Weaver 1469**
Connecticut: Community 1514, Connecticut 1518, Ensworth 1535, Fisher 1542, Hartford 1563, **Seedlings 1645**
Delaware: Crestlea 1701, Crystal 1702, Delaware 1706, Marmot 1728
District of Columbia: Cafritz 1780, **Fannie 1793**, Fowler 1797, Meyer 1834, **Public 1844**
Florida: Beveridge 1907, Community 1948, Elster 1993, Hall 2045, Hicks 2059, **Knight 2097**, Magruder 2125, Martin 2130, Morcom 2144, Sanders 2215, Selby 2230, Stevens 2251, Wilson 2300

Georgia: Anderson 2317, Atlanta 2320, Brown 2331, Community 2355, Exposition 2380, Harris 2408, Tull 2500
Illinois: Amicus 2592, Chicago 2661, Day 2698, Donnelley 2706, Driehaus 2710, Firestone 2729, Hark 2785, **Johnson 2819**, Owens 2929, **Tuohy 3041**, Ward 3056, White 3067
Indiana: Waterfield 3252
Iowa: Krause 3302
Kansas: Hutchinson 3368, Rhoden 3383
Kentucky: Harris 3424
Maine: Berry 3526
Maryland: Columbia 3595, Osprey 3703
Massachusetts: Boston 3812, Cambridge 3828, Clipper 3850, Cogan 3851, Community 3855, EOS 3896, Farnsworth 3899, Hyams 3961, Melville 4034, Parker 4069, Riley 4104, Stevens 4164, Stoico 4166, Worcester 4209
Michigan: Dalton 4266, Grand Rapids 4326, Kalamazoo 4352, Knight 4364, Whiting 4482
Minnesota: Bremer 4523, Butler 4525, Duluth 4556, McKnight 4617, Rochester 4668, Rupp 4669, Schmidt 4673, Thorpe 4701
Mississippi: Oakwood 4760
Missouri: Curry 4802, Gottlieb 4820, Hall 4824, Truman 4919
Nebraska: Weitz 5016, Woods 5018
New Hampshire: Bean 5080
New Jersey: Borden 5138, D'Angelo 5175, Danellie 5177, Gibson 5208, Lanza 5294, Silver 5404, Victoria 5440
New Mexico: McCune 5488, **Pond 5494**
New York: 291 5505, Altman 5542, Charitable 5734, Chautauqua 5738, **Deutsche 5854**, Dove 5878, **Ford 5970**, Gibbs 6024, Horncrest 6200, Knossos 6344, New York 6613, New York 6615, Northern 6639, O'Connor 6645, Pumpkin 6754, Raffiani 6767, REBNY 6780, Rochester 6823, **Surdna 7103**, Taconic 7117, Weezie 7224, Western 7248
North Carolina: BIN 7318, Cemala 7337, Community 7343, Cumberland 7349, Halton 7386, Janirve 7404, Reynolds 7457, Reynolds 7460, Stewards 7485, Triangle 7496, Weaver 7504
North Dakota: Stern 7521
Ohio: Cleveland 7576, Gund 7657, Hamilton 7660, Morgan 7760, Murphy 7768, Schmidlapp 7841, Stark 7867, Watson 7896
Oklahoma: McMahon 7959
Oregon: Carpenter 8003, Jackson 8024, Meyer 8042
Pennsylvania: Briggs 8117, Hulme 8260, Huston 8263, Jaindl 8269, McCune 8332, **Pew 8377**, Philadelphia 8378, Smith 8443, Sovereign 8451, Willary 8503
Rhode Island: CARLISLE 8521
South Carolina: Central 8577, Coastal 8581, Reams 8606
South Dakota: Larson 8627
Tennessee: Community 8662, Johnson 8697, Thompson 8733
Texas: Constantin 8843, Fikes 8899, Frees 8909, Hillcrest 8952, Hoblitzelle 8955, Kempner 8987, Meadows 9049, Prairie 9129, PSH 9137, Waggoner 9256
Utah: Eccles 9320
Virginia: Community 9402, Delmar 9410, English 9414, HRH 9439, **Oak 9488**
Washington: Community 9571, Norcliffe 9650, Satterberg 9677, Tacoma 9693, **Vista 9699**
West Virginia: Kanawha 9723
Wisconsin: Community 9777, Cudahy 9784, Cudahy 9785, **DeAtley 9789**, Hyde 9818, Milwaukee 9876, **Taylor 9947**

Housing/shelter, equal rights
Minnesota: Xcel 4732

Housing/shelter, expense aid
Arizona: Stardust 141

Housing/shelter, home owners
New York: **Heron 6176**
Ohio: Cincinnati 7574
Pennsylvania: Lancaster 8300

Housing/shelter, homeless
California: Firedoll 508, Pacific 970, Smith 1164
Colorado: **Daniels 1362**
Connecticut: **Macauley 1592, Orchard 1619**
Florida: Community 1943
Indiana: Lafayette 3188, Unity 3247
Kentucky: Blue 3407
Maine: **Oak 3552**
Maryland: Mulford 3696
Michigan: Branch 4237, **Degroot 4270**, Mackey 4380
Minnesota: Pax 4648
New Jersey: OceanFirst 5341
New Mexico: Coleman 5470
New York: Dreyfus 5887, Santa 6905
Ohio: Nordson 7781, Osteopathic 7791, Wagler 7893
Tennessee: Plough 8718
Texas: Meadows 9049, NAH 9084
Utah: Bastian 9306

Housing/shelter, information services
California: San Diego 1087

Housing/shelter, owner/renter issues
Minnesota: **Homeownership 4587**

Housing/shelter, public education
California: San Diego 1087
Maryland: Mulford 3696

Housing/shelter, public housing
Illinois: Landau 2847
North Carolina: Reynolds 7458
Washington: Channel 9568

Housing/shelter, public policy
Minnesota: St. Paul 4690

Housing/shelter, rehabilitation
Minnesota: TCF 4699

Housing/shelter, repairs
California: JWS 735
Florida: Smith 2238
Georgia: Spray 2495
Texas: Baron 8774, Reliant 9144

Housing/shelter, research
California: San Diego 1087

Housing/shelter, search services
Massachusetts: Lamm 3994

Housing/shelter, services
California: Ludwick 829
Colorado: Rose 1445
District of Columbia: Spring 1849
Maryland: Viragh 3753
Massachusetts: Melville 4034
Michigan: Shepherd 4435
Minnesota: **Homeownership 4587**, Smikis 4687
Ohio: Davidson 7602
Pennsylvania: Pine 8385

Wisconsin: Argosy 9747, Madison 9854

Housing/shelter, temporary shelter
California: Community 407, Janssen 715, Smidt 1159
Florida: Hayes 2052, Tarrant 2265
Ohio: Reinberger 7815
Tennessee: Plough 8718
Washington: **Weyerhaeuser 9703**

Housing/shelter, volunteer services
Pennsylvania: Willary 8503

Human services
Alabama: Alpha 3, **Altec 4**, AmSouth 5, Anderson 6, Anderson 7, Ard 8, Aronov 9, **Bashinsky 11**, Bedsole 12, Bolden 15, Central 20, Comer 22, Community 23, Community 24, Community 25, Community 26, Community 27, Crampton 30, Daniel 31, Finlay 33, Founders 34, Harrison 36, Hearin 37, Hess 38, Hill 39, Kimerling 41, Lowder 42, Lowder 43, Lowder 44, Lowe 45, May 46, Mayer 47, McMillan 49, McWane 50, Methvin 51, Meyer 52, Mitchell 53, Saks 61, Scrushy 62, Smith 63, Strain 66, Thompson 67, Treadwell 68, **Union 70**, Vines 72, Webb 75, Working 76
Alaska: Alaska 78, Carr 82, Rasmuson 85
Arizona: A.P.S. 86, Arizona 87, Berlin 89, Community 91, Cooper 92, Dee 94, Farrington 97, **Gagarin 99**, Green 102, Halle 103, Hansen 104, Help 105, Herberger 106, **IFS 109**, Jasam 110, **Kleckhefer 113**, Levine 115, Long 118, Marshall 121, Morris 124, Neely 126, Noah's 127, Phelps 129, Pocono 131, Reese 133, Robson 135, **Solheim 139**, Stevens 144, **Tankersley 145**, **Torhjelm 146**, Viad 149, Wilson 152
Arkansas: Arkansas 156, Bradberry 159, **Frueauff 161**, Glass 163, Gleason 164, Murphy 167, Nabholz 168, Northwest 169, Rebsamen 171, Schmieding 175, Smith 176, **Soderquist 177**, Sturgis 178, Tenenbaum 180, Union 183, White 187
California: Aaroe 192, Ackerman 193, Adams 194, Ahmanson 198, Allequash 202, Allergan 203, Altman 210, Amar 213, American 215, **American 217**, Amerman 218, Amgen 219, Anaheim 220, Anderson 222, **Angelica 223**, **Appleton 225**, Applied 226, **Arata 229**, Arbus 231, Argosy 233, **Arkay 235**, Arrillaga 237, Atkins 238, Atkinson 239, **Atkinson 240**, Auen 242, Autry 243, Avery 244, Avery-Tsui 245, **Azus 248**, Bakar 250, Baker 251, **Baker 252**, Baker 253, Barbonchielli 256, Bartman 259, Bauer 261, Bay 264, **Bechtel 269**, Bekins 273, Beneto 277, Bennett 279, Berkshire 283, Berry 284, Bettingen 286, **Bilger 289**, Binder 291, Bireley 292, Black 293, Blackman 294, Bloomfield 295, Blum 297, Blume 298, Bohnett 300, Booth 303, Borchard 304, Borick 305, Borina 306, Borina 307, Bothin 309, Bowes 310, Bowes 311, Bowman 312, Bradley 315, **Brandes 317**, Braun 318, Bravo 319, Brenner 321, Bright 322, Broccoli 326, Brooks 327, Bundy 332, Bunker 333, Burch 334, Burlock 335, Burnett 336, Burnham 337, Burns 338, Byer 339, CAA 341, Cacique 342, Cadence 344, California 345, Campini 353, **Capital 357**, Carsey 361, Carson 362, Caruso 363, Cassin 365, Caufield 367, CEC 368, Center 369, Change 373, Cheeryble 377, Chesed 379, **ChevronTexaco 380**, Chintu 382, Ciocca 387, Cisco 388, CNC 390, Coates 391, Cobb 392, Collins 396, Collins 397, Colombo 398, Commercial 400, Commercial 400, Community 401, Community 403, Community 404, Community 405, Community 406, Community 407, Confidence 411, Connell 412, Connolly 413, Cook 415, Copley 416, Corcoran 417, Cortopassi 419, Cowell 423, Crawford 427, Crean 428, Croul 431, Crummer 432, Cusenza 433, Dachs 435, Daly 437, Danford 438, Davidow 444, Davidson 445, Davies 446, **Day 447**, Deutsch 451, DeVito 452, Dhont 453, Dickinson 454, Disney 456, **Disney 457**, Doelger 459, Doll 461, Douglas 464, **Draper 465**,

Martin 2130, Masters 2131, Michaan 2138, MIDA 2139, Miller 2141, Moore 2142, Moran 2143, Morcom 2144, **Morris 2145**, Morsani 2147, Naples 2151, Nessel 2152, North 2153, O'Neil 2155, Ocean 2156, Olemberg 2157, Overstreet 2159, P & M 2160, Palm Beach 2161, Pamphalon 2162, Pascal 2163, Paulucci 2164, Peacock 2165, **Pearce 2166**, Petway 2167, Phillips 2168, Pinellas 2170, Plangere 2172, Poe 2173, **Pope 2174**, Posnack 2175, Potamkin 2176, Quick 2182, Rales 2184, **Rauenhorst 2185**, **Rawlings 2186**, Rayonier 2189, **Regan 2191**, Resler 2194, Rinker 2196, Rollnick 2203, Rooms 2204, Rosenberg 2206, **Rosser 2208**, Rubin 2211, Ryder 2213, Sanders 2215, Sandler 2216, Sansing 2217, Saunders 2219, Scarpa 2221, Schaefer 2222, Scharlin 2223, Schoenbaum 2227, Schumann 2228, Selby 2230, Sherman 2233, Silverman 2234, Simon 2235, Smith 2238, **Sontag 2239**, Southwest 2240, St. Joe 2244, **Stacy 2246**, Stein 2250, Storer 2252, Stransky 2253, Straz 2254, Sudakoff 2255, **SWS 2260**, Sykes 2261, Taishoff 2262, Taylor 2267, Taylor 2268, Taylor 2269, TECO 2270, United 2276, Victory 2280, Wahlert 2284, Waldbaum 2285, Ware 2287, Weiler 2290, Weintraub 2292, Wellman 2293, Welsh 2295, Westgate 2296, Wilson 2300, Winter 2303, Wolfson 2304, Wolfson 2305, Wollowick 2306

Georgia: Adams 2309, Aflac 2311, Amos 2315, Amos 2316, Anderson 2317, Anncox 2318, Atlanta 2320, Azalea 2322, Beloco 2324, Bradley 2326, Brady 2327, Brain 2328, Brill 2329, Broadfield 2330, Brown 2331, Buisson 2333, Callaway 2336, Camp 2338, Campbell 2339, Carlos 2340, Charter 2345, Chatham 2347, Coca 2350, Colonial 2353, Community 2354, Community 2355, Community 2356, Community 2357, Community 2358, Community 2359, Community 2361, Community 2362, Cooper 2363, Cousins 2365, Covenant 2366, Cox 2367, **Dobbs 2373**, Equifax 2379, Exposition 2380, Faith 2381, Flowers 2384, **Fonda 2385**, Fuqua 2391, Gaines 2393, Glenn 2399, Good 2401, Gordy 2402, Greene 2404, Harris 2408, Harrison 2409, Hertz 2412, Holder 2413, **Hooters 2414**, Imlay 2417, ING 2418, JBS 2420, Jinks 2422, Jones 2424, Knox 2427, Lanier 2428, Lanier 2430, Lanier 2431, Lee 2432, Lewis 2434, Looney 2436, Love 2437, Ma-Ran 2439, Marcus 2440, Millner 2447, Mix 2448, Moeller 2449, **Money 2450**, Moore 2452, Morgens 2453, North 2458, Patterson 2460, Pechter 2461, Pitts 2463, Pittulloch 2464, Poe 2465, Porter 2468, Ramser 2469, Realan 2470, Rice 2471, Rich 2472, Rosenberg 2476, RTM 2477, Russell 2478, Savannah 2480, **Scientific 2482**, **Scott 2483**, Shallenberger 2487, Sheffield 2488, Simpson 2489, Smith 2491, Snodgrass 2492, Spray 2495, Synovus 2497, Terwilliger 2498, Tull 2500, **UPS 2503**, Vogel 2504, Wardlaw 2507, Watkins 2508, Wehadkee 2511, Williams 2517, Williams 2518, Woodruff 2521, Woodruff 2522, Woodward 2523, Young 2527, Zaban 2528, Zeist 2529

Hawaii: Alexander 2530, Anthony 2531, Atherton 2532, Bakken 2534, Bank 2535, Campbell 2536, Ching 2540, Cooke 2541, First 2542, Frear 2543, Geist 2544, Hawaii 2545, Hughes 2548, Kosasa 2549, McInerny 2551, Schuler 2552, Strong 2555, Trimble 2556, Watumull 2558, Wilcox 2559

Idaho: CHC 2566, Cunningham 2567, Idaho 2570, Morrison 2572, Nagel 2573, Simplot 2574, Simplot 2575

Illinois: **Abbott 2579**, Abbott 2580, **Ace 2582**, Adreani 2585, Allegretti 2586, **Allen 2587**, AMCORE 2591, Amicus 2592, **Amsted 2593**, **Andrew 2595**, Andrew 2596, Appleton 2599, Atlas 2603, Barnett 2606, Baskes 2607, Bates 2608, Bauer 2610, Beidler 2613, Bell 2614, Bere 2616, Berner 2617, Bersted 2618, Bersted 2619, Bielfeldt 2620, Blair 2621, Blair 2622, Blowitz 2623, Blum 2624, Blum 2625, Borwell 2627, Brach 2629, **Brach 2630**, Braeside 2631, Bruce 2634, Bruning 2635, **Brunswick 2636**, Buchanan 2637, Buehler 2638, Buffett 2639, **Buntrock 2643**, **Burlington 2644**,

Burnett 2645, Butler 2646, Butterworth 2647, Cabe 2648, Camp 2649, Canning 2650, **Carylon 2652**, Caterpillar 2653, Chaddick 2655, Chapman 2656, Chester 2659, Chicago 2660, Chicago 2661, Chicago 2662, Children's 2664, Christopher 2665, Circle 2666, Citadel 2667, Cless 2668, Cole 2672, Coleman 2673, Combs 2674, Comer 2675, Community 2677, Community 2679, Community 2680, Cooney 2682, Cooper 2683, Corboy 2684, Coydog 2686, Crane 2687, Cressey 2689, Crown 2691, Cuneo 2692, D and R 2693, D.H.R. 2695, Davee 2696, Day 2698, Deere 2699, DeKalb 2701, Dillon 2704, Domanada 2705, Dowdle 2709, Driehaus 2710, Duchossois 2711, Dunard 2712, DuPage 2713, Eisenberg 2716, Elgin 2717, Ellis 2718, Energizer 2721, **Excelsior! 2722**, Feinberg 2727, Field 2728, Firestone 2729, Fites 2730, Flagg 2731, Frank 2733, Frankel 2735, Freehling 2737, Funk 2741, **Gallagher 2744**, Galter 2745, Galvin 2747, Geneseo 2750, Geraldi 2752, Getz 2753, Gidwitz 2756, GKN 2758, Gloyd 2760, Goldberg 2761, Golder 2762, Goldschmidt 2764, **Goodman 2765**, Grainger 2768, Guth 2775, Guthman 2776, H.B.B. 2777, Hales 2778, Hamill 2780, Hark 2785, **Harper 2786**, Harris 2787, Harris 2788, Harris 2789, Harrison 2790, Hartke 2792, Hartmarx 2794, Hendrickson 2796, Hermann 2798, Hirsch 2800, Hobbs 2802, Hochberg 2803, Huizenga 2806, **Hull 2807**, Hunter 2808, Huntington 2809, I and G 2811, Illinois 2813, **JMR 2818**, **Johnson 2819**, Kaplan 2824, Kapoor 2825, Katten 2826, Kazma 2827, Keiser 2828, **Keller 2829**, Kemper 2831, Kendall 2833, Kensington 2836, Kersten 2838, Kipper 2840, Kolschowsky 2843, Kovler 2844, Krueck 2846, Landau 2847, Lange 2848, Lavin 2849, Lea 2850, Lederer 2852, Lee 2853, Leibowitz 2854, Levi 2855, Levy 2856, Lewis 2857, Libra 2858, Louis 2862, Lumpkin 2864, Lyon 2866, Madigan 2869, Magnus 2870, Makray 2871, Martin 2874, Mazza 2877, McGraw 2882, McIntosh 2883, McNally 2885, Mead 2888, Medline 2889, Melman 2891, Melrene 2892, Meyer 2895, Meyer 2896, Millard 2897, Miller 2898, Miller 2899, Mills 2901, Moline 2902, Morton 2905, **Motorola 2906**, Mullen 2907, Negaunee 2909, **Niamogue 2914**, NIB 2915, Nichols 2916, Northern 2918, Nygren 2920, Oak Park 2922, Olin 2925, Omron 2926, Opler 2927, Oppenheimer 2928, Owens 2929, Ozinga 2930, Parmer 2932, PepsiAmericas 2937, Perlman 2938, Perritt 2939, Petersen 2941, Pick 2943, **Ploughshares 2945**, Polk 2946, Prince 2948, Pritzker 2950, **Pritzker 2952**, Pritzker 2955, Regenstein 2962, **Relations 2963**, Retirement 2964, Rhoades 2965, Rosenthal 2970, Rothschild 2971, Ruben 2973, Rubschlager 2975, Russell 2976, Ryan 2977, **Ryan 2978**, Sacks 2979, **Satter 2983**, Schawk 2984, Schield 2985, Schmidt 2986, Schmitt 2987, Schuler 2990, Schwartz 2991, Scully 2992, Seabury 2993, **Searle 2994**, Seid 2996, Seigle 2997, SF 2998, Shaker 2999, Shapiro 3001, **Shaw 3003**, Shirk 3007, Siragusa 3009, Sirius 3010, Snite 3012, Souder 3013, **Square 3018**, Steadley 3020, Steans 3021, Stern 3023, Stone 3025, Stone 3026, Susman 3030, Takiff 3032, Tracy 3037, Trustmark 3039, **Tuohy 3041**, **Tyndale 3042**, United 3044, **United 3045**, USG 3046, Vermilion 3047, **Wadsworth 3050**, Walnut 3054, Walsh 3055, Ward 3056, Weinberg 3061, White 3067, Whitwam 3068, Wieboldt 3069, Willett 3073, **Willow 3074**, Wilson 3075, Wine 3076, Winfrey 3077, Wohlers 3078, Wonderful 3080, **Woodbury 3082**, Woods 3083, Woodward 3085, Worley 3086, WPW 3087, Yulman 3089, Zell 3090, Zerrusen 3091, **Zimmerman 3092**

Indiana: 1st 3094, Adams 3095, Adams 3096, ADL 3097, American 3098, Anderson 3099, Annis 3100, **Anthem 3101**, Anthem 3102, Ball 3103, Ball 3104, Biomet 3106, Blue 3107, Branigin 3109, Brown 3110, **BVM 3112**, Carmichael 3113, Carroll 3114, Cass 3115, Central 3116, Citizens 3118, Clowes 3120, Community 3122, Community 3123, Community 3124, Community 3125, Community

3126, Community 3127, Community 3128, Community 3129, Community 3131, Community 3132, Community 3133, Cornelius 3134, Crown Point 3135, Dearborn 3137, Decatur 3138, DeKalb 3141, Duneland 3143, East Chicago 3144, Elkhart 3145, English 3146, Fairbanks 3147, Froderman 3153, Glick 3155, **Guidant 3159**, Hancock 3160, Harrison 3161, Health 3164, Henry 3165, Heritage 3166, Holiday 3168, Hoover 3169, Hux 3170, Indiana 3173, Irwin 3175, Ispat 3176, Johnson 3178, Jones 3179, Journal 3181, Kimball 3182, Klapper 3183, Koch 3184, Kosciusko 3186, Kuhne 3187, Lafayette 3188, Legacy 3189, Leighton 3190, Lilly 3194, Lincoln 3195, Madison 3197, McAllister 3202, Moore 3207, Morgan 3208, Muselman 3209, Niblick 3212, NiSource 3213, Noble 3214, Noble 3214, Northern 3215, Noyes 3216, Oakley 3217, Ogle 3218, Portland 3223, Pulliam 3225, Raker 3226, Reynolds 3229, Ripley 3230, Rolland 3231, Saemann 3232, Saltsburg 3233, Simon 3239, Simon 3240, Steuben 3241, Tipton 3243, Tobias 3244, Twin 3245, Unity 3247, Valiant 3248, Vectren 3249, Wabash 3250, Watanabe 3251, Wayne 3253, Wells 3255, White 3257, Whitley 3258

Iowa: **AEGON 3259**, Ahrens 3260, Bechtel 3264, Bechtel 3265, Blank 3268, Bright 3269, Butler 3273, Cedar Rapids 3275, Clarinda 3276, Community 3277, Community 3278, Deardorf 3280, Des Moines 3281, Employers 3282, Farver 3283, Figge 3284, Good 3288, Hall 3290, Hanson 3291, HNI 3293, Holden 3294, Holthues 3295, Howe 3296, Hubbell 3297, Iowa 3298, Jacobson 3299, Kinney 3300, Knapp 3301, Kruidenier 3303, Lee 3305, Maytag 3309, Maytag 3310, McCarthy 3311, McDonald 3312, McElroy 3313, Meredith 3314, Mid 3316, Muscatine 3318, **New 3319**, Pella 3323, Poweshiek 3325, Principal 3326, R & R 3327, **Rockwell 3328**, Ruan 3329, Siouxland 3332, United 3338

Kansas: Bane 3345, **Beren 3348**, Capitol 3350, Cessna 3351, Cooper 3353, Deramus 3355, DeVore 3357, Downing 3358, Dreiseszun 3359, Ellis 3361, Garvey 3363, Hutchinson 3368, INTRUST 3369, Joscelyn 3371, Morgan 3377, Payless 3380, Rhoden 3383, Rice 3384, Rudd 3385, Sabatini 3386, Salina 3387, Scroggins 3389, Security 3390, Shannon 3392, Smoot 3394, SYZYGY 3398, Taylor 3399, Topeka 3400, Tyler 3401, V & H 3402, Wichita 3404

Kentucky: Bavarian 3406, Blue 3407, Brown 3408, Brown 3409, **Chase 3413**, Community 3414, Community 3415, Cralle 3416, E.ON 3417, Fischer 3418, Gheens 3421, Hagan Ch 3423, Harris 3424, Horn 3427, **Humana 3428**, **Jones 3430**, Keeneland 3432, Kindred 3434, Klein 3435, Ladner 3436, Norton 3441, Preston 3446, Reed 3447, Sutherland 3451, Young 3454

Louisiana: Adams 3458, Baton Rouge 3462, **Biedenharn 3463**, Booth 3464, Brown 3465, Burton 3467, Community 3469, Coughlin 3470, Deming 3472, Diboll 3473, Factor 3476, Fertel 3477, Frazier 3479, Freeman 3480, Freeport 3481, Goldring 3484, Helis 3486, Heymann 3487, Huie 3488, Institute 3489, Jones 3491, Kabacoff 3492, Keller 3493, Libby 3494, Louisiana 3497, Lupin 3498, Mauboules 3499, **Merkle 3500**, Monroe 3501, New Orleans 3503, Peltier 3504, Pennington 3505, Reily 3506, RosaMary 3507, Scott 3509, Stuller 3510, Wilson 3515, **Woldenberg 3516**, Woolf 3517, Young 3518

Maine: Alfond 3521, Alfond 3522, Burnham 3527, Davenport 3531, Falcon 3532, Fore 3534, Gardiner 3536, **Golden 3538**, Great 3539, Hannaford 3540, Kennebec 3543, Kennebunk 3544, King 3545, Libra 3546, Lunder 3547, Maine 3548, Mulford 3551, TD 3558

Maryland: Abell 3560, Baker 3567, Baltimore 3568, Bank 3569, **Bearman 3570**, Berlitz 3571, **Berman 3572**, Berman 3573, Blades 3574, Blum 3577, Brown 3578, **Brown 3579**, Bunting 3580, Campbell 3582, Capital 3584, **Casey 3585**, Choice 3589, Clark 3590, Clark 3591, Cohen 3593, **Cohen**

Haas 8230, Hall 8232, Hankin 8234, Harsco 8236, Hassel 8237, Heinz 8240, **Henkels 8245**, Herr 8246, Hillman 8249, Hillman 8250, Hillman 8251, Hirtzel 8253, Hodge 8254, Hooper 8256, Hopwood 8257, Hoyt 8259, Hulme 8260, Hunt 8261, Huplits 8262, Huston 8263, Huston 8264, Independence 8266, John 8273, **Johnson 8274**, Johnson 8275, Justus 8276, Kaiserman 8277, Kardon 8279, Katz 8280, Kavanagh 8282, Keystone 8286, Kind 8289, Kinsley 8290, Klein 8291, Kline 8292, Kline 8293, **Knox 8294**, Kunkel 8297, La 8298, Lancaster 8300, Laurel 8301, Lehigh Valley 8303, Lenfest 8304, Les 8306, Levan 8307, Levee 8308, Levis 8309, Lotman 8314, Lutron 8316, Luzerne 8317, Magee 8320, Maguire 8321, Mandell 8322, Massey 8328, McCormick 8329, McCune 8331, McCune 8332, McDonald's 8333, McFeely 8334, Meakem 8341, Mellon 8344, Mellon 8345, Mellon 8346, Mengle 8347, Meshewa 8350, **Metcalf 8351**, Miller 8352, Miller 8353, Miller 8354, Miller 8355, Miller 8356, Murray 8360, Musser 8361, Novotny 8364, Oxford 8367, Palumbo 8368, Peirce 8370, Penn 8371, Perelman 8372, Perelman 8373, Perkin 8375, **Pew 8377**, Philadelphia 8378, Phillips 8380, Phoenixville 8381, Pierce 8382, **Pincus 8384**, Pine 8385, Plankenhorn 8387, PNC 8388, Pollock 8390, Pond 8391, **PPG 8394**, Pryor 8396, PSC 8398, PTS 8399, Reidler 8402, Roberts 8405, Roberts 8406, Roberts 8407, Rohrer 8410, Rosenberg 8412, Rosenfeld 8413, Saint 8419, **Saltsgiver 8420**, Salvaggio 8421, Salvitti 8422, Sampson 8423, Schwab 8430, Scranton 8431, **Seraph 8434**, Shaffer 8436, Simmons 8441, Smith 8443, Smith 8445, Snider 8447, Snyder 8448, Sordoni 8450, Sovereign 8451, Spang 8452, Speyer 8453, Stabler 8455, Stackpole 8456, Staunton 8457, Steinman 8458, Steinman 8459, Stewart 8461, Strauss 8464, Strawbridge 8467, Susquehanna 8471, Taylor 8473, Tecovas 8474, Tippins 8477, Toll 8479, Trexler 8481, Triple 8482, Truman 8483, **United 8487**, **United 8488**, Usher 8489, Vanguard 8490, Warwick 8496, Waters 8498, Weiss 8499, West 8500, Wheeler 8501, Willary 8503, Wolf 8506, **Woods 8508**, Wyomissing 8509, York 8511, Zisman 8513

Rhode Island: Alperin 8516, **Amica 8518**, **Bafflin 8519**, Brooks 8520, Carter 8522, Chace 8523, Champlin 8524, Charter 8525, Citizens 8527, Cuno 8528, Daniels 8530, Fain 8533, **Feinstein 8535**, **FM 8537**, Jackson 8541, Kimball 8542, Kings 8543, Mann 8546, McCarthy 8548, Rhode Island 8551, Roosa 8552, Salem 8554, Sullivan 8558, Usen 8560, van Beuren 8561, Washington 8563

South Carolina: Abney 8564, Arkwright 8565, Bailey 8567, Barnet 8568, Bruce 8571, Central 8577, Coastal 8581, Collins 8582, Community 8583, Community 8584, Daniel 8585, Dintersmith 8586, First 8587, Gibbs 8590, Hipp 8592, Hopewell 8593, Liberty 8597, Montgomery 8600, Phifer 8602, Reams 8606, Smith 8613, Sonoco 8614, South 8615, Spartanburg 8616, TSC 8618, **Wardle 8620**, **Youths' 8621**

South Dakota: Branches 8623, Dakota 8624, Hofer 8626, Larson 8627, Opus 8628, Sioux Falls 8630, South Dakota 8631, Stearns 8632, Vucurevich 8634

Tennessee: 1939 8635, AmSouth 8636, Assisi 8638, Atticus 8639, Ayers 8640, Basler 8641, Belz 8643, Benwood 8644, Briggs 8647, Caldwell 8649, Campbell 8650, Children's 8653, CIC 8656, CLARCOR 8658, Clayton 8659, Community 8661, Community 8662, Conwood 8663, Douglass 8667, Draughon 8668, Dugas 8669, EBS 8672, Eskind 8673, Eskind 8674, Eskind 8675, Frist 8678, Frist 8679, **Garrott 8680**, Gatton 8681, Goldsmith 8682, Gordon 8683, Haslam 8687, Haslam 8688, Hawthorn 8689, Ingram 8694, Jeniam 8695, Johnson 8697, Jones 8698, Lazarus 8700, Martin 8707, Martin 8708, Massey 8709, Melkus 8711, Nelson 8712, Osborne 8714, Pettway 8715, Phillips 8716, Plough 8718, Longleaf 8719, Potter 8720, Ragsdale 8722, Redbird 8723, Schadt 8725, T & T 8731, Tennessee 8732, Thompson

8733, Tucker 8735, Turner 8736, Turner 8737, Turner 8738, Wallace 8740, Washington 8741

Texas: A Glimmer **8747**, Abell 8749, **Adams 8751**, Amarillo 8758, Anderson 8759, Anderson 8760, **Anderson 8761**, Anderson 8762, **AT&T 8765**, Augur 8766, Austin 8768, B & B 8769, Bailey 8771, Baker 8772, Baron 8774, Bass 8777, Beal 8783, Beasley 8784, Behmann 8785, Bergman 8789, Bickel 8790, Bookout 8791, Branch 8794, Bridgeway 8796, Bridwell 8797, Brown 8799, Brumley 8800, Burnett 8801, **C.I.O.S. 8805**, Cailloux 8806, Cain 8809, Cameron 8811, Cameron 8812, Carter 8816, Carter 8817, **CEMEX 8821**, CH 8823, Charitable 8824, Chilton 8826, Christian 8828, Circle 8829, Clayton 8830, Clear 8831, Clements 8832, Coastal 8833, Cockrell 8835, Collins 8837, Collins 8838, Communities 8839, Community 8840, Community 8841, Community 8842, Constantin 8843, Convergence 8844, **Cooper 8846**, Cowden 8848, Cox 8849, Crane 8852, Cullen 8854, Dallas 8855, Dauphin 8856, **Davis 8857**, De Llano 8859, Deakins 8860, Delaney 8862, Dell 8864, di Portanova 8865, Dickson 8866, Diener 8867, Duda 8871, Durrill 8873, Eady 8875, East 8876, **EDS 8877**, Edwards 8880, El Paso 8881, El Paso 8882, Ellwood 8884, Esping 8886, Estill 8888, **ExxonMobil 8889**, Fain 8890, Fair 8891, Farb 8893, Farish 8894, Fasken 8895, Favrot 8897, Fikes 8899, Fisch 8901, Fish 8902, Fleming 8903, Fleming 8904, Folsom 8905, Fondren 8906, Futureus 8912, Gale 8913, Garvey 8914, Gayden 8915, George 8916, GHS Foun 8917, Gill 8919, Gorman 8922, Greathouse 8923, Greathouse 8924, Griffin 8925, Hackett 8928, Haggar 8929, Haggar 8931, Haggerty 8932, Halff 8934, Halsell 8936, Hamill 8937, Hamman 8938, Hanley 8940, **Hartman 8942**, Hawn 8943, Heavin 8945, Hebert 8946, Helm 8947, Herd 8948, Herzstein 8949, Hillcrest 8952, Hirsch 8953, Hobby 8954, Hoblitzelle 8955, Hoglund 8956, Holden 8957, Holthouse 8959, Houston 8961, Hudson 8962, **Hull 8964**, Hunt 8966, Jamail 8969, Jamail 8970, **Jenesis 8971**, Johnson 8972, Johnson 8973, Johnson 8974, Jones 8975, Jonsson 8977, Jordan 8978, Justin 8979, Kahn 8980, Keith 8982, Keithley 8983, Kelleher 8984, Kelley 8986, Kempner 8987, Kennedy 8988, Keown 8989, KFFH 8990, Kimberly 8992, Kinder 8994, King 8995, King 8995, Koehler 9001, Kurth 9003, Lantana 9004, Lard 9005, Lennox 9007, Levit 9009, Light 9011, Lightner 9012, **Link 9013**, Littauer 9014, Looper 9016, Loose 9017, Lord 9018, Lowe 9020, Lubbock 9021, Lyman 9023, Lyons 9024, MacDonald 9025, Marathon 9028, Martin 9031, Martinez 9032, Mayor 9034, Mays 9035, McCoy 9039, McCrea 9040, McCullough 9041, McMillan 9046, McNutt 9048, Meadows 9049, Mechia 9050, Mehta 9052, Mendenhall 9053, Merrick 9055, Meyer 9057, Miller 9061, Miller 9062, Mitchell 9065, Mithoff 9066, Modano 9068, Moncrief 9069, Moody 9070, Moore 9071, Morgan 9073, Morris 9076, Mosbacher 9077, Mundy 9080, Murchison 9081, Murrell 9082, NAH 9084, Navarro 9089, Nightingale 9091, **Notsew 9093**, O'Connor 9094, O'Quinn 9097, **O'Sullivan 9098**, Oehmig 9099, **Onward 9103**, Otter 9105, Owen 9106, Owen 9107, Owsley 9108, Partnership 9110, Paso 9111, Paulos 9112, Pema 9114, Penney 9115, Perkins 9116, Permian 9117, Perot 9118, Perot 9119, Phillips 9122, Pine 9123, Pollock 9127, Powell 9128, Prairie 9129, Priddy 9131, Proctor 9132, Proctor 9132, Prothro 9134, Pryor 9136, Rachal 9138, Rachofsky 9139, Rapoport 9141, Reaud 9143, Richardson 9147, Riddle 9148, Riter 9149, Roach 9150, Roberts 9151, Robinson 9152, Rockjensen 9153, Rockwell 9154, Rosewood 9158, Rowling 9160, RSMIS 9161, San Angelo 9164, San Antonio 9166, Sanders 9167, **Scaler 9170**, Schollmaier 9172, Scurlock 9175, Sharp 9180, **Shell 9181**, Shield 9183, Sidhu 9185, **Silverton 9186**, Simmons 9187, Simmons 9188, Simmons 9189, Smith 9191, Smith 9196, Smith 9198, Snyder 9199,

South 9201, Sowell 9203, Sparrow 9204, Stark 9209, Stemmons 9211, Stewart 9213, Strake 9215, Sturgis 9216, Susman 9220, **Swett 9221**, Swinney 9222, Tapeats 9223, Temple 9227, Temple 9228, **Tenet 9229**, Tennessee 9230, Texas 9232, Thomas 9234, Tolleson 9237, Trull 9240, Turner 9241, Unkefer 9243, USAA 9245, Vale 9246, Valero 9247, Vanberg 9248, Vaughan 9249, Vaughan 9250, Vaughn 9251, Vergara 9253, Waco 9255, Waggoner 9256, Waggoners 9258, Wal 9260, Ward 9262, Ward 9263, Ware 9264, **Waste 9265**, Watson 9266, Weaver 9267, West 9274, Westcott 9278, White 9279, Wichita 9280, Williams 9282, Wise 9284, Wise 9285, Wolens 9286, Wolff 9288, Wolff 9289, Wright 9294, Young 9295, Zachry 9296, Zale 9297, Zeller 9298

Utah: ALS 9301, **ALSAM 9302**, B. Attitudes 9304, Bamberger 9305, Browning 9308, Denkers 9312, Dreamweaver 9314, Eccles 9319, Eccles 9320, Esther 9321, **Force 9322**, Greene 9325, Jones 9330, Lockwood 9333, McGillis 9334, Noorda 9336, Peery 9337, Quinney 9338, Raymond 9339, Savage 9340, Semnani 9341, Simmons 9342, Sorenson 9343, Stewart 9345, Tanner 9347, Watkins 9350, Wing 9352, **Wishnick 9353**, Zions 9354

Vermont: **Green 9358**, Mergens 9360, Vermont 9361

Virgin Islands: Bartner 9362

Virginia: Adams 9366, AMERIGROUP 9369, Arlington 9371, Batten 9374, Batten 9375, Billings 9377, Cabell 9381, Carrington 9386, Cartledge 9388, Charles 9389, Charlottesville 9390, Cole 9397, Community 9400, Constitution 9404, Dalis 9406, Delmar 9410, English 9414, Estes 9415, Flagler 9417, Folger 9418, Foundation 9419, Fralin 9420, Fredericksburg 9423, Friedman 9425, Funger 9426, **Gannett 9428**, **Glenstone 9429**, Golden 9430, Gottwald 9431, Grandis 9432, Graves 9433, Guilford 9434, Gwathmey 9435, Harrison 9436, Herndon 9437, Houff 9438, HRH 9439, Hylton 9440, Joco 9443, **Johnson 9444**, Kegley 9448, Kellar 9449, Kluge-Moses 9451, **Lambert 9453**, LandAmerica 9454, Landmark 9455, Lane 9456, Lawrence 9457, Loeb 9460, Lynchburg 9463, **Malek 9465**, Mars 9466, Massey 9467, McDonnell 9468, McGlothlin 9469, McGue 9470, McNichols 9472, Meador 9473, Memorial 9474, **Modzelewski 9477**, Morgan 9479, N.E.W. 9482, Norfolk 9484, Ochsman 9489, Olsson 9491, Parsons 9493, Perry 9495, Peterson 9497, Portsmouth 9498, Praxis 9500, Ratner 9501, Reynolds 9503, **Riverside 9505**, Robins 9506, Scott 9513, Smith 9517, Snead 9520, Thurman 9526, Titmus 9527, Truland 9528, Ukrop 9529, United 9530, Universal 9531, Virginia Beach 9532, VuBay 9533, Washington 9534, Weil 9535, Weissberg 9536, **WestWind 9538**, Wiley 9539, **Winkler 9542**

Washington: Adams 9548, Allen 9550, Anderson 9551, Archibald 9553, Blue 9559, **Boeing 9560**, Cheney 9569, Community 9570, Community 9571, Community 9571, Crystal 9576, Dimmer 9579, Everard 9582, Evertrust 9583, Ferguson 9585, Forest 9586, Fortune 9587, Foster 9588, Foundation 9589, **Gates 9591**, Geneva 9592, Glaser 9594, Glazer 9596, Grays 9597, Green 9598, Haas 9599, Harvest 9602, Haugland 9603, Hebert 9604, **Hemingway 9606**, Horizons 9608, Howard 9609, Hughes 9610, Hussey 9611, Kaleidoscope 9616, Larson 9624, Laurel 9625, Lauzier 9626, Lematta 9628, Lie 9629, Lochland 9630, Lockwood 9631, Lucky 9632, Lynn 9633, McMillen 9639, Medina 9640, Milgard 9641, Moccasin 9643, Murdock 9644, **Natan 9646**, Nesholm 9647, Neukom 9649, Norcliffe 9650, O'Donnell 9652, OneFamily 9654, **PAH 9657**, PEMCO 9660, Peterson 9662, Positive 9664, Raikes 9668, Raven 9670, **RealNetworks 9672**, **Sage 9674**, Satterberg 9677, Schuler 9678, Schultz 9679, Seattle 9680, Shemanski 9682, Sherwood 9683, Shirley 9684, Shulman 9685, Snyder 9689, T.E.W. 9692, Tacoma 9693, Tamaki 9695, Warren 9700

West Virginia: BB&T 9710, Carter 9712, Chambers 9713, Clay 9714, Community 9716, Daywood 9717, Hollowell 9719, Hunnicutt 9720, Huntington 9721, Jacobson 9722, Kanawha 9723, McDonough 9726, McQuain 9727, Mylan 9728, Parkersburg 9730, Schenk 9732, Whittaker 9737

Wisconsin: Alexander 9740, Alexander 9741, Alliant 9742, Anon 9744, Archer 9746, Argosy 9747, Bader 9749, Baird 9750, Bartlett 9753, Beasley 9755, Beloit 9757, Benidt 9758, Bishop 9759, Bleser 9760, Bolz 9762, Brookbank 9766, Bryant 9768, Bryce 9769, Casper 9770, Chapman 9771, Cleary 9774, Coleman 9775, Community 9776, Community 9777, Community 9778, Community 9779, Community 9780, Cornerstone 9781, Cox 9782, Cudahy 9784, Cudahy 9785, CUNA 9786, Davis 9787, **DeAtley 9789**, Delavan 9790, Demmer 9791, Dudley 9792, Duncan 9793, **Eastman 9794**, Evans 9796, Evjue 9797, **Firestone 9798**, Fond du Lac 9800, Fort 9801, Fotsch 9802, Frautschi 9804, Glover 9805, Gordon 9808, Gould 9809, Green Bay 9810, Handleman 9811, Harley 9812, Helfaer 9813, Hess 9816, Hyde 9818, Johnson 9823, **Johnson 9825**, Johnson 9826, Kadish 9829, Kellogg 9832, Kenosha 9833, Kettering 9835, Kikkoman 9836, Kohl 9837, Krause 9842, Kress 9844, La Crosse 9845, Ladish 9846, Lubar 9851, **Make 9856**, Managed 9857, Manpower 9858, Marcus 9859, Marshall 9860, McBeath 9864, McDonough 9865, McQueen 9866, Mead 9867, **Meehan 9868**, Menasha 9869, Mercy 9871, Merten 9873, Michels 9874, Miller 9875, Milwaukee 9876, MMG 9877, Modine 9878, Morse 9879, Munson 9880, Nicholas 9883, Northwestern 9884, Oshkosh 9887, **Outagamie 9888**, **Palmer 9890**, Pamida 9891, Pangburn 9892, Peck 9894, Peck 9895, Pettit 9897, Phipps 9898, Pick 9899, Pollybill 9900, PPC 9902, Puelicher 9904, Racine 9906, Reinhart 9909, Riordan 9911, **Rockwell 9912**, **Roddis 9913**, Rolfs 9914, Rutledge 9917, Schlegel 9919, Schneider 9920, Schoenleber 9921, Sensient 9922, Seramur 9924, Shattuck 9926, Siebert 9927, **Smith 9929**, Soref 9930, Split 9932, St. Croix 9933, Stackner 9934, Stark 9935, **Stein 9937**, Stone 9940, Stuart 9941, Styberg 9944, Sub 9945, **Taylor 9947**, Taylor 9948, **Thrivent 9949**, Tulsa 9951, Uihlein 9953, Uihlein 9954, Uihlein 9955, **Wagner 9957**, Wagner 9958, Walter 9959, Waukesha 9960, West 9964, Windhover 9966, Wisconsin 9967, Witte 9968, WPS 9970, Wrigley 9971, **Young 9972**

Wyoming: Berry 9975, Chapman 9976, Community 9977, Connemara 9978, Martin 9984, McMurry 9985, Richardson 9987, Sargent 9989, Scott 9991, Stock 9992, Thorson 9994, True 9996, Weiss 9997

Human services, alliance

Massachusetts: Orchard 4062

Human services, emergency aid

Alabama: Community 24
California: Anaheim 220, Fluor 523, Forest 527
Connecticut: Community 1516
Delaware: **Neuberger 1735**
Florida: Conn 1951
Indiana: Central 3116
Maryland: O'Neil 3701
Minnesota: Deluxe 4549, Target 4697
New York: Atticus 5576, R & TP 6764
North Carolina: Southern 7481
Ohio: A Good 7522
Pennsylvania: Plankenhorn 8387
Rhode Island: Rhode Island 8551
Washington: Horizons 9608

Human services, financial counseling

California: Fluor 523, Intuit 696, **Schwab 1110**, **Strauss 1203**, Union 1250

Colorado: Rose 1445
Georgia: ING 2418
Illinois: **Allstate 2588**, Zurich 3093
Iowa: Principal 3326
Maine: TD 3558
Maryland: **Nasdaq 3700**
Michigan: Comerica 4251
Minnesota: RBC 4661, TCF 4699, Xcel 4732
Missouri: American 4773
New Jersey: Prudential 5360
New York: **American 5553**, **Citigroup 5755**, **JPMorgan 6277**, **Merrill 6537**, **Mitsubishi 6560**, New York 6619
North Carolina: **Wachovia 7502**
Ohio: **Key 7700**
Pennsylvania: Blue 8112
Washington: PACCAR 9656
Wisconsin: Johnson 9823, **Thrivent 9949**

Human services, mind/body enrichment

Arizona: Lovell 119
Connecticut: Shei'rah 1649
Massachusetts: Chase 3847
Michigan: Cook 4261, Fetzer 4298, Lachimi 4369
Missouri: **Hana 4827**
New Jersey: **Rippel 5368**
Ohio: **Dewald 7608**

Human services, personal services

California: Santa Barbara 1093

Human services, public education

Virginia: Freddie 9422

Human services, public policy

Illinois: Abbott 2580

Human services, reform

California: Rosenberg 1065

Human services, research

New York: Mangurian, 6482

Human services, travelers' aid

Indiana: Goldstine 3156

Human services, victim aid

California: Keller 752
Florida: Tarrant 2265
New York: Mangurian, 6482, Schnurmacher 6931

Humanities

Alabama: Community 26, Community 27, Moody 54
Arkansas: Arkansas 156
California: Ahmanson 198, Community 407, Lehrer 800, Northrop 942, Osher 961, Pasadena 982, Roth 1071, Sacramento 1080, San Francisco 1088, Sonora 1178
Colorado: Bonfils 1347, Chambers 1354, Community 1357, El Pomar 1374, Gates 1380
Connecticut: Community 1515, Connecticut 1518, **Wiener 1677**
Delaware: Welfare 1762
District of Columbia: Meyer 1834
Florida: Bank 1890, Community 1946, **Kislak 2093**, Tarrant 2265
Hawaii: Atherton 2532, Cooke 2541
Illinois: Chicago 2661, Community 2677, Community 2679, Community 2680, Cressey 2689, Franke 2734, Kaplan 2823, McGraw 2882, Siragusa 3009

Indiana: Ball 3103, Brown 3110, Clowes 3119, Community 3122, **Goodrich 3157**, Lafayette 3188
Kansas: Wichita 3404
Kentucky: Blue 3407, Community 3414
Louisiana: Baton Rouge 3462
Maine: Maine 3548
Maryland: Brown 3578, Knott 3666
Massachusetts: Ayling 3785, Cape Cod 3833, High 3950, Stevens 4163, Worcester 4209
Michigan: Branch 4237, Capital 4243, Community 4253, Community 4255, Grand Rapids 4326, Jackson 4347, **Kresge 4367**, Midland 4392
Minnesota: Andersen 4502, Bigelow 4519, Bush 4524, Butler 4525, Grand Rapids 4574, Minnesota 4624, Saint Paul 4671
Nebraska: Cooper 4954, Fulk 4964, Woods 5018
New Hampshire: New Hampshire 5098, Trust 5103
New Jersey: Aicher 5109, Dodge 5181, Hyde 5247, Kirby 5279, **Newcombe 5338**, **Verizon 5439**
New Mexico: Santa Fe 5496
New York: Achelis 5513, Bodman 5647, Central 5724, Community 5781, Community 5784, **Delmas 5850**, **Frankel 5976**, Glickenhaus 6042, Griffis 6107, **Guggenheim 6119**, Hoyt 6203, Littauer 6434, **Luce 6453**, **Mellon 6525**, **Rockefeller 6826**, Steele 7053, Vidda 7198, **Whiting 7253**
North Carolina: Blumenthal 7320, Community 7343, Cumberland 7349, Harvey 7393, Polk 7449, Triangle 7496
Ohio: Columbus 7580, Community 7583, Dayton 7603, **Deuble 7607**, First 7629, New 7775, Reinberger 7815, Tuscarawas 7890, Wayne 7897
Oklahoma: Bernsen 7925, Williams 7989
Oregon: Jackson 8024, Johnson 8027, Kinsman 8031, Meyer 8042, Swindells 8062
Pennsylvania: **Annenberg 8084**, Barra 8095, Community 8153, Dolfinger 8172, Foundation 8208, Heinz 8242, **Pew 8377**
Rhode Island: **Amica 8518**
South Carolina: Spartanburg 8616
South Dakota: Sioux Falls 8630
Tennessee: Benwood 8644, Community 8662, Hyde 8693
Texas: Constantin 8843, East 8876, El Paso 8881, Hobby 8954, Kempner 8987, Meadows 9049, Permian 9117, **Tenet 9229**, Tennessee 9230, Ward 9263, Zachry 9296
Utah: Eccles 9320
Vermont: Vermont 9361
Virginia: Arlington 9371, Charlottesville 9390, Lynchburg 9463, Virginia Beach 9532
Washington: Blue 9559, Community 9570, Community 9571, Foundation 9589, Seattle 9680, Tacoma 9693
West Virginia: Kanawha 9723
Wisconsin: Alliant 9742, **Bradley 9763**
Wyoming: Chapman 9976, McMurry 9985, Scott 9991

Immigrants/refugees

California: California 345, Grove 625, Haas 637, **Koulaieff 778**, San Francisco 1088, Stern 1195, vanLobenSels 1260, Zellerbach 1326
Colorado: Aspen 1338
District of Columbia: Cafritz 1780, Fowler 1797, Kimsey 1817, Meyer 1834, **Public 1844**
Florida: Dade 1957
Georgia: Goizueta 2400
Illinois: Reese 2961, Washington 3058
Maryland: Meyerhoff 3692
Massachusetts: Boston 3812, Hyams 3961, Stevens 4163, Stevens 4164, **Swensrud 4177**
Michigan: Grand Rapids 4326
Minnesota: Bell 4514, Blue 4521, Bremer 4523, Bush 4524, Grotto 4579, Minneapolis 4623, Phillips 4655
Nebraska: Woods 5018
New Jersey: Victoria 5440
New Mexico: Santa Fe 5496
New York: **Abelard 5508**, **de Hirsch 5840**, **Ford 5970**, **Foundation 5971**, New York 6615
Ohio: Akron 7526

Oregon: Northwest 8048
Pennsylvania: **Pew 8377**
Rhode Island: Rhode Island 8551
Texas: Trull 9240
Vermont: **Ben 9355**
Virginia: **Gannett 9428**
Washington: **Kongsgaard 9620**
Wisconsin: Cudahy 9785

Immunology

Virginia: **de Beaumont 9408**

Immunology research

New York: Vilcek 7199

Indigenous people

California: **Chiron 383**
Virginia: Sacharuna 9509

Infants/toddlers

California: Peninsula 989
Florida: Community 1940
Iowa: Principal 3326
Michigan: Community 4252
New York: Singh 6991
Pennsylvania: CIGNA 8143

International affairs

California: Allequash 202, Amar 213, **American 216**,
   Appleton 225, Becker 271, **Bergstrom 282**,
   Castagnola 366, Draper 465, Edgerton 477,
   Foundation 529, Lee 798, **Saban 1079**, Saga
   1081, **Saje 1084**, Sapling 1094, **Tosa 1240**,
   Unocal 1252
Colorado: McCloskey 1419
Connecticut: Bridgemill 1503, **Richardson 1632**
District of Columbia: Harman 1807
Florida: Catlin 1929, **Morris 2145**
Hawaii: Scott 2553
Illinois: **ARIA 2600**, **MacArthur 2868**, Montgomery
   2903, **Pritzker 2951**, Takiff 3032
Iowa: Holthues 3295
Maryland: Weiss 3760
Massachusetts: Flatley 3911, **Hershey 3949**,
   Morningside 4043, **Sager 4122**
Michigan: Timmis 4459
Minnesota: **Cafesjian 4527**, Kelley 4597, Oswald 4645,
   Sundance 4693
Nevada: **Walsh 5075**
New Jersey: **Hovnanian 5241**, **Johnson 5263**, Weisberg
   5449
New York: **Altria 5545**, **Baker 5594**, Berkowitz 5622,
   Birkelund 5632, Bobst 5646, Bovin 5654, **Bydale
   5694**, **C.O.U.Q. 5695**, Centennial 5722, CJM
   5756, **Daedalus 5821**, **Donner 5873**, **Ford 5970**,
   Furman 6002, GBRG 6008, Gerschel 6019, **Global
   6043**, Gordon 6077, **Guggenheim 6118**, Hurford
   6215, **IAC 6220**, **Isdell 6239**, Janklow 6254, **JEHT
   6257**, Johnson 6271, **Lane 6372**, Loeb 6440,
   M.A.C. 6466, Mitsui 6561, **Phillips 6725**, **Reynolds
   6790**, **Rockefeller 6826**, **Rosen 6843**, Ross 6864,
   Rubin 6874, Seiler 6954, Slifka 7001, Soros 7021,
   Tinker 7143, **United 7185**, Wallach 7210,
   Whitehead 7252, **Zilkha 7300**
Ohio: Fairfax 7621
Pennsylvania: **Carthage 8132**, Ryan 8416, **Scaife 8425**
South Carolina: Ceres 8578
Texas: **A Glimmer 8747**
Virginia: **Parker 9492**
Wisconsin: **Bradley 9763**, Delavan 9790, **Palmer 9890**

International affairs, arms control

California: **Castagnola 366**, **Compton 409**
District of Columbia: **Mott 1836**, **Public 1844**

Illinois: **Shifting 3006**
Maryland: Weiss 3760
New York: **Carnegie 5707**, **Ford 5970**, Glickenhaus
   6042, **Guggenheim 6118**, **HKH 6190**, James
   6252, **New 6621**, **Prospect 6750**, **Rubin 6872**,
   Scherman 6918

International affairs, equal rights

California: **Draper 466**
New Jersey: Jonas 5266
Washington: Channel 9568

International affairs, foreign policy

California: **Compton 409**, Paramitas 977
Connecticut: Bluebell 1496, **Richardson 1632**, **Wiener
   1677**
District of Columbia: **Arca 1767**, **Mott 1836**
Illinois: Cooper 2683, **MacArthur 2868**, Madigan 2869
Massachusetts: Edgerly 3889
New York: Centennial 5722, Coles 5775, **Ford 5970**,
   Guggenheim 6118, **Hauser 6155**, James 6252,
   Kautz 6300, Rose 6839, **Rubin 6872**, **Tinker
   7143**, **United 7185**, **Walter 7211**
Pennsylvania: Hooper 8256
Wisconsin: **Bradley 9763**

International affairs, formal/general education

New York: **Endowment 5931**

International affairs, goodwill promotion

Connecticut: **Wiener 1677**
Georgia: Keough 2426, **Wardlaw 2506**
Illinois: Stuart 3028
Kentucky: C.E. 3412
Minnesota: Duluth 4556
New Jersey: Sweetfeet 5421
New York: **Atlantic 5574**, Banfi 5597, **Bismarck 5633**,
   Centennial 5722, Freeman 5981, Gerschel 6019,
   Grand 6086, Greve 6104, Soros 7024, **Tanaka
   7120**, **Tang 7122**, **Walter 7211**

International affairs, information services

Massachusetts: Colombe 3852

International affairs, national security

New York: **Carnegie 5707**

International affairs, public education

Arizona: **Gagarin 99**

International affairs, public policy

District of Columbia: Kimsey 1817
Minnesota: WEM 4722

International affairs, research

New York: **C.O.U.Q. 5695**

International affairs, U.N.

New York: Central 5723, Loeb 6440, **Woods 7278**

International agricultural development

California: **Bergstrom 282**, Hewlett 671
Colorado: **Working 1476**
Maine: **Sandy 3555**
Texas: **A Glimmer 8748**, Onward 9103
Washington: Channel 9568

International conflict resolution

New Jersey: Sweetfeet 5421
New York: **Carnegie 5707**, Gould 6085

International development

California: **Gere 565**, La Fetra 782, **Tosa 1240**
Connecticut: **Vranos 1673**
District of Columbia: **CityBridge 1783**
Iowa: **Sehgal 3330**
Maryland: O'Neil 3701
Massachusetts: Mazar 4028
Minnesota: **Weyerhaeuser 4725**, Wolohan 4730
Nevada: **SFO 5062**
New Jersey: Orenstein 5344, Reddy 5364
New York: **Altria 5545**, **Bito 5634**, **Children's 5749**,
   Daedalus 5821, **Donner 5873**, **IAC 6220**, **Richman
   6799**, **Rockefeller 6826**, **Saltzman 6900**, **Tsadra
   7169**
Ohio: **Geisse 7646**
Pennsylvania: **Pincus 8384**, Sampson 8423
Tennessee: Lazarus 8700
Texas: **O'Sullivan 9098**
Virginia: **Mousetrap 9480**, **Three 9525**
Washington: Channel 9568, **Gates 9591**
Wisconsin: **Make 9856**

International economic development

California: Atkinson 239, **Bergstrom 282**, **Draper 466**,
   Hewlett 671, **Saje 1084**
Colorado: **Working 1476**
District of Columbia: **Wallace 1858**
Florida: Martin 2130
Illinois: **Fairwyn 2723**
Indiana: West 3256
Massachusetts: **Azadoutioun 3786**
Nevada: **SFO 5062**
New Jersey: **International 5252**
New York: **Children's 5749**, **Echoing 5905**, **Endowment
   5931**, **Ford 5970**, **Open 6665**, **United 7185**
Texas: **A Glimmer 8748**
Washington: Channel 9568, **Stewardship 9691**
Wisconsin: Cudahy 9785

International economics/trade policy

California: Hewlett 671
District of Columbia: **Wallace 1858**

International exchange

New York: **Trust 7168**
Washington: Bezos 9557

International exchange, students

Georgia: **Coca-Cola 2352**
Indiana: **IFSA 3171**
Massachusetts: **Rodgers 4109**

International human rights

California: **Angelica 223**, **Fund 542**, **Gere 565**, Lutz
   833, San Francisco 1088
Colorado: **General 1381**
Connecticut: **Valentine 1669**
District of Columbia: **Arca 1767**, Kimsey 1817, **Moriah
   1835**, **Mott 1836**, **Public 1844**, **Summit 1852**,
   Wallace 1858
Georgia: **Wardlaw 2506**, Weber 2510
Illinois: Keiser 2828, **MacArthur 2868**, **Shifting 3006**
Iowa: Holthues 3295
Maine: Falcon 3532, **Oak 3552**
Maryland: **Blaustein 3575**, Blaustein 3576, **Cohen
   3594**, Osprey 3703
Massachusetts: Carr 3838, **Merck 4036**, **Reebok 4098**
New Jersey: **Johnson 5263**, Knistrom 5282
New Mexico: **Levinson 5486**

Louisiana: Lupin 3498, Monteleone 3502
Maine: Alfond 3521, Alfond 3522, Lunder 3547
Maryland: Abramson 3561, Bank 3569, **Bearman 3570**, **Berman 3572**, Berman 3573, **Blaustein 3575**, Blum 3577, **Brown 3579**, Cohen 3592, Cohen 3593, Crane 3603, **Dahan 3604**, Davis 3607, Davison 3609, Dupkin 3618, England 3622, Epstein 3623, Freeman 3633, Glazer 3635, Goldsmith 3637, Greenberg 3639, Hirschhorn 3650, Hittman 3651, Hoffberger 3652, Kaplan 3659, Klein 3662, Krieger 3668, Lerner 3674, Lerner 3675, Levitt 3676, Meyerhoff 3691, Meyerhoff 3692, **Morningstar 3695**, Myers 3698, Nabit 3699, Polinger 3708, RFI 3716, Rosenbloom 3721, Rothschild 3723, Samuelson 3725, Schifter 3726, Shrensky 3731, Silverman 3733, Small 3734, Small 3735, Stulman 3739, Sylvan 3741, Tauber 3742, Thalheimer 3744, Tucker 3750, Tzedakah 3751, Wasserman 3757, Wasserman 3758
Massachusetts: A.M. 3766, Aaron 3767, Abrams 3768, Ansin 3779, Barron 3792, Berenson 3799, Bernon 3802, Bressler 3815, Casty 3839, Chafetz 3842, Corkin 3861, Cutler 3872, Dana 3873, Demoulas 3878, Fireman 3909, Fireman 3910, Goldberg 3926, Goldberg 3927, Gordon 3928, Grinspoon 3935, Hirschtick 3953, Inavale 3964, Karp 3974, Kobren 3988, Krupp 3991, Landsman 3996, Lappin 3997, Lesser 4002, Levine 4003, Linsey 4010, Lubin 4016, Manzi 4021, Marcus 4022, **Partnership 4071**, Persky 4080, Rabb 4090, Rabb 4091, Rappaport 4093, Ribakoff 4102, Ribakoff 4103, Rubenstein 4116, Sadowsky 4121, Schoen 4130, Shapiro 4135, Sherman 4141, Shillman 4142, Siff 4145, Silverman 4146, Solomont 4152, Spencer 4154, Stoneman 4167, Swartz 4175, Zwanziger 4212
Michigan: Alix 4216, Applebaum 4222, **Berman 4230**, Blumenstein 4234, Brown 4239, DeRoy 4273, Farbman 4294, **Ferber 4296**, Fisher 4299, Ford 4301, Frankel 4312, Frankel 4313, Frankel 4314, Grosfeld 4332, HFF 4342, Kahn 4351, Kogan 4365, Levy 4378, Maas 4379, Manat 4381, Padnos 4406, Pitt 4413, Ravitz 4418, Rogers 4423, **Rosenzweig 4425**, Seligman 4433, Tauber 4454, Wolff 4486
Minnesota: Capp 4529, Deikel 4548, Edelstein 4559, Fiterman 4565, Grossman 4578, Phileona 4654, Phillips 4655, Regis 4664, Sabes 4670, Tankenoff 4696
Missouri: Edison 4808, **Fox 4815**, Gershman 4818, Gottlieb 4820, **Hana 4827**, Jewish 4837, Lopata 4859, Millstone 4867, Pershing 4881, Simon 4903, Sosland 4908, Trio 4918, Uhlmann 4920, Wampus 4923, Wolff 4927
Nebraska: Schrager 5001, Simon 5002, **Slosburg 5003**
Nevada: Bennett 5021, Greenspun 5034, Rochlin 5057
New Hampshire: Trust 5103
New Jersey: Adelson 5108, Bendheim 5126, Berger 5128, Berrie 5130, Bershad 5131, Bildner 5133, Brody 5144, C 5150, Cohen 5166, Cooperman 5168, Croman 5172, Cyh 5173, D & K 5174, Dagish 5176, Drapkin 5185, Eisenberg 5187, Entin 5189, **Eshet 5190**, Fishoff 5195, **Freyer 5197**, Galanta 5202, Gershman 5206, Goldring 5210, Goldstein 5211, Halpern 5220, Harary 5222, Healthcare 5228, **Hess 5231**, Hiller 5237, Holzer 5238, **IDT 5248**, Indian 5250, Isermann 5253, Kaplen 5268, Karma 5269, Katz 5271, Keren 5277, Kerr 5278, Kolatch 5285, Kreitchman 5289, Krieger 5290, L.A.W. 5292, Laurie 5297, **Lautenberg 5298**, Leib 5302, Levy 5306, Mack 5312, **Mack 5313**, Mack 5314, Mamiye 5316, Merkin 5331, NSN 5340, Orenstein 5344, Parnes 5348, Poses 5354, Providence 5358, Rosenbaum 5374, Ross 5375, Roth 5377, Schecter 5385, Schwartz 5392, Schwartz 5393, Schwarz 5394, Seiden 5396, Sierra 5401, Smilowitz 5406, ST2 5410, Steiner 5411, Stern 5412, Straus 5413, Straus 5414, Sutton 5420, Sweetfeet 5421, **Syms 5422**, Taub 5424, Taub 5425, Tolchin 5428, V'Emunah 5437, Werdiger 5451, **Wilf 5455**, Wilf

5456, Zayat 5462, Zimmer 5463, Zobel 5464, Zodiac 5465
New Mexico: **Levinson 5486**
New York: A.R. 5507, Abrons 5511, Abrons 5512, Ades 5516, Adjmi 5518, Adjmi 5519, **Adjmi 5520**, Adnim 5522, Ahava 5526, Ahavas 5527, Alexander 5532, Alff 5533, Alpert 5541, Altman 5542, Altschul 5546, Altus 5547, American 5555, **American 5556**, Apfelbaum 5561, Appleman 5562, Arm 5566, Ashkenazie 5572, Atticus 5576, Auerbach 5578, Azrak 5585, Bachmann 5587, **Baker 5593**, Barrington 5602, Bass 5604, Beker 5613, Belfer 5615, Belfer 5616, Ben-Haim 5617, Benedict 5618, Benenson 5619, **Benenson 5620**, Berg 5621, Berkowitz 5622, Bernstein 5625, Betesh 5627, Betesh 5628, Bialkin 5629, Bildirici 5630, Blankfein 5637, Blue 5641, Blum 5643, Bodner 5648, Botwinick 5653, Bovin 5654, Boxer 5656, Brach 5657, Brand 5658, Braufman 5660, Bravmann 5661, Brodsky 5667, Brodsky 5669, **Bronfman 5672**, **Bronfman 5673**, Buchmann 5681, Burns 5689, Butler 5692, Cambr 5699, Canary 5702, Cappelli 5703, Cayne 5717, Cayre 5718, **Cayre 5719**, Cayre 5720, Centennial 5722, Central 5723, Century 5725, Chai 5727, Chaim 5728, Chanin 5730, Charina 5731, Chasanoff 5735, Chasdei 5736, **Chazen 5739**, Chehebar 5740, Chehebar 5741, Chencinski 5742, Chernow 5744, Chernow 5745, Chesed 5746, Chesed 5747, CJM 5756, **Cogut 5766**, Cohen 5767, Cohen 5768, Cohen 5769, Cohen 5770, Cohen 5771, Cohen 5772, Cohenca 5773, Cole 5774, Cong 5775, Cooper 5788, Corzine 5798, Cowin 5802, Cramer 5804, Croll 5810, **Cummings 5814**, **Dabah 5819**, Dabah 5820, Damial 5823, Danziger 5829, Darivoff 5831, Davenport 5833, Davidowitz 5834, Davidson 5835, **de Hirsch 5840**, Delancey 5849, Diamond 5859, Diker 5862, Dimon 5864, Ditmars 5865, Dobkin 5866, Double 5876, Drexler 5885, Drukier 5890, Dubin 5891, Dweck 5896, Edelman 5906, Edelstein 5907, Educational 5910, Effron 5911, **EHA 5912**, Ehrenkranz 5913, Eig 5914, Einhorn 5915, Einhorn 5916, Eisenreich 5917, Elbogen 5918, Elishis 5921, Elkes 5922, Ellis 5923, Emes 5928, Englander 5933, Equipart 5936, Feil 5949, Feinstein 5951, FIMF 5956, **Fischel 5959**, Fischer 5960, Fisher 5961, Flanzer 5963, Fogel 5965, Franconia 5972, Franklin 5978, Fribourg 5984, Friedberg 5985, Friedman 5986, Friedman 5987, **Friends 5991**, **Fruchthandler 5995**, Fuchs 5996, Fuchsberg 5997, Fuchsberg 5998, Fuld 6000, Fund 6001, Furman 6003, GBRG 6008, Gerschel 6018, Gershwind 6020, Gerson 6021, Gibbs 6024, **Gilbert 6028**, **Gilman 6033**, **Gimprich 6035**, Gindi 6036, Gleberman 6040, Glickenhaus 6042, Godinger 6044, Goldberg 6045, Goldie 6049, Goldman 6051, **Goldman 6052**, Goldschmidt 6058, Goldsmith 6059, Goldsmith 6060, Goldstein 6061, Goldstein 6062, Goldstein 6063, Goldstein 6064, Golub 6070, Goodman 6072, Gordon 6074, Gould 6085, **Grant 6090**, Grateful 6093, Green 6095, Green 6096, Greenberg 6098, Grin 6109, Gross 6110, Gross 6111, Gross 6112, Gruss 6114, Gruss 6115, **Gruss 6116**, Gural 6120, Gurwin 6121, Gutman 6122, Haber 6129, Hager 6131, Hammerman 6139, **Handler 6141**, Harary 6143, Harris 6148, Hartman 6151, **Hasenfeld 6153**, Heisler 6166, **Heller 6167**, Heller 6168, Heller 6169, Hendel 6172, Herman 6174, Hermione 6175, Hersh 6177, Hidary 6181, Hidary 6182, Hilibrand 6184, Hillman 6186, Hirsch 6187, Hochfelder 6191, Hochstein 6192, Hod 6193, Holtzmann 6198, Horowitz 6202, Huberfeld 6205, Huberfeld 6206, Hurst 6216, Icahn 6224, IDF 6225, J G 6244, Jaaaa 6245, Jacobson 6247, Jacobson 6248, **Jaffe 6250**, Jesselson 6259, Joelson 6265, JW 6279, JW 6280, Kalter 6284, Kaminer 6285, Kaplan 6288, Katz 6295, Katz 6296, Katz 6297, Kaylie 6301, Keren 6316, Keren 6318, Keshet 6319, Kingdon 6326, **Kitov 6327**, Klaus 6328, **Klein 6330**, Klein 6331, Klein 6332, Kleinman 6334, **Klingenstein 6335**, Klingenstein 6336, Knafel 6341, **Knopf 6343**, Koppelman 6349,

Kriendler 6358, Kuflik 6360, Kumble 6361, Kupferberg 6363, Kurz 6365, L'Maan 6367, L. & L. 6368, Lambert 6370, Lane 6373, Langer 6376, Lasdon 6378, Lauder 6381, Lauder 6382, **Lauder 6383**, Lawrence 6385, LBC 6386, Lebworth 6390, Leeds 6392, Leffell 6393, Legacy 6394, Leibowitz 6399, Leigh 6400, Lemberg 6401, Levin 6407, Levine 6408, **Levy 6410**, Levy 6411, Levy 6412, Lewis 6415, Lieb 6420, Linden 6424, Lindner 6426, Lipmanson 6431, Lipp 6432, Littauer 6434, Litwin 6436, Loeb 6440, Loewe 6441, Loews 6443, Lopatin 6446, Lostand 6448, Lowinger 6450, Lucerne 6454, Lurie 6459, Lynton 6463, M & E 6464, Magen 6472, **Mailman 6478**, Maleh 6479, Mallah 6481, Manitoba 6483, Mark 6488, Marks 6490, Marmurstein 6491, Marron 6493, Marx 6498, Masada 6500, Mashala 6501, Massry 6502, **Mayer 6509**, Mayore 6511, Melohn 6527, Melohn 6528, Menche 6530, Mercy 6534, **Merlin 6536**, Metropolitan 6543, Meyer 6544, Meyer 6545, Milstein 6554, Milstein 6555, Milstein 6556, Mindel 6557, Mindich 6558, **Monterey 6568**, Morrow 6581, Morton 6585, Moskowitz 6588, Moss 6589, Mosse 6590, MRM 6592, Mullen 6596, Nakash 6600, NAON 6601, **Nash 6602**, Neidich 6606, Nelkin 6608, Netzach 6609, Newman 6626, Olshan 6663, Oppenheimer 6666, Orentreich 6667, Ostreicher 6671, Ostreicher 6672, Paneth 6685, Park 6687, Parker 6690, Parkview 6691, Parshelsky 6693, PBO 6699, Penner 6710, Penson 6711, **Perelman 6716**, Pevaroff 6719, **Phillips 6725**, Pollack 6734, Pollack 6735, Pomeranz 6739, Price 6746, Propp 6749, Providence 6751, Pulier 6753, Quadrangle 6758, Queensgate 6760, R & TP 6764, Raiff 6768, **Ramapo 6769**, Rapaport 6771, Rattner 6773, Rausman 6775, Rechler 6781, Reich 6784, Reiss 6785, Resnick 6787, **Richman 6799**, **Richmond 6801**, Ridgefield 6802, Rieder 6803, Rieger 6805, Rifkind 6806, Riklis 6808, Rohr 6831, Rosansky 6832, Rose 6833, Rose 6836, Rose 6839, Rosedorf 6840, **Rosen 6843**, Rosen 6844, Rosenberg 6846, Rosenberg 6847, Rosenblatt 6848, Rosenblatt 6849, Rosenblum 6850, Rosenthal 6854, Rosenwald 6855, **Rosenwald 6857**, Rosh 6858, Rosner 6860, Ross 6862, Ruben 6868, Rubenstein 6870, Rubin 6871, **Rubin 6874**, **Rukal 6881**, RZH 6885, S.O. 6886, Safra 6893, Saligman 6895, Saltz 6899, **Saltzman 6900**, Sandler 6902, **Sato 6908**, Schafer 6910, Schapiro 6912, Scharf 6913, Schechter 6914, Schenker 6916, Scheuer 6919, Scheuer 6920, **Scheuer 6921**, Schmeelk 6927, Schneider 6929, Schnurmacher 6931, Schon 6933, Schulweis 6936, Schwartz 6938, Schwartz 6942, Schwartz 6945, Schwartz 6946, Schwarz 6947, SDA 6950, Seaver 6952, Seiler 6954, SES 6956, Setton 6957, Seventeen 6958, Shapiro 6959, **Shulamit 6971**, **Sicherman 6973**, Siebert 6975, Siegel 6976, Silberstein 6978, **Silfen 6980**, Silver 6981, Silverman 6982, Silverstein 6984, Silverweed 6985, Simons 6988, Singer 6990, Sisenwein 6993, Sitt 6995, Sitt 6996, Sitt 6997, Skirball 6999, Slant 7000, Slifka 7001, Slovin 7004, SO 7015, Sobel 7016, **Solomon 7017**, Solomon 7018, Solow 7019, Soros 7024, Speyer 7027, Spiegel 7029, **Spiegel 7030**, Srour 7037, SSM 7038, Stanton 7043, Stanton 7045, Stecher 7051, Stein 7055, Stein 7056, Stein 7058, Steinberg 7060, Steinberg 7063, **Steinhardt 7064**, Steinmetz 7066, Steinmetz 7067, Steinmetz 7068, Stern 7070, Stern 7073, Steyer 7077, Stone 7081, Strasser 7083, Straus 7085, Strauss 7087, Sulzberger 7095, Sunrise 7101, Sunrise 7102, Sussman 7104, Sutton 7106, Sutton 7107, Sutton 7108, Sutton 7109, **SVM 7110**, Tarnopol 7123, TBF 7125, Tennenbaum 7129, Terumah 7130, **Tikvah 7140**, Tilles 7141, Tisch 7144, Tisch 7145, Tisch 7146, Tisch 7147, TNG 7151, Traditional 7161, Trump 7167, Tzedaka 7177, Tziterman 7178, **Tzur 7179**, Ushkow 7188, Vogelstein 7201, **Volpert 7202**, Wallach 7210, Walters 7213, Warren 7217, Wasserman 7218, Weiler 7226, Weill 7227,

Weinberg 7228, Weinman 7232, Weiss 7235, Weiss 7236, Weissman 7237, Weissman 7238, Werblow 7245, **Wexner 7249**, Wiener 7257, Winkelried 7265, **Wolfensohn 7270**, Wolk 7271, Yitzchok 7283, Zalaznick 7288, Zankel 7289, Zarin 7290, Zedakah 7291, Zedukah 7292, Zemsky 7294, **Zenkel 7295**, Zichron 7296, Zichron 7297, Zichron 7298, ZIIZ 7299, **Zilkha 7300**, Zucker 7303

North Carolina: Baruch 7311, Blumenthal 7320, Gorelick 7380, Gorelick 7381, High Point 7397, Levine 7421, Nias 7435, Toleo 7495, Tzedakah 7497

Ohio: Beerman 7543, Berkman 7545, Berlin 7546, Binzer 7550, Boymel 7553, Deshe 7606, Diamond 7610, Forest 7634, Gettler 7649, Heiman 7669, Horvitz 7676, Horvitz 7677, Horvitz 7678, Jarson 7686, Jewish 7690, Kaplan 7696, **Lerner 7711**, Levin 7712, Lippman 7719, LKC 7720, M/I 7729, Mandel 7730, Mandel 7731, Mandel 7732, Mayerson 7739, Miller 7752, Miller 7753, Miller 7754, **Ohio 7786**, **PLACE 7805**, Rockwern 7824, Rose 7825, **Sapirstein 7834**, Schottenstein 7844, Shaw 7852, Siegal 7856, Sloat 7861, Stillson 7869, Stone 7871, Toledo 7882, Western 7903, **Wexner 7904**, Wolf 7914

Oklahoma: Gussman 7941, Kaiser 7947, Kaiser 7948, Oxley 7968, **Schusterman 7975**, Sylvan 7981, Zarrow 7992

Oregon: Fohs 8012, Schnitzer 8056, Schnitzer 8057

Pennsylvania: Aaron 8072, Ames 8080, Berger 8101, Berkman 8102, **Berman 8104**, Birnhak 8108, Born 8113, Bronstein 8119, Buncher 8125, Cassett 8133, Chosky 8142, CMS 8148, Cooper 8158, Epstein 8186, Erlbaum 8189, Farber 8194, Farber 8195, **Federation 8197**, Fine 8201, Fox 8210, Giant 8214, Gitlin 8217, Goodstein 8220, Green 8225, Grumbacher 8227, Innisfree 8267, Kaiserman 8277, Kardon 8279, Katz 8281, Klein 8291, Kline 8292, Korman 8296, Levis 8309, Levis 8310, Lubert 8315, Miller 8354, Morris 8359, Neubauer 8363, Novotny 8364, Perelman 8374, Perkin 8375, **Pincus 8384**, Roberts 8405, Roberts 8406, Rosenfeld 8413, Rubin 8415, Satell 8424, Scheller 8430, Schwab 8430, Shapira 8437, Snider 8447, Strawbridge 8467, Toll 8478, Toll 8479, Weiss 8499, Willary 8503, Wimmer 8505

Puerto Rico: **FNZ 8514**

Rhode Island: Alperin 8516, **Alpert 8517**, Fain 8533, Mann 8546, Nelson 8549, Siperstein 8557, Usen 8560

South Carolina: Arnold 8566, Zucker 8622

Tennessee: Belz 8643, Bornblum 8645, Eskind 8674, Eskind 8675, Goldsmith 8682, Gordon 8683, Scheidt 8726

Texas: Ackerman 8750, Alexander 8752, Diener 8867, Essar 8887, Farb 8893, Feinberg 8898, Finger 8900, Gale 8913, Hirsch 8953, Kahn 8980, Kaufman 8981, Kempner 8987, Levit 9009, Mechia 9050, Miller 9061, Nightingale 9091, Oshman 9104, Pollock 9127, Rachofsky 9134, Rosenberg 9157, Rubenstein 9162, Sterling 9212, Susman 9220, Wolens 9286, Wolff 9288, Zale 9297, Zimmer 9300

Utah: McGillis 9334, **Wishnick 9353**

Virginia: Colburn 9395, Dalis 9406, Funger 9426, Golden 9430, Grandis 9432, Kanter 9445, Katzen 9446, Kogod 9452, Lipman 9459, McGue 9470, Ochsman 9489, Ratner 9501, Rosenthal 9508, Sandler 9511, Sandler 9512, Smith 9517, Smith 9518, Taubman 9524, Woodbury 9544

Washington: Glazer 9596, **Kongsgaard 9620**, **Samis 9675**, Sarkowsky 9676, Schultz 9679, Shemanski 9682

Wisconsin: Anon 9744, Bader 9749, Coleman 9775, Goodman's 9807, Handleman 9811, Kohl 9837, Lubar 9851, Peck 9895, Posner 9901, Soref 9930, Zilber 9973

Jewish federated giving programs

Alabama: Kimerling 41
Arizona: Moreno 123, Schwartz 137

Arkansas: Tenenbaum 180
California: 324 190, Alpert 207, Altman 210, **Azus 248**, Becker 271, **Bilger 289**, Black 293, Booth 303, Borick 305, Byer 339, Chais 371, Commercial 400, Davidow 444, **Day 447**, Douglas 464, Edelstein 476, Eichenbaum 478, Eisen 479, Factor 491, Fein 497, Feintech 498, Field 503, Fromm 541, G.T.R. 544, Garb 554, Glickman 582, Gold 589, **Goldberg 592**, Goldman 595, Goldsmith 599, Greenbaum 615, Halperin 640, **Harkham 649**, **Harvey 654**, Hazan 660, Irmas 697, Jolson 727, June 733, Katz 745, **Kayne 749**, Kellerman 753, **Kohl 771**, Koret 775, Koshland 777, Lavine 793, Lehrer 800, Leichtag 801, Levine 809, Marciano 850, Menlo 885, Milken 897, Milken 898, Miller 899, Mitchell 903, Morgenstern 916, Morton 919, Nazarian 932, Ornest 959, Oshman 963, Ostin 964, Pell 987, Pimco 1006, Post 1011, Potiker 1012, Rady Fam 1026, Resnick 1041, Ressler 1042, Rosenberg 1066, Sarver 1095, **Schocken 1105**, Shapell 1135, Shoresh 1147, Simms 1155, Smidt 1159, **Soref 1179**, Stein 1190, Stern 1194, Swig 1220, Tenenbaum 1232, Wagner 1274, Wasserman 1281, Webb 1284, Webster 1286, Williams 1307, Winnick 1310, Wolfen 1316, Wornick 1320, Ziegler 1327

Colorado: Bernstein 1343, Merage 1424, Merage 1425, **Mizel 1427**, Schermer 1449, Strear 1461, Sturm 1462, Tuchman 1467, Wolf 1475

Connecticut: Abramowitz 1478, Berkley 1492, Bodenwein 1497, Davis 1525, Fisher 1542, Gladstein 1555, Heyman 1567, Kohn 1575, Lender 1585, Mandell 1595, Manger 1597, Nirenberg 1613, Robbins 1634, Rogow 1636, Rosenthal 1638

Delaware: Berkley 1691, Hirschl 1721, Phillips 1739, Singer 1753, Sternlicht 1756

District of Columbia: Bender 1772, Bernstein 1775, Dweck 1790, Gewirz 1801, **Goldberg 1802**, Gottesman 1803, Gudelsky 1805, Harman 1807, Lehrman 1821, Reich 1845

Florida: **Abramson 1868**, Adler 1871, Applebaum 1878, Arison 1881, Beaver 1897, Blank 1909, **Braman 1915**, Bronfman 1917, **Coleman 1937**, DuBow 1977, Edelman 1987, **Edelstein 1988**, Einstein 1991, Fisher 1999, **Fiterman 2000**, Five 2001, Gann 2016, Ginsburg 2022, Glazer 2024, Global 2025, Goldstein 2027, Gorin 2032, Greenburg 2034, Gruss 2038, Jaffe 2072, Katz 2081, Kaufman 2082, Kimmel 2091, **KMD 2096**, Kohl 2099, Kramer 2100, Lee 2107, **Levine 2112**, Lorberbaum 2118, Maltz 2126, Marden 2127, Merrill 2136, Meyer 2137, Michaan 2138, MIDA 2139, Miller 2141, Muss 2149, Nessel 2152, Olemberg 2157, Posnack 2175, Rales 2184, Reis 2193, River 2199, Russell 2212, Sandler 2216, Schoenbaum 2227, Seaman 2229, Silverman 2234, Stein 2249, Stein 2250, Taplin 2264, Waldbaum 2285, Weiller 2291, Weintraub 2292, Wollowick 2306

Georgia: Brill 2329, Chatham 2347, Covenant 2366, Hertz 2412, Horowitz 2415, Marcus 2440, Rosenberg 2476, Selig 2484, Zaban 2528

Illinois: Acorn 2583, Anixter 2597, Barancik 2605, Baskes 2607, Blum 2624, Blum 2625, Braeside 2631, **Carylon 2652**, Chapman 2656, Chester 2659, Cole 2672, Feinberg 2727, Freed 2736, Freehling 2737, Galter 2745, Gidwitz 2755, Gidwitz 2756, Goldberg 2761, Golder 2762, **Goodman 2765**, Harris 2788, Harris 2789, Hochberg 2803, **JMR 2818**, Kaplan 2824, Katten 2826, Kersten 2838, Kipper 2840, Knapp 2841, Kovler 2844, Landau 2847, Lederer 2851, Leibowitz 2854, Levy 2856, Mander 2873, Mesirow 2894, Miller 2898, Miller 2899, Oppenheimer 2928, Perlman 2938, Polk 2946, Pritzker 2950, Redhill 2960, Rotonda 2972, Sacks 2979, Seid 2996, Shapiro 3001, Sheba 3005, Sirius 3010, Stein 3022, Stern 3023, Susman 3030, Takiff 3032, Wark 3057, Weinberg 3061

Indiana: **Hasten 3163**, Simon 3236, Simon 3237, Simon 3240, Valiant 3248

Iowa: Blank 3268, Bucksbaum 3271, Mid 3316, Seidler 3331

Kansas: **Beren 3348**, Dreiseszun 3359, Kaplan 3373, Morgan 3377

Kentucky: **Omnicare 3444**

Louisiana: Goldring 3484, Heymann 3487, Lupin 3498, **Woldenberg 3516**

Maryland: Abramson 3561, Bank 3569, **Bearman 3570**, **Berman 3572**, **Blaustein 3575**, Blum 3577, **Brown 3579**, Cohen 3593, Crane 3603, **Dahan 3604**, Davison 3609, Dekelboum 3613, Dupkin 3618, Eliasberg 3620, Epstein 3623, Evergreen 3625, Freeman 3633, Goldsmith 3637, Greenberg 3639, Hackerman 3642, Hecht 3645, Hirschhorn 3650, Hoffberger 3652, Kaplan 3659, Kay 3660, Klein 3662, Krieger 3668, Lerner 3674, Lerner 3675, Levitt 3676, Meyerhoff 3692, Rosenbloom 3721, Rothschild 3723, Small 3734, Wasserman 3757, Wasserman 3758

Massachusetts: Aaron 3767, Barron 3792, Berenson 3799, Casty 3839, Chafetz 3842, Cutler 3872, Dana 3873, Feldberg 3901, Filene 3907, Ford 3913, Goldberg 3926, Goldberg 3927, Jacobson 3967, Kessler 3978, Klarman 3985, Krupp 3991, Lappin 3997, Linsey 4010, Marcus 4022, Marks 4024, Morse 4044, Persky 4080, Rabb 4090, Rabb 4091, Rappaport 4093, Redstone 4097, Ribakoff 4102, Schoen 4130, Shapiro 4135, Shapiro 4136, Sharf 4137, Sherman 4141, Shillman 4142, Siff 4145, Silverman 4146, Solomont 4152, Spencer 4154, **Stern 4162**, Stoneman 4167, Swartz 4175

Michigan: Applebaum 4222, Blumenstein 4234, Brown 4239, DeRoy 4273, Farbman 4294, **Ferber 4296**, Fisher 4299, Frankel 4311, Frankel 4312, Frankel 4313, Frankel 4314, Grosfeld 4332, HFF 4342, Kahn 4351, Kogan 4365, Levy 4378, Maas 4379, Manat 4381, Padnos 4406, Pitt 4413, **Rosenzweig 4425**, Seligman 4433, Tauber 4454

Minnesota: Capp 4529, Deikel 4548, Edelstein 4559, Grossman 4578, Phileona 4654, Phillips 4655, Regis 4664, Sabes 4670, Tankenoff 4696

Missouri: Edison 4807, Edison 4808, Gershman 4818, Gottlieb 4820, Helzberg 4829, Jewish 4837, Lopata 4859, Millstone 4867, Sosland 4908, Uhlmann 4920, Wampus 4923

Nebraska: Friedland 4963, Schrager 5001

Nevada: Rochlin 5057

New Jersey: Adelson 5108, **Allen 5111**, Bendheim 5126, Berrie 5130, Bildner 5133, Brody 5144, Cantor 5152, Cooperman 5168, Croman 5172, Entin 5189, **Freyer 5197**, Halpern 5220, Halpern 5221, Harary 5222, Hiller 5237, Isermann 5253, Katz 5271, Kauffmann 5272, Keren 5277, Kreitchman 5289, L.A.W. 5292, **Lautenberg 5298**, Levin 5304, Levitt 5305, Levy 5306, **Mack 5313**, Mamiye 5316, Merkin 5331, NSN 5340, Riskin 5369, Ross 5375, Roth 5377, Sagner 5381, Schwartz 5392, Schwartz 5393, Schwarz 5394, Seiden 5396, Smilowitz 5406, Stern 5412, Straus 5413, Sudler 5416, **Syms 5422**, Taub 5424, Taub 5425, Tolchin 5428, **Wilf 5455**, Wilf 5456, Zayat 5462, Zodiac 5465

New York: Adjmi 5518, Adnim 5522, Ahavas 5527, Alpert 5541, Altman 5543, American 5555, Apfelbaum 5561, Appleman 5562, Aron 5569, Ashner 5573, **Atran 5575**, **AVI 5582**, Azrak 5585, Bachmann 5587, **Baker 5593**, Barrington 5602, Bass 5604, Beker 5613, Belfer 5615, Belfer 5616, Ben-Haim 5617, Berkowitz 5622, Betesh 5627, Betesh 5628, Bialkin 5629, Blankfein 5637, Braufman 5660, Bravmann 5661, Brodsky 5667, **Bronfman 5672**, Burns 5689, Canary 5702, Cayne 5717, Cayre 5718, Centennial 5722, Century 5725, **Chazen 5739**, Chehebar 5740, Chencinski 5742, Chernow 5745, Chesed 5747, Cohen 5767, Cohen 5768, Cohen 5769, Cohen 5771, Cohen 5772, Cohenca 5773, Colin 5776, Cooper 5788, **Dabah 5819**, Damial 5823, Danziger 5829, Delancey 5849, Diamond 5857, Diker 5862, Ditmars 5865, Dobkin 5866, Drexler 5885, Drukier 5890, Dweck 5896, Eberstadt 5904, Effron 5911, Einhorn 5916, Ellis 5923, Englander 5933, Everett 5941, Fascitelli 5946, Feil 5949, Feinstein 5951,

Fisher 5961, Forchheimer 5968, Franconia 5972, Fribourg 5984, Friedman 5986, Friedman 5987, Fuchs 5996, Fuchsberg 5997, Fuchsberg 5998, Fuld 6000, Furman 6003, Furth 6004, GBRG 6008, Gellman 6013, Gerschel 6018, Gershwind 6020, **Gilbert 6028**, Gindi 6036, Godinger 6044, Goldberg 6045, **Goldman 6052**, Goldring 6057, Goldschmidt 6058, Goldsmith 6060, Goldstein 6062, Goldstein 6063, Goldstein 6064, Golub 6070, Gordon 6074, Gould 6085, Granoff 6089, **Grant 6090**, Green 6096, Greene 6099, Greene 6100, Gross 6110, Gruss 6114, Gural 6120, Gurwin 6121, Gutman 6122, Halis 6136, Hammerman 6139, Harris 6148, Hartman 6151, **Hasenfeld 6153**, **Heller 6167**, Hendel 6172, Hersh 6177, Hidary 6181, Hidary 6182, Hilibrand 6184, Hochfelder 6191, Hochstein 6192, Holtzmann 6198, Horowitz 6202, Hurst 6216, IIMI 6228, Jaaaa 6245, Jacobson 6247, Jesselson 6259, Joelson 6265, JW 6280, Kalter 6284, Kaminer 6285, Kandell 6287, Kaplan 6288, Kaplan 6289, Katz 6294, Katz 6295, Katz 6296, Kaylie 6301, King 6325, Kingdon 6326, Klaus 6328, **Klein 6330**, Klein 6332, Koppelman 6349, Kravis 6354, Kupferberg 6363, Kurtz 6364, L'Maan 6367, Lane 6373, Lasdon 6378, Lastfogel 6380, Leeds 6392, Leffell 6393, Legacy 6394, Leibowitz 6399, Leigh 6400, Lemberg 6401, Leventhal 6406, Levin 6407, **Levy 6410**, Levy 6412, Levy 6413, Lewis 6415, Lieb 6420, Linden 6424, Loeb 6440, Loewenberg 6442, Loews 6443, Lopatin 6446, Lostand 6448, Lucerne 6454, Lurie 6459, M & E 6464, Maleh 6479, Malkin 6480, Manitoba 6483, Mark 6488, Marks 6489, Marks 6490, Marx 6498, Massry 6502, **MBIA 6512**, Melohn 6528, Mercy 6534, Meyer 6544, Millard 6548, Milstein 6556, Mindel 6557, Mindich 6558, **Monterey 6568**, Morse 6582, Moses 6587, Neidich 6606, Nelkin 6608, Neuwirth 6612, **Newhouse 6623**, Newman 6624, Olive 6662, Olshan 6663, Oppenheimer 6666, Orentreich 6667, Ostreicher 6672, **Ostrovsky 6673**, Parker 6690, Parkview 6691, Parshelsky 6693, PBO 6699, Pevaroff 6719, Pollack 6734, Pollack 6735, Pomeranz 6739, Propp 6749, Rapaport 6771, Rausman 6775, Ravitch 6776, Rechler 6781, Reich 6784, Reiss 6785, **Richman 6799**, Ridgefield 6802, **Ritter 6814**, Rohr 6831, Rose 6833, Rose 6836, **Rosen 6843**, Rosenblatt 6849, Rosenthal 6853, Rosenwald 6855, **Rosenwald 6857**, Rosner 6860, Ross 6862, Ruben 6868, Ruben 6869, Rubenstein 6870, Rudin 6879, **Rukal 6881**, S.O. 6886, Sachs 6888, Sackler 6889, Safra 6893, Saligman 6895, Sandler 6902, Schechter 6914, Schenker 6916, Scheuer 6920, Schnurmacher 6931, Schott 6934, Schulhof 6935, Schulweis 6936, Schwartz 6938, Schwartz 6942, Schwartz 6944, Schwartz 6945, SDA 6950, Seaver 6952, Seiler 6954, Siegel 6976, **Silfen 6980**, Silver 6981, Silverman 6982, Singer 6990, Skirball 6999, Slant 7000, Slifka 7001, Slifka 7002, Slovin 7004, SO 7015, **Solow 7020**, Spiegel 7029, **Spiegel 7030**, Spitzer 7034, Srour 7037, Stecher 7051, Stein 7055, Stein 7056, Stein 7057, Steinberg 7060, Steinberg 7061, Steinberg 7063, **Steinhardt 7064**, Stern 7070, Stern 7072, Stern 7073, Stone 7081, Straus 7085, Sunrise 7101, Sutton 7106, Sutton 7108, Sutton 7109, **SVM 7110**, Tarnopol 7123, Tisch 7144, Tisch 7145, Tisch 7146, Tisch 7147, Tisch 7148, Tishman 7150, Trump 7167, Unterberg 7186, Ushkow 7188, Wachtell 7205, Wallach 7210, Wasserman 7218, Weil 7225, Weiler 7226, Weinberg 7230, Weiss 7235, Whispering 7250, Winkelried 7265, Wunsch 7281, **YLRY 7284**, Zalaznick 7288, Zankel 7289, Zemsky 7294, **Zenkel 7295**, **Zilkha 7300**, Zitrin 7302, Zucker 7303, Zuckerberg 7304
North Carolina: Baruch 7311, Blumenthal 7320, Gorelick 7380, Nias 7435, Sklut 7473, Toleo 7495, Tzedakah 7497
Ohio: Beerman 7543, Berkman 7545, Binzer 7550, Boymel 7553, Deshe 7606, Forest 7634, Gettler 7649, Heiman 7669, Horvitz 7676, Jarson 7686, **Lerner 7711**, Lippman 7719, LKC 7720, M/I 7729,

Mandel 7730, Mandel 7731, Mandel 7732, Mayerson 7739, Miller 7753, Miller 7754, Philips 7804, Rockwern 7824, Rose 7825, **Sapirstein 7834**, Schottenstein 7844, Siegal 7856, Watson 7896, **Wexner 7904**, Wolf 7914
Oklahoma: Gussman 7941, Kaiser 7948, **Schusterman 7975**, Schusterman 7976, Sylvan 7981
Pennsylvania: Aaron 8072, Ames 8080, Arete 8088, Berger 8101, Berkman 8102, Birnhak 8108, Born 8113, Bronstein 8119, Buncher 8125, Cassett 8133, Chosky 8142, CMS 8147, CMS 8148, Cooper 8158, Epstein 8186, Erlbaum 8189, Fair 8192, Farber 8194, Farber 8195, Fine 8201, Giant 8214, Kaiserman 8277, Kardon 8279, Klein 8291, Kline 8292, Korman 8296, Levee 8308, Levis 8309, Levis 8310, Lutron 8316, Mandell 8322, Miller 8354, Musser 8361, Novotny 8364, Perelman 8372, Perelman 8374, Perkin 8375, Roberts 8405, Rosenberg 8412, Rosenfeld 8413, Rubin 8415, Satell 8424, Scheller 8426, Schwab 8430, Shapira 8437, Snider 8447, Speyer 8453, Strauss 8464, Strawbridge 8467, Toll 8478, Toll 8479, Wimmer 8505
Rhode Island: Alperin 8516, **Hassenfeld 8540**, Mann 8546, Shaw's 8555, Siperstein 8557, Usen 8560
Tennessee: Belz 8643, Eskind 8673, Eskind 8674, Goldsmith 8682, Gordon 8683
Texas: Diener 8867, Farb 8893, Feinberg 8898, Finger 8900, Gale 8913, Hirsch 8953, Levit 9009, Mankoff 9027, Mechia 9050, Meyerson 9058, Rachofsky 9139, Rapoport 9141, Rosenberg 9157, Wolff 9289, Zimmer 9300
Utah: McGillis 9334, **Wishnick 9353**
Virginia: Colburn 9395, Funger 9426, Grandis 9432, Ochsman 9489, Ratner 9501, Rosenthal 9508, Samberg 9510, Sandler 9511, Sandler 9512, Smith 9517, Woodbury 9544
Washington: Glazer 9596, **Kongsgaard 9620**, **PAH 9657**, Sarkowsky 9676, Schultz 9679, Shemanski 9682, Shulman 9685, Sloan 9687
West Virginia: Jacobson 9722
Wisconsin: Anon 9744, Bader 9749, Coleman 9775, Lubar 9851, Peck 9895, Posner 9901, Stark 9935

Journalism school/education
Iowa: Meredith 3314
New York: Lynton 6463

Kidney diseases
Mississippi: Bower 4736
New York: Westchester 7247
Texas: Bass 8777

Kidney research
California: Cusenza 433
Florida: Kaplan 2079
Louisiana: Diboll 3473
New York: Pulier 6753, Westchester 7247
Pennsylvania: Katz 8280
Texas: Bass 8777

Language (foreign)
Washington: **Blakemore 9558**

Language/linguistics
Colorado: Weckbaugh 1470
Connecticut: Bodenwein 1497, Rosenthal 1638
District of Columbia: Roshan 1847
Illinois: **Tyndale 3042**
New Jersey: Dodge 5181, **Johnson 5263**
New York: **Heineman 6165**, **Kade 6281**, Littauer 6434, **Pforzheimer 6721**, **Wenner 7244**
North Carolina: Cumberland 7349

Law school/education
Alabama: Upchurch 71
Arkansas: Altheimer 155
California: Arata 229, Avery-Tsui 245, Bauer 261, Borina 307, Bravo 319, Brenner 321, Burch 334, Caruso 363, Collins 396, Darling 440, Grand 611, Greenberg 617, Janeway 712, Lamond 785, Lavine 793, Leichtman 802
Colorado: Arsenault 1336
Connecticut: Meriden 1603, Robbins 1634
Florida: Adler 1871, **Levine 2111**, Weintraub 2292
Georgia: Watson 2509
Illinois: Blum 2624, Corboy 2684, **Goodman 2765**
Indiana: Leighton 3191
Louisiana: Gauthier 3482
Maryland: Samuelson 3725
Massachusetts: Cogan 3851, Rubenstein 4116
Michigan: Maas 4379, Wilson 4484
Minnesota: Kelley 4597, **Robins 4667**
Nevada: Boyd 5023, Rufty 5059, Wiegand 5077
New Jersey: Civitas 5163, Hiller 5237, Jockey 5260, L.A.W. 5292, ST2 5410, Straus 5413, Sudler 5416
New York: Berg 5621, Castle 5716, D'Agostino 5818, Diamond 5857, Elkes 5922, F. & J.S. 5942, Goldman 6050, Green 6095, Greenberg 6098, Greene 6100, **Haje 6133**, **Handler 6141**, **Homeland 6199**, Hughes 6209, Huntington 6213, Jacobson 6248, Johnson 6271, Leibowitz 6399, **Levy 6410**, Overhills 6676, Penson 6711, Plant 6731, Richardson 6796, **Rosen 6843**, Rosenkranz 6851, Stecher 7051, **Stempel 7069**, Wachtell 7205, **Walter 7211**, Weil 7225, Werblow 7245
Ohio: M/I 7729, Mellen 7747, Sage 7829, Stark 7867
Pennsylvania: Field 8200
South Carolina: Collins 8582
Texas: Cain 8808, O'Quinn 9097, **Shell 9181**, Sumners 9218, Waggoner 9256
Virginia: Wilkinson 9540
Washington: Peterson 9662, Raven 9670
Wyoming: Allen 9974

Law/international law
California: Jams 711
Michigan: **Fetzer 4297**
New York: **Ford 5970**, **Guggenheim 6118**, **Hauser 6155**, **Open 6665**
Ohio: Dana 7599
Pennsylvania: **Scaife 8425**

Leadership development
California: **Baker 252**, Bechtel 270, California 350, Confidence 411, Flintridge 520, Haas 637, Johnson 725, Los Altos 828, Morgan 915, Pacific 970, Sacramento 1080, San Francisco 1088, Shasta 1139, Sierra 1151, **Strauss 1203**, Stuart 1208, Weingart 1288
Colorado: Gates 1380, Piton 1439, Qwest 1443
Connecticut: Bodenwein 1497, Community 1515
District of Columbia: **Hill 1809**, Meyer 1834, **Moriah 1835**
Florida: Katz 2081
Georgia: AGL 2312, Pittulloch 2464
Hawaii: Hawaii 2545
Illinois: Chicago 2661, Community 2677, Logan 2860, Polk 2946
Indiana: Community 3125, Community 3126, Moore 3207
Iowa: McElroy 3313
Kansas: Kansas 3372
Maine: Horizon 3541, Maine 3548
Maryland: Abell 3559
Massachusetts: Boston 3812, Community 3854, **Krieble 3990**
Michigan: Community 4254, Community 4255, DTE 4289, Grand Rapids 4326, **Kellogg 4357**, **Mott 4399**
Minnesota: Blandin 4520, George 4572, **Land 4602**, Minnesota 4624, Northwest 4637, St. Paul 4690, **SUPERVALU 4695**, West 4723
Mississippi: Foundation 4743

Missouri: Boeing 4785
New Jersey: Community 5167, Cowles 5170, Dodge 5181, Kirby 5279, Prudential 5360, Victoria 5440
New Mexico: McCune 5488
New York: Community 5780, **Ford 5970**, Heckscher 6164, Rochester 6823, **Rockefeller 6825**, Sister 6994, **Wallace 7209**, Wendling 7242
North Carolina: **Babcock 7308**, Cumberland 7349, Foundation 7370, Reynolds 7458, Triangle 7496, Weaver 7504
Ohio: Coshocton 7593, Forest 7634, Middletown 7749, Murphy 7769, Muskingum 7770, Nordson 7781, Stark 7867, Stocker 7870, **Timken 7880**, **Wexner 7904**, Youngstown 7920
Oregon: Johnson 8027, **NIKE 8046**, Oregon 8049
Pennsylvania: American 8079, Dolfinger 8172, **Pew 8377**, Scranton 8431, Stackpole 8456, **Templeton 8475**
Rhode Island: Daniels 8530, Rhode Island 8551
Texas: Cain 8809, **Jenesis 8971**, Kempner 8987, Meadows 9049
Virginia: Landmark 9455
Washington: **Stewardship 9691**, Tacoma 9693
West Virginia: McDonough 9726
Wisconsin: Madison 9854

Learning disorders

California: Alafi 201, Lund 831, Schwab 1109
Connecticut: **Tremaine 1662**
Georgia: Ma-Ran 2439, Rollins 2475
Maine: **Oak 3552**
New York: Butler 5692

Learning disorders research

District of Columbia: **Kennedy 1816**

Legal services

Arizona: Arizona 87
California: Borchard 304, Fein 497, Five 516, Gold 590, Marin 854, Parsons 980, Rosenberg 1065, Sacramento 1080, San Francisco 1088, Stern 1195, vanLobenSels 1260
Connecticut: Bodenwein 1497, Bridgeport 1504, Palmer 1621
District of Columbia: Beech 1771, **Koch 1819**, Meyer 1834, **Public 1844**
Georgia: Goizueta 2400, Spray 2495
Illinois: **Burlington 2644**, **Harper 2786**, Katten 2826, New 2912, Polk 2946
Louisiana: Louisiana 3497
Maryland: Wareheim 3756
Massachusetts: Cogan 3851, Eaton 3888, Edgerly 3889, Mifflin 4038
Minnesota: 1988 4491, Bremer 4523, Leonard 4604, **Robins 4667**
New Jersey: Cantor 5152, Lear 5300, Schering 5387
New York: Abrons 5511, Berg 5621, Charina 5731, Daphne 5830, **Ford 5970**, Fuchsberg 5998, **Greenberg 6097**, **Haje 6133**, Heller 6169, Hughes 6209, Kaplan 6289, Leonhardt 6403, Lipmanson 6431, Miller 6551, New York 6613, Pumpkin 6754, Rhodebeck 6791, Rochester 6823, Scherman 6918, Silverweed 6985, **Spiegel 7030**, Starfish 7046, Weil 7225, Wendt 7243, Western 7248, Zitrin 7302
North Carolina: Reynolds 7458, Triangle 7496
North Dakota: Stern 7521
Oregon: Carpenter 8003
Pennsylvania: Dolfinger 8172, Independence 8266, Philadelphia 8378
Rhode Island: Rhode Island 8551
South Carolina: TSC 8618
Tennessee: **Bridgestone 8646**
Texas: Fikes 8899, Owen 9107, Partnership 9110, Wright 9294
Virginia: **Mousetrap 9480**
Washington: Norcliffe 9650, True 9696
Wisconsin: Milwaukee 9876
Wyoming: Connemara 9978

Legal services, public interest law

Arizona: **Moller 122**
California: **Cortopassi 420**, Friedman 539, Rising 1055, vanLobenSels 1260
District of Columbia: Beech 1771
Georgia: Sapelo 2479
Illinois: Landau 2847
New Jersey: RuthMarc 5380
New York: Green 6095, Johnson 6271
Ohio: Jackson 7685
Pennsylvania: Independence 8266

LGBTQ

California: Bohnett 300, California 345, East 474, Geffen 558, Haas 637, Moonwalk 911, Wunderkinder 1322
Colorado: Community 1358
Florida: Dade 1957
Illinois: Logan 2860, Washington 3058
Massachusetts: Community 3855, Crawford 3867, Harmsworth 3942, **Hostetter 3959**, Hyams 3961
Michigan: **Arcus 4223**, Grand Rapids 4326
Minnesota: Bremer 4523, Grotto 4579, Mossier 4628, Phillips 4655
New Mexico: McCune 5488, Santa Fe 5496
New York: Johnson 6271, Morrow 6581, Rapoport 6772, Richardson 6797, Rose 6834, Snowdon 7012, van Ameringen 7190, Violett 7200
North Carolina: Triangle 7496
Ohio: Akron 7526
Vermont: **Ben 9355**
Virginia: **Gannett 9428**
Washington: **Kongsgaard 9620**
Wisconsin: Gould 9809

Libraries (academic/research)

California: Avery-Tsui 245, Cotsen 421, Hewlett 671
New York: **Magowan 6473**

Libraries (law)

Ohio: Green 7652

Libraries (public)

Alabama: Anderson 6, Crampton 30, Hearin 37, Moody 54
Arkansas: Ross 174
California: Betterworld 285, Engemann 484, Goldwyn 600, Jewett 718, Klein 764, **Mohn 907**, Nestle 935, Schott 1106, Scott 1114, Smittcamp 1168, WHH 1300
Colorado: Bacon 1340
Connecticut: Ambler 1481, Meriden 1603, **Praxair 1629**
Delaware: Hamel 1719
District of Columbia: **Berman 1774**
Georgia: Ma-Ran 2439, Singletary 2490
Illinois: **Allen 2587**, **Buntrock 2643**, GKN 2758, Knox 2842, Lumpkin 2864, Meyer 2895, Sangre 2981, Wilson 3075
Indiana: Annis 3100, Dekko 3142, Marshall 3199, Saemann 3232, Simon 3237, Tobias 3244, Tyson 3246
Iowa: Beckwith 3266, Bright 3269, Hubbell 3297
Kentucky: Preston 3446, Robinson 3449
Maine: Alfond 3522, Hannaford 3540, King 3545, Smith 3556
Maryland: Middendorf 3694
Massachusetts: Caldwell 3827, Fessenden 3903, **Hershey 3949**, **Ruettgers 4119**
Michigan: Frey 4316, Keeler 4355, Mott 4400
Minnesota: Bremer 4523, Garmar 4569, Griggs 4577, Regis 4664, Schmidt 4673
Montana: Browning 4933
New Jersey: Bershad 5131, Nicolais 5339, Sands 5382, Turock 5430
New York: Birkelund 5632, Blythmour 5644, Furth 6004, **Gilder 6030**, Handler 6140, HSBC 6204, Hudson 6207, Katz 6294, Keeler 6306, Marx 6497, Milstein 6556, Quadrangle 6758, Ranger 6770, Rose 6838, Schieffelin 6922, Seevers 6953, Selis 6955, Sheinberg 6963, Stevens 7076, Uphill 7187, Western 7248
North Carolina: Belk 7314, Hommer 7400, Rostan 7467, Woodson 7509
North Dakota: MDU 7517
Ohio: Babcock 7537, Corbett 7590, Hoover 7675, Sky 7859
Oklahoma: Williams 7989
Oregon: Kelley 8030
Pennsylvania: Cotswold 8160, Degenstein 8166, Hooper 8256, Justus 8276, Perkin 8375, S & T 8417, Truman 8483, Vanguard 8490
Rhode Island: Grinnell 8538, Shaw's 8555
Tennessee: Jones 8698, Pettway 8715
Texas: Cameron 8811, Halsell 8936, Holt 8958, Hudson 8962, Kronkosky 9002
Utah: Raymond 9339
Washington: Anderson 9551, Ferguson 9585, Seattle 9680
Wisconsin: Acuity 9739, AnnMarie 9743, Baker 9751, Gordon 9808, Johnson 9823, Krejci 9843, Kress 9844, Managed 9857, Munson 9880, Schoenlein 9921, Smallwood 9928, Taylor 9948, Weill 9962

Libraries (school)

Indiana: Dekko 3142
New Jersey: OceanFirst 5341
North Carolina: Breeden 7324, Goodnight 7377

Libraries (special)

California: **Muth 929**
Colorado: **Avenir 1339**
Connecticut: Berkley 1492
Georgia: Singletary 2490
Illinois: Baskes 2607
Massachusetts: Calderwood 3826, Solomont 4152
New York: Furth 6004
Pennsylvania: Karabots 8278
Texas: Fish 8902, Mays 9035

Libraries, archives

New York: **Carnegie 5707**

Libraries/library science

Alabama: Community 24
Arkansas: Arkansas 156, Murphy 167
California: Ahmanson 198, Anaheim 220, Baker 253, Bartman 259, Brenner 321, Centofante 370, Community 402, Copley 416, Crockett 430, Danford 438, Geschke 568, James 709, Janeway 712, Koontz 773, Lytel 836, Mericos 889, Pelosi 988, Post 1011, Rahimian 1027, Shannon 1133, Sonora 1178, Tesuque 1234, Union 1250
Colorado: El Pomar 1374, Gates 1380, Kinder 1403
Connecticut: Bodenwein 1497, Community 1515, Community 1516, Community 1517, Donchian 1531, Larsen 1579, Mandeville 1596, Palmer 1621, Woodward 1678
Delaware: Crystal 1702, Marmot 1728, Reynolds 1743
Florida: Gainesville 2015, Green 2033, Kirbo 2092, Martin 2130, Rayonier 2189, Rebozo 2190, Spurlino 2242
Georgia: Arnold 2319, Azalea 2322, Callaway 2337, Jones 2424, Porter 2468, Williams 2514
Hawaii: Wong 2560
Idaho: Idaho 2570, Simplot 2575
Illinois: **Andrew 2595**, Brinson 2633, Chicago 2661, Comer 2675, Dillon 2704, Donnelley 2708, Harrison 2790, Harrison 2791, McMullan 2884, McNally 2885, Vermilion 3047
Indiana: Community 3128, Griffith 3158, Simon C 3238
Iowa: Carver 3274, Community 3278, Deardorf 3280
Louisiana: Booth 3464, Huie 3488
Maine: Mulford 3551

Michigan: Mosaic 4398
Minnesota: Chadwick-Loher 4535, Drew 4554, McVay 4620
Nebraska: Weitz 5016
New Jersey: Riskin 5369, Sunup 5419
New York: Harriman 6147, Radio 6765, Schmitt 6928, Vance 7193
North Dakota: MDU 7517
Ohio: Miniger 7756, Morgan 7760, Turben 7888
South Carolina: **Premier 8604**
Tennessee: Atticus 8639, **Bridgestone 8646**
Texas: Heavin 8945, **Hull 8964**, Rapoport 9141
Utah: Bastian 9306
Virginia: **Bansal 9372**
Wisconsin: Johnson 9823, Northwestern 9884

Media, television

Arkansas: Taylor 179
California: American 215, Benificus 278, Center 369, Fluor 523, Rosenfeld 1067, Roth 1071, Sudikoff 1212
Colorado: KBK 1400, Ludlow 1412
Connecticut: Barnes 1488, Chase 1508, Shei'rah 1649, Vervane 1671
Florida: Weiler 2290
Georgia: Amos 2315
Illinois: Frankel 2735, Ward 3056, Wilemal 3070
Indiana: Decio 3139, Martin 3200
Iowa: Gilchrist 3287
Maryland: **Town 3749**
Massachusetts: Black 3808, Fessenden 3903, Hirschtick 3953, Keane 3975, Kingsbury 3982, Schaffer 4129
Michigan: Devereaux 4274, Harding 4337, Riley 4419
Minnesota: Chadwick-Loher 4535
Missouri: Barrows 4781, Carter 4794
Nebraska: Weitz 5016
New Jersey: **Lautenberg 5298**, Riskin 5369
New York: Canary 5702, Centennial 5722, D'Agostino 5818, Davidson 5835, Eberstadt 5904, Green 6095, Harriman 6147, **Jaffe 6250**, JCT 6256, Karmazin 6293, **Magowan 6473**, Marcus 6486, Marron 6493, O'Sullivan 6652, Park 6688, Schafer 6910, Schmitt 6928, Smith 7009, Stuart 7090, Wallach 7210, Walter 7212, WJS 7269
North Carolina: Price 7451
North Dakota: MDU 7517
Ohio: Schiff 7836
Pennsylvania: Dietrich 8170, Mengle 8347
Tennessee: Atticus 8639, **Bridgestone 8646**, Briggs 8647
Texas: Rapoport 9141
Utah: Bastian 9306
Wisconsin: Johnson 9823, Krause 9842, Northwestern 9884

Media/communications

Arizona: **Moller 122**, Soling 140
California: BayTree 265, Becker 271, Bohnett 300, Follis 525, Hitz 676, Knight 768, **LEF 799**, **Marshall 858**, **Omidyar 952**, **Rosengarten 1068**, Rotasa 1070, San Francisco 1088
Colorado: Schermer 1449
Connecticut: **Huisking 1570**, Rosenthal 1638, Shei'rah 1649
Delaware: Presto 1740, Schiff 1750
District of Columbia: Benton 1773, **Wallace 1858**
Florida: Martin 2130, Raygar 2187, Sherman 2233, St. Petersburg 2245
Georgia: **Fonda 2385**, Weber 2510
Illinois: Feinberg 2727, **Harper 2786**, Logan 2860, **MacArthur 2868**, Magnus 2870, O'Connor 2921, Oppenheimer 2928, Rubin 2974, Stuart 3028
Maryland: Deutsch 3616, Eaton 3619, **Town 3749**
Massachusetts: Calderwood 3826, Fraser 3917, Overly 4064, **Ruettgers 4119**, Saltonstall 4126, Tupancy 4186
Minnesota: Bush 4524, Jerome 4595
Missouri: Andrews 4774, Pershing 4880
Nevada: Hawkins 5036

New Jersey: Dodge 5181, **Dow 5184**, **Gulton 5217**, Hickory 5232, **Schumann 5390**, Sweetfeet 5421
New Mexico: **Johns 5482**
New York: Brutsch 5680, Burns 5689, Corning 5794, Davenport 5833, Diller 5863, Downs 5882, Everett 5941, **Ford 5970**, Grand 6086, Haas 6126, **Hauser 6155**, Kellen 6308, Lipp 6432, **MetLife 6542**, **Newhouse 6623**, Newman 6624, **Open 6665**, Park 6688, Pels 6706, Pines 6727, **Popplestone 6741**, Rattner 6773, Revson 6789, Salomon 6897, Skirball 6999, **Time 7142**, Tribune 7163, Walter 7212
North Carolina: Duke 7360
Ohio: Corbett 7590, Dornette 7613, **Freygang 7640**, Luther 7726, McMaster 7744, Reinberger 7815, Wohlgemuth 7913
Oklahoma: **Ethics 7935**, Williams 7989
Pennsylvania: Arkema 8089, Cooper 8158, Kline 8293, Mandell 8322, Vanguard 8490
Tennessee: Schadt 8725
Texas: Meadows 9049, Newman 9090, Paulos 9112, San Antonio 9166, Wright 9294
Utah: Swanson 9346
Virginia: Clark 9393, **Gannett 9428**
Washington: Community 9571, **Glaser 9595**, PEMCO 9660
Wisconsin: Fotsch 9802, Menasha 9869

Medical care, bioethics

New Jersey: Healthcare 5228
New York: Littauer 6434

Medical care, community health systems

Arkansas: Altheimer 155
California: California 350, Sathya 1096
Georgia: Aflac 2311
Illinois: **Astellas 2602**
Indiana: Kosciusko 3185
Iowa: Mid-Iowa 3317
Massachusetts: Chafetz 3842
New Jersey: Large 5295, **Rippel 5368**
New York: Community 5785
Ohio: Osteopathic 7791
Oklahoma: Presbyterian 7969
Pennsylvania: Phoenixville 8381
Virginia: Williamsburg 9541
Wisconsin: Assurant 9748, JKO 9822

Medical care, in-patient care

California: Volentine 1268
Connecticut: **Heimbold 1566**
Florida: **Cobb 1936**, Friedman 2014
Georgia: Cay 2343
Hawaii: First 2542
Louisiana: Brunswick 3466
Maryland: Klein 3662
Massachusetts: Demoulas 3878
Michigan: Ford 4302, McGregor 4389
Minnesota: **Rechelbacher 4662**
Nebraska: Kawasaki 4982
New Jersey: OceanFirst 5341
New York: Ades 5516, Countess 5800, Elkes 5922, **Kreindler 6356**, **Morgan 6577**, Riversville 6815, Rumsey 6882, Vidda 7198
North Carolina: Goodrich 7378
Ohio: **OMNOVA 7789**
Texas: Bickel 8790
Utah: Quinney 9338
Virginia: **DeLaski 9409**, Williamsburg 9541
Washington: De Falco 9578

Medical care, outpatient care

Hawaii: HMSA 2547
Illinois: Goldberg 2761
Minnesota: Oswald 4645
New York: Kellen 6308, Samuels 6901

Medical care, rehabilitation

Alabama: Stallworth 64
Arizona: Dee 94, **Kleckhefer 113**
California: Anaheim 220, Haas 634, Jackson 706, Mericos 889, Patron 983, Sierra 1151, Teichert 1231, Weingart 1288, Williams 1307
Colorado: Boettcher 1344
Connecticut: Bodenwein 1497, Woodward 1678
District of Columbia: Cafritz 1780
Florida: Martin 2130, Rayonier 2189, River 2199
Georgia: Patterson 2460
Illinois: Braeside 2631, Coleman 2673, Community 2677, D and R 2693, Eisenberg 2716, Harris 2788, McNally 2885, Prince 2948, Thoma 3035
Indiana: Bussing 3111
Kentucky: Marshall 3438
Maryland: **Ewing 3626**
Massachusetts: Charlton 3846, Community 3855, Janey 3968
Michigan: Dauch 4268, Fremont 4315, **Tubergen 4463**
Minnesota: Ordean 4643
Missouri: Green 4822
Nebraska: **Union 5012**
Nevada: Nevada 5047, Pennington 5053
New Jersey: Hyde 5247, **International 5252**
New Mexico: McCune 5488
New York: Achelis 5513, Blythmour 5644, Bodman 5647, Charina 5731, Cummings 5815, Goldsmith 6060, **Hearst 6161**, **Hearst 6162**, **Milbank 6547**, Noble 6632, Rosenstiel 6852, **Ross 6863**, Siebert 6975, Western 7248
North Carolina: Cumberland 7349, Reynolds 7457, Roberts 7465, Triangle 7496
Ohio: Dater 7600, Fleming 7631, Ingalls 7684, Murphy 7769
Pennsylvania: Briggs 8117, FISA 8204, Fourjay 8209, Huston 8263, Shenango 8438, Willis 8504
Rhode Island: CVS 8529
South Carolina: Rainey 8605
South Dakota: Larson 8627
Tennessee: Community 8660
Texas: Austin 8768, Constantin 8843, Hillcrest 8952, Hoblitzelle 8955, McKee 9045, Meadows 9049, Rockwell 9154, San Antonio 9166, Shelton 9182, Speas 9206, Sterling 9212, Temple 9227, Temple 9228, Wright 9294
Utah: Eccles 9320
Washington: Community 9571, Foundation 9589, Glaser 9594
Wisconsin: Crump 9783, Four 9803, Rennebohm 9910

Medical research

Alabama: Dixon 32
Arizona: Ottens 128
California: Baker 253, Benbough 276, Booth 302, Commercial 400, Connell 412, Eisen 479, Esseff 488, Feintech 500, Friedman 539, Giannini 572, **Harvey 654**, Magistro 847, Marcus 852, Michelson 896, Miller 899, Neilsen 934, Outhwaite 966, Patron 983, **Reinhard 1037**, Tallen 1225, Valley 1257, WHH 1300
Connecticut: Tow 1661
Delaware: **CTW 1703**
District of Columbia: **CityBridge 1783**, McGowan 1830
Florida: **Anderson 1876**, Batchelor 1893, **Coulter 1955**, **Flight 2002**, Frazier 2011, Gainesville 2015, Gemcon 2019, **SWS 2260**
Georgia: Greene 2404, **Hooters 2414**
Illinois: Arthur 2601, Barnett 2606, Brinson 2633, Cless 2668, Grainger 2768, McGraw 2882, Tellabs 3034, **Tuohy 3041**
Iowa: McDonald 3312, Wallace 3342
Louisiana: Scott 3509
Maryland: Campbell 3582, Hussman 3655, Kerr 3661, **Kluge 3663**, RFI 3716, Tauber 3742, Viragh 3753, **Zickler 3763**
Massachusetts: Charles 3844, **Grass 3931**, **Harris 3944**, Pappas 4067, Shapiro 4136, Smith 4150
Michigan: **ArvinMeritor 4224**, Dow 4286, Perrigo 4410, Ravitz 4418, Stonisch 4449, World 4489
Minnesota: Knowlton 4598, **St. Jude 4689**

Missouri: American 4773, Bodine 4784, **Lockton 4857**, **McDonnell 4864**
New Jersey: Aventis 5120, Brotherton 5145, **Edison 5186**, Hidden 5233, **High 5234**, Integra 5251, **Lafitte 5293**, **Merck 5326**
New York: Behrens 5612, Blythmour 5644, **Borderline 5652**, **Bristol 5666**, Diamond 5860, Dowling 5880, E & WG 5899, Elmezzi 5925, Fisher 5962, Franklin 5978, **Goldman 6052**, **Hearst 6161**, **Hearst 6162**, Icahn 6223, Lowenstein 6449, **Mayer 6510**, **MBIA 6512**, MRM 6592, **Mullen 6595**, Naddisy 6598, New York 6614, New York 6618, **OSI 6670**, Pedersen 6704, Schwartz 6941, Shapiro 6959, **Spirit 7033**, Stanton 7043, **Starr 7048**, Starwood 7049, Stern 7071, Vilcek 7199, Violett 7200
North Carolina: Davis 7353, Lance 7418
Ohio: Akron 7526, **Alpaugh 7527**, **Dewald 7608**, Farmer 7623, Jarson 7686, Midland 7750, Ohio 7785, Reinberger 7815, Reuter 7817, Turben 7888, Western 7903
Oklahoma: Oklahoman 7966, Sarkeys 7974
Oregon: Chambers 8004, Macdonald 8038
Pennsylvania: AMETEK 8081, Drueding 8177, DSF 8178, Hoverter 8258, La 8298, Peterson 8376, PTS 8399, **Seraph 8434**, Spang 8452, Tippins 8477, **United 8487**
Rhode Island: Carter 8522
South Carolina: Bruce 8571
South Dakota: Sioux Falls 8630
Texas: Bass 8777, **ExxonMobil 8889**, Farb 8893, Farish 8894, Kahn 8980, Mitchell 9065, Nash 9085, **Randall 9140**, **RGK 9146**, Riter 9149, Simmons 9188, Smith 9197
Utah: Savage 9340
Virginia: Snead 9520
Washington: Ellison 9581, Foster 9588, Lynn 9633, Sarkowsky 9676
Wisconsin: Joy 9828, Keller 9831, Northwestern 9884, **Smith 9929**

Medical research, association

Arizona: Halle 103
California: Danford 438, Davidson 445, Dickinson 454, Oppenheimer 955, Peterson 995
Illinois: Cole 2672, Traders 3038
Massachusetts: Center 3841
Minnesota: Carlson 4532
Missouri: Rosewood 4894
Montana: Browning 4933
Nevada: Spector 5067
New Jersey: Gershman 5206, Heart 5229
New York: Boisi 5650, Dabah 5820, Finlay 5957, Gould 6085, Mallah 6481, Vogelstein 7201
Ohio: Schott 7842
Pennsylvania: Murray 8360, **Seraph 8434**
Rhode Island: Alperin 8516

Medical research, ethics

New York: **Greenwall 6103**

Medical research, formal/general education

California: Peterson 995
Indiana: Regenstrief 3228

Medical research, information services

Indiana: Regenstrief 3228

Medical research, institute

Alabama: Aronov 9, Methvin 51
Arizona: Aurora 88, Dee 94, Flinn 98, Hermundslie 107, **Kieckhefer 113**, Morris 124, Steele 142, Webb 150
California: **A-T 191**, Arata 229, Arbus 231, **Baker 252**, Barker 257, Bartman 259, Baxter 263, **Beckman 272**, Bell 274, Bireley 292, Brotman 328, Burns 338, Campini 353, **Cantor 354**, Center 369,

Chrysopolae 386, Coates 391, Confidence 411, Daly 436, Danford 438, Davidson 445, Doheny 460, Draper 472, Dwyer 472, Eichenbaum 478, Eisenberg 480, Factor 491, Feintech 498, Femino 501, **Four 532**, Genentech 563, **Glenn 581**, Goldsmith 599, Grammer 610, Guenther 628, Guzik 632, Haas 634, Harrington 652, Hillblom 673, Hoag 678, Irvine 699, Irwin 700, Jameson 710, Jerome 717, Johnson 722, Katzenberg 746, **Keck 750**, Khachaturian 755, Kvamme 781, Leatherby 796, Lehrer 800, Lidow 811, Lincy 812, Mellam 883, Mericos 889, Metta 892, Milken 897, Milken 898, Morgenstern 916, Morton 919, Moss 921, My 930, Norris 940, Oppenheimer 955, Oxnard 969, Petersen 994, Pure Fam 1026, Raintree 1028, Ray 1034, Red 1035, Ressler 1043, Rigler 1051, Robinson 1060, Rogers 1062, **Saban 1079**, San Diego 1087, Shapiro 1137, Shenandoah 1144, Smidt 1159, Smith 1160, Stern 1194, Stevens 1196, Stewart 1199, Towbes 1241, Treadwell 1243, Valente 1255, Valley 1256, Wasserman 1281, Whittier 1304, WWW 1323, Wynn 1324
Colorado: Taylor 1464, Tuchman 1467
Connecticut: **ALFA 1480**, Berkley 1492, Childs 1510, Davis 1525, Donaghue 1529, Gaisman 1551, **Huisking 1570**, Lehrman 1584, **Patterson 1624**, Rosenthal 1638
Delaware: Hall 1718, Hirschl 1721, Rowland 1749, **Schwartz 1751**, Sinsheimer 1754, Watson 1761
District of Columbia: Jones 1813, Lehrman 1821, Merriman 1833
Florida: Abraham 1867, ADFAM 1870, Adler 1871, Amaturo 1873, Applebaum 1878, Avrum 1884, Banbury 1889, Bastien 1892, Chia 1933, Community 1948, **Consolidated 1952**, Coulter 1954, Davis 1961, **Davis 1963**, duPont 1982, Epilepsy 1995, **Fiterman 2000**, **Flight 2002**, Greenburg 2034, **Hayward 2053**, Kennedy 2088, Kimmel 2091, Kramer 2100, Lynn 2120, Maltz 2126, McCann 2132, Moore 2142, Paulucci 2164, Peacock 2165, Price 2177, Rosenberg 2206, **Ross 2207**, Sandler 2216, Taishoff 2262, Taylor 2268, Taylor 2269, **Vollmer 2282**, **von Liebig 2283**, Wells 2294, Wollowick 2306
Georgia: Arnold 2319, Chatham 2347, Cooper 2363, Fraser 2390, Georgia 2394, Harrison 2410, Livingston 2435, Rollins 2475, Rosenberg 2476, Savannah 2489, Simpson 2489
Hawaii: Anthony 2531, Bakken 2534, Hawaii 2545, HMSA 2547
Illinois: Bauer 2609, Berner 2617, Blowitz 2623, Blum 2625, Brach 2629, Buchanan 2637, **Buntrock 2643**, Butler 2646, Eisenberg 2716, Falk 2724, Galvin 2746, Geraldi 2752, Getz 2753, Goldman 2763, Goldschmidt 2764, Grant 2770, **Harper 2786**, Harris 2788, Hochberg 2803, Kovler 2844, Lavin 2849, Lederer 2851, Madigan 2869, McNamara 2886, Miller 2898, Miller 2899, Reese 2961, Retirement 2964, Shapiro 3001, Shaw 3004, Siragusa 3009, Walsh 3055, Washington 3058, Weinberg 3061, Wine 3076
Indiana: Anderson 3099, Griffith 3158, Regenstrief 3228
Iowa: Bucksbaum 3271, Carver 3274, Mid 3316
Kansas: **Muchnic 3379**, Rudd 3385
Louisiana: Booth 3464, Helis 3486, Lupin 3498, Schlieder 3508, Woolf 3517, Zemurray 3519
Maryland: Abramson 3561, **Brown 3579**, Casey 3586, **Ellison 3621**, **Fairchild 3627**, **Hughes 3654**, **Life 3677**, Merrill 3689, Shattuck 3788, Wilson 3761
Massachusetts: Alden 3777, Barron 3792, Bay 3794, Campbell 3830, Cogan 3851, Community 3854, Cox 3863, Cutler 3872, **Fidelity 3904**, Harrington 3943, Henderson 3946, High 3950, Johnson 3970, Kessler 3978, King 3981, Knez 3986, Levy 4005, Marino 4023, Marks 4024, McEvoy 4032, Overly 4064, Pappas 4066, Peabody 4074, Pearce 4075, Rasmussen 4094, Redstone 4097, Rosse 4113, Siff 4145, Smith 4148, **Stern 4162**, Swartz 4175, Tupancy 4186, **Waterman 4198**, Webster 4201

Michigan: Brown 4240, Ford 4303, **Gerber 4321**, Molinello 4395, **Pardee 4407**, Ratner 4417, Schlafer 4429, Thomas 4456, Towsley 4461, **Tracy 4462**, Whiting 4482
Minnesota: Alworth 4499, Carlson 4532, Greystone 4576, **McKnight 4616**, Prospect 4659, Sundet 4694, **Wood 4731**
Missouri: Bellwether 4782, Edison 4807, **Francis 4816**, Gershman 4818, Helzberg 4829, **Mallinckrodt 4860**, Reynolds 4892, Rosewood 4894, Schweppe 4899, Shaw 4901
Nebraska: Perkins 4996
Nevada: Boyd 5023, Fairweather 5032, Fertitta 5033, Lifestyle 5042, Pennington 5053, Redfield 5055, Reynolds 5056, Spector 5067, Wiegand 5077
New Hampshire: **Penates 5099**, Trust 5103
New Jersey: **Allen 5111**, Brody 5144, Capita 5154, **Carolan 5156**, Cowles 5170, Eisenberg 5187, Goldberg 5209, Gund 5218, Healthcare 5228, Hyde 5247, **International 5252**, **Johnson 5263**, Kennedy 5276, Kirby 5279, Kirby 5280, **Lautenberg 5298**, Lazarus 5299, Makk 5315, Orenstein 5344, **Pfeiffer 5351**, **Reeves 5365**, Rose 5373, Taub 5425, Tuchman 5429, Withington 5458, Zobel 5464
New York: Achelis 5513, **Adler 5521**, Alexander 5532, Allyn 5539, Alpern 5540, Altus 5547, American 5555, **Archbold 5563**, Aron 5569, Bachmann 5587, **Berlys 5623**, Bluhdorn 5642, Blum 5643, Bodman 5647, Botwinick 5653, Brodsky 5668, Charina 5731, **China 5750**, Cohen 5770, Community 5780, **Cummings 5813**, **Dana 5826**, **Dana 5827**, Davenport 5833, **de Rothschild 5843**, Decker 5846, DeGeorge 5848, DeMatteis 5852, Diamond 5857, Donaldson 5871, **Dreyfus 5888**, **Duke 5892**, Dunwalke 5894, E & WG 5899, Emerald 5926, **Engelhard 5932**, **Feinberg 5950**, **Friedman 5988**, Fuchsberg 5998, **Gilbert 6028**, Gilman 6032, Glickenhaus 6042, Goldenson 6047, Goldsmith 6060, Goodman 6072, Granoff 6089, Greenberg 6098, Greenhill 6101, Griffis 6107, **Gruss 6116**, **Hearst 6161**, **Hearst 6162**, **Heineman 6165**, Hermione 6175, Hirsch 6187, Hirsch 6188, Hugoton 6210, Johnson 6269, Johnson 6270, **Johnson 6273**, Joy 6276, **Kade 6281**, Kaplan 6289, Karan 6291, **Kaufmann 6299**, Knossos 6344, **Kohlberg 6346**, Kornfeld 6350, Lang 6374, Lasker 6379, Lauder 6381, Leeds 6392, Lewis 6415, Link 6429, Litterman 6435, Litwin 6436, Lookout 6445, Malkin 6480, Manning 6484, **Mapplethorpe 6485**, Marx 6498, **Mayday 6508**, McGonagle 6518, McNulty 6521, Millstein 6553, **Monell 6566**, O'Malley 6647, O'Toole 6653, O'Toole 6654, Ohrstrom 6659, Oishei 6660, **Olayan 6661**, Pascucci 6696, **Peleris 6705**, Perkin 6717, Pope 6740, Pulier 6753, Quick 6762, Raether 6766, **Ramapo 6769**, Rosenblatt 6849, Rosenthal 6853, Rosenwald 6855, **Ross 6863**, Roxe 6867, Rubenstein 6870, Sackler 6892, Saltz 6899, Schlobach 6924, Schnurmacher 6931, Schwartz 6943, SDA 6950, Seaver 6952, Silverman 6982, Smith 7009, Stanton 7044, Starker 7047, Straus 7085, **Summerfield 7097**, Tisch 7145, Tisch 7147, Tisch 7148, Turner 7175, Wagner 7206, Wallach 7210, Weinberg 7230, Wendt 7243, **Whitney 7254**, Woodheath 7274, Zemsky 7294, **Zenkel 7295**
North Carolina: Bryan 7330, **Burroughs 7333**, Foundation 7370, Jones 7408, Van Every 7499, Van Houten 7500
Ohio: Akron 7526, **Armington 7532**, Bell 7544, Berkman 7545, Berlin 7546, Britton 7556, Cleveland 7576, **Freygang 7640**, Horvitz 7678, Ingalls 7684, Jobst 7691, **Kettering 7698**, McBride 7740, Nippert 7777, Prentiss 7806, Schlink 7839, **Warrington 7895**
Oklahoma: Bernsen 7925, Gaylord 7937, Inasmuch 7944, Merrick 7962, Noble 7963, Presbyterian 7969, Puterbaugh 7970, Warren 7987
Oregon: Chiles 8005, Collins 8009, Poznanski 8052, **Schmidt 8055**, Wheeler 8068
Pennsylvania: **Aircast 8074**, Ames 8080, **AO 8085**, Berger 8101, Buncher 8125, Davenport 8164,

Federated 8196, Field 8200, Fleming 8206, Haas 8230, Hirtzel 8253, Kimmel 8288, Kline 8293, Laurel 8301, Mandell 8322, Massey 8328, McCune 8332, McLean 8340, **Merck 8349**, **Seraph 8434**, Smith 8443, **Strawbridge 8465**, Strawbridge 8466, Wheeler 8501, Widener 8502

Rhode Island: **Alpert 8517**, Daniels 8530, Littlefield 8544

South Carolina: Abney 8564, TSC 8618

Tennessee: Belz 8643, Children's 8653, Davis 8665, Massey 8709

Texas: Ackerman 8750, Alexander 8752, Alkek 8753, Alkek 8754, Anderson 8759, Cain 8808, Cain 8809, Charitable 8824, Coates 8834, Cullen 8854, Dauphin 8856, Dickson 8866, Dunn 8872, Edwards 8880, Elkins 8883, Ellwood 8884, Fikes 8899, Fish 8902, Folsom 8905, Franklin 8907, Franklin 8908, Haggar 8930, Haggar 8931, Halsell 8936, Hamill 8937, Hamman 8938, Hankamer 8939, Hawn 8943, Hillcrest 8952, Hobby 8954, Jamail 8969, Kempner 8987, **Kleberg 8999**, Kronkosky 9002, Lightner 9012, MacDonald 9025, McCombs 9037, McDermott 9043, McKee 9045, McMillan 9046, Medallion 9051, Moody 9070, Moss 9078, Owsley 9108, Read 9142, Reynolds 9145, San Antonio 9166, Scurlock 9175, **Shell 9181**, Shivers 9184, Smith 9192, Smith 9193, **Smith 9194**, Smith 9198, Speas 9206, Speas 9207, Strake 9215, Sturgis 9216, Waco 9255, West 9276, Wolff 9289

Utah: **ALSAM 9302**, Bastian 9306, Dialysis 9313, Eccles 9317, Eccles 9319, Eccles 9320, Savage 9340, **Thrasher 9348**

Virginia: Dalis 9406, Jeffress 9442, **Kaufman 9447**, Norfolk 9484, **Scripps 9514**, Titmus 9527

Washington: Anderson 9551, Apex 9552, Coulter 9573, Danz 9577, Dimmer 9579, Glaser 9594, **Hemingway 9606**, Lockwood 9631, Norcliffe 9650, Raven 9670

Wisconsin: Bader 9749, Crump 9783, Evans 9796, Handleman 9811, **Johnson 9825**, Kohl 9837, Reinhart 9909, **Roddis 9913**, Sensient 9922, Stuart 9943

Wyoming: Chapman 9976

Medical research, public education

Connecticut: **Applera 1484**

Medical research, public policy

New York: **Greenwall 6103**
Texas: Stanzel 9208

Medical research, single organization support

Illinois: JYN 2821
New York: Eunice 5939

Medical school/education

Alabama: Alpha 3
Arizona: **Kieckhefer 113**, Morris 124
Arkansas: Altheimer 155
California: Bauer 261, Baxter 263, Boyer 313, Bright 322, DeMille 450, Femino 501, Genentech 563, Gilmore 578, Gold 591, Horn 686, Kanitz 742, Lakiredday 784, Lanni 789, Long 825, MacKenzie 843, Riley 1052, Shayne 1140, Wollenberg 1317
Colorado: Pioneer 1438, Williams 1474
Connecticut: **Aetna 1479**, **ALFA 1480**, Berbecker 1491, Culpeper 1521, **Hoffman 1568**, Larsen 1579, Lynch 1591
Delaware: Beckwith 1689, Hirschl 1721, Schiff 1750, Sinsheimer 1754
District of Columbia: Aid 1765, Cafritz 1780
Florida: **Coulter 1955**, **Davis 1964**, Gerstner 2020, **Goldhammer 2026**, **Jaharis 2073**, Kennedy 2089, Kimmel 2091, Love 2119, MacDonald 2121, Meyer 2137, **Pearce 2166**, Speer 2241, Weintraub 2292
Georgia: Carlos 2340, Cobb 2349, Fonda 2386, Fuqua 2391, Georgia 2394, Jones 2424

Hawaii: Zimmerman 2561
Illinois: Arthur 2601, Davee 2696, **Foundation 2732**, Kemper 2831, Perritt 2939, **Pritzker 2952**, Rice 2966, Rich 2967, Schield 2985, Souder 3013, Washington 3058, Wenske 3063
Indiana: 1st 3094, Ball 3103, Perelman 3222
Iowa: Siouxland 3332
Louisiana: Baton Rouge 3462
Maine: Peters 3553
Maryland: **Hughes 3654**, Krongard 3669, RFI 3716
Massachusetts: Adams 3772, Connell 3856, Ford 3913, Foundation 3915, Gerondelis 3925, Gross 3937, Overly 4064, Pearce 4075, Roddy 4108, Schaffer 4129, Silverman 4146, Stevens 4163, Stevens 4164, Wolfson 4206, Worcester 4209
Michigan: Tauber 4454, Thomas 4456, Towsley 4461
Minnesota: Alworth 4499, Cloverfields 4542
Missouri: Edison 4807, Schweppe 4899
Nevada: Pennington 5053, Wiegand 5077
New Jersey: Aventis 5120, Berger 5128, Cowles 5170, Healthcare 5228, Hyde 5247, Integra 5251, **Johnson 5263**, **Johnson 5265**, Kerr 5278, Levin 5304, Roth 5377, Schecter 5385, Schreyer 5389
New York: Acorn 5515, Allen 5536, Alpern 5540, Arkell 5565, Aron 5569, **Atran 5575**, **Baker 5593**, Belfer 5615, Block 5638, Chanin 5730, Charina 5731, **China 5750**, Chisholm 5752, **Collins 5777**, **Cummings 5813**, Feil 5949, FIMF 5956, Forchheimer 5968, **Friedman 5988**, Goldschmidt 6058, Hall 6137, **Handler 6141**, Horncrest 6200, Icahn 6223, **Institute 6232**, Johnson 6271, Katz 6296, Katz 6297, Kennedy 6314, **Klingenstein 6340**, Kornfeld 6350, Lane 6373, Levin 6407, Lincoln 6423, Lurie 6459, **Macy 6471**, Mallah 6481, McGonagle 6518, Mesdag 6539, Millstein 6553, Milstein 6555, Moore 6573, New York 6618, O'Herron 6646, Paduano 6677, Paestum 6678, Penner 6710, Richardson 6796, **Ritter 6814**, **Robinson 6819**, Rosh 6858, Ross 6864, Roxe 6867, Rudin 6878, Sacerdote 6887, Saunders 6909, Schwartz 6945, SDA 6950, Seaver 6952, Sisenwein 6993, **Smithers 7010**, **Stiefel 7078**, **Tai 7118**, Tarnopol 7123, Tisch 7147, **Weinstein 7233**, Widgeon 7255, Wildwood 7259, Winston 7267, Zalaznick 7288, **Zimmermann 7301**
North Carolina: Brody 7325, Davis 7353, Nias 7435, Smith 7476, Van Houten 7500
Ohio: Brentwood 7555, Cleveland 7576, Coleman 7579, **Dewald 7608**, Mather 7736, Schlink 7839
Oklahoma: Presbyterian 7969
Oregon: Collins 8009, Johnson 8027, Swindells 8062
Pennsylvania: **Aircast 8074**, **AO 8085**, Arete 8088, Blue 8112, Cotswold 8160, Measey 8342, Respironics 8403
Rhode Island: **Alpert 8517**
South Carolina: Abney 8564
Texas: Alexander 8752, Alkek 8754, Cain 8809, CH 8823, Chilton 8826, Elkins 8883, Ellwood 8884, Fikes 8899, Franklin 8907, Gale 8913, Gulf 8926, Hankamer 8939, Hoblitzelle 8955, Hudson 8962, Huffington 8963, Kempner 8987, Meadows 9049, Medallion 9051, Moody 9070, Nash 9085, **Notsew 9093**, Owsley 9108, **Pearle 9113**, San Antonio 9166, Speas 9206, Triad 9239, Vale 9246, Wolff 9289
Utah: Bamberger 9305, Eccles 9317, Eccles 9320
Vermont: Lintilhac 9359
Virginia: Beazley 9376, Moore 9478, Norfolk 9484, Portsmouth 9498, United 9530
Washington: McMillen 9639, True 9696
West Virginia: McDonough 9726
Wisconsin: 1923 9738, Charter 9772, Coleman 9775, Delavan 9790, Demmer 9791, Fotsch 9802, Marcus 9859, McBeath 9864, Mead 9867, Shapiro 9925, Uihlein 9953

Medical specialty research

Louisiana: Pennington 3505
New York: Manning 6484
Pennsylvania: Perelman 8372

Medicine/medical care, public education

Illinois: Brinson 2633, Reese 2961
Massachusetts: Oral 4061
Minnesota: **Medtronic 4622**
New York: Harbor 6144, Pfizer 6720
North Dakota: Leach 7516
Pennsylvania: Blue 8112
Rhode Island: CVS 8529
Tennessee: Pickle 8717

Men

Kansas: Hutchinson 3368

Mental health, addictions

New York: Gordon 6076

Mental health, association

California: Atlas 241, Merage 887
Illinois: Buffett 2640
Maryland: Stulman 3739
Missouri: Baer 4779
Montana: Browning 4933
New York: **Borderline 5652**, Lopatin 6446, Lynton 6463, Stone 7081

Mental health, clinics

Oklahoma: Silas 7978

Mental health, counseling/support groups

Michigan: Doornink 4283

Mental health, depression

Connecticut: **Aetna 1479**
Indiana: **Lilly 3192**
Michigan: World 4489
New York: **Klingenstein 6340**
Pennsylvania: Blue 8112, Peterson 8376
Texas: Bass 8777

Mental health, disorders

Texas: Bass 8777

Mental health, eating disorders

Connecticut: **Davis 1526**
Georgia: **UPS 2503**
New York: Gordon 6076

Mental health, gambling addiction

Tennessee: Harrah's 8685

Mental health, residential care

Maryland: Dupkin 3618, Otenasek 3704

Mental health, schizophrenia

Florida: Hilton 2061
Indiana: **Lilly 3192**
Maryland: Stulman 3739
Minnesota: Wasie 4716
Pennsylvania: Peterson 8376

Mental health, smoking

New Jersey: **Johnson 5265**
New York: **Dynamic 5897**
Pennsylvania: Blue 8112

Mental health, transitional care
Wisconsin: Fleck 9799

Mental health, treatment
Alabama: Community 23
California: Harden 647, Hughes 690
Colorado: McDonnell 1422
Connecticut: Connecticut 1519
Georgia: Marcus 2441
Hawaii: Hawaii 2545
Illinois: Houlsby 2805, Lederer 2852, Shaw 3004
Maryland: **Blaustein 3575**, Stulman 3739
Massachusetts: Community 3854
Michigan: Ravitz 4418
Minnesota: **Weyerhaeuser 4725**
New York: Kenworthy 6315, Nicholas 6627,
    Schnurmacher 6931, Tower 7158, van Ameringen
    7191
Ohio: Reinberger 7815
Pennsylvania: Staunton 8457, Steinman 8459
Texas: Deakins 8860, El Paso 8882
Washington: Lynn 9633
West Virginia: Schenk 9732

Mental health/crisis services
Alabama: McMillan 49, Treadwell 68
Arizona: Arizona 87, Lovell 119, Morris 124
California: Alafi 201, Atkinson 239, **Baker 252**, Barker
    257, Brenner 321, California 350, Community 406,
    Gilmore 578, HealthCare 661, Hughes 690, Irvine
    699, Mental 886, Michelson 895, Norris 940,
    Ornest 959, Patron 983, Sacramento 1080, San
    Diego 1087, San Francisco 1088, Sierra 1151,
    Sonora 1178, Wood 1318
Colorado: Anschutz 1334, Colorado 1356, Rose 1445,
    Summit 1463
Connecticut: **Aetna 1479**, Bodenwein 1497, Bridgeport
    1504, Community 1515, Community 1516,
    Community 1517, Connecticut 1518, Foster 1546,
    Stanley 1652
District of Columbia: Cafritz 1780, Henry 1808, Meyer
    1834
Florida: Bank 1890, Beveridge 1907, Community 1946,
    Gulf 2041, MacDonald 2121, Martin 2130,
    Peacock 2165, Pinellas 2170, Rayonier 2189,
    Southwest 2240
Georgia: Harrison 2410
Illinois: Blowitz 2623, Community 2677, D and R 2693,
    Duchossois 2711, DuPage 2713, Field 2728,
    Illinois 2812, Polk 2946, Retirement 2964, Stern
    3023, **Tuohy 3041**
Indiana: Central 3116, Community 3122, Community
    3124, Kosciusko 3185, Lafayette 3188, **Lilly
    3192**, Vectren 3249, Wayne 3253
Iowa: Siouxland 3332
Kansas: Hutchinson 3368
Kentucky: Gheens 3421, Hayswood 3425
Louisiana: Booth 3464, Institute 3489
Maine: JTG 3542
Maryland: Baker 3567, Blaustein 3576, HRLD 3653
Massachusetts: Cambridge 3828, Crane 3866, High
    3950
Michigan: Acheson 4214, Comerica 4251, Dalton
    4266, Gerstacker 4322, Miller 4393, Pitt 4413,
    Power 4415
Minnesota: Blue 4521, Bremer 4523, Davis 4546,
    Edwards 4561, Ordean 4643, Oswald 4645, Thorpe
    4701
Missouri: Green 4822, H & R 4823, Pott 4886
Nebraska: Steinhart 5005
Nevada: Nevada 5047
New Jersey: Borden 5138, Cowles 5170, Dephillips
    5179, Hyde 5247, **Johnson 5261, Johnson 5265**,
    McGraw 5323, OceanFirst 5341, Schenck 5386,
    Vision 5442
New Mexico: Carlsbad 5469, Frost 5476, McCune
    5488, Santa Fe 5496
New York: Altman 5542, Barker 5600, Cummings 5815,
    Dammann 5824, **EHA 5912**, Glickenhaus 6042,
    Goldman 6053, Green 6096, **Ittleson 6241**, Kealy

6303, Kenworthy 6315, **Klingenstein 6340, Monell
    6566**, Moody's 6569, New York 6613, Parshelsky
    6693, Rhodebeck 6791, **Ritter 6814**, Spingold
    7032, Tower 7158, van Ameringen 7191, Wendt
    7243, Western 7248
North Carolina: Cumberland 7349, Reynolds 7457,
    Ryan 7469, Triangle 7496
North Dakota: North Dakota 7519
Ohio: Akron 7526, Austin 7536, Bicknell 7548,
    Columbus 7580, Coshocton 7593, Fairfield 7622,
    Morgan 7762, Richland 7819, Spaulding 7865,
    Stocker 7870, Toledo 7883, Wodecroft 7912,
    Woodruff 7917
Oklahoma: Zarrow 7991, Zarrow 7992
Oregon: Carpenter 8003
Pennsylvania: **Alcoa 8075**, Annenberg 8083, Central
    8135, Dolfinger 8172, FISA 8204, Fourjay 8209,
    Highmark 8247, Phoenixville 8381, Rockwell 8408,
    Scranton 8431, Smith 8445, Stackpole 8456,
    Staunton 8457, Steinman 8459, Stewart 8461
Rhode Island: CARLISLE 8521, Daniels 8530, Hasbro
    8539
South Dakota: Sioux Falls 8630
Texas: Alexander 8752, Butt 8804, Cameron 8812,
    Ellwood 8884, Fikes 8899, Fisch 8901, Gulf 8926,
    Kempner 8987, Meadows 9049, Paso 9111,
    Speas 9206, Sterling 9212, Swinney 9222, Temple
    9227
Utah: Eccles 9320
Vermont: Vermont 9361
Virginia: Camp 9382, Kellar 9449, Norfolk 9484
Washington: Aven 9554, Casey 9566, Community
    9571, Glaser 9594, **Hemingway 9606**, Medina
    9640, Norcliffe 9650, Seattle 9680, Tacoma 9693
West Virginia: Parkersburg 9730
Wisconsin: Evjue 9797, McBeath 9864, Meng 9870,
    Milwaukee 9876, Northwestern 9884, Sensient
    9922, Stackner 9934

Mental health/crisis services, formal/general education
California: Robertson 1059

Mental health/crisis services, hot-lines
California: vanLobenSels 1260
Pennsylvania: Blue 8112
Texas: Bass 8777, El Paso 8882, NAH 9084

Mental health/crisis services, public education
Connecticut: **Aetna 1479**
Pennsylvania: Blue 8112

Mental health/crisis services, public policy
California: Alliance 204, vanLobenSels 1260,
    Zellerbach 1326
Illinois: **MacArthur 2868**

Mental health/crisis services, rape victim services
Pennsylvania: FISA 8204

Mental health/crisis services, research
New York: Kenworthy 6315, Woodmere 7276

Mental health/crisis services, single organization support
Georgia: Realan 2470
Texas: Bass 8777

Mental health/crisis services, suicide
Illinois: Stewart 3024
Massachusetts: Lindsay 4009

Texas: Bass 8777

Mental health/crisis services, volunteer services
Washington: Lynn 9633

Mentally disabled
California: **Chiron 383**, Fireman's 510, Scully 1116
Delaware: MBNA 1730
Georgia: **UPS 2503**
Illinois: **Burlington 2644**
Maryland: Abell 3560
Minnesota: TCF 4699
New York: Butler 5692
North Carolina: Reynolds 7460
Pennsylvania: FISA 8204
Rhode Island: CVS 8529
Texas: di Portanova 8865

Migrant workers
Florida: Driskill 1975

Military/veterans
New Jersey: Kauffmann 5272
New York: Fisher 5961
Pennsylvania: Hooper 8256
Texas: Cuban 8853

Military/veterans' organizations
California: Borick 305, Esseff 488, **M & T 837**,
    Wunderkinder 1322
Florida: Michaan 2138, **Pope 2174**
Georgia: Jones 2424
Massachusetts: Schaffer 4129
Minnesota: ATK 4509
New York: Fisher 5961, **Robinson 6819**
North Carolina: Cumberland 7349
Ohio: Tetlak 7877
Oklahoma: Share 7977
Pennsylvania: Hooper 8256
Virginia: **Olmsted 9490**

Minorities
Arizona: Arizona 87
Arkansas: Wal-Mart 184
California: Ahmanson 198, **American 217, Atkinson
    240**, California 346, **Chiron 383**, Community 406,
    Confidence 411, Cowell 423, Fleishhacker 518,
    GenCorp 560, Genentech 563, **Getty 570**, Goldwyn
    600, Gumbiner 631, Hewlett 671, **Kaiser 739,
    Living 821**, Mayr 863, Norton 943, Orange 957,
    Peninsula 989, Rosenberg 1065, Sacramento
    1080, San Diego 1087, San Francisco 1088, Sierra
    1151, Soda 1173, **Sun 1214**, Weingart 1288
Colorado: El Pomar 1374, Qwest 1443, St. John's 1456
Connecticut: **Aetna 1479**, Bodenwein 1497,
    Connecticut 1518, Culpeper 1521, Fisher 1542, **GE
    1553**, Hartford 1563, International 1571, Long
    1590, Palmer 1621, **Praxair 1629, Xerox 1680**
District of Columbia: Cafritz 1780, **Hill 1809**, Meyer
    1834, **Public 1844**
Florida: Bank 1890, Beveridge 1907, FPL 2010, Martin
    2130, Rayonier 2189, Ryder 2213, St. Petersburg
    2245, Wilson 2300
Georgia: AGL 2312, BellSouth 2323, **Coca-Cola 2352**,
    ING 2418
Illinois: **Burlington 2644**, Chicago 2661, Community
    2677, Crane 2687, Day 2698, Fry 2740, Kaplan
    2823, Kelly 2830, Oak Park 2922, Olin 2925, Polk
    2946, Prince 2948, Sara 2982, **Shifting 3006,
    State 3019**, Washington 3058, White 3067,
    Woodward 3085
Indiana: Community 3125, Community 3128, **Cummins
    3136**, Griffith 3158, Health 3164, Noyes 3216

Iowa: McElroy 3313, Siouxland 3332
Kansas: Sprint 3395
Maryland: Abell 3559, **Agilent 3563**, Commonweal 3596, **Hughes 3654**
Massachusetts: Boston 3812, Clipper 3850, Community 3855, Millipore 4040, Parker 4069, **Reebok 4098**, Riley 4104, Schrafft 4133, Smith 4150, Stevens 4164, **Technical 4180**, Webster 4201
Michigan: Battle Creek 4228, Binda 4233, Ford 4307, General 4320, **Gerber 4321**, Grand Rapids 4326, **Kellogg 4357**, Mardigian 4386, **Mott 4399**, Wolverine 4488
Minnesota: **3M 4492**, **Andreas 4504**, Bell 4514, Bigelow 4519, Blue 4521, Bremer 4523, Bush 4524, Duluth 4556, General 4570, Grotto 4579, Mardag 4613, **Medtronic 4622**, Minneapolis 4623, Rochester 4668, Saint Paul 4671, **SUPERVALU 4695**
Mississippi: Foundation 4743, Hardin 4747
Missouri: **Anheuser 4776**, Boeing 4785, Butler 4793, **Deer 4804**, Goppert 4819, Hall 4824, Vatterott 4921
Nebraska: Lozier 4988
Nevada: Nevada 5047, Sierra 5064
New Jersey: Berger 5128, **Bonner 5137**, Campbell 5151, Cowles 5170, **Dow 5184**, Fund 5199, Hyde 5247, **Johnson 5265**, Knistrom 5282, **KPMG 5288**, **Lautenberg 5298**, MCJ 5324, **Newcombe 5338**, Princeton 5357, Schering 5387, Unilever 5434, Victoria 5440
New Mexico: Frost 5476, McCune 5488, Santa Fe 5496
New York: **Abelard 5508**, Allyn 5539, Altman 5542, **Bristol 5666**, **Citigroup 5755**, Claiborne 5758, Cummings 5815, **Ford 5970**, Glickenhaus 6042, **Guggenheim 6118**, **Hearst 6161**, **Hearst 6162**, **Heineman 6165**, Hilfiger 6183, Horncrest 6200, I Have 6219, Kealy 6303, Kurtz 6364, Lang 6374, **MetLife 6542**, Moody's 6569, **Morgan 6577**, New York 6615, New York 6619, New York 6620, **Norman 6635**, **Peierls 6705**, **PepsiCo 6714**, Price 6746, Revson 6789, Rochester 6823, Ruffin 6880, **Sloan 7003**, Violett 7200, Wendt 7243, Western 7248
North Carolina: Cemala 7337, Cumberland 7349, Janirve 7404, Reynolds 7458, Triangle 7496, **Wachovia 7502**, Warner 7503
North Dakota: Stern 7521
Ohio: Bruening 7558, **Federated 7624**, Fifth 7626, GAR 7643, Gund 7657, Jubilee 7694, Kroger 7705, Nord 7779, Richland 7819, Schmidlapp 7841, Stark 7867, White 7905, Women's 7916
Oregon: Intel 8022, Jackson 8024
Pennsylvania: **Alcoa 8075**, **Armstrong 8090**, Buck 8123, Buhl 8124, Connelly 8157, Dolfinger 8172, Falk 8193, Hill 8248, **Kennametal 8284**, Mandell 8322, **Pew 8377**, Philadelphia 8378, **PPG 8394**, Smith 8443, United 8486
Rhode Island: Rhode Island 8551
South Carolina: Coastal 8581
South Dakota: South Dakota 8631
Tennessee: Community 8660
Texas: **AT&T 8765**, El Paso 8882, Hoblitzelle 8955, **Jenesis 8971**, Kempner 8987, Kimberly 8992, McDermott 9043, Penney 9115, Powell 9128, **Shell 9181**, Simmons 9188, Sterling 9212, Strake 9215, **Tenet 9229**, Texas 9232, Trull 9240, Wright 9294
Vermont: **Ben 9355**
Virginia: Arlington 9371, Portsmouth 9498
Washington: Community 9571, Glaser 9594, Haas 9599, Norcliffe 9650
Wisconsin: Alliant 9742, Eastman 9795, Madison 9855, Milwaukee 9876, Northwestern 9884, Sensient 9922, Siebert 9927, Stackner 9934

Minorities/immigrants, centers/services

California: Atkinson 239, Community 406, Gumbiner 631, Orange 957, Sacramento 1080, Weingart 1288
Colorado: Qwest 1443, St. John's 1456
Connecticut: Bodenwein 1497, Palmer 1621

District of Columbia: Meyer 1834, **Public 1844**
Florida: Bank 1890, Beveridge 1907, Martin 2130, Ryder 2213, Smith 2238
Georgia: Goizueta 2400
Illinois: Chicago 2661, Fry 2740, Kaplan 2823, Polk 2946, **Shifting 3006**, Woodward 3085
Indiana: Community 3128, **Cummins 3136**
Iowa: Community 3278, Siouxland 3332
Kentucky: Norton 3441
Maryland: Brown 3578
Massachusetts: Boston 3812, Clipper 3850, Community 3855, Parker 4069, Riley 4104, Stevens 4164, **Technical 4180**, Webster 4201
Michigan: Battle Creek 4228, Grand Rapids 4326, **Kellogg 4357**
Minnesota: **Andreas 4504**, Bremer 4523, Rochester 4668, Saint Paul 4671
Mississippi: Foundation 4743
Missouri: Hall 4824
Nevada: Nevada 5047
New Jersey: Cowles 5170, Fund 5199, Hyde 5247, **Lautenberg 5298**, Princeton 5357, Victoria 5440
New Mexico: Frost 5476, McCune 5488
New York: **Abelard 5508**, Abrons 5511, **Ford 5970**, Heckscher 6164, New York 6615, **Peierls 6705**, Reed 6782, Rochester 6823, Sister 6994, Wendt 7243
North Carolina: Cemala 7337, Cumberland 7349, Reynolds 7458, Triangle 7496
Ohio: Gund 7657, Nord 7779, **Ohio 7786**, Stark 7867, Women's 7916
Oregon: Jackson 8024
Pennsylvania: Buck 8123, Dolfinger 8172, **Pew 8377**, Philadelphia 8378, Smith 8443
Rhode Island: Rhode Island 8551
Texas: **Jenesis 8971**, Kempner 8987, **Shell 9181**, Sterling 9212, Trull 9240, Wright 9294
Vermont: Vermont 9361
Virginia: Arlington 9371
Washington: Community 9571
Wisconsin: Stackner 9934

Mormon agencies & churches

Arizona: Trend 147
California: Lindorf 814, Peery 986
Maryland: HRLD 3653
Texas: Estill 8888
Utah: ALS 9301, Ashton 9303, B. Attitudes 9304, Greene 9325, Wadman 9349, Wing 9352
Washington: Crystal 9576

Multiple sclerosis

California: Smidt 1159
Colorado: Richardson 1444
Florida: **Holden 2063**
Illinois: Sheba 3005
Iowa: Krause 3302
Massachusetts: Karp 3974
New York: Brown 5676, Charitable 5733, Goldschmidt 6058, Kaplan 6289
Pennsylvania: Eden 8182, Peterson 8376
Virginia: Universal 9531
Washington: Moccasin 9643, O'Donnell 9652

Multiple sclerosis research

California: Oxnard 969
Florida: Wollowick 2306
Illinois: Barancik 2605
Massachusetts: Perpetual 4078
Ohio: Kramer 7704

Muscular dystrophy

California: Eisen 479
Iowa: Krause 3302
North Carolina: Gipson 7375
Texas: Hebert 8946, Valero 9247
Wisconsin: **DeAtley 9789**, Wagner 9958

Museums

Alabama: AmSouth 5, Barber 10, Blount 14, Hearin 37, McWane 50
Arizona: **Globe 101**, Marley 120, Morris 124
California: Ahmanson 198, Aratani 230, Arbus 231, Autry 243, **Baker 252**, Benbough 276, Booth 303, Bowes 311, Brenner 321, Burnett 336, Campini 353, **Cantor 354**, **Capital 357**, **Castagnola 366**, Caufield 367, **Christensen 384**, Copley 416, Cotsen 421, **Day 447**, DeMille 450, Dickinson 454, Doelger 459, **Field 504**, Fleishhacker 518, Flora 521, Fluor 523, Genentech 563, Getty 569, **Getty 570**, Glickman 582, Gonda 601, Grand 611, Gross 621, Gruber 626, Harman 651, Hills 674, Jackson 706, Johnson 723, Krause 780, Lehrer 800, LLWW 824, Lytel 836, **Marshall 858**, Martin 859, McBean 865, **McConnell 870**, Miller 901, Mudd 924, Nestle 935, **Nimoy 938**, Norton 943, Oppenheimer 955, Osher 961, Otter 965, Paloheimo 974, Pickford 1005, Potiker 1012, Radin 1025, Resnick 1041, Robertson 1059, Rock 1061, Rogers 1062, Sacramento 1080, San Diego 1087, Seaver 1117, Simon 1156, Simpson 1157, Smith 1160, Sprague 1183, Sprague 1184, Springcreek 1185, Stewart 1198, Teel 1230, Union 1250, Van Nuys 1262, Weiss 1290, WHH 1300, Windfall 1309, Zimmerman 1329
Colorado: Boettcher 1344, El Pomar 1374, Gates 1380, Hewit 1391, Hughes 1393, KBK 1400, Schermer 1449, Summit 1463
Connecticut: Bodenwein 1497, Community 1516, Foley 1544, Hartford 1563, **Huisking 1570**, **Kossak 1576**, Larsen 1579, Lynch 1591, Moore 1604, Niblack 1610, Rosenthal 1638, Royce 1639, Tauck 1657, United 1668, Woodward 1678
Delaware: Bishop 1693, Bishop 1694, Cawley 1696, Crestlea 1701, Crystal 1702, Dickenson 1708, **Fair 1713**, Hall 1718, Kingsley 1724, Marmot 1728, **Neuberger 1735**, Parker 1738, **Robinson 1745**, Rowland 1749, Singer 1753
District of Columbia: Brody 1777, Cafritz 1780, **Goldberg 1802**, Lehrman 1821
Florida: Adler 1871, Bank 1890, Behring 1899, Burns 1920, **Cobb 1936**, Duckwall 1978, Edelman 1987, Florida 2003, Gorin 2032, Hunter 2069, **Jaharis 2073**, Kaufman 2082, Martin 2130, Meyer 2137, Palm Beach 2161, **Ross 2207**, SunTrust 2259, United 2276, Winter 2303, Wymbs 2307
Georgia: AEC 2310, Anncox 2318, Carlos 2341, Chatham 2347, Covenant 2366, Cox 2367, Cox 2368, Exposition 2380, Fraser 2390, **Gage 2392**, Harland 2407, Harris 2408, Imlay 2417, Livingston 2435, Moore 2451, Morgens 2453, Patterson 2460, Porter 2468, Synovus 2497, Williams 2514, Young 2527
Hawaii: Ching 2540, Lange 2550, Watumull 2558
Illinois: Abelson 2581, Alsdorf 2590, **Andrew 2595**, Bielfeldt 2620, Buehler 2638, **Buntrock 2643**, **Burlington 2644**, **Carylon 2652**, Cheney 2658, Comer 2675, Comer 2676, Community 2677, Dillon 2704, Donnelley 2708, Field 2728, Galvin 2747, Getz 2753, Gidwitz 2754, Gidwitz 2755, Gidwitz 2756, Grainger 2768, Gray 2771, Guthman 2776, H.B.B. 2777, Halligan 2779, **Hull 2807**, Kaplan 2823, Kaplan 2824, Martin 2874, McCormick 2878, Melrene 2892, Neisser 2910, Nygren 2920, Opler 2927, Polk 2946, **Ryan 2978**, Sara 2982, Sharpe 3002, **Shifting 3006**, Sirius 3010, Stone 3025, Takiff 3032, Woodward 3085
Indiana: Annis 3100, Ball 3103, Cornelius 3134, Griffith 3158, Lilly 3194, Met 3204, Noyes 3216, Perelman 3222, Pulliam 3225, Wayne 3253, White 3257
Iowa: Bechtel 3263
Kansas: **Muchnic 3379**, Sprint 3395, Wiedemann 3405
Kentucky: Brown 3409, Brown 3410, **Brown 3411**, Cralle 3416, Horn 3427, McKellar 3439, Rosenthal 3450, Young 3454, Young 3455
Louisiana: Booth 3464, Diboll 3473, Jones 3491, Lupin 3498, Taylor 3511, **Woldenberg 3516**
Maine: Hannaford 3540, Lunder 3547
Maryland: Brown 3578, **Brown 3579**, Darby 3605, Davison 3609, Eliasberg 3620, FBW 3628, Felburn

3629, Hahn 3643, Kerr 3661, MARPAT 3684, Marriott 3685, Procter 3711, Rothschild 3723, **Shields 3730**, Tucker 3750

Massachusetts: Alvord 3778, Ansin 3779, Bristol 3816, Brookfield 3818, Calderwood 3826, Caldwell 3827, Carney 3837, Connolly 3857, Cox 3862, Cox 3863, Crane 3864, Croll 3868, Donahue 3881, Fraser 3917, Fuller 3918, Goldberg 3927, High 3950, Hopedale 3958, Johnson 3970, Jordan 3971, Knight 3987, Levine 4003, Marks 4024, McEvoy 4032, Morse 4044, Narada 4047, NBT 4048, New 4050, Overly 4064, Peabody 4072, Perry 4079, Putnam 4088, Rogers 4112, Roy 4114, Saltonstall 4126, Shapiro 4136, Smith 4150, Stearns 4160, Stevens 4163, Stevens 4164, Stride 4172, Vance 4191, Vingo 4192, Walske 4196, Weld 4203, Wood 4207, **Wood 4208**

Michigan: Acheson 4214, Besser 4232, Community 4256, DeVos 4276, Fisher 4299, Ford 4300, Ford 4302, Ford 4304, Frankel 4313, Frey 4316, Grand Rapids 4326, Hauenstein 4339, Hurst 4344, Manoogian 4382, Mosaic 4398, Padnos 4406, Saddle 4426, Smith 4441, **Stoddard 4447**, Stryker 4451, Thompson 4457, Van Andel 4467, **Visteon 4472**, Weatherwax 4474, Wege 4476, World 4489

Minnesota: Ankeny 4505, Bell 4514, Bush 4524, Butler 4525, Deluxe 4549, Fiterman 4565, Hubbard 4590, McVay 4620, Slaggie 4686

Mississippi: Community 4737, Mississippi 4758

Missouri: Andrews 4774, Gateway 4817, Gottlieb 4820, H & R 4823, Holekamp 4832, Kemper 4847, Kemper 4848, Laclede 4852, Nichols 4873, Price 4888, **Pulitzer 4889**, Reynolds 4892, **Sayler 4897**, Shaw 4901, Wornall 4929

Montana: Browning 4933

Nebraska: Eihusen 4961, GFH 4966, Hirschfeld 4974, James 4980, Kawasaki 4982, Schrager 5001, **Union 5012**

Nevada: **Bing 5022**, Boyd 5023, Wiegand 5077

New Hampshire: Fuller 5090, Treat 5102

New Jersey: Brady 5141, Cape 5153, Cowles 5170, Dodge 5181, **Edison 5186**, Honickman 5239, Jockey 5260, **Johnson 5263**, Kauffmann 5272, Kerr 5278, **Lautenberg 5298**, Lazarus 5299, Levin 5304, Marianthi 5318, Nicolais 5339, OceanFirst 5341, Roth 5377, Sunfield 5418, Weston 5452

New Mexico: Holt 5480, Hubbard 5481, **Lannan 5484**, McCune 5488, Stockman 5497

New York: Abrons 5511, Alexander 5532, Amicus 5557, Arnhold 5568, Aron 5569, Baird 5592, Barker 5600, Bayne 5607, **Benenson 5620**, Berg 5621, Black 5636, Booth 5651, Brodsky 5669, Butler 5691, Calicchio 5698, Campbell 5700, **Carey 5704**, Chanin 5730, Charina 5731, Chasanoff 5735, **Chazen 5739**, Chisholm 5752, CJM 5756, Clark 5761, Clark 5762, Cohen 5767, Cohen 5770, Cohenca 5773, Coles 5775, Corning 5794, Cornpauw 5795, Cramer 5804, Cullman 5811, Cullman 5812, Davenport 5833, Devlin 5855, Diker 5862, Dobkin 5866, Doran 5875, Double 5876, Ehrenkranz 5913, Emwiga 5930, Epstein 5934, Erpf 5937, Everett 5941, Ferrari 5953, Fisher 5962, **Forbes 5967**, Forchheimer 5968, **Ford 5970**, Fuld 6000, Furth 6004, Gerry 6017, **Gilbert 6028**, Goldberg 6045, Goldring 6057, Goldsmith 6059, Goldsmith 6060, Goldstein 6062, Goldstone 6065, Gould 6082, Greenberg 6098, Greene 6100, Greentree 6102, Haas 6126, Harrison 6149, Haseltine 6152, **Hearst 6161**, **Hearst 6162**, Hillman 6186, **Homeland 6199**, Horowitz 6202, Israel 6240, **Jaffe 6250**, Janklow 6254, Joelson 6265, Johnson 6270, **JPMorgan 6277**, Kandell 6287, Kellen 6308, Kellogg 6311, Klein 6333, Kravis 6353, Kravis 6354, **Kress 6357**, Kriendler 6358, Kurtz 6364, Lasdon 6378, Lauder 6381, Lauder 6382, Lebworth 6390, Lemberg 6401, Leonhardt 6403, Levin 6407, Levy 6413, Levy 6414, Liberman 6419, **Lipchitz 6430**, Litwin 6436, Loeb 6439, **Luce 6453**, **Mapplethorpe 6485**, Marcus 6486, Marks 6489, McCarthy 6516, McGraw 6519, **Mellon 6525**, **Memton 6529**, Metropolitan 6543, Meyer 6544, Meyer 6545, Milstein 6555, Milstein 6556, Model 6565, Morse

6582, Morse 6583, Neidich 6606, Neu 6610, New York 6618, New York 6620, Newman 6625, O'Connor 6645, Ohrstrom 6659, Osborn 6669, **Paley 6679**, Palmer 6683, Pannonia 6686, PBO 6699, Persepolis 6718, Pines 6727, Plant 6731, Propp 6749, Rattner 6773, Resnick 6787, Riedman 6804, Riggio 6807, Rodgers 6828, Rose 6838, Rose 6839, Rosen 6841, **Rosen 6843**, Ross 6864, Rotenstreich 6865, Rudin 6877, Sackler 6891, Saltz 6899, **Saltzman 6900**, Schiff 6923, Schneider 6929, Schulweis 6948, Schwartz 6945, Seevers 6953, Sharp 6961, Sharp 6962, Sheinberg 6963, Shoreland 6968, Siegel 6976, **Silfen 6980**, SO 7015, Sobel 7016, **Solomon 7017**, Stanton 7043, Stern 7070, **Stony 7082**, Straus 7084, Straus 7086, **Teddy 7127**, Three 7135, Tisch 7145, Tober 7152, **Trust 7168**, Tuch 7170, **U.S. 7180**, Ungar 7183, Ushkow 7188, Vance 7193, von der Heyden 7203, Walbridge 7207, Wallach 7210, **Walter 7211**, **Warhol 7215**, Weiler 7226, Weinman 7232, Wendt 7243, Werblow 7245, Western 7248, Williams 7260, Woodmere 7276, Woodward 7279, Wright 7280, Wunsch 7281, Zuckerberg 7304

North Carolina: Broyhill 7328, Cumberland 7349, Dover 7356, Gorelick 7381, Halton 7386, Layden 7419, Martin 7424, North Carolina 7438, O'Herron 7441, Reynolds 7460, Smith 7476, Smith 7478, Spangler 7482, Triangle 7496, Tzedakah 7497, Winston 7507, Woodson 7509

North Dakota: Stern 7521

Ohio: Akron 7526, Charities 7569, Codrington 7578, Community 7583, **Convergys 7587**, **Cooper 7589**, Coshocton 7593, Dayton 7604, Diebold 7611, Dorn 7612, Dornette 7613, Edwards 7618, Frost 7642, Gund 7655, Haile 7659, Hauck 7666, Ingalls 7684, Jackson 7685, Kaplan 7696, Kulas 7706, Lewis 7713, Lindner 7716, McMaster 7744, Miller 7753, Mixon 7757, Murphy 7769, Nord 7780, Ohio 7785, Oliver 7788, Payne 7798, Peninsula 7799, **Perkins 7800**, Philips 7804, Reinberger 7815, Rosenthal 7826, Schiff 7838, Schlink 7839, Seifert 7850, Semple 7851, Stillson 7869, Stranahan 7872, Thendara 7878, Troy 7886, **Vesper 7892**, Watson 7896, Wodecroft 7912, Youngstown 7920

Oklahoma: Gussman 7941, Helmerich 7942, Kerr 7949, Kirkpatrick 7952, Oxley 7968, Williams 7989, Zarrow 7992

Oregon: Bair 7998, Jeld 8025, Johnson 8027, Mentor 8039, Meyer 8042, Schnitzer 8056

Pennsylvania: Ames 8080, Arkema 8089, Bozzone 8114, Briggs 8117, Byers' 8127, **Carpenter 8131**, Dietrich 8170, Dietrich 8171, Dolfinger 8172, Field 8200, **Heinz 8243**, Heinz 8244, Hodge 8254, Janssen 8271, Justus 8276, Karabots 8278, Kardon 8279, Keystone 8286, Kline 8293, Lindback 8312, Mandell 8322, McCune 8332, McLean 8340, **Metcalf 8351**, Miller 8355, Neubauer 8363, Perelman 8373, Perelman 8374, Peterson 8376, **Pew 8377**, Roberts 8407, Rockwell 8408, Schwab 8430, Sherrerd 8439, Simonds 8442, Smith 8445, Speyer 8453, **Strawbridge 8465**, Vanguard 8490

Rhode Island: Alperin 8516, Charlesmead 8525, Daniels 8530, Littlefield 8544, Roosa 8552

South Carolina: Rainey 8605

South Dakota: Sioux Falls 8630

Tennessee: **Bridgestone 8646**, Briggs 8647, CLARCOR 8658, Conwood 8663, Hamico 8684, Jeniam 8695, Johnson 8697, Schadt 8725, Stokely 8730, Thompson 8733, Tucker 8735, Wilson 8744

Texas: Bass 8775, Bass 8777, Benson 8788, Brackenridge 8793, Bridwell 8797, Burnett 8801, **Butt 8803**, Cain 8809, Carter 8816, **Catto 8819**, CH 8823, Clements 8832, Coastal 8833, Coates 8834, Cockrell 8835, Community 8840, Constantin 8843, **Cooper 8846**, Cox 8850, Crane 8852, Delaney 8862, Fikes 8899, Finger 8900, Frost 8910, Garvey 8914, Goodman 8921, Hamill 8937, Hudson 8962, Jones 8975, Kahn 8980, Keith 8982, Kempner 8987, Kilroy 8991, Kimberly 8992, Kronkosky 9002, Kurth 9003, Loose 9017, Luchsinger 9022, Marcus 9029, Mays 9035,

McCrea 9040, McDermott 9043, Meadows 9049, Miller 9061, Mithoff 9066, Moran 9072, Newman 9090, Northen 9092, Rockwell 9154, Rogers 9156, San Antonio 9166, Scurlock 9175, Semmes 9179, Sharp 9180, **Shell 9181**, Sterling 9212, Taylor 9226, Temple 9228, Trull 9240, Waggoner 9256, Waggoner 9257, Wal 9260, **Westbury 9277**, Wise 9285, Wortham 9292, Wright 9294

Utah: Eccles 9320

Virginia: Clark 9393, Delmar 9410, Folger 9418, Grandis 9432, Graves 9433, Guilford 9434, Gwathmey 9435, Herndon 9437, Kanter 9445, Kogod 9452, Lipman 9459, Morgan 9479, Norfolk 9484, **Norfolk 9485**, Olsson 9491, Parsons 9493, Pauley 9494, Portsmouth 9498, Reynolds 9503, Samberg 9510, Scott 9513, Smith 9518, VuBay 9533, Weil 9535

Washington: Anderson 9551, **Blakemore 9558**, Cheney 9569, Community 9571, Dimmer 9579, Ferguson 9585, Kaleidoscope 9616, **Kongsgaard 9620**, Kreielsheimer 9621, Miller 9642, Murdock 9644, **Sage 9674**, Shirley 9684, Tacoma 9693

West Virginia: Daywood 9717, Kanawha 9723, Parkersburg 9730

Wisconsin: Bolz 9762, Chapman 9771, Demmer 9791, Frautschi 9804, Helfaer 9813, Herzfeld 9815, Johnson 9823, Joy 9828, Krause 9841, **Lewis 9850**, Manpower 9858, Marshall 9860, Merrill 9872, Northwestern 9884, Pangburn 9892, Pick 9899, Soref 9930, Steigleder 9936, **Stein 9937**, Stuart 9942, Uihlein 9953, Walter 9959, Windhover 9966, WPS 9970

Wyoming: Sargent 9989, Tozzi 9995, Weiss 9997

Museums (art)

Alabama: Crampton 30, Lowder 42, Mitchell 53, Saks 61

Arizona: Halle 103, Herberger 106

California: Argosy 233, Bakar 250, Bloomfield 295, Booth 303, Broad 323, Brooks 327, Cheeryble 377, D & DF 434, Davies 446, Field 505, Flagg 517, Friedman 539, Friedman 540, Garen 555, Geschke 568, **Good 603**, Greenberg 617, Halperin 640, Mericos 889, Merrill 890, **Mohn 907**, Monkarsh 909, **Nimoy 938**, **Osher 962**, Oshman 963, Outrageous 967, Ovitz 968, Pelosi 988, Robertson 1059, Sebastiani 1119, Segerstrom 1123, **Taub 1227**, Wilbur 1305

Colorado: Bohen 1346, Gooding 1384, Hughes 1393, McCormick 1420, Schermer 1449, Tuchman 1467

Connecticut: Aronson 1485, Chase 1508, Chilton 1511, Davis 1525, Goergen 1556, Heyman 1567, Lee 1582, Pequot 1625, Robbins 1634, **Wiener 1677**

Delaware: Choptank 1699, Newman 1736

District of Columbia: Brody 1777, **Coyne 1788**, HRH 1811, Nef 1839

Florida: **Braman 1915**, Castellani 1928, Cejas 1930, Cisneros 1934, Conese 1950, Edgemer 1989, Fisher 1999, Green 2033, GTE 2040, Hicks 2059, Katcher 2080, Lee 2107, **Levine 2111**, Lorberbaum 2118, MacDougald 2122, Meyer 2137, Miller 2141, River 2199, Sansom 2218, Sherman 2233, Simon 2235, Taplin 2264, Victory 2280, Wolfson 2305

Georgia: Brill 2329, Colonial 2353, Lanier 2431, **Morris 2455**, Rosenberg 2476, Selig 2484, Spray 2495

Illinois: Alsdorf 2590, Anixter 2597, Baskes 2607, Cooper 2683, D.H.R. 2695, Franke 2734, **Galashiels 2742**, Goldberg 2761, Kovler 2844, Krueck 2846, Madigan 2869, Millard 2897, **Niamogue 2914**, Rothschild 2971, Sangre 2981, Schield 2985, Walk 3053

Indiana: Bussing 3111

Iowa: Bucksbaum 3271

Kansas: Downing 3358

Kentucky: Young 3454

Louisiana: Diboll 3473, Heymann 3487

Maryland: Abramson 3561, **Adams 3562**, Baker 3567, Greenberg 3639, Legg 3672, Meyerhoff 3690, Middendorf 3694, Rouse 3724, Shattuck 3728, Small 3735, Wasserman 3758

Massachusetts: Bressler 3815, Brookfield 3818, Cogan 3851, Croll 3868, Evans 3898, Fessenden 3903, Greene 3933, Heide 3945, Keane 3975, Landry 3995, Lee 4001, Manitou 4018, **Middlecott 4037**, Murray 4045, Perry 4079, Sharf 4137, Wheatland 4204

Michigan: Doornink 4283, Dow 4286, Frankel 4312, Frey 4316, Keeler 4355, Meijer 4390, RNR 4420, Schlafer 4429, Wolff 4486, Wolters 4487

Minnesota: Chadwick-Loher 4535, Drew 4554, Griggs 4577

Missouri: Baer 4778, Brauer 4787, Carter 4794, Edison 4808, Pershing 4881

Nebraska: Durham 4959, Swanson 5008

Nevada: Hawkins 5036, Keyser 5039, May 5046, Prim 5054, Wendy's 5076

New Jersey: Amirsaleh 5114, Berlind 5129, Brody 5144, Cendant 5157, Cohen 5166, Geier 5204, **Gulton 5217**, L.A.W. 5292, Levin 5304, Lipper 5308, McMullen 5325, **Parnassus 5347**, Point 5353, Riskin 5369, Segal 5395, Shen 5398, Weny 5450

New Mexico: Phillips 5492, Thaw 5499

New York: A.E. 5506, Abeles 5509, Achilles 5514, Acorn 5515, Allwin 5538, American 5549, Antz 5560, Bachmann 5587, **Baker 5593**, Bayne 5607, Belfer 5615, Birkelund 5632, **Brice 5662**, Brine 5665, Brodsky 5669, Buttenwieser 5693, Canary 5702, Carson 5709, Centennial 5722, Charitable 5733, Chisholm 5753, Cohen 5770, Cornell 5792, **Cornell 5793**, Cowin 5802, Cox 5803, Curry 5817, Debs 5844, Diker 5862, Drukier 5890, Erpf 5937, Gelman 6014, Gerschel 6019, **Gilman 6033**, Goldstein 6064, Green 6095, Gural 6120, Hajim 6134, Harris 6148, Hazen 6159, Hirsch 6188, **Homeland 6199**, Iris 6237, Ivor 6242, **Jaffe 6250**, JCT 6256, Johnson 6271, Katz 6297, Kearns 6304, Kravis 6353, Kravis 6355, L and L 6366, LBC 6386, Lebworth 6390, Loeb 6438, Loeb 6439, Lutece 6460, **Mailman 6478**, Manitoba 6483, Marron 6492, Marron 6493, Matisse 6505, McGraw 6520, Melly 6526, Mesdag 6539, Mindich 6558, **Moore 6571**, Neuwirth 6612, Ogden 6657, Parker 6690, **Pearson 6701**, Pevaroff 6719, Quadrangle 6758, R & TP 6764, **Reed 6783**, Richardson 6796, **Richman 6799**, Riggio 6807, **Rosen 6843**, Rosenkranz 6851, Rosenwald 6856, Ross 6862, **Rothschild 6866**, Sacerdote 6887, Sackler 6892, Saligman 6895, Schapiro 6912, Schwartz 6946, **Silfen 6980**, Smith 7008, Solow 7019, Sosnoff 7025, Speyer 7027, Spiegel 7029, **Spiegel 7030**, Stanton 7043, Straus 7084, Sulzberger 7095, Tisch 7146, Townsend 7159, Trott 7165, Tully 7173, Unanue 7182, Unterberg 7186, Vogelstein 7201, **Volpert 7202**, Weiler 7226, Weinman 7232, Wender 7241, Werblow 7245, **Wigmore 7258**, Wilson 7262, Woodheath 7274, Wunsch 7281, **Zenkel 7295**

North Carolina: Goodnight 7377, Hanes 7388, Holding 7399, Livingstone 7422, Woodward 7510

Ohio: Britton 7556, Callahan 7564, Castellini 7568, **Cooper 7589**, Davidson 7602, DBJ 7605, Gardner 7644, Gund 7656, Horvitz 7677, IHS 7683, Jochum 7692, Lehner 7709, LKC 7720, M/B 7728, Mather 7736, Miller 7753, Miniger 7756, Morley 7763, Peninsula 7799, **PLACE 7805**, Rieveschl 7820, Ritter 7822, Sage 7829, Schiff 7837, Schott 7842, Siegal 7856, Turben 7888, **Warrington 7895**, Williams 7907

Oklahoma: Barnett 7924, Collins 7929, Gussman 7941, Oklahoman 7966, Oxley 7968

Oregon: Bauman 7999, Geary 8017, Jubitz 8029, PGE 8051

Pennsylvania: Alter 8078, Ames 8080, Berkman 8102, Bradley 8115, Cotswold 8160, Fine 8201, Hooper 8256, Hulme 8260, **Johnson 8274**, Kaiserman 8277, Murray 8360, von Hess 8493

Rhode Island: **Bafflin 8519**, Charter 8526

South Carolina: Ceres 8578, South 8615

Tennessee: Atticus 8639, Caldwell 8649

Texas: Bookout 8791, Butler 8802, Cameron 8811, Collins 8838, Gill 8919, Halsell 8936, Hanley 8940, Hudson 8962, Huffington 8963, Jamail

8970, Law 9006, Mays 9035, McNutt 9048, **MFI 9059**, Moncrief 9069, Mosbacher 9077, Once 9101, Oshman 9104, Rachofsky 9139, Ross 9159, Sarofim 9168, Susman 9220, Tobin 9235, Urschel 9244, Vaughan 9249, Vaughan 9250, Waggoner 9256, Ward 9262, Wise 9284, Wolff 9288

Virginia: Connors 9403, **DeLaski 9409**, Fralin 9420, Funger 9426, **Glenstone 9429**, Grandis 9432, Katzen 9446, Kington 9450, Rosenthal 9508, Taubman 9524

Washington: Green 9598, Miller 9642, **PAH 9657**, Raven 9670, Shirley 9684, Wright 9708

Wisconsin: Baker 9751, Brookbank 9766, Chapman 9771, Charter 9772, Community 9779, Helfaer 9813, Hyde 9818, Kohl 9837, Peck 9895, Pollybill 9900, Shattuck 9926, Spire 9931, Uihlein 9953, West 9963, Woodson 9969

Museums (children's)

California: Hoffman 682, Weyrich 1298
Colorado: Hughes 1393, Pioneer 1438
Connecticut: LittleJohn 1588
Delaware: Watson 1761
Florida: Five 2001, Sykes 2261
Georgia: **Morris 2455**
Illinois: **Andrew 2595**, Madigan 2869, New 2912, Souder 3013, Ullrich 3043
Indiana: Indiana 3173, Jones 3179
Kentucky: Rosenthal 3450
Maryland: **Adams 3562**, Rouse 3724
Massachusetts: Inavale 3964
Michigan: Frey 4316
Minnesota: McCarthy 4614
New Mexico: Delle 5474
New York: Geds 6010, Hayden 6158, Kazickas 6302, Lynton 6463, Maheras 6475, Penner 6710, R & TP 6764, **Richmond 6801**, **Rosen 6843**, Tisch 7148, Unterberg 7186
Oregon: Jubitz 8028, Jubitz 8029
Rhode Island: Roosa 8552
Tennessee: Briggs 8647, Jeniam 8695
Texas: Diener 8867, Franklin 8908, **MFI 9059**
Virginia: Grandis 9432, Ukrop 9529
Washington: Danz 9577
Wisconsin: Managed 9857, Reinhart 9909, Stark 9935

Museums (ethnic/folk arts)

California: Shoresh 1147
Colorado: Richardson 1444
Connecticut: Berkley 1492
District of Columbia: Gottesman 1803
Florida: Fisher 1999, Katcher 2080
Indiana: Simon 3239
Michigan: Frey 4316, Schlafer 4429
New Jersey: Indian 5250, Schwarz 5394
New York: Belfer 5615, Brodsky 5669, Canary 5702, Danziger 5829, Gerschel 6018, Goldberg 6045, Goldstein 6064, Jesselson 6259, Lebworth 6390, Milstein 6555, Rubenstein 6870, Saligman 6895, Scheuer 6919, Tarnopol 7123, Weiler 7226
Pennsylvania: Berkman 8102, Fine 8201, Rubin 8415, Toll 8478
Virginia: Ratner 9501

Museums (history)

California: Eisen 479, **Kohl 771**, **Tchang 1229**, Weisman 1289, Wiskemann 1311
Connecticut: Robbins 1634
District of Columbia: Friedman 1799
Florida: Colen 1938
Georgia: Five 2383
Illinois: Knapp 2841
Indiana: Kuhne 3187
Iowa: Kinney 3300
Kansas: SYZYGY 3398
Michigan: Americana 4218, Frey 4316, Harding 4338, Parish 4408
Missouri: Uhlmann 4920
New Jersey: 1772 5106

New York: Fascitelli 5946, Gant 6006, **Gilder 6030**, **Goldman 6054**, Grubman 6113, Habe 6128, Mnuchin 6564
North Carolina: Hayden 7394, Jones 7408, Sklut 7473
Ohio: Lincoln 7715
Oklahoma: Gaylord 7937, Kimmell 7951, Oklahoman 7966
Pennsylvania: Fox 8210, Hooper 8256, McCormick 8329, Meakem 8341, Rubin 8415
Rhode Island: Felicia 8536
Texas: White 9279

Museums (marine/maritime)

California: Outhwaite 966, **Tennity 1233**, Vadasz 1254, Williams 1307
Hawaii: Alexander 2530
Illinois: McNally 2885
Maryland: Kerr 3661
Massachusetts: Fraser 3917
Michigan: Frey 4316
Nebraska: Lincoln 4987
New York: Bovin 5654, McGraw 6519, Ranger 6770, Weinberg 7231
Ohio: Frost 7642
Texas: Benson 8788
Wisconsin: Brotz 9767

Museums (natural history)

Alabama: Mitchell 53
California: Booth 302, Mericos 889, Seinfeld 1124, Williams 1307
Connecticut: Sage 1640
Delaware: Bennett 1690, Reynolds 1743
District of Columbia: Post 1842
Georgia: Lanier 2431
Illinois: **Andrew 2595**, Comer 2676, McNally 2885, Ward 3056, Wilkie 3071
Michigan: Frey 4316
Nebraska: Hubbell 4979
New Jersey: Phipps 5352
New York: **Altman 5544**, **Brokaw 5670**, Corrigan 5796, D'Agostino 5818, Freston 5982, Klingenstein 6337, Pevaroff 6719, Pumpkin 6754, Schwartz 6941, **Solomon 7017**, Speyer 7027, Sulzberger 7095, Walter 7212, Wildwood 7259
Ohio: American 7528, Britton 7556, DBJ 7605, Murch 7766

Museums (science/technology)

Arizona: Dorrance 95
California: Bloomfield 295, Ishiyama 702, Jonsson 729, Koshland 777, Quattrone 1024
Illinois: **Andrew 2595**, Energizer 2721, Farrell 2725, Gidwitz 2755, Ward 3056
Indiana: American 3098
Michigan: Frey 4316
Minnesota: Garmar 4569, Weesner 4720
Missouri: Emerson 4809
New Jersey: 1772 5106, Buehler 5146
New York: Kupferberg 6363, Liu 6437, Smith 7007
North Carolina: Belk 7314, McLean 7425, Smith 7478
Ohio: Miniger 7756, Stillson 7869
Oregon: Hedinger 8019
Pennsylvania: CMS 8147, Keystone 8285, Meakem 8341, Peterson 8376
Texas: Mithoff 9066, Smith 9192
Virginia: Universal 9531
Washington: Green 9598
Wisconsin: Wehr 9961

Museums (specialized)

Arizona: Halle 103
California: Bloomfield 295, Booth 302, Brenner 321, Broccoli 326, Campbell 352, Davidson 445, Greenberg 617, Homer 684, House 687, Johnson 726, Petersen 994, **Schlinger 1102**, Setzer 1130, Witherbee 1312, Wolfen 1316

Colorado: **Avenir 1339**, Wolf 1475
Georgia: Illges 2416, Jones 2424, Woodruff 2522
Illinois: Goldberg 2761, Madigan 2869, Mazza 2877, Wilkie 3071
Indiana: Simon 3236
Iowa: Bucksbaum 3271
Kentucky: Young 3454
Massachusetts: Stamps 4155, Sternberg 4161
Michigan: **Dogwood 4282**, Frey 4316
Minnesota: O'Neil 4638, **Patterson 4647**
New Jersey: 1772 5106, Levin 5304, Levitt 5305, Roth 5377, Smith 5407
New York: Altus 5547, Canary 5702, Charitable 5733, Cohen 5769, Gurwin 6121, Gutman 6122, **Homeland 6199**, Karmazin 6293, Leuschen 6405, Millard 6548, **New 6621**, Overhills 6676, Pollack 6735, Pulier 6753, Resnick 6787, Rosner 6860, Solomon 7018
North Carolina: Davis 7353
Ohio: DBJ 7605, Ferguson 7625
Oklahoma: McCasland 7956
Pennsylvania: Bozzone 8114, Hooper 8256
Tennessee: Sparks 8727
Texas: Holt 8958, Mays 9035, Mechia 9050, Miles 9060, Moncrief 9069, Oshman 9104, Taylor 9226
Virginia: Cartledge 9388, Funger 9426, Moore 9478
Washington: Apex 9552, Archibald 9553, Lematta 9628, Schultz 9679, Shirley 9684
Wyoming: Chapman 9976

Museums (sports/hobby)

Colorado: International 1395
Delaware: **Birch 1692**
Mississippi: Holloway 4749
North Carolina: Ebert 7362
Wisconsin: Uihlein 9955

Native Americans/American Indians

Alaska: Arctic 80, CIRI 83, Doyon 84, Rasmuson 85
Arizona: Ottens 128
California: **American 217**, California 345, Community 406, **LEF 799**, Stern 1195, Wunderkinder 1322
Colorado: Qwest 1443
Connecticut: Culpeper 1521, **Educational 1533**, Woodward 1678
Delaware: **Raskob 1741**
Illinois: **ARIA 2600**, **Burlington 2644**, **State 3019**
Iowa: Siouxland 3332
Maryland: **Hughes 3654**
Massachusetts: Community 3855, High 3950, Hyams 3961
Michigan: Grand Rapids 4326
Minnesota: Bell 4514, Blue 4521, Bremer 4523, Duluth 4556, Grotto 4579, Minneapolis 4623, Phillips 4655
New Jersey: Alcatel 5110, **Carolan 5156**, **Johnson 5265**, **KPMG 5288**, **Newcombe 5338**
New Mexico: Frost 5476, **Lannan 5484**, McCune 5488, New Mexico 5491, Santa Fe 5496
New York: **Abelard 5508**, **Bristol 5666**, **Edouard 5909**, Gould 6083, **Macy 6471**, Oestreicher 6656, **Ross 6863**, Ungar 7183
North Carolina: Cumberland 7349, Easley 7361, Reynolds 7458, Triangle 7496
North Dakota: Stern 7521
Oregon: Intel 8022
Pennsylvania: Moore 8358
South Dakota: South Dakota 8631
Texas: Kempner 8987
Utah: **Wishnick 9353**
Vermont: **Ben 9355**
Virginia: Arlington 9371, Delmar 9410, **Gannett 9428**
Washington: Norcliffe 9650

Neighborhood centers

Alabama: Community 24
Florida: River 2199
Illinois: Beidler 2613, **Goodman 2765**, Hartmarx 2794
Massachusetts: Lappin 3997

Michigan: Knight 4364
Missouri: Simon 4903
New Mexico: Proteus 5495
New York: Dabah 5820, Furth 6004, Heckscher 6164, I Have 6219, Kiernan 6321, Unterberg 7186, Whispering 7250
Ohio: DBJ 7605, Nordson 7781
Oklahoma: Bailey 7923
Texas: Waggoner 9256
Virginia: Colburn 9395

Nerve, muscle & bone diseases

California: Danford 438
Connecticut: **Newman's 1609**, Tow 1661
Florida: Charitable 1931
Indiana: **Lilly 3192**
New York: Effron 5911
Texas: Vale 9246

Nerve, muscle & bone research

Illinois: Miller 2899
New Jersey: Branfman 5142
Pennsylvania: **AO 8085**
South Carolina: TSC 8618
Texas: Veres 9252

Neuroscience

California: Blume 298, **Foundation 530**
Florida: Greenburg 2034
Illinois: **Friedmann 2738**
Massachusetts: **Grass 3931**
Michigan: Levy 4378
Minnesota: McKnight 4617
New York: Schapiro 6912
Pennsylvania: DSF 8178

Neuroscience research

California: Alafi 201, Beneto 277, Blume 298, Coates 391
Colorado: **Avenir 1339**
Illinois: **Buntrock 2643**, **Foundation 2732**, **Friedmann 2738**
Michigan: Dow 4286
New Jersey: Integra 5251, Kauffmann 5272
New York: **Bristol 5666**, Chanin 5730, Diamond 5857, **Essel 5938**, Kaplan 6289, **Klingenstein 6338**
Texas: South 9201
Virginia: Lawrence 9457, **Three 9525**

Nonprofit management

Alabama: Central 20, Community 24
California: **Draper 466**, Flintridge 520, Haas 637, Irvine 698, San Luis 1090, Shasta 1139, Ventura 1264
Connecticut: Bridgeport 1504, Fairfield 1537
District of Columbia: Community 1785
Florida: Bush 1922
Hawaii: Hawaii 2545
Indiana: Vectren 3249
Maine: Maine 3548
Massachusetts: **Bruner 3819**, Cape Cod 3833
Michigan: Knight 4364
Minnesota: Initiative 4593, West 4723
Missouri: Saint Louis 4896
New Mexico: Santa Fe 5496
New York: Area 5564
North Carolina: Community 7346
Ohio: Nordson 7781
Oklahoma: Oklahoma City 7964
Rhode Island: Rhode Island 8551
Texas: Speas 9207
Virginia: Lynchburg 9463

Nursing care

California: McBean 866, Norris 940, Stevens 1196, Weingart 1288
Delaware: Parker 1738
Florida: Langford 2102, Price 2177
Georgia: Moore 2452
Hawaii: Zimmerman 2561
Illinois: VNA 3049, Washington 3058
Iowa: Siouxland 3332
Michigan: Dow 4286
Minnesota: Alworth 4499, Dennis 4550
Missouri: Green 4822, Musgrave 4870
Nebraska: Vetter 5014
Nevada: Fairweather 5032
New Hampshire: Gale 5091
New Jersey: **Johnson 5265**
New York: **China 5750**, **Fuld 5999**, Hugoton 6210, Northern 6639, O'Connor 6645, **Pforzheimer 6721**, Renfield 6786
North Carolina: Reynolds 7457, Van Houten 7500
Ohio: Community 7583, Fleming 7631, Kramer 7704, Murphy 7769, Payne 7798, Schlink 7839
Oklahoma: Goddard 7939
Oregon: Johnson 8027
Pennsylvania: Arcadia 8086, Dolfinger 8172, Fourjay 8209, Independence 8266
Tennessee: Christy 8654, Redbird 8723
Texas: Abell 8749, Cain 8809, Cameron 8812, Franklin 8907, Gulf 8926, Healthcare 8944, Johnson 8974, Meadows 9049, Pollock 9127, Rockwell 9154
Utah: Bamberger 9305, Eccles 9320
Virginia: Camp 9382
West Virginia: Kanawha 9723
Wisconsin: McBeath 9864

Nursing home/convalescent facility

Illinois: Washington 3058
Iowa: R & R 3327
Maryland: Wasserman 3757
Michigan: Knabusch 4362
Nebraska: Vetter 5014
New York: Lindner 6426
North Carolina: Daveler 7351
Pennsylvania: McLean 8340

Nursing school/education

California: Ahmanson 198
Connecticut: Culpeper 1521, Stone 1654
Florida: **Chatlos 1932**
Georgia: Holder 2413
Illinois: Arthur 2601, Washington 3058
Kansas: Scroggins 3389
Louisiana: Baton Rouge 3462, **Live 3495**
Maryland: Johnston 3657
Massachusetts: Greene 3933, Worcester 4209
Missouri: Ballman 4780, Musgrave 4870
New Jersey: Aventis 5120
New York: **Fuld 5999**, Hillman 6186, Kennedy 6314, **Macy 6471**, Orvis 6668, Riley 6809, Rudin 6878, Saligman 6895
North Carolina: Davis 7354, Reynolds 7457, Roberts 7465
Ohio: Wellman 7901
Oregon: Collins 8009, Johnson 8027
Pennsylvania: Independence 8266
Texas: Abell 8749, CH 8823, Healthcare 8944, Johnson 8974, Koehler 9001, San Antonio 9166, Triad 9239
Virginia: Moore 9478
Washington: Coulter 9573
Wisconsin: Shapiro 9925

Nutrition

California: Hughes 690, Irvine 699, Pacific 970, PacifiCare 971, **Saban 1079**, Sierra 1151, Thornton 1235
Colorado: Anschutz 1334, El Pomar 1374
Delaware: Delaware 1706

Minnesota: Adams 4495, Ankeny 4505, Athwin 4508, Bush 4524, Cleveland 4541, Cloverfields 4542, Dasburg 4545, Deluxe 4549, Driscoll 4555, Duluth 4556, General 4570, Griggs 4577, Hubbard 4590, Jerome 4595, Marbrook 4612, McVay 4620, **O'Shaughnessy 4639**, Opperman 4641, Peterson 4652, Red Wing 4663, Sewell 4678, Southways 4688, TCF 4699, Thorpe 4701, **Toro 4702**, **Wood 4731**
Mississippi: Community 4737
Missouri: American 4773, Andrews 4774, Bernoudy 4783, **Bunge 4792**, Curry 4802, Duesenberg 4805, Edison 4808, Gateway 4817, Green 4822, H & R 4823, Hall 4824, Kemper 4847, Kemper 4848, **Pulitzer 4889**, Reynolds 4892, Sosland 4908, Stern 4909, Wornall 4929
Montana: **Edwards 4936**
Nebraska: James 4980, Rogers 4999, Simon 5002, Weitz 5016, Wiebe 5017, Woods 5018
Nevada: **Buck 5025**, Fairweather 5032, Hawkins 5036, Houssels 5038, Wiegand 5077
New Hampshire: Fuller 5090, Trust 5103
New Jersey: Brody 5144, Bulova 5147, Cantor 5152, Cowles 5170, D & K 5174, Dodge 5181, Drapkin 5185, **Hess 5231**, Holzer 5238, Hyde 5247, **Jaqua 5256**, Jockey 5260, **Johnson 5263**, Kerr 5278, Kirby 5279, Levitt 5305, Mack 5312, McGraw 5323, Point 5353, **Puffin 5362**, Riskin 5369, Roth 5377, Sagner 5381, Shen 5398, Shepherd 5399, Silver 5404, Zobel 5464
New Mexico: Maddox 5487, McCune 5488, Santa Fe 5496, Thornburg 5501
New York: Abeles 5509, Acorn 5515, Altus 5547, **American 5553**, Arnhold 5568, Babbitt 5586, Bachmann 5587, Baier 5590, Baird 5592, Balm 5596, **Barth 5603**, **C.O.U.Q. 5695**, Calicchio 5698, Campbell 5700, Carnahan 5706, Cary 5712, Chanin 5730, Chisholm 5752, Clark 5761, Corzine 5797, Cullman 5811, **Dana 5826**, Davenport 5833, Debs 5844, **Delmas 5850**, Diamond 5857, **Dreyfus 5888**, **Duke 5892**, Erpf 5937, Fatta 5947, **Ford 5970**, Friedberg 5985, Gellert 6012, Gerry 6017, **Gilbert 6028**, Gilman 6032, Goldman 6053, Goldring 6057, Goldsmith 6060, Goodman 6072, Gould 6082, Green 6096, Greene 6100, Harkness 6145, Harriman 6147, Harris 6148, **Hauser 6155**, **Hearst 6161**, **Hearst 6162**, **Heineman 6165**, Hillman 6186, **Jaffe 6250**, Joelson 6265, Johnson 6270, Kearns 6304, **Kopf 6348**, Kravis 6353, Krimendahl 6359, L and L 6366, Lang 6374, Lastfogel 6380, Lauder 6382, Lemberg 6401, Leonhardt 6403, Levy 6413, Lindmor 6425, Lindner 6426, Link 6429, Loeb 6439, Loewe 6441, Lostand 6448, **Lucky 6456**, Marks 6489, Mars 6494, MAT 6503, Megrue 6524, **Mellon 6525**, **Memton 6529**, Miller 6550, Morse 6582, Moses 6587, Neidich 6606, Neuberger 6611, New York 6619, New York 6620, O'Connor 6645, O'Toole 6654, Palm 6681, Partridge 6695, Pels 6706, Perkin 6717, **Pforzheimer 6721**, Phaedrus 6722, Pines 6727, Plant 6731, Pumpkin 6754, Reed 6782, Resnick 6787, Richardson 6796, Richenthal 6798, Riggio 6804, Rodgers 6828, Rose 6836, Rose 6837, Rose 6838, Rose 6839, **Rosen 6843**, Rosenkranz 6851, Rosenstiel 6852, Ross 6862, Samuels 6901, Schafer 6910, Scherman 6918, Schlobach 6924, Schneider 6929, Sharp 6961, Sharp 6962, Sheldon 6964, **Shubert 6970**, Siegel 6976, Snow 7011, Sosnoff 7025, Speyer 7027, Sprague 7035, Stein 7057, Steinberg 7061, Stern 7073, Straus 7084, Sussman 7104, **Tanaka 7120**, **Tiffany 7138**, Tisch 7146, Tisch 7148, **Trust 7168**, Tuch 7170, **U.S. 7180**, Van Pelt 7192, Violett 7200, Wallach 7210, Weiler 7226, Weinman 7232, Wendt 7243, Western 7248, Woodheath 7274, Woodland 7275, Zalaznick 7288, Zemsky 7294, **Zilkha 7300**
North Carolina: Adams 7305, Cemala 7337, Cumberland 7349, Goodnight 7377, Graham 7382, Halton 7386, North Carolina 7438, Symmes 7492, Triangle 7496, Woodson 7509
North Dakota: Leach 7516, Stern 7521

Ohio: Akron 7526, Andrews 7530, Bee 7542, Callahan 7564, Charities 7569, Cleveland 7576, Codrington 7578, Columbus 7580, **Convergys 7587**, DBJ 7605, Emery 7619, Fifth 7626, Firman 7628, IHS 7683, Ingalls 7684, Kaplan 7696, **Kettering 7698**, Kettering 7699, Knudsen 7702, Kulas 7706, Lippitt 7718, McMaster 7744, Middletown 7749, Mixon 7757, Morgan 7760, Murphy 7769, Muskingum 7770, Nordson 7781, Reinberger 7815, Rieveschl 7820, Schiff 7838, Schott 7843, Semple 7851, Stark 7867, Stillson 7869, Watson 7896, Wohlgemuth 7913, Youngstown 7920
Oklahoma: Helmerich 7942, Inasmuch 7944, Kerr 7949, Kirkpatrick 7952, McMahon 7959, Silas 7978, Zink 7994
Oregon: Autzen 7997, Bair 7998, Carpenter 8003, Haugland 8018, Jackson 8024, Kelley 8030, Mentor 8039, Meyer 8042
Pennsylvania: **Annenberg 8084**, Baker 8092, **Beneficia 8100**, Bozzone 8114, Brossman 8120, Byers' 8127, **Carpenter 8131**, Cavitolo 8134, Claneil 8144, Dietrich 8170, Dolfinger 8172, Ferree 8199, Fisher 8205, **Forney 8207**, Giant 8214, Heinz 8244, Hillman 8251, Hulme 8260, Huston 8263, Independence 8266, Kaiserman 8277, Kardon 8279, Kline 8293, Laurel 8301, Little 8313, Mandell 8322, Massey 8328, McCormick 8329, McCune 8332, McKinney 8339, McLean 8340, Meakem 8341, Neubauer 8363, Penn 8371, Peterson 8376, **Pew 8377**, PSC 8398, Rees 8401, Rockwell 8408, Rosenfeld 8413, Rubin 8415, S & T 8417, Safeguard 8418, Smith 8445, Strawbridge 8467, Tippins 8477, Vanguard 8490, von Hess 8493, Wyomissing 8509
Rhode Island: Charlesmead 8525, Daniels 8530, Rhode Island 8551, Usen 8560
South Carolina: Liberty 8597
Tennessee: Atticus 8639, Benwood 8644, **Bridgestone 8646**, Community 8660, Frist 8679, Hamico 8684, Johnson 8697, Massey 8709, Ragsdale 8722
Texas: Anderson 8760, Bass 8775, Brown 8798, **Butt 8803**, Cain 8809, Carter 8816, Carter 8817, **Cooper 8846**, Duda 8871, Fikes 8899, Fish 8902, Fleming 8904, Garvey 8914, Hanley 8940, Hoblitzelle 8955, Holthouse 8959, Hudson 8962, Humphreys 8965, Johnson 8973, Kahn 8980, Kempner 8987, Kilroy 8991, Kimberly 8992, Kodosky 9000, Littauer 9014, Marathon 9028, Mithoff 9066, Moody 9070, Mosbacher 9077, O'Connor 9094, Once 9101, Owen 9106, Paulos 9112, Perot 9119, Reynolds 9145, Richardson 9147, Rockwell 9154, Rogers 9156, San Antonio 9166, Scott 9174, Scurlock 9175, **Shell 9181**, Smith 9198, Sterling 9212, Temple 9228, Vanberg 9248, Vaughan 9249, Vergara 9253, Waggoner 9256, Walsh 9261, Wortham 9292, Wright 9294
Utah: Caine 9310, Eccles 9319, Eccles 9320, Quinney 9338, Tanner 9347, **Wishnick 9353**
Virgin Islands: Bartner 9362
Virginia: Arlington 9371, **Bansal 9372**, Cartledge 9388, Columbus 9399, Connors 9403, Constitution 9404, Dalis 9406, Delmar 9410, Folger 9418, Funger 9426, Kanter 9445, Kellar 9449, **Malek 9465**, McNichols 9472, **Norfolk 9485**, Pauley 9494, Reynolds 9503, Wilkinson 9540
Washington: Archibald 9553, Blue 9559, Community 9571, Foster 9588, Kaleidoscope 9616, **Kongsgaard 9620**, Kreielsheimer 9621, Martin 9634, McCaw 9636, McEachern 9638, Nesholm 9647, Norcliffe 9650, O'Donnell 9652, Sarkowsky 9676, Sherwood 9683, Tacoma 9693, Wright 9708
West Virginia: Kanawha 9723, McQuain 9727, Tucker 9736
Wisconsin: Baird 9750, Baker 9751, Banta 9752, Bolz 9762, Briggs 9765, Brookbank 9766, Bryce 9769, Community 9779, Delavan 9790, Johnson 9823, Joy 9828, Kikkoman 9836, Kohler 9840, Lubar 9851, Madison 9854, Mead 9867, Milwaukee 9876, Munson 9880, Northwestern 9884, Pangburn 9892, Peterson 9896, Pick 9899, Sensient 9922, Smallwood 9928, Uihlein 9953, Weill 9962, WPS 9970

Performing arts (multimedia)

Illinois: Alphawood 2589
Ohio: Thendara 7878

Performing arts centers

Alaska: Atwood 81
California: American 215, Carsey 361, Field 503, First 511, Gallo 547, Irvine 698, Jackson 706, Moley 908, Reinhold 1039, Rising 1055, Samueli 1086, Segerstrom 1123, Sodaro 1174
Colorado: Hughes 1393
Connecticut: Chase 1508, Foley 1544
District of Columbia: Gudelsky 1805, Harman 1807, HRH 1811, Johnson 1812, Post 1842
Florida: Kohl 2099, Rales 2184, Rollnick 2203, Saunders 2219, Simon 2235, Sykes 2261, Wolfson 2305
Georgia: Bunzl 2334
Illinois: Bere 2616, Deering 2700, Galvin 2747, Madigan 2869, Millard 2897
Iowa: Fisher 3285
Kansas: Capitol 3350
Kentucky: Reed 3447, Young 3454
Maryland: Baker 3567, Dekelboum 3613, Freeman 3633, Greenberg 3639
Massachusetts: Fireman 3909, Hoffman 3955
Michigan: DeVos 4276, Frey 4316, **Heritage 4340**, Knabusch 4363
Minnesota: Carlson 4532, Chadwick-Loher 4535, Mithun 4626
Nebraska: Hitchcock 4975
New Jersey: Bildner 5133, Geier 5204, Levin 5304, Lipper 5308, Makk 5315, Marianthi 5318, Sagner 5381, Thomas 5427
New Mexico: Bancroft 5467, Messengers 5489
New York: A.E. 5506, Armstrong 5567, Belfer 5615, Black 5636, Centennial 5722, Cordelia 5790, Coulson 5799, Diamond 5857, Diker 5862, Ehrenkranz 5913, Ferrari 5953, Furman 6002, Gellert 6012, Gural 6120, Haas 6126, Hajim 6134, Halis 6136, Harrison 6149, Icahn 6223, Katz 6295, Katzenberger 6298, Kearns 6304, Lauder 6382, Levy 6412, Lipp 6432, Maheras 6475, Morse 6584, Newman 6625, Resnick 6787, **Rubin 6874**, Smith 7007, Snyder 7013, Sternberg 7075, Tarnopol 7123, Weinman 7232
North Carolina: Adams 7305
Ohio: Lincoln 7715, Miller 7753, Peterson 7802, Sage 7829, Wodecroft 7912
Oklahoma: Silas 7978
Pennsylvania: Cassett 8133, Cavitolo 8134, Farber 8195, Field 8200, Kardon 8279, Miller 8354, Peterson 8376, Stewart 8460
Rhode Island: McCarthy 8548
South Carolina: South 8615
Texas: Bass 8777, Carlson 8815, Haggar 8931, Huffington 8963, Mankoff 9027, Sharp 9180
Virginia: Funger 9426
Washington: UNOVA 9697
West Virginia: McDonough 9726
Wisconsin: McQueen 9866, Oshkosh 9887, Weill 9962

Performing arts, ballet

Alabama: Saks 61
California: Brandenburg 316, Corrigan 418, Gill 576, Gillespie 577, Irvine 698, Marcus 852, Martin 860, Peterson 995, Ross 1069, Samueli 1086, Swanson 1217, Webster 1286, Weiss 1290
Colorado: M.D.C. 1413, **Mizel 1427**, Monfort 1428
Connecticut: Lee 1582, Sites 1650
District of Columbia: Harman 1807
Florida: Meyer 2137, Rollnick 2203, Wolfson 2305
Georgia: Holder 2413, Spray 2495
Illinois: Kipper 2840, McIntosh 2883, **Nureyev 2919**
Maryland: Abell 3560
Massachusetts: Casty 3839, Fireman 3910, Wilson 4205
Michigan: Frey 4316
Minnesota: Thorpe 4701
Nevada: **Buck 5025**, Fertitta 5033, Houssels 5038

New Jersey: Lear 5300, Levitt 5305, Point 5353, Sagner 5381
New York: Amicus 5557, Buttenwieser 5693, **C.O.U.Q. 5695**, **Conway 5787**, Cordelia 5790, Friedberg 5985, Gibson 6025, Gollust 6069, Granoff 6089, **Hughes 6208**, Kearns 6304, Leigh 6400, Leventhal 6406, Lipp 6432, Marcus 6486, McGraw 6520, Pittman 6730, Pumpkin 6754, Richardson 6796, Rosenblum 6850, Rosh 6858, Sackler 6892, Stanton 7043, Trott 7165, Vogelstein 7201
Ohio: Bee 7542, Peninsula 7799, Stranahan 7872, Wildermuth 7906
Oregon: Bauman 7999
Pennsylvania: Ryan 8416
Tennessee: Schadt 8725
Texas: Butler 8802, Carlson 8815, Kodosky 9000
Utah: Bastian 9307, Lawson 9332
Washington: **PAH 9657**
Wisconsin: Pangburn 9892

Performing arts, choreography

Illinois: **Nureyev 2919**

Performing arts, circus arts

New York: Antz 5560, Lee 6391

Performing arts, dance

Alabama: Community 25, Lowder 42
California: Copley 416, Fleishhacker 518, Gillespie 577, Hewlett 671, Irvine 698, Osher 961, San Diego 1087, San Francisco 1088, Weiss 1290, Zellerbach 1326
Colorado: Gates 1380
Connecticut: Bridgeport 1504
District of Columbia: Cafritz 1780, Kaye 1815
Florida: Bank 1890, Weaver 2289
Illinois: Abelson 2581, Alphawood 2589, BCS 2612, **Burlington 2644**, Cheney 2658, Community 2677, Kaplan 2823, **Nureyev 2919**, Sara 2982
Maryland: Kay 3660
Massachusetts: Poss 4087, Shapiro 4136
Michigan: Frey 4316
Minnesota: Jerome 4595, Thorpe 4701
Missouri: H & R 4823, Kauffman 4844
Nevada: Fertitta 5033
New Jersey: Cowles 5170, Dodge 5181, **Puffin 5362**
New Mexico: Delle 5474, McCune 5488
New York: Allison 5537, Clark 5761, Cordelia 5790, Diker 5862, **EHA 5912**, Elmaleh 5924, **Ford 5970**, Gibbs 6024, Gilman 6032, Goldsmith 6060, **Haje 6133**, Harkness 6145, Heckscher 6164, **Heineman 6165**, Lipp 6432, Maheras 6475, **Mertz 6538**, Millard 6548, Morse 6582, Moses 6587, Parshelsky 6693, Robbins 6817, Samuels 6901, **Shubert 6970**, **Trust 7168**, **U.S. 7180**, Ungar 7183, Wellin 7240, Western 7248
North Carolina: Biddle 7317, Cumberland 7349, Halton 7386, Triangle 7496
North Dakota: Stern 7521
Ohio: Coshocton 7593, Gund 7655, Murphy 7769
Pennsylvania: Dolfinger 8172, Little 8313, **Pew 8377**, Philadelphia 8378, Rees 8401, Rockwell 8408
South Dakota: Sioux Falls 8630
Tennessee: Community 8660
Texas: Cain 8809, Feinberg 8898, Kempner 8987, San Antonio 9166, Sarofim 9169, **Shell 9181**
Utah: Eccles 9320
Virginia: McGue 9470
Washington: Seattle 9680
West Virginia: Kanawha 9723
Wisconsin: Coleman 9775, Milwaukee 9876

Performing arts, education

California: Lehrer 800
Delaware: Esperance 1710
Illinois: Dunard 2712
Michigan: Frey 4316

New Jersey: Doherty 5182
New York: Chadwick 5726, **Hearst 6161**, **Hearst 6162**, Heckscher 6164, Meyer 6546, Novogratz 6642, Olive 6662, Phaedrus 6722, Rodgers 6828, Steinberg 7060
Ohio: Nordson 7781
Pennsylvania: Field 8200
West Virginia: Clay 9715

Performing arts, music

Alabama: Moody 54
Alaska: Carr 82
Arizona: Morris 124
California: **Bull 331**, Burnett 336, Cantus 355, **Capital 357**, Cassin 365, Chapman 374, **ChevronTexaco 380**, Colburn 394, Community 406, Copley 416, David 443, Femino 501, Fitzgerald 514, Fleishhacker 518, Fresno 537, Getty 569, Gonda 601, Hale 639, Heller 666, Hewlett 671, Isen 701, Jewett 718, Osher 961, San Diego 1087, **Seaver 1118**, Shklar 1146, Simms 1155, Smith 1163, Sonora 1178, Thornton 1235, Wood 1318, Zellerbach 1326
Colorado: Bernstein 1343, Boettcher 1344, El Pomar 1374, Gates 1380, Schermer 1449, **Staley 1457**, Summit 1463
Connecticut: **Bingham 1493**, Bridgeport 1504, Daniell 1523, **Kossak 1576**, Moore 1604
Delaware: Buckner 1695, Crystal 1702, Esperance 1710
District of Columbia: Beech 1771, Bernstein 1775, Cafritz 1780, Dimick 1789, Kaye 1815, Sprenger 1848
Florida: Appleby 1879, Colen 1938, Katcher 2080, Magill 2124, Winston 2302
Georgia: Arnold 2319, Exposition 2380, Flowers 2384, Vogel 2504
Hawaii: Frear 2543
Illinois: Abelson 2581, Alphawood 2589, BCS 2612, Cheney 2658, Dunard 2712, Getz 2753, Gray 2771, Kaplan 2823, Kemper 2831, Krehbiel 2845, Lederer 2852, Negaunee 2909, Rotonda 2972, Sara 2982, Seid 2996, **Shifting 3006**, Walk 3053
Indiana: Clowes 3120, Griffith 3158
Iowa: Fisher 3285, Siouxland 3332
Maryland: **Adams 3562**, Columbia 3595, Hecht 3645, Hittman 3651, Meyerhoff 3690, Rothschild 3723
Massachusetts: Babson 3787, Bressler 3815, Dusky 3885, Filene 3907, High 3950, Hoffman 3955, Kingsbury 3982, Leaves 3999, Lost 4012, Manitou 4018, Overly 4064, Schaffer 4129, Shapiro 4136
Michigan: Burdick 4241, Community 4256, Dalton 4266, Dow 4288, Frey 4316, Harding 4337, Shelden 4434, Westerman 4478, Wolverine 4488
Minnesota: Adams 4495, Bush 4524, Duluth 4556, Jerome 4595, **O'Shaughnessy 4639**
Missouri: Buder 4791, Kauffman 4844, Sosland 4908, Stern 4909
Nevada: **Buck 5025**, Fairweather 5032, Wiegand 5077
New Jersey: Bunbury 5148, Cowles 5170, Dodge 5181, Green 5215, Holzer 5238, **Huntsman 5246**, Makk 5315, OceanFirst 5341, **Puffin 5362**, Smith 5407, Sunfield 5418
New Mexico: Cudd 5472, McCune 5488, Santa Fe 5496, Taos 5498
New York: A.E. 5506, Armstrong 5567, Arrison 5570, Baird 5591, Barrington 5602, Bayne 5607, Botwinick 5653, Burns 5689, Buttenwieser 5693, Carvel 5710, Cary 5712, **Chazen 5739**, Chernow 5744, Clark 5761, **Copland 5789**, Elebash 5919, **Ford 5970**, Gellert 6012, Gerry 6016, Goldsmith 6060, **Grant 6090**, Greene 6099, **Hauser 6155**, **Heineman 6165**, Hillman 6186, Kellen 6308, Krimendahl 6359, Liberman 6419, Lostand 6448, Marcus 6486, **Mercer 6532**, Mercy 6534, **Merlin 6536**, Mesdag 6539, Miller 6550, Morse 6582, Moses 6587, **Newhouse 6623**, **Noble 6633**, O'Malley 6648, Olive 6662, Orvis 6668, Perkin 6717, Phaedrus 6722, Plant 6731, Pope 6740, Rose 6834, Samuels 6901, Scherman 6918, Sharp 6962, Snyder 7013, **Spiegel 7030**, Stiefel

7079, **Trust 7168**, Tuch 7170, Tully 7173, **U.S. 7180**, Vance 7193, Western 7248, Wiener 7257
North Carolina: Bergen 7316, Biddle 7317, Halton 7386, Perkins 7445, Triangle 7496
Ohio: Bee 7542, Callahan 7564, Gund 7655, Gund 7656, Kulas 7706, Mixon 7757, Morley 7763, Muskingum 7770, Nippert 7777, Payne 7798, Rieveschl 7820, Robbins 7823, Sage 7829, Van Wert 7891, Wohlgemuth 7913, Wolf 7914, Youngstown 7920
Pennsylvania: Arcadia 8086, Bradley 8115, Bristol 8118, Campbell 8128, Cassett 8133, Dietrich 8170, Dolfinger 8172, Field 8200, Giop 8216, Hooper 8256, Innisfree 8267, Little 8313, McCormick 8329, Miller 8352, **Pew 8377**, **Presser 8395**, Roberts 8407, Rockwell 8408, Stabler 8455, Steinman 8458, Wyomissing 8509
Rhode Island: Daniels 8530
South Carolina: Central 8577, Montgomery 8600
South Dakota: Sioux Falls 8630
Texas: Cain 8809, Constantin 8843, Fikes 8899, Johnson 8973, **Shell 9181**, **Starling 9210**, Stemmons 9211
Utah: **Huntsman 9329**
Virginia: Delmar 9410, Fralin 9420, Portsmouth 9498
Washington: Community 9571, **Kongsgaard 9620**, Norcliffe 9650, Peach 9659, Seattle 9680
West Virginia: Clay 9715
Wisconsin: Argosy 9747, Pick 9899, Racine 9906, Wilson 9965

Performing arts, music (choral)

California: Webster 1286
Illinois: Hartmarx 2794
Iowa: Krause 3302
Michigan: Frey 4316
New York: **Popplestone 6741**
Ohio: Stranahan 7872

Performing arts, music ensembles/groups

Illinois: Walk 3053
Massachusetts: Lindsay 4009
Michigan: Frey 4316

Performing arts, opera

Alabama: Compass 28
Alaska: Carr 82
California: Colburn 395, Corrigan 418, Davies 446, **Field 504**, Field 505, Fishback 513, **Good 603**, Green 614, Hoag 679, Irvine 698, Leichtman 802, MacNaughton 844, Oshman 963, Panic 976, Pelosi 988, Preuss 1015, Samueli 1086, Segerstrom 1123, Senyei 1127, Stern 1194, Thornton 1235, Webster 1286, Weiss 1290
Colorado: **Avenir 1339**, Hughes 1393
Connecticut: Chase 1508, Grossman 1560
Delaware: Kingsley 1724
District of Columbia: Harman 1807
Florida: **Isenberg 2070**, Leiser 2108, Marden 2127, Meyer 2137, Rollnick 2203, Wolfson 2305
Georgia: Poe 2465
Hawaii: Strong 2555
Illinois: Baskes 2607, Bielfeldt 2620, Farrell 2725, Gidwitz 2755, Katten 2826, Malott 2872, Roberts 2968, Thoma 3035
Iowa: Fisher 3285
Kentucky: Kindred 3434
Maryland: Greenberg 3639, Pohanka 3707, Quinn 3713, Wasserman 3758
Massachusetts: Manitou 4018, Perry 4079, Silverman 4146
Michigan: Frey 4316, HFF 4342
Minnesota: Chadwick-Loher 4535, Drew 4554, Shiebler 4680
Missouri: Centene 4796, Lichtenstein 4855, Lopata 4859
Nebraska: Holland 4977, Hubbard 4978, Simon 5002
Nevada: **Buck 5025**

New Jersey: Cantor 5152, Levitt 5305, Makk 5315, Thomas 5427
New Mexico: **Daniels 5473**
New York: Ades 5516, Allwin 5538, **Baker 5593**, Belfer 5615, Butler 5691, Buttenwieser 5693, Chernow 5744, Chernow 5745, CJM 5756, Cohen 5770, Corey 5791, Cornell 5792, Furman 6003, Gibbs 6024, **Grant 6090**, Harrison 6149, Hermione 6175, **Hughes 6208**, Kennedy 6314, Loeb 6439, McGraw 6520, Mesdag 6539, Miller 6550, Morris 6580, Orvis 6668, **Popplestone 6741**, Richardson 6796, Rotenstreich 6865, Sackler 6892, Samuels 6901, Schwebel 6948, Sculco 6949, Seevers 6953, Snowdon 7012, Sosnoff 7025, Spiegel 7029, **Spiegel 7030**, Stern 7073, Tully 7173, Vilcek 7199, Vogelstein 7201, Weinman 7232
North Carolina: Adams 7305, Smith 7478
Ohio: Kalberer 7695, Miniger 7756, Nord 7780, Peninsula 7799, Pulley 7811, Stranahan 7872, Toulmin 7885
Oregon: Haugland 8018
Pennsylvania: Neubauer 8363
Texas: Clayton 8830, Kodosky 9000, Mankoff 9027, McNair 9047, Owen 9106, Sarofim 9169, Von Seggern 9254
Utah: Lawson 9331
Virginia: **DeLaski 9409**, Kellar 9449, Smith 9518, Taubman 9524
Washington: Wright 9708
Wisconsin: Demmer 9791, Kettering 9835, Morse 9879, Pangburn 9892

Performing arts, orchestra (symphony)

Alabama: Compass 28, Lowder 42, Moody 54, Saks 61, Stephens 65
Arizona: Robson 135
California: Binder 291, Bloomfield 295, Cantus 355, Colburn 394, Connell 412, Corrigan 418, Cortopassi 419, Davies 446, Edgerton 477, **Field 504**, Fluor 523, Gallo 548, Garaventa 553, Geschke 568, Irvine 698, Janeway 712, JL 720, Laurel 792, Lavine 793, Radin 1025, Robertson 1059, Segerstrom 1123, Springcreek 1185, Thornton 1235, Weiss 1290, Zimmer 1328
Colorado: Kern 1402, Newman 1432
Connecticut: Bluebell 1496, Chase 1508, Georgescu 1554, United 1668
District of Columbia: Post 1842
Florida: Edgemer 1989, Stein 2249, SunTrust 2259, Victory 2280, Weiller 2291
Georgia: Adams 2309, Covenant 2366, Cox 2368, Graves 2403, Jones 2424
Hawaii: Anthony 2531
Illinois: Borwell 2627, Charleston 2657, Farrell 2725, Genius 2751, Goldschmidt 2764, Hartmarx 2794, Hobbs 2802, JYN 2821, Kaplan 2824, Lea 2850, Lewis 2857, Melrene 2892, Pasquinelli 2933, Wilemal 3070, Wilson 3075
Indiana: Carmichael 3113, Goldstine 3156, Leighton 3191, Simon 3236, Tobias 3244
Iowa: Gilchrist 3287
Kansas: Sprint 3395
Kentucky: Young 3454
Louisiana: Brunswick 3466
Maine: King 3545
Maryland: Eliasberg 3620, Legg 3672, Meyerhoff 3691, Waidner 3754, Wasserman 3758
Massachusetts: Ansin 3779, BOSE 3810, Fessenden 3903, Fireman 3910, Fraser 3917, Goldberg 3927, Heide 3945, Hoffman 3955, Kingsbury 3982, Lost 4012, Morse 4044, Perry 4079, Rabb 4091, Saltonstall 4126, Sternberg 4161
Michigan: Frey 4316, Harding 4337, HFF 4342, Kogan 4365, Manoogian 4382, Weatherwax 4474, Wolters 4487
Minnesota: Drew 4554, Grossman 4578, Labovitz 4601, Opperman 4641, Sit 4683, Thorpe 4701
Missouri: Barrows 4781, Bodine 4784, Buder 4791, Carter 4794, Centene 4796, Emerson 4809, Gershman 4818, Helzberg 4829, Jordan 4840, Nichols 4873, Reding 4890, Taylor 4916
Nebraska: Gardner 4965, TierOne 5010

Nevada: **Buck 5025**, Hawkins 5036, Houssels 5038
New Jersey: Dealessandro 5178, Marianthi 5318, McCutchen 5322, Upton 5436
New York: Baird 5592, Bayne 5607, Berkowitz 5622, Buchmann 5681, Buttenwieser 5693, **Conway 5787**, **Grant 6090**, Haas 6127, JAM 6251, **Johnson 6273**, Joy 6276, Kearns 6304, Marcus 6486, Martin 6496, Meyer 6546, Novogratz 6642, **Ohga 6658**, Orvis 6668, Pumpkin 6754, Pyewacket 6756, Riordan 6810, Rose 6838, Rosenkranz 6851, Roxe 6867, Schott 6934, Smith 7007, Snyder 7013, Spiegel 7029, **Volpert 7202**, Weinman 7232, White 7251
North Carolina: Haley 7385, Livingstone 7422, Woodward 7510
Ohio: Buenger 7560, Dorn 7612, Frost 7642, Jobst 7691, Jubilee 7694, Kalberer 7695, LKC 7720, M/B 7728, Mellen 7747, Miniger 7756, Mixon 7757, Peterson 7802, Pulley 7811, Siegal 7856, Sky 7859, Stranahan 7872, **Warrington 7895**, Wodecroft 7912
Oklahoma: Crawley 7934, Gussman 7941
Pennsylvania: CMS 8147, Hodge 8254, Hoverter 8258, Neubauer 8363, Ryan 8416, Scheller 8426, Simmons 8441, Smith 8445
Rhode Island: Charter 8526, Usen 8560
South Carolina: Collins 8582, Daniel 8585, South 8615
Tennessee: Basler 8641, Haslam 8687, Unaka 8739
Texas: Bickel 8790, Butler 8802, Halsell 8936, Hobby 8954, Keith 8982, Kodosky 9000, MacDonald 9025, Nation 9087, Rapoport 9141, Roach 9150, Stoffel 9214, Vaughn 9251, Von Seggern 9254, Wolff 9288
Utah: Bastian 9306, Bastian 9307, Gardner 9323, Lawson 9332, Tanner 9347, Zions 9354
Virginia: Grandis 9432, Rosenthal 9508
Washington: Benaroya 9556, Cowles 9574, Green 9598, Kreielsheimer 9621
Wisconsin: Bryce 9769, Demmer 9791, Glover 9805, Hyde 9818, Kettering 9835, Pollybill 9900, Stark 9935

Performing arts, theater

Alabama: Lowder 42
California: Brandenburg 316, Chapman 374, Community 406, Connell 412, Copley 416, Douglas 464, Edgerton 477, Fleishhacker 518, Flintridge 520, Garen 555, Gillespie 577, Grand 611, Hewlett 671, Irvine 698, Kaufman 747, **Marshall 858**, Osher 961, Outrageous 967, Pickford 1005, Quattrone 1024, Rotasa 1070, Sacramento 1080, Samueli 1086, San Diego 1087, Springcreek 1185, **Stangeland 1187**, Stern 1194, **Tennity 1233**, Weiss 1290, Windfall 1309, Witherbee 1312, Wood 1318, Zellerbach 1326
Colorado: El Pomar 1374, Gates 1380, Joy 1399, Summit 1463
Connecticut: Bodenwein 1497, Bossidy 1500, Bridgeport 1504, Chase 1508, **Ettinger 1536**, Foley 1544, Georgescu 1554, Rosenthal 1638, **Seedlings 1645**, Tow 1660, **Xerox 1680**
Delaware: Seevak 1752
District of Columbia: Beech 1771, Cafritz 1780, Loughran 1823, Meyer 1834, **Patterson 1840**, Sprenger 1848
Florida: Bank 1890, Community 1940, Hough 2066, Saunders 2219, Sudakoff 2256
Georgia: Anderson 2317, Blank 2325, Daft 2370, **Gage 2392**, Lee 2432, Marcus 2440, Mix 2448, Patterson 2460, Rich 2472, **Thoresen 2499**
Hawaii: Strong 2555
Illinois: Abelson 2581, **Allen 2587**, Alphawood 2589, **Andrew 2595**, BCS 2612, Bellebyron 2615, **Burlington 2644**, Cheney 2658, Farrell 2725, **Galashiels 2742**, Getz 2753, Gidwitz 2755, **Goodman 2765**, Green 2772, Hitchcock 2801, Kaplan 2823, Kipper 2840, Krueck 2846, Polk 2946, Rubin 2974, Sara 2982, Schield 2985, Seabury 2993, Sirius 3010, Thoma 3035, Walsh 3055
Indiana: Community 3128, Hilbert 3167, Klapper 3183
Kansas: Hutchinson 3368, Morris 3378, Sprint 3395

Kentucky: Brown 3408
Louisiana: **Biedenharn 3463**, Booth 3464, Heymann 3487
Maryland: Abell 3560, Gudelsky 3641, Hecht 3645, Small 3735
Massachusetts: Alvord 3778, Ansin 3779, Babson 3787, Calderwood 3826, Donahue 3881, Hagerty 3938, **Hershey 3949**, High 3950, **Jebediah 3969**, Ladd 3992, Ludcke 4017, Manitou 4018, McCallum 4029, Perry 4079, Shapiro 4136
Michigan: Ann Arbor 4221, Community 4252, Dalton 4266, Dart 4267, **Dogwood 4282**, Dow 4288, Frey 4316, Grand Rapids 4326, Knight 4364
Minnesota: Carlson 4532, Drew 4554, Edelstein 4559, Griggs 4577, Grossman 4578, Jerome 4595, Marbrook 4612, McCarthy 4614, Pacific 4646, Prospect 4659, Rupp 4669, Sewell 4678, Southways 4688, Wells 4721
Missouri: Lopata 4859, Nichols 4873, Orscheln 4877, Pershing 4881, Sosland 4908
Nebraska: Buffett 4949, Gardner 4965
Nevada: Prim 5054, Wiegand 5077
New Jersey: Bildner 5133, Cowles 5170, Dodge 5181, Green 5215, Johnson 5264, Kerr 5278, Laurie 5297, Levitt 5305, OceanFirst 5341, Point 5353, **Puffin 5362**, Schenck 5386, Silver 5404, Sunfield 5418, Tolchin 5428
New Mexico: McCune 5488
New York: Abrons 5512, Amicus 5557, Apfelbaum 5561, Arrison 5570, **AXA 5584**, Babbitt 5586, Baldwin 5595, **Barnett 5601**, Bayne 5607, Buttenwieser 5693, Chasanoff 5735, Clark 5761, Coles 5775, Devlin 5855, Diller 5863, **Dramatists 5883**, Ebb 5903, Emwiga 5930, **Ford 5970**, Furman 6003, Gilliam 6031, Gilman 6032, Goldsmith 6060, Gordon 6076, Granoff 6089, Harrison 6149, **Hayden 6157**, Heckscher 6164, **Heineman 6165**, Hendel 6172, **Homeland 6199**, Janklow 6254, JKW 6262, Joelson 6265, Kadrovach 6282, Kearns 6304, Kimmelman 6322, Krimendahl 6359, Lee 6391, Lieb 6420, Loeb 6439, Loewe 6441, Lortel 6447, **Magowan 6473**, **Mailman 6478**, Marcus 6486, Metropolitan 6543, Meyer 6545, Meyer 6546, Millard 6548, Mindich 6558, Mnuchin 6564, Mosse 6590, Newman 6624, Park 6689, Pels 6707, Pels 6708, **Pforzheimer 6721**, Pittman 6730, Pumpkin 6754, Ranger 6770, Reed 6782, **Reed 6783**, Resnick 6787, Robbins 6817, Samuels 6901, Schaffer 6911, Scherman 6918, Scheuer 6919, **Scheuer 6921**, Schwartz 6945, Sculco 6949, Sharp 6961, Sheldon 6964, SHS 6969, **Shubert 6970**, Silver 6981, Snow 7011, Snowdon 7012, **Solomon 7017**, Sosnoff 7025, Spiegel 7030, Stanton 7043, Stein 7056, Steinberg 7061, Strelsin 7088, Sussman 7104, **Trust 7168**, Tuch 7170, **U.S. 7180**, Unterberg 7186, Vance 7193, Weiler 7226, Weinman 7232, Wendt 7243, Western 7248
North Carolina: Biddle 7317, McLean 7425, Symmes 7492, Triangle 7496
North Dakota: MDU 7517, Stern 7521
Ohio: Gerlach 7648, Heimbinder 7670, Kalberer 7695, LKC 7720, Morgan 7762, Murphy 7769, Outcalt 7792, Payne 7798, Peninsula 7799, **Prulna 7809**, Rosenthal 7826, Stranahan 7873, Watson 7896
Oklahoma: Bernsen 7925
Oregon: Carpenter 8003, Haugland 8018, Poznanski 8052, Wessinger 8067
Pennsylvania: Bozzone 8114, Cassett 8133, Dolfinger 8172, Kaiserman 8277, Laurel 8301, Peterson 8376, **Pew 8377**, Smith 8445, Toll 8478
Rhode Island: Chace 8523, McAdams 8547
South Dakota: Sioux Falls 8630
Tennessee: CLARCOR 8658, Jeniam 8695, Tucker 8735
Texas: Humphreys 8965, Kempner 8987, Littauer 9014, Partnership 9110, Petrello 9121, Proctor 9132, Reaud 9143, San Antonio 9166, **Shell 9181**, Sterling 9212, Vaughn 9251
Utah: Eccles 9320, Lawson 9331, Stern 9344, Zions 9354
Virginia: Cartledge 9388, Delmar 9410, Kanter 9445, McGue 9470, Weissberg 9536

Washington: Community 9571, Glazer 9596, **Kongsgaard 9620**, Kreielsheimer 9621, **Laird 9623**, Norcliffe 9650, Tacoma 9693
Wisconsin: Brotz 9767, Charter 9772, Community 9779, Frautschi 9804, Kettering 9835, Manpower 9858, Martin 9862, Mead 9867, Morse 9879, Pangburn 9892, Parr 9893, Soref 9930, Stark 9935, Weill 9962, Wilson 9965

Performing arts, theater (musical)

California: Dougherty 463
District of Columbia: Harman 1807
Michigan: Frey 4316
New York: Snowdon 7012
Pennsylvania: Alter 8078

Performing arts, theater (playwriting)

Louisiana: Heymann 3487
New York: Butler 5691, Rose 6838

Pharmacy/prescriptions

California: Long 825
Colorado: El Pomar 1374
Hawaii: HMSA 2547, Zimmerman 2561
Kentucky: **Omnicare 3444**
Minnesota: Alworth 4499
North Carolina: Fox 7371, Pharmacy 7446
Pennsylvania: Beaver 8098, Blue 8112, West 8500

Philanthropy/voluntarism

Alabama: Community 25
California: Adams 194, Avery-Tsui 245, Cook 415, **Draper 466**, Flora 521, **Floyd 522, Four 532**, Gerbode 564, Gershman 566, Hamilton-White 642, Hewlett 671, Irvine 698, JL 720, Mann 849, **Mohn 907, Packard 972**, Ramsay 1030, Spiegel 1182, Springcreek 1185, Stewart 1198, Weyrich 1298
Colorado: Anschutz 1334, **Gill 1382, Janus 1396**, Precourt 1441, Rose 1445, Sturm 1462
Connecticut: Cohen 1512, Hartwell 1565, Pequot 1625, Tauck 1657
Delaware: Singer 1753
District of Columbia: **Coleman 1784**, Washington 1860
Florida: Community 1943, **Coulter 1955**, Gainesville 2015, Huizenga 2068, Krauss, 2101
Georgia: North 2458
Illinois: **Carylon 2652**, Cooney 2682, Crane 2687, **Excelsior! 2722**, Logan 2860, Mesirow 2894, **Pritzker 2951**, Steans 3021, Ward 3056
Indiana: Central 3116, Community 3124, Crown Point 3135, Legacy 3189
Iowa: Community 3277
Louisiana: New Orleans 3503
Maryland: Campbell 3582
Massachusetts: Adams 3771, Corcoran 3860, Gross 3936, Jackson 3966, Landry 3995, Levine 4004, Sharf 4137
Michigan: **Fetzer 4297**, Frey 4316, Granger 4329, Kogan 4365
Minnesota: Andreas 4503, Cleveland 4541
Missouri: Saint Louis 4896
Montana: Chutney 4934
New Hampshire: Byrne 5081
New Jersey: **Aspen 5118, Aspen 5118**, Garcia 5203, JHJ 5259, Kean 5274, Schwartz 5393
New York: AHBA 5528, BCHB 5608, Bingham 5631, **CLRC 5765**, Cole 5774, Coulson 5799, DBID 5838, DeGeorge 5848, **Donner 5873**, EMLE 5929, Emwiga 5930, **Falconwood 5943**, Fife 5955, FIMF 5956, **Ford 5970**, Haseltine 6152, Helmsley 6170, Hultquist 6211, Katz 6296, Kiernan 6321, Kimmelman 6322, Kravis 6355, **Kreindler 6356**, Leuschen 6405, PBHP 6698, **Pepsi 6713**, QIBQ 6757, Rogers 6829, Shoreland 6968, Summit 7100, VHIV 7197, Zehner 7293
North Carolina: Duke 7360, Stonecutter 7486
Ohio: Columbus 7580, Olive 7787

Oklahoma: Zink 7994
Rhode Island: Chace 8523
South Carolina: Barnet 8568
South Dakota: Via-Bradley 8633
Tennessee: Community 8661, HCA 8690, Jeniam 8695
Texas: Aragona 8763, Collins 8837, Fikes 8899, McCombs 9037, Meyer 9057, Pema 9114, Sanders 9167, **Search 9176**
Virginia: Constitution 9404
Washington: Sequoia 9681
Wisconsin: Keller 9831, **Rath 9907**, Walter 9959

Philanthropy/voluntarism, administration/regulation

California: Irvine 698

Philanthropy/voluntarism, association

California: Irvine 698, Los Altos 828
Florida: Bush 1922
New York: **Surdna 7103**

Philanthropy/voluntarism, fund raising/fund distribution

California: Peninsula 989

Philanthropy/voluntarism, information services

California: Irvine 698

Philanthropy/voluntarism, management/technical aid

New Jersey: **Aspen 5118**
New York: Dyson 5898
Pennsylvania: York 8511
Tennessee: Frist 8679
Texas: Fikes 8899

Philanthropy/voluntarism, research

Florida: Wells 2294
Indiana: Lilly 3194

Philanthropy/voluntarism, single organization support

California: Peninsula 989

Philosophy/ethics

Illinois: Sheba 3005
Michigan: **Earhart 4291**
Minnesota: Graco 4573
New Jersey: **Merck 5326**

Physical therapy

California: Magistro 847, Marcled 851
Georgia: Woodruff 2522
Maryland: Wasserman 3758
Michigan: Southwest 4442
Minnesota: **Patterson 4647**
New York: SPIA 7028
Ohio: Stillson 7869
Rhode Island: **Bafflin 8519**
Wyoming: **Schultz 9990**

Physical/earth sciences

California: **American 217, Beckman 272, Hertz 670, Keck 750**
Florida: Selby 2230
Minnesota: Alworth 4499
New Hampshire: **Dorr 5086**
New York: **Heineman 6165, Kade 6281, Monell 6566, Vetlesen 7196**

North Carolina: Woodward 7510
Pennsylvania: Society 8449
Virginia: Jeffress 9442
Washington: Murdock 9644

Physically disabled

Arizona: **Johnson 112**
California: **Chiron 383**, Outhwaite 966, **Peterson 996**
Illinois: **Burlington 2644**
Maryland: **Hendricks 3647**
Minnesota: **SUPERVALU 4695**
New York: Butler 5692
North Carolina: Hendrick 7395

Physics

Arizona: **Research 134**
California: **American 217, Beckman 272, Hertz 670**
Minnesota: Alworth 4499
Nevada: Wiegand 5077
New York: **Heineman 6165**

Planetarium

California: Oschin 960
Illinois: Ward 3056

Political science

Connecticut: **Richardson 1632**
Indiana: **Goodrich 3157**
Massachusetts: Colombe 3852
Michigan: **Earhart 4291**
New York: **Aequus 5524, Bydale 5694, Guggenheim 6118**, Littauer 6434, **Monell 6566**, Sackler 6890, **Tinker 7143**, Wendt 7243
Pennsylvania: **Carthage 8132, Scaife 8425**
Texas: Sumners 9218
Washington: Quest 9666
Wisconsin: **Bradley 9763**

Population studies

California: **Compton 409**, Goldman 597, Hewlett 671, Jewett 718, **Packard 972**
Colorado: Aspen 1337, Donnell 1368
Connecticut: **Ettinger 1536, Prentice 1630**
District of Columbia: **Winslow 1863**
Florida: Bronfman 1917, Martin 2130
Georgia: **Turner 2501**
Minnesota: Bell 4514
New Jersey: Cowles 5170
New York: **Dodge 5867, New 6621, Weeden 7223**
North Carolina: Cumberland 7349
Pennsylvania: Laurel 8301
Texas: Fikes 8899, Kempner 8987, Trull 9240

Poverty studies

California: Rosenberg 1065

Pregnancy centers

Georgia: Harrison 2409
Illinois: Hartke 2792
Louisiana: Frazier 3479
Ohio: IHS 7683

Prostate cancer

California: Mozilo 923

Prostate cancer research

California: Wagner 1274
Florida: Lanie 2103
New Jersey: **Carolan 5156**
New York: Handler 6140

Texas: Mischer 9063, Smith 9192
Washington: True 9696

Protestant agencies & churches

Alabama: Bolden 15, Dixon 32, Lowder 43, May 46, McLendon 48, Mitchell 53, Patterson 56, Pleiad 57, Scrushy 62

Arizona: Cooper 92, Gesner 100, Jazzbird 111, Long 118, Marshall 121, Neely 126, Stevens 144

Arkansas: Pruet 170, Smith 176, Taylor 179, Union 183, Whitt 188

California: Altman 210, Atkins 238, **Atkinson 240**, Boeckmann 299, Bunker 333, Cook 415, Daly 436, Eldorado 482, Everlasting 490, **First 512**, Fremont 534, Gill 576, Grimm 619, Hegwer 664, Jameson 710, Jang 713, Leonard 804, **Mac 840**, McCoy 871, Morris 917, Munger 926, Pardee 978, Phelps 1001, Ryan 1076, Schlinger 1103, Schlosser 1104, Smullin 1169, Stamps 1186, **Stangeland 1187**, Stewart 1199, Tomlinson 1238, Vose 1271, Webb 1285, **Whalen 1299**

Colorado: Bowana 1348, Pioneer 1438

Connecticut: Biondi 1494, Georgescu 1554, Oaklawn 1616, Roberts 1635, Wallace 1674, **Waters 1675**, Young 1681, Zimmel 1684

Delaware: **Milliken 1732**, Reynolds 1743

District of Columbia: Washington 1859, Willard 1861, Willoughby 1862

Florida: Schmid 1874, Appleby 1879, Bay 1896, **Believers 1900**, Bell 1901, **Berg 1903**, Beveridge 1907, Burnett 1919, Cobb 1935, **Cobb 1936**, Couch 1953, Dennis 1969, Driskill 1975, Dunspaugh 1981, duPont 1982, Dyer 1984, Faigen 1996, **Hayden 2051**, Hicks 2059, Hollinger 2064, **Jehovah 2075**, Kelly 2086, Kirbo 2092, Krauss 2101, **Levine 2111**, Maren 2128, Masters 2131, Pascal 2163, Petway 2167, Poe 2173, **Rosser 2208**, Schoen 2226, Seneff 2231, Speer 2241, Tatum 2266, **Vanneck 2278**, Ware 2287, Watts 2288, Welsh 2295, Wymbs 2307

Georgia: Amos 2315, Broadfield 2330, Buisson 2333, Camp 2338, Campbell 2339, Community 2354, Cooper 2363, Creel 2369, Day 2371, **Gage 2392**, Graves 2403, Harrison 2409, Harrison 2410, Imlay 2417, Jones 2424, Lewis 2434, Looney 2436, Ma-Ran 2439, Moore 2452, Morgens 2453, Pitts 2463, Porter 2468, Rollins 2475, Russell 2478, SF 2486, Simpson 2489, Snodgrass 2492, South 2493, Terwilliger 2498, Vogel 2504, Williams 2516, Williams 2517, Williams 2518, Young 2527

Hawaii: Atherton 2532, Wilcox 2559

Idaho: Morrison 2572

Illinois: Atlas 2603, Barnett 2606, Bielfeldt 2620, Borwell 2627, Bruning 2635, Butler 2646, Christopher 2665, Combs 2674, D.H.R. 2695, Emerson 2719, Fites 2730, Gantz 2748, Gloyd 2760, **Harper 2786**, Hobbs 2802, Kolschowsky 2843, Parks 2931, Roberts 2968, Schawk 2984, Schmidt 2986, Simmons 3008, Souder 3013, **Spreading 3017**, Sudix 3029, **Tyndale 3042**, Walnut 3054, Weiss 3062, Woods 3083, Worley 3086

Indiana: Hilbert 3167, Hux 3170, Irwin 3175, **Master 3201**, Met 3204, Morgan 3208, Tobias 3244, Valiant 3248

Iowa: Grubb 3289, Krause 3302, **New 3319**, Sukup 3336

Kansas: DeVore 3357, Garvey 3363, Haglage 3365, Joscelyn 3371, McCune 3376, Morris 3378, Rhoden 3383

Kentucky: **Chase 3413**, Hep 3426, Marshall 3438, Preston 3446, River 3448

Louisiana: Burton 3467, Coughlin 3470, Deming 3472, Diboll 3473, Factor 3476, Hardtner 3485, Huie 3488, Jones 3491, **Live 3495**, Lorio 3496, Schlieder 3508, Scott 3509, Wilson 3515, Young 3518

Maine: Berry 3526, Gallagher 3535

Maryland: Clark 3591, deForest 3612, Eliasberg 3620, Rollins 3718

Massachusetts: Benfamil 3797, Byrnes 3821, Charlton 3846, Encourage 3894, **Hostetter 3959**, Inavale

3964, **Jebediah 3969**, McCallum 4029, **Uperetes 4188**, Vinik 4193

Michigan: Dauch 4268, Ford 4302, Ford 4305, **Gast 4317**, Hurst 4344, ICN 4345, **Johnson 4349**, Kay 4354, Knabusch 4362, **Krauss 4366**, Lasko 4373, Mackey 4380, Mott 4400, Slikkers 4439, Turner 4464, Vanderweide 4469

Minnesota: Acorn 4494, Arcee 4506, Caridad 4531, Chadwick-Loher 4535, Garmar 4569, Grossman 4578, Hallett 4582, Mahon 4609, Mithun 4626, Olson 4640, Peterson 4652, Reimer 4665, Sit 4683, Sundet 4694

Mississippi: Luckyday 4752, Mississippi 4756, Peaster 4761, Taylor 4767

Missouri: Bodine 4784, Buckner 4790, Cornelsen 4799, Duesenberg 4805, Herschend 4830, Lemons 4854, **Olofson 4875**, Pearl 4879, PMJ 4885, Reding 4890, Rosewood 4894, **Sayler 4897**

Montana: Bair 4931

Nebraska: Bishop 4946, Buckley 4947, Dunklau 4958, Hawks 4971, Smock 5004, Wiebe 5017

Nevada: Rufty 5059

New Jersey: Bolger 5136, Dephillips 5179, Hugin 5245, **Huntsman 5246**, Kemmerer 5275, Kurr 5291, Lipper 5308, Nicolais 5339, Point 5353, Twin 5432

New Mexico: **Johns 5482**, Walbridge 5503

New York: 1101 5504, Acorn 5515, Bernhard 5624, **Bobolink 5645**, **Burpee 5690**, Campbell 5700, Case 5713, **Chinnick 5751**, Dewar 5856, Fife 5955, Gant 6006, Gerhard 6015, Gilliam 6031, Grubman 6113, Haggin 6132, Iovino 6236, Ivor 6242, **Johnson 6273**, Keeler 6306, Kellen 6308, L and L 6366, **Landegger 6371**, Macdonald 6468, Martin 6496, **Matthews 6507**, Metcalf 6541, Millbrook 6549, **Milliken 6552**, Mostyn 6591, Nagle 6599, Neidich 6606, O'Connor 6645, Peale 6700, **Robertson 6818**, Robison 6821, Rogers 6829, Sandy 6903, Saunders 6909, **Staley 7042**, **Steel 7052**, Stokes 7080, Sugarman 7092, Townsend 7159, Vidda 7198, Walker 7208, Warren 7217, Widgeon 7255, Woodland 7275

North Carolina: Belk 7314, Branan 7322, Braswell 7323, Cannon 7335, Comloquoy 7341, Crutchfield 7348, Dover 7356, Dowd 7357, Duke 7359, Family 7365, Finch 7366, Glenn 7376, Graham 7382, Greensboro 7383, Harvest 7392, Herring 7396, Jenkins 7406, Kulynych 7415, Ladane 7417, Legatus 7420, Martin 7424, McMichael 7426, Morgan 7431, **P & B 7442**, Ragan 7455, Richmond 7463, Simpson 7472, Sloan 7475, Smith 7478, Smith 7479, Stonecutter 7486, Stowe 7487, Summer 7489, Winston 7507, Zelnak 7513

Ohio: Beaverson 7541, Clapp 7575, Cornerstone 7592, DBJ 7605, **Durell 7616**, Geary 7645, Gund 7656, Heavenly 7668, IHS 7683, Jobst 7691, Kalberer 7695, Lindner 7716, Mangano 7733, Ritter 7822, Scotford 7846, Seifert 7850, Sloat 7861, Toledo 7882, Turner 7889, **Warrington 7895**, Wildermuth 7906

Oklahoma: **8:32 7922**, Bailey 7923, Massey 7955, Meinders 7960

Oregon: Bauman 7999, Salem 8054, Wendt 8066

Pennsylvania: Angela 8082, Arcadia 8086, Bradley 8115, Byers' 8127, Cassett 8133, Community 8154, Connelly 8157, **Cornerstone 8159**, Crawford 8162, Crels 8163, Edwards 8183, **Firstfruits 8203**, **Forney 8207**, Grumbacher 8227, Huston 8264, **Knox 8294**, Les 8306, M & S 8318, Maplewood 8324, McCune 8331, McFeely 8334, Oxford 8367, Pollock 8390, Reidler 8402, Sampson 8423, **Seraph 8434**, Snyder 8448, Stabler 8455, Taylor 8473, United 8486

Rhode Island: Chace 8523, Daniels 8530, Roosa 8552

South Carolina: Abney 8564, Arkwright 8565, Campbell 8573, Collins 8582, Gibbs 8590, Hipp 8592, Hopewell 8593, Inman 8595, Lipscomb 8598, Montgomery 8600, Rainey 8605, **Security's 8609**, Smith 8613, TSC 8618

Tennessee: Basler 8641, Dugas 8669, **Garrott 8680**, Harris 8686, Hawthorn 8689, **Maclellan 8704**, Martin 8707, Massey 8709, Nelson 8712, Wallace 8740, Washington 8741, Wilson 8744

Texas: Allison 8757, Aragona 8763, Astin 8764, B & B 8769, Bailey 8771, **C.I.O.S. 8805**, Cain 8808, Cauthorn 8820, Christian 8828, Crain 8851, Dauphin 8856, Deason 8861, Delaney 8862, Estill 8888, Fain 8890, Fair 8891, Fleming 8904, Folsom 8905, Garvey 8914, Gill 8919, Hankamer 8939, Helm 8947, Hobby 8954, Johnson 8972, Kelley 8985, Keown 8989, Mays 9036, McMillan 9046, Morgan 9073, Morris 9076, Nation 9087, O'Connor 9094, O'Quinn 9097, **Oldham 9100**, Paulos 9112, Perkins 9116, Perot 9118, Phillips 9122, Roberts 9151, Rogers 9155, Ross 9159, Scurlock 9175, Sharp 9180, Shelton 9182, Sooch 9200, Sowell 9202, Sterling 9212, Tolleson 9237, Trull 9240, Vaughn 9251, Waggoner 9257, Walsh 9261, Watson 9266, Weaver 9268, Willard 9281, Williams 9283

Utah: GFC 9324

Virginia: Adams 9366, Cartledge 9388, **Doudera 9412**, Estes 9415, Graves 9433, Harrison 9436, Herndon 9437, Lane 9456, Perry 9496, Reynolds 9503, Rice 9504, Titmus 9527

Washington: Anderson 9551, Helstrom 9605, Hughes 9610, Vidalakis 9698

West Virginia: Carter 9712, Hunnicutt 9720

Wisconsin: Alexander 9740, Antioch 9745, Baker 9751, Batterman 9754, Benidt 9758, Bryce 9769, Crump 9783, **DeAtley 9789**, Demmer 9791, Frautschi 9804, Gordon 9808, Johnson 9825, Kellogg 9832, **Kern 9834**, Leake 9849, Martin 9862, MMG 9877, Parr 9893, **Roddis 9913**, Siebert 9927, Stuart 9941, Styberg 9944, **Thrivent 9949**, Wagner 9958, **Young 9972**

Protestant federated giving programs

North Carolina: Daveler 7351
Tennessee: Citizens 8657
Texas: Astin 8764, Paulos 9112, Trull 9240
Wisconsin: Siebert 9927

Psychology/behavioral science

California: **Foundation 530**, Lehrer 800, Ornest 959
Illinois: Lederer 2852
Michigan: Fetzer 4298
New York: **Grant 6092**, **Guggenheim 6118**, **Pioneer 6729**
Pennsylvania: Staunton 8457, Steinman 8459

Public affairs

Alabama: Ard 8, Blount 14, Community 24, Protective 58

Arizona: Arizona 87, Hansen 104

California: Allergan 203, Avery 244, BayTree 265, California 345, Clorox 399, Community 405, Community 406, **Draper 466**, Fluor 523, Furth 543, Gerbode 564, Gilmore 578, Goldman 596, Merage 887, **Omidyar 952**, Pacific 970, Penney 990, San Francisco 1088, Teichert 1231, vanLobenSels 1260

Colorado: **Anschutz 1335**, **Castle 1352**, Community 1358, Pikes 1437, **Staley 1457**

Connecticut: Larsen 1579, Rosenthal 1638, **Xerox 1680**

Delaware: Crestlea 1701, Romill 1747

District of Columbia: **Mott 1836**

Florida: Community 1941, Community 1948, Community 1949, Dunn's 1980, Gulf 2041, Martin 2130

Georgia: **Scientific 2482**, Woodruff 2521

Hawaii: First 2542

Illinois: Abbott 2580, Blair 2621, **Burlington 2644**, Caterpillar 2653, Chicago 2663, Crown 2691, Field 2728, **Friedmann 2738**, **Harper 2786**, Harris 2787, Omron 2926, Steans 3021, Stern 3023, USG 3046, Wieboldt 3069, Woods 3084

Indiana: 1st 3094, Ball 3103, Community 3122, Community 3123, Community 3130, Heritage 3166, Kimball 3182, Koch 3184, Kosciusko 3186,

Recreation, formal/general education
New Jersey: Goldring 5210

Recreation, fund raising/fund distribution
Florida: Castellani 1928

Recreation, government agencies
North Carolina: McMichael 7426

Recreation, parks/playgrounds
Alabama: Community 24
California: Community 402, Fresno 537, Valley 1257
Colorado: Lewis 1410, Richardson 1444
Connecticut: Community 1516, Tsunami 1663
District of Columbia: **Berman 1774**
Florida: Beveridge 1906, Selby 2230
Georgia: **Georgia 2397**, Ma-Ran 2439
Illinois: Anderson 2594, **Aon 2598**, Krueck 2846, Levi 2855, Sirius 3010
Indiana: Community 3124, Community 3131, Journal 3181, Marshall 3199, Michigan 3205, Waterfield 3252
Iowa: Ahrens 3260
Louisiana: Lorio 3496
Maryland: Felburn 3629, Greenberg 3639, Sylvan 3741
Michigan: Dalton 4266
Minnesota: Xcel 4732
Mississippi: Oakwood 4760
Missouri: Barrows 4781, Gateway 4817, Stupp 4910, Ward 4924, Whitaker 4926
Nebraska: TierOne 5010
Nevada: May 5046
New Jersey: **Huntsman 5246**, Nicolais 5339, **Wall 5445**
New York: Goodman 6072, Handler 6140, Heckscher 6164, **JPMorgan 6277**, Klingenstein 6337, Lauder 6382, **Luckow 6455**, **Magowan 6473**, **MetLife 6542**, New York 6616, Northern 6638, Orentreich 6667, **Reed 6783**, Richardson 6797, Tuch 7170, Turn 7174, Vance 7193
North Carolina: Broyhill 7328, **Lowe's 7423**, Woodson 7509
Ohio: Beaverson 7541, Bryan 7559, Community 7583, Davidson 7602, Fox 7638, Slemp 7860, Wilson 7910
Oregon: Salem 8054, Wessinger 8067
Pennsylvania: Degenstein 8166, Eden 8182, Karabots 8278
South Dakota: Larson 8627
Tennessee: **Bridgestone 8646**
Texas: Bass 8777, Belo 8787, Dallas 8855, El Paso 8882, Jones 8976, Keith 8982, Kronkosky 9002
Washington: De Falco 9578
Wisconsin: Duncan 9793
Wyoming: Chapman 9976

Recreation, public education
Pennsylvania: Seiple 8432

Recreation, single organization support
Illinois: Anderson 2594

Recreation, social clubs
Illinois: Gantz 2748
New York: Schneider 6929

Religion
Alabama: **Altec 4**, Bruno 17, Community 26, **Union 70**
Arizona: Stevens 144
Arkansas: Arkansas 156
California: Aratani 230, Auen 242, Bartman 259, Bickerstaff 287, Boeckmann 299, Bowes 311, Callison 351, **Cassin 364**, Conte 414, Doheny 460, Finley 507, Garabedian 552, Gershman 566, **God's**

585, Halsell 641, Hannon 644, Hsin 689, **KLM 767**, Leichtag 801, Lincy 812, MacDonald 841, Marin 854, **Mattel 861**, McLean 880, **Rivendell 1056**, Ryan 1075, Schott 1106, Sclavos 1113, Soda 1173, Stamps 1186, Trust 1246
Colorado: **Crowell 1361**, Weckbaugh 1470
Connecticut: Bodenwein 1497, Mortensen 1605, Palmer 1621, Pequot 1625, Royce 1639
Delaware: Delany 1705, Kent 1723, Laffey 1725, Presto 1740, **Raskob 1741**
District of Columbia: Bernstein 1775, Merriman 1833, Washington 1860
Florida: A Friends' 1866, **Anderson 1876**, Bastien 1892, Beveridge 1907, duPont 1983, Gainesville 2015, Gurtler 2043, Life's 2116, Pinellas 2170, Price 2177, Rinker 2197, Viner 2281, Winter 2303, Zwan 2308
Georgia: Beloco 2324, Bradley 2326, Brown 2331, Campbell 2339, Carlos 2340, Community 2357, Community 2359, Fraser 2390, Gaines 2393, Harland 2407, Lee 2432, North 2458, Patterson 2460, Savannah 2480, **Scott 2483**, Wilson 2519, WinShape 2520
Hawaii: First 2542, Kosasa 2549, Vidinha 2557, Wilcox 2559
Illinois: Eisenberg 2716, Elgin 2717, Hermann 2798, Kern 2837, Lange 2848, Louis 2862, McMullan 2884, **Norris 2917**, Russell 2976, Schawk 2984, Scully 2992, **Spreading 3017**, **Tuohy 3041**, United 3044, Wenske 3063, Woods 3083
Indiana: Crown Point 3135, Hasten 3162, Kimball 3182, Koch 3184, Moore 3207, Muselman 3209, Wabash 3250, Welborn 3254
Iowa: **Andringa 3262**, Butler 3273, Knapp 3301, Kruidenier 3303, Pappajohn 3322, Stark 3334, **Van Wyk 3340**
Kansas: Bane 3345
Kentucky: Blue 3407, Mustard 3440, **Omnicare 3444**, Preston 3446
Louisiana: Almar 3459, Baton Rouge 3462, Booth 3464, Brown 3465, Helis 3486
Maine: Davenport 3531, Gardiner 3536
Maryland: Chaney 3587, Community 3598, Community 3599, Delaplaine 3614, Eliasberg 3620, Hahn 3643, **Smith 3736**, Tucker 3750
Massachusetts: **A & A 3764**, **Afeyan 3773**, Bristol 3816, Demoulas 3878, Hendrickson 3947, High 3950, Highland 3951, Kittredge 3983, Liberty 4006, Lowell 4015, Morningside 4043, Sohn 4151, Weld 4203
Michigan: Ave 4225, DeVos 4279, Ford 4303, Merillat 4391, **Myers 4402**, Westerman 4478
Minnesota: Adams 4495, AHS 4497, Amundson 4500, **Andreas 4504**, Athwin 4508, Fiterman 4565, George 4572, Manitou 4610, Mann 4611, Noreen 4635, O'Neil 4638
Mississippi: Foundation 4743, Maddox 4753, Mississippi 4758, Providence 4762
Missouri: Boswell 4786, Interco 4835, Stupp 4910, Vatterott 4921
Nebraska: Baer 4944, Holland 4977
New Jersey: **Bonner 5137**, Brady 5141, Brotherton 5145, Garcia 5203, Hyde 5247, **Johnson 5263**, Lissak 5309, McGraw 5323, Perrin 5350, Visceglia 5441, **Wilf 5455**, Withington 5458
New York: Achelis 5513, Altus 5547, **Baker 5594**, Bayne 5607, Blythmour 5644, **Bronfman 5671**, Clark 5759, **Engelhard 5932**, Fischer 5960, **Frank 5974**, Frey 5983, Gatto 6007, Jacobson 6247, Johnson 6269, **Klein 6330**, **Klingenstein 6335**, **Lauder 6383**, Littauer 6434, Lostand 6448, Lynch 6462, Maheras 6475, Nagle 6599, **Nicolitch 6630**, O'Connor 6645, O'Malley 6648, Ohrstrom 6659, Richmond 6800, Roxe 6867, Sani 6904, Schlosstein 6925, Schwartz 6940, Schwartz 6943, Seventeen 6958, Siegel 6976, Simon 6987, Sister 6994, Slifka 7001, Steinmetz 7066, Stern 7070, Sternberg 7075, Wendt 7243
North Carolina: **Bank 7310**, Finch 7366, Foundation 7370, Gordon 7379, North Carolina 7438, SunTrust 7491, Woodward 7510, Yeargan 7511, Zelnak 7513

Ohio: **Alpaugh 7527**, Anderson 7529, Ashtabula 7534, **Austin 7535**, Brennan 7554, Bryan 7559, Community 7586, **Durell 7616**, Fairfax 7621, Forest 7634, Gingher 7650, Kaplan 7696, Murdough 7767, Nippert 7777, **Ohio 7786**, Sloat 7861, Toulmin 7885, Wayne 7897, Western 7903, Wolfe 7915
Oklahoma: **8:32 7922**, Bailey 7923
Oregon: Collins 8007, **Foreign 8014**, Johnson 8027, Jubitz 8029
Pennsylvania: 1957 8071, Arcadia 8086, Arete 8088, Ball 8093, Byers' 8127, **Clive 8146**, Community 8153, Crels 8163, Dolfinger 8172, Donnelly 8176, Fair 8192, Federated 8196, Foundation 8208, Hansen 8235, Hopwood 8257, Hunt 8261, Kavanagh 8282, Keystone 8286, Miller 8353, Morris 8359, Rockwell 8408, **Saltsgiver 8420**, Scranton 8431, St. Mary's 8454, Stewart 8460, **Templeton 8475**, United 8486, Weiss 8499
Rhode Island: **Amica 8518**
South Carolina: Liberty 8597, **Security's 8609**, Sonoco 8614
South Dakota: Hofer 8626, Sioux Falls 8630
Tennessee: Citizens 8657, Community 8661, Conwood 8663, Ezell 8676, Stokely 8730
Texas: Ackerman 8750, Alexander 8752, **Allbritton 8755**, Bass 8777, Bookout 8791, Bridgeway 8796, Chatham 8825, Chilton 8826, Edwards 8880, Elkins 8883, Franklin 8907, Frost 8910, Hamman 8938, Hildebrand 8951, Jones 8975, Kelley 8986, Kinder 8994, Looper 9016, Mankoff 9027, McCrea 9040, McKee 9045, Mitchell 9065, Moody 9070, Mosbacher 9077, Mundy 9080, Murrell 9082, O'Connor 9095, Onstead 9102, Paulos 9112, Pryor 9136, Rogers 9155, San Antonio 9166, Scurlock 9175, Smith 9191, Sterling 9212, Strake 9215, Trull 9240, Valero 9247, Vaughan 9249, Ware 9264, Young 9295
Utah: **ALSAM 9302**, Greene 9325, Watkins 9350
Virginia: Beazley 9376, Community 9400, Golden 9430, LandAmerica 9454, Peterson 9497, **Riverside 9505**, Titmus 9527, Ukrop 9529, Washington 9534
Washington: Everard 9582, **Hemingway 9606**, Lynn 9633, Moccasin 9643, **Samis 9675**, Shemanski 9682, Warren 9700
West Virginia: Schenk 9732
Wisconsin: Alexander 9740, Bader 9749, Baird 9750, Hess 9816, Keller 9831, **Meehan 9868**, Nelson 9881, Siebert 9927, U.S. 9952, West 9963
Wyoming: McMurry 9985

Religion, association
New York: Ades 5516
Tennessee: **Maclellan 8704**

Religion, equal rights
Wyoming: Connemara 9978

Religion, formal/general education
California: Ray 1034
Massachusetts: O'Donnell 4059
New Jersey: **Bogoni 5134**
Wisconsin: Vine 9956
Wyoming: Connemara 9978

Religion, fund raising/fund distribution
Wisconsin: **Thrivent 9949**

Religion, interfaith issues
Delaware: Sternlicht 1756
Kentucky: Brown 3408
Maryland: Hirschhorn 3650
Minnesota: AHS 4497
New Hampshire: Levine 5094
New Jersey: Gershman 5206
New York: **Ford 5970**, Slifka 7001

Tennessee: Goldsmith 8682
Texas: Mankoff 9027, Tobin 9235
Virginia: English 9414
Wyoming: Connemara 9978

Religion, management/technical aid
Wisconsin: **Thrivent 9949**

Religion, public policy
New York: **Tikvah 7140**
Pennsylvania: **Pew 8377**

Religion, research
Georgia: Poole 2466
New Jersey: **Bogoni 5134**
Pennsylvania: **Pew 8377**

Religious federated giving programs
Alabama: Wyker 77
California: Keller 752, Price 1017, Wallis 1276
Florida: Masters 2131, Speer 2241
Georgia: Watkins 2508
Illinois: Domanada 2705, **Pritzker 2952**, **Tyndale 3042**
Michigan: **McDonald 4388**, Merillat 4391
Minnesota: **Wallestad 4712**
New Jersey: **Bonner 5137**
New York: O'Connor 6645
North Carolina: Stewards 7485
Oklahoma: Kimmell 7951
Pennsylvania: Dolfinger 8172, Mandell 8322
Texas: Perot 9118
Wisconsin: **Roddis 9913**
Wyoming: Connemara 9978

Reproductive health
California: **Kaiser 739**, Wohlford 1315
Colorado: **Avenir 1339**, **General 1381**
District of Columbia: **Moriah 1835**, **Public 1844**, **Summit 1852**
Illinois: Grant 2770, Harris 2789, **MacArthur 2868**
Iowa: Deardorf 3280
Massachusetts: Gerard 3923, **Merck 4036**
New York: Dickler 5861, **Ford 5970**, Gleacher 6038
Ohio: IHS 7683, Schott 7842
Oregon: **NIKE 8046**
Pennsylvania: CIGNA 8143, Pilgrim 8383

Reproductive health, abortion clinics/services
District of Columbia: **Wallace 1858**

Reproductive health, family planning
Arizona: **Kleckhefer 113**, Morris 124
California: Atkinson 239, Brenner 321, Cheeryble 377, **Compton 409**, Confidence 411, Gellert 559, Gold 590, Goodman 605, Grand 611, Grove 625, Gruber 626, Harman 651, Hewlett 671, HRH 688, Lavine 793, Lehrer 800, Meyer 893, **On 953**, **Packard 972**, San Diego 1087, San Francisco 1088, Springcreek 1185, Steele 1189, Stern 1195, Werner 1296
Colorado: Aspen 1337, **Avenir 1339**, Boettcher 1344, Donnell 1368, **General 1381**, Hughes 1393, KBK 1400
Connecticut: Bodenwein 1497, Community 1515, **Educational 1533**, **Ettinger 1536**, **Niles 1611**, Palmer 1621
Delaware: Beckwith 1689, Crystal 1702, Marmot 1728, Reynolds 1743
District of Columbia: Cafritz 1780, Enfranchisement 1792, **Moriah 1835**, **Mott 1836**, **Public 1844**, Replogle 1846, **Summit 1852**, **Wallace 1858**
Florida: Bank 1890, Henderson 2056, Kennedy 2088, Martin 2130

Georgia: Moore 2452, **Wardlaw 2506**
Illinois: Baskes 2607, Bauer 2609, Beidler 2613, Brach 2629, Community 2677, Harris 2789, Kaplan 2823, New 2912, Prince 2948, **Shifting 3006**
Indiana: Griffith 3158
Iowa: Blank 3268, Knapp 3301
Louisiana: Kabacoff 3492
Maryland: Abell 3559, MARPAT 3684
Massachusetts: Campbell 3830, Community 3855, Fessenden 3903, High 3950, Hyams 3961, **Lalor 3993**, Rappaport 4093, Walske 4196
Michigan: Padnos 4406, Tiscornia 4460, Wolff 4486
Minnesota: Bell 4514, Bremer 4523, Kelley 4597, Prospect 4659
Missouri: Edison 4807, Lopata 4859, Pershing 4881, Sunnen 4913
Nebraska: **Buffett 4950**, Fulk 4964
Nevada: **Bing 5022**, Fairweather 5032, O'Bannon 5049, Smith 5065
New Jersey: Borden 5138, Cowles 5170, **Huber 5244**, Jockey 5260, Riskin 5369, Union 5435, Victoria 5440
New Mexico: McCune 5488
New York: Abrons 5511, Abrons 5512, Allyn 5539, Baird 5591, Block 5638, Clark 5761, Corzine 5798, Dickler 5861, Glickenhaus 6042, Goldsmith 6060, Green 6096, **International 6234**, Johnson 6270, Loeb 6439, Marx 6497, **Moore 6571**, Nichols 6628, **Noble 6633**, Palmer 6683, **Panaphil 6684**, Partridge 6695, **Peierls 6705**, Pevaroff 6719, **Prospect 6750**, Schaffer 6911, Scherman 6918, Schwartz 6941, Spitzer 7034, Sulzberger 7095, Vogelstein 7201, **Wexner 7249**
North Carolina: Cumberland 7349, Gunzenhauser-Chapin 7384, Triangle 7496, Vanderbilt 7501
Ohio: Britton 7556, Columbus 7580, Edwards 7618, **Goatie 7651**, Iddings 7682, Morgan 7760, **Perkins 7800**, Sedgwick 7849, Stocker 7870, Wohlgemuth 7913, Women's 7916
Oklahoma: McGee 7957
Oregon: Johnson 8027
Pennsylvania: Buck 8123, Claneil 8144, Dolfinger 8172, Laurel 8301, Sovereign 8451, Steinman 8458, Steinman 8459, Wyomissing 8509
Rhode Island: Champlin 8524, Daniels 8530
South Carolina: Central 8577, Ceres 8578
Texas: Cain 8809, Clayton 8830, Fikes 8899, Hanley 8940, Jonsson 8977, Kempner 8987, Mankoff 9027, Owsley 9108, San Antonio 9166, Vaughan 9250, Wright 9294
Utah: Eccles 9320, Raymond 9339, **Wishnick 9353**
Vermont: Lintilhac 9359, Vermont 9361
Virginia: Dalis 9406, Delmar 9410, Portsmouth 9499, **WestWind 9538**
Washington: Blue 9559, Community 9571, **Gates 9591**, Horizons 9608, **Kongsgaard 9620**, Moccasin 9643, Neukom 9649, **Wiancko 9704**
Wisconsin: Charter 9772, Evjue 9797, Kettering 9835, Milwaukee 9876, Munson 9880, Pollybill 9900

Reproductive health, fertility
District of Columbia: **Summit 1852**
New York: Green 6096
Virginia: Dalis 9406

Reproductive health, OBGYN/Birthing centers
Tennessee: Clayton 8659

Reproductive health, prenatal care
Alabama: Community 24
Florida: Burns 1920
Ohio: Mehl 7746
Pennsylvania: CIGNA 8143
Texas: **EDS 8877**, Heavin 8945

Reproductive health, sexuality education
District of Columbia: **Summit 1852**, **Wallace 1858**
Florida: Hayes 2052
Minnesota: HRK 4589
New York: **Ford 5970**

Residential/custodial care
Alabama: Treadwell 68
California: American 215
Colorado: **Mercy 1426**
Florida: **Cobb 1936**, Magruder 2125, Smith 2238
Georgia: Cawood 2342, Goizueta 2400, Terwilliger 2498
Hawaii: Hawaii 2545
Illinois: Walsh 3055
Iowa: Bright 3269, Krause 3302
Kansas: Smith 3393
Massachusetts: Ashton 3782, Roddy 4108
Minnesota: Charity 4536, Wolohan 4730
Mississippi: **Seal 4764**
Missouri: Ballman 4780, Emerson 4809
New Jersey: **Anderson 5115**, Kennedy 5276
New York: Black 5636, Davidson 5835
North Carolina: Branan 7322, Reynolds 7460, Woodson 7509
Pennsylvania: Levis 8309
South Carolina: **Security's 8609**
Texas: Anderson 8760, Doss 8869, Garvey 8914, PSH 9137, Waggoner 9256
Wisconsin: Leake 9849, Parr 9893

Residential/custodial care, group home
California: Corrigan 418
Colorado: McDonnell 1422
Texas: Bass 8777, Wolslager 9290
Virginia: Olsson 9491

Residential/custodial care, half-way house
Georgia: Love 2437
Illinois: Genius 2751
New York: Rosenblum 6850

Residential/custodial care, hospices
Alabama: Community 27, McMillan 49
Arizona: **Kleckhefer 113**, Morris 124
Arkansas: Walker 185
California: Atkinson 239, **Atkinson 240**, Auen 242, Christopher 385, Community 406, Copley 416, Cortopassi 419, Dickinson 454, Fireman's 510, Forest 527, Gilmore 578, Gross 621, Harman 651, Irvine 699, **Keck 750**, Laurel 792, Lytel 836, Menard 884, Rady Fam 1026, Sacramento 1080, Sajak 1083, San Diego 1087, Santa Barbara 1093, Scripps 1115, Sonora 1178, Weingart 1288
Colorado: **Benson 1341**, Boettcher 1344, El Pomar 1374, Summit 1463
Connecticut: Connecticut 1518, Culpeper 1521, **Ettinger 1536**, Palmer 1621, Rosenthal 1638, Woodward 1678
Delaware: Crystal 1702, Marmot 1728
District of Columbia: Cafritz 1780
Florida: Appleby 1879, Bank 1890, Bastien 1892, Beveridge 1907, Community 1946, **Foundation 2008**, Gooding 2028, Helow 2055, Kennedy 2088, Petway 2167, Price 2177, Rosenberg 2206, Rubin 2211, Scarpa 2221
Georgia: Community 2362, Cox 2367, Imlay 2417, Jolley 2423, Lewis 2434, Marcus 2440, Moore 2452, Patterson 2460
Hawaii: HMSA 2547, Wilcox 2559
Illinois: Cressey 2689, GKN 2758, Goldberg 2761, Hansen 2782, Kainz 2822, Woodward 3085
Indiana: Garcia 3154, Kosciusko 3185
Kansas: Hutchinson 3368
Kentucky: Fischer 3418
Louisiana: **Biedenharn 3463**

Maryland: Blades 3574, Hahn 3643, Legg 3672, Middendorf 3694
Massachusetts: Bayrd 3795, **Shattuck 4138**
Michigan: **H.I.S. 4334**, Padnos 4406, Ravitz 4418, Wilson 4484
Minnesota: Bremer 4523
Mississippi: Ford 4742
Missouri: Green 4822, Shaw 4901
Nevada: Bennett 5021
New Hampshire: **Penates 5099**
New Jersey: Cowles 5170, Danellie 5177, Geiger 5205, **GHH 5207**, **Johnson 5265**, McCutchen 5322, Smith 5409
New Mexico: Frost 5476, McCune 5488
New York: **Chinnick 5751**, Corning 5794, Lindner 6426, Marx 6498, McGraw 6519, Northern 6638, Northern 6639, Steele 7053, Wendt 7243, Western 7248
North Carolina: Bolick 7321, Cemala 7337, Coffey 7339, Cumberland 7349, Halton 7386, Harvest 7392, **Jefferson 7405**, Legatus 7420, North Carolina 7438, Reynolds 7457, Rostan 7467, Sklut 7473, Stewards 7485, Triangle 7496
North Dakota: Stern 7521
Ohio: Beaverson 7541, Foundation 7636, **HCR 7667**, Heimbinder 7670, M/B 7728, Mangano 7733, McGregor 7742, Miniger 7756, Muskingum 7770, Oliver 7788, Schlink 7839, Stocker 7870, Toledo 7882, Troy 7886, Watson 7896, Youngstown 7920
Oregon: Johnson 8027
Pennsylvania: Arcadia 8086, **Carpenter 8131**, Fourjay 8209, Huston 8263, Ortenzio 8366, Rockwell 8408, Steinman 8459
Rhode Island: Shaw's 8555
South Carolina: Abney 8564, McKissick 8599, **Security's 8609**, TSC 8618
Tennessee: Atticus 8639, Christy 8654, CIC 8656, Massey 8709, Ragsdale 8722, Thompson 8733
Texas: Cameron 8812, Cox 8850, Fasken 8895, Fisch 8901, Hackett 8928, Kempner 8987, McCrea 9040, Meadows 9049, O'Connor 9095, O'Quinn 9097, Prairie 9129, San Antonio 9166, **Shell 9181**, Speas 9206, Sterling 9212, Temple 9227, Wal 9260, Wright 9294
Utah: Bastian 9307
Virginia: Clark 9393, Delmar 9410, Kellar 9449, Peterson 9497, Williamsburg 9541
Washington: Blue 9559, Community 9571, Glaser 9594, Norcliffe 9650, Tacoma 9693
West Virginia: Kanawha 9723
Wisconsin: Bolz 9762, Green Bay 9810, McBeath 9864, Merten 9873, Peterson 9896, Sensient 9922, Sub 9945

Residential/custodial care, senior continuing care

California: Burnett 336
Colorado: KBK 1400, Rose 1445
Connecticut: Ambler 1481
Florida: **Jaharis 2073**
Illinois: Buehler 2638, Knox 2842
Massachusetts: Nichols 4055
New Jersey: **GHH 5207**
New York: Benedict 5618, McNulty 6521
North Carolina: Spring 7483
Ohio: **HCR 7667**, Lincoln 7715
Pennsylvania: DSF 8178
Texas: Kaufman 8981
Wisconsin: Lynn 9853, Madison 9854

Residential/custodial care, special day care

California: PacifiCare 971

Roman Catholic agencies & churches

Alabama: Lowder 44
Alaska: Carr 82
Arizona: Farrington 97, Halle 103, Hansen 104, Lovell 119, Pocono 131

California: Bravo 319, Burns 338, Cacique 342, Centofante 370, Condon 410, Connolly 413, Cusenza 433, Danford 438, Davies 446, Doheny 460, Dougherty 463, Drum 470, Esseff 488, Finley 507, Gallo 547, Gallo 548, Garaventa 553, Geschke 568, Haas 633, Hannon 645, Hayden 657, Jameson 710, JANS 714, Kanitz 742, McFadden 874, Menard 884, Moley 908, Mozilo 923, Muller 925, Murphy 928, Neilsen 934, O'Brien 945, **Oak 947**, Oberndorf 950, Outrageous 967, Rising 1055, Sebastiani 1119, Seeno 1120, Shea 1142, Shea 1143, Snow 1171, Soda 1173, Solari 1176, Trust 1246, Valley 1257, Van Daele 1259, Von der Ahe 1269, Weyrich 1298, **Whalen 1299**, Wiskemann 1311
Colorado: Bacon 1340, Hill 1392, McCormick 1420, Saeman 1448, Weckbaugh 1470
Connecticut: Bossidy 1500, Dartley 1524, Gaisman 1551, **Huisking 1570**, Jeffe 1572, Lynch 1591, Rose 1637, Sullivan 1655
Delaware: Cawley 1696, Hofmann 1722, Laffey 1725, Mastronardi 1729, Morania 1733, **Raskob 1741**, Romill 1747, Wasily 1760
District of Columbia: **Loyola 1825**, Post 1842
Florida: Abraham 1867, Amaturo 1873, Better 1905, Cascone 1926, Charitable 1931, Deaver 1965, Demetree 1967, DiMare 1974, duPont 1982, Fisher 1999, Fortin 2007, Friedman 2014, Gerstner 2020, Gorin 2032, Griffin 2036, Hamilton-Forbes 2046, Hayes 2052, Helow 2055, Hunter 2069, Kelco 2085, **Koch 2098**, **Lewis 2114**, Maren 2128, McKeen 2133, Morrison 2146, O'Neil 2155, Rales 2184, **Regan 2191**, **Rehm 2192**, Rothman 2210, Sanders 2215, Scarpa 2221, **Sullivan 2257**, **Volimer 2282**, Wahlert 2284, Ware 2287
Georgia: Buisson 2333, Hanna 2406, **Keough 2426**, Lewis 2433, Moeller 2449
Illinois: Allegretti 2586, Blair 2621, Bruning 2635, Buffett 2640, Corboy 2684, Crowe 2690, Cuneo 2692, Denny 2703, Dowdle 2709, Endless 2720, Gallagher 2743, **Gavin 2749**, Gidwitz 2754, Kazma 2827, Mazza 2877, McIntosh 2883, O'Connor 2921, Opler 2927, Parmer 2932, Pepper 2936, Perritt 2939, Ryan 2977, **Ryan 2978**, Sangre 2981, Snite 3012, Walgreen 3052, Walsh 3055
Indiana: Bussing 3111, **BVM 3112**, Citizens 3118, Cornelius 3134, Garcia 3154, Hux 3170, Indiana 3173, Valiant 3248
Iowa: Figge 3284, Krause 3302, **Ochylski 3321**, R & R 3327, Stark 3334
Kansas: Sullivan 3396
Kentucky: Bavarian 3406, Fischer 3418, Ladner 3436
Louisiana: Adams 3458, Azby 3460, Booth 3464, Coughlin 3470, Diboll 3473, Lorio 3496, Monroe 3501, Peltier 3504, Stuller 3510, Taylor 3511
Maine: Great 3539
Maryland: Bunting 3580, Darby 3605, Davis 3606, Knott 3666, Linehan 3678, O'Neil 3701, Quinn 3713
Massachusetts: Birmingham 3807, Bradley 3814, Carney 3837, Corcoran 3860, Finnegan 3908, Hagerty 3938, Hyde 3962, Knight 3987, Leclerc 4000, Lost 4012, O'Donnell 4059, Rodgers 4110, Stemberg 4161, Tara 4179, Valerio 4189, Welch 4202
Michigan: Ave 4225, Cold 4250, Cracchiolo 4263, Cracchiolo 4264, Kennedy 4360, LaMothe 4370, Langbo 4371, Riley 4419, **Sage 4427**, Sehn 4432, Stolaruk 4448, Timmis 4459, **Tracy 4462**, Vandomelen 4470, Wheeler 4479, Young 4490
Minnesota: 1988 4491, **A Better 4493**, Adams 4495, Barry 4511, Charity 4536, Christianson 4539, Cloverfields 4542, Dasburg 4545, Gardner 4568, Greycoach 4575, Grundhofer 4580, Kopp 4599, Koran 4600, Maas 4608, Morning 4627, O'Neil 4638, **O'Shaughnessy 4639**, Opus 4642, **Petters 4653**, Sieben 4682, Wolohan 4730
Missouri: Forster 4814, Hauck 4828, McDonnell 4863, Orscheln 4877, Schwartze 4898, Sullivan 4912, Sycamore 4915, Vatterott 4921
Montana: Browning 4933
Nebraska: Buckley 4947, Cope 4955, Dillon 4956, Eagle 4960, **Slosburg 5003**, Sunshine 5007

Nevada: Bennett 5021, Boyd 5023, Engelstad 5031, Fertitta 5033, Hawkins 5036, Ruvo 5060, Wiegand 5077
New Hampshire: Gale 5091, Martin 5097, **Penates 5099**
New Jersey: **Clare 5164**, Creamer 5171, D'Angelo 5175, Dealessandro 5178, Goldberg 5209, Hackett 5219, Healey 5227, Hidden 5233, **International 5252**, Katz 5270, KDK 5273, Kennedy 5276, Lebensfeld 5301, **Marcon 5317**, Olsen 5342, Post 5355, Simon 5405, Smith 5409, Union 5435, Visceglia 5441, **Vollmer 5443**
New Mexico: Coleman 5470
New York: **Altman 5544**, Avanessians 5580, Casey 5714, Chu 5754, Cox 5803, Dewar 5856, Dowling 5880, **East 5900**, Equinox 5935, Fatta 5947, **Halloran 6138**, Hansen 6142, Herdrich 6173, **Homeland 6199**, Hugoton 6210, **Humanitas 6212**, Johnson 6272, Kelleher 6307, **McCaddin 6513**, McCarthy 6515, Meehan 6523, **Meriwether 6535**, **Merlin 6536**, Metcalf 6541, Murphy 6597, O'Herron 6646, O'Neil 6649, O'Shea 6651, O'Toole 6654, Oestreicher 6656, Pascucci 6696, Phelan 6723, Pope 6740, Purchase 6755, Quick 6762, Riley 6809, Ritter 6813, Rudin 6879, Santa 6905, Schieffelin 6922, Schmeelk 6927, Siebens 6974, Steiniger 7065, Straus 7085, Textor 7131, Tully 7173, Weatherup 7222, Weir 7234, Young 7285
Ohio: Bell 7544, Bruening 7558, **Burleigh 7561**, Butler 7562, Cafaro 7563, Cardinal 7566, Castellini 7568, Conway 7588, Downing 7614, H.C.S. 7658, Hamlin 7661, Hatton 7665, Heimbinder 7670, **Kosar 7703**, LaValley 7708, Lehner 7709, M/B 7728, Mather 7736, McBride 7740, O'Neill 7782, Schott 7843, Sloat 7861, Stefanski 7868, Tetlak 7877, Toledo 7882, Trzcinski 7887, Williams 7907
Oklahoma: Collins 7929, Grace 7940
Oregon: Eiting 8011, Frank 8016, **Honzel 8021**, John 8026, Salem 8054
Pennsylvania: Bozzone 8114, Bradley 8115, Connelly 8157, DeGol 8167, Donahue 8174, Donnelly 8176, Eustace 8191, Kavanagh 8282, Kinsley 8290, Maguire 8321, Mandell 8322, Maronda 8325, Mengle 8347, Ortenzio 8366, Ryan 8416, St. Mary's 8454, Stabler 8455, Stewart 8460, Stine 8462, Young 8512
Rhode Island: McCarthy 8548, Routhier 8553
South Carolina: Kane 8596, **Security's 8609**
South Dakota: Dakota 8624, Opus 8628
Texas: Branch 8794, Cameron 8812, **Davis 8857**, Duda 8871, Enrico 8885, Haggar 8930, Haggar 8931, Haggerty 8932, Hankamer 8939, Hebert 8946, Keithley 8983, Kennedy 8988, McCoy 9039, Merrick 9055, **Mevatek 9056**, **MFI 9059**, Mott 9079, O'Connor 9095, South 9201, Sterling 9212, Strake 9215, **Swett 9221**
Virginia: Olsson 9491
Washington: Geneva 9592, Lauzier 9626, Lynn 9633, Snyder 9689, T.E.W. 9692, Tamaki 9695, Vidalakis 9698, Warren 9700
West Virginia: Hoffmann 9718
Wisconsin: Cudahy 9785, Fotsch 9802, Hess 9816, Ladish 9846, Ladish 9847, Managed 9857, Michels 9874, Reinhart 9909, Riordan 9911, Stone 9940, U.S. 9952

Roman Catholic federated giving programs

California: Burns 338, Cassin 365, Drum 470, Gross 621, Hayden 657, Murphy 928, **Muth 929**, Weyrich 1298
Colorado: Hill 1392
Delaware: Laffey 1725, Morania 1733, **Raskob 1741**
Florida: Abraham 1867, Amaturo 1873, Bastien 1892, Cascone 1926, Griffin 2036
Georgia: Amos 2316
Illinois: Katten 2826, Kazma 2827, McIntosh 2883, Walgreen 3052, Ward 3056
Indiana: Hux 3170
Maryland: Lawless 3671, Linehan 3678
Massachusetts: Rodgers 4110, Ruddy 4118
Michigan: **Sage 4427**

California: **American 217**, Amgen 219, Bechtel 270, **Beckman 272**, Blue 296, Brownlee 329, California 349, Callison 351, Confidence 411, Crail 426, Femino 501, **Foundation 530**, GenCorp 560, Hartley 653, **Hewlett 672**, **Kavli 748**, **Keck 750**, Koshland 777, Ludwick 829, **Ludwick 830**, Moore 912, **Moore 913**, Norris 940, Northrop 942, Noyce 944, **Packard 972**, Parsons 980, San Diego 1087, **Schlinger 1102**, Synopsys 1222, Synopsys 1223, Torrey 1239, Union 1250, Wallis 1276
Colorado: Kern 1402, **StorageTek 1460**
Connecticut: **Applera 1484**, Bodenwein 1497, **GE 1553**, Palmer 1621, **Praxair 1629**, Xerox 1680
Delaware: Common 1700, Rowland 1749, **Stroud 1757**
District of Columbia: **Lounsbery 1824**
Florida: Banbury 1889, Coulter 1954, **Flight 2002**
Georgia: Cox 2367
Hawaii: Kosasa 2549
Illinois: Energizer 2721, Galvin 2747, Martin 2874, McGraw 2882, Olin 2925, Tellabs 3034
Indiana: Community 3125
Iowa: **Pioneer 3324**
Kansas: Bane 3345
Kentucky: Foundation 3420
Louisiana: Community 3469
Maine: Libra 3546
Maryland: **Kluge 3663**
Massachusetts: Biogen 3806, **Bosack 3809**, Cabot 3823, Eastern 3886, Ellsworth 3892, Harrington 3943, Lowell 4015, **Technical 4180**
Michigan: Bay 4229, **DaimlerChrysler 4265**, DeVlieg 4275, Dow 4287, General 4320, **Kresge 4367**, Strosacker 4450
Minnesota: **ADC 4496**, Alworth 4499, **Patterson 4647**
Missouri: Boeing 4785, Interco 4835, **Kauffman 4843**, **McDonnell 4864**, Solutia 4907
Montana: Bair 4932
Nevada: Bennett 5021
New Hampshire: **Dorr 5086**
New Jersey: Buehler 5146, **Edison 5186**, **International 5252**, **Johnson 5263**, Knowles 5283, Merck 5327, Monius 5333, **Siemens 5400**, Tuchman 5429
New Mexico: Holt 5480, Santa Fe 5496
New York: Barker 5599, Bright 5664, Community 5780, **Dreyfus 5886**, Golden 6046, **Guggenheim 6118**, **Guggenheim 6119**, **Heineman 6165**, **IBM 6221**, **Memton 6529**, **NEC 6605**, New York 6617, New York 6619, Pfizer 6720, **Vetlesen 7196**
North Carolina: Duke 7360, Goodrich 7378, Kenan 7411, **Lowe's 7423**, **Nickel 7436**, North Carolina 7438, North Carolina 7439, Progress 7453
Ohio: **Durell 7616**, Huntington 7680, Jennings 7688, NFG 7776, Nordson 7781, Schlink 7839
Oregon: Intel 8022
Pennsylvania: Arete 8088, Arkema 8089, Bayer 8096, Buhl 8124, **Clive 8146**, Lehigh Valley 8303, Levis 8309, **Merck 8349**, **Pew 8377**, Rockwell 8408, **Templeton 8475**, **United 8488**, West 8500
Rhode Island: Champlin 8524, Daniels 8530
Texas: Bass 8777, Brown 8799, Elkins 8883, Fikes 8899, Gayden 8915, Hoblitzelle 8955, Jones 8975, Marathon 9028, Mitchell 9064, Moody 9070, National 9088, O'Donnell 9096, Onstead 9102, Phillips 9122, **Shell 9181**, Sturgis 9216
Utah: **Huntsman 9329**
Virginia: Jeffress 9442, **MCI 9471**
Washington: **Boeing 9560**, Murdock 9644, Simonyi 9686
Wisconsin: **Rath 9907**, **Rockwell 9912**, Zilber 9973
Wyoming: Ellbogen 9981

Science, association

Pennsylvania: Glencairn 8219

Science, equal rights

Oregon: Intel 8022
Pennsylvania: PPG 8394

Science, formal/general education

Alabama: **Vulcan 73**
California: **Bechtel 269**, **Chiron 383**, Fluor 523, McCarthy 868, Synopsys 1223
Connecticut: Boehringer 1498
Florida: Rayonier 2189
Georgia: **Scientific 2482**
Idaho: **Micron 2571**
Illinois: Abbott 2580, **Motorola 2906**
Iowa: **Rockwell 3328**
Kansas: Sprint 3395
Maryland: **Agilent 3563**
Massachusetts: Millipore 4040
Michigan: **ArvinMeritor 4224**, Ford 4307
Minnesota: **3M 4492**, **ADC 4496**, Xcel 4732
Missouri: Boeing 4785, **Monsanto 4868**
New Jersey: Alcatel 5110, PSEG 5361, Schering 5387
New York: Afognak 5525, New York 6617, **OSI 6670**, **Toshiba 7156**, **Toyota 7160**
Ohio: Nordson 7781, **OMNOVA 7789**
Oregon: Intel 8022, Mentor 8039
Pennsylvania: Bayer 8096, Comcast 8152, **Dominion 8173**, **PPG 8394**, Rees 8401, Tyco 8485
Texas: **ExxonMobil 8889**, Kodosky 9000, Texas 9232

Science, public education

California: California 349, **ChevronTexaco 380**
Maryland: Rathmann 3715
Missouri: Holekamp 4832
Oregon: Johnson 8027
Virginia: **Ames 9370**
Washington: Simonyi 9686

Science, public policy

District of Columbia: **Lounsbery 1824**

Science, research

California: **Agouron 196**, Jewett 718, Klein 765, **Maxfield 862**, San Diego 1087, **Seaver 1118**
Connecticut: Stone 1654
District of Columbia: Mazda 1828
Illinois: Brinson 2633
Iowa: Carver 3274, Maytag 3310
Maryland: Rathmann 3715
Massachusetts: Millipore 4040
Missouri: JSM 4841, **McDonnell 4864**
New Jersey: Brotherton 5145, **Vollmer 5443**
New York: **Chatterjee 5737**, Johnson 6271, **Mathers 6504**, Oishei 6660, **OSI 6670**, Simons 6989, **Sloan 7003**, Swartz 7112
Ohio: Community 7585
Oklahoma: Communities 7931
Pennsylvania: **Merck 8349**
Utah: **ALSAM 9302**
Virginia: **Three 9525**
Washington: Murdock 9644, Washington 9701

Science, single organization support

Ohio: Ferguson 7625

Secondary school/education

Alabama: Anderson 6
Arizona: Schwartz 137
California: Ackerman 193, Ahmanson 198, Al-Ameen 200, **American 217**, Atkinson 239, Bannerman 255, Barker 257, Burnham 337, Caruso 363, Chapman 374, Community 406, Confidence 411, Copley 416, Cortopassi 419, Crocker 429, Crummer 432, Dachs 435, **Day 447**, de Dampierre 448, Fitzpatrick 515, Fleishhacker 518, Foothills 526, Garaventa 553, Gellert 559, Genentech 563, Geschke 568, Herbst 669, Hills 674, Hofmann 683, Ingold 695, **Keck 750**, Kingsley 761, Koret 774, Lane 787, Lanni 789, Leonard 804, Littlefield 820, **M & T 837**, Magistro 847, Martin 860, Mayr

863, **McConnell 870**, Milken 898, Mosher 920, Muller 925, NBC 933, Norris 940, Oberndorf 950, Outrageous 967, Parsons 980, Philibosian 1003, Rising 1055, Sambar 1085, San Diego 1087, Seeno 1120, Segerstrom 1123, Shea 1143, Smith 1162, Steele 1189, Stuart 1206, Synopsys 1222, Synopsys 1223, Thornton 1236, Van Nuys 1262, Von der Ahe 1269, Ward 1278, Weingart 1288, Westly 1297, Wilson 1308, Witherbee 1312
Colorado: Aspen 1337, **Avenir 1339**, Beren 1342, Donnell 1368, Mater 1417, McCloskey 1419, McCormick 1420, Summit 1463, Taylor 1464, Trueblood 1466, Weckbaugh 1470, Williams 1474
Connecticut: Community 1515, Connecticut 1518, Larsen 1579, Mandeville 1596, Martin 1598, Oaklawn 1616, Palmer 1621, Phoenix 1627, **Seedlings 1645**, **Smart 1651**, Vik 1672, Woodward 1678, Zachs 1682
Delaware: Bartsch 1688, Cawley 1696, Crestlea 1701, Crystal 1702, **CTW 1703**, **Good 1715**, Laffey 1725, Marmot 1728, Mastronardi 1729, Repass 1742
District of Columbia: Cafritz 1780, Dweck 1790, Henry 1808, McGettigan 1829, Meyer 1834, Strong 1851
Florida: Banbury 1889, Bank 1890, **Berg 1903**, Caspersen 1927, Cobb 1935, **Davis 1964**, DiMare 1974, duPont 1983, Henriksen 2057, Kennedy 2088, Kleist 2095, Poe 2173, Ryder 2213, Selby 2230, Wahlert 2284, Winston 2302, Winter 2303
Georgia: Callaway 2337, Camp 2338, Campbell 2339, **Challenge 2344**, **Chesed 2348**, Coca 2350, Exposition 2380, Fraser 2390, Goizueta 2400, Lanier 2431, **Morris 2455**, Patterson 2460, Porter 2468, Robinson 2473, Snodgrass 2492, Tull 2500, WestPoint 2513, Williams 2514, WinShape 2520
Hawaii: Castle 2538, Wong 2560
Idaho: **Micron 2571**
Illinois: Bersted 2618, **Brach 2630**, Brewer 2632, Chicago 2661, Cless 2668, Coleman 2673, Community 2677, Dowdle 2709, Emerson 2719, Energizer 2721, Field 2728, Fry 2740, **Galashiels 2742**, Harrison 2791, Kaplan 2823, Keiser 2828, Kelly 2830, Kemper 2831, McNally 2885, McNamara 2886, **Norris 2917**, Omron 2926, Owens 2929, Pasquinelli 2933, Prentice 2947, Prince 2948, Seabury 2993, Sharpe 3002, Snite 3012, Walsh 3055, Ward 3056, White 3067
Indiana: Adams 3095, Ball 3103, **Cummins 3136**, Dekko 3142, Griffith 3158, Harrison 3161, Jones 3179, Marshall 3199, McAllister 3202, Moore 3207, Muselman 3209, Noyes 3216, Reynolds 3229, Scheumann 3235
Iowa: McElroy 3313
Kentucky: Fischer 3418, Gheens 3421, Justice 3431, Marshall 3438, Norton 3441, Reed 3447
Louisiana: Adams 3458, Baton Rouge 3462, Booth 3464, **Merkle 3500**, Pennington 3505, RosaMary 3507, Scott 3509, Taylor 3511, Young 3518, Zigler 3520
Maine: Alfond 3522, **Ford 3533**, Mulford 3551
Maryland: Commonweal 3596, Crane 3603, **Dean 3610**, **Hughes 3654**, Johnston 3657, Knott 3666, Krieger 3668, Myers 3698, Plitt 3706, Price 3709, Quinn 3713, Sheridan 3729
Massachusetts: Acushnet 3770, Boston 3812, Bristol 3816, Cabot 3825, Connell 3856, Corkin 3861, Cox 3863, Grimshaw 3934, Harrington 3943, Jacobson 3967, Karp 3974, Levy 4005, Mannion 4019, **Massiah 4027**, New 4053, O'Brien 4058, Roddy 4108, Rogers 4112, Schrafft 4133, Shipley 4143, **State 4158**, Sudbury 4173, Van Sloun 4190, Weld 4203, Wood 4207
Michigan: Binda 4233, Herrick 4341, Hurst 4344, Keeler 4355, **Kellogg 4357**, **Sage 4427**, **Skilling 4437**, Stonisch 4449, Van Andel 4467, Young 4490
Minnesota: 1988 4491, Alliss 4498, **Andreas 4504**, Bigelow 4519, Carlson 4532, Edelstein 4559, Greystone 4576, **O'Shaughnessy 4639**, Slaggie 4686, Southways 4688, **Toro 4702**
Mississippi: Ergon 4740
Missouri: Emerson 4809, Forster 4814, Green 4822, H & R 4823, Hall 4824, Kemper 4846, Kemper 4848,

Laclede 4852, McDonnell 4863, Orscheln 4877, Rosewood 4894, Sosland 4908, Sullivan 4912
Montana: First 4937
Nebraska: Arkoosh 4943, Dillon 4956
Nevada: **Bing 5022**, Cord 5029, Keyser 5039, Wiegand 5077
New Hampshire: **Penates 5099**
New Jersey: Cape 5153, **Ceres 5158**, Cowles 5170, Dodge 5181, Gabelli 5200, Geier 5204, Grassmann 5213, Hyde 5247, **James 5254**, Knowles 5283, Marianthi 5318, Martini 5319, Schering 5387, **Siemens 5400**
New Mexico: Holt 5480, Hubbard 5481, McCune 5488
New York: **Adjmi 5520**, Allwin 5538, Altman 5542, Altus 5547, Area 5564, **AXA 5584**, Baird 5591, **Baker 5594**, **Bay 5606**, Bernhard 5624, Booth 5651, Brownington 5677, Carvel 5710, Cohen 5767, **Dodge 5867**, Donaldson 5871, **Engelhard 5932**, Fatta 5947, **Forbes 5967**, **Ford 5970**, **Freeman 5980**, Frohring 5993, **Gelb 6011**, **Goldman 6056**, Goodfriend 6071, Gordon 6075, Gordon 6077, Green 6096, Greene 6099, **Hayden 6157**, Hayden 6158, Ingrassia 6230, **Initial 6231**, Israel 6240, Jephson 6258, Jesselson 6259, Katz 6295, **Keefe 6305**, Kellen 6308, Klein 6332, Link 6429, Lowenstein 6449, Macdonald 6468, Mars 6494, McCann 6514, Mercy 6534, Milstein 6556, Moody's 6569, **Morgan 6577**, Morse 6583, **NEC 6605**, New York 6616, New York 6620, **Newhouse 6623**, Nichols 6628, O'Neil 6649, Ohrstrom 6659, Oishei 6660, Palisano 6680, Parshelsky 6693, **Pforzheimer 6721**, Pope 6740, Rhodes 6792, Riley 6809, Rohatyn 6830, Roxe 6867, Ruffin 6880, Rumsey 6882, Silverman 6982, Sprague 7035, Stern 7071, Strypemonde 7089, **Tang 7122**, **Time 7142**, Tisch 7145, Townsend 7159, Turn 7174, Turner 7175, **United 7185**, Vernon 7195, **Walter 7211**, Weezie 7224, Weinberg 7230, Weiss 7236, Western 7248, Widgeon 7255, Winston 7267
North Carolina: Biddle 7317, Breeden 7324, Cannon 7335, Dickson 7355, Dover 7356, Dowd 7357, Finch 7366, Harvey 7393, Hommer 7400, Reynolds 7458, Stonecutter 7486, Winston 7507, Woodson 7509
North Dakota: MDU 7517
Ohio: Anderson 7529, Andrews 7530, Bicknell 7548, Britton 7556, Buenger 7560, Cleveland 7576, Coshocton 7593, Firman 7628, Frost 7642, GAR 7643, Gund 7657, Hoover 7675, Humphrey 7679, Jennings 7688, Jochum 7692, **Kosar 7703**, LaValley 7708, M/B 7728, Mather 7736, Noble 7778, Nord 7779, O'Neill 7782, Parker 7796, Reynolds 7818, Richland 7819, Robbins 7823, Schott 7843, Stocker 7870, **Timken 7880**, Van Wert 7891, White 7905, Wolfe 7915
Oklahoma: Rapp 7971, Richardson 7973
Oregon: Carpenter 8003, Jubitz 8029
Pennsylvania: Bristol 8118, Buhl 8124, Claneil 8144, Connelly 8157, Dietrich 8171, Dolfinger 8172, Donnelly 8176, Ellis 8184, Fisher 8205, Hillman 8250, IKON 8265, Kelly 8283, **Kennametal 8284**, **Knox 8294**, Laurel 8301, McCune 8331, Mengle 8347, Ortenzio 8366, Penn 8371, Rockwell 8408, Ryan 8416, Sherrerd 8439, Simonds 8442, Smith 8445, Snyder 8448, St. Mary's 8454, Stackpole 8456, Steinman 8458, Steinman 8459, Stewart 8460, Strawbridge 8466, Waters 8498
Rhode Island: Champlin 8524, Daniels 8530, Fain 8533, **Feinstein 8535**, **FM 8537**, Grinnell 8538, Kimball 8542, McAdams 8547
South Carolina: Hipp 8592, **Youths' 8621**
Tennessee: Benwood 8644, Caldwell 8649, Danner 8664, Haslam 8687, Lyndhurst 8703, Martin 8706, Tucker 8735
Texas: Alexander 8752, **Allbritton 8755**, Bailey 8771, Bass 8777, Brackenridge 8793, Cain 8808, Cain 8809, Cameron 8812, Cauthorn 8820, Circle 8829, Collins 8837, Constantin 8843, Dawley 8858, Elkins 8883, Ellwood 8884, Fair 8891, Fikes 8899, Fondren 8906, Haggar 8931, Hillcrest 8952, Hoblitzelle 8955, Kempner 8987, Looper 9016, Lyons 9024, McCrea 9040, McDermott 9043, O'Connor 9095, Peterson 9120, Progress 9133,

Rockwell 9154, Scott 9174, **Shell 9181**, **Smith 9194**, Sterling 9212, Strake 9215, Texas 9232, Trull 9240, Vale 9246, Vergara 9253, Watson 9266, West 9274
Utah: Bastian 9306, Browning 9308, Burton 9309
Vermont: **Green 9358**, Vermont 9361
Virginia: Beazley 9376, Camp 9382, Delmar 9410, Evans 9416, Folger 9418, Hylton 9440, Massey 9467, Perry 9495, Portsmouth 9498, Reynolds 9503
Washington: Ackerley 9547, Haas 9599, Snyder 9689, T.E.W. 9692
West Virginia: Bowen 9711, Hunnicutt 9720, Shott 9733
Wisconsin: Bryce 9769, Fleck 9799, Kohl 9838, Krause 9841, McBeath 9864, **Meehan 9868**, Milwaukee 9876, Pettit 9897, Phipps 9898, Schlegel 9919, Siebert 9927, Stuart 9942, West 9963

Sickle cell disease
Illinois: Kenny's 2835

Skin disorders
Illinois: Bunning 2641
New York: **Stiefel 7078**

Skin disorders research
New York: Johnson 6272, **Stiefel 7078**

Social entrepreneurship
Missouri: **Kauffman 4843**
Oregon: **NIKE 8046**
Pennsylvania: Baker 8092

Social sciences
Alabama: Brock 16
California: Burch 334, Columbia 399, Haynes 659, Sacramento 1080
Colorado: Schermer 1449, **Staley 1457**
Connecticut: Larsen 1579, **Lingnan 1587**, **Richardson 1632**, Rosenthal 1638
Delaware: **Stroud 1757**
Illinois: Community 2677, Retirement 2964
Indiana: Community 3132
Kansas: Garvey 3364
Maryland: **Brown 3579**
Massachusetts: Hopedale 3958, Marks 4024
Michigan: DeVos 4279, **Fetzer 4297**, **Rodney 4422**
Minnesota: **Cafesjian 4527**
Missouri: Craig 4800
New York: **Ford 5970**, **Grant 6092**, **Guggenheim 6118**, **Guggenheim 6119**, Kautz 6300, Littauer 6434, **Luce 6453**, **Ottinger 6674**, Pyewacket 6756, **Sage 6894**, **Starr 7048**
North Carolina: **Richardson 7461**
Pennsylvania: **Pew 8377**
Virginia: Lynchburg 9463
West Virginia: Kanawha 9723

Social sciences, equal rights
Tennessee: Assisi 8638

Social sciences, ethics
Tennessee: Assisi 8638

Social sciences, formal/general education
Massachusetts: Colombe 3852

Social sciences, government agencies
Massachusetts: Colombe 3852

Social sciences, interdisciplinary studies
New Mexico: Proteus 5495
New York: **Grant 6092**

Social sciences, public education
Texas: West 9274

Social sciences, public policy
Alaska: Alaska 79
Arizona: **Rodel 136**
California: Connolly 413, It 704
Connecticut: Lehrman 1584
Florida: Weiler 2290
Maine: Smith 3556
Massachusetts: Colombe 3852
Michigan: **H.I.S. 4334**
Missouri: **Humphreys 4833**
New Jersey: Hickory 5232
New York: Tisch 7144
Ohio: Jackson 7685, Thendara 7878
Texas: Sumners 9218
Utah: ALS 9301
Virginia: **Ames 9370**, **Chase 9391**
Wisconsin: Helfaer 9813

Social sciences, research
Michigan: **Fetzer 4297**
New York: **Grant 6092**, **Pioneer 6729**
Ohio: Jackson 7685
Virginia: **Chase 9391**
Washington: Klorfine 9619

Social work school/education
California: Hutto 693
Kansas: Rhoden 3383

Space/aviation
California: California 349
Florida: Schumann 2228
Michigan: Parish 4408
New Jersey: Buehler 5146
New York: Link 6428, Ueltschi 7181
North Carolina: Davis 7353
Pennsylvania: **United 8487**
Washington: **Boeing 9560**

Speech/hearing centers
Georgia: Ma-Ran 2439, Rollins 2475, Spray 2495, Woodruff 2522
Kentucky: Robinson 3449
Louisiana: Booth 3464
Michigan: Carls 4244
Nevada: Fairweather 5032
Ohio: Fleming 7631, Williamson 7908
Pennsylvania: **Oberkotter 8365**, Smith 8445
Washington: Anderson 9551

Spine disorders
California: Windfall 1309
Georgia: Carlos 2340, JBS 2420, Lanier 2431
New York: **Spinal 7031**

Spine disorders research
New York: Kiernan 6321

Spirituality
California: Angell 224
Michigan: Lachimi 4369
Missouri: **Hana 4827**

Student services/organizations

Connecticut: Nevas 1608
Michigan: **Stoddard 4447**
New York: Heckscher 6164
Pennsylvania: **PPG 8394**
Texas: Kincaid 8993
Wisconsin: Glover 9805

Students, sororities/fraternities

New York: Sigma 6977
Texas: Crain 8851

Substance abuse, prevention

Alabama: Community 24
California: Amerman 218, Community 401
Delaware: Delaware 1706
Florida: Gainesville 2015, Hayes 2052, **Scaife 2220**
Georgia: **Hanley 2405**
Illinois: Brewer 2632
Massachusetts: Crawford 3867
Michigan: Berrien 4231
Missouri: Roblee 4893
Nevada: **Hilton 5037**
New Jersey: Burke 5149, PSEG 5361
New Mexico: Santa Fe 5496
New York: Achelis 5513, Bodman 5647, Carmel 5705, Turn 7174
Ohio: **OMNOVA 7789**, Reinberger 7815
Pennsylvania: Blue 8112, Staunton 8457
South Dakota: Sioux Falls 8630
Texas: Goldsbury 8920, Hebert 8946
Virginia: Williamsburg 9541

Substance abuse, services

Arizona: Arizona 87
Arkansas: Wal-Mart 184
California: Anaheim 220, Atkinson 239, Copley 416, Fireman's 510, Gellert 559, Irmas 697, Irvine 699, Lytel 836, Norris 940, Patron 983, Peninsula 989, San Diego 1087, San Francisco 1088, Santa Barbara 1093, Sierra 1151, Sonora 1178, Warren 1279, Weingart 1288
Colorado: Boettcher 1344, **Daniels 1362**, El Pomar 1374
Connecticut: Bodenwein 1497, Community 1515, Community 1517, Connecticut 1518
District of Columbia: Cafritz 1780, Meyer 1834
Florida: Bastien 1892, Pinellas 2170, Rayonier 2189
Georgia: Patterson 2460
Illinois: Community 2677, Field 2728, Olin 2925, **Tuohy 3041**, **Woodbury 3082**
Indiana: Community 3125, Lafayette 3188, Welborn 3254, West 3256
Iowa: Principal 3326, Siouxland 3332
Kansas: Hutchinson 3368, Topeka 3400
Louisiana: **Merkle 3500**
Maryland: Abell 3559, GEICO 3634
Massachusetts: Community 3855, Ellsworth 3892, Parker 4069
Michigan: Binda 4233, Ford 4304, Fremont 4315, Jackson 4347, Skillman 4438
Minnesota: Butler 4525, Ordean 4643
Nevada: Fairweather 5032, Nevada 5047
New Hampshire: Fuller 5090, **Linnell 5096**
New Jersey: Borden 5138, Cowles 5170, Hyde 5247, **Johnson 5265**, McGraw 5323, Princeton 5357
New Mexico: Frost 5476, Maddox 5487, McCune 5488
New York: Glickenhaus 6042, Hoyt 6203, Joy 6276, **MetLife 6542**, New York 6613, Northern 6638, Northern 6639, O'Connor 6645, Steele 7053, Tower 7158, Wendt 7243, Western 7248
North Carolina: Cumberland 7349, Halton 7386, North Carolina 7438, Reynolds 7457, Triangle 7496
North Dakota: Stern 7521
Ohio: Coshocton 7593, Hamilton 7660, Reuter 7817, Richland 7819, Stark 7867, Troy 7886, Van Wert 7891, Woodruff 7917
Oregon: Carpenter 8003, Jackson 8024, Johnson 8027

Pennsylvania: Beaver 8098, Buck 8123, Connelly 8157, Dolfinger 8172, Eden 8182, Fourjay 8209, Huston 8263, Rockwell 8408, Snee 8446, Stackpole 8456, Staunton 8457
Rhode Island: CARLISLE 8521
South Carolina: Central 8577
Tennessee: Davis 8665
Texas: Abell 8749, Cain 8809, Cameron 8812, Coastal 8833, Constantin 8843, El Paso 8882, Fasken 8895, Hillcrest 8952, Kempner 8987, Meadows 9049, San Antonio 9166, **Shell 9181**, Speas 9206, Sterling 9212, Temple 9227, Trull 9240, Wright 9294
Utah: Eccles 9320
Vermont: Vermont 9361
Virginia: Delmar 9410, Kellar 9449, Norfolk 9484, Portsmouth 9499, Williamsburg 9541
Washington: Casey 9566, Community 9571, Glaser 9594, Norcliffe 9650, Tacoma 9693
West Virginia: Kanawha 9723
Wisconsin: Community 9776, Evjue 9797, McBeath 9864, Milwaukee 9876, Northwestern 9884, Stackner 9934

Substance abuse, treatment

California: Amerman 218, Auen 242, Markkula 856, Riley 1052, Wrather 1321
Florida: Six 2236
Georgia: **Hanley 2405**
Illinois: Bellebyron 2615, D.H.R. 2695, **Woodbury 3082**
Minnesota: Sieben 4682
New Jersey: Schreyer 5389, Tolchin 5428
New York: **Burpee 5690**, Turn 7174
Ohio: Horvitz 7677, Reinberger 7815
Oklahoma: Bailey 7923
Pennsylvania: Staunton 8457
Texas: Proctor 9132
Virginia: Williamsburg 9541
Washington: Lynn 9633
Wisconsin: Beasley 9755, Fleck 9799

Substance abusers

California: Five 516

Surgery

New Jersey: Harrison 5225

Surgery research

New Jersey: Integra 5251

Teacher school/education

California: JL 720, **Peterson 996**, Stuart 1206, Union 1250
Colorado: Rose 1445
Delaware: Robinson 1744
Hawaii: Castle 2538
Illinois: Grand 2769, McDougal 2881
Massachusetts: Pierce 4084
Missouri: Roblee 4893
New Jersey: Knowles 5283
New York: **Carnegie 5707**, Heckscher 6164, Lipmanson 6431
North Carolina: Progress 7453
Texas: Sumners 9218, Vale 9246
Virginia: Moore 9478

Telecommunications

District of Columbia: Benton 1773

Telecommunications, electronic messaging services

California: Kahle 738
Washington: **Gates 9591**, **RealNetworks 9672**

Theological school/education

Alabama: Lowder 42
Arizona: Jazzbird 111
California: **Atkinson 240**, **Bolthouse 301**, Chais 371, Everlasting 490, Gold 589, Jameson 710, **Joseph 730**, Long 827, Menlo 885, **Rivendell 1056**, Shapiro 1137, **Stewardship 1197**, Swanson 1216, Van Daele 1258
Colorado: Beren 1342, **Crowell 1361**, Hill 1392
Connecticut: Bauer 1489, Nirenberg 1613
Delaware: Evelyn 1712
Florida: Catlin 1929, **Chatlos 1932**, **Davis 1964**, Edelman 1987, Forbes 2006, **Morris 2145**, Taplin 2264, Williams 2299
Georgia: Amos 2315, Pittulloch 2464
Hawaii: Atherton 2532
Illinois: Bere 2616, Butler 2646, Combs 2674, Domanada 2705, Dowdle 2709, Grace 2766, Huizenga 2806, Leibowitz 2854, Parmer 2932, Rajchenbach 2958, Susman 3030
Indiana: Lilly 3194, **Master 3201**, Muselman 3209
Iowa: **Andringa 3262**, Grubb 3289, Heerema 3292
Kansas: Morris 3378
Louisiana: Booth 3464
Maine: Gallagher 3535
Maryland: **Berman 3572**, **Calvin 3581**, Denit 3615, Hoffberger 3652, Lerner 3675, **Smith 3736**, Tucker 3750
Massachusetts: Bradley 3814, DeFreitas 3876, Ford 3913, Hendrickson 3947, Manzi 4021, SDSC 4134, **Uperetes 4188**
Michigan: **DeWitt 4280**, **Foundation 4309**, Frankel 4314, Granger 4329, Jurries 4350, **McDonald 4388**, **Myers 4402**, Shepherd 4435, Spoelhof 4443
Minnesota: Greycoach 4575, Hallett 4582, McVay 4620
Mississippi: Hancock 4746
Missouri: Cornelsen 4799, Green 4822, Rosewood 4894
Nevada: Christian 5026
New Hampshire: Martin 5097
New Jersey: Armour 5116, Long 5310, Mamiye 5316, Roth 5377
New York: **American 5554**, Chehebar 5741, Cohen 5767, Englander 5933, **Friends 5991**, Gordon 6077, **Hearst 6161**, **Hearst 6162**, Jesseleson 6259, Kalter 6284, Kaplan 6288, Lopatin 6446, **Luce 6453**, **Mayer 6509**, **McCaddin 6513**, Meyer 6545, Milstein 6556, MRM 6592, Nakash 6600, **Nash 6602**, **Palmer 6682**, Propp 6749, Rausman 6775, Rifkind 6806, **Ripplewood 6812**, Rose 6833, RZH 6885, SO 7015, Stein 7055, Winston 7267, Zichron 7298
North Carolina: Harris 7390, Smith 7476, Woodson 7509
Ohio: Ferguson 7625, Jackson 7685, **Kosar 7703**, Lindner 7716, Parker 7796, **Sapirstein 7834**, Schottenstein 7844
Oklahoma: Crawley 7934, Oxley 7968, Presbyterian 7969
Pennsylvania: Brossman 8120, **Carpenter 8131**, **Cornerstone 8159**, Dolfinger 8172, **Firstfruits 8203**, Neubauer 8363, Rubin 8415, Weiss 8499
South Carolina: Hopewell 8593
Tennessee: Belz 8643, Washington 8741, West 8742
Texas: Baugh 8781, Butt 8804, **C.I.O.S. 8805**, Castle 8818, Clements 8832, Gale 8913, Sparrow 9204, Trull 9240, Weiser 9272
Utah: **ALSAM 9302**
Virginia: **Mustard 9481**
West Virginia: Stout 9734
Wisconsin: Crump 9783, Davis 9787, JKO 9822, McQueen 9866, Merten 9873, Styberg 9944

Theology

Massachusetts: Endowment 3895
New York: **Luce 6453**

Transportation

California: PacifiCare 971, Teichert 1231

Colorado: El Pomar 1374
Connecticut: Bodenwein 1497, Palmer 1621
Illinois: Grand 2769
Maryland: Baltimore 3568
Michigan: **DaimlerChrysler 4265**
Minnesota: McKnight 4617
Missouri: Truman 4919
Pennsylvania: Dolfinger 8172
Texas: Meadows 9049
Washington: Bullitt 9563

Urban League

Puerto Rico: **FNZ 8514**

Urban/community development

Alabama: Webb 75
California: Columbia 399, Hewlett 671, Price 1016, Sacramento 1080, San Francisco 1088
Connecticut: Donchian 1531, Fairfield 1537
District of Columbia: Meyer 1834
Florida: Bank 1890
Georgia: Jinks 2422
Illinois: Borwell 2627, **Burnett 2645**, Community 2677, Firestone 2729, Polk 2946, Steans 3021, White 3067
Kentucky: Brown 3409, C.E. 3412, Young 3455
Maine: Maine 3548
Maryland: **Casey 3585**
Massachusetts: Babson 3787, Boston 3812, **Bruner 3819**, Eaton 3888, Hyams 3961, McDonnell 4031, Walske 4196
Michigan: Community 4252, DTE 4289, Frey 4316, Hudson 4343, Monroe 4396, **Mott 4399**
Minnesota: Bell 4514, Graco 4573, **Homeownership 4587**
Missouri: Gateway 4817, H & R 4823, Hall 4824, Kansas 4842
New Jersey: Community 5167, **International 5252**, PSEG 5361, Victoria 5440
New York: **Abelard 5508**, Clark 5761, **Ford 5970**, **JPMorgan 6277**, **Surdna 7103**, **U.S. 7180**
North Carolina: Cumberland 7349, Triangle 7496
Ohio: Barberton 7539, Cleveland 7576, Cornerstone 7592, First 7629, Gund 7657, Murphy 7769, Nord 7779, **OMNOVA 7789**, Stark 7867, Youngstown 7920
Pennsylvania: Dolfinger 8172, McCune 8332, Mellon 8346, Penn 8371, **Pew 8377**, Philadelphia 8378, Sovereign 8451, Wachovia 8494
Tennessee: Benwood 8644, Community 8660, Tonya 8734
Texas: Meadows 9049, Swinney 9222
Virginia: **Blue 9379**
Wisconsin: Johnson 9823, Milwaukee 9876, Northwestern 9884, Sensient 9922

Venture philanthropy

California: **Google 606**
New York: Blue 5640

Veterinary medicine

California: Craig 425
Kentucky: Keeneland 3432
Nevada: Wendy's 5076

Veterinary medicine, hospital

California: Oppenheimer 955
Florida: Adler 1871
New York: Krimendahl 6359, **Pearson 6701**, **Silfen 6980**

Visual arts

Alabama: Community 25
Arizona: Dee 94

California: Ahmanson 198, **Baker 252**, **Christensen 384**, Community 406, **Coyne 424**, Femino 501, Flagg 517, Fleishhacker 518, Fluor 523, **Getty 570**, Gross 621, LLWW 824, Miller 901, **Nimoy 938**, Norton 943, Oppenheimer 955, Osher 961, Rotasa 1070, Sacramento 1080, San Diego 1087, Sonora 1178, Steele 1189, Webb 1285, Wornick 1320
Colorado: Boettcher 1344, El Pomar 1374, Gates 1380, Summit 1463
Connecticut: Bodenwein 1497, **Kossak 1576**, Martin 1598
Florida: Bank 1890, Community 1948, Dade 1957, Darden 1960, FPL 2010, **Samstag 2214**, Selby 2230
Georgia: Cox 2367, Exposition 2380, Livingston 2435, Moore 2451, SunTrust 2496, Williams 2514
Illinois: Abelson 2581, Alphawood 2589, Cheney 2658, Chicago 2661, Community 2677, Dunard 2712, Kaplan 2823, Lea 2850, Sara 2982, **Shifting 3006**, **Tuohy 3041**
Indiana: Mutual 3210, Vectren 3249, Wayne 3253
Iowa: Krause 3302, Maytag 3309, McElroy 3313
Kansas: Hutchinson 3368, Salina 3387, Sprint 3395
Kentucky: Rosenthal 3450
Louisiana: Booth 3464
Maryland: Abramson 3561, Casey 3586, **Fairchild 3627**, Hecht 3645, **Hendricks 3647**, MARPAT 3684, Rouse 3724
Massachusetts: Ellsworth 3892, High 3950, Johnson 3970, Robbins 4106
Michigan: Ann Arbor 4221, Bay 4229, Fremont 4315, Frey 4316, Schlafer 4429, Skillman 4438
Minnesota: Athwin 4508, Bush 4524, Duluth 4556, General 4570, Jerome 4595, Marbrook 4612, Southways 4688, **SUPERVALU 4695**, **Wood 4731**
Missouri: American 4773, Gateway 4817, H & R 4823, Kemper 4847
Montana: **Edwards 4936**
Nebraska: Woods 5018
Nevada: Wiegand 5077
New Hampshire: Trust 5103
New Jersey: Cowles 5170, Dodge 5181, **Johnson 5263**
New Mexico: **Lannan 5484**, McCune 5488, Santa Fe 5496, Taos 5498
New York: Allwin 5538, **American 5553**, Barker 5600, Clark 5761, **Gilman 6033**, Goldsmith 6060, **Guggenheim 6119**, **Hauser 6155**, **Heineman 6165**, **Kress 6357**, L and L 6366, Lehman 6397, Levy 6413, Link 6429, **Lipchitz 6430**, **Luce 6453**, Mars 6494, MAT 6503, Neuberger 6611, New York 6619, **Pollock 6736**, Reed 6782, Rose 6838, Sheldon 6966, **Solow 7020**, **Tiffany 7138**, **Trust 7168**, **Warhol 7215**, Wendt 7243, Western 7248, Wunsch 7281
North Carolina: Triangle 7496
North Dakota: Leach 7516
Ohio: Charities 7569, Cleveland 7576, **Kettering 7698**, Morgan 7762, Murphy 7769, Reinberger 7815, Stark 7867, Watson 7896, Youngstown 7920
Oklahoma: Kerr 7949, Kirkpatrick 7952
Oregon: Carpenter 8003, Mentor 8039
Pennsylvania: **Annenberg 8084**, Baker 8092, Byers' 8127, Claneil 8144, Dietrich 8170, Heinz 8244, Hillman 8251, Hillman 8252, Independence 8266, Mandell 8322, **Pew 8377**, Safeguard 8418, Smith 8445, Speyer 8453
Rhode Island: Charlesmead 8525
Tennessee: Atticus 8639, Frist 8679, Gordon 8683, Hamico 8684
Texas: Cain 8809, Hoblitzelle 8955, Hudson 8962, Kempner 8987, Marcus 9029, Reynolds 9145, Rockwell 9154, San Antonio 9166, **Shell 9181**, Sterling 9222, Wright 9294
Utah: Caine 9310, Eccles 9319, Eccles 9320, Lawson 9331
Virginia: Delmar 9410, Kanter 9445
Washington: Blue 9559, Community 9571, **Kongsgaard 9620**, Kreielsheimer 9621, Martin 9634, Norcliffe 9650
West Virginia: Tucker 9736

Wisconsin: Johnson 9823, Joy 9828, Kohler 9840, Mead 9867, Milwaukee 9876

Visual arts, architecture

Arizona: Arizona 87
California: **Getty 570**, **LEF 799**
Illinois: Alphawood 2589, **Graham 2767**, Gray 2771, Hyatt 2810, Wilemal 3070
Indiana: **Cummins 3136**
Massachusetts: **Bruner 3819**
Michigan: Binda 4233
Missouri: Gateway 4817
New York: Chisholm 5753, O'Connor 6645, Rosenblum 6850, Solow 7019
Pennsylvania: Heinz 8244
Rhode Island: Felicia 8536
Texas: Meadows 9049
Washington: Norcliffe 9650

Visual arts, art conservation

California: Getty 570
Michigan: Community 4258
New York: **Tiffany 7137**
Virginia: Katzen 9446

Visual arts, design

Alabama: Saks 61
California: **Coyne 424**
Illinois: Driehaus 2710
New Jersey: Point 5353
New York: **Donghia 5872**

Visual arts, drawing

New York: Woodner 7277

Visual arts, painting

Florida: Levine 2113
New York: Avery 5581, **Rothschild 6866**

Visual arts, photography

Georgia: Lubo 2438
Illinois: Krueck 2846
New Jersey: **Puffin 5362**
New York: Apfelbaum 5561, Greenhill 6101, **Mapplethorpe 6485**, **Rothschild 6866**, Werblow 7245, **Zenkel 7295**
Ohio: Women's 7916
Pennsylvania: Ames 8080

Visual arts, sculpture

New York: Avery 5581, **Rothschild 6866**
Texas: Nasher 9086

Vocational education

California: **American 217**, Atkinson 239, Cisco 388, Cowell 423, Lux 834, Nissan 939, Roberts 1058, Sacramento 1080, San Diego 1087, Soda 1173
Colorado: El Pomar 1374
Connecticut: Connecticut 1518
District of Columbia: Jovid 1814, Lehrman 1821, Meyer 1834
Florida: Bank 1890
Georgia: **Georgia 2397**
Illinois: CNA 2670, Galvin 2747, Polk 2946, Woodward 3085
Kansas: Hansen 3366
Massachusetts: Alden 3776, Ratshesky 4095, **State 4158**
Michigan: **DaimlerChrysler 4265**
Minnesota: **Fuller 4567**, **Pentair 4649**, Sundet 4694
Missouri: Green 4822, H & R 4823
New Mexico: McCune 5488

New York: Cummings 5815, **de Hirsch 5840**, Everett 5941, Goldman 6053, Heckscher 6164, O'Connor 6645, Ross 6862, Rubinstein 6876, Statler 7050
North Carolina: Cumberland 7349, Duke 7360, Halton 7386, **Lowe's 7423**, Triangle 7496
Ohio: Murphy 7769, Richland 7819, Troy 7886
Oregon: Johnson 8027
Pennsylvania: Dolfinger 8172, Hill 8248, Scranton 8431, Stackpole 8456
Texas: Constantin 8843, **Cooper 8846**, Hillcrest 8952, Hoblitzelle 8955
Virginia: CarMax 9385, **Gannett 9428**
Washington: Glaser 9594, Norcliffe 9650
Wisconsin: Alliant 9742, Nelson 9882

Vocational education, post-secondary
Illinois: Dillon 2704
Michigan: Grand Haven 4325
Virginia: Kogod 9452

Voluntarism promotion
California: Clorox 389, Crocker 429, Disney 456, Fireman's 510, Fluor 523, Irvine 698, **McConnell 870**, PacifiCare 971, Sacramento 1080, San Diego 1087, San Francisco 1088, Sonora 1178
Colorado: El Pomar 1374, Qwest 1443
Connecticut: Bodenwein 1497, Community 1517
District of Columbia: Cafritz 1780, **CityBridge 1783**, Meyer 1834
Florida: Beveridge 1907, FPL 2010, Rayonier 2189
Georgia: **UPS 2503**
Illinois: Community 2677, **JMR 2818**
Indiana: Community 3125, Lilly 3194, Whitley 3258
Kansas: Hutchinson 3368, Security 3390
Maryland: Lockheed 3682, MARPAT 3684, Sylvan 3741
Massachusetts: Boston 3812, Community 3855, Lowell 4014
Michigan: Fetzer 4298, Grand Rapids 4326, **Kellogg 4357**, **Mott 4399**
Minnesota: Bremer 4523, **Fuller 4567**, Rochester 4668
New Jersey: Campbell 5151, **International 5252**, Johnson 5265, **KPMG 5288**
New York: Everett 5941, Northern 6638, Rochester 6823
North Carolina: Cumberland 7349, Duke 7360, Reynolds 7458, Triangle 7496
Ohio: Cincinnati 7574, Columbus 7580, Mayerson 7739, Stocker 7870
Oregon: Johnson 8027, Oregon 8049
Pennsylvania: **Carnegie 8130**, Comcast 8152, Dolfinger 8172, **Pew 8377**, Scranton 8431, Stackpole 8456
Rhode Island: Rhode Island 8551
Tennessee: Frist 8679
Texas: Abell 8749, Meadows 9049, Speas 9206
Virginia: **Gannett 9428**, **Oak 9488**
Washington: Community 9571, Norcliffe 9650, Tacoma 9693
Wisconsin: Sensient 9922, **Thrivent 9949**
Wyoming: Wyoming 10000

Welfare policy/reform
California: Stuart 1206
Illinois: Woods 3084
New York: Achelis 5513
Pennsylvania: Connelly 8157

Women
Alabama: Hearin 37
Arizona: Halle 103
California: Atkinson 239, Bannerman 255, California 345, Carsey 361, Cohen 393, Community 406, Deutsch 451, Fireman's 510, Grove 625, Gruber 626, Gumbiner 631, Irvine 699, **Kaiser 739**, **Living 821**, Norris 940, Norton 943, Ralphs 1029, San Diego 1087, Soda 1173, Sonora 1178, **Streisand 1204**, Taper 1226, Ventura 1264, Wohlford 1315

Colorado: Boettcher 1344, Community 1359, JFM 1397, Marisco 1416, Weckbaugh 1470
Connecticut: **Aetna 1479**, Bodenwein 1497, Community 1517, Culpeper 1521, **Ettinger 1536**, International 1571, Larrabee 1578, **Xerox 1680**
Delaware: **Gynesis 1717**, Seevak 1752
District of Columbia: Beech 1771, Cafritz 1780, **Hill 1809**, Meyer 1834, True 1854
Florida: Bank 1890, Bush 1922, Ds 1976, Kennedy 2088, Martin 2130, Rayonier 2189, Taylor 2267, Wilson 2300
Georgia: AEC 2310, AGL 2312, Brown 2331, Community 2355, ING 2418, Williams 2515
Illinois: Appleton 2599, **ARIA 2600**, Chicago 2661, Girl's 2757, Guthman 2776, **Hull 2807**, Kipper 2840, **Monticello 2904**, Morton 2905, New 2912, **Niamogue 2914**, Northern 2918, Polk 2946, **Relations 2963**, Sara 2982, **Shifting 3006**, Washington 3058, Winfrey 3077
Indiana: Health 3164, **Lilly 3192**, Pulliam 3224
Kansas: Security 3390
Kentucky: J & L 3429
Louisiana: Baton Rouge 3462, Community 3469
Maine: **Oak 3552**
Maryland: Abell 3560, **Agilent 3563**
Massachusetts: Ashton 3782, Association 3783, Boston 3811, Boston 3812, Chahara 3843, Community 3855, Foundation 3916, Gerard 3923, Goldberg 3927, Grinspoon 3935, High 3950, Hoche 3954, Lee 4001, New 4054, Perpetual 4078, **Schooner 4131**, Swanee 4174, Swartz 4175, **TJX 4183**
Michigan: Grand Rapids 4326, Knight 4364, Nokomis 4404
Minnesota: Andersen 4502, Beim 4513, Bell 4514, Bremer 4523, Bush 4524, Duluth 4556, McVay 4620, Perlman 4651, Phillips 4655, Sexton 4679, WCA 4718
Missouri: Butler 4793, **Deer 4804**, Green 4822, Roblee 4893, Trio 4918
Nebraska: **Global 4967**, Lozier 4988
Nevada: Nevada 5047
New Jersey: Alcatel 5110, Amboy 5112, Borden 5138, Cowles 5170, Healey 5227, Knight 5281, Lear 5300, MCJ 5324, **Newcombe 5338**, **Rippel 5368**, Schering 5387
New Mexico: Frost 5476, McCune 5488, Santa Fe 5496
New York: **Abelard 5508**, **Bristol 5666**, **Bydale 5694**, **Citigroup 5755**, Claiborne 5758, Daphne 5830, Darivoff 5831, **Derossi 5853**, Dobkin 5866, Dreyfus 5887, **Ford 5970**, Goldenson 6047, Gorman 6078, **Hauser 6155**, **Heineman 6165**, Hilfiger 6183, Jewish 6260, Jones 6274, Joy 6276, LCU 6387, **Macy 6471**, Moody's 6569, **NoVo 6641**, O'Connor 6645, Partridge 6695, **Pearson 6701**, Peco 6703, Revson 6789, Richardson 6797, Rochester 6823, **Rubin 6872**, Rubinstein 6876, Sasco 6907, Siebert 6975, Silver 6981, Sister 6994, **Spirit 7033**, Tisch 7147, **Tortuga 7155**, Woodcock 7273
North Carolina: Cumberland 7349, North Carolina 7438, Reynolds 7458, Triangle 7496
Ohio: Akron 7526, Britton 7556, Bruening 7558, Columbus 7580, Community 7582, **Federated 7624**, **Goatie 7651**, Greene 7653, Gund 7657, Kroger 7705, Levin 7712, Morgan 7760, Murphy 7769, Richland 7819, White 7905, Women's 7916
Oklahoma: Communities 7931, McGee 7957
Oregon: Holmes 8020, Intel 8022, Jackson 8024, Wessinger 8067
Pennsylvania: **Alcoa 8075**, Blue 8112, Byers' 8127, Chester 8141, CIGNA 8143, Claneil 8144, Connelly 8157, Dolfinger 8172, Eden 8182, FISA 8204, Heinz 8240, Hillman 8249, Hillman 8250, Simonds 8442, Smith 8443, Smith 8445
Rhode Island: Citizens 8527
Tennessee: Community 8660
Texas: CH 8823, Cockrell 8835, Community 8841, Edwards 8880, El Paso 8882, Frees 8909, Kahn 8980, Lightner 9012, Lowe 9020, Mankoff 9027, McCoy 9038, NAH 9084, Penney 9115, Phillips 9122, **RGK 9146**, Simmons 9188, Smith 9196,

Speas 9206, Sterling 9212, Texas 9232, Waco 9255
Utah: Eccles 9320
Vermont: **Ben 9355**
Virginia: Arlington 9371, **Gannett 9428**, Lynchburg 9463, **Oak 9488**, Rosenthal 9508
Washington: Community 9571, **Kongsgaard 9620**, Norcliffe 9650, Washington 9702
West Virginia: Kanawha 9723
Wisconsin: Charter 9772, Community 9776, Community 9778, Cudahy 9785, Delavan 9790, Meng 9870, Oshkosh 9885

Women's studies
New York: King 6324

Women, centers/services
Alaska: Rasmuson 85
California: Alafi 201, Allequash 202, Arbus 231, **Arkay 235**, Chintu 382, Community 406, Community 407, **Firelight 509**, Five 516, Flora 521, Gruber 626, Gumbiner 631, Listwin 819, **Marisla 855**, Moonwalk 911, Norris 940, Norton 943, San Diego 1087, Shea 1141, Soda 1173, Sonora 1178
Colorado: Boettcher 1344, Chambers 1354, Weckbaugh 1470
Connecticut: Bodenwein 1497, Community 1517, Larrabee 1578
District of Columbia: Cafritz 1780, Meyer 1834
Florida: Bank 1890, Eckerd 1986, Martin 2130, Moore 2142, Pinellas 2170, Wilson 2300
Georgia: Community 2355, Patterson 2460
Illinois: **Allen 2587**, Chicago 2661, Cressey 2689, Polk 2946, Rich 2967, **Shifting 3006**, Sirius 3010, Woods 3083
Kentucky: Harris 3424, J & L 3429
Louisiana: Baton Rouge 3462
Maryland: Abell 3560, Hahn 3643, Osprey 3703
Massachusetts: Ashton 3782, Boston 3812, Community 3855, Goldberg 3927, High 3950, Hoche 3954, Miller 4039, Rubenstein 4116, Stearns 4159, Walske 4196
Michigan: Dow 4288, Grand Rapids 4326, Hahn 4335, Knight 4364, Nokomis 4404
Minnesota: Ankeny 4505, Beim 4513, Bremer 4523, Butler 4525, Minneapolis 4623
Missouri: Green 4822, Roblee 4893
Nebraska: Lozier 4988
Nevada: Nevada 5047, Redfield 5055
New Hampshire: Gale 5091
New Jersey: Borden 5138, **Ceres 5158**, Cowles 5170, Knight 5281, **Wall 5445**
New Mexico: Frost 5476, McCune 5488
New York: **Abelard 5508**, Corning 5794, Dobkin 5866, Dreyfus 5887, **Ford 5970**, Grandison 6087, **Heineman 6165**, Lincoln 6423, New York 6613, **NoVo 6641**, O'Connor 6645, Rochester 6823, Siebert 6975, Sister 6994, Straus 7084, **Tortuga 7155**, Western 7248
North Carolina: Coffey 7339, Cumberland 7349, North Carolina 7438, Reynolds 7458, Triangle 7496
Ohio: Brennan 7554, Britton 7556, Columbus 7580, Gund 7657, Murphy 7769, Richland 7819, Schmidlapp 7840, Stocker 7870, Wohlgemuth 7913, Women's 7916
Oregon: Boyd 8000, Jackson 8024, Johnson 8027
Pennsylvania: Byers' 8127, Connelly 8157, Dolfinger 8172, FISA 8204, Hodge 8254, Pilgrim 8383, Smith 8443, Smith 8445
Rhode Island: Chace 8523
South Carolina: TSC 8618
Texas: Beal 8783, Edwards 8880, El Paso 8882, Lockheed 9015, Lowe 9020, O'Quinn 9097, Sidhu 9185, Simmons 9189, Smith 9196, Sparrow 9205, Speas 9206, Waco 9255, Waggoner 9256
Utah: Bastian 9306, Eccles 9320
Virgin Islands: Prosser 9364
Virginia: Lynchburg 9463

Washington: Channel 9568, Community 9571, Horizons 9608, **Kongsgaard 9620**, OneFamily 9654, Washington 9702
West Virginia: Kanawha 9723
Wisconsin: Delavan 9790, Kettering 9835, Milwaukee 9876, Pettit 9897

YM/YWCAs & YM/YWHAs

Alabama: Finlay 33, Lowder 42, Mitchell 53, Stallworth 64
California: Adams 194, Auen 242, Beattie 267, Brandenburg 316, Brenner 321, Burnham 337, Chambers 372, Davidson 445, Jackson 706, Jerome 717, Klein 764, Martin 860, Phelps 1002, Preuss 1015, Ryan 1075, **Saturno 1097**, Sexton 1132, Tomlinson 1238, Wilkes 1306
Colorado: **Benson 1341**, Schramm 1451
Connecticut: Cohen 1512, Roberts 1635, Rose 1637, **Vasey 1670**, Wallace 1674, **Waters 1675**
Delaware: Beckwith 1689, Bishop 1694, Esperance 1710, Reynolds 1743
Florida: Bond 1913, Eckerd 1986, Jasam 2074, Kiwanis 2094, Life's 2116, Light 2117, Rooms 2204, Spurlino 2242, Sudakoff 2256, Sykes 2261, Weiller 2291, Winter 2303
Georgia: Arnold 2319, Coca 2350, Colonial 2353, Flowers 2384, Harris 2408, Lee 2432, Poe 2465, Singletary 2490
Illinois: Adreani 2585, Barancik 2605, Bersted 2618, Combs 2674, Energizer 2721, Gidwitz 2754, Gloyd 2760, Guth 2775, Lewis 2857, Lyon 2866, McIntosh 2883, Millard 2897, **Norris 2917**, Schmidt 2986, Shirk 3007
Indiana: 1st 3094, Bussing 3111, Holiday 3168, Journal 3181, Kuhne 3187, Scheumann 3235
Iowa: **AEGON 3259**, Bechtel 3264, Krause 3302
Kansas: Joscelyn 3371, Smoot 3394
Kentucky: Preston 3446, River 3448
Maine: Hannaford 3540
Maryland: Community 3600, **Ewing 3626**
Massachusetts: Acushnet 3770, Alden 3776, Bristol 3816, Caldwell 3827, Foundation 3916, Ludcke 4017, Peters 4081, Van Sloun 4190, **Wang 4197**
Michigan: Dart 4267, Duffy 4290, Eddy 4292, Farbman 4294, Granger 4329, Keeler 4355, Knabusch 4362, Paulina 4409, Saddle 4426, Stryker 4451
Minnesota: Ankeny 4505, Hillswood 4586, Knowlton 4598, McCarthy 4614, Olson 4640, Ordean 4643, Red Wing 4663, Sanger 4672, Veden 4707
Mississippi: AmSouth 4733, Ergon 4740
Missouri: Carter 4794
Nebraska: Eihusen 4961, Hirschfeld 4974
Nevada: Wendy's 5076
New Hampshire: Cogswell 5084
New Jersey: Large 5295, Orange 5343, Union 5435, Valley 5438, **Wall 5445**, Weny 5450
New Mexico: **Gorham 5478**
New York: Altus 5547, Behrens 5612, Cappelli 5703, Corning 5794, Cornpauw 5795, Davenport 5833, De La Cour 5842, Gellman 6013, Goldman 6051, Gorman 6078, Gural 6120, Hultquist 6211, Knox 6345, Kupferberg 6363, Lee 6391, Lenna 6402, Mangurian 6482, Niehaus 6631, Palmer 6683, PLM 6732, Schlobach 6924, Sternberg 7075, Stevens 7076, Vernon 7195, von der Heyden 7203
North Carolina: Charlotte 7338, Davis 7352, Harris 7390, Herring 7396, Keith 7410, Livingstone 7422, McLean 7425, Mills 7429, O'Herron 7441, Ryan 7469, Smith 7476, Woodson 7509
Ohio: **Cooper 7589**, DBJ 7605, Frohman 7641, Geary 7645, Gerlach 7648, Home 7672, Hoover 7675, LKC 7720, Luther 7726, Mangano 7733, McBride 7740, Moores 7759, Rieveschl 7820, Ritter 7822, Schiewetz 7835, Schiff 7838, Sky 7859, **Tomkins 7884**, **Warrington 7895**, Wilson 7910
Oklahoma: Goddard 7939, Jones 7946, Oklahoman 7966, Viersen 7985
Oregon: Ackerman 7995, Wendt 8066
Pennsylvania: Bozzone 8114, Brossman 8120, Century 8137, Crawford 8162, Degenstein 8166, Eden 8182, Grumbacher 8227, Hankin 8234, Johnson 8275, Justus 8276, Keystone 8285, Mengle 8347,

Phillips 8380, PSC 8398, S & T 8417, Sampson 8423, Stewart 8461
Rhode Island: Jackson 8541, Washington 8563
South Carolina: Chapin 8579, Hipp 8592, **Security's 8609**, **Wardle 8620**
South Dakota: Dakota 8624
Tennessee: Campbell 8650, CLARCOR 8658, Draughon 8668, Haslam 8688, Hawthorn 8689, Ragsdale 8722, Schadt 8725, Thompson 8733
Texas: Baker 8772, Bass 8777, Beasley 8784, Bosque 8792, Bridwell 8797, Clayton 8830, Estill 8888, Fain 8890, Feinberg 8898, Hunt 8966, Moore 9071, Paulos 9112, South 9201, Sumners 9218, Tolleson 9237, Vaughan 9249, Wise 9284
Utah: Gardner 9323, Jones 9330
Virginia: AMERIGROUP 9369, Cartledge 9388, English 9414, Miller 9475, Ukrop 9529, United 9530, Universal 9531
Washington: Anderson 9551, Fortune 9587, Foster 9588, Hebert 9604, Lochland 9630, UNOVA 9697
West Virginia: Chambers 9713, McDonough 9726
Wisconsin: Bell 9756, Bishop 9759, Bryce 9769, Charter 9772, Davis 9787, Kettering 9835, Kress 9844, Lynn 9853, MMG 9877, Oshkosh 9887, **Outagamie 9888**, Pick 9899, Riordan 9911, Smallwood 9928, Stock 9939, Sub 9945, Walter 9959, West 9963
Wyoming: Whitney 9998

Young adults

Florida: Community 1941
New York: Grigg 6108

Young adults, female

Delaware: **Gynesis 1717**
New York: New York 6613

Youth

Arizona: Piper 130
California: Anaheim 220, Angell 224, **Chiron 383**, Community 401, East 474, Fireman's 510, McKesson 879, Pasadena 982, Solano 1175, Stuart 1208, Teichert 1231
Connecticut: Leever 1583, Tow 1661
District of Columbia: **Hill 1809**
Florida: Community 1944, Community 1946
Georgia: Community 2356, Community 2358, **UPS 2503**
Illinois: Community 2678, Community 2679, Illinois 2813
Indiana: Community 3123, Community 3131, Hancock 3160, Lafayette 3188, Northern 3215, Portland 3223
Iowa: Community 3277, **Rockwell 3328**
Kansas: Sprint 3395
Maryland: Baltimore 3568, Community 3599
Massachusetts: Millipore 4040, **Reebok 4098**, Salem 4125, **Staples 4156**
Michigan: **ArvinMeritor 4224**, Battle Creek 4228, Bay 4229, Berrien 4231, Community 4256, Community 4257, Community 4258, Community 4259, Fremont 4315, Grand 4327, Granger 4328, Lenawee 4376, Masco 4387, Saginaw 4428, Steelcase 4446
Minnesota: **Fuller 4567**, Northwest 4637, RBC 4661
Missouri: American 4773, **Monsanto 4868**, **Nestle 4872**
Montana: Washington 4941
New York: Butler 5692, **Citigroup 5755**, Community 5781, Grigg 6108, Hilfiger 6183, **PepsiCo 6714**
North Carolina: Cumberland 7349
North Dakota: Fargo 7514
Ohio: Community 7586, Stark 7867, Troy 7886
Pennsylvania: Baker 8092, Bayer 8096, York 8511
Rhode Island: CVS 8529
South Dakota: Sioux Falls 8630
Tennessee: Douglass 8667
Texas: Amarillo 8758, Butt 8804, Community 8842, Sterling 9212

Virginia: Lynchburg 9463, **Mitsubishi 9476**, Northern 9486
Washington: **Edwards 9580**, **Starbucks 9690**
Wisconsin: Madison 9854, Oshkosh 9885, Racine 9906, **Thrivent 9949**

Youth development

Alabama: Carson 19, Protective 58, Working 76, Wyker 77
Arkansas: Arkansas 156, Rebsamen 171
California: Aaroe 192, Alpert 208, Amateur 214, Anaheim 220, Anderson 221, Benbough 276, Brandenburg 316, **Brandes 317**, Cadence 344, Campbell 352, Capdevila 356, Clorox 389, Community 403, Cowell 423, Crawford 427, Dreyer's 468, East 474, Fluor 523, Gap 551, Godric 586, Gold 590, Grammer 610, **GSF 627**, Guess? 629, Homer 684, **Jack 705**, Koret 774, Koret 775, Langendorf 788, Long 825, Majestic 848, Marcus 852, **Mattel 861**, McCabe 867, Morgan 915, Nestle 935, PacifiCare 971, Pauley 984, Picerne 1004, Pimco 1006, Pralle 1014, Roth 1071, **Saje 1084**, **Saturno 1097**, Shasta 1139, Sierra 1151, Sierra 1152, Simpson 1157, Smith 1162, Sobrato 1172, Stone 1200, Strauss 1201, **Strauss 1203**, Stuart 1208, Stuart 1208, Swinerton 1221, Teichert 1231, Truckee 1244, Union 1250, **Unocal 1252**, vanLobenSels 1260, **WellPoint 1292**, Wunderkinder 1322, Zellerbach 1326
Colorado: Colorado 1356, Community 1359, **Daniels 1362**, Gates 1380, **Janus 1396**, McDonnell 1422, Piton 1439, **Seay 1453**
Connecticut: American 1482, Bridgeport 1504, Community 1514, Fairfield 1537, Flinn 1543, Foley 1544, Lee 1582, Main 1594, Pequot 1625, Tauck 1657, Tow 1661, Vik 1672
Delaware: Berkley 1691, Cawley 1696, **Neuberger 1735**, Presto 1740
District of Columbia: Block 1776, **Capital 1781**, **CityBridge 1783**, Dimick 1789, **Goldberg 1802**, **Hill 1809**, McGowan 1830, **Summit 1852**, Zients 1865
Florida: Becker 1898, Capital 1924, Cascone 1926, Dade 1957, GTE 2040, Gulf 2041, Gurtler 2043, Jacksonville 2071, Krauss, 2101, Levin 2110, McCann 2132, **Picower 2169**, Walter 2286, **Winn 2301**
Georgia: Campbell 2339, Charter 2345, Community 2355, Community 2359, Community 2361, **Georgia 2397**, Goizueta 2400, ING 2418, Jinks 2422, Porter 2468, WinShape 2520
Hawaii: Castle 2537, Schuler 2552
Idaho: Simplot 2574
Illinois: AMCORE 2591, **Burlington 2644**, Community 2681, Donnelley 2706, Dowdle 2709, Eddema 2714, Elgin 2717, GKN 2758, Grand 2769, **JMR 2818**, Omron 2926, Speh 3014, Tracy 3037, **Wrigley 3088**, Zell 3090
Indiana: American 3098, Citizens 3118, Community 3122, Community 3124, Crown Point 3135, DeKalb 3141, Dekko 3142, Elkhart 3145, Ford 3150, Harrison 3161, Holiday 3168, Irwin 3175, Journal 3181, **Lilly 3192**, Niblick 3212, Northern 3215, Oakley 3217, Simon 3237, Tipton 3243, Unity 3247, Welborn 3254
Iowa: Butler 3273, Carver 3274, Jacobson 3299, Principal 3326, R & R 3327, Ruan 3329, Tye 3337
Kansas: Hutchinson 3368, Sprint 3395
Kentucky: Ford 3419, **Yum! 3457**
Louisiana: Institute 3489, New Orleans 3503, Toms 3512
Maine: Gardiner 3536, TD 3558
Maryland: Allegis 3565, Brown 3578, **Cohen 3594**, Legg 3672, Lockheed 3682, **Shields 3730**
Massachusetts: Bay 3794, Boston 3813, Bristol 3816, Cabot 3825, Demoulas 3874, Essex 3897, Garfield 3921, Grand 3929, Grinspoon 3935, Highland 3951, Merck 4035, Millipore 4040, New 4050, Robb 4105, Salah 4124, Shapiro 4136, **State 4158**, Worcester 4209
Michigan: **ArvinMeritor 4224**, Berrien 4231, Community 4252, Ford 4307, Gilmore 4324,

Granger 4328, Kalamazoo 4352, Mott 4400, Perrigo 4410, Petoskey 4412, Shepherd 4435, **Visteon 4472**
Minnesota: **3M 4492**, **Andersen 4501**, ATK 4509, Bailey 4510, Bemis 4515, Carolyn 4533, **Ecolab 4557**, **Fuller 4567**, Graco 4573, Jostens 4596, Mardag 4613, McKnight 4617, McNamara 4618, Northwest 4637, **Petters 4653**, Red Wing 4663, Star 4691, TCF 4699, **U.S. 4704**
Mississippi: AmSouth 4733, Luckyday 4752
Missouri: Andrews 4774, **Anheuser 4776**, Barrows 4781, **Bunge 4792**, Butler 4793, Express 4811, **Hana 4827**, Interco 4835, Lemons 4854, MFA 4866, Reynolds 4892, Smurfit-Stone 4906, Stupp 4910, Stupp 4911, Trio 4918, Truman 4919
Montana: Washington 4941
Nebraska: Harper 4969, Hawks 4971, Kiewit 4983, **Union 5012**
Nevada: Keyser 5039, Mathewson 5045, Sierra 5064
New Hampshire: Fuller 5090
New Jersey: Alcatel 5110, **Ceres 5158**, Healey 5227, **Lafitte 5293**, New Jersey 5337, OceanFirst 5341, Prudential 5360, Roberts 5371, Rummel 5379, UBS 5433, **Vollmer 5443**
New Mexico: Maddox 5487, Thornburg 5501
New York: Aeneas 5523, **American 5553**, Auchincloss 5577, Black 5636, Blue 5640, Broughton 5675, Butler 5692, **Children's 5749**, **Clark 5760**, Community 5781, Community 5784, ContiGroup 5786, Credit 5807, De La Cour 5842, **Dun 5893**, East 5901, Eig 5914, Fludzinski 5964, **Ford 5970**, Fromkes 5994, Gifford 6026, **Grant 6092**, Hagedorn 6130, Harris 6148, Hayden 6158, Hazen 6160, Heckscher 6164, Hilfiger 6183, King 6325, Lehman 6395, Loews 6443, Luce 6452, Mai 6476, **Merrill 6537**, **MetLife 6542**, **National 6603**, Neu 6610, New York 6613, New York 6617, New York 6618, New York 6619, Pincus 6726, Price 6746, Richardson 6797, Rock 6824, Sacerdote 6887, Schenectady 6915, Steinberg 7060, **Time 7142**, Trump 7167, Weinberg 7229
North Carolina: Comloquoy 7341, Fox 7371, Hayden 7394, Jones 7408, **Sunshine 7490**
Ohio: AK 7525, **Cardinal 7567**, **Convergys 7587**, **Cooper 7589**, Dayton 7603, Findlay 7627, Gingher 7650, LKC 7720, Lubrizol 7725, Morgan 7760, Motorists 7765, Park 7795, **Procter 7807**, Reinberger 7815, Scotford 7846, Sloat 7861, Spaulding 7865, Tait 7875
Oklahoma: Southern 7979
Oregon: Boyd 8000, J.F.R. 8023, Jeld 8025, Jubitz 8028, Meyer 8041, Salem 8054
Pennsylvania: Allegheny 8076, American 8079, Berks 8103, Chester 8141, Claneil 8144, Community 8156, First 8202, Fisher 8205, Hillman 8252, Janssen 8271, Kinsley 8290, Penn 8371, Pittsburgh 8386, Plankenhorn 8387, Rangos 8400, Sovereign 8451, **Templeton 8475**
Rhode Island: **Amica 8518**, Citizens 8527, Shaw's 8555
South Carolina: Campbell 8573, Campbell 8574, Lipscomb 8598
Tennessee: **Bridgestone 8646**, Citizens 8657, Frist 8679, HCA 8690, Johnson 8697, No 8713, Tucker 8735, Wallace 8740
Texas: Carter 8817, Clear 8831, **Dell 8863**, Dynegy 8874, Eady 8875, Edwards 8879, Herzstein 8949, Kelleher 8984, Lard 9005, Moody 9070, Paso 9111, Penney 9115, Priddy 9131, Topfer 9238
Utah: Wadman 9349
Virginia: CarMax 9385, Community 9402, Friedman 9425, Golden 9430, Landmark 9455, United 9530, Weissberg 9536, **WestWind 9538**, Wiley 9539
Washington: **Casey 9567**, Evertrust 9583, Laurel 9625, Lynn 9633, Seattle 9680
Wisconsin: Alliant 9742, Bader 9749, Baird 9750, Bolz 9762, Community 9779, Green Bay 9810, Harley 9812, **Kern 9834**, Ladish 9846, Manpower 9858, Marshall 9860, Michels 9874, Milwaukee 9876, Oshkosh 9887, Stock 9939, Sub 9945

Youth development, adult & child programs

Arizona: Piper 130
California: Community 402, Community 405, Crockett 430, **Draper 466**, Eaton 475, Fluor 523, Pertusati 992, Stuart 1208
Connecticut: Tauck 1657
District of Columbia: **Summit 1852**
Florida: Naples 2151
Illinois: Day 2698, Girl's 2757, Hammersmith 2781, Krehbiel 2845
Iowa: Principal 3326
Kansas: Sprint 3395
Maryland: **Marriott 3686**, Rosenberg 3719, Shultz 3732
New Jersey: OceanFirst 5341, Schering 5387
New York: First 5958, New York 6617
Ohio: Bicknell 7548, Bryan 7559
Oregon: Boyd 8000
Pennsylvania: **PPG 8394**
Texas: **EDS 8877**

Youth development, agriculture

Iowa: Beckwith 3266
Texas: Marti 9030

Youth development, business

Colorado: M.D.C. 1413
Florida: Kiwanis 2094
Indiana: Journal 3181, Oakley 3217
Iowa: Jacobson 3299, McDonald 3312
Michigan: Davenport 4269
Missouri: Emerson 4809
New York: **Goldman 6056**, **Merrill 6537**
Oregon: **NIKE 8046**
Pennsylvania: Ryan 8416

Youth development, centers/clubs

Alabama: **Altec 4**, Harrison 36
California: Center 369, Community 402, Halsell 641, Irvine 698, Long 825, **MacDonald 842**, Parsons 980, Raintree 1028, Ransom 1032, Shannon 1133, Ueberroth 1248
Connecticut: Tauck 1657
Florida: Community 1946, O'Neil 2155, Williams 2299
Illinois: Canning 2650, Clingen 2669, Fasseas 2726, Guth 2775, Kaplan 2824
Indiana: Waterfield 3252
Kansas: Wiedemann 3405
Louisiana: Pennington 3505
Maine: Fore 3534
Massachusetts: Barry 3793
Michigan: Oleson 4405, Wenger 4477
Minnesota: Hudson 4591, Mitchell 4625
Mississippi: Irby 4750
Missouri: Long 4858
New York: ContiGroup 5786, Keeler 6306, Nakash 6600, **Robertson 6818**, **Volpert 7202**, Wilpon 7261
Ohio: Cleveland 7577, Nordson 7781, Schiff 7838, Slemp 7860
Oklahoma: Titus 7983
Pennsylvania: Born 8113, Briggs 8117, Brossman 8120
Tennessee: Day 8666
Texas: Anderson 8759, Barnhart 8773, Cowden 8848, Doss 8869, Jones 8976, Kronkosky 9002, McCombs 9037, Pollock 9127, Temple 9228, Wolslager 9290
Washington: Dimmer 9579, Satterberg 9677
Wisconsin: Anon 9744, Shattuck 9926

Youth development, citizenship

Arkansas: Rockefeller 172
California: Confidence 411
Connecticut: Mandeville 1596
Florida: Price 2177
Illinois: Omron 2926
Massachusetts: Filene 3907

Minnesota: Bremer 4523, **Fuller 4567**
Missouri: Roblee 4893
Nevada: Nevada 5047
New Mexico: McCune 5488
New York: **Carnegie 5707**, Everett 5941, **Memton 6529**, New York 6617, **Pforzheimer 6721**
Ohio: Coshocton 7593, Middletown 7749
Pennsylvania: Connelly 8157, Nelson 8362, **Pew 8377**
South Dakota: South Dakota 8631
Vermont: **Ben 9355**
Wisconsin: **Bradley 9763**, McBeath 9864

Youth development, community service clubs

Connecticut: Tauck 1657
Illinois: Roberts 2968
Massachusetts: Cape Cod 3833
New York: Pincus 6726

Youth development, formal/general education

Washington: Opportunities 9655

Youth development, intergenerational programs

Florida: Community 1939
New York: Butler 5692

Youth development, public education

Texas: Franklin 8908

Youth development, religion

Colorado: Leprino 1408
Maine: Gallagher 3535
Michigan: **H.I.S. 4334**, Spoelhof 4443
New York: Elishis 5921
Washington: **Stewardship 9691**
Wisconsin: Vine 9956

Youth development, scouting agencies (general)

Georgia: JBS 2420
Illinois: Steadley 3020
Massachusetts: Hirschtick 3953, Stemberg 4161
Michigan: **Visteon 4472**
Minnesota: Carlson 4532
New Jersey: Orange 5343
New York: Icahn 6222, Wolk 7271, Woodland 7275
Ohio: Ritter 7822
Oregon: Ackerman 7995
Pennsylvania: Brossman 8120, Musser 8361, Sampson 8423, Stabler 8455
Tennessee: Washington 8741
Texas: Vale 9246
Wisconsin: AnnMarie 9743, Harley 9812, Helfaer 9813, Phipps 9898, Taylor 9948

Youth development, services

Alabama: Russell 60
Arizona: Hickey 108
California: Anaheim 220, Argyros 234, **Baker 252**, Bechtel 270, California 350, Gamble 549, Haas 637, Hoag 678, Irvine 698, Johnson 725, Peery 986, Rest 1044, Riordan 1054, Sacramento 1080, San Francisco 1088, Soda 1173, Stuart 1208, **Tosa 1240**, Weingart 1288
Colorado: Gates 1380, International 1395, Qwest 1443
Connecticut: Bodenwein 1497, Community 1515, Connecticut 1518, Kramer 1577
District of Columbia: **Case 1782**, Community 1785, Meyer 1834, **Public 1844**
Florida: Dunspaugh 1981, Free 2012, Horvitz 2065, **Plan 2171**
Georgia: Blank 2325, Pittulloch 2464, Tull 2500, Young 2527

Illinois: **Brach 2630**, Chicago 2661, Community 2677, D and R 2693, Eisenberg 2716, **Friedmann 2738**, Kenny's 2835, Polk 2946
Indiana: Community 3124, Community 3125, Decatur 3138, Lilly 3194, Moore 3207, Noble 3214
Iowa: Community 3277, McElroy 3313
Kansas: Sprint 3395
Maine: Maine 3548
Maryland: Abell 3559, **Casey 3585**, Eaton 3619
Massachusetts: Ansin 3779, Boston 3812, **Krieble 3990**
Michigan: Community 4254, Community 4255, Ford 4301, Frankel 4313, Grand Rapids 4326, **Kellogg 4357**
Minnesota: Bush 4524, Central 4534, **CHS 4540**, **Land 4602**, Minnesota 4624, Smikis 4687, Wallestad 4713, West 4723
Mississippi: Foundation 4743
Missouri: Long 4858
Nebraska: Dillon 4956
Nevada: Boyd 5023, Lied 5041
New Jersey: Community 5167, Cowles 5170, Gund 5218, Kirby 5279, Martini 5319, PSEG 5361, Victoria 5440
New Mexico: McCune 5488
New York: Bowne 5655, **Clark 5760**, Dimon 5864, Gould 6085, **Hearst 6161**, **Hearst 6162**, **Jaffe 6250**, New York 6615, Richmond 6800, Rochester 6823, Soros 7023, Sweetgrass 7113, Tiger 7139
North Carolina: Cumberland 7349, Davis 7353, Dover 7356, Triangle 7496, Woodson 7509
Ohio: Coshocton 7593, Forest 7634, Hoover 7675, Middletown 7749, Murphy 7769, Muskingum 7770, Stark 7867, Stocker 7870, **Timken 7880**, **Wexner 7904**, Youngstown 7920
Oklahoma: Mabee 7954
Oregon: Oregon 8049
Pennsylvania: Colonial 8151, Comcast 8152, Dolfinger 8172, Huston 8263, Jennings 8272, McCune 8332, McLean 8340, Mellon 8346, **Pew 8377**, Scranton 8431, Stackpole 8456
Rhode Island: Daniels 8530
Texas: Cain 8809, El Paso 8882, Franklin 8908, **Jenesis 8971**, Kempner 8987, Meadows 9049, Reaud 9143
Virginia: Lynchburg 9463, Norfolk 9484
Washington: **Stewardship 9691**, Tacoma 9693
West Virginia: McDonough 9726
Wisconsin: Archer 9746, Madison 9854

Youth development, volunteer services

Connecticut: Tauck 1657

Youth, pregnancy prevention

California: California 350
Colorado: Buell 1350, **General 1381**
Connecticut: **Richardson 1632**
District of Columbia: **Wallace 1858**
Illinois: Kapoor 2825, Prince 2948
Massachusetts: **State 4158**
Michigan: Berrien 4231, Community 4252
Missouri: Roblee 4893
New Jersey: Knistrom 5282, MCJ 5324
New York: Cummings 5815
Pennsylvania: Grable 8221
Virginia: Portsmouth 9499
Washington: Burning 9564, Horizons 9608

Youth, services

Alabama: Protective 58, Webb 75
Arizona: Hickey 108, Laizure 114, Marley 120
California: Ahmanson 198, Amateur 214, Anderson 221, Bay 264, Community 404, Community 406, Copley 416, Crocker 429, Davies 446, Dhont 453, Fein 497, Garaventa 553, Garland 556, Gellert 559, Goldrich 598, Gruber 626, Jameson 710, Johnson 724, Knight 768, Leavey 797, McCabe 867, Monterey 910, Red 1035, Reid 1036, **Reveas 1045**, Schott 1106, **Stewardship 1197**, Stover

1201, Stuart 1206, Tippett 1237, Valley 1256, Ventura 1264, Vons 1270, Webb 1285, Weider 1287, Whittier 1304, Witkin 1313
Colorado: Brett 1349, Community 1359, Coors 1360, Gates 1380, Taylor 1464
Connecticut: Cohen 1512, Ensworth 1535, Matthies 1600, Panwy 1622, Phoenix 1627, Roberts 1635, Woodward 1678
Delaware: **Birch 1692**, Buckner 1695, Longwood 1727
District of Columbia: Graham 1804
Florida: Bastien 1892, Beveridge 1907, Community 1941, Community 1942, Community 1945, Community 1947, duPont 1983, Gulf 2041, **Isenberg 2070**, Kirbo 2092, Martin 2130, **Morris 2145**, Peacock 2165, Price 2177, Publix 2180, Rubin 2211, Selby 2230, Six 2236, Thatcher 2273, Williams 2299
Georgia: Atlanta 2320, Bradley 2326, Buisson 2333, Callaway 2336, Camp 2338, Community 2355, Community 2357, Delta 2372, Fraser 2390, Goizueta 2400, Pittulloch 2464, Ramser 2469, RTM 2477, SunTrust 2496, Wehadkee 2511, WestPoint 2513, Woolley 2525
Hawaii: McInerny 2551
Idaho: Albertson's 2563
Illinois: Chicago 2660, Combs 2674, Community 2679, Meyer 2896, **Niamogue 2914**, Olin 2925, Shapiro 3001, Siragusa 3009, **Square 3018**, Stewart 3024, **Wrigley 3088**
Indiana: Bussing 3111, Cole 3121, Community 3125, Community 3126, Community 3128, **Cummins 3136**, Irwin 3174, Legacy 3189, Met 3204, Muselman 3209, NiSource 3213, Oliver 3219, Saemann 3232, Simon 3240, Wabash 3250, West 3256
Iowa: Ahrens 3260, Bechtel 3263, Hall 3290, Krause 3302
Kansas: Baughman 3346, Capitol 3350, Hansen 3366, Powell 3381, Pritchett 3382
Kentucky: Brown 3409, Novak 3442
Louisiana: Booth 3464, Community 3469, Pennington 3505, Scott 3509
Maine: Kennebec 3543, TD 3558
Maryland: Clark 3591, Dresher 3617, Schifter 3726
Massachusetts: Aaron 3767, Babson 3787, Cape Cod 3833, Clarke 3849, Common 3853, Corkin 3861, Crossroads 3869, Hyams 3961, Johnson 3970, Knight 3987, Peabody 4072, Peabody 4073, **Reebok 4098**, Robbins 4106, Schrafft 4133, Stoddard 4165
Michigan: Citizens 4248, Community 4254, Community 4256, Dalton 4266, DeVlieg 4275, **DeWitt 4280**, Dow 4288, Hurst 4344, **Kellogg 4357**, McGregor 4389, Midland 4392, Tiscornia 4460, Wheeler 4479, Wilson 4485
Minnesota: **3M 4492**, Amundson 4500, **Andreas 4504**, Bieber 4518, Hardenbergh 4583, Mossier 4628, Pax 4648, Rivers 4666, Wedum 4719
Missouri: Ameren 4772, Edison 4807, Emerson 4809, Goppert 4819, Hall 4824, Interco 4835, Jones 4839, Long 4858, **Morris 4869**
Montana: Chutney 4934
Nebraska: Eihusen 4961, Hawkins 4970, Kiewit 4984, Lozier 4988, Omaha 4995, Rogers 4999, Schrager 5001, Sunshine 5007
Nevada: Bretzlaff 5024, Cord 5029, Greenspun 5034, Sierra 5064
New Hampshire: Bean 5080
New Jersey: **Huntsman 5246**, Kirby 5279, National 5335
New York: Altman 5542, Aron 5569, Arrison 5570, **AVI 5582**, Carmel 5705, **Clark 5760**, Corning 5794, Everett 5941, Green 6096, Heckscher 6164, I Have 6219, Knapp 6342, Megrue 6524, Metcalf 6541, Raffiani 6767, Sheldon 6964, Snow 7011, Sugarman 7092, Summit 7100, Task 7124, Union 7184, Weezie 7224, Woodcock 7273, Zucker 7303
North Carolina: Dickson 7355, Finley 7367, Robertson 7466, Summer 7489, Winston-Salem 7508
North Dakota: MDU 7517
Ohio: Butler 7562, Campbell 7565, Cleveland 7576, Columbus 7580, **Durell 7616**, Ferguson 7625,

Foundation 7636, GAR 7643, Kalberer 7695, Middletown 7749, **Ohio 7786**, Stranahan 7872
Oklahoma: Helmerich 7942, Kerr 7949, Mabee 7954, McMahon 7959, Merrick 7962, Waters 7988, Zarrow 7991
Oregon: Ford 8013, Shapira 8058, Wessinger 8067
Pennsylvania: American 8079, Byers' 8127, Donley 8175, First 8202, Grable 8221, Heinz 8240, Hillman 8249, Hooper 8256, Hopwood 8257, Little 8313, Miller 8353, Musser 8361, Phoenixville 8381, Rees 8401, Reidler 8402, Spang 8452, Trees 8480
Puerto Rico: **FNZ 8514**
Rhode Island: Champlin 8524
South Carolina: Campbell 8574, Foothills 8588, Liberty 8597
Tennessee: CLARCOR 8658, Hendrix 8691, Plough 8718, Starfish 8728
Texas: Anderson 8762, Bass 8777, Cameron 8812, Carter 8816, Cauthorn 8820, Communities 8839, **Cooper 8846**, Dodge 8868, East 8876, Edwards 8880, Fair 8891, Fondren 8906, Haggar 8929, Halsell 8936, Kempner 8987, Koehler 9001, Mayor 9034, Miller 9062, NAH 9084, Reliant 9144, Smith 9198, Sumners 9218, Webber 9269, Weekley 9271
Vermont: Vermont 9361
Virginia: Beazley 9376, **Gannett 9428**, Houff 9438, Kogod 9452, Lawrence 9457, Staunton 9521, Wiser 9543
Washington: Allen 9550, Burning 9564, Cheney 9569, Foundation 9589, Shemanski 9682, **Stewardship 9691**
West Virginia: Chambers 9713
Wisconsin: AnnMarie 9743, Cornerstone 9781, Cudahy 9785, Fond du Lac 9800, Janesville 9820, Johnson 9823, Johnson 9824, Keller 9831, Madison 9854, McQueen 9866, Mead 9867, Pick 9899, Prescott 9903, Rutledge 9917, Schlegel 9919, Soref 9930, Stuart 9942, Styberg 9944, Windhover 9966

Zoos/zoological societies

Arizona: Marley 120
California: Amerman 218, Doelger 459, Lehrer 800, Lipinsky 816, Menard 884, Outhwaite 966, Peters 993, Weiss 1290, Witherbee 1312
Colorado: **Hawley 1390**, Wolf 1475
Florida: Petway 2167, Rooms 2204, **Winn 2301**
Georgia: **Morris 2455**
Illinois: Alsdorf 2590, Chaddick 2655, Chicago 2660, Comer 2675, Harris 2788, Hobbs 2802, Kainz 2822, Kemper 2831, Kovler 2844, Makray 2871, Malott 2872, McCormick 2878, McNally 2885, Mullen 2907, Souder 3013, Stewart 3024, Wilemal 3070, Wilson 3075
Indiana: Community 3122, Hilbert 3167, Indiana 3173, Jones 3179, Michigan 3205, Perelman 3222
Iowa: Blank 3268
Kansas: Downing 3358
Maryland: **Brown 3579**, **Head 3644**, Rosenberg 3720
Michigan: Dow 4288, Farbman 4294, Ford 4304, Ford 4305, Frey 4316, Manoogian 4382, Mardigian 4386
Minnesota: McGuire 4615, Weesner 4720
Missouri: Boswell 4786, Brauer 4787, Jones 4839, Lichtenstein 4855, Reding 4890
Nebraska: Baright 4945, Holland 4977, Hubbard 4978, James 4980
New Mexico: Healy 5479, Messengers 5489
New York: Blythmour 5644, Gerschel 6018, Knox 6345, **Magowan 6473**, Stempel 7069, Wolk 7271
Ohio: Bates 7540, DBJ 7605, Dornette 7613, LKC 7720, Luther 7726, Miniger 7756, Reinberger 7815, Schiff 7838, Schott 7842, Shaw 7853, Spaulding 7865, Stillson 7869
Oklahoma: Better 7926, Kerr 7950
Oregon: Ackerman 7995
Pennsylvania: Ryan 8416
South Carolina: First 8587
Tennessee: Beaman 8642, Ragsdale 8722

Texas: Carlson 8815, Duda 8871, Kinder 8994, Kronkosky 9002, McNutt 9048, Moncrief 9069, Paulos 9112, Waggoner 9256

Utah: Lawson 9332
Washington: De Falco 9578, Ferguson 9585

Wisconsin: Demmer 9791, Holz 9817, Merrill 9872

FOUNDATIONS NEW TO THE EDITION

The following foundations appear in this edition of *The Foundation Directory* but had not met criteria for inclusion in the previous edition. The entries for these foundations are highlighted with a star (☆) in the Descriptive Directory section. They are included in all indexes.

Bohlsen Family Foundation, John and Linda, NY, 5649
Bohnert Foundation, Inc., NJ, 5135
Bond Foundation, Inc., The, FL, 1913
Bondi Foundation, The, CT, 1499
Bookout Family Foundation, The, TX, 8791
Booth Foundation, Inc., Alex and Roxanna, FL, 1914
Born Foundation, Walter W., OH, 7552
Bornblum Foundation, The, TN, 8645
BOSE Foundation, Inc., MA, 3810
Bossidy Foundation, Lawrence A., The, CT, 1500
Botwinick-Wolfensohn Foundation, Inc., NY, 5653
Bovin Family Foundation, The, NY, 5654
Bowes Family Foundation, CA, 310
Boyd Foundation, The, NV, 5023
Bradberry Family Foundation, AR, 159
Bradley Foundation, The, CA, 315
Brady Charitable Foundation, Benjamin F., The, GA, 2327
Brady Foundation, NJ, 5141
Brainerd Family Foundation, Inc., Lyman B., The, CT, 1502
Brand Foundation, The, NY, 5658
Brandt Foundation, John H. and Orah I., The, ID, 2565
Braufman Family Foundation, Inc., Daniel L. Nir & Jill E., NY, 5660
Braun/Brown Family Foundation, CA, 318
Breeden Family Foundation, The, NC, 7324
Bressler Family Foundation, The, MA, 3815
Bressler Foundation, Alan S. Bressler and Lorraine D., The, MA, see 3815
Brewer Family Foundation, Robert N., IL, 2632
Brickman Foundation, PA, 8116
Broadcasters Foundation, Inc., CT, 1505
Brookfield Arts Foundation, Inc., MA, 3818
Brotman Family Foundation, WA, 9562
Brown and Charles Seelig Family Foundation, Robin, The, NY, 5676
Brown Charitable Foundation, Alvin I. & Peggy S., MD, 3579
Brown County Community Foundation, Inc., IN, 3110
Brown Foundation, Inc., A. Pat and Kathryne L., The, NC, 7326
Brown Trust 1, Frank E., NC, 7327
Brownell Family Foundation, IA, 3270
Brownlee Foundation, Robert, The, CA, 329
Bryant Foundation, Inc., Edwin E. and Janet L., The, WI, 9768
Bryson Foundation, FL, 1918
Buck Foundation, Peter and Carmen Lucia, The, NY, 5682
Buckner Foundation, MO, 4790
Buffett Early Childhood Fund, NE, 4948
Building Hope...A Charter School Facilities Fund, DC, 1778
Bunning Family Foundation, IL, 2641
Bunning Food Allergy Foundation, IL, 2642
Bunzl Foundation, Inc., Walter & Frances, GA, 2334
Burch Family Foundation, CA, 334
Burch Family Foundation, The, NY, see 5686
Burch Foundation, The, NY, 5686
Burfeind-Codispoti Foundation, Inc., The, NJ, see 5165
Burke Charitable Foundation, Helen Keeler, NY, 5688
Burlock Foundation, Leslie and Walter, CA, 335
Burnett Charitable Foundation, Inc., Al and Nancy, FL, 1919
Burnett Charitable Foundation, Inc., Al, FL, see 1919
Burton Foundation, William T. and Ethel Lewis, The, LA, 3467
Butler Manufacturing Company Foundation, MO, 4793
Butler Memorial Foundation, Robert M., OH, 7562
Butler, Jr. Family Foundation, Inc., Susan C. and James E., GA, 2335
BVM Foundation, Inc., IN, 3112
BWMF Farm, AR, see 187

Cabot Charitable Foundation, Edmund & Betsy, The, MA, 3822
Cadence Foundation, CA, 344
Cain Brothers Foundation, The, NY, 5697
Calicchio Family Foundation, John, The, NY, 5698
Calvin Bible Foundation, Inc., John, MD, 3581
Campbell Foundation, MN, 4528
Canaday Family Charitable Trust, MA, 3831

Cannon Trust, Anne, MD, 3583
CAP Charitable Foundation USA, VA, 9384
Capdevilla/Gillespie Foundation, CA, 356
Capita Charitable Foundation, Emil R., NJ, 5154
Cardinal Brook Trust, MA, 3834
Cardinal Foundation, The, OH, 7566
Carlee Charitable Trust, MA, 3835
Carpenter Family Childrens Foundation, Inc., CA, 360
Carroll Foundation, Leila, The, CO, see 1351
Carse Charitable Family Foundation, Wayne L. Carse & Jimmie L., The, FL, 1925
Carson Foundation, CO, 1351
Cascone Family Foundation, Michael Cascone Jr. and Elizabeth Belyea, The, FL, 1926
Case Family Foundation, NY, 5713
Cassels Foundation, The, SC, 8575
Cassin Foundation, The, CA, 365
Castagnola Family Foundation, George V. and Rena G., CA, 366
Castellani Family Foundation, Lawrence P., FL, 1928
Castle Hills Schools Foundation, Inc., TX, 8818
Casty-Dunn Families Charitable Foundation, MA, 3839
Catalyst Fund, The, ME, 3529
Cato, Jr. Foundation, Inc., Wayland H., SC, 8576
Cavitolo Foundation, Andrea, PA, 8134
Cay Foundation, Inc., GA, 2343
Cayman Conand Foundation, MN, see 4503
CEC Foundation, The, CA, 368
Cejas Family Foundation, Inc., The, FL, 1930
Centene Charitable Foundation, The, MO, 4796
Centofante Foundation, CA, 370
Cesatam Foundation, Inc., The, NJ, 5159
Chancellor Foundation, Inc., IN, 3117
Chaney Foundation, Ltd., Eugene, MD, 3587
Change Happens Foundation, HI, 2539
Channel Foundation, WA, 9568
Chapman Foundation, Norman and Joan, IL, 2656
Charles River Foundation, MA, see 3844
Charles River Laboratories Foundation, Inc., MA, 3844
Charlesmead Foundation, Inc., The, RI, 8525
Charlotte Merchants Foundation, NC, 7338
Charlotte's Web, MD, 3588
Cheesecake Factory-Oscar and Evelyn Overton Charitable Foundation, The, CA, 378
Chencinski Brothers Charitable Foundation, Inc., NY, 5742
Chernin Family Foundation, Inc., The, NY, 5743
Chernow Trust 2, Michael, NY, 5744
Chesed Foundation, NY, 5746
Children's Educational Opportunity Foundation, CA, 381
Children's Family Care, Inc., OH, 7570
Children's Health Fund, CA, see 1044
Childs Charitable Foundation, Roberta M., MA, 3848
Ching Foundation, Hung Wo & Elizabeth Lau, HI, 2540
Chintu Gudiya Foundation, CA, 382
Chiquita Brands International Foundation, OH, 7571
Christopher Foundation, Jay and Doris, IL, 2665
Cinnabar Foundation, The, MT, 4935
Circle Bar Foundation, TX, 8829
Citadel Group Foundation, IL, 2667
Citizens Bank Tri-Cities Foundation, Ltd., TN, 8657
Clarke Trust, John, MA, 3849
Claws Foundation, VA, 9394
Cleveland Foundation, MN, 4541
Clingen Foundation, Ltd., IL, 2669
Clinton Family Foundation, The, NY, 5763
Clive Foundation, Winifred Johnson, PA, 8146
Cloud Mountain Foundation, NY, 5764
Cloverfields Foundation, MN, 4542
CMS Foundation, PA, 8148
CNC Foundation, CA, 390
Cobb Foundation, The, CA, 392
Coca-Cola Enterprises Charitable Foundation, The, GA, 2351
Codispoti Foundation, NJ, 5165
Cohen Charitable Foundation, Inc., Ben & Zelda, MD, 3592
Cohen Family Foundation, Abby and David, The, NY, 5767
Cohen LD Family Foundation, Inc., NY, 5772
Cohenca Foundation, Inc., Jacques & Emy, NY, 5773
Cole Family Foundation, Inc., The, VA, 9396

Coleman Charitable Foundation, Inc., Ruth and Baron, FL, 1937
Coleman Family Foundation, Inc., KS, 3352
Coleman Family Foundation, NM, 5470
Coleman Foundation, Inc., Thomas B. and Robertha K., The, NC, 7340
Collins Foundation, Fred, SC, 8582
Collins, Jr. Foundation, George Fulton, OK, 7930
Collis/Warner Foundation, Inc., The, VA, 9398
Columbia Charitable Foundation, CA, see 1182
Commercial Capital Bank Community Foundation, CA, 400
Common Stream, Inc., MA, 3853
Community Foundation of Acadiana, LA, 3468
Community Foundation of North Florida, Inc., The, FL, 1945
Community Foundation of Portage County, Inc., WI, 9778
Community Foundation of West Georgia, GA, 2362
Community Foundation Partnership, Inc., IN, 3133
Connolly Foundation, G.L., CA, 413
Connors Foundation, John & Kathy, WA, 9572
Conway Foundation, Robert M. & Lois, NY, see 5787
Conway Foundation, Robert M., The, NY, 5787
Corkin Charitable Foundation, Robert Lloyd, MA, 3861
Cornell Memorial Foundation, Joseph and Robert, The, NY, 5793
Cornerstone Foundation, OH, 7592
Cornpauw Foundation, Ltd., NY, 5795
Cotswold Foundation, The, OH, 7594
Countess Moira Charitable Foundation, The, NY, 5800
Countrywide Foundation, The, CA, 422
Cowin Foundation, Inc., Joyce and Daniel, The, NY, 5802
Cox Family Fund, MN, 4543
Cox Trust, Donald & Maria, The, NY, 5803
Craig Foundation, Sid and Jenny, The, CA, 425
Crane Foundation, James R., TX, 8852
Crawford Family Foundation, Inc., FL, 1956
Crawley Family Foundation, OK, 7934
Creel Foundation, The, GA, 2369
Cressey Foundation, Bryan C. & Christina I., The, IL, 2689
Cristaglio Social Responsibility Family Foundation, MA, see 4063
Crockett Foundation, The, ME, 3530
Crotty Family Foundation, Inc., The, MA, 3870
Cuban Foundation, Mark, TX, 8853
Curme Family Foundation, O. & C., The, MA, see 4012
Curran Family Foundation, Michael G., The, NC, 7350
Cyh Foundation, NJ, 5173

D & K Charitable Foundation, NJ, 5174
Dabah Family Foundation, Inc., Barbara & Haim, NY, 5820
Daedalus Foundation, Inc., NY, 5821
Daft Family Foundation, The, GA, 2370
Dahan Family Foundation, Inc., The, FL, 1958
Dahl Family Foundation, Inc., FL, 1959
Dain Rauscher Foundation, MN, see 4661
Dance Charitable Foundation, Harold & Ruth, UT, 9311
Dancing Tides Foundation, Inc., NY, 5828
Daphne Foundation, The, NY, 5830
Darby Foundation, MD, 3605
David Foundation, Ruth and Leo, The, CA, 443
Davies Medical Center, CA, see 533
Davis Charitable Fund, Karen & David, MA, see 3834
Davis Family Foundation, The, MA, 3874
Davis Trust, M. G., NY, 5837
De Llano Charitable Trust, Matias, TX, 8859
Dealessandro Foundation, The, NJ, 5178
DeAtley Family Foundation, Inc., WI, 9789
Decio Foundation, Arthur J., IN, 3139
DeGol Foundation, Bruno & Lena, The, PA, 8167
DeHaan Foundation, Jon Holden, The, FL, 1966
Delancey Foundation, The, NY, 5849
Delle Foundation, The, NM, 5474
Delta Dental Plan of Kansas Foundation, Inc., KS, 3354
DeLuca Family Charitable Trust, The, MA, 3877
Deming Foundation, John W. & Bertie M., LA, 3472
Dennis Foundation, John R. and Maryanne, MN, 4550
Dephillips Foundation, Marion & Silfred, NJ, 5179
Des Femmes International Foundation, DE, see 1717

Deutsch Foundation, Carl & Roberta, CA, 451
Dewald Family Charitable Foundation, Inc., The, OH, 7608
Di Geronimo Foundation, Christine and Guido, The, OH, 7609
di Portanova Charitable Foundation, Enrico & Sandra, TX, 8865
Dial Corp Fund, The, AZ, see 149
Diamond Family Foundation, Jon & Susan, The, OH, 7610
Diamond Family Foundation, Robert & Jennifer, The, NY, 5858
Diamond Foundation, NY, 5859
Dibona Family Foundation, G. Fred & Sylvia, PA, see 8169
Dibona, Jr. Memorial Foundation, G. Fred, PA, 8169
Dickinson Foundation, Inc., The, FL, 1973
Diener Foundation, Robert and Michelle, TX, 8867
DiMaura Charitable Trust, Paul W., MA, 3880
Dinsdale Family Foundation, Inc., NE, 4957
DiPonio Foundation, Angelo & Margaret, The, MI, 4281
Distinguished Service Foundation, CO, 1365
Doherty Foundation, The, NJ, 5182
Dolan Family Foundation, Katherine and Peter, The, NY, 5870
Dolan Family Foundation, NY, 5869
Doll Family Foundation, Dixon and Carol, CA, 461
Dollens Family Foundation, CA, 462
Domanica Foundation, The, NM, 5475
Donnell Initiative Fund, The, CO, 1367
Dornette Foundation, Helen G., Henry F. & Louise T., OH, 7613
Dorothy-Ann Foundation, The, VA, 9411
Douglass Foundation, Terry D. and Rosann B., The, TN, 8667
Dow Foundation, The, NJ, 5183
Dowling Jr. Foundation, William C., NY, 5880
Downs Foundation, The, MA, 3882
Downs Miller Foundation, Inc., Doreen, NY, 5882
Dramatists Guild Fund, Inc., NY, 5883
Drew Family Foundation, CA, 467
Dreyfus Foundation, VA, 9413
Druckenmiller Foundation, NY, 5889
Drue Trust, S. May, NC, 7358
Druker Charitable Foundation, MA, 3883
Drukier Foundation, Inc., The, NY, 5890
Ds Foundation, The, FL, 1976
Dudley Foundation, Inc., WI, 9792
Duff II Scholarship, Lola G. Duff & William H., OH, 7615
Dugas Family Foundation, Laura Jo and Wayne, The, TN, see 8669
Dugas Family Foundation, TN, 8669
Duncan Trust, Louise Head, WI, 9793
Dusky Foundation, The, MA, 3885
Dweck Foundation, Susan & Morris E., NY, 5896
Dwyer Fund for Excellence, Richard F. Dwyer and Eleanor W., The, CA, 472

E & WG Foundation, NY, 5899
Eagle's Wing Foundation, Inc., FL, 1985
East Arkansas Business Development Council, Inc., AR, 160
Easthampton Savings Foundation, MA, 3887
Eaton Family Foundation, Inc., CA, 475
Ebb Foundation, Fred, NY, 5903
Ebrahimi Family Foundation, CO, 1371
Eddema Foundation, IL, 2714
Edelstein Foundation, Inc., Emanuel and Klara, FL, 1988
Edgerton Foundation, CA, 477
Educational Support Foundation, Inc., NY, 5910
Edwards Company Foundation, J. T., OH, see 7618
Edwards Family Foundation, Inc., FL, 1990
Edwards Family Foundation, Jerry and Joan, PA, 8183
Edwards Foundation, Inc., The, OH, 7618
Edwards Foundation, Inc., William, FL, see 1990
Effron Family Foundation, Craig, The, NY, 5911
Eihusen Foundation, Inc., Virgil, NE, 4961
Eihusen-Chief Foundation, Inc., NE, see 4961
Eisenberg Family Charitable Trust, DE, 1709
Elias Foundation, The, NY, 5920
Eliasberg Family Foundation, Inc., The, MD, 3620
Ellbogen Foundation, John P., The, WY, 9981

Ellis Foundation, Danny and Willa, KS, see 3361
Ellis Foundation, Inc., Gail G., IL, 2718
Ellis Foundation, The, KS, 3361
Ellison Foundation, Tom and Sue, WA, 9581
Elqui Valley Foundation, The, MA, 3893
Endowment for Biblical Research, Boston, MA, 3895
Endowment for Vietnamese Education, Inc., The, NY, 5931
Engemann Family Foundation, CA, 484
Engman Foundation, Robert & Mary Jane, CA, 485
Enlight Foundation, CA, 486
Enrico Foundation, Roger and Rosemary, The, TX, 8885
Epstein Family Foundation, Inc., Diana and Michael David, MD, 3623
Equinox Foundation, Inc., NY, 5935
Eshet Chayil Foundation, NJ, 5190
Eskind Family Foundation, Jeffrey and Donna, The, TN, 8675
Esperance Family Foundation, The, DE, 1710
Esther Foundation, The, CO, 1375
Eunice Foundation, The, NY, 5939
Evans Foundation, Edward P., VA, 9416
Evelyn Foundation, The, DE, 1712
Everard Family Foundation, The, WA, 9582
Everett Foundation, Herschel H. & Cornelia N., The, NC, 7364
Evergreen Foundation, Inc., MD, 3625
Evergreen Foundation, OK, 7936

Fabick Charitable Trust, Inc., MO, 4812
Fain Foundation, TX, 8890
Fain Fund Trust, Norman & Rosalie, RI, 8533
Falcon Charitable Foundation, The, ME, 3532
Falkenberg Foundation, The, CO, 1376
Family Development Center, Inc., NJ, 5191
Farb Foundation, Harold, The, TX, 8893
Farrell Foundation, The, IL, 2725
Farver Foundation, Joan Kuyper, IA, 3283
Fassino Foundation, Inc., The, MA, 3900
Fein Foundation, Edward, CA, 497
Feinberg Foundation, Inc., Jac & Eva, NY, 5950
Feinberg Foundation, Inc., TX, 8898
Feinstein Family Fund, RI, 8534
Feinstein Foundation, Edward, CA, see 497
Feintech Family Foundation, Evelyn M. & Norman, CA, 499
Feintech Family Foundation, Irving, CA, 500
Fenwick Foundation, NJ, 5193
Fernandez Family Foundation, Miguel B., FL, 1997
Ferrari Foundation, Andrew U., NY, 5953
Fertel Foundation, Ruth U., LA, 3477
Fetzer Memorial Trust Fund, John E., MI, 4298
Field Fund, Charles D. and Frances K., The, CA, 505
Fine Family Foundation, The, PA, 8201
Finger Foundation, Jerry and Nanette, TX, 8900
Finley Foundation, Ernest L. and Ruth W., CA, 507
First County Bank Foundation, Inc., CT, 1541
First Fruit, Inc., CA, 512
Fishback Family Foundation, Inc., Kathryn C., CA, 513
Fisher Charitable Trust, Zachary and Elizabeth, NY, 5962
Five Smith's Foundation, Inc., GA, 2383
Flagg Creek Foundation, IL, 2731
Flagg Family Foundation, CA, see 517
Flagg Family Foundation, Morgan, CA, 517
Fleming Endowment, TX, 8903
Fleming Foundation, PA, 8206
Flight Attendant Medical Research Institute, Inc., FL, 2002
Flow Foundation, Inc., NC, 7368
Flynt Foundation, Kay Richard and Elizabeth Bates, CA, 524
Focus Foundation, OH, 7632
Foothills Foundation, The, CA, 526
Ford Foundation, Inc., Gordon, KY, 3419
Ford Foundation, Joseph F. and Clara, MA, 3913
Ford, Jr. Scholarship Program, William C., MI, 4308
Forney Family Foundation, Inc., PA, 8207
Foundation for Cardiovascular Research, FL, 2008
Foundation for the Education & Research in Neurological Emergencies, IL, 2732
Foundation Francqui Belgium, NY, see 5973

Foundation in Christ Ministries: 1 Cor. 3:11, Inc., FL, 2009
Foundation M, MA, 3916
Founders Charitable Foundation, Inc., AL, 34
Four Friends Foundation, CA, 532
Fox Family Foundation, CT, 1547
Francqui Foundation, NY, 5973
Frank Foundation, Sidney E., NY, 5975
Frankel Jewish Heritage Foundation, Samuel and Jean, The, MI, 4314
Franklin Benevolent Corporation, CA, 533
Frazier Foundation, The, FL, 2011
Freed Family Foundation, IL, 2736
Freehling Foundation, Norman & Edna, IL, 2737
Fremont Bank Foundation, The, CA, 534
Freston Foundation, Tom and Kathy, NY, 5982
Frey Family Foundation, Inc., NY, 5983
Friedland Family Foundation, NE, 4963
Friedland Foundation, David & Nancy, NE, see 4963
Friends of China Heritage Fund, Ltd., NY, 5989
Fromkes Foundation, Inc., Saul, NY, 5994
Frost Foundation, Pat and Tom, TX, 8910
FSB Foundation, Inc., CT, 1549
Future of Russia, DC, 1800
Futureus Foundation, TX, 8912

Galanta Foundation, Inc., NJ, 5202
Galbraith Foundation, The, VA, 9427
Gale Foundation, Inc., Mary, NH, 5091
Gandy & John H. Sandman Charitable Trust, Virginia Lee, CA, 550
Gantz Family Foundation, IL, 2748
Garaventa Family Foundation, Silvio and Mary, CA, 553
Garcia Family Charitable Foundation Trust, IN, 3154
Gardinor-Prunaret Foundation, MA, 3920
Gardner Foundation, Janice, MN, 4568
Gardner Foundation, Sterling and Shelli, UT, 9323
Garen Family Foundation, CA, 555
Garfinkle Foundation, Inc., Norton, FL, see 2017
Garfinkle-Minard Foundation, Inc., FL, 2017
Garrison Foundation, Thomas & Natalie, The, AR, 162
Gast Charitable Foundation, Warren E. & D. Lou, MI, 4317
Gateway Foundation, The, ME, 3537
Gayden Family Foundation, TX, 8915
Geds Help Fund Foundation, NY, 6010
Geiger Foundation, Inc., NJ, 5205
Gellman Foundation, The, NY, 6013
Georgescu Family Foundation, The, CT, 1554
Georgia Youth Foundation, Inc., GA, 2396
Gershman Foundation, Cynthia, CA, 566
Gerson Family Foundation, Inc., NY, 6021
Gewirz Foundation, Inc., Bernard & Sarah, DC, 1801
GFC Foundation, The, UT, 9324
GHH Foundation, Inc., NJ, 5207
Gibson Charitable Trust, Nancy & Craig, NY, see 6025
Gibson Family Foundation, Inc., NJ, 5208
Gibson Family Foundation, The, NY, 6025
Gibson Hemostasis-Thrombosis Foundation, Mary Rodes, TX, 8918
GII Charities, MI, 4323
Gilbert Foundation, Lewis D. & John J., NY, 6028
Gilbert Foundation, Rosalinde and Arthur, The, CA, 575
Gill Family Foundation, Stephen & Margaret, CA, 576
Ginsburg Family Foundation, Inc., Alan and Harriet, FL, see 2022
Ginsburg Family Foundation, Inc., FL, 2022
Gipson Family Foundation, NC, 7375
GKW Foundation, Inc., GA, 2398
GLA Foundation, WA, 9593
Glassman Foundation, M. B. & Shana, CO, 1383
Gleason Foundation, George and Linda, AR, 164
Glickman Foundation, Inc., Morris, CA, 582
Godric Foundation, CA, 586
Goel Foundation, The, CA, 587
Goldberg Foundation, Inc., Arthur M. Goldberg and Veronica, NJ, 5209
Goldberg Foundation, Inc., Arthur M., NJ, see 5209
Golden Helping Hand Foundation, Inc., Sam and Marion, The, VA, 9430
Golden Rule Foundation, Inc., The, ME, 3538
Goldman Foundation for Fighting Catastrophic Diseases, Judith and George, IL, see 2763

Goldman Foundation, Robert I., NY, 6054
Goldman Philanthropic Partnerships, IL, 2763
Goldschmidt Family Foundation, Inc., Louis Callmann, NY, 6058
Goldstein Charity Fund, Inc., NJ, 5211
Goldstein Family Foundation, NY, 6061
Golkin Family Foundation, Perry & Donna, NY, 6068
Goodes Family Foundation, Inc., Melvin R., NJ, 5212
Goodfriend Foundation, Sidney E. and Amy O., NY, 6071
Gooding Family Foundation, CO, 1384
Goodman's, Inc., WI, 9807
Google Foundation, CA, 606
Gordy Foundation, Evelyn and Frank, The, GA, 2402
Gorelick Family Foundation, Shelton, NC, 7380
Gorman Foundation, The, NY, see 6078
Gorman Testamentary Charitable Trust, Owen T. Gorman & Alice M., NY, 6078
Gotschall Family Foundation, The, CA, 608
Gottlieb Fund, Inc., Lee, NY, 6081
Gould Family Foundation, NY, 6082
Grand Marnier Foundation, The, NY, 6086
Grandview-Steers Foundation, NY, 6088
Grayson Family Foundation, Inc., MA, 3932
Greatbatch Foundation, Eleanor and Wilson, NY, see 5899
Green Foundation, Daniel B. and Florence E., The, PA, 8225
Green Foundation, Howard L., The, NJ, 5215
Green Foundation, Leonard I., CA, see 614
Green Foundation, The, CA, 614
Green Fund, CO, 1385
Green Mountain Coffee Roasters Foundation, VT, 9358
Greensboro Jaycees Charitable Foundation, Inc., NC, 7383
Greenville Area Community Foundation, MI, 4331
Greenville Area Foundation, MI, see 4331
Griffin-Cole Fund, The, NY, 6106
Grin Family Foundation, Inc., NY, 6109
Groff Surgical and Medical Research and Education Charitable Trust, Mary E., The, PA, 8226
Gross Charitable Foundation, Allen I., NY, 6110
Grout Foundation, Gardner, CA, 624
Grumbacher Family Foundation, Nancy and Tim, The, PA, see 8227
Grumbacher Family Foundation, The, PA, 8227
GSF Foundation, CA, 627
GTE Federal Credit Union Charitable Trust, FL, 2040
Guarini Foundation, Inc., Frank J., The, NJ, 5216
Guest House Ministries Foundation, CA, 630
Gulf Power Foundation, Inc., FL, 2042
Gupta Family Foundation, Inc., Jai N., The, DE, 1716
Gural Foundation, Aaron & Marion, NY, 6120
Guthman Fund, Leo S., The, IL, 2776
Gutman Family Foundation, The, NY, 6122
GW Foundation, The, CT, 1561
Gynesis Women's International Foundation, DE, 1717

H.I.S. Foundation, MI, 4334
Habe Foundation, The, NY, 6128
Hager Family Charitable Trust, NY, 6131
Hager Foundation, CA, 638
Haggar Corp. Foundation, TX, 8929
Haglage Charitable Trust Agency, KS, 3365
Hahn Family Foundation, Norman & Elizabeth, The, PA, 8231
Halbert Family Foundation, Jon and Linda, TX, 8933
Halis Family Foundation, NY, 6136
Halloran Foundation, Mary P. Dolciani, NY, 6138
Hamilton-Forbes Charitable Trust, Ruth A., FL, 2046
Hamilton-White Foundation, The, CA, 642
Hammer International Foundation, CA, 643
Hampson Foundation, MI, 4336
Hancock Foundation, Inc., L. D., MS, 4746
Hank, Jr. Charitable Trust, Bernard J. and Joyce M., IL, see 2981
Hankin Foundation, Bernard & Henrietta, PA, see 8234
Hankin Foundation, PA, 8234
Hansen Family Foundation, Inc., NY, 6142
Harary Family Foundation, Jerry and Janet, The, NY, 6143
Harding Family Charitable Trust, OH, 7663
Hardtner Fund, Juliet E., LA, 3485
Harman Family Foundation, CA, 650

Harmon Foundation, Halbert, TX, 8941
Harmon Foundation, Inc., Halbert, TX, see 8941
Harrington Family Foundation, The, FL, 2049
Harris Foundation, Inc., Robinson, The, NJ, 5224
Harris Foundation, Richard V., NV, 5035
Harrison Foundation, Fred G., IL, 2790
Harrison Foundation, Inc., Helen M., IL, 2791
Hartmarx Charitable Foundation, IL, 2794
Harvest Charities, NC, 7392
Haseltine Charitable Foundation, William A., NY, 6152
Haugland Foundation, Rosaria P., OR, 8018
Hawthorn Charitable Foundation, TN, 8689
Hayes Family Charitable Foundation, The, FL, 2052
Haynes Family Foundation, Harold J. & Reta, CA, 658
Hazan Family Foundation, Morris A., The, CA, 660
Head Family Trust, Peyton Samuel, The, WI, see 9793
Healy Foundation, The, NM, 5479
Heart Foundation, The, CA, 662
Heavenly Hands Foundation, OH, 7668
Hebert and Donald Guthrie Charitable Foundation, Elizabeth, The, WA, 9604
Heckmann Family Foundation, The, NY, 6163
Hegwer Foundation, Raymond & Mildred, CA, 664
Heide Foundation Charitable Trust, Ulf B. Heide and Elizabeth C., The, MA, 3945
Heider Family Foundation, Charles and Mary, The, NE, 4972
Heimbinder Family Foundation, OH, 7670
Helen's Hope Foundation, IL, 2795
Heller Foundation, David B., The, NY, 6169
Hellman Family Foundation, CA, 667
Helmsley Foundation, Inc., Harry B., The, NY, see 6171
Helmsley Foundation, Inc., Leona and Harry B., NY, 6171
Help From Above, AZ, 105
Hench Foundation, John C., CA, 668
Hendel Foundation, Stephen and Ruth, NY, 6172
Henderson Foundation, MA, 3946
Hendrick Foundation for Children, NC, 7395
Hendricks Charitable Foundation, John and Maureen, MD, 3647
Hendrickson Foundation, Inc., Stephen J., The, MA, 3947
Hep Foundation Business Trust, The, KY, 3426
Herma Family Foundation, The, WI, 9814
Herman Foundation, Alexander & Charlotte, The, NY, 6174
Herro Charitable Foundation, David, The, IL, 2799
Herschend Family Foundation, MO, 4830
Heuer Foundation, Russell P. & Elizabeth Crimian, The, DE, 1720
Heuer Foundation, The, DE, see 1720
Heyward Memorial Fund, DuBose and Dorothy, The, NY, 6179
Hiawatha Education Foundation, MN, 4585
Hickey Family Foundation, AZ, 108
Hidden Pond Foundation, NJ, 5233
Hightower Foundation, Walter, TX, 8950
Hilfiger Family Foundation, Inc., The, NJ, 5235
Hill Family Foundation, Inc., The, NJ, 5236
Hill Foundation, Margaret M., The, NY, 6185
Hillenbrand Foundation, Roch & Carol, FL, 2060
Hillswood Foundation, MN, 4586
Hilton Family Foundation, FL, 2061
Hinduja Foundation, U.S., The, MA, 3952
Hirsch & Holly S. Andersen Family Foundation, Inc., Douglas A., NY, 6187
Hirsch Family Foundation, TX, 8953
Hirsch Foundation, Neil S., NY, 6188
Hites Family Community College Scholarship Corporation, MO, 4831
Hobbs Foundation, R. C., CA, 680
Hofer Family Foundation, NE, 4976
Hoffritz Charitable Trust, Helen, NY, 6196
Holden Foundation, Inc., Don L. & Julie, TX, 8957
Holden Foundation, Inc., Don L., TX, see 8957
Hollinger Charitable Trust, Pick, FL, 2064
Holloway Foundation, Inc., MS, 4749
Homeownership Preservation Foundation, MN, 4587
Hood Fund, Charles H., MA, 3957
Horizon Charitable Foundation, Inc., NJ, 5240
Horizon Foundation for New Jersey, The, NJ, see 5240
Horne Foundation, Dick, SC, 8594

Horowitz Family Foundation, Inc., GA, 2415
Horowitz Foundation, Inc., Gerald D., GA, see 2415
Hospira Foundation, IL, 2804
Houff Foundation, VA, 9438
Houssels Family Foundation Corporation, NV, 5038
Hoverter Charitable Foundation, Lawrence L. and Julia Z., PA, 8258
Hovnanian Foundation, Kevork and Sirwart, The, NJ, 5242
Hoyt Foundation, Inc., Stewart W. & Willma C., NY, 6203
Hubbell Foundation, Harvey, The, CT, 1569
Hudson Foundation, Laura & Walter, MN, 4591
Hugin Family Foundation, Inc., NJ, 5245
Huntington Foundation, Inc., The, WV, 9721
Huplits Foundation Trust, Myrtle V. C. Huplits & Woodman E., PA, 8262
Hurley-Trammell Foundation, The, NC, 7403
Hussey Foundation, The, WA, 9611
Hussman Foundation, Inc., The, MD, 3655
Hussman Foundation, The, AR, 165
Hutchins Family Foundation, Inc., NY, 6217
Hutton Foundation, Edward L., OH, 7681
Hyde Family Charitable Fund, The, WI, 9818
Hyder Family Foundation, The, WA, 9612

IF Hummingbird Foundation, Inc., NY, 6226
IFSA Foundation, Inc., IN, 3171
IHS Foundation, OH, 7683
Imada Foundation, The, NJ, 5249
Ingrassia Foundation, Elizabeth & Frank, NY, 6230
Innisfree Foundation of Bryn Mawr, Pennsylvania, PA, 8267
International Federation of Red Cross and Red Crescent Societies at the United Nations, Inc., NY, 6233
Irving Foundation, Inc., The, GA, 2419
Irwin Financial Foundation, IN, 3174
Iscol Family Foundation, Inc., The, NY, see 6226
Isen Family Foundation, CA, 701
Issa Family Foundation, CA, 703

Jaaaa Foundation, The, NY, 6245
Jackson Charitable Trust, Daisy B., The, OK, 7945
Jackson Charitable Trust, Ruth H., MA, 3966
Jacobus Family Foundation, Charles D., WI, 9819
Jacoff Foundation, Inc., Sydney & Helen, NY, 6249
Jaeger Foundation, LA, 3490
Jaeger Unruh Foundation, LA, see 3490
Jahn Foundation, Reinhardt H. & Shirley R., IL, 2816
James Foundation, Lawrence R. & Jeanette, NE, 4980
Jams Foundation, CA, 711
Janssen Foundation, Henry, PA, 8271
Janssen/Lagorio Family Foundation, The, CA, 715
Jarson - Stanley & Mickey Kaplan Foundation, Isaac & Esther, OH, 7686
Jarson Charitable Trust, Isaac N. and Esther M., OH, see 7686
Jarx Foundation, Inc., The, NY, 6255
Jeffe Foundation, Robert A. & Elizabeth R., The, CT, 1572
Jeffers Foundation, MN, 4594
Jeg's Quarter Mile Charities, OH, see 7687
Jegs Foundation, The, OH, 7687
Jelks Family Foundation, Inc., The, FL, 2076
Jenkins Foundation, Mervyn W., MO, 4836
Jensam Foundation, Inc., NJ, 5258
Jewish Renaissance Foundation, Inc., NY, 6261
JKO Foundation Charitable Trust, The, WI, 9822
JM Freedom Foundation, IL, 2817
Johnson Family Foundation, George R., TN, 8697
Johnson Family Foundation, Inc., The, NY, 6269
Johnson Family Foundation, J. Stanley and Mary W., CA, 721
Johnson Family Foundation, Violet M., IL, 2819
Johnson Family Foundation, WI, 9824
Jolley Foundation, Leodelle Lassiter, GA, 2423
Jolson Family Foundation, CA, 727
Jones Family Charitable Foundation, Inc., The, KY, 3430
Jones Family Foundation, Inc., The, WA, 9614
Jones Family Foundation, WI, 9827
Jordan Foundation, Inc., The, GA, 2425
JSJN Children's Charitable Trust, MA, 3972
Jubitz Family Foundation, Frederick D. & Gail Y., The, OR, 8029
Judkins Family Foundation, Don & Maxine, The, CA, 732

Juniata Foundation, Inc., The, CA, 734
Justus Trust, Edith C., PA, 8276
JW Foundation, The, NY, 6280
JWS Foundation, Inc., CA, 735

K-Swiss Foundation, The, CA, see 190
Kabcenell Family Foundation, CA, 737
Kalmanovitz Charitable Foundation, CA, 741
Kanitz Scholarship Memorial Fund, Louis J. & Golda I., CA, 742
Kaplan Charitable Foundation, Helen and Sam, KS, 3373
Kaplan Family Foundation, Inc., 1996 M. M., FL, 2078
Kaplan Family Foundation, The, NC, see 7495
Karches Foundation, NY, 6292
Katcher Family Foundation, Inc., The, FL, 2080
Katz Foundation, Inc., Ellen Philips Schwarzman, NY, 6294
Katzen Foundation, Inc., Cyrus, VA, 9446
Kaufman Family Foundation, Ann & Stephen, The, TX, 8981
Kawasaki Good Times Foundation, NE, 4982
Keeler Charitable Trust, Ruth, NY, 6306
Keith Foundation, Greg and India, The, NC, 7410
Keithley Family Foundation, Roy and Cindy, TX, 8983
Keller Foundation, Inc., WI, 9831
Kelly Services, Inc. Foundation, The, MI, 4359
Kennebec Foundation, ME, see 3543
Kennebec Savings Bank Foundation, ME, 3543
Kennebunk Savings Bank Foundation, ME, 3544
Kennedy Family Foundation, John C. & Nancy G., MI, 4360
Kennedy Foundation, Inc., John R., The, FL, 2089
Kenney Watershed Protection Foundation, William C., The, CO, 1401
Kentucky Fund for Healthy Living, Inc., KY, 3433
Keown Charitable Foundation, The, TX, 8989
Keren Yitzchak Foundation, Inc., The, NJ, 5277
Keren Zichron Aron Foundation, The, NY, 6318
Kest Family Foundation, Sol and Clara, CA, 754
Kettering Foundation, Virginia W., The, WI, 9835
Keyser Foundation, Robert S. & Dorothy J., The, NV, 5039
Keystone Nazareth Charitable Foundation, PA, 8285
Keystone Savings Foundation, PA, 8286
Killinger Foundation, Kerry and Linda, The, WA, 9618
Kimerling Foundation, Inc., The, AL, 41
Kimmell Family Foundation, OK, 7951
Kindred Foundation Inc., KY, 3434
King Street Charitable Trust, The, NY, 6325
Kinney-Lindstrom Foundation, Inc., IA, 3300
Kirkland Foundation, Robert E. and Jenny D., TN, 8699
Kiva Foundation, The, MA, 3984
Klapper Family Foundation, Inc., The, IN, 3183
Klein Family Foundation, Lloyd E. Elisabeth, CA, 764
Klein Family Foundation, NY, 6331
Kleinman Family Foundation, The, NY, 6334
Klingenstein Family Fund, Inc., Andrew & Julie, NY, 6335
Kluge Foundation, Patricia M., The, VA, see 9451
Kluge-Moses Foundation, The, VA, 9451
KMD Foundation, FL, 2096
Knabusch Charitable Trust No. 2, Edward M. and Henrietta M., MI, 4363
Knight Foundation, Inc., Faith & James, NJ, 5281
Knott Foundation, Marion, CA, 769
Knowlton Foundation, The, MN, 4598
Kolatch Family Foundation, NJ, 5285
Kommerstad Foundation, The, CA, 772
Kontos Foundation, Inc., Arthur, The, NJ, 5286
Koret Fund, CA, 775
KPB Corporation, NC, 7414
Kramer Charitable Foundation, Arthur B. and Alice, The, CT, 1577
Kraus Family Foundation, The, NY, 6352
Krause Gentle Foundation, IA, 3302
Krauss Charitable Foundation, Jenny H. & Otto F., MI, 4366
Krauss, Miller, Lutz Charitable Trust Foundation, Inc., FL, 2101
Kravis Foundation, Robert Kravis and Kimberly, The, NY, 6355
Krehbiel Family Foundation, IL, 2845

Kreindler Foundation, Lee S., The, NY, 6356
Krejci Trust, Helen and Rudy, WI, 9843
Krieble Foundation, Inc., Vernon K., The, MA, 3990
Krueck Foundation, Anstiss & Ronald, The, IL, 2846
Kuhne Foundation Trust, Charles W., IN, 3187
Kurtz Family Foundation, The, NY, 6364
Kurz Family Foundation, Ltd., The, NY, 6365

Labovitz Foundation, Sharon and Joel, MN, 4601
Lafromboise Foundation, Jean K., WA, 9622
Lamb Foundation, Inc., Robert E., PA, 8299
Lambert Charitable Foundation, Inc., Lucille and Bruce, VA, 9453
Lamond Family Foundation, CA, 785
Landry Charitable Foundation, C. Kevin, MA, 3995
Landsman Charitable Trust, The, MA, 3996
Langbo Foundation, Arnold G. & Martha M., MI, 4371
Langenfelder Charitable Trust, George H., MD, 3670
Langford Foundation, Frances, FL, 2102
Lanier Foundation, Thomas H., The, GA, 2430
Lantana Education Charitable Foundation, TX, 9004
Lapides Foundation, Inc., Allene & Jerome, The, NM, 5485
LaPorte, Jr. Foundation, Ltd., Joe, TN, see 8657
Larson Family Charitable Foundation, The, WA, 9624
Larson Foundation, MN, 4603
Laurel Resources, Inc., CA, 792
Laverack Foundation, William and Cordelia, The, CT, 1580
Lavietes Foundation, Inc., Raymond P., CT, 1581
Lavine Foundation, Richard and Ruth, CA, 793
Lawless Family Foundation, MD, 3671
Lawrence Charitable Foundation, The, NY, 6385
Lawrence County Community Foundation, IN, see 3133
Lea Charitable Trust, The, IL, 2850
Lead International, Inc., NY, 6389
Leadership for Environment & Development International, Inc., NY, see 6389
Leake Charitable Trust, Louise Briley, WI, 9849
Lear Corporation Charitable Foundation, MI, 4374
Lee & George Gund III Foundation, Iara, The, CA, 798
Lee Family Foundation, Daniel and Karen, IL, 2853
Lee Family Foundation, Inc., The, CT, 1582
Legatus Foundation, NC, 7420
Lehrer Family Foundation, CA, 800
Leiser Foundation, Inc., Josephine S., FL, 2108
Lenz Foundation for American Buddhism, Frederick P., The, CA, 803
Leonard Charitable Foundation, George & Wilma, CA, 804
Leslie Family Foundation, CA, 806
Lessing Family Foundation, The, NY, 6404
Let Love Rule Foundation, CA, 808
Levant Foundation, The, TX, 9008
Levi, Ray & Shoup Foundation, IL, 2855
Levine Charitable Foundation, Kenneth and Lorraine, The, MA, 4003
Levine Charitable Foundation, Kenneth and Rachel, The, MA, see 4003
Levine Charitable Fund, Inc., Laurence, FL, 2111
Levine Foundation, Inc., Laurence W., NY, 6408
Levine Foundation, William S. and Ina, AZ, 115
Levinson Foundation, Max and Anna, NM, 5486
Levy Foundation, Frances and Jack, NY, 6411
Levy Foundation, Inc., Shuki, CA, 810
Levy Foundation, Leon, NY, 6414
Lewis Family Foundation, Richard H., CO, 1410
Lewis Foundation, T. W., AZ, 116
Lichtenstein, Jr. Foundation, Morris L., The, TX, 9010
Lie Foundation, Gunnar and Ruth, The, WA, 9629
Lindahl Foundation, TCH, TN, 8702
Lindmor Foundation, The, NY, 6425
Lindner Foundation, Robert D., OH, 7717
Lindorf Memorial Foundation, Bruce, CA, 814
Lindsay Foundation-1989, Margaret Stewart, The, MA, 4009
Link Foundation, The, TX, 9013
Lipchitz Foundation, Inc., Jacques and Yulla, NY, 6430
Lipman Foundation, Eric and Jeanette, The, VA, see 9459
Lipman Foundation, The, VA, 9459
Lipp Family Foundation, The, CA, 818
Little Family Foundation, Inc., The, MD, 3679

Littlefield Foundation, Edmund and Jeannik, CA, 820
Littlefield Foundation, Edmund Wattis, CA, see 820
Living Stones Foundation, CA, 821
Locke Family Foundation, Inc., The, MD, 3680
Lockwood Family Foundation, UT, 9333
Loebs Family Foundation, The, MA, 4011
Logan Foundation, Reva and David, IL, 2860
Looney Foundation, Inc., Martha and Wilton, The, GA, 2436
Lopatin Family Foundation, The, NY, 6446
Lord's Fund, The, TX, 9019
Lost and Foundation, Inc., The, MA, 4012
Louisiana-Pacific Foundation, OR, 8037
Lozick Foundation, Edward A. and Catherine L., OH, 7724
Lozick Foundation, Edward A., OH, see 7724
Lubert Family Foundation, Inc., The, PA, 8315
Luchsinger Family Foundation, The, TX, 9022
Ludcke Foundation, The, MA, 4017
Ludlow-Griffith Foundation, CO, 1412
Ludwig Family Foundation, Inc., The, DC, 1826
Luster Family Foundation, Inc., CA, see 953
Lutece Foundation, Inc., The, NY, 6460
Lynn Foundation, The, CA, 835
Lynton Foundation, The, NY, 6463

M.D.C. Holdings, Inc. Charitable Foundation, CO, 1413
MacDougald Foundation, Inc., The, FL, 2122
Mack Family Foundation, Inc., David & Sondra, The, NJ, 5312
Mack Foundation, Inc., Earle I., The, NJ, 5314
Macrini Foundation, Thomas G. & Nancy J., TX, 9026
Magee Foundation, The, PA, 8320
Magistro Foundation, Inc., CA, 847
Magnus Charitable Trust, IL, 2870
MAH Foundation, NY, 6474
Maheras Foundation, NY, 6475
Mahnken Foundation, Inc., Elizabeth A., The, IN, 3198
Mahon Charitable Foundation, Arthur & Myra, CT, 1593
Mahon Foundation, MN, 4609
Mallory Foundation, NV, 5043
Mangurian Foundation, Inc., The, NY, see 6482
Mangurian, Jr. Foundation, Inc., Harry T., The, NY, 6482
Manitou Fund, MN, 4610
Mann Family Foundation, The, RI, 8546
Many Voices Foundation, MA, 4020
Mapplethorpe Foundation, Inc., Robert, NY, 6485
Marcled Foundation, The, CA, 851
Marcon Foundation, Inc., NJ, 5317
Marcus & Millichap Company Foundation, The, CA, 852
Marcus Family Foundation, George and Judy, The, CA, 853
Marcus Foundation, Edward and Betty, The, TX, 9029
Marden Foundation, Bernard A. & Chris, FL, 2127
Marino Charitable Foundation, Roger M. & Michelle S., The, MA, 4023
Marks Family Foundation, Michael E., CA, 857
Marmurstein Charitable Foundation Trust, Yacov and Rita, The, NY, 6491
Maroone Family Foundation, FL, 2129
Marshall Charitable Foundation, Inc., The, KY, 3438
Marshfield Area Community Foundation, WI, 9861
Martin Charitable Foundation, Steve, The, CA, 859
Martin County Community Foundation, IN, see 3133
Martin Family Foundation, Albert Jay, The, TN, 8706
Martin Foundation, Gilbert J., The, CA, 860
Martin Foundation, Inc., TX, 9031
Martin Memorial Trust, James G., NH, 5097
Masada Foundation, NY, 6500
Maslow Family Foundation, Inc., PA, 8327
Mason Trust, B. A., WI, 9863
Massachusetts Automobile Dealers Charitable Foundation, MA, 4026
Massey Family Foundation, OK, 7955
Master Educational Assistance Foundation, IL, 2875
Masters Foundation, Inc., The, FL, 2131
Mater Dei Foundation, CO, 1417
Max Charitable Foundation, CA, see 1322
May Employees Trust Fund, David, OH, 7738
McCarthy Bush Foundation, IA, 3311
McCaw Family Foundation, Keith & Mary Kay, WA, 9636
McCrea Foundation, TX, 9040
McCune Foundation, Don C. and Florence M., KS, 3376

McDonald Manufacturing Company Charitable Foundation, A. Y., IA, 3312
McDonnell Charitable Foundation, John J. McDonald, Jr. & Marian J., VA, 9468
McGettigan Foundation, Patrick H., The, DC, 1829
McGue Millhiser Family Trust, The, VA, 9470
MCI Education Foundation, VA, 9471
MCI Foundation, VA, see 9471
McKee Foundation, Robert E. and Evelyn, TX, 9045
McLane/Harper Charitable Foundation, Inc., The, MA, 4033
McMullan Foundation, James and Milton, IL, 2884
McNeill Family Foundation, WY, see 9986
McNeill Foundation, Corbin & Dorice S., WY, 9986
McWhinney Foundation, CO, 1423
Mead Charitable Foundation, D. Richard, IL, 2888
Mechia Foundation, TX, 9050
Medleycott Family Foundation, The, PA, 8343
Medline Foundation, The, IL, 2889
Megrue Family Foundation, NY, 6524
Melmac Education Foundation, ME, 3550
Melrene Fund, The, IL, 2892
Melville Foundation, The, CT, 1602
Merage Family Foundation, Paul & Elisabeth, The, CA, 887
Merage Foundation of Nevada, Andre & Katherine, CA, 888
Merck-Schering Plough Patient Assistance Program, NJ, 5329
Meriweather Perpetual Charitable Trust, Tyler, IL, 2893
Meriwether Foundation, The, NY, 6535
Merkle Foundation, Jess, The, LA, 3500
Merrill Foundation, Inc., Julia & Gilbert, FL, 2136
Merrill Foundation, Inc., The, WI, 9872
Merriman Foundation, DC, 1833
Mesirow Charitable Foundation, IL, 2894
Messer Foundation, The, NY, 6540
Metcalf Foundation, Inc., Stanley W., The, NY, 6541
Mevatek Foundation, The, TX, 9056
Meyerson Family Foundation, Morton H., TX, 9058
MFU Training Plan Trust, CA, 894
MIC Foundation, NY, see 6560
Michaan Foundation, J. S. & S., The, FL, 2138
Michelson, M.D. Charitable Foundation, Inc., Gary Karlin, CA, 896
Milagro Foundation, The, TX, see 9056
Miles Foundation, Inc., The, TX, 9060
Miller Charitable Foundation, Mark & Kimberly, PA, 8353
Miller Charitable Trust, James E. & Lila G., OR, 8043
Miller Family Foundation, Barbara and Fred, The, CA, 899
Miller Family Foundation, Ken A. & Gail B., NC, see 7480
Miller Foundation, Alon and Rosana, The, CA, 900
Miller Foundation, Arnold and Suzanne, The, TX, 9061
Miller Foundation, Charles Lawrence Keith and Clara, NY, 6551
Miller Foundation, Jack and Goldie Wolfe, IL, 2899
Miller Foundation, Steve J., The, WI, 9875
Miller Foundation, Steven and Sheila, TX, 9062
Miller Foundation, Tim, VA, 9475
Mills Family Foundation, Inc., NC, 7429
Milton Fine Family Charitable Foundation, PA, see 8201
Mirak Foundation, John, MA, 4041
Mitchell Foundation, Inc., Joan, The, NY, 6559
Mithun Family Foundation, MN, 4626
Mitsubishi International Corporation Foundation, NY, 6560
Mizel Global Cultural Fund, CO, 1427
Mnuchin Foundation, Steven and Heather, The, NY, 6564
Mnuchin Foundation, Steven T., The, NY, see 6564
Moeller Foundation, Joe and Mary, GA, 2449
Monius Institute, Inc., A. M., NJ, 5333
Monteforte Foundation, Inc., The, NY, 6567
Moody Foundation, Inc., Gloria Narramore, AL, 54
Moore Family Foundation, Inc., AL, 55
Moore Family Foundation, Inc., Edward S., NY, 6572
Moore Foundation, Inc., Marion, CT, 1604
Moore Foundation, Sara Giles, GA, 2451
Moore Foundation, Tom and Judy, The, NY, 6574
Moore Fund, Ruth Danley & William Enoch, PA, 8358
Moran Foundations, Inc., Jim, The, FL, 2143

Mordecai Foundation, Daniel and Janet, NY, 6575
Morey Foundation, The, MI, 4397
Morgan Family Foundation, OH, 7760
Morgan Foundation, Inc., Edwin E. & Ruby C., MS, 4759
Morgan Roundation, Inc., John E., NY, 6576
Morrison Foundation, Robert S., OH, 7764
Morrison Knudsen Corporation Foundation, ID, see 2578
Morse Hill Foundation, Inc., NY, 6584
Moss Foundation, Inc., Stephen, NY, 6589
Mossier Foundation, Kevin J., MN, 4628
Mozer Foundation, The, MI, 4401
Mt. Cuba Center, Inc., DE, 1734
Muldoon Fund, Mary, NY, 6594
Mullen Family Foundation, Inc., Donald R., NY, 6595
Murray Foundation, Geraldine M., PA, 8360
Muselman Family Foundation, Inc., Arthur K., IN, 3209
Musser Foundation, Warren V., The, PA, 8361
Mustard Seed Foundation, The, KY, 3440
Mutual Federal Savings Bank Charitable Foundation, Inc., IN, 3210
Mutual of Omaha Foundation, NE, 4993

N.E.W. Charitable Foundation, Inc., The, VA, 9482
N.E.W. Relief Fund, Inc., The, VA, see 9482
Naddisy Foundation, Inc., NY, 6598
Nagle Family Foundation, The, NY, 6599
Nanci's Animal Rights Foundation, Inc., FL, 2150
Nancy and John Foundation, TX, see 9199
Natan Foundation, WA, 9646
National Instruments Foundation, TX, 9088
NBT Charitable Trust, MA, 4048
Neisser Fund, The, IL, 2910
Nelson Family Foundation, Inc., Margaret Irene Taylor Nelson and Mary, MO, 4871
Nevada Partners, Inc., NV, 5048
New Blank Family Foundation, Inc., The, FL, see 1909
New England Patriots Charitable Foundation, Inc., The, MA, 4054
New York Jets Foundation, Inc., NY, 6616
Newcastle Foundation, NY, 6622
Newman Family Foundation, CO, 1432
Newman Foundation, Barnett and Annalee, The, DE, 1736
NFC Foundation, MN, 4633
NFG Foundation, OH, 7776
NFM Charitable Trust, NC, 7434
Nicholas Family Charitable Trust, NY, 6627
Nicholas Foundation, The, CA, 937
Nicholson Family Foundation, MN, 4634
Nicholson Foundation, Richard H. and Nancy B., MN, see 4634
Nickel Producers Environmental Research Association, Inc., NC, 7436
Nickless Family Charitable Foundation, The, MI, 4403
Nicolais Foundation, Inc., The, NJ, 5339
No Other Foundation, TN, 8713
Norcross Family Foundation, Mark A. and Rena R., NC, 7437
North American Rescue Products Foundation, Inc., SC, 8601
North Dade Medical Foundation, Inc., FL, 2153
Northwest Autism Foundation, OR, 8047
Northwest Health Foundation Fund, II, OR, 8048
Northwestern National Insurance Foundation, CT, see 1672
Notsew Orm Sands Foundation, TX, 9093

O'Brien Foundation, Inc., James W., MA, 4058
O'Sullivan Foundation, The, TX, 9098
O'Toole Family Foundation, The, NY, 6653
Oakland Athletics Community Fund, The, CA, 948
Oehmig Foundation, The, TX, 9099
Ohio Casualty Foundation, Inc., OH, 7784
Omega Foundation, The, NV, 5050
Omidyar Network Fund, Inc., CA, 952
On Shore, Inc., CA, 953
One Family-The Innocent Heart Foundation, CA, see 810
Onward & Upward Initiative Charitable Trust, TX, 9103
Oppenheimer Brothers Foundation, CA, 955
Oristaglio Family Foundation, MA, 4063
Orokawa Foundation, Inc., The, MD, 3702

Orr Family Foundation, Robert O. and AnnaMae, OH, 7790
Ortenzio Family Foundation, The, PA, 8366
Orthwein Foundation, William R. Orthwein, Jr. & Laura Rand, The, MO, 4878
Osborn Foundation, The, CO, 1434
Oschin Family Foundation, Mr. & Mrs. Samuel, CA, 960
Oshman Foundation, TX, 9104
OSI Pharmaceuticals Foundation, Inc., NY, 6670
Ostreicher Family Foundation, Harry & Helen, NY, 6671
Ostreicher Family Foundation, Marvin & Susan, NY, 6672
Otenasek Charitable Foundation, Inc., Anne Lindsey, The, MD, 3704
Outcalt Charitable Fund, OH, see 7792
Outcalt Foundation, Jane and Jon, OH, 7792
Outrageous Foundation, Inc., The, CA, 967
Overstreet Foundation, FL, 2159
Ovitz Family Foundation, The, CA, 968
Owen Trust, B. B., TX, 9107
Owens Corning Foundation, OH, 7793
Oxford Area Foundation, The, PA, 8367

Pacific Foundation, MN, 4646
Padnos Foundation, Louis and Helen, MI, 4406
Pamphalon Foundation, Inc., FL, 2162
Paneth Family Charitable Trust, The, NY, 6685
Pannonia Foundation, NY, 6686
Pardee Foundation, J. Douglas & Marian R., The, CA, 978
Park Foundation, The, OH, 7794
Parks Education Foundation, NV, 5052
Parmer Family Foundation, Inc., The, PA, 8369
Parr Family Foundation, Inc., Gary W., The, NY, 6692
Parr Trust, Martha Sue, WI, 9893
Paso del Norte Health Foundation, TX, 9111
Patricelli Family Foundation, Robert & Margaret, The, CT, 1623
Patrick Foundation, Inc., Carl & Frances, The, GA, 2459
Patterson Foundation, Proctor, OH, 7797
Paul Family Foundation, Andrew M., NY, 6697
Paul Foundation, Inc., Terrance and Judith, CO, 1435
Pauley Family Foundation, The, VA, 9494
Paulos Foundation, The, TX, 9112
Paulucci Family Foundation, Jeno & Lois, The, FL, 2164
Paulucci Family Foundation, The, FL, see 2164
PDB Foundation, Inc., IL, 2935
PE Charitable Foundation, CT, see 1484
Peach Foundation, WA, 9659
Pearson-Rappaport Foundation, NY, 6701
Pechter Foundation, The, GA, 2461
Peck Foundation, Ltd., Miriam & Bernard, WI, see 9895
Peck Foundation, Milwaukee, Ltd., WI, 9895
Peirce Family Foundation, Inc., The, PA, 8370
Pelosi Charitable Foundation, Paul & Nancy, CA, 988
Pels International Foundation, Laura, NY, 6708
Peltier Foundation, The, LA, 3504
Penner Foundation, Inc., Arnold S., NY, 6710
Perella Foundation, A. J., The, NY, 6715
Perelman Charitable Foundation, Inc., IN, 3222
Perlman Family Foundation, Harold L., IL, 2938
Perlman Family Foundation, Lawrence and Linda, MN, 4651
Perlman Family Foundation, MN, see 4651
Perlman Foundation, Harold L., IL, see 2938
Perot, Jr. Foundation, Sarah and Ross, The, TX, 9119
Persepolis Foundation, The, NY, 6718
Peters Foundation Corp., Herman & Katherine, The, IL, 2940
Peters Research Foundation, Harvey W., SD, 8629
Peterson Family Foundation, The, WA, 9662
Peterson Foundation, Thomas F., The, OH, 7802
Petitpren Family Foundation, Dean & Diane, MI, 4411
Petrello Family Foundation, TX, 9121
Phelan Foundation, The, NY, 6723
Phelps Family Foundation, CA, 1001
Phillips-Van Heusen Foundation, Inc., NY, 6725
Phoenix Family Foundation, NJ, see 5193
Phoenixville Community Health Foundation, PA, 8381
Picerne Family Foundation, CA, 1004
Picerne Foundation, Ken and Tonya, CA, see 1004
Pickle Charitable Foundation, James W., The, TN, 8717
Piedmont Natural Gas Foundation, NC, 7447

Pigott Scholarship Foundation, Paul, WA, 9663
Pine Foundation, The, TX, 9123
Pioneer Fund, Inc., The, NY, 6729
Pioneer Hi-Bred International, Inc. Foundation, IA, 3324
Piper Jaffray Foundation, MN, 4656
Plus Valia Foundation, The, TX, 9125
Plymouth Rock Foundation, The, MA, 4085
PMJ Foundation, MO, 4885
Podiatry Foundation of Pittsburgh, The, PA, 8389
Pohanka Family Foundation, John J., The, MD, 3707
Polisseni Foundation, Inc., The, NY, 6733
Pollack Family Foundation, Inc., Geri & Lester, The, NY, 6735
Pollack Family Foundation, The, NY, see 6735
Pollock Foundation, PA, 8390
Pollock Foundation, S. Wilson & Grace M., PA, see 8390
Poor Richard's Charitable Trust, PA, 8392
Pope Foundation, John William, NC, 7450
Poses Family Foundation, The, NJ, 5354
Post Family Foundation, Lawrence and Sandra, The, CA, 1011
Post Foundation, John A. & Margaret, NJ, 5355
Postles Scholarship Fund, Wilbur E., PA, 8393
Potamkin Family Foundation I, Inc., FL, 2176
Power Foundation, The, MI, 4415
Poweshiek Community Foundation, Greater, IA, 3325
Praise The Lord Foundation, CA, see 821
Pralle Family Foundation, Robert R. and Helga, The, CA, 1014
Precourt Foundation, The, CO, 1441
Premier Foundation, The, SC, 8604
Prescott Family Foundation, Inc., WI, 9903
Price Charitable Foundation, Tina & Steven, NY, 6745
Price Family Charitable Fund, The, CA, 1016
Price Foundation, Mary Grant, CA, 1018
Price Foundation, Sol & Helen, The, CA, see 1016
Price Foundation, William L., The, CA, 1019
Principato Foundation, Jerold & Marjorie, MD, 3710
Progressive Education Foundation, Inc., IL, 2956
Progressive Insurance Foundation, The, OH, 7808
Promethean Foundation, TN, 8721
Promise Keepers Charitable Foundation, CA, 1023
Prophet Corporation Foundation, MN, 4658
Propp Sons Fund, Inc., Morris and Anna, NY, 6749
Provident Bank Foundation, The, NJ, 5359
Pruet Foundation, The, AR, 170
Pruina Corporation, The, OH, 7809
Pryor Foundation, The, PA, 8396
PSC Charitable Foundation, PA, 8398
PTM Charitable Foundation, The, NY, 6752
Pulier Charitable Foundation, Inc., Benjamin & Seema, NY, 6753
Purple Moon Foundation, Inc., WI, 9905

Quimby Family Foundation, FL, 2183
Quinn Foundation, Inc., John A., MD, 3713
Quinn Foundation, John A., MD, see 3713

R & R Realty Group Foundation, IA, 3327
Rachofsky Foundation, Howard Earl, TX, 9139
Rady Family Foundation, CA, 1026
Rae Charitable Trust, James Arthur, AZ, 132
Raffiani Family Foundation, Inc., NY, 6767
Ragan and King Charitable Foundation, NC, see 7455
Ragan Charitable Foundation, Carolyn King, NC, 7455
Ramsay Family Foundation, CA, 1030
Randall & Dewey Foundation, Inc., TX, 9140
Ranger Family Charitable Trust, The, NY, 6770
Ranney Foundation, P. K., OH, 7813
Rapaport Shallat Foundation, NY, 6771
Ratshesky Foundation, A.C., MA, 4095
Rauenhorst Foundation, Inc., Gerald and Henrietta, FL, 2185
Rav-Noy Family Foundation, Inc., The, CA, 1033
Ravitch Foundation, Inc., Richard, NY, 6776
Raymund Foundation, Inc., FL, 2188
RBC Dain Rauscher Foundation, MN, 4661
Realty Foundation of New York, NY, 6779
REBNY Foundation, Inc., NY, 6780
Rebsamen Fund, AR, 171
Rechelbacher Foundation, Horst M., MN, 4662
Reddy Foundation, Inc., Ravi and Pratibha, NJ, 5364
Reding Family Foundation, MO, 4890

Redstone Charitable Trust, Michael, The, MA, 4097
Reeves Foundation, Inc., Carl Marshall Reeves and Mildred Almen, IN, 3227
Regan Foundation, Inc., John M. Regan, Jr. & Prudence S., The, FL, 2191
Reich Family Charitable Trust, The, NY, 6784
Reimers Family Foundation, The, NY, see 6425
Reinhart Foundation, CA, 1038
Remington Family Foundation, MO, 4891
Repass-Rodgers Family Foundation, Inc., The, DE, 1742
Resch Foundation, Marion G., OH, 7816
Resler Foundation, FL, 2194
ResMed Foundation, CA, 1040
Rest Haven Preventorium for Children, Inc., CA, 1044
Reynolds Foundation, Marjorie Harris, MA, 4101
RFI Foundation, MD, 3716
Ribakoff Charitable Foundation, Eugene J. and Corinne A., MA, see 4103
Ribakoff Family Foundation, MA, 4103
Rice Family Foundation, The, NY, 6794
Rice Foundation, Charles & Catherine B., GA, 2471
Richardson Charitable Foundation, A. E. and Jaunita, OK, 7973
Richardson Foundation, Inc., Blair and Kristin, The, CO, 1444
Riddle Foundation, The, TX, 9148
Rieder Family Foundation, A. & M., The, NY, 6803
Riley Foundation, Susan E., CA, 1052
Rinker Foundation, Harry & Diane, The, CA, 1053
Ripple Foundation, The, NY, 6811
Ripplewood Foundation, Inc., NY, 6812
Rising Family Foundation, CA, 1055
Ritchie Memorial Foundation, Charles E. and Mabel M., The, OH, 7821
Riter, Jr. Family Foundation, A. W., TX, 9149
Ritter Family Foundation, CT, 1633
RNR Foundation, Inc., MI, 4420
Roberts & David Seltzer Charitable Trust, Lisa S., PA, see 8392
Roberts Charitable Foundation, FL, 2201
Roberts Charitable Trust, Belle G., AL, 59
Roberts, Jr. Trust, Percival, NC, 7465
Robideau Foundation, Inc., The, MI, 4421
Robinson Foundation for Hearing Disorders, Inc., CA, 1060
Robinson Foundation, Inc., Jim and Linda, The, NY, 6819
Rochetta-Wessies Scholarship Foundation, The, IL, 2969
Rockjensen Foundation, Inc., The, TX, 9153
Roger's & Betty's Charitable Foundation, CA, see 859
Rogers Foundation Corporation, S. Dennis and Leslie L., MI, 4423
Rogers Private Family Foundation, T. Gary and Kathleen, CA, 1064
Rolfs Foundation, Inc., Robert T., WI, 9914
Rose Foundation, Deborah, The, NY, 6835
Rosen Foundation, Inc., Abner, The, NY, 6842
Rosenberg Foundation, David M. and Marjorie D., The, PA, 8412
Rosenfeld Family Foundation, Gene and Maxine, The, CA, 1067
Rosenwald Foundation, Edward John & Patricia, The, NY, 6856
Ross Foundation, Inc., Bob A., CA, 1069
Rotasa Foundation, CA, 1070
Rothschild Fund, A. Frank and Dorothy B., CA, 1072
Roundy's Foundation, Inc., WI, 9915
Roxe Foundation, The, NY, 6867
Rubenstein Family Charitable Foundation, Harold, MA, 4116
Rubenstein Foundation, Jerry and Maury, The, TX, 9162
Rude Foundation, Inc., Raymond C., NV, 5058
Rupp Foundation, Fran and Warren, The, MN, 4669
Russell Charitable Trust, GA, 2478
Rutledge Charities, Inc., Edward and Hannah M., WI, 9917
Rutledge Charity, Edward, WI, see 9917
Ruvo Family Foundation, The, NV, 5060
Ryan Family Charitable Foundation, CA, 1075
Ryan Foundation, David Claude, CA, see 1075
Ryan Foundation, Patrick G. & Shirley W., IL, 2977
Ryan Foundation, William G. and Mary A., IL, 2978

S.R.C. Education Alliance, NC, 7470
Sachs Family Foundation, NY, 6888
Sadowsky Family Foundation, William, The, MA, 4121
Safety Insurance Foundation, MA, see 4147
Salah Family Foundation for the Town of Canton, Inc., James and Beatrice, MA, 4124
Salem Charitable Trust, Paul and Navyn, RI, see 8554
Salem Five Charitable Foundation, Inc., MA, 4125
Salem Foundation, The, RI, 8554
Salomon Scholarship Fund, William R., NY, 6898
Samaritan Foundation, OH, 7832
Samerian Foundation, Inc., IN, 3234
San Angelo Area Foundation, TX, 9164
San Joaquin Foundation, Inc., CA, 1089
San Simeon Fund, Inc., The, CA, 1091
Sand County Foundation, Inc., WI, 9918
Sanders Family Foundation, Don A., TX, 9167
Sandler Foundation, Mara & Ricky, The, NY, 6902
Sands Foundation, George H. and Estelle M., NJ, 5382
Sandy Hill Foundation, NY, 6903
Sangre De Christo Charitable Trust, IL, 2981
Sani Family Foundation, Inc., NY, 6904
Savage Family Foundation, Neal & Sherrie, The, UT, 9340
Sawnee Mountain Foundation, Inc., GA, 2481
Sawyer Family Foundation, The, NV, 5061
Sayler-Hawkins Foundation, MO, 4897
Schafer Family Foundation, NY, 6910
Scharf Foundation, Inc., Leon & Irene, NY, see 5910
Schecter Family Foundation, Inc., The, NJ, 5385
Scheller, Jr. Family Foundation, Roberta and Ernest, PA, 8426
Scheumann Foundation, Inc., The, IN, 3235
Schiff Family Foundation, Robert C. & Adele R., OH, 7836
Schifter Family Foundation, MD, 3726
Schimmel Foundation, Inc., Stephen Harold, The, CA, 1101
Schippmann Foundation, J. W., FL, 2224
Schmeelk Foundation, Inc., Priscilla & Richard J., NY, 6927
Schmidt Family Charitable Foundation, J. Frank, The, OR, 8055
Schneider Charitable Trust, John D. and Minnie R., IL, 2988
Schneider Charitable Trust, John D., IL, see 2988
Schnitzer/Novack Foundation, OR, 8057
Schocken Foundation, Inc., The, CA, 1105
Scholarships Foundation, Inc., The, NY, 6932
Schott Foundation, Marge & Charles J., OH, 7843
Schuler Family Foundation, Force, WA, see 9678
Schuler Family Foundation, IL, 2990
Schuler Family Foundation, WA, 9678
Schulze Family Foundation, Richard M., MN, 4675
Schusterman Foundation, Dan & Gloria, The, OK, 7976
Schwab Rainess Foundation, PA, 8430
Schwab-Spector-Rainess Foundation, PA, see 8430
Schwartz Family Foundation, Inc., Barry K., NY, 6940
Schwarz Family Foundation, NY, 6947
Schwarzman Foundation, Inc., Ellen Philips, NY, see 6294
Schweers Family Foundation, Geiser, CA, 1112
Scotford Foundation, OH, 7846
Scully Family Foundation, Irene S., CA, 1116
Scully Foundation, Joseph C. and Judith A., The, IL, 2992
SEAKR Foundation, CO, 1452
Seaver Charitable Trust, Richard C., CA, 1117
Seaworld & Busch Gardens Conservation Fund, MO, 4900
Sebastiani Charitable Trust, August, The, CA, 1119
Sedgwick Family Charitable Trust, OH, 7849
Seedlings Foundation, CT, 1645
Seeno, Jr. Family Foundation, Albert D., The, CA, 1120
Seevers Family Foundation, NY, 6953
Seifert Charitable Trust, Dorothy T. & Myron, OH, 7850
Seiple Family Foundation, PA, 8432
Selfon Memorial Fund Charitable Trust, Merle, PA, 8433
Selis Foundation, Inc., Irving and Sara, NY, 6955
Seramur Family Foundation, Inc., WI, 9924
SES Foundation, Inc., The, NY, 6956
Sewell Family Foundation, MN, 4678

Shannon Family Foundation, Ken and Jan, The, KS, 3392
Shannon Foundation, E. L. and Ruth B., The, CA, 1133
Shapira Foundation, David S. and Karen A., The, PA, 8437
Shapiro Foundation, The, CA, 1138
Share Trust, Charles Morton, OK, 7977
Shattuck Charitable Trust, Clinton H. & Wilma T., The, MA, 4138
Shattuck Charitable Trust, S. F., WI, 9926
Shaw Charitable Foundation, Seyfarth, IL, 3003
Shaw Family Foundation, Inc., OH, 7852
Sheba Foundation, The, IL, 3005
Shimek Family Foundation, Dan & Kay, MN, 4681
Shivers Cancer Foundation, TX, 9184
Shklar Foundation, Eugene and Daymel, CA, 1146
Shoolman Children's Foundation, Edith Glick, The, NY, 6967
Short Charitable Foundation, Tommy E., The, CA, 1148
SHP Foundation, CA, 1149
Shrensky Foundation, Inc., MD, 3731
Shulman Family Foundation, Alex, WA, 9685
Sie Foundation, Anna and John J., The, CO, 1455
Siegal Foundation, Alvin and Laura, The, OH, 7856
Siegel Foundation, Ruth and Jerome A., NY, 6976
Sigma Chi Greystone Foundation, Inc., NY, 6977
Silberstein-Boesky Family Foundation, Inc., NY, 6979
Silver Foundation, Jack S. & Shirley M., The, NY, 6981
Silver Foundation, VA, 9516
Silver Mountain Foundation for the Arts, NJ, 5404
Silverman Family Foundation, Inc., Carlynn and Lawrence, The, MD, 3733
Simches Charitable Foundation, Joanne B., MA, 4147
Simmons Family Foundation, The, IL, 3008
Simmons Family Foundation, Virginia and L. E., The, TX, 9187
Simon Charitable Foundation, David E. Simon & Jacqueline S., IN, 3237
Simon Charitable Foundation, NE, 5002
Simon Foundation, Mildred, Herbert and Julian, MO, 4903
Simon, Jr. Foundation, Cynthia L. & William E., NJ, 5405
Simpson Foundation Trust, M. L., The, GA, 2489
Singh Family Foundation, NY, 6991
Siouxland Community Foundation, IA, 3332
Siouxland Foundation, IA, see 3332
Siperstein Charitable Foundation, Mynde & Gary, RI, 8557
Sirrine Textile Foundation, Inc., J. E., SC, 8612
Sit Foundation, Eugene C. & Gail V., The, MN, 4683
Sitt Chesed Fund, David and Marjorie, NY, 6995
Sitt Family Foundation, Morris & Eddie, NY, see 6996
Sitt Family Foundation, The, NY, 6996
Sixty Four Foundation, The, TX, 9190
Skestos Family Foundation, OH, see 7683
Skilling and Andrews Foundation, MI, 4437
Slaggie Family Foundation, MN, 4686
Sloan, Jr. Foundation, O. Temple, NC, 7475
Smidt Family Foundation, CA, 1159
Smith 1990 Charitable Trust, Richard & Susan, MA, 4148
Smith Charitable Foundation, Robert and Dana, MA, 4149
Smith Charitable Trust, R. & S., MA, see 4148
Smith Family Foundation, Inc., G. Gregory, NC, 7477
Smith Family Foundation, Inc., Ian & Margaret, The, NJ, 5407
Smith Family Foundation, Orin, WA, 9688
Smith Family Foundation, Park B. Smith and Carol, The, NY, 7006
Smith Foundation, Inc., George Graham and Elizabeth Galloway, NY, 7007
Smith Foundation, Matthew J. & Anne B., The, NJ, 5409
Smith Foundation, Randall & Kathryn, The, NY, 7008
Smith Foundation, The, MO, 4905
Smith Foundation, William H. and Patricia M., MI, 4441
Smith School of Business Foundation, Inc., Robert H., The, MD, 3737
Smithfield-Luter Foundation, Inc., The, VA, 9519
Smysor Memorial Fund, Harry L. & John L., IL, 3011
Snodgrass Foundation, Inc., The, GA, 2492
Snyder Foundation, Nancy and John, TX, 9199

Sodaro Family Foundation, The, CA, 1174
SOL Foundation Agency, NC, 7480
Soling Family Foundation, AZ, 140
Solomon Testamentary Trust, Alfred Z., NY, 7018
Solve, Inc., CA, 1177
Sooch Foundation, The, TX, 9200
Soros Charitable Foundation, NY, 7021
Soros Foundation-Hungary, Inc., The, NY, 7023
South Family Foundation, Inc., GA, 2493
South Mountain Company Foundation, MA, 4153
Southern Company Charitable Foundation, Inc., GA, 2494
Sowell Charitable Trust, Thomas & Lillian, TX, 9202
Sowell Foundation, James E., TX, 9203
Sparrow Foundation, The, TX, 9205
Spector Family Foundation, The, NV, 5067
Spencer Memorial Foundation, Cheryl, MA, 4154
Speyer Foundation, Alexander C. & Tillie S., PA, 8453
Spiegel Family Foundation, Thomas, CA, 1182
Spirit Foundation, Inc., NY, 7033
Split Rail Foundation, Inc., WI, 9932
Spurlino Foundation, The, FL, 2242
Sragowicz Foundation, Inc., FL, 2243
SSM Foundation, Inc., NY, 7038
St. John's Foundation, CO, 1456
Stallworth Foundation Trust, Mary Elizabeth, The, AL, 64
Stanton Family Foundation, Ruth, The, NY, 7043
Stanton Foundation, Oliver & Elizabeth, The, NY, 7045
Stanton Foundation, Ruth & Oliver, The, NY, see 7043
Star Family Foundation, The, FL, 2248
Star Foundation, Stanley A., FL, see 2248
Stare Fund, The, MA, 4157
Starfish Group, The, NY, 7046
Stark Family Foundation, Ltd., WI, 9935
Stark Foundation, C. Richard Stark, Jr. & Joan E., IA, 3334
Stealth Foundation, CO, 1458
Steel Partners Foundation, The, CO, 1459
Steffens 21st Century Foundation II, NY, 7054
Stein Family Foundation, Inc., Allen A., NY, 7055
Steiner Trust, Lionel, CA, 1191
Steinmetz Foundation, S. & E., NY, 7068
Stephens Christian Trust, TN, 8729
Stephens Foundation Trust, TN, see 8729
Stephens Foundation, AL, 65
Stern Family Foundation, MA, 4162
Stern Foundation, Pauline and Edgar, UT, 9344
Sternberg Charitable Trust, NY, 7075
Sterne-Elder Memorial Trust, AZ, 143
Stevens Kingsley Foundation, Inc., The, NY, 7076
Stevens Point Area Foundation, Inc., WI, see 9778
Stewart Family Foundation, The, NY, see 5931
Stewart Foundation, The, PA, 8460
Stewart, Jr. Foundation, Marlene and J. O., The, TX, 9213
Steyer Family Foundation, Inc., Stanley, NY, 7077
Stoddard Family Foundation, Inc., MI, 4447
Stokes Charitable Trust, H. L., NY, 7080
Stone Family Foundation, Roger and Susan, IL, 3026
Stone Foundation, Irving I., OH, 7871
Stonecutter Foundation, Inc., NC, 7486
Stop & Shop Family Foundation, The, PA, 8463
Stover Foundation, The, CA, 1201
Stowe, Jr. Foundation, Inc., Robert Lee, NC, 7487
Strategic Grant Partners, Inc., MA, 4169
Strauss Foundation, Inc., The, NY, 7087
Stroud Foundation, DE, 1757
Struthers Family Foundation, The, DE, 1758
Sturgis Area Community Foundation, MI, 4452
Sturgis Foundation, MI, see 4452
Sturm Family Foundation, Terri and Roland, NV, 5069
Sub-Zero Foundation, Inc., WI, 9945
Sudakoff Foundation, Inc., Harry, The, FL, 2255
Sugarman Foundation, Jay and Kelly, NY, 7092
Sukup Family Foundation, The, IA, 3336
Sullivan Charitable Trust, Alice I., RI, 8558
Sullivan Family Foundation, The, NY, 7094
Sumitomo Corporation of America Foundation, NY, 7096
Summer Family Foundation, The, OH, 7874
Summer Rest Foundation, NC, 7489
Summerhill Foundation, The, NY, 7098
Summit Foundation, NY, 7100

Sundance Pay It Forward Foundation, MN, 4693
Sundean Foundation, Inc., CA, 1215
Sunrise Klein Foundation, Inc., The, NY, 7102
Sunshine Foundation Trust, NE, 5007
Sunup Foundation, Inc., NJ, 5419
Susman and Asher Foundation, IL, 3030
Sutton Family Foundation, Joe & Eileen, NY, 7107
Sutton Foundation, Celia and Isaac, The, NY, 7108
SVF Foundation, PA, 8472
Swanson & Thomas Foundation, CA, 1216
Swanson Family Foundation, Inc., Gretchen, NE, 5008
Swanson Foundation, Inc., Carl and Caroline, NE, 5009
Swanson, Jr. Foundation, W. Clarke, MO, 4914
Sweet Water Trust, MA, 4176
Swift Foundation, The, CA, 1219
Swigert Foundation, The, OR, 8061
Swinerton Foundation, The, CA, 1221
Syde Hurdus 1992 Charitable Trust, NY, see 7114
Syde Hurdus Foundation, Inc., NY, 7114
Sykes Charitable Foundation, Inc., John H., FL, see 2261
Sykes Family Foundation, NY, 7115
Sykes Foundation, Inc., John H., FL, 2261

T & O Foundation, Inc., WI, 9946
Tabasgo Foundation, The, CA, 1224
Tamaki Foundation, The, WA, 9695
Tamarack Foundation, MN, see 4709
Tandon Family Foundation, Inc., NY, 7121
Tang Family Foundation, Donald and Jean, NV, 5071
Tang Foundation for Education, Inc., Jane and Tom, NJ, 5423
Tankenoff Families Foundation, MN, 4696
Tarrant Foundation, Inc., Amy E., FL, 2265
Tauber Family Foundation, Laszlo N., The, MD, 3742
Taylor Foundation, W. A., MS, 4767
Telos Foundation, Inc., MS, 4768
Templeton Foundation, Richard and Mary, NY, 7128
Ten Talents Foundation, Inc., MD, 3743
Tenenbaum Foundation, AR, 180
Tennessee Health Foundation, Inc., TN, 8732
Tennessee Titans Foundation, TX, 9230
Terry Foundation, The, TX, 9231
Texas Pioneer Foundation, TX, 9233
Thieriot Foundation, Nion Robert, WY, 9993
Thoma Foundation, Carl & Marilynn, The, IL, 3035
Thomas Charitable Foundation, The, NJ, 5427
Thomas Family Foundation, Billie and Gillis, The, TX, 9234
Thomas Foundation, The, TX, see 9234
Thorson Foundation, Harry T., WY, 9994
Tiffany Foundation, Louis Comfort, The, NY, 7138
Tilson Foundation, Willard C., MA, 4182
Timken Company Charitable Trust, The, WI, 9950
Tippett Foundation, William Hall Tippett and Ruth Rathell, The, CA, 1237
Tisch Foundation, Inc., James S. & Merryl H., The, NY, 7144
Tiscornia Foundation, Inc., The, MI, 4460
TNG Charitable Trust, NY, 7151
Tolchin Foundation, Inc., Gary & Tamar, NJ, 5428
Toledo Community Foundation Donor Directed Pooled Fund, OH, 7882
Toleo Foundation, The, NC, 7495
Toms Charitable Foundation, Inc., David, LA, 3512
Toppel Family Foundation, Inc., The, FL, 2274
Toppel Foundation, Harold & Patricia, FL, see 2274
Torray Family Foundation, Robert E. Torray and Anne P., MD, 3748
Torstenson Family Foundation, Robert H., IL, 3036
Touch 'n Tutor Research & Development Foundation, Inc., NY, 7157
Traders Foundation, The, IL, 3038
Traditional Foundation, NY, 7161
Trans-Atlantic Foundation, The, NV, 5073
Trarym Foundation, The, CT, see 1593
Trend Homes Foundation, AZ, 147
Triad Hospitals Private Foundation, The, TX, 9239
Trimble Foundation, The, HI, 2556
Troisi Foundation, Barbara Davies, NY, 7164
Troy Savings Bank Charitable Foundation, Inc., The, NY, 7166
Trueblood Foundation, Harry, The, CO, 1466

Truman Foundation, Mildred Faulkner, PA, 8483
Tsadra Foundation, NY, 7169
Tuchman Family Foundation, CO, 1467
Tully Family Foundation, IL, 3040
Tupperware Children's Foundation, FL, 2275
Turner Charitable Foundation, Inc., Laura G., TN, 8737
Turner Construction Company Foundation, TX, 9242
Turock Family Foundation, The, NJ, 5430
Tyler Charitable Foundation, Robert & Gwen, KS, 3401
Tzedaka Fund Trust, Solomon and Machla, NY, 7177
Tzedakah Foundation, NC, 7497
Tzedakah Fund, The, MD, 3751
Tziterman Memorial Trust, NY, 7178

Uihlein Foundation, Robert A., WI, 9955
Ullrich Foundation Trust, John, IL, 3043
Unaka Foundation, Inc., The, TN, 8739
Unaka Scholarship Foundation, Inc., TN, see 8739
United Brands Foundation, OH, see 7571
United Stationers Foundation, IL, 3045
Unkefer Foundation, TX, 9243
Upchurch, Jr. Charitable Foundation, Samuel E., AL, 71
Uperetes Foundation, MA, 4188
Upton Charitable Foundation, Lucy and Eleanor S., NJ, 5436
USAA Foundation, Inc., The, TX, 9245
Ushkow Foundation, Inc., NY, 7188

Valerio Charitable Remainder Foundation, Michael and Helen, The, MA, 4189
Valley Community Foundation for Lifelong Learning, IA, 3339
Valley Foundation, Inc., The, NJ, 5438
Van Wyk Family Foundation, Arlan J., IA, 3340
Vance Foundation, Lee and Cynthia, NY, 7193
Vandomelen Foundation, William and Katherine, The, MI, 4470
Varadhan Memorial Foundation, Gopal, The, NY, 7194
Vasey Foundation, The, CT, 1670
Vatterott Foundation, MO, 4921
Vaughn-Jordan Foundation, Inc., FL, 2279
Vegesna Foundation, Raju, The, CA, 1263
Vencor Foundation, Inc., KY, see 3434
Vesper Foundation, OH, 7892
Viad Corp Fund, The, AZ, 149
Vickter Foundation, David, The, CA, 1266
Vidalakis Family Foundation, WA, 9698
Vik Brothers Foundation, The, CT, 1672
Vines Foundation, Lanny S., AL, 72
Vintage Foundation, Inc., MN, 4709
Virginia Scrap Iron & Metal Co. Charitable Foundation, Inc., VA, see 9430
Vista Hermosa, WA, 9699
Vogel Family Foundation, Inc., GA, 2504
Vopicka Family Foundation, Inc., NJ, 5444

W.J. Foundation, The, CA, 1273
Waccamaw Community Foundation, SC, 8619
Wadman Foundation, UT, 9349
Waggoners Foundation, The, TX, 9258
Waidner Foundation, Robert A., The, MD, 3754
Walk Fine Arts Foundation, Maurice, IL, 3053
Walker Charitable Foundation, Inc., Willard and Pat, AR, 185
Walters Foundation, William G., The, NY, 7213
Wampus Beth Zion Trust, The, MO, 4923

Wampus Fund, The, MO, see 4923
Warburg Pincus Foundation, The, NY, 7214
Ward Family Foundation, The, TX, 9262
Warner Foundation, Inc., D. Michael, The, NC, see 7503
Warner Foundation, NC, 7503
Warren Charite, OK, 7986
Warren Foundation, Robert C. and Nani S., WA, 9700
Warwick Foundation of Bucks County, The, PA, 8496
Washington Group Foundation, ID, 2578
Watanabe Family Foundation, Inc., IN, 3251
Watson Family Foundation, TX, 9266
Weatherup Family Foundation, The, NY, 7222
Weaver Foundation, William M., TX, 9268
Webb Roven Foundation, CA, see 1070
Webster Charitable Trust, MA, see 3972
Webster Foundation, Helen and Will, CA, 1286
Wedum Foundation, J.A., MN, 4719
Wehadkee Foundation, Inc., GA, 2511
Weiller Foundation, Inc., Ted and Jean, FL, 2291
Weingarten Foundation, Richard and Carol, The, NC, 7505
Weiss Foundation, A. H. and Helen L., PA, 8499
Weiss Foundation, Inc., Joseph H. & Miriam F., The, NY, 7235
Weiss Foundation, Inc., Stephen and Suzanne, The, NY, 7236
Welborn Baptist Foundation, Inc., IN, 3254
Welborn Foundation, Inc., IN, see 3254
Wender Foundation, Joseph H., The, NY, 7241
Wendy's of Montana Foundation, Inc., NV, 5076
Werdiger Family Foundation, The, NJ, 5451
West Family Foundation, TN, 8742
West Suburban Sentinel Corporation, IL, 3065
Westcliff Foundation, MN, 4724
Westlake Health Foundation, IL, 3066
Weyerhaeuser Memorial Foundation, Charles A., The, MN, 4726
Weyerhaeuser/Day Foundation, MN, 4727
Weyrich Family Foundation, CA, 1298
WHH Foundation, CA, 1300
White Family Foundation, Inc., Dean & Barbara, IN, 3257
White Foundation, The, MI, 4481
White Memorial Foundation, Bob, AR, 187
Whitt Foundation, AR, 188
Whitwam Foundation, Inc., David & Barbara, IL, 3068
Wiancko Charitable Foundation, Inc., WA, 9704
Wideman Family Foundation, Steven J., UT, 9351
Wiegers Family Foundation, The, NY, 7256
Wilhite Charitable Foundation, Kate Stamper, CO, 1473
Wilkie Brothers Foundation, IL, 3071
Wilkins Foundation, Inc., IL, 3072
Willard Foundation, Helen Parker, DC, 1861
Willary Foundation, PA, 8503
Williams Foundation, Dave H. & Reba W., NY, 7260
Williams Foundation, Inc., J. L., TX, 9282
Williams, Kastner & Gibbs Foundation in Memorial of J. K. McMullin & W. H. Robertson, WA, 9706
Williams-Corbett Foundation, CA, 1307
Williamsburg Community Health Foundation, VA, 9541
Williamson Family Foundation, OH, 7908
Willoughby Foundation, Ruth S., DC, 1862
Wilson Foundation, Thomas A., OH, 7911
Wing Family Benevolent Agency, H. R., The, UT, 9352
Winkelried Family Foundation, The, NY, see 7265

Winkelried Foundation, Jon and Abby, NY, 7265
Winky Foundation, The, DE, 1763
Winston Charitable Foundation, James H., FL, see 2302
Winston Family Foundation, FL, 2302
Winterhaven, Inc., IA, 3344
Wise Family Foundation, William and Marie, The, TX, 9284
Witkin Charitable Foundation, Bernard E. & Alba, CA, 1313
Witmer Charitable Foundation, Meryl & Charles, The, NY, 7268
Wohlers Family Foundation, IL, 3078
Wolf Charitable Trust, Marie E., IL, 3079
Wolf Foundation, The, PA, 8506
Wolf Mountain Foundation, TX, 9287
Wolfen Family Foundation, CA, 1316
Wolff Family Foundation, Jean & Lewis, MI, 4486
Wolff Foundation No. 2, MO, 4927
Wong Foundation, Harry Chow & Nee-Chang Chock, HI, 2560
Wood Foundation, Charles O. Wood III & Miriam M., MA, 4208
Woods Charitable Foundation, The, PA, 8508
Woods Foundation, Abbey, IL, 3083
Woodward Foundation, Ann Eden, NY, 7279
Working Partners Foundation, CO, 1476
Working Woman's Home Association, Inc., AL, 76
Works of Grace Foundation, The, TX, 9291
WorldCom Education Foundation, VA, see 9471
Worwin Foundation, GA, 2526
WPW Family Foundation, IL, 3087
Wrather Family Foundation, CA, 1321
Wrather Foundation, J. D. & Mazie, CA, see 1321
Wright Family Foundation, William, TX, 9293
Wrigley Foundation, Inc., Julie Ann, WI, 9971
Wunderkinder Foundation, The, CA, 1322
Wunsch Foundation, Inc., NY, 7281
Wyeth Pharmaceutical Assistance Foundation, MO, 4930
Wyker Family Foundation, The, AL, 77

Yeargan Foundation Charitable Trust, The, NC, 7511
Yellow Chair Foundation, NY, 7282
Yitzchok Foundation, Divrei, NY, 7283
Yoder Charitable Foundation, Abner and Esther, The, OH, 7919
Young Family Charitable Foundation, The, NY, 7285
Young Foundation, Inc., Irvin L., WI, 9972
Young Foundation, Jane H. and William D., GA, 2527

Zachs Family Foundation, Inc., The, CT, 1682
Zachs Foundation, Inc., Henry M. Zachs & Judith M., The, CT, see 1682
Zayat Foundation, Inc., NJ, 5462
Zedukah Vechesed Foundation, Inc., NY, 7292
Zelnak Private Foundation, The, NC, 7513
Zephyr Foundation, TX, 9299
Zichron Alter Meir Wilamowsky Foundation, NY, 7296
Zichron Yisroel Vesther Foundation, NY, 7298
Zickler Family Foundation, Inc., MD, 3763
Zimmer Family Foundation, Inc., The, NJ, 5463
Zimmerman Foundation, Myron, CA, 1329
Zisman Family Foundation, The, PA, 8513
Zucker Family Foundation, Inc., Jerry and Anita, The, SC, 8622
Zyskind Charitable Foundation, Morris & Deena, CA, 1330

FOUNDATION NAME INDEX

Numbers following the foundation names refer to the entry sequence numbers in the Descriptive Directory section. The letter "A" following a name refers to Appendix A, which lists foundations that appeared in the previous edition of the *Directory* but no longer qualify.

1101 Foundation, NY, 5504
118 Foundation, The, VA, 9365
1525 Foundation, The, OH, A
1675 Foundation, PA, 8070
1772 Foundation, Inc., NJ, 5106
1923 Fund, WI, 9738
1939 Foundation, TN, 8635
1957 Charity Foundation, PA, 8071
1988 Irrevocable Cochrane Memorial Trust, MN, 4491
1991 Corcoran Foundation, The, MA, see 3860
1st Source Foundation, IN, 3094

2 C 9 Foundation, Inc., GA, A
291 Foundation, NY, 5505

324 Foundation, CA, 190
3M Foundation, MN, 4492

444 Sierra Foundation, WA, see 9546
444S Foundation, WA, 9546

747 Foundation, IL, see 2715

8:32, Inc., OK, 7922
80/20 Fund, The, TX, 8746

A & A Fund, The, MA, 3764
A Better Place, Inc., MN, 4493
A Child Waits Foundation, MA, 3765
A Friends' Foundation Trust, FL, 1866
A Glimmer of Hope Foundation - Austin, TX, 8748
A Glimmer of Hope Foundation, TX, 8747
A Good Day Foundation, OH, 7522
A Good Neighbor Foundation, OH, 7523
A-T Medical Research Foundation, CA, 191
A.E. Charitable Foundation, NY, 5506
A.M. Fund, The, MA, 3766
A.P.S. Foundation, Inc., AZ, 86
A.R. & M.G.R. Charitable Foundation, Inc., NY, 5507
Aaroe Associates Charitable Foundation, Inc., CA, 192
Aaron Family Foundation, The, PA, 8072
Aaron Foundation, The, MA, 3767
Abar Foundation, NJ, 5107
Abbott Charitable Foundation, Ethel S., NE, 4942
Abbott Foundation, Clara, The, IL, 2579
Abbott Laboratories Fund, IL, 2580
ABC Foundation, AR, see 157
ABC Foundation, CA, see 1030
ABC, Inc. Foundation, NY, A
ABE Charitable Foundation, Inc., The, DE, 1686
Abelard Foundation, Inc., The, NY, 5508
Abele Family Charitable Trust, The, WI, see 9747
Abeles Foundation, Inc., Joseph & Sophia, NY, 5509
Abell Foundation, Inc., Charles S., MD, see 3560
Abell Foundation, Inc., The, MD, 3559
Abell Foundation, Inc., William S., MD, 3560
Abell-Hanger Foundation, TX, 8749
Abelson Foundation, Lester S., IL, 2581
Abington Foundation, The, OH, 7524
Abney Foundation, The, SC, 8564
Abraham Foundation, Alexander, The, NY, 5510
Abraham Foundation, Inc., Anthony R., FL, 1867
Abramowitz Family Foundation, CT, 1478

Abrams Foundation, Amy & David, MA, 3768
Abrams Foundation, Talbert & Leota, MI, 4213
Abramson Family Foundation, Inc., MD, 3561
Abramson Family Foundation, The, FL, 1868
Abramson Foundation, Inc., MD, see 3561
Abrons Foundation, Inc., Louis and Anne, NY, 5511
Abrons Foundation, Inc., Richard & Iris, The, NY, 5512
Abrons Foundation, Richard & Mimi, The, NY, see 5512
Ace Hardware Foundation, IL, 2582
ACE INA Foundation, The, PA, 8073
ACE USA Foundation, PA, see 8073
Achelis Foundation, The, NY, 5513
Acheson Foundation, James C., MI, 4214
Achilles Memorial Fund, Edith & F. M., The, NY, 5514
ACK Foundation, Inc., GA, see 2495
Ackerley Foundation, Ginger and Barry, WA, 9547
Ackerman Foundation, Edward & Wilhelmina, TX, 8750
Ackerman Foundation, Thomas C., The, CA, 193
Ackerman Trust, Anna K., OR, 7995
Acorn Foundation, Inc., NY, 5515
Acorn Foundation, MA, 3769
Acorn Foundation, MN, 4494
Acorn Foundation, The, IL, 2583
Acuity Charitable Foundation, Inc., WI, 9739
Acushnet Foundation, The, MA, 3770
Adam Foundation, Inc., FL, 1869
Adams Charitable Foundation, Arthur F. and Alice E., NC, 7305
Adams Charitable Foundation, Inc., The, MD, 3562
Adams Charitable Foundation, Judith and Jean Pape, The, TX, 8751
Adams Charitable Trust, C. F., The, MA, 3771
Adams Charitable Trust, Jessie & Hertha, VA, 9366
Adams County Community Foundation, IN, 3095
Adams Family Foundation, Stephen & Denise, CA, A
Adams Foundation, Moss, WA, 9548
Adams Foundation, Yvonne & Red, LA, 3458
Adams Fund, CA, 194
Adams Memorial Fund, Frank W. and Carl S., MA, see 3772
Adams Trust, Charles E. & Caroline J., MA, 3772
Adams Trust, John & Hester, IN, 3096
Adams, Jr. Charitable Trust, Howell E., GA, 2309
Adams-Mastrovich Family Foundation, MN, 4495
ADC Foundation, MN, 4496
Adelson Family Foundation, NJ, 5108
Ades-Taub Foundation, Inc., Joan & Alan, NY, 5516
ADFAM Charities, Inc., FL, 1870
Adirondack Community Trust, NY, 5517
Adjmi Family Foundation, Inc., Jack, NY, 5518
Adjmi Foundation, Lillian, NY, 5519
Adjmi-Dwek Family Foundation, Inc., The, NY, 5520
Adjuvant Foundation, The, IL, 2584
ADL Charitable Trust, IN, 3097
Adler Community Trust, Leo, OR, 7996
Adler Family Foundation, Inc., FL, 1871
Adler Foundation, Inc., Frederick R., FL, see 1871
Adler Foundation, Inc., NY, 5521
Adler Trust, Leo, OR, see 7996
Administers of the Berwick Health and Wellness Fund, PA, see 8135
Adnim Foundation, NY, 5522
Adreani Foundation, IL, 2585

Adventist World Charitable Trust, CA, 195
Advisory Board Foundation, Inc., The, DC, see 1783
AEC Trust, The, GA, 2310
AEGON Transamerica Foundation, IA, 3259
AEGON USA Charitable Foundation, Inc., IA, see 3259
Aeneas Capital Management Foundation, The, NY, 5523
Aequus Institute, NY, 5524
Aetna Foundation, Inc., CT, 1479
Aetna Life & Casualty Foundation, Inc., CT, see 1479
Afeyan Foundation, Noubar & Anna, MA, 3773
Aflac Foundation, Inc., The, GA, 2311
Afognak Foundation, The, NY, 5525
Agilent Technologies Foundation, MD, 3563
AGL Resources Private Foundation, Inc., GA, 2312
Agostine Trust, Mary H., MA, 3774
Agostino Foundation, Inc., Daniele, The, NY, see 5853
Agouron Institute, The, CA, 196
Agua Fund, Inc., DC, 1764
Agur Foundation, CO, 1332
Ahava Foundation, NY, 5526
Ahavas Chesed Charitable Trust, NY, 5527
AHBA, Inc., NY, 5528
Ahmanson Charitable Community Trust, CA, 197
Ahmanson Foundation, The, CA, 198
Ahrens Foundation, Claude W. & Dolly, The, IA, 3260
AHS Foundation, MN, 4497
Aicher Family Foundation, Inc., NJ, 5109
Aid Association for the Blind of the District of Columbia, DC, 1765
AIG Disaster Relief Fund-New York, NY, 5529
Aikens Family Foundation, Ann and Bob, The, MI, 4215
Aikens Family Foundation, The, MI, see 4215
AirCast Foundation, Inc., PA, 8074
Airdrie Foundation, IL, see 3052
Airport Business Center Foundation, CO, see 1337
AirTouch Communications Foundation, CA, see 1267
AJP Foundation, MO, 4771
AK Steel Foundation, OH, 7525
Akey Charitable Trust, The, OH, see 7597
Akibene Foundation, WA, 9549
Akonadi Foundation, CA, 199
Akron Community Foundation, OH, 7526
Al-Ameen Foundation, The, CA, 200
Alabama Power Foundation, Inc., AL, 1
Alafi Family Foundation, CA, 201
Alaska Community Foundation, The, AK, 78
Alaska Conservation Foundation, AK, 79
Alavi Foundation, NY, 5530
Albertson Foundation, Inc., J. A. & Kathryn, ID, 2562
Albertson's Charitable Foundation, Inc., ID, see 2563
Albertson's Stores Charitable Foundation, Inc., ID, 2563
Albrecht Foundation, FL, 1872
Albuquerque Community Foundation, NM, 5466
Alburger Charitable Trust, H. A. & J. W., FL, A
Alcatel-Lucent Foundation, NJ, 5110
Alchemy Foundation, The, MA, 3775
Alco Standard Foundation, PA, see 8265
Alcoa Foundation, PA, 8075
Alcoholic Beverage Medical Research Foundation, MD, 3564
Alden Trust, George I., The, MA, 3776

Alden Trust, John W., MA, 3777
Alexander & Baldwin Foundation, HI, 2530
Alexander Charitable Foundation, Inc., WI, 9740
Alexander Foundation, Frances, The, NY, 5531
Alexander Foundation, Inc., Joseph, NY, 5532
Alexander Foundation, Inc., Judd S., WI, 9741
Alexander Foundation, Stanford & Joan, The, TX, 8752
Alfa Foundation, AL, 2
ALFA Foundation, The, CT, 1480
Alff Aid, Inc., NY, 5533
Alfiero Family Charitable Foundation, NY, 5534
Alfond Foundation, Harold, ME, 3521
Alfond Foundation, Peter, The, ME, 3522
Alfond Foundation, William and Joan, The, ME, 3523
Alfond Foundation, William L., ME, see 3523
Alice Manufacturing Company, Inc. Foundation, SC, see 8599
Alison Foundation, NY, 5535
Alix Foundation, Jay & Maryanne, MI, see 4216
Alix Foundation, The, MI, 4216
Alkek and Williams Foundation, The, TX, 8753
Alkek Foundation, Albert and Margaret, TX, 8754
Allbritton Foundation, The, TX, 8755
Alleghany Foundation, The, VA, 9367
Allegheny Foundation, PA, 8076
Allegis Group Foundation, Inc., MD, 3565
Allegretti Foundation, Inc., Fred & Jean, IL, 2586
Allen Charitable Foundation, Andrew, The, WY, 9974
Allen Charitable Trust, Adrienne, The, TX, 8756
Allen Family Foundation, Paul G., The, WA, 9550
Allen Foundation, Herbert, The, NY, 5536
Allen Foundation, Inc., MI, 4217
Allen Foundation, Inc., Rita, NJ, 5111
Allen-Heath Memorial Foundation, IL, 2587
Allendale Insurance Foundation, RI, see 8537
Allentown Area Foundation, NC, A
Allequash Foundation, CA, 202
Allergan Foundation, The, CA, 203
Allerton Foundation, Inc., The, PA, 8077
Alliance Healthcare Foundation, CA, 204
Alliant Energy Foundation, Inc., WI, 9742
Alliant Techsystems Community Investment Foundation, MN, see 4509
Allianz Foundation for North America, CA, 205
Allison Family Foundation, Inc., The, NY, 5537
Allison, Jr. Family Foundation, Carolyn J. and Robert J., The, TX, 8757
Alliss Educational Foundation, Charles and Ellora, MN, see 4498
Alliss Educational Foundation, MN, 4498
Allmerica Financial Charitable Foundation, Inc., MA, see 3941
Allred Family Foundation, Inc., Jeffrey & Jennifer, The, GA, 2313
Allstate Foundation, The, IL, 2588
Allwin Family Foundation, The, NY, 5538
Allyn Foundation, Inc., NY, 5539
Almar Foundation, The, LA, 3459
Alon Family Foundation, The, CA, 206
Alpaugh Foundation, The, OH, 7527
Alperin Foundation, The, RI, see 8516
Alperin/Hirsch Family Foundation, The, RI, 8516
Alpern Family Foundation, Inc., NY, 5540
Alpert & Alpert Foundation, The, CA, 207
Alpert Family Foundation, Inc., The, NY, 5541
Alpert Foundation, Herb, The, CA, 208
Alpert Foundation, Raymond & Barbara, CA, 209
Alpert Foundation, Warren, RI, 8517
Alpha & Omega Family Foundation, SD, see 8628
Alpha Foundation, Inc., AL, 3
Alpha Omega Foundation, Inc., FL, see 1905
Alphawood Foundation, IL, 2589
ALS Foundation, The, UT, 9301
ALSAM Foundation, The, UT, 9302
Alsdorf Foundation, IL, 2590
Altec/Styslinger Foundation, AL, 4
Alter Family Foundation, The, PA, 8078
Altheimer Charitable Foundation, Inc., Ben J., AR, 155
Altman Family Foundation, Lisa & Steve, The, CA, 210
Altman Foundation, Inc., Jeffrey A., The, NY, 5543
Altman Foundation, Jenifer, CA, 211
Altman Foundation, NY, 5542
Altman/Kazickas Foundation, NY, 5544

Altria Fund, Inc., NY, 5545
Altschul Foundation, The, NY, 5546
Altus One Fund, Inc., The, NY, 5547
Alvord Family Foundation, MA, 3778
Alworth Memorial Fund, Marshall H. and Nellie, MN, 4499
Amado Foundation, Maurice, CA, 212
Amar Foundation, CA, 213
Amarillo Area Foundation, Inc., TX, 8758
Amateur Athletic Foundation of Los Angeles, CA, 214
Amaturo Family Foundation, Inc., The, FL, 1873
Ambler Trust, Elizabeth Raymond, CT, 1481
Amboy Foundation, Inc., The, NJ, 5112
AMCORE Bank Foundation, IL, 2591
Ameren Corporation Charitable Trust, MO, 4772
American Academy & Institute of Arts and Letters, NY, see 5548
American Academy of Arts and Letters, NY, 5548
American Art Foundation, Inc., The, NY, 5549
American Center for Civil Justice, Inc., NY, A
American Center Foundation, NY, 5550
American Century Companies Foundation, MO, 4773
American Conservation Association, Inc., NY, 5551
American Contemporary Art Foundation, Inc., The, NY, see 5549
American Dream Foundation, Inc., NY, 5552
American Eagle Outfitters Foundation, PA, 8079
American Express Foundation, NY, 5553
American Foundation Corporation, The, OH, 7528
American Foundation for Courtesy and Grooming, CA, 215
American Foundation for Oceanography, CA, see 472
American Friends of Binyan-Av Foundation, Inc., NY, 5554
American Friends of the Citizens Empowerment Center in Israel, CA, 216
American Friends of the Hebrew University Charitable Common Fund, Inc., The, NY, 5555
American Friends of Torah Umesorah of Latino America, NY, 5556
American General Finance Foundation, Inc., IN, 3098
American General Finance, Inc.—Richard E. Meier Foundation, Inc., IN, see 3098
American Honda Foundation, CA, 217
American Mutual Life/AmerUs Charitable Foundation, IA, see 3261
American Savings Charitable Foundation, Inc., CT, see 1482
American Savings Foundation, CT, 1482
American Snuff Company Charitable Trust, TN, see 8663
American Standard Foundation, NJ, 5113
American Woodmark Foundation, Inc., VA, 9368
Americana Foundation, MI, 4218
AMERIGROUP Foundation, VA, 9369
Amerman Family Foundation, CA, 218
AmerUs Group Charitable Foundation, IA, 3261
Ames Charitable Trust, Harriett, PA, 8080
Ames Foundation, K. C., VA, 9370
AMETEK Foundation, Inc., PA, 8081
Amgen Foundation, Inc., CA, 219
Amica Companies Foundation, RI, 8518
Amicus Foundation, IL, 2592
Amicus Foundation, Inc., NY, 5557
Amirsaleh Foundation Trust, Hossein, NJ, 5114
Amos Educational Foundation, Inc., Paul S., GA, 2314
Amos Family Foundation, Daniel P., GA, 2315
Amos Foundation, Inc., Daniel P. and Shannon L., GA, see 2315
Amos Foundation, Inc., John and Elena Diaz-Verson, GA, see 2316
Amos Foundation, Inc., John and Elena, GA, 2316
AMP Foundation, PA, see 8485
AMPCO-Pittsburgh Foundation II, Inc., PA, see 8192
AmSouth Bancorporation Foundation, AL, 5
AmSouth Foundation, MS, 4733
AmSouth/First American Foundation, TN, 8636
Amsted Industries Foundation, IL, 2593
Amundson Charity Foundation, Inc., Lloyd and Barbara, MN, 4500
Anaheim Community Foundation, CA, 220
and Ida Thomas & Walter Schmid Jr. Foundation, Inc., Walter & Louise Schmid, The, FL, 1874

Andersen Family Foundation, G. C., The, NY, 5558
Andersen Foundation, Frank N., MI, 4219
Andersen Foundation, Fred C. and Katherine B., MN, 4501
Andersen Foundation, Hugh J., MN, 4502
Andersen Foundation, Inc., Martin Andersen and Gracia, FL, 1875
Andersen Foundation, MN, see 4501
Anderson Charitable Foundation, Carl C. Anderson, Sr. and Marie Jo, TX, 8759
Anderson Charitable Trust, John R. and Linda L., IL, see 2594
Anderson Charitable Trust, Josephine, TX, 8760
Anderson Children's Foundation, Irene W. & Guy L., CA, 221
Anderson Family Foundation, A. Gary, CA, 222
Anderson Family Foundation, Charles C. and Beth, The, AL, see 6
Anderson Family Foundation, Charlie and Beth, The, AL, 6
Anderson Family Foundation, Lee R., FL, 1876
Anderson Family Gardens Foundation, IL, 2594
Anderson Foundation, Inc., Peyton, The, GA, 2317
Anderson Foundation, John W., IN, 3099
Anderson Foundation, M. D., TX, 8762
Anderson Foundation, NJ, 5115
Anderson Foundation, OH, 7529
Anderson Foundation, Rose-Marie and Jack R., TX, 8761
Anderson Foundation, The, AL, 7
Anderson Foundation, WA, 9551
Anderson Living Trust, Clarence E., The, CA, A
Andersson Children's Foundation, Hanna, OR, A
Andor Capital Management Foundation, CT, 1483
Andrah Foundation, The, MI, 4220
Andreas Foundation, L. & N., MN, 4503
Andreas Foundation, The, MN, 4504
Andrew Family Foundation, The, IL, 2595
Andrew Foundation, Aileen S., IL, 2596
Andrews & McMeel Foundation, MO, see 4774
Andrews Foundation, The, OH, 7530
Andrews McMeel Universal Foundation, MO, 4774
Andringa Family Foundation, Inc., IA, 3262
Angela Foundation, The, PA, 8082
Angelica Foundation, The, CA, 223
Angell Foundation, The, CA, 224
Anheuser Family Foundation, William S., MO, 4775
Anheuser-Busch Foundation, MO, 4776
Animal Assistance Foundation, CO, 1333
Anixter Foundation, L. & R., IL, 2597
Ankeny Foundation, MN, 4505
Ann Arbor Area Community Foundation, MI, 4221
Ann Arbor Area Foundation, MI, see 4221
Anncox Foundation, Inc., GA, 2318
Annenberg Foundation Trust at Sunnylands, The, PA, 8083
Annenberg Foundation, The, PA, 8084
Annis Educational Foundation, R. B., The, IN, 3100
AnnMarie Foundation, WI, 9743
Anon Charitable Trust, WI, 9744
Anonymous Fund, The, NC, 7306
Anschutz Family Foundation, CO, 1334
Anschutz Foundation, The, CO, 1335
Ansin Foundation, FL, 1877
Ansin Foundation, Ronald M., MA, 3779
Ansin Private Foundation, Ronald M., MA, see 3779
Anthem Foundation, Inc., IN, 3101, 3102
Anthony Foundation, Barbara Cox, The, HI, 2531
Antioch Foundation, WI, 9745
Antonovych Foundation, Inc., The, DC, 1766
Antun Foundation, Frank J., The, NY, 5559
Antz Foundation, The, NY, 5560
AO North America, Inc., PA, 8085
AOL Time Warner Foundation, NY, see 7142
Aon Foundation, IL, 2598
Apex Foundation, WA, 9552
Apex Oil Company Charitable Foundation, MO, 4777
Apfelbaum Foundation, Inc., The, NY, 5561
Applebaum Family Foundation, Eugene, The, MI, 4222
Applebaum Foundation, Inc., The, FL, 1878
Appleby Foundation, The, FL, 1879
Appleman Foundation, Inc., The, NY, 5562
Applera Charitable Foundation, Inc., The, CT, 1484

Appleton Foundation, CA, 225
Appleton Foundation, Edith Marie, IL, 2599
Applied Materials Foundation, The, CA, 226
Aquila Foundation, The, CA, 227
Arab Student Aid International Corp., OH, 7531
Aragona Family Foundation, Sandra and Joseph, The, TX, see 8763
Aragona Family Foundation, The, TX, 8763
Aramont Foundation, CA, 228
Arata Brothers Trust, CA, 229
Aratani Foundation, CA, 230
Arbella Charitable Foundation, Inc., MA, 3780
Arbus Foundation, Loreen, The, CA, 231
Arca Foundation, The, DC, 1767
Arcadia Foundation, The, PA, 8086
Arcana Foundation, Inc., The, DC, 1768
Arcee Foundation, Whitney, MN, 4506
Archbold Charitable Trust, Adrian & Jessie, NY, 5563
Archer Charitable Trust, Jacqueline G., WI, 9746
Archer Foundation, PA, 8087
Archibald Charitable Foundation, Norman, WA, 9553
Archstone Foundation, CA, 232
Arctic Education Foundation, AK, 80
Arcus Foundation, MI, 4223
Ard Family Foundation, The, AL, 8
Area Fund, The, NY, 5564
Arete Foundation, PA, 8088
Argosy Foundation, CA, 233
Argosy Foundation, The, WI, 9747
Arguild Foundation, DE, 1687
Argyros Foundation, The, CA, 234
ARIA Foundation, Inc., IL, 2600
Arison Charitable Trust, Ted, FL, 1880
Arison Family Foundation USA, Inc., Ted, FL, 1881
Arison Foundation, Inc., FL, see 1880
Arizona Community Foundation, AZ, 87
Arkansas Community Foundation, Inc., AR, 156
Arkay Foundation, CA, 235
Arkell Hall Foundation, Inc., NY, 5565
Arkema Inc. Foundation, PA, 8089
Arkoosh, Jr. Foundation, Fred G., NE, 4943
Arkwright Foundation, The, SC, 8565
Arlington Community Foundation, VA, 9371
Arm Foundation, NY, 5566
Armfield, Sr. Foundation, Inc., Edward M., The, NC, 7307
Armington Fund, Evenor, The, OH, 7532
Armour-Lewis Family Foundation, NJ, 5116
Armstrong Educational Foundation, Inc., Louis, NY, 5567
Armstrong Foundation, PA, 8090
Armstrong Foundation, The, MS, 4734
Armstrong World Industries Charitable Foundation, PA, see 8090
Arnhold Foundation, Inc., NY, 5568
Arnold Foundation, Inc., NJ, 5117
Arnold Foundation, Norman J., SC, 8566
Arnold Fund, GA, 2319
Arnold Memorial Foundation, Ben, SC, see 8566
Arntz Family Foundation, CA, 236
Arntz Foundation, Eugene S., CA, see 236
Aron Charitable Foundation, Inc., J., NY, 5569
Aronov Family Foundation, Aaron, The, AL, 9
Aronson Family Foundation, The, CT, 1485
Arrillaga Foundation, John, CA, 237
Arrison Family Charitable Foundation, The, NY, 5570
Arsenault Family Foundation, Inc., The, CO, 1336
Arthur Foundation, The, IL, 2601
ArvinMeritor Trust Foundation, MI, 4224
Asbury Foundation of Hattiesburg, Inc., MS, 4735
ASD Foundation, The, MA, 3781
ASDA Foundation, The, NY, 5571
Ashkenazie Foundation, Inc., Jack H., NY, 5572
Ashland Area Cultural and Economic Development Foundation, Inc., Greater, KY, see 3420
Ashland County Community Foundation, OH, 7533
Ashner Family Evergreen Foundation, NY, 5573
Ashtabula Foundation, Inc., The, OH, 7534
Ashton Family Foundation, The, UT, 9303
Ashton Trust, Elisha V., MA, 3782
Aslan Foundation, MN, 4507
Aslan Foundation, The, TN, 8637
Aspen Business Center Foundation, CO, 1337

Aspen Community Foundation, The, CO, 1338
Aspen Foundation, Inc., NJ, 5118
Aspen Valley Community Foundation, CO, see 1338
Asplundh Foundation, PA, 8091
Assisi Foundation of Memphis, Inc., The, TN, 8638
Assisi Foundation, TN, see 8638
Association for the Relief of Aged Women of New Bedford, MA, 3783
Assurant Health Foundation, WI, 9748
Astellas USA Foundation, IL, 2602
Astin Charitable Trust, Nina Heard, TX, 8764
AT&T Foundation, NY, A
AT&T Foundation, TX, 8765
AT&T Global Information Solutions Foundation, OH, see 7773
AT&T National Pro-Am Youth Fund, CA, A
Atchinson Foundation, Robert and Michelle Cooke, The, MA, 3784
Atherton Family Foundation, HI, 2532
Atherton Foundation, Leburta, HI, 2533
Athwin Foundation, MN, 4508
ATK Foundation, The, MN, 4509
Atkins Foundation, Craig S., CA, 238
Atkinson Foundation, CA, 239
Atkinson Foundation, David R. and Patricia D., The, NJ, 5119
Atkinson Foundation, Myrtle L., CA, 240
Atlanta Community Foundation, Inc., Metropolitan, GA, see 2355
Atlanta Falcons Foundation, Inc., GA, see 2383
Atlanta Foundation, GA, 2320
Atlanta Law School, GA, 2321
Atlantic Foundation of New York, The, NY, 5574
Atlas Family Foundation, The, CA, 241
Atlas Foundation, Richard & Lezlie, CA, see 241
Atlas Heritage Foundation, The, IL, 2603
Atofina Chemicals, Inc. Foundation, PA, see 8089
Atran Foundation, Inc., NY, 5575
Atticus Foundation, The, NY, 5576
Atticus Foundation, The, TN, see 8639
Atticus Trust, TN, 8639
Atwood Foundation, Inc., AK, 81
Auchincloss Foundation, Inc., Lily, NY, 5577
Auen Foundation, The, CA, 242
Auen-Bergen Foundation, The, CA, see 242
Auerbach Foundation, Inc., Neil and Judith, The, NY, 5578
Augur Family Foundation, Marilyn, The, TX, 8766
Augur Foundation, Marilyn, The, TX, see 8766
AUL Foundation, Inc., IN, see 3220
Aurora Foundation, AZ, 88
Aurora Foundation, The, FL, 1882
Aurora Foundation, The, IL, see 2680
Aurora Foundation, TX, 8767
Aurora Ministries, Inc., FL, 1883
Aurora Ministries, The, FL, see 1882
Austin Community Foundation for the Capital Area, Inc., TX, 8768
Austin Community Foundation, TX, see 8768
Austin Memorial Foundation, The, OH, 7535
Austin-Bailey Health and Wellness Foundation, OH, 7536
Autry Foundation, CA, 243
Autzen Foundation, The, OR, 7997
Avalon Foundation, NY, 5579
Avanessians Family Foundation, NY, 5580
Ave Maria Foundation, The, MI, 4225
Aven Foundation, WA, 9554
Avenir Foundation, Inc., CO, 1339
Aventis Pharmaceuticals Foundation, NJ, 5120
Aventis Pharmaceuticals Health Care Foundation, NJ, 5121
Avery Arts Foundation, Milton and Sally, NY, 5581
Avery Dennison Foundation, CA, 244
Avery International Foundation, CA, see 244
Avery-Tsui Foundation, CA, 245
AVI CHAI - A Philanthropic Foundation, NY, see 5582
AVI CHAI Foundation, The, NY, 5582
Avis Family Foundation, The, CA, 246
Avon Foundation, NY, 5583
Avon Products Foundation, Inc., NY, see 5583
Avrum Gray Family Fund, FL, 1884
AXA Foundation, Inc., NY, 5584

Axem Foundation, CO, see 1354
Ayers Foundation, TN, 8640
Ayling Scholarship Foundation, Alice S., MA, 3785
Ayoub Foundation Charitable Trust, The, CT, A
Ayrshire Foundation, The, CA, 247
Azadoutioun Foundation, MA, 3786
Azalea Foundation, The, GA, 2322
Azariah Foundation, The, NY, see 6189
Azby Fund, The, LA, 3460
Azeez Foundation, FL, A
Azeez Foundation, Michael and Kathleen, The, FL, see 1885
Azeez Foundation, The, FL, 1885
Azrak and Sons Foundation, Marvin, NY, 5585
Azus Foundation, Inc., CA, 248

B & B Foundation, TX, 8769
B'Seter Foundation, Inc., Matan, NJ, 5122
B. Attitudes Foundation, The, UT, 9304
B.E.L.I.E.F. Foundation, TX, 8770
B.F.Goodrich Foundation, Inc., The, NC, see 7378
Babbitt Family Charitable Trust, NY, 5586
Babcock Foundation, Inc., Mary Reynolds, NC, 7308
Babcock Foundation, Mary E., The, OH, 7537
Babcock Memorial Endowment, William, CA, 249
Babson Foundation, Paul and Edith, The, MA, 3787
Bacardi Foundation, FL, 1886
Bachman Foundation, OH, 7538
Bachmann Foundation, The, NY, see 5587
Bachmann Strauss Family Fund, The, NY, 5587
Bacon Family Foundation, CO, 1340
Bader Foundation, Inc., Helen, WI, 9749
Badgeley Residuary Charitable Trust, Rose M., NY, 5588
Baer Charitable Foundation, Arthur & Helen, MO, 4778
Baer Foundation, Alan and Marcia, NE, 4944
Baer, Jr. Foundation, Sidney R., MO, 4779
Bafflin Foundation, RI, 8519
Bahnik Foundation, Inc., The, NY, 5589
Baier Foundation, Inc., Marie, NY, 5590
Bailey Family Foundation, Inc., The, FL, 1887
Bailey Foundation, Inc., Bobbie, NC, 7309
Bailey Foundation, Larkin, OK, 7923
Bailey Foundation, M D, TX, 8771
Bailey Foundation, P. S. Bailey and Ouida C., SC, 8567
Bailey Nurseries Foundation, MN, 4510
Bain, Jr. Charitable Trust, William W., MA, 3788
Bair Family Trust, Charles M., OR, 7998
Bair Memorial Trust, Charles M., MT, 4931
Bair Ranch Foundation, The, MT, 4932
Baird and Company Foundation, Inc., Robert W., WI, 9750
Baird Foundation, Cameron, The, NY, 5591
Baird Foundation, The, NY, 5592
Bakar Foundation, Gerson, CA, 250
Baker Conservation Trust, The, ME, 3524
Baker Family Foundation, Mr. and Mrs. Robert C., NY, 5593
Baker Family Foundation, Thomas E. and Linda O., NJ, 5123
Baker Foundation, Dexter F. and Dorothy H., PA, 8092
Baker Foundation, Elinor Patterson, The, CT, 1486
Baker Foundation, Howard, The, MI, 4226
Baker Foundation, Inc., Bob, CA, 251
Baker Foundation, Inc., Pat and Jay, WI, 9751
Baker Foundation, R. C., The, CA, 252
Baker Hughes Foundation, TX, 8772
Baker Street Foundation, The, CA, 253
Baker Trust, Clayton, MD, 3566
Baker Trust, George F., The, NY, 5594
Baker, Jr. Memorial Fund, William G., The, MD, 3567
Bakken Foundation, Earl & Doris, The, HI, 2534
Baldwin Charitable Foundation, Inc., A. W., The, MA, 3789
Baldwin Charitable Foundation, Inc., MA, see 3789
Baldwin Family Foundation, Inc., FL, A
Baldwin Foundation, George M., FL, 1888
Baldwin Foundation, Inc., David M. & Barbara, The, NY, 5595
Baldwin Foundation, The, CT, 1487
Balfour Foundation, L. G., MA, 3790
Ball Brothers Foundation, IN, 3103
Ball Family Foundation, G. Carl, IL, 2604

Ball Family Foundation, The, PA, 8093
Ball Foundation, George and Frances, IN, 3104
Ball Foundation, Inc., Edmund F. and Virginia B., IN, 3105
Ball Foundation, Russell C., PA, see 8093
Ballman Family Private Foundation, The, MO, 4780
Ballman Foundation, Ed, AR, A
Balm Foundation, Inc., The, NY, 5596
Baltimore Community Foundation, The, MD, 3568
Baltimore Gas and Electric Foundation, Inc., MD, see 3602
Bamberger Memorial Foundation, Ruth Eleanor Bamberger and John Ernest, UT, 9305
Banbury Fund, Inc., FL, 1889
Bancorp Hawaii Charitable Foundation, HI, see 2535
Bancroft, Jr. Foundation, Hugh, The, NM, 5467
Bandai Foundation, The, CA, 254
Bane Foundation, Earl, KS, 3345
Banfi Vintners Foundation, The, NY, 5597
Bangor Savings Bank Foundation, ME, 3525
Bank Foundation, Inc., Helen S. & Merrill L., MD, 3569
Bank of America Charitable Foundation, Inc., The, NC, 7310
Bank of America Community Foundation, FL, see 1890
Bank of America, N.A. Client Foundation, FL, 1890
Bank of Hawaii Charitable Foundation, HI, 2535
Bank of New York Foundation, The, NY, 5598
BankAtlantic Foundation, Inc., FL, 1891
Banknorth Charitable Foundation, ME, see 3558
Bannerman Foundation, William C., The, CA, 255
Bannerot-Lappe Foundation, PA, 8094
Bansal Foundation, The, VA, 9372
Banta Corporation Foundation, Inc., WI, 9752
Banyan Foundation, Inc., FL, A
Banyan Tree Foundation, DC, 1769
Baptist Community Ministries, LA, 3461
Barancik Foundation, Charles and Margery, IL, 2605
Barber, Jr. Foundation, George W., AL, 10
Barberton Community Foundation, OH, 7539
Barbonchielli and Marie and Manuel B. Perez Foundation, Joseph L., CA, 256
Barbour Foundation, Inc., Bernice, NJ, 5124
Bard Foundation, Inc., C. R., NJ, 5125
Baright Foundation, Hollis and Helen, NE, 4945
Barker Foundation, Coeta and Donald, The, CA, 257
Barker Foundation, Donald R., The, CA, see 257
Barker Foundation, J. M. R., NY, 5599
Barker Welfare Foundation, The, NY, 5600
Barnes Group Foundation, Inc., CT, 1488
Barnet Foundation Trust, The, SC, see 8568
Barnet III Foundation Trust, William, SC, 8568
Barnett Charitable Foundation, Lawrence and Isabel, NY, 5601
Barnett Foundation, Florence L. J. and Howard G., OK, 7924
Barnett Foundation, Gertrude A., IL, 2606
Barnhart Foundation, Joe, TX, 8773
Baron & Blue Foundation, TX, 8774
Barr Foundation, MA, 3791
Barra Foundation, Inc., PA, 8095
Barrington Foundation, Inc., The, NY, 5602
Barron Family Charitable Foundation, The, MA, 3792
Barrows Foundation, Geraldine & R. A., MO, 4781
Barry Charitable Foundation, Richard Allan, MA, 3793
Barry Community Foundation, MI, 4227
Barry Foundation, The, MN, 4511
Barth Family Foundation, CA, 258
Barth Foundation, Inc., Theodore H., NY, 5603
Bartlett Foundation, Edward & Helen, WI, 9753
Bartlett Foundation, Edward E. Bartlett & Helen Turner, WI, see 9753
Bartman Foundation, The, CA, 259
Bartner Family Foundation Trust, VI, 9362
Bartsch Memorial Trust, Ruth, DE, see 1688
Bartsch Memorial Trust, DE, 1688
Baruch Fund, The, NC, 7311
Bas Family Foundation, WA, 9555
Bashinsky Foundation, Inc., AL, 11
Baskes Family Foundation, IL, 2607
Basler Charitable Foundation, Wayne G., TN, 8641
Bass & Edythe & Sol G. Atlas Fund, Inc., Sandra Atlas, NY, 5604
Bass Corporation, Perry and Nancy Lee, TX, 8775

Bass Foundation, Harry W., TX, 8777
Bass Foundation, Lee and Ramona, TX, 8778
Bass Foundation, TX, 8776
Bastian Family Foundation, M., UT, 9306
Bastian Foundation, B. W., The, UT, 9307
Bastien Memorial Foundation, John E. and Nellie J., FL, 1892
Batchelor Foundation, Inc., The, FL, 1893
Bates Foundation, Alben F. & Clara G., IL, 2608
Bates Foundation, John C., The, OH, 7540
Baton Rouge Area Foundation, LA, 3462
Batten Foundation, D. N., The, VA, 9373
Batten Foundation, The, VA, 9374
Batten, Jr. Foundation, Aimee & Frank, VA, 9375
Batten-Rolph Foundation, The, VA, see 9373
Batterman Family Foundation, Inc., Theodore W., WI, 9754
Battle Creek Community Foundation, MI, 4228
Battle Creek Foundation, Greater, MI, see 4228
Battle Family Foundation, CA, 260
Bauer Family Foundation, Ruth & Ted, TX, 8779
Bauer Foundation, Charles T., TX, 8780
Bauer Foundation, Evalyn M., CA, 261
Bauer Foundation, M. R., CA, see 261
Bauer Foundation, M. R., IL, 2609
Bauer Foundation, Modestus, IL, 2610
Bauer Foundation, The, CT, 1489
Baugh Foundation, Eula Mae and John, TX, 8781
Baughman Foundation, KS, 3346
Bauman Family Foundation, Inc., DC, 1770
Bauman Family Foundation, Inc., Robert & Patricia, FL, 1894
Bauman Foundation, William H. Bauman & Mary L., OR, 7999
Baumberger Endowment, TX, 8782
Bausch & Lomb Foundation, Inc., NY, 5605
Bavarian Foundation Trust, KY, 3406
Baxter Allegiance Foundation, The, IL, see 2611
Baxter Family Foundation, Inc., K. & F., CA, 262
Baxter Foundation, Donald E. and Delia B., The, CA, 263
Baxter Foundation, Inc., C. Kenneth and Laura, The, FL, 1895
Baxter International Foundation, The, IL, 2611
Bay and Paul Foundations, Inc., The, NY, 5606
Bay Area Community Foundation, MI, 4229
Bay Bancorp Foundation, Greater, CA, 264
Bay Branch Foundation, The, FL, 1896
Bay State Federal Savings Charitable Foundation, The, MA, 3794
Bayer Foundation, PA, 8096
Bayne Fund, Howard, The, NY, 5607
Bayport Foundation of Andersen Corporation, The, MN, 4512
Bayport Foundation, Inc., MN, see 4512
Bayrd Foundation, Adelaide Breed, MA, 3795
BayTree Fund, CA, 265
BB&T Charitable Foundation, NC, 7312
BB&T West Virginia Foundation, WV, 9710
BCHB, Inc., NY, 5608
BCS Charitable Fund, IL, 2612
Beagle Charitable Foundation, CA, 266
Beal Foundation, The, TX, 8783
Beall Foundation, Donald & Joan, The, CA, A
Beaman Foundation, Alvin and Sally, TN, 8642
Bean Foundation, Norwin S. and Elizabeth N., NH, 5080
Bear Stearns Charitable Foundation, Inc., NY, 5609
Bearman Foundation, Herbert, MD, 3570
Beasley Charitable Trust, Lucy & Emily, WI, 9755
Beasley Foundation, Inc., Theodore and Beulah, TX, 8784
Beattie Foundation, Frances and William H., The, CA, 267
Beattie Foundation, The, CA, see 267
Beatty Trust, Helen D. Groome, PA, 8097
Beaver County Foundation, The, PA, 8098
Beaver Family Foundation, Inc., Donald C., NC, see 7313
Beaver Family Foundation, Inc., NC, 7313
Beaver Street Foundation, Inc., FL, 1897
Beaverkill Foundation, Inc., NY, 5610
Beavers Charitable Trust, CA, 268
Beaverson Foundation, The, OH, 7541
Beazley Foundation, Inc., VA, 9376

Bechtel Charitable Remainder Uni-Trust, Harold R., IA, 3264
Bechtel Charitable Remainder Uni-Trust, Marie H., IA, 3263
Bechtel Charitable Trust, Marie H., IA, see 3263
Bechtel Foundation, CA, see 269
Bechtel Group Foundation, CA, 269
Bechtel Testamentary Charitable Trust, Harold R., IA, 3265
Bechtel, Jr. Foundation, Elizabeth and Stephen, CA, see 270
Bechtel, Jr. Foundation, S. D., CA, 270
Becker Charitable Foundation, Henry E. Becker and Pauline S., The, FL, 1898
Becker Family Foundation, Newton and Rochelle, CA, 271
Beckman Foundation, Arnold and Mabel, CA, 272
Beckwith Charitable Foundation, F. William Beckwith & Leola I., IA, 3266
Beckwith Family Foundation, DE, 1689
Bedell World Citizenship Fund, IA, 3267
Bedminster Fund, Inc., The, NY, 5611
Bedsole Foundation, J. L., The, AL, 12
Bee Fund, Molly, The, OH, 7542
Beech Street Foundation, The, DC, 1771
Beerman Foundation, Inc., The, OH, 7543
Behmann Brothers Foundation, TX, 8785
Behrakis Foundation, The, MA, 3796
Behrend Trust Fund, E. R., PA, A
Behrens and Christopher C. Behrens Foundation, Inc., Mary Taylor, The, NY, 5612
Behring Foundation, FL, 1899
Beidler Foundation, Francis, IL, 2613
Beim Foundation, The, MN, 4513
Beinecke Foundation, Inc., The, NY, see 7255
Beker Foundation, The, NY, 5613
Bekins Foundation, Milo W., CA, 273
Belcher, Jr. Foundation, S. E., AL, A
Beldon Fund, NY, 5614
Beldon II Fund, NY, see 5614
Belfer Family Foundation, Robert A. and Renee E., NY, 5615
Belfer Foundation, Inc., Arthur and Rochelle, The, NY, 5616
Belfer Foundation, Inc., The, NY, see 5616
Believers Foundation, Inc., The, FL, 1900
Belk Educational Foundation, Irwin, NC, 7314
Belk Foundation, The, NC, 7315
Belk-Simpson Foundation, NC, see 7392
Bell Atlantic Foundation, NJ, see 5439
Bell Charitable Foundation, CA, 274
Bell Family Charitable Foundation, Inc., WI, 9756
Bell Family Foundation, FL, 1901
Bell Family Foundation, Inc., IL, 2614
Bell Foundation, Bonne, The, OH, 7544
Bell Foundation, J. G., The, OH, see 7544
Bell Foundation, James Ford, MN, 4514
Bell Trust, TX, 8786
Bella Vista Foundation, CA, 275
Bellamy Memorial Foundation, Inc., Robert R., FL, 1902
Bellebyron Foundation, IL, 2615
BellSouth Foundation, GA, 2323
Bellwether Foundation, Inc., The, MO, 4782
Belo Corporation Foundation, A. H., TX, see 8787
Belo Foundation, The, TX, 8787
Beloco Foundation, Inc., GA, 2324
Beloit Foundation, Inc., WI, 9757
Belz Foundation, TN, 8643
Bemis Company Foundation, MN, 4515
Ben & Jerry's Foundation, Inc., VT, 9355
Ben-Haim Family Foundation, Avi & Jody, The, NY, 5617
Benaroya Foundation, WA, 9556
Benbough Foundation, Legler, The, CA, 276
Bender Foundation, Inc., DC, 1772
Bendheim Foundation, Inc., Siegfried & Nannette, NJ, see 5126
Bendheim Foundation, Inc., The, NJ, 5126
Benedict Foundation, Inc., Helen Andrus, NY, 5618
Benedum Foundation, Claude Worthington, PA, 8099
Beneficia Foundation, PA, 8100
Beneficial Foundation, Inc., DE, see 1703
Benenson Family Foundation, Dr. William O., NY, 5619
Benenson Family Foundation, NY, see 5619

Benenson Foundation, Inc., Frances & Benjamin, NY, 5620
Beneto Foundation, CA, 277
Benfamil Charitable Trust, MA, 3797
Benidt Foundation, Inc., Charles E., WI, 9758
Benificus Foundation, The, CA, 278
Benjamin Charitable Foundation, Inc., Elizabeth and Barets O., The, NJ, 5127
Bennett Family Foundation, The, CA, 279
Bennett Foundation, C. E., DE, 1690
Bennett Foundation, Carl and Dorothy, CT, 1490
Bennett Foundation, The, NV, 5021
Benson Charitable Foundation, Grace and Tom, TX, 8788
Benson Foundation, Alain Ralphs, CA, 280
Benson Foundation, P. Bruce and Virginia C., CO, 1341
Benton Foundation, DC, 1773
Benwood Foundation, Inc., TN, 8644
Benz Trust, Doris L., The, MA, 3798
Berbecker and Lille A. Webb Scholarship Fund, Walter J., CT, see 1491
Berbecker Scholarship Fund, Walter J. Berbecker and Lille A., CT, 1491
Bere Foundation, Inc., IL, 2616
Beren Charitable Trust, Israel Henry, KS, 3347
Beren Foundation, Inc., Robert M., KS, 3348
Beren Trust, Harry H., CO, 1342
Berenson Charitable Foundation, Theodore W. & Evelyn G., MA, 3799
Berg Family Charitable Foundation, FL, 1903
Berg Foundation, Inc., David, The, NY, 5621
Bergen Foundation, Frank and Lydia, NC, 7316
Berger Foundation, David, PA, 8101
Berger Foundation, H. N. & Frances C., CA, 281
Berger Foundation, Sol and Margaret, NJ, 5128
Bergman-Davison-Webster Charitable Trust, TX, 8789
Bergstrom Foundation, A Charitable Trust, Erik E. and Edith H., CA, 282
Berkley Corporation Charitable Foundation, W. R., DE, 1691
Berkley Foundation, Inc., The, CT, 1492
Berkman Foundation, Louis and Sandra, The, OH, 7545
Berkman Foundation, Sybiel B., PA, 8102
Berkowitz Family Charitable Trust, The, NY, see 7125
Berkowitz Foundation, Judy & Howard, The, NY, 5622
Berks County Community Foundation, PA, 8103
Berkshire Bank Foundation, MA, 3800
Berkshire Foundation, CA, 283
Berkshire Hills Foundation, MA, see 3800
Berkshire Taconic Community Foundation, MA, 3801
Berkshire-Taconic Foundation, MA, see 3801
Berlin Family Charitable Corporation, OH, see 7546
Berlin Family Foundation, Inc., OH, 7546
Berlin Foundation, Howard R. & Joy M., AZ, 89
Berlind Foundation, The, NJ, 5129
Berlitz Charitable Trust, August and Marjorie C., MD, 3571
Berlys Foundation, The, NY, 5623
Berman Family Foundation, Inc., Dennis, The, MD, 3572
Berman Family Foundation, Irving & Betty, DC, 1774
Berman Foundation, Inc., Dollye and I. Wolford, The, MD, 3573
Berman Foundation, Inc., Robin and Dennis, The, MD, see 3572
Berman Foundation, Madeleine and Mandell L., MI, see 4230
Berman Foundation, Mandell L. and Madeleine H., MI, 4230
Berman Foundation, Philip and Muriel, The, PA, 8104
Berner Charitable and Scholarship Foundation, The, IL, 2617
Bernhard Foundation, Inc., Arnold, The, NY, 5624
Bernon Family Foundation, Alan J., MA, see 3802
Bernon Family Foundation, Carol and Alan J., MA, 3802
Bernoudy Foundation, Gertrude and William A., MO, 4783
Bernsen Foundation, Grace & Franklin, OK, 7925
Bernstein Family Charitable Foundation, The, FL, 1904
Bernstein Foundation, Inc., Diane & Norman, DC, 1775
Bernstein Foundation, Paula & William, CO, 1343
Bernstein Foundation, Stanley & Vivian, The, NY, 5625
Berrie Foundation, Russell, The, NJ, 5130
Berrien Community Foundation, Inc., MI, 4231

Berry Family Foundation, OH, 7547
Berry Foundation, Archie W. and Grace, WY, 9975
Berry Foundation, Arthur and Doris, ME, 3526
Berry Foundation, Loren M., OH, see 7547
Berry Foundation, Lowell, The, CA, 284
Berry Foundation, Theresa A. and Thomas W., NY, 5626
Bershad Foundation, Inc., David & Susan, NJ, 5131
Bersted Foundation, Grace A., IL, 2618
Bersted Foundation, The, IL, 2619
Berthiaume Family Foundation, Inc., MA, 3803
Bertolon Family Foundation, MA, 3804
Besser Foundation, MI, 4232
Best Buy Children's Foundation, MN, 4516
Bestfoods Educational Foundation, NJ, 5132
Betesh & Sons Foundation, Inc., Sol E., NY, 5627
Betesh Family Foundation, Inc., Eddie and Rachelle, The, NY, 5628
Bethlehem Area Foundation, PA, see 8303
Better Days Foundation, Inc., OK, 7926
Better Way Foundation, Inc., FL, 1905
Betterworld Together Foundation, CA, 285
Bettingen Corporation, Burton G., CA, 286
Betz Foundation, Theodora B., PA, 8105
Beveridge Family Foundation, Inc., The, FL, 1906
Beveridge Foundation, Inc., Frank Stanley, The, FL, 1907
Beverly Foundation, The, MN, 4517
Bezos Family Foundation, WA, 9557
BGB Foundation, WI, see 9768
Bialkin Family Foundation, NY, 5629
Bible Alliance, Inc., FL, see 1883
Bickel & Brewer Legal Foundation, TX, 8790
Bickerstaff Family Foundation, CA, 287
Bickerton Foundation, Susan & Charlie, CA, 288
Bicknell Fund, OH, 7548
Biddle Foundation, Mary Duke, The, NC, 7317
Bieber Family Foundation, The, MN, 4518
Biedenharn Foundation, The, LA, 3463
Bielfeldt Foundation, Gary K. and Carlotta J., The, IL, see 2620
Bielfeldt Foundation, The, IL, 2620
Biesecker Foundation, PA, 8106
Bigelow Foundation, F. R., MN, 4519
Bildirici Hesed Foundation, Gabriel and Sara, NY, 5630
Bildner Family Foundation, NJ, 5133
Bilezikian Family Foundation, Inc., MA, 3805
Bilger Foundation, The, CA, 289
Biller Family Foundation, Sheri Biller & Les, CA, 290
Billings Foundation, Inc., Eric and Marianne, VA, 9377
BIN Charitable Foundation, NC, 7318
Binda Foundation, Guido A. & Elizabeth H., MI, 4233
Binder Foundation, CA, 291
Bing Fund Corporation, NV, 5022
Bing Fund, Inc., NV, A
Bingham 2nd Betterment Fund, William, NY, 5631
Bingham Foundation, William, The, OH, 7549
Bingham Trust, The, CT, 1493
Bingham's Trust for Charity, Mr., CT, see 1493
Binzer Fund, Isadore, OH, 7550
Biogen Foundation, Inc., MA, see 3806
Biogen Idec Foundation Inc., MA, 3806
Biomet Foundation, Inc., The, IN, 3106
Biondi Family Foundation, The, CT, 1494
Birch Foundation, Inc., Stephen and Mary, DE, 1692
Bireley Foundation, The, CA, 292
Birkelund Fund, The, NY, 5632
Birmingham Foundation, Greater, The, AL, see 24
Birmingham Foundation, MA, 3807
Birmingham Foundation, The, PA, 8107
Birnhak Foundation, Marilyn and J. Robert, PA, 8108
Bishop Charitable Trust, A. G., WI, 9759
Bishop Clarkson Episcopal Foundation, NE, 4946
Bishop Foundation, Edward E. and Lillian H., DE, 1693
Bishop Trust A for the SPCA of Manatee County, Florida, Lillian H., DE, 1694
Bismarck Charitable Trust, Mona, NY, 5633
Bissell Foundation, Inc., J. Walton, CT, 1495
Bistricer Foundation, Moric & Elsa, NY, see 6464
Bito and Olivia Carino Foundation, Inc., Laszlo, NY, 5634
BJ's Foundation, Inc., FL, 1908
Black Charitable Foundation, Robert, NY, 5635
Black Charitable Trust, Elizabeth S., OH, 7551

Black Family Foundation, Inc., Leon, NY, 5636
Black Family Foundation, PA, 8109
Black Family Foundation, Stanley and Joyce, The, CA, 293
Black Foundation, Inc., Mary, SC, 8569
Black Mountain Foundation, The, MA, 3808
Blackman Foundation, Inc., Aaron and Marie, The, CA, 294
Blades Foundation, A. T. & Mary H., MD, 3574
Blair & Company Foundation, William, IL, 2621
Blair Foundation, IL, 2622
Blakemore Foundation, WA, 9558
Blanchard III Trust- Dendroica Foundation, Peter P., PA, 8110
Blanchard Trust, Arthur F., PA, 8111
Blandin Foundation, Charles K., MN, see 4520
Blandin Foundation, The, MN, 4520
Blank Charity Fund, Myron and Jacqueline, The, IA, see 3268
Blank Family Foundation, Arthur M., The, GA, 2325
Blank Family Foundation, Inc., The, FL, 1909
Blank Fund, Myron & Jacqueline, IA, 3268
Blankfein Foundation, Lloyd and Laura, The, NY, 5637
Blaustein Foundation, Inc., Jacob and Hilda, The, MD, 3575
Blaustein Foundation, Inc., Morton K. and Jane, The, MD, 3576
Bleser Family Foundation, Inc., WI, 9760
Bless Foundation, Inc., WI, 9761
Bloch Foundation, Henry W. and Marion H., The, MO, A
Block Foundation, Herb, DC, 1776
Block Foundation, Inc., Adele and Leonard, NY, 5638
Blood Family Foundation, The, NY, 5639
Bloomfield Foundation, Inc., Sam & Rie, CA, 295
Blount Educational Charitable Foundation, Inc., Roberts & Mildred, The, AL, A
Blount Educational Foundation, David Strouse, FL, 1910
Blount Foundation, Inc., The, AL, 14
Blount Foundation, Mary K. Archibald, AL, 13
Blowitz-Ridgeway Foundation, The, IL, 2623
Blue & You Foundation for a Healthier Arkansas, AR, 157
Blue Cross and Blue Shield of Minnesota Foundation, Inc., MN, 4521
Blue Cross and Blue Shield of North Carolina Foundation, NC, 7319
Blue Cross and Blue Shield of South Carolina Foundation, SC, 8570
Blue Dot Foundation, VA, 9378
Blue Foundation for a Healthy Florida, Inc., The, FL, 1911
Blue Grass Community Foundation, Inc., KY, 3407
Blue Grass Foundation, Inc., KY, see 3407
Blue Moon Fund, Inc., VA, 9379
Blue Mountain Area Foundation, WA, see 9559
Blue Mountain Community Foundation, WA, 9559
Blue Ribbon Foundation of Blue Cross of Northeastern Pennsylvania, The, PA, 8112
Blue Ridge Foundation New York, NY, 5640
Blue River Community Foundation, Inc., The, IN, 3107
Blue River Foundation, Inc., The, IN, see 3107
Blue Shield of California Foundation, CA, 296
Blue Star Foundation, Inc., NY, 5641
Bluebell Foundation, The, CT, 1496
Bluhdorn Charitable Trust, Charles G. & Yvette, NY, 5642
Blum Family Foundation, CA, 297
Blum Foundation, Harry and Maribel G., IL, see 2844
Blum Foundation, Inc., Edith C., NY, 5643
Blum Foundation, Inc., Walter and Adi, The, FL, 1912
Blum Foundation, Lois and Irving, The, MD, 3577
Blum Foundation, Nathan and Emily S., The, IL, 2624
Blum-Kovler Foundation, IL, 2625
Blume Foundation, CA, 298
Blumenstein Foundation Corporation, Harold & Penny B., MI, 4234
Blumenthal Foundation, The, NC, 7320
Blythmour Corporation, NY, 5644
Bobolink Foundation, The, NY, 5645
Bobst Foundation, Inc., Elmer and Mamdouha, NY, 5646
Bodenhamer Foundation, AR, 158
Bodenwein Public Benevolent Foundation, CT, 1497

Bodine Charitable Trust, Jack and Mary Jane, MO, 4784
Bodman Foundation, The, NY, 5647
Bodner Family Foundation, Inc., NY, 5648
Boeckmann Charitable Foundation, CA, 299
Boehringer Ingelheim Cares Foundation, Inc., CT, 1498
Boeing Company Charitable Trust, The, WA, 9560
Boeing-McDonnell Foundation, MO, 4785
Boettcher Foundation, CO, 1344
Bogoni Operating Foundation, Paul and Irene, The, NJ, 5134
Bohemian Foundation, CO, 1345
Bohen Foundation, The, CO, 1346
Bohlsen Family Foundation, John and Linda, NY, 5649
Bohnert Foundation, Inc., NJ, 5135
Bohnett Foundation, David, CA, 300
Boisi Family Foundation, The, NY, 5650
Bolden Foundation, Herman & Emmie, AL, 15
Bolger Foundation, NJ, 5136
Bolick Foundation, The, NC, 7321
Boll Foundation, John A. & Marlene L., MI, 4235
Bolthouse Foundation, The, CA, 301
Bolz Family Foundation, Eugenie Mayer, WI, 9762
Bond Foundation, Inc., The, FL, 1913
Bondi Foundation, The, CT, 1499
Bonfils-Stanton Foundation, CO, 1347
Bonner Foundation, Inc., Corella & Bertram F., The, NJ, 5137
Bookout Family Foundation, The, TX, 8791
Booth Ferris Foundation, NY, 5651
Booth Foundation, Inc., Alex and Roxanna, FL, 1914
Booth Foundation, Otis, The, CA, 302
Booth Heritage Foundation, Inc., CA, 303
Booth-Bricker Fund, The, LA, 3464
Borchard Foundation, Inc., Albert & Elaine, CA, 304
Borden Foundation, Alec, The, IL, 2626
Borden Memorial Foundation, Mary Owen, The, NJ, 5138
Borderline Personality Disorder Research Foundation, NY, 5652
Boren Foundation, Inc., The, IN, 3108
Borick Foundation, Louis L., CA, 305
Borina Charitable Trust, CA, 306
Borina Foundation, CA, 307
Born Family Charitable Trust, Ross J., PA, 8113
Born Foundation, Walter W., OH, 7552
Bornblum Foundation, The, TN, 8645
Borwell Charitable Foundation, IL, 2627
Bosack and Bette M. Kruger Charitable Foundation, Inc., Leonard X., The, CA, 3809
BOSE Foundation, Inc., MA, 3810
Bosque Charitable Foundation, TX, see 8792
Bosque Foundation, TX, 8792
Bossidy Foundation, Lawrence A., The, CT, 1500
Boston Fatherless & Widows Society, MA, 3811
Boston Foundation, Inc., MA, 3812
Boston Scientific Foundation, Inc., MA, 3813
Boswell Family Foundation, ID, 2564
Boswell Foundation, Inc., MO, 4786
Boswell Foundation, James G., The, CA, 308
Bothin Foundation, The, CA, 309
Botwinick-Wolfensohn Foundation, Inc., NY, 5653
Boulder Area Communities Foundation, CO, see 1358
Bouras Foundation, Inc., Nicholas J. and Anna K., The, NJ, 5139
Boutell Memorial Fund, Arnold and Gertrude, MI, see 4236
Boutell Memorial Fund, MI, 4236
Bovaird Foundation, Mervin, The, OK, 7927
Bovin Family Foundation, The, NY, 5654
Bowana Foundation, CO, 1348
Bowen Foundation, Ethel N., WV, 9711
Bower Foundation, Inc., The, MS, 4736
Bowes Family Foundation, CA, 310
Bowes, Jr. Foundation, William K., CA, 311
Bowman Family Foundation, CA, 312
Bowne Foundation, Inc., Robert, The, NY, 5655
Boxer Foundation, The, NY, 5656
Boyd Charitable Foundation, W. Glen, OR, 8000
Boyd Foundation, The, NV, 5023
Boye Foundation, Inc., The, NJ, 5140
Boyer Foundation, Herbert & Marigrace, The, CA, 313
Boymel Foundation, Sam and Rachel, The, OH, 7553
Bozzone Family Foundation, PA, 8114

BP Amoco Foundation, Inc., IL, see 2628
BP Foundation, CA, 314
BP Foundation, Inc., IL, 2628
Brace Foundation, Donald C., CT, 1501
Brach Family Foundation, Inc., NY, 5657
Brach Foundation, Edwin J., IL, 2629
Brach Foundation, Helen, IL, 2630
Brackenridge Foundation, George W., TX, 8793
Bradberry Family Foundation, AR, 159
Bradley Charitable Foundation, Joseph G., PA, 8115
Bradley Foundation, Inc., Lynde and Harry, The, WI, 9763
Bradley Foundation, The, CA, 315
Bradley, Jr. Charitable Fund, Harry L., MA, 3814
Bradley-Turner Foundation, Inc., GA, 2326
Bradshaw-Knight Foundation, Inc., WI, 9764
Brady Charitable Foundation, Benjamin F., The, GA, 2327
Brady Foundation, NJ, 5141
Braemar Charitable Trust, OR, 8001
Braeside Foundation, The, IL, 2631
Brain Foundation, Inc., Frances Hollis, GA, 2328
Brainerd Family Foundation, Inc., Lyman B., The, CT, 1502
Brainerd Foundation, The, WA, 9561
Braman Foundation, Inc., Norman and Irma, FL, 1915
Branan Trust, Charles I., NC, 7322
Branch County Community Foundation, MI, 4237
Branch Trust, C. B. and Anita, TX, 8794
Branches Foundation, SD, 8623
Brand Foundation, The, NY, 5658
Brand-Boeshaar Foundation, NE, A
Brandenborg Family Foundation, Douglass, The, MN, 4522
Brandenburg Family Foundation, The, CA, 316
Brandes Family Foundation, CA, 317
Brandt Foundation, John H. and Orah I., The, ID, 2565
Branfman Family Foundation, NJ, 5142
Branigin Foundation, Inc., Elba L. and Gene Portteus, The, IN, 3109
Branta Foundation, Inc., NY, 5659
Braswell Trust, James R. and Bronnie L., NC, 7323
Brauer Charitable Trust, Stephen F. and Camilla T., The, MO, 4787
Braufman Family Foundation, Inc., Daniel L. Nir & Jill E., NY, 5660
Braun Trust, Carl F., CA, A
Braun/Brown Family Foundation, CA, 318
Bravmann Foundation, Inc., L., The, NY, 5661
Bravo Foundation, The, CA, 319
Breeden Family Foundation, The, NC, 7324
Breidenthal-Snyder Foundation, The, KS, 3349
Bremer Foundation, Otto, MN, 4523
Bren Foundation, Donald, The, CA, 320
Brencanda Foundation, NY, see 6212
Brennan Family Foundation, OH, 7554
Brenner Foundation, Inc., Mervyn L., The, CA, 321
Brentwood Foundation, OH, 7555
Bressler Family Foundation, The, MA, 3815
Bressler Foundation, Alan S. Bressler and Lorraine D., The, MA, see 3815
Brett Family Foundation, CO, 1349
Bretzlaff Foundation, Inc., Hilda E., The, MI, 4238
Bretzlaff Foundation, Inc., The, NV, 5024
Brewer Family Foundation, Robert N., IL, 2632
Briarcliff Foundation, Inc., The, AL, A
Brice Foundation, Deborah L., NY, 5662
Brickman Foundation, PA, 8116
Bridge Foundation, Inc., The, TX, 8795
Bridgemill Foundation, CT, 1503
Bridgeport Area Foundation, Inc., Greater, The, CT, 1504
Bridgestone/Firestone Trust Fund, The, TN, 8646
Bridgeway Charitable Foundation, TX, 8796
Bridwell Foundation, J. S., The, TX, 8797
Briger Foundation, Peter and Devon, NY, 5663
Briggs & Stratton Corporation Foundation, Inc., WI, 9765
Briggs Foundation, Inc., Thomas W., TN, 8647
Briggs Foundation, Margaret, PA, 8117
Bright Family Foundation, CA, 322
Bright Foundation, The, IA, 3269
Bright Horizon Foundation, NY, 5664

Brill Charitable Trust, Ron and Lisa, GA, 2329
Brindle Foundation, NM, 5468
Brine Charitable Trust, Madeline and Kevin, NY, see 5665
Brine Family Charitable Trust, The, NY, 5665
Brinn Foundation, Elizabeth A., WI, see 9857
Brinson Foundation, The, IL, 2633
Bristol County Savings Charitable Foundation, Inc., MA, 3816
Bristol Fund, Inc., PA, 8118
Bristol-Myers Fund, Inc., The, NY, see 5666
Bristol-Myers Squibb Foundation, Inc., The, NY, 5666
Bristol-Myers Squibb Patient Assistance Foundation, Inc., The, NJ, 5143
Britton Fund, OH, 7556
Broad Art Foundation, The, CA, 323
Broad Foundation, CA, 324
Broad Foundation, Eli & Edythe L., CA, A
Broad Foundation, Inc., Shepard, The, FL, 1916
Broad Reach Foundation, CA, 325
Broadcasters Foundation, Inc., CT, 1505
Broadfield Foundation, The, GA, 2330
Broccoli Charitable Foundation, Dana & Albert R., CA, 326
Brock Foundation, Harry B. & Jane H., The, AL, 16
Brock Foundation, The, AL, see 16
Brockway Charitable Trust, AZ, A
Brodie Charitable Foundation, Donald and Barbara, IL, see 3074
Brodsky Family Foundation, Muriel and Bert, NY, 5667
Brodsky Family Foundation, The, NY, 5668
Brodsky Foundation, Daniel J. and Estrellita, NY, 5669
Brody Brothers Foundation, Inc., NC, 7325
Brody Foundation, Inc., Carolyn & Kenneth D., DC, 1777
Brody Foundation, Sophie & Arthur, NJ, 5144
Brokaw Family Foundation, NY, 5670
Bromley Charitable Trust, The, MA, 3817
Bronfman Family Foundation, Inc., Edgar M., The, NY, see 5672
Bronfman Foundation, Ann L., FL, 1917
Bronfman Foundation, Inc., Andrea and Charles, The, NY, 5671
Bronfman Foundation, Samuel, The, NY, 5672
Bronfman Philanthropies, Inc., Andrea and Charles, The, NY, 5673
Bronstein Foundation, Solomon and Sylvia, The, PA, 8119
Brookbank Foundation, Inc., WI, 9766
Brookfield Arts Foundation, Inc., MA, 3818
Brooks Foundation, Gladys, NY, 5674
Brooks Foundation, Harold, The, RI, 8520
Brooks-Mathews Foundation, CA, 327
Brossman Charitable Foundation, William & Jemima, The, PA, 8120
Brossman Family Charitable Trust for Scholarships, The, PA, 8121
Brotherton Charitable Foundation, Fred J., NJ, 5145
Brotherton Foundation, Inc., Fred J., NJ, see 5145
Brotman Family Foundation, WA, 9562
Brotman Foundation of California, CA, 328
Brotz Family Foundation, Inc., Frank G. and Frieda K., WI, 9767
Brotz Family Foundation, Inc., Frank G., WI, see 9767
Brougher Foundation, Inc., W. Dale, The, PA, 8122
Broughton Charitable Private Foundation, Inc., William Gundry, NY, 5675
Broussard Charitable Foundation Trust, OH, 7557
Broward Community Foundation, Inc., FL, see 1941
Brown & Sons Charitable Foundation, Inc., Alex., MD, 3578
Brown and C. A. Lupton Foundation, Inc., T. J., TX, 8798
Brown and Charles Seelig Family Foundation, Robin, The, NY, 5676
Brown Charitable Foundation, Alvin I. & Peggy S., MD, 3579
Brown Charitable Foundation, Owsley, KY, 3408
Brown Charitable Trust, Dana, MO, 4788
Brown Charitable Trust, Mary L. M., GA, 2331
Brown Charitable Trust, Peter D. and Dorothy S., MI, 4239
Brown County Community Foundation, Inc., IN, 3110
Brown Family Foundation, John and Rosemary, The, MI, 4240

Brown Family Foundation, Warren, GA, 2332
Brown Foundation, Inc., A. Pat and Kathryne L., The, NC, 7326
Brown Foundation, Inc., James Graham, KY, 3409
Brown Foundation, Inc., The, TX, 8799
Brown Foundation, Joe W. & Dorothy Dorsett, LA, 3465
Brown Foundation, W. L. Lyons, KY, 3410
Brown Group, Inc. Charitable Trust, MO, see 4789
Brown Shoe Company, Inc. Charitable Trust, MO, 4789
Brown Trust 1, Frank E., NC, 7327
Brown, Jr. Charitable Foundation, W. L. Lyons, KY, 3411
Brownell Family Foundation, IA, 3270
Browning Charitable Foundation, Val A., UT, 9308
Browning Memorial Fund, L. L., OH, see 7811
Browning-Kimball Foundation, MT, 4933
Brownington Foundation, The, NY, 5677
Brownlee Foundation, Robert, The, CA, 329
Broyhill Family Foundation, Inc., NC, 7328
Bruce and Lee Foundation, Drs., SC, 8571
Bruce Foundation, Julia Harrison, IL, 2634
Bruening Foundation, Eva L. and Joseph M., OH, 7558
Brumley Foundation, The, TX, 8800
Brunckhorst Foundation, The, NY, 5678
Bruner Foundation, Inc., MA, 3819
Brunie Foundation, Jean I. & Charles H., NY, 5679
Bruning Foundation, The, IL, 2635
Bruno Charitable Foundation, Joseph S., The, AL, 17
Brunswick Charitable Foundation, Richard A., LA, 3466
Brunswick Foundation, Inc., The, IL, 2636
Brutsch Charitable Trust, 1994 Sheila Johnson, The, NY, 5680
Bryan Area Foundation, Inc., OH, 7559
Bryan Foundation of Greater Greensboro, Inc., Joseph M., The, NC, 7329
Bryan Foundation, Inc., R. A., NC, 7330
Bryant Foundation, Inc., Edwin E. and Janet L., The, WI, 9768
Bryant Foundation, The, VA, 9380
Bryce Memorial Fund, William and Catherine, WI, 9769
Bryson Foundation, FL, 1918
BT Foundation, NY, see 5854
BTL Foundation, IL, see 3039
Buchanan Family Foundation, The, IL, 2637
Buchmann Charitable Foundation, Josef, The, NY, 5681
Buck Foundation, Carol Franc, NV, 5025
Buck Foundation, Caroline Alexander, PA, 8123
Buck Foundation, Frank H. and Eva B., The, CA, 330
Buck Foundation, Peter and Carmen Lucia, The, NY, 5682
Buckley Trust, Thomas D., NE, 4947
Buckner Charitable Residuary Trust, H. W., DE, 1695
Buckner Foundation, MO, 4790
Bucksbaum Family Foundation, Martin, IA, 3271
Bucksbaum Family Foundation, Matthew and Carolyn, IA, 3272
Bucksbaum Family Foundation, Matthew, IA, see 3272
Bucksbaum Foundation, IA, see 3271
Buddha Dharma Kyokai (Society), Inc., NY, see 5685
Buder Charitable Foundation, G. A., Jr. and Kathryn M., The, MO, 4791
Buehler Family Foundation, IL, 2638
Buehler Foundation, A. C., IL, see 2638
Buehler Perpetual Trust, Emil, NJ, 5146
Buell Foundation, Temple Hoyne, CO, 1350
Buenger Foundation, Clement and Ann, OH, 7560
Buffalo Foundation, The, NY, see 5780
Buffett Early Childhood Fund, NE, 4948
Buffett Foundation, Howard G., IL, 2639
Buffett Foundation, Rebecca Susan, IL, 2640
Buffett Foundation, Susan A., The, NE, 4949
Buffett Foundation, Susan Thompson, The, NE, 4950
Buffett Foundation, The, NE, see 4950
Bugher Foundation, Henrietta B. & Frederick H., NY, 5683
Bugher Foundation, NY, see 5683
Buhl Family Foundation, Inc., The, NY, see 5684
Buhl Foundation, Inc., The, NY, 5684
Buhl Foundation, The, PA, 8124
Building Hope...A Charter School Facilities Fund, DC, 1778
Buisson Foundation, Inc., The, GA, 2333
Bukkyo Dendo Kyokai America, Inc., NY, 5685
Bull Foundation, Henry W., The, CA, 331

Bullard Foundation, George N., TN, see 8701
Bullitt Foundation, The, WA, 9563
Bulova Fund, Inc., Louise and Arde, NJ, 5147
Bumpus Foundation, William and Bernice E., MA, 3820
Bunbury Company, The, NJ, 5148
Buncher Family Foundation, PA, 8125
Bundy Foundation, Bruce and Anne, CA, 332
Bunge Corporation Foundation, MO, 4792
Bunker Foundation, The, CA, 333
Bunning Family Foundation, IL, 2641
Bunning Food Allergy Foundation, IL, 2642
Bunting Family Foundation, Inc., MD, 3580
Buntrock Foundation, Dean L. & Rosemarie, IL, 2643
Bunzl Foundation, Inc., Walter & Frances, GA, 2334
Burch Family Foundation, CA, 334
Burch Family Foundation, The, NY, see 5686
Burch Foundation, The, NY, 5686
Burden Foundation, Florence V., NY, 5687
Burdick-Thorne Foundation, The, MI, 4241
Burfeind-Codispoti Foundation, Inc., The, NJ, see 5165
Burke Charitable Foundation, Helen Keeler, NY, 5688
Burke Family Foundation, PA, 8126
Burke Foundation, Inc., James E. and Diane W., NJ, 5149
Burke Foundation, James E., NJ, see 5149
Burleigh Family Foundation, OH, 7561
Burlington Northern Santa Fe Foundation, IL, 2644
Burlington Resources Foundation, TX, A
Burlock Foundation, Leslie and Walter, CA, 335
Burnett Charitable Foundation, Inc., Al and Nancy, FL, 1919
Burnett Charitable Foundation, Inc., Al, FL, see 1919
Burnett Company Charitable Foundation, Leo, IL, 2645
Burnett Foundation, Andrew H., CA, 336
Burnett Foundation, The, TX, 8801
Burnett-Tandy Foundation, The, TX, see 8801
Burnham Charitable Trust, Margaret E., ME, 3527
Burnham Foundation, CA, 337
Burning Foundation, The, WA, 9564
Burns Foundation, Fritz B., CA, 338
Burns Foundation, Inc., Donald A., FL, 1920
Burns Foundation, Inc., Jacob, NY, 5689
Burpee Foundation, The, NY, 5690
Burress Foundation, J. W., NC, 7331
Burroughs Educational Fund, N. R., NC, 7332
Burroughs Wellcome Fund, NC, 7333
Burt Foundation, MI, 4242
Burton Foundation, Inc., FL, 1921
Burton Foundation, R. Harold, UT, 9309
Burton Foundation, William T. and Ethel Lewis, The, LA, 3467
Bush Charitable Foundation, Inc., Edyth, FL, 1922
Bush Foundation, MN, 4524
Bussing-Koch Foundation, Inc., IN, 3111
Butler Family Foundation, IL, 2646
Butler Family Foundation, Patrick and Aimee, MN, 4525
Butler Family Foundation, The, IA, 3273
Butler Family Fund, Sarah & Ernest, TX, 8802
Butler Family Fund, The, DC, 1779
Butler Foundation, Alice, NC, 7334
Butler Foundation, Inc., Gilbert & Ildiko, NY, 5691
Butler Foundation, Inc., J. E. & Z. B., NY, 5692
Butler Foundation, Inc., NY, see 5691
Butler Manufacturing Company Foundation, MO, 4793
Butler Memorial Foundation, Robert M., OH, 7562
Butler Memorial Scholarship Foundation, J. D. and Alice, NC, see 7334
Butler, Jr. Family Foundation, Inc., Susan C. and James E., GA, 2335
Butnam Foundation, Grace, ME, 3528
Butt Foundation, Charles, The, TX, 8803
Butt Foundation, H. E., TX, 8804
Buttenwieser Foundation, Catherine & Paul, NY, 5693
Butterworth Memorial Trust, William, IL, 2647
Buuck Family Foundation, MN, 4526
Buyse Foundation, The, MN, A
BVM Foundation, Inc., IN, 3112
BWMF Farm, AR, see 187
Bydale Foundation, The, NY, 5694
Byer Foundation, CA, 339
Byerly Foundation, The, SC, 8572
Byers' Foundation, The, PA, 8127
Byrne Foundation, Inc., The, NH, 5081

Byrnes Family Foundation, The, MA, 3821

C Funding, NJ, 5150
C.E. and S. Foundation, Inc., The, KY, 3412
C.I.O.S., TX, 8805
C.M.J. Private Foundation, CA, see 709
C.O.U.Q. Foundation, Inc., The, NY, 5695
C.S. Fund, CA, 340
CAA Foundation, CA, 341
Cabe Foundation, Horace C., IL, 2648
Cabell Foundation, Robert G. Cabell III and Maude Morgan, The, VA, 9381
Cabot Charitable Foundation, Edmund & Betsy, The, MA, 3822
Cabot Corporation Foundation, Inc., MA, 3823
Cabot Family Charitable Trust, MA, 3824
Cabot Foundation, Virginia Wellington, The, MA, 3825
Cacioppo Foundation, Joseph & Mary, The, AZ, 90
Cacique Foundation, CA, 342
Caddock Foundation, Inc., CA, 343
Cadence Foundation, CA, 344
Cader Foundation, Inc., Andrew, The, NY, 5696
Caesars Entertainment Foundation, Inc., TN, 8648
Cafaro Family Foundation, William M. & A., The, OH, 7563
Cafesjian Family Foundation, Inc., The, MN, 4527
Cafritz Foundation, Morris and Gwendolyn, The, DC, 1780
Cailloux Family Foundation, Kathleen, TX, 8806
Cailloux Foundation, Floyd A. & Kathleen C., TX, see 8807
Cailloux Foundation, The, TX, 8807
Cain Brothers Foundation, The, NY, 5697
Cain Foundation, Effie and Wofford, The, TX, 8808
Cain Foundation, Gordon and Mary, The, TX, 8809
Caine Charitable Foundation, Marie Eccles, UT, 9310
Calder Foundation, Louis, The, CT, 1506
Calderwood Charitable Foundation, MA, 3826
Caldwell Foundation, Inc., TN, 8649
Caldwell Foundation, MA, 3827
Caldwell Scholarship Fund, James R., IL, see 2913
Calhoun County Community Foundation, AL, see 23
Calicchio Family Foundation, John, The, NY, 5698
California Community Foundation, CA, 345
California Endowment, The, CA, 346
California HealthCare Foundation, CA, 347
California Masonic Foundation, CA, 348
California Physicians' Service Foundation, CA, see 296
California Space Grant Foundation, CA, 349
California Wellness Foundation, The, CA, 350
Callahan Foundation, M. E. & F. J., OH, 7564
Callaway Foundation, Fuller E., GA, 2336
Callaway Foundation, Inc., GA, 2337
Callaway Foundation, The, TX, 8810
Callison Foundation, The, CA, 351
Calvin Bible Foundation, Inc., John, MD, 3581
Camalott Charitable Foundation, IL, see 2872
Cambr Charitable Foundation Trust, The, NY, 5699
Cambridge Community Foundation, MA, 3828
Cambridge Foundation, The, MA, see 3828
Cameron Foundation, Flora, TX, 8811
Cameron Foundation, Harry S. and Isabel C., TX, 8812
Cammarata Family Foundation, MA, 3829
Camp and Bennet Humiston Trust, Apollos, IL, 2649
Camp Foundation, VA, 9382
Camp Younts Foundation, GA, 2338
Campbell and Adah F. Hall Charity Fund, Bushrod H., MA, 3830
Campbell Charitable Foundation, Estelle S., OH, 7565
Campbell Charitable Trust, Ruth Camp, NY, 5700
Campbell Family Foundation, James & Abigail, HI, 2536
Campbell Family Foundation, The, CA, 352
Campbell Foundation for the Environment, Inc., Keith, The, MD, 3582
Campbell Foundation, Betsy M., SC, 8573
Campbell Foundation, Charles Talbot, PA, 8128
Campbell Foundation, Elizabeth Turner, TN, 8650
Campbell Foundation, J. Bulow, GA, 2339
Campbell Foundation, James & Abigail, HI, see 2536
Campbell Foundation, MN, 4528
Campbell Foundation, Robert S., SC, 8574
Campbell Foundation, Ruth and Henry, VA, 9383
Campbell Foundation, The, FL, 1923

Campbell Foundation, The, OR, 8002
Campbell Foundation, The, TX, 8813
Campbell Soup Foundation, NJ, 5151
Campbell Soup Fund, NJ, see 5151
Campini Foundation, Frank A., CA, 353
Canaday Educational and Charitable Trust, NY, see 5701
Canaday Family Charitable Trust, MA, 3831
Canaday Family Charitable Trust, The, NY, 5701
Canary Charitable Foundation, Inc., The, NY, 5702
Cancer Research Foundation, Inc., The, CA, see 1251
Canning Foundation, The, IL, 2650
Cannon Family Foundation, TN, 8651
Cannon Foundation, Inc., The, NC, 7335
Cannon Trust, Anne, MD, 3583
Cantor Art Foundation, B. G., The, CA, see 354
Cantor Foundation, Iris & B. Gerald, CA, 354
Cantor Foundation, NJ, 5152
Cantus Fund, The, CA, 355
CAP Charitable Foundation USA, VA, 9384
Capdevilla/Gillespie Foundation, CA, 356
Cape Branch Foundation, NJ, 5153
Cape Cod Five Cents Savings Bank Charitable Trust, MA, 3832
Cape Cod Foundation, The, MA, 3833
Cape Fear Community Foundation, Inc., NC, see 7345
Cape Fear Memorial Foundation, NC, 7336
Capecchio Foundation, The, CA, see 419
Capita Charitable Foundation, Emil R., NJ, 5154
Capital Athletic Foundation, DC, 1781
Capital City Group Foundation, Inc., FL, 1924
Capital Gazette Foundation, Inc., MD, 3584
Capital Group Companies Charitable Foundation, The, CA, 357
Capital Region Community Foundation, MI, 4243
Capitol Federal Foundation, KS, 3350
Capote Literary Trust, Truman, The, CA, 358
Capp Foundation, Martin & Esther, MN, 4529
Cappelli Foundation, Inc., Louis R., The, NY, 5703
Cardinal Brook Trust, MA, 3834
Cardinal Foundation, The, OH, 7566
Cardinal Health Foundation, OH, 7567
Cardone Foundation, PA, 8129
Carey Foundation, W. P., NY, 5704
Cargill Foundation, The, MN, 4530
Caridad Corporation, MN, 4531
Caring and Sharing Foundation, Inc., MN, see 4599
Caring Foundation, The, AL, 18
Caring Kids, CA, see 287
Caris Foundation, TX, 8814
Carlee Charitable Trust, MA, 3835
Carleton Family Foundation, Inc., The, MA, 3836
CARLISLE Foundation, The, RI, 8521
Carlos Foundation, Inc., Andrew & Eula, GA, 2340
Carlos Foundation, Thalia & Michael C., GA, 2341
Carls Foundation, The, MI, 4244
Carlsbad Foundation, Inc., NM, 5469
Carlson Charitable Trust, Chester & Dorris, NY, A
Carlson Family Foundation, Inc., NJ, 5155
Carlson Foundation, Curtis L., The, MN, 4532
Carlson Foundation, The, TX, 8815
CarMax Foundation, The, VA, 9385
Carmel Hill Fund, The, NY, 5705
Carmichael Foundation, Inc., IN, 3113
Carnahan-Jackson Foundation, NY, 5706
Carnation Company Foundation, CA, see 935
Carnation Company Scholarship Foundation, WA, see 9648
Carnegie Corporation of New York, NY, 5707
Carnegie Foundation for the Advancement of Teaching, The, CA, 359
Carnegie Hero Fund Commission, PA, 8130
Carney Foundation, Patrick, MA, 3837
Carolan Foundation, Inc., Tina and Richard V., NJ, 5156
Carolina First Foundation, SC, see 8615
Carolyn Foundation, MN, 4533
Carpenter Family Childrens Foundation, Inc., CA, 360
Carpenter Foundation, E. Rhodes & Leona B., PA, 8131
Carpenter Foundation, The, OR, 8003
Carper Foundation, GA, A
Carr Foundation, Inc., Gregory C., MA, 3838
Carr Foundation, Inc., The, AK, 82
Carr Fund, Kristen Ann, The, NY, 5708

Carrington Charitable Trust, Alexander Berkeley Carrington, Jr. and Ruth S., VA, 9386
Carroll Charitable Trust, Florence V., IN, 3114
Carroll Foundation, Leila, The, CO, see 1351
Carrus Foundation, Gerald and Janet, IL, 2651
Carse Charitable Family Foundation, Wayne L. Carse & Jimmie L., The, FL, 1925
Carsey Family Foundation, The, CA, 361
Carson Family Charitable Trust, The, NY, 5709
Carson Foundation, CO, 1351
Carson Foundation, Inc., John W., CA, 362
Carson Pirie Scott Foundation, AL, 19
Cartales Foundation, John A. and Helen M., WA, 9565
Carter Boy Scout Scholarship Fund, Marjorie Sells, CT, 1507
Carter Community Memorial Trust, E. Kemper Carter and Anna Curry, MO, 4794
Carter Community Memorial Trust, MO, see 4794
Carter Family Charitable Trust, The, RI, 8522
Carter Family Foundation, WV, 9712
Carter Foundation, Amon G., TX, 8816
Carter Foundation, Beirne, The, VA, 9387
Carter Star-Telegram Employees Fund, Amon G., TX, 8817
Carthage Foundation, The, PA, 8132
Cartledge Charitable Foundation, Inc., VA, 9388
Caruso Family Foundation, The, CA, 363
Carvel Foundation, Thomas & Agnes, The, NY, 5710
Carver Charitable Trust, Roy J., IA, 3274
Carwill Foundation, The, NY, 5711
Cary Charitable Trust, Mary Flagler, NY, 5712
Carylon Foundation, IL, 2652
Cascade Hemophilia Consortium, MI, 4245
Cascone Family Foundation, Michael Cascone Jr. and Elizabeth Belyea, The, FL, 1926
Case Family Foundation, NY, 5713
Case Foundation, Stephen, The, DC, see 1782
Case Foundation, The, DC, 1782
Casey Family Grants Program, WA, see 9567
Casey Family Programs, WA, 9566
Casey Foundation, Annie E., The, MD, 3585
Casey Foundation, Eugene B., MD, 3586
Casey Foundation, Marguerite, WA, 9567
Casey Foundation, Sophia & William, NY, 5714
Casey Youth Opportunities Initiative, Inc., Jim, MO, 4795
Cash Family Foundation, The, NC, see 7365
Casper Foundation, William J. & Gertrude R., WI, 9770
Caspersen Foundation for Aid to Health and Education, Inc., O. W., FL, 1927
Cass County Community Foundation, Inc., IN, 3115
Cassels Foundation, The, SC, 8575
Cassett Foundation, Louis N., PA, 8133
Cassin Educational Initiative Foundation, CA, 364
Cassin Foundation, The, CA, 365
Castagnola Family Foundation, George V. and Rena G., CA, 366
Castellani Family Foundation, Lawrence P., FL, 1928
Castellini Foundation, OH, 7568
Castelnau Foundation, NY, 5715
Castle Foundation, Harold K. L., HI, 2537
Castle Foundation, NY, 5716
Castle Foundation, Samuel N. and Mary, HI, 2538
Castle Hills Schools Foundation, Inc., TX, 8818
Castle Rock Foundation, CO, 1352
Casty-Dunn Families Charitable Foundation, MA, 3839
Catalyst Fund, The, ME, 3529
Caterpillar Foundation, IL, 2653
Catlin Foundation, Inc., FL, 1929
Cato, Jr. Foundation, Inc., Wayland H., SC, 8576
Catto Charitable Foundation, TX, 8819
Caufield Family Foundation, CA, 367
Caulkins Family Foundation, CO, 1353
Cauthorn Charitable Trust, John & Mildred, TX, 8820
Cavaliere Foundation, Inc., WI, see 9764
Cavitolo Foundation, Andrea, PA, 8134
Cawley Family Foundation, The, DE, 1696
Cawood Foundation, Inc., The, GA, 2342
Cay Foundation, Inc., GA, 2343
Cayman Conand Foundation, MN, see 4503
Cayne Charitable Trust, James E. and Patricia D., The, NY, 5717
Cayre Foundation, Inc., Joseph & Trina, The, NY, 5718

Cayre Foundation, Inc., Kenneth & Lillian, The, NY, 5719
Cayre Foundation, Inc., Stanley & Frieda, The, NY, 5720
Cayre Foundation, Jack & Grace, NY, see 5718
CB&T Charitable Trust, GA, see 2497
CCB Foundation, Inc., NC, see 7491
CEC Foundation, The, CA, 368
Cedar Fund, Inc., NY, 5721
Cedar Hill Foundation, DE, 1697
Cedar Rapids Community Foundation, Greater, The, IA, 3275
Cedar Rapids Foundation, Greater, The, IA, see 3275
Cedar Tree Foundation, MA, 3840
Cejas Family Foundation, Inc., The, FL, 1930
Cemala Foundation, Inc., The, NC, 7337
CEMEX Foundation, TX, 8821
Cendant Charitable Foundation, The, NJ, 5157
Centene Charitable Foundation, The, MO, 4796
Centennial Foundation, NY, 5722
Center Charitable Trust, Hugh Stuart, CA, 369
Center for Biomedical Science & Engineering Trust, MA, 3841
Center for Integrative Health, Medicine and Research, CA, A
Centerior Energy Foundation, OH, see 7630
Centofante Foundation, CA, 370
Central Alabama Community Foundation, Inc., AL, 20
Central Bank Foundation, AL, see 28
Central Carolina Community Foundation, SC, 8577
Central Indiana Community Foundation, Inc., IN, 3116
Central Minnesota Community Foundation, MN, 4534
Central Minnesota Initiative Fund, MN, see 4593
Central National-Gottesman Foundation, The, NY, 5723
Central New York Community Foundation, Inc., NY, 5724
Central Susquehanna Community Foundation, PA, 8135
Central Texas Scholarship Foundation, TX, see 8810
Centre County Community Foundation, Inc., PA, 8136
Century 21 Associates Foundation, Inc., NY, 5725
Century Fund Trust, The, PA, 8137
Ceres Foundation, Inc., The, SC, 8578
Ceres Foundation, NJ, 5158
Cesatam Foundation, Inc., The, NJ, 5159
Cessna Foundation, Inc., KS, 3351
Cestone Foundation, Inc., Michele and Agnese, PA, 8138
Cestone Foundation, Inc., Ralph M., The, PA, 8139
CFP Foundation, TX, 8822
CFVI, VI, see 9363
CGU Charitable Trust, MA, see 4060
CH Foundation, The, TX, 8823
CH2M Hill Foundation, IL, 2654
Chace Fund, Inc., The, RI, 8523
Chaddick Foundation, Inc., Harry F. and Elaine, IL, 2655
Chadwick Fund, Dorothy Jordan, NY, 5726
Chadwick-Loher Foundation, MN, 4535
Chafetz Family Charitable Trust, Irwin, MA, 3842
Chahara Foundation, Inc., The, MA, 3843
Chai X Four Charitable Trust, NY, 5727
Chaim Foundation, NY, 5728
Chais Family Foundation, CA, 371
Challenge Foundation, The, GA, 2344
Chambers Family Foundation, CA, 372
Chambers Family Foundation, OR, 8004
Chambers Family Fund, CO, 1354
Chambers Memorial, James B., WV, 9713
Champlin Foundations, The, RI, 8524
Chana Sasha Foundation, Inc., NY, 5729
Chancellor Foundation, Inc., IN, 3117
Chandler Foundation, AL, see 37
Chaney Foundation, Ltd., Eugene, MD, 3587
Chang Foundation, Robert N., NJ, 5160
Change a Life Foundation, CA, 373
Change Happens Foundation, HI, 2539
Chanin Foundation, Inc., Marcy and Leona, NY, 5730
Channel Foundation, WA, 9568
Chanticleer Foundation, The, PA, 8140
Chapin Foundation of Myrtle Beach, South Carolina, SC, 8579
Chapman Charitable Trust, H. A. and Mary K., OK, 7928
Chapman Family Fund, WY, 9976
Chapman Foundation, Norman and Joan, IL, 2656
Chapman Foundation, WI, 9771

Chapman Foundation, William McCaskey Chapman and Adaline Dinsmore, The, CA, 374

Charina Foundation, Inc., NY, 5731

Charis Foundation, Inc., The, TN, 8652

Charitable and Research Foundation, Inc., The, FL, 1931

Charitable Foundation of the Frost National Bank of San Antonio, The, TX, 8824

Charitable Leadership Foundation, NY, 5732

Charitable Trust dated 4/28/83, NY, 5733

Charitable Venture Foundation, NY, 5734

Charities Foundation, OH, 7569

Charity, Inc., MN, 4536

Charles Charitable Trust Two, Roy R., VA, 9389

Charles Foundation, Inc., NJ, 5161

Charles River Foundation, MA, see 3844

Charles River Laboratories Foundation, Inc., MA, 3844

Charlesbank Homes, MA, 3845

Charlesmead Foundation, Inc., The, RI, 8525

Charleston Area Charitable Foundation, IL, 2657

Charlevoix County Community Foundation, MI, 4246

Charlotte Merchants Foundation, NC, 7338

Charlotte's Web, MD, 3588

Charlottesville Area Community Foundation, VA, 9390

Charlottesville-Albemarle Community Foundation, VA, see 9390

Charlson Foundation, MN, 4537

Charlton, Jr. Charitable Trust, Earle P., MA, see 3846

Charlton, Jr. Discretionary Charitable Trust, Earle P., MA, 3846

Charter Foundation, Inc., The, GA, 2345

Charter Manufacturing Company Foundation, Inc., WI, 9772

Charter One Foundation, The, RI, 8526

Chartwell Charitable Foundation, CA, 375

Chasanoff Foundation, Inc., NY, 5735

Chasdei Yisroel Charitable Trust, The, NY, 5736

Chase & Stuart Bear Family Foundation, Inc., Cheryl, CT, 1508

Chase Charity Foundation, Alfred E., The, MA, 3847

Chase Family Foundation, Inc., Rhoda & David, The, CT, 1509

Chase Family Foundation, Inc., The, CT, see 1509

Chase Family Foundation, KY, 3413

Chase Foundation of Virginia, VA, 9391

Chase Foundation, IL, A

Chase Manhattan Foundation, The, NY, see 6277

Chatham Foundation, The, GA, 2346

Chatham Hill Foundation, TX, 8825

Chatham Valley Foundation, Inc., The, GA, 2347

Chatlos Foundation, Inc., The, FL, 1932

Chattahoochee Valley Community Foundation, Inc., GA, see 2361

Chatterjee Charitable Foundation, NY, 5737

Chautauqua Region Community Foundation, Inc., NY, 5738

Chavez Community Development Fund, Cesar E., CA, 376

Chazen Foundation, The, NY, 5739

CHC Foundation, ID, 2566

Cheeryble Foundation, CA, 377

Cheesecake Factory-Oscar and Evelyn Overton Charitable Foundation, The, CA, 378

Chehebar Family Foundation, Inc., NY, 5740

Chehebar Family Foundation, Joseph, NY, 5741

Chencinski Brothers Charitable Foundation, Inc., NY, 5742

Cheney Foundation, Ben B., WA, 9569

Cheney Foundation, Elizabeth F., IL, 2658

Cherbec Advancement Foundation, MN, 4538

Cherne Foundation, Albert W., MN, A

Chernin Family Foundation, Inc., The, NY, 5743

Chernow Trust 2, Michael, NY, 5744

Chernow Trust, Michael, NY, 5745

Chesed Foundation of America, NY, 5747

Chesed Foundation, CA, 379

Chesed Foundation, NY, 5746

Chesed, Inc., GA, 2348

Chester County Community Foundation, PA, 8141

Chester Foundation, Jack, IL, 2659

Chesterfield Charitable Foundation, NH, 5082

ChevronTexaco Foundation, CA, 380

Chia Family Foundation, Inc., FL, 1933

Chiara Charitable Fund, Inc., Judith L., NY, 5748

Chicago Board of Trade Foundation, IL, 2660

Chicago Community Trust, The, IL, 2661

Chicago Mercantile Exchange Foundation, IL, 2662

Chicago Tribune Foundation, IL, 2663

Chichester duPont Foundation, Inc., DE, 1698

Children's Care Foundation, The, IL, 2664

Children's Educational Opportunity Foundation, CA, 381

Children's Family Care, Inc., OH, 7570

Children's Foundation of Memphis, The, TN, 8653

Children's Health Fund, CA, see 1044

Children's Investment Fund Foundation, The, NY, 5749

Childs Charitable Foundation, Roberta M., MA, 3848

Childs Memorial Fund for Medical Research, Jane Coffin, The, CT, 1510

Chiles Foundation, OR, 8005

Chilton Family Foundation, The, CT, see 1511

Chilton Foundation Trust, The, TX, see 8826

Chilton Foundation, Al and Lenore, The, TX, 8826

Chilton Foundation, The, CT, 1511

China Medical Board of New York, Inc., NY, 5750

Ching Foundation, Hung Wo & Elizabeth Lau, HI, 2540

Chinnick Charitable Foundation, William, The, NY, 5751

Chinquapin Foundation, TX, 8827

Chintu Gudiya Foundation, CA, 382

Chiquita Brands International Foundation, OH, 7571

Chiron Charitable Foundation, The, CA, 383

Chisholm Charitable Trust, M. A., NY, 5752

Chisholm Foundation, The, NY, 5753

Choice Hotels International Foundation, MD, 3589

Choptank Foundation, The, DE, 1699

Chosky Charitable & Educational Foundation, Philip, The, PA, 8142

Chouinard Family Foundation, CA, see 1331

Christensen Fund, The, CA, 384

Christian Evangelical Foundation, MI, 4247

Christian Foundation, Taylor, NH, 5083

Christian Mission Concerns, TX, 8828

Christian Missionary Scholarship Foundation, NV, 5026

Christian Workers Foundation of Alabama, Inc., A., AL, 21

Christianson Foundation, W. G., MN, 4539

Christman Foundation, Anne Kilcawley, OH, 7572

Christopher Foundation, Jay and Doris, IL, 2665

Christopher Memorial Charity Fund, Louis J., CA, 385

Christy-Houston Foundation, Inc., TN, 8654

Chrysalis Foundation, The, TN, 8655

Chrysler Corporation Fund, MI, see 4265

Chrysopolae Foundation, CA, 386

CHS Cooperatives Foundation, MN, see 4540

CHS Foundation, MN, 4540

Chu Foundation, Gina and David, The, NY, 5754

Chubb Foundation, The, NJ, 5162

Church of Christ Foundation, Inc., TN, see 8741

Chutney Foundation, Inc., The, MT, 4934

CIC Foundation, Inc., TN, 8656

Cicala Charitable Trust, IL, A

CIGNA Foundation, PA, 8143

Cimarron Foundation, The, TX, see 8966

Cincinnati Foundation for the Aged, The, OH, 7573

Cincinnati Foundation, Greater, The, OH, 7574

Cincinnati Milacron Foundation, OH, see 7751

Cinergy Foundation, Inc., OH, A

Cinnabar Foundation, The, MT, 4935

Ciocca Charitable Foundation, Arthur & Carlyse, CA, 387

Circle Bar Foundation, TX, 8829

Circle of Service Foundation, IL, 2666

Circuit City Foundation, VA, 9392

CIRI Foundation, The, AK, 83

Cisco Systems Foundation, CA, 388

Cisneros Fontanals Foundation for the Arts, FL, 1934

Citadel Group Foundation, IL, 2667

Citicorp Foundation, NY, see 5755

Citigroup Foundation, NY, 5755

Citizens Bank Mid-Atlantic Charitable Foundation, The, RI, 8527

Citizens Bank Tri-Cities Foundation, Ltd., TN, 8657

Citizens Banking Corporation Charitable Foundation, MI, 4248

Citizens First Foundation, Inc., MI, 4249

Citizens First Savings Charitable Foundation, Inc., MI, see 4249

Citizens Savings Foundation, The, IN, 3118

CityBridge Foundation, Inc., The, DC, 1783

Civitas Foundation, NJ, 5163

CJM Foundation, NY, 5756

Claiborne & Art Ortenberg Foundation, Liz, NY, 5757

Claiborne Foundation, Liz, NY, 5758

Claneil Foundation, Inc., PA, 8144

Clapp Charitable and Educational Trust, Anne L. and George H., The, PA, 8145

Clapp Foundation, M. Roger and Anne Melby, The, OH, 7575

CLARCOR Foundation, TN, 8658

Clare Foundation, David R. Clare & Margaret C., NJ, 5164

Clarinda Foundation, The, IA, 3276

Clark Charitable Foundation, Inc., MD, 3590

Clark Charitable Foundation, James H., NV, 5027

Clark Charitable Fund, NY, see 5759

Clark Charitable Trust, Frank E., NY, 5759

Clark County Community Foundation, WA, see 9570

Clark Family Foundation, Emory T., WI, 9773

Clark Foundation, Edna McConnell, The, NY, 5760

Clark Foundation, Gladys and Franklin, The, VA, 9393

Clark Foundation, Inc., Robert Sterling, NY, 5761

Clark Foundation, The, NY, 5762

Clark-Winchcole Foundation, MD, 3591

Clarke Trust, John, MA, 3849

Claws Foundation, VA, 9394

Clay Foundation, Inc., WV, 9714

Clay Foundation, Lyell B. & Patricia K., WV, 9715

Clayton Family Foundation, The, TN, 8659

Clayton Fund, Inc., The, TX, 8830

Clear Channel Communications Foundation, TX, 8831

Cleary Foundation, WI, see 9774

Cleary-Kumm Foundation, Inc., WI, 9774

Clemens Foundation, The, OR, 8006

Clements Foundation, TX, 8832

Cless Family Foundation, IL, 2668

Cless Foundation, Karl, IL, see 2668

Cleveland Foundation, MN, 4541

Cleveland Foundation, The, OH, 7576

Cleveland Indians Charities, Inc., OH, 7577

Cline Foundation, The, SC, 8580

Clingen Foundation, Ltd., IL, 2669

Clinton Family Foundation, The, NY, 5763

Clipper Ship Foundation, Inc., MA, 3850

Clisby Charitable Trust, The, VA, see 9417

Clive Foundation, Winifred Johnson, PA, 8146

Clorox Company Foundation, The, CA, 389

Cloud Mountain Foundation, NY, 5764

Cloverfields Foundation, MN, 4542

Clowes Charitable Foundation, Inc., Allen Whitehill, IN, 3119

Clowes Fund, Inc., The, IN, 3120

CLRC, Inc., NY, 5765

CME Foundation, IL, see 2662

CMS Endowment Foundation, PA, 8147

CMS Foundation, PA, 8148

CNA Foundation, IL, 2670

CNA Insurance Companies Foundation, IL, see 2670

CNC Foundation, CA, 390

Coastal Bend Community Foundation, TX, 8833

Coastal Community Foundation of South Carolina, SC, 8581

Coastal Villages Investment Fund, AK, A

Coates Charitable Foundation of 1992, Elizabeth Huth, TX, 8834

Coates Foundation, Vincent J., CA, 391

Cobalt Corporation Foundation, Inc., WI, A

Cobb Educational Fund, Ty, GA, 2349

Cobb Family Foundation, Inc., FL, 1935

Cobb Foundation, FL, 1936

Cobb Foundation, The, CA, 392

Coca-Cola Bottlers Foundation, Inc., The, GA, 2350

Coca-Cola Enterprises Charitable Foundation, The, GA, 2351

Coca-Cola Foundation, Inc., The, GA, 2352

Cochran Family Foundation, The, PA, 8149

Cockrell Foundation, The, TX, 8835

Code Family Foundation, The, IL, 2671

Codispoti Foundation, NJ, 5165

Codrington Charitable Foundation, George W., The, OH, 7578

Cody Foundation, The, NY, see 6027

Coffey Foundation, Inc., The, NC, 7339

Cogan Family Foundation, MA, 3851
Cogswell Benevolent Trust, NH, 5084
Cogut Foundation, Inc., Craig & Deborah, The, NY, 5766
Cohen Charitable Foundation, Inc., Ben & Zelda, MD, 3592
Cohen Family Foundation, Abby and David, The, NY, 5767
Cohen Family Foundation, Inc., Ryna and Melvin, The, MD, 3593
Cohen Family Foundation, Michele and Martin, The, NY, 5768
Cohen Foundation for Ovarian Cancer Research, Lynne, CA, 393
Cohen Foundation, Inc., Abraham and Yvonne, NY, 5769
Cohen Foundation, Inc., Joseph M. & Barbara, NY, 5770
Cohen Foundation, Inc., Karen B., NJ, 5166
Cohen Foundation, Jack D., NY, 5771
Cohen Foundation, Naomi and Nehemiah, MD, 3594
Cohen Foundation, Steven A. and Alexandra M., CT, 1512
Cohen LD Family Foundation, Inc., NY, 5772
Cohenca Foundation, Inc., Jacques & Emy, NY, 5773
Colburn Family Foundation, The, VA, 9395
Colburn Foundation, CA, 394
Colburn Fund, Tara, The, CA, 395
Colcom Foundation, PA, 8150
Cold Heading Foundation, The, MI, 4250
Cole Family Foundation, Inc., The, VA, 9396
Cole Foundation, Inc., Jerome and Ilene, IL, 2672
Cole Foundation, Inc., Olive B., IN, 3121
Cole Foundation, Kenneth, NY, 5774
Cole Trust, Quincy, VA, 9397
Coleman Charitable Foundation, Inc., David & Ruth, WI, 9775
Coleman Charitable Foundation, Inc., Ruth and Baron, FL, 1937
Coleman Family Foundation, Inc., KS, 3352
Coleman Family Foundation, NM, 5470
Coleman Foundation, Inc., The, IL, 2673
Coleman Foundation, Inc., Thomas B. and Robertha K., The, NC, 7340
Coleman Foundation, Lester E. & Kathleen A., OH, 7579
Coleman, Jr. Foundation, George E., DC, 1784
Colen Foundation, Inc., The, FL, 1938
Coles Family Foundation, NY, 5775
Colin Foundation, Simon and Eve, NY, 5776
College First Foundation, TX, 8836
Collins Family Foundation, Inc., Calvert K., TX, 8837
Collins Family Foundation, The, CA, 396
Collins Foundation, Carol & James, The, CA, 397
Collins Foundation, Fred, SC, 8582
Collins Foundation, Fulton and Susie, OK, 7929
Collins Foundation, Inc., Calvert K., TX, see 8837
Collins Foundation, James M., The, TX, 8838
Collins Foundation, Joseph, NY, 5777
Collins Foundation, The, OR, 8007
Collins Fund, P. & C., NY, 5778
Collins McDonald Trust Fund, OR, 8008
Collins Medical Trust, OR, 8009
Collins, Jr. Foundation, George Fulton, OK, 7930
Collis Foundation, The, CT, 1513
Collis/Warner Foundation, Inc., The, VA, 9398
Colombe Foundation, MA, 3852
Colombo Charitable Trust, CA, 398
Colombo Charitable Trust, Elsie T. & Josephine, CA, see 398
Colonial Foundation, Inc., GA, 2353
Colonial Oaks Foundation, PA, 8151
Colorado Masons Benevolent Fund Association, CO, 1355
Colorado Trust, The, CO, 1356
Columbia Charitable Foundation, CA, A, see 1182
Columbia Foundation, CA, 399
Columbia Foundation, The, MD, 3595
Columbia Gas Foundation, IN, see 3213
Columbia/HCA Healthcare Foundation, Inc., TN, see 8690
Columbus Foundation and Affiliated Organizations, The, OH, 7580
Columbus Foundation, The, OH, see 7580
Columbus Phipps Foundation, The, VA, 9399
Combined International Foundation, IL, see 2598

Combs Foundation, Earle M. & Virginia M., IL, 2674
Comcast Foundation, The, PA, 8152
Comdisco Foundation, IL, see 2835
Comer Foundation, The, AL, 22
Comer Foundation, The, IL, 2675
Comer Science & Education Foundation, IL, 2676
Comerica Charitable Foundation, MI, 4251
Comloquoy Charitable Foundation, Robert & Sara S., NC, 7341
Commerce Bancshares Foundation, The, MO, 4797
Commerce Foundation, The, MO, see 4797
Commercial Capital Bank Community Foundation, CA, 400
Commercial Federal Charitable Foundation, NE, 4951
Common Stream, Inc., MA, 3853
Common Wealth Trust, The, DE, 1700
Commonweal Foundation, Inc., MD, 3596
Commonwealth Fund, The, NY, 5779
Communities Foundation of Oklahoma, OK, 7931
Communities Foundation of Texas, Inc., TX, 8839
Community Enterprises, Inc., GA, 2354
Community Foundation Alliance, Inc., IN, 3122
Community Foundation for Greater Atlanta, Inc., GA, 2355
Community Foundation for Greater Buffalo, NY, 5780
Community Foundation for Greater New Haven, The, CT, 1514
Community Foundation for Monterey County, CA, 401
Community Foundation for Muskegon County, MI, 4252
Community Foundation for Northeast Georgia, GA, 2356
Community Foundation for Northeast Michigan, MI, 4253
Community Foundation for Palm Beach and Martin Counties, Inc., FL, 1939
Community Foundation for South Central New York, Inc., The, NY, 5781
Community Foundation for Southeast Michigan, MI, 4254
Community Foundation for Southeastern Michigan, MI, see 4254
Community Foundation for Southern Arizona, AZ, 91
Community Foundation for Southwest Washington, WA, 9570
Community Foundation for the Alleghenies, The, PA, 8153
Community Foundation for the Capital Region, Inc., The, NY, 5782
Community Foundation for the Central Savannah River Area, GA, 2357
Community Foundation for the Fox Valley Region, Inc., WI, 9776
Community Foundation for the National Capital Region, The, DC, 1785
Community Foundation for the Ohio Valley, Inc., The, WV, 9716
Community Foundation in Jacksonville, The, FL, 1940
Community Foundation of Abilene, TX, 8840
Community Foundation of Acadiana, LA, 3468
Community Foundation of Ardmore, Inc., OK, 7932
Community Foundation of Boone County, Inc., IN, 3123
Community Foundation of Broward, FL, 1941
Community Foundation of Calhoun County, AL, 23
Community Foundation of Cape Cod, The, MA, see 3833
Community Foundation of Carroll County, Inc., MD, 3597
Community Foundation of Central Florida, Inc., FL, 1942
Community Foundation of Central Georgia, Inc., GA, 2358
Community Foundation of Central Illinois, IL, 2677
Community Foundation of Collier County, FL, 1943
Community Foundation of Decatur/Macon County, The, IL, 2678
Community Foundation of Delaware County, OH, 7581
Community Foundation of Dutchess County, The, NY, see 5564
Community Foundation of Frederick County, MD, Inc., The, MD, 3598
Community Foundation of Gaston County, Inc., NC, 7342
Community Foundation of Grant County, IN, 3124
Community Foundation of Greater Birmingham, The, AL, 24

Community Foundation of Greater Chattanooga, Inc., The, TN, 8660
Community Foundation of Greater Flint, MI, 4255
Community Foundation of Greater Fort Wayne, Inc., IN, 3125
Community Foundation of Greater Greensboro, Inc., NC, 7343
Community Foundation of Greater Jackson, MS, 4737
Community Foundation of Greater Johnstown, The, PA, see 8153
Community Foundation of Greater Lakeland, Inc., The, FL, 1944
Community Foundation of Greater Lorain County, The, OH, 7582
Community Foundation of Greater Memphis, TN, 8661
Community Foundation of Greater New Britain, CT, 1515
Community Foundation of Greater Rochester, MI, 4256
Community Foundation of Greater Tampa, Inc., The, FL, see 1948
Community Foundation of Greenville, Inc., SC, 8583
Community Foundation of Harrisonburg and Rockingham County, The, VA, 9400
Community Foundation of Henderson County, Inc., NC, 7344
Community Foundation of Herkimer & Oneida Counties, Inc., The, NY, 5783
Community Foundation of Howard County, Inc., The, IN, 3126
Community Foundation of Jackson Hole, WY, 9977
Community Foundation of Louisville, Inc., The, KY, 3414
Community Foundation of Madison and Jefferson County, Inc., IN, 3127
Community Foundation of Mendocino County, Inc., The, CA, 402
Community Foundation of Metropolitan Tarrant County, The, TX, see 8841
Community Foundation of Middle Tennessee, Inc., TN, 8662
Community Foundation of Mount Vernon & Knox County, OH, 7583
Community Foundation of Muncie and Delaware County, Inc., The, IN, 3128
Community Foundation of New Jersey, NJ, 5167
Community Foundation of North Central Washington, WA, 9571
Community Foundation of North Central Wisconsin, Inc., WI, 9777
Community Foundation of North Florida, Inc., The, FL, 1945
Community Foundation of North Texas, TX, 8841
Community Foundation of Northern Colorado, CO, 1357
Community Foundation of Northern Illinois, IL, 2679
Community Foundation of Northwest Connecticut, Inc., The, CT, 1516
Community Foundation of Northwest Georgia, Inc., GA, 2359
Community Foundation of Northwest Indiana, Inc., IN, 3129
Community Foundation of Portage County, Inc., WI, 9778
Community Foundation of Riverside County, CA, see 405
Community Foundation of Santa Clara County, CA, see 406
Community Foundation of Santa Cruz County, The, CA, 403
Community Foundation of Sarasota County, The, FL, 1946
Community Foundation of Shelby County, The, OH, 7584
Community Foundation of Shreveport-Bossier, The, LA, 3469
Community Foundation of Sidney and Shelby County, The, OH, see 7584
Community Foundation of South Alabama, The, AL, 25
Community Foundation of South Lake County, Inc., FL, 1947
Community Foundation of South Wood County, Inc., WI, 9779
Community Foundation of Southeast Alabama, AL, 26
Community Foundation of Southeastern Connecticut, The, CT, 1517
Community Foundation of Southeastern Massachusetts, MA, 3854

Community Foundation of Southeastern North Carolina, NC, 7345
Community Foundation of Southern Indiana, IN, 3130
Community Foundation of Southern Wisconsin, Inc., WI, 9780
Community Foundation of Southwest Georgia, Inc., GA, 2360
Community Foundation of St. Clair County, MI, 4257
Community Foundation of St. Joseph County, IN, 3131
Community Foundation of Tampa Bay, Inc., FL, 1948
Community Foundation of the Central Blue Ridge, VA, see 9521
Community Foundation of the Chattahoochee Valley, GA, 2361
Community Foundation of the Chemung County Area and Corning Community Foundation, The, NY, see 5784
Community Foundation of the Dan River Region, VA, 9401
Community Foundation of the Eastern Shore, Inc., MD, 3599
Community Foundation of the Elmira-Corning Area, The, NY, 5784
Community Foundation of the Florida Keys, Inc., FL, 1949
Community Foundation of the Fox River Valley, IL, 2680
Community Foundation of the Great River Bend, IA, 3277
Community Foundation of the Holland/Zeeland Area, The, MI, 4258
Community Foundation of the Lowcountry, SC, 8584
Community Foundation of the Mahoning Valley, OH, 7585
Community Foundation of the Napa Valley, CA, 404
Community Foundation of the Ozarks, The, MO, 4798
Community Foundation of the Texas Hill Country, TX, 8842
Community Foundation of the Upper Peninsula, MI, 4259
Community Foundation of the Virgin Islands, VI, 9363
Community Foundation of Union County, Inc., OH, 7586
Community Foundation of Wabash County, IN, 3132
Community Foundation of Warren County, PA, 8154
Community Foundation of Washington County Maryland, Inc., MD, 3600
Community Foundation of Waterloo/Cedar Falls & Northeast Iowa, IA, 3278
Community Foundation of West Alabama, AL, 27
Community Foundation of West Georgia, GA, 2362
Community Foundation of West Kentucky, KY, 3415
Community Foundation of Western Massachusetts, MA, 3855
Community Foundation of Western Nevada, NV, 5028
Community Foundation of Western North Carolina, Inc., The, NC, 7346
Community Foundation of Westmoreland County, The, PA, 8155
Community Foundation Partnership, Inc., IN, 3133
Community Foundation Serving Boulder County, The, CO, 1358
Community Foundation Serving Coastal South Carolina, The, SC, see 8581
Community Foundation Serving Greeley and Weld County, CO, 1359
Community Foundation Serving Richmond & Central Virginia, The, VA, 9402
Community Foundation Serving Riverside and San Bernardino Counties, The, CA, 405
Community Foundation Silicon Valley, CA, 406
Community Foundation Sonoma County, CA, 407
Community Foundation, Inc., GA, see 2358
Community Foundation, Inc., IN, see 3129
Community Foundation, Inc., MO, see 4798
Community Foundation, Inc., The, MS, 4738
Community Foundation, The, FL, see 1940
Community Health Foundation of Western & Central New York, Inc., NY, 5785
Community Involvement Foundation, PA, 8156
Community Memorial Foundation, IL, 2681
Compass Bank Foundation, AL, 28
Compassion for Animals Foundation, Inc., CA, 408
Compton Foundation, Inc., CA, 409
Con Alma Health Foundation, Inc., NM, 5471

ConAgra Foods Feeding Children Better Foundation, NE, 4952
ConAgra Foods Foundation, NE, 4953
ConAgra Foundation, Inc., The, NE, see 4953
Concordia Foundation, The, MD, 3601
Condon Family Foundation, CA, 410
Conese Foundation, Inc., The, FL, 1950
Confidence Foundation, CA, 411
Conn Memorial Foundation, Inc., FL, 1951
Connecticut Community Foundation, The, CT, 1518
Connecticut Health Foundation, Inc., CT, 1519
Connecticut Mutual Life Foundation, The, CT, see 1599
Connell Charitable Trust, William F., The, MA, 3856
Connell Foundation, Michael J., CA, 412
Connelly Foundation, PA, 8157
Connemara Fund, WY, 9978
Connolly Family Foundation, The, MA, 3857
Connolly Foundation, G.L., CA, 413
Connors Foundation, Inc., The, VA, 9403
Connors Foundation, John & Kathy, WA, 9572
ConocoPhillips Dependent Scholarship Program Trust, OK, 7933
Conservation, Food and Health Foundation, Inc., MA, 3858
Consolidated Anti-Aging Foundation, FL, 1952
Consolidated Natural Gas Company Foundation, PA, see 8173
Consolidated Papers Foundation, Inc., WI, see 9867
Constantin Foundation, The, TX, 8843
Constellation Energy Group Foundation, Inc., MD, 3602
Constitution Foundation, The, VA, 9404
Consumer Action Council on Collective Purchasing, Inc., NY, see 7124
Consumer Health Foundation, DC, 1786
Consumers Energy Foundation, MI, 4260
Consumers Power Foundation, MI, see 4260
Conte Foundation, Sirpuhe & John, The, CA, 414
ContiGroup Companies Foundation, NY, 5786
Continental Grain Foundation, NY, see 5786
Convergence Institute, The, TX, 8844
Convergys Foundation, Inc., The, OH, 7587
Conway Foundation, Inc., Ruth J. & Robert A., OH, 7588
Conway Foundation, Robert M. & Lois, NY, see 5787
Conway Foundation, Robert M., The, NY, 5787
Conway Scholarship Foundation, Inc., Carle C., CT, 1520
Conwood Charitable Trust, TN, 8663
Cook and Signe Otsby Charitable Foundation, Scott, The, CA, 415
Cook Charitable Foundation, MI, 4261
Cook Family Foundation, MI, 4262
Cook Inlet Region, Inc. Foundation, The, AK, see 83
Cook, Sr. Charitable Foundation, Inc., Kelly Gene, TX, 8845
Cooke Foundation, Jack Kent, VA, 9405
Cooke Foundation, Ltd., HI, 2541
Cooney Family Foundation, Robert J. and Loretta W., IL, 2682
Cooper Charitable Foundation, Inc., Frederick E. Cooper and Helen Dykes, GA, 2363
Cooper Family Foundation, AZ, 92
Cooper Family Foundation, IL, 2683
Cooper Family Foundation, Inc., The, NY, 5788
Cooper Foundation, Inc., Harriet & Eli, NY, A
Cooper Foundation, Milton, NY, see 5788
Cooper Foundation, NE, 4954
Cooper Foundation, Richard W., IL, see 2683
Cooper Industries Foundation, TX, 8846
Cooper Tire & Rubber Foundation, OH, 7589
Cooper-Clark Foundation, The, KS, 3353
Cooper-Hohn Family Foundation, NY, see 5749
Cooper-Siegel Family Foundation, The, PA, 8158
Cooperman Family Foundation, Leon and Toby, The, NJ, 5168
Cooperman Foundation, Leon & Toby, NJ, see 5168
Coors Foundation for the Performing Arts, Dallas Morse, DC, 1787
Coors Foundation, Adolph, CO, 1360
Cope Foundation, Ron and Carol, NE, 4955
Copeland Family Foundation, Inc., MA, 3859
Copland Fund for Music, Inc., Aaron, The, NY, 5789
Copley Foundation, Helen K. and James S., CA, 416
Copley Foundation, James S., CA, see 416

Copper Beech Foundation, The, NJ, 5169
Corbett Foundation, The, OH, 7590
Corbin Foundation, Mary S. & David C., OH, 7591
Corboy Foundation, Philip H., IL, 2684
Corcoran Community Foundation, The, CA, 417
Corcoran Family Foundation, John and Mary, The, MA, 3860
Cord Foundation, E. L., The, NV, see 5029
Cord Foundation, The, NV, 5029
Cordelia Corp., NY, 5790
Corey Foundation, The, NY, 5791
Corkin Charitable Foundation, Robert Lloyd, MA, 3861
Corman Foundation, Inc., AL, 29
Cornelius Family Foundation, Inc., IN, 3134
Cornell Foundation, Alverin M., IL, 2685
Cornell Foundation, Henry, The, NY, 5792
Cornell Memorial Foundation, Joseph and Robert, The, NY, 5793
Cornelsen Charitable Foundation, Floy L. and Paul F., The, MO, 4799
Cornerstone Foundation of Northeastern Wisconsin, Inc., WI, 9781
Cornerstone Foundation, OH, 7592
Cornerstone Foundation, PA, 8159
Corning Glass Works Foundation, NY, see 5794
Corning Incorporated Foundation, NY, 5794
Cornpauw Foundation, Ltd., NY, 5795
Corpening, Jr. Memorial Foundation, Maxwell M., NC, 7347
Corrigan Foundation, The, NY, 5796
Corrigan-Walla Foundation, The, CA, 418
Cortopassi Family Foundation, The, CA, 419
Cortopassi Institute, CA, 420
Corzine Foundation, Joanne D., The, NY, 5797
Corzine Foundation, Jon S., The, NY, 5798
Coshocton Foundation, OH, 7593
Cotsen Family Foundation, CA, 421
Cotswold Foundation, The, OH, 7594
Cotswold Foundation, The, PA, 8160
Cottrell Foundation, Frederick Gardner, AZ, 93
Couch Family Foundation, Inc., FL, 1953
Couch Family Foundation, The, NH, 5085
Coughlin-Saunders Foundation, Inc., LA, 3470
Coulson Foundation, Frank L. and Sarah Miller, The, NY, 5799
Coulter Foundation, Inc., Viola Vestal, WA, 9573
Coulter Foundation, Wallace H., FL, 1954
Coulter Trust, Wallace H., FL, 1955
Countess Moira Charitable Foundation, The, NY, 5800
Countrywide Foundation, The, CA, 422
Courts Foundation, Inc., GA, 2364
Cousins Foundation, Inc., The, GA, 2365
Covenant Foundation, Inc., OH, 7595
Covenant Foundation, Inc., The, GA, 2366
Covenant Foundation, Inc., TX, 8847
Covenant Foundation, The, PA, 8161
Cowden Foundation, Louetta M., TX, 8848
Cowell Foundation, S. H., CA, 423
Cowen & Phyllis Green Foundation, Randolph L., NY, 5801
Cowin Foundation, Inc., Joyce and Daniel, The, NY, 5802
Cowles Charitable Trust, The, NJ, 5170
Cowles Foundation, Inc., Gardner and Florence Call, IA, 3279
Cowles Foundation, Inc., Harriet Cheney, WA, 9574
Cowles Foundation, Inc., William H., WA, 9575
Cowles Media Foundation, MN, see 4691
Cox Charity Trust, A. G., WI, 9782
Cox Family Fund, MN, 4543
Cox Foundation of Georgia, Inc., James M., The, GA, 2367
Cox Foundation, Fannie, The, MA, 3862
Cox Foundation, Inc., MA, 3863
Cox Foundation, Jerry & Kay, The, TX, 8849
Cox Foundation, John and Maurine, TX, 8850
Cox Trust, Donald & Maria, The, NY, 5803
Cox, Jr. Foundation, Inc., James M., OH, 7596
Cox, Jr. Foundation, Jim, GA, 2368
Coydog Foundation, The, IL, 2686
Coyne Family Foundation, Richard & Jean, CA, 424
Coyne Foundation, Inc., Marshall B., DC, 1788
Coyote Foundation, Will E., TX, see 9101

Donaldson Charitable Trust, Oliver S. and Jennie R., NY, 5871

Donaldson Foundation, The, MN, 4552

Donchian Charitable Foundation, Inc., Alma Gibbs, CT, 1530

Donchian Charitable Foundation, Inc., Richard D., CT, see 1531

Donchian Foundation, Alma Gibbs, CT, see 1530

Donchian Foundation, Richard Davoud, CT, 1531

Donghia Foundation, Inc., Angelo, NY, 5872

Donley Foundation, The, PA, 8175

Donnell Initiative Fund, The, CO, 1367

Donnell-Kay Foundation, Inc., CO, 1368

Donnelley Foundation, Gaylord and Dorothy, IL, 2706

Donnelley Foundation, R. R., IL, 2707

Donnelley Foundation, The, IL, 2708

Donnelly Foundation, Mary J., PA, 8176

Donner Foundation, William H., The, NY, 5873

Donovan Foundation, NY, 5874

Doornink Foundation, The, MI, 4283

Doran Family Charitable Trust, NY, 5875

Dorea Foundation, MN, 4553

Dorn Foundation, Randolph J. & Estelle M., OH, 7612

Dornette Foundation, Helen G., Henry F. & Louise T., OH, 7613

Dornick Foundation, Inc., CO, 1369

Dorot Foundation, RI, 8531

Dorothy-Ann Foundation, The, VA, 9411

Dorr Foundation, NH, 5086

Dorrance Family Foundation, AZ, 95

Doss Foundation, Inc., M. S., The, TX, 8869

Doty Family Foundation, CT, 1532

Double H Foundation, Inc., The, NY, 5876

Doudera Family Foundation, VA, 9412

Dougherty Family Foundation, CA, 463

Dougherty Foundation, Inc., AZ, 96

Dougherty, Jr. Foundation, Inc, James R., TX, 8870

Douglas Charitable Foundation, CA, see 464

Douglas Foundation, CA, 464

Douglass Foundation, Terry D. and Rosann B., The, TN, 8667

Dove Givings Foundation II, NY, 5878

Dove Givings Foundation, NY, 5877

Dover Foundation, Inc., The, NC, 7356

Dow Chemical Company Foundation, The, MI, 4284

Dow Corning Foundation, MI, 4285

Dow Foundation, Herbert H. and Barbara C., MI, 4286

Dow Foundation, Herbert H. and Grace A., The, MI, 4287

Dow Foundation, The, NJ, 5183

Dow Foundation, The, NY, A

Dow Fund, Alden & Vada, MI, 4288

Dow Jones Foundation, NY, 5879

Dow Jones Newspaper Fund, Inc., NJ, 5184

Dowd Foundation, Inc., NC, 7357

Dowdle Family Foundation, Sally and James, IL, 2709

Dowling Jr. Foundation, William C., NY, 5880

Downey Foundation, Robert N. & Nancy A., NY, 5881

Downing Foundation, Barry L. & Paula M., KS, 3358

Downing Foundation, OH, 7614

Downs Foundation, The, MA, 3882

Downs Miller Foundation, Inc., Doreen, NY, 5882

Doyle Charitable Foundation, The, RI, 8532

Doyon Foundation, The, AK, 84

DPC Community Foundation, VA, see 9401

Dragicevich Wyoming Foundation Trust No. 1, Matthew and Virgie O., WY, 9980

Dramatists Guild Fund, Inc., NY, 5883

Draper Foundation, The, CA, 465

Draper Richards Foundation, The, CA, 466

Drapkin Family Charitable Foundation, NJ, 5185

Draughon Foundation, Louis R., TN, 8668

Dreamweaver Foundation, UT, 9314

Dreiseszun Family Foundation, The, KS, 3359

Dreitzer Foundation, Inc., The, NY, 5884

Dresher Foundation, Inc., The, MD, 3617

Drew Family Foundation, CA, 467

Drew Foundation, Jack, Helen, Louis & Jean, MN, see 4554

Drew Foundation, MN, 4554

Drexler Foundation, Peggy and Millard, NY, 5885

Dreyer's Grand Ice Cream Charitable Foundation, CA, 468

Dreyfus Foundation, Inc., Camille and Henry, The, NY, 5886

Dreyfus Foundation, Inc., Jean and Louis, NY, 5887

Dreyfus Foundation, Inc., Max and Victoria, The, NY, 5888

Dreyfus Foundation, VA, 9413

Driehaus Foundation, Richard H., The, IL, 2710

Driscoll Foundation, MN, 4555

Driskill Charitable Foundation, Walter S. and Lucienne B., FL, 1975

Drown Foundation, Joseph, CA, 469

Druckenmiller Foundation, NY, 5889

Drue Trust, S. May, NC, 7358

Drueding Foundation, PA, 8177

Druker Charitable Foundation, MA, 3883

Drukier Foundation, Inc., The, NY, 5890

Drum Foundation, The, CA, 470

Ds Foundation, The, FL, 1976

DSF Charitable Foundation, PA, 8178

DSSR Charitable Foundation, Inc., The, KS, 3360

DTE Energy Foundation, MI, 4289

Dubin Family Foundation, G. & E., NY, 5891

DuBose Foundation, Inc., Frances and Beverly, The, GA, 2374

DuBow Family Foundation, Inc., FL, 1977

Duchossois Family Foundation, The, IL, 2711

Duchossois Foundation, The, IL, see 2711

Duckwall Foundation, Inc., Frank E., FL, 1978

Duda Family Foundation, The, TX, 8871

Dudley Foundation, Inc., WI, 9792

Duesenberg Foundation, Richard W. and Phyllis B., The, MO, 4805

Duff II Scholarship, Lola G. Duff & William H., OH, 7615

Duffield Family Foundation, The, CA, see 845

Duffy Foundation, The, MI, 4290

Dugas Family Foundation, Laura Jo and Wayne, The, TN, see 8669

Dugas Family Foundation, TN, 8669

Duke Charitable Foundation, Doris, NY, 5892

Duke Endowment, The, NC, 7359

Duke Energy Foundation, NC, 7360

Duke Power Company Foundation, NC, see 7360

Dula Educational and Charitable Foundation, Caleb C. and Julia W., MO, 4806

Duluth-Superior Area Community Foundation, MN, 4556

Dumke Foundation, Dr. Ezekiel R. and Edna Wattis, UT, 9315

Dumke, Jr. Foundation, Katherine W. Dumke and Ezekiel R., The, UT, 9316

Dumont Foundation, CA, A

Dun & Bradstreet Corporation Foundation, The, NY, 5893

Dunard Fund USA, Ltd., IL, 2712

Duncan Trust, Louise Head, WI, 9793

Duneland Health Council, Inc., IN, 3143

Dunklau Foundation, Inc., Rupert, NE, 4958

Dunn Family Charitable Foundation, MA, 3884

Dunn Foundation, Inc., Elizabeth Ordway, FL, 1979

Dunn Foundation, Inc., Robert and Polly, GA, 2375

Dunn Research Foundation, John S., TX, 8872

Dunn's Foundation for the Advancement of Right Thinking, FL, 1980

Dunspaugh-Dalton Foundation, Inc., The, FL, 1981

Dunwalke Trust, Clarence and Anne Dillon, NY, 5894

DuPage Community Foundation, The, IL, 2713

Dupkin Educational and Charitable Foundation, Inc., MD, 3618

duPont Foundation, Inc., Alfred I., FL, 1982

duPont Fund, Jessie Ball, FL, 1983

duPont Religious, Charitable and Educational Fund, Jessie Ball, FL, see 1983

Durell Foundation, George Edward, OH, 7616

Durfee Foundation, The, CA, 471

Durham Foundation, H. W., TN, 8670

Durham Foundation, NE, 4959

Durrill Foundation, Inc., Devary, TX, 8873

Durst Family Foundation, The, NY, 5895

Dusky Foundation, The, MA, 3885

Dwan Family Foundation, The, CO, 1370

Dweck Foundation, Samuel R., The, DC, 1790

Dweck Foundation, Susan & Morris E., NY, 5896

Dwyer Fund for Excellence, Richard F. Dwyer and Eleanor W., The, CA, 472

Dyer Family Foundation, David and Harriet, FL, 1984

Dynamic Strategies Research Foundation, Inc., NY, 5897

Dynegy Foundation, Inc., TX, 8874

Dyson Foundation, NY, 5898

E & WG Foundation, NY, 5899

E.ON U.S. Foundation, KY, 3417

Eady Charitable Trust, J. Tom, TX, 8875

Eagle Foundation, NE, 4960

Eagle's Wing Foundation, Inc., FL, 1985

Earhart Foundation, MI, 4291

Early Medical Research Trust, Margaret E., CA, 473

Easley Foundation, The, NC, see 7361

Easley Trust, Andrew H. & Anne O., NC, 7361

East Arkansas Business Development Council, Inc., AR, 160

East Bay Community Foundation, The, CA, 474

East Chicago Community Development Foundation, Inc., IN, 3144

East Foundation, Inc., Sarita Kenedy, NY, 5900

East Hill Foundation, NY, 5901

East Stroudsburg Savings Association Foundation, PA, see 8190

East Tennessee Foundation, TN, 8671

East Texas Area Foundation, TX, see 8876

East Texas Communities Foundation, Inc., TX, 8876

East West Management Institute, The, NY, A

Eastern Bank Charitable Foundation, MA, 3886

Eastern Star Hall and Home Foundation, Inc., NY, 5902

Easthampton Savings Foundation, MA, 3887

Eastman Chemical Company Foundation, Inc., WI, 9794

Eastman Foundation, Alexander, NH, 5087

Eastman Kodak Charitable Trust, WI, 9795

Eaton Charitable Fund, The, OH, 7617

Eaton Family Foundation, Inc., CA, 475

Eaton Foundation, Inc., MD, see 3619

Eaton Foundation, Inc., Richard, The, MD, 3619

Eaton Foundation, Ralph H. & Frances M., AZ, A

Eaton Memorial Fund, Georgiana Goddard, MA, 3888

Ebb Foundation, Fred, NY, 5903

Eberly Foundation, The, PA, 8179

Eberstadt Foundation, Vera and Walter, The, NY, see 5904

Eberstadt-Kuffner Fund, Inc., NY, 5904

Ebert Charitable Foundation, Horatio B., NC, 7362

Ebrahimi Family Foundation, CO, 1371

EBS Foundation, TN, 8672

ECA Foundation, Inc., CO, 1372

Eccles & Homer M. Hayward Foundation, Nancy, UT, see 9327

Eccles Charitable Foundation, Willard L., UT, 9317

Eccles Family Foundation, Spencer F. & Cleone P., UT, see 9318

Eccles Family Foundation, UT, 9318

Eccles Foundation, George S. and Dolores Dore, UT, 9319

Eccles Foundation, Marriner S., UT, 9320

Echoing Green Foundation, NY, see 5905

Echoing Green, NY, 5905

Eckerd Corporation Foundation, TX, A

Eckerd Family Foundation, Inc., FL, 1986

ECOG Research and Education Foundation, Inc., PA, 8180

Ecolab Foundation, MN, 4557

Ecotrust Foundation, MN, 4558

Eddema Foundation, IL, 2714

Eddy Family Memorial Fund, C. K., MI, 4292

Edelman Family Foundation, Cynthia G., The, FL, 1987

Edelman Family Foundation, Inc., NY, 5906

Edelstein Family Foundation, MN, 4559

Edelstein Foundation, Harold, The, CA, 476

Edelstein Foundation, Inc., Emanuel and Klara, FL, 1988

Edelstein Foundation, Sidney and Mildred, The, NY, 5907

Edelstein Foundation, Sidney M., The, NY, see 5907

Edelweiss Foundation, NY, 5908

Eden Charitable Foundation, PA, 8181

Eden Hall Foundation, PA, 8182

Edgar Charitable Trust, Harold T., NC, 7363

Edgemer Foundation, Inc., The, FL, 1989

Edgerly Foundation, The, MA, 3889

Edgerton Foundation, CA, 477
Edina Realty Foundation, MN, 4560
Edison Foundation, Harry, MO, 4807
Edison Foundation, Inc., Julian I. & Hope R., MO, 4808
Edison Fund, Charles, NJ, 5186
Edmondson Foundation, Joseph Henry, The, CO, 1373
Edouard Foundation, Inc., The, NY, 5909
EDS Foundation, The, TX, 8877
Educational Advancement Foundation, TX, 8878
Educational Foundation of America, The, CT, 1533
Educational Fund for Children of Phillips Petroleum
    Company Employees, OK, see 7933
Educational Support Foundation, Inc., NY, 5910
Edwards Company Foundation, J. T., OH, see 7618
Edwards Family Foundation, Inc., FL, 1990
Edwards Family Foundation, Jerry and Joan, PA, 8183
Edwards Foundation, Inc., Bryant, TX, 8879
Edwards Foundation, Inc., O. P. and W. E., MT, 4936
Edwards Foundation, Inc., The, OH, 7618
Edwards Foundation, Inc., William, FL, see 1990
Edwards Foundation, J. E. S., TX, 8880
Edwards Memorial Trust, MN, 4561
Edwards Mother Earth Foundation, WA, 9580
Edwardson Family Foundation, IL, 2715
Effron Family Foundation, Craig, The, NY, 5911
EG&G Foundation, MA, see 4077
Egan Family Foundation, MA, 3890
EHA Foundation, Inc., NY, 5912
Ehrenkranz Family Foundation, NY, 5913
Eichenbaum Foundation, J. K. & Inez, CA, see 478
Eichenbaum Foundation, Joseph K. & Inez, CA, 478
Eig Family Foundation, Inc., The, NY, 5914
Eihusen Foundation, Inc., Virgil, NE, 4961
Eihusen-Chief Foundation, Inc., NE, see 4961
Einhorn Family Charitable Trust, NY, 5915
Einhorn Family Foundation, The, NY, 5916
Einstein Fund, Albert E. & Birdie W., FL, 1991
Eisen Family Foundation, Harry and Hilda, CA, 479
Eisenberg Family Charitable Trust, DE, 1709
Eisenberg Family Foundation, Inc., Mitzi & Warren, NJ,
    5187
Eisenberg Foundation for Charities, George M., IL, 2716
Eisenberg Foundation for Charities, IL, see 2716
Eisenberg Foundation, Ben B. and Joyce E., CA, 480
Eisenreich Family Foundation, The, NY, 5917
Eisner Foundation, Inc., The, CA, 481
Eiting Foundation, OR, 8011
El Paso Community Foundation, TX, 8881
El Paso Corporate Foundation, TX, 8882
El Paso Energy Foundation, TX, see 8882
El Pomar Foundation, CO, 1374
El-Hibri Charitable Foundation, DC, 1791
Elbogen Family Charitable Trust, NY, 5918
Eldorado Foundation, CA, 482
Elebash Fund, Baisley Powell, NY, 5919
Elec Material Hirtzel Memorial Foundation, PA, see
    8253
Elgin Financial Foundation, IL, 2717
Elias Foundation, The, NY, 5920
Eliasberg Family Foundation, Inc., The, MD, 3620
Eliscu and Sisenwein Fund, Inc., NY, see 6993
Elishis Family Foundation, The, NY, 5921
Elizabethtown Healthcare Foundation, NJ, 5188
Elkes Foundation, The, NY, 5922
Elkhart County Community Foundation, Inc., IN, 3145
Elkins, Jr. Foundation, Margaret & James A., TX, 8883
Ellbogen Foundation, John P., The, WY, 9981
Ellis Foundation, Danny and Willa, KS, see 3361
Ellis Foundation, Inc., FL, 1992
Ellis Foundation, Inc., Gail G., IL, 2718
Ellis Foundation, Inc., Jim, The, GA, 2376
Ellis Foundation, Joseph H. & Barbara I., NY, 5923
Ellis Foundation, The, KS, 3361
Ellis Fund, The, CT, 1534
Ellis Grant and Scholarship Fund, Charles E., PA, 8184
Ellison Foundation, The, MA, 3891
Ellison Foundation, Tom and Sue, WA, 9581
Ellison Medical Foundation, The, MD, 3621
Ellsworth Foundation, Ruth H. and Warren A., MA, 3892
Ellwood Foundation, The, TX, 8884
Elmaleh Foundation, Victor, NY, 5924
Elmar Foundation, Inc., MD, see 3613

Elmezzi Private Foundation, Thomas and Jeanne, NY,
    5925
Elqui Valley Foundation, The, MA, 3893
Elster Foundation, FL, 1993
Ely Foundation, Inc., Sylvia S., MD, A
Emerald Foundation, Inc., NY, 5926
Emerson Charitable Trust, MO, 4809
Emerson Directors and Officers Charitable Trust, IL,
    2719
Emerson Foundation, Inc., Fred L., NY, 5927
Emery Memorial, Thomas J., The, OH, 7619
Emes Foundation Inc., NY, 5928
EMLE, Inc., NY, 5929
Emmerich Foundation Charitable Trust, The, MN, 4562
Employers Mutual Charitable Foundation, IA, 3282
Emwiga Foundation, NY, 5930
Encourage, Inc., MA, 3894
Endless Education, Inc., IL, 2720
Endover Foundation, Inc., The, GA, 2377
Endowment for Biblical Research, Boston, MA, 3895
Endowment for Health, Inc., NH, 5088
Endowment for Vietnamese Education, Inc., The, NY,
    5931
Energizer Charitable Trust, IL, 2721
Energy Foundation, CA, 483
Enfranchisement Foundation, The, DC, 1792
Engelberg Foundation, The, FL, 1994
Engelhard Foundation, Charles, The, NY, 5932
Engelstad Family Foundation, NV, 5031
Engemann Family Foundation, CA, 484
England Family Foundation, Inc., Lois & Richard, The,
    MD, 3622
England Foundation, Inc., Lois & Richard, The, MD, see
    3622
England Trust, Elizabeth R., PA, 8185
Englander Foundation, Inc., NY, 5933
English Foundation, W. C., VA, 9414
English Memorial Fund, Florence C. and Harry L., The,
    GA, 2378
English-Bonter-Mitchell Foundation, IN, 3146
Engman Foundation, Robert & Mary Jane, CA, 485
Enlight Foundation, CA, 486
Enrico Foundation, Roger and Rosemary, The, TX, 8885
Ensworth Charitable Foundation, The, CT, 1535
Entergy Charitable Foundation, LA, 3474
Enterprise Leasing Foundation, MO, see 4810
Enterprise Rent-A-Car Foundation, MO, 4810
Entin Foundation, Lester M. and Sally, The, NJ, 5189
Environment Now Foundation, CA, 487
EOS Foundation, MA, 3896
Epilepsy Research Foundation of Florida, Inc., FL, 1995
Epstein Family Foundation, Inc., Diana and Michael
    David, MD, 3623
Epstein Foundation Trust, Samuel, The, PA, 8186
Epstein Philanthropies, NY, 5934
Equifax Foundation, GA, 2379
Equinox Foundation, Inc., NY, 5935
Equipart Foundation, The, NY, 5936
Equitable Foundation, Inc., The, NY, see 5584
Equitable Resources Foundation, Inc., PA, 8187
Ergon Foundation, Inc., MS, 4740
Erickson Foundation, Inc., The, MD, 3624
Erie Community Foundation, The, PA, 8188
Erlbaum Family Foundation, PA, 8189
Erpf Fund, Inc., Armand G., The, NY, 5937
Eshet Chayil Foundation, NJ, 5190
Eskind and Family Foundation, Jane and Richard, The,
    TN, 8673
Eskind Family Foundation, Annette and Irwin, The, TN,
    8674
Eskind Family Foundation, Jeffrey and Donna, The, TN,
    8675
Esperance Family Foundation, The, DE, 1710
Esping Family Foundation, TX, 8886
ESSA Foundation, PA, 8190
Essar Foundation, TX, 8887
Esseff Foundation, The, CA, 488
Essel Foundation, Inc., NY, 5938
Essex County Community Foundation, Inc., MA, 3897
Estes Foundation, VA, 9415
Esther Foundation, Inc., UT, 9321
Esther Foundation, The, CO, 1375
Estill Foundation, TX, 8888

Ethics & Excellence in Journalism Foundation, OK, 7935
Etnier Charitable Trust, Oliver, DE, 1711
Ettinger Foundation, Inc., The, CT, 1536
Eucalyptus Foundation, The, CA, 489
Eunice Foundation, The, NY, 5939
Eustace Foundation, The, PA, 8191
Evans Charitable Trust, Clyde R., WI, 9796
Evans Family Foundation, Inc., NY, see 5940
Evans Family Foundation, The, MA, 3898
Evans Foundation, Edward P., VA, 9416
Evans Foundation, Inc., R. S., NY, 5940
Evans Foundation, John Michael, NY, see 5715
Evans Foundation, Thomas J., The, OH, 7620
Evelyn Foundation, The, DE, 1712
Everard Family Foundation, WA, 9582
Everett Foundation, Herschel H. & Cornelia N., The, NC,
    7364
Everett Foundation, NY, 5941
Everett Mutual Savings Bank Foundation, WA, see 9583
Evergreen Foundation, Inc., MD, 3625
Evergreen Foundation, OK, 7936
Everhealth Foundation, CA, see 319
Everlasting Private Foundation, CA, 490
Evertrust Foundation, WA, 9583
Evjue Foundation, Inc., The, WI, 9797
Ewing Foundation, Inc., Frank M., MD, 3626
Excelsior! Foundation, The, IL, 2722
Exposition Foundation, Inc., GA, 2380
Express Scripts Foundation, MO, 4811
ExxonMobil Education Foundation, TX, see 8889
ExxonMobil Foundation, TX, 8889
Eye, Ear, Nose and Throat Foundation, LA, 3475
Ezell Foundation, Inc., TN, 8676

F. & J.S. Fund, Inc., NY, 5942
Fabert Foundation, Martin, The, WA, 9584
Fabick Charitable Trust, Inc., MO, 4812
Fabri-Kal Foundation, MI, 4293
Factor Family Foundation, Max, CA, 491
Factor Foundation, Ben E., LA, 3476
Faigen Family Foundation, Inc., FL, 1996
Fain Foundation, TX, 8890
Fain Fund Trust, Norman & Rosalie, RI, 8533
Fair Foundation, R. W., The, TX, 8891
Fair Oaks Foundation, Inc., PA, 8192
Fair Play Foundation, DE, 1713
Fairbanks Foundation, Inc., IN, see 3147
Fairbanks Foundation, Inc., Richard M., IN, 3147
Fairchild Foundation, Inc., Sherman, The, MD, 3627
Fairchild-Martindale Foundation, CA, 492
Fairfax Foundation, The, OH, 7621
Fairfield County Community Foundation, Inc., CT, 1537
Fairfield County Foundation, OH, 7622
Fairweather Foundation, The, NV, 5032
Fairwyn Fund, IL, 2723
Faith Ventures Foundation, Inc., GA, 2381
Falcon Charitable Foundation, The, ME, 3532
Falconwood Foundation, Inc., NY, 5943
Falk Foundation, Dr. Ralph and Marian, TX, A
Falk Foundation, Inc., Michael David, NY, 5944
Falk Fund, Maurice, PA, 8193
Falk Medical Fund, Maurice, PA, see 8193
Falk Medical Research Trust, Dr. Ralph and Marian, IL,
    2724
Falkenberg Foundation, The, CO, 1376
Family Development Center, Inc., NJ, 5191
Family First Foundation, Inc., CA, 493
Family Foundation, The, NC, 7365
Fannie Mae Foundation, DC, 1793
Fansler Foundation, CA, 494
Fant Foundation, The, TX, 8892
Fanwood Foundation, The, NJ, 5192
Farah Foundation, Virginia H., KS, 3362
Farallon Foundation, CA, 495
Farb Foundation, Harold, The, TX, 8893
Farber Family Foundation, Jake and Janet, CA, A
Farber Family Foundation, PA, 8194
Farber Foundation, Inc., PA, 8195
Farbman Family Foundation, The, MI, 4294
Farbman Foundation, The, MI, see 4294
Fargo-Moorhead Area Foundation, ND, 7514
Farish Fund, William Stamps, The, TX, 8894
Farkas Foundation, Howard and Barbara, The, NY, 5945

Farmer Family Foundation, OH, 7623
Farnsworth Trust, Charles H., MA, 3899
Farrell Family Foundation, CA, 496
Farrell Foundation, The, IL, 2725
Farrington Foundation, Alberta B., AZ, 97
Farris Foundation, Inc., The, GA, 2382
Farver Foundation, Joan Kuyper, IA, 3283
Farver Foundation, The, MI, 4295
Fascitelli Family Foundation, The, NY, 5946
Fasken Foundation, The, TX, 8895
Fasseas Foundation, Peter & Paula, IL, 2726
Fassino Foundation, Inc., The, MA, 3900
Fatta Foundation, Inc., The, NY, 5947
Faulconer Scholarship Programs, The, TX, 8896
Faulkner Trust, Marianne G., NY, 5948
Faulkner Trust, Marianne Galliard, NY, see 5948
Favrot Fund, The, TX, 8897
FBW Foundation, MD, 3628
FCCF, CT, see 1537
Federated Department Stores Foundation, OH, 7624
Federated Insurance Foundation, Inc., MN, 4563
Federated Investors Foundation, Inc., PA, 8196
Federation Foundation of Greater Philadelphia, PA, 8197
Feil Family Foundation, The, NY, 5949
Feil Foundation, Inc., Louis & Gertrude, NY, see 5949
Feild Co-Operative Association, Inc., MS, 4741
Fein Foundation, Edward, CA, 497
Feinberg Foundation, Inc., Jac & Eva, NY, 5950
Feinberg Foundation, Inc., TX, 8898
Feinberg Foundation, Joseph and Bessie, IL, 2727
Feinstein Family Foundation, NY, see 5951
Feinstein Family Fund, RI, 8534
Feinstein Foundation, Edward, CA, see 497
Feinstein Foundation, Inc., The, RI, 8535
Feinstein Foundation, Susan & Leonard, NY, 5951
Feintech Family Foundation, CA, 498
Feintech Family Foundation, Evelyn M. & Norman, CA, 499
Feintech Family Foundation, Irving, CA, 500
Felburn Foundation, MD, 3629
Feldberg Family Foundation, The, MA, 3901
Feldman Foundation, The, TX, A
Felicia Fund, Inc., RI, 8536
Felix Foundation, F., MA, 3902
Fels Fund, Samuel S., PA, 8198
Femino Foundation, CA, 501
Fenwick Foundation, NJ, 5193
Feraldo Memorial Fund, William Pablo, MO, 4813
Ferber Foundation, Miriam & Fred, The, MI, 4296
Ferguson Foundation, Bettye Poetz, CA, 502
Ferguson Foundation, Hugh and Jane, The, WA, 9585
Ferguson Foundation, Leonard C. & Mildred F., OH, 7625
Fernandez Family Foundation, Miguel B., FL, 1997
Fernandez Foundation, Inc., The, DC, 1794
Fernleigh Foundation, NY, 5952
Ferrari Foundation, Andrew U., NY, 5953
Ferraro Family Foundation, Inc., FL, 1998
Ferree Foundation, PA, 8199
Ferriday Fund Charitable Trust, The, NY, 5954
Ferris, Baker Watts Foundation, MD, see 3628
Fertel Foundation, Ruth U., LA, 3477
Fertitta Foundation, Ltd., Frank and Victoria, NV, 5033
Fessenden Charitable Foundation, Elizabeth T., The, MA, 3903
Fetzer Foundation, Inc., John E., MI, see 4297
Fetzer Institute, Inc., John E., MI, 4297
Fetzer Memorial Trust Fund, John E., MI, 4298
Feuerman Foundation, Kurt A. and Anne Pelletier, The, CT, 1538
Fidelity Foundation, MA, 3904
Field Family Foundation, Eris & Larry, CA, 503
Field Foundation of Illinois, Inc., The, IL, 2728
Field Foundation, Frances K. & Charles D., The, CA, 504
Field Foundation, Joseph and Marie, PA, 8200
Field Fund, Charles D. and Frances K., The, CA, 505
Fieldcrest Cannon Foundation, TX, A
Fields Pond Foundation, Inc., MA, 3905
Fieldstone Foundation, Inc., MA, 3906
Fieldstone Foundation, The, CA, 506
Fife Family Foundation, Eugene V., NY, 5955
Fifth Third Foundation, The, OH, 7626

Figge Charitable Foundation, V. O. Figge and Elizebeth Kahl, IA, 3284
Fikes Foundation, Inc., Leland, TX, 8899
Filene Foundation, Inc., Lincoln and Therese, MA, 3907
FIMF, Inc., NY, 5956
Finch Foundation, Thomas Austin, NC, 7366
Findlay Hancock County Community Foundation, The, OH, 7627
Fine Family Foundation, The, PA, 8201
Finger Foundation, Jerry and Nanette, TX, 8900
Finish Line Youth Foundation, Inc., IN, 3148
Fink Foundation, Betsy and Jesse, CT, 1539
Finlay Foundation, Francis, NY, 5957
Finlay Foundation, Inc., Curtis, AL, 33
Finley Foundation, Ernest L. and Ruth W., CA, 507
Finley Foundation, Inc., A. E., NC, 7367
Finnegan Charitable Trust, Neal F., MA, 3908
Fippinger Foundation, Inc., Grace J., CT, 1540
Firedoll Foundation, CA, 508
Firelight Foundation, CA, 509
Fireman Charitable Foundation, Paul and Phyllis, The, MA, 3909
Fireman Charitable Foundation, Simon C., The, MA, 3910
Fireman's Fund Foundation, CA, 510
Fireman's Fund Insurance Company Foundation, CA, see 510
Firestone Foundation, Roger S., IL, 2729
Firestone Trust Fund, The, TN, see 8646
Firestone, Jr. Foundation, Harvey, WI, 9798
Firman Fund, OH, 7628
First American Financial Foundation, CA, 511
First American Foundation, TN, see 8636
First Bank System Foundation, MN, see 4704
First Brokers Good Samaritan Fund, NJ, 5194
First Citizens Foundation, Inc., SC, 8587
First Community Foundation of Pennsylvania, PA, 8202
First County Bank Foundation, Inc., CT, 1541
First Data Western Union Foundation, CO, 1377
First Federal of Warren Community Foundation, OH, see 7629
First Fruit, Inc., CA, 512
First Hawaiian Foundation, HI, 2542
First Interstate BancSystem Foundation, Inc., MT, 4937
First National Bank in Wichita Charitable Trust, KS, see 3369
First Niagara Bank Foundation, NY, 5958
First Place Bank Community Foundation, OH, 7629
First Tennessee Foundation, TN, 8677
First Union Regional Foundation, PA, see 8494
FirstEnergy Foundation, OH, 7630
FIRSTFED Charitable Foundation, The, MA, see 4166
Firstfruits Foundation, PA, 8203
FISA Foundation, PA, 8204
Fisch Foundation, Ben & Maytee, TX, 8901
Fischel Foundation, Harry and Jane, NY, 5959
Fischer Family Foundation, KY, 3418
Fischer Foundation, Alan & Laraine, The, NY, 5960
Fischer Foundation, Friderika, The, NY, see 7199
Fischman Scholarship Fund, E. David, MN, 4564
Fish Foundation, Ray C., TX, 8902
Fishback Family Foundation, Inc., Kathryn C., CA, 513
Fisher Brothers Foundation, Inc., The, NY, 5961
Fisher Charitable Foundation, Jerome & Anne C., FL, 1999
Fisher Charitable Trust, Zachary and Elizabeth, NY, 5962
Fisher Foundation, Audrey Hillman, PA, 8205
Fisher Foundation, Gramma, IA, 3285
Fisher Foundation, Inc., CT, 1542
Fisher Foundation, Inc., Max M. and Marjorie S., MI, 4299
Fisher Landau Foundation, The, NY, A
Fisher Memorial Foundation, Inc., Robert M., MD, 3630
Fishoff Family Foundation, NJ, 5195
Fiterman Charitable Foundation, Miles and Shirley, FL, 2000
Fiterman Foundation, Jack and Bessie, The, MN, 4565
Fites Family Charitable Trust, IL, 2730
Fitzgerald Charitable Foundation, Ella, CA, 514
Fitzpatrick Foundation, CA, 515
Five Bridges Foundation, CA, 516
Five Millers Family Foundation, Inc., FL, 2001

Five Smith's Foundation, Inc., GA, 2383
Flagg Creek Foundation, IL, 2731
Flagg Family Foundation, CA, see 517
Flagg Family Foundation, Morgan, CA, 517
Flagler Foundation, The, VA, 9417
Flanzer Charitable Trust, Louis & Gloria, NY, 5963
Flatley Foundation, The, MA, 3911
Fleck Foundation, WI, 9799
Fleckenstein Family Foundation, WI, see 9799
Fleishhacker Foundation, CA, 518
Fleming Charitable Trust, Samuel H., OH, 7631
Fleming Endowment, TX, 8903
Fleming Foundation, PA, 8206
Fleming Foundation, The, TX, 8904
Fletcher Foundation, MA, 3912
Flextronics Foundation, CA, 519
Flight Attendant Medical Research Institute, Inc., FL, 2002
Flinn Foundation, The, AZ, 98
Flinn, Jr. Charitable Trust, Lawrence, The, CT, 1543
Flintridge Foundation, CA, 520
Flora Family Foundation, CA, 521
Florida Rock Industries Foundation, Inc., FL, 2003
Florik Charitable Trust, IL, A
Florman Family Foundation, Inc., The, FL, 2004
Flow Foundation, Inc., NC, 7368
Flowers, Jr. Foundation, Inc., William Howard, GA, 2384
Floyd Family Foundation, CA, 522
Fludzinski Foundation, NY, 5964
Fluor Foundation, The, CA, 523
Flynt Foundation, Kay Richard and Elizabeth Bates, CA, 524
FM Global Foundation, RI, 8537
FNZ Foundation, Inc., PR, 8514
Focus Foundation, OH, 7632
Foellinger Foundation, Inc., IN, 3149
Fogel Foundation, Inc., Aaron and Esther, The, NY, 5965
Fohs Foundation, OR, 8012
Foley Family Charitable Foundation, The, FL, 2005
Foley Family Foundation, Inc., Lawrence & Megan, CT, 1544
Folger Fund, Lee and Juliet, The, VA, 9418
Folger Fund, The, VA, see 9418
Follis Foundation, R. Gwin, CA, 525
Folsom Charitable Foundation, Inc., TX, 8905
Folsom Foundation, Inc., Maud Glover, CT, 1545
Fond du Lac Area Foundation, WI, 9800
Fonda Family Foundation, Inc., The, GA, 2385
Fonda Foundation, Inc., Jane, GA, 2386
Fondren Foundation, The, TX, 8906
Food 4 Less Foundation, The, CA, see 1029
Food Lion Charitable Foundation, Inc., NC, 7369
Foothills Community Foundation, SC, 8588
Foothills Foundation, The, CA, 526
For a Better Life Foundation, IL, see 3077
For HIS Adopted Children, Inc., GA, see 2485
Forbes Charitable Foundation, Mary C., FL, 2006
Forbes Charitable Trust, Herman, NY, 5966
Forbes Foundation, NY, 5967
Force for Good Foundation, The, UT, 9322
Forchheimer Foundation, Leo and Julia, NY, 5968
Forchheimer Foundation, The, NY, see 5968
Ford Family Foundation, The, NY, 5969
Ford Family Foundation, The, OR, 8013
Ford Foundation, David B. & Virginia M., The, NY, see 5969
Ford Foundation, Edward E., The, ME, 3533
Ford Foundation, Inc., Gerald J., The, TX, A
Ford Foundation, Inc., Gertrude C., The, MS, 4742
Ford Foundation, Inc., Gordon, KY, 3419
Ford Foundation, Joseph F. and Clara, MA, 3913
Ford Foundation, The, NY, 5970
Ford Foundation, William & Lisa, MI, 4300
Ford Fund, Benson and Edith, MI, 4301
Ford Fund, Eleanor and Edsel, MI, 4302
Ford Fund, S. N. Ford and Ada, The, OH, 7633
Ford Fund, Walter and Josephine, MI, 4303
Ford Fund, William and Martha, MI, 4304
Ford II Fund, Edsel B., MI, 4305
Ford II Fund, Henry, The, MI, 4306
Ford Meter Box Foundation, Inc., IN, 3150
Ford Motor Company Fund, MI, 4307
Ford, Jr. Scholarship Program, William C., MI, 4308

Fordham Foundation, Thomas B., DC, 1795
Fore River Foundation, ME, 3534
Foreign Mission Foundation, OR, 8014
Foreman Family Foundation, Peter and Virginia, IL, see 3010
Forest City Enterprises Charitable Foundation, Inc., OH, 7634
Forest Foundation, WA, 9586
Forest Lawn Foundation, CA, 527
Forney Family Foundation, Inc., PA, 8207
Forster-Powers Charitable Trust, MO, 4814
Fort Atkinson Community Foundation, WI, 9801
Fort Collins Area Community Foundation, CO, see 1357
Fort Foundation, Inc., Mildred Miller, GA, 2387
Fort Wayne Community Foundation, IN, see 3125
Fortin Foundation of Florida, Inc., The, FL, 2007
Fortis Health Foundation, Inc., WI, see 9748
Fortune Family Foundation, WA, 9587
Foss Memorial Employees Trust, Donald J., OH, 7635
Foster Charitable Foundation, Henry & Lois, MA, 3914
Foster Family Foundation, Louis W. Foster and Gladyce L., The, CA, 528
Foster Foundation, The, WA, 9588
Foster-Davis Foundation, Inc., CT, 1546
Fotsch Foundation, The, WI, 9802
Foulger Foundation, Inc., Sid & Mary, MD, 3631
Foundation for Agronomic Research, Inc., GA, 2388
Foundation for Cardiovascular Research, FL, 2008
Foundation for Child Development, NY, 5971
Foundation for Deep Ecology, CA, 529
Foundation for Enhancing Communities, The, PA, 8208
Foundation for Middle East Peace, DC, 1796
Foundation for Partnerships Trust, MA, see 3889
Foundation for Psycho-cultural Research, CA, 530
Foundation for Research in Cell Biology and Cancer, MA, 3915
Foundation for Roanoke Valley, Inc., VA, 9419
Foundation for Seacoast Health, NH, 5089
Foundation for the Carolinas, NC, 7370
Foundation for the Continuity of Mankind, The, OH, 7636
Foundation for the Education & Research in Neurological Emergencies, IL, 2732
Foundation for the Mid South, MS, 4743
Foundation for the National Capital Region, The, DC, see 1785
Foundation for the Tri-State Community, Inc., KY, 3420
Foundation for Theological Education in Southeast Asia, MI, 4309
Foundation for Worldwide Mercy & Sharing, CO, see 1426
Foundation Francqui Belgium, NY, see 5973
Foundation in Christ Ministries: 1 Cor. 3:11, Inc., FL, 2009
Foundation M, MA, 3916
Foundation Northwest, WA, 9589
Foundation of Faith, Inc., WI, A
Foundation of Greater Greensboro, Inc., The, NC, see 7343
Foundation of the Litton Industries, CA, see 942
Foundation of the Pierre Fauchard Academy, CA, 531
Foundation Source 9 Inc., The, DE, see 1731
Foundation, Inc., Jones, KS, see 3370
Founders Charitable Foundation, Inc., AL, 34
Four County Community Foundation, MI, 4310
Four County Foundation, MI, see 4310
Four D Foundation, Inc., IN, 3151
Four Friends Foundation, CA, 532
Four Way Community Foundation, OR, 8015
Four-Four Foundation, Inc., The, WI, 9803
Fourjay Foundation, PA, 8209
Fowler Memorial Foundation, John Edward, DC, 1797
Fox Charitable Foundation, Harry K. Fox and Emma R., The, OH, 7637
Fox Family Foundation, CT, 1547
Fox Family Foundation, Inc., NC, 7371
Fox Family Foundation, MO, 4815
Fox Foundation, Inc., OH, 7638
Fox Foundation, Richard J., The, PA, 8210
FPL Foundation, Inc., FL, see 2010
FPL Group Foundation, Inc., FL, 2010
Fralin Charitable Trust, Horace G., The, VA, 9420
France Stone Foundation, OH, 7639

France-Merrick Foundation, MD, 3632
Francis Families Foundation, The, MO, see 4816
Francis Family Foundation, The, MO, 4816
Franconia Foundation, Inc., NY, 5972
Francqui Foundation, NY, 5973
Frank Family Foundation, A. J., OR, 8016
Frank Foundation, Inc, Ernst & Elfriede, NY, 5974
Frank Foundation, J. S., IL, 2733
Frank Foundation, Sidney E., NY, 5975
Franke Family Charitable Foundation, IL, 2734
Frankel Family Foundation, Stanley and Judith, MI, 4311
Frankel Foundation, Evan, NY, 5976
Frankel Foundation, IL, see 2735
Frankel Foundation, Julius N., IL, 2735
Frankel Foundation, Maxine and Stuart, MI, 4312
Frankel Foundation, Samuel & Jean, MI, 4313
Frankel Jewish Heritage Foundation, Samuel and Jean, The, MI, 4314
Frankenberg Foundation, Regina Bauer, The, NY, 5977
Frankino Charitable Foundation, Samuel J. & Connie M., NJ, 5196
Franklin Benevolent Corporation, CA, 533
Franklin Charitable Foundation, Inc., Julie and Martin, NY, 5978
Franklin Charitable Trust, Ershel, TX, 8907
Franklin Family Foundation, TX, 8908
Franklin Foundation, Inc., John and Mary, GA, 2389
Franklin Holding Corporation, CA, A
Franklin Southampton Charities, VA, 9421
Franks Foundation, Alta and John, The, LA, 3478
Franks Foundation, The, LA, see 3478
Frasch Foundation for Chemical Research, Herman, NY, 5979
Fraser Family Foundation, Inc., MA, 3917
Fraser-Parker Foundation, The, GA, 2390
Frautschi Family Foundation, Inc., John J., WI, 9804
Frazier Foundation, Inc., LA, 3479
Frazier Foundation, The, FL, 2011
Frear Eleemosynary Trust, Mary D. and Walter F., HI, 2543
Freas Foundation, Inc., CT, 1548
Freddie Mac Foundation, VA, 9422
Fredericksburg Savings Charitable Foundation, VA, 9423
Free Family Foundation Corp., FL, 2012
Freed Family Foundation, IL, 2736
Freed Foundation, The, DC, 1798
Freedom 22 Foundation, IN, 3152
Freedom Forum, Inc., The, VA, 9424
Freehling Foundation, Norman & Edna, IL, 2737
Freeman Charitable Trust, Samuel, NY, 5980
Freeman Foundation, Ella West, The, LA, 3480
Freeman Foundation, Inc., Carl M., The, MD, 3633
Freeman Foundation, NY, 5981
Freeport-McMoran Foundation, LA, 3481
Frees Foundation, The, TX, 8909
Fremont Area Community Foundation, MI, 4315
Fremont Area Community Foundation, NE, 4962
Fremont Area Foundation, The, MI, see 4315
Fremont Bank Foundation, The, CA, 534
Fremont Group Foundation, The, CA, 535
French Family Foundation, Inc., J. L., WI, A
French Fund, Samuel H. French III and Katharine Weaver, CA, 536
Fresno Regional Foundation, CA, 537
Freston Foundation, Tom and Kathy, NY, 5982
Frey Family Foundation, Inc., NY, 5983
Frey Foundation, MI, 4316
Frey Foundation, MN, 4566
Freyer Family Foundation, Inc., Carl & Sylvia, NJ, 5197
Freygang Foundation, Walter Henry, OH, 7640
Fribourg Family Foundation, NY, 5984
Frick Foundation, Helen Clay, PA, 8211
Fricks Private Foundation Trust, The, FL, 2013
Friedberg and Charlotte Moss Family Foundation, Barry, The, NY, 5985
Friedland Family Foundation, NE, 4963
Friedland Foundation, David & Nancy, NE, see 4963
Friedman Family Foundation, CA, 538
Friedman Family Foundation, Frank and Fred, The, AL, 35
Friedman Family Foundation, NY, 5986

Friedman Family Foundation, Richard A. and Susan P., NY, 5987
Friedman Foundation, Frank and Fred, The, AL, see 35
Friedman Foundation, Morton & Marcine, CA, 539
Friedman Foundation, Robert G., FL, 2014
Friedman Foundation, Stephen & Barbara, NY, see 5986
Friedman Fund, Tully and Elise, CA, 540
Friedman New York Foundation for Medical Research, Gerald J. & Dorothy R., The, NY, 5988
Friedman, Billings & Ramsey Charitable Foundation, Inc., VA, 9425
Friedman-French Foundation, Inc., DC, 1799
Friedmann Family Charitable Trust, Philip M., IL, 2738
Friends of China Heritage Fund, Ltd., NY, 5989
Friends of the Congressional Glaucoma Caucus Foundation, Inc., NY, 5990
Friends of Toras Simcha, NY, 5991
Friess Family Foundation, Lynn and Foster, The, WY, 9982
Frieze Family Foundation, Inc., MA, A
Frist Foundation, Dorothy Cate & Thomas F., The, TN, 8678
Frist Foundation, The, TN, 8679
Frist Medical Foundation, The, TN, see 8678
Froderman Foundation, Inc., The, IN, 3153
Froehlich Foundation, Helen V., IL, 2739
Frog Rock Foundation, The, NY, 5992
Frohman Foundation, Sidney, The, OH, 7641
Frohring Foundation, Inc., Paul & Maxine, NY, 5993
Fromkes Foundation, Inc., Saul, NY, 5994
Fromm Fund, Alfred & Hanna, The, CA, 541
Frost Foundation, Ltd., The, NM, 5476
Frost Foundation, Pat and Tom, TX, 8910
Frost-Parker Foundation, The, OH, 7642
Fruchthandler Foundation, Inc., Alex & Ruth, The, NY, 5995
Frueauff Foundation, Inc., Charles A., AR, 161
Fry Foundation, Lloyd A., IL, 2740
FSB Foundation, Inc., CT, 1549
Fuchs Foundation, Gottfried & Mary, The, WA, 9590
Fuchs Foundation, Inc., Shmuel, NY, 5996
Fuchsberg Family Foundation, Inc., Abraham, NY, 5998
Fuchsberg Family Foundation, Inc., NY, 5997
Fuld Health Trust, Helene, NY, 5999
Fuld, Jr. Family Foundation, Inc., Kathy and Richard S., NY, 6000
Fuld, Jr. Foundation, Inc., Richard S., NY, see 6000
Fulk Family Foundation, Inc., NE, 4964
Fuller Company Foundation, H. B., MN, 4567
Fuller Foundation, George F. and Sybil H., The, MA, 3918
Fuller Foundation, Inc., The, NH, 5090
Fullerton Family Charitable Trust, The, CO, 1378
Fullerton Foundation, Inc., The, SC, 8589
Fund for Children of the Americas, The, NJ, 5198
Fund for Life Foundation, Inc., NY, 6001
Fund for New Jersey, The, NJ, 5199
Fund for Nonviolence, CA, 542
Funger Foundation, Inc., The, VA, 9426
Funk Foundation, Paul A., IL, 2741
Fuqua Foundation, Inc., J. B., GA, 2391
Furman Foundation, Inc., Frieda & Roy, NY, 6003
Furman Foundation, Inc., NY, 6002
Furnas Foundation, Inc., IL, see 2782
Furst Foundation, John D., The, TX, 8911
Furth Foundation, Inc., CA, 543
Furth Family Foundation, The, NY, 6004
Fuscone Family Foundation, The, CT, 1550
Future of Russia, DC, 1800
Futureus Foundation, TX, 8912

G & P Foundation for Cancer Research, Inc., The, NY, A
G.T.R. & B. Charitable Foundation, CA, 544
Gabelli Foundation, Inc., NJ, 5200
Gabrieli Family Foundation, The, MA, 3919
Gagarin Trust, The, AZ, 99
Gage Foundation, Philip and Irene Toll, GA, 2392
Gagnon Foundation, Inc., Lois & Neil, The, NJ, 5201
Gaia Fund, CA, 545
Gaines Foundation, Courtney Knight, GA, 2393
Gainesville Community Foundation, GA, see 2458
Gainesville Community Foundation, Inc., FL, 2015

Gaisman Foundation, Catherine and Henry J., The, CT, 1551
Galanta Foundation, Inc., NJ, 5202
Galashiels Fund, Ltd., IL, 2742
Galasso Foundation, NY, 6005
Galbraith Foundation, The, VA, 9427
Gale Foundation, Inc., Mary, NH, 5091
Gale Foundation, The, TX, 8913
Galil Foundation, Inc., CA, 546
Gallagher Charitable Trust, Robert E., The, IL, 2743
Gallagher Family Foundation, Lewis P., The, ME, 3535
Gallagher Foundation, Arthur J., IL, 2744
Gallo Foundation, Ernest, The, CA, 547
Gallo Foundation, Julio R., The, CA, 548
Galter Foundation, The, IL, 2745
Galvin Charitable Trust, Helen M., IL, 2746
Galvin Foundation, Robert W., IL, 2747
Gamble Foundation, The, CA, 549
Gandy & John H. Sandman Charitable Trust, Virginia Lee, CA, 550
Gann Charitable Foundation, Joseph and Rae, FL, 2016
Gannett Communities Fund, VA, see 9428
Gannett Foundation, Inc., VA, 9428
Gant Family Foundation, The, NY, 6006
Gant Foundation, Donald R. & Jane T., NY, see 6006
Gantz Family Foundation, IL, 2748
Gap Foundation, The, CA, 551
GAR Foundation, The, OH, 7643
Garabedian Charitable Foundation, Bertha and John, The, CA, 552
Garaventa Family Foundation, Silvio and Mary, CA, 553
Garb Foundation, Melvin, The, CA, 554
Garcia Family Charitable Foundation Trust, IN, 3154
Garcia Foundation, Inc., Jose M., The, NJ, 5203
Garden Homes Fund, CT, 1552
Gardiner Savings Institution Charitable Foundation, ME, 3536
Gardinor-Prunaret Foundation, MA, 3920
Gardner Family Foundation, James J. and Joan A., The, OH, 7644
Gardner Family Foundation, OH, see 7644
Gardner Foundation, Janice, MN, 4568
Gardner Foundation, NE, 4965
Gardner Foundation, Sterling and Shelli, UT, 9323
Garen Family Foundation, CA, 555
Garfield Foundation, The, MA, 3921
Garfield Street Foundation, NM, 5477
Garfinkle Foundation, Inc., Norton, FL, see 2017
Garfinkle-Minard Foundation, Inc., FL, 2017
Garland Foundation, John Jewett & Helen Chandler, CA, 556
Garmar Foundation, MN, 4569
Garner Foundation, Inc., The, FL, 2018
Garrison Foundation, Thomas & Natalie, The, AR, 162
Garrott Foundation, Thomas M., TN, 8680
Garthwaite Memorial Foundation, Elsie Lee, PA, 8212
Garvey Fund, Jean and Willard, KS, 3363
Garvey Texas Foundation, Inc., TX, 8914
Garvey Trust, Olive White, KS, 3364
Gary-Williams Foundation, The, CO, 1379
Gasser Foundation, Peter A. & Vernice H., CA, 557
Gast Charitable Foundation, Warren E. & D. Lou, MI, 4317
Gates Family Foundation, CO, 1380
Gates Foundation, Bill & Melinda, WA, 9591
Gates Foundation, CO, see 1380
Gates Foundation, William H., WA, see 9591
Gateway Foundation, MO, 4817
Gateway Foundation, The, ME, 3537
Gatto Foundation, Joseph & Susan, The, NY, 6007
Gatton Foundation, Bill, The, TN, 8681
Gauntlett Foundation, Inc., Barbara, The, CA, see 449
Gauthier Family Foundation, Wendell & Anne, LA, 3482
Gavin Foundation, Inc., James & Zita, IL, 2749
Gayar Foundation, The, MI, 4318
Gayden Family Foundation, TX, 8915
Gaylord Foundation, E. L. and Thelma, OK, 7937
GBRG, Inc., NY, 6008
GCP Foundation, PA, see 8159
GE Foundation, CT, 1553
GE Fund, CT, see 1553
Geary Foundation, Inc., Richard and Janet, OR, 8017
Geary, Jr. Memorial Foundation, Henry H., OH, 7645

Gebbie Foundation, Inc., NY, 6009
Geds Help Fund Foundation, NY, 6010
Geffen Foundation, David, The, CA, 558
GEICO Philanthropic Foundation, MD, 3634
Geier Foundation, The, NJ, 5204
Geiger Foundation, Inc., NJ, 5205
Geisse Foundation, John F. and Mary A., OH, 7646
Geisse Foundation, The, OH, see 7646
Geist Foundation, Victoria S. & Bradley L., HI, 2544
Gelb Foundation, Inc., Lawrence M., NY, 6011
Gellert Foundation, Carl Gellert and Celia Berta, The, CA, 559
Gellert Foundation, Carl, The, CA, see 559
Gellert Trust, Michael E., NY, 6012
Gellman Foundation, The, NY, 6013
Gelman Trust, Jacques and Natasha, NY, 6014
Gelvin Foundation, Lyle M., OK, see 7938
Gelvin Foundation, The, OK, 7938
Gemcon Family Foundation, FL, 2019
GenCorp Foundation, Incorporated, CA, 560
Genentech Access To Care Foundation, CA, 561
Genentech Foundation for Biomedical Sciences, CA, 563
Genentech Foundation, CA, 562
Genentech Research Foundation, CA, see 563
General Education Fund, Inc., VT, 9356
General Mills Foundation, MN, 4570
General Motors Cancer Research Foundation, Inc., MI, 4319
General Motors Foundation, Inc., MI, 4320
General Service Foundation, CO, 1381
Generation Trust, The, OH, 7647
Generations Health Care Initiatives, Inc., MN, 4571
Geneseo Foundation, IL, 2750
Geneva Foundation, WA, 9592
Genius Charitable Trust, Elizabeth Morse, IL, 2751
Genuardi Family Foundation, PA, 8213
Genzyme Charitable Foundation, Inc., MA, 3922
George Family Foundation, MN, 4572
George Foundation, Inc., NC, 7372
George Foundation, The, TX, 8916
Georgescu Family Foundation, The, CT, 1554
Georgia Health Foundation, Inc., GA, 2394
Georgia Power Foundation, Inc., GA, 2395
Georgia Scientific and Technical Research Foundation, GA, see 2502
Georgia Youth Foundation, Inc., GA, 2396
Georgia-Pacific Foundation, Inc., GA, 2397
Geraldi Norton Memorial Corporation, IL, 2752
Gerard Health Foundation, MA, 3923
Gerber Companies Foundation, The, MI, see 4321
Gerber Foundation, The, MI, 4321
Gerbode Foundation, Wallace Alexander, CA, 564
Gerdin Charitable Foundation, The, IA, 3286
Gere Foundation, The, CA, 565
Gerhard Foundation, Peter and Kristen, The, NY, 6015
Gerlach Foundation, Inc., OH, 7648
German Protestant Orphan Asylum Association Foundation, LA, 3483
Germeshausen Foundation, Inc., MA, 3924
Gerondelis Foundation, Inc., MA, 3925
Gerry Charitable Trust, NY, 6016
Gerry Charitable Trust, Perry N. & Robert G., NY, see 6016
Gerry Foundation, Inc., NY, 6017
Gerschel Foundation, Laurent and Alberta, NY, 6018
Gerschel Foundation, Patrick A., NY, 6019
Gershman Foundation, Cynthia, CA, 566
Gershman Foundation, Joel and Elaine, NJ, 5206
Gershman Foundation, Joel, NJ, see 5206
Gershman Foundation, MO, 4818
Gershman Foundation, Ronald and Catherine, CA, 567
Gershwind Family Foundation, The, NY, 6020
Gerson Family Foundation, Inc., NY, 6021
Gerstacker Foundation, Rollin M., The, MI, 4322
Gerstner, Jr. Foundation, Inc., Louis V., FL, 2020
Geschke Foundation, Charles M. Geschke and Nancy A., CA, 568
Gesner-Johnson Foundation, AZ, 100
Gettler Family Foundation, The, OH, 7649
Getty Foundation, Ann and Gordon, The, CA, 569
Getty Trust, J. Paul, CA, 570
Getz Foundation, Emma & Oscar, IL, see 2753

Getz Foundation, The, IL, 2753
Gewirz Foundation, Inc., Bernard & Sarah, DC, 1801
Geyer Foundation, Charlotte, SC, 8590
GFC Foundation, The, UT, 9324
GFH & SAH Foundation, The, NE, 4966
Gheens Foundation, Inc., The, KY, 3421
GHH Foundation, Inc., NJ, 5207
Ghidotti Foundation, William & Marian, CA, 571
GHS Foundation, TX, 8917
Giannini Family Foundation, CA, see 572
Giannini Foundation, A.P., CA, 572
Giannini Fund, Claire, CA, 573
Giant Eagle Foundation, PA, 8214
Giant Steps Foundation, The, NY, 6023
Gibbs Charitable Foundation, SC, 8590
Gibbs Foundation, Inc., Malcolm, NY, 6024
Gibney Family Foundation, Inc., The, FL, 2021
Gibson Charitable Trust, Nancy & Craig, NY, see 6025
Gibson Family Foundation, Inc., NJ, 5208
Gibson Family Foundation, The, NY, 6025
Gibson Foundation, Addison H., PA, 8215
Gibson Hemostasis-Thrombosis Foundation, Mary Rodes, TX, 8918
Gidwitz Charitable Foundation, Christina and Ronald, IL, 2754
Gidwitz Family Foundation, IL, 2755
Gidwitz Memorial Foundation, Joseph L. & Emily K., IL, 2756
Gifford Charitable Corporation, Rosamond, The, NY, 6026
Gifford Family Foundation, NY, 6027
Gifford Foundation, Inc., The, CA, 574
GII Charities, MI, 4323
Gilbert Foundation, Lewis D. & John J., NY, 6028
Gilbert Foundation, Rosalinde & Arthur, The, CA, A
Gilbert Foundation, Rosalinde and Arthur, The, CA, 575
Gilbert, Jr. Charitable Fund, Price, NC, 7373
Gilchrist Foundation, IA, 3287
Gilder Foundation, Inc., NY, 6029
Gilder Lehrman Institute of American History, The, NY, 6030
Giles Foundation, Edward C., The, NC, see 7374
Giles Foundation, Lucille P. and Edward C., The, NC, 7374
Gilhousen Family Foundation, MT, 4938
Gill Family Foundation, Stephen & Margaret, CA, 576
Gill Foundation, Pauline Allen, TX, 8919
Gill Foundation, The, CO, 1382
Gillespie Foundation, William, The, CA, 577
Gilliam Foundation, Deane A. and John D., The, NY, 6031
Gilliam Foundation, John D., NY, see 6031
Gilman Foundation, Frank M. & Olive E., VT, 9357
Gilman Foundation, Inc., Howard, NY, 6032
Gilman, Jr. Foundation, Inc., Sondra & Charles, NY, 6033
Gilmore Foundation, Irving S., MI, 4324
Gilmore Foundation, William G., The, CA, 578
Gilo Family Foundation, The, CA, 579
Gimbel Foundation, Inc., Bernard F. and Alva B., NY, 6034
Gimelstob Family Foundation, Inc., Herbert, FL, A
Gimprich Family Foundation, Inc., NY, 6035
Gindi Associates Foundation, Inc., NY, see 5725
Gindi Private Foundation, Ralph S., The, NY, 6036
Gingher State Auto Insurance Companies Foundation, Paul R., OH, 7650
Ginsburg Family Foundation, Inc., Alan and Harriet, FL, see 2022
Ginsburg Family Foundation, Inc., FL, 2022
Giop Charitable Foundation, Sonia Raiziss, PA, 8216
Gipson Family Foundation, NC, 7375
Girard Foundation, CA, 580
Girl's Best Friend Foundation, IL, 2757
Gitlin Family Foundation, Harvey S., The, PA, 8217
GKN Foundation, IL, 2758
GKW Foundation, Inc., GA, 2398
GLA Foundation, WA, 9593
Glades Foundation, The, NY, 6037
Gladstein Foundation, Marsha Lilien, CT, 1555
Glaser Foundation, Inc., WA, 9594
Glaser Foundation, The, WA, see 9595
Glaser Progress Foundation, WA, 9595

Glass Family Foundation, AR, 163
Glassman Foundation, M. B. & Shana, CO, 1383
Glaubinger Foundation, The, FL, 2023
Glaxo Wellcome Foundation, The, NC, *see 7439*
GlaxoSmithKline Foundation, PA, 8218
Glazer Family Foundation, Inc., FL, 2024
Glazer Family Foundation, Lowell & Harriet, MD, 3635
Glazer Family Foundation, Lowell R., MD, *see 3635*
Glazer Foundation, Madelyn L., IA, *see 3307*
Glazer Foundation, Marsha and Jay, WA, 9596
Glazer Philanthropic Fund, Marsha Sloan, WA, *see 9596*
Gleacher Foundation, Anne and Eric, The, NY, 6038
Gleason Foundation, George and Linda, AR, 164
Gleason Foundation, NY, 6039
Gleason Memorial Fund, Inc., NY, *see 6039*
Gleberman Foundation, Joseph & Carson, NY, 6040
Glencairn Foundation, PA, 8219
Glencoe Foundation, Inc., DE, 1714
Glenn Family Foundation, NC, 7376
Glenn Family Foundation, Wilbur and Hilda, The, GA, 2399
Glenn Foundation for Medical Research, Inc., CA, 581
Glenn Foundation for Medical Research, Inc., Paul F., CA, *see 581*
Glenn Foundation, Wadley R., SC, 8591
Glenner Foundation, Sidney and Lisa, IL, 2759
Glens Falls Foundation, The, NY, 6041
Glenstone Foundation, The, VA, 9429
Glick Foundation Corporation, Eugene and Marilyn, IN, 3155
Glickenhaus Foundation, The, NY, 6042
Glickman Foundation, Inc., Morris, CA, 582
Global Environment Project Institute, Inc., CA, 583
Global Quest Foundation, NE, 4967
Global Resource Action Center for the Environment, Inc., NY, 6043
Global Village Charitable Trust, FL, 2025
Globe Foundation, AZ, 101
Glover-Crask Charitable Trust, WI, 9805
Gloyd Family Foundation, IL, 2760
Gluck Foundation, Inc., Maxwell H., CA, 584
GM Foundation, MI, *see 4320*
GMO Charities, Inc., WI, A
Goatie Foundation, The, OH, 7651
God's Gift, CA, 585
Godchaux Foundation, Frank & Mary, LA, *see 3495*
Goddard Foundation Trust, Charles B., The, OK, 7939
Godinger Lefkowitz Memorial Foundation, Inc., The, NY, 6044
Godric Foundation, CA, 586
Goel Foundation, The, CA, 587
Goergen Foundation, Inc., The, CT, 1556
Gogian Family Foundation, John, CA, 588
Goizueta Foundation, The, GA, 2400
Gold Family Charitable Foundation, CA, *see 589*
Gold Family Foundation, CA, 589
Gold Foundation, David B., The, CA, 590
Gold Foundation, Gloria and Peter, CA, A
Gold Foundation, Sheila, CA, 591
Goldbach Charitable Foundation, Inc., WI, *see 9806*
Goldbach Foundation, Inc., Raymond and Marie, WI, 9806
Goldberg Charitable Foundation, Avram & Carol, MA, *see 3927*
Goldberg Charitable Trust, Joseph and Dorothy, CA, 592
Goldberg Family Foundation, Israel and Matilda, MA, 3926
Goldberg Family Foundation, Milton D. and Madeline L., The, IL, 2761
Goldberg Family Foundation, The, MA, 3927
Goldberg Foundation, Frank M. & Lee, The, CA, 593
Goldberg Foundation, Inc., Arthur M. Goldberg and Veronica, NJ, 5209
Goldberg Foundation, Inc., Arthur M., NJ, *see 5209*
Goldberg Foundation, Stephen A. and Diana L., DC, 1802
Goldberg/Nash Family Foundation, NY, 6045
Golden Family Foundation, NY, 6046
Golden Foundation, Robert M., ID, 2568
Golden Helping Hand Foundation, Inc., Sam and Marion, The, VA, 9430
Golden Rule Foundation, Inc., The, ME, 3538

Goldenson Association, Inc., Isabelle and Leonard, The, NY, *see 6047*
Goldenson-Arbus Foundation, Inc., NY, 6047
Golder Family Foundation, IL, 2762
Goldfield Foundation, Jacob, The, NY, *see 6244*
Goldfrank III Foundation, Lionel, The, NY, 6048
Goldhammer Family Foundation, FL, 2026
Goldhirsh Foundation, Inc., Bernard A. and Wendy J., The, CT, *see 1557*
Goldhirsh Foundation, Inc., The, CT, 1557
Goldie-Anna Charitable Trust, The, NY, 6049
Goldman Charitable Trust, Lillian, The, NY, 6050
Goldman Charitable Trust, Sol, The, NY, 6051
Goldman Environmental Foundation, CA, 594
Goldman Family Foundation, Joyce and Irving, NY, 6052
Goldman Foundation for Fighting Catastrophic Diseases, Judith and George, IL, *see 2763*
Goldman Foundation, Herman, NY, 6053
Goldman Foundation, Inc., Irving, NY, *see 6052*
Goldman Foundation, John and Marcia, CA, 595
Goldman Foundation, Robert I., NY, 6054
Goldman Fund, John and Marcia, The, CA, *see 595*
Goldman Fund, Lisa and Douglas, CA, 596
Goldman Fund, Richard and Rhoda, CA, 597
Goldman Philanthropic Partnerships, IL, 2763
Goldman Sachs Charitable Fund, NY, 6055
Goldman Sachs Foundation, The, NY, 6056
Goldman Sachs Fund, NY, *see 6056*
Goldrich Family Foundation, The, CA, 598
Goldring Family Foundation, Inc., The, NJ, 5210
Goldring Family Foundation, LA, 3484
Goldring Foundation, Joseph G., The, NY, 6057
Goldsbury Foundation, The, TX, 8920
Goldschmidt Family Foundation, Inc., Louis Callmann, NY, 6058
Goldschmidt Foundation, Walter & Karla, IL, 2764
Goldseker Foundation of Maryland, Inc., Morris, MD, 3636
Goldsmith Family Foundation, CA, 599
Goldsmith Family Foundation, Inc., The, MD, 3637
Goldsmith Family Foundation, Inc., The, TN, 8682
Goldsmith Foundation, Barbara Lubin, NY, 6059
Goldsmith Foundation, Horace W., NY, 6060
Goldsmith Foundation, The, TN, *see 8682*
Goldsmith-Greenfield Foundation, Inc., The, FL, *see 2035*
Goldsmith-Perry Philanthropies, Inc., NY, *see 6059*
Goldstein Charity Fund, Inc., NJ, 5211
Goldstein Family Foundation, Arnold & Arlene, NY, 6062
Goldstein Family Foundation, NY, 6061
Goldstein Family Foundation, The, NY, 6063
Goldstein Foundation, Inc., Alfred & Ann, FL, 2027
Goldstein Foundation, Leslie & Roslyn, The, NY, 6064
Goldstine Foundation, Inc., Robert, IN, 3156
Goldstone Family Foundation, The, NY, 6065
Goldwasser Family Foundation, Jonathan Plutzik & Lesley, The, NY, 6066
Goldwyn Foundation, Samuel, The, CA, 600
Golisano Foundation, B. Thomas, The, NY, 6067
Golkin Family Foundation, Perry & Donna, NY, 6068
Gollust Foundation, The, NY, 6069
Golub Foundation, Inc., William and Estelle, The, NY, 6070
Golub Foundation, NY, *see 6746*
Gonda Family Foundation, The, CA, 601
Gonda Foundation, The, CA, *see 601*
Good Hope Medical Foundation, CA, 602
Good Samaritan Foundation, Inc., KY, 3422
Good Samaritan, Inc., DE, 1715
Good Shepherds Trust Foundation, The, GA, 2401
Good Trust, Leonard A., IA, 3288
Good Works Foundation, The, CA, 603
Good Works Institute, Inc., The, ID, 2569
Goodes Family Foundation, Inc., Melvin R., NJ, 5212
Goodfriend Foundation, Sidney E. and Amy O., NY, 6071
Gooding Charitable Foundation Trust, Lucy, The, FL, 2028
Gooding Family Foundation, CO, 1384
Gooding Family Foundation, The, CA, 604
Goodman Family Foundation, The, CA, 605
Goodman Family Foundation, The, NY, 6072
Goodman Foundation, Gillian and Ellis, IL, 2765

Goodman Memorial Foundation, Inc., Joseph C. and Clare F., NY, 6073
Goodman's, Inc., WI, 9807
Goodman-Abell Foundation, TX, 8921
Goodnight Educational Foundation, NC, 7377
Goodrich Foundation, Inc., The, NC, 7378
Goodrich Foundation, Pierre F. and Enid, IN, 3157
Goodstein Charitable Trust, Harvey, PA, 8220
Goodwin Foundation, Inc., Leo, FL, 2029
Google Foundation, CA, 606
Goppert Foundation, The, MO, 4819
Gordon Family Foundation, Joel C. and Bernice W., TN, 8683
Gordon Family Foundation, MA, 3928
Gordon Family Foundation, The, NY, 6074
Gordon Foundation, Betsy, The, CA, 607
Gordon Foundation, Gail and Mark, FL, *see 2030*
Gordon Foundation, Gertrude S., WI, 9808
Gordon Foundation, Inc., Michael, The, NY, 6075
Gordon Foundation, Jeff, The, NC, 7379
Gordon Foundation, Mark J., FL, 2030
Gordon Fund, John R. and Kiendl Dauphinot, The, NY, 6076
Gordon Fund, John R., The, NY, *see 6076*
Gordon Fund, The, NY, 6077
Gordon/Rousmaniere/Roberts Fund, The, NY, *see 6077*
Gordy Foundation, Evelyn and Frank, The, GA, 2402
Gore Family Memorial Foundation, FL, 2031
Gorelick Family Foundation, Shelton, NC, 7380
Gorelick Family Foundation, William and Patricia, NC, 7381
Gorham Charitable Foundation, Frank D. Gorham, Jr., and Marie K., NM, 5478
Gorin Foundation, Nehemias, FL, 2032
Gorman Foundation, The, NY, *see 6078*
Gorman Foundation, The, TX, 8922
Gorman Testamentary Charitable Trust, Owen T. Gorman & Alice M., NY, 6078
Gorter Family Foundation, The, NY, 6079
Gotschall Family Foundation, The, CA, 608
Gottesman Fund, The, DC, 1803
Gottlieb Charitable Foundation, Arvin, MO, 4820
Gottlieb Foundation, Inc., Adolph and Esther, NY, 6080
Gottlieb Fund, Inc., Lee, NY, 6081
Gottwald Foundation, VA, 9431
Gould Charitable Trust, Edward S., WI, 9809
Gould Family Charitable Foundation of New York, The, NY, *see 6085*
Gould Family Foundation, NY, 6082
Gould Foundation for Children, Edwin, NY, 6083
Gould Foundation, Florence, The, NY, 6084
Gould Foundation, Joseph B., The, CA, 609
Gould-Shenfeld Family Foundation, The, NY, 6085
GPOA Foundation, LA, *see 3483*
Grable Foundation, The, PA, 8221
Grace Foundation, IL, 2766
Grace Foundation, Inc., W. R., MD, 3638
Grace Living Centers Foundation, Inc., OK, 7940
GRACE, NY, *see 6043*
Graco Foundation, The, MN, 4573
Graduate Health System, Inc., PA, *see 8379*
Graeber Foundation, MS, 4744
Graham Foundation for Advanced Studies in the Fine Arts, IL, 2767
Graham Foundation, The, NC, 7382
Graham Foundation, The, PA, 8222
Graham Fund, Philip L., DC, 1804
Grainger Foundation Inc., The, IL, 2768
Grammer Charitable Foundation, Kelsey, CA, 610
Grand Circle Foundation, Inc., MA, 3929
Grand Foundation, Richard, CA, 611
Grand Haven Area Community Foundation, Inc., MI, 4325
Grand Marnier Foundation, The, NY, 6086
Grand Rapids Area Community Foundation, MN, 4574
Grand Rapids Community Foundation, MI, 4326
Grand Rapids Foundation, The, MI, *see 4326*
Grand Traverse Regional Community Foundation, MI, 4327
Grand Victoria Foundation, IL, 2769
Grandis Family Foundation, Harry and Harriet, VA, 9432

Grandison Foundation, NY, 6087
Grandview-Steers Foundation, NY, 6088
Granger Foundation, MI, 4328
Granger III Foundation, Inc., MI, 4329
Granoff Family Foundation, Inc., Perry and Martin, The, NY, 6089
Granoff Foundation, Leon L., CA, 612
Grant Family Foundation, Eugene and Emily, NY, 6090
Grant Foundation, Charles M. & Mary D., NY, 6091
Grant Foundation, William T., NY, 6092
Grant Healthcare Foundation, IL, 2770
Grantham Charitable Trust, Jeremy and Hannelore, MA, see 3930
Grantham Foundation for the Protection of the Environment, MA, 3930
Grass Family Foundation, PA, 8223
Grass Foundation, The, MA, 3931
Grassmann Trust, E. J., NJ, 5213
Grateful Foundation, Inc., The, NY, 6093
Grauer Foundation, Peter T. and Laura M., NY, 6094
Graustein Memorial Fund, William Caspar, CT, 1559
Graves Charitable Trust, Elizabeth Ireland, VA, 9433
Graves Foundation, Inc., The, GA, 2403
Gray Charitable Trust, PA, 8224
Gray Family Fund, Joseph J., IL, A
Gray Foundation, Richard and Mary, IL, 2771
Graymer Foundation, The, NJ, 5214
Grays Harbor Community Foundation, WA, 9597
Grayson Family Foundation, Inc., MA, 3932
Graziadio Foundation, George and Reva, CA, 613
Great Bay Foundation for Social Entrepreneurship, ME, 3539
Great Lakes Capital Fund Nonprofit Housing Corporation, MI, 4330
Greatbatch Foundation, Eleanor and Wilson, NY, see 5899
Greathouse Charitable Trust, Helen, TX, 8923
Greathouse Foundation, TX, 8924
Green Bay Community Foundation, Inc., Greater, WI, 9810
Green Bay Foundation, NY, see 6079
Green Charitable Foundation, Inc., NY, 6095
Green Charitable Foundation, Preston M., MO, 4821
Green Family Foundation, Inc., FL, 2033
Green Foundation, Allen P. & Josephine B., MO, 4822
Green Foundation, Daniel B. and Florence E., The, PA, 8225
Green Foundation, David Green and Mary Winton, IL, 2772
Green Foundation, George Mason Green & Lois C., The, AZ, 102
Green Foundation, Howard L., The, NJ, 5215
Green Foundation, Inc., Joshua, WA, 9598
Green Foundation, Leonard I., CA, see 614
Green Foundation, Roe, The, OH, 7652
Green Foundation, The, CA, 614
Green Fund, CO, 1385
Green Fund, Inc., The, NY, 6096
Green Mountain Coffee Roasters Foundation, VT, 9358
Green, Jr. Charitable Trust, John P., FL, A
Greenbaum, Jr. Family Foundation, James R., The, CA, 615
Greenberg and Linda Vester Foundation, Glenn, NY, 6097
Greenberg Animal Welfare Foundation, Mary Jo & Hank, CA, 616
Greenberg Foundation, Inc., Maurice R. & Corinne P., The, NY, 6098
Greenberg Foundation, Mayer, The, CA, see 617
Greenberg Foundation, Monica and Hermen, MD, 3639
Greenberg Foundation, The, CA, 617
Greenburg-May Foundation, Inc., The, FL, 2034
Greene Charitable Trust, Helen Wade, MA, 3933
Greene County Community Foundation, OH, 7653
Greene Family Foundation, David and Alan, The, NY, 6099
Greene Foundation, D. Forrest Greene & Gerda M., The, UT, 9325
Greene Foundation, Inc., David J., The, NY, see 6099
Greene Foundation, Inc., Jerome L., NY, 6100
Greene Giving, OH, see 7653
Greene-Sawtell Foundation, The, GA, 2404
Greenfield Foundation, FL, 2035

Greenhill Family Foundation, NY, 6101
GreenPoint Foundation, Inc., The, NY, see 6637
Greensboro Jaycees Charitable Foundation, Inc., NC, 7383
Greenspun Family Foundation, NV, 5034
Greentree Foundation, NY, 6102
Greenville Area Community Foundation, MI, 4331
Greenville Area Foundation, MI, see 4331
Greenwall Foundation, The, NY, 6103
Greer Family Foundation, The, CA, 618
Greve Foundation, Inc., William and Mary, The, NY, 6104
Greycoach Foundation, MN, 4575
Greystone Foundation, The, MN, 4576
Griffin Foundation, Inc., John A., NY, 6105
Griffin Foundation, Inc., The, FL, 2036
Griffin Foundation, Neil and Elaine, The, TX, 8925
Griffin-Cole Fund, The, NY, 6106
Griffis Foundation, Inc., The, NY, 6107
Griffith Foundation, Inc., William Mibra Griffith and Bryne Smith, SD, 8625
Griffith Foundation, W. C., The, IN, 3158
Griffiths Trust, E. S. and M., OH, A
Grigg-Lewis Foundation, Inc., NY, 6108
Griggs and Mary Griggs Burke Foundation, Mary Livingston, MN, 4577
Grim Foundation, S. T., NJ, see 5401
Grimm Family Foundation, Robert A. and Kari L., CA, 619
Grimm Family Foundation, Rodney, The, CA, 620
Grimshaw-Gudewicz Charitable Foundation, MA, 3934
Grin Family Foundation, Inc., NY, 6109
Grinnell Memorial Trust, Russell, RI, 8538
Grinspoon Charitable Foundation, Harold, The, MA, 3935
Griswold Foundation, John C., IL, 2773
Groff Surgical and Medical Research and Education Charitable Trust, Mary E., The, PA, 8226
Grohne Family Foundation, David F. and Margaret T., IL, 2774
Gronewaldt Foundation, Inc., Alice Busch, FL, 2037
Grosfeld Foundation, The, MI, 4332
Gross Charitable Foundation, Allen I., NY, 6110
Gross Charitable Trust, Stella B., CA, 621
Gross Family Charitable Trust, Harold K., MA, A
Gross Family Foundation, J. & H., NY, 6111
Gross Family Foundation, Phillip and Elizabeth, The, MA, 3936
Gross Family Foundation, The, CA, 622
Gross Foundation, Inc., Julia & Seymour, The, MA, 3937
Gross Foundation, Inc., Louis H., MD, 3640
Gross Foundation, Inc., NY, 6112
Grossman Charitable Trust, Sanford J., CT, 1560
Grossman Foundation, N. Bud and Beverly, MN, 4578
Grossman Foundation, N. Bud, MN, see 4578
Grotto Foundation, Inc., MN, 4579
Grousbeck Family Foundation, CA, 623
Grout Foundation, Gardner, CA, 624
Grove Foundation, The, CA, 625
Grubb Charitable Foundation, John R. and Zelda Z., The, IA, 3289
Gruber Family Foundation, CA, 626
Gruber Foundation, Peter, VI, A
Grubman Compton Foundation, The, NY, 6113
Grubman Foundation, Eric P., NY, see 6113
Grumbacher Family Foundation, Nancy and Tim, The, PA, see 8227
Grumbacher Family Foundation, The, PA, 8227
Grundhofer Charitable Foundation, MN, 4580
Grundy Foundation, The, PA, 8228
Gruss Charitable and Educational Foundation, Inc., Oscar and Regina, NY, 6114
Gruss Charitable Foundation, Inc., Emanuel & Riane, NY, 6115
Gruss Foundation, Audrey and Martin, FL, 2038
Gruss Foundation, Martin D., FL, see 2038
Gruss-Lipper Family Foundation, The, NY, 6116
GSB Family Foundation, Inc., FL, 2039
GSF Foundation, CA, 627
GTE Federal Credit Union Charitable Trust, FL, 2040
Gualala Foundation Trust, The, NC, A
Guardian Industries Educational Foundation, MI, 4333
Guarini Foundation, Inc., Frank J., The, NJ, 5216

Gudelsky Family Foundation, Inc., Homer and Martha, The, MD, 3641
Gudelsky Family Foundation, Inc., Isadore and Bertha, The, DC, 1805
Guenther Foundation, Henry L., CA, 628
Guess? Foundation, CA, 629
Guest House Ministries Foundation, CA, 630
Guggenheim Foundation, Daniel and Florence, The, NY, 6117
Guggenheim Foundation, Harry Frank, The, NY, 6118
Guggenheim Memorial Foundation, John Simon, NY, 6119
Guidant Foundation, IN, 3159
Guild Charitable Foundation, Lloyd V., The, PA, 8229
Guilford Foundation, The, VA, 9434
Gulf Coast Community Foundation of Venice, FL, 2041
Gulf Coast Community Foundation, MS, 4745
Gulf Coast Community Foundation, The, FL, see 2041
Gulf Coast Medical Foundation, TX, 8926
Gulf Power Foundation, Inc., FL, 2042
Gulton Foundation, Inc., NJ, 5217
Gumbiner Foundation, Josephine S., CA, 631
Gund 1993 Charitable Foundation, Gordon & Llura, OH, 7654
Gund Foundation, Agnes, The, OH, 7655
Gund Foundation, Geoffrey, OH, 7656
Gund Foundation, George, The, OH, 7657
Gund Foundation, Gordon and Llura, NJ, 5218
Gunzenhauser-Chapin Fund, NC, 7384
Gupta Charitable Foundation, Vinod, NE, see 4967
Gupta Family Foundation, Inc., Jai N., The, DE, 1716
Gural Foundation, Aaron & Marion, NY, 6120
Gurtler Foundation, Inc., John R. and Ruth W., The, FL, 2043
Gurwin Foundation, Inc., J., NY, 6121
Gussman Foundation, Herbert and Roseline, OK, 7941
Guth Foundation Charitable Trust, The, IL, 2775
Guth Foundation, The, IL, see 2775
Guthman Fund, Leo S., The, IL, A, 2776
Gutman Family Foundation, The, NY, 6122
Gutmann Foundation, Leo and Karen, The, NY, 6123
Guttag Foundation, Inc., Irwin & Marjorie, FL, A
Guttman Foundation, Inc., Stella and Charles, NY, 6124
Guzik Foundation, The, CA, 632
Guzzardi/Guzzardi Memorial Foundation, Tina, NC, A
GW Foundation, The, CT, 1561
Gwathmey Memorial Trust, Richard and Caroline T., VA, 9435
Gynesis Women's International Foundation, DE, 1717

H & R Block Foundation, The, MO, 4823
H.B.B. Foundation, The, IL, 2777
H.C.S. Foundation, OH, 7658
H.E.I. Charitable Foundation, HI, see 2546
H.I.S. Foundation, MI, 4334
H.R.C. Foundation, Inc., NY, 6125
Haas Charitable Trust, John C. & Chara C., The, PA, 8230
Haas Foundation, Chuck & Ellen, The, CA, 633
Haas Foundation, Gene, CA, 634
Haas Foundation, Inc., Helen Hotze, The, NY, 6127
Haas Foundation, Inc., Marc, The, NY, 6126
Haas Foundation, Inc., Saul and Dayee G., WA, 9599
Haas Fund, Mimi and Peter, CA, 635
Haas Fund, Miriam and Peter, CA, see 635
Haas Fund, Walter and Elise, CA, 636
Haas, Jr. Fund, Evelyn and Walter, CA, 637
Habe Foundation, The, NY, 6128
Haber Foundation, Amy and James, NY, 6129
Habig Foundation, The, IN, 3182
Hach Scientific Foundation, CO, 1386
Hachar Charitable Trust Fund, D. D., TX, 8927
Hackerman Foundation, Inc., The, MD, 3642
Hackett Family Foundation, TX, 8928
Hackett Foundation, Inc., The, NJ, 5219
Hagan Charitable Foundation, Inc., Virginia Clark, The, KY, 3423
Hagedorn Fund, NY, 6130
Hager Family Charitable Trust, NY, 6131
Hager Foundation, CA, 638
Hagerty Family Foundation, The, MA, 3938
Haggar Corp. Foundation, TX, 8929
Haggar Family Foundation, Ed, TX, 8930

Haggar, Jr. Charitable Foundation, J. M., The, TX, see 8931

Haggar, Jr. Family Foundation, J. M., The, TX, 8931

Haggerty Foundation, Patrick and Beatrice, The, TX, 8932

Haggerty Foundation, TX, see 8932

Haggin Trust in Memory of Her Late Husband, James Ben Ali Haggin, Margaret Voorhies, NY, 6132

Haglage Charitable Trust Agency, KS, 3365

Hahn Charitable Trust, LaVerna, MD, 3643

Hahn Family Foundation, Inc., FL, 2044

Hahn Family Foundation, Norman & Elizabeth, The, PA, 8231

Hahn Foundation, Inc., William and Sharon, MI, 4335

Haile, Jr. Foundation, Carol & Ralph, The, NC, 7659

Haje Foundation, Peter and Helen, NY, 6133

Hajim Family Foundation, The, NY, 6134

Halbert Family Foundation, Jon and Linda, TX, 8933

Halcyon Hill Foundation, NY, 6135

Hale Foundation, Crescent Porter, CA, 639

Hales Foundation, William M., IL, 2778

Haley Family Foundation, MA, 3939

Haley Foundation, Inc., Michael W., NC, 7385

Halff Foundation, G. A. C., TX, 8934

Halis Family Foundation, NY, 6136

Hall 2nd Charitable Trust, Edwin, PA, 8232

Hall Charitable Foundation, D. Ray and Sibyl, FL, 2045

Hall Charitable Trust, Evelyn A. J., DE, 1718

Hall Childhood Diabetes Foundation, George E., The, NY, 6137

Hall Family Foundation, MO, 4824

Hall Family Foundation, The, NV, see 5032

Hall Foundation, Alan and Jeanne, The, UT, 9326

Hall Foundation, Inc., The, IA, see 3290

Hall-Perrine Foundation, Inc., The, IA, 3290

Halle Family Foundation, Bruce T., AZ, 103

Hallett Charitable Trust, E. W., MN, 4581

Hallett Charitable Trust, Jessie F., MN, 4582

Hallett Charitable Trust, MN, see 4582

Halliburton Foundation, Inc., TX, 8935

Halligan Charitable Fund, John R., IL, 2779

Hallmark Corporate Foundation, MO, 4825

Halloran Foundation, Mary P. Dolciani, NY, 6138

Halpern Foundation, Robert and Ruth, CA, 640

Halpern Family Foundation, Inc., Arie and Eva, NJ, 5220

Halpern Family Foundation, Inc., Sam, NJ, 5221

Halsell Foundation, Ewing, The, TX, 8936

Halsell Foundation, O. L., CA, 641

Halton Foundation, Inc., D. F., NC, 7386

Ham Charitable Foundation, Inc., Kendall C. and Anna, MA, 3940

Hamel Family Charitable Trust, D.A., DE, 1719

Hamico, Inc., TN, 8684

Hamill Family Foundation, IL, 2780

Hamill Foundation, The, TX, 8937

Hamilton Community Foundation, Inc., NE, 4968

Hamilton Community Foundation, Inc., The, OH, 7660

Hamilton Family Foundation, Frederic C., The, CO, 1387

Hamilton Family Foundation, The, PA, 8233

Hamilton-Forbes Charitable Trust, Ruth A., FL, 2046

Hamilton-White Foundation, The, CA, 642

Hamlin Foundation, Richard M. & Yvonne, OH, 7661

Hamman Foundation, George and Mary Josephine, TX, 8938

Hammer International Foundation, CA, 643

Hammerman and Fisch Foundation, The, NY, 6139

Hammerman Foundation, Stephen & Eleanor, The, NY, see 6139

Hammersmith Family Foundation, Charles & Carol, IL, 2781

Hammons Foundation, Inc., John Q., MO, 4826

Hampshire Foundation, The, CT, 1562

Hampson Foundation, MI, 4336

Hana Foundation, MO, 4827

Hancock County Community Foundation, Inc., IN, 3160

Hancock Foundation, Inc., L. D., MS, 4746

Handleman Charitable Foundation Trust C, Joseph & Sally, WI, 9811

Handler Family Foundation, The, NY, 6140

Handler Foundation, Milton and Miriam, NY, 6141

Hanes Foundation, John W. and Anna H., The, NC, 7387

Hanes Memorial Fund, James G., NC, 7388

Hanes Memorial Fund/Foundation, James G., NC, see 7388

Haney Memorial Fund, NC, 7389

Hank, Jr. Charitable Trust, Bernard J. and Joyce M., IL, see 2981

Hankamer Foundation, Curtis & Doris K., The, TX, 8939

Hankin Foundation, Bernard & Henrietta, PA, see 8234

Hankin Foundation, PA, 8234

Hankins Foundation, The, OH, 7662

Hanley Family Foundation, Inc., The, GA, 2405

Hanley Foundation, Bryant & Nancy, The, TX, 8940

Hanley Foundation, The, DC, 1806

Hanna Family Foundation, Sally and Frank, The, GA, 2406

Hannaford Charitable Foundation, ME, 3540

Hannon Foundation, Bill, CA, 644

Hannon Foundation, William H., CA, 645

Hanover Foundation, The, CA, see 1137

Hanover Insurance Group Foundation, Inc., The, MA, 3941

Hansen Family Foundation, Inc., NY, 6142

Hansen Foundation, Dane G., KS, 3366

Hansen Foundation, PA, see 8235

Hansen Foundation, Robert and Marie, The, AZ, 104

Hansen Foundation, William Stucki, PA, 8235

Hansen Foundation, Zenon C. R., CO, 1388

Hansen-Furnas Foundation, Inc., IL, 2782

Hanson Family Foundation, Inc., Alice G., IL, 2783

Hanson Foundation, Jack and Vivian, The, NY, A

Hanson Foundation, John K. & Luise V., The, IA, 3291

Hanson Foundation, The, IA, see 3291

Hanus Foundation, George and Barbara, IL, 2784

Happy Hollow Fund, IL, see 2780

HAR-BER Village Foundation, The, AR, A

Harary Family Foundation, Jerry and Janet, The, NY, 6143

Harary Foundation, Inc., Ralph J., NJ, 5222

Harbison Scholarship Trust, CA, 646

Harbor Lights Foundation, NY, 6144

Harbourton Foundation, NJ, 5223

Harcourt Foundation, Inc., Alfred, The, MD, A

Hard Rock Cafe Foundation, Inc., FL, 2047

Harden Foundation, CA, 647

Hardenbergh Foundation, MN, 4583

Harder Foundation, WA, 9600

Hardin Foundation, Phil, MS, 4747

Harding Family Charitable Trust, OH, 7663

Harding Foundation, Charles Stewart, MI, 4337

Harding Foundation, The, MI, 4338

Hardison Family Foundation, The, FL, 2048

Hardtner Fund, Juliet E., LA, 3485

Hargrove Pierce Foundation, The, CA, 648

Hark Foundation, Marguerite Delaney, IL, 2785

Harkham Foundation, CA, 649

Harkness Foundation for Dance, NY, 6145

Harland Charitable Foundation, Inc., John H. and Wilhelmina D., GA, 2407

Harley-Davidson Foundation, Inc., WI, 9812

Harman Family Foundation, CA, 650

Harman Family Foundation, DC, 1807

Harman Foundation, John and Wauna, WA, 9601

Harman Foundation, Reed L. Harman and Nan M., The, CA, 651

Harmon Foundation, Halbert, TX, 8941

Harmon Foundation, Inc., Halbert, TX, see 8941

Harmsworth 1997 Charitable Foundation, Esmond, MA, 3942

Harnischfeger Industries Foundation, WI, see 9828

Harper Family Foundation, The, NE, 4969

Harper Foundation, Philip S., IL, 2786

Harrah's Foundation, The, TN, 8685

Harriman Foundation, Gladys and Roland, NY, 6146

Harriman Foundation, Mary W., NY, 6147

Harrington Family Foundation, The, FL, 2049

Harrington Foundation, Francis A. & Jacquelyn H., MA, 3943

Harrington Foundation, Mark H. & Blanche M., CA, 652

Harris Bank Foundation, IL, 2787

Harris Family Foundation, IL, 2788

Harris Foundation A, Irving, IL, see 2972

Harris Foundation B, Irving, IL, see 2584

Harris Foundation, FL, 2050

Harris Foundation, Inc., Clarence E., GA, 2408

Harris Foundation, Inc., Claude and Betty, The, KY, 3424

Harris Foundation, Inc., J. Ira and Nicki, NY, 6148

Harris Foundation, Inc., Robinson, The, NJ, 5224

Harris Foundation, Irving, The, IL, 2789

Harris Foundation, James J. and Angelia M., NC, 7390

Harris Foundation, Richard V., NV, 5035

Harris Foundation, The, IL, see 2789

Harris Foundation, Will & Jane, TN, 8686

Harris Foundation, William H., MA, 3944

Harrisburg Foundation, Greater, The, PA, see 8208

Harrison Article 11(A) Trust, Mortimer J., NJ, 5225

Harrison County Community Foundation, Inc., IN, 3161

Harrison Family Foundation, Inc., VA, 9436

Harrison Family Foundation, James I., The, AL, 36

Harrison Foundation Trust, Francena T., NY, 6149

Harrison Foundation, Albert E., The, GA, 2409

Harrison Foundation, Fred G., IL, 2790

Harrison Foundation, Helen M., IL, A

Harrison Foundation, Inc., Helen M., IL, 2791

Harrison Foundation, Inc., Luther & Susie, The, GA, 2410

Harrisonburg Rockingham Community Foundation, VA, see 9400

Harsco Corporation Fund, PA, 8236

Hartford Courant Foundation, Inc., The, CT, 1563

Hartford Foundation for Public Giving, CT, 1564

Hartford Foundation, Inc., John A., The, NY, 6150

Hartke Community Foundation, Selma J., The, IL, 2792

Hartley Family Foundation, Fred L., CA, 653

Hartman Family Foundation, Shamai & Richu, NY, 6151

Hartman Foundation, Inc., The, TX, 8942

Hartmarx Charitable Foundation, IL, 2794

Hartquist Foundation, The, NC, 7391

Hartwell Foundation, The, CT, 1565

Harvest Charities, NC, 7392

Harvest Foundation, WA, 9602

Harvey Foundation, Brian and Phyllis, CA, 654

Harvey Foundation, Inc., C. Felix, The, NC, 7393

Harwit Z"L and Manya Harwit-Aviv Charitable Trust, J. Samuel, CA, 655

Hasan Family Foundation, CO, 1389

Hasbro Charitable Trust, Inc., RI, see 8539

Hasbro Children's Foundation, RI, A

Hasbro Children's Fund, RI, 8539

Hascoe Foundation, The, CT, A

Haseltine Charitable Foundation, William A., NY, 6152

Hasenfeld Foundation, Inc., A. & Z., NY, 6153

Haslam Family Foundation, Inc., The, TN, 8687

Haslam Foundation, Inc., The, TN, 8688

Haslinger Family Foundation, Inc., Sandra L. and Dennis B., OH, 7664

Hassel Foundation, The, PA, 8237

Hassenfeld Foundation, RI, 8540

Hasten Family Foundation, Inc., Hart N. and Simona, IN, 3162

Hasten Family Foundation, Inc., Mark and Anna Ruth, IN, 3163

Hatfield Family Foundation, The, CA, 656

Hatton Foundation, E. Kenneth & Esther Marie, OH, 7665

Hau'Oli Mau Loa Foundation, The, NY, 6154

Hauck Charitable Foundation, MO, 4828

Hauck Foundation, John, OH, 7666

Hauenstein Foundation, MI, 4339

Haugland Foundation, Richard P., WA, 9603

Haugland Foundation, Rosaria P., OR, 8018

Haugland Foundation, WA, see 9603

Hauser Foundation, Inc., The, NY, 6155

Havens Relief Fund Society, The, NY, 6156

Hawaii Community Foundation, HI, 2545

Hawaii Medical Service Association Foundation, HI, see 2547

Hawaiian Electric Industries Charitable Foundation, HI, 2546

Hawaiian Foundation, The, HI, see 2545

Hawkins Charitable Trust, NE, 4970

Hawkins Foundation, Robert Z., NV, 5036

Hawks Foundation, The, NE, 4971

Hawksglen Foundation, The, PA, 8238

Hawley Family Foundation, Inc., CO, 1390

Hawn Foundation, Gates Helms, NJ, 5226

Hitchcock Charitable Foundation, Eleanor and Henry, IL, 2801
Hitchcock Foundation, Gilbert M. and Martha H., NE, 4975
Hites Family Community College Scholarship Corporation, MO, 4831
Hittman Family Foundation, Inc., MD, 3651
Hitz Foundation, The, CA, 676
Hixon Fund for Religion and Education, Alexander and Adelaide, MA, see 3764
HKH Foundation, NY, 6190
HMSA Foundation, HI, 2547
HNHfoundation, NH, 5092
HNI Charitable Foundation, IA, 3293
Hoag Family Foundation, CA, 677
Hoag Family Foundation, George, CA, 678
Hoag Foundation, CA, 679, see 678
Hobbs Foundation, R. C., CA, 680
Hobbs Foundation, The, IL, 2802
Hobby Family Foundation, TX, 8954
Hoblitzelle Foundation, TX, 8955
Hochberg Family Foundation, IL, 2803
Hoche-Scofield Foundation, The, MA, 3954
Hochfelder Charitable Foundation, Inc., Peter & Stacy, NY, 6191
Hochschild Fund, Inc., NY, see 5721
Hochstein Foundation, Inc., NY, 6192
Hod Foundation, NY, 6193
Hodge Memorial Fund, Emma Clyde, PA, 8254
Hoechst Marion Roussel Foundation, NJ, see 5120
Hoechst Marion Roussel Health Care Foundation for the III, NJ, see 5121
Hoehn Family Charitable Trust, The, CA, 681
Hoerle Foundation, NY, 6194
Hoernle Foundation, Inc., Count and Countess de, FL, 2062
Hofer Family Foundation, NE, 4976
Hofer Trust, John D. & Edna, SD, 8626
Hoffberger Foundation, Inc., MD, 3652
Hoffman Family Foundation, MA, 3955
Hoffman Foundation, H. Leslie Hoffman and Elaine S., The, CA, 682
Hoffman Foundation, Inc., Maximilian E. & Marion O., The, CT, 1568
Hoffman Foundation, John Ernest, The, MA, see 3955
Hoffman Foundation, Marion O. & Maximilian, NY, 6195
Hoffmann Foundation, August J. & Thelma S., WV, 9718
Hoffritz Charitable Trust, Helen, NY, 6196
Hofmann Article 5 Charitable Trust, DE, see 1722
Hofmann Foundation, K. H., CA, 683
Hofmann Foundation, The, CA, see 683
Hofmann Trust, Renate, Hans & Maria, DE, 1722
Hoglund Foundation, The, TX, 8956
Holdcroft Foundation, Samuel W., VA, A
Holden Charitable Foundation, Inc., Ralph and Nancy, The, FL, 2063
Holden Foundation, Inc., Don L. & Julie, TX, 8957
Holden Foundation, Inc., Don L., TX, see 8957
Holden Foundation, Roland & Ruby, IA, 3294
Holder Construction Foundation, The, GA, 2413
Holding Foundation, Inc., R. P., The, NC, 7399
Holding Foundation, Robert P., The, NC, see 7399
Holekamp Foundation, The, MO, 4832
Holiday Home Foundation of Evansville, Inc., IN, see 3168
Holiday Management Foundation, Inc., IN, 3168
Holland Community Foundation, Inc., MI, see 4258
Holland Foundation, The, NE, 4977
Hollinger Charitable Trust, Pick, FL, 2064
Holloway Foundation, Inc., MS, 4749
Hollowell Foundation, Inc., WV, 9719
Hollowell-Ford Foundation, Inc., WV, see 9719
Hollyhock Foundation, Inc., The, NY, 6197
Holman Charitable Trust, The, MN, see 4627
Holmes Foundation, Charles M., OR, 8020
Holt Foundation, TX, 8958
Holt Foundation, William Knox, NM, 5480
Holthouse Foundation for Kids, The, TX, 8959
Holthues Trust, IA, 3295
Holtzmann Foundation, Jacob L. and Lillian, NY, 6198
Holz Family Foundation, Jerome J. and Dorothy H., WI, 9817
Holzer Memorial Foundation, Richard H., NJ, 5238

Home Savings Charitable Foundation, OH, 7672
Homeland Foundation, Inc., NY, 6199
Homeownership Preservation Foundation, MN, 4587
Homer Family Foundation, CA, 684
Homes Foundation, Shea, CA, 685
Hommer Foundation, Julius and Katheryn, The, NC, 7400
HON INDUSTRIES Charitable Foundation, IA, see 3293
Honda of America Foundation, OH, 7673
Honickman Charitable Fund, The, NJ, 5239
Honickman Foundation, Lynne & Harold, PA, see 8255
Honickman Foundation, The, PA, 8255
Honzel Family Foundation, The, OR, 8021
Hood Foundation, Charles H., MA, 3956
Hood Fund, Charles H., MA, 3957
Hooker Charitable Trust, Janet A., PA, A
Hooper Foundation, Elizabeth S., PA, see 8256
Hooper Foundation, Thorton D. & Elizabeth S., PA, 8256
Hooters Community Endowment Fund, Inc., GA, 2414
Hoover Family Foundation, IN, 3169
Hoover Foundation, Herbert W., The, OH, 7674
Hoover Foundation, The, OH, 7675
Hope Afghanistan Foundation, TN, A
Hope Happens, MO, A
Hopedale Foundation, The, MA, 3958
Hopewell Foundation, Inc., SC, 8593
Hopwood Charitable Trust, John M., PA, 8257
Horejsi Charitable Foundation, Inc., KS, 3367
Horizon Charitable Foundation, Inc., NJ, 5240
Horizon Foundation for New Jersey, The, NJ, see 5240
Horizon Foundation, Inc., ME, 3541
Horizons Foundation, WA, 9608
Hormel Foods Corporation Charitable Trust, MN, 4588
Horn Foundation, Mildred V., KY, 3427
Horn Foundation, The, CA, 686
Horncrest Foundation, Inc., NY, 6200
Horne Foundation, Dick, SC, 8594
Horowitz Cancer Research Foundation, Linda, NY, 6201
Horowitz Family Foundation, Inc., G. & B., The, NY, 6202
Horowitz Family Foundation, Inc., GA, 2415
Horowitz Foundation, Gedale B. and Barbara S., NY, see 6202
Horowitz Foundation, Inc., Gerald D., GA, see 2415
Horton Foundation, Polly, IL, A
Horvitz Family Foundation, Inc., David & Francie, FL, 2065
Horvitz Family Foundation, Inc., William & Norma, FL, see 2199
Horvitz Foundation, Leonard and Joan, The, OH, 7676
Horvitz Foundation, Lois U., OH, 7677
Horvitz Foundation, Richard and Marcy, The, OH, 7678
Horwitch Brothers Foundation, The, AZ, A
Hospira Foundation, IL, 2804
Hospital Service Association of Northeastern Pennsylvania Foundation, PA, see 8112
Hostetter and Alexander N. Habib Foundation, Mark D., The, MA, 3959
Hostetter Foundation, The, MA, see 3791
Houff Foundation, VA, 9438
Hough Family Foundation, Inc., The, FL, 2066
Houlsby Foundation, John R., IL, 2805
House Family Foundation, CA, 687
House Family Foundation, Dave, CA, see 687
House of St. Giles the Cripple, The, NY, see 7041
Houssels Family Foundation Corporation, NV, 5038
Houston Community Foundation, Greater, TX, 8960
Houston Endowment Inc., TX, 8961
Hoverter Charitable Foundation, Lawrence L. and Julia Z., PA, 8258
Hovnanian Foundation, Inc., Hirair and Anna, NJ, 5241
Hovnanian Foundation, Kevork and Sirwart, The, NJ, 5242
Howard Charitable Foundation, WA, 9609
Howe Family Foundation, Inc., Wesley J., The, NJ, 5243
Howe Foundation, The, IA, 3296
Hoyt Charitable Foundation, Franklin and Alice, MA, 3960
Hoyt Foundation, Inc., Stewart W. & Willma C., NY, 6203
Hoyt Foundation, The, PA, 8259
HRH Charitable Foundation, VA, 9439
HRH Family Foundation, OH, see 7677
HRH Foundation, CA, 688
HRH Foundation, DC, 1811

HRK Foundation, MN, 4589
HRLD Foundation, Inc., MD, 3653
HSBC in the Community USA Inc. Foundation, NY, 6204
Hsin Hsin Private Foundation, CA, 689
HTR Foundation, Inc., FL, 2067
Hubbard Broadcasting Foundation, The, MN, 4590
Hubbard Family Foundation, Theodore F. and Claire M., The, NE, 4978
Hubbard Foundation, R. D. & Joan Dale, The, NM, 5481
Hubbard Foundation, The, MN, see 4590
Hubbell Foundation, Harvey, The, CT, 1569
Hubbell Foundation, James W. Hubbell, Jr. & Helen H., IA, 3297
Hubbell-Waterman Foundation, NE, 4979
Huber Foundation, The, NJ, 5244
Huberfeld Family Foundation, Inc., NY, 6205
Huberfeld-Bodner Family Foundation, Inc., NY, 6206
Hubert Charitable Trust, O. C., NC, 7401
Hudgens Family Foundation, Inc., GA, A
Hudson Foundation, Laura & Walter, MN, 4591
Hudson Foundation, M. R. & Evelyn, The, TX, 8962
Hudson River Bancorp, Inc. Foundation, NY, 6207
Hudson-Webber Foundation, MI, 4343
Huffington Foundation, TX, 8963
Hughes Charitable Trust, Mabel Y., CO, 1393
Hughes Family Foundation, Mark, CA, 690
Hughes Foundation, Inc., Geoffrey C., NY, 6208
Hughes Foundation, John C. & Karyl Kay, The, WA, 9610
Hughes Medical Institute, Howard, MD, 3654
Hughes Memorial Foundation, Inc., Charles Evans, The, NY, 6209
Hughes Trust, Teresa F., HI, 2548
Hugin Family Foundation, Inc., NJ, 5245
Hugoton Foundation, NY, 6210
Huie-Dellmon Trust, LA, 3488
Huisking Foundation, Inc., The, CT, 1570
Huizenga Family Foundation, FL, 2068
Huizenga Foundation, Elizabeth I., IL, A
Huizenga Foundation, IL, 2806
Hull Charitable Trust, Elizabeth A., TX, 8964
Hull Family Foundation, IL, 2807
Hull, Jr. Foundation, M. Blair, IL, see 2807
Hulme Charitable Foundation, Milton G., PA, 8260
Hultquist Foundation, Inc., NY, 6211
Humana Foundation, Inc., The, KY, 3428
Humanitas Foundation, The, NY, 6212
Humboldt Area Foundation, The, CA, 691
Hume Foundation, Jaquelin, CA, 692
Humphrey Fund, George M. and Pamela S., OH, 7679
Humphreys Foundation, J. P., MO, 4833
Humphreys Foundation, The, TX, 8965
Huncke Foundation, L. W., ND, 7515
Hunnicutt Foundation, Inc., H. P. and Anne S., The, WV, 9720
Hunt Alternatives Fund, The, MA, see 4174
Hunt Alternatives Fund, The, NY, see 6994
Hunt Family Foundation, The, TX, 8966
Hunt Foundation, Roy A., PA, 8261
Hunt Foundation, Samuel P., NH, 5093
Hunter Foundation, Perkins Malo, IL, 2808
Hunter Trust, Emily S. and Coleman A., FL, 2069
Hunter Trust, Inc., A. V., CO, 1394
Huntington Foundation, The, WV, 9721
Huntington Foundation, James, The, IL, 2809
Huntington Fund for Education, John, The, OH, 7680
Huntington Fund, Lawrence S., NY, 6213
Huntsman Family Foundation, NJ, 5246
Huntsman Foundation, Jon and Karen, The, UT, 9329
Huplits Foundation Trust, Myrtle V. C. Huplits & Woodman E., PA, 8262
Hurdus 1992 Charitable Trust, Syde, NY, 6214
Hurford Foundation, The, NY, 6215
Hurlbut Memorial Fund, Orion L. & Emma B., TN, 8692
Hurley Foundation, J. F., NC, 7402
Hurley-Trammell Foundation, The, NC, 7403
Hurst Family Foundation, NY, 6216
Hurst Foundation, Robert J., The, NY, see 6216
Hurst Foundation, The, MI, 4344
Huss Foundation, Alvin & Miriam, MN, see 4592
Huss Foundation, MN, 4592
Hussey Foundation, The, WA, 9611
Hussman Foundation, Inc., The, MD, 3655
Hussman Foundation, The, AR, 165

Huston Charitable Trust, Stewart, The, PA, 8263
Huston Foundation, The, PA, 8264
Hutchins Family Foundation, Inc., NY, 6217
Hutchins Foundation, Inc., Mary J., NY, 6218
Hutchinson Community Foundation, KS, 3368
Hutto-Patterson Charitable Foundation, CA, 693
Hutton Foundation, CA, 694
Hutton Foundation, Edward L., OH, 7681
Hux Family Charitable Trust, The, IN, 3170
Hyams Foundation, Inc., The, MA, 3961
Hyams Fund, Sarah A., MA, see 3961
Hyatt Foundation, IL, 2810
Hyde and Watson Foundation, The, NJ, 5247
Hyde Family Charitable Fund, The, WI, 9818
Hyde Family Foundations, TN, 8693
Hyde, Jr. Charitable Trust, Lawrence H., The, MA, 3962
Hyder Family Foundation, The, WA, 9612
Hylton Foundation, Inc., Cecil and Irene, The, VA, 9440

I and G Charitable Foundation, IL, 2811
I Have a Dream Foundation - New York, NY, 6219
IAC Foundation, The, NY, 6220
Iacocca Foundation, The, MA, 3963
IASD Health Care Foundation, The, IA, see 3343
IBJ Foundation, Inc., The, NY, see 6562
IBM International Foundation, NY, 6221
IBM South Africa Projects Fund, NY, see 6221
Icahn Charitable Foundation, The, NY, 6222
Icahn Family Foundation, The, NY, 6223
Icahn Foundation, Carl C., The, NY, 6224
ICN Foundation, MI, 4345
Idaho Community Foundation, ID, 2570
Iddings Benevolent Trust, OH, 7682
Iddings Foundation, OH, see 7682
Idema Foundation, Crawford, The, MA, see 3867
IDF Memorial Foundation, NY, 6225
IDT Charitable Foundation, The, NJ, 5248
IF Hummingbird Foundation, Inc., NY, 6226
IFF Foundation, Inc., The, NY, 6227
IFS Family Foundation, Inc., AZ, 109
IFSA Foundation, Inc., IN, 3171
IHS Foundation, OH, 7683
IIMI, Inc., NY, 6228
IKON Office Solutions Foundation, Inc., PA, 8265
Illges Foundation, Inc., John P. and Dorothy S., GA, 2416
Illinois Children's Healthcare Foundation, IL, 2812
Illinois Tool Works Foundation, IL, 2813
Imaca Education Foundation, TX, 8967
Imada Foundation, The, NJ, 5249
Imlay Foundation, Inc., The, GA, 2417
IMMI Word & Deed Foundation, Inc., IN, 3172
Inasmuch Foundation, OK, 7944
Inavale Foundation, Inc., MA, 3964
Independence Community Foundation, MO, see 4919
Independence Community Foundation, NY, 6229
Independence Foundation, PA, 8266
Indian Trail Charitable Foundation, Inc., NJ, 5250
Indiana Chemical Trust, IN, 3173
Indiana Energy Foundation, Inc., IN, see 3249
ING Foundation, GA, 2418
Ingalls Foundation, Inc., Louise H. and David S., The, OH, 7684
Ingold Family Foundation, CA, 695
Ingram Foundation, Martha and Bronson, TN, 8694
Ingram Trust, Joe, MO, 4834
Ingrassia Foundation, Elizabeth & Frank, NY, 6230
Initial Teaching Alphabet Foundation, NY, 6231
Initiative Foundation, MN, 4593
Inman-Riverdale Foundation, SC, 8595
Innisfree Foundation of Bryn Mawr, Pennsylvania, PA, 8267
Institute for Aegean Prehistory, The, PA, 8268
Institute for the Study of Aging, Inc., NY, 6232
Institute of Mental Hygiene of the City of New Orleans, LA, 3489
Integra Foundation, Inc., The, NJ, 5251
Intel Foundation, OR, 8022
Interbel Foundation, CA, A
Interco Inc. Charitable Trust, MO, 4835
Interdenominational Christian Missions, Inc., TX, 8968
Interlake Foundation, IL, see 2758
International Charities, Inc., The, CO, 1395

International Federation of Red Cross and Red Crescent Societies at the United Nations, Inc., NY, 6233
International Foundation, The, NJ, 5252
International Fund for Health & Family Planning, NY, 6234
International Paper Company Foundation, CT, 1571
International Shinto Foundation, Inc., NY, 6235
INTRUST Bank Charitable Trust, KS, 3369
Intuit Foundation, The, CA, 696
Iovino Family Foundation, The, NY, 6236
Iowa Realty Charitable Foundation, IA, see 3301
Iowa West Foundation, IA, 3298
Irby Foundation, Elizabeth M., MS, 4750
Iris Foundation, The, NY, 6237
Irmas Charitable Foundation, Audrey & Sydney, CA, 697
Irvine Foundation, James, The, CA, 698
Irvine Health Foundation, CA, 699
Irving Foundation, Inc., The, GA, 2419
Irwin Charity Foundation, William G., The, CA, 700
Irwin Family Foundation, IL, 2814
Irwin Financial Foundation, IN, 3174
Irwin-Sweeney-Miller Foundation, IN, 3175
Isaac Foundation, Moshe, The, NY, 6238
Isabel Foundation, The, MI, 4346
Iscol Family Foundation, Inc., The, NY, see 6226
Isdell Foundation, NY, 6239
ISE Cultural Foundation, Inc., MD, 3656
Isen Family Foundation, CA, 701
Isenberg Family Charitable Trust, The, FL, 2070
Isermann Family Foundation, Inc., NJ, 5253
ISGO Foundation, IL, see 2761
Ishiyama Foundation, The, CA, 702
Island Foundation, Inc., MA, 3965
Islands Fund, WA, 9613
Ispat Inland Foundation, Inc., IN, 3176
Israel Foundation, Inc., A. C., NY, 6240
Issa Family Foundation, CA, 703
Istock Foundation, Verne G. and Judith A., IL, 2815
It Takes a Family Foundation, Inc., CA, 704
ITT Rayonier Foundation, The, FL, see 2189
Ittleson Foundation, Inc., NY, 6241
Ivor Foundation, NY, 6242

J & AR Foundation, NY, 6243
J & L Foundation, The, KY, 3429
J G Foundation, The, NY, 6244
J.F.R. Foundation, OR, 8023
Jaaaa Foundation, The, NY, 6245
Jack in the Box Foundation, CA, 705
Jackson Charitable Trust, Daisy B., The, OK, 7945
Jackson Charitable Trust, John E. & Sue M., OH, 7685
Jackson Charitable Trust, Marion Gardner, RI, 8541
Jackson Charitable Trust, Ruth H., MA, 3966
Jackson Community Foundation, The, MI, see 4347
Jackson County Community Foundation, The, MI, 4347
Jackson Family Foundation, Ann, The, CA, 706
Jackson Foundation, Greater, MS, see 4737
Jackson Foundation, The, OR, 8024
Jackson Foundation, The, VA, 9441
Jackson Hole Preserve, Inc., NY, 6246
Jacksonville Jaguars Foundation, FL, 2071
Jacobs Engineering Foundation, CA, 707
Jacobs Family Foundation, Inc., CA, 708
Jacobs Foundation, David H. and Barbara M., The, OH, see 7605
Jacobson & Sons Foundation, Benjamin, The, NY, 6247
Jacobson Family Foundation, The, NY, 6248
Jacobson Family Trust Foundation, The, MA, 3967
Jacobson Foundation, Bernard H. and Blanche E., WV, 9722
Jacobson Foundation, Inc., Richard O., IA, 3299
Jacobus Family Foundation, Charles D., WI, 9819
Jacoff Foundation, Inc., Sydney & Helen, NY, 6249
Jaeger Foundation, LA, 3490
Jaeger Unruh Foundation, LA, see 3490
Jaffe Family Foundation, The, NY, 6250
Jaffe Foundation, Inc., Irving and Eleanor, FL, 2072
Jaharis Family Foundation, Inc., The, FL, 2073
Jahn Foundation, Reinhardt H. & Shirley R., IL, 2816
Jaindl Foundation, Fred J., PA, 8269
Jake Foundation, The, PA, 8270
JAM Anonymous Foundation, Inc., NY, 6251
Jamail Family Foundation, David & Sharon, TX, 8969

Jamail Foundation, Joseph D. and Lillie H., The, TX, 8970
James Family Charitable Foundation, The, NJ, 5254
James Family Foundation, CA, 709
James Foundation, Lawrence R. & Jeanette, NE, 4980
James Foundation, Robert & Ardis, NY, 6252
Jameson Foundation, J. W. and Ida M., CA, 710
Jams Foundation, CA, 711
Jandon Foundation, NY, 6253
Janesville Foundation, Inc., WI, 9820
Janeway Foundation, Elizabeth Bixby, CA, 712
Janey Fund Charitable Trust, The, MA, 3968
Jang Foundation, The, CA, 713
Janirve Foundation, NC, 7404
Janklow Foundation, NY, 6254
JANS Foundation, The, CA, 714
Janssen Foundation, Henry, PA, 8271
Janssen Ortho Patient Assistance Foundation, Inc., NJ, 5255
Janssen/Lagorio Family Foundation, The, CA, 715
Janus Foundation, The, CO, 1396
Jaqua Foundation, NJ, 5256
Jarson - Stanley & Mickey Kaplan Foundation, Isaac & Esther, OH, 7686
Jarson Charitable Trust, Isaac N. and Esther M., OH, see 7686
Jarx Foundation, Inc., The, NY, 6255
Jasam Foundation Fund B, AZ, 110
Jasam Foundation, Inc., FL, 2074
Jasper Foundation, Inc., IN, 3177
Jay Foundation, Adalyn, CA, 716
Jazzbird Foundation, The, AZ, 111
JBS Foundation, GA, 2420
JCK Foundation, Inc., GA, 2421
JCM Foundation, TN, see 8709
JCT Foundation, MI, 4348
JCT Foundation, NY, 6256
Jebediah Foundation, The, MA, 3969
JED Charitable Foundation, MA, see 3973
Jeffe Foundation, Robert A. & Elizabeth R., The, CT, 1572
Jeffers Foundation, MN, 4594
Jefferson Smurfit Charitable Corporation, MO, see 4906
Jefferson-Pilot Foundation, NC, 7405
Jeffery Charitable Trust, Clara L. D., NJ, 5257
Jeffress Memorial Trust, Thomas F. and Kate Miller, VA, 9442
Jeffris Family Foundation, Ltd., WI, 9821
Jeg's Quarter Mile Charities, OH, see 7687
Jegs Foundation, The, OH, 7687
Jehovah-Jireh Foundation, Inc., FL, 2075
JEHT Foundation, NY, 6257
Jeld-Wen Foundation, The, OR, 8025
Jeld-Wen, Wenco Foundation, OR, see 8025
Jelks Family Foundation, Inc., The, FL, 2076
Jenesis Group, TX, 8971
Jeniam Clarkson Foundation, The, TN, see 8695
Jeniam Foundation, The, TN, 8695
Jenkins Charitable Foundation, Victoria, NC, 7406
Jenkins Foundation, Inc., George W., FL, see 2180
Jenkins Foundation, Mervyn W., MO, 4836
Jennings Foundation, Martha Holden, The, OH, 7688
Jennings Foundation, Mary Hillman, The, PA, 8272
Jensam Foundation, Inc., NJ, 5258
Jensen Foundation, Janet Jarie, TX, see 8770
Jephson Educational Trust No. 2, NY, 6258
Jergens Foundation, Andrew, The, OH, 7689
Jerome Foundation, CA, 717
Jerome Foundation, MN, 4595
Jesselson Foundation, NY, 6259
Jet Foundation, The, NY, see 5925
Jewett Foundation, George Frederick, CA, 718
Jewish Foundation for Education of Women, NY, 6260
Jewish Foundation of Cincinnati, The, OH, 7690
Jewish Heritage Foundation of Greater Kansas City, MO, 4837
Jewish Renaissance Foundation, Inc., NY, 6261
JFM Foundation, The, CO, 1397
JG Foundation, CA, 719
JHJ Foundation, Inc., NJ, 5259
Jinks Foundation, Ruth T., GA, 2422
JKO Foundation Charitable Trust, The, WI, 9822
JKW Foundation, The, NY, 6262

JL Foundation, CA, 720
JM Foundation, The, NY, 6263
JM Freedom Foundation, IL, 2817
JMR Charities, Inc., IL, 2818
Jobst Foundation, Conrad & Caroline, OH, 7691
Jochum-Moll Foundation, The, OH, 7692
Jockey Club Foundation, The, NY, 6264
Jockey Hollow Foundation, Inc., The, NJ, 5260
Joco Foundation, The, VA, 9443
Joelson Foundation, The, NY, 6265
John Family Foundation, PA, 8273
John Foundation, B. P., Lester and Regina, OR, 8026
John Foundation, B. P., OR, see 8026
Johns Family Foundation, NM, 5482
Johnson & Johnson Family of Companies Contribution Fund, NJ, 5261
Johnson Art and Education Foundation, NJ, 5262
Johnson Charitable Foundation, Willard and Ruth, The, TX, 8972
Johnson Charitable Trust No. 33, 1994 Christopher W., The, NY, 6266
Johnson Charitable Trust, 1994 Elizabeth R., The, NY, 6267
Johnson Charitable Trust, Christopher W., The, NY, see 6266
Johnson Charitable Trust, George R., TN, see 8696
Johnson Controls Foundation, WI, 9823
Johnson County Community Foundation, Greater, IN, see 3178
Johnson County Community Foundation, Inc., IN, 3178
Johnson Endeavor Foundation, Christian A., NY, 6268
Johnson Family Foundation, George R., TN, 8696, 8697
Johnson Family Foundation, Inc., The, NY, 6269
Johnson Family Foundation, J. Stanley and Mary W., CA, 721
Johnson Family Foundation, Violet M., IL, 2819
Johnson Family Foundation, WI, 9824
Johnson Family Fund, The, DC, 1812
Johnson Foundation, Arthur L. & Elaine V., AZ, see 112
Johnson Foundation, Barbara Piasecka, NJ, 5263
Johnson Foundation, Burdine, The, TX, 8973
Johnson Foundation, Carl W., CA, 722
Johnson Foundation, Charles and Ann, CA, 723
Johnson Foundation, Franklin and Catherine, The, CA, 724
Johnson Foundation, Helen K. and Arthur E., CO, 1398
Johnson Foundation, Inc., Geron P., VA, see 9444
Johnson Foundation, Inc., Joyce and Seward, The, NJ, 5264
Johnson Foundation, Inc., Lester & Frances, WI, 9825
Johnson Foundation, Inc., M. G. and Lillie A., TX, 8974
Johnson Foundation, Inc., Sheila C., VA, 9444
Johnson Foundation, Inc., Willard T. C., NY, 6270
Johnson Foundation, Robert Wood, The, NJ, 5265
Johnson Foundation, Samuel S., The, OR, 8027
Johnson Foundation, Suzanne M. Nora Johnson and David G., NY, 6271
Johnson Foundation, The, MI, 4349
Johnson Foundation, The, NY, 6272
Johnson Foundation, Thomas Phillips and Jane Moore, The, PA, 8274
Johnson Foundation, Walter S., CA, 725
Johnson Fund, Edward C., MA, 3970
Johnson Fund, Inc., SC, WI, 9826
Johnson in Memory of Elaine V. Johnson Foundation, Arthur L. "Bud", AZ, 112
Johnson IV Charitable Trust, 1994 Robert W., The, NY, 6273
Johnson Memorial Trust, John Alfred & Oscar, PA, 8275
Johnson Scholarship Foundation, Inc., Theodore R. & Vivian M., FL, 2077
Johnson Wax Fund Inc., SC, WI, see 9826
Johnson, Jr. Foundation, Rupert H., CA, 726
Johnston Foundation, Inc., Willard, OK, see 7972
Johnston Trust for Charitable and Educational Purposes, James M., The, MD, 3657
Jolley Foundation, Leodelle Lassiter, GA, 2423
Jolley Foundation, The, NC, 7407
Jolson Family Foundation, CA, 727
Jonan Foundation, Inc., MD, 3658
Jonas Foundation, The, NJ, 5266
Jones & Co. Foundation, Edward D., The, MO, 4838
Jones Center for Families, Harvey and Bernice, AR, A

Jones Charitable Foundation Trust, Dennis & Judith, MO, see 4839
Jones Charitable Trust, Harvey and Bernice, The, AR, 166
Jones Family Charitable Foundation, Inc., The, KY, 3430
Jones Family Foundation, Dennis M., MO, 4839
Jones Family Foundation, Eugenie and Joseph, LA, 3491
Jones Family Foundation, Inc., Charles H., GA, 2424
Jones Family Foundation, Inc., Seby B., The, NC, 7408
Jones Family Foundation, Inc., The, WA, 9614
Jones Family Foundation, WI, 9827
Jones Foundation, Allan, TN, 8698
Jones Foundation, Daisy Marquis, NY, 6274
Jones Foundation, Emma Eccles, UT, 9330
Jones Foundation, Fletcher, The, CA, 728
Jones Foundation, Fred and Mary Eddy, OK, 7946
Jones Foundation, Herbert B., The, WA, 9615
Jones Foundation, Inc., Helen, TX, 8975
Jones Foundation, Inc., Scott A., The, IN, 3179
Jones Foundation, Inc., W. Alton, VA, see 9379
Jones Foundation, Joseph E. & Marjorie B., The, DC, 1813
Jones Foundation, The, CA, see 728
Jones Foundation, Walter S. and Evan C., KS, 3370
Jones Fund, Paul L., CT, 1573
Jones Testamentary Trust, Walter S. and Evan C., TX, 8976
Jonsson Family Foundation, Kenneth, CA, 729
Jonsson Foundation, Philip R., The, TX, 8977
Jordan Charitable Foundation, Mary Ranken Jordan and Ettie A., MO, 4840
Jordan Foundation, Arthur, IN, 3180
Jordan Foundation, Gerald R., The, MA, 3971
Jordan Foundation, Inc., The, GA, 2425
Jordan Foundation, K. H., TX, 8978
Joscelyn Foundation, Verla Nesbitt, KS, 3371
Joseloff Foundation, Inc., Morris, CT, see 1575
Joseph Foundation, Jim, The, CA, 730
Joshi Foundation, Krishan and Vicky, The, OH, 7693
Jostens Foundation, Inc., The, MN, 4596
Joukowsky Family Foundation, NY, 6275
Journal-Gazette Foundation, Inc., IN, 3181
Jovid Foundation, DC, 1814
Joy Family Foundation, CO, 1399
Joy Family Foundation, NY, 6276
Joy Global Foundation, Inc., WI, 9828
Joyard Foundation, The, CA, 731
Joyce Foundation, The, IL, 2820
JPMorgan Chase Foundation, The, NY, 6277
JSJN Children's Charitable Trust, MA, 3972
JSM Charitable Trust, The, MO, 4841
JSY Foundation, Inc., NJ, 5267
JTG Foundation, ME, 3542
Jubilee Foundation, The, OH, 7694
Jubitz Family Foundation, OR, 8028
Jubitz Foundation, Frederick D. & Gail Y., The, OR, 8029
Judkins Family Foundation, Don & Maxine, The, CA, 732
Julian Foundation, Robert and Carole, NE, 4981
June Foundation, The, CA, 733
Juniata Foundation, Inc., The, CA, 734
Jurodin Fund, Inc., DE, A
Jurries Family Foundation, Jim and Ginger, MI, 4350
Jurzykowski Foundation, Inc., Alfred, NY, 6278
Justice Charitable Foundation, Frank and Mattie, The, KY, 3431
Justin Foundation, Jane and John, TX, 8979
Justus Trust, Edith C., PA, 8276
JVM & JKM Foundation, GA, see 2322
JW & DW Charitable Foundation, Inc., NY, 6279
JW Foundation, The, NY, 6280
JWS Foundation, Inc., CA, 735
JYN Foundation, IL, 2821

K N Energy Foundation, CO, see 1403
K-Swiss Foundation, The, CA, see 190
K.L. Felicitas Foundation, CA, 736
Kabacoff Family Foundation, Lester E., LA, 3492
Kabcenell Family Foundation, CA, 737
Kade Foundation, Inc., Max, NY, 6281
Kadish Foundation, Halbert & Alice, WI, 9829
Kadrovach/Duckworth Family Foundation, NY, 6282
Kahle/Austin Foundation, CA, 738

Kahn Charitable Foundation, Fannie and Stephen, TX, 8980
Kahn Charitable Foundation, MA, 3973
Kahn Family Foundation, MI, see 4351
Kahn Foundation, D. Dan and Betty, The, MI, 4351
Kahn Testamentary Foundation, Robert J., The, PA, A
Kainz Family Foundation, IL, 2822
Kainz Foundation, Joseph A. & Susan J., IL, see 2822
Kaiser Family Foundation, Henry J., The, CA, 739
Kaiser Family Foundation, Inc., Louise and Gerald, The, NY, 6283
Kaiser Foundation, Betty and George, OK, 7947
Kaiser Foundation, Betty E. and George B., OK, see 7947
Kaiser Foundation, Herman G., OK, 7948
Kaiserman Foundation, Kevy K. & Hortense M., PA, 8277
Kalamazoo Community Foundation, MI, 4352
Kalamazoo Foundation, MI, see 4352
Kalberer Foundation, Walter and Jean, The, OH, 7695
Kaleidoscope Foundation, WA, 9616
Kalliopeia Foundation, The, CA, 740
Kalmanovitz Charitable Foundation, CA, 741
Kalter Foundation, Inc., Moshe and Frady, The, NY, 6284
Kaminer Foundation, NY, 6285
Kanas Family Foundation, John and Elaine, NY, 6286
Kanawha Valley Foundation, Greater, The, WV, 9723
Kandell Fund, The, NY, 6287
Kane Foundation, Inc., Eugene I., SC, 8596
Kanitz Scholarship Memorial Fund, Louis J. & Golda I., CA, 742
Kansas City Community Foundation and Affiliated Trusts, Greater, The, MO, see 4842
Kansas City Community Foundation, Greater, MO, 4842
Kansas Health Foundation, KS, 3372
Kansas Health Foundation/Kansas Health Trust, KS, see 3372
Kanter Family Foundation, VA, 9445
Kanzler Foundation, Ernest and Rosemarie, MI, 4353
Kaplan & Robert Fippinger Foundation, Ann F., The, NY, see 5531
Kaplan Charitable Foundation, Helen and Sam, KS, 3373
Kaplan Family Foundation, Inc., 1996 M. M., FL, 2078
Kaplan Family Foundation, Inc., Rita J. and Stanley H., NY, 6288
Kaplan Family Foundation, Mayer and Morris, IL, 2823
Kaplan Family Foundation, The, NC, see 7495
Kaplan Foundation, Charles I. & Mary, MD, 3659
Kaplan Foundation, IL, 2824
Kaplan Foundation, Inc., Lillian Jean, The, FL, 2079
Kaplan Foundation, Robert S., NY, 6289
Kaplan Foundation, The, OH, 7696
Kaplan Fund, Inc., J. M., The, NY, 6290
Kaplen Foundation, The, NJ, 5268
Kapoor Charitable Foundation, IL, see 2825
Kapoor Charitable Foundation, John and Editha, IL, 2825
Kapor Foundation, Mitchell, The, CA, 743
Karabots Foundation, The, PA, 8278
Karan-Weiss Foundation, The, NY, 6291
Karches Foundation, NY, 6292
Kardon Foundation, Samuel and Rebecca, PA, 8279
Karma Foundation, NJ, 5269
Karmazin Foundation, Mel, NY, 6293
Karp Family Foundation, MA, 3974
Karsh Family Foundation, The, CA, 744
Katcher Family Foundation, Inc., The, FL, 2080
Katten Muchin & Zavis Foundation, Inc., IL, see 2826
Katten Muchin Zavis Rosenman Foundation, Inc., IL, 2826
Katz Family Foundation, Harold, The, PA, 8280
Katz Family Foundation, Inc., Eleanor M. and Herbert D., The, FL, 2081
Katz Family Foundation, The, CA, 745
Katz Foundation, Howard & Holly, NY, see 6297
Katz Foundation, Inc., Ellen Philips Schwarzman, NY, 6294
Katz Foundation, Inc., Iris & Saul, The, NY, 6295
Katz Foundation, Inc., M. D., NJ, 5271
Katz Foundation, Jane and Robert, The, NY, 6296
Katz Foundation, NJ, 5270

Katz Foundation, The, NY, 6297
Katz Memorial Fund, Harry, PA, 8281
Katzen Foundation, Inc., Cyrus, VA, 9446
Katzenberg Foundation, Marilyn and Jeffrey, The, CA, 746
Katzenberger Foundation, Inc., The, NY, 6298
Kauffman Foundation, Ewing Marion, MO, 4843
Kauffman Foundation, Muriel McBrien, MO, 4844
Kauffmann Foundation, Inc., Fritz and Adelaide, The, NJ, 5272
Kaufman Americana Foundation, VA, 9447
Kaufman Charitable Foundation, Glorya, The, CA, 747
Kaufman Family Foundation, Ann & Stephen, The, TX, 8981
Kaufman Foundation, Inc., Henry & Elaine, FL, 2082
Kaufmann Foundation, Marion Esser, NY, 6299
Kaul Foundation, Hugh, The, AL, 40
Kaul Foundation, The, FL, 2083
Kautz Family Foundation, NY, 6300
Kavadas Foundation, The, CO, see 1400
Kavanagh Foundation, T. James, PA, 8282
Kavli Foundation, The, CA, 748
Kawasaki Good Times Foundation, NE, 4982
Kay Charitable Trust, Helen L., MI, 4354
Kay Family Foundation, Inc., The, MD, 3660
Kay Foundation, Helen L., MI, see 4354
Kaye Foundation, Danny Kaye and Sylvia Fine, DC, 1815
Kaylie Foundation, Inc., Harvey & Gloria, The, NY, 6301
Kayne Foundation, CA, 749
Kazickas Family Foundation, Inc., The, NY, 6302
Kazma Family Foundation, IL, 2827
KBK Foundation, The, CO, 1400
KBRK, Inc., NY, see 6394
KDK Charitable Trust, NJ, 5273
Kealy Family Foundation, NY, 6303
Kean Revocable Trust, Stewart B., NJ, 5274
Keane Family Foundation, MA, 3975
Kearns Foundation, William H., NY, 6304
Keasbey Memorial Fund, H. G. and A. G., NC, 7409
Keating Family Foundation, FL, 2084
Keck Foundation, W. M., CA, 750
Keck, Jr. Foundation, William M., CA, 751
Keefe Family Foundation, NY, 6305
Keel Foundation, The, MA, 3976
Keeler Charitable Trust, Ruth, NY, 6306
Keeler Foundation, Robert T., OH, 7697
Keeler Foundation, The, MI, 4355
Keeler Fund, Miner S. & Mary Ann, The, MI, see 4355
Keeneland Foundation, Inc., KY, 3432
Kegley Foundation, J. Henry, The, VA, 9448
Keiser Charitable Trust, Michael L. Keiser and Rosalind C., IL, 2828
Keith Foundation Trust, Ben E., TX, 8982
Keith Foundation, Greg and India, The, NC, 7410
Keithley Family Foundation, Roy and Cindy, TX, 8983
Kelben Foundation, Inc., WI, 9830
Kelco Foundation, Inc., FL, 2085
Kellar Family Foundation, The, VA, 9449
Kelleher Charitable Foundation, Denis P. and Carol A., The, NY, 6307
Kelleher Charitable Foundation, Joan and Herb, TX, 8984
Kellen Foundation, Inc., Anna Maria & Stephen, NY, 6308
Keller Family Foundation, IL, 2829
Keller Family Foundation, LA, 3493
Keller Foundation, George M. and Adelaide M., The, CA, 752
Keller Foundation, Inc., WI, 9831
Kellerman Foundation, Jonathan & Faye, CA, 753
Kelley Charitable Foundation, Boyd and Joan, The, TX, 8985
Kelley Charitable Trust, W. D., TX, see 8986
Kelley Family Foundation Trust, Lora L. & Martin N., OR, 8030
Kelley Foundation, Inc., Margaret H. and James E., MN, 4597
Kelley Foundation, W. D., TX, 8986
Kellman Foundation, IL, A
Kellner Foundation, The, NY, 6309
Kellogg Company 25-Year Employees Fund, Inc., MI, 4356
Kellogg Family Foundation, Inc., The, WI, 9832

Kellogg Foundation, Inc., J. C., NY, 6310
Kellogg Foundation, Peter R. & Cynthia K., NY, 6311
Kellogg Foundation, W. K., MI, 4357
Kellogg's Corporate Citizenship Fund, MI, 4358
Kellwood Foundation, The, MO, 4845
Kelly Foundation, Donald P. and Byrd M., IL, 2830
Kelly Foundation, Inc., Ellsworth, NY, 6312
Kelly Foundation, Inc., FL, 2086
Kelly Foundation, Paul E., PA, 8283
Kelly Services, Inc. Foundation, The, MI, 4359
Kelsey Foundation, Forest C. & Ruth V., The, WA, 9617
Kemmerer Family Foundation, Inc., The, NJ, 5275
Kemper Charitable Trust, R. C., MO, 4846
Kemper Charitable Trust, William T., MO, 4847
Kemper Educational and Charitable Fund, IL, 2831
Kemper Foundation, Enid and Crosby, MO, 4848
Kemper Foundation, James S., IL, 2832
Kemper Foundation, William T., MO, 4849
Kemper Memorial Foundation, David Woods, MO, 4850
Kempner Fund, Inc., Harris and Eliza, TX, 8987
Kempner, Jr. Foundation, Thomas L., NY, 6313
Kenan, Jr. Fund for Engineering, Technology and Science, William R., The, NC, 7411
Kenan, Jr. Fund for the Arts, William R., NC, 7412
Kenan, Jr. Fund, William R., The, NC, 7413
Kendall Foundation, George R., The, IL, 2833
Kendall Foundation, Henry P., The, MA, 3977
Kennametal Foundation, PA, 8284
Kennebec Foundation, ME, see 3543
Kennebec Savings Bank Foundation, ME, 3543
Kennebunk Savings Bank Foundation, ME, 3544
Kennedy Charitable Trust, George D. Kennedy & Valerie P., IL, 2834
Kennedy Family Foundation, Inc., Ethel & W. George, The, FL, 2087
Kennedy Family Foundation, John C. & Nancy G., MI, 4360
Kennedy Foundation, Dr. and Mrs. Hugh A., TX, 8988
Kennedy Foundation, Ethel, FL, 2088
Kennedy Foundation, Inc., John R., The, FL, 2089
Kennedy Foundation, Inc., Quentin J., NJ, 5276
Kennedy Foundation, Karen A. & Kevin W., NY, 6314
Kennedy, Jr. Foundation, Joseph P., The, DC, 1816
Kenney Watershed Protection Foundation, William C., The, CO, 1401
Kenny's Kids, IL, 2835
Kenosha Community Foundation, WI, 9833
Kensington Square Foundation, The, IL, 2836
Kent Foundation, Inc., Ada Howe, The, DE, 1723
Kent-Stein Foundation, IA, see 3318
Kentucky Fund for Healthy Living, Inc., KY, 3433
Kenworthy - Sarah H. Swift Foundation, Inc., Marion E., NY, 6315
Keough Foundation, Donald and Marilyn, GA, 2426
Keough Foundation, Donald R., GA, see 2426
Keown Charitable Foundation, The, TX, 8989
Keren Eliyahu, Inc., NY, 6316
Keren Keshet - The Rainbow Foundation, NY, 6317
Keren Yitzchak Foundation, Inc., The, NJ, 5277
Keren Zichron Aron Foundation, The, NY, 6318
Kern Family Foundation, CO, 1402
Kern Family Foundation, Inc., The, WI, 9834
Kern Foundation Trust, IL, 2837
Kerr Family Foundation, Inc., Robert S. and Grayce B., The, WY, 9983
Kerr Foundation, Inc., The, OK, 7949
Kerr Foundation, William A., The, NJ, 5278
Kerr Fund, Inc., Grayce B., MD, 3661
Kerr-McGee Corporation Foundation, OK, see 7950
Kerr-McGee Corporation, OK, 7950
Kerrville Area Community Trust, TX, see 8842
Kersten Family Foundation, IL, 2838
Keshet Foundation, NY, 6319
Kesler Foundation, Inc., Delores Pass, The, FL, 2090
Kessler Family Foundation, MA, 3978
Kest Family Foundation, Sol and Clara, CA, 754
Kettering Family Foundation, The, OH, 7698
Kettering Foundation, Virginia W., The, WI, 9835
Kettering Fund, The, OH, 7699
Key Foundation, OH, 7700
Keyser Foundation, Robert S. & Dorothy J., The, NV, 5039
KeySpan Foundation, The, NY, 6320

Keystone Nazareth Charitable Foundation, PA, 8285
Keystone Savings Foundation, PA, 8286
KFFH, Inc., TX, 8990
Khachaturian Foundation, CA, 755
Khesed Foundation, IL, 2839
Khudari Foundation, The, MA, A
Kibble Family Foundation, CA, 756
Kidder 1996 Charitable Trust, Michael R., MA, 3979
Kidney Care, Inc., MS, see 4736
Kids Care for the Planet Earth, CA, 757
Kieckhefer Foundation, J. W., AZ, 113
Kiernan Foundation, Peter and Eaddo, The, NY, 6321
Kiewit Companies Foundation, NE, 4983
Kiewit Foundation, Peter, NE, 4984
Kiewit Sons', Inc. Foundation, Peter, The, NE, see 4983
Kikkoman Foods Foundation, Inc., WI, 9836
Kilbourne Residuary Charitable Trust, E. H., NE, 4985
Killam Trust, Constance, MA, 3980
Killinger Foundation, Kerry and Linda, The, WA, 9618
Kilroy Foundation, William S. & Lora Jean, TX, 8991
Kim Family Foundation, Steve and Robin, CA, 758
Kim Foundation, Inc., James & Agnes, The, PA, 8287
Kimball Foundation, Horace A. Kimball and S. Ella, RI, 8542
Kimball Foundation, Sara H. and William R., CA, see 759
Kimball Foundation, The, CA, 759
Kimball International—Habig Foundation, Inc., The, IN, 3182
Kimberly-Clark Foundation, Inc., TX, 8992
Kimerling Foundation, Inc., The, AL, 41
Kimmel Foundation, Helen & Martin, The, NY, A
Kimmel Foundation, Inc., Edward & Lucille, The, FL, 2091
Kimmel Foundation, Sidney, The, PA, 8288
Kimmell Family Foundation, OK, 7951
Kimmelman Family Foundation, The, NY, 6322
Kimsey Foundation, DC, 1817
Kincaid Foundation, The, TX, 8993
Kind Family Foundation, Patricia, PA, 8289
Kind World Foundation, The, NM, 5483
Kinder Foundation, Inc., Richard D., TX, see 8994
Kinder Foundation, TX, 8994
Kinder Morgan Foundation, CO, 1403
Kindred Foundation Inc., KY, 3434
King Educational Trust, William Toben, MO, 4851
King Family Foundation, Inc., Charles & Lucille, NY, 6323
King Family Foundation, Jena & Michael, The, CA, 760
King Farm Worker Fund, Martin Luther, CA, see 376
King Foundation, Carl B. and Florence E., TX, 8995
King Foundation, Gioconda & Joseph H., NY, 6324
King Foundation, Inc., Stephen and Tabitha, ME, 3545
King Foundation, Kenneth Kendal, CO, 1404
King Street Charitable Trust, The, NY, 6325
King Trust, Charles A., MA, 3981
Kingdon Fund, Mark and Anla Cheng, NY, 6326
Kings Grant Foundation, RI, 8543
Kings Piont Richmond Foundation, Inc., NY, see 6801
Kingsbury Road Charitable Foundation, MA, 3982
Kingsley Foundation, Lewis A., CA, 761
Kingsley Foundation, The, DE, 1724
Kington Foundation, Inc., The, VA, 9450
Kinney-Lindstrom Foundation, Inc., IA, 3300
Kinsley Family Foundation, PA, 8290
Kinsman Foundation, OR, 8031
Kiplinger Foundation, The, DC, 1818
Kipper Family Foundation, The, IL, 2840
Kirbo Charitable Trust, Thomas M. and Irene B., The, FL, 2092
Kirby Foundation, Inc., F. M., NJ, 5279
Kirby, Jr. Foundation, Inc., A. P., NJ, 5280
Kirchgessner Foundation, Karl, The, CA, 762
Kirkland Foundation, Robert E. and Jenny D., TN, 8699
Kirkpatrick Foundation, Inc., OK, 7952
Kirkwood Family Foundation, CA, see 275
Kirlin Foundation, WA, A
Kislak Foundation, Inc., Jay I., FL, 2093
Kissick Family Foundation, CA, 763
Kitchings Foundation, Chester W., The, CT, 1574
Kitov Foundation, NY, 6327
Kittredge Foundation, The, MA, 3983
Kitzmiller-Bales Trust, CO, 1405
Kiva Foundation, The, MA, 3984

Kiwanis Club of Bradenton Foundation, Inc., FL, 2094
Kiwanis of Michigan Foundation, MI, 4361
Klabzuba Family Foundation, The, TX, 8996
Klapper Family Foundation, Inc., The, IN, 3183
Klarman Family Foundation, MA, 3985
Klarman Foundation, Seth A. & Beth S., The, MA, see 3985
Klaus Family Foundation, Inc., NY, 6328
KLE Foundation, The, TX, 8997
Kleberg Foundation for Wildlife Conservation, Caesar, TX, 8998
Kleberg Foundation, Robert J. Kleberg, Jr. and Helen C., TX, 8999
Klee Foundation, Inc., Conrad and Virginia, The, NY, 6329
Klein Charitable Foundation, Raymond, PA, 8291
Klein Charitable Foundation, Reb Ephraim Chaim & Miriam Rochel, The, NY, 6330
Klein Family Foundation, Inc., Julia & Isadore, KY, see 3435
Klein Family Foundation, Inc., The, KY, 3435
Klein Family Foundation, Lloyd E. Elisabeth, CA, 764
Klein Family Foundation, NY, 6331
Klein Foundation, George & Adele, NY, 6332
Klein Foundation, Inc., Ralph and Shirley, The, MD, 3662
Klein Foundation, Inc., Ruth & Seymour, NY, 6333
Klein Foundation, Jane P. & Charles D., NY, see 6543
Klein, Jr. Foundation, David L., CA, 765
Klein, Jr. Memorial Foundation, Inc., David L., CA, see 765
Kleinman Family Foundation, The, NY, 6334
Kleissner Family Foundation, CA, see 736
Kleist Foundation, Inc., Peter D. & Eleanore A., The, FL, 2095
Kline Foundation, Charles and Figa, PA, 8292
Kline Foundation, Inc., Josiah W. and Bessie H., PA, 8293
Kling Family Foundation, The, CA, 766
Klingenstein Family Fund, Inc., Andrew & Julie, NY, 6335
Klingenstein Fund, Frederick & Sharon, NY, 6337
Klingenstein Fund, Inc., Esther A. & Joseph, The, NY, 6338
Klingenstein Fund, John & Patricia, NY, 6339
Klingenstein Fund, NY, 6336
Klingenstein Third Generation Foundation, The, NY, 6340
KLM Foundation, CA, 767
Klorfine Foundation, WA, 9619
Klosk Foundation, Lawrence, NY, see 6167
Kluge Foundation, John W., The, MD, 3663
Kluge Foundation, Patricia M., The, VA, see 9451
Kluge-Moses Foundation, The, VA, 9451
KMD Foundation, FL, 2096
Knabusch Charitable Trust No. 1, Edward M. and Henrietta M., MI, 4362
Knabusch Charitable Trust No. 2, Edward M. and Henrietta M., MI, 4363
Knafel Family Foundation, NY, 6341
Knapp Charitable Foundation, Jules and Gwen, The, IL, 2841
Knapp Charitable Foundation, William C., IA, 3301
Knapp Educational Fund, Inc., MD, 3664
Knapp Foundation, Inc., The, MD, 3665
Knapp-Swezey Foundation, Inc., NY, 6342
Knez Family Charitable Foundation, MA, 3986
Knight Charitable Foundation, Norman, MA, 3987
Knight Foundation, FL, see 2097
Knight Foundation, Inc., Faith & James, NJ, 5281
Knight Foundation, James A. and Faith, MI, 4364
Knight Foundation, John S. and James L., FL, 2097
Knight Foundation, OR, 8032
Knight-Ridder Fund, Inc., CA, see 768
Knight-Ridder, Inc. Fund, The, CA, 768
Knistrom Foundation, Fanny and Svante, NJ, 5282
Knopf Foundation, Max & Rika, NY, 6343
Knossos Foundation, Inc., The, NY, 6344
Knott Foundation, Inc., Marion I. and Henry J., The, MD, 3666
Knott Foundation, Marion, CA, 769
Knowles Foundation, Inc., Janet H. and C. Harry, NJ, 5283

Knowles Trust B, Leonora H., OH, 7701
Knowlton Foundation, The, MN, 4598
Knox Family Foundation, PA, 8294
Knox Foundation, Seymour H., The, NY, 6345
Knox Foundation, The, GA, 2427
Knox Private Foundation, Winifred H., IL, 2842
Knudsen Charitable Foundation, Earl, OH, 7702
Kobren Family Charitable Trust, The, MA, 3988
Koch Charitable Foundation, Charles G., DC, 1819
Koch Foundation, Fred C., The, KS, see 3374
Koch Foundation, Inc., FL, 2098
Koch Foundation, Inc., Fred C. and Mary R., The, KS, 3374
Koch Foundation, Inc., IN, 3184
Koch Sons Foundation, Inc., George, IN, see 3184
Kodosky Foundation, The, TX, 9000
Koehler Foundation, Marcia & Otto, TX, 9001
Koenig Foundation, Bradford & Lauren, The, CA, 770
Kogan Foundation, MI, 4365
Kogod Family Foundation, Robert P. and Arlene R., The, VA, 9452
Koguan Foundation, Leo, The, NJ, 5284
Kohl Charitable Foundation, Inc., Allen D., CA, 771
Kohl Charities, Inc., Herbert H., WI, 9837
Kohl Educational Foundation, Herb, WI, 9838
Kohl Foundation, Inc., Sidney, FL, 2099
Kohlberg Foundation, Inc., The, NY, 6346
Kohler Charitable Trust, Charlotte & Walter, WI, 9839
Kohler Foundation, Inc., WI, 9840
Kohn-Joseloff Foundation, Inc., CT, 1575
Kolatch Family Foundation, NJ, 5285
Kolschowsky Foundation, Inc., Gerald A. & Karen A., IL, 2843
Komansky Foundation, Inc., The, NY, 6347
Kommerstad Foundation, The, CA, 772
Kongsgaard-Goldman Foundation, WA, 9620
Kontos Foundation, Inc., Arthur, The, NJ, 5286
Koontz Foundation, Dean & Gerda, CA, 773
Kopf Family Foundation, NY, 6348
Kopf Foundation, Inc., NY, see 6348
Kopp Family Foundation, MN, 4599
Koppel Family Charitable Foundation, MD, 3667
Koppelman Family Foundation, The, NY, 6349
Koran Trust, Ida C., MN, 4600
Korein Charitable Trust, Sarah & Isidor, PA, see 8295
Korein Foundation, The, PA, 8295
Koret Foundation, CA, 774
Koret Fund, CA, 775
Korman Family Foundation, Hyman, PA, 8296
Kornfeld Foundation, Emily Davie and Joseph S., NY, 6350
Kornwasser Foundation, Jacob, CA, 776
Kosar Charitable Trust, Bernie J., OH, 7703
Kosasa Foundation, The, HI, 2549
Kosciusko 21st Century Foundation, Inc., IN, 3185
Kosciusko County Community Foundation, Inc., IN, 3186
Koshland Foundation, The, CA, 777
Kossak Foundation, Inc., John & Evelyn, CT, 1576
Koulaieff Educational Fund, Trustees of Ivan V., The, CA, 778
Kovler Family Foundation, IL, 2844
Kovner Foundation, The, NJ, 5287
KPB Corporation, NC, 7414
KPMG Foundation, The, NJ, 5288
KPMG Peat Marwick Foundation, The, NJ, see 5288
Krach Family Foundation, CA, 779
Kraft and J. Hiatt Foundation, Inc., Robert and Myra, MA, see 3989
Kraft Family Foundation, Inc., Robert and Myra, MA, 3989
Kraft Foods Fund, NY, 6351
Kramer Charitable Foundation, Arthur B. and Alice, The, CT, 1577
Kramer Charitable Foundation, Milton A. and Charlotte R., OH, 7704
Kramer Foundation, Inc., C. L. C., FL, 2100
Kratka Foundation, Inc., NJ, A
Kraus Family Foundation, The, NY, 6352
Krause Family Foundation, WI, 9841
Krause Foundation, Charles A., WI, see 9841
Krause Foundation, Inc., WI, 9842
Krause Foundation, The, CA, 780

Krause Gentle Foundation, IA, 3302
Krauss Charitable Foundation, Jenny H. & Otto F., MI, 4366
Krauss, Miller, Lutz Charitable Trust Foundation, Inc., FL, 2101
Kravis Foundation, Inc., Henry R., NY, 6354
Kravis Foundation, Raymond and Bessie, The, NY, 6353
Kravis Foundation, Robert Kravis and Kimberly, The, NY, 6355
Krehbiel Family Foundation, IL, A, 2845
Kreielsheimer Remainder Foundation, WA, 9621
Kreindler Foundation, Lee S., The, NY, 6356
Kreitchman Family Foundation, Inc., The, NJ, 5289
Krejci Trust, Helen and Rudy, WI, 9843
Kresge Foundation, The, MI, 4367
Kress Charities, Inc., George, The, WI, 9844
Kress Foundation, Samuel H., NY, 6357
Krieble Foundation, Inc., Vernon K., The, MA, 3990
Krieger Charitable Trust, NJ, 5290
Krieger Family Foundation, Inc., Abraham and Ruth, The, MD, 3668
Krieger Fund, Inc., The, MD, see 3668
Kriendler Charitable Trust, Jeannette & H. Peter, The, NY, 6358
Krimendahl II Foundation, H. Frederick, The, NY, 6359
Kroger Co. Foundation, The, OH, 7705
Krongard Foundation, Inc., MD, 3669
Kronkosky Charitable Foundation, Albert & Bessie Mae, TX, 9002
Krueck Foundation, Anstiss & Ronald, The, IL, 2846
Krueger Scholarship, Dale, OR, 8033
Kruidenier Charitable Foundation, Inc., IA, 3303
Krupp Family Charitable Foundation, Judith & Douglas, The, MA, 3991
KSM Foundation, NJ, see 5133
Kuflik Charitable Foundation, Mitchell and Karen, NY, 6360
Kuhne Foundation Trust, Charles W., IN, 3187
Kulas Foundation, OH, 7706
Kulynych Family Foundation I, Inc., NC, 7415
Kulynych Family Foundation II, Inc., NC, 7416
Kulynych Foundation, Inc., Petro, NC, see 7415
Kumble Foundation, The, NY, 6361
Kunkel Foundation, John Crain, PA, 8297
Kunstadter Family Foundation, Albert, The, NY, 6362
Kupferberg Foundation, The, NY, 6363
Kurr Foundation, The, NJ, 5291
Kurth, Jr. Charitable Foundation, Ernest L., TX, 9003
Kurtz Family Foundation, Inc., The, NY, 6364
Kurz Family Foundation, Ltd., The, NY, 6365
Kushner Charitable Foundation, Charles and Seryl, NJ, A
Kuyper Foundation, Peter H. and E. Lucille Gaass, IA, 3304
Kvamme Foundation, Jean & E. Floyd, The, CA, 781

L & H Family Foundation, NY, see 6225
L & S Foundation, MD, see 3660
L and L Foundation, NY, 6366
L'Maan Ameinu Foundation, Inc., NY, 6367
L. & L. Foundation, NY, 6368
L. Family Foundation, The, NJ, see 5298
L.A.W. Foundation, Inc., The, NJ, 5292
L.and S. Milken Foundation, CA, see 897
La Crosse Community Foundation, WI, 9845
La Crosse Foundation, WI, see 9845
La Fetra Foundation, The, CA, 782
La Vea Charitable Foundation, James Annenberg, PA, 8298
La Vida Foundation, NM, see 5482
La-Z-Boy Chair Foundation, MI, see 4368
La-Z-Boy Foundation, MI, 4368
Labovitz Foundation, Sharon and Joel, MN, 4601
Lachimi Foundation, The, MI, 4369
Laclede Gas Charitable Trust, MO, 4852
Ladane Foundation, Ltd., The, NC, 7417
Ladd Charitable Corporation, Helen & George, MA, 3992
Ladenburg Foundation, NY, 6369
Ladish Company Foundation, WI, 9846
Ladish Family Foundation, Inc., Herman W., WI, 9847
Ladner Family Foundation, Frank S. and Julia M., KY, 3436
Lafayette Community Foundation, Greater, IN, 3188

Levine Charitable Foundation, Kenneth and Rachel, The, MA, see 4003
Levine Charitable Fund, Inc., Laurence, FL, 2111
Levine Charitable Trust, Caroline C., NH, 5094
Levine Family Charitable Trust, The, MA, 4004
Levine Family Foundation, Hyman, CA, 809
Levine Family Foundation, Mildred & Abner, FL, 2112
Levine Foundation, Inc., A. L., The, FL, 2113
Levine Foundation, Inc., Blanche & A. L., FL, see 2113
Levine Foundation, Inc., Laurence W., NY, 6408
Levine Foundation, Leon, The, NC, 7421
Levine Foundation, William S. and Ina, AZ, 115
Levinson Foundation, Max and Anna, NM, 5486
Levis Family Foundation, Adolph and Rose, The, PA, 8309
Levis Trust, PA, 8310
Levit Family Foundation, Joe, TX, 9009
Levitt Foundation, Inc., Mortimer, NJ, 5305
Levitt Foundation, Madelyn M., IA, 3307
Levitt Foundation, NY, 6409
Levitt Foundation, Richard S., MD, see 3676
Levitt Foundation, The, MD, 3676
Levy Family Foundation, Inc., Ken and Laurie, The, NJ, 5306
Levy Family Foundation, Paul and Karen, The, NY, 6410
Levy Foundation, Chas. and Ruth, IL, see 2840
Levy Foundation, Edward C., MI, see 4378
Levy Foundation, Frances and Jack, NY, 6411
Levy Foundation, Inc., Betty & Norman F., The, NY, 6412
Levy Foundation, Inc., June Rockwell, MA, 4005
Levy Foundation, Inc., Shuki, CA, 810
Levy Foundation, Jerome, NY, 6413
Levy Foundation, Leon, NY, 6414
Levy, Jr. Foundation, Carole & Joseph, The, IL, 2856
Levy, Jr. Foundation, Julie & Edward, MI, 4378
Lewis Charitable Foundation, Martin R., The, NY, 6415
Lewis Family Foundation, Richard H., CO, 1410
Lewis Foundation, Inc., Dorothy V. & Logan, GA, 2433
Lewis Foundation, Inc., Dorothy V. & N. Logan, GA, see 2433
Lewis Foundation, Inc., Frank J., FL, 2114
Lewis Foundation, Inc., J. C., GA, 2434
Lewis Foundation, Inc., Reginald F., NY, 6416
Lewis Foundation, Phoebe R. & John D., WI, 9850
Lewis Foundation, T. W., AZ, 116
Lewis Foundation, The, OH, 7713
Lewis-Sebring Family Foundation, IL, 2857
Lexington Community Foundation, NE, 4986
LG&E Energy Foundation, Inc., KY, see 3417
LGR Charitable Trust, KS, see 3385
LGR Foundation, NY, 6417
Li Foundation, Inc., The, NY, 6418
Libby-Dufour Fund, LA, 3494
Liberman Foundation, Inc., Bertha & Isaac, NY, 6419
Liberty Bank Foundation, Inc., CT, 1586
Liberty Corporation Foundation, SC, 8597
Liberty Mutual Foundation, Inc., The, MA, 4006
Libra Foundation, Inc., FL, 2115
Libra Foundation, ME, 3546
Libra Foundation, The, IL, 2858
Lichtenstein Foundation, David B., MO, 4855
Lichtenstein Foundation, MO, see 4855
Lichtenstein, Jr. Foundation, Morris L., The, TX, 9010
Licking County Foundation, OH, 7714
Lidow Foundation, CA, 811
Lie Foundation, Gunnar and Ruth, The, WA, 9629
Lieb Foundation, Inc., David L., NY, 6420
Liebmann Fund, Dolores Zohrab, The, NY, 6421
Lied Foundation Trust, NV, 5041
Life Enrichment Foundation, WY, see 9982
Life Sciences Research Foundation, MD, 3677
Life's Requite, Inc., FL, 2116
Lifestyle Homes Foundation, NV, 5042
LifeWorks Foundation, TN, 8701
Light Charitable Trust, Jack H. & William M., TX, 9011
Light Foundation, Inc., The, FL, 2117
Lightfoot Foundation, E. L. & B. G., The, OR, 8036
Lightner Sams Foundation, Inc., TX, 9012
Lilliput Foundation, PA, 8311
Lilly and Company Foundation, Eli, IN, 3192
Lilly Cares Foundation, Inc., IN, 3193
Lilly Endowment Inc., IN, 3194
Lilly Foundation, Richard Coyle, MN, 4606

Liman Foundation, Inc., The, NY, 6422
Lincoln Community Foundation, Inc., NE, 4987
Lincoln Electric Foundation, The, OH, 7715
Lincoln Financial Group Foundation, IN, 3195
Lincoln Foundation, Inc., NE, see 4987
Lincoln Fund, The, NY, 6423
Lincoln National Foundation, Inc., The, IN, see 3195
Lincoln-Lane Foundation, The, VA, 9458
Lincy Foundation, The, CA, 812
Lindahl Foundation, TCH, TN, 8702
Lindback Foundation, Christian R. and Mary F., PA, see 8312
Lindback Foundation, The, PA, 8312
Linde Family Charitable Trust, MA, see 4007
Linde Family Foundation, MA, 4007
Linde Foundation, Ronald and Maxine, The, AZ, 117
Linden Family Foundation, Lawrence and Dana, NY, 6424
Linden Foundation, Inc., The, MA, 4008
Linden Root Dickinson Foundation, CA, 813
Lindmor Foundation, The, NY, 6425
Lindner Foundation, Carl H. and Edyth B., The, OH, 7716
Lindner Foundation, Carl H., OH, see 7716
Lindner Foundation, Fay J., The, NY, 6426
Lindner Foundation, Robert D., OH, 7717
Lindorf Memorial Foundation, Bruce, CA, 814
Lindsay Family Foundation, Robert and Teresa, NY, 6427
Lindsay Foundation-1989, Margaret Stewart, The, MA, 4009
Lindsay Trust, Agnes M., NH, 5095
Lindsey Family Foundation, James and Joan, The, CA, 815
Linebery Foundation, Tom & Evelyn, TX, see 9171
Linehan Family Foundation, Inc., MD, 3678
Lingnan Foundation, CT, 1587
Lingnan University, Trustees of, CT, see 1587
Liniger Family Foundation, The, CO, 1411
Link Foundation, The, NY, 6428
Link Foundation, The, TX, 9013
Link, Jr. Charitable Trust, George, The, NJ, 5307
Link, Jr. Foundation, Inc., George, NY, 6429
Linnell Foundation, NH, 5096
Linsey Foundation, Joseph M. and Thelma, MA, 4010
Linsey Foundation, Joseph M., MA, see 4010
Lintilhac Foundation, VT, 9359
Lion Foundation, Albert & Gloria, The, MD, see 3669
Lipchitz Foundation, Inc., Jacques and Yulla, NY, 6430
Lipinsky Family Foundation, CA, 816
Lipinsky Foundation, Bernard and Dorris, CA, see 816
Lipman Family Foundation, Inc., The, CA, 817
Lipman Foundation, Eric and Jeanette, The, VA, see 9459
Lipman Foundation, Inc., Howard and Jean, CA, see 817
Lipman Foundation, The, VA, 9459
Lipmanson Foundation, Inc., Margaret & Richard, NY, 6431
Lipp Family Foundation, The, CA, 818
Lipp Foundation, Inc., Bari, The, NY, 6432
Lipper Family Charitable Foundation, The, NJ, 5308
Lipper Foundation, Kenneth & Evelyn, The, NY, see 6116
Lippitt Foundation, Katherine Kenyon, The, OH, 7718
Lippman Family Foundation, Jerome, OH, see 7719
Lippman Kanfer Family Foundation, OH, 7719
Lipscomb Family Foundation, SC, 8598
Lisabeth Foundation, The, NY, 6433
Lissak Foundation, Inc., The, NJ, 5309
Listwin Family Foundation, The, CA, 819
Littauer Educational Trust, Helen Irwin, TX, 9014
Littauer Foundation, Inc., Lucius N., The, NY, 6434
Litterman Family Foundation, The, NY, 6435
Litterman Foundation, Robert & Mary, The, NY, see 6435
Little Angel Foundation, IL, 2859
Little Angel Perpetual Charitable Trust, IL, see 2859
Little Family Foundation, Inc., The, MD, 3679
Little Family Foundation, The, PA, 8313
Little Foundation, Inc., W. Paul & Lucille Caudill, The, KY, 3437
Littlefield Foundation, Edmund and Jeannik, CA, 820
Littlefield Foundation, Edmund Wattis, CA, see 820
Littlefield Memorial Trust, Ida Ballou, RI, 8544

LittleJohn Family Foundation, The, CT, 1588
Littler Trust, Stephen, MO, A
Litwin Foundation, Inc., The, NY, 6436
Litzsinger Road Ecology Foundation, MO, 4856
Liu Foundation, The, NY, 6437
Live Oak Foundation, LA, 3495
Living Stones Foundation, CA, 821
Livingston Foundation, Inc., GA, 2435
Livingston Memorial Foundation, CA, 822
Livingstone Charitable Foundation, Inc., Betty J. and J. Stanley, The, NC, 7422
LKC Foundation, OH, 7720
Lloyd Charitable Trust, Harry J., KS, 3375
Lloyd Foundation, John M., The, CA, 823
LLWW Foundation, CA, 824
Lochland Foundation, The, WA, 9630
Locke Family Foundation, Inc., The, MD, 3680
Lockhart Vaughan Foundation, Inc., MD, 3681
Lockheed Martin Corporation Foundation, MD, 3682
Lockheed Martin Missiles and Fire Control Employee Charity Fund, TX, 9015
Lockheed Martin Vought Systems Employee Charity Fund, TX, see 9015
Lockport Savings Bank Foundation, NY, see 5958
Lockton Family Foundation, MO, 4857
Lockwood Family Foundation, UT, 9333
Lockwood Foundation, Byron W. and Alice L., WA, 9631
Loeb - Third Point Foundation, Daniel S., NY, 6438
Loeb Foundation, Inc., Arthur L., NY, 6439
Loeb Foundation, Inc., Jesse & Rose, The, VA, 9460
Loeb Foundation, OH, 7721
Loeb, Jr. Foundation, John L., NY, 6440
Loebs Family Foundation, The, MA, 4011
Loewe Foundation, Inc., Frederick, NY, 6441
Loewenberg Foundation, Inc., NY, 6442
Loews Foundation, NY, 6443
Loewy Family Foundation, Inc., The, NY, 6444
Logan Foundation, Reva and David, IL, 2860
Lone Pine Foundation, Inc., CT, 1589
Long Bay Charitable Foundation, The, NJ, 5310
Long Foundation, CA, see 825
Long Foundation, George A. and Grace L., CT, 1590
Long Foundation, Inc., John F., AZ, 118
Long Foundation, J. M., The, CA, 825
Long Foundation, R. A., MO, 4858
Long Foundation, Thomas J., The, CA, 826
Long Foundation, Vera M., CA, 827
Longaberger Foundation, The, OH, 7722
Longleaf Foundation, The, TN, see 8719
Longwood Foundation, Inc., DE, 1727
Lookout Fund, Inc., The, NY, 6445
Looney Foundation, Inc., Martha and Wilton, The, GA, 2436
Looper Foundation, The, TX, 9016
Loose Trust, Carrie J., TX, 9017
Lopata Foundation, Stanley and Lucy, MO, 4859
Lopatin Family Foundation, The, NY, 6446
Lorberbaum Family Foundation, Alan S., The, FL, 2118
Lord Foundation, Inc., Grogan, TX, 9018
Lord Scholarship Fund Trust, Henry C., RI, 8545
Lord's Fund, The, TX, 9019
Lorio Foundation, LA, 3496
Lortel Foundation, Inc., Lucille, The, NY, 6447
Los Altos Community Foundation, CA, 828
Lost and Foundation, Inc., The, MA, 4012
Lostand Foundation, Inc., NY, 6448
Lotman Foundation, Karen & Herbert, PA, 8314
Loughran Foundation, Inc., Mary and Daniel, DC, 1823
Louis Charitable Trust, Michael W., IL, 2861
Louis Foundation, Josephine P. & John J., IL, 2862
Louis Foundation, Sister Mary, MO, see 4853
Louis, Jr. Foundation, John J., IL, see 2862
Louisiana Outside Counsel Health & Ethics Foundation, LA, 3497
Louisiana-Pacific Foundation, OR, 8037
Louisville Community Foundation, Inc., KY, see 3414
Lounsbery Foundation, Inc., Richard, DC, 1824
Love Charitable Foundation, Audrey, FL, 2119
Love Conservation Foundation, Edward K., IL, 2863
Love Family Foundation, Inc., OH, 7723
Love Foundation, Inc., Gay and Erskine, GA, 2437
Lovell Foundation, David and Lura, The, AZ, 119

Lovett/Woodsum Family Charitable Foundation, Inc., MA, 4013
Lowder Family Foundation, J. K., The, AL, 42
Lowder Foundation, James K. and Margaret, AL, see 42
Lowder Foundation, Robert and Charlotte, AL, 43
Lowder Foundation, Thomas H. and Jarman F., The, AL, 44
Lowe Charitable Foundation, Jane K., The, AL, 45
Lowe Foundation, TX, 9020
Lowe's Charitable and Educational Foundation, NC, 7423
Lowell Community Foundation, Greater, MA, 4014
Lowell Institute, The, MA, 4015
Lowenstein Foundation, Alan V. and Amy, NJ, A
Lowenstein Foundation, Inc., Leon, NY, 6449
Lower Pearl River Valley Foundation, MS, 4751
Lowinger Foundation, M. & E., NY, 6450
Loyola Foundation, Inc., The, DC, 1825
Lozick Foundation, Edward A. and Catherine L., OH, 7724
Lozick Foundation, Edward A., OH, see 7724
Lozier Foundation, NE, 4988
LSR Fund, NY, 6451
Lubar Family Foundation, Inc., The, WI, 9851
Lubbock Area Foundation, Inc., TX, 9021
Lubert Family Foundation, Inc., The, PA, 8315
Lubin Charitable Trust, Richard K., The, MA, see 4016
Lubin Family Foundation, Richard K., The, MA, 4016
Lubo Fund, Inc., GA, 2438
Lubrizol Foundation, The, OH, 7725
Luce Charitable Trust, Theodore, NY, 6452
Luce Foundation, Inc., Henry, The, NY, 6453
Lucent Technologies Foundation, NJ, see 5110
Lucerne Foundation, NY, 6454
Luchsinger Family Foundation, The, TX, 9022
Luck Stone Foundation, Inc., VA, 9461
Luckow Family Foundation, Inc., The, NY, 6455
Lucky Seven Foundation, The, WA, 9632
Lucky Star Foundation, NY, 6456
Luckyday Foundation, The, MS, 4752
Ludcke Foundation, The, MA, 4017
Ludington, Inc., VA, 9462
Ludlow-Griffith Foundation, CO, 1412
Ludwick Family Foundation, CA, 829
Ludwick Family Foundation, The, CA, 830
Ludwig Family Foundation, Inc., The, DC, 1826
Lui and Wan Foundation, NY, 6457
Luke Foundation, MN, see 4713
Lumina Foundation for Education, Inc., IN, 3196
Lumpkin Family Foundation, The, IL, 2864
Lund Foundation, Sharon D., The, CA, 831
Lund Foundation, The, CA, see 831
Lunda Charitable Trust, WI, 9852
Lunder Foundation, ME, 3547
Lupin Foundation, The, LA, 3498
Lurcy Charitable and Educational Trust, Georges, NY, 6458
Lurie Family Foundation, Ann and Robert H., IL, see 2865
Lurie Foundation, Ann and Robert H., IL, 2865
Lurie Foundation, Inc., Helen & Rita, The, NY, 6459
Lurie Foundation, Louis R., CA, 832
Luster Family Foundation, Inc., CA, see 953
Lutece Foundation, Inc., The, NY, 6460
Luther Charitable Trust, Frances R., The, OH, 7726
Lutheran Brotherhood Foundation, WI, see 9949
Lutron Foundation, PA, 8316
Lutz Foundation, CA, 833
Lux Foundation, Miranda, CA, 834
Luzerne Foundation, The, PA, 8317
Lyle Foundation, The, NY, 6461
Lyman Charitable Trust, Rachel, TX, 9023
Lyman Lumber Company Foundation, The, MN, 4607
Lynch & Susan Baker Foundation, Michael R., NY, 6462
Lynch Foundation, Ronald P. and Susan E., The, CT, 1591
Lynchburg Community Trust, Greater, VA, 9463
Lyndhurst Foundation, TN, 8703
Lynn Foundation, E. M., FL, 2120
Lynn Foundation, Elizabeth A., WA, 9633
Lynn Foundation, The, CA, 835
Lynn Trust, Charles J., WI, 9853
Lynton Foundation, The, NY, 6463

Lyon Family Foundation, The, IL, 2866
Lyon Foundation, Inc., E. H. and Melody, OK, see 7953
Lyon Foundation, The, OK, 7953
Lyons Foundation, The, TX, 9024
Lytel Foundation, Bertha Russ, CA, 836
LZ Francis Foundation, OH, 7727

M & E Foundation, The, NY, 6464
M & J Foundation, NE, see 4969
M & S Foundation, The, PA, 8318
M & T Charitable Foundation, The, NY, 6465
M & T Foundation, CA, 837
M Health Foundation, The, CA, see 892
M.A.C. Global Foundation, The, NY, 6466
M.D.C. Holdings, Inc. Charitable Foundation, CO, 1413
M.E. Foundation, The, VA, 9464
M.U.S.-J. R. Hyde, Jr. Scholarship Fund, NY, 6467
M/B Foundation, OH, 7728
M/I Homes Foundation, OH, 7729
M/I Schottenstein Homes Foundation, OH, see 7729
Ma-Ran Foundation, GA, 2439
Maag Foundation, Hazel I., CA, 838
Maas Foundation, Benard L., MI, 4379
Maas Foundation, MN, 4608
Mabee Foundation, Inc., J. E. and L. E., The, OK, 7954
Mabie Family Foundation, William and Inez, The, CA, 839
Mac Family Foundation, The, CA, 840
MacArthur Foundation, J. Roderick, IL, 2867
MacArthur Foundation, John D. and Catherine T., IL, 2868
Macauley Foundation, Inc., The, CT, 1592
MacDonald Family Charitable Trust, CA, 841
MacDonald Family Foundation, CA, 842
MacDonald Foundation, Inc., Dr. John T., FL, 2121
Macdonald Foundation, James A., NY, 6468
Macdonald Fund, Maybelle Clark, OR, 8038
MacDonald-Peterson Foundation, TX, 9025
MacDonnell Foundation, The, CA, A
MacDougald Foundation, Inc., The, FL, 2122
Mach-Smjo Foundation, PA, 8319
Macht Foundation, Inc., Morton and Sophia, MD, 3683
Machuga Foundation, Inc., John Victor, The, NJ, 5311
Mack Family Foundation, Inc., David & Sondra, The, NJ, 5312
Mack Family Foundation, Inc., William & Phyllis, The, NJ, 5313
Mack Foundation, C. J., The, NY, see 6469
Mack Foundation, Christy and John, The, NY, 6469
Mack Foundation, Inc., Earle I., The, NJ, 5314
MacKall Trust, Paul MacKall & Evanina, The, NY, 6470
MacKenzie Foundation, The, CA, 843
Mackey Foundation, Harvey and Elizabeth, The, MI, see 4380
Mackey Foundation, The, MI, 4380
Maclellan Foundation, Inc., The, TN, 8704
MacLellan Foundation, Robert L. and Kathrina H., TN, 8705
MacNaughton Family Foundation, CA, 844
MacNeal Health Foundation, IL, see 2601
Macrini Foundation, Thomas G. & Nancy J., TX, 9026
Macy, Jr. Foundation, Josiah, NY, 6471
Maddie's Fund, CA, 845
Maddox Foundation, J. F, NM, 5487
Maddox Foundation, MS, 4753
Made in Dover Foundation, The, NJ, see 5459
Madigan Charitable Foundation, Inc., John J. & Lucille C., FL, 2123
Madigan Family Foundation, IL, 2869
Madison Community Foundation, WI, 9854
Madison County Community Foundation, IN, 3197
Madison Gas and Electric Foundation, Inc., WI, 9855
Magali Foundation, The, CA, 846
Magee Foundation, The, PA, 8320
Magen Ezra Foundation, NY, 6472
Magill Foundation, Arthur and Holly, FL, 2124
Magistro Foundation, Inc., CA, 847
Magnus Charitable Trust, IL, 2870
Magowan Family Foundation, Inc., The, NY, 6473
Magruder Foundation, Inc., Chesley G., FL, 2125
Maguire Foundation, The, PA, 8321
MAH Foundation, NY, 6474
MAHADH Foundation, The, MN, see 4589

Maheras Foundation, NY, 6475
Mahnken Foundation, Inc., Elizabeth A., The, IN, 3198
Mahon Charitable Foundation, Arthur & Myra, CT, 1593
Mahon Foundation, MN, 4609
Mai Family Foundation, The, NY, 6476
Maier Foundation, Inc., WV, 9725
Maier Foundation, Sarah & Pauline, WV, see 9725
Mailman Family Foundation, Inc., A. L., NY, 6477
Mailman Foundation, Inc., The, NY, 6478
Main Street Community Foundation, CT, 1594
Maine Community Foundation, Inc., The, ME, 3548
Maine Health Access Foundation, ME, 3549
Majestic Realty Foundation, CA, 848
Make a Mark Foundation, Inc., WI, 9856
Makk Charitable Foundation, NJ, 5315
Makray Family Foundation, IL, 2871
Maleh-Shalom Foundation, Inc., NY, 6479
Malek Family Charitable Trust, The, VA, 9465
Malkin Fund, Inc., NY, 6480
Mallah Family Foundation, Yvette and Joel, The, NY, 6481
Mallinckrodt, Jr. Foundation, Edward, MO, 4860
Mallon Family Foundation, CO, 1414
Mallory Foundation, NV, 5043
Malone Family Foundation, The, CO, 1415
Malone Foundation, Mary Alice Dorrance, PA, see 8409
Malott Family Foundation, IL, 2872
Maltz Family Foundation, Milton and Tamar, The, FL, 2126
Mamiye Foundation, NJ, 5316
Managed Health Services, Inc., WI, 9857
Manat Foundation, MI, 4381
Mandel Family Foundation, Morton and Barbara, The, OH, 7730
Mandel Foundation, Jack N. and Lilyan, OH, 7731
Mandel Foundation, Joseph and Florence, The, OH, 7732
Mandel Foundation, Morton and Barbara, OH, see 7730
Mandell Family Foundation, Inc., Andrew J. & Joyce D., CT, 1595
Mandell Family Foundation, Inc., The, CT, see 1595
Mandell Foundation, Samuel P., PA, 8322
Mander Foundation, Walter S., IL, 2873
Mandeville Foundation, Inc., CT, 1596
Mangano Foundation, Frank, OH, 7733
Manger Foundation, Inc., B. L., CT, 1597
Mangurian Foundation, Inc., The, NY, see 6482
Mangurian, Jr. Foundation, Inc., Harry T., The, NY, 6482
Manitoba Foundation, The, NY, 6483
Manitou Foundation, Inc., MA, 4018
Manitou Fund, MN, 4610
Mankoff Charitable Foundation, The, TX, see 9027
Mankoff Family Foundation, The, TX, 9027
Mann Family Foundation, Ted, The, CA, 849
Mann Family Foundation, The, RI, 8546
Mann Foundation of Minnesota, Ted and Roberta, MN, 4611
Manning Foundation, Inc., James Hilton Manning and Emma Austin, The, NY, 6484
Mannion Family Foundation, MA, 4019
Manoogian Foundation, Richard & Jane, MI, 4382
Manoogian Simone Foundation, MI, 4383
Manor Care Foundation, Inc., OH, see 7667
Manpower Foundation, Inc., WI, 9858
Mansfield Charitable Foundation, IA, 3308
Mansfield Charitable Foundation, Wesley & Irene, IA, see 3308
Manthei Charitable Trust, MI, 4384
Many Voices Foundation, MA, 4020
Manzi Family Charitable Fund, The, MA, 4021
Maple Hill Foundation, PA, 8323
Maplewood Foundation, PA, 8324
Mapplethorpe Foundation, Inc., Robert, NY, 6485
Marathon Oil Company Foundation, TX, 9028
Marbrook Foundation, MN, 4612
Marciano Family Foundation, Maurice, The, CA, 850
Marcks Foundation, Oliver Dewey, MI, 4385
Marcled Foundation, The, CA, 851
Marcon Foundation, Inc., NJ, 5317
Marcum Foundation, Joseph L. & Sarah S., OH, 7734
Marcus & Millichap Company Foundation, The, CA, 852
Marcus Corporation Foundation, Inc., WI, 9859
Marcus Family Charitable Trust, MA, see 4022

Marcus Family Charitable Trust, William and Cynthia, MA, 4022

Marcus Family Foundation, George and Judy, The, CA, 853

Marcus Foundation, Edward and Betty, The, TX, 9029

Marcus Foundation, Inc., Billi, The, GA, 2440

Marcus Foundation, Inc., The, GA, 2441

Marcus Foundation, James S., The, NY, 6486

Mardag Foundation, MN, 4613

Marden Foundation, Bernard A. & Chris, FL, 2127

Mardigian Foundation, Edward & Helen, MI, 4386

Maren Foundation, Thomas H., FL, 2128

Marianthi Foundation, Inc., The, NJ, 5318

Marietta Community Foundation, OH, 7735

Marin Community Foundation, CA, 854

Marino Charitable Foundation, Roger M. & Michelle S., The, MA, 4023

Mariposa Foundation, Inc., NY, 6487

Marisco Family Foundation, Cydney and Tom, CO, 1416

Marisla Foundation, The, CA, 855

Mark Family Foundation, NY, 6488

Markkula Foundation, The, CA, 856

Marks Charitable Foundation, Nancy Lurie, MA, see 4024

Marks Family Foundation, Michael E., CA, 857

Marks Family Foundation, Nancy Lurie, The, MA, 4024

Marks Family Foundation, NY, 6489

Marks Foundation, Inc., Carl, NY, 6490

Marley Foundation, Kemper and Ethel, The, AZ, 120

Marmot Foundation, The, DE, 1728

Marmurstein Charitable Foundation Trust, Yacov and Rita, The, NY, 6491

Marnell Foundation, The, NV, 5044

Maronda Foundation, The, PA, 8325

Maroone Family Foundation, FL, 2129

MARPAT Foundation, Inc., MD, 3684

Marriott Foundation, Inc., Nancy Peery, MD, 3685

Marriott Foundation, Inc., Richard E. & Nancy P., MD, 3686

Marriott Foundation, J. Willard and Alice S., The, DC, 1827

Marriott Foundation, J. Willard, The, DC, see 1827

Marron Charitable Trust, Donald B., NY, 6492

Marron Foundation, Donald B. & Catherine C., NY, 6493

Mars Foundation, The, VA, 9466

Mars Foundation, Virginia Cretella, NY, 6494

Marsh Biodiversity Foundation, Margot, The, NY, 6495

Marshall & Ilsley Bank Foundation, Inc., WI, see 9860

Marshall & Ilsley Foundation, Inc., WI, 9860

Marshall Charitable Foundation, Inc., The, KY, 3438

Marshall County Community Foundation, Inc., IN, 3199

Marshall Family Foundation, Barbara and Garry, CA, 858

Marshall Foundation, AZ, 121

Marshall Foundation, George Preston, MD, 3687

Marshall Foundation, Thomas, PA, 8326

Marshall Trust in Memory of Sanders McDaniel, Harriet McDaniel, GA, 2442

Marshfield Area Community Foundation, WI, 9861

MARTA Charity Club, GA, 2443

Marti Foundation, TX, 9030

Martin Charitable Foundation, Steve, The, CA, 859

Martin Charitable Trust, Margaret Lee, NC, 7424

Martin County Community Foundation, IN, see 3133

Martin Family Foundation, Albert Jay, The, TN, 8706

Martin Family Foundation, NY, 6496

Martin Family Foundation, R. Brad & Jean L., TN, see 8707

Martin Family Foundation, R. Brad, TN, 8707

Martin Family Foundation, The, WY, 9984

Martin Family Foundation, WI, 9862

Martin Foundation Trust, Charlotte Y., WA, 9634

Martin Foundation, Agnes, NY, A

Martin Foundation, Bert W., IL, 2874

Martin Foundation, Gilbert J., The, CA, 860

Martin Foundation, Inc., The, FL, 2130

Martin Foundation, Inc., TX, 9031

Martin Foundation, John G., The, CT, 1598

Martin Foundation, Rex and Alice A., IN, 3200

Martin Foundation, The, TN, 8708

Martin Marietta Corporation Foundation, MD, see 3682

Martin Memorial Trust, James G., NH, 5097

Martinez Foundation, Guadalupe and Lilia, The, TX, 9032

Martini Foundation, Nicholas, NJ, 5319

Martinson Family Foundation, Inc., NJ, 5320

Marx Foundation, Virginia & Leonard, NY, 6497

Marx Foundation, William, The, NY, 6498

Marx, Jr. Foundation, Page and Otto, The, NY, 6499

Masada Foundation, NY, 6500

Masco Corporation Charitable Trust, MI, see 4387

Masco Corporation Foundation, MI, 4387

Mashala Foundation, Inc., NY, 6501

Maslow Family Foundation, Inc., PA, 8327

Mason Fund, Carlos and Marguerite, The, GA, 2444

Mason Trust, B. A., WI, 9863

Massachusetts 2020 Foundation, Inc., MA, 4025

Massachusetts Automobile Dealers Charitable Foundation, MA, 4026

Massey Charitable Trust, PA, 8328

Massey Family Foundation, OK, 7955

Massey Foundation, Jack C., TN, 8709

Massey Foundation, VA, 9467

Massiah Foundation, Inc., MA, 4027

MassMutual Foundation for Hartford, Inc., The, CT, 1599

Massry Charitable Foundation, Inc., NY, 6502

Master Educational Assistance Foundation, IL, 2875

Master Works Foundation, Inc., IN, 3201

Master's Table, Inc., The, TN, 8710

Masters Foundation, Inc., The, FL, 2131

Mastronardi Charitable Foundation, Charles A., The, DE, see 1729

Mastronardi Foundation, Charles A., The, DE, 1729

MAT Charitable Foundation, Inc., The, NY, 6503

Mater Christi Foundation, The, MI, see 4225

Mater Dei Foundation, CO, 1417

Mather Fund, Elizabeth Ring Mather and William Gwinn, OH, 7736

Mathers Charitable Foundation, G. Harold & Leila Y., The, NY, 6504

Mathewson Foundation, Charles N., NV, 5045

Mathile Family Foundation, OH, 7737

Matisse Charitable Foundation, Pierre and Maria-Gaetana, NY, 6505

Matlin Family Foundation, NY, 6506

Mattel Children's Foundation, CA, 861

Mattel Foundation, CA, see 861

Matthews Foundation, Edward E. & Marie L., The, NY, 6507

Matthies Foundation, Katharine, The, CT, 1600

Mauboules Charitable Trust, Florence, LA, 3499

Max Charitable Foundation, CA, see 1322

Maxfield Foundation, The, CA, 862

Maxwell Foundation, Edmund F., WA, 9635

May Charitable Trust, Ben, The, AL, 46

May Department Stores Company Foundation, Inc., The, MO, see 4861

May Department Stores Foundation, The, MO, 4861

May Employees Trust Fund, David, OH, 7738

May Foundation, Wilbur W., 5046

Maya Corporation, NY, see 7173

Mayborn Foundation, Frank and Anyse Sue, The, TX, see 9033

Mayborn Foundation, Frank W. & Sue, The, TX, 9033

Mayday Fund, The, NY, 6508

Mayer Electric Supply Foundation, Inc., AL, 47

Mayer Family Foundation, Oscar G. and Elsa S., IL, 2876

Mayer Foundation, Frederick R., CO, 1418

Mayer Foundation, Inc., Chaim, NY, 6509

Mayer Foundation, Louis B., The, NY, 6510

Mayerson Foundation, Manuel D. & Rhoda, OH, 7739

Mayor Foundation, Oliver Dewey, TX, 9034

Mayore Foundation, Ltd., NY, 6511

Mayr Trust, George Henry, CA, 863

Mays Family Foundation, TX, 9035

Mays Foundation, TX, 9036

Maytag Corporation Foundation, IA, 3309

Maytag Family Foundation, F., The, IA, 3310

Maytag Family Foundation, Fred, The, IA, see 3310

Mazar Family Charitable Foundation, MA, 4028

Mazda Foundation (USA), Inc., The, DC, 1828

Mazer Foundation, Helen and William, NJ, 5321

Mazza Foundation, IL, 2877

MBIA Foundation, Inc., NY, 6512

MBNA Foundation, The, DE, 1730

McAdams Charitable Foundation, RI, 8547

McAfee Foundation, James T. McAfee, Jr. and Carolyn T., GA, 2445

McAlister Charitable Foundation, Harold, The, CA, 864

McAllister Foundation, Alfred J. McAllister and Dorothy N., IN, 3202

McAshan Foundation, Inc., TX, see 9250

McBean Charitable Trust, Alletta Morris, CA, 865

McBean Family Foundation, CA, 866

McBean Foundation, Atholl, The, CA, see 866

McBeath Foundation, Faye, WI, 9864

McBride, Sr. Family Foundation, Arthur B., The, OH, 7740

McCabe Foundation, B. C., CA, 867

McCaddin-McQuirk Foundation, Inc., The, NY, 6513

McCallum Family Foundation, The, MA, 4029

McCallum Foundation, The, MA, see 4029

McCance Foundation, The, MA, 4030

McCann Charitable Trust and McCann Foundation, Inc., James J., NY, 6514

McCann Foundation, Inc., Joy, FL, 2132

McCann Foundation, NY, see 6514

McCarthy Bush Foundation, IA, 3311

McCarthy Charities, Inc., The, NY, 6515

McCarthy Family Foundation, CA, 868

McCarthy Foundation, Michael W., The, NY, 6516

McCarthy Memorial Trust Fund, Catherine, RI, 8548

McCarthy-Bjorklund Foundation, MN, 4614

McCarty, Jr. Family Foundation, H. F., MS, 4754

McCasland Foundation, OK, 7956

McCaw Family Foundation, Keith & Mary Kay, WA, 9636

McCaw Foundation, Craig and Susan, The, WA, 9637

McCaw Foundation, Wendy P., CA, 869

McClelland Foundation, Stephanie and Carter, The, NY, 6517

McClendon Foundation, Hardin T. & Katie, MO, see 4894

McCloskey Family Charitable Trust, CO, 1419

McCombs Foundation, Inc., TX, 9037

McConnell Foundation, The, CA, 870

McCorkle Foundation, Inc., Bill and Mae, The, OH, 7741

McCormick Charitable Trust, CO, 1420

McCormick Family Foundation, PA, 8329

McCormick Foundation, Chauncey and Marion Deering, IL, 2878

McCormick Trust, Anne, PA, 8330

McCourtney Trust, Flora S., IL, 2879

McCoy Charitable Foundation, Bowen H. & Janice Arthur, The, CA, 871

McCoy Foundation, Emmett and Miriam, TX, 9038

McCoy Foundation, James N., TX, 9039

McCrea Foundation, TX, 9040

McCullough Foundation, Ralph H. & Ruth J., TX, 9041

McCune Charitable Foundation, Marshall L. & Perrine D., NM, see 5488

McCune Charitable Foundation, NM, 5488

McCune Charitable Trust, John R., PA, 8331

McCune Foundation, Don C. and Florence M., KS, 3376

McCune Foundation, PA, 8332

McCune Foundation, The, CA, 872

McCutchen Foundation, The, NJ, 5322

McDaniel Charitable Foundation, TX, 9042

McDaniel Foundation, Ronald L., IL, 2880

McDavid Dental Education Trust, G. N. and Edna, MO, see 4862

McDavid Dental Educational Trust, MO, 4862

McDermott Foundation, Eugene, The, TX, 9043

McDonald Agape Foundation, MI, 4388

McDonald Foundation, Armstrong, NE, 4989

McDonald Foundation, Inc., J. M., CO, 1421

McDonald Manufacturing Company Charitable Foundation, A. Y., IA, 3312

McDonald's Kid's Charities, PA, 8333

McDonnell Charitable Foundation, John J. McDonald, Jr. & Marian J., VA, 9468

McDonnell Douglas Foundation, MO, see 4785

McDonnell Family Foundation, CO, 1422

McDonnell Family Foundation, Inc., James S., MA, 4031

McDonnell Foundation, Inc., MO, 4863

McDonnell Foundation, James S., MO, 4864

McDonough Foundation, Inc., Bernard, WV, 9726

McDonough Foundation, Inc., WI, 9865

McDonough Foundation, The, CA, 873

McDougal Family Foundation, IL, 2881

McDougall Charitable Trust, Ruth Camp, NY, see 5700
McEachern Charitable Trust, D. V. & Ida, WA, 9638
McEachern Charitable Trust, Ida J., WA, see 9638
McElroy Trust, R. J., IA, 3313
McEvoy Foundation, Mildred H., MA, 4032
McFadden Family Foundation, CA, 874
McFeely-Rogers Foundation, PA, 8334
McGee Foundation, Inc., The, OK, 7957
McGee Foundation, The, MO, 4865
McGettigan Foundation, Patrick H., The, DC, 1829
McGill Foundation, Ralph and Frances, OK, 7958
McGillis Charitable Foundation, UT, 9334
McGinnis Charitable Foundation, Gerald E., PA, 8335
McGlothlin Foundation, The, VA, 9469
McGonagle Foundation, Inc., Dextra Baldwin, NY, 6518
McGovern Foundation, John P., TX, 9044
McGowan Charitable Fund, William G., DC, 1830
McGrath Charitable Trust, Callie D., CA, 875
McGraw Foundation, Curtis W., The, NJ, 5323
McGraw Foundation, IL, 2882
McGraw Foundation, Inc., Donald C., The, NY, 6519
McGraw Foundation, Inc., Elizabeth, NY, 6520
McGregor Foundation, The, OH, 7742
McGregor Fund, MI, 4389
McGue Millhiser Family Trust, The, VA, 9470
McGuire Family Foundation, William W. and Nadine M., The, MN, 4615
McGuire Family Foundation, William W. McGuire and Nadine M., The, MN, see 4615
MCI Education Foundation, VA, 9471
MCI Foundation, VA, see 9471
McInerny Foundation, HI, 2551
McInnes Family Foundation, TN, see 8728
McIntire Educational Fund, John, OH, 7743
McIntosh Foundation, Inc., IL, 2883
McIntosh Foundation, The, DC, 1831
McIntyre Foundation, The, CA, 876
MCJ Foundation, The, NJ, 5324
McKaig Foundation, Lalitta Nash, PA, 8336
McKay Foundation, The, CA, 877
McKee Charitable Trust, Thomas M., CO, A
McKee Foundation, Robert E. and Evelyn, TX, 9045
McKeen Fund, FL, 2133
McKellar Charitable Foundation, Jessie Barker, KY, 3439
McKenna Family Foundation, CA, 878
McKenna Foundation, Inc., Katherine Mabis, PA, 8337
McKenna Foundation, Inc., Philip M., PA, 8338
McKenzie Foundation, Inc., The, CT, 1601
McKesson Foundation, Inc., CA, 879
McKesson HBOC Foundation, Inc., CA, see 879
McKinney Charitable Foundation, William V. and Catherine A., PA, 8339
McKissick Foundation, Ellison S. & Noel P., SC, 8599
McKnight Brain Research Foundation, FL, 2134
McKnight Endowment Fund for Neuroscience, The, MN, 4616
McKnight Foundation, Sumner T., The, MD, 3688
McKnight Foundation, The, MN, 4617
McLane/Harper Charitable Foundation, Inc., The, MA, 4033
McLean Contributionship, The, PA, 8340
McLean Foundation, Inc., Thomas R. & Elizabeth E., NC, 7425
McLean Foundation, Mel and Grace, The, CA, 880
McLendon Educational Fund, Violet H., The, AL, 48
McMahon Foundation, The, OK, 7959
McMaster Foundation, Inc., Harold and Helen, The, OH, 7744
McMichael Family Foundation, The, NC, 7426
McMillan Foundation, D. W., AL, 49
McMillan, Jr. Foundation, Inc., Bruce, TX, 9046
McMillen Foundation, Inc., IN, 3203
McMillen Foundation, Robert B., The, WA, 9639
McMullan Foundation, James and Milton, IL, 2884
McMullen Family Foundation, NJ, 5325
McMurry Foundation, The, WY, 9985
McNair Foundation, Robert and Janice, The, TX, 9047
McNair Foundation, TX, A
McNally Charitable Foundation, Andrew & Jeanine, IL, 2885
McNamara Family Foundation, Inc., FL, 2135
McNamara Family Foundation, Richard F., MN, 4618

McNamara Purcell Foundation, The, IL, 2886
McNealy Foundation, Susan Ingemanson, The, CA, see 333
McNeely Foundation, The, MN, 4619
McNeil Foundation, Col. Stanley R., IL, 2887
McNeill Family Foundation, WY, see 9986
McNeill Foundation, Corbin & Dorice S., WY, 9986
McNichols Family Foundation, Inc., Gerald and Paula, VA, 9472
McNulty Foundation, John P. & Anne Welsh, NY, 6521
McNutt Charitable Trust, Amy Shelton, TX, 9048
McQuain Charitable Trust, Hazel Ruby, WV, 9727
McQueen Foundation, Adeline and George, WI, 9866
McRae Foundation, Inc., Selby and Richard, MS, 4755
McRae Foundation, MS, see 4755
McVaney Family Foundation Trust, Kevin E. & Colleen K., CO, see 1409
McVaney-Fernald Family Foundation Trust, CO, see 1430
McVay Foundation, MN, 4620
McWane Foundation, AL, 50
McWhinney Foundation, CO, 1423
MDU Resources Foundation, ND, 7517
Mead Charitable Foundation, D. Richard, IL, 2888
Mead Family Foundation, DC, 1832
Mead Family Foundation, Gilbert and Jaylee, DC, see 1832
Mead Foundation, Giles W. and Elise G., CA, 881
Mead Foundation, Scott & Suling, The, NY, 6522
Mead Witter Foundation, Inc., WI, 9867
Meador Foundation, James A., VA, 9473
Meadowood Foundation, MN, 4621
Meadows Foundation, Inc., The, TX, 9049
MeadWestvaco Foundation, The, OH, 7745
Meakem Foundation, Inc., Glen and Diane, PA, 8341
Measey Foundation, Benjamin and Mary Siddons, The, PA, 8342
Mebane Charitable Foundation, Inc., NC, 7427
Mechia Foundation, TX, 9050
Medallion Foundation, Inc., TX, 9051
Medina Foundation, WA, 9640
Medleycott Family Foundation, The, PA, 8343
Medline Foundation, The, IL, 2889
Medtronic Foundation, The, MN, 4622
Medvedenko Foundation, Stanislav, CA, 882
Meehan Family Foundation, Inc., WI, 9868
Meehan Foundation, Inc., Daniel E., WI, see 9868
Meehan Foundation, Inc., William M. & Miriam F., NY, 6523
Meetinghouse Foundation, Inc., MA, see 3906
Megrue Family Foundation, NY, 6524
Mehl Family Foundation, Inc., George and Deborah, OH, 7746
Mehta Family Foundation, Bhupat and Jyott, TX, 9052
Meijer Foundation, The, MI, 4390
Meinders Foundation, The, OK, 7960
Meinig Family Foundation, OK, 7961
Melkus Family Foundation, The, TN, 8711
Mellam Family Foundation, CA, 883
Mellen Foundation, The, OH, 7747
Mellinger Educational Foundation, Inc., Edward Arthur, IL, 2890
Mellon Family Foundation, R. K., PA, 8344
Mellon Financial Corporation Foundation, PA, see 8345
Mellon Financial Corporation Fund, PA, 8345
Mellon Foundation, Andrew W., The, NY, 6525
Mellon Foundation, Richard King, PA, 8346
Melly Foundation, Alice Pack Melly and L. Thomas, The, NY, 6526
Melly Foundation, L. Thomas, NY, see 6526
Melmac Education Foundation, ME, 3550
Melman Foundation, Richard & Martha, IL, 2891
Melohn Foundation, Inc., The, NY, 6528
Melohn Foundation, Johny, NY, 6527
Melrene Fund, The, IL, 2892
Melville Charitable Trust, The, MA, 4034
Melville Foundation, The, CT, 1602
Memorial Foundation for Children, The, VA, 9474
Memton Fund, Inc., The, NY, 6529
Menard Family Foundation, CA, 884
Menasha Corporation Foundation, WI, 9869
Menche Family Charitable Trust, NY, 6530
Mendenhall Foundation, Trini and O. C., TX, 9053

Mendocino County Community Foundation, Inc., CA, see 402
Meng, Inc., John and Engrid, WI, 9870
Mengle Foundation, Glenn and Ruth, PA, 8347
Menlo Foundation, Inc., CA, 885
Menschel Family Foundation, Robert and Joyce, The, NY, 6531
Menschel Foundation, Robert and Joyce, The, NY, see 6531
Mental Insight Foundation, The, CA, 886
Mentor Graphics Foundation, OR, 8039
Merage Family Foundation, Paul & Elisabeth, The, CA, 887
Merage Foundation of Nevada, Andre & Katherine, CA, 888
Merage Foundation, Andre & Katherine, CO, 1424
Merage Foundation, David and Laura, CO, 1425
Merancas Foundation, Inc., NC, 7428
Mercer Foundation, Johnny, The, NY, 6532
Merchants Fund, PA, 8348
Merchants-Oliver Fund, PA, see 8348
Merck Company Foundation, The, NJ, 5326
Merck Family Fund, MA, 4035
Merck Fund, John, The, MA, 4036
Merck Genome Research Institute, Inc., The, PA, 8349
Merck Institute for Science Education, Inc., NJ, 5327
Merck Patient Assistance Program, Inc., NJ, 5328
Merck-Schering Plough Patient Assistance Program, NJ, 5329
Mercury Foundation of New York, Inc., NY, 6533
Mercy and Sharing, CO, 1426
Mercy Works Foundation, Inc., WI, 9871
Mercy, Jr. Foundation, Inc., Sue and Eugene, The, NY, 6534
Meredith Corporation Foundation, IA, 3314
Meredith Foundation, Edwin T., IA, 3315
Meredith Foundation, TX, 9054
Meredith Private Foundation, TX, see 9059
Mergens Foundation, George W., VT, 9360
Mericos Foundation, CA, 889
Meriden Foundation, The, CT, 1603
Merillat Foundation, Orville D. & Ruth A., MI, 4391
Merillat Private Foundation, Richard D. & Lynette S., NJ, 5330
Meritor Automotive, Inc. Trust, MI, see 4224
Meriweather Perpetual Charitable Trust, Tyler, IL, 2893
Meriwether Foundation, The, NY, 6535
Merkin Foundation, Inc., Leib and Hermann, NJ, 5331
Merkle Foundation, Jess, The, LA, 3500
Merlin Foundation, NY, 6536
Mermans Foundation, Inc., NC, see 7428
Merrick Family Foundation, TX, 9055
Merrick Foundation, Inc., NE, 4990
Merrick Foundation, The, OK, 7962
Merrill Family Foundation, Inc., OR, 8040
Merrill Family Foundation, Steven L., The, CA, 890
Merrill Foundation, Inc., Julia & Gilbert, FL, 2136
Merrill Foundation, Inc., The, MD, 3689
Merrill Foundation, Inc., The, WI, 9872
Merrill Lynch & Co. Foundation, Inc., NY, 6537
Merriman Foundation, DC, 1833
Merten Charitable Trust, Walter L., WI, 9873
Mertz Gilmore Foundation, NY, 6538
Mertz-Gilmore Foundation, Joyce, NY, see 6538
Mesdag Family Foundation, The, NY, 6539
Meshewa Farm Foundation, PA, 8350
Mesirow Charitable Foundation, IL, 2894
Messengers of Healing Winds Foundation, NM, 5489
Messer Foundation, The, NY, 6540
Met Foundation, Inc., IN, 3204
Metabolife Foundation, CA, 891
Metabolife International Foundation, The, CA, see 891
Metcalf Charitable Foundation, Dorothy A., The, PA, 8351
Metcalf Foundation, Inc., Stanley W., The, NY, 6541
Methvin Foundation, Tom & Amy, The, AL, 51
MetLife Foundation, NY, 6542
Metris Companies Foundation, IL, A
Metropolitan Life Foundation, NY, see 6542
Metropolitan Philanthropic Fund, Inc., NY, 6543
MetroWest Community Health Care Foundation, Inc., MA, A
Metta Fund, CA, 892

Mevatek Foundation, The, TX, 9056
Meyer Charitable Foundation, Barry and Wendy, The, CA, 893
Meyer Charitable Foundation, The, IL, 2895
Meyer Charitable Trust, Fred, OR, see 8042
Meyer Family Foundation, C. Louis, IL, 2896
Meyer Family Foundation, Paul & Jane, TX, 9057
Meyer Family Foundation, Paul J., TX, see 9057
Meyer Foundation, Alice Kleberg Reynolds, TX, see 9145
Meyer Foundation, Eugene and Agnes E., DC, 1834
Meyer Foundation, Fred, The, OR, 8041
Meyer Foundation, Inc., Bert & Mary, GA, 2446
Meyer Foundation, Inc., Edward & Sandra, NY, 6544
Meyer Foundation, Robert R., AL, 52
Meyer Foundation, Roslyn Milstein Meyer and Jerome, NY, 6545
Meyer Foundation, Roslyn Milstein, NY, see 6545
Meyer Foundation, The, NY, 6546
Meyer Memorial Trust, OR, 8042
Meyer Private Charitable Foundation, Arthur I. and Sydelle F., The, FL, 2137
Meyer/Smith Foundation, Fred, OR, see 8041
Meyerhoff Foundation, Inc., Robert & Jane, MD, 3690
Meyerhoff Fund, Inc., Harvey M., The, MD, 3691
Meyerhoff Fund, Inc., Joseph, The, MD, 3692
Meyerson Family Foundation, Morton H., TX, 9058
MFA Foundation, MO, 4866
MFI Foundation, TX, 9059
MFU Training Plan Trust, CA, 894
Miami County Foundation, OH, 7748
MIC Foundation, NY, see 6560
Michaan Foundation, J. S. & S., The, FL, 2138
Michels Family Foundation, Dale R. & Ruth L., WI, 9874
Michelson Foundation, The, CA, 895
Michelson, M.D. Charitable Foundation, Inc., Gary Karlin, CA, 896
Michigan Capital Fund for Non-Profit Housing Corporation, MI, see 4330
Michigan City Community Enrichment Corporation, IN, 3205
Micron Technology Foundation, Inc., ID, 2571
Mid-America Foundation, IA, 3316
Mid-America Foundation, MO, see 4802
Mid-Iowa Health Foundation, IA, 3317
Mid-Nebraska Community Foundation, Inc., NE, 4991
Mid-Shore Community Foundation, Inc., MD, 3693
MIDA Foundation, The, FL, 2139
Middendorf Foundation, Inc., MD, 3694
Middlecott Foundation, MA, 4037
Middletown Community Foundation, OH, 7749
Midland Area Community Foundation, MI, 4392
Midland Company Foundation, OH, 7750
Midland Foundation, MI, see 4392
Mifflin Memorial Fund, George H. & Jane A., MA, 4038
Milacron Foundation, OH, 7751
Milagro Foundation, The, TX, see 9056
Milbank Foundation for Rehabilitation, NY, 6547
Miles Foundation, Inc., The, TX, 9060
Miles Inc. Foundation, PA, see 8096
Milgard Family Foundation, Gary & Carol, WA, see 9641
Milgard Family Foundation, Gary E., WA, 9641
Milken Family Foundation, Lowell, CA, 897
Milken Family Foundation, The, CA, 898
Millard Charitable Foundation, Robert & Bethany, NY, 6548
Millard Charitable Foundation, Robert B., NY, see 6548
Millard Charitable Trust, Adah K., IL, 2897
Millbrook Tribute Garden, Inc., NY, 6549
Miller Charitable Foundation, Howard E. & Nell E., PA, 8352
Miller Charitable Foundation, Mark & Kimberly, PA, 8353
Miller Charitable Foundation, Pendleton and Elisabeth Carey, WA, 9642
Miller Charitable Trust, James E. & Lila G., OR, 8043
Miller Charitable Trust, Phillip S., OR, 8044
Miller Design Foundation, Herman, OH, see 7694
Miller Education Foundation, Larry H., UT, 9335
Miller Family Charitable Foundation, Audrey and Jack, IL, 2898
Miller Family Foundation, Alan B., The, PA, 8354

Miller Family Foundation, Barbara and Fred, The, CA, 899
Miller Family Foundation, Inc., FL, see 2141
Miller Family Foundation, Inc., Stuart A., FL, 2140
Miller Family Foundation, Inc., The, NY, 6550
Miller Family Foundation, Ken A. & Gail B., NC, see 7480
Miller Family Foundation, OH, 7752
Miller Family Foundation, The, OH, 7753
Miller Family Fund, Inc., Samuel H., OH, 7754
Miller Foundation, Alon and Rosana, The, CA, 900
Miller Foundation, Arnold and Suzanne, The, TX, 9061
Miller Foundation, Arnold M. & Sydell L., OH, see 7752
Miller Foundation, Charles Lawrence Keith and Clara, NY, 6551
Miller Foundation, Earl B. & Loraine H., CA, 901
Miller Foundation, Herman and Frieda L., MA, 4039
Miller Foundation, Howard, MI, 4393
Miller Foundation, Inc., Albert L. and Louise B., MI, see 4394
Miller Foundation, Inc., FL, 2141
Miller Foundation, Jack and Goldie Wolfe, IL, 2899
Miller Foundation, James F. & Marion L., OR, 8045
Miller Foundation, Steve J., The, WI, 9875
Miller Foundation, Steven and Sheila, TX, 9062
Miller Foundation, The, CA, see 901
Miller Foundation, The, MI, 4394
Miller Foundation, Tim, VA, 9475
Miller Foundation, William R. & Irene D., The, NY, see 6550
Miller Private Foundation, Inc., John & Tammy, The, DE, 1731
Miller, Jr. Family Foundation, Marlin, PA, 8355
Miller-Worley Charitable Foundation, PA, 8356
Milliken Foundation, Gerrish H., The, DE, 1732
Milliken Foundation, NY, 6552
Millikin Trust, James, IL, 2900
Millipore Foundation, The, MA, 4040
Millner Foundation, Inc., Ginny, GA, 2447
Mills Family Charitable Foundation, IL, 2901
Mills Family Foundation, Inc., NC, 7429
Millstein Family Foundation, Ira M. and Diane G., NY, 6553
Millstone Foundation, MO, 4867
Milstein Foundation, Edward L., NY, 6554
Milstein Foundation, Howard P., NY, 6555
Milstein Foundation, Inc., NJ, 5332
Milstein Foundation, Paul and Irma, NY, 6556
Milton Fine Family Charitable Foundation, PA, see 8201
Milwaukee Foundation, Greater, WI, 9876
Milwaukee Foundation, WI, see 9876
Mindala Family Foundation, OH, 7755
Mindel Foundation, The, NY, 6557
Mindich Family Foundation, The, NY, 6558
Mine Safety Appliances Company Charitable Foundation, PA, 8357
Miniger Memorial Foundation, Clement O., OH, 7756
Minneapolis Foundation, The, MN, 4623
Minnesota Community Foundation, MN, 4624
Minnesota Foundation, MN, see 4624
Minnesota Mining and Manufacturing Foundation, MN, see 4492
Minnesota Mutual Foundation, MN, see 4677
Mintz Scholarship Trust, Jessie, AZ, A
Mirak Foundation, John, MA, 4041
Mischer Foundation, Walter M. Mischer & Mary A., The, TX, 9063
Mississippi Common Fund Trust, MS, 4756
Mississippi Hospital Association Educational Foundation, MS, see 4757
Mississippi Hospital Association Health, Research and Educational Foundation, MS, 4757
Mississippi Power Foundation, Inc., MS, 4758
Mistlin and Family Private Foundation, Tony, The, CA, 902
Mitchell Family Foundation, Edward D. and Anna, CA, 903
Mitchell Family Foundation, Wildey H., MN, 4625
Mitchell Foundation, Cynthia & George, The, TX, 9064
Mitchell Foundation, Inc., A. S., AL, 53
Mitchell Foundation, Inc., Joan, The, NY, 6559
Mitchell Foundation, Inc., The, AL, see 53
Mitchell Foundation, The, TX, 9065

Mithoff Family Charitable Foundation, Richard Warren, TX, 9066
Mithun Family Foundation, MN, 4626
Mitsubishi Electric America Foundation, VA, 9476
Mitsubishi International Corporation Foundation, NY, 6560
Mitsui U.S.A. Foundation, The, NY, 6561
Mitte Foundation, Roy F. and Joann Cole, TX, 9067
Mix Memorial Fund, Inc., Charles L., GA, 2448
Mixon Foundation, A. Malachi Mixon III & Barbara W., OH, 7757
Mizel Global Cultural Fund, CO, 1427
Mizuho USA Foundation, Inc., NY, 6562
MJPM Foundation, NY, 6563
MJR Fund, TX, see 8827
MMG Foundation, Inc., WI, 9877
Mnuchin Foundation, Steven and Heather, The, NY, 6564
Mnuchin Foundation, Steven T., The, NY, see 6564
Mobile Community Foundation, The, AL, see 25
Moccasin Lake Foundation, WA, 9643
Modano Foundation, Inc., Mike, TX, 9068
Model Foundation, Inc., Leo, NY, 6565
Modglin Family Foundation, The, CA, 904
Modine Manufacturing Company Foundation, Inc., The, WI, 9878
Modzelewski Charitable Trust, VA, 9477
Moeller Foundation, Joe and Mary, GA, 2449
Mogharebi Family Foundation, CA, 905
Moh Foundation, Celia, The, CA, 906
Mohn Family Foundation, The, CA, 907
Moley Family Foundation, CA, 908
Moline Foundation, The, IL, 2902
Molinello Family Foundation, MI, 4395
Moller Foundation, Dorothy D. and Joseph A., AZ, 122
Moncrief Foundation, William A. and Elizabeth B., TX, 9069
Monell Foundation, Ambrose, The, NY, 6566
Money-Arenz Foundation, Inc., GA, 2450
Monfort Charitable Foundation, CO, see 1429
Monfort Charitable Foundation, Inc., Kenneth and Myra, CO, 1428
Monfort Family Foundation, CO, 1429
Monius Institute, Inc., A. M., NJ, 5333
Monk Cancer Research Foundation, Donald, The, TX, A
Monkarsh Family Foundation, Joy and Jerry, CA, 909
Monroe Foundation (1976), J. Edgar, LA, 3501
Monroe-Brown Foundation, MI, 4396
Monsanto Fund, MO, 4868
Monsweag Foundation, MA, 4042
Montana Community Foundation, MT, 4939
Monteforte Foundation, Inc., The, NY, 6567
Monteleone Family Foundation, LA, 3502
Monterey Fund, Inc., NY, 6568
Monterey Peninsula Foundation, CA, 910
Monterey Peninsula Golf Foundation, CA, see 910
Montgomery Area Community Foundation, Inc., AL, see 20
Montgomery County Community Foundation, IN, 3206
Montgomery Foundation, Kenneth & Harle, IL, 2903
Montgomery Foundation, OH, 7758
Montgomery Foundation, Rose & Walter, SC, 8600
Monticello College Foundation, The, IL, 2904
Moody Foundation, Inc., Gloria Narramore, AL, 54
Moody Foundation, The, TX, 9070
Moody's Foundation, The, NY, 6569
Moonwalk Fund, Silva Watson, CA, 911
Moore Charitable Foundation, Claude, The, VA, 9478
Moore Charitable Foundation, Inc., The, NY, 6570
Moore Family Foundation, CA, 912
Moore Family Foundation, David and Katherine, NY, 6571
Moore Family Foundation, Inc., AL, 55
Moore Family Foundation, Inc., Edward S., NY, 6572
Moore Foundation for Otologic Research, James A., NY, 6573
Moore Foundation, Allen Lovelace Moore and Blanche Davis, TX, 9071
Moore Foundation, Gordon and Betty, CA, 913
Moore Foundation, IN, 3207
Moore Foundation, Inc., Edward S., CT, A
Moore Foundation, Inc., Marion, CT, 1604
Moore Foundation, Inc., Martha G., FL, 2142

Moore Foundation, Sara Giles, GA, 2451
Moore Foundation, Tom and Judy, The, NY, 6574
Moore Fund, Ruth Danley & William Enoch, PA, 8358
Moore Memorial Foundation, Inc., James Starr, GA, 2452
Moores Foundation, Harry C., OH, 7759
Moran Foundation, Inc., Jim, The, FL, 2143
Moran Foundation, W. T. & Louise J., The, TX, 9072
Morania Foundation, Inc., DE, 1733
Morcom Foundation, Inc., FL, 2144
Mordecai Foundation, Daniel and Janet, NY, 6575
Morehead Foundation, John Motley, The, NC, 7430
Moreno Family Foundation, AZ, 123
Morey Foundation, The, MI, 4397
Morgan Charitable Foundation, Inc., TX, 9073
Morgan City Fund, The, LA, see 3518
Morgan Family Foundation, Inc., CA, 914
Morgan Family Foundation, James and Rebecca, CA, 915
Morgan Family Foundation, OH, 7760
Morgan Family Foundation, The, KS, 3377
Morgan Foundation, Burton D., The, OH, 7761
Morgan Foundation, Charles P. and Roxanna L., The, IN, see 3208
Morgan Foundation, Inc., Edwin E. & Ruby C., MS, 4759
Morgan Foundation, Inc., The, NC, 7431
Morgan Foundation, Margaret Clark, The, OH, 7762
Morgan Foundation, Pete, CO, 1430
Morgan Foundation, The, IN, 3208
Morgan Foundation, Todd and Cheri, CA, A
Morgan Foundation, TX, 9074
Morgan Roundation, Inc., John E., NY, 6576
Morgan Stanley Dean Witter Foundation, NY, see 6577
Morgan Stanley Foundation, NY, 6577
Morgan, Jr. Foundation, Marietta McNeill Morgan & Samuel Tate, VA, 9479
Morgens East Foundation, The, NY, see 7259
Morgens West Foundation, GA, 2453
Morgenstern Foundation, Morris, CA, 916
Morgridge Family Foundation, CA, see 1240
Moriah Fund, DC, 1835
Morley Family Foundation, John C. and Sally S., OH, 7763
Morning Foundation, The, MN, 4627
Morning Star Family Foundation, The, TX, 9075
Morningside Foundation, The, MA, 4043
Morningside-Springfield Foundation, Inc., MA, see 4043
Morningstar Foundation, The, MD, 3695
Morrill Charitable Foundation, Inc., IL, A
Morris Charitable Foundation, E. A., NC, 7432
Morris Charitable Trust, Charles M., PA, 8359
Morris Communications Foundation, Inc., GA, 2454
Morris Family Foundation, Inc., The, GA, 2455
Morris Family Foundation, Mark and Bette, KS, 3378
Morris Foundation, Allen, The, FL, 2145
Morris Foundation, Inc., Michael A., The, GA, see 2455
Morris Foundation, Inc., Norman M., NY, 6578
Morris Foundation, Inc., William T., The, NY, 6579
Morris Foundation, Johnny, MO, 4869
Morris Foundation, Margaret T., AZ, 124
Morris Foundation, The, CA, 917
Morris Foundation, The, TX, 9076
Morris Foundation, William C. and Susan F., The, NY, 6580
Morris Fund, Inc., Philip, NY, see 5545
Morrison Family Foundation, FL, 2146
Morrison Foundation, Inc., Harry W., ID, 2572
Morrison Foundation, Robert S., OH, 7764
Morrison Knudsen Corporation Foundation, ID, see 2578
Morrow Foundation, Inc., Allan, The, NY, 6581
Morsani Foundation, Inc., Frank and Carol, FL, 2147
Morse Charitable Trust, Elizabeth, The, WI, 9879
Morse Family Foundation, Inc., NY, 6582
Morse Foundation, Richard P. & Claire W., MA, 4044
Morse Foundation, The, NY, 6583
Morse Hill Foundation, Inc., NY, 6584
Morse, Jr. Foundation, Inc., Enid & Lester S., NY, see 6582
Mortensen Foundation, William & Alice, The, CT, 1605
Morton Foundation, CA, 918
Morton Foundation, Inc., Peter A., CA, 919
Morton Foundation, Inc., The, NY, 6585

Morton Memorial Fund, Mark, IL, 2905
Mosaic Foundation of R. & P. Heydon, The, MI, 4398
Mosaic Fund, The, NY, 6586
Mosbacher Foundation, Inc., TX, 9077
Mosbacher, Jr. Foundation, Inc., Emil, CA, see 1098
Moses Fund, Inc., Henry and Lucy, NY, 6587
Mosher Foundation, Samuel B. and Margaret C., CA, 920
Mosher Foundation, Samuel B., CA, see 920
Mosher Foundation, The, CA, see 920
Moskowitz 1999 Family Foundation, Henry & Rose, The, NY, 6588
Moss Foundation, CA, 921
Moss Foundation, Inc., Stephen, NY, 6589
Moss Heart Trust, Harry S., TX, 9078
Mosse Foundation for Education and the Arts, The, NY, 6590
Mosse Foundation, Hilde L., The, NY, see 6590
Mossier Foundation, Kevin J., MN, 4628
Mostyn Foundation, Inc., NY, 6591
Mote Scientific Foundation, Inc., FL, 2148
Motherwell Foundation, Inc., NY, see 5847
Motorists Insurance Group Foundation, The, OH, 7765
Motorola Foundation, IL, 2906
Mott Charitable Trust, Stewart R., DC, 1836
Mott Charitable Trust/Spectemur Agendo, Stewart R., DC, see 1836
Mott Foundation, Charles Stewart, MI, 4399
Mott Foundation, Inc., Peach, TX, 9079
Mott Foundation, Ruth, MI, 4400
Mount Vernon/Knox County Community Trust, The, OH, see 7583
Mourier Family Foundation, CA, 922
Mousetrap Foundation, The, VA, 9480
Mozer Foundation, The, MI, 4401
Mozilo Family Foundation, The, CA, 923
MRK Foundation, MA, A
MRM Foundation, Inc., NY, 6592
Mt. Cuba Center, Inc., DE, 1734
Muchemore Foundation, G. Robert, NE, 4992
Muchnic Foundation, KS, 3379
Mudd Foundation, Mildred E. & Harvey S., CA, 924
Muehlstein Foundation, Inc., Herman, The, NY, A
Muirfield Foundation, PA, see 8439
Mulago Foundation, NY, 6593
Muldoon Fund, Mary, NY, 6594
Mulford Foundation, Vincent, MD, 3696
Mulford Trust, Clarence E., The, ME, 3551
Mullen Family Foundation, Inc., Donald R., NY, 6595
Mullen Family Foundation, The, IL, 2907
Mullen Foundation, Hilda, The, NY, 6596
Muller Family Foundation, CA, 925
Muller, Sr. Foundation, Frank, CA, see 925
Multiple Sclerosis Center of Atlanta, The, GA, A
Mundi Foundation, Salus, IL, 2908
Mundy Family Foundation, The, TX, 9080
Munger Foundation, Alfred C., CA, 926
Munson Foundation, Curtis & Edith, DC, 1837
Munson Foundation, W. B., WI, 9880
Munzer Foundation, Rudolph J. & Daphne A., The, CA, 927
Murch Foundation, The, OH, 7766
Murchison Foundation, Ginger, The, TX, 9081
Murdock Charitable Trust, M. J., WA, 9644
Murdough Foundation, The, OH, 7767
Murdough Foundation, Thomas G. & Joy P., OH, see 7767
Murphy Family Foundation, The, OH, 7768
Murphy Foundation, Dan, CA, 928
Murphy Foundation, John P., OH, 7769
Murphy Foundation, Katherine John, GA, 2456
Murphy Foundation, Philip D. & Tammy S., The, NY, 6597
Murphy Foundation, The, AR, 167
Murr Family Foundation, WA, 9645
Murray Family Charitable Foundation, The, MA, 4045
Murray Foundation, Geraldine M., PA, 8360
Murray Foundation, Jerome S. & Grace H., MD, 3697
Murray Foundation, Stuart and Eulene, GA, 2457
Murray, Jr. Foundation, James B. and Bruce R., The, VA, see 9500
Murrell Fund, J. Campbell, TX, 9082

Muscatine Foods Corporation Charitable Foundation, IA, 3318
Muse Educational Foundation, The, TX, 9083
Muselman Family Foundation, Inc., Arthur K., IN, 3209
Musgrave Foundation, MO, 4870
Mushett Family Foundation, Inc., NJ, 5334
Muskegon County Community Foundation, Inc., MI, see 4252
Muskingum County Community Foundation, OH, 7770
Muss Foundation, Inc., Stephen, The, FL, 2149
Musser Foundation, Warren V., The, PA, 8361
Musser Fund, Laura Jane, The, MN, 4629
Musser Fund, The, MN, see 4629
Mustard Seed Foundation, Inc., VA, 9481
Mustard Seed Foundation, The, KY, 3440
Muth Foundation, Peter & Mary, The, CA, 929
Mutual Federal Savings Bank Charitable Foundation, Inc., IN, 3210
Mutual of Omaha Foundation, NE, 4993
MWC Foundation, Inc., MA, 4046
My Brother Joey Foundation, CA, 930
Myer Foundation, Inc., Diane Lenfest, The, PA, see 8077
Myers Charitable Foundation, David G. & Carol P., MI, see 4402
Myers Foundation, David & Carol, MI, 4402
Myers Foundation, Inc., Israel & Mollie, The, MD, 3698
Mylan Charitable Foundation, The, WV, 9728

N.E.W. Charitable Foundation, Inc., The, VA, 9482
N.E.W. Relief Fund, Inc., The, VA, see 9482
Nabholz Charitable Trust, Robert D. & Barbara, AR, 168
Nabisco Foundation Trust, NY, see 6351
Nabit Foundation, Inc., The, MD, 3699
Naddisy Foundation, Inc., NY, 6598
Nadeau Charitable Foundation, Inc., The, FL, A
Nagel Foundation, CO, 1431
Nagel Foundation, Edward M., CA, 931
Nagel Foundation, John F., The, ID, 2573
Nagle Family Foundation, The, NY, 6599
NAH Foundation, The, TX, 9084
Nakash Family Foundation, NY, 6600
Nanci's Animal Rights Foundation, Inc., FL, 2150
Nancy and John Foundation, TX, see 9199
NAON, Inc., NY, 6601
Naples Children and Education Foundation, Inc., FL, 2151
Narada Foundation, Creighton, The, MA, 4047
Nasdaq Stock Market Educational Foundation, Inc., The, MD, 3700
Nash Charitable Trust, Beth Nash & Joshua, NY, see 6045
Nash Family Foundation, Inc., The, NY, 6602
Nash Long Life Foundation, Ted, The, TX, 9085
Nasher Foundation, The, TX, 9086
Nashville Community Foundation, Inc., TN, see 8662
Nason Foundation, Inc., Alex G., CT, 1606
Natan Foundation, WA, 9646
Nation Foundation (Corporation), TX, 9087
National Academy of Education, The, DC, 1838
National Bank of Commerce Foundation Inc., FL, see 2259
National Distillers Distributors Foundation, MN, 4630
National Hockey League Foundation, NY, 6603
National Institute of Torah Foundation, DC, see 1781
National Instruments Foundation, TX, 9088
National Organization for Hearing Research Foundation, PA, A
National Starch and Chemical Foundation, Inc., NJ, 5335
National Video Resources, Inc., NY, 6604
Nationwide Foundation, OH, 7771
Nationwide Insurance Enterprise Foundation, OH, see 7771
Navarro Community Foundation, TX, 9089
Nazarian Family Foundation, Y. & S., CA, 932
NBC Universal Foundation, CA, 933
NBI Healthcare Foundation, Inc., NJ, see 5228
NBT Charitable Trust, MA, 4048
NCC Charitable Foundation II, OH, see 7772
NCC Charitable Foundation, OH, 7772
NCR Foundation, The, OH, 7773
Neal Family Foundation, The, NC, 7433
NEC Foundation of America, NY, 6605

Needham Trust, Marie D., NC, A
Needmor Fund, The, OH, 7774
Neely Charitable Foundation, C. W. and Modene, AZ, 125
Neely Foundation, Otto & Edna, AZ, 126
Nef Foundation, Evelyn Stefansson, DC, 1839
Negaunee Foundation, Ltd., The, IL, 2909
Neidich & Brooke Garber Foundation, Daniel M., NY, 6606
Neighborhood Partners Fund, Inc., MA, 4049
Neilsen Foundation, Craig H., CA, 934
Neilson Foundation, George W., MN, 4631
Neiman Foundation, Inc., Leroy, NY, 6607
Neisser Fund, The, IL, 2910
Nelkin Foundation, The, NY, 6608
Nelson Family Foundation, Inc., Margaret Irene Taylor Nelson and Mary, MO, 4871
Nelson Family Foundation, Inc., The, WI, 9881
Nelson Family Foundation, Jonathan M., RI, 8549
Nelson Family Foundation, The, MN, 4632
Nelson Foundation, Grace S. & W. Linton, PA, 8362
Nelson Foundation, Hermoine and Glen, The, TN, 8712
Nelson Foundation, James & Aune, IL, 2911
Nelson Scholarship Fund, Victor and Mary D., WI, 9882
Nesholm Family Foundation, WA, 9647
Nessel Charitable Foundation, Melvin B., The, FL, 2152
Nestle Purina PetCare Trust Fund, MO, 4872
Nestle Scholarship Foundation, WA, 9648
Nestle USA Foundation, CA, 935
Netter Foundation, Inc., Edward and Barbara, CT, 1607
Netzach Foundation, NY, 6609
Neu Family Foundation, Inc., John L., The, NY, 6610
Neubauer Foundation, The, PA, 8363
Neuberger Berman Foundation, The, DE, 1735
Neuberger Foundation, Inc., Roy R. and Marie S., NY, 6611
Neukom Family Foundation, WA, 9649
Neuwirth Foundation, Inc., NY, 6612
Nevada Community Foundation, Inc., NV, 5047
Nevada Partners, Inc., NV, 5048
Nevas Family Foundation, Inc., Leo & Libby, CT, see 1608
Nevas Family Foundation, Inc., Leo, CT, 1608
New Albany Community Foundation, OH, 7775
New Balance Foundation, MA, 4050
New Blank Family Foundation, Inc., The, FL, see 1909
New Breeze Foundation, MA, 4051
New Britain Foundation for Public Giving, CT, see 1515
New Cycle Foundation, NM, 5490
New England Biolabs Foundation, MA, 4052
New England Foundation, The, MA, 4053
New England Patriots Charitable Foundation, Inc., The, MA, 4054
New Hampshire Charitable Foundation, The, NH, 5098
New Haven Foundation, The, CT, see 1514
New Haven Savings Bank Foundation, Inc., The, CT, A
New Hope Foundation, IA, 3319
New Horizon Foundation, WA, A
New Horizons at Choate, Inc., MA, see 3871
New Jersey Natural Gas Foundation, NJ, 5336
New Jersey Nets and Devils Foundation, NJ, 5337
New Jersey Nets Foundation, Inc., NJ, see 5337
New Jersey Resources Foundation, Inc., NJ, see 5336
New Mexico Community Foundation, The, NM, 5491
New Orleans Foundation, Greater, The, LA, 3503
New Prospect Foundation, IL, 2912
New York Community Trust, The, NY, 6613
New York Crohns Foundation, NY, 6614
New York Foundation, NY, 6615
New York Jets Foundation, Inc., NY, 6616
New York Life Foundation, NY, 6617
New York Mercantile Exchange Charitable Foundation, NY, 6618
New York Stock Exchange Foundation, Inc., NY, 6619
New York Times Company Foundation, Inc., The, NY, 6620
New-Land Foundation, Inc., The, NY, 6621
Newcastle Foundation, NY, 6622
Newcombe Foundation, Charlotte W., The, NJ, 5338
Newell Rubbermaid Scholarship Fund, The, IL, 2913
Newhall Foundation, Henry Mayo, The, CA, 936
Newhouse Foundation, Inc., Samuel I., NY, 6623

Newman Assistance Fund, Inc., Jerome A. and Estelle R., NY, 6624
Newman Charitable Foundation, Lizbeth & Frank, The, NY, 6625
Newman Family Foundation, CO, 1432
Newman Foundation, Barnett and Annalee, The, DE, 1736
Newman Foundation, Clinton E., IN, 3211
Newman Foundation, John and Florence, TX, 9090
Newman's Own Foundation, Inc., CT, 1609
Newman-Tanner Foundation, NY, 6626
NFC Foundation, MN, 4633
NFG Foundation, OH, 7776
NFM Charitable Trust, NC, 7434
Ng Charitable Foundation, Anna F., CA, A
Niamogue Foundation, IL, 2914
Nias Foundation, Inc., Henry, NC, 7435
NIB Foundation, IL, 2915
Niblack Foundation, The, CT, 1610
Niblick Family Foundation, Daniel M., IN, 3212
Nicholas Family Charitable Trust, NY, 6627
Nicholas Family Foundation, WI, 9883
Nicholas Foundation, The, CA, 937
Nichols Charitable Foundation, Miller, MO, 4873
Nichols Family Foundation, John D. & Alexandria C., IL, 2916
Nichols Foundation, Inc., N. Woodburn, MA, 4055
Nichols Foundation, Inc., NY, 6628
Nicholson Family Foundation, MN, 4634
Nicholson Foundation, NY, 6629
Nicholson Foundation, Richard H. and Nancy B., MN, see 4634
Nickel Producers Environmental Research Association, Inc., NC, 7436
Nickless Family Charitable Foundation, The, MI, 4403
Nicolais Foundation, Inc., The, NJ, 5339
Nicolitch Charitable Trust, Dragomir, The, NY, 6630
Niehaus Foundation, Robert and Kate, The, NY, 6631
Nightingale Code Foundation, The, TX, 9091
NIKE Foundation, OR, 8046
NIKE P.L.A.Y. Foundation, OR, see 8046
Niles Foundation, Henry E., CT, 1611
Niles Foundation, Laura J., CT, 1612
Nimoy Foundation, The, CA, 938
Nippert Charitable Foundation, Inc., L. and L., OH, 7777
Nirenberg Family Charitable Foundation, Inc., CT, see 1613
Nirenberg Foundation, Inc., CT, 1613
Nirman Foundation, VA, 9483
NiSource Charitable Foundation, IN, 3213
Nissan Foundation, The, CA, 939
No Other Foundation, TN, 8713
Noah's Family Foundation, AZ, 127
Noble Charitable Foundation, Inc., Donald E. and Alice M., OH, see 7778
Noble Charitable Trust, John H. and Ethel G., NY, 6632
Noble County Community Foundation, IN, 3214
Noble Foundation, Inc., Donald and Alice, OH, 7778
Noble Foundation, Inc., Edward John, NY, 6633
Noble Foundation, Inc., Samuel Roberts, The, OK, 7963
Nokomis Foundation, The, MI, 4404
Noonan Memorial Fund, Deborah Munroe, RI, 8550
Noonan Trust, Frank M., RI, see 8550
Noorda Foundation, Ray and Tye, The, UT, 9336
Nooril-Iman Charitable Foundation, Inc., MA, 4056
Norcliffe Foundation, The, WA, 9650
Norcliffe Fund, The, WA, see 9650
Norcross Family Foundation, Mark A. and Rena R., NC, 7437
Norcross Wildlife Foundation, Inc., NY, 6634
Nord Family Foundation, The, OH, 7779
Nord Foundation, Eric and Jane, The, OH, 7780
Nordick Foundation, R. B., The, ND, 7518
Nordson Corporation Foundation, The, OH, 7781
Nordstrom Charitable Foundation, Illsley B., WA, A
Noreen Family Charitable Trust, MN, 4635
Norfolk Foundation, The, VA, 9484
Norfolk Southern Foundation, VA, 9485
Norman Foundation, Inc., NY, 6635
Normandie Foundation, Inc., NY, 6636
Norris Foundation, Dellora A. & Lester J., IL, 2917
Norris Foundation, Kenneth T. and Eileen L., The, CA, 940

North American Rescue Products Foundation, Inc., SC, 8601
North Carolina Community Foundation, NC, 7438
North Carolina GlaxoSmithKline Foundation, The, NC, 7439
North Central Massachusetts Community Foundation, Inc., MA, 4057
North Central Michigan Community Foundation, MI, see 4253
North Dade Medical Foundation, Inc., FL, 2153
North Dakota Community Foundation, ND, 7519
North Dakota Natural Resources Trust, Inc., ND, 7520
North Dakota Wetlands Trust, Inc., ND, see 7520
North Fork Foundation, NY, 6637
North Georgia Community Foundation, GA, 2458
North Manchester Community Foundation, IN, see 3132
North Pacific Marine Science Foundation, WA, 9651
Northeast Iowa Charitable Foundation, IA, 3320
Northeast Michigan Community Foundation, MI, see 4253
Northeast Utilities Foundation, Inc., CT, 1614
Northen Endowment, Mary Moody, TX, 9092
Northern California Scholarship Foundation and the Scaife Scholarship Foundation, The, CA, see 941
Northern California Scholarship Foundation, The, CA, 941
Northern Chautauqua Community Foundation, Inc., NY, 6638
Northern Indiana Community Foundation, Inc., IN, 3215
Northern New York Community Foundation, Inc., NY, 6639
Northern Trust Company Charitable Trust, The, IL, 2918
Northern Virginia Community Foundation, VA, 9486
Northrop Grumman Foundation, The, CA, 942
Northwest Area Foundation, MN, 4636
Northwest Arkansas Community Foundation, AR, 169
Northwest Autism Foundation, OR, 8047
Northwest Florida Improvement Foundation, Inc., FL, see 2244
Northwest Health Foundation Fund, II, OR, 8048
Northwest Minnesota Foundation (NWMF), MN, 4637
Northwestern Mutual Foundation, WI, 9884
Northwestern Mutual Life Foundation, WI, see 9884
Northwestern National Insurance Foundation, CT, see 1672
Norton Company Foundation, PA, see 8419
Norton Family Foundation, Peter, CA, 943
Norton Foundation, Inc., George W., The, KY, see 3441
Norton Foundation, Inc., The, KY, 3441
Norwest Foundation, CA, see 1294
Norwood Foundation, The, CO, 1433
Notsew Orm Sands Foundation, TX, 9093
Novak Foundation, Inc., David C. and Wendy L., The, KY, 3442
Novartis US Foundation, NY, 6640
NoVo Foundation, NY, 6641
Novogratz Family Foundation, The, NY, see 6642
Novogratz-Caceres Family Foundation, The, NY, 6642
Novotny Charitable Trust, Yetta Deitch, PA, 8364
Noyce Foundation, The, CA, 944
Noyes Foundation, Inc., Jessie Smith, NY, 6643
Noyes, Jr. Memorial Foundation, Inc., Nicholas H., IN, 3216
NSN Foundation, Inc., NJ, 5340
Nuclear Threat Initiative, Inc., DC, A
Nucor Foundation, NC, 7440
Nuhn Charitable Trust, Jane W., NY, 6644
Numero-Steinfeldt Foundation, MN, A
Nureyev Dance Foundation, Rudolf, IL, 2919
Nutting Foundation, The, WV, 9729
Nye Scholarship Trust, Grace Swift Nye & Alfred Gibbs, CT, 1615
Nygren Charitable Foundation, William & Sara, IL, see 2920
Nygren Foundation, Bill, IL, 2920
NYMEX Charitable Foundation, NY, see 6618

O'Bannon Foundation, Michael A., NV, 5049
O'Brien Foundation, Dennis and Gloria, CA, 945
O'Brien Foundation, Inc., Cornelius and Anna Cook, WI, A
O'Brien Foundation, Inc., James W., MA, 4058
O'Connor & Hewitt Foundation, The, TX, 9094

O'Connor Foundation, A. Lindsay and Olive B., NY, 6645
O'Connor Foundation, Carroll and Nancy, CA, 946
O'Connor Foundation, Dorothy, TX, see 9094
O'Connor Foundation, Kathryn, The, TX, 9095
O'Connor Foundation, William F., The, IL, 2921
O'Donnell Charitable Trust, Joseph & Katherine, MA, 4059
O'Donnell Family Charitable Foundation, WA, 9652
O'Donnell Foundation, TX, 9096
O'Gara Foundation, Thomas M. & Victoria, CO, A
O'Herron Family Foundation, The, NY, 6646
O'Herron Foundation, Inc., NC, 7441
O'Herron Foundation, Jonathan & Shirley, NY, see 6646
O'Keeffe Charitable Foundation, Esther B., FL, 2154
O'Malley Foundation, Inc., T. D. & M. A., The, NY, 6647
O'Malley Foundation, Inc., The, NY, 6648
O'Neil Foundation, Casey Albert T., The, MN, 4638
O'Neil Foundation, Cyril F. and Marie E., NY, 6649
O'Neil Foundation, M. G., The, FL, 2155
O'Neil Foundation, W., The, MD, 3701
O'Neill Brothers Foundation, The, OH, 7782
O'Neill Foundation, Inc., William J. and Dorothy K., The, OH, 7783
O'Neill Foundation, Timothy J. and Linda D., The, NY, 6650
O'Quinn Foundation, John M., TX, 9097
O'Quinn Foundation, The, TX, see 9097
O'Shaughnessy Foundation, Inc., I. A., MN, 4639
O'Shaughnessy-Hurst Memorial Foundation, Inc., The, VA, 9487
O'Shea Family Foundation, The, NY, 6651
O'Shea Foundation, Robert J. and Michele K., The, NY, see 6651
O'Sullivan Children Foundation, Inc., The, NY, 6652
O'Sullivan Foundation, The, TX, 9098
O'Toole Family Foundation, The, NY, 6653
O'Toole Foundation, Theresa and Edward, NY, 6654
Oak Foundation U.S.A., The, ME, 3552
Oak Hill Fund, VA, 9488
Oak Park/River Forest Community Foundation, IL, 2922
Oak Tree Philanthropic Foundation, The, CA, 947
Oakland Athletics Community Fund, The, CA, 948
Oaklawn Foundation, The, CT, 1616
Oakleaf Foundation, IL, see 2896
Oakley Foundation, Inc., Hollie & Anna, IN, 3217
Oakley Foundation, Inc., Mary, The, CA, 949
Oakwood Foundation Charitable Trust, MS, 4760
Oberkotter Foundation, PA, 8365
Oberndorf Foundation, CA, 950
Oberweiler Foundation, IL, 2923
Ocean Federal Foundation, NJ, see 5341
Ocean Reef Community Foundation, FL, see 2156
Ocean Reef Foundation, Inc., FL, 2156
OceanFirst Foundation, NJ, 5341
Oceanic Heritage Foundation, The, MO, 4874
Ochsman Foundation, Inc., The, VA, 9489
Ochylski Family Foundation, IA, 3321
OCLO, Inc., NY, 6655
October Hill Foundation, The, CT, 1617
Odell Fund, Robert Stewart Odell and Helen Pfeiffer, CA, 951
Oehmig Foundation, The, TX, 9099
Oestreicher Foundation, Inc., Sylvan and Ann, NY, 6656
Offield Family Foundation, The, IL, 2924
Ogden Foundation, Inc., Ralph E., NY, 6657
Ogle Foundation, Inc., Paul, IN, 3218
Ohga Foundation, Norio, The, NY, 6658
Ohio Casualty Foundation, Inc., OH, 7784
Ohio National Foundation, The, OH, 7785
Ohio Savings Association Charitable Foundation, OH, 7786
Ohrstrom Foundation, Inc., The, NY, 6659
Oishei Foundation, John R., The, NY, 6660
Oki Charitable Foundation, The, WA, see 9653
Oki Foundation, The, WA, 9653
Oklahoma City Community Foundation, Inc., OK, 7964
Oklahoma Communities Foundation, Inc., OK, see 7931
Oklahoma Gas and Electric Company Foundation, Inc., OK, 7965
Oklahoman Foundation, The, OK, 7966
Olayan Charitable Trust, NY, 6661
Oldham Little Church Foundation, TX, 9100

Olemberg Private Foundation, Isaac Olemberg and Nieves, The, FL, 2157
Oleson Foundation, MI, 4405
Olin Corporation Charitable Trust, IL, 2925
Olive Branch Foundation, Inc., The, OH, 7787
Olive Bridge Fund, Inc., NY, 6662
Oliver Family Foundation, The, OH, 7788
Oliver Memorial Trust Foundation, IN, 3219
Olmsted Foundation, George and Carol, The, VA, 9490
Olofson Foundation, Tom W. and Jeanne H., MO, 4875
Olsen Foundation, a New Jersey Nonprofit Corporation, The, NJ, 5342
Olshan Foundation, Morton & Carole, NY, 6663
Olson Foundation, Earl B., MN, 4640
Olson Foundation, The, CT, 1618
Olsson Memorial Foundation, Elis, VA, 9491
Omaha Community Foundation, NE, 4994
Omaha World-Herald Foundation, The, NE, 4995
OMC Foundation, The, WI, A
Omega Foundation, The, NV, 5050
Omidyar Foundation, The, CA, A
Omidyar Network Fund, Inc., CA, 952
Omnicare Charitable Foundation, KY, 3443
Omnicare Foundation, KY, 3444
OMNOVA Solutions Foundation Inc., OH, 7789
Omron Foundation, Inc., IL, 2926
On Shore, Inc., CA, 953
On Top of the World Foundation, Inc., The, FL, see 1938
Once Upon A Time Foundation, TX, 9101
One Light-The Innocent Heart Foundation, CA, see 810
One Valley Bank Foundation, Inc., WV, see 9710
OneAmerica Foundation, Inc., IN, 3220
OneBeacon Charitable Trust, MA, 4060
OneFamily Foundation, WA, 9654
ONEOK Foundation, Inc., OK, 7967
Onstead Foundation, Robert R. and Kay M., The, TX, 9102
Onward & Upward Initiative Charitable Trust, TX, 9103
Opatrny Family Foundation, The, NY, 6664
Opatrny, Jr. Charitable Foundation, Donald C. and Judith T., NY, see 6664
Open Doors International, Inc., CA, 954
Open Society Institute, NY, 6665
Open Spaces, Sacred Places, MD, see 3747
Opler Foundation, Edmond and Alice, IL, 2927
Opler Foundation, Edmond, IL, see 2927
Opler Foundation, Scott, FL, 2158
Oppenheimer & Flora Oppenheimer Haas Foundation, Leo, NY, 6666
Oppenheimer Brothers Foundation, CA, 955
Oppenheimer Family Foundation, Gerald and Virginia, CA, see 956
Oppenheimer Family Foundation, Gerald, CA, 956
Oppenheimer Family Foundation, The, IL, 2928
Oppenstein Brothers Foundation, MO, 4876
Opperman Foundation, Dwight D., The, MN, 4641
Opportunities for Education Foundation, WA, 9655
Opus Foundation, MN, 4642
Opus Prize Foundation, SD, 8628
Oral Health Services Foundation, Inc., MA, 4061
Orange County Community Foundation, CA, 957
Orange Orphan Society, The, NJ, 5343
Orange Tree Foundation, The, DE, 1737
Orchard Farm Foundation, The, CT, 1619
Orchard Foundation, The, MA, 4062
Ordean Foundation, MN, 4643
Oregon Community Foundation, The, OR, 8049
Orenstein Foundation, Inc., Henry and Carolyn Sue, NJ, 5344
Orentreich Family Foundation, The, NY, 6667
Orfalea Family Foundation, The, CA, 958
Oristaglio Family Foundation, MA, 4063
Orleton Trust Fund, KY, 3445
Ornest Family Foundation, CA, 959
Orokawa Foundation, Inc., The, MD, 3702
Orr Family Foundation, Robert O. and AnnaMae, OH, 7790
Orscheln Industries Foundation, Inc., MO, 4877
Orson A. Hull & Minnie E. Hull Educational Foundation, MN, 4644
Ortenberg Foundation, The, NY, see 5757
Ortenzio Family Foundation, The, PA, 8366

Orthwein Foundation, William R. Orthwein, Jr. & Laura Rand, The, MO, 4878
Orvis Foundation, Arthur Emerton, The, NY, see 6668
Orvis Foundation, Inc., Arthur and Mae, The, NY, 6668
Osborn Charitable Trust, Edward B., NY, 6669
Osborn Foundation, The, CO, 1434
Osborne Foundation, Inc., Weldon F., TN, 8714
Oschin Family Foundation, Mr. & Mrs. Samuel, CA, A, 960
Oser Foundation, Margaret E., The, CA, A
Osher Foundation, Bernard, CA, 961
Osher Pro Suecia Foundation, Barbro, The, CA, 962
Oshkosh Area Community Foundation, WI, 9885
Oshkosh B'Gosh Foundation, Inc., WI, 9886
Oshkosh Foundation, WI, see 9885
Oshkosh Truck Foundation, Inc., WI, 9887
Oshman Family Foundation, The, CA, 963
Oshman Foundation, TX, 9104
OSI Pharmaceuticals Foundation, Inc., NY, 6670
Osprey Foundation, The, MD, 3703
Osteopathic Heritage Foundations, OH, 7791
Ostin Family Foundation, CA, 964
Ostreicher Family Foundation, Harry & Helen, NY, 6671
Ostreicher Family Foundation, Marvin & Susan, NY, 6672
Ostrovsky Family Fund, Inc., NY, 6673
Oswald Charitable Foundation, MN, see 4645
Oswald Family Foundation, MN, 4645
Otenasek Charitable Foundation, Inc., Anne Lindsey, The, MD, 3704
Ottens Foundation, John and Sophie, The, AZ, 128
Otter Cove Foundation, CA, 965
Otter Island Foundation, TX, 9105
Ottinger Foundation, The, NY, 6674
Ottley Trust-Watertown, Marian W., CT, see 1678
Outagamie Charitable Foundation, Inc., WI, 9888
Outcalt Charitable Fund, OH, see 7792
Outcalt Foundation, Jane and Jon, OH, 7792
Outhwaite Charitable Trust, June G., CA, 966
Outrageous Foundation, Inc., The, CA, 967
Overbrook Foundation, The, NY, 6675
Overhills Foundation, NY, 6676
Overlock Family Foundation, NY, see 5930
Overly Foundation, Edith H., MA, 4064
Overstreet Foundation, FL, 2159
Overture Foundation, WI, 9889
Ovitz Family Foundation, The, CA, 968
Owen Foundation, Dian Graves, TX, 9106
Owen Trust, B. B., TX, 9107
Owenoke Foundation, The, CT, 1620
Owens Corning Foundation, OH, 7793
Owens Foundation, The, IL, 2929
Owens Foundation, Thomas M. & Mary M., IL, see 2929
Owsley Foundation, Alvin and Lucy, TX, 9108
Oxford Area Foundation, The, PA, 8367
Oxford Foundation, Inc., GA, see 2428
Oxley Foundation, The, OK, 7968
Oxnard Foundation, CA, 969
Ozinga Foundation, Inc., The, IL, 2930

P & B Foundation, NC, 7442
P & M Charities, Inc., FL, 2160
PACCAR Foundation, WA, 9656
Pace Foundation, Inc., Dorothy, MA, 4065
Pacific Foundation, MN, 4646
Pacific Life Foundation, CA, 970
Pacific Mutual Charitable Foundation, CA, see 970
Pacific Power/Rocky Mountain Power Foundation, OR, see 8050
PacifiCare Health Systems Foundation, CA, 971
PacifiCorp Foundation For Learning, OR, see 8050
PacifiCorp Foundation, OR, 8050
Packard Foundation, David and Lucile, The, CA, 972
Packard Humanities Institute, The, CA, 973
Padnos Foundation, Louis and Helen, MI, 4406
Paduano Family Foundation, Daniel P. and Nancy C., NY, 6677
Paducah Area Community Foundation, KY, see 3415
Paestum Foundation, Inc., The, NY, 6678
PAH Foundation, WA, 9657
PaineWebber Foundation, NJ, see 5433
Palestine Temple Charities Trust, RI, see 8556
Palestroni Foundation, Inc., Alfiero and Lucia, NJ, 5345

Paley Foundation, Inc., William S., NY, 6679

Palin Foundation, The, NC, 7443

Palisano Foundation, Vincent and Harriet, The, NY, 6680

Palm Beach Community Trust Fund, FL, 2161

Palm Beach County Community Foundation, FL, see 1939

Palm Foundation, Michael, NY, 6681

Palmer Foundation, Francis Asbury, The, NY, 6682

Palmer Foundation, Inc., The, NY, 6683

Palmer Foundation, The, WI, 9890

Palmer Fund, Frank Loomis, The, CT, 1621

Paloheimo Foundation, CA, 974

Palumbo Charitable Trust, A. J. & Sigismunda, PA, 8368

Pamida Foundation, WI, 9891

Pamphalon Foundation, Inc., FL, 2162

Panaphil Foundation, The, NY, 6684

Panda Charitable Foundation, The, CA, 975

Paneth Family Charitable Trust, The, NY, 6685

Pangburn Foundation, The, WI, 9892

Panic, Jr. Foundation, Milan, CA, 976

Pannonia Foundation, NY, 6686

Panwy Foundation, Inc., CT, 1622

Pappajohn Scholarship Foundation, John & Mary, IA, 3322

Pappas Charitable Foundation, Inc., Thomas Anthony, MA, 4066

Pappas Foundation, Arthur M. & Martha R., MA, 4067

Paramitas Foundation, CA, 977

Parasol Community Foundation, Inc., NV, see 5051

Parasol Foundation, Inc., NV, 5051

Pardee Foundation, Elsa U., MI, 4407

Pardee Foundation, J. Douglas & Marian R., The, CA, 978

Pardoe Foundation, Samuel P., MA, 4068

Parish Foundation, Suzanne D., MI, see 4408

Parish Foundation, Suzanne Upjohn Delano, MI, 4408

Park Charitable Trust, NY, 6687

Park Foundation, Inc., NY, 6688

Park Foundation, NY, see 6687

Park Foundation, The, NY, 6689

Park Foundation, The, OH, 7794

Park National Bank Foundation, The, OH, see 7795

Park National Corporation Foundation, The, OH, 7795

Park Place Foundation, Inc., TN, see 8648

Parker Family Foundation, NJ, 5346

Parker Foundation, Inc., Jack, The, NY, 6690

Parker Foundation, Mary E., The, DE, 1738

Parker Foundation, The, CA, 979

Parker Foundation, Theodore Edson, The, MA, 4069

Parker Foundation, VA, 9492

Parker-Hannifin Foundation, The, OH, 7796

Parkersburg Area Community Foundation, WV, 9730

Parks Education Foundation, NV, 5052

Parks Foundation, Dorothy C. and Richard A., IL, 2931

Parks Foundation, Fred & Mabel R., TX, 9109

Parkview Foundation, NY, 6691

Parlin Trust, Albert N., MA, 4070

Parmer Family Foundation, Inc., The, PA, 8369

Parmer Private Foundation, John C. & Carolyn Noonan, The, IL, 2932

Parnassus Foundation, NJ, 5347

Parnes Foundation, Inc., E. & H., NJ, 5348

Parr Family Foundation, Inc., Gary W., The, NY, 6692

Parr Trust, Martha Sue, WI, 9893

Parshelsky Foundation, Moses L., NY, 6693

Parsons - W.D. Charities, Inc., Vera Davis, FL, see 1961

Parsons Foundation, Alison J. & Ella W., The, VA, A

Parsons Foundation, Mary Morton, The, VA, 9493

Parsons Foundation, Ralph M., The, CA, 980

Parsons Memorial Foundation, Ann, NY, 6694

Partnership for Excellence in Jewish Education, MA, 4071

Partnership Foundation, The, TX, 9110

Partridge Foundation, The, NY, 6695

Parvin Foundation, Albert, The, CA, 981

Pasadena Area Residential Aid, A Corporation, CA, A

Pasadena Community Foundation, CA, 982

Pasadena Foundation, CA, see 982

Pascal International, Inc., FL, 2163

Pascale/Sykes Foundation, Inc., NJ, 5349

Pascucci Family Foundation, NY, 6696

Paso del Norte Health Foundation, TX, 9111

Pasquinelli Family Foundation, IL, 2933

Patricelli Family Foundation, Robert & Margaret, The, CT, 1623

Patrick Foundation, Inc., Carl & Frances, The, GA, 2459

Patron Saints Foundation, The, CA, 983

Patterson Dental Foundation, MN, see 4647

Patterson Family Charitable Foundation, The, AL, 56

Patterson Foundation, Cissy, The, DC, 1840

Patterson Foundation, MN, 4647

Patterson Foundation, Proctor, OH, 7797

Patterson Trust, Robert Leet Patterson & Clara Guthrie, CT, 1624

Patterson-Barclay Memorial Foundation, Inc., GA, 2460

Paul Family Foundation, Andrew M., NY, 6697

Paul Foundation, Inc., Josephine Bay Paul and C. Michael, NY, see 5606

Paul Foundation, Inc., Terrance and Judith, CO, 1435

Pauley Family Foundation, The, VA, 9494

Pauley Foundation, Edwin W., The, CA, 984

Paulina Foundation, Anna, MI, 4409

Paulos Foundation, The, TX, 9112

Paulson, Jr. Foundation, Henry M. & Wendy J., NY, see 5645

Paulucci Family Foundation, Jeno & Lois, The, FL, 2164

Paulucci Family Foundation, The, FL, see 2164

Paulus Family Foundation, WA, 9658

Pax Christi Foundation, MN, 4648

Payless ShoeSource Foundation, KS, 3380

Payne Family Foundation, Inc., Karen & Christopher, CA, 985

Payne Foundation, Frank E. Payne and Seba B., IL, 2934

Payne Fund, The, OH, 7798

PBHP, Inc., NY, 6698

PBO Fund, Inc., NY, 6699

PDB Foundation, Inc., IL, 2935

PE Charitable Foundation, CT, see 1484

Peabody Charitable Fund, Amelia, MA, 4072

Peabody Foundation, Amelia, MA, 4073

Peabody Foundation, Inc., The, MA, 4074

Peabody Foundation, Mary K., IN, 3221

Peach Foundation, WA, 9659

Peacock Foundation, Inc., FL, 2165

Peale Foundation, Inc., NY, 6700

Pearce Foundation Trust, Mary Elizabeth, MA, 4075

Pearce Foundation, Inc., Dr. M. Lee, The, FL, 2166

Pearl Foundation, The, MO, 4879

Pearle Vision Foundation, Inc., TX, 9113

Pearson-Rappaport Foundation, NY, 6701

Peaster Foundation, MS, 4761

Pechter Foundation, The, GA, 2461

Peck Foundation, Inc., Milton and Lillian, WI, 9894

Peck Foundation, Ltd., Miriam & Bernard, WI, see 9895

Peck Foundation, Milwaukee, Ltd., WI, 9895

Peckham Family Foundation, NY, 6702

Peco Foundation, NY, 6703

Pedersen Charitable Trust, Peer & Mary, NY, 6704

Peeler Charitable Trust, R. G. and Claudine Pope, TX, A

Peery Charitable Foundation, Louis Scowcroft, The, UT, 9337

Peery Foundation, CA, 986

Peierls Foundation, NY, 6705

Peirce Family Foundation, Inc., The, PA, 8370

Pell and Mark Winkelman Foundation, Dorinda, NY, see 7028

Pell Family Foundation, CA, 987

Pella Rolscreen Foundation, IA, 3323

Pelosi Charitable Foundation, Paul & Nancy, CA, 988

Pels Charitable Trust, Donald A., NY, 6706

Pels Foundation, Laura, The, NY, 6707

Pels International Foundation, Laura, NY, 6708

Peltier Foundation, The, LA, 3504

Pema Foundation, TX, 9114

PEMCO Foundation, WA, 9660

Penates Foundation, The, NH, 5099

Pendleton Charitable Trust, James B., WA, 9661

Penick Fund, Albert, NY, 6709

Peninsula Community Foundation, CA, 989

Peninsula Foundation, The, OH, 7799

Penn Community Trust, Annie, NC, 7444

Penn Foundation, William, The, PA, 8371

Penner Foundation, Inc., Arnold S., NY, 6710

Penney Company Fund, Inc., J. C., TX, 9115

Penney Family Fund, CA, 990

Pennington Foundation, Irene W. & C. B., LA, 3505

Pennington Foundation, William N. and Myriam, NV, 5053

Pennington Foundation, William N., NV, see 5053

Penson Foundation, Shannon and Andrew S., NY, 6711

Pentair Foundation, The, MN, 4649

Penzance Foundation, NY, 6712

People in Business Care, Inc., MN, 4650

Peoria Area Community Foundation, IL, see 2677

Pepper Family Foundation, IL, 2936

Peppercorn Foundation, MA, 4076

Peppers Foundation, Ann, The, CA, 991

Pepsi Bottling Group Foundation, Inc., The, NY, 6713

Pepsi-Cola of Charlotte Foundation, Inc., NC, see 7386

PepsiAmericas Foundation, IL, 2937

PepsiCo Foundation, Inc., The, NY, 6714

Pequot Capital Foundation, Inc., The, CT, 1625

Pequot Community Foundation, Inc., The, CT, see 1517

Perdue Foundation, Inc., Arthur W., MD, 3705

Perella Foundation, A. J., The, NY, 6715

Perelman Charitable Foundation, Inc., IN, 3222

Perelman Community Foundation, Raymond & Ruth, PA, 8372

Perelman Education Foundation, Raymond & Ruth, PA, 8373

Perelman Family Foundation, NY, 6716

Perelman Judaica Foundation, Raymond & Ruth, PA, 8374

Perkin Fund, The, NY, 6717

Perkin Perpetual Charitable Trust, Sylvia, PA, 8375

PerkinElmer Foundation, MA, 4077

Perkins Charitable Foundation, The, OH, 7800

Perkins Foundation, Kitty M., NE, 4996

Perkins Memorial Fund, James J. and Mamie R., NC, 7445

Perkins-Prothro Foundation, TX, 9116

Perlman Family Foundation, Harold L., IL, 2938

Perlman Family Foundation, Lawrence and Linda, MN, 4651

Perlman Family Foundation, MN, see 4651

Perlman Foundation, Harold L., IL, see 2938

Permian Basin Area Foundation, TX, 9117

Perot Foundation, The, TX, 9118

Perot, Jr. Foundation, Sarah and Ross, The, TX, 9119

Perpetual Trust for Charitable Giving, MA, 4078

Perrigo Company Charitable Foundation, MI, 4410

Perrin Family Foundation, The, CT, 1626

Perrin Foundation, The, NJ, 5350

Perritt Charitable Foundation, Richard A., IL, 2939

Perry Foundation, Edward Lee and Slocumb Hollis, The, MA, 4079

Perry Foundation, Inc., VA, 9495

Perry Foundation, Patricia and Douglas, VA, 9496

Persepolis Foundation, The, NY, 6718

Pershing Charitable Trust, MO, 4880

Pershing Place Foundation, MO, 4881

Persky Foundation, Joseph, MA, 4080

Personality Disorder Research Corp., NY, see 5652

Pertusati Charitable Trust, Joseph & Evelyn, CA, 992

Peters Foundation Corp., Herman & Katherine, The, IL, 2940

Peters Foundation, Inc., Leon S., CA, 993

Peters Foundation, Lovett, OH, see 7801

Peters Foundation, Ruth and Lovett, OH, 7801

Peters Medical Education Trust Fund, Dr. Clinton N. & Alice F., ME, 3553

Peters Research Foundation, Harvey W., SD, 8629

Peters Trust, Frank R., MA, 4081

Petersen Foundation, Esper A., IL, 2941

Petersen Foundation, Margie & Robert E., CA, 994

Peterson Charitable Foundation, Alan & Mildred, IL, 2942

Peterson Family Foundation, Inc., VA, 9497

Peterson Family Foundation, Jeffrey and Karen, The, CA, 995

Peterson Family Foundation, The, WA, 9662

Peterson Foundation, G. & D., MN, 4652

Peterson Foundation, Hal & Charlie, TX, 9120

Peterson Foundation, Inc., Fred J., WI, 9896

Peterson Foundation, Patricia Price, The, CA, 996

Peterson Foundation, The, PA, 8376

Peterson Foundation, Thomas F., The, OH, 7802

Petitpren Family Foundation, Dean & Diane, MI, 4411

Petoskey-Harbor Springs Area Community Foundation, MI, 4412
Petrello Family Foundation, TX, 9121
Petrie Foundation, Carroll and Milton, The, NY, A
Petters Family Foundation, Thomas J., MN, 4653
Petteys Memorial Foundation, Jack, The, CO, 1436
Pettit Foundation, Inc., Jane and Lloyd, WI, see 9897
Pettit Foundation, Jane Bradley, WI, 9897
Pettus Foundation, MO, 4882
Pettus, Jr. Foundation, James T., MO, see 4882
Pettway Foundation, Jane L., TN, 8715
Petway Family Foundation, Inc., The, FL, 2167
Pevaroff Cohn Family Foundation, The, NY, 6719
Pew Charitable Trusts, The, PA, 8377
Pfaffinger Foundation, CA, 997
Pfau Foundation, Daniel and Susan, The, OH, 7803
Pfeiffer Research Foundation, Gustavus and Louise, NJ, 5351
Pfizer Foundation, Inc., The, NY, 6720
Pfleger Foundation, George T., CA, 998
Pfleger Foundation, Harriet E., The, CA, 999
Pforzheimer Foundation, Inc., Carl and Lily, The, NY, 6721
PG&E Corporation Foundation, The, CA, 1000
PGE Foundation, OR, 8051
PGE-Enron Foundation, OR, see 8051
Phaedrus Foundation, NY, 6722
Pharmacy Network Foundation, Inc., The, NC, 7446
Phelan Foundation, The, NY, 6723
Phelps Dodge Foundation, AZ, 129
Phelps Family Foundation, CA, 1001
Phelps Foundation, Wilson W., CA, 1002
Phifer/Johnson Foundation, SC, 8602
Philadelphia Foundation, The, PA, 8378
Philadelphia Health Care Trust, PA, 8379
Phileona Foundation, The, MN, 4654
Philibosian Foundation, Stephen, The, CA, 1003
Philips Foundation, Jesse and Caryl, The, OH, 7804
Philips Industries Foundation, OH, see 7884
Phillips Charitable Trust, Dr. & Mrs. Arthur William, PA, 8380
Phillips Family Foundation, Charles G., The, NY, 6724
Phillips Family Foundation, Inc., L. E., The, DE, 1739
Phillips Family Foundation, Jay and Rose, The, MN, 4655
Phillips Family Foundation, TX, 9122
Phillips Foundation, Dr. P., The, FL, 2168
Phillips Foundation, Edwin, MA, 4082
Phillips Foundation, Inc., DC, 1841
Phillips Foundation, Louie M. & Betty M., TN, 8716
Phillips Foundation, The, MN, see 4655
Phillips Foundation, Waite and Genevieve, NM, 5492
Phillips Memorial Charitable Trust, Stephen, MA, 4083
Phillips-Van Heusen Foundation, Inc., NY, 6725
Phipps Foundation, Howard, NJ, 5352
Phipps Foundation, William H., WI, 9898
Phoenix Family Foundation, NJ, see 5193
Phoenix Foundation, Inc., The, CT, 1627
Phoenixville Community Health Foundation, PA, 8381
Physicians New Orleans Foundation, LA, see 3498
Picerne Family Foundation, CA, 1004
Picerne Foundation, Ken and Tonya, CA, see 1004
Pick Charitable Trust, Melitta S., WI, 9899
Pick, Jr. Fund, Albert, The, IL, 2943
Pickett & Hatcher Educational Fund, Inc., GA, 2462
Pickford Foundation, Mary, CA, 1005
Pickle Charitable Foundation, James W., The, TN, 8717
Picower Foundation, Jeffry M. & Barbara, The, FL, see 2169
Picower Foundation, The, FL, 2169
Piedmont Natural Gas Foundation, NC, 7447
Pieperpower Foundation, Inc., WI, see 9902
Pierce Charitable Trust, Harold Whitworth, The, MA, 4084
Pierce Family Foundation, L. W., The, PA, 8382
Pigott Scholarship Foundation, Paul, WA, 9663
Pikes Peak Community Foundation, CO, 1437
Pilchard Foundation, A. Franklin, IL, 2944
Pilgrim Foundation, The, PA, 8383
Pillsbury Foundation, Ed and H., MO, 4883
Pillsbury Foundation, Harriet, MO, 4884
Pillsbury Foundation, William, MO, see 4884
Pimco Foundation, The, CA, 1006

Pincus Charitable Fund, The, PA, 8384
Pincus Family Fund, The, NY, 6726
Pine Foundation, The, TX, 9123
Pine Tree Foundation, PA, 8385
Pinellas County Community Foundation, FL, 2170
Pines Bridge Foundation, The, NY, 6727
Pinkerton Foundation, The, NY, 6728
Pioneer Foundation, NV, see 5042
Pioneer Fund, Inc., The, NY, 6729
Pioneer Fund, The, CO, 1438
Pioneer Hi-Bred International, Inc. Foundation, IA, 3324
Piper Charitable Trust, Virginia G., The, AZ, 130
Piper Foundation, Minnie Stevens, TX, 9124
Piper Jaffray Foundation, MN, 4656
Piqua-Miami County Foundation, OH, see 7748
Piton Foundation, The, CO, 1439
Pitt Charitable Trust, Murray C. and Ina C., MI, 4413
Pitt Foundation, Inc., William H., The, CT, 1628
Pitt III Foundation, Inc., William H., The, CT, see 1628
Pittman Family Foundation, The, NY, 6730
Pitts Foundation, William I. H. and Lula E., GA, 2463
Pittsburgh Foundation, The, PA, 8386
Pittulloch Foundation, Inc., The, GA, 2464
Pitzer Family Foundation, CA, 1007
PLACE Fund, OH, 7805
Plan for Social Excellence, Inc., FL, 2171
Plangere Foundation, Inc., FL, 2172
Plankenhorn Foundation, Inc., Harry, The, PA, 8387
Planseon Foundation, Louis, NC, 7448
Plant Memorial Fund, Inc., Henry B., NY, 6731
Pleiad Foundation, AL, 57
Plitt Trust, Clarence Manger & Audrey Cordero, MD, 3706
PLM Foundation, NY, 6732
Plough Foundation, TN, 8718
Ploughshares Foundation, IL, 2945
Plus Valia Foundation, The, TX, 9125
Plym Foundation, MI, 4414
Plymouth Rock Foundation, The, MA, 4085
PMI Foundation, The, CA, 1008
PMJ Foundation, MO, 4885
PNC Bank Foundation, PA, see 8388
PNC Foundation, The, PA, 8388
PNM Foundation, Inc., NM, 5493
Pocono Charitable Foundation, The, AZ, 131
Podiatry Foundation of Pittsburgh, The, PA, 8389
Poe Charitable Trust, Parker, GA, 2465
Poe Foundation, William F., FL, 2173
Poetry Foundation, The, IL, A
Pogue Family Foundation, The, TX, 9126
Pohanka Family Foundation, John J., The, MD, 3707
Pohlad Family Foundation, Carl and Eloise, MN, 4657
Point Gammon Foundation, NJ, 5353
Polak Charitable Foundation, Vasek and Anna Maria, CA, 1009
Polinger Family Foundation, Howard and Geraldine, MD, 3708
Polinger Foundation, Howard and Geraldine, MD, see 3708
Polinsky-Rivkin Family Foundation, The, CA, see 1057
Polisseni Foundation, Inc., The, NY, 6733
Polk Bros. Foundation, Inc., IL, 2946
Polk County Community Foundation, Inc., The, NC, 7449
Pollack Family Foundation, Inc., Geri & Lester, The, NY, 6735
Pollack Family Foundation, Inc., The, NY, see 6735
Pollack Family Foundation, Inc., Yvonne & Leslie, NY, 6734
Pollard Foundation, Samuel, CA, 1010
Pollock Foundation, PA, 8390
Pollock Foundation, S. Wilson & Grace M., PA, see 8390
Pollock Foundation, TX, 9127
Pollock-Krasner Foundation, Inc., The, NY, 6736
Pollybill Foundation, Inc., WI, 9900
Polo Ralph Lauren Foundation, The, NY, 6737
Polsky Foundation, Inc., Hazen, The, NY, 6738
Polsky Foundation, Inc., The, NY, see 6738
Pomeranz Trust, Sam, NY, 6739
Pond Foundation, C. Northop Pond and Alethea Marder, The, PA, 8391
Pond Foundation, NM, 5494
Ponzio Foundation, June and Craig, The, CO, 1440
Poole Family Charitable Trust, The, GA, 2466

Poor Richard's Charitable Trust, PA, 8392
Poorvu Foundation, William J. & Lia G., MA, 4086
Pope Foundation, Generoso, The, NY, 6740
Pope Foundation, John William, NC, 7450
Pope Foundation, The, GA, 2467
Pope Foundation, The, NY, see 6740
Pope Life Foundation, Lois, The, FL, 2174
Poplar Foundation, The, TN, 8719
Popplestone Foundation, The, NY, 6741
Port Charitable Foundation, NY, see 5667
Porter Testamentary Trust, James Hyde, GA, 2468
Portland Foundation, The, IN, 3223
Portsmouth Community Foundation, The, VA, 9498
Portsmouth General Hospital Foundation, VA, 9499
Poses Family Foundation, The, NJ, 5354
Positive Transitions Foundation, The, WA, 9664
Posnack Family Foundation of Hollywood, FL, 2175
Posner Foundation, Inc., Gene & Ruth, WI, 9901
Poss Family Foundation, The, MA, 4087
Poss Kapor Familly Foundation, The, MA, see 4087
Post and Courier Foundation, SC, 8603
Post Family Foundation, Lawrence and Sandra, The, CA, 1011
Post Foundation, John A. & Margaret, NJ, 5355
Post Foundation, Marjorie Merriweather, The, DC, 1842
Postles Scholarship Fund, Wilbur E., PA, 8393
Potamkin Family Foundation I, Inc., FL, 2176
Potiker Family Foundation, CA, see 1012
Potiker Family Foundation, Hughes and Sheila, CA, 1012
Potlatch Foundation for Higher Education, WA, 9665
Pott Foundation, Herman T. & Phenie R., MO, 4886
Potter Foundation, Justin & Valere Blair, TN, 8720
Potter Foundation, Philip E., The, NY, 6742
Potter's Wheel Foundation, Inc., The, NY, 6743
Pottruck Family Foundation, The, CA, 1013
Pottruck Scott Family Foundation, The, CA, see 1013
Powell Crown Foundation, MO, 4887
Powell Family Foundation, The, KS, 3381
Powell Foundation, The, TX, 9128
Power Foundation, The, MI, 4415
Powers Family Foundation, The, NY, 6744
Poweshiek Community Foundation, Greater, IA, 3325
Poynter Fund, The, FL, see 2245
Poznanski Foundation, OR, 8052
PPC Foundation, WI, 9902
PPG Industries Foundation, PA, 8394
Prairie Foundation, The, TX, 9129
Praise The Lord Foundation, CA, see 821
Pralle Family Foundation, Robert R. and Helga, The, CA, 1014
Praxair Foundation, Inc., CT, 1629
Praxis Foundation, The, VA, 9500
Precourt Foundation, The, CO, 1441
Premier Foundation, The, SC, 8604
Prensky Family Foundation, Inc., The, NY, A
Prentice Foundation, Inc., Abra, IL, 2947
Prentice Foundation, Inc., The, CT, 1630
Prentiss Foundation, Elisabeth Severance, The, OH, 7806
Presbyterian Health Foundation, OK, 7969
Prescott Family Foundation, Inc., WI, 9903
Presser Foundation, The, PA, 8395
Presto Foundation, The, DE, 1740
Preston Family Foundation, Raymond B., KY, 3446
Preuss Family Foundation, Inc., The, CA, 1015
Price Associates Foundation, Inc., T. Rowe, MD, 3709
Price Charitable Foundation, Tina & Steven, NY, 6745
Price Chopper's Golub Foundation, NY, 6746
Price Family Charitable Fund, The, CA, 1016
Price Family Foundation, CA, 1017
Price Family Foundation, Inc., The, NY, 6747
Price Family Foundation, Julian, The, NC, 7451
Price Foundation, Carol Swanson, MO, 4888
Price Foundation, Inc., John E. & Aliese, The, FL, 2177
Price Foundation, Inc., Louis and Harold, The, CO, 1442
Price Foundation, Inc., Michael F., NJ, 5356
Price Foundation, Mary Grant, CA, 1018
Price Foundation, Sol & Helen, The, CA, see 1016
Price Foundation, William L., The, CA, 1019
Prichard School, Board of Trustees of the, WV, 9731
Prickett Fund, Lynn R. and Karl E., NC, 7452
Priddy Charitable Trust, Robert & Ruby, TX, 9130

Priddy Foundation, The, TX, 9131
Priem Family Foundation, The, CA, 1020
Prim Foundation, Wayne L., NV, 5054
Prince Charitable Trusts, IL, 2948
Prince Foundation, Edgar and Elsa, MI, 4416
Prince Foundation, IL, 2949
Prince Foundation, MI, see 4416
Princeton Area Community Foundation, Inc., NJ, 5357
Princeton Area Foundation, Inc., The, NJ, see 5357
Principal Financial Group Foundation, Inc., IA, 3326
Principato Foundation, Jerold & Marjorie, MD, 3710
Priority Healthcare Foundation, Inc., FL, 2178
Pritchard Charitable Trust, Maude, NY, see 6748
Pritchard Charitable Trust, William E. and Maude S., NY, 6748
Pritchett Foundation, KS, 3382
Pritzker Charitable Distribution Fund, Colonel (IL) James N., IL, see 3033
Pritzker Family Foundation, Anthony, The, IL, 2950
Pritzker Family Foundation, Margot & Thomas, IL, 2951
Pritzker Family Foundation, The, CA, 1021
Pritzker Family Fund, John and Lisa, The, CA, 1022
Pritzker Foundation, IL, 2952
Pritzker Foundation, Jay, The, IL, 2953
Pritzker Pucker Family Foundation, The, IL, 2954
Pritzker Traubert Family Foundation, The, IL, 2955
Procter & Gamble Cosmetics and Fragrance Foundation, Inc., The, MD, see 3711
Procter & Gamble Cosmetics Foundation, Inc., The, MD, 3711
Procter & Gamble Fund, The, OH, 7807
Proctor Charitable Trust, Hahl, TX, 9132
Professional Athletes Foundation, DC, 1843
Progress Energy Foundation, Inc., NC, 7453
Progress Foundation, TX, 9133
Progressive Education Foundation, Inc., IL, 2956
Progressive Insurance Foundation, The, OH, 7808
Promethean Foundation, TN, 8721
Promise Keepers Charitable Foundation, CA, 1023
Prophet Corporation Foundation, MN, 4658
Propp Sons Fund, Inc., Morris and Anna, NY, 6749
Prospect Creek Foundation, MN, 4659
Prospect Hill Foundation, Inc., The, NY, 6750
Prosser ICC Foundation, Inc., VI, 9364
Protective Life Foundation, AL, 58
Proteus Foundation, NM, 5495
Prothro Foundation, Vin & Caren, TX, 9134
Providence Charitable Foundation, Inc., The, NJ, 5358
Providence Charitable Foundation, NC, see 7454
Providence Foundation, Inc., NY, 6751
Providence Foundation, MS, 4762
Providence Journal Charitable Foundation, TX, 9135
Provident Bank Foundation, The, NJ, 5359
Provident Bank/Skip Johnson Charitable Foundation, Inc., MD, 3712
Provident Benevolent Foundation, NC, 7454
PRR Foundation, Inc., NY, see 7074
Prudential Foundation, The, NJ, 5360
Pruet Foundation, The, AR, 170
Pruina Corporation, The, OH, 7809
Pruitt Foundation, Inc., J. Crayton, FL, 2179
Prusoff Foundation, William H., CT, 1631
Pryor Charitable Trust, Myra Stafford, TX, 9136
Pryor Foundation, The, PA, 8396
Psalm 103 Foundation, The, PA, 8397
PSC Charitable Foundation, PA, 8398
PSEG Foundation, Inc., NJ, 5361
PSH Foundation, The, TX, 9137
PTM Charitable Foundation, The, NY, 6752
PTS Foundation, PA, 8399
Public Service Electric and Gas Company Foundation, Inc., NJ, see 5361
Public Welfare Foundation, Inc., DC, 1844
Publix Super Markets Charities, FL, 2180
Puelicher Foundation, Inc., WI, 9904
Puerto Rico Community Foundation, Inc., PR, 8515
Puffin Foundation, Ltd., NJ, 5362
Pugliese Charitable Foundation, Charles M. & Thelma M., OH, 7810
Pulier Charitable Foundation, Inc., Benjamin & Seema, NY, 6753
Pulitzer Foundation, Inc., Ceil & Michael E., The, MO, 4889

Pulitzer Foundation, Inc., Michael E., The, MO, see 4889
Pulley Foundation, OH, 7811
Pulliam Charitable Trust, Myrta J., IN, 3224
Pulliam Charitable Trust, Nina Mason, IN, 3225
Pullman Educational Foundation, George M., IL, 2957
Pumpkin Foundation, The, NY, 6754
Purcell Foundation, Anne McNamara, The, IL, see 2886
Purchase Fund, The, NY, 6755
Purple Moon Foundation, Inc., WI, 9905
Puterbaugh Foundation, The, OK, 7970
Putnam Foundation, NH, 5100
Putnam Investments Foundation, The, MA, 4088
Putnam Prize Fund for the Promotion of Scholarship, William Lowell, MA, 4089
Pyewacket Foundation, NY, 6756

QIBQ Foundation, NY, 6757
Quadrangle Group Foundation, Inc., NY, 6758
Quantum Foundation, FL, 2181
Quarry Hill Foundation, NY, 6759
Quartet Foundation in Honor of David and Mary W. Green, IL, see 2772
Quattrone Foundation, Frank and Denise, CA, 1024
Queensgate Foundation, NY, 6760
Quercus Fund, Inc., The, NJ, 5363
Quest for Truth Foundation, WA, 9666
Quick Charitable Trust dated December 29, 1986, Thomas C., The, FL, 2182
Quick Charitable Trust Foundation, Leslie C. Quick, Jr. & Regina A., NY, 6762
Quick Charitable Trust, Patricia, NY, 6761
Quigley Family Foundation, NJ, see 5163
Quimby Family Foundation, FL, 2183
Quinn Foundation, Inc., John A., MD, 3713
Quinn Foundation, John A., MD, see 3713
Quinn Foundation, Stephen D., The, NY, 6763
Quinney Foundation, S. J. & Jessie E., UT, 9338
Quixote Foundation, Inc., WA, 9667
Qwest Foundation, CO, 1443

R & R Realty Group Foundation, IA, 3327
R & TP Family Foundation, Inc., NY, 6764
R.T. Foundation, OH, 7812
Rabb Charitable Foundation, Sidney & Esther, MA, 4090
Rabb Charitable Trust, Sidney R., MA, 4091
Rabb Family Trust, Esther V. & Sidney R., MA, see 4091
Rachal Foundation, Ed, TX, 9138
Rachofsky Foundation, Howard Earl, TX, 9139
Racine Community Foundation, Inc., WI, 9906
Racine County Area Foundation, Inc., WI, see 9906
Radichel Foundation, William D., MN, 4660
Radin Foundation, CA, 1025
Radio Drama Network, Inc., NY, 6765
Radley Family Foundation, The, MA, 4092
Rady Family Foundation, CA, 1026
Rae Charitable Trust, James Arthur, AZ, 132
Raether 1985 Charitable Trust, NY, 6766
Raffiani Family Foundation, Inc., NY, 6767
Ragan and King Charitable Foundation, NC, see 7455
Ragan Charitable Foundation, Carolyn King, NC, 7455
Ragsdale Family Foundation, The, TN, 8722
Rahimian Family Foundation, CA, 1027
Raiff Foundation, The, NY, 6768
Raikes Family Foundation, WA, 9668
Rainey Foundation, Callie & John, SC, 8605
Rainier Pacific Foundation, WA, 9669
Raintree Foundation, The, CA, 1028
Rajchenbach Family Foundation, IL, 2958
Raker Foundation, Inc., M. E., IN, 3226
Rales Foundation, Norman R. Rales and Ruth, The, FL, 2184
Ralphs—Food 4 Less Foundation, The, CA, 1029
Ralston Purina Trust Fund, MO, see 4872
Ramapo Trust, NY, 6769
Ramsay Family Foundation, CA, 1030
Ramser Charitable Foundation, Inc., Forrest & Helen, GA, 2469
Rancho Santa Fe Community Foundation, CA, see 1031
Rancho Santa Fe Foundation, CA, 1031
Randall & Dewey Foundation, Inc., TX, 9140
Randleigh Foundation Trust, NC, 7456
Randolph Foundation, NC, see 7461
Ranger Family Charitable Trust, The, NY, 6770

Rangos Charitable Foundation, John G., PA, 8400
Ranney Foundation, P. K., OH, 7813
Ransom Foundation, Nancy Buck, CA, 1032
Rapaport Shallat Foundation, NY, 6771
Rapoport Foundation, Bernard and Audre, TX, 9141
Rapoport Foundation, Inc., Paul, The, NY, 6772
Rapp Foundation, Robert Glenn, OK, 7971
Rappaport Charitable Foundation, Jerome Lyle, MA, 4093
Raskob Foundation for Catholic Activities, Inc., DE, 1741
Raskob Foundation, Inc., Bill, The, MD, 3714
Rasmuson Foundation, AK, 85
Rasmussen Foundation, V. Kann, MA, 4094
Rath Foundation, Inc., WI, 9907
Rathmann Family Foundation, The, MD, 3715
Ratner Family Foundation, The, VA, 9501
Ratner Foundation, Milton M., MI, 4417
Ratshesky Foundation, A.C., MA, 4095
Rattner and P. Maureen White Foundation, Inc., Steven L., NY, 6773
Rauch Foundation, NY, 6774
Rauenhorst Foundation, Inc., Gerald and Henrietta, FL, 2185
Rausman Foundation, N. & D., NY, 6775
Rav-Noy Family Foundation, Inc., The, CA, 1033
Raven Trust Fund, WA, 9670
Ravitch Foundation, Inc., Richard, NY, 6776
Ravitz Foundation, The, MI, 4418
Rawlings Foundation, Inc., The, FL, 2186
Ray of Light Foundation, CA, 1034
Raygar Foundation, FL, 2187
Raymond Family Foundation, UT, 9339
Raymund Foundation, Inc., FL, 2188
Rayonier Foundation, The, FL, 2189
Razore Family Foundation, W., WA, 9671
RBC Dain Rauscher Foundation, MN, 4661
RCI Foundation, IN, see 3140
Read 1985 Charitable Trust, Norman H., TX, 9142
Reader's Digest Foundation, NY, 6777
Reader's Digest Partners for Sight Foundation, NY, 6778
READY Foundation, Inc., NJ, see 5367
Realan Foundation, Inc., GA, 2470
RealNetworks Foundation, WA, 9672
Realty Foundation of New York, NY, 6779
Reams Foundation, Inc., The, SC, 8606
Reaud Charitable Foundation, Inc., The, TX, 9143
REBNY Foundation, Inc., NY, 6780
Rebozo Foundation, Inc., Carmen, FL, 2190
Rebsamen Fund, AR, 171
Rechelbacher Foundation, Horst M., MN, 4662
Rechler Family Foundation, Inc., The, NY, 6781
Rechler Foundation, Inc., Morton & Beverley, NY, see 6781
Records-Johnston Family Foundation, Inc., The, OK, 7972
Red Acre Farm, Inc., MA, 4096
Red Bird Hollow Foundation, IL, 2959
Red Husky Foundation, CA, 1035
Red Wing Shoe Company Foundation, MN, 4663
Redbird Foundation, TN, 8723
Reddy Foundation, Inc., Ravi and Pratibha, NJ, 5364
Redfield Foundation, Nell J., NV, 5055
Redhill Foundation - Rothberg Family Charitable Trust, IL, 2960
Reding Family Foundation, MO, 4890
Redskin Foundation, Inc., MD, see 3687
Redstone Charitable Trust, Michael, The, MA, 4097
Reebok Foundation, The, MA, see 4098
Reebok Human Rights Foundation, The, MA, 4098
Reed Foundation, Inc., The, NY, 6782
Reed Foundation, John & Cynthia, NY, 6783
Reed Foundation, KY, 3447
Reeder Foundation, The, MA, 4099
Rees Charitable Foundation, John Nesbit Rees and Sarah Henne, PA, 8401
Reese Family Foundation, David E., AZ, 133
Reese Health Trust, Michael, IL, 2961
Reese Hospital Foundation, Michael, IL, see 2961
Reeves Foundation, Inc., Carl Marshall Reeves and Mildred Almen, IN, 3227
Reeves Foundation, Inc., The, NJ, 5365

Rochetta-Wessies Scholarship Foundation, The, IL, 2969

Rochlin Foundation, Abraham and Sonia, NV, 5057

Rock Foundation, The, CA, 1061

Rock River Foundation, Inc., NY, 6824

Rock Springs Foundation, The, MD, 3717

Rockdale Foundation, Inc., The, GA, 2474

Rockefeller Brothers Fund, Inc., NY, 6825

Rockefeller Foundation, The, NY, 6826

Rockefeller Foundation, Winthrop, The, AR, 172

Rockefeller Fund, Inc., David, The, NY, 6827

Rockefeller Trust, Winthrop, AR, 173

Rockford Community Foundation, IL, see 2679

Rockjensen Foundation, Inc., The, TX, 9153

Rockwell Automation Charitable Corp., WI, 9912

Rockwell Collins Charitable Corporation, IA, 3328

Rockwell Foundation, The, PA, 8408

Rockwell Fund, Inc., TX, 9154

Rockwern Charitable Foundation, The, OH, 7824

Roddis Foundation, Inc., Hamilton, WI, 9913

Roddy Foundation, Inc., Fred M., MA, 4108

Rodel Foundation, AZ, 136

Rodgers Family Foundation, Inc., The, NY, 6828

Rodgers Foundation, Richard and Dorothy, NY, see 6828

Rodgers Trust, Elizabeth Killam, MA, 4109

Rodgers, Jr. Family Foundation, Thomas A., MA, 4110

Rodman Ford Sales, Inc. Charitable Trust, MA, 4111

Rodney Fund, The, MI, 4422

Roe Foundation, The, SC, 8607

Roemer Foundation, The, PA, 8409

Roger's & Betty's Charitable Foundation, CA, see 859

Rogers Family Foundation, CA, 1062

Rogers Family Foundation, The, MA, 4112

Rogers Foundation Corporation, S. Dennis and Leslie L., MI, 4423

Rogers Foundation, David & Tricia, The, NY, 6829

Rogers Foundation, Mary Stuart, CA, 1063

Rogers Foundation, NE, 4999

Rogers Foundation, The, TX, 9155

Rogers Fund for the Arts, Russell H., TX, 9156

Rogers Fund for the Arts, Russell Hill, TX, see 9156

Rogers Private Family Foundation, T. Gary and Kathleen, CA, 1064

Rogow Birken Foundation, Inc., The, CT, see 1636

Rogow Greenberg Foundation, Inc., The, CT, 1636

Rohatyn Foundation, Felix G., NY, see 6830

Rohatyn Foundation, Inc., Felix and Elizabeth, The, NY, 6830

Rohr Foundation, Inc., George, The, NY, 6831

Rohrer Charitable Foundation, William G., PA, 8410

Rohrman Autombile Dealership Foundation, Inc., Bob, The, NJ, see 5442

Rolfs Foundation, Inc., Robert T., WI, 9914

Rolland Foundation, Inc., Ian & Mimi, IN, 3231

Roller-Bottimore Foundation, The, VA, 9507

Rollins Foundation, O. Wayne, GA, 2475

Rollins Foundation, R. Randall and Margaret H., GA, see 2439

Rollins-Luetkemeyer Charitable Foundation, Inc., The, MD, see 3718

Rollins-Luetkemeyer Foundation, Inc., MD, 3718

Rollnick Foundation, William D. and Nancy Ellison, FL, see 2203

Rollnick Foundation, William D. Rollnick and Nancy Ellison, FL, 2203

Romill Foundation, DE, 1747

Rooms to Go Children's Fund, FL, 2204

Roosa Family Foundation Trust, RI, 8552

Rordor Foundation, The, MI, 4424

Rorer Foundation, Inc., The, PA, 8411

RosaMary Foundation, The, LA, 3507

Rosansky Foundation, Aaron, Martha, Isidore & Blanche, The, NY, 6832

Rose Community Foundation and Affiliates, CO, 1445

Rose Family Foundation, Inc., Marshall, NY, 6833

Rose Family Foundation, Stuart, OH, 7825

Rose Foundation, Adam R., NY, 6834

Rose Foundation, Deborah, The, NY, 6835

Rose Foundation, Frederick P. & Sandra P., NY, 6837

Rose Foundation, Inc., Billy, NY, 6838

Rose Foundation, Inc., Clare, The, CT, 1637

Rose Foundation, Inc., Jill & Marshall, NY, see 6833

Rose Foundation, Inc., Susan and Elihu, NY, 6836

Rose Foundation, The, NJ, 5373

Rose Fund, Inc., Daniel and Joanna S., NY, 6839

Rosedorf Foundation, NY, 6840

Rosen Family Foundation, Benjamin M., The, NY, 6841

Rosen Foundation, Inc., Abner, The, NY, 6842

Rosen Foundation, Inc., Harris, The, FL, 2205

Rosen Foundation, Inc., Joseph, NY, 6843

Rosen Fund, Inc., Reb Moishe, NY, 6844

Rosenbaum Family Foundation I, Meyer, NJ, 5374

Rosenberg Family Foundation, Inc., GA, 2476

Rosenberg Family Foundation, Inc., William, FL, 2206

Rosenberg Foundation, CA, 1065

Rosenberg Foundation, David M. and Marjorie D., The, PA, 8412

Rosenberg Foundation, Inc., Henry and Ruth Blaustein, The, MD, 3719

Rosenberg Foundation, Inc., Sunny and Abe, NY, 6845

Rosenberg Foundation, Inc., Thomas Jefferson, NY, 6846

Rosenberg Foundation, Marcus & Ann, TX, 9157

Rosenberg Foundation, Murray & Sydell, NY, 6847

Rosenberg Foundation, Murray M., NY, see 6847

Rosenberg, Jr. Family Foundation, Louise and Claude, The, CA, 1066

Rosenberg, Jr. Foundation, Inc., Dorothy L. & Henry A., The, MD, 3720

Rosenblatt Family Foundation, Inc., NY, 6848

Rosenblatt Foundation, Inc., Louis & Emanuel G., NY, 6849

Rosenbloom Foundation, Inc., Ben & Esther, MD, 3721

Rosenblum Family Foundation, Inc., Daniel, NY, 6850

Rosenfeld Family Foundation, Gene and Maxine, The, CA, 1067

Rosenfeld Foundation, Mary and Emmanuel, PA, 8413

Rosengarten Horowitz Fund, CA, 1068

Rosenkranz Foundation, Inc., The, NY, 6851

Rosenstiel Foundation, The, NY, 6852

Rosenthal Family Foundation, Marion & Robert, The, VA, 9508

Rosenthal Foundation, Benjamin J., IL, 2970

Rosenthal Foundation, Inc., Juliet, NY, 6853

Rosenthal Foundation, Inc., The, KY, 3450

Rosenthal Foundation, Lois and Richard, OH, 7826

Rosenthal Foundation, Richard and Hinda, The, CT, 1638

Rosenthal Fund, The, NY, 6854

Rosenwald Family Fund, Inc., William, The, NY, 6855

Rosenwald Foundation, Edward John & Patricia, The, NY, 6856

Rosenwald Foundation, Inc., NY, 6857

Rosenzweig Coopersmith Foundation, The, MI, 4425

Rosewood Foundation, MO, 4894

Rosewood Foundation, The, TX, 9158

Rosh Foundation, NY, 6858

Roshan Cultural Heritage Institute, DC, 1847

Roslyn Savings Foundation, The, NY, 6859

Rosner Foundation, Inc., Leo, NY, 6860

Ross Family Charitable Foundation, NY, 6861

Ross Family Foundation, Elizabeth M., FL, see 2207

Ross Family Foundation, Richard M. and Elizabeth M., FL, 2207

Ross Family Fund, NY, 6862

Ross Foundation, Dale and Deborah, The, TX, 9159

Ross Foundation, Dorothea Haus, The, NY, 6863

Ross Foundation, Eric F., NJ, 5375

Ross Foundation, Inc., Arthur, NY, 6864

Ross Foundation, Inc., Bob A., CA, 1069

Ross Foundation, Lynn & George M., NY, see 6862

Ross Foundation, The, AR, 174

Ross Loan Fund, The, PA, 8414

Ross, Jr. Charitable Foundation, Inc., E. Burke, NJ, 5376

Rosse Family Charitable Foundation, The, MA, 4113

Rosse Family Charitable Foundation, Thomas A., MA, see 4113

Rosser Charitable Trust, FL, 2208

Rostan Family Foundation, NC, 7467

Roswell Foundation, Inc., Elizabeth B. and Arthur E., MD, 3722

Rotasa Foundation, CA, 1070

Rotenstreich Foundation, Inc., Jon & Susan, The, NY, 6865

Roth Family Foundation, CA, 1071

Roth Foundation, Daryl & Steven, NJ, 5377

Rothberg Family Charitable Foundation for Children's Diseases, FL, 2209

Rothman Foundation, The, FL, 2210

Rothschild Charitable Foundation, Inc., The, MD, 3723

Rothschild Foundation, Hulda B. & Maurice L., IL, 2971

Rothschild Foundation, Judith, The, NY, 6866

Rothschild Fund, A. Frank and Dorothy B., CA, 1072

Rotonda Foundation, IL, 2972

Rotto Family Foundation, TX, A

Roundy's Foundation, Inc., WI, 9915

Rouse Company Foundation, Inc., MD, 3724

Routhier Foundation, E. J. & V. M., RI, 8553

Routhier Foundation, Edward J. & Virginia M., RI, see 8553

Rowan Family Foundation, Henry M., NJ, 5378

Rowe Family Foundation, DE, 1748

Rowland Foundation, Inc., DE, 1749

Rowland Foundation, Inc., Pleasant T., WI, 9916

Rowling Foundation, TX, 9160

Roxe Foundation, The, NY, 6867

Roy Foundation, Adelard A. and Valeda Lea, MA, 4114

Royce Family Fund, Inc., CT, 1639

RSMIS Foundation, TX, 9161

RTM Foundation, Inc., The, GA, 2477

Ruan Foundation Trust, John, IA, 3329

Ruane Family Fund, NY, see 5705

Ruben Foundation, Dennis and Joyce, The, IL, 2973

Ruben Foundation, Lawrence, NY, 6868

Ruben Foundation, Selma and Lawrence, The, NY, see 6868

Ruben Foundation, Selma, The, NY, 6869

Rubenstein Charitable Foundation, Lawrence J. and Anne, MA, 4115

Rubenstein Family Charitable Foundation, Harold, MA, 4116

Rubenstein Family Foundation, Marilyn and Barry, The, NY, 6870

Rubenstein Foundation, Jerry and Maury, The, TX, 9162

Rubicon Foundation, NY, see 5640

Rubin Charitable Foundation, Ronald and Marcia J., PA, 8415

Rubin Family Foundation, Inc., The, NY, 6871

Rubin Family Fund, Inc., Cele H. and William B., MA, 4117

Rubin Foundation, Inc., J. M., FL, 2211

Rubin Foundation, Inc., Samuel, NY, 6872

Rubin Foundation, Inc., Shelley & Donald, The, NY, 6873

Rubin Foundation, Jacob & Mae D., The, NY, see 6874

Rubin Foundation, Nancy & Miles, The, NY, 6874

Rubin Foundation, Robert E. & Judith O., IL, 2974

Rubin-Henry Family Foundation, The, NY, 6875

Rubinstein Foundation, Inc., Helena, NY, 6876

Rubschlager Foundation, Paul A. and Joan S., IL, 2975

Rudd Family Foundation, CA, 1073

Rudd Foundation, KS, 3385

Ruddy Charitable Trust, Raymond & Marilyn, MA, 4118

Rude Foundation, Inc., Raymond C., NV, 5058

Rudin Family Foundation, Inc., May and Samuel, NY, 6877

Rudin Foundation, Inc., Louis and Rachel, The, NY, 6878

Rudin Foundation, Inc., The, NY, 6879

Ruettgers Family Charitable Foundation, The, MA, 4119

Ruffin Foundation, Inc., Peter B. & Adeline W., NY, 6880

Rufty Foundation, Archibald C. and Frances F., NV, 5059

Rukal Foundation, Inc., NY, 6881

Rumbaugh Foundation, J. H. & R. H., NC, 7468

Rummel Foundation, Fred C., The, NJ, 5379

Rumsey Foundation, Mary A. H., NY, 6882

Rupe Foundation, Arthur N., CA, 1074

Rupe Foundation, CA, see 1074

Rupp Foundation, Fran and Warren, The, MN, 4669

Rupp Foundation, Richard W., The, NY, 6883

Russell Charitable Foundation, Inc., Tom, IL, 2976

Russell Charitable Trust, GA, 2478

Russell Charitable Trust, Josephine Schell, The, OH, 7827

Russell Educational and Charitable Foundation, Inc., Benjamin and Roberta, AL, see 60

Russell Family Foundation, The, OH, 7828

Russell Family Foundation, The, WA, 9673

Russell Foundation, Benjamin and Roberta, AL, 60
Russell Memorial Foundation, Robert, FL, 2212
Russer Foods/Zemsky Family Trust, NY, *see* 7294
Rust Foundation, The, TN, 8724
RuthMarc Foundation, Inc., The, NJ, 5380
Rutledge Charities, Inc., Edward and Hannah M., WI, 9917
Rutledge Charity, Edward, WI, *see* 9917
Ruvo Family Foundation, The, NV, 5060
Rx Foundation, MA, 4120
Ryan Family Charitable Foundation, CA, 1075
Ryan Family Charitable Foundation, MA, *see* 4131
Ryan Family Foundation, David & Robin, CA, 1076
Ryan Foundation, David Claude, CA, *see* 1075
Ryan Foundation, Inc., Nina M., The, NY, 6884
Ryan Foundation, Patrick G. & Shirley W., IL, 2977
Ryan Foundation, The, NE, 5000
Ryan Foundation, William G. and Mary A., IL, 2978
Ryan Memorial Foundation, PA, 8416
Ryan Trust, Ida Alice, NC, 7469
Ryder System Charitable Foundation, Inc., The, FL, 2213
Ryzman Foundation, Inc., CA, 1077
RZH Foundation, NY, 6885

S & G Foundation, Inc., WY, 9988
S & T Bancorp Charitable Foundation, PA, 8417
S.G. Foundation, CA, 1078
S.O. Charitable Trust, NY, 6886
S.R.C. Education Alliance, NC, 7470
Saban Family Foundation, CA, 1079
Sabatini Family Foundation, KS, 3386
Sabes Family Foundation, Moe and Esther, The, MN, *see* 4670
Sabes Family Foundation, The, MN, 4670
Saccomanno Higher Education Foundation, CO, 1446
Sacerdote Foundation, Peter M., The, NY, 6887
Sacharuna Foundation, VA, 9509
Sachs Family Foundation, NY, 6888
Sachs Foundation, CO, 1447
Sackler Charitable Foundation, Else, The, NY, 6889
Sackler Foundation, Inc., Elizabeth A., The, NY, 6891
Sackler Foundation, Inc., Mortimer D., NY, 6890
Sackler Fund for the Arts & Sciences, Raymond & Beverly, NY, 6892
Sacks Family Foundation, IL, 2979
Sacramento Region Community Foundation, CA, 1080
Sacramento Regional Foundation, CA, *see* 1080
Saddle Foundation, MI, 4426
Sadowsky Family Foundation, William, The, MA, 4121
Saeman Family Foundation, Inc., CO, 1448
Saemann Foundation, Franklin I. and Irene List, IN, 3232
Saemann Foundation, Franklin I., IN, *see* 3232
Safdeye & Sons Foundation, Inc., Ellis A., NY, A
Safeguard Scientifics Foundation, PA, 8418
Safety Insurance Foundation, MA, *see* 4147
Safra Foundation, Inc., NY, 6893
Saga Foundation, CA, 1081
Sage Cleveland Foundation, The, OH, 7829
Sage Foundation, Inc., The, CT, 1640
Sage Foundation, MI, 4427
Sage Foundation, Russell, NY, 6894
Sage Foundation, WA, 9674
Sager Family Traveling Foundation and Road Show, Inc., The, MA, 4122
Saginaw Community Foundation, MI, 4428
Sagner Family Foundation, The, NJ, 5381
Sai Ram Foundation, The, CA, 1082
Saigh Foundation, The, MO, 4895
Sailors' Snug Harbor of Boston, Inc., MA, 4123
Saint Louis Community Foundation, Greater, MO, 4896
Saint Luke's Foundation of Cleveland, Ohio, OH, 7830
Saint Paul Foundation, Inc., The, MN, 4671
Saint-Gobain Corporation Foundation, PA, 8419
Sajak Foundation, Lesly & Pat, The, CA, 1083
Saje Foundation, The, CA, 1084
Saks Incorporated Foundation, AL, 61
Salah Family Foundation for the Town of Canton, Inc., James and Beatrice, MA, 4124
Salem Charitable Trust, Paul and Navyn, RI, *see* 8554
Salem Community Foundation, Inc., OH, 7831
Salem Five Charitable Foundation, Inc., MA, 4125

Salem Foundation, The, OR, 8054
Salem Foundation, The, RI, 8554
Saligman Charitable Trust, Robert, NY, 6895
Salina Community Foundation, Greater, KS, 3387
Sall Family Foundation, Inc., NC, 7471
Salmon Foundation, Inc., The, NY, 6896
Salomon Family Foundation, Inc., Richard, The, NY, 6897
Salomon Foundation, Inc., Richard & Edna, NY, *see* 6897
Salomon Scholarship Fund, William R., NY, 6898
Saltonstall Charitable Foundation, Richard, MA, 4126
Saltsburg Fund Charitable Trust, IN, 3233
Saltsgiver Family Foundation, PA, 8420
Saltz Foundation, Inc., Gary, The, NY, 6899
Saltzman Foundation, Inc., NY, 6900
Salvaggio Family Foundation, PA, 8421
Salvitti Family Foundation, PA, 8422
SAM'S CLUB Foundation, AR, *see* 184
Samaritan Foundation, OH, 7832
Samaritan Foundation, The, IL, 2980
Sambar Private Foundation, CA, 1085
Samberg Family Foundation, VA, 9510
Samerian Foundation, Inc., IN, 3234
Samis Foundation, WA, 9675
Sample Foundation, Inc., The, MT, 4940
Sampson Family Foundation, Myles D. and J. Faye, PA, 8423
Sams Foundation, Inc., Earl C., TX, 9163
Samstag Fine Arts Trust, Gordon, FL, 2214
Samueli Family Foundation, The, CA, *see* 1086
Samueli Foundation, The, CA, 1086
Samuels Foundation, Inc., Fan Fox and Leslie R., The, NY, 6901
Samuelson Foundation, Herman and Walter, The, MD, 3725
San Angelo Area Foundation, TX, 9164
San Angelo Health Foundation, TX, 9165
San Antonio Area Foundation, TX, 9166
San Diego Community Foundation, CA, *see* 1087
San Diego Foundation, The, CA, 1087
San Francisco Foundation, The, CA, 1088
San Joaquin Foundation, Inc., CA, 1089
San Luis Obispo County Community Foundation, CA, 1090
San Simeon Fund, Inc., The, CA, 1091
Sand County Foundation, Inc., WI, 9918
Sandercock Trust, Marian, CA, A
Sanders Family Foundation, Don A., TX, 9167
Sanders Foundation, Inc., Lawrence A., FL, 2215
Sandler Foundation, Inc., Art and Annie, VA, 9511
Sandler Foundation, Inc., Harvey and Phyllis, FL, 2216
Sandler Foundation, Inc., Steve and Toni, VA, 9512
Sandler Foundation, Mara & Ricky, The, NY, 6902
Sandoz Foundation of America, NY, *see* 6640
Sands Foundation, George H. and Estelle M., NJ, 5382
Sandy Foundation, George H., CA, 1092
Sandy Hill Foundation, NJ, 5383
Sandy Hill Foundation, NY, 6903
Sandy River Charitable Foundation, The, ME, 3555
Sanger Family Foundation, MN, 4672
Sangre De Christo Charitable Trust, IL, 2981
Sani Family Foundation, Inc., NY, 6904
Sankey Family Foundation, OH, 7833
Sansing Foundation, Inc., FL, 2217
Sansom Foundation, Inc., FL, 2218
Santa Barbara Foundation, CA, 1093
Santa Cruz County Community Foundation, Greater, CA, *see* 403
Santa Fe Community Foundation, NM, 5496
Santa Fe Pacific Foundation, IL, *see* 2644
Santa Maria Foundation, Inc., NY, 6905
Sapelo Foundation, Inc., The, GA, 2479
Sapelo Island Research Foundation, Inc., GA, *see* 2479
Sapirstein Foundation of Cleveland, Jacob, The, OH, *see* 7834
Sapirstein-Stone-Weiss Foundation, The, OH, 7834
Sapling Foundation, The, CA, 1094
Sapp Family Foundation, The, NY, 6906
Saquish Foundation, MA, 4127
Sara Lee Foundation, IL, 2982
Sarasota County Community Foundation, Inc., The, FL, *see* 1946

Sargent Foundation, Newell B., WY, 9989
Sarkeys Foundation, OK, 7974
Sarkowsky Family Charitable Foundation, Herman and Faye, The, WA, 9676
Sarkowsky Family Charitable Foundation, WA, *see* 9676
Sarofim Foundation, Louisa Stude, TX, 9169
Sarofim Foundation, TX, 9168
Sarver Charitable Foundation, Penny and Robert, CA, 1095
Sasco Foundation, NY, 6907
Satell Family Foundation, PA, 8424
Sathya Sai Foundation of America, CA, 1096
Sato Family Foundation, Inc, The, NY, 6908
Sato Foundation, NJ, 5384
Satori Foundation, VA, *see* 9378
Satter Family Foundation, The, IL, 2983
Satterberg Foundation, WA, 9677
Saturno Foundation, CA, 1097
Saunders Foundation, NY, 6909
Saunders Foundation, The, FL, 2219
Savage Family Foundation, Neal & Sherrie, The, UT, 9340
Savage, Jr. Foundation, Ruth F. Savage and Harlow D., The, CT, 1641
Savannah Community Foundation, The, GA, 2480
Savannah Foods Foundation, GA, *see* 2346
Savannah Foundation, The, GA, *see* 2480
SAW Community Foundation, VA, *see* 9521
Saw Island Foundation, Inc., CA, 1098
Sawnee Mountain Foundation, Inc., GA, 2481
Sawyer Charitable Foundation, MA, 4128
Sawyer Family Foundation, The, NV, 5061
Say Yes to Education, Inc., CT, 1642
Saybrook Charitable Trust, CT, 1643
Sayler-Hawkins Foundation, MO, 4897
Saylor Foundation, The, VA, *see* 9404
SBC Foundation, TX, *see* 8765
SBM Charitable Foundation, Inc., CT, 1644
Scaife Charitable Foundation, PA, *see* 8178
Scaife Family Foundation, FL, 2220
Scaife Foundation, Inc., Sarah, PA, 8425
Scaife Scholarship Foundation, The, CA, 1099
Scaler Foundation, Inc., TX, 9170
ScanSource Charitable Foundation, SC, 8608
Scarborough-Linebery Foundation, TX, 9171
Scarpa Foundation, John F., The, FL, 2221
Schadt Foundation, Inc., The, TN, 8725
Schaefer Family Foundation, Inc., Rowland & Sylvia, FL, 2222
Schaeffer Family Foundation, CA, 1100
Schafer Family Foundation, NY, 6910
Schaffer Foundation, Inc., H., The, NY, 6911
Schaffer Foundation, Michael & Helen, The, MA, 4129
Schapiro Fund, M. A., NY, *see* 6912
Schapiro Fund, Morris and Alma, The, NY, 6912
Scharf Foundation, Inc., Leon & Irene, NY, *see* 5910
Scharf Foundation, Inc., Morris & Dvora, NY, 6913
Scharlin Family Foundation, Inc., The, FL, 2223
Schawk Family Foundation, Clarence W. and Marilyn G., The, IL, 2984
Schechter Foundation, Inc., Harold & Blanche, The, NY, 6914
Schecter Family Foundation, Inc., The, NJ, 5385
Scheidt Family Foundation, Inc., TN, 8726
Scheller, Jr. Family Foundation, Roberta and Ernest, PA, 8426
Schenck Fund, L. P., NJ, 5386
Schenectady Foundation, The, NY, 6915
Schenk Charitable Trust No. 1, Albert Schenk III & Kathleen H., The, WV, 9732
Schenker Family Foundation, The, NY, 6916
Schepp Foundation, Leopold, NY, 6917
Schering-Plough Foundation, Inc., NJ, 5387
Scherman Foundation, Inc., The, NY, 6918
Schermer Foundation, Adler, The, CO, 1449
Schermer Foundation, Betty A. & Lloyd G., The, CO, *see* 1449
Scheuer Family Foundation, Inc., Richard J. & Joan G., NY, 6919
Scheuer Family Foundation, Inc., S. H. and Helen R., NY, 6920
Scheuer Foundation, Inc., Steven H. and Alida Brill, The, NY, 6921

Scheumann Foundation, Inc., The, IN, 3235
Schieffelin Residuary Trust, Sarah I., NY, 6922
Schield Family Foundation, Inc., The, IL, 2985
Schiewetz Foundation, Inc., The, OH, 7835
Schiff Family Foundation, Robert C. & Adele R., OH, 7836
Schiff Foundation, Dorothy, The, DE, 1750
Schiff Foundation, John J. and Mary R., OH, 7837
Schiff Foundation, Robert C. & Adele R., OH, 7838
Schiff Foundation, The, NY, 6923
Schifter Family Foundation, MD, 3726
Schimmel Foundation, Inc., Stephen Harold, The, CA, 1101
Schippmann Foundation, J. W., FL, 2224
Schlafer Foundation, Shirley K., The, MI, 4429
Schlegel Foundation, Oscar C. & Augusta, WI, 9919
Schlessman Family Foundation, Inc., CO, 1450
Schlessman Foundation, Inc., CO, see 1450
Schlieder Educational Foundation, Edward G., LA, 3508
Schlinger Foundation, CA, 1102
Schlinger Foundation, Warren & Katherine, CA, 1103
Schlink Foundation, Albert G. and Olive H., OH, 7839
Schlosser Family Foundation, Nancy B. and C. William, CA, 1104
Schlosstein Hartley Foundation, NY, 6925
Schlumberger Foundation, Inc., NY, 6926
Schmeelk Foundation, Inc., Priscilla & Richard J., NY, 6927
Schmidlapp Fund, C., OH, see 7840
Schmidlapp Fund, Charlotte R., OH, 7840
Schmidlapp Trust No. 1 and No. 2, Jacob G., OH, 7841
Schmidlapp Trust No. 1, Jacob G., OH, see 7841
Schmidt Charitable Foundation, William E., IL, 2986
Schmidt Family Charitable Foundation, J. Frank, The, OR, 8055
Schmidt Family Foundation, FL, 2225
Schmidt Foundation, Carl and Verna, MN, 4673
Schmieding Foundation, Inc., The, AR, 175
Schmitt Foundation, Arthur J., IL, 2987
Schmitt Foundation, Inc., Kilian J. and Caroline F., The, NY, 6928
Schneider Charitable Trust, John D. and Minnie R., IL, 2988
Schneider Charitable Trust, John D., IL, see 2988
Schneider Foundation, Inc., Helen & Irving, NY, 6929
Schneider National Foundation, Inc., WI, 9920
Schnitzer CARE Foundation, Harold & Arlene, OR, 8056
Schnitzer/Novack Foundation, OR, 8057
Schnurmacher Foundation, Inc., Adolph & Ruth, NY, 6930
Schnurmacher Foundation, Inc., Charles & Mildred, NY, 6931
Schock Foundation, Clarence, The, PA, 8427
Schocken Foundation, Inc., The, CA, 1105
Schoen Family Foundation, MA, 4130
Schoen Foundation, FL, 2226
Schoenbaum Family Foundation, Inc., The, FL, 2227
Schoenecker Foundation, MN, 4674
Schoenleber Foundation, Inc., WI, 9921
Scholarship Foundation, The, NJ, 5388
Scholarships Foundation, Inc., The, NY, 6932
Scholl Foundation, Dr., IL, 2989
Scholler Foundation, The, PA, 8428
Schollmaier Foundation, TX, 9172
Schon Family Foundation, NY, 6933
Schooner Foundation, The, MA, 4131
Schoonmaker - Sewickley Valley Hospital Trust, J. & L., PA, 8429
Schott Foundation, Inc., Caroline & Sigmund, MA, see 4132
Schott Foundation, Joseph J., OH, 7842
Schott Foundation, Lewis, NY, 6934
Schott Foundation, Marge & Charles J., OH, 7843
Schott Foundation, Stephen C. & Patricia A., CA, 1106
Schott Fund, Caroline & Sigmund, MA, 4132
Schottenstein Foundation, Jay and Jean, The, OH, 7844
Schottenstein Foundation, Jay L., OH, see 7844
Schow Foundation, The, CA, 1107
Schowalter Foundation, Inc., The, KS, 3388
Schrafft Charitable Trust, William E. Schrafft and Bertha E., MA, 4133
Schrager Foundation, Phillip and Terri, NE, 5001

Schrager Foundation, Phillip, NE, see 5001
Schramm Foundation, The, CO, 1451
Schreyer Foundation, The, NJ, 5389
Schreyer Foundation, William A. & Joan L., The, NJ, see 5389
Schuler Family Foundation, Force, WA, see 9678
Schuler Family Foundation, IL, 2990
Schuler Family Foundation, WA, 9678
Schuler Foundation, James and Patricia, The, HI, 2552
Schuler Foundation, Ruth Epstein, CA, 1108
Schulhof Family Foundation, NY, 6935
Schultz Family Foundation, WA, 9679
Schultz Foundation, Arthur B., The, WY, 9990
Schulweis Family Foundation, The, NY, 6936
Schulze Family Foundation, Richard M., MN, 4675
Schumann Center for Media and Democracy, Inc., The, NJ, 5390
Schumann Foundation, Florence and John, The, NJ, see 5390
Schumann Foundation, Inc., FL, 2228
Schumann Fund for New Jersey, Inc., The, NJ, 5391
Schurgot Foundation, Inc., Paul D., The, NY, 6937
Schusterman Family Foundation, Charles and Lynn, OK, 7975
Schusterman Foundation, Dan & Gloria, The, OK, 7976
Schutte Foundation, Victor E. & Caroline, TX, 9173
Schwab Corporation Foundation, Charles, The, CA, see 1110
Schwab Foundation, Charles and Helen, CA, 1109
Schwab Foundation, Charles, The, CA, 1110
Schwab Raines Foundation, PA, 8430
Schwab-Rosenhouse Memorial Foundation, CA, 1111
Schwab-Spector-Raines Foundation, PA, see 8430
Schwan's Corporate Giving Foundation, MN, 4676
Schwartz Family Foundation Trust, Peter A. and Marion W., NY, 6941
Schwartz Family Foundation, Inc., Barry K., NY, 6940
Schwartz Family Foundation, Jess & Sheila, The, AZ, 137
Schwartz Family Foundation, NY, 6938, 6939
Schwartz Family Foundation, Theodore G. and M. Christine, IL, see 2991
Schwartz Family Foundation, Theodore G., IL, 2991
Schwartz Foundation, Alvin & Dorothy, NJ, 5392
Schwartz Foundation, Bernard Schwartz and Robert, The, NJ, see 5393
Schwartz Foundation, Donna and Marvin, The, NY, 6943
Schwartz Foundation, Inc., Bernard & Irene, NY, 6944
Schwartz Foundation, Inc., Bernard Lee, The, DE, 1751
Schwartz Foundation, Inc., David, NY, 6945
Schwartz Foundation, Inc., The, NJ, 5393
Schwartz Foundation, Jack and Billie, The, NY, 6946
Schwartz Foundation, NY, 6942
Schwartze Community Foundation, A. J., MO, 4898
Schwarz Family Foundation, NY, 6947
Schwarz Foundation, NJ, 5394
Schwarzman Foundation, Inc., Ellen Philips, NY, see 6294
Schwebel Foundation, Inc., Irene & Mac, NY, 6948
Schweers Family Foundation, Geiser, CA, 1112
Schweppe Foundation, The, MO, 4899
Scientific-Atlanta Foundation, Inc., GA, 2482
Scioto County Area Foundation, The, OH, see 7845
Scioto Foundation, The, OH, 7845
Sclavos Family Foundation, CA, 1113
Scotford Foundation, OH, 7846
Scott Charitable Trust, Alton N., AL, A
Scott Charitable Trust, Kenneth A., OH, 7847
Scott Foundation, Homer A. & Mildred S., WY, 9991
Scott Foundation, Inc., GA, 2483
Scott Foundation, Inc., LA, 3509
Scott Foundation, Virginia Steele, CA, 1114
Scott Foundation, William E., TX, 9174
Scott Foundation, William H., John G., and Emma, The, VA, 9513
Scott Scholarship Fund - Gertrude S. Straub Trust Estate, M. M., HI, 2553
Scranton Area Foundation, Inc., The, PA, 8431
Scripps Foundation, Edward W. and Betty Knight, The, VA, 9514
Scripps Foundation, Ellen Browning, The, CA, 1115
Scripps Howard Foundation, OH, 7848

Scroggins Foundation, Inc., Arthur E. & Cornelia C., The, KS, 3389
Scrushy Charitable Foundation, Inc., Richard M., AL, 62
Sculco Foundation, Thomas P. & Cynthia D., The, NY, 6949
Scully Family Foundation, Irene S., CA, 1116
Scully Foundation, Joseph C. and Judith A., The, IL, 2992
Scurlock Foundation, TX, 9175
SDA Foundation, The, NY, 6950
SDSC Global Foundation, The, MA, 4134
Seabury Foundation, The, IL, 2993
SEAKR Foundation, CO, 1452
Seal, Jr. Family Foundation, Leo W., MS, 4764
Sealark Foundation, Inc., The, NY, 6951
Sealed Power Foundation, NC, see 7484
Seaman Family Foundation, Inc., The, FL, 2229
Search Foundation, The, TX, 9176
Searle Freedom Trust, IL, 9679
Seattle Foundation, The, WA, 9680
Seaver Charitable Trust, Richard C., CA, 1117
Seaver Foundation, Beatrice & Samuel A., NY, 6952
Seaver Institute, The, CA, 1118
Seaworld & Busch Gardens Conservation Fund, MO, 4900
Seay Foundation, CO, 1453
Sebastian Foundation, MI, 4430
Sebastiani Charitable Trust, August, The, CA, 1119
Secchia Family Foundation, MI, 4431
Secchia Foundation, Peter F., MI, see 4431
Securian Foundation, MN, 4677
Security Benefit Life Insurance Company Charitable Trust, KS, 3390
Security's Lending Hand Foundation, SC, 8609
Sedgwick Family Charitable Trust, OH, 7849
Seedlings Foundation, CT, 1645
Seeno, Jr. Family Foundation, Albert D., The, CA, 1120
Seevak Family Foundation, DE, 1752
Seevers Family Foundation, NY, 6953
Segal Charitable Trust, Barnet, CA, 1121
Segal Family Foundation II, IL, 2995
Segal Foundation, George & Helen, NJ, 5395
Segerstrom Family Foundation, Hal and Jeanette, CA, 1122
Segerstrom Foundation, The, CA, 1123
Sehgal Family Foundation, IA, 3330
Sehn Foundation, The, MI, 4432
Sei Burning Bush Fund One, TX, 9177
Seibel Foundation, Abe and Annie, The, TX, 9178
Seid Foundation, Barbara and Barre, IL, 2996
Seid Foundation, Barre, IL, see 2996
Seiden Foundation, Norman and Barbara, NJ, 5396
Seidenberg Foundation, Ivan, The, CT, 1646
Seidler Foundation, The, IA, 3331
Seifert Charitable Trust, Dorothy T. & Myron, OH, 7850
Seigle Family Foundation, IL, 2997
Seiler Family Foundation, Inc., Nathan & Lena, NY, 6954
Seinfeld Family Foundation, The, CA, 1124
Seiple Family Foundation, PA, 8432
Selby Foundation, William G. Selby and Marie, FL, 2230
Seldon Foundation, The, NY, see 6433
Self Family Foundation, The, SC, 8610
Self Foundation, The, SC, see 8610
Selfon Memorial Fund Charitable Trust, Merle, PA, 8433
Selig Foundation, The, GA, 2484
Seligman Family Foundation, The, MI, 4433
Selis Foundation, Inc., Irving and Sara, NY, 6955
Sells Foundation, Carol Buck, NV, see 5025
Semel Charitable Foundation, The, CA, 1125
Semmes Foundation, Inc., TX, 9179
Semnani Foundation, UT, 9341
Semple Foundation, Louise Taft, The, OH, 7851
Sence Foundation, The, CA, 1126
Seneff Family Foundation, Inc., FL, 2231
Senior Services of Stamford, Inc., CT, 1647
Sensient Technologies Foundation, Inc., WI, 9922
Sentry Foundation, Inc., WI, see 9923
Sentry Insurance Foundation, Inc., WI, 9923
Senyei Family Foundation, The, CA, 1127
Sequoia Foundation, WA, 9681
Seramur Family Foundation, Inc., WI, 9924
Seraph Foundation, The, PA, 8434
Serenity Fund, CA, 1128

Servant Foundation, KS, 3391

Servant Leadership Foundation, The, CO, 1454

Servant's Heart Foundation, Inc., GA, 2485

Servants' Charitable Trust, The, CA, 1129

ServiceMaster Foundation, The, IL, see 2723

SES Foundation, Inc., The, NY, 6956

Setton Foundation, The, NY, 6957

Setzer Foundation, The, CA, 1130

Seven Woods Foundation, WA, A

Seventeen Torah Foundation, Inc., NY, 6958

Severns Family Foundation, CA, 1131

Sewall Foundation, Elmina B., CT, 1648

Sewell Family Foundation, MN, 4678

Sexton Foundation, Gwendolyn, The, CA, 1132

Sexton Foundation, MN, 4679

SF Foundation II, The, GA, 2486

SF Foundation, IL, 2998

SFC Charitable Foundation, MO, see 4904

SFO Foundation, The, NV, 5062

SGM Scholarship Foundation, NY, see 7024

Shackelford Charitable Trust, Margaret F., FL, 2232

Shadyside Academy Fund, The, PA, 8435

Shaffer Family Charitable Trust, PA, 8436

Shaheen Foundation, Inc., David and Linda, The, NV, 5063

Shakarian Foundation, David & Lois, The, NJ, see 5310

Shaker Family Foundation, Joseph R. and Helen, IL, 2999

Shaker Family Foundation, The, IL, see 2999

Shallenberger Trust Fund, William F., GA, 2487

Shannon Family Foundation, Ken and Jan, The, KS, 3392

Shannon Foundation, E. L. and Ruth B., The, CA, 1133

Shapell Foundation, David and Fela, CA, 1134

Shapell Foundation, Nathan & Lilly, CA, 1135

Shapell-Guerin Foundation, Inc., CA, 1136

Shapira Charitable Foundation, Anne And Eli, OR, 8058

Shapira Foundation, David S. and Karen A., The, PA, 8437

Shapiro Charity Fund Trust, Abraham, MA, 4135

Shapiro Family Charitable Foundation, CA, 1137

Shapiro Family Foundation, Carl and Ruth, MA, 4136

Shapiro Family Foundation, Joseph and Libby, NY, 6959

Shapiro Family Foundation, Lester & Edna, IL, 3000

Shapiro Foundation, Carl and Ruth, MA, see 4136

Shapiro Foundation, Herman and Gwen, WI, 9925

Shapiro Foundation, Inc., Charles and M. R., IL, 3001

Shapiro Foundation, Inc., Fern G. Shapiro, Morris R. Shapiro, and Charles, IL, see 3001

Shapiro Foundation, The, CA, 1138

Shapiro-Silverberg Foundation, NY, 6960

Share Foundation, KS, see 3375

Share Trust, Charles Morton, OK, 7977

Shared Earth Foundation, The, MD, 3727

Sharf Fund, Jean S. & Frederic A., MA, 4137

Sharkey Family Foundation, Thomas & Ruth, NJ, 5397

Sharp Foundation, Evelyn, The, NY, 6961

Sharp Foundation, Inc., Ruth C. and Charles S., TX, 9180

Sharp Foundation, NY, see 6962

Sharp Foundation, Peter Jay, The, NY, 6962

Sharp Foundation, The, VA, 9515

Sharpe Family Foundation, The, IL, 3002

Shasta Regional Community Foundation, CA, 1139

Shattuck Charitable Trust, Clinton H. & Wilma T., The, MA, 4138

Shattuck Charitable Trust, S. F., WI, 9926

Shattuck Family Foundation, Inc., The, MD, 3728

Shaw (U.S.) Foundation, The, HI, 2554

Shaw Charitable Foundation, Seyfarth, IL, 3003

Shaw Charitable Trust, Mary Elizabeth Dee, The, AZ, 138

Shaw Family Foundation, Inc., OH, 7852

Shaw Foundation, Arch W., MO, 4901

Shaw Foundation, Gardiner Howland, MA, 4139

Shaw Foundation, Harold W. & Mary Louise, The, OH, 7853

Shaw Foundation, Walden W. & Jean Young, IL, 3004

Shaw's Market Trust Fund, RI, see 8555

Shaw's Supermarket Charitable Foundation, RI, 8555

Shayne Foundation, CA, 1140

Shea Foundation, Edmund and Mary, CA, 1142

Shea Foundation, John & Dorothy, The, CA, 1143

Shea Foundation, Peter and Carolyn, CA, 1141

Sheakley Family Foundation, Rhonda & Larry A., OH, 7854

Sheba Foundation, The, IL, 3005

Sheehan Family Foundation, MA, 4140

Sheffield-Harrold Charitable Trust, GA, 2488

Shei'rah Foundation, Inc., The, CT, 1649

Sheinberg Foundation, Eric P., NY, 6963

Shelden Fund, Elizabeth, Allan and Warren, MI, 4434

Sheldon Foundation, Inc., Ralph C., NY, 6964

Shell Companies Foundation, Inc., TX, see 9181

Shell Oil Company Foundation, TX, 9181

Shelter Insurance Foundation, MO, 4902

Shelton Family Foundation, TX, 9182

Shemanski Testamentary Trust, Tillie and Alfred, WA, 9682

Shen Family Foundation, The, NJ, 5398

Shenandoah Foundation, CA, 1144

Shenango Valley Community Foundation, PA, 8438

Shenango Valley Foundation, PA, see 8438

Shepherd Foundation, NJ, 5399

Shepherd Foundation, The, MI, 4435

Sheraton Foundation, Inc., The, NY, see 7049

Sheridan Foundation, Hope, The, NY, 6965

Sheridan Foundation, Inc., Thomas B. and Elizabeth M., The, MD, 3729

Sheridan Foundation, James & Chantal, NY, A

Sherman Family Charitable Trust, George and Beatrice, MA, 4141

Sherman Family Foundation, FL, 2233

Sherman Private Foundation, Betsy R. and George M., The, FL, see 2233

Sherrerd Foundation, PA, 8439

Sherwin-Williams Foundation, The, OH, 7855

Sherwood Trust, WA, 9683

Shiebler Family Foundation, MN, 4680

Shield-Ayres Foundation, TX, 9183

Shields Foundation, Inc., George L., The, MD, 3730

Shifting Foundation, The, IL, 3006

Shiley Foundation, The, CA, 1145

Shillman Foundation, The, MA, 4142

Shimek Family Foundation, Dan & Kay, MN, 4681

Shipley Family Foundation, Inc., The, MA, 4143

Shirk Foundation, Russell and Betty, The, IL, 3007

Shirley Foundation, Jon and Mary, The, WA, 9684

Shiva Foundation, Susan Stein, NY, 6966

Shivers Cancer Foundation, TX, 9184

Shklar Foundation, Eugene and Daymel, CA, 1146

Shoemaker Foundation, Edwin J. & Ruth M., MI, 4436

Shoemaker Trust for Shoemaker Scholarship Fund, Ray S., PA, 8440

Shoolman Children's Foundation, Edith Glick, The, NY, 6967

Shoreland Foundation, The, NY, 6968

Shoresh Foundation, CA, 1147

Short Charitable Foundation, Tommy E., The, CA, 1148

Shott, Jr. Foundation, Hugh I., WV, 9733

Shouse Foundation, Catherine Filene, VA, A

SHP Foundation, CA, 1149

Shrensky Foundation, Inc., MD, 3731

Shriners of Rhode Island Charities Trust, RI, 8556

SHS Foundation, The, NY, 6969

Shubert Foundation, Inc., The, NY, 6970

Shulamit Foundation, Inc., Rachel Bat, NY, 6971

Shulman Family Foundation, Alex, WA, 9685

Shultz Foundation, Inc., Bernard E., The, MD, 3732

SI Bank & Trust Foundation, NY, 6972

Sicari Charitable Trust, Joseph & Agatha, MA, 4144

Sicherman Family Foundation, Inc., The, NY, 6973

SICO Foundation, The, PA, see 8427

Sidhu-Singh Family Foundation, The, TX, 9185

Sie Foundation, Anna and John J., The, CO, 1455

Siebel Foundation, Thomas and Stacey, The, CA, 1150

Sieben Foundation, Inc., MN, 4682

Siebens Charitable Foundation, Inc., Harold W., NY, 6974

Siebert Foundation, Inc., Muriel F., NY, 6975

Siebert Lutheran Foundation, Inc., WI, 9927

Siegal Foundation, Alvin and Laura, The, OH, 7856

Siegel Foundation, Ruth and Jerome A., NY, 6976

Siemens Foundation, NJ, 5400

Sierra Foundation, Inc., NJ, 5401

Sierra Health Foundation, CA, 1151

Sierra Pacific Foundation, CA, 1152

Sierra Pacific Resources Charitable Foundation, NV, 5064

Siff Charitable Foundation, MA, 4145

Sigma Chi Greystone Foundation, Inc., NY, 6977

Silas Foundation, OK, 7978

Silberman Foundation, Curt C. & Else, NJ, 5402

Silbermann Foundation, Inc., Rosanne H., The, NJ, 5403

Silberstein Foundation, Inc., William & Sylvia, The, NY, 6978

Silberstein Foundation, Stephen M., The, CA, 1153

Silberstein-Boesky Family Foundation, Inc., NY, 6979

Silfen Foundation, David and Lyn, The, NY, 6980

Silk Charitable Foundation, Fred F., OH, 7857

Silver Foundation, Jack S. & Shirley M., The, NY, 6981

Silver Foundation, VA, 9516

Silver Giving Foundation, The, CA, 1154

Silver Lining Foundation, The, CA, see 1154

Silver Mountain Foundation for the Arts, NJ, 5404

Silverman Family Foundation, Inc., Carlynn and Lawrence, The, MD, 3733

Silverman Family Foundation, Inc., FL, see 2234

Silverman Foundation, Inc., Barry & Judy, FL, 2234

Silverman Foundation, Inc., Harvey, The, NY, 6982

Silverman Foundation, Inc., Lois and Norman, MA, 4146

Silverman Foundation, Marty and Dorothy, NY, 6983

Silverstein Family Foundation, Inc., Raine & Stanley, The, NY, 6984

Silverthorn Foundation, Robert S. and Marilyn I., TX, see 9161

Silverton Foundation, Inc., TX, 9186

Silverweed Foundation, Inc., NY, 6985

Simches Charitable Foundation, Joanne B., MA, 4147

Simmons Family Foundation, R. P., PA, 8441

Simmons Family Foundation, The, IL, 3008

Simmons Family Foundation, UT, 9342

Simmons Family Foundation, Virginia and L. E., The, TX, 9187

Simmons Foundation, Harold, TX, 9188

Simmons Foundation, The, TX, 9189

Simms Foundation, Ronald A. and Victoria Mann, The, CA, 1155

Simon Charitable Foundation Number One, Melvin and Bren, The, IN, 3236

Simon Charitable Foundation, David E. Simon & Jacqueline S., IN, 3237

Simon Charitable Foundation, Deborah Joy, IN, 3238

Simon Charitable Foundation, Max, The, IN, 3239

Simon Charitable Foundation, NE, 5002

Simon Family Foundation, Herbert, The, IN, 3240

Simon Family Foundation, IL, see 2998

Simon Family Foundation, Inc., Arnold, The, NY, 6986

Simon Foundation, Inc., William E. & Carol G., NY, see 6987

Simon Foundation, Inc., William E., NY, 6987

Simon Foundation, Lucille Ellis, The, CA, 1156

Simon Foundation, Mildred, Herbert and Julian, MO, 4903

Simon Foundation-Florida, Sidney, Milton and Leoma, The, FL, 2235

Simon, Jr. Foundation, Cynthia L. & William E., NJ, 5405

Simonds Foundation, Juliet L. Hillman, PA, 8442

Simone Foundation, Louise Manoogian, MI, see 4383

Simons Family Charitable Trust No. 2, Carl and Fay, NY, 6988

Simons Foundation, The, NY, 6989

Simonyi Fund for Arts and Sciences, Charles, WA, 9686

Simplot Company Foundation, Inc., J. R., ID, 2574

Simplot Foundation, Inc., J. R., ID, 2575

Simpson Foundation Trust, M. L., The, GA, 2489

Simpson Foundation, The, NC, 7472

Simpson PSB Fund, CA, 1157

Sims Foundation, Inc., J. Marion, SC, 8611

Singer Family Foundation, Paul, The, DE, 1753

Singer Foundation, Inc., Herbert & Nell, NY, 6990

Singer Foundation, Paul & Linda, The, DE, see 1753

Singh Family Foundation, NY, 6991

Singing for Change, MO, 4904

Singletary Foundation, Inc., Lewis Hall & Mildred Sasser, GA, 2490

Sinsheimer Fund, Alexandrine and Alexander L., The, DE, 1754

Sioux Falls Area Community Foundation, SD, 8630
Siouxland Community Foundation, IA, 3332
Siouxland Foundation, IA, see 3332
Siperstein Charitable Foundation, Mynde & Gary, RI, 8557
Siragusa Foundation, The, IL, 3009
Sirius Fund, IL, 3010
Sirrine Textile Foundation, Inc., J. E., SC, 8612
Sirus Fund, The, NY, 6992
SISB Community Foundation, NY, see 6972
Sisenwein Fund, Inc., Branna and Irv, NY, 6993
Sisler McFawn Foundation, The, OH, 7858
Sister Fund, The, NY, 6994
Sit Foundation, Eugene C. & Gail V., The, MN, 4683
Sit Investment Associates Foundation, MN, 4684
Sites Charitable Foundation, Cindy and John, The, CT, 1650
Sitt Chesed Fund, David and Marjorie, NY, 6995
Sitt Family Foundation, Morris & Eddie, NY, see 6996
Sitt Family Foundation, The, NY, 6996
Sitt Foundation, Isaac, The, NY, 6997
Six Pillar Foundation, Inc., The, FL, 2236
Sixty Four Foundation, The, TX, 9190
Sjolund Foundation, Paul & Dawn, MN, 4685
Skadden Fellowship Foundation, Inc., The, NY, 6998
Skadden, Arps, Slate, Meagher & Flom Fellowship Foundation, NY, see 6998
Skelly Charitable Foundation, Gertrude E., The, FL, 2237
Skelton Charitable Foundation, Homer, MS, 4765
Skestos Family Foundation, OH, see 7683
Skilling and Andrews Foundation, MI, 4437
Skillman Foundation, The, MI, 4438
Skirball Foundation, NY, 6999
Sklut Foundation, Lori L., NC, 7473
Skoll Foundation, The, CA, 1158
Sky Foundation, OH, 7859
Sky View Foundation, OR, 8059
Skywords Family Foundation, CA, A
Slaggie Family Foundation, MN, 4686
Slant/Fin Foundation, Inc., The, NY, 7000
Sleeper Vision Mission Supporting Organization, VA, see 9370
Slemp Foundation, The, OH, 7860
SLEN Foundation, NY, see 6454
Slick Family Foundation, NC, 7474
Slifka Foundation, Inc., Alan B., NY, 7001
Slifka Foundation, Inc., Joseph & Sylvia, NY, 7002
Slikkers Foundation, MI, 4439
Sloan Foundation, Alfred P., NY, 7003
Sloan Foundation, The, WA, 9687
Sloan, Jr. Foundation, O. Temple, NC, 7475
Sloat Foundation, Edward and Betty, OH, 7861
Slosburg Family Charitable Trust, NE, 5003
Slovin Foundation, NY, 7004
SMA Foundation, NY, see 7031
Small Foundation, Inc., Albert & Lillian, MD, 3734
Small-Alper Family Foundation, MD, 3735
Smallwood Foundation, Frances C. & William P., WI, 9928
Smallwood Foundation, WI, see 9928
Smart Family Foundation, The, CT, 1651
SMBC Global Foundation, Inc., NY, 7005
Smidt Family Foundation, CA, 1159
Smikis Foundation, MN, 4687
Smilowitz Private Foundation, Herbert, NJ, 5406
Smith & Athalie R. Clarke Foundation, Joan Irvine, CA, 1160
Smith 1990 Charitable Trust, Richard & Susan, MA, 4148
Smith Benevolent Association, Buckingham, FL, 2238
Smith Charitable Foundation, Clara B. and W. Aubrey, TX, 9191
Smith Charitable Foundation, Lester H., TX, 9192
Smith Charitable Foundation, Robert and Dana, MA, 4149
Smith Charitable Trust, May and Stanley, CA, 1161
Smith Charitable Trust, R. & S., MA, see 4148
Smith Charitable Trust, Stella B., AR, 176
Smith Charitable Trust, Sybil H., AL, 63
Smith Charitable Trust, W. W., PA, 8443
Smith Charities, Inc., John I., NC, 7476
Smith Family Foundation, Arthur L. & Carra J., MI, 4440

Smith Family Foundation, Charles E., VA, 9517
Smith Family Foundation, Hal & John, GA, 2491
Smith Family Foundation, Inc., Eddie and Jo Allison, NC, see 7478
Smith Family Foundation, Inc., G. Gregory, NC, 7477
Smith Family Foundation, Inc., Ian & Margaret, The, NJ, 5407
Smith Family Foundation, Inc., Winthrop H. & Margaret D., The, NJ, 5408
Smith Family Foundation, Inc., Winthrop H., The, NJ, see 5408
Smith Family Foundation, Orin, WA, 9688
Smith Family Foundation, Park B. Smith and Carol, The, NY, 7006
Smith Family Foundation, Richard and Susan, MA, 4150
Smith Family Foundation, Robert H., VA, 9518
Smith Family Foundation, The, NH, 5101
Smith Family Foundation, Will and Jada, CA, 1162
Smith Foundation for Neurological Research, Vivian L., TX, 9193
Smith Foundation for Restorative Neurology, Vivian L., TX, see 9193
Smith Foundation, Bob and Vivian, TX, 9194
Smith Foundation, David H., MA, see 3840
Smith Foundation, Dr. Bob and Jean, TX, 9195
Smith Foundation, Gordon V. & Helen C., MD, 3736
Smith Foundation, H. Russell, The, CA, 1163
Smith Foundation, Hal L. & Julia T., GA, see 2491
Smith Foundation, Hoxie Harrison, PA, 8444
Smith Foundation, Inc., A. O., WI, 9929
Smith Foundation, Inc., Edward C. Smith, Jr. & Christopher B., NC, 7478
Smith Foundation, Inc., George Graham and Elizabeth Galloway, NY, 7007
Smith Foundation, J. M., SC, 8613
Smith Foundation, Jody & Layton, VA, A
Smith Foundation, Kelvin and Eleanor, The, OH, 7862
Smith Foundation, Kenneth L. & Eva S., KS, 3393
Smith Foundation, Lon V., CA, 1164
Smith Foundation, Margaret Chase, The, ME, 3556
Smith Foundation, Matthew J. & Anne B., The, NJ, 5409
Smith Foundation, Morris S., NV, 5065
Smith Foundation, Ralph L., TX, 9196
Smith Foundation, Randall & Kathryn, The, NY, 7008
Smith Foundation, The, MO, 4905
Smith Foundation, The, PA, see 8444
Smith Foundation, Vivian L., TX, 9197
Smith Foundation, Will, CA, see 1162
Smith Foundation, William A. and Madeline Welder, The, TX, 9198
Smith Foundation, William H. and Patricia M., MI, 4441
Smith Fund, Barbara, CA, 1165
Smith Fund, Inc., George D., NY, 7009
Smith Horticultural Trust, Stanley, The, CA, 1166
Smith Memorial Fund, Ethel Sergent Clark, PA, 8445
Smith School of Business Foundation, Inc., Robert H., The, MD, 3737
Smith Trust, General William A., The, NC, 7479
Smith Trust, May and Stanley, The, CA, 1167
Smith, Jr. Charitable Trust, Jack J., The, OH, 7863
Smith, M.D. Foundation, Bob, TX, see 9195
Smithers Foundation, Inc., Christopher D., The, NY, 7010
Smithfield-Luter Foundation, Inc., The, VA, 9519
SmithKline Beecham Foundation, PA, see 8218
Smittcamp Family Foundation, The, CA, 1168
Smock Foundation, Frank L. and Laura L., NE, 5004
Smoot Charitable Foundation, KS, 3394
Smucker Foundation, Willard E., OH, 7864
Smullin Foundation, Patricia D. and William B., CA, 1169
Smurfit-Stone Container Corporation Charitable Fund, MO, 4906
Smysor Memorial Fund, Harry L. & John I., IL, 3011
Smythe Family Foundation, William D., CA, 1170
Snead Family Foundation, VA, 9520
Snee-Reinhardt Charitable Foundation, PA, 8446
Snider Foundation, The, PA, 8447
Snite Foundation, Fred B., IL, 3012
Snodgrass Foundation, Inc., The, GA, 2492
Snook Foundation, AL, A
Snow Foundation, Phoebe, CA, 1171
Snow Memorial Trust, John Ben, NY, 7011

Snowdon Foundation, Ted, The, NY, 7012
Snowdon Foundation, The, NY, see 7012
Snyder Charitable Fund, G. Whitney, PA, 8448
Snyder Foundation, Beatrice, NY, 7013
Snyder Foundation, Frost and Margaret, WA, 9689
Snyder Foundation, Inc., Ruth B. and Willard B., KS, see 3349
Snyder Foundation, Nancy and John, TX, 9199
Snyder Fund, Valentine Perry, NY, 7014
SO Charitable Trust, The, NY, 7015
Sobel and Marcia Dunn Foundation, Jonathan, The, NY, 7016
Sobrato Family Foundation, CA, 1172
Society for Analytical Chemists of Pittsburgh, PA, 8449
Society Foundation, OH, see 7700
Soda Foundation, Y & H, CA, 1173
Sodaro Family Foundation, The, CA, 1174
Soderquist Family Foundation, The, AR, 177
Sohn Foundation, Donald R., The, MA, 4151
SOL Foundation Agency, NC, 7480
Solano Community Foundation, CA, 1175
Solari Charitable Trust, Richard & Mary, CA, 1176
Solheim Foundation, AZ, 139
Solid Waste Management Foundation, MI, see 4267
Soling Family Foundation, AZ, 140
Solomon Foundation, Peter J. & Linda N., NY, see 7017
Solomon Foundation, Peter J., NY, 7017
Solomon Testamentary Trust, Alfred Z., NY, 7018
Solomont Family Foundation, Alan D. and Susan Lewis, MA, 4152
Solow Foundation, Inc., Sheldon H., NY, 7020
Solow Foundation, NY, 7019
Solutia Fund, MO, 4907
Solve, Inc., CA, 1177
Sonoco Foundation, SC, 8614
Sonoma County Community Foundation, The, CA, see 407
Sonora Area Foundation, CA, 1178
Sontag Foundation, Inc., FL, 2239
Sooch Foundation, The, TX, 9200
Sophia Foundation, The, TX, see 9176
Sordoni Foundation, Inc., PA, 8450
Soref Charitable Trust, Daniel M., WI, 9930
Soref Foundation, Samuel and Helen, CA, 1179
Soref Foundation, Samuel M. Soref & Helene K., CA, see 1179
Sorensen Foundation, Harvey L. & Maud C., CA, 1180
Sorenson Legacy Foundation, The, UT, 9343
Soros Charitable Foundation, NY, 7021
Soros Foundation, Paul & Daisy, NY, 7022
Soros Foundation-Hungary, Inc., The, NY, 7023
Soros Fund Charitable Foundation, NY, 7024
Sosland Foundation, The, MO, 4908
Sosnoff Foundation, Martin and Toni, NY, 7025
Sosnoff Foundation, Martin T., NY, see 7025
Souder Family Foundation, IL, 3013
South Central Iowa Community Foundation, IA, 3333
South Dakota Community Foundation, SD, 8631
South Family Foundation, Inc., GA, 2493
South Financial Group Foundation, The, SC, 8615
South Lake County Community Foundation, Inc., FL, see 1947
South Mountain Company Foundation, MA, 4153
South Texas Charitable Foundation, TX, 9201
Southdown Foundation, TX, see 8821
Southeastern Group Foundation, Inc., IN, see 3102
Southern Bank Foundation, NC, 7481
Southern Company Charitable Foundation, Inc., GA, 2494
Southern Foundation, Inc., KS, see 3355
Southern Oklahoma Memorial Foundation, OK, 7979
Southways Foundation, The, MN, 4688
Southwest Florida Community Foundation, Inc., The, FL, 2240
Southwest Gas Corporation Foundation, The, NV, 5066
Southwest Michigan Rehab Foundation, MI, 4442
Sovereign Bank Foundation, PA, 8451
Sowell Charitable Trust, Thomas & Lillian, TX, 9202
Sowell Foundation, James E., TX, 9203
Spang and Company Charitable Trust, PA, 8452
Spangler Foundation, Inc., C. D., NC, 7482
Sparks Foundation, The, TN, 8727
Sparrow Charitable Foundation, The, TX, 9204

Sparrow Foundation, The, TX, 9205
Spartanburg County Foundation, The, SC, 8616
Spaulding Foundation, Joseph H., OH, see 7865
Spaulding Foundation, The, OH, 7865
Speas Foundation, Victor E., TX, 9206
Speas Memorial Trust, John W. and Effie E., TX, 9207
Spector Family Foundation, The, NV, 5067
Speer Foundation, Roy M., FL, 2241
Speh Foundation, Albert J. & Claire R., IL, 3014
Spencer Foundation, The, IL, 3015
Spencer Foundation, W. L. S., The, CA, 1181
Spencer Memorial Foundation, Cheryl, MA, 4154
Sperry Fund, The, NY, 7026
Speyer Family Foundation, Inc., The, NY, 7027
Speyer Foundation, Alexander C. & Tillie S., PA, 8453
SPIA Foundation, The, NY, 7028
Spiegel Family Foundation, Inc., Jerry and Emily, NY, 7029
Spiegel Family Foundation, Thomas, CA, 1182
Spiegel Foundation, Inc., Jerry, NY, see 7029
Spiegel Foundation, Sam, NY, 7030
Spilka Family Foundation, Inc., The, DE, 1755
Spinal Muscular Atrophy Foundation, NY, 7031
Spingold Foundation, Inc., Nate B. and Frances, NY, see 7032
Spingold Foundation, Inc., The, NY, 7032
Spire Foundation, Inc., Nancy Woodson, WI, 9931
Spirit Foundation, Inc., NY, 7033
Spirit Foundation, The, NY, see 6641
Spitzer Charitable Trust, Inc., Bernard & Anne, The, NY, 7034
Spitzer Foundation, Inc., Bernard & Anne, The, NY, see 7034
Split Rail Foundation, Inc., WI, 9932
Spoelhof Foundation, John and Judy, MI, 4443
Spokane Inland Northwest Community Foundation, WA, see 9589
Sprague Educational and Charitable Foundation, Seth, The, NY, 7035
Sprague Foundation, Robert R., CA, 1183
Sprague Memorial Institute, Otho S. A., The, IL, 3016
Sprague, Jr. Foundation, Norman F., CA, 1184
Spray Foundation, Inc., The, GA, 2495
Spreading the Good News of Salvation Foundation, IL, 3017
Sprenger-Lang Foundation, The, DC, 1848
Spring Charitable Trust, NC, 7483
Spring Creek Foundation, The, DC, 1849
Springcreek Foundation, CA, 1185
Springfield Foundation, The, OH, 7866
Springs Close Foundation, Inc., The, SC, 8617
Springs Foundation, Inc., SC, see 8617
Sprint Foundation, KS, 3395
Spunk Fund, Inc., The, NY, 7036
Spurlino Foundation, The, FL, 2242
SPX Foundation, NC, 7484
Square D Foundation, IL, 3018
Sragowicz Foundation, Inc., FL, 2243
Srour Foundation, Inc., Toufic, NY, 7037
SSM Foundation, Inc., NY, 7038
St. Croix Foundation, MN, see 4583
St. Croix Valley Community Foundation, WI, 9933
St. Deny's Foundation, Inc., MI, 4444
St. Faith's House Foundation, NY, 7039
St. George's Society of New York, NY, 7040
St. Giles Foundation, NY, 7041
St. Joe Community Foundation, Inc., FL, 2244
St. John's Foundation, CO, 1456
St. Jude Medical Foundation, MN, 4689
St. Louis Community Foundation, MO, see 4896
St. Mary's Catholic Foundation, PA, 8454
St. Paul Companies, Inc. Foundation, The, MN, see 4690
St. Paul Travelers Foundation, MN, 4690
St. Petersburg Times Scholarship Fund, FL, 2245
ST2 Foundation, Inc., NJ, 5410
Stabile Foundation, Vincent A., FL, A
Stabler Foundation, Donald B. and Dorothy L., The, PA, 8455
Stackner Family Foundation, Inc., WI, 9934
Stackpole-Hall Foundation, PA, 8456
Stacy Foundation, Inc., Festus and Helen, FL, 2246
Stafford Foundation, John R. and Inge P., The, FL, 2247

Staley Educational Foundation, Richard Seth, The, CO, 1457
Staley Foundation for Psychological Development, Richard Seth, CO, see 1457
Staley Foundation, Thomas F., NY, 7042
Stallworth Foundation Trust, Mary Elizabeth, The, AL, 64
Stamps Family Charitable Foundation, Inc., MA, 4155
Stamps Foundation, Inc., James L., CA, 1186
Standard Products Foundation, The, OH, see 7829
Stange Charitable Trust, Mary G., MI, 4445
Stangeland Foundation, Roger and Lilah, The, CA, 1187
Stanley Foundation, Theodore & Vada, CT, 1652
Stanton Family Foundation, Ruth, The, NY, 7043
Stanton Family Foundation, The, NY, 7044
Stanton Foundation, Oliver & Elizabeth, The, NY, 7045
Stanton Foundation, Ruth & Oliver, The, NY, see 7043
Stanzel Family Foundation, Inc., The, TX, 9208
Staples Foundation for Learning, Inc., MA, 4156
Star Family Foundation, The, FL, 2248
Star Foundation, Stanley A., FL, see 2248
Star Tribune Foundation, MN, 4691
Starbucks Foundation, The, WA, 9690
Stardust Foundation, Inc., AZ, 141
Stare Fund, The, MA, 4157
Starfish Foundation, TN, 8728
Starfish Group, The, NY, 7046
Stark Community Foundation, OH, 7867
Stark County Foundation, Inc., The, OH, see 7867
Stark Family Foundation, Ltd., WI, 9935
Stark Foundation, C. Richard Stark, Jr. & Joan E., IA, 3334
Stark Foundation, Nelda C. and H. J. Lutcher, TX, 9209
Starker Family Foundation, Inc., The, NY, 7047
Starling Foundation, Dorothy Richard, TX, 9210
Starr Foundation, The, NY, 7048
Starwood Foundation, Inc., The, NY, 7049
State Farm Companies Foundation, IL, 3019
State Street Foundation, MA, 4158
Statler Foundation, The, NY, 7050
Staton Foundation, Jocelyn Botterell, GA, see 2420
Staton Foundation, Robert W. and Bernice Ingalls, ID, 2576
Stauffer Charitable Trust, John, CA, 1188
Stauffer Communications Foundation, GA, see 2454
Staunton Augusta Waynesboro Community Foundation, VA, 9521
Staunton Farm Foundation, PA, 8457
STB Family Foundation, The, FL, see 2272
Steadley Memorial Trust, Kent D. & Mary L., IL, 3020
Stealth Foundation, CO, 1458
Steans Family Foundation, IL, 3021
Stearns Charitable Foundation, Inc., Anna B., MA, 4159
Stearns Charitable Trust, MA, 4160
Stearns Foundation, Inc., Gwendolyn L., SD, 8632
Stecher Foundation, Esta and Jamie, The, NY, 7051
Steel Family Foundation, Robert K., The, NY, 7052
Steel Partners Foundation, The, CO, 1459
Steelcase Foundation, MI, 4446
Steele Foundation, Harry and Grace, The, CA, 1189
Steele Foundation, Inc., The, AZ, 142
Steele-Reese Foundation, The, NY, 7053
Steere Foundation, William & Lynda, CT, 1653
Stefanski Charitable Foundation, Ben S. & Gerome R., OH, 7868
Steffens 21st Century Foundation II, NY, 7054
Steigleder Charitable Trust, Bert L. and Patricia S., WI, 9936
Stein Family Foundation, Eugene and Marilyn, CA, 1190
Stein Family Foundation, Inc., Allen A., NY, 7055
Stein Family Foundation, Inc., Joseph F., NY, 7056
Stein Foundation Trust, Jay, FL, 2249
Stein Foundation, Avy and Marcie, IL, 3022
Stein Foundation, Inc., Fred & Sharon, The, NY, 7057
Stein Foundation, Inc., Jack & Joan, WI, 9937
Stein Foundation, Louis & Bessie, FL, 2250
Stein Memorial Foundation, Lazar, The, NY, 7058
Steinbach Fund, Inc., Ruth & Milton, NY, 7059
Steinberg 1992 Charitable Trust, Joseph S. & Diane H., NY, 7060
Steinberg Charitable Trust, Harold & Mimi, The, NY, 7061
Steinberg Family Foundation, Inc., Meyer & Jean, NY, 7062

Steinberg Family Fund, Inc., The, NY, 7063
Steinberg Foundation, Inc., Meyer, NY, see 7062
Steiner Charitable Trust, David S. and Sylvia, The, NJ, 5411
Steiner Trust, Lionel, CA, 1191
Steinhardt Foundation, Judy and Michael, The, NY, 7064
Steinhart Foundation, Inc., The, NE, 5005
Steiniger Charitable Foundation, Edward & Joan B., NY, 7065
Steinman Foundation, James Hale, PA, 8458
Steinman Foundation, John Frederick, PA, 8459
Steinmetz Foundation, B.& M., NY, 7066
Steinmetz Foundation, CA, 1192
Steinmetz Foundation, D. & E., NY, 7067
Steinmetz Foundation, S. & E., NY, 7068
Steiro Foundation, Inc., The, NY, see 7056
Stemberg Family Charitable Trust, The, MA, 4161
Stemmons Foundation, TX, 9211
Stempel Foundation, Ernest L., NY, 7069
Stephens Christian Trust, TN, 8729
Stephens Foundation Trust, TN, see 8729
Stephens Foundation, AL, 65
Stephenson Foundation, CA, 1193
Sterling-Turner Foundation, TX, 9212
Stern Family Foundation, Alex, ND, 7521
Stern Family Foundation, Inc., Jerome L., NY, 7070
Stern Family Foundation, MA, 4162
Stern Family Foundation, The, CA, see 1194
Stern Family Foundation, The, NJ, 5412
Stern Family Foundation, Thomas D. & Denise R., NY, 7071
Stern Family Fund, Philip M., VA, see 9522
Stern Family Fund, VA, 9522
Stern Foundation for the Arts, Richard J., MO, 4909
Stern Foundation, Bernice and Milton, NY, 7072
Stern Foundation, Inc., Gustav and Irene, NY, 7073
Stern Foundation, Inc., Gustav, NY, see 7073
Stern Foundation, Inc., Jean L. and Robert A., NY, 7074
Stern Foundation, Inc., Jerome L. and Jane, NY, see 7070
Stern Foundation, Irvin, IL, 3023
Stern Foundation, Marc and Eva, The, CA, 1194
Stern Foundation, Pauline and Edgar, UT, 9344
Stern Memorial Trust, Sidney, CA, 1195
Sternberg Charitable Trust, NY, 7075
Sternberger Foundation, Inc., Sigmund, NC, see 7493
Sterne-Elder Memorial Trust, AZ, 143
Sternlicht Family Foundation, Inc., The, DE, 1756
Steuben County Community Foundation, IN, 3241
Stevens Foundation, Abbot and Dorothy H., The, MA, 4163
Stevens Foundation, Georgiana G., CA, 1196
Stevens Foundation, Inc., Ida Mae, FL, 2251
Stevens Foundation, Jess L. and Miriam B., OK, 7980
Stevens Foundation, Nathaniel and Elizabeth P., The, MA, 4164
Stevens Foundation, Winifred L., AZ, 144
Stevens Kingsley Foundation, Inc., The, NY, 7076
Stevens Point Area Foundation, Inc., WI, see 9778
Stewards Fund, The, NC, 7485
Stewardship Foundation, CA, 1197
Stewardship Foundation, The, WA, 9691
Stewardship Trust, WI, 9938
Stewart Education Foundation, UT, 9345
Stewart Educational Foundation, Donnell B. and Elizabeth Dee Shaw, UT, see 9345
Stewart Family Foundation, The, NY, see 5931
Stewart Foundation, CA, 1198
Stewart Foundation, Faye & Lucille, OR, 8060
Stewart Foundation, IL, 3024
Stewart Foundation, Sarah A., CA, 1199
Stewart Foundation, The, PA, 8460
Stewart Trust, Alexander and Margaret, DC, 1850
Stewart, Jr. Foundation, Marlene and J. O., The, TX, 9213
Stewart, M.D. Foundation, Alexander, PA, 8461
Steyer Family Foundation, Inc., Stanley, NY, 7077
Stiefel Foundation for Dermatological Research, Inc., NY, 7078
Stiefel Foundation, Ernst C., The, NY, 7079
Stillson Foundation, OH, 7869
Stine Family Foundation, IA, 3335

Stine Foundation, James M. and Margaret V., PA, 8462
Stock Foundation, Inc., K. C., WI, 9939
Stock Foundation, Paul, WY, 9992
Stocker Foundation, The, OH, 7870
Stockman Family Foundation Trust, NM, 5497
Stoddard Charitable Trust, The, MA, 4165
Stoddard Family Foundation, Inc., MI, 4447
Stoffel Foundation, Gayle and Paul, TX, 9214
Stoico/FIRSTFED Charitable Foundation, Robert F., MA, 4166
Stokely, Jr. Foundation, William B., The, TN, 8730
Stokes Charitable Trust, H. L., NY, 7080
Stolaruk Foundation, Vivian Vivio Stolaruk and Steve, The, MI, 4448
Stone Family Foundation, Jerome H., IL, 3025
Stone Family Foundation, Roger and Susan, IL, 3026
Stone Foundation, Inc., The, CT, 1654
Stone Foundation, Inc., The, NY, 7081
Stone Foundation, Inc., The, WI, 9940
Stone Foundation, Irving & Jean, CA, A
Stone Foundation, Irving I., OH, 7871
Stone Foundation, The, VA, see 9537
Stone Foundation, W. Clement & Jessie V., CA, 1200
Stone Pier Foundation, MN, 4692
Stonecutter Foundation, Inc., NC, 7486
Stoneman Charitable Foundation, Inc., Anne and David, MA, see 4168
Stoneman Charitable Fund, James and Selma, MA, see 4167
Stoneman Charitable Fund, James M., MA, 4167
Stoneman Family Foundation, MA, 4168
Stonisch Foundation, MI, 4449
Stony Point Foundation, The, NY, 7082
Stop & Shop Charitable Foundation, The, MA, see 3767
Stop & Shop Family Foundation, The, PA, 8463
StorageTek Foundation, CO, 1460
Storehouse Charitable Trust, The, IN, 3242
Storer Foundation, Inc., George B., FL, 2252
Storz Foundation, Robert Herman, NE, 5006
Stout Foundation, Charles H., WI, 5068
Stout Scholarship Fund, O. J., WV, 9734
Stover Foundation, The, CA, 1201
Stowe, Jr. Foundation, Inc., Robert Lee, NC, 7487
Strain Foundation, AL, 66
Strake Foundation, TX, 9215
Stranahan Foundation, OH, 7872
Stranahan, Jr. Charitable Trust, Robert A., OH, 7873
Stransky Foundation, Robert J., FL, 2253
Strasser Foundation, Jonathan, NY, 7083
Strategic Grant Partners, Inc., MA, 4169
Stratford Foundation, The, MA, 4170
Straus Charitable Trust, Melville, The, NY, 7084
Straus Family Foundation, Daniel E. and Joyce G., The, NJ, 5413
Straus Family Foundation, Daniel E., The, NJ, see 5413
Straus Family Foundation, Zahava and Moshael J., The, NJ, 5414
Straus Foundation, Inc., Aaron Straus & Lillie, The, MD, 3738
Straus Foundation, Inc., Martha Washington Straus & Harry H., NY, 7085
Straus Foundation, Inc., Philip A. and Lynn, The, NY, 7086
Straus Quintas Foundation, IL, 3027
Strauss Foundation, Inc., The, NY, 7087
Strauss Foundation, Leon, CA, 1202
Strauss Foundation, Levi, CA, 1203
Strauss Foundation, PA, 8464
Strawbridge Charitable Trust, Maxwell, PA, see 8467
Strawbridge Foundation of Pennsylvania I, Inc., Margaret Dorrance, PA, 8465
Strawbridge Foundation of Pennsylvania II, Inc., Margaret Dorrance, PA, 8466
Strawbridge Foundation, Maxwell, PA, 8467
Straz, Jr. Foundation, David A., FL, 2254
Strear Family Foundation, Inc., The, CO, 1461
Streisand Foundation, The, CA, 1204
Strelsin Foundation, Inc., Dorothy, The, NY, 7088
Stride Rite Charitable Foundation, Inc., The, MA, 4171
Stride Rite Philanthropic Foundation, The, MA, 4172
Strong Foundation, Hattie M., DC, 1851
Strong Foundation, The, HI, 2555
Strosacker Foundation, Charles J., The, MI, 4450

Stroud Foundation, DE, 1757
Strouss Charitable Testamentary Trust, Mildred V., CA, 1205
Strowd Roses, Inc., NC, 7488
Struthers Family Foundation, The, DE, 1758
Stryker and William D. Johnston Foundation, Ronda E., The, MI, 4451
Stryker Foundation, Jon L., MI, see 4223
Stryker-Short Foundation, The, CO, see 1345
Strypemonde Foundation, NY, 7089
Stuart Charitable Foundation, G. B., PA, 8468
Stuart Christian Charitable Trust, Hesta, WI, 9941
Stuart Family Foundation, IL, 3028
Stuart Family Foundation, Inc., The, NY, 7090
Stuart Foundation, Barbara and Robert, The, IL, see 3028
Stuart Foundation, CA, 1206
Stuart Foundation, Elbridge and Evelyn, WI, 9942
Stuart Foundation, Elbridge, CA, see 1206
Stuart Foundation, Hadley and Marion, CA, 1207
Stuart Trust, W. B. & Ellen Gordon, WI, 9943
Stuart Youth Foundation, Dwight, CA, 1208
Studenica Foundation, CA, 1209
Studley Foundation, Julien J., The, NY, 7091
Stuller Family Foundation, LA, 3510
Stulman Charitable Foundation, Inc., Leonard and Helen R., MD, 3739
Stulsaft Foundation, Morris, The, CA, 1210
Stupp Bros. Bridge & Iron Company Foundation, MO, 4910
Stupp Foundation, Norman J., MO, 4911
Stupski Family Foundation, CA, see 1211
Stupski Foundation, CA, 1211
Sturgis Area Community Foundation, MI, 4452
Sturgis Charitable & Educational Trust, Roy & Christine, The, AR, 178
Sturgis Charitable and Educational Trust, Roy and Christine, TX, 9216
Sturgis Foundation, MI, see 4452
Sturm Family Foundation, CO, 1462
Sturm Family Foundation, Terri and Roland, NV, 5069
Styberg Foundation, Inc., E.C., WI, 9944
Sub-Zero Foundation, Inc., WI, 9945
Subaru of America Foundation, Inc., NJ, 5415
Sudakoff Foundation, Inc., Harry, The, FL, 2255
Sudakoff Foundation, Inc., Roberta Leventhal, FL, 2256
Sudbury Foundation, MA, 4173
Sudikoff Family Foundation, The, CA, 1212
Sudix Foundation, IL, 3029
Sudler Charitable Trust, Samuel and Claire, The, NJ, see 5416
Sudler Foundation, The, NJ, 5416
Sugarman Foundation, Jay and Kelly, NY, 7092
Sukup Family Foundation, The, IA, 3336
Sullivan & Cromwell Foundation, The, NY, 7093
Sullivan Charitable Foundation, Charles A., KS, 3396
Sullivan Charitable Foundation, KS, see 3396
Sullivan Charitable Trust, Alice I., RI, 8558
Sullivan Family Foundation, The, NY, 7094
Sullivan Foundation, Algernon Sydney, The, MS, 4766
Sullivan Foundation, Inc., Tom & Glory, FL, 2257
Sullivan Foundation, Ray & Pauline, CT, 1655
Sullivan, Jr. Foundation, John J., MO, 4912
Sulzberger Foundation, Inc., The, NY, 7095
Sumasil Foundation, Inc., NY, A
Sumitomo Bank Global Foundation, NY, see 7005
Sumitomo Corporation of America Foundation, NY, 7096
Summer Family Foundation, The, OH, 7874
Summer Rest Foundation, NC, 7489
Summerfield Foundation, Inc., Solon E., NY, 7097
Summerhill Foundation, The, NY, 7098
Summerlee Foundation, The, TX, 9217
Summers Foundation, Inc., John and Jayne, The, NY, 7099
Summit Area Public Foundation, The, NJ, 5417
Summit Charitable Foundation, Inc., The, DC, see 1852
Summit Foundation, NY, 7100
Summit Foundation, The, CO, 1463
Summit Foundation, The, DC, 1852
Sumners Foundation for the Study and Teaching of Self-Government, Inc., Hatton W., TX, 9218
Sumners Foundation, Hatton W., TX, see 9218

Sun Foundation, David and Diana, The, CA, 1213
Sun Hill Foundation, CT, 1656
Sun Microsystems Foundation, Inc., The, CA, 1214
Sundance Pay It Forward Foundation, MN, 4693
Sundean Foundation, Inc., CA, 1215
Sunderland Foundation, KS, 3397
Sunderland Foundation, Lester T., KS, see 3397
Sundet Foundation, MN, 4694
Sunfield Foundation, Inc., NJ, 5418
Sunnen Foundation, MO, 4913
Sunnyside Foundation, Inc., TX, 9219
Sunnyside, Inc., TX, see 9219
Sunrise Charitable Foundation Trust, MD, 3740
Sunrise Foundation Trust, The, NY, 7101
Sunrise Klein Foundation, Inc., The, NY, 7102
Sunshine Foundation Trust, NE, 5007
Sunshine Foundation, FL, see 2258
Sunshine Lady Foundation, Inc., The, NC, 7490
Sunshine Natural Wellbeing Foundation, FL, 2258
SunTrust Bank Memphis Foundation, FL, 2259
SunTrust Bank, Atlanta Foundation, GA, 2496
SunTrust Carolinas Group Foundation, Inc., NC, 7491
SunTrust Foundation MidAtlantic, VA, 9523
Sunup Foundation, Inc., NJ, 5419
Superior-Pacific Fund, PA, see 8283
SUPERVALU Foundation, MN, 4695
Surdna Foundation, Inc., NY, 7103
Surgala Trust, M. J., PA, 8469
Susman and Asher Foundation, IL, 3030
Susman Family Foundation, TX, 9220
Susquehanna Foundation, PA, 8470
Susquehanna Pfaltzgraff Foundation, PA, 8471
Sussman Foundation, Inc., Laurie Tisch, The, NY, 7104
Sussman Fund, Edna Bailey, NY, 7105
Sutherland Foundation, Inc., The, KY, 3451
Sutton Charitable Foundation, Norma, NY, 7106
Sutton Family Foundation, Joe & Eileen, NY, 7107
Sutton Foundation, Celia and Isaac, The, NY, 7108
Sutton Foundation, Inc., Joseph & Eileen, The, NJ, 5420
Sutton, Abe Dweck, and Isaac Saff Family Foundation, Sam and Jack, The, NY, 7109
SVF Foundation, PA, 8472
SVM Foundation, NY, 7110
Swalm Foundation, TX, A
Swanee Hunt Family Foundation, MA, 4174
Swanson & Thomas Foundation, CA, 1216
Swanson Family Foundation, Inc., Dr. W. C., UT, 9346
Swanson Family Foundation, Inc., Gretchen, NE, 5008
Swanson Foundation, Inc., Carl and Caroline, NE, 5009
Swanson Foundation, The, CA, 1217
Swanson, Jr. Foundation, Gertrude and Walter E., IL, 3031
Swanson, Jr. Foundation, W. Clarke, MO, 4914
Swartz Foundation Trust, The, NY, 7111
Swartz Foundation, MA, 4175
Swartz Foundation, The, NY, 7112
Sweet Water Trust, MA, 4176
Sweetfeet Foundation, Inc., NJ, 5421
Sweetgrass Foundation, NY, 7113
Sweig Foundation, Michael, NV, 5070
Swenson Family Foundation, CA, 1218
Swensrud Charitable Trust, Sidney A., MA, see 4177
Swensrud Foundation, Sidney A., MA, 4177
Swett Foundation, Ralph & Eileen, TX, 9221
Swift Foundation, The, CA, 1219
Swig Foundation, CA, 1220
Swigert Foundation, The, OR, 8061
Swindells Charitable Trust, Ann and Bill, OR, 8062
Swinerton Foundation, The, CA, 1221
Swinney Trust, Edward F., TX, 9222
Switzer Foundation, ME, see 3557
Switzer Foundation, Robert and Patricia, ME, 3557
SWS Charitable Foundation, Inc., FL, 2260
Sycamore Foundation, Inc., The, TN, see 8688
Sycamore Tree Trust, MO, 4915
Syde Hurdus 1992 Charitable Trust, NY, see 7114
Syde Hurdus Foundation, Inc., NY, 7114
Sykes Charitable Foundation, Inc., John H., FL, see 2261
Sykes Family Foundation, NY, 7115
Sykes Foundation, Inc., John H., FL, 2261
Sylvan Foundation, Dave & Barbara, OK, 7981
Sylvan Learning Foundation, Inc., The, MD, see 3741

Toledo Community Foundation, Inc., OH, 7883
Toleo Foundation, The, NC, 7495
Toll Foundation, Bruce E. and Robbi S., The, PA, 8478
Toll Foundation, Bruce E., The, PA, see 8478
Toll Foundation, Robert and Jane, The, PA, 8479
Tolleson Family Foundation, The, TX, 9237
Tombros Foundation, The, CT, 1659
Tomkins Corporation Foundation, OH, 7884
Tomlinson Foundation, CA, 1238
Tomorrow Foundation, NY, 7153
Toms Charitable Foundation, Inc., David, LA, 3512
Tomsich Foundation, OH, see 7812
Toner Foundation, Kevin C., NY, see 6239
Tonya Memorial Foundation, Inc., TN, 8734
Topeka Community Foundation, KS, 3400
Topfer Family Foundation, Morton & Angela, The, TX, see 9238
Topfer Family Foundation, TX, 9238
Toppel Family Foundation, Inc., The, FL, 2274
Toppel Foundation, Harold & Patricia, FL, see 2274
Torhjelm Foundation, AZ, 146
Tormondsen Foundation, John R. and Barbara A., The, NY, 7154
Toro Foundation, The, MN, 4702
Torray Family Foundation, Robert E. Torray and Anne P., MD, 3748
Torrey Foundation, CA, 1239
Torrington Area Foundation for Public Giving, CT, see 1516
Torstenson Family Foundation, Robert H., IL, 3036
Tortuga Foundation, NY, 7155
Tosa Foundation, CA, 1240
Toshiba America Foundation, NY, 7156
Touch 'n Tutor Research & Development Foundation, Inc., NY, 7157
Toulmin Charitable Foundation III, V.B., OH, 7885
Tow Charitable Trust, Inc., Leonard & Claire, The, CT, 1660
Tow Foundation, Inc., The, CT, 1661
Towbes Foundation, The, CA, 1241
Tower Foundation, Peter and Elizabeth C., The, NY, 7158
Town Creek Foundation, Inc., MD, 3749
Towne Scholarship Fund, C. E., CA, 1242
Townsend Family Foundation, The, NY, 7159
Towsley Foundation, Harry A. and Margaret D., The, MI, 4461
Toyota USA Foundation, NY, 7160
Tozer Foundation, Inc., MN, 4703
Tozzi Foundation, John R. & Georgene M., The, WY, 9995
Tracy Family Foundation, IL, 3037
Tracy Family Foundation, Thomas J., The, MI, 4462
Traders Foundation, The, IL, 3038
Traditional Foundation, NY, 7161
Trager Family Foundation, Inc., KY, 3452
Trans-Atlantic Foundation, The, NV, 5073
Trarym Foundation, The, CT, see 1593
Traubert and Penny Pritzker Charitable Foundation, Bryan, The, IL, see 2955
Travelli Fund, Charles Irwin, MA, 4184
Treadwell Charitable Foundation, Joseph, The, AL, 68
Treadwell Foundation, Nora Eccles, The, CA, 1243
Treat Foundation, NH, 5102
Trebor Foundation, Inc., GA, see 2521
Trees Charitable Trust, Edith L., PA, 8480
Trefler Foundation, MA, 4185
Trellis Fund, DC, 1853
Tremaine Foundation, Inc., Emily Hall, CT, 1662
Tremble Foundation, Inc., MI, see 4444
Trend Homes Foundation, AZ, 147
Trexler Trust, Harry C., PA, 8481
Triad Foundation, Inc., NY, 7162
Triad Hospitals Private Foundation, The, TX, 9239
Triangle Community Foundation, NC, 7496
Tribune New York Foundation, NY, 7163
Tricon Foundation, Inc., KY, see 3457
Trimble Foundation, The, HI, 2556
Trinity Foundation, AR, 181
Trio Foundation of St. Louis, MO, 4918
Trio Foundation, MO, see 4918
Triple T Foundation, The, PA, 8482
Trippe Trust, Inc., William D., AL, 69

Troisi Foundation, Barbara Davies, NY, 7164
Trott Family Foundation, The, NY, 7165
Troy Foundation, The, OH, 7886
Troy Savings Bank Charitable Foundation, Inc., The, NY, 7166
Truckee Tahoe Community Foundation, CA, 1244
True and Linda Brown Foundation, Lawrence, WA, 9696
True Foundation, Alice and Russell, DC, 1854
True Foundation, WY, 9996
True North Foundation, CA, 1245
Trueblood Foundation, Harry, The, CO, 1466
Truhlsen Family Foundation, Inc., Stanley M., NE, 5011
Truland Foundation, The, VA, 9528
Trull Foundation, The, TX, 9240
Truman Foundation, Mildred Faulkner, PA, 8483
Truman Heartland Community Foundation, MO, 4919
Trump Foundation, Donald J., The, NY, 7167
Trust Company of Georgia Foundation, GA, see 2496
Trust Family Foundation, The, NH, 5103
Trust for Mutual Understanding, The, NY, 7168
Trust Funds Incorporated, CA, 1246
Trustmark Foundation, IL, 3039
Trzcinski Foundation, The, OH, 7887
Tsadra Foundation, NY, 7169
TSC Foundation, Inc., SC, 8618
Tsunami Foundation, CT, 1663
Tubergen Foundation, Jerry L. & Marcia D., MI, 4463
Tuch Foundation, Inc., Michael, NY, 7170
Tuchman Family Foundation, CO, 1467
Tuchman Foundation, Inc., The, NJ, 5429
Tucker Charitable Trust, Rose E., OR, 8065
Tucker Community Endowment Foundation, WV, 9736
Tucker Foundation, Inc., Marcia Brady, MD, 3750
Tucker Foundation, The, TN, 8735
Tudor Foundation, Inc., The, CT, 1664
Tufenkian Foundation, Inc., The, NY, 7171
Tuft Family Foundation, NY, 7172
Tull Charitable Foundation, The, GA, 2500
Tully Charitable Trust, Daniel P. and Grace I., CT, 1665
Tully Family Foundation, IL, 3040
Tully Foundation, Alice, The, NY, 7173
Tulsa Community Foundation, OK, 7984
Tulsa Foundation, The, WI, 9951
Tuohy Foundation, Alice Tweed, CA, 1247
Tuohy Foundation, Walter & Mary, IL, 3041
Tupancy-Harris Foundation of 1986, The, MA, 4186
Tupperware Children's Foundation, FL, 2275
Turben Foundation, Susan and John, OH, 7888
Turn 2 Foundation, Inc., NY, 7174
Turner 95 Charitable Trust, Harry and Violet, OH, see 7889
Turner Charitable Foundation, Inc., Laura G., TN, 8737
Turner Charitable Foundation, James Stephen, TN, 8736
Turner Charitable Foundation, TX, see 9212
Turner Charitable Trust, Courtney S., TX, 9241
Turner Construction Company Foundation, TX, 9242
Turner Family Foundation, Cal, The, TN, 8738
Turner Family Foundation, PA, 8484
Turner Foundation, Inc., GA, 2501
Turner Foundation, Inc., Jane Smith, MI, 4464
Turner Foundation, The, OH, 7889
Turner Fund, Inc., Ruth, NY, 7175
Turock Family Foundation, The, NJ, 5430
Turrell Fund, NJ, 5431
Tuscany Research Institute, NV, 5074
Tuscarawas County Community Foundation, OH, 7890
Tuttle Fund, Isaac H., NY, 7176
Twin Chimney, Inc., NJ, 5432
Twin City Education Foundation, Inc., IN, 3245
TWL Foundation, LA, 3513
TWS Foundation, The, CT, 1666
Tyco Electronics Foundation, PA, 8485
Tye Foundation, Martha-Ellen, IA, 3337
Tye Medical Aid Foundation, Ray, MA, 4187
Tyler Charitable Foundation, Robert & Gwen, KS, 3401
Tyndale House Foundation, IL, 3042
Tyrrell Foundation, Inc., The, CT, 1667
Tyson Foundation, Inc., AR, 182
Tyson Fund, IN, 3246
Tzedaka Fund Trust, Solomon and Machla, NY, 7177
Tzedakah Foundation, NC, 7497
Tzedakah Fund, The, MD, 3751

Tziterman Memorial Trust, NY, 7178
Tzur Foundation, Inc., Maoz, NY, 7179

U S WEST Foundation, CO, see 1443
U.S. Bancorp Foundation, Inc., MN, 4704
U.S. Friends of Shine, NY, A
U.S. Oil/Schmidt Family Foundation, Inc., WI, 9952
U.S. Trust Corporation Foundation, NY, 7180
UAL Foundation, IL, see 3044
UBS Foundation U.S.A., NJ, 5433
Ueberroth Family Foundation, CA, 1248
Ueltschi Foundation, Albert L., NY, 7181
Uhlmann Foundation, John W., MO, 4920
Uihlein Charitable Foundation, Inc., David and Julia, WI, 9953
Uihlein Foundation, Henry Uihlein II & Mildred A., WI, 9954
Uihlein Foundation, Robert A., WI, 9955
Ukrop Foundation, The, VA, 9529
Ullrich Foundation Trust, John, IL, 3043
Ultramar Diamond Shamrock Foundation, TX, see 9247
Unaka Foundation, Inc., The, TN, 8739
Unaka Scholarship Foundation, Inc., TN, see 8739
Unanue Foundation, Inc., C. & J., The, NY, 7182
Ungar Foundation, The, NY, 7183
Unger Memorial Foundation, Clara Buttenwieser, NY, see 6336
UniHealth Foundation, CA, 1249
Unilever United States Foundation, NJ, 5434
Union Bank Foundation, CA, see 1250
Union Bank of California Foundation, CA, 1250
Union County Community Foundation, Inc., AR, 183
Union County Foundation, OH, see 7586
Union Electric Company Charitable Trust, MO, see 4772
Union Foundation, NJ, 5435
Union Pacific Foundation, NE, 5012
Union Planters Community Foundation, AL, 70
Union Square Awards, NY, 7184
Union Square Fund, Inc., The, NY, see 7184
United Airlines Foundation, IL, 3044
United Brands Foundation, OH, see 7571
United Cancer Front, CA, 1251
United Coal Company Charitable Foundation, VA, see 9530
United Community Foundation, Inc., WI, see 9780
United Company Charitable Foundation, The, VA, 9530
United Fire Group Foundation, IA, 3338
United Health Foundation, MN, 4705
United Illuminating Foundation, The, CT, 1668
United Service Foundation, Inc., PA, 8486
United Space Alliance Foundation, PA, 8487
United States Steel Foundation, Inc., PA, 8488
United States Sugar Corporation Charitable Trust, FL, 2276
United States Trust Company of New York Foundation, NY, see 7180
United States-Japan Foundation, NY, 7185
United Stationers Foundation, IL, 3045
United Telecommunications Foundation, KS, see 3395
United Vision Foundation, NJ, A
Unity Foundation of La Porte County, Inc., IN, 3247
Universal Foundation, Inc., The, FL, see 2167
Universal Leaf Foundation, VA, 9531
Universal Studios Foundation, Ltd., CA, see 933
University Financing Foundation, Inc., The, GA, 2502
University of Phoenix Alumni Network, AZ, 148
University of Phoenix Network for Professional Development, AZ, see 148
Unkefer Foundation, TX, 9243
Unocal Foundation, CA, 1252
UNOVA Foundation, The, WA, 9697
Unterberg Foundation, Inc., Marjorie & Clarence E., NY, 7186
Upchurch, Jr. Charitable Foundation, Samuel E., AL, 71
Uperetes Foundation, MA, 4188
Uphill Foundation, NY, 7187
Upjohn Foundation, Harold and Grace, MI, 4465
Upper Peninsula Community Foundation Alliance, MI, see 4259
UPS Foundation, The, GA, 2503
Upton Charitable Foundation, Lucy and Eleanor S., NJ, 5436
Upton Foundation, Frederick S., MI, 4466

Urschel Foundation, Charles and Betty, The, TX, 9244
USA Networks Foundation, Inc., NY, see 6220
USAA Foundation, a Charitable Trust, The, TX, A
USAA Foundation, Inc., The, TX, 9245
Usen Family Charitable Foundation, Irving and Edyth S., The, RI, 8560
USG Foundation, Inc., IL, 3046
Usher Charitable Foundation, Thomas and Sandra, PA, 8489
Ushkow Foundation, Inc., NY, 7188
USX Foundation, Inc., PA, see 8488
Ute City Charitable Trust, CA, 1253
Utica Foundation, Inc., NY, see 5783

V & H Charitable Foundation, KS, 3402
V'Emunah Foundation, Inc., Emet, The, NJ, 5437
V.F. Foundation, NC, 7498
Vadasz Family Foundation, The, CA, 1254
Vail Valley Foundation, Inc., CO, 1468
Vale-Asche Foundation, The, TX, 9246
Valente Foundation, George and Lena, The, CA, 1255
Valentine Charitable Foundation, Inc., The, NY, 7189
Valentine Foundation, Lawson, CT, 1669
Valerio Charitable Remainder Foundation, Michael and Helen, The, MA, 4189
Valero Energy Foundation, TX, 9247
Valiant Foundation, Inc., IN, 3248
Vallejo Ventures Private Foundation, CA, see 278
Valley Community Foundation for Lifelong Learning, IA, 3339
Valley Foundation, Inc., The, NJ, 5438
Valley Foundation, The, CA, 1256
Valley Foundation, Wayne & Gladys, CA, 1257
Valmont Foundation, The, NE, 5013
Valspar Foundation, The, MN, 4706
van Ameringen Foundation, H., NY, 7190
van Ameringen Foundation, Inc., NY, 7191
Van Andel Foundation, Jay and Betty, MI, 4467
van Beuren Charitable Foundation, Inc., RI, 8561
Van Curler Foundation, MI, 4468
Van Daele Family Foundation, Mike and Linda, CA, 1258
Van Daele Family Foundation, Patrick and Robin, CA, 1259
Van Every Foundation, Philip L., NC, 7499
Van Houten Memorial Fund, Edward W. and Stella C., The, NC, 7500
van Loben Sels Foundation, CA, see 1260
van Loben Sels/RembeRock Foundation, CA, 1260
Van Lunen Charitable Foundation, Richard D., MD, 3752
Van Nuys Charities, J. B. and Emily, CA, 1261
Van Nuys Foundation, I. N. & Susanna H., CA, 1262
Van Pelt Foundation, NY, 7192
Van Sloun Foundation, MA, 4190
Van Vleet Foundation, FL, 2277
Van Wert County Foundation, The, OH, 7891
Van Wyk Family Foundation, Arlan J., IA, 3340
Vanberg Family Foundation, TX, 9248
Vance Charitable Foundation, Robert C., MA, 4191
Vance Foundation, Lee and Cynthia, NY, 7193
Vanderbilt Trust, R. T., NC, 7501
Vanderweide Foundation, Robert & Cheri, MI, 4469
Vandomelen Foundation, William and Katherine, The, MI, 4470
Vanguard Group Foundation, The, PA, 8490
Vanneck-Bailey Foundation, The, FL, 2278
VanVlack Family Charitable Trust, MI, A
Varadhan Memorial Foundation, Gopal, The, NY, 7194
Vasey Foundation, The, CT, 1670
Vaterstetten Foundation, DC, 1855
Vatterott Foundation, MO, 4921
Vaughan Family Foundation, Rosemary Haggar, TX, 9249
Vaughan Foundation, Inc., Susan, TX, 9250
Vaughan Foundation, MI, 4471
Vaughn Foundation, Jim M., TX, 9251
Vaughn Foundation, The, TX, see 9251
Vaughn-Jordan Foundation, Inc., FL, 2279
Vectren Foundation, Inc., IN, 3249
Veden Charitable Trust, Frank W., MN, 4707
Vegesna Foundation, Raju, The, CA, 1263
Vencor Foundation, Inc., KY, see 3434
Venne Foundation, Clarence J., PA, 8491
Ventura County Community Foundation, CA, 1264

Veres Charitable Trust, Andrew F. & Barbara, TX, 9252
Vergara Trust, Lamar Bruni, TX, 9253
Verizon Foundation, NJ, 5439
Vermeer Charitable Foundation, Inc., IA, 3341
Vermilion Healthcare Foundation, IL, 3047
Vermont Community Foundation, VT, 9361
Vernon Foundation, Inc., Miles Hodsdon, NY, 7195
Versacare, Inc., CA, 1265
Vervane, Inc., CT, 1671
Vesper Foundation, OH, 7892
Vest Foundation, The, MN, 4708
Vetlesen Foundation, G. Unger, The, NY, 7196
Vetter Foundation, NE, 5014
VH1 Save The Music Foundation, NY, A
VHIV, Inc., NY, 7197
Via-Bradley College of Engineering, South Dakota, SD, 8633
Viad Corp Fund, The, AZ, 149
Vibern Foundation, IL, 3048
Vickridge Private Foundation, Inc., CO, see 1395
Vicksburg Hospital Medical Foundation, MS, 4769
Vickter Foundation, David, The, CA, 1266
Victoria Foundation, Inc., NJ, 5440
Victory Foundation, Inc., FL, 2280
Vidalakis Family Foundation, WA, 9698
Vidda Foundation, The, NY, 7198
Vidinha Charitable Trust, A. & E., HI, 2557
Viersen Family Foundation, Inc., Sam, OK, 7985
Vik Brothers Foundation, The, CT, 1672
Vilcek Foundation, Inc., The, NY, 7199
Villa Banfi Foundation, The, NY, see 5597
Vince Club Family Foundation, The, IL, see 2954
Vincent Trust, Anna M., PA, 8492
Vine and Branches Foundation, Inc., WI, 9956
Viner Family Foundation, Clifford and Jill, The, FL, 2281
Vines Foundation, Lanny S., AL, 72
Vingo III Trust, The, MA, 4192
Vinik Family Foundation, MA, 4193
Vintage Foundation, Inc., MN, 4709
Violett and Mary P. R. Thomas Foundation, Ellen M., NY, 7200
Violett Foundation, Inc., Ellen M., NY, see 7200
Viragh Family Foundation, MD, 3753
Virginia Beach Foundation, The, VA, 9532
Virginia Environmental Endowment, VA, A
Virginia Scrap Iron & Metal Co. Charitable Foundation, Inc., VA, see 9430
Visceglia Foundation, Frank, NJ, 5441
Vision of Hope Foundation, NJ, 5442
Visiting Nurse Association of Chicago, IL, see 3049
Visiting Nurse Association of Houston Foundation, TX, see 8944
Vista Hermosa, WA, 9699
Visteon Fund, The, MI, 4472
Vitale Family Foundation, Inc., The, DE, 1759
VNA Foundation, IL, 3049
Vodafone-US Foundation, CA, 1267
Vogel Family Foundation, Inc., GA, 2504
Vogelstein Charitable Trust, John L., NY, 7201
Volentine Foundation, Myatt W., CA, 1268
Volkswagen of America Foundation, MI, 4473
Vollmer Foundation, Inc., Alberto, FL, 2282
Vollmer Foundation, Inc., NJ, 5443
Volpert Foundation, Barry & Teri, NY, 7202
Von der Ahe Foundation, CA, 1269
von der Heyden Foundation, The, NY, 7203
von Hess Foundation, Richard C., The, PA, 8493
von Liebig Foundation, Inc., William J., The, FL, 2283
Von Seggern Charitable Foundation, E. F., TX, 9254
von Weber Trust, Madelaine G., NH, 5104
Vons Charitable Foundation, The, CA, 1270
Vons Companies Charitable Foundation, Inc., The, CA, see 1270
Vopicka Family Foundation, Inc., NJ, 5444
Vose Foundation Trust, Clara Edith, CA, 1272
Vose Foundation, Clara Edith, CA, 1271
Vradenburg Foundation, DC, 1856
Vranos Family Foundation, The, CT, 1673
VuBay Foundation, VA, 9533
Vucurevich Foundation, John T., SD, 8634
Vulcan Materials Company Foundation, AL, 73

W.J. Foundation, The, CA, 1273

W.M. Foundation, MN, 4710
Wabash Valley Community Foundation, Inc., IN, 3250
Waccamaw Community Foundation, SC, 8619
Wachenheim Foundation, Sue and Edgar, NY, 7204
Wachovia Foundation, Inc., The, NC, 7502
Wachovia Regional Foundation, PA, 8494
Wachtell, Lipton, Rosen & Katz Foundation, The, NY, 7205
Waco Foundation, The, TX, 9255
Wadleigh Foundation, Inc., George C., MA, 4194
Wadleigh Home for Aged Men, Inc., George C., MA, see 4194
Wadman Foundation, UT, 9349
Wadsworth Golf Charities Foundation, IL, 3050
Waggoner Charitable Trust, Crystelle, TX, 9256
Waggoner Foundation, Inc., E. Paul and Helen Buck, TX, 9257
Waggoners Foundation, The, TX, 9258
Wagler Charitable Foundation, Phil, The, OH, 7893
Wagner and George Hosser Scholarship Fund Trust, Edward, RI, 8562
Wagner Family Foundation, Inc., The, CA, 1274
Wagner Foundation, Ltd., R. H., WI, see 9957
Wagner Foundation, Ltd., The, WI, 9957
Wagner Foundation, Melvin F. and Ellen L., WI, 9958
Wagner Foundation, Melvin F., WI, see 9958
Wagner Foundation, Todd, TX, 9259
Wagner Trust, Leonard, NY, 7206
Wahlert Foundation, FL, 2284
Waidner Foundation, Robert A., The, MD, 3754
Waitt Family Foundation, CA, 1275
Wal-Dot Foundation, TX, 9260
Wal-Mart Foundation, AR, 184
Walbridge Foundation, Doris Goodwin, NM, 5503
Walbridge Fund, The, NY, 7207
Waldbaum Family Foundation, Inc., I., FL, 2285
Waldorf Educational Foundation, The, PA, 8495
Walgreen Benefit Fund, IL, 3051
Walgreen Foundation, Kathleen and Charles R., The, IL, 3052
Walk Fine Arts Foundation, Maurice, IL, 3053
Walker Charitable Foundation, Inc., Willard and Pat, AR, 185
Walker Foundation, Archie D. and Bertha H., MN, 4711
Walker Foundation, Earl E. Walker and Myrtle E., The, MO, 4922
Walker Foundation, Inc., Stanley D. and Kay B., GA, 2505
Walker Foundation, MS, 4770
Walker Foundation, W. E., MS, see 4770
Walker III Foundation, Thomas B., NY, 7208
Wall Foundation, Inc., Vance, NJ, 5445
Wallace Charitable Memorial Foundation, Inc., Fred & Alice, OH, 7894
Wallace Educational Trust, Allyrae, AL, 74
Wallace Foundation, George R., The, MA, 4195
Wallace Foundation, Inc., Jean and David W., The, CT, 1674
Wallace Foundation, Louise B., TN, 8740
Wallace Foundation, The, NY, 7209
Wallace Genetic Foundation, Inc., DC, 1857
Wallace Global Fund, DC, 1858
Wallace Research Foundation, The, IA, 3342
Wallace-Reader's Digest Funds, NY, see 7209
Wallach Foundation, Miriam G. and Ira D., NY, 7210
Wallerstein Foundation for Geriatric Life Improvement, NJ, 5446
Wallerstein Institute, Johanette, NJ, 5447
Wallestad Foundation, MN, 4712
Wallestad Foundation, Phadoris, MN, 4713
Wallin Foundation, MN, 4714
Walling Family Foundation, Halbert, TX, see 8814
Wallis Charitable Trust, Dorothy Wagner, MD, 3755
Wallis Foundation, CA, 1276
Walnut Foundation, IL, 3054
Walsh Foundation, Dale & Edna, The, NV, 5075
Walsh Foundation, The, IL, 3055
Walsh Foundation, TX, 9261
Walske Charitable Foundation, The, MA, 4196
Walske-Longtine Foundation, MA, see 4196
Walter & Lorenz Foundation, Inc., NY, see 7211
Walter Corporation Foundation, Jim, FL, see 2286
Walter Family Trust, Byron L., WI, 9959

FOUNDATION NAME INDEX